ENCYCLOPÆDIA
BRITANNICA

The Encyclopædia Britannica
is published with the editorial advice and consultation
of the faculties of The University of Chicago
and of a committee of members of the faculties of Oxford, Cambridge
and London universities

*

"LET KNOWLEDGE GROW FROM MORE TO MORE
AND THUS BE HUMAN LIFE ENRICHED."

ENCYCLOPÆDIA BRITANNICA

A New Survey of Universal Knowledge

Volume 19

RAYNAL to SARREGUEMINES

17 68

WILLIAM BENTON, Publisher

ENCYCLOPÆDIA BRITANNICA, INC.

CHICAGO · LONDON · TORONTO

ENCYCLOPÆDIA BRITANNICA

Volume 19

RAYNAL to SARREGUEMINES

RAYNAL, GUILLAUME THOMAS FRANÇOIS (1713–1796), French writer, was born at Saint Geniez, Rouergue, on April 12, 1713. He was educated at the Jesuit school of Pezenas, and received priest's orders, but he was dismissed for unexplained reasons from the parish of Saint-Sulpice, Paris, to which he was attached, and thenceforward he devoted himself to society and literature. The Abbé Raynal wrote for the *Mercure de France,* and compiled a series of popular but superficial works, which he published and sold himself. These—*L'Histoire du stathoudérat* (The Hague, 1747), *L'Histoire du parlement d'Angleterre* (London, 1748), *Anecdotes historiques* (Amsterdam, 3 vol., 1753–54)—gained for him access to the salons of Mme. Geoffrin, Helvétius, and the baron d'Holbach. He had the assistance of various members of the *philosophe* coteries in his most important work, *L'Histoire philosophique et politique des établissements et du commerce des Européens dans les deux Indes* (Amsterdam, 4 vol., 1770). Diderot indeed is credited with a third of this work, which was characterized by Voltaire as "du réchauffé avec de la déclamation." The other chief collaborators were Pechméja, Holbach, Paulze, the farmer-general of taxes, the Abbé Martin, and Alexandre Deleyre. The "philosophic" declamations constituted its chief interest for the general public, and its significance as a contribution to democratic propaganda. The *Histoire* went through many editions, being revised and augmented from time to time by Raynal; it was translated into the principal European languages, and appeared in various abridgments. Its introduction into France was forbidden in 1779; the book was burned by the public executioner, and an order was given for the arrest of the author, whose name had not appeared in the first edition, but was printed on the title page of the Geneva edition of 1780. Raynal escaped to Spa, and thence to Berlin, where he was coolly received by Frederick the Great, in spite of his connection with the *philosophe* party. At St. Petersburg he met with a more cordial reception from Catherine II, and in 1787 he was permitted to return to France, though not to Paris. He was elected by Marseilles to the states-general, but refused to sit on the score of age. Raynal now realized the impossibility of a peaceful revolution, and, in terror of the proceedings for which the writings of himself and his friends had prepared the way, he sent to the constituent assembly an address, which was read on May 31, 1791, deprecating the violence of its reforms. This address is said by Sainte-Beuve (*Nouveaux lundis,* xi) to have been composed chiefly by Clermont Tonnerre and Pierre V. Malouet, and it was regarded, even by moderate men, as ill-timed. The published *Lettre de l'abbé Raynal à l'Assemblée nationale* (Dec. 10, 1790) was really the work of the comte de Guibert. During the Terror Raynal lived in retirement at Passy and at Montlhéry. On the establishment of the Directory in 1795 he became a member of the Institute of France. He died in the next year on March 6, at Chaillot.

See A. Feugère, *Un Précurseur de la Révolution: L'abbé Raynal* (1922).

RAYNALD OF CHÂTILLON (d. 1187), a knight in the service of Constance, princess of Antioch, whom she chose for her husband in 1153, four years after the death of her first husband, Raymund (*q.v.*). One of Raynald's first acts was a brutal assault on the patriarch of Antioch; while two years later he made an unjustifiable attack on Cyprus, in the course of which the island was ravaged. The act brought its punishment in 1159, when he had to humiliate himself before the emperor Manuel, doing homage and promising to accept a Greek patriarch; and when Manuel came to Antioch in the same year, and was visited there by Baldwin III, Raynald led his horse into the city. Later in the year he was captured by the Mohammedans, during a plundering raid against the Syrian and Armenian peasants of the neighbourhood of Marash, and confined at Aleppo. His captivity lasted 17 years. Released in 1176, he married Stephanie, the widow of Humphrey of Toron, and heiress of Krak and Mont Royal, to the southeast of the Dead Sea—fortresses which controlled the trade routes between Egypt and Damascus, and gave him access to the Red Sea. In Nov. 1177, at the head of the army of the kingdom, he won a victory over Saladin, who only escaped with difficulty from the pursuit. But in 1181 the temptation of the caravans which passed by his fortress proved too strong, and in spite of a truce between Saladin and Baldwin IV he began to plunder. Saladin demanded reparations from Baldwin IV. Baldwin could only reply that he was unable to coerce his unruly vassal. The result was a new outbreak of war between Saladin and the Latin kingdom (1182). In the course of the hostilities Raynald launched ships on the Red Sea, partly for buccaneering, partly, it seems, with the design of attacking Mecca, and of challenging Mohammedanism in its own holy place. His ships were captured by one of Saladin's officers; and at the end of the year Saladin himself attacked Raynald in his fortress of Krak, at a time when a number of guests were assembled to celebrate the marriage of his stepson, Humphrey of Toron. The siege was raised, however, by Count Raymund of Tripoli; and till 1186 Raynald was quiet. In that year he espoused the cause of Sibylla and Guy de Lusignan against Count Raymund, and his influence contributed to the recognition of Guy as king of Jerusalem. His policy at this crisis was not conceived in the best interests of the kingdom; and a step which he took at the end of the year was positively fatal. Hearing of a rich caravan, in which the sister of Saladin was travelling, he swooped down from his fortress upon it. Thus, for the second time, he broke a truce between the kingdom and Saladin. Guy could not extort from him the satisfaction which Saladin demanded: Raynald replied that he was lord in his lands, and that he had no peace with Saladin to respect. Saladin swore that Raynald should perish if ever he took him prisoner; and next year he was able to fulfil his oath. He invaded the kingdom, and, at the battle of Hittin, Raynald along with King Guy and many others fell into his hands. They were brought to his tent; and Saladin, after rebuking Raynald strongly for his treachery, offered him his life if he would become a Mohammedan. He refused, and Saladin either slew him with his own hands or caused him to be slain (for accounts differ) in the presence of his companions.

The death of Raynald caused him to be regarded as a martyr; his life shows him to have been only a brigand of great capacity. He is the apotheosis of the feudal liberty which the barons of the Holy Land vindicated for themselves; and he shows, in his reckless brigandage, the worst side of their character. Stevenson, *Crusades in the East* (Cambridge, 1907), takes a most favourable view of Raynald's career: *cf.* especially pp. 240-241. But his whole life seems to indicate a self-willed and selfish temper.

RAYNAUD'S DISEASE, a malady first described by P. Edouard Raynaud in 1862 in a paper on "Local Asphyxia and Symmetrical Gangrene of the Extremities." It is a disease of childhood or early adult life, and females are more frequently affected than males. Raynaud attributed the symptoms to an arrest of the passage of blood to the affected parts, and considered this caused by a spasm of the arterioles. That the skin capillaries in the various stages correspond with this view has been shown by G. E. Brown but the more fundamental aetiology is unknown. If the spasm be sufficiently prolonged and intense to close completely the arterial channels, gangrene of the part may result.

The local symptoms are divided into three well-marked stages. The first is *local syncope,* in which the affected parts become temporarily bloodless, white, cold and anaesthetic. The condition is familiar in what is termed a "dead finger," and is usually bilateral. After a variable time the circulation may become restored with a tingling sensation, or the disease may progress to the second stage, that of *local asphyxia.* In this condition some part of the body, usually a finger, toe or the whole hand or foot, becomes painful, bluish-purple or mottled, and cold. The discoloration may deepen until the skin is almost black, the tactile sense being lost. After several hours, the attack may pass off. Such attacks of local asphyxia may return every day for a time. Sometimes severe abdominal pain is present, accompanied by haematuria. In the third stage, that of *local gangrene,* the involved areas assume a black and shrivelled appearance, livid streaks marking the course of the arteries; blebs may form containing bloody fluid. The degree of destruction varies from the detachment of a patch of soft tissue down to the loss of even a whole limb, the part becoming separated by a line of demarcation as in senile gangrene.

In Raynaud's disease the patients have been noticed to be very susceptible to cold; the extremities must be kept warm; and the activity of the circulation roused by douches and exercise; by these means an attack may be prevented. Should local asphyxia have taken place, one of the best treatments to lessen pain and obtain the return of the natural colour is the application of the constant current, the limb being placed in a bath of warm salt and water. Cushing's method of inducing active hyperaemia has been attended with much success. This treatment is only applicable when the vascular spasm affects the extremities, and consists in the artificial constriction of the limb by the application of a tourniquet or Esmarch's bandage for a few minutes daily. This is followed by hyperaemia and increased surface temperature, and affords much relief to the pain of the stage of asphyxia. Drugs which dilate the peripheral vessels, such as amyl nitrite and trinitrine, have also been recommended. The disease tends toward recovery with more or less loss of tissue if the stage of gangrene has been reached.

See G. E. Brown, *Arch. Int. Med.,* 1925, xxxv, 56.

RAYNOUARD, FRANÇOIS JUSTE MARIE (1761–1836), French dramatist and *savant,* was born at Brignoles (Provence), on Sept. 8, 1761. He was educated for the bar and practised at Draguignan. In 1791 he went to Paris as deputy to the legislative assembly, but after the fall of the Girondists, he was imprisoned in Paris. During his imprisonment he wrote his play *Caton d'Utique* (1794). *Les Etats de Blois* and *Les Templiers* were accepted by the Comédie Française. *Les Templiers* was produced in 1805, and, in spite of the protests of Geoffroy, had a great success. Raynouard was admitted to the academy in 1807, and from 1817 to 1826 he was perpetual secretary. He was admitted to the Academy of Inscriptions in 1816. His later life was spent in studying the Provençal language and literature. His chief works are *Choix de poésies originales des troubadours* (6 vol., 1817–22), of which the sixth volume, *Grammaire comparée des langues de l'Europe latine dans leurs rapports avec la langue des troubadours* (1822), was separately published; and *Lexique roman* (6 vol., 1838–44). He died at Passy on Oct. 27, 1836.

RAYON: see SYNTHETIC FIBRES.

RAYONNANT STYLE, in architecture, the fully developed French Gothic style (*see* GOTHIC ARCHITECTURE) of the latter half of the 13th and the first three quarters of the 14th centuries. It is characterized by a complete mastery of the structural ideas of the Gothic vaulted church; great skill in stone cutting; the elimination of wall surface; the reduction in area of all supports to the minimum; thorough development and lavish use of bar tracery (*q.v.*) based on geometric forms; reduction in size and importance of the triforium gallery, and a general attempt to accent all vertical lines. In carved ornament the spherical crocket of the earlier Gothic was replaced by a fully opened, upturned leaf, and naturalistic foliage decorated capitals, string courses and the like. Figure sculpture was lavishly used around entrance doors, and in its combination of decorative validity and realistic presentation, it approached Greek sculpture of the 5th century B.C. Toward the end of the period, realism in sculpture became dominant and the decorative value of the work diminished. Characteristic examples are: later portions of Amiens cathedral (apse completed 1269, side chapels 1292–1375); transept and side chapels of Notre Dame at Paris (1258–1315); Sainte Chapelle, Paris (1245–48); S. Urbain at Troyes (1262–76), famous for its delicate tracery and enormous window area; the Portail des Libraires at Rouen cathedral (1280); and the east end of the great abbey church of S. Ouen at Rouen (choir and transepts begun 1318).

RAYY, one of the great cities of Iran, the ancient Ragha, Latin *Rhages.* The expedition of the Boston and Pennsylvania museums disclosed a prehistoric settlement on the site dating from the third millennium B.C. Rayy is mentioned in the Avesta as a sacred place and is also mentioned in the Apocrypha. The city was well known to classical authors, who referred to it frequently. It was less important in Sasanian times, but in the 9th century, the Caliph Al-Mahdi became governor and there his son, Haroun-al-Rashid, was born. Under Al-Mahdi's rule the city rapidly became a magnificent metropolis, rivalled in western Asia only by Damascus and Baghdad. It covered at least 25 sq.mi., and according to Mustawfi it contained 20,000 mosques, 2,750 minarets, innumerable baths and colleges. Yaqut refers to it as a city of extraordinary beauty, built largely of fired brick, brilliantly ornamented with blue faience, but he also speaks of the dark and crooked streets which made the city a formidable obstacle to invaders. It continued to be a city of political, commercial and artistic importance through Seljuk times. In the 12th century it was tormented and greatly weakened by the fury of rival religious sects, was overcome by the Mongols in 1220 and, according to some probably much exaggerated reports, completely destroyed and the inhabitants massacred. Mongol occupation, however, terminated the dominance of Rayy. It was famous for its decorated silks of an unsurpassed *finesse* and artistic perfection, of which fragmentary examples are to be found in the world's principal museums. Rayy has been wrongly credited with the bulk of the luxurious type of Persian pottery of the 12th and 13th centuries. (*See* POTTERY AND PORCELAIN: *Persia and the Near East.*) Only one architectural monument, the tower of Toghrul (1137) survives. The centre of Rayy was situated about 6 mi. S. of the modern Tehran.

BIBLIOGRAPHY.—Lestrange, *Lands of the Eastern Caliphate*, espec. pp. 214–217; 227–29; Barbier de Maynard, *Dict. Geographique*, pp. 273–80; P. Schwarz, *Iran im Mittelalter*, pp. 740–809; Minorsky, "Raiy," *Encyclopedia of Islam; Survey of Persian Art*, espec. vol. ii, pp. 1541, ff.

RAZIN, STENKA (STEPHEN TIMOFEEVICH) (d. 1671), Cossack hetman and rebel, whose parentage and date and place of birth are unknown. We first hear of him in 1661 on a diplomatic mission from the Don Cossacks to the Kalmuck Tatars, and in the same year we meet him on a pilgrimage of 1,000 miles to the great Solovetsky monastery on the White Sea "for the benefit of his soul." After that all trace of him is lost for six years, when he reappears as the leader of a robber community established at Panshinskoe, among the marshes between the rivers Tishina and Ilovlya, from whence he levied blackmail on all vessels passing up and down the Volga. His first considerable exploit was to destroy the "great water caravan" consisting of the treasury barges and the barges of the patriarch and the wealthy merchants of Moscow. He then sailed down the Volga with a fleet of 35 galleys, capturing the more important forts on his way and devastating the country. At the beginning of 1668 he defeated the voivode Jakov Bezobrazov, sent against him from Astrakhan, and in the spring embarked on a predatory expedition into Persia which lasted for 18 months. Sailing into the Caspian, he ravaged the Persian coasts from Derbend to Baku, massacred the inhabitants of Resht, and in the spring of 1669 established himself on the isle of Suina, off which, in July, he annihilated a Persian fleet sent against him. Stenka, as he was generally called, had now become a potentate with whom princes did not disdain to treat. In Aug. 1669 he reappeared at Astrakhan, and accepted a fresh offer of pardon from the tsar there. In 1670 Razin rebelled against the government, captured Cherkask, Tsaritsyn and other places, and on June 24 burst into Astrakhan. After massacring all who opposed him, and giving the rich bazaars of the city over to pillage, he converted Astrakhan into a Cossack republic. After a three weeks' carnival of blood and debauchery Razin quitted Astrakhan with 200 barges full of troops to establish the Cossack republic along the whole length of the Volga, as a preliminary step toward advancing against Moscow. But his forces were stayed by the resistance of Simbirsk, and after two bloody encounters close at hand on the banks of the Sviyaga (Oct. 1st and 4th), Razin was ultimately routed and fled down the Volga.

But the rebellion was by no means over. The emissaries of Razin, armed with inflammatory proclamations, had stirred up the inhabitants of the modern governments of Nizhniy-Novgorod, Tambov and Penza, and penetrated even so far as Moscow and Great Novgorod. It was difficult to rouse the oppressed population by the promise of deliverance from their oppressors. Razin proclaimed that his object was to root out the boyars and all officials, to level all ranks and dignities, and establish cossackdom, with its corollary of absolute equality, throughout Muscovy. Even at the beginning of 1671 the issue of the struggle was doubtful. Eight battles had been fought before the insurrection showed signs of weakening, and it continued for six months after Razin had received his quietus. At Simbirsk his prestige had been shattered. Even his own settlements at Saratov and Samara refused to open their gates to him, and the Don Cossacks, hearing that the patriarch of Moscow had anathematized Stenka, also declared against him. In 1671 he was captured at Kagalnik, his

last fortress, and carried to Moscow, where, on June 6, after bravely enduring unspeakable torments, he was quartered alive.

See N. I. Kostomarov, *The Rebellion of Stenka Razin* (Rus.) (2nd ed. Petersburg, 1859); S. M. Solovev, *History of Russia* (Rus.), vol. ii (Petersburg, 1895, etc.); R. N. Bain, *The First Romanovs* (London, 1905). (R. N. B.)

RAZMAK, a military cantonment in Waziristan region, North-West Frontier province, Pakistan, was opened after suppression of the Waziristan rebellion which followed the Afghan war of 1919. It is some 6,500 ft. above the sea, on the borders of Mahsud and Waziri territory.

RAZOR. The razor is an instrument used for shaving. The early razor of modern times was made of steel which had a wedge-shaped section, with straight sides tapering to a sharp edge, and although simple in form it was a good and durable instrument for its purpose. Early in the 19th century, the practice was introduced of hollowing out the sides of the blade by grinding, to facilitate sharpening the blade, and improve fineness of the cutting edge. At first the degree of hollowness, or concavity of the sides of the blade was small, but with great skill, hollow-grinding has been carried considerably further, increasing the lightness and flexibility of the blade. The full hollow blade is thinner in the centre than nearer the cutting edge. Hollow-grinding is performed by using grinding wheels of successively diminishing diameters. The processes of the production of the blade are:—forging under the hammer, marking with name of maker, drilling the hole for the pin, then hardening and tempering of the blade; grinding and hollowing; glazing and buffing on small leather-covered wheels with polishing material. The blade is then etched, fitted with handle, whetted to a fine sharp edge. Etching is sometimes elaborate.

Safety Razor.—The razor is naturally considered a dangerous instrument, and many attempts have been made to make it safe. Not until the introduction of the "Gillette" type of razor, at the beginning of the 20th century, was a satisfactory solution found. The principle of the "safety" razor is to place a guard between skin and cutting edge of the razor blade, so that the guard permits the edge to pass over the uneven surface of the part to be shaved, removing the hair without cutting the skin. In some cases devices are provided to enable the user to strop or resharpen the blades. The quality of the steel strip supplied by the steelmaker for use as blades in the safety razor is the result of a combination of the highest grade of skill and experience on the part of the steelmaker and the rolling-mill engineer. Cutting edges of the blade are formed by whetting on suitable wheels.

Other types of safety devices are based on the desire to retain the general form of the ordinary razor, while rendering it safe in use. These take the form of fitting a suitable guard to the blade of the ordinary razor, or the substitution of a holder, carrying an adjustable blade of the strip-steel type.

Electric Razor.—With the invention of the Schick Dry Shaver by the late Lieutenant Colonel Jacob Schick, U.S.A., retired, an entirely new technique was introduced to the art of shaving. This dry shaver consists of a shearing head mounted on a powerful little motor encased in a handle made of some suitable substance, such as bakelite. The shearing head includes an outer and an inner member—the outer member having a very thin shear plate with openings or slots in it to rest against the skin, while the inner member has teeth which co-operate with the nether edges of the walls of the shear plate slots or openings in a shearing action. The toothed inner member is held up tightly against the inside surface of the shear plate by means of springs or other appropriate means and is made to reciprocate very rapidly underneath the shear plate by the motor at approximately 7,200 times a minute. The hairs of the face which penetrate the openings or slots in the shear plate are thus sheared off by the reciprocating motion of the inner member in co-operation with the nether edges of the slot walls of the stationary shear plate. The electric dry shaver operates without the use of sharp blades, soaps, brushes, creams and lotions.

RAZORBILL or RAZOR-BILLED AUK, *Alca torda*, a member of the Auk family, known also as Marrot, Murre, Scout, Tinker or Willock; some of these names it shares with the Guillemot (*q.v.*), and Puffin (*q.v.*). It is a common sea bird of the north Atlantic, resorting in vast numbers to certain rocky cliffs for breeding, and returning to the open sea for the rest of the year. It is in many respects intermediate between the guillemot and the garefowl (q.v.). In habits the razorbill agrees with the guillemots, laying its single egg on ledges of cliffs. It breeds on both sides of the north Atlantic, wandering as far south as the Mediterranean on the east and Long Island on the west in winter. It feeds on fish.

RAZZIA (an adaptation of the Algerian Arabic *ghāziah*, from *ghasw*, to make war), a foray or raid made by African Moslems. As used by the Arabs, the word denotes a military expedition against rebels or infidels, and razzias were made largely for punishment of hostile tribes or for the capture of slaves. English writers in the early years of the 19th century used the form *ghrazzie*, and Dixon Denham in his *Travels* (1826) styles the raiding force itself the ghrazzie. The modern English form is copied from the French, while the Portuguese variant is *gazia, gaziva.*

RÉ, ÎLE DE, an island 1½ mi. off the port of La Pallice in the southwestern part of France. The island, with a northwest-southeast length of 15 mi. and an average width of 2¼ mi., is separated from the coast of Vendée to the north by a shallow bay, the Pertuis Breton, 6 mi. broad, and from the island of Oléron to the south by another, the Pertuis d'Antioche, 7½ mi. broad. The Atlantic coast is reef-fringed, but there are small-craft harbours on the landward side. The most important of these is La Flotte. The largest shore indentation on the east coast, the Fier d'Ars, nearly divides the island, leaving an isthmus only 230 ft. wide to maintain the island's continuity. Dunes and salt marshes cover a large part of the northern end of the island. Many salt pans for the collection of salt by evaporation have been built along the landward shore. Industries are fishing, oyster cultivation, and the collection of seaweed for fertilizer. The island has some cropland which is in vineyards or in early spring vegetables. Île de Ré is included in the department of Charente-Maritime. Population of the island (1946), 7,908.

REA, SAMUEL (1855–1929), U.S. railroad official, was born at Hollidaysburg, Pa., on Sept. 21, 1855. In 1871 he entered the service of the Pennsylvania railroad as chainman and rodman. From 1875 to 1877 he was assistant engineer on construction of the Monongahela river bridge at Pittsburgh. He was next appointed assistant engineer for the Pittsburgh and Lake Erie railroad and returned to the Pennsylvania lines in 1879 in a similar capacity. In 1888 he was appointed assistant to the second vice-president of the Pennsylvania railroad, which position he retained until 1889 when he was made chief engineer on construction of the belt line tunnel under Baltimore for the Baltimore and Ohio railroad.

In 1892 he again returned to the Pennsylvania railroad as assistant to the president, and became first vice-president in 1911. In 1913 he was elected president. He was in charge of the construction of the Pennsylvania station in New York city (completed in 1910), the connecting tunnels under the Hudson and East rivers, the New York Connecting railroad and Hell Gate bridge over the East river (opened in 1917). In 1917 he became a member of the executive committee on national defense of the American Railway association, known as the Railroads War Board. He retired from the presidency of the Pennsylvania railroad on Sept. 30, 1925. He died at Gladwyne, Pa., on March 24, 1929. He wrote *The Railways Terminating in London* (1888).

REACTION KINETICS is that branch of physical science which deals with the determination and interpretation of the rates of chemical change. The subject includes the consideration of the rates both of everyday but complicated reactions such as hard-boiling an egg (an example of protein coagulation) and of simpler but less commonplace reactions such as the one between hydrogen and chlorine. Rates have been measured for slow reactions (*e.g.*, the disintegration of ordinary uranium, only half of which will decompose in 5,000,000,000 years) and for fast reactions (*e.g.*, the dissociation of oxygen from haemoglobin, which is almost complete in a tenth of a second). An attempt is made in each case to show quantitatively the effect of changes in the experimental conditions upon the reaction velocity, and to describe in as much detail as possible the behaviour of the molecules at the moment of their reaction.

Many familiar processes involve chemical reactions which proceed at measurable rates. For example, the rusting of iron, the fermentation of sugar, the "drying" of paint, the hardening of plaster of Paris, the baking of bread and the growth of plants, all involve chemical reactions of greater or lesser complexity, and for each example there is considerable interest in the rate of reaction. In general, these familiar processes are very complex, partly because many of the materials are not single pure compounds, but mixtures. It is well known, however, that the rusting (oxidation) of iron requires both air and water, and that the reaction proceeds much more rapidly near the ocean (where salt is deposited on the iron) than it does elsewhere. The rate of rusting also depends upon the composition of the metal (pure iron and stainless steel corrode less rapidly than do cast iron and mild steel) and on temperature (corrosion is rapid in a stream of steam and air). (*See* CORROSION AND OXIDATION OF METALS.)

Scientists have been largely concerned with measuring the rates of reactions such as the decomposition of ozone, the oxidation of sulphur dioxide and the nitration of hydrocarbons; they assume that an understanding of these and similar reactions of pure chemicals will eventually lead to an understanding of more complex (if more familiar) reactions.

Studies of reaction velocity have not only played a fundamental role in the growth of theoretical chemistry; the concepts developed in these studies have also been highly fruitful in industry, especially in the field of catalysis (*q.v.*). A case in point is the Haber process for the manufacture of ammonia (*q.v.*), which is based in part on studies of reaction kinetics. Both theoretical and practical research in the field of reaction kinetics was by mid-century under way in hundreds of laboratories.

A specific example of a rate study is the work on the decomposition of hydrogen iodide to form hydrogen and iodine.

$$2HI \longrightarrow H_2 + I_2 \tag{1}$$

This reaction proceeds at a rate convenient for measurement in the neighbourhood of 320° C., at which temperature not only the hydrogen and hydrogen iodide but even the iodine is gaseous. (This reaction is a reversible one; however, for the moment, it is better to postpone discussion of this complication and to consider only the reaction as written.) The rate of decomposition of hydrogen iodide increases as the quantity of hydrogen iodide per unit volume is increased; quantitatively, the rate is proportional to the square of the concentration of hydrogen iodide. The rate increases by a factor of 1.9 when the temperature is increased from 320° C. to 330° C. The reaction occurs within the body of the gas, and not on the glass walls of the vessel in which the experiment is performed.

The facts just cited have been interpreted to indicate that when two molecules of hydrogen iodide collide, a chemical change occurs only if the velocity of one of them with respect to the other exceeds 2.4 km./sec. (about 5,000 m.p.h.). The average diameter (so far as collision is concerned) of these hydrogen iodide molecules can also be calculated from the kinetic data; it is of an order of magnitude (0.8 × 10⁻⁸ cm.), roughly consistent with the results of other measurements of the sizes of molecules. The effective collisions (*i.e.*, those which lead to reaction) result in a simple interchange of atoms; here the hydrogen and iodine atoms in each of the two colliding molecules of hydrogen iodide separate; simultaneously, the two hydrogen atoms combine to form a hydrogen molecule, and the two iodine atoms combine to form an iodine molecule.

For the discussion of even the simple example of the decomposition of hydrogen iodide, it has been necessary to employ the elementary concepts of chemistry (*q.v.*) and of the kinetic theory (*q.v.*) of matter. For the more detailed treatment of reaction kinetics which follows, a somewhat more extensive knowledge of these subjects is assumed. In the last sections of this article, a precise presentation is attempted.

History.—Gross differences in the rates of chemical reactions have long been recognized. By the beginning of the 19th century, several instances were known where the rate of a chemical change could be greatly increased by adding to the reacting system a small quantity of some apparently inert material. For example, it was discovered in 1796 that the dehydrogenation of alcohols proceeds much more rapidly in the presence of metals than it does in their absence. In 1836, Jons Jakob Berzelius grouped together many reactions of this type and gave the name "catalysts" to the materials which accelerate chemical change. (The modern definition of catalysts is given below.) Although the qualitative concept of reaction rate was by that time well established, the first quantitative measurement and mathematical formulation of reaction velocity is generally credited to L. F. Wilhelmy, who, in 1850, measured the rate of "inversion" (hydrolysis) of cane sugar.

Definitions.—Chemical reactions can be classified as homogeneous or heterogeneous. Homogeneous reactions are those (like the decomposition of hydrogen iodide) which occur completely within one phase (gaseous, liquid or solid). Heterogeneous reactions are those (like the reaction between a metal and an acid) where the reactants are components of two or more phases (solid and gas, solid and liquid, two mutually immiscible liquids, etc.) or where one or more reactants undergo chemical change at an interface; i.e., on the surface of a solid catalyst.

Reactions may also be classified as "reversible" or "irreversible." An irreversible reaction is one in which the reactants, if mixed in the proper proportions, are almost completely converted to the reaction products; a reversible reaction is one in which appreciable quantities of all the reactants and of all the reaction products are present in the system no matter how long the reaction is allowed to proceed. The mixture eventually formed in such a reversible reaction is called the equilibrium mixture; the same equilibrium mixture may be prepared from suitable amounts of either the reactants or the reaction products. For example, the same equilibrium mixture of hydrogen, iodine and hydrogen iodide (at definite temperature and pressure) can be prepared by starting either with equivalent quantities of hydrogen and iodine or with pure hydrogen iodide. If the definition of equilibrium is that adopted in thermodynamics (q.v.), then every reaction is, in principle, reversible. There are reactions, however, where the extent of the reverse reaction is too small to be detected by any experimental means at present known; such reactions are usually regarded, for the purposes of kinetics, as irreversible.

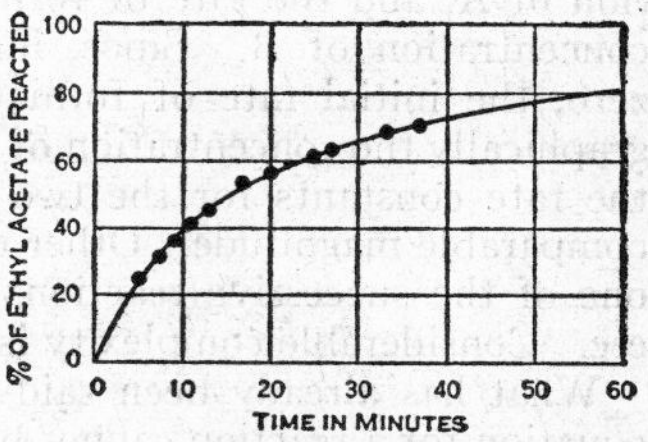

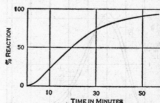

FIG. 1.—SAPONIFICATION OF 0.01M ETHYL ACETATE WITH 0.01M NaOH AT 25° C. CIRCLES, EXPERIMENTAL POINTS, LINE, THEORETICAL FOR k = 6.5 MIN⁻¹ (M/1)⁻¹

"Order" of Reaction.—The fundamental law of reaction kinetics was developed by C. M. Guldberg and P. Waage around 1867 (an independent and similar formulation was made by Jacobus Henricus van't Hoff). These authors assumed that, at constant temperature, the rate of any simple chemical reaction is proportional to the product of the concentrations of the various reacting substances. They showed in a general way that their law of chemical change is consistent with the kinetic molecular theory of matter, and that the data for many chemical reactions could be formulated quantitatively in terms of their theory. Since 1870, the concepts of Guldberg and Waage have been extended and modified, but most of reaction kinetics is still based upon their work.

Consider the simple homogeneous, irreversible reaction between two compounds, A and B (the reactants), to form C and D (the reaction products).

$$A + B \longrightarrow C + D \qquad (2)$$

An example of this sort of reaction is the saponification of ethyl acetate by alkali:

$$CH_3CO_2C_2H_5 + OH^- \longrightarrow CH_3CO_2^- + C_2H_5OH \qquad (2')$$
$$\quad A \qquad\qquad B \qquad\qquad C \qquad\qquad D$$

Equations (2) and (2') as written represent the stoichiometry of the chemical change; i.e., the equations show the relationship between the weights of the initial reactants and those of the final products. The reaction rate may be proportional to the concentrations of the reactants which appear in the stoichiometric equation; if, however, the reaction occurs in several consecutive chemical steps, or requires a catalyst, the kinetics may be more complicated

(see below) than those which could be implied from the stoichiometry. The treatment for a simple case follows.

At the beginning of the reaction, the compounds A and B are present in definite concentrations, say a_0 and b_0 moles per litre respectively[1]; the concentrations of C and D are zero. As the reaction proceeds, the concentrations of A and B decrease, whereas the concentrations of C and D increase. If the concentrations of A and B at any instant are represented by the symbols (A) and (B), then the law of Guldberg and Waage states that wherever equation (2) represents the true kinetic course of the reaction, the reaction velocity, v, is proportional to (A) and to (B). This statement in mathematical form is

$$v = k(A)(B) \qquad (3)$$

where k, the proportionality factor, is called the rate constant. Note that the rate of reaction, v, and the rate constant, k, are not the same, but are connected by an equation of the form of (3).

An equation such as (3) may accurately describe the rate of a chemical reaction. Unfortunately, however, a good experimental method for directly measuring the rate, v, of a reaction is usually not to be found. The quantities which can usually be determined experimentally are the time and the concentrations of the reactants or reaction

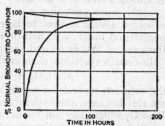

FIG. 2.—RATES AT WHICH EQUILIBRIUM IS ESTABLISHED BETWEEN THE TWO FORMS OF BROMONITROCAMPHOR

products. An equation such as (3) can be transformed by the methods of calculus (q.v.) into an equation expressing a relationship between these concentrations and time. Although the details of this transformation are in no way necessary for the succeeding argument, they are nevertheless presented here for the sake of continuity.

If the concentration of C at any instant is represented by x, then the rate, v, of formation of C is dx/dt, the derivative of x with respect to time; and equation (3) can be replaced by (3').

$$v = \frac{dx}{dt} = k(A)(B) = k(a_0 - x)(b_0 - x) \qquad (3')$$

The integrated form of equation (3) is

$$\log_e \frac{b_0(a_0 - x)}{a_0(b_0 - x)} = kt(a_0 - b_0) \qquad (4)[2]$$

where t is the time measured from the beginning of the reaction; the other symbols have been previously defined. In principle, it should be possible to obtain for every reaction an equation, analogous to (4), from which the concentrations of the various reactants and products at any moment may be calculated.

One method of testing experimentally whether equations (3) and (4) adequately describe the rate of any particular reaction is to measure x (the concentration of C) at several different times, t. An attempt is then made to choose a single value for the rate constant k such that all the sets of corresponding values of x and t satisfy equation (4). If this attempt is successful, the experiment is then repeated at the same temperature but with different initial concentrations (a_0 and b_0) of A and B. If and only if these new data also satisfy equation (4) with the rate constant k unchanged, the demonstration that the reaction obeys the rate equations (3) and (4) is complete. The constant, k, is thus independent of the initial concentrations of A and B; it is, however, a function of the temperature and it depends of course

FIG. 3.—SUCCESSIVE FIRST ORDER REACTIONS, WHERE THE RATE CONSTANT OF THE SECOND IS FOUR TIMES AS GREAT AS THAT OF THE FIRST (DIAZOTIZATION OF PHENYL MERCURIC NITRATE IN 20% HNO₃ WITH 0.16 M/1 HNO₂)

---

[1] For reactions in the gas phase, the partial pressure of each gas is used as a measure of its concentration.

[2] Where $a_0 = b_0$, the corresponding equation is $\frac{x}{a_0(a_0 - x)} = kt$ (4')

upon the chemical nature of the reactants A and B. Fig. 1 is a graphical representation of equation (4) for the saponification of ethyl acetate.

If the equations for various chemical reactions are treated as was equation (3) for reaction (2′), then these reactions fall into a number of different classes. A reaction, the rate of which may be described by an equation of the form

$$v = k(A) \qquad (5)$$

is called a first order reaction; one described by an equation of the form

$$v = k(A)^2 \quad \text{or} \quad v = k(A)(B) \qquad (6) \text{ or } (6')$$

is called a second order reaction, etc. In general, a reaction the rate of which may be described by the equation

$$v = k(A)^m(B)^n(C)^p(D)^q \ldots \ldots \qquad (7)$$

is called a reaction of order r, where $r = m + n + p + q +$ .... Such a reaction is said to be of order m with respect to A, of order n with respect to B, etc. (Some reactions may be of nonintegral order; e.g., half-order. The majority of known reactions are of first or second order.)

In certain reactions, such as the inversion of cane sugar,

$$C_{12}H_{22}O_{11} + H_2O \longrightarrow 2C_6H_{12}O_6 \qquad (8)$$

the rate is proportional to the concentration of some substance (in this instance, the hydronium ion of the acid) (see Acids and Bases), which does not appear among either the reactants or the reaction products in the chemical equation; the reaction cited (equation [8]) is said to be catalyzed by hydronium ion H_3O^+, or hydrated hydrogen ion.

$$v = k(C_{12}H_{22}O_{11})(H_3O^+) \qquad (9)$$

If the catalyst is one of the reaction products, the reaction is said to be autocatalyzed.

Reversible Reactions.—The reactions hitherto described have been assumed to be irreversible, in the sense defined above. If the reaction between the compounds A and B, on the one hand, and C and D, on the other, is reversible, then equation (2) must be rewritten.

$$A + B \rightleftharpoons C + D \qquad (2'')$$

Wherever equation (2″) represents the true kinetic course of the reactions, the rates v_f of the "forward" and v_r of the "reverse" reactions are given by equations (10) and (10′).

$$v_f = k_f(A)(B) \qquad (10)$$
$$v_r = k_r(C)(D) \qquad (10')$$

If the reaction is begun by mixing A and B (either pure or in solution), the initial concentrations of C and D are each zero; hence the rate, v_r, of the reverse reaction is also zero. However, as A and B react to form C and D, these products in turn react to regenerate A and B. The net rate at which C and D are formed is therefore the difference between v_f and v_r.

$$v = v_f - v_r = k_f(A)(B) - k_r(C)(D) \qquad (11)$$

The net rates of the forward and reverse reactions for a particular case are shown graphically in fig. 2. In the reaction in question, a mixture of the two tautomers (see Isomerism: Tautomerism) of bromonitrocamphor is formed both from the normal (N) and from the pseudo (P) isomer. The rate at which the equilibrium mixture is formed from pure N is shown in the upper curve; the rate at which the equilibrium mixture is formed from pure P is shown in the lower curve.

As the latter reaction proceeds, P is converted into N; hence, the forward rate decreases and the reverse rate increases. Eventually, the two rates become equal, and the net rate, v, is zero; thus, a dynamic equilibrium is achieved. This state of dynamic equilibrium is not a condition in which no reaction occurs, but is

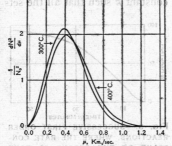

FIG. 4A.—MAXWELL-BOLTZMANN DISTRIBUTION OF PAIRS OF MOLECULES OF HYDROGEN IODIDE (AT 300° C. AND AT 400° C.). THE VELOCITY OF ONE MEMBER OF ANY PAIR RELATIVE TO THE OTHER MEMBER OF THE PAIR IS μ

one in which the rates of the forward and reverse reactions are equal. This kinetic concept of dynamic equilibrium has been experimentally verified by the use of radioactive tracers (see Isotopes).

When, for a reaction which follows equation (2″), the forward and reverse reactions proceed at equal rates, it is seen that

$$v_f = v_r = k_f(A)(B) = k_r(C)(D) \qquad (12)$$

From equation (12) it follows that

$$\frac{(C)(D)}{(A)(B)} = \frac{k_f}{k_r} = K_e \qquad (13)$$

where K_e, the ratio of the rate constants for the forward and reverse reactions, is called the equilibrium constant. Equation (13) gives the relative concentrations of the compounds A, B, C, and D at equilibrium; these concentrations need not be even approximately equal, for in general the rate constants of the forward and reverse reactions differ considerably from one another.

An equation analogous to (13) but more general is obtained by a parallel treatment of a reaction (7). Although this more general expression is correct as a first approximation, it nevertheless disagrees with the precise thermodynamic definition of equilibrium. Consideration of this and similar difficulties is postponed to the sections on collision theory and on activated-complex theory.

Complex Reactions.—The reactions so far considered are of simple types; all sorts of combinations of these types are possible. For example, reactions sometimes occur in several steps.

$$A \longrightarrow B \longrightarrow C \qquad (14)$$

Here the rate of formation of B is proportional to the concentration of A, and the rate of formation of C is proportional to the concentration of B. Since, initially, the concentration of B is zero, the initial rate of formation of C is zero. Fig. 3 shows graphically the concentration of C at any time, t, in a system where the rate constants for the two consecutive reaction steps are of comparable magnitude. Other cases of interest are those in which one of the successive reactions is reversible, or of second order, etc. Considerable complexity is not only possible but common.

What has already been said makes it evident that the kinetic equation for a reaction cannot be inferred from the chemical equation, which gives only the relationship between the weights of reactants which will combine with one another and the weights of the final products (i.e., the stoichiometric relations). The kinetic expression, it is true, must account for the stoichiometric findings, but it should do more than that. Usually more than one reaction path between the initial reactants and the final products is conceivable. Under favourable conditions kinetic considerations permit the selection of just one of these reaction paths, and kinetic measurements demonstrate that the path selected, and no other, is the one which the reaction takes. Under less favourable conditions, kinetic considerations are insufficient to eliminate all reaction paths but one. Even here, however, they serve to rule out many of those paths which from mere stoichiometric considerations might be considered possible.

A simple example will illustrate the ideas just expressed. A chemist might investigate an irreversible reaction, the stoichiometric expression for which is $A \rightarrow C$. This expression means that each molecule of the reactant A is converted (eventually) into one molecule of the product, C. It does not tell whether each molecule of A is converted directly into a molecule of C or whether each molecule of A is converted first into a molecule of an intermediate, B, which is in turn converted into a molecule of C. In the former instance, the proper kinetic expression for the reaction $A \rightarrow C$ may coincide with the stoichiometric expression. In the latter instance, the proper kinetic expression is $A \rightarrow B \rightarrow C$. Measurements of the extent of the reaction at various stages in its course are often sufficient to decide questions of the kind here raised. In the particular instance cited, if the reaction followed a curve of the sort shown in fig. 3, that fact would show that the kinetic expression for the reaction was $A \rightarrow B \rightarrow C$. If, on the other hand, the reaction followed a curve predicted from equation (5), and somewhat resembling the one shown in fig. 1, that fact would show that the kinetic expression for the reaction was $A \rightarrow C$, coinciding with the stoichiometric expression.

This fact alone would not rule out compound B as an intermediate, but it could be an intermediate in the reaction only under certain special circumstances (*i.e.*, the reaction B → C would have to be very fast as compared with the reaction A → B).

If any individual reaction is to be thoroughly understood, its reaction kinetics must be investigated. The object in view is to determine by inference from the kinetic measurements whether the reaction proceeds in one or more stages, to determine the order of each reaction stage with respect to each one of the reactants, and to determine for each particular stage whether or not it is catalyzed by some substance (possibly an ion) which does not appear in the stoichiometric expression for the over-all reaction. It should, however, be stated that kinetic considerations by themselves, although they greatly aid in the treatment of the problem stated, are often insufficient for its solution in all details.

If a kinetic study shows that two molecules (of the same or of different compounds) react with one another directly, then the reaction is said to be bimolecular. In a many-stage reaction, some individual step may be bimolecular, although the over-all reaction is not of second order and may indeed (like [14]) be of no definite order. It is likewise possible for a reaction to be of the second order, but to contain no single step which is truly bimolecular. The interpretation of the reaction kinetics for any individual reaction is thus a difficult matter, and for many important reactions the conclusions are still tentative.

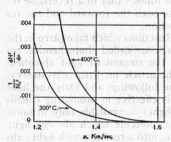

FIG. 4B.—EXPANDED SCALE DRAWING OF HIGH-VELOCITY END OF FIG. 4A

Application of the Kinetic Molecular Theory.—Guldberg and Waage assumed that the rate of any reaction is proportional to the product of the concentrations of the reactants (equation [7]); they interpreted this hypothesis in terms of the kinetic molecular theory. The number of collisions between the molecules of compound A and the molecules of compound B is proportional to the product (A)(B) of their concentrations; Guldberg and Waage's law amounts then to a statement that molecules react only if they collide, and that the rate at which they react is proportional to the number of collisions per second.

But although reaction between two molecules cannot occur unless these molecules collide, it does not follow that reaction must occur every time two molecules collide, even though these are molecules of substances which can react chemically one with another. For most reactions, it has been fully determined that the vast majority of collisions are "elastic"; *i.e.*, that the molecules rebound from one another without chemical reaction. It is possible by means of the kinetic molecular theory to compute the number of collisions per second between the molecules of two compounds which are present in a solution or a gas in known concentrations. For example, the number of collisions between pairs of molecules of hydrogen iodide at a temperature of 320° C. and a total pressure of one atmosphere is approximately 10^{28} per cubic centimetre per second. Under the conditions stated, there are only about 10^{19} molecules of hydrogen iodide in a cubic centimetre of gas. Hence, if every collision between two molecules of hydrogen iodide led to chemical change, the reaction would be over in a small fraction of a second, too short a time indeed to measure. It has been computed that in the system described, only one collision in about 10^{15} leads to chemical change.

Temperature Coefficients of Reaction Rates.—Another (and historically older) consideration leading to the conclusion that not all collisions cause reaction is based on the increase of reaction rates with increase in temperature. According to kinetic-molecular theory, the number of collisions between molecules of two compounds present at definite concentrations increases as the square root of the absolute temperature. For example, the number of collisions at 25° C. (298° absolute) is only about 1.5% greater than the number at 15° C. (288° absolute). But the rates

of most reactions increase by a factor of two or more when the temperature is raised by 10° C.; as much material may react in an hour at 100° C. as in a year at 0° C. In some instances, such as the denaturation of egg albumin, the reaction rate increases one hundredfold when the temperature is raised 10° C.

However, the assumption that only those molecules which collide with high energy of impact react with one another not only furnishes an explanation for the high temperature coefficients of reaction rates, but also accounts for the fact that collisions effective in bringing about chemical change are usually rare. To bring out the connection between the assumption and the conclusions, it is necessary to consider the velocity of one molecule relative to another. This relative velocity is not the same for all colliding pairs, but there is a determinable probability that for any one particular pair the relative velocity will lie close to any chosen value, *u*, of the relative velocity. This probability is calculated from the Maxwell-Boltzmann distribution curve (*see* KINETIC THEORY OF MATTER) shown in figs. 4a and 4b for hydrogen iodide at 300° C. and 400° C. The horizontal co-ordinate represents the velocity, μ, in km./sec., of one molecule of hydrogen iodide relative to the one with which it collides; the vertical co-ordinate represents the probability that the relative velocity is μ. (More precisely, the ordinate is equal to $1/N_0 \cdot d(N^2)/d\mu$, where N_0 is the total number of molecules under consideration, and $d(N^2)$ is the number of pairs of molecules with velocity lying between μ and $\mu + d\mu$.) Fig. 4b is an enlargement in vertical scale of part of fig. 4a. Figs. 4a and 4b indicate (1) that only a minute number of molecular pairs have relative velocities in excess of the 2.4 km./sec. required for reaction (*see* above), and (2) that, although the average value of the relative velocity is not greatly increased by raising the temperature from 300° C. (573° absolute) to 400° C. (673° absolute), the number of molecular pairs with high relative velocities is increased by a large factor. Thus the assumption that reaction is limited to molecular pairs with high relative velocities at the moment of collision qualitatively explains both the fact that few collisions are "effective" in producing reaction and the fact that the rates of most chemical reactions increase sharply with increase in temperature.

The complete equation (24) for the reaction rate derived from the kinetic collision theory is given in the next to last section of this article. Here it is sufficient to say that this complete equation is consistent (within experimental error) with an empirical equation (15) advanced by Svante August Arrhenius in 1889 which has proved useful.

$$\log_e \frac{k_2}{k_1} = \frac{Q}{R}\left(\frac{1}{T_1} - \frac{1}{T_2}\right) \tag{15}$$

In equation (15) k_1 and k_2 are the rate constants at the absolute temperatures T_1 and T_2 respectively, Q is a constant called the activation energy, and R is the gas constant (1.98 cal./mole degree) ($\log_e$ refers to natural logarithms). The larger the value of Q, the more sensitive is the reaction rate to changes in temperature. Reactions with values of Q varying from less than 500 up to about 100,000 cal./mole have been discovered. Q divided by the number of molecules in a mole (Avagadro's number) is (roughly) equal to the relative kinetic energy of a molecular pair which is just sufficient to make the members of the pair react upon collision.

Reaction Mechanism.—In this section, it will be shown how reaction kinetics may be used to determine the path or mechanism of a somewhat puzzling reaction. The example chosen is the reaction in aqueous solution between acetone and bromine. Here the stoichiometric

$$CH_3COCH_3 + Br_2 \longrightarrow CH_3COCH_2Br + HBr \tag{16}$$

expression (16) is of the same form as equation (2). In 1904, however, A. Lapworth discovered that the rate of this reaction is proportional to the concentration of the acetone and of the hydrogen bromide (one of the reaction products) but independent of the concentration of the bromine and of all other substances known to be present in the system. The kinetic equation, therefore, is

$$v = k(CH_3COCH_3)(HBr) \tag{17}$$

These facts suggest the hypothesis that the acetone is slowly converted into some reactive intermediate by the action of the acid;

this reactive intermediate then combines rapidly with bromine. The hypothesis has more recently been elaborated as follows:

$$(CH_3)_2CO + H_3O^+ \rightleftharpoons (CH_3)_2COH^+ + H_2O \text{ ("steady state"} \quad (18)$$
$$\text{rapidly reached)}$$

$$(CH_3)_2COH^+ + H_2O \longrightarrow CH_3\underset{\underset{OH}{|}}{C} = CH_2 + H_3O^+ \text{ (slow reaction)} \quad (18')$$

$$CH_3\underset{\underset{OH}{|}}{C} = CH_2 + Br_2 \longrightarrow CH_3COCH_2Br + HBr \text{ (rapid reaction)} \quad (18'')$$

The proposed reaction between the catalyst and the acetone results in the transformation of the acetone into a reactive intermediate (the "enolic" modification of acetone; see ISOMERISM: *Tautomerism*), which subsequently reacts rapidly with bromine. The rate, v, of the entire reaction is equal to that for the slowest step in the process, namely reaction (18'). The kinetic equation for this step is

$$v = k'((CH_3)_2COH^+) \quad (19)$$

The concentration of water is essentially constant and does not enter into equation (19); its concentration can be included in the rate constant, k'. The ion $(CH_3)_2COH^+$ would be in equilibrium with the acetone and acid present in the solution if it were not for the reactions (18') and (18'') which slowly but essentially irreversibly remove some of this ion. The ion $(CH_3)_2COH^+$ is described as in pseudoequilibrium with acetone and acid, or as in a "steady state." The "steady state" concentration of the ion is given to a good approximation by the equilibrium expression

$$\frac{[(CH_3)_2COH^+]}{[(CH_3)_2CO][H_3O^+]} = K \quad (19')$$

When the theoretical equations (19) and (19') are combined, the experimentally verified kinetic equation (17) for the bromination of acetone is obtained; the rate constant k is the product of k' and K.

Not only does the mechanism presented in equations (18), (18') and (18'') agree with equation (17), but it will further explain many other facts. It is consistent, for example, with the observation that acetone reacts with chlorine, or with iodine at the same rate as it does with bromine. This is in accord with the proposed mechanism, since equation (18'), which does not involve the halogen at all, is postulated as the rate-determining step in the halogenation.

A more detailed investigation of the reaction has revealed that it is catalyzed not only by hydronium ion but also by molecules of un-ionized acids; it is also catalyzed by bases. The catalysis by un-ionized acid molecules can be accounted for by substituting equation (18''') for equation (18')

$$(CH_3)_2COH^+ + B \longrightarrow CH_3\underset{\underset{OH}{|}}{C} = CH_2 + BH^+ \quad (18''')$$

where B represents a molecule of any base. (The detailed mathematical analysis needed to prove the above statement, although beyond the scope of this article, is treated by L. P. Hammett in *Physical Organic Chemistry*.)

The proposed mechanism is thus consistent with a large and varied selection of quantitative kinetic evidence. This is a necessary condition, but not a sufficient one to establish the mechanism; it does, however, make the proposed mechanism quite probable.

Catalysis.—A catalyst is defined as a substance which increases the rate of a chemical reaction, but which can be recovered quantitatively and unchanged at the end of the reaction. There are many substances which (for specified reactions) approach this definition closely. Typical examples of homogeneous catalysis are the action of acids to increase the rate of hydrolysis ("inversion") of cane sugar, the action of bases to increase the rate of polymerization in the preparation of bakelite, the action of oxides of nitrogen in the chamber process for manufacturing sulphuric acid. Typical examples of heterogeneous catalysis are the action of finely divided iron to increase the rate at which nitrogen and hydrogen combine to form ammonia, the action of vanadium pentoxide to increase the rate at which sulphur dioxide and oxygen combine to form sulphur trioxide in the contact process for manufacturing sulphuric acid, and the action of finely divided nickel to increase the rate at which hydrogen combines with vegetable oils to form solid fats (*e.g.*, "Crisco"). (For a discussion of theory, manufacture and use of catalysts see CATALYSIS.)

Catalysts accelerate chemical reactions in various different ways. The bromination of acetone (cited above) illustrates one of the most common modes of action. Here the acid which in this case is the catalyst combines with one of the reactants (acetone) to form an intermediate chemical compound. Then, in a later step of the complex reaction, the catalyst is regenerated and so becomes available for further reaction. In this way the catalyst goes through a complete cycle, and a trace of catalyst increases the rate at which a large amount of material reacts.

It is interesting to note that a catalyst can increase the rate of a chemical reaction but cannot change its point of equilibrium. If this statement were not correct, it would be possible to construct a perpetual motion machine. Since perpetual motion is an impossibility (see THERMODYNAMICS), it follows that in a reversible reaction the catalyst must accelerate both the forward and the reverse rate and in the same proportion.

Photochemical Reactions.—Reactions which take place in the presence of light but not in the dark are called photochemical reactions; their rate depends upon the amount of light absorbed. This subject is treated fully in the article on PHOTOCHEMISTRY. The principles here needed are the following: (1) Only the light which is absorbed by the system is effective in promoting chemical change; (2) radiant energy (light) is available only in units called quanta (see LIGHT); (3) a molecule which absorbs light and is thereby activated (*i.e.*, enters into a reaction with light) absorbs one and only one light quantum (A. Einstein). Subsequently, the activated molecule may enter into other, more complicated chemical reactions.

Chain Reactions.—Hydrogen gas reacts with chlorine at room temperature provided that the mixture is illuminated; the reaction (except under special circumstances, see below) does not occur in the dark. The form of the equation for the chemical reaction

$$H_2 + Cl_2 \longrightarrow 2HCl \quad (20)$$

resembles that of the reaction for the formation of hydrogen iodide (reverse of equation 1); the kinetics of the two reactions are, however, quite different. The reaction between hydrogen and chlorine proceeds when visible light is used. Since light of this wave length is absorbed by chlorine, but not by hydrogen, it follows that chlorine is the reactant affected by the light. Measurements have shown that as many as 1,000,000 molecules of hydrogen chloride are produced for every light quantum absorbed. Evidently a very special mechanism must be postulated to account for this fact. It has been assumed (W. Nernst, M. Bodenstein) that, as an indirect or direct result of the illumination, the molecules of Cl_2 which absorb light quanta are dissociated into chlorine atoms (21). These atoms then react as shown in equations (21') and (21'').

$$Cl_2 \longrightarrow 2Cl \quad (21)$$
$$Cl + H_2 \longrightarrow HCl + H \quad (21')$$
$$H + Cl_2 \longrightarrow HCl + Cl \quad (21'')$$

Each chlorine atom obtained by the illumination reacts with a molecule of hydrogen to produce a molecule of hydrogen chloride and an atom of hydrogen (21'); the latter in turn reacts with a molecule of chlorine to produce another molecule of hydrogen chloride and to regenerate an atom of chlorine (21''). The cycle is then repeated. Reactions characterized by such cycles are called chain reactions. If there were no side reactions to destroy the intermediate hydrogen and chlorine atoms, then, in principle, one chlorine atom could convert all the hydrogen and chlorine in the system to hydrogen chloride. In fact, the chain length varies from a few units to a million, depending upon the experimental conditions. The chains are broken (or terminated) when the chlorine or hydrogen atoms are removed. There are several means of removing these reactive atoms. For example, oxygen combines with either chlorine or hydrogen atoms, and traces of oxygen are effective in decreasing the rate of the reaction in question. In this reaction then, oxygen acts as a negative catalyst, or an inhibitor, or a chain breaker. (These terms are not, however, exactly synonymous.) Another means of breaking the chain is the combination of hydrogen atoms and chlorine atoms present in the gas mixture to form hydrogen chloride. Such combination occurs on the walls of the vessel, or when a hydrogen atom and a chlorine atom, in what is called a three-body collision, collide simultaneously with some third particle (such as a chlorine molecule); interestingly, the combination does not occur when only a hydrogen and a chlorine atom collide. Such a combination independent of the wall or of any third particle would violate either the law of the conservation of momentum or the law of the conservation of energy, or both. (See MECHANICS.) The fact that no such combination is observed simply means that the molecular system in question obeys the laws of mechanics, as do the molecular systems in all similar reactions which have been carefully studied.

The validity of the proposed chain mechanism for the reaction between hydrogen and chlorine is supported (1) by the high photochemical yield of the reaction (i.e., the large amount of hydrogen chloride produced per quantum of light absorbed), (2) by the fact that kinetic equations based upon the chain mechanism adequately describe the reaction velocity and (3) by experiments showing that the reaction can be initiated in the dark by the introduction into the reaction mixture of hydrogen or chlorine atoms from some outside source. There is good reason to believe that hydrogen atoms are produced by an electric arc discharge in hydrogen gas, and that chlorine atoms are produced in the reaction between sodium vapour and chlorine. If the products from either of these reactions are rapidly introduced into a mixture of hydrogen and chlorine, the formation of hydrogen chloride is initiated.

Reaction kinetics has provided much evidence to show that many reactions either in the gas phase or in solution proceed by chain mechanisms.

Heterogeneous Reactions.—Heterogeneous reactions include the solution of solids in solvents, and the reverse process, the crystallization of solids from solution. The reaction of metals with acids and problems of corrosion are part of the subject of heterogeneous reactions. However, by far the majority of the research on heterogeneous reactions is devoted to heterogeneous catalysis (e.g., reactions between gases or liquids catalyzed by solids, etc.). For example, finely divided iron greatly accelerates the rate at which nitrogen and hydrogen unite to form ammonia. Recent studies have shown that iron adsorbs nitrogen in such a fashion as to activate it (by a reaction analogous to the formation of iron nitride); the hydrogen subsequently reacts with the adsorbed nitrogen. Although heterogeneous reactions of this sort are of considerable theoretical and practical interest (see ADSORPTION; CATALYSIS) the present article is devoted largely to a consideration of homogeneous reactions.

Enzymes.—Almost the earliest chemical reactions known are the fermentations by which sugar is converted to alcohol or vinegar (fermentation) or lactic acid (souring of milk). These and similar reactions occur in the presence of living organisms, such as yeasts, fungi, etc. In 1897 E. Buchner discovered that, in the fermentation of sugar, the function of the living yeast is to produce a catalyst for the reaction. He destroyed the yeast cells by grinding them with sand. The filtered juice, although it contained no living organisms, nevertheless rapidly converted sugar to alcohol. The complex organic catalysts produced by living cells are called enzymes; those so far investigated in detail have proved to be protein complexes.

The extensive investigation, largely by methods of reaction kinetics, of the fermentation of sugar has revealed the fact that the reaction is a complex one in which many enzymes take part. Active research is at present under way to elucidate the path of many enzymatic processes, and to determine if possible the detailed mechanisms by which enzymes function as catalysts.

There are enzymatic systems which convert starch into sugar and sugar into alcohol; others hydrolyze proteins into a mixture of amino acids; still others synthesize proteins in the body; such systems are responsible for the conversion (by a form of combustion) of sugar to carbon dioxide and water, with the liberation of energy. The accelerating effect of some of these enzyme systems is enormous. For example, one part of beef catalase can be de-

tected in 25,000,000 parts of water by the acceleration it produces in the decomposition of hydrogen peroxide. Since the mechanism of enzyme action is unknown, and since the kinetics of enzyme action differs considerably from the kinetics of reactions accelerated by ordinary catalysts, direct comparisons are difficult and likely to be inaccurate. As a rough first approximation, however, catalase is about 10,000 times as active a catalyst as is an equal weight of ferrous ion in catalyzing the decomposition of hydrogen peroxide, and urease is about 10,000 times as active (at 20° C. and in neutral solution) as is an equal weight of sodium hydroxide in accelerating the hydrolysis of urea.

Explosions.—Chemical explosions are rapid reactions which are strongly exothermic; that is to say, these reactions are very rapid ones which evolve large quantities of heat. The hot gases formed in the chemical reaction, or the air heated by the energy released, produce a region of high pressure near the site of the explosion. This region of high pressure travels outward through the air in the form of an explosion wave which usually causes much of the destruction resulting from the explosion (see COMBUSTION; EXPLOSIVES). It is of interest to inquire what are the necessary conditions, and what are the possible mechanisms for a reaction which consumes many pounds of material in (say) 10^{-5} seconds. There are two well-known types of mechanism for explosions: the chain branching mechanism and the thermal mechanism. The latter type was suggested by Van't Hoff, the former by N. N. Seminoff; examples of both types have been discovered.

The theory of the chain-branching mechanism is that, during the early stages of a chain reaction, more chains are initiated per unit time than are terminated. The most spectacular example of an explosion caused by chain branching is the fission of atomic nuclei, such as occurs in atomic bombs. Here the disintegration of a particular sort of uranium, U^{235} (or of plutonium) is initiated by neutrons, but, in the disintegration, neutrons are also produced. (See ATOMIC ENERGY; ISOTOPES; NUCLEUS.) If exactly one neutron were produced from each disintegrating nucleus of U^{235}, a chain reaction analogous to the reaction between hydrogen and chlorine would result. In fact, however, more than one neutron is produced by each nuclear disintegration; the average number is probably about two. An equation for the atomic disintegration is

$$U + n \longrightarrow I + Y + 2n \qquad (22)$$

where U, n, I and Y are the symbols for uranium, the neutron, iodine, and yttrium, respectively. (Other elements besides iodine and yttrium are also produced in the disintegration; the principles involved are, however, the same.) The faster the reaction proceeds, the more rapidly are neutrons produced and the more rapidly does the reaction rate increase. Since the disintegration of the uranium is accompanied by a large evolution of energy, the reaction is an explosion.

The second type of explosion mechanism is the thermal one. Most chemical reactions are carried out under conditions such that the heat evolved (or absorbed) by the reaction is taken away (or supplied) by the surrounding medium. If, however, a highly exothermic reaction is carried out under conditions such that the heat is not carried away by the surroundings, the reaction mixture must become hotter. At the more elevated temperature, the rate of the reaction is much greater; the rate of heat evolution, therefore, becomes much greater also, and the reaction mixture rapidly becomes still hotter. Such a reaction must necessarily lead to an explosion. The question whether a particular exothermic reaction will lead to an explosion is thus largely a question of the conditions under which the reaction is carried out. If the reaction can be made to proceed at such a rate that the heat lost to the surroundings per unit time is small compared with the heat input caused by the chemical reaction during the same interval, a thermal explosion ensues.

Reactions of Isotopes.—In general, the reaction rates of compounds which differ only in that they contain different isotopes of the same element are identical within experimental error. When, however, one of the lighter elements is involved, this need not be the fact. A compound which contains atoms of C^{14} (radioactive carbon) may react at a rate which differs appreciably (e.g., by 10%) from that of a compound identical except that it contains only normal carbon atoms. The rate of the reactions of compounds containing deuterium (heavy hydrogen) may, in certain cases, differ from those of the corresponding compounds of light hydrogen by a factor as large as eight. These large differences in rate, which may occur when a bond to a hydrogen atom is formed or broken, arise from an effect (zero-point vibrational energy) predicted by quantum mechanics (*q.v.*). Although a discussion of the theory of this effect is out of place here, the phenomenon is proving a most useful tool in investigations of reaction mechanisms.

The Collision Theory.—In the theory of reaction kinetics as so far presented, several difficulties have been noted. The present section is devoted to a discussion of these difficulties and the methods of avoiding them; a knowledge of physical chemistry on the part of the reader is assumed.

The ratio of the rates of a forward and of the corresponding reverse reactions gives an approximate expression for the equilibrium constant of the reaction in question, as shown for a special case by equation (13). In the more general case, an analogous treatment of the reaction

$$mA + nB + pC + \ldots \rightleftarrows gR + hS + iT + \ldots \quad (23)$$

leads to equation (24).

$$\frac{(R)^g(S)^h(T)^i \ldots}{(A)^m(B)^n(C)^p \ldots} = K_c \quad (24)$$

The ratio of concentrations on the left side of equation (24) is obtained even if the kinetic equation for the reaction is a complex one. For example, if the reaction is catalyzed, the catalyst concentration appears in the expression for the rate of both the forward and the reverse reaction; it thus cancels out in equation (24). Careful inspection shows that other possible complexities are likewise of no effect on K_c. But equation (24) is nevertheless not precisely correct. The true equilibrium expression (*see* THERMODYNAMICS) is defined in terms of the "activities," not the concentrations, of the reactants and reaction products. Although in dilute solutions the concentration of any substance closely approaches its activity, the two functions are by no means identical. (An analogous statement applies to gases at low pressure.) It is therefore clear that the law of Guldberg and Waage, although approximately correct, is not and cannot be uniformly valid.

The difficulty noted cannot be avoided by the assumption that reaction rates are proportional to activities rather than to concentrations; this assumption has been proved false by investigations of the rates of ionic reactions. The ratio of the activity of any substance to its concentration defines its activity coefficient. The activity coefficients of ions depend upon the ionic strength of the solution in which they occur (*see* SOLUTIONS, *Solutions of Electrolytes*). This ionic strength is a function of the concentrations and of the charges on all the ions present; in dilute solutions the activity coefficients of all ions decrease with increasing ionic strength. But the rates of reactions between two ions of like charge increase with increase of ionic strength; only for reactions between ions of opposite charge do the rates (like the activity coefficients) decrease with increasing ionic strength. Thus the rate of a reaction is not proportional to the "activities" of the reactants; it has already been shown that only as a first approximation is this rate proportional to the ionic concentrations.

The difficulty, at least insofar as ionic reactions are concerned, has been resolved by the assumption that reaction rates are proportional not to concentrations or activities, but to the number of collisions per second between the reacting ions. The number of collisions between charged particles should not be strictly proportional to the product of their concentrations. Let W be the ratio between the number of collisions among the reacting ions and the product of the ionic concentrations. Then, because of interionic effects, W should increase with increasing ionic strength for reactions between ions of like charge, and decrease with increasing ionic strength for reactions between ions of unlike charge. This predicted behaviour is in qualitative agreement with the anomaly in ionic reaction rates already cited.

J. A. Christiansen's calculation (1924) based on the theory of P. Debye and E. Hückel, accounts quantitatively for the observed rates of ionic reactions in dilute solution. Further, although the forward and reverse rates, taken separately, are not proportional to the activities of the reactants and reaction products, the expression obtained by setting equal the rates of the forward and reverse reactions (corrected to account for interionic effects) yields the thermodynamic equilibrium expression in terms of activities, not concentrations. How this happens is made clearer in the consideration (*see* below) of the activated-complex theory of reaction velocity. In general, it has been assumed that consideration of the actual number of collisions always leads to corrections for the law of Guldberg and Waage, such that the dynamic and thermodynamic equilibrium constants become equal.

It should be pointed out that interionic and other forces not only affect the change in the number of collisions with change in concentration; they also affect the actual number of collisions per unit time. Thus, in a reaction between two positively charged ions, forces of electrostatic repulsion lower the number of collisions far below that computed from the kinetic molecular theory. Furthermore, it is not true that every collision between reactant particles moving, relative to one another, with a velocity greater than the critical one, u_0, leads to chemical change. There must also be a definite orientation of the molecules with respect to one another at the moment of collision. This consideration holds especially for complex molecules, which may be capable of reacting only at one end. The collision theory is thus considerably less precise than may at first have appeared.

Application of kinetic molecular theory to a simple bimolecular reaction (*e.g.*, the decomposition of hydrogen iodide) leads to equation (25), which relates the rate constant, k, with u_0 the minimal velocity at collision, necessary for reaction:

$$k = \frac{4N^2d^2}{c^2}\sqrt{\frac{\pi kT}{m}}\left(1 + \frac{mu_0^2}{2kT}\right)e^{-mu_0^2/2kT} \quad (25)[8]$$

$$\frac{1}{\mu} = \frac{1}{m_1} + \frac{1}{m_2} \quad (26)$$

Here N molecules of effective diameter d and weight m are present at a concentration of c moles per litre and at an absolute temperature T. The symbol e is the base of the system of natural logarithms, and k is Boltzmann's constant, 1.38×10^{-16} ergs/degree. If the values of k are experimentally determined for a series of temperatures, the values of both u_0 (the minimal velocity of one molecule relative to another required for effective collisions) and of d (the effective diameter of the particles) can be determined. The difficulties previously discussed then appear as anomalously large or small values of d^2. That is to say, when the reacting particles attract each other, the cross sections of the molecules (proportional to d^2) which are "effective" for collisions, will be large compared to these cross sections as determined by other methods; conversely, when the particles repel one another, or when a preferred orientation is necessary for reaction, the "effective" cross section will be small. The latter condition holds (although not to a marked degree) for the hydrogen iodide reaction.

An alternative description of the reaction process may be obtained by computing a collision number on the basis of the best available estimates for molecular cross sections and by replacing equation (25) by (27), to which it is approximately equivalent.

$$k = PZe^{-Q/RT} \quad (27)$$

Here Z is the "normal" collision factor, P is the "probability" factor defined by equation (27), and Q is the activation energy which does not differ greatly from $\frac{1}{2}Mu_0^2$, where M is the molecular weight of the substance in question. The difficulties of the collision theory are then contained in the factor P, and the problem of obtaining precise agreement between theory and experiment is reduced to that of computing P correctly.

One additional aspect of collision theory deserves attention. Some reactions (as previously stated) are of the first order. Such reactions would seem to be independent of collisions. In what way can these reactions be correlated with collision theory? Some first-order reactions probably cannot be so correlated. The disintegration of radium is strictly of the first order; the rate of the

---

[8] If the two molecules which react are not identical, this expression must be somewhat modified. Among other modifications, the reduced mass μ replaces m. If the masses of the two molecules in question are m_1 and m_2, then the reduced mass μ is defined by equation (26).

reaction depends upon changes in the radium nucleus, which are unaffected by collisions of the molecule as a whole. But in ordinary chemical, as opposed to nuclear, reactions, the energy necessary for reaction is probably acquired by the decomposing molecule through previous collisions.

The Activated-Complex Theory.—An alternative general theory of reaction kinetics is formulated in terms of the so-called "activated complex." (S. A. Arrhenius, J. N. Brönsted, N. Bjerrum, H. Eyring). In this theory, it is assumed that all the reactants are in pseudoequilibrium with an activated complex, X,

$$mA + nB + pC + \ldots \rightleftharpoons X \longrightarrow \text{products} \qquad (28)$$

which in turn decomposes to give the reaction products. The activated complex X is not a true molecule; it is merely a stage in the process by which the reactants become the reaction products. Hence, the activated complex is not in true equilibrium with the reactants. The activated-complex theory, however, is founded on the assumption that the concentration of the activated complex may be computed just as if it were a real, stable chemical compound. The rate of reaction is then the product of the concentration of X multiplied by the rate at which it decomposes. This rate can be computed by the general methods of quantum mechanics (q.v.); it is the same for all activated complexes, regardless of the materials out of which they have been formed. For a reaction such as (23), the activated-complex theory leads to equation (29)

$$v = \kappa \frac{kT}{h} K^*(A)^m(B)^n(C)^p \ldots \frac{\gamma_A{}^m \gamma_B{}^n \gamma_C{}^p}{\gamma_X} \qquad (29)$$

where **k** is the Boltzmann constant, h is Planck's constant, K^* is the equilibrium constant for the formation of the activated complex (its decomposition into the reaction products being disregarded), and $\gamma_A, \gamma_B, \gamma_C, \ldots \gamma_X$ are respectively the activity coefficients of the reactants and of the activated complex. The constant κ is called the transmission coefficient; it is usually nearly unity. When the activated-complex theory is used to describe a reversible reaction, a distinction must be drawn between the activated complex formed from the reactants and that formed from the reaction products. The two complexes, although structurally the same, differ with respect to the materials from which they have been formed and into which they are decomposing. Unless the distinction in question is made, the theory is self-contradictory.

Equation (29) contains γ_X, the activity coefficient for the activated complex. Although this coefficient cannot be measured (since the activated complex is not a stable entity) it can be estimated for the complexes which occur in ionic reactions. The charge on the activated complex must be the sum of the charges on the reactants; furthermore, the charge on an ion, as a first approximation, determines its activity coefficient. Equation (29) correctly predicts the rates of ionic reactions; it leads to results identical with those obtained by Christiansen. Although in particular instances the collision theory may be more convenient to apply than is the activated complex theory, or vice versa, the two always lead to the same results; they are, in essence, two different languages in which the same phenomena may be described.

At equilibrium, the rates of the forward and reverse reactions are equal. When two rate expressions analogous to (29) are used, an equation (30) is obtained from which the activity coefficient of the activated complex and the transmission coefficients have been eliminated.

$$\frac{(R)^q(S)^h(T)^i \ldots (\gamma_R)^q(\gamma_S)^h(\gamma_T)^i \ldots}{(A)^m(B)^n(C)^p \ldots (\gamma_A)^m(\gamma_B)^n(\gamma_C)^p \ldots} = K \qquad (30)$$

Here K is the true thermodynamic equilibrium constant, expressed in terms of activities (concentrations multiplied by activity coefficients).

The pseudoequilibrium constant, K^*, of equation (29) is related to the free energy of activation, ΔF^*, the heat of activation ΔH^*, and the entropy of activation ΔS^*, by equation (31).

$$-RT \log_e K^* = \Delta F^* = \Delta H^* - T \Delta S^* \qquad (31)$$

The heat of activation, ΔH^*, corresponds roughly with the energy of activation, Q, of the collision theory; the entropy of activation, ΔS^*, may be roughly related to the logarithm of the "probability"

factor, P, of equation (27).

The thermodynamic concept of entropy has been interpreted, through statistical mechanics, in terms of molecular vibrations. Likewise, entropy of activation can often be interpreted in terms of the geometry and of the estimated vibrational frequencies of the activated complex.

The application of the activated-complex theory depends upon the computation of the pseudoequilibrium constant, K^*. Thus, the kinetic problem is replaced by a thermodynamic one, and all the powerful tools of thermodynamics and of statistical mechanics become immediately available for its solution. It is possible in principle (always) and in practice (occasionally) to calculate the rate of a chemical reaction without the use of any experimentally determined kinetic data. The difficulties reside principally in the selection of appropriate constants for the activated complex. For the reaction between a hydrogen atom and a hydrogen molecule (which has been investigated by the use of ortho- and parahydrogen and of deuterium), the absolute reaction rate has been computed by methods related to the activated-complex theory (E. Wigner). Most reactions are, however, too complex for complete mathematical solution by methods now known.

BIBLIOGRAPHY.—H. S. Taylor and S. Glasstone, *Treatise on Physical Chemistry* (1942); L. P. Hammett, *Physical Organic Chemistry* (1940); J. B. Sumner and G. F. Somers, *Chemistry and Methods of Enzymes* (1943); N. N. Semenov, *Chemical Kinetics and Chain Reactions* (Oxford, 1935); H. D. Smyth, *Atomic Energy for Military Purposes* (1945); C. N. Hinshelwood, *Kinetics of Chemical Change in Gaseous Systems* (Oxford, 1940); S. Glasstone, K. J. Laidler and H. Eyring, *The Theory of Rate Processes* (1941). (F. H. WR.)

READE, CHARLES (1814-1884), English novelist and dramatist, the son of an Oxfordshire squire, was born at Ipsden, Oxfordshire, on June 8, 1814. He entered Magdalen college, Oxford, proceeded B.A. in 1835, and became a fellow of his college. He was subsequently dean of arts, and vice-president of Magdalen college, taking his degree of D.C.L. in 1847. His name was entered at Lincoln's Inn in 1836; he was elected Vinerian fellow in 1842, and was called to the bar in 1843. He kept his fellowship at Magdalen all his life, but after taking his degree he spent the greater part of his time in London. He began as a dramatist, and it was his own wish that "dramatist" should stand first in the description on his tombstone.

His first comedy, *The Ladies' Battle*, appeared at the Olympic theatre in May 1851. It was followed by *Angelo* (1851), *A Village Tale* (1852), *The Lost Husband* (1852) and *Gold* (1853). But Reade's reputation was made by the two-act comedy, *Masks and Faces*, in which he collaborated with Tom Taylor. It was produced in Nov. 1852, and later was expanded into three acts. By the advice of the actress, Laura Seymour, he turned the play into a prose story which appeared in 1853 as *Peg Woffington* as did also *Christie Johnstone*, a study of Scottish fisher folk. In 1854 he produced, with Tom Taylor, *Two Loves and a Life* and *The King's Rival*; and, unaided, *The Courier of Lyons*—well known under its later title, *The Lyons Mail*—and *Peregrine Pickle*. In 1855 appeared *Art*, afterward known as *Nance Oldfield*.

He made his name as a novelist in 1856, when he published *It's Never Too Late to Mend*, a novel written with the purpose of reforming abuses in prison discipline and the treatment of criminals. Five minor novels followed in quick succession—*The Course of True Love Never Did Run Smooth* (1857), *Jack of All Trades* (1858), *The Autobiography of a Thief* (1858), *Love Me Little, Love Me Long* (1859), and *White Lies* (1860), dramatized as *The Double Marriage*. In 1861 his masterpiece, *The Cloister and the Hearth*, appeared, relating the adventures of the father of Erasmus. It is one of the finest historical novels in existence. Returning from the 15th century to modern English life, he produced another novel with a purpose, *Hard Cash* (1863), in which he directed attention to the abuses of private lunatic asylums. Three other novels "with a purpose" were *Foul Play* (1869), in which he exposed the iniquities of ship-knackers, and paved the way for the labours of Samuel Plimsoll; *Put Yourself in His Place* (1870), in which he grappled with the trade unions; and *A Woman-Hater* (1877), on the degrading conditions of village life. *The Wandering Heir* (1875), of which he also wrote a version for the stage, was suggested by the Tichborne trial.

Outside the line of these moral and occasional works Reade produced three elaborate studies of character—*Griffith Gaunt* (1866), *A Terrible Temptation* (1871), *A Simpleton* (1873). The first of these was in his own opinion the best of his novels. His greatest success as a dramatist attended his last attempt—*Drink*—an adaptation of Zola's *L'Assommoir*, produced in 1879. In that year his friend Laura Seymour, who had kept house for him since 1854, died. Reade's health failed from that time, and he died on April 11, 1884, leaving behind him a completed novel, *A Perilous Secret,* which showed no falling off in the arts of weaving a complicated plot and devising thrilling situations. Reade was an amateur of the violin, and among his works is an essay on Cremona violins with the title, *A Lost Art Revived.*

It was characteristic of Reade's open and combative nature that he admitted the public freely to the secrets of his method of composition. By his will he left his workshop and his accumulation of materials open for inspection for two years after his death. He had collected an enormous mass of materials for his study of human nature, from personal observation, from newspapers, books of travel, blue books of commissions of inquiry, and from miscellaneous reading. This vast documentation, and Reade's use of it, show him as a precursor of the school of Zola.

BIBLIOGRAPHY.—Charles L. Reade and Compton Reade, *Charles Reade, a Memoir,* 2 vol. (1887); A. C. Swinburne, *Miscellanies* (1886); John Coleman, *Charles Reade as I Knew Him* (1903); Walter C. Phillips, *Dickens, Reade and Collins, Sensation Novelists* (1919); M. Elwin, *Charles Reade* (London, 1931); J. F. Quinn, *Charles Reade: Social Crusader* (1946).

READING, RUFUS DANIEL ISAACS, 1ST MARQUESS OF (1860–1935), British statesman, was born on Oct. 10, 1860, in London, the second son of Joseph Isaacs, merchant. He was educated at University College school, London, and abroad. At the age of 16 he went to sea, his parents believing that the discipline would be good for him. A subsequent venture on the stock exchange was a failure. He then read for the bar and was called in 1887; his legal career was unbroken and successful.

He entered parliament as a Liberal Imperialist, winning a seat for his party at Reading in a by-election in 1904, which he retained until he went to the house of lords. His party had the highest opinion of him and he became attorney general in 1910, and in 1912 was given a seat in the cabinet, which no attorney general had held before. Then followed the great Marconi shares scandal, in which he and Lloyd George were alleged to be involved. The substance of the charge was that he had bought American Marconi shares, some of which he sold to Lloyd George, while the British Marconi company was contracting with the government. It was investigated by a committee of the house and his reputation was certainly vindicated. On Oct. 22, 1913, he was made lord chief justice, and in Jan. 1914 was created Baron Reading of Erleigh. In this office he distinguished himself by humanity in the conduct of criminal cases and by the establishment of the principle that the court of criminal appeal should act as a real court of revision, upsetting verdicts or reducing sentences even of the individual high court judges. He presided over the trial of Sir Roger Casement during World War I.

After the outbreak of the war in Aug. 1914, he assisted in the drafting and the administration of those measures which saved England from financial ruin. The most sensational of these was the granting of the British guarantee to the great accepting houses, to bills amounting to many hundred millions of pounds. In 1915 he was president of the Anglo-French Loan commission to the United States, where he succeeded in floating a great war loan. On June 26, 1916, he was created Viscount Reading of Erleigh.

In 1917 he was appointed high commissioner and special envoy to the United States, and in November of that year was created an earl. In 1918 he was appointed high commissioner and special ambassador at Washington.

Lord Reading's term as viceroy of India began in 1921. At that time he was faced immediately by four acute problems. First, the dyarchy system of the Montagu-Chelmsford Government of India act, devised as a step in advance toward complete self-government, was definitely rejected by the leaders of the united Hindu and Mohammedan educated population, who in the movement known as

Swaraj had resolved to make it unworkable. The second was the influence of Mahatma Gandhi, one of the most remarkable men of all time, who had inflamed millions of Indians to a boycott of the west by the east and a kind of gigantic movement of passive resistance, in which both British products and British government were to be alike rejected. The third was that the national temper of India had been aroused by prohibitions and indignities put upon Indians in other parts of the empire. The fourth, the story of the Punjab rebellion and the slaughter at Amritsar in 1919, with the support of Gen. Reginald Dyer's action there by the governing classes in England, had excited a feeling of such fierce resentment through the length and breadth of the peninsula as might have caused a general uprising. In dealing with the revolt against the dyarchy, he was compelled to imprison the two Mohammedan leaders, the brothers Ali. And although he was able to establish some kind of self-government in most of the local provinces and even something like friendly co-operation in the central legislative council, the constitution broke down in the Central Provinces and had to be suspended in Bengal, with a return to complete autocratic government. In the case of the boycott of the west the viceroy, after attempts at reconciliation with Gandhi, authorized his prosecution for inciting to mass civil disobedience.

Upon Lord Reading's return to England in April 1926 he was created a marquess, the first commoner to be so created since the duke of Wellington. He was secretary of state for foreign affairs, Aug.–Nov. 1931, in Ramsay MacDonald's national government. He died Dec. 30, 1935. (*See* INDIA: *History.*)

See Gerald Rufus Isaacs, 2nd marquess of Reading, *Rufus Isaacs, First Marquess of Reading* (London, 1942–45).

READING, a county and parliamentary borough and the county town of Berkshire, Eng., 38 mi. W. of London by road. Pop. (1951) 114,196. Area 14.2 sq.mi. Reading is an important junction of railways running west from London and south from the midlands, and the Kennet and Avon canal, to Bath and Bristol, and the Thames afford it connections by water. It lies on the Kennet river near where it joins the Thames. All the ancient churches are restored: Greyfriars church, formerly monastic, was completed early in the 14th century and after the dissolution of the monasteries served successively as a town hall, a workhouse and a jail, being restored to its proper use in 1864; St. Mary's was rebuilt in 1551 from the remains of a nunnery founded by Aelfthryth in expiation of the murder of her stepson Edward the Martyr; St. Laurence's is a Perpendicular building with Norman and Early English features; St. Giles's was much damaged during the siege of 1643 by the parliamentary forces and is almost wholly rebuilt. Public gardens occupy most of the site of the Benedictine abbey.

A University college was opened in 1892 and affiliated to Oxford; its success led to the gathering of an endowment fund and it became an independent university with a charter in 1926. Its researches into agriculture, horticulture and dairying are of special importance. The National Institute of Research in Dairying, established in 1912, is part of the university. At the grammar school, founded in 1485 and now occupying modern buildings, Archbishop Laud (a native of Reading) was educated. There is also a bluecoat school (1656) now just outside the borough at Sonning. The municipal museum, besides an art gallery and other exhibits, includes Roman relics from Silchester (*q.v.*) and finds from the Thames.

Reading early became a place of importance. In 871 the Danes encamped there, and in 1006 it was burned by Sweyn. It consisted of only 30 houses at the time of the Domesday survey. It is thought that a fortification existed there before the Conquest, and Stephen built a masonry castle which Henry II destroyed. On the foundation of a Benedictine abbey in 1121, the town, hitherto demesne of the crown, was granted to the abbey by Henry I. Henry VIII converted the abbey, whose church was among the largest in the country, into a palace and it was destroyed during the Civil War. From the 12th until the 16th century, Reading's history was that of the struggle as to rights and privileges between the abbey and the merchants' guild. A 16th-century account of the merchants' guild shows that many trades were then carried on, but John Leland says the town "chiefly stondith by clothing." By the 17th century the trade had begun to decline; the bequest of the clothier John Kendrick (d. 1624) did little to revive it, and it was greatly injured by the Civil War. In the 18th century the chief trade was in malt.

The first town charter is that of Henry III (1253), confirmed and amplified by succeeding sovereigns. The governing charter until 1835 was that of Charles I (1639), incorporating the town under the title of the mayor, aldermen and burgesses. The market, chiefly held on Saturday, can be traced to the reign of Henry III; four fairs granted by the charter of 1562 are still held.

Reading is an agricultural centre with famous nursery gardens. Its biggest and best-known industry is biscuit manufacture, but there is much business in printing, iron foundries, engineering works, malting and brewing. The sale of corn, cattle and flour is carried on extensively, and there are pottery and brick works, together with riverside boatbuilding yards. The parliamentary borough, which used to return two members before the Reform act of 1885, regained that privilege in 1948.

READING, a city of Hamilton county, O., U.S., on federal highway 52 and served by the Pennsylvania railroad; 12 mi. N. of Cincinnati. Population was 7,836 in 1950 and 6,079 in 1940. Reading was founded in 1797 and incorporated in 1851.

READING, a city of southeastern Pennsylvania, U.S., the county seat of Berks county; on the Schuylkill river, 58 mi. N.W. of Philadelphia. It is on federal highways 22, 222, 422 and 120; has a municipal airport; and is served by the Pennsylvania and the Reading railways, by Capital and Trans World air lines, motorbus and truck lines. Pop. (1950) 109,320; (1940) 110,568 by federal census. An unusually large proportion of the population are natives of the state, and the "Pennsylvania German" element predominates. The city occupies 9.5 sq.mi. on the east bank of the river, at an altitude ranging from 242 to 1,100 ft. To the east rises Mt. Penn (1,100 ft.) and to the south Neversink mountain (878 ft.). There are several summer hotels and sanatoria on the neighbouring hills. The city's parks and playgrounds cover 2,500 ac. Penn common (50 ac.) is a recreation ground in the heart of the city, reserved for the public when the town was laid out. On the eastern slope of Mt. Penn is a park of 1,200 ac., and a boulevard winds along the southern slope of the mountain to the pagoda on the summit, which commands a wide view of the surrounding country. Among the interesting landmarks in the environs are several colonial farmhouses, the Conrad Weiser farm and sites of early forts and iron furnaces.

The public-school system comprises continuation, evening and summer schools, in addition to the usual instruction from kindergarten through high school. Pennsylvania State college and the University of Pennsylvania maintain extension centres in Reading, and it is the seat of Albright college (Evangelical; 1856). The public library contains more than 100,000 volumes and has three branch stations; the county historical society has a building full of interesting exhibits; and the public museum and art gallery occupy a beautiful building completed in 1926. Among the displays in the museum is a fine collection of butterflies. The city supports a symphony orchestra. It is also noted for the cultivation of rare peonies and irises. There are two daily papers; weeklies published in Polish and Italian and one devoted to the interests of labour and socialism; and the monthly organ of the retail coal merchants of Pennsylvania.

Reading adopted a commission form of government in 1912. The city is the centre of Pennsylvania's first superpower system, which supplies electric current to the region extending from Harrisburg to eastern New Jersey. The water supply is filtered mountain water, stored in reservoirs with a capacity of 216,000,000 gal., and the city's daily consumption averages 20,000,000 gal. Reading has a large retail and wholesale trade, and is an important shipping point for agricultural produce. It is within a short haul of the anthracite fields, and also of some of the richest bituminous coal fields of the state. The classification yards of the Reading company are a vast distributing centre for anthracite shipments consigned to the east, west and south. There are about 700 manufacturing establishments in the city and its immediate suburbs, including the shops of the Reading railway and large plants producing hardware, brick, underwear, full-fashioned hosiery, glass doorknobs, goggles, optical goods, pretzels, children's shoes, narrow silk fabrics and certain kinds of hosiery-knitting machines and lacemaking machinery.

Reading was founded in 1748 by Thomas and Richard, sons of William Penn, and was named after the native city and shire of the Penns. It was incorporated as a borough in 1783, as a city in 1847. Though there were many Germans among the first settlers, the control of local affairs remained in the hands of the English colonists until the outbreak of the Revolutionary War, after which, as the English were largely loyalists, it passed to the Germans. In the French and Indian Wars Reading became a military base for a chain of forts along the Blue mountains. During the Revolution it was a depot of military supplies, and was the site of a prison camp in which the Hessians taken at the battle of Trenton were detained. This region was one of the first in America to manufacture iron and iron products. Cannon for use in the Revolution were made there, and Reading supplied much of the heavy ordnance used by the northern army in the Civil War. The first cooking stove made in America was cast in the Hereford furnace, 20 mi. E. of the city, in 1767. The industrial development of the town was greatly stimulated by the opening of the Schuylkill canal to Philadelphia in 1824 (abandoned in 1922), the Union canal to Lebanon and Middletown in 1828 (abandoned about 1880) and the Philadelphia and Reading railway in 1838. A company of Reading and Berks militiamen was the first unit to report to General Washington at Cambridge in response to the call for troops by the second continental congress; and the Ringgold light artillery (later known as "the First Defenders"), largely recruited from Reading and Berks county, was the first volunteer company to reach the national capital when Lincoln called for troops.

READING is the mental process of securing and reacting to an author's message represented by written or printed symbols. To read, one must recognize words, know the meaning of the words, understand the ideas expressed by the author, sense the mood and tone of the selection, evaluate the accuracy of the ideas and use or apply them.

Children in the primary grades usually learn to read simple materials. These abilities are expanded and refined in the middle and upper grades. Many high schools in the United States began to teach reading between 1930 and 1950 and a number of colleges initiated courses to improve reading. By the mid-1950s many adult education courses included reading improvement classes, and some industrial concerns were offering reading courses to their employees. It is recognized that one learns to read, then reads to learn, and that the growth of these two abilities continues from childhood into adulthood.

Stages in Learning to Read.—Studies show that pupils' attainments in reading at various grade levels differ widely. Some at the end of first grade may be reading as well as the average of those in third grade. By the fourth grade a few pupils are reading at first-grade level, others at second, several at third and many at fourth. In addition, a number will attain scores at fifth, several at sixth and a few at seventh and eighth grades. Arthur I. Gates pointed out that all pupils go through the same stages in learning to read, but that individuals vary in the rate at which they master successive stages. Usually the stages are not clear-cut, but each merges gradually into the next.

The first stage is called reading readiness, or preparation for learning to read. Much of this preparation takes place in the home, but kindergarten is also an effective aid. Pupils who are not judged ready to read usually have additional preparation in first grade. Mental, social, emotional and language maturity appropriate to the average pupil of six years is considered optimal. An interest in books and in printed words is usually exhibited at this time.

The second stage is that of learning to read. During this period, children learn to recognize about 300 words by sight. In addition, their interest in reading increases, and they become thoughtful about what is read. Gradually, as this stage progresses, children learn to read simple books independently.

During the third stage there is considerable progress in learning to do good oral reading and rapid silent reading which is fully understood. Sight vocabulary increases to 1,500–2,000 words. Concurrently, pupils learn the skills necessary to figure out independently the words in their speaking vocabulary. At this stage pupils begin to use reading as a tool in other school subjects, to satisfy their curiosity and for pleasure.

The fourth stage is characterized by the acquisition of more mature reading interests and tastes. During this period all of the previously learned abilities are refined and enhanced. Word recognition is gradually increased; knowledge of meanings is extended and precision of meaning is acquired. Understanding or ability to interpret grows as the reader secures a better background against which to evaluate what he reads. He is able to apply new knowledge acquired from his reading to assist him in adjusting his attitudes and behaviour. His reading interests become broader and, in worthwhile areas, more intensified. He begins to become what William S. Gray described as the mature reader.

Methods of Instruction.—One of the earlier methods of teaching reading in most parts of the western world was the so-called ABC method. Children first memorized the names of the letters. Then the letters were combined to form syllables and words. Words were combined to form sentences, and sentences to form paragraphs. Since saying the names of the letters in a word often bears little resemblance to the sound of the word when it is pronounced, learning was largely by memory and without much meaning. According to Nila B. Smith there was a vigorous protest against the ABC method between 1840 and 1850, although this method continued to be used long afterward.

However, experimentation turned in two directions. One involved learning words as units, since they have more meaning for young children than do letters. There were a staggering number of words for pupils to learn by sight without methods for attacking unfamiliar words. A second method developed in just the opposite direction. Instead of learning the names of letters, the sounds of the letters were taught. This was known as the phonetic method. Because some English letters have two or more sounds, a great deal more drill was required to learn all the combinations than was necessary in learning the names of the letters. However, the advantage of the phonetic method was that words could be built or dissected if the proper sounds were known. Several highly formalized phonetic systems were devised and used extensively.

Oral reading predominated during the early periods. Books were scarce and expensive, so reading was shared by many through listening. Early in the 20th century, scientific studies revealed that the processes of oral and silent reading were different. In the meantime, many educators criticized word calling which was done without a knowledge of the meanings expressed. Beginning about 1920, emphasis was placed on silent reading and oral reading was not considered important. Standardized tests of reading had been devised and were used to appraise growth in reading by different methods. Furthermore, studies of learning revealed that young children tend to grasp ideas or units as a whole and later to identify the elements composing the unit. Based on this concept, a different method became prevalent.

The experience method begins when all of the pupils have an experience which is interesting and exciting to them. For example, they may visit a farm or a park or a zoo. Then, as the children talk about this experience, the teacher prints their story on the blackboard. Pupils take turns in reading back to the class the story they have composed. Thus, meaning is emphasized to a greater extent, and the words are viewed as carriers of meaning. Additional experiences use many of the same words and some new ones. Gradually, the sentences are divided into phrases, and finally words per se are identified. After a sufficient number of words are learned in this fashion, children begin to read simple books called preprimers. New words are learned and pupils read their primers, first readers, etc. Subsequently, pupils are introduced to the most common sounds of the letters by being shown the similarity of familiar words which begin and end alike. In later stages, emphasis is placed on the phonetic elements and their application. The pupil is taught to guess what a new word might be to make sense in the story and then to check the sounds to be sure that he has identified the correct word. The names of the letters are learned in connection with spelling, and the order of the alphabet is learned when pupils must use the dictionary.

The experience method seems to appeal to children and most of them learn rapidly as soon as they are ready for this stage. If progress is not satisfactory, teachers may place greater emphasis on visual, auditory or kinaesthetic clues to words. The first reading experiences are oral but silent reading is taught as soon as possible.

Recognition of words is basic to the other skills in reading, but it is useless unless the meanings of words are known. Thus in effective teaching word meanings, often called vocabulary, are taught throughout school. Not only in the reading period is this true, but teachers of all subjects in which reading is used teach the meanings of unfamiliar words. Best results are achieved when children and young people have direct rather than incidental instruction in word meanings. However, independence must be developed as pupils progress in school so that they may continue to expand their reading vocabularies throughout life.

Comprehension and interpretation of printed and written materials are taught from the early school levels on through high school, and sometimes in college. At first the materials used are simple and within the realm of experience of the pupils. Gradually, the materials become more difficult, less familiar and even abstract. A variety of adaptations must be made. For example, in literature a student may read one selection to get the general idea; another to sense the mood and tone of the author; another to study the characters and plot; and poetry may be read orally for the beauty of the language. Thus, comprehension and interpretation may include reading to get the main idea, details, to follow directions, to arrive at conclusions, to interpret the author's ideas and feelings, to evaluate for accuracy or bias or for the appreciation of the literary expression and content.

As word recognition, word meanings and comprehension improve, rate of reading usually increases accordingly. The first-grade pupil reads silently and orally at about the same rate. By third grade the average pupil begins to read silently at a rate more rapid than when he reads orally. Rate of reading for the mature adult should vary with the difficulty of the material and the purpose for reading it. For example, a person might read a novel for sheer pleasure at 300 words per minute. The same person might read an article dealing with politics at 200 words per minute. A technical article on the atom bomb might be read at 100 words per minute. Thus, the mature reader has many reading rates.

Teachers encourage pupils to read large amounts of materials of interest to them and at an appropriate level of difficulty. Thus, children learn to read widely for information, to solve problems, and for pleasure. At the upper school levels, young people are guided, by teachers and librarians, to better literature, and to sources designed to help them solve their personal and social problems. It is the aim of schools and colleges to develop refined reading tastes, and permanent reading interests.

Reading Interests.—Many studies of reading interests have been made of school children, young people and adults. The results show certain trends. In the primary grades, children are usually interested in familiar experiences and enjoy stories about other children of their ages and about animals. They prefer narrative to other types of materials.

In the preadolescent period, the majority of boys exhibit an interest in adventure, descriptions of "how-to-do-it," hero worship, hobbies and science. At the same period, girls' interests turn toward home and family life and fantasy and some interest is shown in adventure. It is significant that girls will often choose boys' books while boys do not like girls' books. Near the end of this period most pupils do more free reading than at any time in their school careers.

Adolescent boys are interested in reading about mysteries, sports and recreational activities. On the other hand, girls frequently turn to romance and stories of teen-age problems. The reading interests of adults are varied and complex. Douglas Waples and Ralph W. Tyler concluded that "international attitudes and problems" and "personal hygiene" were the only two topics of interest to all the groups they studied. Otherwise, the reading interests of adults vary with sex, years of schooling, occupation, age and environment. Ease of securing reading materials is also related to interests. Newspapers and magazines are read more frequently than books.

Effects of Reading.—The emphasis on teaching and use of reading reflects the confidence that reading contributes to personal and social development, either positively or negatively. The widespread concern about reading crime and thrill comic books about the middle of the 20th century bears witness to the negative effects assigned to reading. On the positive side, studies summarized by William S. Gray revealed that reading influences the extent and accuracy of information, the attitudes, morale, beliefs, judgments and actions of readers.

Bibliotherapy, which is the personal interaction between the reader and literature, has been shown to be one method of therapy for some maladjusted persons. Librarians report progress in the adjustment of young people when books dealing with adolescent tasks are read and discussed.

Propaganda in reading materials has been shown to be an effective tool unless people learn to think critically about what they read and to evaluate sources carefully.

Reading Retardation.—Some pupils who grow physically and mentally at the same rate as their age mates make little or no progress in learning to read. Others move through one or more stages of growth and do not progress to the next stage. Such persons are known as retarded readers. Causes for reading retardation include visual difficulties, emotional disturbances, home and family problems, school methods improperly adapted to individuals and, in a few instances, other factors, according to Helen M. Robinson. In most cases, an examination of the retarded reader by a reading specialist results in charting a course for correcting the difficulty. Reading clinics or centres are staffed by persons especially qualified to prescribe and carry out the kind of instruction which results in adequate reading progress. In general, the methods are similar to those used to teach all children, but special adaptations are made for each learner.

Retarded readers are found in elementary schools, high schools, colleges and in adult life. While most of them are retarded in all aspects of reading, some have deficiencies in specific areas such as comprehension or rate of reading.

About the middle 1930s Guy T. Buswell and others demonstrated that many adults could increase their rates of reading without loss of comprehension. A widespread interest in rate improvement followed. Several manufacturers made instruments designed to increase reading rate. Practice has shown the value of the instruments when used wisely with the proper persons.

It seems quite likely that most adults can learn to read better and more rapidly if they want to do so. Reading is best improved by motivated practice with a purpose in mind and a strong desire to secure the information available on the printed page. There is no substitute for a teacher and for books.

BIBLIOGRAPHY.—Nila B. Smith, *American Reading Instruction* (New York, 1934); Arthur I. Gates, *Teaching Reading* (Washington, D.C., 1953); William S. Gray, "Nature of Mature Reading" in *Promoting Maximal Reading Growth Among Able Learners*, p. 11–15, Supplementary Educational Monographs no. 81 (Chicago, 1954), "The Social Effects of Reading," *School Review*, lv, pp. 269–277 (May, 1947);

Douglas Waples and Ralph W. Tyler, *What People Want to Read About* (Chicago, Cambridge, 1931); Helen M. Robinson, *Why Pupils Fail in Reading* (Chicago, Cambridge, 1946); Guy T. Buswell, *Remedial Reading at the College and Adult Levels,* Supplementary Educational Monographs no. 50, (Chicago, 1939).   (H. M. Rn.)

READYMONEY, SIR COWASJI JEHANGIR (1812–1878), "the Peabody of Bombay," belonged to a family descended from Parsee merchants of the early 18th century who had adopted their nickname of "Readymoney" as a surname. At the age of 15 he entered the firm of Duncan, Gibb & Co. as "gowdown keeper" or warehouse clerk. In 1846 he began trading on his own account. He was made a J.P. for the town and island of Bombay, and a member of the board of conservancy, and in 1866 was appointed a commissioner of income tax. He was made C.S.I. in 1871, and in 1872 K.B. His donations to the institutions of Bombay amounted to close to £200,000.

See J. Cowasji Jehangir, *Sir Cowasji Jehangir Readymoney* (1890).

REAGAN, JOHN HENNINGER (1818–1905), U.S. politician, was born in Sevier county, Tenn., on Oct. 8, 1818. He moved to Texas in 1839, was admitted to the bar in 1846, and in 1857–61 was a representative in congress. His political views were determined by the ultrademocratic influence of Andrew Jackson and the state-sovereignty philosophy of John C. Calhoun. In 1861 he was appointed postmaster general in Pres. Jefferson Davis' cabinet, and served in this capacity throughout the Civil War. He was captured with the Davis party on May 10, 1865, and was imprisoned in Ft. Warren, Boston harbour, until the following October. While in prison he wrote the "Fort Warren letter" (Aug. 11), in which he urged the people of Texas to recognize their defeat, grant civil rights to the freedmen and try to conciliate the North. From 1875 to 1887, when he entered the U.S. senate, he was again a representative in congress. In 1891, believing that his first duty was to his state, he resigned from the senate to accept the chairmanship of the newly established state railway commission. In 1901 he retired from public service. He died at Palestine, Tex., on March 6, 1905.

See his *Memoirs; With Special Reference to Secession and the Civil War,* ed. by W. F. McCaleb (1906).

REALGAR, a mineral species consisting of arsenic monosulphide, AsS, and occurring as monoclinic crystals of a bright red colour. There is a perfect cleavage parallel to the plane of symmetry; hardness is 1.5–2, specific gravity 3.55. On exposure to light the crystals crumble to a yellow powder. The mineral usually occurs with ores of silver and lead in mineral veins. Realgar has been used as a pigment and in pyrotechny for producing a brilliant white fire; but it is now replaced by the artificially prepared compound. The other native arsenic sulphide, As_2S_3, is known as orpiment.   (L. J. S.)

REALISM, a philosophical term used in two opposite senses. The older of these is the scholastic doctrine that universals have a more "real" existence than things. Universals are, in scholastic language, *ante res, in rebus* and *post res.* In the most extreme form realism denies that anything exists in any sense except universals. It is opposed to nominalism (*q.v.*) and conceptualism (*q.v.*). For the history of the doctrine, *see* SCHOLASTICISM. In this sense, realism has been called "an assertion of the rights of the subject," and some part of the teaching of Socrates concerns itself with the scholastic doctrine of realism. The modern application of the term is to the opposing doctrine that there is a reality apart from its presentation to consciousness. In this sense it is opposed to idealism (*q.v.*), whether the purely subjective or that more comprehensive idealism which makes subject and object mutually interdependent. In its crude form it is known as "Natural" or "Naïve" Realism. It appears, however, in more complex forms, *e.g.*, as Ideal Realism (or Real Idealism), which combines epistemological idealism with realism in metaphysics. Again, Kant distinguishes "empirical" realism, which maintains the existence of things in space independent of consciousness, from "transcendental" realism, which ascribes absolute reality to time and space. (*See* PHILOSOPHY, HISTORY OF.)

In literature and art "realism" again is opposed to "idealism" in various senses. The realist is (1) he who deliberately declines to select his subjects from the beautiful or harmonious, and, more especially, describes ugly things and brings out details of an unsavoury sort; (2) he who deals with individuals, not types; (3) most properly, he who strives to represent the facts exactly as they are.

REALITY: *see* LOGIC; ONTOLOGY.

REAL PRESENCE: *see* TRANSUBSTANTIATION and EUCHARIST.

REAL PROPERTY AND CONVEYANCING: *see* LAWS OF REAL PROPERTY AND CONVEYANCING.

REAPING, the cutting of ripe grain, began as soon as prehistoric man grew crops. By the Late Stone Age his rudimentary sickle consisted of three saw-toothed flint blades set in a straight wooden shaft about 2 ft. long. Among artifacts of Europe and England are curved flint knives whose shape suggests that they were sickles or reaping hooks. Bronze sickles of various shapes were also common among later remains. The tomb paintings (*c.* 1400 B.C.) at Thebes, Egypt, include the oldest pictorial record of reaping. This painting shows that the grain was either cut low, a handful at a time, and then bound into sheaves or pulled up by the roots and the heads stripped off with a hackle. The Egyptian sickles were made of bronze or iron. The early form consisted of a slightly curved blade fastened at one end to a straight handle; a later type had a serrated blade shaped more nearly like a modern sickle.

Although variants of the Egyptian sickle were used by the Babylonians, Assyrians, Hebrews, Greeks and Romans, the latter were the first to develop the two-handed scythe, which they used only for mowing. Varro described three ways of reaping in his *Rerum rusticarum* (37 B.C.): the grain was cut close to the ground with a sickle and bound in sheaves; it was cut halfway down the stalk and laid in a swath; or the heads were stripped from the stalks leaving the straw standing. A special device, the header, was used for this operation.

Both Pliny and Palladius described the header as a Gallic invention, consisting of a two-wheeled cart with a saw-toothed blade set across the open front. As an ox pushed the cart, the teeth adjusted to the height of the grain stripped the heads from the stalks, and they fell into the cart. The straw was cut later. The header was important as the first of a long series of attempts to lessen the labour and time involved in reaping.

Throughout the middle ages reaping continued to be done with sickle and scythe, but both implements were improved in design and material. An intermediate form, the Hainault scythe, was a Flemish invention. It was a wide blade about 2 ft. long attached to a short handle. Although more efficient than a sickle, it was surpassed by the later forms of the scythe. The most important improvement in the scythe was the addition of the cradle to lay the cut grain in a swath. Although the date of origin is unknown, Thomas Tusser mentioned a barley cradle in 1557. The colonists brought the cradle to America, where it reached its ultimate form—a frame of five tapering wooden fingers paralleling the blade and attached to the snath of the scythe. With a cradle, grain could be cut much faster than with the sickle, so that reaping with the sickle was finally abandoned. However, the sickle and scythe are still used on small, hilly fields throughout the world.

The modern reaper was developed gradually and simultaneously on both sides of the Atlantic. In Europe there was no progress until a deliberate attempt was made to stimulate agricultural inventions. The demand for grain grew with increased population, and agriculture had to compete with industry for labour. Consequently there was an increasing need for machinery to replace the disappearing migratory harvest hands. At the same time rural labour was deeply prejudiced against reapers. In America, where there had always been a labour shortage, the development of the great wheat-growing areas depended on the invention of a satisfactory mechanical reaper, and the U.S. Civil War hastened its adoption because the drain of manpower to the army made mechanical reaping imperative.

English Contributions.—When the London Society of Arts offered a gold medal for the introduction of a reaping machine in 1780, Capel Lofft brought forth Pliny's and Palladius' accounts of the Gallic header and suggested certain improvements in the simple mechanism. Following this same idea, William Pitt of Pendeford, Eng., in 1786 constructed a header with a revolving cylinder armed with rows of teeth that caught the heads and dropped them into the box of the machine. Like its Roman prototype, Pitt's machine was pushed through the grain. The header, however, was a failure, and nothing further was done with the design in England.

The first English patent for a reaper was taken out by Joseph Boyce in 1799. His machine had a revolving knife protected by guards but no reel and no device for laying the cut grain in gavels or in a swath. As invention followed invention, first one feature and then another was tried, so that a shear-action cutter, elementary dividers and fingers, a simple reel, a platform consisting of an endless apron with rollers, a main wheel to support the weight of the machine, and pulling instead of pushing had all been experimented with before Henry Ogle constructed his reaper in 1822. It was drawn from the front and side and carried on two main wheels. The cutter consisted of a straight-edged knife blade. The reel, resembling the modern form, pushed the grain back upon a platform behind the cutter. The platform was hinged so that it could be tilted and serve as a dropper. Although Ogle's machine never became popular, his principle of the cutter and reel was adopted in all subsequent successful designs.

In 1826 Patrick Bell, a Scottish minister, invented a reaper with a shear-action cutter. Twelve movable blades about 15 in. long and 4 in. wide at the base, fastened on pivots, moved back and forth over 13 stationary blades of about the same size and produced a clipping movement like that of shears. The cut grain fell upon an endless apron that carried it to the side and deposited it in a continuous swath. The model had a reel and dividers and was pushed, not pulled. Bell's reaper remained the most important English contribution but received little attention until U.S. designs were taken to England in 1851.

U.S. Contributions.—Although the first U.S. patent was granted in 1803, no machine of any importance was patented until 1822, when Jeremiah Bailey brought out a model that was both mower and reaper. The revolving cutter was shaped like a low-crowned hat, the knife being the edge of the brim. A shoe regulated the distance of the knife from the ground and was the first indication of the principle of a flexible bar. The next invention worthy of mention was that of William Manning in 1831. His cutter bar, made up of spear-shaped cutters sharpened on both edges, reciprocated over guard teeth 6 in.–8 in. long. The machine also had a divider, the first on record in America. Manning's cutter anticipated the designs used by Hussey and Mc-Cormick. Obed Hussey and Cyrus H. McCormick experimented with their reapers simultaneously, but McCormick had his at work by 1831. Hussey, however, was the first to secure a patent—on Dec. 31, 1833. Hussey's machine was fairly simple in construction. Back of the two ground wheels and to the side was the platform supported by a roller. The cutter, original in design, had slotted fingers or guards about 8 in. long fixed solidly to the front edge of the platform. Through these vibrated a number of flat triangular knives riveted to an iron bar, thus forming a coarse-toothed saw.

McCormick's machine, patented the next year, was more complicated and not so well built. A single drive wheel furnished the power for the reciprocating knife. The knife, about 4½ ft. long with a smooth or serrated edge, oscillated through wires designed to act as fingers to hold the grain. Behind this was a platform 5 ft.–6 ft. long made of thin plank from which the cut grain was raked by a man walking behind the machine. A cloth-covered frame served as a divider to separate the cut from the uncut grain. A revolving reel, 6 ft.–7 ft. in diameter and as long as the knife, was fastened over the cutter. The cutters in both these machines represented the new element added to reaper design. Neither functioned very well at first as they had a tendency to clog, but subsequent improvements obviated this difficulty. In 1851 both men sent models to England, where their performance was acclaimed. As soon as a successful reaper had appeared on the market, inventors turned their attention to providing an automatic device that would deliver the cut grain in a form suitable for binding; thus the self-rake and the dropper were next added to the reaper. From 1850 to 1870 the self-raking reaper held the field, but by the middle 1870s the self-rakes in turn were being replaced by harvesters.

The main difference between harvesters and reapers is that the former include special mechanisms to handle and bind the cut grain into sheaves or bundles ready to be set up in shocks. The early attempts to produce machines that would bind as well as reap were very crude, and the actual binding with straw, wire or twine still had to be done by hand. C. W. and W. W. Marsh patented the first successful harvester in 1858. A canvas delivered the cut grain over the drive wheel to a box from which it was taken and bound by two men riding on the machine. This change in design set the pattern for future harvesters. However, a successful binding mechanism was still lacking. Because twine was very expensive, the first binders used wire, but the farmers and millers complained so much about the damage to cattle and machinery that these binders never became popular. John F. Appleby made a successful twine binder in 1858, but it was not put on the market until 1880, when the price of twine was sufficiently low to make its use economical. Thus the McCormick cutting principle, the Marsh frame and the Appleby binder were combined to produce the successful modern harvester.

The header, also belonging to the harvester class, was developed in the United States, Canada and Australia, where the weather permits grain to stand a considerable time after ripening. As early as 1844, George Esterly patented a header that worked very well, and a few were manufactured. The following year in Australia a header was invented that cut and threshed the grain in one operation. The Haines Illinois harvester, patented in 1849, was widely used in the United States until it was replaced by better types of harvesters. Combined harvesters and threshers are used wherever the threshed grain is dry enough to store. On large wheat farms a huge combine can head, thresh, separate and sack the grain from 60 ac. to 125 ac. per day, or about 1,700 bu. to 3,000 bu. Before tractors were available these combines were propelled either by steam engines or horses. For smaller farms in the Great Plains of the United States, the "baby" combine, cutting a 5-ft. or 6-ft. swath and operated by one man, was introduced in 1935. By the 1940s a "midget" combine, cutting only a 40-in. swath, was being used by small farmers to lower harvest costs. (*See also* HARVESTING MACHINERY.)

BIBLIOGRAPHY.—R. L. Ardrey, *American Agricultural Implements* (1894); Merritt Finley Miller, "The Evolution of Reaping Machines," U.S. Department of Agriculture, Office of Experiment Stations *Bulletin* 103 (1902); William T. Hutchinson, *Cyrus Hall McCormick* (New York, 1930–35); Leo Rogin, *The Introduction of Farm Machinery in Its Relation to the Productivity of Labor* (Berkeley, Calif., 1931).
(H. L. E.)

REAR VAULT, in architecture, a vault supporting the thickness of the wall inside a window or door opening, usually with a splayed or sloped surface, and often laid out upon a different curve from that of the arch over the window or door itself. In Gothic architecture, especially in England, the rear vault is usually decorated at its inner edge by a projecting rib known as a scoinson rib, which is itself often supported by colonnettes known as scoinson shafts, at the inner edges of the opening.

RÉAUMUR, RENÉ ANTOINE FERCHAULT DE

(1683–1757), French scientist, was born on Feb. 28, 1683, at La Rochelle, where he received his early education. In 1703 he came to Paris, where he continued the study of mathematics and physics, and in 1708 was elected a member of the Académie des Sciences. In 1710 he was charged with the official description of the useful arts and manufactures of France, which led him to many practical researches that resulted in the establishment of new manufactures and the revival of neglected industries. For discoveries regarding iron and steel he was awarded a pension of 12,000 livres; but he requested that the money should be secured to the Académie des Sciences for the furtherance of experiments on improved industrial processes. In 1735 family arrangements obliged him to accept the post of commander and intendant of the royal and military order of Saint-Louis; he discharged his duties with scrupulous attention, but declined the emoluments. Réaumur died at La Bermondière, Maine, on Oct. 17, 1757. He bequeathed his manuscripts, which filled 138 portfolios, and his natural history collections to the Académie des Sciences.

Réaumur's papers deal with nearly all branches of science. He examined and reported on the auriferous rivers, the turquoise mines, the forests and the fossil beds of France. He devised the method of tinning iron that is still employed, and investigated the chemical differences between iron and steel. His book on this subject (1722) was translated into English and German. The thermometric scale by which he is now best remembered was constructed on the principle of taking the freezing-point of water as 0°, and graduating the tube of the thermometer into degrees each of which was one-thousandth of the volume contained by the bulb and tube up

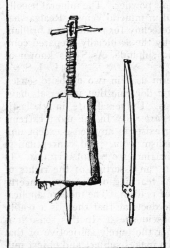

AN ARABIAN REBAB AND BOW

to the zero mark. It was an accident dependent on the coefficient of expansion of the particular quality of alcohol employed which made the boiling-point of water 80° R.; and mercurial thermometers the stems of which are graduated into eighty equal parts between the freezing- and boiling-points of water are Réaumur thermometers in name only. Réaumur wrote widely on natural history, his best known work on this subject being the *Mémoires pour servir à l'histoire des insectes* (6 vols., 1734–42).

REBAB or **RABAB,** an ancient stringed instrument, sometimes plucked and sometimes played with a bow, having a body either pear-shaped or boat-shaped and the characteristics of vaulted back and the absence of neck; also a generic modern Arabic term applied by the Mohammedans of northern Africa to various stringed instruments played with a bow. The rebab exercised a very considerable influence on the history of stringed instruments in Europe, and was undoubtedly the means through which the bow was introduced to the West, though whether it may be accepted as the ancestor of the violin, as is held by some, is another matter. The bowed instruments of the middle ages fall naturally into two distinct classes, according to the principles observed in construction. One is the type having a body formed on the model of a Greek or a Roman cithara, with back and sound board connected by ribs, from which it was evolved by the addition of a neck and finger-board (*see* GUITAR and GUITAR FIDDLE). The other is the type derived from the Eastern rebab, with vaulted back attached directly to the sound board, which has never attained to any serious artistic development.

For the European development of the rebab, *see* REBEC.

REBATES, DEFERRED. A deferred rebate is a discount on the invoice price returned after a lapse of time to a trader, on certain conditions, as a means of maintaining monopoly and keeping out would-be competitors from the trade. The system is in use in many branches of British trade and industry. It consists in returning to the trader (merchant or retailer) at the end of every six or 12 months a rebate equal to perhaps 10 or 15% on his purchases, on condition that he shall not, during the period, have sold, displayed (or, it may be, offered) any of the kind of goods produced by the combination except those made by the combination. The effect of the arrangement is that if at any time during that period the customer is offered an article of better value by an outside maker or by a new firm starting in the industry, the buying of that article will cost him anything from one to 12 months' accumulated rebates on his association purchases and may result in his being placed on the association's "black list," which means that he shall not again be supplied with association goods except at prices which will yield an insufficient profit on resale. The reasons advanced by combinations for the use of the deferred rebate are not altogether reasons of monopoly. They contend that steadiness and continuity of custom are essential to economical manufacture; that by maintaining an even level of prices (which, as the market fluctuates, may be temporarily under-profitable as sometimes over-profitable) they are serving the best interest of the customer; and that these mutual advantages cannot be secured if the customer is left free to trade with the combination when its prices are below average, and go elsewhere when they are above. The most notable example of the use of the deferred rebate is to be found in the case of the shipping companies operating liner services, where the fluctuating competition of the "tramp" and the great importance of securing a steady volume of freights if a regular service is to be maintained lend particular weight to the arguments quoted above. In the manufacturing industries there is less agreement among members of combinations as to the advantage of the deferred rebate, and instances have occurred of the system being voluntarily abandoned. (J. H.)

REBEC or **REBECK,** a mediaeval stringed instrument played with a bow, derived from the Oriental rebab, and sometimes regarded as the ancestor of the viol and violin. Like the rebab (*q.v.*), the rebec assumed at first one of two forms—the pear-shaped body with a wide base, strung with three strings, or the long, narrow pear- or boat-shaped body with two strings and, in addition, the other Oriental characteristics of the rebab, *i.e.,* the vaulted back, the absence of ribs, and pegs set in the back of the head. Except for the addition of a fingerboard, what is now recognized as the rebec underwent no structural development and never entered the domain of art, despite the wide favour which it enjoyed throughout the middle ages.

REBECCA RIOTS, the name given to some disturbances which occurred in 1843 in South Wales. The rioting was directed against the charges at the toll-gates on the public roads, and the rioters took as their motto the words in Gen. xxiv. 60, "And they blessed Rebekah, and said unto her, Thou art our sister, be thou the mother of thousands of millions, and let thy seed possess the gate of those which hate them." Many of the rioters were disguised as women and were on horseback; each band was led by a captain called "Rebecca," his followers being known as "her daughters." They destroyed not only the gates but also the toll-houses, the work being carried out suddenly and at night, but usually without violence to the toll-keepers, who were allowed to depart with their belongings. Emboldened by success, the Rebec-caites turned their attention to other grievances. The govern-

ment despatched soldiers and police to south Wales, and the disorder was quelled. South Wales was relieved from the burden of toll-gates, while the few rioters who were captured were only lightly punished. The movement was separate from Chartism (*q.v.*), but was supported by the same class and arose from the same economic causes.

REBELLION, the act of one who engages in armed resistance to the government to which he owes allegiance. For instance the supporters of the Old Pretender in 1715 and of the Young Pretender in 1745 were regarded and punished as rebels. In the American Civil War of secession, the Federal Government continued for two years to regard the Confederates as rebels although they had been recognized as belligerents by neutral states. And in the South African War of 1899–1902 it was held by the Supreme Court of the Cape of Good Hope that rebels who joined the Burgher forces, and thus committed high treason, remained liable to be punished for criminal offences, although the Burghers had been recognized as belligerents; *Rex* v. *Louw* 21 C. G. H. Supreme Court Rep. 36 (1905). *See* LAWS OF WAR.

REBIKOV, VLADIMIR (1866–1920), Russian composer, was born at Krasnoyarsk in 1866, and studied in Moscow, Berlin and Vienna. He then went to live at Odessa, where, in 1894, his first opera, *The Thunderstorm,* was produced. Other dramatic works are *The Christmas Tree* (1903); *Narcissus, The Fables of Krylov* (his best-known work); *Prince Charming,* a fairy opera; and the pantomime *Snow-White* (1909). He also wrote suites for pianoforte, including the *Mélomimiques,* and mimetic vocal pieces. His music makes no appeal to the popular mind, and is difficult to grasp because of its harshness and lack of form. Rebikov's literary work includes a translation of Gevaert's *Traité d'Instrumentation* (1899) and *La musique de 1960.*

REBOUX, PAUL (1877–   ), French author, was born in Paris on May 23, 1877. Editor of several Paris newspapers, *Le Journal, Paris Soir,* etc., and a well-known broadcaster, his chief novels were: *Liszt ou les amours romantiques* (1940), *Le Phare* (1907) and *Trio* (1924). His historical romances, *Lady Hamilton, Marie Stuart, Meyerling* (1948), *Louis XIV* and *La Grande Catherine,* are successful reconstitutions of atmosphere and period. As an essayist, Reboux became known for a mixture of humour and sound information, for example, *Le Nouveau Savoir-vivre* (Monaco, 1930). His books on gastronomy include *Savoir-manger* and *Plats nouveaux* (1927); books on medical subjects include *Sens interdit, Trop d'enfants* (1951) and *Tuberculeux, on ne veut pas vous guérir* (1952). One of his most popular works is *A la manière de,* a series of satirical imitations of well-known literary works, begun in collaboration with Charles Müller in 1908 and continued by Reboux after Müller's death in action (1914); a volume was published in 1951.

REBUS, a sort of riddle consisting of the representation of some sentence or thing by means of pictures or words, or a combination of both. Rebuses first became popular in France, where they were at first called *rébus de Picardie,* that province, according to G. Ménage (1613–92), having been the scene of their origin. Camden mentions an instance of this kind of wit in a gallant who expressed his love to a woman named Rose Hill by painting in the border of his gown a rose, a hill, an eye, a loaf, and a well; this, in the style of the rebus, reads "Rose Hill I love well." A specimen of a modern rebus is given here, the solution of which is: "Be independent but not too independent" (B in D pendant, butt knot 2 in D pendant).

FROM "WORLD'S BEST WORD PUZZLES"

SPECIMEN REBUS, SOLUTION OF WHICH IS GIVEN IN THE TEXT

The name is also applied to arrangements of words in which the position of the several vocables is to be taken into account in divining the meaning. Thus "I understand you undertake to overthrow my undertaking" makes the rebus

Stand	take	to	taking
I	you	throw	my.

A simple French rebus is expressed by the two letters G a, which may be read, *J'ai grand appétit* (G grand, a petit).

"Rebus" (or "allusive arms"), in heraldry (*q.v.*), is a coat of arms which bears an allusion to the name of the person—as three castles for Castleton, three cups for Butler.

Ben Jonson happily ridiculed this kind of wit in his description of Abel Drugger's device in the *Alchemist.*

RECALL, a device by which the voters may remove an official from office before the expiration of his regular term. It is based upon the principle that officials are properly mere agents of the popular will, and as such should be constantly subject to their control. Under the plan, if a specified percentage of the electorate are dissatisfied with an official's conduct and sign a petition for his removal, the officer must face a general election to determine the majority opinion.

Like the initiative and referendum the recall originated in Switzerland where it is applicable not only to individuals but to the entire legislature. In the United States where its widest use is now found, it first appeared in 1903 in the city charter of Los Angeles. It was soon adopted by many cities with the commission form of government as the most effective way to control the commissioners into whose hands such large powers were put. It was first adopted with State-wide application in Oregon in 1908, followed by California in 1911, Arizona, Idaho, Washington, Colorado and Nevada in 1912, Michigan in 1913, Louisiana, North Dakota and Kansas in 1914. Most of these were States with a large number of elective officers, who, since they were not subject to removal by the governor, were, in effect, beyond control during their term of office. In one State, Kansas, the recall extends to appointed as well as elected officials. In four of the eleven, Idaho, Louisiana, Michigan and Washington, it is not applicable to judges on the ground that the judiciary should be independent of popular passions and political issues.

Though the general principle of the recall is simple, there are many variations in its practical application, which considerably alter its effect. For instance under some plans the question of removal may be decided in one election, and the question of a successor in a subsequent election. For economy's sake the two are often combined into one election in which the official whose conduct is under question may stand as a candidate if he desires. In the latter case the question of his record is evidently complicated by the element of his comparative popularity. The vote required to remove an official may be a simple majority or a higher percentage. The percentage of signatures required to force an election ranges widely, the average being about 25%; and the methods by which it is permissible to secure signatures may vary sufficiently to affect the result. The recall has, in fact, been but seldom resorted to and then almost entirely for local officers. Only twice has it found State application, notably in North Dakota in 1921 when the governor, attorney-general and commissioner of agriculture were removed. Only a few instances of its being applied to judges are on record, all of them in minor courts. In its State-wide application it becomes too cumbersome to be frequently resorted to. Its chief value is perhaps not to be measured by the frequency with which it is applied, but by the restraining influence which its existence may exercise.

See W. E. Rappard, "Initiative, Referendum and Recall in Switzerland," *Annals of the Amer. Acad. of Political and Social Science* (Sept. 1912); W. B. Munro, *The Initiative, Referendum and Recall* (1912); J. D. Barnett, *Operation of the Initiative, Referendum and Recall in Oregon* (1915). The argument against the recall of judges is presented by W. H. Taft in his veto of the enabling act for the admission of Arizona, whose Constitution allowed such a recall (*House Ex. Doc. No. 106*, 62nd Cong. 1st Sess.).

RÉCAMIER, JEANNE FRANÇOISE JULIE ADÉLAÏDE (1777–1849), a famous Frenchwoman in the literary and political circles of the early 19th century, was born on Dec. 4, 1777, at Lyons. Her maiden name was Bernard. She was married at fifteen to the banker Jacques Récamier (d. 1830), who was more than old enough to be her father. From the early days of the consulate to almost the end of the July monarchy her salon in Paris was one of the chief resorts of literary and political society that pretended to fashion. The *habitués* of her house included many former royalists, with others, such as Bernadotte and General Moreau, more or less disaffected to the government. Through her friend Madame de Staël, Madame Récamier became acquainted with Benjamin Constant (*q.v.*). She was eventually exiled from Paris by Napoleon's orders. After a short stay at Lyons she proceeded to Rome, and finally to Naples, where she was on good terms with Murat and his wife, who were then intriguing with

the Bourbons. She persuaded Constant to plead the claims of Murat in a memorandum addressed to the congress of Vienna, and also induced him definitely to oppose Napoleon during the Hundred Days. Her husband had sustained heavy losses in 1805, and she visited Madame de Staël at Coppet in Switzerland. In her later days she lost most of the rest of her fortune; but she continued to receive visitors at the Abbaye-aux-Bois, the old Paris convent to which she retired in 1814. Here Chateaubriand was a constant visitor, and in a manner master of the house; but even in old age, ill-health and reduced circumstances Madame Récamier never lost her attraction. She numbered among her admirers Mathieu de Montmorency, Lucien Bonaparte, Prince Augustus of Prussia, Ballanche, J. J. Ampère and Constant, but none of them obtained over her so great an influence as did Chateaubriand, though she suffered much from his imperious temper. Her sincerest affection seems to have been for Prosper de Barante, whom she met at Coppet. She died in Paris on May 11, 1849.

There are well-known portraits of her by Louis David in the galleries of the Louvre, and by François Gérard in the possession of the préfecture of the Seine. In 1859 *Souvenirs et correspondances tirés des papiers de Madame Récamier,* was edited by Mme. Lenormant. *See* Mme. Lenormant's *Madame Récamier, les amis de sa jeunesse et sa correspondance intime* (1872); Mme. Mohl, *Madame Récamier,* with a sketch of the history of society in France (1829 and 1862); also Guizot in the *Revue des deux mondes* for December 1859 and February 1873; H. Noel Williams, *Madame Récamier and her Friends* (London, 1901); E. Herriot (Eng. trans., by Alys Hallard), *Madame Récamier et ses amis* (1904) (elaborate and exhaustive); L. de Launay, *Un amoureux de Madame Récamier; journal de J. J. Ampère* (1927).

RECANATI, a city of the Marches, Italy, in the province of Macerata, 8 mi. direct N.N.E. of the city of that name. Pop. (1936) 5,354 (town); 16,823 (commune). It has a station on the railway $17\frac{1}{2}$ mi. S. of Ancona, and distant $4\frac{1}{2}$ mi. from the town, which is built on a hill, 931 ft. above the sea. It was the birthplace of the poet Leopardi (1798–1837). It possesses a Gothic cathedral, built towards the close of the 14th century and dedicated to S. Flavianus, patriarch of Constantinople. The churches of S. Maria dei Mercanti and San Domenico contain pictures by Lorenzo Lotto, as also does the municipal palace, with a fine old battlemented tower, while the palace of Cardinal Venier has a fine Renaissance portico by Giuliano da Maiano. The help given the popes in their struggles with the Sforza caused the decline of the city which suffered from an earthquake in 1741 and from wars (1797–99).

RECEIPT, in law, an acknowledgment in writing that a sum of money or other valuable consideration has been received by the person signing the acknowledgment in discharge of a debt or other obligation. Such a receipt is *prima facie* evidence of payment. By the Stamp Act of 1891 a duty of 1d. was imposed on every receipt or form of writing discharging a debt of £2 or upwards; the payment of the duty is denoted by affixing a stamp to the document, and the cancelling of the same by the person giving the receipt. By s. 103 if a person gives a receipt, liable to duty, not duly stamped, or refuses to give a receipt, liable to duty, duly stamped or, on payment to the amount of £2 or upward, gives a receipt for a less sum than £2 or divides the amount paid with intent to evade the duty, he is liable to a fine of £10. A receipt not duly stamped may be stamped at the Inland Revenue Office within 14 days on payment of a fine of £5 or within one month on payment of £10. By the Finance Act of 1920 the receipt stamp was increased to 2d.

American Law.—There are no stamp duties on receipts in the United States. On the effect of a receipt in full, given against payment of less than the amount due, see *Discharge.* On receipts for goods given by transportation or storage agencies see *Bill of Lading, Warehouse Receipt.* The commercial practice of a debtor requiring a receipt on paying a debt has, curiously, no warrant in law except in particular cases: a debtor paying a negotiable instrument (*see* BILL OF EXCHANGE) is entitled to have it surrendered to him, which serves as a receipt; and a mortgagor paying off a mortgage is entitled to receive from the mortgagee a "satisfaction piece" which serves as evidence that the obligation and the mortgage are discharged. In other cases, in general, the debtor's assurance of procuring a receipt rests partly on business custom, partly on the creditor's practical desire to collect his debt and on his willingness to accept payment by check, which will then serve as a receipt.

RECEIVER, in English and American law, a person appointed by a court to administer property for its protection, to receive rent or other income and to pay authorized outgoings. Receivers may be either appointed *pendente lite* or by way of equitable execution, *e.g.*, for the purpose of enabling a judgment creditor to obtain payment of his debt, when the position of the real estate is such that ordinary execution will not reach it. Formerly receivers were appointed only by the court of chancery, but by the Judicature Act of 1873 it is now within the power of all divisions of the High Court to appoint receivers. Their powers and their duties are set forth by Kerr, *On Receivers* (5th ed., 1905), who classifies the cases in which they may be appointed under the following heads: (*a*) infants; (*b*) executors and trustees; (*c*) pending litigation as to probate; (*d*) mortgagor and mortgagee; (*e*) debtor and creditor; (*f*) public companies; (*g*) vendor and purchaser; (*h*) covenanter and covenantee; (*i*) tenant for life and remainderman; (*j*) partners; (*k*) lunacy; (*l*) tenants in common; (*m*) possession under legal title, and (*n*) other cases. The appointment of receivers is entirely within the discretion of the courts. In bankruptcy practice a receiver, termed official receiver, is an officer of the court who in this capacity takes possession of all a debtor's assets. In the United States the appointment of receivers lies within the jurisdiction of courts that are invested with equity powers and in exercise of their equity jurisdiction. Under statutes in many States the power to appoint receivers has been extended to actions at law in various types of cases. (*See* BANKRUPTCY.)

RECEIVING: *see* LARCENY.

RECEIVING SET, the equipment that reproduces speech, music, visible messages or signals from radio waves. (*See* RADIO; RADIO RECEIVER; TELEVISION.)

RECHABITES or **SONS OF RECHAB,** a sort of religious order among the Israelites, analogous to the NAZARITES (*q.v.*), with whom they shared the rule of abstinence from wine. They eschewed settled life, and lived in tents, refusing to sow grain or plant vineyards. They represented a protest against the contemporary civilization and a reaction towards simplicity of life. Their "father," or founder, was that Jehonadab (or Jonadab) son of Rechab, who encouraged Jehu to abolish the Tyrian Baalworship (2 Kings x.). The "house of Rechab" fled for protection into Jerusalem at the approach of Nebuchadrezzar (Jer. xxxv.), and Jeremiah promised them, as a reward of their adherence to the ordinance of Jehonadab, that they should never lack a man to represent them (as a priest) before Yahweh. Later Jewish tradition states that the Rechabites intermarried with the Levites.

RECHBERG-ROTHENLÖWEN, JOHANN BERNHARD, COUNT (1806–1899), Austrian statesman, was the second son of the Bavarian statesman Count Aloys von Rechberg-Rothenlöwen (1766–1849). Johann Bernhard was destined for the Bavarian public service, and he was educated at the universities of Strasbourg and Munich, but incurred the displeasure of King Louis I. by the part he played as second in a duel, and in 1828 transferred to the Austrian diplomatic service. After being attached to the embassies in Berlin, London and Brussels, he was appointed envoy at Stockholm (1841) and at Rio de Janeiro (1843). Returning to Europe in 1847, on the outbreak of the revolution of 1848 in Vienna he accompanied and assisted Prince Metternich in his flight to England. In July 1848 he was appointed Austrian plenipotentiary in the German federal diet at Frankfort, and in 1851 became Austrian *internuncius* at Constantinople, and in 1853 Radetzky's civilian colleague in the government of Lombardo-Venetia. In 1855 he returned to Frankfort as Austrian representative and president of the federal diet. Here his constant disputes with Bismarck, at that time Prussian envoy at the diet, were much sharpened by Rechberg's choleric temper, and on one occasion nearly led to a duel. Bismarck, however, always expressed a high appreciation of his character and abilities. In May 1859, on the eve of the war with Italy, he was appointed Austrian minister of foreign affairs and minister president, surrendering the latter post to the archduke Rainer next year.

The five years during which Rechberg held the portfolio of foreign affairs covered the war with Italy and France, the insurrection in Poland, the attempted reform of the German Confederation through the Frankfort *Fürstentag*, and the Austro-Prussian war with Denmark. Their story is told elsewhere. (*See* AUSTRIA, EMPIRE OF; EUROPE.) In the German question Rechberg's policy was one of compromise, and he generally advocated peaceful arrangement between Prussia and Austria as the indispensable preliminary to a reform of the Confederation. In the Schleswig-Holstein question he was, however, consistently outwitted by Bismarck, and on Oct. 27, 1864, Rechberg resigned. He received the Golden Fleece from the emperor as a sign of special favour. He had been made an hereditary member of the Upper House of the *Reichsrat* in 1861, and as late as 1879 continued occasionally to take part in debates. He died at his Kettenhof near Vienna on Feb. 26, 1899.

See the biography by Franz Ilwof in *Allgemeine Deutsche Biographie*, B. 53. *Nachträge* (Leipzig, 1907).

RECIDIVISM, a disposition or tendency to relapse into crime. While such a disposition may not be a matter of habit but the consequence of mental disorder or congenital defect, the term recidivist is, in criminology, usually employed interchangeably with "habitual offender" (*q.v.*).

RECIFE or PERNAMBUCO, a city and seaport of Brazil, capital of the state of Pernambuco, in 8° 3′ S. and 34° 51′ W., near the easternmost point of South America. The *municipio* of Recife, which is divided into two *distritos* and has an area of 60 sq.mi., had a population of 534,468 in 1950. The city had a population of 522,466.

At the mouth of the Capibaribe river, the city is comprised of four separate parts (Recife, Santo Antonio, São José and Boa Vista) which are integrated by numerous bridges.

The district of Recife occupies the southern end of the Olinda peninsula and is the principal commercial centre of the city. In addition to warehouses and terminal facilities, there are the customhouse, observatory, naval arsenal, government offices, several of the consulates and many of the more important banks, business houses and retail stores.

Santo Antonio, known as Mauritia or Mauritzstad during the period of Dutch occupation, is on an island of the same name. Among the important institutions and public buildings in this part of the city are the government palace, the state treasury, the courthouse, the state museum, public library, several fine churches, including the city's famous church of São Francisco de Assis, the Santa Isabel theatre and many historic landmarks.

São José embraces a large district on the mainland and is chiefly residential in character. The Dutch fort of Cinco Pontas is in this section of the city, as is Restoration square, which commemorates the end of Dutch domination.

Boa Vista, also on the mainland, is both a commercial and residential district and contains many of the educational institutions of Recife, including a normal school and schools of law, medicine, engineering, commerce and fine arts.

Because of the waterways which separate the component parts of the city, Recife is often referred to as the "Venice of America."

Its position near the equator and low elevation combine to produce a hot climate which, however, is mitigated somewhat by the southeast trade winds. July, the coolest month, has a mean temperature of 77°, whereas from December through March it is 82°. The total annual rainfall, based upon a 47-year record, is 65 in., more than 80% of which falls from March through August.

The port of Recife is one of the most important of Brazil because of its proximity to Europe and its convenience for vessels passing around the east shoulder of the continent. Its harbour consists of a narrow body of water, about 2 mi. in length, which is sheltered on the east by a reef and breakwater. The latter extends about 3,600 ft. in a north and northeasterly direction from the reef—an ancient beach of firmly consolidated materials. A second breakwater (Olinda Mole), about 2,500 ft. in length, runs in a southeasterly direction from the mainland and forms the other wing of the entrance channel. The distance between the heads of these two breakwaters is about 900 ft. The northern part of the harbour is approximately 1,600 ft. in width and has been dredged to a low water depth of 32 ft. The southern part is considerably smaller and has been dredged to a depth of but 25 ft. The quay is along the eastern margin of the peninsular district of Recife. The port is equipped with a modern coaling plant and grain conveyor, each having a capacity of 300 tons per hour, a sugar conveyor having a capacity of 1,600 bags per hour and more than 50 electric and steam cranes, the largest of which (floating) has a 50-ton capacity. Three sets of tracks, which connect with the Great Western of Brazil railway, serve the wharf and warehouses. There are 15 concrete warehouses having a total floor space of approximately 400,000 sq.ft., a cold storage warehouse, a warehouse for commodities which create a public hazard and 15 tanks for petroleum products and alcohol. The terminal facilities are operated by a state *directoria* under the authority of the federal government.

The principal imports of Recife are coal, petroleum and wheat; total imports in 1949 amounted to 571,174 short tons. Exports consist largely of sugar (the state of Pernambuco being the second largest producer in Brazil), cotton and other agricultural products. The total outbound traffic in 1949 amounted to 77,542 short tons.

More than 1,600 mi. of railways serve the states of Pernambuco, Alagoas, Paraíba and Rio Grande do Norte, having outlet through Recife, and a well-developed system of surfaced roads provides additional transportation facilities.

Recife, served by Panair do Brasil, a subsidiary of Pan American World Airways, as well as by several other national and European air lines, has national and international cable connections and radio, telegraph and telephone communications. Recife was settled about 1535, when Duarte Coelho Pereira landed there to take possession of the captaincy granted him by the Portuguese crown. The site of Coelho's capital was Olinda, but Recife remained its port and did not become an independent *vila* (town) until 1710.

Down to the close of the 18th century, when Rio de Janeiro became important, Recife was the second city of Brazil and for a time its most important port. It was captured and plundered in 1595 by the English privateer James Lancaster. It was also captured by the Dutch in 1630 and remained in their possession till 1654, during which time the island of Santo Antonio was occupied and the town greatly improved. At the end of the Dutch war the capital was removed from Olinda to Recife, where it has since remained.

RECIPROCATING ENGINE: *see* STEAM ENGINE.

RECIPROCITY, the condition or state of being reciprocal, *i.e.*, where there is give and take, mutual influence, or correspondence between two parties, persons or things (Lat. *reciprocus*, returning back the same way, alternating, probably from *re* back and *pro* forward). In a more particular sense, reciprocity refers to the commercial policy under which a country grants special tariff advantages to imports of another country in return for special tariff advantages granted to it by the other country. In American usage the terms "reciprocity" and "reciprocity agreements" have acquired a highly specialized meaning as a result of the tariff policy formerly pursued by the United States, particularly under the tariff acts of 1890 and 1897, in the negotiation of tariff agreements with other countries. In this specialized sense, a reciprocity agreement is one in which the contracting states grant to each other particular tariff concessions, in return for particular tariff concessions, without the intention or expectation that these concessions will be generalized, *i.e.* extended to third countries. Reciprocity agreements are to be distinguished from reciprocal trade agreements concluded by the United States since 1934, in which the tariff reductions made by the United States (except in the Cuban agreement) have been generalized to all countries except those found to be discriminating against American trade. (H. F. G.)

RECKLINGHAUSEN, a town in the province of North Rhine-Westphalia, Germany, 22 mi. N.W. of Dortmund. Pop. (1950) 104,791. The county of Recklinghausen belonged to the archbishopric of Cologne until 1803, when it passed to the duke of Arenberg. It was known as the West Recklinghausen. After 1815 the duke of Arenberg held it as a fief under Prussian sovereignty. In the neighbourhood of Recklinghausen are extensive coal-mines, iron and tin foundries and brick works, and the industries embrace the manufacture of linen, beer, spirits, cement, soap and ammonia.

RECLAMATION OF LAND: *see* LAND RECLAMATION.

RECLUS, JEAN JACQUES ELISÉE (1830–1905), French geographer, was born at Sainte-Foy la Grande (Gironde), on March 15, 1830, the second son of a Protestant pastor. He was educated at the Protestant college of Montauban, and studied geography under Karl Ritter at the University of Berlin. Leaving France in December 1851, he spent six years (1852–57) visiting the British Isles, the United States, Central America, and Colombia. During the siege of Paris, Reclus shared in Nadar's aerostatic operations. He was taken prisoner on April 5, 1871, while serving in the National Guard, now in open revolt, and on Nov. 16 sentenced to transportation for life; but the sentence was commuted in Jan. 1872 to perpetual banishment. After a short visit to Italy, he settled at Clarens, in Switzerland, where he resumed his literary labours, and, after producing the *Histoire d'une montagne* (a companion to *Histoire d'un ruisseau*), wrote nearly the whole of his great work, *La Nouvelle Géographie universelle, la terre et les hommes*, 19 vols. (1875–94). This is a stupendous compilation, profusely illustrated with maps, plans and engravings, and was crowned with the gold medal of the Paris Geographical Society in 1892. An English edition appeared simultaneously, also in 19 vols., the first four by E. G. Ravenstein, the rest by A. H. Keane. Extreme accuracy and brilliant exposition form the leading characteristics of all Reclus's writings, which thus possess permanent literary and scientific value. In 1882 Reclus initiated the "Anti-Marriage Movement," in accordance with which he allowed his two daughters to marry without any civil or religious sanction. This resulted in government prosecutions, instituted in the High Court of Lyons, against the anarchists, members of the International Association, of which Reclus and Prince Kropotkin were designated as the two chief organizers. The prince was arrested and condemned to five years' imprisonment, but Reclus, being resident in Switzerland, escaped. In 1892 he became professor of comparative geography in the University of Brussels. Reclus died on July 4, 1905.

His works are: *Histoire d'un ruisseau* (1869); *La Terre: description des phénomènes de la vie du globe* (2 vols., 1867–1868); *Histoire d'une montagne* (1880); *La Nouvelle Geographie universelle, la terre et les hommes* (19 vols., 1875–1894); *L'Homme et la terre* (1905); and many contributions to scientific journals.

RECOGNIZANCE, a term of common law usually employed to describe an obligation of record, entered into before some court or magistrate duly authorized, whereby the party bound acknowledges that he owes a personal debt to the Crown, with a defeasance, *i.e.*, subject to a condition that the obligation to pay shall be avoided if he shall do some particular act—as if he shall appear at the assizes, keep the peace, or the like. Recognizances are now used almost solely with reference to criminal proceedings. The security given by a receiver appointed by the High Court is still in the form of a recognizance acknowledging a debt to named officers of the court, and securing it on the real and personal estate of the receiver.

There is a general jurisdiction on conviction of misdemeanour both at common law and by statute to put the offender under recognizances to keep the peace and (or) be of good behaviour in addition to or in substitution for other punishment. On refusal to enter into recognizances as above, the court may order imprisonment for the refusal, limited in cases within the Acts to 12 months, and in cases within the Act of 1879 to six months.

The recognizances above described may be described as a form of punishment or a judicial security for good conduct. Recognizances are, however, most used with reference to proceedings before conviction and judgment. In preliminary enquiries into indictable offences the enquiring justices take recognizances to ensure the attendance of the accused if liberated during any adjournment, and on committal for trial take the recognizances of the accused (if allowed bail) to attend the court of trial and take his trial, and of the prosecutor and the witnesses for the prosecution or defense to attend and prosecute or give evidence. Recognizances taken are returnable under penalty to the court of trial, which orders their estreat (*q.v.*) if the conditions are breached. Similar powers as to the recognizances of persons prosecuted summarily were given by the Summary Jurisdiction acts, 1848 and 1879, amended by the Criminal Justice act, 1925.

By the Land Charges act, 1925, a recognizance, whether obtained or entered into on behalf of the crown or otherwise, did not operate as a charge on land or on any interest on land or on the unpaid purchase money for any land, unless a writ or order for the purpose of enforcing it was registered in the office of the land registry. This enactment was clearly applicable to receivers' recognizances; and on purchases of land search was made for registered recognizances and an official certificate could be obtained affirming or negativing the existence of a registered entry.

In the U.S.A., the states allow by either common law or statutes recognizances in much the same way as in England.

RECONNAISSANCE, a military term for reconnoitring or examination of an enemy's position or movements. A topographical reconnaissance is a survey of a tract of country or route by officers with small patrols, escorts or assistants. Strategical reconnaissance was formerly carried out by cavalry formations or squadrons, but it has now been taken over almost entirely by aircraft. Tactical reconnaissance falls to the lot of troops of all arms, whether in contact with the enemy or for self-protection. A reconnaissance by a large force of all arms with the idea of provoking an enemy into showing his hand, if necessary by fighting, is called a reconnaissance in force.

RECONSTRUCTION FINANCE CORPORATION. The Reconstruction Finance corporation in the United States was established by congress on Jan. 22, 1932, "to provide emergency financing facilities for financial institutions, to aid in financing agriculture, commerce and industry." After a few years of unprecedented depression and steady price declines, an institution was required which could pump dollars into financial institutions, railroads, etc., to enable them to meet their commitments. The RFC in turn was to obtain dollars from the federal government. In moderating the epidemic of bankruptcies in the 1930s, the RFC helped lay the groundwork of recovery.

The RFC was to operate as an independent agency, not subject to political influences. Every application would be considered on its merits, not on political considerations. It was also generally assumed that loans would be made on the condition that private financing was not available and that an important public interest would be served.

In the early years Jesse Jones, chairman of the board of directors, managed the institution without much interference. But as the functions of the RFC grew, and particularly as the RFC, even in the 1930s, began to assume responsibility for disbursing huge sums of money for other government agencies, without the delays incident to the voting of funds through the appropriation committees of the congress, the agency tended to become involved in politics.

By the 1940s the situation had become precarious. The Hoover commission in 1949 noted that "direct lending by the government to persons or enterprises opens up dangerous possibilities of waste and favoritism. . . . It invites political and private pressures, or even corruption" (*Report on Federal Business Enterprises*, March 31, 1949). As early as 1948 a congressional committee (Senate Committee Report no. 974 on the RFC act) had noted that attempts to influence the business judgments of RFC by the use of political influence, even though well intended, were a constant menace to sound administration. In a report in 1951, the senate banking and currency committee (Report no. 649) complained of the increasing practice of applicants seeking direct access to the directors of the RFC through members of the Democratic national committee; and many cases of corruption were aired.

Despite this, the Democratic majority of the banking and currency committee in 1951 proposed only to correct abuses, not to destroy the RFC, for the majority emphasized the important financing contributions of the RFC in a financial market that was imperfect at best. Once the Republicans came into power in 1953, however, they provided for a quick liquidation of the RFC (RFC Liquidation act, July 30, 1953). By the latter part of 1954 all but a few hundred millions of dollars of assets had been liquidated.

Contributions of the RFC.—During 21 years and 8 months of RFC lending, more than $12,000,000,000 was disbursed in RFC's

RFC Activities, First Ten Years

Activity	Amount
Banks, investments in (7,000 banks)	$3,400,000,000
Insurance companies, loans and purchases of securities (for more than 100 insurance companies)	145,000,000
Railroads, loans and purchases of securities	1,100,000,000
Municipalities and other public agencies, purchases of securities	1,300,000,000
Disaster victims (30,000 victims)	69,000,000
Home mortgages, purchases (500,000 mortgages)	2,200,000,000

Source: *RFC (in Liquidation), Report to the Congress* (June 30, 1954).

lending programs. When, in Sept. 1953, its lending authority was terminated, it had $800,000,000 outstanding in loans, securities and commitments. Aside from its peacetime activities, the RFC under legislation in 1940 and 1950 had assumed large military responsibilities; *e.g.*, purchases of strategic items, building of plant facilities. (S. E. H.)

RECORDER. The principal legal officer of an English city or borough having a court of quarter sessions. He must be a barrister of five years' standing, appointed by the crown. The recorder holds once in every quarter of a year, or oftener if he thinks fit, a court of quarter sessions in and for the borough. He is sole judge of the court, "having cognizance of all crimes, offences, and matters cognizable by courts of quarter sessions for counties in England," except that he may not allow or levy any borough rate or grant licences (s. 165). He is not eligible to serve in parliament for the borough or to be an alderman or councillor, or stipendiary magistrate for the borough, though he is eligible to serve in parliament except for the borough. He may be appointed recorder for two or more boroughs conjointly. Appeals from the city and borough justices and under the Rating and Valuation act, 1925, are to the recorder as sole judge.

The recorder of London is judge of the lord mayor's court and one of the commissioners of the central criminal court. (*See* QUARTER SESSIONS, COURT OF.)

In the United States most of the states have county recorders elected by the voters of the county. In some of the states the duties of the recorder fall upon the clerk of one of the courts. In all of the states provision is made by constitution or statutes for some official to record deeds and other legal instruments. In New York the recorder is one of the criminal court judges.

RECORDER, FIPPLE FLUTE or ENGLISH FLUTE, a mediaeval flute, blown by means of a whistle mouthpiece and held vertically in front of the performer like a clarinet. It consisted of a wooden tube which was at first cylindrical or nearly so but became, as the instrument was developed and improved, an inverted cone.

Being very easy to play, the recorder enjoyed great popularity in all countries after the middle of the 18th century until the greater possibilities of the transverse flute turned the tide against it.

After 1800 a smaller variety, called the flageolet, played a certain role as an amateur instrument in England (where even double and triple flageolets were built). In the 20th century an increased interest in ancient music brought forth a renaissance of the recorder, produced in various sizes.

RECORDING, PHONOGRAPHIC: *see* GRAMOPHONE.

RECREATION. Recreation is easier to describe than to define. It has been variously characterized by different writers as any activity engaged in voluntarily just for the pleasure and satisfaction that it brings to the participant, whether through relaxation, refreshment of strength after toil, renewal of spirit, the opportunity for self-expression, relief from boredom, release of emotional tension, the provision of an outlet for repressed impulses, the testing of one's powers, the attainment of a sense of achievement, the forgetting of one's worries, sheer fun or the mere strengthening of the ego that comes from feelings of adequacy and self-esteem. Recreation is more than activity as such, however. It is activity plus an attitude on the part of the reacting individual and, of these two ingredients, the attitude of the individual is the more important.

Properly defined, the term recreation has an even broader meaning than implied thus far, for it can occur in the absence of any discernible activity. To virtually exhausted players, for example, the quiescent break that occurs between the periods of an athletic contest is likely to be recreative. Similarly, to one who has long toiled without respite, a vacation with pay spent mainly at just resting could be highly recreative.

But inactivity is not always recreative. It is the total situation and how the individual feels with reference thereto that determines what is and what is not recreation. For example, a patient sitting in a dentist's waiting room who is scheduled to have a tooth extracted is not likely to find the period of waiting recreative. Similarly, during an economic depression, an individual long unemployed and eager to find profitable employment is likely to find his involuntary leisure not recreative but crushing. Thus, because the attitude of the individual concerned is so important, the same objective situation can be either recreative or quite the opposite.

Although recreation is sometimes defined as consisting of activities in which the individual engages just because he wants to, this statement has limitations. At certain times an individual may eat, sleep, etc., just because he wants to. Most people, however, would not regard such activities as recreation per se. But most of the remaining activities in the behaviour stream (when such reactions as eating, sleeping, etc., are eliminated) in which the individual takes part of his own volition are considered his recreation.

Though not usually regarded as recreation, even eating and sleeping can provide a convivial background and even be essential parts of a gala occasion. This holds true, for example, for birthday parties, banquets, Christmas dinners and informal treats enjoyed with friends. At so-called "slumber parties," a popular pastime among teen-age girls in the United States, it is not the forty winks of sleep but the entire occasion that is recreative. Although we may identify one element as more prominent than another, it would be futile to try to analyze and isolate the specific elements that are recreative and those that are not. In such matters it is the total event that is recreative.

Although activities which are enjoyed by large numbers of people are usually labelled recreations, these activities are recreative only to individuals who find them so. Recreation, therefore, is more than a mere list of activities and festive occasions. Because of individual differences in tastes and preferences, no specific activity is recreative to everyone. On the other hand, under suitable circumstances such as might be found in dramatic play, for example, almost every conceivable human activity can be recreative to someone.

Recreation is sometimes defined as the physical recuperation of adults, and play as characteristic childish activity. These interpretations make a distinction between recreation and play largely because of the fact that small children often start to play immediately upon waking in the morning when they are not in need of physical recuperation. Despite the possible validity of this distinction, in order to avoid the monotonous repetition of any one word, the terms recreation, play, diversion and pastime will be employed interchangeably.

Because thousands play at what is work for professionals, it is impossible to make a sharp distinction between work and play. This fact is well illustrated by the endless amateur-professional controversy. Who is an amateur and who is not depends largely upon what game one plays, the country in which one plays it, and the decade during which it is played. Although various committees have attempted to specify who is and who is not an amateur, the definitions of all such committees have been arbitrary and unsatisfactory, and so have failed to gain general world-wide acceptance.

This discussion implies that, desirable though it might be from the viewpoint of the ardent behaviourist, recreation cannot be defined objectively in a way that gains general acceptance. It in-dicates also that it is impossible to make any accurate computation of the total time devoted to recreation or its total monetary cost. This is revealed by the great disparity in the estimates made. For example, one writer held that 5% of the money annually spent by U.S. consumers went for recreation, while another estimated that, broadly interpreted, not far from 25% of the entire U.S. national income was expended for play and recreation.

Obviously, such estimates are based on different definitions of the term recreation. The specific recreational activities engaged in by different individuals are determined by such factors as chronological age, sex, the social and geographic environment, the season of the year, economic status, the available facilities and equipment, fads and fashions and the skills and abilities of the participants.

Spectator Versus Active Participant Activities.—Recreations are sometimes divided into two general types: those which imply direct participation and those which involve looking on or listening to. The claim is sometimes made that witnessing games, viewing them on television or listening to radio accounts, is less beneficial than direct participation. Others challenge this allegation arguing that we misunderstand the nature of recreation when we try to impose our recreation values upon others. No one but the individual concerned is able to decide whether the role of spectator or that of active participant is more satisfying to him and hence more recreative. Relaxation, it has been argued, is one of the benefits to be obtained from recreation and it would be difficult to prove that, for those engaged in physical occupations, direct participation always provides more real relaxation from the strain of modern productive effort than does appreciative observation. Active participation is often not so much a form of recreation as an ordeal. Either because they are unqualified to perform skilfully or because they feel inadequate to play in a manner that enhances their opinions of themselves, millions are unable to enjoy direct participation, but this need not and should not preclude them from enjoying, as witnesses, the expert performances of others. Moreover, since no trustworthy method for measuring recreative values is available, the relative worth of active participation and of observation are matters of conjecture.

With reference to this entire subject, the Educational Policies commission of the National Education association maintained that it is idle to quarrel over the relative values of participation and observation. Both are important and both should be encouraged, for in the modern urban environment it is difficult to provide the space and the equipment for all who might wish to participate actively in certain kinds of activities. Therefore, many persons must engage in certain forms of recreation vicariously or not at all.

The Change in Attitude and Practice.—In earlier times the attitude of many persons was that play was wasteful and to some it was even wrong. This attitude was, in part, the product of religious convictions and was modified only gradually. The influences of Jean Jacques Rousseau, Friedrich Wilhelm Froebel, John Dewey and others were potent forces in effecting this change. By the beginning of the 20th century, the belief had gained wide acceptance that it is both undesirable and impossible to suppress either the need or the perfectly normal tendency to play; carefully planned leisure-time investment can be a direct and potent educational agent; and, if society does not provide opportunity for wholesome recreation and train the individual's capacity for seeking and finding it, the suppressed drives will frequently find various socially objectionable outlets.

It seems important, therefore, that efforts be made to enable both children and others to engage in those recreational activities which they will pursue whether they are instructed or uninstructed in them. In 1918 the National Education association adopted "worthy use of leisure" as one of seven cardinal principles of education, and in 1946, the Educational Policies commission of the National Education association stated that education for recreational pursuits is imperative. Modern schools, provide after-school and recess recreational opportunities for those of school age and by means of an expanding extracurricular program teach skills and interests that can be used by the pupils as recreation after graduation.

The legal function of the schools has been extended to include the right to provide facilities, purchase supplies and equipment, and employ leaders for many kinds of community recreation. School auditoriums are supplied with stages for dramatics and portable school furniture is installed so that classrooms can readily be cleared for social occasions. In some communities classes in arts and crafts are provided for adults as well as for children, and neighbourhood clubs are permitted to use the school facilities for their recreational activities.

Churches came to assume favourable attitudes toward recreation, and some sponsor their own youth groups in which a social and recreational program receives major emphasis. Although its main purpose is religious, it is not uncommon for a church to own separate quarters that can be used for basketball, parties, dramatics, social dancing, etc. For many persons church work is a major social and recreational activity, and in some small communities and rural districts the church is the centre of the community's recreational life.

Recreation has assumed an increasingly vital role in the program of various churches, partly because it can be a powerful tool in developing church loyalty, partly because by promoting wholesome forms of recreation, the church can more effectively combat and lessen some of the depravities of civilization, and partly because of the general change in public opinion regarding man's basic need for recreation, including that of ecclesiastic authorities themselves.

Interrelations With Other Aspects of Living.—Recreation is so closely associated with other kinds of human endeavour that it is almost impossible to tell where it begins or ends. For example, most voluntary youth-serving organizations such as the Boy Scouts, the 4-H clubs, and a host of others, do not regard recreation as their main function. Nevertheless, it is an important feature in the program of all such groups, and it undoubtedly has much to do with their success in attracting and retaining members. This is true also for many adult organizations, such as women's clubs, fraternal orders, veterans' organizations and service clubs. The existence of numerous noonday luncheon clubs in the U.S. is probably due largely to a desire on the part of the members not merely to eat at regularly specified times but also to talk to congenial companions.

Wholesome recreation is a correlate of mental and physical health. For example, well-adjusted persons have more hobbies and they pursue them with more zest than do psychiatric patients. Although this correlation does not prove that good mental health is caused by recreational interests, many mental hygienists believe that such interests can help to direct troublesome feelings into socially approved channels and that they thus can be a valuable morale builder and a preventative of mental ill health.

During World War II, both as a morale builder and for reasons of social hygiene, the special services division of the U.S. army, for example, provided recreation for 8,000,000 men scattered all over the world by means of movies, athletics, soldier shows, handicrafts, library service, post exchange services, games, clubs and rest camps.

Juvenile Delinquency and Recreation.—Research has shown that legally recognized delinquents differ from nondelinquents in their play behaviour, the delinquents participating more often in desultory, unguided and socially undesirable leisure-time pursuits. Although recreation is often heralded as a sovereign remedy for juvenile delinquency, it is a product of so many unfavourable causative factors that it probably cannot be eliminated by any one preventative measure. The case for recreation is sometimes hurt by overstatement of what it can do. Planned recreation can provide the opportunity for character development, but it cannot work miracles. Indeed, when the conditions are unfavourable, the participant in sports and games may learn not honesty but dishonesty.

Commercial Recreation.—Commercial recreations are those operated for monetary profit. Examples are the theatre, amusement parks, motion-picture theatres, radio and television, horse and dog races, prize fights, wrestling matches and professional sports. Although some fine programs are operated by commercial interests, the tawdry and even vicious nature of certain others resulted in widespread criticism and popular demand for their more rigorous control. Activities and devices most often criticized are unregulated burlesque shows, pulp magazines, bingo games, fraudulent pinball machines which exploit the gullible, slot machines, sadistic comic books, roadhouses, taxi-dance halls and similar questionable resorts. Pool and billiards are sometimes condemned but chiefly because of the unsavory setting in which it is alleged they are played. When played under properly supervised conditions, such games of skill are unlikely to elicit objections.

The chief value of commercial recreation is that its promoters can provide equipment and facilities for specific types of recreation at a time when the call for them is still too slight to justify public expenditure. When public demand has increased and the need justifies the cost, public facilities can be provided. This has happened in the case of golf, tennis and several other recreations which are now offered in many communities by both commercial and public agencies.

Public Recreation.—Playgrounds were first established in the U.S. by philanthropic agencies to help keep underprivileged children off the streets. The Playground Association of America was organized in 1906 and renamed the National Recreation association in 1930. By means of its publications, field studies, consulting and advisory service and annual meetings, this organization led in the drive for a better understanding of community recreation systems, and also served as a public forum for the exchange of ideas and information regarding

recreation in general. Any list of outstanding individual promoters of the U.S. play movement would have to include among others Henry S. Curtis, Luther Halsey Gulick, George E. Johnson and Joseph E. Lee.

Governmental responsibility for recreation was accepted in the United States on the national, state and local levels. Because leisure-time interests are far too numerous for any one agency to handle, about 35 different federal agencies rendered one or more types of recreational service in the 1950s, such as the preservation of areas of natural scenic beauty, the conservation, development and extension of fish and wildlife resources, the maintenance of national parks and forests and a host of others.

North Carolina, Vermont, Washington and California were the first states to accept recreation as a separate service of state government. Each of them created a State Recreation commission empowered by law to aid local communities in developing their recreational resources. Practically every state passed enabling legislation permitting local communities to conduct recreational programs with public funds, and some states established game refuges and bird sanctuaries, as well as state parks and forests. Many also operate roadside parks and picnic areas, provide camping sites for tourists and furnish swimming, boating and other facilities.

Provisions for recreation in local communities throughout the U.S., many of which have continuous year-round, tax-supported programs, are implemented by means of municipal and school playgrounds, athletic fields, golf links, school gardens, field houses, community centres and, most important, the employment of trained leaders.

Outlook For the Future.—Modern industrial efficiency has provided man with: a bewildering array of possibilities for entertaining himself; more income per family with which to pay the cost; more leisure time in which to play; and more congested urban areas where children do not perform the daily chores that occupied their grandparents and where their opportunities for wholesome recreation are much curtailed. Although the machine has greatly increased man's free time, it cannot solve his problem of what to do with it. Therefore, leisure is not only an opportunity, but a social problem.

Recreation has become far more than mere diversion. It is an important social force. Its pattern is incredibly complex. It is, among other things, a big business. In many countries of Europe and in certain states of the United States the tourist or recreation business is among the most important economic assets. Recreation pulls in many directions. It merges with other things so gradually that its boundaries are hard to locate. Perfectly respectable places of entertainment shade off imperceptibly into notorious subterfuges. This poses a problem in policing but government faces serious difficulties when it attempts to operate in the field of morals or of good taste.

Recreation can be used to promote industrial efficiency, to bind the people of a nation to some political system, or to prepare a country for war. In Italy, for example, prior to World War II, the national government assumed control over most aspects of recreation, made them auxiliary organizations of the Fascist party, and used them for the indoctrination of Fascist ideas. One recalls in this connection the Nazi motto, *Kraft durch Freude* ("Strength through Joy"), and how the Nazis channelled the recreation of the entire German nation in harmony with Nazi purposes. It has been said that from 1952 recreative sports were used by the U.S.S.R. as an important political weapon in its drive for international prestige.

Sports have long been considered useful in promoting social cohesion and as agencies for social direction. Since there probably will be even more leisure in the future than heretofore, the modern community faces no more serious responsibility than that of making adequate provision for ways in which both children and adults can fill their free time with constructive and healthful recreational activities. Just how should the individual evaluate the actual worth of his possible recreations?

BIBLIOGRAPHY.—Frank G. Menke, *The New Encyclopedia of Sports* (New York, 1947); Federal Security Agency, *Recreation—A National Economic Asset* (Washington, D.C., 1945); Stuart Chase, "Play," pp. 332–353 in Charles A. Beard, ed., *Whither Mankind* (New York, 1928); Harvey C. Lehman and Paul A. Witty, *The Psychology of Play Activities* (New York, 1927); William C. Menninger, "Recreation and Mental Health," pp. 38–49 in *Proceedings of the 30th National Recreation Congress* (New York, 1948); Joseph W. Byron, "Army Lessons From a Global Recreation Program," pp. 22–29 in *Recreational Congress: National Recreation Association Proceedings 1946* (New York, 1946); The Athletic Institute, *Recreation for Community Living: Guiding Principles by Participants in National Recreation Workshop*, (Chicago, 1952); John L. Hutchinson and G. M. Gloss, "Recreation," pp. 1005–1016 in Walter S. Monroe, ed., *Encyclopedia of Educational Research*, rev. ed. (New York, 1950).

PLAY THERAPY

Since play is the child's easiest and most natural medium of self-expression and an outlet for feelings which he cannot otherwise express, clinical psychologists have experimented extensively with play therapy as a method useful for diagnosing and treating children who have grave emotional problems and personality disturbances. In play therapy the ability of the pre-school child to employ toys and dramatic play as a medium for expressing his phantasy life is utilized. For example, a play situation is arranged in which dolls represent the several members of the child's family. The child is asked to tell something about the dolls or to do something with them. Or he may be requested to complete a partly-finished story pertaining to the dolls, or to interpret a picture.

The purpose here is to provide a means whereby the young child may indirectly and perhaps unwittingly reveal his real attitudes toward the members of his own family or toward others. In employing this technique, the therapist tries to create a permissive atmosphere which will encourage the child to express his deepest feelings, either by means of words or gestures, movements, clay-modelling, finger painting, etc. The proponents of such therapy maintain that the child's play often gives insights into family situations which can be obtained by no other means. They report also that this psychotherapy often dissipates the child's unconscious conflicts and improves his self-expression, thus leading to better personal adjustment.

Play therapy has also been employed for understanding and helping children who have reading problems. Investigators even reported that, for children suffering from severe emotional conflicts, significant increases in intelligence test scores were obtained. The explanation offered for this increase was that the play therapy frees children from paralyzing inhibitions resulting from their emotional problems and that, as one result of this, the children are enabled to employ their capacities more freely and adequately. More research and analysis along these lines was needed in order that these claims might be further tested and verified.

See Virginia Mae Axline, *Play Therapy* (Boston, 1947); Clark E. Moustakas, *Children in Play Therapy* (New York, 1953).

(H. C. Ln.)

RECTIFIER, as used in radio, consists of a device for the direct conversion of an alternating-current wave into a unidirectional wave.

RECTOR, a title given to the bearers of certain ecclesiastical and academical offices. In the Roman empire, after Constantine, the title rector was borne by governors of provinces subordinate to the prefects or exarchs. In the middle ages it was given to certain secular officials (*e.g.*, the podestas of some Italian towns), but more especially to the heads of the universities, the representatives and rulers of the *universitas magistrorum et scholarium,* elected usually for a very short time. After the humanistic movement of the Renaissance the style rector was also given to the chief masters of schools containing several classes, and in some parts of Germany (*e.g.*, Saxony, Württemberg) it is still thus used instead of the more modern title of director. Rector is also still the title of the heads of the Scottish universities (lord rector) and of the German universities (*Rector Magnificus*). Rector is the title of the heads of Exeter and Lincoln colleges, Oxford. The heads of all Jesuit colleges are also known as rectors. As an ecclesiastical title rector was once loosely used for rulers of the church generally, whether bishops, abbots or parish priests, but it is now confined, as in Poland and Spain, to a priest with a cure of souls, in England to the incumbent of a parish where the tithes are not impropriate and in the U.S. to the Protestant Episcopal clergyman in charge of a parish.

RECUSANT (Lat. *recusare,* "to refuse"), the name given in the 16th and 17th centuries to persons, particularly to adherents of the Roman faith, who persisted in refusing to attend the services of the English Church and became thereby liable to prosecution and penalties.

RED BANK, a borough of Monmouth county, New Jersey, U.S., on an estuary called the Shrewsbury river, 6 mi. from the Atlantic ocean and 25 mi. S. of New York city. Pop. was 12,743 in 1950; 10,974 in 1940 by the federal census. It is served by the Central Railroad Company of New Jersey and the Pennsylvania railroad and by motorbus lines. It is a residential suburb, a summer resort and the trade centre of a rich farming region; and has fish industries, canneries, nurseries and various manufacturing plants.

The name Red Bank was applied to this locality as early as 1734, and by 1780 there were several buildings within the limits of the present borough.

REDBREAST or EUROPEAN ROBIN, *Erithacus rubecula* (Linnaeus), is the sole member of its genus, which is included in the thrush family of birds (Turdidae). The species is divided into a number of races in the Palaearctic region. The British race, *melophilus* Hartert, is famous for its close association with man and enjoys a unique place in affection and folklore. Hence British colonists overseas have bestowed its name on various small red-breasted birds (*e.g.*, the American robin). Actually the breast is orange, which colour extends over the face, being divided from the olive-brown upper parts by a narrow blue-gray border. The underparts are white; the legs, bill and iris brown. The sexes are alike, and there is little difference in summer and winter. The juvenile plumage is speckled. The robin is originally a woodland bird and remains so on the European continent. Many British robins breed in woodland or its edge and winter near houses. Continental robins are migratory in the north of their range, partly so in the middle and resident in the south; in Great Britain many females, but few males, appear to migrate.

Both the biology and the folklore of the robin were intensively studied by David Lack in the period 1935–50 and his books, *The Life of the Robin* (rev. ed., London, 1947) and *Robin Redbreast* (Oxford, 1950) are standard works. Lack's technique of marking individual birds with coloured rings followed pioneer work by J. P. Burkitt in Northern Ireland. The robin shows highly developed territorial behaviour.

In the breeding season each pair defends an area containing the nest against others of their own species; in winter each bird maintains a territory with equal rigidity, except in very severe weather. Robins are therefore extremely aggressive, and Lack, using stuffed dummies, was able to separate and analyze the complicated threat and courtship displays.

Robins usually nest from March to June, rearing two broods from clutches typically of five or six white, pink-spotted eggs. Nests in natural woodland sites are hard to find, but many are built in holes of walls, creepers, tins, nestboxes and various bizarre situations. Robins feed on invertebrate animals, especially worms, and on berries and food scraps.

The song is simple but melodious and can be heard almost throughout the year; after a break at midsummer it is resumed with a slightly changed quality. (B. C.)

REDBUD: see JUDASTREE.

REDCAR, a municipal borough in the Cleveland parliamentary division of the North Riding of Yorkshire, Eng., on the northeast coast 8 mi. E.N.E. of Middlesbrough. Pop. (1951) 27,516. Area is 8.1 sq.mi. Lying midway along the continuous stretch of sand between the Tees estuary and Saltburn, it serves as residential town and holiday resort for the industrial population of south Tees-side.

Incorporated in 1922, Redcar was growing rapidly in the 1950s. Huge industrial developments on its western boundaries include chemical works, a steel rolling mill and docks on the borough's frontage to the Tees river.

Kirkleatham hall, in the lovely village of Kirkleatham, was the home of the Turner family from the 17th century until 1948 after which it was demolished.

RED CEDAR: see JUNIPER.

RED CROSS, the national and international agency whose primary purpose is to care for the sick, the wounded and prisoners in time of war. The Red Cross movement, especially after 1919, showed a world-wide tendency to regard the prevention and alleviation of all human suffering as within the purview of Red Cross activity.

Origins of the Movement.—The fundamental idea associated with the Red Cross resulted from the publication by Henri Dunant, at Geneva, Switz., in 1862, of a booklet entitled *Un Souvenir de Solférino.*

Dunant had witnessed appalling scenes of bloodshed during the war of 1859 in Italy, and his booklet gave a shocking account of the distress of the wounded left to die on the battlefield for lack of medical assistance. He urged the necessity of constituting permanent societies for the aid of the wounded, with the purpose of forming detachments of volunteer helpers, and expressed the hope that "the leaders of the military art of different nationalities agree upon some sacred international principle, sanctioned by convention, which, once signed and ratified, would serve as the basis for the creation of societies for the aid of the wounded in the different European countries."

Dunant's appeal quickly found its echo. The Société Genevoise d'Utilité Publique had as president Gustave Moynier, who was impressed by the importance of the suggestions set forth in Dunant's booklet. At his request Dunant attended a meeting of this society and explained his ideas. The society thereupon named a commission to study ways to improve the condition of the wounded in war. The members of this commission, destined to become the Comité International de la Croix-Rouge, were: Gen. Guillaume Dufour, commander in chief of the Swiss army, Gustave Moynier, Henri Dunant, Louis Appia and Theodore Maunoir.

After drafting an agreement providing for the formation of national committees to assist army medical services by creating voluntary aid corps, they held an international meeting at Geneva from Oct. 26 to 29, 1863. Thirty-six experts and government delegates met at the Palais de l'Athénée, and there enunciated the fundamental principles of the Red Cross.

The International committee was urged to continue the mission it had assumed as guardian of the principles laid down in the convention, and to foster the formation of national societies in all countries to develop the Red Cross movement and organize aid for wounded soldiers and other victims of war.

The next step was to secure international legal status for the movement thus set on foot, ensuring the wounded themselves, the personnel engaged in their care and the medical supplies set aside for their use against attack, the whole being protected by a single recognized emblem. The difficulties were enormous, but they were successfully overcome through the prestige of General Dufour, the activity of Henri Dunant (who personally approached the authorities in a number of countries) and the organizational work of Gustave Moynier. Napoleon III brought his influence to bear in favour of the work, and the International committee induced the Swiss federal council to convoke in Geneva on Aug. 8, 1864, a diplomatic conference at which 26 governments were represented. The outcome of this conference was the Geneva convention, which laid down certain principles: the wounded were to be respected; military hospitals to be regarded as neutral; the personnel and material of the medical services were accorded protection; and the symbol of this protection was to be a white flag bearing a red cross (the emblem of the Red Cross throughout the world). The Geneva convention, as revised July 6, 1906, was extended to sea warfare at The Hague in 1907, to the treatment of prisoners of war in 1929, and was further extended and modernized at Geneva in 1949.　　　　　　　　　　　　　　　　(J. T. Nn.)

INTERNATIONAL COMMITTEE OF THE RED CROSS

The objects of the International Committee of the Red Cross (Comité International de la Croix-Rouge) are to maintain the essential principles of the Red Cross, to recognize new national Red Cross societies after verification of the basis upon which they are founded, to work for the observance and development of international humanitarian conventions (especially the Geneva conventions) and to act as benevolent intermediary between governments and national Red Cross societies in time of international or civil war; in addition, in wartime, to establish information agencies concerning prisoners of war, to visit the prisoners in their camps and to improve their material and moral situation by using all available influence; and finally, both in wartime and in peacetime, to act as benevolent intermediary between governments, Red Cross societies and other relief organizations for the purpose of carrying out itself, or enabling others to carry out, the humanitarian task of relieving suffering caused by war and calamities.

The International committee's headquarters are at Geneva, where it was founded in 1863. Recruited by co-optation, the committee possesses juridical personality. The term "international" describes the nature of the committee's work, which is international in scope, while its composition is wholly Swiss (25 members elected by co-optation) to ensure neutrality of its activities in all countries. The committee's activities are governed by the principles upon which the Red Cross rests: absolute impartiality and independence, especially in political and religious matters, and equality as between all members of the great Red Cross family. A link between the committee and national societies is provided by the *Bulletin international de la Croix-Rouge* (from 1864) and the *Revue internationale de la Croix-Rouge* (from 1919).

The committee also publishes books, pamphlets, etc., dealing with Red Cross principles and activities.

In 1928, the 13th International Red Cross conference, at The Hague, established the statutes of the International Red Cross, which comprises the national societies, the International committee and the League of Red Cross Societies. These three elements are the basis of the universal Red Cross movement, whose assembly, the International conference, normally takes place every four years.

The committee was entrusted by the International Red Cross conference with the periodical distribution of Florence Nightingale medals, awarded to the most deserving nurses of all countries. In 1917 and again in 1944 it was awarded the Nobel peace prize.

World War I.—In successive European conflicts from 1864 the committee established agencies for information and the relief of wounded and sick combatants. Relief for prisoners of war was an accessory concern of the Red Cross in 1870 and was not recognized officially before 1912 (Balkan War). At the outbreak of World War I the committee opened the International Prisoners of War agency in Geneva with a staff, mainly voluntary, of about 1,200 persons. Forty-one delegates visited 524 internment camps, and facilities were obtained for the evacuation of civilians from occupied regions (northern France) and the repatriation or accommodation in neutral countries of sick and wounded combatants and medical personnel. The work relative to the eastern front was delegated to the Danish Red Cross, which set up an extensive information bureau for this purpose in Copenhagen.

The work of the committee and its agency in this war showed the insufficiency of treaty stipulations governing the situation of prisoners of war (ruled only by the regulations annexed to the fourth Hague convention of 1907), and contributed materially to the drafting and adoption in 1929 of the Geneva Prisoners of War convention.

Activities Between World Wars I and II.—After the war, the International committee organized the repatriation of 450,000 prisoners of war of all nationalities from Russia and from central Europe; it also effected the exchange of hostages in Upper Silesia, the return of Bulgarians interned in Greece and the exchange of prisoners between Greece and Turkey. In medical relief and reconstruction work in war-stricken countries, the committee co-operated actively with numerous Red Cross societies and other organizations.

After the treaty of Versailles, world opinion was largely dominated by the belief that the covenant of the League of Nations had banished war. The committee's specific function being inseparable from the circumstance of war, certain circles at that time held its continued existence to be at best an anachronism, and at worst a connivance at future attempts to revert to arms. From 1919 to 1929 the committee went through a critical period, withstanding widespread opposition in its refusal to yield to premature and dangerous optimism, and its insistence that so long as even a remote possibility of war remained the Red Cross was pledged to preparedness for its fundamental wartime tasks.

World War I had revealed grave deficiencies in international law, notably with regard to the treatment of prisoners of war and civilian internees, and had shown the urgent need of bringing civilians under protection. Ten years' intensive preparation led in 1929 to the revised convention for the relief of sick and wounded combatants, and the adoption of a new convention relative to the treatment of prisoners of war. At the 15th International Red Cross conference in Tokyo, Jap. (1934), a draft convention for the protection of civilians was approved, but the diplomatic conference convened for 1940, at which these proposals would have become law, was prevented by the outbreak of World War II. The Tokyo draft, however, served the committee to obtain the granting by all belligerents in World War II of prisoner-of-war status to interned enemy aliens. The 16th International Red Cross conference (London, 1938) put forward proposals on the following subjects: revision of the Geneva convention of 1929 (prisoners of war), and of the Hague convention of 1907 for the adaptation of the Geneva convention to war at sea; draft conventions: (1) for adaptation of the same to aerial warfare; (2) for medical and security zones in wartime; and (3) concerning the condition and protection of civilians of enemy nationality in enemy or enemy-occupied territory.

Both the Gran Chaco War in the early 1930s and the Spanish Civil War (1936–39) called into action one of the International committee's most important humanitarian functions—to persuade belligerents not legally bound by conventions to accept their terms nevertheless. Combatants and civilians were thus spared much suffering as a result of the committee's intervention, through its delegates, in the above conflicts. The committee's services were also called upon during the wars in Ethiopia and China.

Numerous legal problems arising out of Red Cross functions and activities permanently occupy the committee in peacetime. Its work in connection with the subjects of the draft conventions and other measures for mitigating the destruction of life and property in wartime proved of great practical and moral value during World War II, either in obtaining good-will concessions, or as the basis of appeals to belligerent powers.

World War II.—In pursuance of article 79 of the Prisoner of War convention the committee opened the Central Prisoner of War agency in Geneva in Sept. 1939. As from 1940, the agency was considerably extended; all the other activities of the committee increased steadily and several new departments were added, especially in the field of relief supplies and transport by sea and land. The committee's staff, which in Sept. 1939 numbered 20, totalled 3,921 in June 1945, half of them voluntary workers. The committee's delegations in all countries numbered 81, comprising 179 delegates who paid more than 11,000 visits to prisoner-of-war camps.

At the end of 1946, the card index of the agency relating to prisoners of war and internees included about 39,000,000 cards. Incoming mail items had totalled 58,701,000, outgoing 60,393,000; telegrams received were 346,696, dispatched 218,582. Civilian messages for correspondence between free civilians in countries at war reached nearly 24,000,000. Close to 1,500,000 printed volumes for recreation or study, contributed by various relief organizations, had been forwarded to the camps. Relief supplies for prisoners and internees reached a total weight of 445,702 tons, valued at 3,400,000,000 Fr. (Swiss). Expenditure for the period 1940–46 amounted to 54,875,909 Fr. and contributions totalled 51,797,768 Fr., half of which were subscribed by Switzerland.

Relief for civilian war victims—particularly women and children—was the purpose of the Joint Relief commission of the International Red Cross, created in July 1941 (at the committee's suggestion) by the International committee and the League of Red Cross Societies. Foodstuffs, clothing and pharmaceutical supplies bought and dispatched by the Joint commission were distributed in the war-stricken countries by national Red Cross societies and other welfare organizations in the presence, whenever possible, of a delegate of the committee. From 1941 to 1946, the Joint Relief commission purchased and forwarded 83,000 tons of supplies valued at 340,000,000 Fr. The chief countries benefited were Belgium, France, Greece, Yugoslavia, the Netherlands, Norway and Poland. The commission's most notable relief schemes were for Belgian children in 1941 and for the famine-stricken Greek population during the winter of 1941–42. This last project was carried out conjointly with the Swedish government and the Swiss Red Cross society, and with the assistance of the Turkish Red Crescent. Organized by delegates at Athens, it saved the lives of 5% to 10% of the population of that city, and enabled 40% of the population to sustain life.

The strictness of the blockade and counterblockade, the scarcity of neutral shipping available and the vast extension of the relief scheme led to the creation of a Red Cross maritime transport system. The Foundation of the Organization of Red Cross Transports, set up by the committee in April 1942, had a fleet of 12 ships operating in the Atlantic, the Mediterranean and later in the North sea. These ships, sailing under neutral colours, were always accompanied by the committee's agents. The ships owned by the foundation ("Caritas I," "Caritas II," "Henry Dunant") or chartered by it made in all 350 round trips and carried 202,965 tons of relief supplies between April 1942 and Dec. 31, 1946.

This cargo represented tonnage equal to that carried by 20,000 railway cars or 500 trains of 40 cars each.

Special Problems.—Total warfare called in question the fundamental principles embodied in the Red Cross conventions and the international humanitarian agreements. Unforeseen problems and complex situations arose which were not provided for, but had to be dealt with as they presented themselves, sometimes on a vast scale and with extreme urgency.

Breaches alleged by one party were communicated to the other by the committee acting as an intermediary between Red Cross societies, the latter being requested to inform their respective governments. The committee received many appeals to investigate and protest against alleged breaches of the rules of war and international law, but was unable on principle to entertain any such application, unless it emanated from all the governments concerned. On the other hand, the committee made spontaneous appeals to belligerent governments in behalf of war victims and in support of humanitarian principles, such action on its part being implied in its function as guardian of essential Red Cross principles.

During World War II, the committee's main task in this field was to secure progressive improvement in the implementing of the conventions, especially as regards the treatment of prisoners of war. To this end, the committee made almost daily application to the detaining powers.

While the Tokyo draft paved the way for the protection of interned enemy aliens, the civilian populations subjected to evacuation, deportation and the rigours attending military occupation remained outside the scope of existing conventions. As to concentration camps, it should be stressed that the committee had no legal basis whatever in international law which could enable it to intervene. These camps were regarded by the detaining authorities as a purely internal affair, and remained absolutely closed to the committee's delegates. Repeated applications to the authorities, however, enabled the committee, in the autumn of 1943, to send food parcels to civilian detainees whose exact addresses were known. During the last days of the war, several of the committee's delegates managed to enter certain concentration camps and succeeded at great personal risk in saving the lives of many thousands.

Two chief belligerents, the U.S.S.R. and Japan, had not ratified the Geneva Prisoner of War convention of 1929. Despite constant efforts during several years, the committee was unable to bring about agreements between Russia and Germany which would have allowed it to forward relief supplies to prisoners of war of either country detained by the other. In the far east, the greatest obstacles were raised to any systematic relief work by Geneva, and the committee's delegates had access only to a limited number of camps in Japan proper, Shanghai and Hong Kong.

After World War II.—Although its wartime services were gradually closing down, the committee was still engaged at mid-century in the following tasks:

1. Aid and protection for many prisoners of war and civilian internees who were detained, despite the close of hostilities and steps in view of their repatriation. This department was particularly active until the end of 1948. The number of reports on visits to prisoner-of-war camps after the armistice in Europe was nearly 2,500.

2. Aid to civilian populations suffering from the consequences of war.

3. Preparatory work for the revision of the Geneva conventions and the establishment of a new convention for the protection of civilians in time of war. This work included the meeting in Geneva of a preliminary Red Cross conference (July–August 1946) and of government experts (April 1947). The drafts prepared by the committee were approved, after slight amendment, by the 17th International Red Cross conference (Stockholm, Swed., Aug. 1948) and were subsequently accepted as a working document by the diplomatic conference of government delegates in Geneva (April 20–August 12, 1949). The Geneva conventions of Aug. 12, 1949 (for the amelioration of the condition of the wounded and sick in armed forces in the field; for the amelioration of the condi-

tion of the wounded, sick and shipwrecked members of armed forces at sea; relative to the treatment of prisoners of war; relative to the protection of civilian persons in time of war), were signed by 63 states.

4. The committee's subsequent interventions were in connection with events in Indochina, Indonesia, Kashmir, Greece, Palestine, Bengal and Korea. (M. H.)

LEAGUE OF RED CROSS SOCIETIES

The League of Red Cross Societies was formed in 1919 on the proposal of H. P. Davison, president of the War Council of the American Red Cross, by the Red Cross societies of France, Great Britain, Italy, Japan and the United States, to develop and intensify the humanitarian activities of the Red Cross in time of peace. By 1951 the league included 68 national Red Cross societies. Its statutes defined among its duties the following:

To act as a permanent liaison agent between national Red Cross societies.

To co-operate in all spheres of their work, especially for the improvement of health, the prevention of disease and the mitigation of suffering.

To represent and to speak for the national societies on the international level in accord with resolutions adopted by the board of governors.

To encourage and facilitate the establishment and the development of the activities of national societies.

To be the guardian of the integrity and interests of the member societies.

The league has a board of governors comprising one representative of each member society, and the board, when not in session, delegates its authority to an executive committee consisting of the chairman and vice-chairmen of the board, together with 12 other societies designated by the board. The board meets biennially and the executive committee at least twice a year. The expenses of the league are met by the voluntary contributions of member societies.

The international activities of the league are supervised by the chairman of the board of governors and carried out by an international secretariat with headquarters at Geneva. In addition to the various branches of the secretary-general's office, there are technical divisions on disaster relief, health, nursing, social service and Junior Red Cross corresponding to the principal peacetime activities of member societies.

The foundation of the league preceded by a few weeks the signing of the covenant of the League of Nations, of which article 25 read as follows:

The Members of the League agree to encourage and promote the establishment and co-operation of duly authorized voluntary national Red Cross organizations having as purposes the improvement of health, the prevention of disease and the mitigation of suffering throughout the world.

This confirmation in the covenant of the central points in the league's program was indicative of the widespread sentiment which caused the national Red Cross societies after World War I to extend their activities to the relief of all preventable suffering. The most immediate tangible result of this decision, and of the consequent activities of the League of Red Cross Societies, was the extension of the Red Cross movement to many countries where it had not previously penetrated—in particular to Latin America. There the association of the Red Cross with war had not found favour, but the idea of an international movement grouping the principal elements that sought to protect mankind against its natural enemies in time of peace made an immediate appeal.

Parallel with this growth in the number of societies came an increase in the Red Cross membership. By the early 1950s it was estimated that the number of Red Cross members in the world (including junior members) totalled 100,000,000.

Since the league functions essentially as a clearinghouse, to enable the national Red Cross societies to use each other's experience and to co-operate readily when need arises, the secretariat has given special attention to creating opportunities for frequent and regular contact between Red Cross representatives from different countries. In 1922 a program of study visits was begun under which delegates visit the headquarters of the league and the headquarters of such national societies as can readily afford facilities for the study of the particular phase of Red Cross activity in which they are interested. This system is supplemented by regular visits by officers of the secretariat to the headquarters of the national societies. Still more important was the establishment of regional conferences. The Red Cross societies of the far east were first brought together in conference in Bangkok, Thai., in 1922 and again at Tokyo in 1926. The first regional conference for central and eastern European societies was held in Warsaw (Warszawa), Pol., in 1923, the second in Vienna, Aus., two years later and, after World War II, in Belgrade, Yugos., in 1947. Inter-American conferences started in Buenos Aires, Arg., in 1923. These meetings facilitate exchange of views and techniques concerned with problems common to the geographic, economic and social conditions of the respective countries and make possible collective action toward the solution of problems which transcend political boundaries.

The Relief Bureau.—The activities of the league in the technical fields already referred to (disaster relief, health, nursing, social service and Junior Red Cross), led to steady developments, especially in the improvement of standards. The important place of relief, especially disaster relief, in the league program can be attributed in large measure to the creation in 1924 of a special relief division which enabled Red Cross societies to handle disaster relief problems in their respective countries with less outside help. Nevertheless, in major natural disasters when outside help is requested, the necessary appeal is issued and the resultant relief activities co-ordinated by the league either on its own responsibility or in conjunction with the International Committee of the Red Cross. The first such joint appeals were occasioned by the Russian famine of 1921 and in connection with earthquakes in Iran, Japan and Central America. During World War II the magnitude of the distress and the extent of relief made available by national societies and other organizations caused the two international organizations of the Red Cross to create a Joint Relief bureau. In 1951 the league appeal on behalf of the victims of the floods in the Po river valley, Italy, yielded more than $1,000,000 in money or commodities given by member societies.

The Health Bureau.—The Health bureau of the league secretariat after World War II acted primarily in the co-ordination of the medical and public health activities of the national societies and in providing health education materials. In 1951 priority was given to first aid, accident prevention, blood banks, standardization of blood transfusion equipment, tuberculosis control, maternal and child health, mental health and the training of health teachers. Co-operative relations existed with the World Health organization of the United Nations, the United Nations International Children's Emergency fund, the International Union Against Venereal Diseases, the International Blood Transfusion society, the International Union for Child Welfare and other governmental and intergovernmental agencies.

Nursing and Social Service Bureau.—This bureau, whose nursing activities are guided by an advisory committee composed of world leaders in the field, was set up originally in 1919 as a nursing bureau; in 1951 steps were taken to include a social service section. From its inception the bureau has assisted national societies to develop their public health or visiting nurse programs, acting in various ways as a co-ordinating agent. Higher standards for nurse training were developed and programs to include instruction in home care of the sick were extended. A significant contribution was made when the league established an international nursing centre in London in 1920 with the co-operation of Bedford College for Women and the College of Nursing.

Under the auspices of the Florence Nightingale foundation, sponsored in part by the league and with the collaboration of the British Red Cross society, graduate nurses from all over the world were given supplementary training. In 1944 responsibility for the centre was transferred to the International Council of Nurses but with the league represented on the governing body. The Nursing and Social Service bureau set up an extensive information service, including documents collected or compiled for the use of national societies, and introduced a quarterly in English, French, German and Spanish. It also helps select candidates for Red Cross scholarships and study visit grants and helps arrange suitable training for accepted candidates. A priority program in 1951 was guidance in the organization of Red Cross nursing schools, in the training of nurses' aides, the teaching of home nursing and the enrolment of qualified nursing personnel.

Junior Red Cross Bureau.—This bureau co-ordinates and promotes the work of Junior Red Cross sections in national societies throughout the world. By the early 1950s there were such sections in 60 countries with more than 40,000,000 members and many of those sections were becoming the Red Cross of the elementary and secondary schools. In others, the membership continued to be maintained in units outside the schools. Through a newsletter published in four languages assistance was being given to the organization and content of Red Cross activities appropriate for the several age groups and for adaptation to the needs, resources and cultures of the different countries. School correspondence, albums and art exchanges were facilitated.

Office of International Relations.—This office was established so that the secretariat could maintain co-operative relationships with international governmental organizations with objectives related to Red Cross activities, such as the World Health organization, United Nations Educational, Scientific and Cultural organization, Food and Agriculture organization, International Refugee organization, International Children's Emergency fund, etc.

NATIONAL RED CROSS SOCIETIES

The national Red Cross societies were originally constituted in most countries to support and assist the army and navy medical services in time of war. Charters granted them by governments, public demand or the absence of other resources to meet great social needs caused them to widen their activities. A national Red Cross society, to obtain official recognition, was required to fulfil the following conditions:

The government of its country must have adhered to the Geneva conventions; the society must have been recognized by its legal government as an auxiliary of the public authorities in the sense of the Geneva conventions; it must adopt the name and emblem of the Red Cross (except in Mohammedan countries the Red Crescent, and in Iran the symbol of the Red Lion and Sun); its activity must extend throughout the country and its dependencies; its membership must be open to all citizens of the country irrespective of sex, politics or religion; and, finally, it must undertake to maintain regular contact with the other national societies and with the International Committee of the Red Cross at Geneva. Only one national Red Cross society may be recognized in each country. Each national society is directed by a central committee and includes a suitable number of regional and local committees which assist the central committee and ensure co-operation from all sections of the country. In most cases there are general meetings once a year of delegates from each local branch.

National Red Cross societies are autonomous and independent within their own territory. The first national Red Cross societies came into existence in Europe immediately following the Geneva conference of 1863, and by 1951 there were 68, with headquarters and founding dates as follows:

Albanian Red Cross; Tirana (Tiranë); 1921.
American National Red Cross; Washington, D.C.; 1881.
Argentine Red Cross; Buenos Aires; 1880.
Australian Red Cross; Melbourne; 1914.
Austrian Red Cross; Vienna; 1867.
Belgian Red Cross; Brussels; 1864.
Bolivian Red Cross; La Paz; 1917.
Brazilian Red Cross; Rio de Janeiro; 1908.
British Red Cross society; London; 1870.
Bulgarian Red Cross; Sofia; 1885.
Burma Red Cross society; Rangoon; 1937.
Canadian Red Cross society; Toronto; 1896.
Chilian Red Cross; Santiago de Chile; 1903.
Chinese Red Cross society; Peking; 1904.
Colombian Red Cross society; Bogotá; 1915.
Costa Rican Red Cross; San José; 1885.
Cuban Red Cross society; Havana; 1909.
Czechoslovak Red Cross; Prague; 1919.
Danish Red Cross; Copenhagen; 1876.
Dominican Red Cross; Ciudad Trujillo; 1927.
Ecuadorian Red Cross; Quito; 1923.
Egyptian Red Crescent society; Cairo; 1912.
Ethiopian Red Cross; Addis Ababa; 1935.
Finnish Red Cross; Helsinki; 1920.
French Red Cross; Paris; 1864.
Greek Red Cross; Athens; 1877.
Guatemalan Red Cross; Guatemala; 1923.
Haitian Red Cross; Port au Prince; 1932.
Honduran Red Cross; Tegucigalpa; 1937.
Hungarian Red Cross; Budapest; 1879.
Icelandic Red Cross; Reykjavik; 1924.
Indian Red Cross society; New Delhi; 1919.
Indonesian Red Cross; Jakarta (Batavia); 1945.
Iranian Red Lion and Sun society; Tehran; 1922.
Iraq Red Crescent society; Baghdad; 1932.
Irish Red Cross; Dublin; 1939.
Italian Red Cross; Rome; 1864.
Japanese Red Cross society; Tokyo; 1877.
Jordanian Red Crescent society; Amman; 1947.
Lebanese Red Cross; Beirut; 1945.
Liechtenstein Red Cross; Vaduz; 1945.

Luxembourg Red Cross; Luxembourg; 1914.
Mexican Red Cross; Mexico, D.F.; 1907.
Monacan Red Cross; Monaco; 1948.
Netherlands Red Cross; The Hague; 1867.
New Zealand Red Cross society; Wellington; 1915.
Nicaraguan Red Cross; Managua, D.N.; 1934.
Norwegian Red Cross; Oslo; 1865.
Pakistan Red Cross society; Karachi; 1947.
Panamanian Red Cross; Panamá; 1917.
Paraguayan Red Cross; Asunción; 1919.
Peruvian Red Cross society; Lima; 1879.
Philippine National Red Cross; Manila; 1947.
Polish Red Cross; Warsaw; 1919.
Portuguese Red Cross; Lisbon; 1865.
Rumanian Red Cross society; Bucharest; 1876.
Salvadorian Red Cross; San Salvador; 1885.
South African Red Cross society; Johannesburg; 1913.
Spanish Red Cross; Madrid; 1864.
Swedish Red Cross; Stockholm; 1865.
Swiss Red Cross; Berne; 1866.
Syrian Red Crescent; Damascus; 1947.
Thailand Red Cross; Bangkok; 1893.
Turkish Red Crescent; Ankara (Angora); 1868.
Uruguayan Red Cross; Montevideo; 1897.
U.S.S.R., Alliance of Red Cross and Red Crescent Societies of; Moscow; 1925.
Venezuelan Red Cross society; Caracas; 1895.
Yugoslav Red Cross; Belgrade; 1876.

In the course of years, a few societies ceased to exist where states in which they operated lost sovereign authority and where others had federated into a single society, following political changes.

War Work.—The discharge by national societies of their primary duty as auxiliaries to the medical services of the armed forces began early. The first opportunity for the relief of the wounded by Red Cross societies occurred in the Dano-Prussian War of 1864. In the Seven Weeks' War of 1866, the Franco-German War of 1870–71, the Russo-Japanese War of 1904–05 and the Balkan Wars of 1912–13 the Red Cross societies of the belligerent countries provided ambulances, hospitals and medical and nursing personnel to the combatant forces.

World War I naturally led to a vast expansion of Red Cross activity. The American Red Cross alone mobilized 23,000 nurses, 55,000 nurses' aides and 6,000,000 voluntary helpers, and set up canteens, hospitals, etc., for U.S. troops. The British Red Cross, in collaboration with the Order of St. John of Jerusalem and the dominion societies, provided trained nurses, voluntary aid detachments, ambulances and hospitals wherever British forces were engaged. Motor ambulance convoys were organized by the British Red Cross for the evacuation of wounded, in addition to ambulance trains and (in Mesopotamia) motor ambulance launches. Similar energy was shown by the Red Cross societies of other belligerents, notably the French, German, Belgian, Italian, Austro-Hungarian, Russian, Serbian and Turkish societies. The Red Cross societies of neutral countries (Switzerland, the Netherlands, Sweden, Denmark, Norway and Spain) also provided assistance to prisoners of war, hospital facilities for serious cases of wounds and sickness, and food for the occupied territories.

In World War II, the work of the Red Cross societies again increased enormously. Although the activities were generally within the categories of World War I, many adaptations to a more total form of war were made. For instance, in World War II, the United States armed forces, not the American Red Cross as in World War I, operated their own hospitals and maintained their own nursing services. However, 70,500 nurses were assigned and certified to the military by the American Red Cross. The canteen service of World War I developed by the American Red Cross in World War II into nearly 1,000 overseas clubs, many of which, in addition to recreation facilities, offered meals and billets. The total expenditures by the national organization from 1939 to 1946, not including the chapters, in services to the armed forces alone amounted to $365,816,818. Another new service was the blood plasma program, to which the American people gave 13,000,000 pints of blood for their fighting forces.

Again in World War II the British Red Cross and the Order of St. John of Jerusalem operated as a joint war organization and their welfare workers served with British forces in all theatres of operation. Home services were adapted and increased to the needs of the moment. County committees met requests for comfort items for hospitalized sailors, soldiers and airmen. Hundreds of thousands were trained in first aid, many of whom joined the Air Raid Precaution organization. Although originally formed to relieve suffering among the sick and wounded of the fighting forces, the British Red Cross in 1940 extended many of its activities to civilian victims of the war. Outstanding among its many activities was packing parcels for the 180,000 prisoners of war who received them regularly. In all their services for prisoners of war through the International Committee of the Red Cross, the British Red Cross and the societies of the dominions worked in close co-operation with the American Red Cross and the societies of the allied nations.

After World War II.—The extent of suffering following World War II brought into being intergovernmental agencies financed by governments, such as the United Nations Relief and Rehabilitation administration. Consequently, to guard against duplication, Red Cross societies which had conducted vast civilian relief programs internationally during and immediately following World War II gradually restricted their civilian relief work to victims of natural disasters. On behalf of the famine-stricken population of India in early 1951, the American Red Cross sent $200,000 worth of processed foods, powdered milk and vitamins, half of which was given by the American Junior Red Cross. The Australian Red Cross sent 53 tons of wheat. Many other societies followed suit preliminary to assistance extended by the government of the United States and others. In the Po river floods of the same year, more than $1,000,000 in cash and commodities were sent to the Italian Red Cross by sister societies. However, aid was not always restricted to the victims of natural disasters. Where war-created human needs were not being met by intergovernmental action, as for instance in Korea, Red Cross societies supplied welfare teams and great quantities of relief commodities to the United Nations command.

Other Services.—At the peak of World War II the American Red Cross had more than 6,000,000 trained volunteers. In many national societies emphasis has been placed on the training of nurses' aides, visiting housekeepers and mothers' assistants. The British Red Cross did much of its work through Voluntary Aide detachments, especially in dealing with emergencies.

First-aid, accident-prevention and water-safety activities are many and varied. They often include ambulance service for emergencies, highway, beach and riverside aid stations, training in first aid, aquatic safety and swimming, and public education in accident prevention.

Maternal and child welfare centres and clinics, such as those of the Iranian Red Lion and Sun and the infants' clinics of the Guatemalan Red Cross, are maintained by many societies. The Indian Red Cross also trains midwives. Some societies specialize in service for handicapped children, such as that of the Australian Red Cross to spastic children. School hygiene is emphasized by many. Summer colonies and preventoria are operated and some societies also have homes for orphans and deserted children.

Assistance to servicemen, such as that of the American Red Cross, includes welfare and communications service between all military installations in the United States and the homes of those in the armed forces; service of the same kind to which recreation is added in military hospitals; home services to the dependents of servicemen; and financial assistance. Assistance to ex-servicemen and their dependents is also a primary responsibility of the Red Cross, and especially in the American, Australian and Philippine societies. It sometimes includes aid in the settlement of veterans' claims, retraining of the disabled, financial assistance, supplying orthopaedic appliances, etc.

Hospitals, clinics and dispensaries are the major programs of many societies, particularly in the Latin-American countries, and mobile clinics for rural work are often featured.

Nurses' training schools vary from the postgraduate training provided by the French Red Cross to those conducted by the British Red Cross for the training of voluntary auxiliary aides for civil defense. The training and enrolment of nurses and of personnel specialized in ambulance, pharmaceutical, radiological, poliomyelitic and tuberculosis work are activities of many societies. Public health nursing is also a growing activity in many societies.

Health education is likewise part of the Red Cross campaign. Lectures and pamphlets are offered. Exhibitions are arranged as part of campaigns against tuberculosis, poliomyelitis, cancer, venereal diseases, etc. Care of the sick and household hygiene are also taught.

Blood for the treatment of the sick and wounded is yet another activity in many Red Cross societies. Some societies maintain blood banks; others may limit their blood program to recruiting donors. Some furnish blood and blood derivatives to the armed forces as well as to civilians. Outstanding examples of comprehensive blood programs are those of the American and Canadian Red Cross societies.

Outpost work is featured by many societies in a variety of ways, such as the mobile clinics for child welfare of the British Red Cross in the Gold Coast, the visiting housekeepers for isolated areas of the Australian Red Cross, the first-aid posts and clinics of the South African society, the air ambulances of the Swedish Red Cross and those of the British Red Cross for service to the mines of Tanganyika, the east coast of Africa, Kenya and Uganda.

THE AMERICAN RED CROSS

The American Association of the Red Cross, as it was then known, was incorporated in 1881. The following year Pres. Chester A. Arthur obtained unanimous ratification of the Geneva convention in the senate, for which Clara Barton had struggled for ten years. In 1905, following relief work that included the Michigan forest fires of 1881, the floods of the Ohio and Mississippi rivers in 1884, the Johnstown, Pa., floods of 1889, the famine in Russia of 1892 and the Spanish-American War, the American National Red Cross became incorporated with the president of the United States as its president and the war department as its auditor. With the grant of the congressional charter, largely the work of Mabel T. Boardman, the American National Red Cross was recognized as an instrumentality of the United States government and the only relief agency with official permission to work for the armed forces in wartime.

The duties prescribed in the charter were not altered even though the charter itself was amended by the congress and approved by the president on May 8, 1947. The amendments did permit structural changes which gave a board of governors of 50 "all powers of government, direction and management" and made membership open to all people of the United States upon payment of $1.

For two years before the United States declaration of war on April 6, 1917, the American Red Cross was revamping the peacetime program it had conducted for many years into active mobilization that it might be prepared to fulfil its wartime duties. Early in World War I, offers of the aid of its trained personnel and contributions, particularly medical and hospital supplies, were accepted by almost all belligerents. The value of those supplies before the United States entered the war was more than $1,500,000. In May 1917, after U.S. entry into the war, Pres. Woodrow Wilson appointed a special Red Cross war council under H. P. Davison to direct the wartime activities of the organization. A popular campaign for a special war fund yielded $100,000,000 within a week. Before the war ended in 1918, contributions for the wartime work exceeded $400,000,000. With these funds the American Red Cross—among other activities—recruited, organized and equipped 50 base hospitals, 40 ambulance units, assisted in the care of the sick and wounded in emergencies and provided 23,000 nurses for the army and navy, a volunteer motor corps of 14,000, 92 convalescent homes in training and embarkation camps, 130 canteens, 24 military hospitals and 12 convalescent hospitals in France, 33 canteens in Italy, 28 military hospitals and 82 canteens in Belgium. Civilian relief to the European victims of the war was on a vast scale; $1,000,000 monthly was spent in France alone. Substantial assistance was also given in Russia, Belgium, Italy, Rumania, Serbia and Greece. The value of relief articles produced by volunteers during the war exceeded $100,000,000.

At the close of the war a peacetime program was inaugurated that continued relief work in Europe, provided aid to disabled veterans and enlarged the scope of various services, especially in communities. Outstanding in this program was the comprehensive development of a disaster relief service making possible instant response to calls for help which, beginning in 1941, averaged 300 per year. Financial aid was given also to scores of other countries suffering disasters which they were unable to handle alone. Other services at mid-20th century included enrolment of nurses, home-nursing courses, instruction in first aid, water safety and accident prevention; service to veterans and servicemen; a consultative nutrition and medical service; supervision of civilian relief in communities where the Red Cross chapter is the only relief agency; the blood program; and the Junior Red Cross.

All but the blood program had been offered to American communities through more than 3,700 chapters and their branches before the outbreak of hostilities in Europe in 1939. The blood program became an additional war measure and provided all plasma, whole blood and blood derivatives used by the armed forces of the United States when it became a belligerent. During the decade 1941–51 more than $1,000,000,000 was contributed to and administered by the American National Red Cross for its work; $428,000,000 was spent for welfare services of the armed forces. Approximately $108,000,000 went for aid to the dependents of servicemen. Volunteers averaged more than 2,000,000 per year. About 300,460 tons of supplies were distributed by Red Cross workers overseas to military personnel through camps, clubs, clubmobiles and hospitals, to prisoners of war and to civilians.

At the close of World War II, the American National Red Cross adjusted its activities, its staff and structure of organization to what had been hoped would be an era of peace. A surplus of about $100,000,000 was used to carry on Red Cross services and assistance. In June 1950, the efforts at readjustment were being concluded when hostilities broke out in Korea. Thereafter the American National Red Cross had to serve a greatly increased military establishment while maintaining its usual community services and, in addition, becoming the official co-ordinating agency for the procurement of all blood needed by the military establishment.

During the year ending June 30, 1951, Red Cross activities were conducted by 3,738 chapters and their 4,384 branches. Of these chapters, 1,300 were entirely operated by volunteers. Membership in 1951 was 37,425,000, of whom 19,334,800 were junior members.

BIBLIOGRAPHY.—Annual reports of the League of Red Cross Societies and the American National Red Cross; Hilary St. George Saunders, *The Red Cross and the White* (1949); Foster Rhea Dulles, *The American Red Cross* (1950). (J. T. NN.)

RED DEER (*Cervus elaphus*), the male of which, the stag, *par excellence,* reaches a height of 4 ft. 6 in. at the shoulder. The antlers are rounded, possessing bez tines and in well-developed animals at least 12 points, the record number for a British wild specimen being 20, though an ancient Irish skull was found bearing 34 and a park specimen had 39. The tail is rather long and the coat is spotted in the young and occasionally even in the adult. The males, which alone bear antlers, often have a "mane" on the throat, and in the breeding season utter a roaring cry. There are numerous local races of the red deer, which inhabit Europe, northern Africa, Asia Minor and north Iran; the species has been successfully introduced into New Zealand. Typically a woodland animal, the red-deer in Britain is now confined to open mountain-sides in the highlands of Scotland, Exmoor and a few other localities, and to parks; as a result, there has been a decided decline in the size and condition of the Scottish animals, which cannot compare with those from the Continent. (*See* DEER.)

REDDITCH, a town and urban district in Worcestershire, England, 15½ mi. S. of Birmingham by the L.M.S.R. Pop. (est. 1938) 22,560. Area, 18.8 sq.mi. It is the centre for the manufacture of needles, fishhooks and fishing tackle; and there is a large motorcycle and cycle works.

REDESDALE, JOHN FREEMAN-MITFORD, BARON (1748–1830), English lawyer and politician, younger son of John Mitford (d. 1761) and brother of the historian William Mitford, was born in London on Aug. 18, 1748. Having become a barrister of the Inner Temple in 1777, he wrote *A Treatise on the Pleadings in Suits in the Court of Chancery by English Bill,* which has been reprinted several times. In 1788 Mitford became M.P. for Beeralston in Devon, and in 1791 he introduced the important bill for the relief of Roman Catholics, which was passed into law. In 1793 he became solicitor-general, becoming attorney-general six years later, when he sat for East Looe, in Cornwall. In Feb. 1801 he was chosen speaker of the House of Commons. A year later, he was appointed lord chancellor of Ireland with the title of Baron Redesdale. Being an outspoken opponent of Roman Catholic emancipation, Redesdale was unpopular in Ireland. In Feb. 1806 he was dismissed on the formation of the ministry of Fox and Grenville. Although Redesdale declined to return to official life, he was an active member of the House of Lords both on its political and its judicial sides. He died on Jan. 16, 1830.

See O. J. Burke, *History of the Lord Chancellors of Ireland* (Dublin, 1879); J. R. O'Flanagan, *Lives of the Lord Chancellors of Ireland* (1870); Sir J. Barrington, *Personal Sketches of His Own Times* (1869); Sir S. E. Brydges, *Autobiography* (1834); and C. Abbot, Lord Colchester, *Diary and Correspondence* (1861).

REDFERN: *see* SYDNEY, AUSTRALIA.

RED INDIANS: *see* NORTH AMERICA: *Ethnology.*

RED JACKET (Sagoyewatha—"he who keeps them awake") (*c.* 1751–1830) was a Seneca Indian chief born near Geneva, N.Y., about 1751. He was an eloquent orator—whence his Indian name —and possessed considerable influence over his people. He fought for the British during the Revolution and because of his ability as a runner was a favourite among the officers, one of whom presented him with a heavily embroidered red coat. This made him conspicuous among his people and he was henceforth known as Red Jacket. He first appeared as a conspicuous figure when he made a notable speech in opposition to the treaty which was signed at Ft. Stanwix in 1784 by the United States and the Six Nations. In 1792 he went to Philadelphia, then the capital, to conclude a treaty of friendship with the United States, and President Washington presented him with a medal. Under his leadership the Senecas allied themselves with the Americans against the British in the War of 1812. Red Jacket understood the whites well and became more and more hostile to them as he realized their overwhelming power. "You are a kind-hearted people, seeking your own advantages," he said in one of his speeches. He tried to consolidate his people and preserve their ancient ways and rites, but by his stand only lost his leadership. He died in Seneca village, N.Y., on Jan. 20, 1830.

See J. Hubbard, *An Account of Sagoyewatha* (1886); Buffalo Historical Society, *Red Jacket* (1885).

REDLANDS, a city of San Bernardino county, Calif., U.S., at the foot of the San Bernardino mountains, 65 mi. E. of Los Angeles, on federal highways 70 and 99. It has an airport and is served by the Pacific Electric, the Santa Fe and the Southern Pacific railways and by motor-coach lines in all directions. The population in 1950 was 18,411 and in 1940 was 14,324 by federal census.

It lies at an altitude of from 1,200 to 2,100 ft., surrounded on three sides by peaks more than 10,000 ft. high (Mts. San Jacinto, San Antonio or "Old Baldy" and San Gorgonio or "Grayback") in the midst of the largest navel orange growing district in the world. From 4,500 to 7,000 carloads of citrus fruit are produced and shipped from Redlands each season. The University of

Redlands (opened in 1907) has an enrolment of more than 1,100. A settlement called "Lugonia" was established there in 1874 but the present city was founded in 1887 by New Englanders and incorporated in 1888. The city is governed by an elected board of five trustees.

REDLICH, JOSEPH (1869–1936), Austrian historian and politician, was born in Göding, Moravia, on June 18, 1869. He studied jurisprudence and history in Vienna, travelled extensively, especially in England, and in 1901 published his first work, *Die englische Lokalverwaltung* (*Local Government in England,* 1904). He afterwards became Professor at Vienna University, and sat in the Austrian parliament till 1911 as deputy for his birthplace. Both in the Austrian parliament in Vienna and the Moravian diet he did much to further the idea of an understanding between the German and Czech races. In 1905 he published another study of English political life: *Recht und Technik des englischen Parlamentarismus* (1905), Eng. trans., *The Procedure of the House of Commons,* 3 vols. (1907), a standard work on the subject and indispensable to the student. During the World War he was politically active, and in 1918 was appointed minister of Finance in the Lammasch Cabinet. He then retired from active politics, to produce *Das oesterreichische Staats- und Rechtsproblem* (vol. 1 1920, vol. 2 1926), a history of Austrian domestic policy from 1848 onward. His other works include *Das Wesen der oesterreichischen Kommunalverfassung* (1910); *The Common Law and the Case Method in American University Law Schools* (1914); *Oesterreichische Regierung und Verwaltung im Weltkriege* (English and German, 1925) and a biography, *Franz Joseph von Oesterreich* (1928). Redlich's attitude was usually rather that of a student of political theory and practice than of a pure historian, and his works were apt to be too voluminous to be easily read; but they were founded on encyclopaedic knowledge, most carefully presented, and were exhaustive.

RED LODGE, a city of southern Montana, U.S.A., 15 mi. from the Wyoming state line; the county seat of Carbon county. It is on federal highway 12 and is served by the Northern Pacific railway. Pop. (1950) 2,715; (1940) 2,950. It is the centre of one of the principal coal mining regions of the state, and there are also gold and silver mines and oil and gas fields in the vicinity. The Beartooth National forest lies a few miles to the west.

REDMAYNE, SIR RICHARD AUGUSTINE STUDDERT (1865–   ), K.C.B. (1914), was born at Gateshead-upon-Tyne, on July 22, 1865, and educated privately and at the Durham College of Science, Newcastle. In 1883 he became under-manager at a colliery firm in Durham, and eight years later went to South Africa. On his return in 1893 he was appointed manager of the Seaton Delaval collieries, Northumberland (1893–1902). He then obtained an appointment at Birmingham university, as professor of mining. He acted as chairman on numerous Government committees on questions affecting the mines, and in 1908 was appointed chief inspector of mines, a post which he held until 1920. He was chairman and governor of the Imperial Mineral Resources bureau (1918–25), and chairman of the advisory council on minerals to the Imperial institute (1925–35). His writings include *Men, Mines and Memories* (1942), *The Problem of the Coal Mines* (1945) and many official reports on mining.

REDMOND, JOHN EDWARD (1856–1918), Irish politician, son of W. A. Redmond, M.P., was born at Ballytrent. He was educated at Trinity college, Dublin, and was called to the bar at Gray's Inn in 1886, and subsequently to the Irish bar, though he never practised. He was a clerk in the vote office of the House of Commons before he entered parliament in 1881 as member for New Ross. From 1885 to 1891 he represented North Wexford. As party whip he rendered great service to the Irish members by his thorough grasp of the procedure of the House. At the time of the rupture of the Irish party consequent on the Parnell scandals, Redmond was the most eloquent member of the minority who continued to recognize his leadership, and in 1891 he became the accredited leader of the Parnellites. In 1900 the two nationalist parties were amalgamated under his leadership. He contested Cork unsuccessfully in 1891, but was elected for Waterford, where he was re-elected in 1906. (For the political events under his leadership of the Irish parliamentary party up to 1910, *see* IRELAND: *History;* ENGLISH HISTORY, etc.).

Redmond obtained for the first time a position of real power in parliament after the general election in Jan. 1910. Though he had amalgamated the two Irish Nationalist parties under his own lead in 1900, he had never hitherto been able, owing to the large Unionist majority of 1900 and the Liberal majority of 1906, to hold that balance of power in the House of Commons which had proved such a formidable weapon in the hands first of O'Connell and then of Parnell. But the reduction of the Liberal forces in Jan. 1910 made it impossible that Asquith's Government should long continue unless it found favour with Redmond.

The first use which he made of this new authority was to insist that Lloyd George's famous budget of 1909, on which the dissolution had turned, should be postponed till after the constitutional resolutions directed against the House of Lords—his one object being to remove the veto of the Upper House, which was the main barrier against Home Rule. This order of procedure was also demanded by the Labour party and by the Radicals; and the Government complied. But Redmond pressed further for an assurance that the royal prerogative would be at the prime minister's disposal to overbear any rejection by the Lords of the veto resolutions. He was impatient at the constitutional conference called in the summer at the beginning of King George's reign to endeavour to discover a solution by consent, and went to America to secure sympathy and funds. The conference having broken down, he conducted a strenuous campaign on behalf of the ministerial programme for the second general election of the year, in spite of a harassing movement on his flank by a small party of independent Nationalists under O'Brien and Healy, who accused him of having sold the Irish vote to the government.

When the result of the polling had confirmed Redmond in his tenure of the balance of parliamentary power, he forwarded the progress of the Parliament bill in 1911 by the steady vote of his party. In the autumn he was regularly consulted on the details of the forthcoming Home Rule bill, and when the bill was introduced, in April 1912, he procured its enthusiastic acceptance from a nationalist convention in Ireland. His speeches during its passage through parliament were, on the whole, moderate; he disclaimed separation but denounced any attempt to take Ulster out of the bill as a mutilation of Ireland. In token of the union of feeling between Nationalists and Liberals, he attended the meeting of the National Liberal Federation at Nottingham in Nov. 1912, and spoke for the first time on the same platform as Asquith. When the determined attitude of Ulster began to suggest to the Liberals the advisability of compromise, Redmond was very loth to agree, denouncing the Unionists and Ulster as engaged in "a gigantic game of bluff and blackmail." He insisted that Asquith's county option scheme was the extreme limit of concession. He was being pressed in Ireland by the rising power of Sinn Feiners and other extremists who had raised, in reply to Ulster, a great body of 100,000 nationalist volunteers, over whom Redmond only obtained control in June 1914 after a sharp struggle. Nevertheless he took part, at the end of July in the abortive Buckingham Palace Conference.

Then came the World War, and in the debate succeeding Sir E. Grey's famous declaration on Bank Holiday, Aug. 3, Redmond created a profound sensation by a speech in which he declared that the events of recent years had completely altered the Nationalist feeling towards Great Britain. The Government, he said, might withdraw its troops from Ireland, whose coasts would be defended by her own sons, Nationalist volunteers joining with Ulster volunteers in the task. This generous attitude was met by the decision of the Government to pass the Home Rule bill into law, suspending its operation till after the war. Redmond took an active part in promoting recruiting in Ireland, and stood on the platform in Dublin Mansion House on Sept. 25 by the side of the prime minister and the lord lieutenant. Unfortunately, his efforts were only moderately successful, but he refused Asquith's offer to join the first Coalition Government, and he successfully opposed all attempts to apply conscription to Ireland. It was a stunning blow to him when the smouldering

dissatisfaction of southern Ireland broke out into a blaze in the Dublin rebellion of Easter 1916. He expressed in the House of Commons his detestation of the crime, and lent his assistance to the attempt which was made by the Government in the summer through Lloyd George to arrange an agreed settlement of the Irish question.

But the effort failed; Duke, a Unionist, was appointed chief secretary; and Redmond treated the whole transaction as a fresh outrage on Ireland, moving on Oct. 18 a resolution (which was, of course, rejected) charging ministers with maintaining a system of Government in that country inconsistent with the principles for which the Allies were fighting in Europe. Next year he threatened a return of his party to the old obstructionist opposition; but when in May 1917 Lloyd George, as prime minister, suggested an Irish convention to produce a scheme of self-government, Redmond agreed; and in the convention he played a conciliatory part. During its sittings, however, his health failed. He died of heart failure in London on March 6, 1918.

See I. G. Redmond Howard, *John Redmond* (1910); *Home Rule: Speeches of John Redmond, M.P.* edit. by R. Barry O'Brien (1919); S. Gwyn, *John Redmond's Last Years* (1919).

REDMOND, WILLIAM HOEY KEARNEY (1861–1917), younger brother of John Redmond (*q.v.*), intended, as a young man, to adopt the army as his profession, and in 1881 he was a lieutenant in the Co. Wexford militia battalion of the Royal Irish regiment. But he resigned his commission to take part in the Land League movement and was imprisoned as a "suspect" in Kilmainham. He was returned for Wexford borough in 1883, and sat in parliament, though for different constituencies, from that time till his death. He was of an ardent and ebullient temper, which resulted in his spending three months in Wexford gaol in 1888 for inciting, at an eviction, to resistance to the sheriff, and in many agitated scenes at different times in the house of commons, where, however, he was personally very popular. Like his brother, in the Nationalist split he adhered to Parnell, and also like his brother, on the outbreak of World War I he instantly recognized the duty of Ireland to fling herself into it on the side of the Allies. Though 53 years old he joined at once the Irish division, receiving a commission in the Royal Irish regiment. He was promoted major for services at the front and mentioned in dispatches. In his intervals of service he made two thrilling speeches in the house of commons, advocating conciliation and a new start between England and Ireland. He died of wounds in France June 7, 1917.

See Memorial Volume, *Major William Redmond* (1917); W. H. K. Redmond, *Trench Pictures from France* (1917); T. P. O'Connor, *The Parnell Movement* (1886).

RED OAK, a city of southwestern Iowa, U.S.A., 50 mi. S.E. of Omaha, Neb., on the Nishnabotna river, federal highway 34 and the Burlington railroad; the county seat of Montgomery county. Pop. (1950) 6,451. Manufactured products include batteries, furnaces, concrete pipe, water tanks, flour and feeds; popcorn and alfalfa are processed. The city was founded in 1855 and incorporated in 1869.

It has a council form of government.

REDON, a town of western France, capital of an *arrondissement* in the department of Ille-et-Vilaine, 45 mi. S.S.W. of Rennes by rail. Pop. (1946) 5,710. Redon grew up round a monastery founded in the 9th century. In the 14th century the abbot Jean de Tréal surrounded the town with walls, of which a portion remains. Redon stands on the right bank of the Vilaine, above the confluence of the Oust and the canal from Nantes to Brest. The church of St. Sauveur, a former abbey, has a square Romanesque central tower with rounded angles. A fine 14th century tower with a stone spire stands isolated from the church, from which it was separated by fire in 1782. The 13th century choir, with ambulatory and radiating chapels, is notable.

REDONDA, an island in the British West Indies. It is a dependency of Antigua, Leward Islands, and lies 25 mi. S.W. of it, in 25° 6′ N. and 61° 35′ W. It is a rocky mountain, rising abruptly from the sea to a height of 1,000 ft.; area ½ sq.mi. Phosphate of alumina (discovered in 1865) was formerly exploited, with an annual output of about 7,000 tons.

REDONDO BEACH, a city of Los Angeles county, California, U.S.A., on the Pacific ocean, 19 mi. S.W. of Los Angeles and 10 mi. N.W. of the Los Angeles and Long Beach harbour. It is on federal highway 101 and is served by two bus systems. Pop. 25,208 in 1950 and 13,092 in 1940 by the federal census. In a natural amphitheatre facing the ocean, the city slopes gently upward from its silvery crescent-shaped beach to an elevation of 250 ft., with Los Angeles and the San Gabriel mountains in the background. It is a pleasure and health resort and a residential centre for workers in the adjacent oil fields and industrial districts. The city owns a mile of the water front, including Moonstone beach. A harbour enclosed by a breakwater provides yacht anchorage. The city was incorporated in 1892.

REDPOLL, the name given to several birds of the finch family (*Fringillidae*), allied to the linnet (*q.v.*), and possessing a reddish head. The best known is the lesser redpoll (*Carduelis linaria*). The mealy redpoll is a subspecies with a more northern range, visiting England in the winter. The type ranges over the whole of the north temperate zone. There are three additional subspecies in America, but these rarely reach the United States.

RED RIVER, the name of two American rivers, one emptying into the Mississippi near its mouth, and the other emptying into Lake Winnipeg.

1. The Red river, sometimes called the Red River of Louisiana, is the southernmost of the large tributaries of the Mississippi. It rises in northern Texas, in the northern part of the High Plains, or Llano Estacado, flows east by south in Texas, between Texas and Oklahoma, and to Fulton, in south-western Arkansas, there turns south-east and continues in a general south-easterly direction through Louisiana to the bank of the Mississippi, where it discharges partly into the Mississippi and partly into the Atchafalaya. Its length is estimated at 1,200 m. or more; its drainage basin has an area of at least 90,000 sq.m.; and its discharge ranges from 3,500 cu.ft. to 180,000 cu.ft. per second. Its middle and lower course is laden with a reddish silt from which it takes its name. From an elevation on the High Plains of about 2,450 ft., the river plunges into a canyon which is about 60 m. long and has nearly perpendicular walls of sandstone and gypsum formation 500 to 800 ft. high. Immediately below the canyon the river spreads out over a broad and sandy bed and flows for about 500 m. through a semi-arid plain. It narrows on entering the alluvial bottom lands, through which it pursues a sluggish and meandering course for the last 600 m. A shifting channel, deposits of silt and fallen trees have always hindered navigation. In 1828 the trees which the river had felled formed the great "Red River raft" extending from Loggy Bayou, 65 m. below Shreveport, Louisiana, to Hurricane Bluffs, 27 m. above Shreveport. Congress began in that year to make appropriations for the removal of the raft, and by 1841 Henry M. Shreve had opened a channel. The river was neglected from 1857 to 1872 and another raft, 32 m. in length, formed above Shreveport. A channel was opened through this in 1872–73, and the complete removal of the obstruction a few years later so improved the drainage that a large tract of waste land was reclaimed. In its course through Louisiana the river has built up a flood-plain with silt deposits more rapidly than its tributaries, with the result that numerous lakes and bayous have been formed on either side, and Cypress has been so flooded that boats ply between Shreveport, Louisiana, and Jefferson, Texas, 66 m. apart. The main river is navigable for small draught boats from the mouth to Fulton, Ark., a distance of 508.6 m.; however, there is little commerce above the mouth of the Black.

During the Civil War, in March and April 1864, Major-General Nathaniel P. Banks conducted a combined military and naval expedition up the Red river in an attempt to open a Federal highway to Texas, but on April 8, the vanguard of his army was repulsed with heavy loss at Sabine Cross-Roads by the Confederates under Lieut-Gen. Richard Taylor and the expedition was abandoned; the gunboats commanded by Rear Admiral D. D. Porter were held above Alexandria by the lowness of the river, but it was flooded by a hurriedly built dam, and they escaped.

See R. B. Marcy and G. B. McClellan, *Exploration of the Red River of Louisiana* (Washington, 1853), and the annual *Reports* of the Chief of Engineers of the U.S. Army.

2. The Red river, commonly called the Red River of the North, rises in the lake region of western Minnesota, not far from the headwaters of the Mississippi, flows north between Minnesota and North Dakota, continues northward through the Canadian province of Manitoba, and discharges into Lake Winnipeg. It has cut a gorge 20 to 50 ft. deep through clay deposits throughout the greater part of its course; it drains a region that is famous for the production of wheat; and much water-power has been developed on its tributaries.

RED RIVER SETTLEMENT, a Scottish colony founded in 1811 near the present city of Winnipeg by a philanthropic Scottish nobleman, Lord Selkirk, who at that time controlled the Hudson's Bay company and received from it a grant of 113,000 sq.mi. in the basin of the Assiniboine and Red rivers. Quarrels soon arose with the French and half-breed employees of the North-West Fur company, and were fostered by its officials. On June 19, 1816, in a fight between the rivals, Governor Semple of the Hudson's Bay company and 20 of his 27 attendants were killed, an affair known as the Battle of Seven Oaks. New settlers were sent by Selkirk, and founded the village of Kildonan, now part of Winnipeg. In 1821 the rival companies united, and in 1836 repurchased from Selkirk's heirs all rights to the territory. In 1821 and in 1835 two forts, known as Lower and Upper Fort Garry, were built to command the junction of the Red and Assiniboine rivers. The purchase in 1869 of the territorial rights of the company by the Dominion of Canada led to a rebellion, and the setting up of a provisional government under Louis Riel, which was dispersed.

BIBLIOGRAPHY.—J. J. Hargrave, *Red River* (1869); George F. G. Stanley, *Birth of Western Canada* (1936); Vera Kelsey, *Red River Runs North* (1951).

REDRUTH, a market town in Cornwall, England, 17 mi. E.N.E. of Penzance, on the G.W. railway. Pop. with Camborne (*q.v.*) 34,920 (1938). It lies high, on the northward slope of the central elevation of the county, with bare rocky moors to the south. It is the chief tin-mining town in Cornwall, and the bulk of the population is engaged in the mines or at the numerous tin-streaming works. A large quantity of the tin is sold by public auction at the mining exchange, the sales being known as tin-ticketings. There are manufactures of safety fuses, breweries, tanning, iron foundries and railway works, and near by are numerous stone quarries. The parish church of St. Uny, of which only the tower is ancient (Perpendicular), stands outside the town to the west, at the foot of Carn Brea. On the summit of this hill, near a small ancient castle, prehistoric remains are traceable.

RED SEA, a narrow strip of water extending south-south-east from Suez to the Strait of Bab el Mandeb in a nearly straight line, and separating the coasts of Arabia from those of Egypt, Nubia and Abyssinia. Its total length is about 1,200 m., and its breadth varies from about 250 m. in the southern half to 130 m. in 27° 45′ N., where it divides into two parts, the Gulf of Suez and the Gulf of Aqaba, separated from each other by the peninsula of Sinai. Structurally, the Red sea is part of a great rift-valley system forming one of the most marked features of the earth's crust. The rift valley of the Jordan and the Dead sea is continued southward by the Wadi el Araba, and its submerged southern section gives the Gulf of Aqaba. This well marked north-north-east to south-south-west line meets the north-north-west to south-south-east line, already marked in the Gulf of Suez, and together they form, to the south, the main basin of the Red sea. The rift may be traced still farther southward among the great African lakes.

This great structural depression is probably of Tertiary age, being let down between two ancient Archaean blocks—Arabia and North Africa. Secondary and Tertiary deposits appear on both flanks in Egypt and Arabia, while Archaean material appears at the surface in many places on the Red sea coast. These extensive earth movements were accompanied by much volcanic activity, traces of which are still evident. A group of volcanic islands occurs in 14° N., and on Jebel Teir, farther north, a volcano has only recently become extinct. The margin of the Red sea itself consists, on the Arabian side, of a strip of low plain backed by ranges of barren hills of coral and sand formation, and here and there by mountains of considerable height. The greater elevations are for the most part formed of limestones, except in the south, where they are largely volcanic. The coasts of the Gulf of Aqaba are steep, with numerous coral reefs on both sides. On the African side there are, in the north, wide stretches of desert plain, which towards the south rise to elevated tablelands, and ultimately to the mountains of Abyssinia. The shores of the Red sea are little indented; good harbours are almost wanting in the desert regions of the north, while in the south the chief inlets are at Massawa, and at Kamaran, almost directly opposite. Coral formations are abundant; immense reefs, both barrier and fringing, skirt both coasts, often enclosing wide channels between the reef and the land.

Depths.—The mean depth of the Red sea is 267 fathoms. The Gulf of Suez is shallow, and slopes regularly down to the northern extremity of the Red sea basin, which has a maximum depth of 640 fathoms, and then over a shoal of 60 fathoms goes down to 1,200 fathoms in 22° 7′ N. The Gulf of Aqaba is separated from the Red sea by a submarine bank only 70 fathoms from the surface, and in 28° 39′ N. and 34° 43′ E. it attains the depth of 700 fathoms. South of the 1,200-fathom depression a ridge rises to 500 fathoms in the latitude of Jeddah, and, south of this again, a similar depression goes down to 1,190 fathoms. Throughout this northern part, *i.e.*, to the banks of Suakin and Farsan in 20° N., the 100-fathom line keeps to a belt of coral reef close inshore, but in lower latitudes the shallow coral region, 300 m. long and 70 to 80 m. across, extends farther and farther seaward until, in the latitude of Hodeida, the deep channel (marked by the 100-fathom line) is only 20 m. broad, all the rest of the area being dangerous to navigation, even for small vessels. In the middle of the gradually narrowing channel three depressions are known to exist; soundings in two of these are: 1,209 fathoms in 20° N. and 890 fathoms in 16° N., a little to the north of Massawa. To the north-west of the volcanic island of Zebayir the depth is less than 500 fathoms; the bottom of the channel rises to the 100-fathom line at Hanish island (also volcanic), then shoals to 45 fathoms, and sinks again, in about the latitude of Mokha, in a narrow channel which curves westward round the island of Perim (depth 170 fathoms), to lose itself in the Indian ocean. This western channel is 16 m. wide in the Strait of Bab el Mandeb; the eastern channel of the strait is 2 m. broad and 16 fathoms deep. Estimates of the total area of the Red sea vary considerably, but it may be taken at 177,030 sq.st.m. approximately, and the volume at 53,700 cb.st.m. approximately.

Meteorology.—In the northern part, down to almost 19° N., the prevailing winds are north and north-west. The middle region, to 14°–16° N., has variable winds in an area of low barometric pressure, while in the southern Red sea south-east and east winds prevail. From June to August the north-west wind blows over the entire area; in September it retreats again as far as 16° N., south of which the winds are for a time variable. In the Gulf of Suez the westerly, or "Egyptian," wind occurs frequently during winter, sometimes blowing with violence, and generally accompanied by fog and clouds of dust. Strong north-north-east winds prevail in the Gulf of Aqaba during the greater part of the year; they are weakest in April and May, sometimes giving place at that season to southerly breezes. The high temperature and great relative humidity in summer, make it a difficult region for active life.

The mean annual temperature of the surface waters near the head is 77°; it rises to 80° in about 22° N., to 84° in 16° N., and drops again to 82° at the Strait of Bab el Mandeb. Daily variations of temperature are observable to a depth of over 50 fathoms. Temperature is, on the whole, higher near the Arabian than the Egyptian side, but it everywhere diminishes with increase of depth and latitude, down to 380 fathoms from the surface; below this depth a uniform constant temperature of 70.7° is observed throughout. In the Gulf of Suez temperature is relatively low, falling rapidly from south to north. The waters of the Gulf of Aqaba are warmer towards the Arabian than the Sinai coast; a uniform temperature of 70.2° is observed at all depths below

270 fathoms.

Salinity.—The salinity of the waters is relatively great, the highest reading being 41 per mille (Gulf of Suez), and the lowest 36.5 near Perim island. The distribution is, speaking generally, the opposite to that of temperature; salinity increases from the surface downwards, and from the south northwards, and it is greater towards the western than the eastern side. This statement holds good for the Gulf of Suez, in which the water is much salter than in the open sea; but in the Gulf of Aqaba the distribution is exceedingly uniform, nowhere differing much from an average of 40 per mille.

The movements of the waters are of great irregularity and complexity, rendering navigation difficult and dangerous. Two features stand out with special distinctness; the exchange of water between the Red sea and the Indian ocean, and the tidal streams of the Gulf of Suez. From the observations of salinity it is inferred that a surface current flows inwards to the Red sea in the eastern channel of the Strait of Bab el Mandeb, while a current of very salt water flows outward to the Indian ocean, through the western channel, at a depth of 50 to 100 fathoms from the surface. In the Gulfs of Suez and Aqaba, almost the only part of the Red sea in which tidal phenomena are well developed, a sharply-defined tidal circulation is found. Elsewhere, the surface movements at least are controlled by the prevailing winds, which give rise in places to complex "transverse" currents, and near the coast are modified by the channels enclosed by the coral reefs. During the prevalence of the north and north-west winds the surface level of the northern part is depressed by as much as 2 feet.

The Red sea was important in Egyptian maritime commerce at least as early as the 2nd millennium B.C. (*see* QOSEIR, EL) and it had associations with India early in the 1st millennium B.C. Under the Arabs the Red sea was an important highway of trade with connections to India, Persia and East Africa. This sea helped to keep Islam in touch with the thinkers of the East and with the glories of the ancient world during "the dark ages" in the West; with the revolutions in shipping and movement by sea that followed "the age of discovery" the Red sea seemed to retreat into the background; but with the cutting of the Suez canal (1869) and the shortening of the route to India, Australia and the East, the Red sea not only recovered its former importance but became one of the greatest commercial highways in the world.

BIBLIOGRAPHY.—A. Issel, *Morfologia e genesi del Mar Rosso. Saggio di Paleogeografia, Congresso Geogr. Ital.* (Florence, 1899); "Die Korallenriffe der Sinai-Halbinsel," *Abhandl. Math.-phys. Gesell. Wiss.,* vol. xiv. (Leipzig, 1888); *Meteorological Charts of the Red Sea* (Meteorological Office, 1895); *Report of the Voyage of the Russian Corvette "Vitiaz"* (1889); "Berichte der Commission für oceanographische Forschungen," 6th series, 1898, in vol. lxv. of the *Denkschriften der K.K. Akademie der Wissenschaften* (Vienna); also various notes and preliminary reports in the *Sitzungsberichte* of the Vienna Academy of Sciences; *Report of the Voyage of H.M.S. "Challenger,"* "Oceanic Circulation," p. 30; J. Hann, *Klimatologie,* vol. iii. p. 76 (1897).

REDSHANK, the name of a bird, *Tringa totanus,* so called from the colour of its long legs. In suitable localities it is abundant throughout the greater part of Europe and Asia, retiring southward for the winter, though a considerable number remain along the coasts of some of the more northern countries. The body of the redshank is as big as a snipe's, but its longer neck, wings and legs make it appear larger. Above, the general colour is greyish-drab, freckled with black, except the lower part of the back and a conspicuous band on each wing, which are white, while the flight-quills are black. The bird nests in inland localities as well as by the sea. The males in spring have a beautiful song-flight, rising and falling with quivering wings, and a striking courtship on the ground. They are very pugnacious, fights often continuing for over an hour. The redshank is very wary, and is disliked by shore gunners for giving the alarm to other species. The nest is generally concealed in a tuft of rushes or grass in the swamp whence the bird gets its sustenance, and contains four eggs of a warmly tinted brown with blackish spots or blotches.

The black, dusky or spotted redshank (*T. erythropus*) is a larger and less common bird, and in the greater part of Europe it only occurs on its passage to or from its breeding-grounds, which are south of the Arctic circle. The spot chosen for the nest is nearly always in forests and at some distance from water. In breeding-dress the head, neck, shoulders and lower parts are black, the back and rump white, while the legs become crimson. At other times of the year the plumage is similar to that of the common redshank and the legs are of the same light orange-red.

REDSTART or **FIRETAIL** (*Phoenicurus phoenicurus*), a small bird which is a summer visitor to Europe, where it haunts gardens, orchards, and old buildings. Its habit of flirting its red tail, and the white forehead, black throat, and bay breast of the cock are distinguishing features; the hen is more plainly coloured; but the characteristic colouring and action of the tail pertain to her equally as to her mate. The nest is almost always placed in a hole of a tree or building, and contains from five to seven eggs of a delicate greenish blue, occasionally sprinkled with faint red spots. The young on assuming their feathers present a great resemblance to those of the redbreast (*q.v.*) at the same age; but the red tail, though of duller hue than in the adult, forms even at this early age an easy means of distinguishing them. The redstart breeds regularly in all the counties of England and Wales. It also reaches the extreme north of Scotland; but in Ireland it is very rare. It appears throughout the whole of Europe in summer, and is known to winter in the interior of Africa. Several very nearly allied forms occur in Asia; and one, *P. aurorea*, is found in Japan. The black redstart (*P. ochrurus*) is darker than the preceding, with a more southerly range. Like the last, however, it winters in Africa. It often haunts the vicinity of houses. The males of the black redstart seem to be more than one year in acquiring their full plumage. Allied to the redstarts are the bluethroats (*q.v.*). These groups belong to the subfamily *Turdinae* of the thrushes. The American redstart (*Setophaga ruticilla*) belongs to the purely New World family *Mniotiltidae*, and ranges from Canada (in summer) to Bolivia, but is rare on the Pacific coast. The salmon of the breast, wings, and tail of the male are replaced by yellow in the female. The painted redstart (*S. picta*) has a deep red breast and belly. It inhabits the Mexican plateau, extending north to Arizona and New Mexico.

REDUCTION: *see* OXIDATION AND REDUCTION.

RED WING, a city of Minnesota, U.S., on the Mississippi river, below the mouth of the Cannon and above the head of Lake Pepin; 50 mi. S.E. of St. Paul; county seat of Goodhue county; on federal highways 61 and 63, state highways 19 and 58. It is served by Chicago Great Western and Chicago, Milwaukee, St. Paul and Pacific railways, bus and barge lines. Pop. (1950) 10,645. In 1695 Pierre Charles le Sueur established a post on Prairie Island, 8 mi. above Red Wing, and in 1727 René Boucher built a fort (abandoned in 1753) on the shore of Lake Pepin. A village of the Dakotas had long occupied the site of the city when in 1837 two Swiss missionaries established a mission which they maintained until 1846. In 1848 a second mission was established by the American board. The city was platted in 1853; chartered in 1857. Red Wing is the name of the Dakota chief who settled his people there, and who is buried on the top of Barn bluff. Red Wing produces shoes, leather, pottery, flour, marine motors, etc.

REDWING, a species of thrush (*q.v.*), *Turdus musicus*, a winter visitor to the British islands, arriving in autumn about the same time as the fieldfare (*q.v.*). It is very similar to the song-thrush, but with a white streak over the eye, and the sides of its body, inner wing-coverts and axillaries reddish-orange. The redwing breeds in colonies in woods in subarctic Europe and Asia to Lake Baikal. In winter it migrates as far south as North Africa and the Himalayas. Its song has often been praised, but is disappointing in comparison with that of the song-thrush or blackbird. In its winter quarters it often gives a peculiar inward song in early spring, while still in flocks. Its nest and eggs resemble those of the blackbird.

REDWOOD, SIR BOVERTON (1846–1919), British chemist, was born on April 26, 1846, and educated at University College school, London. He was trained as a pharmacist, but early specialized in the study of petroleum, becoming in 1869 secretary of the Petroleum association and subsequently studying oil conditions at first hand in many parts of the world (1883–86). He served on several important Government commissions both before

and during the World War. Founder of the Society of Petroleum Technologists, he became its first president 1913–14 and he was also a member of many other societies in pure and applied science. He was knighted in 1905, was made a baronet in 1911 and died in London on June 4, 1919. Redwood wrote widely on his subject, including *Petroleum*, 3 vol. (1913).

REDWOOD (*Sequoia sempervirens*) a valuable, gigantic, coniferous tree extending along the Pacific coastal forests from southern Oregon to near Santa Barbara, California. The largest tree upon which accurate measurements have been made is 364 ft. tall and 12 ft. 7 in. in diameter at breast height. It is seldom found more than 35 mi. inland or above 3,000 ft. in elevation. An unusual feature of this tree is its ability to develop thrifty, vigorous, stump sprouts which attain commercial proportions in a relatively short time. While coppice sprouts of this sort are a common feature of broad-leaved species, their occurrence among conifers is relatively rare. The allied bigtree, *Sequoia gigantea* (syn. *Sequoiadendron giganteum*) also of California (discovered in 1850 in the Sierra Nevada) develops a much more massive bole but not quite the stature of coastal species (*see* SEQUOIA).

REDWOOD CITY, a town of California, U.S.A., on Redwood creek, 27 mi. S. by E. of San Francisco; the county seat of San Mateo county. It is on federal highway 101, and is served by the Southern Pacific Ry. Pop. 25,342 in 1950 by federal census. It was settled about 1856 and incorporated in 1867.

REDWOOD HIGHWAY, an American highway 479 mi. long commencing at San Francisco, Calif., and terminating at Grants Pass, Ore. From Crescent City, Calif., to Eureka, the highway passes close to the Pacific coast, now high up on the cliffs and again down by the sea. It passes through 100 mi. of ancient redwood forests 20 mi. wide, whose trees are 200 and 300 ft. high, very straight, and as much as 30 ft. in diameter. South of Eureka the principal points touched are Fortuna, the Humbolt State Redwood park, Ukia and Santa Rosa.

RED WOODS, INSOLUBLE. Under this designation, sanderswood (*Pterocarpus santalinus*, Tropical Asia), barwood (*Baphia nitida*, West Coast of Africa) and camwood come into commerce. These closely resemble one another in tinctorial property, and contain colouring matters which are sparingly soluble in water. They may be applied to wool without the aid of a mordant, though in general the material is first dyed and a mordant, usually bichromate of potash, added to the dye-bath. The shade given with sanderswood and barwood is dull red brown, with camwood a more violet tint. Both sanderswood and barwood still find employment for "topping" indigoes, *i.e.*, the indigo-dyed woollen material is treated in a boiling bath with one or other of these dyewoods. Little is known of the chemical structure of the colouring matters of these dyewoods.

REED, JOSEPH (1741–1785), American politician, was born in Trenton, N.J., on Aug. 27, 1741. He graduated at Princeton in 1757, studied law in 1763–65 at the Middle Temple, London, and then practised in Trenton until his removal to Philadelphia in 1770. He was aide-de-camp and military secretary to Gen. Washington in 1775–76, and was adjutant general in 1776–77. In 1777–78 he was a delegate to the Continental Congress. From 1778 to 1781 he was president of the State executive council. During his administration the proprietary rights of the Penn family were abrogated (1779), and provision was made for the gradual abolition of slavery (1780). Reed was elected to Congress in 1784, but died in Philadelphia on March 5, 1785.

The Life and Correspondence of Joseph Reed (Philadelphia, 1874), by his grandson, William B. Reed, is based upon the family papers. It pictures Reed as an heroic patriot and statesman; George Bancroft, on the other hand, in the ninth volume (p. 229) of his *History* (1866) and in *Joseph Reed: an Historical Essay* (1867), pictures him as a trimmer of the most pronounced type. Bancroft withdrew his most specific charge in the 1876 edition of his *History*, in which, however, his tone towards Reed was unchanged.

His grandson, WILLIAM BRADFORD REED (1806–76), graduated at the Pennsylvania university in 1822. He was professor of American history in the University of Pennsylvania in 1850–56, United States minister to China in 1857–58, and in 1858 negotiated a treaty with China, proclaimed in 1860.

REED, THOMAS BRACKETT (1839–1902), American statesman, was born in Portland, Me., on Oct. 18, 1839. He graduated at Bowdoin college in 1860, and in 1865 was admitted to the bar. He was a member of the Maine House of Representatives in 1868–69 and of the State Senate in 1870, was attorney-general of the State in 1870–72, and was city solicitor of Portland in 1874–77. He was a Republican member of the National House of Representatives from 1877 until 1899, of which he was speaker in 1889–91 and in 1895–99. He was a "strong" speaker in his control of the proceedings, and he developed an organized committee system, making the majority of the committee on rules consist of the speaker and chairman of the committees on ways and means and on appropriations. The "Reed rules," drawn up by him, William McKinley and J. G. Cannon, were adopted on Feb. 14, 1890; they provided that every member must vote, unless pecuniarily interested in a measure, that members present and not voting may be counted for a quorum, and that no dilatory motion be entertained by the speaker. His parliamentary methods were bitterly attacked by his political enemies, who called him "Tsar Reed." His rules and methods of control of legislation were adopted by his successors in the speakership, and the power of the rules committee was greatly increased. After the war with Spain Reed broke with the administration on the issue of imperialism. He resigned his seat in 1899 and practised law in New York city. He died in Washington on Dec. 7, 1902. Reed was a remarkable personality, of whom many good stories were told, and opinions varied as to his conduct in the chair; but he was essentially a man of rugged honesty and power.

Reed's Rules were published as a parliamentary manual. He edited with others a *Library of Modern Eloquence* (1901). *See* the chapter on Reed in H. B. Fuller's *Speakers of the House* (Boston, 1909).

REED, WALTER (1851–1902), American bacteriologist, was born in Gloucester county, Va., on Sept. 13, 1851, and was educated at the University of Virginia and Bellevue Medical school (M.D., 1870). In 1874 he entered the medical corps of the U.S. army as assistant surgeon, with rank of lieutenant. In 1893 he was promoted to surgeon, with the rank of major, and made professor of bacteriology in the newly-organized Army Medical school. In 1898, when the Spanish American War opened, he was appointed chairman of a committee to investigate the causation and mode of propagation of typhoid fever, an epidemic of which had broken out among the soldiers. His *Report on the Origin and Spread of Typhoid Fever in U.S. Military Camps* (1904) revealed a number of points concerning the disease not before known, and emphasized others which had been little appreciated. In 1897 he and an associate proved the theory of Sanerelli—that the bacillus icteroides was the specific cause of yellow fever—erroneous. In 1899, when the disease was especially severe in Cuba, he was made chairman of a committee to investigate its cause and method of transmission. His observation of many cases led him to discount the then prevalent idea that the disease was transmitted by fomites in bedding, clothing, etc., of patients suffering from yellow fever, and to revive the discarded notion of Dr. Carlos Finlay that the yellow fever parasite was carried only by the mosquitoes. Since the disease was not taken by animals there was no method of proof except by experiment upon human beings. By a thorough set of experiments, in which some of Reed's co-workers sacrificed their lives for the cause, he proved to a sceptical world that the yellow fever parasite was carried only by the mosquito *Stegomyia fasciata* and that its bite caused the disease only under certain conditions. Possessed of this knowledge, American sanitary engineers eradicated the yellow fever from Cuba, and it has since been largely eliminated from civilized portions of the world. Reed died at Washington, D.C., on Nov. 23, 1902.

See H. A. Kelly, *Walter Reed and Yellow Fever* (1906), which contains a bibliography of Reed's publications; also P. De Kruif, *Microbe Hunters*, pp. 311–333 (1926).

REED, a term applied to several distinct species of large, water-loving grasses. The common or water-reed, *Phragmites communis*, occurs along the margins of lakes, fens, marshes and placid streams, not only throughout Great Britain and the United States, but widely distributed in Arctic and also in temperate regions, extending into the tropics. Another very important species is *Ammophila arenaria* (also known as *Psamma arenaria*), the sea-reed or marram-grass, a native of the sandy shores of Europe and north Africa. Both species have been of notable geological importance, the former binding the soil and so impeding denudation, and actually converting swamp into dry land, largely by the aid of its tall (5 to 10 ft.) close set stems. The latter species, of which the branching rootstocks may be traced 30 or even 40 ft., is of still greater importance in holding sand-dunes against the sea, and for this purpose has not only been long protected by law, but has been extensively planted on the coasts of Norfolk, Netherlands, Gascony, etc. Other reeds are *Calamagrostis* (various species), *Gynerium argenteum* (pampas grass), etc., also *Arundo donax,* the largest European grass (6 to 12 ft. high), which is abundant in Europe. Reeds have been used from the earliest times in thatching and in other branches of construction, and also for arrows, the pipes of musical instruments, etc. Reed pens are still used in the East. Plants belonging to other orders occasionally share the name, especially the bur-reed (*Sparganium*) and the reed-mace (*Typha*), both belonging to the family Typhaceae. The bulrushes (*Scirpus*), belonging to the family Cyperaceae are also to be distinguished.

REEDBUCK, a foxy-red South African antelope (*Redunca arundineum*) of medium size, with a bushy tail, a bare gland-patch behind the ear, and in the male short horns which bend forwards in a regular curve. There are several other species of the genus *Redunca* to which the name of reedbuck is also applied, one of these ranging as far north as Abyssinia, and another inhabiting west Africa.

REED INSTRUMENTS, a class of wind instruments in the tubes of which sound-waves are generated by the vibrations of a reed mouthpiece. Reed instruments fall into two great classes: (1) those blown directly by the breath of the performer, who is thus able to control more or less the character of the expression; (2) those in which the wind supply is obtained by mechanical devices, such as the bag of bagpipe instruments or the bellows of such keyboard instruments as the organ and harmonium.

Directly-blown reed instruments comprise the section of modern wind instruments known as the "wood wind," with the exception of flute and piccolo; and they are classified according to the kind of reed vibrator of which the mouthpiece is composed. There are three kinds of reed mouthpieces: (1) the single or beating reed; (2) the double reed; (3) the free reed, all of which perform the function of sound-producer. (For illustration *see* FREE REED VIBRATOR.) The reed used consists of a thin tongue or strip of reed, cane or some elastic material, thinned gradually to a delicate edge. It is adapted to the tube in such a manner that when it is at rest the opening at the mouthpiece end of the tube consists only of a very slight aperture or chink, which is periodically opened and closed by the pulsations of the reed when acted upon by the compressed breath of the player. This principle is common to all reed mouthpieces, and the difference in timbre is in a measure due to the manner in which the pulsations are brought about and the degree of elasticity permitted.

THE ANCIENT SYRINX OR PIPES OF PAN, CONSISTING OF TUBES OF VARYING LENGTHS, BOUND TOGETHER

The *single* or *beating reed* consists of a single blade bevelled at the edge and placed over a table or frame communicating with the main bore of the instrument, against which it beats, causing a series of pulsations. The single reed is common to all the members of the clarinet family, consisting, besides the clarinet, of the basset-horn or tenor, and of the bass and pedal clarinets; of the batyphone, an early bass clarinet, and of the saxophone. The ancient Greek aulos (*q.v.*) was also undoubtedly used with a beating reed during some period of its history.

The *double reed* consists of two blades of reed or other suitable material tightly bound together by many turns of waxed silk, so that above the construction the tube formed by the two blades has an oval section, while below, where it communicates with the main bore of the instrument, it is strictly cylindrical. The chink in this case is thus formed by two thin walls of reed of equal elasticity (*see* OBOE, BASSOON). The double reed is common to the members of the oboe family, consisting, besides the oboe, of the cor anglais or tenor, of the fagotto or bassoon, and of the contra fagotto or double bassoon; and it is also used in the sarrusophone family, instruments of brass but classed with the wood wind on account of the mouthpiece and fingering.

The *free reed* is not represented among members of the modern wood wind, and, as adapted to a directly blown instrument, only finds application in the Chinese cheng, the prototype of the harmonium, and in the mouth-organ or harmonica.

The reed in wind instruments produces a peculiar tone quality to which it has given its name; it varies in the three different kinds of mouthpieces without losing its fundamental reedy timbre.

For reed instruments of the second class, viz., those indirectly blown by mechanical means, *see* under the names of the individual instruments—BAG-PIPE; CONCERTINA; HARMONIUM; ORGAN; etc.

REEVE, CLARA (1729–1807), English novelist, was born at Ipswich, Suffolk, in 1729. She was an industrious writer and produced many works in prose and verse, including a history of fiction, the *Progress of Romance* (1785). Her only eminent success, however, was the novel *The Old English Baron* (1777), originally published under the title of *The Champion of Virtue*.

She died at Ipswich on Dec. 3, 1807.

REEVE, HENRY (1813–1895), English publicist, younger son of Henry Reeve, a Whig physician and writer of Norwich, was born at Norwich on Sept. 9, 1813. He was educated at the Norwich grammar school under Edward Valpy. During his holidays he saw a great deal of the young John Stuart Mill. In 1829 he studied at Geneva and mixed in the then brilliant Genevese society, which included the Sismondis, Charles Victor de Bonstetten, Augustin Pyrame de Candolle, Zygmunt Krasinski (his most intimate friend), and Adam Mickiewicz, whose *Faris* he translated.

During a visit to London in 1831 he was introduced to William Makepeace Thackeray and Thomas Carlyle, while through the Austins he met other men of letters. The next year in Paris he met Victor Hugo, Victor Cousin and Sir Walter Scott. He became in 1835–36 a frequenter of Madame de Circourt's salon, and numbered among his friends Alphonse de Lamartine, Jean Lacordaire, Alfred de Vigny, Louis Adolphe Thiers, François Guizot and Charles de Montalembert. He was also a friend of Alexis Charles de Tocqueville, of whose books, *Démocratie en Amérique* and the *Ancien régime,* he made standard translations into English. In 1837 he was made clerk of appeal and later registrar to the judicial committee of the privy council.

From 1840 to 1855 he wrote for *The Times,* his close touch with men like Guizot, Christian Charles Bunsen, Lord Clarendon and his own chief at the privy council office, Charles Greville, enabling him to write with authority on foreign policy during the period from 1848 to the end of the Crimean war. Upon the promotion of Sir George Cornewall Lewis to the cabinet early in 1855, Reeve was asked to edit the April number of the *Edinburgh Review,* to which his father had been one of the earliest contributors, and in the following July he became the editor. His friendship with the Orleanist leaders in France survived all vicissitudes, and he was appealed to for guidance by successive French ambassadors. He was more than once the medium of private negotiations between the English and French governments.

In April 1863 he published what was perhaps the most important of his contributions to the *Edinburgh*—a review of Alexander William Kinglake's *Crimea;* and in 1872 he brought out a selection of his *Quarterly Review* and *Edinburgh* articles on eminent Frenchmen, entitled *Royal and Republican France.* Three years later appeared the first of three installments (1875, 1885 and 1887) of his edition of the famous *Memoirs* which Greville had placed in his hands a few hours before his death in 1865.

A purist in point of form and style, of the school of Thomas Babington Macaulay and Henry Milman, Reeve outlived his literary generation, and eventually became one of the most reactionary of the old Whigs. Yet he continued to edit and, on the whole, to maintain the reputation of the *Edinburgh* until his death at his seat of Foxholes, in Hampshire, on Oct. 21, 1895. During his lifetime, he had been elected a member of "The Club" in 1861, was made a doctor of civil law by Oxford university in 1869, a Companion of the Bath in 1871 and a corresponding member of the French Institute in 1865.

His *Memoirs and Letters* (2 vol., with portrait) were edited by Sir J. K. Laughton in 1898.

REEVE, a bailiff, steward or business agent; in early English history, one entrusted with the administration of a division of a country; also the chief magistrate of a town or district. The name survives in Canada for the president of a village or town council and in the United States, in composition, as port-reeve, town-reeve, etc.

REEVES, SIMS (1818–1900), English vocalist, was born at Woolwich, Sept. 26, 1818, as John Reeves and received his musical education from his father, a musician in the royal artillery. He studied with J. W. Hobbs and T. Cooke, and appeared at Drury Lane (1841–43) in subordinate tenor parts. He studied under G. M. Bordogni in Paris and A. Mazzucato in Milan, where his debut in Italian opera was made at the Scala theatre as Edgardo in Donizetti's *Lucia di Lammermoor.* His career on the English operatic stage began at Drury Lane in Dec. 1847 in the same part, under the conductorship of Berlioz. At the Norwich festival (1848) he made a great sensation in "The enemy said," from *Israel in Egypt.* He was recognized as the leading English tenor; and the tenor parts in M. Costa's *Eli* and *Naaman* were written for him. His first Handel festival was that of 1857.

He died at Worthing on Oct. 25, 1900.

REEVES, WILLIAM PEMBER (1857–1932), New Zealand administrator, was born at Canterbury, New Zealand, on Feb. 10, 1857, and educated at Christchurch, N.Z. He read for the law and was called to the New Zealand bar, but eventually took up journalism, becoming editor of the *Canterbury Times* and the *Lyttelton Times.*

In 1887 Reeves entered parliament, and held office from 1891 to 1896 as minister of education. He published several volumes on the history of New Zealand, and one volume of verse, and contributed to the 10th and later editions of the *Encyclopædia Britannica.*

RE-EXPORTS: *see* EXPORTS.

REFECTORY, the dining hall of a monastery, convent, etc. There frequently was a sort of ambo, approached by steps, from which to read the *legenda sanctorum,* etc., during meals. The refectory was generally situated by the side of the south cloister, so as to be removed from the church but contiguous to the kitchen.

The word is also sometimes applied to any large hall used for community meals, as in a college, school, etc.

REFEREE, a person to whom anything is referred; an arbitrator. The court of referees in England was a court to which the house of commons committed the decision of all questions as to the right of petitioners to be heard in opposition to private bills. Consisting of the chairman of ways and means, the deputy chairman and not less than seven other members of the house appointed by the speaker, the court was charged with the duty, as defined by a standing order, to decide upon all petitions against private bills, or against provisional orders or provisional certificates, as to the rights of the petitioners to be heard upon such petitions. In the high court of justice, under the Judicature act of 1873, cases might be submitted to three official referees, for trial, inquiry and report, or assessment of damages. Inquiry and report might be directed in any case, trial only by consent of the parties, or in any matter requiring any prolonged examination of documents or accounts, or any investigation which could not be tried in the ordinary way.

United States.—The term referee is commonly applied to persons to whom a court sends a cause or some question therein for determination or for the purpose of taking evidence and reporting upon the same. In this connection it is synonymous with such terms as auditor, commissioner, arbitrator, assessor, etc.

In some states the term is applied to a master, who is appointed in equity suits pursuant to statute as distinguished from masters appointed pursuant to the old equity practice. (*See* EQUITY.)

REFERENDUM AND INITIATIVE, two methods by which the wishes of the electorate may be expressed with regard to proposed legislation. They exist in a variety of forms. The referendum may be obligatory or optional. Under the former type certain classes of actions by a legislature are required, ordinarily by constitutional provision, to be referred to a popular vote for approval or rejection. Amendments to constitutions proposed by legislatures are subject in most states of the United States, for example, to an obligatory referendum. Under the optional (or facultative) referendum a specified number of voters by petition may demand a popular vote on a law passed by a legislative body. By this means the actions of a legislature may be overruled.

The referendum may also be constitutional or legislative depending on the nature of the matter referred. In the United States questions subject to the obligatory referendum are mostly constitutional while those subject to the optional referendum are invariably legislative. The obligatory and optional forms are to be distinguished from the submission by legislative bodies of particular questions to a referendum or plebiscite, the effect of which may be determinative of the issue or only advisory to the legislature.

By the initiative a specified number of voters may invoke a popular vote on a proposed law or constitutional amendment. In its direct form a proposal supported by the requisite number of voters is submitted directly to a popular vote for decision. Under the indirect form the legislature has an opportunity to enact such a proposal. If rejected, the proposition is submitted to a popular vote, in some instances with an alternative proposal by the legislature or with a statement of its reasons for rejection.

The initiative and referendum came into common use in Switzerland in the liberal reaction after the Paris revolution of 1830. In 1831 St. Gall first adopted the facultative referendum (then and for some time after called the veto), and its example was followed by several cantons before 1848. The obligatory referendum appears first in 1852 and 1854 respectively in the Valais and the Grisons, when the older system was reformed, but in its modern form it was first adopted in 1863 by the canton of rural Basle. The initiative was first adopted in 1845 by Vaud. In the case both of the facultative referendum and of the initiative each canton fixes the number of citizens who have a right to exercise this power. Both institutions have been used freely in federal and cantonal matters.

Swiss experience with the devices of direct legislation was influential in the adoption of the initiative and the optional referendum in U.S. states and municipalities.

British Commonwealth.—*Australia.*—The Australian commonwealth constitution provides for neither the initiative nor the optional referendum, but the obligatory referendum exists with respect to amendments to the constitution proposed by parliament. In fact the Australian electorate has proved surprisingly hostile to constitutional innovation. In the first half-century of the commonwealth's life only 12 amendments were submitted to the people by referendum and of these only four were carried. The first in 1906 altered the date of senate elections, the second in 1910 enabled the commonwealth to take over state debts, the third in 1927 set up a Loan council and the fourth in 1946 confirmed the commonwealth's power to legislate upon certain social services. Proposals rejected included conscription for overseas service in 1916 and 1917, federal rent and price control in 1948, and anti-Communist legislation in 1951. The referendum has also been used by the state governments.

New Zealand has used the machinery of the referendum in repeated endeavours to secure the passage of prohibition—always without success. In 1949 proposals to amend the licensing laws were rejected, but off-the-course betting and the introduction of conscription were both carried by referendum.

Canada has no such obligatory referendum as Australia and has in fact used the device on a national scale on only two occasions, in 1898 on the temperance issue and in 1942 when the government sought and obtained release from its pledge not to introduce conscription for service overseas. At the provincial and municipal level the referendum has been much used for securing decisions on the control of liquor, resulting first in the imposition and later in the removal of prohibition in the western provinces. It has also been employed in local government for the submission of bylaws to the electorate. In Newfoundland in 1948 the voters were polled on the constitutional question of whether they wished to continue under commission government, or regain dominion status, or confederate with Canada. They chose the last-named course.

Ireland.—The Irish Free State constitution of 1922 made a referendum mandatory in cases of constitutional amendment and allowed for referenda on nonconstitutional issues in certain circumstances. There was also a provision for an optional initiative. In 1928 the constitutional referendum was suspended, and the optional referendum and initiative were abolished. The 1937 constitution, however (itself ratified by plebiscite), restored the referendum (though not the initiative) in its 1922 form.

European Countries.—Formal adherence to democratic doctrines in drafting new constitutions in various European countries after World War I led to frequent provision for use of the initiative and referendum. Thus Germany's Weimar constitution of 1919 made generous provision for referenda in certain contingencies, although in fact they were little employed. The same was true of Austria. Less enthusiasm for direct democracy was felt by constitution-makers after World War II, but some use of the referendum was provided for. In France the constitution originally proposed for the French republic was rejected by referendum in 1946 and its successor accepted five months later. The constitution later adopted required that any amendment must be submitted to the people unless it has obtained a two-thirds majority of the lower house of the French parliament or a three-fifths majority of both houses. In Italy the post-World War II constitution provided that 50,000 electors may present a proposal to the legislature, and, if 500,000 voters or five regional councils request it, a referendum must be held on the question of abrogating a law. There is also some provision for using the referendum as part of the amending process. Neither in France nor in Italy, however, had any of these provisions been put to the test of use by the latter 1950s.

The United States.—The obligatory referendum on amendments to state constitutions proposed by state legislatures, first adopted by Connecticut in 1818, has become the prevailing method for the amendment of state constitutions. In some states a referendum is obligatory on bond issues and a like rule is widespread in local government for bond issues, tax questions and related matters. Because of the detailed nature of state constitutions and the necessity for their frequent amendment, many issues not of a nature to arouse great interest among the voters are referred to them for amendment.

In U.S. usage, initiative and referendum or direct legislation refers not to the obligatory referendum but to the optional referendum on legislation and to the initiation of laws or constitutional amendments by the voters (with the assumption that a popular vote or referendum on the initiated measure will follow). These devices were adopted in the U.S. under the leadership of groups hostile to machine rule, distrustful of legislatures and with a deep faith in democracy. The belief was that by granting the people a means to overrule legislative action and to initiate popular votes on legislation, abuses at the time characteristic of state legislatures might be prevented. Conservative groups were hostile to the adoption of the institution of direct legislation. The chief use of direct legislation has been in the western states, and it has not fulfilled the hopes of its advocates or the fears of its opponents. In practice the referendum is used by groups which consider themselves aggrieved by an action of the legislature and feel that they might persuade a majority of the electorate to support them in their demand that the law not go into effect. The initiative tends to be used by groups which have been unable to induce the legislature to enact a desired law. By the initiative they can seek direct action by the electorate.

The initiative and referendum proved much less important than the obligatory referendum in bringing issues to the voters. Moreover, a large proportion of the instances of their use occurred in California and Oregon. In the legislative process as a whole the initiative and referendum are comparatively unimportant in so far as the volume of legislation directly affected is concerned. The devices may be regarded, in the words of Woodrow Wilson, as a "gun behind the door" to be used when abuses arise in the legislative body.

BIBLIOGRAPHY.—H. L. McBain and L. Rogers, *The New Constitutions of Europe* (New York, 1923); A. L. Lowell, *Public Opinion and Popular Government* (New York, 1926); W. E. Rappard, *The Government of Switzerland* (New York, 1937); G. Sauser-Hall, *The Political Institutions of Switzerland* (Oxford, 1946); Nicholas Mansergh, *The Irish Free State* (London, New York, 1934); A. Brady, *Democracy in the Dominions,* 2nd ed. (Toronto, 1952; Oxford, 1953); J. D. Barnett, *Operation of the Initiative, Referendum and Recall in Oregon* (New York, 1915); V. O. Key, Jr. and W. W. Crouch, *The Initiative and Referendum in California* (Berkeley, Calif., 1939); J. K. Pollock, *The Initiative and Referendum in Michigan* (Ann Arbor, Mich., 1940); H. F. Gosnell and M. J. Schmidt, "Popular Law Making in the United States, 1924–36," in *Problems Relating to Legislative Organization and Powers,* New York State Constitutional convention (1938).
(V. O. K.; H. G. N.).

REFLECTION. When waves of any kind travelling in one medium arrive at another in which their velocity is different, part of their energy is, in general, turned back into the first medium. This is termed reflection. If the surface of separation is smooth, *i.e.,* if the irregularities in it are small compared with the wave length of the incident disturbance, the reflection is *regular;* if the surface is rough each facet reflects the rays incident upon it in accordance with the laws of regular reflection (*see* LIGHT) and the reflection, as a whole, is *irregular* or *diffuse.* Consider, for example, the reflection of light at smooth and ruffled water surfaces. From the ruffled surface rays enter the eye after reflection from suitably inclined facets distributed over a wide area on the surface and a diffuse band of light is seen, while from the smooth surface only those rays reflected at the requisite angle from a small area on the surface can reach the eye. In the first case the optical system of the eye focuses the water surface on the retina just as it does all other rough surfaces. In the latter the rays appear to come from a laterally inverted replica of the luminous source situated as far below the surface as the source itself is above, and it is this *image* which is then focused on the retina.

The diffusion of light by matt surfaces in general is an example of the same phenomenon differing only in the number and size of the facets which scatter the light.

Echoes and reverberations are caused by the reflection of sound (*q.v.*) and the "fading" of wireless signals (in part) by variations in the conditions under which the electromagnetic waves are reflected by the Heaviside layer in the upper atmosphere. (*See* WIRELESS TELEGRAPHY.)

REFLECTORS: *see* ILLUMINATING ENGINEERING.

REFORMATION. This word, like "Catholic," is in itself a question-begging term; but both are adopted, if only under protest, in the general speech of the present day. By "Reformation," then, we mean that religious revolution of the 16th century which has divided western Christendom into two camps, the Catholic and the Protestant. This was in itself a very complex movement, due to a multiplicity of causes which may be grouped under four main headings: *moral, doctrinal, economic* and *political.*

Moral Causes.—These were the most important of all, for they lay at the very root. From St. Bernard at the beginning of the 12th century to Bishop Fox, who founded Corpus Christi college at Oxford in 1516, there is no generation from which we cannot choose orthodox and distinguished churchmen who urged the crying need for Church reform in language which might seem harsh from the pen of a modern Protestant. From Innocent III. in 1215 to Leo X. in 1512, nine great world-councils were held, with Church reform in the forefront of their programme; yet

each in turn confessed the failure of its predecessors, and the Council of Trent (1545) testified to the impotence of them all.

The attempt to saddle the Black Death (1348–50) with this state of things is grossly unhistorical. Two of the greatest cardinals of the 13th century, St. Bonaventura (d. 1274) and Hugues de St. Cher (d. 1260) were among the most outspoken of all our witnesses against the clerical morals of their day. Even plainer is the testimony of another very distinguished bishop, Guillaume Durand, who was consulted for the Council of Vienne (1311). In his long memorial, he drew a terrible picture of the reigning and growing abuses, and concluded that the thing most needful was "a reformation in head and in members," that is, from the pope and his court downwards; and this became a watchword not only at succeeding councils, not only among outside critics, but sometimes of popes. It is acknowledged on all hands that the abuses emphasized at the council of 1215 were in many respects even more rampant in 1512, and that the discipline so often demanded was never realized until after the Council of Trent had completed its long work (1564).

The celibacy of the clergy had presented great and continual difficulties. (*See* CELIBACY.) Even so energetic a reformer as St. Anselm was practically compelled to abandon his design of separating the English clergy from their partners. A visitation of the diocese of Hereford in 1397 shows 52 concubinary clergy known to the bishop out of 281 parishes. Another of Lausanne diocese in 1416–17 shows, among 273 communities, more than 80 clergy known as concubinary. The Oxford chancellor Gascoigne (1450), a strong anti-Lollard, tells us that the bishop of St. Asaph of his day was earning 400 marks (the equivalent of something like £5,000 a year in modern money) from the licences for concubinage that he sold to his priests; and, though these figures are doubtless greatly exaggerated, yet Sir Thomas More does not deny that there was something of the same system in Ireland; and similar evidence comes to us from other parts of Europe.

It is rare to find any mediaeval author who, if he generalizes about monks, friars and nuns at all, fails to complain of the immoral example which they too frequently set.[1] St. Bernardino of Siena (d. 1444) tells us that "very many" men of his day had no belief in Heaven, and looked upon the Christian scriptures as merely interesting figments, because of the evil lives of cloisterers and other clergy. Pope Gregory X. had said the same at the council of Lyons (1274), and by about 1500 it had become a commonplace that the lives of the clergy were mainly responsible for the increase of heresy. And some of the most distinguished mediaeval witnesses, such as Cardinal Hugues de St. Cher (d. 1260) and St. Catharine of Siena (d. 1380) point out that clerical vices were naturally reflected and even exaggerated in the laity. Again, long before Luther's appearance, orthodox Catholics were emphasizing the abusive side of many Church ceremonies and practices; the sale of indulgences (*q.v.*), the multiplication of holy-days and the vice and riot which often marked these festivals; the abuse of the mass and of the consecrated oils for witchcraft; and the extent to which clerical immunities encouraged crimes. The laity of the later middle ages, with all their faults, were improving far more rapidly than the clergy; and this gave a proportionally increasing impetus to criticism.

Doctrine.—Here the clergy had once been supreme, and would probably have had little difficulty in maintaining their authority if they had kept unquestioned moral superiority. Few people are really interested in pushing theological enquiries very far, and, so long as men's conduct corresponds to their doctrine, the vast majority of mankind are willing to accept this at least as a working theory, and are under no temptation to question the speculative basis of practices which they approve. So long as there was no deep gulf between what the clergy actually were and what the people had a right to expect of them, free-thought was mainly limited to a few philosophers here and there, to a few weavers at their loom or cobblers at their bench, and to that dead weight of indifference, of resistance against idealism of any kind, which

[1] More than 100 orthodox witnesses are cited on pp. 379–419 of G. G. Coulton's *Five Centuries of Religion,* vol. ii.

has prevailed in every generation among the masses who need to concentrate so much of their thoughts and their labour upon the elementary problems of daily bread. We have abundant proof that the majority of the mediaeval population were not actively religious; but for a long time the enthusiastic churchman had generally nothing worse to struggle with than inertia and complacent ignorance. About the year A.D. 1000, there came a revival comparable almost to that which we call the Renaissance. With this revival we also find signs of free-thought and religious friction; an ice-bound world was now thawing; therefore it moved less regularly and under less strict control than might have been desired. Many features of the then existing dogmatic scheme had been created less by profound philosophy than by popular feeling or by comparatively unreflecting impulses. All men, for instance, had gradually grown to assume that we must take that text "many are called, but few are chosen," in its most baldly literal sense. Even in the 13th century, and in a philosopher so remarkable for balance and moderation as St. Thomas Aquinas, we find that the "few" who shall be saved are directly contrasted with the "very many" who shall go to hell. His contemporary, the Franciscan Berthold of Regensburg, whom Roger Bacon singles out as the greatest preacher of the day, actually commits himself in one passage to a rough numerical calculation; only about one in 100,000 shall be saved; and few mediaeval theologians put it more favourably than one in 1,000.

Moreover, they exerted all their imagination and their rhetoric to impress upon their hearers the terrible significance of this separation between the sheep and the goats. All was to depend upon the last moment of life; and, even there, it must depend mainly upon the faith in which the sinner died. Berthold asks his hearers to imagine themselves writhing white-hot within a white-hot universe until the day of judgment, when the pains will be greatly increased. Let them imagine this continuing for as many years as all the hairs that have grown upon all the beasts in this world since the creation; and, even then, the sinner will be only at the beginning of his torments. Yet Berthold was one of the kindliest of men; if he defended the current dogma with this ferociously implacable logic, it was because he had inherited it as part of the deposit of faith, and because he now found himself faced by an opposition which no student of the Reformation can afford to ignore.

Heresy.—The first half of the 12th century had witnessed the rise of several powerful heretical sects, which even the eloquence and influence of men like St. Bernard could not extinguish, though the leaders could be taken and slain. All these sects were more or less antisacerdotal; and more than one held among its chief tenets that the personal unworthiness of the priest impairs or destroys the value of the sacrament which he administers, a doctrine to which some colour had been lent by the very methods taken to combat clerical concubinage by the great pope Gregory VII. (d. 1085).

Towards the end of the century, these popular and comparatively unlearned revolts were succeeded by others of very different intellectual weight. The Waldensians [1175] took their stand upon the Bible; this they read in the vernacular, and committed to memory with a diligence which, as even their persecutors complained, ought to have shamed the orthodox out of their ignorance.

About the same time, the complete works of Aristotle began to filter into the University of Paris through translations from the Arabic, and, a little later, through more accurate versions made by orthodox scholars. The Bible led the Waldensians to deny any essential distinction between clergy and laity; but they long persisted in regarding themselves as orthodox Catholics. The new Aristotle, and especially his Arabic translators and commentators, led a certain number of Paris teachers to adopt the teaching of Averroes (*q.v.*), and thus to deny such fundamental doctrines as the personality of God, the creation, and the immortality of the soul.

But stern measures of repression, first by bishops and clergy and then by the Inquisition (*q.v.*), prevented the general diffusion of these doctrines. In southern France, indeed, about 1200, it was complained that the heretics outnumbered the Catholics; but Innocent III. exterminated them in a merciless crusade; and the new orders of friars, instituted soon afterwards, did almost as much as the sword and the Inquisition to crush movements which were necessarily sporadic and disorganized, since there was no chance of bringing that side of university scholarship into quiet and steady co-operation with the less articulate impulses of the multitudes. Moreover, from the very first, there was naturally a good deal of base leaven in these revolts; and even the Waldensians, whose original tenets resembled modern Quakerism in a good many respects, were gradually compelled, under persecution, to make common cause with other rebels whom they had begun by opposing.

Orthodoxy.—Society as a mass was not ripe for revolution; the nonconformists had too little of a positive programme to substitute for that of the conformists. For the orthodox had gradually set themselves to systematize the theology which they had inherited. Peter Lombard, bishop of Paris (d. 1164) compiled his *Sentences, i.e.,* texts from the Bible and from the fathers, arranged with comments so as to present a fairly consistent foundation upon which most of later mediaeval theology was built. St. Thomas Aquinas (d. 1274) built up a powerful constructive plea for Christianity in his *Summa contra Gentiles* and a wonderfully complete synthesis of Christian tradition with Aristotelian philosophy in his *Summa totius Theologiae.*

From the mid 13th century onwards, there was a tendency in official circles to look upon the intellectual and social equilibrium as complete; philosophers were less concerned to advance than to hold the positions already gained and to strengthen the outworks from generation to generation. Roger Bacon, the slightly older contemporary of Aquinas, might indeed criticize this imposing philosophical structure in terms which almost anticipate Huxley; it rested (he said) upon a Bible misunderstood, and an Aristotle misunderstood, and upon an almost total neglect of the physical and mathematical sciences. But Bacon exaggerates so far as Aristotle is concerned; and he, like those few who thought with him, had no chance in face of the Inquisition; therefore, though a great deal of Averroism survived at the universities, and we have evidence throughout the later middle ages for groups of "intellectuals" who treated Christianity as an outworn superstition, it was improbable that these men would ever have led a revolt. The academic tendency was rather to evade serious issues under shelter of the theory of "double truth"; things (they said) might be theologically true even while they were philosophically false. Far more important was the gradual change of thought among the masses. These, as zealous teachers complained, had always looked too grossly for tangible and immediate results. Saints' images which refused to work expected miracles might be scorned or maltreated; the failure of St. Louis' crusade led common folk to say "nowadays, Mohammed is stronger than Christ." The Black Death inflicted a terrible shock, from which all vital things recovered rapidly, but which shook all mere conventions to their base; to that extent, it must certainly be counted among the hastening factors of the Reformation.

The popes, by their voluntary desertion of Rome for Avignon, did much to impair their prestige, especially in England, where they seemed necessarily partisans of France in the Hundred Years' War. This was expressed in popular rhymes: "The pope is a Frenchman now, but Jesus is English; let us see who will do most, Jesus or the pope!" Then came the Great Schism, with 39 years of struggle between rival popes upon whose claims, though historians are mostly in agreement, the Roman church has never pronounced so clearly and unequivocally as to render it a question settled for all time. Among contemporaries, St. Catharine of Siena was certain that Urban was true pope, and Clement a pretender. But the Spaniard, St. Vincent Ferrer, proves with every reinforcement of scholastic logic, not only that Clement is true pope, but that no man who, having heard the pleas in his favour, decides for Urban, can hope for heaven. The effect of this upon the masses can scarcely be exaggerated; it was the schism, perhaps, which lent its greatest force to the heresy of Wycliffe. For, at the same time, popular devotions and a popular theology were growing up under the wing of the Church, yet in considerable independence of the priesthood.

Piers Plowman is only one of many books which show how pious and thoughtful folk, outside the hierarchy, were exercised by such problems as predestination, or the damnation of virtuous non-Christians, or the papal doctrine of indulgences (*q.v.*). The multiplication of books of popular piety in the last generations before the Reformation is enormous. For good or for evil, the people were beginning to outgrow clerical tutelage. Even in the foundation of schools and hospitals, the laity were beginning not only to pay their money, as they had done for long past, but to demand control of their own foundations. There was new life everywhere about 1500; but the gains were far more secular than sacerdotal.

Economic Causes.—During the later centuries of the middle ages, clerical possessions were enormous; churchmen owned a proportion which has been variously estimated at one-fifth or one-third of the whole landed property; yet they claimed to be free of taxation by the state. This naturally led to extreme friction; the preamble of Boniface VIII.'s celebrated bull *Clericis Laicos* (1296), in which he strongly asserted this claim for immunity, runs: "That the laity are bitterly hostile to the clergy is a matter of ancient tradition which is also plainly confirmed by the experience of modern times."

Equal friction arose from the farther claim, which had gradually grown up and was finally fixed by John XXII. (1316–34), that all Church benefices belong to the pope, who may appoint whom he will. This naturally led to a systematic trade in benefices at the Roman court: "Nothing is to be had at Rome without money," wrote Aeneas Silvius, the future pope Pius II. (1458–64). The popes took from each bishop half of his year's income (annates), and proportionately from abbots of great monasteries. Justice was sold in all the Church courts even more frequently than by secular judges; from at least the 12th century onwards, it was notorious that the archdeacons derived a large proportion of their income from bribes. These economic causes for reformation are most pithily summed up in the *Hundred Grievances of the German Nation*, laid before Adrian VI. (1522–23) by the German princes.

The Inquisition.—Moreover, the Inquisition itself, by its very constitution, had become a terrible economic burden. It had always paid its way by wholesale confiscations; even "reconciled" heretics must lose their goods. Therefore, when heresy had been nearly stamped out among rich and conspicuous folk, and the few that remained were such as had procured some sort of illegal protection, then (as we are frankly told by the Inquisitor Eymeric, writing about 1350) princes ceased to take an interest in the Inquisition, and it languished for want of funds.

In the later middle ages, the Inquisition directed much of its energies to the suppression of witchcraft; for an enormous number of heathen customs still survived, especially among the peasantry, who formed the overwhelming majority of the population. Many peasants, said Berthold of Regensburg (1250), and especially many peasant women, cannot take any step in life without having recourse to witchcraft. Therefore, easy though it was to raise an outcry against some unpopular individual, any general enforcement of severe measures against witchcraft must have been extremely unpopular. The enormous multiplication of witch-hunts during the 15th century—for on this side Joan of Arc's fate is quite typical—was both symptom and cause of a deep gulf between the ignorant multitude and the theology of leaders like Aquinas. "Every Inquisitor whom [the Church] commissioned to suppress witchcraft was an active missionary who scattered the seeds of the belief ever more widely" (Lea). A bull of Innocent VIII. in 1484 had the practical effect that thenceforward to question the reality of witchcraft was to question the utterance of the vicar of Christ, "Thus the Inquisition in its decrepitude had a temporary resumption of activity" (Lea). Here again, however, we are to some extent anticipating; for the Inquisition was not only an economic but also a political force.

But, before quitting the economic factors, we must remember that they brought as much weakness as strength into the Reformation movement. It is evident that an economically irreproachable

Church would have been as impregnable as the earliest Christian society had been; but it is equally true that the purity of reform was very early tainted by greed; so that, when force was used on both sides, there was little or no moral difference between a defensive commercialized hierarchy and an aggressive squirearchy eager for plunder.

Political Causes.—The political factor, though by itself it might never have led to actual revolt, came in at the last stage with decisive effect. It was the struggle with Protestantism which evolved the half-way principle of *cuius regio, eius religio;* "the ruler's choice determines the established religion of his territory"; and this in turn has led to our modern toleration of all creeds. But the mediaeval ideal had been one empire with one religion; and the actual conditions cannot be better described than in the words of the jurist-historian F. W. Maitland (*Canon Law in the Ch. of England*, p. 100), "We could frame no acceptable definition of a State which would not comprehend the [mediaeval] Church. What has it not that a State should have? It has laws, law-givers, law-courts, lawyers. It uses physical force to compel men to obey the laws. It keeps prisons. In the 13th century, though with squeamish phrases, it pronounced sentence of death. It is no voluntary society; if people are not born into it they are baptized into it when they cannot help themselves. If they attempt to leave they are guilty of *crimen laesae maiestatis,* and are likely to be burned. It is supported by involuntary contributions, by tithe and by tax. And, it may be added, it claims to override, all the world over, the power of the secular State."

Much of this power came to the Church by a process as legitimate as that which could be claimed by most of the civil Governments. The Church had consciously modelled her organization on that of the Roman empire; and she survived when the empire went to wreck. At first there was no question of serious rivalry with the earthly state. Gregory I., in face of an imperial edict or law which he might have been excused for interpreting as a trespass upon Church privileges, had no doubt about his duty of publishing the edict as he was commanded, even while he protested against it; "What am I," he wrote to the imperial council, "but dust and a worm? . . . a man set under authority."

It was only by degrees, and not without many reactions, even under Charles's weak successors, that the popes reached a position which rendered possible the claims of Gregory VII., a man of commanding genius and rare courage. Starting from Augustine's theory of the City of God, founded by Christ, in its contrast with the earthly city, founded by Cain, Gregory insists that the papal power of binding and loosing places him above all earthly sovereigns. It enables him to annul all oaths made contrary to God's will (of which the pope is interpreter) and to absolve all subjects from allegiance to an emperor whom the pope has deposed. Innocent III. (d. 1216) reasserted these claims both in theory and in practice; and at the death of the Emperor Frederick II. in 1250 the long struggle between papacy and empire was virtually decided in favour of the former.

National Spirit.—Yet the papacy now found a more formidable rival in the growing spirit of nationalism, which, no less than imperialism, must necessarily find itself in conflict with a non-national authority claiming moral dictatorship, and therefore political dominion, over the whole western world. It has sometimes been asserted that nationalism was unknown to the middle ages; that the one Church, with one Latin tongue for all educated Europe, effaced merely national divisions. This, however, is a very superficial view. In proportion as the heterogeneous mediaeval populations consolidated into nations, they developed also the consciousness of nationality; divisions became fewer than in the dark ages, but deeper; we may say that the papacy and the Latin tongue had scarcely more to do with the ending of the Hundred Years' War than with its outbreak; and Marsilius of Padua (1324) was on unassailable historical ground when he asserted that popes had very frequently been the authors of European wars.

France was the greatest nation in the 14th century; therefore she was nationally one of the most self-conscious; and it is she who came into directest conflict with the papacy. Boniface VIII.

(d. 1302) attempted to forbid taxation of the clergy by the State; again, he claimed that "all law is enclosed in the casket of the pope's breast." In his bull *Unam Sanctam,* he proclaimed to the world: "We declare that all human beings are subject to the pontiff of Rome; and we assert, define and pronounce this tenet to be essential and necessary to salvation." This attitude led to a conflict with Philippe-le-Bel of France, in which Boniface was humbled; this, again was a prelude to the transference from Rome to Avignon, where the popes in fact, though not in pretension, became virtually subjects of the French king. Even in England, where it might be argued that the clergy themselves were becoming more papalist than ever, and where Archbishop Arundel could proclaim that it was heresy to dispute any papal decretal (1408), yet king and parliament were putting very definite limits to papal control by their Statutes of Provisors and of Praemunire. Other sovereigns presently protected themselves by similar measures.

Publicists.—For, meanwhile, in the first half of the 14th century, publicists like Marsilius of Padua and William of Ockham (*see* OCCAM) enunciated theories which probably represented what a good many thinkers had long since been saying confidentially to each other in universities like Paris, and in great self-governing cities like Padua. For Marsilius and Ockham, the Bible is the great rule of life for Christendom; the supreme power resides in a council of the whole Church, to which Ockham, apparently, was ready to admit women, and which may judge the pope. Indeed, Ockham is ready to conceive a Christendom without the pope; true, there are certain functions which it would be difficult to arrange otherwise, but the papacy is not essential to the Church of Christ. These speculations formed a fitting prelude to the conciliar epoch (1414–57) during which, mainly at Constance (*q.v.*) and Basel, the Church attempted to put definite constitutional limits to papal autocracy. Both councils decreed, and compelled popes practically to admit, that a general council may judge and depose even a supreme pontiff, and that the pope cannot legislate without conciliar approval.

It is true that the constitutionalists here, as in the England of 1642, over-reached themselves, and the later mediaeval papacy profited by a reaction which rendered it despotic again within the Church. But the laity never forgot; and temporal princes grew more and more accustomed to maintain their own interests in open conflict with the pope.

Two factors contributed farther to this political independence. The monastic reforms decreed by the councils of Constance and Basel, in so far as they were carried out at all, owed much of their success to the secular authorities; in this field, at any rate, it became increasingly plain that the Church was not likely to reform herself merely from within. Again, the later mediaeval popes were predominantly politicians. The papacy had become an Italian principate; the pontiffs constantly involved themselves in those civil wars which made Italy a "hostelry of pain" (Dante); and they showed no less selfishness and duplicity than the princes with whom they were contending. They were ready to go any lengths to secure a little more authority or a few more square miles of territory; as when Clement V. (1309) decreed that the resisting Venetians should be sold into slavery, and Gregory XI. and Sixtus IV. decreed the same for the Florentines and Julius II. for both Florence and Bologna. The bull by which Nicholas V. (1442) encouraged Portugal to what became the organized trade in negro slaves did not immediately show these disastrous results; but when, in 1538, Paul III. decreed slavery against all Englishmen who should dare to support Henry VIII. against the pope, nobody was deceived as to the selfishness of this political move. (For evidence on these points *see* articles SLAVERY and INQUISITION; also T. Brecht, *Kirche und Sklaverei,* p. 156.) A quarrel with this spiritual autocrat, however moral or religious might be the original cause of difference, became *ipso facto* a political quarrel. Therefore, in 1500, any spark might have kindled a general conflagration.

Martin Luther.—This spark, when it came, was in fact moral and religious; but it at once kindled the mass of inflammable politico-economic material. The pope was working his indulgences to an excess which strained loyalty to the breaking-point. Ber-

thold of Regensburg, long ago [1250], had complained that "many thousands" went to hell because they thought themselves to have bought absolution from these "penny-preachers." Gascoigne, the great Oxford chancellor [1450], wrote even more strongly, in proportion to the growing evil: "Sinners say nowadays 'I care not how many or what evils I do in God's sight; for I can easily and quickly get plenary remission of all guilt and penalty by an absolution and indulgence granted me by the pope, whose written grant I have bought for 4d or 6d, or have won as a stake for a game of tennis.' " (*Lib. Veritatum,* p. 86; full translation in G. G. Coulton, *Social Life in Britain,* p. 204.)

Then, in 1517, the rupture came. A scandalous archbishop of Mainz promised Leo X. 10,000 ducats as a bribe for permission to hold three archbishoprics at the same time. This money was to be paid in part from the sums which here, as everywhere else, were being raised by the sale of indulgences for the building of St. Peter's at Rome. An Augustinian friar and university professor of Wittenberg, Martin Luther, expressed the general indignation by drafting 95 theses on the indulgence system, on which he challenged dispute with all comers.

We may say "the general indignation," for Germany was thoroughly prepared for this revolt. She had many flourishing cities, and a high general level of education for that time; the printing press had long been active; several editions of the vernacular Bible had been published, and very many little books of popular piety. The Greek and Latin classics were being studied busily, and in a far less pagan spirit than in Italy. The Inquisition, again, was comparatively inoperative in Germany; there was little chance of its nipping any doctrine in the bud before it had time to gain popular support. And, lastly, the weakness of the central Government was favourable to Luther; it was the patronage of a few local princes that sheltered his movement in its first stages.

GERMANY

The political complications were here very great; the empire contained more than 300 separate states, small and great, which often rendered little more than nominal obedience to the emperor. Luther was first summoned to Rome and then commanded to present himself before the papal legate at Augsburg (Oct. 1518). Finding that the legate practically demanded submission without discussion, Luther published his account of the interview as an appeal to the German people (*Acta Augustana*). Leo X. then sent an envoy, Miltitz, who was so tactful that a reconciliation might conceivably have been effected but for the Leipzig disputation on the papal primacy and supremacy (June 1519), to which Luther was challenged by the Dominican friar Johann Eck. Luther, in his months of preparation for this debate, discovered how many forgeries there were among the documents which seemed to tell most against him; and Eck, by driving him to the admission that not all the tenets of the Hussite heretics were wrong, widened the breach still farther. The younger university teachers were now on Luther's side; and, encouraged by the growing approbation of all classes among the laity, he began to appeal unhesitatingly and unceasingly through the pulpit and the press.

In three great treatises (1520) he took up a position from which he never after retreated on any essential point. For he had a positive programme; a national Church, free from papal interference; inspection of monasteries; limitation of holy-days and pilgrimages, and marriage for the priesthood as the best remedy for the standing disgrace of concubinage.

Leo X. met this programme with a bull (*Exsurge Domine,* June 1520) in which he condemned 41 propositions attributed to Luther. One of these is all the more significant because the condemnation was repeated in other papal letters: Luther had said "It is against the will of the [Holy] Spirit that heretics should be burned." The pope condemns even the least harmful of these 41 propositions as "scandalous or offensive to pious ears or calculated to lead simple minds astray": those who hold or preach any of them are henceforward excommunicate and liable, unless they repent, to all the pains and penalties of heresy. This bull was entrusted to Luther's enemy Eck; but it overshot the mark. Universities and bishops would not or dared not publish it, and

Luther received encouragement from many quarters.

He was now excommunicate, and his writings were solemnly burned; he retaliated by burning the papal decretals with equal publicity. Luther had great virtues and great faults; but at this crisis even his faults had a value for the world; for his courage and self-assertion precipitated the crystallization of a thousand thoughts and impulses with which society had gradually become saturated, but which had remained in solution until now.

This Church quarrel now became the most burning question in all German politics. The young Emperor Charles V. was crowned in Oct. 1520, and fixed January for his first Diet, at Worms. He had followed the fight, and was determined to uphold the traditions of his ancestors. The princes insisted that Luther should not be placed under the ban of the empire without being heard in his defence; he was therefore summoned under a safe conduct. He decided to go, "even though there were as many devils at Worms as tiles on the house-roofs." Nearly 2,000 people came out from the city to welcome him. He was brought before the Diet (April 17) and asked whether he would retract his books and their contents; he requested a day to consider his answer. His reply on the 18th was clear and decided: "The duty that I owe to my Germany will not allow me to recant." Pressed still farther: "It is impossible for me to recant unless I am proved to be in the wrong by the testimony of Scripture or by evident reasoning." Pressed farther again, while the torches began burning down to their sockets, as to the infallibility of general councils (the infallibility of the pope was not yet a necessary article of faith) he replied that these had sometimes erred by contradicting Holy Scripture, and he could prove it. At this, the emperor made a sign to break up the meeting.

The Credo of Charles.—Next day Charles read to the diet his own profession of faith; he stressed the authority not of popes but of councils; and upon that he was firm; here is a single friar now setting up his private judgment against 1,000 years of Catholicism, and "I have therefore resolved to stake upon this cause all my kingdoms and lordships, my friends, my body and my blood, my life and my soul." He called upon the diet to help him in this crusade; but "many turned paler than death." For the antagonism was here clearly stated; Luther was ready to stake all upon his own personal convictions, and the emperor upon his own loyalty to tradition. Here, then, was the clear parting of the ways. Both sides relied, fundamentally, upon the Bible. St. Thomas Aquinas had been as convinced as any later Protestant theologian that the Bible was inerrant not only in its spiritual teaching but even on matters of historical fact.

Authority and Judgment.—The real question which had gradually grown up during the Christian centuries, and which had now come to a point, was not as to the infallibility of the Bible but as to the methods of interpretation: was the book sufficient in itself, with no light beyond God's grace and the earnest searcher's conscience, or could it be rightly interpreted only in the light of ancient tradition, and by certain divinely-constituted teachers who, whenever they met in solemn conclave, were inerrant? Luther, in asserting that general councils had sometimes contradicted the Bible, had thrown down the gauntlet; at that point the emperor had naturally dissolved the assembly but only to take up the gauntlet solemnly next day; if the princes then turned pale, it was because they saw war imminent, and knew neither where it would end nor even (in most cases) on which side they must range themselves. To many, it seemed impossible to accept the existing constitution of Church and society as sacrosanct, to the extent of condemning all radical reform as sacrilegious, and all radical reformers as faggots for the stake.

Yet, on the other hand, they saw how intimately this treatment of nonconformity as heresy, this distrust of free discussion, and these methods of physical coercion, had grown into the whole social fabric, and therefore how great was the fear lest the edifice should collapse if once a friar were allowed to publish his own biblical interpretations against those of the councils, and to persuade the community that the burning of heretics is against the will of the Holy Spirit. Therefore, in the struggle that now follows, all other questions, however important in themselves, are subordinate to this one fundamental antithesis between authority and private judgment. Did the princes desire a world in which the deposit of faith might safely be entrusted to the reason and religious feeling and good sense of the majority, or must physical force be held over men's heads everywhere and always as a menace, and be very frequently employed in fact? Were most men so firmly assured of the fundamentals that all contrary pleas of a small minority might be mainly left to work out their own confusion (as in More's *Utopia*) or was orthodox assurance so wavering that the centre of gravity might shift under the shock of a friar's contradictions, and the Church might turn upside down, and the State with it? The risk was plainly enormous; here was Luther, willing to take that risk for himself and for the world; but few of the politicians could have faced the crisis without serious misgivings.

The Wartburg.—No compromise between Luther and the emperor was now possible; on the 26th, it was announced that his safe-conduct would expire in 21 days. He left Worms; but he was seized by the advice and with the connivance of the elector of Saxony, and carried off to the elector's castle of the Wartburg near Eisenach. The emperor signed Luther's condemnation as a pestilent heretic (May 26); but his secretary wrote to a friend in Spain: "I am persuaded this is not the end, but the beginning. . . . Since [the Emperor's edict], Luther's books are sold with impunity at every step and corner of the streets and market places."

Luther spent nearly ten months in hiding at the castle of the Wartburg, his "Patmos," as he afterwards called it. Here his pen was unceasingly busy with controversial pamphlets and his translation of the New Testament. But his body suffered from want of exercise, and his mind from natural doubts; could so many past generations and so many estimable contemporaries have been wrong, while he, the mere friar, was right as against them all? Might he not be dragging thousands down to hell with himself? Yet his convictions constantly returned more strongly than ever; and, by a natural reaction, he felt increasing confidence in his divine commission; to doubt of this, or to remain treacherously silent, would be to incur damnation. The gulf between authority and private judgment was thenceforward too wide to be bridged; and Luther emerged from the Wartburg as a determined revolutionary. Yet he was a conservative revolutionary; and this it was which brought him out of his retirement.

His doctrines had been spreading widely; the statistics of the German press are most eloquent here; in 1517 only 37 vernacular books were printed; in 1518 there were 71, and by 1523 the number had risen to 498, of which 180 were by Luther himself. For here was a population which, far beyond all others in Europe, had already been gaining a certain familiarity with the Bible in the vernacular. Fourteen editions in High German, and four in Low German, had appeared before 1518; and, though these editions were doubtless limited and therefore expensive, yet they must have done something to permeate popular thought. Most of the great cities were becoming Lutheran; the new doctrines spread, naturally enough, in Luther's own religious order (the Austin Friars) and in his University of Wittenberg.

Here, in fact, things went too fast. One of the Wittenberg professors, Andrew Bodenstein (Carlstadt), pushed matters to extremes; he lectured and preached and wrote against almost all the traditional ceremonies.

Momentum.—At the same time, and only 60 miles away, the populous weaving centre of Zwickau was in still greater religious commotion; three of the Zwickau enthusiasts came to Wittenberg, and Carlstadt persuaded the magistrates to publish an epoch-making ordinance, which practically transferred the whole direction of Church affairs to the laity, who at the same time undertook the poor relief and the moral discipline of the city. Carlstadt went even farther, and started an iconoclastic crusade. Luther's friend and colleague Melanchthon (q.v.) disapproved strongly, but could do nothing. The elector also was seriously troubled; other princes were taking the Wittenberg disturbances as a text for armed intervention; and Luther risked his own personal safety to return and restore order. He preached at Wittenberg on eight successive days: "I will preach reform, I will talk about it, I will write about it, but I will not use force or compulsion with any one. . . . The word will drop into one heart to-day, and to-morrow into another, and so will work that each will forsake the mass."

A new pope came to the throne in 1522, Adrian VI., a pious man sincerely anxious for reform. At the diet of the empire held at Nuremberg (1522-3) his nuncio pressed that serious measures should be taken against Luther, since Charles V.'s decree, however decisively worded, was practically a dead letter. The members of the diet answered by presenting a list of 100 grievances against the Church; the nuncio reported to the pope that "among a thousand men scarcely one could be found untainted by Lutheran teaching." Then Adrian died suddenly, and was succeeded by Clement VII., a Medici by birth and by nature interested less in reform than in papal prestige. His legate, Campeggio, though a most dexterous diplomatist, could effect very little. The Diet of Speyer (1524) began to plan a Church council for Germany, which would have separated from Rome and anticipated England in the formation of a national Church.

The Peasants' War.—It is from this moment that we must date "the beginning of the separation of Germany into two opposite camps of Protestant and Roman Catholic, although the real parting of the ways actually occurred after the Peasants' War" (T. M. Lindsay). That war, though precipitated by the Lutheran revolt, was essentially a mere continuation of the struggles described above. Luther's message was democratic; his language displayed the defects of his qualities; its extraordinary force and directness constantly tempted him into exaggeration, and added fuel to the social discontent which had smouldered for generations side by side with anti-clericalism.

Seven years after Luther's attack on the indulgence system, the peasants' revolt broke suddenly out (June 1524). It began on the upper Rhine, encouraged doubtless by the successful assertion of freedom by the Swiss. In a few weeks the conflagration spread as far north as the Harz, and eastward to Tirol and Styria; cities, knights, and even princes made terms with the insurgents or joined their ranks. But the want of efficient leadership and discipline soon made itself felt; other princes and knights, with trained soldiers at their back, beat the insurgents in one battle after another, and the main revolt was subdued before the end of 1525, leaving the peasants in a worse plight than before, though the Tirolese held out longer and gained real concessions. Luther at first had sympathized with the insurgents and protested against harsh measures; he even risked his life by going among them and preaching peace and moderation.

But soon their excesses angered and dismayed him; his tract *Against the murdering, thieving hordes of peasants* breathed fire and slaughter. Its pitiless tone may be explained, though never excused, by the disastrous reaction of this social revolt upon Luther's own revolution; the more so, since the rebels had in nearly all cases claimed religious sanctions for the movement. It was thenceforth evident that the Reformation was bound to emphasize political and social differences. Hitherto it might have been called a national movement in Germany, but henceforward it was a party-question in every sense of the word.

A Religion of State.—The story is complicated by the multiplicity and kaleidoscopic changes of these 300 German States, and especially by the confusion between the two Saxonys. Catholicism and Protestantism were exposed to all the gusts of party politics. In Luther himself the prophet often gave way to the politician; and he, who in 1525 had at first insisted that the peasants must be met not with blows but with reasons, was soon ready to call upon secular princes to draw the sword against all enemies of the Reformation. He had begun by insisting on responsibility to God alone; but now with most of the Reformers, he ended by subordinating Church to State. In July 1525, a league of Catholic princes was being formed to quench the Reformation in blood; in October, the landgrave Philip of Hesse began to frame a defensive league of Protestant princes. This support could be bought only by abandoning absolute freedom of private judgment and by allowing many ecclesiastical endowments to be secularized. In order to avoid offending the landgrave, Luther, Melanchthon and Bucer

agreed in allowing him to commit bigamy; a concession which may be paralleled by a few similar licences from popes, but which, coming from these Reformers, justly scandalized the public more than the papal actions. On both sides, Catholic and Protestant, self-interest now played a very great part.

The ups and downs may be very briefly summarized. The Diet of Augsburg (Dec. 1525) did little. That of Speyer (June 1526) refused to execute the edict of Worms, and procured the decision that each prince should so act in matters of faith as to be able to answer for his conduct to God and the emperor. This gave the Reformers a most valuable breathing space, but the Catholic States were presently provoked into organizing persecution against heretical subjects; the emperor, having now made up his private quarrel with the pope, was determined to fight the innovators, and a diet at Speyer (1529) altered the tolerant decree of 1526. Six princes and 14 cities read a solemn protest at the diet against this vote; and the action of this small minority gave to the party that name of Protestant by which it has ever since been known.

Schmalkalden.—For the Diet of Augsburg (June 1530) Melanchthon drew up a confession, which minimized the differences between Lutherans and Catholics, and exaggerated those which separated Luther from the more radical Swiss reformer Zwingli. The emperor granted a respite till April 15, 1531. By that date, eight princes and 11 cities had formed at Schmalkalden a defensive league for six years. The emperor, more and more hampered by the Turkish peril, finally granted the Peace of Nuremberg (July 1532) which guaranteed the Protestants from molestation until the next general council of the Church. But Clement VII. was in no haste to call such a council; he feared the emperor's encroachments scarcely less than Luther's heresy; and, meanwhile, Protestantism gained much ground, though in Switzerland it had received a check in the death of Zwingli. When at last the general council, in spite of dissensions among the orthodox, seemed imminent, the Protestant princes refused to attend it; they renewed the Schmalkaldic League (1537) and were joined by fresh allies. The emperor formed a counter-league (Nuremberg, 1538) and war seemed imminent, when a compromise was arranged at the Diet of Frankfort (1539).

A series of conferences, from 1540 onwards, produced no real agreement. In 1544 the Peace of Nuremberg was formally prolonged for another five years; but the continual spread of Protestantism, not always without a violence equal to that which their enemies were prepared to exercise, precipitated a struggle. The long-delayed council of the Church had at last met (Trent, 1542); but the Protestants refused to attend it. The emperor declared war; the Protestants were beaten at Mühlberg (1547), and promised to send representatives to Trent, but were freed from that undertaking by Catholic dissensions. At the Diet of Augsburg (1548), Charles drew up on his own responsibility a sort of compromise, the *Interim;* and in 1551 the Protestants sent representatives to Trent.

But the Interim was naturally unpopular on both sides; and, next year, Maurice of Saxony took advantage of the emperor's twofold embarrassments with France and Turkey to turn suddenly against him; he almost succeeded in taking him prisoner. Charles, foreseeing defeat and shrinking from the humiliation, soon transferred to his brother Ferdinand of Austria the direction of German affairs (1554). Maurice was killed in the moment of victory at Sievershausen; John Frederick of Saxony died soon afterwards; but Protestantism was too deeply rooted to be shaken.

"Cuius regio, eius religio."—While the Diet of Augsburg was hesitating to grant religious peace, a rival assembly at Naumburg was attended by more princes than the diet itself, and decided to abide by the confession of Augsburg (1555). (*See* AUGSBURG, CONFESSION OF.) The diet, after many struggles, agreed to one of those compromises which leave seeds for future war. It consecrated the principle *cuius regio, eius religio;* each prince might choose for himself between Catholicism and Protestantism; his subjects must submit to that choice unless they preferred to emigrate. We must here end the story of the Reformation in Germany. The mere fact that Catholicism had been compelled, over and over again, to negotiate with Protestantism on something like equal terms, was a death-blow to the mediaeval conception of the Church. Now, by this Peace of Augsburg, Protestantism was actually legalized for about half the population of Germany; and this proportion has since maintained itself with little alteration.

SWITZERLAND

Switzerland had broken loose from the empire in 1499; and here was plenty of fuel for Luther's spark. Ulrich Zwingli (b. 1484) was ordained priest in 1506 and soon distinguished himself as an opponent of moral abuses both in the Church and among the laity. In 1518 he succeeded in expelling the indulgence-seller of St. Peter's from the canton of Schwyz; and was promoted to the great minster of Zürich. Here his learning and zeal, aided by the strongly democratic tendencies of this city of Zürich, made him into a combination of prophet, priest and politician. The burghers of Zürich had long exercised a disciplinary control over their clergy which was far from usual; and here also was an important printing press. Zwingli, in his campaign against the wholesale enlistment of young Switzers as mercenaries for foreign countries, was bold enough to preach also "that it is no sin to eat flesh on a fast day, though it is a great sin to sell human flesh for slaughter." This brought him into conflict with the bishop of his diocese (Constance). In 1522, by a custom general among the Swiss clergy, he contracted a connection with the widow of a citizen, and joined with ten other priests in a petition to the bishop against the law of celibacy, on the ground that this was commonly broken in Switzerland. In April 1524 he married her publicly, in defiance of the Church.

Meanwhile the magistrates had arranged a public disputation between orthodox and innovators (Jan. 1523). More than 600 clergy and representative laity attended, and the magistrates decided in Zwingli's favour. In consequence of a second disputation in the autumn, all church pictures and images were abolished; presently the monasteries were disendowed, and their funds devoted to schools and the poor. The neighbouring canton of Lucerne sent to warn Zürich against its heresies; threats were added, and Zürich began to prepare for war. In 1525 a new form of liturgy was prescribed, severely puritanical; and in 1529 the Catholic worship was forbidden.

Division.—Meanwhile the revolt spread to other cantons. At a disputation at Baden (May 1526), which Zwingli refused to attend, 82 clerical representatives voted for the conservative side, as against 20 reformers. Yet the movement went rapidly forward, in spite of Zwingli's quarrel with the more conservative Luther, and of the set-back which followed here, as in Germany, upon the Peasants' Revolt. The forest cantons, with their comparatively primitive and scattered peasantry, were naturally on the conservative side; they had formed an anti-heretical league (April 1524); and in Zwingli the prophet became more and more overshadowed by the politician. Between 1527 and 1530 Zürich succeeded in creating a league of the greater Protestant towns, to which the five forest cantons replied by a "Christian Union" (April 1529). Each party was ready to ally itself with the foreigner; Zürich with France, the Union with Austria. The Swiss confederacy was thus broken up into two opposing camps. The Catholics were unable to accept the full principle of mutual tolerance; and Zürich also was aggressive and intolerant. The two armies faced each other at Kappel, but peace was patched up (June 1529). This was only a truce; they met again at Kappel, where Zwingli was defeated and slain (1531). The peace now made granted to each canton the choice of its own religion, and did much also to protect minorities. The country soon settled into much the same division which still obtains: Catholicism reigned mainly in the mountains and Protestantism in the more fertile lands and in the great cities.

Geneva.—Geneva (not yet in Switzerland) deserves separate mention: it owed everything to its neutral position and to the personality of John Calvin (q.v.). The Genevese had lived for centuries under a prince-bishop, though with a good deal of democracy in their civic constitution; thus State and Church were more closely interwoven here than in most other cities. In 1530 the city rebelled against its bishop; in 1534 it entered into a contract for joint citizenship with Protestant Berne; in 1536 it formally committed itself to Protestantism, and two months later Calvin settled in the city. He was a man of precociously wide and exact scholarship, bred in the law, and touched with inspiration from Erasmus and Luther at the age of 24 (1533).

Calvin's "Institution."—Next year he fled from France; in 1535 he was at Basel, where he wrote in Latin his *Institution of Christian Religion*, which he afterwards turned into French. This epoch-making book has often been misrepresented. Calvin's insistence upon the torments of hell is merely the orthodox mediaeval doctrine, in a far milder form than we find it (for instance) in St. Bernardino of Siena. His insistence upon predestination does not go far beyond St. Thomas Aquinas, whose actual words are often softened down by his modern exponents. The great value of Calvin's book was that it gave a clear and logical structure to a hitherto formless and disorganized Protestant thought, much as St. Thomas and his fellows had constructed a logical synthesis from the heterogeneous mass of Catholic traditions.

In July of 1536 Calvin passed through Geneva, where the reformer Guillaume Farel persuaded him to stay. He introduced into the city, now an independent republic, a discipline which, like his *Institution*, may easily be misunderstood. His supervision of morals and expenses and amusements was no new thing; there is practically no detail in that field which had not been insisted upon by orthodox mediaeval theologians for centuries past, and written in town statute-books, and sometimes even enforced in practice. Here, Calvin's innovation was to substitute stern regularity for impulse and caprice. For the matter was now in the hands of business men; the bishop having been driven out, this enforcement of discipline devolved upon the town council as wielders both of ecclesiastical and of secular authority.

And behind that was another revival from the past. Anxious as Calvin was to revert to the Christianity of the earliest days, and finding as he did in the Lord's Supper the central Christian rite, he insisted on the rejection of unworthy communicants. This regulation proved too stringent for many others besides the "libertines"; and Calvin, with his two chief colleagues, was banished in 1538. The city recalled him in 1541, and he obeyed, most unwillingly, for the sake of what he regarded as a great public work. His *Ecclesiastical Ordinances* and his institution of the *Consistory*, became in one sense the parents of Presbyterianism (q.v.). The discipline which had always been advocated was now actually enforced; and nonconformists were punished, sometimes even to the death; the world will never forget how this rebel Calvin burned the Unitarian Servetus. But he saw that a Protestant ministry could never hold its ground without solid learning; therefore he wrote a catechism which should teach even children to give reasons for their faith; moreover, he founded a grammar-school and an academy which attracted able men from all lands, and which sent missionaries out in all directions.

FRANCE

In France, as in Switzerland, the germ of the Reformation is pre-Lutheran. The concordat of 1516 had put the French Church practically under royal authority; the Renaissance (q.v.) was rapidly sapping mediaeval conventions; and one very remarkable man devoted himself with equal enthusiasm to religious reform and to learning. This was Jacques Lefèvre (Faber Stapulensis), who in 1512, at the age of about 55, published a Latin translation of the Pauline epistles, with a commentary which roughly anticipated Luther's theory of grace and his denial of transubstantiation. In 1524 Lefèvre revised a French translation of the New Testament, as a foretaste of the whole Bible. He was now under the protection of his old pupil Briçonnet, bishop of Meaux, who had set his heart on the reformation of morals and religion within that diocese. With the help of other pupils, such as Guillaume Farel, Lefèvre created a whole school of students and evangelical preachers.

Meanwhile Luther's doctrines were spreading in France and had been formally condemned (1521); and in 1523 the bishop of

Meaux found himself obliged to fulminate against Luther by name, and against certain doctrines held by Farel and other extremists. Then the *parlement* took strong measures against the innovators: Lefèvre's Testament was burned, while he and his friends found safety in flight. Heresy spread rapidly, and Francis I. favoured or punished it according to the changes of the political weathercock. At the end of 1533 he decreed instant burning against any man convicted by two witnesses of being a Lutheran; but the next January he signed a secret treaty with the Protestant princes of Germany.

Then the excesses of the wilder reformers, who placarded Paris with an offensive broadside against the mass and the priests, caused a natural reaction among the people and at court. In two months, nearly 200 heretics were in the Paris prisons, and eight had been burned. When Lefèvre died (1536) "partly from the timidity of the leaders and partly from the rashness of the rank and file, the first or Evangelical phase of Protestantism in France had failed to bring about a reform of the Church" (A. A. Tilley in *Camb. Mod. Hist.*, vol. II.).

In that same year Calvin published his *Institution,* with which the second, or Calvinistic, phase began. The book supplied the Protestants with a clear and detailed theory of religion; on the other hand, it involved a considerable recoil from two most important principles: it set definite limits both to free enquiry and to individualism. Thenceforward French reformers shared the strength and the weakness of institutionalism. More truly in France than in any other great country, Geneva now became "the Protestant Rome."

The Waldensians.—After a lull, persecution became more severe again (1538-40). The theological faculty of Paris drew up 26 articles of faith in answer to the *Institution,* which Calvin had now published in French, and which was solemnly burned in 1544; meanwhile, many Calvinists were burned here and there. In 1530, the Waldensians (Vaudois) who had survived from mediaeval persecutions in a group of 30 remote mountain villages along the Durance, affiliated themselves to the Lutherans; therefore in 1545, after varying negotiations, an army was sent against them without warning; 22 villages were burned and 3,000 men, women and children were killed.

A still deeper impression was made by the *auto-da-fé* of Meaux (1546) because this was a solemn and judicial act. Sixty persons were here arrested for the crime of having celebrated the Lord's Supper in Protestant fashion; all but ten were punished; 14 were tortured and burned. Even this did not drive the new doctrines altogether underground; other executions took place elsewhere; but meanwhile missionaries and pedlars were secretly preaching and distributing forbidden pamphlets in every province except far-off Brittany. After ten years of this, Francis I. died, and Henry II. sharpened the persecution, by creating an anti-heretical committee of the *parlement* of Paris, which became known as the *chambre ardente.* This condemned at least 100 persons to death in 3 years; and the provincial *parlements* followed suit.

Yet Protestantism still grew; and in 1555 it began to organize itself; churches were founded on the model which Calvin had framed for Strassburg, and in 1559 a General Synod met, representing from 40 to 50 churches. The Government now procured papal approbation for an Inquisition after the Spanish model; but the Paris *parlement* was not prepared to go so far. Meanwhile the new doctrines were taken up by some of the higher nobility; they thus acquired the advantage and the disadvantage of becoming both fashionable and political. The execution of a distinguished member of the *parlement,* Anne du Bourg, for merely protesting against persecution (1559), could be described by an eyewitness as "doing more harm to the Catholic Church than 100 ministers could have done." But the "tumult of Amboise," next year, redressed the balance. The Government, during the boyhood of Francis II., had fallen into the hands of the Guise family; and a number of Protestant nobles conspired at Amboise to arrest and imprison these unpopular rulers. The plot failed and brought natural discredit upon the religious cause.

A Political Party.—Protestantism was now becoming almost as definitely a political party in France as Catholicism; therefore,

a council was held at Poissy, virtually representing the whole nation, to find a *modus vivendi* on the basis of mutual toleration. The Protestants were represented by 12 ministers and 20 laymen; the Catholics by six cardinals and 64 prelates or doctors; the king presided, with the queen mother and princes of the blood. The conference failed to effect a compromise between irreconcilable doctrines; but it was followed by an edict granting liberty of conscience within certain definite limitations. This, however, without fully satisfying the Protestants, was enough to exasperate the Catholics.

In March 1562, the former were holding a religious service in a barn at Vassy, in spite of the edict which forbade their worship in any walled town. The duke of Guise, passing through the town, sent his men to expel them. They resisted, and the soldiers stormed the barn, killing 63 of the worshippers and wounding 100 or more. The example of this "massacre of Vassy" was followed in many other places; henceforward the Wars of Religion begin, and we can no longer treat the French Reformation as a purely spiritual movement. The massacre of St. Bartholomew was a natural sequel to the tumult of Amboise and the massacre of Vassy. But, before quitting this subject, we must note that the "Presbyterian" constitution owes even more, directly, to the French Protestants than to any other source. Their "confession of faith" and their "book of discipline," though founded essentially upon Calvin, have more directly influenced the Dutch, Scottish and American churches, than Calvin's own constitution at Geneva.

THE NETHERLANDS

When we have thus followed the German, Swiss and French Reformations, we find little that is new in other Continental countries. The Netherlands were well prepared for Protestantism by their busy civic life, their early welcome of the printing-press, their vernacular translation of the Bible (1477), and the educational work of the *Brethren of the Common Life* or *Common Lot* (*see* BROTHERS OF COMMON LIFE; GROOT, GERHARD). Luther's writings were welcomed at once; and the Bible was frequently printed in Dutch, Flemish and French between 1513 and 1531.

Charles V. began with public burnings of Lutheran books *en masse,* and then established the Inquisition (1522). Burnings for heresy began early; but the emperor's edicts, though severe and frequently repeated, were difficult to enforce in face of the growing opposition. Special severity and peculiar tortures were reserved for the Anabaptists, who were intercepted and slaughtered in large numbers even when they attempted to emigrate. At last, in 1534, they were provoked to strike back, but with the natural result of severer persecution. Under Philip II., political and religious oppression were intertwined. When, in 1565, he insisted on the publication of the decrees of the Council of Trent, not in the pope's name but in his own, Holland and Brabant protested against this as an infringement of their constitutional liberties. Next year, a confederacy of nobles and leading citizens pledged themselves to resist the Inquisition, and adopted the nickname of *Gueux* (*q.v.*) which the courtiers had fastened upon them.

In July, Philip promised to withdraw the Inquisition and grant such tolerance as his conscience would permit; but the secret archives of Simancas show that he wrote simultaneously to the pope and explained this promise as a mere ruse to gain time. At that point, a series of iconoclastic outrages by the Protestant mob gave a legitimate handle to the Catholics. The duke of Alva was then made vicegerent by Philip II.; he proclaimed heresy as high treason and inaugurated a reign of terror (1567); from that time forth the struggle became political; religious discussion was merged in civil war.

DENMARK AND SWEDEN

In Scandinavia the revolution was comparatively bloodless. King Christian II. of Denmark imported a Lutheran preacher in 1519, and would have welcomed Luther himself; he published new codes of law which no pope could approve. But he became unpopular, fled from his kingdom in 1523, and was reconciled to the pope in 1529. Meanwhile Frederick I., proclaimed as his successor, made peace with the clergy; but Lutheran doctrines still spread; and, Frederick believing himself to have been tricked by the pope in the matter of the archbishopric of Lund, was confirmed in his own growing inclinations towards Protestantism.

His son Christian and his son-in-law Albert of Brandenburg had already declared themselves and in 1527 Frederick met the solemn remonstrances of the bishops with the reply that faith is free, and that each man must follow his own conscience. In 1530, 21 Lutheran preachers, accused of heresy, offered to dispute publicly in Danish against the accusing bishops, who, however, refused to discuss religious questions in the vernacular. Frederick's son Christian III., in 1536, abolished the bishops' authority, seized their possessions, and imported a disciple of Luther, Bugenhagen, as his chief ecclesiastical adviser. Much of the ancient ritual was preserved; and, though there was inevitable friction between the two parties, this systematic and authoritative change of official religion avoided civil war, and brought Denmark higher in commerce and in learning than she had ever stood before. Frederick and Christian made corresponding changes in their subject lands of Norway and Iceland; but here the ancient abuses had been less crying; the people were less ready for change; so that the revolution thus forced upon them from above caused perhaps as much evil as that which it professed to remedy.

In Sweden also the royal initiative secured a bloodless change. Gustavus Vasa (1523–60) had made the acquaintance of Lutheran preachers before his accession; and political necessities led him to look towards disendowment of the Church. A public disputation in the king's palace (1524) went in favour of the reformers; between 1526 and 1541 the whole Bible was published in the vernacular; and men could henceforth judge better for themselves between the rival claims. The diet of 1527 decided in favour of Lutheranism and disendowment. The next king showed some preference for Calvinism; and John III. (1568–92) proposed reunion with Rome. John's son had adopted Catholicism; therefore the people resolved to secure themselves before his formal accession. A synod of lay folk and clergy was held at Uppsala; it decided to accept the Bible as the supreme authority, adopted the Augsburg confession, and restored Luther's catechism as the foundation of all religious teaching.

ITALY AND SPAIN

In Southern Europe, in Italy and Spain, Protestantism enjoyed no princely protection of any importance, nor (perhaps on that account) did it ever spread far enough to gain a hold upon the people. Here, as elsewhere, orthodox reformers constantly fell under suspicion because orthodoxy and radical reform were so difficult to reconcile in practice. The celebrated *Counsel for Amendment of the Church*, drawn up in 1537 by a papal commission of cardinals and other distinguished theologians, insisted that dispensations from Church law should not be so frequent, and should never be given for money. Yet one of these same cardinals, Caraffa, when raised to the papacy as Paul IV., condemned the document in 1559 to his Index of Prohibited Books, while three of the other cardinals (Sadoleto, Contarini and Pole) fell under suspicion of unorthodoxy in later years. Many Italian reformers were thus driven over the line; others protested their loyalty to the last.

The Triumph of Orthodoxy.—The Inquisition, in both countries, was a deciding factor. Into Italy it was reintroduced in 1542 by Cardinal Caraffa, who, when raised to the papacy, worked it with increasing severity. Although Naples and Venice refused to grant it full powers, yet, even there, it was strong enough to prevent any real organization of Protestantism; while in the principalities of Ferrara, Modena and elsewhere heresy was always struck down before it could mature; at Modena 14 persons were burned in the single year 1568. Many fled abroad; in Switzerland there grew up a considerable Italian community; some of these, persecuted by Calvin for their extreme radicalism, fled into Poland and contributed to the spread of Unitarianism.

In Spain, orthodoxy triumphed still more easily. Cardinal Ximenes (d. 1517) had, by the most drastic disciplinary action,

raised the Spanish clergy far above the general European level of morals and learning: consequently there was a strong party which could accuse even Erasmus of wild exaggeration in his attack upon Church abuses; distinguished men were condemned for favouring "Erasmic" propositions. Secret communities of Protestants gradually formed at Seville (where we are told of nearly 1,000 members) and at Valladolid. But two *autos da fé* (1559–60) burned 24 men and women at Seville; two others (1559) burned 27 at Valladolid; there were other sporadic executions, and the Spanish non-conformists, like the Italian, could find safety only in flight. In Portugal, where the Inquisition was even more rigorous, we can scarcely guess what might have been the result if anything like private judgment had been possible for the people; what actually happened was that the country produced very few Protestants.

GREAT BRITAIN AND IRELAND

The English story is peculiar in one most important particular. In its beginnings, the Reformation was strongly political, yet not anti-Catholic; Henry VIII.'s ideal was "the papacy without the pope."

Here, as in Germany, the ground was well prepared. Lollardy had been driven underground; but it was still very far from complete extinction. The clergy were, on the whole, unpopular, especially in London. The bishop of London wrote to Wolsey in 1515: "Assured am I, if my chancellor be tried by any [jury of] 12 men in London, they be so maliciously set in favour of heretical pravity that they will cast and condemn any cleric, though he were as innocent as Abel." And Charles V.'s envoy, Chapuys, reported to his master from London in 1529: "Nearly all the people here hate the priests." Here, therefore, as in many other parts of Europe, the mediaeval concordat between Church and State was already breaking down.

And here also the Renaissance had already begun to undermine the old fabric. In 1516, More told Erasmus that the *Epistolae Obscurorum Virorum*, a bitter satire upon the monks and the traditional philosophy, was "read everywhere" in England. Erasmus's own writings had enjoyed great popularity; and Colet, dean of St. Paul's, supported the new learning against tradition with a boldness which naturally started other men upon still bolder courses; moreover, More's *Utopia*, published in 1516, was almost as revolutionary on the theological as on the social and political side. All religions are tolerated in Utopia, and almost all religious discussion. For in this country "nothing is seen or heard in the churches, but that which seemeth to agree indifferently with them all. If there be a distinct kind of sacrifice peculiar to any several sect, that they execute at home in their own houses." Wider knowledge of the universe was beginning to break down that mediaeval condemnation of all non-Christians to hell; and this breakdown must, sooner or later, involve a break with yet other mediaeval tenets.

The "Defender of the Faith."—Therefore, when Luther came forward, his works found an early welcome in England; and in 1521 Henry wrote a Latin treatise against the heresiarch which earned him from the pope the solemn title of "Defender of the Faith." Heretical books were burned in St. Paul's churchyard, and four heretics were burned in the diocese of Lincoln, while 50 more abjured their creed. But Lutheran groups began to form at the two universities, especially at Cambridge; which produced eight leaders of the new movement. Here, in 1525, the prior of the Austin Friars, Dr. Barnes, preached a sermon which caused his prosecution for heresy; he was compelled to abjure at St. Paul's, in company with four German merchants. But, a year later, the king was planning a divorce and remarriage, since it was politically necessary for him to have a definite heir to the throne.

This has often been represented as a mere piece of sensuality; but the facts speak plainly to the contrary. There was nothing to prevent Henry, if he had wished it, from keeping a harem like those of his contemporary Francis I. in France and his successor Charles II. in England. Moreover, before the question of Catharine's divorce came up, Henry was already taking very strong measures in another direction; he heaped honours upon his one

REFORMATION

known illegitimate son, Henry Fitzroy, and planned, with the advice of his council, the proclamation of this six-year-old boy as heir to the throne. But the plan broke down and Henry's attachment to Anne Boleyn now contributed to suggest the other expedient of a divorce from Catharine. (In the strict technical sense it was not a *divorce*, but a *decree of nullity;* however, the briefer term was very commonly used then, as since.)

This complicated story may be reduced to a few simple issues. In the minds of all the principal actors except Catharine, the problem was mainly or wholly political. The king needed a male heir; he and his counsellors augured disaster to the kingdom from a female or a disputed succession. So also with Rome; Clement VII. himself was long in making up his mind as to the Catharine case; and, most significant of all, he actually suggested in 1530 that the problem might be solved without divorce, by allowing Henry two wives at once. (A. F. Pollard, *Henry VIII.* [1905], p. 207.) Even if, as some of Henry's advisers suggested, this was merely a diplomatic feint, it is no less significant in this present connection. Henry had thought of the proposal seriously at an earlier stage, and based it upon Old Testament precedents. As Pollard points out, Eugenius IV. had actually granted similar licence to Henry IV. of Castile, for similar political reasons, in 1437. For the pope's real difficulty was not in the moral problem of the Boleyn marriage but in the political problem of the divorce, since Catharine was aunt to the most powerful sovereign in Europe, and the one from whom Clement had most to fear personally. Therefore the pope evaded all definite decisions, shifting in response to the shifting political situation, for three years (1527–29), when at last he transferred the case to Rome.

Then, at Cranmer's advice, Henry appealed to the universities, and, apart from Oxford and Cambridge, eight of the greatest in Europe decided for him (Paris, Orléans, Bourges, Toulouse, Bologna, Ferrara, Pavia and Padua). However much we may discount these verdicts by royal pressure and other evidence which suggests bribery by both parties, yet on the whole "these opinions must stand for the general opinion of the learned, unless the divines of France and Italy were more generally venal than is commonly supposed" (H. M. Gwatkin).

Supreme Head.—Already in 1529 Henry had begun to permit the circulation of anti-papal German pamphlets as a threat to the pope; and had even allowed his envoy to hint at further Lutheran developments. Next year, the bishop of Norwich complained of the impossibility of destroying heretical books so long as many folk believed the king to favour them. But at that very moment Henry was taking public measures against heresy, burning Tyndale's New Testament, and forbidding all English Bibles until a version should be made "by great, learned and Catholic persons." This last (as More confessed about the same time) was a great desideratum; yet no such orthodox version was made, or even attempted until long after England had broken finally with Rome (1582–1609).

Already, in 1529, Henry had begun an attack upon the clergy, probably upon the advice of his new minister, the adventurer Thomas Cromwell. Taking advantage of their notorious unpopularity, Henry considerably curtailed the clerical exactions of which lay folk were complaining, and restricted the evils of plurality and non-residence. It was made a penal offense to evade this statute by seeking dispensation from Rome.

Next year, came a still plainer step. Henry, under form of law and without real justice, condemned the clergy of England for having allowed the papal legate to set up his court in England, in violation of the Statute of Praemunire. He extorted not only an enormous fine, but also an acknowledgment in the convocation of Canterbury that the king is "only and supreme lord [of the clergy], and, as far as the law of Christ allows, even supreme head." But this weapon rested in its sheath until the parliament of 1532.

In this parliament, by means which cannot be palliated except on the plea that they were usual in the politics of that day, and that his adversaries were not more scrupulous, Henry first forced convocation, the parliament of the clergy, to accept three articles which definitely submitted Church to State in England. He then procured from parliament a statute abolishing "annates," one of the most lucrative sources of papal revenue from England: this, however, he held in his hand at first only as a menace to Rome, until he had procured papal bulls of approval for the election of Cranmer as archbishop of Canterbury. Next, he procured a statute declaring the king supreme head of Church and State, and forbidding all appeals to Rome. Then, by a capitulation even more humiliating than the previous "submission of the clergy," convocation, at Henry's demand, declared the nullity of Catharine's marriage. There was a mock-trial of the case at Dunstable, and Henry, who had already secretly married Anne Boleyn, was now free to make her his queen. How he then succeeded in defying papal excommunication, and in preventing any papal crusade being launched against him by the Catholic princes of Europe, is a purely political story. Before parliament dissolved, it passed a statute forbidding all further payments of any kind to "the bishop of Rome," and "an act for the submission of the clergy to the king's majesty."

The rest of Henry's reign was spent in ruthless warfare against heretics who believed in mediaeval Catholicism less than he did, and against others who believed more than he. His "six articles" of 1539 rehearsed nearly all the main points of the mediaeval creed; to deny transubstantiation was made heresy, and therefore punishable with burning; to deny any of the other five was felony. Consequently the king was burning heretics on the one hand, while on the other he was enforcing obedience to the royal supremacy by beheading Fisher and More.

The Monasteries.—Three causes led him to strike at the monasteries. They were pro-papal, wealthy, and not popular enough to find many defenders. Among the few points of importance upon which historians on both sides are agreed, are two which concern us here: that the monasteries necessarily considered their own cause bound up with the pope's and that one of the most remarkable features of Henry's despotic reign is the absence of organized or determined resistance on the part of the clergy, whether cloistered or not. Henry was extravagant; he wanted money; and here was a comparatively easy prey. Everywhere else in Europe, the civil authority had already been obliged to interfere in the cause of monastic reform.

The articles of reform for English monasteries, which Cromwell issued by Henry's orders, do not deserve the blame which has sometimes been cast upon them. Not only the majority of them, but the most important, were taken straight from the Benedictine rule or from the decrees of popes and other orthodox reformers in the past. When, for instance, Cromwell prescribes "that no monk, or brother of this monastery, by any means go forth of the precinct of the same," he is here only summarizing the plain prohibition in chapter 66 of St. Benedict's rule. When, again, he goes on to command that "women, of what state or condition soever they be, be utterly excluded," this is one of the most time-honoured and frequently repeated of monastic statutes. The only real novelties in this Cromwellian document are the command to accept and preach royal supremacy, and the freedom given to subject monks to complain against superiors who neglect or contravene any of this long list of injunctions.

But Cromwell's visitation of the monasteries is open to far more serious criticism. He chose base agents, who did their work in a base and hasty fashion. It is quite possible that they invented much of their evidence; yet we have irrefragable orthodox testimony to the fact that this unfavourable evidence did not violate probability. The spoils of the monasteries were devoted partly to public purposes, but mainly to pay Henry's courtiers: here England compares very unfavourably with Scotland and some of the German states, where the money went in a large measure to education. Yet, apart from all this which must be said against Henry's unjust and wasteful methods, his dissolution of the monasteries is justified by the experience of other European countries, all of whom, sooner or later, have been compelled to do the same. In Italy and Spain, where Protestantism has been virtually nonexistent; in France, where Louis XIV. drove out thousands of Huguenots, and the pastor François Rochette was condemned and hanged in 1761 for exercising his pastoral office; in Austria, where the small minority of Protestants was either driven into exile or submitted to the same leaden, crushing tyranny which England exercised over the Irish Catholics; in all these countries there has been a wholesale dissolution and disendowment.

The Tudor monasteries were probably in much the same state as that Oxford which Gibbon describes in his autobiography: and, if the universities of Gibbon's day had been entrenched behind all sorts of extra-legal privileges; if the students had been as numerous as the Tudor Religious were; and if they had successfully resisted, for at least three centuries, all serious efforts for reform, then we can hardly doubt that they also would have been disestablished and disendowed before now. The dissolution was one of many causes for a rising in Lincolnshire, and for the "Pilgrimage of Grace," in the north, where the people were poorest and least educated, and the monasteries would most be missed. Henry here showed himself a perfidious negotiator and took a very cruel vengeance; but his cause had been supported by many of the higher nobility; and he had no difficulty in getting the shire levies of the south to march against the northern rebels (1536).

Edward VI.—Under Edward VI. religious changes came far more rapidly. Henry VIII. had ended by not only permitting but enjoining the popular study of the vernacular Bible (1536–38) and, though the permission was limited in 1543 to the higher classes of society, yet even this implied a freedom of private judgment quite incompatible with mediaeval tradition, and gave an enormous, if not intentional, impetus to Protestantism. Politics, however, played almost more part in the Reformation under Edward VI. than under his father. Reformers were dominant on the council of regency which Henry had appointed; Edward's two tutors, Cheke and Cox, had both been reformers. Under the protector Somerset the chantries were suppressed and confiscated; many of them had also been scholastic foundations in a small way; and thus, though mediaeval England had never possessed an educational system in the modern sense, Edward VI. did far more harm to the schools than he atoned for by a few foundations of his own (1545).

Then, in 1548, came deliberate iconoclasm. The party which looked upon images as a hindrance to true religion was stronger now than those who found them edifying, and much regrettable violence was exercised; yet, when we take a wide view, we find that the orthodox Catholic Montalembert is right in pointing out that a larger proportion of mediaeval Gothic architecture has survived in England than in France. Edward VI. introduced an English liturgy and a Protestant confession of faith in 42 articles (since reduced to 39); and he permitted marriage to the clergy.

A Return to Rome.—His early death put the Catholic Mary upon the throne, while the country in general was still halting between the rival creeds. She communicated immediately with Rome; Cardinal Pole was sent as papal legate; and both houses of parliament answered affirmatively to Mary's question whether they would return to papal obedience. They next rescinded all the anti-papal legislation of Henry VIII. and Edward VI., and revived the statutes against heresy. Mary was now free for all violent measures.

She had promised, and perhaps intended, leniency; but here was a death-struggle between two incompatible ideals, and, in an age when scarcely anybody believed in toleration, Mary had only one choice. She executed 210 Protestants in her last three years; and, at her death, this rate was rather rising than falling. This was fatal; her very first victim, John Rogers, had been so heartily cheered by the London crowd "that he seemed to be going to his marriage," so wrote the French ambassador to his master. This sympathy, strong from the first, grew in proportion as the queen's desperate efforts intensified. Moreover, a new generation was growing up which was far more widely educated than its ancestors; and this was especially noteworthy with the women.

Elizabeth.—The country welcomed Elizabeth; and, though she was not tolerant in the modern sense, she and her ministers carried through one of the most successful compromises in history, the "Reformation settlement." Elizabeth herself would possibly have preferred a moderate form of non-papal Catholicism, though one of her earliest acts was very significant; she forbade the bishop who said mass in her presence to elevate the Host, and went out of the chapel when

he disobeyed. Many of her subjects were convinced and determined Catholics. But she recognized that Protestantism had come to stay; and she so managed that it should have far more freedom than in any Catholic land, while the Catholics, on the other hand, had as much liberty as the Protestant non-conformists.

Death was the legal penalty for obstinate refusal to take the oath of royal supremacy; but in fact no Catholic who refrained from political plots needed to fear more than a shilling fine for each refusal to attend Sunday service, until after the pope had excommunicated her and decreed her deposition. Scarcely one-fiftieth of the Marian clergy were deprived of their livings for refusing the oath. Therefore the nation settled down rapidly; and the result was a more rapid national advance in learning, in literature and in commerce than at any period since the Conquest. One set of figures may be quoted as typical of the rest. The religious quarrels told very heavily upon the universities. The number of degrees fell sadly at Oxford under Henry VIII, and rose again under Mary to the mediaeval average; at Cambridge, however, they fell under Mary. From 1555 to 1558 they averaged only 28 a year; but in 1570 they had risen to 170, and in 1583 to 277, or three times the mediaeval average.

Scotland and Ireland.—The Scottish Reformation went on side by side with the English; each assisted the other. John Knox and Elizabeth were far from complete agreement; but they had sufficient sense and self-control to work together. This religious Concordat went far to obliterate ancient enmities; "Knox included in his liturgy a prayer that there might nevermore be war between Scotland and England; and that prayer has been fulfilled" (F. W. Maitland in *Camb. Mod. Hist.*, vol. II). In 1560 the Scottish parliament did what the English had done a year before; mass and papal authority were formally rejected. Knox's *Book of Discipline,* founded mainly on Calvin's *Institution* and on the organization already adopted by French Protestantism, fixed Scotland in "presbyterianism."

The democratic character of the Scottish Reformation, and Knox's own zeal for education, go far to explain the subsequent love of learning and the high level of general education in Scotland; though the greed of the barons frustrated the hope of endowing a whole system of schools and colleges from confiscated Church property.

England's treatment of Ireland is a black page in Reformation history. The country was conquered, and the conquerors dealt with it after the brutal fashion of that time. Few Catholics lost their lives for religion pure and simple, as apart from political revolts; but a series of unjust penal statutes were enacted, and these, although seldom enforced in their full theoretical strictness, were relaxed far too slowly in the face of advancing civilization; instead of weakening, they strengthened the attachment of the Irish to their religion.

GENERAL RESULTS

It has sometimes been argued that the present religious equilibrium, or something better, might have been obtained without revolution. But this contention seems scarcely reconcilable either with previous or with subsequent history.

We have seen how long this revolution had been brewing. It would be difficult to find any institution which has been so severely criticized by so many of its most devoted adherents, through so many centuries, as the mediaeval Church. At the very beginning of the 12th century, St. Bernard had emphasized weaknesses which, if not remedied, must necessarily bring disaster; yet orthodox churchmen of 1500 frequently quote St. Bernard's actual words as exactly applicable to the Church of their own day. Some scandals had been abated; but others were even more rampant. Such improvements as had taken place were mainly due to pressure from the laity; and friction between clergy and their flocks seemed increasing rather than decreasing.

Subsequent history, again, seems to point even more decisively in this same direction. We have seen that the real question at issue was that of private judgment. Nearly all reformers had two fundamental points in common with the orthodox; they wanted to save souls and they believed in the inerrancy of the Bible. But on one fundamental point they differed; is the Bible to be interpreted by the individual for his own soul's sake, or by the Church for the individual's soul's sake? The reformers acted on the former principle; and this opened the floodgates for the rest; so, although the full claim of private judgment was not the basis on which the reformers consciously took their stand, yet it was implicit in their original theories and actions.

Private Judgment.—Between authority and private judgment, no agreement seems possible except the agreement to differ; yet even that was essentially impossible under the mediaeval regime. To differ publicly from any solemn pronouncement of the Church was a crime; obstinately to differ was a capital crime. Therefore no orthodox mediaeval churchman could grant to others the right of nonconformity, or could really escape from the responsibility (however much he might personally shrink from it) of denouncing and punishing all dissenters. Yet, by 1500 at least, it was becoming quite obvious that considerable numbers of Christians were trusting more to private judgment, confessedly or implicitly, than to the traditional teaching of their priests.

The Inquisition had driven the nonconformists underground for nearly three centuries, very much as early Christianity had been driven underground for nearly three centuries by imperial persecution; but it was now emerging with irresistible force. The pope could not now do what Constantine had done in 324, reversing at a single stroke the policy of his predecessors. To Constantine, this religious question had been only one of many debatable issues, and he may even have looked upon it as one of the least important of his political problems; therefore, a reversal at that point need not in the least imply reversal of the whole imperial machine. To the pope, on the other hand, this question of private judgment was absolutely fundamental.

Moreover, even the strongest of popes was always far more at the mercy of his predecessors' traditional policy, of his court and of his officials, than a strong emperor. The pope had no means of coming to terms with Protestantism but by accepting the basic tenet of Protestantism; the Protestants, again, could have come to terms only by abandoning a tenet which, implicitly at least, was absolutely necessary to their position. And the fact that, after a century of strife, Christendom was, and has since remained, pretty equally divided between these two irreconcilable principles, would seem to prove that no human ingenuity could have kept the parties permanently within one fold.

And, indeed, this division of parties seems to have worked more than any other factor towards that tolerance which is one of the greatest gains of modern civilization. The general mass of European society had improved greatly, in many important respects, between 1100 and 1500; but in this one matter of toleration there had been painful and continual retrogression. The Reformers, again, at their earliest stage, were compelled to plead for impunity; but, once in power, they proved as untrue to this principle as the Christian Church had proved when the emperors raised it from a persecuted minority to a persecuting majority.

Mutual Toleration.—Lord Acton, in one of his most plain-spoken essays, has insisted on the wickedness of this *volte-face*, and has pointed out that the innovators Martin Luther and John Calvin lacked that palliation which may be pleaded for persecutors who had persecuted in defense of tradition. But, whether we agree or disagree with him in condemning the individual persecuting Protestant more severely than the individual Catholic, the fact remains that the principle of private judgment is logically inseparable from the principle of toleration, and that no institution can survive, in the face of a powerful enemy, if it acts in public and systematic and continual violation of its own fundamental principle. There is a painful truth in the contention that both sides have learned toleration only under outside pressure; yet that pressure itself has resulted from the assertion of a principle irreconcilable with mediaeval theory and practice.

Private judgment brought half of Europe into conflict with the traditions of centuries; the resultant wars were indecisive; it became evident that neither side could exterminate the other; thenceforward both were obliged to seek some way of living together in the same world. The one party has never granted the individual's right to interpret Scripture otherwise than it was interpreted by the mediaeval hierarchy. Even Protestantism, for many generations, did not advance from the claim for individual interpretation of the Bible to the wider modern claim of rejecting, when necessary, some things that are plainly written in the Bible. But Catholics and Protestants and men of many other creeds live together in modern times in far less discord than that which often reigned in the middle ages among professing Catholics.

The Reformation thus becomes one of the most remarkable episodes in world history, whether we regard it in bulk or in detail. It is rich in striking incidents and in display of human character, both on the Catholic and on the Protestant side; we may find here the loftiest heroism and the lowest depths of turpitude. It exemplifies all the problems of daily life, magnified in proportion to the greatness of the issues here involved. And from the heat of this conflict between two irreconcilable ideals one principle has slowly emerged, theoretically repudiated by one side and too often violated by the other in practice, yet finally victorious through the mere force of circumstances; the principle of religious toleration. The experience of centuries has now suggested that the main differences which separate many minds from the teaching of the mediaeval Church are rooted in human nature itself; and that, however near the two parties may draw to each other in the distant future, no such *modus vivendi* was possible in 1517.

BIBLIOGRAPHY.—L. v. Ranke, *History of the Reformation in Germany,* tr. by S. Austin (1845); C. Beard, *The Reformation in Relation to Modern Thought* (1883, republished 1927); F. v. Bezold, *Geschichte der deutschen Reformation* (1890); J. Janssen, *History of the German People at the Close of the Middle Ages,* 17 vol., tr. by M. A. Mitchell and A. M. Christie (1896-1910); E. Armstrong, *Charles V* (1902); J. Gairdner, *History of the English Church in the 16th Century* (1902); *Cambridge Modern History,* vol. ii (1903); A. F. Pollard, *Henry VIII* (1905); H. A. L. Fisher, *History of England 1485-1547* (1906); T. M. Lindsay, *History of the Reformation* (1907); A. O. Meyer, *England and the Catholic Church Under Elizabeth,* tr. by J. R. McKee (1916); H. M. Gwatkin, *Church and State in England* (1917); R. H. Tawney, *Religion and the Rise of Capitalism* (1926). (G. G. C.)

REFORMATORY SCHOOL, an institution for the vocational training of juvenile offenders. In Great Britain this means offenders over 12 and under 16 years of age, who have been convicted of offenses which, in the case of adults, would be punishable by penal servitude or imprisonment. The schools are supported in the main from public funds. The departmental committee on young offenders recommended, in 1927, the substitution of 17 for 16 as the upper limit of age at the time of committal to a reformatory school and the abolition of the distinction between these and industrial schools. (*See also* BORSTAL SYSTEM.) (X.)

UNITED STATES

The reformatory system of the United States, as distinguished from the penitentiary or prison system, may be considered under two heads: (1) reform schools and industrial schools for youths under 16 or 18 committed for violations of the criminal law or for the want of proper guardianship; and (2) reformatories for persons between the ages of 16 or 18 and 30 convicted of criminal acts. The former is an outgrowth of the houses of refuge, which developed in the early part of the 19th century, under private and charitable organizations.

The latter development was a reaction to the earlier Pennsylvania and Auburn prison systems which through the 19th century had converged to produce a specific prison philosophy with a companion architectural style. This distinctive American penology called for a system of punishment designed to chasten and make penitent through the agency of a fortresslike maximum security institution.

The failure of these prisons to either reform the inmates or make them penitent gave rise to a movement emphasizing and reexamining the conditions necessary for reformation. This new "reformatory movement" stressed the development of penal methods designed to produce positive and constructive changes among the reformatory inmates. The new emphasis found specific affirmation with the organization of the National Prison association in Cincinnati in 1870. The 1870 meetings of the association called for new prison methods including good conduct rewards, educational and industrial training, professionalizing of penal personnel and other measures which it was believed would encourage the reformation of the offender.

Beginning with the last quarter of the 19th century, a number of states established industrial schools or state homes for the correction and training of their delinquent youths. The first reformatory for older adolescents was created in New York in 1869, when the legislature of that state enacted a law and appropriated funds to establish the New York State reformatory at Elmira. The Elmira reformatory was opened in 1876 under Zebulon R. Brockway, who accepted the position of superintendent with the understanding that the new institution would emphasize rewards for good conduct and provide industrial training and education. Furthermore, it would receive only inmates under an indeterminate sentence who would be eligible for release under parole.

The reformatory system developed rapidly after the New York innovation and by 1901, 11 states had added a reformatory to their penal systems. Thereafter, through the mid-1950s, 10 other reformatories were built in 9 states and the District of Columbia.

In practically all cases the system of discipline, training and release established at Elmira was more or less followed. The indeterminate sentence is an integral part of the U.S. reformatory system. Beginning with 1925 there was a decided trend toward specialized vocational training in connection with the educational work of all U.S. reformatories.

In some of the more progressive reformatories the academic and vocational programs have been guided by clinical techniques involving psychological, sociological and psychiatric services. However, these developments have been generally handicapped by limited resources and they have resulted in improved classification and training of prisoners in only a few institutions. In these institutions, greater emphasis is being placed upon clinical studies in determining fitness for release.

The U.S. government opened its first federal reformatory for adolescent male offenders in March 1926 at Chillicothe, Ohio. In 1927 the first Federal Industrial Institution for Women was opened at Alderson, W.Va. Prior to this time, federal offenders of all types over 16 years were received at the federal penitentiaries. The federal government now maintains five reformatories for younger improvable offenders. In addition, it continues to follow the practice of boarding a number of its younger offenders in state and local institutions.

The "reformatory movement" represents a historic phase in the development of the U.S. penal system. For the most part, the changes introduced have been adopted by the penal system at large and it is no longer possible to clearly distinguish between prisons and reformatories by their programs. The optimism engendered with the spread of the reformatory system has been offset by the reports of recent surveys. These studies indicate that the primitive and repressive measures of an earlier day have not yet been replaced or even seriously challenged by the reformatory movement. Follow-up studies indicate no appreciably greater amount of successful adjustment among the releasees of the reformatories of the U.S. as compared with the releasees from the "senior" penal institutions.

BIBLIOGRAPHY.—F. H. Wines, *Punishment and Reformation* (1895); Z. R. Brockway, *Fifty Years of Prison Service* (1912); B. G. Lewis, *The Offender and His Relations to Law and Society* (New York, 1917); *Annual Reports* of the American Prison Association; O. F. Lewis, *The Development of American Prisons and Prison Customs* (1922); H. H. Lou, *Juvenile Courts in the United States* (Chapel Hill, N.C., 1927); Fred E. Haynes, *The American Prison System* (New York, 1939); William Healy and B. S. Alper, *Criminal Youth and the Borstal System* (New York, London, 1941); U.S. Department of Justice, Bureau of Prisons, *Handbook of Correctional Institution Design and Construction* (Washington, D.C., 1949); Paul W. Tappan, *Contemporary Correction* (New York, 1951); Harry E. Barnes and Negley K. Teeters, *New Horizons in Criminology* (New York, 1951). (J. D. LN.)

REFORMED CHURCHES, THE, are those European churches which during the Reformation undertook to reform their faith and life, as they declared, "according to the Word of God," under the leadership of such men as Huldreich Zwingli, Martin Bucer, John Calvin, Heinrich Bullinger and John Oecolampadius. The movement first began in German-speaking Switzerland and in the Rhineland, spreading quickly to French-speaking Switzerland, France, the Netherlands, Hungary and other European countries. The churches are now world-wide in distribution. The Presbyterian Churches of Great Britain share, in part, these same origins, but are also distinctly British in other ways. The Presbyterians, however, classify themselves as Reformed Churches because of the common heritage. The Reformed Churches call their ecclesiastical polity the "presbyterian" system. The name "Reformed" was originally used by all the Reformation churches, as were the names "Evangelical" (*i.e.*, based on the Evangel, the Gospel) and "Lutheran." Only after the serious controversy over the Lord's Supper (after 1529) did the followers of Martin Luther become known distinctly as the Lutherans and the non-Lutheran Reformation bodies as the Reformed.

Though the term "Calvinistic Churches" has become synonymous with the name "Reformed Churches," John Calvin of Geneva was not the original leader of this phase of the Reformation. Rather he, coming after the first great leaders, Zwingli, Bucer, Oecolampadius, etc., took up their ideas, systematized them, adapted them and improved upon them. He is, therefore, the greatest figure in the history of these churches. Not all his distinctive ideas were adopted by all the Reformed Churches.

Switzerland.—The Reformation in Switzerland may properly be said to have been begun by Zwingli in 1519 at Zürich. Zwingli had been deeply influenced by Desiderius Erasmus, and stood closer to Renaissance Humanism than did any of the other great Reformation leaders. His outright break with the Roman Church did not come until 1522. It came then in a form which was to become virtually standard for the entire Swiss Reformation and which was to have consequences of the utmost importance. Switzerland had become a federation of cantons each of which had almost total autonomy in internal affairs. A democratically elected council, or other body, controlled all matters. Ecclesiastically episcopal authority had become vague in most cantons.

When controversy broke out between the reforming preachers and the Roman priests, the council of Zürich assumed jurisdiction. Zwingli demanded that a public disputation be held between the reformers and the Roman clergy, and that thereafter the people themselves, through their officers, should decide which religion to follow. This pattern of debate followed by a vote of the people was used in almost every Swiss city or canton which became Evangelical (Protestant). The civil authorities were established

in this manner as the heads of the churches, though they had actually controlled church affairs in great measure before. This control once established came to have serious consequences.

Zürich became fully Evangelical after a series of major disputations, 1523–25. Basle, following a similar pattern, led by Wolfgang Capito, Oecolampadius and Guillaume Farel, voted in the Evangelical faith the same year. Berne, the most powerful of all the cantons, followed suit in 1528. St. Gallen, Biel and others also made the change in the same manner. Opposition from those cantons which remained Roman Catholic grew, and Zürich and Berne led in the formation of the Christian Civic league in defense of the Evangelical Reformation. Eventually even German cities such as Strasbourg joined, and Hesse and Württemberg became interested. The Roman forces now joined in the Christian union. In the two wars which followed, the Evangelical forces were finally defeated, Zwingli was killed, and the Evangelical advance all but permanently halted. Moreover, political leadership in Swiss Protestantism passed from Zürich to Berne (1531). Evangelical and Roman groups agreed to recognize the right of the other to exist. Heinrich Bullinger succeeded Zwingli at Zürich.

Meanwhile, the controversy over the Lord's Supper (after 1529) had broken the Swiss reformers away from the German reformers led by Luther and had brought the Strasbourg reformers led by Bucer into the role of unsuccessful mediators. After Zwingli's death, Bullinger and the other Swiss reformers came to an understanding with Bucer and even with Philipp Melanchthon, but could not do so with Luther. Henceforth no one theological mind dominated the Reformation of the Swiss-German Rhineland, and a great area of tacit agreement came into existence. These reformers remained more Humanistic than Luther was or than Calvin was to be (though he was to be deeply influenced by them).

Berne took over and pushed the policy laid out by Zürich of advancing the Reformation by open debate and elections. In the furtherance of this policy it had as agents a number of Evangelical preachers who went everywhere, protected by Berne, preaching and debating in Roman Catholic areas. Guillaume Farel was one of the leaders of these preachers. So successful were their efforts that in 1532 it was possible to call a synod of 230 Evangelical preachers at Berne. Bucer was present as an adviser.

Farel turned his attention to Geneva in 1532 but found progress slow and hard. Only after riots and threats of force by both Catholic and Protestant cantons did Geneva finally agree to hold a public disputation in 1532. The Catholic forces led by the prince-bishop besieged Geneva. Berne by coming into the war saved Geneva and crushed the house of Savoy's forces. This brought Geneva somewhat under Berne's tutelage, with Farel as the religious leader. Farel was unable to get an Evangelical church life established in any real measure at Geneva the first year.

Farel saved the situation by persuading John Calvin, a young French Evangelical refugee, to become his assistant. Calvin had been associated with the "group of Meaux," and perhaps also with the Strasbourg reformers. He had, in addition to great theological and pastoral gifts, unusual organizing abilities. Geneva had become Evangelical for political reasons and wished to do as Berne, Zürich and other Swiss cities had; namely, control, and use, the church. Calvin and the other Genevan pastors demanded independence for the church in religious matters and the right to criticize, on moral and religious grounds, the acts of the government and the moral life of the city. The church was, however, to have no authority in civil matters. After three years Farel and Calvin were dismissed by the civil authorities from their pastorates because of this clash of ideas (1538). Calvin became a pastor in Strasbourg.

Geneva dared not return to Roman Catholicism because it would mean the loss of its independence to the prince-bishop of the house of Savoy. Yet, religiously and politically the situation in the city deteriorated. The second year Calvin was asked to return, but he refused. In 1541 Calvin's friends persuaded him to come back. He returned as pastor and teacher.

Work was now begun on the reforming of the church in Geneva. Calvin desired a church based on the Gospel and free to conduct its own affairs, including the right to discipline its members, if need be, by excommunication. Also, he desired no civil office, but the right to preach and teach on civic issues. No civil officer was to have any hold on the church. The government, however, wished still to control, and to use, the church. In the end, the government temporized, leaving the pulpit free, with no civic office for ministers; but the government of the city constituted the government of the church, thus controlling it in the final analysis. Thus, the civil authorities hired the ministers also, whereas Calvin had wished the people to have this right. Because Geneva did have certain serious moral problems, the authorities gave the church large disciplinary power backed by civil penalties as well as religious. The mediaeval "blue laws" and many other regulations were imposed at once in order to reform the city.

Civil and religious authorities worked together well for a time. However, when the church attempted to discipline members of the upper, ruling class trouble came from the civil authorities. Also, Calvin's insistence upon making Geneva a centre for Evangelical refugees caused great resentment among the "old Genevese" party which resented the coming in of these "foreigners." The group in the city for which the religious change from Catholicism to Evangelicalism had been essentially a part of the move for civic independence made common cause with those who resented religious reform. In 1553 Calvin's cause seemed defeated.

Michael Servetus appeared in Geneva at that very time. He had just escaped from the Inquisition at Lyons, Fr., where he had been condemned for Unitarian views. He was an able and well-known freethinker. In Geneva he was arrested for heresy and tried before the civil authorities. At once this became the test case of the whole struggle between Calvin and his opponents. The trial lasted more than a month. Servetus eventually demanded that he be acquitted and that Calvin be put to death and Calvin's property awarded to himself. As other issues were interjected into the case, Calvin and several other ministers resigned and prepared to leave the city. The authorities now temporized and decided to circularize a number of other European churches asking for advice. The mediaeval idea that heretics were disrupters of society and dangerous prevailed, and all these churches recommended death for Servetus. The opposition now not only lost the Servetus test case but was in a hopeless strategic position. The city authorities burned Servetus, though Calvin and others urged a less cruel death.

Two years later (1555) the civil authorities gave up all control over the internal life of the church, but still held out on the issue of the refugees. When the leaders of the opposition to Calvin were found to be in secret negotiations with the French king their whole cause collapsed. Calvin was then free to settle church affairs, found the University of Geneva, train refugee ministers for service all over Europe and make Geneva the Evangelical centre of Europe. He held no office other than that of pastor of the church, though his influence was enormous. Gradually leadership of the various Reformed Churches passed to Geneva. Calvin died in 1564, and his successor, Theodore Beza, was the acknowledged leader of French Protestantism. Under his successors Genevan leadership declined wholly. By the 18th century Geneva was dominated by the Enlightenment. German Switzerland came to greater prominence. French Reformed leadership was never again great.

During the Reformation most Swiss cantons had each its own state church. This pattern has never been dropped. During the 20th century most of the churches were disestablished in greater or lesser measure, without losing their character of national churches. The presbyterian form of government in general prevails in these churches. No particular creed is used by any of them, though, in general, they follow the Reformed tradition.

Switzerland has become the international centre of world Protestantism, and the Reformed Churches have contributed much to this ecumenical work. During World Wars I and II the Swiss Churches did much to hold together Evangelical Churches in the warring world. In 1948 the Swiss Reformed Churches formed a federation which included roughly three-fifths the population of Switzerland.

Germany.—Matthew Zell, who had been influenced by Zwingli,

began preaching Evangelical doctrine in Strassbourg as early as 1521. Soon he was joined by Capito from Basle, and others. Martin Bucer, who had become an Erasmian reformer, met Luther in 1518 and became an Evangelical. In 1524 he went to Strasbourg and shortly was made pastor. Subject now to influences from Zürich, Basle and France, he gradually moved away from Luther. At the Diet of Augsburg, 1530, he led a small group of Germans and others who sought a middle ground between Luther's and Zwingli's groups. From then on he followed a policy of mediation, first between the various reforming groups, and then between the Reformed groups and the Roman groups. When the Interim was forced on Germany (1548), Strasbourg was compelled to become Roman Catholic, and the Reformed leaders were exiled. Bucer and others went to England, and some went to Switzerland. When the Interim was lifted Strasbourg was made exclusively Lutheran until 1789.

The course of the Reformed system in Strasbourg was, therefore, limited to the period 1521-49. However, during that period some decisive things took place. Strasbourg became the centre, within Germany, of Swiss Reformation thought. All down the Rhine valley Swiss-Strasbourg influences moved, even into the Netherlands. Calvin found refuge in Strasbourg 1538-41, and both gave and received lasting contributions. English Puritans before, during and after the "Marian exile" were permanently affected by this theology of the Rhineland, and Bucer eventually went to England. Without Strasbourg's role as a channel the influence of Zürich, Basle and Geneva upon the outside world might well have been rather small. The so-called Reformed Churches might have been limited to Switzerland and France.

Francis Lambert of Avignon, who had been at both Wittenberg and Strasbourg, led a brief attempt at a Reformed Church in Hesse. At the Synod of Homberg in 1526 the Reformed plan of pastors, elders and deacons elected by the people had been projected. The church soon became Lutheran, but the ideas set in motion by the synod continued to permeate other regions.

The city of Emden became Evangelical under Reformed leadership in 1526-29. Difficulties abounded until a Polish noble, Jan Laski the younger, who had become a Reformed minister took charge in 1542. He introduced a system which blended German Swiss-Rhineland views with those of Calvin. This form of Reformed thought had a wide influence, since Laski was twice a refugee pastor in England and later settled in the Rhineland.

Elector Frederick III of the Palatinate was, in many ways, the one who really gave the German Reformed Church its great opportunity. During the later years of Melanchthon's life, and for some time thereafter, grievous controversy raged among Lutherans between an ultra-Lutheran faction and a more moderate group of Melanchthon's followers. The latter were continually accused of being Calvinists, and Melanchthon was friendly toward Calvin and the Reformed groups. The violence of the controversy turned many minds toward Calvinism, or the Reformed views.

Frederick made Heidelberg university a centre of Reformed thought, bringing to it men such as Zacharias Ursinus and Kaspar Olevianus. Ursinus had been first a Melanchthonian Lutheran and had later come under Peter Martyr and Farel. Frederick commissioned these men to draft a constitution for the Palatinate which would more nearly express the Reformed views. The Heidelberg Catechism (1563) which they drew up quickly became the catechism (in many ways the creed) of all the Reformed Churches. In clarity, depth, simplicity and warmth it excelled any other Reformed confession or catechism. Theologically it was an able harmony of all current Reformed thought. Moreover, while it was not based on the then rising Federal theology, with which Olevianus was shortly to side, it could be fitted into that scheme. In view of its many virtues it is not surprising that it replaced, in time, all other Reformed catechisms.

Ursinus and Olevianus prepared also a directory for public worship for the Palatinate. It was definitely Reformed, being a guide to the right ordering of public worship and not a stated, required liturgy whose forms must be used. Altars and vestments were dispensed with, and the communion table was brought in. The pulpit became the focus of the church's public worship, because from it the Gospel was proclaimed.

The Heidelberg Catechism was attacked fiercely by the ultra-Lutherans. Soon it was being asserted that those who held its views had no right to toleration under the terms laid down in the Peace of Augsburg, 1555. Frederick fought the issue to a successful conclusion at the Diet of Augsburg, 1566, thus gaining a clear-cut admission that the Reformed Churches had the right to exist parallel to the Lutheran Churches allowed by the diet of 1555. With a persuasive statement of faith, a great university, the legal right to exist and a powerful elector as their champion, the Reformed Churches enjoyed a period of growth and success.

Despite temporary or local losses, or both, the Reformed Churches spread down the Rhine. The Wetterau counties became Reformed, and at Herborn a famous Reformed university was founded. Bremen also became Reformed, and then Brandenburg (1613) with its capital Berlin. Other smaller areas scattered over the German states also became Reformed.

The Thirty Years' War brought the Reformed territories almost to ruin, and at the Peace of Prague, 1635, the Reformed groups were so wholly betrayed that the war was resumed. The Peace of Westphalia, 1648, recognized explicitly the Reformed Churches and restored the lands of the Reformed nobles. It also recognized Switzerland's independence of the empire. The war, therefore, had been an important event for the Reformed Churches. The revocation of the Edict of Nantes (1685) brought into Germany about 60,000 Huguenot refugees. These greatly strengthened the Reformed Churches. During this same period the French ravaged the Palatinate and greatly reduced the Reformed Churches, which were saved only by the intervention of Brandenburg. Yet, until 1802 serious hardship was their fate.

During the 18th century Pietism, coupled with the Federal theology, gained almost total allegiance among the German Reformed Churches. The form of Pietism was that of the Dutch Churches, and drew these two Reformed groups closer together. Pietism, in turn, was followed by the Enlightenment. (F. D. E. Schleiermacher was of the Reformed Church.)

Beginning in 1817, Prussia united, by three stages, the Reformed and Lutheran Churches in its territories. The first stage was federation, the second (1830) a common liturgy, and the third (1834) allowed each congregation the right to use whichever creed and liturgy it wished (Reformed or Lutheran). The territories were those where the Reformed groups had their greatest strength, Brandenburg, Prussia, Pomerania, Silesia, Posen, Westphalia and the Rhine provinces. Those provinces which joined Prussia after 1817, Hanover, Nassau and electoral Hesse, were not compelled to unite their churches, although Nassau had done so previously at its own order. Small local unions were made in these areas, however. Nonunion Reformed Churches remained in Bremen, Lippe, Alsace-Lorraine, Lower Saxony, etc. Generally speaking the Reformed tradition was overshadowed by the Lutheran in the union.

In 1861 Reformed leaders began to revive, but within the various union agreements, a greater appreciation for the Reformed tradition and ethic. Inner mission work among the poor, sick, etc., also was pushed, as were foreign missions, youth work, etc. A vigorous literature on the Reformed ideals began to appear. World War I and the years immediately following wrought havoc on all German Churches. Old cultural patterns disappeared, and the industrialized, modern secular society emerged. The close connections of all the churches with the German state had become a hindrance, and disestablishment under the Weimar republic was in itself good. However, it came when the churches could least afford the financial and other losses which it entailed.

Beginning in 1918–21 a vigorous theological renewal took place in Germany. The Reformed federation, led by August Lang, brought Karl Barth to Göttingen university. He quickly became the leading Reformed theologian of modern times. As the nazi regime took over, Barth and Otto Weber of the Reformed federation became leaders in the struggle of the German Churches against Hitler and neopaganism.

World War II brought serious losses to the Reformed Churches. Those regions of Germany where they were strongest fell into the soviet zone of occupation. Moreover, many Lutherans, pressed by the remembrance of the nazi persecutions, demanded unqualified adherence to (Lutheran) traditional creeds as a guarantee of future strength for the church. This meant the denunciation of the union in fact if not in law. In Hesse, the Ruhr and other regions of west Germany the Reformed Churches recovered slowly after the war, aided by United States Presbyterian and Reformed Churches.

Prior to World War I the German Protestant Churches, working through numerous missionary societies, had a vast foreign missionary work. After 1918 it was necessary, for financial reasons, that churches in other nations take over this work.

During the height of Germany's power, German Reformed groups spread out over a large part of Europe and also into Russia. Sizeable churches were established in Austria (Vienna), Yugoslavia, and Slovakia; smaller bodies were found among the German settlers in Russia, Lithuania and Latvia. In the territories which were alternately Polish and German in the 19th and 20th centuries there were large Reformed groups. The status of all these groups deteriorated seriously after World War II.

The Netherlands.—Reforming interest emerged in the Netherlands early in the Reformation era. Erasmus did much of his best work at Rotterdam. Moreover, the Brethren of the Common Life and other mystical groups had been active in these areas. From 1513 to 1531 about 25 different translations of the Bible, or parts of it, into Dutch, Flemish or French were published in the Netherlands. Much of the early English Reformation literature also was printed in the Low Countries.

Erasmian and mystical types of reform were soon followed by Zwinglian and Lutheran influences. Communications, and other interests also, bound the Rhineland and the Netherlands together. Hence the Swiss-Rhineland type of reform came to predominate. The Anabaptists and the other reform movements seldom if ever merged, and their influences were felt more at a later period. Charles V, who controlled the Netherlands, instituted the Inquisition there against the Reformation as early as 1522.

The struggle for freedom from Spain was begun by the Dutch as a protest in demand of greater liberties, especially religious, within Charles's empire. Charles was determined to wipe out all heresy, and, while frustrated in Germany, he gave himself to the task in his own hereditary provinces, the Netherlands, with the more fanatic zeal. Eventually, the Dutch nobles (c. 1566), led by William the Silent of Orange, turned against him. When he finally abdicated in defeat and despair, Philip II took over his father's crusade against heresy, but with even fewer prospects of success. One of Philip's generals, the duke of Alva, became a notorious symbol of blind and merciless despotism. William was murdered by a hired assassin in 1584, but by that time the Spanish-Roman Catholic cause had been defeated. The Netherlands became free, and the Reformed Church was established.

During the long struggle the religious situation had also become clarified. The leaders in the war for freedom had been deeply influenced by French Huguenot-Calvinist political and religious thought. Lutheran and Erasmian ideas had given way to a theology blended from Rhineland, Genevan Calvinist and French Huguenot influences and ideas drawn from Jan Laski's work. The Belgic Confession of 1561 became the standard creed. Church organization was patterned most nearly after the forms of Laski and the Huguenots, two forms of Calvinistic presbyterian polity. However, the church was not a national church. The Netherlands was a federation of states with great local autonomy in each state. Each had its own church over which the local authorities had almost complete powers. National synods were provided for in the church's system but were seldom allowed by the various states.

Civic peace had scarcely been achieved before a theological revolution took place in the Dutch Church. Calvinists, in their controversies with Lutherans and Catholics, had carried their philosophical development of Calvin's religious view of predestination (which he shared with Luther) to great lengths. Some Reformed thinkers began to object, among them a Dutch theologian named Jacobus Arminius. Other issues also were involved, especially Dutch political issues. The leader of the ultrapredestinarian Calvinists in the Dutch Reformed Churches was Franz Gomarus.

To solve the issue a synod of representatives of Reformed Churches in all lands was called by the civil authorities. Representatives came from several European countries. James I of England took peculiar interest in the synod and sent representatives from the Church of England. The synod met at Dort in 1618, condemned Arminius' mild views, rejected Gomarus' extreme views and stated in more or less classical form the quasi-Calvinistic view which had become the badge of Calvinists in their polemics with other theologians. The term "Arminianism" became a very broad designation in Europe for any deviation from any essential aspect of Calvinistic orthodoxy, whether or not connected with Arminius' followers or with the original points of controversy.

Though scholastic Calvinistic orthodoxy won the struggle with Arminius it failed to nurture the life of the Reformed Church. Dutch Pietism (anterior to and more churchly and theological than German Pietism) and the Federal theology soon dominated the Dutch scene. In these movements the Canons of Dort were always honoured but also made harmless in practice.

By the 19th century the extreme orthodox groups in the Dutch Church were disaffected by the influences of the Enlightenment upon the church. A series of schisms took place which eventually gave Holland three Reformed Churches, each professing to be the successor of historic Reformed Christianity in the Netherlands. The original church bears the name the Netherland Reformed Church. Two early secessionist groups were the Christian Reformed Church (1834) and the Low German Mourning Reformed Church (1886). These merged in 1892 as the Reformed Churches in the Netherlands. A minority of the early secession, however, constituted itself the Christian Reformed Church (Restored). None of these three churches is now a state church, although the original body is still regarded, in some measure, as the national church. During World War II and the German occupation of the Netherlands much progress was made toward healing these old schisms. After the peace most of this gain was lost.

On all matters of Dutch colonial policy the old original church became a leader of enlightened opinion in postwar times. Political parties and labour unions usually follow confessional lines in the Netherlands. Accordingly the various Reformed Churches have their corresponding political parties and labour unions. This structure has tended to fix the distance between the church and all degrees and forms of left-wing thought.

The Netherland Reformed Church had (in 1948) 1,500,000 members, 1,400 congregations and 2,500 additional preaching points, 1,550 ministers, 4,500 elders and 169 missionaries at 65 stations in the Netherlands Indies and Malaya.

The Reformed Churches in the Netherlands had (in 1948) 324,621 members, 810 congregations and 801 ministers. Missionary work was being done in the Netherlands Indies.

The Christian Reformed Church (Restored) had (in 1948) approximately 35,000 members.

The Dutch Churches followed the colonial expansion of the Netherlands. In the Union of South Africa they became the principal Christian Churches. This, together with the Dutch tendency to have political parties follow confessional lines, threw upon these churches a very large responsibility. With few exceptions, these churches reflected the views of the Dutch South Africans. The post-World War II premier, Daniel Malan, who led the campaign for the total segregation of the population and areas of South Africa on racial and colour lines, was an ordained Reformed minister. The South African Reformed Churches officially approved his policy.

Controversy over doctrinal issues divided the church in South Africa also. There were five distinct bodies in South Africa (in 1948) with an aggregate (white) membership of approximately 895,000 members. A mission church for nonwhite missionary converts had (in 1948) a membership of 132,096.

The Netherlands Indies, prior to its independence, had a Dutch Church of about 300,000 members.

France.—From the beginning the Reformation made slow progress in France. And yet, reforming movements within the Roman Catholic Church had been early in appearing. Before Luther had emerged as a reformer, French Humanists had created much interest in biblical studies and had aroused a concern for a purer type of Christianity. In time Marguerite d'Angoulême, the sister of Francis I, became the centre of a Humanistic group known as the "group of Meaux." While this group never broke with the Roman Church, and never became outright Evangelical, it did create great interest in reform. Also, members of it, such as Jacobus Faber, contributed much by their writings to biblical and theological studies which the Evangelicals could and did use. Again, a number of the group—Nicolas Cop, Guillaume Farel, etc.—as individuals, left the group and became outright Evangelicals. Moreover, because of her position and her influence, Marguerite was often of aid to all degrees of reforming interests.

Not until 1555 was any real attempt made to organize Evangelical congregations in France. Until that time some had hoped for reform from within the Roman Church, others had looked to the group of Meaux and others had thought the Evangelical cause too weak to organize. Calvin, Farel and Beza, all Frenchmen then active in Geneva, had maintained a deep interest in the French Reform movement. Hundreds of students had been sent from Geneva to evangelize France. By 1560 it was estimated that there were about 300,000 Evangelicals in France, and there were at least 49 organized congregations.

Geneva had indeed been the spiritual guide of these churches, but not their ruler. When, in 1559, these churches moved to draw up a confession of faith, Calvin had demurred, thinking the move too hasty. Nonetheless they proceeded, and informed him that they had used his brief confession of 1557 as a basis, although they had altered it somewhat. This pattern of relationships was to continue to the bitter end: Calvin urging patience, the French Reformed Churches (called the Huguenots) impetuous and often violent. In general the Huguenots followed Calvin's views, yet on many critical matters they made such changes as they wished and when they wished.

The Huguenot alterations on Calvin which became of greatest significance were two: in political theory and in church polity. Calvin had been resolute but cautious on the right of revolution against a civil government. He believed that when a tyrannical king or government attempted to force men to live contrary to the will of God, then, and then only, men might resist—but only through the next lowest, willing, legally constituted, official body or group (*i.e.*, usually a parliament against a king, or a league of cities against a king, etc.). The Huguenots urged that when men felt oppressed in any serious regard by a king, they might individually, or collectively in extralegally constituted groups, resist, revolt and even use tyrannicide.

The second alteration on Calvin's views made by the Huguenots was in the realm of church polity, or government. Calvin's adaptation of presbyterian church government had been worked out for the church of a small city-state. The Huguenots adapted it quite successfully to a national scale. The local congregation elected its minister and a body of elders and deacons who, with the pastor, formed the consistory. These consistories then constituted the provincial synod by electing members to it. The provincial synods again constituted by elected representatives the national synod. Nearly all subsequent forms of presbyterian church organization—European, British, U.S., etc., are directly or indirectly modelled on this Huguenot adaptation of Calvin's Genevan system (which in turn had not been original with Calvin).

Frances I had been no friend of the Huguenots, but under Frances II the Guises and their Roman Catholic followers harried the Huguenots. They in turn leaned, to their great loss, upon certain high nobles. Finally, against Calvin's objections, they organized as a political and military force. In a long series of civil wars (1562–94) which followed, they gained and lost as the fortunes of war came and went. Finally peace came when the Huguenot leader, Henry of Navarre, became King Henry IV of France as a Roman Catholic. This satisfied the Roman Catholic groups, and Henry promulgated the Edict of Nantes, 1598, which guaranteed the Huguenots virtual freedom of religion. During this era of strife had occurred the greatest horror of the Reformation, the massacre of thousands of Huguenots throughout France on St.

Bartholomew's night, 1572.

The French Reformed Churches recovered in great measure from these frightful persecutions after 1598. However, the Edict of Nantes was revoked in 1685. Untold sufferings preceded and succeeded this act by Louis XIV. Despite laws against emigration, more than 250,000 Huguenots fled to Germany, the Netherlands, England, Switzerland and the new world. Those who remained persisted as a virtual underground movement and did not regain their full rights until the Revolution of 1789.

Since the Revolution France as a nation has been quite indifferent to all religions. The French Reformed Churches have grown slowly under great handicaps. The theological upheavals of the 19th century broke these churches into two main bodies, the National Union of Evangelical Reformed Churches (conservative) and the National Union of Reformed Churches in France (liberal). In addition, the Reformed Churches of Alsace-Lorraine were grouped separately under that name. A union of the conservative and liberal unions was achieved in 1939, the Reformed Church of France. The churches of Alsace-Lorraine remained distinct and enjoyed state support, whereas the churches of France proper did not after 1905. A small group of the old conservative union continued under its old name.

The Reformed Church of France had (in 1948) approximately 150,000 members, 528 congregations, 600 ministers and 5,000 elders; missionary work was done through interdenominational bodies rather than through exclusive confessional agencies.

The Reformed Church of Alsace-Lorraine had (in 1948) 22,073 members, 50 congregations, 84 additional preaching points, 47 ministers and 280 elders; missionary work done as by the Reformed Church of France.

Hungary.—The influence of the Reformation was felt early in Hungary. A synod at Erdod adopted the Augsburg Confession in 1545. By 1567 Reformed views had become so well known that the Synod of Debrecen adopted the Heidelberg Catechism and the Second Helvetic Confession, thus becoming a Reformed Church. Except for minor reverses the Evangelicals made progress in Hungary until 1677. The Magyars had become almost all Reformed. The Counter Reformation era was one of severe persecution for all Evangelicals. Not until Joseph II promulgated the Edict of Toleration in 1781 did respite come. Nevertheless, the Reformed Church had not been destroyed by the persecution. Within the old Austro-Hungarian empire the Reformed Church was of two wings, the Magyar (the larger) and the German. The Magyar people spread rather widely through the old empire, carrying their church with them. Theologically the Reformed Churches were much influenced by German theological scholarship. Within the empire they built up a very large system of schools, elementary to university, and did much for Hungarian cultural life. Through state aid and through other sources the church became possessed of much landed property which was used for income purposes (a familiar pattern in Hungarian life).

World War I broke up the old Austria-Hungary, and the nation of Hungary which emerged after the peace of Versailles was approximately one-third the size of the old Hungary. The Hungarian Reformed Church was now shattered. Within the new nation of Hungary there remained about one-half the church. The other half was now minority groups in unfriendly or even hostile countries. The largest segment, 780,000 in Rumania, suffered grievously for both religious and cultural reasons. The 210,000 in Slovakia suffered less. The small group of 40,000 in Yugoslavia had a precarious existence.

The effect of this dismemberment in Hungary was to foster an extreme type of nationalism, to which the church in part fell prey also. Many of the upper middle class, the professional, the government and the military leaders were in the Reformed Church, Adm. Nicholas Horthy de Nagybanya among them. World War II brought a terrible defeat to Hungary and to all hopes of reuniting the Magyar people and their church. Moreover, it brought about a changed outlook among Reformed leaders. When the Communist government nationalized all church lands (Evangelical and Catholic), Reformed leaders urged that land reform must not be resisted; the church must give up its old privileges, etc. So,

also, the church gave up its schools without strife when all church schools were nationalized. This reaction away from its pre-World War II upper-class nationalism and toward a better understanding with, and vigorous evangelism among, the Communist-controlled working classes caused much international comment. The war losses of the church in life and property were severe.

The Reformed Church in Hungary had (in 1948) 973,393 members, 1,203 congregations and 2,016 additional preaching points, 1,850 ministers (100 of whom were women) and 22,000 elders.

The Reformed Church in Rumania (Hungarian Magyar) had (in 1948) 380,000 members, 719 congregations, 686 ministers and 10,200 elders.

The Reformed Church in Slovakia (Hungarian Magyar) had (in 1948) 20,000 members, 31 congregations and 23 additional preaching points, 31 ministers and 588 elders.

Yugoslavia had approximately 40,000 Magyar Reformed Christians in 1948.

Czechoslovakia.—The Reformed Churches of Czechoslovakia are, as the nation itself, of varied origins. The Czech Reformed body is the Evangelical Church of Bohemian Brethren. The Slovak Reformed body is a wing of the Hungarian Magyar Reformed family (*see* above under *Hungary*).

John Huss's attempt at reforming the church ended at the stake in 1415. His followers were crushed in 1434, but underground the cause persisted. During the 16th-century reforming movement the Bohemian Brethren emerged again to flourish for a brief period. In 1547 they were again suppressed, and the Jesuits were given charge of religious affairs in Bohemia. A Bohemian revolt in 1618 began the Thirty Years' War in Europe, and thereafter the house of Habsburg and the Counter Reformation held sway in Bohemia. Thousands of Evangelicals fled the country, and the patriot and the Evangelical leaders were executed. During this Thirty Years' War the population of Bohemia was reduced from 3,000,000 to 800,000 by the frightful excesses of the conquest.

Not until 1781 were Evangelical groups again tolerated in Bohemia. Then only bodies holding either of the two German Protestant symbols (Augsburg or Heidelberg) were tolerated. The old native Czech Bohemian Church was still banned. It remained in existence, however, underground. Moreover, the cause of Czech independence and of the Bohemian Church became intertwined.

When the nation of Czechoslovakia was created by the peace of Versailles the Evangelical Church of Czech Brethren was freed. It became the leading Evangelical, or Protestant, Church in the nation. Its leadership in theological education, social work, etc., was marked. During the crises preceding World War II, Czech patriotism and the Bohemian Brethren again made common cause. When the nazi army seized Czechoslovakia the consequences for this Reformed Church were severe. Many of its leaders, Joseph Hromadka among them, had to flee. After the war the nation came under a Communist government and the church faced a new crisis. The church had been predominantly middle and upper class, with no great hold on the classes now influenced by communism. Under the leadership of Hromadka the church strove to come to an understanding with the government and with the proletariat in an effort to overcome its previous social stratification and isolation. Considerable criticism was directed at this move from other nations.

The church had (in 1948) 90,000 members, 218 congregations and 296 additional preaching points, 186 ministers and 2,616 elders.

Other European Countries.—Small Reformed Churches, often only a few scattered congregations, are found in Belgium, the Scandinavian countries, Greece, Spain and Portugal. Also, the ancient Waldensian Churches of Italy, together with their branches in Uruguay and Paraguay, have come within the orbit of the Reformed Churches, though preserving their own character.

United States.—*The Reformed Church in America.*—Dutch settlers were brought to the New York area in 1624 by the Dutch West India company. The first church was founded, subject to the church of the homeland, in 1628. When the English conquered the colony in 1664 they allowed the church of the Netherlands to continue in the area. In 1629 a slight amount of power was granted by the home church to a local governing body of churches called a "classis."

Early in the 18th century new movements came, colonial self-consciousness, the "Great Awakening" revival of religion, etc. The Dutch Church was divided into two groups, one favouring great freedom from the home church, supporting the revival, a local college and the free use of the English language. The other group was extremely conservative and wished to remain a part of the Dutch culture. The colonial group grew more rapidly, and founded Queen's college (later Rutgers university) in 1766.

The two factions reunited in 1771 under a plan which left ultimate authority in the Netherlands but gave great local autonomy. After the Revolutionary War the church became wholly independent under a constitution drafted 1784–92. By 1820 the Dutch language had ceased to be in use. The name Reformed Protestant Dutch Church was changed in 1867 to the Reformed Church in America.

A large migration of Dutch people into the United States about the middle of the 19th century added greatly to the church. Most of these settled in Michigan and other midwestern areas. The church had, therefore, two integrally related though rather distinct groups, one centred in New York and New Jersey, the other in Michigan.

The church had (in 1948) 181,299 members, 743 congregations, 899 ministers and 114 missionaries in Arabia, China, India, Japan and Mesopotamia.

The Christian Reformed Church.—In 1822 a small group withdrew from the Reformed Protestant Dutch Church because of doctrinal disagreements. When the mid-century migrations brought many Hollanders who were members of the Christian Reformed Church of the Netherlands into the United States, these united to form the Christian Reformed Church in America. A new secession from the Reformed Church in America in 1882 brought added strength.

The church had (in 1948) 74,778 members, 312 congregations, 268 ministers and 28 missionaries in China.

The Evangelical and Reformed Church.—(This body was formed in 1934 by the union of the Reformed [German] Church in the United States, and the Evangelical Synod of North America. It maintains contact officially with the other Reformed Churches in the United States and elsewhere, although by the union it became both Lutheran and Reformed.)

Palatinate Germans, driven out by the wars between France and Germany, came to the American colonies early in the 18th century. The Reformed Church in the Netherlands aided them for a time. They settled in Pennsylvania and in the Valley of Virginia. Attempts to unite them to the Dutch Church and to the Presbyterian Church failed. Gradually they emerged as a self-sustaining church, 1791–93.

During the 19th-century migrations and the expansion of the American west, new German Reformed bodies arose only loosely connected with the eastern parent body. In 1863 these united in one. Efforts to unite with the Dutch Reformed Churches failed in 1891. Later attempts to unite with the Presbyterian Church in the U.S.A. failed also. Union with the Evangelical Church was achieved in 1934. In 1950 the church was in process of merging with the Congregational Christian Church, although some legal hindrances had appeared. (*See* also CALVIN, JOHN; PRESBYTERIANISM; REFORMATION.)

BIBLIOGRAPHY.—T. M. Lindsay, *History of the Reformation*, 2 vol. (1906–07); *Cambridge Modern History*, vol. 3–6; W. Pauck, *Heritage of the Reformation* (1950); A. Keller and G. Stewart, *Protestant Europe* (1927); *American Church History Series*, vol. viii (1895); C. E. Corwin, *Manual of the Reformed Church in America*, 5th ed., rev. (1922); J. H. Dubbs, *Historical Manual* (1902); W. W. Sweet, *Story of Religion in America*, rev. ed. (1939). (L. J. T.)

REFORMED EPISCOPAL CHURCH, a Protestant community in the United States, dating from Dec. 1873. The influence of the Tractarian movement began to be felt at an early date in the Episcopal Church of the United States, and the ordination of Arthur Carey in New York, July 1843, a clergyman who denied that there was any difference in points of faith between the Anglican and the Roman Churches and considered the Reformation an unjustifiable act, brought into relief the antagonism between the evangelical Protestant clergy and those who sympathized with the position of Carey. The struggle went on for a generation and with increasing bitterness. The climax was reached when George D. Cummins (1822–76), assistant bishop of Kentucky, was angrily attacked for officiating at the united communion service held at the meeting of the sixth General Conference of the Evangelical Alliance in New York, Oct. 1873. This prelate resigned his charge in the Episcopal Church on Nov. 11, and a month later, with seven other clergymen and a score of laymen, constituted the Reformed Episcopal Church, and consecrated Charles E. Cheney (1836–1916), rector of Christ church, Chicago, Ill., to be bishop.

The church recognizes no "orders" of ministry; the episcopate is an office, not an order, the bishop being the chief presbyter, *primus inter pares. See* also ENGLAND, THE CHURCH OF.

REFORM MOVEMENT, the name given in history to that movement toward parliamentary electoral reform, active in England between 1769 and 1832, and in France between 1832 and 1848. Different as the two movements were in character, time (the principal phase of the English struggle was over in 1832, when the movement in France was, strictly, only beginning) and result (the ultimate desideratum of manhood suffrage was achieved in France in 1848 and in England only in 1918), the march of events in either country had a profound effect upon the movement in the other. The following article sketches the course of the movement in the two countries. (X.)

THE MOVEMENT IN ENGLAND

The ultimate, if long delayed, success of "reform," embodied in the great act of 1832 was due to an unanalysable blend of political theory and the logic of concrete fact. The political, social and economic structure of Great Britain had, in short, been revolutionized between 1780 and 1830 before the revolution was expressed in a decisive formative statute. The act of 1832 did not so much impose the new system of an ardent minority on an unprepared country as it translated into the organization of self-government the appropriate machinery for achieving what a majority had already accepted as inevitable.

The System in 1714.—The system of representation existing in 1714 was, like every other major organ of the national life, the deposit of a prolonged historic development of at least eight centuries. The House of Commons in 1714 consisted of 558 members, of whom 513 represented England and Wales and 45 represented Scotland. Ireland (with 100 members) was not included until the Act of Union of 1800, which abolished the separate Irish legislature. The Scottish representation had only been introduced in 1707 by the Act of Union. Of the 513 English representatives 94 represented counties, 415 boroughs, and four the two universities of Oxford and Cambridge; 30 members represented Scottish counties and 15 Scottish boroughs. The English franchises for the counties, and the boroughs differed fundamentally. The county franchise, with trifling exceptions, was based on a 40s. freehold, assessed to the land tax. The borough franchise was amazingly varied and defied reduction to a single principle. Four groups can broadly be distinguished: (i.) The "Scot and lot" and "pot walloper" boroughs, where the voters, roughly, were residents rated to Church and poor rate; (ii.) the boroughs where every freeman, *i.e.,* enjoying the freedom of the borough, had a vote; (iii.) the burgage-boroughs with the franchise attaching to a certain holding or burgage, and (iv.) the corporation-boroughs, where a close corporation was the privileged electoral organ.

The county franchise dated back to 1430. The borough franchise was the haphazard result of five centuries of piecemeal development. The electoral map of 1714 emphasized the enormous preponderance of voting power in the borough representatives. The distribution of the boroughs roughly represented the distribution of population at the end of the 16th century. But by 1650 this distribution had altered, and since then had been altering rapidly, even before the radical redistribution and growth caused by the "Industrial Revolution" (*q.v.*). The "Reform of Parliament" embodied in "The Instrument of Government" of the Cromwellian period (1654), demonstrated very clearly by its redistribution the admitted hiatus between the existing system and the actual facts. The elaborate analyses made by the "Reformers" of the 18th century revealed these bewildering anomalies. Apart from the contradictions of the borough franchise, which allowed a vote in one borough that was denied in another, custom degenerating into caprice, or avowed manipulation, the distribution of seats resulted in the most astonishing paradoxes. Cornwall, for example, paying 16 out of 513 parts of the land-tax, returned 42 members (two county, 40 borough members); Lancashire, paying ten times as much, returned 14 (two county and 12 borough members). The City of London returned four, as did, also, the united boroughs of Weymouth and Melcombe Regis, with neither landed nor economic interests. In Yorkshire, York city and 13 boroughs, with a total of 7,000 voters, returned 28, while the county, with a total of 16,000 voters, returned two members.

The disabilities imposed by law severely restricted both the electors and the elected. Apart from women, children, lunatics, paupers or convicted criminals, the Nonconformists, the Roman

Catholics, the Quakers, the Jews and agnostics could neither vote nor be elected. In the counties neither leaseholders nor copyholders, however wealthy, could vote. Prosperous cities such as Birmingham or Manchester, which had come into existence since 1600, had no representation, while Old Sarum with seven, or Dunwich, half under the sea, with 14 voters, returned respectively two members apiece. Even in 1714 it was abundantly clear that members of parliament did not represent their constituencies, and that the constituencies still more did not represent the nation. It was estimated in 1793 that, with a population of some eight and a half millions, 257 members (*i.e.*, a majority of the House of Commons) were returned by 11,075 electors; that in 51 constituencies there were less than 50 voters, and that 130 boroughs had less than 300 electors apiece; and that whereas 92 county members were returned by 130,000 voters, 84,000 electors in the boroughs had 421 representatives. "The rotten boroughs," *i.e.*, those which were completely under the control of the Crown or a patron, were admittedly the most indefensible parts of this parody of principles and facts.

The Society of the Friends of the People undertook, in 1793, to prove that the lords of the Treasury, 71 peers and 82 commoners could together nominate 306 out of 558 members, *i.e.*, make a decisive majority. The influence of the Crown, *i.e.*, of the Government—through the patronage of the navy, army, Church, judiciary, civil and colonial services—was enormous, and secured the steady voting support in the Commons without which no administration considered itself safe or even possible. In 1770 there were 192 place-holders in the Commons. "Vested interests" in the whole system, indeed, were so strong and deeply-rooted that nothing short of a complete organic change in the social and economic structure could compel a House of Commons to accept "reform" which meant the extirpation of a half of those who sat in it, with the lucrative possibilities that membership offered. It follows from this brief summary that the would-be "reformer" of the 18th century, with so large and easy a target to attack, but which covered such a variety of interests, had really to prove that the "system" resulted in bad government, and that in the major issues of the national life the welfare of the unrepresented was more important than the welfare of the minority and was being continually sacrificed to it. Before the political theory of Locke, Blackstone and Burke could be dissolved a new political theory had to be created and absorbed. The Reform movement had by 1830 produced such a new theory, with a re-interpretation both of the ends and methods of popular government and civil society under a limited monarchy—but it was not until 1790 when Whiggism had been dissolved once and for all by the corrosive acids of the Industrial and French Revolutions that the school of Godwin, Priestley and Price, above all of Adam Smith and Bentham, had captured the best minds alike of the old gentry and the new individualists. In 1832 a true revolution was accomplished with less bloodshed and disturbance than "the glorious revolution" of 1688, and as in 1688 so in 1832, the monarchy entered on a new lease of life, influence and prestige.

The First Phase (1714–65).—In the Walpole and Bolingbroke era (1714–40) "reform" was the cry of the broken and discredited Tories or the schismatic Whigs, who denounced the corruption by which they asserted Walpole maintained his power, or who demanded the repeal of the Septennial Act and a return of the Triennial Act, or even to the annual parliaments of a "golden middle-age." The agitation, which had no support outside Westminster, had no effect on the general acquiescence in parliaments with a legal duration of seven years, and resulted only in a very limited Place bill, disfranchising a few hundreds of place-men. The elder Pitt gave a new life and a new power to the Reform movement, due to his prestige, his disinterestedness, the splendour of his achievements, and his criticism of effete or flabby government. But Pitt was neither a consistent political thinker nor a practical and constructive administrator, capable of creating and leading a party with a coherent and thought-out programme of internal reform. He accepted the Whig view that "representation was not of persons but of property," and that "the share of national burdens (*i.e.*, taxation of *property*) should decide the weight it

ought to have in the political balance." He accepted "the rotten boroughs" (for one of which he had sat) as "the natural infirmity of the Constitution." "Amputation might be death." Pitt's sole remedy for "the corruption of the people and the ambition of the Crown" was to add a third member to the county representation, "the purest part of the system," and to revert to triennial parliaments. Neither of these remedies was seriously pressed, though they became a traditional formula for the Chathamite and Rockingham Whigs.

Cartwright, 1763–80.—John Wilkes, demagogue and the popular hero of the struggle against general warrants, for the rights of the electors in the Middlesex election and for the right to report debates in parliament, with John Cartwright, the brother of the inventor of the power-loom, were, in 1776, the joint but independent "fathers" of the real Reform movement, *i.e.*, a demand not merely to eliminate the rotten elements, but by an extension of the franchise and a redistribution of seats to secure "a just and equal representation of the people." Wilkes and Cartwright pinned reform down to these points—disfranchisement, enfranchisement and redistribution—on the basis of two democratic principles, that government was for the good of the governed and that rich and poor alike had equal rights and an equal interest in determining laws and government affecting their lives, fortunes and happiness. The Reform Act of 1832 was thus foreshadowed in embryo in 1776, the year of the Declaration of American Independence, of Adam Smith's *Wealth of Nations,* and Bentham's *Fragment on Government.* Cartwright, also, by founding *The Society of the Supporters of the Bill of Rights* was the parent of a new political method, the organized league for propaganda, education and consolidation of a group with a defined and agreed programme. Radicalism, in short, as a theory of political life and a constructive political machine, was born in 1776. Cartwright's society was the fruitful mother of many leagues, societies and federations down to the Free Trade League of 1837, the "Birmingham Caucus" of 1878, and the party organizations of to-day.

The Whigs and Economic Reform.—The Whigs, under the influence of Dowdeswell and of Burke, would have none of either Wilkes' and Cartwright's principles, or of "demagogic" methods. The genius of Burke, reverencing the Constitution as almost a Divine gift to a chosen people, dreading organic change as the betrayal of a mighty heritage, and already, in 1780, scenting in the political theory of the American rebels and of the English Radicals the Jacobinical poison which the French Revolution was to let loose, saw in "economic reform" the supreme remedy for purging a sound organism afflicted by a temporary but paralysing disease in the corrupting influence of the Crown. The Yorkshire Association and the famous Yorkshire Petition of 1780 were methods borrowed from the Radicals, but "the economic reform" for which they pressed kept clear of the Radical demand for organic reconstruction of the representative system. Burke and the Rockingham Whigs succeeded in disfranchising contractors and revenue officers, in abolishing sinecures and in reducing places and a swollen pension list, but in accomplishing this valuable result they had shot their bolt. They had not attempted to deal either with the legal disabilities which excluded whole classes from representation, or with the rotten boroughs which were far more demoralizing and far-reaching in their control of parliament than the "corrupt influence" of the Crown.

The Younger Pitt (1780–1785).—The mantle of Chatham fell, and the hopes of Radicalism concentrated on Chatham's son, the younger Pitt, who, in 1781, moved for "a Committee to enquire into the Present State of the Representation" and was defeated only by 20 votes—the best division the Reformers had between 1780 and 1831. As prime minister, in 1785, Pitt endeavoured to introduce a Reform bill, his intention being to disfranchise 36 rotten boroughs, establish a fund of £1,000,000 for compensating the owners of borough "property," and assign the 72 seats set free by the disfranchised 36 boroughs to the counties, London, Westminster and the chief unrepresented towns. "Leave to introduce" was, however, refused by a majority of 79 votes. Henceforward Pitt was lost to the Reform movement. It was his first and his last effort as a constructive Reformer and the French Revolution shortly converted him into an obstinate antagonist to all or any change.

The Fourth Phase (1785–1807).—The movement really gained in the long run by this set-back. Had Pitt's milk-and-water proposals been carried the old system would have been given a new lease of existence. Pitt, equally with Burke, accepted the inherited past, and his acceptance of the rotten boroughs as a form of property, the disfranchisement of which required compensation, was rightly rejected as immoral and indefensible on any theory of national representation, by the Reformers of 1831. The Whigs had never really believed in reform, and it now became the monopoly of the "doctrinaire Radicals." For seven years the stars in their courses fought for Radicalism. The American War had given an immense stimulus to political thinking and a new school of political philosophy came into existence; the Industrial Revolution was steadily sapping the bases of 18th century society and of the economic fabric. In 1788 the centenary of 1688 was celebrated by the ardent Radicals and the young minds of the country outside politics. In 1789 the outbreak of the French Revolution galvanized all these currents into enthusiastic activity, and The London Revolution Society—the leading organization of the Reformers, of which Price and Godwin were vigorous members—entered into direct connection with the National Assembly in France and the Constitutional Revolutionists in Paris.

Fox, who hailed the French Revolution with joy, professed to be a Reformer, but he was in reality too deeply saturated with the old Whiggism to accept with conviction the new Radicalism. The real leaders in parliament were the young Charles Grey (the Earl Grey who carried the Reform Act in 1832) and Erskine. But all the ardent aspirations of 1789–91 were doomed to disastrous extinction, for which four main causes were responsible. First, the September massacres, the execution of Louis XVI. and Marie Antoinette, and the Reign of Terror not only paralyzed the moderate Reformers with a chill of disillusionment, but sent a series of waves of panic through Great Britain. Reform was promptly identified with revolution on the French model. Secondly, once Great Britain was at war with France (1793), reform was regarded as sedition and treason. Even the mildest critic of existing institutions was denounced as a Jacobin and a traitor. Thirdly, the opposition to reform found in Burke a thinker of genius whose "Reflections on the French Revolution" became the Bible, not only of Toryism, but of three-fourths of thinking or unthinking England. To Burke the new democratic philosophy of Price, Goodwin and Paine, even of Bentham and Mackintosh, was anathema, and the "Rights of Man" were exposed as the pseudo-scientific basis of a creed which would logically end in the downfall of the monarchy, a Jacobin Reign of Terror and a military dictatorship on the French model. The extremists on the Left of the Reform movement, with the bravado that extremists enjoy, were powerful allies of reaction. For 15 years Great Britain lived in the hurricane of a European convulsion, and Wyndham's phrase as to the folly "of repairing your house in the hurricane season," for all its shallowness, correctly summed up the mood of three-fourths of Great Britain, shown in the "loyalist" riots at Birmingham, Manchester and other industrial centres. Fourthly, the irreparable breach between Burke and Fox not only split the parliamentary opposition but drove one-half of the Whigs into coalition with Pitt and the Tory Party.

The war at first was popular; prosecutions for sedition followed, and the judiciary, especially in Scotland, where a great awakening of political activity had followed the French Revolution, were ready to strain the law of treason and to lay it down from the Bench that all criticism of existing institutions was calculated to bring the Government into contempt, and was, therefore, seditious treason. The proposal to hold at Edinburgh a British convention for the discussion of reform whetted the panic of the Government and the convention was dissolved. The trials and condemnation of "the Scottish martyrs," such as Tytler, Stewart, Callender, Muir, Palmer, Margarot, Gerrald, Watt and Downie, and, in England, of Frend, Frost, Eaton and Winterbotham, make a soiled page in the history of British law. Thanks to

Erskine's splendid advocacy, the acquittal of Hardy and Horne Tooke brought some sanity into the supercharged atmosphere of indiscriminate terror and proscription. But until 1799 liberty of opinion ceased to exist in Great Britain, and in this valley of black shadows the numerous political societies, the chief of which were *The London Corresponding Society* and the *Society of United Scotsmen*, withered at the roots and were easily and finally suppressed by governmental action (1794–98). There would have been general and resentful astonishment could the memorial to "the Scottish Martyrs," on the Calton hill, at Edinburgh, erected by public subscription have been foreseen in 1800. Muir's "blasphemous" prediction that "the cause would ultimately prevail" was accepted as a platitude by a reformed and grateful Great Britain in 1844.

It "prevailed" for three reasons. First, the existing system of parliamentary representation provided its own condemnation when men could once more use their eyes, unblurred by panic and war-fever. Secondly, every five years of the changes made by "the Industrial Revolution" threw up a new and unrepresented population, creating a new wealth which paid three-fourths of the taxes but, under the old system, was not "property" with any political rights. Thirdly, the real Reformers retained their faith, and the new and abhorred creed of "democracy" was being hammered out by powerful minds, and could be proved to have a better scientific basis for the theory of a reborn, civilized and progressive society than the philosophy of Burke. To the England of 1807 and onwards the old Whig creed of 1688 was not to be regarded as a climax and a terminus, but simply a stage in an inexhaustible development.

The Fifth Phase (1807–1815).—A new point of departure was made in 1807. The Westminster election of that year brought Sir Francis Burdett, a wealthy and ardent Reformer, into the House of Commons to be the fearless and effective champion of the new Radicalism. The indefatigable Cartwright, who lived until 1824 and saw the dawn of the new day, was ready to join with Cobbett, "orator Hunt," Bentham, the stubborn and aristocratic Whig, Coke of Holkam, the "King of Norfolk," of whose respectability and place in the great gentry there could be no doubt. Reform had, in fact, its increasing adherents alike in the peerage, the intelligentsia and "the people." It only needed now two further acquisitions—the conversion of the official Whig Opposition and a first-rate organizer. The latter was found in Francis Place, the tailor of Charing Cross, whose career and gifts make a fascinating chapter in the history of British politics. Place, if any man, was the "organizer of victory." The conversion of the Whigs, led by Grey (who had succeeded to the earldom in 1807) was accomplished in 1820, when Lord Russell definitely associated the Whig party with the cause. Russell was ably supported by Brougham, and even more effectively by the aristocratic Radical, Lambton (later Lord Durham of the "Durham report"). Cartwright, in 1823, predicted that reform would "come suddenly." He did not live to see the passing of the Nonconformist Emancipation Act in 1828, of Roman Catholic emancipation by a Tory minister in 1829, or the triumphant passage of the Reform Act of 1832, nine years after his prediction. It was, indeed, in the irony of history that the French Revolution of 1789 should have shattered "the cause," and that a second revolution in France in 1830 should convert Great Britain to enthusiastic support of the Whig Reform bill of 1831.

BIBLIOGRAPHY.—The reform movement is treated in all the general histories and text books, notably by W. E. H. Lecky, *A History of England in the Eighteenth century* (1878–90; new ed., 7 vols., 1892). The best special books are: E. and A. G. Porritt, *The Unreformed House of Commons. Parliamentary Representation before 1832*, 2 vols. (1903); G. S. Veitch, *The Genesis of Parliamentary Reform* (1913); J. R. M. Butler, *The Passing of the Great Reform Bill* (1914). See also T. E. May, Baron Farnborough, *The Constitutional History of England since the Accession of George the Third; 1760–1860*, 2 vols. (1861; edit. and cont. to 1911 by F. Holland, 3 vols., 1912); W. R. Anson, *The Law and Custom of the Constitution*, vol. i., "Parliament" (1886–92; 5th ed. by M. L. Gwyer, 1922). Of the numerous biographies, *see* particularly: G. Wallas, *The Life of Francis Place* (1918); and G. M. Trevelyan, *Lord Grey of the Reform Bill: being the life of Charles, second Earl Grey* (1920).　　　　　(C. G. Ro.)

THE MOVEMENT IN FRANCE

If the political history of France be compared with that of England, it will be seen that the political system of both countries underwent similar changes, and arrived at approximately the same result—the main features of which were a responsible ministry and popular suffrage.

The political organization which was created both in France and in England was based on three essential elements: (1) an elected assembly capable of imposing an effective limitation on the power of the monarch; (2) a council of ministers subject to the control of the assembly; (3) an electorate capable of maintaining the control of the nation over the assembly. Three things were thus necessary in order to establish responsible government: the arbitrary power of the king must be restricted by an assembly independent of the court; the assembly must obtain effective control of the Government by transforming the king's ministers into agents for carrying out the will of the assembly; and the electoral system must be such as to ensure that the members of the assembly were representative of the will of the people.

In France the power of the king was so great that the people, who possessed no institutions through which they could exercise their action, were unable to impose any limitation on his authority. At a period when Great Britain already had a government responsible to an elected parliament, France had no political assembly, no franchise, and no check on the arbitrary power of ministers. The latter were simply the instruments through which the king exercised his personal authority.

It was impossible to modify this system, as had been done in England, by introducing successive improvements in the method of government, because there was no machinery in France through which control could be exercised. The change was made, without transition, by revolution; the old system of government was destroyed, and a new one had to be improvised. In devising a new system of government in this way it was of course necessary to proceed according to a general plan and to apply uniform rules of a legal and abstract character, whereas the British constitution was rather in the nature of a body of customs built up by a series of historical precedents. The difference in the method followed in the two countries has generally been attributed to a difference of national temperament, the Englishman being more phlegmatic, conservative and practical, and the Frenchman more passionate, revolutionary and fond of abstract ideas. It may however be more naturally explained by the different conditions under which the transformation of the political system was effected in the two countries. England already possessed an elected parliament which tended by gradual development to establish its control over the ministry; all that the English had to do was to reform their archaic electoral system. The French nation had to improvise an entire political system, and could only do so by the application of general rules.

The Revolution.—The French Revolution was initiated by the action of the royal Government itself in calling a meeting of the States General for the purpose of voting money. The meeting of the States General was not however, like the English parliament, an institution with the force of tradition behind it. The meeting called in 1789 under the old name of the States General was in reality a new assembly, summoned by a procedure created expressly for it.

Thus the question of the electoral system, which was the last to be settled in England, was in France the one which arose earliest. The system adopted was uniform for the whole country, and thus more logical than that of England. Voting was by secret ballot and by absolute majority. As the Government had extended the right to vote to all tax-payers, including the very numerous peasant class, the election of the deputies of the Third Estate was carried out by indirect suffrage. A system of indirect suffrage of two degrees, with a secret ballot and absolute majority, was applied to all elections of legislative bodies throughout the Revolution period.

The assembly, converted into a "National Assembly," declared that it would not separate until it had given France a Constitution; the royal power was thus limited by an elected body representing the nation as a whole. After the fall of Louis XVI. it became necessary to vest all powers in a single body, which was given the name of the Convention, a term borrowed from the United States. When the Convention desired to restore a regular political order conforming to the doctrine of the separation of powers, all that it could do was to replace the king by an executive Directory.

The third question, that of the qualifications and functions of ministers, had been settled under the pressure of practical necessities in 1789, when it had had to be decided whether ministers might also be members of the Assembly. The Constituent Assembly had been apprehensive of the influence which ministers might exercise over the legislative body; it feared the ambition of one of its members, Mirabeau. Ministers, as members of the executive, were therefore forbidden to be at the same time members of the Legislative Assembly; and this made it impossible to establish a system of responsible government in France.

The Restoration.—The institutions created by the Revolution were abolished by Napoleon, who reduced assemblies, elections and ministers to the position of instruments through which the absolute authority of the emperor was exercised. At the Restoration, however, a fresh attempt was made to create an organized political system. Louis XVIII. accepted the limitation of the royal power by a constitution and its control by an assembly. The three questions which had had to be considered in 1789 thus arose again in 1814; this time they were settled on lines directly copied from Great Britain.

Under the imperial regime there had been two chambers; Louis XVIII. maintained them under different names. The senate became a hereditary chamber of peers; the Legislative Assembly became the chamber of deputies, and the king had power to dissolve it, as in England. The chamber adopted a number of the practices of the British parliament, such as the King's speech, the voting of the Address, and the procedure for voting on ways and means.

The method of selecting ministers was not regulated by the Charter of 1814, just as there were no formal rules on the subject in England. Ministers were responsible, but only in the case of action contrary to the constitution, when they were liable to a procedure copied from the English system of impeachment. Thus France did not yet enjoy responsible government in the sense in which the term is understood in English-speaking countries at the present day. Louis XVIII. however generally followed the practice of forming the ministry in agreement with the majority of the chamber, and when Charles X., in 1829, appointed ministers who were definitely unpopular, the majority made an official protest, the "address of the 221," in which it enunciated the theory of responsible government.

The dispute led to an insurrection in Paris, and the Revolution of 1830 was the result. The new king, Louis Philippe, formally recognized the sovereign rights of the nation, and accordingly did not contest the principle of the responsibility of ministers to the Chamber. France thus adopted the principle of the political responsibility of ministers, according to which a minister is obliged to resign as soon as he is in disagreement with the elected Chamber.

"The Reform Movement."—The electoral system in France had been a constant subject of party controversy from 1814 onwards. The practice of holding elections had been introduced as a new departure in 1789; it was not a long-standing tradition as it was in England, and it had not struck deep root in the political life of the nation. The Charter of 1814, which was hastily drafted, only contained a single provision dealing with the electoral system; no one was entitled to vote unless he paid not less than 300 francs in direct taxes. This represented a much more limited franchise than that in force in England, and the result was to deprive the elections of their popular character.

It was not until later that legislation was adopted fixing the minimum tax payment constituting the electoral qualification and the procedure for elections. The act of 1831, which was passed after the Revolution, merely lowered the electoral qualification from 300 to 200 francs. This resulted in increasing the number of electors from 87,000 to 166,000; a maximum of 249,000 was reached in 1847.

One section of opinion in France regarded this reform as insufficient, since the large majority of citizens were still excluded from political life. Demands for the extension of the franchise were therefore put forward. At the time when in England the reform movement which had been initiated 60 years earlier was at last achieving success in the Reform Acts of 1832, agitation for the same object in France was only beginning. It is to the movement of 1832–48 that the term "reform" is applied in France.

Neither in France nor in England were the supporters of an extended franchise able to agree on the scope of the desired reform. Universal suffrage, which had been advocated in England as early as 1780, was not at first proposed in France except by a few isolated republicans. The *Société des Droits de l'Homme,* an association consisting mainly of young Parisian students and workmen, referred to universal suffrage in its manifesto of 1833 as an instrument for bringing about social revolution and improving the position of the proletariat; this attitude corresponded to that of the English Chartists.

The supporters of a less radical measure of reform put forward their demand for an extended franchise in the form of petitions to parliament, as had been done in England. The movement did not attain real political importance until 1838, when the National Guard of Paris, in which nearly the whole of the lower middle class population was enrolled, organized a petition asking that all members of the National Guard should be given the right to vote. A committee of deputies was formed to direct operations in the provinces; public manifestations were arranged, in which the National Guards marched in procession to greet the deputy with cries of "Vive la Réforme." The same cry was raised on June 14, 1840 at a review of the National Guard by Louis Philippe. The petition obtained about 240,000 signatures.

The opposition accused the Government of corrupting those deputies who were in the Government service by promises of promotion, and the electors by granting them personal favours. As a remedy for the "corruption" of deputies it demanded "parliamentary reform," *i.e.,* that civil servants should be forbidden to sit in the chamber. As a remedy for "electoral corruption" it demanded "electoral reform." These were the terms which had been employed in England in the time of George III.

Universal suffrage was at no time demanded by more than a very small minority, much less numerous than the Chartists in England. Almost its only champion in the chamber was the lawyer Ledru-Rollin, who founded a journal entitled *La Réforme* in 1843. Ledru-Rollin represented political reform as a necessary condition for social reform. *La Réforme* did not however have a circulation of more than 2,000.

The campaign for reform was carried on in the chamber principally by the party which was opposed to the dynasty. For some years the question formed the subject of debates which led to no practical result. Guizot, the virtual head of the ministry, always replied that the introduction of reform measures was inexpedient. Louis Philippe himself took part in the dispute. "There will be no reform," he said in Jan. 1848; "I will not have it. If the Chamber of Deputies votes for it, I have the Chamber of Peers to reject it. Even if the Chamber of Peers adopted it, I have my veto."

The restrictions imposed on the press by the legislation of 1835 made it difficult for the opposition to state its views in the newspapers. A means of expression was found in the organization of a series of public dinners by opposition deputies and journalists; some 70 such dinners were held in 1847 and 1848, and toasts were drunk in honour of Reform. The Government, by prohibiting a public dinner in Paris, provoked the revolt which led to the Paris insurrection of Feb. 23 and the overthrow of the monarchy. The provisional Government, composed of deputies representing the small republican minority, at once introduced universal male suffrage. Thus electoral reform, which was only begun in England after half a century of agitation, was consummated in France in a few days in its most radical form. (C. Se.)

BIBLIOGRAPHY.—F. V. A. Aulard, *Histoire politique de la Révolution française* (1901), Eng. trans. B. Miall, *The French Revolution, a political history* (1910); *Histoire de la France contemporaine* (ed. E. Lavisse, vols. i. to v., 1920–22), with bibliography.

REFRACTION. When waves of any kind travelling in one medium enter another, in which their velocity is different, their direction is, in general, changed; the rays, *i.e.,* the lines perpendicular to the wave surfaces (in isotropic media) along which the energy travels, being bent or refracted at their point of incidence on the second medium. The change in direction is such that the sine of the angle formed by the incident ray and the normal to the surface of separation bears the same ratio to the sine of the angle formed by the refracted ray and this normal, as the velocity of the waves in the first medium to their velocity in the second. This ratio, known as the refractive index, may depend on the frequency of the wave vibrations. If such be the case, each frequency in the incident disturbance gives rise to a separate refracted ray—a phenomenon known as Dispersion. (*See* LIGHT.)

Mirage is due to the refraction of light by layers of air of gradually varying temperature and density. A similar variation, due to convection currents, is responsible for the flickering appearance seen, *e.g.,* above asphalt and sand on a hot day, and also for the twinkling of the stars. (*See* STAR.) The refraction of rays of light entering the earth's atmosphere from heavenly bodies is known as Astronomical Refraction; it has the effect of making such bodies appear higher above the horizon than they really are. (*See* ASTRONOMY: *Spherical.*)

REFRACTOMETER, an optical instrument for the measurement of refractive index. The refractive index, n, of a substance is a property which depends on the velocity of light, V_s, within that substance relative to its velocity, V_m, in some other medium; $n = V_m/V_s$. Each pure substance has a unique value of n under standard conditions of temperature, pressure and wave length. In refractometry the measurement of light velocity is performed indirectly and relative to some standard medium, usually air or, in the case of gases, vacuum.

Historical.—Refractometers have occupied an important place in the chemical laboratory and in industry since 1874, when E. Abbe introduced the first instrument adapted to the routine investigation of liquids and solids. The Abbe refractometer was soon made commercially available by the C. Zeiss optical works. In 1887 C. Pulfrich brought out his refractometer for chemists, which had the advantage of allowing a precise and convenient measurement of the optical dispersion, an important property related to the change in refractive index accompanying a change in the wave length of the light. The Abbe and Pulfrich refractometers were based on the critical-angle principle of refraction, suggested in 1800 by P. S. Laplace as a means of determining accurately refractive index, and applied first by W. Wollaston in 1802. As early as 1856 an interference refractometer for determining small differences of refractive index had been devised by J. Jamin, who used the principles of light wave interference established earlier by T. Young (1801–04), A. J. Fresnel (1815–19) and D. F. J. Arago (1816–19). In 1896 Lord Rayleigh constructed an interferometer to study the behaviour of the newly discovered gas argon; the accuracy and convenience of his design stimulated further interest in the interferometric method. However, it was not until 1910 that this type of refractometer was generally applied; in that year F. Haber and F. Löwe made significant improvements and shortly thereafter practical models were placed on the market.

Prior to these developments of the late 19th century, refractometric measurements were performed with spectrometers or other devices originating in spectroscopy; these instruments were not well suited to the kinds of samples encountered in chemical investigations, and they required such careful manipulation as to discourage widespread use. The earliest work in refractometry goes back to the 17th century, when W. Snell established the basic law of refraction. Subsequently, on the occasion of his first scientific publication, Isaac Newton made a historic advance by showing that the refractive index depends on the colour (now interpreted as wave length) of the light used. Also, in Newton's

Opticks (1704) is to be found the first widely circulated publication of a table giving the refractive indexes of various fluids; he correlated these data with the densities of the substances and also noted some influence of chemical composition on the values of refractive index per unit density. An earlier table of refractive indexes compiled by Snell at Leyden was seen by only a few

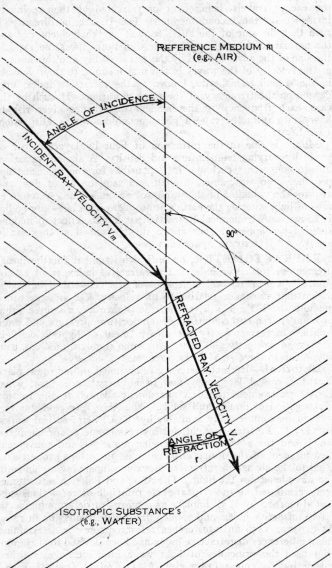

FIG. 1.—SNELL'S LAW OF REFRACTION. SUBSTANCE *s* HAS THE REFRACTIVE INDEX $n\lambda = \sin i/\sin r$, RELATIVE TO THE MEDIUM *m*, FOR LIGHT OF A GIVEN WAVE LENGTH λ. THE VALUE OF $n\lambda$ IS A UNIQUE CHARACTERISTIC OF THE SUBSTANCE WHEN *m* AND *s* ARE MAINTAINED AT SOME STANDARD TEMPERATURE AND PRESSURE. WHEN *s* = WATER AND *m* = AIR UNDER ORDINARY CONDITIONS, n = 1.33 FOR YELLOW SODIUM LIGHT (λ = 5,893 ANGSTROMS). IN THIS CASE, r = 32° FOR i = 45°

scientists, including Newton's great contemporary C. Huygens, before the manuscript was lost.

Uses.—Refractometers have found wide application as a rapid means of identifying substances and quantitatively analyzing solutions. In various industrial processes, such as petroleum refining and food canning, the concentrations of certain ingredients are kept within specified limits by means of refractometric analyses. For example, the sugar content of syrups is accurately controlled in this way. Many of the analytical problems continually arising in scientific research are solved by refractometric techniques.

Methods of analysis have shown an increasing tendency to depend on accurately measurable physical properties rather than chemical reactions and separations. The availability of the pre-

cision refractometer considerably promoted this tendency. Even after the development of important physical tools for directly identifying molecular structures, such as spectrophotometry, the refractometer continued to occupy a prominent place. Its usefulness is primarily derived from the extreme sensitivity which can be attained and from the ease of manipulation. For example, differences in refractive index as small as 1 part per 1,000,000 can be determined with the ordinary interference refractometer; only a few minutes are required for filling the sample chambers and making the observations. This makes possible the detection of very small amounts of dissolved impurities.

Although the refractive index does not give direct information about the kind of molecular species present in a substance, refractometric studies of pure substances and of known mixtures have an importance for certain theoretical questions relating to chemical forces and molecular structure. The well-known ion deformation theory (1923–52), developed by K. Fajans and others, is based largely on refractometric data.

Optical Principles.—Refractometers generally fall into two broad classes, the deviation type and the interference type, each corresponding to an observable change in a light wave when it passes from one medium to another. These changes are connected with the difference of wave velocities in the two media and consist of: (1) a change in direction (unless the ray travels perpendicular to the boundary surface) and (2) a change in phase of vibration of the light wave. A third type of refractometer depends on the intensity of light reflected from the surface between two mediums, relative to the incident intensity. The principle of such a photometric refractometer was apparent ever since the derivation (*c.* 1820) of Fresnel's equations of reflection, but it was not until 1946 that a practical instrument was achieved. At that time the development of sensitive photoelectric cells had reached a stage which allowed the rapid detection of small changes in refractive index by the photometric method.

Basic to all *deviation-type refractometers* is Snell's law of refraction: $n = \sin i/\sin r$ (fig. 1). Snell's law means that the refractive index can be determined from the angle of incidence i and the angle of refraction r which the light ray makes with respect to a normal (*i.e.*, perpendicular) line passing through the boundary surface. The angles i and r are usually found indirectly from the observed deviations of a bundle of rays which traverse not only the sample but one or more prisms and lenses of the refractometer as well. In principle this method is reducible to measurements of the positions of pointers on a circular scale, corresponding to the directions of incident and refracted rays. In the spectrometer type of deviation instrument the incident rays come from a narrow slit so that, with a proper lens arrangement, the refracted rays can be located precisely. The spectrometer is ordinarily used with the principle of minimum deviation which states that a prism can be oriented to give a minimum angle, Δ, between incident and emergent rays (fig. 2); under these conditions, $i = e$ and the refractive index of the prism is $n = \sin \frac{1}{2}(\beta+\Delta)/\sin (\beta/2)$, where β is the angle between refracting faces of the prism.

Critical-angle refractometers make use of a more convenient method of locating the incident and refracted rays. The critical angle of refraction, C, is the maximum value of r which can be attained by any ray which passes from a less to a more refractive medium (fig. 3). In harmony with Snell's law, C corresponds to those incident rays which just graze the surface of the more refractive medium ($i = 90°$). All other refracted rays come closer than C to the normal direction. In critical-angle refractometers a prism of known refractive index, n_p, is used as the more refractive medium. A beam of light is passed through the sample in a direction parallel to the boundary between sample and prism. On viewing the refracted rays through a telescope, there is observed a sharp critical boundary between a dark and a light region, shown in fig. 3, which very precisely defines the rays having the angles $i = 90°$ and $r = C$. The refractive index of the sample is $n = \sin \alpha \cos \beta - \sin \beta \sqrt{n_p^2 - \sin^2\alpha}$, where α (fig. 3) is the critical angle as modified by passage of the refracted rays from the prism into air and n_p is measured relative to air.

The *interference-type refractometer* depends on a set of interference bands, produced by the convergence of two light beams coming from the same slit source (fig. 4). If a transparent substance having a refractive index n is placed in the path of one such beam while the other beam traverses a comparable thickness of some other substance of index n_o, there is a visible displacement of the interference bands. The interference refractometer allows a determination of the difference $n - n_o$ through measurement of this displacement.

The relationship between refractive index and band displacement can be understood by considering two converging wave fronts (fig. 4). If they come from the same slit source, there is a set of points for which the crest of one wave is exactly superimposed on that of the other; *i.e.*, the waves are in phase and a maximum of light intensity exists at these points. At other points crests are superimposed on troughs, resulting in the complete absence of light. At still other points the relation between crests and troughs is intermediate. Thus, when the region of convergence of the waves is viewed through a lens, a series of alternately dark and light areas is seen; these constitute the interference bands. The bands usually appear as narrow vertical bars having fairly sharp edges. Consider now the change which takes place at the position, P, of the central bright band when one of the two waves is slowed down somewhat before reaching the region of convergence; *i.e.*, when one wave is made to traverse a slightly more refractive medium than the other. In this case the crest of the retarded wave arrives at P too late to coincide exactly with the crest of the unretarded wave; the position of maximum intensity will have shifted to another point, O, such that both waves take the same amount of time to reach O. The distance between P and O is greater, the greater the difference in velocity of the two waves. On continuing to decrease the velocity of one wave—by interposing, for example, more and more of some gas having a greater refractive index than that traversed by the other wave—the region originally occupied by band P becomes darker and darker until the retardation corresponds to one-half wave length. For a retardation of one whole wave length this region becomes bright again, and so on. Under these conditions the bands appear to be moving continuously from the field of view. The magnitude of the band displacement is related to refractive index by the formula $n - n_o = \lambda N/t$, where λ is the wave length of the light, t is the thickness of the interposed sample and N is the band displacement, expressed in number of band widths.

Usage, Construction and Performance of Instruments.—A number of variables must be carefully controlled in using precision refractometers. These are mainly temperature, wave length of light and alignment of parts. An increase in temperature of

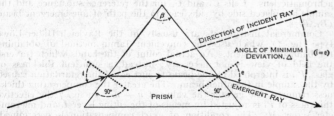

$1°$ C. causes, for most liquids, a decrease in n of several units in the fourth decimal. The refractive index of a colourless substance measured with red light may be as much as several units in the second decimal smaller than when measured with violet light. The most widely used monochromatic light source is the sodium lamp; unless otherwise stated, values of n refer to the average wave length of the yellow sodium spectral lines (5,893 angstroms). Electric discharge tubes containing elements such as helium, hydrogen, cadmium or mercury provide a series of well-defined wave lengths, useful for determining the optical dispersion.

For instruments designed to give fourth- or fifth-decimal ac-

curacy the highest quality workmanship is required in making the optical and mechanical alignments. Reliable refractometric measurements require frequent calibrations of the instrument with

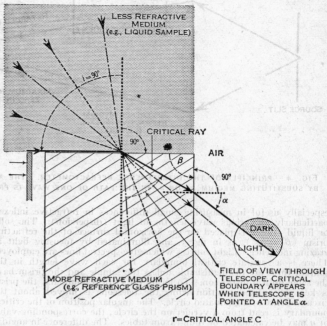

FIG. 3.—CRITICAL ANGLE OF REFRACTION. RAYS HAVING AN ANGLE OF INCIDENCE OF EXACTLY 90° APPEAR IN THE VIEWING TELESCOPE AT THE SHARP BOUNDARY BETWEEN A LIGHT AND A DARK REGION, HENCE THEIR ANGLE OF REFRACTION CAN BE MEASURED ACCURATELY

known standards. The greatest accuracy is obtained when a direct comparison of the unknown with a similar known substance is made. The Pulfrich and the interference-type refractometers allow this kind of technique, known as the differential method. Easily purified liquids, such as water, serve as convenient standards of comparison; glass test plates are also used. In 1944 the U.S. national bureau of standards made available a series of pure hydrocarbons with refractive indexes certified to the fifth decimal.

A variety of refractometers has been made commercially available by optical manufacturers in Europe and the United States; in addition, many others have been constructed in laboratories and described in detail in the scientific literature. Of the types on the market, the critical-angle principle is the most widely used.

The *Abbe refractometer* (fig. 5) is perhaps the most popular critical-angle instrument. The ordinary model is rugged, compact (about the size of a microscope) and is capable of fourth-decimal accuracy. Only a few drops of liquid sample are required, and a determination may be completed in less than five minutes. Liquid samples are confined to a thin film between the surfaces of the refracting prism P ($\beta = 60°$) and an adjacent auxiliary prism P'. The latter prism also serves as a window; its roughened surface scatters into the sample some light along the direction of grazing incidence, required for the critical boundary. For convenience white light can be used but in this case the critical boundary is not inherently sharp and has the appearance of a rainbow because of the different refraction for rays of different wave length. Most Abbe models are provided with a pair of compensating prisms, mounted in the barrel of the telescope, which remove nearly all the boundary colour and improve the accuracy. The amount of rotation of one compensating prism relative to the other, required for achromatizing the boundary, is a rough measure of the dispersion of the sample. The compensating system is designed to give refractive indexes corresponding to an average wave length near that of the yellow sodium lines. The refracting prism, located at the base, can be rotated with respect to the telescope axis (*see* point R, fig. 5). With an illuminated solid or liquid sample on the lower face of this prism, the critical boundary can be made to coincide with the cross hairs in the telescope, using a slow-motion screw to rotate the prism. A pointer attached to an arm (alidade) of the prism-mount indicates the degree of rotation on a goniometer scale attached to the telescope. The scale reads directly in terms of refractive index or, as desired, in terms of concentration of some solute. Each instrument is limited to a given range, depending on the glass of the prism. Usually values of n from 1.3 to 1.7 can be covered.

The *Pulfrich refractometer* is a versatile critical-angle instrument

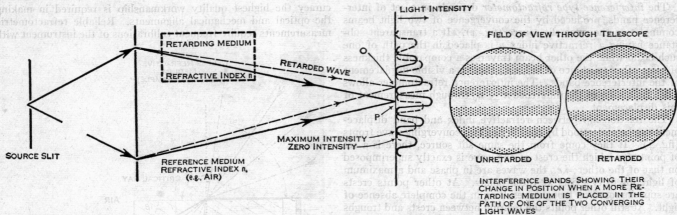

FIG. 4.—PRINCIPLE OF THE INTERFERENCE REFRACTOMETER. THE AMOUNT OF THE DISPLACEMENT OF THE BANDS (DISTANCE $P-O$) CAUSED BY SUBSTITUTING MEDIUM n FOR n_0 IN THE PATH OF ONE WAVE IS PROPORTIONAL TO THE REFRACTIVE INDEX DIFFERENCE $n-n_0$

especially useful in measuring small differences in refractive indexes, particularly at various wave lengths of light (dispersion). The solid or liquid sample is placed on the horizontal surface of the refracting prism ($\beta = 90°$), as in fig. 3, and illuminated by focusing light at grazing incidence. Light sources which give spectral lines are employed. There is a separate critical boundary for each wave length in the source; these are distinguishable unless the sample and the prism have the same optical dispersion. To locate the critical boundary, the prism is kept in a fixed position while the telescope is moved about the circumference of a graduated circle. The angular position of the critical boundary is read from a vernier on the circle; the corresponding value of n may be calculated or found from tables. The difference in angular position of two fairly close critical boundaries is measured with a graduated micrometer screw which moves the telescope. In this way the differences in refractive index for various wave lengths are found with fifth-decimal accuracy.

The *dipping* or *immersion refractometer* resembles the Abbe instrument. The refracting prism, compensating prisms and telescope are mounted in a single tube, giving a compact, portable unit. The prism is directly immersed in liquid samples and the critical boundary is located with respect to a movable eyepiece scale. The dipping refractometer is ordinarily used by making a calibration of scale readings v. concentration of some solute. The accuracy is only slightly better than that of the Abbe, but it has the advantage of a greater range through interchangeability of prisms.

Deviation-type instruments which do not use the critical-angle principle have certain important advantages. For example, *spectrometers* cover an unlimited range of refractive indexes and, when properly equipped, can be used with ultra-violet or infra-red light. An accurately shaped prism mounted at the centre of a movable graduated circle constitutes the basic element of the spectrometer. The prism consists of, or contains, the sample under investigation. Monochromatic or polychromatic light from a narrow slit source is rendered parallel

by a collimating lens before traversing the prism. For each wave length an image of the refracted light source is located by means of a telescope mounted on the circle. The many necessary careful adjustments make the spectrometer inconvenient for routine applications. However, its principle is employed in a number of simple *image-displacement refractometers*. These may be designed for rapid measurement of very small quantities of liquid samples with third-decimal accuracy. The sample is made into a tiny prism by placing a droplet between an appropriate set of glass surfaces. If an illuminated object, say a slit, is viewed through such a prism, its apparent position is shifted from the true position by an amount which depends on the refractive index of the sample and of the glass. The amount of image displacement can be observed on a scale mounted behind the prism; the scale is usually calibrated in terms of n. A convenient application of this principle is found in the Nichols refractometer, which uses a microscope for observing the image displacement. The ordinary microscope itself is capable of being used as a simple refractometer of this type.

Interference refractometers are indispensable for finding the refractive indexes of gases; they can also be used for liquids and some solids. The interferometric method offers the most convenient means of determining the concentration of a substance in an extremely dilute solution. Differences in refractive index as small as 1 part per 1,000,000 can be detected without elaborate precautions and still higher sensitivities have been achieved. Even such small differences may be of practical importance, as in the industrial analysis of air. Portable interference refractometers have been used to detect traces (0.1%) of methane (marsh gas) in coal mine air as a means of preventing explosions.

The basic elements of the *Rayleigh interference refractometer* (fig. 7) are two achromatic lenses of long focal length, the first for rendering parallel the light from a narrow slit source, the second for bringing about convergence of two beams, B_I and B_{II}, emerging from two broad slits in front of the first lens. The interference bands are generally viewed with a cylindrical lens focused on the focal plane of the second achromatic lens. Cells C_1 and C_2 for the reference substance and the sample are placed side by side, each in the path of one emergent beam (B_I, B_{II}).

Commercial instruments are usually of the Rayleigh-Haber-Löwe type (fig. 7), which uses the convenient Jamin method of obtaining the band displacement. An actual count of the bands which traverse the field of view is not necessary; instead, a sufficient thickness of glass, P_1, is interposed in one beam to just equal the retardation caused by the sample in the other beam. The greater the compensating thickness required, the greater the value of $n - n_0$. In fig. 7 the effective thickness of P_1 is adjusted by means of the tilting lever L and micrometer screw M. The condition of exact compensation is determined, using white light, by turning the micrometer screw M until the central band is brought back to the position it had before the sample was introduced. The central band can be recognized because it is the only one having a pure white colour. Its position is located by matching with a fixed auxiliary set of interference bands formed by two reference beams, b_1 and b_{II}. The reference beams traverse equivalent paths of glass and air so that instrument distortions shift both bands in the same way and errors of alignment are minimized. The prism Pr in fig. 7 serves to bring the two sets of bands closer together for ease of comparison. Improved interference refractometers have achieved a sensitivity of one in the eighth decimal, corresponding to the effect of adding one milligram of salt to a litre of water. Such accuracy involves the use of monochromatic light, which, however, allows no visible distinction to be made between the central band and the others. This difficulty has been overcome in several ways, the most reliable being based on the rotating chamber device developed by W. Geffcken. In this apparatus the two sample cells are rotated with respect to the beam direction while a count is made of the number of bands traversing the field of view. There is a known relation between refractive index

FIG. 5.—ABBE REFRACTOMETER (SCHEMATIC)

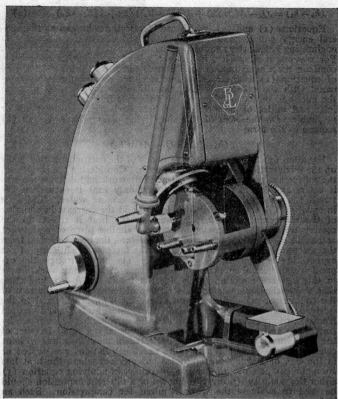

FIG. 6.—ABBE REFRACTOMETER

and the number of bands for a given angle of rotation.

Modern trends in interference refractometry show a revival of interest in the early instrument of Jamin, as modified by E. Mach and L. Zehnder (1891).

Certain technical drawbacks were overcome by H. Kuhn and G. A. Wheatley in 1945. Outstanding contributions to aerodynamics have been made by using the Jamin-type interference refractometer to study local variations in the density of air flowing at high speed past solid surfaces.

Automatic recording refractometers are in the early stages of development and show promise of widespread application in science and industry as a means of rapidly detecting or controlling small changes in flowing liquids or gases. Any of the three types of refractometers may be adapted to automatic recording by substitution of a photo-

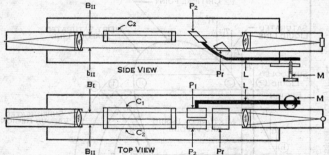

FIG. 7.—RALEIGH-HABER-LÖWE INTERFERENCE REFRACTOMETER (SCHEMATIC)

electric cell for the human eye, since the electric current produced by such a cell is a measure of the intensity of light falling on the cell at a precisely known location.

BIBLIOGRAPHY.—Sir Richard Tetley Glazebrook (ed.), *Dictionary of Applied Physics,* vol. iv (1923); W. E. Williams, *Applications of Interferometry* (1930); A. E. Dunstan (ed.), A. L. Ward, S. S. Kurtz and W. H. Fulweiler, *Science of Petroleum,* vol. iii (1938); T. R. P. Gibb, *Optical Methods of Chemical Analysis* (1942); N. Bauer and K. Fajans, "Refractometry," chap. xvi of *Physical Methods of Organic Chemistry,* vol. i., 2nd ed., ed. by A. Weissberger (1949); H. Kuhn, *Reports on Progress in Physics,* ed. by A. C. Stickland (1951).
(No. Br.)

REFRIGERATION AND ITS APPLICATIONS.

Refrigeration is the process of producing within an insulated enclosure temperatures below that of the enclosure's surroundings. The process of refrigeration of an enclosure and its contents consists of extracting heat from the space the temperature of which is to be lowered and rejecting it to the surroundings (or some other external medium) which are at a higher temperature. As heat will not flow spontaneously from a region of low temperature to one at higher temperature, it is necessary to expend either mechanical work or heat energy from an external source depending on the nature of the mechanical equipment used for this purpose. Refrigeration technology draws its basic knowledge from three interrelated yet distinct areas of science, namely: thermodynamics, heat transfer and fluid flow. In the following sections the underlying principles of operation of major refrigeration systems are discussed, drawing on the basic sciences only to the extent necessary to achieve better understanding and clarity.

The application of refrigeration is so extensive and diverse that a complete coverage is not possible within a limited scope. Cold storage, transportation of foods, ice making and comfort air conditioning are discussed briefly and many other interesting applications are mentioned.

WORKING PRINCIPLES OF REFRIGERATION SYSTEMS

In all refrigeration systems the working fluid used to carry away the heat from the region to be cooled is known as the refrigerant. The boiling temperature of refrigerants, as that of any other liquid, depends on the pressure at which the boiling takes place, the boiling temperature decreasing with decreasing pressure. This boiling temperature v. pressure characteristic of refrigerants is used to advantage in all refrigeration systems and can be said to constitute the main principle of operation. Fig. 3 illustrates the boiling temperature v. pressure characteristics of some commonly used refrigerants. It is to be noted that, at a given pressure, the phenomena of boiling and condensation take place at the same temperature, one process being the reverse of the other.

MECHANICAL COMPRESSION REFRIGERATION SYSTEMS

The most widely used refrigeration cycle is the mechanical compression refrigeration cycle which is schematically illustrated in fig. 1. Referring to fig. 1, high-pressure refrigerant vapour is discharged from the compressor (point 1) in a superheated state (a state having a temperature higher than the boiling temperature at that pressure) and enters a heat exchanger known as the condenser. In the condenser the refrigerant vapour is condensed, essentially at constant pressure, by giving up its latent heat to the cooling water flowing through coils or tubes, as shown in the figure, or to the surrounding atmosphere as is often the case in small size machines. The saturated liquid refrigerant (liquid at the boiling temperature corresponding to the condensing pressure) is collected into a receiver tank which in the case of water-cooled condensers may consist of the lower portion of the condenser shell itself as indicated in fig. 1. At point 2 the saturated liquid refrigerant at high pressure enters the expansion valve, also known as the throttling valve or reducing valve, and its pressure is reduced to a much lower value at point 3. Simultaneous with the reduction in pressure an associated reduction in temperature takes place, the new temperature corresponding to the boiling temperature at this lower pressure. The actual mechanism which accounts for this lowering of the liquid refrigerant temperature consists of the flashing into vapour of a portion of the liquid, and as there exists no external source of heat, the energy for this evaporation is supplied by the liquid refrigerant itself, thus causing its temperature to drop. At point 3 in fig. 1 the low-temperature liquid refrigerant, with a small fraction of its vapour, is admitted into a heat exchanger known as the evaporator. Within the evaporator (which may be constructed in a variety of designs) the liquid refrigerant is evaporated by heat transferred to it from the comparatively warmer space to be refrigerated. The flow rate of the refrigerant is so adjusted by the thermostatic expansion valve that at the exit of the evaporator, at point 4 in the system, all the liquid refrigerant is in the saturated vapour state (vapour at the boiling temperature corresponding to the evaporator pressure). The vapour leaving the evaporator enters the suction side of the compressor and is compressed to a higher pressure. The work of compression raises both the pressure and temperature of the refrigerant vapour which is discharged in the superheated vapour state and ready to repeat the entire cycle over again.

A cycle of the type described above is known as a steady flow thermodynamic cycle because at any one point in the cycle refrigerant conditions (*i.e.,* flow rate, temperature, pressure, etc.) do not change with time, while heat and work are received by the refrigerant in the evaporator and compressor, respectively, and heat is rejected in the condenser. It is to be noted that the cycle discussed above operates between two levels of pressure and two corresponding levels of temperature. The high-pressure half of the cycle extends from the discharge of the compressor to the inlet of the expansion valve and the low-pressure side extends from the discharge of the expansion valve to the inlet of the compressor.

Thermodynamic Analysis of Compression Refrigeration Cycles.

The evaluation of the performance of the various components of the refrigeration cycle discussed above requires a knowledge of some of the laws of thermodynamics which govern the interconversion

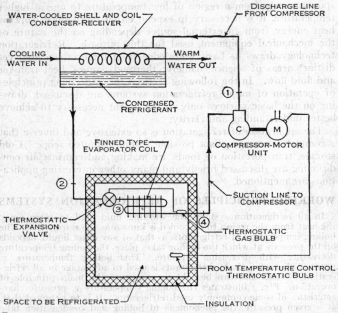

FIG. 1.—SCHEMATIC FLOW DIAGRAM OF A MECHANICAL REFRIGERATION SYSTEM

of heat and work and enable the calculation of the thermal properties of substances. It suffices to state here that extensive tables of thermodynamic properties of all commonly used refrigerants have been prepared and are available in tabular or graphical form readily usable in engineering calculations (see HEAT; THERMODYNAMICS).

From the principle of conservation of energy it can be stated that for a fluid in steady flow the summation of all its energy quantities (its total energy) entering a system (compressor, heat exchanger, etc.) must be equal to the summation of all its energy quantities leaving the system. For a unit mass flowing in and out of a system per unit time this principle can be written in symbolic form as:

$$u_1 + A(P_1 v_1) + A(V_1^2/2g) + AZ_1 + {_1}Q_2 = u_2 + A(P_2 v_2) + A(V_2^2/2g) + AZ_2 + A({_1}Wk_2) \qquad (1)$$

In the above relation subscripts 1 and 2 refer respectively to the magnitudes of the various quantities as the fluid enters and leaves the system. The magnitude of the various quantities can be expressed in any consistent set of units such as the British system of engineering units employed here. The above symbols are defined as follows: u = internal energy of the fluid, its value depending on the temperature and pressure of the fluid, expressed in the units of B.T.U./lb. (one B.T.U. [British thermal unit] is the quantity of heat required to raise the temperature of one pound of water by one degree Fahrenheit [from 63° F. to 64° F.]); P = pressure of the fluid, in lb./sq.ft.; v = specific volume of fluid, in cu.ft./lb.; V = velocity of the fluid, in ft./sec.; Z = elevation of the inlet to the system measured from an arbitrary reference level, in ft.; $_1Q_2$ = heat transferred to or away from the fluid from the time it enters to the time it leaves the system, in B.T.U./lb. of fluid flowing (by convention, $_1Q_2$ is taken as positive if the fluid receives heat and negative if it gives up heat); $_1Wk_2$ = external work done by the fluid or on the fluid from the time it enters to the time it leaves the system, in ft.-lb./lb. of fluid flowing (by convention, $_1Wk_2$ is taken as positive if it is performed by the fluid and negative if it is performed on the fluid); g = gravitational acceleration whose standard value is 32.2 ft./sq.sec.; A = the mechanical equivalent of heat, a universal constant used to convert units of work into units of heat and vice versa ($A = \frac{1}{778}$ ft.lb./B.T.U.).

Examining equation (1) further, the term (Pv), the product of the pressure by the volume, represents the magnitude of the flow work necessary to set the fluid in motion; the term $V^2/2g$ represents the kinetic energy caused by motion; and Z represents the potential energy of the moving fluid measured above a given arbitrary reference datum plane. In thermodynamics, because of the frequent simultaneous occurrence of the terms u and (Pv), a new term called enthalpy is defined as $h = u + Pv$. Hence, the quantity $(u_1 + AP_1 v_1)$ can be written as h_1 and $(u_2 + AP_2 v_2)$ as h_2. Making these substitutions and transposing some of the terms, equation (1) can be rewritten in the form

$$(h_2 - h_1) = {_1}Q_2 - A({_1}Wk_2) + A(V_1^2 - V_2^2)/2g + A(Z_1 - Z_2) \qquad (2)$$

Equations (1) and (2), which are identical, are known as the general energy equations for steady flow and are used extensively in engineering calculations involving the interchange of heat and work. For reasons of simplicity, in the analysis of refrigeration cycles it is common practice to neglect the last two terms on the right-hand side of equation (2) as their magnitude is either zero or negligible compared with the others. Indeed, the difference in elevation between the inlet and outlet openings or the difference in velocity between the inlet and outlet of compressors or heat exchangers is either nil or negligible. On the basis of this simplifying assumption equation (2) reduces to the form

$$(h_2 - h_1) = {_1}Q_2 - A({_1}Wk_2) \qquad (3)$$

Equation (3) may be applied to any one of the components that make up the refrigeration system shown in fig. 1. Considering the condenser, the refrigerant receives no external or shaft work and delivers none as it enters and leaves this equipment and only heat is exchanged between the condensing refrigerant and the cooling water. Therefore in equation (3) the quantity $_1Wk_2$ is zero and the decrease in enthalpy of the refrigerant, $(h_2 - h_1)$, is equal to the heat it rejects to the cooling water, $_1Q_2$. The evaporator is a similar piece of equipment and again there is no work involved; therefore, the heat absorbed from the space to be refrigerated is equal to the increase of enthalpy of the evaporating refrigerant, $_3Q_4 = (h_4 - h_3)$. The flow through the expansion valve involves neither the exchange of heat nor work, hence in this instance equation (3) yields the result $h_3 - h_2 = 0$, indicating that the refrigerant undergoes no change of enthalpy. In the case of the compressor a definite amount of work, $_4Wk_1$, is delivered to the refrigerant vapour being compressed. While some heat, $_4Q_1$, is dissipated from the compressor cylinder head to the surrounding atmosphere by convection and radiation, this quantity is usually a small fraction of the total work input and may be neglected in most instances without causing serious error. Where more exact calculations are desired or in the case of jacketed water-cooled compressors where the heat loss from the compressor cylinder is appreciable, in applying equation (3) either the quantity $_4Q_1$ must be known or a different expression should be used to evaluate the work required for compression. Such an expression has the general form

$$Wk_{comp.} = [n/(n-1)]P_4 v_4 [1 - (P_1/P_4)^{(n-1)/n}] \qquad (4)$$

where all symbols are as defined before and n is a constant which depends on the nature of the refrigerant, the type of compression (the extent of heat loss during compression) and the pressure range over which the compression takes place. Values of n are determined experimentally and are reported in reference works on refrigeration. An important observation to be made in equation (4) is the fact that the work of compression depends primarily on the pressure ratio of compression and not on the absolute values of the inlet or discharge pressures.

The Thermodynamic Diagram.

In the solution of refrigeration problems it is most helpful to trace the processes the refrigerant undergoes on a chart of thermodynamic properties of the refrigerant. Such a chart most frequently used in refrigeration work is the pressure

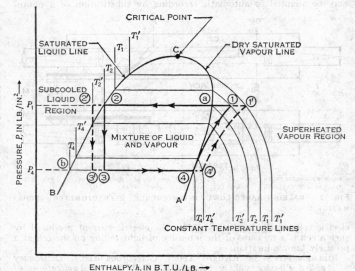

FIG. 2.—SKELETAL THERMODYNAMIC DIAGRAM ILLUSTRATING THE REFRIGERANT CYCLE FOR THE SYSTEM SHOWN IN FIG. 1 (NUMBERS CORRESPOND TO POINTS IN FIG. 1)

v. enthalpy chart shown in skeletal form in fig. 2 where the interrelationship between three of the most frequently used properties of refrigerants (pressure, enthalpy and temperature) is graphically depicted. The properties pressure and enthalpy are chosen as the co-ordinates for the figure and their variation with temperature is represented by the family of constant temperature lines T_4, $T_{4'}$, $T_{2'}$, T_2, T_1, $T_{1'}$, in order of increasing temperature. The dome A-C-B is known as the saturation dome. Points along the curve A-C represent states of dry saturated vapour and along B-C states of saturated liquid. The saturated vapour and saturated liquid curves meet at point C which is known as the critical point. At this unique temperature and pressure the liquid and vapour phases of the refrigerant are indistinguishable and therefore possess identical properties known as the critical properties of the refrigerant. The region to the right of the saturated vapour curve A-C represents states of superheated vapour and that to the left of the saturated liquid curve B-C represents states of subcooled (or compressed) liquid (liquid at a temperature lower than the condensation temperature corresponding to the same pressure). The region within the dome A-C-B (wet vapour region) represents states of mixtures of liquid and vapour refrigerant. The per cent by weight of vapour in the mixture at any point within the dome is obtained by taking the ratio of the horizontal distance between the saturated liquid curve and the point in question to the total distance between the two saturation curves (measured at the same pressure). For example, at point 3 (fig. 2) the per cent of vapour in the mixture is given by the ratio of distances (b to 3)/(b to 4) or $(h_3-h_b)/(h_4-h_b)$. This fraction is called the quality of the wet vapour and is designated by the symbol x. On this basis, the vapour at point 4 on the saturated vapour curve would have a quality $x=100\%$. At a given pressure, or temperature, the difference in enthalpies between the saturated vapour and saturated liquid is known as the latent heat of evaporation (or condensation) representing the quantity of heat required to evaporate completely a unit mass of refrigerant from the saturated liquid state to saturated vapour state (at constant temperature and pressure). It should be noted that within the saturation dome A-C-B the constant temperature lines are horizontal and coincide with the corresponding saturation constant pressure lines.

The Thermodynamic Cycle.—The cycle of the refrigerant corresponding to the simple refrigeration system of fig. 1 is traced on this thermodynamic chart with corresponding points on the flow diagram being labelled by matching numbers on fig. 2. Referring to fig. 2, the trace 1-2-3-4 represents this cycle. At point 1 the compressed and superheated refrigerant vapour (at temperature T_1 and pressure P_1) leaves the compressor and enters the condenser. As heat is transferred in the condenser to the cooling water the superheated vapour is cooled at constant pressure and its temperature drops from T_1 to T_2 (same as T_a). At point a the saturated vapour begins to condense and upon further heat transfer condensation continues between points a and 2, the vapour giving up its latent heat of condensation until at point 2 all of the vapour is completely liquefied and is collected in the lower part of the condenser (or a receiver) as saturated liquid. At point 2 the saturated liquid refrigerant enters the expansion valve and its pressure is reduced from P_1 (same as P_2) to P_3 ($P_3=P_4$). As shown earlier, the enthalpy of the refrigerant entering and leaving the expansion valve is the same, i.e., $h_2=h_3$. As a result of this pressure drop the temperature of the refrigerant is reduced to T_3 (same as T_4) at the expense of some of the liquid flashing into vapour. The fraction of the liquid flashed (the quality) is given by the ratio $x_3=(h_3-h_b)/(h_4-h_b)$. At point 3 the refrigerant (mixture of liquid and vapour) enters the evaporator and as it absorbs heat from the refrigerated space and its contents it continues to evaporate at constant pressure and temperature until at point 4 all of the refrigerant is completely evaporated and leaves the evaporator as saturated vapour. The dry saturated vapour enters the compressor at point 4 and by means of external work it is compressed along the path 4-1 and is discharged at 1 to repeat the cycle. The cycle just described is known as the simple saturation ideal cycle because the refrigerant entering the expansion valve and the compressor consists of saturated liquid and saturated vapour, respectively. It is called ideal because of the simplifying assumption that no pressure drop takes place in any of the piping, the heat exchangers, or at the inlet and outlet of the compressor.

In actual practice it is nearly always the case that the liquid refrigerant leaving the condenser is somewhat subcooled and the vapour leaving the evaporator is somewhat superheated. Such a cycle is shown in fig. 2 by the trace 1'-2'-3'-4'. All other things being the same the effect of subcooling is to increase the refrigeration effect per pound of refrigerant circulated in the system and is therefore desirable. On the other hand, superheating of the vapour entering the compressor increases the work of compression and should be kept to a minimum. A slight amount of superheating is encouraged in practice as a safety measure to protect the compressor by preventing any liquid from entering the compressor cylinder.

All previous discussion and analysis has been based on one pound of refrigerant circulating in the system. In the design and analysis of actual systems certain information and requirements are given the engineer at the outset. For instance, the refrigeration load (demand) is specified and the temperature at which this refrigeration effect is desired is stated. The temperature of the available condenser cooling water (or ambient air) is also specified. Starting with this information the first step is to determine the condensation and evaporation tem-

peratures and pressures for the refrigeration cycle. In practice, it is customary to assume an average temperature difference between the cooling medium and the condensing refrigerant of the order of 10° F. A similar figure is taken for the temperature difference between the evaporating refrigerant and the refrigerated medium. The smaller the temperature differential, the larger becomes the required size of the heat exchanger needed to accomplish a given heat transfer. Hence, the actual selection of temperature differentials to be used is based on both engineering and economic considerations. In general one can write, therefore,

$$T_c=(T_{c.w.})_{av.}+(\Delta T)_c \text{ and } T_e=T_r-(\Delta T)_e \qquad (5)$$

where T_c, T_e and T_r are the temperatures of the condensing and evaporating refrigerant and refrigerated medium, respectively; $(T_{c.w.})_{av.}$ is the average cooling water or air temperature; $(\Delta T)_c$ and $(\Delta T)_e$ are the design temperature differentials between the cooling water and condensing refrigerant and between refrigerated medium and evaporating refrigerant, respectively; all temperatures being expressed in degrees F.

At this point the choice of a refrigerant must be made. The proper refrigerant selection is dependent primarily on the condenser and evaporator temperatures. A desirable refrigerant should not give rise to either unduly high condenser pressures or very low evaporator pressures. Some of the characteristics of refrigerants are discussed in a later section. Having decided on the refrigerant to be used and having determined the condensing and evaporating temperatures, the respective pressures are directly obtained by looking up the saturation pressures corresponding to these two temperatures. The next step in the analysis is the determination of the flow rate of refrigerant necessary to provide the desired refrigeration. Refrigeration load is commonly expressed in the unit of tons of refrigeration. In the U.S., 1 ton of refrigeration is equal to a cooling rate of 288,000 B.T.U./24-hour day or 200 B.T.U./min. The ton as the unit of refrigeration derives its name from the fact that to freeze 1 ton of water per day (1 U.S. ton equals 2,000 lb.) from 32° F. liquid to 32° F. solid requires approximately 288,000 B.T.U. In Great Britain and Europe the ton of refrigeration is sometimes defined either on the basis of the long ton (2,240 lb.) or taken equal to a cooling rate of one kilocalorie per second. These units are larger than the U.S. ton by 12% and 18.8% respectively. Referring to the cycle 1-2-3-4 of fig. 2, the refrigeration performed per pound of refrigerant is given by (h_4-h_3), in B.T.U./lb.; hence, the required refrigerant flow rate, w, is

$$w=(\text{tons of refrigeration}) \ 200/(h_4-h_3), \text{ lb./min.}$$

The work necessary for compression is obtained from the relation

$$Wk_{comp.}=w(h_1-h_4)/42.42, \text{ h.p.}$$

where 42.42 is a conversion factor between heat units and horsepower (1 h.p.=42.42 B.T.U./min.).

A final quantity of interest in the analysis of refrigeration cycles is the efficiency of performance of the cycle. The efficiency of refrigeration cycles, which is known as the coefficient of performance

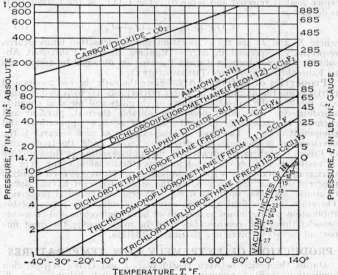

FIG. 3.—PRESSURE AND TEMPERATURE RELATIONSHIP OF SOME REFRIGERANTS

(C.O.P.), is defined as the ratio of the refrigeration effect produced in the evaporator to the compressor work necessary to bring about this refrigeration effect. In symbolic form this may be expressed as

$$C.O.P.=w(h_4-h_3)/w(h_1-h_4)=(h_4-h_3)/(h_1-h_4)$$

The C.O.P. of all mechanical refrigeration cycles is greater than 1. Since the magnitude of the C.O.P. is not directly indicative of the degree of perfection attained by an actual refrigeration system, it is

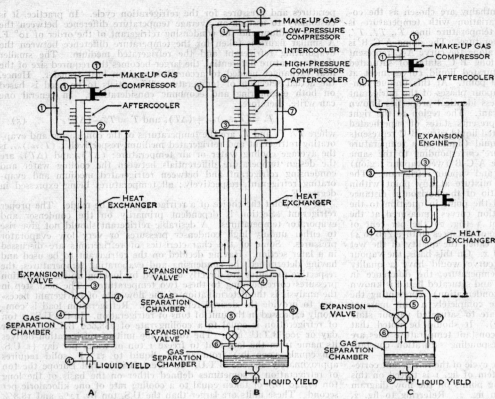

FIG. 4.—SCHEMATIC FLOW DIAGRAMS OF GAS LIQUEFACTION CYCLES. (A) SIMPLE LINDE CYCLE; (B) IMPROVED LINDE CYCLE; (C) CLAUDE CYCLE

often compared with the C.O.P. of an ideal cycle operating between the same condensing and evaporating temperatures. Such an ideal cycle is the Carnot cycle, named after its originator, Nicolas Léonhard Sadi Carnot, the French engineer. It can be shown in thermodynamics that a refrigeration system operating on the Carnot cycle requires the least amount of work per unit of refrigeration. It can further be shown that the C.O.P of the Carnot cycle is independent of the type of refrigerant used and is fixed solely by the two temperatures at which heat is rejected and received. The C.O.P. of the Carnot cycle is defined as

$$(C.O.P.)_{Carnot} = T_e/(T_c - T_e) \qquad (6)$$

where T_e and T_c are the evaporation and condensation temperatures, respectively, expressed in degrees Rankine (degrees Fahrenheit Absolute). Temperatures in degrees Rankine are obtained by adding 460 to Fahrenheit degrees (see THERMOMETRY).

Properties of Refrigerants.—Since the early days of mechanical refrigeration the number of available refrigerants has increased steadily as a result of the consistent efforts of chemists and physical chemists searching for new fluids possessing suitable thermal, physical and chemical characteristics to meet demands of new applications and equipment design. The most striking example of such research is the development of the series of refrigerants known under the trade name of Freons. With rapid advances in the understanding of the structure of matter it has become possible to synthesize almost any type of refrigerant suitable for a specific application. However, even scientific progress was not able to produce the ideal refrigerant having simultaneously optimum thermodynamic, physical and chemical properties. Therefore, in the final analysis, refrigerant suitability for a specific application is determined as a result of both engineering and economic considerations, and compromises must be made among the most important factors involved in a particular situation.

PRODUCTION OF EXTREMELY LOW TEMPERATURES

During the period between World Wars I and II few refrigeration applications existed requiring temperatures much below —40° F. except on a relatively small scale in the field of liquefaction of air and some of the other so-called permanent gases: oxygen, nitrogen, argon, hydrogen, helium. During and after World War II the field of very low temperature refrigeration received a great impetus primarily because of military demands and to a much lesser extent of new peacetime industrial applications. As a result of this interest in extremely low temperatures a new area of specialization developed known as the field of cryogenic engineering. For purposes of definition, it can be said that the field of cryogenics concerns itself primarily with the production of temperatures below that of liquid oxygen (—297° F., at atmospheric pressure) all the way to near absolute zero. The more

important permanent gases having normal liquefaction temperatures (at atmospheric pressure) below that of oxygen are: argon, —302° F.; air, —318° F.; nitrogen, —320° F.; hydrogen, —424° F.; and helium, —453° F. The liquefaction of these gases is accomplished by using either one or both of two simple thermodynamic phenomena; namely: the Joule-Thomson effect (also known as Joule-Kelvin effect) and the adiabatic expansion (involving no heat loss or gain) in an expansion engine. These processes and their application to gas liquefaction are discussed below (see LIQUEFACTION OF GASES).

It is a well-known fact that when a gas at high pressure is throttled down to a lower pressure, depending on the initial value of its temperature, it may undergo an increase or a decrease in temperature. There exists for each gas a maximum temperature below which a gas must be cooled prior to expansion in order to experience a cooling effect upon expansion. This temperature is known as the maximum inversion temperature. The maximum inversion temperature for many gases is above room temperature so that no special precooling of the gas is necessary prior to expansion. For instance, if air is compressed to a pressure of 200 atm. (1 atm. = 14.7 lb./in.²) and a temperature of 125° F., then, upon throttling to a pressure of 1 atm., it will be cooled to 73° F. On the other hand, if helium, originally at 200 atm. and 125° F., is throttled to 1 atm., its temperature will rise to 147° F. The inversion temperature of some common permanent gases are: argon, 842° F.; nitrogen, 658° F.; air, 626° F.; hydrogen, —96° F.; helium, —382° F. approximately. From these figures it is seen that hydrogen and helium need considerable precooling prior to expansion in order to obtain a Joule-Thomson cooling effect. This necessary precooling is accomplished either by means of external refrigeration or by the use of an expansion engine as stated above.

The adiabatic expansion of a gas within a reciprocating engine or turbine always produces a decrease in temperature, no matter what its initial temperature. If, therefore, hydrogen or helium are made to do external work adiabatically through the medium of an engine or a turbine, then they could be made to achieve a temperature below their respective inversion temperatures. Both the Joule-Thomson expansion and the adiabatic work production methods of self-cooling in gases have their advantages and disadvantages. The former is most effective (*i.e.*, greatest temperature drop for a given drop in pressure) when used at low temperatures (near the critical temperature of the gas) and utilizes a very simple device (in the form of a needle valve without any moving parts), but thermodynamically it is a very inefficient process. On the other hand, the adiabatic expansion in an engine is most effective at higher temperatures and has high thermodynamic efficiency, but it requires an engine which is rather complex in design as its moving parts must operate at very low temperatures without the benefit of conventional lubrication. Three basic low-temperature gas liquefaction cycles, using the two methods of cooling just discussed, are schematically illustrated in fig. 4.

Simple Linde System.—The apparatus shown in fig. 4A was first used by Carl von Linde in 1895 to produce liquid air on a commercial scale. This is the simplest type of liquefaction system consisting of three basic components: a compressor, an expansion valve and a heat exchanger. Compressed air at 200 atm. pressure, after being cooled in the aftercooler by atmospheric air or water to essentially room temperature, enters the centre tube of a counterflow heat exchanger (point 2). As this compressed air passes through the expansion valve (point 3) and its pressure is reduced to 1 atm. (point 4) the amount of cooling is not sufficient at first to bring about liquefaction. So the low-pressure cold air is returned back to the compressor through the outer annulus of the heat exchanger, thus cooling the high-pressure air flowing toward the expansion valve. After a time, when steady state conditions are reached, the compressed air entering the heat exchanger (point 2) is cooled by the returning cold gas to about —243° F. (point 3) and is further cooled and partially liquefied after it passes through the expansion valve. Under the conditions of pressure and temperature mentioned above about 10% of the air is liquefied (point 4") as it leaves the expansion valve and the remaining unliquefied portion (point 4') is returned through the cold side of the heat exchanger to the compressor, leaving the heat exchanger (point 1) 2° or 3° below room temperature. The system produces liquid air continuously by receiving make-up air (point 1) at the same weight rate of flow as liquid air is taken out of the system. Because of its simplicity of construction and operation this type of liquefier is often used when small quantities of liquefied gas are needed whose inversion temperature is above room temperature.

Improved Linde Cycle.—In the preceding discussion it was pointed out that the work of compression of a gas is a function of the pressure ratio of compression, becoming greater with increasing pressure ratio (see equation [4]). It was also pointed out, in this section, that the Joule-Thomson cooling effect is greater when the initial temperature of the expanded gas is low. Taking advantage of these two factors, the efficiency of the simple Linde cycle is improved

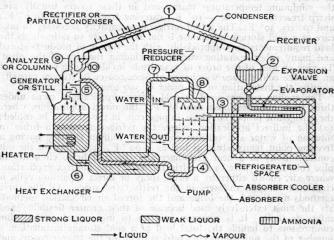

FIG. 5.—SCHEMATIC FLOW DIAGRAM OF AQUA-AMMONIA ABSORPTION REFRIGERATION CYCLE

appreciably by carrying out the compression of the gas in two stages (two compressors) instead of one and by using two expansion stages; where all the gas is first expanded to an intermediate pressure undergoing cooling and then part of this cold gas is further expanded, resulting in much greater additional cooling and partial liquefaction. Referring to fig. 4B, air at atmospheric pressure and temperature (point 1) is compressed by the low-pressure, first-stage compressor to an intermediate pressure of 40 atm. and after being cooled to atmospheric temperature in the intercooler (point 2) it is compressed from 40 to 200 atm. in the high-pressure, second-stage compressor. The air at 200 atm. and atmospheric temperature enters the centre tube (point 2) of a three-channel counterflow heat exchanger, and upon leaving the heat exchanger (point 4) its pressure is reduced to 40 atm. (point 5) as it passes through the first expansion valve. At this point about 20% of the cooled air is further expanded from 40 to 1 atm. (point 6) through the second expansion valve, resulting in additional cooling. At the start of operation the amount of cooling obtained by these two expansions is not sufficient to produce any liquefaction. So 80% of the cold gas at intermediate pressure (point 5) and the colder gas at 1 atm. pressure (point 6') are returned to the compressor through the inner and outer annuli of the heat exchanger, respectively, thus cooling the high-pressure gas approaching the first expansion valve. After a time, when steady state conditions are reached, the high-pressure air entering the heat exchanger (point 2) is cooled by the two returning cold gas streams close to its critical temperature of −221° F. At the end of the first expansion liquefaction may or may not occur depending on the temperature reached at this point. Of this cold air 80% is returned to the heat exchanger and then to the second-stage compressor while the other 20% is further expanded to produce partial liquefaction. Under the conditions of pressure and temperature stated above about 8% of the air going through the second expansion valve is liquefied and the unliquefied portion is returned to the heat exchanger and first-stage compressor.

The Claude Cycle.—Because of the poor thermodynamic efficiency of the Joule-Thomson throttling process, Georges Claude conceived the idea of liquefying gases by the method of adiabatic expansion in an engine, as discussed above. A liquefaction cycle based on this principle was first employed by Claude in 1902 to liquefy air. Claude soon realized that it would be mechanically impractical to have the liquefaction take place within the engine itself because of the enormous difficulties encountered in lubricating the expansion engine. He resorted to a happy compromise of using the expansion engine at relatively high temperatures and pressures and completing the expansion by means of an expansion valve to produce liquefaction of the gas. Such a system, combining both the adiabatic expansion in an engine and the Joule-Thomson effect of gas cooling, is known as the Claude system. In the Claude cycle, shown in fig. 4C, the gas is compressed to about 40 atm. and after being cooled essentially to room temperature in the

aftercooler enters the centre tube (point 2) of the counterflow heat exchanger. Part way down the heat exchanger the gas stream separates into two parts, 20% continuing its way down the heat exchanger to the expansion valve and expanding to 1 atm. and the remaining 80% passing through the expansion engine and being cooled by expanding from 40 to 1 atm. At the start, the cooling effects thus produced are not sufficient to bring about liquefaction of the gas. After a time, when steady state conditions are reached, the low-pressure cold gas from the expansion valve (point 6'), flowing up the heat exchanger and being joined by the cold gas from the expansion engine (point 4), cools down the high-pressure gas sufficiently to enable partial liquefaction to take place at the exit of the expansion valve (point 6).

The Claude cycle can be used to liquefy any gas irrespective of its inversion temperature, and it is used with slight modifications and refinements to liquefy hydrogen and helium efficiently and practically. The most outstanding example of such work is the Collins helium liquefier, developed by S. C. Collins of the Massachusetts Institute of Technology, Cambridge, just prior to World War II. The Collins liquefier is a compact, self-contained unit comprising a three-stage compressor, a reciprocating expansion engine, an expansion valve, counterflow heat exchangers, Dewar flasks, vacuum pumps and all switches and gauges necessary for an automatic refrigeration plant.

Two other low-temperature systems of some prominence are the Heylandt system and the cascade system (see LIQUEFACTION OF GASES).

ABSORPTION REFRIGERATION SYSTEMS

Absorption refrigeration systems use heat energy directly through the medium of a generator-absorber-pump circuit which replaces the complex mechanical compressor. In some absorption refrigerators a small liquid pump constitutes the only moving part in the entire system and in others even this is eliminated resulting in a system with no moving parts whatsoever. Two of the most prominent types of absorption systems are discussed below.

The Ammonia-Water Absorption Refrigeration Cycle.—The most common absorption system is the two-fluid, water-ammonia (also known as aqua-ammonia) system. The operation of this system is based on the particular relationship between the temperature, pressure and concentration of a mixture of two fluids, such as ammonia and water, while it undergoes a change of phase. When a mixture of ammonia and water boils at a given pressure, the vapour phase is much richer in ammonia (the more volatile of the two components) than the liquid phase in contact with it. Conversely, when condensing a mixture of ammonia and water vapour the condensate is poorer in ammonia than the vapour mixture in contact with it. It is also observed that at a given pressure the boiling point temperature of the mixture decreases with increasing concentration of ammonia. This behaviour can be interpreted to mean that at low temperatures the mixture can hold more ammonia in solution than at high temperatures. Increasing the pressure on the mixture at constant temperature has the same effect. Finally, as is the case with single-component liquids, at a given concentration the boiling temperature of the mixture increases with increasing pressure. These basic behaviour characteristics of binary (two-component) mixtures will help in the understanding

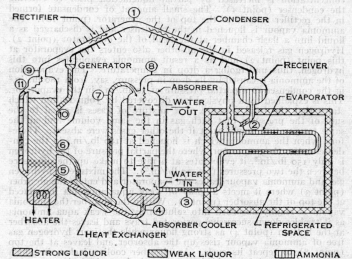

FIG. 6.—SCHEMATIC FLOW DIAGRAM OF ELECTROLUX ABSORPTION REFRIGERATION CYCLE

of the operation of the absorption system schematically shown in fig. 5 (see SOLUTIONS). Liquid ammonia (point 2) at about 85° F. and 160 lb./in.² is expanded through the expansion valve to about 22 lb./in.² and 15° F. and enters the evaporator where it evaporates, absorbing heat from the space to be refrigerated. This ammonia vapour is discharged into the absorber (point 3) where it meets a shower (point 8) of weak liquor (about 30% ammonia) which absorbs the ammonia vapour into solution as it trickles down successive trays, thus forming a solution stronger in ammonia (about 38%). This strong liquor is pumped from the absorber to the top of the analyzer (point 5), being partly heated on its way as it passes through the heat exchanger. In the analyzer this strong liquor trickles down trays against a current of vapour of ammonia and water rising from the boiling solution in the generator below it. The heater (electric, gas or low-pressure condensing steam) boils the ammonia-water liquor and the hot vapour (about 220° F.) rises up the analyzer counterflow to the cold strong liquor. As a result of this distillation process the vapour at the top of the analyzer (point 9) obtains a concentration of about 94%. This concentration is further increased as the vapour continues its way through the rectifier where partial condensation takes place and the vapour is enriched to about 99.5% ammonia as it enters the condenser at about 125° F. (point 1). The small amount of condensate (about 60% ammonia) formed in the rectifier flows back to the top of the analyzer (point 10). As the liquor boils in the generator the part weak in ammonia gravitates to the bottom of the generator from where it is taken to the absorber through a pressure reducer (point 7). On its way to the absorber this weak liquor is partly cooled in the heat exchanger as it heats up the strong liquor. The C.O.P. of absorption systems is much lower than that of mechanical refrigeration systems (about 0.5); however, this disadvantage is offset by the fact that they can be made to operate on inexpensive, low-grade energy. Also, the fact that they have no major moving parts makes for quiet and vibration-free operation, a feature desirable in some applications.

Electrolux Absorption Refrigeration System.—An ingenious modification of the absorption cycle shown in fig. 5 is the Electrolux absorption system in which the refrigerant is taken around the refrigeration cycle without employing any machinery with moving parts. This system, which is schematically illustrated in fig. 6, was invented by two Swedish engineers, Carl Munters and Baltzar von Platen, while they were still undergraduates at the Royal Institute of Technology in Stockholm. Comparing fig. 5 and 6 it is seen that the Electrolux system is in all respects identical to the ammonia-water absorption system with the exception that the strong-liquor pump, the expansion valve and the pressure-reducer valve shown in fig. 5 are all eliminated. In the Electrolux system the ammonia is transported from the absorber to the generator by going into solution in water and the aqua ammonia being circulated by gravity and thermal siphon effect. The functions of the expansion and pressure-reducer valves are performed by an inert atmosphere of hydrogen gas (insoluble in water or ammonia) which circulates between the evaporator and the absorber, transporting the ammonia vapour with it. Referring to the flow diagram of fig. 6, heat is supplied to the generator which forces slugs of strong aqua-ammonia solution and its vapour into the standpipe to the left of the generator and lifts the liquid in the same way as a coffee percolator operates. As this stream discharges into the top of the generator (point 11) the liquid and vapour separate and the concentrated ammonia vapour enters the rectifier (point 9) where the concentration is increased by partial liquefaction prior to entering the condenser (point 1). The small amount of condensate formed in the rectifier returns to the top of the generator (point 10). The ammonia vapour is liquefied in the condenser and is discharged as a liquid into a flash chamber at the head of the evaporator (point 2). Hydrogen gas released in the absorber also enters the evaporator at this point (point 2) and as a result ammonia evaporates into this hydrogen, thus undergoing a drop in temperature. The evaporation of the ammonia is caused by its drop in pressure, say, from 180 lb./in.² in the condenser to a partial pressure of 30 lb./in.² in the evaporator. This is explained by a physical law discovered by John Dalton which states that the total pressure of a mixture of gases is equal to the sum of the pressures that each gas in the same volume and at the same temperature would exert if the other gases were absent. Therefore, when the ammonia which is liquefied at 180 lb./in.² in the condenser enters the evaporator, where the partial pressure of the hydrogen is only 150 lb./in.², it evaporates at a rate to make up the difference between the two pressures (i.e., 30 lb./in.²). The mixture of hydrogen gas and ammonia vapour leaves the evaporator and enters the absorber (point 3) where it meets a spray of weak aqua ammonia introduced at the top of the absorber (point 7). Within the absorber the ammonia vapour is readily absorbed into solution by the weak aqua ammonia as it trickles down successive perforated trays and leaves the absorber at the bottom (point 4) as strong liquor while the inert hydrogen gas free of ammonia vapour rises up the absorber and leaves at the top (point 8) to repeat its cycle. An absorber cooling jacket, in which water is circulated, is provided to remove the heat of solution generated by the absorption of ammonia vapour by the weak liquor. The strong liquor leaving the absorber (point 4) proceeds to the generator (point 5), being partially heated on its way in the heat exchanger by the hot weak liquor coming from the generator (point 6) on its way to the absorber (point 7). It is seen that in this system the total pressure in all its parts is the same (except for minor friction losses). While the partial pressure of the refrigerant varies from a minimum in the evaporator to a maximum in the condenser, a compensating variation in the partial pressure of the hydrogen gas enables the maintenance of the same total pressure throughout.

APPLICATIONS OF REFRIGERATION

Mechanical refrigeration occupies a position in everyday life as an indispensable necessity. The applications of refrigeration are so numerous and varied that it is impossible to touch even briefly upon each of them here. Because a large portion of refrigeration machinery and accessories produced is used for the preservation of food, this phase of application is treated in some detail while a number of others are briefly mentioned.

Cold Storage Warehouses.—Cold storage warehouses vary in capacity from 1,000,000 to 6,000,000 or more cubic feet of storage space devoted on the average two-thirds to freezer space and one-third to cooler space. Unless special provisions are made for quick freezing, the minimum temperatures maintained in these spaces usually are: sharp freezers, —15° to —10° F.; carrying freezers, —10° to 0° F.; and coolers, 30° F. The actual refrigeration capacity necessary to take care of a cold storage warehouse is not always easy to estimate as the load requirements vary appreciably with the nature of products stored and many other operating variables including the size of the plant. To give an idea of the order of magnitude involved, one can say that an average cold storage warehouse of 6,000,000 cu.ft. storage capacity requires the installation of the order of 300 tons of refrigeration.

The cooling systems used in cold storage applications come under three main classifications; namely: (1) the direct application, where the refrigerant proper circulates in pipe coils in the space to be cooled; (2) the indirect application, where the refrigerant cools a brine (a solution of water and calcium chloride or sodium chloride having a freezing point temperature as low as —60° F., depending on the salt concentration) in a heat exchanger and the cold brine circulates in pipe coils in the space to be refrigerated; (3) the indirect application, where air, cooled either by a brine spray or direct expansion coils, is circulated through diffusers in the refrigerated space. Of the three methods mentioned, the brine and the forced-air circulation methods are the most extensively used because of their greater flexibility and safety features. It is common practice to use several refrigeration compressors to handle the total load of a cold storage installation, a number of the units supplying refrigeration for the freezer rooms and others for the coolers, with at least one unit kept as a stand-by or spare to be used in the event one of the operating units breaks down.

Another type of installation somewhat similar to the cold storage warehouse but much smaller in capacity and more specialized in function is the frozen food locker plant, where foods are frozen and held in storage for families and other groups of a community.

Refrigerated Food Transportation.—*Trucks and Trailers.*— The distribution of refrigerated foods from major storage centres to retailers and even the long-distance hauling from farms and food processing centres to cities is handled to a large extent by refrigerated trucks and trailers. In the main, two types of truck bodies are constructed: those maintaining 35° to 40° F. for carrying fresh meat, vegetables and dairy products; and those holding about 0° F. for ice cream and frozen foods. Numerous types of mechanical refrigeration systems are used in both trucks and trailers, the source of power being obtained either by a separate internal-combustion engine or from the truck engine itself, either by a crankshaft extension at the front end or by a power take-off from the transmission. Besides mechanical refrigeration, water ice and dry ice (solid carbon dioxide) are extensively used in refrigerated transportation, where these are charged in conveniently located bunkers either at the end or near the ceiling of the truck body and air is circulated past them and through the body by means of a small blower. The use of dry ice in refrigerated transportation (truck, trailer and rail) was steadily increasing in the later 1950s despite its much higher cost per pound. Because of its low temperature it is ideal for frozen food transportation. When dry ice is used in the shipment of fresh foods, the carbon dioxide gas in the atmosphere immediately surrounding the product serves as a means of reducing the oxygen content of the air, thus minimizing possible deterioration resulting from oxidation. Also, it inhibits the growth and development of bacteria and various moulds which cause spoilage. It is often the practice to precool the interior of the truck as well as the fresh produce prior to or at the time of loading.

Refrigerated Railroad Cars.—Despite the tremendous volume of perishables transported by trucks and trailers and their increasing competition with the railroads, the main bulk of long-distance refrigerated transportation was still handled by rail in the 1950s. The earliest known use of refrigeration by the railroads was in July 1851, when several tons of butter were shipped from Ogdensburg, N.Y., to Boston, Mass., in a wooden boxcar insulated with sawdust and stocked with ice. More than a century later water ice was still more or less the universal cooling medium in refrigerated freight and express cars. In the U.S. alone in the mid-1950s the railroads used about 17,000,000 tons of ice annually or nearly one-third of the total ice production of that country. The modern standard refrigerator car in the U.S. is 40 ft. long and of the end-bunker type, equipped with fans and having about 4 in. insulation. Some cars, 50 ft. long and with 6 in. insulation, using 30% by weight sodium chloride salt with water ice giving a bunker temperature of —3° F., are used in the transportation of frozen foods. The use of mechanical refrigeration on railroads was still more or less in the developmental stage in the 1950s. Considerations of high

REFRIGERATION EQUIPMENT AND MACHINERY FOR MAKING ICE

1. Refrigerating equipment for air conditioning the Capitol, Washington, D.C.

2. Refrigerant compressor (foreground) installed in building for air conditioning. In the background is an evaporative cooler for the hot refrigerant gases

3. Ammonia compressor for ice making. Two compressors are coupled to a single synchronous motor

4. Freezing tank filled with brine for making ice. Ammonia pipes absorb heat from the brine. A group of cans filled with water is placed in the tank and their contents are frozen to a solid

5. Can-filling apparatus. The cans are conveyed by the crane to the freezing tank

6. Cans are emptied, and the blocks of ice are transferred on a conveyor to storage

first cost (about $16,000 per car) and high maintenance costs were expected to delay wide-scale mechanical installations. The few mechanically refrigerated freight cars in operation were mostly equipped with Freon-12 compressors run by diesel-electric drives. Each of these cars had a refrigeration capacity of about seven tons and they were used mainly by the frozen food and frozen concentrate industry.

Marine Refrigeration.—The early history of mechanical refrigeration as applied to food transportation finds its origin in marine refrigeration. In the summer of 1880 the steamer "Strathleven" brought to England the first successfully carried refrigerated meat cargo. Early shipboard installations were equipped with dense-air machines, later being replaced by carbon dioxide and ammonia systems. In modern installations Freon refrigerants are used extensively, primarily as a result of development work carried out in the U.S. Design conditions and other basic principles are not greatly different in marine refrigeration from those in cold storage warehouse practice. All equipment and installations must be specified as complying with the rules and regulations of the classification societies (American Bureau of Shipping or *Lloyd's Register* or both, etc.), the U.S. coast guard, the U.S. public health service and the American Society of Refrigerating Engineers Standard 26, "Recommended Practice for Installations on Shipboard."

Manufacture of Water Ice.—Despite the tremendous increase in the use of fractional-horsepower mechanical refrigeration units for household and other commercial refrigeration uses, the manufacture of water ice remained a major industry. The method most extensively used is the can method, using treated or untreated raw (tap) water. Galvanized steel ice cans, usually of about 320 lb. capacity, 11 x 12 in. at the top and 50 in. in depth with an over-all taper of $\frac{1}{2}$ in. in their length, are submerged in a well-insulated (10 to 12 in. granulated cork) tank in which cold brine is circulated. Tank depths are usually about 52 in. for 320-lb. ice cans, and width and length seldom exceed 40 and 120 ft. The brine is cooled by direct-expansion evaporator coils normally placed between rows of cans. The velocity of the brine flowing past the cans and the brine temperature determine the time required for freezing. Brine velocities should not exceed about 35 ft. per minute and variations of temperature should be kept less than 1° F. For a given brine velocity, the time required to freeze a given thickness of ice is determined first by the brine temperature. As most raw waters, treated or untreated, crack upon freezing at temperatures below 10° F., the freezing temperatures are in general somewhat above this figure. The rate of freezing drops rapidly as the ice becomes thicker. An 11 x 12-in. can holding 320 lb. of water in 12° F. brine takes 24 hours to freeze the first 280 lb. of ice and requires an additional 14 hours to freeze the last 40 lb. When raw water is used in the manufacture of ice it is necessary to agitate the water in the cans during freezing to obtain clear ice. This is done by bubbling dry air, usually at about 15 to 18 lb./in.^{2} gauge pressure, at the centre of each can, thus rejecting most of the dissolved minerals into the unfrozen centre core. Near the completion of freezing the concentrated core, consisting of about three to four gallons, is sucked out and replaced with chilled fresh water to complete the freezing of the complete block. The refrigeration required to manufacture ice depends on many factors, such as initial water temperature, brine temperature, insulation of brine tank, efficiency of refrigeration compressors, size of plant, etc. A good figure for a well-constructed plant of 30- to 50-ton daily ice capacity using 60° F. water and 12° F. brine is 1.52 tons of refrigeration per ton of ice.

Despite the large amount of ice consumption in all countries of the world, the methods for handling and processing ice have not changed significantly over the years. Even in the U.S., where more than 50,000,000 tons of ice were used annually in the 1950s, representing about 85,000,000 tons of mechanical refrigeration actually produced for this purpose, only in the decade following World War II had mechanization of ice making become widespread. There was then a definite trend toward increased sales of ice in small sizes (cubed, crushed and sized and shaved) aside from the manufacture of block ice. Installation of scoring machines, cubing machines, sizing machines and packing machines for automatic vending stations expanded rapidly. In the U.S. the production of crystal clear ice cubes (about 1⅜ in. along the sides) by fully automatic machines, particularly for beverage purposes, reached nearly 1,000,000 tons a year.

Comfort Air Conditioning.—In its strictest definition, comfort air conditioning must incorporate the following features: control of temperature, humidity, air distribution (ventilation), odour, air cleanliness and in some instances air sterilization. All comfort conditioning applications are functionally similar whether the space under consideration be a residential dwelling, large building, hotel or restaurant. In large installations, involving sometimes 1,000 or more tons of refrigeration capacity, the central system design is adapted. However, the majority of installations run in sizes starting from $\frac{1}{3}$ or $\frac{1}{2}$ ton for window air-conditioning units to 5, 10 or 25 tons for small stores, restaurants, etc. Most of these installations are equipped with self-contained factory-assembled package units ready to plug in for operation. These units are complete with motor, compressor, evaporator, condenser, blower, thermostat and all necessary controls for automatic operation. The enclosing cabinets are usually elaborate and smart in appearance and are often provided with integral adjustable air-distribution registers near ceiling height and return openings close to the floor. In sizes of five tons and smaller the majority of these units

are equipped with hermetic motor-compressor assemblies requiring the minimum of service, if any. The condensers on these units are either air or water cooled. On sizes larger than five-ton capacity, the compressors are normally of the open-head type, with water-cooled condensers for improved efficiency. The package units described above are quite adequate for normal applications but they do not provide humidity control independent of temperature control. Humidity control, completely independent of temperature conditions, can only be obtained by the use of a reheater coil following the evaporator cooling coil whereby the air is first cooled sufficiently, producing a degree of dehumidification which upon reheating will result in the required relative humidity at the desired temperature. This type of design is usually found only in the more elaborate year-around air-conditioning installations.

The heat-pump system, designated more correctly as the reverse-cycle refrigeration system, is a conventional refrigeration system where the heat rejected by the refrigerant at the condenser is utilized for heating during the winter while the evaporator absorbs heat from the outside air, ground or any other low-grade heat source (river, well, etc.) conveniently available at no cost. The heat rejected at the condenser is the sum of the heat energy equivalent of the work input to the compressor plus the heat absorbed by the evaporator. Hence, for a mechanical refrigeration system having a C.O.P. of five it is seen that for every kilowatt of electrical energy consumed by the system the equivalent of six kilowatts of heat energy is obtained at the condenser for heating purposes. In summer operation the functions of the evaporator and condenser are reversed and the refrigeration system performs its normal functions of cooling and dehumidification. The heat-pump system of year-around air conditioning has become well established and close to 3,000 installations, large and small, were in successful operation, mostly in the more temperate regions of the U.S., England and Europe, in the mid-1950s. In some sections of the U.S. where utility rates were low (around 1 cent per kilowatt hour) and the winter climate not extreme, the heat pump was already competitive from the operating cost standpoint with conventional heating and cooling systems.

Other Applications.—The following constitutes only a partial illustrative list of the many diverse applications where refrigeration is used extensively: food processing and manufacturing: dairy products (butter, ice cream, cheese), beverages (beer, wine and other alcoholic and carbonated beverages), bakery, etc. (*see also* REFRIGERATORS [HOUSEHOLD]); industrial and engineering applications: liquefied storage and transportation of industrial gases (oxygen, nitrogen, hydrogen), manufacture of dry ice, textile industry (synthetic and natural yarn processing and weaving), petroleum refining and chemical processes, metallurgical processes, engineering construction (freezing of sliding silty soils in the construction of dams, tunnels, shaft sinking, curing of large masses of poured concrete), low-temperature testing facilities, wind-tunnel cooling, etc.; industrial air conditioning: printing and paper manufacture, precision machining and assembly of metal machine parts, confectionery processing, deep mine cooling, preservation of valuable books, paintings, tapestry, etc., in libraries and museums, etc. (*See also* AIR CONDITIONING, HEATING AND VENTILATION.)

BIBLIOGRAPHY.—The American Society of Refrigerating Engineers, *Air Conditioning Refrigerating Data Book—Design Volume* (New York, 1953–54), and *Applications Volume* (New York, 1954–55); American Society of Heating and Air Conditioning Engineers, *Heating, Ventilating, Air Conditioning Guide* (New York, 1955); B. F. Raber and F. W. Hutchinson, *Refrigeration and Air Conditioning Engineering* (New York, London, 1945); M. Ruhemann, *The Separation of Gases* (London, 1940; New York, 1941); Mark Waldo Zemansky, *Heat and Thermodynamics,* 3rd ed. (New York and London, 1951).

(Y. S. T.)

REFRIGERATORS (HOUSEHOLD). Mechanical or automatic refrigerators may be either of the compressor or absorption type. Both have a closed system in which the refrigerant circulates. In the evaporator, the part of the system inside the refrigerator, the liquid refrigerant changes to a gas, removing heat from the food chamber in the process. In the condensing coils it is cooled by air passing over the coils and changed to a liquid again. A thermostat (*q.v.*) may be regulated to produce the temperature desired.

The compressor system uses a small motor, $\frac{1}{4}$ to $\frac{1}{8}$ h.p., to start the cycle of operation. It forces the gaseous refrigerant from the evaporator into the condensing coils. From the coils it passes through a valve into the evaporator. The valve may be the expansion type, through which the refrigerant is sprayed into the evaporator in such a fine stream that it is partially vaporized immediately, or a float type which allows a relatively large amount of liquid refrigerant to collect in the evaporator. The cycle then repeats itself.

The functioning of the absorption system depends upon the fact that water absorbs ammonia gas in the cold but is easily separated from it again in the presence of heat.

Heat, usually from a gas or oil flame, is used in the generator to bring about the separation. The ammonia, free from the water, passes into the condensing coils, is liquefied and flows into the evaporator, where a medium of hydrogen reduces the pressure sufficiently to allow ready evaporation. From the evaporator the ammonia-hydrogen gas combination passes into the absorber, where a spray of water from the condenser absorbs the ammonia. The insoluble hydrogen returns to the evaporator. The ammonium hydroxide flows to the generator to start the cycle again. Heat and cold exchangers complicate the construction of the system, but increase its efficiency.

As has been noted, ammonia, because of its affinity for water, is the refrigerant used in the absorption system. Sulphur dioxide and recently dichlordifluoromethane are most commonly used in the compression system.

Certain characteristics are desirable in a refrigerant. It should be stable under frequent change of state, noninflammable and nontoxic. It should have moderately high latent heat, a low condensing pressure and no effect on metals or lubricating oils.

None of the refrigerants used complies with all the requirements, but those mentioned have the necessary latent heat and usable operating pressure to meet the demands of construction in household-size refrigerators. Dichlordifluoromethane is nontoxic. Ammonia and sulphur dioxide are considered nontoxic in the amounts present in five to eight cubic foot boxes, under usual home ventilating conditions. (See REFRIGERATION AND ITS APPLICATION.)   (L. J. P.; X.)

REFUGEES AND THE EXCHANGE OF POPULA-
TIONS. In the early history of European civilization wars and conquests were often followed or accompanied by considerable movements of population. Sometimes the two went necessarily together, because the motive for war was the desire for richer lands on which the conquerors wished to live; sometimes the movement of population resulted from the ferocity of the invaders who drove whole populations away from the countries which they had inhabited.

For a long period this feature of warfare disappeared, but with World Wars I and II it once more recurred. The events of 1914–18 caused greater movements of population from one place to another than there had been for centuries before. In some cases, it is true, these movements, though large, were only temporary. For example, although the Belgian refugees who fled from the German invaders in 1914 were very numerous, and although practically all of them remained away from their homes until the end of 1918, they did not attempt to create a new life or to establish new homes outside their native land; their migration was only temporary, like that of the refugees who fled from the invaded provinces of France, Italy and Rumania, and to a smaller extent from all the territories occupied by enemy troops during World War I.

But in other cases, great masses of refugees who left their homes when the tide of war swept over them had little prospect of ever returning or of recreating their previous life there. This was the situation, for example, of a considerable proportion of the inhabitants of the Balkan peninsula.

MOVEMENTS IN VARIOUS COUNTRIES, WORLD WAR I

Excluding such temporary movements as those of the Belgians, the emigrations of war refugees of different nationalities were roughly as follows:

Russians.—Between 1917 and 1920 nearly 1,500,000 political refugees from Russia were thrown upon the charity of Europe. Some of these refugees were prisoners taken by the Germans and Austrians during the war, who refused to return to Russia. A great number were members of the defeated armies of Koltchak, Wrangel, Denikin and others. Many of the refugees were women and children who fled from the bolshevist revolution. In the earlier days of their exile they were dispersed as follows: Germany 300,-000, Poland 400,000, France 400,000, Constantinople 100,000, Yugoslavia 50,000, Bulgaria 30,000, Czechoslovakia 26,000, Rumania and Greece 50,000, Baltic states 100,000. In addition a large number, at least 100,000, fled eastward into China.

Greeks.—As the result of warlike operations there fled into Greece between 1915 and 1922 1,250,000 Greek refugees from Asia Minor and eastern Thrace and 50,000 from Bulgaria. In addition there came under treaties for the exchange of population from Bulgaria a further 50,000; from Asia Minor approximately 100,000.

Armenians.—From the year 1915 onward there were expelled from their dwellings in Asia Minor some hundreds of thousands of Armenians. Great numbers of them perished in their wanderings in the mountains; some thousands succeeded in making journeys on foot as far as Mesopotamia; others sought protection in the Russian empire. In 1921 the independent Armenian republic of Erivan, with an Armenian population of 800,000, adopted the soviet régime and became part of the Union of Soviet Socialist Republics. To its original population, 300,000 to 400,000 additional refugees from Turkish Armenia were shortly added, and in spite of their great suffering, they were absorbed with remarkable rapidity into the economic system of the country. It was further estimated that more than 300,000 other Armenians were scattered more or less in destitution over Russia and the near east, particularly Bulgaria and Greece. In 1921 100,000 fled to Syria, many of whom became Syrian subjects in the territory then under French mandate; more than 60,000 fled in the following year to Greece, 35,000 to Bulgaria and 20,000 to 30,000 more fled to the republic of Erivan.

Bulgars.—From 1918 onward a large number of minorities of Bulgarian or quasi-Bulgarian race and language fled from their homes in the Dobruja, in Macedonia and in eastern and western Thrace. It was calculated by the Bulgarian government that their total number amounted to almost 500,000. In addition, about 75,000 Bulgars voluntarily emigrated to Bulgaria from Greece under the terms of the Greco-Bulgarian Exchange of Populations treaty.

Turks.—Approximately 50,000 Turks fled from eastern Thrace and Smyrna when these territories were occupied by Greek forces in 1919, but returned to their homes in 1922. In addition approximately 350,000 to 400,000 Turks were moved from Greece (most of them from Macedonia, Crete and western Thrace) to Asia Minor under the terms of the Exchange of Populations treaty made at Lausanne in 1923.

Effects.—Broadly speaking, the general features of these movements of population during and following World War I may be summarized as follows:

The great emigration of Russian political refugees was, in the first instance, regarded as an almost unmixed evil both for Europe and for the refugees themselves. Their great suffering was not, in the early stages, compensated by any considerable political or economic gain. This is not equally true, however, of the movement of population in the Balkans and in the near east. These movements at least accomplished a great deal toward effective unmixing of the populations in these areas. The mixture of populations had led to so much political trouble in modern times that this unmixing process must be regarded as a very considerable advantage.

Further, in certain countries the influx of refugees, while at first it appeared to be a disaster, in the long run proved to be a source of strength. This was particularly true of Greece, where, thanks to arrangements which will be mentioned shortly, the refugees were absorbed very quickly into the economic system of the country, where they immensely increased the agricultural production and imported industries formerly unknown. There is no doubt that they thus improved the political position of Greece by giving it a homogeneous and vigorous new population and by increasing the economic wealth of the nation as a whole.

In Bulgaria, however, the process was much slower, as the refugees showed less inclination to accept their exile as definitive and to settle down in new homes, than did those who went from Asia Minor to Greece.

Another result of general importance which followed the movement of population caused by World War I was that Asia Minor was left almost exclusively to the Turks. Hitherto inhabited by a very mixed population, including elements which continued the traditions of the ancient civilization of Byzantium, there were now few of these elements left. Furthermore it should be noted that the Russian emigration, which, as already stated, was regarded as an unmixed evil for the refugees and for the countries offering them hospitality began under the guidance of the League of Nations and the International Labour office, in certain countries, especially France, to constitute an important reconstructive economic factor.

Treaties of Exchange.—Under these treaties, the most important of which were the Greco-Turkish and the Greco-Bulgarian, impartial committees consisting of one representative from each government and two or three impartial experts appointed by the League of Nations supervised or actually carried out the transportation of the persons moved from one country to the other, valued their property, kept an exact record of it and established their claim for this value against the government of the country to which they went. These treaties of exchange worked with varying success.

So far as the Greco-Turkish treaty was concerned, its principal and most necessary effect was to make room in Greece, by the removal of 350,000 Turks, for a great part of the incoming flood of refugees, who found in the evacuated Turkish properties fields and houses ready for their use. Without this treaty of exchange, and without a refugee settlement loan floated under the auspices of the League, the absorption of the Greek refugees into productive employment in their motherland could never have been done.

On the other hand, the fate of the Turks transported under the treaty from Greece into Turkey and in the absence of such a loan, appears to have been less happy. Official information was not disclosed, but it is obvious that the arrival of 350,000 refugees in a country whose total population did not exceed 5,000,000, necessarily imposed a heavy burden on its resources already straitened by many years of war.

Of the Greco-Bulgarian treaty of exchange, it is enough to say that while the working of its machinery was slow, it laid the foundation for an unmixing of the population in Greek Macedonia and in parts of Bulgaria.

Work of the League of Nations.—The other personal and economic problems which were raised by the refugee movements above described were dealt with partly by individual governments and partly by the League of Nations. To take the Russians first, many governments throughout Europe accorded them particular privileges and gave them much state help, estimated at £2,000,000 per annum—in particular Yugoslavia, Czechoslovakia and Bulgaria deserve mention. The League of Nations and the International Labour office also played a considerable part through the action of the delegations established in Constantinople and in the Baltic states, Rumania, China, Bulgaria, Greece, Serbia, Germany, Poland, France and other countries, in breaking up the most disastrous congestions of refugees in places where no employment could be found, for example, in Constantinople and Greece; in placing some hundreds of thousands in employment in no fewer than 50 different countries; in securing for the refugees in many countries legal protection, freedom of movement in search of employment and a new form of so-called "League of Nations passport" which secured the recognition of over 50 governments, under which they were enabled to travel from one country to another; and even in securing for a small number who desired it, repatriation to their native land. Under the auspices and with the help of these League offices, large movements of Russian refugees were carried out to France, where some thousands were settled as tenant farmers and in industry, to the United States, to Canada, to South America and to other countries where employment could be found.

For the Greek refugees the League did still more. Through its machinery a loan of £12,000,000 for their settlement in agricultural and other employment was obtained, and under the international control of a League commission this settlement was carried out with remarkable success.

For the Armenians, who did not enjoy the protection of the government of the Turkish republic, the same passport privileges and legal protection were obtained through the machinery of the League as had previously been obtained for the Russians.

(F. Na.; X.)

CONDITIONS BETWEEN WARS

The death of Fridtjof Nansen in May 1930 was a distinct loss to the refugees whose problems had absorbed his attention during the last ten years of his life. After a year of study and uncertainty the League of Nations established in 1931 the Nansen International Office for Refugees to carry on the work which Dr. Nansen had initiated.

The League, while accepting responsibility for the legal protection of refugees, had always considered its interest in refugee problems to be of a temporary nature. Consequently the new Nansen office was established as an autonomous body under the authority of the League of Nations with mandates to conclude its affairs by 1938 and to restrict its humanitarian activities to the co-ordination of the efforts of private organizations engaged in administering relief to refugees.

In order that the legal protection of refugees might be assured after the closing of the Nansen office, the League of Nations provided, through the medium of the convention of. Oct. 28, 1933, for the issuance of Nansen identity certificates by the governments signing the convention and for rights of residence and employment and other benefits for Russians, Armenians and assimilated refugees then under the protection of the Nansen office. In 1938, after the Nansen office had concluded its activities, the League constituted a new high commissioner to deal with refugees hitherto coming under the Nansen office and the office of the high commissioner for refugees coming from Germany.

Saar.—After the plebiscite in the Saar in 1935 approximately 7,000 former residents of the Saar left that territory, most of them to settle in France. This new group of refugees was added by League action to those already under the protection of the Nansen office and a recommendation was made to the governments that Nansen identity certificates be issued to them.

China.—The war in China beginning in 1937 precipitated one of the largest internal migrations in modern history. It was estimated that approximately 30,000,000 Chinese fled before the Japanese armies in two substantial movements from the coast areas to the agricultural hinterland—one from central China and the southeast to the southwest and the other from the northeast to the northwest. Apart from the problem of internal displacement in China the Chinese government was later concerned, at the end of the war, with accomplishing the return of 135,000 overseas Chinese driven back to China by the war to their former homes in countries of southeast Asia. These overseas Chinese had played an important role in the economy of China and the resumption of their trading activities was a matter of importance to China's economic recovery.

Germany.—When the nazi party assumed control of the German government in 1933, thousands of new refugees were dispersed over central and western Europe in the beginning of a movement which later gained momentum during World War II. Those in Germany who opposed the nazi political philosophy—non-Aryans according to the Nürenberg laws, scientists, intellectuals, authors, artists, the members of other liberal professions and labour leaders—were first removed from government posts and later from private positions in the universities, publishing houses and business, were arrested and confined in concentration camps, deprived of their property and citizenship and finally driven from Germany, to find new places of livelihood as best they could in other countries.

Neighbouring countries—Austria, Hungary, Poland, Czechoslovakia, Switzerland, Belgium, the Netherlands and France—accepted the refugees, often in flight over their borders at night, in the expectation of extending hospitality to them for a temporary period until they could emigrate to places of permanent residence overseas. Approximately half of the Jewish refugees who left Germany in the early days of the persecution migrated to Palestine.

The German *Anschluss* with Austria in March 1938 added new thousands to the stream of central European refugees, who were already taxing the capacities of the countries of temporary refuge of western Europe. In an effort to substitute planned migration for the chaotic dispersion of refugees, President Franklin D.

Roosevelt summoned 32 governments to the Evian conference of July 1938.

Offers to receive refugees for permanent settlement were not forthcoming at Evian, however, with the exception of the Dominican Republic, which offered to accept 100,000 for settlement in agriculture.

The Intergovernmental Committee on Refugees, composed of the governments which had met at Evian in July was organized in London in Aug. 1938. It was believed at that time that the committee, lacking refugee-producing countries in its membership and free, in comparison with the high commissioners of the League of Nations, to negotiate on behalf of refugees who had not yet left their countries of origin but were under pressure to do so, would soon be able to resettle the refugees from Germany and Austria and an additional 185,000 from Czechoslovakia on a pro rata basis in receiving countries. This expectation was not realized.

Spain.—On the collapse of the loyalist army in Spain in Feb. 1939 some 340,000 refugees burst over the border into France. While at first there was indecision in France with respect to admitting the refugees, the final decision was to intern them in refugee camps at Argelès-sur-Mer and Cyprien. Since many of the refugees were fleeing primarily from military action, repatriation to Spain started immediately after the end of the war. However, some 40,000 were political refugees who could not return to Spain with safety and they eventually were placed in labour camps and absorbed in French industry. Others migrated to North Africa, Mexico, the Dominican Republic and Latin and South American countries.   (J. G. McD.; X.)

REFUGEES IN WORLD WAR II

Poland.—The German invasion of Poland in Sept. 1939 precipitated an eastward movement of refugees far larger in volume and more rapid and violent in action than the westward movement which had been in process since 1933. Poland's population of 3,000,000 Jews constituted the majority of those affected by the advance of the German armies eastward, but as the war was fought more bitterly, distinctions between the treatment of Jews and Poles at the hands of the Germans became less marked. Fewer than 100,000 refugees from Poland escaped into the Baltic countries and southward into Rumania, Hungary and Bulgaria. More than 1,175,000 Jews became subject to German control in the area of former Poland that was incorporated into the German reich and in Government-General Poland.

Unknown numbers of Polish and Jewish refugees who resided in or fled into the area of former Poland which was occupied by the forces of soviet Russia were moved eastward to Siberia and southeastern Asiatic Russia.

The conquest of Poland also created numerous cross currents of population movements. The policy of the German reich was to repatriate German minorities in eastern and southwestern Europe to the *Altreich*. A treaty concluded with Italy in the fall of 1939 providing for the return of some 270,000 Germans from the south Tirol was the first effort to implement this policy. Later similar treaties were signed with Latvia and Estonia for the return of approximately 75,000 Baltic Germans.

Some 300,000 Germans were also repatriated from Bukovina, Bessarabia and Rumania.

As the members of these German minorities in other countries returned to Germany they crossed the paths of the 300,000 to 400,000 Jewish refugees from Germany, Austria and Czechoslovakia who were constantly being deported eastward to the ghettos established in Warsaw, Lublin and Lwów. These constituted the remainder of the refugees who had been unable to escape from central Europe before the outbreak of the war. The last to escape had gone by boat to Shanghai or through Poland and across Siberia to Harbin and Vladivostok and thence on to the Philippines or to the western hemisphere through Kobe and Yokohama.

As western Poland was incorporated into the reich both Poles and Jews were driven eastward into Government-General Poland. It was estimated by Polish sources that more than 1,200,000 Poles had been moved into Government-General Poland by Germany by the end of 1939. Germans in Government-General Poland were returned to Germany. Germans were also moved from southern and eastern Poland occupied by soviet Russia to Germany.

From this area Poles and Jews were evacuated far eastward into Russia to be replaced by a Russian infiltration westward.

Finland.—Finns from the Karelian isthmus, ceded to Russia by the peace treaty between Russia and Finland after the winter war of 1939–40, were resettled in the diminished area of that hard-pressed country. More than 400,000 people had to be placed on the land or in industry at a time when the resources of the Finnish government were exhausted by the war.

Some assistance was provided by private funds raised in the United States.

Norway.—Norway faced a similar problem of internal resettlement after the German invasion. Approximately 400,000 people were moved from the coast defense areas into the interior of the country, including many who had resisted the invasion in the short-lived defense of their country.

Low Countries and France.—The advance of the German armies into the Low Countries of western Europe in the spring of 1940 uprooted civilian populations on a scale comparable to that precipitated but a few months earlier by the invasion of Poland. This movement of about 3,000,000 Dutch, Belgian and French people in flight to southern France in advance of the German armies was joined by some 140,000 refugees from central Europe who had found temporary respite in the Netherlands, Belgium and France.

The great majority who had fled to safety from military actions returned to their homes after the signing of the armistice between France and Germany, which illustrated the generally temporary character of such war refugee movements.

England after the flight of its defeated army from Dunkerque found itself harbouring some 70,000 central European refugees in addition to the members of the military forces of its allies who had escaped with its own forces. The threat of an impending German invasion from the continent and the fear of "fifth columnists" among the refugees, understandably resulted in the internment of all. Later, when the defenses against invasion were strengthened, the great majority of the refugees were released.

Balkans.—In the late summer and fall of 1940, Germany in its efforts to bind allies in the Balkan countries more closely to the axis cause did not hesitate to utilize minority groups as pawns in its strategy. In Vienna in Aug. 1940, Hungary was awarded part of the coveted area of Transylvania and approximately 2,500,000 people. The fact that many Rumanians were included in the transfer demonstrated again the difficulties involved in legislating boundaries in order to achieve racial homogeneity in the confused pattern of racial strains in southeastern Europe.

South Dobruja was allotted to Bulgaria, which agreed to repatriate 65,000 Bulgarians from north Dobruja. The transfer to Rumania of Rumanians in south Dobruja was also planned. Slovakia undertook to repatriate Slovaks from the protectorate of Bohemia and Moravia.

Luxembourg and Lorraine.—In the west, Luxembourg and Lorraine were incorporated as provinces into the German reich. Again non-Aryan refugees, members of the government of Luxembourg and political refugees were forced to flee. Some 20,000 of the French population of Lorraine were expelled without warning into France and only vigorous protest by the Vichy government prevented the expulsion of larger numbers from their homes. In Nov. 1940, 10,000 Jewish refugees were driven from Baden and the Palatinate into southern France.

U.S.S.R.—The advance of the German armies into soviet Russia in the summer and fall of 1941 drove before it the greatest migration of a decade in which the history of uprooted populations had exceeded in stark tragedy all previous records of modern history. No authentic figures were available, but conservative estimates placed the numbers driven eastward as between 10,000,000 and 20,000,000. More than 2,000,000 inhabitants of the invaded soviet areas survived the hardships and cruelties of the labour camps in which they were confined during the war in eastern Europe. Similar numbers were estimated to have succumbed under the conditions of work which could only result in exhaustion and death.

German Forced Labour.—Apart from the dispersal and flight of political refugees, the transfers of German minorities in pursuit of concepts of racial purism, the transfer of minority groups as political pawns and the flight of masses of civilians from military action, the most outstanding movement of people during World War II was the draft into Germany of more than 8,500,000 workers from countries occupied by the German armies. One-fifth of these slave labourers were women. In addition, 4,000,000 workers were employed away from their homes and often outside their own countries in industrial or military labour in the occupied countries of Europe. Included in this group were many former Polish and French prisoners of war whose status under the Geneva prisoner of war convention was violated by one device or another.

After the occupation of western Europe efforts were made to enlist such labour voluntarily by inducements of high wages and promises of food rations. French prisoners of war were in the first instance returned from Germany to France and released from custody only to be confronted by various pressures to return to Germany immediately as labourers. As the demands of the German war machine increased, legal and proper methods of recruiting were abandoned for more forceful methods.

The conditions of work of the labourers from the east, chiefly Russians and Poles, were deplorable in the early years of the war. On the other hand, efforts were made by the Germans to provide better conditions of work and wages for workers from the western European countries. Finally as the sources of forced labour were exhausted, food, wages and working conditions were equalized for all in desperate efforts to secure maximum production. This policy continued until toward the end of World War II, when deterioration in German organization and control became evident and conditions in the labour camps degenerated to those prevailing in the concentration camps, where the policy appeared to be to drive the inmates to exhaustion by long hours of heavy work with inadequate provisions for food and shelter.

Included among the 8,500,000 workers drawn into Germany were approximately 2,000,000 Russians, 2,000,000 French, 1,500,000 Poles, 500,000 Belgians, 500,000 Dutch, 600,000 Italians and smaller numbers of Czechs, Balts, Hungarians, Rumanians, Danes and Norwegians.

As the German armies disintegrated in the spring and early summer of 1945 these millions of slave labourers were released by the Allied armies as were also the inmates of the concentration camps. In the early days of liberation they provided a problem for the Allied armies intent upon the final destruction of all German resistance. Food and means of care and transport were lacking. The liberated workers trekked homeward as best they could, living on the land; many were in such advanced stages of malnutrition that even hospital care which was soon organized could not save their lives.

POSTWAR PROBLEMS OF DISPLACED PERSONS

Gradually as the occupying armies stabilized conditions within Germany and Austria, orderly means of repatriation were developed. The displaced persons were removed to their home countries by train, truck and air.

Their eagerness to reach home was matched by the necessity of the Allied armies to repatriate them or to organize supply lines to feed them where they were. It proved more practical to repatriate them quickly than to move food and clothing to them in central Europe. Within six months after the cessation of hostilities in the summer of 1945 between 6,500,000 and 7,000,000 United Nations nationals had been returned to their home countries in Europe.

Repatriation slowed down substantially in the winter months of 1945 and 1946 owing to the lack of heated transportation equipment and inadequate reception facilities in the receiving countries. Efforts to re-establish the flow of repatriation in the spring and summer months of 1946 proved unavailing. By that time it appeared that many among the former workers and concentration camp victims were unwilling to return to their countries of origin because of the political changes which had taken place in those countries during the war. More than 1,000,000 displaced persons, including approximately 600,000 Poles, 75,000 to 100,000 Yugoslavs, 250,000 former Baltic nationals and 50,000 Ukrainians, were unwilling to return. They were maintained in displaced persons assembly centres in Germany, Austria and Italy provided by the occupying military authorities and administered by the personnel of the United Nations Relief and Rehabilitation administration which in 1946 undertook the responsibility for further repatriations.

The Jewish refugees included among the foregoing total constituted a special group. They had suffered particularly at the hands of the nazis and were reluctant to return to home areas where so many of their relatives and coreligionists had perished during the war. At the end of the war it was estimated that no more than 1,250,000 Jews remained out of a prewar population of approximately 5,500,000 in Europe excluding soviet Russia.

The numbers of Jewish refugees in central Europe was slightly under 100,000 at the end of hostilities in 1945. However, these numbers were swollen by postwar infiltrations from Poland, Hungary and Rumania to 200,000 by the end of 1946. More than 90% expressed the desire for emigration to Palestine.

The displacements of German and Austrian nationals in Germany and Austria at the end of the war were substantial. These had resulted from the dispersion of industry during the war, evacuations from bombed areas and the flights of civilians from final military action. One of these general movements was westward from the Baltic countries, Poland and East Prussia to Denmark and southwestward toward Austria and Switzerland. Some 200,000 Germans in this movement remained interned in Denmark because of the overcrowding and lack of housing facilities in Germany until late 1948.

Following the cessation of hostilities, political pressures and hatreds aroused by the war resulted in the expulsion from Poland, Czechoslovakia and Hungary under the Potsdam agreement (1945) of more than 6,000,000 members of the German prewar minorities in those countries. This substantial movement severely strained the limited housing facilities in Germany resulting from the destruction in the final stages of the war. There were similar expulsions of German minorities totalling 250,000 persons into Austria from Yugoslavia and Rumania which were not covered by the Potsdam agreement.

The presence in Germany, Austria and Italy of more than 1,000,000 United Nations refugees and displaced persons who were unwilling to accept repatriation to their home countries was disturbing to the peace and order of central Europe and a cause of political friction between friendly allied governments. The eastern European governments took the position that their nationals should return to their countries.

The position of the western democracies was that the individual should have complete freedom of choice with respect to repatriation. This principle was formally adopted by the general assembly of the United Nations in its resolution of Feb. 12, 1946 on the subject.

International Refugee Organization.—In Dec. 1946 the general assembly of the United Nations adopted the constitution of the International Refugee organization (I.R.O.) which was to take over from U.N.R.R.A., the Intergovernmental Committee on Refugees and the military authorities of the occupying powers in Germany and Austria the task of providing care and maintenance for United Nations refugees and displaced persons and of accomplishing their repatriation or resettlement. The I.R.O. came into formal existence on Aug. 20, 1948. Its constitution made no provision for the disposition of the displaced German minorities in Germany and Austria.

The preparatory commission for I.R.O. assumed the responsibility for the disposition of over 1,000,000 displaced persons in central Europe on July 1, 1947. In the first three years of operation of the preparatory commission and I.R.O. from July 1, 1947, to June 30, 1950, these governments contributed a total of approximately $360,000,000 for the operations of I.R.O. From July 1, 1947, to Jan. 1, 1950, the combined efforts of governments, voluntary organizations and the I.R.O. resulted in the resettlement of 760,000 United Nations refugees from central Europe. The United States accepted approximately 160,000; Israel, 131,000; the United Kingdom, 100,000; Australia, 103,000; Canada, 78,000; France, 41,000; Brazil, 27,000 and Venezuela 14,000. In the same period 68,000 had been repatriated to their countries of origin. During this two and a half year period I.R.O. had maintained more than 900,000 persons in camps for varying periods of time and provided medical care, hospitalization, vocational training, food and clothing.

In anticipation of the termination of I.R.O. services by March 31, 1951 the general assembly of the United Nations in Dec. 1949 adopted a resolution providing for the establishment of an office of high commissioner for refugees to continue the work of protection of refugees to be relinquished by the I.R.O.

Palestine.—The U.N. general assembly in 1948 was concerned with the plight of 750,000 Arab refugees resulting from the conflict in Palestine. These refugees had fled from Palestine into Lebanon, Syria, Iraq, Hashemite Jordan and Egypt and in the fall of 1948 were without means of livelihood or organized assistance.

The general assembly thereupon created the United Nations relief for Palestinian refugees and requested its government members to contribute sufficient funds for relief.

Japan.—Japanese infiltration into other countries of the far east prior to and during World War II was substantial. More than 2,000,000 Japanese were in China at the end of the war, larger numbers in Manchuria, 800,000 in Korea, 500,000 in southeast Asia and 200,000 in Australia and New Guinea. The total of displacement in Japan proper was estimated at 12,000,000 including 2,000,000 Korean labourers and their families. The repatriation of these large numbers of Japanese and Koreans began before the war was over and continued under the direction of the Allied military forces.

These infiltrations and later repatriations had their respective effects on the economies of the areas involved and left serious problems of reconstruction behind which complicated the task of postwar economic and political reorganization.

BIBLIOGRAPHY.—Sir John Hope Simpson, *The Refugee Problem* (1939) and *Refugees, A Review of the Situation since September 1938* (1939), issued under the auspices of the Royal Institute of International Affairs; "Refugees," *The Annals of The American Academy of Political and Social Science* (May 1939); Louise W. Holborn, "The Legal Status of Political Refugees, 1920–1938," *American Journal of International Law* (1938); *Russian, Armenian, Assyrian, Assyro-Chaldean and Turkish Refugees,* Report by the Secretary-General on the Future Organisation of Refugee Work. (A.28, 1930, XIII) (Ref. G.A.C. 15, 1930) (Series of League of Nations Publications 1930, XIII, 2); *Convention Relating to the International Status of Refugees,* Geneva, Oct. 28, 1933 (C.650. M.311, 1933) (Ser. L.o.N.P. Official Journal, page 109); *Nansen International Office for Refugees Report on the Liquidation of the Office,* Geneva, June 14, 1937 (A.11, 1937, XII) (C.226, 1937, XII); *Convention Concerning the Status of Refugees Coming from Germany,* Geneva, Feb. 10, 1938 (C.75.M.30, 1938, XII) (Ser. L.o.N.P. XII, B. International Bureaux 1938, XII, B.1.). Eugene M. Kulischer, *The Displacement of Population in Europe* (1943) and *Europe on the Move* (1948); Jane Perry Clark Carey, "Displaced Populations in Japan at the End of the War," *Department of State Bulletin,* vol. XIII, no. 328 (Oct. 7, 1945); Joseph B. Schechtman, *European Population Transfers 1939–1945* (1946); George L. Warren, "The Office of High Commissioner for Refugees," *Department of State Bulletin,* vol. XXI, no. 546 (Dec. 19, 1949).   (G. L. W.; X.)

REFUSE DISPOSAL, the general term employed in the United States for the collection and disposal of the solid wastes of a community, including garbage, rubbish and ashes. (For British practice *see* DESTRUCTORS.) Garbage may be defined as the waste matter resulting from the preparation, cooking and consumption of food. Rubbish is the miscellaneous material discarded by a community as being no longer of use or value. It includes paper, rags, crockery, glassware, rubber, tin cans, wood, etc. The term ashes, as generally used, refers only to the residue resulting from the operation of heating plants in homes and small business establishments or offices. In the average city (there are wide differences in various cities) of the United States, gar-

bage comprises about 13% by weight and 18% by volume of all refuse; rubbish amounts to only 7% by weight, but to 25% by volume; ashes form approximately 80% by weight and 57% by volume of the total. Garbage weighs from 1,000 to 1,200 lb. per cubic yard, the weight varying with the season, temperature, rainfall and other factors. Of the total weight of garbage, from 60% to 65% is moisture while the combustible matter amounts to 15% or 20%. A pound of dry garbage contains about 8,500 heat units, and 40 to 60 lb. of grease per ton can be extracted from raw garbage. Garbage attracts vermin, is unstable and decomposes quickly, producing nuisance. Rubbish breaks down more slowly and relatively without objection; it has considerable fuel value, the volatile matter ranging from 40% to 70% of the total. Ashes collected from residences and small business establishments also have some fuel value.

Quantity of Waste.—Where the collection service is good, the average daily amount of garbage collected ranges from 0.5 to 1 lb. per person. The amount of garbage appears to be increasing, and data collected from 17 cities where careful and reliable records have been kept showed that in 1936 the average production was more than 274 lb. per person per year, compared to previous figures ranging from 150 to 200 lb. The daily production varies markedly with the season. In the southern states, watermelon rinds form a large part of the garbage during the late summer months. The amount of rubbish collected ranges from 50 to 175 lb. per person per year, averaging about 75 lb. The collections of rubbish remain fairly uniform throughout the year, increasing slightly during the spring and fall months. Ashes, in the northern cities, compose a large part of the refuse collected, but where climatic conditions are milder, the amount may become unimportant. Street sweepings, night soil, manure, dead animals and other wastes vary in amount according to local conditions and local regulations governing their collection. However, the collection and disposal of these wastes are not, in most cities, functions of the general refuse collection organization, but are performed by special departments. Therefore, they will not be considered here. The total amount of refuse collected per person per year ordinarily amounts to 1,200 to 2,000 lb. but because of the many factors influencing collection, the amounts reported by typical cities range from 1,000 to 2,500 lb.

Collection of Wastes.—The collection of waste is generally considered to include both the actual gathering of the garbage, rubbish and ashes, and the subsequent transportation to the points of disposal. The methods of collection vary; in *separate* collection, garbage is collected separately and apart from the other wastes which may or may not be collected together; in *mixed* collection, garbage and rubbish, or sometimes garbage, rubbish and ashes are collected at one time and from a common receptacle. A survey of 84 cities and villages showed that garbage was collected separately in 39, while in 45 it was collected with other material. The trend since 1930 has been toward mixed collection of waste. The practice of separate collection is based upon either utilization of the garbage, as in feeding to swine or reduction, or on cheaper disposal of the less objectionable components of the wastes. In many cities, rubbish and ashes may be dumped or used for filling within the city limits, while garbage disposal must be accomplished at some distant point. In such cases, the saving in hauling and handling costs may be much more than the extra cost occasioned by separate collection. Where garbage is collected separately, it is the usual practice to collect it twice a week in the summer and once or twice a week in the winter; a few cities collect more frequently; many make daily collections in the business sections.

Mixed refuse, because decomposition is slower, is usually collected once or twice a week. Ashes and rubbish are generally collected weekly.

Most of the large cities and about half the smaller ones employ municipal collection, contract collection being used otherwise except in the smallest places.

Satisfactory collection and handling of refuse is impossible without proper receptacles for the storage of waste materials, and most cities have regulations covering the size, material of construction and quality of garbage receptacles. They are usually required to be watertight, of impervious materials and to have a tight cover. The usual capacity is 9 to 15 gallons. Few cities require any special receptacle for rubbish or ashes, but generally provide that the former be tied in bundles, or placed in boxes or barrels; ashes should be placed in non-combustible, covered containers. Receptacles may be placed at the back door, at the alley

BY COURTESY OF THE DECARIE INCINERATOR CORP.

CHARGING FLOOR OF ONE OF NEW YORK CITY'S CENTRAL GARBAGE DUMPS, WHERE GARBAGE, MIXED WITH DRY REFUSE, IS DUMPED DIRECTLY INTO THE FURNACE

line or at the curb line. It costs more to collect from the back door, but it is the usual practice in the United States, only about 30% of the cities requiring that garbage and refuse be placed at the curb, which is aesthetically objectionable.

Collection Equipment.—Motor trucks are used almost exclusively for the collection of wastes, and the sizes of trucks used are increasing. The larger cities have found that 2 to 3-ton trucks are more advantageous and economical when equipped with 8 to 12-yard bodies. In the smaller communities, the light trucks with 3 to 6-yard water level capacity bodies predominate. Increased attention has been given to the development of tight, covered bodies; excellent larger units have been produced, but there is still a need for better equipment for use with small trucks.

Disposal.—Many methods of refuse disposal are in use in the United States, probably due to the differing conditions existing. The methods in use include dumping on land and in water, filling, ploughing under, burial, feeding to hogs, incineration, reduction, sorting and utilization. Garbage from cities is relatively rich in food values. If these values can be reclaimed, the net cost of disposal may be reduced. In addition to the food value of the garbage, the facilities for the cheap and ready disposal of rubbish and

BY COURTESY OF THE CITY OF N.Y DEPT. OF STREET CLEANING

LOADING GARBAGE WHICH CANNOT BE BURNED ON SCOWS TO BE TAKEN 20 MILES OUT IN THE OCEAN AND DUMPED

ashes and the availability of easily accessible sites for incinerators will be factors in the choice of the method to be used.

Disposal of refuse by filling-in low places is common; in the larger cities and in closely built-up metropolitan areas, sites for dumps are increasingly difficult to find, requiring longer hauls, higher hauling costs and dump control costs, and increasing the cost. Garbage cannot be dumped satisfactorily, unless extreme precautions are taken, and disposal in this manner is rare, except in cases of emergency. For satisfactory disposal by dumping, garbage must be treated with a deodorant or disinfectant, spread out

in thin layers, and covered immediately with earth, ashes or other inorganic material. Ashes make good filling material and are used in many cities for making fills. Rubbish is frequently dumped, but because of the time required for the fill to compact, and the miscellaneous material composing rubbish, it is not as generally satisfactory. Dumps are almost certain to catch fire, resulting in objectionable fumes. To obviate this, many cities burn the combustible matter as it comes to the dump. Paper is often collected, baled and sold. Picking over the materials on the dump is quite a general custom and usually affords some slight revenue.

Sorting.—In few cities is there any organized attempt to recover materials of value in refuse, experience having shown that it is not possible to pay the cost of labour and overhead. Milwaukee has attempted salvaging, primarily to conserve dumping space which at the present rate of use will be exhausted in a few years. It has been found that ash volume can be cut in half, and that enough saleable material can be salvaged to pay much of the expense. By weight, refuse consists of 48% fine ash, 38% combustible ash, 6% tin cans and metal, 1% paper and 4% miscellaneous. Combustible ash has been used for heating city buildings.

Burial.—Few cities dispose of their garbage by burial. In case of the breakdown of other methods of disposal, burial is sometimes employed as a temporary measure. The usual practice is to place the garbage in trenches about 3 ft. deep and 3 or 4 ft. wide, the garbage being deposited in layers from 12 to 18 in. deep. Before covering, the garbage should be sprayed liberally with disinfectant

A REFUSE COLLECTION TRUCK IN SERVICE

or crude oil. A cover of 18 to 24 in. of earth appears to give best results. For winter disposal, the trenches must be dug before the ground freezes, and covering can be done in early spring. Sandy, well-drained soil is most suitable, and where conditions are favourable, the land can be reused in 3 to 5 years. Ploughing under of garbage is a little used method. The cover secured is very thin, and men with hoes must follow the plough.

Feeding to Swine.—This is probably the most prevalent method of garbage disposal, especially in the smaller communities. Initial costs are low and there is some return for the food value in the garbage. It is estimated that 50lb. of garbage will produce 1lb. of pork. Based on a live market price of six cents a pound for pork, garbage is therefore worth $2.40 per ton, less the cost of extra haul, labour, and final disposal of the residue resulting from feeding. Recent studies by the U.S. Public Health Service have shown incidence of trichinosis in garbage-fed swine is three to five times as great as in grain-fed swine, and in view of the high human trichina infestation, the influence of public health authorities may adversely affect this method of disposal.

For utilization of the garbage by hog feeding, frequent collection is necessary. In the summer, collections should be made at least three times a week. Careful separation of the garbage is necessary, since its value as a food depends upon the care with which rubbish, glass, crockery, soap and other harmful materials are excluded. It is always difficult to find a suitable situation for a farm, as there is always objection to its establishment in settled areas; as a result an isolated place usually must be chosen, with a resultant long and costly haul. Dry and well-drained sites, preferably with sandy or gravelled soil, and with plenty of water, are almost a necessity. Hogs should be fed on platforms, which should be of impervious materials, and so arranged as to reduce spillage and waste. The refuse remaining from the feeding, which,

BY COURTESY OF THE CITY OF N.Y. DEPT. OF STREET CLEANING

A SWEEPER AT WORK CLEANING THE WILLIAMSBURG BRIDGE OF SNOW

with the droppings from the pigs, amounts to 40 to 50% of the original volume of the garbage, must be removed daily. Disposal of this waste is difficult; composting, burial and incineration have been used in various places with some success. Cooking of the garbage is not desirable, as the hogs are less able to choose the materials most suited to them. Hogs fed on garbage are liable to suffer from cholera, and immunization is necessary to prevent loss.

Incineration.—The complete destruction by fire of all wastes in specially constructed furnaces called incinerators has several advantages. It permits the collection of mixed refuse, thereby

BY COURTESY OF THE DECARIE INCINERATOR CORP.

A SECTION OF A GARBAGE DESTRUCTOR SHOWING DIFFERENT PARTS

reducing the complexity and difficulty of the collection service; incinerators frequently can be situated near the centres of the largest sources of production of waste, thus reducing the length of haul and the cost; the possibility of having several plants placed at suitable locations throughout the city permits still greater reduction in haul and provides insurance against complete interruption of all disposal facilities. Some slight revenue is occasionally available from steam and from clinker, but this is unimportant. In the United States incineration is employed for the disposal of mixed refuse and of garbage alone. The mixed refuse will normally burn

without added fuel, but when garbage is burned, some additional fuel must be supplied. When garbage alone, or very wet refuse is to be burned, a drying hearth is provided upon which the garbage or wet refuse is placed. The flames from the burning material on the grate pass over this material, drying it.

Either natural or forced draft may be employed in operation, but, unless the refuse is unusually heavy and compact, natural draft is sufficient, the air being supplied to the furnace pre-heated to a temperature of about 400° F. The furnace is commonly mechanically charged.

Both high and low temperature incinerators are used, local conditions usually dictating the choice of type. With the high temperature plants in which the interior of the furnace is maintained at 1,600 to 2,000° F, odours are effectively destroyed; low temperature plants operate at 1,250 to 1,400° F, which does not always prevent the emission of odours. The high temperature plant, therefore, is especially suited for use in closely built up sections where discharge of odours cannot be permitted. Low temperature plants do not emit odours at all times, but may do so when the fire is cooled below the safety point. In 1939, there were about 700 municipal incinerator plants in use in the United States.

Disposal of Garbage with Sewage.—If garbage is ground into minute particles, it may be discharged into the sewers and carried to the sewage treatment plant. If domestic grinders are in use, collection is eliminated; if a municipal grinding plant is established, other disposal methods are unnecessary. The added burden of organic matter tends to overload the sewage treatment plant and, under most conditions, enlargement is necessary; and these enlargements may cost more than garbage disposal facilities. Many municipalities do not permit the discharge of ground garbage into the sewers. In 1939, there were about 6,000 household garbage grinders in use in some 235 cities, but the volume contributed by them is too small to affect sewage treatment.

Reduction.—Some of the fats and food values in garbage may be recovered by the reduction process. The products of reduction are grease and tankage. The grease, which is of low grade, is used in making soap, candles and similar products, while tankage forms a base or filler for fertilizer. Reduction is applicable only to garbage and dead animals, and other wastes must be collected and disposed of separately. Because of the costly and complicated equipment required for this process, the necessity for skilled operation, and the large overhead costs, reduction is not commercially feasible for cities having a population less than about 100,000. In 1939, there were 14 reduction plants in the United States.

There are two general processes of reduction, the *drying method* and the *cooking method*. Though the latter process is higher in first cost and operating cost, more grease is recovered and the by-products are in somewhat better condition. The yield of grease ranges from 2 to 3% of the original weight of the garbage, while from 150 to 225 lb. of tankage per ton are produced. The value of the grease varies with the market; tankage value is determined by its content of ammonia, potash and bone phosphate of lime, which carry the same values as in commercial fertilizers. To be saleable, tankage must contain less than 10% of moisture.

Solid and liquid wastes result from reduction processes. The former consist largely of the rubbish sorted from the garbage, and are usually buried or burned. The liquid wastes include floor washings, waste liquors and drainings. They may be discharged into the sewer system or treated in an individual plant. Because of odours, reduction plants must be situated in thinly settled areas. This requirement necessitates long hauls, which increase the cost of disposal. (W. A. Har.)

BIBLE REGAL, A PORTABLE ORGAN WHICH FOLDS UP LIKE A BOOK

REGAL, a small late-mediaeval portable organ, furnished with beating-reeds and having two bellows like a positive organ; also in Germany the name given to the reed-stops (beating-reeds) of a large organ, and more especially the "vox humana" stop. During the 16th and 17th centuries the regal was a very great favourite, and although, because of the civil wars and the ravages of time, few specimens now remain, the instruments are often mentioned in old wills and inventories.

REGALIA: *see* Crown Jewels or Regalia; Coronation.

REGENCE STYLE, in architecture and the decorative arts, a name sometimes given to a style transitional between the classic grandeur of the Louis XIV work and the freely imaginative rococo of the developed Louis XV period; so-called from the fact that from 1715 to 1723 France was under the regency of Philip, duke of Orleans. (*See* Louis Styles.)

REGENERATION. Terminology.—The term regeneration is usually defined as the process by which organisms replace structures or organs which have been lost by accident or mutilation. This definition is not quite adequate because its wording does not cover two phenomena which belong undoubtedly to the category of regeneration phenomena. In some invertebrates, as for instance the fresh-water polyp, *Hydra,* and the flatworm, *Planaria,* and in the starfish, a small fragment of the body can restore a complete, whole organism, rather than a structure or organ. Furthermore, many animals can restore structures which are lost in the normal course of life processes rather than by accident. The periodic moulting of feathers in birds, the shedding of fur in mammals, of the exoskeleton in arthropods or of the epidermal cornified scales in reptiles are followed by a regeneration of the discarded structures. The uppermost cornified skin layers in mammals including man are constantly worn off in small bits and replaced by active, proliferating cell layers in the deeper strata of the skin. The same holds for the continuous replacement of hair, nails and claws. The teeth are replaced only once in mammals including man, but there is a continuous succession of teeth in lower forms, such as the dogfish and shark. The antlers of deer are shed at regular intervals, and then regenerated. The periodic changes in the genital tracts of female mammals, during menstruation and oestrus should also be included here. All these instances in which replacements are part of the normal life functions are called "physiological" or "repetitive" regeneration, in distinction to "restorative" or "reparative" regeneration which follows injury. The present article deals primarily with the latter type.

There are wide differences in the regenerative capacity of different animals. The one extreme is represented by the above-mentioned invertebrates in which a part of the body can restore a whole organism. In higher organisms, as for instance, the salamanders among the vertebrates, and many crustaceans and insects, only single organs, such as limbs can regenerate, and mammals can not restore entire organs, but they can repair damage to tissues, such as bone fractures, skin and muscle injuries and peripheral nerve loss. These phenomena of tissue repair are, of course, included under the general heading, regeneration.

It has long been recognized that regeneration can be accomplished in two ways: by outgrowth of new tissue from the wound surface, or by the transformation and reorganization of the remaining parts, without an outgrowth of new material. In the former case, a regeneration bud, or "blastema," is formed at the wound surface (fig. 4). It is usually cone-shaped and consists of an embryonic type of cells which gradually form the adult structures by processes of cell differentiation and growth, much in the fashion of the embryonic development. The regeneration of limbs and tails in salamanders are examples of this type of regeneration, for which the term "epimorphosis" (T. H. Morgan, 1901) has been coined. The second type of regeneration, the remodelling of old parts, has been called "morphallaxis" (Morgan, 1901). Very small fragments of a fresh-water or marine polyp, or of a planarian, undergo a change in shape instead of growing blastemas; they break down old structures, and build in their place new ones of a smaller proportion. All regeneration processes in protozoans are of this type. Occasionally, both types of regeneration take place simultaneously, and there may be no fundamental difference between them. The term "regeneration" is almost universally adopted as the all-inclusive term, with "epimorphosis" and "morphallaxis" as subheadings. C. M. Child (1941) proposes "reconstitution" as the general term to cover all related phenomena. He uses "regeneration" in a narrow sense, synonymously with epimorphosis as reconstitution by outgrowth, and the term "reorganization" as reconstitution by internal changes.

The aim of regeneration is to maintain or restore the fitness of an organism after the loss of parts. This aim is best accomplished by a replacement of precisely those structures which were lost. However, a number of cases are known in which more than, or less than, the lost part is regenerated, and other cases in which the regenerate is structurally different from the lost part. The term "heteromorphosis" covers all types of atypical regeneration. The term "homoeosis" is used for those atypical regenerations in which the regenerate represents an organ which is different from the original. For instance, in crabs, an amputated eye stalk will, under certain conditions, be replaced by an antenna. Another type of atypical regeneration has been given special attention; namely, those instances in which the polarity of the regenerate is changed. For example, the posterior cut surface of a piece of planarian will, under certain conditions, regenerate a head instead of a tail (see *Polarity; Polar Heteromorphosis*). This type of polarity change is called "polar heteromorphosis."

Theoretical Considerations.—When a regeneration blastema differentiates into the head of a planarian or into the limb of a salamander, the processes which go on in the blastema are fundamentally of the same nature as the embryonic developmental processes which created these organs to begin with. Although the regeneration processes are rarely exact replicas of the corresponding developmental processes, they are alike in some fundamental aspects. Both require a building material of plastic, undifferentiated embryonic-type cells, and a set of specific organizing factors which direct and control the moulding and differentiation of such building materials. In this sense, regeneration can be defined as the revival, or reactivation, of developmental potencies in organisms which have passed the embryonic stages of development.

If one adopts this point of view, then the close affinity of regeneration processes with asexual reproduction becomes evident. In fact, in some instances it is difficult to draw the line between the two. For instance most protozoans reproduce asexually, by fission. The daughter individuals restore by regeneration those structures which they do not contain at the start of the fission. If a protozoan is cut in two by a fine instrument, the result is the same—each half regenerates the missing structures. In this instance, fission and regeneration differ primarily in the factors which set these processes in motion. Similarly, some flatworms and annelids (segmented worms) which possess high regenerative powers reproduce regularly by transverse fission or by a budding process at their posterior ends. Their regenerative potencies are, so to speak, placed in the service of reproduction. Budding is another mode of asexual reproduction particularly common among colonial forms. It is practised by coelenterates and tunicates among animals and by plants. A bud is an outgrowth on an adult organism which is an expression of the revival of growth potentialities at a localized area of the body. The parallel to regeneration is obvious. In many marine coelenterates one can readily produce a lateral regeneration bud by making a cut in the body wall (laceration). Again, the main difference between regeneration and spontaneous budding lies in the initiating stimuli.

If we consider the ability for regeneration as a residual developmental capacity which a number of organisms retain throughout adult life, we imply that regeneration is the manifestation of a universal and basic property of all organisms; namely, the capacity for growth and development. This point of view which is generally adopted did not always prevail. It was seriously contested during the second half of the 19th century. Under the impact of the theory of natural selection, another theory of regeneration was strongly advocated by August Weismann and others. This theory emphasized the usefulness and adaptive value of regeneration; it stressed the point that regeneration was apparently limited to those organs and structures which are particularly in danger of being injured or mutilated by enemy attacks. Hence, it was assumed that regeneration is not part of a basic equipment of all organisms, but is acquired secondarily as a special adaptation wherever the ability to regenerate was of crucial survival value in the struggle for existence. It was held that the all-powerful natural selection was instrumental in creating and improving the regenerative capacity. A just objection has been raised against this theory, namely, that in many instances inner organs regenerate which are not liable to injuries, as for instance, the crystalline lens of the amphibian eye, or the liver. Furthermore, we are now aware that natural selection can not create a property like regeneration, but can, at best, only improve an existing regenerative power by selecting consistently those hereditary variants which possess high regenerative capacity. For these and other reasons, Weismann's theory in its extreme form is untenable. However, its valid element, namely, the emphasis of natural selection as a mechanism for increasing preexisting limited regenerative capacity, can be readily incorporated in the residual growth theory of regeneration.

In the following section it will be shown that, generally speaking, lower organisms have a better regenerative power than higher organisms, but that the regenerative capacity is distributed sporadically among animals and that in many instances closely related forms differ widely in their regenerative capacity. A theory of regeneration has to explain this scattered distribution of regeneration. Natural selection can not account for it, because there is apparently no close correlation between liability to injury and the regenerative power. The residual growth theory, which assumes that regeneration is a manifestation of a universal property of all organisms, has to account for the fact that this potentiality is lost in a great many forms. Two prerequisites must be fulfilled if a successful regeneration is to occur; there must be available the necessary building material in the form of embryonic-like cells, capable of growth and differentiation, and the necessary organizing factors must be present which direct the development of these cells. Regeneration may be prevented by the loss of either one or of both. The necessary building material may be lost in the normal course of development, during which embryonic cells undergo a differentiation into highly specialized tissues. This differentiation is undoubtedly irreversible in most instances, and the transformation of all cell materials into an irrevocably differentiated form is probably one reason for the lack of regeneration in highly organized animals. Some authors maintain that in some instances a differentiated tissue can dedifferentiate and rejuvenate under certain conditions, and thus become available as a source of regeneration material. Furthermore, in a number of invertebrates and lower chordates, certain embryonic cells remain in an undifferentiated embryonic condition and form a reservoir for regeneration and asexual reproduction (see below). It is obvious that regeneration is impossible in all those organisms which possess neither reserve cells nor tissues capable of de- and redifferentiation. The organizing or "field" factors for regeneration will be discussed below. Their loss, in the course of embryonic development, may be an alternative cause for a lack of regenerative power. Finally, an amputation stump may be potentially capable of regenerating but be prevented from doing so either by a deficiency in one of the many subsidiary agents necessary for regenerative growth, such as hormones or nerve-produced agents, or by a block from a rapidly overgrowing skin or wound scar which would prevent the outgrowth of the blastema cells. In the latter instances an appropriate treatment of the stump may call forth a regeneration where it would not occur under ordinary conditions.

DESCRIPTION
REGENERATION IN DIFFERENT ANIMAL GROUPS

The following survey is by no means complete. Only such cases were selected in which regeneration was observed in the laboratory, since the evidence from incidental findings of regeneration in animals which were caught in the field is often ambiguous and inconclusive.

Protozoa (see review by W. Balamuth, 1940).—Most Protozoa reproduce asexually by longitudinal or transverse fission, or by other modes of division. Fission requires a reorganization

and new formation of structures in the daughter individuals, and this process can be considered as a physiological regeneration. The power to rebuild structures is therefore inherent in all protozoans, and it is not surprising to find that most Protozoa can regenerate parts which were lost by accident or removed in an experiment. In all instances, the presence of nuclear material is a necessary prerequisite for successful regeneration. In ciliates which possess a macro- and a micronucleus, the former is essential; the latter is not. In forms, like *Stentor*, in which the macronucleus is represented by a beadlike chain, small segments of the chain are sufficient to enable a fragment to regenerate. In *Amoeba*, which is the most primitive protozoan in that it has no highly specialized organelles, a nonnucleate fragment can grow and survive up to 30 days, but it can not divide. The most highly differentiated Protozoa, the ciliates, have been the subject of extensive studies on regeneration; *Paramecium* and *Stentor* are the favourite materials. Their regenerative power is excellent. Fragments as small as 1/64 of an individual can form a complete new organism. The new organelles are formed, either by a remodelling of the remnants of the old ones, or by breakdown of the latter and rebuilding of entirely new structures. In parasitic Protozoa the regeneration capacity seems to be poor or entirely missing.

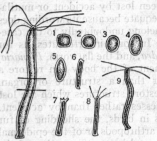

FROM KORSCHELT, AFTER MORGAN

FIG. 1.—REGENERATION IN THE FRESH-WATER POLYP, HYDRA. THE SHORT PIECE BETWEEN THE TWO LINES (AT LEFT) REGENERATES INTO A NEW POLYP. 1 TO 9 ARE STAGES IN THE REGENERATION PROCESS

Porifera (Sponges).—The regeneration of amputated parts in Porifera does not seem to be very extensive. However, a series of interesting experiments has revealed a remarkable capacity of the sponge cells to reorganize themselves into a whole organism, following a complete breakup of their organization. Sponges were strained through bolting-silk and thus completely dissociated. Following this treatment, small cell groups reunited into larger aggregates which reorganized themselves and formed eventually a typical sponge.

Coelenterata.—They occur in the forms of polyps and medusae (jellyfish). The well-known fresh-water form *Hydra* takes its name from the Greek mythological nine-headed monster which was believed to regenerate two heads in the place of each amputated head. The regenerative power of our native *Hydra* is at least as startling as that of its namesake. It was in this form that the Swiss naturalist Abraham Trembley made the first planned regeneration experiments (1744), which aroused a tremendous interest and were soon followed by those of R. A. F. de Réaumur, Lazaro Spallanzani and others. Small fragments of the body can regenerate a whole individual (see fig. 1). One tentacle with a small portion of the hypostome is capable of forming a new individual. The regenerative power of other hydroids differs in different species. *Tubularia* and other marine forms have been widely used for experiments on the physiology of regeneration (see below).

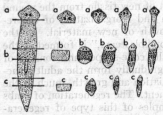

FROM KORSCHELT, AFTER MORGAN

FIG. 2.—REGENERATION IN THE FLATWORM, PLANARIA. THE THREE ROWS SHOW THE REGENERATION OF THREE SHORT PIECES, a, b, c, OF THE ANIMAL AT THE LEFT

The regenerative capacity of the medusae (jellyfish) is much restricted. The Anthozoa (sea anemones and corals) have a considerable regenerative capacity.

Platyhelminthes (Flatworms).—This phylum includes the planarians, which have an exceedingly high regenerative capacity, and which have therefore been used more than any other form for regeneration experiments. A planarian may be cut in any direction by one or more transverse, longitudinal or oblique sections, and each fragment will regenerate a whole, though smaller, individual (*see* fig. 2). Planarians possess complex structures such as eyes, brain and pharynx. Any or all of these can be rebuilt from a fragment not containing them. It is of interest to note that of three closely related groups which are mainly distinguished by differences in the shape of the intestine (Rhabdocoela, Triclads, polyclads), only the triclads to which planarians belong have a high regenerative power, and even within this group there are great differences with respect to the ability to regenerate.

The entirely parasitic Trematoda (flukes) and Cestoda (tapeworms) have not been thoroughly investigated. They seem to lack regenerative power.

Annelida.—Regeneration in the common earthworm is well known. It can regenerate many segments at the posterior part of the body, but the regeneration of the anterior part is limited. Up to five segments can be completely restored; but, if more are removed, less than the normal number are rebuilt; no regeneration takes place if 15 or more anterior segments are amputated. Some relatives of the earthworm can do better. For instance, the fresh-water worm *Criodrilus* regenerates as many as 25 anterior segments. In another fresh-water form, *Nais*, two isolated segments can regenerate a whole worm. One of the remarkable features in these annelid regenerations is the formation of gonads in the regenerated segments, although the stumps which give rise to the regenerates may not contain a trace of gonad material. The regenerative power of the more highly specialized marine polychaetes is, in general, lower than that of the earthworm and its relatives (oligochaetes). It is very low in the Hirudinea (leeches).

Echinodermata.—The arms of Asteroidea (starfish) and Ophiuridea (brittle star) can regenerate a whole individual in some instances, even if the amputated arm contains no trace of the central disc. Occasionally, one finds on the seashore an odd-looking starfish with one or two normal-sized and several very short arms (*see* fig. 3). The latter are in the process of regeneration. Echinids (sea urchins) can repair damage in the skeleton and restore tube feet and spines.

It is of interest to note that, according to several experimenters, the sea urchin and starfish larvae (pluteus) have little regenerative power.

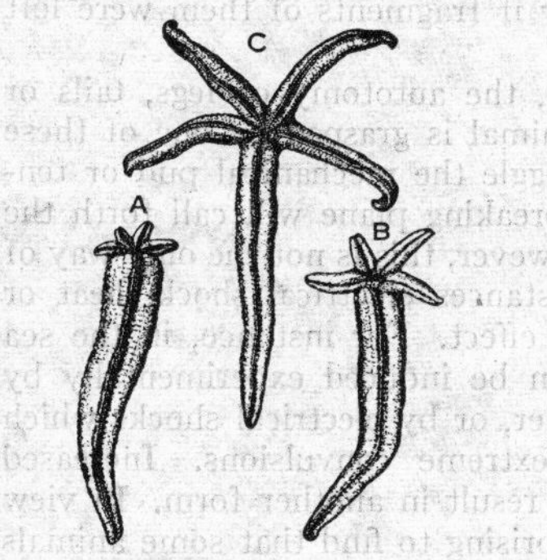

Mollusca.—Those Gastropoda (snails) and Lamellibranchia (clams and relatives) which are protected by a shell can replace parts of the latter. Damage can be repaired at the margin, at which the shell is formed, and also in central parts. The mantle and the foot can likewise regenerate. Some snails have highly complex eyes at the tips of tentacles. The amputation of a tentacle at its base results in its regeneration, including the eye. However, the entire head of a snail can not be regenerated. Cephalopoda (squid, octopus and cuttlefish) can regenerate amputated arms.

FROM KORSCHELT
FIG. 3.—REGENERATION IN THE STARFISH. ONE ARM REGENERATES A WHOLE STARFISH

Arthropoda.—The body of an arthropod has many appendages such as legs, wings, antennae, stalked eyes, mandibles and tail appendages. They are all readily exposed to accidental damage, and most of them can be regenerated when lost. This holds particularly for the best-known and most thoroughly investigated groups, the Crustacea (crayfish, crab, lobster, etc.) and the Insecta. All arthropods moult periodically, that is, they shed their chitinous exoskeleton. Its replacement may well be considered as a type of physiological regeneration. The regeneration of lost parts is, by and large, limited to those phases of their lives in which moulting occurs. For instance, insects with very few exceptions, do not moult after metamorphosis. Their regenerative power is high during larval and pupal stages but greatly reduced in the adult. The regeneration of structures like wings or legs of adult insects is either limited and incomplete or, in other

forms, entirely impossible. On the other hand crustaceans continue to moult throughout adult stages, and they are capable of regenerating organs which are as complex as are some types of legs or eyes. Some inner organs can be regenerated in insects, as, for instance, parts of the intestine and of the gonads.

Tunicata (Sea squirts, etc.).—A high regenerative power is found in the sedentary ascidians. A small part of the body can regenerate a whole individual.

Vertebrata.—In the Teleostei (bony fishes) the regenerative capacity is limited. They can regenerate the tail fins and the other paired and unpaired fins. A few other structures are known to be capable of regeneration, such as the operculum (gill cover), parts of the gills and of the lower jaw.

Amphibia.—The tailed Amphibia, or Urodela (salamanders and newts), have by far the most extensive regenerative potency of all vertebrates and have, therefore, been the favourite material for experiments on vertebrate regeneration. In particular, the limb regeneration of salamanders has been analyzed in many respects, ever since it was discovered by Spallanzani in 1768 (*see* below). Any part of a foot or hindlimb can be regenerated; one of the remarkable features is the precision with which the missing part is restored. If the foot is amputated (*see* fig. 4, level *b*), only this part is replaced; if the leg is removed at its base (*see* fig. 4, level *a*), it will be replaced in its entirety.

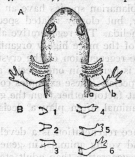

(A) FROM HAMBURGER, "MANUAL OF EXPERIMENTAL EMBRYOLOGY" (UNIVERSITY OF CHICAGO PRESS); (B, 1-6) BY COURTESY OF VIKTOR HAMBURGER

FIG. 4.—A, ARM REGENERATION IN A SALAMANDER. B, 1-6 ARE REGENERATION STAGES, FOLLOWING AMPUTATION AT *a*: BLASTEMA AT 1 AND 2

How is limb regeneration accomplished in a salamander? (*See* fig. 4.) The wound heals within 12 hours. During the first three days, the tissues near the wound surface, particularly the skeleton and musculature, undergo histolysis and dedifferentiate into mesenchymelike cell types. Beginning with the fourth day, a blastema is formed which is composed of densely packed cells of embryonic appearance. The blastema grows out into a cone, and by the 12th day the toes appear at its tip. With further lengthening, the different parts of the limb become outlined. Meanwhile, the blastema cells differentiate into skeleton, musculature and other tissues. Apart from the first, regressive phase, the process resembles closely the original process of embryonic limb formation.

Other organs can regenerate equally well, for instance, the tail, parts of the snout and eyes and parts of inner organs such as lungs and gonads. The regenerative capacity of salamander larvae and of young specimens exceeds even that of full-sized specimens. In the tailless Amphibia, the Anura (frogs, toads), the regenerative capacity is limited to larval stages, the tadpoles. They can readily regenerate a tail which is clipped at the tip or even near the base. The hindleg regeneration proceeds rapidly and efficiently in young tadpoles, but this capacity subsides when the larva approaches metamorphosis. Adult frogs do not regenerate limbs, contrary to a common belief. Usually, the stumps heal without regenerating. Recently, it has been found that if the arm of an adult frog is amputated and the wound surface is bathed repeatedly in a saturated sodium chloride solution, the stump will proceed to form a regenerate. However, the regenerated arm is never complete and normal. It is assumed that in untreated adult frogs the thick skin closes up rapidly over the wound surface and suppresses regeneration.

Reptilia.—Vertebrates higher than Amphibia have greatly reduced regenerative potentialities. The tail of a lizard is the only highly specialized structure in reptilians which can regenerate. The animal makes occasional use of this capacity. When captured by its tail, it shakes the tail off and leaves the foe behind with its token booty. Lizards with regenerated tails are occasionally encountered in the field. However, tail regenerates are never complete; their inner structures are atypical. Amputated limbs of lizards do not regenerate.

Aves (Birds).—The regeneration of fragments of beaks has been reported for several birds. The periodic renewal of the plumage after each moult is a type of physiological regeneration, and the growth of a feather from a feather germ resembles other regenerative processes.

Mammalia.—These present numerous instances of physiological regeneration, but very little, if any, evidence for the regeneration of complex structures. The change of hair, of teeth and of red blood cells and the regeneration of antlers in deer illustrate physiological regeneration. Reparative regeneration, following an amputation, is limited to tissues, such as bone, muscle, skin or peripheral nerves. Whole organs can not be regenerated.

What general concepts can be derived from this survey? In the first place, it brings into proper relief a point which has been emphasized by students of regeneration since the early days, that there is a correlation between regeneration potentiality and level of organization; *i.e.*, lower organisms have a high regenerative power and the latter decreases with increase in complexity. Mammals, including man, pay for their high organization with an almost complete loss of regenerative capacity. The relation between regenerative power and level of organization, however, holds only in a general way and breaks down in numerous special instances. For example, some planarian species have an exceptionally high regenerative power, but closely related species have none. The same holds for Annelida. The regenerative ability of the fishes is lower than that of the more highly organized tailed amphibians, the Urodela. The regeneration of the crystalline lens of the eye of salamanders is perfect in one species and entirely absent in a closely related species. These examples could be easily multiplied. They show that factors other than the general level of organization of the animal often play a decisive role.

It has also been asserted that since regeneration is a developmental process, embryos, larvae and young animals, in general, should be more readily capable of regeneration than adult stages of the same animal. This expectation is fulfilled in many instances, but again it is not a rigid rule. It is true that salamander larvae regenerate limbs and tails more rapidly and more perfectly than adults do, and lens regeneration in some salamander species is limited to larvae. Frog tadpoles can regenerate a hindlimb, but an adult frog can not. On the other hand, we have mentioned the seemingly paradoxical instance of the sea urchin and starfish larvae which do not regenerate, in contrast to the adults. The same holds for annelids and for tunicates. Again, factors other than age determine the limitation of regenerative power in these forms. Finally, one would expect that external organs and appendages which are readily exposed to injury and loss would show a higher regenerative capacity than inner organs. This, again, holds in a general way. However, several examples have been mentioned of the regeneration of inner organs which are rarely subject to injury during the normal course of life.

AUTOTOMY

A number of animals, when attacked and apprehended by a leg or tail, save their lives by casting off this appendage. The organ which is sacrificed can usually be restored by regeneration. This act of self-amputation is called autotomy. We find instances of autotomy in a number of different animal groups, such as Coelenterata, Mollusca, Echinodermata, Annelida, Arthropoda and others, although this means of escape is used only by a few representatives of these phyla and by no means by all of them. The only case of autotomy in vertebrates, and perhaps the best known of all, is that of the autotomy of the tail in lizards. Anybody who has tried to catch a lizard by its tail has had the experience of finding himself left with a wiggling tail while the animal escaped; and one occasionally finds lizards in nature which show unmistakable signs of a regenerated tail. The facility with which the tail breaks off is astounding. This is because of a special structural adaptation. A breaking plane is prepared at the base of the tail along which it is severed when grasped. Several vertebrae are split across their middle. The halves are held together by cartilage which ruptures readily. The regeneration usually begins at the breaking plane. The regenerated tail is not quite typical. It contains no vertebrae but merely a cartilaginous skeletal axis. The muscle and nerve distribution is likewise atypical. Nevertheless, such a regenerated tail can regenerate a second time.

Many Crustacea (crabs), insects and spiders have a similar device to facilitate autotomy, namely, a preformed breaking plane at the base of legs or antennae. The chitinous exoskeleton is soft and thin at certain levels, and the muscle arrangement expedites self-amputation. It is not always the same segment of the leg at which such a breaking place is prepared, but the mechanism is apparently similar in all species. In the walking stick, all three pairs of legs are adapted for autotomy. Quite frequently, special care is taken to avoid an excessive loss of blood: the skin contracts over the wound and closes it off. A few other instances of autotomy may be mentioned: some actinians (sea anemones) let go of a tentacle when it is strongly stimulated; starfishes cast off an arm voluntarily and some annelids (segmented worms) can autotomize the hindmost body segments, and regenerate them subsequently.

One of the most startling instances of autotomy is the self-evisceration in holothurians (sea cucumbers). They belong to the Echinodermata and have the appearance of a cucumber-shaped, leathery bag. When strongly stimulated, they cast off their anterior ends, including tentacles, lantern and the water-vascular system and, at the same time, eviscerate through the anus the intestine and attached structures, such as gonads. The discarding of the inner organs is accomplished by strong muscle contraction. The nearly empty hull composed of skin and muscles is capable of regenerating the autotomized organs. *Thione,* which is found at the Atlantic seashore, can accomplish this feat within a month. The formation of the new intestine starts at the remnants of the mesenteries (linings of the body cavities) which were left behind. The body wall is instrumental in rebuilding the anterior organs. The gonads can be replaced only if fragments of them were left behind in the bag.

Under ordinary circumstances, the autotomy of legs, tails or antennae will occur when the animal is grasped by one of these appendages. In the ensuing struggle the mechanical pull or tension exerted on the preformed breaking plane will call forth the separation of the appendage. However, this is not the only way of eliciting autotomy. In many instances electrical shock, heat or chemical stimuli have the same effect. For instance, in the sea cucumber, *Thione,* autotomy can be induced experimentally by placing it in dilute ammonia water, or by electrical shocks which throw the body muscles into extreme convulsions. Increased water temperature has the same result in another form. In view of this observation, it is not surprising to find that some animals cast off a structure, seemingly spontaneously, but actually in response to adverse environmental conditions. For instance, some coelenterates autotomize a polyp head, and some holothurians eviscerate, when the water in which they live deteriorates.

There is only one step from this type of "spontaneous" autotomy to spontaneous fission for the purpose of asexual reproduction. For instance, certain starfishes and certain sea cucumbers break apart at more or less regular time intervals and the fragments regenerate a whole individual. Likewise, in certain annelids and flatworms, posterior parts of the body are constricted off and the fragments regenerate into new individuals. This performance has been established as a regular mode of reproduction. The close affinity of regeneration and reproduction in lower animals is thus again affirmed.

HETEROMORPHOSIS

A regenerate is ordinarily a replica of the original structure; but a number of cases are known in which regeneration is atypical in that either less or more than was lost is regenerated. Occasionally, the regenerate represents an organ entirely different from the one which it replaces. All forms of atypical regeneration are called heteromorphosis. The last mentioned category of heteromorphic regenerations is called homoeosis (William Bateson):

(1) *Incomplete regeneration* is frequent both in naturally occurring and in experimentally induced regeneration. Regenerated tails of lizards invariably show certain structural deficiencies, such as the absence of normal vertebrae. Regenerated salamander limbs frequently have a reduced number of digits or even greater deficiencies. Those of arthropods may have a reduced number of segments. Several species of annelids can regenerate only a limited number of head segments. If more are amputated, the total segment number of the worm after completed regeneration will be subnormal. Planarians occasionally regenerate a head with two fused eyes, or only one eye, or eyeless heads, instead of the normal head with two separate eyes. Such atypical head regenerates can be produced experimentally by exposing the regenerating animals to any one of a number of chemical agents which are known to impair developmental processes in a general, non-specific way.

(2) Among the *super-regenerations*, those of greatest interest are ones in which a single organ is replaced by a duplicated or multiple formation. Instances of such monstrosities have been observed in practically all regenerating animal forms, as, for instance, in hydranths of *Hydra* and of its marine relatives, in heads and tails of planarians and annelids, in tails of lizards and limbs or digits of amphibians and particularly frequently in appendages of arthropods. Double claws of crabs or lobsters, double legs and antennae of beetles and of other insects have been described. Starfishes with bifurcated arms and holothurians with duplicated body parts have also been observed. Triplicate appendages are most frequent in arthropods and occasionally found in other forms. They originate probably in most instances in the following way: a leg, or a claw or an antenna ruptures at a joint without breaking off completely. As a result, two wound surfaces are exposed, each of which begins to regenerate the distal parts. The two new formations, together with the persisting original structure, form the triple monstrosity. It was found that such triplicate structures follow a definite rule of symmetry relations (Bateson's rule): two adjacent components, namely, the middle one and one of the marginal components, are mirror images of each other, whereas the two marginal parts have the same symmetry pattern.

It is often difficult or impossible to decide whether double or triple monstrosities found in nature have been brought about by regeneration, or whether the duplication has already occurred in early embryonic development. Therefore, experimental methods were devised which permit us to study the origin of duplications by regeneration under controlled conditions. An expedient way of accomplishing this is to create a wound surface which will produce two separate blastemas instead of one. For instance, if the tail of a tadpole is amputated by two oblique cuts, in the form of an arrowhead (instead of making one transverse cut), then two blastemas and tails will grow out, each with its main axis perpendicular to the oblique, cut surface (Barfurth's rule). Multiple digits in salamander legs were produced in the same fashion, by making two oblique transections. Two-headed planarians (*see* fig. 5) can be obtained by making a longitudinal fission in the median plane through the anterior part of the animal, and a subsequent amputation of the two halves of the head. Each separate anterior body half then regenerates the missing lateral parts and in addition, a whole head at the anterior surface. By repeating this procedure, animals with multiple heads (up to ten) were obtained. In the same way, planarians with double tails can be produced experimentally.

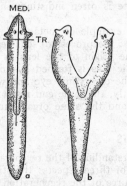

FROM HAMBURGER, "MANUAL OF EXPERIMENTAL EMBRYOLOGY" (UNIVERSITY OF CHICAGO PRESS)

FIG. 5.—REGENERATION OF A DOUBLE HEAD IN PLANARIA. THE ANIMAL IS SPLIT ALONG LINES MED. AND TR. REGENERATED TISSUE IS UNSTIPPLED

(3) *Homoeosis.* This category of atypical regenerations includes all those instances in which the regenerate represents a structure different in type from the original. Homoeosis occurs mainly in arthropods. It is a characteristic of this phylum that most of the numerous body segments bear appendages which are of different types in different body regions (*e.g.*, antennae, mandibles, claws, thoracic legs, abdominal appendages). In homoeosis, the appendage of one type substitutes for another type. A few examples may serve as illustrations: in crustaceans (crayfish, lobster, crab), a thoracic leg with claws was regenerated in place of a maxilliped; in other cases an abdominal leg was found in place of a thoracic leg. A leg may be regenerated in place of an antenna or of a mandible, and vice versa. An anterior wing of a butterfly or moth may replace a posterior wing. Of particular interest is the regeneration of an antenna in place of a stalked eye, which was observed in the marine decapod crustaceans of the genus *Palinurus, Palaemon* and in others (fig. 6). This case was analyzed experimentally by Curt Herbst (University of Heidelberg). He discovered that if the optic ganglion which is located at the base of the eye stalk is removed along with the eye, an antenna grows out, but if the optic ganglion is left intact and the eye alone is amputated, a normal eye stalk and eye regenerate. The ganglion, then, determines the quality of the regenerate.

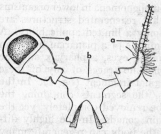

FROM MORGAN, "REGENERATION" (COLUMBIA UNIVERSITY PRESS)

FIG. 6.—HOMOEOSIS IN THE SHRIMP, PALAEMON. THE EYE (e) WITH ITS STALK WAS AMPUTATED AT THE RIGHT SIDE. AN ANTENNA (a) REGENERATED IN ITS PLACE. b= BRAIN

ORIGIN OF THE REGENERATION MATERIAL

Students of the process of regeneration have been chiefly concerned with two problems: the source of the material out of which the regenerates are formed, and the factors which determine the formation of typical organs and structures out of the raw material.

Early investigators were of the opinion that each tissue in the regenerate was formed by tissue outgrowth. For instance, in the regeneration of a salamander limb, the skeleton exposed at the amputation surface would regenerate skeleton, the muscle of the stump would give rise to new muscle. In other words, each tissue would be formed by tissue of its own kind. This idea was based on the assumption that differentiated tissues of the adult organism are highly specific and, therefore, not capable of transformation into other types of tissue; and, furthermore, that no other sources of regeneration material were available. Later investigations have led to a considerable modification of this point of view. Although some regenerated structures undoubtedly originate from their own kind, there is also some evidence to show that old tissue of the regeneration stump can dedifferentiate into embryonic cell types and then redifferentiate into a structure different from what it had been before. This transformation is called "metaplasy." Furthermore, a third source of regeneration material has been discovered; in several animal groups certain types of reserve cells were found which are stored in different parts of the body and mobilized when the need for regeneration arises. We have, then, three modes of origin for regeneration material, and it is, of course, possible that several of them are combined in the same regeneration process. In many instances, it is difficult to distinguish between them, and our information concerning this entire problem is not far advanced.

Tissue Outgrowth.—The best example of the origin of a regenerating structure from its own kind is the nerve regeneration in vertebrates (*see* below, *Nerve Regeneration*). The nerves of a regenerated salamander limb or tail invariably originate by outgrowth of nerve fibres from the cut nerves of the amputation surface. The same holds for nerve regeneration following transection in higher vertebrates and in man. Also, the skin which closes over the amputation wound in salamanders and in many invertebrates is derived from the old skin of the stump, and it is retained as the covering of the outgrowing regenerate. The regeneration of bone, muscle, liver and other tissue in higher vertebrates and in man is likewise accomplished by remnants of their own kind. Salamanders have the remarkable capacity to regenerate an eye but are able to do so only if a fraction of the original eye tissue is left behind. These examples could easily be multiplied. Yet a glance at some of the regeneration phenomena in lower organisms convinces us that the principle that regenerated structures are derived from their own kind has only a limited applicability. A narrow transverse piece from the middle of a planarian body can regenerate a new individual, including eyes, a pharynx and the complex copulatory organs, although no traces of any of these structures were present in the original fragment (fig. 2). In the earthworm and in other annelids, the segments containing the gonads and other sex organs can be removed completely, yet the newly regenerated segments contain gonads. In the highly differentiated tunicates, any part of the body can regenerate many structures which it does not itself contain. Although these examples demonstrate beyond doubt that in lower organisms an organ or a structure can be formed anew, one would hesitate to attribute to vertebrates a similar versatility unless one were offered a crucial experimental proof. Such evidence has been provided for the skeleton regeneration of the salamander limb. At first, a long bone was carefully removed, as for instance the humerus, but the other tissues were left intact. After the wound had healed, the limb which merely lacked a humerus was amputated by a transverse cut in the upper arm. Although the amputation stump contained no bone, regeneration proceeded normally, and the regenerated distal part contained the normal skeletal elements. They originated by differentiation from the blastema, without direct contact with the old bone. A similar proof was given for the origin of the deep layer of the skin, the so-called dermis.

Reserve Cells.—Many invertebrates solve the problem of the formation of organs *de novo* with the help of "reserve cells" or "regeneration cells." These are cell types which have retained the characteristics and potentialities of embryonic cells; that is, they have not undergone a differentiation into specialized tissues. In hydra, and related coelenterates, the interstitial cells, a type of mesenchyme cells, are scattered throughout the body, except for the tentacles. According to many investigators, these cells assemble at a cut surface and become the chief, or exclusive, source of regeneration material. In a number of annelids, a type of particularly large cell has been found in different regions of the body. They are called "neoblasts" and play the same role as the interstitial cells of *Hydra*. They migrate toward the cut surface and there undergo a differentiation into different structures. They are apparently concerned with the new formation of muscles, of the pharynx, of blood vessels and of the walls and septa of the body cavities of regenerating segments, whereas the nervous system and some other structures originate by proliferation of the epidermis, and the new intestine is formed by outgrowth from the old intestine. Here we have an instance of a double source of regenerative material, from reserve cells and from old structures of the amputation surface. The exact share of both is still disputed. The Turbellaria (flatworms) contain similar formative or regeneration cells in the mesodermal parenchyma of the body. They belong in the same category with the interstitial cells and neoblasts. It was found that planarians with a high regenerative capacity contain more of these cells than do related species which have little regenerative power. Similar cell types have been described in Porifera (sponges) and Tunicates.

It is difficult to determine the origin of these reserve cells, and their share in regeneration, on the basis of microscopic studies alone. Despite much effort of a large number of careful investigators, many issues remain controversial. In this situation, the presentation of new evidence obtained by an entirely different technique was of great value. It was found that regeneration can be suppressed in both invertebrates and vertebrates, by radiation with X-rays, radium or other rays. A careful examination of the X-rayed tissues in hydra, flatworms and annelids showed that the

reserve cells or neoblasts are particularly sensitive to radiation and killed by a dosage which does not interfere seriously with the life processes of the animal as a whole. In this way it is possible to eliminate the reserve cells selectively without killing the animal. A close correlation was found between the loss of reserve cells and the loss of regenerative power; different dosages of irradiation resulted in a proportional reduction of reserve cells, and also a proportional reduction in regenerative capacity. These experiments seem to establish firmly the role of reserve cells in the regeneration of these forms.

Metaplasy.—The regeneration blastemas of amphibians which form limbs, tails or other regenerates are composed of undifferentiated cells which are densely packed and which give rise to most structures of the regenerate. Irradiation experiments have shown that in amphibians, in contrast to the above-mentioned invertebrates, the blastema cells are of local origin and do not migrate from other parts of the body. Careful histological studies have given satisfactory evidence that muscle and skeletal cells near the amputation surface can dedifferentiate and assume the appearance of undifferentiated, embryonic cells; and there is but little doubt that these cells contribute to the blastema material. It would be of a great general interest to know whether such cells redifferentiate into the same type of tissue from which they originated, or whether a true metaplasy of one type of tissue into a different one is possible. Another question remains to be solved: whether these dedifferentiated cells are the only source of material for the blastema. Connective tissue cells which are undifferentiated and resemble embryonic mesenchyme undoubtedly exist in adult amphibian organs. They may well have properties similar to the reserve cells of lower animals. It is possible that they are likewise mobilized for the formation of the blastema, and that the latter is, therefore, of a double origin.

A clear case of metaplasy occurs in the regeneration of the crystalline lens of salamander eyes. It is possible to remove the lens carefully with fine instruments without injuring the eye to any extent. If this is done, lens regeneration sets in at the upper margin of the iris. The iris is the pigmented part of the eye bordering on the pupil and adjacent to the lens. The first change which is observed in the iris following lens extirpation is the loss of pigment, that is, a process of dedifferentiation. Next, the two tissue layers which form the iris split, separate and expand at the rim to form a vesicle. This vesicle grows toward the pupil which it eventually fills. It differentiates into the transparent fibrous structure, characteristic of the lens, and becomes eventually detached from the iris. The regenerate is often indistinguishable from a normal lens.

Apart from its importance as an example of metaplasy, this case is of interest in another respect: the process of lens regeneration is entirely different from the origin of the lens in embryonic development. The embryonic lens is formed by an infolding of the epidermis overlying the embryonic eye and without participation of the iris. Evidently, the same end result can be achieved in two different ways, and the same organ can be derived from two different sources.

ANALYSIS

The Initial Stimulus.—An understanding of the regeneration process is based on a consideration of three aspects: the stimulus which starts regeneration, the source of the regeneration material and the organizing factors which direct the differentiation of this material into specific organs. The second question has been discussed above. Little information is available concerning the first problem. Ordinarily, an injury is necessary to start the process of regeneration. The trauma plays a role similar to that of fertilization in embryonic development. Undoubtedly, amputation upsets cellular physiological and biochemical equilibria at the wound surface, but we do not know which of these disturbances provides the essential stimulus. In the case of amphibian limb and tail regeneration, it was found that an initial phase of tissue breakdown near the amputation surface is the first reaction; it precedes blastema formation. As would be expected, the concentration of proteolytic enzymes, in particular cathepsin, is excessively high near the amputation surface and in the young blastema. How the histolytic processes prepare the ground for the synthetic processes is unknown.

A trauma is not necessary in all instances for the initiation of regeneration. In the case of lens regeneration in salamanders (*see above, Metaplasy*), the removal of the lens without injury to the upper iris activates the regeneration process in the latter. A series of ingenious experiments has shown that a chemical equilibrium exists between substances produced by the retina of the eye and substances produced by the lens. This equilibrium is upset by the removal of the lens and the ensuing change in the chemical milieu of the iris serves as the stimulus for its regeneration, in the place of a mechanical injury.

Determination: General.—The organizing factors for regeneration remain to be considered. Since we know little concerning the factors which govern regeneration by internal reconstitution (morphallaxis), the following discussion will be limited to regenerations which proceed by way of blastemas (epimorphosis). Limb and tail regenerations in urodelan amphibians have been the objects of the most intensive analysis of these factors.

In a causal analytical approach which tries to penetrate more deeply into the nature of regeneration than a pure description can do, problems of the following kind become pertinent. What are the potentialities and properties of the blastema? In which way, and by which agents, is its destiny determined? Where do the factors reside which bring it about that one blastema forms a limb and another one forms a tail? This type of question has been suggested to the student of regeneration by the experimental embryologist who has analyzed the embryonic process from a similar point of view (for the following discussion *see* EXPERIMENTAL EMBRYOLOGY). It was found that, at least in amphibians and other vertebrates and in some invertebrate embryos, early embryonic cells are relatively indifferent for a considerable period, and pluripotent, that is, capable of differentiation (*q.v.*) along any one of several different lines. Their potentialities become gradually limited and their final fates determined by interaction with so-called "inductors," by hormonal influences and by other agents. We shall see that in all probability the same holds for regeneration blastemas. This process of gradual fixation of the final fate of cell groups is called "determination." Whereas regeneration blastemas, as well as embryonic primordia, receive their essential and immediate determining influences from factors residing within the organism, the external milieu can modify the direction of regeneration and of developmental processes. This holds particularly for lower invertebrates, such as coelenterates and planarians. The influence of the chemical environment, of temperature and so forth on the regeneration process can be considered as subsidiary determining factors.

Experimental embryology has devised the methods and techniques for the analysis of such problems. It is obvious that causal-analytical questions concerning determination can be answered only by experimental methods. The factors of the external milieu can be studied relatively easily in controlled experiments, in which one factor is varied quantitatively, and all others are kept constant. The methods of microsurgery which have been devised in experimental embryology for the study of internal factors were found to be applicable to regeneration as well. They are: "extirpation," that is, the complete removal of an organ or structure for the purpose of studying the effect of its absence on adjacent or other parts; "transplantation" of structures from one part of the body to the other, for the purpose of studying tissue interactions, and "isolation" in tissue culture or otherwise, for the purpose of studying the inherent potentialities of an isolate.

The Potentialities of the Blastema.—The following discussion refers to regeneration in amphibians. A number of experiments support the view that the early limb and tail blastemas are relatively indifferent, or undetermined, during the earliest phase of their growth. To prove this, it is necessary to show that they can be induced to form structures which they would not form in the normal course of their development; in other words, that they are pluripotent. If a young forelimb blastema, a few days old, without the underlying stump parts, is transplanted onto a

hindlimb amputation stump, it forms a hindlimb. If the same experiment is done with a forelimb blastema nine days old or older, it forms a forelimb. The two experiments demonstrate that the blastema is relatively indifferent during the first week, whereupon its fate becomes irreversibly fixed. Other experiments give further proof of the pluripotency of young tail blastemas. They can be induced to form structures entirely foreign to their normal fate, such as a crystalline lens or an ear vesicle, if they are brought under the influence of the so-called inductors for these structures. Finally, the occurrence of duplications on a single regeneration stump illustrates the same point of relative indeterminacy of the young blastemas.

Regeneration Fields.—These experiments suggest that the decisive factors for the determination of the blastemas must be sought outside of the blastemas themselves. The following experiments show that they reside in the amputation stump. If a forelimb is transplanted to the flank between the fore- and hindlimb position and then amputated in its middle, the stump regenerates a forelimb. Even a transplanted small slice of a forelimb amputation stump suffices to bring about forelimb regeneration at a foreign location. Similar results were obtained with hindlimb and tail transplants. One may ask: what is the extent of the areas which contain the limb or tail determining agents? If a limb is amputated at its base, the shoulder or pelvic region is still capable of restoring the limb. However, if the girdles are also extirpated, regeneration fails to occur. The capacity for limb regeneration is obviously limited to a well-circumscribed area. The same was shown for tail and snout regeneration. Likewise, an eye or a gill can be regenerated only if a remnant of these organs is left behind. An area which is capable of organizing the regeneration of a specific organ is called a "field-district," and the organizing factors within such a district constitute its "field." We speak of a limb, or tail, regeneration field, etc. Paul Weiss (University of Chicago) and E. Guyenot (Geneva university) are mainly responsible for the development of the regeneration-field concept. One of its theoretical implications is this: all experiments show clearly that it is not the whole animal which regenerates a limb or an eye, but it is the limb or eye regeneration-field which restores its lost parts. It would, therefore, be misleading to consider regeneration merely from the teleological point of view.

The field concept has been fruitfully applied to embryonic development. More or less definitely delimited embryonic areas which contain the factors for the determination of a specific organ, such as ear or eye, are called embryonic or "morphogenetic" fields. In some instances, an embryonic field is carried over into adult stages as a regeneration field.

One of the outstanding characteristics of a field is that it is a unit, or a whole, and not merely the sum of the cellular materials of which it is composed. This property is illustrated best in those instances in which a field is split in half, whereupon each half gives rise to a whole organ. For instance, the amputation stump of a limb can be split lengthwise, and one lateral half removed. The remaining half cross section of the stump then regenerates a whole foot rather than a half foot. All double and multiple regenerations illustrate the same point. Likewise, two blastemas which are fused together and implanted on one stump give rise to one harmonious limb. Generally speaking, the field with its organizing capacities remains undisturbed if the cellular material which it controls under normal circumstances is diminished or enlarged. The unit-character of the field finds its clearest manifestation in these regulative properties.

The Role of the Nervous System.—It has been established beyond doubt that the presence of peripheral nerves is necessary for amphibian limb regeneration. The experiments which prove this are usually set up as follows: the limb nerves are transected at the shoulder or pelvic region, and the limb is amputated more distally, for instance at the elbow, or knee, respectively. Limb regeneration is then inhibited. However, the nerves have the capacity to regenerate, and as soon as the regenerated nerve fibres have reached the amputation surface, the regeneration of the limb begins. If the nerve regeneration is prevented by repeated nerve transections at the base of the limb, then the limb regeneration is not only blocked permanently but the amputation stump, including its skeleton and musculature, undergoes regression, and the entire limb is eventually resorbed. These and similar experiences lead to the belief that it is the function of the nervous system to stop the resorption at the amputation stump, which is the first phase in the regeneration process, and to promote the subsequent synthetic activities. At any rate, the role of the nervous system in regeneration is not that of an inductor of specific structural characters but of a trophic agent. The question as to which component of the peripheral nerves, sensory, motor or sympathetic, plays the essential role has led to a great amount of experimental work since the beginning of the 20th century, but has not been settled. It is possible that not any one specific component but merely a certain quantity of nerve fibre material is required for regeneration.

The nervous system is likewise essential in the regeneration of some invertebrates, but dispensable in others. The regeneration of the earthworm head seems to be dependent on the presence of the ventral nerve cord at the amputation surface. The influence of the nervous system on eye regeneration in the marine decapod crustaceans was mentioned above (under homoeosis). If the eye and eye stalk are amputated but the eye ganglion at its base is left intact, then a normal eye regenerates. If the eye ganglion is also removed, then an antenna is formed instead of an eye (fig. 6). However, this case can not be considered as representative of all arthropod regenerations.

For instance, in the praying mantis, regenerations of normal legs and of normal antennae were observed after removal of their ganglia, and similar instances of regeneration in the absence of innervation are known to occur in other arthropods.

Polarity; Polar Heteromorphosis.—Polarity refers to the regional differences along the main axis of an organism; it is clearly expressed in head formation at one end and tail formation at the other. It is also expressed in the formation of the tentacle-bearing polyp (hydranth) at the distal end of the stem of *Hydra* and its marine relatives and of a stolon at the other (fig. 8). Polarity is ordinarily retained in regeneration. For instance, a transverse piece of a planarian from the middle of the body regenerates a head at the anterior cut surface and a tail at the posterior amputation surface. A stem piece of *Hydra,* or of any other coelenterate, regenerates a hydranth at its distal surface. However, reversal of polarity does occur occasionally, as for instance in the formation of two heads on both ends of a regenerating piece of planarian (fig. 7) or of two hydranths at both ends of a stem piece of the marine coelenterates, *Tubularia* and *Corymorphora.* Instances of polarity reversal are called polar heteromorphosis. We shall see that they can be produced experimentally.

Gradient Theory.—These atypical cases bring into focus the question of the nature and determination of polarity. Older theories which explained polarity and its maintenance in regeneration on the basis of different concentrations at different levels of head- or tail-determining substances or stuffs have been completely abandoned. It is generally recognized that a dynamic concept of polarity is necessary to explain such fundamental aspects as this: that the same body level of a planarian regenerates a tail if it happens to be the posterior cut surface of an anterior piece, or a head, if it happens to be the anterior level of a posterior piece. The gradient theory of C. M. Child (formerly of the University of Chicago) offers the most satisfactory dynamic con-

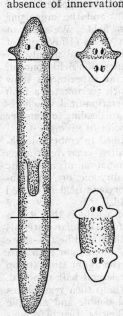

FIG. 7.—POLAR HETEROMORPHOSIS (REVERSAL OF POLARITY) IN THE FLATWORM, PLANARIA. AN AMPUTATED HEAD, OR A SHORT POSTERIOR BODY PIECE MAY REGENERATE A HEAD, WHERE A TAIL WOULD BE EXPECTED. REGENERATED TISSUE UNSTIPPLED

cept of polarization. According to this theory, the structural polarity is the manifestation of a gradation of physiological or metabolic activities which are highest at the anterior end and lowest at the posterior end. The existence of axial physiological gradients (*q.v.*) has been demonstrated by several methods, as, for instance, by the differential disintegration of animals when exposed to toxic agents. According to this theory, a head, or hydranth, regenerates at that region of an isolated piece which has the highest metabolic activity, and the tail, or stolon, at the region of lowest activity. Since in a transverse piece of a planarian the cut surface which was originally nearest the head has a higher activity than any other level of the piece, it will be the one which regenerates a head. In other words, the fate of a regeneration blastema is not determined by specific structural conditions at the cut surface but by its relative position in the whole regenerating system. The polar heteromorphoses, which occur predominantly in very short pieces (fig. 7), are explained by the assumption that in such short pieces no differential, or gradient, is established between the two surfaces, and that their metabolic levels are equally high.

The concepts of "physiological dominance" and of "physiological subordination" are an important corollary to the axial gradient theory. It is postulated that the region of highest metabolic activity, apart from forming head, or hydranth, suppresses at the same time the head or hydranth formation in any other part of the regenerating system; it sets itself up as a "dominant region."

One of many experiments which demonstrate "physiological dominance" may illustrate this concept (fig. 8). In the marine coelenterate, *Tubularia,* a piece of the stem was isolated and the distal amputation surface which normally would have regenerated the hydranth was separated from the rest of the piece by a tight ligature. As a result, the other end of the stem which was in this way released from the inhibiting effect of the dominant region, set itself up as a new dominant region and formed a hydranth. In this way the original polarity was reversed and a polar heteromorphosis produced. The ligature experiment has made it possible to analyze dominance quantitatively; it has led to an interpretation of the dominance relation in terms of competition for available substances (*see* W. G. Barth, 1940). In other experiments, it was possible to obliterate the polarity of a stem piece completely by exposing it to adverse environmental conditions. As a result, it undergoes involution and forms a spherical aggregate of cells. In the subsequent regeneration of such amorphous masses, a new polarity is developed which has no relation to the original polarity. In accordance with Child's concepts, it should be possible to control the polarization of such fragments by raising the metabolic activity locally, which would make this particular region the dominant hydranth-forming region. This can be done in the following way: pieces of *Tubularia* and *Corymorpha* are sensitive to oxygen tensions, and free access to oxygen is a necessary condition for their regeneration. If depolarized aggregates are placed on the bottom of a dish, the new hydranth is formed at the contact-free surface. According to Child, those cells which are freely exposed to sea water are raised to the relatively highest level of metabolic activity and, consequently, set themselves up as hydranth-forming, dominant regions. Many other phenomena of regeneration and asexual reproduction, particularly in lower animals, have been interpreted in terms of the gradient theory. For an exhaustive presentation

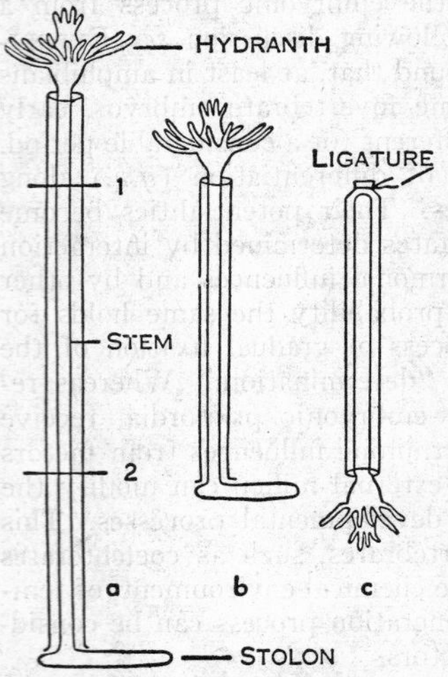

FIG. 8.—EXPERIMENTAL REVERSAL OF POLARITY IN THE MARINE POLYP, TUBULARIA. A PIECE 1-2 (a) REGENERATES NORMALLY A HYDRANTH AT 1 AND A STOLON AT 2. (b) IF A LIGATURE IS MADE AT 1, A HYDRANTH REGENERATES AT 2 (c)

of the subject *see* Child, 1941.

NERVE REGENERATION

The process of nerve regeneration is of great practical importance in medicine and deserves special consideration. It has been studied extensively by biologists and clinicians, in higher animals and in the human being. World Wars I and II have given additional incentive to its exploration.

It should be realized that nerve regeneration is limited to the peripheral nerves; the central nervous system, including brain, spinal cord and ganglia can not restore a loss of nerve cells.

For an understanding of nerve regeneration, it is necessary to give a brief account of the structure of peripheral nerves. They are composed of bundles of nerve fibres held together by connective tissue. Each nerve fibre has a rather complex structure. Its most essential part, the central axon, is a delicate protoplasmic thread which was spun out in early embryonic development by one of the nerve cells located in the central nervous system. It terminates in an effector (muscle, gland) or in a sense organ. The axon remains part of the cell body from which it originated. It is dependent in its metabolic activities on a continuity with its cell body and nucleus, and any part of the axon which is cut off from it degenerates. In the case of accidental or experimental severance of a peripheral nerve, all portions of the axons distal, or peripheral, to the transection are broken down. Nerve regeneration is accomplished by a revival of growth activities at the proximal, or central, ends of the severed axons which retained their connections with their cell bodies. Most peripheral axons are covered by a noncellular myelin sheath which gives them a whitish, glistening appearance and all of them are surrounded by an outer sheath, the so-called Schwann sheath, formed by delicate, nucleated cells. In myelinated fibres the Schwann sheath cells cling tightly to the surface of the myelin sheath, but at times they are capable of migration, and they play an important role in regeneration. The term "nerve fibre" is applied to the axon and its sheaths.

If a nerve is severed by a cut or an injury, its first reaction is a degeneration process which sets in at the proximal as well as at the distal stump. However, degeneration at the proximal end is limited to a short stretch near the amputation surface and is soon superseded by regenerative processes, whereas the entire distal nerve part breaks down eventually, including the nerve endings. Degeneration results in a complete disintegration of the axons and of their myelin sheaths; the debris are gradually removed by macrophages. The cells of the Schwann sheath are not only not affected by this degeneration but, on the contrary, stimulated to new activities. They become instrumental in preparing the pathways for the newly outgrowing nerve fibres both in the gap, or scar, and along the entire length of the peripheral nerve stump. Shortly after nerve transection, they begin to proliferate abundantly, and large numbers of them migrate from the two cut ends into the gap. Together with connective tissue cells (fibroblasts), they become arranged in more or less parallel strands which the regenerating fibres use later on as tracks to reach the distal stump. At the same time, the Schwann cells within the distal stump undergo an equally active proliferation and line up in rows to form long protoplasmic strands, the so-called "bands of Büngner" (after O. von Büngner, who discovered them in 1891). These bands eventually fill the spaces formerly occupied by the degenerated axons and myelin sheaths. They form an ideal substrate and guiding structure for the regenerating nerve axons, which will subsequently enter the distal stump. All changes in the latter, up to this point, are called "Wallerian degeneration" (after A. Waller, who gave the first classical description of this process, in 1852). This term is somewhat misleading since it includes, in its present connotation, not only the degenerative phase but also the simultaneous formation of the bands of Büngner, which is a decidedly constructive process preparatory to reinnervation.

The regeneration process in the true sense of the word, namely, the sprouting of the axons from the proximal nerve ends, starts soon after nerve severance. The cut ends branch profusely and begin to traverse the gap. The course of these fibres is at first rather irregular, but under favourable conditions, parallel strands of regenerating fibres may reach the distal end of the gap as early as 15 days after transection. How do the fibres find the distal stump? Why are they not lost in the scar? It has been claimed repeatedly that the peripheral stump attracts the fibres by a chemical agent (neurotropism), but all experimental evidence is against such chemotropism; galvanotropism is likewise ruled out as a guiding mechanism. The view which is rather generally adopted is that the nerve fibres are not directed by agents acting at a distance but that they merely follow tracks which they find in the substrate on which they grow and to which they cling ("contact guidance," P. Weiss). The Schwann sheath cells and fibroblasts, which are aligned in parallel strands in the scar and which form a bridge between the two nerve ends, supply a suitable track system for the sprouting nerves. Once the peripheral stump is reached, the bands of Büngner with their linear orientation provide an ideal guiding structure all the way through the peripheral stump to the end organs. The first fibres which reach the periphery are thin, and few in number. Before a regenerated nerve is able to carry impulses effectively, the fibres must increase in thickness and in numbers, and they must become myelinated. In man, this process takes several months, depending, of course, on the distance of the end organ from the wound.

It is evident that nerve regeneration faces its greatest hazard in the crossing of the gap, or scar. Functional repair can be successful only if the gap is not too extensive and if the out-growing nerves find in the scar a substrate with longitudinal orientation of cells or micelles. It is at this point that the surgeon can lend a helping hand. To reduce the hazards, nerve ends are usually connected with sutures, or by a so-called "tubulation," that is, by fitting the ends together with a sleeve made from a piece of artery or of other organic or inorganic materials. Larger gaps are sometimes closed by an autoplastic nerve transplant (that is, a piece of another nerve from the same individual). The transplanted piece supplies, of course, merely a suitable guiding structure and not the nerve material proper. None of these methods is ideal, but a continued experimental analysis of the mechanism of nerve regeneration will undoubtedly bring about advances in the surgery of nerve repair.

BIBLIOGRAPHY.—W. Balamuth, "Regeneration in Protozoa," *Quart. Rev. of Biol.*, Vol. 15 (1940); W. G. Barth, "The Process of Regeneration in Hydroids," *Biol. Rev.*, Vol. 15 (1940); C. M. Child, *Patterns and Problems of Development* (1941); E. Korschelt, *Regeneration und Transplantation*, Vol. 1 (1927); T. H. Morgan, *Regeneration* (1901); O. Schotte, *The Origin and Morphogenetic Potencies of Regenerates*, Growth Suppl. (1940); P. Weiss, *Principles of Development* (1939); J. Z. Young, "The Functional Repair of Nervous Tissue," *Physiol. Rev.*, Vol. 22 (1942).   (V. H.)

REGENERATIVE or **RECUPERATIVE FURNACE:** *see* FURNACE, METALLURGICAL.

REGENSBURG (RATISBON), a city and episcopal see of Germany, in the *Land* of Bavaria, and the capital of the government district of the Upper Palatinate. Pop. (1939) 97,924. It is situated on the right bank of the Danube, opposite the influx of the Regen, 86 mi. by rail N.E. from Munich, and 60 mi. S.E. of Nuernberg. The pre-Roman settlement of *Radespona* was chosen by the Romans, who named it *Castra Regina,* as the centre of their power on the upper Danube. It afterward became the seat of the dukes of Bavaria and was the focus from which Christianity spread over southern Germany. St. Emmeran founded an abbey there in the middle of the 7th century, and St. Boniface established the bishopric about 100 years later. Regensburg acquired the freedom of the empire in the 13th century, and was for a time the most flourishing city in southern Germany. It became the chief seat of the trade with India and the Levant, and the boatmen of Regensburg are frequently heard of as expediting the journeys of the crusaders. Numerous imperial diets were held there in the middle ages, and after 1663 it became the regular place of meeting of that body. The Reformation found only temporary acceptance at Regensburg and was met by a counter-reformation inspired by the Jesuits. Before this period the city had almost wholly lost its commercial importance because of the changes in the great highways of trade. Regensburg is said to have suffered in all no fewer than 17 sieges. In 1810 the town and bishopric were ceded to Bavaria. In 1809 the French reduced a great part of the city to ashes.

Across the river is Stadt-am-Hof, connected with Regensburg by a stone bridge of the 12th century. One of the most characteristic features in its architecture is the number of strong loopholed towers attached to the more ancient dwellings.

The cathedral, though small, is an interesting example of pure German Gothic. It was founded in 1275 and completed in 1634, with the exception of the towers, which were finished in 1869. Adjoining the cloisters are two chapels of earlier date than the cathedral itself, one of which, known as the "old cathedral," goes back perhaps to the 8th century. The church of St. James —also called Schottenkirche—a plain Romanesque basilica of the 12th century, derives its name from the monastery of Irish Benedictines ("Scoti") to which it was attached. The old parish church of St. Ulrich is a good example of the Transition style of the 13th century. Examples of the Romanesque basilica style are the church of Obermünster, dating from 1010, and the abbey church of St. Emmeran, built in the 13th century, and remarkable as one of the few German churches with a detached belfry. The cloisters of the ancient abbey, one of the oldest in Germany, are still in fair preservation. In 1809 the conventual buildings were converted into a palace for the prince of Thurn and Taxis. The town hall, dating in part from the 14th century, contains the rooms occupied by the imperial diet from 1663 to 1806. Among the chief manufactures are pottery, parquet flooring, musical instruments, furniture, sugar, chemicals, tobacco and lead pencils.

REGENT, one who rules or governs, especially one who acts temporarily as an administrator of the realm during the minority or incapacity of the king. This latter function, however, is one unknown to the English common law. "In judgment of law the king, as king, cannot be said to be a minor, for when the royal body politic of the king doth meet with the natural capacity in one person the whole body shall have the quality of the royal politic, which is the greater and more worthy and wherein is no minority." But for reasons of necessity a regency, however anomalous it may be in strict law, has frequently been constituted both in England and Scotland. The earliest instance in English history is the appointment of the earl of Pembroke with the assent of the loyal barons on the accession of Henry III.

Lord Coke recommends that the office should depend on the will of parliament (*Inst.,* vol. iv. p. 58), and in modern times provision for a regency has always been made by Act of parliament. As late as 1704 provision was made for a regency after the death of Anne. The earliest regency in England resting upon an express statute was that created by 28 Hen. VIII. c. 7, under which the king appointed his executors to exercise the authority of the crown till the successor to the crown should attain the age of 18 if a male or 16 if a female.

The Act of 5 Geo. III. c. 27 vested in the king power to appoint a regent under the sign manual, such regent to be one of certain named members of the royal family. Owing to the king's insanity in 1810 the Act of 51 Geo. III. c. 1 was passed, appointing the prince of Wales regent during the king's incapacity. The royal assent was given by commission authorized by both Houses of Parliament. By this Act no council of regency was appointed. There was no restriction on the regent's authority over treaties, peace and war, or over giving assent to bills varying the Act of Settlement or the Act of Uniformity, as in the previous Regency Acts, but his power of granting peerages, offices and pensions was limited. By 10 Geo. IV. c. 7 the office of regent of the United Kingdom cannot be held by a Roman Catholic. A similar disability is imposed in the great majority, of Regency acts, if not indeed in all of them.

In the State of New York, a Regent is a member of the corporate body known as the University of the State of New York.

REGER MAX (1873–1916), German composer, was born at Brand, Bavaria, on March 19, 1873. He studied at Weiden, Sondershausen and Wiesbaden, and taught at the Royal academy, Munich, from 1905–07, when he became a teacher at the Leipzig conservatorium, a post which he retained until his death, on May 11, 1916. His early piano works, Variations on a Theme from Bach, Variations on a Theme from Beethoven, the Passacaglia and Fugue, and later the violin sonata in F sharp minor, which show already his individuality and remarkable technical powers, were followed by his first orchestral work, *Sinfonietta* (1906). After moving to Leipzig he wrote the violin concerto and piano concerto, with the powerful Symphonie Prologue to a Tragedy and the Comedy Overture, a number of choral pieces including *Die Nonnen, Der römische Triumphgesang* and *Die Weihe der Nacht,* the fine motets written for the Thomaner-Chor and the *Schlichte Weisen* sonatinas. From the period 1911–13, when he was also director of the court orchestra at Meiningen, there dates the Romantische Suite, Böcklin Suite, Ballet Suite, and later, Variations on a Theme from Mozart. From 1914 onwards his numerous compositions include many chamber works, pieces for choir and orchestra, for the piano and for the organ, and songs.

Reger was one of the most prolific and, in some respects, remarkably gifted composers of his day. His fertility was extraordinary, and he turned out work after work, often on the largest scale and in the most complex forms, with astonishing ease. His powers as a contrapuntist were especially noteworthy, and the fugue was one of his favourite forms. But as to the value of his immense output critical opinion is sharply divided.

A list of Reger's works is given in Grove's *Dict. of Music* (3rd ed., 1928). *See also* K. Hasse, *Max Reger* (Leipzig, 1921); E. Segnitz, *Max Reger* (Leipzig, 1922); and R. Würz, *Max Reger* (Munich, 1920).

REGGIO DI CALABRIA (anc. *Regium, q.v.*), a town and archiepiscopal see of Calabria, Italy, capital of the province of Reggio, on the Strait of Messina, 248 mi. S.S.E. from Naples by rail. Pop. (1936) 60,342 (town); 119,804 (commune). It is the terminus of the railways from Naples along the west coast, and from Metaponto along the east coast of Calabria. The straits are here about 7 mi. wide, and the distance to Messina nearly 10 mi. The ferryboats to Messina therefore cross by preference from Villa S. Giovanni, 8 mi. N. of Reggio, now included within its communal boundary, whence the distance is only 5 mi. In 1894 the town suffered from an earthquake, though less severely than in 1783. It was totally destroyed, however, by the great earthquake of December 1908; in the centre of the town about 35,000 out of 40,000 persons perished. The cathedral, which dated from the 17th century, and the ancient castle which rose above it, were wrecked. Great damage was done by a seismic wave following the shock. The town was heavily bombed in 1943.

REGGIO NELL'EMILIA, a city and episcopal see of Emilia, Italy, the capital of the province of Reggio Nell'Emilia (till 1859 part of the duchy of Modena), 38 mi. by rail N.W. of Bologna. Pop. (1906) 19,681 (town) 64,548 (commune); (1936) 49,069 (town) 93,913 (commune). The town is in the shape of a diamond. The cathedral, originally erected in the 12th century, was reconstructed in the 15th and 16th; the façade shows traces of both periods, the Renaissance work by Prospero Spani (1516–1584) being complete only in the lower portion. The Madonna della Ghiara, built in 1597–1619 in the form of a Greek cross, is beautifully proportioned and finely decorated in stucco and with frescoes of the Bolognese school of the early 17th century. S. Prospero has a good façade of 1753. There are several good palaces of the early Renaissance, a fine theatre (1857) and a museum containing important palaeo-ethnological collections, ancient and mediaeval sculptures, and the natural history collection of Lazzaro Spallanzani. Lodovico Ariosto, the poet (1474–1533), was born in Reggio, and his father's house is still preserved. The industries embrace the making of railway locomotives and carriages and tramcars, and of cheese.

Regium Lepidi was probably founded by M. Aemilius Lepidus during the construction of the Via Aemilia (187 B.C.), on which it lay half-way between Mutina and Parma. It was during the Roman period a flourishing town. The bishopric dates perhaps from the 4th century A.D. Under the Lombards the town was the seat of dukes and counts; in the 12th and 13th centuries it formed a flourishing republic, busied in surrounding itself with walls (1229), controlling the Crostolo and constructing navigable canals to the Po. About 1290 it first passed into the hands of Obizzo d'Este, and the authority of the Este family was finally recognized in 1409.

REGICIDE, the name given to anyone who kills a sovereign (Lat. *rex,* a king, and *caedere,* to kill). Regicides is the name given in English history at the Restoration of 1660 to those persons who were responsible for the execution of Charles I. The number of regicides was estimated at 84, this number being composed of the 67 present at the last sitting of the court of justice, 11 others who had attended earlier sittings, four officers of the court and the two executioners.

The trial of the regicides before a court of 34 commissioners took place in Oct. 1660. Twenty-nine were condemned to death, but only ten were actually executed, the remaining 19 with six others being imprisoned for life. The ten who were executed at Charing Cross or Tyburn, London, in Oct. 1660, were Thomas Harrison, John Jones, Adrian Scrope, John Carew, Thomas Scot and Gregory Clement, who had signed the death-warrant; the preacher Hugh Peters; Francis Hacker and Daniel Axtel, who commanded the soldiers at the trial and the execution of the king; and John Cook the solicitor who directed the prosecution.

In Jan. 1661 the bodies of Cromwell, Ireton, and Bradshaw were exhumed and hanged at Tyburn, but Pride's does not appear to have been treated in this way. Of the nineteen or twenty regicides who had escaped and were living abroad, three, Sir John Barkstead, John Okey and Miles Corbet, were arrested in Holland and executed in London in April 1662; and one, John Lisle, was murdered at Lausanne. The last survivor of the regicides was probably Edmund Ludlow, who died at Vevey in 1692.

BIBLIOGRAPHY.—Ludlow's *Memoirs,* edited by C. H. Firth (Oxford, 1894), give interesting details about the regicides in exile. *See also* D. Masson, *Life of Milton,* vol. vi. (1880), and M. Noble, *Lives of the English Regicides* (1798); L. E. Welles, *History of the Regicides* (1927).

REGILLUS, an ancient lake of Latium, Italy, famous in the legendary history of Rome as the lake in the neighbourhood of which occurred (496 B.C.) the battle which finally decided the hegemony of Rome in Latium. Of the various sites proposed, the best is Pantano Secco, some 2 m. N. of Frascati.

REGINA, the capital city of the province of Saskatchewan, Canada, situated at 104° 36′ W. and 50° 27′ N., and 357 mi. W. of Winnipeg. Pop. (1951), 69,928. After the Canadian Pacific railway was completed in 1885, the necessity for a place of government on the railway line pressed itself upon the federal government. The Northwest Territories were but little settled then, but a central position on the prairies was necessary, where the mounted police might be stationed and where the numerous Indian bands might be easily reached. The minister of the interior at Ottawa, afterward Gov. Edgar Dewdney, chose this spot, and for a number of years Regina was the seat of the territorial government. The governor took up his abode on the adjoining plain, and the North-West council met each year, with a show of constitutional government about it. On the formation of the province of Saskatchewan in 1905 the choice of capital was left to the first legislature of the province. Prince Albert, Moose Jaw and Saskatoon all advanced claims, but Regina was decided on as the capital.

The city has a large distributing trade and is the central market for an agricultural region. It is on the Canadian Pacific and Canadian National railways, and has several radiating lines. There are many mills, banks, wholesale houses and factories, including a large oil refinery. Regina is the western headquarters of the Royal Canadian Mounted Police.

REGINON, or REGINO OF PRÜM, mediaeval chronicler, was born at Altripp near Spires, and was educated in the monastery of Prüm. Here he became a monk, and in 892, just after the monastery had been sacked by the Danes, he was chosen abbot. In 899, however, he was deprived of this position and he went to Trier, where he was appointed abbot of St. Martin's. He died in 915, and was buried in the abbey of St. Maximin at Trier, his tomb being discovered there in 1581.

Reginon wrote a *Chronicon,* dedicated to Adalberon, bishop of Augsburg (d. 909), which deals with the history of the world from the commencement of the Christian era to 906, especially with the affairs in Lorraine. The chronicle was first published at Mainz in 1521; another edition is in Band I. of the *Monumenta Germaniae historica. Scriptores* (1826); the best is the one edited by F. Kurze (Hanover, 1890); German trans. by W. Wattenbach (Leipzig, 1890). Reginon also drew up at the request of his patron, Radbod, archbishop of Trier (d. 915), a collection of canons, *Libri duo de synodalibus causis et disciplinis ecclesiasticis;* this is published in Migne's *Patrol. Lat.* t. 132.

See H. Ermisch, *Die Chronik des Regino bis 813* (Göttingen, 1872); P. Schulz, *Die Glaubwürdigkeit des Abtes Regino von Prüm* (Hamburg, 1894); C. Wawra, *De Reginone Prumensis* (Breslau, 1901).

REGIOMONTANUS (1436–1476), German astronomer, was born at Königsberg in Franconia on June 6, 1436. His name originally was Johann Müller, but he called himself, from his birthplace, Joh. de Monteregio, an appellation which became modified into Regiomontanus. At Vienna, from 1452, he was the pupil and associate of George Purbach (1423–1461), and they jointly undertook a reform of astronomy rendered necessary by the errors they detected in the Alphonsine Tables. In this they were much hindered by the lack of correct translations of Ptolemy's works; and in 1462 Regiomontanus accompanied Cardinal Bessarion to Italy to study a copy of the *Almagest.* He rapidly mastered Greek at Rome and Ferrara, lectured on Alfraganus at Padua, and completed at Venice in 1463 Purbach's *Epitome in Cl. Ptolemaei magnam compositionem* (printed at Venice in 1496), and his own *De Triangulis* (Nuremberg, 1533), a treatise on trigonometry. In 1468 he returned to Vienna, and was thence summoned to Buda by Matthias Corvinus, king of Hungary, for the purpose of collating Greek manuscripts. He also finished his *Tabulae Direc-*

tionum (Nuremberg, 1475), essentially an astrological work, but containing a valuable table of tangents.

In 1471 Regiomontanus settled at Nuremberg. Bernhard Walther, a rich patrician, became his pupil and patron; and they together equipped the first European observatory, for which Regiomontanus himself constructed instruments of an improved type (described in his posthumous *Scripta,* Nuremberg, 1544). His observations of the great (Halley's) comet of 1472 supplied the basis of modern cometary astronomy. At a printing-press established in Walther's house by Regiomontanus, Purbach's *Theoricae planetarum novae* was published in 1472 or 1473; a series of popular calendars issued from it, and in 1474 a volume of *Ephemerides* calculated by Regiomontanus for thirty-two years (1474–1506), in which the method of "lunar distances," for determining the longitude at sea, was recommended and explained. In 1472 Regiomontanus was summoned to Rome by Pope Sixtus IV., to aid in the reform of the calendar; and there he died on July 6, 1476.

See P. Gassendi, *Vita Jo. Regiomontani* (Parisiis, 1654); and the general histories of astronomy.

REGIONAL PLANNING, a term used by community planners, engineers and geographers to describe a comprehensive ordering of the natural resources of a community, its material equipment and its population for the purpose of laying a sound physical basis for the "good life." In America the term has also been used to describe plans for city extension over wide metropolitan areas; this type of planning should properly be called metropolitan planning. Regional planning involves the development of cities and countrysides, of industries and natural resources, as part of a regional whole.

The programme of regional planning has grown out of a multitude of fresh initiatives; the activities of foresters and conservationists with forest working plans, of engineers with water power plans, of municipal engineers with plans for city extensions and parkways, and finally, of a great school of regional geographers, who, under Vidal de la Blache in France, Herbertson in England, Fenneman, Smith and others in the United States, have established the region as a definite unit, with its special individuality of geologic formation, climate, vegetation, landscape and human culture. The method of the regional plan can perhaps best be grasped by considering its simpler prototype, that which covers but a single aspect of regional life. Take an actual forest working plan for an area in the State of Washington, between the Cascade range and Puget sound: it is about the size of Rhode Island. Except for the mountain barrens and narrow strips of agricultural land along the rivers, the whole region is under forest. The plan divides this area into six "cutting-blocks," each block to be cut within a ten year period and the logs hauled to a central saw mill. When the last block has been cut over the first is ready to be cut again. The central mill and the houses provided for its working force are permanent fixtures.

This plan brings out the essential characteristics of every regional plan, whether specialized or comprehensive. (1) It deals with a geographic area; (2) it surveys that area and discovers its natural characteristics and resources; (3) it suggests a method of conserving its resources and developing its economic life; (4) it erects relatively permanent seats of human habitation, with all the social facilities that derive from such stability. Lacking such a plan and such a public policy, current commercial methods of exploitation would cut over the entire area in one operation, would provide only temporary employment and temporary habitations, would make no provision for natural reforestation, and would, as a result, permit the soil of the timber-mined area to be washed away, degrading the whole region and making further human activity difficult, if not impossible in it.

The Means to an End.—A regional plan, if it is really a plan and not a description, deals not only with a geographic area but with a force or "flow" or group of activities taking place within it. This flow may consist of water or electricity or commodities like lumber, wheat, dairy produce, manufactured articles—some product required for human sustenance. The flow may also be that of population; this includes industrial plant and social institutions—schools, libraries, churches, colleges, museums, hospitals

—in short, a flow of civilization. We usually regard these things as static; actually, they are always in motion, improving, deteriorating, changing their position, if not from year to year, then from decade to decade. Regional planning would direct and modify these changes to the advantage of the whole community, instead of simply letting them "happen." A comprehensive regional plan involves not merely the forces of man's industrial life but his cultural activities as well; for plans that concern themselves solely with the means of life are in danger of defeating man's cultural activities, which express his aims or objectives. In contrast to the view of industrial production almost universally accepted during the 19th century, regional planning recognizes that the means must be subordinate to the ends. Thus, in utilizing sites along a river, the regional planner may reserve for recreation a spot that would ordinarily be dedicated to heavy manufacturing; or between two possible types of industry, he may select that which has a higher civilization-value. Regional planning, following Ruskin, recognizes as the ultimate product of industry not money or commodities but human life. Briefly, regional planning deals with the ecology of the human community. Just as plant ecology treats of the climate, soil, the plant and insect partnerships necessary to the existence of a species of plants, so regional planning deals with the climate, vegetation, minerals, power resources, landscape, economic and social institutions necessary to a flourishing human community. It is not an effort to make a region self-subsistent; it *is* an attempt to bring it into the highest state of economic and human cultivation. No region is a self-contained unit. Except for islands and isolated mountain areas, there are no self-contained units even in the narrow geographic sense, whilst economically and culturally no region has existed without contact with other regions. Inter-regional relationships are just as important as internal ones, and of as much concern to the regional planner. Thus it has been pointed out that the only fundamental solution of New York's congestion of population and traffic involves a redistribution of the flow of commodities through the Atlantic ports, decreasing the share that now falls to New York, and redistributing part of New York's growing population in regional cities outside the immediate metropolitan area. Such a programme was partly sketched out in the final report of the New York State Housing and Regional Planning commission (1926).

Aspects.—In the countries where there is regional planning one aspect or another has usually been dominant, although regional planning involves every aspect of a region's life. In France, for example, the necessity for political administrative units that bear some relation to economics, history and geography has made the political side dominant; similar considerations have governed the drawing up of new governmental units in Siberia. Regional survey brings out the arbitrary nature of a great many political boundaries, and suggests the possibility of re-drawing them, or of co-operatively ignoring them, as in the constitution of the New York-New Jersey port authority. Economically, regional planning seeks the fullest development of local resources and skills, without the extravagant waste and degradation that accompanied this process in the past; in America this aspect of regional planning has been uppermost in the work of foresters and conservationists like Gifford Pinchot and Liberty Hyde Bailey. Socially, regional planning attempts to curb the growth of metropolitan slums and to create independent cities in more effective relationship with nature and industry and to take care of further increments of population: in England, the garden city movement, which has built Letchworth and Welwyn, has emphasized this side of regional planning. In reports on the Deeside and the Doncaster districts in England, and the newly found coal-areas in Kent, as well as in the final report of the New York State Housing and Regional Planning commission, these various aims have been co-ordinated and focussed. Regional rather than metropolitan development has been aided by motor transport and the aeroplane, by the radio, telephone, and giant power; and regional planning tends to make the fullest use of these. Similar reports and surveys have been made for the Ruhr district in Germany, for the French Alps, and, on a smaller scale, for agricultural communities in the Caucasus.

Among the precursors and intellectual preceptors of the modern regional planning movement, one must note Auguste Comte and Frédéric Le Play in political decentralization, Henry Thoreau in philosophy, George Perkins Marsh, author of *The Earth as Modified by Human Action,* Reclus, Ratzel and Shaler in geography, Kropotkin in economics, and Patrick Geddes, whose social studies and technical initiatives as city planner have touched every part of it. The first conception of dealing with the administration of modern utilities like electricity on a regional, rather than a national or local scale, was embodied in a Fabian pamphlet in the "New Heptarchy Series" on *Municipalization by Provinces;* the first definitive project for a regional city was that issued by Sir Ebenezer Howard in *Tomorrow* (*see* GARDEN CITIES).

See Benton MacKaye, *The New Exploration, A Philosophy of Regional Planning;* Victor Branford and Patrick Geddes, *The Coming Polity;* C. B. Fawcett, *The Provinces of England;* J. Charles-Brun, *Le Régionalisme;* J. Russell Smith, *North America;* J. M. Mackinder, *Britain and the British Seas;* the "Regional Planning" number of the *Survey Graphic,* May 1925; and the *Report* of the New York State Housing and Regional Planning Commission (1926).

(B. MACK.; L. MU.)

REGISTRATION: *see* BIRTH; SHIPPING: REGISTRATION, CLASSIFICATION AND STATE REGULATION; BILL OF SALE; ELECTORAL SYSTEMS; COMPANY AND CORPORATION LAW; FRIENDLY SOCIETIES; BUILDING SOCIETIES; PRESS LAWS; COPYRIGHT; TRADE MARKS; PATENTS; LAND TITLES.

REGIUM, a city of the territory of the Bruttii in South Italy, on the east side of the strait between Italy and Sicily (*see* REGGIO DI CALABRIA). A colony, mainly of Chalcidians, partly of Messenians from the Peloponnesus, settled at Regium in the 8th century B.C. About 494 B.C. Anaxilas, a member of the Messenian party, made himself master of Regium (apparently with the help of the Samians: *see* MESSINA) and about 488 joined with them in occupying Zancle (Messina). In 433 Regium made a treaty with Athens, and in 427 joined the Athenians against Syracuse, but in 415 it remained neutral. An attack which it made on Dionysius I of Syracuse in 399 was the beginning of a great struggle which in 387 resulted in its complete destruction and the dispersion of its inhabitants as slaves: but it soon recovered its prosperity. In 280, Pyrrhus invaded Italy, the Regines admitted within their walls a Roman garrison of Campanian troops; these mercenaries revolted, massacred the male citizens, and held the city till in 270 they were besieged and put to death by the Roman consul Genucius. The city remained faithful to Rome throughout the Punic wars, and Hannibal never succeeded in taking it.

It took the name Regium Iulium under Octavius (Augustus); and the pedestal of a statue erected in his honour (as Augustus) has been found there. It continued to be a Greek city even under the empire. Toward the end of the empire it was made the chief city of the Bruttii.

See P. Larizza, *Rhegium Chalcidense* (Rome, 1905); Orsi in *Notizie degli scavi,* 1922, 151 *sqq.*

REGIUM DONUM or ROYAL GIFT, an annual grant formerly made from the public funds to Presbyterian and other Nonconformist ministers in Great Britain and Ireland. In 1690 William III. made a grant of £1,200 a year to the Presbyterian ministers in Ireland as a reward for their services during their struggle with James II. Owing to the opposition of the Irish House of Lords the money was not paid in 1711 and some subsequent years, but it was revived in 1715 by George I., who increased the amount to £2,000 a year. Further additions were made in 1784 and in 1792, and in 1868 the sum granted to the Irish Presbyterian ministers was £45,000. The Regium Donum was withdrawn by the act of 1869 which disestablished the Irish church. Provision was made, however, for existing interests therein, and many Presbyterian ministers commuted these on the same terms as the clergy of the church of Ireland.

In England the Regium Donum proper dates from 1721, when Dr. Edmund Calamy (1671-1732) received £500 from the royal bounty "for the use and behalf of the poor widows of dissenting ministers." Afterwards this sum was increased to £1,000 and was made an annual payment "for assisting either ministers or their widows," and later it amounted to £1,695 per annum. It was given to distributors who represented the three denominations, Presbyterians, Baptists and Independents, enjoying the grant. Among the Nonconformists themselves, however, or at least among the Baptists and the Independents, there was some objection to this form of state aid, and it was withdrawn in 1857.

See J. Stoughton, *History of Religion in England* (1901); J. S. Reid, *History of the Presbyterian Church in Ireland* (Belfast, 1867); and E. Calamy, *Historical Account of my own Life*, edited by J. T. Rutt (1829–30).

REGLA, formerly an important suburb of Havana, Cuba, opposite that city, on the bay; now a part of Havana and an independent municipality. Pop. (1943), 23,037. It was formerly the scene of the Havana bullfights. The church is one of the best in Cuba; the building dates mainly from 1805, but the church settlement goes back to a hermitage established in 1690. Regla is the shipping point of the Havana sugar trade. It has enormous sugar and tobacco warehouses, fine wharves, a dry dock, foundries and an electric railway plant.

Regla is the western terminus of the eastern line of the United Railways of Havana and is connected with the main city of Havana by ferry. A fishing village was established there about 1733. At the end of the 18th century Regla was a principal centre of the smuggling trade, and about 1820 was notorious as a resort of pirates. It first secured an *ayuntamiento* (city council) in 1872; annexation to Havana occurred in 1899.

REGNARD, JEAN FRANÇOIS (1655–1709), French comic dramatist, was born in Paris on Feb. 7, 1655. His masterpieces are *Le Joueur* (Théâtre Français, Dec. 19, 1696), and *Le Légataire universel* (1708). Regnard died on Sept. 4, 1709.

Besides many plays Regnard wrote miscellaneous poems, the autobiographical romance of *La Provençale*, and several short accounts in prose of his travels, published posthumously under the title of *Voyages*.

The first edition of Regnard's works was published in 1731 (5 vols., Rouen and Paris). There is a good selection of almost everything important in the Collection Didot (4 vols., 1819). A selection by L. Moland appeared in 1893. See also a *Bibliographie et iconographie des oeuvres de J. F. Regnard* (Paris, Rouquette, 1878); *Le Poète J. F. Regnard en son chasteau de Grillon*, by J. Guyot (Paris, 1907).

REGNAULT, HENRI (1843–1871), French painter, born at Paris on Oct. 31, 1843, was the son of Henri Victor Regnault (*q.v.*). He studied successively under Montfort, Lamothe and Cabanel, and in 1864 exhibited two portraits at the Salon. In 1866, he gained the *Grand Prix* with "Thetis bringing the Arms forged by Vulcan to Achilles" (Beaux-Arts). In Rome Regnault came under the influence of the modern materialistic Hispano-Italian school. His paintings include an imaginative picture of Marshal Prim at the head of his troops, inspired by a glimpse of his subject, received when travelling in Spain; "Judith" (1870), "Salome" and the realistic "Execution without Hearing under the Moorish Kings," painted at Tangiers. Regnault was killed in the Franco-German War on Jan. 19, 1871, while serving under Buzenval.

See *Correspondance de H. Regnault*; Duparc, *H. Regnault, sa vie et son œuvre*; Cazalis, *H. Regnault, 1843–1871*; C. Blanc, *H. Regnault.*

REGNAULT, HENRI VICTOR (1810–1878), French chemist and physicist, was born on July 21, 1810, at Aix-la-Chapelle. His early life was a struggle with poverty, he worked in a drapery establishment in Paris until 1829. Then he entered the École Polytechnique, and passed in 1832 to the École des Mines. A few years later, after studying under Justus von Liebig (*q.v.*), he was appointed to a professorship of chemistry at Lyons. His most important contribution to organic chemistry was a series of researches, begun in 1835, on the halogen and other derivatives of unsaturated hydrocarbons. He also studied the alkaloids and organic acids, introduced a classification of the metals and effected a comparison of the chemical composition of atmospheric air from all parts of the world. In 1840 he became professor of chemistry in the École Polytechnique, Paris; he was elected a member of the Académie des Sciences, and in 1841 he succeeded Pierre Louis Dulong (*q.v.*), professor of physics in the Collège de France. In 1847 he published a four-volume treatise on *Chemistry* which has been translated into many languages. Regnault's work in physics was remarkably accurate and painstaking. He designed

apparatus for a large number of measurements which is the standard apparatus of the present.

Regnault executed a careful redetermination of the specific heats of many solids, liquids and gases. (*See* CALORIMETRY.) He investigated the expansion of gases by heat, and showed that, contrary to previous opinion, no two gases had precisely the same coefficient of expansion. By delicate experiments he proved that Boyle's law is only approximately true for real gases. He studied the subject of thermometry (*q.v.*) critically; he introduced the use of an accurate air-thermometer, and compared its indications with those of a mercurial thermometer, determining the absolute expansion of mercury as a step in the process. He also paid attention to hygrometry and devised Regnault's hygrometer.

In 1854 he was appointed as director of the porcelain manufactory at Sèvres. He carried on his great research on the expansion of gases in the laboratory at Sèvres, but all the results of his latest work were destroyed during the Franco-German War, in which also his son Henri (noticed above) was killed. Regnault never recovered from the double blow, and, although he lived until Jan. 19, 1878, his scientific labours ended in 1872. Regnault's most important work is collected in vols. 21 and 26 of the *Mémoires de l'Académie des Sciences.*

RÉGNIER, HENRI FRANÇOIS JOSEPH DE (1864–1936), French poet and novelist, was born at Honfleur (Calvados) on Dec. 28, 1864, and was educated in Paris for the law. In 1885 he began to contribute to the Parisian reviews, and his verses found their way into most of the French and Belgian periodicals favourable to the symbolist writers. Having begun, however, to write under the leadership of the Parnassians, he retained the classical tradition, though he adopted some of the innovations of Moréas and Gustave Kahn. His gorgeous and vaguely suggestive style shows the influence of Stéphane Mallarmé. His first volume of poems, *Lendemains*, appeared in 1885, and among numerous later volumes are *Poèmes anciens et romanesques* (1890), *Les Jeux rustiques et divins* (1890), *Les Médailles d'argile* (1900), the most famous and the most read of his books of verse, and *La Cité des eaux* (1903). He is also the author of a series of realistic novels and tales, among which are *La Canne de jaspe* (2nd ed., 1897), *La Double Maîtresse* (5th ed., 1900), and *Les Amants singuliers* (1905).

His later works include: *L'Amphisbène* (1912); *La Pécheresse* (1920); *Vestigia Flammae* (7th ed., 1921); *Le Divertissement Provincial* (1925); *Proses datées* (1925); *L'Escapade* (1926).

See also E. Gosse, *French Profiles* (1905); van Bever and Leautaud, *Poètes d'aujourd'hui* (1900); H. Berton, *Henri de Régnier, le poète et le romancier* (1910); A. Lowell, *Six French Poets* (1915); and R. Honnert, *Henri de Régnier, son oeuvre* (1923).

RÉGNIER, MATHURIN (1573–1613), French satirist, was born at Chartres on Dec. 21, 1573, the son of Jacques Régnier, and Simone Desportes, sister of the poet. Little is known of his youth, except that he received the tonsure at eight years old, and it is chiefly conjecture which fixes the date of his visit to Italy in a humble position in the suite of the cardinal, François de Joyeuse, in 1587. Régnier found his duties irksome, and when, after many years of constant travel in the cardinal's service, he returned definitely to France about 1605, he took advantage of the hospitality of Desportes. In 1606 Desportes died and Régnier obtained a pension of 2,000 livres, chargeable upon one of Desportes' benefices. He was also made in 1609 canon of Chartres through his friendship with the lax bishop, Philippe Hurault, at whose abbey of Royaumont he spent much time in the later years of his dissipated life. The death of Henry IV. deprived him of his last hope of great preferments. He died at Rouen at his hotel, the Écu d'Orléans, on Oct. 22, 1613.

His undoubted work falls into three classes: regular satires in alexandrine couplets, serious poems in various metres, and satirical or jocular epigrams and light pieces, which often, if not always, exhibit considerable licence of language. The real greatness of Régnier consists in the vigour and polish of his satires, contrasted and heightened as that vigour is with the exquisite feeling and melancholy music of some of his minor poems. In these Régnier is a disciple of Ronsard (whom he defended brilliantly against Malherbe), without the occasional pedantry, the affectation or the undue fluency of the Pléiade; but in the satires he seems to have had no master except the ancients, for some of them were written before the publication of the satires of Vauquelin de la Fresnaye, and the *Tragiques* of D'Aubigné did not appear until 1616. Régnier was an acute critic, and the famous passage (Satire ix., *À Monsieur Rapin*) in which he satirizes Malherbe contains the best denunciation of the merely "correct" theory of poetry that has ever been written. All his merits are displayed in the masterpiece entitled *Macette ou l'Hypocrisie déconcertée,* which does not suffer even on comparison with *Tartuffe;* but hardly any one of the sixteen satires which he has left falls below a very high standard.

Les Premières Oeuvres ou satyres de Régnier (1608) included the *Discours au roi* and ten satires. There was another in 1609, and others in 1612 and 1613. The author had also contributed to two collections—*Les Muses gaillardes* in 1609 and *Le Temple d'Apollon* in 1611. In 1616 appeared *Les Satyres et autres oeuvres folastres du sieur Régnier,* with many additions and some poems by other hands. Two famous editions by Elzevir (Leiden, 1642 and 1652) are highly prized. The chief editions of the 18th century are that of Claude Brossette (printed by Lyon & Woodman, London, 1729), which supplies the standard commentary on Régnier, and that of Lenglet Dufresnoy (printed by J. Tonson, London, 1733). The editions of Prosper Poitevin (Paris, 1860), of Ed. de Barthélemy (Paris, 1862), and of E. Courbet (Paris, 1875), may be specially mentioned. The last, printed after the originals in italic type, and well edited, is perhaps the best. *See* also Vianey's *Mathurin Régnier* (1896); M. H. Cherrier, *Bibliographie de Mathurin Régnier* (1884); Jean-Marc Bernard, *L'introducteur de la satire en France: Mathurin Régnier* (1913); Emile Roy, *Notes sur les deux poètes Jean et Mathurin Régnier* (1910).

REGNITZ, a river of Germany, 126 m. long, and a left-bank tributary of the Main. It rises in the Jurassic rocks of the Frankish Jura, but its course is along the Trias, through an undulating vine-clad country, past Fürth, Erlangen, Baiersdorf and Forchheim, from which point it is navigable, and joins the Main at Bischberg, below Bamberg. The Ludwigs canal connects it with the Main and the Danube. Its main tributaries are the Pegnitz, on which is Nurnberg, the Gründlach and the Wiesent (right) and the Zenn, the Aurach and the Aisch (left). (*See* Main and Rhine.)

REGRATING, in English criminal law, was the offence of buying and selling again in the same market, or within four miles thereof (O. Fr. *regrater,* to sell by retail). (*See* Engrossing.)

REGULA, the Latin word for a rule, hence particularly applied to the rules of a religious order. (*See* Monasticism.) In architecture the term is applied to a rule, a square and the short fillet or rectangular block, under the taenia (*q.v.*) on the architrave of the Doric entablature. (*See* Order.)

REGULAR (Lat. *regularis,* from *regula,* a rule, O.Fr. *reule*), orderly, following or arranged according to a rule, steady, uniform, formally correct. Until the sixteenth century the adjective was applied exclusively to the discipline and customs of religious orders bound by a rule, and to their members, who constituted the "regular" as opposed to the "secular" clergy. Thus, as a substantive, "regular" means a monk or friar; while there were bodies of canons regular and canons secular. In more recent military usage, the regular forces was the name for the standing army organised on a permanent system, as opposed to "irregulars," levies raised on a voluntary basis.

REGULATION, AUTOMATIC. Modern processing is required in the production of most of the articles of clothing, foodstuffs, and other items that are used in every day life. Processing requires proper conditions not only in workrooms but in the endless variety of boilers, ovens, furnaces, dryers, sterilizers and other types of apparatus. To insure the proper conditions the automatic regulation of *temperature, pressure, humidity, timing, liquid level, flow, specific gravity* of the substance being processed and *speed of moving parts* is of great importance. These eight conditions will be dealt with. *Voltage* (which must be regulated in many devices), *current density* (in electroplating, etc.) and other electrical conditions are discussed under Instruments, Electrical, and Electricity. No discussion is here given of the regulators, controllers or governors incorporated in engines, turbines, generators and other such machines, since these devices as conceived, designed, built, sold, installed and maintained with the machines, belong to their machines and seldom can function on others.

Automatic regulation of the eight conditions listed above is, however, a science, and the proper application of standardized automatic regulators to improve products and effect economies is a prominent branch of engineering.

Development of Automatic Regulation.—For every industry it has been established that there is one best set of conditions for operation and manufacture. Before the World War, in searching for this "one best way," workers were frequently required to watch indicators and manipulate valves and levers constantly in order to maintain proper conditions, until a fairly suitable automatic device was purchased or painstakingly contrived. To-day (1929) specialists may install the required automatic devices as soon as the particular requirements are known. One of the factors that have made this possible is the spread of knowledge of formerly secret processes. This has led to "professional divisions" within the larger engineering societies and to co-operative industrial "institutes" and research bureaux. Competition between industries has also led to the exchange of formulae and data on automatic processes. Instrument-makers have pursued an increasingly active policy of scientific research into processes, with two objectives: (1) the development and standardization of classes and types of automatic regulators, based on industrial requirements; (2) the improvement and standardization of processes through methods worked out by their research staffs.

All these tendencies point to the need of an agency for the systematic utilization of scientific achievements. A central "institute" under the auspices of instrument makers may ultimately be developed. The progress of the last decade will undoubtedly be eclipsed when manufacturers thus combine their research and present their united facilities to the instrument-using industries. For example, the standardization of bulbs, connections, protective sockets, thermocouples, charts, scales, ranges, etc., has been initiated in the United States, but as yet only on a small scale.

Types of Automatic Regulators.—All regulators require some form of power to operate a valve, damper, etc., in order to maintain the optimum condition.

Self-operating regulators requiring no auxiliary power are directly installed (*i.e.,* on a steam line) and usually consist of a globe or balanced valve operated by a bellows; the expansion of the bellows being obtained in temperature regulators by the dilation or evaporation of a liquid in a sensitive bulb, and in pressure regulators by the pressure which is to be regulated. This group of devices includes thermostats and damper regulators.

Air-operated regulators are the most wide-spread in industrial process service. They utilize the ample and flexible power of compressed air, controlling its flow to an operative mechanism which usually embodies an elastic diaphragm. Pilot valves add extreme sensitiveness to ample power, obviating the use of bellows—a small capsular or spiral spring or Bourdon tube being sufficient. (*See* Plate, figs. 6 and 7.)

Electrically operated regulators function on the relay principle and actuate standardized electrical mechanisms. Heavy work may be performed through their agency but their on-and-off action produces the frequently objectionable "saw-tooth" record. On a temperature application, for instance, the steam valve would "hunt" whereas air-operated regulators can provide exact throttling regulation. (*See* Plate, fig. 1.)

Steam-operated regulators utilize the power of the steam which they control. They embody the sensitive bulb, capillary tube and capsular spring. This latter operates a pilot valve so located that the pressure above a steam diaphragm may be varied with respect to the pressure below it. Pressure fluctuations of the steam supply cannot destroy accuracy, for the differential principle is used. Valves up to 4 in. are successfully operated by diaphragms up to 11 in. diameter. (*See* Plate, figs. 3 and 4.)

Temperature Systems. *Fixed Stem.*—It is sometimes possible to use the "solid expansion" principle, and the sensitive member then consists of a bimetallic stem (or of a carbon or quartz rod

BY COURTESY OF (1, 2, 4) THE C. J. TAGLIABUE MANUFACTURING COMPANY, (5) THE BROWN INSTRUMENT COMPANY, (3) THE REPUBLIC FLOW METERS COMPANY, (6, 7) THE FOXBORO COMPANY

INSTALLATIONS OF AUTOMATIC CONTROLLERS IN VARIOUS INDUSTRIES

1. Process controller in milk pasteurization. The automatic cycle controller, on the pedestal to left, regulates the filling of each of the separate pasteurization vats, to the right, with the proper quantity of milk; holds the fluid for the required length of time; maintains the proper heat at a uniform temperature, and empties the vats when the cycle has been completed. 2. Process controller in tyre manufacturing. Automatic combination controllers which maintain the correct cure temperature and the time in tyre vulcanization. 3. Regulating and indicating instruments in a modern boiler room, indicating and regulating the flow of steam, air, water and gas. 4. Steam-operated temperature controllers on a bottle washing machine. 5. Decorating lehr, or heated oven, in a glass plant. High grade perfumery bottles are passed through the lehr for annealing and burning on the enamel decorations. An automatic control pyrometer governs the motor driven valve in the rectangular box to the right. 6. Interior of a temperature recorder-controller. Air-operated recorder showing helical tubes which actuate a flapper valve, one for heat control and the other for vapour or humidity control. All temperature variations are recorded graphically. 7. Diaphragm temperature control valve, air-operated. Among other uses the valve may be installed in an oil still, dyeing machine, tyre press, or pasteurization vat

within a metal tube) to which the instrument "head" with its graduated dial is directly attached. The great majority of applications, however, demand a *remote* bulb or thermocouple with either a closed system or an electrical system.

Closed Systems consist of bulb, capillary tube and Bourdon tube or capsular spring. They are either *completely* filled with mercury, another liquid or a gas; or *partially* filled with a volatile liquid the vapour pressure of which is utilized.

Electric Systems possess three advantages: (1) applicability to high temperature work, (2) practicability of long distance regulation, (3) replaceability of sensitive element. *Radiation Pyrometric Systems* are seldom used for automatic regulation. *Resistance Systems* are applicable for temperatures up to 300° F with base metal (nickel) elements and up to 1,500° F with platinum. *Thermoelectric Systems* may be of the galvanometric or potentiometric type. The latter has several advantages for "medium" temperatures. Usual range limitations are 300° to 1,800° F with base metal and 1,000° to 2,500° F with rare metal couples.

Other Conditions. *Pressure.*—The majority of pressure regulators are of the self-operating type, but for process work the air-operated type is being increasingly adopted. "Absolute pressure" and "differential pressure" regulators are in use in gas and by-product plants.

Humidity.—In general, instruments regulating the humidity in dryers consist of a pair of automatic temperature regulators of the closed system type—the bulb of one being affected by "air temperature" while the bulb of the other is enclosed in a constantly moistened porous sleeve exposed to the cooling effect of fairly rapid air circulation. The dry-bulb regulator unit controls the source of heat, while the wet-bulb unit controls the "spray." Many ingenious humidity regulators have recently appeared, including models which provide a "drying schedule."

Timing.—The first automatic regulators for this purpose were "modified alarm clocks." Modern ones dependably perform the complex cycles of operations required in vulcanization, dyeing, pasteurization of milk, etc. (*See* ROBOT.)

Liquid Level.—An "automatic liquid level regulator" is to be found in every modern bathroom, but the industrial types necessarily differ. They utilize auxiliary power to operate large valves. Extra heavy and corrosion-resisting models are used in petroleum refineries and chemical plants under severe temperature and pressure conditions.

Flow.—While flow meters are being increasingly adopted in power plants and numerous industries, the demand for automatic regulation of flow has not as yet brought about the full development of special instruments.

Specific Gravity.—Two types of devices which automatically regulate the density of the substance being processed are commercially manufactured. One utilizes the hydrometric principle and embodies a float chamber; the other utilizes the electrical resistance of the substance being processed.

Speed.—Standardized commercial devices consist essentially of tachometers provided with electric contacts or other means of operating levers, rheostats or other appliances.

See *The Instrument World* (London) and *Instruments* (Pittsburgh, Pa.).   (M. F. Bé.)

REGULUS, MARCUS ATILIUS, Roman general and consul (for the second time) in the ninth year of the First Punic War (256 B.C.). He was one of the commanders in the naval expedition which shattered the Carthaginian fleet at Ecnomus, and landed an army on Carthaginian territory (*see* PUNIC WARS).

The other consul was recalled, Regulus being left behind to finish the war. After a severe defeat at Adys near Carthage, the Carthaginians were inclined for peace, but the terms proposed by Regulus were so harsh that they resolved to continue the war. In 255, Regulus was completely defeated and taken prisoner by the Spartan Xanthippus. There is no further trustworthy information about him. According to tradition, he remained in captivity until 250, when after the defeat of the Carthaginians at Panormus he was sent to Rome on parole to negotiate a peace or exchange of prisoners. On his arrival he strongly urged the senate to refuse both proposals, and returning to Carthage was

tortured to death (Horace, *Odes*, iii. 5). The story is insufficiently attested; it may have been invented to excuse the treatment of Carthaginian prisoners at Rome but it served to make Regulus the type of heroic endurance to the later Romans.

See Polybius i, 25–34; Florus ii, 2; Cicero, *De Officiis*, iii, 26; Livy, *Epit.* 18; Valerius Maximus ix, 2; Sil. Ital. vi, 299–550; Appian, *Punica*, 4; Zonaras viii, 15; *see also* O. Jäger, *M. Atilius Regulus* (1878).

REHABILITATION, MEDICAL AND VOCATIONAL. Medical rehabilitation has frequently been termed the third phase of medicine, following preventive medicine and curative medicine and surgery. In contrast to convalescence, the period in which the patient is left alone to let nature and time take their course, rehabilitation assists the patient in reaching the maximum of his physical, emotional, social and vocational potentials.

The first objective of medical rehabilitation is to eliminate the physical disability if that is possible; the second, to reduce or alleviate the disability to the greatest extent possible; and the third, to retrain the person with a residual physical disability to live and work within the limits of his disability and to the extent of his capabilities. Much of the interest in expanding rehabilitation opportunities and services for the handicapped resulted both directly and indirectly from World War II when attention was focused on the problems of disabled servicemen. Such advances, however, were not entirely due to this impetus, as the growth of rehabilitation services for the handicapped had become a part of a total pattern of an expanding community, national and global consciousness of social welfare, which was reflected in similar advances in all educational, health and social services.

Except in a few isolated instances, the physically handicapped person must be retrained to walk and travel, to care for his daily needs, to use normal methods of transportation, to use ordinary toilet facilities, to apply and remove his own prosthetic devices, and to communicate orally or in writing. These are such simple things that they are frequently overlooked, but the personal, vocational and social success of the handicapped person is dependent upon them.

Some outstanding rehabilitation programs in various parts of the world have demonstrated that rehabilitation to the point of self-care and even to full or limited employment is possible for many of the chronically ill who have been hospitalized for long periods.

Paraplegia.—Paraplegia is a condition resulting from the severing of the spinal cord in which the patient is left without the power of motion or feeling below the level of the severance. Formerly, most patients suffering such disabilities died within a relatively short time from kidney infections, decubitus ulcers (bed sores) or other complications. Of the 400 United States veterans of World War I thus disabled, only two were alive 20 years later. With the 2,500 United States paraplegic veterans of World War II, however, the story was different. More than 80% of them were at work or in school in the late 1950s.

The advances in paraplegic rehabilitation for disabled veterans in Great Britain and the United States were extended to the far greater number of civilians who suffer the same condition as a result of automobile accidents, surf and diving accidents and disease. Although paralyzed from the waist down, these people have demonstrated that with the proper rehabilitation training they could once again take their places in society as self-sufficient, productive citizens.

Hemiplegia.—One of the major causes of disability throughout the world, and particularly in the northern European and North American countries, is hemiplegia, or paralysis of one side, following stroke of apoplexy. Stroke was formerly believed to be a hopeless situation and the patient was relegated to the chronic hospital or the back bedroom to wait until a second, third or fourth attack came. This concept, however, was proved to be invalid.

In a study reported in 1949, it was noted that 90% of the strokes suffered by individuals in the older age groups were caused by thrombosis, or a blocking of the blood supply. For those surviving six to eight weeks after the initial attack, life expectancy was soon the same as for others of their age who had not had strokes. The 1949 study found only a 2% to 3% recurrence. Thus, even a severe stroke need not mean the end of a productive useful life. In a 1953 study at Bellevue hospital, New York city, among 1,000 patients who underwent modern rehabilitation training after strokes, 90% were able to walk, meet all the needs of daily living and live noninstitutional lives, and 40% were able to return to some gainful work.

In modern methods of treating patients who have had strokes caused by thrombosis, early ambulation or walking is practised just as it is in modern surgery. Exercise is started as soon as the patient becomes conscious, and walking training instituted as rapidly as is medically feasible. Most patients with hemiplegia resulting from strokes can be rehabilitated in an average of two months.

About half require a small brace on the lower leg, and a considerable percentage have a persistent lack of function in the affected hand. The overwhelming majority are capable mentally and physically of taking their places back in active life again.

Cerebral Palsy.—An almost totally neglected disability until the late 1940s, cerebral palsy thereafter gained attention throughout the world. Cerebral palsy is a neuromuscular disability caused by damage to the motor centres of the brain. This damage, which may occur before or during infancy, causes varying disturbances of motor function such as spasticity, weakness, inco-ordination, athetosis, rigidity or tremors.

These neuromuscular dysfunctions may be accompanied by mental retardation, sensory disorders, convulsions, ear and eye disabilities, and disorders of behaviour. The condition apparently occurs more frequently in premature children, the first-born and those with heavy birth weight where prolonged labour is more frequent. It occurs more often in infants of older women and in boys than girls. This may be caused by the fact that older women, on the average, have heavier babies, and boys, on the average, weigh more than girls at birth. The condition also seems to occur more frequently among white than among Negro children. This may stem from the average smaller size of Negro newborn and the lower incidence of the Rh-negative factor in the blood of Negroes. With these exceptions, there seem to be no economic, social or geographic predilections for cerebral palsy.

The only logical approach to the problem is to consider each child individually, provide him with the specialized medical, rehabilitation and educational services he needs and then make an evaluation of his mental capacities on the basis of his ability to profit by these opportunities.

Multiple Sclerosis.—This is a chronic, crippling disease of the nervous system which strikes particularly persons between the ages of 20 and 40; it also was once considered a hopeless disease. There was no specific diagnostic test; its cause and cure were unknown and the disease was progressive and unpredictable. The myelin surrounding the nerves is destroyed in patches and replaced by scar tissue. As a result, nerve impulses do not pass properly from the brain to the muscles and other organs which they activate.

Although the disease is progressive and crippling, the life span of most multiple sclerosis patients is not much less than that of the average person. In a study completed in 1951 at the Mayo clinic, Rochester, Minn., it was found that 79% of more than 400 patients observed were still living ten years after the diagnosis of the disease. Many of these patients undoubtedly had the disease for some time before it was diagnosed. This compared favourably with the 95% survival rate in the United States at that time for the general population.

Nor does the fact that the disease is progressively crippling mean necessarily that the patient cannot continue to earn a livelihood. The same study showed that of the patients who were working and walking at the beginning of the 10-year period, 42% were still able to continue these activities at the end of the period.

Unfortunately, because of the lack of facilities throughout the world for rehabilitation and the prejudice and misunderstanding that still surrounded this disease in the late 1950s, most multiple sclerotic patients do not have the opportunity for rehabilitation training and employment, even though activity and holding employment seem to be the best possible form of therapy for this condition.

Epilepsy.—One of the world's most misunderstood medical conditions, epilepsy is a fairly common disease with an incidence rate in the developed parts of the world about the same as that of tuberculosis and diabetes. Studies show that among all epileptics, about two-thirds are of average or above average intelligence, 23% are of slightly below average intelligence, and only 16% are mentally deficient. Unfortunately, most of the popular concepts about epilepsy have had their origins with this latter group, most of whom are institutionalized.

Epilepsy is fundamentally a disorder of the brain cell metabolism, but its exact cause was still unknown in the 1950s. The condition itself is not inherited, but a predisposition or susceptibility may be. With the electroencephalograph, an electronic precision instrument which records the electric potentials of the brain, predisposition or susceptibility may be determined. Among the factors which may precipitate epilepsy are brain damage resulting from injuries prior to or during birth, subsequent head injuries, tumours, circulatory changes or infection following such diseases as encephalitis, measles, meningitis or whooping cough.

As a result of research centred around the use of the electroencephalograph, drugs were developed to control completely seizures in about 50% of all cases and to reduce markedly the number and intensity of seizures in another 30%.

Despite the great strides in bringing epilepsy under control medically, there were not similar social advances in casting aside the misunderstanding, social stigma and prejudice surrounding the disease.

Summary.—The degree of actual medical control in these conditions, and such other conditions causing chronic disability as arthritis, disease of the heart and circulation, diabetes, amputations, Parkinson's disease, muscular dystrophy, poliomyelitis and tuberculosis, varies, as does their physical effect upon the patient. Some persons, for example, suffering the residual effects of poliomyelitis may have only a slight limp which goes unnoticed. Others may be so severely affected that they must spend the remainder of their lives in the respirator or iron lung. Regardless of the disease causing the disability or the degree of disability within the individual, experience has shown that there are few, if any, disabled persons for which something cannot be done through rehabilitation to assist them in reaching a higher level of physical, social or emotional adjustment.

BIBLIOGRAPHY.—Howard A. Rusk and Eugene J. Taylor, *New Hope for the Handicapped* (New York, Toronto, 1949); United Nations, *Modern Methods of Rehabilitation of the Adult Disabled* (New York, 1952); *Rehabilitation of the Handicapped*, Social Welfare Information Series, special issue (New York, 1953); Edith Buchwald *et al.*, *Physical Rehabilitation for Daily Living* (New York, 1952); *Disabilities, How to Live With Them* (London, 1952); Roger G. Barker *et al.*, *Adjustment to Physical Handicap and Illness* (New York, 1953); Henry Redkey, *Rehabilitation Centers in the United States* (Chicago, 1953); Henry H. Kessler, *Rehabilitation of the Physically Handicapped* (New York, London, 1953); *Proceedings,* Sixth World Congress, International Society for the Welfare of Cripples, 1954 (New York, 1955); Howard A. Rusk and Eugene J. Taylor, *Living with a Disability* (New York, Toronto, 1953).   (H. A. Rk.; E. J. Tr.)

REHOBOAM, son and successor of king Solomon (*q.v.*), began to reign *c.* 931 B.C. He was not acceptable to the northern tribes of Israel, who recalled Jeroboam from his exile in Egypt and made Rehoboam's contemptuous refusal of their demands the occasion for instituting a rival kingdom under Jeroboam (I Kings xii). It is probable that this was done with the encouragement of Egypt. Shishak of Egypt attacked the kingdom of Judah *c.* 930, and despoiled the temple at Jerusalem of its treasures. Rehoboam's reign was marked by constant conflict with the kingdom of Israel. An unfavourable judgment is pronounced on him by the editor of Kings because he favoured customs connected with Baal worship.

The fact that his mother was an Ammonitess may in some measure account for this. He was succeeded after a reign of 17 years by his son Abijah (in I Kings, Abijam) of whom little is known save a victory over Jeroboam.

REICHENAU, a picturesque island in the Untersee or western arm of the lake of Constance, 3 mi. long by 1 mi. broad, and connected with the east shore by a causeway ¾ mi. long. It is in the *Land* of Baden, Ger. It had 2,606 inhabitants in 1933. The soil is fertile, and excellent wine is produced in sufficient quantity for exportation. The Benedictine abbey of Reichenau, founded in 724, was long celebrated for its wealth and for the services rendered by its monks to the cause of learning. In 1540 the abbey, which had previously been independent, was annexed to the see of Constance, and in 1799 it was secularized. The abbey church, dating in part from the 9th century, contains the tomb of Charles the Fat (d. 888), who retired to this island in 887, after losing the empire of Charlemagne.

REICHENBACH, a town in the Prussian province of Silesia, Ger., on the Peile, at the foot of the Eulengebirge, a spur of the Riesengebirge, 30 mi. S.W. of Breslau by rail. Pop. (1939) 17,045. Among its industries are dyeing, brewing and machine building and the manufacture of chemicals and glass buttons, and there is a considerable trade in grain and cattle. Here was held, in 1790, the congress which resulted in the convention of Reichenbach—between Great Britain, Prussia, Austria, Poland and Holland—guaranteeing the integrity of Turkey. Here, too, in 1813, was signed the treaty for the prosecution of the war against France.

REICHENBACH, a German town in Saxony, situated in the Vogtland, 11 mi. S.W. of Zwickau, at the junction of the main lines of railway Dresden-Leipzig-Hof. Pop. (1939) 31,266. The earliest mention of the town occurs in a document of 1212. Woollen manufacture was introduced in the 15th century, and took the place of the mining industry. The industries include the manufacture of textile goods and machinery and dyeing.

REICHENBERG: *see* LIBEREC.

REICHENHALL, German town in Upper Bavaria, on the river Saalach, 1,570 ft. above sea level, 9 mi. S.W. of Salzburg. Pop. (1939) 13,156. The brine springs of Reichenhall are mentioned in a document of the 8th century and were perhaps known to the Romans; but almost all trace of antiquity of the town was destroyed by a conflagration in 1834. The brine conduit to Traunstein dates from 1618. The water of some of the springs, the sources of which are 50 ft. below the surface, is so strongly saturated with salt (up to 24%) that it is at once conducted to the boiling houses, while that of the others is first submitted to a process of evaporation.

Reichenhall is the centre of the four chief Bavarian saltworks: Berchtesgaden, Traunstein and Rosenheim. In the 19th century it became an important health resort.

REICHSBANK: *see* BANKING.

REICHSTADT, NAPOLEON FRANCIS JOSEPH CHARLES, DUKE OF (1811–1832), known by the Bonapartists as Napoleon II, was the son of the Emperor Napoleon I and Marie Louise, archduchess of Austria. He was born on March 20, 1811, in Paris at the Tuileries palace. He was at first named the king of Rome, after the analogy of the heirs of the emperors of the Holy Roman Empire. By his birth the Napoleonic dynasty seemed to be finally established; but in three years it crumbled in the dust.

At the time of the downfall of the empire (April 1814) Marie Louise and the king of Rome were at Blois with Joseph and Jerome Bonaparte, who wished to keep them as hostages. This design, however, was frustrated. Napoleon abdicated in favour of his son; but events prevented the reign of Napoleon II from being more than titular.

While Napoleon repaired to Elba, his consort and child went to Vienna; and they remained in Austria during the Hundred Days (1815), despite efforts made by the Bonapartists to carry off the prince to his father at Paris.

In the settlements of 1814 and 1815 (*see* MARIE LOUISE), the powers opposed all participation of the prince in the affairs of his mother's duchy of Parma. He therefore remained at Vienna.

From this time onward he became, as it were, a pawn in the complex game of European politics, his claims being put forward sometimes by Metternich, sometimes by the unionists of Italy, while occasionally malcontents in France used his name to discredit the French Bourbons. In November 1816 the court of Vienna informed Marie Louise that her son could not succeed to the duchies. This decision was confirmed by the treaty of Paris

of June 10, 1817. The title of "duke of Reichstadt" was conferred on him on July 22, 1818, by way of compensation. Thus Napoleon I, who once averred that he would prefer that his son should be strangled rather than brought up as an Austrian prince, lived to see his son reduced to a rank inferior to that of the Austrian archdukes.

His education was confided chiefly to Count Dietrichstein, who found him precocious, volatile, passionate and fond of military affairs. His nature was sensitive, as appeared on his receiving the news of the death of his father in 1821. The upheaval in France in 1830 and the disturbances which ensued led many Frenchmen to turn their thoughts to Napoleon II; but though Metternich dallied for a time with the French Bonapartists, he had no intention of inaugurating a Napoleonic revival.

The duke's indulgence in physical exercise far beyond his powers aggravated a natural weakness of the chest, and he died on July 22, 1832.

See A. M. Barthelemy and J. P. A. Méry, *Le Fils de l'homme* (Paris, 1829); Baron G. I. Comte de Montbel, *Le Duc de Reichstadt* (Paris, 1832); J. de Saint-Félix, *Histoire de Napoléon II* (Paris, 1853); Guy de l'Hérault, *Histoire de Napoléon II* (Paris, 1853); Count Anton von Prokesch-Osten, *Mein Verhältniss zum Herzog von Reichstadt* (Stuttgart, 1878); H. Welschinger, *Le Roi de Rome* (Paris, 1897); E. de Wertheimer, *The Duke of Reichstadt* (Eng. ed., 1905); C. Tschudi, *Napoleon's Son* (Eng. tr., 1912); H. Fleischmann, *Le Roi de Rome et des femmes* (1910); M. Rostand's *L'Aiglon;* Marie Louise, consort of Napoleon I, *Private Diaries* (1922).

REID, SIR GEORGE (1841–1913), knighted in 1902, Scottish artist, was born in Aberdeen on Oct. 31, 1841. He was apprenticed in 1854 for seven years to Messrs. Keith & Gibb, lithographers in Aberdeen. In 1861 Reid took lessons from an itinerant portrait-painter, William Niddrie, who had been a pupil of James Giles, R.S.A., and afterward entered the school of the Board of Trustees in Edinburgh. His first portrait of interest was that of George Macdonald, the poet and novelist, now the property of the university of Aberdeen. In 1865 he went to Utrecht to study under A. Mollinger, whose work he admired for its unity and simplicity. For some years after this his work failed to please the Scottish authorities, but after his further studies under Yvon in Paris and Josef Israëls at The Hague, Reid's success was assured.

A typical landscape is his "Whins in Bloom," which combines great breadth with fine detail. His flower pieces, such as "Roses," were brilliant, but his most individual work is found in his portraits, which show great insight.

REID, SIR GEORGE HOUSTON, K.C.M.G., 1909 (1845–1918), Australian politician, was born on Feb. 25, 1845, at Johnstone, Renfrewshire, and emigrated in 1852 to Australia. He practised as a barrister in Sydney and was elected to the New South Wales parliament in 1880. In 1883–84 he was minister of public instruction and from 1891–94 was leader of the free-trade party. In 1894 he became premier and retained that office until 1899.

Reid played a conspicuous part in the federation movement and was a member of the first commonwealth parliament in 1901, leading the free-trade opposition to Sir Edmund Barton. In 1904 he became prime minister, but he stood for a program which was unacceptable to a predominantly protectionist country, and after his fall in the following year he never again held office. He led the opposition from 1905–08 and in the latter year retired from Australian politics. In 1909 he was appointed high commissioner in London; and on the expiration of his term entered the house of commons as Conservative member for St. George's, Hanover Square, London. He published *My Reminiscences* in 1917. He died on Sept. 12, 1918.

REID, ROBERT (1862–1929), American artist, was born at Stockbridge, Mass., on July 29, 1862. He studied at the art schools of the Boston Museum of Fine Arts, the Art Students' league, New York, and under Boulanger and Lefebvre in Paris. His early pictures were figures of French peasants, painted at Étaples, but subsequently he became best known for mural decoration and designs for stained glass. He contributed with others to the frescoes of the dome of the Liberal Arts building at the

Columbian exposition, Chicago, in 1893. Other work is in the Congressional library, Washington, D.C., the Appellate court house, New York, and the State house, Boston, where are his three large panels, "James Otis Delivering his Speech against the Writs of Assistance," "Paul Revere's Ride" and the "Boston Tea Party." He executed a panel for the American pavilion at the Paris exhibition, 1900, and in 1906 he completed a series of ten stained glass windows for a church at Fairhaven, Mass., for the Rogers memorial. In 1906 he became a full member of the National Academy of Design. He died at Clifton Springs, New York, on December 2, 1929.

REID, THOMAS (1710–1796), the founder of the "Scottish School" of philosophy, was born on April 26, 1710, at Strachan in Kincardineshire, where his father was minister. He graduated at Aberdeen in 1726, remained there as librarian for ten years, and was presented to the living of Newmachar near Aberdeen in 1737. His first philosophical work, *Essay on Quantity, occasioned by reading a Treatise in which Simple and Compound Ratios are applied to Virtue and Merit,* denying the possibility of mathematical treatment of moral subjects, appeared in the *Transactions* of the Royal Society (1748). In 1740 Reid married a cousin, the daughter of a London physician. In 1752 he became professor of philosophy at King's college, Aberdeen. The Aberdeen Philosophical Society (the "Wise Club"), which numbered among its members Campbell, Beattie, Gerard and Dr. John Gregory, was mainly founded by Reid, who was secretary for the first year (1758). Reid propounded his point of view in the *Enquiry into the Human Mind on the Principles of Common Sense* (1764). In this year, Reid succeeded Adam Smith as professor of moral philosophy at Glasgow.

After 17 years he retired to complete his philosophical system. The *Essays on the Intellectual Powers of Man* appeared in 1785, and their ethical complement, the *Essays on the Active Powers of the Human Mind,* in 1788. These, with an account of Aristotle's *Logic* appended to Lord Kames's *Sketches of the History of Man* (1774), conclude the list of works published in Reid's lifetime. He died of paralysis on Oct. 7, 1796.

The key to Reid's philosophy is to be found in his revulsion from the sceptical conclusions of Hume. In several passages of his writings he expressly dates his philosophical awakening from the appearance of the *Treatise of Human Nature.* In the dedication of the *Enquiry,* he says: "The ingenious author of that treatise upon the principles of Locke—who was no sceptic—hath built a system of scepticism which leaves no ground to believe any one thing rather than its contrary. His reasoning appeared to me to be just; there was, therefore, a necessity to call in question the principles upon which it was founded, or to admit the conclusion." Having decided that the rationalist philosophy was subversive of religion and morals he examined the doctrine, which he declared to be contrary to experience. He appealed not to eternal truths, but to the testimony of experience. He maintained that we do not start with "ideas," and afterwards refer them to objects; we are never restricted to our own minds, but are from the first immediately related to a permanent world. There are certain presuppositions unassailable by doubt which are older and more authoritative than any philosophy. Among these he places the belief in a material external world and in the existence of the soul. Reid has a variety of names for the principles which, by their presence, lift us out of subjectivity into perception. One of these, "principles of common sense," which became the current one, conveyed a false impression of Scottish philosophy. Reid did not merely appeal from the reasoned conclusions of philosophers to the unreasoned beliefs of common life. His real mode of procedure is to redargue Hume's conclusions by a refutation of the premises inherited by him from his predecessors. Reid everywhere unites common sense and reason, making the former "only another name for one branch or degree of reason." Reason, as judging of things self-evident, is called common sense to distinguish it from ratiocination or reasoning. And in regard to Reid's favourite proof of the principles in question by reference to "the consent of ages and nations, of the learned and unlearned," it is only fair to observe that this argument assumes a much more

scientific form in the *Essays,* where it is almost identified with an appeal to "the structure and grammar of all languages." "The structure of all languages," he says, "is grounded upon common sense." To take but one example, "the distinction between sensible qualities and the substance to which they belong, and between thought and the mind that thinks, is not the invention of philosophers; it is found in the structure of all languages, and therefore must be common to all men who speak with understanding" (Hamilton's *Reid,* pp. 229 and 454).

BIBLIOGRAPHY.—The best edition of Reid's *Works* is that by Sir William Hamilton (2 vols.). *See* also "Reid and the Philosophy of Common Sense" in J. F. Ferrier's *Lectures,* ed. Grant and Lushington (1866); A. C. Fraser, *Thomas Reid* ("Famous Scots Series," 1898); K. Peters, *Thomas Reid als Kritiker von David Hume* (Leipzig, 1909); O. M. Jones, *Empiricism and Intuitionism in Reid's Common Sense Philosophy* (1927).

REID, THOMAS MAYNE (1818–1883), better known as MAYNE REID, British novelist, the son of a Presbyterian minister, was born at Ballyroney, Co. Down, Ireland, on April 4, 1818. His own early life was as adventurous as any boy reader of his novels could desire. When 20 years old he went to America in search of adventure. He traded on the Red river, studying the ways of the red man and the white pioneer; he made acquaintance with the Missouri in the same way. In Philadelphia, where he was engaged in journalism from 1843 to 1846, he made the acquaintance of Edgar Allan Poe. When the war with Mexico broke out in 1846 he obtained a captain's commission, was present at the siege and capture of Vera Cruz, and led a forlorn hope at Chapultepec, where he sustained such severe injuries that his life was despaired of. In one of his novels he says that he believed theoretically in the military value of untrained troops, and that he had found his theories confirmed in actual warfare. He offered his services to the Hungarian insurgents in 1849, raised a body of volunteers, and sailed for Europe, but arrived too late. He then settled in England, and began his career of a novelist with the publication, in 1850, of the *Rifle Rangers.* This was followed next year by the *Scalp Hunters.* He never surpassed his first productions, except perhaps in *The White Chief* (1859) and *The Quadroon* (1856); but he continued to produce tales of self-reliant enterprise and exciting adventure with great fertility. He died in London on Oct. 22, 1883.

See *Memoir* (1890) by his widow, Elizabeth Mayne Reid.

REID, WHITELAW (1837–1912), American journalist and diplomatist, was born of Scotch parentage, near Xenia, O., on Oct. 27, 1837. He graduated at Miami University in 1856, and spoke frequently in behalf of John C. Frémont, the Republican candidate for the presidency in that year. In 1860 he became legislative correspondent at Columbus for several Ohio newspapers, including the Cincinnati *Gazette,* of which he was made city editor in 1861. He was war correspondent for the *Gazette* in 1861–62, serving also as volunteer aide-de-camp to generals Thomas A. Morris, William S. Rosecrans in West Virginia, and was Washington correspondent of the *Gazette* in 1862–68. In 1868 he became a leading editorial writer for the New York *Tribune,* in the following year was made managing editor, and in 1872, upon the death of Horace Greeley, became the principal proprietor and editor-in-chief. In 1905 Reid relinquished his active editorship of the *Tribune,* but retained financial control. He served as minister to France in 1889–92, and in 1892 was the unsuccessful Republican candidate for vice president on the ticket with Benjamin Harrison. In 1897 he was special ambassador of the United States on the occasion of Queen Victoria's jubilee; in 1902 was special ambassador of the United States at the coronation of King Edward VII., and in 1905 became ambassador to Great Britain. In 1881 he married a daughter of Darius Ogden Mills (1825–1910), a prominent financier. He died in London on Dec. 15, 1912.

His publications include *After the War* (1867); *Ohio in the War* (1868); *Some Consequences of the Last Treaty of Paris* (1899); *Our New Duties* (1899); *Later Aspects of Our New Duties* (1899); *Problems of Expansion* (1900); *The Greatest Fact in Modern History* (1906); *How America Faced its Educational Problem* (1906); *The Scot in America and the Ulster Scot* (1912), and posthumously, *American and English Studies* (1913).

See Royal Cortissoz, *The Life of Whitelaw Reid* (1921).

REIDSVILLE, a town of Rockingham county, North Carolina, U.S.A., in the northern part of the state, at an altitude of 822 ft.; on the Southern railway and federal highway 29 and state highways 158, 67 and 68; 24 mi. S.W. of Danville, Va. Pop. 11,760 in 1950. It is a tobacco marketing and shipping point; has cotton and silk mills, cotton bags, leather preservative and woodworking plants. One plant makes 100,000,000 cigarettes daily. The city was founded about 1829 and incorporated in 1873. It has a commission-manager form of government.

REIGATE, a market town and municipal borough in the Reigate parliamentary division of Surrey, England, 24 mi. S.W. of London by the S.R. Pop. (est. 1938) 36,630. Area, 16 sq.mi. Reigate (Cherchefelle, Regat, Reygate), at a cross-road on the Pilgrim's Way, at the foot of the North Downs, had a castle, a stronghold of the Warennes in the 12th, 13th and 14th centuries. On the death of Edith, the widow of Edward the Confessor, to whom it belonged, William I secured the manor of Cherchefelle. It was granted by William Rufus to Earl Warenne, through whose family it passed in 1347 to the earls of Arundel. The name Reigate occurs in 1199. Burgesses of Reigate are mentioned in a close roll of 1348, but no early charter is known. The town was incorporated in 1863. It returned two members to parliament from 1295 till 1831, and afterwards one member until 1867, when it was disfranchised for corruption. Of the old castle (destroyed *c.* 1648), there remains only the entrance to a cave beneath, 150 ft. long and from 10 to 12 ft. high, excavated in the sandstone, which was used as a guardroom. The grounds are laid out as a public garden. The old town hall (1708) is on the site of an ancient chapel dedicated to St. Thomas Becket. In the chancel of the parish church of St. Mary (Transitional Norman to Perpendicular) is buried Lord Howard, the commander of the English navy against the Spanish Armada. The grammar school was founded in 1675. The borough, which was considerably extended in 1933, contains the modern town of Redhill.

REIMARUS, HERMANN SAMUEL (1694–1768), German philosopher and man of letters, was born at Hamburg, on Dec. 22, 1694. He was educated by his father and by the famous scholar J. A. Fabricius, whose son-in-law he became, and later at Jena. He was professor of Hebrew and Oriental languages in the high school of his native city from 1727 till his death. His house was the centre of the highest culture, and a monument of his influence in that city still remains in the *Haus der patriotischen Gesellschaft,* where the learned and artistic societies partly founded by him still meet. He died on March 1, 1768.

Reimarus's reputation as a scholar rests on the valuable edition of Dio Cassius (1750–52) which he prepared from the materials collected by J. A. Fabricius. He also published *Abhandlungen von den vornehmsten Wahrheiten der natürlichen Religion* (Hamburg, 1754, 6th ed. 1791); *Vernunftlehre* (Hamburg and Kiel, 1756, 5th ed., 1790); *Betrachtungen über der Kunsttriebe der Thiere* (Hamburg, 1762, 4th ed., 1798). But his best-known work is his *Apologie oder Schutzschrift für die vernünftigen Verehrer Gottes* (kept back during his lifetime) from which, after his death, Lessing published certain chapters under the title *Wolfenbüttel Fragments* (see LESSING, GOTTHOLD EPHRAIM). Other portions were published by "C. A. Schmidt" (1787) and D. W. Klose (1850–52). The original MS. is in the Hamburg town library.

The standpoint of the *Apologie* is that of pure naturalistic deism. Miracles and mysteries, with the exception of the Creation, are denied, and natural religion is put forward as the absolute contradiction of revealed. The essential truths of the former are the existence of a wise and good Creator and the immortality of the soul. These truths are discoverable by reason, and are such as can constitute the basis of a universal religion and lead to happiness. A revealed religion could never obtain universality, as it could never be intelligible and credible to all men.

See the "Fragments" as published by Lessing, reprinted in vol. xv. of *Lessing's Werke,* Hempel's edition; D. F. Strauss, *H. S. Reimarus und seine Schutzschrift für die vernünftigen Verehrer Gottes* (1862, 2nd ed., 1877); C. Voysey, *Fragments from Reimarus* (1879) (a translation of Strauss's book, with the second part of the seventh fragment, on the "Object of Jesus and his Disciples"); R. Schettler, *Die Stellung d. Philos. Reimarus zur Religion* (Leipzig, 1904), and J. Engert, *Reimarus als Metaphysiker* (Paderborn, 1909).

REIMS (RHEIMS), a city of north-eastern France, chief town of an arrondissement of the department of Marne, 98 mi. E.N.E. of Paris, on the Eastern railway. Pop. (1946) 110,749. Reims stands in a plain on the right bank of the Vesle, a tributary of the Aisne, and on the canal which connects the Aisne with the Marne. South and west rise the "montagne de Reims" and vine-clad hills.

Before the Roman conquest Reims, as *Durocortorum,* was capital of the Remi, from whose name that of the town was subsequently derived. The Remi made voluntary submission to the Romans, and by their fidelity secured the special favour of their conquerors. Christianity was established in the town by the middle of the 3rd century, at which period the bishopric was founded. The consul Jovinus, an influential supporter of the new faith, repulsed the barbarians who invaded Champagne in 336; but the Vandals captured the town in 406 and slew St. Nicasus, and Attila afterwards put it to fire and sword. Clovis, after his victory at Soissons (486), was baptized at Reims in 496 by St. Remigius. Later kings desired to be consecrated at Reims with the oil of the sacred phial which was believed to have been brought from heaven by a dove for the baptism of Clovis and was preserved in the abbey of St. Remi. Meetings of Pope Stephen III. with Pippin the Short, and of Leo III. with Charlemagne, took place at Reims; and here Louis the Débonnaire was crowned by Stephen IV. Louis IV. gave the town and countship of Reims to the archbishop Artaldus in 940. Louis VII. gave the title of duke and peer to William of Champagne, archbishop from 1176 to 1202 and the archbishops of Reims took precedence of the other ecclesiastical peers of the realm.

In the 10th century Reims had become a centre of intellectual culture, Archbishop Adalberon, seconded by the monk Gerbert (afterwards Pope Silvester II.), having founded schools where the "liberal arts" were taught. Adalberon was also one of the prime authors of the revolution which put the Capet house in the place of the Carolingians. The most important prerogative of the archbishops was the consecration of the kings of France—a privilege which was exercised, except in a few cases, from the time of Philip Augustus to that of Charles X. Louis VII. granted the town a communal charter in 1139. The treaty of Troyes (1420) ceded it to the English, who had made a futile attempt to take it by siege in 1360; but they were expelled on the approach of Joan of Arc, who in 1429 caused Charles VII. to be consecrated in the cathedral. A revolt at Reims, caused by the salt tax in 1461, was cruelly repressed by Louis XI. The town sided with the League (1585), but submitted to Henry IV. after the battle of Ivry. In the foreign invasions of 1814 it was captured and recaptured; in 1870–71 it was made by the Germans the seat of a governor-general and impoverished by heavy requisitions.

Reims suffered severely during World War I. The town was heavily bombarded by the Germans in September 1914, and the population took shelter in the huge subterranean wine cellars, occupying old chalk quarries, where dormitories were made, schools were held and a daily paper was published. In 1917 the civilian population which remained was evacuated; in 1918 the town was one of the objectives of the Germans, but it was held until freed by the Allied offensive in October. Reims was then in ruins, and the cathedral was severely damaged, especially on the southwest side. The work of restoration of the cathedral, to the cost of which there was a large American contribution, took many years to complete. The statue of St. Joan of Arc, which stood in front of the cathedral, was removed during World War I for safety and replaced in 1921; many of the art treasures, tapestries, etc., were also saved.

The oldest monument in Reims is the Mars Gate (so called, from a temple to Mars in the neighbourhood), a triumphal arch 108 ft. in length by 43 ft. in height, consisting of three archways flanked by columns. It is popularly supposed to have been erected by the Remi in honour of Augustus when Agrippa made the great roads terminating at the town, but probably belongs to the 3rd or 4th century. In its vicinity a curious mosaic, measuring 36 ft. by 26, with thirty-five medallions representing animals and gladiators, was discovered in 1860. To these remains must be added a Gallo-Roman sarcophagus, said to be that of the consul Jovinus and preserved in the archaeological museum in the cloister of the abbey of St. Remi.

The cathedral of Notre Dame, where the kings of France used to be crowned, replaced an older church (burned in 1211) built on the site of the basilica where Clovis was baptized by St. Remigius. The cathedral, with the exception of the west front, was completed by the end of the 13th century. That portion was erected in the 14th century after 13th-century designs—the nave having in the meantime been lengthened to afford room for the crowds that attended the coronations. In 1481 fire destroyed the roof and the spires. The façade was one of the most perfect masterpieces of the middle ages. The three portals are laden with statues and statuettes. The central portal, dedicated to the Virgin, was surmounted by a rose-window framed in an arch itself decorated with statuary. The rose-window, the statue of the smiling angel, the still more famous "Beau Dieu" statue were all severely damaged in World War I. The gallery of the kings above the rose-window survived but the angel spire was destroyed.

The archiepiscopal palace, built between 1498 and 1509, and in part rebuilt in 1675, was almost completely destroyed. The church of St. Remi (11th, 12th, 13th and 15th centuries) still retains intact its façade and two Romanesque towers; the nave and choir were ruined, and the mausoleum of St. Remigius (1847), containing the reliquary of the saint, behind the high altar, had to be reconstructed.

Reims is the seat of an archbishop, a court of assize and a sub-prefect, and a tribunal and a chamber of commerce. It is an important centre for the combing, carding and spinning of wool and the weaving of flannel, merino, cloth and woollen goods of all kinds. The manufacture of and trade in champagne are also very important. The wine is stored in large cellars tunnelled in the chalk. Other manufactures are linoleum, safes, capsules, bottles, casks, candles, soap and paper. The town is well known for its cakes and biscuits.

REINACH, JOSEPH (1856–1921), French author and politician, was born in Paris on Sept. 30, 1856. After leaving the Lycée Condorcet he was called to the bar in 1887. He attracted the attention of Gambetta by articles on Balkan politics published in the *Revue bleue*, and in Gambetta's *grand ministère* Reinach was his secretary. In the *République française* he waged a steady war against General Boulanger which brought him three duels, one with Edmond Magnier and two with Paul Déroulède. Between 1889 and 1898 he sat for the Chamber of Deputies for Digne. He brought forward many reform bills, advocated complete freedom of the theatre and the press, the abolition of public executions, and denounced political corruption. But he is best known as the champion of Captain Dreyfus. At the time of the original trial he attempted to secure a public hearing of the case, and in 1897 he allied himself with Scheurer-Kestner to demand its revision. He denounced in the *Siècle* the Henry forgery, and Esterhazy's complicity. His articles in the *Siècle* aroused the fury of the anti-Dreyfusard party, especially as he was himself a Jew and therefore open to the charge of bias. He lost his seat in the Chamber of Deputies, and, having refused to fight Henri Rochefort, eventually brought an action for libel against him. Finally, the "affaire" being terminated and Dreyfus pardoned, he undertook to write the history of the case, the first four volumes of which appeared in 1901. This was completed in 1905. In 1906 M. Reinach was re-elected for Digne. He died in Paris on April 18, 1921.

SALOMON REINACH (1858–1932), born at St. Germain-en-Laye on Aug. 29, 1858, brother of Joseph Reinach (*q.v.*), was educated at the École Normale Supérieure, and joined the French school at Athens in 1879. He made valuable archaeological discoveries at Myrina near Smyrna in 1880–82, at Cyme in 1881, at Thasos, Imbros and Lesbos (1882), at Carthage and Meninx (1883–84), at Odessa (1893) and elsewhere. He received in 1886 an appointment at the National Museum of Antiquities at St.

Germain; in 1893 he became assistant keeper, and in 1902 keeper of the national museums. In 1903 he became joint editor of the *Revue archéologique,* and in the same year officer of the Legion of Honour. The lectures he delivered on art at the École du Louvre in 1902–3 were published by him under the title of *Apollo.*

His other works include: *Manuel de philologie classique* (1880–1884); *La Nécropole de Myrina* (1887), written with E. Pottier; *Répertoire de la statuaire grecque et romaine* (3 vols., 1897–98); *Répertoire de peintures du moyen âge et de la Renaissance 1280–1580* (1905, etc.); *Répertoire des vases peints grecs et étrusques* (1900). In 1905 he began his *Cultes, mythes et religions;* and in 1909 he published a general sketch of the history of religions under the title of *Orpheus.*

REINCARNATION: see METEMPSYCHOSIS.

REINDEER, a large Arctic and sub-Arctic deer, the American species of which is called caribou. The reindeer constitutes the

genus *Rangifer*, characterized by the possession of antlers by both sexes, though those of the male are larger and more complex. Reindeer are clumsily built animals, with large lateral hoofs, hairy muzzles, and a curious type of antler with the brow-tine directed downwards. The compact, dense coat is clove-brown in colour above and white below, with a white tail-patch. The ears and tail are short and the throat is maned. A tarsal gland is present. The lateral metacarpal bones are represented only by their lower extremities (*see* DEER).

BY COURTESY OF THE N.Y. ZOOLOGICAL SOCIETY
REINDEER (RANGIFER TARANDUS) It inhabits Arctic and sub-Arctic regions

The type of the genus (*R. tarandus*) is the Scandinavian wild form. In America the barren ground caribou are forms of the old world species. The woodland caribou (*R. caribou* and *R. novaterrae*) are other species. All caribou move around and many herds undertake great migrations in the spring and autumn. A small species (*R. platyrhynchus*) inhabits Spitzbergen and Novaya Zembla.

The reindeer has been domesticated by the Lapps and introduced as a domestic animal into Arctic Canada and Alaska. Reindeer feed largely on lichens, one species of which is the so-called "reindeer moss." The brow-tine is not used to scrape away snow; this is done with the hoofs, the horns being shed before spring.

BIBLIOGRAPHY.—B. Laufer, "Reindeer and its Domestication," *Mem. Amer. Anthrop. Assn.*, vol. 4, p. 91–147 (1917); G. Hatt, "Reindeer Nomadism," *Ibid.*, vol. 6, p. 75–133 (1919); L. J. Palmer, "Raising Reindeer," *U.S. D. Ag. Misc. Pub.* 207 (1934).

REINDEER MOSS (*Cladonia rangiferina*), a species of lichen found in great abundance in Arctic lands. It is an erect, much branched plant, a few inches in height, which covers immense areas somewhat in the manner of pasture grasses in the temperate regions. In many districts it forms the chief food of the reindeer, and it also provides forage for the barren-ground caribou and the musk-ox. (See LICHENS.)

REINECKE, CARL HEINRICH CARSTEN (1824–1910), German composer and pianist, was born at Altona, June 23, 1824. He studied music with his father, with Mendelssohn and with Schumann. From 1846–48 he was court pianist to Christian VIII of Denmark and later taught until 1860, when he became conductor of the Leipzig Gewandhaus, a post he held for 35 years. He died in March 1910. His piano playing was characterized by grace and neatness and at one time he was probably unrivalled as a Mozart player and an accompanist. He wrote a grand opera, *König Manfred*, a comic opera, *Auf hohen Befehl*, a cantata, *Hakon Jarl*, and an overture, which were once frequently played but his most valuable works were those written for educational purposes.

REINFORCED CONCRETE: see FERRO-CONCRETE.

REINFORCED GLASS: see GLASS, SAFETY.

REINHARDT, MAX (1873–1943), Austrian theatrical producer, was born in Baden, near Vienna, Austria, on Sept. 9, 1873. He was educated at the Untergymnasium and later studied for the stage under Emil Burde, and at the School of Acting of the Vienna Conservatorium (1890). He began his professional career in 1893 at the Stadt theatre in Salzburg, where his characterization of elderly rôles attracted the attention of Otto Brahm, who engaged him for the Deutsches theatre, Berlin, in 1894. There he met with notable success, creating such rôles as Baumert in Hauptmann's *The Weavers;* Akim in Tolstoy's *The Power of Darkness;* Engstrand in Ibsen's *Ghosts;* and many others. In 1903 he left the Brahm ensemble to begin his career as a director at the Neues theatre, Berlin, with the production of Shakespeare's *A Midsummer Night's Dream,* in which he assumed leadership of the neoromantic movement against the prevailing school of naturalism. He soon transferred his activities to the Deutsches theatre, where he subsequently produced practically all the plays of Shakespeare, Molière, Goethe, Strindberg, Wedekind, Ibsen, Shaw and others, as well as musical comedies and operas, turning from the purely literary and historical conception of stage management to one essentially dramatic. In 1902, he opened his Kleines theatre, and in 1906 his Kammerspielhaus. He first produced *The Miracle* in 1911. After resigning from the Kammerspielhaus in 1932, he went to the U.S.A., where he produced a film version of *A Midsummer Night's Dream* (1935), Franz Werfel's *The Eternal Road* (1937) and *Rosalinda,* based on Johann Strauss' *Die Fledermaus.* He became a U.S. citizen in 1940. He died in New York city, Oct. 31, 1943. See *Max Reinhardt and His Theatre,* ed. Oliver M. Sayler (1924).

REINKENS, JOSEPH HUBERT (1821–1896), German Old Catholic bishop, was born at Burtscheid, near Aix-la-Chapelle on March 1, 1821. He became professor of ecclesiastical history at Breslau, and in 1865 rector of the university. In 1870, Reinkens opposed the proclamation of the dogma of papal infallibility. He signed the Declaration of Nüremberg in 1871, and took a conspicuous part in the Bonn conferences with the Orientals and Anglicans in 1874 and 1875. The Old Catholics having decided on secession, Reinkens was chosen their bishop in Germany at Cologne in 1873 (*see* OLD CATHOLICS). His best-known theological work is his treatise on Cyprian and the Unity of the Church (1873). In 1881 Reinkens visited England, and in 1894 he defended the validity of Anglican orders against his co-religionists, the Old Catholics of Holland. He died at Bonn on Jan. 4, 1896.

See *Joseph Hubert Reinkens,* by his nephew, J. M. Reinkens (Gotha, 1906).

REINSURANCE. Reinsurance is the term used to denote the transaction whereby a person who has insured a risk insures again a part or the whole of that risk with another person. The purpose of reinsurance is to relieve the original insurer from a liability which is too heavy for him to carry. There is no privity of contract between the reinsurer and the original insured, so that the latter could not sue the former to recover any part of a loss, but the insured could recover in respect of a loss against the original insurer up to the full amount of the policy, notwithstanding that part of it had been reinsured.

In a reinsurance transaction the company which reinsures is called the ceding company, the accepting company is called the reinsurer, and the transaction itself is termed a cession.

It is not known when reinsurance was first practised, though there is evidence of its existence at least as early as the first half of the 18th century. In the early days of insurance insurers did not, as a rule, insure for greater amounts than they were prepared to keep for themselves, and, even when this rule began to be relaxed, the arrangements whereby they relieved themselves of heavy commitments partook more of the nature of co-insurance than of reinsurance. Under such arrangements the original insured was in contractual relationship with each of the insurers.

However, in marine business reinsurance was known nearly 200 years ago, for in 1746 an act of parliament made it illegal, a prohibition which was not raised until 1864. It is thought by some that the Act of 1746 really prohibited double insurance; *i.e.,* where the insured covered his property twice, but the word used in the act is "reassurance." However this may be, it is certain that the growth of reinsurance in various sections of the business was slow until well into the 19th century, and it is only during the past 30 years or so that it has developed into its present important and widespread position.

Reinsurance may be divided into two main branches:— Facultative (or optional) and Treaty (or automatic or obligatory).

Facultative Reinsurance.—This was the original form. By this method each risk is offered for reinsurance separately and the ceding company has a free choice as to where it will offer the business. Similarly the reinsurer has freedom to accept or decline. The term facultative is derived from the power of choice, which this method implies. This system of reinsurance is cumbersome, as each risk reinsured has to be handled separately. The particulars of the risk are first shown to the reinsurer on a slip, which it initials for the share it is prepared to accept. This is followed by a request note; *i.e.,* a formal demand issued by the ceding company to the reinsurer for the specified reinsurance. Upon this the reinsurer issues its take note, which is its official acceptance given pending the issue of a reinsurance policy. This last is the final stage in the transaction, and forms the contract between the parties in respect of the risk reinsured.

The facultative system served its purpose at a time when insurance was transacted on a small scale, and when the need for reinsurance cover was neither great nor urgent. But the need arose in course of time for some more efficient method, and this was eventually found in the reinsurance treaty.

Reinsurance by Treaty.—A treaty is an obligatory arrangement, under which the ceding company binds itself to cede, and the reinsurer binds itself to accept, a fixed share of every risk, of a nature as defined in the contract, which the ceding company has to reinsure. A treaty, therefore, provides not for the reinsurance of an individual risk, but for all the risks of a given class. The power of choice is here eliminated. The two parties are reciprocally bound, one to cede and the other to accept.

This is an advantage to both, since the ceding company knows in advance that it can place the reinsurances and the reinsurer can rely on receiving a regular flow of business under the treaty. It is a condition of all treaties that, as soon as a reinsurance is placed thereunder the reinsurer's liability commences from the same moment as the liability of the ceding company, while the obligation to cede prevents the ceding company placing some of its reinsurances with one reinsurer and some with another, or favouring one at the expense of another. In both these particulars reinsurance by treaty differs from and represents a considerable advance over the older facultative method.

It is extremely rare for a ceding company to place a treaty with only one reinsurer, for this would be to entrust too great a responsibility to one undertaking. It is therefore customary to arrange a treaty so that a number of reinsurers share in it, each accepting only a proportionate part of the business ceded.

There are three kinds of reinsurance treaty in general use:— Quota-share or Open Treaties; Surplus Treaties; and Excess of Loss Treaties.

Quota-Share Treaty.—A quota-share treaty is one under which the ceding company agrees to cede a fixed share of every risk which it accepts from its clients. There is a necessary tendency for reinsurance business to comprise risks of a second class nature, since the better the risk the more the ceding company keeps for itself. But in a quota-share treaty this feature is not present. Every risk must be reinsured, whether it be good or bad, large or small. For this reason the quota-share treaty is not greatly used, except by small companies, which can obtain sound reinsurance cover only by offering attractive terms.

Surplus Treaty.—The surplus treaty is that in common use. Under this the ceding company first fixes the amount it will keep, which is called its retention, and the remainder of the amount insured constitutes the surplus. This is divided amongst the treaty reinsurers according to their due proportion. The whole surplus is usually divided into percentages, each reinsurer taking 1% or more as agreed of every surplus. But the amount which can be ceded is always governed by the ceding company's retention.

Excess of Loss Treaty.—An excess of loss treaty is an agreement under which no part of any individual risk is reinsured, but the ceding company arranges to cover only the excess of any one loss over and above an agreed figure. This is a treaty to guard against catastrophe. A ceding company may arrange to cover itself by reinsurance against the excess of loss over £50,000 in respect of any one fire, the cover to run, say, up to £100,000; i.e., a further £50,000. Then if one fire results in a loss to that company of £50,000, or less, the reinsurers pay nothing, but if the cost of the fire exceeds that figure the reinsurers pay the amount of the excess, according to their agreed proportions. This kind of treaty is largely used in motor insurance; but in fire insurance its use is a modern development. In that branch it is operated independently of and in addition to the surplus treaty. The ceding company must still use its surplus treaty to limit its liability on individual risks, taking out an excess of loss cover only to protect itself against heavy conflagrations.

Conditions of Reinsurance.—The conditions applying to a reinsurance are, as a rule, the same as those which apply to the original insurance. Thus the reinsurer receives the same rate of premium and must pay its proportionate share of any claim. There are, however, exceptions to this rule. Under an excess of loss treaty the reinsurer receives no specific premium, but is paid a percentage of the total premium income derived by the ceding company from the class of business to which the treaty applies. In marine reinsurance there is a practice to reinsure risks which are affected by a possibility of loss, and in such cases much higher premium may be paid than under the original policy.

The share of premium payable to the reinsurer is subject to a deduction of commission, which varies from 20% to 35% or in rare cases, 40% or 45%. Reinsurance commission has to cover not only the agent's commission paid on the original insurance but also a part of the ceding company's expense of obtaining and dealing with the business. The rate of reinsurance commission depends partly on the level of the expense of dealing with the business and partly on the quality of the treaty. Treaties giving consistently good results can command better terms than poor treaties. As well as commission deducted from premium, the reinsurer has to pay a commission—usually 10%—on the profits. In this way the profitable treaty automatically receives better terms than the bad one. The profit on a treaty is computed after making due provision for all claims and liabilities outstanding at the end of the year. The commission is payable on the average of the profit of the year of account, and of the two preceding years, so that a reinsurer shall not be required to pay away part of its profits in a year which follows a year showing a heavy loss.

The reinsurer, being liable to pay its share of all losses, is entitled to a like share of any amounts recovered as salvage. The ceding company has the control of all loss settlements and may settle a loss or contest a claim as it thinks fit. The reinsurer is bound to follow the fortunes of the ceding company in this matter.

Disputes arising between the parties to a reinsurance treaty, as to any matter coming thereunder, are almost invariably settled by arbitration.

Bordereaux.—Particulars of cessions made under a treaty are advised by the ceding company to the reinsurer by means of bordereaux. A bordereau is a statement giving the name and address of the insured, the nature of the risk, the sum insured, the premium, the amount reinsured and the reinsurance premium. No reinsurance policies are issued under treaties, as the reinsurance cover operates under the treaty contract. In marine business, however, properly stamped policies have to be issued even for reinsurance, under the provisions of the Stamp Act, 1891, and the Marine Insurance Act, 1906.

Retrocession.—A reinsurer, receiving particulars of its cessions by bordereaux, will itself deal with the business so received, and will in its turn arrange treaties to cede off its own surplus lines. A reinsurance of a reinsurance is called a retrocession. Retrocession is an important part of reinsurance business because where a reinsurer has a share of many treaties it will frequently receive a share of the same risk under many of its different treaties and must needs relieve itself by retrocession of the accumulation of risk.

(C. E. G.)

United States.—The U.S. reinsurance business grew rapidly during the 20th century. As in the European countries facultative and the three kinds of treaty insurance are used, but the percentage of facultative is rapidly diminishing because of delay and uncertainty.

What may be called a variation of the fixed treaty is the "pool" or "syndicate." Here as many as 35 companies will enter into an agreement to share all insurance in a given territory on a basis of certain agreed proportions both in regard to premiums and losses.

In order to facilitate the placing of reinsurance and to bring about greater uniformity of practice, reinsurance clearing houses or exchanges were established. Here the detailed reinsurance agreement is subscribed to by the member companies who are all represented by a manager.

Many of the life insurance companies continued to use the facultative plan of reinsurance.

There are two ways of reinsuring. The smaller companies will reinsure the amount at risk with term insurance. Most of the larger companies use the coinsurance plan, whereby the reinsurance company receives a proportionate part of the premium and guarantees a proportionate part of all payments including expenses and taxes.

There are many insurance companies whose business is entirely reinsurance.

(R. RET.; X.)

REISKE, JOHANN JACOB (1716–1774), German scholar and physician, was born on Dec. 25, 1716, at Zörbig in Electoral Saxony. From the Waisenhaus at Halle he passed in 1733 to the university of Leipzig, and there spent five years. He bought Arabic books, and when he had read all that was then printed he thirsted for manuscripts, and in March 1738 started on foot for Hamburg. At Hamburg he got money and letters of recommendation from the Hebraist Wolf, and took ship to Amsterdam. Reiske refused a generous offer from d'Orville at Amsterdam for his services as amanuensis. Ultimately he got free access to the Leiden collection, which he re-catalogued—the work of almost a whole summer, for which the curators rewarded him with nine guilders. D'Orville and Schultens helped him to find teaching and reading for the press. On the advice of Schultens he qualified as a doctor, after which, in 1746 he returned to Leipzig.

But he failed to secure any medical practice at Leipzig, and lived, as before, on ill-paid literary hack work. Although the electoral prince gave him the title of professor he was not permitted to lecture. At length in 1758 the magistrates of Leipzig rescued him from poverty by giving him the rectorate of St. Nicolai, and, though he still met with hostility in the university, he enjoyed the esteem of Frederick the Great, of Lessing, Karsten Niebuhr, and many foreign scholars. The last decade of his life was made cheerful by his marriage with Ernestine Müller, who shared all his interests and learned Greek to help him with collations. Reiske died on Aug. 14, 1774, and his ms. remains passed, through Lessing's mediation, to the Danish minister Suhm, and are now in the Copenhagen library.

Reiske surpassed all his predecessors in the range and quality of his knowledge of Arabic literature. In the *Adnotationes historicae* to his Abulfeda (*Abulf. Annales Moslemici*, 5 vols., Copenhagen, 1789–91), he collected a veritable treasure of sound and original research; he knew the Byzantine writers as thoroughly as the Arabic authors, and was alike at home in modern works of travel in all languages and in ancient and mediaeval authorities. He was interested too in numismatics, and his letters on Arabic coinage (in Eichhorn's *Repertorium*, vols. ix.–xi.) form, according to De Sacy, the basis of that branch of study.

In Leipzig Reiske worked mainly at Greek. His corrections are often hasty and false, but a surprisingly large proportion of them have since received confirmation from MSS. His German translations shew more practical insight than was usual in his time.

For a list of Reiske's writings *see* Meusel, xi. 192 *seq.* His chief Arabic works (all posthumous) have been mentioned above. In Greek letters his chief works are *Constantini Porphyrogeniti libri II. de ceremoniis aulae Byzant.*, vols. i. ii. (Leipzig, 1751–66), vol. iii. (Bonn, 1829); *Animadv. ad Graecos auctores* (5 vols., Leipzig, 1751–66) (the rest lies unprinted at Copenhagen); *Oratorum Graec. quae supersunt* (8 vols., Leipzig, 1770–73); *App. crit. ad Demosthenem* (3 vols., *ib.*,

1774-75); *Maximus Tyr.* (*ib.*, 1774); *Plutarchus* (11 vols., *ib.*, 1774-79); *Dionys Italic.* (6 vols., *ib.*, 1774-77); *Libanius* (4 vols., Altenburg, 1784-97). Various reviews in the *Acta eruditorum* and *Zuverl. Nachrichten* are characteristic and worth reading. Compare *D. Johann Jacob Reiskens von ihm selbst aufgesetzte Lebensbeschreibung* (Leipzig, 1783).

REITH, JOHN CHARLES WALSHAM REITH, 1ST BARON, OF STONEHAVEN (1889–   ), British civil engineer, served in the royal engineers during World War I. He was director-general of the British Broadcasting corporation (1927–38), first chairman of the British Overseas Airways corporation (1939–40), minister of information (1940) and director of the combined operations material department for the admiralty during World War II (1943–45), and became chairman of the Commonwealth Communications council in 1946. He was created baron in 1940.

RÉJANE, GABRIELLE (CHARLOTTE RÉJU) (1857–1920), French actress, was born in Paris and made her debut in 1875. Her first great success was in Henri Meilhac's *Ma camarade* (1883), and she soon became known as an emotional actress of rare gifts, notably in *Décore, Germinie Lacerteux, Ma cousine, Amoureuse* and *Lysistrata.* Her performances in *Madame Sans Gêne* (1893) made her as well known in England and America as in Paris, and in later years she was particularly successful in *Zaza* and *La Passerelle.* She opened the Théâtre Réjane in Paris in 1906. She died in Paris on June 14, 1920.

REJANG, a tribe of Proto-Malayan or mixed Indonesian stock, partly akin to the Achinese, Bugis (*qq.v.*) and Mangkassaras. Though now Muslim they were formerly influenced by Indo-Javanese culture and retain an alphabet derived from that source, speaking a language of the Austronesian family. Their alphabet has been described as "pure Phoenician," but is intimately related to others derived from the Indo-Javan culture. Ideas of ancestor-worship are strong, and metempsychosis (*q.v.*) is vaguely believed in, tigers in particular being regarded as embodying the souls of the dead. Worship of the sea also prevails. It is believed that invulnerability can be acquired. Teknonymy is practised, and persons object to mentioning their own names. The dead are buried in a chamber excavated to one side of the grave. Betel is chewed. In blood-tariffs the value of a woman is nearly double that of a man except in the case of chiefs, only the highest of whom are rated higher than their wives.

See Marsden, *History of Sumatra* (1783). (J. H. H.)

REJERIA, the Spanish form of open-work screens made from combinations of wrought and cast iron work. The word *reja* is used for a screen, individually; *rejeria* properly signifies this whole class of iron work. A magnificent example is the *reja* of the Capilla Mayor of Seville cathedral (1518–33). Many beautiful examples of this type are found as window guards in Spanish Renaissance houses.

REJUVENATION. In all multicellular animals the process of regeneration, growth and rejuvenation is constant as is shown typically by the hair and nails. It is now possible to cultivate tissues in suitable media (*see* TISSUE CULTURE) and to keep them alive long after the death of the parent organism. This proves that death is not the inevitable end of cellular vitality, but is in every case the result of unfavourable conditions to which the cells are subjected at a given moment.

The endocrine glands produce substances (hormones), which they pour into the circulatory system and thereby influence the metabolic processes, the growth and morphology of the cells. One of these glands should have as its special function the secretion of a substance which gives tone and stimulus to cellular vitality during a certain period of life and ceases to do this on the approach of old age. This cannot be the special function of the thyroid, parathyroid, pituitary or suprarenal glands, since they continue to act during old age. The only gland which constitutes an exception to this rule is the genital gland. It plays a double rôle. It secretes spermatozoa externally, and it secretes internally hormones which it passes into the blood stream, actively at puberty and during maturity, but less and less thereafter, so that the diminution and disappearance of its activity correspond with old age.

Examination of male vertebrate animals, including man, after removal of the genital glands shows distinctly the nature of the influence of the internal secretion of these glands on the whole organism as affecting, not only the secondary male sexual characters, but also the growth and development of the body as a whole, the brain and skin cells, the bones and tissues. The physical and intellectual qualities of animals and of man are as intimately conditioned by the hormone secreted by the testicles as are the secondary sexual characters.

There can thus be no doubt as to the nature of the relation between the general reduction of the forces of the organism and the disappearance of the internal secretion of the testicles. No organ can keep its vital energy and yield a full return if the cells are not stimulated and vivified by the testicular hormone. It acts more or less directly on other endocrine glands, since castration is followed by hypertrophy of the anterior lobe of the pituitary gland and by regression of the thyroid body and epiphysis. If the genital glands remained active in old age, were they not the only glands which cease to secrete hormones, old age would certainly be delayed.

Eunuchs in Cairo who had been castrated at an early age and had therefore never been exposed to the activity of the testicular hormones, were never known to have been more than 60 at death. All had the appearance of old men, with desiccated skins, haggard eyes, bent, and looking like centenarians.

It is obvious that the deprivation of the internal secretion of the testicles accelerates the advance of old age and shortens life. The only remedy is to graft a young testicle, whether that of a young human being or of an ape, by which the tone-giving substance is provided, so as to increase the vitality of all the cells which are weakened but are not yet atrophied and therefore still able to renew themselves, and thus effectively to rejuvenate the whole organism. So long as an organism, however old, continues to exist, its cells continue to be renewed and rejuvenated. Unfortunately, in old age this process of rejuvenation is slowed down, a certain number of the functional cells regress and are replaced by conjunctive tissue. The cells which escape this are renewed more slowly, but continue to be renewed to the extreme limit of their vitality.

With a rich addition of the testicular hormone, the cells acquire new energy, grow more rapidly, proliferate more intensely and rejuvenate the whole system. At the end of several years the beneficent action of the grafted gland is exhausted because the grafts in turn are subject to positive regression. The organism is again deprived of the stimulating hormones and the symptoms of old age reappear. In most cases testicular grafting is adequate, but in some cases thyroid grafts have to be added. *See* S. Voronoff, *Rejuvenation by Grafting* (1925). (S. V.)

RELANDER, LAURI KRISTIAN (1883–1942), president of Finland, born May 31, 1883, and educated at Helsingfors university. He was a member of the central committee of the agrarian party in 1909, sat in the diet from 1910 to 1913, and 1917–19, when he became its speaker. From 1925 to 1931, he was president of the republic. He died Feb. 9, 1942.

RELAPSING FEVER (*Febris recurrens*), the name given to a specific infectious disease occasionally appearing as an epidemic in communities suffering from scarcity or famine. It is characterized mainly by its sudden invasion, with violent febrile symptoms, which continue for about a week and end in a crisis, but are followed after another week, during which the patient is fairly well, by a return of the fever. In exceptional cases, second, third and even fourth relapses may occur.

This disease has received many other names, the best known of which are famine fever, seven-day bilious relapsing fever, and spirillum fever. Like typhoid, relapsing fever was long believed to be simply a form of typhus. The distinction between them appears to have been first clearly established in 1826, in connection with an epidemic in Ireland.

In 1873 Obermeier discovered in the blood of persons suffering from relapsing fever minute spiral filaments of the genus *Spirochaete*, having rotatory or twisting movements. This organism received the name of *Spirillum obermeieri.* Fritz Schaudinn brought forward evidence that it is an animal parasite. Relapsing fever is most commonly met with in the young. One attack does not appear to protect from others, but rather, according to some authorities, engenders liability. The incubation of the disease is about one week.

The mortality in relapsing fever is comparatively small, about 5% being the average death-rate in epidemics (Murchison). The fatal cases occur mostly from the complications common to continued fevers. The treatment is essentially the same as that for typhus fever. Löwenthal and Gabritochewsky by using the serum of an immune horse succeeded in averting the relapse in 40% of cases.

RELATIONSHIP TERMS. Relationship terms are studied by the anthropologist not merely as so many words inviting philological analysis and comparison, but as correlates of social custom. Broadly speaking, the use of a specific kinship designation, *e.g.*, for the maternal as distinguished from the paternal uncle, indicates that the former receives differential treatment at the hands of his nephews and nieces. Further, if a term of this sort embraces a number of individuals, the probability is that the speaker is linked to all of them by the same set of mutual duties and claims, though their intensity may vary with the closeness of the relationship. Sometimes the very essence of a social fabric may be demonstrably connected with the mode of classifying kin. Thus, kinship nomenclature becomes one of the most important topics of Social Organization.

In the daily routine of savage life, relationship terms are not only important as at once ticketing the status of the person addressed or mentioned with reference to the speaker, but also because often there is no other mode of address. This is because of the widespread prejudice against the vocative use of personal names, for which accordingly kinship appellations are substituted, even to the extent of assuming a relationship where none exists.

CLASSIFICATION OF KINSHIP TERMINOLOGIES

The foundation of the scientific study of this subject was laid by Lewis H. Morgan in his *Systems of Consanguinity and Affinity of the Human Family* (Smithsonian Contributions to Knowledge, XVII., Washington, 1871). In this great work were assembled comprehensive schedules for every major area of the globe except Africa and Australia, for which data were largely or wholly inaccessible to the author. Morgan grouped all terminologies under two main heads—the descriptive and the classificatory. The descriptive system, ascribed to the Aryan, Semitic and Uralian families, "describes collateral *consanguinei*, for the most part, by an augmentation or combination of the primary terms of relationship" (pp. 12, 468). The classificatory system never describes *consanguinei* by a combination of primary terms but ranges them into great classes or categories: "All the individuals of the same class are admitted into one and the same relationship, and the same special term is applied indiscriminately to each and all of them" (p. 143). Two varieties of the classificatory type were recognized—the Malayan, which merged all kindred of one generation irrespective of proximity in one category; and the Turanian-Ganowanian, in which only some of the collateral kin of a generation were merged with the lineal, the remainder being separated by distinctive terms.

This dichotomy is unacceptable. As Kroeber[1] and Rivers[2] remark, *our* words for uncle, aunt and cousin likewise range *consanguinei* into large classes, so that the absoluteness of the distinction breaks down. Furthermore, Rivers notes[3] that "descriptive" does not strictly apply to the English and related terminologies, which rarely augment or combine the primary terms. That epithet may be properly reserved for such Norwegian words as *farbror* and *morbror* for father's and mother's brother, respectively; and hence for certain nomenclatures, *e.g.*, the Arabic, which largely employ expressions of this order. Thus, Rivers supplanted Morgan's dualism with a tripartite scheme, recognizing denotative, descriptive and classificatory types. Elsewhere he suggests the

appellations family, kindred and clan systems, the "kindred" being a major bilateral unit.[4] These latter terms are, however, objectionable since they inject the inferential basis of a system into its descriptive definition. There are clanless tribes with clan systems in Rivers' sense, and the result would be confusion. Apart from this terminological difficulty, the scheme fails to obviate a logical fault in Morgan's earlier effort. "Descriptive" and "classificatory" do not relate to the same logical universe, hence are not complementary terms. "Classificatory" relates to the number of individuals defined, "descriptive" to the technique of defining a relationship. It is possible to augment or combine primary terms and then apply the resultant to an indefinitely large class of persons. The antithesis to "classificatory" is the concept "individualizing," as Morgan felt, though he failed to express it.

But the purging of the traditional terminology does not carry us very far. How shall we characterize our simple English system if it embodies both individualizing *and* classificatory principles? The answer is provided in Kroeber's above-cited essay: a kinship terminology is not a logically coherent whole but must be resolved into the several categories recognized. Those enumerated by Kroeber are: the difference of generations; the difference between lineal and collateral kin; the difference of age within one generation; sex; the speaker's sex; the connecting relative's sex; the difference between consanguinity and affinity; and the life or death of the connecting relative.

This pioneer attempt requires both revision and amplification. The last mentioned feature, *e.g.*, is of purely local significance in western North America and of limited application where found. The differentiation between elder and younger sibling (brother *or* sister) means psychologically simply the intercalation of two additional generations. On the other hand, the reciprocity principle, linking by a common term distinct generations, merits independent status. Cognizance must also be taken of the frequent duplication of terms in address and mere reference, the mode of classification itself sometimes differing. Extra-American terminologies also suggest that the categories laid down by Kroeber might be materially increased. Even as it stands, however, his sketch furnishes a valuable instrument for the precise definition and comparison of distinct systems.[5]

In the present state of our knowledge it is impracticable to do more than concentrate upon an unequivocally significant feature as a basis for classification in a world-wide survey, and to refine areally by supplementary characteristics. The trait that obtrudes itself on our notice is the treatment of collateral as compared with lineal kin in the first ascending and descending generations. It is implicitly the phenomenon that impressed Morgan; it has a bearing on Tylor's and Rivers' theories (*see* below); and constitutes one of Kroeber's categories. Practically, the data usually suffice to characterize systems from this point of view.

The logical possibilities are as follows: (a) Collateral lines are wholly merged in the lineal within a particular generation (generation system); (b) each generation is bisected so that only half the collateral kin are merged in the lineal (bifurcate merging system); (c) the immediate collateral lines are distinguished from the lineal *and from each other* (bifurcate collateral system); (d) collateral lines are distinguished from the lineal, but *not from each other* (lineal).

In standard samples of these four systems logical coherence prevails: *if* the father's brother is called father, he addresses his brother's son as son; *if* there is a separate word for mother's brother, there is likely to be one for nephew. However, discrepancies occur, and a system must sometimes be classed by the preponderance of its affiliations. Taking the classification of uncles for illustration, the scheme may be illustrated by the table on page 85.

The second system, which Morgan and Rivers genetically connect with the first (though in a reverse sense), is not one whit farther from the third; and the bifurcate collateral system sets off the immediate family as sharply from the rest of the universe as

[1]A. L. Kroeber, "Classificatory Systems of Relationship," *Journal Royal Anthrop. Instit.*, 1909, 39: 77–84.
[2]W. H. R. Rivers, *Social Organization*, 1924, 51–77.
[3]Id., article "Kin. Kinship" in Hastings' *Encyclopaedia of Religion and Ethics*.

[4]*Social Organization*, 55 sq.
[5]E. W. Gifford, *California Kinship Terminologies* (Univ. Cal. Pub., vol. 18, 1922).

System	Relatives			Criterion
	Father	Father's Br.	Mother's Br.	
Generation . .	Father	Father's Br.	Mother's Br.	One "father" term
Bifurcate Merging .	„	„ „ „	„ „	Two terms; partial merging
Bifurcate Collateral .	„	„ „ „	„ „	Three terms; no merging
Lineal . . .	„	„ „ „	, ,	Two terms; merging only of collaterals

our English lineal system. All four systems actually occur in primitive communities, notwithstanding the widespread notion that they have only the first two, corresponding to Morgan's classificatory types.

With this provisional scheme it is possible to characterize the main areas of the globe. Since regional summaries are available for Australia and North America, it will be best to begin with these continents.

AUSTRALIA

Australian kinship terminologies follow the bifurcate merging plan.

Certain other traits are characteristic. Among these is the use of separate terms for maternal and paternal grandparents. Thus, the Kakadu in Northern Australia call the father's father *kaga,* but the mother's father *peipi.* With many tribes this trait is coupled with the reciprocity principle: in Arunta, *arunga* designates simultaneously the father's father and the son's child. Again, the world-wide distinction between the speaker's elder and younger siblings often displays refinement, so that in Arunta the father's elder brother's sons are "elder brothers," while the father's younger brother's sons are "younger brothers." More rarely, as among the Mungarai, the uncles and aunts themselves are distinguished with reference to their age as compared with the speaker's parents.

While these features have parallels in remote areas, others seem distinctive. According to Radcliffe-Brown, all nomenclatures of the region conform to two types, correlated with distinct forms of marriage law. In type I., as found among the West Australian Kariera and the Urabunna of the Lake Eyre region, the father's father is classed with the mother's mother's brother; by the correlated matrimonial rule a man is prohibited from marrying any woman unless she stands to him in the relation of a mother's brother's daughter. In type II., the mother's mother's brother is distinguished from the father's father, being often classed with the mother's mother; here the prescribed marriage is between the children of two female cross-cousins, a man marrying his mother's mother's brother's daughter's daughter. This second type is of wider distribution than the first, having been discovered among the Dieri, the Central tribes generally, from the Arunta northward to the Anula and Mara, and among such West Australians as the Mardudhunera.[1]

Probably most of the tribes substitute relationship terms for personal names in ordinary intercourse, but the central Australians only tabu sacred appellations, while secular names are used in address, interchangeably with the kinship terms.[2]

A feature worth noting is the absence of terms of affinity. This is evidently to be correlated with the fact that in Australia marriage is prescribed with definite blood relatives. Accordingly there is no necessity for coining new words for connections by marriage. This same trait may be expected to occur in greater or lesser degree in other parts of the world where corresponding forms of marriage with blood relatives are either obligatory or at least preferred.

[1]A. R. Radcliffe-Brown, "Three Tribes of Western Australia," *Journ. Royal Anthrop. Instit.,* 1913, vol. 43, 143–194.
[2]For Australia in general *cf.* Radcliffe-Brown in Walter Hutchinson, ed., *Customs of the World,* 160. B. Spencer and Gillen, *The Native Tribes of the Northern Territory of Australia,* 1914, 65–82, and *The Native Tribes of Central Australia,* 1898, 66–91, 637.

NORTH AMERICA

North America north of Mexico may be split into two main divisions. Among the Eskimo, in southern British Columbia, the Basin states, Washington, Oregon, and part of California, there are predominantly lineal or bifurcate collateral systems; in the remainder of the continent the terminologies are bifurcate merging. These two main areas correspond roughly to a social organization on the family basis and a clan organization, respectively.

Two Australian features, the reciprocity principle and the discrimination of maternal and paternal grandparents, occur exclusively, or nearly so, in the Far West. However, they do not appear with bifurcate merging traits.

Primarily on the basis of cousin grouping Spier has established eight varieties of nomenclature.[3] The Iroquois type maintains the separation of generations, treats parallel cousins as siblings, and designates cross-cousins by a specific cousin term. The Mackenzie Basin type drops distinctions between cousins, treating all alike as siblings. The Eskimo type resembles the foregoing in merging parallel and cross-cousins, but separates them from siblings. The Omaha systems, embracing several Californian as well as Central tribes, distinguish among cross-cousins. The father's sister's children are regarded as sister's children, which classes them (on bifurcate merging principles) as children if the speaker is a woman. Correlatively, the mother's brother's daughter is classed as a mother, while the mother's brother's son is equated with the mother's brother. In the Crow type the reverse confusion of generations occurs; the father's sister's son is a "father" and addresses his mother's brother's children as his "children"; the father's sister's daughter is a father's sister.

Spier's remaining varieties rest on other principles. His Salish type diverges in displaying lineal features. The Acoma type is segregated by virtue of its three grandparental terms,—one for a man's grandfather, another for a woman's grandmother, a third for a grandparent of the opposite sex. Finally, the Yuman variety is characterized by a refinement of age distinctions,—the father's elder brothers and mother's elder sisters being distinguished from their younger siblings, while parallel cousins are sometimes classed as elder or younger siblings according to their parents' rather than their own ages.

Spier's types avowedly embrace tribes neither geographically nor linguistically close to their eponyms. Thus, the Iroquois type embraces the Iroquois, Ojibwa, Cree, Dakota, some Californian groups, and the Tsimshian of British Columbia.

Based on different principles, Spier's findings (for which he deprecates any interpretation) are not at once wholly convertible into our terminology. However, the Salish case, which he refuses to class by the cousin criterion as of the Mackenzie Basin category, is coextensive with the lineal type. Moreover, both his Omaha and Crow types are varieties of the bifurcate merging type. This, in its classical Seneca form, largely coincides with Spier's Iroquois type, though his stressing of cousin terminology leads to the admission of several tribes who do not merge parents' siblings and parents. In Spier's scheme, the Eskimo are segregated because they use a distinctive cousin term for all cousins. Their separation is undoubtedly warranted. Morgan himself, though describing their system as "classificatory," shows that the nomenclature has "but two, out of ten, of the indicative features of the system of the Ganowanian family" and that "in the greater and most important fundamental characteristics of this system it is wanting."[4] On Morgan's evidence, the use of individualizing terms for the parents and the segregation of maternal from paternal uncles and aunts, would place the Eskimo under the bifurcate collateral head; more recent data for another local division are confirmatory.[5]

Spier's Acoma and Yuman varieties, logically outside his own scheme, hardly merit separate categories, as he himself admits in the Acoma case.

A summary classification of the North American systems thus leads to the following tentative scheme:

[3]L. Spier, *The Distribution of Kinship Systems in North America,* Univ. of Washington Pub. in Anthropology, Seattle, 1925, vol. 1, 69–88.
[4]Morgan, *op. cit.,* p. 277.
[5]D. Jenness, *The Life of the Copper Eskimos,* Ottawa, 1922.

1. Bifurcate Merging	(a)	Iroquois; Dakota; Ojibwa
	(b)	Omaha; Menomini, Sauk; Miwok, Wintun
	(c)	Crow; Pawnee; Creek; Cherokee; Hopi; S. Pomo; Tlingit
2. Bifurcate Collateral		Eskimo, Monc
3. Lineal		Salish; Nootka, Kwakiutl

The Generation system is lacking. Faintly adumbrated, it appears in Spier's Mackenzie Basin type, but the generation principle is restricted in application, so that there is no approach to the Hawaiian scheme. Various Californian and Basin tribes classed by Spier as of the Mackenzie pattern appropriately fall under the bifurcate collateral group, deviating from the norm only in the grouping of cousins. Such tribes as the Northwestern Maidu belong to the same category and show how this may approach the merging type: parallel cousins here coincide with siblings, while cross-cousins are separated by a special term.[1] The gap between this Maidu and the Iroquois system is thus reduced to the distinction the former maintains between the father and his brother, the mother and her sister.

Sporadically, instances occur in otherwise bifurcate merging systems of a partial failure to bifurcate. Thus, the Crow, though only in direct address, use one term for the mother and either kind of aunt.

Personal names are generally eschewed in address.

CENTRAL AND SOUTH AMERICA

Central American systems are known mainly through such sources as Gilberti's *Diccionario de la lengua Tarasca* (1559), Molina's *Vocabulario de la lengua Mexicana* (1571), and Beltran's *Arte del idioma Maya* (1742).[2] The distinction of elder and younger sibling is general, and so is the use of reciprocal terms between different generations. Thus, Maya *mam* is applied to the maternal grandfather and the daughter's son. The principle of reciprocity occurs among the Miskito of Nicaragua, *dapna* designating father-in-law and son-in-law, as well as mother-in-law and daughter-in-law in female speech. The former classification is shared by the Chibcha of Colombia. In the Ucayali region, the Sipibo apply the word *rayos* to parent-in-law and son-in-law, while the words for maternal uncle and sister's son—*cuca* and *cucu* suggest a common stem.[3] In America there is thus a fairly continuous distribution of the reciprocity principle extending from British Columbia through the Pacific and Basin States into Mexico and northern South America.

Several tribes in Latin America recognize to an unusual extent Kroeber's category of the speaker's sex. While a Cakchiquel man calls his son *cahol* and his daughter *mial*, a woman uses *val* and *vixocal*.

From the scanty material accessible it is not clear how commonly bifurcate merging systems occur south of the Rio Grande. Molina's Nahuatl nomenclature is Hawaiian in grouping all uncles with the father, *tlatli*; but it is lineal in segregating aunts, *auitl* from the mother, *nantli*, and all nepotic kin as *machtli* from the son *tepitlzin* and daughter, *teichpuch*. The Cakchiquel use of *tata* for father and paternal uncle is true to the bifurcate merging type, but the reported classification of the *paternal* aunt with the mother, *te*, while both maternal aunt and uncle are called *vican* is so anomalous as to call for corroboratory evidence.[4]

Lineal uncle and aunt terms are reported for the Pomeroon Arawak. On the whole, the frequency of lineal and bifurcate collateral features arrests our attention. Thus, the Miskito, while using for the maternal aunt a word from the stem for mother (*yapti*; mother's sister: *yaptislip*), call the father *aisa*, the paternal uncle *urappia*, the mother's brother *tarti*. A glossary of Arawakan languages shows no discrimination between paternal and maternal uncles except in Siusi; there the bifurcate collateral rather than the bifurcate merging principle obtains since the father's brother is not identified with the father. A single term for aunt (distinct

from mother) indicates either inconsistency or inaccurate reporting.[5] The Tupi generic terms exist for aunt and uncle (*aixe* and *tutyra*), but the father term is said to be applicable to all the father's male kin. In short, there is a mingling of lineal and merging features.[6] More consistently, the Sipibo separate the father, *papa*, from both the father's brother, *eppa*, and the maternal uncle, *cuca*, and similarly segregate the mother from the maternal as well as the paternal aunt (*tita, huasta, yaya*, respectively; it is not clear to what extent the matter is complicated by the use of separate words by men and women). The Araucanian terminology is in part bifurcate collateral: the father, *chao*, is distinguished from his brother, *malle* and his brother-in-law, *huecu*; while the mother's sister is designated by a derivative from the mother term.[7]

It cannot be denied that there are nomenclatures of the usual "classificatory" type. According to Ruiz de Montoya (1640), the Guarani was of this order.[8] Nevertheless, the South American tendency toward collateral or lineal usage cannot be ignored.

ASIA

In Asia the wide distribution of status terms expressive of relative seniority is noteworthy, differences of generation being sometimes disregarded, while again the relative seniority of relatives other than those immediately concerned may be significant. The system of the Turkic Yakut of northern Siberia illustrates some of the relevant complications. Radically of the bifurcate merging type, it groups together as *agas* the elder sister and all older women in the speaker's clan, those younger being designated as *babys*, and the words for elder brother are similarly extended. But the seniority idea overrides the generation principle when *ini* designates not only younger brother or cousin within the clan, but also, the father's younger brother and his son; or when *ogom* is applied indifferently to a child, a grandchild, and even to younger people without reference to relationship. Again, while the father's elder brother is called by a derivative from the father term, this same word is extended by the seniority principle to the mother's father; and while *tay* marks off the maternal from the paternal uncles, the mother's sisters are called according to their age with reference to the mother, *tay agas* and *tay babys*. Thus, since the mother is *yä*, there is in so far forth bifurcation without merging.[9]

When the two parental lines are discriminated and the parents' siblings are set off from the parents by mere modifiers of the primary "parent" stem, it seems legitimate to speak of a basically bifurcate merging system. The primitive Sinitic languages in part present this phenomenon and suggest that the proto-Chinese system may have conformed to this model. Its present form is puzzling. Morgan vacillated between calling it Malayan or Turanian, *i.e.*, a generation or a bifurcate merging system. If we stress the specialization of, say, uncles by modifiers rather than the use of a common primary stem, it would be recognized as collateral; otherwise it might rank as a generation system. Some traits however, such as the classing of brother's sons by males indicate bifurcation. It is evident that emphasis on status and seniority would cause a drift from the bifurcate merging toward the generation pattern. Of the primitive members of the Sinitic stock, the Sema, Ao, Angami and Lhota fall rather clearly under the bifurcate merging division, some of them definitely presenting the Omaha variety. Thus, Lhota *omo*, Sema *angu*, Chongli Ao *okhu* mean the maternal uncle *and* his son; Sema *atikeshiu*, Lhota *orrho*, and Chongli *anok* refer to the sister's son and the father's sister's son in male speech.

---

[1]E. W. Gifford, *Californian Kinship Terminologies*, Univ. of Cal. Pub., 1922, 18:43.

[2]A. C. Breton, "Relationships in Central America," in *Man*, Dec. 1919, 186–192. R. H. Lowrie, *Culture and Ethnology*, 1917, 125f.

[3]K. von den Steinen, *Diccionario Sivibo*, Berlin, 1904.

[4]Breton, *l.c.*

[5]W. E. Roth, *An Introductory Study of the Arts, Crafts and Customs of the Guiana Indians* (38th Rept. Bur. Amer. Ethnol.; 1924, p. 674). Th. Koch-Grünberg, *Aruak-Sprachen Nordwestbrasiliens u. der angrenzenden Gebiete*, Mitteill der Anthrop. Gesell. in Wien, 1911, 41:83 *sq.*

[6]C. F. Th. von Martius, *Beiträge zur Ethnographie u. Sprachenkunde Amerikas, zumal Brasiliens*, Leipzig, 1876, 1:353.

[7]Otto Bürger, *Acht Lehr- und Wanderjahre in Chile*, Leipzig, 1909, 86.

[8]S. A. Lafone Quevedo, *Los términos de parentesco en la organización social sud-americana*, Revista de la Univ. de Buenos Aires, 1917, 37:32 *sq.*

[9]M. A. Czaplicka, *Aboriginal Siberia*, 1914, p. 59.

The complete lack of certain kinship terms in some Assamese tribes is remarkable; in Angami, for example, parallel cousins can be designated only by their personal names. The Chinese *may* combine such names with the specific kinship terms.[1]

Typical nomenclatures of the bifurcate merging type occur among the peoples of Southern India (including the Toda) and the Vedda of Ceylon. Here, and in other tribes of the area showing this pattern in obscured form, the terminology is affected by cross-cousin marriage. Since a Kachin seeks to marry the daughter of his maternal uncle, he calls his father-in-law and his mother's brother alike *tsa;* while in Mikir the sister's son and the son-in-law are both a man's *osa,* and the wife's brother is his *òng-so* or "little maternal uncle," in other words, his maternal uncle's son.[2]

The two Negrito tribes of Southern Asia differ radically inasmuch as in address the Semang of the Malay Peninsula avoid personal names, while the Andamanese use them exclusively. They resemble each other in stressing status in their nomenclature. Indeed, it seems doubtful whether the Andamanese have any true kinship terms. Though a parent may be individualized by prefixing the personal pronoun to an appropriate noun, this by itself expresses no bond of consanguinity but simply the status of being *some one's* parent. Correspondingly, other words denote relative seniority in varying degrees: *mama* extends to all considerably older persons such as grandparents and parents-in-law. The Andamanese nomenclature lacks bifurcation completely and might be treated as a variety of the generation system; this feature, linked with the vocative use of names, suggests affiliation with Polynesia, where however, generation terms are limited to actual kin. The Semang system is not so well known, but bifurcation seems undeveloped. From *ai,* father, designations for *either* parent's elder and younger brother are formed by the addition of age-suffixes; the word for mother with the appropriate suffix means *either* parent's elder sister, while a new stem designates a younger sister of father or mother. We shall not go far wrong in assigning this system also to the generation category.[3]

In western Asia the Semitic tribes have been treated as typical of the "descriptive" pattern. As has been shown, the descriptive *technique* is wholly consistent with a "classificatory" meaning. The Arabic terminology is on the face of it bifurcate collateral. It is partly shaped by the custom of parallel-cousin marriage, so that father's brother and father-in-law are identified in fact and in masculine speech. The absence of a common word for paternal uncle in Semitic languages has suggested the hypothesis, as yet awaiting confirmation, that the proto-Semitic system was of the merging type.[4]

Lineal systems occur in northeastern Siberia among the Koryak and Chukchee, where clans are lacking. Both tribes distinguish younger and elder siblings, and the Chukchee have even a separate term for "middle" brother. The Yukaghir terminology presents disparate features. In a sense, the parents are individualized, the children are set off from nepotic kin, and the distinction between paternal and maternal uncles indicates a bifurcate collateral system. However, some of the uncle-aunt words are etymological derivatives from the parent terms, suggesting a merging principle. In addition, the seniority principle of the Yakut order plays a large part, putting both grandmothers in the same class with the father's elder sister, both grandfathers with the elder brother. The technique is sometimes denotative, sometimes descriptive. It is plausible to regard this medley as at least partly the result of

distinct culture layers. An archaic system resting on the family may have been complicated by a bifurcate merging system, stressing the seniority idea. In other words, a palae-Asiatic layer may have had Yakut-like accretions.[5]

AFRICA

In the southern half of the continent bifurcate merging systems prevail. The Hottentot nomenclature approximates the Iroquois pattern, though the occasional classification of the mother's brother's son with the maternal uncle marks a deviation in the Omaha direction. For the Bushmen, data are inadequate, though reported suggestions of a "classificatory system" indicate another sample of the Iroquois form. With modifications of a minor character this holds for most of the Bantu. There is little to support Morgan's interpretation that the terminology is "Malayan." His guess that the stem for mother's brother was a recently evolved substitute for the father term is refuted by its occurrence in much the same form among the Thonga and Wayao, while the concept is attested for as far north as Uganda and the Congo. The very fact cited by Morgan that a single word denotes the paternal aunt and the father proves the stress on bifurcation, even to the detriment of sex distinctions. The generation factor doubtless asserts itself in the classification of all cousins with siblings, but this is far from universal in Bantu speech. The Wayao, *e.g.,* distinguish cross-cousins from parallel cousins by a distinctive designation. Moreover, the very essence of the generation principle is ignored by a number of tribes. The Thonga, like the Hottentot, *may* call the mother's brother's son *malume,* like the maternal uncle, while the daughter of the mother's brother is a "mother," and sometimes the grandchild and the sister's child fail to be distinguished.

Again, the wife's parent and the wife's elder sibling fall into the same Thonga category, and sometimes the grandfather term embraces the maternal uncle. Finally, the Wayao have a reciprocal term for parent-in-law and child-in-law. There is thus no warrant for putting the Bantu with the Polynesians: their system is basically of the bifurcate merging type, modified locally by various causes, sometimes along Omaha lines.[6]

The Hamitic and Hamitoid tribes are generally credited with "descriptive" systems. In fact, the descriptive technique may be employed to an unusual degree, so that the 'Afar of the East Horn call a brother "mother's son." This, however, does not preclude a classificatory meaning for the descriptive designation, much less for other parts of the same nomenclature. Galla *abba,* for example, may be applied not only to the father but as an honorific appellation to any old man. The Somali system is definitely bifurcate collateral. Among the Masai the paucity of genuine kinship terms is no less remarkable than certain correlated usages. While father's and mother's siblings are distinguished from the parents by descriptive phrases, this discrimination extends only to reference, while in address the father's brother is a father. Most kinsmen, however, are not called by terms of consanguinity or affinity but according to the livestock they have received from the speaker: if he has presented a man with a bull (*ainoni*), the beneficiary is called *b-ainoni,* etc. Generations often fail to be separated: *koko* embraces aunt *and* grandmother, and with a suffix the word is applied to a woman's grandson. Similarly, a reciprocal stem embraces grandfather and a man's grandson.[7]

Among the Sudanese negroes a great diversity obtains. The Timne terminology is lineal, the words for aunt and uncle being generic and distinct from the parent terms, while cousins in a lump

[1] Ching-Chao Wu, "The Chinese Family: Organization, Names and Kinship Terms," *Amer. Anthrop.,* 1927, 316 *sq.* L. H. Morgan, *Systems,* 413 *sq.* F. W. Baller, *A Mandarin Primer,* 1911, 369. J. H. Hutton, *The Angami Nagas,* 1921, 132; *id., The Sema Nagas,* 1921, 138, 382. J. P. Mills, *The Lhota Nagas,* 1922, 93; *id., The Ao Nagas,* 1926, 164.

[2] E. Stack and Sir Ch. Lyall, *The Mikirs,* 20f. C. G. Seligmann, *The Veddas,* 1911, 64. W. H. R. Rivers, *The Todas,* 1906, 484. O. Hanson, *The Kachins,* Rangoon, 1913, 215 *sq.*

[3] A. R. Brown, *The Andaman Islanders,* 1922, 53–69. P. Schebesta, *Bei den Urwaldzwergen von Malaya,* 1927, 108.

[4] C. S. and B. Z. Seligman, *The Kababish, a Sudan Arab Tribe,* Harvard African Studies, II., 1918, 123. B. Z. Seligman, "Studies in Semitic Kinship," *Bull. School of Oriental Studies,* London Institution, III., pt. 1, 1923, 51–68, 263–279.

[5] W. Jochelson, "The Koryak," *Mem. Amer. Mus. Nat. Hist.,* X., 1905–08, 759; *id.* "The Yukaghir and the Yukaghirized Tungus," *ibid·,* XIII., 1910, 68. W. Borogas, *The Chukchee, ibid.,* XI., 1907, 538.

[6] A. W. Hoernlé, "The Social Organization of the Nama Hottentots of Southwest Africa," *Amer. Anthrop.,* 1925, 1–24. I. Schapera, *South African Journal of Science,* 1926, XXIII., 847. Morgan, *Systems,* 465. H. Junod, *The Life of a South African Tribe,* 1912 I., 217 *sq.* H. S. Stannus, *The Wayao of Nyasaland,* Harvard African Studies, III., 1922, 281. E. W. Smith and A. M. Dale, *The Ila-speaking Peoples of Northern Rhodesia,* 1920, I., 316 *sq.* R. S. Dennett, *At the Back of the Black Man's Mind,* 1906, 35. B. Z. Seligman, "Marital Gerontocracy in Africa," *Journal Royal Anthrop. Inst.,* 1924, 231 *sq.*

[7] Ph. Paulitschke, *Ethnographie Nordost-Afrikas,* 1893, I., 188. M. Merker, *Die Masai,* 1904, p. 41.

are separated from siblings. Some of the languages display an amazing paucity of primary stems, lacking even distinct vocables for siblings. Thus, in Ewe "brother" is designated by the descriptive compound "mother's-child-male," and the Edo construct descriptive compounds for "brother" according to whether he is fellow-child through the father or the mother. However, the bifurcate merging principle is by no means eliminated since even in Edo the paternal uncle is frequently classed with the father in address. Nor are typical systems on the bifurcate merging plan lacking. The Susu nomenclature conforms to the Iroquois standard, and this essentially holds for the Ashanti also. Here, however, cross-cousin marriage in some measure has affected classification and the rather extensive use of reciprocal terms partly breaks down the barriers between generations. Thus, *ase* means spouse's parent *or* child's spouse; *nana* is applied to the grandparent and his sibling *or* to the grandchild and the sibling's grandchild. Some relatives *may* be designated descriptively, but this does not interfere with the "classificatory" use of the phrase. For example, the father's brother's child is called either "brother" or "father's child" without any individualization of meaning in either case.[1]

Finally, the Lango terminology is of the bifurcate merging type, the partial use of the descriptive technique being once more consistent with "classificatory" meanings. A noteworthy feature is the anomolous designation of cousins. The maternal uncle's son and daughter are designated by descriptive compounds; a distinct stem, with varying vocalic sex-prefix (*okeo, akeo*), is applied to the paternal aunt's children; another stem, similarly varied, denotes the mother's sister's son and daughter; while the father's brother's children are treated as siblings. Thus, neither the two kinds of cross-cousins nor the two kinds of parallel cousins are grouped together. The classification of the father's sister's children with the sister's children exhibits an element of the Omaha variety, while other deviations from the generation principle can be derived from rules of widow-inheritance. The occasional designation of a father's sister's son as father is contingent on inheritance of a maternal uncle's widow, making her children the heir's step-children. The Lango nomenclature has been partly shaped by loans from Hamitic neighbours, which have been engrafted on the old Nilotic nomenclature.[2]

INDONESIA AND OCEANIA

Morgan based his "Malayan" type on Polynesian terminologies. For the Malay branch of the Malayo-Polynesian family he had a single incomplete report from Borneo, which seemed, however, to conform to the Hawaiian norm. There is still great dearth of material for this area. In the Philippines, bifurcation is generally lacking and approximation to the generation system frequently results. But even there the Tinguian, Professor Fay-Cooper Cole states, distinguish uncles and aunts from parents, *i.e.*, fall into the lineal category. This is at least partly true of some "Pagan" systems from Borneo, where aunt and mother are indeed merged, but where the father is distinguished from uncles generally. The importance some Malayans attach to status is probably significant; where a parent is addressed teknonymously and a grandfather receives an appropriate title, people are on the high-road to stratifying society in terms of generation. However, the Mentawei islanders, representative of archaic Malayan culture, radically differ from the Polynesians in not using personal names in address. They exhibit conflicting tendencies toward a generation, a bifurcate merging, and a bifurcate collateral system: while "ina" is the term of address for mother and father's sister alike, the latter has a separate term in non-vocative use; the maternal uncle is distinguished from the paternal, and the latter is distinguished from the father except vocatively.[3]

[1] N. W. Thomas, *Anthropological Report on Sierra Leone*, I: *Law and Customs of the Timne and other Tribes*, 1916, 103 sq.; *id., Anthropological Report on the Edo-speaking Peoples of Nigeria*, I., 1910, 112 sq. R. S. Rattray, *Ashanti*, 1923, 24 sq.

[2] J. H. Driberg, *The Lango, a Nilotic Tribe of Uganda*, 1923, 178 sq.

[3] Morgan, *Systems*, 451. Ch. Hose and Wm. McDougall, *The Pagan Tribes of Borneo*, I., 80 sq. Kroeber, *Kinship in the Philippines*, Anthrop. Papers, American Museum of Natural History, XIX., 1919, 75 sq. E. M. Loeb, ms. on the Mentawei Islands.

For most of Oceania Rivers has given a convenient summary. Broadly, the Melanesians refrain from using personal names whenever there is a suitable term of relationship, while the Polynesians use personal names even for the closest relatives.

Of the Papuans, the Bánaro, settled on a tributary of the Augusta River, have been accurately described. The differentiation of the maternal uncle suggests a bifurcate merging system, but in other respects they have developed on generation lines, though anomalous matrimonial customs colour the terminology. An interesting distinction is drawn between a paternal aunt who has and one who has not been exchanged for the speaker's mother: the former is called "mother," the latter "maternal uncle's wife." In the contemporary generation, siblings are distinguished according to seniority, cousins are treated as siblings, but are designated in accordance with the relative seniority of the connecting *parents*. This feature is shared by such Melanesians of New Guinea as the Jabim. These tribes fall into the bifurcate merging category. Reciprocal terms occur for grandfather and grandson, maternal uncle and sister's son, parent-in-law and child-in-law.[4]

HISTORICAL AND SOCIOLOGICAL INTERPRETATIONS

Morgan inaugurated both historical and sociological interpretations of the facts he scheduled. Starting from the axioms that kinship classifications were "independent of the mutations of language" (p. 506) and that they could not be diffused except if the phonetic symbols themselves were borrowed, he accepted the similarity of systems as proof of *racial* identity. He thus inferred the unity of the Dravidians and the American Indians, and that of the Zulu and the Hawaiians (p. 466). Apart from the questionableness of the premises this argument would lead to the absurd conclusion that the Eastern North American Indians stood racially much closer to the Melanesians and various Africans than to their congeners of the Basin area. However, by his collation of specific resemblances, Morgan paved the way for sound historical conclusions. For example, he recognized the likeness of certain Central Algonkian and southern Siouan systems (p. 179)— a fact now interpreted as the result of diffusion. Diffusion evidently is the only possible explanation of the concentration west of the Rockies of such features as the discrimination between paternal and maternal grandparents.

Sociologically, Morgan viewed his nomenclatures as indices of family life. The "Malayan" as the simplest was considered the earliest; and since it failed to distinguish the mother's brother from the father, Morgan concluded that the two were identical, *i.e.*, that a man had access to his own sister when the system originated. The introduction of a term for maternal uncle was said to result from the prohibition of such unions when the Turanian-Ganowanian system arose. Finally, the "descriptive" terminology, failing to merge *any* collateral relatives with the direct line of descent, was correlated with the rise of property rights and the parents' insistence on transmitting them only to direct descendants (p. 492f.). The scheme thus forms part of an evolutionary theory explaining the gradual rise of our civilized family out of more or less promiscuous beginnings.

These interpretations are now recognized as basically wrong. Morgan was not warranted in assuming that the Polynesian term translated "father" implied procreation: the facts simply reveal a common status term for all kindred of one generation. Simplicity here, as in many other linguistic phenomena, is a late development, not a badge of antiquity. Three independent investigators, Sternberg in Siberia, Rivers in Oceania, Lowie in North America, have been able to show recent transformations of bifurcate merging nomenclatures in the direction of generation systems.

Morgan's extravagance led Kroeber to reject sociological interpretations almost *in toto*. In reply to criticism by Rivers, he has long since receded from this position, specifically admitting the correlation of certain terminological features with cross-cousin terminology. The issue was thus reduced to a difference in philosophical attitude toward cultural phenomena. Rivers championed a rigid determinism, contending that "not only has the

[4] R. Thurnwald, *Die Gemeinde der Bánaro*, 1921, 60 sq. C. G. Seligman. *The Melanesians of British New Guinea*, 1910. 66, 481, 707.

general character of systems of relationship been strictly determined by social conditions, but every detail of these systems has also been so determined." On the other hand, Kroeber insisted that "the infinitely variable play of the variable factors forbids any true determinations of causality of a sweeping character."[1]

Kroeber was unquestionably right in rejecting Rivers' extreme claim, and in maintaining that since kinship terms were linguistic phenomena, they were subject to alterations of a linguistic character, *e.g.*, extensions in meaning, independently of social conditions. However, he did not sufficiently consider that language represents reality and that in so far as it related to social phenomena it is likely to mirror them, even though imperfectly. The empirical facts of distribution indicate that the correlation between social custom and nomenclature is indeed far from perfect, but fairly high.

First of all, there is an undeniable tendency to designate by separate terms relatives with distinctive social functions. It is not sheer accident that Polynesians generally lack a term for the maternal uncle, but that a term appears with the avunculate. Furthermore, the same term applied to different individuals is an index of their sharing the same duties and claims, as Radcliffe-Brown has pointed out for Australia.

Secondly, how are we to interpret the data of geographical distribution? Rivers found that neighboring Oceanians often differed more widely in their kinship systems than remote tribes. A survey of the world establishes this fact on a broader basis. Morgan's solution of resemblances in Dravidian and Iroquois nomenclature is impossible, but he put his finger on a real problem. When the Omaha of Nebraska resemble the Californian Miwok far more than their fellow-Siouans; when specific Omaha features crop up in some Assamese tribes and again on the upper Nile, the fact naturally arouses curiosity and calls for explanation. If the same social factors uniformly accompany the terminological resemblance, a genuine correlation is established. Thus, the grouping of the mother's brother's son with the maternal uncle in the tribes cited is linked with paternal descent, while the classification of the father's sister's son with the father, and of the father's sister's daughter with the paternal aunt generally accompanies maternal descent. We are not dealing with a simple causal nexus, for there are matrilineal tribes like the Seneca and patrilineal tribes like the Ojibwa who do not override the generation principle in this fashion. But a functional relationship remains. It is conceivable that the Omaha and Crow varieties of the bifurcate merging type depend on additional factors that may some time be discovered.

That, without prejudice to other functional relations, a high correlation obtains between a clan organization and the bifurcate merging system, seems certain. Clanless tribes like the Andamanese, Chukchee, Basin Shoshoneans, Hawaiians, have no terminologies of this type; characteristic clan organizations are almost uniformly coupled with them. Tylor's generalization, corroborated by Rivers and Lowie for Oceania and North America, respectively, seems to hold.[2] Yet it is possible to derive the terminology from the joint effect of the levirate and the sororate, institutions probably quite as widely distributed as the clan organization. True, they do not explain why in the common Iroquois variety of the type parallel cousins of the same sex are grouped together, while cross-cousins of the same sex are segregated under a common term of their own. Tylor's idea that the moiety represents the primeval clan does explain this; but large sections of the world with the bifurcate merging nomenclature—notably Africa—lack moieties.

In the present state of our knowledge, then, we may say that while social correlations of terminological features are undeniable,

we are not usually in a position to determine a simple cause-effect relationship. There are often alternative explanations: the mother's brother may be identified with the father's sister's husband because of cross-cousin marriage *or* because they both belong to the same exogamous moiety or because two households arrange to marry off their respective daughters to the boys in the other household (Rivers). The safe rule is to reject any social determinant of a nomenclatorial trait unless it is reported as extant in the tribe or at least in the general area in question.

Other phases of the problem must be considered. An institution may be overshadowed by coexisting institutions or it may not yet have had time to assert itself terminologically. The Miwok, *e.g.*, practise cross-cousin marriage but their terminology shows a far deeper impress of rival forms of marriage. It seems a fair conclusion that the latter are of greater antiquity.[1]

Diffusion presents a further complication. While harmony between the nomenclature and the social structure is frequent, there are discrepancies that can be most readily interpreted by borrowing. To exemplify, there are tribes with a bifurcate merging terminology that lack clans, but their location suggests that they have borrowed a neighbor's nomenclature. It would be dangerous to infer that they had at one time been organized into clans, unless extraneous data so suggest.

Finally, there are the linguistic factors stressed by Kroeber. When nearly all Siouan languages have a separate term for paternal aunt, the lack of such a word (in address only) among the Crow must be interpreted as a late development; and the use of the "mother" word appears as a characteristic sample of linguistic extension,—the same phenomenon as when English uses "wife" as a special term of affinity while the cognate German *Weib* applies to woman generically. The reality of such phenomena militates against any attempt to reduce the whole of kinship terminology to social causes. There will always be residual phenomena resisting interpretation on any but linguistic lines. This means that they are in a sense unique facts that can be understood after they have been observed but that could not be deduced from general principles.[2]

These cautions limit but do not destroy the sociological significance of relationship terminologies. When all allowances are made for disturbing factors, a host of correlations remain between kinship features and sociological factors. When more intensive studies of large linguistic families shall be available, it will be possible to balance with greater nicety the relative importance of sociological and other factors as determinants.   (R. H. Lo.)

RELATIVITY. The progress of natural science in the first quarter of the present century was especially noteworthy through the appearance of the doctrine of relativity, and its almost immediate acceptance by the scientific world in general. The need for some such theory had long been felt and was becoming continually more urgent. As far back as 1887 Michelson and Morley, experimenting for quite another purpose, had obtained results which obstinately refused to fit into 19th-century conceptions of the general nature of the universe. Experiments in other directions soon indicated that the difficulties thus revealed were not isolated difficulties confined to one special corner of science, but extended throughout a large part of electrical and optical science. Theoretical discussions by Lorentz, Larmor and others drew attention to the serious nature and extent of the difficulties which had arisen, and pointed, although somewhat vaguely, to the direction in which a solution was likely to be found.

The first intimation of the revolution in thought which had now become necessary was given by Henri Poincaré, who, in an address delivered before the International Congress of Arts and Science at St. Louis on Sept. 24, 1904[3], formulated a "principle of relativity," namely, that the laws of physical phenomena ought to be the same for any two observers, one of whom has a movement of uniform translation relative to the other; so that we can not by any

[1]Rivers, *Kinship and Social Organization,* 1914; id., *History of Melanesian Society,* II., 11, *passim.* Kroeber, *Classificatory Systems of Relationship,* 1909; id., "California Kinship Systems," *Univ. of Cal. Pub.,* vol. 12, no. 9, p.p. 385–396 (1917).

[2]E. B. Tylor, "On a Method of Investigating the Development of Institutions, applied to Laws of Marriage and Descent," *Jour. Anthrop. Inst.* XVIII., 1889, 245–272. Rivers, *Kinship and Social Organization.* Lowie, "Exogamy and the Classificatory System of Relationships," *Am. Anth.,* 1915, 223–239.

[1]E. W. Gifford, "Miwok Moieties," *U. Cal. Pub.,* 1916, 12, 139–194, esp. 181 *seq.* (1916).

[2]R. H. Lowie, "The Kinship Systems of the Crow and Hidatsa," *Proc. 19th Intern. Congr. Americ.,* p. 340 (1917).

[3]Published in *Bulletin des sciences math.* (2) 28:302 (1904).

means discover whether we are or are not partaking in such a movement. After examining the results of observation and experiment in the light of this principle, Poincaré declared that an entirely new type of dynamics was required, characterized by the law that no velocity could exceed that of light. The program thus indicated was carried out in 1905[1] by Albert Einstein, then professor of theoretical physics in the University of Berne.

At this time gravitation held obstinately aloof from all other physical phenomena; an ether had been devised which explained optical and electrical phenomena with fair success, but it refused to find room for the phenomenon of gravitation. In 1915 Einstein published further papers which showed that gravitation admitted of a very simple explanation in terms of the new ideas as to the nature of space and time. The gravitation which was explained in this way was, however, just a shade different from the gravitation of Sir Isaac Newton. When it was realized that the gravitation of nature was also just a shade different from that of Newton, and it was further discovered that nature ranged herself completely with Einstein in this matter, then the acceptance of Einstein's theory was universal and complete.

While gravitation fitted quite naturally into the new scheme of nature demanded by the theory of relativity, it was found to be less easy to fit in the general phenomena of electromagnetism. The years after 1918 saw a great deal of discussion as to the way in which these must be joined on to Einstein's general theory of relativity and, as we shall see below, the issue is still in doubt.

General Nature of the Principle.—Science advances in two ways, by the discovery of new facts, and by the discovery of mechanisms or systems which account for the facts already known. The outstanding landmarks in the progress of science have all been of the second kind. Such, for instance, was the Copernican system of astronomy, which explained the already known motions of the planets; such was the Newtonian mechanism (the force of gravitation) which explained the elliptic orbits of the planets and the earth's pull on terrestrial bodies; such was the Darwinian mechanism of natural selection, which explained the survival of some species and the extinction of others. Such also is the theory of relativity.

The scientist's desire to discover mechanisms or systems arises no doubt primarily from the constitution of the human mind; our intellects, unsatisfied with a mere accumulation of facts, impel us ever to search for the causes underlying the facts: *Vere scire est per causas scire.* But to the working scientist the discovery of a mechanism has an additional and more practical value. When he has found a mechanism which will account for certain laws, he can proceed to examine the complete set of laws which the mechanism demands. If his mechanism corresponds with sufficient closeness to reality he may in this way be led to the discovery of new natural laws. On the other hand, the new laws deduced from the supposed mechanism may be false. If the falsity of the new laws is not at once revealed science may for a time be led into wrong paths. When more accurate experimenting or observation discloses that the new laws are not true a recasting of ideas becomes necessary, and the branch of science concerned may experience a time of revolution followed by a period of rapid growth.

An obvious illustration of these general statements is provided by the history of astronomy. The laws of the motions of the planets, as observed from the earth, were tolerably well-known to the Greeks. They had also evolved an explanatory mechanism starting from the premise, which seemed to them to be necessary on metaphysical grounds, that the paths of the planets must necessarily be circles. The earth was the centre of the universe and round this revolved spheres to which the planets were attached. The retrograde motion of the outer planets was explained by supposing that they were attached to secondary spheres revolving about points on the primary spheres which in turn revolved about the earth. This mechanism of cycles and epicycles as an explanation of planetary motion held the field for 18 centuries. Finally the observations of Tycho Brahe provided a test which

revealed the falsity of the whole structure. The position of Mars was found to differ from that required by the mechanism of epicycles by an amount as great as 8 min. of arc. "Out of these eight minutes," said Johann Kepler, "we will construct a new theory that will explain the motions of all the planets."

The history of the succeeding century of astronomy need not be recapitulated here. The earth yielded its place as the centre of the universe, and the structure of cycles and epicycles crumbled away. The laws of planetary motion were determined with a precision which for the time appeared to be final. The mechanism underlying these laws was supposed to be a "force" of gravitation. This force was supposed to act between every pair of particles in the universe, its intensity varying directly as the product of the masses of the particles and inversely as the square of the distance separating them—the famous law of Newton.

In science, history repeats itself and, in recent years, the theory of relativity has provided a further instance of the general processes we have been considering. Under the Newtonian mechanism every planet would describe a perfect ellipse about the sun as focus, and these elliptic orbits would repeat themselves indefinitely except in so far as they were disturbed by the gravitational forces arising from the other planets. But, after allowing for these disturbing influences, Urbain Leverrier found that the orbit of the planet Mercury was rotating in its own plane at the rate of 43 sec. a century. Various attempts have been made to reconcile this observed motion with the Newtonian mechanism. The gravitational forces arising from the known planets were demonstrably unable to produce the motion in question, but it was possible that Mercury's orbit was being disturbed by matter so far unknown.

Investigations were made as to the disturbance to be expected from various hypothetical gravitating masses—a planet or a ring of planets between Mercury and the sun, a ring of planets outside the orbit of Mercury, a belt of matter extended in a flattened disk in a plane through the sun's centre, an oblateness greater than that suggested by the shape of the sun's surface, in the arrangement of the internal layers of the sun's mass. In every case the mass required to produce the observed disturbance in the motion of Mercury would have also produced disturbances not observed in the motions of the other planets. The solution of the problem came only with the theory of relativity. Just as Tycho's 8 min. of arc, in the hands of Kepler and Newton, revolutionized mediaeval conceptions of the mechanism of the universe, so Leverrier's 43 sec. of arc, in the hands of Einstein, has revolutionized our 19th-century conceptions, not only of purely astronomical mechanism, but also of the nature of time and space and of the fundamental ideas of science. The history of this revolution is in effect the history of the theory of relativity. It falls naturally into three chapters, a first narrating the building of the earlier physical theory of relativity, a second dealing with the extension of that theory to gravitation, and a third, which is still in process of being written, attempting to include electromagnetism in the physical system presented by the existing theory of relativity.

THE PHYSICAL THEORY OF RELATIVITY

The earliest successful attempt to formulate the laws governing the general motion of matter is found in Newton's laws. The first law states that:—

Every body perseveres in its state of rest or of uniform motion in a right line unless it is compelled to change that state by forces impressed thereon.

In this law no distinction is made between rest and uniform motion in a straight line, and the same is true of the remaining laws. Hence follows the property to which Newton draws explicit attention in his fifth corollary to the laws of motion:—

The motions of bodies included in a given space are the same among themselves, whether that space is at rest, or moves uniformly forwards in a right line without any circular motion.

As a concrete application of his principle, Newton instances "the experiment of a ship, where all motions happen after the same manner whether the ship is at rest or is carried uniformly forward in a right line." Just as a passenger on a ship in a still

[1]Einstein's paper, *Ann. d. Phys.* 17:841 (1905) is dated June 30, 1905.

sea could not determine, from the behaviour of bodies inside the ship, whether the ship was at rest or moving uniformly forward, so we cannot determine from the behaviour of bodies on our earth whether the earth is at rest or not. We believe the earth to be moving round the sun with a speed of about 30 km. a second, so that there can be no question of the earth being permanently at rest, but we are unable to determine whether it is at rest at any specified point of its orbit, or, in the probable event of its not being at rest, what its absolute velocity may be. There is no more reason for thinking the sun, than the earth, to be at rest. Newton wrote as follows:—

"It is possible that in the remote regions of the fixed stars, or perhaps far beyond them, there may be some body absolutely at rest, but impossible to know, from the positions of bodies to one another in our regions, whether any of these do keep the same position to that remote body. It follows that absolute rest cannot be determined from the position of bodies in our regions."

The above quotations are all from the first book of the *Principia Mathematica*. Previous to them all Newton writes: "I have no regard in this place to a medium, if any such there is, that freely pervades the interstices between the parts of bodies." The two centuries which elapsed after the publication of the *Principia* witnessed a steady growth of the belief in the reality of such an all-pervading medium. It was called the ether, or aether, and by the end of these two centuries (1887) it was almost universally believed that light and all electromagnetic phenomena were evidence of actions taking place in this ether. Light from the most distant stars was supposed to be transmitted to us in the form of wave motions in the ether, and we could see the stars only because the sea of ether between us and these stars was unbroken. It had been proved that if this sea of ether existed it must be at rest, for the alternative hypothesis that the ether was dragged about by ponderable bodies in their motions had been shown to be incompatible with the observed phenomenon of astronomical aberration and other facts of nature. On this view it was no longer necessary to go to Newton's "remote regions of the fixed stars, or perhaps far beyond them," to find absolute rest. A standard of absolute rest was provided by the ether which filled our laboratories and pervaded all bodies. Owing to our motion it would appear to be rushing past us, although without encountering any hindrance—"like the wind through a grove of trees," to borrow the simile of Thomas Young. The determination of the absolute velocity of the earth was reduced to the problem of measuring the velocity of an ether current flowing past us and through us.

In this same year (1887) the first experimental determination of this velocity was attempted by the Chicago physicist Michelson. The velocity of light was known to be, in round numbers, 300,000 km. a second, a velocity which was interpreted as representing the rate of progress of wave motion through the ether. If the earth were moving through the ether with a velocity of 1,000 km. a second, the velocity of light relative to a terrestrial observer ought to be only 299,000 km. a second when the light was sent in exactly the direction of the earth's motion through the ether, but would be 301,000 km. a second if the light was sent in the opposite direction. In more general terms, if the earth were moving through the ether, the velocity of light, as measured by a terrestrial observer, would depend on the direction of the light, and the extent of this dependence would give a measure of the earth's velocity. The velocity of light along a single straight course does not permit of direct experimental determination, but the same property of dependence on direction ought to be true, although to a less extent, of the average to-and-fro velocity of a beam of light sent along any path and then reflected back along the same path.

It was through this property that Michelson attempted to measure the earth's velocity through the ether. The apparatus was simple in principle. A circular table ABCD (*see* fig. 1) was arranged so as to be capable of slow rotation about its centre O.

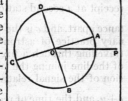

FIG. 1.—DIAGRAM OF MICHELSON'S APPARATUS Designed to ascertain the earth's velocity through the ether

Light sent along CO was divided up at O into two beams which were made to travel along perpendicular radii OA, OB. The arms OA, OB were made as equal as possible and mirrors were placed at A and B to reflect the beams of light back to O. An extremely sensitive optical method made it possible to detect even a very slight difference in the times of the total paths of the two beams from O back to O. There would in any case be a difference owing to the necessarily imperfect equalization of the lengths of the arms OA, OB, but if the earth is moving through the ether in some direction OP, and if the table is made to rotate slowly about O, then this difference ought itself to vary on account of the earth's motion through the ether. Michelson, and afterwards Michelson and Morley in collaboration, attempted to estimate the amount of this variation. No variation whatsoever could be detected, although their final apparatus was so sensitive that the variation produced by a velocity through the ether of even 1 km. a second ought to have shown itself quite clearly.

Thus to the question "What is our velocity through the ether?" nature appeared to give the answer "None." It was never suggested that this answer should be accepted as final; this would have brought us back to a geocentric universe. Clearly either the question had been wrongly framed or the answer wrongly interpreted. It was pointed out in 1893 by George F. FitzGerald, and again independently, in 1895, by Lorentz, that the *null* result of the Michelson-Morley experiment could be explained if it could be supposed that motion through the ether altered the linear dimensions of bodies. They both showed that the experiment would invariably and of necessity give a *null* result if every body moving through the ether with a velocity u was contracted in the direction of its motion in the ratio $\sqrt{1 - \dfrac{u^2}{c^2}}$, c being the velocity of light. The supposition that such a contraction occurred was not only permissible—it was almost demanded by electrical theory. Indeed, Lorentz had already shown that if matter were a purely electrical structure, the constituent parts would of necessity readjust their relative positions when set in motion through the ether and the final position of equilibrium would be one showing precisely the contraction just mentioned.

On this view, there was no prima facie necessity to abandon the attempt to measure the earth's velocity through the ether. The answer to the problem had merely been pushed one stage farther back, and it now became necessary only to measure the shrinkage of matter produced by motion. It was obvious from the first that no direct material measurement could disclose the amount of this shrinkage, since any measuring rod would shrink in exactly the same ratio as the length to be measured; but optical and electrical methods appeared to be available. Experiments to this end were devised and performed by Lord Rayleigh, De Witt Brace, Frederick T. Trouton and H. R. Noble, Trouton and Alex O. Rankine and others. In every case a *null* result was obtained. It appeared then that if the earth moved through the ether this motion was concealed by a universal shrinkage of matter, and this shrinkage was in turn concealed by some other agency or agencies.

At this time the word "conspiracy" found its way into the technical language of science. There was supposed to be a conspiracy on the part of the various agencies of nature to prevent man from measuring his velocity of motion in space. If this motion produced a direct effect x on any phenomenon, the other agencies of nature seemed to be in league to produce a countervailing effect $-x$. A long train of experiments had not revealed, as was intended, our velocity through the ether; they had merely created a conviction that it was beyond the power of man to measure this velocity. The conspiracy, if such there was, appeared to have been perfectly organized.

A perfectly organized conspiracy of this kind differs only in name from a law of nature. The inventor who tries to devise a perpetual-motion machine may come to the conclusion that the forces of nature have joined in a conspiracy to prevent his machine from working, but wider knowledge shows that he is in conflict not with a conspiracy, but with a law of nature—the conservation of energy. In 1904 Poincaré crystallizing an idea which must have been vaguely present in many minds, propounded the hypothesis that the apparent conspiracy might be in effect a law of nature. He suggested that there might be a true law to the effect that "it is of necessity impossible to determine absolute motion by any experiment whatever." This hypothetical law may again be put in the equivalent form: "The phenomena of nature will be the same to two observers who move with any uniform velocity whatever relative to one another." As we have seen, Poincaré called this the principle of relativity. It belongs to the class of statements which have been named by Edmund T. Whittaker postulates of impotence; these are statements which assert the impossibility of achieving something, even though there may be an infinite number of ways of trying to achieve it. The second law of thermodynamics, the principle of uncertainty in quantum mechanics and the principle of the indistinguishability of electrons are of this nature.

The hypothesis in itself was not of a sensational character. Indeed, from the quotations which have already been given from Newton's works, it appears probable that Newton himself would have accepted the hypothesis without hesitation: he might even have regarded it as superfluous. The true significance of the hypothesis can only be understood by a reference to the scientific history of the two centuries which had elapsed since Newton. The Newtonian view that absolute rest was to be found only "in the remote regions of the fixed stars, or perhaps far beyond them," had given place to a belief that absolute rest was to be found all around us in an ether which permeated all bodies. What was striking about the hypothesis was its implication—either that we could not measure the velocity relative to ourselves of a medium which surrounded us on all sides, or else that no such medium existed.

The hypothesis demanded detailed and exhaustive examination. It was for the mathematician to test whether it was in opposition to known and established laws of physics and to this task Einstein, Lorentz and others set themselves. If the hypothesis proved to be in opposition to a single firmly established law, then of course it must be abandoned. It was unlikely that such an event would occur among the well-established laws, for if it did, the phenomena governed by that law would enable direct measurement to be made of the earth's velocity through the ether, a measurement which had so far eluded all attempts of experimenters. It was among the more obscure and less well-established laws, if anywhere, that discrepancies were to be looked for.

It is impossible here to give a complete account of the many tests to which the relativity hypothesis has been subjected. The result of all can be summed up in one concise and quite general statement:—Wherever the hypothesis of relativity has appeared to be in conflict with known or suspected natural laws, further experiment, where possible, has without a single exception shown the laws to be erroneous, and has moreover shown the alternative laws suggested by the hypothesis of relativity to be accurate. It is only in somewhat exceptional cases that the hypothesis of relativity suffices of itself to determine fully the form of a natural law; these cases constitute the most striking triumphs of the theory. As instances may be mentioned the determination of the law connecting the mass of an electron with its velocity; of the law expressing the velocity of light through a transparent medium in motion (Armand Fizeau's water-tube experiment); and of the formulae for the magnetic forces on moving dielectric media (experiments of A. Eichenwald and H. A. Wilson).[1]

Before leaving this general statement, particular mention must be made of one special case. A natural law which, at an early stage, was seen to be in conflict with the hypothesis of relativity was Newton's famous law of gravitation—namely, that every particle of matter attracts every other particle with a force proportional to the product of the two masses, and to the inverse square of their distance apart. Either, then, Newton's great law had to be abandoned or else the hypothesis of relativity had to be discarded, in which case it would immediately become possible, in

---

[1]For references to the original papers dealing with these and other tests of the hypothesis of relativity *see* E. Cunningham, *The Principle of Relativity*, or J. H. Jeans, *Mathematical Theory of Electricity and Magnetism* (4th or 5th ed.).

theory at least, to determine the earth's velocity through space by gravitational means. It is the choice between these two alternatives that has led to the most surprising developments of the theory of relativity; and to these we shall return later.

The hypothesis of relativity, as has already been explained in this section, postulates that the phenomena of nature will be the same to two trained observers moving relative to one another with any uniform velocity whatever. The hypothesis has been so amply tested as regards all optical and electromagnetic phenomena that no doubt is felt, or can rationally be felt, as to its truth with respect to these phenomena. The hypothesis can be examined and developed in two opposite directions. We may, on the one hand, proceed from the general hypothesis to the detailed laws implied in it; this has already been done with completely satisfactory results as regards confirmation of the hypothesis. Or regarding the hypothesis of relativity as being itself a detailed law, we may attempt to generalize upward to something still wider. It is this possibility which must for the moment claim our attention.

In 1905 Einstein examined in full the consequences of the hypothesis that one simple optical phenomenon—namely, the transmission of a ray of light in free space—was, in accordance with the hypothesis of relativity, independent of the velocity of the observer. If an ether existed, and provided a fixed framework of reference, then light set free at any instant would obviously travel with a velocity which would appear to an observer at rest in this ether to be the same in all directions, and the wave front at any instant would be a sphere having the observer as centre. On the hypothesis of relativity the phenomenon of light transmission must remain unaffected by the motion of the observer, so that the light must appear, to a moving observer also, to travel with a uniform velocity in all directions, and thus to the moving observer also the wave front must appear to be a sphere of which he is the centre. It is, however, quite obvious that the same spherical wave front cannot appear, to each of two observers who have moved some distance apart, to be centred round himself, unless the use either of the common conceptions of science or of the ordinary words of language is greatly changed. In fig. 2 it is not possible, in ordinary language, that both O and P should be at the same instant be at the centre of the sphere ABC. The change to which Einstein was forced is one which has an intimate bearing upon our fundamental conceptions of the nature of space and time; this change it will be necessary to explain in some detail.

Suppose that two observatories, say Greenwich and Paris, wish to synchronize their clocks, with a view to, let us say, an exact determination of their longitude difference. Paris will send out a wireless signal at exact midnight as shown by the Paris clock, and Greenwich will note the time shown by the Greenwich clock at the instant of receipt of the signal. Greenwich will not, however, adjust its clock so as to show exact midnight when the signal is received; a correction of about .001 sec. must be made to allow for the time occupied by the signal in traversing the distance from Paris to Greenwich. To turn to mathematical symbols, if t_0 is the time at which a signal is sent out from one station, the time of receipt at a second station is taken to be $t_0 + \dfrac{x}{c}$, where x is their distance apart, and c is the velocity of light. This represents the ordinary practice of astronomers, but it is clear that if the earth is travelling through a fixed ether with a velocity u in the direction of the line joining the two observatories, the velocity of transmission of the signal relative to the two observatories will not be c but $c + u$, and the time of receipt at the second station will be $t_0 + \dfrac{x}{c+u}$. Thus it appears that it is impossible to synchronize two clocks unless we know the value of u, and that the ordinary practice of astronomers will not, as they expect, synchronize their clocks, but set them at an interval apart equal to

$$x\left(\frac{1}{c} - \frac{1}{c+u}\right)$$

which may, to an approximation, be put equal to $\dfrac{ux}{c^2}$.

According to the hypothesis of relativity, it is impossible ever to determine the value of u, and so it is impossible ever truly to synchronize two clocks. Moreover, according to this hypothesis, the phenomena of nature go on just the same whatever the value of u, so that the want of synchrony cannot in any way show itself —in fact, if it did, it would immediately become possible to measure the effect and so arrange for true synchrony.

As the earth moves in its orbit, the value of u changes, so that its value in the spring, for instance, will be different from its value in the autumn. One pair of astronomers may attempt to synchronize a pair of clocks in the spring, but their synchronization will appear faulty to a second pair who repeat the determination in the autumn. There will, so to speak, be one synchrony for the spring and another for the autumn, and neither pair of astronomers will be able to claim that their results are more accurate than those of their colleagues. Different conceptions of synchrony will correspond to different velocities of translation.

These elementary considerations bring us to the heart of the problem which we illustrated diagrammatically in fig. 2. The observer at O in the diagram will have one conception of simultaneity, while the second observer who moves from O to P will, on account of his different velocity, have a different conception of simultaneity. The instants at which the wave front of the light signal from O reaches the various points A, B, C in the diagram will be deemed to be simultaneous by the observer who remains at O, but the observer who moves from O to P will quite unconsciously have different ideas as to simultaneity. At instants which he regards as simultaneous the wave front will have some form other than that of the sphere ABC surrounding O. If the hypothesis of relativity is to be true in its application to the transmission of light signals, this wave front must be a sphere having P as its centre. Einstein examined mathematically the conditions that this should be possible. A precise statement of his conclusions can only be given in mathematical language.

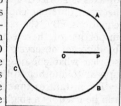

FIG. 2.—DIAGRAM OF MOTION OF OBSERVER AND LIGHT SIGNAL

The observer who remains at O in fig. 2 may be supposed to make exact observations and to record these observations in mathematical terms. To fix the positions of points in space he will map out a "frame of reference" consisting of three orthogonal axes, and use Cartesian co-ordinates x, y, z, to specify the projections along these axes of the radius from the origin to any given point. He will also use a time co-ordinate t which may be supposed to specify the time which has lapsed since a given instant, as measured by a clock in his possession. Any observations he may make on the transmission of light signals can be recorded in the form of equations between the four co-ordinates x, y, z, t. For instance the circumstance that light travels from the origin with the same velocity c in all directions will be expressed by the equation (of the wave front):—

$$x^2 + y^2 + z^2 - c^2 t^2 = 0 \quad .. \quad .. \quad .. \quad (1)$$

The second observer who moves from O to P will also construct a frame of reference, and we can simplify the problem by supposing that his axes are parallel to those already selected by the first observer. His co-ordinates, to distinguish them from those used by the first observer, may be denoted by the accented letters x', y', z', t'. If his observations also are to show light always to travel with the same velocity c in all directions, the equation of the wave front, as observed by him, must be:—

$$x'^2 + y'^2 + z'^2 - c^2 t'^2 = 0 \quad .. \quad .. \quad .. \quad (2)$$

A 19th-century mathematician would have insisted that x, y, z, t must necessarily be connected with x', y', z', t' by the simple relations:—

$$\left. \begin{array}{l} x' = x - ut \\ y' = y \\ z' = z \\ t' = t \end{array} \right\} \quad .. \quad .. \quad .. \quad (A)$$

Indeed, he would have been unable to imagine that there should be any other relation connecting these quantities. It is, however, obvious that if these relations hold, then equation (1) cannot trans-

form into equation (2). Einstein showed that equation (1) will transform into equation (2) provided the co-ordinates x, y, z, t of the first observer are connected with the co-ordinates x', y', z', t' of the second observer by the equations:—

$$\left. \begin{array}{l} x' = \beta (x - ut) \\ y' = y \\ z' = z \\ t' = \beta \left(t - \dfrac{ux}{c^2} \right) \end{array} \right\} \quad .. \quad .. \quad .. \quad (B)$$

where β stands for $\left(1 - \dfrac{u^2}{c^2} \right)^{-\frac{1}{2}}$.

To form some idea of the physical meaning of these equations, let us consider the simple case in which the first observer is at rest in the ether while the second moves through the ether with velocity u. The points of difference between equations (B) and (A) then admit of simple explanation. The factor β in the first of equations (B) is simply, according to the suggestion of FitzGerald and Lorentz already mentioned, the factor according to which all lengths parallel to the axis of x must be adjusted on account of motion through the ether with velocity u. The moving observer must correct his lengths by this factor, and he must correct his times by the same factor in order that the velocity of propagation of light along the axis of x may still have the same velocity c; this explains the presence of the multiplier β in the last of equations (B). The one remaining difference between the two sets of equations, namely, the replacement of t in (A) by $t - \dfrac{ux}{c^2}$ in (B), represents exactly the want of synchrony which, as we have already seen, is to be expected in the observations of two observers whose velocity differs by a velocity u.

Although the equations admit of simple illustration by considering the case in which one observer is at rest in a supposed ether, it will be understood that the equations are more general than the illustration. They are in no way concerned with the possibility of an observer being at rest in an ether, or indeed the existence of an ether at all. Their general interpretation is this: If one observer O, having any motion whatever, finds, as a matter of observation, that light for him travels uniformly in all directions with a constant velocity c, then a second observer P, moving relative to O with a constant velocity u along the axis of x, will find, as a matter of observation, that light, for him also, travels uniformly in all directions with the same constant velocity c, provided he uses, for his observations, co-ordinates which are connected with the co-ordinates of O by equations (B).

This is the meaning that was attached to the equations by Einstein in 1905, but the equations had been familiar to mathematicians before this date. They had in fact been applied to the equations of vibratory motions in 1887 by Woldemar Voigt, and had been rediscovered by Lorentz in 1895 as expressing the condition that all electromagnetic phenomena, including of course the propagation of light, should be the same for an observer moving through the ether with velocity u as for an observer at rest in the ether. For this reason the transformation of co-ordinates specified by these equations is universally spoken of as a "Lorentz transformation." What Einstein introduced in 1905 was not a new system of equations but a new interpretation of old equations. The two observers who used the co-ordinates x, y, z, t and x', y', z', t' had been regarded by Lorentz as being one at rest in an ether and one in motion with a velocity u; for Einstein they were observers moving with any velocities whatever subject to their relative velocity being u. Lorentz had regarded t as the true time and t' as an artificial time. If the observer could be persuaded to measure time in this artificial way, setting his clocks wrong to begin with and then making them gain or lose permanently, the effect of his supposed artificiality would just counterbalance the effects of his motion through the ether. With Einstein came the conception that both times, t and t', had precisely equal rights to be regarded as true time. The measure t' of time is precisely that which would be adopted naturally by any set of observers, or race of men, who disregarded their steady motion through space; their adoption of it would be above criticism if, as Einstein suggested, their motion through space had no influence on material phenomena, and it represents, as we have seen, the usual practice of astronomers in comparing time at different places. From this point of view neither measure of time is more accurate or more logical than the other. There are as many ways of measuring time as there are observers, and all are right.

The investigator who is trying to discover laws of nature will, in general, require to measure both time and space either directly or indirectly. If, to take a simple case, he is studying the motion of a single particle, he will measure out the position of the particle at definite instants as determined by his clock. He may specify the position of the particle at any instant by three measurements in space—for instance, he may say that two seconds after his particle started it was 6 ft. to the E. of the point from which it started, 9 ft. to the N. and 12 ft. vertically upward. The mathematician would express this by taking axes x, y, z to the E., to the N. and vertically upwards, and saying that at time $t = 2$ the particle had co-ordinates $x = 6$, $y = 9$, $z = 12$. Or he might, putting his time co-ordinate t on the same footing as the space co-ordinates x, y, z, simply say that $x = 6$, $y = 9$, $z = 12$, $t = 2$ represented one position of the particle. A complete set of readings of this type, each consisting of values of four co-ordinates, would give the complete history of the motion of the particle.

Such sets of simultaneous measurements form the common material of investigations in both pure and applied science. For instance, the engineer may measure the extension of a sample of steel corresponding to different loads; the electrician may measure the amount of light given by an electric filament corresponding to different amounts of current passed through it. In each of these cases there are only two quantities to be measured simultaneously, and an investigator can conveniently represent the result of the whole series of his measurements in graphical form; a single reading is represented by a point whose distances from two fixed perpendicular lines represent the quantities measured, and the curve obtained by joining these single points will give all the information contained in the whole set of readings.

We have seen that, in studying the motion of a particle in space, four sets of quantities must be measured, so that the results obtained cannot be plotted graphically on a piece of paper. Their proper representation demands a four-dimensional space, in which x, y, z and t are taken as co-ordinates. The practical importance of such graphical representation is *nil*, since it is impossible to construct a four-dimensional graph, but its theoretical importance to the theory of relativity is immense. For if the hypothesis of relativity is true, then the four-dimensional graphs of any natural event constructed by all observers, no matter what their relative motions, will be identical. The influence of their motion will be shown only in that the axes of x, y, z and t will be different for different observers, and the relations between these sets of axes will be those given by the foregoing equations (B).

The importance of this conception can hardly be overestimated, and it may be well to consider it further with the help of an illustrative example. Imagine a number of aeroplanes flying over England, and, in order to eliminate one of the three directions in space—the vertical—let us limit them to fly always at the same height, say 1,000 ft. above sea-level. Imagine a number of similar plates of glass prepared, each marked faintly with an outline map of England and with lines of latitude and longitude. Suppose that at 12 hr. 0 min. G.M.T. a plate is taken and the position of each aeroplane marked by a thick black dot. At 12 hr. 1 min. let a second plate be taken and similarly marked, and let this be done every minute for an hour. The 60 plates so marked will constitute a record of the motion of each aeroplane within this hour. If, now, we place the plates in order, one above the other, on a horizontal table, the mass of glass so formed will present a graphical representation, in three dimensions, of the motions of all the aeroplanes. In this graph the two horizontal co-ordinates represent motions in any two rectangular directions over England, say east and north, while the third co-ordinate—the vertical—represents

time. The individual black dots which represent the positions of any one aeroplane will form a dotted curve, and this curve gives a graphical representation of the motion of the particular aeroplane. Our rectangle of glass contains the history, for one hour, of all the aeroplanes in graphical form.

To represent the motion of particles in the whole world of space a four-dimensional graph is required. The four-dimensional space in which it is constructed may, following the usual terminology, be spoken of as a four-dimensional continuum. The history of any particle in the universe—just as that of any aeroplane flying over England—will be represented by a continuous line in the continuum, and this is called the "world line" of the particle. If the hypothesis of relativity is true, the same continuum and the same world lines will represent the history of the particles of the universe equally well for all observers, the influence of their motions being shown only through their choosing different axes in the continuum for their axes of space and time. Thus the continuum must be thought of as something real and objective, but the choice of axes is subjective and will vary with the observer, the relation between different choices being expressed mathematically by our equations (B), the equations of the Lorentz transformation. An inspection of these equations shows that the sets of axes chosen by different observers have different orientations in the continuum, so that what one observer describes as a pure space interval will appear to another to be a mixture of time and space.

The instant of time and point in space at which any event occurs can be fixed by a single point in the continuum, so that the interval between two events will be represented by a finite line. The events and the interval between them are absolute, but the interval will be split up into time and space in different ways by different observers. The interval between any two events, such as the great fire of London and the outburst on the star Nova Persei, may be measured by one set of observers as so many years and so many millions of miles, but another set of observers may divide the interval quite differently. For instance a terrestrial astronomer may reckon that the outburst on Nova Persei occurred a century before the great fire of London, but an astronomer on the Nova may reckon with equal accuracy that the great fire occurred a century before the outburst on the Nova. A third astronomer may insist that the events were simultaneous. All may be equally right, although none will be right in an absolute sense. At this stage we may notice one respect in which our pile of glass plates failed to represent the true continuum. The mass of glass was stratified into different plates which represent different times for one particular observer. To obtain a section which would represent what an observer in motion relative to this first observer could regard as simultaneous positions of the aeroplanes, we should have to cut the mass of glass on the slant. The continuum is more closely represented by our plates of glass if they are annealed into a solid mass from which all trace of the original stratification is made to disappear. All observers, no matter what their motion, are then equally free to cut a section to represent their individual ideas of simultaneity.

Thus space and time fade into subjective conceptions, just as subjective as right or left hand, front and behind, are in ordinary life. The continuum alone is objective and may be thought of as containing an objective record of the motion of every particle of the universe. The curve in which this record is embodied is spoken of as the world line of the particle in question. To use the words of Hermann Minkowski: "Space in itself and time in itself sink to mere shadows, and only a kind of union of the two retains an independent existence."

GRAVITATION AND RELATIVITY

Since all the phenomena of light and of electromagnetism are believed, on almost incontrovertible evidence, to be in accordance with the hypothesis of relativity, it is necessarily impossible to determine absolute velocity by optical or gravitational means. On the other hand, as we have already mentioned, the Newtonian law of gravitation is readily seen to be inconsistent with the hypothesis of relativity. Three alternatives are open:

(i) The Newtonian law may be true, in which case it must be

possible to determine absolute velocity by gravitational means.

(ii) The Newtonian law may be untrue in its original form, but may become true when amended so as to conform to the relativity hypothesis.

(iii) Neither of the foregoing possibilities may be true.

Alternative (i) was explored by Sir Oliver Lodge, who, assuming the exact truth of the Newtonian law of gravitation, deduced that the observed motion of the perihelion of Mercury could be accounted for if the sun were moving through space with a velocity of about 70 km. a second in a certain direction. This investigation had to be abandoned when Sir Arthur Eddington pointed out that a similar discussion of the motions of the other planets would lead to vastly different values for the sun's velocity. Alternative (ii) was explored by Einstein and others, but was found to lead to a motion of the perihelion of Mercury equal only to one-sixth part of that actually observed.

Alternative (iii) remained with its innumerable possibilities. Einstein commenced his attack on the problem by eliminating all possibilities which did not conform to two general principles. The first of these was the principle of relativity. Inasmuch as all physical phenomena except gravitation were believed to conform to this principle, it was natural to try as a working hypothesis, the effect of assuming gravitation also to conform. The second principle was the so-called principle of equivalence, and this demands a word of explanation.

To our children we explain that an apple falls to the ground because a force of gravitation inherent in the earth's mass impels the apple towards the centre of the earth. Most schoolboys know that this is not quite the whole story; the path of the apple is more accurately determined by supposing the apple to be acted on simultaneously by two forces—a gravitational force of attraction towards the earth's centre and the centrifugal force arising from the earth's rotation. It is only because the earth's rotation is comparatively slow that the conception of an attraction towards the earth's centre gives a tolerably plausible account of the fall of the apple. If the earth rotated at 17 times its present rate objects would not fall, even approximately, towards the earth's centre; they would fall always parallel to the earth's axis, and the inhabitants of the northern hemisphere might explain this as arising from a force of repulsion inherent in the pole star. If the earth rotated many times faster even than this, bodies would fall always perpendicularly away from the earth's axis, and this might be interpreted as arising from a gravitational repulsion residing in the earth's axis.

These illustrations will show that it is easy to confuse acceleration arising from the earth's rotation with gravitational attraction. We may go further and say that it is impossible to distinguish between the effects of gravitational attraction and the effects of acceleration of any kind whatever. Every aviator knows this to his sorrow; it is inherently impossible to devise any instrument which shall show the direction of the vertical in an aeroplane since an acceleration of the aeroplane produces on any instrument whatever, effects which are indistinguishable from those of gravity. From such considerations Einstein was led to his principle of equivalence, which may be enunciated as follows:—

"A gravitational field of force at any point of space is in every way equivalent to an artificial field of force resulting from acceleration, so that no experiment can possibly distinguish between them."

Guided by these two principles—relativity and equivalence—Einstein was led to the view that all gravitational "fields of force" must be illusions. The apparent "force" arises solely from acceleration and there is no other kind of gravitational force at all. In this statement, as in the statement of the principle of equivalence above, the word acceleration is used in its widest sense. Acceleration results not only from change in the amount of a velocity, but from a change in its direction also. For instance a motorcyclist riding in a circle at a uniform speed of 60 mi. an hour will be the subject of an acceleration towards the centre of the circle. He knows that the apparent force so produced is just as real in its effects as gravitation, and to save himself from falling as a result of its influence he must incline the direction of his machine to the vertical.

It is clear that the acceleration or curvature of path which figures as gravitation cannot be an acceleration or curvature in ordinary three-dimensional space. Before the apple starts to fall from the tree there is neither acceleration nor curvature and yet the apple is undoubtedly acted on by gravitation. Moreover, this three-dimensional space is, as we have seen, different for different observers—it is a subjective and not an objective conception, and the gravitation resulting from such a curvature could not conform to the relativity condition. Einstein was accordingly led to suppose that gravitation arose from curvature in the four-dimensional space, or continuum, in which time formed the fourth dimension. This continuum, as has been seen, is objective and if the path of the particle can also be made objective, the resulting gravitation will conform to the relativity principle. The path of the particle in the continuum is, however, simply its "world line," which we have already had under discussion. This world line is determined by natural laws, and if these are to be objective the specification of the world line must also be objective. There is, however, only one specification of world lines in the continuum which is objective in the sense that the same specification will give the same world lines to observers moving with different velocities. It is that every world line must be so drawn as to represent the shortest path between any two points on it. Mathematically, lines which satisfy this condition are known as *geodesics*. Thus Einstein was led to suppose that world lines must be geodesics in the four-dimensional continuum.

Consider for a moment a page of this volume as presenting a two-dimensional analogy of the continuum. The shortest distance between any two points is of course the straight line joining them, so that the geodesics are simply straight lines. These possess no curvature of path, and if they formed a true analogy to the geodesics in the continuum there could clearly be no explanation of gravitation of the type we have been contemplating. There is, however, another type of two-dimensional surface. It is represented by the surface of a solid body such as a sphere—say the earth. On the earth's surface the geodesics are the great circles; every mariner or aviator who desires to sail the shortest course between two points sails along a great circle. To take a definite instance, the shortest course from Panamá to Ceylon is not along the parallel of lat. (about 9°N.) which joins them—the aviator who wishes to fly the shortest course between the two countries will fly northeast from Panamá, he will pass over England and finally reach Ceylon from the northwest. The reader may rapidly verify this by stretching a thread tightly over the surface of an ordinary geographical globe. Let him now trace out the course on an ordinary Mercator chart, and it will be found to appear very curved indeed—the course of the aviator will look surprisingly like that of a comet describing an orbit under the attraction of a sun situated somewhere near the middle of the Sahara.

The reader who performs these simple experiments will understand how Einstein was led to suppose that gravitation could be explained by a curvature inherent in the continuum. The world lines of particles are geodesics but the space itself, so to speak, provides the curvature. The curvature of path is thrust upon the particle by the nature of the continuum, but we, who until recently have been unaware even of the existence of the continuum, have been tempted to ascribe it to the action of a special agency which we have invented *ad hoc* and called "gravitation." According to Einstein's view of the nature of gravitation, it is no more accurate to say that the earth attracts the moon than to say that the pockets of an uneven billiard table attract or repel the balls.

Perhaps this train of thought may seem artificial. If so, the reason is that we have not been able to explore the other possibilities which have branched off our main line of thought. In point of fact, Einstein found himself practically limited to the conclusion we have stated. Not only so, but the actual type and degree of curvature in the continuum prove to be uniquely fixed in terms of the masses of the gravitating bodies. Thus Einstein, knowing the mass of the sun, was able to predict absolutely what the discrepancy in the motion of the perihelion of Mercury must be. It was found to be 42.9″ a century, a figure which agreed with observation to well within the limits of error of the observations. The motions of the other planets as predicted by the theory of relativity, have also been found to agree with those observed to within the errors of observation. This latter test is not a very stringent one, since the departures from the motion predicted by the Newtonian law are too small to admit of very precise measurement.

Effect of Gravitation on Light.—Einstein's theory requires that the world line of a ray of light also shall be a geodesic in the continuum. In interstellar space and regions remote from gravitating masses, this merely means that light travels in straight lines. But a star or other massive body distorts the continuum in its neighbourhood by an amount which is proportional to its mass. In the neighbourhood of such a body a ray of light does not travel in a straight line; it is deflected by the gravitational field of the body by an amount which is directly proportional to the mass of the body, and also, of course, depends on how closely the ray approaches the body. Einstein calculated that a ray of light which comes from a distant star and passes near the edge of the sun on its journey must be bent, in its passage past the sun, by an angle which should be 1.745″ if the ray just grazes the sun, and would be less, in proportion to the inverse distance from the centre of the sun, for other rays.

The observatories of Greenwich and Cambridge dispatched expeditions to test this prediction at the eclipse of 1919. It was found that the stars which appeared near to the sun at the instant of eclipse showed an appreciable displacement, as compared with their normal positions, of the type required by Einstein's theory. Exact measurement confirmed that the displacement varied approximately as the inverse distance from the sun, and that the displacement at the limb was sensibly equal to Einstein's predicted value of 1.745″. The Cambridge observers, hampered by cloudy weather, obtained for this quantity the value 1.61″ but with a probable error of 0.30″. The Greenwich observers obtained a value of 1.98″ with a probable error of 0.12″, but Prof. H. N. Russell subsequently pointed out that their photographs contained intrinsic evidence of a horizontal and vertical scale difference of the order of one part in 12,000 almost certainly due to a distortion of the coelostat mirror under the sun's rays, and if the measures are corrected for this the result is brought much closer to the theoretical prediction. Three years later an expedition, sent out by Lick observatory to observe the 1922 eclipse, was favoured by good weather and obtained for the displacement at the sun's limb, a value of 1.72″ with a probable error of 0.11″. On the other hand, Potsdam observers at the Sumatra eclipse of 1929 found a deflection of 2.2″ instead of the predicted value of 1.75″; and E. Freundlich inferred from a re-examination of the Lick observations of 1922 that they agreed with this. The question must be regarded as still unsettled in 1945. None of the expeditions had of course measured the deflections of stars actually at the sun's limb; most of the stars were several diameters away from the limb, the observed deflections being corrected so as to bring them to the limb.

The Gravitational Shift of Spectral Lines.—The theory makes one further prediction which admits of experimental test. The atoms of any element, say calcium, may be supposed to be formed according to a definite specification, the terms of which depend neither on the velocity of a particular observer nor on his position relative to the gravitational fields of the universe. It can be deduced that the light received from a calcium atom situated in the intense gravitational field near the sun's surface ought to be of slower period, and therefore of redder colour, than the similar light emitted by terrestrial atoms. To be more precise, the Fraunhofer lines in the solar spectrum ought to show a displacement to the red; this displacement ought to be homologous, and should be of amount 0.008 Å units at the cyanogen band λ 3883 at which observations have been chiefly made. Early attempts to test this prediction led to strangely discordant results. All observers found some effect of the kind predicted, but its amount was generally substantially less than the predicted amount, varying from almost *nil* (Charles E. St. John, 1917) to nearly the full amount to be expected (John Evershed, 1918 and 1923,

L. Grebe and Albert Bachem, 1919). The latest measurements of the displacement are those of Evershed (1927). Measuring the mean displacement shown by the lines of 29 prominences, Evershed found that the H and K lines of calcium showed the same mean displacement of 0.009 Å, as compared with 0.008 Å required by theory.

The want of success of the earlier observations is explained by the circumstance that the relativity shift of 0.008 Å is liable to be masked by larger shifts of uncertain amount arising from other causes. Larger shifts would be expected in stars which were of larger mass than the sun or of smaller radii. Many known stars have masses far larger than the sun, but they also have larger radii, and so ought to show only about the same spectral shift as the sun. On the other hand the class of stars known as "white dwarfs" have masses comparable with that of the sun, but far smaller radii. For instance, calculation shows that the companion to Sirius, a star whose radius is only about $\frac{1}{35}$ of that of our sun, ought to show a shift of as much as 0.30 Å. On putting the matter to the test at Mount Wilson observatory, Walter S. Adams found an actual shift of 0.32 Å. It is not possible any longer to doubt that the spectral shift predicted by Einstein really exists.

ELECTROMAGNETIC FORCES

The restricted physical theory of relativity introduced a revolution into the foundations of scientific thought by destroying the objectivity of time and space. The gravitational theory has effected a hardly less important revolution by destroying our belief in the reality of gravitation as a "force." The physicist has, however, to deal with other "forces" besides those of gravitation, namely, the electromagnetic forces which are concerned in all electrical, magnetic and chemical phenomena, and the question inevitably arises as to whether these also must be regarded as illusions, arising only from our faulty interpretation of the special metrical properties of the continuum. Analysis makes it clear that the continuum as imagined by Einstein has no capacity for simulating any forces beyond those of gravitation. If electromagnetic forces are evidence of special geometrical properties of the continuum, then the continuum is more complicated even than Einstein imagined.

In a brilliant paper published in 1918 (*Berlin Sitzungsber.*, p. 465 [1918]) Hermann Weyl proved that Einstein's geometry is far from being the most general geometry which is consistent with the general principle of relativity, and showed that certain at least of the forces of electromagnetism could be explained very naturally by adding an extra degree of complexity to the geometry of the continuum. In the continuum as imagined by Einstein, the length of a measuring rod might change as it was moved about in a gravitational field, but its length at any instant would depend solely on its position in space. In the geometry of Weyl, this concept of length is abandoned—that is to say, a vector with given components at a given point no longer has a definite length, but the concept of length is admitted in a modified form; namely, when by an arbitrary act of choice we have fixed the meaning of the word "length" at a point P, we can derive a definite meaning for the word "length" at a neighbouring point P', provided a certain vector function of position is given. And this vector function is identified by Weyl with the electromagnetic potential-vector.

In 1921 Eddington extended Weyl's geometry into a still more general system of geometry, in which even lengths at the same point were not assumed to be capable of direct comparison. This geometry had a certain advantage over Weyl's original geometry in that the terms which were ultimately called on to explain electromagnetic phenomena occurred naturally as a necessary development of the geometry. In Weyl's geometry the necessary terms are shaped to fill a gap, and it is then found that they fit exactly. In Eddington's geometry no shaping is necessary, or, rather, the shaping process is performed off the stage or before the curtain rises. The gravitational and electromagnetic forces are accounted for by the symmetrical and antisymmetrical parts of a single tensor, so that an electromagnetic field appears almost to be a necessary accompaniment to a gravitational field. But

Eddington's geometry, like that of Weyl, predicts precisely the same phenomena as James Clerk Maxwell's classical electromagnetic theory, so that experimental test is impossible.

Both these geometries are successful in interpreting the electromagnetic field in free space in terms of geometry, but show less success in interpreting the ponderomotive forces on charged bodies, electrons, protons, etc. Many other forms of unified field theory were published after 1920; but none of them won general acceptance from theoretical physicists, although many of them furnished contributions of great value to the pure mathematical science of differential geometry.

In 1943, however, Erwin Schrödinger remarked that a method of unifying the gravitational and electromagnetic fields which had been proposed in 1923 by Einstein, but afterward abandoned, was worthy of renewed attention; and in a series of papers in 1943–44 he showed that it was capable of representing mathematically the "meson-field" as well as the gravitational and electrical fields. Another attempt at a unified theory is a theory of "bivector fields," put forward by Einstein and V. Bargmann in 1944, and developed in 1945 by Schrödinger and F. Mautner. In this the fundamental field variables, unlike the gravitational potentials of Einstein's original theory, depend on the combination of the coordinates of two points.

The Position of the Ether.—It is clear that the doctrine of relativity must profoundly affect our views of the ether and its function in the scheme of the universe. At one stage in the history of science, there was a tendency to imagine space filled with innumerable ethers, to the extent almost of one ether for every set of phenomena requiring explanation. That stage passed, and by the end of the 19th century only one ether received serious consideration, the so-called electromagnetic ether of Michael Faraday and Maxwell. This ether gave a plausible mechanical explanation of electrostatic phenomena, although it was more than doubtful whether it could account for the electromagnetic phenomena from which it took its name, and it was comparatively certain that it could not account for gravitation. It gave, however, a satisfactory explanation of the propagation of waves of light—they were simply waves in the ether which travelled with an absolute velocity c determined once and for all by the structure of the ether. On this view it was quite certain that an observer moving through the ether with a velocity u would measure the velocity of light travelling in the same direction as himself as $c-u$. Relativity, teaching that this velocity is always precisely c, dismisses the particular type of ether imagined by Faraday and Maxwell. Whether any new ether will be devised to replace it remains to be seen, but none appears to be necessary. Any ether which can be imagined would appear to depend upon an objective separation of time and space. Relativity does not deny that such an objective separation may, in the last resort, really exist, but it shows that no material phenomena are concerned with such a separation. By a very slight turn of thought, the primary postulate of relativity may be expressed in the form that the material world goes on as though no ether existed.

To the relativist the essential background to the picture of the universe is not the varying agitation of a sea of ether in a three-dimensional space but a tangle of world lines in a four-dimensional space. Only the intersections of the world lines are important. An intersection at a point in the continuum represents an event, while the part of a world line which is free from intersections represents the mere uneventful existence of a particle or a pulse of light. And so, since our whole knowledge of the universe is made up of events, it comes about that the tangle of world lines may be distorted and bent to any degree we please; so long as the order of the intersections is not altered, it will still represent the same universe. Thus the last function of the ether, that of providing a scale of absolute measurements in space, becomes a superfluity. To the physicist who urges that space measurements without an underlying ether become meaningless, the relativist can reply that time-measurements without an underlying "time-ether" are equally meaningless. A "time-ether" has never been regarded as a necessity, and the relativist may fairly argue that the "space-ether" has no greater claim to retention.

Probably, however, final judgment on this, as on other similar questions, must be suspended until the position of electromagnetic forces in the general scheme of relativity is better understood than it is now.

COSMOLOGY

According to the simple views of space and time which prevailed before the advent of relativity, time had no properties except duration, and space had no properties except extension. Every instant of time was, in its essence, precisely similar to every other instant of time, so that time must go on forever unless it was stopped by something different from time; it could not end of itself, for this would require the last instant of time to have different properties from all other instants of time. Similarly all elements of space were supposed to be intrinsically of the same nature and to have Euclidean properties, which required that space should extend to infinity in all directions.

Einstein's theory of relativity changed all this. According to this theory the space-time in the neighbourhood of a gravitating mass is essentially different from space-time which is far away from all masses; the former is curved, while the latter, at least if all gravitating masses are infinitely far away, is not. The curvature of the space-time in the neighbourhood of the sun causes the planets to describe ellipses, whereas if all masses were infinitely removed, they would describe straight lines. When it is once admitted that all elements of space-time are not intrinsically similar, no reason remains either why space should be of infinite extent or why time should be of infinite duration.

In 1917 Einstein added to the differential equations of the gravitational field a term containing a constant which is called the "cosmical constant." The effect of this term is to cause a mutual repulsion or scattering of the stars, which is opposed by their gravitational attraction or tendency to aggregate. If we consider a universe occupied by material particles (representing the stars), the presence of the matter produces a curvature of the space, and a solution exists in which the space is closed (*i.e.*, finite in volume), the density of matter and the radius of curvature being constant and uniform and the gravitational attraction being balanced exactly by the cosmical repulsion, so that the system remains permanently at rest in equilibrium. This is called an "Einstein universe."

Besides the Einstein world there is another solution of the equations which likewise is statical (*i.e.*, it does not vary with the time), discovered by Willem de Sitter and known as the "De Sitter universe": this is entirely empty of matter. Certain nonstatical types of universe found by G. A. Friedman and the abbé G. Lemaître are intermediate between Einstein's and De Sitter's; and it was shown by Eddington in 1930 that the Einstein universe is unstable and, when disturbed, assumes in succession forms of these intermediate types, the volume continually increasing. This is the theory of the "expanding universe." In the limit when the expansion has reduced the density so much that the mutual influences of the particles are negligible, the universe tends to the De Sitter type.

An observer situated on any one of the particles (*i.e.*, stars) would see all the other particles receding from him on account of the expansion, the rate of recession increasing uniformly with the distance, since the universes at different times are geometrically similar to each other; if a is the distance of another star at time t, the quantity $\frac{1}{a}\frac{da}{dt}$ tends to a fixed limit as the expansion proceeds, and this limit was shown by Lemaître to be $\frac{c}{R\sqrt{3}}$ where R denotes the radius of curvature of the Einstein world and c the velocity of light. This remarkable theory is confirmed by the observed recession of the extra-galactic nebulae, which is exactly of the type predicted. By combining measurements of the recession with Lemaître's formula, the value of R can be obtained; it is found to be of the order of 10^{27} cm.

The total mass M of the universe may then be deduced by use of a formula derived from the theory of the Einstein world, namely,

$$\gamma M = \tfrac{1}{2}\pi c^2 R$$

where γ denotes the Newtonian constant of gravitation and c

the velocity of light. The value of the mass of the universe thus obtained is of the order of 10^{55} gr. These values of R and M have been independently confirmed by other investigations of Eddington.

Nonmathematicians are liable to misunderstand the nature of the expanding universe, conceiving of it as being like a globular star cluster which is expanding into the empty space around it. This is wrong; there is no empty space around the material universe. At any instant, the whole of space is occupied by matter of (on the average) uniform density; but space is closed and of finite volume (proportional to the cube of its radius of curvature at the instant), and it is this volume which is expanding.

In 1933 a new type of cosmological research was initiated by Edward A. Milne. He considered a universe of particles, and described two particle observers A and B as "equivalent" when the totality of observations A can make on B can be described by A in the same way as the totality of observations which B can make on A can be described by B. The universe is then said to satisfy the "cosmological principle" when, if A and B are two equivalent members of the system, A's description of the whole system (in terms of his clock-measures or associated co-ordinates) is identical with B's description of the whole system (in terms of B's clock-measures or associated co-ordinates). Milne has deduced the fundamental properties of a universe which satisfies the cosmological principle, obtaining a comprehensive theory of dynamical, gravitational and electromagnetic phenomena. Some of his conclusions are discussed in the article SPACE-TIME.

PROGRESS IN OTHER DIRECTIONS AFTER 1930

In 1931 and following years the concept of distance in curved space-time and the displacement of the spectral lines of distant sources was examined, with special reference to the relation between theoretical expressions and observed quantities. If an observer O in a general space-time makes an assertion regarding the "spatial distance" of a star S from himself, he is really stating a relation between the world point of S at the instant when light left it, and his own world point at the instant when the light arrives. In other words, he is dealing with a relation between two world points which lie on the same null geodesic. This statement brings into sharp relief the contrast between spatial distance and the "interval" of general relativity; for between two points on the same null geodesic the interval is always zero. Thus, spatial distance exists when, and only when, the interval is zero.

Now the distance of a remote star from the earth is generally determined by finding the square root of the ratio of its absolute brightness to its apparent brightness (i.e., the brightness as actually seen by the observer), and the translation of this method into the language of geometry furnished a definition of spatial distance which was given by Whittaker in 1931 and led to the subsequent developments. It may be expressed as follows: the spatial distance between a star S and an observer O (on the same null geodesic) is proportional to the square root of the two-dimensional cross section made by a thin pencil of null geodesics, with vertex S and passing near O, on the instantaneous three-dimensional space of the observer. The factor of proportionality is fixed by requiring that when O and S are near one another the spatial distance shall reduce to the ordinary Euclidean distance.

An important book published by Richard C. Tolman in 1934 under the title *Relativity, Thermodynamics and Cosmology* broke fresh ground in many directions, particularly in the formulation of the second law of thermodynamics in general relativity. He showed *inter alia* that the tendency of a system undergoing irreversible changes, to attain a final state of maximum entropy, can no longer be regarded as inevitable in all cases.

In a series of memoirs published from 1928 to his death in 1944 Eddington developed his work on relativity in an entirely new direction, leading ultimately to a complete revision of the foundations of physics. His first achievement was to predict that the reciprocal of the fine-structure constant must have the exact value 137—a result which seemed at the time to be irreconcilable with the observed value, but which is now generally accepted.

Subsequently, he found a quadratic equation whose roots are the masses of the proton and the electron, a theoretical value for the ratio of the gravitational to the electrostatic force between a proton and an electron, and predictions of many other natural constants, connecting in a remarkable way the properties of the atom with the structure of the cosmos. As a mathematical tool for the purposes of the investigation he devised a noncommutative algebra with 16 units, which may be described as the square of quaternion algebra. The theory in its definitive form is given in his posthumous book.

The extremely difficult problem of n bodies in general relativity was advanced somewhat in 1938 by Eddington and G. L. Clark, who succeeded in evaluating the "total mass" of a system of particles which are in relative motion and which interact with each other. They defined the mass M of the system as equal to the mass of a single particle, having the position and acceleration of the centre of the mass, which would produce the same gravitational field at a great distance from the system. If M is changing, the time to which this value refers is earlier than the time of comparison at the distant point by the time taken by light to traverse the intervening distance. With this definition, the formula established is

$$M = M_0 + 3K + 2V$$

where M_0 is the sum of the proper-masses of the particles, K the kinetic energy and V the internal potential energy. This theorem interprets and amplifies the general statement that "mass is energy"; but though it can be obtained only after lengthy calculations, it is only an approximation, and there is much need for further investigation on the subject.

In 1942–44 George D. Birkhoff originated a new theory of matter, electricity and gravitation, in which matter was taken to be a perfect fluid in the flat space-time of special relativity, the velocity of disturbance in the matter being that of light. On this theory he was engaged at the time of his death in Nov. 1944; it has been further developed by Manuel Vallarta and others (*Proc. Nat. Ac. Sci.*, 1943 and 1944; *Phys. Rev.*, 1944).

BIBLIOGRAPHY.—In the first place should be named a series of seven books published in succession during 24 years by Sir Arthur Eddington: *Space, Time, and Gravitation* (1921), *The Mathematical Theory of Relativity* (1923), *The Nature of the Physical World* (1928), *The Expanding Universe* (1933), *Relativity Theory of Protons and Electrons* (1936), *The Philosophy of Physical Science* (1939), *The Combustion of Relativity Theory and Quantum Theory* (1943). A posthumous book, *Fundamental Theory*, was published in 1946. Other works, whose point of view or subject matter differs from that of Eddington's books are: E. A. Milne, *Relativity, Gravitation, and World-Structure* (1935); H. P. Robertson, "Relativistic Cosmology," *Rev. Mod. Phys.*, 5: 62 (1933); E. Schrödinger, *Proc. R. Irish Acad.*, 49 (1943–44), 50 (1945); R. C. Tolman, *Relativity, Thermodynamics, and Cosmology* (1934); A. N. Whitehead, *The Principle of Relativity* (1922); E. T. Whittaker, "The Outstanding Problems of Relativity," *Nature*, 120 (1927). A textbook of the mathematical theory is P. G. Bergmann, *Introduction to the Theory of Relativity* (1942). (J. H. J.; E. WR.)

RELATIVITY: PHILOSOPHICAL CONSEQUENCES.

The most important philosophical consequence of the theory of relativity is the clarification it has brought into the relations between science and philosophy. The position may be briefly summarized as follows. Up to the 17th century the subject matter of these studies formed a unity, the rudiments of that which we now call science being simply a part of a larger whole. A rift then appeared and gradually widened until, by the beginning of the 20th century, science and philosophy had become quite distinct and a person expert in one was usually very inexpert and ill-informed in the other. The effect of the relativity theory was to re-establish physics on a philosophical basis and thereby to elucidate certain bewildering implications of current research.

More particularly, the position was this. The general problem of philosophy is to give a rational account of experience with the minimum of presuppositions. Consequently it was not originally presupposed that physical experience must be regarded as an effect on our senses of an objectively existing external world having certain definite and ascertainable properties: that was a matter for discussion, and both affirmative and negative answers were given. Modern science, however, originated in the determination to ignore the metaphysical question and to accept experience as an object of study, whether or not it was "real." Thus Galileo discovered the law of falling bodies by measuring how the space covered varied with the time of fall. By carrying out certain processes of measurement he obtained results which stood in a certain relation to one another, and this relation remained true whatever metaphysical status one assigned to motion.

This became the origin and type of a large body of investigation which, by reason of its distinctive character and its rapid growth and success, came to be regarded as something other than traditional philosophy and was given the name "science." Nevertheless, it was still an attempt to give a rational account of experience with the minimum of presuppositions. Moreover, although it needed no supplement, it was in fact coupled from the beginning with a particular view of what the measurements signified. Galileo, for instance, supposed that they represented the magnitudes of certain characteristics of the external world which he regarded as possessing only mechanical properties such as size, shape, position, motion; other qualities (*e.g.*, colours, sounds, temperatures) he thought were not properties of the bodies which seemed to possess them but were contributed by the observing subject. This view was tenable in his day since he was unable to measure such things; but after the invention of thermometers, spectroscopes, etc., there remained no reason for distinguishing these so-called secondary qualities so fundamentally from motions and shapes, and they were gradually put back into the external world and included among the objectively existing properties of bodies, which science investigates.

The progress of physics from Galileo's time up to the beginning of the 20th century had therefore a twofold aspect: in practice it was a faithful prosecution of the program of carrying out certain operations of measurement and finding relations between their results; in theory it was an investigation of the metrical properties of an external world. While the latter view was of almost indispensable assistance in pointing the way to the most profitable operations of measurement to perform, the achievements of physics can clearly stand in their own right if it is abandoned and if no suppositions at all are made about the metaphysical status of the measurements performed. So instinctive, however, had this particular metaphysical interpretation of physics become that when, in 1887, the Michelson-Morley experiment (*q.v.*) gave an incredible result, it occurred to no one for nearly 20 years to inquire whether the root of the anomaly might not lie in the invalidity of that interpretation. That this was actually so is the essential point of Albert Einstein's *special* relativity theory of 1905.

In the Michelson-Morley experiment a comparison was made between the passage of light along material bars in different states of uniform motion. The bars, when relatively at rest, were equal in length, and since, according to the metaphysical view just described, its length is an objective property of a bar, they were equal in length when in uniform relative motion, for uniform motion, according to Newtonian mechanics, can have no mechanical effect. But if that view is rejected, the "length of a bar" is not an objective property but simply the result obtained when a particular operation of measurement is made. Now the operation for measuring length was well-known, but it required that the body measured must be at rest with respect to the measuring scale; it was inapplicable if the body was moving along the scale. Hence one had no right to speak of the "length" of a moving bar. This was not because the length, an objectively existing property, could not, because of practical difficulties, be ascertained. It was because one had no right to use the word until one had the result of a particular operation to which to apply it, and no such operation had been devised for a moving body.

The theory of relativity prescribed an appropriate operation, and the experiment was then satisfactorily explained. This belongs to physics, but one aspect of it has philosophical implications. The reason why the ordinary operation for measuring length was inapplicable to a moving body was that the scale readings for the two ends of the bar varied with time when the body was moving. To get a definite result, therefore, they had to be taken simultaneously. Hence one had to know how to determine that two events at different places occurred at the same time, and on analysis it appeared that this was impossible without some arbitrary stipulation.

Here again, then, the idea of something existing objectively which physical measurement revealed had to be given up. It was not that, because of practical limitations, we could not determine which of a number of spatially separated events were simultaneous. There was no meaning in speaking of the simultaneity of such events until one had prescribed a process for determining it, and there was a wide degree of liberty in prescribing such a process.

Physics was thus thrown back on the unadorned description of itself as the discovery of relations between the results of chosen operations of measurement. This description adequately covered the whole of physics from Galileo's basic discoveries onward; but the metaphysical accompaniment that had provided the imagination with a model and the experimenter with a guide was now proved misleading. The philosopher must henceforth interpret physics in terms of operations and their results alone, leaving external existences out of account. But the physicist, finding a picture of an external world indispensable, began to devise a better one. In the old picture the world consisted of pieces of matter, measured essentially by their mass, moving about, without thereby becoming changed, in an infinite extension called space and an independent extension called time. According to the revised picture, matter, space and time are no longer independent but merge into a single continuum, space-time—a device made possible by the fact that, according to the definitions adopted for the length of moving bodies and the time relations of separated events, a certain combination of the space and time separations of events is independent of the state of motion which we choose to assign to any one of the bodies concerned. We can thus suppose that this combination of our measurements measures some absolute quality of events, just as we previously thought that the measurement of length indicated some absolute quality of a body. The masses of bodies, however, still change with motion; but going farther in the same direction, the *general* theory of relativity succeeds in prescribing a combination of space, time and mass measurements that is independent of motion altogether and so—for the time being, at any rate—can pose as an aspect of an external world of which physical measurements provide a quantitative description. From the philosophical point of view, however, it would be exceedingly unwise to forget, as pre-relativity physics did, that all such pictures are but an aid to investigation and have no fundamental significance whatever. It has been shown, indeed, that when the phenomenon of radiation is treated in the same manner as the phenomenon of motion, an "entropy-time" emerges which is of precisely similar character to the space-time of mechanics. Neither of these concepts is to be regarded as objective in the way that space and time were formerly thought to be.

The general effect of all this on the philosophy of science has been to emphasize the distinction between the empirical and the rational. It was the theory of relativity that chiefly inspired the Vienna circle, later known as the logical positivist school, to formulate their verification principle, according to which the meaning of any statement is determined by the empirical steps necessary to verify it. Statements that are not susceptible of empirical verification (or falsification) are either rational (*i.e.*, tautological) or nonsensical. The absolute simultaneity of separated events is a typical example of a nonsensical concept since it is neither empirically determinable nor a rational necessity.

Precisely the same classification was made by Sir Arthur Eddington, who also was inspired primarily by the relativity theory; but whereas the logical positivists have developed their views in the direction of an analysis of language in general, without special reference to physics, Eddington undertook the detailed examination of physical theory. He was led to the conclusion that the whole scheme of physical law was rational in nature and could have been derived without any experience at all of actual events. In other words, although, as a historical fact, the laws have been derived by studying the results of measurements, they are actually so abstract that they characterize only the nature of the processes of measurement and are therefore independent of the particular results that applications of those processes have yielded.

Eddington's views on this point are not generally accepted, but it must be acknowledged that they are either not understood or misunderstood by the majority of critics—a fact for which Eddington himself is not entirely blameless. His mathematical work is not without error, and his gift for picturesque language led him at times to sacrifice rigour of expression for the sake of a vivid metaphor. He himself advanced, as the crucial argument for his view, the claim that he had derived all the dimensionless constants of physical theory from purely rational considerations; but the derivation involved such a wealth of little-known mathematical processes that a lengthy analysis was required before it could be finally appraised. One common misunderstanding, however, can here be removed: he did not claim that the whole course of physical experience could have been predicted; on the contrary, he held that none of it could. The laws of physics, he believed, were not the laws of behaviour of observed bodies but those of postulated entities. Only when observed bodies were identified with such entities were the laws applicable to them, and any lack of agreement would indicate, not a failure of the laws, but false identification.

BIBLIOGRAPHY.—P. A. Schilpp (ed.), *Albert Einstein: Philosopher-Scientist,* 2nd ed. (New York, Cambridge, 1952); A. S. Eddington, *The Philosophy of Physical Science* (Cambridge, New York, 1939); H. Dingle, *The Special Theory of Relativity,* 3rd ed. (London, New York, 1950).   (H. D.)

RELEASE, in law, the term applied to the discharge of some obligation, by which it is extinguished (*see* DEBT), and to the conveyance of an estate or interest in real or personal property to one who has already some estate or interest therein. For the special form of conveyancing known as "lease and release," *see* LAND TENURE: ECONOMIC AND AGRARIAN ASPECTS, *Leases.*

RELICS, any objects once connected with the person of a departed saint, especially the body or parts of the body. Veneration of the relics of saints, especially of martyrs, appears at an early date both in the Eastern and in the Western Church. St. Thomas Aquinas formulates the doctrinal principles thus: "It is clear . . . that he who has a certain affection for anyone, venerates whatever of his is left after death, not only his body and the parts thereof, but even external things, such as his clothes and such-like. Now it is manifest that we should show honour to the saints of God, as being members of Christ, and children and friends of God, and our intercessors. Wherefore in memory of them we ought to honour any relics of theirs in a fitting manner: principally their bodies, which were temples, and organs of the Holy Spirit dwelling and operating in them, and are destined to be likened to the body of Christ by the glory of the resurrection. Hence God Himself fittingly honours such relics by working miracles at their presence." (*Summa Theol.,* iii, q. 25, art. 6.)

The council of Trent, in its 25th session, solemnly affirmed the same doctrine, while condemning those who hold the practice in contempt, and modern canonical legislation was framed in accordance with these principles (*Codex Iuris Canonici,* especially canons 1276–89). It is noted expressly that relics are to be honoured with a veneration that looks beyond the relics to the saints themselves, whom the relics commemorate (canon 1255 § 2). Further prescriptions attempt to assure the authenticity of relics exposed for public veneration (canons 1283–86); the fabrication of false relics, their sale or distribution, or their exposition for public veneration involves *ipso facto* excommunication (canon 2326). The Old Testament refers to the cult of relics, in the religious character of the burial of saintly persons (Gen. xxxv, 19, 20; l, 25, 26; Exod. xiii, 19), in the miraculous power of Elijah's mantle (IV [II] Kings, ii, 13, 14) and the bones of Elisha (*ibid.,* xiii, 21); but the practice assumes its definitive form in the New Law (*see* Matt. ix, 20–22; Acts xix, 11, 12). St. John Chrysostom refers frequently to the relics of the martyrs as sources of divine favours (Eulogy of St. Eustathius, in J. P. Migne, *Patrol. Graeca,* l, 600; Homily on the Martyrs, *ibid.,* 648, 649; Eulogy of St. Julian, *ibid.,* 670–672). St. Augustine makes clear reference to the practice (for example in *De Civitate Dei,* in Migne, *Patrol. Lat.,* xli, 255), and indeed all the great doctors of early Christianity extolled the veneration of the relics of the saints. Inevitably, the insatiable demand of churches and of private persons led to a traffic in relics, both genuine and spurious, and to other abuses, which ecclesiastical authority constantly strove to hold in check. Already in 386, the Theodosian code legislated against the traffic in relics of the martyrs, and the sale of relics was forbidden by the fourth Lateran council in 1215 (canon 62) and by the council of Trent.

The veneration of relics is a practice rooted in ecclesiastical tradition and in human psychology. It is to be understood and judged by reference to its doctrinal foundations, rather than to its abuses.

See article "Reliques," by P. Sejourne, in the *Dictionnaire de théologie catholique,* ed. by A. Vacant *et al.,* vol. xiii (Paris, 1937); and the article "Reliques et reliquaires," by H. Leclercq, in the *Dictionnaire d'archéologie chrétienne et de liturgie,* ed. by F. Cabrol and H. Leclercq, fasc. clx–clxi (Paris, 1947).

RELIEF. The term "relief" is used in sociology and social work to denote aid given to needy persons who would otherwise suffer without it. It is contrasted with work relief and social insurance. Relief as a generic term is used to cover all forms of aid, in cash and in kind, public and private, to needy persons. As a specific term it is sometimes used in the United States to distinguish aid given on a noncategorical, undifferentiated and emergency basis from the types of public assistance for which federal funds are given under the Social Security act. In both Great Britain and the United States, the term relief was being replaced in the 1950s by the word "assistance."

Relief has been provided in ancient as well as modern forms of society. Helping one another in a time of emergency such as sickness, orphanhood or old age was practised in simpler and early societies. (For early history, *see* CHARITY.) Private forms of relief exist through individuals and voluntary institutions.

UNITED STATES

Responsibility for providing relief was, in accordance with the tradition and statutes of Great Britain, accepted by the American colonists as a local governmental responsibility. (*See* POOR LAW.) During the period 1910–30 state governments in the United States began to take financial and administrative responsibility to assist the localities for various categories of needy persons such as the aged, the blind, and dependent children. In 1932–33 the federal government began to assume responsibility for aid in the relief of human need and suffering. An important and far-reaching development was the enactment in 1935 of the Social Security act, which provided for the establishment of federal old-age insurance and state programs of unemployment insurance which greatly reduced the need for relief. (*See* SOCIAL SECURITY.) In addition the federal government made grants to the states for "assistance" to the needy aged, blind, and dependent children. In 1939 the federal old-age insurance program was broadened to include survivors insurance and in 1950 to add a fourth category of assistance to needy persons who are permanently and totally disabled. In 1954 the federal old-age and survivors insurance program was expanded to cover virtually all persons who work for a living. As a result of these legislative changes, the increase in the aged and child population, and the relatively high levels at which the economic system operated, the role of relief in the American economy changed in important respects after 1932.

Relief Programs in 1932.—There was no system of federal relief in existence when the depression began in the United States in 1929. Public relief was provided under state "poor laws," and was usually limited to almshouse care, medical care, burial and small amounts of relief, financed by towns and counties. In structure, social theory and method of administration, this system of local public relief had remained practically unchanged from the days of Elizabethan England. This kind of public relief was supplemented by private charity.

For three years after 1929, notwithstanding the rapid growth of unemployment (which rose from an estimated 2,000,000 to 15,000,000), the federal government held that the relief of unemployment was a local problem, to be handled by state and local governmental resources supplemented by private charity. Two successive committees were set up by Pres. Herbert Hoover to co-ordinate private and local governmental relief efforts—the president's emergency committee for employment, and the president's organization on unemployment relief.

Appeals for federal relief, however, became more and more insistent. The Reconstruction Finance corporation, a new federal agency which was making loans to distressed banks, railroads and businesses, was authorized by congress in July 1932 to make loans for relief purposes to states and municipalities. Because of the various restrictions imposed on such relief loans, only $80,000,000 was disbursed by Jan. 1, 1933.

Federal Emergency Relief Administration, 1933–35.— With the inauguration of Franklin D. Roosevelt as president in

March 1933, the principle of federal participation in relief was immediately broadened. Instead of a financial agency making loans to states and municipalities in distress, a new social agency, the Federal Emergency Relief administration, was created to undertake a program of federal grants-in-aid to states. While the grants were made to the state governments, the actual administration of relief was primarily in the hands of the local communities to which the state government granted the available federal funds, together with state appropriations where such had been made. The FERA assumed a major share of the cost, the rest being borne by states and local communities.

The FERA attempted to set up minimum standards for relief administration, under penalty of withholding the federal grants. It also had authority, which it exercised only in exceptional circumstances, of administering federal relief directly in those states where it met with no co-operation. In addition, the FERA earmarked a portion of the grants to the states for a number of special programs, for classes of persons whose needs could not be met effectively by the general relief program. These included transient relief, education, college student aid and rural rehabilitation.

One of the objectives of the FERA from the beginning was the development on a national scale of the system of work programs for employable persons that had been initiated by some state relief administrations. During the first six months, however, comparatively little was accomplished along that line because of the pressure of the more elementary needs of the unemployed for food, shelter and clothing. The early state work projects were in some cases poorly conceived, for it took time to realize that there was certain work the unemployed could do that would be socially useful and not compete with private industry. There was generally a shortage of funds for materials since only local funds—not federal moneys —could at the beginning be used for that purpose.

Civil Works Administration, 1933–34.—The deficiencies of the local work relief programs, the critical unemployment situation and the need of stimulating business recovery by large scale governmental expenditures prompted President Roosevelt to start a new works program in the fall of 1933. This was the program of the Federal Civil Works administration, instituted within two weeks after the creation of the agency on Nov. 9, 1933. While the civil works program was directly administered by the federal government through a nationwide organization, most of the projects were initiated and sponsored by local governments.

Workers were paid on the basis of the work performed rather than on the "budgetary deficiency" basis which characterized local work relief projects.

Within two months of its organization, the civil works program reached a peak employment of 4,200,000, roughly half of the workers being taken from the relief rolls. The greater part of the program was terminated at the end of March 1934. The program resulted in total expenditures of $951,600,000, of which the federal government contributed $860,400,000, the local communities $85,-000,000, and the states the remainder.

Though hastily organized, the civil works program for the first time revealed the large variety of socially useful projects that could be operated with unemployed labour. Its field of activity embraced the repair and construction of roads and streets, the rehabilitation and new construction of school buildings, recreational facilities, the building of new sanitation works, and a wide array of white-collar and service projects.

During the period of the CWA program, the FERA continued to function as an agency subsidizing the state relief agencies, although local work relief programs were very much curtailed. With the discontinuance of the CWA, the FERA, in co-operation with the states, set out to develop a more adequate work relief program than had been in operation in 1933. Those CWA projects which had not been finished were taken over and completed. New projects were developed on the same principles. Thus, federal funds were made available for the purchase of materials; better supervision of projects was instituted.

Wages in the FERA work program were based on the principle of "budgetary deficiency." A relief family's sources of available private income were determined by the social service staff and de-

ducted from the estimated budgetary needs. The principal breadwinner was given as many hours of work as would yield the requisite income deficiency.

In the case of large families, work relief earnings were often supplemented by direct relief. In addition, surplus foods were sometimes furnished to general relief cases through the Federal Surplus Relief corporation, which was largely financed with FERA funds. (It later became an agency in the U.S. department of agriculture.)

In 1935 congress and the administration made an important change in the method of dealing with the problem of unemployment relief. This new method involved, first, the turning over of direct relief to the states and local communities and, second, the setting up of a large federal works program to provide emergency employment, particularly to employable heads of families on relief rolls.

The decision to take the federal government "out of the business of relief" was made at the moment a comprehensive social security system was set up. This system made provision not only for unemployment and old-age insurance, but for old-age assistance, aid to the blind and aid to dependent children, to be administered by the states with matching grants by the federal government. It was felt that once these three categories of destitution were taken care of, and once the federal government assumed responsibility for the employment of employables on relief, the remaining direct relief problem could be handled by the states and local communities with their own resources.

WPA, 1935–39.—The new feature in the reoriented programs of 1935 was the introduction of a broad program of project work, comprising locally planned and sponsored undertakings that were, however, to be federally directed and in large measure federally financed. Workers were to be removed from the relief rolls and paid fixed monthly security wages. The security wages represented a compromise between the CWA principle of regular wages and the FERA principle of budgetary needs. Monthly wages were fixed at the same level for the same type of work regardless of family diversities, but the wages for the different classifications of skills and different regions of the country represented less than the corresponding normal earnings in private industry. Most of the work projects were directed by the newly created Works Progress (later Work Projects) administration, which was originally intended to serve as a co-ordinating agency for the entire works program but which became the principal operating agency as well.

In addition to the system of work projects, the works program of 1935 continued the emergency employment programs on heavy public works carried on by the bureau of public roads and the Public Works administration. These phases of the work program were carried on by the contract method. At first these agencies were required to see to it that contractors selected their crews as far as possible from the relief rolls—a requirement that proved difficult to enforce and was later dropped. The 1935 works program also continued the program of the Civilian Conservation corps, which provided employment and training to needy youths between 18 and 25. A National Youth administration was established within the WPA, which, in addition to providing aid for high school, college and graduate students, developed work projects for needy youths between 16 and 25.

The cost of WPA operations was borne largely by the federal government. But since the work projects concentrated on local needs, it was felt desirable that local communities should suggest and sponsor the projects that were put in operation and should at the same time pay part of the cost. Sponsors' contributions varied with the financial resources of the community, the character of the public improvements it desired to carry out and the gravity of the local unemployment problem. Contributions averaged about 20% for the nation as a whole after July 1937. Beginning Jan. 1, 1940, the average of sponsors' contributions for each state was required by law to be 25% of the total cost of projects subsequently approved and initiated.

A few federal projects (notably the arts projects) were operated by the WPA on a nationwide basis with relatively small contributions from co-sponsors. The Emergency Relief Appropriation act of 1939 provided that the WPA could not itself sponsor projects.

Thereafter the arts projects were continued where state and local governments were interested in sponsoring and sharing in the cost of the work. The theatre projects were entirely discontinued on July 1, 1939, by act of congress.

About 80% of WPA activities were in the construction field, while 20% represented goods projects (canning projects and sewing rooms for women) and white-collar projects.

Surplus Farm Commodity Distribution.—Surplus farm commodities were first distributed to needy persons in 1933 under emergency relief legislation. Nearly 13,000,000 received such surplus farm commodities in 1939. The department of agriculture was assigned the responsibility for delivering the commodities in carload lots to state and local welfare agencies which distributed them in accordance with state or local eligibility standards. At the end of 1954, about 2,500,000 needy persons were receiving such commodities, of whom about one-fourth were persons on the public assistance rolls. Schools and charitable institutions were also made eligible for surplus farm commodities.

Public Assistance Under the Social Security Act, 1935–54.—The provisions of the public assistance titles of the Social Security act of 1935 were designed to overcome some of the major limitations of the earlier relief programs. The selection of the term "assistance" instead of "relief" was intended by those who drafted the act to distinguish the categorical forms of aid as a more liberal, humane and modern form of aid in contrast with restrictive, harsh and haphazard forms of relief. The Dill-Connery bill for federal aid to needy aged persons, which was favourably considered by the house of representatives in 1934, used the terms "relief" and "assistance." But the proposal recommended to the congress by Pres. Roosevelt's committee on economic security in 1935 adopted the term "assistance," which was accepted by the congress and written into the federal law without debate or controversy.

The Social Security act also included the specific language that assistance meant "money payments" to the needy individuals. This limited the federal funds to cash payments and was intended to limit and discourage payments in kind such as grocery orders and direct distribution of commodities. The unrestricted cash payment was intended to eliminate the restrictive control exercised by local authorities in the granting of aid. In 1950 congress made an exception to the principle of unrestricted money payments to the individual by amending the federal act to permit payment of federal funds within certain maximums in cases where states paid medical bills directly to the doctor, hospital or to others providing medical care. The special characteristics of medical care—particularly irregularity and unpredictability—distinguish it from other types of needs.

The Social Security act of 1935 also required as a condition of receipt of federal aid that the state make a financial contribution to the program, a single state agency administer each program, the state have a "state plan" in effect in all political subdivisions of the state, and the individual be given the opportunity for a fair hearing if his claim for assistance is denied. Each of these requirements was aimed at eliminating certain provincial and discriminatory methods of administering relief to needy persons.

Congress also provided that no federal funds could be used to pay assistance to any adult in a public institution or to any child in any institution. This was the outgrowth of dissatisfaction with county homes, almshouses, orphan asylums and other large institutions. (*See* COUNTY HOME.) As a result, the assistance program encouraged aiding persons in their own homes and in practically eliminating almshouses. In 1950, however, congress amended the law to permit federal funds for payment of assistance to adults in certain types of public medical institutions. A growing number of chronically-ill aged persons came to be cared for in public and private nursing homes operating under standards established and maintained by the states. The 1950 amendments also required the states to establish and maintain standards for private or public institutions if the state plan includes payments to individuals in such institutions.

In 1939 congress amended the law to require the states to select and promote their personnel in accordance with a merit system so that the programs would be administered on a professional basis.

Another requirement added to the law by the congress in 1939 provided that the states establish safeguards which restrict the use or disclosure of information concerning applicants and recipients to purposes directly connected with administration of assistance. This provision was the subject of much controversy in 1951 and congress amended the law to permit states to enact legislation prescribing any conditions under which public access might be permitted to records of disbursements if such legislation prohibited the use of any list of names for commercial or political purposes.

Enactment of the federal assistance programs and the requirement for the establishment of a single state agency for the administration of each program helped accelerate the trend toward the establishment of state departments of welfare and the co-ordination of all state welfare functions in one state agency. The result was an improvement in welfare programs through the leadership, standard-setting, research and community organization and planning undertaken by the state welfare departments. While conditions continued to vary widely in the various states, there was a substantial measure of progress. Since in many states the state departments of public welfare also help finance or administer the general assistance or relief programs, there has been a tendency for standards in the general relief programs to be administered to some extent along the same lines as the categorical programs for which federal funds are received and federal standards maintained. However, in the states which left the entire general assistance problem to the localities, there still remained in the 1950s a great deal of the same type of inadequacies which existed prior to the enactment of the social security program.

Numerous groups which studied the assistance, relief and related programs in the United States made recommendations for changes in the federal and state legislation. Perhaps the most important in helping reduce the need for assistance and relief was the expansion and liberalization of the federal old-age and survivors insurance program in 1950, 1952 and 1954, and of the federal and state provisions for unemployment insurance. Increased coverage under private pension, health and welfare plans, particularly as a result of collective bargaining, also aids in reducing the need for assistance and relief. The number of aged persons receiving old-age insurance became larger than the number of aged persons receiving assistance for the first time in 1951. The year 1953 was a turning point in the history of public assistance. The number receiving old-age and survivors insurance benefits at the end of 1953 was larger than the number receiving all four types of public assistance (including general assistance). At the end of 1954, there were about 6,800,000 persons receiving insurance benefits compared with 5,700,000 receiving assistance.

General Assistance.—General assistance, often called general relief in the United States, is supported by the localities and the states with no participation by the federal government. It is the only recourse of needy persons in want who are ineligible for one of the four federal-state assistance programs. General assistance also is provided to some extent to recipients of the special types of public assistance when the maximum amounts of categorical aid they can get are insufficient to meet their needs.

In some states the general assistance program is integrated with all or some other assistance programs at the local level. In other states general assistance is administered separately. The amount of financial aid and supervision supplied by the state welfare departments to the local units varies greatly from state to state. In 10 states in 1954, the state paid the entire bill for general assistance. At the opposite extreme were 16 states where the localities met the full cost. In the other states, the localities and the state shared the cost in varying degrees. Total expenditures for general assistance in the mid-1950s were shared approximately 50% by the localities and 50% by the states.

In most states with little or no state financial participation, each locality decides for itself who shall be eligible for aid and how much assistance in cash or kind he shall get. Thus the place where a needy person lives is likely to be a primary determinant of the adequacy with which his needs are met. In many places throughout the nation a needy person deemed employable can get assistance only if he is in the direst straits—and then only for a temporary period. In such places in most cases the breadwinner is suffering from acute illness or disability that is not sufficient in degree to qualify him for aid to the permanently and totally disabled. Some states still have local settlement laws which originated before the days of modern transportation and high mobility of population. On the other hand, in some states general assistance is available at substantially the same standard as the special types of public assistance for any needy person for whom there is no other provision.

Consideration has been given from time to time to providing federal funds and federal standards for general assistance. In 1948, an Advisory Council on Social Security recommended such legislation and the congress considered such a proposal in 1949. Congress did not adopt the proposal but did add a fourth category of assistance to the Social Security act in 1950 for persons permanently and totally disabled, thus narrowing the scope of general assistance. A large number of the disabled persons were transferred from general assistance to the disabled category. General assistance tended to decline in terms of its role in the total assistance picture. In 1940 expenditures for general assistance represented about 40% of expenditures for all forms of public assistance; but by 1950, they had dropped to about 13% and by 1954 they were only about 7%.

Medical Care.—A large proportion of the number of persons receiving public assistance are disabled or chronically ill and require medical care. The states vary in the extent to which they provide medical care to needy persons. This variation depends upon the availability of funds, and the extent of available hospital care and services from physicians. About $200,000,000 was paid annually in the mid-1950s by public assistance agencies directly to doctors, hospitals and other suppliers of medical care for medical services for assistance recipients. About one-quarter of all expenditures for general assistance at that time was for payments directly to such suppliers of medical care. Medical care to public assistance recipients improved slowly in both coverage and scope after 1950 when the Congress earmarked a limited amount of federal funds for this purpose. However, because of the many inadequacies, Pres. Dwight D. Eisenhower in 1955 recommended that the Congress earmark additional federal funds for medical care for public assistance recipients.

Status of Relief and Assistance Programs.—Total relief and assistance expenditures in the United States reached a peak of $300,000,000 a month in 1938–39. Expenditures for these purposes declined sharply during the World War II years 1942–45. As a result of increased population—particularly aged persons and children—increased prices and more adequate standards of assistance, expenditures began to increase after World War II. Nevertheless, measured as a per cent of the national income, relief and assistance expenditures were substantially below the proportions for the years immediately prior to 1940. During the fiscal year ending June 30, 1954, nearly $2,800,000,000 was expended for all five forms of public assistance and their administration. This amount was equivalent to about 1% of all personal incomes in the nation, or $16 per capita for the year. The federal government assumed about 52% of total assistance payments made under all five programs; the states 37%; and the localities 11%.

Approximately 5,700,000 persons were receiving public assistance at the end of 1954. Of this number about 2,500,000 were receiving old-age assistance, 2,000,000 persons were receiving aid to dependent children, 100,000 aid to the blind, 300,000 aid to the permanently disabled and about 800,000 general assistance.

OTHER COUNTRIES

Programs of public assistance or relief for the general population or for some categories of needy people are in operation in many countries. Although there are some common features, there are notable differences among the countries in such matters as the method of determining need, the extent of local and national administrative and financial responsibility, and the age, residence and other requirements.

While in most of western Europe social welfare functions are delegated to the provincial and local governments, in some countries of the British Commonwealth relief is a function of the central government. Thus, in the United Kingdom a national assistance board administers the principal assistance programs, which, except for certain institutional and welfare services, are nationally financed and have standardized payments.

Australia and Canada, which have a federal form of government like the United States, employ some different methods than either Great Britain or the United States. In Australia, the Commonwealth Department of Social Services administers social security and relief for needy persons not eligible for any of the categorical payments. In

Canada, the general relief function remains in the hands of the local governments. The provinces pay mothers' pensions and administer and share the financing with the national government of the system of old-age assistance for persons aged 65–69, inclusive. (*See also* CHARITY; COUNTY HOME; PENSIONS; POOR LAW; SOCIAL SECURITY; and SOCIAL SERVICE.)

BIBLIOGRAPHY.—Edward T. Devine, *The Principles of Relief* (New York, 1904); Edith Abbott, *Public Assistance* (Chicago, Oxford, 1940); Josephine C. Brown, *Public Relief, 1929–1939* (New York, 1940); Karl de Schweinitz, *England's Road to Social Security, 1349 to 1942* (Philadelphia, 1943; Oxford, 1944); Eveline M. Burns, *The American Social Security System* (New York, 1949); *Methods of Administering Assistance to the Needy,* United Nations (1952); *Social Security Bulletin* (monthly). (WR. J. C.)

RELIEF, literally, the projection of forms from a ground; in sculpture, a work in which figures or ornaments are shown as projecting from a ground. The height of elevation may vary. In a low relief (*basso-rilievo* or bas-relief) the design is more or less of a piece with the ground, projecting but slightly and with little, if any, undercutting of outlines. In a high relief (*alto-rilievo*) the forms are made to stand out more detachedly and may in parts be completely disengaged from the ground, so as to approximate sculptures in the round. But a reference to and, in most cases, physical connection with the ground must be taken to be a constituent feature of all representations in relief, in contrast to statuary which is not related to any ground and can be viewed from all sides. The 19th century tendency to employ the term "bas-relief" indiscriminately for all kinds of relief, high as well as low, is unjustified linguistically, and seems now to be subsiding.

Rarer forms of relief are the "sunk reliefs," especially of ancient Egypt, where the forms are carved in and beneath the surrounding ground rather than rising from it. Intaglio (*q.v.*), likewise, is a hollow relief, but carved as a negative image like a mould instead of a positive form. Actually the most common use of intaglio is in engraved seals of precious stones or metal, designed to produce a positive imprint when pressed into a plastic material such as heated wax. However, intaglio techniques may also be used without such a purpose; *e.g.*, in the decoration of transparent materials such as glass (*q.v.*).

Modes of representation and composition in relief are always determined by their dependence on the ground plane from which the forms emerge, or on which they are superimposed. In this important respect reliefs are more nearly related to painting than to the detached roundness of statuary. Ancient Egyptian art, which differentiated the various branches of art in the most systematic manner, from the beginning applied the same basic principles of representation to reliefs as to painting. Usually the design stands out from the ground in very low relief, however carefully modelled. Figures are shown sidewise, standing on base lines, and precisely outlined in conformity to the plane surface from which they are carved. As to their methods of representation, and regardless of their materials—wood, soft stones, hard stones or metal—they must therefore be classified with painting. Similar observations are true of other early arts, like those of Mesopotamia and the ancient near east. (*See* BABYLONIA AND ASSYRIA.)

High reliefs first became common in Greek art; notable examples are the Attic tomb reliefs, with individual figures or family groups shown almost in the round, of the 4th century B.C. On the whole the Greek reliefs, also, follow rather closely the development of contemporary painting. Sculptured friezes were often used in architectural decoration. A doubt may arise regarding the famous pedimental sculptures of Greek classical temples which are composed of large figures worked singly, and not physically connected with the ground, thus resembling free statues. (*See* AEGINA; GREEK ART; OLYMPIA; PARTHENON; and others.) However, since these figures were placed in the pediments and consequently not seen freely but against a background wall, their compositions must in effect be regarded as a kind of high reliefs. Likewise in Roman art, the pictorial character of the reliefs is undeniable. (*See* ROMAN ART.) A rich field of study for the relation between ground and figures in classical reliefs can be found in the numerous sculptured sarcophagi which constitute one of the most representative achievements of Roman art during the 2nd and 3rd centuries A.D. Excellent examples of ancient relief are also available in the minor arts, both of Greece and Rome, especially in silver and ivory. (*See* Silversmiths' and Goldsmiths' Work.) Moreover the rapid expansion of the classical style in and beyond the Mediterranean area after the Hellenistic period gave rise to a flowering art of relief sculpture in the far east, first of all in the religious art of India (*See* Indian and Sinhalese Art and Archaeology.)

It appears as a natural consequence of the classical tradition that during the early middle ages, a period which generally exhibits a marked preference for painting over statuary, the emphasis in sculpture was definitely on relief work. This statement holds good of Byzantine no less than western art. Not only does a wealth of very fine reliefs appear in the minor arts, Byzantine as well as western mediaeval, but French Romanesque art, especially, reached a new height of relief sculpture in architectural decoration. Some of the most outstanding examples of mediaeval art are among the Romanesque portals ("tympana"), sculptured capitals of columns and other reliefs decorating the ecclesiastic buildings of France, England and other European countries. (*See* Byzantine Art; Stone Carving.) The Gothic period continued this tradition, often preferring a higher relief than the Romanesque, in accordance with the renewed interest in statuary typical of the later middle ages. Reliefs were much in demand also for funeral monuments of bronze or stone, a number of which include some of the finest works of the period. The latest examples of Gothic relief art are the frequent carved altars, mostly of wood, and other church furniture of the "international style" shown in churches all over western and central Europe from Spain to Poland. (*See* Pisano, Andrea; Pisano, Niccola; Stoss, Veit; Wood-Carving: *Gothic*.)

During the Italian Renaissance period the status of relief work among the total output of art begins to change. Between painting and statuary the number of reliefs decreases, except perhaps in the minor arts. No longer are certain places traditionally reserved for decoration in relief, as was true of the mediaeval church buildings. On the other hand the condition of representations in relief now became subjected to new studies and experimentation with a revisory intent, as a task of art different from both painting and statuary. The first striking results of the new trend are the bronze doors which L. Ghiberti created for the famous baptistery of Florence. Characteristic is the free play between high and low relief, from which a strikingly illusionistic style of composition can be derived, supporting the new interest in space as a subjective, visual experience. Donatello further exploited these experiments, adding to the interplay of high and low relief the contrasts between rough and smooth surfaces, as well as between forms shown fully modelled and others only indicated in an almost painterly, impressionistic state of incompleteness. As a result, Florentine artists after Donatello pursued for a while two rather different trends regarding the treatment of reliefs. Typical of the one are the delicate and low reliefs in marble and terra cotta, for which Desiderio da Settignano and Mino da Fiesole became best known. The other, more contrasting trend became incorporated in the relief style of Bertoldo and later, Michelangelo.

Baroque art continued these experiments, often on a very large scale. Characteristic are large compositions—a kind of marble painting—of which the Roman churches, especially, hold many excellent specimens. These compositions, because of their large size and high relief, often approach the effect of *tableaux vivants* shown in deep boxlike frames and special, stagelike conditions of lighting. L. Bernini's "Ecstasy of Sta. Theresa," with figures carved almost fully in the round but encased in a marble altar, in the church of Sta. Maria della Vittoria, Rome, offers a most impressive example.

Neoclassic art of the early 19th century, following a more puritan attitude toward artistic principles, temporarily revived experimentation with low reliefs, relying for effect on fine surface modelling and clarity of design. The works of Antonio Canova and Bertel Thorwaldsen are typical. However, on the whole the Renaissance concept of relief prevailed. Its dramatic and impressionistic possibilities were sensed keenly and employed vigorously by subsequent sculptors of the 19th century such as F. Rude ("The Marseillaise," decorating the Arc de Triomphe in Paris) and

later, most famously, A. Rodin ("Portal of Hell" and other reliefs). In continuation of these trends relief techniques came to be used in modern art, not only for representational but also for abstract compositions which exploit freely the spatial element as well as the contrasts of light and shade, in reliefs conceived as a succession of overlapping planes. The latter concept, by its nature, often leads to a greater emphasis of the pictorial qualities inherent in relief art. It is typical of this situation that modern painters not infrequently show an interest in the art of relief as did Picasso, among others, during the evolution of his Cubism. (*See* also Sculpture; Sculpture Technique; etc.)

Bibliography.—C. R. Post, *A History of European and American Sculpture From the Early Christian Period to the Present Day* (Cambridge, Mass., 1921); A. Toft, *Modelling and Sculpture*, rev. ed. (London, New York, 1950); A. Miller, *Tradition in Sculpture* (London, Toronto, 1949). (O. J. Bl.)

RELIGION (AND THEOLOGY), ARTICLES ON.

For the purpose of enumerating the main articles in this section, a division will be made into (1) Christian, and (2) Non-Christian.

(1) CHRISTIAN

The number of articles on the different aspects of Christian doctrine, faith and Church is so great that nothing beyond a casual selection of titles can be made here. Anything approaching a complete guide to the separate religious divisions would be a lengthy index of titles of differing merit. To begin with, all the prophets of the Old Testament, all the disciples of the New Testament, and all the books of the Bible have separate articles under their own headings. Special terms occurring in the Scriptures, such as Alpha and Omega; Armageddon; Apostle; Angel, etc., have articles to themselves, where their meaning and connection with other passages in Holy Writ are given in some detail. The article Bible is divided, for convenience of reference, into sections and sub-sections, with appropriate subheads and sideheads to mark out the main points of interest. Concordance is exhaustively treated, and the article Jesus Christ deals with the life of the Founder of Christianity and all His activities and influences. Joseph (husband of Mary) and Mary (the Mother of Jesus), are important articles, and those such as Apocalypse and Pastoral Epistles are deserving of attention. Vulgate; Atheism; Deism; Immortality; Miracle; Mysticism; Eschatology; Apologetics; Dogma, Dogmatic Theology; Absolution; Antichrist; Apostasy; Atonement; Baptism; Benediction; Catechism; Catholic; Church; Confession; Confirmation; Creeds; Excommunication; Extreme Unction; Fasting; Grace; Martyr; Preaching; Relics; Sacrament; Sin and Worship, are all important articles well worthy of special attention. The different sects and divisions of Christian practice and worship are treated under their own headings.

Church History is a long article suitably sub-divided for convenience of reference. The different councils (*e.g.*, Basel, Council of, etc.) are treated in separate articles apart from the main article Council. The synods, too, have special articles under the names they usually bear, as is also the case with the different courts. The famous heresies are also treated under their separate names. There is also a large article Papacy.

The chief saints of the Church Calendar are noted and details are given under their respective names. The popes have biographies, and are also treated in connection with their special work in separate articles where there is historical mention of their times. The reader should refer to Apostolic Constitutions; Apostolic Canons; Didache, The, etc., for the Christian documents required.

There are comprehensive articles on the religious orders. (*See* for example, Ambrosians; Benedictines; Capuchins, etc.) In addition to the main article Roman Catholic Church, all important sub-divisions of this aspect of Christian worship have articles under their own headings, *e.g.*, Immaculate Conception; Indulgence; Penance, etc. All the main Eastern Churches have articles devoted specially to them. All relationships of the Church of England and the modern Continental Churches, their special forms of worship and attitude to problems of belief and practice, are treated under their own headings. Ecclesiastical offices are treated under separate headings, *e.g.*, Abbess; Acolyte; Archbishop; Archdeacon, etc. The ecclesiastical seasons have all their own headings, and this is also the case with Ecclesiology and its sub-divisions. Bible and Biblical Criticism is a section which contains important articles on the prophets and books of the Old Testament, and the Apostles and books of the New.

2. NON-CHRISTIAN

In this section appear such major articles as Babylonian and Assyrian Religion; Greek Religion; Roman Religion; Hinduism; Ancestor-Worship; Zoroaster (for Zoroastrianism); Asceticism, etc. Apart from the main articles on Greek and Roman Religion, there are numerous short articles on the gods and goddesses of the ancient classical world. Such articles as Animism; Anthropomorphism; Demonology; Divination; Exorcism; Fetishism; Dead, Disposal of the; Idolatry; Lycanthropy; Mythology; Priest; Ritual and Witchcraft are the main supports of the non-Christian religious programme.

In addition to these there are numerous accounts, each under its own heading, of the gods and spirits of Brahmanism, Buddhism, etc., and the early faiths of Scandinavia, Europe, and the two divisions of America.

RELIGION. The treatment of this subject will fall into two distinct sections, *A. Primitive Religion* and *B. The Higher Religions.*

A. PRIMITIVE RELIGION

I. Definition of Primitive Religion.—Amongst the numberless definitions of religion that have been suggested, those that have been most frequently adopted for working purposes by anthropologists are Tylor's and Frazer's. Sir E. B. Tylor in *Primitive Culture* (1), i. 424, proposes as a "minimum definition" of religion "the belief in spiritual beings." Objections to this definition on the score of incompleteness are, firstly, that, besides belief, practice must be reckoned with (since, as W. Robertson Smith has made clear in his *Lectures on the Religion of the Semites*, 18 *sqq.*, ritual is in fact primary for primitive religion, whilst dogma and myth are secondary); secondly, that the outlook of such belief and practice is not exclusively towards the spiritual, unless this term be widened until it mean next to nothing, but is likewise towards the quasi-material, as will be shown presently. The merit of this definition, on the other hand, lies in its bilateral form, which calls attention to the need of characterizing both the religious attitude and the religious object to which the former has reference. The same form appears in Sir J. G. Frazer's definition in *The Golden Bough* (3rd ed.), i. 222. He understands by religion "a propitiation or conciliation of powers superior to man which are believed to direct and control the course of nature and of human life." He goes on to explain that by "powers" he means "conscious or personal agents." It is also to be noted that he is here definitely opposing religion to magic, which he holds to be based on the (implicit) assumption "that the course of nature is determined, not by the passions or caprice of personal beings, but by the operation of immutable laws acting mechanically." His definition improves on Tylor's in so far as it makes worship integral to the religious attitude. By regarding the object of religion as necessarily personal, however, he is led to exclude much that the primitive man undoubtedly treats with awe and respect as exerting a mystic effect on his life. Further, in maintaining that the powers recognized by religion are always superior to man, he leaves unclassed a host of practices that display a bargaining, or even a hectoring, spirit on the part of those addressing them (*see* Prayer). Threatening or beating a fetish cannot be brought under the head of magic, even if we adopt Frazer's principle (*op. cit.* i. 225) that to constrain or coerce a personal being is to treat him as an inanimate agent; for such a principle is quite inapplicable to cases of mere terrorism, whilst it may be doubted if it even renders the sense of the magician's typical notion of his mode of operation, viz., as the bringing to bear of a greater *mana* or psychic influence (*see* below) on what has less, and must therefore do as it is bidden. Such definitions, then, are to be accepted, if at all, as definitions

of type, selective designations of leading but not strictly universal features. An encyclopaedic account, however, should rest rather on an exterior definition which can serve as it were to pigeon-hole the whole mass of significant facts. Such an exterior definition is suggested by E. Crawley in *The Tree of Life*, 209, where he points out that "neither the Greek nor the Latin language has any comprehensive term for religion, except in the one ἱερά and in the other *sacra,* words which are equivalent to 'sacred.' No other term covers the whole of religious phenomena, and a survey of the complex details of various worships results in showing that no other conception will comprise the whole body of religious facts." It may be added that we have here no generalization imported from a higher level of culture, but an idea or blend of ideas familiar to primitive thought. An important consequence of thus giving the study of primitive religion the wide scope of a comparative hierology is that magic is no longer divorced from religion, since the sacred will now be found to be coextensive with the magico-religious, that largely undifferentiated plasm out of which religion and magic slowly take separate shapes as society comes more and more to contrast legitimate with illicit modes of dealing with the sacred. We may define, then, the religious object as the sacred, and the corresponding religious attitude as consisting in such manifestation of feeling, thought and action in regard to the sacred as is held to conduce to the welfare of the community or to that of individuals considered as members of the community.

II. Aspects of the Nature of the Sacred.—To exhibit the general character of the sacred as it exists for primitive religion it is simplest to take stock of various aspects recognized by primitive thought as expressed in language. If some, and not the least essential, of these aspects are quasi-negative, it must be remembered that negations—witness the Unseen, the Unknown, the Infinite of a more advanced theology—are well adapted to supply that mystery on which the religious consciousness feeds with the slight basis of conceptual support it needs. (1) *The sacred as the forbidden.* The primitive notion that perhaps comes nearest to our "sacred," whilst it immediately underlies the meanings of the Latin *sacer* and *sanctus,* is that of a *taboo,* a Polynesian term for which equivalents can be quoted from most savage vocabularies. The root idea seems to be that something is marked off as to be shunned, with the added hint of a mystic sanction or penalty enforcing the avoidance. Two derivative senses of a more positive import call for special notice. On the one hand, since that which is tabooed is held to punish the taboo-breaker by a sort of mystic infection, taboo comes to stand for uncleanness and sin. On the other hand, since the isolation of the sacred, even when originally conceived in the interest of the profane, may be interpreted as self-protection on the part of the sacred as against defiling contact, taboo takes on the connotation of ascetic virtue, purity, devotion, dignity and blessedness. Primary and secondary senses of the term between them cover so much ground that it is not surprising to find taboo used in Polynesia as a name for the whole system of religion, founded as it largely is on prohibitions and abstinences. (2) *The sacred as the mysterious.* Another quasi-negative notion of more restricted distribution is that of the mysterious or strange, as we have it expressed, for example, in the Siouan *wakan,* though possibly this is a derivative meaning. Meanwhile, it is certain that what is strange, new or portentous is regularly treated by all savages as sacred. (3) *The sacred as the secret.* The literal sense of the term *churinga,* applied by the Central Australians to their sacred objects, and likewise used more abstractly to denote mystic power, as when a man is said to be "full of *churinga,*" is "secret," and is symptomatic of the esotericism that is a striking mark of Australian, and indeed of all primitive, religion, with its insistence on initiation, its exclusion of women, and its strictly enforced reticence concerning traditional lore and proceedings. (4) *The sacred as the potent.* Passing on to positive conceptions of the sacred, perhaps the most fundamental is that which identifies the efficacy of sacredness with such mystic or magical power as is signified by the *mana* of the Pacific or *orenda* of the Hurons, terms for which analogies are forthcoming on all sides. Of *mana* R. H. Codrington in *The Melanesians*, 119 *n.*, writes: "It essentially belongs to personal beings to originate it, though it may act through the medium of water, or a stone or a bone. All Melanesian religion consists . . . in getting this *mana* for oneself, or getting it used for one's benefit." E. Tregear's *Maori-Polynesian Comparative Dictionary* shows how the word and its derivatives are used to express thought, memory, emotion, desire, will—in short, psychic energy of all kinds. It also stands for the vehicle of the magician's energy—the spell; which would seem likewise to be a meaning, perhaps the root-meaning, of *orenda* (*cf.* J. N. B. Hewitt, *American Anthropologist*, N.S., iv. 40). Whereas everything, perhaps, has some share of indwelling potency, whatever is sacred manifests this potency in an extraordinary degree, as typically the wonder-working leader of society, whose *mana* consists in his cunning and luck together. Altogether, in *mana* we have what is *par excellence* the primitive religious idea in its positive aspect, taboo representing its negative side, since whatever has *mana* is taboo, and whatever is taboo has *mana*. (5) *The sacred as the animate.* The term "animism," which embodies Tylor's classical theory of primitive religion, is unfortunately somewhat ambiguous. If we take it strictly to mean the belief in ghosts or spirits having the "vaporous materiality" proper to the objects of dream or hallucination, it is certain that the agency of such phantasms is not the sole cause to which all mystic happenings are referred (though ghosts and spirits are everywhere believed in, and appear to be endowed with greater predominance as religious synthesis advances amongst primitive peoples). Thus there is good evidence to show that many of the early gods, notably those that are held to be especially well disposed to man, are conceived rather in the shape of magnified non-natural men dwelling somewhere apart, such as the Mungan-ngaur of the Kurnai of S.E. Australia (*cf.* A. Lang, *The Making of Religion*, x. *seq.*). Such anthropomorphism is with difficulty reduced to the Tylorian animism. The term, however, will have to be used still more vaguely, if it is to cover all attribution of personality, will or vitality. This can be more simply brought under the notion of *mana*. Meanwhile, since quasi-mechanical means are freely resorted to in dealing with the sacred, as when a Maori chief snuffs up the sanctity his fingers have acquired by touching his own sacred head that he may restore the virtue to the part whence it was taken (R. Taylor, *Te Ika a Maui*, 165), or when uncleanness is removed as if it were a physical secretion by washing, wiping and so forth, it is hard to say whether what we should now call a "material" nature is not ascribed to the sacred, more especially when its transmissibility after the manner of a contagion is the trait that holds the attention. It is possible, however, that the savage always distinguishes in a dim way between the material medium and the indwelling principle of vital energy, examples of a pure fetishism, in the sense of the cult of the purely material, recognized as such, being hard to find. (6) *The sacred as the ancient.* The prominence of the notion of the *Alcheringa* "dreamtime," or sacred past, in Central Australian religion illustrates the essential connection perceived by the savage to lie between the sacred and the traditional. Ritualistic conservatism may be instanced as a practical outcome of this feeling. Another development is ancestor-worship, the organized cult of ancestors marking, however, a certain stage of advance beyond the very primitive, though the dead are always sacred and have *mana* which the living may exploit for their own advantage.

III. The Activity of the Sacred.—The foregoing views of the sacred, though starting from distinct conceptions, converge in a single complex notion, as may be seen from the many-sided sense borne by such a term as *wakan*, which may stand not only for "mystery," but also for "power, sacred, ancient, grandeur, animate, immortal" (W. J. McGee, *15th Report of U. S. Bureau of Ethnology*, 182). The reason for this convergence is that, whereas there is found great difficulty in characterizing the elusive nature of the sacred, its mode of manifesting itself is recognized to be much the same in all its phases. Uniform characteristics are the fecundity, ambiguity, relativity and transmissibility of its activity. (1) *Fecundity.* The mystic potency of the sacred is

no fixed quantity, but is big with possibilities of all sorts. The same sacred person, object, act, will suffice for a variety of purposes. Even where a piece of sympathetic magic appears to promise definite results, or when a departmental god is recognized, there would seem to be room left for a more or less indefinite expectancy. It must be remembered that the meaning of a rite is for the most part obscure to the participants, being overlaid by its traditional character, which but guarantees a general efficacy. "Blessings come, evils go," may be said to be the magico-religious formula implicit in all socially approved dealings with the sacred, however specialized in semblance. (2) *Ambiguity.* Mystic potency, however, because of the very indefiniteness of its action, is a two-edged sword. The sacred is not to be approached lightly. It will heal or blast, according as it is handled with or without due circumspection. That which is taboo, for instance, the person of the king, or woman's blood, is poison or medicine according as it is manipulated, being inherently just a potentiality for wonder-working in any direction. Not but what primitive thought shows a tendency to mark off a certain kind of mystic power as wholly bad by a special name, *e.g.*, the *arungquilta* of Central Australia; and here, we may note, we come nearest to a conception of magic as something other than religion, the trafficker in *arungquilta* being socially suspect, nay, liable to persecution, and even death (as amongst the Arunta tribe, *see* Spencer and Gillen, *The Arunta*, ii. 414 *n.*), at the hands of his fellows. On the other hand, wholly beneficent powers seem hardly to be recognized, unless we find them in beings such as Mungan-ngaur ("father-our"), who derive an ethical character from their association with the initiation ceremonies and the moral instruction given thereat (*cf.* Lang, *l.c.*). (3) *Relativity.* So far we have tended to represent the activity of the sacred as that of a universal force, somewhat in the style of our "electricity" or "mind." It remains to add that this activity manifests itself at numberless independent centres. These differ amongst themselves in the degree of their energy. One spell is stronger than another, one taboo more inviolable than another. W. H. R. Rivers (*The Todas*, 448) gives an interesting analysis of the grades of sanctity apparent in Toda religion. The gods of the hill-tops come first. The sacred buffaloes, their milk, their bells, the dairies and their vessels are on a lower plane; whilst we may note that there are several grades amongst the dairies, increase of sanctity going with elaboration of dairy ritual (*cf. ibid.* 232). Still lower is the dairyman, who is in no way divine, yet has sanctity as one who maintains a condition of ceremonial purity. (4) *Transmissibility.* If, however, this activity originates at certain centres, it tends to spread therefrom in all directions. F. B. Jevons (in *An Introduction to the History of Religion*, vii.) distinguishes between "things taboo," which have the mystic contagion inherent in them, and "things tabooed," to which the taboo-infection has been transmitted. In the former class he places supernatural beings (including men with *mana* as well as ghosts and spirits), blood, new-born children with their mothers, and corpses; which list might be considerably extended, for instance, by the inclusion of natural portents, and animals and plants such as are strikingly odd, dangerous or useful. Any one of these can pass on its sacred quality to other persons and objects (as a corpse defiles the mourner and his clothes), nay to actions, places and times as well (as a corpse will likewise cause work to be tabooed, ground to be set apart, a holy season to be observed). Such transmissibility is commonly explained by the association of ideas, that becoming sacred which as it were reminds one of the sacred; though it is important to add, firstly, that such association takes place under the influence of a selective interest generated by strong religious feeling, and, secondly, that this interest is primarily a collective product, being governed by a social tradition which causes certain possibilities of ideal combination alone to be realized, whilst it is the chief guarantee of the objectivity of what they suggest.

IV. The Exploitation of the Sacred. A. Methods.—It is hard to find terms general enough to cover dealings with the sacred that range from the manipulation of an almost inanimate type of power to intercourse modelled on that between man and man. Primitive religion, however, resorts to either way of approach so indifferently as to prove that there is little or no awareness of an inconsistency of attitude. The radical contrast between mechanical and spiritual religion, though fundamental for modern theology, is alien to the primitive point of view, and is therefore inappropriate to the purposes of anthropological description. (1) *Acquisition*. Mystic power may be regarded as innate so far as skill, luck or queerness are signs and conditions of its presence. On the whole, however, savage society tends to regard it as something acquired, the product of acts and abstinences having a traditional character for imparting magico-religious virtue. An external symbol in the shape of a ceremony or cult-object is of great assistance to the dim eye of primitive faith. Again, the savage universe is no preserve of man, but is an open field wherein human and non-human activities of all sorts compete on more or less equal terms, yet so that a certain measure of predominance may be secured by a judicious combination of forces. (2) *Concentration*. Hence the magico-religious society or individual practitioner piles ceremony on ceremony, name of power on name of power, relic on relic, to consolidate the forces within reach and assume direction thereof. The transmissibility of the sacred ensures the fusion of powers drawn from all sources, however disparate. (3) *Induction*. It is necessary, however, as it were, to bring this force to a head. This would appear to be the essential significance of sacrifice, where a number of sacred operations and instruments are made to discharge their efficacy into the victim as into a vat, so that a blessing-yielding, evil-neutralizing force of highest attainable potency is obtained (*see* H. Hubert and M. Mauss, "Essai sur la nature et la fonction du sacrifice" in *L'Année sociologique,* ii.). (4) *Renovation*. An important *motif* in magico-religious ritual, which may not have been without effect on the development of sacrifice, is, as Frazer's main thesis in *The Golden Bough* asserts, the imparting of reproductive energy to animals, plants and man himself, its cessation being suggested by such phenomena as old age and the fall of the year. To concentrate, induce and renovate are, however, but aspects of one process of acquisition by the transfusion of a transmissible energy. (5) *Demission*. Hubert and Mauss show in their penetrating analysis of sacrifice that after the rite has been brought to its culminating point there follows as a pendant a ceremony of re-entry into ordinary life, the idea of which is preserved in the Christian formula *Ite, missa est*. (6) *Insulation*. Such deposition of sacredness is but an aspect of the wider method that causes a ring-fence to be erected round the sacred to ward off casual trespassers at once in their own interest and to prevent contamination. We see here a natural outcome of religious awe supported by the spirit of esotericism, and by a sense of the need for an expert handling of that which is so potent for good or ill. (7) *Direction*. This last consideration brings to notice the fact that throughout magico-religious practice of all kinds the human operator retains a certain control over the issue. In the numberless transitions that, whilst connecting, separate the spell and the prayer we observe as the accompaniment of every mood from extreme imperiousness to extreme humility an abiding will and desire to help the action out. Even "Thy will be done" preserves the echo of a direction, and, needless to say, this is hardly a form of primitive address. At the bottom is the vague feeling that it is man's own self-directed mysterious energy that is at work, however much it needs to be reinforced from without. Meanwhile, tradition strictly prescribes the ways and means of such reinforcement, so that religion becomes largely a matter of sacred lore; and the expert director of rites, who is likewise usually at this stage the leader of society, comes more and more to be needed as an intermediary between the lay portion of the community and the sacred powers.

V. Results.—Hitherto our account of primitive religion has had to move on somewhat abstract lines. His religion is, however, anything but an abstraction to the savage, and stands rather for the whole of his concrete life so far as it is penetrated by a spirit of earnest endeavour. The end and result of primitive religion is, in a word, the consecration of life, the stimulation of the will to live and to do. This bracing of the vital feeling takes place by means of imaginative appeal to the great forces man perceives

stirring within him and about him, such appeal proving effective doubtless by reason of the psychological law that to conceive strongly is to imitate. Meanwhile, security against any clashing of conceptions to inhibit the tendency of the idea of an acquired "grace" to realize itself in action, is assured by the complete unanimity of public opinion, dominated as it is by an inveterate custom. To appreciate the consecrating effect of religion on primitive life we have only to look to the *churinga*-worship of the Central Australians (as described by Spencer and Gillen in *The Native Tribes of Central Australia,* [1] *The Northern Tribes of Central Australia* and *The Arunta*). Contact with these repositories of mystic influence "makes them glad" (*Nat. Tr.* 165); it likewise makes them "good," so that they are no longer greedy or selfish (*North. Tr.* 266); it endows them with second sight (*ibid.*); it gives them confidence and success in war (*Nat. Tr.* 135); in fact, there is no end to its "strengthening" effects (*ibid. n.*). Or, again, we may note the earnestness and solemnity that characterize all their sacred ceremonies. The inwardness of primitive religion is, however, non-existent for those who observe it as uninitiated strangers; whilst, again, it evaporates as soon as native custom breaks down under pressure of civilization, when only fragments of meaningless superstition survive: for which reason travesties of primitive religion abound.

It remains to consider shortly the consecration of life in relation to particular categories and departments. (1) *Education*. Almost every tribe has its initiation ceremonies, and in many tribes adult life may almost be described as a continuous initiation. The object of these rites is primarily to impart mystic virtue to the novice, such virtue, in the eyes of the primitive man, being always something more than social usefulness, amounting as it does to a share in the tribal luck by means of association with all it holds sacred. Incidentally the candidate is trained to perform his duties as a tribesman, but religion presides over the course, demanding earnest endeavour of an impressionable age. (2) *Government*. Where society is most primitive it is most democratic, as in Australia, and magico-religious powers are possessed by the whole body of fully initiated males, age, however, conferring increase of sacred lore and consequently of authority; whilst even at this stage the experts tend to form an inner circle of rulers. The man with *mana* is bound to come to the top, both because his gifts give him a start and because his success is taken as a sign that he has the gift. A decisive "moment" in the evolution of chiefship is the recognition of hereditary *mana,* bound up as this is with the handing on of ceremonies and cult-objects. Invested, as society grows more complex, with a sanctity increasingly superior to that of the layman, the priest-king becomes the representative of the community as repository of its luck, whilst, as controller of all sacred forces that bear thereon, he is, as Frazer puts it, "dynamical centre of the universe" (*The Golden Bough* [3rd ed.], iii. 1). Only when the holy man's duty to preserve his holiness binds him hand and foot in a network of taboos does his temporal power tend to devolve on a deputy. (3) *Food-supply*. In accordance with the principle of Renovation (*see* above), the root-idea of the application of religion to economics is not the extorting of boons from an unwilling nature, but rather the stimulation of the sources of life, so that all beings alike may increase and multiply. (4) *Food-taking*. Meanwhile, the primitive meal is always more or less of a sacrament, and there are many food-taboos, the significance of which is, however, not so much that certain foods are unclean and poisonous as that they are of special virtue and must be partaken of solemnly and with circumspection. (5) *Kinship*. It is hard to say whether the unit of primitive society is the tribe or the group of kinsmen. Both are forms of union that are consolidated by means of religious usages. Thus in Australia the initiation ceremonies, concerned as they partly are with marriage, always an affair between the kin-groups, are tribal, whilst the totemic rites are the prime concern of the members of the totem clans. The significance of a common name and a common blood is immensely enhanced by its association with mystic rights and duties, and the pulse of brotherhood beats faster. (6) *The Family*. Side by side with the kin there is always found the domestic group, but the latter institution develops fully only as the former weakens, so that the one comes largely to inherit the functions of the other, whilst the tribe too in its turn hands over certain interests. Thus in process of time birth-rites, marriage-rites, funeral-rites, not to mention subordinate ceremonies such as those of name-giving and food-taking, become domestic sacraments. (7) *Sex.* Woman, for certain physiological reasons, is always for primitive peoples hedged round with sanctity, whilst man does all he can to inspire awe of his powers in woman by keeping religion largely in his own hands. The result, so far as woman is concerned, is that, in company with those males who are endowed with sacredness in a more than ordinary degree, she tends as a sex to lose in freedom as much as she gains in respect. (8) *Personality.* Every one has his modicum of innate *mana,* or at least may develop it in himself by communicating with powers that can be brought into answering relation by the proper means. Nagualism, or the acquisition of a mystic guardian, is a widely distributed custom, the essence of which probably consists in the procuring of a personal name having potency. The exceptional man is recognized as having *mana* in a special degree, and a belief thus held at once by others and by himself is bound to stimulate his individuality. The primitive community is not so custom-bound that personality has no chance to make itself felt, and the leader of men possessed of an inner fund of inspiration is the wonder-worker who encourages all forms of social advance.

VI. Psychology of the Primitive Attitude Towards the Sacred.—We are on firmer ground when simply describing the phenomena of primitive religion than when seeking to account for these in terms of natural law—in whatever sense the conception of natural law be applicable to the facts of the mental life of man. One thing is certain, namely, that savages stand on virtually one footing with the civilized as regards the type of explanation appropriate to their beliefs and practices. We have no right to refer to "instincts" in the case of primitive man, any more at any rate than we have in our own case. A child of civilized parents brought up from the first amongst savages is a savage, neither more nor less. Though race may count for something in the matter of mental effectiveness—and at least it would seem to involve differences in weight of brain—it clearly counts for much less than does *milieu,* to wit, that social environment of ideas and institutions which depends so largely for its effectiveness on mechanical means of tradition, such as the art of writing. The outstanding feature of the mental life of savages known to psychologists as "primitive credulity" is doubtless chiefly due to sheer want of diversity of suggestiveness in their intellectual surroundings. Their notions stick fast because there are no competing notions to dislodge them. Society suffers a sort of perpetual obsession, and remains self-hypnotized as it were within a magic circle of traditional views. A rigid orthodoxy is sustained by means of purblind imitation assisted by no little persecution. Such changes as occur come about, not in consequence of a new direction taken by conscious policy, but rather in the way that fashions in dress alter amongst ourselves, by subconscious, hardly purposive drifting. The crowd rather than the individual is the thinking unit. A proof is the mysterious rapid extinction of savages the moment that their group-life is broken up; they are individually so many lost sheep, without self-reliance or initiative. And the thinking power of a crowd—that is, a mob, not a deliberative assembly—is of a very low order, emotion of a "panicky" type driving it hither and thither like a rudderless ship. However, as the students of mob-psychology have shown, every crowd tends to have its *meneur,* its mob-leader, the man who sets the cheering or starts the running-away. So too, then, with the primitive society. Grossly ignorant of all that falls outside "the daily round, the common task," they are full of panicky fears in regard to this unknown, and the primary attitude of society towards it is sheer avoidance, taboo. But the mysterious has another face. To the mob the mob-leader is mysterious in his power of bringing luck and salvation; to himself also he is a wonder, since he wills, and lo! things happen accordingly. He has *mana,* power, and by means of this *mana,* felt inwardly by himself, acknowledged by his fellows, he stems the social impulse

to run away from a mystery. Not without nervous dread—witness the special taboo to which the leader of society is subject —he draws near and strives to constrain, conciliate or cajole the awful forces with which the life of the group is set about. He enters the Holy of Holies; the rest remain without, and are more than half afraid of their mediator. In short, from the standpoint of lay society, the manipulator of the sacred is himself sacred, and shares in all the associations of sacredness. An anthropomorphism which is specifically a "magomorphism" renders the sacred powers increasingly one with the governing element in society, and religion assumes an ethico-political character, whilst correspondingly authority and law are invested with a deeper meaning.

VII. The Abuse of the Sacred.—Lest our picture of primitive religion appear too brightly coloured, a word must be said on the perversions to which the exploitation of the sacred is liable. Envy, malice and uncharitableness are found in primitive society, as elsewhere, and on their behalf the mystic forces are not infrequently unloosed by those who know how to do so. To use the sacred to the detriment of the community, as does, for instance, the expert who casts a spell, or utters a prayer, to his neighbour's hurt, is what primitive society understands by magic (*cf. arungquilta,* above), and anthropology has no business to attach any other meaning to the word if it undertakes to interpret the primitive point of view. On the other hand, if those in authority perpetrate in the name of what their society holds sacred, and therefore with its full approval, acts that to the modern mind are cruel, silly or revolting, it is bad science and bad ethics to speak of vice and degradation, unless it can be shown that the community in which these things occur is thereby brought nearer to elimination in the struggle for existence. As a matter of fact, the earlier and more democratic types of primitive society, uncontaminated by our civilization, do not present many features to which the modern conscience can take exception, but display rather the edifying spectacle of religious brotherhoods encouraging themselves by mystical communion to common effort. With the evolution of rank, however, and the concentration of magico-religious power in the hands of certain orders, there is less solidarity and more individualism, or at all events more opportunity for sectional interests to be pursued at other than critical times; whereupon fraud and violence are apt to infect religion. Indeed, as the history of the higher religions shows, religion tends in the end to break away from secular government with its aristocratic traditions, and to revert to the more democratic spirit of the primitive age, having by now obtained a clearer consciousness of its purpose, yet nevertheless clinging to the inveterate forms of human ritual as still adequate to symbolize the consecration of life—the quickening of the will to face life earnestly.

BIBLIOGRAPHY.—The number of works dealing with primitive religion is endless. The English reader who is more or less new to the subject is recommended to begin with Sir E. B. Tylor, *Primitive Culture* (4th ed., Lond. 1903), and then to proceed to Sir J. G. Frazer, *The Golden Bough* (3rd ed., Lond. 1911–15), together with his other works *The Belief in Immortality* 1913; *Folk-Lore in the Old Testament,* 1919; *The Worship of Nature,* 1926. Only second in importance to the above are W. Robertson Smith, *Lectures on the Religion of the Semites* (3rd ed. with Introd. and additional notes by Dr. S. A. Cook, Lond. 1927); A. Lang, *Myth, Ritual and Religion* (2nd ed., Lond. 1899), and *Magic and Religion* (Lond. 1902); E. S. Hartland, *The Legend of Perseus* (Lond. 1894–96); F. B. Jevons, *An Introduction to the History of Religion* (2nd ed., 1902); E. Crawley, *The Tree of Life* and *The Mystic Rose* (2nd ed. Lond. 1927). The two last-mentioned works perhaps most nearly represent the views taken in the text, which are also developed by the present writer in *The Threshold of Religion* (2nd ed., 1909) and *Psychology and Folk-Lore,* 1920. *See also* H. Hubert and M. Mauss, "Essai sur la nature et la fonction du sacrifice," *L'Année sociologique,* ii.; and "Esquisse d'une théorie générale de la magie," *ibid* vii.; E. Durkheim, *Les formes élémentaires et la vie religieuse,* Paris, 1912; L. Levy-Bruhl, *Les fonctions mentales dans les sociétes inférieures,* Paris, 1912; R. H. Lowie, *Primitive Religion,* 1925, E. Westermarck, *Ritual and Belief in Morocco,* 1926; R. Briffault, *The Mothers,* 1927.
Side by side with works of general theory, first-hand authorities should be freely used. To make a selection from these is not easy, but the following at least are very important: R. H. Codrington, *The Melanesians* (Oxford, 1891); W. B. Spencer and F. J. Gillen, *The*

Native Tribes of Central Australia (Lond. 1899); *The Northern Tribes of Central Australia* (Lond. 1904); *The Arunta* (Lond. 1927); A. W. Howitt, *The Native Tribes of South-Eastern Australia* (Lond. 1904); A. C. Haddon, *Reports of the Cambridge Anthropological Expedition to Torres Straits* (Cambridge, 1904, vol. v.); A. B. Ellis, *The Tshi-Speaking Peoples of the Gold Coast* (Lond. 1897); *The Ewe-Speaking Peoples of the Slave Coast* (Lond. 1890); *The Yoruba-Speaking Peoples of the Slave Coast* (Lond. 1894); Miss M. H. Kingsley, *Travels in West Africa* (Lond. 1898), and *West African Studies* (Lond. 1899); R. S. Rattray, *Ashanti* (1923); *Religion and Art in Ashanti* (1927); E. Westermarck, *Ritual and Belief in Morocco* (1926); A. C. Hollis, *The Masai* (1905); W. Crooke, *The North-West Provinces of India* (Lond. 1897); W. H. R. Rivers, *The Todas* (1906). An immense amount of valuable evidence is to be obtained in the *Reports of the Bureau of Ethnology*, Smithsonian Institution, Washington. *See* Nos. 2, 5, 6, 7, 8, 9, 11, 13, 14, 15, 16, 18, 19, 21, 22, 23, and specially J. O. Dorsey, *A Study of Siouan Cults*, in No. 11; A. C. Fletcher, *The Hako*, in No. 22; and M. C. Stevenson, *The Zuñi Indians*, in No. 23. Though dealing primarily with a more advanced culture, J. J. M. de Groot, *The Religious System of China* (1892–1901), will be found to throw much light on primitive ideas. Finally let it be repeated that there is offered here no more than an introductory course of standard authorities suitable for the English reader. (R. R. M.)

B. THE HIGHER RELIGIONS

No attempt can here be made to deal in detail with the Higher Religions. These are treated elsewhere under their respective headings. The different Higher Religions will only be considered in so far as they exhibit general principles. The main object of this section will be to show the lines on which the higher religious consciousness has developed, the broad features which it discloses, and the way in which it gives expression to human needs.

I. THE BASIS OF HIGHER RELIGION

Higher religions have developed on a pre-existing basis, in response to an impulse of the religious spirit seeking better self-expression. They have grown out of primitive religion, and all of them exhibit traces of their lineage. The survival of primitive traits in developed religion is a recurring phenomenon.

Evidently a higher religion can only emerge from a lower by a process of selection and development. Certain elements in early religion were intractable to development, while others were capable of it. To the former must be reckoned the strongly local character and particularist tendency of primitive religion. Spirits or powers attached to a definite spot, or embodied in a specific object are not easily elevated or expanded. Sentiment is conservative, and the being reverenced is too much lacking in individual quality to be readily transformed into a personal god. On the other hand, though the feeling of the clan that its objects of worship belong to it resists absorption in a larger cult, the strong sense of affinity with divine powers is capable of being elevated to a higher religious relationship. The same holds of primitive rites of communion. So too primitive ideas of Tabu and Interdiction have naturally passed into conceptions of the sacred and not-sacred, the pure and the impure, ideas that play a great part in developed religion. Again the cult of the dead, passing into that of family ancestors (*see* ANCESTOR-WORSHIP) easily expands with the enlargement of society: it has contributed important elements to national religion as in the case of China and ancient Rome. There are then higher possibilities in primitive religion, but they can only come to fruition with the emergence of new needs and a wider outlook.

II. THE RISE AND GROWTH OF POLYTHEISM

Higher religions emerge after the tribal has been superseded by the national culture. The transition to the more developed stage was the outcome of social changes which were reflected in the growth of man's inner life. This enrichment of personal life carried with it the need of a revised idea of the objects of worship and of the religious relation. The old spiritism, with its multitude of indefinite powers and capricious daemons, no longer corresponded to man's better ordered life and his varied and specialized interests. The larger and more constant values of a social order based on agriculture required divine beings capable of responding to its wants, and the rise of polytheism was the answer to these religious demands. The polytheistic system was the ex-pression of man's vision of the world, a world of diverse departments and manifestations though not a real unity. But polytheism marks an advance. For it helped (a) to liberate religion from its bondage to purely local associations. And (b), it replaced the colourless powers or *numina* of older belief by a number of divine beings of more specific character and with more or less definite spheres of activity. A god, as distinguished from a spirit, is a being with determinate qualities which embody the values of which men are conscious.

(1) *The Emergence of Gods.*—The formless spirits supply only a shifting and uncertain basis on which to evolve a god. It has been suggested that the Greek deities Hermes and Artemis were developed in this way, and the Roman goddess Juno has been construed as the general personification of the fertility *numen* or Juno of every woman. In any case such a process is infrequent. And the instances in which a totem has grown into a god, if they do occur at all, are extremely rare. What is clear is, that many of the greater gods have a connection with the phenomena of nature, and show traces of this relationship. Sometimes the connection is quite definite. Thus the Egyptian Ra and the Babylonian Shamash are sun-gods. The Greek Zeus, to whom corresponds the Vedic Dyaus, is a sky-god, and Ushas of the Vedic Hymns is a dawn-goddess. But there are many instances where the connection of a deity with nature cannot be precisely stated, though the general fact is not in doubt. Thus it remains uncertain what the natural basis of the Egyptian Osiris is; and we cannot say more of the Vedic Varuna and Vishnu than that they are connected with light and the heaven. The later development of a deity usually furnishes a very slender clue to his real origin. Moreover when the identification of a deity with a phenomenon of nature is transparent and precise, it is difficult for the god to develop by assuming new and higher qualities.

But while the greater phenomena of nature, by the fact that they possess a kind of physical universality, were a means of helping the mind to rise to the conception of deities of wider range and power, all gods are not to be explained thus. For some of them have their origin in the cult. The Hindu Soma is the power of the sacrificial libation, and Brahma the power of the sacrificial prayer personified. The Greek Hestia and the Roman Vesta (*q.v.*) have grown out of the sacred hearth as the centre of family life. Again, aspects of the cultural life, such as war and agriculture, have suggested deities who preside over them. In some cases men remarkable for their power and deeds have been exalted to the rank of divine, or semi-divine beings, *e.g.*, the Greek Herakles and Asklepios. (*See* AESCULAPIUS and HERCULES.) The motives which develop polytheism are complex.

(2) *The Characterization of the Gods.*—As social life expands, its values become more varied, and the representations of the gods gain correspondingly in content. A god takes on new qualities and aspects in response to the needs and desires of his worshippers, and this process appears in all religions. Few gods have acquired so varied qualities and offices as the Greek Apollo. His identification with the sun is comparatively late, and his original character obscure. But he came to figure as the lord of flocks and herds, the master of oracles and prophecy, the god of healing, of purification, and of poesy. The imaginative process which predicated diversified attributes to a deity at the same time expressed the interests and aspirations of his worshippers. And the cultus was the chief medium by which these tendencies were developed and took concrete form.

The problem of organization is urgent where a religion arises out of the fusion of different cultures. Conspicuous instances are Babylonian and Greek religion. The Semitic invaders of Babylonia absorbed the older Sumerian culture, and found a place for Sumerian deities within their own pantheon. Greek civilization, as we now know, was the result of a fusion of two races, a race of Aryan invaders with the "Helladic" race. And it is almost certain that some of the Hellenic deities, *e.g.* Athene, Artemis, and Aphrodite, were adopted by the Greeks from the older culture. Yet it is always hard to achieve organization in the religious complex of polytheism even when a fusion of cultures seems to render it essential. The local associations and the cult-interests of the deities of the conquered race resist absorption. This difficulty may be overcome by fitting them into the enlarged pantheon as sons or servants of greater gods. Even then the older cults and beliefs will linger on. Homeric religion is no doubt an example of organisation; but it is artificial and literary, it does not fairly represent the actual beliefs and cult-practices in Greece. Still, however imperfectly the process may work itself out, there is behind polytheistic religion an impulse towards order and system. The development of social life, with its well-marked departments and functions, prompted the mind to conceive the divine world after the pattern of the human. The needs of worship, where not dominated by magical ideas, led in the same direction. For worship at the higher level cannot be easily apportioned among a number of divine beings whose mutual relations are quite indefinite. Some order and gradation are necessary.

III. THE CULTUS IN HIGHER RELIGIONS

The cultus is the focus of a religion: here it is concentrated and symbolized. As the focus of religious life the cultus becomes the point at which the sense of the sacred is most concentrated and intense. Radiating from this centre the sacred suffuses associated elements, investing with religious significance things and persons, places and times.

(1) *The Sacred Place.*—In early religion a place or thing became sacred through the presence in it of a spirit or power: *numen inest.* But when men began to build houses, when the house became the centre of family life, the thought lay to hand that there must be a house for the deity to be the focus of his worship. So the temple arose, reared often on sacred spots or "high places," hallowed by immemorial associations. As the deity was supposed to be more intimately present in his temple, it often became a centre of oracles and prophecy.

(2) *Sacred Men: the Priesthood.*—To holy places correspond holy men. The priest has his precursor in the wizard of the lower culture. The priest is a man endowed with a special knowledge of the cultus, is possessed of ritual purity, and embodies in his person the power of the sacred. At first priestly functions were not the exclusive privilege of a class. The head of the family, or the king as head of the people, offers sacrifice, so in the old Hebrew and Roman religions. But with the growing value attached to sacred functions there was the tendency to assign the priestly office to a particular class, as in the Hebrew, Persian and Hindu religions. Nowhere have the priests formed a more strict and exclusive caste than in Brahmanism.

(a) *Prayer.*—Perhaps nowhere does the spirit of a religion reveal itself more intimately than in its prayers. Yet even in the higher religions the idea of prayer as the free outpouring of the soul to the divine comes late. Primitive prayer is closely allied to the spell, and it must take a fixed form of words to be effective. The elevation of prayer comes with the development of inner life and an enhanced sense of ethical and spiritual values. Some knowledge of the kind of prayers offered in the cultus may be gathered from liturgical forms, *e.g.* from the sacrificial hymns of the Gathas and the Vedas. Prayer as petition to the gods is universal. But only in a few religions do we find prayers containing confessions of sin *e.g.* in the penitential psalms of the Hebrew and the Babylonian religions. Nowhere is the mysterious potency of prayer so exalted as in Brahmanism. Here prayer becomes a cosmic power which constrains the gods, and is finally construed as the divine principle of things. But wherever prayer ceases to be the expression of a fundamental dependence on the Divine, it loses its essential meaning and value. An intrinsically efficacious form of words is really a reversion to the magic spell. (*See* PRAYER.)

(b) *Sacrifice.*—Sacrifice springs from a deep-rooted impulse of the religious nature. It plays a part in early religion, and is present in some form in all the higher religions. The purpose of sacrifice is to maintain and strengthen, or to restore, fellowship with divine powers, and it takes a central place in the cultus. In the burnt-offering the sacrifice is wafted to the gods. In the bloody offering the victim, through contact with the altar, becomes charged with the sacred, and its sprinkled blood has aton-

ing virtue. The idea of substitutionary atonement is later and is due to reflection. In sacrifices of purification and atonement there is an ethical element which may lead to the higher development of religion. Just as with prayer, however, sacrifice may evolve in a way which is detrimental to the religious relation. What lifts sacrifice to an ethical and spiritual level is the conception of the righteousness of God. Where this obtains it is the inner side of the sacrificial act which is emphasised, the offering of the contrite heart and the obedient will. (*See* SACRIFICE.)

IV. RELIGIONS OF OBSERVANCE AND PROPHETIC RELIGIONS

The ritual aspect of religion tends to grow with the increasing complexity of the social order. When this tendency prevails religion takes on the specific character of legal observance.

(1) *Religions of Observance and Law.*—The idea of fixed observances or rules binding on the faithful develops where the idea of ritual purity is emphasised. The roots of the conception of the clean and unclean go back to primitive ideas of the sacred and of the dangerous with the associated apotropaic rites of expulsion. The growth of a sacral system leads to the fuller definition of the clean and unclean, and rules and forms are prescribed to preserve purity and remove impurity. In many higher religions there are detailed methods and a ritual of cleansing. In Roman religion we have lustration, which combined cathartic and apotropaic rites, and in Greece cathartic rites were specially connected with Apollo, the god of ritual purity. It is, however, in later Persian religion that rites of purification receive the most comprehensive and detailed expression, and nowhere is the notion of purity so dominant and pervasive. To all the numerous defilements that are possible correspond stated cleansings, and the Vendidad itself has been described as a kind of sin-codex. With this we may compare the laws of purity and impurity in the book of Leviticus, a book which embodies the cathartic ritual of post-Exilic Judaism. When a higher religion has developed a complicated system of ritual observance it brings the sense of the sacred into close and constant relation with the varied details of life. On the other hand, the religion itself is exposed to great dangers. The magical beliefs, which are a heritage of older religion, always tend to reassert themselves, and the religious rites readily degenerate to a mechanical performance which has intrinsic efficacy. When this happens the way to spiritual development is closed, and the later Persian and Jewish religions did not wholly escape the danger.

(2) *Prophetic Religion.*—Religion as piety has its centre within. The prophetic spirit proclaims this principle, and is itself the issue of personal and moral conviction. The prophet turns from the formal and external side of religion to emphasize its inner life, and when such a movement appears within a national religion it involves a loosening of religion from the social and political system. Great religious reforms and renewals arise from an individual or individuals for whom religion has become an intense and personal concern. Such a prophetic figure was Zarathustra. As we picture him from the Gathas he was a man of burning conviction, for whom Ahura Mazda was a supreme and moral deity whose cause is the right as against the lie. In this conflict the prophet calls men to fight and freely to choose the good. A like intense moral conviction and faith in the righteousness of Jahveh appears in the eighth century prophets of Israel linked with an even greater stress on the inner side of piety. The same note recurs in the teaching of Jesus that the vision of God is for the pure in heart.

It is curious to find an emphasis on the inner side of religion appearing within Hinduism. It emerges in the doctrine of Bhakti which has its classical expression in the *Bhagavad Gita.* Here we have the doctrine that trust and devotion, faith and love, to the divine power are a means of salvation. Religion assumes a personal colour. With Buddha this principle appears in the form of an extreme subjectivism. Within man himself lies the secret of salvation.

The work of the prophetic spirit makes possible the high stages of spiritual religion. Apart from its vivifying influence institutional religion tends to grow formal and fixed, and its inner life to ebb. "Where there is no vision the people perish." The uprising of the prophet is a token that a religion which seems dead has still within it the springs of life.

V. REDEMPTIVE RELIGIONS

The prophetic movement is one symptom of the enhanced sense of personal and religious values, and the emergence of religions of salvation or redemption is another. Both indicate a slackening of the tie which binds religion to the national and political structure. For the official religion which men share simply as citizens of the state, a religion concerned with external observance rather than inner spirit and motives, no longer satisfies the more personal needs of which men are becoming aware. Corresponding to this increasing self-consciousness there grows up a craving for a more intimate and individual relation with the divine Power, a craving which the traditional religious forms cannot meet. And this feeling is deepened by the personal sense of the evils and sufferings of life. This longing for deliverance finds no fulfilment in the customary and external religion that a man inherits from his social group. Some better way is necessary; and the personal consciousness of the need of salvation carries with it a sense of responsibility for realizing it. So men seek some mode of expressing the religious spirit which shall embody their choice and preference, for religion must be in a more intimate sense their own. As the new movement takes its rise from broadly human needs, the form of religion which meets these needs cannot be merely local and particular: in its meaning at least it will be universal. This implies that the form of the religious relation is reconstituted, and this carries with it a differentiation of the religious community from political society. There now come into being religious associations or churches, where membership is based on a voluntary adherence to a particular religion or cult. This principle of a sacred society or church, clearly distinguished from secular society, is of great significance in the evolution of religion. For only under such conditions can the other-worldly or transcendent element in faith come to its due, and religion itself be delivered from bondage to political and secular interests. The idea of the sacred gains spiritual significance: the sacred community is united not merely in the observance of sacred rites but by a common disposition of the mind and will toward a religious good. And this good is not mundane but supramundane.

The new tendency finds expression in different ways. It appears as a movement which, without deliberately breaking with existing religion, takes form in religious associations which minister to felt religious wants. Again it appears as a philosophic gospel which offers spiritual deliverance to elect souls. Finally it manifests itself in the birth of a new religion, a religion which originates with a personal founder who proclaims a message of salvation. To the first class belong the various forms of mystery religions which were common in Greek and Mediterranean lands for a period of eight centuries B.C. One of the best known is the Orphic mysteries, a cult open at least to all Hellenes who underwent initiation. This cult held out the prospect of immortality and union with the divine. The body was a kind of tomb ($\sigma\hat{\omega}\mu\alpha$, $\sigma\hat{\eta}\mu\alpha$) from which the soul had to win deliverance. The way of salvation was by purification, abstinence and sacramental rites. The idea of something peculiarly sacred, in which the initiated participate, is common to mystery religions. The later mystery cults, like those of Attis, Isis and Mithras, which were widespread in eastern Mediterranean lands in the post-Alexandrian period, set in the foreground the spectacle of the dying and reviving god. Their votaries, through baptism, purification and a sacramental meal, somehow shared in the being of the god and with him rose to new life.

In the philosophic sphere, Neoplatonism proclaims the deliverance of the soul through an ecstatic union with the One that transcends rational thinking. Philosophic Brahmanism likewise has a doctrine of salvation, but a salvation through knowledge of the identity of the self with the Absolute or Brahman.

In Buddhism and in Christianity the spirit of redemptive religion is most fully expressed. In Buddhism the principle is seen taking an extreme subjective form. Buddha discards the metaphysics of Brahmanism, though he shares with it the idea that salvation comes through knowledge. The Enlightened, the Arahat, knows that thirst, with its attendant desire and suffering, is the evil of life, and by following the Noble Eightfold Way he advances to that indefinable goal, Nirvana. Redemption is thus a negative process: it is a gospel for the monk who breaks with the world rather than for the ordinary man who has to live in the world. Christian redemption is a richer and more positive conception. The deliverance sought is from moral evil or sin, and it is conditioned by repentance and faith. The end is not the extinction of personality but its enrichment through the power of a divine life, and it has corporate expression in life in the Kingdom of God which overcomes the evil in the world. Christian redemption is marked by its theistic basis, its sense of personal values and its positive character. The religious society of Buddhism is a monkish community: that of Christianity is the church, or the fellowship of the faithful united in the service of God.

VI. PANTHEISM, MYSTICISM AND MONOTHEISM

These are features found only in the higher religious culture. They all claim to be an advance on some existing religious system. (1) *Pantheism.*

Pantheism is in the main a result of the development of reflective thinking. In the many it finds merely the passing appearances of the One. If pantheism is a late development, it was at least foreshadowed at earlier stages of religious evolution. Men soon became dimly conscious of a unity pervading the cosmic order and everywhere operative throughout it. In the Hindu conception of Rita and of Karma we have the idea of a power behind all things working by inflexible law. The ancient Chinese Tao conveys a sense of the eternal order and way of the universe. The Greek Moira and the Persian Asha contain the same ideas. This belief in a universal principle, when applied to polytheism, leads to the notion of a common power behind the gods and suggests that the various gods are only forms of the one Reality. Thus during the middle kingdom in Egypt reflective thinking treated the various gods as manifestations of Ra, and among the priesthood there was an esoteric pantheism.

The trend toward pantheism works itself out more readily when the gods are not sharply defined in their specific character and attributes. This was the case with the Vedic gods, since the qualities of one were often transferred to another. In the avatars of Vishnu one god assumes many divine forms. So by an easy process of transition the pantheism of the Upanishads and the Vedanta is reached. Here pantheism is thoroughgoing. All cosmic and psychical phenomena are unified in the one real Being: Brahman-Atman, the soul and the Absolute, are identical. *Tat tvam asi:* "that art thou." The multiplicity of the phenomenal world is only Maya or illusion; it disappears with knowledge. In contrast the clear-cut gods of Greece resisted a process of fusion. The Stoic pantheism, which identified Zeus with the universal and immanent reason or Logos, was rather an independent speculative theory than a development of Greek religion.

Religious pantheism is in the main a reflective development resulting from rational demands. If consistent, it is not a working religious creed, for it abolishes the religious relation by reducing it to an identity. (*See* PANTHEISM.)

(2) *Mysticism.*

Mysticism, like pantheism, in the strict sense is a phenomenon of highly developed religion. Individualistic in character, it is the outcome of a longing for intimate communion with the Divine. The mystery religions show a mystic tendency in their doctrine of union with the god through the sacramental meal. The same is perhaps true of Hindu Yoga which is a method of inducing religious ecstasy by concentration and absorption of mind. The Yogin became for others a kind of supernatural being. But mysticism proper is a conscious reaction against the externality of a merely intellectual knowledge of God: its goal is a perfect union with the Deity in which the element of difference implied in thinking is overcome. The Neoplatonic union of the soul with the One is a purely mystical experience. The same spiritual movement appeared within Islam in Sufism, which no doubt was influenced by Neo-Platonism. The sufi sought to purge his mind of all that was not God, and the perfect man attained to absorption in God. The great mediaeval mystics sought the same consummation, an *unio mystica* achieved by transcending the form of thinking. Mysticism is loosely related to official and institutional religion. Possessing a "more excellent way," it can dispense with the recognized means of mediation. But if it invests religion with a new warmth and intimacy, it is deficient as a social power. And mysticism is always exposed to the danger of falling into pantheism. (*See* MYSTICISM.)

(3) *Monotheism.*

Monotheism is a late phenomenon of religion. The hypothesis of a primitive monotheism lacks foundation, and is intrinsically improbable. Beyond doubt the spirit and meaning of religion attain their fullest and best expression in some form of monotheistic faith. Polytheism disperses the religious interest: intimacy of worship and the confidence of trust are only possible when there is one, and only one, object of religious devotion. The trend towards monotheism was gradual, and it had preparatory stages. The first stage was what is called monarchianism. After the analogy of human society one deity is exalted above the rest, and becomes the king of the gods. A familiar example is the Homeric Zeus who stands supreme over all the gods and looks down on the conflicts of mortals among whom his will is accomplished. (Διὸς δ' ἐτελείετο βουλή.) The Babylonian Marduk and the Egyptian Ra are illustrations of the same phenomenon of one deity attaining a position of undisputed sovereignty. A rather more advanced stage is that of monolatry, where other gods are admitted to exist, but worship is reserved for one. This we find in Hebrew religion in the pre-prophetic period.

The earliest attempt—an abortive one—to introduce a pure monotheism, in this case a solar monotheism, is that of the Egyptian Amenhotep IV. in the XIVth century B.C. More impressive is the monotheism of Zarathustra, perhaps some eight hundred years before our era. This monotheism rests on a comprehensive view of the world. The physical and moral order derive from the one God, his will is right, and all the pure elements of life belong to his kingdom. The pronounced dualism of the later Avesta is absent from the prophet's teaching. With the eighth century prophets of Israel the earlier monolatry became a true monotheism. This monotheistic universalism finds its clearest utterance in the work of Deutero-Isaiah. From this heritage of Hebrew religion Christianity derived its pure monotheism, and the same influence is manifest in the monotheism of Islam.

Monotheism is the ripest expression of the religious consciousness. It rests on the conviction that the ethical and religious values must have a sufficient ground, and this is the one God on whom all existence and value depend.

VII. REVELATION AND THEOLOGY

Belief in the communication of truth to man from a divine source is common in religions. This kind of communication usually concerns the future, and may be subject to a process of interpretation. Hence the practices of divination, the reading of omens and auspices, and star-lore. But the communication may be in and to the individual, for instance through visions and dreams.

(1) *Revelation.*

More especially is revelation thought to come through inspiration or "possession" by a divine power. The words spoken by the individual thus "possessed" are identified with the utterances of the god. The Greek Apollo was the god of prophecy, and the words spoken by his inspired priestess at Delphi were deemed to be the authentic voice of the god himself. The religious value of revelation depends on the character of the deity who is believed to reveal; and it is the consciousness of ethical values leading to an ethical idea of deity which purifies the content of revelation. Revelation in the large and comprehensive sense is linked with monotheistic religion. So Zarathustra proclaimed the message communicated to him by Ahura Mazda, and Mohammed in his

visions had the truth revealed to him by Allan. The divine word came to the prophets of Israel, and the preface to their message was, "Thus saith the Lord." What they spoke Jahveh had caused them to know. At this level revelation centres in an experience or illumination within. But these inspired utterances were afterwards written down and collected: in the form of sacred books they came to be regarded as objective statements of divine truth. Hence the claims made for the Avesta, the Veda, the Koran, and the Old and New Testaments. Books which were accepted as statements of revealed truth naturally became authoritative, and as expressing authoritatively the content of a religion they furnished a basis for theology.

(2) *Theology.*

Theology grows out of the beliefs contained in an historic religion: it is an endeavour to state what is involved in a definite religious type of experience in general propositions or doctrines. The earliest anticipation of this is the myth framed to explain the meaning of something done in the cult. Theology is not detached like speculation, it is a natural and necessary outgrowth from the life of religion itself. It is the product of a mature religion, and commonly has its basis in the sacred books which record its religious experience. We find theological developments in Judaism and Buddhism, but in a more complete form in Islam and in Christianity. The Islamic and the Christian theologies claim to interpret the authoritative revelation contained in their sacred scriptures. In both instances the growth of theology was stimulated by the presence of beliefs judged to be heretical. The Mutazalite movement, with its doctrines of faith and free-will and its criticism of tradition, impelled the orthodox party in Islam to define the true doctrine of Allah and his attributes. In a like way the Gnostic heresies provoked the growth of a Christian theology which sought to expound the doctrines involved in Christian faith and practice. The Islamic conception of religion, however, is too much interwoven with what is external and political to furnish a favourable field for theological development. Christianity, on the other hand, has developed a body of religious experience of a wealth and amplitude capable of sustaining an impressive body of doctrine.

The function of theology is primarily to interpret. As contrasted with speculation it leans on authoritative revelation, and stands in organic relation to a specific historic religion. (*See* THEOLOGY.)

VIII. ETHICS AND ESCHATOLOGY

The ethical element is of fundamental importance in determining the quality of a religion: it is a powerful factor in elevating the object of worship, the religious relation, and the religious life. At the pre-deistic stage the sacred is interpenetrated with magical beliefs, and ethical principles have their lowly precursor in the sanctity of tribal custom. When through the growth of social culture the moral virtues are recognized as values, they are made to qualify the character of the gods.

(1) *Ethics.*

The process may not be easy when the deity has a pronounced natural basis, but still it does occur, as in the case of the Vedic Varuna and the Babylonian Shamash. On the other hand, the Persian Ahura Mazda became a definitely ethical god who demands pure living and right thinking. At a later date Mithra was revered as the god of truth and loyalty. The Greek Zeus acquired moral functions, and Δική, or Justice, was proclaimed to be his daughter. The feeling for the moral element in religion appears in the saying of Euripides: "If the gods do aught that is shameful, they are no gods." A profound appreciation of the moral values is seen in the Hebrew prophets who passionately declared that Jahveh is a righteous God who demands righteousness in his people. And when men cherish the conviction that the divine Power is righteous, the efficacy of sacrifice is made to depend on moral conditions.

Through the interpenetration of ethics with religion the sphere of the sacred is enlarged, and the moral life becomes an aspect of the religious vocation. Moral laws rank as divine commands, and ethical duty as a religious obligation. On the other hand, when the notion of divine personality is weak or lacking, ethics inevitably assume a worldly or a negative character. Chinese religious ethics, for instance, founds on the idea of Tao or world-order, and man's duty is to reflect this order in his life. The ethical ideal is one of conformity, propriety and measure. A like utilitarianism is present in the Roman *pietas,* the knowledge of the *jus divinum* which enables a man to keep on profitable terms with the divine powers. The negative conception of ethics is strongly marked in Buddhism, which, in its original form, had no deity. The ideal of the Arahat is merely an ascetic discipline by which the dominion of desire and sense may be extinguished and Nirvana attained. In strong contrast is Christian ethics which rests on an ethical monotheism. Here the ideal is positive, the development of man's ethical life as a member of the Kingdom of God.

(2) *Eschatology.*

The problem of eschatology is the ultimate destiny of man and the world. It is a problem which lies in the background of the religious consciousness, though eschatological motives may powerfully affect the working of religion. Thus eschatology looms large in the old Egyptian, the Christian and the Islamic religions, but it plays a feeble part in the Babylonian, the old Hebrew and the early Greek religions. There is no side of religion where the survival of old ideas is more apparent, or where the presence of inconsistent elements is more conspicuous. This is intelligible; for eschatological ideas do not lend themselves to verification in religious experience, and they offer an ample field for religious imagination.

Primitive eschatological ideas gather round the fate of the dead, and are unleavened by ethical elements. Two factors promote the growth of eschatology in higher religions, a quickened moral consciousness and the sense of the value of the individual. If ethical ideas, however, be cast in a utilitarian mould, the eschatological interest may be slender; and even though they are of a higher order, as in Hebrew Prophetic religion, the merging of the individual in the people as the religious unit has the same result. Post-Exilic Judaism gained a new sense of the value of the individual, and felt the need of retribution, and this led to decided eschatological developments. In Buddhism, where ethics are negative and personality an obstruction rather than a value, eschatological doctrine is nebulous in the extreme.

Of the ethical ideas which promote eschatology the most prominent is that of justice, for it directly suggests the notion of future rewards and punishments. Justice, it is felt, is only imperfectly done on earth. The Osiris-Religion of Egypt figured the soul of the dead man ushered into the judgment-hall of Osiris, where his deeds were weighed in a balance. Those who pass the test go to serve Osiris in the fields of Earu. In the Avesta, Shraoshi, the guide of souls, is said to lead the just over the heavenly bridge to the gate of paradise. Orphism taught that the initiated were rewarded by a happy life in the Elysian Fields, while the wicked were cast into Tartarus. In the Persian, Christian, and Islamic religions, along with the judgment of the individual there is conjoined the idea of a world-judgment and the final separation of the good from the wicked.

The fuller development of eschatological doctrines belongs to the ethical and redemptive religions. But no religion has done this consistently, and eschatology remains the most backward aspect of religion. Here the material and the ethical, the sensuous and the spiritual, are often incongruously blended, and old beliefs survive in an alien environment. The Islamic eschatology, for instance, is on a lower level than that of a religion of salvation. And Christian eschatology, at least in its traditional form, is only imperfectly spiritualized. The problem of a consistent eschatology is a difficult one. (*See* ESCHATOLOGY; IMMORTALITY.)

IX. CLASSIFICATION OF RELIGIONS

Various attempts have been made to classify religions, but with only partial success, and there is no generally accepted scheme. Every religion is a complex of many elements, and there is no one specific feature which adequately characterizes it. One of the earlier classifications is that of Hegel into Nature-Religions, Religions of Spiritual Individuality, and Absolute Religion. But he arbitrarily groups together very disparate materials, and in the light of modern knowledge the scheme is unworkable. Edward Caird's revision into Objective, Subjective, and Absolute or Universal Religion is less open to this objection, but it is too vague and too much dependent on a particular philosophic construction of religion. Tiele adopts a very broad classification into Nature-Religions and Ethical Religions, while Siebeck groups religions into Primitive Religions, Morality-Religions, and Redemptive Religions. The latter scheme is certainly suggestive, though the distinction between ethical religions and redemptive religions can hardly be carried out consistently. Even the broad distinction between natural and ethical religion would have to be applied rather arbitrarily.

In the classification of religions into Tribal, National, and Universal, the line of demarcation is much more distinct and can be more easily used. But it may be objected to this classification that it is based on a principle which gives no clue to the character and content of the religions. Moreover it may be said that no religion is *de facto* universal. And from an evolutionary standpoint it is a defect in a classification that it ignores the principle of valuation.

The complexity and variety of the materials render a complete and consistent classification impracticable. But it is always possible to apply different criteria in surveying the religious field. Religions may be grouped according to their conception of the Divine, according to the types of piety they foster, or according to the ideal after which they strive. But such classifications will be merely provisional: though suitable for the purpose on hand, they cannot claim to be comprehensive and final.

BIBLIOGRAPHY.—Monographs dealing with particular religions will be found under the respective headings. The literature on religion is vast, and only a few of the works likely to be useful are noted here.
(a) *Histories of Religion.*
The most compact and complete history, embodying the results of recent research, is the *Lehrbuch der Religionsgeschichte,* edited by Bertholet and Lehmann, 2 vols. 1925. G. F. Moore, *History of Religions,* 2 vols., 1914, 1920. A. Menzies, *History of Religion* (1st ed., 1895, and later editions). Toy, *Introduction to the History of Religions* (1913). The *Religionsgeschichtliche Lesebuch* (1908), ed. by Bertholet, gives a translation of extracts from the chief religious classics. A new edition is appearing. There is also the *Textbuch zur Religionsgeschichte* (1912), by E. Lehmann.
(b) *The General Development of Religion.*
E. Caird, *The Evolution of Religion* (1894). Tiele, *Elements of the Science of Religion* (2 vols., 1897 & 1899). Bousset, *Das Wesen der Religion* (1904); Galloway, *Principles of Religious Development* (1909). King, *The Development of Religion* (1910). Farnell, *Greece and Babylon* (1911), and *Attributes of God* (1925). Wundt, *Mythus und Religion* (1909). G. F. Moore, *The Birth and Growth of Religion* (1923). Some works of more restricted scope are valuable for the light they cast on religious development, *e.g.* W. R. Smith's *Religion of the Semites* (3rd ed. 1927), Nilsson's *History of Greek Religion* (1925), and Warde Fowler's *Religious Experience of the Roman People* (1911).
(c) *Psychology and Philosophy of Religion.*
For the Psychology of Religion James's *Varieties of Religious Experience* (1902), Stratton's *Psychology of the Religious Life* (1911), Pratt's *The Religious Consciousness* (1923), will be found useful, and other works equally deserve mention.
Hegel's *Philosophie der Religion* (1840) is historically important. Among other works on the subject are those of J. Caird, Rauwenhoff, Höffding, Siebeck, Pfleiderer, Galloway and Ladd.   (G. GA.)

RELIGION, WARS OF (1562-1609).

The so-called Wars of Religion opened with the massacre of sixty Huguenots at Vassy in 1562, and ended with the declaration of the twelve years' truce between Spain and Prince Maurice of the Netherlands in 1609. They included eight civil wars in France, the revolt of the Netherlands, and a number of less important rebellions. Though outwardly religious in character, inwardly they were influenced by economic and financial causes, constituting as they did a revolt against the fiscal policy of the mediaeval papacy.

Causes and Personalities.—During the Crusades the Church became an all-controlling power, establishing its own law courts, its own tax collectors and its own prisons in nearly every European country. As long as the various kings were occupied in mastering their feudal nobility the papacy remained all-powerful, but once control over them was established the next conflict was between the more progressive of the kings and the pope. This quarrel centred round the questions of appointments, taxation, "benefit of clergy" and the interference of the pope in national government. In 1296, Edward I. of England demanded one-fifth of the personal property of the clergy, and four years later Philip the Fair of France openly quarrelled with Boniface VIII. over taxation. A religious-economic conflict then began which lasted until the peace of Westphalia in 1648.

In England, John Wycliffe began to preach reform about 1366. Eleven years later the papacy moved back from Avignon to Rome, and the whole question of papal control was thrown into the melting-pot. Then arose the question of whether a general council of Christendom was not superior to the papacy. This question gave rise to the Council of Constance in 1414, which, in 1415, condemned Hus, a Bohemian reformer influenced by Wycliffe, to be burnt. This in turn brought about the Hussite wars (1419-1436)—the forerunner of the wars of religion.

By the opening of the 16th century discontent against the Church was general, especially so in Germany, and all that was wanting were leaders. These, as is always the case during revolutionary periods, soon came to the fore. The most prominent were Erasmus, a Dutchman (1469-1536); Luther, a German (1483-1546); Zwingli, a Swiss (1484-1531), and Calvin, a Frenchman (1509-1564). Erasmus was an evolutionary, he believed in a slow and steady change; Luther was the reverse, he wanted immediate change, and his doctrine of "justification by faith" sent a thrill of horror through the Catholic Church. He was a democrat and an economist as well as a religious reformer. He attacked "indulgences," and said: "Since the pope is rich as Croesus, why does he not build St. Peter's with his own money, instead of taking that of the poor man?" In 1520 he was excommunicated, and this same year at Wittenberg he threw the Papal bull into the flames. He was of opinion that the power of the papacy rested on money, and if money were withheld in two years the papacy would vanish.

Turmoil.—The results of his teachings led to a peasants' war in Germany in 1525. In Switzerland, Zwingli (the originator of the name Protestant) attacked the Church, and the first conflict between Protestants and Catholics took place at Kappel, in 1531. In France Calvin's doctrines, based on the infallibility of the Bible in place of that of the Church and pope, gave rise to the Huguenot and Presbyterian movements. Meanwhile, in England, out of Henry VIII.'s first divorce arose a quarrel with Rome which ended in 1534 in the revolt of the English Church from the pope and in the closing of the monasteries, whereby Henry enriched himself.

The greatest part of Europe was now thrown into a spiritual and economic turmoil. On one side stood religious freedom confronted by papal infallibility, on the other fiscal control faced by papal anathema. Nations, cities, villages and families were divided. A general Council of the Church was held at Trent in 1545, but the Protestants refused to attend. The "Society of Jesus," founded by Loyola in 1538, gained strength, its scientific system of propaganda rousing the fury of the Reformed Church.

Hostilities in France.—The first clash came in France which had been stirred by the preaching of Lefevre (1450-1537). Henry II. (1547-1559) swore to extirpate the Protestants, and burnt them in hundreds. He was succeeded by his son Francis II., a boy of sixteen married to Mary Queen of Scots. As Francis was too young to rule, the duke of Guise put himself at the head of the army, and when Francis died, in 1560, the duke was reluctant to surrender his power so that a conflict soon arose between him and the Huguenots under Coligny, merging, in 1562, into the First Civil War. An indecisive battle was fought at Dreux; then two other civil wars followed, in which battles were fought at St. Denis in 1567, and Jarnac and Moncontour in 1569. These were concluded by the peace of St. Germain, according to which the Huguenots were to be tolerated, Coligny being received on friendly terms by Charles IX. of France and his mother, Catharine de' Medici.

The Catholic party of the Guises, determining to put an end to this friendship, plotted and carried out the massacre of St. Bartholomew on August 23, 1572. The result was the Fourth Civil

War which was followed by the fifth, sixth, seventh and eighth. The last of these known as the war of the three Henrys—Henry III., Henry of Navarre and Henry of Guise—ended with the assassination of the first and third, leaving Henry of Navarre, now Henry IV., the national hero. In 1590, he won the battles of Arques and Ivry, and to put an end to the war, in 1593, re-entered the Catholic Church. In 1598, he issued the Edict of Nantes by which the Calvinists were permitted to worship as they chose, and to be eligible to hold government appointments. Meanwhile an even more terrible war was being waged in the Netherlands.

Spain and the Netherlands.—In the second half of the 16th century, the chief ally of the pope was Philip II., son of the emperor Charles V. Charles though a firm Catholic was not a fanatic; Philip's attitude was very different, for he was willing to sacrifice everything so long as the Protestants were exterminated. In 1555 Charles abdicated, handing over his Habsburg possessions to his brother Ferdinand, and Spain, the American Colonies, the Two Sicilies and the Netherlands to his son Philip. For ten years the Dutch suffered Philip's rule. Then in 1566, five hundred of the nobles protested against his policy. Thereupon Philip sent the duke of Alva to the Low Countries. William of Orange fled to Germany and thousands of Flemish weavers sought refuge in England. Alva's administration was a veritable reign of terror. Though not unaccustomed to persecution, for Charles V. had burnt many of them, the people revolted and found their leader in William, Prince of Orange and Count of Nassau (1533-1584), who in 1568 collected together a small army and opened the wars of religion with Spain. Defeated again and again he was never conquered, and in 1572 the northern provinces of Holland chose William as their governor.

After six years of tyranny Alva was recalled, but this did not improve things as his leaderless soldiers committed every possible atrocity. The north, guided by William, now refused to recognise Philip as their king, and the Union of Utrecht followed in 1579, by which the United Provinces were constituted. Two years later these provinces declared themselves independent of Spain. Philip realising that William was the heart and soul of the revolt offered a patent of nobility and a large sum of money to anyone who would assassinate him, with the result that the great patriot was shot at Delft in 1584.

His son, Maurice of Nassau (1567-1625) succeeded him, and was made stadtholder. When Queen Elizabeth of England decided to send troops to his assistance, Philip was so enraged that he determined on the conquest of England, and, in 1588, equipped and despatched the "Armada." Its defeat and destruction as well as the failing resources of Spain were of the greatest assistance to Maurice, who soon showed himself to be a general far in advance of any of his contemporaries. A great campaign was fought in 1597. From then onwards to 1609 battles were waged and sieges undertaken, and though Maurice was by no means always successful, as was notably the case in 1605, the power of Spain was definitely on the decline, and in 1609 a twelve years' truce was concluded and the United Provinces took their place in the European system "as a free and independent State."

This truce was but an interlude in the struggle for freedom, for in 1618 the Thirty Years' War (q.v.) broke out, and it was not until it ended with the Treaty of Westphalia in 1648, that once and for all the semi-religious conflict of nearly 100 years was brought to an end, Europe emerging out of the night into the daylight of modern history.

BIBLIOGRAPHY.—The bibliography of this period is extensive, and the reader is referred to *The Cambridge Modern History*, vol. iii., 1904, and especially to the full list of books at the end of the volume.

(J. F. C. F.)

RELIGIOUS AND MEMORIAL ARCHITECTURE.

The earliest religious buildings were not so much congregational as shelters for the mysteries or provisions for the rite, sometimes consisting merely of an altar; and the earliest memorials were a stone or a mound. Even the Egyptian temple, with its court guarded by pylons or towers and approaching avenue of sphinxes or colossal human figures, was a sanctuary for kings and priests rather than a place of worship for the people; and the pyramids were the tombs of kings, furnished with the necessities of the future life (*see* EGYPTIAN ARCHITECTURE). The Greek temple, with its central shrine for a statue of the god or goddess, porticoes to front and rear, and flanking colonnades, was more like a place of worship as we understand it to-day. It was at least a public building. Greek memorials were generally tombs (*see* GREEK ARCHITECTURE). The Roman temple, of which the construction was determined by the blending of the Greek columnar system with the Etruscan arch, came nearer than the Greek to the Christian church in plan; the *cella*—used as a treasury or as a museum of sculpture and frequently occupying the whole width of the building—corresponding to the chancel or sanctuary, and the deep portico and steps of the entrance anticipating the west front. A favourite form of Roman memorial, reflecting a proud spirit, was the triumphal arch (*see* ROMAN ARCHITECTURE).

Early Christian and Mediaeval.—It is probable that the earliest Christian churches, in countries under Persian rule, were humble structures of wood, clay, or at the most brick concrete, in the form of a shrine for an altar where two or three might be gathered together. Such churches, of which remains have been found in Syria, Palestine, Armenia and north Africa, were concentric in plan—that is to say, square, circular, octagonal or cruciform—and roofed with a dome. With the conversion of Rome to Christianity in the 4th century, and the establishment of Constantine's new capital at Byzantium, a more congregational form of church was evolved by adjustments between the domed, concentric shrine and the plan derived from the Roman basilica, or hall of justice. In the Eastern empire the interactions between East and West were extremely complicated, and authorities still differ about the respective shares of Greek, oriental and Roman influence in forming the religious architecture that we call Byzantine. The result, however, was a square, circular, octagonal or cruciform church of brick and concrete, with a central space covered by the principal dome, and arms or extensions covered by subsidiary domes. One arm was provided with an apse for the altar—now removed from the centre of the building—and another with a narthex, or porch. Decoration took the form of a continuous sheathing or "skin" of marble and mosaic. St. Sophia, Constantinople, and St. Mark's, Venice, are famous surviving examples.

In the Western empire development was simpler, and the earliest Christian churches in Rome itself were copies or even adaptations of Roman buildings, frequently embodying fragments of pagan temples in their construction, following, with internal modifications, the plan of the basilica. The usual arrangement of basilican churches was that of nave and aisles, divided by arcades, with a semi-circular apse for the altar and a choir enclosed by low screen walls at one end, and a covered narthex, or porch, preceded by an open court, or atrium, at the other. From the basilica, with some reflection from the East, was evolved the form known as Romanesque. The addition of transepts and the prolongation of the sanctuary resulted in a cruciform plan, and the flat wooden roof of the basilica was gradually exchanged for vaulting in stone. In northern Italy conditions favoured a mixed style, so that it is sometimes difficult to say whether a particular building should be described as Byzantine or Romanesque, but in passing down the Rhine and extending into France and Germany Romanesque became more clearly defined, reaching England finally in the form we know as Norman. (*See* BYZANTINE AND ROMANESQUE ARCHITECTURE.)

Gothic, which may be dated from the 12th century, proceeded logically from Romanesque by the substitution of the pointed for the round arch and the development of rib vaulting—changes which enabled unequal spans to be vaulted to the same height and smaller units of inferior materials to be used for filling the spaces between the ribs. With the progress of Gothic the onus of stability tended to be put more and more upon the stone skeleton, with its elaborate system of thrust and counterthrust, the downward pressure of the nave vaulting being met externally by buttresses and flying buttresses, while the inactive wall-spaces were pierced by larger and larger traceried window openings filled with stained glass. Architecturally the Gothic church was a collaboration of many kinds of craftsmen—masons, carvers, painters and glaziers—organized into guilds and working more or less "freehand" under a master mason, and ecclesiastically it was adapted to the requirements of a powerful priesthood. Its characters can be studied to advantage in Chartres and Reims cathedrals in France, and Westminster Abbey and Canterbury and Wells cathedrals in England.

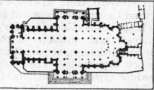

FROM BAUDOT AND PERRAULT, "CATHÉDRALES DE FRANCE" (LAURENS)

FIG. 1.—PLAN OF CHARTRES CATHEDRAL

Gothic memorials were almost exclusively religious, in such forms as "Eleanor" and market crosses (*see* GOTHIC ARCHITECTURE). In the 20th century the Gothic, because of its aspiring verticality, has sometimes been adapted to tall, non-religious buildings (*see* ARCHITECTURE).

Renaissance.—In Northern Europe, at any rate, the Renaissance and the Reformation went hand in hand in deciding the form and character of churches. As was natural, the revival of Roman architecture began in Italy, where the tradition survived, and it gradually spread to the rest of Europe with local modifications due to the resistance of native styles. For our purposes the critical example is St. Paul's cathedral, designed by Sir Christopher Wren and built between 1675 and 1710. Disliking Gothic, which he called "barbarous," Wren observed that the chief requirement of the Reformed religion was a preaching space or auditorium. His first design for St. Paul's was a Greek cross in plan, and though clerical opposition compelled the adoption of a Latin cross he carried out his ideas to some extent in the great space under the dome at the crossing of the transepts. His other city churches, of which St. Stephen, Walbrook, and St. Mary-le-Bow are examples, were frankly rectangular sermon halls with at most a shallow recess for the communion table. The plan of church introduced by Wren persisted through the 18th century, as may be seen in St. Mary, Woolnoth, by Wren's pupil Hawksmoor, and St. Martin-in-the-Fields and St. Mary-le-Strand, by James Gibbs.

Even on the Continent, in countries untouched by the Reformation, the revival of Roman architecture restored a similar plan, as we see in the Pantheon and the churches of St. Sulpice and the Madeleine, Paris. In Italy and Spain the Renaissance passed into Baroque, with its free handling of form without reference to construction, and florid ornament, characters which have been associated with the religious movement known as the Counter-Reformation (*see* BAROQUE ARCHITECTURE). The memorials of the Renaissance period are chiefly sculptured tombs, in which Christian and classical sentiment are blended (*see* RENAISSANCE ARCHITECTURE).

In England the general tendency of the Renaissance in church designing was interrupted by the Gothic revival. Its earliest phase, like that of the Renaissance itself, appears to have been purely literary and romantic, but as time went on it became associated with the definitely religious Oxford Movement of High Anglicanism. Contributing causes were undoubtedly the scientific materialism of the 19th century, which sharpened and stiffened the religious attitude in opposition, and the observed effects of the industrial revolution, which made men like Ruskin look for a remedy in the revival of handicrafts (*see* MODERN ARCHITECTURE: *18th and 19th Centuries*).

FROM BIRCH, "LONDON CHURCHES OF THE 17TH AND 18TH CENTURIES" (BATSFORD)

FIG. 2.—PLAN OF ST. MARY-LE-BOW

The Orient.—The many examples of religious and memorial architecture in the countries of Asia are treated in the articles CHINESE ARCHITECTURE; INDIAN ARCHITECTURE; JAPANESE ARCHITECTURE; MOHAMMEDAN ARCHITECTURE. It is interesting to note here that the aspiring quality of the Gothic is also expressed in religious architecture in the Orient.

THE MODERN PERIOD

For present purposes the modern period may be regarded as the last 60 years, with special emphasis upon the first half of the 20th century. When considering the causes which led to the more practical designing of churches after the Gothic revival we are inclined to give first place to the decline of materialism as a respectable philosophy and the consequent easing of the conflict between science and religion. Pressure removed, there was not the same need for the church to insist upon the outward forms of its past. At the same time there was a change in the spirit of industry. It began to be recognized that though craftsmanship—in the mediaeval sense—could not be revived, self-interest required that mechanical skill should be given its best opportunity. The result, in religious architecture, was a broader system of planning, to the actual requirements of the religion of the day rather than to advertise its historical claims, and a more intelligent use of the mechanical skill that survived, instead of a hankering after a craftsmanship impossible to restore.

Great Britain.—The first important result of the new spirit in religious architecture in Great Britain was the Roman Catholic cathedral of Westminster, designed by John Francis Bentley (1839–1902) and begun in 1894. Bentley himself would have preferred a Gothic design, but several good reasons were given for the Byzantine building decided upon: a wide nave and a view of the sanctuary best adapted to the congregational needs of a metropolitan cathedral; economy—since the whole space could be covered and the whole building erected, apart from decoration and ornament, which in other styles would form a substantial and costly part of the structure itself; avoidance of hopeless competition with Westminster Abbey; an opportunity to suggest an international character by the use of a style associated with inclusive primitive Christianity up to the 9th century. Externally Westminster cathedral is remarkable for its tall campanile, and for the bold use of brick and stone in alternating bands. The interior consists of a vast nave of three bays, 60 ft. square, each surmounted by a saucer-shaped concrete dome. A fourth bay, with a more elaborate dome, 52 ft. in diameter and pierced for the admission of light, forms the sanctuary, and behind it is the apse, with a raised retro-choir visible from the whole of the nave. Each bay of the nave is divided by lesser piers and again by monolith columns, forming an arcaded aisle.

With Liverpool cathedral, designed by Sir Giles Gilbert Scott, R.A. (b. 1880) at the age of 22, and begun in 1904, there was a return to Gothic, but Gothic with a difference. Liverpool cathedral is an example of designing in mass instead of in line, the style being a free interpretation of Decorated or 14th century Gothic (*see* DECORATED PERIOD) and the material a warm red

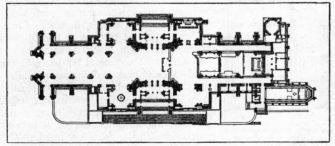

FIG. 3.—PLAN OF LIVERPOOL CATHEDRAL

sandstone, with dressings of lighter stone. Standing on the summit of a rocky mass, St. James's Mount, in the heart of the city, the building when completed will consist of a central square space rising into a great tower crowned with an octagonal lantern, with eastern and western transepts and two oblong extensions, nearly equal in length, forming the nave and choir. In a side view the central mass formed by the tower and transepts will be absolutely, and the whole building nearly, symmetrical, the choir having a different termination to that of the nave. A striking feature of Liverpool cathedral is the great size of the bays which make up

the nave and choir—three only occupying the space which in older buildings would be divided into something nearer ten. Each bay is lighted by a single two-light window, and the aisles are reduced to passage-ways through the return walls, continuous with the buttresses outside, which divide the bays.

In the space of a short article dealing with the modern religious and memorial architecture of the world it is not possible to select more than a few significant examples, preferably those with the most modern characteristics. From this point of view there is a special interest in churches associated with town-planning schemes (*see* TOWN AND CITY PLANNING). Earliest in order of date are the church of St. Jude's-on-the-Hill and the free church in the Hampstead garden suburb, designed by Sir Edwin Lutyens R.A. The strongly domestic flavour of these, with their deep tiled roofs and cornices at the level of those of the surrounding houses, is in keeping with the communal ideals of a garden suburb. Naturally it is in the neighbourhood of London, with its rapid growth of population, that some of the most characteristically modern churches are to be found. St. Catherine Coleman, Hammersmith, designed by Robert Atkinson F.R.I.B.A., is essentially a rectangular auditorium with short chancel, both barrel vaulted by means of steel arches embedded in concrete, faced externally with London "stock" bricks and roofed with pantiles, and finished off internally with a surface of rough plaster. The stylish allusion is Byzantine, which appears to be the natural consequence of brick and concrete building for congregational needs. Within a few hundred yards of St. Catherine Coleman there is an exceptionally beautiful church, St. Saviour's, designed by Edward Maufe F.R.I.B.A. for the Royal Association in Aid of the Deaf and Dumb. In this church, which is of brick in a free interpretation of Decorated or 14th century Gothic, everything is adapted to sight to the exclusion of hearing. There is no organ and no provision for a choir, the clergy seats being in two "ambos" set at an angle to keep the occupants in full view, the nave walls splay in to the chancel, the floor rakes as in a theatre, and there is a western gallery. A feature of the interior is restful colour decoration.

St. Barnabas mission church, Dalston, designed by Prof. C. H. Reilly F.R.I.B.A. and built about 1910, is an example of an urban building so closely surrounded that it can be seen only as an interior. This, of London "stock" bricks, is of almost startling grandeur; the brick being used, not as by Bentley at Westminster as a support for marble sheathing, but for its own decorative effect; the full colour value being brought out by the use of white metal instead of brass for candlesticks, chancel gates and other fittings. Unlike most modern churches below cathedral rank, St. Barnabas has what amounts to a choir, formed by the crossing of the shallow transepts, saucer-domed in concrete above and separated from the barrel-vaulted nave of three bays by a wooden screen of four columns supporting the rood beam. The special point about St. Andrew's, Ilford, designed by Sir Herbert Baker, A.R.A., is that it is an exercise in brick and timber construction, giving full opportunity to the native craftsmanship in these materials, the only stone employed being in the chancel flooring, the corbels supporting the roof timbers and the font. Characteristically modern is the addition of decorative details by prominent artists and craftsmen; an altar and reredos carved by Lawrence Turner, a triptych painted by Colin Gill, a lunette of glazed pottery—in the baptistery—by the Poole Potteries, and, externally, a bronze figure of the angel of peace by Charles Wheeler.

Mention must be made of a few other recent churches in England of special architectural interest. In the neighbourhood of Liverpool and elsewhere Sir Giles Gilbert Scott has designed several churches in his characteristic manner of moulded Gothic—as it might be called in distinction from the stone skeleton construction of the middle ages—St. Paul's, Derby lane, Liverpool, being a good example.

As an instance of planning to requirements, combining the maximum of space and unimpeded movement, sight and hearing with a dignified architectural effect, special mention must be made of the new church at Hindley, Lancashire, designed by Robert Atkinson F.R.I.B.A

CHURCHES AND MEMORIALS

Top left: Kruiskerk (Church of the Cross), Amstelveen, Neth.; Marius Duintjer, architect. More than 900 small windows covering three walls substitute for the few large windows in conventional church design

Top centre: Memorial in a cemetery at Milan, It.; Belgiojoso, Peressutti and Rogers, architects. Constructed of steel and marble, the cube presents a design of the cross on each face

Top right: The Church of the Advent, Copenhagen, Den.; Erik Moller, architect. A single square room designed to serve all functions of the church

Centre left: Christ Evangelical Lutheran church, Minneapolis, Minn.; Saarinen, Saarinen and Associates, architects. Design was dictated by the scientific demands for the best in acoustics, lighting and heating

Centre right: St. Josef's church, Hindenburg, Ger.; D. Böhm, architect. An 11th-century church plan adapted to a 20th-century design

Bottom right: Protestant church, Basle, Switz.; Egender and Burckhardt, architects. A feature of design was the use of trees planted along a paved terrace and flanking the entrance to the church

With the exception of Westminster cathedral which has already been described all the buildings we have been discussing belong to the Established Church of England. To a certain extent the characters described—congregational plan, and construction in terms of contemporary labour and most readily available materials—are common to the modern churches of all creeds and sects, but every creed has its particular requirements. Naturally the Roman Catholic Church puts the emphasis upon its Roman tradition, with a preference for the basilica form, and the somewhat exuberant Baroque of the Brompton oratory, by Herbert A. K. Gribble, finds more sober echoes elsewhere. Beyond dispensing with the chancel the Protestant Free Churches of England do not follow the lead, peculiarly suitable to their requirements, given to them by Wren, but rather surprisingly cling to Gothic, though here and there, as in the Broadway Congregational church, Hammersmith, by Cecil M. Quilter, the plan of the sermon hall is frankly adopted.

Christian Science, however, has followed a bolder policy, and all its churches in England are designed as auditoriums, with a platform for the "readers" and a screened organ chamber in place of a chancel, and generally a raking floor, as in a theatre. One of the most recent examples, the Eleventh Church of Christ, Nutford place, Bryanston square, by Oswald P. Milne F.R.I.B.A., seems to have arrived at a perfect adjustment between form and requirement, and is in every respect an admirable building, proclaiming at a glance its purpose and construction as an auditorium with a very wide span of roof, buttressed at each corner by a tower-like bastion or pavilion containing a staircase. The interior, which will seat 900, is designed to allow complete circulation of the building without disturbing the congregation.

In memorial architecture the most extensive work in England during the period under review is the memorial to Queen Victoria, in front of Buckingham palace, designed by Sir Aston Webb R.A. Otherwise the memorial architecture of the period resolves itself inevitably into war memorials. Of these by far the most important, by reason of its wide appeal, is the cenotaph in Whitehall, designed by Sir Edwin Lutyens R.A., the stone of remembrance by the same architect, and the memorial cross by Sir Reginald Blomfield R.A. Modifications and combinations of these three architectural forms have been used as war memorials in several provincial centres.

Many war memorials, however, have taken the form of halls and chapels, either as new structures or as additions to existing buildings. The Scottish national war memorial is a reconstruction of part of Edinburgh castle, designed by Sir Robert Lorimer, A.R.A. On the site of an old barrack, and improving the general outline of the castle from a distance, the memorial is in the form of the letter E, with a heptagonal shrine, containing the memorial casket supported by a marble table, projecting at the back in line with the middle limb, which thus forms a porch allowing a vista into the shrine. The stem of the E forms a gallery of honour, with a bay for each of the 12 Scottish regiments; and, by means of stained glass, moulded bronze, carved stone and wood, metalwork and painting, the place is made a museum of illustrative symbolism—not only every type of soldier and the women's services, but even animals and carrier pigeons and the actual arms and materials used in the War being recorded.

Though not on English soil, reference must be made to the several important memorials designed by English architects for war areas in France and Belgium. Three in particular claim attention: the memorial to the missing at St. Quentin, by Sir Edwin Lutyens R.A.; the Menin gate memorial to the missing, Ypres, by Sir Reginald Blomfield R.A.; and the memorial to the missing, Ploegsteert wood, by H. Chalton Bradshaw, A.R.I.B.A. The last is a circular pavilion, the others taking the form of the triumphal arch with the provision of extensive surfaces for the inscription of names by means of vaulted passages.

The British Dominions.—With one exception religious architecture in the oversea dominions of the British empire cannot be said to show any very interesting modern developments. The noteworthy exception is Africa, chiefly through the initiative of Sir Herbert Baker A.R.A., whose cathedrals of Cape Town, Pretoria and Salisbury, Rhodesia, and other churches, show a most interesting adaptation to local materials and conditions, working out, at Pretoria and Salisbury, as a spacious Romanesque-Byzantine type of building, with the exclusion of light except that from comparatively small clerestorey windows. Among works in memorial architecture produced by or for the dominions must be named the "All India" war memorial, Delhi, in the form of a triumphal arch, by Sir Edwin Lutyens R.A.; the South African war memorial, Delville wood, France, by Sir Herbert Baker A.R.A.; and the Australian war memorial, Villers-Bretonneux, France, by William Lucas. The national war memorial for New Zealand is to take the form of an art gallery and museum, with a campanile and a hall of memories. In the mandatory country of Palestine there is the Jerusalem war cemetery, by Sir John Burnet R.A.

The Continent of Europe.—During the last 50 years, religious and memorial architecture all over the world has been moulded by the same influences: a less dogmatic attitude in religion and science alike, a decline in the social authority of the churches, a growth of the democratic spirit, and a progressive mechanization of labour accompanied by the discovery of new materials and methods of construction.

In France the modern period may be said to open with the basilica of the Sacré Coeur, Paris, designed by Abadie and begun in 1875. Standing on the summit of the Butte Montmartre, it forms a conspicuous object in the northern approach to Paris, and closes impressively the vistas of streets ascending from the main boulevards. Romanesque-Byzantine in style, the Sacré Coeur represents the first important break with the Renaissance tradition in France. Otherwise recent religious architecture in France is remarkable chiefly for daring experiments in reinforced concrete. The best known examples are the churches of St. Denis, Paris, Notre Dame, Raincy, and St. Thérèse, Montmagny, by the brothers Auguste and Gustave Perret, in which an attempt has been made to work out forms proceeding logically from the material itself, used constructively, with very slender internal supports, and an elaborate tracery—or rather trellis—of concrete at the windows. In the Byzantine church at Vincennes, by J. Marast, which is faced externally with brick, the vaulting is carried out with deep concrete ribs, dividing the roof into panels, and dispensing with intermediate supports. Other interesting examples of religious architecture in France are the church of St. François, St. Etienne, entirely of reinforced concrete, the columns being supported by screw-jacks to allow compensation for movements caused by mining operations below, and the tower of St. Louis, Villemomble, by Paul Tournon, with sculptured decoration in concrete.

In Germany also, the chief interest is in the use of concrete, as in the churches by Prof. Dominikus Böhm at Neu-Ulm and Bischofsheim, near Mainz. In them concrete has been employed more solidly than in the French examples, with more emphasis upon the plastic mass of concrete than upon the steel supports, in a system of parabolic vaulting which, with its projecting ribs, intersecting to form complicated patterns in the roof, suggests a true translation of Gothic principles into the new material. Other recent German churches to be noted are St. Gabriel's, Munich, by O. Kurz and E. Herbert, in Byzantine-Romanesque, and the Protestant church at Ellingen, by Bestelmeyer, which is octagonal in plan, with circular galleries, and has a bulb-domed minaret or campanile.

Common to all the countries of Europe is an attempt to recover a national style from the Gothic and Classic revivals, which all have experienced in some degree, embodying the principles of both without their stylish accidents; the energy of Gothic and the order and proportion of Classic. In Holland this takes the form of a development of the native brick construction, an excellent example being the church at Bussum, by Cuypers, a domed structure with round arches and vaulting ribs in brick. Other modern churches in Holland which call for mention as formal essays in brick construction are those at The Hague, by Kropholler, Bussum, by Rueter, and Utrecht, by Slothouwer.

In Scandanavia the modern impulse appears to have originated in Denmark, where there are several interesting new churches, a stepped gable, on both tower and transepts, being a characteristic feature. The church of St. Hans Tveje, Odensee, and Grundtvig's church—associated with a housing scheme—Copenhagen, by P. V. J. Klint, are striking examples. With their tall fluted towers, ending in stepped gables, they have a curiously organ-like effect. Among smaller and simpler buildings may be named Gurre church, by Carl Brunner, the church at Aarhus, by K. Gottlieb and A. Frederiksen, and the church at Frederiksberg, by Hanning and Frederiksen.

In Sweden the national style that is emerging from the various "revivals" in response to the modern spirit appears to be —paradoxical as it may sound—a fusion of the Byzantine and the Baroque, at any rate in religious architecture, with a substitution of lean and angular forms for the full curves we associate with Baroque in the South. Two famous examples are the Saltsjöbaden church, by Ferdinand Boberg, and Högalid church, Stockholm, by Ivar Justus Tengbom. Both churches are without aisles, the Saltsjöbaden church, which contains interesting sculpture in bronze and alabaster by Carl Milles, having a polygonal apse and a single tower; while the other, which is vaulted internally, the ribs being rectangular in section, has twin towers, rather oriental in character, with bulbous domes. Masthuggs church, Gothenburg, by Sigfrid Ericson, with its massive tower and open timbered roof; Engelbrecht church, Stockholm, by L. T. Wahlman, a high-shouldered, cruciform edifice, vaulted in parabolic curves; and the small chapels by Gunnar E. Asplund and Sigurd Lerverentz, the one circular and the other like a little Corinthian temple, in the cemetery at Enskede, are other interesting buildings.

In Czechoslovakia there is a vigorous architectural revival, with such results as the Palladian basilica of St. Venceslaus, Smichov, by V. Barvitius, and the Romanesque church of Stechovice, by Kamil Hilbert.

Italy and Spain, being Catholic countries, have kept more or less on traditional lines in their religious architecture. In Italy a revival of Byzantine-Romanesque was followed by a return to Roman, of a simple and massive character, and under the present régime the Roman tradition is likely to be emphasized. Spain's most striking contribution to the modern period is the fantastic church of the Sagrada Familia, Barcelona.

As regards memorial architecture Italy provides the most important example in Europe in the memorial to Victor Emmanuel II., Rome. Designed by Count G. Sacconi and begun in 1885, it takes the form of a great loggia, with columns 48 ft. high and end pavilions, with pediments, supporting sculptured groups. In front steps ascend to a platform bearing an equestrian statue of the king. Closing a vista at the end of the Corso Umberto, it is one of the most impressive monuments ever erected to one man. All the combatant countries of Europe have their share of war memorials, taking the forms already described and generally associated with sculpture. In Sweden note must be taken of the several recent memorials, mostly in the form of fountains, by Carl Milles. Though they are the work of a sculptor they are essentially architectural in general design.

The United States.—To an extent which does not prevail in any other country religious architecture in the United States of America is affected by two conditions: the upward growth of cities, and the shading off of religious beliefs into ethical systems. The first is leading inevitably to the incorporation of places of worship in business districts or in office buildings. Projects for churches in skyscrapers like the Broadway Temple, New York, begun by the late Donn Barber have been much publicized and in some cases even built in some of the principal cities; the second creates an intermediate type of building, something between the church and the lecture or concert hall, of which the Christian Science Church may be quoted as an example. Allowing for these special conditions religious architecture in America during the last 50 years has developed on very much the same lines as in England. The "colonial" version of the type of church instituted by Wren has persisted in the Congregational and Unitarian communities, Roman Catholic churches incline to the Lombard, or Romanesque-Byzantine form, and Christian Science prefers Classic; but Episcopalians and Presbyterians generally prefer

Gothic. To a certain extent, the broadening and simplification of Gothic associated in England with the names of Bodley, Temple Moore and Sir Giles Gilbert Scott, have been repeated in America, particularly by the late Bertram G. Goodhue and his associates Cram and Ferguson. Churches which may be named in this connection are St. Thomas', New York City; the chapel of the U.S. Military Academy, West Point; Emmanuel church, Cleveland, O.; and the First Baptist church, Pittsburgh, all by Cram, Goodhue and Ferguson; All Saints, Peterboro, N.H., by Cram and Ferguson; church of the Holy Innocents, Brooklyn, by Helmle and Corbett; and Washington Episcopal church, originally designed by Vaughan and Bodley and carried on by Frohman, Robb and Little.

The cathedral is a comparatively recent institution in the United States, and two important examples are now in course of construction.

In 1893 Congress granted a charter for the establishment and maintenance of a cathedral and institutions of learning within the District of Columbia for the promotion of religion, education and charity. Mt. Saint Alban, 400 ft. above the Potomac river, was chosen as the site for Washington cathedral; to-day the cathedral close occupies 67½ acres. Dr. George F. Bodley, of London, and Henry Vaughan, of Boston, his pupil, both of whom have since died, were the original architects chosen and their plan was accepted in 1907; the present architects are Frohman, Robb and Little, of Boston, with Cram and Ferguson, also of Boston, as consulting architects. The cathedral will be cruciform in shape with two impressive transepts, forming the arms of the cross. The total length will be 534 ft., the width at the transepts 215 ft., the area 71,000 square feet. The central tower will be 262 ft. and the western towers 195 ft. high. The entire foundation is now structurally complete. Three chapels in the crypt, together with the vaulted connecting passages, are now open. On the main floor the apse has risen, and the choir and crossing, including the great piers to support the central tower, are approaching completion. Through the western portal, the effect promises to be a vaulted vista of more than 500 ft., through the nave, the crossing and the choir to the sanctuary. The vaulting of the nave will rise 95 ft. from the floor, and the height of the inner aisles, flanking the nave, will be 45 feet. The nave will consist of nine bays and the choir of five. The plans call for more than 800 statues, some 300 stained

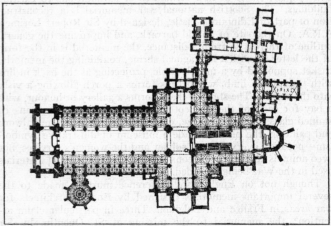

FIG. 4.—PLAN OF THE WASHINGTON CATHEDRAL

glass windows and more than 1,000 sculptured bosses or keystones of the vaulted arches. The landscape work within the cathedral close combines two distinct elements: (1) that of the cathedral itself and its adjacent buildings, which is in the spirit of old world gardens; (2) that of the wooded slope of Mt. Saint Alban, preserving its natural beauty and increasing its dogwood, laurel, wild azalea and choice undergrowth. Ultimately the cathedral close will contain some 30 auxiliary buildings, harmonizing in design with the central edifice. Among these will be the chapter house, synod hall, cloisters, sacristy, choir rooms and administration building, the dean's residence, six canons' and six minor canons' residences, 12 retired clergy residences, a library and librarian's residence, a guest house, additional buildings for St. Albans, the National Cathedral School for Boys, and the National Cathedral School for Girls, the College of Preachers and the lodges for the cathedral employees, an amphitheatre, a gymnasium and an athletic field. A stone wall with 12 gates, named after the 12 apostles, will ultimately surround the entire group.

The cathedral of St. John the Divine, on Morningside Heights, New York, when completed, will be third in area among the cathedrals of the world. Founded by the sixth bishop of New York, Bishop Horatio Potter, who obtained a charter to build it in 1873, the cathedral was originally designed by Heins and Le Farge, with a French Romanesque exterior and a Byzantine interior, the first corner stone being laid on St. John's day, 1892. Even during construction efforts were made at a greater unity of style, and the exterior of the choir was made Gothic; and when, in 1911, Dr. Ralph Adams Cram was appointed consulting architect, he reconsidered the whole design and recommended the adoption of French Gothic for both exterior and interior. In its final form St. John the Divine will be a five-aisled structure, three aisles being included within the clerestorey walls, the triforium and clerestorey being carried, not by the piers of the nave, but over those separating the inner from the outer aisles. The narrow outer aisles take the place of the chain of chapels to be found in most Continental cathedrals. There will be nine bays in the nave, with alternating large and small piers, but the roof vaulting will be in four huge bays, with internal buttressing by means of arches and wing-walls pierced by "roses" across the upper part of the inner side aisles. Owing to the narrowness of the outer aisles there will be no need for external flying buttresses. Externally St. John the Divine will have a central spire, or lantern, and twin west towers.

Other recent churches in the United States which deserve mention are Emmanuel church, Boston, Mass., by Allen and Collens; St. John's, Cambridge, Mass., by Maginnis and Walsh, and St. Bartholomew's, New York, by Goodhue, both Romanesque-Byzantine; the Renaissance Presbyterian church, Madison square, New York, by McKim, Mead and White; the Second Reformed Church, New Brunswick, N.J., by Ludlow and Peabody; and the Tabernacle Presbyterian church, Indianapolis, by J. W. C. Corbusier and R. F. Daggett. Synagogues naturally refer back to their Eastern origin, and the Byzantine Temple Tifereth Israel, Cleveland, O., by Charles R. Greco; Temple Ben Israel, Cincinnati, O., by Tietig and Lee; Temple Emanu-El, San Francisco, Cal., by Bakewell and Brown; and Isaiah temple, Chicago, Ill., by Alfred S. Alschuler, may be quoted as examples. The characteristic form and style of Christian Science churches in America is well illustrated by First Church of Christ, New York, by Carrère and Hastings, and Third Church of Christ, Park avenue, New York, by Delano and Aldrich. In California there have been some interesting experiments in concrete churches, without, however, any very determined attempt—as in France and Germany—to give formal expression to the method of construction, but rather a simplified imitation of bygone styles in the new material. Thus, the church of St. John, by Pierpont and Walter Davis, Wilshire Boulevard church, by Allison and Allison, and St. Paul's cathedral, by Johnson, Kauffman and Coate, all in Los Angeles, are Byzantine, while St. Vincent's church, by Albert C. Martin, in the same city, is in the Baroque of the Spanish mission.   (C. Ma.)

In the United States it is quite common to dedicate buildings of all types as memorials to persons or causes. Memorials in the form of monuments of honorary types were erected in great quantities after the Civil War and again by almost every community at the end of the World War of 1914-18. Aside from these which are noteworthy primarily for their quantity, a few distinguished architectural monuments exist. An outstanding example is the Lincoln Memorial at Washington, D.C. (Henry Bacon, architect, 1914-22). Its design combines the dignity of a Greek temple with the grandeur of a landscape setting inspired by the French Renaissance. The Lincoln Memorial has been placed not far from a striking, older memorial, the Washington Monument designed by Robert Mills. The great strength and simplicity of this simple white marble obelisk 555ft. high make it a structure ageless in spirit and strong in character. Among the World War memorials, the Liberty Memorial of Kansas City, Mo. (H. van Buren Magonigle, architect) is outstanding for its freedom from the mere application of the classic forms which constituted the vocabulary of architects of that period. Its simple shaft crowned by an urn and flanked by two isolated pavilions on a high terrace, makes a strong impression. A memorial to Thomas Jefferson in the form of a classic, domed structure when undergoing construction in 1938 brought about extended controversy as to the advisability of building another costly monument in the classic style at a period when the spirit for classic revivalism was well passed.

BIBLIOGRAPHY.—A. L. Drummond, *The Church Architecture of Protestantism* (1934); E. J. Weber, *Catholic Ecclesiology* (1927); R. A. Cram, *American Church Building of Today* (1929); J. G. Wattjes, *Moderne Kerken en Europa, en Amerika* (1931); Arnaud d'Agnet, *L'art Religieux Moderne* (1936); F. R. Webber, *The Small Church* (1938); *Architectural Record*, vol. 85 (April 1939), vol. 86 (July 1939); G. H. Edgell, *The American Architecture of To-day* (1928). Periodicals: *The Architectural Review* and *The Architects' Journal* (England); *The Architectural Forum* (America); *Bauformen* (Germany).   (W. F. B.)

REMAGEN, a town in the Prussian Rhine Province, on the left bank of the Rhine, 12 m. above Bonn, by the railway from Cologne to Coblenz, and at the junction of the railway to Adenau. Pop. (1933) 5,834. Its Roman name was Rigomagus and many Roman remains have been found here. It passed to Prussia from the duchy of Jülich. The (Roman Catholic) parish church is remarkable for a gate dating from the 12th century. Just below the town, on a height overlooking the Rhine, stands the Apollinaris church, built 1839–53 on the site of a chapel formerly dedicated to St. Martin.

REMAINDER, REVERSION. In the view of English law a remainder or reversion is classed either as an incorporeal hereditament or, with greater correctness, as an estate in expectancy. That is to say, it is a present interest subject to an existing estate in possession called the particular estate, which must determine before the estate in expectancy can become an estate in possession. A remainder or reversion is in strictness confined to real estate, whether legal or equitable, though a similar interest may exist in personalty. The particular estate and the remainder or reversion together make up the whole estate over which the grantor has power of disposition. Accordingly a remainder or reversion limited on an estate in fee simple is void. The difference between a remainder and a reversion, stated as simply as possible, is that the latter is that undisposed-of part of the estate which after the determination of the particular estate will fall into the possession of the original grantor or his representative, while a remainder is that part of the estate which under the same circumstances will fall into the possession of a person other than the original grantor or his representative. The subject is too technical for further treatment, for which reference must be made to legal text books.

The State laws of the United States affecting remainders will be found in Washburn, *Real Property*, ii. bk. ii. As a general rule contingent remainders have been rendered of little practical importance by enactments that they shall take effect as executory devises or shall not determine on determination of the particular estate.

REMAINDER THEOREM, a theorem of particular value in the study of polynomials and equations. If we divide

$$2x^2+3x+6 \text{ by } x-2,$$

for example, the quotient is $2x+7$ and the remainder is 20. The remainder, however, can be found by substituting 2 for x in the polynomial. This gives:

$$2\cdot2^2+3\cdot2+6=8+6+6=20.$$

More generally, to find the remainder arising from dividing $f(x)$ by $x-r$, substitute r for x in $f(x)$. This evidently amounts simply to evaluating $f(x)$ for some special value (r) of x. This is conveniently done by following the plan shown at the right. This work reveals not only the remainder (20) but also the coefficients (2+7) of the quotient ($2x+7$). When

$$\begin{array}{ccc|c} 2 & +3 & +6 & \underline{\,2\,} \\ & 4 & 14 & \\ \hline 2 & +7; & 20 & \end{array}$$

used for this latter purpose it is known as synthetic division. This method of dividing is very helpful in finding the roots of numerical higher equations.

REMAND, a term of English law meaning the return of a prisoner by order of a court to the custody from which he came to the court. Where trials or indictments are not concluded at a single sitting the court of trial has power to remand the accused into proper custody during any necessary adjournment. If the remand is for more than three days the order must be in writing (Indictable Offences Act 1848). Similar powers of remand or committal to prison during adjournments are given to justices in the exercise of their summary criminal jurisdiction (Summary Jurisdiction Acts 1848 and 1879).

In the case of charges against children or young persons the remand must be to a "place of detention" unless released on bail or certified unfit for such a place of detention (Children Act 1908). For this purpose homes have been established under the act.

In the United States the term is used in two senses. The first is where a prisoner is returned to custody to await the resumption of the preliminary hearing or the commencement of the trial. The second is where a cause of action is returned to the original court after the same had been transferred or appealed.

REMBRANDT (1606–1669). REMBRANDT HARMENS VAN RIJN, Dutch painter, was born in Leyden on July 15, 1606. It is only within the past 50 years that we have come to know anything of his real history. A tissue of fables formerly represented him as ignorant, boorish and avaricious. These fictions, resting on the loose assertions of Houbraken (*De Groote Schouburgh*, 1718), have been cleared away by the untiring researches of Scheltema and other Dutchmen, notably by C. Vosmaer, whose elaborate work (*Rembrandt, sa vie et ses oeuvres*, 1868, 2nd ed., 1877) is the basis of our knowledge of the man and of the chronological development of the artist.

Rembrandt was born at No. 3 Weddesteg, on the rampart at Leyden overlooking the Rhine. He was the fourth son of Gerrit Harmens van Rijn, a well-to-do miller. His parents resolved that he should enter a learned profession. With this view he was sent to the Latin School and was enrolled on May 20, 1620, as a student of the University at Leyden, but the boy soon determined to be a painter. Accordingly he was placed for three years under Swanenburch, an architectural painter trained in Italy. He then went to Peter Lastman in Amsterdam for six months, after which time he returned to Leyden where he remained from 1626—the date on his earliest picture—to 1631. During the early years of his life at Leyden, Rembrandt seems to have devoted himself entirely to studies, painting and etching the people around him, every picturesque face and form he could get hold of. Life, character, and above all light were the aims of these studies. His mother was a frequent model, and we can trace in her features the strong likeness to her son, especially in the portraits of himself at an advanced age. Eleven portraits of his father are catalogued by Hofstede de Groot. One of his sisters also frequently sat to him. Hofstede de Groot catalogues also 62 existing portraits of himself, most of them painted in youth and in old age.

Rembrandt's earliest pictures were painted at Leyden, from 1627 to 1631. They are chiefly paintings of single figures, as "St. Paul in Prison" and "St. Jerome"; but now and then compositions of several, as "Samson in Prison" and "Presentation in the Temple." The prevailing tone of all these pictures is a greenish grey, the effect being somewhat cold and heavy. The gallery at Cassel gives a typical example of his studies of the heads of old men, firm in workmanship and full of detail, the effects of light and shade being carefully thought out. His work was now attracting the attention of lovers of art in the great city of Amsterdam; and, urged by their calls, he removed about 1631 to live and die there. At one bound he leaped into the position of the first portrait painter of the city, and received numerous commissions. During the early years of his residence there are many portraits from his hand, firm and solid in manner and staid in expression. The excellent painter Thomas de Keyser was then in the height of his power, and his influence is to be traced in some of Rembrandt's smaller portraits. Pupils also now flocked to his house in the Bloemgracht, among them Gerard Douw, who was nearly of his own age. The first important work executed by Rembrandt in Amsterdam is "Simeon in the Temple," of The Hague museum, a fine early example of his treatment of light and shade and of his subtle colour. The concentrated light falls on the principal figures while the background is full of mystery. The surface is smooth and enamel-like; the action of light on the mantle of Simeon shows how soon he had felt the magical effect of the play of colour. In the life-sized "Lesson in Anatomy" of 1632 we have the first of the great portrait subjects— Tulp the anatomist, the early friend of Rembrandt, discoursing to his seven associates, who are ranged with eager heads round the foreshortened body. The subject had been treated in former years by the Mierevelts, A. Pietersen and others, for the Hall of the Surgeons. But it was reserved for Rembrandt to make it a great picture by the grouping of the expressive portraits and by the completeness of the conception. The colour is quiet and the handling of the brush timid and precise, while the light and shade are somewhat harsh and abrupt. But it is a marvellous picture for a young man of twenty-five, and it is generally accepted as marking a new departure in the career of the painter.

In recent times the number of pictures painted by Rembrandt has been variously estimated. Smith, in his *Catalogue Raisonné* (1836) lists 614 pictures; Bode's *Catalogue* (Paris, 1897, *seq.*) lists some 550; Wurzbach's *Lexicon* (1910) has about 500; Hofstede de Groot's *Catalogue* (1916) has 988 numbers; and recently J. C. Van Dyke (*Rembrandt and his School*, New York, 1923) has reduced the number of undoubtedly genuine examples painted by the master's own hand to 48. It is impossible here to notice more than the prominent works. Besides the Pellicorne family portraits of 1632, now in the Wallace collection, we have the caligraphist Coppenol of the Cassel gallery, interesting in the first place as an early example of Rembrandt's method of giving permanent interest to a portrait by converting it into a picture. He invests it with a sense of life by a momentary expression as Coppenol raises his head towards the spectator while he is mending a quill. The same motive is to be found in the "Shipbuilder," 1633 (Buckingham Palace), who looks up from his work with a sense of interruption at the approach of his wife. Coppenol was painted and etched by the artist. The two small pictures of "The Philosopher" of the Louvre date from 1633, delicate in execution and full of mysterious effect.

In 1634 Rembrandt married Saskia van Uylenborch, a beautiful, fair-haired Frisian maiden of good connections. Till her death in 1642 she was the centre of his life and art. Saskia brought him a marriage portion of 40,000 guilders. She bore him four children, Rumbartus and two girls, successively named Cornelia after his mother, all of whom died in infancy, and Titus, named after Titia, a sister of Saskia. We have several noble portraits of Saskia, a good type of the beauty of Holland, all painted with the utmost love and care, at Cassel (1633), at Dresden (1641), and a posthumous one (1643) at Berlin.

One of Rembrandt's greatest portraits of 1634 is the superb full-length of Martin Daey, which, with that of Madame Daey, painted according to Vosmaer some years later, formed one of the ornaments of the Van Loon collection at Amsterdam. Both now belong to Baron Gustave de Rothschild. From the firm detailed execution of this portrait one turns with wonder to the broader handling of the "Old Woman" (Françoise van Wasserhoven), aged 83, in the National Gallery, of the same year, remarkable for the effect of reflected light and still more for the sympathetic rendering of character.

The life of Samson supplied many subjects in these early days. The "Samson Menacing his Father-in-Law" is forced and violent in its action. One of the prominent examples of Rembrandt's work is the "Marriage of Samson," of the Dresden gallery, painted in 1638. Here Rembrandt gives the rein to his imagination and makes the scene live before us. Except the bride (Saskia), who sits calm and grand on a dais in the centre of the feast, with the full light again playing on her flowing locks and wealth of jewels, all is animated and full of bustle. Samson, evidently a Rembrandt of fantasy, leans over a chair propounding his riddle to the Philistine lords. In execution it is a great advance on former subject pictures; it is bolder in manner, and we have here signs of his approaching love of warmer tones.

The story of Susannah also occupied him in these early years, and he returned to the subject in 1641 and 1653. "The Bather" of the National Gallery may be another interpretation of the same theme. In all of these pictures the woman is coarse in type and lumpy in form, though the modelling is soft and round, the effect which Rembrandt always strove to gain. Beauty of form was outside his art. But the so-called "Danae" (1636) at Leningrad is a sufficient reply to those who deny his ability ever to appreciate the beauty of the nude female form. It glows with colour and life, and the blood seems to pulsate under the warm skin. In the picturesque story of Tobit Rembrandt found much to interest him, as we see in the beautiful small picture of the d'Arenberg Collection at Brussels. Sight is being restored to the aged Tobias, while with infinite tenderness his wife holds the old man's hand caressingly. In the Berlin gallery he paints the anxiety of the parents as they wait for the return of their son. In 1637 he painted the fine picture now in the Louvre of the "Flight of the Angel." Reverence and awe are shown in every attitude of the Tobit family. A similar lofty treatment is to be found in the "Christ as the Gardener," appearing to Mary, of 1638 (Buckingham Palace).

We have now arrived at the year 1640, the threshold of his second manner, which extended to 1654, the middle age of Rembrandt. During the latter part of the previous decade we find the shadows more transparent and the blending of light and shade more perfect. There is a growing power in every part of his art. The coldness of his first manner had disappeared, and the tones were gradually changing into golden-brown. He had attained to a truer, calmer form of dramatic expression, of which the "Manoah" of Dresden is a good example (1641). The portraits painted "to order" became more rare about this time, and those which we have are chiefly friends of his circle, such as the "Mennonite Preacher" (C. C. Ansloo) and the "Gilder," a fine example of his golden tone, in the Havemeyer collection, New York. His own splendid portrait (1640) in the National Gallery illustrates the change in his work. It describes the man well—strong and robust, with powerful head, firm and compressed lips and determined chin, with heavy eyebrows, separated by a deep vertical furrow, and with eyes of keen penetrating glance—altogether a self-reliant man. He has now many friends and pupils, and numerous commissions, even from the stadtholder; he has bought a large house in the Breedstraat, in which during the next 16 years of his life he gathers his large collection of paintings, engravings, armour and costume which figure afterwards in his inventory. His taste was wide and his purchases large, for he was joint owner with picture-dealers of paintings by Giorgione and Palma Vecchio, while for a high-priced Marcantonio Raimondi print he gave in exchange a fine impression of his "Christ Healing the Sick," which has since been known as the "Hundred Guilder Print." The stadtholder was not a prompt payer, and an interesting correspondence took place between Rembrandt and Constantin Huygens, the poet and secretary of the prince. The Rembrandt letters which have come down to us are few, and these are therefore of importance. Rembrandt puts a high value on the picture, which he says had been painted "with much care and zeal," but he is willing to take what the prince thinks proper; while to Huygens he sends a large picture as a present for his trouble in carrying through the business. There is here no sign of the grasping greed with which he has been charged, while his unselfish conduct is seen in the settlement of the family affairs at the death of his mother in 1640.

The year 1642 is remarkable for the great picture formerly known as the "Night Watch," but now more correctly as the "Sortie of the Banning Cock Company," in which 29 life-sized civic guards are introduced issuing pell-mell from their clubhouse. Such gilds of arquebusiers had been painted admirably before by Ravesteyn and notably by Frans Hals, but Rembrandt determined to throw life and animation into the scene. The domi-

nant colour is the citron yellow uniform of the lieutenant, wearing a blue sash, while a Titian-like red dress of a musketeer, the black velvet dress of the captain, and the varied green of the girl and drummer, all produce a rich and harmonious effect. The background has become dark and heavy, and the scutcheon on which the names are painted is scarcely to be seen.

But this year of great achievement was also the year of his great loss, for Saskia died in 1642, leaving Rembrandt her sole trustee for her son Titus, but with full use of the money till he should marry again or till the marriage of Titus. The words of the will express her confidence in her husband. With her death his life was changed. There is a pathetic sadness in his pictures of the Holy Family—a favourite subject at this period of his life. All of these he treats with the naïve simplicity of Reformed Holland, giving us the real carpenter's shop and the mother watching over the Infant reverently and lovingly, with a fine union of realism and idealism.

The street in which he lived was full of Dutch and Portuguese Jews, and many a Jewish rabbi sat to him. He accepted or invented their turbans and local dress as characteristic of the people. But in his religious pictures it is not the costume we look at; what strikes us is the profound perception of the sentiment of the story, making them true to all time and independent of local circumstance. A notable example of this feeling is to be found in the "Woman Taken in Adultery" of the National Gallery, painted in 1644 in the manner of the "Simeon" of The Hague. It commands our attention from the grand conception of the painter who has invested Christ with majestic dignity. A similar lofty ideal is to be found in his various renderings of the "Pilgrims at Emmaus," notably in the Louvre picture of 1648. From the same year we have the "Good Samaritan" of the Louvre, the story of which is told with intense pathos. The helpless suffering of the wounded man, the curiosity of the boy on tiptoe, the excited faces at the upper window, are all conveyed with masterly skill. In these last two pictures we find a broader touch and freer handling, while the tones pass into a dull yellow and brown with a predilection for a note of deep rich red.

Rembrandt touched no side of art without setting his mark on it, whether in still life, as in his dead birds or the "Slaughtered Ox" of the Louvre (with its repetitions at Glasgow and Budapest), or in his drawings of elephants and lions, all of which are instinct with life. But at this period of his career we come upon a branch of his art on which he left, both in etching and in painting, the stamp of his genius, viz., landscape. Roeland Roghman, but ten years his senior, evidently influenced his style, for the resemblance between their works is so great that, as at Cassel, there has been confusion of authorship. Hercules Seghers also was much appreciated by Rembrandt, for at his sale eight pictures by this master figure in the inventory, and Vosmaer discovered that Rembrandt had worked on a plate by Seghers and had added figures to an etched "Flight into Egypt." The earliest pure landscape known to us from Rembrandt's hand is that at the Rijks museum (1637–38), followed in the latter year by those at Brunswick, Boston (U.S.A.) and "The River Scene," formerly in the collection of Marcus Kapfel, Berlin. Better known is the "Winter Scene" of Cassel (1646), silvery and delicate. As a rule in his painted landscape he aims at grandeur and poetical effect, as in the "Repose of the Holy Family" of 1647 in the National gallery, Dublin, a moonlight effect, clear even in the shadows. The "Canal" in the Rijks museum, Amsterdam, is also conceived in this spirit. A similar poetical vein runs through the "Landscape with Ruins" of Cassel, in which the beams of the setting sun strike on the ruins while the valley is sunk in the shades of approaching night. More powerful still is the weird effect of the "Windmill," with its glow of light and darkening shadows. In all these pictures light with its magical influences is the theme of the poet-painter. From the number of landscapes by himself in the inventory of his sale, it would appear that these grand works were not appreciated by his contemporaries. The last of the landscape series dates from 1655 or 1656, the close of the middle age or manhood of Rembrandt, a period of splendid power. In the "Joseph Accused by Potiphar's Wife" of 1655 we have great dramatic vigour and perfect mastery of expression, while the brilliant colour and glowing effect of light and shade attest his strength. To this period also belongs the great portrait of himself in the Fitzwilliam museum at Cambridge.

But evil days were at hand. The long-continued wars and civil troubles had worn out the country, and money was scarce; and we find Rembrandt borrowing considerable sums of money on the security of his house. Then, in this year of 1654, we find him involved in the scandal of having a child by his servant Hendrickje Jagers or Stoffels, as appears by the books of the Reformed Church at Amsterdam. He recognized the child and gave it the name of Cornelia, after his mother, but there is no proof that he married Hendrickje, who seems to have continued to live with him, for we find her claiming a chest as her property at his sale in 1658.

The beautiful portrait of the "Lady" in the Salon Carré of the Louvre and the "Venus and Cupid" of the same gallery may represent Hendrickje and her child. Both pictures belong to this date, and by their treatment are removed from the category of Rembrandt's usual portraits. But if this is conjecture, we get nearer to fact when we look at the picture to which tradition has attached the name of "Rembrandt's Mistress," now in the Edinburgh National Gallery. At a glance one can see that it is not the mere head of a model, as she lies in bed raising herself to put aside a curtain. In 1654 he painted the famous "Portrait of Jan Six," the future burgomaster, consummate in its ease and character, as Six descends the steps of his house drawing on his glove. The connection between Rembrandt and the great family of Six was long and close. In 1641 the mother of Six, Anna Wymer, had been painted with consummate skill by Rembrandt, who also executed in 1647 the beautiful etching of Six standing by a window reading his tragedy of *Medea*, afterwards illustrated by Rembrandt. Now he paints his portrait in the prime of manhood. In 1656 Rembrandt's financial affairs became more involved, and the Orphan's Chamber transferred the house and ground to Titus, though Rembrandt was still allowed to take charge of Saskia's estate. Nothing, however, could avert the ruin of the painter, who was declared bankrupt in July 1656, an inventory of all his property being ordered by the Insolvency Chamber. The first sale took place in 1657 in the Keizerskroon hotel; and the second in 1658, when the larger part of the etchings and drawings were disposed of—"collected by Rembrandt himself with much love and care," says the catalogue. The sum realized, under 5,000 guilders, was but a fraction of their value. Driven thus from his house, stripped of everything he possessed, even to his table linen, Rembrandt took a modest lodging in the Keizerskroon hostelry (the amounts of his bills are on record), apparently without friends and thrown entirely on himself.

But this dark year of 1656 stands out prominently as one in which some of his greatest works were produced, as, for example, "Jacob blessing the Sons of Joseph" of the Cassel Gallery, and "John the Baptist Preaching" of the Berlin gallery, though this picture is sometimes ascribed to an earlier period of about 1635. Instead of the brilliancy of 1654 we have for two or three years a preference for dull yellows, reds and greys, with a certain uniformity of tone. The handling is broad and rapid. There is less caressing of colour for its own sake, even less straining after vigorous effect of light and shade. To the same year belongs the "Lesson in Anatomy of Johann Deyman," in the museum at Amsterdam. The subject is similar to the great Tulp of 1632, but his manner and power of colour had advanced so much that Sir Joshua Reynolds, on his visit to Holland in 1781, was reminded by it of Michelangelo and Titian. The same period gives us the "Adoration of the Magi" of Buckingham Palace.

After the sale of the house in the Breedstraat, Rembrandt retired to the Rosengracht, an obscure quarter at the west end of the city. We are now drawing to the splendid close of his career in his third manner, in which his touch became broader, his impasto more solid and his knowledge more complete. We may mention the "Old Man with the Grey Beard" of the National Gallery (1657) leading up to the great portraits of the "Syndics of the Cloth Hall" of 1661.

In his old age Rembrandt continued to paint his own portrait as assiduously as in his youthful days. Fine examples are in the Louvre, in the National Gallery, London, and in the Frick collection, New York. All show the same self-reliant expression, though broken down by age and the cares of a hard life.

About the year 1668, Rembrandt painted the (so-called) "Jewish Bride" of the Rijks museum in Amsterdam, and the "Family Group" of Brunswick, the last and perhaps the most brilliant works of his life, bold and rapid in execution and marvellous in the subtle mixture and play of colours in which he seems to revel.

In 1668 Titus, the only son of Rembrandt, died, leaving one child, and on Oct. 4, 1669, the great painter himself passed away, leaving two children, and was buried in the Wester Kerk. He had outlived his popularity, for his manner of painting was no longer in favour with a people who preferred the smooth trivialities of Van der Werff and the younger Mieris.

We must give but a short notice of Rembrandt's achievements in etching. Here he stands out by universal confession as first excelling by his unrivalled technical skill, his mastery of expression and the lofty conceptions of many of his great pieces, as in the "Death of the Virgin," the "Christ Preaching," the "Christ Healing the Sick" (the "Hundred Guilder Print"), the "Presentation to the People," the "Crucifixion" and others. So great is his skill simply as an etcher that one is apt to overlook the nobleness of the etcher's ideas, and this tendency has been doubtless confirmed by the enormous difference in money value between "states" of the same plate, rarity giving in many cases a factitious worth in the eyes of collectors. The points of difference between these states arise from the additions and changes made by Rembrandt on the plate; and the prints taken off by him have been subjected to the closest inspection by Bartsch, Gersaint, Wilson, Daulby, De Claussin, C. Blanc, Seymour Haden, Middleton, Dutuit, Rovinski, Singer, Hind and lately by J. C. Van Dyke and Coppier, who have described them, and to whom the reader is referred. The classification of Rembrandt's etchings adopted till lately was according to the subject, as biblical, portrait, landscape, and so on; until Vosmaer attempted the more scientific and interesting line of chronology. This method has been developed by Sir F. Seymour Haden and Middleton.

The great period of his etching lies between 1639 and 1661, after which the old painter seems to have renounced the needle. In these 20 years were produced his greatest works in portraiture, landscape and Bible story. They bear the impress of the genius of the man. Rembrandt's drawings are done almost exclusively in pen and wash, though he used red and black chalk sometimes in his early period. His line, apparently haphazard, is extremely suggestive, expressive and sure, and by a few strokes of the pen he suggests scenes full of life and feeling. The publication *Original Drawings by Rembrandt* (1888–1906) was issued in three series of eight volumes. The first series, with 200 drawings edited by F. Lippmann with the help of Bode, Colvin, Seymour Haden and Heseltine, contains the best drawings. The following two series completed by Hofstede de Groot contain many doubtful pieces. Recently attempts have been made to distinguish the master's work from that of his pupils by W. R. Valentiner and by J. C. Van Dyke (the *Rembrandt Drawings and Etchings*, New York, 1927). But agreement has not been reached.

For bibliography and general *see*: C. Vosmaer, *Rembrandt* (2nd ed., The Hague, 1877); W. Bode, *Studien zur Geschichte der Holländischen Malerei* (Brunswick, 1883); E. Michel, *Rembrandt* (Paris, 1893; London, 1906); W. Bode and C. H. de Groot, *Rembrandt* complete work 8 vols. (1897–1906); W. Bode, *Rembrandt und seine Zeitgenossen* (Leipzig, 1906); C. H. de Groot, *Die Urkunden* (The Hague, 1905); J. Baldwin Brown, *Rembrandt* (1907); W. R. Valentiner, *Rembrandt und seine Umgebung* (Strasbourg, 1905).

For reproductions of Rembrandt's work *see*: the monumental folios compiled by Dr. Bode, in smaller form the volume on Rembrandt in the series *Klassiker der Kunst* (3rd ed. by Dr. Valentiner, Stuttgart, 1908); with a supplementary volume of recently discovered Rembrandts issued in 1921; and the volumes of Rembrandt's etchings compiled by H. W. Singer (1906) and of Rembrandt's drawings compiled by W. R. Valentiner (1924–   ) in the same series; and the volumes of Rembrandt's etchings arranged by A. M. Hind (1912 and 1923).

For appreciations of Rembrandt's work *see* E. Fromentin, *Maîtres d'autrefois* (1904); D. Langbehn, *Rembrandt als Erzieher* (Leipzig, 1890); P. G. Hamerton, *Rembrandt's Etchings* (1894); W. Weisbach, *Rembrandt* (1926). (J. F. W.)

REMEMBRANCER, the name of certain officials who compiled the memoranda rolls and prepared the business for the barons of the exchequer, and so "reminded" them of the matter with which they must deal. There were at one time three clerks of the remembrance, styled king's remembrancer, lord treasurer's remembrancer and remembrancer of first-fruits. The latter two offices have become extinct. At the present moment (1929) the King's remembrancer is required to be a master of the court of exchequer, and by the Supreme Court of Judicature (Officers) Act, 1879, he is a master of the supreme court. The office is usually filled by the senior master. The king's remembrancer still assists at certain ceremonial functions. His duties are set out in the *Second Report of the Legal Departments Commission* (1874).

"Remembrancer" is also the title of an official of the corporation of the City of London, whose principal duty is to represent that body before parliamentary committees and at council and treasury boards.

REMIGIUS, ST. (*c.* 437–533), bishop of Reims and the friend of Clovis, whom he converted to Christianity. According to Gregory of Tours, 3,000 Franks were baptized with Clovis by Remigius on Christmas Day, 496, after the defeat of the Alamanni. A good many fictions grew up around his name, *e.g.*, that he anointed Clovis with oil from the sacred ampulla, and that Pope Hormisdas had recognized him as primate of France. The *Commentary on the Pauline Epistles* (ed. Villalpandus, 1699) is not his work, but that of Remigius of Auxerre.

For authorities *see* H. Jadart, *Bibliographie des ouvrages conc. la vie et le culte de S. Remi . . .* (Reims, 1891).

REMINGTON, FREDERIC (1861–1909), American artist, was born at Canton (N.Y.), on Oct. 4, 1861. He was a pupil of the Yale Art School, and of the Art Students' League, New York, and became known as an illustrator, painter and sculptor. Having spent much time in the West, where he went for his health, and having been with the United States troops in actual warfare, he made a specialty of rendering the North American Indian and the United States soldier as seen on the western plains. In the Spanish-American War he was with the army under General Shafter as war correspondent. He died Dec. 26, 1909, near Ridgefield (Conn.). His statuettes of soldiers, Indians, cowboys and trappers are full of character, while his paintings have been largely reproduced. He wrote several volumes of stories, including *Pony Tracks* (1895), *Crooked Trails* (1898), *Sundown Leflare* (1899), and *John Ermine of the Yellowstone* (1902).

REMIREMONT, a town of eastern France, in the department of Vosges, 17 m. S.S.E. of Épinal by rail, on the Moselle, below its confluence with the Moselotte. Pop. (1936) 10,242. Remiremont (*Romarici Mons*) is named after St. Romaric, a companion of St. Columban of Luxeuil, who in the 7th century founded a monastery and a convent on the hills above the present town. In 910 an invasion of the Hungarians drove the nuns to Remiremont, which had grown round a villa of the Frankish kings, and in the 11th century they settled there. Enriched by dukes of Lorraine, kings of France and emperors of Germany, the ladies of Remiremont attained great power. The abbess was a princess of the empire, and received consecration at the hands of the pope. The fifty canonesses were selected from the nobility. On Whit-Monday the neighbouring parishes paid homage to the chapter in a ceremony called the "Kyrioles"; and on their accession the dukes of Lorraine, the immediate suzerains of the abbey, had to come to Remiremont to swear to continue their protection. The "War of the Scutcheons" (Panonceaux) in 1566 between the duke and the abbess ended in favour of the duke, and terminated the abbess's power. The monastery and nunnery were both suppressed in the Revolution. Remiremont is surrounded by forest-clad mountains. The 13th cent. abbey church has a crypt of the 11th century. The abbatial residence (which now contains the *mairie*, the court-house and the public library) has been twice rebuilt in the original plan in modern times. Some of the houses of the canonesses (17th and 18th centuries) remain. Remire-

mont has a board of trade-arbitrators and a chamber of arts and manufactures. Its industries include cotton-spinning and weaving, the manufacture of embroidery, iron and copper founding and the manufacture of brushes.

REMIZOV, ALEXEI (1877–   ), Russian novelist, was born June 24, 1877, in Moscow and brought up amid factory surroundings and in the strict observance of Orthodox Church rites, with frequent pilgrimages to monasteries. He thus gained an intimate knowledge of national habits, monastic life and old religious legends. He studied natural science and economics at Moscow University, took part in revolutionary activities, and was imprisoned and spent years of exile in Vologda. He subsequently went to live in Paris. The influences of his varying surroundings contributed to the formation of his unique fantastic personality, uniting the whimsical mischievousness of some fairy-tale sprite with a deep spirit of pity. His literary life dates from 1902; from that time until 1920 he published 36 volumes of fiction: novels, tales, short stories and fairy-tales, miracle plays, etc.

The most remarkable of Remizov's works are *The Pond* (1905), a powerful and gloomy picture of vulgarity, vice and crime among the Moscow bourgeoisie and the monasteries; *The Clock* (1908, Eng. trans. 1924); *The Fifth Pestilence*, two stories of provincial life (Eng. trans. by A. Brown 1927); *The Sisters of the Cross* (1910), a novel of St. Petersburg life; also *The Cockerel* and stories relating to the revolution of 1905, and several plays.

REMONSTRANTS, the name given to those Dutch Protestants who, after the death of Arminius (*q.v.*), maintained the views associated with his name, and in 1610 presented to the states of Holland and Friesland a "remonstrance" in five articles formulating their points of departure from stricter Calvinism. These were: (1) that the divine decree of predestination is conditional, not absolute; (2) that the Atonement is in intention universal; (3) that man cannot of himself exercise a saving faith; (4) that though the grace of God is a necessary condition of human effort it does not act irresistibly in man; (5) that believers are able to resist sin but are not beyond the possibility of falling from grace. The Remonstrants were assailed both by personal enemies and by the political weapons of Maurice of Orange, who executed and imprisoned their leaders for holding republican views. In 1618–19 the synod of Dort (*see* DORT, SYNOD OF), from which the thirteen Arminian pastors headed by Simon Episcopius (*q.v.*) were shut out, established the victory of the Calvinist school. The judgment of the synod was enforced by the deposition and in some cases the banishment of Remonstrant ministers; but the government soon became convinced that their party was not dangerous to the state, and in 1630 they were formally allowed liberty to reside in all parts of Holland and build churches and schools. Henceforth, however, their importance was more theological than ecclesiastical; and their liberal school of theology, which naturally grew more liberal and even rationalistic, has reacted powerfully on the state church and on other Christian denominations.

REMORA or **SUCKING-FISH,** a name given to fishes of the family Echeneididae, remarkable for having the spinous dorsal fin transformed into a transversely laminated suctorial disc, placed on top of the head. There are about a dozen species from warm seas; they attach themselves to sharks, turtles, and large fish, and are transported by them, but they detach themselves and swim when searching for food.

REMPHAN (in A.V., *Rephan* in R.V.) a word found in Acts vii. 43 ('Ρομφά, Westcott and Hort). The writer is quoting the Septuagint of Amos v. 26 ('Ραιφάν), where the Hebrew has *Kiyyun* (כיון). This is probably a mistake for *Kewan*, the Babylonian name for the planet Saturn. The Greek form may be an error of the transliterator.

REMSCHEID, a town in the Prussian Rhine Province, Germany, 6 mi. by rail S. of Barmen, in an industrial area heavily bombed in World War II. Pop. (1939) 103,437. It is a centre of the hardware industry, and makes large quantities of tools, scythes, drills and other small articles in iron, steel and brass.

REMSEN, IRA (1846–1927), American chemist, was born in New York city on Feb. 10, 1846, and educated at the College of the City of New York (B.A., 1865), College of Physicians and Surgeons (Columbia—M.D., 1867) and at the Universities of Munich and Göttingen (Ph.D., 1870). He spent the two years 1870–72 at the University of Tübingen as assistant to Fittig and here began the investigations into pure chemistry upon which his later fame was chiefly based. He was professor of chemistry at Williams college in 1872–76 and in 1876 was one of the original faculty of the new Johns Hopkins university. Here he was professor of chemistry 1876–1913, director of the chemical laboratory 1876–1908, secretary of the Academic Council 1881–1901 and president of the university 1901–1913. He was president emeritus and professor emeritus 1913–1927, during which time he travelled widely and worked on government pure food commissions. He brought to Johns Hopkins many of the German laboratory methods and as a teacher he soon became famous. A long series of students trained in intimate association with him became widely scattered and influential. He founded the *American Chemical Journal* in 1879 and continued to edit it almost to the time of his death. In it most of his scientific papers were published. In the first volume he described the preparation and properties of a new compound, subsequently to become widely known as saccharine, which he and a pupil discovered. Another long series of studies led to the discovery and enunciation of Remsen's law. He also became widely known for his series of text-books, *Principles of Theoretical Chemistry* (1876) passing through five editions and being translated into German, Russian and Italian. Others of like popularity were *An Introduction to the Study of the Compounds of Carbon* (1885; 5th rev., 1922); *Elements of Chemistry* (1888); *Inorganic Chemistry* (1889); *A College Text-book of Chemistry* (1908). Remsen died at Carmel, Cal., on Mar. 5, 1927.

See B. Harrow, *Eminent Chemists of Our Time* (1920); "Impressions of Ira Remsen," in *Johns Hopkins Alumni Magazine*, vol. xvi. pp. 215–226 (1928); "Ira Remsen" in *Science*, N.S. vol. lxvi. (1927), pp. 243–246.

RÉMUSAT, CHARLES FRANÇOIS MARIE, COMTE DE (1797–1875), French politician and man of letters, was born in Paris on March 13, 1797. He was called to the bar, and became an active journalist. He signed the journalists' protest against the Ordinances of July 1830, and in October was elected deputy for Haute Garonne. He then ranked himself with the *doctrinaires,* and supported measures of restriction on popular liberty.

Rémusat held office under Thiers in the reign of Louis Philippe. He took no part in politics under the Empire until 1869. In Aug. 1871 he succeeded Favre as minister of foreign affairs. He died in Paris on Jan. 6, 1875.

His works include: *Abélard* (2 vols., 1845); *Saint Anselme de Cantorbéry* (1854); *L'Angleterre au XVIIIème siècle* in 1856 (2nd ed. enlarged, 1865); *Bacon, sa vie, son temps,* etc. (1858); *Channing, sa vie et ses oeuvres* (1862); *John Wesley* (1870); *Lord Herbert de Cherbury* (1874) *Histoire de la philosophie en Angleterre depuis Bacon jusqu'à Locke* (1875).

RÉMUSAT, JEAN PIERRE ABEL (1788–1832), French Chinese scholar, was born in Paris on Sept. 5, 1788. He was educated for the medical profession, but a Chinese herbal in the collection of the Abbé Tersan led him to study Chinese. His *Essai sur la langue et la littérature chinoises* (1811) won him the patronage of Silvestre de Sacy, and in 1814 he was appointed to the chair of Chinese founded in that year at the Collège de France. His contributions from Chinese sources to the history of the Tatar nations claims special notice. Rémusat became an editor of the *Journal des savants* in 1818, and founder and first secretary of the Paris Asiatic Society in 1822; he also held various Government appointments. He died at Paris on June 4, 1832. A list of his works is given in Quérard's *France littéraire* s.v. Rémusat.

RENAISSANCE, THE. The "Renaissance" or "Renascence" is a term used to indicate a well-known but indefinite space of time and a certain phase in the development of Europe. On the one hand it denotes the transition from that period of history which we call the middle ages (*q.v.*) to that which we call modern. On the other hand it implies those changes in the intellectual and moral attitude of the Western nations by which the transition was characterized. If we insist upon the literal and etymological meaning of the word, the Renaissance was a re-birth;

and it is needful to inquire of what it was the re-birth. The metaphor of Renaissance may signify the entrance of the European nations upon a fresh stage of vital energy in general, implying a fuller consciousness and a freer exercise of faculties than had belonged to the mediaeval period. Or it may mean the resuscitation of simply intellectual activities, stimulated by the revival of antique learning and its application to the arts and literatures of modern peoples. Upon our choice between these two interpretations of the word depend important differences in any treatment of the subject. The former has the disadvantage of making it difficult to separate the Renaissance from other historical phases—the Reformation for example—with which it ought not to be confounded. The latter has the merit of assigning a specific name to a limited series of events and group of facts, which can be distinguished for the purpose of analysis from other events and facts with which they are intimately but not indissolubly connected. In other words, the one definition of Renaissance makes it denote the whole change which came over Europe at the close of the middle ages. The other confines it to what was known by our ancestors as the Revival of Learning. Yet, when we concentrate attention on the recovery of antique culture, we become aware that this was only one phenomenon or symptom of a far wider and more comprehensive alteration in the conditions of the European races. We find it needful to retain both terms, Renaissance and Revival of Learning, and to show the relations between the series of events and facts which they severally imply. The Revival of Learning must be regarded as a function of that vital energy, an organ of that mental evolution, which brought into existence the modern world, with its new conceptions of philosophy and religion, its reawakened arts and sciences, its firmer grasp on the realities of human nature and the world, its manifold inventions and discoveries, its altered political systems, its expansive and progressive forces. Important as the Revival of Learning undoubtedly was, there are essential factors in the complex called the Renaissance with which it can but remotely be connected. When we analyse the whole group of phenomena which have to be considered, we perceive that some of the most essential have nothing or little to do with the recovery of the classics. These are, briefly speaking, the decay of those great fabrics, church and empire, which ruled the middle ages both as ideas and as realities; the development of nationalities and languages; the enfeeblement of the feudal system throughout Europe; the invention and application of paper, the mariner's compass, gunpowder, and printing; the exploration of continents beyond the ocean; and the substitution of the Copernican for the Ptolemaic system of astronomy. Europe in fact had been prepared for a thorough-going metamorphosis before that new idea of human life and culture which the Revival of Learning brought to light had been made manifest. It had recovered from the confusion consequent upon the dissolution of the ancient Roman empire. The Teutonic tribes had been Christianized, civilized and assimilated to the previously Latinized races over whom they exercised the authority of conquerors. Comparative tranquillity and material comfort had succeeded to discord and rough living. Modern nationalities, defined as separate factors in a common system, were ready to co-operate upon the basis of European federation. The ideas of universal monarchy and of indivisible Christendom, incorporated in the Holy Roman empire and the Roman Church, had so far lost their hold that scope was offered for the introduction of new theories both of state and church which would have seemed visionary or impious to the mediaeval mind. It is, therefore, obvious that some term, wider than Revival of Learning, descriptive of the change which began to pass over Europe in the 14th and 15th centuries, has to be adopted. That of Renaissance, Rinascimento, or Renascence is sufficient for the purpose, though we have to guard against the tyranny of what is after all a metaphor. We must not suffer it to lead us into rhetoric about the deadness and the darkness of the middle ages, or hamper our inquiry with preconceived assumptions that the re-birth in question was in any true sense a return to the irrecoverable pagan past. Nor must we imagine that there was any abrupt break with the middle ages. On the contrary, the Renaissance was rather the last stage of the middle ages emerging from ecclesiastical and feudal despotism, developing what was original in mediaeval ideas by the light of classic arts and letters, holding in itself the promise of the modern world. It was, therefore, a period and a process of transition, fusion, preparation, tentative endeavour. And just at this point the real importance of the Revival of Learning may be indicated. That rediscovery of the classic past restored the confidence in their own faculties to men striving after spiritual freedom; revealed the continuity of history and the identity of human nature in spite of diverse creeds and different customs; held up for emulation master-works of literature, philosophy and art; provoked inquiry; encouraged criticism; shattered the narrow mental barriers imposed by mediaeval orthodoxy. Humanism[1], a word which will often recur in the ensuing paragraphs, denotes a specific bias which the forces liberated in the Renaissance took from contact with the ancient world—the particular form assumed by human self-esteem at that epoch—the ideal of life and civilization evolved by the modern nations. It indicates the endeavour of man to reconstitute himself as a free being, not as the thrall of theological despotism, and the peculiar assistance he derived in this effort from Greek and Roman literature, the *litterae humaniores,* letters leaning rather to the side of man than of divinity.

In this article the Renaissance will be considered as implying a comprehensive movement of the European intellect and will toward self-emancipation, toward reassertion of the natural rights of the reason and the senses, toward the conquest of this planet as a place of human occupation, and toward the formation of regulative theories both for states and individuals differing from those of mediaeval times. The Revival of Learning will be treated as a decisive factor in this process of evolution on a new plan. To exclude the Reformation and the Counter-Reformation wholly from the survey is impossible. These terms indicate moments in the whole process of modern history which were opposed, each to the other, and both to the Renaissance; and it is needful to bear in mind that they have, scientifically speaking, a quite separate existence. Yet, if the history of Europe in the 16th century of our era came to be written with the brevity with which we write the history of Europe in the 6th century B.C., it would be difficult at the distance of time implied by that supposition to distinguish the Italian movement of the Renaissance in its origin from the German movement of the Reformation. Both would be seen to have a common starting-point in the reaction against long dominant ideas which were becoming obsolete, and also in the excitation of faculties which had during the same period been accumulating energy.

Chronology.—The Renaissance, if we try to regard it as a period, was essentially the transition from one historical stage to another. It cannot therefore be confined within strict chronological limits. There is one date, however, which may be remembered with advantage as the starting-point in time of the Renaissance, after the departure from the middle ages had been definitely and consciously made by the Italians. This is the year 1453, when Constantinople, chosen for his capital by the first Christian emperor of Rome, fell into the hands of the Turk.[2] One of the survivals of the old world, the shadow of what had been the Eastern empire, now passed suddenly away. Almost at the same date that visionary revival of the Western empire, which had imposed for six centuries upon the imagination of mediaeval Europe, hampering Italy and impeding the consolidation of Germany, ceased to reckon among political actualities; while its more robust rival, the Roman Church, seemed likely to sink into the rank of a petty Italian principality. It was demonstrated by the destruction of the Eastern and the dotage of the Western empire and by the new papal policy which Nicholas V. inaugurated, that the old order of society was about to be superseded. Nothing remained to check those centrifugal forces in state and church which substituted a confederation of rival European Powers for the earlier ideal of

[1] To the humanists themselves "humanitas" meant nothing more nor less than "culture."

[2] Most scholars now deny that the fall of Constantinople had any appreciable influence on the culture of Western Europe. For Symonds' date of 1453 they would substitute the date of the invention of printing about 1440.

universal monarchy, and separate religious constitutions for the previous Catholic unity. At the same time the new learning introduced by the earlier humanists awakened free thought, encouraged curiosity, and prepared the best minds of Europe for speculative audacities from which the schoolmen would have shrunk, and which soon expressed themselves in acts of cosmopolitan importance. If we look a little forward to the years 1492–1500, we obtain a second date of great importance. In these years the expedition of Charles VIII. to Naples opened Italy to French, Spanish and German interference. The leading nations of Europe began to compete for the prize of the peninsula, and learned meanwhile that culture which the Italians had perfected. In these years the secularization of the papacy was carried to its final point by Alexander VI., and the Reformation became inevitable. The same period was marked by the discovery of America, the exploration of the Indian seas, and the consolidation of the Spanish nationality. It also witnessed the application of printing to the diffusion of knowledge. Thus, speaking roughly, the half-century between 1450 and 1500 may be termed the culminating point of the Renaissance. The transition of the mediaeval to the modern order was now secured if not accomplished, and a rubicon had been crossed from which no retrogression to the past was possible. Looking yet a little farther to the years 1527 and 1530 a third decisive date is reached. In the first of these years happened the sack of Rome, in the second the pacification of Italy by Charles V. under a Spanish hegemony. The age of the Renaissance was now closed for the land which gave it birth. The Reformation had taken firm hold on northern Europe. The Counter-Reformation was already imminent.

THE MIDDLE AGES

It must not be imagined that so great a change as that implied by the Renaissance was accomplished without premonitory symptoms and previous endeavours. In the main we mean by it the recovery of freedom for the human spirit after a long period of bondage to oppressive ecclesiastical and political orthodoxy—a return to the liberal and practical conceptions of the world which the nations of antiquity had enjoyed, but upon a new and enlarged platform. This being so, it was inevitable that the finally successful efforts after self-emancipation should have been anticipated from time to time by strivings within the ages that are known as dark and mediaeval. It is, therefore, part of the present inquiry to pass in review some of the claimants to be considered precursors to the Renaissance.

First of all must be named the Frank in whose lifetime the dual conception of universal empire and universal church, divinely appointed sacred and inviolable, began to control the order of European society. Charles the Great (Charlemagne) lent his forces to the plan of resuscitating the Roman empire at a moment when his own power made him the arbiter of Western Europe, when the papacy needed his alliance, and when the Eastern empire had passed under the usurped regency of a female. He modelled an empire, Roman in name, but essentially Teutonic, since it owed such substance as its fabric possessed to Frankish armies and the sinews of the German people. As a structure composed of divers ill-connected parts it fell to pieces at its builder's death, leaving little but the incubus of a memory, the fascination of a mighty name, to dominate the mind of mediaeval Europe. As an idea, the Empire grew in visionary power, and remained one of the chief obstacles in the way of both Italian and German national coherence. Real force was not in it, but rather in that counterpart to its unlimited pretensions, the Church which had evolved it from barbarian night, and which used her own more vital energies for undermining the rival of her creation. Charles the Great, having proclaimed himself successor of the Caesars, was obscurely ambitious of imitating the Augusti also in the sphere of letters. He caused a scheme of humanistic education to be formulated, and gave employment at his court to rhetoricians of whom Alcuin was the most considerable. But very little came of the Revival of Learning which Charles is supposed to have encouraged; and the empire he restored was accepted by the mediaeval intellect in a crude theological and vaguely mystical spirit. We should, however, here remember that the study of Roman law, which was one important precursory symptom of the Renaissance, owed much to mediaeval respect for the empire as a divine institution. This, together with the municipal Italian intolerance of the Lombard and Frankish codes, kept alive the practice and revived the science of Latin jurisprudence at an early period.

Speculation and Heresy.—Philosophy had tried to free itself from the trammels of theological orthodoxy in the hardy speculations of some schoolmen, notably of Scotus Erigena and Abelard. These innovators found, however, small support, and were defeated by opponents who used the same logical weapons with authority to back them. Nor were the rationalistic opinions of the Averroists without their value, though the Church condemned these deviators from her discipline as heretics. Such mediaeval materialists, moreover, had but feeble hold upon the substance of real knowledge. Imperfect acquaintance with authors whom they had studied in Latin translations made by Jews from Arabic commentaries on Greek texts, together with almost total ignorance of natural laws, condemned them to sterility. Like the other schiomachists of their epoch, they fought with phantoms in a visionary realm. A similar judgment may be passed upon those Paulician, Albigensian, Paterine and Epicurean dissenters from the Catholic creed who opposed the phalanxes of orthodoxy with frail imaginative weapons, and alarmed established orders in the state by the audacity of their communistic opinions. Physical science struggled into feeble life in the cells of Gerbert and Roger Bacon. But these men were accounted magicians by the vulgar; and, while the one eventually assumed the tiara, the other was incarcerated in a dungeon. The schools meanwhile resounded still to the interminable dispute upon abstractions. Are only universals real, or has each name a corresponding entity? From the midst of the Franciscans who had persecuted Roger Bacon because he presumed to know more than was consistent with human humility arose John of Parma, adopting and popularizing the mystic prophecy of Joachim of Flora. The reign of the Father is past; the reign of the Son is passing; the reign of the Spirit is at hand. Such was the formula of the Eternal Gospel, which as an unconscious forecast of the Renaissance, has attracted retrospective students by its felicity of adaptation to their historical method. Yet we must remember that this bold intuition of the abbot Joachim indicated a monastic reaction against the tyrannies and corruptions of the Church, rather than a fertile philosophical conception. The Fraticelli spiritualists, and similar sects who fed their imagination with his doctrine, expired in the flames to which Fra Dolcino Longino and Margharita were consigned. To what extent the accusations of profligate morals brought against these reforming sectarians were justified remains doubtful; and the same uncertainty rests upon the alleged iniquities of the Templars. It is only certain that at this epoch the fabric of Catholic faith was threatened with various forms of prophetic and Oriental mysticism, symptomatic of a widespread desire to grasp at something simpler, purer and less rigid than Latin theology afforded. Devoid of criticism, devoid of sound learning, devoid of a firm hold on the realities of life, these heresies passed away without solid results and were forgotten.

Naturalism.—We are apt to take for granted that the men of the middle ages were immersed in meditations on the other world, and that their intellectual exercises were confined to abstractions of the schools, hallucinations of the fancy, allegories, visions. This assumption applies indeed in a broad sense to that period which was dominated by intolerant theology, and deprived of positive knowledge. Yet there are abundant signs that the native human instincts, the natural human appetites, remained unaltered and alive beneath the crust of orthodoxy. In the person of a pope like Boniface VIII. those ineradicable forces of the natural man assumed, if we may trust the depositions of ecclesiastics, well acquainted with his life, a form of brutal atheistic cynicism. In the person of an emperor, Frederick II., they emerged under the more agreeable garb of liberal culture and Epicurean scepticism. Frederick dreamed of remodelling society upon a mundane type, which anticipated the large toleration and cosmopolitan enlightenment of the actual Renaissance. But his efforts were defeated by

the unrelenting hostility of the Church, and by the incapacity of his contemporaries to understand his aims. After being forced in his lifetime to submit to authority, he was consigned by Dante to hell. Frederick's ideal of civilization was derived in a large measure from Provence, where a beautiful culture had prematurely bloomed, filling southern Europe with the perfume of poetry and gentle living. Here, if anywhere, it seemed as though the ecclesiastical and feudal fetters of the middle ages might be broken, and humanity might enter on a new stage of joyous and unimpeded evolution. This was, however, not to be. The Church preached Simon de Montfort's crusade, and organized Dominic's Inquisition; what Quinet calls the "Renaissance sociale par l'Amour" was extirpated by sword, fire, famine and pestilence. Meanwhile the Provençal poets had developed their modern language with incomparable richness and dexterity, creating forms of verse and modes of emotional expression which determined the latest mediaeval phase of literature in Europe. The naturalism of which we have been speaking found free utterance now in the fabliaux of jongleurs, lyrics of minnesingers, tales of trouvères, romances of Arthur and his knights—compositions varied in type and tone, but in all of which sincere passion and real enjoyment of life pierce through the thin veil of chivalrous mysticism or of allegory with which they were sometimes conventionally draped. The tales of Lancelot and Tristram, the lives of the troubadours and the Wachtlieder of the minnesingers, sufficiently prove with what sensual freedom a knight loved the lady whom custom and art made him profess to worship as a saint. We do not need to be reminded that Beatrice's adorer had a wife and children, or that Laura's poet owned a son and daughter by a concubine, in order to perceive that the mystic passion of chivalry was compatible in the middle ages with commonplace matrimony or vulgar illegitimate connections. But perhaps the most convincing testimony to the presence of this ineradicable naturalism is afforded by the Latin songs of wandering students, known as Carmina Burama, written by the self-styled Goliardi. In these compositions, remarkable for their facile handling of mediaeval Latin rhymes and rhythms, the allegorizing mysticism which envelops chivalrous poetry is discarded. Love is treated from a frankly carnal point of view. Bacchus and Venus go hand in hand, as in the ancient ante-Christian age. The open-air enjoyments of the wood, the field, the dance upon the village green are sung with juvenile light-heartedness. No grave note, warning us that the pleasures of this earth are fleeting, that the visible world is but a symbol of the invisible, that human life is a probation for the life beyond, interrupts the tinkling music as of castanets and tripping feet which gives a novel charm to these unique relics of the 13th century. Goliardic poetry is further curious as showing how the classics even at that early period were a fountain-head of pagan inspiration. In the taverns and low places of amusement haunted by those lettered songsters, on the open road and in the forests trodden by their vagrant feet, the deities of Greece and Rome were not in exile, but at home within the hearts of living men. Thus, while Christendom was still preoccupied with the Crusades, two main forces of the Renaissance, naturalism and enthusiasm for antique modes of feeling, already brought their latent potency to light, prematurely indeed and precociously, yet with a promise that was destined to be kept.

The Mediaeval Attitude.—When due regard is paid to these miscellaneous evidences of intellectual and sensual freedom during the middle ages, it will be seen that there were by no means lacking elements of native vigour ready to burst forth. What was wanting was not vitality and licence, not audacity of speculation, not lawless instinct or rebellious impulse. It was rather the right touch on life, the right feeling for human independence, the right way of approaching the materials of philosophy, religion, scholarship and literature that failed. The courage that is born of knowledge, the calm strength begotten by a positive attitude of mind, face to face with the dominant over-shadowing sphinx of theology, were lacking. We may fairly say that natural and untaught people had more of the just intuition that was needed than learned folk trained in the schools. But these people were rendered licentious in revolt or impotent for salutary action by ignorance, by terror, by uneasy dread of the doom declared for heretics and rebels.

The massive vengeance of the Church hung over them, like a heavy sword suspended in the cloudy air. Superstition and stupidity hedged them in on every side, so that sorcery and magic seemed the only means of winning power over nature or insight into mysteries surrounding human life. The path from darkness to light was lost; thought was involved in allegory; the study of nature had been perverted into an inept system of grotesque and pious parablemongering; the pursuit of truth had become a game of wordy dialectics. The other world, with its imagined heaven and hell, haunted the conscience like a nightmare. However sweet this world seemed, however fair the flesh, both world and flesh were theoretically given over to the devil. It was not worth while to master and economize the resources of this earth, to utilize the good and ameliorate the evils of this life, while everyone agreed, in theory at any rate, that the present was but a bad prelude to an infinitely worse or infinitely better future. To escape from these preoccupations and prejudices except upon the path of conscious and deliberate sin was impossible for all but minds of rarest quality and courage; and these were too often reduced to the recantation of their supposed errors no less by some secret clinging sense of guilt than by the Church's iron hand. Man and the actual universe kept on reasserting their rights and claims, in one way or another; but they were always being thrust back again into Cimmerian regions of abstractions, fictions, visions, spectral hopes and fears, in the midst of which the intellect somnambulistically moved upon an unknown way.

THE REVIVAL OF LEARNING IN ITALY

At this point the Revival of Learning intervened to determine the course of the Renaissance. Mediaeval students possessed a considerable portion of the Latin classics, though Greek had become in the fullest sense of the phrase a dead language. But what they retained of ancient literature they could not comprehend in the right spirit. Between them and the text of poet or historian hung a veil of mysticism, a vapour of misapprehension. The odour of unsanctity clung around those relics of the pagan past. Men bred in the cloister and the lecture room of the logicians, trained in scholastic disputations, versed in allegorical interpretations of the plainest words and most apparent facts, could not find the key which might unlock those stores of wisdom and of beauty. Petrarch first opened a new method in scholarship and revealed what we denote as humanism. In his teaching lay the twofold discovery of man and of the world. For humanism, which was the vital element in the Revival of Learning, consists mainly of a just perception of the dignity of man as a rational, volitional and sentient being, born upon this earth with a right to use it and enjoy it. Humanism implied the rejection of those visions of a future and imagined state of souls as the only absolute reality, which had fascinated the imagination of the middle ages. It involved a vivid recognition of the goodliness of man and nature, displayed in the great monuments of human power recovered from the past. It stimulated the curiosity of latent sensibilities, provoked fresh inquisition into the groundwork of existence and strengthened man's self-esteem by knowledge of what men had thought and felt and done in ages when Christianity was not. It roused a desire to reappropriate the whole abandoned provinces of mundane energy, and a hope to emulate antiquity in works of living loveliness and vigour. The Italians of the 14th century, more precocious than the other European races, were ripe for this emancipation of enslaved intelligence. In the classics they found the food which was required to nourish the new spirit; and a variety of circumstances among which must be reckoned the pride of a nation boasting of its descent from the *populus Romanus,* rendered them apt to fling aside the obstacles that had impeded the free action of the mind through many centuries. Petrarch not only set his countrymen upon the right method of studying the Latin classics, but he also divined the importance of recovering a knowledge of Greek literature. To this task Giovanni Boccaccio addressed himself; and he was followed by numerous Italian enthusiasts, who visited Byzantium before its fall as the sacred city of a new revelation. The next step was to collect manuscripts, to hunt out, copy and preserve the precious relics of the past.

In this work of accumulation Guarino da Verona and Francesco Filelfo, Giovanni Aurispa and Poggio took the chief part, aided by the wealth of Italian patricians, merchant princes and despots, who were inspired by the sacred thirst for learning. Learning was then no mere pursuit of a special and recluse class. It was fashionable and it was passionate, pervading all society with the fervour of romance. For a generation nursed in decadent scholasticism and stereotyped theological formulas it was the fountain of renascent youth, beauty and freedom, the shape in which the Helen of art and poetry appeared to the ravished eyes of mediaeval Faustus. It was the resurrection of the mightiest spirits of the past. "I go," said Cyriac of Ancona, the indefatigable though uncritical explorer of antiquities, "I go to awake the dead!" This was the enthusiasm, this the vitalizing faith, which made the work of scholarship in the 15th century so highly strung and ardent. The men who followed it knew that they were restoring humanity to its birthright after the expatriation of ten centuries. They were instinctively aware that the effort was for liberty of action, thought and conscience in the future. This conviction made young men leave their loves and pleasures, grave men quit their countinghouses, churchmen desert their missals, to crowd the lecture rooms of philologers and rhetoricians. When Greek had been acquired, manuscripts accumulated, libraries and museums formed, came the age of printers and expositors. Aldus Manutius in Italy, Joannes Froben in Basle, the Étiennes in Paris committed to the press what the investigators had recovered. Nor were there wanting men who dedicated their powers to Hebrew and Oriental erudition, laying, together with the Grecians, a basis for those biblical studies which advanced the Reformation. Meanwhile, the languages of Greece and Rome had been so thoroughly appropriated that a final race of scholars, headed by Politian, Jovianus Pontanus, Lorenzo Valla, handled once again in verse and prose both antique dialects, and thrilled Europe with new-made pagan melodies. The Church itself at this epoch lent its influence to the prevalent enthusiasm. Nicholas V and Leo X, not to mention intervening popes who showed themselves tolerant of humanistic culture, were heroes of the classical revival. Scholarship became the surest path of advancement to ecclesiastical and political honours. Italy was one great school of the new learning at the moment when the German, French and Spanish nations were invited to its feast.

It will be well to describe briefly, but in detail, what this meeting of the modern with the ancient mind effected over the whole field of intellectual interests. In doing so, care must be taken to remember that the study of the classics did but give a special impulse to pent-up energies which were bound in one way or another to assert their independence. Without the Revival of Learning the direction of those forces would have been different; but that novel intuition into the nature of the world and man which constitutes what we describe as Renaissance must have emerged. As the facts, however, stand, it is impossible to dissociate the rejection of the other world as the sole reality, the joyous acceptance of this world as a place to live in and act in, the conviction that "the proper study of mankind is man," from humanism. Humanism as it actually appeared in Italy was positive in its conception of the problems to be solved, pagan in its contempt for mediaeval mysticism, invigorated for sensuous enjoyment by contact with antiquity, yet holding in itself the germ of new religious aspirations, profounder science and sterner probings of the mysteries of life than had been attempted even by the ancients. The operation of this humanistic spirit has now to be traced.

Dante, Petrarch, Boccaccio and Villani.—It is obvious that Italian literature owed little at the outset to the Revival of Learning. The *Divine Comedy,* the *Canzoniere* and the *Decameron* were works of monumental art, deriving neither form nor inspiration immediately from the classics but applying the originality of Italian genius to matter drawn from previous mediaeval sources. Dante showed both in his epic poem and in his lyrics that he had not abandoned the sphere of contemporary thought. Allegory and theology, the vision and the symbol, still determine the form of masterpieces which for perfection of workmanship and for emancipated force of intellect rank among the highest products of the human mind. Yet they are not mediaeval in the same sense as the song of Roland or the Arthurian cycle. They proved that, though Italy came late into the realm of literature, her action was destined to be decisive and alterative by the introduction of a new spirit, a firmer and more positive grasp on life and art. These qualities she owed to her material prosperity, to her freedom from feudalism, to her secularized church, her commercial nobility, her political independence in a federation of small states. Petrarch and Boccaccio, though they both held the mediaeval doctrine that literature should teach some abstruse truth beneath a veil of fiction, differed from Dante in this, that their poetry and prose in the vernacular abandoned both allegory and symbol. In their practice they ignored their theory; Petrarch's lyrics continue the Provençal tradition as it had been reformed in Tuscany, with a subtler and more modern analysis of emotion, a purer and more chastened style than his masters could boast; Boccaccio's tales, in like manner, continue the tradition of the fabliaux, raising that literary species to the rank of finished art, enriching it with humour and strengthening its substance by keen insight into all varieties of character. The *Canzoniere* and the *Decameron* distinguish themselves from mediaeval literature, not by any return to classical precedents, but by free self-conscious handling of human nature. So much had to be premised in order to make it clear in what relation humanism stood to the Renaissance since the Italian work of Dante, Petrarch and Boccaccio is sufficient to indicate the re-birth of the spirit after ages of apparent deadness. Had the Revival of Learning not intervened, it is probable that the vigorous efforts of these writers alone would have inaugurated a new age of European culture. Yet, while noting this reservation of judgment it must also be remarked that all three felt themselves under some peculiar obligation to the classics. Dante, mediaeval as his temper seems to us, chose Virgil for his guide, and ascribed his mastery of style to the study of Virgilian poetry. Petrarch and Boccaccio were, as we have seen, the pioneers of the new learning. They held their writings in the vernacular cheap, and initiated that contempt for the mother tongue which was a note of the earlier Renaissance. Giovanni Villani, the first chronicler who used Italian for the compilation of a methodical history, tells us how he was impelled to write by musing on the ruins of Rome, and thinking of the vanished greatness of the Latin race. We have, therefore, to recognize that the four greatest writers of the 14th century, while the Revival of Learning was yet in its cradle, each after his own fashion acknowledged the vivifying touch upon his spirit of the antique genius. They seem to have been conscious that they could not give the desired impulse to modern literature and art without contact with the classics; and, in spite of the splendour of their achievements in Italian, they found no immediate followers upon that path.

Scholarship and Literature.—The fascination of pure study was so powerful, the Italians at that epoch were so eager to recover the past, that during the 15th century we have before our eyes the spectacle of this great nation deviating from the course of development begun in poetry by Dante and Petrarch, in prose by Boccaccio and Villani, into the channels of scholarship and antiquarian research. The language of the *Canzoniere* and *Decameron* was abandoned for revived Latin and discovered Greek. Acquisition supplanted invention; imitation of classical authors suppressed originality of style. The energies of the Italian people were devoted to transcribing the codices, settling texts, translating Greek books into Latin, compiling grammars, commentaries, encyclopaedias, dictionaries, epitomes and ephemerides. During this century the best histories—Bruni's and Poggio's annals of Florence, for example—were composed in Latin after the manner of Livy. The best dissertations, Landino's *Camaldunenses,* Valla's *De Voluptate,* were laboured imitations of Cicero's *Tusculans.* The best verse, Pontano's elegies, Politian's hexameters, were, in like manner Latin; public orations upon ceremonial occasions were delivered in the Latin tongue; correspondence, official and familiar, was carried on in the same language; even the fabliaux received, in Poggio's *Facetiae,* a dress of elegant Latinity. The noticeable barrenness of Italian literature at this period is referable to the fact that **men** of genius and talent devoted themselves to

erudition and struggled to express their thoughts and feelings in a speech which was not natural. Yet they were engaged in a work of incalculable importance. At the close of the century the knowledge of Greece and Rome had been reappropriated and placed beyond the possibility of destruction; the chasm between the old and new world had been bridged; mediaeval modes of thinking and discussing had been superseded; the staple of education, the common culture which has brought all Europe into intellectual agreement, was already in existence. Humanism was now an actuality. Owing to the uncritical veneration for antiquity which then prevailed, it had received a strong tincture of pedantry. Its professors, in their revolt against the middle ages, made light of Christianity and paraded paganism. What was even worse from an artistic point of view, they had contracted puerilities of style, vanities of rhetoric, stupidities of wearisome citation. Still, at the opening of the 16th century, it became manifest what fruits of noble quality the Revival of Letters was about to bring forth for modern literature. Two great scholars, Lorenzo de'Medici and Politian, had already returned to the practice of Italian poetry. Their work is the first absolutely modern work—modern in the sense of having absorbed the stores of classic learning and reproduced those treasures in forms of simple, natural, native beauty. Boiardo occupies a similar position by the fusion of classic mythology with chivalrous romance in his *Orlando Innamorato.* But the victor's laurels were reserved for Ariosto whose *Orlando Furioso* is the purest and most perfect extant example of Renaissance poetry. It was not merely in what they had acquired and assimilated from the classics that these poets showed the transformation effected in the fields of literature by humanism. The whole method and spirit of the mediaeval art had been abandoned. That of the *cinque cento* is positive, defined, mundane. The deity, if deity there be, that rules in it, is beauty. Interest is confined to the actions, passions, sufferings and joys of human life, to its pathetic, tragic, humorous and sentimental incidents. Of the state of souls beyond the grave we hear and are supposed to care nothing. In the drama the pedantry of the Revival which had not injured romantic literature made itself perniciously felt. Rules were collected from Horace and Aristotle. Seneca was chosen as the model of tragedy; Plautus and Terence supplied the groundwork of comedy. Thus in the plays of Rucellai, Trissino, Sperone and other tragic poets, the nobler elements of humanism, considered as a revelation of the world and man, obtained no free development. Even the comedies of the best authors are too observant of Latin precedents, although some pieces of Machiavelli, Ariosto, Aretino, Cecchi and Gelli are admirable for vivid delineation of contemporary manners.

Fine Arts.—The relation of the plastic arts to the Revival of Learning is similar to that which has been sketched in the case of poetry. Cimabue started with work which owed nothing directly to antiquity. At about the same time Niccola Pisano (d. 1278) studied the style of sculpture in fragments of Graeco-Roman marbles. His manner influenced Giotto, who set painting on a forward path. Fortunately for the unimpeded expansion of Italian art, little was brought to light of antique workmanship during the 14th and 15th centuries. The classical stimulus came to painters, sculptors and architects chiefly through literature. Therefore there was narrow scope for imitation; and the right spirit of humanism displayed itself in a passionate study of perspective, nature and the nude. Yet we find in the writings of Ghiberti and Alberti, we notice in the masterpieces of these men and their compeers Brunelleschi and Donatello, how even in the 15th century the minds of artists were fascinated by what survived of classic grace and science. Gradually, as the race became penetrated by antique thought, the earlier Christian motives of the arts yielded to pagan subjects. Gothic architecture, which had always flourished feebly on Italian soil, was supplanted by a hybrid Roman style. The study of Vitruvius gave strong support to that pseudoclassic manner which, when it had reached its final point in Palladio's work, overspread the whole of Europe and dominated taste during two centuries. But the perfect plastic art of Italy, the pure art of the *cinque cento,* the painting of Raphael, Da Vinci, Titian and Correggio the sculpture of Donatello, Michelangelo and Sansovino, the architecture of Bramante, Omodeo, and the Venetian Lombardi, however much imbued with the spirit of the classical revival, take rank beside the poetry of Ariosto as a free intelligent product of the Renaissance. That is to say, it is not so much an outcome of studies in antiquity as an exhibition of emancipated modern genius fired and illuminated by the masterpieces of the past. It indicates a separation from the middle ages, inasmuch as it is permanently natural. Its religion is joyous, sensuous, dramatic, terrible, but in each and all of its many-sided manifestations strictly human. Its touch on classical mythology is original, rarely imitative or pedantic. The art of the Renaissance was an apocalypse of the beauty of the world and man in unaffected spontaneity, without side thoughts for piety or erudition, inspired by pure delight in loveliness and harmony for their own sakes.

Science and Philosophy.—In the fields of science and philosophy humanism wrought similar important changes. Petrarch began by waging relentless war against the logicians and materialists of his own day. With the advance made in Greek studies scholastic methods of thinking fell into contemptuous oblivion. The newly aroused curiosity for nature encouraged men like Alberti, Da Vinci, Toscanelli and Da Porta to make practical experiments, penetrate the working of physical forces, and invent scientific instruments. Anatomy began to be studied, and the time was not far distant when Titian should lend his pencil to the epoch-making treatise of Vesalius. The middle ages had been satisfied with absurd and visionary notions about the world around them, while the body of man was regarded with too much suspicion to be studied. Now the right method of interrogating nature with patience and loving admiration was instituted. At the same time the texts of ancient authors supplied hints which led to discoveries so far-reaching in their results as those of Copernicus, Columbus and Galileo. In philosophy, properly so called, the humanistic scorn for mediaeval dullness and obscurity swept away theological metaphysics as valueless. But at first little beyond empty rhetoric and clumsy compilation was substituted. The ethical treatises of the scholars are deficient in substance, while Ficino's attempt to revive Platonism betrays an uncritical conception of his master's drift. It was something, however, to have shaken off the shackles of ecclesiastical authority; and, even if a new authority, that of the ancients, was accepted in its stead, still progress was being made toward sounder methods of analysis. This is noticeable in Pomponazzo's system of materialism, based on the interpretation of Aristotle, but revealing a virile spirit of disinterested and unprejudiced research. The thinkers of southern Italy, Telesio, Bruno and Campanella, at last opened the two chief lines on which modern speculation has since moved. Telesio and Campanella may be termed the predecessors of Bacon. Bruno was the precursor of the idealistic schools. All three alike strove to disengage their minds from classical as well as ecclesiastical authority, proving that the emancipation of the will had been accomplished. It must be added that their writings, like every other product of the Renaissance, except its purest poetry and art, exhibit a hybrid between mediaeval and modern tendencies. Childish ineptitudes are mingled with intuitions of maturest wisdom and seeds of future thought germinate in the decaying refuse of past systems.

Criticism.—Humanism in its earliest stages was uncritical. It absorbed the relics of antiquity with omnivorous appetite and with very imperfect sense of the distinction between worse and better work. Yet it led in process of time to criticism. The critique of literature began in the lecture-room of Politian, in the printing house of Aldus, and in the school of Vittorino. The critique of Roman law started under Politian's auspices, upon a more liberal course than that which had been followed by the powerful but narrow-sighted glossators of Bologna. Finally, in the court of Naples arose that most formidable of all critical engines, the critique of established ecclesiastical traditions and spurious historical documents. Valla by one vigorous effort destroyed the False Decretals and exposed the Donation of Constantine to ridicule, paving the way for the polemic carried on against the dubious pretensions of the papal throne by scholars of the

Reformation. A similar criticism, conducted less on lines of erudition than of persiflage and irony, ransacked the moral abuses of the Church and played around the foundations of Christianity. This was tolerated by men who repeated the witty epigram, attributed to Leo X, "What profit has not that fable of Christ brought us!" The same critical and philosophic spirit working on the materials of history produced a new science, the honours of which belong to Machiavelli. He showed, on the one side, how the history of a people can be written with a recognition of fixed principles, and at the same time with an artistic feeling for personal and dramatic episodes. On the other side, he addressed himself to the analysis of man considered as a political being, to the anatomy of constitutions and the classification of governments, to the study of motives underlying public action, the secrets of success and the causes of failure in the conduct of affairs. The unscrupulous rigour with which he applied his scientific method, and the sinister deductions he thought himself justified in drawing from the results it yielded, excited terror and repulsion. Nevertheless a department had been added to the intellectual empire of mankind, in which fellow-workers, like Guicciardini at Florence, and subsequently Sarpi at Venice, were not slow to follow the path traced by Machiavelli.

Education.—The object of the foregoing paragraphs has been to show in what way the positive, inquisitive, secular, exploratory spirit of the Renaissance, when toned and controlled by humanism penetrated the regions of literature, art, philosophy and science. It becomes at this point of much moment to consider how social manners in Italy were modified by the same causes, since the type developed there was in large measure communicated together with the new culture to the rest of Europe. The first subject to be noticed under this heading is education. What has come to be called a classical education was the immediate product of the Italian Renaissance. The Universities of Bologna, Padua, and Salerno had been famous through the later middle ages for the study of law, physics and medicine; and during the 15th and 16th centuries the first two still enjoyed celebrity in these faculties. But at this period no lecture-rooms were so crowded as those in which professors of antique literature and language read passages from the poets and orators, taught Greek, and commented upon the systems of philosophers. The mediaeval curriculum offered no defined place for the new learning of the Revival, which had indeed no recognized name. Chairs had therefore to be founded under the title of rhetoric, from which men like Chrysoloras and Guarino, Filelfo and Politian expounded orally to hundreds of eager students from every town of Italy and every nation of Europe their accumulated knowledge of antiquity. One mass of Greek and Roman erudition, including history and metaphysics, law and science, civic institutions and the art of war, mythology and magistracies, metrical systems and oratory, agriculture and astronomy, domestic manners and religious rites, grammar and philology, biology and numismatics, formed the miscellaneous subject-matter of this so-styled rhetoric. Notes taken at these lectures supplied young scholars with hints for further exploration; and a certain tradition of treating antique authors for the display of general learning, as well as for the elucidation of their texts, came into vogue, which has determined the method of scholarship for the last three centuries in Europe. The lack of printed books in the first period of the Revival, and the comparative rarity of Greek erudition among students, combined with the intense enthusiasm aroused for the new gospel of the classics, gave special value to the personal teaching of these professors. They journeyed from city to city, attracted by promises of higher pay, and allured by ever-growing laurels of popular fame. Each large town established its public study, academy or university—similar institutions under varying designations—for the exposition of the *literae humaniores*. The humanists, or professors of that branch of knowledge, became a class of the highest dignity. They were found in the chanceries of the republics, in the papal curia, in the council chambers of princes, at the headquarters of condottieri, wherever business had to be transacted, speeches to be made and the work of secretaries to be performed. Furthermore, they undertook the charge of private education, opening schools which displaced the mediaeval system of instruction and taking engagements as tutors in the families of despots, noblemen and wealthy merchants. The academy established by Vittorino da Feltre at Mantua under the protection of Gian Francesco Gonzaga, for the training of pupils of both sexes, might be chosen as the type of this Italian method. His scholars who were lodged in appropriate buildings met daily to hear the master read and comment on the classics. They learned portions of the best authors by heart, exercised themselves in translating from one language to another and practised composition in prose and verse. It was Vittorino's care to see that while their memories were duly stored with words and facts their judgment should be formed by a critical analysis, attention to style and comparison of the authors of a decadent age with those who were acknowledged classics. During the hours of recreation suitable physical exercises, as fencing, riding, and gymnastics, were conducted under qualified trainers. From this sketch it will be seen how closely the educational system which came into England during the reign of the Tudors, and which has prevailed until the present time, was modelled upon the Italian type. English youths who spend their time at Eton between athletic sports and Latin verse, and who take a first class in *Literae Humaniores* at Oxford are pursuing the same course of physical and mental discipline as the princes of Gonzaga or Montefeltro in the 15th century.

The humanists effected a deeply penetrating change in social manners. Through their influence as tutors, professors, orators and courtiers, society was permeated by a fresh ideal of culture. To be a gentleman in Italy meant at this epoch to be a man acquainted with the rudiments at least of scholarship, refined in diction, capable of corresponding or of speaking in choice phrases, open to the beauty of the arts, intelligently interested in archaeology, taking for his models of conduct the great men of antiquity, rather than the saints of the Church. He was also expected to prove himself an adept in physical exercises and in the courteous observances which survived from chivalry. The type is set before us by Castiglione in that book upon the courtier which went the round of Europe in the 16th century. It is further emphasized in a famous passage of the *Orlando Innamorato* where Boiardo compares the Italian ideal of an accomplished gentleman with the coarser type admired by nations of the north. To this point the awakened intelligence of the Renaissance, instructed by humanism, polished by the fine arts, expanding in genial conditions of diffused wealth, had brought the Italians at a period when the rest of Europe was comparatively barbarous.

Defects of the Renaissance.—This picture has undoubtedly a darker side. Humanism in its revolt against the middle ages was, as we have seen already, mundane, pagan, irreligious, positive[1]. The Renaissance can, after all, be regarded only as a period of transition in which much of the good of the past was sacrificed while some of the evil was retained, and neither the bad nor the good of the future was brought clearly into fact. Beneath the surface of brilliant social culture lurked gross appetites and savage passions, unrestrained by mediaeval piety, untutored by modern experience. Italian society exhibited an almost unexampled spectacle of literary, artistic and courtly refinement crossed by brutalities of lust, treasons, poisonings, assassinations, violence. A succession of worldly pontiffs brought the Church into flagrant discord with the principles of Christianity. Steeped in pagan learning, desirous of imitating the manners of the ancients, thinking and feeling in harmony with Ovid and Theocritus, and at the same time rendered cynical by the corruption of papal Rome, the educated classes lost their grasp upon morality. Political honesty ceased almost to have a name in Italy. The Christian virtues were scorned by the foremost actors and the ablest thinkers of the time, while the antique virtues were themes for rhetoric rather than moving springs of conduct. This is apparent to all students of Machiavelli and Guicciardini, the profoundest analysts of their age, the bitterest satirists of its vices, but themselves infected with its incapacity for moral goodness. The Italians were not only vitiated; they had also become impotent for action and re-

[1] But there was also a great school of Christian humanists intent upon reconciling the gospel with the Greek philosophers.

sistance. At the height of the Renaissance the five great Powers in the peninsula formed a confederation of independent but mutually attractive and repellent states. Equilibrium was maintained by diplomacy, in which the humanists played a foremost part, casting a network of intrigue over the nation which helped in no small measure to stimulate intelligence and create a common medium of culture, but which accustomed statesmen to believe that everything could be achieved by wire-pulling. Wars were conducted on a showy system by means of mercenaries, who played a safe game in the field and developed a system of bloodless campaigns. Meanwhile the people grew up unused to arms. When Italy between the years 1494 and 1530 became the battlefield of French, German and Spanish forces, it was seen to what a point of helplessness the political, moral and social conditions of the Renaissance had brought the nation.

Spread of the New Learning.—It was needful to study at some length the main phenomena of the Renaissance in Italy, because the history of that phase of evolution in the other Western races turns almost entirely upon points in which they either adhered to or diverged from the type established there. Speaking broadly, what France, Germany, Spain and England assimilated from Italy at this epoch was in the first place the new learning as it was then called. This implied the new conception of human life, the new interest in the material universe, the new method of education, and the new manners, which we have seen to be inseparable from Italian humanism. Under these forms of intellectual enlightenment and polite culture the renascence of the human spirit had appeared in Italy, where it was more than elsewhere connected with the study of classical antiquity. But that audacious exploratory energy which formed the motive force of the Renaissance as distinguished from the Revival of Learning took, as we shall see, very different directions in the several nations who now were sending the flower of their youth to study at the feet of Italian rhetoricians.

The Renaissance ran its course in Italy with strange indifference to consequences. The five great Powers, held in equilibrium by Lorenzo de' Medici, dreamed that the peninsula could be maintained *in statu quo* by diplomacy. The Church saw no danger in encouraging a pseudo-pagan ideal of life, violating its own principle of existence by assuming the policy of an aggrandizing secular state, and outraging Christendom openly by its acts and utterances. Society at large was hardly aware that an intellectual force of stupendous magnitude and incalculable explosive power had been created by the new learning. Why should not established institutions proceed upon the customary and convenient methods of routine, while the delights of existence were augmented, manners polished, arts developed and a golden age of epicurean ease made decent by a state religion which no one cared to break with because no one was left to regard it seriously? This was the attitude of the Italians when the Renaissance, which they had initiated as a thing of beauty, began to operate as a thing of power beyond the Alps.

GERMANY

Germany was already provided with universities, seven of which had been founded between 1348 and 1409. In these haunts of learning the new studies took root after the year 1440, chiefly through the influence of travelling professors, Peter Luder and Samuel Karoch. German scholars made their way to Lombard and Tuscan lecture-rooms, bringing back the methods of the humanists. Greek, Latin and Hebrew erudition soon found itself at home on Teutonic soil. Like Italian men of letters, these pioneers of humanism gave a classic turn to their patronymics: unfamiliar names, Crotus Rubeanus and Pierius Graecus, Capnion and Lupambulus Ganymedes, Oecolampadius and Melanchthon, resounded on the Rhine. A few of the German princes, among whom Maximilian, the prince cardinal Albert of Mainz, Frederick the Wise of Saxony, and Eberhard of Württemberg deserve mention, exercised a not insignificant influence on letters by the foundation of new universities and the patronage of learned men. The cities of Strasbourg, Nuremberg, Augsburg, Basle, became centres of learned coteries which gathered round scholars like Wimpheling, Brant, Peutinger, Schedel, and Pirckheimer, artists like Dürer and Holbein, painters of the eminence of Froben. Academies in imitation of Italian institutions came into existence, the two most conspicuous named after the Rhine and the Danube, holding their headquarters respectively at Heidelberg and Vienna. Crowned poets, of whom the most eminent was Conrad Celtes Protucius (Pickel!) emulated the fame of Politian and Pontano. Yet though the Renaissance was thus widely communicated to the centres of German intelligence, it displayed a different character from that which it assumed in Italy. Gothic art, which was indigenous in Germany, yielded but little to southern influences. Such work as that of Dürer, Vischer, Cranach, Schöngauer, Holbein, consummate as it was in technical excellence, did not assume Italian forms of loveliness, did not display the paganism of the Latin races. The modification of Gothic architecture by pseudo-Roman elements of style was incomplete. What Germany afterwards took of the Palladian manner was destined to reach it on a circuitous route from France. In like manner the new learning failed to penetrate all classes of society with the rapidity of its expansion in Italy, nor was the new ideal of life and customs so easily substituted for the mediaeval. The German aristocracy, as Aeneas Sylvius had noticed, remained for the most part barbarous, addicted to gross pleasures, contemptuous of culture. The German dialects were too rough to receive that artistic elaboration under antique influences which had been so facile in Tuscany. The doctors of the universities were too wedded to their antiquated manuals and methods, too satisfied with dullness, too proud of titles and diplomas, too anxious to preserve ecclesiastical discipline and to repress mental activity, for a genial spirit of humanism to spread freely. Not in Cologne or Tübingen but in Padua and Florence did the German pioneers of the Renaissance acquire their sense of liberal studies. And when they returned home they found themselves encumbered with stupidities, jealousies and rancours. Moreover the temper of these more enlightened men was itself opposed to Italian indifference and immorality; it was pugnacious and polemical, eager to beat down the arrogance of monks and theologians rather than to pursue an ideal of aesthetical self-culture. To a student of the origins of German humanism it is clear that something very different from the Renaissance of Lorenzo de' Medici and Leo X. was in preparation from the first upon Teutonic soil. Far less plastic and form-loving than the Italian, the German intelligence was more penetrative, earnest, disputative, occupied with substantial problems. Starting with theological criticism, proceeding to the stage of solid studies in the three learned languages, German humanism occupied the attention of a widely scattered sect of erudite scholars; but it did not arouse the interest of the whole nation until it was forced into a violently militant attitude by Pfefferkorn's attack on Reuchlin. That attempt to extinguish honest thought prepared the Reformation; and humanism after 1518 was absorbed in politico-religious warfare.

Humanism and the German Reformation.—The point of contact between humanism and the Reformation in Germany has to be insisted on; for it is just here that the relation of the Reformation to the Renaissance in general makes itself apparent. As the Renaissance had its precursory movements in the mediaeval period, so the German Reformation was preceded by Wycliffe and Huss, by the discontents of the Great Schism, and by the councils of Constance and Basel. These two main streams of modern progress had been proceeding upon different tracks to diverse issues, but they touched in the studies stimulated by the Revival, and they had a common origin in the struggle of the spirit after self-emancipation. Johann Reuchlin, who entered the lecture-room of Argyropoulos at Rome in 1482, Erasmus of Rotterdam, who once dwelt at Venice as the house guest of the Aldi, applied their critical knowledge of Hebrew and Greek to the elucidation and diffusion of the Bible. To the Germans, as to all nations of that epoch, the Bible came as a new book, because they now read it for the first time with eyes opened by humanism. The touch of the new spirit which had evolved literature, art and culture in Italy sufficed in Germany to recreate Christianity. This new spirit in Italy emancipated human intelligence by the classics; in Ger-

many it emancipated the human conscience by the Bible. The indignation excited by Leo X.'s sale of indulgences, the moral rage stirred in Northern hearts by papal abominations in Rome were external causes which precipitated the schism between Teutonic and Latin Christianity. The Reformation, inspired by the same energy of resuscitated life as the Renaissance, assisted by the same engines of the printing-press and paper, using the same apparatus of scholarship, criticism, literary skill, being in truth another manifestation of the same world-movement under a diverse form, now posed itself as an irreconcilable antagonist to Renaissance Italy. It would be difficult to draw any comparison between German and Italian humanists to the disparagement of the former. Reuchlin was no less learned than Pico; Melanchthon no less humane than Ficino; Erasmus no less witty and far more trenchant than Petrarch; Ulrich von Hutten no less humorous than Folengo; Paracelsus no less fantastically learned than Cardano. But the cause in which German intellect and will were enlisted was so different that it is difficult not to make a formal separation between that movement which evolved culture in Italy and that which restored religion in Germany, establishing the freedom of intelligence in the one sphere and the freedom of conscience in the other. The truth is that the Reformation was the Teutonic Renaissance. It was the emancipation of the reason on a line neglected by the Italians, more important indeed in its political consequences, more weighty in its bearing on rationalistic developments than the Italian Renaissance, but none the less an outcome of the same ground-influences. We have already in this century reached a point at which, in spite of stubborn Protestant dogmatism and bitter Catholic reaction, we can perceive how the ultimate affranchisement of man will be the work of both.

The Counter-Reformation.—The German Reformation was incapable of propagating itself in Italy, chiefly for the reason that the intellectual forces which it represented and employed had already found specific outlet in that country. It was not in the nature of the Italians, sceptical and paganized by the revival, to be keenly interested about questions which seemed to revive the scholastic disputes of the middle ages. It was not in their external conditions, suffering as they were from invasions, enthralled by despots, to use the Reformation as a lever for political revolution. Yet when a tumultuary army of so-called Lutherans sacked Rome in 1527, no sober thinker doubted that a new agent had appeared in Europe which would alter the destinies of the peninsula. The Renaissance was virtually closed so far as it concerned Italy, when Clement VII. and Charles V. struck their compact at Bologna in 1530. This compact proclaimed the principle of monarchial absolutism, supported by papal authority, itself monarchially absolute, which influenced Europe until the outbreak of the Revolution. A reaction immediately set in both against the Renaissance and the Reformation. The Council of Trent, opened in 1545 and closed in 1563, decreed a formal purgation of the Church, affirmed the fundamental doctrines of Catholicism, strengthened the papal supremacy, and inaugurated that movement of resistance which is known as the Counter-Reformation. The complex onward effort of the modern nations, expressing itself in Italy as Renaissance, in Germany as Reformation, had aroused the forces of conservatism. The four main instruments of the reaction were the papacy, which had done so much by its sympathy with the revival to promote the humanistic spirit it now dreaded, the strength of Spain, and two Spanish institutions planted on Roman soil—the Inquisition and the Society of Jesus. The principle contended for and established by this reaction was absolutism as opposed to freedom—monarchial absolutism, papal absolutism, the suppression of energies liberated by the Renaissance and the Reformation. The partial triumph of this principle was secure, in as much as the majority of established powers in Church and State felt threatened by the revolutionary opinions afloat in Europe. Renaissance and Reformation were, moreover, already at strife. Both, too, were spiritual and elastic tendencies toward progress, ideals rather than solid organisms.

SPAIN

The part played by Spain in this period of history was determined in large measure by external circumstance. The Spaniards became one nation by the conquest of Granada and the union of the crowns of Castile and Aragon. The war of national aggrandizement being in its nature a crusade, inflamed the religious enthusiasm of the people. It was followed by the expulsion of Jews and Moors, and by the establishment of the Inquisition on a solid basis, with powers formidable to the freedom of all Spaniards from the peasant to the throne. These facts explain the decisive action of the Spanish nation on the side of Catholic conservatism, and help us to understand why their brilliant achievements in the field of culture during the 16th century were speedily followed by stagnation. It will be well, in dealing with the Renaissance in Spain, to touch first upon the arts and literature, and then to consider those qualities of character in action whereby the nation most distinguished itself from the rest of Europe. Architecture in Spain, emerging from the Gothic stage, developed an Early Renaissance style of bewildering richness by adopting elements of Arabic and Moorish decoration. Sculpture exhibited realistic vigour of indubitably native stamp; and the minor plastic crafts were cultivated with success on lines of striking originality. Painting grew from a homely stock, until the work of Velasquez showed that Spanish masters in this branch were fully abreast of their Italian compeers and contemporaries. To dwell here upon the Italianizing versifiers, moralists and pastoral romancers who attempted to refine the vernacular of the *Romancero* would be superfluous. They are mainly noticeable as proving that certain coteries in Spain were willing to accept the Italian Renaissance. But the real force of the people was not in this courtly literary style. It expressed itself at last in the monumental work of *Don Quixote*, which places Cervantes beside Rabelais, Ariosto and Shakespeare as one of the four supreme exponents of the Renaissance. The affectations of decadent chivalry disappeared before its humour; the lineaments of a noble nation, animated by the youth of modern Europe emerging from the middle ages, were portrayed in its enduring pictures of human experience. The Spanish drama, meanwhile untrammelled by those false canons of pseudo-classic taste which fettered the theatre in Italy and afterwards in France, rose to an eminence in the hands of Lope de Vega and Calderon which only the English, and the English only in the masterpieces of three or four playwrights, can rival. Camoens in the *Lusiad,* if we may here group Portugal with Spain, was the first modern poet to compose an epic on a purely modern theme, vying with Virgil, but not bending to pedantic rules, and breathing the spirit of the age of heroic adventures and almost fabulous discoveries into his melodious numbers. What has chiefly to be noted regarding the achievements of the Spanish race in arts and letters at this epoch is their potent national originality. The revival of learning produced in Spain no slavish imitation as it did in Italy, no formal humanism, and, it may be added, very little of fruitful scholarship. The Renaissance here, as in England, displayed essential qualities of intellectual freedom, delight in life, exultation over rediscovered earth and man. The note of Renaissance work in Germany was still Gothic. This we feel in the penetrative earnestness of Dürer, in the homeliness of Hans Sachs, in the grotesque humour of *Eulenspiegel,* and the *Narrenschiff,* the sombre pregnancy of the Faust legend, the almost stolid mastery of Holbein. It lay not in the German genius to escape from the preoccupations and the limitations of the middle ages, for this reason mainly that what we call mediaeval was to a very large extent Teutonic. But on the Spanish peninsula, in the masterpieces of Velasquez, Cervantes, Camoens, Calderon, we emerge into an atmosphere of art definitely national, distinctly modern, where solid natural forms stand before us realistically modelled, with light and shadow on their rounded outlines, and where the airiest creatures of the fancy take shape and weave a dance of rhythmic, light, incomparable intricacy. The Spanish Renaissance would in itself suffice, if other witnesses were wanting, to prove how inaccurate is the theory that limits this movement to the revival of learning. Touched by Italian influences, enriched and fortified by the new learning, Spanish genius walked firmly forward on its own path. It was crushed only by forces generated in the nation that produced it, by the Inquisition and by despotic Catholic absolutism.

In the history of the Renaissance, Spain and Portugal represent the exploration of the ocean and the colonization of the other hemisphere. The voyages of Columbus and Vespucci to America, the rounding of the Cape by Diaz and the discovery of the sea road to India by Vasco da Gama, Cortés's conquest of Mexico and Pizarro's conquest of Peru, marked a new era for the human race and inaugurated the modern age more decisively than any other series of events has done. It has recently been maintained that modern European history is chiefly an affair of competition between confederated states for the possession of lands revealed by Columbus and Da Gama. Without challenging or adopting this speculation, it may be safely affirmed that nothing so pregnant of results has happened as this exploration of the globe. To say that it displaced the centre of gravity in politics and commerce, substituting the ocean for the Mediterranean, dethroning Italy from her seat of central importance in traffic, depressing the eastern and elevating the western Powers of Europe, opening a path for Anglo-Saxon expansiveness, forcing philosophers and statesmen to regard the Occidental nations as a single group in counterpoise to other groups of nations, the European community as one unit correlated to other units of humanity upon this planet, is truth enough to vindicate the vast significance of these discoveries. The Renaissance, far from being the re-birth of antiquity with its civilization confined to the Mediterranean and the Hercules' Pillars beyond which lay Cimmerian darkness, was thus effectively the entrance upon a quite incalculably wider stage of life on which mankind at large has since enacted one great drama. While Spanish navies were exploring the ocean, and Spanish paladins were overturning empires, Charles V headed the reaction of Catholicism against reform. Stronger as king of Spain than as emperor, for the Empire was little but a name, he lent the weight of his authority to that system of coercion and repression which enslaved Italy, desolated Germany with war, and drowned the Low Countries in blood. Philip II, with full approval of the Spanish nation, pursued the same policy in an even stricter spirit. He was powerfully assisted by two institutions in which the national character of Spain expressed itself, the Inquisition and the Society of Jesus. Of the former it is not needful to speak here. But we have to observe that the last great phenomenon of the Spanish Renaissance was Ignatius Loyola, who organized the militia by means of which the Church worked its Counter-Reformation. His motto, *Perinde ac cadaver,* expressed that recognition of absolutism which papacy and monarchy demanded for their consolidation. (*See* JESUS, SOCIETY OF and LOYOLA, ST. IGNATIUS OF.)

FRANCE

The logical order of an essay which attempts to show how Renaissance was correlated to Reformation and Counter-Reformation has necessitated the treatment of Italy, Germany and Spain in succession; for these three nations were the three main agents in the triple process to be analysed. It was due to their specific qualities, and to the diverse circumstances of their external development that the re-birth of Europe took this form of duplex action on the lines of intellectual and moral progress, followed by reaction against mental freedom. We have now to speak of France, which earliest absorbed the influence of the Italian revival, and of England which received it latest. The Renaissance may be said to have begun in France with Charles VIII.'s expedition to Naples, and to have continued until the extinction of the house of Valois. Louis XII. and Francis I. spent a considerable portion of their reigns in the attempt to secure possession of the Italian provinces they claimed. Henry II.'s queen was Catherine of the Medicean family; and her children, Charles IX. and Henry III., were Italianated Frenchmen. Thus the connection between France and Italy during the period 1494–1589 was continuous. The French passed to and fro across the Alps on military and peaceful expeditions. Italians came to France as courtiers, ambassadors, men of business, captains and artists. French society assumed a strong Italian colouring, nor were the manners of the court very different from those of an Italian city, except that externally they remained ruder and less polished. The relation between the crown and its great feudatories, the military bias of the aristocracy, and the marked distinction between classes which survived from the middle ages, rendered France in many vital points unlike Italy. Yet the annals of that age, and the anecdotes retailed by Brantôme, prove that the royalty and nobility of France had been largely Italianized.

Architecture.—It is said that Louis XII. brought Fra Giocondo of Verona back with him to France and founded a school of architects. But we need not have recourse to this legend for the explanation of such Italian influences as were already noticeable in the Renaissance buildings on the Loire. Without determining the French style, Italian intercourse helped to stimulate its formation and development. There are students of the 15th century in France who resent this intrusion of the Italian Renaissance. But they forget that France was bound by inexorable laws of human evolution to obey the impulse which communicated itself to every form of art in Europe. In the school of Fontainebleau, under the patronage of Francis I., that Italian influence made itself distinctly felt; yet a true French manner had been already formed, which, when it was subsequently applied at Paris, preserved a marked national quality. The characteristic of the style developed by Bullant, De l'Orme and Lescot, in the royal or princely palaces of Chenonceaux, Chambord, Anet, Écouen, Fontainebleau, the Louvre and elsewhere is a blending of capricious fancy and inventive richness of decoration with purity of outline and a large sense of the beauty of extended masses. Beginning with the older castles of Touraine, and passing onward to the Tuileries, we trace the passage from the mediaeval fortress to the modern pleasure-house, and note how architecture obeyed the special demands of that new phenomenon of Renaissance civilization, the court. In the general distribution of parts these monumental buildings express the peculiar conditions which French society assumed under the influence of Francis I. and Diane de Poitiers. In details of execution and harmonic combinations they illustrate the precision, logic, lucidity and cheerful spirit of the national genius. Here, as in Lombardy, a feeling for serene beauty derived from the study of the antique has not interrupted the evolution of a style indigenous to France and eminently characteristic of the French temperament.

Painting and Sculpture.—During the reign of Francis I. several Italian painters of eminence visited France. Among these Del Rosso, Primaticcio, Del Sarto and Da Vinci are the most famous. But their example was not productive of a really great school of French painting. It was left for the Poussins and Claude Lorraine in the next century, acting under mingled Italian and Flemish influences, to embody the still active spirit of the classical revival. These three masters were the contemporaries of Corneille, and do not belong to the Renaissance period. Sculpture, on the contrary, in which art, as in architecture, the mediaeval French had been surpassed by no other people of Europe, was practised with originality and power in the reigns of Henry II. and Francis I. Ponzio and Cellini, who quitted Italy for France, found themselves outrivalled in their own sphere by Jean Goujon, Cousin and Pilon. The decorative sculpture of this epoch, whether combined with architecture or isolated in monumental statuary, ranks for grace and suavity with the best of Sansovino's. At the same time it is unmistakably inspired by a sense of beauty different from the Italian—more piquant and pointed, less languorous, more mannered perhaps, but with less of empty rhythmical effect. All this while the minor arts of enamelling, miniature, glass-painting, goldsmith's work, jewellery, engraving, tapestry, wood-carving, pottery, etc., were cultivated with a spontaneity and freedom which proved that France, in the middle point between Flanders and Italy, was able to use both influences without a sacrifice of native taste. It may indeed be said in general that what is true of France is likewise true of all countries which felt the artistic impulses of the Renaissance. Whether we regard Spain, the Netherlands, or Germany at this epoch, we find a national impress stamped upon the products of the plastic and the decorative arts, notwithstanding the prevalence of certain forms derived from the antique and Italy. It was only at a later period that the formalism of

pseudo-classic pedantry reduced natural and national originality to a dead unanimity.

Literature.—French literature was quick to respond to Renaissance influences. De Comines, the historian of Charles VIII.'s expedition to Naples, differs from the earlier French chroniclers in his way of regarding the world of men and affairs. He has the perspicuity and analytical penetration of a Venetian ambassador. Villon, his contemporary, may rather be ranked, so far as artistic form and use of knowledge are concerned, with poets of the middle ages, and in particular with the Goliardi. But he is essentially modern in the vividness of his self-portraiture, and in what we are wont to call realism. Both De Comines and Villon indicate the entrance of a new quality into literature. The Rhétoriqueurs, while protracting mediaeval traditions by their use of allegory and complicated metrical systems, sought to improve the French language by introducing Latinisms. Thus the Revival of Learning began to affect the vernacular in the last years of the 15th century. Marot and his school reacted against this pedantry. The Renaissance displayed itself in their effort to purify the form and diction of poetry. But the decisive revolution was effected by Ronsard and his comrades of the Pléiade. It was their professed object to raise French to a level with the classics, and to acclimatize Italian species of verse. The humanistic movement led these learned writers to engraft the graces of the antique upon their native literature, and to refine it by emulating the lucidity of Petrarch. The result of their endeavour was immediately apparent in the new force added to French rhythm, the new pomp, richness, colouring and polish conferred upon poetic diction. French style gradually attained to fixity, and the alexandrine came to be recognized as the standard line in poetry. D'Aubigné's invective and Régnier's satire, at the close of the 16th century, are as modern as Voltaire's. Meanwhile the drama was emerging from the mediaeval mysteries; and the classical type, made popular by Garnier's genius, was elaborated, as in Italy, upon the model of Seneca and the canons of the three unities. The tradition thus formed was continued and fortified by the illustrious playwrights of the 17th century. Translation from Greek and Latin into French progressed rapidly at the commencement of this period. It was a marked characteristic of the Renaissance in France to appropriate the spoils of Greece and Rome for the profit of the mother tongue. Amyot's *Plutarch* and his *Daphnis and Chloe* rank amongst the most exquisite examples of beautiful French prose. Prose had now the charm of simplicity combined with grace. To mention Brantôme is to mention the most entertaining of gossips. To speak of Montaigne is to speak of the best as well as the first of essayists. In all the literary work which has been mentioned, the originality and freshness of the French genius are no less conspicuous than its saturation with the new learning and with Italian studies. But the greatest name of the epoch, the name which is synonymous with the Renaissance in France, has yet to be uttered. That, of course, is Rabelais. His incommensurable and indescribable masterpiece of mingled humour, wisdom, satire, erudition, indecency, profundity, levity, imagination, realism, reflects the whole age in its mirror of hyper-Aristophanic farce. What Ariosto is for Italy, Cervantes for Spain, Erasmus for Holland, Luther for Germany, Shakespeare for England, that is Rabelais for France. The Renaissance cannot be comprehended in its true character without familiarity with these six representatives of its manifold and many-sided inspiration.

The Reformation.—The French Renaissance, so rich on the side of arts and letters, was hardly less rich on the side of classical studies. The Revival of Learning has a noble muster-roll of names in France: Turnebus, the patriarch of Hellenistic studies, the Étiennes of Paris, equalling in numbers, industry and learning their Venetian rivals; the two Scaligers; impassioned Dolet; eloquent Muret; learned Cujas; terrible Calvin; Ramus, the intrepid antagonist of Aristotle; De Thou and De Bèze; ponderous Casaubon; brilliant young Saumaise. The distinguishing characteristics of French humanism are vivid intelligence, critical audacity and polemical acumen, perspicuity of exposition, learning directed in its applications by logical sense rather than by artistic ideals of taste. Some of the names just mentioned remind us that in France, as in Germany and Holland, the Reformation was closely connected with the revival of learning. Humanism has never been in the narrow sense of that term Protestant; still less has it been strictly Catholic. In Italy it fostered a temper of mind decidedly averse to theological speculation and religious earnestness. In Holland and Germany with Erasmus, Reuchlin and Melanchthon it developed types of character, urbane, reflective, pointedly or gently critical, which left to themselves would not have plunged the north of Europe into the whirlpool of belligerent reform. Yet none the less was the new learning, through the open spirit of inquiry it nourished, its vindication of the private reason, its enthusiasm for republican antiquity, and its proud assertion of the rights of human independence, linked by a strong and subtle chain to that turbid revolt of the individual consciousness against spiritual despotism draped in fallacies and throned upon abuses. To this rebellion we give the name of Reformation. But while the necessities of antagonism to papal Rome made it assume at first the form of narrow and sectarian opposition, it marked in fact a vital struggle of the intellect towards truth and freedom, involving future results of scepticism and rationalistic audacity from which its earlier champions would have shrunk. It marked, moreover, in the condition of armed resistance against established authority which was forced upon it by the Counter-Reformation, a firm resolve to assert political liberty, leading in the course of time to a revolution with which the rebellious spirit of the Revival was sympathetic. This being the relation of humanism in general to reform, French learning in particular displayed such innovating boldness as threw many of its most conspicuous professors into the camp at war with Rome. Calvin, a French student of Picard origin, created the type of Protestantism to which the majority of French Huguenots adhered. This too was a moment at which philosophical seclusion was hardly possible. In a nation so tumultuously agitated one side or the other had to be adopted. Those of the French humanists who did not proclaim Huguenot opinions found themselves obliged with Muret to lend their talents to the Counter-Reformation, or to suffer persecution for heterodoxy like Dolet. The Church, terrified and infuriated by the progress of reform, suspected learning on its own account. To be an eminent scholar was to be accused of immorality, heresy and atheism in a single indictment; and the defence of weaker minds lay in joining the Jesuits as Heinsius was fain to do. France had already absorbed the earlier Renaissance in an Italianizing spirit before the Reformation made itself felt as a political actuality. This fact, together with the strong Italian bias of the Valois, serves to explain in some degree the reason why the Counter-Reformation entailed those fierce entangled civil wars, massacres of St. Bartholomew, murders of the Guises, regicides, treasons and empoisonments, that terminated with the compromise of Henry IV. It is no part of the present subject to analyse the political, religious and social interests of that struggle. The upshot was the triumph of the Counter-Reformation, and the establishment of its principle, absolutism, as the basis of French government. It was a French king who, when the nation had been reduced to order, uttered the famous word of absolutism, *"L'État, c'est moi."*

THE NETHERLANDS

The Renaissance in the Low Countries, as elsewhere, had its brilliant age of arts and letters. During the middle ages the wealthy free towns of Flanders flourished under conditions not dissimilar to those of the Italian republics. They raised miracles of architectural beauty, which were modified in the 15th and 16th centuries by characteristic elements of the new style. The Van Eycks, followed by Memling, Metsys, Mabuse, Lucas van Leyden, struck out a new path in the revival of painting and taught Europe the secret of oil-colouring. But it was reserved for the 17th century to witness the flower and fruit time of this powerful art in the work of Porbus, Rubens and Vandyck, in the Dutch schools of landscape and home-life, and in the unique masterpieces of Rembrandt. We have a right to connect this later period with the Renaissance, because the distracted state of the Netherlands during the 16th century suspended, while it could not extinguish,

their aesthetic development. The various schools of the 17th century, moreover, are animated with the Renaissance spirit no less surely than the Florentine school of the 15th or the Venetian of the 16th. The animal vigour and carnal enjoyment of Rubens, the refined Italianizing beauty of Vandyck, the mystery of light and gloom on Rembrandt's panels, the love of nature in Ruysdael, Cuyp and Van Hooghe, with their luminously misty skies, silvery daylight and broad expanse of landscape, the interest in common life displayed by Ter Borch, Van Steen, Douw, Ostade and Teniers, the instinct for the beauty of animals in Potter, the vast sea spaces of Vanderveldt, the grasp on reality, the acute intuition into character in portraits, the scientific study of the world and man, the robust sympathy with natural appetites, which distinguish the whole art of the Low Countries, are a direct emanation from the Renaissance.

The vernacular in the Netherlands profited at first but little by the impulse which raised Italian, Spanish, French and English to the rank of classic languages. But humanism, first of all in its protagonist Erasmus, afterwards in the long list of critical scholars and editors, Lipsius, Heinsius and Grotius, in the printers, Elzevir and Plantin, developed itself from the centre of the Leyden university with massive energy, and proved that it was still a motive force of intellectual progress. In the fields of classical learning the students of the Low Countries broke new ground chiefly by methodical collection, classification and comprehensive criticism of previously accumulated stores. Their works were solid and substantial edifices, forming the substratum for future scholarship. In addition to this they brought a philosophy and scientific thoroughness to bear on studies which had been pursued in a more literary spirit. It would, however, be uncritical to pursue this subject further; for the encyclopaedic labours of the Dutch philologers belong to a period when the Renaissance was overpast. For the same reason it is inadmissible to do more than mention the name of Spinoza here.

The Netherlands became the battlefield of Reformation and Counter-Reformation in even a stricter sense than France. Here the antagonistic principles were plainly posed in the course of struggle against foreign despotism. The conflict ended in the assertion of political independence, as opposed to absolute dominion. Europe in large measure owes the modern ideal of political liberty to that spirit of stubborn resistance which broke the power of Spain. Recent history, and, in particular, the history of democracy, claims for its province the several stages whereby this principle was developed in England and America, and its outburst in the frenzy of the French Revolution. It is enough here to have alluded to the part played by the Low Countries in the genesis of a motive force which may be described as the last manifestation of the Renaissance striving after self-emancipation.

ENGLAND

The insular position of England combined with the nature of the English has allowed the country to feel the vibration of European movements later and with less of shock than the continental nations. Before a wave of progress has reached its shores there has been the opportunity of watching it as spectators, and of considering how to receive it. Revolutions have passed from the tumultuous stages of their origin into some settled and recognizable state before we have been called upon to cope with them. It was thus that England took the influences of the Renaissance and Reformation simultaneously, and almost at the same time found herself engaged in that struggle with the Counter-Reformation which, crowned by the defeat of the Spanish Armada, stimulated the sense of nationality and developed the naval forces of the race. Both Renaissance and Reformation had been anticipated by at least a century in England. Chaucer's poetry, which owed so much to Italian examples, gave an early foretaste of the former. Wycliffe's teaching was a vital moment in the latter. But the French wars, the Wars of the Roses and the persecution of the Lollards deferred the coming of the new age; and the year 1536, when Henry VIII. passed the Act of Supremacy through parliament, may be fixed as the date when England entered definitely upon a career of intellectual development abreast with the foremost nations of the continent. The circumstances just now insisted on explain the specific character of the English Renaissance. The Reformation had been adopted by consent of the king, lords and commons; and this change in the state religion, though it was not confirmed without reaction, agitation and bloodshed, cost the nation comparatively little disturbance. Humanism, before it affected the bulk of the English people, had already permeated Italian and French literature. Classical erudition had been adapted to the needs of modern thought. The hard work of collecting, printing, annotating and translating Greek and Latin authors had been accomplished. The masterpieces of antiquity had been interpreted and made intelligible. Much of the learning popularized by the poets and dramatists was derived at second hand from modern literature. This does not mean that England was deficient in ripe and sound scholars. More, Colet, Ascham, Cheke, Camden were men whose familiarity with the classics was both intimate and easy. Public schools and universities conformed to the modern methods of study; nor were there wanting opportunities for youths of humble origin to obtain an education which placed them on a level with Italian scholars. The single case of Ben Jonson sufficiently proves this. Yet learning did not at this epoch become a marked speciality in England. There was no class corresponding to the humanists. It should also be remembered that the best works of Italian literature were introduced into Great Britain together with the classics. Phaer's *Virgil*, Chapman's *Homer*, Harrington's *Orlando*, Marlowe's *Hero and Leander*, Fairfax's *Jerusalem Delivered*, North's *Plutarch*, Hoby's *Courtier* —to mention only a few examples—placed English readers simultaneously in possession of the most eminent and representative works of Greece, Rome and Italy. At the same time Spanish influences reached them through the imitators of Guevara and the dramatists; French influences in the versions of romances; German influences in popular translations of the Faust legend, *Eulenspiegel,* and similar productions. The authorized versions of the Bible had also been recently given to the people—so that almost at the same period of time England obtained in the vernacular an extensive library of ancient and modern authors. This was a privilege enjoyed in like measure by no other nation. It sufficiently accounts for the richness and variety of Elizabethan literature, and for the enthusiasm with which the English language was cultivated.

Art, Letters, and the Drama.—Speaking strictly, England borrowed little in the region of the arts from other nations, and developed still less that was original. What is called Jacobean architecture marks indeed an interesting stage in the transition from the Gothic style. But, compared with Italian, French, Spanish, German and Flemish work of a like period, it is both timid and dry. Sculpture was represented in London for a brief space by Torrigiani; painting by Holbein and Antonio More; music by Italians and Frenchmen of the Chapel Royal. But no Englishman rose to European eminence in these departments. With literature the case was very different. Wyat and Surrey began by engrafting the forms and graces of Italian poetry upon the native stock. They introduced the sonnet and blank verse. Sidney followed with the sestine and terza rima and with various experiments in classic metres, none of which took root on English soil. The translators handled the octave stanza. Marlowe gave new vigour to the couplet. The first period of the English Renaissance was one of imitation and assimilation. Academies after the Italian type were founded. Tragedies in the style of Seneca, rivalling Italian and French dramas of the epoch, were produced. Attempts to Latinize ancestral rhythms, similar to those which had failed in Italy and France, were made. Tentative essays in criticisms and dissertations on the art of poetry abounded. It seemed as though the Renaissance ran a risk of being throttled in its cradle by superfluity of foreign and pedantic nutriment. But the natural vigour of the English genius resisted influences alien to itself, and showed a robust capacity for digesting the varied diet offered to it. As there was nothing despotic in the temper of the ruling classes, nothing oppressive in English culture, the literature of that age evolved itself freely from the people. It was under these conditions that Spenser gave his romantic epic to the world, a poem which derived its allegory from the middle ages, its decorative richness from the Italian Renaissance, its sweetness, purity, harmony and imaginative splendour from the most poetic nation of the modern world. Under the same conditions, the Elizabethan drama, which in its totality is the real exponent of the English Renaissance, came into existence. This drama very early freed itself from the pseudo-classic mannerism which imposed on taste in Italy and France. Depicting feudalism in the vivid colours of an age at war with feudal institutions, breathing into antique histories the breath of actual life, embracing the romance of Italy and Spain, the mysteries of German legend, the fictions of poetic fancy and the facts of daily life, humours of the moment and abstractions of philosophical speculation, in one homogeneous amalgam instinct with intense vitality, this extraordinary birth of time, with Shakespeare for the master of all ages, left a monument of the Renaissance unrivalled for pure creative power by any other product of that epoch. To complete the sketch, we must set Bacon, the expositor of modern scientific method, beside Spenser and Shakespeare, as the third representative of the Renaissance in England. Nor should Raleigh, Drake, Hawkins, the semi-buccaneer explorers of the ocean, be omitted. They, following the lead of Portuguese and Spaniards, combating the Counter-Reformation on the seas, opened for England her career of colonization and plantation. All this while the political policy of Tudors and Stuarts tended towards monarchial absolutism, while the Reformation in England, modified by contact with the Low Countries during their struggles, was narrowing into strict reactionary intolerance. Puritanism indicated a revolt of the religious conscience of the nation against the arts and manners of the Renaissance, against the encroachments of belligerent Catholicism, against the corrupt and Italianated court of James I., against the absolutist pretensions of his son Charles. In its final manifestation during the Commonwealth, Puritanism won a transient victory over the mundane forces of both Reformation and Renaissance, as these had taken shape in England. It also secured the eventual triumph of constitutional independence. Milton, the greatest humanistic poet of the English race, lent his pen and moral energies during the best years of his life to securing that principle on which modern political systems at present rest. Thus the geographical isolation of England, and the comparatively late adoption by the English of matured Italian and German influences, give peculiar complexity to the phenomena of Reformation and Renaissance simultaneously developed on our island. The period of our history between 1536 and 1642 shows how difficult it is to separate these two factors in the re-birth of Europe, both of which contributed so powerfully to the formation of modern English nationality.

THE NEW EUROPE

It has been impossible to avoid an air of superficiality and the repetition of facts known to every schoolboy in this sketch of so complicated a subject as the Renaissance—embracing many nations, a great variety of topics, and an indefinite period of time. Yet no other treatment was possible upon the lines laid down at the outset, where it was explained why the term Renaissance cannot now be confined to the Revival of Learning and the effect of antique studies upon literary and artistic ideals. The purpose of this article has been to show that, while the Renaissance implied a new way of regarding the material world and human nature, a new conception of man's destiny and duties on this planet, a new culture and new intellectual perceptions penetrating every sphere of thought and energy, it also involved new reciprocal relations between the members of the European group of nations. The Renaissance closed the middle ages and opened the modern era—not merely because the mental and moral ideas which then sprang into activity and owed their force in large measure to the revival of classical learning were opposed to mediaeval modes of thinking and feeling, but also because the political and international relations specific to it as an age were at variance with fundamental theories of the past. Instead of empire and church, the sun and moon of the mediaeval system, a federation of peoples, separate in type, and divergent in interests, yet bound together by common tendencies, common culture and common efforts came into existence. For obedience to central authority was substituted balance of power. Henceforth the hegemony of Europe attached to no crown, imperial or papal, but to the nation which was capable of winning it, in the spiritual region by mental ascendancy, and in the temporal by force.

That this is the right way of regarding the subject appears from the events of the first two decades of the 16th century, those years in which the humanistic revival attained its highest point in Italy. Luther published his thesis in 1517, 64 years after the fall of Constantinople, 23 years after the expedition of Charles VIII. to Naples, ten years before the sack of Rome, at a moment when France, Spain and England had felt the influences of Italian culture but feebly. From that date forward two parties wrestled for supremacy in Europe, to which may be given the familiar names of Liberalism and Conservatism, the party of progress and the party of established institutions. The triumph of the former was most signal among the Teutonic peoples. The Latin races championed by Spain and supported by the papacy fought the battle of the latter, and succeeded for a time in rolling back the tide of revolutionary conquest. Meanwhile that liberal culture which had been created for Europe by the Italians before the contest of the Reformation began continued to spread, although it was stifled in Italy and Spain, retarded in France and the Low Countries, well-nigh extirpated by wars in Germany and diverted from its course in England by the counter-movement of Puritanism. The *autos da fé* of Seville and Madrid, the flames to which Bruno, Dolet and Paleario were flung, the dungeon of Campanella and the seclusion of Galileo, the massacre of St. Bartholomew and the faggots of Smithfield, the desolated plains of Germany and the cruelties of Alva in the Netherlands, disillusioned Europe of those golden dreams which had arisen in the earlier days of humanism, and which had been so pleasantly indulged by Rabelais. In truth the Renaissance was ruled by no *Astraea redux* but rather by a severe spirit which brought no peace but a sword, reminding men of sternest duties, testing what of moral force and tenacity was in them, compelling them to strike for the old order or the new, suffering no lukewarm halting between two opinions. That, in spite of retardation and retrogression, the old order of ideas should have yielded to the new all over Europe—that science should have won firm standing-ground and political liberty should have struggled through those birth-throes of its origin—was in the nature of things. Had this not been, the Renaissance or re-birth of Europe would be a term without a meaning. (J. A. S.)

While Symonds' article on the Renaissance, originally contributed to the 9th edition of the *Encyclopædia Britannica* remains the classical exposition of a certain view of the subject, more recent research has brought out other aspects of the matter. It is noteworthy, however, that in some important points the very latest investigators have returned to Symonds' conception of the Renaissance, from which historians of the generation immediately following him had departed.

Our continually growing knowledge of the middle ages has thrown the Renaissance into a very different perspective from that in which it was once viewed. Less and less are the centuries preceding the 15th seen as the "Dark Ages" in contrast to the sudden sunrise of modern times. Indeed, many scholars now speak of a Carolingian Renaissance in the 8th century, an Ottonian Renaissance in the 10th, and of the Renaissance of the 12th century, in order to emphasize the constant stream of light and progress throughout the millennium once regarded as a long night of gloom and decadence. On the other hand, many scholars have emphasized even more than did Symonds the extreme gradualness of the efflorescence of the Italian Renaissance and the long persistence in it of mediaeval and Germanic elements. The extreme position is taken by Mr. Henry O. Taylor, who is so impressed by the slowness of the transition from mediaeval to modern times that he would abolish the term "Renaissance" altogether. This proposal, however, has commended itself to few other scholars; there *was* a re-birth of the human mind in the 15th century, though it was not so sudden and decisive as once thought.

In another way our view of the Renaissance has been greatly modified by the economic historians who have stressed the material antecedents of the great political and intellectual movements of the 14th, 15th and 16th centuries. Symonds, like nearly all his contemporaries, wrote almost as if the change in the mental habit of the race were a first cause, unexplained by any alteration in social conditions. But it is now generally accepted that the intellectual change was but the natural result of material conditions altered by the growth of wealth, of commerce, and of city communities. The humanists and artists were dwellers in the cities and in the marts of trade; their patrons were largely found in the newly powerful bourgeoisie of the Italian and German cities. Of course the Renaissance had its intellectual as well as its material antecedents; it was produced by the happy creation in the commercial revolution of a wealthy and leisured class just at a time when discoveries and inventions were thrilling the mind of Western Europe with interest and curiosity. It was no accident that individualism, humanism, and Italian painting attained their majority in the age which saw the invention of printing and the great geographical discoveries of Diaz, of Vasco da Gama, and of Columbus.

Of all the positions taken by Symonds that most subject to attack has been his assertion of the close connection and similar purpose of the Renaissance and Reformation. Like most historians of the 19th century, Symonds regarded them both as liberal movements, emancipations of reason so nearly alike that the Reformation might be called "the Teutonic Renaissance." Just as he was writing, however, Friedrich Nietzsche, basing his opinion on Janssen's *Geschichte des deutschen Volkes seit dem Ausgang des Mittelalters*, which represented the Reformation as a blight on German Catholic civilization, proclaimed that "the Reformation was a reaction of backward minds against the Italian Renaissance": and this view gained ground until it was adopted by Catholic historians like Lord Acton, Protestant historians like Ernst Troeltsch, and generally by the majority of scholars. They have pointed out that the humanists and Reformers came to blows, that the spirit of the Renaissance was largely secular and that of the Reformation intensely religious, that the former was tolerant and often indifferent and sceptical and that the latter was usually intolerant, devout, and sometimes superstitious, that the humanists were aristocratic and the Reformers democratic in method, and that Puritanism proved hostile to and often destructive of the artistic and pleasure-seeking interests of the Renaissance. In criticism of this view, however, it has been contended that the Renaissance was not, any more than the Reformation, consciously progressive; rather did both movements find their ideal in the past, the one in the golden age of Rome and the other in the primitive age of Christianity. It has been further shown that the humanists did little in principle to emancipate the reason from authority; they were closely bound by their own authorities in the classical poets and orators, and could only attack the schoolmen on the basis of the ancient pagans as the Reformers attacked them from the standpoint of the ancient Fathers. In conclusion one may say that neither movement was a conscious appeal to reason or an intentional step forward and away from the past, but that each accomplished, undesignedly, a great work of emancipation and that each created new cultural values.

BIBLIOGRAPHY.—The special articles on the several arts and literatures of modern Europe, and on the biographies of the great men mentioned in this essay, will give the details of necessity here omitted. Of general works, with bibliographies, may be mentioned Jakob Burckhardt, *Die Cultur der Renaissance in Italien*, called by Lord Acton, "the most penetrating and subtle treatise on the history of civilization that exists in literature" (Leipzig, 1st ed. 1860; 20th ed., revised by L. Geiger, 1919; Eng. trans. by S. G. C. Middlemore, 1875); W. H. Pater, *Studies in the History of the Renaissance* (1873); J. A. Symonds, *The Renaissance in Italy* (1875–88); *Cambridge Modern History*, vol. i, "The Renaissance" (1902); A. Tilley, *The Literature of the French Renaissance* (1904); J. E. Sandys, *Harvard Lectures on the Revival of Learning* (1905) and a *History of Classical Scholarship*, vol. ii. (1908); W. H. Hudson, *The Story of the Renaissance* (1912); K. Burdach, *Reformation, Renaissance, Humanismus* (Berlin, 1918); H. O. Taylor, *Thought and Expression in the Sixteenth Century* (1920); P. Monnier, *Le Quattrocento: essai* sur l'histoire ütteraire due XVe siècle italien (2nd ed. 1920); F. J. Mather, *History of Italian Painting in the Renaissance* (1922); J. Huizinga, *The Waning of the Middle Ages* (1924); G. Scott, *The Architecture of Humanism* (2nd ed. 1924); F. J. C. Hearnshaw, *The Social and Political Ideas of some Great Thinkers of the Renaissance and Reformation* (1925); E. Troeltsch, "Renaissance und Reformation" in *Historische Zeitschrift* (Munich, vol. cx. pp. 519 ff.); F. Clement, ed., *Civilization of the Renaissance* (1929).   (P. S.)

RENAISSANCE ARCHITECTURE.

During the 15th, 16th and 17th centuries the structural and decorative elements of Roman architecture (*q.v.*), revived after long disuse, were adapted to the requirements of contemporary buildings throughout Europe. The column and the arch, the dome and groin vault, the arabesque and the rinceau, were conventions from which, in infinite combinations, architects developed their designs. The unity of centralized space and mass, the power of great scale and weight, the repose and completeness of definite and simple development of planes, passages and profiles, and the splendour of richly modelled and coloured surfaces, were the effects most often strived for. Yet Renaissance (*q.v.*) architects did not reproduce, even remotely, a single Roman building; the conditions of life had changed too much for Roman buildings to be practicable.

New Forms.—New and magnificent forms in structure, and in decoration applied to it, were developed. The dome raised on a drum, free from its abutments and crowned with a cupola, was one; when such a dome was raised, by means of pendentives, on four great arches, new and noble harmonies in spatial and mass composition resulted. Façades in which a classic ordinance is adapted to the basilican profile; barrel-vaulted or domed naves; campaniles which end in columned belfries; and vertical spires, encrusted with delicately modelled classic forms, are among the striking inventions of the period. The public buildings of the 15th and 16th centuries—the libraries, town halls, theatres and civic monuments—were utterly different from those of Rome. New combinations of the arch and the column, new rhythms in space, new arrangements in mass, new variations in ornament, had continually to be invented in order to fit the discovered architecture of ancient times to these new uses. Country houses—chateaux and villas, with their gardens—offered another field for adaptation and development; the design of public squares and streets and of buildings in ensembles another; and the vast palaces of the monarchs of France and Spain and England, and of the pope and the princes of the Church another. After three centuries of experiment and growth the Renaissance architect, in the façades of palaces, public buildings and houses, still expressed new ideas in the language of the column and the arch.

In the sixteenth century Europe was neither homogeneous nor centralized. Spain, Italy, Holland, England each had a native culture, a peculiar heritage from the mediaeval world, and each followed a course of development that was, at least in part, independent of all others. Spain, which had defended the Catholic faith against the Moors and which was flooded with the gold of Mexico and Peru, placed on her Renaissance forms a stamp very different from that of commercial and insular England. Monarchical France, rich with the heritage of the 13th century cathedrals, gave necessarily a different metamorphosis to the Italian tradition from Protestant and democratic Holland. Climate, building materials, prosperity, intellectual growth and inherited types of architecture such as the patio of Spain and the timber-roofed hall of England, the turreted chateau of the Loire and the balconied palace of Venice—these and many similar differences in civilization gave the Renaissance a distinctive colour, a special character in each locality.

Great Architects.—Finally there was the influence of individual genius. No period is so crowded with great architects and at no time have architects been so free to impress on their designs the imprint of a great personality. The Roman tradition has been called a tradition of formula and of precedent, yet no tradition has proved so flexible in the hands of a master. It lent itself with equal facility to the requirements of Bramante and of Bernini, of Christopher Wren and Juan de Herrera, of Mansart and of Alessi. It embraced within the limits of a single convention the delicate and gracious lyricism of Lescot, the agitated and passionate declamation of Churriguera, the clear and vigorous rhythms of Inigo Jones, and the mighty harmonies conceived in the illimitable imagination of Michelangelo.

See also ARCHITECTURE and PERIODS OF ART.

BIBLIOGRAPHY.—L. B. Alberti, *re edificatoria* (Architecture in Ten Books, 1726);* Andrea Palladio, *I Quattro Libri dell' architectura* (The Five Books of Architecture, 1740);* Giacomo Barozzi da Vignola, *Regola delle Cinque Ardini* (1742);* Sebastino Serlio, *I Cinque libri d'Architecttura* (1770);* A. B. Scamozzi, *Le Fabbriche e i Desequi di Andrea Palladio* (1776);* Giorgio Vasari, *Lives of the Most Eminent Sculptors, Painters and Architects* (1778);* H. D'Espouy, *Fragments d'Architecture de la Renaissance* (1897); J. Buhlman, *Die Architektur der Renaissance* (1904); F. M. Simpson, *A History of Architectural Development,* vol. iii. (1911).   (J. HUD.)

*The dates are those of first English editions.

I. RENAISSANCE ARCHITECTURE IN ITALY

Owing to the small hold which the principles of Gothic architecture (*q.v.*) were able to obtain in Italy it is a fair generalization to look upon the architecture of that country from the 3rd century A.D. to the beginning of the 15th as a gradually failing struggle of the builders to retain Roman order and dignity in their undertakings. The early Christian period (*see* BYZANTINE AND ROMANESQUE ARCHITECTURE), no doubt produced, largely through the influence of Byzantine, much brilliant craftsmanship and a great deal of beautiful decoration, but on the whole it is safe to say that all this was applied to buildings in which the structure was decadent Roman. Later on, in what is generally called the Romanesque period the problems of Roman vaulting, now that the art of making concrete was lost, were solved by what to the Romans would have seemed the makeshift arrangement of surface ribs of stone in place of their own buried reinforcements. The clearness of the lines and surfaces of the Roman vaults were thereby interrupted, as were the wall surfaces, by a decoration of pilaster strips and thin arcading. It was the function then of the Renaissance builders—architects we may call them because they did their work with a greater foresight and seriousness of purpose—to bring back the Roman orderliness and precision. In the process they became no mere copiers of the antique. They invented many lovely forms and motives which had, as far as we know, no Roman precedents. As has often been pointed out there is far more difference between a Renaissance church and a Roman temple than between a Roman temple and a Greek one. On the other hand it must be admitted that, even more than in the other arts, there was a strong determination to recover Roman methods both of design and construction. Once the possibility of this was realized the remains of Roman buildings and monuments must have produced a great effect on the imagination. With their far greater scale, if not always greater mass, they must have seemed like the work of a race of giants, no longer to be shunned as something evil but instead, with the striking ambition of a time that produced figures like Galileo and Christopher Columbus, to be equalled and surpassed. The serious study of actual Roman buildings, which was started with Brunelleschi in 1403, gradually gave place, however, after the discovery of the works of Vitruvius, and their dissemination in numberless editions, to an academic interest in his system of proportions for columns, cornices and other details, which stifled real design until the latter was rescued and revivified by Michelangelo and the other giants of the Baroque movement (*see* BAROQUE ARCHITECTURE). The history of the Italian Renaissance, as far as architecture is concerned, is the history of a school of ordered design, which receiving its initial impetus from the antique set out on a new and adventurous career of its own until it was finally bogged by misapplied scholarship.

Brunelleschi.—An appropriate date from which to start is therefore 1403 when Filippo Brunelleschi, a Florentine metal worker by trade and some 26 years of age, having failed in the competition for the bronze doors of the baptistery, left his native town for Rome with the express purpose of studying the Roman remains in that city. The young Donatello, then 16, afterwards to be the famous sculptor, accompanied him "to hold the other end of the tape" as we should say to-day. They stayed away four years and on his return Brunelleschi, with the reputation his knowledge of Roman work gave him, persuaded the council to allow him to finish the Duomo, which still lacked a covering to the great crossing. For this he designed his famous dome, the first great dome to be raised on a drum. A dome raised on a drum was not a Roman form; neither was Roman construction used; which shows that Brunelleschi's Roman studies had not fettered his imagination. The great raised dome, like that of St. Peter's at Rome, was to become one of the most magnificent and distinctive products of the Renaissance and this Florentine one at the start was one of the largest and boldest.

The more distinctive work of Brunelleschi in the new manner, however, is to be found in the smaller buildings that he carried on at the same time, such as the Pazzi chapel in the cloister of Santa Croce—the first completed ecclesiastical building of the Renaissance. It is a small structure, some 70 ft. square, containing an open loggia, an oblong main compartment (60 by 30 ft., approximately) and a square chancel with a square sacristy on either side. The loggia is a Roman barrel vault with coffering carried on six lofty Corinthian columns the centre bay of which is larger than the rest and the vault is there carried up on pendentives as a small dome. Above the entablature of the columns the exterior consists of a broad panelled surface and it and the entablature alike are boldly broken by a semi-circular arch joining the two groups of columns. Above this again is an open belvedere under the eaves of an overhanging tile roof and above again the main dome of the chapel. This composition then has no likeness to the façade of a Roman temple although in size it equals many of them. While using elements derived from Rome it is a light and graceful structure in which all the ordered parts of the design are made subservient to the main climax of the great central arch. The same remarks apply to the interior. The construction is very like that of the loggia, a dome intersecting a barrel vault. It is in white plaster, dark stone pilasters and entablatures outlining the architectural forms. Its note, like that of the façade, is lightness and elegance in which Roman forms and details have been used with a new delicacy. In place of the heavy tramp of Romanesque bays and piers we have here a building unified by its central dome and by its orderly arrangement of columns and pilasters, spiritualized and made light and beautiful by the purity of its lines and the delicacy and charm of its detail. It is a new thing neither Roman nor Romanesque, but nevertheless with Roman completeness and unity. The Pazzi chapel has been dealt with at this length because probably more than any other building of its time it gives the Renaissance outlook with its modern feeling for orderliness and perfection combined with the suggestion of Roman grandeur.

Types of Building.—The two chief types of building on which the Italian Renaissance was to found itself were palaces and churches. In mediaeval times the Italian cities were full of lofty stone palaces presenting cliff-like walls to the streets and surrounding central, arcaded courts. They were a feature of Italian urban civilization with its city states. Buildings with flat street façades almost necessarily have an orderly arrangement of windows. To such buildings, therefore, it was easy for the Renaissance architect, thinking in a Roman system of units, based on the regular setting out of colonnades and their super-imposition, to apply his new ideas. The great overhanging eaves of the roof could be transformed to a crowning cornice, the pointed windows turned to semi-circular ones, the rough stonework reduced to a graded system of storeys, gradually approaching a clear ashlar face from which the main cornice could spring. Order was there already. All that had to be done was to introduce a higher sense of unity by seeing that every part bore some tangible relation to the whole. In this way we get palaces like Michelozzi's Riccardi and Majano and Cronaca's Strozzi in Florence in which the strength of the cliff wall is enhanced by contrast with fine detail and a higher sense of unity and power is reached.

The next stage in the development was the actual application to the wall surface of a series of pilasters recalling the Roman system of super-imposed colonnades. These were first used at the Rucellai palace in Florence by Alberti. The columns and their entablatures are here very tentative and are planted on top of the strong stone jointed face, which still dominates. A next step would be the grouping of such pilasters in pairs as at the Palazzo Giraud or the Cancellaria in Rome, both by Bramante. Following this idea through we have, in the more luxurious atmosphere of Venice, columns at each storey taking the place of pilasters and used in great profusion either singly or in pairs with one quarter of their thickness apparently buried in the wall. The palaces on the Grand canal offer many examples, but it will be noticed that even in the richest the wall plane is carefully preserved and the cliff-like face, however articulated, remains. Florentine palaces, however, were never to go beyond applied pilasters until the Baroque period (see BAROQUE ARCHITECTURE) arrived. Indeed, it shed even them and produced in the 16th century the astylar palace in which all orders or columns, apart from those to windows or doors, are implicit. A Florentine architect, Antonio Sangallo, carried the idea to Rome with the Farnese palace from whence it has spread over the world.

The architectural quality of orderliness which produced the great palaces and stately churches of the Renaissance did not for a long time, however, destroy the lightness and fancy which the carvers, goldsmiths and painters who turned their attention to building brought to their new task. The smaller details of all early Renaissance buildings, such as wall monuments, balconies and screens in the churches, the furniture in the palaces, show, not only in Florence but in most towns in the north of Italy, a profusion of exquisitely drawn and modelled ornament based on classical motives but used with great freshness and originality. A Renaissance doorway would be applied to, or carved on, a Gothic church, as at Como cathedral, and it would not only form a delightful composition in itself, often in several planes, but would make an extraordinarily rich and delicate piece of decoration against its coarser surroundings. In such work, especially in Lombardy, pilasters and architraves were filled with delicate arabesques. Indeed, in many minds this rich highly carved detail constitutes the chief characteristic of Renaissance work. Those who think this, however, mistake the flower for the tree. The organic relation of all parts to each other and to the whole, based on the Roman system of axial relationship while making use of simple Roman shapes, is the essential trait.

Development.—From Florence the movement of architecture "in the antique manner" spread to every town in Italy and, as in painting, each town produced its school centred round one or two first-rate artists. In Milan, Bramante carried out his early but very accomplished work before Rome absorbed him for St. Peter's. His church of Santa Maria delle Grazie piles up in the simple logical way of applied masses, which the Renaissance always implied, while its detail remains fanciful and in parts Romanesque in character. A great difference between Renaissance architecture in Italy and similar work in France or England is that in the former country the movement attacked from the beginning the plan forms and the structural shape of buildings, whereas in the latter countries it began by an application of the new fashioned detail to buildings which remained Gothic both in plan and structure.

The first half of the 16th century saw the migration to Rome of the best artists from Florence, Milan and other centres attracted by the superior opportunities that city offered under such patrons of the arts as Popes Julius II. and Leo X. Even the sack of Rome in 1527 did not stay building activities. It was there, under the shadow of the great monuments of antiquity, that the full use of the Roman orders (see ORDER) was recovered but without any attempt at imitating Roman buildings. This culminating period produced no Parthenon as a climax. The great scheme for St. Peter's, however, started on its career at this time with magnificent and entirely novel plans for the Greek cross building piling up to a great central dome. Bramante laid down the general lines and began the actual structure. Sangallo and Peruzzi followed with modifications of his plan and finally after further vicissitudes Michelangelo took hold of the work and carried it through. His great structure rightly belongs to the Baroque period, though the basic idea on which he worked was that of Bramante and the earlier architects mentioned, and though the building as far as its orderly procession of parts both in plan and section is a Renaissance structure. If, however, St.

Peter's, by the majestic simplicity of its major parts and by its great dome—the best example of the finest architectural invention of the Renaissance—has a claim to a place in that movement it is in smaller buildings in Rome like the Farnese and Massimi palaces, by Antonio Sangallo and Baldassare Peruzzi respectively, that the full flavour of the culminating period is to be tasted. In them is to be found not only complete mastery of plan, by which all apartments flow together to make a whole out of well-shaped units, but both exteriors and interiors that show a similar mastery of classical detail while maintaining the traditional form and expression of an Italian nobleman's house.

From Rome this mastery of classical forms and their adaptation to modern purposes, which makes Italian Renaissance architecture of importance to us to-day, flowed back to the provincial towns. In Bologna, his native city, Peruzzi built a number of astylar houses simple in composition yet completely unified and with detail almost Greek in its refinement. In Verona, Sanmichele, architect and military engineer, fortified the town, his birthplace, and gave to the palaces he built in it and in Venice qualities of strength and scale which are unsurpassed in the works of any master. Through his military engineering work he apparently learnt economy of means in obtaining his effects; for instance, in his series of great gateways through the walls of Verona he reduced cornices to mere bands except in the central portion of his design in order to enforce his climax. His work shows a strength, grandeur and scale that surpasses in its finest qualities Roman work itself. His Grimani palace on the Grand canal at Venice is the strongest and most impressive of those built during the Renaissance.

In the library of St. Mark's at Venice, by Jacopo Sansovino, architect and sculptor, who like so many of his profession started life in Florence, the culminating period of the Renaissance reaches a note of greater richness if not greater grandeur. In its façades of two main storeys, each with fully developed order and arch in the Roman manner, Sansovino succeeded in combining these storeys into one whole by means of an enlarged frieze to the upper order, by low thin steps to the lower and by a crowning balustrade with statues. By the depth of his reveals and the doubling of his subsidiary order in the thickness of the wall, by his overlay of rich, sculptured ornament, he produced here perhaps the richest building before the full advent of the Baroque period. The building, nevertheless, with the assistance of the broad surfaces of its unfluted columns, carries its richness with complete assurance and dignity. There is no feeling that it is overloaded. It is no wonder, therefore, that its façades have formed the main motives of many an opera house and theatre throughout the world, including the most famous, Garnier's great opera house in Paris.

Palladio and Vignola.—The freer use of the orders was carried a step further still by Andrea Palladio who practised chiefly in the small town of Vicenza in the second half of the 16th century but whose name nevertheless became more widely known than that of any of his contemporaries. Indeed, his use in his later buildings of a single order of columns or pilasters for a façade gave rise to the term Palladian in English architecture. So great was his fame, assisted by his book, that Vicenza became a centre of pilgrimage for English architects in the 17th and 18th centuries from Inigo Jones onwards. His written work like that of Serlio, Vignola and other Italian architects who wrote on their art, followed Vitruvius and was largely concerned in establishing a system of proportions for the orders and their accessories. Palladio's buildings, however, are better than his writing. The Palazzo Consiglio, for instance, facing his more famous basilica, where he used a powerful Corinthian order of four columns running up the face of the building, with the cornice returned round each column as in the form of Nerva, shows the hand of the master in the modelling of his small building so that its scale throughout lives up to the giant size set by his columns. In the comparatively poor town of Vicenza to obtain the great effects he sought he was reduced to building in brick covered with stucco and no doubt it was the fluidity of this latter material which gave to his buildings their slight sense of unreality. His stone churches in Venice including the great composition of San Giorgio Maggiore with church, campanile, monastery, harbour and lighthouses in one scheme, facing the town across the lagoon, are sounder architecture because they are sounder building.

Giacomo Barozzi da Vignola, commonly called Vignola, was much the same type of architect as Palladio and, like him, published his designs and his rules of proportion. As Palladio ruled in England so Vignola did in France. Working chiefly in Rome and the neighbourhood during the latter half of the 16th century he stood like Palladio as a bulwark against the increasing power of the Baroque. Michelangelo seems to have little influence upon him, except perhaps in the dramatic quality of his compositions, such as that of his great pentagonal villa at Caprarola and the magnificent climax achieved in his small one for Pope Julius III. in the Borghese gardens.

With these two men, Palladio and Vignola, the work of the Italian Renaissance may be said to have reached the utmost limit of revived and revivified Roman architecture. The motives and orders of the Romans could be exploited no further. For fresh advance it required the genius of Michelangelo and the other founders of the Baroque, who, lifting Italian architecture from its orderly Roman basis of assembled units in plan and elevation, gave it new freedom by considering structure rather as so much plastic material for the fancies of the modeller than so much cubic content in rooms and walls for the imagination of the architect. While, however, the Baroque for a time conquered the known world, with perhaps the single exception of England, as new problems arose in later centuries calling for new solutions the whole of the Western world, including America, turned again to the architecture of the Italian Renaissance, for refreshment, for guidance and, most important of all, for sanity and clearness of expression.

BIBLIOGRAPHY.—L. B. Alberti, *De re aedificatoria*, or *I dieci Libri de l'architettura* (1458, trans. by Leoni as *Architecture in Ten Books*, 3 vols., 1726); L. Gruner, *Fresco Decorations and Stuccoes of Churches and Palaces of Italy*, 2 vols., plates in folio and text in 4to. (1854); H. G. Nicolai, *Das Ornament der Italienischen Kunst des XV. Jahrhunderts* (1882); W. J. Anderson, *Architectural Studies in Italy* (1890); A. Schutz, *Die Renaissance in Italien*, 4 vols. (1891-95); W. J. Anderson, *The Architecture of the Renaissance in Italy* (1927); J. Burckhardt, *Geschichte der Renaissance in Italien* (1912); G. Gromort, *Histoire abrégée de l'architecture de la Renaissance en Italie* (1912); J. Durm, *Baukunst der Renaissance in Italien* (Handbuch der Architektur, 1914); H. Willich, *Baukunst der Renaissance in Italien* (1914); G. Biagi, *The Architecture of the Renaissance in Italy;* H. Strack, *Central- und Kuppelkirchen der Renaissance in Italien*, 2 vols.

Florence: F. Ruggieri, *Scelti di Architettura della Città di Firenze*, 4 vols. (1738); A. H. V. Grandjean de Montigny et A. Famin, *Architecture Toscane* (1874); H. von Geymuller and A. Widman, *Die Architektur der Renaissance in Toscana* (1885-1908); J. C. Raschdorff, *Toscana* (1888).

Milan and Genoa: M. P. Gauthier, *Les Plus beaux édifices de la ville de Gênes*, 2 vols. (1818); G. and F. Durelli, *La Certosa di Pavia* (1853); F. Callet et J. B. C. Lesueur, *Architecture italienne: édifices publics et particuliers de Turin et Milan* (1855); T. V. Paravicini, *Die Renaissance Architektur der Lombardei* (1878); R. Reinhardt, *Genua* (1886); O. Grosso, *Portali e Palazzi di Genova*.

Rome: A. Palladio, *I Quattro Libri dell' Architettura* (1570. The best English editions are those of Leoni and Ware); D. de Rossi, *Studio d'Architettura Civile della Città di Roma*, 3 vols. (1720-21); O. B. Scamozzi, *Fabbriche e Disegni di Andrea Palladio*, 4 vols. (1776-83); C. Percier and P. F. L. Fontaine, *Choix de plus Célèbres Maisons de Plaisance de Rome et de ses Environs* (1809); T. F. Suys et L. P. Haudebourt, *Palais Massimi à Rome* (1818); H. von Geymuller, *Les Projets primitifs pour la Basilique de St. Pierre de Rome*, 2 vols. (1875-80); Letarouilly, *Le Vatican et la Basilique de Saint Pierre de Rome*, 2 vols. (1882); H. von Geymuller, *The School of Bramante* (trans. 1891); H. Strack, *Baudenkmaeler Roms des XV.-XIX. Jahrhunderts* (1891); C. Ricci, *Baroque Architecture and Sculpture in Italy* (1912); M. S. Briggs, *Baroque Architecture* (1913).

Venice: G. Leoni, *The Architecture of Andrea Palladio* (1715, 1721, 1742); P. Paoletti, *L'Architettura e la Scultura del Rinascimento in Venezia*, 3 vols. (1893); O. Raschdorff, *Palast-architektur von Ober-Italien und Toscans-Venedig* (1903); A. Haupt, *Palast-architektur von Ober-Italien und Toscana* (1908).   (C. H. R.)

II. RENAISSANCE ARCHITECTURE IN SPAIN

Towards the latter part of the 15th century, the decorative motives of the Italian Renaissance began to make their appearance in the ornamentation of Spanish buildings. The prosperity which followed the conquests of Peru and Mexico and the national exaltation which accompanied the end of the long wars with the Moors had found expression in the construction of great Gothic cathedrals, but for the decoration of these, and especially for the construction of minor works of architecture such as tombs, altars, retablos and rejeria (iron screens), Italian artisans were employed. These artisans, bringing with them many examples of Renaissance design, taught their art to the Spanish and Moorish craftsmen. The patronage of wealthy ecclesiastics who, travelling in Italy on some business of the Church, had fallen under the spell of Italian art, gave an added impetus to this new school of ornamentalists. From the chapels of the cathedrals the new style was introduced into the palaces of the archbishops and into the universities and hospitals established by the Church; the wealthy families of Burgos, Toledo and Salamanca soon adopted it for the decoration of their patios and the façades of their houses; and by the second decade of the 17th century it had become the accepted style of ornament throughout Spain, profoundly modifying the character of Spanish architecture.

Plateresque.—This decoration, which in its delicacy of scale and the exquisite perfection of its workmanship resembles silversmith's work—the work of artisans rather than of architects—has been called Plateresque (from *platero,* silversmith). The motives used are the arabesque, the rinceau, the grotesque, the candelabrum shaft, the panelled pilaster and the richly moulded entablature; and with these Italian forms there are mingled the geometric patterns inherited from the Moors and, not infrequently, Gothic forms such as the pinnacle, the crocket, cresting and the pierced balustrade. Moorish influence is felt, also, in the use of elaborate wood carvings, especially on the ceilings which are splendidly enriched with carved ornament and colour, and in the use of tiles, in superb coloured patterns, for walls and for stairs. Gothic influence survives in the occasional use of the ribbed vault. The use of the undraped human figure is infrequent except in the forms of children, but representations of animals in action, accurately observed and vigorously executed, are used in great profusion. Heraldry is also a source of many ornamental enrichments.

The exuberance of ornament, the fine craftsmanship and the refinement in modelling, in line and in the distribution of light and shade, are the architectural expression of a wealthy and proud aristocracy, which had discovered in Italy a new vocabulary of pleasure-giving forms. These forms were employed, oftentimes, with little understanding of their relation to structure; nor were they used, as in Italy, to give accent and significance to a composition in mass or space. They were used rather to enliven and enrich the textures of walls—an embroidery applied to surfaces—as if the house, or the tomb, were an added garment worn by its owner to express his taste and his importance. Like the costumes of the time, the buildings are embellished with rich patterns, applied with an exquisite tact and with a fine feeling for rhythm and contrast in spacing. The masterpiece of the period is undoubtedly the Ayuntamiento, or city hall, of Seville (1527–35), a building whose ornament is not excelled in Europe in fertility of invention or in facility of execution.

Second Phase.—The Plateresque architecture in Spain resembles the 15th century architecture of Lombardy and Venetia, and, like it, was succeeded by a colder and more monumental manner of building more correctly based upon Roman precedents. This change was due in part to the increasing knowledge of Roman art and to an admiration for the splendid monumental achievements of the 16th century masters, Bramante, Sangallo and Sanmichele, newly revealed to Spain. Her armies had overrun Italy; she had taken, and sacked, the city of Rome itself. But the change is also due to a change in the temper of the Spanish aristocracy. An architecture that was merely an embroidery applied to buildings could not, however lovely in itself, satisfy men who were masters of the world and who desired to express in an enduring form the grandeur and permanence of the political fabric that they had created. The colder and more abstract architecture of ancient Rome, vast in scale and in weight, an architecture, not of ornament

but of mass and of proportion, seemed more in keeping with the arrogant imperialism of Charles and Philip.

At any rate when these monarchs had extended their power over Spain, the Empire, Holland, Naples, Burgundy and America, Renaissance architecture in Spain entered, quite abruptly, its second phase. Monumental building succeeded ornamental. Architecture became once more a form-giving art. Buildings seem no longer to have been addressed to the social spirit of man, to seek to charm, to become a pleasing amenity in civic and ecclesiastical life; rather they seem to have been intended to overawe, to express in plastic form the energy and might of a stupendous Government. The palace built by Charles V. at Granada is a fine example of this political architecture. A part of the Alhambra was destroyed to make room for it. One regrets, of course, the oriental palace, full of sensuous charm and aristocratic loveliness, but the newer palace is not less beautiful. Still more impressive is the great Escorial (1560–84), a vast monastery built around a votive church and a mausoleum. This granite pile, which measures 675 ft. by 530 ft., achieves a majestic and awe-inspiring character by sheer size and weight. The grandeur and consistency of the remarkably unified design, the dramatic setting against the mountains and above the plain of Madrid, make of this monument a sublime symbol of the union of Spanish power and Catholic faith. The interior of the great cathedral of Granada, the Lonja, or exchange of Seville, and the hospital of San Juan Bautista, Toledo, are other examples of this second phase of the Spanish Renaissance, which are not unworthy of comparison with the best work of contemporary Italy. This phase did not last long beyond the close of the 16th century. (*See* BAROQUE ARCHITECTURE.)

Churrigueresque.—An architecture more congenial to the artistic spirit of Spain and derived from that of Fontana and Borromini appeared in the early part of the 17th century. It is characterized by a free plastic handling of masses, a broken or undulating skyline, an irregular, capricious distribution of light and shade, and a vast profusion of ornament; structure, geometric form and classic precedent are smothered under a lavish encrustation of luxuriant detail. At times this detail recalls that of the Plateresque; more often it differs from it altogether. It is bolder with far greater depths of broken shadow and vigorous projections; it is more fluid, the forms and planes melting into each other in rounded forms and an intricacy of curved lines; and there is lacking altogether the delicacy of line and shadow and the exquisite refinement in modelling that give distinction to the plateresque. The joyousness, the youth, of the early 16th century was replaced by a self-conscious and sophisticated spirit. Architecture was not, as in the Plateresque, a source of direct sensuous enjoyment; it was a language that attempted to translate passion and mysticism into plastic forms. The vocabulary of this new language is like that of Baroque Italy: there is the same prodigal use of volutes and consoles, of broken and scrolled pediments, of twisted columns, of reversed balusters and of elaborately modelled finials. The cartouche, enmeshed in a fantastic frame of volutes and scrolls, and the human figure, emotionally rendered and set in a niche, are characteristic forms of ornament, and there is a lavish abundance of flowers, of modelled draperies, shells and festoons, often executed (in an altar or retablo) in onyx, lapis lazuli, bronze or some other richly coloured material. This Baroque style in Spain is often called the Churrigueresque, from the name of its most successful practitioner, José Churriguera. It reaches its fullest development in altar-pieces and in the decoration of doorways. The west front of the Cathedral of Marcia, although not completed until the 18th century, is a characteristic example of the Spanish Baroque.

BIBLIOGRAPHY.—*Monumentos arquitectónicos de España* (1859–81); Andrew Prentice, *Renaissance Architecture and Ornament in Spain* (1890); C. Uhde, *Baudenkmaler in Spanien und Portugal* (1892); M. Junghandel, *Die Baukunst Spaniens* (1898); A. Shubert, *Der Barock in Spanien* (1908); A. Byne and M. Stapley, *Spanish Architecture in the Sixteenth Century* (1917); C. Moncanut (editor), *Arte y Decoración en España* (1922); A. Whittlesey, *Architecture of Southern Spain and Architecture of Northern Spain* (1922); Vicente Lampérez Romea, *Arquitectura Civil Española* (1922).   (J. HUD.)

RENAISSANCE ARCHITECTURE OF SPAIN

Garuza

PHOTOGRAPHS, (1, 2, 3) E.N.A., (4) EWING GALLOWAY

1. Façade of the Hospicio Provincial, Madrid
2. Detail of the Palace of Charles V, near the Alhambra. Granada
3. The Ayuntiamento, or the town hall, of Seville (1527–32), designed by Diego de Riano and Martin
4. The Escorial, near Madrid; built 1563–93 by Philip II. Juan Bautista de Toledo, architect. The building comprises a palace, a church, a monastery, and a mausoleum

PLATE II

RENAISSANCE ARCHITECTURE

PHOTOGRAPHS, (1, 3, 4) COLLECTION ARCHIVES PHOTOGRAPHIQUES, (2) F. FRITH AND COMPANY, LTD.

RENAISSANCE ARCHITECTURE OF FRANCE AND ENGLAND

1. The church of the Sorbonne, Paris. 18th century
2. St. Paul's Cathedral, London, built 1675–1710, Sir Christopher Wren, architect
3. Ecole Militaire, Paris. Façade on the Champs de Mars. Built 1752; Jacques IV. Ange Gabriel, architect
4. The Château at Blois, showing a gallery of the Louis XII. wing facing the courtyard (late 15th century)

PHOTOGRAPHS, (1) F. R. YERBURY, (2-6) ALINARI

ARCHITECTURE OF THE ITALIAN RENAISSANCE

1. The Cathedral of Florence, showing the dome (1420–61) designed by Filippo Brunelleschi, and at the left the Campanile, or bell-tower, begun by Giotto in 1334. and continued by Andrea Pisano and by Fr. Talenti

2. The Pazzi Chapel (1429) in the cloister of Santa Croce, Florence, designed by Filippo Brunelleschi

3. The Palazzo Strozzi, Florence, begun in 1489 by Benedetto da Maiano, and continued by Cronaca

4. Cancelleria Palace, Rome, early 16th century, designed by Bramante and others

5. The Palazzo Massimi alle Colonne, Rome, 1532, with convex façade; designed by Baldassare Peruzzi

6. The church of San Giorgio Maggiore, Venice, rebuilt by Palladio in 1565–80, and completed by Scamozzi in 1610

PLATE IV   RENAISSANCE ARCHITECTURE

ARCHITECTURE OF THE ITALIAN RENAISSANCE

1. The Libreria Vecchia, or old library of St. Mark's, opposite the Doge's palace, Venice. Built 1536–82; one of the greatest works of the architect Sansovino
2. Courtyard of the Farnese palace, Rome, erected early 16th century, by Antonio da Sangallo, the Younger, and completed by Michelangelo
3. Palazzo Grimani, Venice (c. 1550), designed by Michele Sanmichele, one of the greatest designs of the Renaissance

III. RENAISSANCE ARCHITECTURE IN FRANCE

It has become customary to include under the classification of Renaissance architecture all the architecture produced in a country after the Graeco-Roman revival in Italy from the 15th century to the end of the 18th. In the course of three centuries, as must be clear, the types of buildings, their planning and their construction—*i.e.*, all that is vital and fundamental in the character of architecture—must vary widely, to meet the demands of changing social systems; and thus the only characteristic common to such dissimilar types of architecture as, for instance, that of the time of Francis I. and that of the period of 1750, is the employment of the classic orders as elements of the decorative design. Bearing this in mind, then, the following divisions for the periods of French Renaissance architecture are essential:

Renaissance Proper (1475–1610).—Covering the period from the introduction of the Italian-revival classicism through the reigns of Charles VIII., Louis XII., Francis I., Henry II. and his successors, up to 1589, and including, as a transitional period, the period of reconstruction, after the religious wars, of Henry IV. (1589–1610).

Seventeenth Century, Baroque and Academic.—Covering the period of the development of French classic art, from its formation in the first half of the century (reign of Louis XIII., 1610–43) through 1660, when the personal influence of Louis XIV. (1643–1715) was dominant, and up to about 1700.

Eighteenth Century, Rococo and Classical Reaction.—Covering the last phase of the Louis XIV. period, the Regency, and the return, in the second half of the century, to the more academic style which terminated at the Revolution.

Renaissance Proper (1475–1610).—In the last quarter of the 15th century the importations of Italian works of art increased steadily; the French nobles ordered funeral monuments and cabinet work in Italy, and brought over skilled Italian workmen; the military expeditions into Italy had familiarized many Frenchmen with the Italian Renaissance and created the desire to produce at home the masterpieces admired abroad. But the Gothic art (*see* GOTHIC ARCHITECTURE), though dying, was by no means dead, and Gothic edifices continued to be built as late as the 17th century. The Italian influence, therefore, did not find a clear course, but asserted itself simply in the replacement of certain Gothic forms of decoration by Renaissance details. A compromise was thus effected between the old and new traditions, and the work of building went on as before under the guidance of the French master-builders (heads of the various gilds). The plan of a building, and its vaults, high roofs, dormer windows and decorative chimneys followed the Gothic tradition; while on every space suitable for carving appeared the arabesques of the Italian pilaster, the medallions with profiles of the Caesars, and the capitals, mouldings and ornaments inspired by Roman precedent. This dualism of structure and ornament is the essential characteristic of French Renaissance architecture.

Authorship of Buildings.—The authorship of the principal buildings of this first period has been the subject of long and violent controversies; but the argument of those who attribute it almost exclusively to Italian architects is not overwhelmingly convincing. This argument runs to the effect that "the ignorant master-builders whose names appear on the records were incapable of producing the work of the early Renaissance." But these same "ignorant" master-builders had been, and were still, building masterpieces of Gothic architecture. The work of French designers is clearly marked by its *fluency* in the prevailing Gothic construction, and its *uncertainty* in the Italian vocabulary of ornamentation. To ascribe it, therefore, to Italian builders, compels the strange assumption that the Italian, in crossing the Alps, had forgotten the very rudiments of forms of which his knowledge was regarded as authoritative, while acquiring with the same miraculous suddenness a complete knowledge of French Gothic forms!

Buildings.—From the end of the 15th century to the reign of Francis I., the buildings—late Gothic in everything but the introduction of Italian ornamental detail—are the work of a transitional period. Then, in the reign of Francis I., the Gothic elements of the façade were supplanted by new features. As yet there was no clear understanding of the essence of classic architecture, *i.e.*, unity and purity of form, and a definite relationship of all the elements of a composition to a common standard of measure, but there was an effort to attain harmonious distribution of these elements. The king was building, or remodelling, Villers-Cotteret, Fontainebleau, Chambord, Madrid, St. Germain, La Muette and Blois, and, at his example, Renaissance forms were adopted for Écouen, Ancy-le-Franc, St. Pierre at Caen, St. Eustache and St. Étienne du Mont. The nobles, with the necessity for security decreasing as the king's power grew, abandoned their old fortresses or transformed their family seats by large windows pierced in the towers, and by the addition of new wings. The plan of city residences remained Gothic, however, with the master's dwelling standing between the garden and the courtyard in front; the services were arranged at the sides of the courtyard, and the house faced the garden side; this disposition *entre cour et jardin* remained a favourite in France as late as the 19th century. Within the dwelling, the walls—unless covered with tapestries—still showed their masonry, and the rooms still had Gothic timber-work ceilings, but the huge fireplaces were adorned, on their pilasters and niches, with the new arabesques (*e.g.*, chimneys of Blois and Hôtel D'Alluye).

By the middle of the 16th century, the Gothic finally disappeared from domestic architecture, although in religious architecture—where evolution is always slower—the planning still remained flamboyant Gothic (*e.g.*, Brou, Troyes, transepts of Beauvais, and St. Nizier at Lyons). Then, in the period from 1547 to the beginning of the reign of Henry IV. (1589) there was an amazing development—the antique system of proportions was mastered. The use of the Roman orders became general, but they were adapted to conditions so different from those prevailing in Italy that they acquired a character peculiarly French. Such innovations as open stair-wells, alternation of ordinances of pilasters and projecting columnated motives, and the French order of Philibert de l'Orme, are contributions to the architectural repertory that were widely used later. The *giant order,* embracing two storeys, was developed simultaneously in France and in Rome.

The names of three architects dominate this period: Philibert de l'Orme (1510–70), who built the Château d'Anet, part of Chenonceau and the earliest portion of the Tuileries; Pierre Lescot (1510?–78), who built a portion of the Cour du Louvre; and Jean Bullant (1525–78), who built at Fère-en-Tardenois, at Chantilly (Châtelet), additions to Écouen, and a part of the Tuileries. With the passing of this generation of great architects, the brilliant period closes,—having lasted for only 20 years,—and is succeeded by a period of sterility, due to religious wars and anarchy.

Reign of Henry IV. (1589–1610).—The architecture of the short interval between the time of the entrance of Henry IV. into Paris and his death (1595–1610), may be called the architecture of a reconstruction period. It is characterized by a simplicity and effectiveness attained, not by the use of expensive ornament, but by brick and stone employed in the old French tradition, the façades being decorated by quoins of rustication instead of by the orders—a somewhat severe treatment which was softened by the mellow colour of the walls under the firm silhouette of the slate roofs. The outstanding contribution to architecture, however, was the king's great undertaking to remodel the city, which had grown up haphazardly—an undertaking such as had not been attempted since the days of imperial Rome. To achieve his end, he made laws regulating the heights of buildings and the paving and widening of streets, and prohibiting the overhanging upper stories of the middle ages. Finally, by the contribution of such schemes of civic planning as the Place Royale (now the Place des Vosges) and the Place Dauphine, he inaugurated a school which, after reaching its apogee in the 18th century, furnishes models for city-development to-day. Examples of this period are the important additions to Fontainebleau, the château of St. Germain-en-Laye and portions of the Louvre.

Seventeenth Century.—At the beginning of the century, there was an unprecedented activity in building; the long period of wars had brought about the usual changes in private fortunes, and the "nouveaux riches" had to provide themselves with splendid habitations. The architecture of this time excels in the planning of town residences (hôtels), with their admirable arrangements of the cour d'honneur, service courts and noble garden elevations. The larger houses retained the "galeries" of the earlier Renaissance for the display of art treasures. The country estates are notable for their fine gardens, decorated with statues, basins and balustrades. In ecclesiastical architecture, the Jesuits cast the weight of their influence in favour of the adoption of Renaissance forms, and the churches and chapels designed by members of their order are inspired by the Gesu and the 16th century Italian examples (e.g., St. Paul and the Novitiate in Paris). To the influence of the Jesuit architecture and that of the Italian Baroque, rather than to the Flemish, may be ascribed the exuberant ornamentation prevalent in the early part of the century. Architects of the first rank were numerous, among whom the first is François Mansart (1598–1666), by far the greatest architect of his time, and, according to Blondel (a competent critic of the 18th century), "the most skillful architect France has ever produced." Among other notable works he designed the wing added by Gaston d'Orléans at Blois, with its magnificent stairway, the additions to the Hôtel Carnavalet with their exquisite refinement of detail, the Château de Maisons and the Val-de-Grâce, a masterpiece which one has only to compare to St. Eustache, built 50 years before, to realize that French architecture had reached maturity. The palace of the Luxembourg, by Salomon de Brosse, the magnificent composition of the town and palace of Richelieu, the chapel of the Sorbonne, by Le Mercier, the Château de Tanlay (Burgundy), by Pierre le Muet, with its beautiful park, antedating the compositions of Le Nôtre, and finally the work of Louis Le Vau, who created the style of Versailles and Vaux-le-Vicomte, of the Hôtel Lambert and the Collège des Quatre Nations, and who represents the transition from the period of Louis XIII. to that of Louis XIV., are some of the outstanding compositions of the early 17th century.

Louis XIV. Period.—The *grand monarque* placed the artists of his time under a discipline administered strictly by Colbert and Le Brun. The Academy of Painting and Sculpture was re-founded in 1666 and the Academy of Architecture created in 1671. There followed a reaction from the empiricism of the preceding period, strengthened by the reverence of the academies for their classic doctrines, and by the king's disdain of foreign influences. The academies were as suspicious of artistic independence as the king of political heterodoxy. The striking feature of this period is a curious contrast between the classic composition of exteriors, free from the earlier experimental fantasies, and the elaborate ornamentation of interiors. There was a simplification both of the masses of a building, and of outward ornament, even to the silhouette of the roofs. The combining of few elements with unerring taste resulted in a stately dignity of proportion that lends even to the most unambitious work in provincial towns the noblesse of the greater constructions. On the other hand, the interiors were often overloaded with decoration. Le Brun, the court painter from 1664 to 1690, was in full authority at Versailles; a great decorator, he had the weaknesses of this aspect of his talent. Thus, refinement and intensity of expression were often sacrificed in the attempt to combine architecture, painting and sculpture into a single homogeneous effect.

Among the principal architects of the time, are Claude Perrault (1613–83), who, besides the Porte St. Antoine, and the Observatoire, designed the three façades of the Louvre which have been praised and attacked beyond all measure, and the excellence of which is readily seen by a comparison with Bernini's project for the same work; François Blondel (1618–86), who designed the beautiful Porte St. Denis; Jules Hardouin Mansart (1646–1708), architect of Marly, the Grand Trianon, Place Vendôme, Place des Victoires and the "Dôme des Invalides," and who designed all the work at Versailles after 1676; and Liberal Bruant (1637–97), whose simple, powerful architecture may be seen in the Hôtel des Invalides and La Salpêtrière. A résumé of 17th century architecture would hardly be complete without a mention of Le Nôtre (1613–1700), who brought to its highest development the composition of the formal garden.

Eighteenth Century.—The change that began to make itself perceptible in the last period of the reign of Louis XIV. and up through the first half of the succeeding century, is the further simplification of exteriors, coupled with a still more striking change of interiors. The classic doctrine, with the orders, is still asserted in the designs of the façades; but there appeared a bolder use of blank surfaces, relieved by chains of rustication, and more restraint in the use of mouldings. Thousands of houses of this period are still to be seen, with quiet elevations whose harmonious proportions are their only bid to attract attention, and with skilful interior planning which still serves as a model. The treatment of these 18th century interiors forms a striking contrast with the Baroque splendours of the heyday of Louis XIV. A reaction had set in against the conservatism, and the theatrical pomp of the 17th century, in which people moved like actors on a stage; the new tendency was toward greater freedom in the adaptation of the classic formulas, and lightness and elegance of effect, and *intimacy*. Even at Versailles, stately apartments were broken up into groups of smaller rooms, and houses were planned with corridors and an arrangement of rooms convenient to their uses. The wood panelling, which replaced the marble inlay of palaces or the bare walls of simpler dwellings, was treated as woodwork, with a scale of moulding and decoration suitable to the material and without imitation of stone architecture motives. Fabric and paper were introduced as wall coverings; the ceilings were no longer designed to imitate vaulting—the open beams and joists disappeared and plasterwork was treated frankly as such. The stairways were decorated only by their railings of admirably wrought ironwork. In these interiors there is a complete emancipation from Graeco-Roman motives, pilasters, cornices, etc. The curved line prevails. It is the style of the Rococo.

The examples of the architecture of this period are so numerous that only a few can be mentioned here: e.g., the stables of Chantilly, and the Hôtel Biron by Aubert, la Malgrange (Nancy) and the Hôtel d'Amelot by Boffrand, the Palais Bourbon, by Giardini and l'Assurance. The work of public buildings and city planning counts in its first ranks the admirable ensemble at Nancy (Places Stanislas, de la Carrière and du Gouvernement) by Boffrand and Héré de Corny, the bridges at Nantes and Blois by J. J. Gabriel, the Place Royale at Bordeaux (Gabriel), and the Place Bellecour at Lyons (De Cotte). The religious architecture is exemplified by some imposing monasteries, which acquire with the excellent qualities of the domestic designing a certain touch of worldliness. Examples are St. Étienne at Caen, St. Ouen at Rouen, and the bishops' palaces of Toul, Verdun and Strasbourg.

Second Period.—Madame de Pompadour and her artistic advisers, such as Cochin and M. de Caylus, the archaeologists, and the architects Gabriel and Blondel had never looked with favour upon the infringements of the antique formulas that were committed in the Louis XV. period, and the new discovery of antiquities at Herculaneum and Pompeii infused the supporters of the classic doctrine with fresh conviction. Toward 1750, then, the fashion reverted to the close imitation of a Graeco-Roman style, newly baptized "à la Grecque." De Caylus's *"Recueil d'Antiquités,"* published in 1762, Leroy's *"Ruines des plus beaux Monuments de la Grèce"* (1754), Soufflot's work on Paestum, and Piranesi's engravings, encouraged and facilitated the return to antique example by giving more precise documentation. Among the representative works of the architecture of the time are the Petit Trianon, the École Militaire, the wings of the entrance court and the opera at Versailles, and the Place de la Concorde, by J. A. Gabriel, the Hôtel-Dieu at Lyon, the church of Ste. Geneviève at Paris, now the Pantheon, by Soufflot, and the works of Antoine, Mique, Ledoux, Victor Louis, Rousseau, (theatre of Bordeaux, mint and Palais de Justice at Paris).

BIBLIOGRAPHY.—C. Daly, *Motifs Historiques* (1870); L. Palustre, *La Renaissance en France* (1881); H. von Geymuller, *Baukunst der Renaissance in Frankreich* (1898); M. Fonquier, *Les Grands Châteaux de France* (1907); C. Martin, *La Renaissance en France* (1911); W. H. Ward, *Architecture of the Renaissance in France* (1926); P. Vitry, *Hôtels et Maisons de la Renaissance Française* (1912); Reginald Blomfield, *A History of French Architecture—1494 to 1661* (1912), and *A History of French Architecture, 1661 to 1774* (1921); Georges

Gromart, *L'Architecture de la Renaissance en France (XVIe, XVIIe et XVIIIe Siècles)* (1930). (P. P. CR.; X.)

IV. GERMANY, FLANDERS AND HOLLAND

In the 16th century, Germany resisted, more than France or Spain, the Italian influence. The classic spirit in art was apparently less congenial to her civilization, which lacked the Latin basis, and she had not suffered, like France and Spain, the disintegrating influences of a long destructive war which, by weakening the mediaeval and national traditions, had prepared the way for a new and alien art. The Italian motives appeared sporadically—for example, in a Florentine belvedere built in Prague in 1536 and in the Lombardesque wing of the castle at Heidelberg, built in 1556—but the Renaissance had to await the end of the 16th century to win a wide acceptance north of the Alps.

About 1580 the Baroque forms of Alessi were introduced into Germany. These forms, which were understood more as a system of decoration than as elements in mass composition, became immediately popular in the South German cities: broken pediments, scrolls, consoles, cartouches, the human figure placed in a niche, began to appear in profusion on the façades of churches and houses which in composition were still mediaeval. This fusion of Gothic picturesqueness with the sophisticated Baroque ornament gave to this first phase of German Renaissance an altogether unique character. The great stepped gables of town houses and the transept ends or façades of churches, wholly mediaeval in mass and line, flower out at the top into a rich encrustation of modelled form in which all the elements of classic architecture seem to be melted together. Examples of such designs are the Merienkirche, at Wolfenbuttel, the Gewendhaus at Brunswick (1592) and the Pellerhaus, in Nuremberg (1625).

After the Thirty Years' War, which ended in 1648 and devastated the greater part of the Rhine countries, German Renaissance architecture entered a new phase. The Baroque spirit gained a more complete ascendancy and in many localities mediaevalism entirely disappeared. Naturally the Baroque was more completely accepted in the southern and Catholic countries where Italian architects, brought into Germany by the Jesuits, built, or helped to build, many churches and palaces. Along the Rhine the French influence was felt, but it was not until the 18th century (*see* MODERN ARCHITECTURE: *18th and 19th Centuries*) that Germany turned directly to France for artistic inspiration. In that century the architecture of Versailles was widely imitated in the German courts, achieving there a compromise, or fusion, with the Italian Baroque. The result was a vigorous and original style, often piquant and full of that element of "surprise" which is a result of Baroque freedom and movement.

Germany, having a larger number of capital cities—there were more than 300 in the 16th century—developed a greater variety of local styles than any other country. Vienna was of course the most important centre. The relief that was felt when in 1685 the Turks were driven from before her walls, the prosperity fostered by Leopold I. and Charles VI., and the renewed faith of the Catholic reaction, found expression there in a series of remarkable monuments. Fischer von Erlach and Lukas von Hildebrandt, the two great architects of Vienna, transformed the mediaeval city, as Bernini had transformed Rome, with fountains and public places, with majestic churches, vast palaces and astonishing gardens. In their hands the exuberant Baroque, touched with an oriental fantasy, reached a magnificence altogether consonant with the gorgeous imperialism and the fervid piety of the times. The Karlskirche (1717–37) and the Hofbibliothek (1736), by von Erlach, and the Belvedere (1713–16), by Hildebrandt, are the most famous and perhaps most characteristic examples of this Viennese Renaissance.

After Vienna, the smaller courts of Dresden and Munich furnished important opportunities for the Renaissance architect. In Dresden, Pöpplemann (1662–1736) built the court of the Zwinger palace (1711–22), an extraordinary assembly of fantastic pavilion, bizarre planting and agitated sculpture. The Frauenkirche, in Dresden (1726–43), by George Bähr, is an original, free and virile design, perhaps the greatest achievement of the German

Renaissance. In Munich, where the Italian architect Agostino Barelli had built a Neapolitan church, the Theatinerkirche (1667–75), the Wittelsbachs employed the French architect, François Cuvilliers, to add to their somewhat grandiose palace the altogether delightful Residenz-theatre (1752–60). Salzburg, with its cathedral (1614–34), its University church, and its Mirabel-Schloss, is one of the loveliest of Baroque towns; Prague has the great Wallenstein palace (1673–1730), the work of the Italian Marini, as well as the more Teutonic Kinsky palace, the work of the talented architect Kilian Ignaz Dientzenhofer; and in Potsdam, where, under Frederick the Great, French influence is most felt, the palace of Sans Souci (1716) achieves a delicacy and graceful freedom certainly not excelled in contemporary France.

To this architecture of the city and court there is added the architecture of the monasteries. Placed picturesquely among the hills of the Danube or the Rhine, these vast buildings offered opportunities most congenial to the spirit of 17th century architecture. Melk (1707–36) is perhaps the most impressive; a colossal mass which commands the Danube from the top of a mighty cliff and throws against the sky a superb tangle of modelled spire and dome.

In Flanders and Holland the development of architecture in the Renaissance was not essentially different from that of North Germany. The Jesuit influence was felt in Flanders and the development of churches of the Il Gesu type, such as the church of St Michael, in Louvain (1650) was parallel to the contemporary development in South Germany and France. In Holland, as in Germany, the stepped gables of the town houses were transformed by the addition of Baroque detail but the use of brick and of quoins and the need of economy often gave them a more sober aspect than their Germanic cousins. At times the French influence was felt, as, for example, in the Hôtel de Ville in Antwerp (1561), a design in which superimposed columns enframe round-arched windows with a gracefulness and distinction in detail that recalls the work of Lescot.

BIBLIOGRAPHY.—W. Lubke, *Geschichte der Renaissance in Deutschland* (1882); A. Ortwein and A. Scheffer, *Deutsche Renaissance* (1871–88); K. E. O. Fritsch, *Denkmaler deutsche Renaissance* (1891); Gron Bezold, *Die Baukunst der Renaissance in Deutschland, Holland, Belgien, und Dänemark* (1908); Herman Popp, *Die Architektur der Barock in Deutschland und in der Schweiz* (1913); Karl Horst, *Die Architektur der Deutschen Renaissance* (1928). (J. HUD.)

V. RENAISSANCE ARCHITECTURE IN ENGLAND

The Renaissance architecture of England may be conveniently divided into two phases which correspond roughly to the 17th and 18th centuries, to the period of the Stuarts and the period of the Georges. In the first phase the genius of two great architects, Inigo Jones and Christopher Wren, created for England a new system of design, based upon elements imported from Italy. In the second phase a host of other architects, highly talented but less original, imitated and developed the architecture formulated by Jones and Wren. The 17th century supplied a mine of architectural motives and enriched England with a few supremely great masterpieces; the 18th century made use of that mine to create a great number of brilliant designs, no one of which quite achieves greatness. (*See* MODERN ARCHITECTURE: *18th and 19th Centuries*.)

There are not lacking in England many examples of the use of Renaissance forms before the 17th century, but the spirit of her architecture remained essentially mediaeval. In the Tudor period, when the cathedral-building impulse had come to an end, when the monasteries ceased to exist and when the building of great country houses had become the chief preoccupation of architects, there grew up a certain simplicity and breadth of handling, a horizontal tendency in composition, which presaged the Renaissance. At the same time the ornamental motives of Italy appeared on the mantelpieces and around the doorways of the Elizabethan houses; and the craftsmen of Flanders, then numerous in England, employed these motives in their decorative work in plaster or carved wood.

Inigo Jones.—The failure of the national style of England to resist the imported Italian style is one of the remarkable circumstances of Renaissance architecture. Travel in Italy, where the cultivated Englishman might compare the masterpieces of Bramante and Michelangelo with the formless Tudor of his own land, and the importation of Italian books, prepared the way no doubt for the new architecture, but they do not explain its immediate success. That success appears to have been due to the genius and force of one man: Inigo Jones. Jones, almost single-handed, put an end to the mediaeval tradition and set up a national movement that rescued English architecture from the Tudor chaos and brought it back to the Roman road along which progress was possible. His supreme accomplishment was to revive in England the conception of architecture as a form-giving art, having an academic and intellectual basis, and to get this accepted as the foundation of a new, national development.

This conception of architecture, rigorously developed by the somewhat intransigent architects of the 18th century, brought into English architecture a certain artificiality which is no doubt the cause of much that is deplorable in the English tradition. A lack of vitality and saliency results when architecture becomes, as it did in Georgian England, a wholly academic art, when the authority of books and of the Italian masters replaces a tradition in building to which the usages of the people, the needs of institutions, the climate and the temper of the nation have contributed. Nor did England develop great sculptors and mural painters to soften, as in France, the austerity of the Roman column and vault. The traditions of fine craftsmanship in plaster and in wood carving remained but they did not suffice to give English Renaissance architecture the warmth, the feeling of having become wholly assimilated, wholly expressive of a national temperament, that one finds in the Renaissance of Italy or Spain.

The reputation of Inigo Jones rests in no small degree on the designs that he made for the great palace at Whitehall in the years 1619–25. This palace is comparable in size to the great projects of the Louvre and the Vatican. The design is splendid and monumental and the palace, had it been erected, would without doubt have been unrivalled, except perhaps by the Escorial, in grandeur of effect. The façades of its seven courts abound in original motives, in which Palladian architecture is skilfully made comformable to English needs. In this, as in all his designs, Jones displays the correctness in proportion and the vigorous and unaffected handling of space and detail, that give his style a nobility and strength excelling that of any other English architect. The Banqueting hall, which is the only part of the palace of Whitehall actually executed, is an embodiment of these qualities.

Christopher Wren.—On the foundation laid by Jones, Sir Christopher Wren built the great masterpieces of English architecture. To the strength and sensitive feeling for proportion possessed by Jones, he added one of the most active and resourceful imaginations in the history of architecture. To a solid basis of Palladianism—that is to say, to correctness in academic design—Wren added the freedom and movement, the piquancy and drama, of the Baroque. He could unite in one ensemble the two currents into which architecture had divided in the 17th century, the academic and the ingenious, so that they flowed together into a reservoir of original and expressive motives that the 18th century was to find inexhaustible. Very characteristic of this compromise are the 51 parish churches that Wren built in London after the great fire of 1666. Among his secular buildings are important additions to Hampton Court, the library of Trinity college, Cambridge, and the great hospital at Greenwich.

In the city churches Wren created a wholly new type. Built for congregational use, with galleries, shallow chancels and meagre provision for services, they occupy irregular congested sites in the midst of crowded streets. The exteriors had to be severely plain, since funds were scarce; red brick and plaster for the interior were the materials employed. Yet with all these discouragements Wren produced interiors oftentimes full of charm, and exteriors that play a commanding part in their civic environment. These exteriors, plain and even box-like, have slender towers so placed as to be most effective in the street-picture and modelled at the top into delicate spires or lanterns over which there is an encrustation of classic forms.

The secular buildings were more conventional in character. The additions made to Hampton Court (c. 1690) constitute a sober essay in brick-and-stone architecture, somewhat crowded in effect and lacking the repose that marks their Italian prototypes. The Cambridge library (1678) follows the lines of the library at Venice, but is without the piquant proportion and wealth of sculptured ornament that give the Venetian façades so much distinction and grace. Greenwich hospital is more imaginative, having a masterly plan in which four palatial masses are grouped on an axis about two courts. Two domed pavilions are introduced to give the design unity and add life to the façades.

All of these buildings, although exceedingly diverse and original, are of less importance than the great cathedral of London. The ruins of the Gothic cathedral having been cleared away after the Great Fire, Wren was commissioned in 1668 to construct a new St. Paul's in accordance with a Renaissance design that he submitted. During the period from 1675, when the first stone was laid, to 1710, when the work was completed, Wren made many departures from this accepted design, which grew steadily in imaginative power and monumental unity, but at no time did he abandon his central idea, a classic monument contrasted with forms taken from the Baroque. The greatness of St. Paul's is derived, not from the perfection of detail, which is frequently open to criticism, but from the consistency and grandeur with which it realized this idea. The central dome, definite and geometric in mass and in silhouette, imposing in scale, rises from a wide podium and is preceded, at the western end, by two spirited campaniles whose modelled surfaces, profuse shadow and broken silhouette contrast dramatically with the simpler forms with which they are associated.

Eighteenth Century.—After the death of Wren there remained the academic basis which Jones had established for English architecture and the compromise which Wren had brought about between the Palladianism and the virile and free Baroque. These two traditions dominated English architecture and gave direction, in more or less equal degree, to its development during the 18th century. But gradually the academic triumphed. The largeness of conception, the grandiose effect, is forsaken towards the middle of the century in favour of purity and repose.

John Vanbrugh (1664–1726), who did not begin to practice architecture until after the age of 35, was the most robust and daring of Wren's successors and most resembled him in the power and breadth of his imagination. He was the builder of vast country houses, such as Blenheim (1710), 856 ft. long, and Castle Howard (1702), a private dwelling with a dome 100 ft. high. These are monstrous buildings, with innumerable faults of technique and propriety, but magnificent in conception, piling up huge geometric masses around the perimeters of immense courts in a kind of intoxication of architecture.

Nicholas Hawksmoor (1661–1736), a pupil of Wren and an assistant of Vanbrugh, found fewer opportunities than either. For his fine Christ church, Spitalfields, he combined the most original and spirited tower in England with an interior almost unrivalled in formal elegance and classic beauty. The façade that he built for Westminster Abbey is more successful than might have been expected from an age so out of tune with the mediaeval spirit. His rugged and simple work contrasts strangely with that of his more successful and versatile contemporary, James Gibbs (1682–1754). Gibbs, like Hawksmoor, a builder of churches in the Wren tradition, shows great facility in adapting and developing motifs taken from Wren; but his care for correct detail and for elegance in technique oftentimes lessens the breadth and virility of his work. The church of St. Mary-le-Strand, in London, is a good example of his style. The Radcliffe library, Oxford, is a more monumental building, but executed with less *address*. St. Martins-in-the-Fields, London, has a magnificent spire thrust through the roof of a Roman portico; a conception worthy of the greatest Baroque designers, boldly carried out and combined with an interior full of dignity and feeling.

Gibbs was a scholarly architect, possessing that thorough training in Palladian design which is characteristic of the 18th century designers, but he found in Wren a source of vitality which counteracted, to some extent at least, the frigidity of the master of Vincenza. Gibbs' contemporaries were often less fortunate: Lord Burlington, a wealthy amateur whose actual accomplishments are still a subject of controversy; Colin Campbell (d. 1734), his protégé and the author of the *Vitruvius Britannicus;* and William Kent (1684–1748), who resided in Burlington House, form a group of academic architects to whom adherence to the Italian model seemed more to be desired than individuality of manner or a continuation of the English tradition of Wren. All were builders of great country houses.

Kedleston Hall, by James Paine (1716–89), recovers to some extent the spirit of Vanbrugh, speaking the language of abstract architectonic form, rather than that of ornament. It is planned in the grand manner, with a porticoed central block flanked by smaller blocks, in which all the parts echo those of the centre. On the major axis are two Roman rooms, one peristyled and one domed. Harewood House, Yorkshire, by Carr of York (1723–80), in which there is, as at Kedleston, a central block flanked by wings, illustrates further the rigid purity of the classic taste of the middle of the century, when the tradition of Wren was disappearing and correct proportion was allowed to take the place of inspiration. The Palladian bridge at Wilton, by Robert Morris, and the house at Prior park, Bath, by John Wood, are other examples.

The last of the Renaissance architects were William Chambers (1726–96) and Robert Adam (1728–92). To the former fell the greatest opportunity of the century, the building of the immense Somerset palace in London. A man of pure taste and of unusual executive powers, he succeeded in creating one of the finest palatial façades in Europe; a façade, however, which has the excellence of scholarliness and of technique rather than that of inspiration and power. Adam, who practised in partnership with his brother James, was even more academic in his outlook; his style is, on his exterior designs, simple, tenuous and dry in the extreme. His interiors, which often take unusual shapes in plan and in the modelling of ceilings, are enriched by a delicate and graceful system of decoration which, when skilfully executed, attains a unique loveliness. His influence was enormous and under his leadership the architecture of the Renaissance came to an end.

BIBLIOGRAPHY.—J. A. Gotch, *Renaissance Architecture in England* (1894); Belcher and MacCartney, *Later Renaissance Architecture in England* (1897); R. Bloomfield, *History of Renaissance Architecture in England* (1897); H. Field and M. Bunny, *English Domestic Architecture of the 17th and 18th Centuries* (1904); J. A. Gotch, *The Growth of the English House* (1908); MacCartney, *English Houses and Gardens of the 17th and 18th Centuries* (1908); J. A. Gotch, *Early Renaissance Architecture in England* (1914); P. L. Dickensen, *Georgian Mansions in Ireland* (1915); S. A. Ramsay, *Small Georgian Houses* (1919).   (J. HUD.)

RENAISSANCE ART. The revival of classic learning in Italy, which was so marked a feature of Italian culture during the 15th century, was paralleled by an equal passion for the beauty of classic design in all the artistic fields; and when this eager delight in the then fresh and sensuous graciousness that is the mark of much classic work—to the Italians of that time, seemingly the expression of a golden age—became universal, complete domination of the classic ideal in art was inevitable.

This turning to classic models was less sudden and revolutionary than it seemed. Throughout the history of Romanesque and Gothic Italian art, the tradition of classic structure and ornament still remained alive; again and again, in the 12th and 13th centuries classic forms—the acanthus leaf, moulding ornaments, the treatment of drapery in a relief—are imitated, often with crudeness, to be sure, but with a basic sympathy for the old imperial Roman methods of design. (*See* GOTHIC ART; ROMANESQUE ART.) How much more at home seems the mediaeval Italian artist, who carved the spiralling acanthus leaves on the doors of Pisa cathedral (11th century) than the designer of the laboured and stupid, crocketted capitals of the cathedral in Florence (14th century), or the contorted and unconvincing buttress pinnacles of Milan cathedral (begun 1386). The best of Italian Gothic art is always that which is least like northern Gothic, and is usually dominated by ideals, essentially those of earlier Italian building, like the Byzantinesque palaces of Venice. Niccolo Pisano (c. 1206–1280) was but the first of many Italian

artists, particularly sculptors, to turn definitely to Roman sculpture for inspiration.

It was therefore only natural that Brunelleschi (1377–1476) should study the ruins of ancient Rome, and that, following his example, the whole artistic world of Florence turned to the same source of inspiration almost unanimously. Brunelleschi's famous cupola over the cathedral of Florence completes the work of the preceding age and is not yet a Renaissance manifestation. The new style was displayed in the Pazzi chapel and in the plans for San Lorenzo and San Spirito.

Florence was the great centre of this early Renaissance; whence it spread throughout Italy in the 15th century; the greater number of artists were Florence-trained. The enthusiastic patronage of art of the new type by Cosimo dei Medici (1389–1464), and Lorenzo dei Medici (1449–1492), who founded the famous Platonic Academy, gave a tremendous impetus to the movement, and the general Florentine method of art training, through *bottege,* or craftsman shops, assured the fact that the Renaissance was not confined to architecture and sculpture, but spread to all the industrial arts as well.

Another element besides the influence of ancient Rome becomes evident as the Renaissance matured in such of the minor arts as textiles, pottery and metal work. This was the influence of the Near East. Commerce between Italy and the Turkish dominions was constant and large in amount, and Oriental pottery and textiles were much sought after. When the Italians started manufacturing their own goods to compete with this foreign source, limitation and adaptation of the Oriental patterns was natural. Thus the controlling designs of Venetian velvets and brocades, down to the 18th century, owe much to the carnation and the palmette of Persia, and in 16th and 17th century armour and silver-ware, there occur the spear-head shapes and bifurcated leaves and intricate interlaces of fine lines which characterize the inlaid brass, copper and steel of Damascus or Constantinople.

By the beginning of the 16th century the tentative and experimental characteristics of the earlier Renaissance had, in Italy, given way to the mature, knowing, and facile use of classic forms which constitutes the High Renaissance or cinquecento (*q.v.*). In architecture, the orders were used with entire command; in the minor arts the decorative exuberance of the 15th century was yielding to sounder and more dignified conceptions. Yet the development of this polished classicism was limited and eager; creative imaginations refused to be bound by it. The result was the resurgence of untrammelled and, at times, unlicensed individualism in design, which is known as the Baroque or late Renaissance. Already, in the work of Michelangelo, 1474–1564, and Cellini, 1500–71 (*see* SILVERSMITHS' AND GOLDSMITHS' WORK), Baroque elements are obvious, and by the year 1600 the ideals of climax, broken curves, magnificent composition and dynamic contrasts, which constitute the Baroque movement, were universally accepted, and the classic forms became merely an inspirational frame-work for individual development and creation. The Baroque was a style curiously turgid, often gigantesque, theatrical, often denying or falsifying structural framework, yet magnificently alive; producing alike such over lavish and ill considered decorations as those of Andrea Pozzo (1642–1709) for the church of S. Ignazio in Rome and the dignified and monumental colonnades of the Piazza of S. Peter's, by Bernini (1598–1680). During the 18th century the vitality of the Baroque degenerated into a chaos of contorted forms, to be in turn replaced, at the end of the century, by a recrudescence of stern, cold and rather sterile classicism. Yet the Renaissance in Spain was no mere copy of the Italian.

Renaissance feeling was introduced into Spain during the latter years of the 15th century by wandering Italian sculptors, but a school of native artists soon developed, and during the 16th century an individual school of Renaissance dominance was complete, despite the Italian impetus given by the campaign of Charles V., 1500–58, and the fanatical Romanism of his son Philip II., 1527–1598, whose palace monastery, the Escorial, by Juan Bautista (16th century) and Juan de Herrera (1530–97), is a stark and lonely monument to Philip II.'s Italian taste. Elsewhere, the Moorish influence was so strong as to modify the Italian forms profoundly; Moorish craftsmen controlled the potteries and often built the buildings. Moreover, perhaps due to the bleak and sombre character of so large a part of the Spanish territory, the emotional quality of the Spanish Renaissance work has a sharp pungency quite different from the usual graciousness of the Italian feeling. The style in Spain may be divided into three parts—the early Renaissance, or Plateresque (*q.v.*), in which Moorish influence is marked; the classic or Griego-Romano, a short and sterile attempt to introduce strict Italian classicism; and the Baroque or Churrigueresque, so-called from one of its main exponents, Jose Churriguera (died 1725). It was in this final style that the Spanish temperament found itself most at home. Particularly characteristic of the Spanish Renaissance is the work in certain of the minor arts, especially in iron work, as shown in the magnificent church screens, or rejeria (*q.v.*); in furniture, in which iron and wood were frequently combined; and in stamped leather, for which Spain was famous.

In France, the history of the early Renaissance shows a style originally essentially an imported court fashion, gradually permeating all French life. The Italian campaigns of Charles VIII, 1470–1498, Louis XII, 1462–1515, and Francis I, 1494–1547, had given the French court an intimate knowledge of the comparative luxury, cleanliness and monumentality of the Italian cities. Italian artists were invited to the court; Italian decorators and architects helped Francis I in his great building schemes. Yet this court fashion had to compete with a vivid and vital flamboyant, late Gothic style, and much of the charm of the early French Renaissance results from the naive, yet brilliantly executed combinations of the two influences. During the reign of Henry II, 1519–1559, the classic ideal was dominant, though Gothic forms were still in use. Under Henry IV, 1553–1610, though the Gothic had at last passed away, Baroque freedom controlled design, and under Louis XIII, Louis XIV, Louis XV and Louis XVI whose reigns stretched from 1610 to 1793, there was a continual see-saw between academic classicism and imaginative freedom. (*See* LOUIS STYLES.)

From the beginning a court style, the French Renaissance remained essentially a luxurious style. All of the arts of luxury flourished. Rich textiles—tapestries and brocades—are characteristic, and the lavish furniture was copied all over Europe, especially during the 18th century. The development of pottery, first privately, and later under government auspices, culminated in the magnificent porcelains of Sèvres.

The development of the Renaissance in the rest of Europe was marked by common features. In England and the Teutonic countries, there was not only a late vital Gothic style, but definite characteristics of national taste and vastly different climatic and geographical conditions. Yet the humanistic impetus of the Renaissance existed almost everywhere and the beauty of the naturalistic painting and sculpture, as well as the exquisite productions of Italian goldsmiths, formed a continual invitation toward a change in artistic ideals. Thus, despite occasional purely classic work by Italian artists, such as Torregiano's tomb of Henry VII in Westminster abbey, London (1515), the early Renaissance in north Europe is chiefly characterized by the gradual creeping in of misunderstood classic decorative forms, often caricatured. In none of these countries did classicism become dominant until the 17th century, and even then it is coloured by local taste. Thus in Germany, the picturesqueness of late Gothic decorative design controlled all of the arts down to the 18th century and even the pseudoclassic of the French inspired Rococo embodied many picturesque elements. In England, due to the influence of Inigo Jones, 1572–1652, and Sir Christopher Wren, 1632–1723, at least in architecture, classic forms were used with purity and unusual correctness. In Germany and Flanders, on the other hand, Baroque elements were favoured, especially in woodcarving and the minor arts generally; and through the diffusion of Flemish craftsmen consequent upon the confused religious and political conditions during the 17th century, these northern varieties of Baroque forms were broadcast over Europe, influencing markedly the later Renaissance work

in England and recognizably, though to a less extent, that of France and Spain. This confusion of international influences marked the Renaissance of the 18th century, the style movements in France being generally paralleled by those in other countries. Yet the erratic swing between licence and classicism was indicative of a decaying style vitality, and new archaeological discoveries were giving to the classicism of the end of the century a motivation quite different from the simpler Renaissance tradition that was dying. With the fall of the French court, in the French revolution, more than a political system was swept away, for with it went the last vestiges of Renaissance tradition. *See* BAROQUE ARCHITECTURE; BRONZE AND BRASS ORNAMENTAL WORK; INTERIOR DECORATION; PAINTING; POTTERY AND PORCELAIN; RENAISSANCE ARCHITECTURE; ROCOCO; LOUIS STYLES; RUGS AND CARPETS; SILVERSMITHS' AND GOLDSMITHS' WORK; TAPESTRY.

(T. F. H.)

RENAIX (Flem. *Ronse*), town, province of East Flanders, Belgium, 8 mi. S. of Oudenarde, at the foot of the hills of Flanders. It has yielded many pre-Roman and Roman finds. There are manufactories for woollen and linen goods. Pop. (1939) 25,491.

RENAN, ERNEST (1823–1892), French philosopher and orientalist, was born on Feb. 27, 1823, at Tréguier. His father's people were of the fisher-clan of Renans or Ronans. He was only 5 years old when his father died, and his sister Henriette, 12 years older than Ernest, a girl of remarkable character, was henceforth morally the head of the household. Ernest was educated in the ecclesiastical college at Tréguier. In the summer of 1838 he carried off all the prizes at the college. Through his sister, who was teaching in Paris, Felix Dupanloup heard of him, and sent for him at once, and placed him in the new ecclesiastical college of St. Nicolas du Chardonnay. He then proceeded to study for the priesthood at the Seminary of Issy, then at St. Sulpice, and finally he found his way to Stavistas, a lay college of the Oratorians. He soon found himself torn between his desire to lead the life of a Catholic priest and his intellectual inability to accept in its entirety the ordinary presentation of Catholic doctrine, or to submit to ecclesiastical authority. Even at Stavistas he found himself too much under the domination of the church, and, after a few weeks there, he reluctantly broke the last tie which bound him to the religious life, and entered M. Crouzet's school for boys as an usher. There he made the acquaintance, in 1846, of the chemist Marcellin Berthelot, then a boy of 18. To the day of Renan's death their friendship continued. Renan was occupied as usher only in the evenings. In the daytime he continued his researches in Semitic philology. In 1847 he obtained the Prix Volney for his *General History of Semitic Languages*.

The revolution of 1848 confronted him with the problems of democracy. The result was an immense volume, *The Future of Science*, which remained in manuscript until 1890. *L'Avenir de la science* is an attempt to conciliate the privileges of a necessary *élite* with the diffusion of the greatest good of the greatest number. In 1849 the French government sent him to Italy on a scientific mission. In Italy the artist in him awoke and triumphed over the savant and the reformer. On his return to Paris Renan lived with his sister Henriette. A small post at the National library, together with his sister's savings, furnished him with the means of livelihood. In the evenings he wrote for the *Revue des deux mondes* and the *Débats* the exquisite essays which appeared in 1857 and 1859 under the titles *Études d'histoire religieuse* and *Essais de morale et de critique*. In 1852 his book on *Averroès* had brought him not only his doctor's degree, but his first reputation as a thinker. In his two volumes of essays Renan shows himself a liberal, but no longer a democrat. Nothing, according to his philosophy, is less important than prosperity. The greatest good of the greatest number is a theory as dangerous as it is illusory. Man is not born to be prosperous, but to realize, in a little vanguard of chosen spirits, an ideal superior to the ideal of yesterday. Only the few can attain a complete development. Yet there is a solidarity between the chosen few and the masses which produce them; each has a duty to the other. The acceptance of this duty is the only foundation for a moral and just society. The aristocratic idea has seldom been better stated.

BY COURTESY OF (3, 5) THE METROPOLITAN MUSEUM OF ART, NEW YORK, (4) THE DIRECTOR OF THE BERNE MUSEUM, (6) A. E. BULLOCK FROM "GRINLING GIBBONS AND HIS COMPEERS" (JOHN TIRANTI AND CO.); PHOTOGRAPHS, (1) ANDERSON, (2) ALINARI

DECORATIVE DETAILS OF THE RENAISSANCE

1. "The creation of Adam and Eve and their expulsion from Paradise," a panel in bronze by Lorenzo Ghiberti (1378–1455) in the famous east door made for the Baptistery in Florence between 1425 and 1452, a masterwork of early Renaissance decorative sculpture

2. Vault of the Scala d'Oro in the Doges' Palace, Venice, designed by Jacopo Sansovino (1486–1570)

3. Glazed polychrome terra cotta, "Assumption of the Virgin" by Luca della Robbia (1400–82), characteristic of the early Florentine Renaissance in its perfect blend of architecture and sculpture as well as in the exquisite delicacy of its modelling. In the Metropolitan Museum of Art, New York

4. Swiss room, 17th century, the woodwork characteristic in its free handling of Baroque motives. Now in the Berne Museum

5. Swiss panelled room, 17th century, with rich Baroque woodwork and a magnificent porcelain stove. Now in the Metropolitan Museum of Art, New York

6. The seat for the Archbishop of Canterbury incorporated in the choir stalls of St. Paul's cathedral, London, executed by the wood carver Grinling Gibbons (1648–1720) in collaboration with the architect Sir Christopher Wren (1632–1723). It is characteristic in its dignified combination of restrained Baroque forms with figures, heads and naturalistic foliage

PLATE II   RENAISSANCE ART

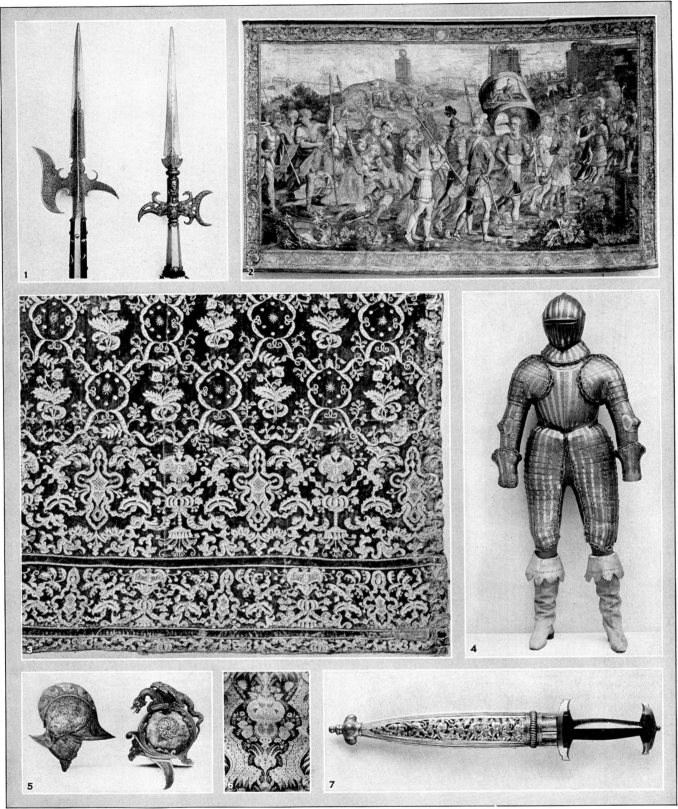

APPLIED ARTS OF THE RENAISSANCE

1. Halberds: left, German, 16th century, characteristic in its fine decoration on the surface of the metal; right, Italian, 16th century, showing greater amount of modelling in the round and strong Baroque elements. 2. Louis XIV. tapestry, French, of the last half of the 17th century, showing the return of the Sabine women with the Roman soldiers; probably one of a set woven at the royal looms of the Gobelins. 3. Embroidered Italian altar frontal, with touches of naturalistic ornament, in the manner of Louis XIII. and early Louis XIV. textiles. 4. A three-quarter suit of Italian armour, etched and gilded, and showing the arms of the Barberini family, probably once the property of Taddeo Barberini, middle 17th century. It illustrates the lavishness of ornament applied to arms and armour in the Baroque period. 5. French Renaissance helmets: on the left, period of Henry II., showing the strong classic influence; on the right, period of Louis XIV. with typically fantastic outline. 6. French silk brocade of about 1700, showing a characteristic Louis XIV. mixture of Baroque line and naturalistic detail. 7. A dagger and scabbard, dated 1567, of Swiss manufacture

Renan now began to frequent more than one Parisian salon, and especially the studio of Ary Scheffer, whose niece and adopted daughter, Cornélie, he proposed to marry in 1856. Henriette consented not only to the marriage, but to make her home with the young couple, whose housekeeping depended on the sum that she could contribute. The history has been told by Renan in the memorial essay, *Ma Soeur Henriette*. In 1859 appeared his translation of the *Book of Job* with an introductory essay, followed in 1859 by the *Song of Songs*.

Renan was now a candidate for the chair of Hebrew and Chaldaic languages at the Collège de France. The Catholic party, upheld by the empress, would not appoint an unfrocked seminarist, a notorious heretic, to a chair of Biblical exegesis. Yet the emperor wished to conciliate Ernest Renan. He offered to send him on an archaeological mission to Phoenicia. Leaving his wife at home with their baby son, Renan left France, accompanied by his sister, in the summer of 1860. Madame Renan joined them in January 1861, returning to France in July. The mission proved fruitful in Phoenician inscriptions which Renan published in his *Mission de Phénicie*. They form the base of his *Corpus Inscriptionum Semiticarum*. At Amshit, near Byblos, Henriette Renan died of intermittent fever on Sept. 24, 1861. Her brother, himself at death's door, was carried unconscious on board a ship waiting in harbour and bound for France. On Jan. 11, 1862, the Minister of Public Instruction ratified Renan's election to the chair of Hebrew. But his opening lecture, in which, amid the applause of the students, Renan declared Jesus Christ "an incomparable Man," alarmed the Catholic party. Renan's lectures were pronounced a disturbance of the public peace, and he was suspended. He refused the librarian's post he was offered in exchange, and thenceforth lived by his pen.

Vie de Jésus.—Henriette had told him to write the life of Jesus. They had begun it together in Syria, she copying the pages as he wrote them, with a New Testament and a *Josephus* for all his library. The book is filled with the atmosphere of the East. It is the work of a man familiar with the Bible and theology, and no less acquainted with the inscriptions, monuments, types and landscapes of Syria. But it is scarcely the work of a great scholar. Renan still used his literary gifts to pursue a scientific ideal. He produced the *Apostles* in 1866, and *St. Paul* in 1869, after having visited Asia Minor with his wife. His object was "to evoke from the past the origins of Christianity." In *St. Paul*, as in the *Apostles*, Renan shows his concern with the larger social life, his sense of fraternity, and a revival of the democratic sentiment which had inspired *L'Avenir de la science*.

The Franco-German War was a turning-point in Renan's history. Germany had always been to him the asylum of thought and disinterested science. Now his heart turned to France. In *La Réforme intellectuelle et morale* (1871) he endeavoured at least to bind her wounds, to safeguard her future. At the same time the irony always perceptible in his work grows more bitter. His *Dialogues philosophiques*, written in 1871, his *Ecclesiastes* (1882) and his *Antichrist* (1876) (the fourth volume of the *Origins of Christianity*, dealing with the reign of Nero) show a disenchanted and sceptical temper. Gradually he aroused himself from his disillusioned mood, and observed with genuine interest the struggle for justice and liberty of a democratic society. The fifth and sixth volumes of the *Origins of Christianity* (the *Christian Church* and *Marcus Aurelius*) show him reconciled with democracy, confident in the gradual ascent of man.

Later Works and Death.—In 1883 he published *Souvenirs d'enfance et de jeunesse*, which have the Celtic magic of ancient romance and the simplicity, naturalness and veracity prized in the 19th century. But his *Ecclesiastes*, published a few months earlier, his *Drames philosophiques*, collected in 1888, give a more adequate image of his fastidious, critical, disenchanted, yet not unhopeful spirit. They show the attitude towards uncultured Socialism of a philosopher liberal by conviction, by temperament an aristocrat. We learn in them how Caliban (democracy), the mindless brute, educated to his own responsibility, makes after all an adequate ruler; how Prospero (the aristocratic principle, or, if we will, the mind) accepts his dethronement for the sake of

greater liberty in the intellectual world, since Caliban proves an effective policeman, and leaves his superiors a free hand in the laboratory; how Ariel (the religious principle) acquires a firmer hold on life, and no longer gives up the ghost at the faintest hint of change. Religion and knowledge are as imperishable as the world they dignify. Thus out of the depths rises unvanquished the essential idealism of Ernest Renan.

At sixty years of age, having finished the *Origins of Christianity,* Renan began his *History of Israel* (3 vol., 1887–91) based on a lifelong study of the Old Testament and on the *Corpus Inscriptionum Semiticarum*, published by the Académie des Inscriptions under his direction from the year 1881 till the end of his life. He died on Oct. 12, 1892.

There is no collected edition of Renan's works. There is an English translation of the *Vie de Jésus* in Everyman's Library (1927). His *Correspondance* has been edited in 2 vol. (Paris, 1926–28). For Henriette Renan *see* Prof. Giraud, *Soeurs de grands hommes* (1926) and Renan's *Lettres Intimes* (1923).

See Desportes and Bournand, *E. Renan, sa vie et son oeuvre* (1892); E. Grant Duff, *Ernest Renan, in memoriam* (1893); Séailles, *E. Renan, essai de biographie psychologique* (1894); G. Monod, *Les maîtres de l'histoire* (1894); Allier, *La Philosophie d'E. Renan* (1895); M. J. Darmesteter, *La vie de E. R.* (1898); Platzhoff, *E. Renan, ein Lebensbild* (1900); Brauer, *Philosophy of Ernest Renan* (1904); W. Barry, *Renan* (1905); Sorel, *Le Système historique de R.* (1905–06); J. M. Robertson, *Ernest Renan* (1924).

RENARD THE FOX: *see* REYNARD THE FOX.

RENAUD DE MONTAUBAN (Rinaldo di Montalbano), one of the most famous figures of French and Italian romance. His story was attached to the *geste* of Doon of Mayence by the 13th-century *trouvère* who wrote the *chanson de geste* of *Renaus de Montauban*, better known perhaps as *Les quatre fils Aymon*. The four sons of Aymon give their name to inns and streets in nearly every town of France, and Renaud's sword Floberge, and his horse Bayard passed with him into popular legend. The poem opens with the dissensions between Charlemagne and the sons of Doon of Mayence, Beuves d'Aigremont, Doon de Nanteuil and Aymon de Dordone.

The rebellious vassals are defeated by the imperial army near Troyes, and, peace established, Aymon rises in favour at court, and supports the emperor, even in his persecution of his four sons, Renaud, Alard, Guichard and Richard. At the end of the usual series of violent adventures and catastrophes, Renaud gives himself up to religion, working as a mason on the church of St. Peter at Cologne, where he receives martyrdom at the hands of his jealous fellow labourers.

The connection of the four brothers with Montessor, Dortmund, Mayence and Cologne, and the abundant local tradition, mark the heroes as originating from the region between the Rhine and the Meuse. Nevertheless, their adventures in Gascony, with the king of which they take service against the Saracens, are corroborated by historical evidence, and this section of the poem is the oldest. The enemy of Renaud was Charles Martel, not Charlemagne; King Yon was Odo of Gascony; the victory over the Saracens at Toulouse, in which the brothers are alleged to have taken part, was won by him in 721, and in 719 he sheltered refugees from the dominions of Charles Martel, Chilperic II, king of Neustria, and his mayor of the palace, Raginfred, whom he was compelled to abandon.

In a local chronicle of Cologne it is stated that St. Reinoldus died in 697, and in the Latin rhythmical *Vita* his martyrdom is said to have taken place under Bishop Agilolf (d. 717). Thus the romance was evidently composite before it took its place in the Carolingian cycle.

In Italy Renaud had his greatest vogue, and many episodes were added, as well as the personage of the hero's sister, Bradamante. Rinaldo di Montalbano had been the subject of many Italian poems before *Il Rinaldo* of Tasso.

BIBLIOGRAPHY.—The *chanson* of *Maugis d'Aigremont* and the prose romance of the *Conqueste de Trebizonde* belong to the same cycle. The prose *Ystoire de Regnault de Montauban* (Lyons, *c.* 1480) had a great vogue. It was generally printed as *Les quatre fils Aymon*, and was published in English, *The Foure Sonnes of Aymon*, by William Caxton, and subsequently by Wynkyn de Worde and William Copland. See *Hist. litt. de la France*, xxii., analysis by Paulin Paris; *Renaus de Montauban* (Stuttgart, 1862), ed. H. Michelant; *Storia di Rinaldino*, ed. C. Minutoli (Bologna, 1865); F. Wulff, *Recherches sur les sagas de Magus et de Geirard* (Lund, 1873); *Renout von Montalbaen*, ed. J. C. Matthis (Groningen, 1873); *Magus saga*, ed. G. Cederschiöld (Lund, 1876); A. Longnon, in *Revue des questions historiques* (1879); R. Zwick, *Über die Sprache des Renaut von Montauban* (Halle, 1884); *The Four Sonnes of Aimon* (E. E. Text Soc., ed. Octavia Richardson, 1884); F. Pfaff, *Das deutsche Volksbuch von den Heymonskindern* (Freiburg im Breisgau, 1887), with a general introduction to the study of the saga; a special bibliography of the printed editions of the prose romance in L. Gautier's *Bibl. des chansons de geste* (1897); rejuvenations of the story by Karl Simrock (Frankfurt, 1845), and by Richard Steele (1897).

RENAUDOT, THÉOPHRASTE (1586?–1653), French physician and philanthropist, was born at Loudun (Poitou), and studied surgery in Paris. He was only 19 when he received, by favour apparently, the degree of doctor at Montpellier. In 1612 he was summoned to Paris by Richelieu and was appointed to organize a scheme of public assistance. Many difficulties were put in his way, however, and until 1625 he spent most of his time in Poitou, though Richelieu made him "commissary general of the poor" in 1618.

In 1630 he opened an information bureau in Paris at the sign of the Grand Coq near the Pont Saint-Michel. This *bureau d'adresse* was a combined labour bureau, intelligence department, exchange and charity organization; and the sick were directed to doctors prepared to give them free treatment.

Renaudot established (1635) a free dispensary despite the opposition of the faculty in Paris, which refused to accept the new medicaments proposed by the heretic from Montpellier, restricting themselves to the old prescriptions of bloodletting and purgation.

Under the protection of Richelieu, Renaudot started the first French newspaper, the *Gazette* (1631). In 1637 he was authorized to add pawnbroking to the activities of the *bureau d'adresse*, and *monts de piété* were opened.

In 1640 the medical faculty, headed by Guy Patin, started a campaign against Renaudot. After the death of Richelieu and of Louis XIII the parliament of Paris refused to allow him to practise medicine in Paris. The *Gazette* remained, and in 1646 Renaudot was appointed by Mazarin historiographer to the king. He died on Oct. 25, 1653.

BIBLIOGRAPHY.—E. Hatin, *Théophraste Renaudot* (Poitiers, 1883); G. Bonnefont, *Un Oublié, Théophraste Renaudot* (Limoges, n.d.); Arturo Castiglioni, *History of Medicine*, trans. by E. B. Krumbhaar, p. 575 (Toronto, 1941).

RENAULT, LOUIS (1843–1918), French jurist, was born on May 21, 1843, at Autun. From 1868 to 1873 he was professor of Roman and commercial law at the University of Dijon. From 1873 until his death he was professor in the faculty of law at the University of Paris, where in 1881 he became professor of international law. In 1890 he was appointed jurisconsult of the ministry of foreign affairs, a post specially created for him, and thereafter French foreign policy was scrutinized by him in the light of international law. He served at numerous conferences in this capacity, notably at the two Hague conferences in 1899 and 1907, and at the London naval conference of 1908–09.

Renault was prominent as an arbitrator, his more famous cases being the Japanese House Tax case of 1905, the Casa Blanca case of 1909, the Sawarkar of 1911, the Carthage of 1913 and the Manouba of the same year. Among his writings are numerous articles and monographs on the specialized topics of international law. Together with his friend and colleague, C. Lyon-Caen, he produced a compendium of commercial law in two volumes, a treatise in eight volumes, and a manual which ran to many editions.

In 1879 Renault published his *Introduction to the Study of International Law*, and in 1917 *The First Violations of International Law by Germany*, concerning the invasion of Belgium and Luxembourg in breach of Germany's treaty obligations. In 1907 he was awarded a Nobel peace prize for his services to international law. He died on Feb. 7, 1918, at Barbizon.   (E. H. Ld.)

RENDERING, ARCHITECTURAL. Architectural rendering is a pictorial art whose object is to visualize architectural conceptions. When an architect is employed to design a building, it is desirable that he provide his client, in advance, with an accurate impression of the appearance of the proposed structure. Since words cannot adequately convey the architectural story, paintings or drawings are employed to render it, as it were, clear to the eye; they serve as a kind of communication. This is the most familiar application of the art; and, when so used, rendering may be defined as the medium whereby the renderer communicates a sense of the reality of a structure in advance of its concrete materialization. Occasionally, however, the architect has a rendering made in the course of his own work and as an aid to his own study. When an architectural conception first forms in the background of his mind, it has, of necessity, a certain nebulous character. But with the effort of expressing it on paper, in actual lines and tone values, it emerges, so to speak, and crystallizes. When so employed, rendering serves as a definite step in the evolution of architectural conceptions.

Rendering has a third use; viz., in connection with already existing buildings. When so used, renderings—as distinguished from the miscellaneous paintings and drawings that refer only incidentally to architecture—have, as their chief or sole concern, to render clear the strictly architectural nature of the subject. By this selection of architectural factors, they may enable the layman to grasp the significance of a building more readily than when faced by its multitudinous and irrelevant details. At the same time, they may serve as a faithful record of the historic course of architectural design. In these three ways, rendering fulfills a recognized function, and has done so over a long period.

In the last quarter of a century, there has developed an aspect of architectural and engineering practice that involves rendering on a more extended scale—town and city planning (*q.v.*). A comprehensive plan for the future building development of any large community is never the conception of a single mind; many minds must collaborate in it. Nor is it materialized in a few years, but in many years. In these circumstances, it becomes impractical for its whole purport to be carried only in any single given mind, or for an accurate image to be postponed until the whole long scheme has been consummated. The various contributory ideas and suggestions must be assembled, in definitive terms, on the paper or canvas of the rendering, in order that the prophecy may assume sufficient reality to serve as a criterion and a guide.

Another factor, which more clearly reveals the contemporary field of rendering, is that Western architecture, as a whole, is passing through a period of transition and, therefore, of experiment (*see* ARCHITECTURE). It is true that the practice of many of the most prominent architects is to continue constructing mere copies, or very slightly modified copies, of those classic styles which, in their impressionable years, they were led to regard as being the very body of architectural culture; their effort is to emulate the classic designers in all respects, save, perhaps, the latter's logic, sense of congruity and ability to fashion novel forms. Their public, accordingly, has been wont to feel the presence of architecture only in a building to which the architect has added a Greek colonnade, a Roman dome or a Gothic spire. In all this, professional rendering has been able to play but a small part, since the picture has been regarded as an end in itself simply to be made as attractive as possible; it could scarcely be employed as a means of rendering forth a new truth, more especially as the appearance of these styles of architecture has been known for centuries.

In recent years, however, definite changes have occurred in methods of construction and the manufacture of materials, as well as in the general social and economic situation; and one notices that in the larger centres of Western civilization a distinct type of designer is making his presence in the architectural profession more and more strongly felt. These designers are inspired not so much by the traits of an architectural heredity as by the needs of contemporary environment. For them, the tremendous environmental changes that have occurred imply and demand a corresponding change in the architectural approach. They do not—to choose one example—employ a new material, steel, to support façades, which have developed in other materials and can be logical only therein. They are engaged, briefly, in developing new types of architecture. Certain limitations lie upon these practising

EXAMPLES OF VARIOUS TYPES OF RENDERINGS

1. Carbon pencil drawing on cameo paper: made to visualize a proposed structure; effect of mass remaining dominant in spite of thoughtful delineation of detail; sense of relation to surroundings. By Chester B. Price. **2.** Crayon drawing: made to visualize proposed structure; arbitrary handling of tone values, details and entourage resulting in an unusual impression of mass. By Gilbert P. Hall. **3.** Wash: made to visualize a proposed structure; grasp of architectural factors, sensitive feeling, conveyed through a cultured technique. By H. VanBuren Magonigle

PLATE II

RENDERING, ARCHITECTURAL

BY COURTESY OF (1) B. G. GOODHUE

EXAMPLES OF RENDERINGS, VARIOUS AS TO MEDIUM, USE, CONTENT AND STYLE

1. Water colour: made to convey general impression of a proposed structure in relation to its natural surroundings; adequate consideration of material reality of the general scene; architectural elements handled impressionistically with detail omitted; pictorial values predominating; emphasis on atmosphere and colour. By Birch Burdette Long

2. Lithograph: made to vivify an historical subject; cautious delineation of material facts; intelligent exaggeration of scale, conveying emotion of dignity, mystery, spaciousness. By David Roberts

3. Pencil drawing, with wash: made to visualize proposed structures; fine discrimination between essentials and details, resulting in a convincing sense of reality both as to structural and human factors. By Thomas R. Johnson

4. Water colour over pencil layout: made to visualize proposed interior; fidelity to material detail. By Houghson Hawley

5. Pencil drawing on tracing paper with water colour used after mounting: made to visualize proposed addition to existing structure; complete comprehension of architectural factors conveyed by a perfected technique. By Otto Eggers

6. Water colour and pencil: straightforward sensing of material facts, intelligent subduing of detail to dominant, absence of emotional bias resulting in credible visualization. By Cyril Farey

PROGRESSIVE VIEWS OF A RENDERING

A rendering by Hugh Ferriss, showing: 1. Lines drawn, tentatively suggesting a mass in space. 2. Additional lines added as material for tone values. 3. Lines rubbed together with paper stump, producing tone values to confirm indication of mass. 4. The form further modelled by use of kneaded eraser on right hand planes. 5. Principal subdivisions of the mass delineated, also by use of (1) pencil, (2) paper stump and (3) kneaded eraser. 6. Minor items introduced, same process. (*See* section of article on *Procedure.*)

RENDERINGS IN VARIOUS MEDIUMS

1. Engraving: structural factors, accurately sensed, recomposed with a virile imagination, conveying powerful emotional impression. By Piranesi. 2. Pencil drawing, coffee wash: made to visualize a civic project; primarily concerned with the architectural conception, yet adequate attention given to pictorial values. By Eliel Saarinen. 3. Etching: imaginary composition on historical motif; highly stimulating impressions. By William Walcot.

4. Pastel: selection of architectural factors from an existing building; thoughtful composition of subject matter, affectionate attention to technique. By T. de Postels. 5. Pencil: example of a one minute sketch made to convey an architect's conception to his assistants; attention centred on essentials of the design (which were later constructed as sketched). By Cass Gilbert

and experimental architects. It is sometimes too hazardous to test a novel conception by actually carrying it out in a building which, whether a success or a failure, must stand for many years. But the conception may be quite thoroughly tested in a series of conscientious renderings. For example, the modern American zoning laws involved a radical departure in the general forms of buildings, and into the strange spaces created by these laws some architects proceeded without pause to force the classical images with which their minds were filled. More cautious architects sought to discover the basic structural types that the laws admitted; for this purpose, renderings were employed. Another limitation is that the projects of architects are practically bound by the ideas and the financial resources of their clients; they cannot actually build in advance of their clients' prepossessions. In renderings, however, they may freely express their real intentions, and these renderings, when duly exhibited can, and in fact do, make a distinct contribution to the progress of architectural design. A third limitation is that no practising architect, however fortunate, has time to build more than a very few influential buildings during his lifetime. He may, however, record himself in soundly fashioned drawings and paintings whose content, though at first existing in only two dimensions, may, in due time, be realized in three.

In addition to the functions thus far mentioned, rendering has a rôle to play in what is doubtless the greatest concern of architecture—the psychological influence it exerts on human life. A few people, it is true, are fully conscious of the impressions that they receive in the face of noble buildings; the more pertinent and important fact is that the vast majority of human beings are continually, if unconsciously, influenced by the architectural forms and spaces with which they come in contact. Architects themselves are often unaware of the extent of this influence; that is to say, the influence which is unconsciously received is unconsciously initiated. Perhaps it is in consequence of this that the haphazard and miscellaneous architectural scene which is presented by most modern cities, and which is constantly before the population, is left to impress the corresponding qualities upon the human psyche. On the other hand, there have been periods in the past—the "great periods" of architecture—when the designers must have been quite aware of the influence, and utilized it for conscious purposes. In the Gothic cathedrals, for example, there is embodied, in terms of form and space (terms safely beyond the vicissitudes of any particular church) a potent and lasting influence for the betterment of mankind. Buildings of the first category—depressing or distracting buildings—are legion; those of the second—buildings which arrest or elevate—are rare. But the more significant forms may be repeatedly delineated and interpreted in drawings and paintings by whose agency they may be widely exhibited, published and, so to speak, broadcast. Rendering, in short, by allying itself with the conscious and objective forces in architectural work, may serve, by paraphrase, to bring home the laconic message of architecture.

To sum up, rendering has six principal objects. The first three have long been recognized: to convey advance realizations of proposed structures, to aid in crystallizing ideas in the architect's mind and to interpret the architectural significance of existing structures. The other three remain largely for future development: to serve as criterion and guide in city planning, to assist in evolving new types of architecture and to strengthen the psychological influence of architecture on human values.

Whichever of these a given rendering is to serve, the renderer—having comprehended *why* the drawing is being made—is faced with two fundamental considerations. The first is to grasp *what* is the nature of the architectural subject to be rendered, to so ponder it as to exclude non-essentials. The second is *how* to employ the various devices of draughtsmanship so as to communicate this realization to others. Between these two items—the nature of the subject and the process of rendering—there exists the distinction between ends and means, and it is important that the renderer have this distinction clearly in mind at the outset. As a matter of common practice, this distinction is often not made. The painting or drawing is often regarded as being an end

in itself, and discussion of it centres, in consequence, on purely technical questions: interest of composition, nicety of line, cleverness of brushwork, etc. Many such works are contributions to the subject of technique and justify the enthusiasm of technicians; but, lacking architectural significance, they are not, strictly speaking, architectural renderings.

It is also a common practice to regard rendering as indeed a means but to substitute for its authentic and natural ends, ends that are special or perverted. For example,—as in the Beaux Arts curriculum—projects are often rendered in elevation (*i.e.*, the representation is of but one façade of the building as this would appear were the eye directly opposite each and every point thereon). This, obviously, produces a form which can exist only on paper; it is not the form which the human eye would perceive in the building itself. Such a treatment serves a purpose, in that an architect, when reading its conventionalized and inexact statement, can translate it, in his trained mind, into at least an approximation of the truth. But just because it requires a translation, and is, in itself, foreign to reality, it may be classified as a special practice.

Another common practice, of a different category, is to accomplish, by means of a picture, an end which is positively opposed to architectural fact. The renderer may be called on to exaggerate certain aspects of a proposed building in order to create a more favourable advance impression; or to exaggerate certain factors of an existing building in a way to advertise them. The architect or advertiser may wish such a rendering as a result of deliberate calculation or because his personal interest in particulars is so great as to obscure from his view the real appearance of the building in its entirety. In any case, the executing of such commissions falls rather into the class of commercialized art and may be excluded from a discussion on rendering.

The twofold criterion of values remains to be applied to all renderings: first, comprehension of the architectural essentials involved in the subject; second, effectiveness in pictorial communication.

ESSENTIALS TO BE RENDERED

Mass.—From the renderer's point of view a building is, in the first place, a material mass. While it is not, in actuality, a mass in the sense that a mountain is a mass, *i.e.*, it is not a solid, nevertheless the effect of solidity is essential to it. And while, in constructing a building, this effect may be the last to be realized, in drawing a building it is logically the first. The renderer must realize the presence of mass before he can fully realize the presence of any appurtenant form. It may be likened to the clay which a sculptor must grasp before any particular shape can be given or any details modelled. The first necessary attribute of a convincing architectural rendering is, correspondingly, an adequate suggestion of mass. Without this primary effect of solidity, all details which may be delineated later must appear without body and the presentation as a whole must lack substance.

Form.—Being imbued with a sense of the substantial nature that his subject, in general, possesses, the renderer addresses himself to a study of its particular form. It is generally taken for granted that if accurate floor plans and elevations are available, an accurate image of the building can be produced by following the rules of perspective draughtsmanship—those rules are said to have originated with Leonardo and are commonly accepted as being correct and comprehensive. The fact is, however, that there is considerable question as to how forms really look. It is quite doubtful if the system of perspective draughtsmanship which we accept as a science, is more than a convention—a convention which, indeed, is usually of great help to accurate representation and yet, in numerous instances, is a specific hindrance. The forming, in the human eye of images of buildings appears, in fact, to involve factors with which we, as renderers, have not yet adequately dealt (*see* PERSPECTIVE).

The Single Viewpoint.—One item to be considered in this connection is that, in laying out perspectives the draughtsman habitually assumes that the subject is being viewed from a single viewpoint. He establishes, on his draughting board, a specific point, termed the "viewpoint" and his operations proceed from this base. But this assumption is inadequate to the extent that the appearance which a building actually produces on a one-eyed man is inadequate as compared to that produced on a two-eyed man. In some cases, the discrepancy is not remarkable—as, for example, small forms viewed at considerable distances. But, in forms which are closely scrutinized, the discrepancy becomes pronounced; there is a definite lack of the three-dimensional quality to the single-eyed vision, and there is a corresponding flatness to the general run of perspectives laid out from the single viewpoint.

The Stationary Viewpoint.—A second item is that a draughtsman in laying out his perspective assumes, according to the convention, that his single viewpoint is stationary. In reality, however, an observer in forming his image of a building, assumes a series of viewpoints. In seriously studying a building, one will purposefully view it from many different angles; but even if the interest is only casual one will instinctively look at it more than once—always from a viewpoint which is, of necessity, slightly altered. In all cases, it may be said that the image which the observer takes away with him is not the single first impression received from a literally stationary viewpoint, but is a composite of several distinct impressions. This composite quality of the image is an essential which demands the renderer's attention: how he may, by a cunning draughtsmanship, convey this aspect of the case is considered in this article under the heading of "Procedure."

The foregoing consideration involves a problem that often appears in rendering; viz., one is often faced with the necessity of choosing between a truthful pictorial statement of the building which is being drawn and a truthful statement of the viewpoint which happens to have been chosen.

It is usually held that when a viewpoint has once been selected, it is demanded by honesty that all items of the scene (including adjoining buildings) must be delineated exactly as they appear; that if one arbitrarily makes alterations (as, for example, showing adjoining buildings less prominently than they actually are) he is guilty of "faking." Undeniably, many renderings are "faked"; at the same time, there is a distinction to be made. If the alteration has been made for the purpose of conveying a more favourable impression than the actual scene, then the charge of misrepresentation is, obviously, sustained. It often happens, however, that a building possesses a very important feature which, while entirely visible from many points of view, may happen to be screened from the particular point of view that has been chosen. For instance, a building may possess a certain buttressing member which gives its tower integrity, and which may be visible from many viewpoints, but this member may be hidden from the chosen viewpoint by some extraneous and perhaps temporary obstruction. We may assume at the same time, that the renderer's commission is to depict the building as truthfully and completely as possible in a single drawing. In such a case, it would appear that he is not so much permitted as actually required to slight incidental facts of his viewpoint in favour of the essential facts of the subject which he is viewing.

Perspective of Vertical Lines.—Another item demanding the renderer's attention is that all effects of perspective which a building presents to the human eye apply to its vertical as well as to its horizontal extension. Although this is obviously so, the current convention of perspective generally disregards it, the horizontal lines, only, being drawn to meet in a "vanishing point," but the vertical lines being arbitrarily drawn parallel to each other. In the case of very low buildings, the discrepancy is not important; but in the cases, now so numerous, of very tall buildings, the inaccuracy is serious. The convention not only produces distorted drawings, but so habituates onlookers to distortion that they become disinclined to recognize normal appearances.

Method of Construction.—The renderer may, to a considerable degree, express in his drawing such differences of appearance as exist, for example, between a building of solid masonry and one of steel grille construction. His medium allows considerable variety of indication of texture characteristic of stone, brick, terracotta, glass, etc.

Atmospheric Conditions.—Buildings are, of necessity, seen through a physical atmosphere and a suggestion of reality obviously cannot be conveyed in a drawing in which an atmospheric condition is not convincingly suggested; some renderings, for instance, fail by conveying the suggestion that the subject was viewed through a vacuum.

The important question of colour belongs to a general study of the painter's art (see PAINTING; WATERCOLOUR PAINTING).

In addition to these material factors, an architectural subject presents others of a psychological nature. A realistic rendering may, indeed, be produced by dealing honestly with only the physical facts; an authentic rendering, however, demands a realistic treatment of intellectual and emotional aspects as well. In this connection, the following experiment is illustrative. An exact perspective was laid out of the form of the Woolworth building, using the architect's blue prints as a basis. A second study was made, sketching from the building itself from an exactly corresponding viewpoint. The building was then photographed from this viewpoint. On comparing the three results it was found that the principal proportions were different in each case. The more striking conclusion was that none of them conveyed the sense of structural logic which the disposition of the steel members themselves conveys to the thoughtful observer; none of them suggested the emotion of soaring aspiration which the form itself suggests to the human onlooker. It becomes, indeed, one of the chief concerns of the renderer to comprehend the nature of the architectural idea which his subject embodies, the trend of thought the architect has expressed. Similarly, the renderer must especially aim to appreciate the emotional tone, the particular mood, of his subject. On entering these outlying psychological domains rendering, like the other arts, may attain its happiest freedom of movement. Yet just here, unfortunately, it must evade competent technical guidance. We have many paintings and drawings which succeed in conveying an isolated thought or an isolated emotion; but too often we find that the renderings which have attained this success have paid in distorted material proportions.

Viewed in this way, renderings as a whole fall into certain rather well-defined groups. The largest, and most familiar, includes those in which the renderer has made a competent presentation of the material facts, but has failed to include any of those elements which, in architecture, stimulate the mind and arouse the emotions. It is as though he worked only with his hands, neither his thought nor feeling having been involved. The result is correct but chilling. A second group is that in which only an emotional aspect of the subject has been fully rendered, just as a third is that in which only an intellectual aspect has been emphasized. Such works, generally labelled "impressionistic," "futuristic," etc., often convey what was intended yet fail of permanent value in that they distort or omit the physical facts of the case. If, for example, the subject be a mausoleum which has, in actuality, an atmosphere of solemnity, such a rendering may—perhaps in a few dark washes—convey an emotion of solemnity but leave the mausoleum itself in doubt. Or, if the subject be a tower notable for its logical growth, the rendering may—perhaps in a few cold lines—suggest logical growth but refer to no particular tower. There follow, naturally, three further groups in which the result is more appealing or convincing: that in which the material facts have been accurately presented in a thoughtful manner; that in which they have been presented with appreciable emotion; and that in which, while the material facts have been presented inexactly, a clear architectural thought appears accompanied by deep feeling. The ideal, which would constitute a seventh group, would be to convey the material, the emotional and the intellectual facts in the same rendering.

Why renderings should fall into these various groups is probably not difficult to ascertain: they do so by following the various personalities of the renderers. A draughtsman naturally draws that aspect of a building which he is by habit inclined to appreciate. From one renderer, we shall almost always get a very correct and cold drawing; from another a very bold and incorrect drawing. This suggests the reason why a perfectly balanced rendering has never been produced. It also suggests a point of interest to the student of rendering. It may well be that he will develop his art not simply by cultivating whatever tendency he happened to exhibit in the beginning, but, rather, by seeking to add to his forces some tendency which was not habitual to him. For example, if he is in the way of being an excellent draughtsman, he might seek to acquire an emotional appreciation of architecture in addition; just as, if he has always had strong feelings about buildings, he might seek to comprehend the pure logic by which all architectural masterpieces are given form. When thus regarded, rendering becomes, for the renderer himself, not so much a matter of self-expression as of self-development.

PROCEDURE

To answer the remaining question—*how* to make a rendering—it is necessary, since there are numerous equally promising methods of procedure, to describe the method employed in a specific case. In the case of the rendering reproduced in fig. 1–6 of Plate III the procedure was as follows:—

A sheet of mounted Whatman paper 27 by 40 in. was tacked to a slightly larger drawing board and placed on a vertical easel. The draughtsman standing before the easel, made the assumption that, for the moment, the paper represented *space*. With the intention of introducing into this space, the presence of *mass*, a number of lines were lightly sketched in, using a 3B Wolff crayon (*see* fig. 1). These lines fall into three groups, according to their direction; they proceed, respectively, from three previously assumed "vanishing points" (*see* PERSPECTIVE). They serve the draughtsman as an adequate notation of the three-dimensionality which characterizes any mass in space. While sketching these generalized lines, he emphasized such as would tentatively indicate the particular form that he intended to give the mass—the form which, until now, had existed only in his mind. The next step was to confirm and solidify these outlines by introducing tone values—produced by drawing, rapidly, a number of freehand lines across the areas to be shaded (*see* fig. 2) and rubbing these lines together into a tone with a gloved finger or a paper "stump" (*see* fig. 3). In the rendering now under consideration, the degree of solidity which was desired at this stage was effected by producing three general tones—the background being the darkest, the planes of the building which face toward the left being intermediary, and the planes which face toward the right being the lightest. The last tone was produced by cleaning the areas with a "kneaded" eraser (*see* fig. 4).

At this point, the draughtsman had before him a visualization, vivid enough for his own purposes, of the basic form of the building. His next step was to identify, in his mind, the principal subdivisions of his preconceived design and to indicate, on the paper, these modifications of the basic form. This involved a repetition, at a smaller scale, of his previous procedure; that is to say, he first sketched in the minor forms in line and then solidified them with tone values, using glove, stump and eraser. At this point another tone value was added to contribute further to the effect of solidity; *i.e.*, the cast shadows (*see* fig. 5). The same process of indicating form in line was repeated again and again—each time dealing with a category of smaller forms—until the building appeared in that degree of detail which seemed best calculated to serve the purposes for which the drawing was undertaken (*see* fig. 6).

Of renderings of this sort, it might be said that the draughtsman begins his task in this spirit: he is, metaphorically, facing a building which, although it exists in its entirety, is completely hidden from him in a mist or fog. As he approaches his subject, however, he begins to discern the principal outlines of its mass. Soon its secondary and tertiary features appear. He is free to continue his approach until the most minute details have become plain. Nevertheless, it is important that he halt at that point where his subject has revealed all that is essential to his inquiry.

The numerous other methods of rendering, all equally useful, can best be studied in reproductions of actual renderings; such material, with explanatory notes, is shown in the accompanying plates. They all point to the same conclusion—the draughtsman's best procedure is first to delineate the essentials of his subject, then to build all indication of detail on this foundation.

BIBLIOGRAPHY.—David A. Gregg, *Architectural Rendering in Pen and Ink* (1891); F. F. Frederick, *Architectural Rendering in Sepia* (1892); Frank A. Hays, ed., *Architectural Rendering in Pen and Ink* (1915); A. L. Guptill, *Sketching and Rendering in Pencil* (1922); H. V. Magonigle, *Architectural Rendering in Wash* (1926); A. L. Guptill, *Drawing with Pen and Ink* (1928). Articles on architectural rendering have also appeared in the following magazines during the years indicated: *Arts and Decoration* (New York, 1920); *Pencil Points* (New York, 1921–25); *Architecture* (New York, 1923). (H. FE.)

RENDSBURG, a town in the Prussian province of Schleswig-Holstein, Germany, on the Eider and on the Kaiser Wilhelm canal, 20 mi. W. of Kiel, on the Altona-Flensburg railway. Pop. (1939) 24,249. Rendsburg came into existence under the shelter of a castle founded by the Danes about the year 1100 and was an object of dispute between the Danish kings and the counts of Holstein. In 1252 it was adjudged to the latter and the town was surrounded with ramparts in 1539. The war of 1848–50 began with the capture of Rendsburg by the Holsteiners and it formed the centre of the German operations. In Nov. 1863 the town was occupied by the Saxon troops acting as the executive of the German Confederation, and it was the base of the operations of the Austrians and Prussians against Schleswig in the spring of the following year. Rendsburg was jointly occupied by Austrian and Prussian military until 1866, when it fell to Prussia. It consists of three parts—the crowded Altstadt, on an island in the Eider; and new towns on the north and south banks of the river. Its importance rests on the commercial facilities afforded by its connection with the North sea and the Baltic through the Kaiser Wilhelm canal, by which transit trade is carried on in grain, timber, Swedish iron and coals. The principal products are dyes, iron, artificial manures, machines and tobacco.

RENÉ I (1409–1480), duke of Anjou, of Lorraine and Bar, count of Provence and of Piedmont, king of Naples, Sicily and Jerusalem, was born at Angers on Jan. 16, 1409, the second son of Louis II, king of Sicily, duke of Anjou, count of Provence, and of Yolande of Aragon. By his marriage treaty (1419) with Isabella, elder daughter of Charles II, duke of Lorraine, the comte de Guise, as he then was, became heir to the duchy of Bar, which was claimed as the inheritance of his mother Yolande, and in right of his wife, heir to the duchy of Lorraine. René, then only ten, was to be brought up in Lorraine under the guardianship of Charles II and Louis, cardinal of Bar, both of whom were attached to the Burgundian party, but he retained the right to bear the arms of Anjou. When Louis of Bar died in 1430 René came into sole possession of his duchy; and in the next year, on Charles II's death, he succeeded to the duchy of Lorraine. But the inheritance was claimed by the heir-male Antoine de Vaudémont, who with Burgundian help defeated René at Bulgnéville in July 1431. The duchess Isabella effected a truce with Antoine de Vaudémont, but the duke remained a prisoner of the Burgundians until April 1432, when he recovered his liberty on parole on yielding up as hostages his two sons, John and Louis of Anjou. His title as duke of Lorraine was confirmed by his suzerain, the emperor Sigismund, at Basle in 1434. This proceeding roused the anger of the Burgundian duke Philip the Good, who required him early in the next year to return to his prison, from which he was released two years later on payment of a heavy ransom. He had succeeded to the kingdom of Naples through the deaths of his brother Louis III and of Joanna II (of Durazzo), queen of Naples, the last heir of the earlier dynasty. Louis had been adopted by her in 1431, and she now left her inheritance to René.

The marriage of Mary, daughter of Charles I of Bourbon and niece of Philip of Burgundy, with John, duke of Calabria, René's eldest son, cemented peace between the two princes. After appointing a regency in Bar and Lorraine, he visited his provinces of Anjou and Provence and in 1438 set sail for Naples, which had been held for him by the duchess Isabella. In 1441 Alphonso of Aragon laid siege to Naples, which he sacked after a six months' siege. René returned to France in the same year; and though he retained the title of king of Naples his effective rule was never recovered.

René took part in the negotiations with the English at Tours in 1444, and peace was consolidated by the marriage of his younger daughter, Margaret, with Henry VI at Nancy. René now made over the government of Lorraine to John, duke of Calabria, who was, however, only formally installed as duke of Lorraine on the death of Queen Isabella in 1453. René had the confidence of Charles VII of France (who had married his sister, Mary of Anjou) and is said to have initiated the reduction of the men-at-arms set on foot by the king, with whose military operations against the English he was closely associated. He entered Rouen with him in Nov. 1449 and was also with him at Formigny and Caen.

After his second marriage (1454) with Jeanne de Laval, daughter of Guy XIV, count of Laval, and Isabella of Brittany, René took a less active part in public affairs and devoted himself more to artistic and literary pursuits. In 1453 he made an unsuccessful attempt on northern Italy. In 1467 his son John took Barcelona from John II of Aragon and held it till his death in 1470 (see ANJOU).

The king of Sicily's fame as an amateur of painting has led to the attribution to him of many old paintings in Anjou and Provence, in many cases simply because they bear his arms. These works are generally in the Flemish style and were probably executed under his patronage and direction, so that he may be said to have formed a school of fine arts in sculpture, painting, gold work and tapestry. Two of the most famous works once attributed to René are the triptych, the "Burning Bush," in the cathedral of Aix, showing portraits of René and his second wife, Jeanne de Laval, and an illuminated Book of Hours in the Bibliothèque Nationale, Paris. The "Burning Bush" was in fact the work of Nicolas Froment of Avignon. Among the men of letters attached to René's court was Antoine de la Sale, whom he made tutor to his son, the duke of Calabria. He encouraged the performance of mystery plays: On the performance of a mystery of the Passion at Saumur in 1462 he remitted four years of taxes to the town; and the representations of the Passion at Angers were carried out under his auspices. He exchanged verses with his kinsman Charles of Orléans. The best of his poems is the idyll of Regnault and Jeanneton, representing his courtship of Jeanne de Laval. *Le Livre des tournois,* a book of ceremonial, and the allegorical romance, *Conqueste qu'un chevalier nommé le Cuer d'amour espris feist d'une dame appelée Doulce Mercy,* with other works, were perhaps dictated to his secretaries or compiled under his direction. He died on July 10, 1480.

BIBLIOGRAPHY.—L. F. de Villeneuve-Bargemont, *Histoire de René d'Anjou,* 3 vol. (Paris, 1825); A. Lecoy de la Marche, *Le Roi René,* 2 vol. (Paris, 1875); M. L. des Garets, *Le Roi René* (Paris, 1946); Y. de Raulin, *Les Peintres de René d'Anjou et de Jeanne de Laval* (Laval, 1938); P. Champion, *Le Roi René écrivain* (Monaco, 1925); E. Trenkler, *Das Livre du cuer d'amours espris des Herzogs René von Anjou* (Vienna, 1946); also René's *Oeuvres,* ed. by Comte de Quatrebarbes, 4 vol. (Paris and Angers, 1845-46.)

RENÉE OF FRANCE (1510–1575), second daughter of Louis XII and Anne of Brittany, was born at Blois on Oct. 25, 1510. After being betrothed successively to Gaston de Foix, Charles of Austria (the future emperor Charles V), his brother Ferdinand, Henry VIII of England, and the elector Joachim II of Brandenburg, she married in 1528 Hercules II of Este, son of the duke of Ferrara, who succeeded his father six years later. Renée's court became a rendezvous of men of letters and a refuge for the persecuted French Calvinists. She received Clément Marot and Calvin at Ferrara, and finally embraced the reformed religion. Her husband, however, who viewed these proceedings with disfavour, banished her friends, took her children from her, threw her into prison, and eventually made her abandon at any rate the outward forms of Calvinism. After his death in 1559, Renée returned to France and turned her duchy of Montargis into a centre of Protestant propaganda. During the wars of religion she was several times molested by the Catholic troops, and in 1562 her château was besieged by her son-in-law, Francis, duke of Guise. She died at Montargis.

See B. Fontana, *Renata di Francia* (Rome, 1889 seq.); and E. Rodocanachi, *Renée de France* (Paris, 1896).

RENFREW, a royal and small burgh and the county town of Renfrewshire, Scot., near the south bank of the Clyde, 5½ mi. W.

by N. of Glasgow by road. A small part of the parish of Govan is included in the burgh boundaries. Pop. (1951) 17,091. Industries include large shipbuilding works, engineering and the manufacture of rubber and paint. The Clyde trust has constructed a large dock and there is a ferry to Yoker. South of the town is the municipal aerodrome and civil airport. Robert III gave a charter in 1396, but it was a burgh (Renifry) at least 250 years earlier. Close to the town, on the site of Elderslie house, Somerled, lord of the Isles, was defeated and slain in 1164 by the forces of Malcolm IV, against whom he had rebelled. Robert III bestowed upon his son James (afterward James I of Scotland) the title of baron of Renfrew, still borne by the eldest son of the sovereign.

RENFREWSHIRE, a southwestern county of Scotland, bounded north by the river and Firth of Clyde, east by Lanarkshire, south, southwest and west by Ayrshire and northwest by the Firth of Clyde. The county has an area of 224.7 sq.mi. The surface is low and undulating, except toward the Ayrshire border on the west, where the principal height is the hill of Stake (1,711 ft.) and the confines of Lanarkshire on the southeast, where a few points attain a height of 1,100 ft. The southwestern hills are formed of volcanic rocks, basalts, porphyrites, tuffs and agglomerates of the age of the Calciferous Sandstone series. Practically all the area west of these rocks is occupied by the Carboniferous Limestone series. Boulder clays and glacial gravels and sands cover extensive areas. Much of the higher land in the centre is well wooded. In the northwest Loch Thom and Gryfe reservoir provide Greenock with water, and southeast of Barrhead Balgray reservoir and Glen reservoir reinforce the water supply of the Glasgow area. Castle Semple loch and other lakes are situated in the south and southeast. Strathgryfe is the only large vale in the shire; the scenery at its head is wild and bleak, but the lower reaches are pasture land. The wooded ravine of Glenkilloch, to the south of Paisley, is watered by Killoch burn, on which are three falls.

Greenock, Gourock, Wemyss bay and Inverkip are holiday resorts on the northwestern coast of the county.

History.—At the time of the Roman advance from the Solway the land was peopled by the British tribe of Damnonii. To hold the natives in check the conquerors built in 84 the fort of Vanduara on high ground now covered by houses and streets in Paisley; but after the Romans retired (410) the territory was overrun by Cumbrian Britons and formed part of the kingdom of Strathclyde, the capital of which was situated at Alclyde, the modern Dumbarton. In the 7th and 8th centuries the region practically passed under the supremacy of Northumbria, but in the reign of Malcolm Canmore became incorporated with the rest of Scotland. During the first half of the 12th century, Walter Fitzalan, high steward of Scotland, ancestor of the royal house of Stuart, settled in Renfrewshire on an estate granted to him by David I. Until their accession to the throne the Stuarts identified themselves with the district, which, however, was only disjoined from Lanarkshire in 1404. In that year Robert III erected the barony of Renfrew and the Stuart estates into a separate county, which, along with the earldom of Carrick and the barony of King's Kyle (both in Ayrshire), was bestowed upon his son, afterward James I. From their grant are derived the titles of earl of Carrick and baron of Renfrew, borne by the eldest son of the sovereign. Apart from such isolated incidents as the defeat of Somerled near Renfrew in 1164, the battle of Langside in 1568 and the capture of the 9th earl of Argyll at Inchinnan in 1685, the history of the shire is scarcely separable from that of Paisley or the neighbouring county of Lanark.

Agriculture and Industries.—The hilly tract contains much peat moss and moorland, but over those areas which are not thus covered the soil, which is a light earth on a substratum of gravel, is deep enough to produce good pasture. In the undulating central region the soil is better, particularly in the basins of the streams, while on the flatlands adjoining the Clyde there is a rich alluvium which, intensively used for arable and horticultural cropping as well as dairying, yields heavy crops. Near the populous centres some orchards and market gardens are found, and an increasing acreage is under wood. Most of the cattle are maintained in connection with dairying. Sheep farming, though on the increase, is not so important as in the other southern counties of Scotland, and pig raising is on the decline.

In point of commercial and manufacturing importance Renfrewshire is second only to Lanark. Granite, limestone and sandstone are quarried. The thread industry at Paisley is very extensive. Cotton and flax spinning, printing, bleaching and dyeing are carried on at Paisley, Renfrew, Barrhead and elsewhere; woollens and worsteds are produced at Greenock and Renfrew. Engineering works and iron foundries are at Greenock, Port Glasgow, Paisley, Renfrew, Barrhead and Johnstone. Sugar is a staple article of trade in Greenock and there are chemical works at Cathcart, Paisley, Hurlet and Nitshill. Brewing and distilling are carried on chiefly at Greenock. Jams and preserves are made at Paisley. Shipbuilding is especially important at Greenock and Port Glasgow. Paper mills are established in Greenock, Johnstone and Linwood. There are tanning industries at Bridge of Weir and Barrhead. Numerous miscellaneous industries—such as the making of starch, cornflour, earthenware and soap are important in Paisley and elsewhere. Trade and fisheries are centred at Greenock. Barytes and fireclay are mined and there are limestone and sandstone quarries.

The trading estate at Hillington, 2½ mi. east of Paisley, was the first to be established in Scotland as part of a plan to attract new industries to the area. The municipal aerodrome and civil airport, near Renfrew and about 7 mi. west of central Glasgow, serves all parts of the world.

Population and Administration.—The population in 1951 was 324,660 and Gaelic and English were spoken by 2,044 persons. Thus, though the shire is but 27th in point of size of the 33 Scottish counties, it is third in population. The large burghs are Paisley (1951 pop. 93,711), Greenock (76,292), Port Glasgow (21,618). The small burghs are Johnstone (15,660), Barrhead (12,971), Gourock (9,107) and Renfrew (17,091), which is the only royal burgh. (*See* separate articles on each burgh.) There are five county districts.

The shire returns one member to parliament for the eastern, and another for the western division. Paisley and Greenock each return one member. Renfrewshire forms a sheriffdom with Argyll, and there is a resident sheriff-substitute at Paisley and one at Greenock.

RENNENKAMPF, PAUL (1854–1918), Russian general, was born in 1854 and entered the army in 1873. In 1882 he was appointed to the general staff. Promoted to the rank of general in 1900, he distinguished himself in the Russo-Japanese war (1904–05). In 1913 he was appointed to command of the troops in the Vilna military district. In Aug. 1914 he commanded the I army which invaded eastern Prussia. His inaction during the battle of Tannenberg, where the neighbouring army of Samsonov was destroyed on Aug. 26–29 was a bitter disappointment, and he was even suspected of treachery. Personally brave, Rennenkampf, as an army commander, showed himself in the strategic sphere alternately rash and timid, owing to his inability to grasp the situation as a whole. At the beginning of 1915 he was recalled, and later under the pressure of public indignation, dismissed from the service.

In 1918 Rennenkampf was killed by the Bolsheviks.

RENNER, KARL (1870–1950), Austrian politician, was born on Dec. 14, 1870, the son of a peasant, at Dolni-Dunajovice (Unter-Tannowitz), Moravia. He studied law at the university of Vienna and early attached himself to the Social Democratic party. He advocated the transformation of the Habsburg empire into a federal democratic commonwealth based on equal political and cultural rights for all nationalities. He was elected deputy to the Austrian *reichsrat* (parliament) in 1907 and, after the collapse of the empire, he became, on Nov. 12, 1918, the first chancellor of the Austrian republic. He then supported the idea of a union of Austria with a democratic federal Germany.

Renner was largely responsible for the decrees of the *nationalrat* (lower chamber) which called for the dethronement of the dynasty of Habsburg-Lorraine and the banishment of all members of this house if they did not submit entirely to the laws of the republic,

and he was in charge of the negotiations which led to the former emperor Charles's leaving Austria in March 1919. On May 12, 1919, Renner went to Paris as head of the Austrian delegation to receive the conditions of peace. As the foreign minister, Otto Bauer (*q.v.*), resigned rather than take the responsibility for certain provisions of the treaty, Renner took over the conduct of foreign affairs and on Sept. 10, 1919, signed the Treaty of St. Germain by which Austro-German union (*Anschluss*) was prohibited.

The first coalition ministry had been succeeded in Oct. 1919 by a second, in which Renner was again chancellor and secretary for foreign affairs. Relations between the Austrian government and Hungary, which since the regime of the revolution had been succeeded by a reaction, were very strained. Renner, who as a Social Democrat, was inimical to the nationalist Hungarian government, refused to grant demands put forward to extradite the Hungarian revolutionaries who had fled to Vienna. This brought him into conflict with the Christian Democrats and their representatives in the cabinet. The coalition dissolved in June; but Renner remained in charge of foreign affairs until Oct. 1920. When in 1930 the Social Democrats became the stronger party, Renner was elected president of the *nationalrat;* he resigned in 1933.

After the annexation of Austria to Germany in 1938, Renner remained unmolested. In a public statement a few days before the plebiscite of April 10, 1938, he had recalled that he had already supported the *Anschluss* idea in 1918.

After the occupation of Vienna by the Soviet army, Renner obtained approval from the Russians for the formation of an Austrian democratic government and on April 29, 1945, became chancellor of the second Austrian republic. On Dec. 20, 1945, the newly elected *nationalrat* nominated him president of the republic. He died at Doebling, near Vienna, on Dec. 31, 1950.

His principal works are *Grundlagen und Entwicklungsziele der Österreichisch-ungarischen Monarchie* (1906); *Oesterreichs Erneuerung* (1919); *Die Wirtschaft als Gesamtprozess und die Sozialisierung* (1924).

(A. F. P.; X.)

RENNES, a town of western France, formerly the capital of Brittany and now the chief town of the department of Ille-et-Vilaine. Pop. (1946) 113,781. Rennes is situated at the meeting of the Ille and the Vilaine and at the junction of several lines of railway connecting it with Paris (232 mi. E.N.E.), St. Malo (51 mi. N.N.W.), Brest (155 mi. W.N.W.). Rennes, the chief city of the Redones, was formerly (like some other places in Gaul) called Condate (hence *Condat,* Condé), probably from its position at the confluence of two streams. In Roman times it was in Lugdunensis Tertia and became the centre of Roman roads. The oldest chronicles named it *Urbs Rubra* from the bands of red brick in the foundations of its first circuit of walls. Conan le Tort, count of Rennes (late 10th century), subdued the whole province, and his son and successor, Geoffrey, first took the title duke of Brittany. The dukes were crowned at Rennes; and before entering the city by the Mordelaise gate, they had to swear to preserve the privileges of the church, the nobles and the commons of Brittany. In 1356–57 Bertrand du Guesclin saved it from capture by the English. The parlement of Brittany, founded in 1551, held its sessions at Rennes from 1561, they having been previously shared with Nantes. Henry IV entered the city in state on May 9, 1598. In 1675 an insurrection at Rennes, caused by the taxes imposed by Louis XIV, was cruelly suppressed. The parlement was banished to Vannes till 1689, and the inhabitants punished. At the beginning of the Revolution Rennes was again the scene of bloodshed, caused by the discussion about doubling the third estate for the convocation of the states-general. In Jan. 1789 Jean Victor Moreau (afterwards general) led the law students in their demonstrations on behalf of the parlement against the royal government. It was the centre of the operations of the Republican army against the Vendeans. The bishopric, founded in the 5th century, in 1859 became an archbishopric, a rank to which it had previously been raised from 1790 to 1802.

The town was for the most part rebuilt of dark granite on a regular plan after the seven days' fire of 1720. The old town or Ville-Haute occupies a hill bounded on the south by the Vilaine, on the west by the canalized Ille. The Vilaine flows in a deep hollow bordered with quays and crossed by six bridges leading to the new town or Ville-Basse on its left bank. The cathedral of Rennes was rebuilt between 1787 and 1844 on the site of two churches dating from the 4th century. The Renaissance west façade has twin towers. The archbishop's palace occupies in part the site of the abbey of St. Melaine. The Mordelaise gate is a curious example of 15th century architecture and preserves a Latin inscription of the 3rd century, a dedication by the Redones to the emperor, Gordianus. The finest building in Rennes is the 17th century parliament house, now the law-court.

Rennes is the seat of an archbishop and a prefect, headquarters of the X army corps and centre of an *académie* (educational division). Its university has faculties of law, science and letters and a preparatory school of medicine and pharmacy. The town is also the seat of a court of appeal, of a court of assizes, of tribunals of first instance and commerce, of a board of trade-arbitrators and of a chamber of commerce. Tanning, iron-founding, timber-sawing and the production of furniture and wooden goods, flax spinning and the manufacture of tenting and other coarse fabrics, bleaching and various smaller industries are carried on. Trade is chiefly in butter made in the neighbourhood and in grain, flour, leather, poultry, eggs and honey.

RENNET: *see* CHEESE; NUTRITION: *Chemistry of Digestion.*

RENNIE, JOHN (1761–1821), British engineer, was the youngest son of James Rennie, a farmer at Phantassie, Haddingtonshire, where he was born on June 7, 1761. His first engineering work was the erection of flour mills, but his fame chiefly rests on his achievements in civil engineering. His skill solved the problem of draining and reclaiming extensive tracts of marsh in the eastern counties and on the Solway Firth. As a bridge engineer he built Waterloo, Southwark and London bridges—the last of which he did not live to see completed (*see* BRIDGES).

A noteworthy feature in many of his designs was the flat roadway. Among the harbours and docks in the construction of which he was concerned are those at Wick, Torquay, Grimsby, Holyhead, Howth, Kingstown and Hull, together with the London dock and the East India dock on the Thames, and he was consulted by the government in respect of improvements at the dockyards of Portsmouth, Sheerness, Chatham and Plymouth, where the breakwater was built from his plans. He died in London on Oct. 4, 1821, and was buried in St. Paul's.

See J. Rennie, *Autobiography of Sir John Rennie, F.R.S.* (1875).

RENO, the largest city of Nevada, U.S., and the county seat of Washoe county; on the Truckee river, 14 mi. from the western boundary of the state. It is on federal highways 40, 50 and 395; has a privately owned airport, operated by United Air Lines; and is served by the Southern Pacific and the Western Pacific railways and by freight truck and bus lines. Pop. (1950) 32,378. The city covers 5.9 sq.mi., at an altitude of 4,500 ft., near the foot of the Sierra Nevada range, amid magnificent and varied scenery. It is the financial, educational and professional centre of the state and the commercial centre for the adjacent districts of California as well as for Nevada. The volume of retail business in 1949 was $77,000,000; wholesale, $44,000,000; manufacturing, $30,000,000.

In Sparks, practically adjoining Reno on the east (pop., 1950, 8,170), are extensive shops of the Southern Pacific railroad. Bank debits for the city of Reno totalled $174,300,000 in 1940 while in 1949 the total was $576,336,000.

The University of Nevada (opened at Elko in 1873 and moved to Reno in 1885) occupies a 60 ac. campus on a low plateau overlooking the city. Adjoining the campus is the 60 ac. farm of the agricultural experiment station, given by the citizens of Washoe county to the state in 1899.

The Mackay school of mines was founded in 1907 by Mrs. John W. Mackay and Clarence H. Mackay in memory of John W. Mackay, one of the pioneers of the Comstock lode. Affiliated with the university are the Nevada agricultural experiment station (1887), the state analytical laboratory (1895), the state hygienic laboratory (1909), the state laboratory for pure food and drugs and weights and measures (1909), the state veterinary control service (1915), and one of the 12 experiment stations of the United States bureau of mines, handling all the investigations for the United States on gold, silver, platinum and the rare metals (1919). The state hospital for mental diseases (1882) is located between Reno and Sparks. St. Mary's (Catholic) and Washoe county general (public) hospitals give service covering a wide area. Because of the relative ease with which a divorce may be secured in Nevada (the law recognizing seven grounds for an absolute decree and requiring only six weeks' residence before bringing suit) Reno is the temporary residence of many persons from New York and other states with less liberal laws on the subject. About 25 mi. S.E. of the city are the famous mining camps of Virginia City and Gold Hill, on the Comstock lode. In 1859 (the year the Comstock lode was discovered) a roadhouse was built on the site of Reno for the accommodation of travellers and freight-teams on the Overland Route and to the goldfields. By 1863 the place had become known as Lake's Crossing, and five years later it was chosen for a station on the Central (now the Southern) Pacific railroad, then building through the Truckee valley. It was named after General Jesse Lee Reno (1823–62), a Federal officer in the Civil War. The town was incorporated in 1879, and was chartered as a city in 1899 and again in 1903. In 1873 and in 1879 it suffered from destructive fires.

RENOIR, PIERRE AUGUSTE (1841–1919), French painter, was born at Limoges on Feb. 25, 1841. He was the son of a tailor. At 13 he was apprenticed to a manufacturer of porcelain, and in painting on china he acquired a taste for pure and transparent colour and subtle brushwork. After earning some money in painting fans and blinds he entered the studio of Gleyre, where he became the friend of Sisley and Monet. He was inspired by Courbet to study nature; he was interested in Delacroix's colour technique; and the work of Monet and Corot appealed to him. In his early work he followed, with pronounced modern modifications, certain traditions of the French 18th century school. In the work of a later period colour was made subservient to form under the influence of Ingres, and his search for volume and form induced him at the end of his life to take up modelling. In the '70s he threw himself into the impressionist movement and became one of its leaders. Renoir tried his skill in almost every genre—in portraiture, landscape, flower-painting, scenes of modern life and figure subject; he excelled in painting nude figures of women. His art breathes sensuality, transfigured by lyrical feeling and plastic sense. His finest works rank among the masterpieces of the modern French school. Among these are some of his nude "Bathers," the "Rowers' Luncheon," the "Ball at the Moulin de la Galette," "The Box," "The Terrace," "*La Pensée,*" and the portrait of "Jeanne Samary." He is represented in the Caillebotte room at the Luxembourg, in the collection of M. Durand-Ruel, and in most of the collections of impressionist paintings in France, in the United States, in Germany and in the Tate gallery, London.

Renoir died on Dec. 17, 1919, at Cagnes in Provence, where he had settled in 1900.

See A. Vollard, *La Vie et L'oeuvre de Pierre-Auguste Renoir* (1919) and *Impressionism;* F. Fosca, *Renoir* (Eng. trans., 1924).

RENOUF, SIR PETER LE PAGE (1822–1897), Egyptologist, was born in Guernsey, on Aug. 23, 1822. He was educated at Elizabeth College there, and proceeded to Oxford, which, upon his becoming a Roman Catholic, under the influence of Dr. Newman, he quitted without taking a degree. He took an active part in church controversy, and his treatise (1868) upon the condemnation of Pope Honorius for heresy by the council of Constantinople in A.D. 680 was placed upon the index of prohibited books. After holding various educational posts he became in 1866 Keeper of Oriental Antiquities in the British Museum, in succession to Samuel Birch. He was also elected in 1887 president of the Society of Biblical Archaeology, to whose *Proceedings* he contributed, among other important papers, the translation of *The Book of the Dead,* with a commentary. He retired in 1891, and died in London on Oct. 14, 1897.

RENOUVIER, CHARLES BERNARD (1815–1903), French philosopher, was born at Montpellier on Jan. 1, 1815, and died on Sept. 1, 1903. His two leading ideas are a dislike for the unknowable, and a reliance on the validity of personal experience

The former accounts for his acceptance of Kant's phenomenalism, combined with rejection of the "thing in itself." It accounts, too, for his polemic on the one hand against a Substantial Soul, a Buddhistic Absolute, an Infinite Spiritual Substance; on the other hand against the no less mysterious material or dynamic substratum by which naturalistic Monism explains the world. He holds that nothing exists except presentations, which are not merely sensational, and have an objective aspect no less than a subjective. To explain the formal organization of our experience he adopts a modified version of the Kantian categories. The insistence on the validity of personal experience leads Renouvier to a yet more important divergence from Kant in his treatment of volition. Liberty, he says, in a much wider sense than Kant, is man's fundamental characteristic. Human freedom acts in the phenomenal, not in an imaginary noumenal sphere. Belief is not intellectual merely, but is determined by an act of will affirming what we hold to be morally good. In his religious views Renouvier makes a considerable approximation to Leibnitz. He holds that we are rationally justified in affirming human immortality and the existence of a finite God who is to be a constitutional ruler, but not a despot, over the souls of men. He would, however, regard atheism as preferable to a belief in an infinite Deity. His chief works are: *Essais de critique générale* (1854–64); *Science de la morale* (1869); *Uchronie* (1876); *Esquisse d'une classification systématique des doctrines philosophiques* (1885–86); *Philosophie analytique de l'histoire* (1896–97); *Histoire et solution des problèmes métaphysiques* (1901); *Victor Hugo: Le Poète* (1893); *Le Philosophe* (1900); *Les Dilemmes de la métaphysique pure* (1901); *Le Personnalisme* (1903); *Critique de la doctrine de Kant* (1906, published by L. Prat).

See L. Prat, *Les Derniers entretiens de Charles Renouvier* (1904); M. Ascher, *Renouvier und der französische Neu-Kriticismus* (1900); E. Janssens, *Le Néocriticisme de C. R.* (1904); A. Darlu, *La Morale de Renouvier* (1904); G. Séailles, *La Philosophie de C. R.* (1905); A. Arnal, *La Philosophie religieuse de C. R.* (1907).

RENSSELAER, a city of Rensselaer county, New York, U.S.A., on the east bank of the Hudson river, opposite Albany.

It is on federal highways 9 and 20 and is served by the New York Central railway; it is a part of the deep-water port of Albany (*q.v.*) and shares in the other transportation facilities of that city.

The population in 1950 was 10,856; in 1940 it was 10,768 by federal census. It has large railroad shops; among the leading manufactures are chemicals, dyes, shirts, woollen products and petroleum.

A settlement called Greenbush was established there in 1631, on the large tract known as Rensselaerwyck. In 1810 a square mile of land within the present city limits was acquired by a speculator, who divided it into lots and offered them for sale, and in 1815 the village was incorporated. In 1897 it was chartered as a city under its present name.

RENT. Various species of rent appear in Roman law (*q.v.*). In English law rent is a certain and periodical payment or service made or rendered by the tenant of a corporeal hereditament and issuing out of (the property of) such hereditament. Its characteristics, therefore, are (1) certainty in amount; (2) periodicity in payment or rendering; (3) the fact that rent is *yielded* and is, therefore, said "to lie in *render*," as distinguished from *profits à prendre* in general, which are taken, and are, therefore, said to lie in *prendre;* (4) that it must issue out of (the profits of) a corporeal hereditament. A rent cannot be reserved out of incorporeal hereditaments. But rent may be reserved out of estates in reversion or remainder (*see* LAWS RELATING TO REAL PROPERTY AND CONVEYANCING) which are not purely incorporeal. It is not essential that rent should consist in a payment of money. Apart from the rendering of services, the delivery of hens, horses, wheat, etc., may constitute a rent. But at the present day, rent is generally a sum of money paid for the occupation of land. It is important to notice that this conception of rent was attained at a comparatively late period in the history of the law. The earliest rent seems to have been a form of personal service, and was fixed by custom. Rent service is the oldest kind of existing rent. It is the only one to which the power of distress

attaches at common law, giving the landlord a preferential right over other creditors exercisable without the intervention of judicial authority (*see* DISTRESS). The increasing importance of socage tenure, arising in part from the convenience of paying a certain amount, whether in money or kind, rather than comparatively uncertain services, led to the gradual evolution of the modern view of rent as a sum due by contract between two independent persons.

Classes of Rents.—Rents, as they now exist in England, are divided into two great classes—rent service and rent charge. A rent service is so called because by it a tenure by means of service is created between the landlord and the tenant. The service is now represented by fealty, and is nothing more than nominal. Rent service is said to be incident to the reversion—that is, a grant of the reversion carries the rent with it (*see* REMAINDER). A power of distress is incident at common law to this form of rent. A rent charge is a grant of an annual sum payable out of lands in which the grantor has an estate. It may be in fee, in tail, for life—the most common form—or for years. A rent charge may also be granted out of another rent charge (Law of Property Act, 1925, s. 7, 122 [1]). A rent charge must be created by deed or will, and might be either at common law or under the Statute of Uses (1536). As from Jan. 1, 1926, a rent charge may be created or reserved without the intervention of a use (Law of Property Act, 1925, ss. 65, 187). The grantor has no reversion, and the grantee had at common law no power of distress, though such power was given him by the instrument creating the rent charge. Annual sums charged on land by way of rent charge may be recovered (*a*) if unpaid for 21 days, by distress; (*b*) if unpaid for 40 days, by entry into possession of the land and appropriation of income, and/or demise. By s. 45 of the Conveyancing Act, 1881, a power of redemption of certain perpetual rents in the nature of rent charges is given to the owner of the land out of which the rent issues. Rent charges granted since April 26, 1855, otherwise than by marriage settlement or will for a life or lives or for any estate determinable on a life or lives were required, in order to bind lands against purchasers, mortgagees or creditors, to have been registered in the Land Registry in Lincoln's Inn Fields (Judgments Act, 1855). After 1925, however, rent charges of this character became equitable interests only, and as such are overreached by conveyances to purchasers of a legal estate in lands (Law of Property Act, 1925, s. 2). There was no need, therefore, to provide for the registration of such rent charges, and the Land Charges Act, 1925, enacted that after Jan. 1, 1926, they should not be entered in the register of annuities (s. 4 [1]). Rent charges in possession charged on land perpetually or for a term of years absolute are "legal estates," registrable as such under the Land Registration Act, 1925 (ss. 2, 3, viii., xxv.); and certain classes of rent charge may be entered in the register of land charges under the Land Charges Act, 1925 (s. 10). Rent charges are barred by nonpayment or non-acknowledgment for 12 years (Limitation Act, 1874). The period of limitation for arrears of rent is six years. As to the colonies see Burge, *Col. and For. Laws* (by Bewes, iv., pt. 2, 460).

Forms of rent charge of special interest are *tithe rent charge* (*see* TITHES), and the rent charges formerly used for the purpose of creating "faggot votes." The device was adopted of creating parliamentary voters by splitting up freehold interests into a number of rent charges of the annual value of 40s., so as to satisfy the freeholders' franchise. But such rent charges were rendered ineffective by the Representation of the People Act, 1884, s. 4, which enacted (subject to a saving for existing rights and an exception in favour of owners of tithe rent charge) that a man should not be entitled to be registered as a voter in respect of the ownership of any rent charge.

A rent charge reserved without power of distress is termed a *rent-seck (reditus siccus)* or "dry rent," from the absence of the power of distress. But, as power of distress for *rents-seck* was given by the Landlord and Tenant Act, 1730, the legal effect of such rents has been since the act the same as that of a rent charge.

Other Varieties of Rent.—*Rents of assize* or *quit rents* are a relic of the old customary rents. They are presumed to have been established by usage, and cannot be increased or diminished. Provision was made in 1922 for the extinction after 1925 of quit rents and other manorial incidents (Law of Property Act, 1922, ss. 138, 144).

Fee farm rents are rents reserved on grants in fee. They, like quit rents, now occur only in manors, unless they existed before the statute of *Quia Emptores* was enacted or created by the Crown. A rent which is equivalent or nearly equivalent in amount to the full annual value of the land is a *rack rent*. As to ground rent, *see* GROUND RENT. A *dead rent* is a fixed annual sum paid by a person working a mine or quarry, in addition to royalties varying according to the amount of minerals taken.

The object of a dead rent is twofold—first, to provide a specified income on which the lessor can rely; secondly (and this is the more important reason), as a security that the mine will be worked, and worked with reasonable rapidity. *Rents in kind* still exist to a limited extent. All *peppercorn*, or nominal, rents seem to fall under this head. The object of the peppercorn rent is to secure the acknowledgment by the tenant of the landlord's right. In modern building leases a peppercorn rent is sometimes reserved as the rent for the first few years. *Labour rents* are represented by those cases, not unfrequent in agricultural leases, where the tenant is bound to render the landlord a certain amount of team work or other labour as a part of his rent.

As to the apportionment of rents, *see* APPORTIONMENT, and as to the rent of apartments, etc., *see* LODGER AND LODGINGS.

Payment of Rent.—Rent is due in the morning of the day appointed for payment, but a tenant is not in arrears until after midnight on that day. Rent made payable in advance by agreement between a landlord and his tenant is called *forehand rent*. It is not uncommon in letting a furnished house, or as to the last quarter of the term of a lease of unfurnished premises, to stipulate that the rent shall be paid in advance. As soon as such rent is payable under the agreement the landlord has the same rights in regard to it as he has in the case of ordinary rent. Where a cheque in payment of rent is lost in the course of transmission through the post, the loss falls on the tenant, unless the landlord has expressly or impliedly authorized it to be forwarded in that way: and the landlord's consent to take the risk of such transmission will not be inferred from the fact that payments were ordinarily made in this manner in the dealings between the parties. A tenant may deduct from his rent (i.) the "landlord's property tax" (on the annual value of the premises for income tax purposes), which is paid by the tenant, if the statute imposing the tax authorizes the deduction (which should be made from the rent next due after the payment); (ii.) taxes or rates which the landlord had undertaken to pay but had not paid, payment having thereupon been made by the tenant; (iii.) payments made by the tenant which ought to have been made by the landlord, *e.g.*, rent due to a superior landlord; (iv.) compensation under the Agricultural Holdings Act, 1923 (s. 37), and Landlord and Tenant Act, 1927 (s. 11 [2]).

A landlord's main remedy for non-payment of rent is *distress* (*q.v.*). Besides distress the landlord has his ordinary remedy by action. In addition, special statutory remedies are given in the case of tenants holding over after the expiration of their tenancy (*see* EJECTMENT). Under the Rent Restriction Acts, 1920–25, landlords of dwelling houses to which these statutes apply were prevented during their continuance from effectually raising the rents above specified limits, and except in certain cases from recovering possession on the termination of the tenancy. The act of 1920 expired in England on Dec. 25, 1927, and in Scotland on May 28, 1928. The provisions of Pt. II. of the act of 1923 continue in force for five years from the expiration of the act of 1920. (*See* further LANDLORD AND TENANT.)

Under the Landlord and Tenant Act, 1927, the landlord of trade premises may offer a renewal of the tenancy at such rent as, failing agreement, the statutory tribunal may consider reasonable, as an alternative to compensation for improvements (s. 2 [1] [d]) or goodwill (s. 4 [1]). The tenant of such premises may also apply for a new lease at a rent similarly approved (s. 5).

Scotland.—Rent is properly the payment made by the tenant to the landlord for the use of lands held under lease (*see* LANDLORD AND TENANT). In agricultural tenancies the legal terms for the payment of rent are at Whit Sunday after the crop has been sown, and at Martinmas after it has been reaped. But a landlord and tenant may substitute conventional terms of payment, either anticipating (*fore* or *forehand rent*) or postponing (*back* or *backhand rent*) the legal term. The rent paid by vassal to superior is called *feu-duty* (*see* FEU). Its nearest English equivalent is the *fee farm rent*. The remedy of distress does not exist in Scots law. Rents are recovered (i.) by summary diligence, proceeding on a clause, in the lease, of consent to registration for execution; (ii.) by an ordinary petitory action; (iii.) by an action of "maills and duties" (the rents of an estate in money or grain: "maills" was a coin at one time current in Scotland) in the Sheriff Court or the Court of Session; and (iv.) in non-agricultural tenancies by procedure under the right of hypothec, where that still exists; the right of hypothec over land exceeding two acres in extent let for agriculture or pasture was abolished as from Nov. 11, 1881; it was also excluded, by the House-letting and Rating (Scotland) Act, 1911 (s. 10), in lets to which that act applies, from all bedding material and all implements of trade used by the occupier and his family and from furniture selected by him up to £10 value (*see* DISTRESS; HYPOTHEC); (v.) by action of removing (*see* EJECTMENT). Arrears of rent prescribe after the expiration of a period of five years reckoned from the time of the tenant's removal from the land.

Labour or service rents were at one time very frequent in Scotland. The events of 1715 and 1745 showed the vast influence over the tenantry that the great proprietors acquired by such means. Accordingly acts of 1716 and 1746 provided for the commutation of services into money rents. Such services may still be created by agreement, subject to the summary power of commutation by the sheriff given by the Conveyancing Act, 1874 (ss. 20, 21). They will no longer be eligible from and after Jan. 1, 1935 (Conveyancing [Scotland] Act, 1924, s. 12 [7]). The Conveyancing (Scotland) Act, 1924, provides (s. 12) for the abolition or commutation of feu-duties payable in grain or other fungibles.

United States.—The law is in general accordance with that of England, apart from statute. The tendency of modern State legislation is unfavourable to the continuance of distress as a remedy. In the New England States, attachment on mesne process has, to a large extent, superseded it. Alabama, Colorado, Missouri, Montana, North Carolina and Oklahoma have refused to recognize the right of distress upon the ground that the landlord's rights have been secured by the substitution of other remedies. In the District of Columbia, Indiana, Minnesota, New York and Wisconsin it has been abolished by statute. "In those (states) in which it still exists, it has been modified by statutes, the general tendency of which is more or less to withdraw the control of the proceedings from the landlord and to rest it in public officials, thus assimilating it to the process of attachment." (2 Tiffany, Landlord and Tenant, section 325.)

Other Countries.—Under the French Code Civil (art. 2,102) the landlord is a privileged creditor for his rent. If the lease is by authentic act, or under private signature for a fixed term, he has a right over the year's harvest and produce, the furniture of the house and everything employed to keep it up, and (if a farm) to work it, in order to satisfy all rent due up to the end of the term. If the lease is not by authentic act nor for a specified term, the landlord's claim is limited to the current year and the year next following (*see* law of Feb. 12, 1872). The goods of a sub-lessee are protected: and goods bailed or deposited with the tenant are in general not liable to be seized. The French law is in force in Mauritius, and has been reproduced in substance in the Civil Codes of Quebec (arts. 2,005 *seq.*) and St. Lucia (arts. 1,888 *seq.*). There are analogous provisions in the Spanish Civil Code (art. 1,922). The subject of privileges and hypothecs is regulated in Belgium by a special law of Dec. 16, 1851; and in Germany by ss. 1,113 *seq.* of the Civil Code. The law of British India as to rent (Transfer and Property Act, 1882) and distress (cf., e.g., Act 15 of 1882) is similar to English law. The British dominions generally tend in the same direction. See, e.g., New South Wales (the consolidating Landlord and Tenant Act, 1899, and Act 66 of 1915); Union of South Africa (Act 30 of 1921); Newfoundland (Act 4 of 1899); Ontario (Act 1 of 1902, s. 22, giving a tenant five days for tender of rent and expenses after distress); Jamaica (Law 17 of 1900, certification of landlord's bailiffs); Queensland (Act 15 of 1904). English rent restriction legislation was followed in British India (e.g., Bombay, No. 3 of 1925; Burma, No. 1 of 1925) and in many of the colonies and dominions (e.g., Hongkong, No. 8 of 1925; Malta, No. 1 of 1925; New Zealand, No. 3 of 1925).

BIBLIOGRAPHY.—English Law: W. M. Fawcett, *A Concise Treatise on the Law of Landlord and Tenant* (3rd ed., 1905); E. Foà, *Landlord and Tenant* (6th ed., 1924); W. Woodfall, *Treatise on the Law of Landlord and Tenant* (21st ed., 1924). Scots Law: R. Hunter, *A Treatise on the Law of Landlord and Tenant* (4th ed., 1876); J. Erskine, *Principles of the Law of Scotland* (21st ed., 1911); Sir J. Rankine, *Law of Landownership in Scotland* (4th ed., 1909) and *A Treatise on the Law of Leases in Scotland* (3rd ed., 1916); W. M. Gloag and R. C. Henderson, *Introduction to the Law of Scotland* (1927). American Law: Herbert Thorndike Tiffany, *Landlord and Tenant* (1910); John N. Taylor, *The American Law of Landlord and Tenant* (9th ed., 1904); D. MacAdam, *The Rights, Remedies and Liabilities of Landlord and Tenant* (4th ed., 1910). (A. W. R.)

RENT: IN ECONOMICS.

In economics, rent is the name given to the income which the owner of a productive instrument gets by using it himself or by exacting a payment from another user. Much of the importance of the general theory of rent in economics comes from its application to the special case of income derived from land ownership. In the case of the incomes yielded by the ownership of reproducible instruments of production the principle of rent is subordinate, in the long run, to the principles which govern the rate of interest on capital, for the supply of such instruments will be maintained and increased if, but only if, the prospective return is sufficient to induce the investment of capital. At any given time, however, the income-yielding power of reproducible instruments of production is determined, not by what they cost, but by the value of their productive uses. That is, it is governed by the laws of rent. The specific hypothesis upon which the significance of the principle of rent depends is that the supply of the productive instruments which yield rent may be assumed to be given or fixed, so that the question remains only of how they may best be used.

Rent is generally held to have two distinguishing characteristics: first, it is a differential or graded return; second it is a surplus above costs. That it is a differential return depends upon the circumstance that productive instruments are described or measured in units (e.g., acres) which are not themselves units of productive efficiency. It is obvious that if one acre of agricultural land is better (more fertile or nearer to the market) than another it will command a larger rent. It is also obvious that the rent which any given piece of land commands may be taken to be a measure of its differential superiority over land which just falls short of being good enough to be worth using. That rent may be regarded as a surplus over costs is a consequence of the circumstance that the supply of rent-yielding instruments is taken as given. Even if they were produced or improved (as land is improved) at a cost in the past, their past costs have no relevance to the practical question of how and for what purposes the instruments shall be used. The only costs which need to be taken into account are the costs of using them.

Rent's Relation to Product.—Why, then, should rent be paid? The reason is that rent-yielding productive instruments, including rent-yielding land, exist in limited quantities, in the sense that if any one unit of them were withdrawn from use the aggregate product would be smaller. The rent of a given piece of land or of a given farm tends to be approximately equal to the value of the amount of product which is dependent upon using it. This amount can be determined by comparing the product which the given piece of land or farm will yield under proper cultivation with the product which could be got by employing the same amount of capital and labour on the best land which is not good enough to yield a rent (i.e., at the "extensive margin of cultiva-

tion") or by employing it in cultivating rent-yielding lands more intensively (i.e., at the "intensive margin of cultivation"). When the supply of a particular class of rent-yielding productive agents cannot be increased as rapidly as the demand for the products which they yield increases, they will command higher rents. Furthermore, unless there are compensating improvements in productive technique, production can be increased under such circumstances only by using instruments which had previously been below the level of profitable use or by making more intensive use of the latter instruments, i.e., by increasing the labour and other types of instruments used in conjunction with them. Whichever method is followed, increasing costs are encountered. This circumstance is the basis of the doctrine that with a fixed supply of land an increased agricultural product can be had only at the expense of a more than proportionate outlay of labour and capital—a doctrine to which the name, "law of diminishing returns," has been given.

When economists refer to some other form of income or gain, not derived from the ownership of land or of other productive instruments, as rent, they generally mean either that it may be looked upon as a differential return or that it may be conceived to be a surplus above costs. Thus, "rent of ability" is a name sometimes given to the differential element in personal earnings. "Entrepreneur's rent" denotes the profits of an ably-managed and successful enterprise, conceived of as a differential above the return secured by a marginal undertaking which is barely able to meet its costs. "Consumer's rent" is the difference between the amount which the consumer pays and the value which he attaches to what he buys, as measured by the maximum amount which he would have been willing to pay if required. Similarly, "producer's rent" is the difference between what the state of the market enables the producer to get for his goods and the amount which would have sufficed to induce him to produce them. (*See* also ECONOMICS and LAND.) (A. Yo.)

RENTON, a manufacturing town in Cardross civil parish, Dumbartonshire, Scotland. Pop. (1931) 4,562. It is on the Leven, 2 mi. N.N.W. of Dumbarton by the L.M.S. & L.N.E. railways. The leading industry is Turkey red dyeing, and calico-printing and bleaching are also carried on. The town was founded in 1782 by Mrs. Smollett (sister of Tobias Smollet); it was named after Cecilia Renton who became her daughter-in-law.

RENTON, a city in King county, western Washington, U.S., about 12 mi. S.E. of Seattle.

It is on U.S. highway 10 and is served by the Chicago, Milwaukee, St. Paul and Pacific, the Northern Pacific and the Pacific Coast railroads.

The population of Renton was 16,039 in 1950; it was 4,488 in 1940 and 4,062 by the census of 1930.

Renton, which is in a fertile area covering the flats of the Cedar river and on the south shore of Lake Washington, is an important trading centre as well as an industrial and agricultural community. A large plant of the Boeing Airplane company is located there. Lumber, shingles, steel products, railroad freight and refrigerator cars, logging machinery and stokers are also manufactured, and there are clay pits, coal mines and railroad shops.

Truck farming is carried on and there is some poultry farming.

Coal was discovered there in the middle of the 19th century, and in 1873 a coal company began to operate the mines. Prominent in the foundation of the company was William Renton, for whom the city is named. Renton, which is incorporated, is administered by a mayor-council form of government with direct popular election.

RENTSCHLER, HARVEY CLAYTON (1881–1949),

U.S. physicist, was born at Hamburg, Pa., on March 26, 1881. He was graduated from Princeton university, Princeton, N.J., in 1903 and took his master's degree there the following year. He received the Ph.D. degree from Johns Hopkins, Baltimore, Md., in 1908. Immediately afterwards, he became an instructor in physics at the University of Missouri, Columbia, Mo., and remained there until 1917, rising to the rank of associate professor.

He then accepted the position of director of research in the lamp division of the Westinghouse Electric and Manufacturing Co. at Bloomfield, N.J. There, out of experimental work in photochemistry on the case hardening of steel came his important contribution to medicine and food preservation, the sterilamp ("Bactericidal Effect of Ultraviolet radiation," *J.Bact.* 41:745–774, 1941). The lamp is a gaseous-conductor tube generating radiant energy, *i.e.*, ultra-violet rays with a wave length of 2,537 angstrom units. Such irradiation prevents spoilage through mould and yeast spores, and after tests proved satisfactory, lamps were installed in the processing and storage places of meat, bakery, dairy and brewing establishments. Although the work, which was done in association with Dr. Robert F. James, a biochemist at Westinghouse, was carried on with food preservation in mind, its medical application was also considered. In surgery, though the staff and materiel be germfree, the air contains bacteria which may infect the patient. Lamps were installed experimentally in the operating room of the Duke university hospital. Results proved postoperative infection and temperatures to be lower, and the lamps were subsequently installed at the Mayo Clinic, the N.Y. Medical Center and elsewhere. Dr. Rentschler also developed an ultra-violet light meter and conducted researches on the photoelectric emission from metals, the preparation and properties of ductile thorium and uranium, and the resonance and ionization of monatomic gases. He was made honorary D.Sc. by Princeton university in 1941, and the following year the honorary degree of doctor of laws was conferred on him at Ursinus college, Collegeville, Pa. His early researches with the refinement of uranium were credited with Westinghouse Electric's ability to provide the first batches of that element for atom bomb experiments in 1943. He died March 23, 1949, at East Orange, N.J.

RENWICK, EDWARD SABINE (1823–1912), U.S. inventor, was born in New York city on Jan. 3, 1823, the youngest son of James Renwick (*q.v.*) (1792–1863). He was graduated from Columbia college in 1839 and took his master's degree there in 1842. After several years of employment as an engineer, he went to Washington, D.C., where in 1849 he became associated with Peter H. Watson as patent expert in the U.S. circuit courts. Six years later he returned to New York where he worked independently in the same field. Renwick was also an inventor of some note. Among his accomplishments were a self-binder to improve the McCormick reaper (1851–53), an automatically heated and ventilated incubator for the raising of chicks and a chicken brooder (1877–86). He died at Short Hills, N.J., on March 19, 1912.

RENWICK, JAMES (1662–1688), Scottish covenanting leader, was born at Moniaive in Dumfriesshire, on Feb. 15, 1662, the son of a weaver, Andrew Renwick. Educated at Edinburgh university, he joined the section of the Covenanters known as the Cameronians about 1681 and soon became prominent among them. Afterwards he studied theology at the university of Groningen and was ordained a minister in 1683. Returning to Scotland "full of zeal and breathing forth threats of organized assassination," says Andrew Lang, he became one of the field-preachers and was declared a rebel by the privy council. He was largely responsible for the "apologetical declaration" of 1684 by which he and his followers disowned the authority of Charles II; the privy council replied by ordering every one to abjure this declaration on pain of death. Unlike some of his associates, Renwick refused to join the rising under the earl of Argyll in 1685; and in 1687, when the declarations of indulgence allowed some liberty of worship to the Presbyterians, he and his followers, often called Renwickites, continued to hold meetings in the fields, which were still illegal. A reward was offered for his capture, and early in 1688 he was seized in Edinburgh. Tried and found guilty of disowning the royal authority and other offenses, he refused to apply for a pardon and was hanged on Feb. 17, 1688. Renwick was the last of the covenanting martyrs.

See R. Wodrow, *History of the Sufferings of the Church of Scotland*, vol. iv (Glasgow, 1838); and A. Smellie, *Men of the Covenant* (1904); also Renwick's life by Alexander Shields in the *Biographia Presbyteriana* (1827).

RENWICK, JAMES (1792–1863), educator and engineer, was born in Liverpool, England on May 30, 1792, of Scottish descent. He emigrated to the United States with his parents in 1794. Two of his sons, Henry Brevoort (1817–1895) and Edward Sabine (*q.v.*) were also engineers, and his second son, James (*q.v.*), a distinguished architect. Renwick was graduated from Columbia college in New York city in 1807 and then travelled through Europe with his good friend Washington Irving. Three years later he earned his master's degree from Columbia. In 1812 he taught natural philosophy there during the illness of Prof. John Kemp, serving without pay. He entered government service as topographical engineer with the rank of major and three years later was commissioned colonel of engineers in the state militia. In 1820 he was appointed to the chair of natural philosophy and experimental chemistry at Columbia, which position he held until his retirement in 1853 to become the first emeritus professor of that college. In addition to his regular courses at Columbia, he also lectured on geology, mineralogy, practical mechanics and astronomy. While teaching he was also active in many public engineering projects on which his expert advice was increasingly sought. President Van Buren appointed him in 1838 to the commission of three which tested inventions designed to safeguard steam engine boilers against explosions. Two years later he was a member of the commission appointed to survey the northeast boundary between the United States and New Brunswick; these findings were later incorporated in the Webster-Ashburton treaty. Prof. Renwick was a frequent contributor to the best current periodicals and wrote a number of books on scientific and mechanical problems including *Outlines of Natural Philosophy* (2 vols., 1822–23); *Treatise on the Steam-Engine* (1830); and biographies of David Rittenhouse (1839), Robert Fulton (1845), and Count Rumford (1848) for Sparks's *Library of American Biography*. He also translated from the French, Lallemand's *Treatise on Artillery* (2 vols. 1820) and edited American editions of books on chemistry and mechanics. He died on Jan. 12, 1863.

RENWICK, JAMES (1818–1895), U.S. architect, was born in the section of New York city then known as Bloomingdale, on Nov. 1, 1818, the second son of James Renwick (*q.v.*) (1792–1863). He was graduated from Columbia college in 1836 at the precocious age of 17, and became an engineer for the Erie railroad. Later, as assistant engineer on the Croton aqueduct, he supervised the construction of a distributing reservoir in what is now the midtown area of Manhattan. His career in architecture began in 1843 when his plans won in the competition for the design and erection of Grace church at Broadway and 10th street. By the time of its completion in 1846, Renwick, still a very young man, had established his reputation as an architect. His early commissions were mainly for churches, including Calvary, St. Stephen's, and St. Bartholomew's. In 1853 the plans he entered in the competition for the designing of the Roman Catholic St. Patrick's cathedral were chosen, and in 1858 the work of more than 20 years was begun. This example of Gothic revival in the heart of the city is now one of its landmarks and occupies the square block bounded by Fifth and Madison avenues, and 50th and 51st streets. In addition to his ecclesiastical designs, Renwick was also architect for many public and private structures, the most outstanding being the Smithsonian institution and Corcoran gallery in Washington, Vassar college at Poughkeepsie, and numerous hotels, theatres and fashionable residences in New York city and elsewhere. As architect for the Board of Governors of Charities and Correction of New York city, he also built a number of asylums and hospitals. Renwick's early work was mainly Gothic or Romanesque. Later his designs took on a more eclectic character with occasional bad results, but he had imagination and his planning was usually sound. He was a noted connoisseur and acquired a fine collection of paintings and *objets d'art*. He died in New York city on June 23, 1895.

REP, REPP or **REPS**, cloth made of silk, wool or cotton. The name is said to have been adopted from the French *reps*, a word of unknown origin; it has also been suggested that it is a corruption of "rib." It is woven in fine cords or ribs across the width of the piece. In various forms it is used for dresses, and to some extent for ecclesiastical vestments. In wool and cotton it is also used for upholstery purposes.

REPARATIONS. Reparations are a levy upon defeated nations to compensate the victorious powers in some measure for the costs of war. The word came into general use after 1918 to describe the economic obligations of the Central to the Allied and Associated Powers and was meant to replace the older conception of war indemnities which were exacted as a punitive measure as well as in payment for war losses. The word reparations was used again after World War II to designate part of the payments which the United Nations participating in the war demanded of the defeated countries, mainly Germany, Japan and Italy. The levying and payment of reparations involves ethical and economic considerations of a complex kind, calling for the determination of the exact responsibility of the defeated nations, for appraising their ability to make reparation and estimating the capability of the victorious nations to accept it.

There are two practicable ways in which a defeated country can make reparation. It can pay over in cash or kind a portion of the goods and services it is currently producing; *i.e.*, a part of its national income. Or it can pay over in cash or kind some of its capital in the form of machines, tools, rolling stock, merchant shipping and the like, which is a part of its national wealth. The payment of gold or other universal money is not a practicable method of paying reparations. The supposed consequence of reparations is a decrease in the income, and hence level of living, of the defeated nation, and an increase in the income of the victorious nation, the capitalized value of the increase being equal to its war costs. However, there is no warrant for these suppositions in either the economics of reparations or in historical experience with them. Experience suggests that the smaller the reparations levy the more likely it is to be paid, and conversely that large levies are unlikely to be collected. In both World Wars I and II the failure to obtain desired reparations was unmistakable. Indeed, some of the victorious nations eventually had to make payments to the defeated in the interests of restoring economic and political stability. After both wars the initial policy of the victors was the imposition of severe reparations. Though understandable, this attitude had little justification and gradually changed by force of circumstances to a policy of making the conquered nations self-supporting as quickly as possible.

Magnitude of Reparations.—The size of the defeated nation's liability cannot be determined by the war costs for which it is directly or indirectly responsible. These costs are of two kinds, economic and social. The economic cost of war is the value of civilian goods and services which must be foregone in order that resources can be used for war production, plus the capital destruction resulting from war. The social cost of war is the burden created by loss of life and disorder in social institutions. The loss of life has economic implications, but its cost cannot be measured because the labour value of human life is not capitalized as, say, the income value of equipment can be capitalized. Estimates can be made of the economic costs of war, and they are usually much in excess of the capacity of the defeated nation to make reparation. For example, after World War II the principal belligerents submitted claims of $320,000,000,000 against Germany. This sum was more than ten times greater than the total prewar national income of Germany (at constant prices) and an even greater multiple of German income at the end of the war.

Since the magnitude of reparations cannot be determined by war costs, it must be determined by the defeated nation's ability to pay, and this is much less than its imputed liability. Its ability to pay is dependent on three factors: (1) its national wealth or alternatively its national income; (2) the ability of either the occupying powers or the government of the defeated nation to organize the economy for the payment of reparations; and (3) the capacity of the victors to organize their economies for the productive use of reparation receipts. The first of these is most important. In the two world wars, the economic resources of all belligerents were destroyed or depleted more rapidly than they could be replaced. Each side destroyed the capital of the other at a great capital cost to itself; and the capital which escaped destruction was not maintained with the same care devoted to it in peacetime.

The political instability which usually follows a war makes it difficult to organize the defeated economy for the payment of reparations. Authority is diffuse and uncertain; there are conflicts among the victorious nations, and the populace of the defeated country is, to say the least, unco-operative, particularly in the matter of transferring its capital or income to recent enemies. Finally, the payment of reparations depends on the willingness and ability of the victorious countries to accept the new economic structure attendant upon transfers of income or capital. Here occurred the paradoxes of reparations history in the 20th century. Following World War I, some of the Allied Powers were able to conceive of no limit to a justifiable tribute from Germany, but when payments out of income began the Allies found the imports competing with domestically produced goods and services and thereupon took measures which prevented Germany from honouring its obligations. After World War II, the transfers of capital from Germany and Japan so threatened to dislocate the economic structure of Europe and Asia that measures were taken to reduce reparation liabilities; by 1950 payments had virtually ceased.

METHODS OF PAYMENT

The payment of reparations in kind or cash out of income or capital constitutes an export surplus; *i.e.*, the paying nation sends out of the country more goods and services than it imports. Reparations are impossible without this surplus, and it is for practical purposes more dependent on increasing exports than on decreasing imports. The fact that reparations are possible only via an export surplus should not be obscured by the financial mechanics of reparations. The defeated nation usually compensates the private owners of capital for the export of the goods which constitute reparations, and to do this it taxes or borrows from its citizens. But reparations cannot be paid out of revenue raised internally; the revenue must be converted into income or capital for transfer to the victor nation or into the currency of that nation. After World War I, reparations were designed to be paid mainly in cash out of income. After the second war, they were meant to be paid in kind, mainly out of capital.

Payments in Kind.—If payments in kind are made out of capital, the defeated nation pays over to the victors specific assets within the defeated economy and titles to assets held abroad. After 1918, the Allies obtained the largest vessels in the German merchant marine and a small amount of additional capital. After 1945, the United Nations seized merchant vessels and industrial equipment in Germany and Japan, acquired German and Japanese owned assets within the victor countries and sought to obtain axis-owned assets within neutral countries. Most of the owners of this property were compensated by revenue raised within the defeated nations, the effect being to distribute the burden of the loss among enemy nationals whether property owners or not.

Reparations in the form of capital transfers in kind have certain, though limited, advantages. They avoid some of the more complex monetary problems of cash payments. They are adaptable to a general program of economic disarmament whereby victor nations dismantle and remove industrial equipment of actual or potential military value. Some of this equipment may be of immediate peacetime value to the victorious economies, relieving critical shortages and assisting in reconstruction. Against these advantages must be set the complex economic problems created by the transfers. It is difficult if not impossible to distinguish between industrial equipment of military value and that which can be used only to produce peacetime goods. The steel industry may be used for peaceful purposes or it may become the centre of the munitions industry. The war potential of an industry may be reduced by limiting its capacity but this also limits its peaceful uses. An even greater problem is the dislocation of economic structure which capital removals produce. Reducing plant capacity or eliminating it is a complex technical and economic undertaking. A slight error in removing too much of one kind of equipment can produce a great loss in another industry which in consequence must operate at undercapacity. Even with complete technical consistency in scaling down plant facilities there can be unnecessary losses when the reduced output is measured in monetary (*i.e.*, economic) units. The removal and transportation of capital is expensive, and if any of the labour is done by enemy nationals there is likelihood of additional expense through sabotage. Capital removals require a reallocation of resources in both the defeated and victorious countries. During the process there is a loss of income resulting from installation costs and partial unemployment. Meanwhile the defeated country may become a charge on its conquerors, requiring relief of various kinds until it can become self-supporting. These problems are present in the most ideal circumstances which can be supposed.

In the conditions likely to be present, capital reparations mean a very long-term reduction in income for the victorious nations as well as the defeated. This is probable because capital is removed from an economy where it has been used efficiently with trained labour to one where it must be used less efficiently for a considerable time. The net effect is then a lower income for all countries, victorious as well as defeated. This consequence is avoidable only by the creation of a perfect mechanism for the transfer of capital and by supposing that the recipient nations will be able to use it as efficiently as the paying nation. Such conditions are improbable. This being so, reparations are apt to produce quite the opposite of their intended effect. This was the experience after World War II.

Following World War I there was some payment of reparations in kind out of income. There were other instances of this method. Out of its annual production, a paying country exports certain commodities to its creditors or performs certain services for them. It can, for example, ship specified quantities of raw material, fuel or manufactured goods, and it may perform transportation and labour services. It may send numbers of its workers to the victorious nation to restore areas damaged by the war and repatriate them when the work is completed. The difficulties encountered in a scheme of capital reparations are present here also but on a lesser scale. The excessive export of current output may force a reduction in plant operations within the defeated countries. The receipt of these goods and services by the victors disturbs their normal exchange pattern. After World War I, the immigration of German workers into France to restore the devastated areas caused French workers to protest that their wages were being reduced by the increased labour supply. After World War II, some British trade unions resisted the attempt of the Labour government to use German prisoners of war to relieve critical labour shortages. Similarly, some U.S. manufacturers complained that the import of Japanese goods on reparations account was driving down prices in the U.S.

Cash Payments.—Prior to World War II, reparations were more often made as cash payments than as transfers in kind. It was believed that such a method was easier to organize and more productive of a successful settlement (a viewpoint which was reversed after World War II). Cash payments can be made out of accumulated capital, in which case the paying country sells certain of its assets held either at home or abroad, converts the proceeds into the currency of the victorious nation and pays it over to the latter's government. The effect of capital transfers via cash payments need not be quite as disturbing as that of capital transfers in kind, though in practice both may produce much the same result. A conceivable advantage of the former is the greater opportunity given the paying nation to dispose of its capital at a minimum loss; it may sell it on the highest paying market and convert the receipts into the currency of the victor nation, while capital transfers in kind must be made directly to the victor nation and valued realistically at the worth to it.

After World War I, the bulk of reparations levied on Germany were to consist of cash payments out of income over a period of years. The successful execution of this plan called for an export surplus in the paying country and conversion of the surplus into the currency of the receiving nations. The effect was a reduction in the income of the paying nation and an increase

in that of the recipients. Cash payments produce distinctive effects which are not present when reparation is made in kind; they arise because the debtor country must obtain the currency of the creditor nation. The nature and importance of the effects depend on the size of reparations in relation to the national income of the debtor and creditor countries, on the sensitivity of their price levels to expenditures and receipts from imports and exports, on the flexibility of their foreign exchange rates and on the money supply together with the rate at which it is spent. As these factors are highly variable when taken separately or together, it is impossible to generalize precisely about the effect of cash reparations, depending as it does on the magnitude and interrelations of the variables. If any one result is more probable than others, it is a fall in the foreign value of the paying nation's currency and a concomitant rise in that of the receiving country. This in turn increases the real cost of reparations to the debtor and creates a corresponding gain to the creditor. Because its money buys less of the money of the creditor, the debtor must offer a greater quantity of exports in order to obtain a given quantity of the creditor's money. It is to be repeated that this is a probable, not an invariable, consequence.

There are two major conditions for the successful settlement of cash reparations. Payments must be within the defeated nation's ability to pay after full account is taken of their monetary effects, and payments must be acceptable to the receiving country. The latter must either increase its net imports from the paying nation or from a third nation which is in debt to the paying nation. The inherent complexities of a reparations program of any kind usually have been made more troublesome by the imposition of controls over the economies of the defeated and victorious nations. This was significant after World War II when the German and Japanese economies were closely regulated and when there was regulation in every important victorious nation excepting the U.S. Control over prices, the movement of goods and labour represent a comprehensible wish to soften the rigours of reconstruction and of readjustment from war. This, however, does not alter the fact that control removes from the economy the price mechanism whereby gains and losses from alternative lines of action can be compared. This was recognized after 1945 when an effort was made to remove Japanese industrial equipment to nonindustrial nations of Asia and the Pacific. As the Japanese economy was controlled there was no realistic way of appraising the final results of the transfer, nor was there any method of measuring the usefulness of the equipment to the recipient nations because they too controlled their economies. Eventually it was concluded that the transfers had no economic justification.

REPARATIONS AND WORLD WAR I

The history of reparations after 1918 does not disclose any great appreciation of their economic implications, although prior to that reparations were not the complex problem they later became. Indemnities (as the payments were then called) were levied in the Napoleonic, Franco-Prussian and the Russo-Japanese Wars. The amounts were moderate and were paid mainly by the surrender of foreign-held assets and from the proceeds of foreign loans, the transfers being made in a relatively short time.

Germany's Liability.—Following World War I, however, the problem of reparations was never completely solved. Without specifying the exact amount to be paid, the treaty of Versailles held Germany responsible for all damages to civilians and their dependents; for losses caused by the maltreatment of prisoners of war; for pensions to veterans and their dependents; and for the destruction of all nonmilitary property. Following a series of conferences in 1920, Germany's liability was fixed tentatively at a minimum of 3,000,000,000 gold marks annually for 35 yr. with maximum payments not to exceed 269,000,000,000 marks. Germany immediately declared it was unable to pay even the minimum, and there followed successive reductions culminating in the decision of the London conference of 1921, which fixed the liability at 132,000,000,000 (all figures in gold marks) to be paid in annuities, or annual instalments, of 2,000,000,000 marks plus an amount equal to 26% of Germany's annual exports. Germany's default brought the occupation of the Ruhr in 1923 by French and Belgian troops in order to collect reparations by force. Dispossessed of this important area, Germany was unable to make payments and each attempt to convert marks into foreign currency drove down their value. The result was the disastrous inflation of 1923 when the mark fell to a billionth of its par value.

In 1924 the Allies sponsored the Dawes plan which stabilized the nation's internal finances by a reorganization of the Reichsbank; a transfer committee was created to supervise reparations payments. The total liability was left to later determination, but standard annuities of 2,500,000,000 marks were set subject to increase. The plan was initiated by a loan of 800,000 marks to Germany. The Dawes plan worked so well that by 1929 it was believed that the stringent controls over Germany could be removed and total reparations fixed. This was done by the Young plan, which set reparations at 121,000,-000,000 marks to be paid in 59 annuities. But hardly had the Young plan started operation than the world depression of the 1930s began and Germany's ability to pay dwindled to the vanishing point. In 1932 the Lausanne conference proposed to reduce reparations to the token sum of 3,000,000,000 marks, but the proposal was never ratified. Adolf Hitler came to power in 1933, and within a few years all important obligations under the treaty—political as well as economic—were repudiated.

Obstacles to Settlement.—Two circumstances were mainly responsible for the failure of reparations. One was the political instability of Germany and its refusal to accept responsibility for the war. A more fundamental circumstance was the unwillingness of the creditor nations to accept reparation payments in the only practicable way they could be made—by the transfer of goods and services. The attitude of the creditors had its origin in the notion that a nation is injured by importing more than it exports. Through the 1920s the creditor nations tried to exclude Germany from world trade and simultaneously to increase their exports to Germany (on credit, of course). By the logic of its position Germany was committed to failure.

Germany's Actual Payments.—The total of reparations paid is not exactly known because of uncertainty over payments between 1918 and 1924, their probable value being, however, 25,000,000,000 marks. From 1924 to 1931 Germany paid 11,100,000,000 marks, making total payments about 36,100,-000,000 marks. During the postwar period, however, Germany borrowed 33,000,000,000 marks from abroad; its net payments to the rest of the world were therefore 3,100,000,000 marks. The reparations program was most successful during the period of greatest borrowing, between 1924–31, when Germany paid 11,100,000,000 marks on reparations account and borrowed 18,000,000,000 marks, the net transfer being 6,900,000,000 marks to Germany. Although reparations often were called the cause of Germany's postwar difficulties, their direct effects were actually negligible. The following table shows that reparations were never a sizable portion of any important economic magnitude.

German Reparations, 1924–30
(in millions of marks)

	1924	1925	1926	1927	1928	1929	1930
Reparations payments	1,000	1,220	1,500	1,584	1,999	2,501	1,253
National income	49,000	55,000	50,000	67,500	65,000	65,650	54,600
Governmental expenditures	3,725	4,450	4,848	5,917	6,300	7,475	7,153
Exports	6,552	9,290	10,414	10,801	12,276	13,483	12,300
Reparations as a percentage of national income	2.04	2.02	2.72	2.28	2.77	3.43	3.44
Reparations as a percentage of governmental expenditures	26.86	27.42	30.94	26.77	31.73	33.46	17.52
Reparations as a percentage of exports	15.28	13.15	12.48	14.67	16.29	18.55	10.19

REPARATIONS AND WORLD WAR II

Reparations for the second war were viewed in two distinct ways. In one they were made incidental to a program of economic disarmament and were to be paid out of capital of: (1) actual or potential military value; and (2) that in excess of the amount permitted the defeated nations by the victorious powers. In the other view, reparations were regarded in the conventional way as payments in compensation for the costs of war and were to be made in kind out of capital and income. These two views were both enunciated in the policy laid down by the major Allies in conferences at Yalta and Potsdam in 1945.

The two conceptions are not wholly consistent, and the attempt to apply both of them created confusion and conflict. Removals of capital reduce the economic power of the defeated nation but they do not necessarily increase the power of the recipient nation correspondingly, so that the loss of income by the defeated nation may be (and usually is) greater than the gain to the victors. With each removal of capital, the ability to pay and receive reparations is lessened. If, on the other hand, maximum reparations are wanted by the victorious nations they cannot disarm the defeated nation of its economic power. These difficulties of the Allied reparations program were later complicated by two additional factors: the disagreement between the U.S.S.R. and U.S., which prevented the conclusion of peace treaties with the major defeated nations; and the establishment by the U.S. of the Economic Cooperation administration (ECA) for the purpose of capital reconstruction and development in Europe and Asia.

German Reparations.—The express policy was formulated at Potsdam in 1945. Uniform control was to be established over the entire German economy and administered jointly by four powers in their zones of occupation. The purpose was to dismantle German industry in order that the nation never again could engage in war. Dismantlement was to be limited by two considerations: the German level of living was not to be less than the average living level of other European countries excepting Britain and Russia; and Germany was to be left with sufficient capital in order to pay for its essential imports and so be self-supporting. Reparations were to be paid out of the difference between total German capital and the permissible amount. The distribution of reparations was to be made by the Inter-Allied Reparations agency established in 1945. A "level of industry" plan was formulated to specify the kind and amount of reparations available to claimant nations. It soon was recognized that the initial claims of $320,000,000,000 could not be satisfied, and the Allies announced their satisfaction with reparations which would "compensate in some measure for the loss and suffering caused by Germany."

Shortly after the end of the war, the political disagreement between eastern and western Allies made unified control impossible over the German economy. Its division into eastern and western areas curtailed the useful exchange of agricultural for industrial products and removed the possibility of Germany's supporting itself. The division also increased the difficulties of capital removals since there was no way of appraising their effect on the total economy. The western powers sought to unify control over their zones in order to advance the reparations program, but here too there was disagreement over the amount of capital to be removed, France insisting on maximum removals in order to disarm Germany completely and Britain and the United States maintaining that Germany should be allowed enough industrial power to assist in the recovery of the entire economy of western Europe. In 1947 the U.S. offered large loans to European countries if they in turn would co-operate by increasing their output and by reducing trade barriers. The conditions were accepted and the ECA (originally called the Marshall plan) was begun. It was quickly discovered that European reconstruction would be assisted by allowing the Germans to retain the capital in their western areas (no assistance was given to the eastern area). There was then a conflict between the program for reparations and that for reconstruction. This was resolved by reducing reparations to a token amount, and by 1950 payments had virtually ceased. Moreover, the economy of western Germany had so increased in importance that the Allies by this time were extending loans to Germany for reconstruction. In the eastern zone, the Russians found that capital removals did not yield the expected value. They were halted, and reparations in kind were collected out of income.

The net effect of German reparations could not be determined because reliable information was lacking. It was known that the value of capital removals was much less than expected and the costs of occupation (not including ECA loans) higher than anticipated. The U.S.S.R. and Poland together obtained approximately 25% of the arable land of Germany by transfers of territory; the former in 1945–46 took approximately $500,-000,000 of German income, a part of which was to go to Poland. It is probable that after World War II the total of reparations paid by Germany was negative, that payments to Germany by victor nations exceeded receipts from Germany. Reparation payments from other European nations could not be estimated, again because reliable information was wanting. Italy was required to pay the U.S.S.R. $100,000,000 in kind out of capital and income; against this must be set a considerably larger though unknown sum representing relief payments to Italy by western powers.

Japanese Reparations.—The initial policy was identical with that for Germany and the consequences quite similar. Japan was to be disarmed of its economic power but left with enough capital to become self-supporting and to maintain a living level equal to that of other Asiatic countries. Reparations were to consist of capital in excess of the permissible amount. To this end an inventory of surplus capital was taken in 1945 and large-scale removals were planned. The Pauley report embodying the program was challenged and its conclusions were later modified, reducing Japan's liability. The major recipients were to be Asiatic countries which Japan had occupied during the war.

As in Germany, the collection of reparations was more expensive than expected and their value to the recipients less than expected. The claimant nations were unable to agree on their proper shares, which delayed execution of the program. Meanwhile, reparations capital in Japan was allowed to deteriorate, and Japan continued as a deficit economy supported mainly by the U.S. as the major occupying power. The continued deficit caused the U.S. to suspend all reparations deliveries in May 1949. To that date, total reparations paid out of assets held within Japan were 153,000,000 yen or $39,000,000 (at 1939 values). In addition, an unspecified sum was paid out of Japanese assets held in foreign countries. Offsetting total receipts from reparations was a considerably larger sum representing relief and occupation costs of the victor nations. As in Germany, occupation costs in Japan were not allocated as reparations receipts were. Some nations therefore obtained net reparations. Taken together, however, Allied reparations from Japan were also negative; net payments were made to Japan as well as to Germany. That these payments might have been still larger had no reparations whatever been collected is a moot question; it is to be noted that some of the payments were necessitated by the reparations program itself.

BIBLIOGRAPHY.—Reparations Commission, *Reparations Papers*, no. 1–23 (1922–30); H. G. Moulton and Leo Pasvolsky, *War Debts and World Prosperity* (1932); Hans Neisser, *The Problem of Reparations* (1944); Edwin W. Pauley, *Report on Japanese Reparations to the President of the U.S.* (1946); David Ginsburg, *The Future of German Reparations* (1947); Inter Allied Reparation Agency, *Report of the Secretary General, for the Year 1947* (1948).   (W. D. G.)

REPEAL, the abrogation, revocation or annulling of a law. The word is particularly used in English history of the movement led by Daniel O'Connell (*q.v.*) for the repeal of the act of Union and in the United States for the repeal of the 18th (Prohibition) amendment of the constitution.

REPERTORY THEATRE: see DRAMA.

REPHAIM (Heb. shades, ghosts), a race of reputed giants mentioned in the Bible as the prehistoric inhabitants of Canaan before the land was conquered by the Israelites. Rephaim are often held to be inclusive of the other Biblical giants, namely the Emim, Zuzim, Anakim and Horim. The giant legend, as well as that of longevity, is common in ethnic myths which tend to ascribe extraordinary powers and qualities to extinct forbears. The concept of larger than human proportions is also held to have arisen from the sight of ancient ruins and tombs. For example, the sarcophagus of Og, the king of "Bashan which was called the land of the giants" (Deut. 3:11) is described as being giant sized. In the later books of the Bible (Psalms 88:11; Job 26:5, etc.) Rephaim is the Hebrew word used to denote the shades of the dead which dwell in Sheol, similar to the ghosts (*gigim, gidim*) of Sumerian mythology. The valley of the Rephaim was a plain in Judah where David twice conquered the Philistines (II Sam. 5:17–25).

REPIN, ILYA YEFIMOVICH (1844–1930), Russian painter, was born in 1844 at Chuguyev in the department of Kharkov, the son of parents in straitened circumstances. He learned the rudiments of art under a painter of saints named Bunakov, for three years gaining his living at this humble craft. In 1863 he obtained a studentship at the Academy of Fine Arts of St. Petersburg (Leningrad), where he remained for six years, winning the gold medal and a travelling scholarship which enabled him to visit France and Italy. He returned to Russia after a short absence, and devoted himself exclusively to subjects having strong national characteristics. In 1894 he became professor of historical painting at the St. Petersburg academy. Repin's paintings are powerfully drawn, with not a little imagination and with strong dramatic force and characterization. He died at Kuokkala in Finland on Sept. 29, 1930.

His chief pictures are "Procession in the Government of Kiev," "The Arrest," "Ivan the Terrible's murder of his Son," and, best known, "The Reply of the Cossacks to Sultan Mahmoud IV."

REPINGTON, CHARLES A'COURT (1858–1925), British military critic, was born on Jan. 29, 1858, and commissioned in the Rifle Brigade in 1878. After serving with distinction in the Afghan War, the Sudan and South Africa, he was appointed military attaché at Brussels and The Hague in 1900, being then a lieutenant colonel. Two years later his military career ended abruptly through domestic causes, and he took up journalism, becoming military correspondent of the *Times* in 1904. In 1915, after staying with the British commander-in-chief in France, he came home to call attention to the shell shortage. In Jan. 1918 a divergence of views caused him to leave the *Times* for the *Morning Post,* and after World War I he became military correspondent of the *Daily Telegraph,* a post which he held till his death at Hove, Sussex, on May 25, 1925.

His works include *Vestigia* (1919); *The First World War, 1914–18; Personal Experiences* (1920); *After the War; A Diary* (1922); *Policy and Arms* (1924).

REPINGTON (or REPYNGDON), **PHILIP** (d. 1424), English bishop and cardinal, was educated at Oxford and became an Augustinian canon at Leicester before 1382. A man of some learning, he came to the front as a defender of the doctrines taught by John Wycliffe; for this he was suspended and afterwards excommunicated, but in a short time he was pardoned and restored by Archbishop William Courtenay, and he appears to have completely abandoned his unorthodox opinions. In 1394 he was made abbot of St. Mary de Pré at Leicester, and after the accession of Henry IV to the throne in 1399 he became chaplain and confessor to this king, being described as "clericus specialissimus domini regis Henrici." In 1404 he was chosen bishop of Lincoln, and in 1408 Pope Gregory XII made him a cardinal. He resigned his bishopric in 1419. Some of Repington's sermons are in manuscript at Oxford and at Cambridge.

REPLEVIN, a term in English law signifying the recovery by a person of goods unlawfully taken out of his possession by means of a special form of legal process; this falls into two divisions—(1) the "replevy," the steps which the owner takes to secure the physical possession of the goods, by giving security for prosecuting the action and for the return of the goods if the case goes against him, and (2) the "action of replevin" itself. The jurisdiction in the first case is in the county court (*q.v.*); in the second case the supreme court has also jurisdiction in certain circumstances. At common law, the ordinary action for the recovery of goods wrongfully taken would be one of detinue (*q.v.*); but no means of immediate recovery was possible till the action was tried, and until the Common Law Procedure Act 1854 the defendant might exercise an option of paying damages instead of restoring the actual goods.

United States.—In the United States the action of replevin is almost entirely regulated by statute in each jurisdiction, and is materially different from the use and construction of the common law action of replevin in England. The action is laid upon a wrongful taking and a wrongful detaining or a wrongful detaining alone. It is a proceeding *in rem* to recover goods and chattels, *i.e.,* every kind of personal property to which the plaintiff has the right to present possession, and also, by statute, a proceeding *in personam*, to recover damages for either the detention or both the caption and detention, according to the wording of the statute. It is a possessory action, the gist of which is the right of possession in the plaintiff, but in nearly all cases the title is determined since the owner is entitled to possession, and possession by verdict where the title is in question awards title. It will not lie to recover real property or fixtures attached to the freehold, nor can it be maintained in any case in which the object sought is the determination of title to land. In some jurisdictions all damages growing out of the wrongful taking and detention may be assessed in the replevin action; in others, where the statute limits the recovery of damages to detention only, a separate subsequent action may be brought to recover compensatory and punitive damages sustained by a malicious wrongful taking (*Crockett* v. *Miller*, 112 Federal 729; *Petrie* v. *Wardman-Justice Motors*, Sup. Ct. D. C. No. 71,338). This is a rule peculiar to replevin, where so regulated by statute, and is at variance with the general rule of law requiring the adjudication in one cause of action of all claims and demands growing out of a single tort.

REPNIN, ANIKITA IVANOVICH, Prince (1668–1726), Russian general, and one of the collaborators of Peter the Great. He took part in all the principal engagements of the Great Northern War. Defeated by Charles XII. at Holowczyn, he was degraded to the ranks, but was pardoned as a reward for his valour at Lyesna and recovered all his lost dignities. At Poltava he commanded the centre. From the Ukraine he was transferred to the Baltic Provinces and was made the first governor-general of Riga after its capture in 1710. In 1724 he succeeded the temporarily disgraced favourite, Menshikov, as war minister. Catherine I. created him a field-marshal.

See A. Bauman, *Russian Statesmen of the Olden Time* (Rus.), vol. i. (St. Petersburg, 1877).

REPNIN, NIKOLAI VASILIEVICH, Prince (1734–1801), Russian statesman and general, grandson of the preceding, served during the Rhenish campaign of 1748 and subsequently studied in Germany. Peter III. sent him as ambassador in 1763 to Berlin. The same year Catherine transferred him to Warsaw, with instructions to form a Russian party in Poland from among the dissidents, who were to receive equal rights with the Catholics. Repnin convinced himself that the dissidents were too poor and insignificant to be of any real support to Russia, and that the whole agitation in their favour was factitious. At last, indeed, the dissidents themselves even petitioned the empress to leave them alone. The attempt had failed, and Repnin went to fight the Turks. At the head of an independent command in Moldavia and Walachia, he prevented a large Turkish army from crossing the Pruth (1770); distinguished himself at the actions of Larga and Kagula; and captured Izmail and Kilia. In 1771 he received the supreme command in Walachia and routed the Turks at Bucharest. A quarrel with the commander-in-chief, Rumyantsev, then induced him to send in his resignation, but in 1774 he participated in the capture of Silistria and in the negotiations which led to the peace of Kuchuk-Kainarji. In 1775–76 he was ambassador at the Porte. On the outbreak of the war of the Bavarian Succession he led 30,000 men to Breslau, and at the subsequent congress of Teschen, where he was Russian plenipotentiary, compelled Austria to make peace with Prussia. During the second Turkish war (1787–92) Repnin was, after Suvarov, the most successful of the Russian commanders. He defeated the Turks at Salcha, captured the whole camp of the *seraskier*, Hassan Pasha, shut him up in Izmail, and was preparing to reduce the place when he was forbidden to do so by Potemkin (1789).

On the retirement of Potemkin (*q.v.*) in 1791, Repnin succeeded him as commander-in-chief, and immediately routed the grand vizier at Machin, a victory which compelled the Turks to accept the truce of Galatz (July 31, 1791). In 1794 he was made governor-general of the newly acquired Lithuanian provinces. The emperor Paul raised him to the rank of field-marshal (1796), and, in 1798, sent him on a diplomatic mission to Berlin and Vienna in order to detach Prussia from France and unite both Austria and Prussia against the Jacobins. He was unsuccessful, and on his return was dismissed from the service.

See A. Kraushar, *Prince Repnin in Poland, 1764–8* (Pol.) (Warsaw, 1900); "Correspondence with Frederick the Great and others" (Rus. and Fr.), in *Russky Arkhiv* (1865, 1869, 1874, Petersburg); M. Longinov, *True Anecdotes of Prince Repnin* (Rus.) (St. Petersburg, 1865).

REPORTING, the business of reproducing, mainly for newspapers, but also for such publications as the *Parliamentary* or *Law Reports*, the words of speeches, or of describing the events in contemporary history by means of the notes made by persons known generally as reporters. There was no systematic reporting until the beginning of the 19th century, though there was parliamentary reporting of a kind almost from the time when parliaments began, just as law reporting in the middle ages began in the form of notes taken by lawyers of discussions in court. The first attempts at parliamentary reporting, in the sense of seeking to make known to the public what was done and said in parliament, were made by the *Gentleman's Magazine* in 1736. Access to the houses of parliament was obtained by Edward Cave (*q.v.*), the publisher of this magazine, and some of his friends, and they took surreptitiously what notes they could. These were subsequently put into shape for publication by another hand. Such reporting was a violation of the standing order of the house, passed in 1728, declaring the publication of any of its proceedings to be a breach of privilege, and on the attention of the house being called in 1738 to the reports in the *Gentleman's Magazine* it threatened to proceed with the utmost severity against the offenders. Thereupon Cave published his reports as "Debates in the Senate of Lilliput," and instead of giving the first and last letters of each speaker's name, employed such barbaric terms as "Wingul Pulnub" for William Pulteney. Dr. Johnson composed the speeches for the *Gentleman's Magazine* from 1740 to 1743, the names of the speakers being given in full. Though he said he took care not to let the "Whig dogs" get the best of it, he really dealt out argument and eloquence to both political parties.

In the latter half of the century the newspapers began to report parliamentary debates more fully, with the result that, in 1771 several printers, including those of the *Morning Chronicle* and the *London Evening Post*, were ordered into custody for publishing debates of the house of commons. A bitter struggle between the house and the public ensued. In 1772 the newspapers published the reports as usual, and their right to do so has never again been really questioned. Early in the 19th century, greater freedom of access to both houses was given to newspaper reporters. Special galleries for their accommodation were provided in the legislative chambers of the new palace of Westminster erected in place of the old which was burned down in 1834. The press gallery of the house of lords was first used in 1847, and the press gallery of the house of commons in 1852. At this time the London newspapers had a virtual monopoly of parliamentary reporting, since only their representatives were admitted to the galleries.

The *Times* established a supremacy for the best parliamentary report, which has never been shaken. The other London papers, however, gave less and less attention to the debates while the leading provincial newspapers began to publish full reports of debates of local interest. They employed reporters in the service of the London journals but their reports were printed a day late. Then telegraphic wires from London were placed at the disposal of provincial newspapers from six o'clock at night till three o'clock in the morning. The arrangement was first made by the *Scotsman* and by other newspapers in Scotland in the 1860s. When the telegraphs were taken over by the state in 1870 the facilities for reporting were increased in every direction. News agencies undertook to supply the provincial papers, but the reports which any agency supplied were identical. In 1880 a select committee of the house of commons was appointed to consider whether the gallery should continue to be closed to all save the London papers and the news agencies. It reported in favour of the extension of the gallery and of the admission of provincial papers. The press gallery of the house of commons was accordingly enlarged and representatives of the leading provincial newspapers were admitted at the opening of the session of 1881. At this period the *Times* first established telephonic communication with the gallery. In 1951 that paper introduced a new tool of parliamentary reporting—the system of teletypesetting, by which a compositor in the palace of Westminster could set type by remote control of a linotype machine in the offices of the *Times.* This system had been used in the United States and by the *Scotsman* and the *Glasgow Herald* between London and their head offices.

What is commonly called "descriptive reporting" has in some cases nearly shouldered the reporting of speeches out of newspapers. The special correspondent or the war correspondent is a "descriptive reporter." The "interviewer" came into great prominence during the 1880s and 1890s. In 1900 in the English case of *Walter* v. *Lane* it was decided on the final appeal to the house of lords that the reporter of a speech, printed verbatim in a newspaper, was under the Copyright act of 1842 to be considered the "author." Absurd as it might seem to call the reporter the author of another man's speech, the decision gave effect to the fact that it is his labour and skill which bring into existence the "copy" to which alone can right of property attach. Strictly speaking, he is the author of the *report* of the speech; but for literary purposes the report *is* the speech. Any other persons present when the speech was made could equally have obtained copyright in *their* report of it; there may be more than one verbatim report, and therefore more than one "author." The effect of *Walter* v. *Lane* was not, it was considered, affected by subsequent legislation of the law of copyright.

Law reports have a special place in the English judicial system. When a new point of law is determined in a lawsuit, that case becomes in theory a precedent for future cases in which the same point arises. Whether a case in fact becomes a precedent depends mainly, however, on whether it is reported, and the reporting of cases has always been in private, or at least unofficial hands. Any law report made by a barrister may be cited in court—those, for instance, appearing in the *Times* are frequently so cited when no fuller report is available—but it is usual to cite reports specially prepared for the purpose. These should begin with a headnote stating succinctly the point determined, usually by reference to the facts found, followed by a full statement of the relevant facts, the arguments of counsel, and the judgment of the court on the law. Reports in this form date back to the time of Lord Mansfield, chief justice, in the late 18th century, and thereafter a strict doctrine of *stare decisis* evolved requiring the judges invariably to follow the decision of at least a higher court in future similar cases. In 1865 the Council of Law Reporting was set up, a non-profit-making body publishing the *Law Reports,* but a host of series of reports published commercially, mostly defunct by the mid-1950s, competed with them, often printing more cases. Accordingly in 1953 the council instituted the *Weekly Law Reports,* at least as full as any private series, only select cases of which appear finally in the *Law Reports.* The *Law Reports* alone set out the arguments of counsel, which add considerable value to a report; for if a point was missed it may be raised again in a future case to show that the reasoning of the court was wrong—*per incuriam.* The odd fact remains that the great majority of cases are never reported at all, and the selection of those so reported remains in unofficial hands. Comparison with other countries (such as the United States), where cases are generally reported, shows that the principle of *stare decisis* works better under the English system.

See also COPYRIGHT; NEWSPAPERS; PRESS LAWS; SHORTHAND; TELEGRAPH. (R. P. Cx.)

UNITED STATES

The first known reporting of news for current publication in America consisted of an account of a Guatemalan earthquake printed in a Mexican newssheet. The first known such publication in what is now the United States was in a broadside published in Boston in 1689 and entitled "The Present State of the New-English Affairs"; the reporter was Increase Mather, who told of what was being done in England in regard to the Andros revolution.

Because colonial papers were made up chiefly of articles taken from other newspapers issued in England and other colonial towns, essays, political documents, etc., direct reporting by newsmen connected with their respective papers was limited to brief pieces about the most important local happenings written by the editor or a friendly contributor. It was not until the rise of the "penny press" in the 1830s, with its emphasis on local news, that reporting came into its own as the most essential part of newspaper work. In 1851, Horace Greeley, one of the greatest U.S. editorial writers of the time, testifying before a British house of commons committee, insisted that U.S. readers gave far more attention to news than editorials. William Rockhill Nelson, founder (1880) of the *Kansas City Star,* declared, "The reporter is the essential man on the newspaper; he is the big frog in the puddle."

Types of News Reporting.—Most important of all are the local reporters, because (1) they outnumber those of any other category, and (2) local news is always regarded as of primary importance. A local reporter sometimes does little or no writing. A "leg man" telephones his news to a "rewrite man," and may visit the office of his paper only occasionally. A "cub" reporter is a beginner and usually has a routine "beat," while a "star" reporter receives from his editor the most important special assignments.

The capital, or state house, correspondent reports news of the state government. In states containing large cities, handling such news for metropolitan papers is a big task, especially during sessions of the legislature.

Washington correspondents cover the news of the national government. Their task is complicated, exacting, responsible. They cover the capitol, the White House, the various departments and bureaus, etc. There has been increasing insistence on "digging out" news of situations instead of waiting for its development in events, or merely collecting "handouts." There were about 1,400 reporters, including photographers, covering Washington in the 1950s, three-fifths serving daily newspapers, one-fifth radio and television and one-fifth periodicals.

Foreign correspondence is the goal of many ambitious reporters, but in peacetime United States papers and news agencies keep only about 300 full-time U.S. reporters abroad. When they work in war areas, these men and women become war correspondents, accredited by military, naval, or air commands. During World War II, the U.S. war department accredited 1,186 U.S. correspondents and news officials, and the navy department 460 more—a total of 1,646 newsmen for all media.

Distribution by Media.—In modern communication, reporting is by no means limited to the men and women who gather and write the news. Gathering is essential to the process, but the reporter may write, picture, or speak the news for newspapers, magazines, books, radio, television, or motion pictures.

Newsphotography has been a means of reporting ever since the American Civil War pictures of Mathew B. Brady, and movie news shorts have been used ever since the Spanish War motion pictures of J. C. Hemment. With the development of the inexpensive halftone engraving process in the last two decades of the 19th century, pictures as news made an increasingly important contribution to reporting.

Beginning with an amateur broadcast of election returns in 1916, radio gradually came to play a large and essential part in the news distribution system, and all large broadcasting stations include on their staffs local newsmen who make direct reports. The networks have their own reporters at Washington and abroad, and radio reporters have seats in the senate and house press galleries.

Reportorial Ethics.—Strides toward professional standing have been made by reporting, through (1) better training in schools of journalism and liberal arts colleges, and growing acceptance of specialized training for journalism by employing editors; (2) increasing group solidarity through organization and the recognition of such codes as the Canons of Journalism of the American

Society of Newspaper Editors and Walter Williams' "Journalist's Creed"; and (3) a better wage scale, largely through the efforts of the American Newspaper Guild, organized in 1933. (F. L. Mt.)

REPOUSSÉ (Fr. "driven back"), the art of raising designs upon metal by hammering from the back, while the "ground" is left relatively untouched. The term is often loosely used, being applied indifferently to "embossing." Embossing is also called *repoussé sur coquille* and *estampage,* but the latter consists of embossing by mechanical means and is therefore not to be considered as an art process. Moreover, it reverses the method of repoussé, the work being done from the front, and by driving down the ground leaving the design in relief.

Repoussé—a term of relatively recent adoption, employed to differentiate the process from embossing—has been known from remote antiquity. Nothing has ever excelled, and little has ever approached, the perfection of the bronzes of Siris (4th century B.C., in the British Museum), of which the armour-plate—especially the shoulder-pieces—presents heroic figure-groups beaten up from behind with punches from the flat plate until the heads and other portions are wholly detached—that is to say, in high relief from the ground of which they form a part. Yet the metal, almost as thin as paper, is practically of constant thickness, and nowhere is there any sign of puncture.

The art was not only Greek and Graeco-Roman in its early practice; it was pursued also by the Assyrians, the Phoenicians, and other oriental peoples, as well as in Cyprus and elsewhere, and was carried forward, almost without a break, although with much depreciation of style and execution, into mediaeval times. In the 11th century the emperor Henry II. presented as a thank-offering to the Basle cathedral the altar-piece, in the Byzantine style, decorated with fine repoussé panels of gold (representing Jesus Christ with two angels and two saints), which is now in the Cluny Museum in Paris. Up to this time, also, repoussé instead of casting in metal was practised for large work, and Limoges became a centre for the manufacture and exportation of sepulchral figures in repoussé bronze. These were affixed to wooden cores. By the time of Benvenuto Cellini the art was confined almost entirely to goldsmiths and silversmiths (who, except Cellini himself, rarely cast their work); and to them the sculptors and artists of to-day are still content to relegate it.

The elementary principle of the method, after the due preparation and annealing of the plate, was to trace on the back of it the design to be beaten up, and to place it face downwards upon a stiff yet not entirely unresisting ground (in the primitive stage of development this was wood), and then with hammers and punches to beat up the design into relief. According to Cellini, his master Caradosso da Milano would beat up his plate on a metal casting obtained from a pattern he had previously modelled in wax; but he is not sufficiently explicit to enable us to judge whether this casting was a hollow mould, which would result in true repoussé, or in the round, which is tantamount to *repoussé sur coquille,* or embossing.

Nowadays the plate is laid upon and affixed to a "pitchblock," a resinous ground docile to heat, usually composed of pitch mixed with pounded fire-brick, or, for coarser work such as brass, with white sand, with a little tallow and resin. This compound, while being sufficiently hard, is elastic, solid, adhesive and easy to apply and remove. Gold and silver are not only the densest and most workable but the most ductile metals, admitting of great expansion without cracking if properly annealed. The tools include hammers, punches (in numerous shapes for tracing, raising, grounding, chasing and texturing the surfaces), together with a special anvil called in French a *recingle* or *ressing,* in English "snarl." The *recingle,* or small anvil with projecting upturned point, was known in the 16th century. This point is introduced into the hollow of the vase or other vessel such as punch and hammer cannot freely enter, which it is desired to ornament with reliefs. A blow of a hammer on that part of the anvil where the prolongation first projects from it, produces, by the return spring, a corresponding blow at the point which the operator desires to apply within the vase. The same effect is produced by the modern "snarl" or "snarling iron"—a bar of steel, with an inch or two of the smaller end upturned and ending in a knob—held firmly in a tightly screwed-up vice, whereby the blow is similarly repeated or echoed by vibration. The repoussé work, when complete, is afterwards finished at the front and chased up. (*See also* EMBOSSING; BRONZE AND BRASS ORNAMENTAL WORK; SILVERSMITHS' AND GOLDSMITHS' WORK.) (M. H. S.)

REPRESENTATION, a concept with the broad general connotation of making present something or somebody that is not present; but more especially the term is used in a political meaning and pertains to modern government as a method of solving the problem of how to enable a very large number of people to participate in the shaping of legislation and governmental policy.

Representation in the broadest sense has roots which link it with the world of beliefs called magic, a world in which mysterious connections were regularly assumed to prevail between distinct persons and beings, both natural and supernatural. Without going into the historical evolution of the various meanings of "represent," "representation" and "representative," it is worth noting that the modern governmental meaning was not attached to these expressions until the 16th century, when the modern parliamentary development began. Sir Thomas Smith, in his *De Republica Anglorum* (1583), uses the expression freely in describing parliamentary institutions.

It must be admitted, however, that a magical element remained in spite of the continuous effort to rationalize the relationship spoken of as representation. Some writers, like Jean Jacques Rousseau, simply denied that representation of the will of the people is possible. While few would be willing to follow Rousseau, it is generally agreed that representation of the electorate in modern representative assemblies poses very real problems, because the views both of the representative and of those represented are likely to undergo change as the situation changes.

Theoretical Problems of Representation.—In large modern countries the people cannot, of course, assemble in the market place as they did in Athens or Rome. If, therefore, the people are to participate in government, they must select and elect a small number from among themselves to represent them and act for them. Through the course of a long historical evolution, the methods for such elections have been rationalized. The extended struggle over electoral reform in England was fought over this issue; rotten boroughs, patrons and other features of aristocratic nepotism were eliminated. In these reforms, Jeremy Bentham's rational principle of utility prevailed against Edmund Burke's earlier defense of traditional practices. Direct general elections are accepted as the most rational method for choosing representatives, whether they be legislative or executive. For executives are also representatives of the people. The view that this is not so is a survival of attitudes developed during the monarchical age, when progressive forces fought the crown as unrepresentative. It is important that executives be included among the people's representatives because of the paramount role the executive establishment plays in modern government. Public policy in most modern democratic governments is shaped as much by the executive as by the legislative. Since parties are usually led by the chief executive, their role in determining the pattern of representation strengthens the executive's representative position.

Somewhat different are the role and position of the courts. The thorough legal knowledge required of a good judge has stood in the way of choosing judges by election. Wherever judicial bodies have been elective, much dissatisfaction has developed. In most jurisdictions, judges are ordinarily selected on the basis of technical competence—a relatively objective standard. Elections have not seemed a rational method. The supreme court of the United States would seem to most people less representative if elected by the people. The reason for this is that all representation involves ideas; for only through an idea can the making present of one thing or person by another be conceived.

The deepest and most obscure aspect of representation is its ideological foundation. It has always been in controversy between those who would have the representatives of the people act as delegates carrying out instructions and those who would have them be free agents acting in accordance with their best ability and understanding. The latter alternative was stated by Edmund Burke in his celebrated speech to the electors at Bristol:

My worthy colleague [Burke's opponent for the seat] says his will ought to be subservient to yours. If that be all, the thing is innocent. If government were a matter of will upon any side, yours, without question, ought to be superior. But government and legislation are matters of reason and judgment, and not of inclination; and what sort of reason is that, in which the determination precedes the discussion; in which one set of men deliberate and another decide . . . ? To deliver an opinion is the right of all men; that of constituents is a weighty and respectable opinion, which a representative ought always to rejoice to hear; and which he ought always most seriously to consider. But *authoritative* instructions; *mandates* issued, which the member is bound blindly and explicitly to obey, to vote and to argue for, though contrary to the clearest conviction of his judgment and conscience; these are things utterly unknown to the laws of this land, and which arise from a fundamental mistake of the whole order and tenor of our constitution. Parliament is not a *congress* of ambassadors from different and hostile interests, which interests each must maintain, as an agent and advocate, against other agents and advocates; but parliament is a *deliberative* assembly of *one* nation, with *one* interest, that of the whole; where not local purposes, not local prejudices ought to guide, but the general good. . . .

Pushing the matter one step farther, Burke also stated:

Certainly, gentlemen, it ought to be the happiness and glory of a representative to live in the strictest union, the closest correspondence, and the most unreserved communication with his constituents. Their wishes ought to have great weight with him; their opinion high respect; their business unremitted attention. . . . But his unbiased opinion, his mature judgment, his enlightened conscience, he ought not to sacrifice to you, to any man, or to any set of men living. These he does not derive from your pleasure; no, nor from the law and the constitution. They are a trust from Providence, for the abuse of which he is deeply answerable.

Burke's idealistic conception accords neither with the reality of popular politics nor yet with the democratic ideal that the will of the people should prevail. The issue as to whose will is to prevail and is therefore to be taken as the will of the whole cannot be sidestepped by asserting, as Burke does, that parliament represents *one* nation, with *one* interest. While this is true in the abstract, the issue at hand is who is to say what that general interest is at a given time. For the conflict of various interests and their possible relation to a more comprehensive public interest is the real issue. Abstractly considered, a special mandate cannot be admitted, since it would make the members of representative assemblies into mandatories for special interests. But there is a great difference between a special mandate and a broad indication as to the general line of policy to be pursued.

It is possible to study the representativeness of representative assemblies in terms of the votes as they correlate with the known desires and views of the electorate. In 1928 Stuart Rice made an interesting investigation along these lines in the United States. He correlated the progressiveness of Minnesota legislators with the progressiveness of their districts. The result of his study showed, as might be expected, that there was a correlation, although "the coefficient of correlation was no higher than could be reasonably expected." Similar results were obtained when Rice inquired into the common assumption that men elect as representatives men "of their own kind." Using nationality as a factor, Rice found that Minnesota and Wisconsin legislators, more than 100 of whom were foreign-born, were favoured by those of their own nationality and that there existed "a well-marked disposition on the part of foreign-born voters to elect men of their own nationality." (Stuart Rice, *Quantitative Methods in Politics*, Appleton-Century-Crofts, Inc., 1928.) As a result of opinion polls, rich materials exist for further detailed correlation between the opinions and behaviour of representatives and those they represent. Perhaps further study will show that the preoccupations and prejudices of the voters themselves convert the representative into a delegate.

The reason that the elected representatives of a party can be said to represent their electorate is basically that these representatives and those whom they represent are bound together by a world of ideas and beliefs which they share. Consequently, it can be assumed that any conclusion the representatives come to with regard to a new issue is likely to be the same as the conclusion the electorate would have come to had it been able to consider the new facts. But we get lost in metaphysics of a rather shady sort when

we claim that the majority represents the minority in any concrete sense. It is the majority and the minority together who represent the people as a whole and their general interest. But what about the single chief executive? All attempts to lift a chief executive above parties have proved abortive. A disastrous example is provided by the institution of the presidency under the German republican (Weimar) constitution, where the superpartisan president eventually betrayed the republic. The third (French) republic narrowly averted a similar fate. Such insistence upon the nonpartisan character of the chief executive is a result of the persistence of ideas prevalent during the monarchical age, when the king or the crown was supposed to be the preordained representative of all.

Dual Nature of Representation.—Historically speaking, representative assemblies developed in most European countries in the course of the later middle ages as an important part of the mediaeval constitutional order. Though great variations existed, the three estates were usually composed of nobility, clergy and the merchants of the cities (the burgesses). In the English parliament the higher nobility was joined with the higher clergy in "the lords spiritual and temporal," while the lower squirearchy and the burgesses together constituted the commons. This system of two estates proved more viable than the commoner continental system of three. The representatives of the lower estate were originally called by the crown in order to secure additional financial support over and above the feudal dues. (*See* FEUDALISM.) Quite naturally, these representatives when gathered together proceeded to present complaints and petitions in an effort to strike a bargain. Such bargains were in favour of their own class. They represented their class as agents of the local powers and acted under instructions or mandates. But when, after the deal was struck, the king and the two houses of parliament acted together as "the king in parliament," they were taken to represent the whole realm. This historical background shows clearly that we are not justified in drawing the sharp distinction Burke had in mind between agents with definite instructions and representatives speaking for one nation. An elected body is both: a deliberative assembly from *one* nation with *one* interest, that of the whole, *and* a congress of ambassadors from different and hostile interests. We cannot escape from this dualism in political representation. Many political philosophers have tried to do it, but with unsatisfactory results. Thomas Hobbes's monistic conception, like that of fascists and Communists, is forced into seeking some kind of religious or inspirational sanction, deifying the state, or the proletariat, or the folk and their respective leaders. The dualism of representing both the whole and one or another of its parts lies deeply embedded in representative schemes.

Representation Defined.—In the light of the foregoing, it is possible to suggest a definition of political representation: Representation is the process through which the attitudes, preferences, viewpoints and desires of the entire citizenry or a part of them are, with their expressed approval, shaped into governmental action on their behalf by a smaller number among them, with binding effect upon those represented.

Some features of this difficult definition require further comment. We speak advisedly of attitudes, preferences, viewpoints and desires, rather than of will, influence or control, because the large citizen bodies of modern times do not possess a clearly defined will in most matters of public policy, because of lack of knowledge. We use the general expression "governmental action," rather than legislation or policy, because all kinds of governmental activity are expressive of popular reactions. Perhaps the most important part of this definition is the phrase "with their expressed approval." Since such approval can be secured only periodically, it must be in a form covering a specified period of time. No setting such as that of the German National Socialist regime can be called truly representative; for although the original grant of power was secured for four years, Adolf Hitler set this limitation aside and no one was able to challenge him. Hence, nothing done after 1937 can be called representative of the German people at large. Finally, it is essential for genuinely representative action that it be accepted by those represented as theirs and hence binding upon them in all its consequences—a result which flows from their expressed approval. But while periodic elections are the commonest method for demonstrating expressed approval, there are exceptions, such as courts, where the expressed approval may be found in a constitution adopted by common consent, or in a special interest represented, as in so-called economic councils.

SOME HISTORICAL AND CONSTITUTIONAL ASPECTS OF REPRESENTATION

Representative systems of the rationalized type are a modern growth. They certainly were not found, as Montesquieu implied, in the forests of ancient Germany. We have seen that political representation arose as part of the mediaeval constitutional order. Like so many mediaeval institutions, this political representation drew its inspiration from the church, whose vast body of the faithful was presumably represented by the great councils in which all Christian people were believed to be present.

Reasons for the Late Appearance of Representation.—But why did representation appear so late in the history of mankind? Essentially, the answer must be that it was not needed before modern times. The great empires of Asia had been animated by religious beliefs in which the individual human being counted for little and his personal preferences for less. In classical antiquity, with its city-states in which the personalist sense of man's dignity first crystallized, the small number of citizens permitted personal participation. Aristotle deemed this participation so vital that he opposed altogether a political framework larger than the average city-state. This necessity for personal participation became impossible of fulfilment whenever such a city-state expanded beyond the local unit. Attempts to solve the problem through federal organization foundered because of the lack of an ideological base upon which a representative scheme might have been evolved. The Romans undertook to embody the citizenry of each city of their Latin federation in the Roman citizenry by using various fictions, but the system broke down when Rome expanded and the Romans adopted the Asiatic technique of deifying the emperor. Still, the Roman constitution unquestionably contained elements of genuine representation. These elements were crippled, however, by the ascendancy of the unrepresentative senate. By contrast, the spirit of corporate solidarity in the mediaeval towns, shires, monasteries and cathedrals was sufficiently developed to render the group willing to exercise its participation in the larger community through representatives. Unless such solidarity provides a common base of ideas, true representation cannot take place.

Representation and Constitutional Government.—Except in small communities, constitutional government is impossible without a system of representation. Constitutional government is government in which the use of power is restrained by a constitution which defines the functions of various authorities. Restraint is indissolubly connected with dividing governmental power. Undivided power is unlimited power.

From a historical standpoint, the need for securing responsibility in government is the central objective in all the various schemes of representation. This is true even of completely supernatural and irrational schemes, such as that by which a king is supposed to represent God on earth. For this notion may be the most powerful restraint upon him and provide an impulse for him and his officials to act justly and avoid abuse of power. Examples abound not only in the experience of Europe but in such systems as the sultanate of Turkey or the empire of China. But this scheme works only as long as the faith lasts. If the ruler becomes an unbeliever, the most arbitrary tyranny easily develops.

The division of power may take many different forms. Perhaps the two most important modern forms are the so-called separation of powers, and federalism. For both, representation is of vital importance. Distinct federal divisions of the electorate, created and maintained under a constitution, require the selection of distinct groups of representatives among whom the several functions of government may be divided. The same is true under any kind of separation of powers; it presupposes a variety of representatives for different constituencies. Looked at from this angle, these schemes for dividing "power" really amount to dividing the people in a number of different ways and then giving these several subdivisions a voice in shaping governmental action through different representatives who are kept from abusing their power by holding each other in check. Such a plan could, of course, have no practical effect unless the community were actually divided into a number of groups, parties and classes.

Not only does constitutional government depend upon representation, but representation in turn depends upon constitutionalism. For unless the community is ready to agree upon and live by a basic charter in accordance with which authority is exercised, plans for representation are liable to break down, as they did in Italy and Germany. The representative quality rests upon a belief in common ground as far as doing things is concerned, and while there is no need for agreement on fundamentals other than the constitutional mores themselves, the latter, which have sometimes been called constitutional morality, are indeed of paramount importance. Representation, we might say, is a game in which the rules are prescribed by the constitution as approved by the people.

Representation and Legislation.—Ever since the 16th century, legislation has been considered the most important phase of governmental action. Legislation involves the making of rules binding upon the whole community. Such general rules, it was felt, should bear the closest possible relation to the community's general beliefs. The higher law which Sir Edward Coke and others expounded as the yardstick for evaluating parliamentary statutes was believed immutable, a precious heritage of principles upon which all legislation should be based. At this point, the Protestant idea that one cannot force men in matters of belief, now generally accepted by all Christians as well as by many other faiths, suggested the necessity of consent in matters of general legislation. A specific act of government may be justified in terms of a specific emergency, but no general rule can be considered valid unless assented to by those to whom it is to apply. Since the citizenry is too large, representation becomes essential. "No taxation without representation" is a vivid expression of this general view.

There is another aspect which suggests the use of representative assemblies as the natural agents for the purpose of making laws. A general rule presupposes that there is a series of events which have certain aspects in common. There must be a normal situation. If an event is recurrent, time elapses. Time is available, therefore, for deliberation to determine what is right and proper. Deliberative processes are therefore well suited to the relatively slow procedure of representative bodies. Nevertheless, the procedure of a well-organized representative assembly is so arranged as to result in action; namely, the adoption of a general rule. The enactment of such a general rule requires careful co-ordination of conflicting viewpoints; really workable compromises need to be reached. Through argument and discussion the area of agreement is determined in the representative legislature. It symbolizes the consent which legislation presupposes, if it is to be compatible with the dignity of man's autonomy in matters of basic conviction and belief.

ELECTORAL SYSTEMS AND REPRESENTATION

In our discussion so far we have spoken of electing representatives as if an election were as simple a thing as throwing a stone. Actually, some of the most difficult problems of representation cluster around elections. Should elections be secret or public? Should limiting qualifications be required of those participating in the elections? How should the country be divided so as to make it possible for people to vote? These and similar issues have all been sharply debated at one time or another, with a view to their bearing upon the central issue of making the results representative.

To the ancients, democracy meant that the whole citizenry met in the market place and decided all matters of common concern. To the modern world, democracy means that the whole citizenry goes regularly to elect representatives, after having read about their platforms in the newspapers or listened to them in a meeting or over the radio or television. But there is a great difference between those elections in which the citizen is confronted by a clear-cut alternative between electing either A or B, and thereby supporting either party X or party Y, and elections in which he must choose among A, B, C, D, E, F and so forth and thus align himself with one of at least half a dozen parties, none of which has any chance of securing a majority.

The English and U.S. System.—The so-called two-party system has long been traditional in the United States and Great Britain. British parliamentary government rested for a long time upon a strictly traditional system of elections. It abounded with abuses of all kinds, such as rotten boroughs. Through a series of reforms Britain eventually arrived, in 1884–85, at the single-member constituency, though the constituencies continued to lack uniformity of size and structure. Elections thereafter were decided in England by relative majority or plurality. This means that the candidate who secures the largest number of votes wins the seat. The elections are secret, though before 1885 they were public, with much brawling and rioting. The British electoral system is thus clearly directed toward the goal of dividing each constituency, and thereby all of the United Kingdom, into two parts: the majority which is to govern and the minority which is to criticize. This may mean permanent minority status for a man who belongs to the wrong party in a particular constituency. As the English economist Walter Bagehot (1826–77) once wrote (in *The English Constitution* [1873]), "I have myself had a vote for an agricultural county twenty years, and I am a Liberal; but two Tories have always been returned, and all my life will be returned." A Democrat in Vermont or a Republican in Alabama is in the same situation.

The main criticism brought against this system of single-member constituencies is that the number of representatives elected is usually not proportional to the ratio of votes cast. This is virtually certain to be the case, because in many constituencies one of the parties may predominate, as Democrats do in the southern states of the United States or Tories do in many rural constituencies in England. It may even happen that a minority of votes secures a majority of representatives.

Gerrymandering ("Electoral Geometry").—If the desirability of a majority (plurality) system of elections be conceded, the issue of how to divide the electorate appropriately is of great importance. As long as the population shifts, periodic readjustments of the boundaries of electoral districts are necessary, if gross injustices such as rotten boroughs are to be avoided. In the United States and elsewhere this issue is a familiar one; there is a recurrent political fight over reapportionment. Even with skilful and competent handling, there are bound to be lags. Under adverse conditions, reapportionment becomes a football of party politics. Since in order to gain a seat all a party needs is a small majority of votes, it is very tempting for the party in power to redraw the political map, that is, the boundaries of districts, wards and other subdivisions, so as to distribute its voting power most effectively. The resulting shapes of electoral subdivisions are often fantastic and not even always contiguous. Because a salamanderlike sprawling district was first constructed under a governor of Massachusetts, Elbridge Gerry, in 1812, this practice is known as gerrymandering. It is easy to construct cases which illustrate how the same electorate may give a majority to opposing parties as a result of adroit electoral geometry.

The Issue of Proportional Representation.—The nonproportionality of single-member constituencies electing representatives by pluralities as well as gerrymandering has given rise to a series of proposals for proportional representation which seek to remedy these defects. The idea first appeared in the French national convention in 1793, without practical results. It was further elaborated by the mathematician Joseph Diez Gergonne (1820) and developed independently by an English schoolmaster, Thomas Wright Hill, whose son took the idea to Australia (1839). At about the same time, in 1842, Victor Prosper Considérant proposed to the council of Geneva a proportional-representation scheme entitled *De la sincérité du gouvernement, lettre à MM. les*

membres du grand conseil . . . de Genève. Two years later Thomas Gilpin published a pamphlet *On the Representation of Minorities of Electors to Act with the Majority in Elected Assemblies* (1844). About 12 years later the Danish minister of finance, Carl Andrae, worked out a system resembling the Australian plan, but using ballots. Finally, in 1857, Thomas Hare expounded the plan definitively in *The Machinery of Representation,* which he developed more fully in 1859 in his *Treatise on the Election of Representatives, Parliamentary and Municipal.*

From this rapid survey it is clear that proportional representation responded to a widely felt need. The underlying idea of all the various proposals was to secure a representative assembly reflecting with more or less mathematical exactness the various divisions in the electorate. Why should such divisions be reflected? "The voice of minorities should be heard," is the answer.

The most penetrating philosophical argument in support of this general idea was set forth by John Stuart Mill in his *Considerations on Representative Government* (first published in 1861), in which he called it "one of the very greatest improvements yet made in the theory and practice of government." After briefly outlining Hare's scheme of proportional representation, Mill set forth its "transcendent advantages." "In the first place, it secures a representation, in proportion to numbers, of every division of the electoral body: not two great parties alone . . . but every minority in the nation. . . . Secondly, no elector would be nominally represented by someone whom he had not chosen. Every member of the House would be the representative of an unanimous constituency." Mill stresses the strong tie, the complete identification, the weakening of localism, the higher intellectual qualification of the representatives and the avoidance of collective mediocrity. Finally, Mill sees it as a check on "the ascendancy of the numerical majority" by offering "a social support for individual resistance. . . . a rallying point for opinions and interests which the ascendant public opinion views with disfavour." In his enthusiasm, Mill calls proportional representation "personal representation" which offers a refuge to the "instructed elite." No objections of real weight could be seen by Mill, though in his usual deliberate manner he examines a few which he finds wanting. Yet it is obvious that his whole argumentation rests upon certain unexplained major premises. His is an extreme individualist argument which he reinforces by the undemocratic preoccupation with the enlightened few who might be lost in the shuffle of the ignorant mass.

But the key assumption is that there can be no representation of the whole without a representation of each of the whole's parts. What actually is the primary function of a representative assembly? Is it to represent or is it to do something else? To put the question is to answer it. The primary function is to participate in governing. In order to be able to do that, a representative assembly needs a measure of cohesion. It cannot be, as we have seen, solely a congress of ambassadors from different and hostile interests. It must be able to reach decisions.

The elusive quality of Mill's approach is made evident by the opposing view of Walter Bagehot, another eminent writer on government and a liberal like Mill, albeit more to the right. Bagehot, in rejecting proportional representation, put the following question: What will proportional representation do to the *functioning* of a parliament as we know it? Bagehot was a practical man, a banker, and his great achievement in this debate was to spell out what everyone knew in practice, namely, that the function of a parliament was twofold: (1) for the majority to support the cabinet in its conduct of the government, and (2) for the minority to criticize the actions of the government. This combination of action and criticism enables a parliament to represent the people as a whole.

Bagehot considers the basic difference between election by majority and proportional representation the fact that proportional representation makes the constituency voluntary—each voter individually is able to choose his own constituency. He votes as a voluntary member of a group which has no other tie. A constituency being the group or segment of voters which is entitled to send a member to parliament or congress, this is indeed the basic point, although the language of proportional-representation advocates often obscures it. To put Bagehot's point another way, all proportional schemes suggest saying to the electorate: If a certain number among you, say 10,000, can agree upon a candidate, that candidate shall be elected. The majority system implies this approach: A certain number among you shall constitute an electoral district, and the one for whom the largest number among you vote shall be considered elected. "Under the compulsory form of constituency the votes of the minorities are thrown away. . . . Again this plan gets rid of all our difficulties as to the size of constituencies. . . . Again the admirers of a great man could make a worthy constituency for him." But central party organizations would acquire an overweening influence. "The crisis of politics would be not the election of members, but the making of the constituency. . . . The result of this would be the return of party men mainly. . . . Upon this plan, in theory voluntary, you would get together a set of members bound hard and fast with party bands and fetters infinitely tighter than any members now. . . ." These are brief bits from a memorable passage in Bagehot's *The English Constitution* which anticipated with remarkable clairvoyance some of the troubles that arose when proportional-representation schemes were actually tried. These arguments do not, of course, exhaust the problem. They are focused upon the issues which arise when the cabinet governs with the support of the majority of a parliament. They also fail to take into account the problems which arise when the divisions or cleavages among the electorate have gone so far that failure to represent them adequately would undermine the belief of the people in the justice of the constitution.

Theory and practice suggest that the truth lies somewhere between the lines of argument taken by Bagehot and Mill. There are situations, such as in multinational Switzerland, where proportional representation is probably to be preferred, but then parliamentary government should be discarded or at any rate considered very difficult of operation. There are others, such as in Great Britain, where the later evolution of parliamentary government, with its increasing emphasis on executive leadership, would seem to make a majority system advisable. In the United States the trend is in the same direction.

The Problem of Justice.—A broader philosophical issue which deserves special consideration is the justice of a representative system. Mill, in his plea for proportional representation, laid considerable stress upon this aspect. "There is a part," he wrote in *Considerations on Representative Government,* "whose fair and equal share of influence in the representation is withheld from them; contrary to all *just* government. . . . The injustice and violation of principle are not less flagrant because those who suffer by them are a minority. . . ." Mill considers this matter of justice to the minority so obvious that he proclaims representation in proportion to numbers the first principle of democracy. What kind of justice and democracy is this? Discarding for the sake of argument the extreme and atomistic individualism of Mill's approach, let us assume for the moment that representation should be that of individuals and that it is unjust to a minority not to be "represented," or "represented adequately." If there were only one such minority, perhaps it would not be too bad, although the number of representatives who would criticize rather than help to decide would be increased. It would mean less action, rather than different action. If there were many such minorities, so that no group any longer had a majority, it might mean complete inaction for long periods. This situation arose toward the end of the German republic and spelled its doom. It arose in France in the 1930s with disastrous effects, and again in the early 1950s. What then about justice for the majority? Is it not a question of competing claims? Why should the question of what is just to the minorities be given precedence over what is just to the majority? Admittedly, the majority wants some action. If such action is, through proportional representation, delayed or altogether prevented, what is the justice of that? Problems of justice are problems of adjustment between conflicting claims.

The election of representatives, therefore, always involves the paring down of some claims; justice can be achieved only through a careful balancing of these. Presumably the majority's claims are weightier than those of any minority. Representation is a broad thing: The majority participates through acting, the minority through discussion and criticism. Proportionalists fail to consider the possibility that there might not be any majority at all, in spite of the fact that the need for action, and hence the existence of a majority, may be paramount. A just government is above all a government which governs. No government which fails to do that can possibly be just.

Experience with Proportional Representation.—As contrasted with the time when Mill and Bagehot wrote, we possess today a substantial body of experience with the workings of proportional representation. But the conclusions to be drawn from this experience divide the experts. On the one hand we have the enthusiasts for the proportional scheme, who contend that it is the only truly democratic method which at the same time solves the problem of gerrymandering and other forms of corruption.

On the other hand, there are scholars like Ferdinand Aloys Hermens who have been inclined to blame proportional representation for the collapse of the German republic, as well as the general tendency toward the anarchy of multiple parties and boss rule. A detailed analysis of the experience of Belgium, the Netherlands, the Scandinavian kingdoms, Switzerland and Ireland, as well as local experience in the United States and in the British Commonwealth, makes it difficult for the detached observer to agree with either of these views. Leaving aside the rigid list system used in the German republic, and generally condemned, it would seem that all these countries achieved substantial stability and a great deal of social progress under proportional representation, whether combined with parliamentary government or not.

The systems differ from each other in many interesting details. In Belgium lists are used, but the voter can indicate personal preference for individual candidates; in the Netherlands the same is true, but there is also a national pool; in Norway and Sweden there are likewise lists in use, but the voter himself determines how the candidates on the lists are ranked. In Denmark a complicated plan of combining single-member constituencies with proportional representation by way of a transferable vote is employed. Switzerland makes use of a list system which gives the voter extreme freedom in making up his list and an almost mathematical representation of views in the community is achieved; yet the resulting complex party structure in the representative assembly permits effective action, because the Swiss do not use a parliamentary system of government. Finally, Ireland adopted the single transferable vote system long advocated by the British Proportional Representation society, with virtually every county an electoral district. A critical evaluation of the different systems must be looked for in the special works suggested in the bibliography below. Suffice it to say that these countries found proportional representation compatible with their governmental tasks and settled down to a general acceptance of it. The same may be said of quite a few U.S. municipalities.

The conclusion regarding proportional representation is not simple. It all depends upon the group and class structure of the community, the constitution and pattern of the government at large, the extent to which foreign policy is vital and imposes its requirements of integration and consistency. The fact that Switzerland does well under proportional representation does not prove that the United States would do well also. Newton D. Baker, referring to the experiment with proportional representation in Cleveland, wrote as follows: "We have groups of all sorts and kinds, formed around religious, racial, language, social and other contentious distinctions. Proportional representation invites these groups to seek to harden and intensify their differences by bringing them into political action where they are irrelevant, if not disturbing. A wise election system would invite them to forget these distracting principles." (*Cleveland Plain Dealer,* July 25, 1935.)

This is one side of the medal. The other side is that proportional representation does provide an opportunity for political self-expression to minorities which are already crystallized as politically self-conscious groups. If the representative assembly is capable of integrating these conflicting groups, either by foregoing the task of "supporting" the government, as in Switzerland, or by remaining content to co-operate with a monarchical head, as in the Scandinavian countries and the Netherlands, proportional representation may work better than a majority system. In many U.S. cities the city manager has provided a neutral balance wheel which enables a city council proportionally elected to function effectively.

In the last analysis, the problem of representation under modern conditions should be seen functionally in relation to the task assigned to the representatives. Legislation is one function, executive direction and leadership another, judicial and administrative determination something else again. Any system of representation, electoral or other, which works will be acceptable to the people at large and considered just; any system which fails to do so will be rejected or, as in Germany, will become a fatal flaw which may bring on the collapse of the entire governmental system. For technical as the problems of representation may seem, they relate to the very core of modern popular government: Unless the people can be made present in their thought, their opinions and their will, democratic government becomes impossible.

BIBLIOGRAPHY.—Beside the broad philosophical discussions and some continental legal studies, there are only rather partisan analyses. The broad treatments of comparative government contain general analyses. Here might be mentioned Carl J. Friedrich, *Constitutional Government and Democracy*, chs. XIV, XV and XX (1950), and Herman Finer, *Theory and Practice of Modern Government* (1932). Special treatments are to be found in G. H. Hallett and C. G. Hoag, *Proportional Representation—the Key to Democracy* (1937), and F. A. Hermens, *Europe Between Democracy and Anarchy* (1951). An important source is still the *Report of the Royal Commission Appointed to Enquire into Electoral Systems*, Cd. 5163, and its *Minutes of Evidence*, Cd. 5162 (1910). For the U.S. system, *see* C. E. Merriam and H. F. Gosnell, *The American Party System* (1940).   (C. J. FH.)

REPRESENTATIVE GOVERNMENT: *see* REPRESENTATION.

REPRISALS, acts of retaliation by one belligerent to compel the other belligerent to refrain from committing unlawful acts of war, and to comply with the recognized laws and customs of war. Reprisals should only be taken in the last resource. They should not be excessive and in no case be of a barbarous character. They should consist of a repetition of the same or similar acts, and, so far as possible, should be inflicted, not vicariously, but on the actual wrongdoer. The only authoritative rule is to be found in the *Oxford Manual of the Laws and Customs of War on Land* (1880) of the Institute of International Law. For the extent to which neutrals may be involved, *see* NEUTRALITY.

Certain measures of redress, short of war, are also termed reprisals. At the present time they usually take the form of the occupation of a port or some part of the territory of the offending state, or the seizure of its customs duties, or the detention of its vessels lying in the territorial waters of the injured state, or the institution of a pacific blockade. (*See* also BLOCKADE.)

See P. Cobbett, *Leading Cases on International Law* (1885); A. D. McNair, *The Legal Meaning of War and the Relation of War to Reprisals,* Grotius Transactions vol. ii (1926).

REPRODUCTION, the process by which a living thing, whether plant or animal, gives rise to another of its kind, is commonly cited as one of the outstanding characteristics of living matter. In so far as biologists have ever been able to discover, all life comes from pre-existing life. No living thing has ever been found to arise directly from nonliving matter. The only possible exception may be the filterable viruses, so-called because, being particles too minute to be visible under the highest powers of the microscope, they have their size estimated by the smallness of the pores through which they will filter. Such viruses apparently possess most of the characteristics of living matter including that of reproduction. The reproduction may be, however, merely the capacity for duplication from the products of their own chemical activities, or for reorganization of the several ingredients of the nutritive matrix in which they are located. In other words, they may be operating merely as centres of crystallization, as it were, of the various constituents of the surrounding medium into an organization similar to their own. This power is seemingly possessed by various nonliving fermentlike substances. How such synthetic duplication differs from ordinary protoplasmic reproduction—if it does—is by no means clear, since we still know so little about the chemical basis of the latter.

By Division and Growth.—At some point in their life cycle living things give rise to other living things like themselves or which will become like them through a process of development. In one-celled animals and in the simpler many-celled types, reproduction commonly consists in a division of a parent form into two or sometimes into several descendants. True protoplasmic growth is increase of living substance, and inasmuch as reproduction is a continuation of such substance in the form of new individuals, it may be looked upon as a process of overgrowth.

For purposes of emphasis and discussion it is common practice to state the two great aims or ends of all living organisms as: (1) preservation of the individual, and (2) perpetuation of the race, but since these are both based fundamentally on nutrition they do not stand wholly apart. Growth is the outcome of nutrition, and reproduction may be regarded as a form of discontinuous growth. Constructive metabolism proceeds to a certain limit, and then the organism divides, or part of it is detached and continues life activities as a separate individual. Or to state it another way, reproduction is a means by which metabolic activities established in a given individual are passed on to be continued in the form of new individuals.

By Germ Cells.—In more complex creatures reproduction is manifested by the giving off of special cells termed germ cells, or gametes, which either alone, or more commonly after pairing, give rise to new individuals. Germ cells which pair (fig. 6) are usually differentiated into macrogametes and microgametes, and commonly, particularly in animals, come to be borne by different parents which are then designated as male and female.

The Multicellular Body.—In unicellular organisms the new individuals may continue to live apart as independent cells, but in the more complex plants and animals the division products remain associated, growing and functioning as components of a more highly specialized order (fig. 11). The advantage in this is evident, since each unit cell, although in a large measure retaining its identity, can, together with certain of its fellows, specialize in the perfection of some particular function, while depending on neighbouring groups of cells for the more effective carrying-out of other functions necessary to the organism as a whole. Just as in human society it is advantageous to have such specialists as carpenters, electricians, shoemakers, bakers, merchants, teachers, doctors and others, so in cell aggregates specialization in different directions, as for motion, digestion, sensation and the like, permits of the development of a more complex and efficient organism.

Although certain unicellular forms and certain nutritive cells, such as egg cells, may be visible to the unaided eye, cells for the most part are of microscopic dimensions. The clue to their small size, and possibly to the reproduction of organisms by division in the first place, lies apparently in the physical necessity of maintaining a certain ratio between surface and mass in a functioning body. It is a physical law that surface increases as the square, and mass as the cube. Or to put it more concretely, when a cell doubles in diameter the mass to be nourished increases eightfold but the surface through which nourishment is to be absorbed and wastes discharged increases only fourfold. It is evident, therefore, that with any considerable increase in size, the supply of foodstuffs and oxygen from without and the elimination of wastes from within must fall below the needs of the cell since the surface becomes insufficient to provide for the exchange. The cell solves this problem by dividing, thus reducing mass and increasing surface. This necessity of maintaining a certain balance between mass and surface, indeed, is probably back of the first protoplasmic reproduction. As already noted, it is essentially a matter of overgrowth and division, or, in other words, discontinuous growth.

The Rise of Sex.—Superimposed upon this original method of direct reproduction, however, we find, even in the firstlings of life, the foreshadowing of sex. Beginning with the simplest organisms, temporary or permanent pairing of two individuals may occur before initiation of reproduction. Out of this has grown sex, and as a result unquestionably much of the complexity and diversity of all higher organisms, whether plant or animal.

To understand the significance of reproduction and the intricacies imposed upon it through sex, it is well to begin with its initial expressions in the unicellular organisms, most of which are too small to be seen without the aid of a microscope. Probably the simplest living things are the blue-green algae. Examining the one-celled body of the most primitive of these, one sees a homogeneous granular-looking material which is really of jelly-like consistency. This is the essential living substance or protoplasm (*q.v.*). In these simple algae it is suffused by two pigments, a blue and a green, and is encased within a protecting and supportive wall—a lifeless product of the protoplasm itself termed cellulose. The green component, chlorophyll, is a pigment which is present in all green plants. Chlorophyll has the remarkable capacity of enabling plant protoplasm to utilize in the synthesis of food the energy supplied by sunlight. Out of the two simple raw materials, carbon dioxide (CO_2) and water (H_2O), which

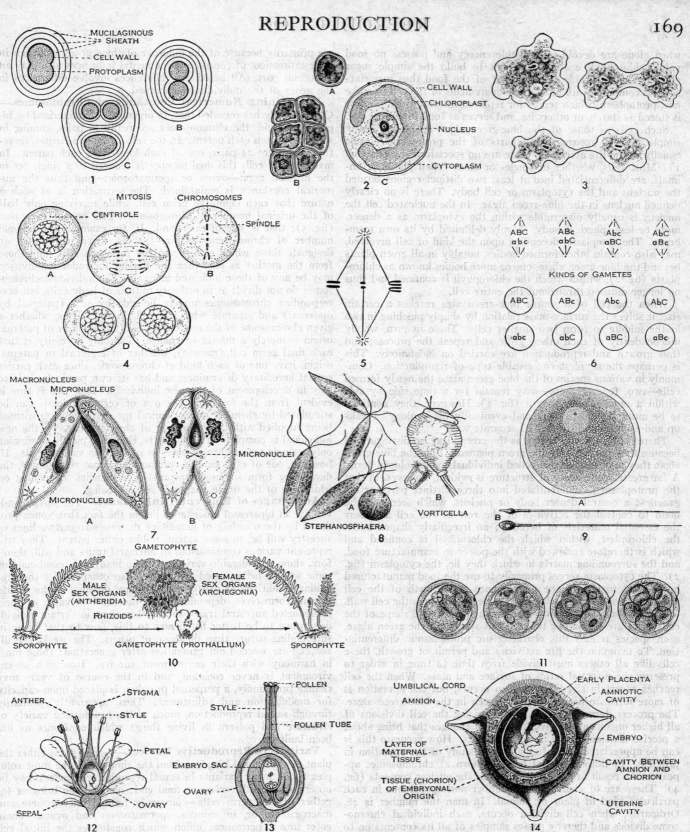

Fig. 1. Division stages of a blue-green alga (*Gloeothece*). Fig. 2. A, single cell; B, colony of green alga (*Pleurococcus*); C, highly magnified *Pleurococcus* showing cell organs. Fig. 3. Amoeba reproducing by division. Fig. 4. Mitosis in a cell possessing six chromosomes (three pairs): A, chromatin diffusely distributed in nucleus (resting stage); B, equatorial plate stage with chromatin concentrated into six chromosomes ready for division (precocious division before alignment on spindle is not uncommon); C, divergence of divided chromosomes and beginning of cytoplasmic division; D, division completed. Fig. 5. Chromosomes arranged for reduction division. Fig. 6. Eight kinds of gametes may result from the reduction divisions of a germ cell possessing three pairs of chromosomes (ABC from one parent, abc from the other). Fig. 7. A, beginning of conjugation in *Paramecium caudatum*; B, diagram of two conjugating paramecia (the macronuclei disintegrate; after several micronuclear divisions, all micronuclei but two disappear in each individual; one of these then passes to the opposite individual and fuses with the residual micronucleus; the animals then separate and after several divisions each descendant resumes the original state with one micronucleus and one macronucleus). Fig. 8. A, fusion of two protozoa (*Stephanosphaera*) of equal size; B, fusion of two of unequal size (*Vorticella*) to form a new individual. Fig. 9. Human ovum and human spermatozoon (showing different aspects of latter). Fig. 10. Alternation of generations in the fern; left and right, sporophyte stages; centre, the gametophyte (prothallium). Fig. 11. Two-, three-, four- and eight-celled stages in the cleavage of the monkey ovum (drawn from photographs of the living cells by Lewis and Hartman). Fig. 12. Parts of the flower. Fig. 13. Enlarged ovary of flower showing path of fertilization and the greatly reduced gametophyte. Fig. 14. Schematic illustration of very young human embryo in the uterus

when alone are devoid of available energy and possess no food value, chlorophyll enables the plant to build the simple sugar glucose, rich in usable energy. Part of the food thus manufactured is combined with nitrogenous ingredients of the cell to make new protoplasm, which serves for replacement and growth; some is stored as starch, or otherwise, and serves as food for future use.

Such cells as those of the blue-green algae are exceptionally simple in that apparently all parts of the protoplasm engage equally in the life activities; there are no specialized regions (fig. 1). Most cells, whether of single- or many-celled plants or animals, are differentiated into at least two distinct regions termed the nucleus and the cytoplasm or cell body. There is no clearly defined nucleus in the blue-green algae. In the nucleated cell the nucleus is usually discernible within the cytoplasm as a denser, more or less spherical body, sharply delimited by its own membrane. The cytoplasm, depending upon the kind of cell involved, may also contain other formed bodies, notably in all green plants beyond the blue-green algae, one or more bodies known as chloroplasts (fig. 2), within which the chlorophyll is confined and thus no longer diffused throughout the entire cell.

When the cell of a simple blue-green alga reaches a certain size, it solves the surface-mass relation by simply pinching in two in the middle to form two smaller cells. These in turn, wholly independently of each other, grow and repeat the process; and thus growth and reproduction are carried on indefinitely. This is perhaps the simplest conceivable type of reproduction. Commonly in various species of the blue-green algae the newly formed cells—two, four or more—may remain for a time side by side within a mucilaginous sheath (fig. 1). However, they continue to be mutually independent and eventually the "colony" breaks up and each individual goes its separate way.

There is also a group known as the green algae, so distinguished because they possess only the green pigment. Like the blue-green algae they may exist as one-celled individuals or in colonial form. A far greater complexity of structure is evident, however, in that the protoplasm is differentiated into three distinct parts or organelles: a central denser body or nucleus, which seems in the main to control the activities of the rest of the cell and bear the essential materials of heredity; an irregularly shaped body, the chloroplast, within which the chlorophyll is confined and which is therefore endowed with the power to manufacture food, and the surrounding matrix in which they lie, the cytoplasm (fig. 2). The cytoplasm serves primarily to use the food manufactured by the chloroplast in the maintenance and growth of the cell and to regulate the interchange of materials through the cell wall.

Mitosis and the Genes.—Although the size and shape of the cell varies greatly among the different species of the green algae, each species retains this characteristic protoplasmic differentiation. To maintain the life activities and permit of growth, these cells like all others must divide from time to time in order to preserve the essential ratios of surface and mass. When the cell reaches a certain size-limit division occurs, but the operation is of more intricate nature than that seen in the blue-green algae. The process, termed mitosis, characterizing the cell divisions of all higher organisms, involves a series of changes that bring about a precise division of the nuclear contents. How accurate this is can be appreciated only after a careful study of the operation in progress. In mitosis special bodies known as chromosomes appear as the result of a rearrangement of the nuclear contents (fig. 4). These are of characteristic number and appearance in each particular kind of plant or animal. In man the number is 48. Ordinarily, when cell division occurs, each individual chromosome divides and thereby passes samples of all its contents on to the new cells. Painstaking studies by means of the highest powers of the microscope have revealed that each chromosome carries, chainlike, a series of still smaller units, the chromomeres, representatives of each of which are contributed to the new generation of cells. Evidence from various sources establishes that the fundamental units of heredity, the genes, reside in these individual particles or chromomeres, and that thus with their division and regrowth each newly formed cell gets a full contribution of the inheritance mechanism. All characteristics of living organisms

are primarily because of the influence of these genes, although in their expression, of course, environmental influences also play an important part. All hereditary differences involve differences in the genes of the individuals concerned.

Maintaining Numerical Constancy of Chromosomes.—Careful study has revealed that, in organisms characterized by biparental origin, the chromosomes are really in pairs, coming in single sets from each parent. In the cells of human tissues, therefore, there are 24 pairs, one of each kind from each parent. In mature germ cells this dual number is reduced to a single set in the finished germ—ovum or spermatozoon—and thus the numerical constancy is maintained. The separation is of such a nature that each definitive germ cell, while receiving only half of the original number of chromosomes, gets one of each pair (fig. 5); that is, one of each kind. If, for example, the original number of chromosomes is six—that is, three pairs—and we designate those which come from the father as ABC and those from the mother as abc, then the line-up for reduction-division may be any of those indicated in fig. 6. The individual chromosomes do not divide as in ordinary mitosis of body cells, but corresponding chromosomes merely lie side by side (paternal by maternal) and separate when the cell divides. Thus, whether a given chromosome of the reduced set is of maternal or of paternal origin is merely a matter of chance. The only necessity is that each final germ cell (gamete), whether of maternal or paternal origin, have one of each kind of chromosome, since each carries special hereditary determiners and has its own particular role to play in development of the new individual. That this is true is evident from the fact that the ova of certain animals can be stimulated by chemical or mechanical means to develop without being supplied with the second set of chromosomes, yet the new individual is complete in all its parts, though typically possessing only a single set of chromosomes in each of its various cells. If, however, one of each kind of chromosome is not represented, the developing form shows characteristic deficiencies, depending on which one of the single (haploid) set is missing.

Advantages of Biparental Inheritance.—The obvious advantage in biparental inheritance lies in the fact that young produced by the mingling of hereditary materials from two lines of ancestry will be, to some extent, unlike either parent. They will represent various combinations of ancestral traits and will, therefore, show considerable variety. Of the many new combinations some will be better fitted to survive than others under the prevailing conditions of existence. As many different paths of life present themselves, depending upon the survival value of their commingled ancestral traits, the combinations in certain individuals prove to be better fitted now to this, now to that niche in surrounding nature than do those of others. The weak, the ill-adapted are weeded out generation after generation; those most in harmony with their environment survive. Inasmuch as environment is never constant, and in the course of years may change profoundly, a perpetual premium is placed upon capacity for modification and adjustment. Thus, apparently, primarily through sexual reproduction, much of the bewildering variety of structure and pattern in living things which confronts us has been built up.

Variants in Reproductive Devices.—As one scans either the plant or the animal kingdom from the simplest to the most complex types, many variants in sexual reproductive devices may be observed. But all serve one final end; namely, the bringing together of two germ cells—commonly termed microgamete and macrogamete or, in animals, spermatozoon and ovum. These enter into a permanent union which constitutes the initial cell from which, through a succession of cell divisions, the new organism will arise. It is important to remember that no matter how discrepant these pairing gametes may be in size, they each carry the same number of chromosomes and therefore contribute the same number of genes.

In the simplest plants or animals the cells which unite may be of similar size; but, as forms rise higher in the scale of life, discrepancy in size becomes apparent until in the most complex organisms it may be extreme. The human ovum, for instance, although itself only about 1/125 of an inch in diameter, has a volume about 35,000 times that of the sperm (fig. 9), yet each contributes 24 chromosomes to the zygote.

Advantages of Dimorphic Gametes.—Apparently it has been found advantageous in organisms of biparental origin to have one of the gametes conserve stores of food for consumption of the newly developing form. But, since such increased bulk diminishes activity, a compensatory reduction in size commonly accompanied by motility develops in the opposite or male gamete. Moreover, inasmuch as the burden of effecting union has fallen largely to the microgametes, they have come to be produced in prodigious numbers, thus ensuring that one will reach and fertilize the more inactive macrogamete. In witness of this one has only to recall the countless millions of pollen grains, each bearing a microgamete, produced by a flowering plant, or the equally great numbers of spermatozoa carried in a single milligram of semen.

The occurrence of sex throughout the whole range of life, from all but the simplest organisms to man, is self-evident expression of its importance. It so pervades the make-up of the higher animals and plants that the significance of much of their structure and behaviour is interpretable only in terms of it. The reciprocal sexual structures and activities between the two forms we designate as male and female, whether in plants or animals, have come to their present state of mutual adaptation through millions of years of selection, and either set of such differences would be wholly meaningless without the other. Not only have special structures arisen which are connected with the reproductive system, but innumerable secondary characters such as devices to ensure pollination in plants, or ornaments which serve for allurement or sex-identification in animals, have appeared. There was much less intricacy in the make-up of living organisms during the millions of years of their existence before the coming of sex, but from that time on increasing complexities appeared in many groups and in many directions so that diversity of form and structure multiplied rapidly. It seems improbable, indeed, that living things could have become so remarkably complex without the establishment of sex.

Although the fundamental factors involved in reproduction, whether asexual or sexual, are readily discernible, the secondary differences in structures, activities and mutually adaptive relations which appear in both the plant and the animal kingdom become bewildering in their diversity. While most of these are interpretable in terms of special environing conditions, the paths of procedure are often very circuitous and the processes understandable only in terms of the distant ancestry from which modern forms have been derived.

In Unicellular Organisms.—Among one-celled organisms, whether plant (Protophyta) or animal (Protozoa), some form of division—equal fission as in the amoeba (fig. 3), budding or spore formation—is the dominant procedure even though it may be alternated, especially in the higher types, with occasional pairing analogous to the sexual unions of multicellular forms (Metazoa). In some members of the most primitive of the main groups of Protozoa (Rhizopoda, forms which can acquire large surface by the flowing out of pseudopodia) sex is possibly in a way foreshadowed in some in the coalescence of amoebulae into plasmodia as in the slime molds (Mycetozoa) from time to time. And the multiple conjugation seen in some Heliozoa and other protozoa, as well as in certain algae, may be a still further advance of the same nature. Such multicellular formations, through confluence of a number of individual cells, however, seem early to have given place to the union of only two cells, as seen in all higher organisms, and therewith the development of the bisexual form of reproduction characterized by the appearance of male and female types. In such protozoa as the colonial flagellate *Stephanosphaera,* the total fusion (conjugation) of two indistinguishable units (isogamy) occurs (fig. 8a); in others, such as *Vorticella,* the conjugating units differ in size (anisogamy, fig. 8b). In many different kinds of protozoa (for example, the radiolarians), special reproductive units (gametes) arise by division of the ordinary vegetative units. Such gametes are commonly dimorphic, and they unite in pairs to form a zygote, which may either grow into the original form or subdivide into many smaller individuals.

In any discussion of the evolution of sexual reproduction the situation seen in paramecium, a member of the most complex class of protozoa, the Infusoria, is interesting and instructive. Paramecium (fig. 7) possesses a large oval nucleus (macronucleus) and, in a small depression in its side, a tiny, spherical micronucleus. The macronucleus seems to be wholly nutritive; the micronucleus, reproductive in function. Commonly the elongate animal reproduces by a simple transverse fission into two. After a number of such divisions—usually several hundred—the process is interrupted ordinarily by a temporary union of two individuals during which, after disintegration of the macronucleus and elaborate preparations of the micronucleus, micronuclear material is exchanged. The animals then separate and resume reproduction by division. Regrowth is rapid and, under favourable conditions, 4 divisions in 24 hr. may occur. Calculations show that a single paramecium could thus produce 268,000,000 offspring in one month.

Investigations have shown that although the individuals of a particular species of paramecium may look alike, nevertheless they are divided into mating types. Individuals of the one type, commonly the progeny of a single individual (clone), ordinarily will not unite with each other but will conjugate actively with members of other strains. In some species such as *Paramecium bursaria,* as many as eight distinct mating types have been identified, members of any one of which, though not conjugating together, would conjugate readily with members of any of the other seven types. Variants are known, however, in which members of one mating type will conjugate with only one or a few of the other mating types.

In nonconjugating strains of paramecium, however, a process of internal nuclear reorganization, known as endomixis, occurs from time to time which apparently effects a physiological readjustment similar to that following conjugation. This suggests that some form of occasional constitutional reorganization is necessary. Although usually secured through nuclear exchange, under unusual conditions it may thus by endomixis be otherwise accomplished.

The exhaustive studies of Prof. H. S. Jennings and his associates, made to determine in what respect conjugating and nonconjugating members of the same stock differ, are enlightening. One of the fundamental experiments was to divide a given strain into two parts and keep them under identical conditions, except that conjugation was permitted in one line and prevented in the other. The nonconjugating strains maintained about the same even rate of division, with no evidence of decline. In the conjugating strains, however, marked differences in division rate appeared in different families. Thus, hereditarily diverse families arose even though the conjugating strains were all derived from the same parental stock. Evidently great variety resulted from the new combinations of hereditary characters incident to the interchange of nuclear materials between the two conjugants. Some of the new strains thus secured were vigorous, others weak. Obviously, such combinations as possessed survival value under the conditions prevailing would result in the perpetuation of the fortunate strains. It is significant, furthermore, that unfavourable changes of the conditions under which these infusoria live usually induce conjugation.

Such facts among the protozoa bear out the inference already reached regarding the relation between sex and heredity in the higher animals, namely, that there is enormous insurance value in the constitutional diversity brought about by biparental inheritance—insurance that, in a changing environment, at least some of the variants will probably prove fit.

Rejuvenescence.—It is believed by some biologists that sexual reproduction not only results in a diversified progeny but that the fusion of the two germ cells, or the exchange of reproductive nuclei in protozoa, also commonly induces an actual rejuvenescence—a restoration of youth, as it were—to the protoplasm of the newly formed zygote. Professor G. N. Calkins has shown, for example, that in the protozoan *Uroleptus mobilis* actual rejuvenescence follows conjugation. In this species, after about

200 or more divisions, in the absence of conjugation, the division rate slows down and the individuals pass into a decline followed by structural degeneration and death. Conjugation, however, renews the waning activities of the protozoon and initiates a new cycle of active growth and division.

Asexual Reproduction in Multicellular Organisms.—In the lower levels of many-celled animals and extensively throughout the plant kingdom, it is common for more or less of the parent body to separate off as a new individual which may or may not become wholly free. In some instances, as in the sea anemone, the entire body may split longitudinally into two. The fresh-water *Hydra* buds off new individuals when food is abundant. On the other hand, a starving hydra may reabsorb its own buds. Certain species of starfish multiply by separating off their arms (*see* REGENERATION). And various wormlike forms, especially among the flatworms and the nemertine worms, may divide into several pieces, each of which develops into a completely functioning individual. In certain cases the asexual multiplication leads to the formation of colonies in which the individuals remain attached, as in the zoophytes and corals, the polyzoa and the compound tunicates.

Among plants an endless variety of asexual reproduction is evident, ranging from the innumerable forms of bulbs or bulblike structures to the new individuals produced through the sending out of runners, as in the strawberry, which root at intervals.

Hermaphroditism.—Many common animals, such as hydras, flatworms, earthworms, leeches and snails may have both ovary and testis present in the same individual (hermaphroditism), though not uncommonly the ova and the spermatozoa mature at different times, so that in spite of their double sex there is cross-fertilization. In such forms as the earthworm, for example, when two individuals enter into sexual union, they pair in such a way that the sperm receptacles of each conjugant are stocked with spermatozoa from the other, and when the eggs are shed they are thus fertilized by spermatozoa from the other individual. In various of the internal parasites, such as the liver flukes and tapeworms, there is self-fertilization (autogamy).

Alternation of Generations.—Although the asexual mode of reproduction is common in all except the highest metazoa and in the great majority of the metaphyta, these all, for the most part, also exhibit sexual reproduction. The latter becomes of increasing importance in the ascending scale of structural complexity. The highest animals which show asexual reproduction in the adult stage are the Tunicata. Here, in the salps, a solitary, so-called nurse buds off a chain of sexual individuals which eventually separate. The alternation of a nonsexual polyp form with a sexual medusa form, seen in the Coelenterata, is one of the most commonly cited examples of alternation of generations (metagenesis). Hydroid colonies are formed in such small branching colonial animals as Obelia, for example, by growth and budding from an original free-swimming planula larva which has become attached. To the human eye such colonies look like minute branching plants attached to submerged objects in the shallow water along the seashore. At the end of each branch is a nutritive polyp. From time to time cylindrical individuals (gonangia) arise which come to bear small lateral medusa buds. These eventually mature and are set free as minute medusae or jellyfish. The free-swimming medusae produce ova and sperm and thus reproduce sexually. Each fertilized ovum grows into a polyp, which again by budding produces the original nonsexual colonial type.

A classical example of metagenesis also frequently pictured in textbooks is that of a much larger kind of jellyfish known as *Aurelia*. A free-swimming embryo becomes attached and develops into a polyp which, through a system of transverse budding (asexual reproduction), eventually becomes subdivided into a stack or column of saucer-shaped young medusae (ephyrae). These become free and swim away as individual jellyfish that produce ova and sperm and thus reproduce sexually. From the fertilized ova the new generation of polyps is produced. Not all coelenterates, however, exhibit such alternations of polyp and medusa generations. Many medusae are known in the life cycle of which there is no polyp form and the entire great group of

anemones and corals, though for the most part reproducing by division as well as by eggs, have no medusa stage.

In the early developmental stages of even the highest vertebrates, however, twins or even quadruplets may arise by division of a single egg or embryo. Identical twins in man, for example, are believed by some embryologists to arise in this way. And in such simpler mammals as the armadillo the quadruplets which constitute the usual litter are definitely known to have been derived from a single ovum. The same is true of the multiple embryos which spring from a common source (polyembryony) in such parasitic insect forms as *Encyrtus*. In such vertebrates as the amphibia it is a relatively simple laboratory experiment to separate the first two cleavage cells of the dividing ovum and demonstrate that each will then develop into a complete and normal larva instead of the half of one it would have been without the operation.

In plants alternation of sexual with asexual generations is conspicuous in mosses and ferns. In such plants one phase in the life history (sporophyte) has to do with the production of spores—special reproductive cells which develop without fertilization. The second phase (gametophyte) is characterized by the production of macrogametes and microgametes, corresponding to the ova and spermatozoa of animals. Such gametophytes, therefore, constitute the sexual generation. In ferns, for example, spores are discharged from spore cases located on the fronds. Such as land on moist soil or sometimes on the fern frond itself, develop into small sexual plants termed prothallia (gametophytes). These eventually develop the usual two types of sex cells, the macrospores and the microspores (fig. 10). When the egg cell of such a prothallus is fertilized by a sperm cell (antherozoid) it grows into the familiar fern plant (sporophyte). In flowerless plants, and in the primitive flowering plants known as cycads and gingkos, the male cell (antherozoid) is locomotor as in most animals.

In flowering plants such alternate occurrence in one life history of two or more distinctive forms is not so obvious as in ferns and mosses, but close inspection shows that the male and female gametophytes exist in much reduced form as minute structures dependent on the sporophyte. The pollen grain, for example, is not itself a male germ cell but is really a minute gametophyte or bearer of the functional sperm cell. Likewise, the functional egg cell is borne by a female gametophyte or embryo sac which is a part of the flower itself (fig. 13). Looked at from the standpoint of alternation of generations the plant body which bears the flowers is the sporophyte, while special parts of the flower represent the gametophytes. Usually, an eight-celled structure, one cell of which is the egg cell, constitutes the female gametophyte (macrogametophyte); and (2) an even more reduced structure consisting of two sperm nuclei and a pollen tube nucleus constitutes the male gametophyte (microgametophyte).

The microspores form within the anthers (fig. 12) and upon nuclear division become pollen grains. The dehiscence of the pollen sacs frees the pollen. Shortly before or after being shed, a tube nucleus and two sperm nuclei arise from an earlier nucleus. One sperm nucleus eventually unites with the egg to form the fertilized egg or zygote; the other unites with the so-called fusion nucleus (*see* centre of embryo sac, fig. 13) to form a triple-fusion nucleus made up of three haploid sets of chromosomes. The zygote germinates to form the young sporophyte. The triple-fusion nucleus, in some seeds, gives rise to a nutritive endosperm around the embryo.

Where alternation of asexual with sexual generation occurs in either the plant or the animal world, it is usually associated with some advantageous hastening of productivity in favourable seasons of the year or under other special environing conditions. In the competitions of living things the struggle is severe, and great numbers must be produced in order that a select few, adapted to the prevailing conditions, may survive and maintain the race. Commonly, the quickest and easiest way to get numbers is through asexual reduplication, leaving it to the slower and more intricate methods of sexual reproduction to establish from time to time that variability which is necessary as the basis for adaptive selection.

Dual Hosts.—Some of the most complicated life cycles are found under specially hazardous conditions of existence, where the chances against successful propagation are meagre. Numerous examples occur among the internal animal parasites. If parasites increased in too great numbers within a given host, not only would the host be destroyed but with it often the parasites themselves. This is avoided commonly by the utilization of two hosts, part of the life cycle being passed in one, part in the other. Thus, in such human parasites as malaria, for example, female mosquitoes from any of the several species of *Anopheles* are the sources of infection in man. Spindle-shaped cells (sporozoites), which invade the human red blood corpuscles, are injected from the saliva of the mosquito when she bites. These multiply by division within the red blood cells. Liberated through destruction of the corpuscles they enter new red cells, and the process is repeated until a large number of red blood corpuscles have thus been destroyed and the number of parasites enormously increased. Such reproduction in the blood cells of man (primary host) are asexual. Eventually male and female gametocytes are formed, but these undergo their final transformations and conjugation only if withdrawn from the blood of man into the stomach of the anopheles mosquito (secondary host). The resulting zygotes penetrate to the outer wall of the mosquito's stomach where, in saclike pockets, they undergo repeated nuclear divisions with the eventual formation of numerous spindle-shaped sporozoites. With the rupture of the surrounding sac, the sporozoites make their way through the body spaces to the salivary glands of the mosquito whence they are injected with the saliva into the human host.

Many similar examples of alternate hosts might be cited among both vertebrates and invertebrates, and the various devices hit upon for securing transmission from one host to another afford some of the most complex and perplexing chapters in the study of animal relations. In the common pork tapeworm (*Taenia solium*), for example, man, the primary host, becomes parasitized by eating underdone pork (secondary host) which contains the encysted larvae. When taken into the human alimentary canal, the small head, bearing suckers and a circlet of hooks, attaches to the intestinal wall and the worm begins to grow rapidly in length by the formation of segments. These increase in size from the anterior toward the posterior end, new segments arising in the narrow neck region. The whole chain is regarded by zoologists as a colony of individuals. Without mouth or alimentary canal of its own, the parasite is wholly dependent upon the digested food in the intestine of its host. The terminal segments, filled with embryos, are shed from time to time and pass from the body of the host. When the embryos are swallowed by a pig, they become freed as six-hooked larvae which bore their way out of the intestinal tract and encyst as so-called "bladder-worms" in the muscles or other structures of the pig. They attain their adult form only when such infected flesh is eaten and they are released into the human intestinal tract. The chances against the perpetuation of such forms are obviously great, yet there is an abundance of both pork and beef tapeworms.

The Life Span.—In unicellular organisms there seems to be no death from old age. When an alga or an amoeba reaches a certain size and nutritional state, it simply divides and what was one living individual now is two (fig. 3). If death occurs, it is because of some harmful condition in the environment such as lack of food, existence of enemies or the like. The protozoon we view through our microscope has no dead ancestors; it is the direct descendant of the original of its kind. With the establishment of a body as distinct from the germ, natural death enters the scene. The cells which jointly constitute what we might call the vegetative individual eventually perish; only the reproductive individuals known as germ cells maintain continuity between successive generations.

Although, if we may judge from what we see in nature, the penalty paid for a body is death, the higher realizations of living matter could not have been attained without that combination of diversity and unity made possible through the association of spe-

cialized cells which make up the bodies of the more complex organisms. Under these circumstances, from the standpoint of survival value of the species, it is desirable for the individuals of today to give place eventually to those of tomorrow, because environing conditions are never constant for extensive periods, and it is only by giving the reproductive variants a chance that new fitnesses may be established and prolonged survival be made possible. Insurance of the welfare of the species is the all-important accomplishment.

What determines the life span of any one particular species is not always evident, but it may be safely said that in general organisms live only long enough to ensure their continuance as a race or stock (*see* LONGEVITY). Duration of life is, within generous limits, automatically adjusted to survival of the species. Where the hazards of existence are numerous or outstanding, the rate of reproduction is high and the number of offspring produced is great; where the risks are fewer and the individual is better prepared to cope with them, the rate is low (fig. 14). In general there is an automatic adjustment between length of life of the individual and the chances of the young for survival. Any extraordinary increase in numbers, as may happen with unusual abundance of food, favourable weather conditions or removal of natural checks, is eventually offset by such factors as competition within the group itself for food, disease incident to propinquity and by the multiplication of enemies which feed upon its members. Either sudden increase or decrease in numbers is likely to prove disastrous. Slight fluctuations which do not upset the so-called "balance of nature" are more likely to prove safe.

BIBLIOGRAPHY.—H. S. Jennings, *Life and Death, Heredity and Evolution in Unicellular Organisms* (1920); H. H. Newman, *The Physiology of Twinning* (1923), *Multiple Human Births* (1940); E. B. Wilson, *The Cell in Development and Heredity* (1925); M. J. D. White, *The Chromosomes* (1937); Hans Spemann, *Embryonic Development and Induction* (1938); M. C. Coulter, *The Story of the Plant Kingdom* (1938); C. H. Waddington, *Organizers and Genes* (1940); F. R. Moulton, ed. (many contributors), *The Cell and Protoplasm* (1940); A. S. Romer, *Man and the Vertebrates* (1941); Bentley Glass, *Genes and the Man* (1943); M. F. Guyer, *Animal Biology* (1941). (M. F. G.)

PHYSIOLOGY OF REPRODUCTION

It is common knowledge that the majority of animals and plants have more or less definite times at which they breed, though the ova (estimated at 200,000 in man) are possibly preformed at birth. These depend often upon seasonal or environmental conditions and it is well known that spring and summer are the times for reproductive activity among birds, insects and a host of other animals. Unusual warmth or cold may hasten or check the periodic development of sexual activity and the accompanying internal and external changes which take place in the body. The connection between breeding and food supply is also generally realized. Moreover, where climatic and nutritive conditions are approximately uniform throughout the year, periodicity in the breeding habits of animals is often obliterated. Thus, Semper states that sexual periodicity is absent among molluscs, insects and other land animals in the Philippine Islands. On the other hand, the regularity of the migratory movements, which directly relate to changes in the reproductive organs and the instincts for breeding, occurs to a great extent independently of temporary climatic conditions, though not wholly so. (*See* BIRDS, MIGRATION OF.) It is clear, however, that, broadly speaking, the factors which control the periodic changes in the generative system in association with breeding are of two kinds, the external ones referred to above, and internal factors inherent in the animals themselves, and particularly in the essential reproductive organs. Before attempting to describe these changes and the manner in which they occur it will be well, briefly, to describe the reproductive organs, referring more particularly to the higher animals.

The Generative System.—Among vertebrates the sexes are nearly always separate, although a few species are hermaphrodite. The usual arrangement, however, is for each individual to have its own characteristic sexual organs, those of the other sex, it represented at all, failing to develop or undergoing early degeneration. In the male of all lower vertebrates (including birds) the *testes* lie dorsally inside the body cavity and discharge their products, the spermatozoa, along with fluid secretions, into ducts communicating with the exterior by a passage (the *cloaca*) common to the urogenital and alimentary systems. In most mammals, on the other hand, the testes lie outside the main body cavity in a double sac (the *scrotum*) between the anus (or opening of the gut) and the penis. The testes are largely composed of tubules whose walls give rise to the spermatozoa and these latter are budded off into the interior as in other animals. Between the seminiferous tubules are *interstitial cells*. These give rise to chemical substances (hormones, *q.v.*) which pass internally into the blood. (*See* ENDOCRINOLOGY.) There is strong evidence that these internal secretions by their power of stimulation are responsible for the growth and development of the distinctively male characters and instincts. Thus, the presence of the testes is commonly regarded as the test for maleness.

In all mammals the spermatozoa pass out from the testis by a number of short ducts (the *efferent ductules*) into a coiled tube lying alongside it (the *epididymis*). This acts as a storehouse for the spermatozoa until they are ejaculated. Spermatozoa may remain alive within the epididymis and still be capable of fertilizing ova for 30 days (rabbit). The epididymis is a long coiled tube with muscular walls and the coils lie in juxtaposition so that the whole forms one discrete body closely applied to the testis. From each epididymis a duct (the *ductus deferens*) passes back through the *inguinal canal* (a passage connecting the scrotum with the body cavity). The two *vasa deferentia* open close together in the common channel with which the urinary bladder also communicates. This passage (the *urethra*) is continued within the erectile copulatory organ or *penis*, at the end of which it opens to the exterior. In addition to these organs there are several accessory glands communicating with the common urogenital passage. These are the *seminal vesicles*, the *prostate gland* and *Cowper's glands*, all of which contribute fluid substances to the semen in which the spermatozoa swim; the secretions are believed also to cleanse the urethra of urine prior to the ejaculation of semen. The above description applies more especially to man, but in the majority of the lower mammals the organs are similarly arranged.

The ovaries, the essential reproductive organs of the female, likewise serve a double function. They produce the ova and also elaborate internal secretions comparable to those of the testes; these secretions are responsible for initiating the development of the female characters, as well as being a necessary factor in the sexual and reproductive processes. In the lower vertebrates the ova are large because of the amount of food substances (yolk) contained in them (as with the egg of the fowl), but in mammals they are microscopic, each being about $\frac{1}{125}$ in. in diameter (this, however, is considerably bigger than a spermatozoon, which is about $\frac{1}{500}$ in. in length). The ova are contained within little sacs (Graafian follicles). These begin by being very small, but as they approach maturity their cavities enlarge until they protrude from the surface of the ovary; eventually (unless, as often happens with many of them, they have degenerated) they discharge their ova to the exterior in *ovulation*.

The ovaries are attached, one on either side, to the dorsal wall of the abdominal cavity by the *broad ligament*. The tubes which convey the ova to the exterior are also suspended by this ligament, a double fold of tissue arising from the wall of the body cavity. In the lower vertebrates the oviducts are provided with glands secreting albumen or egg white which coats the ovum as it passes down the tube. The egg shell in those animals in which it is formed is also secreted by a gland; in birds this is at the posterior end of the oviduct just in front of where it opens into the common urogenital passage. At the anterior end each oviduct has a fimbriated trumpet-shaped aperture which expands at ovulation and receives the eggs as they pass into the body cavity. The interior of the expanded end is provided with cilia which direct the passage of the ova into and down the tubes. The oviducts are usually paired to correspond with the ovaries, but in birds only the left ovary and oviduct are present. In mammals and birds the ova are usually fertilized by the spermatozoa in the passage of the oviduct, but in the lower vertebrates (*e.g.,* most

fish) this often occurs outside the body. In mammals, the oviducts (small, somewhat-coiled tubes) swell out posteriorly to form the *cornua uteri*, or womb. These may continue double throughout their entire length and open separately into the vagina (rabbit) or after continuing separate for a considerable distance may unite together to form the *corpus uteri* or body of the uterus (cow, sheep, mare, bitch, etc.) or they may extend for only a short distance before opening into the corpus uteri, which is a sac or bag (man). At the hind end the corpus uteri narrows down to form a neck (*cervix*) and this opens into the vagina by the *os uteri*. The uterus is the organ which contains the developing young during pregnancy. It has thick muscular walls on the outside and a mucous membrane with numerous glands lining the cavity inside. These secrete a fluid which helps to nourish the developing embryo during pregnancy and supplies a medium in which the spermatozoa swim after copulation. The *vagina* is the broad urogenital passage which extends backward through the pelvis and opens to the exterior at the *vulva*. The latter is constituted by all the female generative organs visible externally. The lateral boundaries are the *labia*, or lips. The *clitoris* is a small rod-like erectile structure and corresponds to the penis of the male but is solid.

The mammary glands, although not directly concerned with the reproductive processes, are dependent upon the ovaries for growth. They consist of milk-secreting tissue and are provided with ducts which convey the milk to the nipple, whence it can be drawn off.

The Reproductive Cycle.—At the approach of the breeding season in most animals the gonads (testes and ovaries) undergo marked growth. This is very pronounced in fishes and is hardly less marked in birds. Thus, in the sparrow in winter the testis is no larger than a grain of mustard seed but at the breeding season it reaches the size of a small cherry.

The male breeding season, when it occurs, is called the season of *rut*. The increase in the size of the testes which occurs prior to rut is accompanied by activity not only of the cells which give rise to the spermatozoa (the spermatogenetic tissue of the seminiferous tubules) but also of the interstitial cells. In some mammals the testes are not permanently retained in the scrotum but descend thither at the beginning of rut and are withdrawn into the abdomen again after the rutting season is over (*e.g.,* many rodents). In insectivores (*e.g.,* mole and hedgehog) the testes descend periodically into temporary receptacles. In the mole it is estimated that the testes increase in size 64 times, and the seminal vesicles, prostate and other accessory glands likewise show enormous growth. The time for sexual intercourse is continuous throughout rut, there being no short periods of quiescence within the breeding season as in the females of many species. Among domestic animals generally there is no special season of rut, the male being capable of service throughout the year, the semen evacuated normally containing an abundance of spermatozoa. In this respect these species differ from their wild ancestors, for in the undomesticated state the male usually experiences a rutting season at the same time as the breeding season in the female.

In the female mammal the times for sexual intercourse, instead of extending continuously over a season of considerable duration, as with the male, are restricted to periods of "heat" or oestrus. These may recur at rhythmical intervals within one breeding season (mare, cow, ewe, sow) or there may be only one oestrus to the season (bitch). The former condition has been described by Walter Heape as polyoestrous, the latter as monoestrous. The whole cycle of changes is known as the oestrous cycle. In the case of a typical monoestrous mammal, such as the dog, the oestrous cycle is divided as follows: anoestrum (period of rest); pro-oestrum (period of growth and preparation); oestrus (period of desire); pregnancy or (alternatively) pseudopregnancy.

During the anoestrum the reproductive system is, relatively speaking, quiescent. The Graafian follicles which contain the ova probably undergo slow growth and ripening, but they do not become conspicuous upon the ovarian surface until near the end of the anoestrum. The uterus is relatively anaemic and the glands inactive. The mammary glands are also inactive unless lactation is in progress after recent pregnancy. The entire anoestrum in the bitch lasts about three months.

The pro-oestrum is marked by increased activity of the generative system generally. It is the time of coming on heat. The follicles come to protrude visibly from the surface of the ovaries. The uterus also undergoes growth, the blood vessels increase in size and number and the glands in the mucous membrane elaborate more secretion. At a slightly later stage a definite haemorrhage occurs in the uterus and blood is passed out to the exterior at the vulva. The mammary glands may also become slightly congested. The entire pro-oestrum lasts from one to two weeks and external bleeding may go on for ten days, but it is usually slight, consisting of no more than a sanguineo-mucous flow.

Oestrus or heat is the period at which (and, ordinarily, only at which) sexual intercourse takes place. It is marked internally by ovulation, that is, the rupture of the Graafian follicles and the discharge of the ova, which then become mature and ready for fertilization by spermatozoa. The wall of the uterus undergoes repair at this time but the glandular secretion is abundant and more liquid in character, to provide a suitable medium for the spermatozoa. In the bitch oestrus lasts about a week.

Oestrus is succeeded by either pregnancy or pseudopregnancy. Each of these periods in the bitch lasts about two months. At their termination the uterus and the generative organs pass back to a condition of rest, and so the oestrous cycle is repeated. The complete cycle takes about six months in the bitch, there being typically two cycles and two oestrous periods in the year but there is a good deal of individual and racial variation.

If pregnancy takes place as a result of fertilization of the ova, discharged during oestrus, these segment and become attached to the inside wall (mucous membrane) of the uterus, which grows around each of them. The structure formed in this way is highly vascular and serves as the organ of nourishment for the developing embryos to which the ova give rise. (*See* VERTEBRATE EMBRYOLOGY.) This organ is the *placenta* and is characteristic of nearly all mammals. The embryos are attached to the placenta of the mother by the outer of a number of membranes, and vascular processes (*villi*) grow out from this membrane (the *chorion*) into the hypertrophied uterine mucous membrane now forming the maternal placenta. Thus, a close connection is formed between the embryo and the mother and the placenta acts as an organ of respiration, supplying the developing young with oxygen brought thither in the maternal blood, and an organ of excretion, getting rid of carbon dioxide and the waste nitrogenous products, besides supplying the necessary nutriment. During pregnancy also the uterine muscles undergo a great hypertrophy, and are responsible for a great part of the increased weight which occurs in that organ. Thus, in the human subject, the virgin uterus weighs about 30 grams, whereas the same organ at the close of pregnancy, apart from the contained young, weighs 1,000 grams. It is through the rhythmical contraction of the uterine muscles that the young are expelled in parturition (the act of giving birth). The mammary glands undergo great development during pregnancy in preparation for the secretion of milk at its close.

If the ova discharged at ovulation are not fertilized during oestrus (as when coition does not occur) they die in the uterus and disintegrate. Nevertheless, in the bitch and many other mammals the uterus and mammary glands pass through growth-changes which, though not so pronounced, are similar in character to those during pregnancy. Thus, the mucous membrane becomes highly vascular and the glands greatly enlarge. The mammary glands also undergo marked development and toward the end of the period secrete milk. Even virgin bitches secrete milk freely about two months after the cessation of oestrus. At the end of this pseudopregnancy the generative system as a whole subsides into a condition of rest.

The ovarian changes (at any rate in the bitch) are also similar in both pregnancy and pseudopregnancy. The Graafian follicle, after parting with its ovum, becomes converted into the *corpus luteum,* or yellow body, so called because of a pigmented fat (lutein) formed inside it. The yellow body is formed by the

rapid hypertrophy of the cells surrounding the cavity of the follicle; this is so great that the individual cells increase in size 16 or 20 times. This structure, which plays an important part during pregnancy, lasts throughout that period (and correspondingly during pseudopregnancy) and then undergoes degeneration.

In polyoestrous animals there is a succession of oestrous periods within a single breeding season, that is to say, that if coition does not take place at the first oestrus, or if for some other reason the ova discharged at ovulation are not fertilized, the animal, instead of experiencing a prolonged pseudopregnancy followed by an anoestrum (as with the bitch), undergoes a short period of apparent quiescence, called by Heape the dioestrum, and then comes on heat again. Thus, with the sheep, the ewe, if she fails to become pregnant at her first oestrus, comes back to the ram (as the shepherds say) after about 15 days, and if she again fails, may experience a third oestrus after another 15 days, and so on for a succession of cycles until the breeding season is over or the ewe succeeds in becoming in-lamb. This short (or dioestrous) cycle in the sheep is therefore 15 days. The number of dioestrous cycles which the animal is capable of experiencing depends partly on the breed and partly on the environment, whether favourable or otherwise. Among sheep of all breeds there is a complete gradation between the monoestrous condition of certain wild varieties and the extreme of polyoestrum exhibited by certain merinos, in which there may be no anoestrum (even in the nonoccurrence of pregnancy) but (in the absence of the ram) an unbroken succession of dioestrous cycles which last the whole year. Many wild animals (*e.g.,* rodents) are polyoestrous and the dioestrous cycle may last for only a few days.

In polyoestrous animals ovulation typically occurs during oestrus and is followed by the formation of the corpus luteum. The time of persistence of this structure varies according to whether or not pregnancy occurs. In the absence of pregnancy the corpus luteum persists for the duration of the dioestrum and then begins to degenerate as if to make way for the ripening of a fresh batch of follicles in the ovary and a new oestrous period. If, however, pregnancy takes place the corpus luteum continues in the ovary until parturition as in monoestrous animals. In reality, the dioestrum, instead of being a period of complete rest, is of the nature of a very abbreviated pseudopregnancy, and the uterus undergoes some growth changes in association with the presence of the corpus luteum in the ovary.

In man there is typically no anoestrum (except among the Eskimos in winter) and the menstrual cycles, each lasting about a month, correspond to the dioestrous cycles of the polyoestrous lower mammal. The actual menstrual phenomena probably represent the degenerative changes at the end of an abbreviated pseudopregnancy (or dioestrum) telescoped into the pro-oestrum of a new cycle. Ovulation takes place most commonly about the 14th day after the beginning of the menstrual flow but it may occur at other times, though rarely, in the week or ten days before the beginning of menstruation.

In some animals (rabbit, ferret) ovulation takes place only after coition. The actual process can be demonstrated in an anaesthetized rabbit whose ovaries have been exposed to view (J. Hammond). It is possible that in man also ovulation may sometimes require the additional stimulus set up by coition. In most domestic animals (bitch, sow, ewe, cow, mare) ovulation takes place spontaneously at or about the time of oestrus.

The Testis and Ovary as Organs of Internal Secretion.— It has been mentioned that the testis, besides producing the spermatozoa, is also an organ elaborating an internal secretion which is discharged into the blood. A similar statement may be made about the ovary. The evidence for these conclusions falls under three heads: (1) the effects of removing these organs (castration and spaying); (2) the effects of transplanting the testis or ovary into animals whose own gonads have previously been removed and (3) the result of injecting tissue extracts prepared from testes or ovaries.

The general effect of castration in all vertebrate animals is to prevent the development of the secondary characters of sex, that is, of those characters which, while correlated with the sex in question, are not directly concerned with reproduction. This statement applies to ovariotomy or the extirpation of the ovaries in the female as well as to castration in the male. It is essential, however, that this operation should be performed early in life to have its full effect. It not only ensures permanent sterility (whenever it is done) but if performed on the young stops the development of superficial sexual characters as well as the accessory reproductive organs (prostate gland, etc.). Thus, in man, castration prevents the growth of hair on the face and various parts of the body and arrests the enlargement of the larynx and the consequent deepening of the voice normally characteristic of puberty in the male. In stags castration inhibits the growth of the antlers and in those breeds of sheep which are horned in the male and hornless in the female it prevents development of the horns; moreover, the horn growth is arrested at any stage of development at which castration is performed. With fowls, castration is followed by an arrest of the development of the erectile structures about the head (comb, wattles, etc.). Castration has been practised on the domestic animals from the earliest times, for it improves the quality of the flesh and favours fattening in meat-producing animals and is conducive to a greater tractability in working animals since the disturbing effects of sexual desire no longer occur.

If the testes are removed from the normal position and grafted to an abnormal one (or if the testes of another male are transplanted immediately after castration), the organs exert their usual influence on the secondary sexual characters and accessory sexual glands, although their normal nerve connections have been severed. Since, then, the influence of transplanted organs can not be through intermediation of the nervous system it would seem that it must operate through chemical substances passed into the blood and so into the general circulation. Thus, in experiments upon fowls the testes have been removed and broken up into pieces, which have attached themselves to different parts of the alimentary canal or the wall of the body cavity, and the birds have developed into typical cocks with comb, wattle, etc., male voice and sexual and combative instincts. Furthermore, the experiments of Eugen Steinach and others have shown that the grafting of testes into females whose ovaries had been removed may cause the development of secondary male characters and bring about a partial or complete reversal of sex. For the successful implantation of testis tissue, as with most other organs in higher vertebrates, the material to be transplanted must come from an animal of the same species; in salamanders and frogs sometimes grafts may become incorporated and persist in the host organism when the living transplant has come from a donor of different species. Mammalian testis grafts will secrete hormone when they are incorporated into any locality in the host organism, but the grafts will produce spermatozoa only when transplanted into the scrotum or in the anterior chamber of the eye. In these two localities the body temperature is sufficiently low to permit formation of completed spermatozoa. The scrotum functions as a heat regulator, effectively reducing the temperature below ordinary body temperatures. Testes of mammals that fail to descend into the scrotum, or are located as grafts in the abdomen, are unable to produce spermatozoa because of the higher temperature in this locality. Testes of birds, which have even higher body temperatures than do mammals, are more heat resistant; however, active division of the germinal cells of the testis apparently occurs almost exclusively at night during periods of sleep in which the body temperature falls by several degrees.

Ovariotomy leads to the suppression of the distinctly female characters. If done before puberty the uterus and mammary glands do not develop and the general bodily form tends toward a neutral condition not dissimilar to that of the castrated male. If performed after puberty ovariotomy is followed by cessation of the oestrous or menstrual cycles and the uterus undergoes atrophy in much the same way as occurs normally at the menopause (climacteric) or time of permanent cessation of reproductive activity (in women at from 45 to 50). If, however, the ovaries (or one of them) instead of being removed are grafted to an abnormal position such as the ventral wall of the body

cavity or into a kidney the oestrous cycle is continued and the uterus remains normal. Since the ovary in such a position is without its normal nerve supply it is presumed that its influence on the organism is because of internal secretions passed into the circulation. The corpus luteum is also known to be an organ of internal secretion serving the special function of secreting into the blood substances essential for maintaining the raised nutrition of the uterus during pregnancy and for the development of the mammary glands, for if this structure be removed surgically pregnancy can not continue, the uterus lapses and the mammary glands fail to develop. The corpus luteum also plays some part in controlling the short or dioestrous cycle, for so long as it is present in its integrity heat can not occur; but if it is extirpated some days before a new oestrous period is normally due, the period occurs shortly after the operation of removal. Thus, Hammond, by squeezing out the corpus luteum of a cow, has induced oestrus after 9 days instead of the usual 19 to 21.

Internal Secretions and the Control of Reproductive Processes.—An understanding of the role exercised by internal secretions in the first establishment of a functional reproductive system at the age of puberty, and in the control of the rhythmical processes occurring during reproductive life, is largely a development of the 20th century. Internal secretions from the sex glands, while immediately responsible for the principal functional changes, are themselves regulated by the secretory activity of other endocrine glands, especially those from the pituitary gland.

Analyses of the oestrous cycles in the guinea pig, repeated approximately every 15th day, were made by C. R. Stockard and G. N. Papanicolaou in 1917, and five-day cycles in the rat were carefully described by J. A. Long and H. M. Evans in 1922. The inactive period of the cycle, or dioestrum, gradually changes to the pro-oestrum as renewed growth of follicles occurs in the ovary. The entire female reproductive tract—oviducts, uterus and vagina—become more vascular, increase in size and show active changes in their glands; the vaginal epithelium exhibits renewed cellular activity under the old epithelial wall, which is rather precipitously cast off into the cavity of the vagina. The period of oestrus, or acceptance of the male, in these small rodents is restricted to a few hours in comparison with several days for larger mammals; it occurs as follicular size approaches the maximum and as samples of the castoff vaginal cell wall show nucleated epithelial cells mixed with the old cornified cells of the vaginal epithelium. Ovulation occurs approximately 10 hr. after the first mating is permitted. The growth, or estrogenic, phase of the cycle is followed by the luteal or regressive phase and this involution period is indicated by the character of cells appearing in a smear taken from the vagina. The cornified cell stage of the smear is gradually superseded by one in which scattered leucocytes appear and the final quiescent stage of the dioestrum is characterized by a scanty smear composed of cells almost exclusively made up of leucocytes.

Thus, the state of the reproductive cycle can be diagnosed rapidly from the living female by means of examining a smear made from the open vagina. The known correlations between the character of the smear and the ovarial condition makes it possible to understand the condition of the ovary simply from microscopic observations of the vaginal smear. Since removal of the ovaries abolishes all cyclical phenomena as well as recurrent phases of activity on the part of the uterus and vagina, the vaginal smear technique provides a rapid test for the estrogenic hormones involved in these changes in the reproductive tract, and thereby has aided tremendously in efforts to identify the source and to follow the procedures of isolation of these hormones.

The fundamental activities of the sex glands (testes and ovaries) are not self-regulating phenomena, but were shown clearly to be dependent upon secretions from the anterior lobe of the pituitary gland by Philip E. Smith and Earl T. Engle in 1927. This sex-gland activity involves both the formation of mature germ cells and the hormone secretion by the respective sex gland. Removal of the pituitary gland (hypophysectomy) in the adult animal leads to immediate involution of the sex glands, with loss of capacity to mature sex cells and inability to secrete hormones. Conversely, the introduction under the skin of a normal animal of finely ground fresh pituitary substance, or extracts made from fresh or dried pituitary tissue, rapidly stimulates excessive activity on the part of the gonads. Defective secretion of pituitary hormones introduces defective activity on the part of the testis or ovary.

Some notion of the delicacy of interaction between the gonads and pituitary body can be appreciated from a knowledge of the regularity in the short recurrent oestrous cycles, and such phenomena as menstruation in the human females, as well as from the regularity in the strictly annual breeding cycles. In many wild mammals the gonads are active for but a short span of the year. During the periods of low gonadal, or reproductive, activity the pituitary gland is far less potent in stimulating sex-gland activity when introduced into a test animal than it is at the approach of the breeding season. Also, since the sex glands of the sexually inactive seasonal breeding animal can be stimulated rapidly into intense activity it becomes evident that the problem of the control of the seasonal sexual activity is essentially the problem of seasonal pituitary activity. What, then, is responsible for the secretory activity of the pituitary gland that regulates the seasonal sexual cycle?

The external environment as well as internal conditions both play a role in these reproductive processes and in the secretory activity of the pituitary body. Different elements in the external environment are involved in the regulatory mechanism of different species of animals and probably in the same one. The relative lengths of day and night have marked influences on the reproductive state of birds especially, as well as of some mammals, whereas other animals, particularly hibernating ones, appear to be less responsive to light changes. The experiments of William Rowan (1926) on the small migrant bird, the junco, in the Canadian northwest pointed to light as a factor of greater significance than food or temperature in the control of seasonal sexual activity. Males of this small bird show high testicular activity in the month of May, and after the mating season they experience severe involution of the testes. When captive birds in outdoor aviaries were maintained over winter, testes were small and inactive until the month of February or March, but with a gradual daily increase in the length of the light period, provided by electric bulbs for periods of 10 min., beginning in fall the testes became fully active and produced spermatozoa in November and December in temperatures as low as $-40°$ F. From this sexually active condition the sex glands underwent regression as the days were gradually shortened. Jacques Benoit (1937) demonstrated clearly that the effect of added light was indirect in that it incited the pituitary gland of light-treated ducks to greatly increased secretory activity.

In similar manner the breeding season of several wild game birds (wild turkey, pheasant, quail), some mammals and fish have been tremendously modified. Other animals respond apparently to temperature changes as one factor in the environment that regulates the breeding season and still other unknown elements probably play a part.

The secretion of substances (hormones) by the pituitary gland in the adult animal, that so markedly affect the reproductive system, is modified by factors other than light. The nutritive state of the animal is important. Simple inanition or starvation affects the secretory activity of the gland; lack of vitamin B_2 (lactoflavin or riboflavin) in the diet has a similar effect. The concentration of sex hormones in the circulation tends to inhibit secretion of the substances acting upon the gonads, hence a reciprocal gonadal-hypophyseal interaction constitutes at least one contributory element in the intimate control of the reproductive cycles.

The initiation of sexual activity, or the condition commonly known as puberty, depends upon the secretory activity of the pituitary gland. Prepuberal animals can be thrown into reproductive activity long before it normally occurs if pituitary secretions are merely introduced under the skin. Young hatched male chicks receiving pituitary extract for the first 12 days after hatching develop enormously enlarged combs and wattles, utter squeaky crowing sounds and attempt to tread their young pen mates.

Other organs of internal secretion than the pituitary gland probably play a definite role in the control of breeding cycles. This appears to be true for the thyroid secretions in some animals and less definitely for other products of internal secretion.

Fertility and Sterility.—The number of spermatozoa discharged in a normal ejaculation of human semen is estimated at 226,000,000, whereas the number of ova ejected at one ovulation is usually only 1. For mammals generally the number of ova discharged is on an average only slightly more than the average number of young in a litter. It follows that the female rather than the male controls the size of the litter. (On the other hand, Sanders has shown for horses that a reduction in the number of spermatozoa may reduce the chances of the ovum being fertilized.) The sheep discharges one or two (sometimes three and rarely more) ova at oestrus, but by flushing the ewes, that is supplying them with extra or stimulating food before and during breeding, the number may be increased and consequently a higher proportion of lambs obtained. This is an example of the influence of favourable nutrition upon fertility. Too high feeding (resulting in adiposity), however, promotes atrophy of the ova in the ovary and so is conducive to sterility. There is evidence also that sterility may be caused by the absence of certain essential accessory food substances or vitamins (*q.v.*) and that one such vitamin is present in green food (Herbert Evans). Degeneration of ova in the ovary may therefore be caused by faulty nutrition of various kinds, but some degeneration is normal.

Sterility may result from coition at an inappropriate time, that is, at too long an interval before or after ovulation, for Hammond has shown in the rabbit that the ova are not capable of being fertilized for longer than four hours after their release from the ovary, and that the spermatozoa in the female passages do not retain their power of fertilization for more than two days. (In the male passage, where they are quiescent, they retain this power for 30 days.) It is probable that in many other mammals the duration of viability of the spermatozoa and ova is not widely different. In animals such as the mare, which has a prolonged oestrus (a week or more), sterile unions may well be the result of this cause (Hammond).

Artificial insemination is sometimes successfully resorted to in cases where sterility has been because of an abnormal constriction of the *os uteri* or to the presence of an acid secretion in the vagina. The practice is to inject the semen directly into the *os uteri*, thus avoiding the constriction or escaping the action of the abnormal secretion. Walton has found that the semen of rabbits may be kept in a fertile condition in tubes outside the body at a medium temperature for more than five days and that after a journey by post from Cambridge to Edinburgh the spermatozoa contained therein could still successfully fertilize ova with normal pregnancy as a result.

Fertility, like other characters, is capable of being transmitted from one generation to another. Thus, rams which were twin lambs may hand on the tendency to produce twins to the next generation of ewes, and by breeding from rams which were twins the fertility of a flock may be increased.

BIBLIOGRAPHY.—F. H. A. Marshall, *An Introduction to Sexual Physiology* (1925); *The Physiology of Reproduction* (1922); J. Hammond, *Reproduction in the Rabbit* (1925), *The Physiology of Reproduction in the Cow* (1926); A. Lipschütz, *The Internal Secretions of the Sex Glands* (1924); J. S. Fairbairn, *Obstetrics* (1927); E. Allen, C. H. Danforth and E. A. Doisy, *Sex and Internal Secretions* (1939); J. Benoit, *Bull. Biol.*, 71 (fasc. 4):394-437 (1937); J. Long and H. M. Evans, *Memoirs University of California*, vol. 6 (1922); C. R. Stockard and G. N. Papanicolaou, *Amer. J. Anat.*, 22: 225-264 (1917); Philip E. Smith and Earl T. Engle, *Am. J. Anat.*, 40: 159 (1927); William Rowan, *Proc. Boston Soc. Natural Hist.*, 39: 151 (1926). (F. H. A. M.; C. R. Me.)

REPRODUCTIVE SYSTEM. The reproductive system in some parts of its course shares structures with the urinary system (*q.v.*).

MALE REPRODUCTIVE SYSTEM

The scrotum is a pouch of integument which is divided into two compartments by a median septum. Each compartment contains a testis, an epididymis and a portion of the spermatic cord. The left half of the scrotum reaches a somewhat lower level than the right half in conformity with the comparative positions of the two testes. The integument contains coarse scattered hairs and well-developed sudoriparous and sebaceous glands. The deeper layers contain smooth muscle fibres, the dartos; contraction of these fibres draws the scrotum up and produces a corrugated appearance. Internal to the dartos there is a layer of laminated connective tissue, the intercolumnar (external spermatic) fascia, which is continuous at the abdominal inguinal ring with the intercrural fibres. The next layer, the cremasteric fascia, contains bundles of muscle fibres, the abdominal cremasteric muscle; these fibres are derived from the internal abdominal oblique muscle; contraction of the cremasteric muscle tends to draw the testis toward the abdominal cavity. The subsequent layer of fascia, tunica vaginalis communis, is relatively thin and is derived from the transversalis fascia of the abdomen. The innermost layer, the tunica vaginalis propria, is a double layer forming the serous investment of the testis; it is derived from the peritoneum. The outer layer (parietal) is closely adherent to the tunica vaginalis communis, the inner layer (serous) completely invests the testis and a portion of the epididymis, when it dips between the testis and epididymis it forms a pocket, the sinus epididymidis.

During the development of the foetus an outpouching of the lower part of the abdominal wall occurs on each side to form the genital swellings; these later become the scrotum in the male and the labia majora in the female. With the descent of the testes into the outpouching, the ductus (vas) deferens and vessels and nerves of the testes are carried through the abdominal wall as the spermatic cord. The passage way thus formed is referred to as the inguinal canal; it is at first widely open but eventually forms only a flat-sided passage in the abdominal wall and is somewhat more than 3 cm. ($1\frac{1}{2}$ in.) in length. The entrance to the canal, the abdominal inguinal ring, is formed by the funnel-shaped expansion of the transversalis fascia as it envelops the spermatic cord; the exit from the canal, the subcutaneous inguinal ring, is surrounded by the aponeurosis of the external abdominal oblique muscle. The layers of the anterior abdominal wall are carried into the scrotum as coverings of the testes and spermatic cord.

The testes or testicles, the essential male organs of reproduction, are contained within the scrotum. Each is oval, about 4–5 cm. ($1\frac{1}{2}$–2 in.) in length and 2.5–3 cm. (1 in.) in width, and has a strong fibrous coat (tunica albuginea), from which septa penetrate into the substance, dividing it into lobules in which the seminiferous tubules are coiled. The tubules of each lobule form a single duct (tubuli recti) which extends toward the mediastinum and there forms a plexus of tubules (rete testis). In this way the secretion of the gland is carried to its upper and back part, where from 15 to 20 small tubules (ductuli efferentia) pass to the epididymis. Each of these is convoluted before opening (conus vasculosus). Microscopically the seminiferous tubules consist of a basement membrane surrounding several layers of epithelial cells, some of which are constantly being transformed into spermatozoa or male sexual cells.

The epididymis is a soft body covering the entire posterior margin and the adjacent part of the outer surface of the testis. It is enlarged above to form the head (caput) and below is a lesser swelling the tail (cauda). The entire epididymis is made up of a convoluted tube about 6–7 m. (18–21 ft.) long. Between the head and the testis two small vesicles are often found (appendix testis and appendix epididymidis).

The ductus deferens is the continuation of the tube of the epididymis and extends from the tail of the epididymis to its termination on the posterior surface of the prostate, where it joins the seminal vesicle to form the ejaculatory duct. The ductus deferens ascends on the inner (medial) side of the epididymis to the subcutaneous inguinal ring, being joined in this part of its course by testicular arteries, veins, lymphatics and nerves to form the spermatic cord. After entering the subcutaneous inguinal ring, these structures pass obliquely through the abdominal wall, lying in the inguinal canal, until the abdominal inguinal ring is reached. There they separate and the ductus deferens passes down the side of the pelvis and turns inward along the posterior wall of the bladder to the prostate, at which point it meets its fellow of the opposite side. It is remarkable for the thickness of its muscular walls. The ductus deferens presents a uniform diameter of 2 to 3 mm. until it reaches the seminal vesicle; there it broadens out and forms the ampulla ductus deferentis, the lumen of which presents numerous sacculations (diverticula ampullae). Immediately before joining the excretory duct of the seminal vesicle the ductus deferens again becomes rounded and slender.

The seminal vesicles (vesiculae seminales) are two saclike appendages of the ductus deferens that lie upon the posterior surface of the bladder, parallel and lateral to the corresponding ductus deferens. The vesicle is a tubular structure, 10 to 12 cm. long, which is folded back and forth on itself to be contained within a fibromuscular capsule. Arising from the main tube are a varying number of blind pockets or diverticula. The excretory duct of the seminal vesicle joins the ductus deferens to form the ejaculatory duct; these are narrow and thin-walled, and run side by side through the prostate to open into the floor of the prostatic urethra.

The prostate is situated just below the bladder and is traversed by the urethra and the ejaculatory ducts; it is somewhat conical with the base upward in contact with the bladder. The vertical dimension is from 2.15–3.0 cm. (1–$1\frac{3}{8}$ in.), the transverse diameter from 3.5–4.0 cm. ($1\frac{3}{8}$–$1\frac{3}{4}$ in.), and a thickness from 2–2.5 cm. ($\frac{4}{5}$–1 in.); the size is liable to great variation with marked increase in elderly individuals. The prostate is composed of both glandular and muscular tissue and is enclosed by a fibrous capsule from which it is separated by the prostatic plexus of veins anteriorly. Microscopically it consists of masses of long, slender, slightly branching glands, embedded in unstriped muscle and fibrous tissue; these glands open by delicate ducts (about 20 in number) into the prostatic urethra.

The urethra is the canal which begins at the bladder and runs through the prostate and perineum to the penis, which it traverses

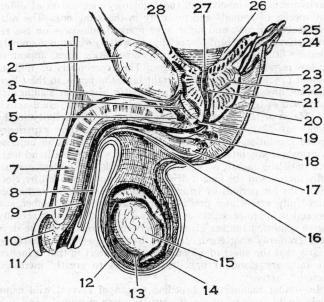

FROM MORRIS'S "HUMAN ANATOMY," IOTH ED. (BLAKISTON CO.)

FIG. 1.—MIDSAGITTAL SECTION (DIAGRAMMATIC) SHOWING MALE BLADDER, URETHRA AND RELATED STRUCTURES. 1. SUPERFICIAL ABDOMINAL FASCIA. 2. SYMPHYSIS PUBIS. 3. DORSAL VEIN OF PENIS. 4. UROGENITAL DIAPHRAGM (SUPERIOR LAYER). 5. UROGENITAL DIAPHRAGM (INFERIOR LAYER). 6. DEEP PERINEAL FASCIA. 7. PENIS. 8. TUNICA DARTOS. 9. URETHRA. 10. GLANS PENIS. 11. PREPUCE. 12. TUNICA DARTOS. 13. CAV. TUNICA VAGINALIS. 14. SCROTUM. 15. TESTIS. 16. DEEP PERINEAL FASCIA. 17. BULB. 18. BULBOURETHRAL GLAND. 19. EXTERNAL URETHRAL SPHINCTER. 20. PROSTATE. 21. UTRICULUS PROSTATICUS. 22. EJACULATORY DUCT. 23. DUCTUS DEFERENS. 24. SEMINAL VESICLE. 25. URETER. 26. URETERAL ORIFICE. 27. INTERNAL URETERAL ORIFICE. 28. BLADDER WALL

as far as the tip. It serves for the passage of both urine and seminal fluid. The urethra is divided into a prostatic, a membranous and a cavernous part. The prostatic urethra is about 2–3 cm. ($\frac{3}{4}$–$1\frac{1}{4}$ in.) in length; there is a longitudinal ridge (urethral crest) on its posterior wall, on each side of which the numerous ducts of the prostate open. Near the lower part of the urethral crest is a little pouch, the prostatic utricle, which is regarded as the morphological equivalent of the vagina and uterus. Close to the opening of the utriculus the ejaculatory ducts have very small openings. The part of the urethra above the openings of these ducts really belongs to the urinary system only, though it is convenient to describe it here. After leaving the prostate the urethra runs forward for about 1 cm., lying between the two layers of the urogenital diaphragm, both of which it pierces. This is known as the membranous urethra; it is the shortest, narrowest and least distensible of the segments and is surrounded by the fibres of the sphincter urethrae muscle. The cavernous urethra is that part which is enclosed within the penis after piercing the inferior layer of the urogenital diaphragm. Its length varies, but averages about 14 cm. ($5\frac{1}{2}$ in.). At first it lies in the substance of the bulb and, later, in the body of the corpus cavernosum, while finally it passes through the glans. In the greater part of its course it is a transverse slit, but in traversing the glans it enlarges considerably to form the fossa navicularis and there, in transverse section, it looks like an inverted T, then an inverted Y, and finally at its opening (external meatus) a vertical slit. Into the whole length of the urethra, mucous glands (urethral glands of Littré) open. As a rule the meatus is the narrowest part of the whole canal.

Opening into the cavernous urethra, where it passes through the bulb, are the ducts of two small glands known as Cowper's glands (bulbourethral glands), which lie on each side of the membranous urethra.

The penis, the male organ of copulation, is made up of three cylinders of erectile tissue, covered by skin and subcutaneous tissue without fat. In a transverse section two of these cylinders (the corpora cavernosa penis) are above, side by side, while the third (the corpus cavernosum urethrae) is below. At the root of the penis the two corpora cavernosa penis diverge, become more and more fibrous in structure, and are attached on each side to the inner border of the pubic arch, while the corpus cavernosum urethrae enlarges to form the bulb. The whole length of the latter corpus is traversed by the urethra. The anterior part of the penis is formed by the glans, a bellshaped structure, continuous with the corpus cavernosum urethrae and having the conical ends of the corpora cavernosa penis fitted into depressions on its proximal surface. On the dorsum of the penis the rim of the glans projects beyond the level of the corpora cavernosa penis (corona glandis). The skin of the penis forms a fold which covers the glans (prepuce or foreskin); when this is drawn back a median fold, the frenulum praeputii, is seen running to just below the meatus. After forming the prepuce the skin is reflected over the glans and there looks like mucous membrane. The structure of the corpora cavernosa penis consists of a strong fibrous coat, the tunica albuginea, from the deep surface of which trabeculae penetrate the interior and divide it into a number of spaces which are lined by endothelium and communicate with the veins. Between the two corpora cavernosa penis the sheath is incomplete and, having a comblike appearance, is known as the septum pectiniforme. The structure of the corpora cavernosa urethrae and glans resembles that of the corpora cavernosa penis, but the trabeculae are finer and the network closer.

Blood Supply.—The superficial layers of the scrotum are supplied partly by the perineal branches of the internal pudendal artery and partly by the external pudendal branches of the femoral artery. The deep layers are supplied by the spermatic branches of the femoral artery. The veins accompany the arteries.

The testis and epididymis receive blood by way of the internal spermatic, a direct branch of the abdominal aorta and also from the deferential artery, a branch of the superior vesicle. The veins accompany the arteries.

The deferential artery supplies the ductus deferens; the deferential vein accompanies the ductus deferens to the base of the bladder, where it breaks up into a plexus and communicates with the pudendal plexus.

The seminal vesicle receives its blood supply from branches of the inferior vesicle and deferential arteries. The veins drain into the seminal vesicle plexus.

The penis is supplied blood chiefly by branches of the internal pudendal artery; however, the proximal part of the integument is supplied by the external pudendal arteries. The veins of the integument collect to form the superficial dorsal vein which later bifurcates to drain into the great saphenous vein of each side. The deep veins from the corpora cavernosa drain into a median deep dorsal vein which terminates in the pudendal plexus but

communicate with the internal pudendal veins.

The prostate receives its arterial blood supply from branches of the inferior vesical and middle haemorrhoidal, both of which are direct branches of the hypogastric artery. The veins form a rich prostatic plexus which communicates with both the hemorrhoidal plexus and vesical plexus, the blood eventually reaching the hypogastric vein.

Lymphatics.—The lymphatics of the scrotum terminate in the inguinal nodes. Those from the testis and epididymis unite to form several large stems that pass upward in the spermatic cord and terminate in the lower lumbar nodes. The lymphatics from the ductus deferens pass to the external iliac and hypogastric nodes. The hypogastric nodes also receive the lymphatics from the seminal vesicle. The superficial and deep lymphatics of the penis terminate in the superficial inguinal nodes with the exception of those from the glands and urethra which drain into the deep inguinal and external iliac nodes. The lymphatics of the prostate are very abundant and pass into the hypogastric nodes.

Nerve Supply.—The male reproductive system receives sympathetic fibres from the hypogastric plexus; those with fibres from the third and fourth sacral plexus constitute the nervus erigens, so called since stimulation of it produces erection of the organ. The following nerves supply ordinary sensation to the scrotum and penis: the external spermatic branch of the genitofemoral, the dorsal nerve of the penis and perineal branches of the pudendal, scrotal branches of the ilioinguinal, and perineal branches of the posterior femoral cutaneous. (C. M. Cs.)

FEMALE REPRODUCTIVE SYSTEM

Functional Anatomy.—In the human species as in most other vertebrates, the female reproductive system consists of a pair of ovaries within the body cavity and a tubular canal or duct which leads to the exterior. The ovary produces egg cells (ova) and sex hormones. The canal receives the egg cell and harbours the product of conception (embryo and its surrounding membranes) during the prenatal period of life. Different parts of the canal are specialized for particular functions. Its chief divisions (fig. 2) are: (1) right and left oviducts (uterine or Fallopian tubes) each associated with the corresponding ovary. They serve to conduct eggs directly into (2) the womb (uterus) where the embryonic membranes become attached and where the embryo is nourished until birth. The uterus lies in the midline and consists of a body

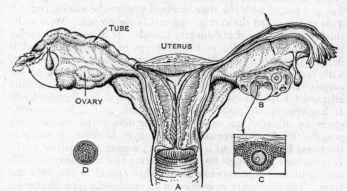

FROM CORNER, "OURSELVES UNBORN" (YALE UNIVERSITY PRESS)

FIG. 2.—A. DIAGRAM OF HUMAN OVARIES, OVIDUCTS (FALLOPIAN TUBES), AND UTERUS, AS SEEN FROM THE REAR. THE RIGHT TUBE AND THE UTERUS ARE DRAWN AS IF OPENED BY REMOVAL OF THEIR REAR WALLS, TO SHOW THE CANAL OF THE TUBE AND THE CAVITY OF THE UTERUS. THE ARROWS AT THE LEFT INDICATE THE COURSE OF THE OVUM FROM OVARY THROUGH TUBE TO UTERUS. B. A RIPE FOLLICLE IN THE OVARY, WITH EGG CELL (NOT TO SCALE) IN ITS WALL. C. ENLARGED VIEW OF THE EGG HILLOCK OF THE FOLLICLE IN SECTION. D. EGG CELL (OVUM) EXTERNAL ASPECT, MAGNIFIED ABOUT 30 DIAMETERS

(corpus uteri) and neck (cervix uteri) which opens into (3) the vagina, an organ of copulation.

The attachments of ovary, oviduct and uterus are such as to permit free and independent movements. All three are bound together by the sheetlike broad ligament which suspends them from the walls of the pelvis; through it blood vessels, lymphatics and nerves reach them from below. The ovary has another ligament which supports blood vessels that enter from above. The two sets of vessels communicate so that blood may reach the organs by either route. The ligaments are so disposed that ovary and oviduct are screened off from the intestines and other pelvic organs. A muscular band (round ligament) passes from the uterus out of the body cavity and is attached to the outer skin. It corresponds to the gubernaculum testis of the male.

The mature ovary is a firm organ, about the size of a large almond shell, with a scarred or wrinkled surface. It lies within the body cavity and is suspended from the body wall so as to be freely movable. Near the surface there are many minute egg cells which have remained dormant since birth. Each is surrounded by a layer of flattened follicle cells; together they constitute a primordial follicle. More than 200,000 such microscopic follicles were counted in each ovary of a 22-yr.-old girl. From time to time, even before birth, certain primordial follicles begin to grow. As the egg cell enlarges slowly the follicle cells multiply rapidly, forming a thick wall about it. Fluid soon appears between the follicle cells and as this accumulates a small blisterlike sac is formed, the ovarian or Graafian follicle (figs. 2B and 3). The egg cell lies in its wall, the cells which immediately surround it forming a domed projection into the fluid which fills the follicular cavity. There may be several hundred such follicles in an adult ovary. The great majority degenerate but they are not useless since they are concerned in the production of ovarian hormones. Less than 400 follicles of the available thousands are likely to produce mature egg cells during a woman's reproductive period.

The oviduct is a tube of involuntary muscle with a cavity about 6 in. long, lined by a folded mucous membrane. The end toward the ovary is open, with a thin wall flared out like a funnel (infundibulum tubae uterinae). Its edges are frilled and folded; only one of the frills is anchored, being attached to the ovary. The rest of the tube has thick walls and like the funnel it can change its shape and position. It narrows near the uterus and where it passes through the thick muscular wall of the uterus its cavity is very small. Ciliated cells in the lining of the oviduct maintain a constant current of fluid from the body cavity toward the uterus.

The uterus, when not pregnant, resembles a flattened pear in size and shape, with the stem directed toward the vagina (fig. 2). This end is called the cervix; the rest is the corpus. Most of its thick wall consists of involuntary muscle. It has a slitlike cavity which extends laterally to the openings of the oviducts and is flattened from before backward. The cavity is triangular in form with the lower angle at the cervix (fig. 2). The lining of the corpus (endometrium) is a mucous membrane which is specially adapted for the reception and development of the fertilized egg. It has remarkable powers of regeneration, and it is constantly changing in structure and appearance during the reproductive period. In the nonpregnant state it may increase 10 times in thickness in the space of a month, i.e., during a menstrual cycle. It is covered by a single layer of secreting and ciliated cells which are continuous with tubelike glands that extend to the muscular layer. The glands are embedded in an embryonic type of connective tissue richly supplied with blood vessels. The superficial zone where the fertilized egg develops has a distinct set of arteries (fig. 3) which alternately dilate and contract so that the supply of blood varies rhythmically. The corpus is usually bent forward so that it lies upon the urinary bladder and is thus at an angle with the cervix, which is firmer than the corpus and less movable. It is cylindrical in shape and has many glands which secrete mucus. Its cavity is narrowed by interlocking folds of mucous membrane. At its lower end it protrudes into the vagina with which it communicates by a narrow slit (orificium externum uteri).

The vagina is a flattened muscular tube, its folded lining resembling the outer skin (epidermis) in structure. There are no glands but the surface is moistened by secretions from the uterus. At its lower end a thin fold of mucous membrane, the hymen, narrows the external opening in virgins. The external genitalia

(pudendum) consist of (1) a pair of skin folds, the lesser labia, which lie on either side of (2) a shallow trough, the vestibule, into which the vagina, the urethra (from the urinary bladder) and various small glands open. At the upper end of the vestibule is the clitoris, a small erectile organ, counterpart of the penis. These organs are usually completely covered by a pair of thick folds of hair-covered skin, the greater labia, which correspond to the scrotum of the male.

Development of Reproductive Function in Woman.—Before birth the infant's genital organs are stimulated by hormones which reach it from the placenta (q.v.). Such influences necessarily cease at birth and there is a regression which is particularly obvious in the cervix. During childhood there are no signs of activity but at the beginning of adolescence (8 to 12 years) the ovaries are activated by the hypophysis to the production of large follicles and hormones. The latter stimulate all parts of the reproductive tract and in addition the bony pelvis, breasts, hair (crines) and fat depots begin their progress toward maturity. There is a rhythmic alternation in the dominance of the hormones of the hypophysis and ovary. Eventually the hormonal tides attain a height which results in bleeding from the endometrium (menstruation), and the first menstrual period (menarche) appears.

Menstrual Cycles.—During the child-bearing period the sequence of events in the cycle is usually as follows: Under stimulation from the hypophysis at intervals of about a month, an ovarian follicle outstrips its fellows in growth and in a few days attains a diameter of about half an inch. Usually only one follicle enters upon this final growth period but rarely more may ripen. The enlarged follicle soon protrudes from the ovary like a clear blister. The ripened egg cell has become loosened from the follicle wall, and soon the outer wall of the follicle bulges, breaks, and the viscid follicular fluid wells out, carrying the egg along with it. This event is called ovulation. At about this time the hormone estrin reaches a peak in the blood stream and the oviducts, uterus and vagina are stimulated to great activity. It has been possible to peer into the body cavity of monkeys at such a time and see the thin-walled folds at the end of the oviduct wrapped closely about the ovary while both organs moved rhythmically. If spermatozoa are present the egg may be fertilized as soon as it is liberated. In any case it is swept into the oviduct where it is slowly moved along, reaching the uterus by the fourth day. The endometrium in the interim has been growing thick through cell division and the accumulation of fluid in the tissue. The glands have been secreting a watery mucus which moistens the surface. At about the time of ovulation the vessels are so dilated that the surface appears bright red and some blood corpuscles often leak out. The glands of the cervix have produced a quantity of mucus

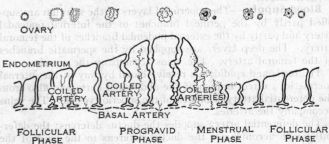

G. W. BARTELMEZ IN MAXIMOW-BLOOM "TEXTBOOK OF HISTOLOGY," 5TH ED. (W. B. SAUNDERS CO.)

FIG. 3.—A DIAGRAM TO INDICATE THE CHANGES IN OVARY AND ENDOMETRIUM DURING THE SUCCESSIVE DAYS OF THE MENSTRUAL CYCLE. IN THE UPPER ROW THE FIRST TWO FIGURES SHOW A GROWING FOLLICLE, THE NEXT ITS RUPTURE WITH THE LIBERATION OF THE EGG (OVULATION), THE TWO FOLLOWING REPRESENT THE FORMATION OF THE CORPUS LUTEUM FROM THE COLLAPSED FOLLICLE, AND THE LAST THREE SHOW THE DEGENERATION OF THE CORPUS LUTEUM WITH THE CONCOMITANT GROWTH OF A NEW FOLLICLE WHICH MARKS THE BEGINNING OF THE NEW CYCLE. BELOW THE CHANGES IN THE GLANDS AND ARTERIES OF THE ENDOMETRIUM ARE SHOWN, ASSOCIATED AT FIRST WITH THE HORMONES OF THE FOLLICLE AND CORPUS LUTEUM AND THEN WITH THEIR REDUCTION WHICH RESULTS IN SHRINKING OF THE ENDOMETRIUM FOLLOWED BY BLEEDING FROM ITS DEGENERATING SURFACE

which plays a role in the survival of spermatozoa. The lining of the vagina has thickened by rapid cell division. This period is called the follicular phase of the cycle because it is dominated by the hormones of the ovarian follicle and is associated with its growth and rupture. Ovulation may occur as early as 7 days after the beginning of a menstrual period or it may be delayed for 18 days or even more.

The next phase of the cycle is called the luteal (or progravid) phase because it is dominated by an organ of internal secretion which arises from the walls of the ruptured follicle. It is called the corpus luteum, because in the human species it soon becomes yellow in colour. While the egg is in the oviduct, the thin walls of the collapsed follicle thicken rapidly. The cells enlarge and a meshwork of thin-walled vessels develops between them. The healing of the rupture point permits some fluid to accumulate in the cavity. The distinctive hormone of the corpus luteum, progesterone, produces changes in the uterus which make it a most favourable site for the reception and development of an embryo. The same changes occur whether the egg has been fertilized or not. During this time the contractions of the uterus are slowed down, the endometrium becomes more succulent, its glands become contorted and swell up with a secretion rich in nutrient substances. The arteries continue to grow and become more closely coiled. They play an important role in the subsequent events as was demonstrated by observations on the living endometrium in monkeys which have menstrual cycles very similar to the human cycle. If conception has not occurred the corpus luteum remains active for only 10 to 14 days. With the decline in its hormone output the blood flow to the uterus is reduced and the endometrium begins to shrink. Its superficial zone suffers particularly, for it is supplied by the coiled arteries which constrict for minutes at a time. This was observed in pieces of endometrium which had been transplanted to the eye where they could be watched continuously for hours at a time. In this location they may continue to show the cyclic changes for years. The reduced circulation and shrinkage were seen to persist for days in some instances, for shorter periods in others. This is called the ischaemic phase. Sooner or later superficial weakened vessels break and blood pours out into the tissue. Blood blisters may form which soon drain into the cavity of the uterus. This marks the beginning of menstruation (menstrual phase). The blood-soaked tissue soon loosens and sloughs off, leaving a raw wound surface. These observations illuminate many conditions that are found in microscopic preparations of human menstruating endometrium removed surgically. The endometrium continues to shrink during menstruation, and the processes of repair are rapid. Sometimes there is a period of relative inactivity before a new ovarian follicle enters on its final growth and initiates the changes of the next cycle.

Menstrual cycles continue more or less regularly unless interrupted by pregnancy. They are accompanied by various general bodily changes. A sudden fall followed by a rise in the basal temperature, for example, and a sense of exhilaration may be noted about the middle of the cycle when ovulation is most apt to occur. Rarely is abdominal pain experienced at this time. The relations between hypophysis and ovary may be affected by other hormones and by the nervous system as well. Changes in climate, living conditions, infections or psychic disturbances may consequently affect the rhythm. When the responses of the ovaries begin to wane at the age of 45 to 50 years, marked changes appear in the economy of the body as a whole and the hormonal balance is upset. (*See* also MENSTRUATION.)

BIBLIOGRAPHY.—F. L. Adair (ed.), *Obstetrics and Gynecology* (1940); E. Allen *et al.*, *Sex and Internal Secretions*, 2nd ed. (1939); G. W. Corner, *The Hormones in Human Reproduction* (1942); C. G. Hartman, *Time of Ovulation in Women* (1936); E. C. Hamblen, *Endocrinology of Woman* (1945); F. H. A. Marshall, *Physiology of Reproduction* (1922).   (G. W. B.)

EMBRYOLOGY

The development of the reproductive organs is closely interwoven with that of the urinary system (*q.v.*). It will here be convenient to take up the development at the stage in which the

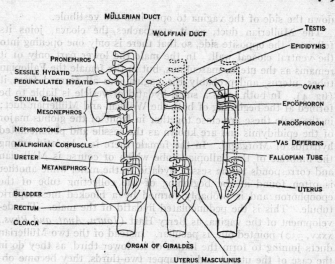

FIG. 4.—DIAGRAM OF THE FORMATION OF THE GENITO-URINARY APPARATUS (SUPPRESSED PARTS ARE DOTTED)

genital ridge is seen on each side of the attachment of the mesentery; external to this, and forming another slight ridge of its own, is the Wolffian duct, while a little later the Müllerian duct is formed and lies ventral to the Wolffian. Until the fifth or sixth week the development of the genital ridge is very much the same in the two sexes, and consists of cords of cells growing from the epithelium-covered surface into the mesenchyme, which forms the interior of the ridge. In these cords are some large germ cells which are distinguishable at a very early stage of development. It must, of course, be understood that the germinal epithelium covering the ridge, and the mesenchyme inside it, are both derived from the mesoderm or middle layer of the embryo. About the fifth week of human embryonic life the tunica albuginea appears in the male, from which septa grow to divide the testis into lobules, while the epithelial cords form the seminiferous tubes, though these do not gain a lumen until just before puberty. From the adjacent mesonephros, or perhaps, coelomic epithelium, cords of cells grow into the attached part of the genital ridge, or testis, as it now is, and from these the rete testis is developed.

In the female the same growth of epithelial cords into the mesenchyme of the genital ridge takes place, but each one is distinguished by a bulging toward its middle, in which alone the large germ cells are found. Eventually this bulging part is broken up into a series of small portions, each of which contains one germ cell or ovum and gives rise to a Graafian follicle. Mesonephric cords appear as in the male; they do not enter the ovary, however, but form a transitory network (rete ovarii) in the mesovarium. As each genital gland enlarges it remains attached to the rest of the intermediate cell mass by a constricted fold of the coelomic membrane, known as the mesorchium in the male, and the mesovarium in the female. Lying dorsal to the genital ridge in the intermediate cell mass is the mesonephros, consisting of numerous tubules which open into the Wolffian duct. This at first is an important excretory organ, but during development becomes used for other purposes. In the male, as has been shown, it may form the rete testis, and certainly forms the vasa efferentia and globus major of the epididymis: in addition to these, some of its separate tubes probably account for the ductus aberrans and the organ of Giraldès (*see* fig. 4). In the female the tubules of the epoöphoron represent the main part, while the paroöphoron, like the organ of Giraldès in the male, is probably formed from some separate tubes (*see* fig. 4).

The Wolffian duct, which, in the early embryo, carries the excretion of the mesonephros to the cloaca, forms eventually the body and tail of the epididymis, the ductus (vas) deferens, and ejaculatory duct in the male, the vesicula seminalis being developed as a pouch in its course. In the female this duct is largely done away with, but remains as the collecting tube of the epoöphoron, and in some mammals as the duct of Gärtner, which runs down the side of the vagina to open into the vestibule.

The Müllerian duct, as it approaches the cloaca, joins its fellow of the opposite side, so that there is only one opening into the ventral cloacal wall. In the male the lower part only of it remains as the uterus masculinus, but in the female the Fallopian tubes, uterus, and probably the vagina, are all formed from it (fig. 4). In both sexes a small hydatid or vesicle is liable to be formed at the beginning of both the Wolffian and Müllerian duct; in the male these are close together in front of the globus major of the epididymis and are known as the sessile and pedunculated hydatids of Morgagni. In the female there is a hydatid among the fimbriae of the Fallopian tube which of course is Müllerian and corresponds to the sessile hydatid in the male, while another is often found at the beginning of the collecting tube of the epoöphoron and is probably formed by a blocked mesonephric tubule. This is the pedunculated hydatid of the male. The development of the vagina, as Berry Hart (*Journ. Anat. and Phys.*, xxxv, 330) pointed out, is peculiar. Instead of the two Müllerian ducts joining to form the lumen of its lower third, as they do in the case of the uterus and its upper two-thirds, they become obliterated, and their place is taken by two solid cords of cells, which later become canalized and the septum between them is obliterated.

The common chamber, or cloaca, into which the alimentary, urinary and reproductive tubes open in the foetus, has the urinary bladder (the remains of the allantois) opening from its ventral wall (*see* PLACENTA; URINARY SYSTEM).

During development the alimentary or anal part of the cloaca is separated from the urogenital. According to F. Wood Jones, the anal part is completely shut off from the urogenital and ends in a blind pouch which grows toward the surface and meets a new ectodermal depression, the permanent anus, not being part of the original cloacal aperture, but a new perforation. This description is in harmony with the malformations occurring in this region.

The external generative organs have at first the same appearance in the two sexes and consist of a swelling, the genital eminence, in the ventral wall of the cloaca. This in the male becomes the penis and in the female the clitoris. Throughout the generative system the male organs depart most from the undifferentiated type and in the case of the genital eminence two folds grow together and enclose the urogenital passage, thus making the urethra perforate the penis, while in the female these two folds remain separate as the labia minora. Sometimes in the male the folds fail to unite completely and then there is an opening into the urethra on the under surface of the penis—a condition known as hypospadias.

In the undifferentiated condition the integument surrounding the genital opening is raised into a horseshoelike swelling with its convexity over the pubic symphysis and its concavity toward the anus; the lateral parts of this remain separate in the female and form the labia majora, but in the male they unite to form the scrotum. The median part forms the mons Veneris or mons Jovis.

It has been shown that the testis is formed in the loin region of the embryo close to the kidney, and it is only in the later months of foetal life that it changes this position for that of the scrotum. In the lower part of the genital ridge a fibromuscular cord is formed which stretches from the lower part of the testis to the bottom of the scrotum; it is known as the gubernaculum testis, and by its means the testis is directed into the scrotum. Before the testis descends, a pouch of peritoneum called the processus vaginalis passes down in front of the gubernaculum through the opening in the abdominal wall, which afterward becomes the inguinal canal, into the scrotum, and behind this the testis descends, carrying with it the mesonephros and mesonephric duct. These, as has already been pointed out, form the epididymis and ductus deferens. At the sixth month the testis lies opposite the abdominal ring, and at the eighth reaches the bottom of the scrotum and invaginates the processus vaginalis from behind. Soon after birth the communication between that part of the processus vaginalis which now surrounds the testis and the general cavity of the peritoneum disappears, and the part which remains forms the tunica vaginalis. Sometimes the testis fails to pass beyond the inguinal canal, and the term "cryptorchism" is used for such cases.

In the female the ovary undergoes a descent like that of the testis, but it is less marked since the gubernaculum becomes attached to the Müllerian duct where that duct joins its fellow to form the uterus. Thus, the ovary does not descend lower than the level of the top of the uterus, and the part of the gubernaculum running between it and the uterus remains as the ligament of the ovary, while the part running from the uterus to the labium is the round ligament. In rare cases the ovary may be drawn into the labium just as the testis is drawn into the scrotum.   (F. G. P.)

REPTILES (*Reptilia*) is the name given to a class of vertebrates which hold a position in the animal kingdom intermediate between the amphibians and the birds, and the mammals. The group arose, perhaps in Lower Carboniferous times, from the Labyrinthodont Amphibia, and was already varied at the end of the Carboniferous. During Permian times the class branched out into many orders, one of which included the ancestors of the Mammalia, whilst from another the birds, crocodiles, Sphenodon, and perhaps the lizards and snakes arose. The tortoises are the descendants of another early group. In a recent survey by Nopcsa, it is pointed out that, of the 125 families into which he divides the reptiles, only 18 are represented by living forms, whilst of the 19 orders only four are extant. The modern forms fall into the orders Crocodilia, including the crocodiles and alligators; the Squamata, the lizards and snakes; the Rhynchocephalia, represented only by the Tuatera lizard of New Zealand, and the Chelonia, the tortoises and turtles. These living forms are characterized as follows:

(1.) The animal breathes air by lungs.

(2.) The body temperature is variable.

(3.) The skin is covered with horny scales formed by the epidermis.

(4.) Fertilization is internal, and an egg, consisting of a yolk surrounded by albumen and contained in a shell, is usually laid and hatched by the heat of the sun or of decaying vegetation. In some cases reptiles are viviparous.

(5.) In the brain the cerebral hemispheres are comparatively small. Their roof tends to become thinned and may be almost membranous. There is a well-developed hypopallium which becomes assimilated to the corpus striatum, losing the original stratification of the neurones. The mid-brain is relatively large and its roof forms a pair of large optic lobes.

(6.) The olfactory organ has its surface increased by a simple turbinal or concha, and there is a well-developed Jacobson's organ

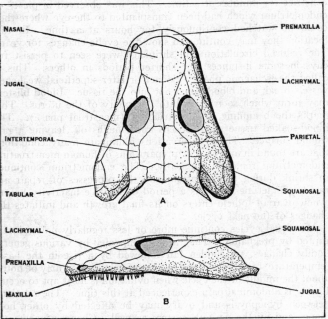

FROM PHILOSOPHICAL TRANSACTIONS OF THE ROYAL SOCIETY

FIG. 1.—SKULL OF THE EMBOLOMEROUS AMPHIBIAN PALAEOGYRINUS; (A) FROM ABOVE. (B) FROM THE LEFT SIDE

The posterior nares may be immediately below the external nostrils or may be carried back to the hinder end of the head.

The eyes are usually present, but may be hidden in burrowing forms. The retina normally contains both rods and cones, but may consist exclusively of either type. There is a pecten in the form of a folded sheet projecting into the vitreous humour.

The internal ear shows a more marked separation of *sacculus* and *utriculus* than obtains in Amphibia, a lagena always occurs and is associated with a perilymphatic duct, in some cases so as to form a rudimentary cochlea. The tympanic cavity lies high up and the tympanic membrane is either superficial or lies at the end of a short external auditory meatus. The membrane is connected to that closing the *fenestra ovalis* by a straight rod, whose inner end, the columella, is bony, whilst the outer half, the extra-columella, is often four-rayed, a short dorsal process being connected to the end of the paroccipital process and a ventral process often continued into the hyoid.

(7.) There is a well-developed tongue capable of free movement. The mid-gut has the usual structure; there is a cloaca and an urinary bladder of allantoic origin. The lungs are more elaborate than those of Amphibia and less than those of mammals.

(8.) The heart is three- or four-chambered, there being two auricles and a ventricle more or less completely divided into two. There is no bulbus; three arteries arise from the ventricle; of these one is the right systemic, another the pulmonary, whilst the third is the left systemic and both carotids. The posterior cardinals have both almost disappeared as such, the post-caval vein returning most of the blood from the posterior part of the animal to the heart. There is a coronary circulation.

(9.) The functional kidney in the adult is a metanephros discharging by a ureter into the cloaca. The ovary is often single and the egg always large. The oviduct is provided with glands which secrete albumen and a shell. A copulatory organ is usually present in the male, but is variable in structure.

(10.) The pre-sacral part of the vertebral column is usually less clearly divided into regions than in mammals and birds. There are two sacral vertebrae and a longer or shorter series of caudals. The atlas consists of a pair of neural arches, a single inter centrum and a centrum which forms an odontoid, though it may not be fused to the axis. There is sometimes a pro-atlas. The vertebra of the rest of the column always consists of a neural arch and a centrum with inter-centra forming chevron bones in the tail. Small inter-centra may be present throughout the column. Ribs are usually present on all vertebrae except the posterior caudals; they may be single or double headed. A true sternum is usually present, connected to some of the dorsal ribs by sternal ribs.

The neural cranium is generally incompletely ossified, a good deal of the lateral walls anteriorly being membranous. It is often movably connected to the dermal bones of the skull roof and palate. There is a single occipital condyle, mainly basi-occipital but with contributions from the ex-occipital. A supra-occipital is present and articulates with the parietals. The inner ear lies within the opisthotic, usually fused with the ex-occipital, the prootic and the supra-occipital. An ossification in front of the prootic, in the side wall of the cranium, is absent in only two orders. There is an ossified basi-sphenoid, but the unossified pre-sphenoid is usually underlain by a para-sphenoid.

The dermal bones of the skull form a roof, which may be very incomplete or, indeed, absent, over the masticatory muscles, whilst the orbit is surrounded by a ring of bones which are continuous with the maxillae and nasals which enclose the anterior end of the head. In the palate the pterygoids are always large bones articulating with the basi-sphenoid and extending back to the quadrate. Pre-vomers and palatines are always present and ectopterygoids usually so. In many forms an epipterygoid is ossified. The lower jaw is complex, it articulates with the quadrate by an articular bone of endochondral origin, and at least five membrane bones contribute to its structure.

Fore and hind limbs are usually present, but either or both may be absent. The shoulder girdle consists of a pair of scapulae and "coracoids," both contributing to the glenoid cavity. There are generally clavicles and an inter-clavicle. The hand and foot are primitively pentadactyl, the fourth digit being the longest.

(11.) Segmentation of the egg is incomplete (meroblastic). No primitive streak is formed and a rudimentary archenteron with both roof and floor may be established. There is an amnion and an allantois, membranes developed for the protection, nutrition and respiration of the embryo.

Amphibian Ancestry.—The Amphibia, which were the ancestors of the reptiles, spent the greater part of their life in water, probably crawling on to land only to pass from one pool to another. They laid small eggs, which were fertilized after they had passed out from the body of the mother. These eggs developed into an aquatic larva which breathed by means of gills; subsequently, when this larva had reached a relatively large size, the gills were absorbed and the animal became dependent on the air for the main bulk of its oxygen. An aquatic animal may have, and in the case of the Amphibia did have, a soft skin which can only remain healthy if it be kept moist. Living Amphibia secure this condition by pouring out mucus and water from glands in their skin, which is therefore slimy. An animal which adopts this method has great difficulty in roaming far from water, the possibility of dying from desiccation being always present. Thus one of the first changes necessary to make an effectively terrestrial animal from an amphibian is to alter the character of its skin in such a way that it becomes water-tight, and has a dry outer surface. Such a change in a vertebrate is most readily achieved by thickening the epidermis and laying down keratin in its outer layers; continuation of this process leads to the formation of the horny scales of reptiles, which are made by localized patches of skin exceptionally active in the production of keratin. As such a skin does not require to be kept moist, glands are very poorly developed in the skin of reptiles.

During the transition from water to air the sense organs necessarily undergo great modifications. The olfactory organ, which had become adapted to the relatively large amounts of odorous substances which could come to it in solution in water, had to be made capable of recognizing the much smaller amounts brought to it as vapour through the air. In the intervening stage of the Amphibia the nose becomes double, one part of it, Jacobson's organ, functioning in water, the rest in air. When the reptiles became completely terrestrial, Jacobson's organ took on the new function of smelling the material lying in the mouth, and the rest of the organ became the normal organ of smell.

The eye, adapted for focussing objects under water, has to be so

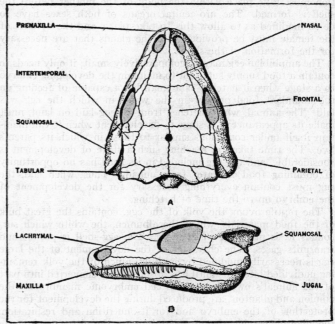

FROM PHILOSOPHICAL TRANSACTIONS OF THE ROYAL SOCIETY

FIG. 2.—SKULL OF THE COTYLOSAUR SEYMOURIA, (A) FROM ABOVE, (B) LEFT SIDE

changed in its proportions as to see its surroundings through air.

That part of the ear whose function is to determine the position of the animal with respect to gravity and to recognize changes in position, can remain unaltered, but the lagena, which, with its associated structures, the columella, middle ear and tympanic membrane, is concerned with hearing in the ordinary sense, necessarily undergoes changes on account of the very different specific gravity of the mediums, water or air, through which sound waves come to it.

Aquatic Amphibia have, in common with fish, a special sense, whose organ is the lateral line, which is concerned with the recognition of movements in water; with the transition to land this sense is entirely lost.

Any animal living in water is so nearly floating that the proportion of its weight which has to be supported by the limbs is extremely small. As soon as it comes out of water practically the whole of its weight falls on the legs. Thus the skeleton and musculature necessarily become more powerful.

The most serious changes, however, are those in the mode of reproduction. An amphibian which lays its eggs in the water can fertilize them there, but a terrestrial animal can only lay an egg

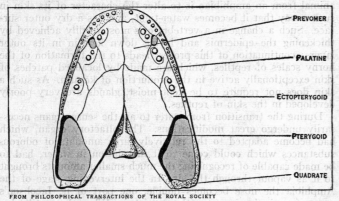

PREVOMER

PALATINE

ECTOPTERYGOID

PTERYGOID

QUADRATE

FROM PHILOSOPHICAL TRANSACTIONS OF THE ROYAL SOCIETY

FIG. 3.—PALATE OF THE EMBOLOMEROUS AMPHIBIAN, BAPHETES

if it be included in a shell which will protect it from mechanical injury and, a matter of more importance, from drying up. Such a shell cannot be perforated by a spermatozoan, so that fertilization must take place within the body of the mother before the shell is formed. The uro-genital organs of both sexes have to be so modified as to allow this to take place, and the oviduct of the female must be provided with the glands that are necessary for the formation of the shell.

The amphibian egg may be comparatively small; it only needs to contain a food supply sufficient to maintain the developing embryo to a stage when it hatches as a small larva capable of feeding on the abundant food present in the water in which the egg was laid. The animal, which hatches from an egg laid on land, must make its appearance at a stage in development when it can maintain itself under conditions similar to those in which its parents live. The time taken in reaching such a stage of development is considerable, and the egg included in its shell has no opportunity of obtaining food or water from outside. Thus, when laid, the egg must contain everything necessary for the development of the embryo up to the time of hatching.

The reptile ovum, the yolk of the egg, contains the great bulk of the food materials, whilst the albumen, the white which surrounds it, is mainly a water store. The egg-shell is porous and transmits gases. The character of the development of the large egg is necessarily modified by its bulk, much of the yolk remaining undivided into cells until it is absorbed and converted into part of the animal's own tissues. Special embryonic membranes, the amnion and allantois, are produced during the development for the protection of the embryo and for its nutrition and respiration, the allantois serving also as a reservoir for the nitrogenous waste products produced by its metabolism.

The great majority of these changes, including all those which are of the greatest importance, cannot be determined from fossil material, and we are driven back for the discrimination between fossil reptiles and fossil amphibians to the use of technical points mainly of little functional importance to the animal. The break between the Amphibia and Reptilia was regarded by Huxley and other early workers as the most important in the vertebrate phylum; such contrasted terms as Ichthyopsida and Sauropsida, Anamniota and Amniota emphasize its importance. None the less we now know an animal, Seymouria, from the lowest Permian of Texas, which is regarded by one group of students as an amphibian and by another as a reptile. As the osteology of this

animal is very completely known, the doubt which exists as to its systematic position illustrates vividly the completeness with which the gap between these two divisions has been bridged.

Seymouria is a small animal about 2 ft. in length, with a comparatively small head, no visible neck, a somewhat stumpy body, and a short tail. The limbs were very muscular, but short. The hands and feet were placed far away from the middle line, and the stride was exceedingly small. Each limb has five digits.

The skull of Seymouria consists of two parts, which could have easily been separated from one another. These are the brain case, made of bones which have replaced the cartilage which existed in the embryonic skull, and a superficial coating covering the whole outer surface of the head (except for the nostrils, orbits and pineal foramen), and the roof of the mouth, made of bones which have developed in the lower layers of the skin. The pattern formed by these dermal bones is identical with that which is found in the more primitive Labyrinthodont Amphibia, and is important, because from it the structure of the corresponding parts of the skulls of all other reptiles can be derived, by a process of reduction. The palate of Seymouria is, in essence, identical with that of an Embolomerous Labyrinthodont. The brain case, however, differs somewhat from those of the Amphibia. For example, the single occipital condyle is convex instead of being concave, and there is a large fenestra ovalis leading into the ear which does not exist in the Embolomeri. There are also variations in other details of the structure of the otic region. In the lower jaw, Seymouria is identical with an amphibian, but the vertebral column is very different.

In the amphibian the first vertebra articulates with the condyle by a disc-shaped inter-centrum followed by a disc-shaped centrum, of the same character as those which succeed it. In Seymouria the rounded condyle articulates below with a concavity on an inter-centrum which represents only the lower half of that of the amphibian, and with facets carried on the lower ends of the two halves of the neural arch. The centrum of the atlas is a curious trefoil-shaped bone which fits in between the three elements which articulate with the condyle; this arrangement is completely reptilian. The structure of a vertebra from the middle of the back of Seymouria is quite peculiar. There is a small cylindrical centrum separated from the next by an inter-centrum having the shape of half a disc. The neural arch is enormously heavy, it articulates with the centrum alone and the pre- and post-zygopotheses are produced laterally as masses of bone which overhang the much smaller centrum. The articulating faces are quite flat and placed horizontally, so that the back, although free to move from side to side, must have been extremely stiff dorso-ventrally.

Vertebrae of this type are known in no amphibian, but in a less exaggerated form occur in many of the more primitive reptiles. It is reasonable to believe that they were evolved as a clumsy method of giving that stiffness to the back which is necessary to an animal which, living in air, has to support the whole of its weight. The ribs of Seymouria do not differ essentially from those of some Labyrinthodonts. The limb girdles and limbs are of the amphibian pattern except in one or two details, e.g., the occurrence of an ent-epi-condylar foramen piercing the humerus, and the number of the phalanges, which is two, three, four, five, three, the characteristic reptilian number.

Thus it is possible to be in doubt whether an extinct animal whose skeleton is completely known is an amphibian or a reptile, the break between the two being completely bridged so far as the skeleton is concerned. From a skeleton similar to that of Seymouria it is possible to derive those of all later reptiles, and in this way, by sorting out separate evolutionary lines to establish a classification which may express not only differences of structure existing between the animals contained in it, but something of their phylogenetic relationships.

Evolutionary Development.—The reptiles, as a whole, with a few doubtful exceptions, divide into two great branches, the mammal-like reptiles and the rest. The differences between the members of these two groups are to be found mainly in the structure of the brain case and the back of the skull. In all the mammal-like reptiles the inner ear lies in the lower part of the side wall of the brain case, the brain extending far above it, while in all other reptiles the ear extends throughout the whole of the side wall of the cranium and is not exceeded in height by the brain. In *Seymouria* the tympanic membrane is stretched across a notch on the outer surface at the back of the skull; in the mammal-like reptiles this notch is destroyed, so that the occipital surface of the skull is flat and the tympanic membrane, if it exists at all, lies ventrally in the neighbourhood of the hinder end of the lower jaw, to one of whose elements it is attached. In the remaining reptiles the tympanic or otic notch is preserved, bounded above by a special process of the squamosal or tabular bone, and by the free distal extremity of the paroccipital. The tympanic membrane, when present, lies high up on the side of the head, far removed from the lower jaw. In the mammal-like reptiles the stapes is attached directly to the quadrate bone, while in the others it is continued by an extra columella which is inserted into the tympanic membrane.

It is customary to recognize a primitive group of reptiles, the Cotylosauria, which includes the most primitive members of each division of the reptiles. The animals included in it agree with *Seymouria* in that the dermal bones of the outer surface of the skull form a continuous sheet, perforated only by the nostrils, orbits and pineal foramen. This group is restricted to Permian and Triassic time, and its members thus possess very primitive limbs and limb-girdles. They are usually devoid of a neck, the shoulder-girdle lying immediately behind the head. The back is short and the vertebrae of which it is composed have very massive neural arches which articulate with one another by horizontal surfaces. The centra are perforated and transmit a continuous notochord. There is usually a series of intercentra throughout the column. The shoulder girdle has three bony elements, the scapula, procoracoid and coracoid in each side of the cartilage girdle; all of them contribute to the glenoid cavity. Cleithra are often present, and clavicles and large inter-clavicles are universal. The fore leg is short and massive, the humerus projecting out at right angles to the animal's body and lying in a plane parallel to the ground. It can only be moved backwards and forwards, and is incapable of rotation. The elbow joint is flexible, so that the fore arm has much freedom of movement. The hand has five fingers, the number of the phalanges being 2, 3, 4, 5, 3, in the digits from 1 to 5. The pelvis consists of an ilium, pubis and ischium on each side, these bones meeting one another in continuous sutures, so that the whole structure is "plate-like." The hind limb projects out laterally and the knee is relatively inflexible; it could be stretched out straight, but, in many cases, could not be closed even to a right angle. The foot has five toes with a digital formula 2, 3, 4, 5, 4.

This super-order can be divided into three sub-groups, as follows:—(A.) *Seymouria morpha,* primitive forms represented by three genera, *Solenodonsaurus,* from the Upper Carboniferous of Czechoslovakia; *Seymouria,* from the basal Permian of Texas, and *Kotlassia,* from the Upper Permian of Russia, which may not properly belong to the group.

These animals possess skulls which very greatly resemble those of the Embolomerous Amphibia. (*See* AMPHIBIA.) These skulls have a narrow otic notch differing from that of all other reptiles; the neural cranium is peculiar in that the powerful paroccipital processes which arise from the sides of the brain case extend outwards and upwards to support the tabular bones. The basioccipital, together with the exoccipitals, form a rounded condyle. There are well marked basisphenoidal tubera and the basipterygoid processes of the basisphenoid are short, and in *Seymouria* support the pterygoid, not directly, but through the intervention of the epipterygoid. The parasphenoid is short and narrow. The palate is almost completely roofed with bone, there being small palatal nostrils and sub-temporal fossae in addition to a very conspicuous inter-pterygoid vacuity. The palatine bears a large tusk, the marginal teeth in the upper jaw form a uniform unbroken series and exhibit an indefinite replacement. The lower jaw is built up from nine bones, dentary, splenial, post splenial, angular, sur-angular on the outer surface, the series of three coronoids between the pre-

articular and dentary, and an articular bone which, unlike that of all contemporary Amphibia, is not a mere part of the sur-angular. With this exception, the jaw is identical with that of a Labyrinthodont.

The vertebral column is massive, there is no distinction of neck, trunk, and lumbar region, all the vertebrae from the atlas back to the sacrum bearing two-headed ribs; there is one sacral vertebra. In the shoulder girdle a coracoid is absent, the lower part of the primary structure being ossified entirely as a pre-coracoid. The glenoid cavity has the characteristic screw-shaped form of the early Tetrapod. The humerus is an extraordinary bone, nearly as wide as it is long, while the fore arm is short. The hand is short and broad, the five fingers ending in small claws.

The pelvis is plate-like, the pubes and ischia being exceptionally large elements; the femur, short, broad and unusually massive, exactly resembles that of contemporary Amphibia. The fibula is widened distally, and the tarsus is remarkable among reptiles in possessing three bones in its proximal row, the intermedium being still separate from the tibiale. The foot is five toed, with the normal formula.

The mammal-like members of the Cotylosauria belong to the group (B.) Captorhinomorpha. This group includes a considerable number of reptiles, all of Lower Permian age, which vary a good deal in their general structure. The most typical are Captorhinus and its descendant, Labidosaurus. These animals are comparatively small, with no neck, rather long bodies and not excessively long tails. They had a straddling gait, the ventral surface touching the ground and the feet being placed well away from the side of the body. The head is pointed, the face in front of the eyes narrow, while the temporal region is wide. The skull is completely roofed and there is no trace of an otic notch, the head having a square cut appearance posteriorly. The brain case seems to be high, and is loosely connected with the rest of the skull by the summit of the supraoccipital and the ends of the paroccipital process. The stapes is very massive and extends from the fenestra ovalis, which is placed below the level of the brain, to the quadrate to which it is attached.

The lower jaw differs from that of *Seymouria* by a lateral compression of its hinder half, and by the reduction of the coronoids to one.

The vertebral column is characterized by the massiveness of the neural arches and the obsolescence of the neural spines. The

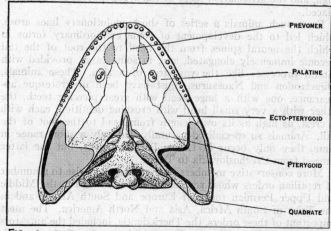

FIG. 4.—SKULL OF THE COTYLOSAUR SEYMOURIA (AFTER WATSON)

centra are small and perforated, the intercentra much reduced. All the ribs are single-headed. The remainder of the skeleton does not differ materially from that of *Seymouria,* which has been described above.

The earliest and most primitive members of the group of mammal-like reptiles belong to the order Pelycosauria. The most primitive members of this group, such as Varanosaurus and Mycterosaurus are small, rather slender animals, with elongated pointed heads. They had no visible neck, the shoulder girdle being placed behind the skull. The body was long and the tail even longer. Their skulls differ from those of the Captorhino-morpha most obviously in that the dermal roof is no longer complete, but is perforated by a large lateral vacuity which is bounded by the jugal, postorbital and squamosal bones. This opening serves to give room for the thickening of the masticatory muscles, which necessarily occurs when they are shortened so as to close the mouth.

Another important difference is that the supraoccipital bone becomes so widened that, with the overlying interparietal and tabu-

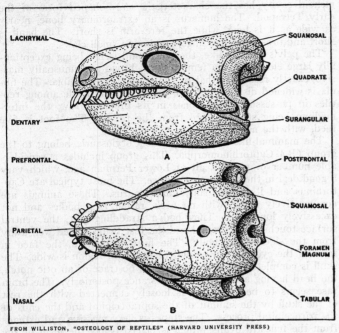

FROM WILLISTON, "OSTEOLOGY OF REPTILES" (HARVARD UNIVERSITY PRESS)

FIG. 5.—SKULL OF THE CALYLOSAUR, DIADECTES; (A) LEFT SIDE WITH LOWER JAW, (B) FROM ABOVE

lar, it forms a plate on the hinder surface of the skull, which reduces the post-temporal fossae to very small proportions.

The only important changes in the post cranial skeleton are that the neural arches become light and narrow, the neural spines high, and the articulation faces of the zygapophyses are obliquely placed.

From such animals a series of short evolutionary lines arose, which led to the development of some extraordinary forms in which the neural spines from the head to the root of the tail become immensely elongated, and, in some cases, provided with lateral processes like the yard-arm of a ship. These animals, Dimetrodon and Naosaurus, must have been of grotesque appearance, one with a huge head with great piercing teeth, the other with a very small head with crushing dentition, each with a crest, as high as its own length from head to the root of the tail. Animals so specialized naturally had only a short range in time, they only occur in Lower Permian rocks, but the latter ranged from Czechoslovakia to Texas.

More conservative members of the group gave rise to a number of reptilian orders whose remains have been found in the Middle and Upper Permian rocks of Europe and South Africa, and in the Trias of South Africa, Asia and North America. The most important of these orders, the Theriodontia, included the ancestors of the mammals, and its members exhibit a series of stages which seem to bridge the structural gap between a Pelycosaur and a mammal very completely.

Some of these changes are illustrated by a comparison of the skulls of Scymnognathus and Cynognathus.

The skull of Scymnognathus, a Gorgonopsid, differs from that of a primitive Pelycosaur in that in it the whole head is flattened, the temporal vacuity, instead of facing laterally, is directed upward and is greatly increased in size; this change implies that the muscles which close the mouth had changed, an originally rather simple mass splitting up into pterygoidal, temporal and

masseter muscles. In order to give room for this powerful development the side of the roof of the skull, formed by the jugal postorbital and squamosal, is bowed out, with the result that the quadrate and quadrato-jugal, being fixed in position by their articulation with the lower jaw, become detached from the side of the head and remain inserted in a depression on the front face of the squamosal, within the temporal vacuity. At the same time they are somewhat reduced in size.

The enlarged masticatory muscles require a more extensive area of attachment on the lower jaw, to provide which the upper and hinder end of the dentary becomes free and grows upward. At the same time, the hinder half of the jaw, composed of the surangular, angular, articular and prearticular bones, become converted into a thin sheet by a lateral compression, and the lower border of the angular is notched, a special lamina of the bone being reflected over the outer surface of its posterior part. To this reflected lamina the lower edge of the tympanic membrane seems to have been attached.

The palate, though it still has the posterior nares placed far forward, is advanced because it is very much vaulted, owing to the downgrowth of the maxillae on each side of it. Posteriorly, the pterygoids, with a parasphenoid held between them, form a narrow girder which connects the basisphenoid with the anterior part of the palate.

The stapes still articulates with the quadrate. The brain case is incompletely ossified in front of the point of exit of the fifth cranial nerve. The branches of that nerve pass on each side of the rod-like epipterygoid, and the cerebral hemispheres are enclosed in a single ossification homologous with the sphenethenoid of a frog.

Cynognathus has advanced beyond Scymnognathus in that the face has become deeper and more rounded, and the nostrils larger. The temporal vacuity has enlarged so that it is bounded above by the parietal, and this bone is drawn up into a deep sagittal crest which allows of longer temporal muscles. The quadrate and quadrato-jugal have become greatly reduced in size, but retain their position and function.

The coronoid process of the dentary has increased enormously, and now overlaps the rest of the lower jaw so greatly that it has nearly, but not quite, acquired an independent articulation on the squamosal.

The hinder part of the lower jaw, though still retaining all its constituent bones, has become so small that it seems inadequate to resist the very great stresses to which it might be subjected during feeding. The reflected lamina of the angular is still present in the form of a slender downturned process.

The palate has changed greatly, the original roof of the median area is still present in part, but it is concealed from view by a secondary palate exactly like that of a mammal, which is formed by ingrowths from the maxillae and palatines. By this change the posterior nares are driven so far backward that they open behind the cheek teeth, and the animal became capable of breathing whilst the mouth was full of food undergoing mastication. The ectopterygoid is greatly reduced, and the posterior part of the pterygoid, the quadrate ramus, has vanished altogether, its place being taken by a process which grows backward from the root of the epipterygoid.

The side walls of the brain case have become bony by a widening of the upper end of the epipterygoid, now recognizable as the homologue of the mammalian alisphenoid. This arrangement involves the inclusion in the cranial cavity of a space, the cavum epiptericum, which in most other reptiles lies outside the cranium. By a continuation of changes in the same direction as those which converted a Gorgonopsid such as Scymnognathus into the Cynodent Cynognathus, a primitive mammalian structure is easily reached.

The face changes little, a disappearance of the internarial processes throws the bony nostrils into one, the prefrontal and postorbital disappear, and the orbit becomes confluent with the temporal fossa.

Further growth of the dentary leads to the development of a new temporo-mandibular joint between that bone and the squamosal, and the quadrate and hinder part of the jaw, freed from any function in connection with the jaw, become available as auditory ossicles. The stapes persists, little changed, the quadrate, further reduced in size, becomes the incus. The articular is the malleus, and the prearticular its processus folianus. The angular, to which the tympanic membrane has been attached for a very long period, becomes the tympanic, and the surangular disappears.

This account of the origin of the mammalian auditory ossicles is confirmed by the mode in which those bones develop in every mammal; indeed, all marsupials are still born in a stage in which the lower jaw still moves on the old reptilian joint between the incus and malleus, and the musculus tensor tympani still functions as a jaw muscle.

The palate of *Cynognathus* requires very few modifications to become typically mammalian. The already minute ectopterygoid vanishes, the great flanges of the pterygoids, which exist to ensure the accurate closure of the mouth, become unnecessary when the new temporo-mandibular joint is established, and vanish, and the posterior ramus of the alisphenoid becomes the tympanic process.

The skull of *Scymnognathus* is connected to the complex atlas by a single condyle composed of the basi and exoccipitals, that of *Cynognathus* has a mammal-like pair of exoccipital condyles.

More serious modifications have to be made in the ear region and brain case. The opisthotic and pro-otic of *Cynognathus* house only part of the inner ear, the summit of that organ lying in the supraoccipital. In mammals, the whole lies in a single bone, the periotic. The mammalian periotic is a much smaller bone than the pro- and opisthotics of a cynodont, and, unlike them, it is comparatively unimportant as a buttress for the squamosal. None the less, it is not impossible to homologize the different regions of the two sets of structures.

The post-cranial skeleton of Cynodonts shows a similar resemblance to that of mammals, some of the more important features of the evolution being discussed in the section *Locomotion* of this article. Thus we know in considerable detail the evolutionary stages which lie between the structure of an embolomerous amphibian and that of a mammal. Unfortunately, we can trace no such ancestry for the birds. We are certain that they sprang from a group of reptiles very remote from the mammal stock, but we are still faced by a considerable gap.

Classification.—The classification of reptiles is necessarily based on skeletal characters, and is still in a state of flux. The existing divergences of view are not very important; they relate to the phylogenetic position of a few orders, and do not seriously affect the main outline.

Class Reptilia.—Tetrapodous vertebrates, which breathe air throughout their life. The body temperature is variable. The heart possesses a sinus venosus, two auricles and a ventricle incompletely or completely divided into two; there is no conus arteriosus. Both systemic arches persist. The red blood corpuscles are nucleated, oval and biconvex. The kidney is a metanephros, and there is an allantoic bladder, in most forms. There is a cloaca, which in living reptiles is divided into a series of regions. The skin is either naked or covered with scales, never with feathers or hair. It includes very few glands, always placed in special situations, and not generally distributed. The skeleton is ossified. The skull comprises a cranium, of cartilage bones, and an extensive series of bones, which, dermal in origin, sink in and become membrane bones in the later forms. The occipital condyle is single or double. The lower jaw articulates with a quadrate bone and is built up of a number of bones. There is a rod-like columella auris. The vertebrae consist mainly of centra and neural arches, intercentra, when present, being small. Ribs occur on all precaudal vertebrae, those in the thoracic region joining to form a sternum in the mid-ventral line.

The pectoral girdle, when fully developed, includes at least a scapula and precoracoid, clavicles and an interclavicle. The pelvic girdle, except in one or two cases, articulates with two or more sacral ribs. The limbs are primitively pentadactyle and the phalangeal formula 2, 3, 4, 5, 3 or 4.

Fertilization is internal, the eggs are large and yolk laden, usu-

ally laid, when they are surrounded by a coat of albumen and a shell which is often calcified. Cleavage is meroblastic, a primitive streak is not formed, the embryo is surrounded by an amnion and an allantois is developed.

Super-order. Cotylosauria. Archaic reptiles in which the temporal region of the skull is completely covered by a continuous roof of dermal bones. Stapes either articulating with the quadrate or ending in a tympanic notch. Lower jaw usually with more than one coronoid. Presacral vertebrae (except in Pantylus) with very heavy neural arches with horizontal zygapophysial articular faces. Ribs one or two headed. No ossified sternum. Abdominal ribs sometimes present as fine bony rods. Shoulder girdle with scapula and precoracoid at least, a coracoid usually present in addition. Cleithra usually, clavicles and an interclavicle always present. Humerus with (usually) a screw-shaped head, short and with widely expanded extremities. Pelvis, plate-like, the suture between the pubis and ischium extending from the acetabulum to the middle line.

Order 1. Seymouriamorpha. Cotylosaurs in which the skull greatly resembles in all external features that of the Embolomerous Labyrinthodonts, the dermal bones are sculptured and the otic notch extends far forward below the tabular and supratemporal, so that the quadrate slopes backward. Stapes ending in the otic notch. Fenestra ovalis low down on the cranium, below the level of the base of the brain. Intercentra present and very large, ribs one or two headed. Only one sacral vertebra. Shoulder girdle without coracoid or cleithrum, limbs primitive.

Upper Carboniferous to Upper Permian. Families, *Seymouriidae, Kotlassiidae.*

Order 2. Captorhinomorpha. Cotylosaurs in which the otic notch has been obliterated by a movement backward of the upper end of the quadrate. Dermosupraoccipitals and tabulars, when present, restricted to the occipital surface. Stapes articulating

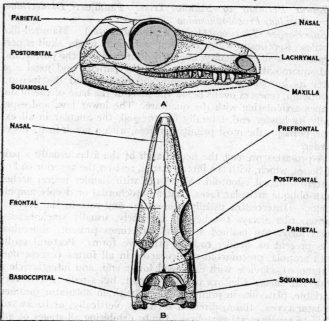

FIG. 6.—SKULL OF PELYIOSAUR MYCTEROSAURUS; (A) RIGHT SIDE WITH LOWER JAW, (B) SKULL FROM ABOVE

distally with the quadrate. Brain case behind the incisura pro-oticum short and high, fenestra ovalis ventrally situated. Intercentra usually present. One or two sacral vertebrae. Shoulder girdle with both precoracoid and coracoid. Cleithrum present or absent. Limbs primitive, though sometimes slender.

Lower Permian. Families *Captorhinidae, Pantylidae, Limnoscelidae.*

Order 3. Diadectomorpha. Cotylosaurs in which the otic notch is enlarged by a movement forward of the lower end of the quadrate, dermosupra occipitals and tabulars when present on the

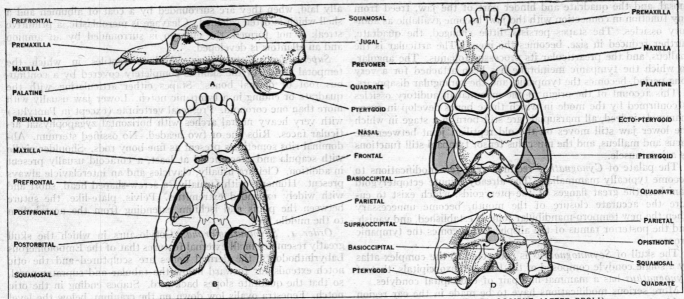

FIG. 7.—SKULL OF PLACODUS: (A) LEFT SIDE, (B) FROM ABOVE, (C) FROM BELOW, (D) OCCIPUT (AFTER BROLI)

upper surface of the skull, the latter overhanging the otic notch. Stapes terminating freely in the otic notch. Brain case long, fenestra ovalis placed at about the middle of its height. Intercentra usually present. Two to four sacral vertebrae. Shoulder girdle with a scapula alone or with three cartilage bones. Cleithrum usually present. Humerus always with expanded ends but often of advanced structure. Ilium sometimes backwardly directed.

Lower Permian to Middle Trias. Families: *Diadectidae, Pariasauridae, Procolophonidae*

Super-order Theromorpha (or *Anomodontia*). Mammal-like reptiles. Reptiles in which the temporal region of the skull is perforated by a single vacuity, bounded primitively by the postorbital and squamosal, but enlarging so that the parietal and jugal also enter its borders. Cranium short and high behind the incisura prooticum, fenestra ovalis below the level of the base of the brain. Stapes articulating with the quadrate. The lower jaw, and especially its hinder end, laterally compressed, the angular in all except, perhaps, the most primitive forms, with a notch in its lower border.

A pro-atlas present, the neural arch of the atlas usually a pair of bones, which, with the intercentrum, rest on the anterior end of a trefoil-shaped odontoid. Vertebrae with slender neural arches with oblique articular faces, centra notochordal or deeply amphicoelous. Intercentra usually present, at any rate in the cervical region, ribs always two-headed anteriorly, usually single-headed posteriorly. An ossified sternum sometimes present, abdominal ribs present as slender rods in primitive forms. Pectoral girdle with scapula, precoracoid and coracoid in all forms (except one, Varanops), clavicle with expanded lower end, and interclavicle a wide flat sheet. Cleithra usually present, but small. Pelvis very variable, plate-like in primitive forms, with an obturator foramen in later types. Ilium, directed forwards, vertically, or backward. Two to seven sacral vertebrae. Limbs exhibiting all stages of advance from primitive cotylosaur-like organs to a pro-mammalian condition. Digital formula primitively 2, 3, 4, 5, 3 or 4 reduced to 2, 3, 3, 3, 3 in later forms.

Order 1. Pelycosauria. Primitive Theromorpha in which the pterygoids articulate with the basipterygoid processes of the basisphenoid by a movable joint. The quadrate is relatively large and the quadrato-jugal forms part of the lateral surface of the skull. The shoulder girdle has a screw-shaped glenoid cavity shared by the scapula, coracoid and precoracoid, and the limbs are primitive. The pelvis is plate-like.

Upper Carboniferous and Lower Permian. Families: *Poliosauridae, Ophiacodontidae, Sphenacodontidae, Edaphosauridae, Caseidae, Bolosauridae, Palaeohatteriidae.*

Order 2. Deinocephalia. Theromorpha in which the pterygoids are attached to the basisphenoid by an immovable joint. The basioccipital and basisphenoid are produced downward below the occipital condyle as a thick sheet of bone. The quadrate is unreduced and the quadrato-jugal is on the lateral surface. The shoulder girdle in early forms has the glenoid cavity borne only to a very slight extent on the precoracoid, but it is screw-shaped; in later forms this structure disappears and the glenoid cavity is restricted to the scapula and coracoid. The limbs are of modernized type. The pelvis is plate-like, the ilium being attached to four sacral ribs.

Middle Permian. Families: *Tapinocephalidae, Titanosuchidae.*

Order 3. Dromosauria. Small Theromorpha in which the facial region of the skull is very short, the temporal fossa is bounded above by the postorbital and squamosal and the zygomatic arch is reduced to a narrow rod so that the quadrate and quadrato-jugal project below it. Shoulder girdle with the glenoid cavity on the scapula and coracoid, precoracoid large. No cleithra. Pelvis plate-like. Limbs very long and slender, digital formula 2, 3, 3, 3, 3.

Upper Permian. One family only.

Order 4. Dicynodontia (or *Anomodontia*). Theromorpha in which the preorbital part of the skull is very short, whilst the temporal vacuity is greatly enlarged. The latter is bounded above by the postorbital and squamosal. The quadrate and quadrato-jugal are reduced, and rest in a recess in the front face of the lower end of the T-shaped squamosal, which is widely expanded laterally so as to form a sheet in the plane of the occipital surface. The pterygoids are rigidly fixed to the basisphenoid, and are not produced into transverse flanges. The premaxillae are fused and toothless, the maxillae may have a large canine or a series of small cheek teeth, or both, or be toothless. A horny beak like that of a tortoise was always present. The articular of the lower jaw always has the unique feature of a convex articular surface. Intercentra are absent except in the atlas and axis. The tail is short. The glenoid cavity is entirely, or almost entirely, restricted to the scapula and to the coracoid. There is an acromium on the scapula which also shows the beginnings of a mammal-like scapular spine.

There is an obturator foramen in the pelvis. The limbs are short and powerful, the track wide, and the digital formula 2, 3, 3, 3, 3.

Upper Permian to Middle Trias. Division into families not yet carried out.

Order 5. Theriodontia. Theromorpha in which there is a differentiation of the dentition into incisors, canine and cheek teeth. The face is usually long, the temporal fossa, short in primitive forms, elongated in the more advanced types, the parietal entering into its border.

Quadrate and quadrato-jugal, fused, much reduced and carried in a recess on the front face of the squamosal.

Pterygoids forming great transverse flanges, behind which they suddenly contract to form a narrow girder extending back to the basisphenoid. Palate at first with the large posterior nares placed anteriorly, becoming vaulted, the air passage being finally cut off from that for the food by a secondary palate. The dentary, always extending above the surangular, in a free coronoid process. Limbs and their girdles variable.

Sub-order 1. Gorgonopsia. Primitive Theriodonts, with the postorbital and squamosal meeting above the temporal fossa. Single occipital condyle: No sub-orbital vacuities. No secondary palate. Scapula without acromion, plate-like pelvis, digital formula (of hand) 2, 3, 4, 5, 3.

Upper Permian.

Sub-order 2. Cynodontia. Advanced Theriodonts, with the parietal entering the temporal fossa. No sub-orbital vacuities. A secondary palate. Pair of exoccipital condyles. Scapula with acromion. Pelvis with an obturator foramen. Limbs modernized, digital formula 2, 3, 3, 3, 3.

Top of the Permian and Lower Trias.

Sub-order 3. Therocephalia. Primitive Theriodonts with large temporal vacuities into whose border the parietal always enters. Large sub-orbital vacuities. No secondary palate or vaulting of the mid line of the anterior part of the palate. Single occipital condyle.

Upper Permian.

Sub-order 4. Bauriamorpha. Advanced Theriodonts, with the parietal forming part of the temporal fossa. Large sub-orbital vacuities, a secondary palate. Single occipital condyle.

Lower to Upper Trias.

Order 6. Thalattosauria. A group of marine reptiles, still incompletely known, but perhaps allied to the Pelycosauria. If so interpreted they may be defined by the following characters:—Skull with a very elongated face formed by the maxillae and premaxillae, nostrils dorsal and immediately in front of the large orbit, nasals small. The large temporal fossa is entirely lateral and is bounded above by the postorbital and squamosal. Quadrate large. A supratemporal present. Parietals short and wide. Vertebrae with biconcave centra which are short cylinders, ribs single-headed. Scapula and coracoid incompletely ossified. Humerus with expanded ends and a twisted shaft. Radius and ulna short flattened bones.

Upper Trias.

Super-order Archosauria (Diaptosauria). Reptiles in which the temporal region of the skull is perforated by two vacuities, the upper of these, the supratemporal fossa is bounded by the parietal, supratemporal, squamosal and postorbital the lower, the infratemporal fossa lies between the postorbital squamosal, quadrato-jugal and jugal bones.

The brain, at any rate in the later forms, is completely enclosed by bone, a pair of latero-sphenoids surrounding the cerebral hemispheres and stretching back to have a suture with the pro-otic. The epipterygoid forms no part of the wall of the cranial cavity. The fenestra ovalis lies half way up the wall of the brain case. There is always a distinct neck, often of eight vertebrae.

The pectoral girdle contains a scapula and precoracoid on each side, the true coracoid never appearing. Cleithra are never present. The sternum usually ossifies from a pair of centres. The limbs are never of the primitive Cotylosaurin character, and are often very highly modified. The digital formula is 2, 3, 4, 5, 4 or 3.

Order 1. Thecodontia. Primitive Archosauria in which a supratemporal, tabular and interparietal may be present in the skull. A preorbital vacuity may be present or absent. The ribs may have one or two heads and a sternum if ossified is paired.

Clavicles and an interclavicle are always present, the pelvis is plate-like, and there are only two sacral vertebrae.

Upper Permian to Upper Trias. Families: *Eosuchidae, Phytosauridae, Pseudosuchidae, Erythrosuchidae, Erpetosuchidae* and others not yet defined.

This order is, in a sense, artificial, it includes the ancestors, for the greater part unknown, of the remainder of the orders of Archosauria, and in addition contains a number of animals which belong to short-lived unsuccessful side branches.

Order 2. Crocodilia. Archosaurs usually of medium or large size, and adapted more or less completely to an aquatic habit. The skull is characterized most clearly by the fact that the quadrate is very large, and lies at a very low angle with the horizontal. The wedge-shaped otic cavity so formed is closed behind by a downgrowth of the squamosal, which, with the overlapping "exoccipital" reaches the quadrate. The tympanic membrane lies some distance below the outer surface, and the external auditory meatus can be closed by a muscular flap. The elongated face is chiefly formed by the maxillae, the external nostrils, usually confluent in the bony skull lying quite anteriorly. There is always a secondary palate, the choanae lying posteriorly between the palatics or pterygoids. The vertebrae are amphiplatean or procoelous, the ribs double-headed throughout the presacral part of the column, the dorsal ribs articulating entirely with the neural arch. The coracoid is elongated, clavicles are absent; and the sternum is unossified. The ilium is a small bone supported by two sacral ribs, and the pubis is excluded from the acetabulum.

The hand is five-fingered, the foot has the fifth toe reduced to a stump of its metatarsal.

Lower Jurassic (Upper Trias) to Recent. Families: *Teleosauridae, Metriorhynchidae, Dyrosauridae, Goniopholidae, Libycosuchidae, Pholidosauridae, Stomatosuchidae, Gavialidae, Crocodilidae.*

It is not improbable that the Crocodilia sprang from the family *Erpetosuchidae* of the order Thecodontia.

Order 3. Saurischia (Deinosauria parts) Archosauria, with a well-developed preorbital vacuity. The neck is sharply marked off from the trunk. The presacral ribs are two-headed, and the dorsal ribs articulate only with the neural arch. Clavicle and interclavicle are lacking, the coracoid is short. There are three or more sacral vertebrae. The pubis and ischia form diverging rods, primitively the pelvis is plate-like, but the bones separate from one another in later forms. The acetabulum is perforate. The fore limb is shorter than the hind, and the femur moves in a plane parallel to the animal's length. The body is thus held well above the ground, and the animal is often bipedal.

Sub-order Theropoda. Carnivorous Saurischia, in which the dentition consists of a single series of the codont, laterally compressed teeth in the premaxillae and maxillae. The cervical vertebrae may be opisthocoelus. The fore limb is often very much smaller than the hind, and the animals are usually bipedal. The hand tends to be reduced to the first three fingers, which are provided with powerful claws, and the foot becomes functionally tridactyl and symmetrical about the third toe.

Middle Trias to Upper Cretaceous.

Families: *Hallopidae, Podokosauridae, Coeluridae, Compsognathidae, Ornithomimidae, Plateosauridae, Zanclodontidae, Anchisauridae, Megalosauridae, Spinosauridae.*

Sub-order Sauropoda. Herbivorous Saurischia, usually of gigantic size. The skull is extremely small, and the dentition feeble. The cervical and many or all the dorsal vertebrae opisthocoelic. Accessory articulating faces are developed in the neural arch of the dorsal vertebrae. The dorsal centra are excavated laterally, so that they may be reduced to mere shells of bones.

The animals are quadrupedal, and walk on the ends of the metapodials, both feet are five toed, but some of the digits have a reduced number of phalanges and most lack claws.

Middle Jurassic to Upper Cretaceous. Families: *Cetrosauridae, Allantosauridae, Camarosauridae, Diplodocidae, Titanosuchidae.*

Order 4. Ornithischia (Deinosauria pars). Archosauria of herbivorous diet. The preorbital fossa is usually small or absent, the nostrils very large. The quadrate, unless secondarily fixed, is movable, a spherical head on its upper extremity resting in a cup in the squamosal. Premaxillae usually toothless, and covered with a horny beak, which opposes a similar structure carried by a special predentary bone in the lower jaw. Posterior end of the dentary raised into an upstanding coronoid process. The pubis bifid, a prepubic process stretching forward along the belly, and a posterior part passing downward and backward parallel to the

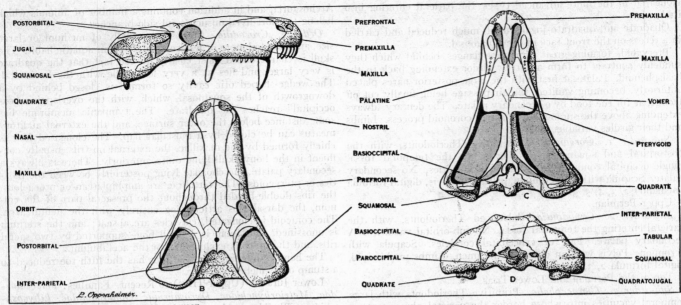

Labels on figure (left skull A, top-left): POSTORBITAL, JUGAL, SQUAMOSAL, QUADRATE, NASAL, MAXILLA, ORBIT, POSTORBITAL, INTER-PARIETAL

Labels (centre-top, right of A/B): PREFRONTAL, PREMAXILLA, MAXILLA, PALATINE, NOSTRIL, BASIOCCIPITAL, PREFRONTAL, SQUAMOSAL, BASIOCCIPITAL, PAROCCIPITAL, QUADRATE

Labels (right side, C/D): PREMAXILLA, MAXILLA, VOMER, PTERYGOID, QUADRATE, INTER-PARIETAL, TABULAR, SQUAMOSAL, QUADRATOJUGAL

L. Oppenheimer.

BY COURTESY OF THE ZOOLOGICAL SOCIETY OF LONDON

FIG. 8.—SKULL OF THE GORGONOPSID REPTILE, SCYMNOGNATHUS
A. Right side, B. from above, C. from below, D. occiput

ischium. Ilium elongated anteroposteriorly. Acetabulam perforate. Fore leg shorter than the hind, the animal being often bipedal. Hand usually pentadactyl, foot often tridactyl.

Rhaetic to Upper Cretaceous.

Super-family Ornithopodidae. Families: *Hypsilophodontidae, Camptosauridae, Ignanodontidae, Trachodontidae. Super-family Stegosauridae.* Families: *Scelidosauridae, Stegosauridae, Acanthopholidae, Polocanthidae. Super-family Ceratopsidae,* with one family.

Order 5, Pterosauria. Archosauria fully adapted for flight. The vertebrae and many long bones are hollow and, where occupied by air sacs, arising no doubt, like those of birds, by extension of the bronchi. Skull elongated, triangular in plan, and peculiar in that the quadrato-jugal excludes the jugal from the border of the infra temporal fossa. Teeth may extend throughout the jaws, be restricted to their anterior ends, or be absent altogether.

Cervical vertebrae large, procoelous, and very freely movable, head carried nearly at right angles to the neck. Dorsal vertebrae small, sometimes largely fused, sacrum of four to 10 vertebrae, tail either very short or greatly elongated and quite stiff.

Scapula and coracoids elongated slender rods, the latter articulating with a large shield-shaped sternum. Clavicular arch absent. Ilium long, pubis and ischium fused with it and with each other, not meeting in a median symphysis. Prepubic bones present. Fore limb supporting a wing, which is formed by a fold of skin arising from the side of the body and stretched between the upper arm, fore arm and greatly extended fourth finger, and the hind leg. Fingers one to three, present and clawed.

Sub-order Rhamphorhynchoidae. Pterosaurs, with a long tail, wing metacarpal short, fifth toe well developed.

Upper Trias? Lower Lias to Upper Jurassic.

Sub-order Pterodactyloidae. Pterosaurs, with a short tail, wing metacarpal long, and fifth toe reduced or absent.

Upper Jurassic to Upper Cretaceous. Families: *Pterodactylidae, Ornithocheiridae.*

The birds, class Aves, are certainly descendants of Archosaurian reptiles; had the group become extinct in Cretaceous time it would be regarded as an order equivalent to those listed above.

The remaining reptilian orders cannot usefully be grouped into super-orders.

Order Rhynchocephalia. Reptiles in which the temporal region is perforated by two fossae; the supratemporal fossa seems to differ from that of Archosauria in that the post frontal enters into its margin, whilst the infratemporal fossa differs by the exclusion of the quadratojugal.

The preorbital part of the skull is short, and there is no preorbital opening. The fenestra ovalis is placed high in the skull. The dentary bears a single series of acrodont teeth which bite into a groove between the similar teeth on the maxilla and palatine, so that with use they acquire a wedge-shaped section. The vertebrae have amphicoelous centra, and all the ribs are single-headed. An unossified sternum is present. The shoulder girdle includes scapulae, precoracoids, clavicles and an interclavicle.

The pelvis has an ilium attached to two sacral vertebrae and directed downward in front. The pubis and ischia are plate-like in primitive forms, but diverge widely in later times. The limbs are pentadactyl, and the fifth metatarsal has a hook-shaped upper extremity.

One group of Rhynchocephalia, the *Champsosauridae,* became highly adapted to an aquatic life in estuaries.

Middle Trias to Recent. Families: *Rhynchosauridae, Sauranodontidae, Sphenodontidae, Champsosauridae.*

Order Squamata. (The following account does not include the characters of the reptile Pleurosaurus, which is, perhaps, a member of the order.)

Reptiles in which the dermal roof of the temporal region is so far reduced that only a single temporal arcade, or none at all, remains. The quadrate is thereby freed so that it can move, its rounded head articulating with one or two bones which are connected with the parietal. If two bones be present the inner is firmly applied to the front face of the posterior wing of the parietal, and rests against and may even be firmly fixed by suture to the front face of the end of the paroccipital process. This bone is either the supratemporal or squamosal, or, very improbably, tabular. The outer bone is fixed to the lateral surface of the inner, often overlapping it on to the parietal; it stretches forward as the hinder part of the temporal arcade, and meets the postorbital and sometimes the jugal. This bone is either the squamosal or quadrato-jugal. In the palate the pterygoid no longer reaches the prevomers, and the whole is often very lightly constructed.

The vertebrae are usually procoelous, but may be amphicoelous; there are two sacrals or none. Ribs are single-headed throughout. The shoulder girdle, if present and fully developed, consists of scapulae and precoracoids, often enlarged and notched or fenestrated, clavicles, an interclavicle and a sternum. The pelvis has a forwardly and downwardly directed ilium, the pubes and ischia are divergent rods. The limbs are pentadactyl primitively, but may be reduced or absent.

Sub-order Lacertilia (Lizards). Squamata in which a temporal arcade is usually present, and in which the two rami of the lower jaw are connected suturally at the symphysis. An epipterygoid is present in the normal position and the anterior part of the brain case is very little ossified. The pterygoid articulates with the basipterygoid process of the basisphenoid.

Upper Jurassic to Recent.

Division Ascalabota.

Section Gekkota.

Families: *Ardeosauridae, Gekkonidae, Uroplatidae.*

Section Iguania. Families: *Iguanidae,* and *Agamidae.*

Section Rhiptoglossa. Family *Chamaeleontidae.*

Division Antarchoglossa. Section Scincomorpha. Families: *Xantusiidae, Scincidae, Anclytropiidae, Flyliniidae, Dibamidae, Gerrhosauridae, Lacertidae, Tejidae, Amphisbaenidae.* Section Anguimorpha. Families: *Euposauridae, Varaniidae, Dolichosauridae, Aigialosauridae, Mosasauridae, Pygopodidae, Glyptosauridae, Helodermatidae, Anguidae, Xenosauridae, Anniellidae, Zonuridae.*

Sub-order Ophidia (Snakes). Squamata in which the temporal arcade has completely vanished, and the quadrate is very freely movable. The pterygoids have lost all connection with the basisphenoid, and the palate has become mobile, connected to the cranium only by ligaments and by its connection with the maxillae and quadrate. Much of the palate and the maxillae may vanish in burrowing forms. The brain case is completely ossified, the epipterygoid being absorbed into it. The two halves of the lower jaw are loosely connected by an extensible ligament.

The vertebral column is extraordinarily long, in one case containing 565 vertebrae. Each vertebra has a procoelous centrum and a heavy neural arch, on which additional articulating faces, the zygosphenes, and zygantra, are developed. The single-headed ribs are long and are very freely movable antero-posteriorly; by such movements they cause the transversely widened ventral scales to catch the ground, and force the animal along. There is never any trace of a fore limb or its girdle. All three elements of the pelvic girdle may be present in one family, the Glauconidae, but in most this limb is entirely absent. Upper Cretaceous to Recent.

Families: *Typhlopidae, Glauconiidae, Ilysiidae, Uropeltidae, Boidae* (boa constrictors), *Xenopeltidae, Colubridae.* As the last family contains nine-tenths of all known snakes it is subdivided into the series Aglypha (harmless snakes), Opisthoglypha (poisonous but little dangerous to man) and Proteroglypha (typical poisonous snakes).

Sub-order Pleurosauria. A small group of extinct reptiles including only one or two genera, which may be related to the Squamata; if so, these are not, as usually held, derived from the Archosauria. Aquatic reptiles with a very long body and lizardlike limbs partially adapted for swimming. Limb girdles of Lacertilian type. Skull elongated and depressed, quadrate short and immovable. There is a single temporal fossa, bounded below by a broad arcade composed of the squamosal, postorbital and jugal. There is no supratemporal, and the outer surface of the quadrate is covered by a quadrato-jugal. Upper Jurassic. One family.

Order Sauropterygia (Plesiosauria). Reptiles which show a progressive adaptation to a marine life.

Skull with a single temporal vacuity surrounded by the parietal, squamosal, postorbital and post-frontal, and therefore apparently homologous with the upper temporal vacuity of Rhynchocephalia, and not with the single fossa of Theromorpha and Squamata. The single temporal arcade is formed almost entirely by the squamosal and postorbital, the jugal being a small bone wedged in between the postorbital and the hinder end of the maxilla. A quadrato-jugal is absent. The fenestra ovalis lies high in the side wall of the brain case. The palate is primitive, the posterior nares being anterior, and the pterygoids reaching the prevomers.

Except in Placodonts, the neck is long, often exceedingly so (76 vertebrae in Elasmosaurus), the back is long and the tail short; there are usually three sacral vertebrae, but may be more. The cervical ribs, though double-headed in early forms, articulate only with the centra, the single-headed dorsal ribs being supported entirely by the long transverse process of the neural arch.

The pentadactyl limbs are large, and are more or less completely converted into paddles by a flattening and shortening of the radius and ulna and tibia and fibula, and an increase in the number of phalanges. The shoulder girdle consists of scapulae and coracoids, which meet one another in median suture. Clavicles are probably always present, an interclavicle usually so. The ilium is small, the pubis and ischium, though separated by an obturator foramen, are expanded into flat sheets of bone. A strong plastron of abdominal ribs is always present.

Sub-order 1. Trachelosauria. A single, small reptile, with a long neck consisting of 20 vertebrae whose centra support two-headed ribs. Dorsal ribs single-headed and articulating with the long transverse processes of the dorsal neural arches.

Ilium and femur like those of a land reptile.

Lower Trias.

Sub-Order 2. Nothosauria. Sauropterygia in which the limbs are still incompletely converted into paddles, the elbow and knee joints still being flexible. Phalangean formula 2, 3, 4, 5, 3 or 4.

In the skull the opisthotic is enlarged distally, and articulates with the squamosal quadrate and pterygoid, so as to close the middle ear cavity behind. Clavicular arch powerful; coracoids

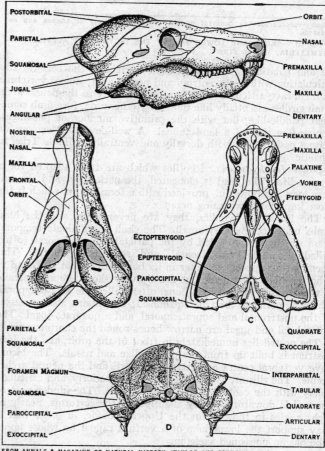

FROM ANNALS & MAGAZINE OF NATURAL HISTORY (TAYLOR AND FRANCIS)

FIG. 9.—SKULL OF THE CYNODONT, CYNOGNATHUS
A. From the right side, with lower jaw, B. from above, C. from below, D. occiput

meeting in a short symphysis, which lies behind a line joining the glenoid cavities. Ilium articulating with both pubis and ischium.

Middle Trias, perhaps just appearing in the Lower Trias. Families not discriminated.

Sub-Order 3. Plesiosauria. Sauropterygia in which the limbs are completely converted into paddles, with no freedom of movement at any joint; the number of phalanges in the five fingers and toes is increased, reaching 6, 13, 15, 13, 9 or more. The distal end of the opisthotic is slender, resting on the hinder surface of the squamosal. Clavicular arch, when present, reduced to flat sheets of bone, supported by the greatly enlarged acromia of the scapulae. Coracoids with a symphysis which extends forward between the glenoid cavities. Ilium articulating only with the ischium. Rhaetic to Upper Cretaceous. Families not yet discriminated.

Sub-order 4. Placodontia. Sauropterygia in which the skull has become modified to support great crushing teeth in the maxil-

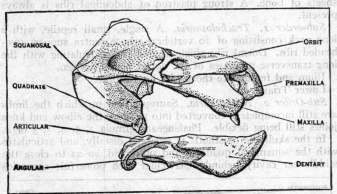

FROM "PROCEEDINGS" BY COURTESY OF THE ZOOLOGICAL SOCIETY OF LONDON AND DR. PEARSON

FIG. 10.—SKULL AND LOWER JAW OF THE DICYNODONT REPTILE KANNEMEYERIA, RIGHT SIDE

lae and palatines. Neck with eight vertebrae, the cervical ribs articulating with both centrum and neural arch; dorsal vertebrae with concave articulations, ribs attached solely to the neural arch. Limb girdles essentially like those of Nothosauria, fore limb somewhat paddle-like, but with the primitive number of phalanges, Femur like that of a land animal. A well-developed armour of dermal ossifications both dorsally and ventrally. Middle Trias to Rhaetic.

Order Ichthyosauria. Reptiles which are fully adapted for a marine life. The head is elongated, the neck short and the tail very long and powerful, provided with a terminal fin, which is the most important swimming organ.

The limbs are paddles, they are never large, and the hind limbs may become very small. The skull has a single temporal fossa which is surrounded by the parietal, supratemporal (often called squamosal) postfrontal, and sometimes frontal. This opening thus appears to differ in its boundaries from all found in other reptiles. The deep, but usually very short temporal arcade is very largely formed by a bone, often called the supratemporal, which is, perhaps, the true squamosal; it contains also processes of the postfrontal and supratemporal, and a quadrato-jugal. The postorbital and jugal are narrow bones round the enormous orbit.

The nostril lies immediately in front of the orbit, and the long rostrum is built up from the premaxillae and nasals. The biconcave vertebral centra are extremely short, and the neural arches feeble. The ribs are two-headed at least anteriorly, and articulate solely with the centra. There is no sacrum. The hinder part of the tail is downturned very slightly in Triassic forms, nearly at right angles in those from the Upper Jurassic, in order that it may support the lower lobe of a vertical caudal fin whose upper lobe has an unossified skeleton.

The shoulder girdle consists of scapulae and coracoids which meet in a powerful median symphysis between the glenoid cavities, and a rigid clavicular arch. The pelvis has a narrow ilium and pubis and ischia, separated by an obturator foramen, but expanded into great sheets in Triassic forms. In both fore and hind limbs the proximal bone is very short and widened distally, the remainder of the limb, in the later forms, being reduced to an interlocking mass of polygonal bones. The number of fingers is often increased to seven or more, and the phalanges increase to a very great number.

Middle Trias to Upper Cretaceous. Families: *Mixosauridae, Ichthyosauridae.*

Order Chelonia. Reptiles in which the trunk is enclosed in a shell built up from a series of dermal bones, with which the neural arches and ribs become continuous. The limb girdles are unique, in that they lie entirely within the ribs. Skull without any temporal vacuity, but the continuous sheet of bone which, in the primitive forms, overlies the temporal muscles may be emarginated either from the back or from below, or from both, so that in extreme cases the squamosal may be left without connection with any other bones of the skull roof. The powerful vertically-placed quadrate is then only supported by its abutment in the pro-otic opisthotic and pterygoid.

Postfrontals and lachrimals are always, nasals usually absent, and the external nares are confluent. Except in Triassochelys, the jaws are toothless, and they always support a horny beak. There is often a small secondary palate, not homologous with that of mammals or crocodiles, formed by extensions of the palatines and prevomers. The eight cervical vertebrae are so formed that the neck is flexible, bending into a vertical loop in Cryptodeira, and into a horizontal S in Pleurodeira.

The dorsal vertebrae are ten in number, the first being free, or nearly so, from the shell, whilst the rest are fixed immovably by their attachment to the neural plates of the carapace; the two sacral vertebrae are similarly attached. The posterior dorsal vertebrae are peculiar, in that each of their neural arches rests on two centra.

The shoulder girdle consists of a scapula, whose acromian process is produced into a long rod lying horizontally, and approaching its fellow in all forms except Triassochelys, and a coracoid which form a curious pedunculate glenoid cavity. Cleithra are present only in Triassochelys. Clavicles and an interclavicle are entirely detached from the shoulder girdle and form part of the plastron.

The ilium usually articulates, not with the sacral ribs, but with the carapace; the pubis and ischium are lacertilian-like. The limbs are much modified, in order to reach the girdles which lie within the shell, and to allow of their withdrawal in the more primitive forms. The fifth metatarsal is hook shaped. Both feet are pentadactyl, the phalangeal formula never exceeding 2, 3, 3, 3, and being sometimes reduced to 2, 2, 2, 2, 0.

The shell, in its fullest development, consists of a dorsal carapace, built up from a median row of nuchal, preneural, eight neural and two suprapygal bones, and lateral rows, each of eight costals, articulating with the neurals, a variable development of supra marginals may occur secondarily; in their absence the costals articulate with a continuous chain of marginals which connect carapace and plastron.

The plastron consists of three plates anteriorly, the epiplastra which are clavicles, and an entoplastron, the interclavicle; a pair of hyoplastra, two pairs of mesoplastra, one pair of hypoplastra and one of xiphiplastra. The neural bones are co-ossified with the neural spines of the dorsal vertebrae, the costals with the ribs of the second to ninth dorsals.

Sub-order Amphichelydia. Chelonia with no power of completely withdrawing the head within the shell, mesoplastra present, pelvic girdle not fused with the plastron. Families not yet discriminated. Middle Trias to Eocene.

Sub-order Pleurodeira. Chelonia which withdraw the head sideways. Mesoplastra usually present, pelvic girdle fused with the carapace, and usually with the plastron. Families: *Pelomedusidae, Chelyidae, Miolanidae, Plesiochelyidae.* Jurassic to Recent.

Sub-order Cryptodira. Chelonia which withdraw the head vertically. Mesoplastra absent, pelvic girdle never fused with the plastron. Families: *Thalassemydidae, Chelydridae, Testudinidae, Cinosteriidae, Platysternidae, Cheloniidae, Protostegidae, Dermochelyidae, Dermatemydidae, Trionychiidae.* Jurassic to Recent.

There is a considerable number of small Palaeozoic reptiles which do not fall into any of the 19 orders defined above. Of these the more important are: Eosaurus from the Coal Measures of the United States, which may be Cotylosaurian; Eunotosaurus from the Upper Permian of South Africa, which may be an ancestor of the Chelonia; Broomia from the Upper Permian of South Africa, which may be an ancestral lizard; and Araeoscelis, from the Lower Permian of Texas, which has also been regarded as a lizard ancestor.

Limbs and Locomotion.—The Lower Permian reptiles of all groups possess limbs which either belong to a definite characteristic type or are clearly simple derivatives of it.

In all of them a distinct neck is absent, the body is of circular section, although variable in length, and the tail is usually of considerable size.

The fore limbs were attached to the body immediately behind the head, the upper arm lies parallel to the ground, and was capable of being moved backward and forward only. The elbows were thus pointed directly outward. The forearm lay nearly parallel to the principal plane of the animal, and made a very small angle with the ground. The wrist was large in comparison with the forearm, and the hand possessed five somewhat spreading digits. The hind leg was attached to the body at a considerably higher level than the fore leg. The thigh projected freely from the body, almost at right angles, and the lower leg made a wide angle with it, indeed the stiff knee could not, in many cases, be bent to a right angle. The ankle joint was flexible, and the five toes greatly resemble the fingers of the same animal.

As the large head makes the load carried by the fore legs rather larger than that on the hind, the hand is generally larger than the foot.

These animals, like the lizards and salamanders of to-day, threw their backbones into lateral waves as they walked. Their procedure was as follows:—When the animal is standing with its right fore leg advanced to the greatest possible extent, and the right hand on the ground, the head is turned to the left, and the left hand lies near to it but is ready to be lifted. The trunk is thrown over to the right side and the base of the tail to the left. This body flexure implies that the right hind leg is turned somewhat backward and the left hind leg is directed forward. The left hand is then lifted from the ground by movement at the elbow, and carried forward not only by a movement of the upper arm on the shoulder girdle and a straightening of the elbow, but also by a bending of the backbone so that the head becomes directed to the right. This movement of the back involves a corresponding twist of the pelvis, which brings the left hind leg to its backward position, and makes it necessary to lift the right foot from the ground. The right hind leg is then swung forward by motion, mainly at the hip joint, and the foot placed down as far ahead as possible. During these movements the animal, as a whole, has travelled forward and the right hand is ready to be raised. Its movements agree exactly with those of the left, and it is followed in turn by the left hind foot.

Thus the animal progresses with a waddling gait, the head and body being constantly thrown from side to side of the line along which the animal is moving. The feet are moved one at a time, so that the animal is never standing on less than three of them, and are placed wide apart. This mode of walking must have been extremely slow and clumsy; measurements suggest that a reptile about a yard in length, without the tail, must have made a track 15 in. in width, with a stride of some 6 or 8 inches.

Fossil materials enable us to trace the steps whereby the later reptiles gradually improved their modes of walking, until on one line, they became like the more primitive mammals, walking with their bodies raised high above the ground, the feet brought in towards the middle line and the stride long, whilst along a second course they became bipedal, striding along on their hind legs, with their heads raised high in the air.

The nature of the skeleton and musculature which is associated with the primitive type of locomotion is as follows:—The shoulder girdle consists of the pair of primary elements, each of which is in the most primitive forms, *Seymouria* and *Varanopus*, ossified as two bones, the dorsal scapula and ventral precoracoid. The glenoid cavity has a characteristic shape in that its articular surface is a rather narrow screw-shaped strip of a cylinder whose axis is nearly vertical. The glenoid cavity is shared nearly equally by the two bones. The two halves of the primary shoulder girdle do not touch one another in the mid line ventrally; but are held in position with respect to one another by the powerful

clavicular arch. This consists of pairs of cleithras and clavicles and an interclavicle. Each cleithrum is firmly attached to the front edge, and sometimes to the upper end of the scapula. The clavicle is firmly attached to the front face of the lower end of the cleithrum and has no contact with the scapula; its lower end is turned inward so as to underlie the thorax, and is usually widened, its lower end underlying the lateral margin of the interclavicle. The interclavicle is usually a thin flat bone, with a widely expanded anterior end, and a narrower shaft projecting posteriorly under the sternum, which is unossified.

The whole girdle was held in position by muscles, the serrati passing from the ribs to the inner surface of the scapula and by others, sternomastoids and cleidomastoids passing from the head to the clavicular arch. Posteriorly, the coracoid is attached to the ventral surface of the abdomen.

The humerus of these reptiles has its extremities very much widened and placed nearly at right angles to one another. The articular surface of the head is screw-shaped, and fits the glenoid cavity so accurately that the bone cannot be rotated, and is restricted to a to-and-fro motion along a definite track. The widened proximal end allows the muscles which pass from the humerus to the ventral part of the animal, the pectoral and coraco-brachials, to have a mechanically favourable insertion. The widened lower end of the humerus similarly secures a

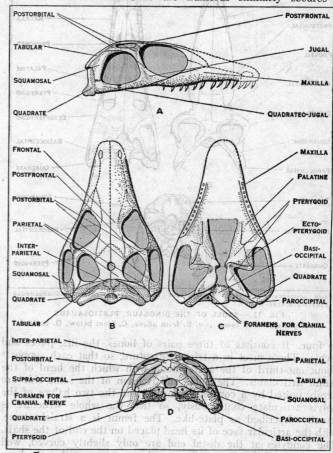

FIG. 11.—SKULL OF THE PRIMITIVE THECODONT, YOUNGURA
A. Right side, B. from above, C. from below, D. occiput

favourable insertion for the flexor muscles which pass from it to the palmar surface of the hand and forearm, and take the whole weight of the anterior part of the body.

The lower end of the humerus bears a hemispherical boss on its front face, with which the head of the radius articulates, and a cylindroid articulation on its end which fits into the sigmoid notch of the ulna. The distal ends of the radius and ulna are widely separated; they articulate with the four bones: radiale, intermedium, ulnare and pisiform, of the proximal row of the carpus. The middle row of the wrist usually consists of only two bones, the centralia, one of which forms part of the inner border, whilst the other separates the intermedium from the distal row. This consists of five bones, of which the fourth, which articulates with the ulnare, is the largest. The metacarpals articulate directly with the corresponding carpals and the number of phalanges is 2, 3, 4, 5, 3 respectively. This ensures that the ends of the fingers lie in a straight line at right angles to the animal, when the hand is placed on the ground.

The pelvis is attached to the vertebral column by the sacral ribs, which vary in number in Lower Permian reptiles from one

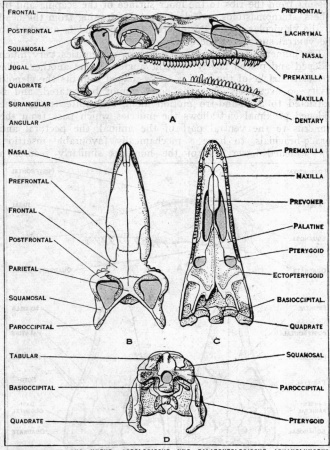

FROM POMPECKJ AND HUENE, "GEOLOGISCHE UND PALAEONTOLOGISCHE ABHANDLUNGEN" (GUSTAV FISCHER)

FIG. 12.—SKULL OF THE DINOSAUR, PLATIOSAURUS
A. Right side with lower jaw, B. from above, C. from below, D. occiput

to four. It consists of three pairs of bones, the ilia, pubes and ischia. These meet in a triradiate suture, so that each supports about one-third of the acetabulum, with which the head of the femur articulates. The pubis and ischium of the same side are firmly united by a continuous suture and the two halves of the pelvis articulate continuously, so that the whole structure is usually described as plate-like. The femur is a straight bone, with the articular face of its head placed on the end of the shaft. The condyles at the distal end are only slightly curved, well separated and placed at such an angle as to suggest that the knee could neither be extended into a straight line nor flexed beyond a right angle.

The tibia is a bone with an expanded upper end, and is always shorter than the fibula, which is unusually massed. At their lower ends the two bones are widely separated. The tarsus, in one case (*Seymouria*) has a proximal row of three bones, the tibiale intermedium and fibulae, corresponding with those of the carpus, but in nearly all other reptiles and their descendants, the mammals and birds, the intermedium is no longer found as an independent bone, even during development, and has fused with the tibiale to form an astragalus. As a result of this fusion the tibia

articulates only with the astragalus, whilst the fibula impinges on both astragalus and fibulare or calcaneum. The calcaneum is always in direct contact with the fourth and fifth (if present) distal tarsal, whilst the astragalus is separated from the first three distal tarsals by a row of two or more, usually one, centrale, the mammalian navicular. There are primitively five digits, the fourth being the longest. The phalangeal formula is 2, 3, 4, 5, 4.

The great majority of the changes which take place in the structures of these limbs during the evolution of the reptiles can be explained by a consideration of the mechanics of the structures under modified conditions of locomotion.

In the line of the mammal-like reptiles, and also in some of the other forms, the first change which takes place in the shoulder girdle is the addition of a bone, the coracoid, to the two existing in the primary shoulder girdle. These animals then acquire a pectoral girdle which resembles the pelvis in that the facet for articulating the proximal bone of the limb is carried almost equally on three bones. The glenoid cavity at first retains its screw shape, the humerus being restricted in its motion to an excursion along an arc lying nearly parallel to the ground. Gradually, as an integral part of the whole process whereby these animals acquired a more rapid and less clumsy gait, the plane of this glenoid cavity becomes twisted round, so that the humerus moves freely in a dorso-ventral direction and the elbow is no longer directed outward, but is drawn in toward the side of the body, nearly to the stage in which it exists in the more primitive mammals. This change results in the restriction of the glenoid cavity to the scapula and coracoid alone, the precoracoid no longer contributing to it.

Concurrently with this change, the humerus took up a more vertical position, so that the muscles connecting it with the coracoid could become smaller, in part because the forces they had to exert were actually reduced and, in part, because their insertion became more favourable. Thus the coracoid and precoracoid suffer steady reduction compared with the scapula. Finally, in order to secure a larger surface for its attachment, one muscle, which serves to support the animal's weight and to drive the humerus downwards, migrates on to the inner surface of the scapula, the tendon by which it is attached to the humerus passing over a notch in the front border of the scapula below the point at which the clavicle is attached to that bone. In this way a definite acromium becomes established, and the upper part of the anterior border of the scapula becomes recognizable as the homologue of the spine of a mammalian scapula.

The most important change in the clavicular arch is the gradual reduction and final complete disappearance of the cleithrum. The other bones sink in from their original position in the skin, so that they become surrounded by muscles on all sides, but otherwise they suffer comparatively little change during the evolution of the mammals.

The great changes in the position of the fore limb during the development of the mammal-like reptiles necessitate corresponding modifications of the structure of the humerus and other limb bones. Of these, the most striking is the gradual narrowing of the two ends of the humerus and their rotation until they become nearly parallel.

In the hand, the number of phalanges in the third and fourth fingers is reduced to three, so that the formula becomes that characteristic of mammals, 2, 3, 3, 3, 3. It is evident that this change is associated with a new pose in which the third finger, which becomes the longest, lies parallel to the mid line of the animal and the others are symmetrically placed on each side of it.

In the pelvis, the most important changes are a widening of the upper part of the ilium associated with an increase in the number of vertebrae in the sacrum, and the development of an obturator foramen, a gap lying in the suture between the pubis and ischium.

The femur so changes its shape that it can lie with the knee directed as much forward as outward, and the lower leg become capable of much freer movement. At the same time the astragalus and calcaneum shorten so that the tibia and fibula rest partly on their upper surface, thus forming an ankle joint which is on the way to a mammalian structure and the phalangeal formula of the foot becomes reduced to 2, 3, 3, 3, 3.

The non-mammal-like reptiles exhibit so many different types of adaptation that a full analysis of the structures of their limbs is impossible; indeed, it has not yet been systematically attempted. Some of the main types of life are here discussed with reference to a particular case.

Nondescript.—The majority of lizards and Rhynchocephalia exhibit a simple modification of the mode of locomotion found in the most primitive reptiles. In them the body and tail are thrown into lateral waves, which pass steadily backward so that each point along the back swings from side to side across the animal's track as the creature moves forward. The hands and feet are widely separated, the body only just raised off the ground, and only one foot is moved at a time. In detail there is much variety; both fore and hind feet may be much everted, so that the first digits point forward and the toes increase in length from one to four, so that when in the natural position their claws end on a straight line at right angles to the body. In some cases, however, the fingers are directed forward and the hand is nearly symmetrical about the third finger, and even the foot is less asymmetrical than in the more primitive forms. Nevertheless, these animals always retain the original phalangeal formula.

These animals have a primary shoulder girdle consisting of a scapula and precoracoid, the glenoid cavity has lost all trace of the screw shape of primitive reptiles and permits considerable freedom of motion. In the larger and more advanced lizards the anterior part of the scapula and coracoid is much enlarged, and these bones are perforated by fenestrae.

The clavicles have an expanded, and sometimes fenestrated, lower end, and the interclavicle is usually cross-shaped. There is a large sternum, which is usually calcified although not ossified, with whose antero-lateral borders the precoracoids articulate.

The pelvis of these reptiles is of very characteristic pattern, the ilia are narrow rods with an expanded lower end which contributes to the acetabulum. It slopes downward and forward and is firmly held by its articulation with the two sacral ribs. The pubis and ischium are separated by a large obturator foramen which, in many cases in the bony skeleton, is confluent with that of the opposite side. The hind limb presents few features of interest, but it may be noted that a patella is sometimes present, and that most of the motion at the ankle-joint takes place between the two rows of tarsals and not, as in mammal-like reptiles, between the tarsus and lower leg.

One universal and unexplained feature of the hind foot of these reptiles is that the fifth distal tarsal is absent, and that the upper end of the fifth metatarsal has moved up into contact with the calcaneum, and has become much widened so that the whole bone is hook-shaped. As a result, the fifth toe tends to be widely separated from the other four.

This feature occurs in Rhynchocephalia, Thecodontia, Crocodilia, Dinosauria, Squamata, and Chelonia, and has been held to imply a close relationship between these orders.

Cursorial Progression.—The only group of non-mammal-like reptiles which became highly adapted for rapid progress on hard land was the Dinosauria. They arose from Thecodonts whose general body proportions and gait generally resembled those of certain lizards. These animals possessed slender scapulae and small precoracoids, clavicles and interclavicle were present, and there was, in some cases, a sternum with a single pair of ossifications. The fore limb was slender, the hand small and with five fingers. The pelvis had an ilium which was antero-posteriorly extended, but so low that the acetabulum lay on the level of the vertebrae. The pubis and ischium were plate-like, but much elongated and directed largely downward. The hind legs were much longer and more massive than the fore, a condition made possible to a quadripedal animal by the presence of a long tail, which acted as a counterpoise to the body. Although it is certain that these animals had a straddling gait, it is probable that the feet were placed unusually near to the middle line and the feet were not so asymmetrical as those of most lizards.

From such reptiles the Saurischia, the carnivorous dinosaurs arose by an increase in the length of the hind legs, and concurrent reduction of the arms. They became predominantly bipedal, a habit which necessitates the raising of the body so far above the ground that the whole animal balances about the pelvis. This pose can only be attained if the thighs are turned in until they lie parallel to the body of the animal, and the feet are placed on the line which marks the middle of the track. Such an arrangement ensures that the body need no longer be thrown from side to side, as it is in all more primitive reptiles.

A further result is that, as the powerful muscles which are used for propelling the animal forward no longer press the heads of the femora into the acetabula, this depression no longer needs a floor and becomes perforated. At the same time, in order to lengthen the muscles attached to them and thus enable the leg to swing through a larger arc, the pubis and ischium, both elongated, stretch downwards and away from one another, meeting only at the acetabulum. The reduction in size of the forelimb, which occurs because it is no longer required to carry the weight of the body, results in a reduction and final loss of the clavicular arch, and in a reduction in size of the precoracoid. Subsequently, certain carnivorous dinosaurs increased greatly in size and became quadripedal again, retaining in many parts of their skeleton features which arose during the bipedal stage in their ancestry.

The long limbs which are necessary for a bipedal cursorial life, involve elongated feet. These are secured by lifting the heel entirely off the ground, so that the animal walks on the ends of the metatarsals, the toes stretching out along the ground as they do in birds. As the foot is placed directly under the body it tends to become symmetrical about the middle third toe, and rapidly becomes either functionally or actually tridactyl. The hand, which serves as a grappling hook for catching the prey, is reduced to three fingers, all provided with claws, that on the thumb becoming very large indeed in the latest forms.

The other group of dinosaurs, the Ornithischia, pursue a somewhat similar course of modifications; they also become bipedal, some of them secondarily returning to a quadripedal life. But in them the extension of the pubis and ischium into long downwardly directed rods, which is necessary to afford suitable muscle attachments, takes place in such a way that the pubis acquires two branches, one directed downward and forward, the other directed backward so that it lies parallel to the ischium. The early stages of this arrangement are not known, but it persists throughout the whole group.

Flight.—One group of lizards, the genus Draco, has the habit of living in trees and of passing from tree to tree by making great

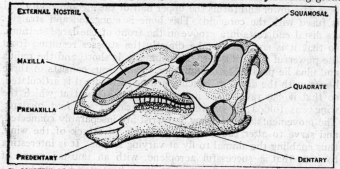

FIG. 13.—SKULL AND LOWER JAW OF THE ORNITHOPODOUS DINOSAUR KRITOSAURUS

leaps, whose length is extended by the presence of a parachute, made by flaps of skin which project from the sides of the body and are supported by the much elongated ribs. Such gliding is scarcely flight in any true sense, it cannot be maintained by any action of the animal whilst in the air, and its extent is limited by the speed acquired at the original jump and by the height of the point of departure. A similar gliding habit, carried out without any elaborate mechanism by a mere concavity of the ventral surface, is exhibited by certain arboreal snakes from Borneo. The only reptiles which have acquired true flight were the extinct Pterodactyls.

There are two series of the animals, in one of which the tail is extremely short and probably functionless, whilst in the other the tail is a very long stiff rod bearing a horizontal fin at its hinder end. The presence of this fin renders the maintenance of the body on an even keel much easier than it can have been in the tailless forms. The wing of every pterodactyl consists of a fold

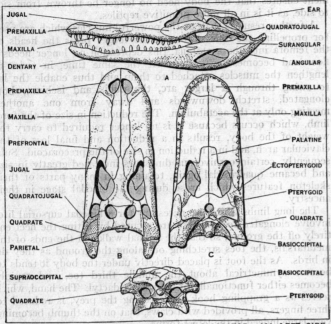

FIG. 14.—SKULL OF A CROCODILIAN, THE ALLIGATOR; (A) LEFT SIDE, WITH LOWER JAW, (B) FROM ABOVE, (C) FROM BELOW, (D) OCCIPUT (AFTER ANDREWS)

of skin which is supported by the greatly extended fourth finger and by the hind leg; it may or may not have connected the hind legs together, either directly or by passing on to the base of the tail. The structure of the fore limbs, which enabled these animals to perform automatically the many carefully-adjusted movements which are necessary for flight, is so strictly determined by mechanical considerations that it is practically uniform in all known species of the group.

In all of them, the scapula is an elongated narrow rod of bone which may articulate with the neural spine of the dorsal vertebrae. Its lower end forms the upper half of the glenoid cavity and is fused with the coracoid. This bone is elongated and straight, its distal end rests in a groove in the front of the large sternum, so that it is enabled to take directly the stresses resulting from the powerful wing muscles. The humerus is short, and the radius and ulna lie parallel to one another. The carpus consists of three bones, with the distal of which the wing metacarpal is articulated, so that it can revolve on its axis. The main joint at which the wing was folded lay between the metacarpal and first phalanx. The movements at the elbow and wrist are inseparably connected, and serve to alter the camber and angle of attack of the wing, thus enabling the animal to fly at varying speeds. It is interesting to note that a successful aeroplane, with an unusual range of flying speed, has been designed on lines suggested by the tailless pterodactyls.

Swimming.—Two extreme modes of swimming are open to a tetrapod. It may convert its limbs into paddles by whose actions it rows itself through the water, or it may use its tail as a propeller, either flattening it and causing waves to pass along its length or producing a fin at the extreme tip, which can be used like a screw propeller. Both types are found in reptiles.

The Chelonia include amongst the fresh water tortoises a number of animals which swim well with limbs which, except for the webbing of the toes, are much like those of a land animal. But in the marine turtles and in the fresh water Carettochelys from New Guinea, the limbs are transformed into paddles, mere bags

of skin surrounding the whole of the elongated digits.

The Plesiosaurs carried this principle to its limit; in them each limb is a rigid oar, flattened and widened distally, circular in section where attached to the body. It was feathered when brought forward, then turned so that its broad plane was vertical for the swimming stroke.

The crocodiles, the semi-marine lizard Amblyrhynchus, and the sea snakes are the living exponents of the second mode of swimming. In them the powerful tail is laterally flattened, and is swung from side to side so that a series of waves passes along its length. The limbs are used for steering and for maintaining stability in the water. The only groups of reptiles which have formed a caudal fin are the Ichthyosaurs and the marine crocodiles of the family Metriorhynchidae. In each case the end of the vertebral column is suddenly turned down so that it passes into the lower lobe of a forked fin whose upper lobe is supported only by non-ossified structures. These animals show a reduction of the limbs, the pelvic limb of Ichthyosaurs and the pectoral limb of the crocodiles being reduced to a tiny paddle.

Limblessness.—Many lizards belonging to unrelated families, but chiefly of burrowing or sand living habits, exhibit a reduction of limbs associated with an elongation of the body. The process takes place gradually, all stages being known in one or other form between normally developed limbs and their complete absence. In snakes the reduction is always complete in the case of the fore limbs, whilst the hind limbs may be represented by a claw-like spur on each side of the vent. In some cases all three bones of the pelvis and the femur may be present. Normally, all trace of limbs, except for a rudimentary nerve plexus, is lost.

Skin.—The fact that the reptiles were originally distinguished from the amphibians by their more completely terrestrial habits, implies that in them the skin had become capable of withstanding desiccation, and the serious wear to which it became exposed.

The skin of amphibians is maintained in good condition by a coat of mucus, poured out from glands which lie all over it; that of reptiles is dry and covered by a watertight layer of horn, very well adapted for resisting abrasion. The horny layer, though continuous, is not of the same thickness throughout, but is divided into specially thickened areas, the scales which are connected by flexible regions. The scales may be flat, fitting together like a mosaic or separated widely, or they may be prolonged backwards so that they overlap and are overlapped by others, like slates on a roof. The scales often have a definite arrangement, which is used in the classification of Squamata.

The skin, as in other Amniotes, consists of a compound squamous epithelium which rests on a corium built of connective tissues. The actual scale consists of the keratinized outer layers of the epidermis, its thickness is increased by additions to its inner surface, and it grows in area either all round or at one end. The area of the scale is always raised by a special papilla of the corium, which may project so far that the scale overlaps that behind it. The scale is colourless, its transparency allowing the pigment in the cutis to show through.

The outer layer of the keratinized epithelium is worn away in crocodiles and Chelonia, but in the Rhynchocephalia and Squamata it comes away either in flakes or, in some lizards and snakes, in one piece. Such cast skins exhibit perfectly the continuity of the horny skin, which in them even covers the eyes. This process of shedding the skin is facilitated in some or all of these reptiles by a special mechanism which allows the head to be distended with blood. The papilla of the corium which fills the centre of each scale may, in crocodiles, some lizards and many fossil reptiles, be ossified as a bony scute.

The carapace and plastron of the Chelonia consist essentially of such scutes. Each ossifies in the corium, the bone finally occupying nearly the whole thickness of that layer, leaving only a thin sheet of connective tissue to support the peritoneum, and a similar sheet containing pigment cells below the epidermis in which the horny shields are developed. The originally dermal ossifications of the carapace extend so far down into the body of the animal that, in the end, they completely surround the middle parts of the ribs, which first calcify and are then ossified by extension of membrane bone from the scute.

Most of the glands found in the skin of reptiles are scent glands, which give to these animals their characteristic odour of musk, which has, no doubt, a sexual significance. All these glands are sac-shaped, multicellular structures opening by a pore on the surface, and their secretion is set free by disruption of cells.

The musk glands have the following distribution:—In crocodiles there is a pair which open by longitudinal slits on the inner sides of the lower jaws, and another pair lie within the lips of the cloaca; these are present in both sexes. Crocodiles possess also a row of small sac-like glands without external openings along each side of the back.

In Chelonia there is a pair of inguinal glands opening near the hypoplastra, and sometimes an anterior pair similarly related to the hyoplastra. Sphenodon has a pair of cloacal glands. Lizards have cloacal glands and, in addition, in certain forms there are the so-called femoral pores, which extend along the lower and hinder surface of the thigh to pass on to the belly in front of the cloaca. They are present in both sexes, but best developed in males. Each pore opens in the middle of a scale and leads into a canal which ends in a pocket with many shallow diverticula. The cells of the walls of these become detached, filling up the lumen of the gland and duct, and forming a rod which may project beyond the surface of the skin. It is possible that these structures are of assistance in copulation.

Muscular System.—No useful account of the muscles of reptiles can be given here, the functional effects of those used in locomotion are described in the section *Locomotion*.

Body Cavity.—The body cavity of reptiles is always more or less completely divided into sacs. A completely closed pericardium is always present. In lizards, a post-hepatic septum built up by special folds of the mesentery and suspensory ligament of the liver, may reach the ventral surface and bring about an almost complete division of the peritoneal cavity into two. In snakes, similar folds enclose the two lobes of the liver and the stomach in separate sacs. In Chelonia, the lungs lie above a fold of peritoneum which reaches the liver, excluding them from the general cavity. In crocodiles, there are two pleural cavities and a combination of other folds connected with the liver forms a complete transverse partition separating the pericardium, lungs and liver from the rest of the peritoneal cavity. This sheet is muscular, and probably functions in respiration like the non-homologous mammalian diaphragm.

Digestive System: Teeth.—The teeth of reptiles may be found on the pre-maxillae, maxillae, on all the bones of the palate, and on the dentary and coronoid bones of the lower jaw. Individual teeth are generally simple cones with a conical pulp which produces dentine and an enamel cap. They may be set in sockets (thecodont) or fused to their supporting bone (acrodont or pleurodont). In the majority of reptiles they are shed periodically, and replaced as often as necessary. In reptiles, the marginal teeth of both jaws appear to belong to two series, whose members alternate with one another, and in primitive forms were functional alternately.

Thus, in these animals two teeth are usually separated by an empty emplacement in which a new tooth will arise, the original pair being shed together when it has grown to its full size. When the original teeth have been shed a new dental papilla passes outward from the lingual side to the empty socket and there produces a new tooth. In crocodiles this process has already happened before the tooth is shed, so that these new tooth crowns may often be found in the pulp cavity of the original tooth. Sphenodon, and some other recent reptiles with acrodont teeth, exhibit no replacement after maturity has been reached. The mammal-like reptiles in their various orders show all stages in the reduction of tooth change from the primitive unlimited replacement of all teeth to a mammalian condition in Cynodonts, where the incisors, canines and pre-molars are replaced once during the animal's life, and the molars, when once formed, are never shed.

The dentition of reptiles is usually homodont, that is, uniform or regularly varying from front to back of the jaw, but the Theriodont dentition is heterodont and mammal-like. The tooth crown may be elaborated into a crushing mechanism, in Placodonts, some Ichthyosaurs, and very effectively in the Trachodont dinosaurs, where several successive series of teeth are in use at one time, forming a splendid triturating surface, in Cotylosaurs, Theromorpha, and even, though imperfectly, in some lizards. The peculiarly specialized fangs of poisonous snakes are described in the article on these animals.

Tongue.—A tongue is present in all reptiles. In crocodiles and Chelonia, it is a short, broad, fleshy structure attached to the floor of the mouth over a large area. In crocodiles, a fold on the hinder margin of the tongue engages with a similar structure of the palate, so as completely to separate the air passage from that for food. In lizards the tongue may be flat, broad and not protrusible; it may be narrow, cylindrical and capable of being extended out of the mouth, or its cylindrical anterior half may telescope into the posterior portion, so that the whole can be projected far in front of the snout. This last type reaches its climax in the chameleon (*q.v.*).

Buccal Glands.—The only salivary gland of universal occurrence in reptiles is a sub-lingual. Upper and lower labial glands occur only in lizards and snakes, where they are arranged in rows between the lips and the teeth. The poison glands of the lizard Heloderma, and of the snakes, are special developments of such upper labial glands. They are described in the article SNAKE.

Gut.—In Chelonia, Sphenodon, lizards and snakes, the oesophagus passes gradually into the stomach, which is, in them, usually spindle-shaped, with its openings widely removed from one another. In crocodiles, the stomach is placed more transversely, the opening of the oesophagus and the pylorus being approximated. This stomach is an oval sac whose proximal portion is very muscular, recalling, in its arrangement, the gizzard of a bird; indeed, it customarily contains pebbles used for triturating food. The pyloric end of the stomach is distinct. The stomach always contains gastric glands.

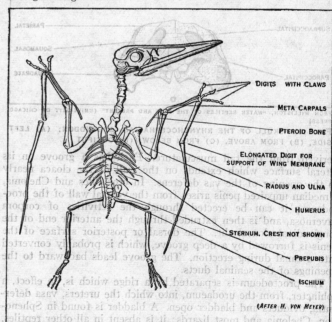

DIGITS WITH CLAWS

META CARPALS

PTEROID BONE

ELONGATED DIGIT FOR SUPPORT OF WING MEMBRANE

RADIUS AND ULNA

HUMERUS

STERNUM. CREST NOT SHOWN

PREPUBIS

ISCHIUM

(AFTER H. VON MEYER)

FIG. 15.—PTERODACTYLUS SPECTABILIS FROM THE LITHOGRAPHIC STONE

A pyloric valve usually exists, and the duodenum is not usually sharply marked off from the rest of the small intestine; only in crocodiles does it form a loop round the pancreas as it does in birds and mammals. The walls of the mid gut are usually thrown into folds or ridges, but seem to contain few or no glands. There is usually or always an ilio-colic valve separating the mid from the hind gut; immediately beyond this the latter gives rise to a caecum in some lizards and snakes. The rectum ends in a cloaca which is usually of elaborate structure.

Cloaca.—The cloacal opening leads into a proctodeum, a chamber whose walls give origin to the copulatory organ or organs in the male, and their representative in the female duct to the pair of anal glands; the peritoneal canals when present open into it.

Copulatory organs are absent in Sphenodon, in Squamata they are a pair of papillae capable of being protruded through the lateral ends of the transverse cloacal slit, and of being retracted, being turned inside out by the contraction of special muscles

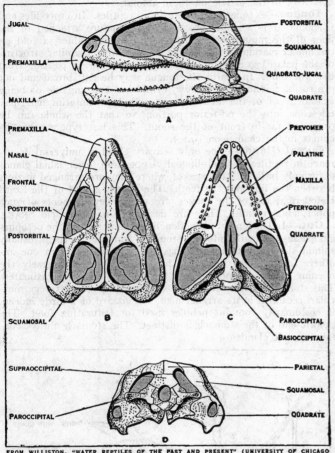

FROM WILLISTON, "WATER REPTILES OF THE PAST AND PRESENT" (UNIVERSITY OF CHICAGO PRESS)

FIG. 16.—SKULL OF THE RHYNCHOCEPHALIAN, SPHENODON; (A) LEFT SIDE, (B) FROM ABOVE, (C) FROM BELOW, (D) OCCIPUT

derived from the tail musculature. Each has a groove on its lateral surface which extends on the wall of the cloaca nearly to the opening of the vas deferens. In crocodiles and Chelonia, a median unpaired penis arises from the ventral wall of the proctodeum; it can be erected through the activities of corpora cavernosa, and is then extruded through the anterior end of the longitudinal cloacal slit. The dorsal or posterior surface of the penis is furrowed by a deep groove, which is probably converted into a canal during erection. The groove leads backward to the openings of the seminal ducts.

The proctodeum is separated by a ridge which is, in effect, a sphincter, from the urodaeum, into which the ureters, vasa deferentia, oviducts and bladder open. A bladder is found in Sphenodon, Chelonia and most lizards; it is absent in all other reptiles. The urodaeum is partially subdivided in many reptiles; in snakes a dorsal recess receives the ureters and gonoducts; in crocodiles they open into the dorsal side of the urodaeum, whilst in Chelonia they discharge directly into the neck of the bladder. In Sphenodon, lizards and snakes, the oviducts open rather dorsally, in crocodiles and Chelonia ventrally, the vasa deferentia having a similar opening in all forms.

The urodaeum is, in some aquatic Chelonia, produced into a pair of their walled sacs on the dorsal side, which are constantly filled and emptied of water, thus serving as accessory respiratory **organs**. In all reptiles except crocodiles and Chelonia there is

an additional cloacal chamber, the coprodeum, which serves for the storage of faeces.

Urogenital System.—The kidney of an adult reptile is always a metanephros, discharging by a single ureter. The kidney may be elongated and its surface furrowed, or it may be a small compact organ. The urine of Chelonia and Crocodilia is fluid, that which is voided by snakes and lizards contains crystals of insoluble urates, an arrangement which prevents waste of water in these animals, which often live in very arid surroundings.

The ovaries are always paired, and large owing to the size of the yolky eggs. Interstitial tissue is small in amount. The oviducts have independent funnel-shaped ostia, and are usually provided with glandular walls which secrete the albumen and shell. In some viviparous forms they can combine with the faetal membranes to form a placenta. The elongated testes are connected with an epididymis of mesonephric origin.

Respiratory System.—All reptiles breathe by lungs. These are always produced by the elaboration of a median ventral outgrowth of the pharynx. The glottis lies immediately behind the tongue and is sometimes protected by a rudimentary upstanding epiglottis. There is a larynx, supported by arytenoid and cricoid cartilages, there being no thyroid cartilages; muscles passing from the laryngeal cartilages to the "hyoid" enable the glottis to be opened and closed. There are often vocal chords, which give to Sphenodon, crocodiles, some tortoises and lizards a voice, usually a grunt or squeak. The trachea is often long and its cavity is kept open by cartilaginous rings. The bronchi may be very short in Sphenodon or very long in tortoises. The lung is very variable in its structure; it may be almost as primitive as in Amphibia or become comparable to that of a bird.

In Sphenodon and snakes the cavity of the lung is single, but the walls are divided up into a series of cells by upstanding ridges or septa. In some lizards certain of these septa elongate so that the original single sac begins to be cut up into lobes, each with cellular walls. In crocodiles, this process has gone on so far that the lung is definitely divided into a number of chambers each of which receives a number of wide side canals, the parabronchi, in whose walls lie the alveoli. In Chelonia this process has gone so much further that the whole lung is spongy, the alveoli, through walls whose walls the whole of the respiratory exchange takes place, being connected with an irregularly branched series of bronchial tubes.

Not only is the actual structure of the lung altered in this way, but reptiles show an advance over the Amphibia in an increased size of the lung resulting from the development of a special anterior projection, the prebronchial part, which, very small in Sphenodon, becomes much more extensive in more advanced reptiles. In chameleons, long, hollow non-respiratory process of the lungs pass backward among the viscera; they are important as morphological forerunners of the air sacs of birds and Pterodactyls. In elongated legless reptiles one of the lungs is usually reduced, and may be absent.

The mode of respiration in Reptilia is not well known. In all except the Chelonia, movements of the ribs may be expected to draw air into the lungs, whilst the muscular post-hepatic diaphragm of crocodiles is, no doubt, used as is the comparable structure in mammals. In Chelonia, and probably also in other reptiles, air is actively forced down into the lungs by movements of the floor of the buccal cavity brought about by the hyoid and its musculature. In Chelonia, the protrusion and withdrawal from the shell of the neck and legs gives a pumping action which, by creating a virtual vacuum, draws air into the lungs.

Vascular System.—The heart of reptiles lies in the thoracic region, usually between the lungs. There is a sinus venosus, at least in most, which opens by a valve guarded slit into the right auricle. Right and left auricles are completely separated, and open independently into the ventricle or ventricles. The lower edge of the interauricular septum is expanded laterally into, usually, very large right and left membranous valves, which direct the arterial blood to the left, the venous to the right side of the ventricular cavity. The ventricle is incompletely, or, in Crocodilia, completely divided by an upstanding ridge into right and left halves. Except for a possible relic in Sphenodon, there is no trace of a conus arteriosus nor of a truncus. Three arteries arise independently from the ventricle, and are then twisted round one another like a rope, so that they cross one another. That vessel whose origin is most to the right is the left systemic arch, the next is the pulmonary arch, and the third is the right systemico-carotid, from which arise both carotids. As a result of this arrangement, in Chelonia the pulmonary arch arises from a partially separated cavum pulmonale, and the two systemics from a cavum venosum, which has to be traversed during systole by the blood from the left auricle, which is originally discharged into the cavum arteriosum on the left side of the ventricle. In crocodiles, the right systemico-carotid alone leaves the left ventricle, whilst both pulmonary arch and left systemic come off from the venous right ventricle: but in them the left and right systemics are connected by a special opening, the foramen of Panizzi at the point where they cross. Although it has been shown by the electrocardiograph that the nature of the contraction of the heart in tortoises is much as in mammals, very little is known of its general physiology.

Arterial System.—The pulmonary arch soon divides into two branches, one to each lung; in Sphenodon and some lizards it gives off a paired laryngotracheal artery which is a relic of a

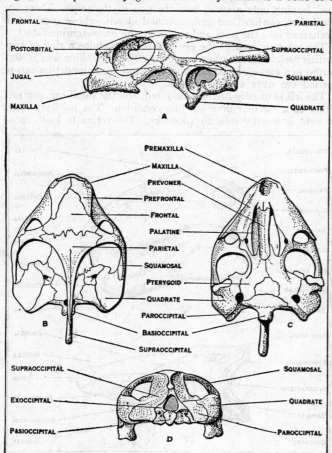

FIG. 17.—SKULL OF A TORTOISE, TESTUDO
A. Left side, B. from above, C. from below, D. occiput

Urodela structure. The systemic arches unite to form the dorsal aorta; from one or both of them arise coronary arteries to the heart. From the right come off both subclavians, and the left usually gives off a coelic branch. The carotids may arise independently from the right systemico-carotid, or may be formed by the branching of a single primary carotid. In snakes the right carotid is usually much reduced or absent.

Venous System.—The venous system is exceedingly complicated, differing in details in the four orders but with a common ground plan. The pulmonary veins pass straight from the lungs

into the left auricle.

The venous blood is returned to the heart by the pair of precaval, and single postcaval veins which open into the sinus venosus. The branches of the precavals come from the head and fore limb, the subclavian often receiving an azygous vein from the anterior part of the body wall which represents part of the embryonic posterior cardinal. Nearly the whole of the blood which

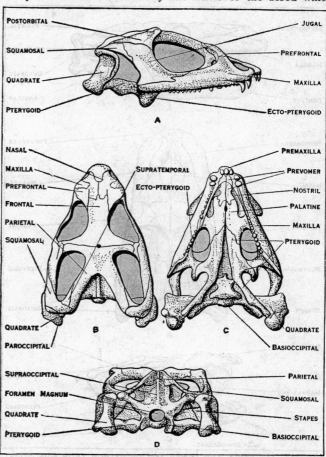

FIG. 18.—SKULL OF THE LIZARD CHAMYDOSAURUS
A. Right side, B. from above, C. from below, D. occiput

enters the heart through the postcaval has previously passed through one of the portal systems.

The renal portal system drains the tail, and part of the hind limbs, the afferent renals arising from the bifurcated anterior end of the caudal vein and the iliacs. The efferent renals open into the postcaval, whose hinder end is formed by them. The supra renal portal system consists of a series of afferent veins which come from the body wall; the efferents discharge with the gonadial veins into the postcaval.

The hepatic portal system includes the series of veins from the gut, which form the true hepatic portal vein and also the median anterior abdominal vein, which is originally formed by a fusion in the middle line of pelvic veins, themselves built up from the iliacs and a series of vessels from the hinder part of the body wall of the abdomen. The anterior abdominal passes along in a mesenteric sheet in the ventral part of the body cavity to enter the liver and there receive the hepatic portal or a branch from it. Finally, the whole of the blood in the liver passes by the hepatic veins into the posterior cardinal.

Lymphatic System.—Definite lymphatic canals are well developed in reptiles; those of the head unite into thoracic ducts which open into the innominate veins. There is a pair of posterior lymph hearts discharging into the iliacs.

Blood.—The red blood corpuscles are oval, biconvex and nucleated; they are larger than those of birds and mammals, smaller than those of Amphibia.

"Ductless Glands."—A spleen is constantly present in reptiles, placed near the stomach or within the loop of the duodenum behind the pancreas. The reptilian thyroid is a median structure placed somewhere on the ventral surface of the trachea.

There are two pairs of thymuses in Sphenodon and lizards, derived from the second and third pharyngeal pouches in the latter. In snakes there are usually two pairs derived from the

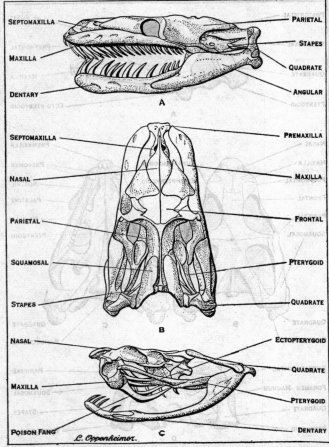

FIG. 19.—(A) SKULL AND LOWER JAW OF PYTHON (NON-POISONOUS), (B) SAME FROM ABOVE, (C) LEFT SIDE OF SKULL AND LOWER JAW OF RATTLESNAKE (POISONOUS)

dorsal extremities of the fourth and fifth pouches. A variable series of epithelial bodies, either dorsal or ventral, is present, and there is an ultimobranchial body of the left side, at any rate, in lizards.

Nervous System: *Sense Organs.*—Skin. Tactile corpuscles are found in the cutis of all reptiles. In crocodiles a group of them lies at the bottom of a pit, filled with non-conified cells near the anterior border of each of the large ventral scales. In Chelonia they lie in the thin layer of connective tissue between the epidermal scutes and the bony shell. In certain Agamids some of the scales of the dorsal surface bear long rod-like projections and are surrounded by nerve endings so that they may function as specialized tactile organs as do some mammalian hairs.

Taste.—It is clear that some sense of taste exists, the taste buds being probably on the tongue.

Smell.—The sense of smell is well developed in all recent reptiles, although it was much reduced or absent in the later Pterodactyls.

The external nostril, often provided with a valve, leads into a short vestibule, which opens out into the true olfactory chamber, whose wall is lined with the sensory epithelium which contain the olfactory cells. The area of the surface of this epithelium is increased by the presence of a ridge, the concha, which stretches into the cavity from the outer side. In crocodiles there is an additional concha, and there are reasons for believing that in Cynodonts, ethmo- and naso-turbinals were developed as in

mammals. The nasal cavity finally opens to the palate by the internal nostril, which may be carried far back by the formation of a secondary palate.

Jacobsen's organ is, in Chelonia, a mere diverticulum of the ventral part of the nasal cavity. In Squamata it becomes an independent chamber, separated from the nasal cavity by the septomaxillary bone; it then has a special opening to the palate and may be very highly developed, receiving a large proportion of the olfactory nerve fibres. Its function is clearly to smell food after it has been taken into the mouth.

Jacobsen's organ soon vanishes in crocodiles. A special nasal gland is developed in the concha of reptiles, and the naso-lachrimal duct opens on the lateral wall of the nasal cavity.

Eye.—The eyes of reptiles are normally provided with movable upper and lower eyelids, and a nictitating membrane which is usually transparent and can be drawn across the cornea. The nictitating membrane may vanish in some lizards; in snakes it is permanently drawn across the eye, fuses with the remnant of the upper eyelid, and has a cornified scale on its outer surface, which is shed with the rest at ecdysis.

In some desert lizards the lower eyelid has a transparent window in the middle and is fused with the upper. In chameleons there is no nictitating membrane, and the upper and lower eyelids fuse, leaving only a small hole the size of the pupil. There are Harderian, conjunctival and lachrimal glands, whose secretion is discharged into the nose and palate by the naso-lachrimal duct.

The sclerotic coat of the eye ball often contains a ring of supporting ossicles, the cornea is convex. The crystalline lens is supported in a capsule by ciliary muscles, and accommodation can be carried out over a wide range.

The iris is usually brightly-coloured, and the pupil can contract either to a circular or a slit-like condition. The pupilary reflex to light is usually difficult to evoke. The retina is built up of

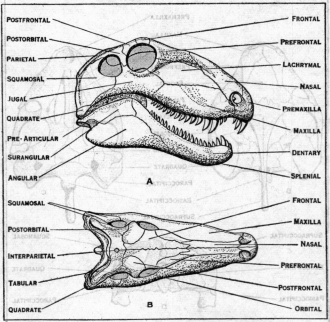

FROM "CONTRIBUTIONS FROM THE WALKER MUSEUM, CHICAGO UNIVERSITY"

FIG. 20.—SKULL OF THE PELYIOSAUR, SPHENACODON; (A) RIGHT SIDE, WITH LOWER JAW, (B) FROM ABOVE

small elements, both rods and cones being present in some forms, rods or cones alone in others. The retina, like that of birds, often contains pigmented oil granules, yellow, red, green, and, in Chelonia, blue and violet. Nutrition of the contents of the eye ball is secured, in many reptiles, by the presence of a pecten, a pigmented vascular projection, at first conical and when more highly developed fanshaped which arises from the fundus. A pecten is absent in Sphenodon and rudimentary in Chelonia. In snakes its place is taken functionally by a vascularization of the choroid. In chameleon there is a macula and fossa like that of birds or primates. The eyes of reptiles are always laterally directed, but can be moved through a small arc of about 20°. They possess the normal series of six eye muscles and a retractor bulbi in addition. Reptiles appear to possess a colour sense, but accurate observations are lacking.

Pineal Eye.—In Sphenodon and lizards the epiphysis of the brain lies in a foramen between the parietal bones, and is covered by a transparent scale. It ends in a vesicle whose outer wall is lens-shaped, whilst the lower surface is a pigmented retina. It appears to exhibit no perception of light. The immense size of the pineal foramen in some fossil reptiles suggests that the pineal eye was functional in them.

Ear.—All reptiles have an inner and middle ear, an outer ear being present in crocodiles and the extinct Cynodonts. The inner ear is more advanced than that of Amphibia in that the utriculus is connected to the swollen sacculus by a duct from which the endolymphatic duct rises. There is a lagena which, in crocodiles, becomes much elongated and provided with a rudimentary organ of Corti seated on a basilar membrane.

The endolymphatic duct ends blindly, usually within the skull, but in Geckos is extended into a sac under the skin of the neck. There is a special perilymphatic duct which forms a closed tube definitely associated with the lagena. In crocodiles this begins to form definite scalae comparable to those of the mammalian cochlea.

The cavity of the middle ear is formed by an upgrowth from the first visceral pouch; in Sphenodon and lizards the cavity communicates with the pharynx by a wide opening, in Chelonia by a narrow Eustachian tube. In crocodiles the Eustachian tubes of the two ears meet and form a duct running in a special canal between the basisphenoid and basioccipital to open in the middle line just behind the choanae; lateral branches from the duct pass in canals between the basisphenoid and the pterygoids up into the supraoccipital and cranial roof, there enlarging into air spaces which again communicate with the tympanic cavities. Finally, a tube rising from each cavity leads air down into the quadrate and lower jaw. The history of this elaborate arrangement can be made out from fossil materials. In snakes, the tympanic cavity is totally obliterated. The outer wall of the tympanic cavity is the tympanic membrane, which, in crocodiles and most lizards, is a thin sheet sunk below the surface of the head at the lower end of an external auditory meatus. In Sphenodon and Chelonia it lies flush with the surface, and its outer surface is indistinguishable from that of the neck. In snakes and chameleons it is absent.

The tympanic membrane is connected with the fenestra ovalis by a rod, whose inner end is an ossified columella or stapes, whilst the unossified outer end is the extra columella. This is small and simple in Chelonia, absent in snakes, where the end of the stapes articulates with the quadrate, and in Amphisbaenans. In lizards, the extra columella has a dorsal process attached to the end of the paroccipital process, and often detached, a ventral process applied to the quadrate, and a plate for insertion in the tympanic membrane. The whole structure is of hyoidean origin, and the hyoid articulates with the end of the paroccipital process. In Sphenodon it fuses with the end of the extra columella, and in crocodiles it arises from its shaft to pass down the air canal to the lower jaw and become continuous with Meckel's cartilage.

Most or all reptiles are capable of hearing, but we know nothing of their ability to discriminate musical notes.

Peripheral Nervous System.—The spinal nerves of reptiles agree in all important characters with those of other Tetrapods, the only interesting peculiarity being the presence in snakes of rudimentary pectoral and pelvic plexuses, relics of the limbs of their ancestors.

The sympathetic system presents an advance over that of most Amphibia in that many of the ganglia in the thoracic region are fused into a single large ganglion, and that the cervical sympathetic is separated into deep and superficial portions, each running continuously from the ganglion of the vagus to the thorax, the details varying in different orders. This arrangement is derived from that of Urodeles and leads directly to birds.

The cranial nerves of reptiles differ from those of living Amphibia in the absence of all trace of the lateral line system, except the auditory nerve, in the presence of a spinal accessory nerve XI. and in the fact that the hypoglossal nerve XII. passes out through the exoccipital bone.

Brain.—The reptilian brain is larger proportionately than that of an amphibian of the same size. The cerebral hemispheres

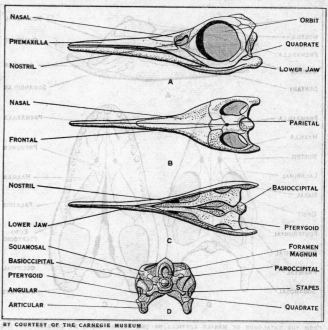

BY COURTESY OF THE CARNEGIE MUSEUM

FIG. 21.—SKULL AND LOWER JAW OF THE ICHTHYOSAUR OPHTHALMO-SAURUS; (A) LEFT SIDE, (B) FROM ABOVE, (C) FROM BELOW

are pointed and usually pass gradually into the olfactory lobes. Their hinder ends are free and often project posteriorly so as to conceal the diencephalon.

In Sphenodon and in Chelonia the whole of the upper surface of the hemisphere, from the hippocampus on the inner surface to the lateral face, is covered by a pallium, devoted to the sense of smell. This layer of cells then turns inward from the surface, and lies on the top of the corpus striatum, forming a hypopallium. In lizards, and especially in crocodiles, the dorsal surface of the hemisphere becomes less and less nervous until, in birds, it is a mere membrane playing no part in the functioning of the brain. In these reptiles the hypopallium becomes broken up by a penetration of nerve fibres, loses its pallial appearance and becomes assimilated to the corpus striatum. Thus, presumably in these animals, and certainly in birds, behaviour is controlled and memory exercised by a part of the brain quite different from that which fulfils these functions in mammals. In some reptiles, at any rate, the first trace of the neopallium, which is the important and developing part of the brain in mammals, is represented by a small cortical area in which alone other senses than smell gain a direct representation.

The mid brain of reptiles has its roof thickened and raised into a pair of optic lobes, which not only receive the endings of the optic nerves from the retina but are the motor area, stimulation of which brings about movements of the body.

The cerebellum of reptiles is always larger and better developed than that of Amphibia, though in living forms it is not externally divided into regions, as is that of a bird or mammal.

The brain of the extinct pterodactyls is interesting because, in the reduction of the olfactory lobe, the large size of the cerebellum and the lateral position of the optic lobes, it exactly resembles that of a bird, is indeed more like that of recent birds than is the brain of Archaeopteryx, which is the most primitive member of that class.

Reproduction.—Fertilization of the reptilian egg always takes place internally, in contrast to the condition in many Amphibia.

The egg is always large and provided with so large a store of food materials in the form of yolk that the growing embryo, without any additional materials, can hatch in a form capable of fending for itself, and is, indeed, usually a miniature copy of its parents.

This ovum is surrounded by a semi-fluid layer of albumen, and enclosed in a membranous shell which may be calcified as is

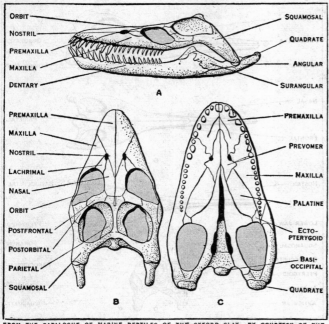

FROM THE CATALOGUE OF MARINE REPTILES OF THE OXFORD CLAY, BY COURTESY OF THE BRITISH MUSEUM

FIG. 22.—SKULL OF THE PLESIOSAUR, MURAENOSAURUS
A. From the left side, B. from above, C. from below

that of a bird. Usually the egg is laid before development has gone far, but in some cases it is retained within the oviduct until the foetus is ready to be born. These animals, including many lizards and snakes, are thus viviparous. In their case the egg shell is thin, and food materials may pass through it; indeed, in some cases it is practically absent, and the little lizard secures nourishment from its mother through a special placenta.

Cleavage is meroblastic, resulting only in the formation of a primitive plate of cells. Gastrulation involves an actual invagination, resulting in the formation of an archenteron which has both floor and roof. The process is, indeed, similar in principle to that in the Gymnophionan Amphibia. No primitive streak is formed behind the blastopore in Chelonia, Sphenodon, lizards or snakes.

The later development much resembles that of birds or monotremes. A headfold is formed, followed by tail and lateral folds, which gradually raise the embryo from the yolk and extra-embryonic structures. An amnion arises from the extra embryonic somatopleure, as in birds, and an allantois is formed later by a ventral outpushing of the hind gut. It serves not only as a reservoir for the excretory products of the embryo, but also as a respiratory organ. The embryo breaks its way out of the shell by the aid either of an egg-tooth, placed mesially on its nose or of a caruncula on its head.

Further details will be found in the article VERTEBRATE EMBRYOLOGY.

Mode of Life.—No general statements can be made about the habits of reptiles. If the extinct forms be taken into account it will be found that they have occupied all the habitats which are to-day filled with mammals, except that they are excluded from polar regions by the impossibility of hatching their eggs there, and in extreme cases of achieving a sufficiently high rate of metabolism. The temperature of the body of reptiles, like that of Amphibia, and unlike that of the birds and mammals, is determined by that of their surroundings, rising when the animal is in a warm place, and sometimes becoming very high in bright

sunlight, and falling at night, perhaps to freezing point. The animal's muscular activity always keeps it a very few degrees above the air temperature. Some idea of the variety of habit of reptiles may be gathered from the section on *Locomotion* in this article, and further facts from the articles: LIZARD, TURTLE, CROCODILIAN, and SNAKES.

Geographical Distribution.—Apart from the limitation imposed by temperature, no general statements can be made about reptilian distribution; any useful account would occupy much space, and involve a discussion of the interrelationships of the families of lizards and snakes, a disputed field.

Geological Distribution.—The earliest bone which has been referred to a reptile is an isolated femur from the Lower Carboniferous of Scotland. Eosauravus, from the Upper Carboniferous (Middle Coal Measures) of Ohio, is probably a reptile, and Solenodonsaurus, from the top of the Upper Carboniferous of Czechoslovakia is certainly one.

The evolution of the reptiles was rapid, nearly all orders being fully established by the end of Triassic times. Several important orders became extinct at the end of the Trias, but the reptiles were the dominant group of vertebrates to the end of the Mesozoic, when, within a short period though not simultaneously, many orders became extinct, leaving only the four which still survive.

Economic Importance.—Reptiles are of slight importance to man. Poisonous snakes are responsible for many deaths of man and domesticated animals in all tropical and some temperate regions.

The marine turtle, *Chelone midas,* found in tropical waters of the Atlantic, Indian and Pacific oceans, provides the best of all soups; several other forms found in fresh water are often eaten, the most familiar of these being the terrapins, of the genus *Chrysemys.* The eggs of various species are also eaten by uncivilized peoples.

The skins of crocodiles, and of certain of the larger lizards and snakes, are tanned and used as leather. This consists only of the cutis, the horny epidermis being removed. This leather is extraordinarily tough and wear resisting, and the presence in it of the papillae which underlie the scales gives it a most attractive surface. The pigment, or at any rate such of it as

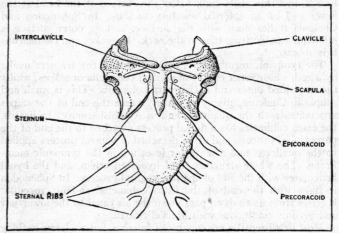

FIG. 23.—SHOULDER GIRDLE OF A LIZARD AMBLYRHYNCHUS FROM BELOW, SHOWING THE RELATIONS OF THE CLAVICLES, INTERCLAVICLE PRECORACOID AND STERNUM TO ONE ANOTHER

is melanine, may remain in the leather and give it characteristic patterns. The use of reptilian leathers for ladies' shoes and handbags has become popular and led to the destruction of many of these animals. That of alligators, however, is derived in part from animals bred for the purpose.

Further information about reptiles will be found in the separate articles: CROCODILIAN, DINOSAURIA, LIZARD, SNAKES, ICHTHYOSAURIA, PLESIOSAURUS, PTERODACTYL, TURTLE, etc., and in the general articles, EMBRYOLOGY, PHYSIOLOGY, ZOOLOGICAL GEOGRAPHY, etc.   (D. M. S. W.)

REPTON, a township in Derbyshire, Eng., 8 mi. S.W. of Derby, on the London Midland Region railway. Population 1,518. Its famous school was founded in 1557 by Sir John Port. Its modern buildings incorporate considerable portions (restored as a memorial to old Reptonians who fell in World War I) of an Augustinian priory established in 1172. There was a monastery in the 7th century, the first bishop of Mercia being established there. The parish church of St. Wystan retains pre-Conquest work in the chancel.

REPUBLIC, a term denoting (1) a state not ruled by a monarch or emperor, generally a public interest and not a private or hereditary property; (2) a state where power is not directly in the hands of or subject to complete control by the people, in contrast with a democracy; (3) more loosely, any regime where government depends actually or nominally on popular will. The latter meaning is implied more generally in the adjective, "republican," than it is in the noun.

"Republic" derives from the Latin words *res publica,* public affair or thing. That concept was in turn loosely equivalent to the classical Greek *ta koinonia,* common things or property, a term originally applied in the early city-state to the city's treasure, the public funds, and then by analogy coming to symbolize and denote the common interests. From these root origins derive in turn the concepts of commonwealth, which was the official title of Great Britain under Oliver Cromwell's rule, the first republic in the English-speaking world, and common weal or common welfare, at that same time a widely held designation of the proper end or purpose of government.

The term republic has generally been applied by historians first to the government of ancient Rome after the expulsion of the Etruscan kings, the Tarquins, and prior to the establishment of the empire by Augustus. During that period, indeed, political institutions, constitutional arrangements and the locus of effective political power varied widely, though the regime might be generally described as one of aristocratic, or patrician, ascendancy moderated by popular, or plebeian, influence and assent. But the dual concepts which subsequently characterized the republican idea, absence of monarchy and a collective public interest and business, were present.

Some historians have also applied the term to the ancient Greek city-state. There, however, governments were normally classified by the numbers exercising power, such as monarchy, aristocracy and democracy, and their perversions, tyranny, oligarchy and ochlocracy (or, frequently, again democracy), where rule was arbitrary rather than directed by the principle of the good of the city. Nevertheless, one root idea of a republic, that of common interest and participation, was present in the contrast between Greek city-state and barbarian empires, with their irresponsible rulers and submissive mass of subjects.

In any event, republic, when applied to ancient governments, has implied some popular and collective power and the absence of hereditary or autocratic rule, as contrasted with government by kings or emperors.

The modern usage of "republic" derives from these dual ideas, absence of monarchy, and some degree of avowed concern for the common welfare of the state and for public control or participation. During the later middle ages there were established some brief-lived local republics, consequent on revolt. But it was in certain city-states of Italy during the Renaissance, of which the most celebrated are Venice and Florence (during a limited period after the expulsion and before the return of the Medici) that the republic re-emerged as a meaningful designation and form of government. Here again absence of monarchy, of an established lordly ruling family or of a self-imposed absolute ruler was the first test. In such republics a share in control of government was often confined to noble or wealthy privileged families, while the form of government tended to be by a small group, co-opted or elected on a narrow franchise, though sometimes with a titular head of state, such as the doge in Venice. On occasion, too, as a result of popular pressure or revolt, government might for a while come to rest on a broader base, and to include representatives of at least the lesser burghers and the artisans.

But republics which combined the ideas of absence of monarchy, a realm of public affairs and popular consent or participation first emerged, generally as temporary phenomena, in the 17th and 18th centuries. Cromwell's commonwealth, though it developed into rule by one man not unlike the more moderate modern dictatorships, had its genesis in antimonarchical doctrines and forces, expressed in the Civil War against Charles I. During that conflict, too, the concept of the interest of the community at large in government became firmly associated with the republican idea. The Dutch republic, though it was headed by a stadholder, initially the equivalent of a modern strong president, combined opposition to monarchy (and to Catholicism) with a concept of independence not unlike the later idea of national self-determination, with implications of a common collective interest and a certain degree of public participation and control. Similar considerations also played a part in the early evolution of the Swiss republic, which after many vicissitudes became the modern federal republic of Switzerland. Here, however, the independent city-states of the Reformation, republican even when theocratic and in some cases free still earlier, provided a foundation.

The antimonarchical idea constituted a major element in both the American and the French Revolutions. The former created a lasting republic, the United States of America, while the second created a temporary republic in France but firmly established the republican idea and spread it throughout most of western Europe. In both revolutions the twin ideas of consent of the governed and the rights of man played a major part. A little later the separation of the Spanish-American colonies from Spain produced numerous republics which rested on similar ideas. During the 19th century, however, the moral significance of the republican idea declined in Europe, where monarchies continued and republics remained the exception. Constitutional government spread in the monarchies, and by the early 20th century the term "republic" no longer connoted the substance and content of political institutions and practice. "Democracy" tended to supplant "republic" in describing governments free from arbitrary and imposed authority. Democracy was widespread in Great Britain (also the British Commonwealth) and the Scandinavian countries—all monarchies. In Latin America, on the other hand, nominal republics were often dictatorships on behalf of oligarchies.

In these and other instances, the term "republic" had been stripped of its earlier appeal as the alternative to divine-right monarchy and autocracy.

After World War I, the emergence of dictatorships, which might function formally within a monarchical state (fascism in Italy), might reject the idea of a republic without restoring monarchy (Francisco Franco's Spain), though restoring the title of empire (Hitler's third reich), or might continue nominally as republics, rendered the classification of regimes into monarchies or republics practically meaningless. After World War II, moreover, the term had still less relevance. The United States of America, Franco's anti-Communist dictatorship in Spain and Joseph Stalin's Communist dictatorship in the U.S.S.R. were all nominally republics. In essence, the basic classification of governments was into constitutional governments and dictatorships, a division which corresponded in ethos to the former opposition of republic and monarchy. The term republic no longer had a manifest connection with struggles over liberty, authority and sovereignty.

The adjective "republican," however, was still sometimes used with connotations equivalent to its ancient meaning in political ethics.

In the United States the term "republic" has special connotations and is frequently used with supposed historical justification to contrast with democracy and as a ground for denial that the U.S. is technically a democracy. The bases for this contrast are (1) the ancient and purist use of the term "democracy" to denote small-scale direct democracy; (2) the classical fear, which continued at least to the end of the 18th century, of such democracy as unstable and fickle; (3) the Ciceronian interpretation, which widely influenced the U.S. founding fathers, of the Roman republic as a mixed and balanced government; and (4) the revival by

Montesquieu in the 18th century of the idea of democracy as direct and small-scale, and his insistence that democracy was impossible in a larger state, which could be at best a representative republic. These ideas were studied and combined by a number of the founding fathers, and especially by James Madison, who used the term "republic" (1) as a technical designation for representative government as opposed to direct democracy and (2) to insist on the necessity for a system of checks and balances against the dangers of straight majoritarian decision in a legislature elected by majority on a single principle of representation. The insistence that republic is not synonymous with democracy either as direct democracy or as absolute majoritarian democracy, but rather is synonymous with constitutional democracy, is correct in the specific U.S. context, though that usage is a narrowing of the wider use of the term to denote any nonmonarchical regime. The guarantee to the states of the union of a republican form of government (in a nation whose given title deliberately excluded the designation republic) seemingly refers primarily to the more generic usage. It does not imply specific forms or checks, although some later extensions to the states of limitations on the federal government by guaranteed individual rights might be taken inferentially to imply more specific connotations of republican, even though those extensions were not, in constitutional interpretation, in any way related to that guarantee.

BIBLIOGRAPHY.—Charles A. Beard, *The Republic: Conversations on Fundamentals* (1943); Zera S. Fink, *The Classical Republicans* (1945); H. A. L. Fisher, *The Republican Tradition in Europe* (1911); Henry Mann, *Ancient and Medieval Republics* (1879).   (T. I. C.)

REPUBLICAN PARTY, THE, in the United States was organized in 1854. Intense opposition in nonslave states to the further extension of the slavery system, and the breakdown of the compromise policy of Henry Clay, with the Kansas-Nebraska bill and repeal of the Missouri Compromise as the incidental causes, brought the party into being. The first actual meeting was possibly the one at Ripon, Wis., Feb. 28, 1854. The first convention was held at Jackson, Mich., July 6, 1854. All opposed to slavery extension were welcome. An informal gathering, national in scope, meeting in Pittsburgh, Pa., Feb. 22, 1856, planned the first national convention, which assembled in Philadelphia, Pa., June 17.

The chairman, E. D. Morgan of New York, declared the party's purpose to be to determine "not whether the South is to rule or the North . . . but whether the broad national policy our fathers established, cherished and maintained is to be permitted to descend to her sons."

Opposition to slavery extension and to polygamy, the imperative necessity of a railroad to the Pacific ocean, and approval of congressional appropriations for improvement of rivers and harbours were the platform subjects. Gen. John C. Frémont of California and William L. Dayton were the nominees, but were defeated after a vigorous campaign. Many events rapidly consolidated and intensified the antislavery movement, and on May 16, 1860, probably the most historic of all Republican national conventions assembled in the "Wigwam" at Chicago, Ill. It established a majority rule for nominations in contrast with the Democratic two-thirds. Threats of secession were denounced by the platform, which favoured restriction of slavery, opposed reopening the slave trade and favoured a protective tariff. Abraham Lincoln was elected president, Hannibal Hamlin vice-president. The story of the Lincoln administration is very largely the story of the Civil War. Preservation of the union at any cost was Lincoln's policy, and emancipation and other policies were largely incidental. During the war, however, the Republican congress found time to organize a national banking system under the National Bank act (Feb. 25, 1863); to pass a high tariff law and internal revenue acts; and to take steps toward the construction of the first transcontinental railway. Despite earlier doubts, the result of opposition to the extent of the war and its terrific cost in life, President Lincoln was renominated by acclamation and re-elected in 1864, Andrew Johnson of Tennessee being selected as vice-president to secure the border states' support. The war was continued to a successful conclusion, but the assassination of Lincoln, who died on April 15, 1865, quickly terminated the celebrations of victory.

Reconstruction.—Johnson's outstanding problems, and those of the two following administrations were concerned with the so-called "reconstruction" of the seceded states. A marked difference of opinion as to the treatment to be accorded these states developed. Johnson's policy was not rigorous to the extent demanded by powerful congressional leaders. The result was a conflict between the executive and congress, culminating in Johnson's impeachment and acquittal by one vote.

"Let us have peace" was the slogan under which Gen. Ulysses S. Grant was elected president in 1868, with Schuyler Colfax of Indiana as vice-president. The problems of reconstruction, enactment of bills designed to enforce provisions of the 14th amendment and the signing of a treaty with Great Britain (1871), called the treaty of Washington, which made provisions for settling diplomatic controversies between the two countries, were outstanding features of Grant's administration. The senate refused to ratify a treaty to annex Santo Domingo.

In 1872 certain Republicans opposed Grant's re-election and a new party, known as the Liberal Republican, nominated Horace Greeley to run against him. The Democratic national convention endorsed Greeley, but only six states were carried by the fusion ticket. Despite two troublesome years, with panic and scandal, there was much of credit in constructive achievement and U.S. foreign policies won respect abroad. In 1874 President Grant vetoed an inflation bill and a year later approved the resumption of specie payments.

Making capital out of scandals and with the slogan, "Turn the rascals out," the Democratic party won the house in 1874 and almost won the presidential election of 1876. Rutherford B. Hayes of Ohio, Republican nominee for president, won after an electoral commission, especially created, had decided one of the most bitter political contests. William A. Wheeler of New York became vice-president. President Hayes completed reconstruction in the south by withdrawing federal troops, a policy which brought him northern criticism because immediately after the troops were withdrawn Democratic leaders in southern states inaugurated the policy of Negro disfranchisement. Specie payments were resumed.

Domestic Questions.—James A. Garfield of Ohio was elected president in 1880, and upon his assassination in 1881, Chester A. Arthur of New York succeeded. Enactment of a national civil service law, establishment of the bureau of labour, two-cent first-class postage rates, and the beginnings of a new navy were brought about. The campaign of 1884 was most bitter in personal recriminations, both nominees, James G. Blaine, Republican, and Grover Cleveland, Democrat, suffering unparalleled attacks. Certain Republican elements refused to support Blaine, and at the end one famous phrase, "rum, Romanism and rebellion," lost for him the state of New York by 1,149 votes and he consequently lost the electoral college.

In 1888 Benjamin Harrison of Indiana defeated Cleveland, and Levi P. Morton of New York became vice-president. The tariff was a chief issue, but enactment of a higher rate bill, known as the McKinley act, was delayed until just before the election of 1890. It was unpopular and an overwhelming Republican defeat followed. The Harrison administration was noted for enactment of the Sherman Antitrust law, additional coinage of silver, admission of several new states, among them Wyoming with the first provision for woman suffrage, and the famous Reed enforcement of new rules in the house designed to prevent minority obstruction.

Personal dislike of the president by certain prominent leaders was a factor in bringing about Harrison's defeat for re-election in 1892, when Cleveland was returned to office with his party in control of both houses of congress for the first time since the Civil War. One of the worst panics and unemployment periods in U.S. history occurred and a lower tariff bill was enacted. The tariff was included in the Republican platform as an issue in the campaign of 1896, but as this battle approached, much greater prominence was given the question of the coinage of silver in relation to gold. William McKinley of Ohio was nominated by the Republicans on a gold standard platform, with Garret A. Hobart of New Jersey, vice-president. William Jennings Bryan of Nebraska won the Democratic nomination and stood upon the issue of free coinage of silver at the ratio of 16 to 1. McKinley won. Soon after he took office, higher protective rates in the Dingley bill were enacted. There was a tremendous revival of business and general prosperity during his administration.

Expansion Abroad.—The outstanding event of the McKinley administration, however, was the war with Spain over Cuban liberation. As a result, the United States acquired the Philippines, Puerto Rico, Guam and other possessions; Hawaii was annexed. The policy of continental isolation came to an end with this expansion, and citizens of the United States began to take an interest in problems abroad. With McKinley's assassination, after his re-election, Theodore Roosevelt of New York became president, and he was also the successful candidate in 1904. One of the most popular and vigorous men ever in the presidency, Roosevelt adopted a number of strong policies: emphasis on conservation of national resources; beginning of the Panama canal; enactment of legislation for pure food and meat inspection; enlargement of the functions of the Interstate Commerce commission so it could regulate railway rates against discriminatory practices; settlement of the anthracite coal strike; intervention to bring peace in the Russo-Japanese War; creation of a monetary commission; and sending of the U.S. fleet around the world. Seldom has a president or an administration promoted so many issues that appealed generally to the people.

William Howard Taft of Ohio was elected president in 1908 and James S. Sherman of New York, vice-president. A new tariff law failed to appeal to the people as making good party pledges for lower rates, and a Democratic house was elected in 1910. The house was the scene of a so-called war against Cannonism, with modified powers for the speaker resulting. The 16th amendment to the constitution, making possible a national income tax law, was submitted, and the parcel post system was established. A division of the party came between the followers of Roosevelt and Taft in 1912, and the formation of the Progressive party with Roosevelt as leader contributed to the election of Woodrow Wilson, Democratic candidate for president in 1912. The Democrats won control of both houses of congress and retained it for four years for the first time since 1860. A lower tariff bill was enacted and the federal reserve system was created.

World War I.—World War I occupied the attention of the world from 1914 to 1918. The rallying cry, "He kept us out of war," proved sufficient to re-elect Wilson in 1916, but the Democrats suffered losses in membership in both houses of congress. When President Wilson asked for participation of the U.S. in the war in 1917, the Republicans joined Democrats in support of the war program. Wilson appealed to the country for a Democratic congress in 1918, but the Republicans gained control of both houses in the 66th congress—by a narrow margin in the senate but by a decided majority in the house. The president went to Europe and participated in the treaty negotiations at Versailles; his influence caused the incorporation in the treaty of provisions for a League of Nations. The Covenant of the League was considered by numerous leaders, some Republicans, some Democrats, as failing to protect U.S. interests, but proposed clarifying reservations were refused by President Wilson. A long fight resulted, and the issue was projected into the campaign of 1920. The result was a Republican victory, electing Warren G. Harding of Ohio, president, and Calvin Coolidge of Massachusetts, vice-president.

President Harding's administration made a separate peace treaty with Germany and Austria, summoned the naval arms limitation conference in Washington, made vast reductions in government personnel, established the budget system and generally emphasized the need of national economy. Loans were made to relieve agriculture and a higher tariff law was passed.

Upon the death of President Harding in Aug. 1923, Calvin Coolidge became president and was nominated and elected for a full term in 1924. Charles G. Dawes of Illinois was elected vice-president. Coolidge's administration was noted especially for its insistence upon governmental economy and the payment of the national debt. The senate approved the adherence of the U.S. to the world court but with reservations that proved unacceptable to the other nations. Some damage to the party's reputation resulted from the uncovering of scandals in the preceding administration, notably in connection with the letting of oil leases. Coolidge was urged to stand for re-election in 1928, but he declined. When efforts to draft him failed, the nomination went to his secretary of commerce, Herbert Hoover of California. The Republicans also nominated Charles Curtis of Kansas for vice-president.

Depression and World War II.—In the election which followed, the party won a great victory, winning even the "solid south" Democratic states of Virginia, North Carolina, Tennessee, Florida and Texas. Less than a year later came the financial crash, in Oct. 1929, followed by the great depression. Hoover sought to check the downward course of business by following a conservative financial and economic policy. The depression continued, however, and he went down to defeat at the presidential election of 1932, when Franklin Delano Roosevelt was the successful Democratic candidate.

In 1936 the Republican candidates, Alfred M. Landon of Kansas and Frank Knox of Illinois, met overwhelming defeat, carrying only two states, Maine and Vermont, in the electoral college. In 1940 the candidates, Wendell L. Willkie of Indiana and Charles L. McNary of Oregon carried ten states. The election of 1944 was also lost, the candidates being Thomas E. Dewey of New York and John W. Bricker of Ohio, who won only 12 states. In 1946, however, the Republicans gained majority control over both the senate and the house of representatives for the first time in 16 years.

In 1948 the Republican national convention again nominated Dewey for president, with Gov. Earl Warren of California for vice-president. In spite of vigorous opposition, Pres. Harry S. Truman was nominated to succeed himself, with Alben W. Barkley of Kentucky for vice-president. The public opinion polls forecast a Republican victory, but President Truman entered upon a remarkable personal campaign in all parts of the country. The result was an unprecedented "upset," with Truman carrying 28 states and Dewey 16, while the electoral vote was Truman 303, Dewey 189 and J. Strom Thurmond 39.

Republican Victory of 1952.—At the Republican convention of 1952 in Chicago, Gen. Dwight D. Eisenhower was nominated on the first ballot for president, with Sen. Richard M. Nixon as his running mate. The Eisenhower–Nixon ticket carried the nation on Nov. 4 by a landslide, winning 442 of the 531 electoral votes.

BIBLIOGRAPHY.—William Starr Myers, *The Republican Party; A History* (1931); Wilfred E. Binkley, *American Political Parties* (1943); Peter Odegard and E. Allen Helms, *American Politics* (1938); Arthur N. Holcombe, *Political Parties of To-day* (1924).　　(F. B. W.; X.)

REQUEST, LETTERS OF. The legal terms "letters rogatory," or "of request" (*commission rogatoire*), express a request made by one judge for the assistance of another in serving a citation, taking the deposition of a witness, executing a judgment, or the doing of any other judicial act. The only trace of such a practice to be found in England or the United States, independent of statutory enactment, is in the admiralty doctrine that

the sentence of a foreign court of admiralty may be executed on letters of request from the foreign judge or on a libel by a party for its execution. *See* the authorities collected by Sir R. Phillimore in *The City of Mecca*, 5 P.D. 28. The British and United States courts issue commissions to private persons, generally, however, to consular officers, but sometimes to foreign judges in their private capacities, for the purpose of taking the depositions of witnesses. Many countries object to this process and require letters of request, which have to be forwarded through diplomatic channels (see *Rules of the Supreme Court*, O.37). In ecclesiastical law, letters of request are issued for the purpose of sending causes from one court to another. Letters of request are also issued for other purposes: to examine witnesses who are out of the jurisdiction, to enforce a monition, etc.

REQUESTS, COURT OF, originally a committee of the king's council in England. Petitions of poor persons were heard by the justices in eyre and on the fall of the eyre were referred by the council to the chancery. By an Order in Council of 1390 these petitions were transferred to a committee of the council and the lord privy seal became its president. At first the court followed the king, but about 1516 Wolsey assigned to it a permanent seat in Whitehall, when it became known as the court of Whitehall or the court of poor men's causes. Lastly, it obtained its official title of the court of requests. The judges were at first those privy councillors who happened to be present, together with judges and masters as assessors. Eventually four privy councillors, known as masters of requests, were appointed at fixed salaries. *See* I. S. Leadam, *Select Cases in the Court of Requests* (Selden Society, 1898).

REQUISITION OF SHIPPING: see SHIPPING, MINISTRY OF; SHIPPING CONTROL COMMITTEE.

REREDOS (rēr'dǒs), an ornamental screen of stone or wood built up, or forming a facing to the wall behind an altar in a church. Reredoses are frequently decorated with representations of the Passion, niches containing statues of saints, and the like. In small churches the reredos is usually replaced by a hanging or parament behind the altar, known as a dossal or dorsal. (*See* also ALTAR.) The use of the word reredos for the iron or brick back of an open fireplace is obsolescent.

RESACA DE LA PALMA, a battlefield of the war between Mexico and the United States (1846–48), about 4 mi. north of Brownsville, Texas. On the morning of May 9, 1846, the day after the battle of Palo Alto, which had been indecisive, the United States troops under Brig. Gen. Zachary Taylor, ready to renew the conflict, were surprised to see the column under the Mexican Gen. Mariano Arista disappearing through the *chaparral* toward Matamoras. Unable to pursue with more than a few hundred men, because he must first put his wagon train in a state of defense, Taylor was slow in following his adversary. The latter had entered a dense growth that continued interruptedly to the Rio Grande, 7 mi. to the south.

After having marched about halfway through the thickets, Arista disposed his command behind an old river channel which crossed the road at right angles. The bed (Resaca de Guerrero) was full of ponds and mud, impassable in many places. The Americans, about 1,700, came upon the Mexican guns planted in the road and almost immediately thereafter there was a collision. The dense growth of mesquite and cactus made it impossible for companies to see each other and it was difficult for Taylor's artillery to operate. His soldiers, losing touch with one another, floundered and hacked their way toward their enemy. Although there was little direction or plan to the encounter, the discipline and training of his subordinates kept them pressing forward. The vigour of the U.S. troops in their assault dismayed the Mexicans. When one of Arista's flanks was accidentally turned, a panic seized his whole force. It is estimated that about 4,000 out of some 5,000 succeeded in reaching the river where many were drowned in crossing. The American loss was comparatively small.

BIBLIOGRAPHY.—J. H. Smith, *The War with Mexico*, vol. i (1919); G. B. McClellan, *The Mexican War Diary* (1917); C. M. Wilcox, *History of the Mexican War* (1892); W. A. Ganoe, *The History of the United States Army* (1924); Original correspondence and reports in

RESCHEN SCHEIDECK. This Alpine pass is in a way the pendant of the Brenner pass, but leads from the lower Engadine to the upper valley of the Adige. Near the summit (4,944 ft.) is the hamlet of Reschen, while some way below is the former hospice of St. Valentin auf der Haid, mentioned as early as 1140. Starting from Landeck, the motor road runs up the Inn valley to Pfunds, whence it mounts above the gorge of Finstermünz to the village of Nauders (27¼ mi.) joining the road from the Swiss Engadine (53½ mi. from St. Moritz). Thence it mounts gently to the pass and then descends, with the Adige, to Mals (15½ mi.), whence the pass is sometimes wrongly named Malserheide. The road now descends the upper Adige valley, or Vintschgau, past Meran (37¼ mi.) to Botzen (20 mi. from Meran) where the Brenner route is joined.

RESEARCH, INDUSTRIAL. The use of tools and machines to wring a living out of nature and to gain a measure of comfort and security reaches back to the earliest times, but until the late 18th century the tools were simple and progress was slow. The Industrial Revolution, made possible by the invention of machines to produce what had previously come from handcraft and the introduction of steam power, gave a new scope to living. It transformed Great Britain from a predominantly agricultural community into an industrial one, and affected every aspect of social and economic life.

The Beginnings of Organized Scientific Research.—A century and a half earlier Francis Bacon had turned men's minds from mediaeval theorizing to observation, experiment and measurement, and scientific research (as the term is understood today) began to establish itself as a new force enabling man to understand the nature of things and turn this knowledge, if he chose, to his material advantage. The pioneers of the Industrial Revolution did not wait for research to grow up, so that before long experiment began to overhaul empiricism and in due course the application of knowledge obtained from scientific research became a powerful factor in creating, step by step, our modern standard of living.

Relation Between Industrial and Fundamental Research.—It is usual to speak of the research which has been directly associated with producing these results as industrial research, but although the term is well justified and generally understood, there is in fact no hard and fast dividing line between the various categories of research. It is truer to say that scientific research is a spectrum shading from fundamental research at one end to technical advance at the other. But just as the difference between one part of the spectrum and another can be recognized, so can the difference between fundamental research, pursued without concern or regard for material advantage, and industrial research which is undertaken for the economic, social and other advantages which are to be obtained from it. Nevertheless, it is fundamental research that produces the great discoveries and ultimately revolutions. Michael Faraday's researches on electromagnetic induction opened up the road to modern power stations; and after J. J. Thomson had coaxed the secret of the electron out of matter, Ernest Rutherford could begin to pick the lock of the atomic nucleus. J. A. Fleming's discovery of the thermionic valve arose from sheer scientific curiosity about the blackening of the carbon filament lamp, but it led to the creation of new industries—radio, radar and television—based on electronics.

But if fundamental research is the goose that lays the golden eggs, the goose is quite incapable of hatching them out. This is the business of the industrial scientist and technologist who, between them, make it possible for the industrial machines to deliver their products in an ever-increasing stream of abundance. Industrial research is not, however, concerned only with exploiting fundamental discovery. It bases itself squarely on the accumulated store of natural knowledge, attends to the need of the particular industry it serves and through its work in the laboratory and workshop brings new manufacture a stage nearer. This may be simply an improvement of an existing process, but it may be an entirely new one and the product may be new also.

Industrial research has extended its scope to include the systematic study of industrial operations, the handling of materials and the layout of plant. And since it is concerned broadly with the economic efficiency of industry, it works to raise the level of productivity through the better use of resources, human and material. Technological advance is apt to conflict with habits of work and current conceptions of management, and the industrial scientist finds himself involved increasingly in the deep and largely uncharted sea of human relations.

INDUSTRIAL RESEARCH IN GREAT BRITAIN, EUROPE AND THE COMMONWEALTH

Research in Industry.—By far the greater part of industrial research in Great Britain is undertaken by industry in its own laboratories. Accurate figures are not available but in a survey made by the Federation of British Industries in 1950–51 (see *Bibliography*) a questionnaire was sent to 1,400 firms and the 361 replies indicated that 301 firms spent £23,779,000 on research and development as compared with the following figures of earlier surveys. Thus, in 1930, £1,736,000 was spent on research and development; in 1935, £2,696,000; in 1938, £5,442,000; and in 1945–46, £21,815,000. In the 1945–46 survey it was concluded that the total amount spent by all firms could be estimated as of the order of £30,000,000. The figure in 1955 was certainly not less than £50,000,000.

There are no corresponding figures available for the European countries, but as in Great Britain, large industrial research staffs are maintained by the leading manufacturing firms and particularly those in the newer industries which have sprung from research or have been, from the beginning, dependent on the laboratory; e.g., oil, chemical, electrical and synthetic fibres. The main emphasis is on applied research and development, but it is recognized that a certain proportion of fundamental research should be undertaken, both for its own sake and to attract and retain scientific staff of good quality. This is not only important in itself, but exercises a beneficent influence throughout the company, extending to the development and production departments. Development is many times more costly than the research itself, but any comparison of costs must take into account the fact that all research does not end in development. Many research projects do not turn out as expected and in any event costs and the market have the final say in the choice of which projects should be developed.

There is no way of evaluating the results of research in terms of accountancy. Most good industrial research laboratories can point to some outstanding achievements over a period of years and claim rightly that if they had done nothing else they would have paid for themselves handsomely. But although this may inspire confidence it does not enable a board of a company to determine how much of its profits it should devote to research. Research expenditure in industry is frequently expressed as a proportion of annual turnover, and the proportions, as would be expected, vary greatly from industry to industry (3% is not uncommon in firms in the newer science-based industries). There is, however, no logical justification for comparing or estimating research expenditure on this basis; experience and judgment are the only guides, and boards of companies who are alive to the needs of the times endeavour to maintain a level of research which will enable them to remain competitive in world markets.

The Role of the Government in Industrial Research.—The government has a smaller but nevertheless distinctive place in industrial research because of its special and general responsibilities. In Great Britain, government departments are concerned, directly or indirectly, with maintaining health and safety; adequate housing; methods of growing, storing and distributing food; transport by road, rail and air; the maintenance of communications; the provision of electricity and gas; the development of atomic energy; and the provision of fuel and its economical use to meet the requirements of the nation. The government has general responsibilities also for the maintenance of physical and engineering standards and for promoting a high level of industrial productivity.

The realization at the beginning of the 20th century of the loss caused by the profusion of standards used by engineers and the advantages to be gained by a system based on accurate measurement and a careful investigation of the properties of materials led in 1901 to the setting up of the British Engineering Standards committee. In this work the National Physical laboratory, which was founded at about the same time, co-operated and continues to co-operate very fully. The scope of the committee's activities gradually widened, and in 1931 the British Standards institution came into being as the approved body for the preparation and promulgation of national standards.

George V, then prince of Wales, showed a keen perception of the needs of his time when he opened the National Physical laboratory in 1902 with these words: "The object of the scheme is, I understand, to bring scientific knowledge to bear practically upon our everyday industrial and commercial life, to break down the barrier between theory and practice, to effect a union between science and commerce. . . ." The aims of industrial research could not be more tersely expressed.

These aims were furthered in 1915 by the creation of a committee of the privy council, with the lord president of the council presiding, "to direct, subject to such conditions as the Treasury may from time to time prescribe, the application of any sums provided by Parliament for the organization and development of scientific and industrial research." Simultaneously, an advisory council was established to consider and report on proposals for instituting specific researches; for establishing or developing special institutions for the scientific study of problems affecting particular industries or trades; and for the establishment and award of research studentships and fellowships. To serve these bodies the department of scientific and industrial research was established in Dec. 1916 as a separate department of state with its own parliamentary vote, or grant. The new department assumed responsibility, jointly with the Royal society, for the National Physical laboratory, and later the geological survey of Great Britain became part of it. Separate establishments were formed to cover other main fields of applied research. In addition, a scheme was planned for co-operative research associations to be set up by various industries with financial assistance from the government; and a system of grants to young graduates to enable them to undergo training in research was instituted.

In 1955 the department of scientific and industrial research controlled 14 research establishments and financed in partnership with industry 42 co-operative research associations. Its grants to universities for special researches and its maintenance allowances to students for postgraduate training in research amounted to more than £700,000 annually. The gross expenditure of the department in 1953–54 was slightly less than £6,000,000.

The principle on which the department of scientific and industrial research is based has been followed in varying degrees and by various means both in European countries and the commonwealth. National research councils have been set up in some countries which not only act as policy-making co-ordinating bodies but in some cases undertake programs of research on their own account. A detailed analysis of the different types of organization was made by the United Nations Educational, Scientific and Cultural organization in 1952. (See *Bibliography*.)

National programs of industrial research undertaken under direct government control may vary according to local conditions but the general pattern conforms to what may be called the prototype organization, the U.K. department of scientific and industrial research. The principal national organizations are listed in the table; fuller details will be found in two surveys by O.E.E.C. and the British Commonwealth Scientific conference (see *Bibliography*). In some countries the government controls research directly, through these organizations; in others the organization does not itself undertake research, but sponsors it by means of grants.

In Great Britain and several other commonwealth countries steps were taken after World War II to develop research results of potential value arising in government laboratories or elsewhere as the national interest required. In Great Britain the National Research Development corporation was set up under the Development of Inventions act, 1948, as a national corporation with funds available for investing in any development work required "in the public interest." Its functions were slightly modified in 1954.

Chief Organizations for Industrial Research in Europe and the Commonwealth

Country	Organization and date of foundation*
Australia†	Commonwealth Scientific and Industrial Research Organization 1949 (1926)
Belgium‡	L'Institut pour L'Encouragement de la Récherche Scientifique dans l'Industrie et l'Agriculture (*I.R.S.I.A.*), 1944
Canada†	National Research Council, 1916
Denmark‡	Der Teknisk-Videnskabelige Forskningstaad, 1946
France†	Centre National de la Récherche Scientifique (C.N.R.S.), 1939 (1901)
German Fed. Rep.‡	Deutsche Forschungsgemeinschaft, 1949 (1920)
Great Britain†	Department of Scientific and Industrial Research, 1916
India†	Council of Scientific and Industrial Research, 1942
Italy†	Consiglio Nazionale delle Ricerche (C.N.R.), 1923
Netherlands†	Nederlandse Centrale Organisatie voor Toegepast Natuurwetenschappelijk Onderzoek (T.N.O.), 1932
New Zealand†	Department of Scientific and Industrial Research, 1926
Norway†	Norges Teknisk-Naturvitenskapelige Forskningsrad (N.T.N.F.), 1946
Pakistan†	Council of Scientific and Industrial Research, 1953
South Africa†	Council for Scientific and Industrial Research, 1945
Spain†	Consejo Superior de Investigaciones Cientificas, 1939
Sweden‡	Statens tekniska Forskningsrad, 1942
Switzerland‡	Fonds National Suisse de la Récherche Scientifique, 1952

*Date of foundation of earlier organization from which the present one developed is given in brackets. †Undertakes research directly. ‡Sponsors research by grants.

A further aspect of development is illustrated by projects undertaken jointly, to spread the cost of the work, by several European countries under the auspices of the Organization for European Economic Cooperation. International co-operation in research increased greatly during and after World War II.

Co-operative Research Associations.—In this field Great Britain was again a pioneer, as the department of scientific and industrial research from the time of its establishment in 1916 encouraged and supported research in individual industries through the setting up of co-operative research associations, financed partly by the industry concerned and partly by the government. The initial intention was that ultimately the associations should depend solely on industrial sources, but this principle was abandoned in 1945 when it was announced that government grants would form a permanent part of the normal income. The grants are reassessed at five-year intervals and the general tendency is to increase progressively the proportion of industrial income to government grant as the research association becomes established. On the industrial side, members' subscriptions are assessed by the association generally in relation to the size of each firm. After the passing of the Industrial Organization and Development act in 1947, some of the research associations derived their industrial income from a statutory levy, while other industries introduced a voluntary levy for the same purpose. Contributions from nationalized industries are regarded as industrial contributions. The nationalized industries largely assumed their predecessors' responsibilities and commitments to the research associations.

The co-operative research association type of organization has proved particularly suited to Great Britain. It has been successfully adopted in certain industries in several of the other Commonwealth countries, notably New Zealand, South Africa and India.

Co-operative research groups also exist in Belgium, Denmark, France, the German Federal Republic, the Netherlands, Norway and Sweden and other European countries. Methods of financing vary according to the country, but in most cases industrial income is supplemented by government grants. Details are given in the O.E.E.C. survey mentioned previously. Norway and Sweden have introduced a novel feature in that they provide in addition a central establishment where equipment and services are placed at the disposal of various industrial research groups for definite programs, generally for limited periods of a few years. Each group has its own staff and finances its own work. There is no rent, but a service charge is made covering 50% of the cost, the rest being met by state grants.

Independent Industrial Research Organizations.—In contrast with the growth of co-operative research organizations in Great Britain and Europe, centralized research services for industry in the United States have developed on different lines, the emphasis after 1945 being on the provision of facilities for confidential sponsored work. The rapid growth of nonprofit sponsored research institutes in the United States, of which Mellon, Battelle and Armour were the first to be established, was not reflected to any considerable extent elsewhere, but some of the U.S. institutes began to open branches in Europe. Thus the Battelle Memorial institute established in 1952 a European counterpart known as Battelle International with branches in Switzerland and Germany.

In Great Britain after 1945, two sponsored research organizations, the Fulmer Research institute and the Sondes Place Research institute, were opened and were well established by 1955, but neither was operating on the scale of the larger American institutes.

Education for Research.—An adequate supply of scientists and technologists is one of the first requirements of any industrial community. Germany was one of the first countries to realize this and toward the end of the 19th century established a series of technical high schools which played an important part in its industrial development. Other European countries later established similar institutions, while in the United States colleges such as the Massachusetts Institute of Technology, Cambridge, filled a similar role.

In Great Britain there are many educational institutions which provide training in technologies as well as academic and commercial courses. Most of them have strong regional associations, and often specialize in education for practice in local industries. Some, however, are truly national institutions, and a few work in close association with universities. Most of the universities themselves cater for some branches of technology, but on the whole they give greater emphasis to training in basic science. After World War II increased attention was given by the ministry of education, the University Grants committee, the Advisory Council on Scientific Policy, the Federation of British Industries and others to the urgent necessity for increasing the supply of science teachers in the schools and of the scientists and technologists needed by industry where there is a considerable leeway to make up. The importance of higher technological education was repeatedly stressed and the need to extend facilities for the teaching and study of the applied sciences and technologies was accepted by the government. Policy became not to create completely new technological institutes of university status, but rather to expand and develop certain existing institutions of which the first would be the Imperial College of Science and Technology, London, where due emphasis would be placed on the development of postgraduate work. Other major expansions were planned at Manchester, Glasgow, Leeds and Birmingham.

BIBLIOGRAPHY.—Organization for European Economic Cooperation, *The Organization of Applied Research in Europe, the United States and Canada,* 3 vol. (Paris, 1954); "Survey of National Research Councils for Pure and Applied Science in the Member States of UNESCO," and A. King, "International Scientific Co-operation—Its Possibilities and Limitations," *Impact of Science on Society,* vol. iv, no. 4 (UNESCO, Paris, winter 1953); Federation of British Industries, *Scientific and Technical Research in British Industry: a Statistical Survey by the F.B.I. Industrial Research Secretariat* (London, July 1947); *Research and Development in British Industry: a Survey of Expenditure on Industrial Research and Development in the Year 1950–51* (London, 1952); British Commonwealth Scientific Conference, *The Application of Results of Research* (London, 1954). (B. Lr.)

GROWTH OF U.S. INDUSTRIAL RESEARCH

The object of industrial research is the discovery and invention of useful processes and products. Hence this discussion of industrial research should be read collaterally with the article INVENTIONS AND DISCOVERIES.

It is impossible to make an important scientific discovery or to invent a process or machine without engaging in experimentation. Even a discovery made by accident must usually be developed by experimentation before it can be adopted. The prehistoric savage who first made pottery or thought of fashioning a basket or learned how to use heat in a hundred different ways engaged in the kind of experimentation that is still the mark of the empirical investigator and inventor but nevertheless deserves to be classed as research. In this broad sense industrial research is as old as man.

Industrial research in the modern sense is organized, planned, skilfully directed, continuous and as self-perpetuating as industry itself. It has been a powerful factor in the astounding industrial growth of the United States since 1900. It gained momentum with the disappearance of the last frontiers and the depletion of natural resources once supposed to be inexhaustible. It accounts in part for the transformation of the United States from an agricultural into an industrial nation.

There is no question that the flowering of scientific discovery in the latter half of the 19th century had much to do with the rise of organized industrial research. Such successful inventions as the telegraph, the telephone, the electric incandescent lamp, the generation and distribution of electric energy had sprung from the discoveries of such men as Michael Faraday (1791–1867) and had been reduced to something approaching commercial practice by imaginative, dogged empiricists of the Edison type. Industry had little more to do than make the most of these discoveries and inventions. Its next obvious step was to make the discoveries themselves, and this it cautiously proceeded to do.

Industrial research was individualistic in Europe until about the middle of the 19th century and in the United States until about 1900. The individual investigators were independent inventors of the Morse-Bell-McCormick-Edison type or occasional chemists and mechanics in the employ of the few manufacturing companies that could not dispense with expert technical guidance. There is no industry in which a chemist cannot be advantageously employed, yet industry showed no great interest in chemistry. University chemists were long distrusted largely for the reason that they knew little about the industrial processes that they were to improve. It was not until 1902 that E. I. du Pont de Nemours instituted organized chemical research—the first in its field to do so. Because of this distrust of the chemist the United States lagged behind Europe in organized industrial chemistry. Not until 1889 did the U.S. petroleum industry employ its first professional chemist, William Burton, who devised a cracking process once important in oil refining.

Before the beginning of the 20th century it was still possible for a gifted mechanic to acquire the knowledge and skills that he needed to evolve important inventions in widely different fields. With the advance of science and technology the "universal genius" found himself unable to cope with problems that could be solved only by highly trained mathematicians, physicists, chemists and scientists drawn from a dozen different disciplines. Yet it is from a kind of "universal genius," the individualistic Thomas A. Edison (1847–1931), that American industry learned how industrial research could create inventions on which whole new enterprises could be built. His private laboratory with its machine shop, its facilities for making instruments and models and its large reference library was something new in the annals of professional, individualistic invention. The 70-odd men who were employed in this laboratory in the 19th century were not formally organized, yet they constituted an organization because they all worked under Edison's direction on different portions of a common problem. Edison therefore deserves the credit of having set an example. Despite his frank dislike of "theorists" and university professors and his reliance on the try-and-try-again method, which might compel him to suffer a thousand failures before he achieved success, he employed good physical chemists and mathematical physicists, among them Arthur E. Kennelly (1861–1939), who was an independent discoverer with Oliver Heaviside (1850–1925) of the ionosphere, a layer in the sky that reflects radio waves over oceans and continents to their destination.

The great industrial laboratories of today all have their theorists. The General Electric company sprang in 1892 out of Edison's work and the enterprises that he founded or with which he was associated. The company's laboratory was the first in American industry to cultivate fundamental research.

The growth of industrial research has been uneven. The older the industry the more backward is it likely to be scientifically and technologically and the newer, the more active. Such new industries as electrical communications, telephony, radio, petroleum refining and television have sedulously fostered research almost from their beginnings, and such old industries as coal mining have been laggard. Mass-production industries (again automobiles, petroleum, electrical communications, electrical machinery) spend the most money on research and employ the greatest number of scientists, engineers and laboratory technicians. Research policies are determined partly by the spirit of an industrial organization, partly by the character of the industry and the pressure of competition.

Edison's example and success do not alone explain the rise of industrial research in the United States. A high-tariff policy was also a factor; for high tariffs assured large profits, so that there was no great incentive to improve industrial products and processes through research. The merits of a new invention or discovery had to be almost glaringly obvious before a businessman would buy it. Neither he nor his banker could turn to specialists who could appraise the potentialities of an innovation. Hence the individualistic inventor was of necessity a gambler, who usually spent his own money in carrying out his ideas and took the risk of recouping himself with what profits he could make. Organized and planned industrial research has not taken all the risk out of discovery and invention but it has reduced it, so that millions are poured into experimentation with the strong probability that the harvest will be reaped in 20 or 30 years. The problems to be studied and the ends sought are usually determined by managerial policy. Directors of research are frequently responsible executives and sit on boards of directors. Indeed so intimate is the relation of the laboratory to manufacturing and selling that investors of large sums are as much concerned with research policies of the companies in which they may take a financial interest as they are in balance sheets. Research is probably the most powerful factor in the growth of an industrial enterprise, and the possibility of growth always receives the shrewd investor's attention.

The growth of the trust also had much to do with the rise of industrial research in the United States. Federal courts had interpreted the patent laws with the utmost liberality so as to carry out the constitution's purpose of encouraging invention. These interpretations made it possible for a patentee to do what he pleased in fixing prices, limiting markets geographically, granting licences, stipulating what materials should be used by the licensee in carrying out the patented process or making the patented product. The federal courts have for years been curtailing the monopolistic privileges granted to patentees. Under the patent law, as it was generously interpreted, it was possible to do legally for 17 years (the life of a patent) what was illegal under the antitrust law. Hence the great corporations turned to the patent monopoly. Patents imply invention and discovery and hence research. This is one reason why after 1900 more and more industrial laboratories were established.

Another reason, perhaps the most important, was the influence of the state on industry in such emergencies as war. The continental blockade prompted Napoleon to encourage French production of materials that could no longer be imported. The effect of military pressure on industry was always apparent. In the United States, the National Academy of Sciences was chartered in 1863 "to investigate, examine, experiment and report upon any subject of science or art desired by any department of Government." In World War I Pres. Woodrow Wilson implemented this purpose by establishing the National Research council (see *Co-operating Agencies* below), a body that has played a conspicuous part in the development of the United States as a military power, though its activities are by no means restricted to military matters. In World War II the amalgamation of government and industry was virtually complete. Every university, every research laboratory was under contract to the government to conduct research of both military and industrial importance. In total war it is impossible always to separate military from industrial purpose. The far-flung research activities of the federal government were largely under the direction and control of the Office of Scientific Research and Development. The invention of the atomic bomb by scores of organized physicists and chemists called for the creation of the industrial communities of Oak Ridge, Tenn., and Hanford, Wash., and the laboratories of Los Alamos, N.M. So huge was this undertaking that it had to be separately administered. In addition the army and navy maintained their own research establishments. In other words, science was completely mobilized, no matter where

it was pursued or by which organization. This mobilization did not disintegrate with the end of World War II. The so-called "cold war" waged by the U.S.S.R. in its successful aggressions and the fear of western democratic nations that they would have to fight for their freedoms and their manner of life made it necessary to preserve the system of government-controlled industrial and other research that had evolved in World Wars I and II.

Industrial research has long been a major industry in itself. By the 1950s more than $2,500,000,000 was being spent annually by American industrial laboratories, according to a survey made by the Research Development board of 2,000 companies which together spent about 85% of the funds available for research. These 2,000 companies employed about 100,000 engineers who were engaged in what may be truly called research. Two out of every three of the 100,000 were on the payrolls of companies with 5,000 or more employees.

The larger the company the more self-sufficient is it likely to be. In other words it makes in its own shops about everything that the research laboratory may need, with the exception of special instruments. The smaller the company the more likely it is to contract with outside organizations for the building of experimental machinery and apparatus. The research laboratories of these smaller companies specify clearly yet broadly what is wanted but leave the preparation of working drawings and the production of prototype equipment to the contractor. The number of workers required to support a research scientist or engineer was 1.5 on the average in the mid-1950s, but as low as 0.9 for companies with less than 500 employees and as high as 1.6 for companies with 5,000 or more employees.

The expansion of industrial research and development in the United States after World War I and again after World War II was without precedent. It is difficult to separate industrial research from applied research as a whole, in which term must be included research carried on for military, agricultural, medical and other purely utilitarian purposes, so that government cannot always be separated from industrial participation. In 1951, for example, the federal government paid for nearly half of the cost of industrial research and development. The total cost of research undertaken by industry, including $1,400,000,000 paid by the government, was $2,500,000,000 in 1952. The government's share of expenditures ranged from 85% in aircraft production to as little as 3% in petroleum refining.

Statistics show that fundamental or basic research, on which industry must depend for its own improvement, was still neglected in the 1950s; that military necessity had forced the federal government to direct the course of industrial research into certain channels; and that research paid for by industry was highly concentrated in a few industries and in the large corporations. Industrial research, whether carried on with government or with private support, is still enormously concerned with practical results and very little with fundamental science. Despite its remarkable technical progress the United States was utterly dependent on European discoveries in basic science in meeting the industrial demands of peace and war. When it was found that the European stock of knowledge had been virtually exhausted and that it could not be rapidly replenished because of the destruction wrought in World War II and the loss of many scientists, the United States at last created the National Science foundation and charged it, among other things, with the task of cultivating fundamental science. It is the only agency that can appraise the effect of all the specialized programs of the federal government and aid the president and congress in appraising the government's scientific policies.

There is no question that military necessity did much to stimulate organized industrial research in every advanced country. One powerful stimulus came from World War I in which new and importunate demands were made on American industry. So it happened that the number of industrial laboratories in the United States increased from about 300 to more than 2,200 between 1920 and 1940.

Individualistic and organized industrial research both call for the application of fundamental scientific knowledge or "theory" to the production of goods. The purpose of fundamental or theoretical research in any branch of science is to add to the sum total of human knowledge regardless of practical results or profits. In the early days of organized industrial research it was not considered the function of the laboratory to engage in fundamental or theoretical research. Most industrial organizations' research laboratories continue to adhere to this principle and insist on practical results and profits. A few of the very large corporations engage on a fairly large scale in what may be properly called fundamental or theoretical research. Thus the Eastman Kodak company devotes much attention to the theoretical problems of photochemistry, the Bell Telephone laboratories study sound and speech, the General Electric company the chemical transformations that occur in exhausted lamp bulbs and vacuum tubes and the generation of light by means that have no immediate commercial chance of success. Technological progress is hardly possible unless theories are developed and new principles and laws discovered in the university, industrial, government or other laboratory. If a process breaks down in the effort to improve it, if a product is faulty for no apparent reason it is fair to assume that the basic theory applied must be discarded or corrected to reach the industrial goal in view. Though it is concerned primarily with practical results, industrial research is too often belittled as a mere exploitation of the conclusions reached by idealistic theoretical scientists who are not concerned with profits. The distinction between fundamental and applied or industrial research is not sharp. At best it is merely a convenience too often overstressed. For example, before it was possible to arrive at an experimental plane that could travel faster than sound (that is, at a speed higher than about 730 m.p.h. at sea level) an immense amount of fundamental research in aerodynamics had to be conducted; yet always a practical result was kept in view. Science is science whether it is pursued in the factory or the university laboratory. In fact, fundamental and applied science are interdependent. Advance in one affects the other. The interdependence is manifest in the increasingly important part played by universities in solving the scientific and technological problems of industry.

The results of practical research carried on by universities for industry or for the federal government have been impressive and have changed the pattern of technical education. That change is not approved by scholars who cling to tradition. University professors often patent their inventions and discoveries and assign the patents to their universities. The royalties collected are an aid in meeting educational obligations. The argument that these activities distract attention from fundamental research is hardly supported by the available evidence. In some of the schools the royalties are turned back into research or used to expand the technical teaching program. Nevertheless, educators are alarmed at a trend which reduced the funds available in colleges and universities by nearly $4,000,000 in 1951–52, whereas in the same period the funds available for applied research useful to industry increased by $50,000,000.

Most of the money given to the universities for applied research comes from the department of defense or its close affiliates. In fact the department is the principal support of applied scientific research in the United States.

More important is the virtual conscription of university professors of science and technology to carry on military or industrially useful research for the government on a contract basis. The amount of federal money thus expended runs into the millions, as the figures presented earlier indicate. The chief objection to this method of subsidizing the universities, in the opinion of some observers, is a whittling away of academic freedom or, more specifically, of the right of the university scientist to publish what he has discovered. The exigencies of military secrecy prevent publication. There is no doubt that science, particularly nuclear physics, has been held back by this contractual system. Not only must most of the advances made be kept secret but the professor who engages in research for the government is thoroughly examined to make certain that he is not what is called a "security risk." This invasion of academic freedom aroused resentment in many quarters and engendered fears for the future of university education.

BIBLIOGRAPHY.—DeWitt C. Dearborn, Rose W. Kneznek and

Robert N. Anthony, *Spending for Industrial Research, 1951–52* (Boston, 1953); Lincoln T. Work, "The Philosophy and Economics of an Industrial Research Program," in *Research Operations in Industry*, ed. by David B. Hertz and Albert H. Rubenstein (New York, 1953); David B. Hertz, *The Theory and Practice of Industrial Research* (New York, London, 1950); D. H. Killeffer, *The Genius of Industrial Research* (New York, London, 1948); T. A. Boyd, *Research, the Pathfinder of Science and Industry* (New York, 1935); J. B. Steelman, *Science and Public Policy*, vol. i, *A Program for the Nation* (Washington, D.C., 1947); E. R. Weidlein and W. A. Hamor, *Science in Action* (New York, London, 1931); C. C. Furnas, *Research in Industry* (New York, London, 1948); C. E. K. Mees and J. A. Leermakers, *The Organization of Industrial Scientific Research*, 2nd ed. (New York, London, 1950); Don K. Price, *Government and Science: Their Dynamic Relation in American Democracy* (New York, 1954); National Resources Planning Board, *Research—a National Resource*, vol. i and ii (Washington, D.C., 1941).   (W. Kt.)

Industrial Research by Companies.—One of the largest research establishments in the United States is the Bell Telephone Laboratories, Inc., which employs numerous physicists, chemists and engineers for original investigation and development of new forms and improvement of existing forms of apparatus and equipment for electrical communication. In the laboratories of E. I. du Pont de Nemours and company, Wilmington, Del., chemists and engineers have studied problems of the heavy chemical, paint, lacquer, solvent, plastics, textile, dye, rubber and explosive industries. Other great laboratories were established by the Aluminum Company of America at New Kensington, Pa.; Dow Chemical company, Midland, Mich.; Eastman Kodak company, Rochester, N.Y.; General Electric company, Schenectady, N.Y., Lynn and Pittsfield, Mass., and Cleveland, O.; General Motors corporation, Detroit, Mich.; Gulf Research and Development company, Harmarville, Pa.; Hercules Powder company, Wilmington, Del.; Monsanto Chemical company, St. Louis, Mo.; Radio Corporation of America Manufacturing company, Harrison and Camden, N.J.; Standard Oil Development company, Linden, N.J.; and Westinghouse Electric corporation, East Pittsburgh, Pa., and Bloomfield, N.J.

Numerous companies have taken advantage of the industrial fellowship system of Mellon Institute of Industrial Research in Pittsburgh, Pa., as a means of solving problems in manufacturing practice. In 1954, for example, 80 fellowships were sustained by as many different companies, largely chemical manufacturers, and other fellowships were supported by trade associations.

A large number of companies in the field of chemical industry make research grants to educational institutions, chief among them being E. I. du Pont de Nemours and company. Other firms making many grants to universities include E. R. Squibb and Sons; Merck and company; Standard Oil Company of California; Upjohn company; and Standard Brands, Inc.

Many college laboratories are used not only for purposes of instruction but also to a great extent for industrial research work and for commercial testing.

A considerable number of companies, mostly small concerns that have no laboratories of their own or larger companies that encounter few problems or are engaging in research for the first time, are regular or occasional clients of consulting laboratories. There are several hundred commercial laboratories in the country, and some of them are strongly staffed and excellently equipped for scientific investigation, particularly in specific industries. For example, a firm of consultants which has a main laboratory and also branches in other cities employs a large staff of scientists and their assistants for varied research. Most of these commercial organizations do testing as well as research work.

Trade Association Research.—The U.S. department of commerce has expressed the opinion that "among constructive activities of trade associations none is more fitting nor more profitable than scientific research." The study of production and distribution problems to evolve more efficient and more economical methods has in fact become a leading association activity. We shall describe here associative industrial or technological research, and not commercial or economic investigations which, while entirely different in nature, are often related to the former.

Five different procedures have been applied with success in conducting associative industrial research: (1) a number of associations co-operate with government departments and bureaus in accordance with the research associate plan; (2) other associations sustain scientific investigations in Mellon Institute of Industrial Research at Pittsburgh, Pa., in Battelle Memorial institute, Columbus, O., or in other research foundations; (3) some associations support fellowships or scholarships in educational institutions; (4) still others carry on research in commercial establishments, such as the laboratories of professional consultants; (5) a number of associations have founded their own laboratories.

Federal Government Research.—For many years the scientific and technical research facilities of various government departments have been available, by legislative enactment, to duly qualified workers (Supp. Rev. Stat., 2, 71–2, 1532; Stat. L., 27, 1010; Bureau of Standards *Circular No. 296*). This plan has been developed especially in the national bureau of standards, where various research associates are employed by associations or specific groups. Each associate is subject to the bureau's regulations and has most of the rights and privileges of the members of the bureau staff. The investigational results are immediately accessible to the industry concerned and are published by the bureau. Specialists on the bureau's staff may be consulted by the association and its research worker, and the latter is also permitted to use the scientific equipment, special laboratories and shops of the institution.

In general this flexible, closely co-operative plan was successfully applied. There are in fact not a few notable instances of economic savings to technology from research in the bureau. It has been reported (Department of Commerce, "Trade Association Activities," *Domestic Commerce Series No. 20*, 1927) that great savings have come to industry and the public from the bureau's brakelining research, from its tire investigations and from its motor fuel studies. Research in the bureau eventuated in the founding of a dextrose industry in the U.S. The following are among the outstanding investigations: constitution of petroleum, colour standardization, dental materials, silver, nonferrous alloys, soldered plumbing fittings, aviation lighting, railroad signal glasses and portland cement.

Many agencies of the federal government do research and development. The agricultural research service and the Forest Products laboratory of the department of agriculture and the bureau of mines of the department of the interior have advanced technology by researches on behalf of various industries. The bureau of mines conducts various investigations in mining, metallurgy, health and safety, and on the economics of the production, preparation and utilization of minerals. The laboratory of the National Advisory Committee for Aeronautics has maintained for years a central research plant serving the industries concerned and government alike. Certain researches of the public health service of the department of health, education and welfare—investigations of dusty trades, sewage disposal, water purification, illumination of buildings and motor fuels—have also benefited industry.

The research and development work of the Atomic Energy commission is especially wide and important. Action toward national security accounted for 85% of the total government research and development budget in the mid-1950s. About 87% of this activity was in the realm of physical sciences. The National Science foundation, which conducted a wide survey of current industrial research, fosters much pure science investigation that promised to be basically useful to technology. Operations research with its multilateral scientific approach is supplementing physical science investigation in attacking comprehensive problems of industrial management.

Industrial Fellowship System.—Some of the research of Mellon institute is sustained by associations of manufacturers, according to the institution's industrial fellowship system. These association fellowships pertain to air pollution control, industrial hygiene, refractories and other fields, embracing water pollution abatement. The multiple fellowship of the Industrial Hygiene Foundation of America represented a collective effort by 350 companies in behalf of employee health. Fundamental research in industrial health is nurtured and member companies are provided with practical plant applications to prevent industrial illness. The water pollution fellowship aimed to make both basic investigations and practical studies of any subjects promising to improve the water economy of the U.S. The American Refractories institute's multiple fellowship, established in 1917, was continued without interruption thereafter. Its incumbents enriched both refractories technology and metallurgy by their studies of the evaluation of refractories for specific purposes and by the improvements effected in manufacturing and testing methods.

An association fellowship of this type enables direct research service to a number of industrial concerns instead of to an individual company. Its activities also give rise to stable relations of co-operation among the members of the association by the exchange of technical experience and research results. An association fellowship usually acts as a clearing house of information for the sustaining organization and gives technical assistance and scientific advice to the members. One of the prominent advantages of association research is that it enables a small manufacturer, who cannot afford to have a research laboratory of his own, to profit from the investigational work in the same way as a larger manufacturer. Association research reduces the cost factor to a minimum and thus promotes the welfare of manufacturers in the field concerned, without respect to size. Moreover, problems may be studied that require more time and expense than should be borne by a single manufacturer or company in view of the wider application of the results. The correlation of research effort, such as is done in the fellowships supported by associations, prevents unnecessary duplication in scientific inquiries.

Association Fellowships in Educational Institutions.—This class of research became important in many industrial fields. It serves to train technical specialists as well as to aid in solving production problems. The Illinois Institute of Technology, Chicago, Purdue university, West Lafayette, Ind., Ohio State university, Columbus, Columbia university, New York city, Iowa State college, Ames, and the universities of Illinois (Urbana), Michigan (Ann Arbor), Wisconsin (Madison), Minnesota (Minneapolis), Chicago, Cincinnati (O.) and Pittsburgh (Pa.) led in encouraging industrial research by associations and also by individual companies. Various trade associations sustained such investigational work, the American Petroleum institute being a leader in making educational grants.

Association-Owned Laboratories.—Industrial research is not conducted in any set type of laboratory nor in accordance with any fixed plan. The nature of the problems, the financial support available and the uses to which the research findings are to be put determine the method. If problems are extensive and association members are so appreciative of the value of research that they will contribute to the building and maintenance of a laboratory, it is often advisable for an association to do its own research.

Co-operating Agencies.—The National Research council serves as a general clearinghouse of information on research work undertaken throughout the country. Its division of engineering and industrial research endeavours to co-ordinate the scientific resources of the nation as regards engineering and secures the co-operation of engineering agencies in which investigational facilities are available. It works in co-operation with the Engineering foundation and various national engineering and technical societies. Associations or companies undertaking research may ascertain from the council what work has been done or is in progress along similar lines, thus avoiding duplication of effort.

The American Standards association, the American Society for Testing Materials and the American Engineering council are some of the organizations whose effectiveness depends in many cases on the collaboration that they receive from trade associations as well as individual concerns that carry on research.

BIBLIOGRAPHY.—W. A. Hamor, "Progress in Industrial Research," news edition of *Industrial and Engineering Chemistry*, vol. 16, pp. 1-2, and vol. 17, pp. 1-9 (1938-39); National Research Council, *Industrial Research Laboratories of the United States*, 10th ed. (Washington, D.C., 1955); Callie Hull, "Research Supported by Industry Through Scholarships, Fellowships, and Occasional Grants," news edition of *Industrial and Engineering Chemistry*, vol. 17, pp. 155-160 (1939); Mellon Institute, *A Trip Through the New Building of Mellon Institute*, 2nd ed. (1939); National Resources Committee (later the National Resources Planning Board), *Research—a National Resource* (Washington, D.C., 1938 *et seq.*); E. O. Rhodes, "The American Way in Industrial Research," *Industrial and Engineering Chemistry*, vol. 31, pp. 549-556 (1939); E. R. Weidlein, 42nd *Annual Report* of Mellon Institute (1955); E. R. Weidlein and W. A. Hamor, *Glances at Industrial Research* (New York, 1936). A valuable bibliography of research management was published by American University, Washington, D.C. (1954). (W. A. HA.)

RESEDACEAE, in botany, the mignonette family, dicotyledonous plants, mostly xerophytic herbs. There are six genera and about 70 species.

Reseda odorata is the mignonette (*q.v.*); *R. lutea* is dyer's woad. (*See* WOAD.)

See F. Bolle, "Resedaceae," Engler and Prantl, *Die Natürlichen Pflanzenfamilien* 17b: 659-692, fig. 427-432 (1936).

RESENDE, ANDRE DE (1498-1573), the father of archaeology in Portugal, began life as a Dominican friar but about 1540 passed over to the ranks of the secular clergy. He travelled in Spain, France and Belgium, where he corresponded with Erasmus and other learned men. He was also intimate with King John III and his sons, and acted as tutor to the Infante D. Duarte.

In Portuguese Resende wrote: (1) *Historia da antiguidade da cidade de Evora* (1553); (2) *Vida do Infante D. Duarte* (1789). His chief Latin work is the *De Antiquitatibus Lusitaniae* (Evora, 1593).

See the Life in Farinha's *Collecção das antiguidades de Evora* (1785).

RESENDE, GARCIA DE (1470-1536), Portuguese poet and editor, was born at Evora, and began to serve John II as a page at the age of ten, becoming his private secretary in 1491. He was present at his death at Alvor on Oct. 25, 1495. He continued to enjoy the same favour with King Manoel, whom he accompanied to Castile in 1498 and from whom he obtained a knighthood of the Order of Christ. In 1514 Resende went to Rome with Tristão da Cunha, as secretary and treasurer of the famous embassy sent by the king to offer the tribute of the east at the feet of Pope Leo X. In 1516 he was given the rank of a nobleman of the royal household and became *escrivão de fazenda* to Prince John, afterward King John III, from whom he received further pensions in 1525. Resende built a chapel in the monastery of Espinheiro near Evora, the pantheon of the Alemtejo nobility, where he was buried.

Resende collected the best court verse of the time in the *Cancioneiro Geral*, probably begun in 1483 though not printed until 1516.

The *Cancioneiro* is redeemed from complete insipidity by Resende, and his fine verses on the death of D. Ignez de Castro inspired the great episode in the *Lusiads* of Luis de Camoens (*q.v.*). Resende is the compiler of a gossiping chronicle of his patron John II., which, though plagiarized from the chronicle by Ruy de Pina, has a value of its own. Resende's *Miscellanea*, a rhymed commentary on the most notable events of his time, which is annexed to his *Chronicle*, is a document full of historical interest, and as a poem not without merit.

His *Cancioneiro* appeared in 1516, and was reprinted by Kausler at Stuttgart (3 vols., 1846–52). A new edition was published by the Hispanic Society of America in 1904. The editions of his *Chronicle* are those of 1545, 1554, 1596, 1607, 1622, 1752 and 1798. For a critical study of his work, *see* Antonio de Castilho, *Excerptos, seguidos de uma noticia sobre sua vida e obras, um juizo critico, apreciação de bellezas e defeitos e estudo da lingua* (Paris, 1865). Also Anselmo Braamcamp, *As sepulturas do Espinheiro* (1901) *passim*, especially pp. 67–80, where the salient dates in Resende's life are set out from documents recently discovered; and Dr. Sousa Viterbo, *Diccionario dos Architectos . . . Portuguezes*, ii. 361–74.

RESERVE: *see* ARMY and the sections *Defence* of FRANCE, GERMANY, UNITED STATES and other countries.

RESERVES: *see* BANKING AND CREDIT.

RESERVES, NATURAL: *see* PHYSICAL RESOURCES.

RESERVOIRS. These may be divided into two classes, "impounding reservoirs" and "service reservoirs," the latter being concerned with the distribution of water (*see* WATER SUPPLY).

Impounding Reservoirs.—Owing to the fact that the flow of streams and rivers varies greatly throughout the year, it is necessary to provide works to store water if any substantial use is to be made of the annual discharge. Such works are known as impounding reservoirs, their function being to store water when the stream flow is ample for the purpose of augmenting the natural flow in dry weather.

The urgency for the construction of such reservoirs must have become apparent in very early times in countries where the climatic conditions were such that the streams ran dry for a portion of the year, and records exist of one being made in Ceylon as early as 504 B.C. Anciently reservoirs were formed by an embankment across the valley through which a stream flowed, and were sometimes of vast extent, the Padavil-Colan Tank in Ceylon, for instance, having an embankment 11 m. long and, in parts, 70 ft. high.

Storage.—Having selected a catchment area capable of yielding sufficient water, the capacity of the reservoir has next to be determined. This will depend upon the incidence and intensity of the rainfall and the loss by evaporation and absorption, conditions which vary within wide limits. In countries subject to long periods of drought, the necessary capacity will be greater than in those enjoying a temperate climate, and in India, for instance, where the rain falls only during monsoon periods, two years' storage of the daily quantity may be necessary.

Few records exist of the flow of streams in the British Isles taken over a sufficiently lengthy period to be of service, and recourse has generally to be made to the annual rainfall records, from which the annual discharge of the stream is deduced. Long period rainfall gaugings show that the rainfall of the driest year is about two-thirds, the mean fall of the two driest years about three-quarters, and the rainfall of the three driest consecutive years about four-fifths, of the average annual rainfall. Notwithstanding the wide variation of climatic conditions, these proportions hold fairly well over a large portion of the land surface of the globe (*see* "The Variations of Rainfall," by A. R. Binnie, *Proc. Inst. C.E.*, vol. 109).

As storage increases in relation to the average flow of a stream, the maintainable yield increases in a decreasing ratio until a maximum is reached where there would be little advantage in further increase, and in the British Isles the economic limit is generally taken as that capacity which would be sufficient to equalize the flow of the three driest consecutive years.

The average annual rainfall of the three driest consecutive years, being approximately four-fifths of the average annual rainfall; and the average annual loss by evaporation and absorption being about 14 inches; the average annual discharge of the stream during the three driest consecutive years would be that due to $\frac{4}{5}$ average rainfall—14 inches running off the catchment area, which may be denoted by f. The formula known, from its author, as the Hawksley Formula gives the number of days

storage which should be provided to maintain this flow $= \frac{1000}{\sqrt{f}}$. In many cases it is not necessary to provide so large a storage, as some quantity may be required which is less than the average flow of the stream during the three driest consecutive years.

Fig. 1 gives the relation between the maintainable yield and the capacity to be provided for catchment areas in the British

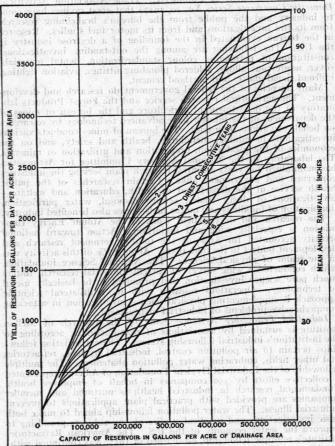

FIG. 1

Isles having a mean annual rainfall varying from 100 to 30 in., and is due to the investigations of Dr. G. F. Deacon. The capacity of the reservoir in gal. per ac. of catchment area is shown on the base line, and the yield of the reservoir in gal. per ac. per diem is given by the length of the vertical line between that capacity and the curve of average rainfall, the yield in gal. per ac. per diem being read from the vertical scale at the left-hand side. The storage required for any particular average rainfall to balance the average stream discharge during different series of consecutive dry years, is given by the diagonal lines which intersect the curve of rainfall on the diagram.

The diagram gives the capacity above the lowest draw-off level of the reservoir, and as it is undesirable to abstract muddy water for supply, this level should be well above the bottom of the reservoir. The loss by evaporation from a water surface is greater than the loss on the catchment area, and in the British Isles the depth of the reservoir should be about 6 in. more than would be required to give the gross storage, whereas in tropical countries the allowance may be as much as 6 ft.

TYPES OF DAMS

Dams may be divided into two classes, masonry or embankments; and the selection of the particular type will depend upon the nature of the materials on which they will rest, and which are available for construction.

Where good sound rock exists at no great depth from the surface, a masonry dam is to be preferred, but where the rock can only be reached at a considerable depth, the cost is prohibitive.

Masonry Dams.—Masonry dams should be arched in plan concave to the water face where the length of the dam is not too great, as such a form adds to the stability, and the pressure of the water tends to close temperature or contraction cracks at right angles to the axis of the dam. It is desirable to slope the foundations towards the water face, especially where the depth below the surface is moderate, as this reduces the tendency to slide on the foundations and the possibility of overturning due to the uplifting pressure of water penetrating between the masonry and the rock. The design should avoid the development of tension in the masonry, tending to rupture the dam on a horizontal plane; and the maximum pressure at any point in the masonry should be limited to 10–15 tons per sq.ft., depending on the materials used for construction and the nature of the underlying rock. Prof. Rankine pointed out the importance of avoiding tension, and evolved the theory on which most modern dams have been designed, viz.: that the resultant pressure due to the weight of the masonry and the water thrust must fall within the inner third of the dam if tension is to be avoided. Any fissure developing at the water face due to tension tends to increase owing to the water pressure, and may ultimately lead to the failure of the dam (*see* Prof. Unwin, *Proc. Inst. C.E.*, vol. 126, and E. P. Hill, vol. 129).

The masonry of a dam is not isotropic as horizontal planes of weakness, where new work is superimposed upon that which has set, are difficult to avoid. It is advisable therefore to step the masonry at the water face so as to avoid the construction of a horizontal joint between old and new work.

The arched form of dam is economical when the radius of curvature is comparatively small, as the sectional area can be decreased by designing the dam as a horizontal arch transmitting the water thrust to its abutments. For reasons of economy modifications of the simple type of masonry dam have been introduced; these dams are of ferro-concrete construction, the pressure of the water being transmitted to buttresses by means of steel reinforced slabs or arches.

Earth Embankments.—The profile of the embankment requires careful study of the materials of which it will be composed, and slips have frequently occurred, leading to the complete or partial failure of banks, due to lack of local study and the adoption of a design which was unstable. Light sandy soils will stand at a high angle of repose, but clays or plastic materials require flatter slopes, the inclination decreasing as the base of the embank-

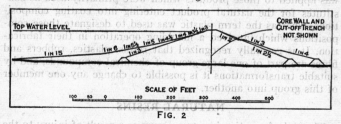

TOP WATER LEVEL

CORE WALL AND CUT-OFF TRENCH NOT SHOWN

1 IN 15

SCALE OF FEET

FIG. 2

ment is approached. On fig. 2 the inner line profile would apply to good banking material, and the outer line to clay or plastic material.

Care must be exercised to prevent the saturation of the outer slope of the bank, and when possible it should be composed of freely draining material. When such materials are not available, the outer portion should rest on a layer of stone terminating in a stone toe, vertical drains of dry stone being carried up through the bank at intervals.

Cut-off Trench.—In order to prevent percolation below the bottom of the embankment, a trench is first excavated across the valley bottom, carried down—if possible—to an impermeable substratum and continued into the hillsides, so as to cut off any percolation below top water level. This is filled with impermeable material, preferably concrete, so as to form a barrier to percolation below the bank; and an impermeable core wall is brought up in continuity with this barrier to prevent percolation through the bank.

Core Walls.—Puddle is the material generally used in the British Isles to form the core wall, and reinforced concrete in America. Puddle is not an absolutely impermeable material, and the thickness of a puddle core wall must be much greater than that of a concrete core wall. The use of concrete core walls has been limited in the British Isles owing to the apprehension that such walls would crack under pressure due to unequal settlement of the embankment. That such fears are unfounded is proved by the numerous successful examples of such construction in America.

The very greatest care must be exercised in the construction of a puddle core wall to prevent the occurrence of any layer through which water could pass owing to the erosion which may take place, causing the formation of a cavity and the failure of the bank; whereas no erosion of the concrete would take place, and a crack would soon be sealed by earth carried in suspension by the water.

Tunnel Outlets.—It is necessary to divert the stream during construction, and for this purpose it is advisable to construct a tunnel round one end of the bank through which the stream may flow, and through which the supply pipe can ultimately be laid from the Valve Tower. A cheaper form of construction is to build a culvert under the bank, but many cases of whole or partial failure of such culverts have occurred due to the varying earth pressure. (*See* C. J. Wood, "Tunnel Outlets," *Proc. Inst. C.E.*, vol. 59.)

Flood Works.—When a reservoir formed by a masonry dam overflows, water passes harmlessly over the top of the masonry into the stream below. It is obvious, however, that water cannot be allowed to overflow an earth embankment, as the material would rapidly erode, leading to the failure of the bank. It is therefore necessary to allow for the escape of flood water in such a way that the water level can never rise to a height that would endanger the bank.

The usual flood escape is provided by a weir of such a length and placed at such a level below the top of the bank as will ensure that the water in the reservoir can never rise above it, the weir discharging into a masonry channel placed in the hillside at one end of the bank. Another and more economical escape consists of a vertical shaft communicating below with the tunnel through which the stream was diverted during construction and terminating above in a bell-mouthed opening, the periphery of which forms the overflow weir.

Flood Intensity.—The maximum intensity of the flood discharge over the weir will depend on the extent of the catchment area, the maximum intensity of rainfall during a period bearing relationship to that area, and many other factors, such as the

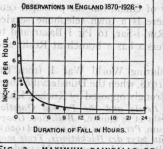

OBSERVATIONS IN ENGLAND 1870-1926

INCHES PER HOUR

DURATION OF FALL IN HOURS

FIG. 3.—MAXIMUM RAINFALLS OF RARE INTENSITY

inclination of the valley, the steepness of the slopes, the permeability of the surface, and the presence of lakes or obstructions which would delay the discharge. It is impossible to determine the exact effect of many of these factors, and therefore recourse must be made to actual records of the maximum discharge from catchments of different areas.

The main factor in determining the maximum intensity of a flood must obviously be the amount of rain which fell in a given period, a condition which varies so widely in different parts of the globe, that records of flood discharge in one country would not be applicable to another.

The curve on fig. 3 shows the relationship between rainfall and period, and is derived from the formula determined by Prof. Talbot as applicable to the Eastern United States for maximum rainfalls during different periods. The small circles show actual observations made in the British Isles, from which it appears that Talbot's curve fits British conditions fairly well. This fact is of importance as indicating that records of floods in the Eastern

States are of assistance in arriving at the maximum intensity of discharge from different catchment areas in the British Isles. The larger the catchment, the smaller is the flood discharge per unit of area.

Unfortunately, the estimates of maximum flood discharges from small catchment areas, are scanty and not very reliable. Most reservoirs are placed at comparatively high altitudes, where the catchment area is small, in order to impound water free from pollution and to furnish water to the district of supply by gravity. Failures of such reservoirs, due to insufficient provision for the discharge of flood water, are not infrequent, and demand serious consideration owing to the consequent loss of life and property.

The formula $Q = 750/\sqrt[3]{M}$, where Q denotes the maximum flood intensity in cu.ft. per sec. per sq.mi. and M the drainage area in sq.mi., agrees fairly well with the records of maximum flood intensity in Great Britain. (*See* also WATER SUPPLY; DAMS; CATCHMENT AREAS.)   (W. J. E. B.)

RESHT, the capital of the province of Gilan in Iran, in 37° 17′ N., and 49° 36′ E., on the left bank of the Siah Rud which is a branch of the Safid Rud and flows into the *murdab* or lagoon of Pahlavi (Enzeli). Population (census of 1940) 121,625.

During the Bolshevik invasion in 1920 about 8,000 refugees left the town, but later returned; and a large part of the bazaar was burnt. The town is situated in low malarious ground and was originally buried in jungle, but the Russians during their occupation of the place in 1723–24, cleared most of the jungle and it is now surrounded by rice fields. The summer climate is damp, sultry and unhealthy, with an average minimum temperature of 84.5° F. in August and a rainfall of 32 to 59 inches. The houses are mostly of handsome, though soft, red brick, are red-tiled or thatched, and often raised from the ground, with broad verandahs and overhanging eaves.

Most of the streets are paved with cobble stones, an improvement which was begun in 1910. There are many caravanserais in the city.

Resht is the centre of important roads in Gilan. The metalled road from Tehran (226 mi. distant) via Kazvin to Pahlavi skirts the town on the east, upon which a regular motor transport service is in operation. There is a similar road to Pir i Bazar (4 mi. up the river of the same name which runs into the lagoon), whence there is a regular daily service of flat-bottomed sailing boats to Pahlavi. Launches also run between the bar at the mouth of the Pir i Bazar river and Pahlavi. A narrow gauge railway runs alongside the Resht-Pir i Bazar road. A good motor road also runs laterally from Kasma through Resht to Lahijan, Langarud and Rud-i-Sar on the Caspian sea, following in great part a raised causeway through rice fields, with innumerable wooden bridges over irrigation canals. Resht is a centre of the rice trade and of the activities of the silk industry of Gilan, but the principal centre of the latter is Lahijan. There is a town telephone service with trunk lines to Pahlavi, to Rud-i-Sar, to Pir i Bazar and to Tehran. The Imperial bank of Persia has a branch at Resht and the town is lit by electric light.

Resht suffered a good deal during World War I from the Russian army and, afterwards in 1918, when the Dunsterville force had to fight its way to Pahlavi, strongly opposed by Kuchak Khan.

BIBLIOGRAPHY.—G. N. Curzon, *Persia and the Persian Question* (1892); G. Ferrand, "Notes sur Resht et le Guilan," *Bull. Soc. Geogr. d'Alger* (1902); A. V. Williams Jackson, *Persia past and present* (1906); H. R. d'Allemagne, *Du Khorassan au pays des Backhtiaris. Trois mois de voyage en Perse* (1911); H. L. Rabino, "A journey in Mazanderan (from Resht to Sari)," *Geogr. J.* (1913); L. C. Dunsterville, "From Baghdad to the Caspian in 1918," *Geogr. J.* (1921); and *The Adventures of Dunsterforce* (1920); L. S. Fortescue, "The western Elburz and Persian Azerbaijan," *Geogr. J.* (1924); and "Les provinces caspiennes de la Perse," *La Géographie* (1925).   (P. Z. C.)

RESIDENCE, in general, a place of abode. In law, it usually means continuance in a place. The ordinary meaning of the word has been defined as "the place where an individual eats, drinks and sleeps, or where his family or his servants eat, drink and sleep" (*R. v. North Curry*, 1825, 4 B. & C. 959). For certain purposes, however, a man may be said to have his residence not only where he sleeps, but also at his place of business. (*See* ABODE; DOMICILE.)

RESIDENT, a political agent or officer representing the Indian government in certain native states in India; he resides in the state and advises on all matters of government, legislative or executive. In certain other dependencies or protectorates of the British Empire the representative of the government is termed a resident or political agent, notably in Nepāl, Aden, Sarawak, British North Borneo, etc. In general, where the state to which a resident is attached is not an independent one, he exercises consular and magisterial functions.

For "Resident" as the title of a diplomatic agent *see* DIPLOMACY.

RESINS. Prior to the introduction of synthetic resins, the term resin was applied exclusively to certain sticky substances which exude in the form of yellow or brown deposits from certain trees, particularly from the pine and the fir. As knowledge gradually accumulated concerning the nature of such natural resinous products as well as the means by which similar compositions could be made by known chemical reactions, a large and ever-increasing number of products have been included in the category of resins. At first these products of the laboratory were hesitatingly referred to as resinlike products, then as artificial resins and as resin substitutes and finally as synthetic resins. In almost every respect, the natural resin can be replaced by one of the synthetic varieties in many of the industrial applications, especially in the moulding and the coating industries. Through the study of chemical reactions which lead to resinification, a better insight was gained concerning the chemical transformation which takes place in the natural product with the result that, in certain instances, it became possible to combine chemically the natural and the synthetic product leading to the formation of a new material possessing unique properties.

At one time resins were recognized by certain well-known attributes, that is, by their transparency and amorphousness and by their brittleness and conchoidal fracture. Synthetic resins of all types are known, and certain of them fail to exhibit any of these characteristics. Some of the latter preparations are tough and colourless, whereas others are opaque and crystalline. There appears to be only one property which is common to both natural and synthetic resinous products—in one stage of their existence both products are plastic.

The distinction between resins and plastics is at best arbitrary since many of the later synthetic materials can be called both resins and plastics. Historically, it appears that the term resin was applied to those products which were primarily used as substitutes for the natural product entering into coating compositions, whereas the term plastic was used to designate those compositions which involved a moulding operation in their fabrication. It is generally recognized that resins, plastics, rubbers and fibres are part of one large group of chemical compounds, and by suitable transformations it is possible to change any one member of this group into another.

NATURAL RESINS

The resin formation in a tree occurs as a result of injury to the bark inflicted by wind, fire, lightning or other means. Initially this secretion is fluid in nature and appears in the form of an oleoresin or as a balsam. In contact with air certain of the more volatile components evaporate, and the residue oxidizes, polymerizes and gradually converts to a soft, resinous product which is readily soluble in appropriate media. As the natural resin gets older, it becomes more insoluble. When the resin flow from the tree is copious, some of the secretion passes into the ground, with the result that many of the fossil resins are found as buried deposits. Even in the case of the recent fossil resins, the chemical reaction leading to resinification may have proceeded for thousands of years. For example, the kauri pines are known to attain an average age of 1,000 years; and since resin can now be found in areas where the original forest has wholly disappeared, it is obvious that the resin must be extremely old. This resin is still soluble. The fossil resin, amber, is of a less soluble type. The very existence of this resin indicates that the process and time of polymerization from the oleoresin to resin, to recent fossil resin, to fossil resins must, in the case of amber, be reckoned in geological periods.

Resinous deposits are found in many parts of the world, and many varieties derive their names from the locality where they are collected. Not only are these products derived from many lands, but they have been known and used technically for long periods of time. Certain tree emanations were utilized by the Chinese and the Japanese in their preparation of oriental lacquers. There is reason to believe that the Incas and the Egyptians used varnishlike materials. The Carthaginians, Phoenicians and Greeks were acquainted with resinous products, and the association between resins and varnishes can be seen in the derivation of the word varnish. This term appears to originate from Berenice, queen of Cyrene, the name the Greeks applied to amber. The term Berenice became corrupted gradually to Pheronice and then Verenice and Vernis.

Amber is not used in the preparation of varnishes but is mainly employed in the fabrication of beads and in decorative wear. In certain respects amber can be handled in very much the same manner as that employed in the fabrication of cast plastics.

Any mucilaginous exudation of a tree is considered a gum. Shellac is a distinctive product inasmuch as it is an insect secretion. True gums, as distinct from varnish gums, are soluble in water; for example, gum arabic which is used in the manufacture of adhesives. The true gums are related to sugars and carbohydrates. These products are soluble in water and insoluble in organic liquids and on heating decompose without fusion. They differ from glues in that they are soluble in cold water. Varnish gums, on the other hand, are resinous materials related to terpenes and essential oils. They are soluble in oils and organic liquids but are insoluble in water. On heating they generally melt and decompose and become more readily soluble. Although the tendency has been to decry the use of the word gum for varnish resins, the term is too well established to be eradicated. Moreover, there are certain natural products which take on the properties of both gums and varnish resins. From Indian frankincense or olibanum, a water-soluble gum has been isolated as well as terpenes and a resinlike product.

Natural varnish resins, as has been noted, can be recognized by their transparency and translucency, by their brittleness and conchoidal fracture and by their brown or yellow coloration. As a rule they possess no taste or smell in the solid state. On heating they melt and often give off a distinctive aromatic odour; on burning they yield a smoky flame. Certain of these gums will dissolve directly in various organic liquids such as alcohol or turpentine. In dispersing the more insoluble resins in oils, it is necessary to preheat the resin—a process referred to as running or sweating. No generalization can be made concerning the chemical changes which occur during the running operation, but it involves complex and deep-seated chemical rearrangements such as cracking, decarboxylation and dehydration. All of these changes are accompanied by a loss in weight; it is by such heat treatment that the resins become more readily dispersible in oil.

Solubility and hardness are the chief criteria used technically in classifying resins, and on the basis of solubility resins can be divided into the spirit-soluble and oil-soluble types. Spirit-soluble means what the word implies, solubility in commercial spirit or ethyl alcohol. Many new powerful organic solvents have been developed for the preparation of cellulose lacquers, and a number of these liquids can likewise be employed in the preparation of solutions of natural resins. Congo is substantially insoluble in all liquids. Kauri and Manila are soluble in alcohols but are insoluble in hydrocarbons. Dammar is soluble in hydrocarbons but only partly insoluble in alcohols. Accroides and sandarac are soluble in alcohol but insoluble in hydrocarbons, whereas mastic and elemi are soluble in aromatic hydrocarbons.

Spirit-Soluble Resins.—As the name balsam implies, these resins are of a fluid character and have found their chief use in healing preparations as well as for other phases of materia medica. Certain of the more aromatic varieties have been incorporated into incense. Balsams are generally considered to be solutions of resins dispersed in benzoic- or in cinnamic-acid esters, whereas

oleoresins are considered to be solutions of resins in essential oils. However, it is difficult to draw a rigid distinction between balsams and oleoresins, although the latter are usually considered to be slightly more fluid. Canada balsam, which is used in cementing lenses, is not a true balsam in that it does not contain benzoic acid or its ester, but is really an oleoresin derived from *Abies canadensis*. Certain of the true balsams are the balsam of Tolú, the balsam of Peru, as well as the Sumatra and Siam benzoins and storax. The storax balsam is of particular interest from the standpoint of synthetic resins in that it was from this material that M. Bonaster in 1831 first isolated styrene, and doubtlessly this product arose through decarboxylation under heat of the cinnamic acid present in the balsam. Another variety of balsam is derived from the grass trees of Australia, and these products are referred to as the Xanthorrhoea balsams. The most important varieties are the yellow and red types, often referred to as accroides gum. This resin contains phenolic bodies which appear to possess some medicinal values, particularly for treating infections of the mucous membranes.

As stated above, oleoresins are solutions of resins dispersed in essential oils; various of these oleoresins are known as turpentines. Venice turpentine is a pale green, viscous liquid which is collected from the larch (*Pinus larix, Larix decidua*). A liquid of lemonlike odour known as Strasbourg turpentine is derived from the *Pinus picea,* whereas Bordeaux turpentine is an oleoresin derived from the *Pinus maritima* or pinaster. The chief American varieties yielding oil of turpentine are the loblolly pine, *Pinus taeda,* and the slash pine, *Pinus caribaea.* On evaporation of the oleoresin a solid resin results, together with a volatile component or spirit of turpentine. The residue from distilling Bordeaux turpentine is known as Burgundy pitch and is used in medicinal plasters.

Mastic is a soft resin melting at about 105° C. and is derived from the tree of the *Pistacia* genus which grows in the islands of the Greek archipelago. When dissolved in turpentine, it is used as a varnish for the protection of paintings; and when dispersed in bodied linseed oil, it is known as megilp and is used as a colour vehicle. Dragon's blood is a black-brown resin in bulk, but in thin films it is transparent and of a deep crimson-red colour. The resin is found on the fruits of the rattan palm growing in the East Indies. It is soluble in alcohol and benzene, but not in ether or turpentine. The resin has been used as a varnish by Italian violin makers and as a dye to colour spirit varnishes a deep red. Another resin used as a colour vehicle and in medicine is gamboge.

Dammar is one of the harder resins and is usually secured in the form of clear, pale-yellow beads, melting at about 140° C. Various other coloured varieties are obtained from the *Dammara orientalis,* which is indigenous to Malaya and the East Indies. The resin is insoluble in alcohol but dissolves in both aliphatic and aromatic hydrocarbons. Excellent varnishes can be made from these solutions, and the resulting films have a light colour and a good lustre. The resin is also readily soluble in oils without preliminary thermal processing. This resin in combination with nitrocellulose enabled the formulation of rapid-drying lacquers.

From the cypress pine, *Callistris,* which grows in Australia, North Africa and North America, one can obtain the hard resin called sandarac which is soluble in alcohol as well as in the more-powerful lacquer solvents. The resin melts at 150° C. and is used as a spirit varnish for coating paper, leather and metal. Although the initial film is somewhat brittle, it can be readily modified to yield elastic films by the addition of elemi.

Shellac has been considered a zoochemical substance, inasmuch as it is a secretion of an insect known as *Laccifer lacca.* The word lac appears to be derived from *laksa,* an early Sanskrit word meaning 100,000. The term shellac has been used incorrectly to cover generically all of the lac products. Insects growing on certain of the trees of the genus *Acacia* produce a scaly substance known as stick-lac. This material is ground, washed and filtered hot, the filtrate passing onto water-cooled drums from which it is removed in the familiar flakelike form. The button lac is a lac which has been allowed to fall on a flat surface. Lac is one of the widely used resins in industry. It is also used in electric insulation as a coating for wood and metal and as a binding agent for moulding composition. Certain varieties are incorporated into sealing waxes. The bulk of the shellac manufactured bears the mark T.N.

Chemically, shellac consists of a mixture of polyhydroxy acids. Two varieties have been isolated, one a hard lac and the other a softer material which appears to act as a plasticizer for the harder component. The softer portion consists primarily of uncombined acids, whereas the harder material consists of polyesters. A major portion of the hard lac was found to be a monobasic ester which could be made to undergo hydrolytic fission to aleuritic acid and lacollic lactone. Other acids which have been isolated from shellac are a tetrahydroxy acid known as kerrolic acid, as well as shellolic acid, together with a natural yellow dyestuff known as erythrolaccin. Aleuritic acid is considered to be 9,10,16-hexadecanetriol acid ($HO-CH_2-(CH_2)_5-(CHOH)_2-(CH_2)_7-COOH$). Although the solubility of shellac is usually associated with alcohol, it is also dispersible in aqueous solutions. There appears to be some indication that on long standing alcohol may react with shellac. A white variety can be made by a bleaching process from which colourless, transparent lacquers can be made.

Oil-Soluble Resins.—Upon distillation of the oleoresin from the longleaf pine two materials are obtained: one a volatile component or spirit of turpentine and the other a nonvolatile, resinous residue or rosin. The word rosin is used for this product rather than resin because the latter is a term used generically to cover all of the compounds of this type. Depending on the source of the oil of turpentine, it is possible to have either gum turpentine and gum rosin or wood turpentine and wood rosin; the former variety originates from the turpentine which is secured by tapping the trees. By solvent extraction of the stumps, wood rosin is obtained, and this is generally of a darker colour. Various designations are employed to distinguish the colour of the product. The colour of French rosin is designated by the letter A, and the greater the number of As used the paler the grade. The U.S. designation is more arbitrary, and the better classes are known as WW (water-white) and WG (window glass). Rosin is a brittle resin which powders readily and becomes sticky when warm. Its specific gravity is about 1.070 to 1.080, and it dissolves in the usual organic liquids. Rosin is also known by the name of colophony or colophonium (from the Greek Kolophonios). The suggestion that the term was derived from two Greek words meaning sound-glue because of its use for treating violin bows does not appear satisfactory.

At one time much of the rosin was used untreated, but the trend is to subject it to chemical processing before it is offered for sale. The chief constituent of rosin is an acid known as abietic acid, and many of the uses of rosin are dependent upon its acidic properties. Combined with alkalies or with metallic oxides, soaps are obtained. The sodium soap is water dispersible and is employed in sizing paper. Sodium abietate is mixed with other alkali soaps in the manufacture of laundry soap. The lime and zinc salts find use as so-called gloss oils in the paint industry, whereas the metallic soaps derived from lead, cobalt and manganese are used as driers in paints and varnishes. When rosin is esterified with glycerol (glycerine), the resulting product is known as ester gum. Somewhat harder esterification products are made through a conjoint ester of rosin with glycerol and with phthalic anhydride. Partial decarboxylation of acid occurs when rosin is heated to elevated temperatures; such products are known as rosin oils.

The acids isolated from rosin include abietic acid,

pimaric acid,

and laevopimaric acid,

It will be noted that certain of these acids appear to possess a system of conjugated double bonds which may account for the ease with which rosin oxidizes when it is exposed to air. By chemically combining rosin with hydrogen it is possible to obtain a product which exhibits greater stability and is less subject to discoloration on storage. The abietic acid in rosin can be made to undergo hydrogen disproportionation leading to the so-called dehydrogenated rosin. This type of chemically modified rosin, as the sodium soap, was used extensively during World War II as the emulsifying agent in the preparation of synthetic rubber. The properties of the modified rosin were such that it could be allowed to remain in the coagulated rubber. Hydrogenation and disproportionation both cause rosin to crystallize more readily, and consequently the hydrogenation is carried only to the point where satisfactory stability can be secured without crystallization. By combining rosin chemically with certain unsaturated types of dibasic acids, such as maleic and fumaric acid, it is possible to destroy the unsaturation without inducing crystallization. It is probable that the character of the varnish which can be made from China wood oil, and rosin derivative may reside in the chemical combination that takes place between the unsaturated components of both products.

The copals form an important group of varnish resins. The word copal appears to have been derived from the Spanish or Mexican word *copalli*—incense. Various types of products are known—the recent varieties as well as the fossil types. Soft Manila copal is readily soluble in organic solvent liquids and in oils or, as in the case of the pontianak variety, it requires running before it can be dispersed in oil. There are several varieties which are employed in the varnish trade: kauri copal, melting at about 150° C., is derived from the New Zealand pine; Congo copal originates in the Belgian Congo; while Zanzibar copal is dug from the mainland opposite the island of Zanzibar. Some of the South American copals derived from Brazil and Colombia have attracted some attention. Copal has been esterified with glycerol in a manner similar to that employed in making ester gum. Because of the high melting point of the copal gum, it is necessary to conduct this thermal decomposition to a point much further than is customarily employed when the resin is to be dissolved in oil, and temperatures as high as 330° C.–340° C. are employed. Two acids have been isolated from Congo copal; one is the dibasic congocopalic acid ($C_{36}H_{58}(COOH)_2$), and the other is the monobasic congocopalolic acid ($C_{27}H_{32}(OH)COOH$).

Amber, the hardest natural resin known, finds little use in the varnish industry because of its lack of solubility. When it is incorporated in oil, so much discoloration takes place during the running operation that the resulting varnish is of a poor colour. The resin is found in the so-called blue earth, in east Prussia in the Baltic region. The fact that it is derived from a variety of *Pinus* indicates that over a sufficiently long period of time under appropriate conditions an oleoresin can be converted into a heat-infusible product.

Oriental lacquers are a distinct product derived from the *Rhus vernicifera*, a tree which is indigenous to China. The process was introduced into Japan and remained secret for centuries. A milk-like emulsion secured from the tree is concentrated by evaporation to a viscous liquid which resembles a bodied oil. When this is applied as a thin film, it hardens in about a day to form a tough skin. The composition is peculiar in that it will dry only in the dark and in a moist atmosphere; exposed to light and warmth, the varnish remains tacky. The varnish contains a skin irritant, and this material may be the urishiol which is similar to a product isolated from the *Rhus toxicodendron* or poison ivy, which is common in the United States.

Another product containing phenolic bodies is derived from the nuts of the cashew tree (*Anacardium occidentale*); the oil known as the cashew-shell-nut oil possesses materials which lead to vesicant action, but by appropriate chemical treatment the irritant is destroyed. This product has found some commercial importance in the United States.

SYNTHETIC RESINS

Synthetic resins possess most of the physical characteristics of natural resins and in addition have many unique properties of their own. Chemically there is a certain degree of resemblance between the synthetic resins of phenol-formaldehyde and the natural phenolic resins found in oriental lacquer and in accroides gum. Moreover, one can trace a certain amount of resemblance between the polyester resins known as alkyds and the polyesters found in shellac. Although it has usually been considered that the synthetic resins possess the unique characteristic of becoming insoluble and infusible on heat treatment, it is known that shellac will become insoluble on prolonged heating, and the same phenomenon has been observed with certain of the other gums. The synthetic resins are of industrial interest not only as substitutes for natural resins in the coating industry but also because they find extensive use as adhesives, textile impregnants, binders, as agents for removing ions from water solutions and as binders in the plastics moulding industry (*see* PLASTICS).

Thermoplastic and Thermosetting Resins.—Physically it is possible to classify synthetic resins according to their solubility. There are those resins which remain permanently soluble and those which are initially soluble but become insoluble and infusible under the action of heat. The first type is known as the thermoplastic type of synthetic resin, whereas the latter is known variously as heat hardenable, thermosetting or thermocuring resins.

Linear and Three-dimensional Resins.—The permanently soluble or thermoplastic resins consist of molecules which are more or less linear in form. During solution in an organic medium, the solvent penetrates between the threadlike molecule; irrespective of the size of the resin molecule, solution will eventually occur. Under the influence of heat the threadlike molecules can be forced to move, and on cooling the impressed form is retained. On the other hand, the thermosetting resins consist of resinous molecules which are tied together three-dimensionally into a network pattern. In the initial stages where the network is small, solvent can readily penetrate the interstices of the network, but after chemical combination has taken place and a large three-dimensional network is formed, the resin becomes insoluble. Since the network is tied together rigidly, the resulting molecular structure is infusible.

Condensation and Polymerization Resins.—Two main classes may be distinguished under chemical classification: first, the condensation resin, such as the phenol-formaldehyde or melamine-formaldehyde type, in which the molecules unite with the elimination of water; and second, the polymerization resin, in which chemical reaction takes place through loss of unsaturation, without the evolution of any low-molecular-weight material.

Coating Resins: 1. Phenol-Formaldehyde Resins.—The chemical combination of phenols with aldehydes was noted by many investigators in the 19th century. Among the organic chemists who had studied the reaction were C. F. Gerhardt (1853), Adolf

von Baeyer (1872) and A. Michael (1883), but it was only after the advent of cheap formaldehyde in 1891 that a more extensive investigation was made toward the commercial utilization of this resin. Various investigations were made by W. Kleeberg, by A. Smith and by A. Luft, and certain of the methods employed resembled the technology which had proved successful with thermoplastic nitrocellulose plastics but which failed when such procedures were extended to thermosetting compositions. The first successful work in this field was carried out by L. H. Baekeland. Through a study of the various stages of resinification and through the utilization of a so-called bakelizer, he was able to mould many products, and in 1910 he organized the General Bakelite company. Much of the plastic entered into electrical goods. Meanwhile, the possibility of employing this condensation product to replace shellac in phonograph records was considered by J. W. Aylsworth of East Orange, N.J. On the basis of his development work, the Condensite Company of America was established at about the same time. Still another concern for the manufacture of phenolic resins was started by the Redmanol Chemical Products company, based on the studies of L. V. Redman. After much patent litigation these various companies pooled their resources.

In spite of the marked commercial success of these resins in moulding, in casting and in laminating, they were not suitable for coating compositions. While it was possible to make a phenolic varnish for laminating purposes, this varnish could be dissolved only in alcohol and could not be dispersed in cheap solvents or in drying oils. The first successful attempt to use phenol-formaldehyde resins directly as substitutes for natural resins in coating composition was the result of the work of Dr. K. Albert of Germany. He found that by a preliminary heating or fluxing of the phenol-formaldehyde resin with rosin or colophony, it was possible to disperse the resulting mixture in drying oils. These products, when dispersed in China wood oil, possessed rapid drying characteristics and formed films possessing good durability.

In 1928 the first so-called oil-soluble phenolic resin appeared on the market. Through the use of appropriately substituted phenols and the combining of such substituted phenols with formaldehyde, it was possible to obtain a resin which was directly soluble in oil without preliminary fluxing with rosin. These oil-soluble phenolic resins found wide acceptance in the varnish field. Among the phenols useful for such purposes are phenyl, phenol I, tertiary butylphenol II and cyclohexylphenol III, as well as certain of the

tar acids which boil in the xylenol range. The resins are incorporated into the oil by adding resin in increments at a rate at which frothing can be controlled. After addition of the resin the temperature is raised until satisfactory increase in viscosity occurs. The European procedure favours the addition of the resin to the pretreated oil, and, while it appears to yield lighter coloured and less viscous products, the resulting films appear to be less resistant chemically. Other combinations are known, certain of which consist in substituting an alkyd resin for a part of the drying oil. Durable finishes have been made from alkyd-phenol-formaldehyde oil combinations.

2. Alkyd Resins.—These resins are reaction products of polyhydric alcohols and polybasic acids, and various modifications can be made by adding monohydric alcohols or monobasic acids to the polyester composition. The derivation of the term alkyd becomes apparent when it is pointed out that the "cid" from acid was changed to "kyd" for the sake of euphony. J. J. Berzelius prepared glycerol tartrate in 1847; J. M. van Bemmelen prepared a resin by reacting succinic acid with glycerol in 1856; M. P. E. Berthelot esterified glycerol and sebacic acid in 1854; while M. A. von Lourenço prepared a resin from glycerol and citric acid in 1863. The most important dibasic acid employed in the manufacture of alkyd resins is phthalic acid. The phthalic acid (or phthalic anhydride) is obtained readily by the catalytic oxidation of naphthalene, and once this synthesis was properly worked out a ready source of this valuable commodity was available at a reasonable price. While the reaction product of glycerol and phthalic anhydride is of limited utility by itself, it is upon this structural vertebra that such ingredients as natural resin acids as well as drying and nondrying varieties of vegetable fatty-oil acids can be hung. Other dibasic acids are used where specialized properties are required. Maleic acid is obtained by the vapour-phase oxidation of benzene, while its geometrical isomer, fumaric acid, is obtained either by rearrangement of the maleic acid or by fermentation processes. Succinic acid can be prepared by the reduction of maleic acid. Sebacic acid and azelaic acids are incorporated into alkyd resins where exceptional flexibility is required, and these acids are manufactured commercially by treatment of castor oil or cottonseed oil, respectively, with caustic at elevated temperatures. Adipic acid is also available by the oxidation of cyclohexanol, which in turn can be derived from phenol. Glycerol is by far the most important polyhydric alcohol used, but ethylene glycol, diethylene glycol and pentaerythritol are used for merits of their own.

The drying-type alkyd resins first came into commercial prominence when it was demonstrated by R. H. Kienle that it was possible to form a new type of product by recombining the component parts of a drying oil, that is, the glycerol and the drying-oil acid in the presence of a saturated dibasic acid such as phthalic. Under these conditions, the cocondensation of glycerol, phthalic acid (as anhydride) and a drying-oil acid yielded a high-molecular-weight resinous condensation product in which the unsaturation of the drying-oil acid was substantially unimpaired. The result was that the resin would dry in a manner similar to the natural drying oil. Such resins in organic liquids yield solutions which resemble varnish and can be used as such. Since the resins could be dispersed in relatively cheap organic liquids, these varnish solutions found wide acceptance in coating various metals, as priming paints and as enamels. They are used to finish transportation equipment such as automobiles, streetcars and railway coaches and, because of their good chemical resistance, find acceptance as enamels for coating refrigerators and washing machines. Similar resin solutions are used in ornamental hardware, to coat metal furniture, metal signs and farm equipment, and, because of good heat resistance, these resins are employed to cover radiators, smokestacks and light reflectors. They find wide acceptance as architectural enamels, traffic paints and as printing-ink ingredients.

These resins are often used alone, but they show excellent compatibility characteristics with a wide variety of other film-forming agents such as nitrocellulose, natural resins, phenolic resins and urea and melamine-formaldehyde resins. With nitrocellulose it is possible to secure films possessing toughness, hardness and durability, as well as good gloss. It was this combination with nitrocellulose and alkyd resins which initially permitted the formulation of automotive finishes possessing an enamel-like quality and having excellent outdoor durability. When these resins are modified with natural resins, the melting point and hardness are increased; since such compositions release solvent very readily, they are used as rubbing and sanding vehicles. When mixed with urea-formaldehyde and melamine-formaldehyde condensation products, the alkyd resin becomes harder and more mar-resistant.

3. *Polyester Resins.*—While closely related to alkyd resins, the polyester materials differ from the conventional alkyd resins in that the cure is associated with a low-molecular-weight unsaturated organic liquid. The polyester resins, or anhydrous thermosetting resins, usually comprise an unsaturated alkyd resin prepared from a polyhydric alcohol with an unsaturated acid such as maleic or fumaric acid. This alkyd resin is then dispersed in an organic liquid such as monomeric styrene or with diallyl phthalate. This solution, appropriately stabilized for shipping, is treated with a peroxide catalyst just before use. The catalyzed resinous material is then employed in saturating various fibrous materials such as fabric or glass fibre. The cured composite structure of resin and glass fibre found use in such widely differing applications as plastic armour, trays, radar housings, luggage and light-weight boats.

4. *Urea-Formaldehyde Resins.*—The chemical condensation of urea and formaldehyde yields resins which are of great value both in the moulding and in the coating industry. The resins are characterized by extremely light colour, and products fabricated from such materials can be made into mouldings which are colourless. The fundamental chemical investigations of Hanns John laid the foundation for the use of this resin in the plastics industry; but in so far as coating resins are concerned, it was the observation of Kurt Ripper that proved most valuable. He found that under suitable conditions the water-soluble condensation product of urea and formaldehyde could be dispersed in organic liquids. To make the resin soluble in varnish solvents for coating use, it was first necessary to conduct the condensation of urea and formaldehyde in a solvent such as alcohol and then to remove the water of condensation as an azeotrope with the alcohol. The resin thus formed in alcoholic solution could then be diluted with aromatic solvents.

By themselves, films and coatings of the unmodified urea resins are hard and mar-proof and possess good colour and gloss but lack distensibility. From the standpoint of their use in enamels the resins are neutral, and consequently any type of pigment can be admixed with them. When these urea resins are blended with alkyd resins, they become flexible and adhere to metal surfaces. This combination of urea-formaldehyde resins and alkyd resins is in many ways a unique combination whereby the urea resins improve certain of the deficiencies of the alkyd resins such as increasing hardness and eliminating the tendency of the oil-modified alkyd resins to wrinkle on rapid drying. The urea-formaldehyde resins under the influence of heat contribute hardness, colour and gloss to the cured film, while the alkyd resins produce flexibility, drying ability and adhesion to metal surfaces.

5. *Melamine-Formaldehyde Resins.*—Many of the excellent characteristics exhibited by the urea-formaldehyde resins in coatings are also shown by the melamine-formaldehyde resins. Melamine, or polymerized (trimerized) cyanamide, is a heterocyclic compound which reacts with and cures rapidly in combination with formaldehyde. Unlike urea, which is low melting and soluble in water, melamine possesses a high melting point (354° C.) and dissolves very slightly in water. It is characterized by an exceptionally stable ring system of alternate carbon and nitrogen atoms —a stability which is reflected in the resins made from it. The melamine and formaldehyde resin can be dispersed in organic solvents by procedures similar to those employed for the urea-formaldehyde condensation product. When used in admixture with alkyd resins a much faster heat cure can be secured than when urea-formaldehyde is used. The outstanding characteristics which urea resins supply to films are further enhanced with melamine resins; these are superior in resistance to various chemical reagents, outdoor durability and colour retention on exposure to both heat and light. These properties, in addition to porcelain-like appearance and resistance to abrasion, enabled such finishes to enter into automotive coatings and industrial finishes on a large scale.

6. *Coumarone-Indene Resins.*—From the light oils present in the distillation of coal tar, it is possible to secure a fraction rich in indene, coumarone and related isomers. This mixture can be polymerized by means of sulphuric acid into resins of soft or hard consistency. These synthetic resins are one of the oldest-known synthetic products and have been available from the time of the initial investigations of G. Kraemer and A. Spilker in 1890. The resins exhibit good compatibility characteristics with a wide variety of other polymeric products, both synthetic and natural, and have been used in coating of concrete, in the manufacture of antifouling ship-bottom paints, as additives to paraffin

wax, in admixture with bitumens and as compounding agents in butadiene-styrene synthetic rubber.

7. Silicones.—The silicone resins are based on the silicon-oxygen skeleton rather than upon the carbon-oxygen chains or upon the carbon chain found in the conventional resins. This siloxane linkage, as the silicon-oxygen combination is called, introduces a degree of resistance to heat that is not found in those chains possessing carbon atoms exclusively. Naturally, those same reagents which can break the silicon-oxygen bridge in silicate minerals are also instrumental in causing the silicone resins to undergo cleavage; both hydrofluoric acid and strong caustic will cleave the siloxane chain in the silicone resins. Through the proper choice of ingredients, groupings can be introduced into the molecular structure whereby growth may be made to occur essentially linearly as, for example, through the introduction of saturated dialkyl-siloxy groups, or three-dimensionally through the utilization of the monoalkyl-siloxy groupings.

Various silicones can be made by changing the nature of the alkyl group, but most of the commercial production is restricted to the methyl silicones. Various polymeric structures have been made, certain of which are viscous liquids, others resinous; and even rubbery products have been produced. The liquids have found use as hydraulic oils and as instrument and transformer oils. Some of the higher-molecular-weight materials have found further application as varnishes as well as in high-temperature-resisting paints and enamels and as coatings for electrical insulation. When applied to the surfaces of glass or ceramics and baked, the silicones yield surfaces which are water repellent.

Resin Adhesives: 1. Plywood Adhesives.—Prior to the introduction of synthetic resins for plywood construction, laminated wood was susceptible to deterioration by water and high humidity. The natural protein products such as albumin and casein could not be rendered insoluble to the same extent as later became possible with various condensation products such as phenol-formaldehyde, urea-formaldehyde and melamine-formaldehyde resins. The new resin adhesives permit the construction of plywood in which the glue line is strong, resistant to water and immune to attack by the action of fungi, moulds and vermin. Such plywood can be used not only for architectural and automotive purposes but also for aeronautical and marine construction. Phenolic-resin adhesives became commercially available about 1935, while the urea condensation products were introduced about two years later.

Two types of synthetic glues are manufactured—cold-setting and hot-setting. Certain of the resins are supplied in powder form which requires solution prior to use, whereas other types are already dispersed in a liquid medium. Extenders such as cereal flour and wheat flour are sometimes employed where maximum strength and waterproofness are not essential. Phenolic resins yield an especially durable bond, but the resin is coloured, and the colour may bleed through thin veneers. Such colour is also a disadvantage where the glued edges are exposed. The urea resin is characterized by a rapid cure at low temperature and is widely employed in the preparation of cold-setting adhesives. The urea-resin, moreover, is colourless and will not change the colour of the wood. Melamine resins likewise possess excellent colour characteristics, and in addition the glue line formed from this resin is resistant to cold as well as to boiling water.

Keeping pace with the development of new adhesives were new fabricating and moulding techniques which allowed the construction of complicated shapes particularly necessary in aeronautics and in boat construction. Flat sheets can be "post-formed" into simple curves, but for construction of compound curved surfaces a moulding procedure is preferred. This is accomplished by applying the glue to the veneers and allowing them to dry in order to permit easy handling. A mould is constructed with the exact contours needed in the finished assembly, and the coated wood veneers are placed in the mould and fastened by staples. The laminates are enclosed in a rubber bag which is evacuated in order to keep the veneers rigidly in place, and the assembly is placed in an autoclave and heated in order to render the resin insoluble and infusible. Such procedures enabled rapid construction of large aircraft parts, pontoons and motor torpedo boats.

2. Wood Impregnation.—Wood which has been subjected to reduced atmospheric pressure to remove occluded air can be impregnated with various resin solutions dissolved in water or in alcohol. After drying, the temperature is raised, whereupon curing of the resin occurs in the interior of the wood, rendering it harder, stronger and more resistant to water and water vapour. Through the addition of appropriate accelerators prior to impregnation the cure can be effected at a lower temperature with less damage to the structure of the wood. Phenol-formaldehyde, urea-formaldehyde and a mixture of the two resins have been employed for this purpose.

3. Other Adhesive Applications.—Many other resinous and rubbery compositions, dispersed in water or dissolved in organic liquids, are used to bind metals, plastics, glass, rubber, paper, brickwork, leather, fabrics and cork. Others are used in the manufacture of shoes, gaskets, furniture construction, lighting assemblies, sound insulation and upholstery. Certain of these adhesives have natural or synthetic rubber as a base, whereas others involve the use of synthetic thermoplastic and thermosetting resins. During World War II the reinforcement of starch by urea-resin adhesives in paperboard manufacture allowed the fabrication of paper containers which had a high resistance to water.

Resins for Textile Applications: 1. Continuous Coating.—One of the methods of separating electrical conductors is by means of a covering of cotton or silk, and so long as anhydrous conditions exist such insulation is satisfactory. In a humid atmosphere, the textile absorbs water, and its insulating efficiency is markedly decreased. To overcome this disadvantage, the dried fabric is treated with a varnish subsequently cured, thereby sealing the fabric. The varnish is selected in order that the water vapour transmission through the film of resin will be as small as possible. Among the resins which have been employed, the phenolic resins are the best known, although almost every type of natural and synthetic resin has been tested at some time or another for this type of insulating varnish.

2. Impregnation of Fabrics.—Resins are applied to fabrics for purposes other than to produce insulation; for instance, to improve the finish of cotton and rayon and to render them non-shrinking and crushproof. Resins have also been employed to bind pigments to the fabric, to minimize bleeding and crocking of dyes and as mordants for dyeing cellulosic fibres with wool dyes (animalized cellulose). Since no resin discoloration can be tolerated in uses of this type, the thermosetting resins which have enjoyed widest acceptance in this field are the urea-formaldehyde condensation products. In numerous applications, superior results can be secured only with the melamine-formaldehyde resins. Among the more notable achievements of the latter resin, the following may be mentioned: shrinkage control of cotton and wool; improvement in the crease resistance of cotton and rayon; production of durable glazes on chintz; preparation of binders to prevent thread slippage; and minimizing of gas fading of acetate colours. Many of these effects are achieved by treating textiles with low-molecular-weight water-soluble condensation products and then causing resin formation to occur on the fabric.

Quite different effects are secured by using high-molecular-weight water-insoluble thermoplastic resins which are dispersed in water. Such resins render the fabric stiff, crisp and full, and when properly formulated such properties are not destroyed by the laundering operation. Other thermoplastic resins impart good draping characteristics and improve the abrasion resistance of the textile, whereas still others are employed for upholstery finishing, raincoats, shower curtains and other waterproofing applications.

Resins Possessing Ionic Charges: 1. Ion-Exchange Resins.—By the introduction of strong acid groupings such as carboxyl and sulphonic acid into a three-dimensional polymer, high-molecular-weight resins can be made up where the resin is ionic in character and where the ion is chemically bound in the resin molecule. These ionic resins in the form of sodium salt can be used as a means of softening water whereby the calcium ions of the hard water are replaced by the sodium ions from the resin. In this respect the synthetic ion-exchange resins, generally known as cation resins, behave like the natural zeolites; and, like the zeolites, the resins when used under such conditions do not change the amount of dissolved salt in the water.

Condensation products can also be prepared synthetically where basic groupings such as amino- and guanido- are bound in the resin molecule, and these so-called anion resins can replace anions. It follows that a combination of the acidic and basic resins or a cation and an anion resin can completely eliminate the mineral content of water by first allowing the cation-exchange resin in the form of a free acid to react with the salt and subsequently reacting the effluent with an anion exchanger.

Once the resins become saturated with minerals, they can be regenerated chemically and used over again as often as required. The process works most expediently where the concentration of a mineral matter is low, but the scavenging is so complete that the method has found favour not only in producing a so-called demineralized distilled water but in numerous industrial processes where the removal of ionic impurities is not possible by distillation. Ion-exchange resins have been used to remove mineral impurities from pharmaceutical preparations, dyestuffs, sugar, syrups, enzyme preparations, emulsions and glycols and formaldehyde. Other industrial uses include the recovery of valuable metals and various other inorganic and organic materials from industrial wastes. The resins have also been employed as catalysts in chemical reactions, particularly in the inversion of sugar.

2. *Resins for the Treatment of Paper.*—Another resinous ion which has attracted attention is the cationic melamine-formaldehyde resin. Unlike the ion-exchange resins, the cationic melamine resin is initially dispersible in water solution. The large ion is attracted toward and adheres to the cellulose fibre. It can be incorporated into paper by adding—as an acidic dispersion to a paper-pulp suspension and after migration to the paper fibre, the resin becomes insoluble and infusible during the drying of the paper stock. The resulting product is characterized by superior fold resistance and by a nonlinting behaviour when dry, and when wet it does not disintegrate as does untreated paper. Water-dispersible urea resins with ionic properties have been developed and can be added to paper stock in a similar manner. Certain of these resins are anionic, *i.e.,* they contain sulphonic acid groups and are flocculated on the fibres through the use of aluminum sulphate while others are cationic and need no flocculation agent.

BIBLIOGRAPHY.—H. W. Chatfield, *Varnish Constituents* (London, 1944); Carleton Ellis, *The Chemistry of Synthetic Resins* (1935); N. Heaton, *Outlines of Paint Technology* (London, 1928); R. Houwink, *Chemie und Technologie der Kunststoffe* (Leipzig, 1939); J. J. Mattiello (ed.), *Protective and Decorative Coatings*, vols. I–V (1941–42); R. S. Morrell and others (eds.), *Synthetic Resins and Allied Plastics* (London, 1937), *Varnishes and Their Components* (London, 1924); J. Scheiber and K. Sändig, *Artificial Resins* (London, 1931).

(E. L. KA.)

RESISTANCE, MEASUREMENT OF: *see* INSTRUMENTS, ELECTRICAL.

RESONANCE, a term used in physics and related fields originally denoting a prolongation or increase of sound because of sympathetic vibration of some body capable of moving in the proper period. An example is the oscillation induced in a violin or piano string of a given pitch when a musical note of the same pitch is sung or played nearby. For resonance in acoustical theory and experiment, *see* SOUND; in rooms and buildings, *see* ACOUSTICS OF BUILDINGS; as a theory of hearing, *see* HEARING; in violin construction, *see* VIOLIN.

The term has been extended by analogy to the familiar selective mechanical resonance of a springboard or bridge to certain frequencies of jumping or walking; and to the selective electrical resonance of a tuned radio circuit to the radio frequency transmitted by a single radio station. At the high frequencies used in microwaves and radar (*q.v.*), the tuned circuit is actually constructed most easily in the form of a small metal cavity resonator not unlike the cavity of an acoustical resonator such as an open-mouthed bottle. (J. R. Pt.)

RESONANCE, THEORY OF, in chemistry, is an extension of the theory of valence (*q.v.*), which contributed greatly to the understanding of the structure of molecules and the structural interpretation of the chemical and physical properties of substances.

The concept of resonance has been applied in chemistry in the elucidation of the nature of the covalent bond, of the partial ionic character of bonds and of other aspects of valence. Its most important chemical applications have been to aromatic molecules, molecules containing conjugated systems of double bonds, hydrocarbon free radicals, and other molecules to which no satisfactory single structure in terms of single bonds, double bonds and triple bonds can be assigned.

For many molecules it is possible to formulate valence-bond structures which are so reasonable and which account so satisfactorily for the properties of the substances that they are generally accepted and are used as the basis for chemical reasoning. Examples of such molecules are:

hydrogen,   H—H   or H:H

methane,   H—C—H   or H:C:H

ethylene,   C=C   or C::C

acetylene,   H—C≡C—H   or H:C:::C:H

chloroform,   Cl—C—H   or :Cl:C:H

It is sometimes found, however, that a choice cannot be made between two or more conceivable structures which are expected to be about equally stable and of which no one accounts in a completely satisfactory way for the properties of the substance. The concept of quantum-mechanical resonance provided the solution to this problem; namely, the actual normal state of such a molecule can be described as corresponding not to any one of the alternative reasonable structures but rather to a combination of them, their individual contributions being determined by their nature and stability. The molecule is then said to resonate among the several valence-bond structures or to have a structure which is a resonance hybrid of these structures. The molecule is stabilized by this resonance, its energy being less than the energy which would be expected for any one of the structures among which it resonates. This stabilization is characteristic of the phenomenon of quantum-mechanical resonance, which was discovered by Werner Heisenberg in 1926 (*see* below). The physical and chemical properties of the substance and the configuration of the molecule are determined by the nature of the resonating structures; these properties are, however, not the properties averaged for the resonating structures but are instead the averaged properties as influenced also by the effects of resonance and in particular by the additional stability resulting from the resonance energy.

The aromatic substance benzene provides not only an illuminating but also the most important example of the application of the concept of the resonance of molecules among two or more valence-bond structures. The formulation of the structure of benzene as a six-membered ring of carbon atoms with attached hydrogen atoms was made by F. A. Kekulé in 1865. To make the structure compatible with the quadrivalence of carbon he introduced alternating single and double bonds in the ring, and later, in 1872, in order to account for the nonobservance of isomeric orthodisubstituted benzenes (differing in having a single bond or a double bond between the substituted carbon atoms), he introduced the idea of an oscillation between two structures.

The Kekulé structure for benzene is unsatisfactory in that the substance does not show the properties of unsaturation to be expected for a molecule containing double bonds; and, after a period during which the centric structure of H. E. Armstrong and Adolf von Baeyer, the diagonal structure of A. Claus and the structure of J. Thiele based on his theory of partial valence were proposed, an important advance was made in the years following 1920 in the theory of intermediate stages proposed by F. Arndt and the theory of mesomerism developed by Sir Robert Robinson, C. K. Ingold and other English and U.S. chemists. The suggestion of these investigators, induced from the facts of chemistry, was that the true state of a molecule may be intermediate between those represented by several different valence-bond structures. Complete clarification of the structure of benzene was then provided in 1931 through the application of the theory of resonance and the consideration of the effect of resonance energy. According to the quantum-mechanical discussion of the structure of benzene, the normal state of this molecule can be represented as a hybrid of the two Kekulé structures ⬡ and ⬡ and three diagonal structures of the form ⬡ ⬡ ⬡ (the para bond in these structures being a weak bond, almost equivalent to a free valence on each of the para carbon atoms) and other structures which make smaller contributions. The configuration of the molecule should be a suitable average of those configurations corresponding to the individual structures. Because of the resonance the six carbon-carbon bonds are equivalent, and because of the stereochemical properties of a double bond the molecule as a whole is planar; hence the benzene molecule is predicted to be a planar hexagonal molecule, in agreement with observations made by the electron diffraction, X-ray diffraction and spectroscopic methods. Moreover, each carbon-carbon bond should be intermediate in length between a single carbon-carbon bond and a double carbon-carbon bond, the lengths of which, in molecules represented by a single valence-bond structure, are 1.54 Å and 1.33 Å, respectively. The observed value in benzene, 1.39 Å, is compatible with this prediction. Moreover, the benzene molecule is predicted from the quantum-mechanical considerations to be stabilized by resonance energy to the extent of about 40 kg.cal. per mole, relative to the value expected for one of the Kekulé structures. The amount of resonance stabilization can be estimated experimentally by measurement of the heat of combustion or heat of hydrogenation of benzene and related substances. For example, the heat of hydrogenation of cyclohexene is 28.6 kg.cal. per mole; if each of the three double bonds in benzene were the same as the double bond in cyclohexene, the heat of hydrogenation of benzene would be 85.8 kg.cal. per mole, whereas in fact the observed value is 49.8, indicating that the benzene molecule is stabilized relative to a Kekulé structure by the amount of energy 36 kg.cal. per mole, in approximate agreement with the quantum-mechanical prediction. The characteristic chemical stability and non-reactivity shown by benzene, relative to simpler unsaturated substances, may be attributed to this stabilization by resonance. It is possible, moreover, by the detailed consideration of the resonating structures to explain in a reasonably satisfactory way the other striking chemical properties of benzene, such as the influence of one substituent in determining the position of attachment of further substituents to the ring.

The structures of polynuclear aromatic hydrocarbons are similar. Naphthalene, for example, can be described as resonating among the three structures ⬡⬡ , ⬡⬡ and ⬡⬡ , with small contributions from other structures analogous to the *para*-bonded structures of benzene, and the resonance energy of naphthalene is found to be about 75 kg.cal. per mole.

The stabilization of the aromatic heterocyclic molecules such as thiophen results from resonance of the most important structure

with structures such as

The resonance energy for thiophen is about 30 kg.cal. per mole.

The characteristic properties of substances which contain conjugated systems of double bonds can be readily accounted for by the theory of resonance. A molecule such as biphenyl, ⬡—⬡ , is stabilized not only by Kekulé resonance but also by the resonance energy of conjugation, resulting from the contributions of the somewhat less stable structures of type ⬡=⬡ .

For biphenyl, phenylethylene and butadiene the resonance energy of conjugation is about five kg.cal. per mole. There are two stereochemical effects of this conjugation: the carbon-carbon distance for the single bond involved in the conjugated system is decreased from the single-bond value, 1.54 Å, to about 1.48 Å, as the result of the contribution of the conjugated structures with a double bond in this position; and the double-bond character of this bond also finds expression in the tendency to hold the adjacent bonds in the planar configuration. These molecules are observed to be planar or nearly planar, except when planarity is prevented by the arrangement of valence bonds or by steric effects, in which case the properties of the substance show that there is interference with the conjugation.

The phenomenon of resonance can be invoked in the discussion of the colour of dyes and other organic substances. The normal state of the cation of malachite green, for example, involves resonance among all structures of the sort shown below, in which the positive charge is located on different atoms within the molecule:

The excited states of the molecule are similar resonating states involving these structures. The absorption of light by the molecule, with its transition from the normal state to an excited state, occurs with great ease; the quantum-mechanical molecule can be compared with a classical oscillator in which a positive charge is resonating through a large amplitude, from one nitrogen atom across to the other, and from this comparison it can be predicted that the molecule should show intense absorption of light of suitable wave lengths.

Resonance also provides an explanation of the properties of many inorganic substances. For example, the carbon-monoxide molecule is a far more stable molecule than would be expected from the apparent bivalence of carbon, and there was formerly discussion as to whether its structure should be written as $:C=\ddot{O}:$, containing a double covalent bond, or as $:C\equiv O:$, similar to the nitrogen molecule. The molecule can be assigned a hybrid structure based upon these structures, and its stability can be attributed to resonance stabilization. For carbon dioxide the structure $:\ddot{O}=C=\ddot{O}:$ was for many years accepted without question; later, however, evidence of interatomic distances and other properties showed that this structure is in resonance with the two structures $:O\equiv C-\ddot{O}:$ and $:\ddot{O}-C\equiv O:$. Nitric oxide, which is surprisingly stable for a molecule containing an odd number of electrons, can be described as achieving this stability through resonance between the structures $:\dot{N}=\ddot{O}:$ and $:\ddot{N}=\dot{O}:$, and may be said to have a double bond plus a three-electron bond between its two atoms. The nitrate ion, NO_3^-, resonates among the three structures

making each of the nitrogen-oxygen bonds a hybrid between a single bond and a double bond.

The general rules regarding the resonance of a molecule among alternative valence-bond structures are the following: Equivalent structures contribute equally to the normal state of the resonating molecule. The more stable structures in general make larger contributions to the normal state, and less stable structures make smaller contributions. The electronic state of the resonating molecule applies to a definite configuration of the atomic nuclei; accordingly the energy values of the individual structures to be considered in connection with the foregoing statements are those calculated for the nuclear configuration of the actual state of the molecule and not for nuclear configurations which would be the most stable for the individual structures. The strain involved in this change in configuration in some cases makes structures unimportant which otherwise might be important. All of the structures which contribute to a resonance hybrid structure must have the same number of unpaired electrons; significant resonance does not occur, for example, between a structure with no unpaired electrons (singlet state) and a structure with two unpaired electrons (triplet state).

The basis of the theory of resonance is the fundamental principle of quantum mechanics that the wave function representing a stationary state of a system can be expressed as a sum of wave functions which correspond to hypothetical structures for the system, and that, in particular, the wave function representing the normal state of a system is that sum which leads to a minimum calculated energy of the system. The concept of resonance was introduced into quantum mechanics by Werner Heisenberg in an illuminating discussion of the stationary states of the helium atom (*Z. f. Physik*, vol. 38, p. 411; vol. 39, p. 499 [1926]). Heisenberg discussed certain excited states of this two-electron atom in terms of structures in which one electron occupies an inner orbit, close to the helium nucleus, and the second electron occupies an outer orbit; and he showed that an actual stationary state can be represented by a wave function obtained by adding to or subtracting from the wave function for this structure another wave function, representing the structure in which the second electron occupies the inner orbit and the first electron the outer orbit. On the basis of anology with the classical system of resonating coupled harmonic oscillators, he assigned the name quantum-mechanical resonance to this concept (*see* ATOM; QUANTUM MECHANICS; SPECTROSCOPY).

The special usefulness of the harmonic oscillator in the interpretation of quantum mechanics results from the fact that when this system is treated by the methods of classical mechanics and the old quantum theory, with the number $\frac{1}{2}$ added to the integral values of the quantum number, many of the calculated properties of the system are the same as those given by quantum mechanics. The simplest system illustrating resonance consists of two equivalent harmonic oscillators with a weak Hooke's-law coupling between them. The potential energy for this system may be represented by the expression $2\pi^2 m v_o^2 x_1^2 + 2\pi^2 m v_o^2 x_2^2 + 4\pi^2 m \lambda x_1 x_2$, and the kinetic energy by $\frac{1}{2}m\dot{x}_1^2 + \frac{1}{2}m\dot{x}_2^2$, where m is the mass of each oscillator, x_1 and x_2 are the displacements of the oscillators from their positions of rest, v_o is the characteristic frequency of oscillation of each oscillator when there is no coupling ($\lambda=0$), and λ is a parameter determining the strength of the coupling. The classical equations of

motion for this system can be solved in terms of the normal co-ordinates $\xi = \sqrt{\frac{1}{2}}(x_1+x_2)$ and $\eta = \sqrt{\frac{1}{2}}(x_1-x_2)$. Each of these normal co-ordinates varies harmonically with the time, t, the integrated equations of motion being
$$\xi = \xi_o \cos\left(2\pi\sqrt{v_o^2+\lambda}\,t + \delta_\xi\right)$$
and
$$\eta = \eta_o \cos\left(2\pi\sqrt{v_o^2-\lambda}\,t + \delta_\eta\right)$$
in which ξ_o, η_o, δ_ξ and δ_η are the constants of integration. It is seen that the characteristic frequencies for ξ and η, $\sqrt{v_o^2+\lambda}$ and $\sqrt{v_o^2-\lambda}$ respectively, differ from v_o. The co-ordinates x_1 and x_2 are then given by the equations
$$x_1 = \frac{\xi_o}{\sqrt{2}}\cos\left(2\pi\sqrt{v_o^2+\lambda}\,t + \delta_\xi\right) + \frac{\eta_o}{\sqrt{2}}\cos\left(2\pi\sqrt{v_o^2-\lambda}\,t + \delta_\eta\right),$$
and
$$x_2 = \frac{\xi_o}{\sqrt{2}}\cos\left(2\pi\sqrt{v_o^2+\lambda}\,t + \delta_\xi\right) - \frac{\eta_o}{\sqrt{2}}\cos\left(2\pi\sqrt{v_o^2-\lambda}\,t + \delta_\eta\right).$$
If η_o is zero, the two oscillators carry out, exactly together in phase, a simple harmonic motion with amplitude $\frac{\xi_o}{\sqrt{2}}$ and frequency $\sqrt{v_o^2+\lambda}$; and if ξ_o is zero, they carry out, with phase difference π, a similar harmonic motion with amplitude $\frac{\eta_o}{\sqrt{2}}$ and frequency $\sqrt{v_o^2-\lambda}$; but if neither η_o nor ξ_o vanishes, each of the oscillators vibrates in a complex way, the amplitude changing slowly from $\frac{\xi_o+\eta_o}{\sqrt{2}}$ to $\frac{|\xi_o-\eta_o|}{\sqrt{2}}$. This is the phenomenon described as classical resonance.

The rules of the old quantum theory with zero-point energy lead to the value $(n_\xi+\frac{1}{2})\,h\sqrt{v_o^2+\lambda} + (n_\eta+\frac{1}{2})\,h\sqrt{v_o^2-\lambda}$ for the energy of this system, and to the equations
$$\xi_o = \left\{(n_\xi+\frac{1}{2})h/2\pi^2 m\sqrt{v_o^2+\lambda}\right\}^{\frac{1}{2}}$$
and
$$\eta_o = \left\{(n_\eta+\frac{1}{2})h/2\pi^2 m\sqrt{v_o^2-\lambda}\right\}^{\frac{1}{2}}$$
for the amplitudes. Each of the quantum numbers n_ξ and n_η can assume the values 0, 1, 2, $\ldots$. Since neither ξ_o nor η_o can vanish, even when the quantum number is zero, the oscillators show the phenomenon of classical resonance in every quantized state.

The stationary states of a harmonic oscillator in quantum mechanics are described by wave functions $\psi_o(x)$, $\psi_1(x)$, $\psi_2(x)$, $\ldots,\psi_n(x)$, $\ldots$, corresponding to the energy values $(n+\frac{1}{2})hv_o$, with integral values for the quantum number n. The wave functions $\psi_n(x)$ are the successive Hermite orthogonal functions. The system of two equivalent coupled harmonic oscillators (with the same frequency) can be treated rigorously by use of the co-ordinates ξ and η, and the correct wave functions for the system are $\psi_{n_\xi}(\xi)\psi_{n_\eta}(\eta)$, the energy values being the same as for the old quantum theory, as given above. In this discussion of the system there is no need to mention resonance. However, the system may also be treated by a perturbation method, based on the wave functions $\psi_{n'}(x_1)\psi_{n''}(x_2)$ for the unperturbed system, with no coupling between the oscillators. For the normal state of the system, with $n'=n''=0$, there is only one wave function. There are, however, two independent wave functions, $\psi_o(x_1)\psi_1(x_2)$ and $\psi_1(x_1)\psi_o(x_2)$, for the next energy level; these functions correspond to states in which one oscillator has small energy, $\frac{1}{2}hv_o$, and the other has larger energy, $3/2hv_o$. It is found on treating the system of coupled oscillators that these functions are not satisfactory approximations to the correct wave functions representing the two slightly different energy levels of the system, but that their normalized sum and difference, $\frac{1}{\sqrt{2}}[\psi_o(x_1)\psi_1(x_2)+\psi_1(x_1)\psi_o(x_2)]$ and $\frac{1}{\sqrt{2}}[\psi_o(x_1)\psi_1(x_2)-\psi_1(x_1)\psi_o(x_2)]$, are satisfactory; the first wave function, symmetrical in the two co-ordinates x_1 and x_2, represents the more stable of the two states, and the second, antisymmetrical in x_1 and x_2 (changing sign when x_1 and x_2 are interchanged), represents the less stable state. Each of these states is a hybrid of the two structures represented by $\psi_o(x_1)\psi_1(x_2)$ and $\psi_1(x_1)\psi_o(x_2)$, and, from analogy with the classical system, it has become customary to describe these hybrid states as resonance hybrids. This description is applied also to other quantum-mechanical systems which are conveniently discussed by a similar perturbation method, even though there is no close classical analogue for them.

The arbitrary nature of quantum-mechanical resonance is evident from the foregoing paragraphs. The system of coupled harmonic oscillators can be treated rigorously without mentioning resonance. It is for convenience, resulting from knowledge of the unperturbed wave functions, that these functions are used in the perturbation treatment. Quantum-mechanical resonance is not a property of a system, but of a system in relation to structures which are assumed as the basis for its discussion. In chemistry the theory of resonance is used primarily as an aid in discussing the structure and properties of complex molecules in terms of simple molecules. Simple structures similar to those which have been assigned to simple molecules are assumed as the basis for the discussion of complex molecules; and often when no one of the simple structures is satisfactory, a resonance hybrid can be formulated which represents the complex molecule in a satisfying and useful way.

The arbitrariness mentioned above is not characteristic of the theory of resonance in chemistry, but is shared by it with other branches of structural theory. It is recognized now that the structures of molecules may be correctly described by the quantum-mechanical wave functions pertaining to their normal states, and that the structural formulas assigned by chemists are symbols for the wave functions. For nearly a century chemists have written the simple valence-bond formulas $H-H$ for molecular hydrogen, $Cl-Cl$ for molecular chlorine and $H-Cl$ for hydrogen chloride. The dash in the formulas $H-H$ and $Cl-Cl$ is a symbol for wave functions describing the normal states of these diatomic molecules formed of identical atoms. The normal state of the hydrogen chloride molecule is, of course, correctly described by its wave function, and this wave function is not rigorously related to the wave functions of the hydrogen molecule and the chlorine molecule. Nevertheless, chemists have found it convenient to assign the structural formula $H-Cl$ to the molecule with use of a dash like that used in the formulas $H-H$ and $Cl-Cl$, and to describe the hydrogen chloride molecule, like the hydrogen molecule and the chlorine molecule, as involving a single valence bond. Thus the valence-bond structural theory, which has been of great value in the development of chemistry, is an arbitrary approximate representation of the wave functions that alone correctly represent the molecules. It is conceivable that a system of symbols much different from the valence-bond dashes could be developed that would correspond just as well to the wave functions, but in fact a satisfactory alternative system of this sort has not been discovered, and chemists continue to use the valence-bond theory.

The theory of resonance in chemistry has been subjected to criticism because of its arbitrariness. The critics may not have recognized that, as mentioned above, the same criticism applies to the whole of structural theory. A structural formula for a nonresonating molecule such as ethane is a rough description of the wave function in terms of wave functions involving first a hydrogen nucleus, a carbon nucleus and a pair of electrons, and second two carbon nuclei (each with its inner shell of K electrons) and a pair of electrons. In the same way the structural formula for the resonating molecule benzene is a rough description of the wave function of benzene as a sum of valence-bond wave functions similar to the one assigned to ethane; the two Kekulé structures and other structures that are hybridized in the resonance representation of the benzene molecule do not correspond separately to states of the benzene molecule, but are symbols that, taken together, provide a rough description of the wave function of the molecule in its normal state.

The theory of resonance is of value in chemistry in the discussion not only of the configuration of molecules, interatomic distances, electric dipole moments, force constants of bonds and similar molecular-structural properties, but also of thermodynamic stability (as of aromatic substances, conjugated systems, free radicals), strengths of acids and bases, existence of tautomers, and chemical properties in general.

BIBLIOGRAPHY.—L. Pauling, *The Nature of the Chemical Bond and the Structure of Molecules and Crystals* (2nd ed., 1940); G. W. Wheland, *The Theory of Resonance and Its Application to Organic Chemistry* (1944).   (L. C. P.)

RESONANCE ENERGIES, also resonance potentials, are general expressions denoting energy differences between the stationary states of atoms, molecules and atomic nuclei. The term resonance was first applied because of the apparent analogy between acoustical or electrical resonance (*q.v.*) and the selective absorption or emission of certain light frequencies by these microscopic systems. Since the energy absorbed is proportional to the frequency, the microscopic system can only absorb or emit particular selected amounts of energy, which carry it from one stationary state of internal energy (or potential) to another; this holds whether the energy is the radiant energy in a particle of radiation or the kinetic energy of motion in a colliding particle of matter which hits the microscopic system.

In structural chemistry, however, the "resonance energy" of a molecule has quite a different meaning. It refers to the deviation of the energy of formation of a molecule from a hypothetical ideal energy which is conceived as the sum of the energies of its parts. Here the term resonance is supposed to be drawn from a branch of quantum theory and is only distantly related to acoustical or mechanical resonance.   (J. R. Pt.)

RESORCINOL, also called resorcin, is metadihydroxybenzene, $C_6H_4(OH)_2$. It was first obtained in 1864 by H. Hlasiwetz and L. Barth by the potash fusion of certain natural resins (galbanum, asafoetida, etc.). It crystallizes in colourless rhombic prisms or plates, which dissolve readily in water, alcohol or ether and sparingly in benzene. It melts at $110°$ C. and boils at $276.5°$ C. at 759.7 mm., or $178°$ C. at 16 mm.; its density is 1.287 at $15°$ C. It has a sweet taste, and its aqueous solution gives a deep-violet coloration with ferric chloride.

Resorcinol is an important commercial product and is manufactured in large quantities from benzene. The general procedure consists in sulphonating benzene with fuming sulphuric acid to benzene metadisulphonic acid and fusing the sodium salt of this acid with caustic soda at a relatively high temperature. The crude resorcinol is ex-

tracted, preferably with ether, from an aqueous solution of the fusion mass neutralized with a mineral acid. Technical resorcinol is obtained by boiling off the solvent and vacuum distilling the crude resorcinol. It is purified by sublimation or by recrystallization from a strong aqueous solution.

Resorcinol is used in the manufacture of resins, plastics, adhesives, dyes, explosives, cosmetics, pharmaceuticals and as an intermediate in the synthesis of many other organic compounds.

By the second half of the 20th century, the biggest use for resorcinol was in making adhesive resins and plastics. These resorcinol-formaldehyde-type resins are cold setting and are used with a catalyst or hardener. They will bond wood and many other materials at contact pressure. Although these resins had been known for a long time, the technique of controlling them was not solved until the early 1940s. During World War II they played an important part in marine, aircraft and other types of construction.

Resorcinol is a component in some azo dyes. It couples readily with diazo compounds. Two moles of diazo compound can be coupled in succession with one mole of resorcinol. It is also condensed with phthalic anhydride to produce fluorescein, and through this the various dyes of the eosin and rhodamine types. By condensing with *p*-nitrosodimethylaniline hydrochloride (on the fibre) it yields an oxazine dye. The dinitroso derivative of resorcinol is fast green or Alsace green.

Resorcinol has some antiseptic properties and is used in solutions and ointments for chronic skin diseases such as psoriasis and eczema and as a urinary antiseptic. In large doses resorcinol causes giddiness, deafness, salivation, sweating and convulsions. When applied externally to large surfaces it is dangerous and even fatal. Appreciable quantities of resorcinol are used in making hexylresorcinol, an antiseptic of germicidal value; beta-methyl-umbelliferone, a sun-screening agent; and lead styphnate, the lead salt of trinitroresorcinol, a powerful detonator used in the manufacture of sporting ammunition.

BIBLIOGRAPHY.—I. M. Heilbron, ed., *Dictionary of Organic Compounds* (1934–38); A. Davidson, *Intermediates for Dyestuffs* (1926); P. H. Groggins, ed., *Unit Processes in Organic Synthesis*, 2nd ed. (1938), *Plastics and Resins* (Dec. 1944); *Plastics News Letter*, vol. 5, p. 1 (1945); *J.A.C.S.*, vol. 43, p. 348 (1921), vol. 48, p. 1688 (1926); *J. Ind. and Eng. Chem.*, vol. 12, p. 857 (1920).   (C. B. Bl.)

RESPIGHI, OTTORINO (1879–1936), Italian composer, was born at Bologna on July 9, 1879, and studied at the Liceo of Bologna, at St. Petersburg (Leningrad) under Rimsky-Korsakov and in Berlin under Max Bruch. In 1913 he was made professor at the Conservatorio di S. Cecilia in Rome, and in 1923 director. The operas *Semirama* (1910) and *La Bella addormentata* (1922) were followed by the successful *Belfagor* (1923), which reflects in the eclecticism of its style the cosmopolitan character of the composer's training. His orchestral music includes the symphonic poems *Fontane di Roma* (1917), *Pini di Roma* (1924) and *Vetrate di chiesa* (1927); in the way of chamber music he wrote a sonata for violin and pianoforte and two string quartets, while a *Concerto gregoriano* for violin and orchestra may also be mentioned.

RESPIRATION. The conception of life is so closely bound up with that of respiration that the very word "expiration" has come to connote the extinction of life, and "inspiration" its elevation to a superhuman level. Respiration is a process common to all forms of animal life, the reason for which is that the chemical basis of life is essentially an oxidation of tissue. Rightly, we speak of the "flame" of life, for in the body, as in the fire, material is all the while being consumed, with concurrent consumption of oxygen, and the production of carbon dioxide. Respiration consists essentially in the transport of oxygen from the air to the place where the oxygen is used up by the body, and the transport of carbon dioxide from the place where it is produced to the external air. Many animals, of course, live in water; indeed, life presumably began in that medium. But even for them the ultimate source of oxygen is the atmosphere; from it the water acquires fresh stocks of oxygen as the animals which inhabit it use up the gas. The oxygen in water is for the most part in solution, not in bubbles; but in the sea the constant breaking of the waves has a most potent effect in oxygenating the surface layers of the water. In the primitive forms of life respiration is simple. In the amoeba, which is little more than a minute particle of jelly, the respiratory process is carried on in this way: the amoeba lives in water, from the water oxygen soaks into the body of this animalcule, where it is always being used up, and because it is always being so used the potential of oxygen inside the amoeba is always less than the potential of oxygen in the water outside. The oxygen, therefore, by a simple process of diffusion, is ever tending to migrate from the place of higher to that of lower potential, *i.e.*, from the water to the interior of the amoeba, so a constant stream of gas is maintained. So also with the carbon dioxide; it is produced in the amoeba, from the interior of which it diffuses out, through the surface into the surrounding water.

In the higher forms of life, there is no different principle involved, so far as is known, from that of the amoeba. The apparatus for effecting respiration becomes more complicated, but the actual process is the same, namely, the *diffusion* of gas, oxygen or carbon dioxide from the place of higher to the place of lower potential.

THE SUPPLY OF BLOOD TO THE LUNG

The necessity for some definite system of transport arises partly from the greater size of animals as compared with the amoeba, and partly from the greater intensity of their oxidative processes. The inhabitants of an island a mile square would need no special transport system for the carriage of their fish, but the population of a continent does, and not only the mere machinery for moving the fish but all the accessory apparatus of cold storage and the rest for moving it in good condition. Moreover, if the continent be inhabited by persons with an insatiable craving for fish the capacity of the transport system must be correspondingly increased.

In the more lowly organized aquatic animals the system of transport is as follows: A circulation is maintained throughout the animal of fluid which differs little from seawater. At some point, known as the gill, this circulation comes very near to the surface, being only separated from the seawater by the wall of the vessel in which it is coursing. That wall is no thicker than the body of the amoeba, and so the gases, oxygen and carbon dioxide, have no difficulty in diffusing into and out of the circulating fluid. The amount of gas which can be dealt with depends principally on the extent of the surface of circulating fluid that can be exposed at any one time to the water. Therefore, for the purpose of creating the maximal surface, the gills of some creatures take on curious and feathery forms. Such are those of the lobster, which may be seen by breaking away the shell at the side. Indeed, the surface is so great that the water around the gill would be completely denuded of oxygen were there not a special mechanism for ensuring a constant circulation of fresh water, carrying a continuous supply of oxygen-charged water over the surface of the gill feathers.

The gill system of the lobster exhibits the principles on which the respiratory systems of almost all the higher animals are based, *i.e.*, the exposure of a large surface of fluid which circulates in the animal (the blood) to a corresponding large surface of either air or water which is constantly being replenished. The oxygen-containing medium and the circulating blood are not in actual contact, but are separated from one another by a membrane through which the oxygen (and carbon dioxide) must diffuse. One section of the animal kingdom has attempted a respiratory system on different lines, namely, the insects. In them the air is piped all over the interior body to, or almost to, the actual functioning cells. There is no intermediary circulating fluid. The whole tissues of the insects are therefore permeated by an elaborate system of tubes, the tracheae, with walls stiff enough to prevent their collapsing. The tracheal tubes are often extremely narrow in bore. This system has grave limitations. The rate at which gases can diffuse along very fine tubes is very slow, and sufficient oxygen can only penetrate, therefore, for a short length. No portion of the insect, therefore, can be far removed from the external air, and for that reason all insects are small; the largest development of which they seem capable is that of the dragon fly, which has a relatively long but extremely attenuated body. Developmentally the insects are side-tracked.

To return to the normal line of development, the principles of respiration are simply portrayed in such an air breathing animal as the newt (fig. 1a). Imagine a grape with a tubular stalk and with air inside the skin instead of fruit, and you have something like the lung of the newt. In the substance of the wall the blood circulates, a large surface being exposed in a close network of capillaries to the air in the lung, which air is intermittently forced in and out of the lung by swallowing movements on the part of the newt, the stalk of the lung (or trachea) being an outgrowth of the gullet.

Leaving for the moment the consideration of the circulating fluid, we may follow two other lines of development: (1) the mechanism for increasing the amount of surface of fluid exposed to air and (2) the mechanism for perfecting the ventilation of the lung.

Mechanism for Increasing Exposed Surface of Fluid.— In the lung of the frog a much larger surface of blood can be exposed than in that of the newt, for the inner surface of the lung is thrown up into ridges, called septa. These again give rise to secondary and even tertiary septa, as is shown in fig. 1b. All these septa are richly supplied with blood capillaries.

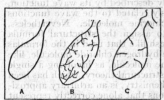

FIG. 1.—SCHEMATIC REPRESENTATION OF SECTIONS THROUGH LUNGS (A) Lung of the newt with no septa, (B) lung of frog showing primary, secondary and tertiary septa, (C) infundibulum of human lung showing primary septa

The lung of the warm blood animals is more complicated still. It may be likened, not to a grape, but to a bunch of grapes—indeed to several bunches of grapes. The unit corresponding to a single grape is called the infundibulum. That corresponding to a bunch the lobule. Each infundibulum is intermediate in structure between the whole lung of the newt and that of the frog. It contains septa, but only primary septa (fig. 1c). These divide the margin of the infundibulum into a number of chambers, the alveoli. The interior of the infundibulum is, therefore, a sort of honeycomb, the alveoli corresponding to the cells of the comb; indeed, they are often called the air cells. In microscopical sections of the lung the air cells are cut across in all sorts of quite irregular ways, but the general appearance much resembles that of a section of a rather broken honeycomb (fig. 2).

Before birth the whole lung is folded up, the opposing walls of the air cells are in contact with one another and there is, of course, no air in the lung. Such a lung will sink if thrown into water, in which respect it is in marked contrast to the normal organ. It is one of the abiding mysteries of creation, that, when the new born child expands his lungs for the first time, the whole system of lobulae, infundibula and alveoli unfolds and fills with air. From that time onwards air is always passing into and out of the lung. The quantity taken in at each respiration is called the tidal air and is normally about 300–550 cu.cm. Of this about 150 cu.cm. never goes further than the respiratory passages; the remainder becomes mixed up with the air in the air cells (alveolar air) of which there is, perhaps, three litres in the lung. The following table gives the percentage composition of inspired and alveolar air:—

Component	CO_2	N_2	O_2	H_2O (vapour)
Inspired air . .	0·04	79	20·94	1
Alveolar air . .	5·3	74·1	14·4	6·2

There are several ways of measuring the composition of alveolar air. That of Haldane and Priestley consists of blowing with extreme suddenness and force down a rubber tube about 5 ft. in length and about 1 in. in diameter. The air from the respiratory passages passes first along the tube and is washed out by the air from the deeper parts of the lung. If the subject has emptied his lung to the maximum the tube, or at least, the portion next to his mouth will contain pure alveolar air. Immediately after the expiration, the tube is closed with the tongue. To it, about 1 in. from the mouth, is fitted a vacuous sampling tube; by the opening of a tap a sample of the air in the alveolar air tube can be taken into the sampling tube for analysis.

Residual air is the volume of air remaining in the chest after the most complete respiratory effort. It ranges from 1,600–2,100 cu.cm.

Reserve or *Supplemental Air* is the volume of air which can be expelled from the chest after an ordinary quiet respiration—about

1,500 cu.cm.

Complemental air is the volume of air that can be forcibly inspired over and above what is taken in by normal inspiration and is 1,600–2,100 cu.cm.

Vital capacity is the quantity of air which can be expelled from the lungs by the deepest possible expiration, after the deepest possible inspiration. It obviously includes the complemental, tidal and reserve airs. The vital capacity of 73 Air Force pilots in the British army, tabulated by Col. Flack, varied between 5,500 cu.cm. and 2,800 cu.cm. Considerable importance is attached to the vital capacity as an index of the suitability of pilots for high flying. *Vital capacity* is measured by means of a *spirometer*, a graduated gasometer into which air is blown from the lungs.

FIG. 2.—SECTION OF A NORMAL LUNG OF GOAT (B) The termination of a small branchiole

Lung Surface.—The whole surface presented by the walls of all the alveoli of a single human lung has been computed at about 1,000 sq.ft.; over the whole of this there is a compact network of capillaries, spread like a close pattern on a carpet. The blood in this vessel is separated from the air in the alveoli only by a membrane of almost inconceivable thinness.

Minute Volume of Blood.—The quantity of blood which reaches the lung in man is variously computed as being from 3–7 litres per minute during rest, and may be increased probably to 20 or 30 litres per minute or even more during exercise and in athletic persons. This blood comes from the right side of the heart, along the pulmonary artery, and parts with about 50 cu.cm. of carbon dioxide per litre in its transit of the lung. Simultaneously it picks up about the same amount of oxygen or rather more.

Provision, therefore, is required for air to ventilate the lung in sufficient quantity to carry off about 250 cu.cm. of carbon dioxide per minute during rest, and to supply about 300 cu.cm. of oxygen. Moreover this oxygen must be contributed without so far depleting the air itself as seriously to reduce the rate of diffusion.

In practice, the level of carbon dioxide in air of the alveoli is not allowed to rise above 5·5%, nor the oxygen to sink below about 14% at the sea level.

THE SUPPLY OF AIR TO THE LUNG

To accomplish these ends a ventilation through the respiratory system of about 7 litres of air per minute must be maintained during rest, which may be increased up to something like 100 litres per minute during violent exercise. The primitive method of ventilation is quite inadequate for the needs of warm blooded animals. The frog carries out the following routine: (1) It fills its mouth with air; (2) closes its nostrils; (3) forces the air in the mouth into the lungs, which become distended; (4) opens the nostrils and lets out the air so that the lung partially collapses. Both the bird and the mammal have invoked the muscles of the body for the purpose of evolving special and efficient mechanisms

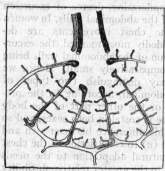

FIG. 2A.—DIAGRAM OF BRONCHIOLAR TERMINATION OR ATRIUM WITH INFUNDIBULA OPENING OFF

by which to ventilate the lungs. Their mechanisms are, however, very different, not to say contrary. The bird, like the mammal, possesses a trachea which branches into bronchi, but whereas in the vertebrate each bronchus supplies one lung and that alone, in the birds each bronchus leads not only to a lung but to a series of air sacs which ramify over a great part of the body, even penetrating the bones (see *Diverticula* in fig. 3), which gives an idea of the size and situation of the air sacs. The function of the air sacs appears to the present author to be incompletely understood. The following quotation expresses the state of knowledge on the subject:—

"In the bird the chest does not exist as a separate chamber. Expiration is effected by the thoracic and abdominal muscles,

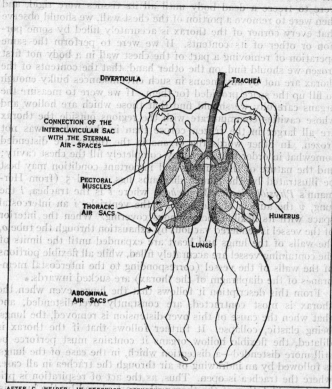

FIG. 3.—DIAGRAM OF THE LUNGS AND AIR SACS OF THE PIGEON

which compress the thorax and abdomen, driving the air from the air sacs, through the lungs and trachea. Inspiration is effected by the elastic expansion of the thorax and abdomen on relaxation of the muscles; this expansion causes an inrush of air along the

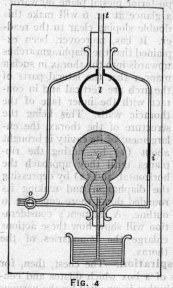

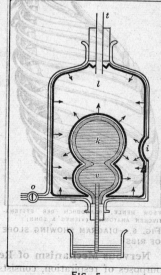

FIG. 4.

FIG. 5.

trachea and lungs into the air sacs, the lungs being thus filled with fresh air." The above description, given by Marshall and Hurst, refers to the bird at rest; when flying the movements of the wings probably have an important effect on inflating and deflating the chest.

Mechanics of Respiration.—The mammal has elaborated a very special mechanism for the inhalation and exhalation of air.

By means of the diaphragm the portion of the body cavity which contains the lungs, the heart and the great vessels is shut off from the rest. The thorax is practically a closed box entirely filled by the lungs, heart and other structures contained within it. If we were to freeze a dead body until all its tissues were rigid, and then were to remove a portion of the chest wall, we should observe that every corner of the thorax is accurately filled by some portion or other of its contents. If we were to perform the same operation of removing a part of the chest wall in a body not first frozen we should find, on the other hand, that the contents of the thorax are not by any means in such circumstances bulky enough to fill up the space provided for them. If we were to measure the organs carefully we should find that those which are hollow and whose cavities communicate with the regions outside the thorax are all larger in the frozen corpse than in that which was not frozen. In other words the organs in the thorax are distended somewhat in order that they may completely fill the chest cavity; and the nature of this curious and important condition may best be illustrated by the simple diagrams figs. 4 and 5 (from Hermann's *Physiologie des Menschen*) where *t* is the trachea, *l* the lung, *v* the auricle of the heart, *k* the ventricle, *i* an intercostal space with its flexible membranous covering. When the interior of the vessel is rendered vacuous by exhaustion through the tube *o*, the walls of the lungs and heart are expanded until the limits of the containing vessel are accurately filled, while all flexible portions of the walls of the vessel (corresponding to the intercostal membranes of the diaphragm of the thorax) are sucked inwards.

From this description it follows that the lungs, even when the thorax is most contracted, are constantly over-distended, and that when the cause of this over-distension is removed, the lungs, being elastic, collapse. It further follows that if the thorax is dilated, the flexible hollow organs it contains must perforce be still more distended—a distention which, in the case of the lungs, is followed by an indrawing of air through the trachea in all cases where the trachea is open. Thus, as the act of respiration is primarily a dilatation of the thorax, the part played by the lungs is, as Galen knew, a purely passive one.

How is dilatation of the thorax effected? It has been pointed out that the rib-planes decline from the horizontal in two directions, viz., from behind forwards, and from the antero-posterior mesial plane outwards; a glance at fig. 6 will make this double sloping clear to the reader. It has, moreover, been explained that the diaphragm arches upwards into the thorax in such a manner that the lateral parts of the arch are vertical and in contact with the inner face of the thoracic walls. This being the structure of the thorax, the enlargement of its cavity is brought about (1) by raising the rib-planes until they approach the horizontal, and (2) by depressing the diaphragm and making its rounded dome more cone-like in outline. A moment's consideration will show how these actions enlarge the boundaries of the thorax.

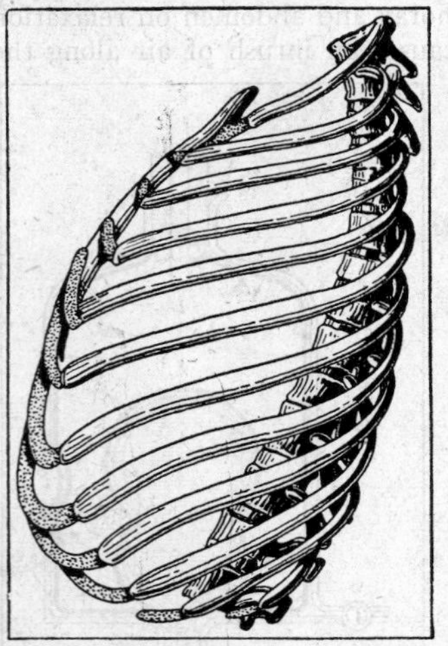

FROM HENLE, "HANDBUCH DER SYSTEMA-TISCHEN ANATOMIE" (VIEWEG & SOHN)
FIG. 6.—DIAGRAM SHOWING SLOPE OF RIBS

Nervous Mechanism of Respiration.—The chest, then, for purposes of respiration, consists of a box which dilates and contracts rhythmically; the actual rhythm is supplied by the nervous system. Physiologists are not agreed as to the precise rôle which the brain plays, but the following conception has much to recommend it. There is in the medulla oblongata a "centre," *i.e.*, something analogous to a telephone exchange from which rhythmical messages pass down the nerves which connect it with the muscles of respiration. The principal nerves in question are the phrenic (4th cervical) nerves which supply the diaphragm and the intercostal nerves which supply the intercostal muscles. If the mechanism consisted merely of this centre and the motor nerves which it operates, respiration would be of a very curious type; for, apart from controlling influences, the natural rhythm of the centre is one which produces a series of gasps at slow intervals. Pursuing the analogy of the telephone exchange, the particular centre immediately responsible for the primitive gasping type of respiration, and known as the "respiratory" centre, is of the nature of a local exchange and is governed by two other centres in the brain, each of which modifies the natural gasping rhythm. One such centre imparts an inspiratory bias to the gasping rhythm, so that the respiration of an animal possessing these two centres, and these only, consists of infrequent respiratory efforts between which the lung is distended and therefore full of air. The third centre in the brain imparts the smoothness and a rate which gives respiration a more normal character.

Even so, there are other influences which conspire to impart the usual rhythm to breathing. They come from without the central nervous system, and the most important of them arrive from the lung itself, along the vagus nerve.

As has been shown by Hering and Breuer, and by Head, at each phase of respiration a message is sent from the lung up the vagus. The precise nature of this message is unknown, whether it merely demands the termination of that particular phase, or whether it demands the initiation of the next, or both, is uncertain; the certain thing is that the change from inspiration to expiration (and vice versa) which would take place in time apart from vagus influences, is accelerated by them, so that respiration is more rapid and less deep with the vagi intact than with them cut. Animals will, however, live for a long time without their vagi, and when they die it is not because the power of respiration is deficient. Of the other nerves which lead to the brain, that which most influences respiration is the fifth cranial nerve, as is shown when strong ammonia is placed beneath the nose. The sensory nerves from almost any part of the skin, too, can influence respiration, as when cold water is suddenly dashed on to the surface of the body.

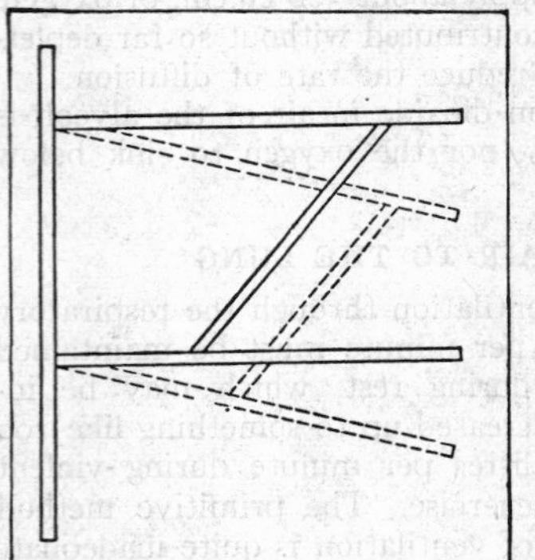

FIG. 7.—MODEL OF PAIR OF RIBS

Types of Respiration.—The visible characters of respiration in man vary considerably according to age and sex. In men, while there is a moderate degree of upheaval of the chest, there is a considerable, although not preponderating, degree of excursion of the abdominal walls. In women the chest movements are decidedly most marked, the excursion of the abdominal walls being comparatively small. Hence we may distinguish two types of respiration, the costal and the abdominal, according to the preponderance of movement of one or the other part of the body wall. In forced respiration the type is costal in both sexes, and so it is also in sleep. The cause of this difference between men and women has been variously ascribed (*a*) to constriction of the chest by corsets in women, (*b*) to a natural adaptation to the needs of childbearing in women, and (*c*) to the greater relative flexibility of the ribs in women permitting a wider displacement under the action of the inspiratory muscles.

In healthy breathing the mouth should be closed and the ingoing current should all pass through the nose. When this happens the nostrils become slightly expanded with each inspiration, probably by the action of the M. dilatores naris. In some people this movement is hardly perceptible unless breathing be heavy or laboured. As the air passes at the back of the throat behind the soft palate it causes the velum to wave very gently in the current; this is a purely passive movement. If we look at the glottis or opening into the larynx during respiration, as we may readily do with the help of a small mirror held at the back of the throat, we may notice that the glottis is wide open during inspiration and that it becomes narrower by the approximation of the vocal chords during expiration. This alteration is produced by the action of the laryngeal muscles. Like the movements of the nostril, those of the larynx are almost imperceptible in some people during ordinary breathing, but are very well marked in all during forced respiration.

GASEOUS EXCHANGE

The extent of gaseous exchange in man varies greatly with the size and age of the person, the degree of activity, etc.

	O_2 consumption in cu. cm. per min. at o° C and 76 mm. (Haldane)	CO_2 production in cu. cm. per min. at o° C and 76 mm. (Haldane)	Litres of air breathed per min. at 37° C, moist and at the prevailing barometric pressure
Rest in bed . . .	237	197	7·67
Rest—standing . . .	328	264	10·4
Walking on grass:			
2 miles an hour . .	780	662	18·6
3 ,, ,, ,, . .	1,065	992	24·8
4 ,, ,, ,, . .	1,595	1,398	37·3
4½ ,, ,, ,, . .	2,005	1,788	46·5
5 ,, ,, ,, . .	2,543	2,386	60·9

The absolute minimum of oxygen consumption for any person is known as the basal metabolism and is that which takes place when the person is at rest in bed some ten hours after a meal. The basal metabolism in persons of different size, but otherwise comparable, varies not proportionately to the weight but to the body surface (*see* ANIMAL HEAT) and is therefore expressed in calories (*i.e.*, in units of heat produced) or in oxygen consumed per square metre of body surface per hour.

The basal metabolism varies with age, thus:

Mean age (years)	Basal metabolism per sq. metre per hour	
	Calories	Oxygen used litres (approx.)
6	57·5	11·7
12·6	50·4	10·3
13·7	49·4	10·1
16·5	43	8·73
19·25	40·7	8·30

In warm blooded animals the total ventilation varies with the size of the organism, being more intense the smaller the creature.

	Man	Goat	Rabbit	Guinea pig	Rat	Mouse
Total ventilation in litres per kg. per minute	·1	·2	·4	·6	1·5	5·1

The reason is as follows: The capacity for heat loss depends upon the superficial area of the animal. The heat production naturally must equal the heat loss; therefore the heat production must also vary with the superficial area, *i.e.*, in some way proportionally to the square of the linear dimensions on the animal. The weight, however, bears in proportion not to the square but to the cube; therefore, as the animal gets larger its area becomes relatively less proportionally to its weight, *i.e.*, the heat production, and therefore the degree of oxidation per gram of animal diminishes as the size increases. If the amount of oxygen required per gram of animal diminishes, the whole mechanism for its supply and therefore the total ventilation will diminish correspondingly.

The exchange of gases in the lung is regarded by almost all authorities as being a process of *diffusion*, the oxygen diffusing from the alveolar air through the pulmonary epithelium into the blood which circulates through the capillaries in the alveolar wall. (The most notable opponents of this view are Dr. J. S. Haldane, F.R.S., and some of those who have been associated with him. His views are fully set forth in his book *Respiration*.) The carbon dioxide likewise is regarded as passing by diffusion out of the

blood into the alveolar air.

Transport of the Oxygen.—Oxygen constitutes about 14% of the moist air which fills the pulmonary alveoli and therefore exerts a pressure of a little over 100 mm. of mercury. In order that blood exposed to so low a pressure should carry away any considerable quantity of the gas, it must needs be a fluid possessing very special qualities. These qualities blood owes to the red pigment in the corpuscles—haemoglobin. This material can unite with large quantities of oxygen at a pressure not exceeding 100 mm. of mercury and so leaves the lung charged with oxygen. But what is more remarkable—haemoglobin gives up this oxygen again when exposed to lower oxygen pressures. Thus, at about 30 mm. of mercury the blood surrenders one-half of the oxygen united to it; at 20 mm. it gives up about three-quarters and so on. The curve which represents the relation between the quantity of oxygen united with the haemoglobin in blood, and the pressure of oxygen to which the blood is exposed, is called the oxygen dissociation curve.

There is one synthetic substance which attaches oxygen to itself if exposed to more than a certain critical pressure of that gas and from which the oxygen escapes if the oxygen pressure drops below the critical point—that substance which has recently been discovered by Prof. Moureu is rubrine, a complicated hydrocarbon. Though rubrine and haemoglobin seem to unite with oxygen after a manner not wholly dissimilar and, so far as other oxides are concerned, unique, they are otherwise not at all alike. Rubrine consists of three benzine rings united in a way not at present ascertained. Haemoglobin consists of a protein united with haematin, a substance which contains iron on the one hand and four pyrrol rings on the other. Moreover, it is clear from spectroscopic and other evidence, that the attachment of the oxygen to the haemoglobin has some relation both to the iron and to the pyrrol constitution of the substance. The constitution and properties of haemoglobin are of great theoretical importance because, but for it, the warm blooded animal could never have developed the high degree of vitality which he possesses. Oxy-

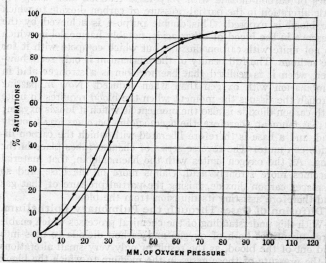

FIG. 8.—OXYGEN DISSOCIATION CURVES—ARTERIAL BLOOD AND VENOUS BLOOD (ADAPTED FROM HALDANE)
Ordinate represents percentage and saturation with oxygen, Abscisse, pressure of oxygen in mm. of mercury

gen is so insoluble in water that, apart from haemoglobin, blood could only carry to the tissues about one-sixtieth part of the quantity of oxygen which it does; therefore to maintain oxidation in the tissues at its normal level 60 times as much blood would have to circulate as at present. As the blood already forms one-fifteenth of the weight of the body, without haemoglobin it must needs form four times the weight of the rest of the body—an impossible burden. There are in the lower forms of life some respiratory pigments not altogether dissimilar from haemoglobin. In the blood of some worms, for instance, is found a material chlorocruorin, which is really a form of haemoglobin, but possessed of a somewhat different scaffold of porphyrin. In some of the molluscs is found haemocyanin, also a protein body containing not iron but copper, and which, moreover, contains no porphyrin. These bodies like haemoglobin possess the power of condensing, transporting and yielding oxygen under suitable conditions. The exact affinity of haemoglobin for oxygen is an example of nice adjustment of the conditions under which the haemoglobin is found to the needs of the body. The affinity varies according to the saline concentration of the medium in which the haemoglobin is dissolved, according to the hydrogen ion concentration and according to the temperature. Moreover, there appears to be an assortment of haemoglobins specific to the forms of life in which they are found, and which have affinities for oxygen suitable to those forms of life.

Transport of the Carbon Dioxide.—Carbon dioxide, unlike oxygen, is carried largely in the plasma; a small quantity is in physical solution, but the major portion is in chemical combination as sodium bicarbonate. The relative quantities in solution and in chemical combination regulate the reaction (degree of acidity or alkalinity) of the blood. The equation which connects the concentration of hydrogen ions c_H to the concentration of carbon dioxide (CO_2) in solution, V_{CO_2} and in chemical combination B_{CO_2} is

$$c_H = k_1 \frac{V_{CO_2}}{B_{CO_2}}$$

It is often expressed logarithmically as:

$$-P_H = Pk_1 + \log V_{CO_2} - \log B_{CO_2}.$$

To say that the carbon dioxide is present chiefly in chemical combination as sodium bicarbonate ($NaHCO_3$) gives but a partial picture of its relation to the blood. Such a combination by itself would be very stable, and while it might provide a medium of suitable hydrogen ion concentration would not present the all-important property of absorbing and parting with large quantities of carbon-dioxide with very little reaction and with very little alteration in the partial pressure of carbon dioxide to which the blood is exposed. This double purpose is achieved by the presence in the blood of other acids, notably haemoglobin, which do not unite with carbon dioxide, but which compete with it for the sodium. The full beauty of the mechanism is only seen, however, when it is realized that haemoglobin is a stronger acid in combination with oxygen than when reduced. Now in passing through the tissues the moment when the blood requires to unite with carbon dioxide is also the moment at which it looses oxygen; at that moment, therefore, the haemoglobin becomes less strongly acid, and a base is therefore liberated with which the carbon dioxide can unite. The reverse series of changes takes place in the lung. As the oxygen unites with the haemoglobin, that material becomes more strongly acid, claims more of the base, and so displaces carbon dioxide, raising the partial pressure of that gas and therefore assisting its diffusion from the blood.

Diffusion of Gases Through the Pulmonary Epithelium.—With this understanding of the chemical processes which enable large quantities both of oxygen and carbon dioxide to pass into and out of the blood, as the result of only very small alterations in the pressure of those gases in the medium to which the blood is exposed, let us return to the proof of the general thesis that the passage of gases through the pulmonary epithelium is due simply to diffusion.

The basal principle of diffusion is that the quantity of gas which passes through a given membrane depends upon the difference of pressure of the gas on the two sides of the membrane. Regarding the lung as a membrane through which gas diffuses, Q being the quantity of oxygen which will pass through it per minute, P the pressure of oxygen in the pulmonary alveoli, T the mean pressure of oxygen in the capillaries of the lung, and k a coefficient depending upon the area and nature of the lung, then

$$Q = k(P - T);$$

k may be defined as the quantity of gas in cubic centimetres which will pass through the pulmonary epithelium per minute, with a difference of pressure of 1 mm. of mercury between the oxygen on the two sides of the membrane.

If the diffusion theory is correct, then not only must P be always greater than T, but their relations must be such as to allow of quantities of oxygen ranging from 200 cu.cm. at rest to perhaps 3,000 during extreme activity, being driven through the pulmonary epithelium per minute. As all the quantities Q, k, P and T are susceptible of independent measurement, it should be possible to form a judgment of the applicability of the equation. The simplest case is the condition of rest. The following measurements of k are given for 11 men, all of good physique at rest.

DIFFUSION COEFFICIENT OF LUNG CU.CM. OF O2

Individual	(1)	(2)	(3)	(4)	(5)	(6)	(7)	(8)	(9)	(10)	(11)
D. C. of L.	25	32	36	38	42	43	43	43	45	45	65

Assuming that each of these men was absorbing 250 cu.cm. per minute, the mean difference of pressure ($P - T$) between the oxygen in the alveolar air and capillary blood would have to be

MEAN DIFFERENCE OF PRESSURE IN MM.

Individual	(1)	(2)	(3)	(4)	(5)	(6)	(7)	(8)	(9)	(10)	(11)
Mean	10	8	7	7	6	6	6	6	6·5	5·5	4

These figures lead to the conclusion that at rest the pressure of oxygen in the alveolar air exceeds the average pressure in the capillary blood by about 6 mm. of mercury in the majority of well-developed persons. The average pressure in the capillaries is, of course, less than the pressure in the arteries and greater than that in the veins. Other data known concerning the individuals on whom these experiments were made lead to the conclusion that 6 mm. for the value of ($P - T$) when Q is 250 cu.cm. may likely enough be correct. Greater difficulties arise when Q becomes, say, 2,500 cu.cm. during degrees of activity of which probably all the above persons would have been capable. If the diffusion coefficient still remains on the average 40 cu.cm. the value of ($P - T$) would become 62·5 mm. It is hardly possible that the pressure of oxygen in the lungs should exceed the average pressure in the capillaries by so great an amount. We are therefore thrown back upon the position that in violent exercise the diffusion coefficient must alter, and there seems little doubt that an alteration on a sufficient scale takes place.

The Regulation of Respiration.—When active exercise is taken both the depth and the rate of respiration are as a rule increased. The increase is effected by one or both of two mechanisms; of these the first to be considered is nervous, the second chemical. The nervous factor in the regulation of respiration has been well illustrated by the following experiment, devised by Krogh and Lindhart. The subject is placed on a bicycle ergometer of a special type, *i.e.*, a bicycle which, instead of progressing, is made to work against a brake, the actual work done being measured by the brake. In this case the brake was an electromotor, the resistance to the worker and hence the work which he performed in overcoming it could be regulated by adjustment of the current passed through the motor. When work was commenced there was an immediate increase in the rate of depth of respiration and also in the pulse rate. Had these alterations been due to the stimulating action of chemical products formed in the muscle on the respiratory centre, enough time must have elapsed to allow of the products being taken up by the blood, carried to the heart, passed through the lungs and driven to the brain. These processes would have occupied upwards of half a minute. In point of fact, the augmentation of respiration came about much more quickly—in about five seconds from the commencement of the exercise. An even more striking experiment of the same sort was the following: The apparatus being as before the subject was led to suppose that the load on the machine (and consequently the exercise he was to take) was to be suddenly and largely increased by throwing in a powerful current. Actually the current was not thrown in, though the pantomime of closing the switches, etc., was gone through. The pulse and respirations were augmented as before, though no extra work was done by the subject. Clearly, therefore, the increased respiratory efforts were not due to chemical products produced by the work.

The chemical regulation of respiration was first clearly set forth by Haldane and Priestly, the demonstration of it following immediately on their discovery of a satisfactory method of determining the composition of alveolar air. The essential point emerged that at various altitudes which ranged between that of the top of Ben Nevis and the bottom of the Dolcoath mine, although the percentage of carbon dioxide in the alveolar air alters, the percentage becoming lower as the barometric pressure increases, the actual partial pressure of carbon dioxide in the alveoli and hence the concentration of that gas in the blood remains at such altitudes almost unchanged. This constancy of the pressure of carbon dioxide in the alveolar air means that the greater the barometric pressure the more the carbon dioxide produced by the body is diluted in the lung. As the carbon dioxide produced by the body is approximately constant in amount, the total ventilation of the lung, and hence the respiratory efforts must be greater the higher the barometer and the lower the altitude. Any effort to increase the carbon dioxide pressure in the blood, as by inhaling carbon dioxide or shedding it into the blood as the result of muscular exercise, has the effect of stimulating the respiratory centre and increasing the respiratory efforts more especially as regards the depth of respiration.

Controversy has ranged round the question of whether carbon dioxide is a specific stimulus to the respiratory centre, or whether its presence in the blood acts indirectly and, by increasing the concentration of hydrogen ions, stimulates the centre; the hydrogen ions and not the carbon dioxide acting as the stimulus. In favour of the latter view is the fact that after violent exercise, when the hydrogen ion concentration of the blood is increased and concentration of carbon dioxide diminished (lactic acid being present in considerable quantities), breathing may still be very laboured. It is certain also that, as shown by Winterstein, the administration of other acids to animals will cause dyspnoea (laboured breathing). On the other hand, other acids do not produce at all so striking an effect as carbon dioxide.

It is probable that CO_2 does act not specifically but by virtue of its power of increasing the hydrogen ion concentration in the brain; and that its potency in this respect is due to the ease with which it diffuses from the blood into the tissue of the brain itself. It is ultimately the hydrogen ion concentration inside the nerve cells which constitute the respiratory centre which would affect their stimulation—a fact which has been stressed by Gesell. According to his conception, if the activity of the respiratory centre is heightened as the result of nervous impulses playing upon it, the cells themselves will work harder, produce more CO_2 and undergo a sort of secondary stimulation. In the language of wireless, the original nervous stimulus will be "amplified." Similarly, if the carbon dioxide in the blood be increased, that produced by the cells will be unable to escape and will stimulate the centre.

In the above description it has been assumed that the irritability of the cells, i.e., the degree of response which any particular stimulus will provoke, remains constant. This is not so in all circumstances. Many drugs, such as morphia, depress the centre, but the most interesting case of altered irritability of the centre is that of oxygen want (see ANOXAEMIA). If the respiratory centre be insufficiently supplied with oxygen over considerable periods of time the irritability is heightened, a given amount of exercise will then produce a much greater degree of breathlessness than it evokes in normal circumstances.

Temperature has an important effect upon respiration. This is less marked in man than in animals, which do not sweat; if the dog or goat, for instance, lies in the sun, shortly the respiration will become very rapid and shallow, a great volume of air will pass in and out of its respiratory passages, but the amount of air which ventilates the alveoli is not correspondingly increased. This alteration in the type of respiration (tachypnoea) may, in part be due to rise in the temperature of the blood. If this blood, as it passes through the carotid artery to the brain be warmed, tachypnoea results. But tachypnoea is probably also helped by a reflex nervous mechanism initiated by the actual heating of the skin, for it is claimed that the temperature of the blood may even be lowered. The purpose is clear. The heat loss is, of course, proportional to the amount of aqueous vapour which leaves the body, and the aqueous vapour in its turn is roughly proportional to the total ventilation. Therefore, by establishing a large total ventilation the body temperature is kept from rising, but if there were also a large alveolar ventilation the loss of carbon dioxide would be too great, the respiration being, however, shallow the alveolar ventilation is not greatly increased.

(J. BAR.)

Tissue Respiration is the consumption of oxygen accompanied by the production of carbon dioxide that occurs on combustion of foodstuffs by the tissues. The complete combustion of carbohydrates ends with the uptake of oxygen and production of CO_2 in equal quantities giving a respiratory quotient (R.Q. $= \frac{CO_2}{O_2}$) of one. $(C_6H_{12}O_6 + 6O_2 = 6CO_2 + 6H_2O)$. Combustion of fats and proteins give lower R.Q. values. Tissue respiration is measured according to methods devised by O. Warburg. Tissue respiration values, Q_{O_2}, Q_{CO_2}, are given as cubic millimetre per milligram dry weight per hour. The table gives values for respiration of rat tissues. Tissues of man give lower values.

Tissue (slices)	Q_{O_2}
Retina	30.5
Kidney	18.0
Heart, ventricle	12.6
Brain	12.0
Liver	10.0
Submaxillary gland	10.0
Small intestine	12.0
Lung	7.7
Diaphragm	7.0
Skeletal muscle	4.0
Skin	0.9

Oxygen is transported from the lungs to the tissues by the haemoglobin of the red blood cells, a ferroporphyrin protein, which combines reversibly with O_2 (haemoglobin $+ O_2 \rightleftharpoons$ oxyhaemoglobin). In muscle it is also transported by another pigment, myoglobin. Diffusion of oxygen from haemoglobin to the tissues and of CO_2 from the tissues to the blood is a rapid process regulated by the oxygen tension at the capillaries.

Since tissue respiration provides the energy necessary for the performance of cellular activities, respiration increases when the tissue is at work. The best example is muscle: at rest, respiration is low, 720 cu.mm. O_2 per gram per hour; during exercise it is increased threefold to fivefold. On the other hand, it has not yet been possible to measure the increase of respiration caused by brain activity. The increased oxygen requirement is met by an increase in the capillary bed, as shown by A. Krogh. In the resting organ relatively few of the capillaries are open; as the activity of the organ increases the number of open capillaries increases so that diffusion of oxygen to the tissues is greatly facilitated (for the mechanism by which the quantity of blood to organs is regulated, see VASCULAR SYSTEM). This process is also best seen in muscle. At the start of strong exercise the muscle, not having enough oxygen supply, is obliged to use fermentation (lactic acid formation) to provide energy for contraction, and an oxygen debt accumulates. After a time when the closed capillaries have opened and their surface is greatly increased, the oxygen supply becomes adequate and the lactic acid that accumulated disappears.

Tissues respond differently to changes in oxygen pressure, the brain and the heart being the most sensitive to low oxygen pressure (anoxia). Acute mountain sickness, which occurs on going to high altitudes, seems to be caused by the effect of anoxia upon the brain and the heart.

The combustion of foodstuff by oxygen is catalyzed by enzymes, which are systems—large in number—made up of a specific protein (dehydrogenase) and coenzymes (such as water-soluble vitamins of the B group—thiamin, riboflavin, niacin, pyridoxine, folic acid, pantothenic acid). Among these coenzymes riboflavin as flavoproteins, niacin as pyridine nucleotides, and iron-porphyrin-proteins as cytochromes and cytochrome oxidase perform the oxidation process, which is carried out step by step so as better to utilize the energy produced on oxidation. This stepwise oxidation is illustrated by the oxidation of a phosphorylated sugar, glucose, 6-phosphate. It is oxidized by triphosphopyridine nucleotide (step 1); the reduced nucleotide is oxidized by a flavoprotein (step 2); the reduced flavin is oxidized by cytochrome C (step 3); reduced cytochrome is oxidized by cytochrome oxidase (step 4); and, finally, reduced cytochrome oxidase is oxidized by oxygen (step 5). Hydrogen peroxide, which is produced during oxidation of foodstuff, is utilized by two iron-porphyrin enzymes: peroxidase, which catalyzes the oxidation of phenols and of aromatic amines by H_2O_2; and catalase, which catalyzes the oxidation of ethyl and methyl alcohols by H_2O_2 and also decomposes H_2O_2 into water and oxygen. Part of the energy provided by respiration is stored in the form of high-energy phosphate compounds, and part goes as heat. Tissue respiration is regulated by a number of factors, among which the hormones play the predominant role.

See O. Warburg (ed.), *Metabolism of Tumours* (London, 1930); A. Krogh, *Anatomy and Physiology of Capillaries* (1929).

(E. S. G. B.)

THE RESPIRATION OF INJURIOUS ATMOSPHERES

Carbon Dioxide.—Until within recent years it was supposed that carbon dioxide was harmful when inhaled even in small quantities. In any but the most recent textbooks the estimates of the quantity of air necessary for the efficient ventilation of a room are based on the assumption that the carbon dioxide present must not rise above a certain level. The figure usually given is 0·1%. This rule is probably not a bad one, but it is now known that carbon dioxide in such small quantities is quite innocuous and even in much greater quantities would have to be breathed before an injurious level was reached. Men can inhale 5% for some hours without suffering from much more than discomfort, and untutored persons would not be conscious of the presence of 2% of carbon dioxide in the air if it were otherwise pure.

The rule that the air of dwelling rooms should not contain more than 0·1% carbon dioxide is therefore useful, because air laden beyond that limit with carbon dioxide is also probably laden with other things to an injurious degree.

Meaning of "Ventilation."—Indeed the connotation of the word "ventilation" has been rendered somewhat vague by the more recent discoveries of science. If the use of the word be stretched to cover such sources of health as may be secured by the practice of opening the window, there are at least four such. (1) The removal of aqueous vapour; (2) the movement of air over the skin; (3) the removal of germs, and (4) the admission of ultra-violet rays of light.

Considering the above points, the benefits of ultra-violet rays are treated elsewhere (LIGHT AND RADIATIONS IN RELATION TO HEALTH). Here it is only necessary to say that ordinary window glass is relatively opaque to ultra-violet light and even specially manufactured glasses are often much less penetrable than is the open window. The beneficial effects of changing the air in a room on the disposition of germs has been demonstrated beyond dispute by experiments carried out by Leonard Hill. He dissipated a certain number of germs into a room with the windows shut; 20 min. later he exposed a plate of gelatine and found on it 39 germs. On a second occasion he dissipated the same number of germs into the room, opened the windows, and on exposure of the plate after 20 min. only one germ settled on it.

The advantage of keeping the air in motion may be illustrated by the following experience. On two successive days (on each of which the outside air was hot and still) a small over-crowded room was occupied for 8 hours by 11 typewriting clerks at work, a doctor and two experimenters. On the first day all avenues of ventilation were as far as possible closed, the chimney stuffed up, curtains put over the doors, etc., but the air in the room was actively circulated by electric fans. The percentage of carbon dioxide rose to about 2%. On the second day the fans were not in motion, but panes were abstracted from the windows. Chemical analysis showed that the air, though still, was pure. The stenographers who were unaware of the point of the experiment agreed

that the conditions were more tolerable the first day than the second, and examination of their work bore out that statement. The benefits of movement are probably due to two causes: (1) the actual stimulating effect of moving air passing over the skin, and (2) the fact that moving air evaporates moisture from the skin much more readily than still air. The relative importance of these factors probably differs much in different persons. The moral of the above experiment is not to disparage purity. It is to emphasize the necessity of combining purity with movement.

Carbon Monoxide and Coal Gas.—For the theory of carbon monoxide poisoning see ANOXAEMIA and BLOOD. Here it need only be said that the following are given as the percentages of carbon monoxide in the air which must be inhaled to produce the results stated.

Time and concentration	=	300 or less, no perceptible effect
,, ,, ,,	=	600, a just perceptible effect
,, ,, ,,	=	900, headache and nausea
,, ,, ,,	=	1,500, dangerous.

In the above table time is measured in hours and the concentration in parts of carbon monoxide per million of air. The figures assume that the subject is at rest and inhaling about seven litres of air per minute. If he is active and therefore inspiring greater quantities of air, the time necessary to produce death or unconsciousness is cut down directly in proportion to the magnification of the quantity of air breathed per minute.

In practice it is not easy to attain the concentrations of carbon monoxide necessary to produce fatal results. The experiments of Haldane have shown that the walls of ordinary dwelling rooms are quite permeable to the gas. This fact, together with the gradual movement of air, even through ill-ventilated rooms, as a rule prevents dangerous concentration of carbon monoxide being maintained, even where there is a slight escape of gas.

High Atmosphere Pressure.—Where men work under water at considerable depth, it is necessary to supply them with air at a pressure as great as, or greater than, the combined pressure of the atmosphere and of the water under which they are working. Unless the pressure be very high this in itself has no injurious effects and men may go confidently and quickly into such pressures; great care, however, must be exercised in emerging from a high atmospheric pressure into a normal one. The danger is due to the nitrogen dissolved in the blood. The quantity of this gas held in solution in the blood depends upon the pressure of oxygen to which the body is exposed. Normally, each litre of blood holds about 15 cu.cm. of nitrogen; at depths of 33 ft. under water the pressure of air in the diving apparatus would be two atmospheres, in which case each litre of blood would hold 30 cu.cm. of gas in solution. As the gas is not removed by the formation of any chemical compounds with other materials in the body, when the pressure is lowered it forms minute bubbles of nitrogen in the plasma. These bubbles when carried to the capillaries form emboli. Indeed, the danger is not confined to the blood, for if the worker be long enough exposed to the high pressure, all juices which permeate all the tissues of the body become charged with abnormally large quantities of nitrogen which, when the pressure is reduced, renders itself evident by the formation of small bubbles. These appear in many situations in the body, notably in nerve cells in the brain and elsewhere. Such bubbles are the cause of the condition known as "bends" associated with pain and paralysis, which may be even fatal.

Chlorine.—The inhalation of chlorine in concentration of more than one part per million of air for an indefinite period is dangerous; for half-an-hour the maximum allowable is four parts per million; 40 to 60 even for short periods is dangerous. Chlorine is typical of a number of gases which produce inflammation of the lungs, death being due not directly to the gas, but to asphyxia. It is of particular historic interest as being the first gas used on a large scale as a lethal weapon in war; clouds of the gas being liberated from cylinders in the German lines were carried by the favourable wind over to the lines of the Allied armies, where it produced the most devastating effect. More potent asphyxiants than chlorine, but much less used in commerce, are phosgene and chloropicrin. Other gases which act similarly are sulphuretted hydrogen, sulphur dioxide, nitrous acid and acid fumes.

Other Gases Having Deleterious Effects.—*Hydrocyanic or Prussic Acid* is much used for the fumigation of passenger steamers in port; for while poisonous to practically all forms of animal life, including vermin, it does not attack paint work. It is invisible and though it has a distinctive odour, the nose rapidly becomes deadened to the smell, so that persons may easily walk into stronger concentrations of the gas, being deceived by his nose into the idea that he is walking out of it. When the ship is opened up after fumigation particular care must be taken that fatal concentrations of the gas do not remain in pockets. Canaries are much more sensitive to HCN than men, and may be used to detect the gas.

Aniline, Nitrobenzine and other bodies which contain NH₂, NO, and NO₂ groups, are met with in the dye industry and in the manufacture of explosives; their action is to appropriate the haemoglobin of the blood, turning it temporarily into methaemoglobin. (*See* ANOXAEMIA.) The following table gives an idea of their toxicity.

	Parts per million of air		
	Nitrobenzine	Aniline	Toluidine
Slight symptoms after several hours exposure. Maximum amount that can be inhaled for 1 hour without serious disturbance . . .	0·2–0·4	7·0–26·0	6–23
	1·0	105–170	91–140

Sulphides of Arsenic, Phosphorus and Hydrogen.—*Arsene* sometimes contaminates the air in the vicinity of storage batteries, for the charging of which impure sulphuric acid is being used. Thus in submarines whole crews may be affected. The poison is a cumulative one; small quantities inhaled accumulate in the body until a toxic concentration is reached. *Phosphine* is evolved when water acts on calcium phosphide and is used as an illuminating gas, in buoys, etc. *Hydrogen sulphide* may contaminate the air in chemical works, but is more frequently the cause of accident in sewers, where sewer gas may accumulate in pockets. Toxicity:

	Parts per million parts of air		
	Arsine	Phosphine	Hydrogen sulphide
Maximum amount which can be inhaled for one hour . . .	50	100–200	200–300
Rapidly fatal . . .	250	2,000	1,000–3,000

Dichlordiethylsulphide—the so-called "mustard gas" or "Yperite"—was by far the most devastating gas used in the World War. It owed its potency largely to the fact that it was extremely indestructible, contaminating the ground and giving off small quantities of vapour which, if breathed for long periods of time, produced an inflammation of the respiratory passages which was either itself fatal or was liable to doom the lung to subsequent infection by bacteria. This gas also caused intense inflammation of the eyes and blistering of the skin.

Toxic Smokes such as dichlorarsine and dicyanarsine which when inhaled caused intense irritation of the nose and throat, leading to uncontrollable fits of sneezing and coughing, were also used as shell fillings in the World War.

Respirators.—Both in war and in industry the entry of poisonous gases into the respiratory system is prevented by the use of respirators. These are of two general types:

1. *The oxygen breathing set* consists of an air-tight mask (*a*) connected to a cylinder supplying oxygen; and (*b*) containing a cartridge of soda-lime or some other absorbent of carbon dioxide. The whole apparatus is self-contained, so that the subject has not and need not have access to the outer air. This form of ap-

paratus is particularly useful in atmospheres containing carbon monoxide, *e.g.*, the air in mine galleries after an explosion, and is indispensable to rescue parties.

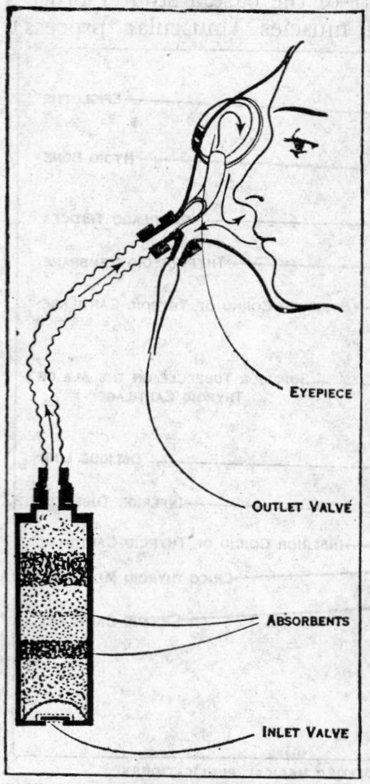

2. In various forms of respirators the mask is attached to a canister containing some chemical absorbent. The outer air is inhaled during inspiration, but on its way this air is filtered through the absorbent and so rid of the poisonous principle. The expired air passes out from the mask through a valve. Naturally the absorbent employed depends upon the nature of the poison to be met.

EYEPIECE

OUTLET VALVE

ABSORBENTS

INLET VALVE

FIG. 9.—GAS MASK IN SECTION

BIBLIOGRAPHY.—E. H. Starling, *Principles of Human Physiology* (1912; 4th ed., 1926); J. Barcroft, *The Respiratory Function of the Blood* (1914; 2nd ed. 1925); J. S. Haldane, "Respiration," *Silliman Memorial Lectures* No. 14 (New Haven, 1922); L. E. Hill, *Sunshine and Open Air* (1924; 2nd ed., 1925); J. C. Meakins and H. W. Davies, *Respiratory Function in Disease* (1925); C. A. L. Evans, *Recent Advances in Physiology* (1925; 2nd ed., 1926); Y. Henderson and H. W. Haggard, *Noxious Gases and the Principle of Respiration Influencing their Action* (1927). *See* also Medical Research Council, "The Medical Problem of Flying," Rep. No. 53 (H.M.S.O., 1920), and "The Acid-Base Equilibrium of the Blood," Rep. No. 72 (H.M.S.O., 1922). (J. BAR.)

RESPIRATORY SYSTEM, ANATOMY OF. The respiratory tract consists of the nasal cavities, pharynx, larynx, trachea, bronchi and lungs. For the first two parts *see* OLFACTORY SYSTEM and PHARYNX.

Larynx.—The *larynx* is the upper part of the air tube specially modified for the production of notes of varying pitch, though it is not responsible for the whole of the voice. Its framework is made up of cartilages which are moved on one another by muscles, and it is lined internally by mucous membrane. The larynx is situated in the front of the neck and corresponds to the fourth, fifth and sixth cervical vertebrae.

The *thyroid cartilage* is the largest in the larynx and consists of two plates or *alae* joined in the mid-ventral line. At the upper part of their junction is the *thyroid notch* and just below that is a forward projection, the *pomum Adami* ("Adam's apple"), best marked in adult males. From the upper part of the posterior border of each *ala* the *superior cornu* rises up to be joined to the tip of the great cornu of the hyoid bone by the *lateral thyrohyoid ligament*, while from the lower part of the same border the *inferior cornu* passes down to be fastened to the cricoid cartilage by the *crico-thyroid* capsule.

From the upper border of each ala the *thyro-hyoid membrane* runs up to the hyoid bone, while near the back of the outer surface of each the *oblique line of the thyroid cartilage* runs downward and forward.

The *cricoid cartilage* (*see* figs. 1 and 2) is something like a signet ring with the seal behind; its lower border, however, is horizontal. To the mid-ventral part of its upper border is attached the mesial part of the *crico-thyroid membrane*, which attaches it to the lower border of the thyroid cartilage; the lateral parts of this membrane pass up internally to the thyroid cartilage and their upper free edges form the true *vocal cords*. On the summit of the signet part of the cricoid are placed the two *arytenoid cartilages* (*see* fig. 2), each of which forms a pyramid with its apex upward. The base articulates with the cricoid by a concave facet, surrounded by the *crico-arytenoid capsule*, and the two arytenoids can glide toward or away from one another, while each can rotate round a vertical axis. From the front of the base a delicate process projects which is attached to the true vocal cord (*vocal process*), while from the outer part of the base a stouter process attaches the two crico-arytenoid muscles (muscular process).

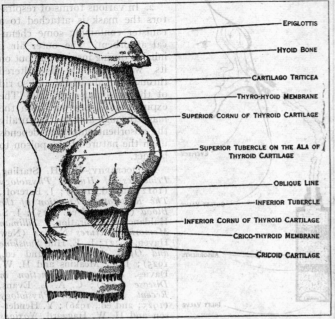

EPIGLOTTIS

HYOID BONE

CARTILAGO TRITICEA

THYRO-HYOID MEMBRANE

SUPERIOR CORNU OF THYROID CARTILAGE

SUPERIOR TUBERCLE ON THE ALA OF THYROID CARTILAGE

OBLIQUE LINE

INFERIOR TUBERCLE

INFERIOR CORNU OF THYROID CARTILAGE

CRICO-THYROID MEMBRANE

CRICOID CARTILAGE

FROM CUNNINGHAM, "TEXTBOOK OF ANATOMY" (OXFORD MEDICAL PUBLICATIONS)

FIG. 1.—PROFILE VIEW OF CARTILAGES AND LIGAMENTS OF LARYNX

The *epiglottis* (*see* fig. 3) forms a lid to the larynx in swallowing; only the box moves up to the lid instead of the lid moving down to the box. It is leaf-shaped, the stalk being attached to the junction of the thyroid cartilages inside the larynx, while the anterior surface of the leaf is closely attached to the root of the

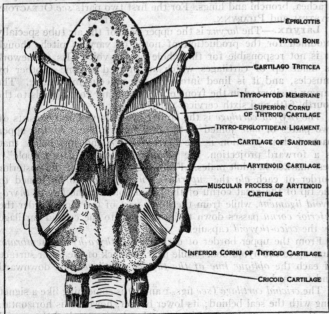

EPIGLOTTIS

HYOID BONE

CARTILAGO TRITICEA

THYRO-HYOID MEMBRANE

SUPERIOR CORNU OF THYROID CARTILAGE

THYRO-EPIGLOTTIDEAN LIGAMENT

CARTILAGE OF SANTORINI

ARYTENOID CARTILAGE

MUSCULAR PROCESS OF ARYTENOID CARTILAGE

INFERIOR CORNU OF THYROID CARTILAGE

CRICOID CARTILAGE

FROM CUNNINGHAM, "TEXTBOOK OF ANATOMY" (OXFORD MEDICAL PUBLICATIONS)

FIG. 2.—CARTILAGES AND LIGAMENTS OF LARYNX SEEN FROM BEHIND

tongue and body of the hyoid bone. The posterior or laryngeal surface is pitted for glands. All the cartilages of the larynx are of the hyaline variety except the epiglottis, the cornicula laryngis and the cuneiform cartilages, which are yellow elastic. The result is that all except these three tend to ossify as middle age is approached.

The *muscles of the larynx* are: (1) the *crico-thyroids*, attached to the lower border of the thyroid and the anterior part of the

cricoid, by pulling up which they make the upper part of the signet, with the arytenoids attached to it, move back and so tighten the vocal cords. (2) The *thyro-arytenoids* (*see* fig. 4), which run back from the junction of the thyroid alae to the front of the arytenoids and side of the epiglottis; they pull the arytenoids toward the thyroid and so relax the cords. (3) The single

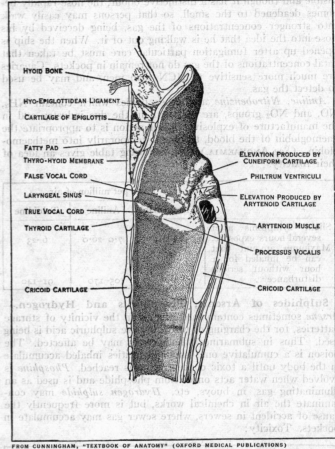

HYOID BONE

HYO-EPIGLOTTIDEAN LIGAMENT

CARTILAGE OF EPIGLOTTIS

FATTY PAD

THYRO-HYOID MEMBRANE

FALSE VOCAL CORD

LARYNGEAL SINUS

TRUE VOCAL CORD

THYROID CARTILAGE

CRICOID CARTILAGE

ELEVATION PRODUCED BY CUNEIFORM CARTILAGE

PHILTRUM VENTRICULI

ELEVATION PRODUCED BY ARYTENOID CARTILAGE

ARYTENOID MUSCLE

PROCESSUS VOCALIS

CRICOID CARTILAGE

FROM CUNNINGHAM, "TEXTBOOK OF ANATOMY" (OXFORD MEDICAL PUBLICATIONS)

FIG. 3.—MESIAL SECTION THROUGH LARYNX TO SHOW OUTER WALL OF RIGHT HALF

arytenoideus muscle, which runs from the back of one arytenoid to the other and approximates these cartilages. (4) The *lateral crico-arytenoids* (*see* fig. 4) which draw the muscular processes of the arytenoids forward toward the ring of the cricoid and, by so doing, twist the vocal processes, with the cords attached, inward toward one another; and (5) the *posterior crico-arytenoids* (*see* fig. 4) which run from the back of the signet part of the cricoid to the back of the muscular processes of the arytenoid and, by pulling these backward, twist the vocal processes outward and so separate the vocal cords. All these muscles are supplied by the recurrent laryngeal nerve, except the crico-thyroid which is innervated by the external branch of the superior laryngeal (*see* NERVE: *Cranial*).

The *mucous membrane of the larynx* is continuous with that of the pharynx at the *aryteno-epiglottidean folds* which run from the sides of the epiglottis to the top of the arytenoid cartilages (*see* fig. 3). To the outer side of each fold is the *sinus pyriformis* (*see* PHARYNX). From the middle of the junction of the alae of the thyroid cartilage to the vocal processes of the arytenoids the mucous membrane is reflected over, and closely bound to, the true vocal cords which contain elastic tissue and, as has been mentioned, are the upper free edges of the lateral parts of the crico-thyroid membrane. The chink between the two true vocal cords is the *glottis* or *rima glottidis*. Just above the true vocal cords is the opening into a recess on each side which runs upward and backward and is known as the *laryngeal saccule;* its opening is the *laryngeal sinus.* The upper lip of this slit-like opening is called the *false vocal cord*.

The mucous membrane is closely bound down to the epiglottis and to the true vocal cords, elsewhere there is plenty of submucous tissue. In the upper part of the front and sides of the larynx and over the true vocal cords the mucous membrane is lined by squamous epithelium, but elsewhere the epithelium is columnar and ciliated: it is supplied by the superior laryngeal

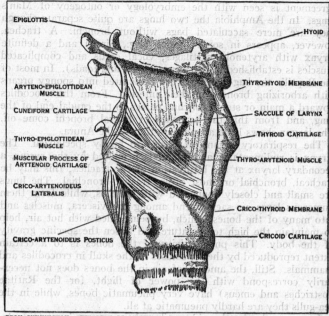

EPIGLOTTIS

HYOID

ARYTENO-EPIGLOTTIDEAN MUSCLE

THYRO-HYOID MEMBRANE

CUNEIFORM CARTILAGE

SACCULE OF LARYNX

THYRO-EPIGLOTTIDEAN MUSCLE

THYROID CARTILAGE

MUSCULAR PROCESS OF ARYTENOID CARTILAGE

THYRO-ARYTENOID MUSCLE

CRICO-ARYTENOIDEUS LATERALIS

CRICO-THYROID MEMBRANE

CRICO-ARYTENOIDEUS POSTICUS

CRICOID CARTILAGE

FIG. 4.—DISSECTION OF THE MUSCLES IN LATERAL WALL OF LARYNX SHOWN WITH THE RIGHT ALA OF THE THYROID CARTILAGE REMOVED

branch of the vagus nerve and above the glottis is peculiarly sensitive.

Trachea.—The *Trachea* or windpipe (*see* fig. 5) is the tube which carries the air between the larynx and the bronchi; it is from four to four and a half inches long and lies partly in the neck and partly in the thorax. It begins where the larynx ends at the lower border of the sixth cervical, and divides into its two bronchi opposite the fifth thoracic vertebra. The tube is kept always open by rings of cartilage, which, however, are wanting behind, and, as it passes down, it comes to lie farther and farther from the ventral surface of the body, following the concavity of the thoracic region of the spinal column. In the whole of its downward course it has the oesophagus close behind it, while in front are the isthmus of the thyroid, the left innominate vein, the innominate artery and the arch of the aorta. On each side of it and touching it is the vagus nerve.

The cervical part of the tube is not much more than an inch in length, but it can be lengthened by throwing back the head. This is the region in which tracheotomy is performed, and it should be remembered that in children, and sometimes in adults, the great left innominate vein lies above the level of the top of the sternum.

The trachea is made up of an external fibro-elastic membrane in which the cartilaginous rings lie, while behind, where these rings are wanting, is a layer of unstriped muscle which, when it contracts, draws the hind ends of the rings together and so diminishes the calibre of the tube. Inside these is plentiful submucous tissue containing mucous glands and quantities of lymphoid tissue, while the whole is lined internally by columnar ciliated epithelium.

Bronchi.—The *Bronchi* (*see* fig. 5) are the two tubes into which the trachea divides, but the branches, which these tubes give off later, are also called bronchi. Put shortly, they are two long tapering tubes which run from the bifurcation of the trachea to the lower and back part of each lung, and give off a series of large ventral and small dorsal branches. The upper part of each

of these long tubes or *stem bronchi* is outside the lung and in the middle mediastinum of the thorax, the lower part embedded in the substance of the lung. The structure of the bronchi is practically identical with that of the trachea. (*See* G. S. Huntington's "Eparterial Bronchial System of the Mammalia," *Am. Journ. Med. Sci.* [Phila. 1898]. *See* also Quain's *Anatomy*, London, last edition.)

Lungs.—The *Lungs* are two pyramidal, spongy, very vascular organs in which the blood is oxygenated. They are pink normally, but, often in city dwellers are slate-coloured from local deposition of soot particles. Each lies in its own side of the thorax and is surrounded by its own pleural cavity (*see* COELOM AND SEROUS MEMBRANES), and has an *apex* which projects into the side of the root of the neck, a *base* which is hollowed for the convexity of the diaphragm, an outer surface which is convex and lies against the ribs, an inner surface concave for the heart, peri-

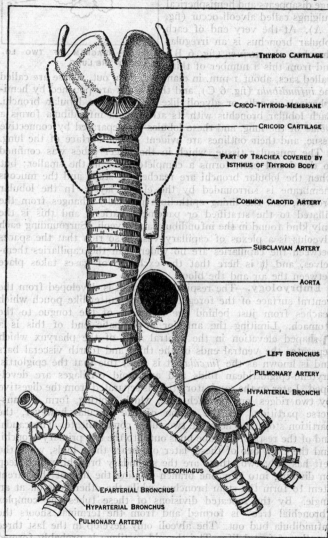

THYROID CARTILAGE

CRICO-THYROID-MEMBRANE

CRICOID CARTILAGE

PART OF TRACHEA COVERED BY ISTHMUS OF THYROID BODY

COMMON CAROTID ARTERY

SUBCLAVIAN ARTERY

AORTA

LEFT BRONCHUS

PULMONARY ARTERY

HYPARTERIAL BRONCHI

OESOPHAGUS

EPARTERIAL BRONCHUS

HYPARTERIAL BRONCHUS

PULMONARY ARTERY

FIG. 5.—TRACHEA AND BRONCHI, INDICATING THE THYROID BODY BY A DOTTED LINE

cardium and great vessels, a sharp anterior border which overlaps the pericardium and a broad, rounded posterior border which lies at the side of the spinal column. Each lung is nearly divided into two by a *primary fissure* which runs obliquely downward and forward, while the right lung has a *secondary fissure* which runs horizontally forward from near the middle of the primary fissure. The left lung has therefore an *upper* and *lower or basal lobe*, while the right has *upper*, *middle* and *lower* lobes. On the inner surface of each lung is the *root* or *hilum* at which alone its vessels, nerves and ducts (bronchi) can enter and leave it.

The structures contained in the root of each lung are the branches and tributaries of (1) the *pulmonary artery*, (2) the *pulmonary veins*, (3) the *bronchi*, (4) the *bronchial arteries* which supply the substance of the lung, (5) the *bronchial veins*, (6) the *bronchial lymphatic vessels and glands*, (7) the *pulmonary plexuses of nerves*. Of these the first three are the largest and, in dividing the root from in front, the veins are first cut, then the arteries and last the bronchi. As the bronchi become smaller and smaller by repeated division, the cartilage completely surrounds them and tends to form irregular plates instead of rings—they are therefore cylindrical, but when the terminal branches (*lobular bronchi*) are reached, the cartilage disappears and hemispherical bulgings called alveoli occur (fig. 6 A). At the very end of each lobular bronchus is an irregular chamber, the *atrium* (fig. 6 B), and from this a number of thin-walled sacs, about 1 mm. in diameter, open out. These are called the *infundibula* (fig. 6 C), and their walls are pouched by hemispherical air-cells or alveoli like those in the lobular bronchi. Each lobular bronchus with its atrium and infundibula forms a *lobule* of the lung, and these lobules are separated by connective tissue, and their outlines are evident on the surface of the lung.

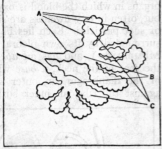

FIG. 6.—DIAGRAM OF TWO LOBULES OF THE LUNG

The muscular tissue, which in the larger tubes was confined to the dorsal part, forms a complete layer in the smaller; but when the lobular bronchi are reached, it stops and the mucous membrane is surrounded by the elastic layer. In the lobular bronchi, too, the lining epithelium gradually changes from the ciliated to the stratified or pavement variety, and this is the only kind found in the infundibula and alveoli. Surrounding each alveolus is a plexus of capillary vessels so rich that the spaces between the capillaries are no wider than the capillaries themselves, and it is here that the exchange of gases takes place between the air and the blood.

Embryology.—The respiratory system is developed from the ventral surface of the foregut as a long gutter-like pouch which reaches from just behind the rudiment of the tongue to the stomach. Limiting the anterior or cephalic end of this is a ∩-shaped elevation in the ventral wall of the pharynx which separates the ventral ends of the third and fourth visceral bars and is known as the *furcula;* it is from this that the epiglottis, aryteno-epiglottidean folds and arytenoid cartilages are developed. Later on the respiratory tube is separated from the digestive by two ridges, one on each side, which, uniting, form a transverse partition. In the region of the furcula, however, the partition stops and here the two tubes communicate. The caudal end of the respiratory tube buds out into the two primary bronchi, and the right one of these, later on, bears three buds, while the left has only two; these are the secondary bronchi, which keep on dividing into two, one branch keeping the line of the parent stem to form the stem bronchus, while the other goes off at an angle. By the repeated divisions of these tubes the complex "bronchial tree" is formed and from the terminal shoots the infundibula bud out. The alveoli only develop in the last three months of foetal life. The thyroid cartilage is probably formed from the fourth and fifth bronchial bars, while the cricoid seems to be the enlarged first ring of the trachea. Before birth the lungs are solid and much less vascular than after breathing is established. (For further details *see* Quain's *Anatomy*, vol. i., Lond. 1908.)

Comparative Anatomy.—In the lower vertebrates respiration is brought about by the blood vessels surrounding the gill clefts (*see* PHARYNX). In the higher fishes (Ganoids and Teleosteans) the "swim bladder" appears as a diverticulum from the dorsal wall of the alimentary canal, and its duct sometimes remains open and at others becomes a solid cord. In the former case it is probable that the blood is to some extent oxygenated in the vascular wall of this bladder. In the Dipnoi (mud-fish) the opening of the swim bladder shifts to the ventral side of the pharynx and the bladder walls become sacculated and very vascular, so that, when the rivers are dried up, the fish can breathe altogether by means of it. In the S. American and African species of mud-fish the bladder or lung, as it may now be called, is divided by a longitudinal septum in its posterior (caudal) part into right and left halves. In this sub-class of Dipnoi, therefore, a general agreement is seen with the embryology or ontogeny of Man's lungs. In the Amphibia the two lungs are quite separate though they are mere sacculated bags without bronchi. A trachea, however, appears in some species (*e.g.*, Siren) and a definite larynx with arytenoid cartilages, vocal cords and complicated muscles is established in the Anura (frogs and toads). In most of the Reptilia the bag-like lungs are elaborated into spongy organs with arborizing bronchi in their interior. From the crocodiles upward a main or stem bronchus passes to the caudal end of the lung, and from this the branches or lateral bronchi come off. The larynx shows little advance on that of the Anura.

The respiratory organs of birds are highly specialized. The larynx is rudimentary, and sound is produced by the *syrinx,* a secondary larynx at the bifurcation of the trachea; this may be tracheal, bronchial or, most often, tracheo-bronchial. The lungs are small and closely connected with the ribs, while from them numerous large air sacs extend among the viscera, muscles and into many of the bones, which, by being filled with hot air, help to maintain the high temperature and lessen the specific gravity of the body. This pneumaticity of the bones is to a certain extent reproduced by the air sinuses of the skull in crocodiles and mammals. Still, the amount of air in the bones does not necessarily correspond with the power of flight, for the Ratitae (ostriches and emeus) have very pneumatic bones, while in the sea-gulls they are hardly pneumatic at all.

In mammals the thyroid cartilage becomes an important element in the larynx, and in the Echidna the upper and lower parts of it, derived respectively from the fourth and fifth bronchial bars, are separate (R. H. Burne, *Journ. Anat. and Phys.* xxxviii. p. xxvii.). The whole larynx is much nearer the head than in Man, and in young animals the epiglottis projects up behind the soft palate. This prevents the milk trickling into the larynx during suckling, and is especially well seen in the Marsupials and Cetacea, though evidences of it are present in the human embryo. In the lower mammals an inter-arytenoid cartilage is very frequent (*see* J. Symington, "The Marsupial Larynx," *J. Anat. and Phys.* xxxiii. 31, also "The Monotreme Larynx," *ib.* xxxiv. 90).

The lungs show much variation in their lobulation; among the porcupines forty lobes have been counted in the right lung, while in other mammals no lobulation at all could be made out. The *azygous lobe* of the right lung is a fairly constant structure and is situated between the post-caval vein and the oesophagus. It is supplied by the terminal branch of the right stem bronchus and, although it is usually absent in Man, the bronchus which should have supplied it is always to be found.   (F. G. P.)

RESPIRATORY SYSTEM, DISEASES OF. In almost all the diseases of the respiratory system, five symptoms are present either singly or in groups—cough, expectoration, pulmonary haemorrhage, pain in the chest and shortness of breath. Prompt cognizance of these symptoms aids early diagnosis and proper treatment.

Dry cough lasting more than a month may portend tuberculosis or cancer of the lung. Cough with wheeze occurs in asthma, closure of the air passage by tumour, foreign body, ulceration and bronchitis. Hollow or brassy cough indicates pressure upon the larynx by tumour, aneurysm or disease of the vocal cords. Ear wax, a long uvula and tonsillitis cause cough, especially in children. Expectoration of rust-coloured sputum usually means pneumococcal pneumonia. In Friedländer's pneumonia, the sputum is extraordinarily sticky. In abscess and bronchiectasis it is fetid, and in congestion frothy and blood-tinged.

Haemorrhage from the lung occurs most frequently in bronchiectasis, pulmonary tuberculosis, cancer of the lung, abscess, heart disease, fungous and parasitic diseases, pneumonias (particularly Friedländer's bacillus pneumonia), diseases of the blood, formation of clots in the blood vessels of the lungs, scurvy and blast injuries to the lungs.

Pain in the chest signifies irritation of the parietal pleura and is common in infectious diseases, particularly tuberculosis and pneumonia. The pain is sharp and stabbing in nature, aggravated by breathing, and usually is localized in the side or the front part of the chest. Pleurisy is often followed by the formation of fluid in the pleural space. If the fluid is blood-tinged, it suggests strongly cancer of the lung. In cancer the pain may be deep-seated and difficult to localize. When the pleura covering the diaphragm is irritated, the pain may be felt on the shoulder, side of the neck or in the abdomen simulating appendicitis. Thoracic pain may be brought about by diseases of the heart, aorta and gall bladder, injury to the ribs, intercostal neuralgia and shingles.

Shortness of breath indicates an inadequate supply of oxygen to the body. It may be mild and apparent only on exertion as in early emphysema, or severe and constant as in congestion of the lungs in heart failure. Obstruction in the larynx and trachea by a foreign body, tumour, swelling, infections (especially diphtheria), tuberculosis and syphilis cause varying degrees of shortness of breath. Enlarged thyroid, thymus and lymph glands, aortic aneurysm and tumours of the oesophagus and mediastinum cause shortness of breath by pressure upon the air passage. Tracheobronchitis, pneumonia, asthma, pulmonary fibrosis, tuberculosis, fungous infections, congestion of the lungs, inhalation of noxious fumes and dusts and the collection of air, blood, pus and other fluids between the lungs and the chest wall also induce breathlessness. When it is pronounced there is associated bluish discoloration of the lips and the nail beds. This is seen in congestion, fibrosis, tuberculosis, emphysema, injuries to the chest and collection of fluid or air or both in the pleural space.

A careful evaluation of the symptoms, physical and roentgenologic findings, direct visualization of the larynx, trachea and bronchi by means of a bronchoscope, microscopic studies of the sputum and other laboratory procedures aid in establishing a correct diagnosis.

Diseases Caused by Infections.—Influenza, common colds and pneumonias are discussed elsewhere (see COLD; INFLUENZA; PNEUMONIA).

Bacterial infections of the accessory nasal sinuses may follow common colds, swimming and diving and dental abscesses. Bed rest, nasal shrinkage, application of heat, analgesics and sedatives are indicated. In suppurative sinusitis surgical drainage and antibiotics are sometimes necessary (see also SINUS).

Inflammation of the larynx with hoarseness of the voice may follow infections of the upper respiratory tract, injudicious use of the voice, alcohol and tobacco and inhalation of chemical fumes. In children it causes nocturnal episodes of harsh cough, respiratory difficulty and exhaustion. Abstinence from speaking and inhalation of steam are helpful. The laryngitis (q.v.) in tuberculosis and syphilis improves only when the latter diseases respond to treatment. Laryngeal stridor without fever occurs among boys from six months to two years of age with rickets.

Acute bronchitis often begins with common colds. Influenza viruses and other organisms in the nasopharynx and bronchi may be responsible. In children and debilitated persons, pneumonia may supervene. Whooping cough, typhoid and typhus fevers (qq.v.), viral pneumonia and fungous infections may begin with bronchitis. When there is fever, the patient should remain in bed, and the diet should be simple. Forcing fluids and purgation are unwise. Steam inhalation and codein relieve the cough. Antibiotics usually are unnecessary, and vitamins and vaccines are useless as prophylactic measures. Bronchitis lasting more than a month may be due to tuberculosis, cancer, emphysema and other pulmonary diseases (see also BRONCHITIS).

Bronchiectasis (q.v.) is a disease characterized by dilatation and infection of the bronchi. This disease may be congenital or acquired. Bronchial obstruction by a foreign body, neoplasm, tuberculosis, chronic sinusitis and other infections are important causes. Unpleasant breath, chronic cough, profuse expectoration of foul sputum, bouts of pulmonary haemorrhage, and enlarge-

ment of the tips of the fingers and toes are the features. In some the disorder remains symptomless only to be discovered unintentionally. Cough sedatives and antibiotics are of no permanent value. Postural and bronchoscopic drainages afford temporary relief. Early diagnosis with surgical removal of the diseased portion of the lung is recommended.

Abscess of the lung may follow aspiration of food particles, liquids and other foreign bodies, infected tissues and other matters during an operation in the mouth and throat under general anaesthesia, implantation of septic emboli after abdominal and pelvic operations, new growths of the lungs and oesophagus, pulmonary inflammation, injuries to the chest with penetration of the lungs and certain forms of pneumonia. Cough, fetid sputum, blood-spitting, pain in the chest, irregular fever and enlargement of the fingertips are the common features. Roentgenologic and bronchoscopic examinations, and laboratory study of the sputum and blood help in determining the cause. Some lung abscesses heal spontaneously. The younger the patient, the better is the outlook. Bed rest in fresh air with a nutritious diet is essential. Penicillin and other antibiotics are of great value. Operation is indicated when the abscess does not respond promptly to medical treatment.

Fungous infections of the lungs are caused by three main varieties of simple filamentous plants: a mouldlike form causing aspergillosis, a yeastlike form causing moniliasis, histoplasmosis, coccidioidomycosis, sporotrichosis and blastomycosis, and a higher variety producing actinomycosis.

Pulmonary mycoses have in common fever, chronic cough, expectoration of purulent sputum, haemorrhage, pain in the chest and loss of weight and strength. An acute infection resembles pneumonia and a chronic form of pulmonary tuberculosis.

Histoplasmosis has been seen in Central America, the south Pacific islands and the United States, particularly along the Mississippi river. The diagnosis is made by roentgenologic examination of the chest, skin test and by finding the fungus in the blood, lymph nodes and other tissues. Spontaneous healing and calcification of the foci occur in mild infections. When the infection is severe, the outlook is poor. There is no satisfactory treatment.

Coccidioidomycosis is endemic in the San Joaquin valley of California and in other southwestern regions of the United States. It probably occurs in other parts of the world. The infection occurs frequently during the dry season and in dusty conditions; the disease follows the inhalation of spore-laden dusts. It is not transmissible from person to person. The inhabitants of the endemic region receive the infection during the first year of residence and develop some degree of immunity. The primary infection has a high morbidity but a low mortality rate. In the acute stage the disease resembles viral pneumonia, and in the chronic stage it simulates tuberculosis. A positive diagnosis is made by finding the fungi in the sputum, lymph glands and other infected tissues. In mild cases, bed rest, a bland diet, proper elimination and measures to control the cough are all that is required. In severe infections, treatment is unsatisfactory. Vaccines, sulfonamides and antibiotics are of no value.

Actinomycosis (q.v.) frequently forms abscesses and draining sinuses through the chest wall. In the lung the infection resembles chronic pulmonary tuberculosis. A definite diagnosis is made by finding the fungi in the pus and tissues about the abscesses and sinuses. The general health of the patient should be cared for by a nutritious diet and rest in bed. Penicillin combined with sulfadiazine appears beneficial. Vaccines and iodides are valueless. Surgical operation facilitates the drainage of pus.

The mortality from tuberculosis (q.v.) in the United States declined from 200 deaths per 100,000 of the population in 1900 to less than 25 in 1950. A similar decline was noted in England. Paradoxically, there was an apparent increase in the number of new cases reported in the United States, Canada, England and Wales. To a certain extent, this paradox could have been due to the increased interest in roentgenologic surveys for tuberculosis. There was no doubt as to the increased frequency with which tuberculosis was found among the aged at mid-century. In many of these the disease appears as acute tuberculous pneumonia. The roentgenologic surveys during World War II of the military personnel, college students and large industrial groups revealed that slightly less than 1% examined showed significant pulmonary tuberculosis. In the United States it was estimated that 70,000,-000 people were infected with tuberculosis at mid-century and of these, 600,000 were actually ill. About 60,000 were dying annually from the disease.

Early diagnosis and proper treatment consisting of bed rest, nutritious diet, collapse therapy, lobectomy, pneumonectomy streptomycin and para-aminosalicylic acid prolong lives. Nicotinic acid hydrazide was introduced experimentally in the 1950s. As long as the patient has active disease with tubercle bacilli in the sputum, it would be wise for him to be in an institution. Treatments can be carried out most effectively if the patient is in a hospital. Dry climate and high altitude are not prerequisites for cure.

Those who have been exposed to tuberculosis should have semi-annual examinations for any evidence of disease. Immunization against tuberculosis by the general use of BCG vaccine for all infants, children and tuberculin-negative persons in the United States is not recommended. Doctors, medical students and nurses who are exposed to the infection, all hospital, sanatorium and laboratory personnel who come in close contact with tuberculous patients, individuals who are exposed to tuberculosis in their homes, patients and employees in mental institutions, prisons and other custodial institutions, and children and adults considered to have inferior resistance to tuberculosis are advised to be vaccinated.

Diseases Caused by New Growths.—Cancer of the lung originates usually in the bronchus. It appeared to be increasing in incidence at mid-20th century. In the United States there were about 500,000 people under care for cancer at that time, and of these approximately 13,000 had cancer of the lung. Eight thousand or more new patients with this disease were seen each year. The greatest incidence was occurring in the fifth, sixth and seventh decades of life, predominantly in males.

The cause remained unknown, but its greater prevalence among residents of urban areas suggested bronchial irritation as a cause. Smoking as a factor had been emphasized. Radioactive particles when inhaled may produce new growths. The incidence of bronchogenic carcinoma is greater among uranium miners and chromate workers than in the general population.

Cough is the most common symptom. At the onset the cough is dry, but later it becomes productive of mucopurulent sputum frequently streaked with blood. Pulmonary haemorrhage, wheezing respiration, chest pain, fever, loss of weight and strength, hoarseness and breathlessness are other accompanying symptoms.

Roentgenologic examination of the chest, a careful consideration of the symptoms and signs, direct visualization of the bronchial tract by means of a bronchoscope and microscopic examination of the bronchial secretion for cancer cells are necessary for a correct diagnosis.

Early diagnosis and removal of the entire involved lung offer the only hope. Even after complete removal of the lung, only 20% live as long as five years. Frequently by the time the patient seeks medical advice, the disease has already progressed too far for successful surgery.

New growths may originate in the mucous membrane of the nasopharynx and in the pleura. Surgical removal with radium therapy is recommended. Cancer of the larynx developing in the vocal cords has a fair outlook, whereas that originating in the mucous membrane covering the cartilages or the wall of the larynx is poor.

Persistent hoarseness in an individual apparently in good health should arouse suspicion. Early removal of the growth and irradiation offer much hope. (*See* also CANCER.)

Diseases Caused by Inhalation of Dusts and Fumes.—Prolonged inhalation of silica created in such industries as mining, drilling, sand-blasting, stone-cutting, rock-crushing, the manufacture of scouring powders and other operations in which quartz, sand, granite, sandstone and marble are processed, results in silicosis (*q.v.*), causing damage to the lungs by fibrosis.

Shortness of breath, particularly on exertion, cough, expectoration, haemoptysis, chest pain, loss of weight and strength are the symptoms. In far-advanced silicosis, emphysema, pleural thickening, heart failure and pulmonary tuberculosis develop frequently. The usual treatment for pulmonary tuberculosis is ineffective in the presence of advanced silicosis.

Proper ventilation and the use of a mask do much in the prevention of silicosis. The efficacy of inhaled aluminum hydroxide as a preventative is not generally accepted. Once silicosis is well-established, no treatment has any value and life expectancy is considerably shortened.

Asbestos is hydrated silicate of magnesium and is used in the manufacture of insulating materials. Asbestos fibres, upon inhalation, tend to obstruct the terminal portions of the air passages and set up areas of fibrosis. Long continued exposure to the dusts causes widespread fibrosis of the lungs. The onset of the disease is gradual with the appearance of cough, expectoration, breathlessness, loss of weight and strength. Two frequent complications are pulmonary tuberculosis and heart failure. There is no effective treatment for asbestosis and its sequelae. In the manufacture of fluorescent lights the workers may be exposed to beryllium. This compound, upon inhalation, produces acute tracheobronchitis, pneumonia, pulmonary oedema or fibrosis.

Inhalation of bagasse (the residue of sugar cane after extraction, extensively used in the manufacture of building materials) causes bronchitis and occasionally pneumonia, and the condition is termed bagassosis.

Inhalation of cotton fibres may produce pulmonary changes termed byssinosis. Dyes, synthetic rubber, furs, hairs and the dusts in threshing grain are also injurious. Fumes of ammonia, formaldehyde, sulphur dioxide, chlorine, oxides of nitrogen and cadmium when inhaled in sufficient concentration cause chemical pneumonia. Mustard gas, lewisite, chloropicrin, acetates in strong concentration may bring about sudden death from pulmonary inflammation, oedema and asphyxia. Prevention of the hazards is possible in large measure by proper ventilation and the use of masks. In cases of acute inflammation, the patient must be treated by emergency measures.

In patients with pneumonia or lung abscess, the management is the same as for these conditions.

Diseases Caused by Disturbed Circulation.—Infections of the lungs, inhalation of chemical irritants, alcoholic, barbiturate and other intoxications, diseases of the heart and injuries to the chest, head and spine cause pulmonary congestion producing breathlessness, cough and frothy and blood-tinged sputum. Bed rest, application of moderate heat to the body, morphine and oxygen inhalation are indicated. A correction of the underlying cause is essential for effective treatment. The blood vessels within the lung may be occluded by clots giving rise to infarction. Cough, expectoration, chest pain and blood-spitting are the symptoms. When a main pulmonary artery is blocked by a large clot, sudden death usually ensues. Such a complication may occur after injuries to the limbs and after abdominal and pelvic operations. When the pulmonary vessels become thickened, giving rise to pulmonary hypertension, the patient has constant shortness of breath with bluish discoloration of the lips and fingertips. The outlook is poor.

Diseases Caused by Allergy.—Allergic rhinitis and sinusitis are characterized by perennial colds, difficulty in breathing, paroxysmal attacks of sneezing and nasal discharge. Allergic factors are animal epidermal substances, pollens, moulds, house dusts, foods and occupational dusts. Whenever possible, the specific excitants should be identified by means of sensitivity tests. Avoidance of known allergic agents, desensitization and antihistaminic drugs are helpful.

Hay fever (*q.v.*) is caused by sensitiveness to air-borne pollens. Pollens of the oak, elm, hickory, poplar, ash and birch are responsible in the spring, beginning in March and ending in May. The pollens of grasses, plantain and sorrel are the causes in May, June and July. In August and September ragweed, mountain cedar, amaranths and artemesia are the factors. Those suffering in the autumn may find relief in Europe, California, the White mountains and the coast of Maine. No locality affords complete relief in the spring and summer except upon the ocean. Antihistaminic drugs control the symptoms to a certain extent. Specific treatment with pollen extracts is helpful.

Transitory pulmonary infiltration known as allergic pneumonia may occur in those suffering from asthma, hay fever and allergic rhinitis. This is not a serious condition, but may be mistaken for tuberculosis and other serious diseases (*see also* ALLERGY; ANAPHYLAXIS; ASTHMA).

Emergencies.—Coins, pins, nails, screws, buttons, dentures, nuts and other objects may lodge in the air passages, producing atelectasis. These accidents cause gagging, choking and coughing with bluish discoloration of the face. Small metallic objects may remain within the bronchus for some time without producing symptoms, whereas vegetable matter such as a peanut, because of rapid swelling, brings about early symptoms such as wheezing, cough, pain in the chest, blood-spitting and fever. Treatment is removal of the object by means of a bronchoscope.

Close proximity to explosion causes diffuse haemorrhages in the lungs, particularly in persons in closed spaces. Prostration, cough, expectoration of blood-tinged sputum, shortness of breath, pain in the chest and rapid heart action are the usual symptoms. Bed rest, external heat, oxygen, transfusions and morphine are beneficial. Crushing injuries and penetrating wounds of the chest produce symptoms like those seen in lung blast and the treatment is the same. When large amounts of blood, with or without air, accumulate in the pleural space, it may be necessary to withdraw it lest serious interference with circulation and respiration occur. Fracture of the rib is best treated by rest in bed and drugs to relieve pain. Splinting the chest may aggravate the discomfort. In atomic bombing, if vomiting, diarrhoea, fever and prostration occur on the day of injury, the outlook is hopeless. If vomiting occurs on the day of the bombing followed by a period of asymptomatic interval, survival is possible. If there is no vomiting on the day of bombing, the victim will most likely recover. (*See also* EAR, NOSE AND THROAT, DISEASES OF THE.)

BIBLIOGRAPHY.—Hobart A. Reimann, "Diseases of the Lungs," *Textbook of Medicine*, edited by Russell Cecil and Robert F. Loeb (1951); Council on Pharmacy and Chemistry, "Status of BCG Vaccine," *J.A.M.A.*, 144:1260 (1950); J. Wilson and R. Tunbridge, "Pathologic Findings in a Series of Blast Injuries," *Lancet*, 1:257 (1943).

(R. CR.)

RESTAURANT. This term was first used for an establishment where refreshments and meals were provided by one Boulanger, or Champ d'Oiseau, who opened the first establishment of the kind in the rue des Poulies, Paris, about 1765. The success of the house was almost instantaneous, and brought imitators, other restaurants being opened by chefs and stewards who left their employers. A notable advance followed the Revolution, when ruined aristocracy could no longer afford large retinues. Amongst the early restaurants was one managed by Antoine Beauvilliers.

The "Ordinary."—The earliest predecessors in England of the modern restaurant were the old coffeehouses and taverns which had a daily "ordinary"—a mid-day dinner or supper, generally noted for a particular dish, and served at a common table at a fixed price and time. Some of the more ancient of these arose in the middle of the 17th century. The first coffeehouse was opened in St. Michael's alley, Cornhill, by Pasqua Rosee, a Greek. This youth was the first to teach the method of roasting coffee and to introduce the drink into England.

Nearly 100 years before it was burnt down in the Great Fire of 1666, the Castle ordinary, off Paternoster Row, was a great place for booksellers and literary men. It was rebuilt after the Great Fire, and attained its greatest fame as Dolly's Chop House, in Queen's Head Passage, Paternoster Row, when "Dolly," a proprietress, introduced pretty serving maids in place of men. For 150 years it was famous for its beef steaks and gill ales, and among its customers were Fielding, Defoe, Smollett, Richardson, Swift, Dryden, Pope, Gainsborough and Handel. It was demolished in 1885. Jonathan's Coffee House in Change alley, opened at the time of the South Sea Bubble speculation, was a luncheon rendezvous for stock jobbers long prior to the establishment of the

Stock Exchange, and similarly Lloyds' Coffee House in Lombard street and Abchurch lane was the underwriters' headquarters and the cradle of Lloyds of to-day.

Other famous ordinaries were the Rainbow, in Fleet street, frequented by Dr. Johnson, Boswell and other notables, the Old Cock, Nando's, the Goose and Gridiron, also near St. Paul's, which, as the Mitre, was the first "musick house," and Simpson's Fish Dinner House, Bird-in-Hand court, Cheapside. The last-named was founded in 1723. It served a 2/- "fish ordinary" of soup, three fish courses, haunch of mutton and cheese 200 years ago, and was doing the same in 1929. Though no ordinary is served there, the Cheshire Cheese in Fleet street retains the atmosphere, and the steak, kidney, lark and oyster pudding of the days of Dr. Johnson.

Reference to the "ordinaries" may be found as long ago as 1577 (Hollinshed). In the 17th century the more expensive ordinaries were frequented by men of fashion, and gambling usually followed, so that the term "ordinary," by which was understood either the establishment or the meal was then more synonymous with the gambling house than the tavern. In the early part of the 18th century, however, the character changed again, and the choice of such establishments was great in number and varied in quality. Steele in the *Tatler* (1709) refers to a board being hung out of a window announcing "an excellent ordinary on Saturdays and Sundays." In the *Journey through England* (1714) it is remarked, "At two we generally go to dinner. Ordinaries are not so common here as abroad yet the French have set up two or three good ones in Suffolk street, where one is tolerably well served." Pontack's was considered one of the finest, and Defoe says that dinner there cost from 4s. to 5s. each, or anything up to a guinea. In addition a man could "dive," take his food in a mixed company of footmen and chair men for 2½d., have a sausage at a "farthing fry," or go to one of the taverns where the real "ordinary," a very good dinner of several courses, was served at from 6d. to 1s. Johnson records that he used to dine regularly for 7d. The usual hours for the meal were between 1 and 4, and there were 33 taverns serving ordinaries in the area between Threadneedle and Lombard streets and Gracechurch and Bishopgate streets.

Some of these have lasted until now, but the majority have had to give way to bank and office premises. Of the old ones, Birch's, formerly in Cornhill, dates from 1700, and Stone's Chop House in Panton street W., from 1770.

The restaurant habit as known to-day in London dates from the later decades of the 19th century when large fashionable hotels began to cater to the needs of fastidious diners on an elaborate scale. Suppers after the theatre became popular, and the establishments attached to hotels competed at widely varying prices while small restaurants sprang up in Soho, run by French and Italian proprietors, and provided good dinners tastefully served, at reasonable prices.

Modern grill rooms are an even later offshoot of the hotels and restaurants, and owe their existence largely to the travelling American who, with his own ideas of comfort, felt he did not wish to dress every night, but that otherwise he would be out of place in a fashionable restaurant. The grill room made no demand for dress, and offered an excellent dinner, long or short as required, served with rapidity in luxurious surroundings. London's first grill room was opened by Spiers and Pond in the '60s under the arch at Ludgate Hill, and the Savoy hotel was the first of the large hotels to inaugurate a similar room. One of the first restaurants in London was that opened at Whiteleys in 1873, purely for the benefit of customers, but that it was not enthusiastically received is shown in the first year's loss of £183 on £1,629 turnover. But from then on the idea grew in favour and the takings annually. Soup or fish, meat and vegetables were served for 1s. 6d.

In 1884 the first A.B.C. teashop was opened near London Bridge Station, and was ridiculed, the coffeeshops with their high-backed benches being still popular. Ten years later J. Lyons and Co. (*See* LYONS, SIR JOSEPH) opened at 213 Piccadilly, their first teashop.

All the larger restaurants have banqueting halls and other rooms where Masonic, regimental, club and other festival dinners may be had at varying prices. Among the "classic" restaurants are the Carlton, Savoy, Berkeley, Ritz, Claridge's, Oddenino's, Romano's, and the Café Royal, and latterly the May Fair, the Dorchester, and the Grosvenor House.

UNITED STATES

The word restaurant in America was first applied to the dining rooms of the better class hotels and to a few high class à la carte restaurants. As establishments of different types came into being their character was fixed by some such expression as coffee-house, as in England. Then came cafés, lunch rooms, dairy lunch rooms, cafeterias, tea rooms, waffle houses, fountain lunches, sandwich shops and many others, all included in the general use of the word restaurant.

The early American eating places were patterned after the inns, taverns and coffee houses in England and on the Continent. In Philadelphia there was the Blue Anchor Tavern, opened as early as 1683 or 1684. Ye Coffee House was opened in 1700, the proprietor being Henry Flower, who was also the postmaster of the province. In fact, the Coffee House was in all probability used as the post office for a time. The London Coffee House, opened in 1702, and the second London Coffee House, established in 1754 by William Bradford, printer of the Pennsylvania journal, and the City Tavern (1773) were meeting places for the sea captains, merchants and others who went there to transact their business, as well as social gathering places for the leading citizens. The City Tavern, later known as the Merchants Coffee House, was long considered the largest and best coffee house in America.

Ye Crown Coffee House, in Boston, was built in 1711 on the Boston Pier, or Long Wharf, by Jonathan Belcher.

In New York the famous old Fraunces' Tavern at Broad and Pearl streets near the Battery still stands, only the ground floor being used as a restaurant. Upstairs the Sons of the Revolution protect the collection of mementoes of Washington's life and times in the room in which he said farewell to his officers. Brown's Chop House was famous for many generations not only for its chops and steaks but for its unique collection of old photographs, prints and autographs. For years it was the rendezvous of journalists, authors, actors and painters. The Old St. Denis on Broadway at 11th street in the 90's; Fleischman's Vienna Garden, opposite the St. Denis, with its continental touch; Dorlon's on 23rd St., famous for its sea food; the old Hoffman House; Café Martin and the Holland House should be at least mentioned. But supreme over all until Sherry opened was Delmonico, first built on Broad street, later moved to 26th street and finally to 44th street and Fifth avenue. Soon after Delmonico moved to 44th street, Sherry opened diagonally across the avenue and, attracting the younger generation, threatened for a time to usurp the crown so long worn by Delmonico. But the two great restaurants were both destined to go. Delmonico closed its doors, and the Sherry of to-day is not the old-time Sherry.

Bégué's, opened over 60 years ago in New Orleans for the butchers of the city, is now a fashionable rendezvous.

Don's and the El Dorado House, famous for their Spanish cooking, were the earliest eating places in San Francisco in the pioneer days. Lavish feasts and exorbitant prices were the order of the day. The most fashionable restaurant was the Iron House made of sheet iron which had been brought in a sailing vessel around the Horn. Unique among the restaurants was the Bazzuro, opened by an Italian. The first restaurant by that name was a sailing vessel which had run aground in the bay. Later this spot was filled in with land and a house built on the same site. The restaurant is still run by members of the original family.

Other eating places of special interest were the Tehama House, frequented by the army and navy officers; Marchand's, where the food was cooked in the window to entice the passerby; and the Mint, which boasted an old Southern mammy in the kitchen. Few of these famous places survived the San Francisco fire of 1906.

See also CAFETERIA.

RESTIF, NICOLAS EDME (1734–1806), called RESTIF DE LA BRETONNE, French novelist, son of a farmer, was born at Sacy (Yonne) on Oct. 23, 1734. He was educated by the Jansenists at Bicêtre, and on the expulsion of the Jansenists was received by one of his brothers, who was a curé. Owing to a scandal in which he was involved, he was apprenticed to a printer at Auxerre, and, having served his time, went to Paris. Here he worked as a journeyman printer, and in 1760 he married Anne or Agnes Lebègue, a relation of his former master at Auxerre. Restif produced about two hundred volumes, many of them printed with his own hand, on almost every conceivable subject. He drew on the episodes of his own life for his books, which display an extraordinary licence in choice of subject and in treatment. They provide useful documents for the history of the underworld of the period. They include: *Le Pied de Fanchette,* a novel (1769); *Le Pornographe* (1769), a plan for regulating prostitution which is said to have been actually carried out by the Emperor Joseph II., while not a few detached hints have been adopted by continental nations; *Le Paysan perverti* (1775), a novel with a moral purpose, sufficiently horrible in detail; *La Vie de mon père* (1779); *Les Contemporaines* (42 vols., 1780–1785), a vast collection of short stories; *Ingénue Saxancour,* also a novel (1785); and, lastly, the extraordinary autobiography of *Monsieur Nicolas* (16 vols., 1794–1797; the last two are practically a separate and much less interesting work), in which at the age of sixty he has set down his remembrances, his notions on ethical and social points, his hatreds, and above all his numerous loves, real and fancied. The original editions of these, and indeed of all his books, have long been bibliographical curiosities owing to their rarity, the beautiful and curious illustrations which many of them contain, and the quaint typographic system in which most are composed. Just before his death (Feb. 2, 1806) Napoleon gave him a place in the ministry of police.

See J. Assézat's selection from the *Contemporaines,* with excellent introductions (3 vols., 1875), and the valuable reprint of *Monsieur Nicolas* (14 vols., 1883–84); also Eugen Dühren, *Rétif de la Bretonne, der Mensch, der Schriftsteller, der Reformator* (Berlin, 1906), and *Rétif-Bibliothek* (Berlin, 1906).

RESTITUTION: *see* DIVORCE; LARCENY.

RESTRAINT, in law, a restriction or limitation. The word is used primarily in four connections:

Restraints on Alienation.—When real property is conveyed in fee simple, restricting the right of the grantee to alienate it, thereby derogating from the grant, it was considered by the common law so inimicable to the policy of permitting the ready transfer of land that such restrictions were stricken down by the courts as illegal. A general restraint upon alienation was thus void, though the courts would uphold restraint limited with reference to time or to a class of persons. *See* Gray, *Restraints on the Alienation of Property* (2nd ed. 1895).

Restraints on Anticipation.—A restraint on anticipation consists of an attempt by the grantor of an estate for life to prevent the grantee from anticipating the income by alienating it voluntarily or involuntarily prior to its acquisition. In England such restraints are invalid save with reference to restraints imposed upon a married woman as to her separate estate during the period of coverture. *See* Conveyancing Act, 1881, s. 39; Married Women's Property Act, 1883, s. 29. In the United States such restraints accompanying the creation of a spendthrift trust are valid in many States. *See* TRUST AND TRUSTEES.

Restraint of Marriage.—A gift or bequest to a person may have a condition attached in restraint of marriage. A condition in general restraint of marriage is void, as being contrary to public policy, although a condition in restraint of a second marriage is not void. A condition in partial restraint of marriage is valid, and may be either to restrain marriage with a particular class of persons, *e.g.,* a papist, a domestic servant or a Scotsman, or under a certain age.

Restraint of Trade.—A contract in general restraint of trade was deemed void at common law as against public policy (*Mitchel v. Reynolds,* 1 P. Wms. 181 [1711]), though a contract in partial restraint of trade accompanying the sale of a business or the employment of an individual is valid (*United States* v. *Addyston Pipe and Steel Co.,* 85 Fed. 271 [1898]). The modern attitude, however, is that the test that should determine the validity of contracts in restraint of trade should be whether they are reasonably necessary to protect the interests of the parties and not unnecessarily harmful to the general public (*Nordenfelt* v. *Nordenfelt Guns and Ammunition Co.* [1894], Appeal Cases 535). Legislation and judicial decision in recent years widely affected the doctrines of restraint of trade.

See TRUST AND TRUSTEES.

BIBLIOGRAPHY.—W. Berge, *Cartels: Challenge to a Free World* (1944); E. T. Grether, *Price Control under Fair Trade Legislation* (1939); G. C. Henderson, *The Federal Trade Commission* (1927); H. L. Purdy, *Corporate Concentration and Public Policy* (1942); S. A. Weigel, *The Fair Trade Acts* (1938).

RESURRECTION PLANT (*Anastatica hierochuntina*), a small herb of the family Cruciferae, called also rose of Jericho, native to Arabia, Iran and Egypt. Upon the ripening of the seeds during the dry season, the leaves fall off and the branches curve inward so that the dry plant assumes a globular form. It then rolls about in the manner of a tumbleweed (*q.v.*), until the rainy season. When wetted the branches unfold and it assumes for a time the appearance of a living plant. The name is also given to two other plants. One is the mosslike *Selaginella lepidophylla* which also dries up into a ball and expands when wetted. It is called also bird's-nest moss and is found from Texas southward to Peru. The other is the resurrection fern (*Polypodium polypodioides*), the commonest epiphytic fern in Florida.

RESZKE, JEAN DE (1850–1925), operatic singer, was born at Warsaw, Pol., on Jan. 14, 1850. His parents were Poles; his father was a state official and his mother a capable amateur singer, their house being a recognized musical centre. He studied law before adopting singing as his profession and going to Italy to study. He made his first public appearance, as a baritone, at Venice in Jan. 1874, as Alfonso in *La Favorita*, and in the following April he sang for the first time in London, appearing at Drury Lane theatre, and a little later in Paris. He was not entirely successful and retired for a further period of study, during which his voice gained remarkably in the upper register; so that when he made his first reappearance at Madrid in 1879 it was as a tenor, in the title-role of *Robert le Diable*. His great fame as a singer, especially in Wagnerian parts, dates from this time. He appeared at the Metropolitan Opera house, New York, N.Y., from 1893 to 1899. In 1904 he retired, but he continued teaching almost to the day of his death on April 3, 1925.

RETABLE, a term of ecclesiastical art and architecture, applied in modern English usage to an altar ledge or shelf, raised slightly above the back of the altar or communion table, on which are placed the cross, ceremonial candlesticks and other ornaments.

Retables may be lawfully used in the Church of England (*Liddell & Beale*, 1860, 14 P.C.).

RETAILING is that part of the distributive process which is concerned with selling goods directly to the ultimate consumer. The term "retailing," therefore, is broad. For example, it embraces even the direct-to-consumer sales activities of a producer who sells through his own retail stores, or by house-to-house canvassers, or by mail order, or by a combination of these methods; for such a producer is performing the retailing function.

The direct sale of goods to the individual or to the individual as a member of the family and for purposes of ultimate consumption constitutes the retailing activity. The ultimate consumer is the aim and contact of that activity. The goods sold may be bought by the seller, or handled on consignment, or produced. The types of goods sold in largest unit volume at retail are food products, clothing, clothing accessories, home furnishings and home equipment.

The principal activities involved in retailing are: (1) buying—providing stocks to meet consumer demand, quantitative and qualitative; (2) receiving and storing—checking, recording, marking prices on goods, caring for stock; (3) selling; (4) publicizing merchandise stocks—creating interior store and window displays, advertising, executing sales promotion programs; (5) providing customer services—delivering, caring for telephone and mail or-

ders, adjusting complaints, exchanging merchandise, maintaining customer restaurants, rest rooms, etc.; (6) managing the store personnel—employing, training, paying, supervising, executing welfare programs, etc.; (7) purchasing and caring for supplies—providing, stocking and controlling the use of such accessory materials as wrapping paper, bags, boxes, price tags, twine, tape, printed forms, etc.; (8) maintaining and caring for the building and its equipment; (9) financing the retailing operations; and (10) accounting for and controlling the operations.

The essential difference in the performance of these activities in large or small establishments lies in the much greater division of labour and organization possible in the large establishments.

While retailing is not exclusively confined to the four walls of a retail store, it is in the retail store that most retailing transactions take place (for example, probably not more than 2% of the total retail dollar volume is made up of sales by house-to-house canvassers). Using merchandise carried as a basis, retail stores are classified as: (1) single-line stores—groceries, or meats, or hardware, etc.; (2) multiple-line stores—combination food markets including meats, green vegetables, etc., and the modern drug store with its cigars, stationery, luncheonette and household convenience goods; (3) specialty stores—single-line stores carrying selected merchandise and catering to limited customer groups; and (4) department stores—stores that carry dry goods, apparel, furniture, housewares and almost any other type of consumer goods and that are departmentalized as to location, management and accounting. Still another useful classification—based upon ownership and control—is as follows: (1) independently-owned stores; (2) branch stores; (3) centrally-owned chain stores; (4) "voluntary" chain stores—units of independently-owned stores, associated with or without wholesaler affiliations for the purpose of conducting joint merchandising activities; and (5) consumers' co-operative stores.

A growing emphasis upon style, design and colour became characteristic of consumer demand and rapid changes in fashion affected retail stocking problems. The retailer has found it necessary to do an increased amount of "hand-to-mouth" buying (the ratio of year-end inventory to sales in retailing has generally decreased). There has been a steady increase in sales on "open account" and only an occasionally-interrupted gain in instalment retail sales in relation to total retail sales.

The department store failed to match the percentage increases in total retail sales in years of expansion and found it necessary to continue to affiliate and combine for the purpose of reducing overhead through research and merchandise costs through group or central buying. In those fields where the centrally-owned chain is strong, the independent retailer continued to associate with other independents and with wholesalers in "voluntary" chains to practice joint merchandising. In the food field there occurred the very spectacular rise of the supermarket under independent, old-line centrally-owned chain, and "new" chain sponsorship. There was a sharp decline in the number of true single-line retail stores and an increased experimentation with retailing a wide variety of merchandise at limited prices. The history of retailing in the U.S. has been one of experiment, improvement and progress. The department store, the mail-order house, the centrally-owned chain store, the "voluntary" chain, the supermarket, each in its turn, represents a new development in retailing to meet new needs under reasonably free competition. In the 1930s particularly there were increasing legislative restraints and regulations in the field of retailing.

However, even the discriminatory tax measures levelled at the centrally-owned chain stores, and so often widely supported by the independent retailer, failed to cripple the affected type of retailing or even to place it in a rigid mould. No important recession of "chain" business occurred in those states that taxed the centrally-owned chain. In the taxing states, the national food chains reduced the number of their outlets (most chain taxation is based upon the number of store units owned and operated) only slightly more than in the tax-free states. None of the three measures—size, sales or profits—suggested a general decline or "freezing" of the national centrally-owned chains. Flexibly, they shifted from "long" systems (a large number of unit stores) to "large" systems (fewer units, but large volumes), from neighbourhood to shopping area, from limited merchandise assortments to wide varieties, even from complete central ownership to an affiliation of independents.

In retailing, whether conducted by chain or independent, by large establishment or small, the principal management problem was to find ways and means of spreading an increasing amount of overhead over as large a sales volume as possible. Enhanced wage levels, the trend toward shorter hours, social security burdens and increased taxes, all played a part in this problem. Moreover, there was the constant threat of higher prices that might represent more than gradual and nominal increases and that might restrict expansion in sales volume.

Successful retailing, therefore, demands an efficient functioning on the side of the ultimate consumer as his purchasing agent, rather than as a convenient storage depot or as a promoter of goods that some producer wants to sell. Careful buying, the assembly of broad assortments from which the customer can choose, the building of harmonious ensembles and merchandise relationships, the provision of qualities suited to utilitarian needs, the training and supervising of retail sales people with the aim of improving their assistance to the ultimate consumer in making wise choices—these are the essentials of profitable retailing. *See* CHAIN STORE; DEPARTMENT STORE.   (G. R. C.; X.)

BIBLIOGRAPHY.—*Market Data Book, Consumer Markets Edition* (1941 *et seq.*); Curtis Publishing Co., *Where People Buy* (1941); C. W. Barker, *Principles of Retailing* (1941); N. A. Brisco, *Retailing* (1935).

RETAINER, properly the act of retaining or keeping for oneself, or a person or object which retains or keeps; historically, a follower of a house or family, and particularly used of armed followers attached to the barons of the middle ages.

Retainer of Counsel.—When it is considered desirable by a litigant that the services of any particular counsel (barrister) should be obtained for the conduct of his case, it is necessary to deposit with counsel a form of retainer together with the necessary fee in cash, from which time counsel is bound to give the party who has thus retained him the first call on his services in the matter in which he has been retained. Retainers are either general or special. A general retainer retains counsel for all proceedings in which the person retaining is a party. A special retainer is one which only applies to some particular cause or action. In the United States the retainer is much less formal than in England, and is used to refer to the preliminary fee given a counsel to take or defend proceedings.

See ADVOCATE; BARRISTER.

Retainer of Debt.—In connection with the administration of an estate under a will, it is the right of the personal representative—whether executor or administrator—of a deceased person to retain in respect of all assets which have come into his hands a debt due to himself in his own right whether solely or jointly with another person as against creditors of an equal degree, and this even though his debt is barred by the Statutes of Limitation (*see* Administration of Estates Act 1925, s. 34; *Taylor* v. *Deblois*, Fed. Cas. no. 13,790). The appointment of a receiver deprives the representative of his right except in regard to assets which came to his hands prior to the appointment of the receiver.

RETENE, an aromatic hydrocarbon occurring in wood tars and obtained by distilling resinous woods. It crystallizes in colour-

less plates melting at 98.5° C. and boiling at 394° C. Chromic acid oxidizes the hydrocarbon to retene quinone (an ortho-diketone) and permanganate oxidizes the quinone to 3-hydroxy-isopropyldiphenyl-1:1′:2′-tricarboxylic acid. These reactions show that retene is ethylisopropylphenanthrene, $C_{18}H_{18}$, with the adjacent structural formula.

See A. E. Everest, *The Higher Coal Tar Hydrocarbons* (1927).

RETFORD (officially EAST RETFORD), a market town and municipal borough in the Bassetlaw parliamentary division of Nottinghamshire, England, 138½ mi. N.W. from London on the Eastern Region Railway route. Pop. (est. 1938) 15,190. Area, 7.3 sq.mi. Retford (Redforde, Ratford) owes its importance to its position near one of the Roman roads and on the river Idle, where there was a ford. In 1086 the archbishop of York owned a mill at Retford, and Roger de Busli had rights there. Retford was a borough by prescription, and was in the hands of the crown when, in 1276, Edward I granted it to the burgesses in fee-farm with the right of electing bailiffs. This charter was confirmed by Edward III, Henry VI and Elizabeth I. In 1607 James I granted a charter of incorporation, under which the town was governed until 1835, when it was reincorporated. East Retford returned two members to parliament in 1315, and again from 1572 till 1885, when it was disfranchised.

There is a large trade in corn and cheese, and the town possesses iron foundries and works, paper and corn mills and rubber works. Coal is mined in the vicinity.

RETHEL, ALFRED (1816–1859), German historical painter, was born at Diepenbend near Aix-la-Chapelle on May 15, 1816. At the age of 13 he executed a drawing which procured his admission to the academy of Düsseldorf, where he studied for several years. In 1836 he moved to Frankfürt, and was selected to decorate the walls of the imperial hall in the Römer with figures of famous men. Four years later he was commissioned to ornament the restored council house of his native city with frescoes from the life of Charlemagne, but the execution of this work was delayed for about six years. Meanwhile Rethel occupied himself with the production of easel pictures and drawings. In 1842 he began a striking series of designs dealing with the "Crossing of the Alps by Hannibal," in which the weird power which animates his later art became apparent. In 1844 Rethel visited Rome, executing, along with other subjects, an altar-piece for one of the churches of his native land.

Returning to Aix, in 1846, he commenced his Charlemagne frescoes. But mental derangement, remotely attributable to an accident in childhood, began to manifest itself. While he hovered between madness and sanity, Rethel produced some of his most impressive works. He painted "Nemesis Pursuing a Murderer," a flat stretch of landscape, with a slaughtered body, while in front is the assassin speeding away into the darkness and above an angel of vengeance. Another design which Rethel executed was "Death the Avenger," a skeleton appearing at a masked ball scraping daintily, like a violinist, upon two human bones; in contrast he produced "Death the Friend." Rethel also executed a powerful series of drawings—"The Dance of Death"—suggested by the Belgian insurrections of 1848. He died at Düsseldorf on Dec. 1, 1859.

His "Peter and John at the Beautiful Gate of the Temple," is in the Leipzig museum, and his "St. Boniface" and several cartoons for the frescoes at Aix are in the Berlin National gallery.

See his *Life*, by Wolfgang Müller von Königswinter (1861); *Art Journal*, Nov. 1865; monograph by Max Schmid in Knackfuss's *Künstlerbiographien*, vol. 32 (1898).

RETHEL, a town of France, capital of an arrondissement in the department of Ardennes, on the Aisne and the Ardennes canal, 31 mi. S.W. of Mézières by rail. Pop. (1946) 4,715. Rethel, of Roman origin, was from the 10th century the seat of a countship held successively by the families of Flanders, Burgundy, Clèves, Foix and Gonzaga. The

In 1581 it was erected into a duchy in favour of the latter. In 1663 it was sold by Charles VI de Gonzaga to Mazarin, whose family held it until the Revolution. Rethel has a subprefecture, a board of trade arbitrators, chamber of arts and manufactures, and carries on wool spinning, the weaving of light woollen fabrics and the manufacture of farm implements.

RETREAT, a withdrawal, especially of a body of troops after a defeat or in face of a superior enemy. In military usage, retreat is the term for the ceremony at military posts of lowering the flag at or about sunset and also refers to the signal of the ceremony given by bugle or drum.

In religious usage, a retreat is a period and place set aside for prayer, self-examination and other spiritual exercises.

The word is also used of an institution or home where insane persons or habitual inebriates may be treated.

RETRENCHMENT, an act of cutting down or reduction, particularly of expenditure. A technical use of the term is in fortification, where it is applied to a work or series of works constructed in the rear of existing defenses in order to bar the further progress of the enemy should he succeed in breaching or storming these. For example, during the siege of Port Arthur in 1904, the Russians, after Fort Panlung fell to the Japanese, connected the two adjacent first-line forts to a fort in the rear by new works; the retrenchment remained in Russian hands until the fall of the whole line of forts.

RETZ, JEAN FRANÇOIS PAUL DE GONDI, Cardinal de (1614–1679), French churchman and agitator, was born at Montmirail in 1614. The family was one of those which had been introduced into France by Catherine de' Medici, but it acquired great estates in Brittany and became connected with the noblest houses of the kingdom. Retz himself always spelled his designation "Rais." He was the third son and was destined for the church. The family of Retz had military traditions, but it had also much church influence, and despite the unclerical leanings of the future cardinal, which were not corrected by the teachings of his tutor St. Vincent de Paul, the intentions of his family never varied respecting him.

He studied at the Sorbonne, and when he was scarcely 18 wrote the remarkable *Conjuration de Fiesque*, a little historical essay, of which he drew the material from the Italian of Augustino Mascardi, but which is all his own in the negligent vigour of the style and the audacious insinuation, if nothing more, of revolutionary principles. Retz received no preferment of importance during Richelieu's life, and even after the minister's death, though he was presented to Louis XIII and well received, he found difficulty in attaining the coadjutorship with reversion of the archbishopric of Paris. But almost immediately after the king's death, Anne of Austria appointed him to the coveted post on All Saints' Eve, 1643.

Retz acquired great influence with the Parisians, which he gradually turned against Jules Mazarin. No one had more to do than Retz with the outbreak of the Fronde in Oct. 1648, and his history for the next four years is the history of that confused and, as a rule, much misunderstood movement. Of the two parties who joined in it Retz could only depend on the bourgeoisie of Paris. But although he had some speculative tendencies in favour of popular liberties, and even perhaps of republicanism, Retz represented no real political principle, and when the breakup of the Fronde came he was left in the lurch, having more than once in the meantime been in no small danger from his own party. One stroke of luck, however, fell to him before his downfall. He was made cardinal almost by accident and under a misapprehension on the pope's part.

In 1652 he was arrested and imprisoned, first at Vincennes, then at Nantes; he escaped, however, after two years' captivity, and for some time wandered about in various countries. He made his appearance at Rome more than once, and had no small influence in the election of Alexander VII. In 1662, he was received back again into favour by Louis XIV and on more than one occasion he served as envoy to Rome. Retz, however, was glad in making his peace to resign his claims to the archbishopric of Paris. In compensation he received the rich abbacy of St. Denis and restoration to his other benefices with the payment of arrears.

The last 17 years of Retz's life were passed partly in his diplomatic duties (he was again in Rome at the papal election of 1668), partly at Paris, partly at his estate of Commercy, but latterly at St. Mihiel in Lorraine. His debts were enormous, and in 1675 he resolved to make over to his creditors all his income except 20,000 livres, and, as he said, to "live for" them. He died in Paris on Aug. 24, 1679.

One of the chief authorities for the last years of the life of Retz is Madame de Sévigné, whose connection he was by marriage. Retz's *Memoirs* were certainly not written till the last ten years

of his life, and they do not go farther than the year 1655. They are addressed in the form of narrative to a lady who is not known, though guesses have been made at her identity, some even suggesting Madame de Sévigné herself. In the beginning there are some gaps. They display, in a rather irregular style and with some oddities of dialect and phrase, fine narrative skill and a high degree of ability in that special art of the 17th century—the drawing of verbal portraits or characters.

Retz sketched the early barricade of the Fronde in which the writer had so great a share, the hesitations of the court, the bold adventure of the coadjutor himself into the palace and the final triumph of the insurgents.

Beside these memoirs and the youthful essay of the *Conjuration de Fiesque*, Retz left diplomatic papers, sermons, Mazarinades and correspondence.

The *Memoirs* of the Cardinal de Retz were first published in a very imperfect condition in 1717 at Nancy. The first satisfactory edition was that which appeared in the twenty-fourth volume of the collection of Michaud and Poujoulat (Paris, 1836). They were then re-edited from the autograph manuscript by Géruzez (Paris, 1844), and by Champollion-Figeac with the Mazarinades, etc. (Paris, 1859). In 1870 a complete edition of the works of Retz was begun by M. A. Feillet in the collection of *Grands Écrivains*. The editor dying, this passed into the hands of M. Gourdault and then into those of M. Chantelauze, who had already published studies on the connection of St. Vincent de Paul with the Gondi family, etc. (1882). *See also* L. Batiffol, *Le Cardinal de Retz* (1927).

REUBEN, according to Gen. xxix, 32, was the eldest son of Jacob, by his first wife, Leah. From this it may be inferred that at one time Reuben ranked as the foremost of the Hebrew tribes. But for reasons which are obscure the tribe lost this pre-eminence at an early period of the history. In Gen. xxxv, 22 Reuben is said to have been intimate with his father's concubine, and the story, which breaks off abruptly, probably went on to record a curse pronounced upon him in consequence. This would be regarded as a sufficient explanation of the decline of the tribe (*cf.* Gen. xlix, 4, and *see* I, Chron. v, 1). It is possible that the story may be a personification of some aggressive move made by the tribe Reuben against the Bilhah clan. The subsequent history of the tribe is obscure. The territory which later traditions assign to it east of the Dead sea is not clearly delimited or distinguished from the territories of Gad and Moab. A Reubenite name is found on the west of the Jordan (Josh. xv, 6; xviii, 17), and the reference to Reuben in the Song of Deborah (Judges v, 15–17) would naturally mean that Reuben was a pastoral tribe on the west of the Jordan, since of the next tribe mentioned it is definitely stated "Gilead abode beyond Jordan."

See C. F. Burney, *Israel's Settlement in Canaan*, pp. 50–52.

(W. L. W.)

REUCHLIN, JOHANN (1455–1522), German humanist and Hebraist, was born on Feb. 22, 1455, at Pforzheim in the Black Forest, where his father was an official of the Dominican monastery. The name was graecized by his Italian friends into Capnion. Reuchlin constantly writes himself Phorcensis. He learned Latin at the monastery school at Pforzheim, and spent a short time in 1470 at the university of Freiburg. His fine voice gained him a place in the household of Charles I, margrave of Baden, and he was chosen to accompany to the University of Paris the young prince Frederick. In Paris he learned Greek, and he attached himself to the leader of the Paris realists, Jean Heynlin, or à Lapide (d. 1496), whom he followed to the vigorous young university of Basel in 1474. At Basel Reuchlin took his master's degree (1477), and began to lecture, teaching a more classical Latin than was then common in German schools, and also explaining Aristotle in Greek. His Greek studies were continued at Basel under Andronicus Contoblacas, and he became acquainted with the bookseller, Johann Amorbach, for whom he prepared a Latin lexicon (*Vocabularius Breviloquus*, 1st ed., 1475–76). Reuchlin soon left Basel to study under George Hieronymus at Paris. He then studied law at Orleans (1478), and at Poitiers, where he became licentiate in July 1481. On his return to Germany he was engaged as interpreter by Count Eberhard of Württemberg, for a tour in Italy. They started for Florence and Rome in February 1482. His connection with the count became permanent, and after his return to Stutigart he received important posts at Eberhard's court. About this time he appears to have married, but little is known of his married life. He left no children; but in later years his sister's grandson Melanchthon was almost as a son to him till the Reformation estranged them.

In 1490 he was again in Italy. Here he saw Pico della Mirandola, to whose Cabbalistic doctrines he afterwards became heir, and also made the friendship of the pope's secretary, Jakob Questenberg. On an embassy to the emperor Frederick at Linz in 1492, he began to read Hebrew with the emperor's Jewish physician Jakob ben Jehiel Loans. In 1494 his rising reputation had been greatly enhanced by the publication of De Verbo Mirifico.

In 1496 Eberhard of Württemberg died, and Reuchlin was glad to accept the invitation of Johann von Dalberg (1445–1503), bishop of Worms, to Heidelberg, which was then the seat of the "Rhenish Society." In this court of letters Reuchlin made translations from the Greek authors. He was during a great part of his life the real centre of all Greek teaching as well as of all Hebrew teaching in Germany. Reuchlin pronounced Greek as his native teachers had taught him to do, i.e., in the modern Greek fashion. This pronunciation, which he defends in Dialogus de Recta Lat. Graecique Serm. Pron. (1519), came to be known, in contrast to that used by Erasmus, as the Reuchlinian.

At Heidelberg Reuchlin had many private pupils, among whom Franz von Sickingen is the best known name. With the monks he had never been liked; at Stuttgart also his great enemy was the Augustinian Conrad Holzinger. On this man he took a scholar's revenge in his first Latin comedy Sergius, a satire on worthless monks and false relics.

Through Dalberg, Reuchlin came into contact with Philip, elector palatine of the Rhine, who employed him to direct the studies of his sons, and in 1498 sent him on a mission to Rome. He came back laden with Hebrew books, and found when he reached Heidelberg that a change of government had opened the way for his return to Stuttgart, where his wife had remained all along. His friends had now again the upper hand, and knew Reuchlin's value. In 1500, or perhaps in 1502, he was given high judicial office in the Swabian League, which he held till 1512, when he retired to a small estate near Stuttgart.

For many years Reuchlin had been increasingly absorbed in Hebrew studies, which had for him more than a mere philological interest for as a good humanist he could not rest satisfied with the Vulgate text of the Old Testament. In 1506 appeared his epoch-making De Rudimentis Hebraicis—grammar and lexicon—mainly after Kimhi, yet not a mere copy of one man's teaching. The edition was costly and sold slowly. One great difficulty was that the wars of Maximilian I. in Italy prevented Hebrew Bibles coming into Germany. But for this also Reuchlin found help by printing the Penitential Psalms with grammatical explanations (1512), and other helps followed from time to time. But his Greek studies had interested him in those fantastical and mystical systems of later times with which the Cabbala has no small affinity. Reuchlin's mystico-cabbalistic ideas and objects were expounded in the De Verbo Mirifico, and in the De Arte Cabbalistica (1517).

Unhappily many of his contemporaries thought that the first step to the conversion of the Jews was to take from them their books. This view had for its chief advocate the bigoted Johann Pfefferkorn (1469–1521), who secured the ear of the emperor Maximilian. In 1510 Reuchlin was summoned in the name of the emperor to give his opinion on the suppression of the Jewish books. He proposed that the emperor should decree that for ten years there be two Hebrew chairs at every German university for which the Jews should furnish books. The other experts proposed that all books should be taken from the Jews; and, as the emperor still hesitated, the bigots threw on Reuchlin the whole blame of their ill success. Pfefferkorn circulated at the Frankfort fair of 1511 a gross libel (Handspiegel wider und gegen die Juden) declaring that Reuchlin had been bribed; and Reuchlin retorted as warmly in the Augenspiegel (1511). His adversary's next move was to declare the Augenspiegel a dangerous book; the Cologne theological faculty, with the inquisitor Jakob von Hochstraten (d. 1527), took up this cry, and on Oct. 7, 1512, they obtained an imperial

order confiscating the Augenspiegel. Reuchlin was timid, but he was honesty itself. He was willing to receive corrections in theology, which was not his subject, but he could not unsay what he had said; and as his enemies tried to press him into a corner he met them with open defiance in a Defensio contra Calumniatores (1513). The universities were now appealed to for opinions, and were all against Reuchlin. Even Paris (August 1514) condemned the Augenspiegel, and called on Reuchlin to recant. Meantime a formal process had begun at Mainz before the grand inquisitor, but Reuchlin by an appeal succeeded in transferring the question to Rome. Judgment was given in July 1516; and then, though the decision was really for Reuchlin, the trial was simply quashed. The result had cost Reuchlin years of trouble and no small part of his modest fortune, but the obscurantists received a crushing blow in Germany. No party could survive the ridicule that was poured on them in the Epistolae Obscurorum Virorum.

Reuchlin did not long enjoy his victory in peace. In 1519 Stuttgart was visited by famine, civil war and pestilence. Reuchlin sought refuge in Ingolstadt and taught there for a year as professor of Greek and Hebrew. He was now called to Tübingen and again spent the winter of 1521–22 teaching in his own systematic way. He died at the baths of Liebenzell on June 30, 1522, leaving in the history of the new learning a name only second to that of his younger contemporary Erasmus.

See L. Geiger, Johann Reuchlin (1871), which is the standard biography; also D. F. Strauss, Ulrich von Hutten; S. A. Hirsch, "John Reuchlin, the Father of the Study of Hebrew among the Christians," and his "John Pfefferkorn and the Battle of Books," in his Essays (London, 1905). Some interesting details about Reuchlin are given in the autobiography of Conrad Pellicanus (q.v.), which was not published when Geiger's book appeared. See also the article on Reuchlin in Herzog-Hauck, Realencyklopädie, and literature there cited.

RÉUNION, an island and French overseas département in the Indian ocean, 425 mi. S.E. of Tamatave, Madagascar, and 130 mi. S.W. of Port Louis, Mauritius. It is elliptical in form and has an area of 970 sq.mi. It lies between 20° 51′ and 21° 22′ S. and 55° 15′ and 55° 54′ E.

The coast line is little indented, high and difficult of access, and the harbours are usually sunken craters. The narrow coastlands, from $\frac{2}{3}$ to 2 mi. wide, are succeeded by hilly ground which gives place to mountain masses and tableland, occupying most of the island. The main axis and watershed runs northwest-southeast, and divides the island into windward (eastern) and leeward (western) districts. The whole relief is complex because of its volcanic nature. First was formed a mountain whose summit is approximately represented by Piton des Neiges (10,069 ft.), an immense denuded crater, and later another crater opened toward the east, piling up the mountain mass of Le Volcan. The oldest erupted rocks belong to the type of the andesites; the newest are varieties of basalt. The two massifs are united by high tablelands. In the older massif the most striking features are now three areas of subsidence—the cirques or mountain amphitheatres of Salazie, Mafatte and Cilaos—which lie northwest and south of Piton des Neiges. The first, which may be taken as typical, is surrounded by high, almost perpendicular walls of basaltic lava. Somewhat lower plateaus (the Plaine des Cafres and the Plaine des Palmistes) extend between Piton des Neiges and Le Volcan.

The second massif, Le Volcan, is cut off from the rest of the island by two "enclosures," each about 500 or 600 ft. deep. The outer enclosure runs across the island in a north and south direction; the inner forms a kind of parabola with its arms stretching east to the sea and embracing not only the volcano proper but also the great eastward slope known as the Grand Brûlé. The 30 mi. of mountain wall round the volcano is perhaps unique in its astonishing regularity. It encloses an area of about 40 sq.mi. known as the Grand Enclos. There are two principal craters, each on an elevated cone—the more westerly, now extinct (8,596 ft.), and the more easterly, called the Burning Crater or Fournaise (8,294 ft.). Eruptions, though not infrequent (30 were registered between 1735 and 1860), are seldom serious. The volcano is of Hawaiian type and its lava runs down to the sea. Following 40 years' inactivity, it reawakened in 1925 and erupted several times thereafter. Hot mineral springs are found on the flanks of Piton des Neiges; the Source de Salazie, 2,860 ft. above sea level, has a temperature of 90° F., and discharges water impregnated with bicarbonate of soda, carbonates of magnesium, lime, iron, etc.; that of Cilaos is 3,650 ft. above the sea with a temperature of 100°; and that of Mafatte at 2,238 ft. and 87°.

Climate.—The year divides into two seasons—that of heat and rain from November to April, that of dry and more bracing weather from May to October. The prevailing wind is the southeast trade wind, which sometimes veers around to the south and more frequently to the northeast; the west winds are not so steady (307 days of east to 58 of west wind in the year). As over all the Indian ocean, cyclonic storms are frequent at the change of seasons. The relief of the land causes appreciable climatic differences, the leeward side getting much less rain than the windward. On the coast and lower zones on the windward side the mean temperature is about 73° in the "winter" and 78° in the "summer." On the leeward side the heat is somewhat greater. In the Salazie cirque the mean annual average is 66°; on the Plaine des Palmistes 62°. On the mountain heights snow falls every year. Hill stations (Hellbourg, Cilaos) have been established in the cirques.

Flora and Fauna.—The heat, humidity and fertility of the volcanic soil have given Réunion an abundant and varied vegetation. In the forest region of the island there is a belt, from 4,500 to 5,000 ft. above the sea, characterized by the prevalence of dwarf bamboo (*Bambusa alpina*); and above that is a similar belt of *Acacia heterophylla*. Besides this last the best timber-trees are *Casuarina laterifolia, Foetida mauritiana, Elaeodendron orientale, Calophyllum spurium* (red tacamahac), *Terminali borbonica, Parkia speciosa.* A species of coffee plant is indigenous. Fruits grown include banana, coconut, breadfruit and jackfruit. Forests originally covered nearly the whole island; most of the land has been cleared, but the administration in part replanted the higher districts with eucalyptus and rubber trees.

The fauna of Réunion is not very rich in variety of species. Among the mammals are several bats, a wildcat, the tenrec (*Tenrec ecaudatus*), introduced from Madagascar, rats, etc. Among the more familiar birds are the Bourbon flycatcher (*Tchitrea bourbonnensis*), the Réunion merle (*Mieroscelis borbonica*), the Bourbon manioc bird (*Malacirops borbonicus*), the cardinal (*Foudia madagascariensis*), various swallows, ducks, etc. Lizards and frogs of more than one species are common, but only one snake (*Lycodon aulicus*) is known in the island. Various species of gobies, a gray mullet that goes into fresh water, a freshwater mullet (*Agonostomus eyprinoides*), *Doules fuscus* in brackish water and *Osphronamus olfax* (introduced into the island) are among the fishes found.

History.—Réunion is usually said to have been discovered on Feb. 9, 1513, St. Apollonia's day, by the Portuguese navigator Pedro Mascarenhas, and his name is still applied to the Mascarene Islands, the archipelago of which Réunion forms a part. The island itself was at first called Santa Apollonia or Mascarenhas. The French later called it Bourbon, then, after the Revolution, "la Réunion des Patriotes." When in 1638 the island was taken possession of by Captain Goubert, of Dieppe, it was uninhabited.

The first inhabitants were a dozen mutineers deported from Madagascar by Jacques Pronis. In 1664 the Compagnie des Indes Orientales initiated a regular colonization scheme. In 1717 there were only about 2,000 inhabitants, of whom 1,100 were Malagasy and Kaffir slaves. They lived on excellent terms with the pirates who frequented Madagascar. Mocha coffee, introduced at that time, quickly made the island prosperous. At the end of the century sugar replaced it as the principal crop.

From 1810 to 1815 the island was occupied by the English. In the enthusiasm of the 1848 revolution slavery was abolished. At that time there were 105,000 inhabitants, including 60,000 slaves who now received French citizenship. Under the Second Empire Indian coolies were brought in. Réunion became an overseas *département* of France in 1946.

Réunion has been called *colonie colonisatrice* because its inhabitants were among the first French settlers in Mauritius, Rodriguez and the Seychelles (in the 18th century), Madagascar and the Austral Islands of the Indian ocean (in the 19th). People from

Réunion have also gone as colonists to Cochin-China and New Caledonia. It is also called "l'île des poètes": extolled by André de Chénier, it was the birthplace of the Vicomte de Parny, Antoine de Bertin, Leconte de Lisle and Léon Dierx.

Inhabitants.—Réunion, strictly speaking, has no indigenous population. The inhabitants include Creoles, mulattoes, Negroes, Indians and other Asians. The Creole population is descended from the first French settlers, chiefly Normans and Bretons. Much of the population is of mixed descent. Three kinds of Creole are recognized—those of the towns and coasts, those of the mountains and the *petits blancs,* originally a class of small farmers living in the uplands, now reduced to a condition of poverty and dependence on the planters. The *créoles de villes,* the typical inhabitants of the island, are in general of a somewhat weak physique, quick-witted and of charming manners, and very proud of their island. The Creole patois is French distorted by Malagasy and Bantu pronunciation. The population numbered 242,067 at the 1946 census (1950 est., 261,647). The density is 270 persons to the square mile or, if only the settled areas are counted, 645 to the sq.mi.; the birth rate is high. Madagascar has been a receiving country for Réunionais emigrants, but overpopulation remains a problem. Indians and Chinese together number about 30,000.

Towns and Communications.—St. Denis (pop., 1950 est., 39,057), the capital of the island, lies on the north coast. It is built in the form of an amphitheatre, and has several fine public buildings and centrally situated botanic gardens. The only anchorage for vessels is an open roadstead. St. Pierre (pop. 24,652), the chief town on the leeward side of the island, has a small artificial harbour. Between St. Pierre and St. Denis, and both on the leeward shore, are the towns of St. Louis (pop. 23,925) and St. Paul (pop. 27,585). A few miles north of St. Paul on the south side of Cap Pointe des Galets is the port of the same name, the only considerable harbour in the island. It was completed in 1886, covers 40 ac., is well protected and has 28 ft. of water. A railway serving the port goes around the coast from St. Pierre, by St. Paul, St. Denis, to St. Benoît.

A road runs around the island. Lateral roads give access to the cirques and the hill stations.

Agriculture and Industry.—Most of the coastal region is occupied by sugar-cane plantations, vanilla and cocoa. Sugar cane, introduced in 1711 by Pierre Parat, is now the staple crop. In the 18th century the first place belonged to coffee (introduced from Arabia in 1715) and to the clove tree, brought from the Netherlands Indies by Pierre Poivre at the risk of his life. Both are now cultivated on a limited scale. Vanilla, introduced in 1818, is cultivated mostly in the more humid eastern part. In the highlands, which have a Mediterranean climate, geraniums and vetiver (from which essential oils for perfumes are extracted), maize, legumes and fruit trees are cultivated.

The sugar industry suffered greatly from the competition with beet sugar, the effects of bounties and antiquated methods of manufacture. It was not until 1906 that steps were taken to set up central sugar mills and refineries. By 1954 the industry was concentrated into 13 well-equipped plants. This concentration of industry is paralleled by a concentration of property: an aristocracy of millowners and big proprietors employs a proletariat of tenant farmers and farm workers. Rum is distilled and forms an important item of export.

Administration.—Réunion is a *département* of France. It sends three deputies and two senators to the French legislature, and a councillor to the assembly of the French union. All nonalien inhabitants are French citizens. At the head of the local administration is a prefect who is assisted by a secretary-general, a *procureur général* and a *conseil général* elected by the suffrage of all citizens, which, after 1946, had powers no greater than those of *conseils généraux* of French metropolitan *départements.* The technical services are administered by the several metropolitan ministries, and French metropolitan legislation as a whole extends to the island. For administrative purposes the island is divided into two *arrondissements,* the Windward, with five cantons and nine communes, and the Leeward, with four cantons and seven communes. The towns are subject to the French municipal law.

The island's revenue and expenditure are wholly accounted for within the French metropolitan budget.

Economy.—The Banque de la Réunion issues notes valued in francs Colonies Françaises d'Afrique (1 fr. C. F. A. = 2 fr. metropolitan). Exports in 1953 were valued at 5,354,000,000 fr. C. F. A., including 4,487,000,000 fr. C. F. A. for sugar (149,557 metric tons), 334,000,000 fr. C. F. A. for rum (41,614 hl.), 452,000,000 fr. C. F. A. for geranium and other essences (112 metric tons) and 51,000,000 fr. C. F. A. for vanilla (34 metric tons). The main destinations of exports were France (3,374,000,000 fr. C. F. A.), Indochina (503,000,000 fr. C. F. A.) and Morocco. Réunion's imports cost 6,415,000,000 fr. C. F. A. in 1953. Almost all foodstuffs are imported, notably rice and meat from Madagascar (6,415,000,000 fr. C. F. A.). Nearly all manufactured goods come from France (3,984,000,000 fr. C. F. A. in 1953).

BIBLIOGRAPHY.—G. Bory de St. Vincent, *Voyage dans les quatre principales îles des mers d'Afrique* (Paris, 1804); G. Azéma, *Histoire de l'île Bourbon* (Paris, 1859); I. Guët, *Les Origines de l'île Bourbon . . . etc.*, new ed. (Paris, 1888); J. de Cordemoy, *Flore de l'île de la Réunion* (Paris, 1895); P. Hermann, *Histoire et Géographie de l'île Bourbon* (Paris, 1909); A. Lacroix, *Minéralogie de Madagascar*, vol. iii (Paris, 1923); R. Barquissau *et al.*, *L'Île de la Réunion* (Paris, 1925); "Madagascar—Réunion" in *Encyclopédie maritime et coloniale*, vol. ii (Paris, 1947); R. Decary, "Réunion," in *Côte des Somalis, Réunion, Inde* (Paris, 1948); A. Brunet, *Trois Cents ans de colonisation, la Réunion* (Paris, 1948); P. Isnard, "La Réunion," in *La France de l'Ocean Indien* (Paris, 1952).   (Hu. De.)

REUNION, CHURCH. The modern divisions of the Christian world date from the 5th century when the so-called Monophysite and Nestorian Churches split from the rest partly for doctrinal and partly for political reasons. The 11th century witnessed the completion of the division between the Christian east and the west, while in the 16th century the Christian west was itself riven asunder by the Reformation and its aftermath. Since that time there have been divisive tendencies constantly apparent in Christendom which have resulted in the increase of Protestant sects.

The first half of the 20th century saw the spread of a worldwide movement for church reunion or for greater Christian unity in one form or another. This movement, sometimes called the ecumenical movement, was focused in the World Council of Churches, established at Amsterdam at a world assembly in 1948 (*see* below). The Roman Catholic Church is not associated with the council, and some Orthodox Eastern Churches, including the Russian Orthodox Church, withheld their support. The council represents most of non-Roman Christianity, however.

Two main factors lay behind 20th-century attempts to unite Christendom. The first was a renewed awareness of the part which the conception of unity played in the minds of the New Testament writers and particularly in that of Jesus Himself, together with the fact that the acute doctrinal issues which sundered men in earlier centuries no longer played a prominent part in their belief. The second reason was both evangelistic and theological: there was a widespread impatience with the failure of Christians to make an adequate impression on the world because of their failure to act together. This failure was especially acutely felt in the mission field. First attempts at a working agreement in mission areas in fact aggravated the problem they were meant to solve. In order to avoid direct competition many missions agreed to confine their efforts to one area each, but the result was to make unity even more necessary since it was impossible to confine each brand of Christian to the area where his particular church was in operation.

Position of the Roman Catholic Church.—The Roman Catholic Church does not take part in the above movements toward church unity, but it does not stand altogether outside them. The Council of Florence in 1438–39 was the most notable pre-Reformation effort to heal the breach between east and west. As, however, the claims of the Roman pontiff increased and the government of the church became more centred in the person of the pope, so did it become less possible for Rome to discuss common concerns about unity on the same level as other Christians. Its dogmatic position is such that there can be no terms of Christian reunion apart from surrender to the claims of the pope.

Nevertheless there has been increased interest in good relations with other Christians among Roman Catholics, and there are many religious orders and individuals whose prayers are devoted to this cause. The Church Unity octave, a week in which prayers are offered for Christian unity (Jan. 18–25) each year, has received much support from Roman Catholics all over the world.

World War I stimulated interest in Christian unity, and one result was a series of conversations at Malines, Belg., between a group of theologians of the Church of England and a similar body of Roman Catholic scholars led by Désiré Cardinal Mercier of Belgium. These talks were at first private and unofficial; later they were carried on with the knowledge both of the pope and of the archbishop of Canterbury. They earned however the intense disapproval of the Roman Catholic hierarchy in England, who had not been consulted about them, and subsequent decisions of the Holy See officially discouraged any further similar discussions. At the end of 1949 however the holy office at Rome issued an instruction about the ecumenical movement permitting discussions between Roman Catholics and other Christians under control of the local bishop, and also permitted common prayer at such mixed gatherings, again under control. Roman Catholic bishops differ widely about such common activities. Official Roman Catholic observers were appointed to attend the third World Conference on Faith and Order at Lund, Swed., in 1952, but were forbidden to attend the second Assembly of the World Council of Churches at Evanston, Ill., in 1954.

Orthodox Eastern Churches.—The Orthodox Eastern Churches in the 20th century have come into closer contact with western Christianity than for centuries, partly because of the large numbers of members of the Orthodox Churches who have fled to the west as refugees. After World War I thousands of Orthodox Russians fled to the west, and even larger numbers did so after World War II, as did Orthodox Serbs and Ukrainians. The west therefore had the opportunity of learning more about these ancient churches, especially through the work of the Russian Institute of St. Sergius in Paris.

The Church of England had had occasional contacts with the Orthodox Churches since the 17th century, and in the 20th attempts were made to create closer links. After consultations in 1920 the ecumenical patriarchate in 1922 announced "recognition" of Anglican orders. Strictly speaking, the Orthodox Churches consider their own orders as the only fully constituted ministry. This recognition of Anglican orders officially stated that Anglican orders exhibited all the necessary external conditions to make them authentic. The Orthodox Churches do not normally consider the question of orders in quite the same terms as do Roman Catholics, but this recognition involved the statement that the apostolic succession had been retained in the Church of England, a point which was considered to be of importance after the papal condemnation of Anglican orders in 1896. The recognition was also given later by the patriarch of Jerusalem, the Church of Cyprus, the patriarchate of Alexandria and the Church of Rumania. In a consideration of the question at a conference of Orthodox Churches in Moscow in 1948 the need for doctrinal agreement was particularly stressed, however. No final conclusion could be reached without a general synod of the Orthodox Churches, which political divisions made difficult. The large numbers of Orthodox Eastern Christians in the United States have thrown the Orthodox into close contact with Christians of western traditions, and there have been many instances of close but unofficial mutual ministrations especially between Orthodox and Anglicans there.

There have, however, been serious dissensions among *émigré* Russian Orthodox Christians since the end of World War I. After World War II the number of Orthodox in emigration considerably increased, and differences about the attitude to be adopted to the Orthodox Churches in Communist-dominated countries caused further division among them. During the first half of the 20th century the lesser Eastern Churches (Armenian, Coptic, Ethiopian, Syrian Orthodox in the middle east and in south India, and Assyrian) came into closer contact with each other and with other Christians, especially through the ecumenical movement.

Relations Among Other Churches.—The 19th century witnessed the beginning of a new movement toward close cooperation among Christians of churches affected by the Reformation. Two practical movements—the British and Foreign Bible society and the Young Men's Christian association—set the pattern for a new kind of co-operation among evangelical Christians of different bodies. Although not concerned with ecclesiastical relations, the work of these organizations brought Christians together and demonstrated the advantages of common action.

The 19th century also witnessed in England the rise of the Oxford movement, which exhibited a heightened interest in reunion of the churches from a theological point of view. The proclamation of the dogma of the infallibility of the pope in 1870 caused secessions that strengthened the Old Catholic Churches, which were particularly interested in achieving reunion with the Orthodox Church and later with the Anglican Churches.

In 1931 and 1932 an agreement for full intercommunion was reached between the Old Catholic Churches and the Church of England, which was subsequently endorsed by almost all the other Anglican Churches. In the United States it brought intercommunion between the Protestant Episcopal Church and the Polish National Catholic Church there. This agreement is the only concordat which has achieved full intercommunion between churches of an episcopal polity and is therefore of importance. It rests on three simple principles: (1) mutual recognition of one another's catholicity and independence; (2) mutual admission of each other's members to communion; (3) freedom to vary in doctrinal opinion and liturgical practice where essentials are not in question.

The retention of episcopal traditions and government in the Lutheran Churches of Scandinavia prompted attempts at closer relations with the Church of England, and formal relationships were established of a friendly nature but falling short of the full intercommunion achieved with the Old Catholics.

There have been many discussions with a view to creating union between episcopal and nonepiscopal churches in which Anglican Churches have been involved. Negotiations have been conducted on the Anglican side on the basis of the "Lambeth Quadrilateral" as approved in the Lambeth conference of all Anglican bishops in 1920. This consisted of four points on the acceptance of which might be based the future reunion of Christendom, namely: the Holy Scriptures as the standard of faith, the Nicene and Apostles' creeds as a sufficient statement of the Christian faith, the use of the two sacraments of baptism and the holy communion, and a ministry universally recognized in the form of the historic episcopate.

This "Appeal to all Christian People" was dispatched to churches throughout Christendom and led to discussions with free churches in England, which however had not reached a favourable outcome by 1939, although free church leaders had publicly recognized that the episcopate was the only form of the Christian ministry which would have general acceptance.

In 1946 the archbishop of Canterbury appealed to the free churches to seek advance by taking episcopacy into their systems rather than by constitutional reunion. This initiated a series of discussions culminating in the report *Church Relations in England* issued in Sept. 1950. It revealed considerable accord on almost all matters except the ministry. There were divergencies as to the use of creeds and sacraments, yet it was recorded that "On the doctrines of God the Father, the Person and Work of Christ, the Person and mission of the Holy Spirit, the Trinity, and the Life Everlasting we have found nothing which separates any one of these Communions from another. All acknowledge the apostolic faith as contained in the Scriptures and expressed in the Apostles' and Nicene Creeds."

The difficulty of the ministry remained, for no method was discovered whereby an episcopal ministry could be introduced without in some way implying that nonepiscopally ordained ministers were inferior to those ordained by bishops. There were also other important obstacles such as the custom in some free churches of permitting laymen to celebrate the holy communion. It seemed probable that advance must depend on negotiations between individual churches which already had affinities, such as the Church of England and the Methodist Church.

Whatever the outcome of efforts aimed at reunion there was a remarkable growth in friendliness and understanding between the Anglican and free churches in England, which after 1942 had an organ of co-operation in the British Council of Churches.

In 1947 a successful conclusion was reached to 28 years' discussions with the inauguration of the Church of South India, an organic union of Christians from Anglican, Presbyterian, Congregationalist and Methodist traditions which included the acceptance of a full episcopal ministry. The main difficulty of the reordination of ministers previously ordained in the constituent churches was overcome by an escape clause permitting ministers to remain active ministers of the new church without reordination for 30 years. Then the church would decide what exceptions, if any, would be permitted to episcopal ordination.

In 1948 the Anglican Church in America undertook the consecration of bishops for the Philippine Independent Church, thus establishing a special connection between that church and the Protestant Episcopal Church of the United States.

There remains the field of relations among Protestant Churches in which no question of the historic episcopate arises, and in this area there were a number of successful reunions. In Scotland in 1900 the Free Church of Scotland and the United Presbyterian Church became the United Free Church of Scotland, and in 1929 this church united with the Church of Scotland under the latter's name. In 1938 four bodies united to form the Reformed Church of France. The Dutch Reformed Church united two bodies in 1946, and in Switzerland in 1943 two Reformed Churches of Neuchâtel reunited.

There have also been organic unions achieved among Lutherans in Brazil (1950), Madagascar (1950) and the Netherlands (1951). Much closer relations among the Lutherans have been reached in the United States. Three U.S. Methodist Churches combined in 1939 to form the Methodist Church, and in 1955 they were engaged in conversations about close relations with other U.S. Protestants.

There have also been successful mergers of Protestants of different confessions. The following bodies are the outcome of such unions: the Church of Christ in Japan (1941), the Church of Central Africa in Rhodesia (1945), the Evangelical United Brethren Church (U.S.) (1946) and the United Church of Christ in the Philippines (1948). The Evangelical Church in Germany (1948), while not constituting a church strictly speaking, represents more than a simple federation.

The United States exhibits a particular zeal for closer Christian co-operation. The churches there for the most part co-operate in common programs through the National Council of the Churches of Christ in America (originally the Federal council), which includes Orthodox Churches as well as most of the other non-Roman Catholic churches. The situation in the United States was worse than in many other countries owing to the fragmentation of Protestant Churches there caused by the fact that many of those who emigrated did so for religious reasons and thus took all the divisions of the old world with them.

Development of the World Council of Churches.—The most important single organization facilitating unity among the churches is the World Council of Churches, which represented at the time of its second world assembly at Evanston in 1954 no fewer than 163 churches from 48 nations. A significant advance toward its development was the holding of the world missionary conference in Edinburgh, Scot., in 1910, where were first seen the possibilities of co-operation among Christians on the grand scale.

Two main strands contributed to the foundation of the World Council of Churches. The first was a theological strand, springing from a desire to discuss, and if possible to overcome, the differences of belief which divided Christians, many of them heritages from past history rather than immediate issues of the day. A movement was initiated to bring Christian theologians together to discuss doctrinal questions: this was the Faith and Order movement, owing much to the effort of Bishop Charles Brent of the Protestant Episcopal Church of the United States. In 1910 a committee in the United States first spoke of the possibility of a world conference. The first World Conference on Faith and Order was held at Lausanne, Switz., in 1927, and, although the Roman Catholic Church declined to attend, all the other main traditions of Christendom were represented. A second world conference was held at Edinburgh in 1937 and a third at Lund in 1952.

Parallel to this movement was another, the chief inspiration of which was Nathan Soderblom, archbishop of Uppsala, Swed. His interest was to bring representatives of Christianity together in practical co-operation for the peace and benefit of mankind. A World Conference on Life and Work was first held under his chairmanship at Stockholm in 1925; a second was held at Oxford in 1937 immediately before the Faith and Order conference.

At the Oxford and Edinburgh conferences it was agreed that the two movements should be amalgamated to form a World Council of Churches. Preliminary plans were laid in 1939, but the outbreak of World War II prevented further action. A skeleton staff in Geneva with W. Visser 't Hooft as general secretary did great work during the war in keeping Christians on both sides in touch with one another. It was only after the war that the first constitutive assembly could be held at Amsterdam in 1948.

The World Council of Churches has no power over the churches. It is a means of initiating common discussion and action and of providing the churches with a centre of information and co-ordination. The council as such is not concerned with church re-union, since that is for the churches themselves. Nevertheless the whole activity of the council brings Christians together and makes them aware of the need for unity both in theory and in practice.

BIBLIOGRAPHY.—Ruth Rouse and Stephen Charles Neill (eds.), *A History of the Ecumenical Movement 1517-1948* (London, 1954); Stephen Neill, *Towards Church Union, 1937-1952* (London, Chicago, 1952); the *Ecumenical Review,* quarterly (Geneva, 1948–); *International Review of Missions,* quarterly (London, 1912–).
(H. M. W.)

REUS, a city of northeast Spain, in the province of Tarragona, on the Saragossa-Tarragona railway, 4 mi. N. of Salou, its port on the Mediterranean. Pop. (1950) 35,950 (mun.). Reus consists of two parts, the old and the new, separated by the Calle Arrabal, which occupies the site of the old city wall. The earliest records of Reus date from about the middle of the 13th century. Its modern prosperity is traced to about the year 1750, when a colony of English settled there and established a trade in woollens, leather, wine and spirits. The principal incidents in its political history arose out of the occurrences of 1843 (*see* SPAIN: *History*), in connection with which the town received the title of city, and Generals Zurbano and Prim were made counts of Reus. The city was the birthplace of General Prim (1814–70) and of the painter Mariano Fortuny (1839–74). The city has important flour, wine and fruit export houses.

REUSCH, FRANZ HEINRICH (1823–1900), German theologian, was born at Brilon, Westphalia, on Dec. 4, 1823. He studied general literature at Paderborn and theology at Bonn, Tübingen and Munich, where he was a friend and pupil of Döllinger. In 1854, he became *Privatdozent* in the exegesis of the Old Testament in the Catholic theological faculty at Bonn; in 1858 he was made extraordinary and in 1861 ordinary professor of theology in the same university. From 1866 to 1877 he was editor of the *Bonner Theologisches Literaturblatt.* In the controversies on the infallibility of the Pope, Reusch, who had been ordained priest in 1849, attached himself to Döllinger's party, and he and his colleagues Hilgers, Knoodt and Langen were interdicted by the archbishop of Cologne in 1871 from pursuing their courses of lectures. In 1872 he was excommunicated. For many years after this he held the post of Old Catholic *curé* of Bonn, as well as the position of vicar-general to the Old Catholic bishop Reinkens, but resigned both in 1878, when, with Döllinger, he disapproved of the permission to marry granted by the Old Catholic Church in Germany to its clergy. He was made rector of Bonn university in 1873. In 1874 and 1875 he was official reporter of the reunion conferences held at Bonn. He produced with Döllinger the *Geschichte der Moralstreitigkeiten in der Römisch-Katholischen Kirche seit dem XVI. Jahrhundert* and the *Erörterungen über Leben und Schriften des hl. Liguori.* He died on March 3, 1900.

REUSS, ÉDOUARD GUILLAUME EUGÈNE (1804–1891), German Protestant theologian, was born at Strasbourg on July 18, 1804. He studied philology in his native town (1819–22); theology at Göttingen under J. G. Eichhorn; and oriental languages at Halle under Wilhelm Gesenius, and afterward at

Paris under Silvestre de Sacy (1827–28). He taught at Strasbourg from 1828 until 1888, for 60 years, having become full professor in 1836. His most important works are: *Geschichte der heiligen Schriften Neuen Testaments,* (1842), *Histoire de la théologie chrétienne au siècle apostolique* (1852); *L'Histoire du canon des saintes écritures dans l'église chrétienne* (1863); *La Bible, nouvelle traduction avec commentaire* (1874, etc.); and *Geschichte der heiligen Schriften Alten Testaments,* a veritable encyclopaedia of the history of Israel from its earliest beginning till the taking of Jerusalem by Titus. He died at Strasbourg on April 15, 1891. For many years Reuss edited with A. E. Cunitz (1812–86) the *Beiträge zu den theologischen Wissenschaften.* With Cunitz and J. W. Baum (1809–78), and after their deaths alone, he edited the monumental edition of Calvin's works (38 vol., 1863 ff.). His critical edition of the Old Testament appeared a year after his death.

See the article in Herzog-Hauck, *Realenzyklopädie,* and *cf.* Otto Pfleiderer, *Development of Theology in Germany Since Kant* (1890).

REUSS, the name of two former German principalities (Reuss-Greiz and Reuss-Schleiz-Gera) which after 1918 were amalgamated into Thuringia (*q.v.*).

History.—The princes of Reuss traced their descent to Henry (d. about 1120), who was appointed by the emperor Henry IV imperial bailiff (Ger. *Vogt,* from Lat. *advocatus imperii*) of Gera and of Weida. His descendants called themselves lords of Weida. The land under their rule gradually increased in size, and it is said that the name of Reuss was applied to it because of the fact that one of its princes married a Russian princess, their son being called *der Russe,* or "the Russian." In 1564 the family was divided into three branches by the sons of Henry XVI (d. 1535). One of these died out in 1616, but those of Reuss-Greiz and Reuss-Schleiz-Gera survived as sovereign houses till the revolution of 1918. The lords of Reuss took the title of count in 1673; the head of the elder line became a prince of the empire in 1778, and the head of the younger line in 1806. In 1807 the two princes joined the confederation of the Rhine, and in 1815 the German confederation. In 1866 both principalities became members of the north German confederation.

A curious custom prevailed in the house of Reuss. The male members of both branches of the family all bore the name of Henry (Heinrich), the individuals being distinguished by numbers.

See H. von Voss, *Die Ahnen des reussischen Hauses* (Lobenstein, 1882); O. Liebmann, *Das Staatsrecht des Fürstenthums Reuss* (1884); C. F. Collmann, *Reussische Geschichte: Das Vogtland im Mittelalter* (Greiz, 1892); B. Schmidt, *Die Reussen, Genealogie des Gesamthauses Reuss* (Schleiz, 1903).

REUTER, FRITZ (1810–1874), German novelist, made Plattdeutsch a literary language. Born Nov. 7, 1810, at Stavenhagen, in Mecklenburg-Schwerin, he studied at Rostock and at Jena, where he was a member of the political students' club, or German Burschenschaft, and in 1833 was arrested in Berlin by the Prussian government. Although the only charge which could be proved against him was that he had been seen wearing the Burschenschaft colours, he was condemned to death for high treason. The sentence was commuted to imprisonment for 30 years in a Prussian fortress. In 1838, through the personal intervention of the grand duke of Mecklenburg, he was handed over to the authorities of his native state, and in 1840 was set free by a general amnesty.

In 1850 he settled as a private tutor at the little town of Treptow in Pomerania. There he married Luise Kunze, the daughter of a Mecklenburg pastor. Reuter's first publication was a collection of miscellanies, written in Plattdeutsch and entitled *Läuschen un Riemels* ("Anecdotes and Rhymes," 1853; a second collection followed in 1858). There followed *Polterabendgedichte* (1855) and *De Reis' nah Belligen* (1855). In 1856 Reuter left Treptow and established himself at Neubrandenburg. His next book (published in 1858) was *Kein Hüsung,* an epic in which he presents with great force and vividness some of the least attractive aspects of village life in Mecklenburg. This was followed, in 1860, by *Hanne Nüte un de lütte Pudel,* the best of his verse compositions. In 1860 he published the first series of his *Olle Kamellen* ("Old Stories of Bygone Days"), which contained *Woans ick tau'ne Fru kam* and *Ut de Franzosentid.* Later volumes were entitled *Ut mine Festungstid* (1861); *Ut mine Stromtid* (3 vols. 1864); and *Dörchläuchting* (1866)—all written in the Plattdeutsch dialect of the author's home. *Ut mine Stromtid* is by far the greatest of Reuter's writings. *Ut de Franzosentid* describes the deep national impulse under which Germany rose against Napoleon. *Ut mine Stromtid* deals with the revolution of 1848.

In 1863 Reuter moved to Eisenach; and here he died on July 12, 1874.

Reuter's *Sämtliche Werke,* in 13 vols., were first published in 1863–68. To these were added in 1875 two volumes of *Nachgelassene Schriften,* with a biography by A. Wilbrandt; and in 1878 two supplementary volumes to the works appeared. A popular edition in 7 vols. was published in 1877–78 (new edition, 1902); there are also editions by K. F. Müller (18 vols., 1905), and W. Seelmann (7 vols., 1905–06). See *Briefe F. Reuters an seinen Vater,* ed. F. Engel (2 vols., 1895); A. Römer, *F. Reuter in seinem Leben und Schaffen* (1895); G. Raatz, *Wahrheit und Dichtung in Reuters Werken* (1895); E. Brandes, *Aus F. Reuters Leben* (1899); K. F. Müller, *Der Mecklenburger Volksmund und F. Reuters Schriften* (1902). A complete bibl. will be found in the *Niederdeutsche Jahrbuch* for 1896 and 1902.

REUTER, GABRIELE (1859–1941), German novelist, was born at Alexandria, Egypt, on Feb. 8, 1859. Her first novel, *Glück und Geld,* appeared in 1888. One of her early novels, *Aus guter Familie,* had reached its 25th edition in 1907. Among her works are *Frauenseelen* (1901); *Jugend eines Idealisten* (1916); and *Benedikta* (1923). She died at Weimar in Nov. 1941.

REUTER, PAUL JULIUS, BARON DE (1816–1899), founder of Reuters news agency, was born at Cassel, Germany. At the age of thirteen he became a clerk in his uncle's bank at Göttingen, where he met Gauss, whose experiments in telegraphy were then attracting some attention. In 1849 there was a gap between the end of the new German telegraph line at Aix-la-Chapelle and that of the French and Belgian lines at Verviers. Reuter organized a news-collecting agency at each of these places and bridged the interval by a pigeon-post. On the establishment of through telegraphic communication, Reuter endeavoured to start a news agency in Paris, but finding that the French government's restrictions would render the scheme unworkable, removed in 1851 to England and became a naturalized British subject. The first submarine cable—between Dover and Calais—had just been laid, and Reuter opened a news office in London. At first, however, his business was practically confined to the transmission of private commercial telegrams to places not connected with the new system. He appointed agents at the telegraph termini on the Continent to forward these despatches by rail or pigeon-post to the addresses. His efforts to induce the English papers to publish his foreign news telegrams were unsuccessful, until in 1858 *The Times* published the report of an important speech by Napoleon III. forwarded by Reuter's Paris agent.

Reuter now extended his sphere of operations all over the world. He laid down a special cable from Cork to Crookhaven, Ireland, which enabled him to circulate news of the American Civil War several hours before steamers could reach Liverpool. A concession for a cable beneath the North Sea to Cuxhaven was granted him by the king of Hanover in 1865, and in the same year a concession was granted him for a cable between France and the United States, the line being worked jointly by Reuter and the Anglo-American Telegraph Company. Reuter was in 1871 given the title of baron by the duke of Saxe-Coburg and Gotha, and by a special grant of Queen Victoria he and his heirs were authorized to have the privileges of this rank in England. Reuter died at Nice on Feb. 25, 1899.

REUTERHOLM, GUSTAF ADOLF, BARON (1756–1813), Swedish statesman. After a brief military career he was appointed *Kammerherr* to Sophia Magdalena, queen consort of Gustavus III., and became intimately connected with the king's brother, Charles, then duke of Sudermania. He was imprisoned for a time in 1789 with other malcontents opposed to Gustavus III. On the death of Gustavus and the assumption of the regency by Charles he was made a member of the council of state and one of the "lords of the realm." His policy became increasingly reactionary and on the accession of Gustavus IV. he was expelled from Stockholm. He died in exile in Schleswig on Dec. 27, 1813.

See *Sveriges Historia* (Stockholm, 1877–81), vol. v.

REUTERS, the principal British and international news agency, founded in 1849 by Baron Paul Julius de Reuter (*q.v.*), who established a system of offices and correspondents throughout the world. He concentrated in London the news from these correspondents and then redistributed it. In 1865 Reuter transferred his business to a joint stock company, of which he became the governing director; he was succeeded in 1879 by his elder son, Baron Herbert de Reuter (1852–1915). Mark F. Napier was chairman of the company from 1910 to 1919, and in conjunction with him, Sir Roderick Jones, chairman and managing director, for national reasons arising out of World War I, converted the agency from a public company into a private trusteeship. This involved buying out the then existing shareholders for a sum of considerably over half a million sterling. Ten years later Sir Roderick reorganized the trusteeship in conjunction with the Press Association to ensure the passage ultimately of the complete ownership of Reuters to the newspapers of the United Kingdom. The principal news agency in every country in the world is affiliated with Reuters. Reuters' correspondents resident in the respective countries enjoy the exclusive call for Reuters' purposes upon the news of these agencies.

Where Reuters do not supply their telegrams direct to the newspapers, they deliver their service to these agencies to be disposed of by them in their territories. In addition to their services of imperial and foreign political news Reuters have greatly extended, especially to the Continent, to the East, the Far East and to the empire their services of commercial and financial prices and intelligence. (H. B. C.; X.)

REUTLINGEN, a German town, in the Swabian Alps of Württemberg, on the Echatz, an affluent of the Neckar, 36 mi. by rail S. of Stuttgart. Pop. (1939) 38,870. Reutlingen, which is first mentioned in 1213, became a free imperial town in the 13th century and was fortified by the emperor Frederick II. It came into the possession of Württemberg in 1802. Its industries include cotton spinning and weaving, dyeing and bleaching; also the manufacture of leather and machinery.

REVAL: see TALLINN.

REVELATION, BOOK OF: *see* APOCALYPSE.

REVELSTOKE, city, British Columbia, on the Columbia river, a key point on the Trans-Canada highway and a divisional station on the Canadian Pacific railway, 245 mi. N.E. of Vancouver. Pop. (1951) 2,908.

It is the supply centre for a mining and lumbering district, with railway shops, and is surrounded by rich fruit growing and ranching country.

A scenic motor road leads up Mt. Revelstoke to 5,000 ft. above the town.

REVENTLOW, CHRISTIAN DITLEV FREDERICK, COUNT (1748–1827), Danish statesman and reformer, born on March 11, 1748, was educated at Sörö and Leipzig, and made an extensive tour of western Europe to study economic conditions before he returned to Denmark in 1770. In 1774 he held a high position in the *Kammerkollegiet,* or board of trade, and two years later he entered the Department of Mines, and in 1781 he was a member of the *Overskattedirectionen,* or chief taxing board.

In 1784, he was placed at the head of the *Rentekammeret,* which took cognizance of everything relating to agriculture. He appointed a small agricultural commission to better the condition of the crown serfs, and among other things enable them to turn their leaseholds into freeholds.

Reventlow induced the Crown Prince Frederick, in July 1786, to appoint a grand commission to take the condition of all the peasantry in the kingdom into immediate consideration. This agricultural commission resulted in a series of reforms of the highest importance. The ordinance of June 8, 1787, modified the existing leaseholds, greatly to the advantage of the peasantry; the ordinance of June 20, 1788, abolished villeinage and completely transformed the much-abused *hoveri* system whereby the feudal tenant was bound to cultivate his lord's land as well as his own; and the ordinance of Dec. 6, 1799, did away with *hoveri* altogether. Reventlow also started public credit banks enabling small cultivators to borrow money on favourable terms.

But the financial distress of Denmark, the jealousy of the duchies, the ruinous political complications of the Napoleonic period, and, above all, the Crown Prince Frederick's growing jealousy of his official advisers, prevented Reventlow from completing his reforms. On Dec. 7, 1813, he was dismissed, and retired to his estates in Laaland, where he died on Oct. 11, 1827.

See Adolph Frederik Bergsöe, *Grev. C. D. F. Reventlows Virksomhed* (Copenhagen, 1837); Louis Theodor Alfred Bobe, *Efterl. Papirer fra den Reventlowske Familiekreds* (Copenhagen, 1895–97).

REVENUE, income, return, or profit; more particularly the receipts from all sources of a Government or State (O. Fr. *revenu,* from *revenir,* to return). The revenue of a State is largely made up of taxation, and the general principles of taxes are discussed in TAXATION and in a number of articles to which a guide will be found under FINANCE, ARTICLES ON. In some countries public or State domain may contribute substantially to the revenue, as do the forests in Russia, while in other countries important contributions are made from the State railways, post and telegraph services, etc. (*See* EXCISE; ESTATE DUTIES; INCOME TAX; INHERITANCE TAX; STAMP DUTY; TARIFFS; etc.)

REVERBERATORY FURNACE: *see* FURNACE, METALLURGICAL.

REVERE, PAUL (1735–1818), American engraver and patriot, was born in Boston, Mass., on Jan. 1, 1735. He had a meagre schooling, and in his father's shop learned the trade of a gold- and silversmith. In 1756 he was 2nd lieutenant of artillery in the expedition against Crown Point, and for several months was stationed at Ft. Edward, in New York. He became a proficient copper engraver, and engraved several anti-British caricatures in the years before the American revolution. He was one of the Boston grand jurors who refused to serve in 1774 because parliament had made the justices independent of the people for their salaries; was a leader in the Boston Tea Party; was one of the 30 north end mechanics who patrolled the streets to watch the movements of the British troops and Tories; and in Dec. 1774 was sent to Portsmouth, N.H., to urge the seizure of military stores there, and induced the colonists to attack and capture Ft. William and Mary—one of the first acts of military force in the war. His midnight ride from Charlestown to Lexington on April 18–19, 1775, to give warning of the approach of British troops from Boston, is Revere's most famous exploit; it is commemo-

BY COURTESY OF THE HALLIDAY HISTORICAL PHOTOGRAPH CO., BOSTON

THE HOUSE OF PAUL REVERE IN BOSTON, MASS.; BUILT ABOUT 1676, THE DIAMOND WINDOW PANES BEING A RESTORATION

rated by Longfellow, who, however, has "paid little attention to exactness of fact" (Justin Winsor). In 1775 Revere was sent by the Massachusetts provincial congress to Philadelphia to study the working of the only powder mill in the colonies, and although he was allowed only to pass through the building, obtained sufficient information to enable him to set up a powder mill at Canton. He was commissioned a major of infantry in the Massachusetts militia in April 1776; was promoted to the rank of lieutenant-colonel of artillery in November; was stationed at Castle William, defending Boston harbour, and finally received command of this fort.

He served in an expedition to Rhode Island in 1778, and in the following year participated in the unsuccessful Penobscot expedition. After his return he was accused of having disobeyed the orders of the commanding officer, was tried by court martial, and was acquitted. After the war he engaged in the manufacture of gold- and silverware, and became a pioneer in the production in America of copper-plating and copper spikes for ships. In 1795, as grand master of the Masonic fraternity, he laid the cornerstone of the new State House in Boston. He died in Boston on May 10, 1818.

See Charles F. Gettemy, *The True Story of Paul Revere* (Boston, 1905); E. Forbes, *Paul Revere and the World He Lived In* (1942).

REVERE, a city of Suffolk county, Massachusetts, U.S.A., on Massachusetts bay, adjoining Boston on the north-east. It is served by the Boston and Maine railway. The population of Revere in 1950 was 36,763; in 1940 it was 34,405; and in 1930 it was 35,680 by the federal census. It is primarily a residential suburb and resort, with some light manufacturing. Revere beach, extending from the promontory of Winthrop on the south to the Point of Pines on the north, is to Boston what Coney Island is to New York city. The first settlement there (called Rumney Marsh) was made in 1626. It was part of Boston until 1739, and then of the town of Chelsea until in 1846 North Chelsea was set off and incorporated as a separate town. In 1871 North Chelsea changed its name to Revere (in honour of Paul Revere) and in 1914 it was incorporated as a city.

REVEREND, a term of respect or courtesy, now especially used as the ordinary prefix of address to the names of ministers of religion of all denominations. The uses of Med. Lat. *reverendus* do not confine the term to those in orders; Du Cange (*Glossarium s.v.*) defines it as *titulus honorarius, etiam mulieribus potioris dignitatis concessus,* and in the 15th century in English it is found as a term of respectful address.

In the Church of England deans are addressed as "very reverend," bishops as "right reverend" and archbishops as "most reverend." The moderator of the Church of Scotland is also styled "right reverend."

REVERSING LAYER, of the sun or stars, the layer where the absorption indicated by the dark lines in the spectrum occurs. The reversing layer proper lies near the top of the photosphere where the pressure is usually about one ten-thousandth atmosphere; but some of the dark lines are caused by absorption at higher levels in the chromosphere.

REVERSION, in biology, the phenomenon of an organism "throwing back" to some remote ancestor.

For reversion in law, *see* REMAINDER.

REVILLA GIGEDO, an isolated, uninhabited group of rocky islands in the North Pacific, 18° N., 112° W., belonging to Mexico and forming part of the state of Colima. They are about 420 mi. from the Mexican coast and comprise the large island of Socorro (San Tomás), 24 mi. long by an average of 9 mi. wide, and the three widely separated islets of San Benedicto, Roca Partida and Clarion, with a total area of 320 sq.mi. The island of Socorro has an extinct volcano 3,660 ft. high. The archipelago derives its name from the Spanish viceroy who governed Mexico from 1746 to 1755.

REVIVAL, RELIGIOUS, is a renewed interest in religion, coming, as a rule, after a period of indifference or decline. Revivalism and evangelism are frequently used as identical terms, but evangelism has a definite doctrinal connotation, emphasizing the objective atonement of Christ, the necessity of a new birth or conversion, and salvation through faith. Revivalism, on the other hand, connotes certain methods of presenting evangelical doctrine, and the religious awakening resulting therefrom.

Revivalism, in the modern sense, has its roots in 18th-century pietism, with its emphasis upon Christianity as an inner experience and a way of life. It was taken to the English colonies of America by pietistic Dutch, German Reformed and Lutheran pastors in the first third of the 18th century. The colonial revival began in 1725, under the preaching of Theodorus J. Frelinghuysen, a Dutch Reformed pastor in central New Jersey. Largely through the influence of William Tennent and the graduates of his "log college" the revival spread to the Scots-Irish settlers swarming across the

Atlantic. Gilbert Tennent, Jonathan Dickinson (the first president of the College of New Jersey) and Aaron Burr, Sr., spearheaded this phase of the revival, which brought Presbyterianism to a place of prime significance in the colonies. The New England revival began in 1734 under the preaching of Jonathan Edwards, the Congregational minister at Northampton, Mass., and resulted in more than 300 conversions in that frontier village. This was but the beginning of a movement which swept through New England and continued for ten years, resulting in adding at least 25,000 members to the Congregational churches and the creation of 150 new congregations. The last phase of the colonial awakenings was the southern revival, which began as a Presbyterian movement in Virginia under the leadership of Samuel Davies (1750); it continued as a Baptist movement after 1760, and its final phase marked the beginning of Methodism in America, under the leadership of the Anglican evangelical clergyman Devereux Jarratt, George Shadford and Francis Asbury.

These several phases of the colonial revival were tied together by the activities of George Whitefield who made seven evangelistic tours of America between 1738 and 1770. He co-operated with all revivalists without distinction, preaching always to immense crowds.

The Wesleyan revival in England was also rooted in pietism. It may be said to have begun with the conversion experiences of John and Charles Wesley and Whitefield in 1738. The revival as a movement centred in John Wesley as its organizer. The methods used to bring vital religion to the unchurched masses, especially those living in towns, was through a system of itinerant preachers, who travelled definite circuits, preaching wherever opportunity offered and then gathering the converts into small groups for encouragement and instruction, called classes under appointed leaders. The whole work in the British Isles and in America was completely under John Wesley's control until his death. He superintended the work in Britain personally by travelling 6,000-8,000 mi. a year; he toured Ireland 19 times during the course of his long life. The Methodist revival was, until the death of John Wesley, a movement within the Church of England, and a strong and permanent evangelical party arose within the church. Methodism became a separate ecclesiastical body in America in 1784 and in England after 1800.

One of the most remarkable revivals of modern times was that which swept over the western part of the United States from 1797 to 1805, often called the Great Western Revival. It had its beginnings among the Presbyterians, but the Methodists and Baptists soon joined in the movement and it eventually affected all the Protestant bodies. Great meetings were held in the woods, often attended with emotional excitement. From the western revivals came the camp meeting, begun by the Presbyterians but eventually taken over by the Methodists and developed into an institution of large social and religious significance. The eastern phase of this revival, sometimes called the second awakening, was centred in the colleges under such leaders as Timothy Dwight, president of Yale, and resulted in the raising up of a new leadership in the revivalistic churches.

The two most outstanding revivalists of the 19th century were Charles G. Finney (1792-1875) and Dwight L. Moody (1837-99). Finney set the revivalistic pattern for the generation previous to the Civil War, Moody for the generation following. Finney's converts led in the great reform movements of the 1830s and 1840s; Moody and his imitators, J. W. Chapman, R. A. Torrey and William A. Sunday, were chiefly concerned with fighting the paganism of the fast-growing cities in the U.S. A sweeping revival occurred in Wales (1904-06), and the English revivalist Gipsy Smith conducted revivalistic campaigns on both sides of the Atlantic after the turn of the century.

The Salvation Army, founded in England by William Booth in 1878, was immediately taken to the United States and introduced its continuous revivals into every U.S. city. The decline of the revivalistic emphasis in the great evangelical churches was a main factor in the springing up of numerous revivalistic sects, such as the Churches of God and the Nazarenes. Modern psychology gave considerable attention to the study of conversion and the revival, especially after the appearance of E. D. Starbuck's *Psychology of Religion* (1899) and William James's *Varieties of Religious Experience* (1902).

BIBLIOGRAPHY.—Jonathan Edwards, *Some Thoughts Concerning the Present Revival of Religion in New England* (1742); Joseph Tracy, *The Great Awakening: A History of the Revival of Religion in the Time of Edwards and Whitefield* (1842); A. Ritschl, *Geschichte des Pietismus* (1880-86); J. H. Overton, *Evangelical Revival in the Eighteenth Century* (1886); F. M. Davenport, *Primitive Traits in Religious Revivals* (1905); H. E. Lewis, *With Christ among the Miners* (1907); C. C. Cleveland, *The Great Revival in the West, 1797-1805* (1916); C. H. Maxson, *The Great Awakening in the Middle Colonies* (1920); W. M. Gewehr, *The Great Awakening in Virginia, 1740-1790* (1930); S. G. Dimond, *The Psychology of the Methodist Revival* (1926); Gamaliel Bradford, *D. L. Moody, a Worker in Souls* (1927); W. W. Sweet, *Revivalism in America, Its Origin, Growth and Decline* (1944); Ola Elizabeth Winslow, *Jonathan Edwards, 1703-1758* (1940). (W. W. S.)

REVOLUTIONARY TRIBUNAL, THE (*le tribunal révolutionnaire*), a court instituted in Paris by the Convention during the French Revolution for the trial of political offenders, which became one of the most powerful engines of the Terror. The news of the failure of the French arms in Belgium gave rise in Paris to popular movements on March 9 and 10, 1793, and on March 10, on the proposal of Georges Jacques Danton, the Convention decreed the establishment in Paris, in addition to the ordinary civil and criminal courts, of an "extraordinary" criminal court, which received the official name of the "revolutionary" tribunal by a decree of Oct. 29, 1793. It was composed of a paid jury, a public prosecutor and two substitutes, all nominated by the Convention, and from its judgments there was no appeal. With M. J. A. Hermann as president and Antoine Quentin Fouquier-Tinville as public prosecutor, the tribunal preserved, at first at least, the forms of a court of justice, dealing with political offenses by royalists, refractory priests and all agents of counterrevolution. The excesses of the Revolutionary tribunal increased with the growth of Robespierre's ascendancy in the Committee of Public Safety, and on June 10, 1794, was promulgated, at his instigation, the Law of 22 Prairial, which forbade prisoners to employ counsel for their defense, suppressed the hearing of witnesses and made death the sole penalty. Before 22 Prairial the Revolutionary tribunal had pronounced 1,220 death sentences in 13 months; during the 49 days between the passing of the law and the fall of Robespierre 1,376 persons were condemned, including an increasing proportion of ordinary citizens and government officials. The lists of prisoners to be sent before the tribunal were prepared by the public prosecutor and signed, after revision, by the Committee of General Security and the Committee of Public Safety jointly.

The Revolutionary tribunal was suppressed May 31, 1795. Its celebrated victims included Marie Antoinette, the Hébertists, the Dantonists and finally the Robespierrists.

BIBLIOGRAPHY.—C. Berriat Saint-Prix, *La Justice révolutionnaire à Paris, Bordeaux, Brest, Lyons, Nantes . . .* (1861) and *La Justice révolutionnaire (août 1792-prairial an II) d'après des documents originaux* (1870); E. Campardon, *Le Tribunal révolutionnaire de Paris*, 2nd ed. (1866); H. A. Wallon, *Histoire du tribunal révolutionnaire de Paris* (1880-82); G. Lenôtre, *Le Tribunal révolutionnaire* (1908); G. Walter, *Histoire de la Terreur* (1937).

REVOLVER: see PISTOL.

REVUE: see MUSICAL COMEDY.

REWA, formerly a princely state within the Central India agency. In 1948 it became a part of the union of Vindhya Pradesh (*q.v.*), dominion (later republic) of India, the maharaja being appointed *rajpramukh*, or prince-president, of the union. Rewa had an area of 12,830 sq.mi.; its population, mainly Hindu, was 1,820,445 in 1941. Many of the inhabitants of the hilly tracts are Gonds and Kols.

More than one-third of the area is covered with forests, yielding timber and lac; the region also possesses valuable coal deposits in the Umaria field. The capital, Rewa city, is 70 mi. S.S.W. of Allahabad, Uttar Pradesh; pop. (1951) 29,623. The history of the state, until it came under British guarantee in 1812, was a record of almost continuous warfare. In the mutiny of 1857, the ruler aided the British. The maharaja's family is a Rajput of the Baghela branch of the Solianki race. The present Rewa district (pop., 1951, 633,706) is 2,513 sq.mi. in area.

REWARD. In English law the offering of rewards presents two distinct aspects: (1) with reference to the nature of the information or act for the giving or doing of which the reward is offered; (2) with reference to the nature of the relation created between the person offering and the person claiming the reward.

1. Courts of assize and quarter sessions are empowered to order the payment of rewards to persons who have been active in or toward the apprehension of persons charged with certain specified crimes against person and property (criminal law, 1826, secs. 28, 29; Criminal Justice Administration act, 1851, secs. 7, 8). The rewards are payable according to a scale fixed by the home secretary. (See LARCENY.)

2. Where a reward is lawfully offered for information the person who first supplies the required information (i.e., satisfies the conditions on which the reward is payable) is entitled to recover by action the reward offered. Performance of the conditions is an acceptance of the offer (Carlill v. Carbolic Smoke Ball Co., 1893, 1 Q.B. 256,270).

In the United States the law is practically the same.

REWARI, a municipality, Gurgaon district, Punjab, India. The town (pop. 1951, 34,082), about 55 mi. S.W. of Delhi, is an important rail and trade centre, and produces brassware.

REWBELL, JEAN FRANÇOIS (1747–1807), French politician, was born at Colmar (then in the department of Haut-Rhin) on Oct. 8, 1747. He sat in the constituent and legislative assemblies and in the Convention. He took part in the reactionary movement which followed the fall of Robespierre, and became a member of the reorganized committees of public safety and general security. His moderation caused his election by 17 departments to the Council of Five Hundred. Appointed a member of the Directory on Oct. 1, 1795, he became its president in 1796, and retired in 1799. He then entered the Council of Ancients. After the coup d'état of 18 Brumaire he retired from public life, and died at Colmar on Nov. 23, 1807.

See L. Sciout, Le Directoire (1895–97).

REYKJAVIK, the capital of Iceland, is on the northern side of the Seltjarnarnes peninsula on the southeastern corner of the Faxafloi bay in the southwest of Iceland. It stood originally in a hollow between two hills, but has grown far beyond the hills. The harbour is protected on the west by a tongue of land and on the east by a pier; it is open on the north. The first Norse settler to Iceland, Ingolfur Arnarson, built his farm at Reykjavik in the 9th century, and for many centuries Reykjavik had only rural colonization. In 1786 it was licensed by the king of Denmark with privileges of a market town; it numbered, however, no more than 307 inhabitants in 1801.

After the restoration at Reykjavik in 1843 of the mediaeval Icelandic parliament, the althing, the town grew faster (pop. in 1901, 6,682), especially in the 20th century, when its main trade, the fishing industry, was developed by the use of modern vessels and equipment. By mid-20th century Reykjavik had textile, oilskin, rope, shipbuilding, fishmeal, margarine, chocolate, biscuit and beer industries, and most of the imports and exports of Iceland went through its harbour. Hot springs at Reykir make hothouse gardening possible and supply a swimming pool and the houses of Reykjavik with warm water.

In 1944 Reykjavik became the capital of the independent republic of Iceland. The residence of the president is at Bessastadir, outside the town. Reykjavik has a theatre, a museum, a library containing about 125,000 volumes and about 8,000 manuscripts, a cathedral (built in 1847), a university and a number of special schools and a state-owned general hospital. It is the seat of the Icelandic bishop. Reykjavik has regular steamship services with the United Kingdom, Norway and Denmark, and there is an airport at Keflavik, 30 mi. W. Its population, mainly Lutheran, was 56,096 in 1950. (H. LN.)

REYMONT, WLADYSLAW STANISLAW (1868–1925), Polish novelist, was born at Kobiele Wielkie in the county of Piotrkow on May 6, 1868. He spent his youth in various occupations, and his first novels were written when he was superintendent of a small railway sector. The Comédienne (1896; Eng. trans. 1921), Ferments (2 vol., 1897) and Lily (1899) were objective novels describing the everyday life of a troupe of provincial actors. In 1899 appeared The Promised Land (2 vol.; Eng. trans. 1928), modelled on Zola and describing industrialism in Lodz. Reymont's best-known work, The Peasants, appeared in four volumes in 1904–09 (Eng. trans. 1925–26). He describes the four seasons' labours of a peasant and brings to light his primitive instincts, inward dignity and almost religious attachment to the land. This great peasant epic brought Reymont the Nobel prize for literature in 1924. While The Peasants was being prepared, a number of novels and short stories appeared, the most important of which are Before Dawn (1902), Komurasati (1903), From a Diary (1903) and The Storm (1907). As a historical novelist, Reymont, primarily an observer of the direct processes of life, was less successful: the trilogy 1794 (The Last Diet, 1913, Nil Desperandum, 1916, and The Insurrection, 1918), though not lacking in literary merit, revealed a lack of historical exactness. He died on Dec. 5, 1925. (See POLISH LITERATURE.)

See I. Matuszewski, Tworczosci Tworcy (Warsaw, 1904); Z. Debicki, W. S. Reymont (Warsaw, 1925); J. Lorentowicz, Ladislas Reymont, prix Nobel 1924 (1925).

REYNARD THE FOX, a beast epic, current in French, Dutch and German literature. The cycle of animal stories collected round the names of Reynard the Fox and Isengrim the Wolf in the 12th century seems to have arisen on the borderland of France and Flanders. The tales, like those of "Uncle Remus," were amusing in themselves; they were based on widely diffused folklore, and Reynard and his companions were not originally men disguised as animals. Jacob Grimm (Reinhart Fuchs, 1834) maintained their popular origin.

The principal names of the Reynard cycle were German. Reynard himself (Raginohardus, strong in counsel), Bruin the Bear, Baldwin the Ass, Tibert the Cat, Hirsent the She-Wolf, had German names, most of which were used as person names in Lorraine. But it was in France that the cycle obtained its greatest vogue. The Roman de Renart as printed by Méon (4 vol., 1826) runs to more than 40,000 lines. Renart was a popular epic parodying feudal institutions as represented in the romances of chivalry.

The early French originals are lost, the most ancient existing fragments being in Latin. The fable of the lion's sickness and his cure by the wolf's skin occurs in the Ecbasis cujusdam captivi per Tropologiam (ed. by E. Voigt; Strasbourg, 1875), written about 940. Ysengrimus (ed. by E. Voigt; Halle, 1884), a clerical satire written by Nivard of Ghent about 1148, includes the story of the lion's sickness and the pilgrimages of Bertiliana the Goat. Most later versions of Reynard have been derived from the Flemish Van den vos Reinarde (ed. by E. Martin, Paderborn, 1874), written about 1250 in East Flanders by Arnout and Willem. The Flemish epic is a poem of 3,476 lines. The corresponding branch of the French Roman de Renart (for which see FRENCH LITERATURE) is one of the earliest and best of the great French cycle.

The fable was known in England. The English poem of the Fox and the Wolf dates from the 13th century; and the "Nun's Priest's Tale" of Chaucer, in which, however, the fox is Rossel and the ass Brunel, is a genuine Reynard history. A Dutch version of the Reynard poem, Hystorie van Reynaert die Vos, was printed at Gouda in 1479. On this Caxton based his Historye of Reynart the Foxe (reprinted by E. Arber, 1878), which he finished on June 6, 1481. As a satire on the church, especially on monks and nuns, Reynard became popular with reformers, and numerous versions followed in England and Germany. The modern German version (1794) of Goethe has been often reprinted, notably in 1846, with illustrations by Wilhelm von Kaulbach.

BIBLIOGRAPHY.—The best edition of the Roman de Renart is by Ernest Martin, 3 vol. (Strasbourg and Paris, 1881–87). See also Jacob Grimm, Sendschreiben an C. Lachmann über Reinhart Fuchs (Leipzig, 1840); Léopold Sudre, Les Sources du roman de Renard (Paris, 1890); Gaston Paris, "Le Roman de Renard," Journal des savants (Dec. 1894 and Feb. 1895); Kaarle Krohn, Bär und Fuchs (Helsinki, 1888); H. Gagering, Van den Vos Reynaerde (Münster, 1910). A modernized version of Caxton's translation appeared in 1926.

REYNOLDS, JOHN FULTON (1820–1863), U.S. soldier, was born at Lancaster, Pa., Sept. 20, 1820, and graduated from the U.S. Military academy in 1841. He was breveted captain and major for gallantry in the Mexican War. In 1859 he was made commandant of cadets at West Point. At the outbreak of the Civil War in 1861 he was made a lieutenant colonel of infantry and some time later brigadier general of volunteers. In Nov. 1862, after having been in numerous actions, he was commissioned major general of volunteers, and appointed to command the 1st corps of the army of the Potomac, took part in the battle of Fredericksburg and gave General Meade his whole-hearted support in the three critical days preceding the battle of Gettysburg (q.v.). He was placed in command of the left wing and thrown forward to Gettysburg to cover the concentration of the army of the Potomac. The battle which ensued there, July 1, 1863, took its shape from Reynolds' resolution to support Buford's cavalry with the 1st and 11th corps. Reynolds himself was killed very early in the day by a rifle bullet. A bronze statue was placed on the field of Gettysburg and a portrait in the library at West Point by the men of the 1st corps. The state of Pennsylvania erected a granite shaft where he fell, and an equestrian bronze statue stands in Philadelphia.

REYNOLDS, SIR JOSHUA (1723–1792), the most prominent figure in the English school of painting, was born at Plympton Earl, in Devonshire, on July 16, 1723. He received a fairly good education from his father, who was a clergyman and the master of the free grammar school. At 17, the lad was apprenticed in London to Thomas Hudson, a native of Devonshire, who, though a mediocre artist, was popular as a portrait painter. Reynolds remained with Hudson for two years, and in 1743 he returned to Devonshire, where, settling at Plymouth Dock, he employed himself in portrait painting. By the end of 1744 he was again in London. He was well received by his old master, from whom he appears previously to have parted with some coldness. Hudson introduced him to the artists' club that met in Old Slaughter's, St. Martin's Lane, and advised him as to his work. Reynolds now painted a portrait of Captain the Hon. John Hamilton, the first that brought him any notice, with those of other people of some repute.

Meanwhile Reynolds had made the acquaintance of Lord Edgcumbe, who introduced him to Captain (afterwards Viscount) Keppel. Keppel was made aware of Reynolds' desire to visit Italy; and, as he had just been appointed to the command of the Mediterranean squadron, he invited the artist to accompany him in his ship, the "Centurion." The offer was gladly accepted. While Keppel was conducting his negotiations with the dey of Algiers, relative to the piracy with which that potentate was charged, Reynolds resided at Port Mahon, the guest of the governor of Minorca, painting portraits; and in December 1749 he sailed for Leghorn, and then made his way to Rome. Of the early Italians he praises the "simplicity and truth" and observes that they "deserve the attention of a student much more than many later artists." In Venice he made memoranda of the gradations of light and shade in the pictures, "and this without any attention to the subject, or to the drawing of the figures."

After more than two years in Rome, where he caught a severe cold which resulted in permanent deafness, Reynolds, in the spring oi 1752, spent five months in visiting Parma, Florence, Venice and other important cities of Italy. Returning to England, Reynolds, after a brief stay in Devonshire, established himself as a portrait painter in St. Martin's Lane, London, whence he afterwards removed to Great Newport Street, and finally, in 1760, to Leicester Square, where he continued to paint till his death.

In London, Reynolds stepped at once into a foremost position as the fashionable portrait painter of the day. In this he was greatly helped by his success in society. Throughout his career his social occupations claimed the next place to his painting. Lord Edgcumbe was a generous patron, and exerted himself to obtain commissions for his protégé, of whose ability the portraits which he now produced—especially the famous full-length of his old friend Keppel—were sufficient guarantee. In 1755 his clients for the year numbered 120, and in 1757 the number of sittings recorded reached a total of 677. He maintained his position unimpaired. During his year in London he had made the acquaintance of Dr. Johnson, which became a friendship for life. To him Burke and Goldsmith, Garrick, Sterne and Bishop Percy were before long added. Most of them were members of "The (Literary) Club," established at Reynolds' suggestion, in 1764.

In 1760 the London world of art was greatly interested by the novel proposal of the Society of Artists to exhibit its works to the public. In the month of April a successful exhibition was opened, the precursor of many that followed. Reynolds contributed four portraits. In 1765 the association obtained a royal charter, and became known as "The Incorporated Society of Artists"; but much rivalry and jealousy were occasioned by the management of the various exhibitions, and an influential body of painters withdrew from the society. They had access to the young king, George III., who promised his patronage and help. In December 1768 the Royal Académy was founded, and Reynolds, whose adhesion to the movement was for a time doubtful, was hailed by acclamation its first president. In a few months the king signified his approval of the election by knighting the new president, and intimating that the queen and himself would honour him with sittings for portraits to be presented to the Academy. Reynolds did not take any part in the educational work of the new institution, but on the social side he set the Academy on the lines it has followed with the greatest worldly success ever since. At his suggestion the annual banquet was instituted. To the specified duties of his post he added the delivery of a presidential address at the distribution of the prizes, and his speeches on these occasions form the well-known "Discourses." These discourses entitle their author to literary distinction; indeed, when they were first delivered, it was thought impossible that they could be the production of a painter, and Johnson and Burke have been credited with their composition, in spite of Dr. Johnson's indignant exclamation—"Sir Joshua, sir, would as soon get me to paint for him as to write for him!"

Sir Joshua was too successful an artist to escape the jealousy of his less fortunate brethren, and it must be admitted that his attitude towards some of his contemporaries was wanting in generosity. His relations with Gainsborough, who on his part was in fault, would require more space for discussion than can here be afforded, but he was not just either to Hogarth or to Richard Wilson. Cosmo Monkhouse in the Dictionary of National Biography speaks of "the beauty of his disposition and the nobility of his character," but adds: "he was a born diplomatist." In 1784 Reynolds was appointed painter to the king.

In the summer of 1789 his sight began to fail; but he continued occasionally to paint till about the end of 1790, delivering his final discourse at the Academy on Dec. 10. On Feb. 23, 1792, the great artist passed peacefully away.

As a painter Reynolds stands, with Gainsborough, just behind the very first rank. There can be no question of placing him by the side of the greatest Venetians or of the triumvirate of the 17th century, Rubens, Rembrandt, Velasquez. He could not draw the figure properly; nor could he as a rule compose successfully on anything like a monumental scale.

He was all his life devoured by what he calls "a perpetual desire to advance." The weight and power of the art of Reynolds are best seen in those male portraits, "Lord Heathfield," "Johnson," "Sterne," "Goldsmith," "Gibbon," "Burke," "Fox," "Garrick," that are historical monuments as well as sympathetic works of art. In this category must be included his "Mrs. Siddons as the Tragic Muse," now in the Huntington Library and Art gallery, San Marino, Calif. (with a replica at the Dulwich gallery).

In portraits of this order Reynolds holds the field, but he is more generally admired for his studies of women and of children, of which the Althorp portraits of the Spencer family are classic examples. No portrait painter has been more happy in his poses for single figures, or has known better how to control by good taste the piquant, the accidental, the daring, in mien and gesture. "Viscountess Crosbie" is a striking instance. When dealing with more than one figure he was not always so happy, but the "Duchess of Devonshire and her Baby," the "Three Ladies decking a Figure of Hymen," and the "Three Ladies Waldegrave" are brilliant successes. He was felicitous too in his arrangement of drapery. Few painters, again, have equalled the Reynolds in dainty and at the same time firm manipulation of the brush. The richness of his deeper colouring is at times quite Venetian.

In the "Discourses" Reynolds unfolds his artistic theories. The first deals with the establishment of an academy for the fine arts, and of its value as a repository of the traditions of the best of bygone practice. In the second lecture the study of the painter is divided into three stages,—in the first of which he is busied with processes and technicalities, with the grammar of art, while in the second he examines what has been done by other artists, and in the last compares these results with Nature herself. In the third discourse Reynolds treats of "the great and leading principles of the grand style"; and succeeding addresses are devoted to such subjects as "Moderation," "Taste," "Genius," and "Sculpture." The fourteenth has an especial interest as containing a notice of Gainsborough, who had died shortly before its delivery; the concluding discourse is mainly a panegyric on Michelangelo.

His other literary works comprise his three essays in The Idler for 1759–1760 ("On the Grand Style in Painting," and "On the True Idea of Beauty"), notes to Du Fresnoy's Art of Painting, Remarks on the Art of the Low Countries, brief notes in Johnson's Shakespeare, and two singularly brilliant fragments, imaginary conversations with Johnson, which were never intended for publication, but, found among his papers after his death, were given to the world by his niece, the marchioness of Thomond.

Sir Joshua left to his niece, Mary Palmer, the bulk of his property, about £100,000, with works of art that sold for £30,000 more. There were, besides, legacies amounting to about £15,000. His body rests in St. Paul's.

In the United States, of the representative paintings by Reynolds, fourteen are in the Metropolitan Museum of Art, and others are as follows: New York Public Library, "Mrs. Billington as 'St. Cecilia' "; the Frick collection, New York city, "Lady Elizabeth Taylor" and "Lady Selena Skipwith"; the Frick Collection, Prides Crossing (Mass.), "Lady Cecil Rice," "Lady Margaret Beaumont," and "Sir George Howland Beaumont"; the Joseph Widener Collection, Philadelphia, "Portrait of Lady Cornewall" and "Portrait of Nelly O'Brien"; Boston Museum of Fine Arts, "Kitty Fisher" and "Sir Thomas Mills"; A. E. Newton Collection, Philadelphia, "Samuel Johnson"; Chicago Art institute, "Lady Sarah Bunberry"; Cleveland Museum of Art, "Portrait of Mrs. Collyear"; Detroit Institute of Arts, "Sir Brooke Boothby, Bart."

See J. Northcote, *Memoirs of Sir Joshua Reynolds* (1813), and *Supplement* thereto (1815); J. Farrington, *Memoirs of the Life of Sir Joshua Reynolds* (1839); Leslie and Taylor, *Life and Times of Sir Joshua Reynolds* (2 vols., 1865); R. Reynolds, *Life of Joshua Reynolds, by his son* (1839); E. Hamilton, *A Catalogue Raisonné of the Engraved Works of J. Reynolds* (1755–1820) (1874); Graves and Cronin, *A History of the Works of Sir Joshua Reynolds* (4 vols., 1899–1901); Sir Walter Armstrong, *Sir Joshua Reynolds* (1900; also a shorter work, 1905); Lord Ronald Gower, *Sir Joshua Reynolds* (1902). For Reynolds's literary works, see Malone, *The Works of Sir Joshua Reynolds* (3 vols., seven editions 1799–1851); Leisching, *Sir J. Reynolds zur Aesthetik u. Technik der bildenden Künste* (Leipzig, 1893); *Discourses delivered to the Students of the Royal Academy by Sir Joshua Reynolds, Kt.*, ed. by Roger Fry (1905); M. Osborn, *Joshua Reynolds* (Künstler-Monographien, 1908).

REYNOLDS, STEPHEN (1881–1919), English author, was born at Devizes on May 16, 1881, and educated at Manchester university and the École des Mines at Paris. He became subeditor of an Anglo-French review in 1902, and in 1903 began an association with the Woolley brothers, fishermen of Sidmouth, becoming a recognized authority on fisheries. He was a member of the committee of enquiry into Devon and Cornwall Fisheries (1912), of the departmental committee on Inshore Fisheries (1913), and in that year was appointed adviser on Inshore Fisheries to the Development commission. In 1914 he became resident inspector of fisheries for the southwestern area. He died at Sidmouth on Feb. 14, 1919. His books include *A Poor Man's House* (1908), a classic in its own kind; *Alongshore* (1910); *The Lower Deck, the Navy and the Nation* (1912); *The Holy Mountain* (a novel, 1909).

REYNOLDS, WALTER (d. 1327), archbishop of Canterbury, was the son of a Windsor baker, and became a clerk, or chaplain, in the service of Edward I. In 1307 Reynolds was appointed treasurer of England; in 1308 he became bishop of Worcester and in 1310 chancellor. When Robert Winchelsea, archbishop of Canterbury, died in May 1313 Edward II prevailed upon Pope Clement V to appoint his favourite to the vacant archbishopric, and Reynolds was enthroned at Canterbury in Feb. 1314. He continued the struggle for precedence between the archbishops of Canterbury and of York and in 1317 he laid London under an interdict after William de Melton (d. 1340), archbishop of York, had passed through its streets with his cross borne erect before him. Reynolds remained in general loyal to Edward II until 1324, when with all his suffragans he opposed the king in defense of the bishop of Hereford, Adam of Orlton. In the events which concluded Edward's life and reign the archbishop played a contemptible part. Having fled for safety into Kent he returned to London and declared for Edward III, whom he crowned in Feb. 1327. He died at Mortlake on Nov. 16 following.

REZÁNOV, NICOLAI PETROVICH DE (1764–1807), Russian administrator under Catherine II, Paul I and Alexander I. He was the first Russian to represent his country in Japan (1804), and instigated the first attempt of Russia to circumnavigate the globe (1803), commanding the expedition himself as far as Kamchatka. But Rezánov's monument for many years after his death was the great Russian-American Fur company; and his interest to students of history centres round the policy involved in that enterprise.

Meeting (in 1788) Shelikov, chief of the Shelikov-Golikov Fur company, Rezánov became interested in the merchant's project to obtain a monopoly of the fur trade in those distant dependencies. He became a partner, and, after the death of Shelikov in 1795, the leading spirit of the company, and resolved to obtain

privileges analogous to those granted by Great Britain to the East India company. He had just succeeded in persuading Catherine to sign his charter when she died, and he was obliged to begin again with the ill-balanced and intractable Paul. Rezánov's skill, subtlety and address prevailed, and shortly before the assassination of Paul he obtained his signature to the instrument which granted to the Russian-American company, for a term of 20 years, dominion over the coast of N.W. America, from latitude 55° northward; and over the chain of islands extending from Kamchatka northward and southward to Japan. This famous "trust," which crowded out all the small companies and independent traders, was a source of large revenue to Rezánov and the other shareholders, including members of the imperial family, until the first years of the 19th century, when mismanagement and scarcity of food threatened it with ruin. Rezánov, his humiliating embassy to Japan concluded, reached Kamchatka in 1805, and found commands awaiting him to remain in the Russian colonies as imperial inspector and plenipotentiary of the company, and to correct the abuses that were ruining the great enterprise. He travelled slowly to Sitka by way of the islands.

At the end of a winter in Sitka, the headquarters of the company, he sailed for the Spanish settlements in California, purposing to trade his tempting American and Russian wares for foodstuffs, and to arrange a treaty for the provisioning of his colonies twice a year from New Spain. He cast anchor in the harbour of San Francisco early in April 1806, after a stormy voyage which had defeated his intention to take possession of the Columbia river in the name of Russia. Although he was received with courtesy, he was told that the laws of Spain forbade her colonies to trade with foreign powers, and that the governor of all the Californias was incorruptible. Rezánov, had it not been for a love affair with the daughter of the *comandante* of San Francisco, Don José Argüello, and for his personal address and diplomatic skill, with which he won over the clergy to his cause, would have failed again. As it was, when he sailed for Sitka, six weeks after his arrival, the "Juno's" hold was full of breadstuffs and dried meats, he had the promise of the perplexed governor to forward a copy of the treaty to Spain at once, and he was affianced to the most beautiful girl in California. Shortly after his arrival in Sitka he proceeded by water to Kamchatka, where he dispatched his ships to wrest the island Sakhalin of the lower Kurile group from Japan, then started overland for St. Petersburg to obtain the signature of the tsar to the treaty. He died of fever and exhaustion in Krasnoiarsk, Siberia, on March 8, 1807.

The treaty with California, the bare suggestion of which made such a commotion in New Spain, was the least of Rezánov's projects. It was sincerely conceived, for he was deeply and humanely concerned for his employees and the wretched natives who were little more than the slaves of the company. His correspondence with the company betrays a clearly defined purpose to annex to Russia the western coast of North America, and encourage immediate emigration from the parent country on a large scale. Had he lived, he might have accomplished his object. The treaty was never signed, the reforms of Rezánov died of discouragement, the fortunes of the colonies gradually collapsed, the Spanish girl who had loved Rezánov became a nun; and one of the ablest and most ambitious men of his time was forgotten in the cemetery of a poor Siberian town.

See H. H. Bancroft, *History of California* (1889) and *History of Alaska* (1887); Tikhmener, *Istoricheskoye obozryeniye obrazovaniya Rossüsko-Amerikanskoi Kompanii* (1861–63); T. C. Russell, ed., *The Rezánov Voyage to Nueva California* (1926); A. Yarmotinsky, "A Rambling Note on the Russian Columbus," *New York Public Library Bulletin,* vol. xxxi (1927). (G. At.)

REZEKNE, a town of Latvia in 56° 30′ N., 27° 20′ E., at a railway junction between north-south and east-west lines. In spite of its position on the railway, it has not much trading importance and its pop. in 1939 was only 13,139. Founded in 1285, under the name of Roziten, by the Teutonic Knights as a fort against the Lithuanians and Letts, the position of the town has rendered it perpetually subject to attack. In 1561 the Teutonic Knights gave it in pawn to Poland and, though captured by the Russians in 1567 and 1577, and dismantled by the Swedes during the war of 1656–60, it continued Polish till 1773, when White Russia was united with the Russian empire. During 1914–20 the town was in the war zone and suffered severely. Rule passed to Latvia in 1918, the U.S.S.R. in 1940, and Germany in 1941.

REZONVILLE, BATTLE OF. The name given by the French to the battle of Vionville–Mars-la-Tour in the Franco-German War (*q.v.*). *See also* METZ.

RHADAMANTHUS, in Greek mythology, son of Zeus and Europa, and brother of Minos, king of Crete. Homer represents him as dwelling in the Elysian fields (*Odyssey*, iv. 564). According to later legends, on account of his inflexible integrity, he was made one of the judges of the dead in the lower world, together with Aeacus and Minos.

RHAETO-ROMANCE LANGUAGES. The Rhetic, or Rhaetic, idioms consist of several patois which form three distinct groups separated one from another by tracts of territory in which German and Italian are spoken. They represent the Latin spoken in Raetia, whither it was first brought by the legions of Tiberius and Drusus (subjugation of Raetia 15 B.C.), and the Latin spoken in Noricum after the tribes inhabiting that country had been defeated by Publius Sirius (16 B.C.). From the close of the 5th century Raetia and Noricum became the scene of numerous migrations and Germanic invasions; cut off from the neighbouring romance-speaking populations (French and Italian) they pursued an evolution of their own. They fought hard and ceaselessly to maintain themselves against German and Italian inroads and assaults, but the long struggle resulted in a considerable diminution and disaggregation of the once very extensive and compact Rhaeto-romance domain. The study of documents of diverse kinds and resourceful philological device have established the foregoing facts, the data for which have been recently assembled by C. Pult in a paper entitled "Raetia Prima in the Middle Ages."

There is evidence, for instance, of traces of romanization persisting round the Lake of Constance even after the eighth century, while at the same time there were still compact groups of *Romani* in the district of Salzburg. In certain areas of central and eastern Tirol, Ladin held out beyond the 13th century, and in western Tirol beyond the 16th; it subsisted, indeed, later still in various localities round Venosta and Montafon. On the Rhine the country round Ragaz and Pfävers remained almost undilutedly romance down to the 17th century and in this region the Rhetic dialect lived on till the close of the same century. Sargans, Mels and the principality of Liechtenstein were Germanized at an earlier period. The district of Werdenberg up to Buchs as well as Flums with its environs, as regards romanization, appear to have been in like condition with Ragaz. North of Buchs as far as Hirschensprung the traces of romanization are less numerous. In the Glaris canton Germanization did not take place before the 11th century, and romance survived until considerably later in Kerenzerberg, on the south bank of the Lake of Walenstadt. The Unseren valley continued romance beyond the 11th century. In the Grisons canton, Prättigan and Schamfigg retained their Rhetic dialect till the beginning of the 15th century. The chief town of Grisons, Coire (Chur) clung to Ladin till the beginning of the 15th century. The Rhetic dialect is at present in process of extinction in the basins of the Noce and Avisio.

Manifold reasons explain this gradual shrinkage of the Rhetic idioms: their lack of cohesion, the multiplicity of patois presenting exceptional divergences between places not far apart, the impossibility of efficient literary output for lack of any predominant dialect, their state of general inferiority as towards the strongly constituted languages by which they have been ousted. In these circumstances, the activity displayed by the Rhetic idioms is the more remarkable. Their literature, an entirely artificial product, counts many poets of talent.

The three groups of Rhetic idioms are constituted as follows:—
I. WESTERN GROUP.—Till recently this group was subdivided into *Romansh* and *Engadinian*. The classification now adopted is into (1) *Sursilvanian*, from the sources of the Rhine to Trins; (2) *Central Grison*, including *Subsilvanian* and *Surmeirian* (*supermurum*); (3) *Engadinian*, including *Upper Engadinian* and *Lower Engadinian* (with the valley of Münster). A noteworthy fact with regard to this group is that whereas between 1850 and 1890 the population composing it declined from 42,436 to 36,472, it had risen to 37,662 in 1910 and to 39,029 in 1920.

II. CENTRAL GROUP.—This includes the patois of (1) the Burgraviato (Burggrafenamt), (2) the basin of the Noce, (3) the basin of the Avisio, (4) Livinallongo, (5) Ampezzo, (6) Comelico, (7) the basin of the Gardera, (8) Gardena, (9) Pusteria, (10) the valley of the Isarco (11) and of the Rienza; about 12,000 souls

III. EASTERN GROUP.—Constituted by Friulian, at present spoken by some 450,000 persons in the province of Udine. This is divided by C. Battisti as follows:—1. *Friulano del piano*, including (a) the Udinese-goriziano group; (b) the Sacilese group (strongly penetrated with Venetian). 2. *Friulano della Carnia*, including (a) group of the Degano; (b) group of the But; (c) group of the Fella; (d) the Tolmezzano-gemonese group, which might also be called "prealpino." (L. B.)

RHAGES: *see* RAYY.

RHAMNACEAE, the buckthorn family, a group of dicotyledonous plants in the warmer parts of both hemispheres, consisting of 45 genera and about 700 species of shrubs, woody vines and trees. Large genera are *Rhamnus* with about 230 species, *Ziziphus* with 100 species and *Phylicia* with 90 species. Jujube (*q.v.*), or the Chinese date, native of Asia, is the fruit of *Ziziphus jujube* (*Z. vulgaris*), and the Indian jujube is the fruit of *Z. mauritiana*. The bark of various species of *Rhamnus* is utilized in the practice of medicine, cascara sagrada (*q.v.*), being that of the western American *R. purshiana*. *Ceanothus*, a genus highly developed in the western United States, is known as the California lilac. *See also* BUCKTHORN. (E. D. ML.)

RHANKAVÉS (commonly also RHANGABE), **ALEXANDROS RHIZOS** (1810–1892), Greek savant, poet and statesman, was born at Constantinople of a Phanariot family on Dec. 25, 1810. He was educated at Odessa and the military school at Munich. Having served as an officer of artillery in the Bavarian army, he returned to Greece. He subsequently became ambassador at Washington (1867), Paris (1868), and Berlin (1874–1886), and was one of the Greek plenipotentiaries at the congress of 1878. After his recall he lived at Athens, where he died on June 29, 1892. He was the chief of a school of literary men whose object was to restore so far as possible the ancient classical language. Of his various works the most important are *Hellenic Antiquities* (1842–1855), *Archaeologia* (1865–1866), an illustrated *Archaeological Lexicon* (1888–1891), and a *History of Modern Greek Literature* (1877).

A complete edition of his philological works in 19 volumes was published at Athens (1874–90), and his Ἀπομνημονεύματα (Memoirs) appeared posthumously in 1894–95.

See Sandys, *History of Classical Scholarship*, vol. iii.

RHAPSODIST, originally an epic poet who recited his own poetry; then, one who recited the poems of others (*see* HOMER).

THE RHEA (RHEA AMERICANA), FOUND ONLY IN SOUTH AMERICA

RHATANY or **KRAMERIA ROOT,** in medicine, the dried root either of Para or of Peruvian rhatany. Its action is due to rhatania-tannic acid, and resembles that of tannic acid, being a powerful astringent. An infusion is used as a gargle for relaxed throats; and lozenges, particularly those containing rhatany and cocaine, are useful in similar cases. The powdered extract may be applied as a local haemostatic. All preparations of rhatany taken internally are powerful astringents in diarrhoea and intestinal haemorrhage.

RHEA, the American "ostrich," a Ratite bird confined to South America. Three species are recognized: *R. americana*, ranging from Paraguay to Patagonia; *R. darwini*, confined to Patagonia; and *R. macrorhyncha*, of northeast Brazil. Considerably smaller than the ostrich, the rheas are further distinguished by the possession of three toes, the absence of fine plumes and the general brownish colour of the feathers, which, in *R. darwini*, are tipped with white. The feathers have a considerable market value. The rhea is polygamous, and the cock bird performs the duties of incubation. Rheas frequently associate with deer or guanacos to form "mixed herds" similar to those formed by the ostrich with zebras and antelopes. *See* also BIRDS; OSTRICH.

See C. R. Darwin, *Voyage of the Beagle;* Cunningham, *Natural History of the Straits of Magellan.*

RHEA, a Titaness, sister and consort of Cronus and mother of Zeus. For her legend, *see* CRONUS. Very little cult of Rhea existed, but she was commonly identified in historical times with Cybele (*see* GREAT MOTHER OF THE GODS). Hence such legends as that in Virgil (*Aen.,* iii, 111), that Cybele originally came from Crete; and indeed the various mother goddesses of the Mediterranean, while not actually the same, closely resemble one another and are the product of the same class of ideas and practices.

RHEINBERGER, JOSEPH GABRIEL (1839–1901), German composer, was born at Vaduz, Liechtenstein, on March 17, 1839. He studied at the Munich conservatorium from 1851 to 1854, and in 1859 became a professor there. He was from 1860 to 1866 organist of the Michelskirche, and then court conductor. His compositions include the operas *Die sieben Raben* (Munich, 1869) and *Türmers Töchterlein* (Munich, 1873); the oratorio *Christoforus,* op. 120;

BY COURTESY OF THE METROPOLITAN MUSEUM OF ART

A JAR SHOWING RHEA, A GODDESS OF THE GREEKS, ENTRUSTING HER INFANT, ZEUS, TO ONE OF THE PRIESTS OF THE CURETES

the well-known quartet for piano and strings in E flat, op. 38; the nonet for wind and strings, op. 139; and 20 organ sonatas. Rheinberger's organ music is original in method, and breaks loose from the Bach tradition in many points. He died at Munich on Nov. 25, 1901.

RHENANUS, BEATUS (1485–1547), German humanist, was born in 1485 at Schlettstadt in Alsace, where his father, a native of Rheinau (hence the surname *Rhenanus*), was a butcher. He was educated at the famous Latin school of Schlettstadt, and afterward (1503) went to Paris.

In 1511 he removed to Basel, where he became intimate with Erasmus, and took an active share in the publishing enterprises of Joannes Froben (*q.v.*). In 1526 he returned to Schlettstadt, and devoted himself to a life of learned leisure, enlivened with epistolary and personal intercourse with Erasmus (the printing of whose more important works he superintended) and many other scholars of his time. He died at Strasbourg on July 20, 1547.

His earliest publication was a biography of Geiler of Kaisersberg (1510). Of his subsequent works the principal are *Rerum Germanicarum Libri III* (1531) and editions of *Velleius Paterculus* (ed. princeps, from a manuscript discovered by himself, 1522); *Tacitus* (1519, exclusive of the *Histories*); *Livius* (1535); and *Erasmus* (with a life, 9 vol., 1540–41).

See A. Horawitz, *Beatus Rhenanus* (1872) and *Des Beatus Rhenanus literarische Tätigkeit,* 2 vol. (1872); also the notice by R. Hartfelder in *Allgemeine deutsche Biographie.*

RHENIUM (symbol Re, atomic number 75, atomic weight 186.31) is a very rare metallic element discovered by Ida and Walter Noddack in 1925. There are two naturally occurring isotopes with mass numbers: 185, which is stable, and 187, which is radioactive and the more abundant; radioactive isotopes with mass numbers 182, 183, 184, 186 and 188 have been prepared. The arrangement of electrons in the unfilled orbits (O and

P) is: $5s^2$, $5p^6$, $5d^5$, $6s^2$.

Rhenium is widely distributed but only in traces in various minerals and especially in certain sulphide ores containing molybdenum. It is probably present as its stable disulphide, ReS_2. When the ores are smelted, the rhenium becomes concentrated in residues or flue dust, as a result of the volatility of its oxide. The element is extracted from these and finally purified by the recrystallization of potassium perrhenate, $KReO_4$, which is only slightly soluble in water. The metal is obtained as a dark gray or black powder by reducing $KReO_4$ at a moderate temperature in hydrogen. The powder is washed with water to remove KOH and is again reduced at a higher temperature. The careful reduction of ammonium perrhenate gives a better product. Like tungsten, which it resembles, this powder can be compressed and sintered in hydrogen at a temperature near its melting point (3,150° C.) to produce massive metal with a density in excess of 19. The solid metal has a density of 21. It is much harder than tungsten, even at high temperatures. It oxidizes if heated in the air above 150° C. and at high temperatures emits clouds of the volatile oxide, Re_2O_7. This, however, is not poisonous like the volatile oxide of osmium. The metal is not soluble in hydrochloric acid, but dissolves readily in nitric acid, forming perrhenic acid. Numerous salts of this acid have been studied.

Since rhenium forms compounds in which it shows a wide range of valencies, a number of oxides exist in addition to the most stable yellow heptoxide, Re_2O_7. These include the insoluble red trioxide, ReO_3, the black dioxide, ReO_2, and the black sesquioxide, Re_2O_3. Compounds are formed when rhenium is heated in the presence of such elements as sulphur, phosphorus or arsenic. Like tungsten (*q.v.*), it forms numerous anhydrous halides or oxyhalides with fluorine, chlorine or bromine, which are hydrolyzed by water. The trichloride, $ReCl_3$, is a red solid which, on heating, gives a green vapour, from which metal deposits can be obtained on hot filaments of platinum or tungsten by thermal decomposition. A number of alloys containing rhenium are known.

See B. S. Hopkins, *Chapters in the Chemistry of the Less Familiar Elements* (1940); H. J. Emeléus and J. S. Anderson, *Modern Aspects of Inorganic Chemistry* (1938); N. V. Sidgwick, *The Chemical Elements and their Compounds* (1950).   (C. W. BE.)

RHEOBASE: *see* CHRONAXIE.

RHEOSTAT, a device that is used for readily varying the resistance of an electric circuit.

RHESUS MONKEY (*Macaca mulata*), probably the best known of all monkeys, a native of India. It is brown in colour, with long hair and a naked area on the buttocks, and is gregarious. (*See* MACAQUE.)

RHETICUS or RHAETICUS (1514–1576), a surname adopted by GEORGE JOACHIM, German astronomer and mathematician.

Born at Feldkirch on Feb. 15, 1514, Rheticus studied at Tiguri with Oswald Mycone and afterward went to Wittenberg, where he was appointed professor of mathematics in 1537. Being greatly attracted by the new Copernican theory, he resigned the professorship in 1539 and went to Frauenberg to associate himself with Nicolaus Copernicus (*q.v.*); it was because of his enthusiasm that Copernicus completed the *De Orbium Revolutione*. Rheticus now began his great treatise, *Opus Palatinum de Triangulis,* published in 1596, and continued to work at it while he occupied his old chair at Wittenberg, and indeed up to his death at Cassovia in Hungary, on Dec. 4, 1576.

The *Opus Palatinum* of Rheticus was published by Valentine Otho, mathematician to the electoral prince Palatine, in 1596. It gives tables of sines and cosines, tangents, etc., for every ten seconds, calculated to ten places. He had projected a table of the same kind to 15 places, but did not live to complete it. The sine table, however, was afterward published on this scale under the name of *Thesaurus Mathematicus* (Frankfurt, 1613) by B. Pitiscus (1561–1613), who himself carried the calculations of a few of the earlier sines to 22 places. He also published *Narratio de Libris Revolutionum Copernici* (Gedenum, 1540), which was subsequently added to editions of Copernicus' works, and until 1551 *Ephemerides,* which were founded on the Copernican doctrines. He projected numerous other works, as was shown by a letter to

Petrus Ramus in 1568, which Adrian Romanus inserted in the preface to his *Idea of Mathematics*.

RHETORIC, the art of using language in such a way as to produce a desired impression upon the hearer or reader. Rhetoric as an art was taught in Greece by the Sophists (*q.v.*).

The power of eloquent speech is recognized in the earliest Greek writings, but the founder of rhetoric as an art was Corax of Syracuse. In 466 a democracy was established in Syracuse. One of the immediate consequences was a mass of litigation on claims to property, urged by democratic exiles who had been dispossessed by Thrasybulus, Hieron or Gelon. Such claims, going many years back, would often require that a complicated series of details should be stated and arranged. The claimants also, in many instances, would lack documentary support, and rely chiefly on inferential reasoning. Hence the need of professional advice. The facts known as to the "art" of Corax perfectly agree with these conditions. He gave rules for arrangement, dividing the speech into five parts: proem, narrative, arguments ($\dot{\alpha}\gamma\hat{\omega}\nu\epsilon\varsigma$), subsidiary remarks ($\pi\alpha\rho\acute{\epsilon}\kappa\beta\alpha\sigma\iota\varsigma$) and peroration. Next he illustrated the topic of general probability ($\epsilon\grave{\iota}\kappa\acute{o}\varsigma$), showing its two-edged use; *e.g.*, if a puny man is accused of assaulting a stronger, he can say, "Is it likely that I should have attacked him?" If vice versa, the strong man can argue, "Is it likely that I should have committed an assault where the presumption was sure to be against me?" This topic of $\epsilon\grave{\iota}\kappa\acute{o}\varsigma$, in its manifold forms, was in fact the great weapon of the earliest Greek rhetoric and it was further developed by Tisias, the pupil of Corax, as we see from Plato's *Phaedrus*. Its later developments were largely the work of Gorgias and Lysias and in a greater degree of Antiphon and Isocrates (*see* their separate biographies). But the detailed study of the art begins with Aristotle's *Rhetoric* (written 322–320 B.C.)

Aristotle's "Rhetoric."—Aristotle sets out from the proposition that rhetoric is properly an art, because when a speaker persuades, it is possible to find out why he succeeds in doing so. It is, in fact, the popular branch of logic. Hitherto, Aristotle says, writers on rhetoric have concerned themselves mainly with the exciting of emotions. All this is very well, but "it has nothing to do with the matter in hand; it has regard to the judge." The true aim should be to *prove* your point, or seem to prove it.

Aristotle does not sufficiently regard the question: What, as a matter of experience, is most persuasive? Logic may be more persuasive with the more select hearers of rhetoric; but rhetoric is for the many, and with the many appeals to passion will sometimes, perhaps usually, be more effective than syllogism. No formulation of rhetoric can correspond with fact which does not leave it absolutely to the genius of the speaker whether reasoning (or its phantom) is to be what Aristotle calls it, the "body of proof" ($\sigma\hat{\omega}\mu\alpha\ \pi\acute{\iota}\sigma\tau\epsilon\omega\varsigma$) or whether the stress of persuading effort should not be rather addressed to the emotions of the hearers.

His statement, that the master of logic will be the master of rhetoric, is a truism if we concede the essential primacy of the logical element in rhetoric. Otherwise it is a paradox; and it is not in accord with experience, which teaches that speakers incapable of showing even the ghost of an argument have sometimes been the most completely successful in carrying great audiences along with them. Aristotle never assumes that the hearers of his rhetorician are as $o\grave{\iota}\ \chi\alpha\rho\acute{\iota}\epsilon\nu\tau\epsilon\varsigma$, the cultivated few; on the other hand, he is apt to assume tacitly—and here his individual bent comes out—that these hearers are not the great surging crowd, the $\ddot{o}\chi\lambda o\varsigma$, but a body of persons with a decided, though imperfectly developed, preference for sound logic.

What is the use of an art of rhetoric? It is fourfold, Aristotle replies. Rhetoric is useful, first of all, because truth and justice are naturally stronger than their opposites. When awards are not duly given, truth and justice must have been worsted by their own fault. This is worth correcting. Rhetoric is then (1) *corrective.* Next, it is (2) *instructive,* as a popular vehicle of persuasion for persons who could not be reached by the severer methods of strict logic. Then it is (3) *suggestive.* Logic and rhetoric are the two impartial arts; that is to say, it is a matter of indifference to them, as arts, whether the conclusion which they draw in any given case is affirmative or negative. Suppose that I am going to

plead a cause, and have a sincere conviction that I am on the right side. The art of rhetoric will suggest to me what might be urged on the other side; and this will give me a stronger grasp of the whole situation. Lastly, rhetoric is (4) *defensive.* Mental effort is more distinctive of man than bodily effort; and "it would be absurd that, while incapacity for physical self-defence is a reproach," incapacity for mental defense should be no reproach. Rhetoric, then, is corrective, instructive, suggestive, defensive. But what if it be urged that this art may be abused? The objection, Aristotle answers, applies to all good things, except virtue, and especially to the most useful things. Men may abuse strength, health, wealth, generalship.

The Period from Alexander to Augustus.—Aristotle's method lived on in the Peripatetic school. Meanwhile the fashion of florid declamation or strained conceits prevailed in the rhetorical schools of Asia, where, amid mixed populations, the pure traditions of the best Greek taste had been dissociated from the use of the Greek language. The "Asianism" of style which thus came to be contrasted with "Atticism" found imitators at Rome. Hermagoras of Temnos in Aeolis (*c.* 110 B.C.) did much to revive a higher conception. Using both the practical rhetoric of the time before Aristotle and Aristotle's philosophical rhetoric, he worked up the results of both in a new system—following the philosophers so far as to give the chief prominence to "invention." He thus became the founder of a rhetoric which may be distinguished as the scholastic. Through the influence of his school, Hermagoras did for Roman eloquence very much what Isocrates had done for Athens. Above all, he counteracted the view of Asianism, that oratory is a mere knack founded on practice, and recalled attention to the study of it as an art.

Cicero's rhetorical works are to some extent based on the technical system to which he had been introduced by Molon at Rhodes. But Cicero further made an independent use of the best among the earlier Greek writers, and he could draw, at least in the later of his treatises, on a vast fund of reflection and experience. The result is certainly to suggest how much less he owed to his studies than to his genius. Some consciousness of this is perhaps implied in the idea which pervades much of his writing on oratory, that the perfect orator is the perfect man. The same thought is present to Quintilian, in whose great work, *De Institutione Oratoria,* the scholastic rhetoric receives its most complete expression (*c.* A.D. 90). He treats oratory as the end to which the entire mental and moral development of the student is to be directed. Thus he devotes his first book to an early discipline which should precede the orator's first studies, and his last book to a discipline of the whole man which lies beyond them. After Quintilian, the next important name is that of Hermogenes of Tarsus, who under Marcus Aurelius made a complete digest of the scholastic rhetoric from the time of Hermagoras of Temnos (110 B.C.) in five extant treatises, remarkable for clearness and acuteness.

Hermogenes continued for nearly a century and a half to be one of the chief authorities in the schools. Longinus (*q.v.*) (*c.* A.D. 260) published an *Art of Rhetoric* which is still extant; and the more celebrated treatise *On Sublimity* ($\pi\epsilon\rho\grave{\iota}\ \ddot{\upsilon}\psi o\upsilon\varsigma$), if not his work, is at least of the same period. In the later half of the 4th century Aphthonius (*q.v.*) composed the "exercises" ($\pi\rho o\gamma\upsilon\mu$-$\nu\acute{\alpha}\sigma\mu\alpha\tau\alpha$) which superseded the work of Hermogenes. At the revival of letters the treatise of Aphthonius once more became a standard textbook. Much popularity was enjoyed also by the exercises of Aelius Theon (of uncertain date). (*See* further the editions of the *Rhetores Graeci* by L. Spengel and by C. Walz.)

Rhetoric under the Empire.—During the first four centuries of the empire the practice of the art was in greater vogue than ever before or since. First, there was a general dearth of the higher intellectual interests: politics gave no scope to energy, philosophy was stagnant and literature was, as a rule, either arid or frivolous. Then the Greek schools had poured their rhetoricians into Rome, where the same tastes which revelled in coarse luxury welcomed tawdry declamation. The law courts of the Roman provinces further created a continual demand for forensic speaking. The public teacher of rhetoric was called "sophist," which was now an academic title, similar to "professor" or "doctor." In the 4th century B.C. Isocrates had taken pride in the name of σοφιστής, which, indeed, had at no time wholly lost the good, or neutral, sense which originally belonged to it.

Vespasian (A.D. 70–79), according to Suetonius, was the first emperor who gave a public endowment to the teaching of rhetoric. Under Hadrian and the Antonines (A.D. 117–180) the public chairs of rhetoric became objects of the highest ambition. The Rhetorical school (θρόνοι) had two chairs, one for sophistic, the other for political rhetoric. By "sophistic" was meant the academic teaching of rhetoric as an art, in distinction from its "political" application to the law courts. The sophistical chair was superior to the political in dignity as in emolument, and its occupant was invested with a jurisdiction over the youth of Athens similar to that of the vice-chancellor in a modern university. The Antonines further encouraged rhetoric by granting immunities to its teachers. Three sophists in each of the smaller towns, and five in the larger, were exempted from taxation (Dig. xxvii, 1, 6, §2). The wealthier sophists affected much personal splendour. The aim of the sophist was to impress the multitude. His whole stock in trade was style, and this was directed to astonishing by tours de force. The scholastic declamations were chiefly of two classes. (1) The suasoriae were usually on historical or legendary subjects, in which some course of action was commended or censured (cf. Juv. Sat.). These suasoriae belonged to deliberative rhetoric (the βουλευτικὸν γένος, deliberativum genus). (2) The controversiae turned especially on legal issues, and represented the forensic rhetoric (δικανικὸν γένος, iudiciale genus). But it was the general characteristic of this period that all subjects were treated alike in the style and spirit of that third branch which Aristotle distinguished, the rhetoric of ἐπίδειξις or "display." This academic oratory is shown under various aspects, and presumably at its best, by such writers as Dio Chrysostom at the end of the 1st century, Aelius Aristeides (see ARISTEIDES, AELIUS) in the 2nd (the chief rhetorician under the Antonines) and Themistius, Himerius and Libanius in the 4th. Amid much which is tawdry or vapid, these writings occasionally present passages of true literary beauty, while they constantly offer matter of the highest interest to the student.

The Middle Ages and the Renaissance.—In the mediaeval system of academic studies, grammar, logic and rhetoric were the subjects of the trivium, or course followed during the four years of undergraduateship. Music, arithmetic, geometry and astronomy constituted the quadrivium, or course for the three years from the B.A. to the M.A. degree. These were the seven liberal arts. In the middle ages the chief authorities on rhetoric were the latest Latin epitomists, such as Martianus Capella (5th century), Cassiodorus (5th century) or Isidorus (7th century).

After the revival of learning the better Roman and Greek writers gradually returned into use. Some new treatises were also produced. Leonard Cox (d. 1549) wrote *The Art or Craft of Rhetoryke*, partly compiled, partly original, which was reprinted in Latin at Cracow. The *Art of Rhetorique*, by Thomas Wilson (1553), afterward secretary of state, embodied rules chiefly from Aristotle, with help from Cicero and Quintilian. About the same time treatises on rhetoric were published in France by Tonquelin (1555) and Courcelles (1557). The general aim at this period was to revive the best teaching of the ancients. At Cambridge in 1570 the study of rhetoric was based on Quintilian, Hermogenes and the speeches of Cicero viewed as works of art. An Oxford statute of 1588 shows that the same books were used there. In 1620 George Herbert was delivering lectures on rhetoric at Cambridge, where he held the office of public orator. The decay of rhetoric as a formal study at the universities set in during the 18th century. The function of the rhetoric lecturer passed over into that of correcting written themes; but his title remained long after his office had lost its primary meaning. If the theory of rhetoric fell into neglect, the practice, however, was encouraged by the public exercises ("acts" and "opponencies") in the schools. The college prizes for declamations served the same purpose.

Modern Writers on Rhetoric.—The fortunes of rhetoric in the modern world, as briefly sketched above, may suffice to suggest why few modern writers of ability have given their attention to the subject. One of the most notable modern contributions to the art is the collection of commonplaces framed (in Latin) by Bacon, "to be so many spools from which the threads can be drawn out as occasion serves," a truly curious work of that acute and fertile mind, and quite in the spirit of Aristotle's treatise. The popularity enjoyed by Hugh Blair's *Lectures on Rhetoric* in the latter part of the 18th and the earlier part of the 19th century was merited rather by the form than by the matter. Campbell's *Philosophy of Rhetoric*, which found less wide acceptance than its predecessor, was superior to it in depth, though often marred by an imperfect comprehension of logic. But undoubtedly the best modern book on the subject is Richard Whately's *Elements of Rhetoric*. Starting from Aristotle's view, that rhetoric is "an offshoot from logic," Whately treats it as the art of "argumentative composition." He considers it under four heads: (1) the address to the understanding (=Aristotle's λογικὴ πίστις); (2) the address to the will, or persuasion (=Aristotle's ἠθική and παθητικὴ πίστις); (3) style; (4) elocution, or delivery. But when it is thus urged that

All a rhetorician's rules
But teach him how to name his tools,

the assumption is tacitly made that an accurate nomenclature and classification of these tools must be devoid of practical use. The conditions of modern life, and especially the invention of printing, have to some extent diminished the importance which belonged in antiquity to the art of speaking, though modern democratic politics and forensic conditions still make it one which may be cultivated with advantage.

BIBLIOGRAPHY.—Among more modern works are J. Bascom, *Philosophy of Rhetoric* (1885), and numerous books on voice culture, gesture and elocution. For ancient rhetoric *see* Sir R. C. Jebb's translation of Aristotle's *Rhetoric*, ed. by J. E. Sandys (1909), and his *Attic Orators* (1876); also Spengel, *Artium Scriptores* (1828); Westermann, *Gesch. der Beredtsamkeit* (1833–35); Cope, in the *Cambridge Journal of Classical and Sacred Philology* (1855–57); introductions to Cicero's *De Oratore* (A. S. Wilkins) and *Orator* (J. E. Sandys); Volkmann, *Die Rhetorik der Griechen und Römer in system. Übersicht,* 2nd ed. (1885); Norden, *Die Antike Kunstprosa* (1898). (R. C. J.; X.)

RHEUMATIC FEVER is a generalized disease commonest in children between the ages of 5 and 15 but occurring with considerable frequency in young adults. The manifestations, severity, duration and after-effects are highly variable. In a small percentage of patients death may occur because of inflammation of the heart in the acute attack, but in a much larger number the acute attack subsides with a variable amount of cardiac damage. Recurrences of acute attacks are frequent.

Causative Factors.—The exact cause of rheumatic fever was still unknown at mid-20th century, although a close relationship to previous streptococcus infection had been well established. This is based on the high incidence of known streptococcus infection preceding attacks of acute rheumatic fever, the presence of streptococcal antibodies (particularly antistreptolysin) in the blood of patients with the disease, the association of increased incidence of rheumatic fever following streptococcus infections, and the prevention of recurrent attacks of rheumatic fever by the continued use of drugs which prevent streptococcus infection. It is generally believed that the disease results from the reaction of the body to the streptococcus rather than the direct effect of streptococcal infection, since bacteria cannot be regularly recovered from the body during the disease.

Many authorities believe that this illness represents a hypersensitivity reaction somewhat similar to the allergies. Rheumatic fever is not known to occur in any species but man, but pathologic lesions in the heart somewhat similar to those seen in rheumatic fever have been produced in rats and rabbits by repeated injection of foreign proteins.

Pathology.—Although clinical evidences of rheumatic fever may occur in the heart, joints, skin and central nervous system, the most characteristic pathological findings are seen in the heart. On gross examination the heart is usually dilated and the surface may be covered by a stringy material which adheres to the membrane covering the heart (the pericardium). The heart muscle is paler and softer than normal. Microscopic examination shows evidence of a peculiar type of inflammation in the connective tissue. The most characteristic microscopic lesion is the Aschoff nodule, which consists of an accumulation of large pale cells together with smaller cells surrounding degenerating connective tissue fibres. Aschoff nodules are most characteristically found in the connective tissue of various parts of the heart, but similar lesions have been identified in the connective tissues of other organs.

In later stages of the disease the acute inflammation is replaced by scar formation. Such scarring results in deformity of the valves of the heart, bringing about interference with normal function. The mitral valve is most frequently involved, although the aortic valve is also commonly distorted. The tricuspid and pulmonary valves are rarely affected.

Public Health Aspects.—Rheumatic fever frequently occurs in more than one member of a family. This is usually attributed to hereditary susceptibility, although some authorities believe it is the result of common environmental conditions. There was as yet no conclusive evidence at mid-century to decide this question.

Rheumatic fever has been found in many parts of the world in representatives of all races. In the United States (as measured by mortality statistics) it is commoner in the northern half of the country, with the exception of low rates in the northern Pacific states. The highest rates occur in the middle Atlantic and mountain states. The observed rates cannot be correlated simply with latitude, average temperature, altitude or rainfall.

Rheumatic fever is not confined to any socio-economic group, but most studies have indicated a higher mortality in the poorer groups. Mortality rates are higher in the nonwhite than in the white population of the United States.

Rheumatic fever became one of the leading causes of death of children in the U.S. as death rates from infectious diseases declined with improved measures for prevention and treatment. It is difficult to estimate the true incidence because of difficulties in diagnosis and poor reporting. In the U.S. there was evidence of a decline in the death rate of children from rheumatic fever and rheumatic heart disease between 1920 and 1948. In 1948 it was estimated that 2,500 persons between the ages of 5 and 19 years died of acute rheumatic fever and rheumatic heart disease.

Because of the frequent long duration of rheumatic fever, few families are able to meet the financial burden; the disease thus became an important public health problem. In some large cities special hospitals are maintained for the care of children with rheumatic fever and rheumatic heart disease.

One of the earliest community attempts to meet the problem was the development of the London County council's Rheumatism scheme, which provided for both hospital care and a follow-up program for all children with rheumatic fever. The private financial difficulties of the care of rheumatic fever in Great Britain were overcome by the National Health Insurance scheme.

In the United States special programs for the care of children with rheumatic fever were developed after 1939 under the Social Security act. These programs were operated on a state basis with funds provided jointly by the states and the children's bureau of the Federal Security agency. By 1951, 23 states, Alaska, the District of Columbia and Hawaii had such programs. The nature of the services and the manner in which they were administered varied from state to state. The American Council on Rheumatic Fever, organized in 1944 under the leadership of the American Heart association, was instrumental in promoting public and private programs for care, research and education in the disease. Under the National Heart act of 1948 the National Heart institute of the United States public health service began to conduct research on heart disease including rheumatic fever. Through a program of grants-in-aid the Heart institute also supported research, training, demonstration programs and community programs for the control of rheumatic fever.

Clinical Characteristics.—The clinical recognition of rheumatic fever is made difficult by the wide variety of symptoms. The most important evidences are those which result from inflammation of the heart, and, of these, the commonest are certain types of murmurs and increased heart-beat rate. It is frequently difficult to determine whether a given murmur is the result of the

presence of active rheumatic fever or of a previous attack. With more serious heart involvement there may be rapid enlargement of the heart, heart failure resulting in difficulty in breathing, evidence of inflammation of the membranes overlying the heart (pericarditis) and irregularities of the heart beat. Additional evidence of cardiac involvement is sometimes obtained on electrocardiographic tracings. The extent and duration of cardiac inflammation is extremely variable in all age groups, but in general tends to be more severe in younger children than in young adults. Severe cardiac involvement may result in death in a relatively short time.

Involvement of the joints is a common manifestation. This may vary from mild aches and pains to severe swelling, redness, tenderness and limitation of motion. Characteristically several joints are involved, with migration from day to day. Although there may be only mild aches and pains in the joints, these symptoms may occur in so many other diseases that they are insufficient in themselves to establish a diagnosis. The joint symptoms are commoner in patients in the older age groups than in young children. Joint manifestations are commonest in the early stages and never result in permanent impairment of function.

Numerous small nodules may occur in the skin, but rarely before the third or fourth week of disease. A variety of skin rashes may be present in acute rheumatic fever, the most characteristic of which is erythema marginatum, which is considered highly specific for the disease by most authorities.

Chorea (St. Vitus' dance) represents a nervous system manifestation of rheumatic fever. It is characterized by purposeless movements of the arms and legs and inability to perform coordinated movements of muscle groups. Marked emotional disturbances may also be present. The severity and duration of these symptoms are highly variable.

Fever occurs in a relatively large percentage of patients with rheumatic fever, but is not necessarily present. A wide variety of other signs and symptoms may also be present. Among these are nosebleeds, weakness, abdominal pain, chest pain and weight loss. Examination of the blood usually shows an increase in the rate of sedimentation of red blood cells, and frequently shows an anaemia and an increased number of white blood cells.

In typical cases a combination of the above symptoms makes diagnosis relatively certain. Many patients have the disease in a more subtle form, so that the first recognition of the previous rheumatic episode comes from the presence of structural abnormalities of the heart characteristically produced by rheumatic fever.

The length of an individual attack of acute rheumatic fever is highly variable and is sometimes difficult to ascertain. In certain persons symptoms may be transient, while in others the disease remains obviously active for periods of more than a year.

The degree of cardiac damage sustained during an individual attack is not related simply to the severity of the acute attack, but may be more closely related to the total duration of active disease. The interference with normal heart function, usually referred to as rheumatic heart disease, results in the main from distortion of the valve structure. Although such distortion may lead to extreme cardiac disability, patients with rheumatic heart disease may carry on relatively normal lives. The greatest threat to life is reactivation of the rheumatic process. A large percentage of people have no interference with cardiac function following recovery from acute rheumatic fever.

Treatment.—Until 1949 the usual treatment of rheumatic fever consisted of the use of salicylate drugs. There remained some difference of opinion as to whether these drugs have any specific effect on the rheumatic process. In 1949 it was shown that adrenocorticotrophic hormone and cortisone have striking effects on rheumatic fever including cardiac involvement. It was still not clear, however, whether use of these drugs prevents subsequent development of heart disease and has an advantage over salicylate treatment.

Patients with active rheumatic fever are usually kept at bed rest for the duration of their active disease. In patients with severe cardiac failure digitalis, mercurial diuretics, restriction of salt intake, and oxygen are valuable. Adequate nutrition and good nursing care are important. In view of the relationship to streptococcal infection, prevention of infection by this microorganism is important.

The use of small doses of sulfadiazine and penicillin prophylactically has resulted in the reduction of the rate of recurrences in patients with previous attacks.   (A. Dor.)

RHEUMATISM, a general descriptive term meaning discomfort, pain and stiffness in or around muscles and joints. It may be the result of injury, such as strain, or of the inflammatory or degenerative processes affecting the joints or ligaments, the muscles or nerves. More specifically it may refer to rheumatic fever, forms of arthritis and a variety of conditions designated by a descriptive adjective such as articular rheumatism, muscular rheumatism, etc.

(See Joints and Ligaments; Rheumatic Fever; Rheumatoid Arthritis.)   (F. L. A.)

RHEUMATOID ARTHRITIS. Rheumatoid arthritis is a chronic disease, the course of which is generally progressive. Its outstanding manifestations are destructive and deforming inflammation of multiple articulations. In addition, many other organs and systems are affected, notably the musculature, subcutaneous tissues, peripheral nerves, blood and lymphatic structures. Frequently patients with rheumatoid arthritis experience episodes of ophthalmitis, chronic progressive inflammatory carditis, and show multiple subcutaneous nodules. Pronounced vasomotor disturbances are commonly present, evidenced by excessive sweating of hands and feet, with cyanosis of the extremities, or by dilatation of capillaries about the palms and fingertips. Certain serologic, biochemical and haematologic abnormalities are characteristically present. Synonyms for rheumatoid arthritis include atrophic arthritis, chronic infectious arthritis, chronic polyarthritis and arthritis deformans. Rheumatoid arthritis occurs at all ages, being encountered in children, adults and in the aged. The onset occurs most frequently, however, between the ages of 20 and 40. The cause was still unknown at mid-20th century. Search for the responsible agent had at times centred upon investigations of bacteria, metabolic disorders, allergies and inherited abnormalities. Later, attention was directed to the possibility of a hormonal aetiology by the discovery that the adrenocorticotrophic hormone, cortisone, 17-hydroxy, 11-dehydrocorticosterone (Compound E of Kendall) and the pituitary adrenocorticotrophic hormone are capable of relieving symptoms of this disease. This discovery had not disclosed the ultimate mechanism of rheumatoid arthritis, however.

The total incidence of rheumatoid arthritis was not definitely known. Results of a broad survey concerning incidence of chronic diseases in the United States indicated that more than 6,850,000 persons in the United States were suffering with "rheumatism"; of these, 3,000,000 had chronic rheumatism and 1,250,000 were said to be disabled thereby. It was believed that a majority of those disabled had rheumatoid arthritis, and it was estimated, therefore, that in the United States alone there were between 1,000,000 and 2,000,000 sufferers with this disease at mid-century. Rheumatoid arthritis was by far the most important form of joint diseases, causing great economic waste and many serious sociologic problems.

During the first three decades of the 20th century the dominant theory as to cause of rheumatoid arthritis was the infectious theory. Search for a germ, however, generally proved fruitless. Bacterial cultures made from joints usually were sterile, and cultures of the blood and other tissues likewise failed to disclose responsible organisms.

The bacterial theory of causation of rheumatoid arthritis lost favour also when it became evident that removal of so-called infected focuses, such as tonsils and teeth, rarely resulted in cures. Studies of serologic reactions of blood did not produce direct evidence to support the infectious theory.

Abnormal serologic reactions which had been detected were widely considered nonspecific in character. No responsible virus had been identified.

During the next two decades, extensive studies conducted to determine whether a vitamin deficiency was related to the cause of rheumatoid arthritis did not succeed in establishing such a relationship.

At mid-20th century information was acquired which indicated that symptoms of rheumatoid arthritis could be relieved or improved by administering a hormone of the pituitary gland or certain hormones of the cortex of the adrenal gland. This suggested that rheumatoid arthritis might be caused by a biochemical or metabolic disturbance, but such a disturbance if it existed had not yet been detected.

Physicians commonly refer to rheumatoid arthritis as a collagen disease. This suggests that rheumatoid arthritis results from a disturbance of the albuminoid material in white fibres of connective tissue, cartilage and bone. This concept, however, was still a hypothetical one at mid-century.

Two major types of rheumatoid arthritis are encountered. They are not always distinct in their manifestations, and in some cases the disease appears as a mixture of both, with clinical features of one or the other predominating. The first type which affects mainly joints of the extremities has been designated the peripheral type. The second, manifested primarily as an inflammatory disease of the spine, has variously been designated rheumatoid spondylitis, Strümpell-Marie disease, Bechterew's disease, adolescent spondylitis and spondylitis deformans. The peripheral form of rheumatoid arthritis occurs predominantly among females, the incidence being two or three times greater than in males. The spinal variety occurs most commonly in males, the incidence being 10 to 20 times as great as among females.

Characteristically the onset of both types is insidious, although symptoms may begin precipitately, with high fever and severe constitutional symptoms. Generally patients observe stiffness and swelling in several joints and complain of fatigue, loss of weight and pain on motion. Joints become visibly swollen and tender and sometimes show a bluish discoloration. In some instances a few scattered joints are involved at the beginning; more typically, multiple joints are attacked in a symmetrical pattern; for example, fingers of both hands, wrists, metatarsophalangeal joints of both feet, elbows, knees, etc. The clinical course is usually marked by periods of rapid progression and severe symptoms alternating with periods of quiescence and relatively good health. Sometimes patients experience complete remissions from symptoms and may remain in a state of good health for months or years. Recurrences and exacerbations may occur later. In some instances the disease progresses relentlessly to an advanced stage in which the patient presents a picture of great crippling and deformity, inanition, wasting of muscles and various atrophic skin disorders. Some patients may experience febrile periods lasting for weeks or months.

Certain biological data characteristic of rheumatoid arthritis may aid in establishing the diagnosis and provide objective evidence of the severity of the disease. Erythrocyte counts and haemoglobin determinations show moderate secondary anaemia in milder cases and more intense anaemia in severe instances. The rate of sedimentation of erythrocytes through heparinized or oxalated plasma is moderately rapid in mild cases and relatively more rapid in severe cases. Severe cases also show relative increases in level of serum globulins in relation to albumin fractions, thus causing reduction or actual inversion of the albumin-globulin ratio.

In mild cases leucocyte counts are within normal limits, but acute cases may show leucocytosis ranging between 10,000 and 20,000. In cases of long duration, especially where patients are approaching a state of exhaustion, leucocyte counts may be low, ranging between 2,000 and 5,000 per cubic millimetre. In some cases the serum may show elevated titres of agglutinating antibodies against the haemolytic streptococcus. The latter test, however, is considered to be a nonspecific reaction and does not necessarily prove an aetiologic relationship to the streptococcus.

In earlier stages of rheumatoid arthritis roentgenograms may disclose only swelling of soft tissues about joints and atrophy of subarticular epiphyseal bone. As the disease progresses and as inflammatory destruction advances, roentgenograms disclose additional abnormalities, narrowing of articular spaces, erosion and atrophy of articular cartilages and finally destruction of epiphyseal bone, together with various subluxations and deformities.

Special forms of chronic arthritis regarded by most rheumatologists as aberrant forms of rheumatoid arthritis include Still's disease, intermittent hydroarthrosis and Felty's syndrome. Still's disease (juvenile rheumatoid arthritis) affects children. In this condition, articular symptoms are associated with anaemia, enlargement of the spleen, lymph nodes and liver. Intermittent hydroarthrosis is manifested by regularly recurring episodes of painful swelling, affecting mainly the knees and rarely the ankles or other joints. Attacks last three to five days, usually subside completely for varying brief periods of a week or so and recur with clockwork regularity at given intervals. In later years such patients may show progressive involvement of joints as in the commoner variety described above. The term "Felty's syndrome" has been applied to a condition of chronic progressive polyarthritis occurring in adults, associated with enlargement of the spleen and lymph nodes and usually associated with characteristic leucopenia. In other respects, the course of Felty's syndrome is the same as that of classic rheumatoid arthritis.

Pathologists have described distinctive inflammatory reactions in tissues from patients with rheumatoid arthritis. These lesions are highly characteristic of the disease. Synovial membranes show hypertrophy of all elements, proliferation and reduplication of lining endothelial layers and thickening of the subendothelial fibrous tissues. Tiny villus projections normally present on the lining membranes become greatly enlarged and may give to the interior of the joint a shaggy appearance. Blood vessels within these villi and throughout the lining and capsular tissues show evidences of active proliferation and usually are dilated and filled with blood. Lymphocytes and other inflammatory cells accumulate throughout the lining membrane and in some regions lymphocytes collect to form dense follicles similar to the follicles of lymphocytes found normally in spleen and lymph nodes. Small scattered regions of inflammation, somewhat similar to those in synovial membranes, have been found in muscles and nerves. Subcutaneous nodules found in some cases also show a distinctive pathologic picture: central necrotic zones, surrounded by inflammatory cells of the reticulo-endothelial system. The latter cells, elongated and sometimes multinucleated, are arranged side by side, with long axes, perpendicularly to the necrotic zones. This arrangement has been designated palisading. Beyond this layer of palisaded cells appears a zone of inflammatory cellular reaction in a stroma of varying density.

Patients who have rheumatoid arthritis occasionally present signs and symptoms indicating involvement of the heart muscle or valves. Studies made at necropsy revealed that in at least 40% of the cases gross or microscopic lesions are present. These are indistinguishable from the cardiac lesions previously considered specific for rheumatic fever.

No rapidly acting or specific therapeutic agent had been discovered for rheumatoid arthritis by mid-20th century. However, certain remedies are helpful in relieving symptoms, preventing deformity and perhaps in some cases in shortening the course of the disease. Physicians widely experienced in the care of patients with this disease consider it advisable to remove infected focuses, with a view to improving the general health. Regular periods of rest are considered desirable to oppose the symptom of fatigue which is prominent in most cases. For those patients who lose weight and strength, the diet should be generally high in calories. In the presence of obesity, however, weight reduction diets are indicated. Valuable physical measures of treatment include applications of dry or moist heat, contrasting hot and cold applications for the extremities, massages and carefully prescribed exercise. Injections of gold salts are widely used and approved. Distinct improvement and in some cases complete remissions have resulted from such injections. Toxic reactions to gold may occur as with any heavy metal therapy. Usually these reactions are not serious, but occasionally severe and even fatal toxicity has been reported. Severe reactions are usually well controlled by means of Bal (British antilewisite; 2,3—dimercaptopropanol). A dry climate may give temporary relief from symptoms of rheumatoid arthritis,

but results of climate therapy are often disappointing. No one climate has been consistently helpful. Chemotherapeutic and antibiotic agents (sulfonamides, penicillin, streptomycin, aureomycin, chloromycetin, etc.) are valueless against rheumatoid arthritis.

Many remedies formerly in favour were later considered to have little or no value: vaccines, concentrated preparations of vitamins, bee or cobra venom, sulphur compounds, etc.

To improve function in crippled joints, certain nonsurgical and surgical orthopaedic procedures are available: braces, supportive corsets and various plastic operations on joints are used in special cases.

Therapy of rheumatoid arthritis with cortisone (Compound E of Kendall) and with the pituitary adrenocorticotrophic hormone was being widely used at mid-20th century. Therapy with hydrocortisone (Compound F of Kendall) was also being tested. An estimate of the ultimate value of these procedures could not be made, however, because of the brief period of observation. Patients adequately treated with cortisone and pituitary adrenocorticotrophic hormone show notable reduction of inflammatory swellings, increased muscle strength, improvement of anaemia and varying degrees of improvement of abnormal sedimentation rates. Undesirable side effects reported frequently include rounding of facial contours, water retention, growth of hair on the face, and psychoses. The beneficial effects appeared to outweigh in importance the gravity of side effects, however, and many rheumatologists therefore considered further therapeutic application and experimentation with these hormones to be justified.

BIBLIOGRAPHY.—E. W. Boland and N. E. Headley, "Effects of Cortisone Acetate (Adrenal Preparation) on Rheumatoid Arthritis," *J.A.M.A.*, 141:301 (1949); R. L. Cecil, W. H. Kammerer and F. J. dePrume, "Gold Salts in the Treatment of Rheumatoid Arthritis: A Study of 245 Cases," *Ann. Int. Med.*, 16:811 (1942); R. H. Freyberg, "Gold Therapy for Rheumatoid Arthritis," in B. I. Comroe, *Arthritis and Allied Conditions*, ed. by J. L. Hollander *et al.*, p. 258 (1949); F. H. Krusen, *Physical Therapy in Arthritis* (1937); L. M. Lockie, B. M. Norcross and C. W. George, "Treatment of Two Reactions due to Gold; Response of Thrombocytopenic Purpura and Granulocytopenia to BAL Therapy," *J.A.M.A.*, 133:754 (1947); J. L. Miller, "A Critical Review of the Literature on Chronic Rheumatism," *Arch. Int. Med.*, 57:213 (1936); C. Ragan and R. H. Boots, "The Treatment of Gold Dermatitis; Use of BAL (2,3-dimercaptopropanol)," *J.A.M.A.*, 133:752 (1947); E. F. Rosenberg, "The Present Status of Gold Therapy for Rheumatoid Arthritis," *Proc. Staff Meet., Mayo Clin.*, 17:264 (1942), and "Cortisone, ACTH and Other Steroids in Rheumatoid Arthritis," *Med. Clin. No. America*, 35:3 (1951); C. L. Short, "Gold Therapy of Rheumatoid Arthritis," *Bull. New Eng. Med. Center*, 4: 31 (1942); C. J. Smyth, R. H. Freyberg and W. S. Peck, "Roentgen Therapy for Rheumatic Disease," *J.A.M.A.*, 116:1995 (1941); G. W. Thorn *et al.*, "Medical Progress: Studies on the Relation of Pituitary-Adrenal Function to Rheumatic Disease," *New Eng. J. Med.*, 241:529 (1949). (E. F. RG.)

RHEYDT, a town in Nordrheinland-Westfalen, Germany, situated on the Niers, 19 mi. W. of Düsseldorf, on the main line of railway to Aachen, and at the junction of lines to Crefeld and Stolberg. Pop. (1939) 76,823. Rheydt is an ancient place, but its industrial importance is of recent growth, and it only received municipal rights in 1856.

The principal products of Rheydt's numerous factories are silk, cotton, woollen and mixed fabrics, velvet, iron goods, machinery, shoes, cables, soap and cigars. It was frequently bombed in World War II.

RHIANUS, Greek poet and grammarian, a native of Crete, friend and contemporary of Eratosthenes (275–195 B.C.). Suidas says he was at first a slave and overseer of a palaestra but obtained a good education later in life and devoted himself to grammatical studies, probably in Alexandria. Of his works none has been preserved except 11 epigrams. But he was chiefly known as a writer of epics, the most celebrated of which was the *Messeniaca* in six books, dealing with the second Messenian war and the exploits of Aristomenes.

Other similar poems were the *Achaica, Eliaca, Thessalica* and *Heracleia.*

Fragments in A. Meineke, *Analecta Alexandrina* (1843); for Rhianus' work in connection with Homer, see C. Mayhoff, *De Rhiani Studiis Homericis* (Dresden, 1870); also W. Christ, *Geschichte der griechischen Literatur* (1898).

RHIGAS, CONSTANTINE, known as Rhigas of Velestinos (Pherae), or Rhigas Pheraios (1760–1798), Greek patriot and poet, was born at Velestinos, and was educated at Zagora and at Constantinople, where he became secretary to Alexander Ypsilanti. In 1786 he entered the service of Nicholas Mavrogenes, hospodar of Wallachia, at Bucharest, and when war broke out between Turkey and Russia in 1787 he was inspector of the troops at Craiova. Rhigas later became interpreter at the French consulate at Bucharest, where he wrote the famous Greek version of the *Marseillaise*, well known in Lord Byron's paraphrase as "sons of the Greeks, arise." He founded the Hetairia, a society formed to organize Greek patriotic sentiment and to provide the Greeks with arms and money. Believing that the influence of the French Revolution would spread to the near east, he went to Vienna to organize a revolutionary movement among the exiled Greeks and their foreign supporters in 1793, or possibly earlier. There he founded a Greek press, but his chief contribution was the collection of national songs which, passed from hand to hand in manuscript, roused patriotic sentiment throughout Greece. They were printed posthumously in 1814.

While at Vienna Rhigas communicated with Napoleon Bonaparte, to whom he sent a snuffbox made of the root of a laurel tree taken from the temple of Apollo, and eventually he set out with a view to meeting the general of the army of Italy in Venice. But before leaving Vienna he forwarded papers, among which is said to have been his correspondence with Napoleon, to a compatriot at Istria. The papers fell into the hands of the Austrian government, and Rhigas was arrested at Trieste and handed over with his accomplices to the Turkish authorities at Belgrade. Immediately on arrest he attempted suicide. His five companions were secretly drowned, but Rhigas himself offered such violent resistance that he was shot by two Turkish soldiers. Rhigas, who wrote in the popular dialect instead of in classical Greek, has been credited with arousing the patriotic fervour of his contemporaries, and his poems were a serious factor in the awakening of modern Greece.

See Rizos Néroñlos, *Histoire de la révolution grecque* (Paris, 1829); I. C. Bolanachi, *Hommes illustres de la Grèce moderne* (Paris, 1875); and Mrs. E. M. Edmonds, *Rhigas Pheraios* (London, 1890).

RHINE, the most important river in Europe, both historically and commercially, has a course more than 700 mi. in length and drains an area of 76,000 sq.mi. It rises in Switzerland and later follows the Swiss-Austrian, Swiss-German and Franco-German frontiers before crossing, first northwestern Germany and then the Netherlands, to reach the North sea. Its valley has long formed part of the main highways from the North sea to the Mediterranean, across the Alps, and to the Black sea, by way of the Danube. It has always been a zone of contact between central and western Europe.

Course.—From their sources in the Glarus and Adula Alps the two main headstreams, the Vorder Rhein and Hinter Rhein, flow northeastward and unite near Chur (Coire). The river here is a typical alpine torrent, flowing rapidly in a deep, narrow valley and fed mainly by melting snow and ice on the mountains. From Lake Constance to Basle the High Rhine flows westward but still keeps its alpine character, dropping from 1,200 ft. to 800 ft. above sea level. The falls or rapids at Schaffhausen are used to develop electrical power. Midway in this section of its course it is joined by the Aar, bringing the drainage of the northern Alps and the Swiss plateau.

At Basle the river turns abruptly north again and enters the Upper Rhine valley, a tectonic depression formed in late Tertiary times and usually referred to as the Rhine rift valley or *Graben*. This depression is 25 mi. wide and extends northward for 180 mi. between the Vosges and Hardt mountains on the west and the Black Forest and Odenwald on the east. The level of the river falls about 550 ft. between Basle and Bingen. For much of the way it shares the wide valley floor with its left bank tributary, the Ill. Some of the many meanders in this part of its course have been cut across to ease navigation to Strasbourg. For 120 mi., to near Lauterbourg, the main stream forms the boundary between France and Germany. The Neckar and the Main, both right bank tribu-

taries, join the Rhine at Mannheim and Mainz respectively.

The Rift valley is blocked at its northern end by the Taunus range causing the river to turn westward to Bingen and enter the 80 mi. gorge characteristic of the Middle Rhine as it crosses the Rhenish plateaus. From Bingen to Bonn the river is deep and narrow, sometimes occupying the whole width of the valley, and is dominated by many castles. Channels were blasted through the rapids at Bingen to facilitate navigation. Near Coblenz the valley widens for a short distance where the Moselle and Lahn enter, the former with its tributary the Saar draining the area between the Vosges and the Ardennes.

The Lower Rhine begins at Bonn where it enters the Cologne "gulf" and starts its course over the deltaic deposits laid down by the ancient Rhine and Maas (Meuse). Wide terraces cut in the sands and gravels mark former river levels before the marshy flood plain of the modern river is reached at Emmerich and diking becomes necessary. Throughout this section it is a wide sluggish stream. Below Cologne it receives as right bank tributaries the Ruhr and the Lippe flowing across the great industrial region of Westphalia. After the river turns west into the Netherlands it soon breaks up into two main arms of which the Waal carries about two-thirds and the Lek about one-third of its volume. The Maas (Meuse) and Waal waters mingle in the many deltaic channels and finally reach the sea by the Hollandschdiep.

The Regime.—The flow of the Rhine is remarkably regular throughout much of its course. As far downstream as Strasbourg it carries only alpine waters and the range of levels is very high. Both the alpine Rhine and the Aar are fed mainly from the snows and glaciers. Their flow is therefore at a minimum in January but reaches flood heights in June and July when the vigorous melting is often supplemented by heavy rainstorms. At Basle the mean flow of 35,000 cusec. in January may reach 160,000 cusec. in July. The change is very apparent in the Rift valley where the river in winter shrinks to shallow channels through gravel banks all covered in summer. With the entry of the Neckar the regime changes. Melted snow still provides a large proportion of the river waters but, as altitudes are lower and generally continue to decrease northward, this supply is received much earlier in the year. On the Neckar and Main levels are highest in March and lowest from June to September, on the Moselle highest in January and lowest in August. All the middle and lower basins receive more rain than snow water. In this way the unbalance upstream is corrected in the middle course and the lower river has a regular flow. Minor difficulties for navigation are created for short periods from time to time in exceptional seasons. Thus a dry summer may lead to abnormally low levels in autumn and persistent heavy rains on the Rhenish plateaus may cause flooding in the diked country. Freezing occurs on slack water in most winters (at Cologne for an average period of 20 days per year) and may halt river traffic. If the frost has been long and severe, blocking of the river bridges by ice cakes may occur in the thaw period.

Navigation.—Trade from the Netherlands to the Alps has followed the Rhine since prehistoric times. By the early middle ages it was already the scene of a flourishing civilization based on trade, mineral wealth and agriculture. In the 15th century its valley was the most important route in all western Europe. Besides draining nearly a quarter of the area of Germany it also serves Austria, Switzerland, eastern France and the Netherlands as an outlet to the North sea. Before 1939 Rotterdam handled one-fifth of Germany's overseas trade and practically all these imports and exports arrived at or left the port along the Rhine waterway.

Between the Swiss and Dutch frontiers the main river alone provides 440 mi. of navigable waterway and another 110 mi. in Netherlands territory. Its tributaries, the Lippe, Ruhr, Lahn, Moselle, Main and Neckar, all have navigable stretches, some of them of considerable length and capable of carrying barge loads of about 1,000 tons. Seagoing ships pass regularly to Cologne and barge trains of 5,000 tons reach Mannheim. Strasbourg, the real head of navigation, receives barges of up to 2,000 tons. By an artificial channel 600-ton barges can reach Basle at certain times of the year.

The area from which river cargoes are drawn has been considerably extended by the construction of canals linking the Rhine with neighbouring river systems. Thus the Marne-Rhine canal makes possible water transport from Paris and, by branch canals, from the Lorraine ore fields and the Saar basin. The Rhône-Rhine canal gives connection to southern France and Marseilles through the Belfort gap. Through traffic to the Danube is not possible as the Ludwigskanal became obsolete. A new canal route up the Main and then to Regensburg was under construction in the mid-1950s. The Dortmund-Ems canal, though not suitable for the modern large barges gives an alternative route from the Ruhr to the North sea and links with the Mittelland canal, thereby giving a waterway to the Elbe and the east German rivers.

All the Rhine lands thus form a single economic unit with interdependent parts—western Germany, eastern France and the Low Countries. The Rhine with its navigable tributaries, the connecting canals and the railways following their valleys, provides the links which bind them together. On the east and west flanks of the river are the greatest industrial areas of Europe, based on Lorraine iron ore and Ruhr coal respectively. Before 1939 over 40,000,000 tons of shipping crossed the Dutch frontier each year. To serve this heavy traffic harbour accommodation was provided at several points and these are all rapidly recovering their former importance. The river is of course especially suitable for the carriage of bulky cargoes. Duisburg handles one-third of all the water-borne traffic of Germany, importing ore, grain and oil products and dispatching coal both up and down stream. It has separate basins equipped to handle each of these types of cargo. Mannheim-Ludwigshafen ranks second among Rhine ports, dealing with coal for southwestern Germany as well as for its own chemical and other industries. With Strasbourg, which mainly serves the French side of the river, it shares in the landing of coal and grain for Switzerland. Mainz deals with traffic along the Main to Frankfurt-on-Main and Bamberg, while Basle collects and distributes Swiss cargoes. Down-river cargoes are relatively light—mainly timber, potash and iron ore.

BIBLIOGRAPHY.—Sir Halford J. Mackinder, *The Rhine, Its Valley and History* (London, 1908); E. de Martonne, *Conditions physiques et économiques de la navigation rhénane* (Paris, 1921); A. Demangeon and L. Febvre, *Le Rhin, problèmes d'histoire et d'histoire et d'économie* (Paris, 1935); *Les Actes du Rhin: traités, conventions, lois et reglements principaux concernant la navigation sur le Rhin* (Strasbourg, 1947). (T. HER.)

RHINELAND, THE. Before Prussia's dissolution the word "Rhineland" was used to designate the Prussian province of *Rheinprovinz* as well as parts of the Prussian province of Hesse-Nassau, parts of Hesse, the Bavarian Palatinate and most of Baden.

The old Rhenish territory north of Lorraine had been annexed by France in 1801, but after the fall of Napoleon the Congress of Vienna transferred it to Prussia and Bavaria. In 1866 Napoleon III vainly tried to recover the Rhineland by diplomatic bargaining with Bismarck. After the defeat of Germany in 1918, French policy aimed at detaching the left bank of the Rhine from Germany, with the object of protecting itself against a new German attack; but since the region is German in nationality and tradition this was opposed by Great Britain and the United States, and France had to accept a compromise: (1) the left bank remained German; (2) it was to be occupied, together with the bridgeheads, by Allied troops in three zones, the northern zone (Cologne) to be evacuated after 5 years, the middle (Coblenz) after 10, the southern (Mainz) after 15 years, if Germany faithfully carried out the conditions of the peace (Art. 428–29 of the Treaty of Versailles); (3) the left bank of the Rhine and a strip of 50 km. on the right bank were to be completely and permanently demilitarized (Art. 42–44). The occupation was intended to provide both guarantees for the execution of the treaty and security to France against military aggression.

By a separate Rhineland agreement an interallied commission was established, composed of representatives of Belgium, France, Great Britain and the United States, with the right to issue ordinances for the security of the Allied forces. It was not to interfere with the German civil administration, but to erect a customs barrier in order to safeguard the economic interests of the population (Art. 270). Considerable friction developed be-

tween the commission, presided over by Paul Tirard, a Frenchman, and the Germans, particularly over the use of Negro soldiers by the French as part of their occupying troops. The charges of bad conduct against the Negro troops were, however, greatly exaggerated, according to the testimony of the general commanding the American troops. The British and the Americans favoured a lenient policy of occupation, whereas the French and the Belgians were inclined to severity. After the United States failed to ratify the Treaty of Versailles and made a separate peace with Germany (1921), the American troops were withdrawn from Coblenz, and that area was taken over by the French.

France accepted the compromise about the Rhineland because both Great Britain and the United States, simultaneously with the Treaty of Versailles, signed treaties of alliance with France, by which they bound themselves to come to the aid of France "in the event of any unprovoked movement of aggression against her being made by Germany." When these treaties were not ratified by the British and U.S. governments, France felt that she had been victimized, that she had lost the real fruits of victory; subsequent events were to prove the correctness of this view.

As soon as it became clear that the left bank of the Rhine would not be separated from Germany, the French military authorities began to foster separatist movements in the region. An old-established anti-Prussian prejudice of the Catholic population of the Rhine province had been intensified by a fear of the spread of bolshevism, and a genuine movement for decentralization arose, which demanded the creation of a Rhineland state within the German republic. The head of this movement, Dr. Hans Dorten, entered into negotiations with General Charles-Marie Mangin, which killed the movement so far as the Germans were concerned, and since the American authorities would not cooperate, the plan collapsed. Dorten was subsequently abducted and arrested by the Germans, but was released at the demand of the French high commissioner.

The occupation of the Ruhr (*q.v.*) in 1923 by France and Belgium, which extended to Karlsruhe and to the districts between the bridgeheads on the right bank of the Rhine, gave new life to the separatist movement, for the British were in a minority on the Rhineland commission and the French authorities were free to assist the separatists. The first manifestation was a rising in Düsseldorf on Sept. 30, which was easily suppressed by the local authorities. Then came the proclamation on Oct. 21 of a "Rhineland republic" at Aachen (Aix-la-Chapelle), in the Belgian zone; this lasted until Nov. 2, when the Belgian government, under British pressure, disavowed the enterprise. Simultaneously, Dorten and one Matthes organized a *Putsch* at Bonn, Coblenz, Wiesbaden and Mainz, their followers being transported by the Franco-Belgian railway administration. When the two leaders quarreled, their regime collapsed, early in 1924.

More serious was the movement in the Bavarian Palatinate, where it was fathered by General de Metz. On Oct. 25, he declared that the Palatinate had ceased to be part of Bavaria, and the separatists seized the government and ejected about 19,000 German officials. The population retaliated and there was a kind of civil war, in which the separatists fared badly, 15 of them being massacred at Pirmasens. The Rhineland commission proposed to recognize the new state, but under British pressure the French government withdrew its support, and the German officials returned in Feb. 1924. This French policy of encouraging separatism destroyed any sentiment among the Germans in favour of Rhenish autonomy.

In 1924, as a result of the elections which transferred control of parliament from the right to the left, the new French government, under Edouard Herriot, agreed to the Dawes plan (*see* REPARATIONS) for the settlement of the reparation question and to the evacuation of the Ruhr. Germany thereupon looked forward to the evacuation of the northern zone of the Rhineland on Jan. 10, 1925. The Allied governments, however, were convinced that Germany had not carried out her obligations to disarm and postponed the evacuation until the terms of the treaty had been complied with. In order to facilitate the negotiations for evacuation and to prevent another occupation of the Ruhr, the German foreign minister, Dr. Gustav Stresemann, on Feb. 9, 1925, suggested to France a pact between the powers interested in the Rhineland which should provide a mutual guarantee of existing frontiers. The French government accepted the proposals, which were extended to include eastern Europe as well as the Rhineland, and after long negotiations between Germany, Great Britain, France, Italy, Belgium, Poland and Czechoslovakia, the Treaty of Locarno (see LOCARNO, PACT OF) was concluded on Oct. 16 and signed in London on Dec. 1, 1925. Reassured by the feeling of security thus created and mollified by Germany's willingness to carry out her disarmament as prescribed by the interallied commission, France now agreed to the evacuation of the northern zone. The evacuation began on Nov. 30 and was completed on Jan. 31, 1926, more than a year after the date prescribed in the treaty; the interallied commission was largely replaced by a commission of the League of Nations.

For the next few years, Germany continually pressed for complete evacuation of the Rhineland on the ground that she was a member of the League of Nations and had fulfilled her obligations, except as regards reparation, which was the subject of another agreement (the Dawes plan); or at least for a reduction of the Allied garrisons (for the upkeep of which Germany had to pay). France reluctantly agreed to reduce the occupying force to 60,000 men, of whom approximately 50,000 were French, but insisted that complete evacuation must depend, as the treaty stipulated, on Germany's fulfilling her obligations on reparation. Shortly after Germany entered the league, Stresemann and Aristide Briand, the French foreign minister, tried, at Thoiry, to reach an understanding about reparation and the whole economic relationship between France and Germany; but nothing practical resulted, partly because Stresemann shortly afterward raised the question of "war guilt" and aroused fears in France that Germany intended to repudiate the Versailles treaty. By the time, however, that the Young committee met to revise the Dawes plan, it was generally understood that if a satisfactory financial agreement could be reached, evacuation of the Rhineland would be conceded as part of a general settlement with Germany. At the Hague conference in Aug.–Sept. 1929, the French delegates endeavoured to postpone evacuation until Germany had accepted the Young plan and to establish some kind of control in the Rhineland for making sure that the region remained demilitarized; but the new Labour government in England and the Belgian government announced their intentions to withdraw their troops before the end of the year, and France was again compelled to compromise. In place of a commission of control it had to be content with the plan of referring difficulties concerning the Rhineland to arbitration under the Locarno treaty and with maintaining the occupation of the third zone only until the Young plan had gone into operation. The British and Belgian troops were withdrawn before the end of 1929, the Young plan became effective on May 17, 1930, and on June 30 the last Allied troops left the Rhineland. The president of the Rhineland high commission, Tirard, prophetically declared: "All that remains on the Rhine is the word which Germany has given. The future depends on how that word is kept." It was significant of the future that in the November elections for the reichstag, 113 nazis were chosen, whereas they had secured only seven seats in the previous election, for the Allies had surrendered all means of pressure.

Whatever trust France may have had in Germany was shattered by the abortive attempt in 1931 to establish an Austro-German customs union. After the true character of the nazi revolution of 1933 had begun to manifest itself, France in 1935 concluded a five-year pact of mutual guarantee with the soviet union. The German government protested against this pact, declaring that it was inconsistent with the Treaty of Locarno (but refusing to submit the question to arbitration, as proposed by France). Inasmuch, however, as the German foreign minister, Baron Konstantin von Neurath, assured the British government that Germany continued to recognize the Locarno agreements (which had been entered into voluntarily by Germany), the French government decided to ratify the treaty with the soviet union. The chamber of deputies acted on Feb. 27, 1936, but on March 7 the senate

was still considering the matter.

On that day Hitler, in a speech to the *reichstag*, repudiated the Rhineland clauses of the Treaty of Versailles and the whole of the Locarno settlement and announced the entry of German troops into the demilitarized zone, where they were uproariously received. At the same time, he declared that Germany was ready to conclude a 25-year pact of nonaggression with France and Belgium, re-enter the League of Nations, negotiate an agreement concerning disarmament and undertake a project for a Franco-German demilitarized frontier zone to be guaranteed by Great Britain and Italy.

The German action was a "flagrant" violation of both Versailles and Locarno, and a few years before France would certainly have sent its troops into the Rhineland. In March 1936 the French general staff, overestimating the number of German troops (35,000) and not knowing (so it is said) that Hitler had ordered his troops to withdraw if the French marched in, refused to take action unless there was a partial mobilization of the French army; the cabinet refused to sanction this, perhaps because of the cost, and only a few specialized units were moved up to the Maginot line. The French government merely asked the League of Nations and the Locarno powers to take cognizance of the situation.

The British government made clear that it would not take positive action; British public opinion regarded the Rhineland as German territory which German troops might properly enter and refused to comprehend the political or military consequences of Hitler's action. Belgium was weak and helpless. Italy was at war in Africa and secretly approved the German course. Only Poland and Czechoslovakia, among the Locarno powers, were ready to stand by France. The council of the League of Nations and the Locarno powers recorded Germany's violations of its agreements, but, since Hitler offered to make a new agreement, tried to set up a "second Locarno." Negotiations went on for several months but led to nothing. Germany re-established its position in the Rhineland without assuming any new obligations, and soon recovered military ascendancy on the continent. The failure of Britain and France to use force against Germany on this issue proved to be a turning point, for in 1938, at the time of the Sudeten crisis, the western powers did not feel strong enough to challenge Germany on the Rhine and had to accept Hitler's terms at Munich.

The Rhineland was heavily damaged during World War II. After the conclusion of hostilities, it was occupied by British, French and U.S. troops. Thus for a second time the Rhineland was divided between three political jurisdictions until the establishment of the west German government in 1949.

The French government repeatedly tried to have the status of the Rhineland discussed at sessions of the Council of Foreign Ministers. Its program called for the separation of the left bank from Germany, with full self-government for the region, and for permanent occupation by Allied forces. The British and U.S. governments were sympathetic with the French demand for security against renewed German aggression, and were prepared to accept military occupation of the Rhineland for a long period, but they did not agree to political separation of the left bank from Germany. So the question remained in abeyance pending the conclusion of a treaty of peace with Germany.

BIBLIOGRAPHY.—*Documents:* France, *Documents relatifs aux Negociations concernant les Garanties de Sécurité contre une Agression de l'Allemagne (1919–1923)* (Paris, 1924); Great Britain, *Papers Respecting Negotiations for an Anglo-French Pact* (London, 1924), *Papers Respecting the Proposals for a Pact of Security Made by the German Government* (London, 1925); *Correspondence Showing the Course of Certain Diplomatic Discussions Directed towards Securing an European Settlement (June 1934–March 1936),* (London, 1936); *Correspondence with the German Government Regarding German Proposals for an European Settlement (March–May 1936),* (London, 1936); J. W. Wheeler Bennett and Stephen Heald (ed.), *Documents on International Affairs, 1929, 1930, 1936* (Oxford, 1930, 1931, 1937); F. J. Berber, *Locarno: A Collection of Documents (1919–1936),* (London, 1936). *Treaty of Versailles:* R. S. Baker, *Woodrow Wilson and World Settlement* (1923); A. Tardieu, *La Paix* (Paris, 1921); D. Lloyd George, *The Truth About the Peace Treaties* (London, 1938); American ed. *Memoirs of the Peace Conference* (1939); P. Birdsall, *Versailles Twenty Years After* (1941). *The Occupation:* H. T. Allen, *The Rhineland Occupation* (1927); V. Markham, *A Woman's Watch on the Rhine* (London, 1920); P. Tirard, *La France sur le Rhin* (Paris, 1930); K. F. Koehler, *Under the Yoke of Foreign Rule* (Leipzig, 1923); F. Tuohy, *Occupied, 1918–1930: A Postscript to the Western Front* (London, 1931). *Locarno:* K. Strupp, *Das Werk von Locarno* (Berlin, 1926); H. S. Quigley, *From Versailles to Locarno* (1927). *After Locarno:* A. J. Toynbee, *Survey of International Affairs,* annual vol. (Oxford, 1925–1937); M. Monmarché, *Bords du Rhin, Forêt-noire, Pays rhénans* (Paris, 1939). (B. E. S.)

RHINELANDER, a city of northern Wisconsin, U.S.A., on the Wisconsin river, 254 mi. N.N.W. of Milwaukee; the county seat of Oneida county. It is on federal highway 8; has a municipal airport; and is served by the Chicago and North Western and the Soo Line railways. Pop. 8,728 in 1950 and 8,501 in 1940. It is in the midst of the great north pine woods, and there are 232 lakes within a radius of 12 mi. The city has manufacturing industries: paper mills, veneer works, novelty works, plastic products, yeast plant, structural bricks and blocks, burial vaults, boat factory, brewery, bottling plants, flooring factory, bakeries, creameries. Rhinelander was settled in 1882 and chartered as a city in 1894.

RHINE PROVINCE or RHINELAND, the most westerly province of Prussia. The small district of Wetzlar in the midst of the province of Hesse-Nassau also belongs to the Rhine province, which, on the other hand, surrounds the Oldenburg province of Birkenfeld. The Rhine province is 9,995 sq.mi.

The southern and larger part of the Rhine province, belonging geologically to the Devonian formations of the lower Rhine, is hilly. On the left bank are the elevated plateaus of the Hunsrück and the Eifel, separated from each other by the deep valley of the Mosel, while on the right bank are the spurs of the Westerwald and the Sauerland, the former reaching the river in the picturesque group known as the Seven Mountains (*Siebengebirge*). The highest hill in the province is the Walderbeskopf (2,670 ft.) in the Hochwald, and there are several other summits above 2,000 ft. on the left bank, while on the right there are few which attain a height of 1,600 ft. Most of the hills are covered with trees, but the Eifel (*q.v.*) is a barren and bleak plateau. To the north of a line drawn from Aix-la-Chapelle to Bonn the province is flat, and marshy districts occur near the Dutch frontier. The climate varies considerably with the configuration of the surface. That of the northern lowlands and of the sheltered valleys is the mildest and most equable in Prussia, with a mean annual temperature of 50°, while on the hills of the Eifel the mean does not exceed 44°. The annual rainfall varies in the different districts from 18 to 32 inches. Almost the whole province belongs to the basin of the Rhine, but a small district in the northwest is drained by affluents of the Meuse. Of the numerous tributaries which join the Rhine within the province, the most important are the Nahe, the Mosel and the Ahr on the left bank, and the Sieg, the Wupper, the Ruhr and the Lippe on the right. The only lake of any size is the Laacher See, the largest of the extinct crater lakes of the Eifel.

Little except oats and potatoes can be raised on the high-lying plateaus in the south of the province, but on the lower ground cereal crops and fruit are grown, and tobacco, hops, flax, rape, hemp and beetroot (for sugar) are cultivated for commercial purposes. Vine-culture occupies about 30,000 acres, about half of which are in the valley of the Mosel, a third in that of the Rhine itself, and the rest mainly on the Nahe and the Ahr. The choicest varieties of Rhine wine, however, such as Johannisberger and Steinberger, are produced higher up the river, beyond the limits of the Rhine province. In the hilly districts more than half the surface is sometimes occupied by forests, and large plantations of oak are formed for the use of the bark in tanning. Considerable herds of cattle are reared on the rich pastures of the lower Rhine, but the number of sheep is small. The wooded hills are well stocked with deer, and a stray wolf occasionally finds its way from the forests of the Ardennes into those of the Hunsrück. The salmon fishery of the Rhine is very productive, and trout abound in the mountain streams.

The Rhine province is very rich in mineral resources. It contains important deposits of coal near Aix-la-Chapelle. Iron ore is found in abundance near Coblenz, the Bleiberg in the Eifel possesses an apparently inexhaustible supply of lead, and zinc is found near Cologne and Aix-la-Chapelle. The mineral products of the district also include lignite, copper, manganese, vitriol, lime, gypsum, volcanic stones (used for millstones) and slates.

The mineral resources of the Prussian Rhine province, coupled with its favourable situation and the facilities of transit afforded by its great waterway, have made it the most important manufacturing district in Germany. The industry is mainly concentrated round two chief centres, Aix-la-Chapelle and Düsseldorf (with the valley of the Wupper), while there are naturally few manufactures in the hilly districts of the south or the marshy flats of the north. The largest iron and steel works are at Essen, Oberhausen, Duisburg, Düsseldorf and Cologne, while cutlery and other small metallic wares are extensively made at Solingen, Remscheid and Aix-la-Chapelle. The cloth of Aix-la-Chapelle and the silk of Crefeld form important articles of export. The chief industries of Elberfeld-Barmen and the valley of the Wupper are cotton-weaving, calico-printing and the manufacture of turkey red and other dyes. Glass is manufactured in the Saar district and beetroot sugar near Cologne. Though the Rhineland is *par excellence* the country of the vine, beer is largely produced; distilleries are also numerous, and large quantities of sparkling Moselle are made at Coblenz.

The population of the Rhine province in 1939 was 7,392,000. The province contains a greater number of large towns than any other province in Prussia and more than half the population is industrial and commercial. There are universities at Bonn (founded 1786 and refounded 1818) and Cologne (refounded 1918). For purposes of administration the province is divided into the five districts of Coblenz, Düsseldorf, Cologne, Aix-la-Chapelle and Trier. Coblenz is the official capital. The province is a modern creation, formed in 1815 out of the duchies of Cleves, Berg, Gelderland and Jülich, the ecclesiastical principalities of Trier and Cologne, the free cities of Aix-la-Chapelle and Cologne, and nearly 100 small lordships and abbeys.

RHINOCEROS, the name for such perissodactyle mammals (*see* PERISSODACTYLA) as bear one or two median horns on the head, and for their extinct relatives. Rhinoceroses are large, massively built animals, with little intelligence and a bad temper. The horns, which are composed of modified hairs, are borne on the nose and are used as weapons. The animals are dull of sight, but their hearing and scent are very acute. They are vegetarian in diet and largely nocturnal. The skin is very thick and tough. In the Miocene and Pliocene, rhinoceroses inhabited both eastern and western hemispheres, but they are now restricted to tropical Africa and Asia. An interesting feature is that the horn appears to have been independently evolved in several separate groups of rhinoceroses. Living forms fall into four genera: (1) With a single nasal horn and the thick skin raised into folds on the shoulders and thighs. There are two species. The Indian rhinoceros (*Rhinoceros unicornis*), standing 5–5¾ ft. high at the shoulder, with a horn 1 ft. in length, is now confined to the Assam plain. The Javan rhinoceros (*R. sondaicus*) is smaller and in the female the horn is often absent. It inhabits Bengal, Burma, the Malay peninsula, Java, Sumatra and Borneo. It prefers hilly forests. (2) With a large nasal and a small frontal horn and the skin not thrown into folds. The only species is the Sumatran rhinoceros (*Rhinoceros* or *Dicerorhinus sumatrensis*), range as in the Javan species, except it does not extend into Java. It reaches a height of 4½ ft. and inhabits hilly forests. A form with hairy ears and skin is regarded as a local race. (3) With two horns, no skin folds and no lower incisors. This group is

BY COURTESY OF THE N.Y. ZOOLOGICAL SOCIETY

GREAT INDIAN RHINOCEROS (RHINOCEROS UNICORNIS)

confined to Africa and comprises two species. The black rhinoceros (*Diceros bicornis*) is the smaller, weighing just over a ton, with a pointed, prehensile upper lip. It inhabits Africa south of Abyssinia, though in reduced and diminishing numbers, dwelling in the wooded, watered districts. (4) The white rhinoceros (*Cerathotherium simus*) is the largest living land mammal except the elephant and feeds largely on grass. It now inhabits only a reserve in Zululand and the Lado enclave on the Upper Nile. It may stand 5 ft. 8 in. at the shoulder and measure 15 ft. in length, but is very swift of foot. The flesh is said to be excellent to eat, especially in the autumn and winter.

The woolly rhinoceros (*R. antiquitatis*), which inhabited Europe, became extinct during the glacial epoch.

RHINTHON (*c.* 323–285 B.C.), Greek dramatist, son of a potter. He was probably a native of Syracuse and afterward settled at Tarentum. He invented the *hilarotragoedia*, a burlesque of tragic subjects. He was the author of 38 plays, of which only a few titles (*Amphitryon, Heracles, Orestes*) and lines have been preserved chiefly by the grammarians, as illustrating dialectic Tarentine forms. The metre is iambic, in which the greatest licence is allowed. The *Amphitruo* of Plautus, although probably imitated from a different writer (Archippus of the Middle Comedy), may be taken as a specimen of the manner in which such subjects were treated. There is no doubt that the hilarotragoedia exercised considerable influence on Latin comedy, the *Rhinthonica* (*i.e.*, fabula) being mentioned by various authorities among other kinds of drama known to the Romans. Scenes from these travesties are probably represented in certain vase paintings from lower Italy, for which *see* H. Heydemann, "Die Phlyakendarstellungen auf bemalten Vasen," in *Jahrbuch des archäologischen Instituts*, i (1886).

See fragments in monograph by E. Völker (Leipzig, 1887); E. Sommerbrodt, *De Phlyacographia Graecorum* (Breslau, 1875); W. Christ, *Geschichte der griechischen Literatur* (1898).

RHIZOPODA, the name given by Felix Dujardin (*pro parte*, 1838) to a group of Sarcodine Protozoa. They are distinguished by their pseudopods, simple or branched, passing by wide bases into the general surface, never fine radial nor fusing into complex networks; skeleton absent or a simple shell ("test," "theca"), never (?) a calcareous shell, nor represented by a siliceous network, nor spicules. Reproduction is by binary fission; by division or abstriction of buds after the body has become multinucleate; or by the resolution of the body into numerous uninucleate zoospores (amoebulae or flagellulae) which may conjugate as gametes; plasmodium formation unknown; encystment (in "resting cysts" or "hypnocysts") common. Without a knowledge of the history it is impossible to distinguish a naked Lobose from the Amoebula (pseudopodiospore) of a Myxomycete or Proteomyxan. As to the name, Dujardin included the thecate Lobosa, the Filosa and the Reticularia or Foraminifera. For further particulars *see* PROTOZOA.

RHODE ISLAND, popularly known as "Little Rhody," is a North Atlantic state of the United States, belonging to the New England group, and lying between approximately 41° 9′ and 42° 3′ N. and 71° 8′ and 71° 53′ W. It is bounded, north and east, by Massachusetts; south, by the Atlantic ocean; and west, by Connecticut, from which it is separated in part by the Pawcatuck river. Rhode Island is the smallest state in the union, having an extreme length, north and south, of 48 mi., an extreme width, east and west, of 37 mi. and a total area of 1,214 sq.mi., of which 157 sq.mi. are inland water area.

Physical Features.—The region of which Rhode Island is a part was at one time worn down to a gently rolling plain near sea level, but has since been uplifted and somewhat dissected by stream action. As a result the topography is characterized by low, rounded hills but is nowhere mountainous. Since the uplift and stream dissection a slight depression has allowed the sea to invade the lower portions of the river valleys, forming the bays known as Narragansett bay, Providence "river," Sakonnet "river," etc. Glaciation has disturbed the river systems.

In the northwest is Jerimoth hill, which attains an elevation of 812 ft., and is the highest point within Rhode Island. The mean elevation for the entire state is 200 ft. The coast line, including the shores of the bays and islands, is extensive; its western portion is only slightly indented, but its eastern portion is deeply indented by Narragansett bay, a body of water varying in width from 3 to 12 mi., and extending inland for about 28 mi. Within Narragansett bay there are the numerous islands characteristic of an area which has suffered comparatively recent depression, the largest being Rhode Island (or Aquidneck), Conanicut Island and Prudence Island. Of these the most important is Rhode Island, 15 mi. long and 3 mi. wide, which has given the state its name. Lying about 10 mi. off the coast and south of the central part of the state is Block Island.

The rivers of the state are short and of no great volume, but they flow swiftly and are useful in supplying power for manufacturing. The Providence river is really an arm of Narragansett bay, into which flow the waters of the Pawtuxet and the Blackstone rivers. The latter stream at Pawtucket has a fall of about 50 ft., and the Pawtuxet river also has a number of falls along its course. Mount Hope bay is a northeastern arm of Narragansett bay and is also the estuary of the Taunton river. The Sakonnet river is a long bay separating Aquidneck or Rhode Island from the mainland on the east. The Pawcatuck river forms the boundary between Rhode Island and Connecticut.

History.—Rhode Island was founded by refugees from Massachusetts, who went there in search of religious and political freedom. The first settlements were made at Providence by Roger Williams (*q.v.*) in June 1636 and at Portsmouth on the island of Aquidneck by the Antinomians, William Coddington (1601–78), John Clarke (1609–76) and Anne Hutchinson (1591–1643), in March–April 1638. Becoming dissatisfied with conditions at Portsmouth, Coddington and Clarke moved a few miles farther south in April 1639, and established a settlement at Newport. In a similar manner Warwick was founded in Jan. 1643 by seceders from Providence under the lead of Samuel Gorton. The union of Portsmouth and Newport, March 12, 1640, was followed by the consolidation of all four settlements, May 19, 1647, under a patent of March 14, 1644, issued by the parliamentaric board of commissioners for plantations. The particularistic sentiment was still very strong, however, and in 1651 the union split into two confederations, one including the mainland towns, Providence and Warwick; the other, the island towns, Portsmouth and Newport. A reunion was effected in 1654 by Roger Williams, and a charter was secured from Charles II on July 8, 1663.

In the patent of 1644 the entire colony was called Providence Plantations. On March 13, 1644, the Portsmouth-Newport general court changed the name of the island from Aquidneck to the Isle of Rhodes or Rhode Island. The official designation for the province as a whole in the charter of 1663, therefore, was Rhode Island and Providence Plantations. The charter was suspended at the beginning of the Sir Edmund Andros regime in 1686, but was restored again after the revolution of 1689. The closing years of the 17th century were characterized by a gradual transition from agricultural to commercial activities. Newport became the centre of an extensive business in piracy, privateering, smuggling and legitimate trade. Cargoes of rum, manufactured from West Indian sugar and molasses, were exported to Africa and exchanged for slaves to be sold in the southern colonies and the West Indies. The passage of the Sugar act of April 5, 1764, and the steps taken by the British government to enforce the Navigation acts seriously affected this trade.

The people of Rhode Island played a prominent part in the struggle for independence. On June 9, 1772, the "Gaspee," a British vessel which had been sent over to enforce the acts of trade and navigation, ran aground in Narragansett bay and was burned to the water's edge by a party of men from Providence. Nathanael Greene, a native of Rhode Island, was made commander of the Rhode Island militia in May 1775, and a major general in the Continental army in Aug. 1776, and in the latter capacity he served with ability until the close of the war. In the year 1776, Gen. William Howe sent a detachment of his army under Gen. Henry Clinton to seize Newport as a base of operations for reducing New England, and the city was occupied by the British on Dec. 8, 1776. To capture this British garrison, later increased to 6,000 men, the co-operation of about 10,000 men (mostly New England militia) under Maj. Gen. John Sullivan, and a French fleet carrying 4,000 French regulars under Count d'Estaing, was planned in the summer of 1778. On Aug. 9, Sullivan crossed to the north end of the island of Rhode Island, but as the French were disembarking on Conanicut Island, Lord Howe arrived with the British fleet. Count d'Estaing hastily re-embarked his troops and sailed out to meet Howe. For two days the hostile fleets manoeuvred for positions, and then they were dispersed by a severe storm. On the 20th, d'Estaing returned to the port with his fleet badly crippled, and only to announce that he should sail to Boston to refit. The American officers protested but in vain, and on the 30th the Americans, learning of the approach of Lord Howe's fleet with 5,000 troops under Clinton, decided to abandon the island. The British evacuated Newport on Oct. 25, 1779, and the French fleet was stationed there from July 1780 to 1781.

The influence of Roger Williams' ideas and the peculiar conditions under which the first settlements were established have tended to differentiate the history of Rhode Island from that of the other New England states. In 1640 the general court of Massachusetts declared that the representatives of Aquidneck were "not to be capitulated withal either for themselves or the people of the isle where they inhabit," and in 1644 and again in 1648 the application of the Narragansett settlers for admission to the New England confederacy was refused except on condition that they should pass under the jurisdiction of either Massachusetts or Plymouth. Rhode Island was one of the first communities to advocate and to put into practice religious freedom and political individualism.

The individualistic principle was shown in the jealousy of the towns toward the central government, and in the establishment of legislative supremacy over the executive and the judiciary. The legislature migrated from county to county up to 1854, and there continued to be two centres of government until 1900. The dependence of the judiciary upon the legislature was maintained until 1860, and the governor is still shorn of certain powers which are customary in other states. In the main the rural towns have adhered most strongly to the old individualistic sentiment, whereas the cities have kept more in touch with the modern nationalistic trend of thought. This was shown, for example, in the struggle for the ratification of the federal constitution. Under the Articles of Confederation it was principally Rhode Island that defeated the proposal to authorize congress to levy an impost duty of 5% mainly as a means of meeting the debts of the central government. When the Constitutional Convention met in Philadelphia in 1787 to frame a constitution for a stronger federal government, the agriculturists of Rhode Island were afraid that the movement would result in an interference with their local privileges, and the state refused to send delegates, and not until the senate had passed a bill for severing commercial relations between the United States and Rhode Island did the latter, in May 1790, ratify the federal constitution, and then only by a majority of two votes. Rhode Island, like the rest of New England, was opposed to the War of 1812 and the Mexican War. During the Civil War it sent 23,457 men into the service of the Union.

Providence possesses superior water-power facilities and has therefore become one of the leading manufacturing centres of New England, whereas Newport is known as a fashionable summer resort and naval port.

The charter of 1663 and franchise law of 1724 established substantial equality of representation among the towns, and restricted the suffrage to freeholders. In the course of time, therefore, the small towns came to be better represented proportionally than the large cities, and the growing class of artisans was entirely disfranchised. Providence issued a call for a constitutional convention in 1796, and similar efforts were made in 1799, 1817, 1821, 1822 and 1824, but nothing was accomplished. About 1840 Thomas W. Dorr (1805–54), a young lawyer of Providence, began a systematic campaign for an extension of the suffrage, a reapportionment of representation and the establishment of an independent judiciary. The struggle, which lasted for several years, and in fact continued at mid-20th century, was one between the cities and the country, between the manufacturers and the agriculturists.

A convention summoned without any authority from the legislature and elected on the principle of universal manhood suffrage met at Providence, Oct. 4 to Nov. 18, 1841, and drafted a frame of government which came to be known as the People's constitution. A second convention met on the call of the legislature in Feb. 1842 and adopted the so-called Freeman's constitution. On being submitted to popular vote (on Dec. 27, 28 and 29, 1841) the former was ratified by a large majority, while the latter was rejected (on March 21, 22 and 23, 1842), by a majority of 676. At an election held on April 18, 1842, Dorr was chosen governor.

The supreme court of the state and the president of the United States (John Tyler) both refused to recognize the validity of the People's constitution, whereupon Dorr and a few of his more zealous adherents decided to organize a rebellion. They were easily repulsed in an attack upon the Providence town arsenal, and Dorr, after a brief period of exile in Connecticut, was convicted of high treason on April 26, 1844, and was sentenced to imprisonment for life. He was released by act of the assembly in June 1845, and restored to the rights and privileges of citizenship in May 1851.

The Freeman's constitution, modified by another convention, which held its session at Newport and East Greenwich on Sept. 12 to Nov. 5, 1842, was finally adopted by popular vote on Nov. 21–23, 1842. Only a partial concession was made to the demand for reform. The suffrage was extended to nonfreeholders, but only to those of American birth. But a constitutional amendment of 1888 extended to naturalized citizens the right of suffrage in state and national elections, and an amendment of 1909 partially remedied the evils in the system of apportionment.

Inequalities still existed, however, as can best be illustrated by Providence, which, with a population in 1927 of 280,600 out of a total of 740,000, had one member in a senate of 39 and 25 members in a house of representatives of 100. This inequality was somewhat modified by constitutional amendment in 1928. The Republicans controlled the state government, Democrats being elected only occasionally. In 1922 the Democratic candidates for governor, lieutenant governor, attorney general and treasurer were elected, although the Republicans retained control of both branches of the general assembly. A long struggle in the senate culminated in the Republican members leaving for Rutland, Mass., on June 19, 1924, where they stayed until Jan. 5, 1925. The Democratic minority continued to meet daily, however, until the newly elected senate took office. The legislative business of the state was practically at a standstill for a year, and the failure of passage of the annual appropriation bill in 1924 led to the advancing of money to the state by private individuals and by 23 Rhode Island banks.

In common with other New England states Rhode Island's cotton manufacturing industries suffered from southern competition. The south's advantage of raw material and cheap labour was overcome in part, however, by Rhode Island's manufacturing its own mill machinery and by training skilled workers in its textile schools, to produce a higher quality of goods. In 1923 a mother's aid law came into effect; and a state law raising the minimum working age to 15 years (with certain exceptions) came into effect in 1924.

In presidential elections the state was Federalist, 1792–1800; Democratic Republican, 1804; Federalist, 1808–12; Democratic Republican, 1816–20; John Quincy Adams (Republican), 1824–28; National Republican, 1832; Democratic, 1836; Whig, 1840–48; Democratic, 1852; and thereafter Republican, except in 1912, until 1928, when Alfred E. Smith carried the state. The Democrats continued to win in the presidential elections of 1932–48 by large pluralities.

Climate.—Rhode Island has a more moderate climate than that of the northern sections of New England. There are no great extremes of either heat or cold, and a number of the towns and cities, especially Newport and Narragansett Pier, became noted summer resorts. Narragansett Pier has a mean annual temperature of 50° F., a mean summer temperature (for June, July and August) of 68°, and a mean winter temperature (for December, January and February) of 30°. The mean annual temperature at Providence is 50.5°; the mean for the summer, 70.1°; and for the winter, 30.2°; while the highest and lowest temperatures ever-recorded are respectively 102° and –17°. The mean annual precipitation is about 38.68 in.

Population.—The population of Rhode Island in 1790 was 68,825; in 1840 it was 108,830; in 1880, 276,531; in 1910, 542,-610; in 1940, 713,346; and in 1950, 791,896. This last figure represented an increase of 11% over the population in 1940. The population per square mile in 1950 was 749.2, as compared with 674.2 in 1940 and with 50.7 for the U.S. in 1950.

The urban area of Rhode Island in 1940 comprised 7 cities, the smallest having a population of nearly 30,000, and 12 towns (townships) classified as urban under a special rule in accordance with which the entire town was classified as urban in any case where more than half the population of the town lived in a village (or villages) having 2,500 inhabitants or more. This rule was justified by the fact that no provision was made in Rhode Island for the incorporation of places smaller than the cities. The urban population in 1940, under this definition, was 653,383, or 91.6% of the state total. The population of the same area in 1950 was 700,410, or 7.2% more than in 1940, and represented 88.4% of the state total.

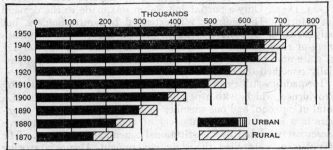

BY COURTESY OF THE U.S. BUREAU OF THE CENSUS
URBAN AND RURAL POPULATION OF RHODE ISLAND: 1870 TO 1950
The vertical-lined section of the 1950 bar represents the amount by which the population that would have been counted as urban under the 1940 definition exceeds the "new" urban population

Prior to the enumeration in 1950, boundaries were set up for the thickly settled suburban area, or "urban fringe," around Providence and Pawtucket, and also for villages outside the urban fringe, so that these might be enumerated separately from the remainder of the town in which they were located. The 1950 urban area comprised all the cities, the urban fringe around the two larger cities and four unincorporated places (villages for which arbitrary boundaries had been set up) of 2,500 or more. Of the 12 special-rule towns of 1940, 1 was found to contain no village of as much as 2,500, 3 contained villages of urban size and 8 were partly within the urban fringe of one of the larger cities. In addition there was one unincorporated place of urban size in another town. The 1950 urban area had thus gained, as compared with that of 1940, by the addition of considerable suburban territory, but not enough to offset the area lost by the dropping of the outlying parts of the 1940 special-rule towns.

The urban population under the new 1950 definition was thus only 667,212, representing 84.3% of the state total, or considerably less than the 1950 population of the 1940 area given above. This situation was in marked contrast with that in most other states, where the new definition resulted in a larger urban area.

Area	Population			Per cent of increase	
	1950	1940	1930	1940–50	1930–40
The state . . .	791,896	713,346	687,497	11.0	3.8
Urban	667,212*	653,383	635,429	2.1	2.8
Rural	124,684*	59,963	52,068	107.9	15.2
Per cent urban	84.3	91.6	92.4		
Principal cities					
Providence . .	248,674	253,504	252,981	-1.9	0.2
Pawtucket . . .	81,436	75,797	77,149	7.4	-1.8
Cranston . . .	55,060	47,085	42,911	16.9	9.7
Woonsocket . .	50,211	49,303	49,376	1.8	-0.1
Warwick . . .	43,028	28,757	23,196	49.6	24.0
Newport . . .	37,564	30,532	27,612	23.0	10.6

*Final figures for 1950 based on new definition. See comment in text.

The number of households in 1950 was 225,487, as compared with 187,706 in 1940. The average population per household had declined from 3.8 in 1940 to 3.5 in 1950.

The population of the state was distributed by colour and nativity in 1950 as follows: 83.8% native white; 14.3% foreign-born white; and 1.9% nonwhite, practically all Negro. Of the

foreign-born white population, 21.5% was born in Italy, 16.9% was Canadian-French and 12.6% was born in England or Wales. There were 98.9 males per 100 females in the native white population and 89.8 in the foreign-born white; 8.8% of the population was 65 years old or over; and 56.0% of the population 14 years old and over was in the labour force.

Of the total number of employed males, 2.1% was engaged in agriculture, 8.2% in construction, 41.3% in manufacturing and 23.2% in transportation and trade.

Government.—Rhode Island is governed under the constitution of 1842, with amendments adopted in 1854, 1864, 1886, 1888, 1889, 1892, 1893, 1900, 1903, 1909, 1911, 1916, 1928, 1930, 1944 and 1948.

Amendments must be passed by both houses of the general assembly and by two consecutive legislatures, and must then be approved by three-fifths of the electors of the state voting thereon.

The executive and administrative officers elected by the people at elections held in November of even-numbered years are a governor, a lieutenant governor, a secretary of state, an attorney general and a treasurer. By an administrative code enacted by the general assembly in 1935 and amended in 1939 and 1949, there are 14 major administrative departments, designated as executive department, department of state, department of the attorney general, treasury department and the departments of finance, social welfare, public works, business regulation, education, labour, agriculture and conservation, health, civil service, and employment security. The first four are headed by the governor, secretary of state, attorney general and treasurer, respectively, the next nine each by a director and the last by an administrator, appointed by the governor with the consent of the senate. Most of the work of administration that was formerly distributed among numerous boards and commissions was consolidated into the departments named above. There remained a few independent agencies, including the sinking fund commission, commission on interstate co-operation, commission on uniform state laws, retirement board, etc.

The powers of the governor were somewhat extended by legislative enactment over their former scope.

The 11 judges of the superior court, the district judges and the juvenile court judges are appointed by the governor with the advice and consent of the senate. The superior court judges hold office during good behaviour, the district judges for a term of three years and the juvenile court judges for a term of ten years.

Finances.—The valuation of rateable property in the several towns and cities, as returned by the boards of assessors on June 15, 1950, was $1,859,036,990.26. The rate of state tax in 1934 was four cents on each $100, but state taxes on cities and towns were repealed on May 31, 1935. For the fiscal year ending June 30, 1950, revenue receipts were $37,058,591.82; expenditures and encumbrances $38,080,727.74; general net debt $40,932,473.59; and sinking fund $5,004,526.41. The net debt increased $4,932,541.43 during the year. The chief sources of revenue were: automobile licences, the gasoline tax, the tax on savings deposits, the financial institutions excise tax, business corporate taxes on net income, corporate excess and franchise tax, inheritance taxes, the tax on insurance premiums, the gross earnings tax on public service corporations, the horse-racing tax, the cigarette tax, the unincorporated business tax and the 1% selective sales tax.

Expenditures for the fiscal year 1949–50 were as follows: executive department $1,316,611.64; department of state $175,866.39; department of the attorney general $125,750.05; treasury department $69,388.06; department of finance $576,624.47; department of social welfare $20,192,453; department of public works $6,868,297.44; department of business regulation $274,467.02; department of education $4,178,408.60; department of labour $281,778.70; department of agriculture and conservation $726,517.17; department of health $2,036,405.24; department of civil service $146,349.89; legislative $181,603.04; judiciary $714,157.05; state colleges $1,336,419.66; other commissions and agencies $163,989.17; pension and retirement salaries $1,526,702.33;

debt service $2,312,677.18; general $4,021,943.37; support of certain organizations $83,950.

On June 30, 1950, there were 30 banking institutions within the state with resources of $1,127,763,804.53 and deposits of $1,007,-427,952.89.

Education.—The public-school system of Rhode Island was established in 1800, abolished in 1803 and re-established in 1828. At the head of it is the director of the department of education appointed by the governor with the consent of the senate to serve at the pleasure of the governor. Each town has a school committee elected by the people and independent of the town or city council. School attendance is compulsory for children between the ages of 7 and 16. An act to promote Americanization was passed in 1919 obliging illiterate minors (16–21) to attend evening school. Rhode Island in 1917 accepted the provisions of the federal vocational act, and a part-time trade school was opened for boys over 14 years of age at Providence and subsequently at Newport, Westerly, West Warwick, Cumberland, Central Falls and Pawtucket. Also there are 10 centres where instruction is given in vocational agriculture, 14 for instruction in home economics and 2 for instruction in the distributive occupations.

The total population between 5 and 17 years of age, as shown by the 1950 school census, was 132,898. The average number attending the public schools in 1949–50 was 90,507; the total expenditure for school purposes in 1949–50 was $19,292,010.47.

The institutions of higher education supported by the state are the Rhode Island College of Education at Providence and Rhode Island State college at Kingston, a land-grant college under the Morrill acts of 1862 and subsequent acts. There are opportunities for training teachers under teacher critics at all the cities of the state—Providence, Central Falls, Cranston, Newport, Pawtucket, Warwick and Woonsocket—and at several of the towns. Training schools for teachers are conducted at Rhode Island State college, Rhode Island College of Education, Brown university, Providence college, Rhode Island School of Design and Bryant college. The state also makes appropriations for state scholarships ($75,000 in 1950) to institutions for higher education other than those supported by the state, viz., Brown university, Rhode Island School of Design, Rhode Island College of Pharmacy and Allied Sciences, Providence college and Bryant college.

Charities and Corrections.—Most of the charitable and penal institutions are administered by the department of social welfare. Those so administered in 1950 were the Exeter school (for feeble-minded) at Exeter; the children's centre of Rhode Island (for dependent children) at Providence; the veterans' home at Bristol; a group of institutions at Cranston, including the state hospital for mental diseases, the state infirmary, the reformatory for women, the state prison and county jail, the reformatory for men, the training school for boys and the training school for girls. In addition to the institutions under the jurisdiction of the department of social welfare, there were the School for the Deaf at Providence under the state department of education and the state sanatorium (for tuberculosis) at Wallum Lake under the state department of health.

Agriculture.—Rhode Island ranks low in the list as an agricultural state, chiefly because of the smallness of the state and the sterile nature of the soil. The boulder clay or hardpan of which most of the surface lands are composed forms a very indifferent support for vegetation. Rhode Island had receipts from sale of principal farm products in 1949 of $23,179,000. The farm acreage declined from 308,000 ac. in 1935 to 222,000 ac. in 1940 and increased to 252,731 ac. in 1949. Of this total only 61,725 ac. were classed as cropland, 81,130 ac. as improved land and 109,876 ac. as pasture and woodland. The number of farms declined from 4,327 in 1935 to 3,014 in 1940 and then increased to 3,600 in 1950. Only 312 or 8.7% of the 3,603 farms in 1945 were cultivated by tenants. The values of farmland and buildings in 1950 were approximately $39,466,560 and $29,494,080 respectively. The chief crop in 1950 was cultivated hay. The 37,000 ac. devoted to hay produced 54,000 tons; potatoes, 5,100 ac. produced 1,275,000 bu.; corn. 8.000 ac. produced 336,000 bu.; oats,

1,000 ac. produced 34,000 bu.; alfalfa, 1,000 ac. produced 2,000 tons. Apples were the principal orchard crop. There were produced apples, 248,000 bu.; peaches, 4,000 bu.; pears, 9,000 bu.; grapes, 270 tons. The livestock products of Rhode Island are of greater value than the field crops. Livestock on the farms on Jan. 1, 1950, consisted of about 1,000 horses, 9,000 swine, 2,000 sheep and 27,000 cattle. Of the latter, 21,000 were kept for dairy purposes. There were 604,000 hens, 5,000 turkeys and 1,000 colonies of bees.

Minerals.—Rhode Island in mineral wealth ranked 47th among the states of the union in 1948. The total value of all mineral products of the state in that year was $1,450,000, and of this total sand and gravel was valued at $728,990 and stone at $536,-651.

Products in order of value were sand and gravel, stone and graphite.

Fisheries.—Whaling was early an established industry in Rhode Island. As late as 1846 about 50 whaling vessels sailed annually from Rhode Island ports; but by the close of the century the industry had become practically extinct. Rhode Island in 1950 ranked third among the New England states in the number of persons engaged, investment and yield of its fisheries. In 1950 the total number of persons employed in all fisheries was 2,275, of whom 1,450 were in the shore and boat fisheries. The year's catch was 26,370,500 lb., of which 19,586,700 lb. were boat fish, value $1,509,179, and 6,783,800 lb. were shellfish, value $3,337,-741. Total value was $4,846,920.

Manufactures.—Rhode Island is essentially a manufacturing state; of the 301,469 persons in the state engaged in gainful occupation in Oct. 1950, 152,778 or 50.7% were employed in manufacturing. Rhode Island is the most industrialized state in the nation, as of 1947, with 172 out of every 1,000 in its population working in factory jobs. Boatbuilding was an early industry, and large vessels were built at Newport. During the Revolutionary War the state offered a premium for every pound of steel made within its boundaries. A company to spin cotton, formed at Providence in 1786, established there in the following year a factory containing a spinning jenny of 28 spindles (the first machine of its kind to be used in the United States), and also a carding machine. The fly shuttle was first introduced at Providence in 1788. In 1790 there was established at Pawtucket a factory equipped with Arkwright machines constructed by Samuel Slater, an immigrant from England. This machine was operated by water power; and from this may be dated the beginning of the factory system in Rhode Island. The first power loom used in the United States was set up at Peacedale in 1814.

The manufacture of jewellery, which was started in Providence in 1784, was greatly promoted ten years later by Nehemiah Dodge's invention of the process of "gold filling," and was still further improved in 1846 by Thomas H. Lowe. Rhode Island's water power has been its only natural resource which has aided its development.

The number of establishments engaged in manufactures was 2,214 in 1947 and 1,399 in 1939; number of production workers was 128,130 in 1947 and 106,089 in 1939; value added by manufacture was $658,420,000 in 1947 and $237,698,000 in 1939. In

Industry	No. of establishments	All employees	Value added by manufacture (000's)
Food and kindred products	216	4,539	$ 22,985
Textile-mill products	374	62,566	282,164
Apparel and related products	81	2,825	9,517
Lumber and products except furniture	38	580	2,476
Furniture and fixtures	34	792	2,918
Paper and allied products	33	1,988	8,467
Printing and publishing	139	3,258	15,925
Chemicals and allied products	59	1,349	10,239
Rubber products	14	6,336	27,163
Leather and leather products	27	430	1,835
Stone, clay and glass products	35	1,053	4,492
Primary metal industries	47	5,099	28,568
Fabricated metal products	231	7,825	38,246
Machinery (except electrical)	192	17,310	69,170
Electrical machinery	26	5,289	24,135
Transportation equipment	20	274	881
Instruments and related products	26	1,712	8,354
Jewellery and silverware	248	10,325	50,888
Costume jewellery	232	8,806	33,632

1947 textiles held the first place among the manufactures of the state. Other important manufactures were jewellery, rubber goods, metal products and machinery. The accompanying table shows the 19 principal manufacturing industries in 1947, the number of active establishments, persons employed and value added by manufacture.

Transportation and Commerce.—The steam railway mileage in Rhode Island never was great because the cities are unfavourably situated to be the termini of interstate railway systems. The total mileage within the state decreased from 205 mi. in 1934 to 185 mi. in 1949. The mileage of electric railways decreased from 183 mi. in 1932 to 86 mi. in 1941 to 82 mi. in 1949.

Much attention was given to the state's highway system. The total mileage in the state system of highways on Jan. 1, 1951, was 1,300 mi.; of this total 839 mi. were surfaced. In 1949 $5,837,517 was spent by the state for the construction and maintenance of roads.

Rhode Island has water outlets at Providence (by far the largest), Newport, Pawtucket, Bristol, Tiverton and Wickford. There are also harbours of refuge at Block Island and Point Judith. The water-borne commerce of the state in 1949 consisted of 717,367 tons of imports, 9,014 tons of exports, 7,044,327 tons of goods received in the coastwise trade and 587,783 tons of goods shipped in that trade, 106,402 tons of goods received in the internal trade and 106,804 tons of goods shipped in that trade. Total water-borne commerce of Rhode Island in 1949 was 8,623,-810 tons; in 1940 it was 6,186,513 tons. The foreign trade of the state in 1940 amounted to 325,208 tons of imports and 32,549 tons of exports.

BIBLIOGRAPHY.—For general physical description *see:* N. S. Shaler, J. B. Woodworth and A. F. Foerste, *Geology of the Narragansett Basin* (1899) and C. T. Jackson, *Report on the Geological and Agricultural Survey of Rhode Island* (1840). For administration *see* the *Rhode Island Manual,* issued biennially by the Secretary of State; C. Carroll, *Outline of Government in Rhode Island,* in Rhode Island educational circulars; and the annual reports of the various state officials, boards and commissions. For general bibliographies *see* J. R. Bartlett, *Bibliography of Rhode Island* (1864); C. S. Brigham, *List of Books upon Rhode Island History* (1908) in Rhode Island Educational Circulars, History Series no. 1; and H. M. Chapin, *Bibliography of Rhode Island* (1914) and *Cartography of Rhode Island* (1915). *History:*—For a considerable time the standard authority on the period before the ratification of the constitution was S. G. Arnold, *History of Rhode Island, 1636–1790* (1859–60, 4th ed., 1894). His work, however, has been practically superseded by I. B. Richman, *Rhode Island: Its Making and Meaning, 1636–1683* (1902) and *Rhode Island; A Study in Separatism* (1905). *See* also, for this period, T. W. Bicknell, *The History of Rhode Island and Providence Plantations* (1920). E. Field (editor), *State of Rhode Island and Providence Plantation at the End of the Century; A History* (1902) is valuable for the later history of the state. Two works of special interest for young readers are H. W. Preston, *Rhode Island's Historic Background* (1930) and A. C. Gleeson, *Colonial Rhode Island* (1926). *See* also A. Gorton, *The Life and Times of Samuel Gorton* (1908); O. S. Straus, *Roger Williams, The Pioneer of Religious Liberty* (1936); A. M. Mowry, *The Dorr War; or the Constitutional Struggle in Rhode Island* (1901); *Records of the Colony of Rhode Island and Providence Plantations, 1636–1792* (1856–65); H. M. Chapin, *Documentary History of Rhode Island* (1916–19); C. S. Brigham, "Report on the Archives of Rhode Island" in the *Annual Report* (1903, vol. i) of the American Historical Association; *Rhode Island Historical Society, Collections* (1827–1941); *Proceedings* (1872–92); *Publications* (1892–1900); *Proceedings* (1900–06); *Rhode Island History* (1941 et seq.); *Rhode Island Historical Tracts, Series I* (1877–84), *Series II* (1889–96); and the publications of the Rhode Island Soldiers and Sailors Historical Society (1878–1915); C. Carroll, *Rhode Island; Three Centuries of Democracy,* 4 vol. (1932); S. H. Brockunier, *The Irrepressible Democrat, Roger Williams* (1940); Federal Writers' Project, WPA, *Rhode Island,* in the "American Guide Series" (1937); *Rhode Island,* Historical Records Survey, Work Projects Administration Publications (1935–42); A. R. Hasse, *Index of Economic Material in Documents of the States of the United States, Rhode Island 1789–1904* (1908); Reports of U.S. Bureau of the Census. **(M. C. ML.)**

RHODES, CECIL JOHN (1853–1902), British colonial and Imperial statesman, was born on the 5th of July 1853, at Bishop Stortford, in Hertfordshire. His father was a clergyman, but he claimed descent from yeoman stock. Cecil John Rhodes was the fifth son in a large family of sons and daughters. The boy was educated at the grammar school of Bishop Stortford, where his father held the living, with the intention of preparing for the Church; but at the age of sixteen his health broke down, and in the latter part of 1870 he joined his eldest brother Herbert, then engaged in farming in Natal. In that year diamonds were discovered in the Kimberley fields. By the end of 1871 Rhodes and his brother were among the successful diggers. The dry air of the interior restored his health, and before he was nineteen he found himself financially independent and physically strong.

Rhodes next spent eight months in a solitary journey through the then little known parts of the country lying to the north of the Orange and Vaal rivers. He went through Bechuanaland to Mafeking, thence to Pretoria, Murchison, Middelburg and back through the Transvaal to Kimberley, passing in an ox-wagon at a rate of some 15 to 20 miles a day, through vast spaces of rolling veld. He saw one of the healthiest countries in the world barely occupied. He knew the agricultural possibilities of Natal and its mineral wealth. The effect of the combined influences on his mind was profound. He was filled with desire that that fine country be secured for occupation by the British race, and that no power but Great Britain be allowed to dominate in the administration of South Africa. He had found an object to which he proposed to devote his life. It was nothing less than the governance of the world by the British race. A will exists written in Rhodes's own handwriting, when he was still only twenty-two, in which he states his reasons for accepting the aggrandizement and service of the British empire as his highest ideal of practical achievement. It ends with a single bequest of everything of which he might die possessed for the furtherance of this great purpose. Five-and-twenty years later his final will carried out, with some difference of detail, the same intention.

The share which he allotted to himself was the extension of the area of British settlement in Africa. He returned to Oxford, where he matriculated at Oriel. In 1873 his health again failed, and he was sent back under what was practically a death sentence. Years afterwards, as an older man, he saw the entry of his own case in the diary of the eminent physician whom he consulted with a note "Not six months to live." South Africa again restored him to health. Three years later he was back at Oxford, and from 1876 to 1878 he kept his terms. During this period he spent the Long Vacation each year in South Africa, where his large financial interests were daily increasing in importance. He was a member of the Cape ministry when after a further lapse of years he kept his last term and took his degree. He did not read hard at Oxford and was more than once remonstrated with in the earlier terms for non-attendance at lectures. But he passed his examinations; and though he was never a student in the university sense of the term, he was to the end of his life a keen devourer of books. He kept always a special liking for certain classic authors. Aristotle was the guide whom as a lad he followed in seeking the "highest object" on which to exercise the "highest activity of the soul." Marcus Aurelius was his constant companion. There exists at Groote Schuur a copy of the *Meditations* deeply scored with his marks.

During this Oxford time and to 1881 Rhodes was occupied with the amalgamation of the larger number of the diamond mines of Kimberley with the De Beers Company, an operation which established his position as a practical financier in the business world. To many admirers who shared his views on public questions his connection with the financial world and his practical success were a stumbling block. It was often wished for him that he "had kept himself clear of all that." But this was not the view he took of the matter. His ideals were political and practical. To him the making of money was a necessary preliminary to the realization of his political ideals, and he was proud of his practical ability in this direction. He was a man of simple tastes. His immense fortune was spent in the furtherance of his ideas, and it has been justly said of him that he taught the world a new chapter of the romance of wealth.

In 1881 Mr. Rhodes entered the Cape assembly as one of the two members for Barkly West and kept the seat for life. It was the year of the Majuba settlement. South Africa was convulsed

RHODES

with questions between the British and the Dutch, and leaders of Dutch opinion at the Cape spoke openly of the formation of a United States of South Africa under its own flag. The British party needed a rallying-ground, when Cecil Rhodes offered to Dutch and British alike the ideal of a South African Federation governing itself within the empire, and extending, by its gradual absorption of native territories, the range of Imperial administration. Local self-government was, in his opinion, the only enduring basis on which the unity of the empire could be built, and throughout his life he was as keen a defender of local rights as he was of Imperial unity. There was a time when his advocacy of the elimination of direct Imperial interference in local affairs caused him to be viewed in certain quarters as a Separatist. Such suspicions were strengthened at a critical moment in the struggle for Home Rule in Ireland by his contributing £10,000 to the funds of the Nationalist party. The subsequent publication of his correspondence on the subject with Mr. Parnell demonstrated, however, that Rhodes's contribution was made strictly subject to the retention of the Irish members at Westminster. He remained of the opinion that the Home Rule movement, wisely treated, would have had a consolidating effect upon the empire.

In South Africa the influence which he acquired over the local independents and over the Dutch vote was subsequently an important factor in enabling him to carry out the scheme of northern expansion which he had fully developed in his own mind at Oxford in 1878. In 1881 the Bechuana territory was a sort of no man's land through which ran the trade routes to the north. It was evident that any power which commanded the trade routes would command the unknown northern territory beyond. The Pretoria Convention of 1881 limited the westward expansion of the Transvaal to a line east of the trade routes; but the irregular overflow into native territories made Rhodes fear that British expansion would be permanently blocked by Dutch occupation. One of his first acts as a member of the Cape assembly was to urge the appointment of a delimitation commission. He served on it in person, and obtained from Mankodoane, who claimed about half of Bechuanaland, a formal cession of his territories to the British government of the Cape. The Cape government refused to accept the offer. In February 1884 a second convention signed in London again defined the western frontier of the Transvaal, Bechuanaland being left outside the republic. With the consent of Great Britain, Germany had occupied, almost at the same time, the territory on the Atlantic coast later known as German South-West Africa. In August 1884 Rhodes was appointed resident deputy commissioner in Bechuanaland, where Boers had ousted the natives from considerable areas and set up the so-called republics of Goshen and Stellaland. An old Dutchman said privately to Rhodes, "This is the key of South Africa." The question at issue was whether Great Britain or the Transvaal was to hold the key. It was a question about which the British public knew and cared nothing. Rhodes made it his business to enlighten them. President Kruger, speaking for the government of the Transvaal, professed to regard the Dutch commandoes as freebooters, whom he was unable to control. Largely as the result of Rhodes's exertions the Warren expedition of 1884–85 was sent out. In the presence of British troops and Rhodes upon the frontier President Kruger withdrew the commandoes without any fighting, and south Bechuanaland became British territory, while a British protectorate was declared over the northern regions up to the 22nd parallel (September 1885).

It was the first round in the long duel between Cecil Rhodes, representative of British interests, and President Kruger, head of the militant Dutch. The score was to Rhodes. The entrance to the interior was secured, but the 22nd parallel was far short of the limits to which Rhodes hoped to see British influence extend, and he feared lest Germany and the Transvaal might together bar his progress. The discovery of gold on the Witwatersrand in 1886, by adding to the wealth and importance of the Transvaal, gave substance to this fear.

The territory north of the 22nd parallel was under Lobengula, chief of the Matabele, a native potentate celebrated alike for his ability and for his despotic character. There were rumours of Dutch and German emissaries at his kraal engaged in persuading him to cede portions of his territory. Portugal also was putting forward shadowy claims to the country. Rhodes conceived the idea of forming a British Chartered Company, which should occupy the territory for trading and mining purposes as far as the Zambezi, and bring the whole under the protection of Great Britain. Rhodes's first emissaries were sent to Lobengula in 1887 and the charter of the British South Africa Company was granted in October 1889. Crossing the Zambezi at the back of the Portuguese settlements, Rhodes obtained permission to extend the territories of the Chartered Company to the southern end of Lake Tanganyika and the British settlements already made in Nyasaland. He hoped to create a connected chain of British possessions which might justify the words, "Africa British from the Cape to Cairo," but the treaty between Great Britain and Germany in 1890, by extending the German sphere of influence to the frontier of the Congo Free State, defeated this hope. But Rhodes did not even then wholly renounce the idea. In 1892 when the question of the retention or abandonment of Uganda hung in the balance at home, he threw all the weight of his influence into the scale of retention, and offered at his own personal expense to connect that territory by telegraph with Salisbury. In 1893, a war with the Matabele added to the British empire about 450,000 square miles of country, of which large portions consist of healthy uplands suitable for white colonization. The pioneer party crossed the frontier at the end of 1889. In six years, though the country had passed through the trial of a war, two native rebellions, and the scourge of rinderpest, it had become Rhodesia, a well-settled province of the British empire, with a white population of some 12,000 persons.

In 1890, Rhodes became prime minister of the Cape. Maintained in power very largely by the Dutch vote, which he spared no pains to conciliate, and having won the confidence of both sections of the colony, he was practically a despot in South Africa. He did much to elevate and to enlarge the field of local politics. He frankly declared and worked for the policy of uniting British and Dutch interests in South Africa; he took a keen interest in local education. He restricted the franchise, introducing an educational test and limiting the vote to men with an income equal to a labourer's wage—thus abolishing, without making any distinction of colour, the abuses of the "blanket" vote.

His native policy was far from being one of simple restriction. He liked the natives; he employed them by thousands in the mining industry, and was successful in dealing with them. The first canon of his native policy was that liquor should be kept from them; the second, that they should be guaranteed the earnings of their labour; the third, that they should be educated in the practical arts of peace. He appreciated the full importance of raising their territorial condition from one of tribal to individual tenure; and while he protested against the uncivilized Kaffir voting on questions of highly civilized white policy, he believed in the principle of self-government in native affairs. Of these views some received practical embodiment in the much-disputed act known as the Glen Grey Act of 1894. In this connection it may also be noted that he was one of the warmest and most convinced supporters of Lovedale, the very successful missionary institution for the education of natives in South Africa.

The position of benevolent despot has obvious drawbacks. In Rhodes's case the dependence which the populations of Cape Colony were led to place on him had its reaction on the public in a demoralizing loss of self-reliance, and for himself it must be admitted that the effect on the character of a man already much disposed to habits of absolutism in thought and action was the reverse of beneficial. Rhodes felt himself to be far stronger than any man in his own surroundings; he knew himself to be actuated by disinterested motives in the aims which he most earnestly desired to reach. He was profoundly impressed by a sense of the shortness of life, and he so far abused his power as to become intolerant of any sort of control or opposition. The inevitable result followed, that though Rhodes did much of great and good work during the six years of his supreme power, he entirely failed during that period to surround himself, as he might have done, with a circle of able men fit to comprehend and carry on the work to which his own best efforts were directed. To work with him was practically impossible for those who were not willing to accept without demur the yoke of dogmatic authority. He had a few devoted personal friends who appreciated his aims and were inspired by his example; but he was lacking in regard for individuals, and a great part of his daily life was spent in the company of satellites and instruments, whom he used with cynical unconcern for the furtherance of his ends.

In 1896 the brilliant period of his premiership was brought to an end by the incident which became famous under the name of the Jameson Raid. The circumstances which led to the raid belong properly to the history of the Transvaal. It is enough to say briefly here that the large alien population which had been attracted to the Transvaal by the phenomenal wealth of the Johannesburg gold fields, conceiving itself to have reason to revolt against the authority of the Transvaal government, resolved toward the end of 1895 to have recourse to arms in order to obtain certain reforms.

Rhodes, as a large mineowner, was theoretically a member of the mining population. In this capacity he was asked to give his countenance to the movement. But as prime minister of a British colony he was evidently placed in a false position from the moment in which he became cognizant of a secret attempt to overturn a neighbouring government by force of arms. He did more than become cognizant. The subsequent finding of a Cape committee, which he accepted as accurate, was to the effect that "in his capacity as controller of the three great joint-stock companies, the British South Africa Company, the De Beers Consolidated Mines, and the Gold Fields of South Africa, he directed and controlled the combination which rendered such a proceeding as the Jameson Raid possible." He gave money, arms and influence to the movement; and as the time fixed for the outbreak of the revolution approached, he allowed Dr. Jameson, who was then administrator of the British South Africa company in Rhodesia, to move an armed force of some 500 men upon the frontier. Here Rhodes' participation in the movement came to an end. It became abundantly clear from the subsequent inquiry that he was not personally responsible for what followed. A cipher correspondence, seized and published by the Boers, left the civilized world in no doubt as to Rhodes' share in the previous preparation, and he was for a time believed to be responsible for the raid itself. Subsequent inquiries held by committees of the Cape parliament and of the British house of commons acquitted him entirely of responsibility for Dr. Jameson's final movement, but both committees found that he had acted in a manner which was inconsistent with his duty as prime minister of the Cape and managing director of the British South Africa company.

He made no concealment of his own share in the catastrophe; he took full responsibility for what had been done by subordinates, and accepted the consequences which ensued. He resigned his premiership of the Cape (Jan. 1896), and turned his attention to the development of Rhodesia. His design was to live in the country and to give all the stimulus of his own presence and encouragement to the development of its resources. The Matabele rebellion of March 1896 intervened, and in June Imperial troops were sent up and drove the natives to a practically impregnable position in the Matoppo hills.

The prospect before the British was one of continued war with a renewal of a costly campaign in the following spring. Rhodes conceived the idea that he might effect singlehanded the pacification which military skill had failed to compel. To succeed, it was essential that he should trust and be trusted. He moved his tent away from the troops to the base of the Matoppo hills, and lay there quietly for six weeks, in the power of the enemy if they had chosen to attack. Word was circulated among the natives that he had come alone and undefended to hear their side of the case. A council was held by them in the very depths of the hills, where no armed force could touch them. He was invited to attend it. It was a case of staking his life on trust. He displayed no hesitation, but mounted and rode unarmed with the messenger. Three friends rode with him. They met the assembled chiefs who

laid the native grievances before them. At the end of a long discussion Rhodes, having exacted such concessions as he thought fit, asked the question, "Now, for the future is it peace or is it war?" And the chiefs, laying down their sticks as a symbol of surrendered arms, declared, "It is peace." Rhodes, riding away, characterized the scene as one of those "which make life worth living."

His life was drawing toward its end. He had still a few years before him, however, and he devoted them with success to the development of the country which bore his name. The railroad was now brought to Bulawayo, and arrangements were made for carrying the line on in sections as far as the south end of Lake Tanganyika, a construction which was part of his pet scheme for connecting the Cape by a British line of communication with Cairo.

Rhodes also concluded arrangements for carrying a telegraphic land line through to Egypt. The mineral development of the country also was fairly started. But the federal union of South Africa, the aim toward which he had always worked as the secure basis of the extension of British rule in the southern half of the continent, was not for him to see. The South African War broke out in 1899. Rhodes took his part at Kimberley in sustaining the hardships of a siege; but his health was broken, and though he lived to see victory practically assured to British arms, peace had not been concluded when, on March 26, 1902, he died at Muizenberg, near Capetown.

His life's work did not end actually with his death. He left behind him a will in which he dedicated his fortunes, as he had dedicated himself, exclusively to the public service. He left the bulk of his vast wealth for the purpose of founding scholarships at Oxford university of the value each of £300 a year, to be held by students from every important British colony, and from every state and territory of the United States of America. The sum so bequeathed was very large; but it was not for the munificence of the legacy that the will was received with acclamation throughout the civilized world: it was for the striking manifestation of faith which it embodied in the principles that make for the enlightenment and peace and union of mankind, and for the fine constancy of Rhodes' conviction that the unity of the British empire, which he had been proud to serve, was among the greatest of organized forces uniting for universal good. The will was drawn up some years before his death. A codicil, signed during the last days of his life, gave evidence of some enlargement of his views as to the association of races necessary in order to secure the peace of the world, and added to the original scheme a certain number of scholarships to be held at the disposal of German students. (See RHODES SCHOLARSHIPS.)

The publication of the will silenced Rhodes' detractors and converted many of his critics. It set a seal which could not be mistaken upon his completed life. The revulsion of sentiment toward him was complete, and his name passed at once into the public estimation to the place which it is probably destined to take in history, as one which his countrymen are proud to count among the great makers of the British empire.

See the *Life* by Sir Lewis Michell (2 vols., London, 1910); Sir T. E. Fuller, *Cecil John Rhodes: A Monograph and a Reminiscence* (London, 1910), "Vindex," *Cecil Rhodes: His Political Life and Speeches* (London, 1900); R. Jourdan, *Cecil Rhodes's Private Life* (1911); also: "Imperialist," *Cecil Rhodes*, with a chapter by Sir L. Starr Jameson (1897); E. T. Cook, *Rights and Wrongs of the Transvaal War* (1902); Sir Charles Dilke, *Problems of Greater Britain* (1890); Scholtz & Hornbeck, *Oxford and the Rhodes Scholarships* (1907); A. F. B. Williams, *Life of Rhodes* (1921); T. G. McDonald, *Life of Rhodes* (1927). (F. L. L.; X.)

RHODES, JAMES FORD (1848–1927), U.S. historian, was born in Cleveland, O., on May 1, 1848. He studied at New York university, at the University of Chicago, and at the Collège de France in 1867–68, and in 1868 served as occasional Paris correspondent to the Chicago *Times*. He then took a course in metallurgy in the School of Mines, at Berlin, Germany; subsequently he inspected iron and steel works in western Germany and in Great Britain; and in 1870 he joined his father in the iron, steel and coal business in Cleveland, becoming a member of the firm in

1874. He retired from business with an ample fortune in 1885, and after two years devoted to general reading and travel he began his *History of the United States From the Compromise of 1850,* which was published in eight volumes in 1893–1917 (rev. ed., 1920).

In 1909 he published a volume of *Historical Essays;* in 1913, *Lectures on the American Civil War;* in 1917, *History of the Civil War;* and in 1922, *The McKinley and Roosevelt Administration 1897–1909.*

The merit of his work earned him numerous honorary degrees in England and America. He died in Brookline, Mass., on Jan. 22, 1927.

BIBLIOGRAPHY.—C. F. Adams, *Some Phases of the Civil War* (Cambridge, Mass., 1905), an appreciation and criticism of Rhodes's history of this period; J. R. Lynch, *Some Historical Errors of James Ford Rhodes* (Boston, 1922); A. W. Lowell, "James Ford Rhodes," *Mass. Hist. Soc. Proc. 1926–27,* vol. lx, pp. 122–128 (Boston, 1927); J. T. Morse, "Memoir of James Ford Rhodes," *ibid.,* pp. 178–192.

RHODES (RODI), the most easterly island of the Aegean sea, about 10 mi. S. of Cape Alypo in Asia Minor (length about 45 mi. from northeast to southwest, greatest breadth 22 mi., area about 545 sq.mi.).

Rhodes were taken by Italy from the Turks in 1912 and became capital of the administration of the Dodecanese (*q.v.*). Under the Allies' peace treaty with Italy in 1947, the island of Rhodes and the other Dodecanese Islands were awarded to Greece. During World War II representatives of the people of the Dodecanese had formally declared their union with Greece.

Population (island) (1936) 61,886; (town) (1936) 25,425, (1951) 23,599.

The island is diversified in its surface and is traversed from north to south by an elevated mountain range, the highest point of which is called Attavyros (It. Attairo; anc. Atabyris or Atabyrium) (3,986 ft.). It commands a view of the elevated coast of Asia Minor toward the north, and of the archipelago, studded with its numerous islands, on the northwest; on the southwest is seen Mt. Ida in Crete, often veiled in clouds, and on the south and southeast the vast expanse of waters which wash the African shore. The rest of the island is occupied in great part by ranges of moderately elevated hills, on which are found extensive woods of ancient pines, planted by the hand of nature. These forests were formerly very thick, but they were subsequently greatly thinned by the Turks, who cut them down and took no care to plant others in their place.

Beneath these hills the surface of the island falls lower, and several hills in the form of amphitheatres extend their bases as far as the sea, forming a series of beautiful pictures.

Rhodes has been famed at all times for its delightful climate. The wind blows from the west, often with violence, for nine months in the year; at other times it blows from the north, moderating the summer heat, except during July and August when hot winds blow from the mainland.

Rhodes, in addition to its fine climate, is blessed with a fertile soil and produces a variety of the finest fruits and vegetables. Around the villages are extensive cultivated fields and orchards containing fig, pomegranate and orange trees. On the sloping hills, carob trees and others, both useful and agreeable, grow abundantly; the vine also holds its place and produces a species of wine which was highly valued by the ancients, though it seems to have degenerated greatly in modern times; a strong red wine is still exported. The valleys afford rich pastures, and the plains produce a wide variety of grain.

Under Turkish rule Rhodes was a distributing centre for European manufactures to the neighbouring islands and mainland, receiving cattle, foodstuffs and other produce in return. Under Italian rule its commercial position changed and became uncertain. Italian, French and Greek steamships call frequently, and tourists became more numerous.

The only large town is the capital, Rhodes, at the northeast extremity, rising from the sea in the form of an amphitheatre, surrounded with walls and towers and defended by a moated castle. These are the work of the Knights of St. John, almost unimpaired. But few traces remain of the splendour of the ancient city, with its regular streets, well-ordered plan and numerous public buildings.

The modern city of Rhodes is in general the work of the Knights of St. John and has a mediaeval aspect. The picturesque fortifications by which the city is surrounded remain as they were in the 15th century, almost without alteration. Principal buildings are the church of St. John, which became the principal mosque; the hospital, transformed into a museum; the palace of the grand master; and the senate house. The picturesque Street of the Knights is perfectly straight, lined by old houses on which remain armorial bearings of members of the order, including those of royal and noble houses of Europe.

Relics of classical antiquity, inscribed altars, bases of statues and architectural fragments are found in courtyards and gardens in the suburbs, the whole of which were within the limit of the ancient city.

The foundations of the moles between the harbours are also of Hellenic works, though the superstructures were erected by the knights.

Rhodes has two harbours. The lesser lies toward the east, and admits cargo steamers, which can also anchor outside in fair weather. The larger is silted and only admits small craft. The two harbours are separated by a mole and at the eastern entrance is the fort of St. Elmo, with a lighthouse.

HISTORY

Archaeological remains of the Late Minoan age show that the early Aegean culture maintained itself in Rhodes comparatively unimpaired until the historic period. Legend also peopled primitive Rhodes with skilful workers in metal, the "Telchines," and with bold navigators, "Children of the Sun." In Homeric legend there was already a Heracleid settlement, and in historic times Rhodes was occupied by a Dorian population, mainly from Argos and subsequent to the Dorian invasion of Greece. The three Homeric cities refounded by these settlers—Lindus, Ialysus and Camirus—belonged to the League of Six Cities, by which Dorian colonists in Asia Minor protected themselves against the neighbouring mainland.

The early history of these towns records brisk commercial expansion and active colonization, illustrated by the rich tombs of Camirus. Rhodian colonies extended not only eastward along the southern coast of Asia Minor, but also to the westernmost parts of the Greek world. Examples are Phaselis in Lycia, Soli in Cilicia, Salapia on the east Italian coast, Gela in Sicily, the Lipari Islands, and Rhoda in northeast Spain. In home waters the Rhodians dominated Karpathos and other islands.

The history of Rhodes during the Persian Wars is obscure. In the 5th century B.C. the three cities were enrolled in the Delian league and were democracies. In 412 the island revolted from Athens and became the headquarters of the Peloponnesian fleet. Four years later the inhabitants concentrated in the newly founded city of Rhodes laid out on an exceptionally fine site according to a scientific plan by the architect Hippodamus of Miletus. This town soon rose to considerable importance and attracted much Aegean and Levantine commerce which had hitherto been in Athenian hands.

In the 4th century B.C. political development was arrested by constant struggles between oligarchs and democrats, who in turn brought the city under the control of Sparta (412–395, 391–378), of Athens (395–391, 378–357) and of the Carian dynasty of Mausolus (357–340).

About 340 it was conquered for the Persian king by his Rhodian admiral, Mentor. In 332 it submitted to Alexander the Great, but on his death the people expelled the Macedonian garrison and henceforth not only maintained their independence but acquired great political influence. The expansion of Levantine trade in the Hellenistic age brought especial profit to Rhodes, whose standard of coinage and code of maritime law became widely accepted in the Mediterranean. Under modified democracy, in which the six πρυτάνεις found a powerful executive, the city long enjoyed a good administration. In foreign politics it prudently avoided the ambitious schemes of Hellenistic monarchs, but gained prestige by energetic interference against all who threatened the balance of power or the security of the seas. Chief incidents were a memorable siege by Demetrius Poliorcetes in 304, who sought in vain to force the city into active alliance with King Antigonus; a severe earthquake in 227, the damages of which all Hellenistic states contributed to repair because they could not afford to see the island ruined; some vigorous campaigns against Byzantine, Pergamene and Pontic kings, who threatened the Black sea trade route (220 *sqq.*), and against the pirates of Crete.

In accordance with their settled policy the Rhodians supported the Romans when they made war on Philip V of Macedon and Antiochus III of Syria on behalf of the minor Greek states. During the Third Macedonian War a false step deprived them of possessions in Lycia and partially diverted their trade to Delos (167). Nevertheless, during the two Mithridatic Wars they remained loyal to Rome and in 88 successfully stood a siege. The Rhodian navy did further good service for Pompey in his campaigns against the pirates and against Julius Caesar. But in 43 G. Cassius besieged and ruthlessly plundered the people for refusing to submit to his exactions and, though Rhodes continued a free town for another century, its commercial prosperity was crippled, and extensive earthquakes after A.D. 155 completed its ruin.

In the days of its greatest power Rhodes became famous as a centre of pictorial and plastic art; it had a school of eclectic oratory whose chief representative was Apollonius Molon, the teacher of Cicero; it was the birthplace of the Stoic philosopher Panaetius; the home of the poet Apollonius Rhodius and the historian Poseidonius.

Protogenes embellished the city with his paintings, and Chares of Lindus with the celebrated colossal statue of the sun-god, which was 105 ft. high. The colossus stood for 56 years, until an earthquake prostrated it in 244 B.C. Its enormous fragments continued to excite wonder in the time of Pliny, and were not removed until A.D. 656, when Rhodes was conquered by the Saracens, who sold the remains for old metal to a dealer, who employed 900 camels to carry them away. The notion that the colossus once stood astride over the entrance to the harbour is a mediaeval fiction. During the later Roman empire Rhodes was the capital of the "province of the islands."

The history of Rhodes under the Byzantine rule is uneventful except for some temporary occupations by the Saracens (653–658, 717–718) and the gradual encroachment of Venetian traders after 1082. In the 13th century the island stood as a rule under the control of Italian adventurers, who were, however, at times compelled to acknowledge the overlordship of the emperors of Nicaea, and who failed to protect it against the depredations of Turkish corsairs.

In 1309 it was conquered by the Knights Hospitallers of St. John of Jerusalem at the instigation of the pope and the Genoese, and converted into a great fortress for the protection of the southern seas against the Turks. Under their mild and just rule both the native Greeks and the Italian residents were able to carry on a brisk trade. But the piratical acts of these traders, in which the knights themselves sometimes joined, and the strategic position of the island between Constantinople and the Levant necessitated its reduction by the Ottoman sultans. A siege in 1480 by Mohammed II led to the repulse of the Turks with severe losses; after a second investment, during which Sultan Suleiman (Soliman) I is said to have lost 90,000 men out of a force of 200,000, the knights evacuated Rhodes under an honourable capitulation (1522). The population henceforth dwindled in consequence of pestilence and emigration, and although the island recovered somewhat in the 18th century under a comparatively lenient rule, it was brought to a very low ebb as a result of the severity of its governor during the Greek revolution.

The sites of Lindus, Ialysus and Camirus, which in the most ancient times were the principal towns of the island, are clearly marked, and the first of the three is still occupied by a small town with a mediaeval castle, both of them dating from the time of the knights, though the castle occupies the site of the ancient acropolis, of which considerable remains were still visible. There are no ruins of any importance on the site of either Ialysus or Camirus, but excavations at both places produced valuable and interesting results

in the way of ancient vases and other antiquities, which were placed in the British Museum and in the local collection at Rhodes.

In mediaeval times Rhodes's pottery, a lustreware at first imitated from Persian, developed into an independent style of fine colouring and rich variety of design. After the Italian occupation in 1912 a considerable modern quarter on European lines grew up west of the city of the knights; carriage roads were constructed and the harbours improved.

BIBLIOGRAPHY.—*See* Pindar, *7th Olympian Ode;* Diodorus, v, 55–59, xiii–xx *passim;* Polybius, iv, 46–52, v, 88–90, xvi, 2–9, xxvii–xxix *passim;* A. Berg, *Die Insel Rhodos* (1862); C. Torr, *Rhodes in Ancient Times* (Cambridge, 1885), *Rhodes in Modern Times* (Cambridge, 1887); C. Schumacher, *De republica Rhodiorum commentatio* (Heidelberg, 1886); H. van Gelder, *Geschichte der alten Rhodier* (Hague, 1900); B. V. Head, *Historia Numorum,* pp. 539–542 (Oxford, 1887); Baron de Balabre, *Rhodes of the Knights* (1909); K. F. Kinch, *Fouilles de Vroulia* (1914); A. Gabriel, *La Cité de Rhodes* (1921).

RHODESIA AND NYASALAND, FEDERATION OF.

The federation consists of three British central African countries: Northern Rhodesia, a protectorate lying north of the Zambezi river; Nyasaland, also a protectorate, east of Northern Rhodesia; and Southern Rhodesia, a self-governing colony to the south of the Zambezi. It is bounded north by Tanganyika and the Belgian Congo, south by Bechuanaland and the Union of South Africa, west by Angola and east by Mozambique (both Portuguese possessions), and has an area of about 487,000 sq.mi. and an estimated population of 6,792,000. English, tribal dialects and (in Southern Rhodesia) Afrikaans are spoken. The native population is predominantly pagan, and there is a Christian minority. Salisbury, in Southern Rhodesia, is the federal capital. The federation is "exclusive" with limited powers, and those primarily affecting only Europeans, allotted to the federal government; Northern Rhodesia and Nyasaland retain their protectorate status under the aegis of the colonial office so far as African affairs are concerned, and the land rights and political prospects of the Africans are specifically safeguarded. The administration is in the hands of a governor general, a prime minister and an executive council (forming the cabinet); there is a federal assembly with speaker and elected majority, and an African Affairs board, a standing committee of the federal assembly, scrutinizes bills involving African interests before their presentation to the assembly. The three component countries retained their prefederation legislative structure. The political foundation of the federation and embryo dominion was declared to be interracial partnership based on equality of economic and political opportunity. The first governor general and prime minister of the federation were, respectively, Lord Llewellin and Sir Godfrey Huggins. The monetary unit is the Southern Rhodesian pound (= £1 sterling).

In this article the history of Rhodesia is treated first, followed by separate sections on Northern Rhodesia and on Southern Rhodesia describing the physical features, administration and economy of each country. Nyasaland is dealt with in the separate article NYASALAND.

HISTORY

The historical records of south-central Africa before the European occupation in the closing years of the 19th century are inevitably scarce, because the African inhabitants built only with poles, grass and mud, could not write and, since they did not have the wheel, made no roads. Yet it is known that the first of them was one of the earliest of men; Rhodesian man, whose skull was discovered at Broken Hill in 1920, was comparable with Neanderthal man who lived in Europe more than 10,000 years ago; and many palaeolithic implements of the type used by Neanderthal man have also been found. When the first wave of Bantu migrants arrived from the north, probably in the 13th century, they found, and drove before them into the southern deserts, Bushmen. These people, who still exist on the upper Zambezi and in the Kalahari desert in considerable numbers, were cave dwellers, hunters and artists. More than 400 of their lively paintings of men and animals have been discovered in the caves and on the rocks of the two Rhodesias. Of non-African culture evidence is provided by the ruins in Southern Rhodesia of at least 400 stone buildings of which Zimbabwe is the largest and most famous. Nobody really knows their date or origin, though theories and legends take the story back to the Sabaeo-Phoenicians and King Solomon's mines ("Ophir" was a generic term meaning any conspicuous source of natural products or merchandise, and most of the gold of those days came from southwestern Arabia), but it seems most probable that they date from the 1st millennium A.D. and that their builders either came from or at least traded with the east. In any case, by the

COMMUNICATIONS AND MINERAL RESOURCES OF RHODESIA AND NYASALAND FEDERATION

time the Portuguese captured the east coast ports from the Arabs between 1500 and 1520, they found that this civilization had already vanished. There was a gold industry of great size and antiquity but it was already in decay. Before this date, it is now estimated, gold to the present value of about £75,000,000 had been mined from the rocks of the Southern Rhodesian plateau, but the Portuguese bought gold only from alluvial workings, brought down to the coast in porcupine quills by the people of Monomotapa. This was the dynastic name of a series of Bantu chiefs who seem to have ruled a very considerable "kingdom" on the plateau until well into the 17th century.

Meanwhile it is probable that a later wave of industrial Bantu discovered and began to mine the other great mineral belt of central Africa, the enormous copper deposits of the Congo-Zambezi watershed. It is not known when they started, but they were still mining the outcrops in the early years of the 20th century.

The curtain of history lifts again in 1798 with the explorations into central Africa of Francisco de Lacerda in search of the *viagem a contracosta,* and the actual crossing of the continent from west to east by two half-castes called Pedro Baptista and A. José in 1802–11; and soon after this began the return to the north of Bantu warrior tribes from south Africa under the impact of Shaka's (Chaka's) tyranny. For one reason or another, but chiefly fear, three of these tribes fled northward during the first half of the century and themselves brought terror and conquest to much of central Africa. The Matabele conquered for themselves a kingdom south of the Zambezi, the Makololo under Sebitoane crossed that river and became the overlords of the Barotse on its upper reaches, and the Angoni went even farther north, to wander and raid and plunder as far afield as the east African hinterland. One branch of them eventually settled on the Luangwa-Lake Nyasa watershed, partly in what was later to become northeastern Rhodesia.

At about the same time, or perhaps a little later, the for the most part quite unmartial tribes north of the Zambezi began to be further afflicted by the inroads of the Arab slave trade. The slavers allied themselves with the Babemba and other warrior tribes and between them for more than a generation they decimated the population.

David Livingstone reached the upper Zambezi in 1851 and discovered the Victoria falls on Nov. 17, 1855. He died at Chitambo's village near Lake Bangweulu on May 1, 1873, during his famous last journey in fruitless quest of the source of the Nile. In the years between he discovered the whole of the Zambezi basin, Nyasaland and the plateau to the south of Lake Tanganyika. He also called the attention of the Christian world to the "open sore" of the east African slave trade, and so started the great missionary developments of the closing years of the century and, indirectly, the occupation and liberation of central Africa from 50 years of war and slavery.

This occupation came from the south. Cecil Rhodes first discussed the possibility of opening up central Africa in a conversation with (later Sir) Sidney Shippard, afterward commissioner in Bechuanaland, in 1878, but it was not until ten years later that he was in a position to act. In 1887 Portugal laid claim to all the interior between Angola and Mozambique (to secure the *viagem a contracosta* which De Lacerda had tried so hard to find 100 years before). This spurred Rhodes, then in Bechuanaland, to action. J. S. Moffat was sent to make a treaty, on Feb. 11, 1888, with Lobengula, chief of the Matabele, binding him to have no dealings with any foreign power; and on Oct. 30 James Rochford Maguire and two other emissaries of Rhodes acquired from the chief a mineral concession covering the whole of the country south of the Zambezi. Rhodes went to London and persuaded Lord Salisbury to entrust him and his associates with the occupation of the whole of central Africa. After some negotiation the British South Africa company received its charter on Oct. 29, 1889. The stated objects of the company were: (1) to extend the railway from Kimberley northward toward the Zambezi; (2) to encourage emigration and colonization; (3) to promote trade and commerce; (4) to secure all mineral rights in return for guarantees of protection and security of rights to the tribal chiefs. Nine months later a pioneer column, led by Lieut. Col. E. G. Pennefather, guided by the great hunter F. C. Selous and consisting of about 200 settlers and 500 police, reached the site of the future capital of Southern Rhodesia and built Fort Salisbury. There was a brush with the Portuguese on the eastern border but in 1891 a treaty was concluded which was still in force in the 1950s; it delineated the frontier and included provision for the building of a railway from Beira and the recognition of the Shiré and Zambezi rivers as international waterways. By 1892 there were 1,500 settlers prospecting in Matabeleland, mostly on the ancient gold workings, and beginning to take up land, but for the next few years they were beset by trouble. In 1893 the Matabele attacked and were only defeated after severe fighting. In 1895 many of the settlers took part in the Jameson raid and were subsequently sent to England for trial; and a few months later the Matabele rose again, 10,000 of them forcing the settlers at Bulawayo to go into laager. Rhodes came out from London by way of Beira and held his famous indaba with the Matabele chiefs at the place in the Matopo hills where his grave now lies.

Meanwhile Rhodes had been energetically trying to secure the hinterland north of the Zambezi for Britain before the Germans, the Belgians or the Portuguese should forestall him. The "scramble for Africa" was on. In 1887 Chief Lewanika of the Barotse on the upper Zambezi had, under the influence of the great missionary, François Coillard, sought Queen Victoria's protection, and after much tortuous negotiation an agreement was arranged by Frank Lochner in 1890. It was followed by a treaty in 1900. This secured for the company rights which were later extended to cover the whole of what was to become northwestern Rhodesia. In the northeast Rhodes's emissaries were Alfred Sharpe and Joseph Thomson who between them, in 1890, made treaties with most of the chiefs in the country. Sharpe tried to secure also a concession from the powerful Chief Msiri in the Katanga hills, but, because of a misunderstanding, he did not succeed and in 1891 the Belgians annexed Msiri's country and so secured the "Congo Pedicle" which contains some of the richest copper mines in the world. The war-like Babemba, south of Lake Tanganyika, refused to parley and continued, in alliance with the Arabs, to raid their weaker neighbours for slaves and ivory. The first European to penetrate their country was a missionary called Père van Oost of the White Fathers but it took several years of intermittent fighting to drive the Arabs from the plateau and to pacify the area. In the east, too, the Angoni, who had given a concession to a German which he in turn sold to the North Charterland Exploration company, rebelled. None of this fighting was very serious, but it was not until 1900 that the *Pax Britannica* was finally secured throughout the chartered company's vast new territories.

In 1899 the Barotseland-Northwestern Rhodesia order in council established a separate protectorate over northwestern Rhodesia with its capital at Kalomo and with Robert Coryndon as its first administrator; and two years later a similar order was made establishing the protectorate of North-Eastern Rhodesia with its capital at Fort Jameson. Robert Codrington, its administrator, and Coryndon in the west were both very remarkable men and were both under 30 years of age when given these high commands.

For the next 14 years the story of all these territories was one of peaceful progress and economic development. The railway had reached Bulawayo five months after the end of the Matabele rebellion and eight years later (two years after Rhodes's death) the Victoria falls. It halted for a while at Broken Hill and finally linked up with the Belgian system on the Katanga border in 1909. In Southern Rhodesia there were 12,506 settlers by 1904. In 1905 gold exports rose to £1,500,000 and by 1909 to £2,623,708. Agricultural development, however, got off to a slower start and it was not until 1907 that steps were taken to make the acquisition of land easier and give help and advice to the farmers. After that, progress improved and £34,810 worth of tobacco was exported in 1911. By then the white population (mainly of British stock) had risen to 23,606.

In the north settlement followed the railway and, because of the remoteness of the country, it was slow to develop. The lead-zinc-vanadium mine at Broken Hill was discovered in 1902 and by 1911 both this and the Bwana Mkubwa copper mine, the forerunner of the Northern Rhodesia copper belt, were in operation. But the prospecters had been active. The outcrops of most of the great copper mines had been discovered, including the Roan Antelope and Nkana, though they attracted little attention. The surface ores were copper oxides which were very expensive to work and the attention of the mining world was fully concentrated on the fabulous discoveries in the Katanga. In 1911 there were still only 1,500 Europeans, including officials and missionaries, in both the northern territories. In that year the two were united into the single protectorate of Northern Rhodesia, with its capital at Livingstone, near the Victoria falls.

In 1914, when the 25-year term of the company's charter was due to expire, the electors in Southern Rhodesia had the choice of either joining the Union of South Africa, supporting the continuation of the charter or pressing for self-government. They chose the middle course and the British government renewed the charter for ten years, provided that self-government should be granted earlier if the settlers showed themselves capable of administering the colony. During World War I all three territories contributed liberally of their manpower to the armed services, and local units played a prominent part in the campaign in East Africa against Gen. Paul von Lettow-Vorbeck. The armistice came at a very timely moment, when the German column, hotly pursued by Northern Rhodesian troops, was moving southward through the Bemba country in the direction of Broken Hill. The formal surrender took place at Abercorn. The Rhodesias, like most other countries, suffered severely from the influenza epidemic in 1918–19 and tens of thousands of Africans died. Meanwhile discussion about the political future of the territories had been going on and a privy council judgment was needed in 1918 to settle a dispute between the legislative council of Southern Rhodesia and the company about the ownership of unalienated land. After the war a royal commission under Lord Buxton was appointed to con-

sider the political problem, as a result of which a referendum was held in 1922 on the choice between entry into the Union of South Africa and self-government. In spite of the offer of generous terms by Gen. Jan Christiaan Smuts 8,774 electors voted for self-government as against 5,989 for joining the Union, and on Sept. 12, 1923, on the 32nd anniversary of the arrival of the pioneers at Fort Salisbury, Southern Rhodesia was annexed to the crown and became a self-governing colony. Northern Rhodesia became a protectorate of the crown under colonial office rule in 1924. The company, which had never yet paid a dividend and had spent great sums on administration and development, received £3,750,-000 in cash, retained its land rights in the north for 40 years, and all its mineral rights in both territories, from which, later, it was to reap a rich reward. At the time of the annexation there were about 34,000 whites in Southern Rhodesia and still only 4,000 in the north, but the dawn of Northern Rhodesia's prosperity was already in the sky. In 1921 Chester Beatty had become interested in the mineral possibilities of the Northern Rhodesian side of the Congo border and had formed a small syndicate called Copper Ventures Ltd. The ventures which it undertook were to lead, during the next four years, to the discovery of the great bodies of copper-sulphide ores underlying the oxide outcrops on the old Roan Antelope and Nkana claims, and to the rapid development of the great copper belt.

The Federation of Rhodesia and Nyasaland.—After 1924 the obvious geographical unity of the three central African territories continually bred discussion about the possibility of their political union. Royal commissions reported on the question in 1927 and 1939 but both of them recommended postponement of any such project, mainly because Southern Rhodesia, as a much more prosperous and self-governing colony, would be too weighty a partner for the two backward protectorates. Northern Rhodesia's revenues, however, leaped from £3,000,000 to £30,000,000 a year between 1945 and 1953 and, in this respect, to equality with the south. In consequence the northern settlers stepped up their agitation for closer union and in 1951 an impartial committee of civil servants from the three territories and the United Kingdom strongly recommended a federation. They rejected outright amalgamation because of the long-expressed opposition of the northern Africans to such a project. Two years of discussion and negotiation followed, marked by considerable opposition from the vocal elements of the African populations of Northern Rhodesia and Nyasaland and sharp party controversy in the British parliament; but a referendum in Southern Rhodesia supported federation; the colonial office remained convinced that it was both essential and urgent, and the necessary legislation was passed in July 1953. The federal assembly met for the first time on Feb. 2, 1954, and by the following July the government had assumed most of the responsibilities allotted to it. Oct. 23 was chosen as "Federation day."

NORTHERN RHODESIA

Northern Rhodesia is a British central African protectorate administered by the colonial office. It is 288,130 sq.mi. in area and is bounded on the north by the Belgian Congo, Lake Tanganyika and Tanganyika, on the east by Nyasaland, on the south by Portuguese East Africa and Southern Rhodesia and on the west by Angola.

Physical Features.—Most of the country consists of undulating plateaus between 3,000 and 4,500 ft. high, rising to more than 5,000 ft. on the Congo-Zambezi watershed along the Congo border, in the hills along the eastern border and in the Muchinga escarpment southeast of Lake Bangweulu (*q.v.*). Most of it is drained by the Zambezi and its two great tributaries, the Luangwa and the Kafue. In the northeast the Chambezi river runs into Lake Bangweulu and this in turn drains into Lake Mweru (*q.v.*) through the Luapula river. The Luangwa and lower Zambezi, below the Victoria falls, run in deep, hot valleys through broken, arid country.

The climate is tropical, with three distinct seasons: hot, August to October; wet, November to April; cool, May to July. Annual rainfall amounts vary, according to altitude, from 25 in. to 50 in.

The plateau country is of the wooded savanna type, though the woodland is heavier along the Congo-Zambezi watershed and in the teak forests on the central Zambezi. Most of the country north of Broken Hill is infested with tsetse fly. For 100 mi. W. of Kafue township the Kafue is bordered by grassy plains about 40 mi. wide, flooded in the rains, the home of thousands of antelope and buffalo. Similar plains occur on the middle Zambezi and near Lake Bangweulu. The westward bend of the Kafue (the "Hook") was made a national park (c. 8,650 sq.mi.) in 1950 and is particularly well stocked with game. Game is fairly plentiful in most of the more thinly inhabited areas, and almost all varieties of south-central African fauna are to be found, including sitatunga, koodoo, sable and roan antelope, wildebeest, rhinoceros, hippopotamus and a few giraffe. Lions are not uncommon and elephant and buffalo abound in certain areas.

Population and Chief Towns.—There were, in 1951, 37,221 Europeans in the country, 2,529 Asiatics, 1,092 coloured people and about 1,700,577 Africans. In 1942 there were estimated to be only about 15,000 Europeans and 1,366,641 Africans. More than 20,000 Europeans are concentrated on the copper belt and most of the remainder live near the railway, with isolated planting communities at Fort Jameson and Abercorn. There are about 60 distinguishable tribes of Africans, among the largest being the Babemba, Achewa, Barotse and Angoni.

The chief towns are Lusaka (cap.), 62,000 (1953 est., 6,000 Europeans); Kitwe 60,926 (6,300 Europeans); Luanshya, 54,127 (4,727); Ndola, 44,120 (5,120); Mufulira, 41,668 (4,247); Chingola, 34,484 (3,384); and Broken Hill 32,810 (4,050).

Education and Health.—For European children there are 22 government and 9 other schools. Seven of them offer secondary education. Education is free. In 1951 approximately 146,000 Africans were attending 1,380 schools, administered either by the government or the missions or the native authorities with government grants. Teacher training and secondary and technical education for Africans are being developed as rapidly as the output of the primary schools permits. The climate is good and, if normal precautions against tropical disease are taken, healthful. Malaria, hookworm, dysentery and similar illnesses are prevalent in rural areas only and there is much malnutrition in the villages. Sleeping sickness occurs in certain, well-defined areas. Hospitals and dispensaries serve all but the remotest districts.

Administration.—Northern Rhodesia is administered by a governor and commander in chief assisted by an executive council of seven official and four unofficial members, one of whom represents African interests. These councillors, including the unofficial members, share between them most of the administrative portfolios and answer for the departments in the legislative council. This consisted in 1953 of a speaker, nine official members, nine (European) elected members and four members nominated to represent African interests, of whom two were Africans. The latter were members of the African representative council which advises on all bills affecting African interests and which stands at the apex of a system of provincial councils and tribal local government. The franchise for the legislative council was limited to British subjects, which virtually means the European population.

Agriculture and Industries.—Copper mining employs about 6,000 European males out of a total labour force of 16,000 and about 40,000 Africans. Apart from civil servants, missionaries, traders and railway workers, most other Europeans are engaged in farming. Along the railway they produce cattle, maize, some wheat and tobacco (which is also grown around Fort Jameson in the east). Coffee is produced on the highlands south of Lake Tanganyika. Except for tobacco, which is exported, the chief market for produce is the copper belt, and after World War II many secondary industries developed, including a big, publicly owned cement factory at Chilanga near Lusaka. Lead, zinc and vanadium are mined at Broken Hill, and there is a considerable output of timber from the Zambezi teak forests. After the war production and trade expanded remarkably. Exports in 1938 were worth £5,114,428; by 1951 the figure had risen to more than £67,000,000. This prosperity was almost entirely the result of the rise in the price of copper of which 309,142 tons were exported in 1951, worth 83% of the total value of the export trade. The African population is mainly

engaged in subsistence farming though maize is grown as a cash crop, mainly in the Southern province, and tobacco and cotton in the Eastern province. There is a big fishing industry on the Luapula river. About 46,000 adult males are usually away working in Southern Rhodesia and many others in South Africa, in addition to those employed on the copper belt and in the farming areas. In many tribal areas less than 30% of the men are to be found in their villages.

Communications.—The Cape to Congo railway runs northward (507 mi.) from the Victoria falls to the Katanga border with a branch-line system serving the copper belt. It provides access to the ports of Lobito Bay in Angola, Beira in Mozambique and all South African ports. Some barges operate on the upper Zambezi but otherwise the rivers are only used for local canoe transport. Mpulungu on Lake Tanganyika is served by a lake steamer operating from East Africa. Main roads (only 300 mi. with a bitumen surface) run northward from Livingstone to the copper belt and northeast to Abercorn (1,100 mi.); eastward from Lusaka to Fort Jameson (392 mi.); westward from Lusaka and Nchanga to Mwinilunga, and from Lusaka to Mongu, and southeastward from Kafue to Chirundu and onward to Salisbury. These are all-weather roads of varying quality. District roads serve all the settled areas and the more densely populated African areas. There are 42 airfields, those at Lusaka and Livingstone being of international standard. Internal and regional air services are provided by Central African airways.

Finance.—Revenue rose from less than £3,000,000 in 1942 to £15,000,000 in 1951 and more than £23,000,000 in 1952, more than half of it being paid in income tax by the mining companies. Expenditure followed suit. A ten-year development plan was expected to cost £36,000,000 and was to be financed by £20,500,000 from revenues, £13,000,000 from loans and £2,500,000 from colonial development and welfare funds.

Customs.—The northern third of the country is in the "Congo basin" where, by international convention, no preferences can be given. Ad valorem duties do not exceed 10%. The rest of the country is covered by customs agreements with Southern Rhodesia and South Africa under which these countries admit their products, except spirits and tobacco, duty free. Goods from overseas may be consigned through to Northern Rhodesia in bond, thus, in some cases, saving the higher duties payable in South Africa.

(K. G. B.)

SOUTHERN RHODESIA

Southern Rhodesia, separated from Northern Rhodesia by the Zambezi river, is bounded on the northeast and east by Portuguese East Africa, on the south by the Transvaal and on the southwest and west by the Bechuanaland protectorate. It consists of Matabeleland and Mashonaland, covering 150,333 sq.mi. The country lies between 15° 36' and 22° 25' S. and 25° 14' and 33° 4' E.

Physical Features.—Southern Rhodesia forms part of the great southern African plateau. The highest part runs from southwest to northeast and forms a broad watershed between the basin of the Zambezi and the basins of the Limpopo and Sabi. It is along this central axis that the railway runs from Plumtree through Bulawayo to Salisbury. In this central area the elevation ranges from more than 4,000 ft. to more than 5,000 ft. On each side the elevation decreases, falling to less than 2,000 ft. about the Zambezi and to less than 1,000 ft. in the southeast. About 24% of the total area lies above 4,000 ft. The surface consists for the most part of gently undulating plains, diversified by steep-sided hill ranges and isolated *kopjes*. The highest point occurs 48 mi. N. of Umtali in Mt. Inyangani, 8,251 ft. There a definite mountain range runs north and south and forms the eastern border of the country.

On the whole the considerable altitude partly compensates for the low latitude. The days are mostly hot throughout the year, the nights frequently cool, and frost is likely to occur during June, July and August. From the middle of August the temperature increases to its maximum in October, when the mean maximum is 85.2° F., taking the country as a whole. Rains and clouds usually appear about October and bring a little coolness. Sometimes the rains are late and the high temperatures continue to be rather trying during November and December. The thermometer may rise to more than 100° F. even on the high veld. Humidity averages 65% over the year, falling to 48% in October and remaining at about 75% from December to March. The rainy season may be said to last from October to March. The annual average rainfall is 28 in.

About two-thirds of the country is covered with trees and shrubs. There are comparatively few open stretches. The prevailing plant association is savanna, forming parklike territory. At favourable spots on the mountainous eastern border, close evergreen forests occur in patches, some of the trees attaining a height of 200 ft. On the upper slopes *Lussonia umbellifera* and *Eugenia* species are dominant, and there they grow to heights up to 80 ft. The so-called Rhodesian teak (native *igusi; Baikiaea plurijuga*) is about 50% harder than real teak. From the bark of the baobab the natives obtain a fine fibre which they use for making nets.

The country is rich in antelopes, the most common species being the duiker, the steinbok and the reitbok. Other herbivorous animals are the buffalo, giraffe, zebra, elephant, rhinoceros and hippopotamus. The Carnivora include the lion, leopard, cheeta and various wildcats. There are crocodiles in the rivers. Beetles, butterflies and moths abound. White ants (termites) and locusts can be troublesome. Among the largest of the birds are ostriches, secretary birds, paauws, knorhaans, cranes, storks, vultures and eagles. Guinea fowl, partridge, duck, geese and teal are shot. Good shooting is to be had, but the following are royal game, and so are protected: eland, elephant, giraffe, gemsbok, hippopotamus, inyala, ostrich and rhinoceros. Animals and plants are protected in eight national parks. (*See also* SOUTH AFRICA, UNION OF.)

Population and Chief Towns.—In 1954 the population consisted of 160,000 Europeans, 2,150,000 Africans and about 12,000 Asian and coloured people. One of the first concerns of the colonial government was to augment the European element. In the first nine months of 1927, 3,574 immigrants were received. In the following year the European population was estimated to be 50,000. After World War II immigration averaged 15,000 a year. The Africans include Amandebele, Amatshangana, Basuto and numerous tribes often grouped together as "Mashona." English is the official language. A certain amount of Afrikaans, however, is spoken in the country districts.

Salisbury (cap.) and Bulawayo are described in separate articles. Umtali, the centre of a gold-mining area, has a European population of 7,000 (1954). Other municipalities are Gwelo, Fort Victoria, Que Que and Gatooma.

Education.—In 1954 there were 116 European government schools and 24 private, 9 European-aided farm schools, 14 Asian and coloured government schools and more than 2,300 mission and government schools for Africans.

Administration.—In the constitution under the letters patent of 1923 legislation affecting the African population, the unalienated land, the railways and the mineral rights of the British South Africa company were subject to disallowance by the crown (there were several important changes later), but in other respects Southern Rhodesia was endowed with the institutions of a self-governing overseas British state. Legislative power is vested in the sovereign, represented by the governor, and an executive council composed of the ministry under the presidency of the governor and responsible to the legislative assembly of 30 members. The first general election was held on April 29, 1924, and the first ministry was then formed by Sir Charles Coghlan. The franchise is extended to all British subjects, including Africans, over 21 years of age and possessing premises to the value of £500 or receiving an income of not less than £240 a year.

Agriculture and Industries.—Farming exists in several forms, from ranching to tobacco growing. Mixed farming is common and dairying is practised on the smaller farms near the towns and mines. The three major agricultural products are tobacco, cattle and maize. The acreage under crops (1953) was: maize 374,500; tobacco 178,200; green manures, legumes and fodders 240,000. Irrigation is rapidly developing. Citrus orchards are extending.

Ranching is favoured by the climate, which allows the cattle to run on the veld throughout the winter. In 1953 there were more than 3,000,000 head of cattle, generally in herds of from 600 to 1,000. African-owned cattle totalled 1,831,735. They are grass-fattened for market or are sent on to agricultural farms for final preparation.

Minerals being mined in the 1950s were gold, chrome, lead, asbestos, mica, tungsten, coal, silver, etc. In 1954 the output of gold was valued at £6,651,000. The total output of minerals was valued at £18,776,000.

The gross output of industries in 1952 was valued at £60,000,000. Exports (1952) were valued at £44,486,182, in the form of produce and manufactures. Tobacco exports were valued at £18,838,300. Imports of general merchandise totalled £88,377,915, chiefly textiles and iron and steel goods. Exports to the U.K. were £19,362,000 (1952); to the U.S., £2,596,484.

Communications.—The railways, with a mileage of nearly 3,000, are operated by a railway commission acting for the two Rhodesias and Bechuanaland (Railway act, 1926). The colony is well served, and is connected with Beira, the nearest port, Lourenço Marques, the Belgian Congo and the Union of South Africa. There is through communication by the Rhodesian system from Cape Town to the Congo border and, via Bulawayo and Salisbury, to Beira on the Indian ocean. The lines, as far as possible, follow the watersheds. The standard gauge is 3 ft. 6 in. More than 2,500 mi. of all-weather roads of full tarmac or on the strip principle reach in all directions from end to end of the country. The approximate mileage of existing motor roads is 15,600.

Finance.—In the budget for Southern Rhodesia for 1954–55 revenue was estimated at £12,346,000 and expenditure at £12,900,000. The national income for 1954 was estimated at £127,600,000. (*See also* NYASALAND.)   (C. L. BK.)

BIBLIOGRAPHY.—Rhodesia (History): David Livingstone, *Last Journals* (London, 1874), *Missionary Travels and Researches in South Africa* (London, 1857); Hugh Marshall Hole, *The Making of Rhodesia* (London, New York, 1926); H. M. Bate, *A Report on the Rhodesias* (London, 1953); N. S. Kane, *The World's View* (London, New York, 1954); Kenneth Bradley, *Copper Venture* (London, 1952). Northern Rhodesia: L. F. G. Anthony, *North of the Zambezi* (London, 1953); W. Cullen Gouldsbury, *An African Year* (London, 1912); Kenneth Bradley, *Diary of a District Officer* (London, 1943). Southern Rhodesia: Robert Moffat, *The Matabele Journals, 1829–1860* ed. by J. P. R. Wallis (London, 1945); Thomas Baines, *Northern Goldfield Diaries, 1869–1872,* (London, New York, 1946); Dore Ogrizek (ed.), *South and Central Africa* in "World in Colour Series," (London, New York, 1954).

RHODES SCHOLARSHIPS, founded in 1902 under the will of Cecil Rhodes. Rhodes provided for the maintenance at Oxford university of men from specified areas overseas. The value of each scholarship eventually rose to £600 a year, for two years in the first instance, and for a third year should the trustees so decide in individual cases. The annual awards in the 1950s were distributed as follows: from Australia, 6 (1 from each state); from Canada 11 (Ontario and Quebec, 2 each; the other provinces, including Newfoundland, 1 each); from New Zealand, 2; from Rhodesia, 3; from South Africa, 8 (including boys from 4 specified schools); and from Bermuda, India, Jamaica, Malta and Pakistan, 1 each. From the United States 32 scholars are elected annually. Five annual scholarships were originally allotted to Germany (because "an understanding between the three great powers will render war impossible and educational relations make the strongest tie") but these were annulled by act of parliament in 1916. The renewed German scholarships were discontinued in 1939.

In his will Rhodes mentions the objects he had in view in founding the different scholarships.

1. *Colonial.* "I consider that the education of young colonists at one of the universities in the United Kingdom is of great advantage to them for giving breadth to their views, for their instruction in life and manners, and for instilling into their minds the advantage to the colonies as well as to the United Kingdom of the retention of the unity of the empire."

2. *United States.* "I also desire to encourage and foster an appreciation of the advantages which I implicitly believe will result from the union of the English-speaking people throughout the world, and to encourage in the students from the United States an attachment to the country from which they have sprung, but without, I hope, with-

drawing them or their sympathies from the land of their adoption or birth."

He defines as follows the principles on which he wished his scholars to be selected: "My desire being that the students who shall be elected to the scholarships shall not be merely bookworms, I direct that in the election of a student to a scholarship regard shall be had to (1) his literary and scholastic attainments; (2) his fondness for and success in manly outdoor sports such as cricket, football and the like; (3) his qualities of manhood, truth, courage, devotion to duty, sympathy for and protection of the weak, kindliness, unselfishness and fellowship; and (4) his exhibition during school days of moral force of character and of instincts to lead and to take an interest in his schoolmates, for those latter attributes will be likely in after life to guide him to esteem the performance of public duties as his highest aim."

Method of Selection.—Subject to ratification by the eight trustees, the nomination of scholars is in the hands of local committees, which are appointed by the trustees, and on which former Rhodes scholars sit, but never preside. Candidates must be citizens of the country which they are to represent, with at least five years' domicile, and unmarried; and they must have passed their 19th and not have passed their 25th birthday by Oct. 1 of the year for which they are elected. Candidates are judged on their records and after a personal interview with the election committee. Save in certain exceptional cases, candidates are obliged to have attended a recognized degree-granting college or university for two years at least. At Oxford the scholars are distributed, as Rhodes desired, among all the colleges of the university, as far as possible in accordance with their own wishes; but acceptance of any scholar is determined by the colleges themselves. More than 3,000 scholars had been elected by 1955.

The 50th anniversary of the first elections (all of which were from South African schools) and the centenary of the founder's birth were celebrated in Rhodes house, Oxford, in 1953.

(P. K.; E. T. Ws.)

RHODIUM is a chemical element (symbol Rh, atomic number 45, atomic weight 102.91) which is a precious silver-white metal, one of the six platinum metals (*q.v.*). The metal has a specific gravity of 12.4 and melts at 1,980° C.; thus it is difficult to fuse or cast. Rhodium is fairly hard and cannot be easily worked at room temperature; but it can be forged above 800° C., a red heat. Its boiling point must be above 2,500° C.

The surface of the metal has a high reflectivity for light and is not corroded or tarnished by the atmosphere at room temperature. It is frequently electroplated onto metal objects and polished to give permanent attractive surfaces for jewellery and other decorative purposes. In particular, the black tarnish of silver is avoided by the use of rhodium plate. Rhodium also serves for the preparation of "silvered" surfaces for reflectors of searchlights and motion-picture projectors.

Rhodium added to platinum in small amounts yields alloys which are harder and lose weight at high temperatures even more slowly than does pure platinum. Therefore crucibles for heating materials in the chemical laboratory are commonly made from these alloys. In the industrial manufacture of nitric acid, gauze catalysts of the rhodium-platinum alloys are used because of their ability to withstand the flame temperature as ammonia is burned to nitric oxide. A wire of the alloy 10% rhodium-90% platinum joined to a wire of pure platinum forms an excellent thermocouple for measuring high temperatures in an oxidizing atmosphere. The International Temperature Scale is defined over the region from 660° to 1,063° C. by the electromotive force of this thermocouple.

The only stable isotope for rhodium has a mass number of 103, *i.e.*, Rh^{103}. Its nuclei possess a high cross section or probability for the capture of neutrons with thermal energies. The Rh^{104} formed by neutron capture is radioactive, and consists of two nuclear isomers (half-lives of 44 sec. and 4.3 min.). In nuclear physics experiments a flux of neutrons can be conveniently and quickly measured by the determination of the amount of radioactivity induced in a thin rhodium foil, exposed for a few minutes to the neutrons.

Rhodium always accompanies platinum in minerals, but only to a minor extent. It was first isolated from crude platinum by William Wollaston, who announced its discovery in 1804. He gave it the name rhodium in consequence of the red colour of a number of its compounds.

Rhodium is almost as resistant as iridium to chemical attack by acids. The massive metal is not dissolved by hot concentrated nitric or hydrochloric acid or even by aqua regia which dissolves gold and platinum. The element dissolves in fused potassium hydrogen sulphate to yield a complex sulphate, soluble in water.

Rhodium, in all well-characterized compounds, possesses the +3 oxidation state. Possibly some compounds of lower oxidation state can form, and strong oxidizing agents yield higher oxidation states of transient stability, probably +4 and +6. All its compounds are readily reduced or decomposed by heating to yield the powdered or sponge metal. Many rhodium compounds contain co-ordination complexes in which ammonia, water, chloride or other groups are bonded covalently to a central rhodium ion. Characteristically, the groups in these complexes are replaced slowly. A series of substituted ammine compounds is analogous to familiar compounds of cobalt (III) (*see* COBALT). A yellow hydrous rhodium hydroxide, soluble in acid or alkaline solutions, can be precipitated, but some conditions will cause a black precipitate to form. Rh_2O_3 is a gray compound, insoluble in acids. $RhCl_3$ can be prepared in a form which does not dissolve in water or acids. Other forms dissolve readily to give solutions whose colour may range from brown to yellow and in which some or all of the chloride is not precipitated by silver nitrate. (D. S. Mn.)

RHODOCHROSITE (from the Greek ρόδο-χρως, rose-coloured), one of the calcite group of rhombohedral carbonate minerals, consisting of manganese carbonate, $MnCO_3$. Extensive substitution of iron and calcium, as well as lesser amounts of magnesium, may occur in place of the manganese. It occurs more commonly as compact crystalline masses and incrustations than as single crystals. When pure it is usually some shade of pink or rose red, with a specific gravity of 3.70 and a hardness of $3\frac{1}{2}$–4.

Rhodochrosite is found in sedimentary deposits, in mineral veins of silver, lead, copper, and zinc minerals formed at moderate temperatures and in high-temperature metamorphic deposits. It is used as a source of manganese for the ferromanganese alloys consumed in steelmaking and in the preparation of other manganese chemicals. (D. L. G.)

RHODODENDRON, a large genus of shrubs and small trees belonging to the heath family (Ericaceae). *Azalea* and *Rhodora* (*qq.v.*), although commonly kept distinct by gardeners, are here considered as species of *Rhododendron* since no adequate botanical distinction can be drawn to separate them.

The rhododendrons are trees or shrubs, never herbs, with simple, evergreen or deciduous leaves and flowers in terminal clusters surrounded in the bud by bud scales but not as a rule by true leaves. The flowers are remarkable for the frequent absence or reduced condition of the calyx. The funnel- or bell-shaped corolla, on the other hand, with its five or more lobes, is usually conspicuous, and in some species so much so as to render these plants greatly prized in gardens. The free stamens are usually ten, with slender filaments and anthers opening by pores at the top. The ovary is five- or many-celled, ripening into a long woody pod which splits from top to bottom into a number of valves, liberating a large number of small branlike seeds.

The species, which exceed 600 in number, are for the most part natives of the mountainous regions of the northern hemisphere, extending as far south as the Malay archipelago and New Guinea but not hitherto found in South America or Australia; none is native to Great Britain. They vary greatly in stature, some of the alpine species being mere pygmies with minute leaves and tiny blossoms, while some of the Himalayan species are moderate-sized trees with huge flowers. Some are epiphytal, growing on the branches of other trees but not deriving their sustenance from them. Several notably handsome species are natives of North America. Among these are the great rhododendron (*R. maximum*), called also great laurel and rose bay, found from Nova Scotia and Ontario and southward to Georgia; the catawba or Carolina rhododendron or mountain rose bay (*R. catawbiense*) of the high Appalachian mountains; the western rhododendron (*R. macrophyllum*), found from British Columbia to California and adopted as the state flower of Washington; and the delicate rhodora (*q.v.*) of the northeastern states. The great laurel and the mountain rose bay are widely planted; less frequently *R. minus* and *R. carolinianum*, both small evergreen shrubs with showy flowers, native to the mountains of the southeastern states, are grown as ornamentals. The varieties grown in gardens are mostly grafted on the Pontic species (*R. ponticum*) and the North American *R. catawbiense*. The common Pontic variety is fine for game covert from its hardiness, the shelter it affords and the fact that hares and rabbits rarely eat it. Variety of colour has been infused by crossing or hybridizing the species first named, or their derivatives, with some of the more richly coloured Himalayan-American varieties. More than 1,000 named horticultural forms comprise some of the finest ornamental shrubs in cultivation.

The hardy evergreen kinds are readily propagated by seed, by layers and by grafting. Grafting is resorted to only for the propagation of the rarer and more tender kinds. Loamy soil containing a large quantity of peat or vegetable humus is essential, the roots of all the species investigated being associated with a fungus partner or mycorrhiza (*q.v.*). An excess of lime or chalk in the soil sooner or later proves fatal to rhododendrons and their allies. The hardy deciduous kinds are valuable for forcing and withstand cold-storage treatment well.

Rhododendrons in America are unsuited to regions of extreme summer heat and deficient rainfall, hence are best cultivated along the Atlantic seaboard, in the Alleghenies or on the Pacific coast, generally north of San Francisco.   (N. Tr.; X.)

RHODONITE, a member of the silicate group of minerals, consisting of manganese metasilicate, $MnSiO_3$, and crystallizing in the anorthic system. It commonly occurs as cleavable to compact masses with a rose-red colour; hence the name, from the Greek ῥόδον (a rose). Crystals often have a thick tabular habit; there are perfect cleavages parallel to the prism faces. The hardness is $5\frac{1}{2}–6\frac{1}{2}$, and the specific gravity 3.4–3.68. Rhodonite is liable to alteration, and in certain cases forms the primary source of very important deposits of ores of manganese, mainly in the form of oxides; such are a considerable part of the manganese ores of India, now exploited on a very large scale.

Rhodonite occurs as large rough crystals with franklinite and zinc ores at Franklin, N.J. Fine-grained rhodonite of clean colour is a desirable gem and ornamental stone. The finest quality is mined near Sverdlovsk, U.S.S.R., in the Urals. Good stone occurs in Siskiyou and Plumas counties in California. It is used for beads, pendants and other ornaments.   (W. F. Fg.)

RHODORA, the common name for *Rhododendron canadense* (formerly *Rhodora canadensis*), a small deciduous shrub of bogs and low-acid soils of the New England states and adjacent areas. It produces beautiful pale to deep rose-purple flowers in April and May. The plant is perhaps best known from Emerson's poem concerning it. (*See* Rhododendron.)   (J. M. Bl.)

RHOECUS, a Samian sculptor and architect of the 6th century B.C. He and his partner Theodorus were especially noted for their work in bronze. Herodotus says that Rhoecus built the temple of Hera at Samos. In the temple of Artemis at Ephesus was a figure of "Night" by Rhoecus, apparently of bronze. The name has been found on a fragment of a vase dedicated to Aphrodite at Naukratis. His sons Theodorus and Telecles made a statue of the Pythian Apollo for the people of Samos.

BY COURTESY OF THE WILD FLOWER PRESER-VATION SOCIETY

RHODORA (RHODORA CANADENSE) A delicate pink flower found in Canada and New England

RHONDDA, DAVID ALFRED THOMAS, 1ST VISCOUNT (1856–1918), British colliery owner and statesman, was born on March 26, 1856, in Aberdare, the son of a grocer, Samuel Thomas, who had enriched himself by colliery speculations. After an education at Clifton college and Caius college, Cambridge university, Thomas joined his father in the coal business, into which he threw himself with great energy and ability. His extraordinary commercial gifts, his insight, his foresight and the sympathy which he brought to bear on conditions of life in the mining industry soon made him a prominent, and eventually the leading, figure in the industrial world of south Wales. His business combinations brought him great wealth, and culminated in the Cambrian super-combine, which produced about 6,000,000 tons of steam coal a year.

Though he had sat as a Liberal for Merthyr Tydfil for 22 years from 1888, and for Cardiff for a few months in 1910, Thomas achieved no political importance till the outbreak of World War I, when Lloyd George invoked his assistance in mobilizing British industrial resources. He considerably expedited U.S. munitions supplies by personal visits to the United States, on one of which he narrowly escaped with his life from the sinking of the "Lusitania." He was created a baron, as Lord Rhondda, for his services, in Jan. 1916; and took office in Lloyd George's ministry in the following December as president of the local government board, passing to the food controllership in June 1917. There, taking strong steps to put an end to speculation in the necessities of life, he gradually fixed prices and brought supplies under control.

He will be mainly remembered as the author of the system of compulsory food rationing, which was carried out with absolute fairness and impartiality. In April 1918 he tendered his resignation; but pressure was put upon him to remain. He died on July 3 at Llanwern, Monmouthshire. Just previously he had been created a viscount. His only child, a daughter (who married Sir Humphrey Mackworth in 1908, and obtained a dissolution of their marriage in 1923), succeeded to the viscounty of Rhondda under a special remainder. In 1921 Lady Rhondda published a *Life* of her father.

RHONDDA, an urban district of Glamorganshire, south Wales, 12 mi. long by about $4\frac{3}{4}$ mi. across at its widest part, comprising two main valleys, named after their respective rivers, Rhondda Fawr and Rhondda Fach. Pop. (1951) 111,389. Area 37.3 sq.mi. The valleys are deeply incised in the coal measures of the south Wales geological basin and their lateral boundaries are formed by hills varying from 560 ft. near Trehafod to 1,340 ft. on the northeast of Maerdy in the Rhondda Fach and 1,742 ft. on the southwest of Treherbert in Rhondda Fawr. The upper end of the latter valley rises to the Rhigos plateau where Craig-y-Llyn (1,969 ft.) is the highest point in Glamorgan. The two valleys are separated by the ridge of Cefn-y-Rhondda, which ranges from 600 ft. above Porth to 1,690 ft. There are tributary valleys where it joins the Rhigos plateau of which Cwmparc, Clydach vale and Cymmer are the chief.

Rhondda is the centre of the eastern division of the south Wales coal field. Coal exploitation there started in 1807 and so it was later than that of the northern sections of the south Wales area where coal was worked early for iron smelting. It was the realization of the steam-raising properties of the Rhondda coal and the opening of the Treherbert pits in 1855 that made the region famous.

With the great demands made for steam coal by the ever-increasing railway traffic, steamship services and navies of the last half of the 19th century, Rhondda from being a purely pastoral upland region was transformed into a densely populated industrial area. No thought was given then, however, to the development of other industries which could provide alternative employment in the event of a setback in the coal-mining industry. With the rapid growth of each township provision was made for miners' libraries and institutes and numerous places of worship, and around these grew and flourished social, religious and cultural activities, particularly in music and drama, which, in turn, led to the creation of a strong community of interest and civic pride.

In 1801 the population was 542, but by 1871 it had reached 23,950; in 1881 it was 55,632 and in 1901 it was 113,735. The peak population figure was 167,900 in 1924 but during the severe industrial depression of the 1930s it fell to 121,940 by 1938. Further migration during World War II reduced the population seriously and by 1951 the figure stood at 111,389.

With the development of the coal exporting trade a number of small railway companies connected Rhondda with Cardiff, Port Talbot and Swansea but all these lines were eventually merged in the Great Western railway, and in 1947 in the Western region of British railways. The slump in world demand for Welsh coal following World War I undermined the prosperity of the area and led to mass unemployment and migration. In 1934, of Rhondda's 61,460 insured men more than 47% were without work. In an attempt to relieve this critical situation two new factories were opened in the area in 1939. After World War II the policy of re-distribution of industry to help depressed areas brought 29 new industries to Rhondda. At mid-century the area had a stable and varied industrial pattern. There are two major schemes of mining reorganization at Maerdy and Treherbert.   (J. C. G. J.)

RHÔNE, a department of southeastern France, formed in 1793 from the eastern portion of the department of Rhône-et-Loire, and comprising the old districts of Beaujolais, Lyonnais, Franc-Lyonnais, Forez and a small portion of Dauphiné. Pop. (1946), 918,866. Area, 1,104 sq.mi. Rhône is bounded north by the department of Saône-et-Loire, east by Ain and Isère and south and west by Loire. The Saône and the Rhône form its natural boundary to the east. The department belongs almost entirely to the basin of the Rhône, to which it sends its waters by the Saône and its tributary the Azergues, and by the Gier. The mountains which cover the surface of the department con-stitute the watershed between the Rhône and the Loire, and from north to south form four successive groups—the Beaujolais mts., the highest peak of which is 3,320 ft.; the Tarare group; the Lyonnais mts. (nearly 3,000 ft.); and Mt. Pilat, the highest peak of which belongs to the department of Loire.

Good agricultural land is found in the valleys of the Saône and Rhône, but for the most part the soil is stony and only moderately fertile. Wheat, oats, rye and potatoes are widely grown, with colza on the banks of the Saône, but they are less important than the vine, the hills of the Beaujolais on the right bank of the Saône producing excellent wines. Mines of copper pyrites and coal and quarries of marble (at Bully) are worked. The production of silk fabrics, the chief branch of manufacture of artificial silk goods, of chemicals and machinery, together with most of the other industries of the department, are concentrated in Lyons (q.v.) and its vicinity. Tarare is a centre for the manu-facture of velvet, muslin and embroidery. Oullins has large rail-way workshops belonging to the P.L.M railway, and there are important glass works at Lyons and at Givors. Cotton-spinning and weaving are carried on in several localities.

The department is served by the P.L.M. railway. The Rhône and the Saône and in the extreme south the canal of Givors are its navigable waterways. Lyons, the capital, is the seat of an archbishop and of a court of appeal and centre of an educational division (*académie*). The department is in the 14th military region. There are two arrondissements (Lyons and Villefranche) subdivided into 33 cantons and 269 communes. The principal places besides Lyons are Givors, Tarare and Villefranche (*qq.v.*).

RHÔNE, one of the most important rivers in Europe, and the chief of those which flow directly into the Mediterranean. It rises at the eastern extremity of the Swiss canton of the Valais, flows through Switzerland and France and enters the Mediterranean at the Gulf of Lyons. Its total length is 500 mi., of which the Lake of Geneva, through which it flows, claims 45 mi.; and its total fall is 5,898 ft. Its course (excluding the Lake of Geneva, q.v.) naturally falls into three divisions: (1) from its source to the Lake of Geneva (105½ mi. and fall 4,679 ft.) (2) from Geneva to Lyons (124 mi. and fall 689 ft.) and (3) from Lyons to the Mediterranean (230 mi. and fall 530 ft.).

From its Source to the Lake the Rhône is a purely Alpine river, flowing through a great trench first in a synclinal structure between the Aar and St. Gothard massifs, then along the front of the Pennine nappes. (*See* ALPS.) It issues as a torrent, at the height of 5,909 ft., from the Rhône glacier at the head of the Valais. It is almost immediately joined (left) by the Mutt tor-rent, coming from a small glacier and then flows past the Gletsch hotel (where the roads from the Grimsel and the Furka pass

unite). About half a mile from the glacier the river descends through a wild gorge to the more level valley, to reach the first village, Oberwald. It preserves a south-westerly direction till Martigny.

The uppermost valley of the Rhône is named Goms, its chief villages being Münster and Fiesch, whilst the river is swollen by mountain torrents, descending from the glaciers on either side, by the Geren (left), near Oberwald; by the Eginen (left), near Ulrichen; by the Fiesch (right), from the Fiesch glacier, at Fiesch; by the Binna (left), near Grengiols; by the Massa (right) from the Aletsch glaciers, above Brig. At Brig the Rhône has descended 3,678 ft. from its source in 28 m., and is already a considerable stream when joined (left) by the Saltine, descending from the Simplon Pass. Its course below Brig is less rapid and lies through wastes of alluvial deposits. The valley is wide and marshy, the river frequently overflowing its banks. Further mountain torrents fall into the Rhône: these are the Visp (left) from the Zermatt valley, at Visp; at Gampel, the Lonza (right) from the Lötschen valley; at Leuk, the Dala (right) from the Gemmi Pass; at Sierre, the Navizen (left) from the Einfisch or Anniviers valley; at Sion, the capital of the Valais, the Borgne (left) from the Val d' Hérens; below Sion, by the Morge (right), from the Sansetsch pass; and at Martigny by the Dranse (left) from the Great St. Bernard and the Val de Bagnes. At Martigny, the river bends sharply to the north-west toward the Lake of Geneva. Opposite Dorénaz it receives the Salanfe (left). Immediately below St. Maurice the Rhône rushes through a narrow and striking defile which commands the entrance of the Valais.

Beyond, the river enters the wide alluvial plain, formerly occupied by the south-eastern arm of the Lake of Geneva, but now marshy. It receives at Bex the Avançon (right) flowing from the glaciers of the Diablerets range, at Monthey the Vièze (left) from Champéry and the Val d' Illiez, and at the Aigle the Grande Eau (right), from the valley of Ormonts-dessus. It passes Port Valais, once on the lake, before expanding into the Lake of Geneva, between Villeneuve (right) and St. Gingolph (left). During all this portion of its course the Rhône is not navigable, but its valley forms an artery into the Alps which is followed by the railways and roads.

The Upper Rhône, being fed by glacial streams, is overladen with sediment, much of which is deposited along the course, the remainder settling down in the Lake of Geneva, in the blue waters of which it is possible to follow the whiter course of the stream for some distance before it disappears.

From Geneva to Lyons.—About ½ m. below Geneva the blue-ness of the water of the Rhône is again disturbed by the Arve (left), from the glaciers of the Mont Blanc range, the two cur-rents for some distance refusing to mix. The Rhône is here forced southward by the sweep of the Jura folds through which it breaks in a number of narrow gorges or *cluses*. It continues southward until joined near Corbelin by the Guier (left), from the Grande Chartreuse mountains and it continues the direction of this tributary thus rounding the southern spur of the Juras.

About 12 m. south of Geneva the Rhône enters France. At Bellegarde the Valserine flows in (right), and then the river resumes its southerly direction, from which a great gorge has deflected it for a while. Some way below Bellegarde, between Le Parc and Pyrimont, the Rhône becomes officially "navigable" though as far as Lyons the navigation consists almost entirely of flat-bottomed boats. Above Seyssel the Usses (left) joins the Rhône, while just below that village the Fier (left) flows in from the Lake of Annecy. Below the junction of the Fier the hills sink on either side, the channel of the river widens and it leaves the mountains for the plains. The Geneva-Paris railway follows the river as far as Culoz. The Rhône receives the waters from Lake Bourget by a canal (left). The last of the *cluses* is at the Pont du Saut or Sault, a little south of Lagnieu. The river now widens but the neighbouring country is much exposed to inun-dations.

It receives the Ain (right), which descends from the French slope of the Jura and is navigable for about 60 m., above its junction with the Saône, just below Lyons. The Saône (*q.v.*) which has received (left) the Doubs, is the real continuation of the lower Rhône, both from a geographical and a commercial point of view, and it is by the means of canals branching off from the course of the Saône that the Rhône communicates with the basins of the Loire, the Seine, the Rhine and the Moselle.

Below Lyons, the Rhône becomes one of the great historical rivers of France. It was up its valley that various civilizations penetrated from the Mediterranean to Lyons. From Lyons downwards the left bank serves as a great medium of commerce by which central France sends its products to the sea. During this half of its course it flows over an alluvium-filled valley resting on Jurassic and Cretaceous rocks, and it can boast of having on its left bank (the right bank is very poor in this respect) such historical cities at Vienne, Valence, Avignon, Tarascon and Arles, while it receives (left) the Isère, the Drôme, the Aygues and the Durance rivers, all formed by the union of many streams from the Dauphiné Alps.

The Ardèche is the only considerable affluent from the right. Near Arles, about 25 m. from the sea, and by rail $175\frac{1}{4}$ m. from Lyons, the river breaks up into two main branches, the Grand Rhône running south-east and the Petit Rhône south-west; they enclose between them the delta of the Camargue, which is cultivated on the banks of the river only, but elsewhere is simply a great alluvial plain, composed of scanty pasturages and of great salt marshes. Changes in sea level have taken place in the Rhône delta in recent times. R. D. Oldham (*Nature,* vol. cxvi. [1925] pp. 16, 52, 100), shows that in Pre-Roman times the sea-level was 15 ft. higher than today. A rise was followed by a subsidence which occurred in about the 8th century when the river ended far inland in a shallow land-locked inlet which it proceeded to fill up with alluvium until in the 17th century it had regained the sea-front. Even since that time it has greatly modified its form by changes of channels, etc.

The Rhône river system is dominated by two tectonic features, the Alps and the Central Plateau of France. Below Chalon-sur-Saône, the Saône-Rhône flows along the eastern side of the central plateau and most of the course is determined by a north to south fault. The remainder of the river system is determined by the structure of the Alps (*q.v.*). The greater length of the river and of its Alpine affluents is parallel to the trend of the structures, as above Martigny, between the Lake of Geneva and Corbelin, the Arve in the Chamonix valley and parts of the Isère and of the Durance. On the other hand other portions flow radially to the trend, as between Martigny and the Lake of Geneva, parts of Isère, the Drôme, the Aygues, the Durance and numerous other tributaries.

RHOXOLANI, a Sarmatian tribe defeated in the Crimea by Diophantus, general of Mithradates, *c.* 100 B.C., and by the Romans on the lower Danube *c.* A.D. 60, and also under M. Aurelius. They seem to have finally succumbed to the Goths.

RHUBARB. This name is applied both to a drug and to a vegetable.

1. The drug has been used in medicine from very early times, being described in the Chinese herbal *Pen-king,* which is believed to date from 2700 B.C. It is still produced in the four northern provinces of China. In England the culture of rhubarb for medicinal purposes began in 1777 at Banbury in Oxfordshire and is still carried on there.

Two varieties of the drug are known, *viz.,* kiln-dried and sun-dried. So-called "Turkey" rhubarb was the Chinese drug which reached Europe from Aleppo and Smyrna, having travelled to Asia Minor by way of Persia and the Caspian.

Chemistry.—The most important constituent of this drug, giving it its purgative properties and its yellow colour, is chrysarobin, $C_{30}H_{36}O_7$, formerly known as rhein or chrysophan. The rhubarb of commerce also contains chrysophanic acid, a dioxymethyl anthra-quinone, $C_{14}H_5(CH_3)O_2(OH)_2$, of which chrysarobin is a reduction product.

Nearly 40% of the drug consists of calcium oxalate, which gives it the characteristic grittiness. There is also present rheo-tannic acid, which is of some practical importance. There are

numerous other constituents, such as emodin, $C_{15}H_{10}O_5$, mucilage, resins, rheumic acid, $C_{20}H_{18}O_9$, aporrhetin, etc.

The dose of rhubarb is from $\frac{1}{2}$ up to 30 grains, according to the action which is desired. The Pulvis Rhei Compositus of the *British Pharmacopoeia,* or Gregory's powder, is composed of 2 parts of rhubarb, 6 of heavy or light magnesia and 1 of ginger. The dose is 20 to 60 gr. The United States *Pharmacopoeia* includes the tincture, syrup and extract of rhubarb.

Rhubarb is occasionally administered in the form of powder, but more commonly it is employed in the form of one of its preparations. Rhubarb and the extract are cathartic, bitter tonic and stomachic, while the aromatic tincture and the aromatic syrup are laxative and to a slight extent astringent. As cathartics they act chiefly on the colon and have a tendency to produce constipation after the initial laxative effect. Hence they are useful in the beginning of diarrhoea as they cause the expulsion of irritating substances and promote a return to normal by their constipating influence.

Some chrysarobin is absorbed and is excreted in the urine, which it slightly increases and colours a reddish brown. The colour is discharged by the addition of a little dilute hydrochloric acid to the urine.

2. The vegetable rhubarb (*Rheum rhaponticum*), also called pie plant (family Polygonaceae), is a hardy Asiatic perennial grown for its large, succulent leafstalks. The plant produces large clumps of enormous leaves, up to 2 ft. across, on proportionately large petioles or leafstalks—an inch or more in diameter and up to 2 ft. or more in length—that arise from a shortened underground stem. These huge leaves arise early in the spring; later in the season a large central flower stalk may appear and bear numerous small white flowers and three-angled or winged fruits containing one seed. The plant is best adapted to the cooler parts of the temperate zones; the roots are quite hardy to cold although the tops are killed in autumn.

Rhubarb seed does not produce plants true to the variety that bears them; therefore it is propagated by dividing the perennial "crown" into pieces each consisting of a root piece and a bud. These are set in the field about 4 or 5 ft. apart each way. The large crowns are sometimes moved into forcing houses in late winter for producing the leafstalks under artificial heat, and in subdued light. A greenhouse is not necessary. Only the fleshy leafstalks are eaten; they are highly acid and contain considerable amounts of oxalates. The leaves should never be eaten since they are sometimes poisonous.

RHYL, a watering-place and urban district of Flint, North Wales, 30 mi. N.W. of Chester on the L.M.S.R. Pop. (1938) 15,680. Area, 2.6 sq.mi. It is situated on a sandy coast near the mouth of the Clwyd. It was originally a small fishing village with a little coastal trade, and is now an important watering-place.

RHYME, more correctly spelled rime, from Provençal word *rim* (its customary English spelling is due to a confusion with *rhythm*), a literary ornament or device consisting of an identity of sound in the terminal syllables of two or more words. In the art of versification it signifies the repetition of a sound at the end of two or more lines in a single composition. This artifice was practically unknown to the ancients, and, when it occurs, or seems to occur, in the works of classic Greek and Latin poets, it must be considered to be accidental. Conscious rhyme came later. The name given to lines with an intentional rhyme in the middle is *Leonine verse,* the invention being attributed to a probably apocryphal monk Leoninus or Leonius, who is supposed to be the author of a history of the Old Testament preserved in the Bibliothèque Nationale of Paris. This "history" is composed in Latin verses, all of which rhyme in the centre. Recent criticism has been inclined to look upon the African church-Latin of the age of Tertullian as the starting-point of modern rhyme, and it is probable that the ingenuities of priests, invented to aid worshippers in hearing and singing long pieces of Latin verse in the ritual of the Catholic church produced the earliest conscious poems in rhyme. It is certain that by the 4th century a school of rhymed sacred poetry had come into existence, classical examples of which we still possess in the "Stabat Mater" and the "Dies Irae." In the course of the middle ages, alliteration, assonance and end-rhyme held the field without a rival in vernacular poetry. After the 14th century, in the north of Europe, and indeed everywhere except in Spain, where assonance held a powerful position, end-rhyme became universal and formed a distinctive indication of metrical construction. It was not until the invention of blank verse (q.v.) that rhyme found a modern rival. Certain forms of poetry are almost inconceivable without rhyme, though efforts have been made to compose even rhymeless sonnets. In the heyday of Elizabethan literature a serious attempt was made in England to reject rhyme altogether, and to return to the quantitative measures of the ancients. The prime mover in this heresy was a pedantic grammarian of Cambridge, Gabriel Harvey (1545?-1630). For a short time he actually seduced no less melodious a poet than Edmund Spenser to abandon rhyme and adopt a system of accented hexameters and trimeters. From 1576 to 1579 the genius of Spenser seems to have been obscured by this error of taste, but he shook it off completely when he composed *The Shepherd's Calendar*. Thomas Campion, in a tract published in 1602, advocated the omission of rhyme from lyrical poetry. By dint of a prodigious effort, he produced some unrhymed odes, which were not without charm, but the best critics of the time, such as Daniel, repudiated the innovation.

In Germany a determined attack on rhyme was made early in the 17th century, particularly by a group of aesthetic critics in the Swiss universities. Lessing recalled the German poets to a sense of the beauty and value of rhyme, but the popularity of Klopstock and his imitators continued to exercise a great influence. Goethe and Schiller, without abandoning rhyme, permitted themselves a great liberty in the employment of unrhymed measures and in imitation of classic metres. This was carried to greater lengths by Platen and Heine, the rhymeless rhythm of the last of whom was imitated in English verse by Matthew Arnold and others. In France, on the other hand, the empire of rhyme has always been triumphant, and in French literature the idea of rhymeless verse could till recently scarcely be said to exist.

In Italian literature the excessive abundance and facility of rhyme has led to a rebellion against its use. It was the influence of German aesthetics which forced upon the notice of Leopardi the possibility of introducing rhymeless lyrical measures into Italian verse, an innovation which he carried out with remarkable hardihood and success. The rhymeless odes of Carducci are also worthy of admiration. At the close of the 19th century, particularly in France, where the rules of rhyme had been most rigid, an effort was made to modify and minimize the restraints of rhyme. The laws of rhyme, like other artificial regulations, may be too severe, but there is no evidence that the natural beauty which pure rhyme introduces into poetry is losing its hold on the human ear or is in any real danger of being superseded by accent, assonance, or rhythm.

See J. B. Schutze, *Versuch einer Theorie des Reimes nach Inhalt und Form* (Magdeburg, 1802); J. Minor, *Neuhochdeutsche Metrik* (Strasbourg, 1893); J. B. Mayer, *A Handbook of Modern English Metre* (1903); Egerton Smith, *The Principles of English Metre* (Oxford, 1923); Henry Lanz, *The Physical Basis of Rime* (1931).

RHYMNEY, an urban district of Monmouthshire, England, on the borders of Glamorganshire, 22 mi. N.W. of Cardiff, on the G.W.R. Pop. (1938) 9,437. Area, 4.25 sq.mi. The Rhymney river, in the upper valley of which this town lies, forms almost throughout its course the boundary between England and Wales (Monmouthshire and Glamorganshire). The district belongs to the south Wales iron field.

RHYNIE: *see* CHERT.

RHYOLITE, the group name of a type of volcanic rock, occurring mostly as lava flows, characterized by a highly acid composition, and so called from Gr. ῥύαξ, to flow (because of the frequency with which they exhibit fluxion structures). They are the most siliceous of all lavas, and, with the exception of the dacites, are the only lavas with free primary quartz. In chemical composition they very closely resemble the granites, the corresponding rocks of plutonic or deep-seated origin; their minerals also present many points of similarity to those of granite though they are by no means entirely the same. Quartz, orthoclase and

plagioclase felspars, and biotite are the commonest ingredients of both rocks, but the quartz of rhyolites is full of glass enclosures and the potash felspar is pellucid sanidine, while the quartz of granite contains dust-like fluid cavities of very minute size and its potash felspar is of the turbid variety which is properly called orthoclase. The granites also are holocrystalline, while in the rhyolites there are usually porphyritic crystals floating in a fine ground-mass. Rhyolites have also been called liparites because many of the lavas of the Lipari Islands are excellent examples of this group. Above all rocks they have a disposition to assume vitreous forms, as when fused they crystallize with great difficulty; the vitreous forms are known as obsidian, perlite and pumice (qq.v.).

Mineral Constituents.—The minerals of the first generation, or phenocrysts, of rhyolite are generally orthoclase, oligoclase, quartz, biotite, augite, or hornblende. The felspars are usually glassy clear, small but of well-developed crystalline form: the potash felspar is sanidine, usually Carlsbad twinned; the soda-lime felspar is almost always oligoclase, with characteristic polysynthetic structure. Both of these may be corroded and irregular in their outlines; their cleavage and twinning then distinguish them readily from quartz. The quartz occurs as blebs or sub-rounded grains, which are corroded double hexagonal pyramids. In some rhyolites apparent crystals of quartz or felspar are found under the microscope to consist of a micrographic intergrowth of the two. Biotite is always deep brown or greenish brown, in small hexagonal tablets, generally blackened at their edges by magmatic corrosion. Muscovite is not known in rhyolites. Hornblende may be green or brown; in the quartz-pantellarites it sometimes takes the form of strongly pleochroic brown crossyrite. Like biotite it is idiomorphic but often corroded in a marked degree. Augite, which is equally common or more common than the other ferro-magnesian minerals, is always green; its crystals are small and perfectly shaped, and corrosion phenomena are very rarely seen in it. Zircon, apatite and magnetite are always present in rhyolites, their crystals being often beautifully perfect though never large. Olivine (fayalite) is never a normal ingredient, but occurs in the hollow spherulites or lithophysae of some rhyolites with garnet, tridymite, topaz and other minerals which indicate pneumatolytic action.

Types of Texture.—The ground-mass of rhyolitic rocks is of three distinct types which are stages in crystalline development, viz., the vitreous, the felsitic or cryptocrystalline, and the microcrystalline. Mixtures of the different kinds occur; thus a vitreous rhyolite has often felsitic areas in its ground-mass, and in the same lava flow some parts may be vitreous while others are felsitic. The vitreous rhyolites are identical in most respects with the obsidians, from which they can only be separated in an artificial classification; and in their glassy base the banded or eutaxitic, spherulitic and perlitic structures of pure obsidians are very frequently present (*see* OBSIDIAN; PERLITE). The felso-liparites or liparites with stony ground-mass are specially common among the pre-Tertiary igneous rocks, as liparite glass is unstable and experiences devitrification in course of time. Many of these felsites have fluxion banding, spherulites and even perlitic cracks, which are strong evidence that they were originally glassy. In other cases a hyaloliparite, obsidian or pitchstone becomes felsitic along its borders and joint planes, or even along perlitic cracks, and we may assume that the once glassy rock has changed into felsite under the action of percolating moisture or even by atmospheric decomposition. In many rhyolites the felsite is original and represents an incipient crystallization of the vitreous material which took place before the rock was cold. The felsite in turn is liable to change; it becomes a fine mosaic of quartz and alkali felspar; and in this way a matrix of the third type, the microcrystalline, may develop. This is proved by the occurrence of the remains of spherulitic and perlitic structures in rocks which are no longer felsitic or glassy. Many microcrystalline rhyolites have a ground-mass in which much felsitic matter occurs; but as this tends to recrystallize in course of time, the older rocks of this group show least of it. Whilst no quartz-bearing rhyolites are known to have been erupted in recent years, Lacroix proved that portions of the "spine" which rose as a great tower or column out of the crater of Mont Pelée after the eruption in 1906 contained small crystals of quartz in the ground-mass. The microcrystalline ground-mass of rhyolites is never micrographic as in the porphyries (granophyres); on the other hand it is often micropoikilitic, consisting of small felspars, often sub-rectangular, embedded in little rounded or irregular plates of quartz.

Changes of Ground-mass.—The ground-mass of rhyolites is liable to other changes, of which the most important are silicification, kaolinization and sericitization. Among the older rocks of this group it is the exception to find that secondary quartz has not been deposited in some parts of them. Often indeed the matrix is completely replaced by silica in the form of finely crystalline quartz or chalcedony; and these rocks on analysis prove to contain over 90% of silica. In the recent rhyolites of Hungary, New Zealand, etc., the deposit of coarse opal in portions of the rock is a very common phenomenon.

Kaolinization may be due to weathering, and the stony dull look of the matrix of many microcrystalline rhyolites is due to the decomposed state of the felspar grains in them; it is even more typically developed by fumarole action, which replaces the felspars with soft, cloudy white products belonging to a mineral of the kaolin group. Sericitization, or the development of fine white mica after felspar, is usually associated with shearing, and is commonest in the older rhyolites.

Vesicular structure is very common in rhyolites; in fact the pumiceous obsidians have this character in greater perfection than any other rocks (*see* Pumice); but even the felso-rhyolites are very often vesicular. The cavities are usually lined with opal and tridymite; in the older rocks they may be filled with agate and chalcedony. The "mill-stone porphyries," extensively used in Germany for grinding corn, are porous rhyolites; the abundance of quartz makes them hard, and their rough surfaces render them peculiarly suitable for this purpose. In some of them the cavities are partly secondary. These rocks are obtained in the Odenwald, Thuringerwald and Fichtelgebirge.

Occurrence.—In Britain a pale grey Tertiary rhyolite occurs at Tardree, Antrim, and in Skye. Felsitic rhyolites occur among the Old Red rocks of Scotland (Pentland Hills, Lorne, etc.), in Devonshire, and in large numbers in North Wales. The Carnarvonshire rhyolites are often much altered and silicified; many of them have a nodular structure which is very conspicuous on weathered surfaces. The spheroids may be two or three in. in diameter; some are built up of concentric shells. Rhyolites are also known from Fishguard, Malvern, Westmorland and Co. Waterford. One of the oldest volcanic rocks of Britain (pre-Cambrian, Uriconian) is the spherulitic rhyolite of the Lea Rock near Wellington, Shropshire. It shows bright red spherulites in great numbers and is probably an obsidian completely devitrified. Perlitic structure is also visible in it.

In other parts of Europe rhyolites have a fairly wide distribution though they are not numerous. In Hungary (Hlinik, etc.) there are many well-known examples; they extend along the margin of the Carpathians and are found also in Siebenburgen. In Italy they occur in the Euganean Hills and in the Lipari Islands; the latter being the principal source of pumice at the present day. Rhyolites of Recent age occur in Iceland (Myvatn, etc.), where they are characterized by the frequent absence of quartz, and the presence of much plagioclase and pyroxene. Some of these rocks have been called trachyte-obsidians, but they seem to be rhyolites which contain an exceptionally large amount of soda The older rhyolites, which are generally called quartz-porphyries in Germany, are mostly of Permian or Carboniferous age and are numerous in the Vosges, Odenwald, Thuringerwald, etc. They are often accompanied by basic rocks (melaphyres). Permian rhyolites occur also at Lugano in Italy. Rhyolites are known also in Asia Minor and the Caucasus, in New Zealand, Colorado, Nevada and other parts of western North America. In the Yellowstone National Park there is a well-known cliff of obsidian which shows remarkably perfect columnar jointing. Some of the rhyolites of Nevada are exceedingly rich in porphyritic minerals, so that they appear at first sight to be holocrystalline rocks, since

the ground-mass is scanty and inconspicuous. To this type the name nevadite has been given, but it is rare and local in its distribution.

In Pantellaria, south-west of Sicily, there are rocks of rhyolitic affinities which present so many unusual features that they have been designated pantellarites. They contain less silica and alumina and more alkalis and iron than do ordinary rhyolites. Their felspars are of the anorthoclase group, being rich in soda together with potash, and are very variable in crystalline development. Aegirine-augite and forms of soda-amphibole are also characteristic of them, while dark brown aenigmatite or cossyrite often occur. Quartz is not very plentiful; other ingredients are olivine, arfvedsonite and tridymite. The ground-mass varies much, being sometimes quite vitreous, at other times a glass filled with swarms of microliths, while in certain pantellarites it is a microcrystalline aggregate of quartz and alkali felspar. The absence of plagioclase and biotite are marked distinctions between these rocks and the rhyolites, together with the scarcity of quartz and the prevalence of soda-bearing pyroxenes and amphiboles. Comendites are practically identical rocks. They occur in Sardinia, Corsica, British East Africa, East Siberia, West Texas and the East Indies.

Among the Palaeozoic volcanic rocks of Germany there is a group of lavas, the quartz-keratophyres, which are of acid composition and rich in alkali felspar. Their dominant alkali is soda: hence their felspars are albite and cryptoperthite, not sanidine as in rhyolites. Quartz occurs sometimes as corroded phenocrysts, but is often scarce even in the ground-mass. Porphyritic biotite or augite are very rare, but occur in the matrix along with felspars and quartz. Micropegmatite is not infrequent in these rocks, and they may be silicified like the rhyolites. As quartz-keratophyres mostly occur in districts where there has been a good deal of folding, they are often crushed and more or less sericitized. They are best known from the Devonian rocks of Westphalia and the Harz, but are also found in New South Wales, and similar rocks have been described (as soda-felsites) from Ireland. The rocks which they accompany are usually dolerites and spilites.

Composition.—The following analyses show the composition of some of the principal types of rhyolites:—

	SiO$_2$	Al$_2$O$_3$	Fe$_2$O$_3$	FeO	CaO	MgO	K$_2$O	Na$_2$O	H$_2$O
I.	76·34	13·22	1·93		1·85	0·21	3·67	2·84	0·61
II.	72·15	13·50	3·12		0·93	0·16	4·54	4·20	0·85
III.	77·59	12·75	0·67	n.f.	0·04	0·16	3·99	2·56	1·54
IV.	67·48	9·70	7·42	2·21	1·45	0·77	2·94	7·21	0·96
V.	70·97	13·84	3·21	0·78	1·26	0·20	1·57	6·27	0·74
VI.	74·76	11·60	3·50	0·19	0·07	0·18	4·92	4·35	0·64

I. Rhyolite, Telki Banya, Hungary.
II. do. Mafahlid, Iceland.
III. do. Omahu, New Zealand.
IV. Pantellarite, Pantellaria.
V. Quartz-keratophyre, Muhlenthal, Harz.
VI. Comendite, Sardinia.

We note in the rhyolites I.–III. the very high silica, with alkalis and alumina also in considerable amount, while lime, magnesia and iron are very low. In the pantellarite, keratophyre and comendite the silica tends to be less abundant, while the alkalis, especially soda, increase; they have less alumina but are richer in iron and magnesia. It is easy to see why the latter types contain less quartz, felspars often very rich in soda, and ferric minerals which contain iron and alkalis in notable amounts such as aegirine, riebeckite and arfvedsonite. (J. S. F.)

RHYTHM, a certain swing or balance in bodily movement, music, verse or prose; often extended by metaphor to apply in other spheres (*e.g.*, "rhythm of life"). The early critic of prosody, Aristoxenus (*c.* 320 B.C.), distinguished three elements in rhythm—the speech (λέξις), the melody (μέλος) and the bodily motion (κίνησις σωματική); but the later tendency has been to separate these elements, and to emphasize more and more the distinction between them. Precision, however, has hardly yet been reached; and there are few subjects on which opinions, even among experts, differ more widely. In a short article it will be necessary to make controversial statements without defending them by argument.

Rhythm in Verse.—The line between rhythm and metre is hard to draw. Aristotle is very vague on the question: Suidas says that rhythm is the father of metre, and Quintilian that rhythm is male and metre female. Such sayings merely prove the difficulty of measuring a delicate instinct by rule of three. It would appear, however, that to the Greeks metre was concerned with the measurements of poetic periods, and rhythm with their effective chanting or recitation; it cannot therefore have depended largely on *ictus* or stress, and the word is therefore often applied to prose as well as to verse. It is probable that, in a quantitative language like Greek, this stress (as it is in modern French) was far less strongly marked than (*e.g.*) in English; but it is a mistake to think it entirely absent, as, conversely, it is a mistake to think that in English, though accent is, of course, predominant, quantity is unimportant.

As Schipper says, "in English long and short syllables have no constant length, no constant relation; they depend on the context. They do not *determine* rhythm, but they help to *regulate* it." No rigid laws, therefore, can be laid down as to the proper employment of rhythmic balance. A subtle *feeling* must govern the periodic progress of sounds in harmony with the emotions it is desired to express. When the ear is satisfied, we feel that the rhythm is adequate; and a very brief study will show us that the ear demands different rhythms for an expression of different emotions. The genius of the poet is, on this side, revealed by the unforced skill with which he selects the appropriate rhythm. Ecstasy, *e.g.*, takes a quick, eager, rising movement; sadness is full, slow and emphatic; meditation deliberate; mystery and suspense are faint, languorous and throbbing; often, indeed, the rhythm is so intimately linked with human feeling that no analysis can disentangle them.

Pauses, again, are an almost essential element in modern rhythm. In Shakespeare and Milton, *e.g.*, a pause may take the place of a whole beat; and the right use of such pauses often lends a variety which increases the beauty of a passage. Still more important is what has been called the "free musical paragraph," of which Milton, in *Paradise Lost*, is so consummate a master. Here the balance, overstepping the limits of the verse-form, and felt over wide spaces, is perhaps the chief glory of the poet's style; and the skill with which one "paragraph" is set against another forms, so to speak, a larger rhythm containing and holding up the smaller rhythms of the single paragraphs and of the verse-form. In rhymed verse this larger rhythm is represented by the progression of the stanza in itself, and by the linking of the stanzas into harmonious wholes. Thus in the full meaning of the term, rhythm depends at least as much on the orderly arrangement of the thought as on the balance of the words.

Rhythm in Prose.—We perceive then that there is a rhythm in prose no less than in verse; and this appears not only in the balance of the sentence, but in the arrangement of the sentences in paragraphs and in the building up of paragraphs into chapters. Here, as in everything else, the art must be concealed. A mechanical, epigrammatic balance, like that of Johnson, is too obvious, and ere long tends to weary. The truly rhythmic prose-writer satisfies at once the ear and the mind as a skilled dancer satisfies at once the ear and the eye, without drawing attention to the means by which the effect is attained.

On the special laws of rhythm in the poetry of different nations—Greek, Hebrew, Old English, and the like—it is impossible to speak here; the works of scholars should be studied.

BIBLIOGRAPHY.—W. Christ, *Metrik der Griechen* (Leipzig, 1874); J. H. H. Schmidt, *Rhythmic and Metric of the Classical Languages* (1879), followed by R. C. Jebb in the metrical introductions to his edition of Sophocles: T. de Banville, *Petit Traité de la Poésie française* (1881); E. Guest, *History of English Rhythms* (2nd ed., 1882); F. B. Gummere, *Handbook of Poetics* (1885); J. Minor, *Neuhochdeutsche Metrik* (Strasbourg, 1893); J. Schipper, *Englische Metrik* (Leipzig, 1895); George Saintsbury, *History of English Prosody* (1906–10), *History of English Prose Rhythm* (1912); *see* also the various works by T. S. Omond. On old English metre, *see* editions of H. Sweet, *Anglo-Saxon Reader* (1897); for the metre of Chaucer *see* the various editions by W. W. Skeat; on Hebrew metre, *International Critical Commentaries*, edit. S. R. Driver, A. Plummer and C. A. Briggs (1910–20); French metre, F. Spencer, *A Primer of French Verse* (1899); L. E. Kastner, *History of French Versification* (1903); E. A. Sonnen-schein, *What is Rhythm?* (1925); W. Thomson, *The Rhythm of Speech* (1923); M. Austin, *American Rhythm* (1923); J. H. Scott, *Rhythmic Verse* (1925), *Rhythmic Prose* (1925). (E. E. K.)

RHYTHM IN MUSIC

Like all artistic categories musical rhythm must be studied historically, to avoid Philistinism towards the rhythms of early periods. But the musical rhythms of the 18th and 19th centuries are so much more familiar to us than any others, and so radically different from speech-rhythms, that we shall do well to analyse them first. Their true relation to speech-rhythms will then become much clearer, and the study of older rhythms will be greatly simplified.

1. **Body-rhythm and Speech-rhythm.**—These are two prehistoric elements in musical rhythm; and in modern music they are in equipoise, though apart from music they are incompatible. Dance-rhythm is too narrow a term for the one, and speech-rhythm is a satisfactory term for the other. We may coin the term body-rhythm as giving the necessary extension to the notion of dance-rhythm. Musical body-rhythm, even in the slowest paces, is enormously stronger than anything known to prosody. It is no exaggeration to say that it is as strong as the pace of a horse. Not even Browning could have recited "How they brought the good news from Ghent to Aix" with comfort while riding a galloping horse; but Schubert's Characteristic Marches (op. 121) do not merely imitate that pace but go far to stimulate it if played to a body of cavalry. Gentler rhythms may be less immediately understood, but, once grasped, are not more easily changed. The music must brace itself up for any abrupt change of its fundamental rhythm. But that fundamental rhythm may be very slow and lie very deep.

In the example on p. 274 (Ex. 1), Haydn uses an underlying rhythm of thrice two beats. The beat is a quaver, for which one second is not too slow a tempo for this particular composition. Its whole group of six beats is invariably $3 \div 2$ and never $2 \div 3$. In this kind of music change from the one division to the other would be impossible without either violence or vagueness; unless it were a permanent change of metre. So important is the notion of $3 \div 2$ that it is not counted as 6 at all, but as **1** & 2 & 3, etc. Of these beats the first bears the chief stress, the second and third bear less, and there is no rule to give either more stress than the other. We are not, at present, considering the case of three beats quick enough to mark the rhythm without subdivision. Obviously the subdivisions (counted by "&") have no accent, except in relation to their own further subdivisions. Musical rhythms are measured from accent to accent; and of pairs of accents the first is stronger than the second. In larger groups, if the rhythm is binary the third accent will be stronger than the second, but not as strong as the first or fifth. At a very quick pace the difference of strength between the first accent and the fifth may become perceptible, but the rhythm would be inartistically stiff if such distinctions were not soon obliterated.

Triple rhythm, whether slow and subdivided or quick and undivided, also falls readily into larger binary periods with the same relative strengths of accent. There is nothing to prevent it from falling into ternary periods, but the mind ceases to apprehend a high power of three rhythmically, for we cannot know that the third period of a slow group is not the first of a new pair.

On these data it is now possible to analyse the rhythm of Ex. 1. It begins on the main accent, with no anacrusis. Between the first and second quaver beats there is a group of grace-notes. In actual time these should come on the second quaver and reduce the length of the second main note instead of that of the first, but they have no accent, and the second main note has its due stress and is not noticed to have arrived late, even if the grace-notes have been taken with some deliberation. They are like the consonants in the word *three*: it is easy to pronounce the word at a given moment, and nobody thinks of dividing it as thr-ee, though the consonants really take an appreciable time.

During the second bar of six beats the accompaniment (not given here) takes its cue from the melody and divides the quaver-beats by 3 (and the crotchets by 6). This motion thereafter pervades the whole composition, sometimes in the melody, and

Ex. 1

---

always in the accompaniment, except when the whole orchestra pauses. These triplet semiquavers become equivalent to the average length of syllables in speech-rhythm, and the mind automatically measures all pauses by them. Besides the indeterminate grace-notes there are definite shorter values.

No rhythm in poetry or prose ever contemplated giving one syllable seven times the length of another, as we see in the double-dotted quavers with their complementary demisemiquavers. But in the fifth bar we have the whole six beats occupied by one sustained note, eighteen times the length of the average syllable. Yet so cogent is the body-rhythm of these long and complex bars that a deviation from the symmetry of an 8-bar period is permissible only when a change of key introduces new topics, as happens immediately after this quotation. But this will lead us to the separate topic of *phrasing*. Irregularities in the lengths of the bars themselves would be quite impossible, except in the case of a dramatic or final pause. Haydn has one opportunity for a dramatic pause in the course of the movement, yet he does not leave it at that, but expands it to two entire normal bars filled with organized rhythms.

Musical rhythm is not often as ornate as this, nor is this elaboration capable of much contrast or development, but the example at once carries us far away from the rhythms of poetry and includes all the musical principles so far mentioned. From it we can move a step nearer towards considering the simple relations between musical and poetic rhythm.

The technical terms of prosody are of no use here, with the solitary exception of the word anacrusis, which may be generalized to mean anything that happens before the first principal accent. When Rockstro tells us that "the theme of Weber's Rondo brillante in E flat (op. 62) is in Anapaestic Tetrameter Brachycatalectic, very rigidly maintained," this tells us less about the music than Weber's brilliant theme tells us about these solemn terms. A more scientific idea of Weber's theme, and of the prosodic technicalities, may be obtained from the following paradigm, to be recited *prestissimo*. Each dash at the end of the line represents a quarter of a beat.

Prestissimo.

Diddle | dum diddledum diddledum diddledum diddle | dum diddledum diddledum:— |
    1   &   2   &   1   &   2   &

Diddle | dum diddledum diddledum diddle | dum diddledum diddledum:— |
    1   &   2   &   1   &   2   &

After which Weber ceases to maintain his anapaestic-etcetera so rigidly, and proceeds for two lines with:—

Diddle | diddle diddle diddle diddle diddle diddle dum dum | dum dum dum dum Di do |
    1   &   2   &   1   &   2

Such rapid rhythms at once remind us of Aristophanes or Gilbert, though they can move faster than syllables can be pronounced. If they coalesce into uniformity for a long period (e.g., *diddle-diddle* for several bars without a single *dum*) they cease to resemble speech-rhythm and subside into vibration, unless melodic interest sets up larger rhythms by illuminating a peak here and there. A common defect in second-rate music is the composer's failure to know when his quick motion has settled down into mere vibration.

2. **Time.**—The body-rhythm underlying Weber's Rondo brillante is an unchangeable binary rhythm, counted (as the paradigm shows) in a slow two or a quick four. Classical music uses only binary and ternary times, which, so long as vertebrate anatomy continues to develop with bilateral symmetry, are the only ones that yield a strong body-rhythm naturally, the elements of triple time giving just enough resistance to be overcome by a pleasant compromise.

The kinds of time, *i.e.*, of invariable rhythmic molecules underlying each continuous piece of music, are classed not only as *duple* and *triple* but also as *simple* and *compound*. Compound time is the result of dividing simple time by three. Division by two is ignored: thus the evidently highly compound time of Ex. 1 is reckoned as simple triple time. All beats are reckoned as binary divisions and subdivisions of the modern standard note, the semibreve: the time-signature given at the beginning of a composition is a fraction, with a numerator showing the number of beats in a bar, and a denominator showing the size of the beat. Thus $\frac{3}{4}$ signifies three crotchets (quarters) in a bar. Compound time does not indicate the main beats at all, but counts the smaller beats as normal fractions of the semibreve. The main beats are written as *dotted* notes, in which the dot lengthens the note by one half. Accordingly $\frac{6}{8}$ is the compound time of two dotted crotchets divided by three quavers; $\frac{9}{8}$ is that of three dotted crotchets: $\frac{12}{8}$ of four. When the division by three is only local, *triplets* are used. Triplets are groups of three equal notes crowded into the time of two.

Binary and ternary subdivision answers every ordinary purpose of musical rhythm, being capable of expressing distinctions far more subtle than have ever been regulated in speech. It is impossible to pronounce a syllable in less than a tenth of a second; but it is easy to play 16 notes in a second on the pianoforte. In such rapid notes a single break twice in a second would have an effect directly measured by the ear. If the broken series were levelled into an even series of fourteen notes a second, the rhythmic effect would be appreciably different, though the actual difference of pace would be only $\frac{1}{56}$ of a second.

The special sign for triplets is readily adapted to other subdivisions. In most cases such adaptation is not meant to produce abstruse rhythms, but to secure an effect of free declamation. Freedom is as necessary in music as it is in speech; but fine playing, whether in obvious *tempo rubato* or in apparent strictness, bases this freedom on the superlative accuracy of good rhythmic notation.

3. **Tempo.**—The time-signature tells us nothing about the pace of the music, for the choice of the denominator is determined by a tangle of historic associations, so that $\frac{3}{8}$ may mean (as in Beethoven's C minor concerto) the slowest movement ever written, and $\frac{3}{4}$ may be a scherzo-tempo in which only one beat in a bar is countable.

The sense of tempo is a larger aspect of the body-rhythm, and in classical music it is very steady. A fundamental law of all musical rhythm is that a hurrying or slackening of tempo has no power to alter the rhythmic organization. If your phrase is too short a *ritardando* will not make it aesthetically any the longer; nor will an *accelerando* get rid of a redundant bar. On the contrary, it is crowded detail that will best profit by slackening, and loose-knit passages that have most to gain by an unobtrusive mending of the pace.

The genuine *tempo rubato* is, as its name implies, a rhythmic robbing of Peter to pay Paul. Chopin said that his left hand conducted in strict time while his right declaimed freely. The truth is that sound is as full of illusions as sight. One such illusion has already been illustrated by the grace-notes of Ex. 1, and other illusions are of much the same kind. The tick of metronome measures average time-intervals; and if it is set to measure a naturally rhythmic performance it will seem to hustle the player in some passages and to drag upon him in others, however carefully we select its pace.

In the classics from Bach to Brahms a movement may give more legitimate scope for *tempo rubato* than some purists care to admit, but it will not drift from one tempo to a radically different tempo, unless towards the end, or as evidence of imminent break-up. The gradual drift from one tempo to another first becomes something better than a weakness when the whole nature of musical movement becomes capable of continuity over hours, as in Wagnerian opera. Then, and not before, can we view one and the same tempo from opposite directions. Thus, in *Tristan und Isolde* the last part of the love-duet in the second act is a quick movement in $\frac{3}{8}$ time. Isolde's *Liebestod* ends the opera with an exact recapitulation of this (differing only in the voice part and absolutely unaltered in the orchestra) in rather slow $\frac{4}{4}$ time. By metronome the two tempi should be identical, though the impulse in the duet is energetic and that of the *Liebestod* reposeful. Wagner merely feels that the broader notation better suits Isolde's dying vision; and the listener, who may know and care nothing about the notation, agrees with Wagner.

Ex. 2
Adagio

Dal-la sua pa - ce la mia di - pen - de

It is partly a question of accent and comes under the heading of phrasing.

4. **The Rhythm of Classical Music in Relation to Poetry.**—We can now return, furnished with new criteria, to the relation between musical and poetic rhythm. Even a simple musical setting of poetry will stretch the words in ways which speech does not normally admit. The naïve poet will unhesitatingly accept this as in the nature of singing. Only the half-baked musical *littérateur* objects, when Mozart makes Ottavio sing *Dalla sua pace la mia dipende* (Ex. 2) five times as slowly as any speaker could naturally utter the words, and then puts the top note and chief accent on the

unimportant *la*. The poet would be glad to sing it that way if he could. It is quite good Italian prosody to give a nearly equal stress to *la* and *mia*: and the climax on *la* is more than counterbalanced by the fact that the important word *mia* falls on a harmonically sensitive note. The grammatical sense might have been clearer if a similar but slighter emphasis had been given to *sua*. But Ottavio is not giving instructions to a servant, but expressing his inmost feelings in solitude. Language does not base its emotional accents on logical analysis. Dr. Johnson corrected a clergyman for saying "Thou *shalt* not steal" instead of "Thou shalt *not* steal." If Johnson was right, how in the world did "shall not" ever become "shan't"?

The sensitive note on *mia* shows one of the four main degrees of freedom in musical accent. There is first the normal time-accent. Many critics of musical declamation seem to know no other forms of stress; but it can be completely eclipsed by putting the highest note of the melody elsewhere. The highest note can in its turn be eclipsed by the longest note. And in Ex. 2, both together are eclipsed by the most sensitive note. Moreover, and without recourse to anything so drastic as syncopation, the weakest note in the phrase may be given a special accent stronger than a main beat. This is beautifully shown in the third bar of Ex. 1, where the accented Eb, normally quite the weakest note in the bar, could certainly bear the chief syllable in a sentence if words for Haydn's wonderful rhythm could be found at all. Lastly, such a displaced accent may have a double meaning, the note retaining its original lightness in spite of its borrowed stress. Weber has been blamed for his bad declamation in the following famous passage:—

Ex. 3   Weber, *Der Freischütz, Act II.*

Trübe Augen, Liebchen, taugen, etc.

But, by your leave, this is a triumph of musical gesture. The lively Aennchen might even point a playful finger at the anxious Agathe with each false accent that Weber so explicitly marks. Meanwhile the orchestra corrects the declamation in waltz-rhythm.

By the interplay of these varieties of accent the strophic song, with the same tune to several stanzas, condemned as lazy and low by our prose critics of music, becomes, as Brahms always maintained, the highest achievement of a song-writer. The interplay does not annihilate right and wrong in declamation, nor does it prove that the classics are infallible; but it forms a musical technique as disciplined as prosody and as unlike prose. In such ways artistic factors reconcile their conflicts, and without such conflicts there is neither art nor life. Wagner and Wolf are perfect masters of a musical declamation that follows the rules of prose; but when we are told that there are no other rules, and that the classics from Bach to Brahms merely blundered insensitively, it is time to point out that musical rhythm cannot be learnt from a bell-metronome nor poetry from a pronouncing dictionary.

Let us now try a few experiments in setting blank verse to music. The first step will be to find a constant musical rhythm to represent the average line. This average rhythm will horrify the poetic ear if it is put forward as a specimen of blank verse, and probably if a line could be found that fitted it exactly that line would be a very ugly one. Still, the fact remains that the musician's average idea of blank verse is accurately represented by the following scheme, which represents two lines:—

Ex. 3a

Now read the first paragraph of *Paradise Lost* rigidly to this scheme at the rate of two syllables to a metronome-beat of 80 to the minute. You will not satisfy the poet's ear; but you will find that the lines accommodate themselves better to this than to any other uniformity; that extra syllables can be managed by grace-notes, and that the interval of two quavers between each line is a natural part of the scheme. We can proceed thus for eight lines, with rheumatic pains but not complete disaster. The imperative "Sing" is a heavy word to put into anacrusis, even of double length, and our three main beats must override many accents in lines that so often have four. Also the interlinear pause of two beats is irksome when the sense runs on. In the ninth line we must alter the scheme, for no anacrusis can digest any part of "In the beginning." So we must "invert" the first foot thus:—

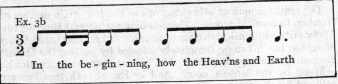

Ex. 3b

In the be-gin-ning, how the Heav'ns and Earth

But before we condemn the scheme let us see how far the torture is mitigated by merely adding musical rise and fall:—

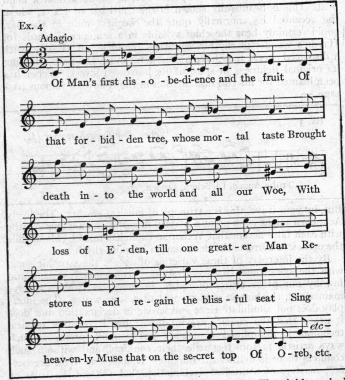

Ex. 4

Adagio

Of Man's first dis-o-be-di-ence and the fruit Of

that for-bid-den tree, whose mor-tal taste Brought

death in-to the world and all our Woe, With

loss of E-den, till one great-er Man Re-

store us and re-gain the bliss-ful seat Sing

heav-en-ly Muse that on the se-cret top Of O-reb, etc.

Blank verse has been worse recited than this. The rigid musical timing proves unexpectedly flexible already; and the rubato of a good singer can go far to improve it without becoming vulgar.

Now let us legalize the singer's rubato, and, without altering the two-quaver intervals between the lines, help the *enjambement* by a pianoforte accompaniment that makes the ear expect the resolution of a discord. Sensitive harmonies will further aid the rhythmic sense. The $\frac{3}{2}$ notation is now becoming troublesome; so that bars are divided into three and the lengths of the notes doubled. But the original $\frac{3}{2}$ scheme is nowhere violated. (*See* Ex. 5.)

After this point any attempt to continue this literal interpretation of the metre would make the music drag hopelessly. Already the first two lines would be the better for running over the pause and doubling the pace of "that forbidden tree." But this would mean using two time-scales and would take us into free composition. The object of this illustration is not to show how these words ought to be set, nor to prove the very doubtful proposition that they are singable to any kind of music; but simply to bring out the most elementary relations between music and verse.

5. **Phrasing.**—The higher art of phrasing is chiefly observable in groups of very much simpler bars than those of our illustra-

tions so far. Two facts, often ignored, must be realized before we can understand phrasing at all. First, music, being in time and not in space, is never apprehended in a *coup d'oeil*, but always in a momentary present connecting a remembered past with an imperfectly anticipated future. Consequently we miss half the aesthetic values of rhythm if we insist on knowing all about it from the first note. Rhythms have as much right to change their meaning while we listen to them as the cats of Wonderland have to grin; and "they all can and most of them do."

The second point is that the bar represents no fundamental rhythmic fact. It did not come into existence so long as music was printed only in parts. When music began to be printed with all the parts ranged legibly on one page, it was necessary to score the pile of parts with vertical strokes to range them in partitions and guide the eye. Hence the word *score*, and the French *partition* and German *Partitur*. The nascent body-rhythm grew stronger and gradually made it convenient that the bars should coincide with the groups indicated by the time-signature, and this gave rise (but only in recent times) to the delusion that the bar was the permanent unit. It is often obviously not so. When Mozart writes in moderate common time his phrasing is sure to make an odd number of half-bars somewhere so that a theme that originally lay on **1**, 2, 3, 4 now lies on 3, 4, **1**, 2. In such a case it is pedantic to say that the accent has changed and still more pedantic to blame Mozart for not either taking shorter bars throughout or changing to them according to the rhythm. If the half-bar displacement is really awkward Mozart will put it right, as when he rebarred the duet "Bei Männern welche Liebe fühlen" in *Die Zauberflöte*. But long bars imply delicate accents and these accents become no harder when the phrasing contracts.

Beethoven writes his scherzos, and some very powerful other movements, in the shortest possible bars, and it is often difficult to tell whether the first of such bars is a main accent or an anacrusis. In the first movement of the C minor sonata (op. 10, No. 1) when we reach bar 22 it becomes manifest that bar 9 must have been in anacrusis; but we cannot have noticed that at the time, for when theorists go back to bar 1 and say that that initial bump was in anacrusis we can only smile. In three late works Beethoven helps the players by the words *Ritmo di tre battute* and *Ritmo di quattro battute*. The most famous of these passages is in the scherzo of the ninth symphony. Why did Beethoven not use there $\frac{6}{4}$ or $\frac{12}{4}$ bars so that his *ritmo di tre battute* became self-evident as a change to $\frac{9}{4}$? Because if you wish to ride this Pegasus you must please to rise on your stirrups once in Beethoven's bar, and not only once in 3 or 4. The change to 3-bar rhythm is obvious enough; but the return to 4 is not, as Grove said, effected by the drums, but comes where nobody can possibly detect it. And Beethoven, having helped the conductor at this point, is quite content, as in earlier works *passim*, that the listeners should gradually become aware that the 3-bar swing is no longer in being. In the trio, Beethoven wishing to indicate that 2 of its crotchets correspond to 3 of the scherzo, first wrote in $\frac{2}{4}$ time. But this made the lilt as unrecognizable as the true proportions of Iceland at the top of a map on Mercator's projection. So he changed it to alla-breve bars $\frac{2}{2}$.

The common sense of the whole matter is that hard accents and soft accents are equally liable in the long run to obliterate the distinction between the first and the third of four beats, and may go far to weaken that between the first and the second. We shall never find that Beethoven's short bars will fit any one interpretation throughout a piece, nor shall we often be able to fix the point at which the rhythmic angle is shifted. And when we have fixed everything some overlap will upset us or some extra bar make us hold our breath. Four-bar rhythm is more important to music than limericks are to literature, but the limerick is hardly more adequate or historically qualified to be taken as the fundamental basis for rhythm. And we must not take a lofty timeless view of rhythmic inequalities and changes. Farmer Giles is mistaken in the idea that the lady he finds sketching in the woods where you can't see round the corner would find a better subject on the top of a hill where you can see six counties.

Ex. 5

Andante con moto ♩ = 54

Of Man's first dis-o-be-di-ence and the fruit Of that for-bid-den tree, Whose mor-tal taste Brought

Pianoforte p

cresc. — — — fp cresc.

death in-to the world and all our Woe, With loss of E-den, till one great-er Man Re-

f dim. p cresc. — — f

store us and re-gain the blissful seat Sing . . . . heavenly Muse . . . that on the se-cret top, etc.

rit. a tempo

rit. a tempo ff etc.

6. Older Musical Rhythms.

—In measuring the distance between the musical rhythms, the most familiar to us and those of the 16th and earlier centuries, the first thing we must dismiss is our strong body-rhythm. Only the lightest ballets and fa-las of our great madrigalists have any such element. The greater part of

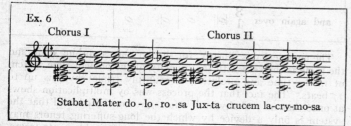

Ex. 6

Chorus I   Chorus II

Stabat Mater do - lo - ro - sa Jux-ta crucem la-cry-mo-sa

the 16th century polyphony is held together by a time system which merely counts semibreves and settles whether the semibreve is to be *perfect* and equal to 3 minims or *imperfect* and equal to 2, and also whether three or only two semibreves are to go to a breve. The law of accent holds with pairs of minims

about as strongly as in modern music, but it is already very much weakened with pairs of semibreves. Examine the first two lines of Palestrina's *Stabat Mater*, which is as wonderful in rhythm as it is in harmony.

The music of the second line is identical with that of the first, and both lines are an exact quantitative rendering of the verses, with longs twice the size of shorts. The time signature tells us that the breve contains 2 semibreves and the semibreve two minims. Accordingly the modern editor draws bar strokes at regular breve-distances throughout the score. Then comes the modern choir master, warm from a rehearsal of *Be Not Afraid* in *Elijah*, and beats four in a bar, down, left, right, up, while the dutiful double choir sings

Sta-bat	Ma-ter do	(sniff) lo ro	Sa jux
1 2 3 4	**1** 2 3 4	**1** 2 3 4	**1** 2 3 4

Ta cru	Cem la (sniff) cry	mo sa
1 2 3 4	**1** 2 3 4	**1** 2 3 4

But now let each singer, at a starting signal from the conductor, merely move one finger regularly up and down in minims, downward for accented beats and upward for unaccented. It will then be found perfectly easy to override these gentle accents whenever the sense dictates, and the choir will find itself declaiming the words beautifully.

Ex. 6a

If bars must be drawn let them come only where there is a normal accent. We must not put a bar line after *mater*, because this would come in the middle of a semibreve, or, as Morley calls it, a stroke. The examples of Victoria and Josquin given in the articles MASS, MOTET and MUSIC are barred freely by these rules, but no such single scoring is adequate for an elaborate

ing of which first appears later in the course of the music, nor with the case of an intentional vagueness. Nor, to return to the 16th century, must we put the unanimous speech-rhythm syncopations of Ex. 6 into the same category as those of the tenor at the end of Ex. 7.

Triple time in the 16th century was very different from what it is in music with a strong body-rhythm. For one thing, it continually obliterates the difference between 2÷3 and 3÷2, as in example 8 by Lasso.

This swing from 3 to a 3 twice as slow is called *hemiole* and survives as late as Bach and Handel. Thus, in the first chorus of *The Messiah* the hemiole which Handel always uses in triple time closes gives the cadential accentuation:

Ex. 8a

the | Lord shall be re - veal - - | ed

Ex. 7

polyphony. Ex. 7 gives a passage from Victoria's *O quam gloriosum* in full score barred so as to display what cannot be shown in the short score given with MOTET.

From this we can see Victoria's Miltonic art of finishing a big paragraph. The lower voices enjoy their own rhythms until the slow swing of the soprano draws the bass along with it. Then the alto joins, and the tenor is compelled to regard his own rhythm as a syncopation against this majority.

Little has been said so far about syncopation, and little now remains to be said. Its main point, even in the 16th century, as

Ex. 8

In ex-ul-ta-ti-o-ne me - - tent

etc-

2nd choir

Ex. 7 shows, is that it requires a strong body-rhythm to contradict. A common fallacy of self-centred composers is to write syncopations that never encounter opposition at all. We must not confuse this with the legitimate case of a rhythm the mean-

The opposite swing from 3/2 to 6/4 with a curious bump in the last ( ) bar characterizes the French courantes of Couperin and Bach.

Before Palestrina we find in England a fairly steady slow triple time (3 divided by 2 or 4) in Tallis; but a little earlier we find Obrecht writing music which abounded in amazing complexities, such as three depths of triple rhythm:

Ex. 8b

thus, 3/4 | over 3/2

and again over 3/1

The complexity is illusory, for the ear makes nothing of it, and the same is the case with the capacity of the ancient time system of mode, time and prolation to multiply triple rhythms up to 27 beats. The fact that the process was by multiplication shows at once that no real rhythmic effects are concerned, and that the system is only a device by which the long-suffering tenors may count out the enormous notes of some unrecognizable *canto fermo*. If we want genuine highly compound times we must leave these multiplication tables and study the last movement of Beethoven's sonata Op. 111, where the theme and first variation are in triple time divided by 3 ($\frac{9}{16}$); the second variation divides the half-beat by 3, producing $\frac{18}{32}$ (which Beethoven misnames $\frac{6}{16}$); the

Ex. 9

third variation divides the quarter-beats, producing $\frac{36}{64}$ (misnamed $\frac{12}{32}$); and the fourth variation returns to $\frac{9}{16}$ time and divides it by a uniform triplet vibration of 27 notes to a bar, afterwards surmounted by the unmeasured vibration of a trill. All this is sublime in its cogent clearness.

Genuine complexity was achieved by Palestrina in the second Kyrie of his *Missa "L'homme armé,"* a work as beautiful as it is ingenious. But Mozart achieved something unsurpassed in the ballroom scene in *Don Giovanni,* putting his vigorous body-rhythms to the supreme test of making the characters actually dance and pass remarks in them.

7. **Recent Rhythmic Developments.**—Rhythms other than binary and ternary cannot develop a very strong ictus, though Holst manages in the ballet of *The Perfect Fool* to make some good dance-rhythms of $\frac{7}{8}$. But they tend to flow like speech-rhythms, and they are very reluctant to change their pattern. A rhythm of 5 falls into either $3+2$ or $2+3$. The famous 5-time movement in Tschaikowsky's *Pathetic* symphony is $2+3$ and is in absolutely square 8-bar rhythm throughout. Again 7-time will be some form of 4 and 3, or will suggest 8 with a beat clipped. Ravel, in his pianoforte trio, showed that it is possible to divide 8 into $3+2+3$ so inveterately that no listener can possibly hear it as $4+4$. The effect is excellent, and other versions of it are used in a much quicker tempo and with more variety by Holst in his Fugal Overture. But we must call things by their right names and not say that a thing is complex when it clings like grim death to its one pattern and falls into phrases of $2+2$ for pages together.

The *Pantoum* of Ravel's trio blends an impish $\frac{3}{4}$ with a sanctimonious $\frac{4}{2}$ very amusingly. An early pianoforte sonata by Cyril Scott attempts to get away from all regularities. Its 13s and 3s do not always succeed in avoiding straightening out into plain $16=4\times4$; and when successful are conscientious rather than impulsive. The rhythms of Greek tragedy, interpreted syllabically, are suggestive, and so are many oriental rhythms. But they are not body-rhythms; and it may be doubted whether any great increase in variety of strong body-rhythms is imminent at present.

(D. F. T.)

RHYTINA: *see* SEA COW.

RIAL. The monetary unit of Persia (Iran), which has a paper currency mainly. There are notes of 5, 10, 20, 50, 100, 500 and 1,000 rials issued by the Bank Melli Iran and subsidiary coins of copper and bronze for 5, 10 and 50 dinars (1 rial = 100 dinars). Authority was given in Dec. 1943 for the minting of 1, 2, 5 and 10 rial coins from an alloy containing 60% silver and 40% copper. Fixed rates of exchange are maintained by virtue of the foreign exchange control law of 1936. The sterling value of the rial in 1944 was slightly under 2d., the rate of exchange being fixed at 128–130 in accordance with the currency law of Nov. 19, 1942, which also provided for the retention of a 60% reserve of gold

and silver against the first 3,500,000,000 rials in circulation and a reserve of 100% in gold or foreign exchange convertible into gold against any circulation in excess of this figure. The circulation on April 20, 1944, was 6,035,000,000 as compared with approximately 800,000,000 in the years 1936–38.   (N. E. C.)

RIAZ PASHA (*c.* 1835–1911), Egyptian statesman, was born about 1835. He was discovered by Ismail Pasha, who made him one of his ministers. When Ismail's financial straits compelled him to agree to a commission of inquiry, Riaz was vice-president of the commission. He filled this office with distinction, but not to the liking of Ismail.

When Ismail attempted to resume autocratic rule, Riaz fled the country. Upon the deposition of Ismail (June 1879), Riaz was sent for by the British and French controllers, and he formed the first ministry under the khedive Tewfik. His administration was overthrown by the agitation which had for its figurehead Arabi Pasha (*q.v.*).

On Sept. 9, 1881, Riaz was dismissed and went to Europe, remaining until the fall of Arabi. He then accepted office as minister of the interior under Sherif Pasha. He wanted the immediate execution of Arabi and his associates; and when the British insisted on clemency to the leaders of the revolt, he resigned (Dec. 1882).

Riaz took no further part in public affairs until 1888 when, on the dismissal of Nubar Pasha (*q.v.*), he was summoned to form a government, remaining in office until May 1891. In Feb. 1892 he again became prime minister under Abbas II. In April 1894 he finally resigned office.

Riaz died on June 18, 1911.

RIBADENEIRA, PEDRO A. (1527–1611), hagiologist, was born at Toledo on Nov. 1, 1527. In Rome on Sept. 18, 1540, he was admitted by Ignatius Loyola as one of the Society of Jesus.

He pursued his studies at Paris (1542) in philosophy and theology. Loyola, in 1555, sent him on a mission to Belgium; in pursuance of it he visited England in 1558. In 1560 he was made provincial of the Society of Jesus in Tuscany. He was transferred as provincial to Sicily in 1563, was again employed in Flanders and from 1571 served in Spain. In 1574 he settled in Madrid, where he died on Sept. 10, 1611. His most important work is the *Life of Loyola* (1572). That Ribadeneira was, though an able, a very credulous writer, is shown by his lives of Loyola's successors Diego Laynez and St. Francis Borgia; and especially by his *Flos Sanctorum* (1599–1610), a collection of saints' lives, entirely superseded by the labours of the Bollandists.

See his autobiography in his *Bibliotheca Scriptorum Societatis Jesu* (1602 and 1608, supplemented by P. Alegambe and N. Sotwell in 1676); H. F. De Puy, *An Early Account of the Establishment of Jesuit Missions in America* (1921).

RIBAULT or **RIBAUT, JEAN** (*c.* 1520–1565), French navigator, was born at Dieppe, about 1520. Appointed by Admiral

Coligny to take French Protestants to America, Ribault sailed on Feb. 18, 1562, with two vessels, and on May 1 landed at Florida at St. John's river, or, as he called it, Rivière de Mai. Having settled his colonists at Port Royal harbour (now Paris Island, S.C.), and built Fort Charles for their protection, he returned to France. In 1563 he appears to have been in England and to have issued *True and Last Discoverye of Florida* (Hakluyt Soc., vol. vii.). In April 1564 Coligny despatched another expedition under René de Laudonnière, but meanwhile Ribault's colony, destitute of supplies, revolted against their governor and attempted to make their way back to Europe in a boat which was happily picked up by an English vessel. In 1565 Ribault was again sent out to satisfy Coligny as to Laudonnière's management of his new settlement, Fort Caroline, on the Rivière de Mai. While he was still there the Spaniards attacked the French ships at the mouth of the river. Ribault set out to retaliate but his vessels were wrecked near Matanzas Inlet and he had to return to Fort Caroline by land. The Spaniards by this time had slaughtered all the colonists except a few who got off with two ships under Ribault's son. Induced to surrender by false assurances, Ribault and his men were put to the sword in Oct. 1565.

BIBLIOGRAPHY.—See E. and E. Haag, *La France protestante* (1846-59); F. Parkman, *Pioneers of France in the New World* (new ed. 1912); J. Ribaut, *The Whole and True Discoverye of Terra Florida*, a reprint of the London ed. of 1563 with notes and biography (Deland, Florida, 1927).

RIBBONFISH: *see* OARFISH.

RIBBONISM, the name given to an Irish secret-society movement which began at the end of the 18th century in opposition to the Orangemen (*q.v.*) and which was represented by various associations under different names, organized in lodges, and recruited all over Ireland from the lowest classes of the people.

The actual name of Ribbonism (from a green badge worn by its members) became attached to the movement later, about 1826; and after it had grown to its height, about 1855, it declined in force, and was practically at an end in its old form when in 1871 the Westmeath act declared Ribbonism illegal.

RIBBONS. By this name are designated narrow webs, commonly of silk or velvet, used primarily for binding and tying in connection with dress, but also applied for innumerable useful, ornamental and symbolical purposes. Along with that of tapes, fringes and other small wares, the manufacture of ribbons forms a special department of the textile industries.

RIBEAUVILLÉ (Rappoltsweiler), a town of France, in the department of Haut-Rhin. Pop. (1936) 4,596. It lies at the entrance of the valley of the Strengbach, under the Vosges mountains, 33 mi. S.W. of Strasbourg on the railway to Basle. It is in part surrounded by ancient walls and has many mediaeval houses and two fine Gothic churches, of St. Gregory and St. Augustine. The Carolabad, a saline spring with a temperature of 64°, made Ribeauvillé a watering-place.

Rappoltsweiler, known in the 8th century as Rathaldovilare, passed from the bishops of Basle to the lords of Rappoltstein, famous nobles of Alsace. The lord of Rappoltstein was the protector of wandering minstrels. When the family became extinct in 1673 this office of king of the pipers (*Pfeiferkönig*) passed to the counts palatine of Zweibrücken-Birkenfeld. The minstrels had a pilgrimage chapel near Rappoltsweiler, dedicated to their patron saint, Maria von Dusenbach, and here they held an annual feast on Sept. 8. Near the town are the ruins of three famous castles, Ulrichsburg, Girsberg and Hohrappoltstein.

RIBEIRA, a town of northwestern Spain, in the province of Corunna, on the extreme southwest of the peninsula formed between the Ria of Muros and Noya and Arosa bay. Pop. (1940) mun., 18,760. Ribeira is in a hilly country, abounding in wheat, wine, fruit, fish and game. Its port is Santa Eugenia de Ribeira.

RIBEIRO, BERNARDIM (1482-1552), the father of bucolic prose and verse in Portugal, was a native of Torrão in the Alemtejo. He studied at the University of Lisbon, was introduced by one of his relatives to the court of King Manoel, and became secretary to King John III. in 1524. Ribeiro's early verses are to be found in the *Cancioneiro Geral* of Garcia de Resende (*q.v.*). He took part in the historic *Serões do Paço,* or palace evening entertainments, which largely consisted of poetical improvisations; there he met and earned the friendship of the poets Sá de Miranda (*q.v.*) and Christovão Falcão, who soon became his literary comrades and the confidants of his romantic passion for a lady who has been variously identified by literary historians. All that is certain is that the upshot of the affair was banishment from court. Ribeiro had poured out his heart in five beautiful eclogues, the earliest in Portuguese, written in the popular octosyllabic verse. He is said to have gone to Italy, and possibly was there when he wrote his moving knightly and pastoral romance *Menina e Moça,* in which he related the story of his passion, personifying himself under the anagram of "Bimnarder," and the lady under that of "Aonia." When he returned home in 1524, the new king, John III, restored him to his former post. But his mind was already unhinged by trouble. About 1534 a long illness supervened, then melancholia. In 1549 the king gave him a pension; in 1552 he died insane in All Saints hospital in Lisbon.

The *Menina e Moça* was not printed until after Ribeiro's death (Ferrara, 1554.) It is divided into two parts, the first of which is certainly the work of Ribeiro (ed. Dr. José Pessanha, Oporto, 1891), while as to the second opinion is divided.

See Visconde Sanches de Baena, *Bernardim Ribeiro* (1895); Dr. Theophilo Braga, *Bernardim Ribeiro e o Bucolismo* (Oporto, 1897); A. F. G. Bell, *Portuguese Literature* (1922).

RIBERA, GIUSEPPE (1588-1652), called LO SPAGNOLETTO or "little Spaniard," a leading painter of the Spanish and partly Neapolitan school. He was born at Játiba near Valencia in Spain on Jan. 12, 1588. He studied painting under Francisco Ribalta (*c.* 1551-1628), the Spanish Caravaggio, whose "tenebroso technique" with marked contrast of light and shade, he acquired. He then proceeded to Italy. In Rome he studied Raphael's frescoes in the Vatican; in Parma Correggio's works; he probably also visited Padua and Venice. Eventually he settled at Naples, where he married Catarina Azzolino, the daughter of a painter, in 1616. His work attracted the attention of the Spanish viceroy, the duke of Ossuna, who favoured him, and whose patronage was continued by his successors, among whom was Count Monterey. For this nobleman he painted the wonderful "Conception" (1635) in the Augustine monastery of Salamanca. After 1637 he was employed on important work in the Carthusian church of S. Martino at Naples. Commissions flowed in upon Ribera. In 1626 he was elected a member of the Academy of St. Luke in Rome; he was decorated by the pope with the insignia of the order of "the Abito di Cristo" in 1644. Velasquez is said to have visited him at Naples. His influence was felt throughout Italy and Spain, and the popularity of the painters known as the *Tenebrosi* and naturalists depended as much on the example of Ribera as on that of Caravaggio. Luca Giordano was his most distinguished pupil. The close of Ribera's career was shadowed by his grief over the abduction of his second daughter by Don Juan of Austria.

Ribera was one of the most able naturalist painters, but he was also a poet. His drawing was precise and also powerful; his figures are true in form but also full of feeling, especially those of old men. In his earlier style, founded on Ribalta (some say on Caravaggio), he displays an excessive love of strong shadows. His later work was more luminous and of a rich golden tone. Pacheco rightly called him one of the great colourists of Spain. Ribera's religious pictures are free from sentimentality and essentially Roman Catholic in spirit. Owing to his realistic rendering of scenes of martyrdom of Christian saints it has been said that he delighted in subjects of horror. Thus to quote Byron: "Spagnoletto tainted his brush with all the blood of all the sainted" (*Don Juan*, XIV. 71). Among Ribera's principal works we may mention: "The Martyrdom of St. Bartholomew" (1630) in the Prado; "The Pietà" (1637) in S. Martino, Naples; "St. Agnes" (1641) in the Dresden gallery; "The Descent from the Cross" (1644) in the Neapolitan Certosa: "St. Januarius emerging from the Furnace" (1646) in the cathedral, Naples; and "The Adoration of the Shepherds" (1650) in the Louvre. He also painted mythological subjects such as "The Silenus" (1626) in the gallery of Naples and "Venus and Adonis" (1637) in the Galleria Nazionale, Rome. He was the author of several fine male portraits such as "The Musician" from the Stroganoff collection now in the museum of Toronto, Canada. The Prado, Madrid, contains no less than 50 of his paintings.

As an etcher he belonged to the Italian school, and his plates all date from a late period (1621–48). They are masterpieces in direct drawing especially "the Drunken Silenus with Satyrs" (1628) and "Don Juan on Horseback" (1648). Bartsch enumerates 18 plates, of which three are studies of features.

See C. Bermudez, *Diccionario Historico;* Dominici, *Vite de' Pittori* (Naples 1840–46); A. L. Mayer, *Ribera* (Leipzig, 1923).

RIBOT, ALEXANDRE FÉLIX JOSEPH (1842–1923), French statesman, was born at St. Omer on Feb. 7, 1842. After a brilliant career at the University of Paris, he rapidly made his mark at the bar. He was secretary of the conference of advocates and one of the founders of the *Société de législation comparée.* After entering the Chamber of Deputies in 1878 he devoted himself especially to financial questions, and in 1882 was reporter of the budget. He became one of the most prominent republican opponents of the Radical party, distinguishing himself by his attacks on the short-lived Gambetta ministry. He refused to vote the credits demanded by the Ferry cabinet for the Tongking expedition, and shared with M. Clémenceau in the overthrow of the ministry in 1885. At the general election of that year he was defeated, but re-entered the chamber in 1887. After 1889 he sat for St. Omer. His fear of the Boulangist movement converted him to the policy of "Republican Concentration," and he entered office in 1890 as foreign minister in the Freycinet cabinet. He gave a fresh direction to French policy by the understanding with Russia, declared to the world by the visit of the French fleet to Cronstadt in 1891, and subsequently ripened into a formal treaty of alliance. He retained his post in the Loubet ministry (Feb.–Nov. 1892), and on its defeat became himself president of the council, retaining the direction of foreign affairs. The government resigned in March 1893 on the refusal of the chamber to accept the Senate's amendments to the budget. On the election of Félix Faure as president of the Republic in Jan. 1895, Ribot again became premier and minister of finance. On June 10 he made the official announcement of a definite alliance with Russia. On Oct. 30 the ministry fell. After the fall of the Méline ministry in 1898 Ribot tried in vain to form a cabinet of "conciliation." The policy of the Waldeck-Rousseau ministry on the religious teaching congregations broke up the Republican party, and Ribot was among the seceders; but at the general election of 1902, though he himself secured re-election, his policy suffered a severe check. He actively opposed the policy of the Combes ministry and denounced the alliance with Jaurès, and on Jan. 13, 1905, he was one of the leaders of the opposition which brought about the fall of the cabinet. Nevertheless, he now announced his willingness to recognize a new régime to replace the Concordat, and gave the government his support in the establishment of the *Associations cultuelles,* while he secured some mitigation of the severities attending the separation.

In June 1914 M. Poincaré summoned Ribot to form a cabinet. He succeeded in doing so but his Government did not survive the first ministerial declaration. He returned to office in Aug. 1914 as minister of finance in M. Viviani's reconstituted ministry of national defence. He held the same office in the ministry formed by M. Briand on Oct. 29, 1915, and again in the reduced cabinet of Dec. 1916. In March 1917 he succeeded M. Briand as prime minister and minister of foreign affairs. He gave way in Sept. of the same year to M. Painlevé, in whose Government he retained the ministry of foreign affairs, which he resigned in the following month. M. Ribot was a member of the Académie Française and of the Académie des Sciences Politiques et Morales. He died in Paris Jan. 13, 1923.

See M. Laurent, *Nos gouvernements de guerre* (1920).

RIBOT, THEODULE ARMAND (1839–1916), French psychologist, was born at Guingamp on Dec. 18, 1839, and died on Dec. 9, 1916. In 1888 he became professor of psychology at the Collège de France. His thesis for his doctor's degree, republished in 1882, *Hérédité: étude psychologique* (5th ed., 1889), is his most important and best known book. Following the experimental and synthetic methods, he collected instances of inherited peculiarities; he pays particular attention to the physical element of mental life, ignoring all spiritual or non-material factors in man.

Of his works the following have been translated into English:— *English Psychology* (1873); *Heredity: a Psychological Study of its Phenomena, Laws, Causes, and Consequences* (1875); *Diseases of Memory: An Essay in the Positive Psychology* (1882); *Diseases of the Will* (1884); *German Psychology of to-day,* tr. J. M. Baldwin (1886); *The Psychology of Attention* (Chicago, 1890); *Diseases of Personality* (Chicago, 1895); *The Psychology of the Emotions* (1897); *The Evolution of General Ideas,* tr. F. A. Welby (Chicago, 1899); *Essay on the Creative Imagination,* tr. A. H. N. Baron (1906).

RICARDO, DAVID (1772–1823), English economist, was born in London on April 19, 1772, of Jewish origin. His father, who was of Dutch birth, was a successful member of the Stock Exchange. In 1786 Ricardo entered his father's office, where he showed much aptitude for business, but in consequence of his adoption of the Christian faith about 1793, when he married Miss Wilkinson, he was separated from his family and thrown on his own resources. He continued a member of the Stock Exchange and by 1797 was sufficiently wealthy to be able to turn to scientific pursuits; but, having read Adam Smith's great work, he threw himself into the study of political economy.

His publication of a tract on *The High Price of Bullion, a Proof of the Depreciation of Bank Notes,* in 1809, gave a fresh stimulus to the controversy respecting the resumption of cash payments, and indirectly led to the appointment of a committee of the House of Commons, commonly known as the Bullion Committee, to consider the question. The report of the committee confirmed Ricardo's views, and recommended the repeal of the Bank Restriction Act, but the House of Commons declared that paper had undergone no depreciation. In 1811 he met James Mill, who, while influencing Ricardo politically, was under obligations to him in the economic field. Mill said, in 1823, that he himself and J. R. M'Culloch were Ricardo's only genuine disciples.

In 1815, when the Corn Laws were under discussion, Ricardo published his *Essay on the Influence of a Low Price of Corn on the Profits of Stock,* directed against a tract by Malthus entitled *Grounds of an Opinion on the Policy of Restraining the Free Importation of Foreign Corn.* His arguments were based on the theory of rent, which, as Ricardo admitted, had been clearly enunciated by Malthus in his *Inquiry into the Nature and Progress of Rent,* and which had earlier been stated by Anderson. In this essay are set forth the essential propositions of the Ricardian system, such as, that an increase of wages does not raise prices; that profits can be raised only by a fall in wages and diminished only by a rise in wages; and that profits, in the whole progress of society, are determined by the cost of the production of the food which is raised at the greatest expense. These ideas were afterwards incorporated in the *Principles of Political Economy.* In the field of the theory of banking and currency some of Ricardo's best work appears. His main ideas are expressed in three pamphlets: (1) *The High Price of Bullion* (1810), in which he discusses the available means of testing the value of paper money, and the power of the Bank of England to regulate the supply. (2) *Proposals for an Economical and Secure Currency* (1816), in which he elucidates the quantity theory, and pronounces in favour of a mono-metallic standard. (3) *A Plea for a National Bank* (1824), which was, in fact, an indictment of the methods of the existing bank, particularly in connection with its issue of paper money.

Ricardo's chief work, *Principles of Political Economy and Taxation,* appeared in 1817. The fundamental doctrine of this work is that, on the hypothesis of free competition, exchange value is determined by the labour expended in production. Ricardo's theory of distribution has been briefly enunciated as follows: "(1) The demand for food determines the margin of cultivation; (2) this margin determines rent; (3) the amount necessary to maintain the labourer determines wages; (4) the difference between the amount produced by a given quantity of labour at the margin and the wages of that labour determines profit." These theorems require much modification to adapt them to real life. His theory of foreign trade has been embodied in the two propositions: "(1) International values are not determined in the same way as domestic values; (2) the medium of exchange is distributed so as to bring trade to the condition it would be in if it were conducted by barter." A considerable portion of the work is devoted to a study of taxation, which requires to be considered as a part of the problem of distribution. A tax is not always paid by those on whom it is imposed; it is therefore necessary to determine the ultimate, as distinguished from the immediate, incidence of every form of taxation. Smith had already dealt with this question. Ricardo, in developing and criticising his results, arrives at the conclusion that a tax on raw produce falls on the consumer, but will also diminish profits; a tax on rents falls on the landlord; taxes on houses will be divided between the occupier and the ground landlord; taxes on profits will be paid by the consumer, and taxes on wages by the capitalist.

Having retired from business and become a landed proprietor, Ricardo entered parliament as member for Portarlington in 1819. He contributed to bringing about the change of opinion on the question of free trade which led to the legislation of Sir Robert Peel on that subject, and made some valuable speeches on economic questions. In 1820 he contributed to the supplement of the *Encyclopædia Britannica* (6th ed.) an "Essay on the Funding System." In this besides giving an historical account (founded on Dr. Robert Hamilton's valuable work *On the National Debt*, 1813, 3rd ed., 1818) of the several successive forms of the sinking fund, he urges that nations should defray their expenses, whether ordinary or extraordinary, at the time when they are incurred, instead of providing for them by loans.

Ricardo died on Sept. 11, 1823, at his seat (Gatcomb Park) in Gloucestershire, from a cerebral affection. James Mill, who was intimately acquainted with him, says (in a letter to Napier of November 1818) that he knew not a better man, and on the occasion of his death published a highly eulogistic notice of him in the *Morning Chronicle*. A lectureship on political economy, to exist for ten years, was founded in commemoration of him, M'Culloch being chosen to fill it.

In forming a general judgment respecting Ricardo, we must have in view not so much the minor writings as the *Principles*, in which his economic system is expounded as a whole. By a study of this work we are led to the conclusion that he was an economist rather than a social philosopher like Adam Smith or John Mill, for there is no evidence of his having had any but the narrowest views of the great social problems. He shows no trace of that sympathy with the working classes which is apparent in the *Wealth of Nations;* and he regards the labourer as merely an instrument in the hands of the capitalist. Ricardo's main contributions to economics relate to foreign trade, money, and paper issues and rent. He was responsible for the doctrine of comparative costs, as applied to foreign trade, a clear statement of the quantity theory, and a rather involved discussion of the nature of rent. His work suffers from ambiguity of expression, which has led to erroneous interpretations by his successors.

The criticisms to which Ricardo's general economic scheme is open do not hold with respect to his treatment of the subjects of currency and banking. These form precisely that branch of economics where the operation of purely mercantile principles is most immediate and invariable. They were, besides, the departments of the study to which Ricardo's early training and practical habits led him to give special attention; and they have a lasting value independent of his systematic construction.

Ricardo's collected works were published, with a notice of his life and writings, by J. R. M'Culloch in 1846. The *Principles* were edited, with an introduction, bibliography, and notes, by G. C. K. Gonner (1891), who also edited the *Economic Notes* (1923). *See also Letters to T. R. Malthus* (ed. J. Bonar, 1887); *Letters to J. R. M'Culloch* (ed. J. H. Hollander, 1895); *Letters to H. Trower and Others* (ed. J Bonar and J. H. Hollander, 1899); *Notes on Malthus' Principles of Political Economy* (ed. J. H. Hollander and T. E. Gregory, 1928). A French translation of the *Principles* by F. S. Constancio, with notes by J. B. Say, appeared in 1818; the whole works, trans. F. S. Constancio and A. Fonteyraud, form vol. xiii. (1847) of the *Collection des principaux economistes*, with important notes. *See also* E. Baumstark, *David Ricardo's Grundgesetze der Volkswirthschaft und die*

Besteuerung *übersetzt und erläutert* (1837), also J. H. Hollander, *David Ricardo* (1910) and A. Graziani, *Ricardo e J. S. Mill* (1921).

RICASOLI, BETTINO, Baron (1809–80), (rē-kah'sō-lĭ), Italian statesman, born at Broglio March 19, 1809. In 1847 he founded the journal *La Patria,* and sent to the grand duke of Tuscany a memorial suggesting remedies for the difficulties of the state. In 1848 he was for a short time gonfaloniere of Florence. As Tuscan minister of the interior in 1859 he promoted the union of Tuscany with Piedmont. Elected Italian deputy in 1861, he succeeded Cavour in the premiership. As premier he admitted the Garibaldian volunteers to the regular army, revoked the decree of exile against Mazzini, and attempted reconciliation with the Vatican; but his efforts were rendered ineffectual by the *non possumus* of the pope. He found himself obliged in 1862 to resign office, but returned to power in 1866. On this occasion he refused Napoleon III.'s offer to cede Venetia to Italy, on condition that Italy should abandon the Prussian alliance, and also refused the Prussian decoration of the Black Eagle because Lamarmora, author of the alliance, was not to receive it. After the French troops left Rome in 1866 he attempted to conciliate the Vatican with a convention, in virtue of which Italy would have restored to the Church the property of the suppressed religious orders in return for the gradual payment of £24,000,000. He conceded the *exequatur* to 45 bishops inimical to the Italian régime. The Vatican accepted his proposal, but the Italian Chamber proved refractory, and, though dissolved by Ricasoli, returned more hostile than before. Without waiting for a vote, Ricasoli resigned office. He died at Broglio on Oct. 23, 1880. His private life and public career were marked by a rigid austerity which earned him the name of the "iron baron."

See Tabarrini and Gotti, *Lettere e documenti del barone Bettino Ricasoli,* 10 vols. (Florence, 1886–94); Passerini, *Genealogia e storia della famiglia Ricasoli* (1861); Gotti, *Vita del barone Bettino Ricasoli* (1894).

RICCATI, JACOPO FRANCESCO, Count (1676–1754), Italian mathematician, was born at Venice on May 28, 1676, and died at Treviso on April 15, 1754. He studied at the University of Padua, where he graduated in 1696. His authority on all questions of practical science was referred to by the senate of Venice. He corresponded with many of the European savants of his day, and contributed largely to the *Acta Eruditorum* of Leipzig. He was offered the presidency of the academy of science of St. Petersburg (Leningrad), but he declined, preferring the leisure and independence of life in Italy. Riccati's name is best known in connection with his problem called Riccati's equation, published in the *Acta Eruditorum,* Sept. 1724. A very complete account of this equation and its various transformations was given by J. W. L. Glaisher in the *Phil. Trans.* (1881).

His works were collected and published by his sons (1758, 4 vols.).

RICCI, MATTEO (1552–1610), Italian missionary to China, was born of a noble family at Macerata in the March of Ancona on Oct. 7, 1552. After some education at a Jesuit college in his native town he went to study law at Rome, where in 1571, in opposition to his father's wishes, he joined the Society of Jesus. In 1577 Ricci and other students offered themselves for the East Indian missions. Ricci, without visiting his family to take leave, proceeded to Portugal. His comrades were Rudolfo Acquaviva, Nicolas Spinola, Francesco Pasio and Michele Ruggieri, all afterwards, like Ricci himself, famous in the Jesuit annals. They arrived at Goa in Sept. 1578. After four years spent in India, Ricci was summoned to the task of opening China to evangelization.

Several fruitless attempts had been made by Xavier, and since his death, to introduce the Church into China, but it was not till the arrival at Macao of Alessandro Valignani on a visitation in 1582 that work in China was really taken up. For this object he had obtained the services first of M. Ruggieri and then of Ricci. After various disappointments they found access to Chow-king-fu on the Si-Kiang or West River of Canton, where the viceroy of the two provinces of Kwangtung and Kwangsi then had his residence, and by his favour were able to establish themselves there for some years. Their proceedings were very cautious and tentative; they excited the curiosity and interest of even the more intelligent Chinese by their clocks, their globes and maps, their books of European engravings, and by Ricci's knowledge of mathematics, dialling and the projection of maps. Eventually troubles at Chow-king compelled them to seek a new home; and in 1589, with the viceroy's sanction, they migrated to Chang-chow in the northern part of Kwangtung, not far from the well-known Meiling Pass.

During his stay here Ricci was convinced that a mistake had been made in adopting a dress resembling that of the bonzes, a class who were the objects either of superstition or of contempt. With the sanction of the visitor it was ordered that in future the missionaries should adopt the costumes of Chinese literates, and, in fact, they before long adopted Chinese manners altogether.

Chang-chow, as a station, did not prove a happy selection, but it was not till 1595 that an opportunity occurred of travelling northward. For some time Ricci's residence was at Nan-changfu, the capital of Kiang-si; but in 1598 he was able to proceed under favourable conditions to Nanking, and thence for the first time to Peking, which had all along been the goal of his missionary ambition. But circumstances were not then propitious, and the party had to return to Nanking. The fame of the presents which they carried had, however, reached the court, and the Jesuits were summoned north again, and on Jan. 24, 1601, they entered the capital. Wan-li, the emperor of the Ming dynasty, in those days lived in seclusion, and saw no one but his women and the eunuchs. But the missionaries were summoned to the palace; their presents were immensely admired, and the emperor had the curiosity to send for portraits of the fathers themselves.

They obtained a settlement, with an allowance for subsistence, in Peking, and from this time to the end of his life Ricci's estimation among the Chinese was constantly increasing, as was at the same time the amount of his labours. Visitors thronged the mission house incessantly; and inquiries came to him from all parts of the empire respecting the doctrines which he taught, or the numerous Chinese publications which he issued. As head of the mission, which now had four stations in China, he also devoted much time to answering the letters of the priests under him, a matter on which he spared no pains or detail. In May 1610 he broke down, and after an illness of eight days died on the 11th of that month.

Ricci's work was the foundation of the subsequent success attained by the Roman Catholic Church in China. When the missionaries of other Roman Catholic orders made their way into China, twenty years later, they found great fault with the manner in which certain Chinese practices had been dealt with by the Jesuits. The controversy burned for considerably more than a century with great fierceness. (For a list of the controversial works *see* Cordier, *Bibliographie de la Chine*.)

Probably no European name of past centuries is so well known in China as that of *Li-ma-teu*, the form in which the name of Ricci (*Ri-cci Mat-teo*) was adapted to Chinese usage, and by which he appears in Chinese records. The works which he composed in Chinese are numerous; a list of them (apparently by no means complete, however) will be found in Kircher's *China Illustrata*, and also in Abel Rémusat's *Nouveaux Mélanges Asiatiques* (ii. 213-15).

The chief facts of Ricci's career are derived from the account brought home by P. Nicolas Trigault, *De Expeditione Christiana apud Sinas Suscepta ab Soc. Jesu*, extracted from Ricci's commentaries and published at Augsburg and at Lyons.　　(H. Y.; X.)

RICCOBONI, MARIE JEANNE, *née* LABORAS DE MÉ-ZIÈRES (1714–1792), French novelist, was born in Paris. She married Antoine François Riccoboni, an actor and dramatist, in 1735 but separated from him soon after. She was also an actress but had no great success on the stage. Her writings are examples of the "novel of sensibility," the nearest English equivalent being the work of Henry Mackenzie. Her works include: *Lettres de Mistriss Fanny Butlerd* (1757); the remarkable *Histoire de M. le Marquis de Cressy* (1758); *Lettres de Milady Juliette Catesby* (1759); *Lettres d'Adelaïde de Dammartin, Comtesse de Sancerre*, 2 vol. (1767); *Lettres d'Elisabeth-Sophie de Vallière*, 2 vol. (1772); Let-

tres de Mylord Rivers, 2 vol. (1777); and *Histoire d'Ernestine* (1783), which J. F. de La Harpe thought her masterpiece. Deprived of her small pension from the crown by the Revolution, she died in great indigence on Dec. 6, 1792.

BIBLIOGRAPHY.—The complete edition of Madame Riccoboni's *Oeuvres*, 9 vol. (Paris, 1826) gives notices by J. F. de La Harpe, Baron von Grimm and Denis Diderot. *See also* J. M. Quérard, *La France littéraire*, vol. vii (Paris, 1835); Julia Kavanagh, *French Women of Letters*, 2 vol. (London, 1862), which gives an account of her novels; Jean Fleury, *Marivaux et le marivaudage* (Paris, 1881); and E. A. Crosby, *Une romancière oubliée* (Paris, 1924).

RICE, EDMUND IGNATIUS (1762–1844), Irish philanthropist, founder of the "Irish Christian Brothers," was born at Westcourt, near Callan, Kilkenny, on June 1, 1762. He abandoned his provision merchant business to devote himself to education and in 1808 he and nine others, meeting at Waterford, took religious vows from their bishop, assumed a "habit" and adopted an additional Christian name, by which, as by the collective title "Christian Brothers," they were thenceforth known. Schools were established in Cork (1811), Dublin (1812), and Thurles and Limerick (1817). In 1820 Pope Pius VII. issued a brief sanctioning the order of "Religious Brothers of the Christian Schools (Ireland)," the members of which were to be bound by vows of obedience, chastity, poverty and perseverance, and to give themselves to the free instruction, religious and literary, of male children, especially the poor. Rice held the office of superior general of the order from 1822 to 1838. He died on Aug. 29, 1844.

RICE, JAMES (1843–1882), English novelist, was born at Northampton on Sept. 26, 1843. Educated at Queens' college, Cambridge, where he graduated in law in 1867, he was called to the bar at Lincoln's Inn in 1871. In the meantime (1868) he had bought *Once a Week*, which proved a losing venture for him, but which brought him into touch with Walter Besant, a contributor. (*See* Besant's preface to the Library Edition [1887] of *Ready-money Mortiboy*.) There ensued a close friendship and a literary partnership between the two men which lasted ten years until Rice's death. The first of their joint works was *Ready-money Mortiboy* (1872), dramatized by them later and unsuccessfully produced at the Court theatre in 1874. In rapid succession followed *My Little Girl* (1873); *With Harp and Crown* (1874); *This Son of Vulcan* (1876); *The Golden Butterfly* (1876); *The Monks of Thelema* (1878) and others. (*See* BESANT, SIR WALTER.) James Rice died at Redhill on April 26, 1882.

RICE, a well-known cereal, is the staple food of hundreds of millions of people in Asia. According to R. J. Roschevicz, cultivated rice, *Oryza sativa*, including all its numerous varieties, originated from wild species which are indigenous to Africa, India and Indo-China. The cultivated rice plant is an annual grass with linear pubescent or glabrous leaves, each provided with a pointed ligule. The spikelets are borne on a loose panicle, which is erect at blooming, but nodding as the grains develop and mature. Each spikelet contains one flower enclosed by the compressed lemma and palea. At the base of each of these organs is a small lance-shaped glume. The flower consists of six stamens and an ovary surmounted by two styles bearing a feathery stigma. The ovary, after fertilization, develops into the fruit or grain, which is enclosed by the lemma and palea or hull. The cultivated varieties are numerous and differ markedly in morphological characters and in physiological behaviour. Most varieties are adapted for growth on submerged land, but others, known as upland rice, are grown on land not submerged.

Rice is grown in coastal plains, tidal deltas and river basins in tropical, semi-tropical and temperate regions where fresh water is available to submerge the land. In the orient, where most of the farms are too small for the use of farm machinery, rice is generally grown by hand labour, although animals, when available, are used in preparing the land. The rice is sown broadcast on well prepared beds, and when the seedlings are 25 to 50 days old they are pulled and transplanted to the field or paddy by hand. Before transplanting, the fields, which are inclosed by levees or bunds, are submerged 2 to 4 in. and the surface soil is thoroughly stirred. Two to five seedlings are placed in hills 3 to 6 in. apart in rows 8 to 12 in. apart. The land is submerged during most of the growing season, and the crop is harvested by hand.

Outside of the orient, farm machinery usually is used for preparing the land, seeding and harvesting. In California, most of the rice is broadcast on the water from aeroplanes. The crop is grown in essentially the same manner as wheat, oats and barley, except that the land is submerged during most of the growing season. About 95% of the world's rice is produced in Asia and the nearby islands. The principal rice-producing countries, outside of the orient, are Egypt, Italy, Spain, Brazil and the United States.

Preparation of Rice.—The kernel of rice as it leaves the thresher is enclosed by the hull or husk, and is known as paddy or rough rice. Rough rice is used for seed and feed for livestock, but most of it is milled for human consumption. Rice is a good energy food, and is consumed in vast quantities in the orient. In the western hemisphere, however, rice is not the staple cereal food, except in certain Caribbean and South Pacific islands. A diet limited largely to well milled rice renders eastern people on a restricted diet liable to beriberi, a deficiency disease caused by a shortage of essential thiamin (vitamin B_1) and minerals. This

BY COURTESY OF THE BRITISH MUSEUM (NATURAL HISTORY)

RICE (ORYZA SATIVA), SHOWING GENERAL HABIT OF GROWTH
A. Single flower with part removed to show branched stigma and 6 stamens
B. Single stamen (Both A and B are enlarged)

disease, however, can be avoided by adding legumes, fish, fruits and vegetables to the diet.

Rough rice that is parboiled and dried prior to milling retains more thiamin and minerals than untreated rice, and hence is less apt to cause beriberi. It appears that in parboiling, the thiamin, which is largely in the germ and bran layers of the kernel, diffuses into and is fixed in the starchy endosperm.

Most of the rice is milled in or near the areas in which it is produced. In modern mills, special machines are used for removing the hull from the kernel, for removing the bran layers by attrition, for polishing, for coating and for grading. The object in milling is to remove the hull and the bran layers of the kernel with as little breakage as possible, for the most valuable product is the whole kernel.

Milled rice often is coated with glucose and talc, or with vegetable oils, to improve its appearance. The by-products, bran and polish, are used as feed for livestock, the broken rice for brewing, distilling, and the manufacturing of starch and rice flour.

The hulls are used for fuel or packing, and the straw is used for feed, for bedding livestock, for thatching roofs, and for mats, garments, packing and broom straws.

United States.—Rice production in the United States, which averaged 37,022,000 bags of 100 lb. each in 1943-52, increased by 1954 to more than 58,850,000 bags. The average yield was 2,447 lb. per acre.

Leading producing states were Texas, Louisiana, Arkansas, California and Mississippi.

World Production.—The world rice crop was estimated at 262,325,000,000 lb. in the mid-1950s, excluding Communist China, the U.S.S.R. and North Korea. Production averaged 229,807,300,-000 lb. in 1945-50 and 224,482,000,000 lb. before World War II. Principal producing countries include India, Pakistan, Japan, Indonesia, Thailand, Burma, Indochina and China.

BIBLIOGRAPHY.—G. Watt, *Dictionary of the Economic Products of India* (1908); W. W. Robbins, *The Botany of Crop Plants* (1924); R. J. Roschevicz, *Kpoznaniiu risa (A Contribution to the Knowledge of Rice) (Russian), Bulletin Applied Botany, Genetics and Plant Breeding* 27(4):1-133, 1931; V. D. Wickizer and M. K. Bennett, *The Rice Economy of Monsoon Asia* (1941).   (J. W. Js.; C. R. Ar.)

RICE, WILD (*Zizania aquatica*), or Indian rice, water oats, also known locally by many other names, is an indigenous, coarse,

annual grass, the grain of which has long been used as an important food by various Indian tribes and early settlers. It is commonly found on muddy bottom in fresh to brackish water along shores, streams or in lakes and swampy places from the Atlantic coast west to the Mississippi Valley and is widely planted as food for waterfowl. A tall, self-sowing grass (4–8 ft.), it is highly variable and regionally marked by three varieties: (1) the short variety of the St. Lawrence river system; (2) the small northern wild rice found along the Canadian border; and (3) the large wild rice of the middle west. The fruiting panicle may be 1–2 ft. long, the lower spreading branches of which bear male flowers whereas the upper erect branches bear female flowers. When well cooked, the slender, round, purplish black, starchy grain (nearly $\frac{3}{4}$ in. long) is excellent food. Among northern Indians "ricing" means harvesting wild rice by canoe and preparing it for winter storage. The primitive methods employed by them still yield a superior product. Unless kept in wet, cool storage, wild rice completely loses its viability.

(T. K. J.)

RICE BIRD: *see* BOBOLINK.

RICE PAPER. The substance which has received this name in Europe, through the mistaken notion that it is made from rice, consists of the pith of a small tree, *Aralia papyrifera*, which grows in the swampy forests of Formosa. The cylindrical core of pith is rolled on a hard flat surface against a knife, by which it is cut into thin sheets of a fine ivorylike texture. Dyed in various colours, rice paper is extensively used for the preparation of artificial flowers, while the white sheets are employed by native artists for water-colour drawings.

RICH, BARNABE (c. 1540–1617), English author and soldier, was a distant relative of Lord Chancellor Rich. He fought in the Low Countries, rising to the rank of captain, and afterward served in Ireland. He shared in the colonization of Ulster, and spent the latter part of his life near Dublin. In the intervals of his campaigns he produced many pamphlets on political questions and romances.

He died on Nov. 10, 1617. His best-known work is *Riche his Farewell to Militarie Profession conteining verie Pleasaunt discourses fit for a peaceable tyme* (1581). Of the eight stories contained in it, five, he says, "are forged only for delight, neither credible to be believed, nor hurtful to be perused." The rest are translations from the Italian. Among his euphuistic tales are *The Strange and Wonderful Adventures of Don Simonides* (1581), with its sequel (1584); and *The Adventures of Brusanus, prince of Hungaria* (1592).

His authenticated works number 24. His works on Ireland include *Allarme to England* (1578); *A New Description of Ireland* (1610); and *The Irish Hubbub, or the English Hue and Crie* (1617), in which he also inveighs against the use of tobacco.

See "Introduction" to the Shakespeare Society's reprint of *Riche his Farewell* (1846); P. Cunningham's "Introduction" to Rich's *Honesty of this Age* (reprinted for the Percy Society, 1844); and the life by S. Lee in the *Dict. Nat. Biog.*

RICH, JOHN (1682?–1761), English theatre manager and actor, made history in both capacities. He was a manager by inheritance, receiving a half-share in Lincoln's Inn Fields theatre from his father, Christopher Rich (d. 1714), and after running this house successfully for 18 years he founded Covent Garden theatre. At both he staged entertainments of a new type based on Italian foundations, known as "pantomime," in which, from 1717 till the year before his death, he played Harlequin (under his stage name of Lun). He has thus a claim to be the inventor of the harlequinade of English pantomime tradition. David Garrick paid tribute, after Rich's death, to the matchless expressiveness of his miming.

Rich has another special claim to be remembered. Some time in 1727 he was offered John Gay's Newgate pastoral *The Beggar's Opera*, which Drury Lane had refused. Rich, though notoriously not an educated man and indeed illiterate, nevertheless appreciated Gay's satire and produced the play on Jan. 29, 1728, at Lincoln's Inn Fields theatre. It had the longest run then known of 62 performances, and, as was said at the time, "made Gay rich and Rich gay."

(W. A. Dn.)

RICH, PENELOPE, Lady (*c.* 1562–1607), the Stella of Sir Philip Sidney's *Astrophel and Stella,* was the daughter of Walter Devereux, 1st Earl of Essex. She was a child of fourteen when Sir Philip Sidney accompanied the queen on a visit to Lady Essex in 1576, on her way from Kenilworth, and must have been frequently thrown into the society of Sidney, in consequence of the many ties between the two families. Essex died at Dublin in Sept. 1576. He had sent a message to Philip Sidney from his deathbed expressing his desire that he should marry his daughter, and later his secretary wrote to the young man's father, Sir Henry Sidney, in words which seem to point to the existence of a definite understanding. But her relative and guardian, Henry Hastings, earl of Huntingdon, secured Burghley's assent in March 1581 for her marriage with Robert Rich, 3rd Baron Rich. Penelope is said to have protested in vain against the alliance with Rich, who is represented as a rough and overbearing husband. The evidence against him is, however, chiefly derived from sources as interested as Sir Philip Sidney's violent denunciation in the twenty-fourth sonnet of *Astrophel and Stella,* "Rich fooles there be whose base and filthy hart." Sidney's serious love for Penelope appears to date from her marriage with Rich. The eighth song of *Astrophel and Stella* narrates her refusal to accept him as a lover.

Lady Rich was the mother of six children by her husband when she contracted in 1595 an open liaison with Charles Blount, 8th Lord Mountjoy, to whom she had long been attached. Rich obtained a legal separation in 1601, and Mountjoy acknowledged her five children born after 1595. Mountjoy was created earl of Devonshire on the accession of James I, and Lady Rich was in high favour at court. In 1605 they legitimized their connection by a marriage celebrated by William Laud, the earl's chaplain. This proceeding, carried out in defiance of canon law, was followed by their banishment from court. Devonshire died on April 3, 1606, and his wife within a year of that date.

See the editions of *Astrophel and Stella* by A. B. Grosart, E. Arber and A. W. Pollard; also the various lives of Sir Philip Sidney, and Mrs. Aubrey Richardson's *Famous Ladies of the English Court* (London, 1899). *See* also references under SIDNEY.

RICH, RICHARD, 1ST BARON RICH (*c.* 1496–1567), lord chancellor of England, was born in the parish of St. Lawrence Jewry, London. His great grandfather, a mercer, had been sheriff of London. Richard, a lawyer of the Middle Temple and M.P. for Colchester (1529), held various minor offices before becoming solicitor general in 1533. He took part in the trials of Sir Thomas More and Bishop Fisher and was one of Thomas Cromwell's agents in the dissolution of the monasteries, himself obtaining large grants of monastic property. In 1536 he was M.P. for Essex and speaker of the house of commons. That year also he was knighted and became the first chancellor of the newly established court of augmentations. By Aug. 1540 he was a privy councillor. He was one of the executors of Henry VIII's will, was created Baron Rich in Feb. 1547, and succeeded the earl of Southampton as lord chancellor in October. In Oct. 1549 he joined the earl of Warwick and Southampton in overthrowing the duke of Somerset, the Protector, over whose trial he presided. He resigned the lord chancellorship, on grounds of ill health, in Dec. 1551, at the time of the final breach between Warwick (now duke of Northumberland) and Somerset. Like other councillors, he had to subscribe Edward VI's settlement of the succession on Northumberland's daughter-in-law, Lady Jane Grey, but after Edward VI's death he soon declared for Mary Tudor, whose religious policy he now supported, although henceforward he did not take a prominent part in public affairs. A "civil servant" rather than a politician he had never been an heroic or a very attractive figure. He died at Rochford, Essex, on June 12, 1567, and was buried in Felsted church.   (R. B. Wm.)

RICH, RICHARD (*fl.* 1610), English soldier and adventurer, the author of *Newes From Virginia,* sailed from England on June 2, 1609, for Virginia, with Capt. Christopher Newport and the three commissioners entrusted with the foundation of the new colony.

In his verse pamphlet he relates the adventures undergone by the expedition, and describes the resources of the new country with the advantages offered to colonists. The only known copy of this tract, dated 1610, is in the Huth library. A reprint edited by J. O. Halliwell-Phillips appeared in 1865.

RICHARD, ST., of Wyche (*c.* 1197–1253), English saint and bishop, was named after his birthplace, Droitwich in Worcestershire. Educated at Oxford, he soon began to teach in the university, of which he became chancellor, probably after he had studied in Paris and in Bologna. About 1235 he became chancellor of the diocese of Canterbury under Archbishop Edmund Rich, and he was with the archbishop during his exile in France. Having returned to England some time after Edmund's death in 1240 he became vicar of Deal and chancellor of Canterbury for the second time. In 1244 he was elected bishop of Chichester, being consecrated at Lyons by Pope Innocent IV. in March 1245, although Henry III. refused to give him the temporalities of the see, the king favouring the candidature of Robert Passelewe (d. 1252). In 1246, however, Richard obtained the temporalities. He died at Dover in April 1253. It was generally believed that miracles were wrought at his tomb in Chichester cathedral, which was long a popular place of pilgrimage, and in 1262 he was canonized at Viterbo by Pope Urban IV.

His life by his confessor, Ralph Bocking, is published in the *Acta Sanctorum* of the Bollandists, with a later life by John Capgrave.

RICHARD (d. 1184), archbishop of Canterbury, was a Norman, who became a monk at Canterbury, where he acted as chaplain to Archbishop Theobald and was a colleague of Thomas Becket. In 1173, more than two years after the murder of Becket, it was decided to fill the vacant archbishopric of Canterbury; there were two candidates, Richard, at that time prior of St. Martin's, Dover, and Odo, prior of Canterbury, and in June Richard was chosen, although Odo was the nominee of the monks. Objections were raised against this election both in England and in Rome, but in April 1174 the new archbishop was consecrated at Anagui by Pope Alexander III., and he returned to England towards the close of the year. The ten years during which Richard was archbishop were disturbed by disputes over the respective rights of the sees of Canterbury and York. Richard died at Rochester on Feb. 16, 1184, and was buried in his cathedral.

See the article by W. Hunt in the *Dict. Nat. Biog.* vol. xlviii. (1896); and W. F. Hook, *Lives of the Archbishops of Canterbury.*

RICHARD I. (1157–1199), king of England, nicknamed "Coeur de Lion" and "Yea and Nay," was the third son of Henry II. by Eleanor of Aquitaine. Born in Sept. 1157, he received at the age of 11 the duchy of Aquitaine, and was formally installed in 1172. In his new position he was allowed, probably from regard to Aquitanian susceptibilities, to govern with an independence which was studiously denied to his brothers in their shares of the Angevin inheritance. Yet in 1173 Richard joined with the young Henry and Geoffrey of Brittany in their rebellion; Aquitaine was twice invaded by the old king before the unruly youth would make submission. Richard was soon pardoned and reinstated in his duchy, where he distinguished himself by crushing a formidable revolt (1175) and exacting homage from the count of Toulouse. In a short time he was so powerful that his elder brother Henry became alarmed and demanded, as heir-apparent, that Richard should do him homage for Aquitaine. Richard having scornfully rejected the demand, a fratricidal war ensued; the young Henry invaded Aquitaine and attracted to his standard many of Richard's vassals, who were exasperated by the iron rule of the duke. Henry II. marched to Richard's aid; but the war ended abruptly with the death of the elder prince (1183).

Richard, being now the heir to England and Normandy, was invited to renounce Aquitaine in favour of Prince John. The proposal led to a new civil war; and, although a temporary compromise was arranged, Richard soon sought the help of Philip Augustus, to whom he did homage for all the continental possessions in the actual presence of his father (Conference of Bonmoulins, Nov. 18, 1188). In the struggle which ensued the old king was overpowered, chased ignominiously from Le Mans to Angers, and forced to buy peace by conceding all that was demanded of him; in particular the immediate recognition of **Richard** as his successor.

But the death of Henry II. (1189) at once dissolved the friendship between Richard and Philip. Not only did Richard continue the continental policy of his father, but he also refused to fulfil his contract with Philip's sister, Alais, to whom he had been betrothed at the age of three. An open breach was only delayed by the desire of both kings to fulfil the crusading vows which they had recently taken. Richard, in particular, sacrificed all other interests to this scheme, and raised the necessary funds by the most reckless methods. He put up for auction the highest offices and honours; even remitting to William the Lion of Scotland, for a sum of 15,000 marks, the humiliating obligations which Henry II. had imposed at the Treaty of Falaise. By such expedients he raised and equipped a force which may be estimated at 4,000 men-at-arms and as many foot-soldiers, with a fleet of 100 transports (1191).

Richard did not return to his dominions until 1194. But his stay in Palestine was limited to 16 months. On the outward journey he wintered in Sicily, where he employed himself in quarrelling with Philip and in exacting satisfaction from the usurper Tancred for the dower of his widowed sister, Queen Joanna, and for his own share in the inheritance of William the Good. Leaving Messina in March 1191, he interrupted his voyage to conquer Cyprus, and only joined the Christian besiegers of Acre in June. The reduction of that stronghold was largely due to his energy and skill. But his arrogance gave much offence. After the fall of Acre he inflicted a gross insult upon Leopold of Austria; and his relations with Philip were so strained that the latter seized the first pretext for returning to France, and entered into negotiations with Prince John (see JOHN, king of England) for the partition of Richard's realm.

Richard also threw himself into the disputes respecting the crown of Jerusalem, and supported Guy of Lusignan against Conrad of Montferrat with so much heat that he incurred grave, though unfounded, suspicions of complicity when Conrad was assassinated by emissaries of the Old Man of the Mountain. None the less Richard, whom even the French crusaders accepted as their leader, upheld the failing cause of the Frankish Christians with valour and tenacity. He won a brilliant victory over the forces of Saladin at Arsuf (1191), and twice led the Christian host within a few miles of Jerusalem. But the dissensions of the native Franks and the crusaders made it hopeless to continue the struggle; and Richard was alarmed by the news which reached him of John's intrigues in England and Normandy. Hastily patching up a truce with Saladin, under which the Christians kept the coast-towns and received free access to the Holy Sepulchre, Richard started on his return (Oct. 9, 1192).

His voyage was delayed by storms, and he appears to have been perplexed as to the safest route. The natural route overland through Marseilles and Toulouse was held by his enemies; that through the empire from the head of the Adriatic was little safer, since Leopold of Austria was on the watch for him. Having adopted the second of these alternatives, he was captured at Vienna in a mean disguise (Dec. 20, 1192) and strictly confined in the duke's castle of Dürenstein on the Danube. His mishap was soon known to England, but the regents were for some weeks uncertain of his whereabouts. This is the foundation for the tale of his discovery by the faithful minstrel Blondel, which first occurs in a French romantic chronicle of the next century. Early in 1193 Leopold surrendered his prize, under compulsion, to the emperor Henry VI., who was aggrieved both by the support which the Plantagenets had given to the family of Henry the Lion and also by Richard's recognition of Tancred in Sicily. Although the detention of a crusader was contrary to public law, Richard was compelled to purchase his release by the payment of a heavy ransom and by doing homage to the emperor for England. The ransom demanded was 150,000 marks; though it was never discharged in full, the resources of England were taxed to the utmost for the first instalments; and to this occasion we may trace the beginning of secular taxation levied on movable property.

Richard reappeared in England in March 1194; but his stay lasted only a few weeks, and the remainder of his reign was entirely devoted to his continental interests. He left England to be governed by Hubert Walter (q.v.), and his personal authority was seldom asserted except by demands for new subsidies. The rule of the Plantagenets was still popular in Normandy and Aquitaine; but these provinces were unable or unwilling to pay for their own defence. Though Richard proved himself consistently the superior of Philip in the field, the difficulty of raising and paying forces to resist the French increased year by year. Richard could only stand on the defensive; the keynote of his later policy is given by the building of the famous Château Gaillard at Les Andelys (1196) to protect the lower courses of the Seine against invasion from the side of France. He did not live to see the futility of such bulwarks. In 1199 a claim to treasure-trove embroiled him with the viscount of Limoges. He harried the Limousin and laid siege to the castle of Châlus; while directing an assault he was wounded in the shoulder by a crossbow bolt, and, the wound mortifying from unskilful treatment or his own want of care, he died on April 6, 1199. He was buried by his own desire at his father's feet in the church of Fontevrault. Here his effigy may still be seen[1]. Though contemporary, it does not altogether agree with the portraits on his Great Seal, which give the impression of greater strength and even of cruelty. The Fontevrault bust is no doubt idealized.

The most accomplished and versatile representative of his gifted family, Richard was, in his lifetime and long afterwards, a favourite hero with troubadours and romancers. This was natural, as he belonged to their brotherhood and himself wrote lyrics of no mean quality. But his history shows that he by no means embodied the current ideal of chivalrous excellence. His memory is stained by one act of needless cruelty, the massacre of over two thousand Saracen prisoners at Acre; and his fury, when thwarted or humbled, was ungovernable. A brave soldier, an experienced and astute general, he was never happier than when engaged in war. As a ruler he was equally profuse and rapacious. Not one useful measure can be placed to his credit; and it was by a fortunate accident that he found, in Hubert Walter, an administrator who had the skill to mitigate the consequences of a reckless fiscal policy. Richard's wife was Berengaria, daughter of Sancho VI., king of Navarre, whom he married in Cyprus in May 1191. She was with the king at Acre later in the same year, and during his imprisonment passed her time in Sicily, in Rome and in France. Husband and wife met again in 1195, and the queen long survived the king, residing chiefly at Le Mans. She died soon after 1230. Berengaria founded a Cistercian monastery at Espau.

BIBLIOGRAPHY.—The more important of the general chronicles are: the Gesta Henrici Secundi, ascribed to Benedict of Peterborough (Rolls Series, 2 vols., 1867); the Chronica of Roger of Hoveden (Rolls Series, 4 vols., 1868–71); the Chronica of Gervase of Canterbury (Rolls Series, 1879); the Imagines Historiarum of Ralph of Diceto (Rolls Series, 2 vols., 1876); the Historia Rerum Anglicarum of William of Newburgh (in Chronicles of the Reigns of Stephen, etc., Rolls Series, 2 vols., 1884–85); the De rebus gestis Ricardi Primi of Richard of Devizes (in Chronicles of the Reigns of Stephen, etc., vol. iii., Rolls Series, 1886); the Chronicon Anglicanum of Ralph of Coggeshall (Rolls Series, 1875); the Flores Historiarum of Roger of Wendover (Rolls Series, 3 vols., 1886–89); the Gesta Philippi Augusti of Rigord (Société de l'histoire de France, Paris, 1882) and of Guillaume le Breton (op. cit.). A detailed narrative of Richard's crusade is given in L'Estoire de la guerre sainte, a rhyming French chronicle by the minstrel Ambroise (ed. Gaston Paris, Paris, 1897), and in the Latin prose version known as the Itinerarium O. Peregrinorum et gesta Regis Ricardi; this last, with some valuable historical letters, is printed in W. Stubbs's Chronicles and Memorials of the Reign of Richard I. (Rolls Series, 2 vols., 1864–65). Of modern works the following are useful: W. Stubbs's preface to vols. iii. and iv. of Hoveden; the same author's Constitutional History of England, vol. i. (Oxford, 1897); Miss K. Norgate's England under the Angevin Kings, vol. ii. (1887) and Richard the Lion Heart (1924); Sir J. H. Ramsay's Angevin Empire (1903); R. Röhricht's Geschichte des Königreichs Jerusalem (1898); W. B. Stevenson's Crusaders in the East (Cambridge, 1907); A. Cartellieri's Philipp II. August (Leipzig, 1899, etc.). (H. W. C. D.)

RICHARD II. (1367–1400), king of England, younger son of Edward the Black Prince by Joan "the Fair Maid of Kent," was born at Bordeaux on Jan. 6, 1367. He was brought to Eng-

[1] The remains of Richard, together with those of Henry II. and his queen Eleanor, were removed in the 17th century from their tombs to another part of the church. They were rediscovered in 1910 during the restoration of the abbey undertaken by the French Government.

land in 1371, and after his father's death was, on the petition of the Commons in parliament, created prince of Wales on Nov. 20, 1376. When Edward III. died, on June 21, 1377, Richard became king. Popular opinion had credited John of Gaunt with designs on the throne. This was not justified; nevertheless, the rivalry of the boy-king's uncles added another to the troubles due to the war, the Black Death and the prospect of a long minority. At first the government was conducted by a council appointed by parliament. The council was honest, but the difficulties of the situation were too great. The ill-considered poll-tax of 1381 was the occasion, though not the real cause, of the Peasants' Revolt in that year. The ministers were quite unequal to the crisis, and when Wat Tyler and his followers got possession of London, Richard showed a precocious tact and confidence in handling it. He met and temporized with the rebels on June 13 at Mile End, and again next day at Smithfield; and with courageous presence of mind, he saved the situation when Tyler was killed, by calling on them to take him for their leader.

From this time Richard began to assert himself. His chief ministers, appointed by parliament in 1382, were the earl of Arundel and Michael de la Pole. Arundel Richard disliked, and dismissed next year, when he began his personal government. Pole, whom he retained as chancellor and made earl of Suffolk, was a well-chosen adviser. But others, and especially his youthful favourite Robert de Vere, promoted to be marquess of Dublin and duke of Ireland, were less worthy. Further, Richard made his own position difficult by lavish extravagance and by outbursts of temper. He chafed under the restraint of his relatives, and therefore encouraged John of Gaunt in his Spanish enterprise.

Thereupon, Thomas of Gloucester, supported by Arundel, attacked his nephew's ministers in the parliament of 1386, and by open hints at deposition forced Richard to submit to a council of control. When Richard, with the aid of his friends and by the advice of subservient judges, planned a reversal of the parliament, Gloucester, at the head of the so-called lords appellant, anticipated him. Richard had been premature and ill-advised. Gloucester had the advantage of posing as the head of the constitutional party. The king's friends were driven into exile or executed, and he himself forced to submit to the loss of all real power (May 1388). Richard changed his methods, and when the lords appellant had lost credit, asserted himself constitutionally by dismissing Gloucester's supporters from office, and appointing in their place well-approved men like William of Wykeham. In the next parliament of 1390 the king showed himself ready to meet and conciliate his subjects. The simultaneous return of John of Gaunt from Spain put a check on Gloucester's ambition. For seven years Richard ruled constitutionally and on the whole well.

In Jan. 1383 Richard had married Anne of Bohemia (1366–1394), daughter of the emperor Charles IV. Her death on June 7, 1394 was a great shock to Richard, and incidentally had important consequences. Richard sought distraction by an expedition to Ireland, the first visit of an English king for more than two centuries. In his policy there he showed a wise statesmanship. At the same time he was negotiating for a permanent peace with France, which was finally arranged in Oct. 1396 to include his own marriage with Isabella, daughter of Charles VI., a child of seven. Gloucester criticized the peace openly, and there was some show of opposition in the parliament of Feb. 1397.

Period of Absolute Monarchy.—But there was nothing to foreshadow the sudden stroke by which in July Richard arrested Gloucester and his chief supporters, the earls of Arundel and Warwick. The others of the five lords appellant, Henry of Boling-broke, afterwards King Henry IV., and the earl of Nottingham, now supported the king. Richard's action was apparently in deliberate revenge for the events of 1387–88. Gloucester, after a forced confession, died in prison at Calais, smothered by his nephew's orders. Arundel, in a packed parliament, was condemned and executed; his brother Thomas archbishop of Canterbury was exiled. The king's friends, including Nottingham and Bolingbroke, made dukes of Norfolk and Hereford, were all promoted in title and estate. Richard himself was rewarded for ten years' patience by the possession of absolute power. He might perhaps have

established it if he could have exercised it with moderation. But he declared that the laws of England were in his mouth, and supported his court in wanton luxury by arbitrary methods of taxation. By the exile of Norfolk and Hereford in Sept. 1398 he seemed to have removed the last persons he need fear. He was so confident that in May 1399 he paid a second visit to Ireland, taking with him all his most trusted adherents.

Rebellion and Deposition.—Thus when Henry landed at Ravenspur in July he found only half-hearted opposition, and when Richard himself returned it was too late. Ultimately Richard surrendered to Henry at Flint on Aug. 19, promising to abdicate if his life was spared. He was taken to London riding behind his rival with indignity. On Sept. 30, he signed in the Tower a deed of abdication, wherein he owned himself insufficient and useless, reading it first aloud with a cheerful mien and ending with a request that his cousin would be good lord to him. The parliament ordered that Richard should be kept close prisoner, and he was sent secretly to Pontefract. There in Feb. 1400 he died: no doubt of the rigour of his winter imprisonment, rather than by actual murder as alleged in the story adopted by Shakespeare. The mystery of Richard's death led to rumours that he had escaped, and an impostor pretending to be Richard lived during many years under the protection of the Scottish government. But no doubt it was the real Richard who was buried without state in 1400 at King's Langley, and honourably reinterred by Henry V. at Westminster in 1413.

Richard II. is a character of strange contradictions. It is difficult to reconcile the precocious boy of 1381 with the wayward and passionate youth of the next few years. Even if it be supposed that he dissembled his real opinions during the period of his constitutional rule, it is impossible to believe that the apparent indifference which he showed in his fall was the mere acting of a part. His violent outbursts of passion perhaps give the best clue to a mercurial and impulsive nature, easily elated and depressed. He had real ability, and in his Irish policy, and in the preference which he gave to it over continental adventure, showed a statesmanship in advance of his time. But this, in spite of his lofty theory of kingship, makes it all the more difficult to explain his extravagant bearing in his prosperity. In appearance Richard was tall and handsome, if effeminate. He had some literary tastes, which were shown in fitful patronage of Chaucer, Gower and Froissart. Richard's second queen, Isabella (1389–1409), was born in Paris on Nov. 9, 1389, and was married to the English king at Calais in October, or November, 1396, but on account of the bride's youth the marriage was never consummated.

When Richard lost his crown in 1399 Isabella was captured by Henry IV.'s partisans and sent to Sonning, near Reading, while her father, Charles VI., asked in vain for the restoration of his daughter and of her dowry. In 1401 she was allowed to return to France; in 1406 she became the wife of the poet, Charles, duke of Orleans, and she died on Sept. 13, 1409.

BIBLIOGRAPHY.—The best contemporary authorities are the *Chronicon Angliae* down to 1388, Walsingham's *Historia Anglicana*, the *Annales Ricardi II.*, Knighton's *Chronicle* (all these in the Rolls Series), the *Vita Ricardi II.* by a Monk of Evesham (ed. T. Hearne), and the *Chronique de la traison et mort* (English Hist. Soc.). Froissart wrote from some personal knowledge. A metrical account of Richard's fall, probably written by a French knight called Creton, is printed in *Archaeologia*, xx. The chief collections of documents are the *Rolls of Parliament* and the *Calendar of Patent Rolls*. H. A. Wallon's *Richard II.* (Paris, 1864) is the fullest life, though now somewhat out of date. For other modern accounts see W. Stubbs, *Constitutional History*, and C. W. C. Oman, *The Political History of England*, vol. iv., and *The Great Revolt of 1381*. (C. L. K.)

RICHARD III. (1452–1485), king of England, youngest son of Richard, duke of York, by Cicely Neville, was born at Fotheringhay on Oct. 2, 1452. After the second battle of St. Albans in Feb. 1461, his mother sent him with his brother George for safety to Utrecht. They returned in April, and at the coronation of Edward IV. Richard was created duke of Gloucester. As a mere child he had no importance till 1469–70, when he supported his brother against Warwick, shared his exile and took part in his triumphant return. He distinguished himself at Barnet and Tewkesbury; according to the Lancastrian story, after the latter battle he murdered the young Edward of Wales in cold blood; this is discredited by the authority of Warkworth (*Chronicle*, p. 18); but Richard may have had a share in Edward's death during the fighting. He cannot be so fully cleared of complicity in the murder of Henry VI., which probably took place at the Tower on the night of May 22, when Richard was certainly present there.

Richard shared to the full in his brother's prosperity. He had large grants of lands and office, and by marrying Anne (1456–1485), the younger daughter of Warwick, secured a share in the Neville inheritance. This was distasteful to George, duke of Clarence, who was already married to the elder sister, Isabel. The rivalry of the two brothers caused a quarrel which was never appeased. Richard does not, however, seem to have been directly responsible for the death of Clarence in 1478; Sir Thomas More, who is a hostile witness, says that he resisted it openly "howbeit somewhat (as men deemed) more faintly than he that were heartily minded to his wealth." Richard's share of the Neville inheritance was chiefly in the north, and he resided usually at Middleham in Yorkshire. In May 1480 he was made the king's lieutenant-general in the north, and in 1482 commanded a successful invasion of Scotland. His administration was good, and brought him well-deserved popularity.

Protectorate.—On Edward's death he was kept informed of events in London by William, Lord Hastings, who shared his dislike of the Woodville influence. On April 29, 1483, supported by the duke of Buckingham, he intercepted his nephew at Stony Stratford and arrested Lord Rivers and Richard Grey, the little king's half-brother. It was in Richard's charge that Edward was brought to London on May 4. Richard was recognized as protector, the Woodville faction was overthrown, and the queen with her younger children took sanctuary at Westminster. For the time the government was carried on in Edward's name, and June 22 was appointed for his coronation. Richard was nevertheless gathering forces and concerting with his friends. In the council there was a party, of whom Hastings and Bishop Morton were the chief, which was loyal to the boy-king. On June 13 came the famous scene when Richard appeared suddenly in the council baring his withered arm and accusing Jane Shore and the queen of sorcery; Hastings, Morton and Stanley were arrested and the first-named at once beheaded. A few days later, probably on June 25, Rivers and Grey were executed at Pontefract. On June 22 Dr. Shaw was put up to preach at Paul's Cross against the legitimacy of the children of Edward IV. On the 25th a sort of parliament was convened at which Edward's marriage was declared invalid on the ground of his precontract with Eleanor Talbot, and Richard rightful king. Richard, who was not present, accepted the crown with feigned reluctance, and from the following day began his formal reign.

Usurpation of the Throne.—On July 6, Richard was crowned at Westminster, and immediately afterwards made a royal progress through the Midlands, on which he was well received. But in spite of its apparent success the usurpation was not popular. Richard's position could not be secure whilst his nephews lived. There seems to be no reasonable doubt that early in August Edward V. and his brother Richard (whom Elizabeth Woodville had been forced to surrender) were murdered by their uncle's orders in the Tower. Attempts have been made to clear Richard's memory. But the report of the princes' death was believed in England at the time, "for which cause king Richard lost the hearts of the people" (*Chronicles of London*, 191), and it was referred to as a definite fact before the French states-general in January 1484. The general, if vague, dissatisfaction found its expression in Buckingham's rebellion.

Richard, however, was fortunate, and the movement collapsed. He met his only parliament in Jan. 1484 with some show of triumph, and deserves credit for the wise intent of its legislation. He could not, however, stay the undercurrent of disaffection, and his ministers, Lovell and Catesby, were unpopular. His position was weakened by the death of his only legitimate son in April 1484. His queen died also a year later (March 16, 1485), and public opinion was scandalized by the rumour that Richard intended to marry his own niece, Elizabeth of York. Thus the feeling in favour of his rival Henry Tudor strengthened. Henry landed at Milford Haven on Aug. 7, 1485, and it was with dark forebodings that Richard met him at Bosworth on the 22nd. The defection of the Stanleys decided the day. Richard was killed fighting, courageous at all events. After the battle his body was carried to Leicester, trussed across a horse's back, and buried without honour in the church of the Greyfriars.

Richard was not the villain that his enemies depicted. He had good qualities, both as a man and a ruler, and showed a sound judgment of political needs. Still it is impossible to acquit him of the crime, the popular belief in which was the chief cause of his ruin. He was a typical man in an age of strange contradictions of character, of culture combined with cruelty, and of an emotional temper that was capable of high ends, though unscrupulous of means. Tradition represents Richard as deformed. It seems clear that he had some physical defect, though not so great as has been alleged. Extant portraits show an intellectual face characteristic of the early Renaissance, but do not indicate any deformity.

BIBLIOGRAPHY.—The chief original authorities are Sir Thomas More's *History of Richard III.*, based on information supplied by Archbishop Morton, and therefore to be accepted with caution; the more trustworthy *Continuation of the Croyland Chronicle* in Fulman's *Scriptores*, the *History* of Polydore Vergil, written in a Tudor spirit; the *Chronicle of London* (ed. C. L. Kingsford, 1905), and its biased expansion in Fabyan's *Chronicle*. See also *Letters and Papers Illustrative of the Reigns of Richard III. and Henry VII.*, ed. J. Gairdner, in Rolls Series. Of later accounts those in Stow's *Annales* (preserving some oral tradition) and George Buck's *Richard III.* ap. Kennet *History of England* deserve mention. Horace Walpole attempted a vindication in his *Historic Doubts* (1768). The best modern account is James Gairdner's *Life of Richard III.* (2nd ed., 1898). The latest and fullest defence is given in Sir Clements Markham's *Richard III., His Life and Character* (1906); G. B. Churchill's *Richard the Third up to Shakespeare* (*Palaestra* x., 1900) is a valuable digest of material.   (C. L. K.)

RICHARD, earl of Cornwall and king of the Romans (1209–1272), was the second son of the English king John by Isabella of Angoulême. Born in 1209, Richard was the junior of his brother, Henry III., by fifteen months; he was educated in England and received the earldom of Cornwall in 1225. From this date to his death he was a prominent figure on the political stage. In the years 1225–27 he acted as governor of Gascony; between 1227 and 1238, owing to quarrels with his brother and dislike of the foreign favourites, he attached himself to the baronial opposition and bade fair to become a popular hero. But in 1240 he took the command of a crusade in order to escape from the troubled atmosphere of English politics. He was formally reconciled with Henry before his departure; and their amity was cemented on his return by his marriage with Sancha of Provence, the sister of Henry's queen (1243). In 1257 a bare majority of the German electors nominated Richard as king of the Romans, and he accepted their offer at Henry's desire.

In the years 1257–68 Richard paid four visits to Germany. He obtained recognition in the Rhineland, which was closely connected with England by trade relations. Otherwise, however, he was unsuccessful in securing German support. In the English troubles of the same period he endeavoured to act as a mediator. On the outbreak of civil war in 1264 he took his brother's side, and his capture in a windmill outside Lewes, after the defeat of the royalist army, is commemorated in the earliest of English vernacular satires; he remained a prisoner till the fall of Montfort. But after Evesham he exerted himself, not without success, to obtain reasonable terms for those who had suffered from the vengeance of the royalist party. He died on April 2, 1272. His end is said to have been hastened by grief for his eldest son, Henry of Almain, who had been murdered in the previous year by the sons of Simon de Montfort at Viterbo.

Authorities.—The original sources and general works of reference are the same as for the reign of Henry III. G. C. Gebauer's *Leben und Thaten Herrn Richards von Cornwall* (Leipzig, 1744), H. Koch's *Richard von Cornwall, 1209–1257* (Strassburg, 1888), and A. Busson's *Doppelwahl des Jahres, 1257* (Münster, 1866) are useful monographs.   (H. W. C. D.)

RICHARD OF CIRENCESTER (*c.* 1335–*c.* 1401), historical writer, was a member of the Benedictine abbey at Westminster, and his name ("Circestre") first appears on the chamberlain's list of the monks of that foundation drawn up in the year 1355. In the year 1391 he obtained a licence from the abbot to go to Rome, and in this the abbot gives his testimony to Richard's perfect and sincere observance of religion for some 30 years. In 1400 Richard was in the infirmary of the abbey, where he died in the following year. His only known extant work is *Speculum Historiale de Gestis Regum Angliae, 447–1066.* The ms. of this is in the university library at Cambridge, and has been edited for the Rolls Series (No. 30) by Professor J. E. B. Mayor (2 vols., 1863–69).

RICHARD OF DEVIZES (*fl.* 1191), English chronicler, was a monk of St. Swithin's house at Winchester. The *Chronicon de rebus gestis Ricardi Primi,* by which Richard of Devizes is chiefly known, is an account of events in England and the Holy Land during the third crusade.

See the editions of the Chronicon de rebus gestis Ricardi Primi by J. Stevenson (Eng. His. Soc., 1838) and by R. Howlett in Chronicles of the Reigns of Stephen, Henry II. and Richard I., vol. iii. (Rolls Series, 1886); the Annales de Wintonia in H. R. Luard's Annales Monastici, vol. ii. (Rolls Series, 1864–69).

RICHARD OF HEXHAM (*fl.* 1141), English chronicler, became prior of Hexham about 1141, and died between 1163 and 1178. He wrote *Brevis Annotatio,* a short history of the church of Hexham from 674 to 1138, for which he borrowed from Bede, Eddius and Simeon of Durham. This is published by J. Raine in *The Priory of Hexham, its Chroniclers, Endowments and Annals* (Durham, 1864–65). More important is his *Historia de gestis regis Stephani et de bello Standardii,* valuable for the history of the north of England during the earlier part of the reign of Stephen, and for the battle of the Standard. It has been edited for the Rolls Series by R. Howlett in the *Chronicles of the Reigns of Stephen, Henry II. and Richard I.,* vol. iii. (1886); and has been translated by J. Stevenson in the *Church Historians of England,* vol. iv. (1856).

RICHARD OF ILCHESTER or OF TOCLYVE (d. 1188), English statesman and prelate, was born in the diocese of Bath, where he obtained preferment. Early in the reign of Henry II., however, he is found acting as a clerk in the king's court, probably under Thomas Becket, and he was one of the officials who assisted Henry in carrying out his great judicial and financial reforms. In 1162, or 1163, he was appointed archdeacon of Poitiers, but he passed most of his time in England, although in the next two or three years he visited Pope Alexander III. and the Emperor Frederick I. in the interests of the English king, who was then engaged in his struggle with Becket. For promising to support Frederick he was excommunicated by Becket in 1166. In May 1173 he was elected bishop of Winchester, being consecrated at Canterbury in October 1174. In 1176 he was appointed justiciar and seneschal of Normandy, and was given full control of all the royal business in the duchy. He died on Dec. 21 or 22, 1188, and was buried in Winchester cathedral.

See the article by Miss K. Norgate in the Dict. Nat. Biog., vol. xlviii. (1896); and W. R. W. Stephens and W. W. Capes, The Bishops of Winchester (1907).

RICHARD OF ST. VICTOR (d. 1173), theologian and mystic of the 12th century. Very little is known of his life; he was born in Scotland or in England, and went to Paris, where he entered the abbey of St. Victor and was a pupil of the great mystic, Hugh of St. Victor. He succeeded as prior of this house in 1162. The best known of Richard's writings are the mystical treatises: *De statu hominis interioris, De praeparatione animi ad contemplationem, De gratia contemplationis, De gradibus caritatis, De arca nuptica,* and his two works on the Trinity: *De trinitate libri sex, De tribus appropriatis personis in Trinitate.* According to him, six steps lead the soul to contemplation: (1) contemplation of visible and tangible objects; (2) study of the productions of nature and of art; (3) study of character; (4) study of souls and of spirits; (5) entrance to the mystical region which ends in (6) ecstasy.

His theory of the Trinity is chiefly based on the arguments of Anselm of Canterbury. The influence of neo-Platonic terminology, as well as of the works of the pseudo-Dionysius, can be clearly detected in his works. In the *Paradiso* Dante has placed Richard among the greatest teachers of the Church. His writings came into favour again in the 16th and 17th centuries, six editions of his works having been printed between 1506 and 1650.

BIBLIOGRAPHY.—*Oeuvres,* edited in the *Patrologia latina* by Migne, vol. cxcvi.; W. Kaulich, "Die Lehren des Hugo und Richard von St. Victor" (*Abhandlungen der K. böhmischen Gesellschaft der Wissenschaften*). V. Folge, vol. xiii. (2nd ed. Paris, 1905), p. 231 (Prague, 1864); P. C. F. Daunou, article in *Histoire littéraire de la France,* tome xiii. (Paris, 1869); G. Buonamici, *Riccardo da S. Vittore* (Alatri, 1899); J. Ebner, *Die Erkenntnislehre Richards von St. Viktor* (Beiträge z. Gesch. d. Phil. vol. 19, Münster, 1917); full bibliography in Überweg, *Gesch. d. Phil.,* Bd. 2 (1928).

RICHARDS, THEODORE WILLIAM (1868–1928), U.S. chemist, was born in Germantown, Pa., on Jan. 31, 1868. He graduated from Haverford college (S.B., 1885) and Harvard university (A.B., 1886; Ph.D., 1888); he also studied at Göttingen, Leipzig and the Dresden Technical university.

He was appointed assistant professor of chemistry at Harvard in 1894 and professor in 1901, and was made director of the Wolcott Gibbs memorial laboratory in 1912. He was best known for his researches on atomic weights which he began in 1883. He greatly improved the technique of gravimetric atomic weight determinations, introducing quartz apparatus, the bottling device and the nephelometer. The values of J. S. Stas had been regarded as standard, but about 1903, physicochemical measurements showed that some of his values were not as accurate as had been supposed. Richards and some of his students revised these figures, lowering the value of silver (Stas's standard) from 107.93 to 107.88. Investigations of the atomic weight of lead from different sources definitely proved the existence of isotopes. The results were generally accepted and "for his accurate determination of the atomic weight of a large number of elements," he received the Nobel prize in chemistry in 1914. He also gave much time to physicochemical investigation.

He died at Cambridge, Mass., on April 2, 1928.

BIBLIOGRAPHY.—G. P. Baxter, *Science* 68:333 (1928); H. Hartley, "Richards Memorial Lecture," *Journal Chemical Society* 133:1937 (1930); B. Harrow, *Eminent Chemists of Our Times* (1927).

(R. E. O.)

RICHARDSON, HENRY HOBSON (1838–1886), American architect, was born in the parish of St. James, La., on Sept. 29, 1838, of a rich family, his mother being a grand-daughter of the famous Dr. Priestley, the English dissenting refugee and man of science. He was graduated from Harvard university in 1859, and went immediately to Paris to study architecture, entering the École des Beaux-Arts. The Civil War, which broke out in the United States while he was in the school, prevented his return to Louisiana, and stripped his family of their possessions. Richardson provided for his own support by working in the offices of practising architects in Paris, till the fall of 1865. He then established himself in New York, where he soon made his way into practice as an architect. In 1878 he moved to Boston, designing there most of the work that made his reputation. He married in 1867 Miss Julia Gorham Hayden of Boston; he died there on April 27, 1886.

Richardson's career was short, and the number of his works was small indeed compared with the attention they attracted and the influence he left behind him. The most important and characteristic are: Trinity church and the so-called Brattle Square church, in Boston; the alterations in the State Capitol at Albany; the county buildings at Pittsburgh; town halls at Albany, Springfield and North Easton; town libraries at Woburn, North Easton, Quincy, Burlington and Malden; Sever hall and Austin hall at Harvard university; the Chamber of Commerce at Cincinnati. Trinity church, the Pittsburgh buildings and the Capitol at Albany were works of great importance, which have had a strong influence on men who followed him.

The best known book about Richardson is Mrs. Schuyler van Rensselaer's *H. H. Richardson and his Works* (Boston, 1888).

RICHARDSON, SIR OWEN WILLANS (1879–   ), English physicist, was born on April 26, 1879, at Dewsbury, Yorkshire. He was educated at Batley Grammar school and at Trinity college, Cambridge, where he became a fellow. He was professor of physics at Princeton university, 1906–13, and Wheatstone professor of physics at King's college, London, 1914–24. He was then appointed a Yarrow research professor by the Royal society and director of research in physics at King's college, a post he held until 1944 when he became emeritus professor of physics of the University of London. Richardson's best-known work was on the emission of electricity from hot bodies. He made this subject peculiarly his own and gave it the name "thermionics." Richardson was elected F.R.S. in 1913 and was knighted in 1939. He was awarded the Nobel prize for physics in 1928. He wrote the standard works: *The Electron Theory of Matter* (1914) and *The Emission of Electricity from Hot Bodies* (1916; 2nd ed. 1921).

RICHARDSON, SAMUEL (1689–1761), English novelist, was the son of a London joiner, who, for obscure reasons, probably connected with Monmouth's rebellion, had retired to Derbyshire, where, in 1689, Samuel was born. He was apprenticed at seventeen to an Aldersgate printer named John Wilde. Here he became successively compositor, corrector of the press, and printer on his own account; married his master's daughter according to programme; set up newspapers and books; dabbled a little in literature by compiling indexes and "honest dedications," and ultimately became Printer of the Journals of the House of Commons, Master of the Stationers' Company, and Law-Printer to the King. Like all well-to-do citizens, he had his city house of business and his "country box" in the suburbs; and, after a thoroughly "respectable" life, died on July 4, 1761, being buried in St. Bride's Church, Fleet Street, close to his shop (now demolished), No. 11 Salisbury Court.

The origin of *Pamela* dates back to a request from Rivington of St. Paul's Churchyard and Osborn of Paternoster Row, two book-selling friends who were aware of Richardson's epistolary gifts, to suggest that he should prepare a little model letter-writer for such "country readers" as "were unable to indite for themselves." The result was *Pamela; or Virtue Rewarded*. He completed it in a couple of months (Nov. 10, 1739 to Jan. 16, 1740). In Nov. 1740 it was issued by Messrs. Rivington and Osborn, who, a few weeks afterward (Jan. 1741), also published the model letter-writer under the title of *Letters written to and for Particular Friends, on the most Important Occasions*. Both books were anonymous. The letter-writer was noticed in the *Gentleman's Magazine* for January, which also contains a brief announcement as to *Pamela*, already rapidly making its way without waiting for the reviewers. A second edition, it was stated, was expected; and such was its popularity, that not to have read it was judged "as great a sign of want of curiosity as not to have seen the French and Italian dancers"—*i.e.*, Mme. Chateauneuf and the Fausans, who were then delighting the town. In February a second edition duly appeared, followed by a third in March and a fourth in May. At public gardens ladies held up the book to show they had got it; Dr. Benjamin Slocock of Southwark openly commended it from the pulpit; Pope praised it; and at Slough, when the heroine triumphed, the enraptured villagers rang the church bells for joy. The other volume of "familiar letters" consequently fell into the background in the estimation of its author, who, though it went into several editions during his lifetime, never acknowledged it.

Such a popularity, of course, was not without its drawbacks. That it would lead to *Anti-Pamelas*, censures of *Pamela* and all the spawn of pamphlets which spring round the track of a sudden success, was to be anticipated. One of the results to which its rather sickly morality gave rise was the *Joseph Andrews* (1742) of Henry Fielding (*q.v.*). But there are two other works prompted by *Pamela* which need brief notice here. One is the *Apology for the Life of Mrs. Shamela Andrews*, a clever and very gross piece of raillery which appeared in April 1741, and by which Fielding is supposed to have alluded to *Joseph Andrews*. The second noteworthy result of *Pamela* was *Pamela's Conduct in High Life* (Sept. 1741), a spurious sequel by John Kelly of the *Universal Spectator*. Richardson tried to prevent its appearance, and, having failed, set about two volumes of his own, which followed in December, and professed to depict his heroine "in her exalted condition." It attracted no permanent attention.

About 1744 we begin to hear something of the progress of Richardson's second and greatest novel, *Clarissa; or the History of a Young Lady*, usually miscalled *Clarissa Harlowe*. The first edition was in seven volumes, two of which came out in Nov. 1747, two more in April 1748 and the last three in December. Upon the title-page of this, of which the mission was as edifying as that of *Pamela*, its object was defined as showing the distresses that may attend the misconduct both of parents and children in relation to marriage. Virtue, in *Clarissa*, is not "rewarded," but hunted down and outraged. The chief drawbacks of *Clarissa* are its merciless prolixity (seven volumes, which cover only 11 months); the fact that (like *Pamela*) it is told by letters; and a certain haunting and uneasy feeling that many of the heroine's obstacles are only molehills which should have been readily surmounted.

Between *Clarissa* and Richardson's next work appeared the *Tom Jones* of Fielding—a rival by no means welcome to the elder writer, although a rival who generously (and perhaps penitently) acknowledged *Clarissa's* rare merits.

> Pectus inaniter angit,
> irritat, mulcet, falsis terroribus implet,
> ut Magus

Fielding had written in the *Jacobite's Journal*. But even this could not console Richardson for the popularity of the "spurious brat" whom Fielding had made his hero, and his next effort was the depicting of a genuine fine gentleman—a task to which he was incited by a chorus of feminine worshippers. In the *History of Sir Charles Grandison*, "by the Editor of *Pamela* and *Clarissa*" (for he still preserved the fiction of anonymity), he essayed to draw a perfect model of manly character and conduct. In the pattern presented there is, however, too much buckram, too much ceremonial—in plain words, too much priggishness—to make him the desired exemplar of propriety *in excelsis*. Yet he is not entirely a failure, still less is he to be regarded as no more than "the condescending suit of clothes" by which Hazlitt unfairly defines Miss Burney's Lord Orville. When Richardson delineated Sir Charles Grandison he was at his best, and his experiences and opportunities for inventing such a character were infinitely greater than they had ever been before. And he lost nothing of his gift for portraying the other sex. Harriet Byron, Clementina della Porretta and even Charlotte Grandison, are no whit behind Clarissa and her friend Miss Howe. *Sir Charles Grandison*, in fine, is a far better book than *Pamela*.

Grandison was published in 1753, and by this time Richardson was sixty-four. Although the book was welcomed as warmly as it predecessors, he wrote no other novel, contenting himself instead with indexing his works, and compiling an anthology of the "maxims," "cautions" and "instructive sentiments" they contained. To these things, as a professed moralist, he had always attached the greatest importance. He continued to correspond relentlessly with a large circle of worshippers, mostly women, whose counsels and fertilizing sympathy had not a little contributed to the success of his last two books. He was a nervous, highly strung little man, intensely preoccupied with his health and his feelings, hungry for praise when he had once tasted it, and afterwards unable to exist without it; but apart from these things, well meaning, benevolent, honest, industrious and religious. Seven vast folio volumes of his correspondence with his lady friends, and with a few men of the Young and Aaron Hill type, are preserved in the Forster library at South Kensington. Parts of it only have been printed. There are several good portraits of him by Joseph Highmore, two of which are in the National Portrait Gallery.

Richardson is the father of the novel of sentimental analysis. As Sir Walter Scott has said, no one before had dived so deeply into the human heart. No one, moreover, had brought to the study of feminine character so much prolonged research, so much patience of observation, so much interested and indulgent apprehension, as this twittering little printer of Salisbury Court. That he did not more materially control the course of fiction in his own country was probably owing to the new direction which was given to that fiction by Fielding and Smollett, whose method, roughly speaking, was synthetic rather than analytic. Still, his influence is to be traced in Sterne and Henry Mackenzie, as well as in Miss Burney and Miss Austen, both of whom, it may be noted, at first adopted the epistolary form. But it was in France, where the sentimental soil was ready for the dressing, that the analytic process was most warmly welcomed. Extravagantly eulogized by the great critic, Diderot, modified with splendid variation by Rousseau, copied (unwillingly) by Voltaire, the vogue of Richardson was so great as to tempt French critics to seek his original in the *Marianne* of a contemporary analyst, Marivaux. As a matter of fact, though there is some unconscious consonance of manner, there is nothing whatever to show that the little-letter author of *Pamela,* who was also ignorant of French, had the slightest knowledge of Marivaux or *Marianne.* In Germany Richardson was even more popular than in France. Gellert, the fabulist, translated him; Wieland, Lessing, Hermes, all imitated him, and Coleridge detects him even in the *Robbers* of Schiller. What was stranger still, he returned to England again under another form. The French *comédie larmoyante,* to which he had given a fillip, crossed the channel as the sentimental comedy of Cumberland and Kelly, which, after a brief career of prosperity, received its death-blow at the hands of Goldsmith and Sheridan.

Richardson's novels were edited by Mangin (19 vols., 1811), and an edition in 12 vols. was published by Sotheran in 1883 with preface by Sir Leslie Stephen. A *Collection of the Moral and Instructive Sentiments,* etc., was published in 1755. A selection from Richardson's *Correspondence* was published by Mrs. A. L. Barbauld in 1804, in six volumes, with a valuable Memoir. Recent lives are by Miss Clara L. Thomson, 1900, and by Austin Dobson (" Men of Letters "), 1902. A convenient reprint of the novels, with copies of the old illustrations by Stothard, Edward Burney and the rest, and an introduction by Mrs. E. M. M. McKenna, was issued in 1901 in 20 volumes.

(A. Do.; X.)

RICHBOROUGH, England, a port on the Stour, in Kent, 1¼ m. from Sandwich. Richborough castle is one of the most remarkable monuments of the Roman occupation of Great Britain. It marked the beginning of Watling street, and guarded the channel of the Wantsum, then separating the Isle of Thanet from the mainland. Richborough was a landing place and base for Roman legionaries. The extant remains of the castle include the north wall of the castellum, 460 ft. long and 22 ft. high. There is a cruciform platform of concrete, 144 ft. long and 104 ft. wide. It is believed to have borne a lighthouse. A subterranean passage runs round the foundations of the platform. In 1926 excavations revealed a double series of ditches surrounding the fortifications. During World War I, to relieve the traffic in military stores through Dover, the old port was re-established. Work began in 1916; the Stour was widened and deepened, a canal cut across a bend, and 250 ac. of marsh were reclaimed. Nearly a mile of wharfage was built and equipped. In six months regular cross-channel services of barges to Calais and Dunkirk were begun. In 1925 the port, with equipment, 1,500 ac. of land and the ferries and barges, was sold for development in connection with the Kent coalfields, but it eventually became derelict.

RICHELIEU, ARMAND EMMANUEL SOPHIE SEPTEMANIE DU PLESSIS, DUC DE (1766–1822), French statesman, was born in Paris on Sept. 25, 1766, the son of Louis Antoine du Plessis, duc de Fronsac and grandson of the marshal de Richelieu (1696–1788). The comte de Chinon, as the heir to the Richelieu honours was called, was married at fifteen to Rosalie de Rochechouart, a deformed child of twelve, with whom his relations were never more than formal. After two years of foreign travel he entered the Queen's dragoons and next year received a place at court, where he had a reputation for Puritan austerity. He left Paris in 1790 for Vienna, and in company with his friend Prince Charles de Ligne joined the Russian army as a volunteer, reaching the Russian headquarters at Bender on the 21st of November. By the death of his father in February 1791, he succeeded to the title of duc de Richelieu. He returned to Paris shortly afterwards on the summons of Louis XVI., but he was not sufficiently in the confidence of the court to be informed of the projected flight to Varennes. In July he obtained a passport from the National Assembly for service in Russia. In 1803

he became governor of Odessa. Two years later he became governor general of the Chersonese, of Ekaterinoslav and the Crimea, then called New Russia. In the eleven years of his administration, Odessa rose from a village to an important city. The central square is adorned with a statue of Richelieu (1826). A magnificent flight of nearly 200 granite steps leads from the Richelieu monument down to the harbours.

Richelieu returned to France in 1814; on the triumphant return of Napoleon from Elba he accompanied Louis XVIII. in his flight as far as Lille, whence he went to Vienna to join the Russian army, believing that he could best serve the interests of the monarchy and of France by attaching himself to the headquarters of the emperor Alexander. As the personal friend of the Russian emperor his influence in the councils of the Allies was likely to be of great service. He refused, indeed, Talleyrand's offer of a place in his ministry, pleading his long absence from France and ignorance of its conditions; but after Talleyrand's retirement he succeeded him as prime minister.

The events of Richelieu's tenure of office are noticed elsewhere. (*See* FRANCE: *History.*) It was mainly due to his efforts that France was so early relieved of the burden of the allied army of occupation. It was for this purpose mainly that he attended the congress of Aix-la-Chapelle in 1818. There he had been informed in confidence of the renewal by the Allies of their treaty binding them to interfere in case of a renewal of revolutionary trouble in France; and it was partly owing to this knowledge that he resigned office in December of the same year, on the refusal of his colleagues to support a reactionary modification of the electoral law. After the murder of the duc de Berry and the enforced retirement of Decazes, he again became president of the council (Feb. 21, 1821); but his position was untenable owing to the attacks of the "Ultras" on the one side and the Liberals on the other, and on Dec. 12 he resigned. He died of apoplexy on May 17, 1822.

Part of Richelieu's correspondence, his journal of his travels in Germany and the Turkish campaign, and a notice by the duchesse de Richelieu, are published by the Imperial Historical Society of Russia, vol. 54. *See also* L. de Crousaz-Crétêt, *Le Duc de Richelieu en Russie et en France* (1897); L. Rioult de Neuville in the *Revue des questions historiques* (Oct. 1897); R. de Cisternes, *Le Duc de Richelieu, son action aux conférences d'Aix-la-Chapelle* (1898).

RICHELIEU, ARMAND JEAN DU PLESSIS DE, CARDINAL (1585–1642), French statesman, was born of an ancient family of the lesser nobility of Poitou. The cardinal's father, François du Plessis, seigneur de Richelieu (d. 1590), fought through the wars of religion, first as a favourite of Henry III., and after his death under Henry IV. His mother, Susanne de La Porte, belonged to a legal family. Armand was the third son and was born in Paris, Sept. 9, 1585. In 1606, at the age of twenty-one, he was nominated bishop of Luçon by Henry IV. As he was under the canonical age, he went to Rome to obtain a dispensation and was consecrated there in April 1607. In the winter of 1608 Richelieu went to his poverty-stricken little bishopric, and for the next six years devoted himself seriously to his episcopal duties. In 1614 he was elected by the clergy of Poitou to the last States-general which met before the Revolution. There he attracted the attention of Marie de' Medici, the queen-mother, and was chosen at its close to present the address of the clergy embodying its petitions and resolutions. After the States-general was dissolved he remained in Paris, and the next year he became almoner to Anne of Austria, the child-queen of Louis XIII. He was appointed in 1616 a secretary of state to the king. But he owed all to Concini, and his taste of power ended with the murder of his patron on Aug. 24, 1617.

The reign which Richelieu was to dominate so absolutely began with his exile from the court. He resigned himself to the post of chief adviser to Marie de' Medici in her exile at Blois. Here he sought to ingratiate himself with Luynes and the king by reporting minutely the actions of Marie and by protestations of loyalty. As this ungrateful work brought no reward, Richelieu retired once more to his bishopric. But he was exiled to Avignon, with his brother and brother-in-law, on April 7, 1618. There he wrote "A Defence of the Main Principles of the Catholic Faith," but the escape of Marie de' Medici from Blois, on Feb. 22, 1619, again opened paths for his political ambition. Luynes and the king recalled him to the post at Angoulême with the queen-mother, who allowed him to sign the treaty of Angoulême with the Cardinal de la Rochefoucauld, acting for the king. By this treaty Marie was given liberty to live wherever she wished, and the government of Anjou and of Normandy with several castles entrusted to her. Richelieu was made a cardinal by Pope Gregory XV., on Sept. 5, 1622.

Luynes's death on Dec. 15, 1621, made possible a reconciliation a month later between the king and his mother. Richelieu seized his opportunity. He furnished Marie de' Medici with political ideas and acute criticisms of the king's ministry, especially of the Brularts. Marie zealously pushed her favourite towards office, and eventually, in 1624, the king named him a member of his council. In August he became chief minister of Louis XIII.

Home Policy.—For the next eighteen years, he worked to make the royal power—his power—absolute and supreme at home, and to crush the rival European power of the Habsburgs. At home there were two opponents to be dealt with: the Huguenots and the feudal nobility. The former were crushed by the siege of La Rochelle and the vigorous campaign against the duc de Rohan. But the religious toleration of the edict of Nantes was reaffirmed while its political privileges were destroyed, and Huguenot officers fought loyally in the foreign enterprises of the cardinal. The suppression of the independence of the feudal aristocracy was inaugurated in 1626 by an edict calling for the destruction of castles not needed for defence against invasion. There was no serious opposition to the new minister. The first serious conspiracy took place in 1626, the king's brother, Gaston of Orleans, being the centre of it. His governor, Marshal D'Ornano, was arrested by Richelieu's orders, and then his confidant, Henri de Talleyrand, marquis de Chalais and Vendôme, the natural son of Henry IV. Chalais was executed and the marshal died in prison. The overthrow of the Huguenots in 1629 made Richelieu's position seemingly unassailable, but the next year it received its severest test. Marie de' Medici had turned against her "ungrateful" minister with a hatred intensified, it is said, by unrequited passion. In September 1630, while Louis XIII. was very ill at Lyons, the two queens, Marie and Anne of Austria, reconciled for the time, won the king's promise to dismiss Richelieu. He postponed the date until peace should be made with Spain. When the news came of the truce of Regensburg Marie claimed the fulfilment of the promise. On Nov. 10, 1630, the king went to his mother's apartments at the Luxembourg palace. Orders were given that no one should be allowed to disturb their interview, but Richelieu entered by the unguarded chapel door. When Marie had recovered breath from such audacity she proceeded to attack him in the strongest terms, declaring that the king must choose between him or her. Richelieu left the presence feeling that all was lost. The king gave a sign of yielding, appointing the brother of Marillac, Marie's counsellor, to the command of the army in Italy. But before taking further steps he retired to Versailles, then a hunting lodge, and there, listening to two of Richelieu's friends, Claude de Saint-Simon, father of the memoir writer, and Cardinal La Valette, sent for Richelieu in the evening, and while the salons of the Luxembourg were full of expectant courtiers the king was reassuring the cardinal of his continued favour and support. The "Day of Dupes," as this famous day was called, was the only time that Louis took so much as a step toward the dismissal of a minister who was personally distasteful to him but who was indispensable. The queen-mother followed the king and cardinal to Compiègne, but as she refused to be reconciled with Richelieu she was left there alone and forbidden to return to Paris. The next summer she fled across the frontiers into the Netherlands, and Richelieu was made a duke. Then Gaston of Orleans, who had fled to Lorraine, came back with a small troop to head a rebellion to free the king and country from "the tyrant." The only great noble who rose was Henri, duc de Montmorenci, governor of Languedoc, and his defeat at Castelnaudary on the 1st of September

1632, was followed by his speedy trial by the parlement of Toulouse, and by his execution. Richelieu had sent to the block the first noble of France, the last of a family illustrious for seven centuries, the head of the nobility of Languedoc. He knew no mercy. The only other conspiracy against him which amounted to more than intrigue was that of Cinq Mars in 1642, at the close of his life. This vain young favourite of the king was treated as though he were really a formidable traitor, and his friend, De Thou, son of the historian, whose sole guilt was not to have revealed the plot, was placed in a boat behind the stately barge of the cardinal and thus conveyed up the Rhone to his trial and death at Lyons.

Foreign Policy.—Richelieu's foreign policy was as inflexible as his home policy. To humble the Habsburgs he aided the Protestant princes of Germany against the emperor, in spite of the strong opposition of the disappointed Catholic party in France, which had looked to the cardinal as a champion of the faith. The year of Richelieu's triumph over the Huguenots (1629) was also that of the Emperor Ferdinand's triumph in Germany, marked by the Edict of Restitution, and France was threatened by a united Germany. Richelieu, however, turned against the Habsburgs young Gustavus Adolphus of Sweden, paying him a subsidy of a million livres a year by the treaty of Bärwalde of Jan. 23, 1631. The dismissal of Wallenstein was of double value to Richelieu when his Swedish ally marched south. After the treaty of Prague, in May 1635, by which the emperor was reconciled with most of the German princes, Richelieu was finally obliged to declare war, and, concluding a treaty of offensive alliance at Compiègne with Oxenstierna, and in October one at St. Germain-en-Laye with Bernard of Saxe-Weimar, he proceeded himself against Spain, both in Italy and in the Netherlands. The war opened disastrously for the French, but by 1642, when Richelieu died, his armies,—risen from 12,000 men in 1621 to 150,000 in 1638—had conquered Roussillon from Spain; they held Catalonia, which had revolted from Philip IV. of Spain, and had taken Turin and forced Savoy to allow French troops on the borders of the Milanese. In Germany Torstensson was sweeping the imperialist forces before him through Silesia and Moravia. The lines of the treaty of Westphalia, six years later, were already laid down by Richelieu; and its epochal importance in European history is a measure of the genius who threw the balance of power from Habsburg to Bourbon.

Personality.—His own personality was his strongest ally. The king himself quailed before that stern, august presence. His pale, drawn face was set with his iron will. His frame was sickly and wasted with disease, yet when clad in his red cardinal's robes, his stately carriage and confident bearing gave him the air of a prince. His courage was mingled with a mean sort of cunning, and his ambition loved the outward trappings of power as well as its reality; yet he never swerved from his policy in order to win approbation, and the king knew that his one motive in public affairs was the welfare of the realm—that his religion, in short, was "reason of state."

No courtier was ever more assertive of his prerogatives. He claimed precedence over even princes of the blood, and one like Condé was content to draw aside the curtains for him to pass, and to sue for the hand of Richelieu's niece for his son, the "Great Condé." His pride and ambition were gratified by the foundation of a sort of dynasty of his nephews and nieces, whose hands were sought by the noblest in the realm. Like all statesmen of his time, Richelieu made money out of politics. He came to court in 1617 with an income of 25,000 livres from his ecclesiastical benefices. In the later years of his life it exceeded 3,000,000 livres. He lived in imperial state, building himself the great Palais Cardinal, now the Palais Royal, in Paris, another at Rueil near Paris, and rebuilding his ancestral château in Poitou. In January 1641 the tragedy of *Mirame,* which was said to have been his own, was produced with great magnificence. Richelieu was anxious for literary fame, and his writings are not unworthy of him. But more important than his own efforts as an author were his protection and patronage of literary men, especially of Corneille, and his creation of the French Academy in 1635. When he died, on Dec. 4, 1642, he was buried in the chapel of the Sorbonne, which still stands as he built it. His tomb, erected in 1694, though rifled at the Revolution, still exists.

Many writings are attributed to Richelieu, although because of his habit of working with substitutes and assistants it is difficult to settle how much of what passes under his name is authentic. *Les Tuileries, La Grande Pastorale, Mirame* and the other plays have long been forgotten; but a permanent interest attaches to his *Mémoires* and correspondence: *Mémoire d'Armand du Plessis de Richelieu, l'année 1607 à 1610,* ed. by A. Baschet (1880); *Histoire de la mère et du fils* (Marie de Medici and Louis XIII), sometimes attributed to Mézeray (Amsterdam, 1730) and, under title *Histoire de la régence de reine Marie de Medici, femme de Henry IV* (The Hague, 1743); *Mémoires sur le règne de Louis XIII,* 1610 to 1638, and of which the earlier portion is a reprint of the *Histoire de la mère et du fils,* Petitot's collection (1823, *seq.*); *Testament politique d'Armand du Plessis, cardinal de R.* (Amsterdam, 1687, *seq.*); *Journal de 1630–31* (1645); "Lettres, instructions diplomatiques, et papiers d'état," publ. in the *Coll. de doc. ined.* (1853–77); these, with the *Mémoires* in J. F. Michaud and J. Poujalat's collections, are the most important sources for Richelieu's statesmanship.

BIBLIOGRAPHY.—M. Topin, *Louis XIII et R.* (1876); B. Zeller, *R. et les Ministres de Louis XIII* (1880); A. Desprez, *R. et Mazarin; leur deux politiques* (1883); G. d'Avenel, *R. et la monarchie absolue* (1884); L. E. Dussieux, *Le Cardinal de R.; étude biographique* (1886); G. Hanotaux, *Hist. du Cardinal de R.,* 2 vol. (1893–1903), "Maximes d'état et fragments politiques," in the *Coll. de doc. ined;* J. H. Mariejol, *Henri IV et Louis XIII* (1905), in Lavisse, *Hist. de la Fr.,* vol. iv; S. Leathes in *Camb. Mod. Hist.,* vol. iv (1906); E. C. Price, *Cardinal de R.* (1912); P. Denis, *Le Cardinal de R. et la réforme des monastères benedictines* (1913); M. Deloche, *Autour de la Plume du Cardinal de R.* (1920); W. Mommsen, *Kardinal R., seine Politik im Elsass und Lothringen,* bibl. (1922); F. C. Palmer, *The Economic Policies of R.,* bibl. (1922) in "Univ. of Illinois Studies in the Social Sciences"; Hilaire Belloc, *Richelieu* (1929).

RICHELIEU, LOUIS FRANÇOIS ARMAND DU PLESSIS, DUC DE (1696–1788), marshal of France, was a grandnephew of Cardinal Richelieu and was born in Paris on March 13, 1696. As ambassador to Vienna (1725–29) he settled in 1727 the preliminaries of peace; in 1733–34 he served in the Rhine campaign. He fought with distinction at Dettingen and Fontenoy; three years afterward he made a brilliant defense of Genoa; in 1756 he expelled the English from Minorca by the capture of the San Felipe fortress; and in 1757–58 he closed his military career by those pillaging campaigns in Hanover which procured him the sobriquet of *Petit Père de la Maraude.* In his early days he was thrice imprisoned in the Bastille: in 1711 at the instance of his stepfather, in 1716 in consequence of a duel, and in 1719 for his share in Alberoni's conspiracy against the regent Orléans. He died in Paris on Aug. 8, 1788.

See H. Noel Williams, *The Fascinating Duc de Richelieu* (1910); L. A. F. Du Plessis, *Mémoires authentiques du Maréchal de Richelieu, 1725–1757* (1918); P. d'Estrée, *Le Maréchal de Richelieu 1696–1788* (1917).

RICHEPIN, JEAN (1849–1926), French poet, novelist and dramatist, the son of an army doctor, was born at Médéa, Algeria, on Feb. 4, 1849. He served as a *franc-tireur* in the Franco-German War and was afterward actor, sailor and stevedore. Richepin became famous with the publication, in 1876, of a volume of verse entitled *Chanson des gueux;* the outspokenness and the revolutionary defiance in these verses resulted in imprisonment and a fine for *outrage aux moeurs.* Later volumes were: *Les Caresses* (1877), *Les Blasphèmes* (1884), *La Mer* (1886), *La Bombarde* (1899). His novels which include *Miarka* (1883), his plays (*Nana Sahib,* 1883; *Monsieur Scapin,* 1886; *Par le glaive,* 1892; *Le Chemineau,* 1897) and the libretti of *Le Mage* (1891; for the music of Jules Massenet) and of *Miarka* (1905; for the music of Alexandre Georges) seem of less interest for posterity. He died on Dec. 11, 1926, when he was director of the Académie Française. His son, Jacques Richepin (1880–1946) also made his mark in the theatre.

RICHERUS (*fl.* 10th century), monk of St. Remi at Reims and a chronicler of the 10th century, studied at Reims under Gerbert, afterward Pope Silvester II. He was still living in 998, but there is no later mention of him. His *Historiae* has a unique value as giving the only tolerably full account by a contemporary of the revolution of 987, which placed the Capets on the throne of France. From 969 Richerus had no earlier history before him, and he is the chief source for the period.

There are French translations by Guadet (1845) and Poinsignon (Reims, 1855).

RICHET, CHARLES (ROBERT) (1850–1935), French physiologist, was born in Paris on Aug. 26, 1850, the son of Alfred Richet, a well-known surgeon. He obtained his M.D. in 1877, but before this he had carried out important researches on the role of conditioned reflexes in the digestive process and had discovered that the acid of gastric juice is hydrochloric acid. In 1881 he was appointed codirector of the *Revue Scientifique* and in 1887 he was nominated professor of physiology in the faculty of medicine of the University of Paris. He worked on the physiology of respiration, on epilepsy and on the treatment of tuberculosis by feeding with raw meat. More important were his researches on immunity. He discovered that an animal can be immunized against an infection by introducing blood taken from another animal that has already been immunized against the infection in question. On Dec. 16, 1890, he gave the first serotherapeutic injection into a human being. Richet's discovery of anaphylaxis followed upon and was connected with his work on serum therapy. He found that the injection of certain protein substances, instead of producing immunity, caused the development of a state of hypersensitivity. Anaphylaxis ("without protection") was recognized as the converse of immunity. Its discovery threw new light on diseases like hay fever and asthma and on drug reactions and serum sickness; and it provided an explanation for many mysterious cases of intoxication and sudden death. For this work—which was of profound significance both for theory and practice—Richet was awarded the Nobel prize for medicine in 1913.

Richet made outstanding contributions in many other fields. He was distinguished not only as a physiologist, bacteriologist, pathologist, psychologist and medical statistician, but also won fame as a pioneer of aviation, as an earnest worker on behalf of peace, as a scientific investigator of occult phenomena and as a poet, novelist and playwright. Among his many works the most outstanding were *Physiologie; Travaux du Laboratoire de C. Richet* (1882–1909); *L'Anaphylaxie* (1911; Eng. trans. 1925); *L'Homme stupide* (1919; Eng. trans. 1925); *Traité de métapsychique* (1922; Eng. trans. 1923); *Le Savant* (1923); and *L'Intelligence de l'homme* (1927). He died in Paris on Dec. 4, 1935.

(W. J. BP.)

RICHMOND, EARLS AND DUKES OF. The title earl of Richmond appears to have been in existence in England a considerable time before it was held in accordance with any strict legal principle. Alan III, duke of Brittany (997–1040), had a brother Eudon who at first disputed the ducal title with him and with his successor Conan II (1040–66) but was eventually satisfied with a partition of the family's lands and the style of "count of Brittany." Two of Eudon's sons, likewise "counts of Brittany," Alan Rufus (d. 1089) and Alan Niger (d. 1093), took part in William the Conqueror's invasion of England.

Alan Rufus was rewarded with grants in various parts of England, including manors formerly held by Earl Edwin in Yorkshire, on one of which he built the castle of Richmond. His possessions there were formed into the honour of Richmond, to which first Alan Niger and after him his youngest brother Stephen (d. 1135 or 1136) succeeded. Stephen, moreover, succeeded to all the Breton lands that had previously been divided among the sons of Eudon. These "counts of Brittany" are often reckoned as earls of Richmond, though they were not so in the strict and later sense. The first to style himself and to be styled earl of Richmond was Stephen's son Alan III Niger (d. 1146).

This Alan married Bertha, daughter and heiress of Conan III, the reigning duke of Brittany; and his son Conan IV (d. 1171), who married Margaret, sister of Malcolm IV of Scotland, asserted his right to Brittany and transferred it in his lifetime to his daughter Constance (d. 1201). As he left no sons the honour of Richmond and his other English possessions passed to Constance. Constance was three times married: first to Geoffrey Plantagenet (1158–1186), son of Henry II, king of England; then to Ranulf de Blundevill, earl of Chester (c. 1172–1232), the marriage with whom Constance treated as null on the ground of consanguinity; and finally to Guy, brother of the viscount of Thouars, who survived her. Geoffrey and Ranulf in turn assumed the title earl of Richmond; and Guy for a time at least acted as if he held the honour. The only son of the first marriage, Arthur of Brittany (1187–1203), was styled earl of Richmond in his mother's lifetime. On his murder at the hands of his uncle, King John, the earldom was resumed by the crown.

By her third husband Constance had two daughters, the elder of whom, Alice, was given in marriage by Philip II Augustus, king of France, to Peter of Braine (Peter of Dreux or Pierre Mauclerc) in 1212, after which date Peter was styled duke of Brittany. In 1219 he received seisin of the lands of the earldom of Richmond; but in 1235 he finally renounced his allegiance to the king of England and thereupon suffered forfeiture of his English earldom.

In 1240 Henry III granted the honour of Richmond to Peter of Savoy (c. 1203–68), uncle of Queen Eleanor, who was thereafter described as earl of Richmond by contemporary chroniclers, though never in official documents. By his will Peter left the honour of Richmond to his niece, the queen consort, who transferred it to the crown. In the same year (1268) Henry III granted the earldom specifically to John, duke of Brittany (1216–86), son of Peter of Braine, in whose family the title continued—though it frequently was forfeited or reverted to the crown and was regranted to the next heir—till 1342, when Edward III granted it to his son John of Gaunt, who surrendered it in 1372. It was then given to John de Montfort, duke of Brittany, but on his death without heirs in 1399 it was seized by the crown.

The earldom now became finally separated from the duchy of Brittany, with which it had been loosely conjoined since the Conquest, although the dukes of Brittany continued to assume the title till a much later date. From 1414 to 1435 the earldom of Richmond was held by John Plantagenet, duke of Bedford, and in 1452 it was conferred on Edmund Tudor, uterine brother to King Henry VI, whose wife, Margaret Beaufort, was the foundress of St. John's college, Cambridge, and of the Lady Margaret professorships of divinity at Oxford and Cambridge. (*See* RICHMOND AND DERBY, MARGARET, COUNTESS OF.) When Edmund Tudor's son Henry ascended the throne as Henry VII in 1485 the earldom of Richmond merged in the crown, but in 1525 Henry Fitzroy, natural son of Henry VIII by Elizabeth Blount, was created duke of Richmond and Somerset and earl of Nottingham, all these titles becoming extinct at his death without children in 1536.

Ludovic Stuart, 2nd duke of Lennox (1574–1624), who also held other titles in the peerage of Scotland, was created earl of Richmond in 1613 and duke of Richmond in 1623. These became extinct at his death in 1624, though his Scottish honours devolved on his brother Esmé, who was already earl of March in the peerage of England. (*See* MARCH, EARLS OF; and LENNOX.) Esmé's son, James, 4th duke of Lennox (1612–55), was created duke of Richmond in 1641, the two dukedoms as well as the lesser English and Scottish titles thus becoming again united. In 1672, on the death of his nephew Charles, 3rd duke of Richmond and 6th duke of Lennox, whose wife was the celebrated beauty called "La Belle Stuart" at the court of Charles II (*see* RICHMOND AND LENNOX, FRANCES TERESA STEWART, DUCHESS OF), his titles became extinct.

In 1675 Charles II created his illegitimate son Charles duke of Richmond, earl of March and Baron Settrington. This Charles (1672–1723), on whom the king bestowed the surname of Lennox, was the son of the celebrated Louise de Kéroualle, duchess of Portsmouth. His son Charles, 2nd duke (1701–50), added to the titles he inherited from his father that of duke of Aubigny in France, to which he succeeded in 1734 on the death of his grandmother the duchess of Portsmouth; these honours continued to be held by his descendants, the later dukes of Richmond.

The 2nd duke, by his marriage with Sarah, daughter of the 1st Earl Cadogan, was father of Lady Caroline Lennox, who eloped with Henry Fox and was the mother of Charles James Fox. Another daughter of the 2nd duke was the beautiful Lady Sarah Lennox (1745–1826) with whom George III fell in love and contemplated marriage, and who afterward married, first, Sir Thomas Bunbury, from whom she was divorced, and second, George Napier, by whom she was the mother of Generals Sir Charles and Sir William Napier.

Charles, 3rd duke of Richmond (1735–1806), was famous for his advanced views on the question of parliamentary reform. Having succeeded to the peerage in 1750 and fought at Minden (1759), he was appointed British ambassador extraordinary in Paris in 1765, and in the following year he became a secretary of state in the Rockingham administration, resigning office on the accession to power of the earl of Chatham. In the debates on the policy that led to the American War of Independence Richmond was a firm supporter of the colonists. Richmond also advocated a policy of concession in Ireland, with reference to which he originated the famous phrase "a union of hearts." In 1779 the duke brought forward a motion for retrenchment of the civil list; and in 1780 he embodied in a bill his proposals for parliamentary reform, which included manhood suffrage, annual parliaments and equal electoral areas. Richmond sat in Rockingham's second cabinet as master general of the ordnance; and from Dec. 1783 he held the same office under William Pitt. He now developed strongly Tory opinions, and his alleged desertion of the cause of reform led to a violent attack on him by Lauderdale in 1792. Richmond died in Dec. 1806 and, leaving no legitimate children, was succeeded in the peerage by his nephew Charles.

The 5th duke (1791–1860), while still known by the courtesy title of earl of March, served on Wellington's staff in the peninsula and fought at Waterloo. He was member of parliament for Chichester (1812–19). He was afterward a vehement opponent in the house of lords of Roman Catholic emancipation, and at a later date a leader of the opposition to Peel's free trade policy.

In 1836, on inheriting the estates of his maternal uncle, the 5th and last duke of Gordon, he assumed the name of Gordon before that of Lennox. On his death in 1860 he was succeeded in his titles by his son Charles Henry, 6th duke of Richmond (1818–1903), a statesman who held various cabinet offices in the Conservative administrations of Lord Derby, Disraeli and the marquess of Salisbury; and who in 1876 was created earl of Kinrara and duke of Gordon. These honours in addition to the numerous family titles of more ancient creation passed on his death to his son Charles Henry Gordon-Lennox (1845–1928) and subsequently to his son's descendants.

BIBLIOGRAPHY.—Sir Robert Douglas, *The Peerage of Scotland*, ed. by Sir J. B. Paul, 9 vol. (Edinburgh, 1904–14); G. E. C(ockaigne), *Complete Peerage*, rev. ed., vol. x (London, 1945); the duke of Richmond, *The Right of the People to Universal Suffrage and Annual Parliaments* (London, 1817), being an edition of the 3rd duke's famous "Letter to Lieut.-Colonel Sharman," originally published in 1783; Lord William Pitt Lennox, *Memoir of Charles Gordon-Lennox, 5th Duke of Richmond* (London, 1862).

RICHMOND, GEORGE (1809–1896), English painter, was born at Brompton (now within Kensington, London), on March 28, 1809. In 1824 he went to study under Henry Fuseli at the Royal Academy schools, there forming friendships with Samuel Palmer and Edward Calvert. Through them, and John Linnell, he met William Blake, who profoundly affected his early life and art. After his runaway marriage in 1831, however, he turned to portraiture for a livelihood, earning a national reputation for work in water colour and crayon. He was a staunch supporter of the Oxford church reformers, and the large group of his works in the National Portrait gallery, London, includes likenesses of John Keble, J. H. Newman and Edward Pusey. Richmond was elected R.A. in 1866. He died in London, March 19, 1896.

His second son, SIR WILLIAM BLAKE RICHMOND (1842–1921), was early a disciple of John Ruskin and the Pre-Raphaelites, later a painter of antique mythological subjects and a successful portraitist. He executed mosaics in the sanctuary of St. Paul's cathedral (1891 ff.). He succeeded Ruskin in the Oxford Slade professorship (1879–83); and was appointed K.C.B. in 1897.

See A. M. W. Stirling (ed.), *Richmond Papers* (London, 1926).

RICHMOND, a municipal and parliamentary borough in Surrey, Eng., 9 mi. W.S.W. of Charing Cross, London. Pop. (1951) 41,944. Area, 6.4 sq.mi. It lies on the right bank of the Thames.

Richmond was anciently called Syenes and afterward Schene and Sheen (a name preserved in the village of East Sheen, adjacent on the London side) until the name was changed in 1500 to Richmond by command of Henry VII, who was earl of Richmond in Yorkshire. It grew up round the royal manor house, of which nothing but a gateway remains. Edward I received the Scotch commissioners at his manor of Sheen in 1300. The palace was rebuilt by Edward III, who died here in 1377. It was frequently used by Richard II, who afterwards caused it to be demolished. By Henry V, however, it was rebuilt, and a great tournament was held here in 1492 by Henry VII, who after its destruction by fire in 1498 restored it. Henry VIII gave it to Wolsey to reside in, after the latter presented him with the new palace of Hampton Court. James I settled it on his son Henry, prince of Wales, who restored it. Charles I added to it the new deer park, Richmond park, 2,258 acres in extent surrounded by a wall. After the execution of the king, the parliament presented the park to the citizens of London, who again presented it to Charles II at the Restoration. Though partly dismantled, the palace was the residence of the queen dowager till 1665, but it was parcelled into tenements about 1720. In the old deer park extending northwards from the site of the palace, Kew observatory was erected in 1769, occupying the site of a Carthusian convent founded by Henry V. The White Lodge was built by George I. A theatre, first established in 1719, was during his later years leased by Edmund Kean. Richmond was incorporated in 1890 and after 1918 returned one member to parliament, the parliamentary borough including Barnes and Ham.

RICHMOND, a municipal borough in the North Riding of Yorkshire, England, 15 mi. S.W. of Darlington by a branch of the L.N.E. railway, of which it is the terminus. Pop. (1951) 6,165. Area 3.9 sq.mi. It is situated on the left bank of the Swale, where the valley is still narrow and steep-sided before it emerges from the Pennines into the Vale of York.

The town is chiefly interesting because of the castle, which occupies the summit of a high cliff. The castle was founded about 1071 by Alan Rufus of Penthièvre in Brittany, who is said to have rebuilt the town on obtaining from William the Conqueror the estates of the Saxon earl Edwin, which embraced some two hundred manors of Richmond and extended over nearly a third of the North Riding. This tract was called Richmondshire at this time, but the date of the creation of the shire is uncertain. William the Lion of Scotland was imprisoned in the castle in the reign of Henry II.; otherwise the town owes its importance chiefly to its lords. It was a valuable possession in the middle ages, and was usually in royal or semi-royal hands. The whole shire reverted to the crown on the accession of Henry VII. Henry VIII. gave it to his son Henry, afterwards Duke of Richmond, and the title was also bestowed upon a son of Charles II. The original castle covered an area of 5 acres, but the only portions remaining are the Norman keep, with pinnacled tower and walls 100 ft. high by 11 ft. thick, and some smaller towers.

The name of Richmond (Richemont, Richemund) has not been traced further back than 1145, but it is probable that there was an earlier settlement on the site. As far as is known, the earliest charter was granted in 1145 giving the burgesses the borough of Richmond to hold for ever in fee farm at an annual rent of £29, but a charter dated 1146 shows that the burgesses had enjoyed some municipal liberties at an earlier period. Other charters were granted in 1150 and in 1268, the latter pointing to the existence of a market at Richmond, but there is no grant of it extant. In 1278, a yearly fair was granted and in 1328, Edward III. gave the first Royal Charter to the town.

A charter of incorporation, under the title of aldermen and burgesses was granted in 1576 by Queen Elizabeth, who also allowed a market each Saturday, an animal market every fortnight, and a fair each year on the vigil of Palm Sunday. In 1668, Charles II. granted a charter under the title of mayor and aldermen. This charter, though superseded later, was restored in the reign of James II., and, until the passing of the Municipal Reform Act of 1835, was regarded as the governing charter of the borough. Although Richmond received a summons as early as 1328, it was not represented in parliament until 1584, from which time it usually sent two members. In 1867, the number was reduced to one, and since 1885 the representation has been

merged in the Richmond division of the North Riding. In 1889, Richmond became the seat of a bishop suffragan in the diocese of Ripon, but the second and last bishop died in 1921.

The church of St. Mary is transitional Norman, Decorated and Perpendicular, and is largely restored. The church of the Holy Trinity is ancient and was restored to use from ruins; only the nave and a detached tower remain. The tower of a Franciscan abbey, founded in 1258, still exists. Close to the town are the ruins of Easby Abbey, a Premonstratensian foundation of 1152, beautifully situated by the river. The remains include a Decorated gateway, an Early English chapel and fragments of the transepts and choir of the church, with sufficient portions of the domestic buildings to enable the complete plan to be traced.

The free grammar school existed in 1390, and was refounded in 1567, but the present building dates from 1850.

The principal trade is in agricultural produce, and as Richmond possesses the only railway station in Swaledale, the market is still important.

See R. Eale, *Registrum Honoris de Richemond* (1722); C. Clarkson, *History and Antiquities of Richmond* (Richmond 1821); T. D. Whitaker, *A History of Richmondshire* (1823); *Victoria County History: Yorkshire.*

RICHMOND, a city of Contra Costa county, California, U.S., on the eastern shore of San Francisco bay, 8 mi. N.E. of San Francisco, with which it is connected by the San Francisco-Oakland bay bridge.

Richmond is served by the Southern Pacific and Santa Fe railways, and has a busy harbour. The population was 99,545 in 1950 and it was 23,642 in 1940 by the federal census. Richmond is an important industrial centre.

Major industries include the assembling of automobiles, petroleum refining, railroad shops, and the manufacturing of building supplies, chemicals, explosives, machinery, tanks, dairy products and many other commodities.

Richmond was established in 1899, when the Santa Fe railway purchased a right-of-way to the bayshore, and was incorporated in 1905.

The city is under the council-manager form of government.

RICHMOND, a city of Indiana, U.S., 68 mi. E. of Indianapolis, near the Ohio state line, on the east branch of the Whitewater river; the county seat of Wayne county. It is on federal highways 27, 35 and 40, and is served by the Chesapeake and Ohio and the Pennsylvania railways, by air lines and motor bus. Population (1950) 39,539. The city has broad, well shaded streets, several parks and substantial public buildings. It is the seat of a state hospital for the insane (1890) and of several charitable institutions under religious auspices. Adjoining its western boundary is the beautiful campus (120 ac.) of Earlham college, established in 1847 by the Society of Friends. Richmond has a large wholesale trade and important manufacturing industries. Richmond was founded by Quakers from North Carolina and Pennsylvania, and for many years was the principal centre of the Society of Friends west of Philadelphia. Settlement began in the vicinity in 1806. In 1816, the year Indiana became a state, Richmond was platted as a town.

Richmond was incorporated as a village in 1818 and chartered as a city in 1840.

RICHMOND, a city of eastern Kentucky, U.S., the county seat of Madison county; 125 mi. S.E. of Louisville, on federal highway 25 and the Louisville and Nashville railroad. Pop. 10,268 in 1950; 7,335 in 1940 by the federal census. It is in the blue-grass region, near the foothills of the Cumberland mountains, about 1,000 ft. above sea level. There is a sulphur spring in the heart of the city. Natural gas is available, and hydroelectric power from the development on the Dix river. Richmond is an important market for thoroughbred livestock and burley tobacco. A miniature-lamp plant is there, and 3 mi. away is Blue Grass ordnance depot, a U.S. ammunition storage installation.

Richmond is the seat of the U.S. Trachoma hospital (1926) and of the Eastern Kentucky state college (1906) with a 50-ac. campus, formerly occupied by Central university (founded 1874, and consolidated in 1901 with Centre college at Danville). The trail marked in 1770 by Squire Boone, who preceded his brother Daniel, passed through Richmond, over what is now the Dixie highway, and one of the huge sandstone slabs on which he cut an inscription is now in the courthouse yard. Along this trail was fought the battle of Richmond (Aug. 30, 1862) when the Confederate Gen. Edmund Kirby Smith won a decisive victory. Fort Boonesborough (erected 1775) and the town founded by Daniel Boone were about 12 mi. S. of Richmond. There are many fine old mansions in the city and its environs.

RICHMOND, the capital and largest city of Virginia, U.S., a port of entry, the county seat of Henrico county (but administratively independent of it) and from 1861 to 1865 the capital of the Confederate States of America; at the head of navigation on the James river, 100 mi. S. by W. of Washington, D.C. It is on federal highways 1, 33, 60, 250, 301 and 360; and is served by the Atlantic Coast Line, the Chesapeake and Ohio, the Richmond, Fredericksburg and Potomac, the Seaboard Air Line, the Norfolk and Western and the Southern railways; also by American, Capital, Eastern, National and Piedmont air lines. Pop. (1950) 229,-906; (1940) 193,042 by federal census.

The city is attractively built around a bend in the James. The original site, embracing seven hills on the north side of the river, has been extended by annexations in all directions (including the city of Manchester on the south side in 1910) until the area is 40 sq.mi. Four highway and four railroad bridges cross the James within the city limits. There are numerous islands, including Belle Isle, the site of a Confederate prison during the Civil War, and Mayo's Island. Projects were completed in 1940 for straightening the bends in the river and deepening the channel to 25 ft. between Richmond and Hampton Roads. The state capitol, standing in a 12-ac. square, was built (1785–92) after designs prepared from a model and plans of the Maison Carrée at Nîmes, which Thomas Jefferson secured while he was minister to France. It contains the Houdon statue of Washington (1796) and a replica of the bust of Lafayette by Houdon, which was presented by Virginia to the city of Paris. In this building Aaron Burr was tried (1807), the Virginia secession convention met (1861) and the sessions of the Confederate congress were held. The oldest building in the city is a stone dwelling erected prior to 1700, now the Edgar Allan Poe shrine. St. John's Episcopal church (1741) was the meeting place of the Virginia convention of 1775, before which Patrick Henry made his famous speech ending, "Give me liberty or give me death!" Jefferson Davis was attending services in St. Paul's church when word reached him (April 2, 1865) from Lee that Richmond must be evacuated. The executive mansion of the Confederacy, occupied by Jefferson Davis 1861–65, a house built in 1819, is now a Confederate museum. The home of Chief Justice John Marshall (built in 1795) and the wartime residence of Lee's family also house historical collections. The Valentine museum, devised by Mann S. Valentine in 1892 as a public trust, includes many books of the 15th and 16th centuries. The state library, completed in 1940, has a collection of old manuscripts. The Father Tabb library commemorates this poet.

Richmond is an important educational centre. The public schools have an annual budget of $6,500,000, not including the Virginia Mechanics' institute, founded in 1856. The University of Richmond (1832), including Richmond college for men, Westhampton college for women, school of business administration and the T. C. Williams school of law, has an extensive campus in the western suburbs of the city. The Union Theological seminary (Presbyterian, 1824) moved to Richmond in 1898. The Medical College of Virginia (1838) is one of the oldest medical schools in the south. Virginia Union university for Negroes (created in 1899) combines Wayland seminary (1865), Richmond Theological seminary (1886) and Hartshorn Memorial college. The Richmond Professional institute has extension classes of the College of William and Mary and the Virginia Polytechnic institute. The daily papers (both Democratic) are the *Times-Dispatch*, formed in 1903 by the consolidation of the *Dispatch* (1850) and the *Times* (1886), and the *News-Leader* (1896).

The city has 18 public parks, covering 908 ac., and 42 playgrounds for children. There are many fine monuments and statues, among them the Washington monument in Capitol square, designed and largely executed by Thomas Crawford, and the noble equestrian statue of Robert E. Lee by M. J. A. Mercié. In Hollywood cemetery are the graves of Jefferson Davis, James Monroe, John Tyler, John Randolph of Roanoke, Commodore Matthew F. Maury, several Confederate generals and 16,000 Confederate soldiers. Oakwood cemetery contains the graves of 18,000 Confederate soldiers. Two miles northeast of the city is a national cemetery with 6,600 graves of Union men, most of whom were killed in the actions around Richmond.

Richmond has a city manager form of government with a city council of nine members elected from the city at large; one of the councilmen serves as honorary mayor. It owns and operates its water, gas and electric plants and had an annual budget of $25,000,000 at mid-20th century. A city plan and zoning ordinances are in effect. The assessed valuation of property subject to taxation was $481,412,077 in 1950. Richmond is the financial and commercial metropolis of a large area of the south and the leading manufacturing city of Virginia. It is the seat of the federal reserve bank of the fifth district. Bank debits in 1950 amounted to $6,151,000,000 and postal receipts totalled $5,389,-000. The wholesale and jobbing houses do an annual business of $650,000,000. Richmond is one of the oldest tobacco markets in the United States. Its principal manufactures are cigars, cigarettes and other tobacco products. More than 100,000,000,-000 cigarettes are produced in the city annually. Principal industries, ranked according to employment, are: cigarettes and tobacco products; chemicals, including rayon and cellophane; food and kindred products; apparel and textiles; paper and paper products; iron and steel; printing and publishing.

History.—Richmond was projected in 1733 by Col. William Byrd, owner of much land along the James, who held important offices in the colony and was the author of some of the best accounts of contemporary scenes and events and whose family has been conspicuous in the history of Virginia since 1637. He was an ancestor of Harry F. Byrd, governor 1926–30, and of Richard E. Byrd (*q.v.*), explorer. An exploring party from Jamestown had sailed up the river in 1607 and erected a cross on one of the small islands there; a short-lived settlement had been made within the present city limits in 1609, and a second had been attempted 3 mi. below by Capt. John Smith on land he bought from the Indians. In 1645 Fort Charles had been built as a frontier defense at the falls. Colonel Byrd (who had been educated in England) called the town Richmond, probably because of the similarity of its site to that of Richmond on the Thames. It was laid out in 1737 by Maj. William Mayo and was incorporated as a town in 1742. In 1777 the public records were brought there from Williamsburg, and in May 1779 Richmond was made the capital of the state. The town was partly burned on Jan. 5, 1781, by British troops under Benedict Arnold. It was chartered as a city in 1782. At the opening of the Civil War it was an important port and commercial centre, with a population of about 38,000. On May 8, 1861, it was made the capital of the Confederacy, and for the next four years was the objective of military operations to which the greatest leaders and the finest armies were devoted. (*See* AMERICAN CIVIL WAR.) The city was defended by three encircling lines of fortifications. On March 1, 1862, President Davis placed it under martial law, together with the environs within a radius of 10 mi. The opening of G. B. McClellan's peninsular campaign (*see* YORKTOWN) in 1862 caused great apprehension in Richmond, and preparations were made to ship the government records to a safer place. On the approach of the "Monitor" and the Union gunboats many persons fled from the city, and President Davis appointed a day of prayer. Confidence was restored by the checking of the fleet at Drewry's bluff on May 15, 1862, the battle of Fair Oaks and the Seven Days (*qq.v.*). In May 1864 Grant began the final campaign against Richmond. (*See* PETERSBURG CAMPAIGN; WILDERNESS.)

On the fall of Petersburg (April 2, 1865), Richmond was evacuated, after the ironclads, the bridges and many of the tobacco and military warehouses had been set on fire. When the Federal troops made their entrance the next morning a serious conflagration was under way, which was not extinguished until a third of the city was in ruins. The Tredegar ironworks, still a leading industry of Richmond, was the principal iron foundry of the Confederacy, where most of the cannon were cast. A tobacco warehouse and ship chandlery (built in 1845 by Luther Libby) was used as a prison, chiefly for Federal officers, throughout the war. In 1888–89 Libby prison was moved to Chicago to be a war museum. Within 25 years after the close of the war the population of Richmond had doubled (reaching 81,388 in 1890). From 1890 to 1920 the population doubled again.

RICHMOND AND DERBY, MARGARET, COUNTESS OF (1443–1509), mother of the English king Henry VII and foundress of St. John's and Christ's colleges at Cambridge, was the daughter and heiress of John Beaufort, duke of Somerset, and was born at Bletsoe on May 31, 1443. She became the child wife (1450) of John de la Pole, later duke of Suffolk, but the marriage was dissolved before March 24, 1453. In 1455 she married Edmund Tudor, earl of Richmond, who died in the following year; she then married Henry (d. 1471), son of Humphrey Stafford, duke of Buckingham, and later Thomas Stanley, afterward earl of Derby. With her husband, Lord Stanley, she aided her son Henry to gain the crown in 1485. Under the influence of her confessor, John Fisher, afterward bishop of Rochester, the countess founded the Lady Margaret professorships of divinity at the universities of Oxford and Cambridge. She completed the foundation of Christ's college, Cambridge, and much of her wealth was left for building and endowing St. John's college. She died on June 29, 1509.

See C. H. Cooper, *Memoir of Margaret, Countess of Richmond and Derby* (Cambridge, 1874); E. M. G. Routh, *Lady Margaret* (London, 1924).

RICHMOND AND LENNOX, FRANCES TERESA STEWART, DUCHESS OF (1648–1702), daughter of a physician in the household of Queen Henrietta Maria when she was in exile after 1649, was born in 1648 and was brought up in France. Henrietta Maria sent her to England, where she was appointed maid of honour to Catherine of Braganza, queen of Charles II. Charles II became infatuated with her, and it is stated that in 1667 he was considering the possibility of obtaining a divorce in order to make her his wife. This was at a time when he feared to lose her as his mistress, since her hand was sought in marriage by Charles Stewart, duke of Richmond and Lennox. In March 1667 she eloped with Richmond and married him secretly; but on her return to court she retained her hold on the king's affections.

See C. H. Hartmann, *La Belle Stuart* (New York, London, 1924).

RICHMOND RIVER AND BASIN, together with the basins of the Tweed and Clarence rivers, forms the largest area of coastal lowland in New South Wales, Australia (c. 125 mi. N.-S.; 20–40 mi. E.-W.). The area is subject to violent rainstorms which cause wide flooding on the lower ground. Electric power is developed on the Nymboida tributary of the Clarence. Dairying, the main feature of local farming, produces about two-thirds of the state production of butter, with large factories at Byron bay, Lismore and Grafton. The whole of the cane sugar produced in New South Wales (about 5% of Australian output) is grown in the area. Yields per ton of cane are somewhat lower than in Queensland and the growing period is nearly double (20–24 months against 12–14 months). The district is linked by rail with Sydney, and by both a through route and a coastal route to Brisbane. (T. HER.)

RICHTER, EUGEN (1839–1906), German politician, was born on July 30, 1839 at Düsseldorf. After attending the universities of Bonn, Heidelberg and Berlin, he entered the government service. In 1864 he was chosen burgomaster of Neuwied; but he was already known for his Liberal opinions, and the government refused to confirm the appointment and transferred him to Bromberg, in East Prussia. In consequence, he resigned from the public service, went to Berlin and entered journalism. A consistent advocate of the economic doctrines of the Manchester school, he was also keenly interested in the working-class co-operative movement, on which he wrote a book. In 1867 he was tried for revolu-

tionary tendencies but acquitted. In 1867 he was elected a member of the Reichstag, and in 1869 of the Prussian parliament. A member of the Progressive party, in 1880 one of the founders, and eventually the leader, of the Freisinnige, he was always in opposition. Next to Ludwig Windthorst he was Bismarck's most dangerous opponent, and leader of the opposition to the introduction of protection, to the new colonial policy introduced after 1878, and to state socialism. He also strongly opposed all increases in the army and navy; and it was his opposition to the army measures of 1893 which finally split his party, leaving him with only a small following. In 1885 he founded the *Freisinnige Zeitung*, which he edited himself; he also wrote many political brochures and works on Prussian finances. He died at Jena, on Jan. 26, 1906.

See his reminiscences *Jugenderinnerungen* (1892) and *Im alten Reichstag* (2 vols., 1894–96).

RICHTER, HANS (1843–1916), Austro-Hungarian musical conductor, born at Györ on April 4, 1843, was the son of the chapel master at the cathedral, whose wife, *née* Josephine Csazinsky, was an operatic singer. He studied (1860–65) at the Vienna Conservatoire and in 1866–67 he assisted Richard Wagner in Switzerland, making a fair copy of the *Meistersinger* score. In 1878 he assisted in the domestic performance of the *Siegfried Idyll.*

In 1871, after holding some minor posts, Richter was appointed conductor of the Hungarian National opera at Budapest, and in May 1875 began his long connection with the Vienna opera, which terminated only with the century. In 1876 he directed the rehearsals and performances of Wagner's *Ring* at Bayreuth, and in 1877 paid his first visit to England to conduct the Wagner concerto at the Albert Hall. In 1879 he founded the Richter concerts in London and quickly established himself as a prime favourite there. Later, in 1882, he conducted a famous series of performances of Wagner's works (including the first in England of *Die Meistersinger* and *Tristan*) at Drury Lane; special performances of German opera were also conducted by him at Covent Garden from 1904 until his retirement. In 1897 he became conductor of the Hallé orchestra in Manchester, doing splendid service in this capacity, while previously in 1885 he had established an equally happy connection with Birmingham as conductor of the Birmingham Triennial festival. His last performance of *Die Meistersinger* was given at Bayreuth in 1912, and his last years were spent in retirement there. He died on Dec. 5, 1916. As a conductor Richter was supreme in the interpretation of Wagner, though hardly less great in that of Mozart, Beethoven, Brahms and other German classical masters. He took no interest in non-German composers, but made an exception of Sir Edward Elgar.

RICHTER, JOHANN PAUL FRIEDRICH (1763–1825), usually called JEAN PAUL, German author, was born at Wunsiedel, in Bavaria, on March 21, 1763. His father was a schoolmaster and organist at Wunsiedel, but in 1765 he became a pastor at Joditz near Hof, and in 1776 at Schwarzenbach, where he died in 1779. After attending the gymnasium at Hof, Richter went in 1781 to the University of Leipzig. Unable to maintain himself at Leipzig he returned in 1784 to Hof, where he lived with his mother. From 1787 to 1789 he served as a tutor at Töpen, a village near Hof; and afterward he taught the children of several families at Schwarzenbach.

Richter's first work was *Grönländische Prozesse* and *Auswahl aus des Teufels Papieren,* the former of which was issued in 1783–84, the latter in 1789. In later life Richter had little sympathy with their satirical tone. His next book, *Die unsichtbare Loge,* a romance, published in 1793, had all the qualities which were soon to make him famous, and its power was immediately recognized. He then produced in rapid succession *Hesperus* (1795), *Biographische Belustigungen unter der Gehirnschale einer Riesin* (1796), *Leben des Quintus Fixlein* (1796), *Blumen- Frucht- und Dornenstücke, oder Ehestand, Tod und Hochzeit des Armenadvokaten Siebenkäs* (1796–97), *Der Jubelsenior* (1797), and *Das Kampaner Tal* (1797). This series of writings won for Richter an assured place in German literature.

In 1797 he went to Leipzig, and in the following year to Weimar, where he had much pleasant intercourse with Herder, by whom he was warmly appreciated. He did not become intimate with Goethe and Schiller, to both of whom his literary methods were repugnant; but in Weimar, as elsewhere, his good talk and genial manners made him a favourite in general society. In 1801 he married Caroline Meyer, whom he met in Berlin in 1800. They lived first at Meiningen, then at Coburg; and finally, in 1804, they settled at Bayreuth. Here Richter spent a quiet, simple and happy life, constantly occupied with his work as a writer. In 1808 he was delivered from anxiety as to outward necessities by the prince-primate, K. T. von Dalberg, who gave him a pension of a thousand florins. Before settling at Bayreuth, Richter had published his most ambitious novel, *Titan* (1800–3); and this was followed by *Flegeljahre* (1804–5), two works which he himself regarded as his masterpieces. His later imaginative works were *Dr. Katzenbergers Badereise* (1809), *Des Feldpredigers Schmelzle Reise nach Flätz* (1809), *Leben Fibels* (1812), and *Der Komet, oder Nikolaus Marggraf* (1820–22). In *Vorschule der Aesthetik* (1804) he expounded his ideas on art; he discussed the principles of education in *Levana, oder Erziehungslehre* (1807); and the opinions suggested by current events in *Friedenspredigt* (1808), *Dämmerungen für Deutschland* (1809), *Mars und Phöbus Thronwechsel im Jahre 1814* (1814), and *Politische Fastenpredigten* (1817). In his last years he began *Wahrheit aus Jean Pauls Leben*, to which additions from his papers and other sources were made after his death by C. Otto and E. Förster. In 1821 Richter lost his only son, and never quite recovered from the shock. He died of dropsy, at Bayreuth, on Nov. 14, 1825.

Schiller said of Richter that he would have been worthy of admiration "if he had made as good use of his riches as other men made of their poverty." And it is true that in the form of his writings he never did full justice to his great powers. In working out his conceptions he found it impossible to restrain the expression of any powerful feeling by which he might happen to be moved. He was equally unable to resist the temptation to bring in strange facts or notions which occurred to him. Hence every one of his works is irregular in structure, and his style lacks directness, precision and grace. But he had an amazingly fertile imagination and a surprising power of suggesting great thoughts by means of the simplest incidents and relations. Richter was a great nature-lover and deeply religious in spirit; to him visible things were but the symbols of the invisible, and in the unseen realities alone he found elements which seemed to him to give significance and dignity to human life. His humour, the most distinctive of his qualities, cannot be dissociated from the other characteristics of his writings. It determined to some extent the form in which he embodied even his most serious reflections. It is sometimes extravagant and grotesque but never harsh or vulgar, and generally it springs naturally from the perception of the incongruity between ordinary facts and ideal laws. With all his wilfulness and eccentricity Richter was a man of a pure and sensitive spirit, with a passionate scorn for pretence and an ardent enthusiasm for truth and goodness.

Richter's *Sämtliche Werke* appeared in 1826–28 in 60 vols., to which were added 5 vols. of *Literarischer Nachlass* in 1836–38. Editions of selected works appeared in 16 vols. (1865), in Kürschner's Deutsche Nationalliteratur (edited by P. Nerrlich, 6 vols., 1884–87). The chief collections of Richter's correspondence are: *Jean Pauls Briefe an F. H. Jacobi* (1828); *Briefwechsel Jean Pauls mit seinem Freunde C. Otto* (1829–33); *Briefwechsel zwischen H. Voss und Jean Paul* (1833); *Briefe an eine Jugendfreundin* (1858); P. Nerrlich, *Jean Pauls Briefwechsel mit seiner Frau und seinem Freunde Otto* (1902). See further the continuation of Richter's autobiography by C. Otto and E. Förster (1826–33); R. O. Spazier, *J. P. F. Richter: ein biographischer Kommentar zu dessen Werken* (5 vols., 1833); F. J. Schneider, *Jean Pauls Altersdichtung* (1901), and *Jean Pauls Jugend und erstes Auftreten in der Literatur* (1906). All Richter's more important works have been translated into English, *Quintus Fixlein* and *Schmelzles Reise*, by Carlyle; see also Carlyle's two admirable essays on Richter.

RICHTHOFEN, FERDINAND, BARON VON (1833–1905), German geographer and traveller, was born near Karlsruhe, Silesia, on May 5, 1833. He was educated at Breslau and Berlin, and in 1856 carried out geological investigations in the Tirol, subsequently extending them to Transylvania. In 1859 he accompanied as geologist the Prussian diplomatic mission to the Far East under Count von Eulenburg, and visited Ceylon, Japan, Formosa,

the Philippines and Java, subsequently making an overland journey from Bangkok to Moulmein and reaching Calcutta in 1862. No important work resulted from these travels, for much of Richthofen's records and collections was lost. China was at the time inaccessible owing to the Taiping rebellion, but Richthofen was impressed with the desirability of exploring it, and after a visit to California, where he remained till 1868, he returned to the East. In a remarkable series of seven journeys he penetrated into almost every part of the Chinese Empire. He returned home in 1872, and a work comprising three large volumes and an atlas, which, however, did not cover the entire field or complete the author's plan, appeared at Berlin in 1877–85 under the title of *China; Ergebnisse eigner Reisen und darauf gegründeter Studien*. In this standard work the author deals not only with geology but with every subject necessary to a general geographical treatise. Notably he paid close attention to the economic resources of the country he traversed; he wrote a valuable series of letters to the Shanghai Chamber of Commerce, and first drew attention to the importance of the coalfields of Shantung, and of Kiaochow as a port. In 1875 Richthofen was elected professor of geology at Bonn, but being fully occupied with his work in China he did not take up professorial duties till 1879; in 1883 he became professor of geography at Leipzig, and in 1886 was chosen to the same office at Berlin, and held it till his death. He died Oct. 16, 1905.

Among his other works are: *Natural System of Volcanic Rocks* (San Francisco, 1867); *Aufgaben und Methoden der heutigen Geographie* (an address delivered at Leipzig, 1883); *Führer für Forschungsreisende* (Berlin, 1886); *Triebkräfte und Richtungen der Erdkunde in neunzehnten Jahrhundert* (address on his election as rector, Berlin, 1903).

RICHWOOD, a city of Nicholas county, West Virginia, U.S., 60 mi. E. of Charleston, on the Baltimore and Ohio railroad. The population was 5,321 in 1950 and 5,051 in 1940 by the federal census.

Richwood is in a farming and timber region in the foothills of the Alleghenies, and has lumber and paper mills, coal mines and wood-working factories. The town was founded and incorporated in 1901, and in 1921 was chartered as a city.

RICIMER (d. 472), master of the Roman Empire in the West during part of the 5th century, was the son of a prince of the Suebi and the daughter of Wallia, king of the Visigoths. His youth was spent at the court of Valentinian III., and he won distinction under Aetius. In 456 he defeated the Vandals in a sea-fight near Corsica, and on land near Agrigentum in Sicily. He then gained the consent of the Roman senate to an expedition against the emperor Avitus, whom he defeated at Piacenza on Oct. 16, 456. Ricimer then obtained from Leo I., emperor at Constantinople, the title patrician, but in 457 set up Majorianus as his own emperor in the West. When, however, Majorianus tried to rule by himself, Ricimer forced him to abdicate and caused his assassination on Aug. 7, 461. The successor whom Ricimer placed upon the throne was Libius Severus, who proved to be more docile than Majorianus. Upon his death in 465—said to be due to the poison of Ricimer—this emperor-maker ruled the West for eighteen months without an emperor, and then accepted Leo's candidate Anthemius. Before long, however, Ricimer moved to Milan, ready to declare war upon Anthemius. St. Epiphanius, bishop of Milan, patched up a truce, but in 472 Ricimer proclaimed as emperor Olybrius, whom Leo had sent to pacify the two enemies, and after three months' siege captured Rome, on July 1, 472. Anthemius was massacred and Rome was a prey to Ricimer's soldiers. He himself, however, died on Aug. 18, 472, of malignant fever.

The main authorities for this period are collected in Mommsen's *Chron. Minora* (3 vols., 1892–98). See also Gibbon ed. Bury (London, 1907) p. 15–49. L. M. Hartmann, *Geschichte Italiens im Mittelalter*, vol. i. (1897).

RICINA, an ancient town of Picenum, Italy, 3 m. N.W. of the modern Macerata, on the banks of the river Potenza, in a fertile valley. After it was refounded by Pertinax and Septimius Severus, it bore the name Colonia Helvia Ricina Pertinax. Considerable ruins of an amphitheatre and remains of baths and other buildings (all of the imperial period) still exist; also the fragments of an ancient bridge over the Potenza.

RICKETS, a disease of children and young animals characterized by deficient calcification of the bones and teeth and by other evidences of perverted nutrition (*see* METABOLIC DISEASES). Rickets most commonly attracts attention about the end of the first year of life but the bony changes are preceded by digestive disorder. The child's appetite is poor, and there is frequent vomiting, with diarrhoea and wasting. A common early symptom is profuse sweating of the head, particularly during sleep, with a tendency in the child to kick off all coverings and expose the limbs. There is great tenderness of the bones, as shown by the pain produced on moving or handling the child. Gradually changes in the shape of the bones become obvious about the epiphyseal lines at the ends of the long bones. Thus in the arm there is enlargement at the wrists, and in the ribs a knobbed appearance at the junction of their ends with the costal cartilages. The bones from their lack of calcium salts become misshapen, by the action of the muscles and the superincumbent weight of the body. Those of the limbs are bent outwards and forwards, and the child becomes "bow-legged" or "in-kneed." The trunk shows alterations and deformities owing to curvature of the spine, flattening of the lateral curves of the ribs, and projection forwards of the sternum ("pigeon breast"). The pelvis undergoes distortion, which may reduce its diameters to a degree that in the female may afterwards lead to difficulties in parturition. The head of the rickety child is large-looking in its upper part, the individual bones of the cranium sometimes remaining long ununited, while the face is small and ill-developed, and the teeth appear late and fall out or decay early. The spleen often is enlarged. Commonly, the disease terminates in recovery, with more or less deformity and dwarfing, the bones although altered in shape becoming firmly ossified. But during the progress of the disease, various intercurrent ailments may cause death, such as the infectious fevers, bronchitis and other pulmonary affections, chronic hydrocephalus, convulsions, laryngismus stridulus, etc. Rickets is now recognized to be largely if not entirely due to deficiency of vitamin D in the food (*see* VITAMINS). The treatment is directed toward the supply of this deficiency, *e.g.*, by cod liver oil, exposure to sunlight or in its absence to ultra-violet light. Recently ergosterol which has been exposed to ultra-violet radiation, has been introduced to replace cod-liver oil. In addition general hygienic and nutritive measures must be adopted. Unduly prolonged suckling and artificial—especially starchy—foods given before the infant is able to digest them, are often noted in the histories of rickety children.

An acute form of rickets of rare occurrence (really a form of scurvy, *q.v.*) has been described, in which all the symptoms develop rapidly, the result in many instances being fatal.

The condition formerly known as foetal rickets (achondroplasia or chondrodystrophia foetalis) is now classed as a separate disease. Its chief characteristics are dwarfism with shortening of the limbs and enormous enlargement of the articulations.

RICKETTS, CHARLES (1866–1931), English artist, was born at Geneva on Oct. 2, 1866, and educated in France. In 1889 he became joint editor with Charles Shannon of the *Dial*. In 1896 he founded the Vale press, the output of which was a series of beautifully designed and printed books. Of his pictures, "The Plague" (1911) is in the Luxembourg at Paris, and "Don Juan" (1916) in the National Gallery. He published *The Prado and its Masterpieces* (1903); *A Bibliography of the Books issued by Hacon and Ricketts* (1904); *Titian* (1906); *Pages on Art* (1913).

RICKMAN, THOMAS (1776–1841), English architect, was born on June 8, 1776, at Maidenhead, Berkshire, and died at Birmingham on Jan. 4, 1841. He designed many churches, the new court of St. John's College, Cambridge and a palace for the bishop of Carlisle. These are all in the Gothic style, but show more knowledge of its outward form than real acquaintance with its spirit. Rickman played a part in the revival of mediaevalism perhaps second only to Pugin. His *Attempt to discriminate the Styles of Architecture in England* ran through many editions.

RICKMANSWORTH, an urban district in Hertfordshire England; 17½ mi. W.N.W. of London by the Met. and L.N.E. Jt. railway; served also by the L.M.S.R. Pop. (1938) 18,700. Area,

12.3 sq.mi. William Penn, founder of Pennsylvania, lived during 1672–76 in Basing house, in the High street, now the council offices. In 1937 the council purchased the mansion and grounds (345 ac.) of Moor park as part of the London Green Belt scheme. The Royal Masonic Institution for girls was opened here in 1934.

RICOCHET, a military term expressing the rebound of a projectile that strikes on a hard surface. The origin of the French word *ricochet* is unknown. Its earliest known use (14th and 15th centuries) was in the sense of "repetition," e.g. *chanson du ricochet,* "an oft-told tale." Hence it came to be applied to the rebound of a flat stone skimmed along the surface of water, known familiarly in English as "ducks and drakes," and so finally in the military sense, which found its way into the English language. The use of the now obsolete "ricochet fire" in war is well illustrated by "ducks and drakes." The shot, striking the ground at a small angle, described for the remainder of its course a succession of leaps and falls. The discovery of this species of fire, usually attributed to Vauban (siege of Ath in 1697), had the greatest influence both on sieges and on operations in the field. In siege warfare, ricochet, especially when combined with enfilade, *i.e.* when directed along the enemy's line of defense, soon became the principal weapon of the besieger, and with the system of parallels gave the attack a superiority so complete that a siege came to be considered as the most certain operation of war. Enfilade fire by itself was neutralized by traverses in the defenses, but by the new method a shot could be so aimed as to skip over each successive traverse and thus to search ground that was immune from direct fire. The application of ricochet fire to operations in the field came somewhat later. In the 18th century field artillery, which was not, before Napoleon's time, sufficiently mobile to close with the enemy, relied principally upon the ricochet of round shot, which, sweeping a considerable depth of ground, took effect upon several successive lines of hostile troops. But once artillery was able to gallop up to the enemy and to use its far more terrible close-range projectile, case-shot, ricochet fire came to be used less and less, until finally, with the general adoption of shell (which, of course, burst at the first contact with the ground), the round shot disappeared altogether from the battlefield. Similarly in siege warfare, as soon as high-angle fire with shells became sufficiently accurate, there was no further need of round shot and ricochet.

The term "ricochet" is now only applied, in modern rifle shooting, to the graze of a bullet that has struck short. A modern bullet that has ricochetted inflicts a very severe wound, as its nickel or other hard envelope is torn and jagged by its contact with the ground. With its high remaining velocity it is dangerous even after more than one ricochet, except at extreme ranges.

RICOLD OF MONTE CROCE (1242–1320), Italian Dominican missionary, was born at Monte Croce, near Florence. In 1267 he entered the Dominican house of Santa Maria Novella in Florence, and in 1272 that of St. Catherine in Pisa. He started for Acre with a papal commission to preach in 1286 or 1287: in 1288 or 1289 he began to keep a record of his experiences in the Levant; this record he probably reduced to final book form in Baghdad. He travelled extensively in Syria, Asia Minor and Persia. In Baghdad he stayed several years, studying the Koran and other works of Moslem theology, for controversial purposes, arguing with Nestorian Christians, and writing. In 1301 Ricold again appeared in Florence: some time after this he proposed to submit his *Confutatio Alcorani* to the pope, but did not. He died on Oct. 31, 1320.

The best edition of the *Itinerary* is by J. C. M. Laurent, in *Peregrinatores Medii Aevi Quatuor*, pp. 105 (101)–41 (Leipzig, 1864 and 1873). The *Epistles* have been edited by R. Röhricht in *Archives de l'orient latin*, vol. ii. part ii. (Documents) pp. 258–96 (Paris, 1884). The *Confutatio Alcorani*, printed at Seville in 1500, at Venice in 1607, adds hardly anything to the sections of the *Itinerary* devoted to Moslem belief, etc. Ricold's *Libellus contra Nationes Orientales* and *Contra errores Judaeorum* have never been printed. *See* also C. Raymond Beazley, *Dawn of Modern Geography*, iii. 190–202, 218, 390–391, 547, 554, 564.

RICOTTI-MAGNANI, CESARE (1822–1905), Italian general and knight of the Annunziata, was born at Borgo Lavezzaro on June 30, 1822. After serving from 1856 to 1859 as director of the artillery school, he became general of division in 1864, commanding the 5th division at the battle of San Martino. In the war of 1866 he stormed Borgoforte, to open a passage for Cialdini's army. Upon the death of General Govone in 1872 he was appointed minister of war, and after the occupation of Rome bent all his efforts to army reform, in accordance with the lessons of the Franco-German War. He shortened the period of military service; extended conscription to all able-bodied men; created a permanent army, a mobile militia and a reserve; commenced the renewal of armaments; and placed Italy in a position to put 1,800,000 men on a war footing. Ricotti fell from power with the Right in 1876, but returned to office with Depretis in 1884, and amended his previous scheme of reform. Resigning in April 1887, he became a member of the senate in 1890, but took little part in public life until 1896, when, after the battle of Adowa, he formed a ministry; he made over the premiership to the marquis di Rudini, retaining for himself the portfolio of war, and sought to consolidate the tactical structure of the army without weakening its fighting power. Ricotti's ideas were not acceptable at court, and he had to resign. Nevertheless, his prestige as creator of the modern Italian army remained unimpaired.

RIDDELL, GEORGE ALLARDICE RIDDELL, 1ST BARON (1865–1934), British newspaper proprietor, was born in London on May 25, 1865, and educated privately. He became a solicitor in 1888 and settled in practice at Cardiff. There he acquired an interest in *The Western Mail*, and he eventually turned his energies mainly to newspaper management. He went to London and obtained control over the Sunday paper *The News of the World*, which he developed on popular lines, so that it obtained a huge circulation during the first decade of the 20th century and made its proprietor a wealthy man. He gradually extended his newspaper connections, becoming a director also of George Newnes Ltd., Country Life Ltd. and C. Arthur Pearson Ltd., etc. In 1909 he received a knighthood. He was a prominent member of the Newspaper Proprietors' Association at the outbreak of the World War, and, owing to his intimate relations with Mr. Lloyd George, he gradually became the principal liaison between the Press and the Government so far as all matters of publicity were concerned. In this capacity he represented the British Press at the Peace Conference in 1919 and at all the important Allied conferences subsequently. He was created a baronet in 1918 and raised to the peerage as Baron Riddell of Walton Heath in 1920. His publications include *Some Things That Matter* (1922) and *More Things That Matter* (1925).

RIDGEFIELD PARK, a village of Bergen county, New Jersey, U.S., 6 mi. W. of the Hudson river, opposite New York city (about 100th street). It is served by the New York, Susquehanna and Western and the West Shore railways and bus lines. Pop. (1950) 11,993. It is a residential and industrial suburb with paper mills and factories on the Hackensack river.

RIDGEWOOD, a village of Bergen county, New Jersey, U.S., 22 mi. N.W. of New York city and 5 mi. N.E. of Paterson on the Erie railroad. Pop. (1950) 17,481; in 1940, federal census, 14,948. It is a parklike residential community in the foothills of the Watchung and the Ramapo mountains. The village, originally called Godwinville, was incorporated in 1894 and in 1911 a commission form of government was established.

RIDGWAY, a borough of northern Pennsylvania, U.S., the county seat of Elk county; midway between Buffalo and Pittsburgh, on the Clarion river at the mouth of Elk creek. It is on federal highways 120 and 219, and is served by the Baltimore and Ohio and the Pennsylvania railways. Pop. (1950) 6,244; (1940) 6,253; (1930) 6,313. The borough has an altitude of 1,380 ft. and covers nearly 3 sq.mi. It is in a natural gas field.

Manufactures include electric motors and generators, glue, ink, lumber products, bearings, brake linings and snow plows. Ridgway was founded in 1824 by Jacob Ridgway of Philadelphia and incorporated in 1880.

RIDING, THRITHING or **THRIDING,** a Scandinavian term for the third part of a shire or county, *e.g.*, the ridings of Yorkshire and of Lindsey in Lincolnshire. In Iceland the third

part of a *thing* which corresponds roughly to an English county was called *thrithjungr*; in Norway, however, the *thrithjungr* seems to have been an ecclesiastical division. To the riding causes were brought which could not be determined in the wapentake, and a matter which could not be determined in the riding was brought into the court of the shire. There is abundant evidence that riding courts were held after the Norman Conquest.

Each of the ridings of Yorkshire has its own lord lieutenant and commission of the peace, and under the Local Government Act of 1888 forms a separate administrative county. They are distinguished as the north, east and west ridings, but the ancient divisions of Lindsey were known as the north, south and west ridings respectively.

See Dugdale, *Monasticon Anglicanum*, vol. vi. ed. by John Caley and others (1846); F. Liebermann, *Die Gesetze der Angelsachsen* (Halle, 1888–89); Stubbs, *Constitutional History of England*.

RIDING: *see* HORSEMANSHIP AND RIDING.

RIDLEY, NICHOLAS (*c.* 1500–1555), English bishop and martyr, was the second son of Christopher Ridley of Unthank Hall, near Willemoteswick, Northumberland. He was sent about 1518 to Pembroke Hall, Cambridge. Having graduated M.A. in 1526 he went to study at the Sorbonne in Paris and at Louvain, and on his return to Cambridge was appointed junior treasurer of his college. In 1534 he was one of the university proctors, and signed the decree of the university against the jurisdiction of the pope in England. Ridley was now chaplain to the university and began to show leanings to the reformed faith. In 1537 he became chaplain to Thomas Cranmer, archbishop of Canterbury, and in April 1538 vicar of Herne, Kent. In 1540 he was chosen master of Pembroke Hall; in 1541 he became chaplain to Henry VIII. and canon of Canterbury. In 1543 he was accused of heretical teaching and practices but acquitted, although just after his exculpation he finally abandoned the doctrine of transubstantiation.

In September 1547 Ridley was nominated bishop of Rochester. He was one of the visitors who were appointed to establish protestantism in the University of Cambridge; in 1548 helped to compile the English prayer book, and in 1549 was one of the commissioners who examined Bishops Gardiner and Bonner. He concurred in their deprivation, and succeeded Bonner in the see of London. Having signed the letters patent settling the English crown on Lady Jane Grey, Ridley, in a sermon preached at St. Paul's cross on July 9th, 1553, affirmed that the princesses Mary and Elizabeth were illegitimate, and that the succession of the former would be disastrous to the religious interests of England. When Lady Jane's cause was lost, however, he went to Framlingham to ask Queen Mary's pardon, but was at once arrested and sent to the Tower of London. From his prison he wrote in defence of his religious opinions, and early in 1554 he, with Cranmer and Latimer, was sent to Oxford to be examined. He defended himself against a number of divines, but was declared a heretic. and excommunicated. He refused to recant, and in Oct. 1555 he was tried for heresy under the new penal laws, being degraded and sentenced to death. With Cranmer and Latimer he met his end at the stake in Oxford on Oct. 16, 1555.

See *Works of Nicholas Ridley D.D.* (ed. H. Christmas, Parker Soc., 1841). His *Life* was written by Dr. Gloucester Ridley in 1763, and there is a memoir of him in Moule's edition of the bishops' *Declaration of the Lord's Supper* (1895).

RIDOLFI or RIDOLFO, **ROBERTO DI** (1531–1612), Italian conspirator, born at Florence on Nov. 18, 1531, settled in London about 1555. In 1570 he set to work on the plot against Elizabeth which is usually associated with his name. His intention was to marry Mary, queen of Scots, to the duke of Norfolk and to place her on the English throne. In 1571 he visited the duke of Alva at Brussels, Pius V. at Rome, and Philip II. at Madrid to explain to them his scheme and to gain their active assistance thereto. His messenger, by name Charles Baillie (1542–1625), was, however, seized at Dover; Norfolk and Lesley were arrested, the former being condemned to death in January 1572. Ridolfi, who was then in Paris, died at Florence on Feb. 18, 1612.

RIEGER, PHILIPP FRIEDRICH VON (1818–1903), Bohemian politician and publicist, was born on Dec. 18, 1818, at

Semil, Bohemia. He first came into prominence as one of the Czech leaders in the revolution of 1848. In 1853 he married a daughter of the historian Palacky. In 1858 he started the *Slovník naučny*, the Czech national encyclopaedia and also helped to found the first Czech political daily newspaper published in Prague (1861), of which he was for a while the editor. After the issue of the "October diploma" of 1860, Rieger, with Palacky, undertook the leadership of the reconstituted Czech party. In 1871 he conducted the negotiations with the Hohenenwarth ministry for a federal constitution of the empire, which broke down owing to his extreme attitude in the matter of Bohemian independence. On the reappearance of the Czechs in the Bohemian diet (1878) and the Austrian *Reichsrath* (1879) Rieger, as chief of the so-called "Old Czechs," supported Count Taaffe's government. In 1891, together with the other "Old Czechs," he was defeated at the poll. In March 1897 he was created a baron (*Freiherr*) and given a seat in the Upper House, but his influence was now at an end. He died on March 3, 1903.

RIEL, LOUIS (1844–1885), Canadian agitator, son of Louis Riel and Julie de Lagemaundière, was born at St. Boniface, on Oct. 23, 1844, according to his own account, though others place his birth in 1847. Though known as a half-breed, or Métis, and though with both Indian and Irish ancestors, his blood was mainly French. From July 1866 he worked for two years at various occupations in Minnesota, returning in July 1868 to St. Vital, near St. Boniface. In 1869 the transfer of the territorial rights of the Hudson's Bay Company to the dominion of Canada gave great uneasiness to the Métis, and in October 1869 a party led by Riel turned back at the American frontier the newly appointed Canadian governor; in November they captured Fort Garry (Winnipeg), the headquarters of the Company, and called a convention which passed a bill of rights.

In December a provisional government was set up, of which on Dec. 29, Riel was made president, and which defeated two attacks made on it by the English-speaking settlers of the vicinity. So far the Métis had been within their rights, but Riel was flighty, vain and mystical, and his judicial murder on March 4, 1870, of Thomas Scott, an Orangeman from Ontario, roused against him the whole of English-speaking Canada. An expedition was equipped and sent out under Colonel Garnet, later Lord Wolseley, which captured Fort Garry on Aug. 24, 1870, Riel decamping.

Riel was not arrested, and on Aug. 4, 1871, urged his countrymen to combine with the Canadians against a threatened attack from American Fenians, for which he was publicly thanked by the lieutenant-governor. In 1872 for religious reasons he changed his name to Louis David Riel. In October 1873 he became member of the dominion parliament for Provencher, came to Ottawa and took the oath, but did not sit. On April 16, 1874, he was expelled from the house, but in September was again elected for Provencher; on Feb. 10, 1875, he was outlawed, and the seat thereby again vacated. In 1877–78 he was for over a year a patient in the Beauport asylum for the insane, but from 1879 to 1884 he lived quietly in Montana.

In 1884 in response to a deputation from the Métis, who had moved west to the forks of the Saskatchewan river, he returned to Canada to win redress for their wrongs. His own rashness and the ineptitude of Canadian politicians and officials brought on a rising, which was crushed after some hard fighting, and on May 15, 1885, Riel surrendered. He was imprisoned at Regina, was tried and on Aug. 1 found guilty of treason, and on Nov. 16 was hanged at Regina, meeting his fate with courage. His death was the signal for a fierce outburst of racialism in Quebec and Ontario, which nearly overthrew the Conservative government.

See J. S. Willison, *Sir Wilfrid Laurier*, vol. i; George Bryce, *History of the Hudson's Bay Company* (1900); and the Canadian daily press for 1885.

RIEMANN, GEORG FRIEDRICH BERNHARD

(1826–1866), German mathematician, was born on Sept. 17, 1826, at Breselenz, near Dannenberg in Hanover.

In 1840 he went to Hanover, where he attended the lyceum and two years later he entered the Johanneum at Lüneburg. The director, Schmalfuss, encouraged him in his mathematical studies by lending him books (among them Euler's works and Legendre's *Theory of Numbers*). In 1846 Riemann entered the university of Göttingen, where, although supposed to be studying theology, he attended lectures on the numerical solution of equations and on definite integrals by M. A. Stern, on terrestrial magnetism by Goldschmidt, and on the method of least squares by K. F. Gauss. In 1847 he went to Berlin, where P. G. L. Dirichlet, C. G. J. Jacobi, J. Steiner and F. G. M. Eisenstein were professors. During this period he formed those ideas on the theory of functions of a complex variable which led to his great discoveries.

In 1850 he returned to Göttingen and in 1851 obtained his doctorate with his celebrated thesis "Grundlagen für eine allgemeine Theorie der Functionen einer veränderlichen complexen Grösse."

In his Habilitationsschrift on the "Representation of a Function by Means of a Trigonometrical Series," Riemann shows his usual originality and refined style. The subject of his trial lecture, chosen by Gauss, was "On the Hypotheses which form the Foundation of Geometry." (*See* GEOMETRY: *Non-Euclidean*.) This wonderful work was published in the *Göttinger Abhandlungen* (1868) and a translation by Clifford in *Nature* (vol. 8).

Riemann's health had never been strong and now under the strain of work he broke down, and retired to the Harz with his friends Ritter and R. Dedekind, where he gave himself up to excursions and "Naturphilosophie." After his return to Göttingen (Nov. 1857) he was made extraordinary professor, and his salary raised to 300 thalers. Before this he had been in very straitened circumstances, and in 1855 was granted a government stipend of 200 thalers. On Dirichlet's death in 1859, Riemann was appointed his successor in Göttingen. He died at Selasca, on Lake Maggiore, on July 20, 1866. Most of his memoirs are masterpieces—full of original methods, profound ideas and far-reaching imagination. *See* RIEMANNIAN GEOMETRY below.

The collected works of Riemann were published by H. Weber, assisted by R. Dedekind (8vo, Leipzig, 1876; 2nd ed., 1892).

RIEMANNIAN GEOMETRY.

Any n independent variables x_i where i takes the values 1 to n, may be thought of as the coordinates of an n-dimensional space, or variety V_n, in the sense that each set of values of the x's defines a point of V_n. In a space as thus defined there is not an *a priori* basis for the determination of magnitude nor for the comparison of directions at two different points. Riemann proposed the study of the metric properties of a general V_n by introducing as the basis for measurement a quadratic differential form

$$\sum_{i, j}^{1,\ldots,n} g_{ij}dx_i dx_j,$$

where the g's are functions of the x's, subject to the restrictions that the determinant of the g's is not zero and that for all values of the differentials the above sum is positive. By definition the distance ds between the points of coordinates x_i and x_i+dx_i is given by

$$ds^2 = \sum_{i, j}^{1,\ldots,n} g_{ij}dx_i dx_j. \qquad (1)$$

This is a generalization of the first fundamental form of a surface in ordinary space when the surface is defined in terms of two parameters, as proposed by Gauss (*see* DIFFERENTIAL GEOMETRY). In this case the metric on the surface is induced by the Euclidean metric of the enveloping space, whereas in a general Riemannian space the metric is assigned.

From the hypotheses concerning (1) it can be shown that at any point

$$\sum_{i, j}^{1,\ldots,n} g_{ij} \frac{dx_i}{ds} \frac{\delta x_j}{\delta s}$$

is less than unity for two different sets of differentials dx_i and δx_i. Consequently a real angle θ is determined by the equation

$$\cos\theta = \sum_{i, j}^{1,\ldots,n} g_{ij} \frac{dx_i}{ds} \frac{\delta x_j}{\delta s}; \qquad (2)$$

by definition it is the *angle* between the directions at the point determined by the two sets of differentials. This is in keeping with the fact that the cosine of the angle between two tangents, at a point, to a surface in ordinary space when expressed in terms of the induced metric, is given by an equation of the form (2).

When we have n independent functions ϕ_i of the x's the equations

$$x'_i = \phi_i(x_1, \cdots, x_n) \qquad (i = 1, \cdots, n)$$

define a transformation of coordinates of the space. If the g's in (1) are such, which is rarely the case, that by a suitable transformation the form (1) is reducible to

$$ds^2 = \sum_i^{1,\ldots,n} (dx'_i)^2, \qquad (3)$$

which is a generalization of the metric of ordinary space in cartesian coordinates, we say that the space is flat, or *plane*; otherwise it is *curved*. The locus of points defined by

$$x_1 = f_1(t), \cdots, x_n = f_n(t)$$

for all values of the parameter t is called a *curve*. When these expressions are substituted in (1), we obtain an expression of the form $ds = F(t)dt$, and then the length of arc of the curve is given by integration. If the result of the integration is $s = \phi(t)$, by means of this equation the coordinates at points of the curve are expressible as functions of the arc s as parameter. The theory of curves involves $n-1$ principal curvatures, which are generalizations of the curvature and torsion of a curve in ordinary space.

Using the terminology of the calculus of variations, we say that the extremals of the integral

$$\int \left(\sum_{i,j}^{1,\ldots,n} g_{ij} \frac{dx_i}{ds} \frac{dx_j}{ds} \right)^{\frac{1}{2}} ds$$

are the shortest lines, or *geodesics*, of the space. The geodesics are found to be the integral curves of a system of differential equations

$$\frac{d^2 x_i}{ds^2} + \sum_{i,k}^{1,\ldots,n} \Gamma^i_{jk} \frac{dx_j}{ds} \frac{dx_k}{ds} = 0 \qquad (i = 1, \cdots, n), \qquad (4)$$

where the Γ's are certain functions of the g's and their first derivatives. When the space is flat and the coordinates are those for which the fundamental form is (3), all the functions Γ vanish identically. Consequently in the coordinate system the equations of the geodesics of the flat space are

$$x_i = a_i s + b_i, \qquad (i = 1, \cdots, n), \qquad (5)$$

where the a's and b's are constants. Thus the geodesics of a Riemannian space are the analogues of straight lines of a Euclidean space. Riemann showed that in a general space a coordinate system exists such that all the geodesics through a given point are defined by $a_i s$ $(i = 1, \ldots n) = 1$, but those through other points are not given by (5). In such a coordinate system the Γ's vanish at the given point, but not their derivatives.

Two sets of differentials dx_i and δx_i determine two directions at a point, and $a dx_i + b \delta x_i$, where a and b are parameters, a linear pencil of directions at the point. The geodesics issuing from a point P in a linear pencil of directions constitute a surface; the Gaussian curvature (*see* DIFFERENTIAL GEOMETRY) of this surface at P was taken by Riemann as the measure of curvature of the space for the given pencil. It is expressed in terms of the directions, and the components of a tensor of the fourth order, which involves the functions Γ^i_{jk} and their first derivatives; it is now known as the *Riemannian curvature tensor* (*see* TENSOR ANALYSIS). Ordinarily the curvature varies with the choice of the pencil. Schur showed that, if it is the same for all pencils at each point of the space, then it has the same value at every point; these are the spaces of constant Riemannian curvature; when, and only when, the constant is zero, the space is flat.

From time to time important contributions to Riemannian geometry were made by Bianchi, Beltrami, Christoffel, Voss and others, and Ricci co-ordinated and extended the theory simultaneously with the development of tensor calculus. These contributions include the study of a sub-space of a Riemannian space analogous to that of a surface in ordinary space. Such a sub-space of order r is the locus of points defined by the equations

$$x_i = \psi_i(u_1, \cdots, u_r) \qquad (i = 1, \cdots, n), \qquad (6)$$

where the u's are independent parameters. When these expressions are substituted in (1), we obtain an induced metric for the sub-space—a generalization of the first fundamental differential form of a surface (*see* DIFFERENTIAL GEOMETRY). There is also a generalized second fundamental form, whose coefficients enter in the relations between the curvatures of a curve in the sub-space relative to the latter and the curvatures of the curve as of the enveloping space. Among the curves of the sub-space there are geodesics, lines of curvature, asymptotic lines and conjugate systems of curves, which are generalizations of these types of curves on a surface in ordinary space. Einstein based his theory of gravitation upon the assumptions that physical space and time constitute a four-dimensional continuum whose metrical character is determined by the presence of matter, and that these spaces are of a particular kind defined in invariantive form by means of the curvature tensor; in this theory the fundamental form (1) is not positive for every choice of the differentials. This and other physical interpretations of differential geometry of spaces have stimulated the development of the theory.

Notable among contributions is the concept of parallelism of vectors in a general Riemannian space as introduced by Levi-Civita (1873–1942). In such a space parallelism is not absolute, as it is in Euclidean space, but is relative to the curve joining the points of application of the vectors. Thus for a curve $x_i = f_i(s)$ each set of solutions of the equations

$$\frac{d\xi^i}{ds} + \sum_{i,k}^{1,\ldots,n} \Gamma^i_{jk} \xi^j \frac{dx_k}{ds} = 0 \qquad (i = 1, \cdots, n) \qquad (7)$$

are the components of a family of vectors at the points of the curve which are parallel to one another with respect to the curves. Certain Riemannian spaces admit one or more fields of vectors, such that any two of them are parallel with respect to any curve joining their points of application. When there are n independent fields of this kind, the space is flat. In particular, the tangents to a geodesic are parallel with respect to the geodesic, as follows from (7) and (4), when we put $\xi^i = \frac{dx_i}{ds}$, geodesics are the straight lines of the space. This concept of parallelism is involved in many of the recent developments of Riemannian geometry and its generalizations have opened up new fields (*see* TENSOR ANALYSIS).

One type of generalization of Riemannian geometry is that in which there is no assigned metric, but the basic concept is a generalization of geodesic lines. These curves, called *paths* by Veblen and Eisenhart, are defined by equations of the form (4), in which now the quantities Γ^i_{jk} are assigned, and not derived as in the case of geodesics from the quadratic form (1). When the same interpretation is put upon the functions Γ^i_{jk} in equations (7), there is thus defined parallelism in this geometry, and the paths are straight lines, in the sense that all the tangents to a path are parallel to one another with respect to the path (*see* AFFINE GEOMETRY). From this basis a geometry has been developed in many respects analogous to Riemannian geometry which Eisenhart termed Non-Riemannian geometry. This term may be applied, however, to other geometries. For example, Finsler in his Goettingen Dissertation in 1918 proposed a metric different from that of Riemann, and there has been considerable study of Finsler spaces. Also Cartan has developed the geometry of metric spaces founded on the notion of area (Paris, 1933).

BIBLIOGRAPHY.—G. Ricci, *Lezioni sulla teoria delle superficie* (Padua, 1898); J. Struik, *Grundzüge, Mehrdimensialen Differentialgeometrie* (1922); J. A. Schouten, *Der Ricci-Kalkül* (1924); E. Cartan, *La géométrie des espaces de Riemann* (1925); L. P. Eisenhart, *Riemannian geometry* (1926); T. Levi-Civita, *The Absolute Differential Calculus* (Eng. trans. 1927); A. J. McConnell, *Applications of the Absolute Differential Calculus* (1931); C. E. Weatherburn, *Riemannian Geometry and the Tensor Calculus* (1938).   (L. P. E.)

RIENZI, COLA DI (*c.* 1313–1354), tribune of the Roman people, was born in Rome, the son of a tavern-keeper named Lorenzo Gabrini. His father's Christian name was shortened to Rienzo, and his own, Nicholas, to Cola; hence the Cola di Rienzi, or Rienzo, by which he is generally known. His early years were passed at Anagni. The study of the Latin writers, historians, orators and poets filled his mind with stories of the glories and the power of ancient Rome, and he dreamed of restoring his native city to its pristine greatness. His zeal was quickened by the desire to avenge his brother, who had been killed by a noble. Rienzi became a notary and a person of some importance in the city, and was sent in 1343 on a public errand to Pope Clement VI. at Avignon. He won the favour and esteem of the pope, who gave him an official position at his court. Returning to Rome about April 1344 he gathered a band of supporters, plans were drawn up, and at length all was ready for the rising. On May 19, 1347, heralds invited the people to a parliament on the Capitol, and on the 20th, Whit-Sunday, the meeting took place. Dressed in full armour and attended by the papal vicar, Cola headed a procession to the Capitol; here he addressed the assembled crowd on "the servitude and redemption of Rome." A new series of laws were adopted by acclamation, and unlimited authority was given to the author of the revolution. The nobles left the city or went into hiding, and a few days later Rienzi took the title of tribune (*Nicholaus, severus et clemens, libertatis, pacis justiciaeque tribunus, et sacre Romane Reipublice liberator*).

The new ruler governed the city with a stern justice, in marked contrast to the recent reign of licence. The tribune moved through the streets of Rome in state, being received at St. Peter's with the hymn *Veni Creator spiritus*. Petrarch wrote to him, urging him to continue his great and noble work, and called him the new Camillus, Brutus and Romulus. In July in a sonorous decree he proclaimed the sovereignty of the Roman people over the empire, but before this he had set to work to restore the authority of Rome over the cities and provinces of Italy, to make the city again *caput mundi*. He invited the cities of Italy to send representatives to an assembly to meet on Aug. 1, when the formation of a great federation under the headship of Rome would be considered. On the appointed day representatives appeared, and after elaborate and fantastic ceremonial Rienzi, as dictator, issued an edict citing the emperor Charles IV., and also the imperial electors and all others concerned in the dispute, to appear before him in order that he might pronounce judgment in the case. On the following day the festival of the unity of Italy was celebrated.

Rienzi's power was recognized in Naples, whence both Queen Joanna and her bitter foe, King Louis of Hungary, appealed to him for protection. On Aug. 15 he was installed tribune with great pomp, wreaths of flowers being placed on his head. Gregorovius says this ceremony "was the fantastic caricature in which ended the imperium of Charles the Great. A world where political action was represented in such guise was ripe for overthrow, or could only be saved by a great mental reformation." Rienzi then seized, but soon released, Stephen Colonna and other barons who had spoken disparagingly of him. But his power was waning. His extravagant pretensions excited ridicule. His government was costly, and he was obliged to lay heavy taxes upon the people. He offended both pope and emperor by his proposal to set up a new Roman empire, resting directly upon the will of the people. In October Clement gave power to a legate to depose him and bring him to trial. The exiled barons gathered some troops, and war began. Rienzi obtained aid from Louis of Hungary and others, and on Nov. 20 his forces defeated the nobles in a battle outside the gates of Rome, where Rienzi's most distinguished foe, Stephen Colonna, was killed. But this victory did not save him. He passed his time in feasts and pageants, while in a bull the pope denounced him as a criminal, a pagan and a heretic, until, terrified by a slight disturbance on Dec. 15, he abdicated and fled from Rome. He sought refuge in Naples, but soon left that city and spent over two years in a mountain monastery.

Emerging from his solitude Rienzi journeyed to Prague, which he reached in July 1350, and threw himself upon the protection of the emperor Charles IV. Denouncing the temporal power of the pope he implored the emperor to deliver Italy, and especially Rome, from their oppressors; but Charles kept him in prison for more than a year in the fortress of Raudnitz, and then handed him over to Clement. At Avignon, where he appeared in August 1352, Rienzi was tried by three cardinals, and was sentenced to death, but this judgment was not carried out, and he remained in prison. In December 1352 Clement died, and his successor, Innocent VI., anxious to strike a blow at the baronial rulers of Rome, pardoned and released his prisoner. Giving him the title of senator, he sent him to Italy with the legate, Cardinal Albornoz, and Rienzi, with a few mercenaries, entered Rome in August 1354. He was received with great rejoicing, and regained his former position. A tumult broke out on Oct. 8. Rienzi attempted to address the mob, but the building in which he stood was fired, and while trying to escape in disguise he was murdered. In 1887 a statue of the tribune was erected at the foot of the Capitoline hill in Rome.

Rienzi's life and fate have formed the subject of a famous novel by Bulwer Lytton, of an opera by Wagner and of a tragedy by Julius Mosen. His letters, edited by A. Gabrielli, are published in vol. vi. of the *Fonti per la storia d'Italia* (Rome, 1890). *See* also Papencordt,

Cola di Rienzo und seine Zeit (Hamburg, 1841); Auriac, *Étude historique sur N. Rienzi* (Amiens, 1885); E. Rodocanachi, *Cola di Rienzi* (Paris, 1888); Kühn, *Die Entwickelung der Bündnispläne Cola di Rienzos im Jahre 1347* (Berlin, 1905); A. von Reumont, *Geschichte der Stadt Rom* (1867–70); and F. Gregorovius, *Geschichte der Stadt Rom im Mittelalter*, vol. vi. (Eng. trans., by A. Hamilton, 1898).

RIESA, a German town, in Saxony, on the Elbe, 30 m. N.W. of Dresden, on the main line of railway to Leipzig, and at the junction of lines to Chemnitz, Elsterwerda and Nossen. Pop. (1939) 29,873. Riesa received municipal rights in 1632, and after a period of decay was again raised to the rank of a town in 1859. The town contains a castle, which is now used as a town hall. There are rolling-mills and saw-mills and ironworks. Other industries are the manufacture of furniture, beer, soap, carriages, marble wares, and bricks. The most important shipping station on the Elbe in Saxony, Riesa is the lading-place for goods to and from Bavaria, and a mart for herrings, petroleum, wood and grain. A passenger steamboat service is maintained with Meissen and Dresden.

RIESENER, JEAN HENRI (1734–1806), French cabinet-maker of the Louis XVI. period, was born at Gladbach near Cologne on July 4, 1734, and died in Paris on Jan. 6, 1806. At an early age he went to Paris, where he entered the workshop in the arsenal of Jean François Oeben. When his master died, Riesener became foreman of the works; two years later he married Mme. Oeben. By 1782 he had accumulated a fortune of about £40,000 and had received the title, formerly Oebens's, of "Ébéniste du Roi." Riesener was unquestionably the greatest of the Louis Seize cabinet-makers. His work is generally bold and graceful. His marquetry presents an extraordinary finish; his chiselled bronzes are of the first excellence. He was especially distinguished for his cabinets, in which he employed many European as well as exotic woods. Wreaths and bunches of flowers form the centres of the panels; on the sides are often diaper patterns in quiet colours. His high-water mark was reached in the Bureau du Roi, conceived by Oeben, finished in 1769 and consequently belonging rather to the Louis Quinze than the Louis Seize period, and a similar cylinder bureau believed to have been made for Stanislas Leszczynski, king of Poland, now in the Wallace Collection. At Buckingham Palace there is a third bureau on the same lines. These pieces are triumphs of marquetry. For long Riesener followed Oeben, but there was a gradual transition to a style more individual, more delicately conceived, with finer but hardly less vigorous lines. By the time he had been working alone for ten years he had completely embraced the Louis Seize manner —he had, perhaps, some responsibility for it. One of the most distinguished of his achievements for the court was the famous flat writing-table now at the Petit Trianon. Some of his creations are vitiated by being mounted with panels of Sèvres, Wedgwood and other china. Such is the beautiful little secretaire in the Jones collection in the Victoria and Albert Museum.

See F. de Salverte, *Les Ébénistes du XVIII. Siècle* (Paris, 1927).

RIESENGEBIRGE or **GIANT MOUNTAINS,** a lofty and rugged group on the boundary between Prussian Silesia and Bohemia, between the upper courses of the Elbe and the Oder. They are continued towards the north-west in the Erzgebirge, the Thuringian Forest and the Harz Mountains. Adjoining the Isergebirge and the Lausitzergebirge on the west, and the Eulengebirge and the Adlergebirge on the east and south-east, the Riesengebirge proper trend south-east and north-west between the sources of the Zacken and the Bober, for a distance of 23 m., with a breadth of 14 miles. They cover an area of about 425 sq.m., three-quarters of which is in Czecho-Slovakia, the rest in Germany. The boundary line follows the crest of the principal ridge (Riesenkamm, average height 4,000 ft.), which stretches along the northern side of the group. The principal peaks are the Reifträger (4,430 ft.), the Hohes Rad (4,950 ft.), the Great Sturmhaube (4,862 ft.), the Little Sturmhaube (4,646 ft.), and, near the east extremity, the Schneekoppe (5,258 ft.), the loftiest mountain in northern or central Germany. Roughly parallel to this northern ridge, and separated from it by a long narrow valley of the Siebengründe, there extends on the south a lower chain, of broad massive "saddles," with comparatively few peaks. The chief heights here are Kesselkoppe (4,708 ft.), the Krkonose (4,849 ft.), the Ziegenrücken and the Brunnenberg (5,072 ft.). From both ridges spurs are sent off, whence a magnificent view is obtained from Breslau to Prague; the lowlands of Silesia, watered by the Oder, and those of Bohemia, intersected by the Elbe and Moldau, appear to lie mapped in relief near the *Schneekoppe*. A group of isolated columnar rocks known as the *Adersbacher Felsen* occur in a valley on the Bohemian side of the Riesengebirge, 9 m. from Braunau.

On its northern side this mountain group has a rugged and precipitous slope from the Hirschberg valley; but on its southern slope, towards Bohemia, a more gradual one. The Bohemian ridge is cleft about the middle by a deep gorge through which pour the headwaters of the river Elbe, which finds its source in the Siebengründe. A great number of small streams also rise among these mountains and small lakes and tarns are not unfrequent. The Great and Little Schneegruben—two deep rocky gorge-like valleys in which snow remains all the year round—lie to the north of the Hohes Rad.

A wide range of rock formations occurs in the Riesengebirge. Archaean gneisses and schists form an important part, but Palaeozoic and Mesozoic rocks (especially Jurassic and Cretaceous) are also important. Variscan and Tertiary folding affected the region and north-easterly faults run along the foot of the Isergebirge and Riesengebirge. Extensive peat moors occupy many of the mountain slopes and valleys. The lower parts of the mountains are clad with forests of oak, beech, pine and fir; above 1,600 ft. only the last two kinds of trees are found, and beyond about 3,950 ft. only the dwarf pine (*Pinus Pumilio*). Various alpine plants are found, some of them having been artificially introduced on the Schneekoppe. Wheat is grown to an elevation of 1,800 ft. above the sea and oats as high as 2,700 feet.

The Riesengebirge is easily accessible by railway, several branches from the main lines on both sides, penetrating the valleys, and thus many spots are a good deal frequented in the summer. The Schneekoppe and other summits are annually visited by numbers of travellers, notably the spas of Warmbrunn (near Hirschberg) and Flinsberg on the Gneis, and Görbersdorf, with its sanatorium. The Riesengebirge is the legendary home of Number Nip (Rübezahl), a goblin of German folklore.

RIETI (anc. *Reate*), a city and episcopal see of Italy, the capital of the province of Rieti, 25½ mi. by rail and 15 mi. direct S.S.E. of Terni, which is 70 mi. by rail from Rome. Population (1936) 14,366 (town), 34,769 (commune). It is 1,318 ft. above sea level on the right bank of the Velino (a torrent subtributary to the Tiber), which at this point issues from the limestone plateau; the old town occupies the declivity and the new town spreads out on the level. While with its quaint red-roofed houses, its old town walls (some Roman fragments, restored about 1250), its cathedral (13th and 15th centuries), its episcopal palace (1283), and its various churches and convents Rieti has much mediaeval picturesqueness; it also displays a good deal of modern activity in corn, vine and olive growing and cattle-breeding. The fertility of the neighbourhood is celebrated both by Virgil and by Cicero.

In 1149 the town was besieged and captured by Roger I. of Sicily. In the struggle between church and empire, it always held with the former; and it defied the forces of Frederick II. and Otho IV. Pope Nicholas IV. long resided at Rieti, and it was there he crowned Charles II. of Anjou king of the Two Sicilies. In the 14th century Robert, and afterwards Joanna of Naples managed to keep possession of Rieti for many years, but it returned to the States of the Church under Gregory IX.

About the year 1500, the liberties of the town, long defended against the encroachments of the popes, were entirely abolished. An earthquake in 1785 was in 1799 followed by the pillage of Rieti by the Neapolitans.

See G. Colasanti, *Rieti* (Perugia. 1911).

RIEVAULX (rē-ę-vō), a village, North Riding, Yorkshire, England, three miles west by north of Helmsley, which is served by the L.N.E. railway. Pop. (1931) 208. It is situated on the River Rye before it emerges from the York moors into the Vale of Pickering. The name is probably a corruption of Rye Vale. Rievaulx abbey, one of the most beautiful ruins in Yorkshire, was founded by the Cistercians in 1131. The principal remains are those of a cruciform church which is mainly Early English in style and is of very fine workmanship. Considerable fragments of the refectory remain and the domestic buildings may be traced.

RIF CAMPAIGNS: see MOROCCO: *History, 19th Century.*

RIFIS, the name given to the Berbers of the Rîf district of Morocco, the mountain region bordering the north coast from Ceuta eastward nearly to the borders of Algeria and forming part of the Atlas range. The Rîf dialect changes the Arabic "l" to "r," and this supports the derivation of "Rifi" from "Libi," "b" and "f" being interchangeable. *See* MOROCCO.

RIFLE: see SMALL ARMS, THE DEVELOPMENT OF.

RIFLE-BIRD or **RIFLEMAN-BIRD,** the name applied to birds of paradise (*q.v.*) of the genera *Ptilorrhis* and *Craspidornis,* probably because their plumage bears some resemblances to the full-dress uniform (green and black) of the British rifle regiments. There are five species, of which one inhabits New Guinea and the others the Australian continent. The best known is *P. paradisea.* See R. B. Sharpe, *Monograph of the Paradiseidae.*

RIGA, a seaport of Latvia, of which it is the capital, in 57° 3′ N., 24° 1′ E. Pop. (1939) 393,211. It is situated at the southern extremity of the Gulf of Riga, 8 mi. above the mouth of the western Dvina, which is connected by means of inland canals with the basins of the Dnieper and Volga. The Gulf of Riga is 100 mi. long and 60 mi. wide, with shallow waters of slight salinity and a greatest depth of 22 fathoms. It is frozen for an average of 127 days in the year. The sea entrance has a depth of 24½ ft. which is dredged constantly to 26 ft. The channel up to the town is 26 ft. deep, and the depth at the quays varies from 18 to 26 ft. There are vast warehouses and a large grain elevator. The port has eight state-owned electric cranes of 2.5 tons as well as seven private ones of larger capacity, including two electric revolving cranes (25 and 10 tons) and floating cranes of 130-, 15- and 5-ton capacity. The Riga Exchange committee's slip dock at Bolderaja is capable of taking ships up to 1,000 tons. Large ships unload at Ust-Dvinsk (formerly Dünamünde). The imports ordinarily are herrings, foodstuffs, clothing, sugar, tobacco, industrial and agricultural machinery, mechanical tools, railway equipment, coal, coke and fertilizers, and the exports flax, timber, wooden goods, dairy produce and meat (pork and ham). The town manufactures paper, wood pulp, cellulose, matches, veneered goods, paints and varnishes, textiles (especially cotton and linen goods), boots and shoes, rubber goods, cement, vegetable oils, tobacco and alcoholic drinks. Manufactures were seriously hampered by the destruction of factories and plants during World War I; Riga was occupied by German troops in September 1917 and held to the end of the war.

Riga consists of four parts—the old town and suburbs on the right bank of the Dvina (Latvian, *Daugava*), and the Mitau suburb on the left bank, the two sides being connected by a floating bridge, which is removed in winter, and by a viaduct, 820 ft. long. The old town still preserves its Hanseatic features—high storehouses, with spacious granaries and cellars, flanking the narrow, winding streets. The only open spaces are the market-place and two other squares. The suburbs, with their broad and quiet boulevards on the site of the fortifications, grew steadily during the period of Latvian independence, 1918–1939.

Few antiquities of the mediaeval town remain. The oldest church, the Dom (St. Mary's), founded in 1215, was burned in 1547, and the present building dates from the second half of the 16th century, but has been thoroughly restored since 1883. Its organ, dating from 1883, is one of the largest in the world. St. Peter's church, with a beautiful tower 412 ft. high, was erected in 1406–9. The castle was built in 1494–1515 by the master of the Knights of the Sword, Walter von Plettenberg, a spacious building often rebuilt. The "House of the Black Heads," a corporation, or club, of foreign merchants, was founded in 1330, and subsequently became the meeting-place of the wealthier youth.

The Livländische Ritterhaus, the former place of meeting of the Livonian nobility, still stands. Near the city are extensive

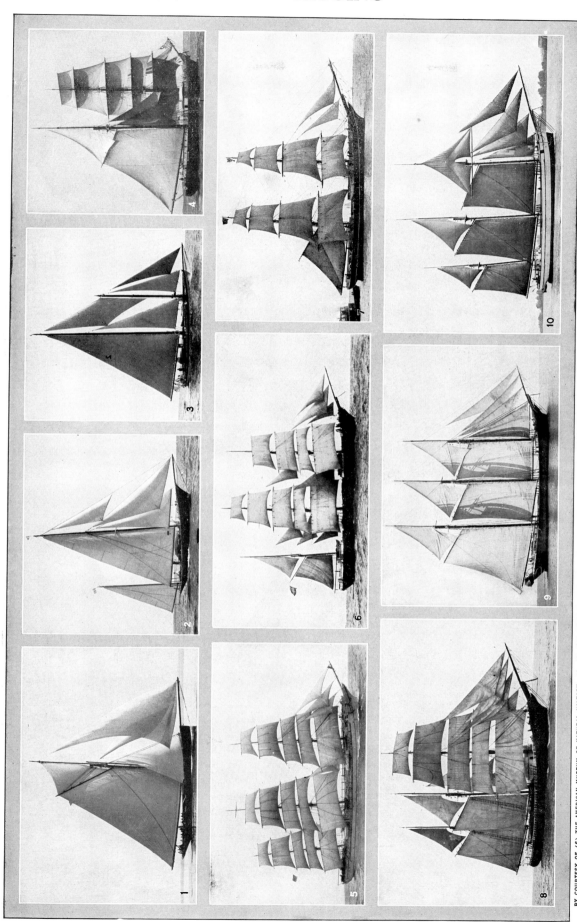

VARIOUS TYPES OF SAILING VESSELS AND THEIR RIGGING

1. A cutter, with gaff-mainsail and topsail
2. A yawl, with Bermuda or jib-headed rig
3. A staysail schooner, so-called because of the staysails between the masts instead of the regular foresail
4. A brigantine, or hermaphrodite brig
5. A full-rigged ship, square-rigged on all three masts
6. A barque, square-rigged on fore and main masts and fore and aft rigged on the mizen
7. A brig; two-masted ship, square-rigged on both masts
8. A barquentine; three-masted ship, square-rigged on foremast only
9. A three-masted schooner, fore-and-aft-rigged on all three masts
10. A Great Lakes schooner, with a raffee or triangular sail on the foremast

PLATE II RIGGING

PHOTOGRAPHS, (1, 2, 3, 7, 8) DONALD MCLEISH, (4, 9) SPORT AND GENERAL PRESS AGENCY, (5) EWING GALLOWAY, (6) THE NAUTICAL PHOTO AGENCY

SAILING BOATS OF DIFFERENT NATIONS

1. Arab dhow with long overhanging forepart, an open waist and high poop
2. Native trading boat of the type frequently found on the River Nile
3. Small fishing boat on an Italian lake
4. Chinese junk
5. Japanese sampans
6. Chinese junk
7. Broad beamed Venetian trading boat
8. Dutch fishing boat as used on the Zuider Zee
9. English fishing smacks

summer bathing beaches, with little wooden chalets. When Dorpat (Tartu) university, which served all the Russian Baltic provinces, became Estonian property in 1919, Riga Polytechnic institute was made a university. In 1939 7,231 students were enrolled.

History.—Riga was founded in 1158, as a storehouse at the mouth of the river, by a few Bremen merchants. About 1190 the Augustinian monk Meinhard erected a monastery there, and in 1199–1201 Bishop Albert I of Livonia obtained from Pope Innocent III permission for German merchants to land at the new settlement, and chose it for his seat, exercising his power over the neighbouring district in co-operation with the Teutonic Knights. As early as the first half of the 13th century the city obtained the right of electing its own magistracy. It joined the Hanseatic League, and from 1253 refused to recognize the rights of the bishop and the knights. In 1420 it fell under the rule of the bishop, who maintained his authority until 1566, when it was abolished in consequence of the Reformation. Sigismund II, king of Poland, took Riga in 1547, and in 1558 the Russians burned its suburbs. In 1561 Gotthard Kettler abdicated his mastership of the order of the Teutonic Knights, and Riga, with southern Livonia, became a Polish possession. After some unsuccessful attempts to reintroduce Roman Catholicism, Stephen Bathory, king of Poland, recognized the religious freedom of the Protestant population. In 1621 Gustavus Adolphus, king of Sweden, took it from Poland, and the Swedes held it when the Poles and Russians besieged it in 1656. During the Northern War between Sweden and Russia, it was defended (1700), but after the battle of Poltava it was taken in July 1710 by the Russians. In 1919 it became the capital of the independent republic of Latvia. During World War II the town was occupied by the Russians, then by the Germans.

RIGAUD, HYACINTHE (1659–1743), French painter, born at Perpignan on July 20, 1659, was the descendant of a line of artists. He was sent to Montpellier to study under Pezet, and afterwards went to Lyons, and in 1681 to Paris. There he obtained the grand prix de Rome, but on the advice of Jean Le Brun he allowed it to lapse and devoted himself to painting portraits. For 62 years he did as many as 30 to 40 portraits a year. But Rigaud, although purely a portrait painter, set his heart on gaining admission to the academy as a historical painter, and succeeded in Jan. 1700. He died on Dec. 27, 1743.

His principal portraits at the Louvre are those of himself and his mother (Marie Serre), of the sculptor Desjardins, of Mignard and Le Brun, of Bossuet and of Louis XIV.

RIGBY, RICHARD (1722–1788), English politician, was the only son of Richard Rigby (d. 1730) of Mistley Hall, Essex, a merchant who made a fortune through his connection with the South Sea company. Young Rigby became an associate of Frederick, prince of Wales, and entered parliament in 1745. He is chiefly known to fame through his connection with John Russell, 4th duke of Bedford, and the "Bloomsbury gang," his audacity earning for him the title of the "brazen boatswain" of the "crew." In 1758 he became secretary to Bedford, who was lord lieutenant of Ireland, and in 1759 he was given the office of master of the rolls for Ireland. Following the political fortunes of the duke he became vice-treasurer of Ireland in 1765, and in 1768 he obtained the position of paymaster-general of the forces. Rigby often spoke in parliament, and in 1769 he shared in the opposition to Wilkes. In 1784 he resigned his position as paymaster-general, and was surprised and embarrassed when requested to pay over the sum of public money which was in his possession. He left a fortune when he died at Bath on April 8, 1788. Wraxall says that Rigby "possessed talents for addressing a popular assembly which were sustained by a confidence that nothing could abash."

RIGEL, the bright star at the heel of the constellation Orion (*q.v.*). It is of magnitude 0.34, being one of the brightest stars in the sky. Its equivalent in the alphabetical series is β Orionis. Rigel is in reality—as well as apparently—one of the brightest stars known. It is a blue supergiant located at a probable distance from the sun of about 1,100 light-years. If Rigel were as close to the sun as the bright star Sirius (nine light-years), it would shine with a brilliancy similar to that of the half-moon. (*See* STAR.)   (W. W. M.)

RIGG, JAMES HARRISON (1821–1909), English Nonconformist divine, was born at Newcastle-on-Tyne on Jan. 16, 1821. In 1845 he entered the Wesleyan ministry, and during the agitation of 1849–52 wrote successfully in exposition and defence of the polity of Methodism. In 1857 he published *Modern Anglican Theology*, an acute criticism of the writings of Coleridge, Hare, Maurice, Kingsley and Jowett. In 1868 Rigg was appointed Principal of the Westminster Wesleyan Training College for day-school teachers, a post which he held for 35 years. In 1870 he was elected on the first School Board for London. In 1886 he sat on the Royal Commission of Education. In 1878 he was elected president of conference—and again in 1892. He resigned his principalship in 1903 and died at Brixton on April 17, 1909.

See *Life* by John Telford (1909). His other works include: *National Education in its Social Conditions and Aspects* (1873); *The Living Wesley* (1875, reissued as *The Centennial Life of Wesley* in 1891); *Character and Life-work of Dr. Pusey* (1893); *Oxford High Anglicanism and its chief Leaders* (1895).

RIGGING (A.S. *wrigan* or *wrihan*, to clothe), the general term, in connection with ships, for the whole apparatus of masts, yards, sails and cordage. (*See* also SHIP; YACHT; SEAMANSHIP.) The word is also used as meaning the cordage only.

SAILING SHIPS

Sailing vessels of all classes are classed according to their "rig," *i.e.*, the particular combination of spars, sails and cordage. "Cutter," "brig," or "ship," are really convenient abbreviations for "cutter-rigged," "brig-rigged," or "ship-rigged."

The basis of all rigging is the mast whether it be composed of one or of many pieces of wood or of steel. The mast is supported against fore and aft or athwartship strains by fore and back stays and by shrouds, known as the "standing rigging," because they are made fast, and not hauled upon. In the case of a mast composed of several parts, including topmast and topgallant mast, the stays, and other ropes which keep the top and topgallant masts in place, are however only comparative fixtures as they may be cast off when these masts are lowered down. The bowsprit, though it does not rise from the deck but projects from the bow, is in the nature of a mast. The masts and bowsprit support all the sails, whether they hang from yards, slung across the mast, or from gaffs, projecting from the mast, or, as in the case of the jibs, or other triangular sails, travelling on the ropes called "stays," which go from the mast to the bowsprit or deck. The bowsprit is subdivided like the masts. The bowsprit proper corresponds to the lower fore-, main- or mizzen-mast. The jib-boom, which is movable and projects beyond the bowsprit, corresponds to a topmast; the flying jib-boom, which also is movable and projects beyond the jib-boom, answers to a topgallant mast. The ropes by which the yards, booms and sails are manipulated for trimming to the wind or for making or shortening sail, are known as the "running rigging." The rigging also provides the crew with the means of going aloft, and for laying out on the yards to let fall or to furl the sail. Therefore the shrouds (*see* below) are utilized to form ladders, the steps of which are called ratlines. Near the heads of the lower masts are the tops—platforms on which men can stand —and in the same place on the topmasts are the "cross-trees," of which the main function is to extend the topgallant shrouds. The yards are provided with ropes, extending from the middle to the extremities or yard-arms, called foot-ropes, which hang down about 2 or 3 ft., and on which men can stand. The material of which the cordage is made differs greatly. Leather has been used but the prevailing materials have been hemp or grass rope, and, in recent days, chain and wire. As the whole of the rigging is divided into standing and running, so a rope forming part of the rigging is divided into the "standing part" and the "fall." The standing part is that which is made fast to the mast, deck or block. The fall is the loose end or part on which the crew haul. The block is the pulley through which the rope runs. A "tackle" (pronounced "taikel") is a combination of ropes and blocks which gives increased power at the lifting or moving end, as distinct from the end which is being "manned." If fig. 1 is followed from the bow to the mizzenmast, it will be seen that a succession

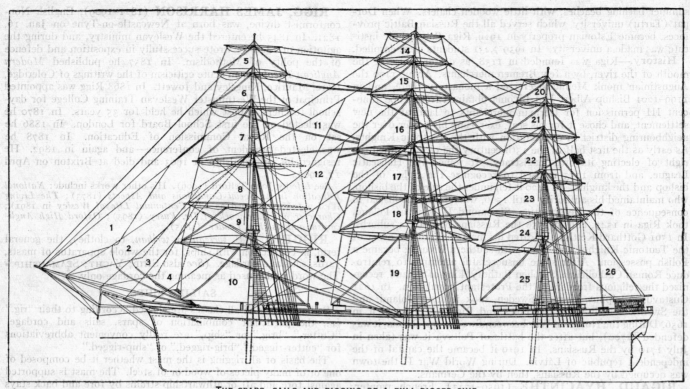

THE SPARS, SAILS AND RIGGING OF A FULL-RIGGED SHIP

1. Flying jib; 2. Outer jib; 3. Inner jib; 4. Jib; 5. Fore skysail; 6. Fore royal; 7. Fore topgallant sail; 8. Fore upper topsail; 9. Fore lower topsail; 10. Foresail; 11. Main royal staysail; 12. Main topgallant staysail; 13. Main topmast staysail; 14. Main skysail; 15. Main royal; 16. Main topgallant sail; 17. Main upper topsail; 18. Main lower topsail; 19. Mainsail; 20. Mizzen skysail; 21. Mizzen royal; 22. Mizzen topgallant sail; 23. Mizzen upper topsail; 24. Mizzen lower topsail; 25. Crossjack; 26. Spanker

of stays connect the masts with the hull of the ship or with one another. All pull together to resist pressure from in front. Pressure from behind is met by the backstays, which connect the topmasts and topgallant masts with the sides of the vessel. Lateral pressure is met by the shrouds and breast-backstays. A temporary or "preventer" backstay is used when great pressure is to be met. The bobstays hold down the bowsprit, which is liable to be lifted by the tug of the jibs and of the stays connecting it with the fore-topmast. If the bowsprit is lifted the fore-topmast loses part of its support.

The running rigging by which all spars are hoisted or lowered and sails spread or taken in may be divided into those which lift and lower—the lifts, jeers, halliards (haulyards)—and those which hold down the lower corners of the sails—the tacks and sheets. A long technical treatise would be required to name the many parts of standing and running rigging and their uses. All that is attempted here is to give the main lines and general principles or divisions.

The vessel dealt with here is the fully rigged ship with three masts. But the principles of others are the same. The simplest of all forms of rigging is the dipping lug, a quadrangular sail hanging from a yard and always hoisted on the side of the mast opposite to that on which the wind is blowing (the lee side). When the boat is to be tacked so as to bring the wind on the other side, the sail is lowered and rehoisted. One rope can serve as halliard to hoist the sail and as a stay when it is made fast on the weather side on which the wind is blowing. The difference between such a craft and the fully rigged ship is that between a simple organism and a very complex one; but it is one of degree, not of kind. The steps in the scale are innumerable. Every sea has its own type. (See Pl. II, figs. 1, 2, 3, 4, 5, 6, 7.) Some in eastern waters are of extreme antiquity, and even in Europe vessels are still to be met with which differ very little if at all from ships of the Norsemen of the 9th and 10th centuries. For a full account of these varieties of rigging the reader may be referred to Mast and Sail in Europe and Asia (London, 1906), by H. Warington Smyth.

When the finer degrees of variation are neglected the types of

rigging may be reduced to comparatively few, which can be classed by the shape of their sail and the number of their masts. At the bottom of the scale is such a craft as the Norse herring boat. This boat has one quadrangular sail suspended from a yard which is hung (or slung) by the middle to a single mast which is placed (or stepped) in the middle of the boat. She is the direct representative of the ships of the Norsemen. Her one sail is a "course" such as is still used on the fore and mainmasts of a fully developed ship; a topsail may be added (above the course) and then we have the beginning of a fully clothed mast. A very similar craft called a Humber keel is used in the north of England. The lug sail is an advance on the course, since it is better adapted for sailing on the wind, with the wind on the side. When the lug is not meant to be lowered, and rehoisted on the lee side, as in the dipping lug mentioned above, it is slung at a third from the end of the yard, and is called a standing lug. A good example of the lug is the junk (Pl. II, figs. 4, 6). The lug is a "lifting sail," and does not tend to press the vessel down as the fore and aft sail does. Therefore it is much used by fishing vessels in the North Sea. The type of the fore and aft rig is the schooner (Pl. I, fig. 9). The sails on the masts have a gaff above and a boom below. These spars have a prong called "the jaws," which fit to the mast, and are held in place by a "jaw rope" on which are threaded beads called trucks. Sails of this shape are carried by fully rigged ships on the mizzenmast, and can be spread on the fore and main. They are then called trysails and are used only in bad weather when little sail can be carried, and are hoisted on the trysail mast, a small mast above the great one. The lateen sail (Pl. II, fig. 2) is a triangular sail akin to the lug, and is the prevailing type of the Mediterranean. These original types, even when unmodified by mixture with any other, permit of large variations. The number of masts of a lugger may vary from one to five, and of a schooner from two to five or even seven. A small lug may be carried above the large one, and a gaff topsail added to the sails of a schooner. A one-masted fore-and-aft-rigged vessel may be a cutter (Pl. I, fig. 1) or sloop. But the pure types may be combined, in topsail schooners, brigantines, barquentines and barques, when the topsail, a quadrangular sail hanging from and fastened to a yard, slung by the middle, is combined with fore and aft sails. The lateen rig has been combined with the square rig to make such a rigging as the xebec—a three-masted vessel square rigged on the main, and lateen on the fore and mizzen. Triangular sails of the same type as the jibs can be set on the stays between the masts of a fully rigged ship, and are then known as staysails. But it can only be repeated that the variations are innumerable. Studding-sails (pronounced "stun-sails") are lateral extensions to the courses, topsails, etc., of a square-rigged ship to increase the spread of sails, that require the support of special yards, booms and tackle.

The development of the rigging of ships is a very obscure subject. It was the work of centuries, and of practical men who wrote no treatises. It has never been universal. A comparison of the four-masted junk given above with the figures of ships on mediaeval seals shows at least much similarity. Yet by selecting a few leading types of successive periods it is possible to follow the growth of the fully rigged ship, at least in its main lines, in modern times.

For a time, and after the use of spritsails had been given up, the spritsail yard continued to be used to discharge the function now given to the gaffs. (*See* Smyth, *Sailor's Word-Book*.) The changes in the mizzen have an obscure history. About the middle of the 18th century it ceased to be a pure lateen. The yard was retained, but no sail was set on the fore part of the yard. Then the yard was given up and replaced by a gaff. The resulting new sail was called the spanker. It was, however, comparatively narrow, and when a greater spread of sail was required, a studding-sail (at first called a "driver") was added, with a boom at its foot. At a later date "spanker" and "driver" were used as synonymous terms, and the studding-sail was called a "ringtail." The studding-sails are the representatives of a class of sail once more generally used. In modern times a sail is cut of the extreme size which is capable of being carried in fine weather, and when the wind increases in strength it is reefed—*i.e.*, part is gathered up and fastened by reef points, small cords attached to the sail. Till the 17th century at least the method was often to cut the courses small, so that they could be carried in rough weather. When a greater spread of sail was required, a piece called a bonnet was added to the foot of the sail, and a further piece called a drabbler could be added to that. It is an example of the tenacious conservatism of the sea that this practice is still retained by the Swedish small craft called "lodjor" in the Baltic and White Sea. It will be easily understood that no innovation was universally accepted at once. Jib and sprit topsail, lateen-mizzen and spanker, and so forth, would be found for long on the sea together.

The history of the development of rigging is one of adjustment. The size of the masts had to be adapted to the ship, and it was necessary to find the due proportion between yards and masts. As the size of the mediaeval ship increased, the natural course was to increase the height of the mast and of the sail it carried. Even when the mast was subdivided into lower, top and topgallant, the lower mast was too long, and the strain of the sail racked the hull. Hence the constant tendency of the ships to leak. Sir Henry Manwayring, when giving the proper proportions of the masts, says that the Flemings (*i.e.*, the Dutch) made them taller than the English, which again forced them to make the sails less wide.

A few words may be added concerning the tops. In the earlier form of ships the top was a species of crow's nest placed at the head of the mast to hold a look-out, or in military operations to give a place of advantage to archers and slingers. They appear occasionally as mere bags attached to one side of the mast. As a general rule they are round. In the 16th century there were frequently two tops on the fore- and main-masts, one at the head of the lower, another at the head of the topmast, where in later times there have only been the two traverse beams which make the crosstrees. The upper top dropped out by the 17th century. The form was round, and so continued to be till the 18th century when the quadrangular form was introduced.

Rigging in Power Ships.—The steam and motor ship still carries one or more masts for supporting derricks, for lifting heavy weights in and out of the ship, for carrying wireless aerials, for providing a platform for look out aloft, for mounting the steaming lights and for visual signalling. In the bigger ships the masts are usually hollow steel structures, occasionally with an internal ladderway, while in some merchant ships they also act as uptake ventilators. Stays are usually provided on the same principle as in sailing days, but dead eyes have given way to bottle screws as rope has to wire. Where masts are provided with ladderways, either internally or externally on the iron structure itself, ratlines on the rigging are dispensed with. Modern battleships, battle cruisers and light cruisers in the British navy usually have a tripod foremast in which the lower mast is supported by two inclined steel struts instead of rigging. This is to give the necessary rigidity for mounting the gun director, (*see* GUNNERY, NAVAL) control top and rangefinder.

The main mast usually carries the main derrick and is stayed on the old lines. Wooden topmasts and sometimes topgallant masts are fitted for wireless and signalling, while one or more signal yards are always carried on the foremast. In light cruisers the main mast is usually a small wooden pole. Destroyers and other light craft are fitted with a light wooden foremast and usually a short main or mizzen mast.

The upper end of the standing rigging is shackled to steel bands round the lower masthead and their lower ends are secured to the deck by bottle screws and slips, the screw being locked by a check piece which prevents it easing back, and together with its slip it is covered with painted canvas.

The topmast rigging, consisting of the usual shrouds, stays and back stays is fitted with insulators so as to avoid interference with wireless and danger from lightning. In the case of ships with a tripod foremast it is set up to projections on a level with the base of the control top instead of being brought right down to deck level. A Jacob's ladder gives access to the masthead, whilst above all is a lightning conductor connected by a copper strap running down the mast to the hull of the ship. Where a masthead flashing lamp is fitted, a gallows is provided for its reception. In flagships a pole 16 feet long is clamped to the fore topmast or fore topgallant mast head to carry the Admiral's flag.

Modern Running Rigging.—The only semblance to running rigging in a modern power ship is as follows:

Gantlines, which can be rove through a sheave in the topmast for tricing weights aloft and general purposes.

Clothes lines and hammock gantlines, used for drying clothes or hammocks, which in warships are of thin flexible steel rope which lead through blocks on a shroud near the fore or main lower mast heads and are set up well forward or well aft.

Dressing lines, leading from the foremast awning stantion over both topmasts and down to the after awning stantion. To these are attached flags for "dressing ship."

Signal halyards, made of light white line led through blocks on the yards and trucks for hoisting signal flags.

BIBLIOGRAPHY.—*A Treatise on Rigging* (about 1625), London, Society for Nautical Research, 1921; Sir Henry Manwayring, *The Seaman's Dictionary* (1644); Darcy Lever, *The Young Sea Officer's Sheet Anchor* (1808); Sir George Nares, *Seamanship* (Portsmouth); Vice-Adm. Edmond Paris, *La Musée de marine du Louvre* (1883); Anderson, *The Rigging of Ships—1600–1720* (Salem, Mass., 1927); *Der geöfnete See-Hafen* (Hamburg, 1700 and 1702); Lescalier, *Traité pratique du Gréement des vaisseaux* (Paris, 1791); *The Elements and Practice of Rigging and Seamanship* (London, 1794); Commander Walker, R.N., *Alston's Seamanship; Manual of Seamanship*, Vol. 1, 1926, H.M. Stationery Office.

RIGHI, AUGUSTO (1850–1920), Italian physicist, was born at Bologna on Aug. 27, 1850. He studied at Bologna, where he afterwards held several posts for the teaching of physics. In 1880 he was appointed professor of physics at Palermo university, and in 1889 to a similar post at Bologna, which he retained until he died, on June 8, 1920.

Righi's researches were on electricity, magnetism and light. He discovered the variation in the resistance of bismuth in a magnetic field, and applied this to the measurement of magnetic fields. Righi extended Kerr's observations on the Kerr effect, and found the variation in the rotation of the plane of polarization with the wave length of the light. He examined the phenomena in a discharge tube and investigated the potential in the neighbourhood of the cathode. Righi observed the discharge of negative electricity from a zinc plate when illuminated by ultraviolet light, and this led him to work on photoelectricity. He worked with electromagnetic waves and designed a Hertzian oscillator known by his name. His principal works are: *Ricerche di elettro-statica* (1873), *La telegrafia senza filo* (with B. Dessau, 1902, etc.), *L'Ottica delle oscillazioni elettriche* (1897), *La moderna teoria dei fenomeni fisici* (1907), *Le nuove vedute sulla struttura della materia* (1907), *I fenomeni elettro-atomici sotto l'azione del magnetismo* (1918).

RIGHT ASCENSION. in astronomy, that co-ordinate of a heavenly body defined by the angle which the meridian passing through it makes with the prime meridian through the vernal equinox (*see* ASTRONOMY).

RIGHT-HANDEDNESS: *see* HANDEDNESS.

RIGHTS OF MAN AND OF THE CITIZEN, DECLARATION OF, a sort of manifesto issued in 1789, by the constituent assembly in the French Revolution, to be inscribed at the head of the constitution when it should be completed. It stated the fundamental principles which inspired the revolution. The declaration was first drafted and proposed by the marquis de Lafayette, who had returned from America full of enthusiasm for the principles proclaimed in the Declaration of Independence. The final text voted by the assembly and accepted by the king on Oct. 5, 1789, is much fuller than the American prototype. It contains a preamble and 17 articles. They proclaim and define political equality and liberty in its various manifestations.

See E. Blum, *La Déclaration des droits de l'homme et du citoyen,* text with commentary (1902); G. Jellinck, *Die Erklärung der Menschen und Bürgerrechte* (Leipzig, 1895). This study was translated into English by Rudolf Tombo, and aroused considerable controversy.

RIGHT WHALE (*Eubalaena*) is found in the northern and southern hemispheres. The allied Greenland whale (*Balaena mysticetus*), also called the bowhead whale, attains a length of 60 ft. to 70 ft., the largest and most valuable of the whalebone whales, a single specimen sometimes furnishing 3,500 lb. of whalebone. It was formerly the mainstay of the whaling trade, but now almost extinct. (*See* CETACEA; WHALE FISHERIES.)

RIGORD (*c.* 1150–*c.* 1209), French chronicler, was probably born near Alais in Languedoc, and became a physician. He entered the monastery of Argenteuil, and then that of St. Denis, and described himself as *regis Francorum chronographus*. Rigord wrote the *Gesta Philippi Augusti,* covering the period 1179–1206. It was abridged and continued by William the Breton.

See Dom Bouquet's *Recueil des historiens des Gaules et de la France* (Paris, 1738–1876); another ed. by H. F. Delaborde (Paris, 1882–85); French trans. in tome xi of François Guizot's *Collection des mémoires relatifs à l'histoire de France jusqu'au XIIIᵉ siècle* (Paris, 1825).

RIGORISM, a philosophical term applied by Immanuel Kant specially to those moralists who take up an antihedonist or ascetic standpoint (Lat. *rigor,* stiffness, firmness). In general the term is opposed to "latitudinarianism" or "indifferentism"—respectively a morality of compromise and a morality of pure indifference— and signifies insistence upon the strictest interpretation of a principle, rule or criterion. Thus, in Roman Catholic theology, a rigorist holds that in cases of conscience the proper course is to adhere to the strict wording of the law in question.

RILA (Bulg. RILSKOE SELO), a village of Bulgaria, 51 mi. S.S.W. of Sofia, which can be reached by rail to Radomir and Decauville. Pop. 3,490. Ten miles farther, up a gorge of the Rila mountains, stands the monastery of Rila, the largest and richest in Bulgaria. It was founded in the 10th century.

RILEY, JAMES WHITCOMB (1849–1916), U.S. poet, was born, of pioneer stock, in Greenfield, Ind., Oct. 7, 1849. "The poet of the common people," Riley was elected to the American Academy of Arts and Letters, received the gold medal of the National Institute of Arts and Letters, was given several honorary degrees and in 1915 had his birthday declared an official holiday throughout his home state in honour of "Indiana's most beloved citizen." After a happy boyhood, which he records in his poems, he found his father's profession of lawyer distasteful and spent several years as an itinerant sign painter, entertainer

and assistant to patent-medicine venders, all valuable experience, for it gave him the opportunity to compose songs and dramatic skits, to gain skill as an actor and to come into intimate touch with the rural folk of Indiana. His first reputation came through his poems contributed to newspapers—*Leonainie,* which purported to be a poem written by Edgar Allen Poe, and the series in Hoosier dialect ostensibly written by a farmer, "Benj. F. Johnson, of Boone," which he contributed to the *Indianapolis Daily Journal* and later published in book form as *The Old Swimmin' Hole and 'Leven More Poems* (1883). Riley was for a short time local editor of the *Anderson* (Ind.) *Democrat,* but his later life was spent in Indianapolis, where he died, July 22, 1916.

Of Riley's numerous volumes, among the most outstanding are: *The Boss Girl and Other Sketches* (1885; republished 1891 as *Sketches in Prose*), *Pipes o' Pan at Zekesbury* (1888), *Old-Fashioned Roses* (1888), *The Flying Islands of the Night* (1891), *A Child-World* (1896), *Home Folks* (1900). Because of reprints under varying titles, it is most satisfactory to read him in one of the collected editions: *Poems and Prose Sketches* (Homestead ed., 16 vol., 1897–1914); the biographical edition prepared by his nephew and secretary E. H. Eitel (6 vol., 1913); and the memorial edition of his *Complete Works* (10 vol., 1916). Hewitt Howland collected Riley's conventional English verse in *The Lockerbie Book* (1911) and his dialect poems in *The Hoosier Book* (1916).

See Clara E. Laughlin, *Reminiscences of James Whitcomb Riley* (1916); also Marcus Dickey, *The Youth of James Whitcomb Riley* (1919) and *The Maturity of James Whitcomb Riley* (1922); and Edgar Lee Masters, "James Whitcomb Riley," *Century Mag.* (Oct. 1927).

RILKE, RAINER MARIA (1875–1926), was born in Prague, Dec. 4, 1875. He studied in St. Pölten, Prague, and in Munich and Berlin, travelled throughout Europe, and frequented artistic circles, acting in 1905–06 as Auguste Rodin's secretary. During World War I he served for a short time in the Austro-Hungarian war department. His work includes both prose and verse, and he became regarded as the foremost German lyric poet of the first half of the 20th century. Russian religious mysticism influenced his philosophical poetry. His poetical style is of a unique delicacy and grandeur. In the last seven years of his life he settled down in Muzot, Switz., and here he was able to bring his work to a fitting end: in Feb. 1922, he finished the 10 *Duinese Elegies* and the 55 *Sonnets to Orpheus.* He found, in the French language, from which he had previously translated, new fields of expression for original poems. He died at Valmont, Switz., Dec. 29, 1926. The first complete collection of his works appeared in 1927 in six vol.; famous single publications are: *Zwei Prager Geschichten* (1899); *Mir zur Feier* (1899); *Geschichten vom lieben Gott* (1900); *Worpswede* (1903); *Auguste Rodin* (1903); *Das Stundenbuch* (1905); *Die Weise von Liebe und Tod des Cornets Christoph Rilke* (1906); *Neue Gedichte* (1907–08); *Requiem* (1909); *Aufzeichnungen des Malte Laurids Brigge* (1910); *Das Marienleben* (1913); *Erste Gedichte* (1913); *Sonette an Orpheus* (1923); *Duineser Elegien* (1923); *Vergers,* poems in French (1925).

BIBLIOGRAPHY.—*Gesammelte Briefe* 6 vol. (1929ff); Lou Andreas-Salomé, *Rainer Maria Rilke* (1928); Marie von Thurn and Taxis-Hohenlohe, *Erinnerungen an Rainer Maria Rilke* (1932); Katharina Kippenberg, *Rainer Maria Rilke* (1942); Dieter Bassermann, *Der spaete Rilke* (1947); Stefan Zweig, *Abschied von Rilke, Eine Rede* (1947); Marga Bauer, *Rilke und Frankreich* (1931); Maurice Betz, *Rilke à Paris* (1941); Edmond Jaloux, *Rainer Maria Rilke* (Paris, 1927); J. R. von Salis, *Rilkes Schweizerjahre* (1938); Federico Olivero, *Rainer Maria Rilke: a Study in Poetry and Mysticism* (1931); Richard von Mises, *Rilke in English: A Tentative Bibliography* (1947); *Publications* of the Rilke-Archiv, ed. by Mrs. Ruth Fritzsche-Rilke (Weimar); E. M. Butler, *Rainer Maria Rilke* (1941); Rainer Maria Rilke and Magda von Hattingberg, *Book of Thanks,* Eng. trans. by Cyrus Brooks (1949); Nora Purtscher, *Rilke: Man and Poet* (1949).

RIMBAUD, JEAN ARTHUR (1854–1891), French poet and adventurer, born at Charleville, in the Ardennes, on Oct. 20, 1854. He was the second son of a captain in the French army who in 1860 abandoned his wife and family. From early childhood Arthur Rimbaud, who was severely brought up by his mother, displayed rich intellectual gifts and a sullen, violent temperament. He began to write when he was ten, and some of the poems which now appear in his works belong to his 15th year.

Before he was 16, in consequence of a violent quarrel with his mother, the boy escaped from Charleville with a packet of his verse, was arrested as a vagabond, and for a fortnight was locked up in the Mazas prison, Paris. A few days after being taken home Rimbaud escaped again, into Belgium, where he lived for some time as a tramp, almost starved, but writing verses with feverish assiduity. In Feb. 1871 he left his mother for a third time and made his way to Paris, where he knew no one, and whence, after very nearly dying of hunger and exposure, he begged his way back to Charleville. There he wrote in the same year the extraordinary poem of *Le Bateau ivre*, which is now hailed as the pioneer of the entire "symbolist" or "decadent" movement in French literature in all its forms. He sent it to Paul Verlaine, who encouraged the boy of 17 (whom he supposed to be a man of 30) to return to Paris. Rimbaud spent from October 1871 to July 1872 in the capital, partly with Verlaine, partly as the guest of Théodore de Banville, and served in the army of the Commune. With Verlaine he travelled for 13 months, after the fall of the Commune, through England and Belgium, where in 1873 he published the only work which he ever printed, *Une Saison en Enfer,* in prose; in this he gives an allegorical account of his extravagant relations with Verlaine, which ended at Brussels by a double attempt of the latter to murder his young companion. On the second occasion Rimbaud was dangerously wounded by Verlaine's revolver, and the elder poet was imprisoned at Mons for two years.

Meanwhile Rimbaud, deeply disillusioned, determined to abandon Europe and literature, and he ceased at the age of 19 to write poetry. He settled for a while at Stuttgart, studying German, and in 1875 he disappeared. He set out on foot for Italy, and after extraordinary adventures found employment as a day-labourer in the docks at Leghorn. Returning to Paris, he obtained a little money from his mother, and then definitely vanished. For 16 years nothing whatever was heard of him, but it is now known that he embarked as a Dutch soldier for the Sunda Isles, and, presently deserting, fled to Sumatra and then to Java where he lived for some time in the forest. Returning to Europe, after a vagabond life in every capital, in 1880 he obtained some menial employment in the quarries of Cyprus, and then worked his way to Aden and up into Abyssinia, where he was one of the pioneers of European commercial adventure. There he settled at Harrar as a trader in coffee and perfumes, to which he afterward added gold and ivory; for the next 11 years, during which he led many commercial expeditions into unknown parts of northern Africa, Shoa and Harrar were his headquarters, and he lived almost entirely with the natives, and as one of them. From 1888 to 1891, having prospered greatly as a merchant, he became a sort of semi-independent chieftain, intriguing for France, just outside the borders of civilization. From documents which were first produced in 1902 it appears that from 1883 to 1889 Rimbaud was in close relations with the Ras Makonnen and with Menelek, then only king of Shoa. At the death of the Negus John, in 1888, he was concerned in the formation of the empire of Ethiopia. From this time Rimbaud had a palace in the town of Harrar and intrigued with the French government in favour of Menelek and against Italy.

Meanwhile, in 1886, believing Rimbaud to be dead, Verlaine had published his poems under the title of *Les Illuminations,* and they had created a great sensation in Paris. In this collection appeared the sonnet on the vowels, attributing a different colour to each: "A noir, E Blanc, I rouge, U vert, O bleu voyelles." But the author, in his Abyssinian hut of palm leaves, was, and remained, quite unconscious of the fact. In March 1891 a tumour in his knee obliged Rimbaud to leave Harrar and go to Europe for surgical advice. He reached Marseilles, but the case was hopeless; the leg had to be amputated, and Rimbaud died there in hospital on Nov. 10, 1891. The poems of Rimbaud all belong to his earliest youth. Their violent originality, the influence which they have exercised upon younger writers, the tumultuous existence of their author, and the strange veil of mystery which still hangs over his character and adventures have given to Rimbaud a remarkable fascination. His life was written by M. Paterne Berrichon (1897), and reminiscences by his sister, Mlle. Isabella Rimbaud. His *Oeuvres* were collected in 1898 by MM. Berrichon and Delahaye, and in 1901 his statue was unveiled at Charleville. (E. G.)

BIBLIOGRAPHY.—*Lettres de Jean Arthur Rimbaud (Égypte, Arabie, Éthiopie)*, 1899, edited by P. Berrichon; Paul Verlaine, *Les Poètes maudits* (1884); George Moore, *Impressions and Opinions: Two Unknown Poets* (1891); A. Symons, *The Symbolist Movement in Literature* (1900); M. Coulon, *Le Problème de Rimbaud, Poète maudit* (Nîmes, 1923); E. Delahaye, *Rimbaud: l'artiste et l'être moral* (1923); E. Rickword, *Rimbaud: the Boy and the Poet* (1924); A. L. Chisholm, *The Art of Arthur Rimbaud* (Melbourne, 1930); W. Fowlie, *Rimbaud, the Myth of Childhood* (1946). His *Oeuvres complètes* were published by the *Mercure de France.* For the great significance of Rimbaud and his influence on postwar French writers *see* CLAUDEL, PAUL.

RIME, a beautiful, white, friable, crystalline ice deposit formed by freezing of supercooled cloud- or fog-water droplets on objects exposed to the cloudy or foggy air. It occurs in two typical shapes: (1) growths of uniformly short, projecting, feathery-branching crystal aggregates on all sides of a freely exposed object, and (2) asymmetrical growths of crystal aggregates in the form of long plumes or flags orientated into the direction held by the wind during the formation of the deposit. The latter type, which may reach a length of 6 ft., is common on exposed upper slopes of mountains in middle and high latitudes; the terms "frozen fog deposit" and "frost feathers" are often applied to the phenomenon in such places. The first type is less common and occurs chiefly in valleys from winter ground fogs with calm air. Under the microscope, rime appears to be a mosaic agglomeration of minute crystal accretions, almost amorphous, with spaces of entrapped air. Often wind-blown snowflakes become embedded in the deposit, giving it a greasy consistency when crushed between the fingers. When the temperature at formation is just below 32° F. the rime becomes a denser, smoother deposit which is hard and tenacious like ordinary ice, sometimes called rough frost, or hard rime, in contradistinction to the more usual types, or soft rime. Some hydrologists and glaciologists claimed that the larger part of the alimentation of the icecaps in such regions as Greenland, Norway, Iceland and Spitzbergen is provided by rime depositing on the surfaces of the mountain snowfields. Field measurements, however, cast some doubt on the general validity of this assumption.

(R. G. SE.)

RIME ROYAL, the name given to a strophe or stanza form, which is of Italian extraction, but is almost exclusively identified with English poetry from the 14th to the early 17th century. It appears to be formed out of the stanza called ottava rima (*q.v.*), by the omission of the fifth line, which reduces it to seven lines of three rhymes, arranged ababbcc. It was earliest employed with skill, if not invented, by Chaucer, who composed his long romantic poem of *Troilus and Cressida* in rime royal, of which the following is an example:

> "And as the new-abashéd nightingale,
> Thet stinteth first when she beginneth sing,
> When that she heareth any herdë tale,
> Or in the hedges any wight stirring,
> And, after, siker doth her voice out-ring,—
> Right so Cresseyda, when her dredë stint,
> Opened her heart, and told all her intent."

In the 15th century this stanza was habitually used, in preference to heroic verse, by Thomas Occleve and John Lydgate, and with more melody and grace, by the unknown writer of *The Flower and the Leaf.* In the 16th century it was regarded as the almost exclusive classical form for heroic poetry in England, and it had long been so accepted in Scotland, where *The King's Quair* of King James I, the *Fables* of Henryson and *The Thistle and the Rose* of Dunbar had closely followed the pattern of Chaucer. After the first decade of the 17th century rime royal went out of fashion. Since then it has been occasionally revived, but not in poems of great length or particular importance. Rime royal should always be written in iambic metre, and be formed of seven lines of equal length, each containing ten syllables.

RIMINI, a town and bishop's see of Italy (anc. *Ariminum, q.v.*), in the province of Forlì, Emilia, on the Adriatic coast, 69 mi. S.E. of Bologna by rail. Pop. (1936): town, 31,505; commune, 64,738. The city is bounded on three sides by water. It faces the Adriatic to the north, has the torrent Aprusa, now called Ausa, on the east, and the river Marecchia, which has been canalized to serve as a harbour for small boats, on the west. It stands in a fertile plain, which on the southern side soon swells into pleasant slopes backed by the jagged peaks of the Umbrian Apennines. The foremost foothill of the range is the steep crag of Monte Titano, crowned by the towers of the republic of San Marino. Rimini attracts numerous visitors for the sea-bathing, and has extended as far as the coast, from which the old town is nearly a mile distant. Apart from its ancient buildings, Rimini has some interesting churches, notably S. Agostino in the Romanesque style (1247) with a lofty campanile; the Palazzi del Podestà (1304) and dell'Aréngo (1204) are good mediaeval buildings; there is a municipal picture gallery and an archaeological museum. The ancient castle of Sigismondo Malatesta is now dilapidated. For the church of S. Francis *see* below.

HISTORY

Rimini is the ancient Ariminum (*q.v.* for its early history and remains). Alternately captured by Byzantines and Goths, it was rigorously besieged by the latter in A.D. 538. They were, however, compelled to retreat before the reinforcements sent by Belisarius and Narses; thus the Byzantines, after various vicissitudes, became masters of the town, appointed a duke as its governor, and included it in the exarchate of Ravenna. It afterward fell into the power of the Longobards, and then of the Franks, who yielded it to the pope, for whom it was governed by counts to the end of the 10th century. Soon after this period the imperial power became dominant in Rimini. In 1157 Frederick I gave it, by imperial patent, the privilege of coining money and the right of self-government; and in the 13th century Rimini was an independent commune waging war on the neighbouring cities.

Rise of the Malatesta.—In the year 1216 Rimini, being worsted by Cesena, granted citizenship to two members of the powerful Malatesta family, Giovanni and Malatesta, for the sake of their aid and that of their vassals in the defense of the state and the conduct of the war. This family quickly struck root in the town, and in 1237 Giovanni was named podesta.

Giovanni Malatesta died in 1247 and was succeeded by his son Malatesta, born in 1212 and surnamed Malatesta da Verrucchio. This chieftain, who lived to be 100 years old, was the real founder of his house. Being repeatedly elected podesta for lengthy terms of office, he at last became the virtual master of Rimini. Pope Boniface VIII not only left Malatesta, as a Guelph champion, unmolested but in 1299 conferred on him fresh honours and estates, so that his power went on increasing to the day of his death in 1312. He had four sons, Malatestino, Giovanni (called the Lame), Paolo and Pandolfo. Giovanni served under Giovanni da Polenta of Ravenna and won the hand of that potentate's beautiful daughter, known to history as Francesca da Rimini. But her heart had been won by the handsome Paolo, her brother-in-law; and the two lovers, being surprised by Giovanni, were murdered by him (1285). This episode has been immortalized in Dante's *Inferno*. Giovanni died in 1304. Thus in 1312 Malatestino became lord of Rimini, and on his decease in 1317 bequeathed the power to his brother Pandolfo.

Pandolfo died in 1326, leaving two heirs, Malatesta and Galeotto. In 1355 the Malatesta were reduced to submission by Pope Innocent VI. The two brothers divided their lands. Galeotto retained the lordship of Rimini, ruling tranquilly and on good terms with the popes, who allowed him to add Cervia, Cesena and Bertinoro to his states. Dying in 1385 at the age of 80, he left two sons—Carlo (1364-1429) and Pandolfo (1370-1427). Carlo left no sons. Of those of Pandolfo, the eldest, Galeotto (1411-32), was an ascetic, gave little or no attention to public business and, dying early, bequeathed the state to his brother Sigismondo Pandolfo. The third son, Novello (1418-65), ruled over Cesena.

Sigismondo Pandolfo.—Sigismondo (1417-68) is the personage to whom Rimini owes its renown during the Renaissance, of which indeed he was one of the strangest and most original representatives. He was born in Brescia, and when called to the succession, at the age of 15, had already given proofs of valour in the field. His knowledge of antiquity was so profound as to excite the admiration of all the learned men with whom he discoursed, even when, as in the case of Pius II, they chanced to be his personal enemies. To him is due the erection of the church of St. Francis, or temple of the Malatesta, the greatest of Rimini's treasures. On assuming power in 1432, Sigismondo was already affianced to the daughter of Count Carmagnola; but when that famous leader was arraigned as a traitor by the Venetians and ignominiously put to death, he promptly withdrew from his engagement and espoused Ginevra d'Este, daughter of the duke of Ferrara, in 1434. In 1440 his wife died. Two years afterward he married Polissena, daughter of the famous *condottiere*, Francesco Sforza, who in 1443 bore him a son named Galeotto Roberto. But by this time he was already madly in love with Isotta degli Atti, and this was the passion which endured to his death. The lady succeeded in gaining an absolute ascendancy over him, which increased with time. She bore him several children, but this did not prevent his having others by different concubines. Such being the nature of the man, it is not astonishing that, as his ardour for Isotta increased, he should have little scruple in ridding himself of his second wife. On June 1, 1450, Polissena died by strangling, and on the 30th of the same month Isotta's offspring were legitimated by Nicholas V.

The Church of St. Francis.—Her marriage with Malatesta did not take place until 1456; but of the ardent affection that had long bound them together there are stronger proofs than the lover's juvenile verses, or than even the children Isotta had borne to him. For, more than all else, the temple of St. Francis has served to transmit to posterity the history of their love. Malatesta decided to build this remarkable church as a thank offering for his safety during a dangerous campaign undertaken for Pope Eugene IV about the year 1445. The first stone was laid in 1446, and the work was carried on with such alacrity that mass was performed in it by the close of 1450. Sigismondo entrusted the execution of his plans to Leon Battista Alberti. The vault was never finished, and still shows its rough beams and rafters. The eight side chapels alone are complete, and their pointed arches spring from Renaissance pilasters planted on black marble elephants, the Malatesta emblem, or on baskets of fruit held by children. Everywhere—on the balustrades closing the chapels, round the base of the pilasters, along the walls, beneath the cornice of both the exterior and the interior of the church—there is one ornament that is perpetually repeated, the interwoven initials of Sigismondo and Isotta. This monogram is alternated with the portrait and arms of Malatesta; and these designs are enwreathed by festoons linked together by the tyrant's second emblem, the rose. The most singular and characteristic feature of this edifice is the almost total absence of every sacred emblem. Rather than to St. Francis and the God of the Christians it was dedicated to the glorification of an unhallowed attachment. Nature, science and antiquity were summoned to celebrate the tyrant's love for Isotta.

Sigismondo understood the science of fortification. He was also the first to discard the use of wooden bombshells and substitute others cast in bronze. As a soldier his numerous campaigns had shown him to be possessed of all the best qualities and worst defects of the free captains of his time. He took part in many hazardous campaigns against adversaries such as the duke of Urbino, Sforza of Milan, Piccinino and, worst of all, the Sienese pope, Pius II, his declared and mortal foe. This time Sigismondo had blundered, and he was driven to make his submission to the pope, but, again rebelling, was summoned to trial in Rome (1460) before a tribunal of hostile cardinals. All the old charges against him were now revived and eagerly confirmed. He was pronounced guilty of rapine, incendiarism, incest, assassination and heresy. Consequently he was sentenced to the deprivation of his state (which was probably the main object of the trial), and to be burned alive as a heretic. This sentence, however, could not easily be executed, and Sigismondo was only burned in effigy. He could afford to laugh at this farce; nevertheless he prepared in great haste for a desperate defense (1462). He knew that the bishop Vitelleschi, together with the duke of Urbino and his own brother, Novello Malatesta, lord of Cesena, were advancing against him in force; and, being defeated at Pian di Marotta, he was forced to go to Rome in 1463, again to make submission to the pope. This time he was stripped of all his possessions excepting the city of Rimini and a neighbouring castle, but the sentence of excommunication was withdrawn. In 1464 he took service with the Venetians and had the command of an expedition to the Morea. In 1466 he was able to return to Rimini, for Pius II was dead and the new pope, Paul II, was less hostile to him. Indeed, the latter offered to give him Spoleto and Foligno, taking Rimini in exchange; but Malatesta was so enraged by the proposal that he went to Rome with a dagger concealed on his person, to kill the pope. But, being forewarned, Paul received him with great ceremony and surrounded by cardinals prepared for defense; whereupon Sigismondo changed his mind, fell on his knees and implored forgiveness. His star had now set forever. For sheer subsistence he had to hire his sword to the pope and quell petty rebellions with a handful of men. At last, his health failing, he returned to his family and died in Rimini on Oct. 7, 1468, aged 51 years.

Roberto Malatesta.—He was succeeded by his wife Isotta and his son Sallustio, who were ousted by an illegitimate elder son (named Roberto Malatesta) by another mother. Isotta and Sallustio both died in 1470 in suspicious circumstances. Roberto died in 1482; his son Pandolfo fled before Cesare Borgia in 1500. Rimini was captured by Pope Julius II after his victory at Ravenna in 1512. Malatesta made more than one attempt to win back his city, but always in vain, for his subjects preferred papal rule; and in 1528 Pope Clement VII became definite master of the town. The history of Rimini practically ends with its independence.

BIBLIOGRAPHY.—Battaglini, *Memorie Storiche di Rimini e de' suoi signori, publicati con note di G. A. Zanetti* (Bologna, 1789); Fossati, *Li tempi di Malatesta di Rimini* (Foligno, 1794); Moroni, *Dizionario di erudizione storico-ecclesiastica* (vol. lvii, *s.v.* "Rimini"); Ch. Yriarte, *Rimini: Un Condottiere au XV. Siècle: Études sur les lettres et les arts à la cour des Malatesta* (1882); Tonini, *Storia di Rimini* (Rimini, 1848–62); E. Hutton, *Sigismondo Malatesta* (1906). (P. V.; L. V.)

RIMSKY-KORSAKOV, NICOLAS ANDREIEVICH (1844–1908), Russian composer, was born at Tikhvin, Novgorod, on March 18, 1844. He spent six years (1856–62) in the Naval college at St. Petersburg, and at the end of that time received a commission and spent three years afloat. But as a cadet he had been one of the musical amateurs who, with Borodin, Cui and Moussorgsky, gathered round Balakirev in St. Petersburg in the days when Wagner was still unknown. During this cruise he had written a symphony (in E minor) which in that year was performed—the first by a Russian composer—under Balakirev's direction, and in 1873 he definitely retired from the navy, having been appointed a professor in the St. Petersburg Conservatoire. The same year witnessed his marriage to a talented pianist, Nadejda Pourgold, and the production of his first opera, *Pskovitianka*. This was followed by *May Night* (1878), *The Snow Maiden* (1880), *Mlada* (1892), *Christmas Eve* (1894), *Sadko* (1895), *Mozart and Salieri* (1898), *The Tsar's Bride* (1899), *Tsar Saltana* (1900), *Servilia* (1902), *Kostchei the Immortal* (1902), *The Tale of the Invisible City of Kitezh* (1905), and *Le Coq d'Or* (1910). For all of these, with the exception of *Mozart and Salieri,* he chose Russian national subjects. But his operas attracted less attention abroad than his symphonic compositions, which show a mastery of orchestral effect combined with a fine utilization of Russian folk-melody. Notable among these works are his first symphony, his second (op. 9) *Antar,* his third (op. 32), and his orchestral suites including the well known *Scheherazade* and overtures. He also wrote a number of beautiful songs, pianoforte pieces, etc., and he eventually took Balakirev's place as the leading conductor in St. Petersburg, where he died on June 20, 1908.

The influence of Rimsky-Korsakov on the Russian composers of his day was very great. His instrumentation was fresh and original; he was direct and clear, with something of a painter's vision, and he brought a wealth of learning and study to bear on his subject. Many came directly under his influence as his pupils at the Conservatoire, while many more studied his great treatise of *The Foundations of Instrumentation.* He did much also to promote the better appreciation of Moussorgsky and others of his fellow Russians, although during recent years he has been severely criticized for his alleged tampering with Moussorgsky's original text in his edition of *Boris Godounov.*

See his own *History of My Musical Life* (which has been translated into English); Stassov, *Rimsky-Korsakov* (1890); Rosa Newmarch, *The Russian Opera* (1914) and Montagu Nathan, *History of Russian Music* (1915); G. E. Abraham, *Studies in Russian Music* (1936).

RINCEAU, from the French, meaning foliage. In architecture and the decorative arts, a decorative form consisting of a continuous wavy stemlike motif from which smaller leafy stems or groups of leaves branch out at more or less regular intervals. Its use is frequent in the friezes of Roman buildings, in the jamb ornament and capitals of Romanesque structures and in friezes and panels of buildings in the various Renaissance styles.

RINDERPEST. A disease, primarily of cattle, which has been known also as steppe murrain, contagious bovine typhus, peste bovine and cattle plague, rinderpest was first recognized in early Christian times. The earliest records of the disease suggest that it originated in Asia or eastern Europe, its incursions into western Europe having followed the paths of invading armies in the periodic sweeps of barbarous tribes from the east. Rinderpest reached Africa in the latter half of the 19th century and, after spreading throughout that continent with disastrous effect, was eventually cleared from the southern half but remained endemic

or enzootic in the northern parts, its southernmost extension being in Tanganyika territory. The disease is also endemic in India and certain parts of southeastern Asia. In all these areas rinderpest is considered a major obstacle to development of the livestock industry, and in unmechanized sections, particularly those in which the water buffalo is used as the principal beast of burden, agriculture in general is retarded.

Characteristics.—Rinderpest is an acute, highly contagious disease of ruminants characterized by an unusually rapid course and a high mortality in areas where the disease is not endemic. The causative agent is an ultravisible virus, provisionally named *Tortor bovis.*

When infection is introduced into a herd of susceptible animals, signs of illness appear after an incubation period of three to five days. Early signs are depression, loss of appetite and a staring coat. These are accompanied by a pyrexia generally of the order of 105° to 107° F. In the midcourse of the disease, ocular and nasal discharges and salivation with buccal ulceration and a disagreeable fetid odour are characteristic. Profuse diarrhoea with progressive emaciation and dehydration occur, often with dysentery and eventually marked tenesmus.

In many cases, a cutaneous, eruptive condition termed streptothricosis develops on the back and flanks. In the terminal stages of fatal cases, prostration, coma and death supervene generally after 10 to 14 days.

Autopsy of such an animal shows involvement of the mucous membrane of the entire alimentary tract. This is usually most marked in the mouth, where ulcers containing cheesy deposits are often found, and in the abomasum, ileum, cecum, colon and rectum, where deep congestion and sometimes ulceration occur. In the lower bowel the congestion is often in well-defined, dark streaks and has been referred to as zebra marking. Pneumonia frequently is seen as a complication, and often cystitis and vaginitis are present. Diagnosis is made on the clinical appearance of the disease and autopsy findings, but, since these may be similar to those found in certain other diseases, virus transmission and cross-immunity tests are necessary for confirmation.

Spread of the Disease.—The virus is generalized in the animal body and is passed out in all the secretions. It gains access to the tissues of a susceptible animal via the mucous membranes, most probably those of the nostrils. In areas where the disease is endemic, wild animals play an important part in the epidemiology. Many species of wild ruminants, together with wild pigs and warthogs in such areas as Tanganyika and Uganda, have been found to be susceptible to rinderpest. These animals, in competition with domestic animals for limited grazing and water, present great difficulties in the way of control. It is seen, therefore, that control of the disease is complicated by the maintenance of the virus in wild animals which form vast reservoirs of infection. Eradication in areas where wild animals exist in large numbers is dependent on the control of the disease in these animals or the elimination of their contact with the domestic animal populations.

Control.—Control of rinderpest has been attempted by several methods. Strict quarantine measures alone can be effective, provided the control of susceptible wild animals can be assured. However, it was early recognized that some form of immunization combined with quarantine was the most promising method of control, and efforts were made to find effective immunogens. As recovery from an attack of the disease leaves a durable immunity, early workers experimented with serum of recovered animals. Later, the bile of infected animals was tried. The former produced only a transient or passive immunity, while the latter caused a manifestation of the disease, often mild, which left an active immunity. The "serum simultaneous" method which comprised the simultaneous inoculation of virulent virus and sufficient immune or hyperimmune serum to modify the reaction, proved the most satisfactory of the early methods of artificial immunization used. The use of this method, however, has some serious disadvantages, the major one being that an animal reacting to this treatment is virtually suffering from rinderpest and is a possible source of infection to other susceptible animals, and so the use of this method may set up new focuses of infection. Later work gave rise to the production of vaccines made from virulent tissues, principally spleens, in which the virus is inactivated by means of some chemical agent. These so-called inactivated vaccines produce a solid immunity which, however, lasts only for a matter of months; nevertheless, they were of great value in the control of rinderpest. Although still used in some regions under special circumstances at mid-20th century, they had been superseded by the use of living rinderpest virus which had been attenuated by repeated passage in a species other than the bovine. The first step in this direction was taken with the adaptation of bovine virus to goats, followed by the widespread use of the so-called caprinized virus in India and east Africa. Other workers, by adaptation of the virus to the rabbit and to the developing chick embryo, opened the way to the possible use of new vaccines. (J. A. BR.; J. K. H. W.)

RING, a band of circular shape, made of any material and for various purposes, but, particularly, a circular band of gold, silver or other precious or decorative material used as an ornament, not only for the finger, but also for the ear (*see* EAR-RING), or even for the nose, as worn by certain races in India and Africa.

Egyptian Rings.—The earliest existing rings are those found in the tombs of ancient Egypt. The finest examples date from about the 18th to the 20th dynasty; they are of pure gold, simple in design, very heavy and massive, and have usually the name and titles of the owner deeply sunk in hieroglyphic characters on an oblong gold bezel. Rings worn in Egypt by the poorer classes were made of less costly materials, such as silver, bronze, glass or pottery covered with a siliceous glaze and coloured brilliant blue or green with various copper oxides. Some of these had hieroglyphic inscriptions impressed while the clay was moist. Other examples have been found made of ivory, amber and hard stones, such as carnelian. Another form of ring used in the 12th and subsequent dynasties of Egypt had a scarab in place of the bezel, and was mounted on a gold hoop which passed through the hole in the scarab and allowed it to revolve.

Cylinders.—In ancient Babylonia and Assyria the signet took the form of a cone seal or of a cylinder cut in crystal or other hard stone and perforated from end to end. A cord was passed through the cylinder, and it was worn on the wrist like a bracelet.

Within the limits necessarily imposed by its purpose the finger ring assumed a considerable variety of form, according to its date and place of origin.

In the Cretan and Mycenaean periods a characteristic form of ring had a broad flat bezel, not organically connected with the hoop, and having an incised design in the gold. The use of inset stones hardly occurs, but rings from Enkomi and Aegina of the late Mycenaean period have inset paste decorations.

The Phoenician type of ring was primarily intended to carry a scarab or scarabaeoid, usually in a box setting on a swivel, called for by the fact that the flat base of the scarab would be wanted for sealing purposes, but in wear would be most conveniently turned inward. Strength being necessary, the hoop became massive. A similar arrangement of the signet-scarab is found attached to a twisted ring, which, from its shape, must have been meant to be suspended, and which is shown thus worn on some of the Cypriote terra cottas.

The Greek ring of an early period has a characteristic flattened bezel, for an intaglio design in the gold. An alternative form was a swivel ring for a scarab or scarabaeoid.

Etruscan Rings.—The Etruscans used very largely the gold swivel ring mounted with a scarab, a form of signet probably introduced from Egypt. Some found in Etruscan tombs have real Egyptian scarabs with legible hieroglyphs; others, probably the work of Phoenician or native engravers, have rude copies of hieroglyphs, either quite or partially illegible. A third and more numerous class of Etruscan signet rings have scarabs, cut usually in sard or carnelian. One from Etruria, now in the British Museum, is formed by two minutely modelled lions whose bodies form the hoop, while their paws hold the bezel, a scarab engraved with a lion of heraldic character. An alternative type of Etruscan ring has an incised design on the gold bezel, or a flat stone set in the rigid bezel.

Roman Rings.—The Romans appear to have imitated the simplicity of Lacedaemonia. Throughout the republic none but iron rings were worn by the bulk of the citizens, and even these were forbidden to slaves. Ambassadors were the first who were privileged to wear gold rings, and then only while performing some public duty. Next senators, consuls, equites and all the chief officers of state received the *ius annuli aurei*. In the Augustan age many valuable collections of antique rings were made, and were frequently offered as gifts in the temples of Rome. One of the largest and most valuable of the *dactyliothecae* was dedicated in the temple of Apollo Palatinus by Augustus' nephew Marcellus (Pliny, *H.N.* xxxvii, 5).

Different laws as to the wearing of rings existed during the empire: Tiberius made a large property qualification necessary for the wearing of gold rings in the case of those who were not of free descent; Severus conceded the right to all Roman soldiers; and later still, all free citizens possessed the *ius annuli aurei,* silver rings being worn by freedmen and iron by slaves. Under Justinian even these restrictions passed away.

Early Christian Rings.—Most early Christian rings date from the 4th century onward. Generally of bronze or gold they are often engraved with acclamations and invocations and occasionally with the owner's bust or with Christian symbols.

Celtic Rings.—Large numbers of gold rings have been found in many parts of Europe in the tombs of early Celtic races. They are usually of pure gold, often penannular in form, that is, with a slight break in the hoop so as to form a spring. They are often of gold wire formed into a sort of rope, or else a simple bar twisted in an ornamental way. Some of the quite plain penannular rings were used in the place of coined money.

Throughout the middle ages the signet ring was a thing of great importance in religious, legal, commercial and private matters.

Episcopal Rings.—The episcopal ring was solemnly conferred upon the newly made bishop together with his crozier, a special formula for this being inserted in the Pontifical. In the earliest references to rings worn by bishops, there is nothing to distinguish them from other signet rings. In A.D. 610 the first mention has been found of the episcopal ring as a well-understood symbol of dignity. It is clear that it was derived from the signet. It was only in the 12th century and onward that it was brought into mystical connection with the marriage ring. In the time of Innocent III (1194) the ring was ordered to be of pure gold mounted with a stone that was not engraved; but this rule appears not to have been strictly kept. It was the custom upon the death of a bishop for his ring to be handed over to the royal treasurer but many rings with all the appearance of consecration rings have been discovered in the coffins of bishops. Among the collection of rings formed by the naturalist Edmund Waterton, and now in the South Kensington museum, is a fine gold episcopal ring decorated with niello, and inscribed with the name of Alhstan, bishop of Sherborne from 824 to 867. In many cases an antique gem was mounted in the bishop's ring, and often an inscription was added in the gold setting of the gem to give a Christian name to the pagan figure. The monks of Durham, for example, made an intaglio of Jupiter Serapis into a portrait of St. Oswald by adding the legend CAPVT S. OSWALDI. In other cases the engraved gem appears to have been merely regarded as an ornament without meaning—as, for example, a magnificent gold ring found in the coffin of Seffrid, bishop of Chichester (1125–1151), in which is mounted a Gnostic intaglio.

Papal Rings.—The papal "Ring of the Fisherman" (*annulus piscatoris*) bears the device of St. Peter in a boat, drawing a net from the water. The first mention of it, as the well-understood personal signet ring of the pope, that has been found, occurs in a letter of Clement IV in 1265. After the middle of the 15th century it was no longer used as the private seal of the popes, but was always attached to briefs. After the death of a pope the ring is broken. A new ring with the space for the name left blank is taken into the conclave, and placed on the finger of the newly elected pontiff, who thereupon declares what name he will assume, and gives back the ring to be engraved. (*See* Waterton, *Archaeologia,* 40, p. 138.)

The so-called papal rings, of which many exist dating from the 15th to the 17th centuries, are very large thumb rings, usually of gilt bronze coarsely worked, and set with a foiled piece of glass or crystal. On the hoop is usually engraved the name and arms of the reigning pope, the bezel being without a device. They are sometimes described as rings of investiture and according to another hypothesis they were carried as credentials by envoys. Such cumbrous ornaments could not have been worn by the popes and cardinals themselves.

Other Varieties.—The giving of a ring to mark a betrothal was an old Roman custom. The ring was probably a mere pledge, *pignus,* that the contract would be fulfilled. In Pliny's time conservative custom still required a plain ring of iron, but the gold ring was introduced in the course of the 2nd century. This use of the ring, which was thus of purely secular origin, received ecclesiastical sanction, and formulas of benediction of the ring exist from the 11th century. The exact stages by which the wedding ring developed from the betrothal ring can no longer be traced. Gold marriage rings enriched with niello date from the 5th century though they may not have been used in the actual ceremony of marriage.

Posy rings, so called from the "poesy" or rhyme engraved on them, were specially common in the same centuries. The name "posy ring" does not occur earlier than the 16th century. A posy ring inscribed with "Love me and leave me not" is mentioned by William Shakespeare (*Mer. of Ven.*, act v, sc. 1). The custom of inscribing rings with mottoes or words of good omen dates from a very early time. Greek and Roman rings exist with words such as ZHCAIC, XAIPE, KAAH, or *votis meis Claudia vivas*. In the middle ages many rings were inscribed with words of cabalistic power, such as *anam sapta*, or Caspar, Melchior and Balthasar, the supposed names of the Magi.

In the 17th century memorial rings with a name and date of death were frequently made of very elaborate form, enamelled in black and white; a not unusual design was two skeletons bent along the hoop, and holding a coffin which formed the bezel.

Cramp rings were much worn during the middle ages as a preservative against cramp. They derived their virtue from being blessed by the king; a special form of service was used for this, and a large number of rings were consecrated at one time, usually when the sovereign touched patients for the king's evil.

Decade rings were not uncommon, especially in the 15th century; these were so called from their having ten knobs along the hoop of the ring, and were used, after the manner of rosaries, to say nine Aves and a Pater Noster.

In the 15th and 16th centuries signet rings engraved with a badge or trademark were much used by merchants and others; these were not only used to form seals, but the ring itself was often sent by a trusty bearer as the proof of the genuineness of a bill of demand. At the same time private gentlemen used massive rings wholly of gold with their initials cut on the bezel, and a graceful knot of flowers twining round the letters. Other fine gold rings of this period have coats of arms or crests with graceful lambrequins.

Poison rings with a hollow bezel were used in classical times; as, for example, that by which Hannibal killed himself, and the poison ring of Demosthenes. Pliny records that, after Crassus had stolen the gold treasure from under the throne of Capitoline Jupiter, the guardian of the shrine, to escape torture, "broke the gem of his ring in his mouth and died immediately." The mediaeval *anello della morte*, supposed to be a Venetian invention, was actually used as an easy method of murder. Among the elaborate ornaments of the bezel a hollow point made to work with a spring was concealed; it communicated with a receptacle for poison in a cavity behind, in such a way that the murderer could give the fatal scratch while shaking hands with his enemy. This device was probably suggested by the poison fang of a snake.

(*See* also GEM; JEWELLERY; SEALS.)

BIBLIOGRAPHY.—Fortunius Licetus, *De Annulis antiquis* (Udine, 1645); Kirchmann, *De Annulis* (Schleswig, 1657); King, *Antique Gems and Rings* (1872); F. H. Marshall, *Catalogue of Finger Rings, Greek, Roman and Etruscan in the British Museum* (1907); O. M. Dalton, *Catalogue of Finger Rings, Early Christian, Byzantine, Teutonic, Mediaeval and later in the British Museum* (1912); G. F. Kunz, *Rings* (1917); Cabrol, *Dictionnaire d'archéologie chrétienne, s.v.* "Anneaux"; articles of Waterton in *Archaeologia* and *Archaeological Journal*.

(J. H. MI.; A. H. SM.; X.)

In Mathematics.—In mathematics the term "ring" is used for an important type of algebraic system. By a ring R is meant a set of elements in which two compositions, called addition ($+$) and multiplication (.), are defined in such a way that the following conditions obtain:

A 1 $a+b$ is in the set R.
A 2 $(a+b)+c=a+(b+c)$.
A 3 $a+b=b+a$.
A 4 There is an element O in R such that $a+O=a$ for all a in R.
A 5 For each a in R there is an element $-a$, called the negative of a, such that $a+(-a)=O$.
M 1 ab is in R.
M 2 $(ab)c=a(bc)$.
D 1 $a(b+c)=ab+ac$.
D 2 $(b+c)a=ba+ca$.

The conditions A 1 to A 5 imply that R is a commutative group (*see* GROUPS) relative to the addition operation. Conditions M 1 and M 2 imply that R is a system of the type called a semigroup relative to multiplication, and D 1 and D 2 are the distributive laws connecting the two operations of addition and multiplication.

The concept of a ring is used in advance developments in algebra and details of such work may be found in the treatises listed in the bibliography.

BIBLIOGRAPHY.—A. A. Albert, *Modern Higher Algebra* (1937) and "Structure of Algebras," *American Mathematical Society Colloquium*, vol. xxiv (1939); E. Artin, C. J. Nesbitt and R. M. Thrall, *Rings with Minimum Condition* (1944); G. Birkhoff and S. MacLane, *A Survey of Modern Algebra* (1941); M. Deuring, *Algebren, Ergebnisse der Mathematik und ihrer Grenzgebiete*, vol. 4 (Berlin, 1935); E. Hecke, *Theorie der algebraischen Zahlen* (Leipzig, 1923); N. Jacobson, "Theory of Rings," *American Mathematical Society Surveys*, vol. ii (1943); W. Krull, *Idealtheorie, Ergebnisse der Mathematik und ihrer Grenzgebiete*, vol. 4 (Berlin, 1935); C. C. MacDuffee, *An Introduction to Abstract Algebra* (1940); B. L. van der Waerden, *Moderne Algebra*, vol. i and ii (Berlin, 1st ed. 1931, 2d ed. 1937 and 1940); H. Weyl, *Algebraic Theory of Numbers* (1940). (N. J.)

RINGWOOD, a market town in Hampshire, England, $103\frac{1}{2}$ mi. W.S.W. of London by the Southern Region Railway route.

Pop. (1931) 5,052. It lies on the river Avon, which here divides into numerous branches. The church of SS. Peter and Paul, of the 13th century, was almost entirely reconstructed in 1854. An agricultural trade and the manufacture of agricultural implements are carried on.

RINGWORM or TINEA TONSURANS, a disease mainly affecting the scalp; it consists of bald patches, usually round, and half an inch up to several inches across, the surface showing the broken stumps of hairs and a fine whitish powdering of desquamated epidermic scales. The disease is caused by a group of fungi distinguished, among other features, by the size of the spores they form. In London and Paris *Microsporon audovini* causes about three-quarters of all cases of ringworm. If one of the broken hairs is plucked out with forceps and pressed flat under a cover glass in a drop of dilute caustic potash, the microscope will show it to be occupied by long rows of minute oval spores, very uniform in size. Forms of ringworm are also met with in lower animals (*e.g.*, cat and dog) but according to J. G. Hare and P. Tate there is little evidence that these infect children. (*Journ. Hygiene*, 1927, xxvii, 32).

Modern treatment is by X-ray (*see* RADIOLOGY) and is very effective. Thallium acetate has also been recommended. (*See* also FAVUS.)

RIO BRANCO, one of five federal territories of Brazil provided for in the constitution of 1937 and created by decree law in Sept. 1943. Other territories established by this decree were Amapá, Guaporé, Ponta Porã and Iguassú (the last two abolished in 1946).

Governed by federal interventors (as were all the states from 1937), the territories came under the direct administration of the government. Situated along Brazil's sparsely inhabited frontiers, the territories have been ostensibly created for purposes of national defense, selective colonization, and economic development. Rio Branco, formerly a part of northern Amazonas, is bounded northeast by British Guiana, southeast by the Anauá and Branco rivers, south (between the mouths of the Branco and Padauarí rivers) by the Rio Negro, southwest by the Rio Padauarí, and northwest and north by Venezuela. Its area is 97,438 sq.mi.; population (1950) 17,623. (R. W. RD.; X.)

RÍO CUARTO, a town of Argentina in the province of Córdoba, 140 mi. S. of the city of that name, and about 385 mi. N.W. of Buenos Aires. Pop. (1943) 48,233. It stands 1,440 ft. above sea level and about halfway across the great Argentine pampas, on the banks of a river of the same name which finds an outlet through the Carcarañal into the Paraná near Rosario. The town is built on the open plain and is surrounded with attractive suburbs.

It is the commercial centre of a large district and has a large and lucrative trade. Its geographical position gives it great strategical importance, and the government maintains there a large arsenal and a garrison of the regular army. Previous to the activities of General Ivanovski in 1872 this region was overrun by the Ranqueles, a warlike tribe of Indians. The surrounding country belongs to the partially arid pampas region and is devoted to stock raising agriculture. Irrigation is employed in its immediate vicinity. There are some manufacturing industries in the town, although it is primarily an agricultural centre.

The San Martin and the Mitre railways pass through Río Cuarto, giving railway communication with Buenos Aires, Rosario, Tucumán, Córdoba, San Luis, Mendoza and other cities.

RIO DE CONTAS or VILLA DE CONTAS, a town of Brazil, in the state of Bahia, 230 mi. S.W. from the city of Salvador (Bahia), on a headwater stream of the Rio de Contas, which rises on the eastern slope of the neighbouring Serra de Santo Onofre, and flows southeast and east to the Atlantic coast at Barra do Rio de Contas.

The population of the town in 1950 was 1,466; municipality 16,186. Stock raising was formerly an important industry there. The town was founded in 1715 by some "Paulistas" who discovered gold there in the sands of the river. It became a *vila* in 1724, but was soon afterward moved down the river five miles to its present site.

RIO DE JANEIRO, a maritime state of Brazil, bounded north by Minas Gerais, east by Espírito Santo and the Atlantic, south by the Atlantic and west by São Paulo. It is one of the smaller states of the republic: area 16,087 sq.mi.; pop. (1950) 2,326,201. The state is traversed longitudinally by the Serra do Mar, which divides it into a low, narrow, irregular coastal zone and a broad elevated river valley through which the Paraíba flows eastward to the Atlantic. The eastern part of this valley widens out into a great alluvial plain on which are some of the richest sugar estates of Brazil. The well-watered Paraíba valley is celebrated for its fertility, and is an important centre of coffee production. Stock raising developed slowly after the abolition of slavery (1888). Manufacturing was developed largely because of the water power supplied by mountain streams; manufactures are cotton, woollen, silk and jute fabrics, brick, tile and rough pottery, sugar, rum, vehicles, furniture, beer and fruit conserves. Railways include the Central do Brasil, Leopoldina, Melhoramentos and Rio do Ouro. The Central line runs from the city of Rio de Janeiro north-northwest across the Serra do Mar to the Paraíba valley, where it divides into two branches at the station of Barra do Piraí, one running west to São Paulo and the other east and north into Minas Gerais. Besides these there are a number of short railways called the Teresópolis, União Valenciana, Rio das Flores, Bananal and Vassourense lines. The total extension of these railways in the state in 1949 was 1,681 mi. Other than Niterói, the ports of the state are São João da Barra, Macaé or Imbetiba, Cabo Frio and Paratí, visited only by the smaller coasting vessels.

The capital of the state is Niterói, pop. (1950) 174,535, on the east side of the Bay of Rio de Janeiro; other cities and towns, with populations of the *municípios* in which they are located, are: Campos (240,829; city 63,384) on the lower Paraíba in a rich sugar-producing region; Rio Bonito (25,528); Itaboraí (30,489); Barra Mansa (72,458) on the upper Paraíba; Resende (35,414), in a fertile district of the upper Paraíba; Petrópolis (109,531; city 61,843); Cantagalo (21,898), in a rich coffee district of the Serra do Mar; Paratí (9,459), a small port on the west side of the Bay of Angra dos Reis; Valença (36,544); Vassouras (60,114); São Fidelis (44,154), a river port on the lower Paraíba having steamboat communication with Campos; Macaé (53,292), an old port on the eastern coast of the state at the mouth of the Macaé river whose original anchorage has been filled with silt, and that of Imbetiba, in the vicinity, with which it is connected by tramway, is used by vessels both for the town and the Macaé and Campos railway; Barra do Piraí (45,549), an important station and junction of the Central do Brasil railway on the north side of the Serra do Mar, with large manufacturing and commercial interests; Paraíba do Sul (22,439), in a fertile, long-settled district in the northeast part of the state; Maricá (19,255); Cabo Frio (17,169); and Nova Friburgo (48,682).

RIO DE JANEIRO (in full, São Sebastião do Rio de Janeiro, colloquially shortened to Rio), a city and port of Brazil, capital of the republic and seat of an archbishopric, on the western side of the Bay of Rio de Janeiro, or Guanabara, in lat. 22° 53′ 42″ S., long. 43° 13′ 22″ W. (the position of the observatory). The city occupies about 60 sq.mi. in the southeast angle of the Federal District, an independent district or commune with an area of 451 sq.mi., detached from the province of Rio de Janeiro in 1834. The city stands in great part on an alluvial plain formed by the filling in of the western shore of the bay, which extends inland from the shore line in a northwesterly direction between a detached group of mountains on the south known as the Serra da Carioca, and the imposing wooded heights of the Serra do Mar on the north. The spurs of the Carioca range project into this plain, in some places close up to the margin of the bay, forming picturesque valleys within the limits of the city. Some of the residential quarters follow these valleys up into the mountains and extend up their slopes and over the lower spurs, which, with the hills covered with buildings rising in the midst of the city, give the city a distinctive charm. At the entrance to the bay is the Sugar Loaf (Pão de Açucar), a conical rock rising 1,200 ft. above the water level and forming the terminal point of a short range

between the city and the Atlantic coast. The culminating point of that part of the Carioca range which projects into and partly divides the city is the Corcovado (Hunchback), a sharp rocky peak, 2,100 ft. above the Botafogo inlet, on whose narrow summit towers the imposing statue of Christ the Redeemer, the construction of which was completed in 1931. The Corcovado, approachable either by road or inclined railway, provides a point of vantage from which the entire capital, the bay and its surrounding districts may be viewed. Considerably beyond the limits of the city on its southwest side, but within the Federal District, is the huge isolated flat-topped rock known as the Gávea, 2,575 ft. high, which received its name from its resemblance to the square sail used on certain Portuguese craft. The sky line of this range of mountains, as seen by the approaching traveller several miles outside the entrance to the bay, forms the rough outline of a reclining figure called "the sleeping giant."

The entrance to the bay, between the Sugar Loaf on the west and the Bico do Papagaio (Parrot's Beak) on the east, with the fortress of Santa Cruz on one side and the fort of São João on the other, is about a mile wide. Although the entrance is free from obstructions, dangerous swells are produced by a deeply submerged bar whenever storms come out of the south or southwest. Almost midway in the channel is the little island and fort of Lage, temporary site of the first Huguenot settlement in Rio de Janeiro. On the west is the semicircular bay of Botafogo, round which are grouped the residences of one of the wealthiest suburbs; on the east, the almost landlocked bay of Jurujuba. (*See* Nictheroy [Niterói].)

The bay extends northward about 16 mi. from the entrance channel, opening to a maximum width of about 15 mi. near its head. The irregular shore line was modified by the construction of sea walls and the filling in of shallow bays. Close to the shore are the islands of Villegaignon (occupied by the national naval academy), Cobras (occupied by fortifications, naval storehouses, hospital and dry docks), Santa Bárbara and Enxadas.

The oldest part of the city, which includes the commercial section, lies between Castle and Santo Antonio hills on the south, and São Bento, Conceição and Livramento hills on the north, and extends inland to the Praça da República, though the defensive works in colonial times followed a line much nearer the bay. This section was extended southward along the bay shore during the 19th century and led to the development of a string of suburbs such as Catete and Botafogo, with that of Laranjeiras behind Catete in a pretty valley of the same name, Leme, Copacabana, Ipanema and Gávea, the last including Rio's famous botanical garden, which dates from the early 19th century. The major trend of later development was northward and westward, where are to be found the suburbs of Cidade Nova, São Cristovão, Engenho Novo, Praia Formosa, Pedregulho, Vila Isabel, Tijuca, Rio Comprido, Cajú and others, some of which are residential, while others are essentially industrial. The outlying, poorer suburbs are reached by the Central do Brasil railway; those closer in are served by street railways and buses. The population of the Federal District, according to the census of 1950, was 2,413,152; and of the city 2,335,931.

Climate.—The climate of Rio de Janeiro is warm and humid, the average temperature for the year being about 74° F., with July, the coolest month, having an average temperature of 68.7°. The rainfall averages about 44 in. annually, with July and August being the least rainy months. Formerly the low-lying and poorly drained areas which are marginal to the bay, plus the lack of adequate sanitary facilities, created a serious health problem in Rio de Janeiro, which was, however, in no way connected with the climate. Yellow fever, the first recorded appearance of which was in Dec. 1849, was for many years almost a regular occurrence, and the mortality from it was exceedingly high. This and other dangerous diseases disappeared as epidemics as a result of improved sanitary conditions following the notable work begun by Oswaldo Cruz, under whose direction Rio de Janeiro was made one of the most healthful of tropical cities.

Streets and Parks.—Some of the most modern streets were laid out with Spanish-American regularity, but much the greater part seems to have sprung into existence without any plan. Most of the streets of the old city are parallel and cross at right angles, but they are narrow and enclose blocks of unequal size. Each suburb is laid out independently, with straight streets where the ground permits, and crooked ones where the shore line or mountain contour compels. From the beginning of the 20th century, large sums were expended on new avenues, the widening and straightening of old streets and the improvement of the water front between the Passeio Público and the southern extremity of the Praia de Botafogo by the construction of a grand boulevard, partly on reclaimed land. One of these improvements consists of a central avenue (Avenida Rio Branco) cut across the old city from a point on the water front near the Passeio Público northward to the Saúde water front. More than a mile long from north to south, it is lined with fine private and public buildings. The military, naval and jockey clubs are situated there, and also the offices of some of the principal newspapers, besides fashionable shops, cafés and business places. The shore line boulevard, called the Avenida Beira Mar, is more than 4 mi. long, the wider parts being filled in with gardens. Toward the south, outside the Guanabara bay, the shore along the beaches of Leme, Copacabana and Ipanema was built into one of the most fashionable resorts of the continent.

The Mangue canal, originally designed as an entrance to a central market for the boats plying the bay, is used for drainage purposes. The canal is nearly 2 mi. long, enclosed with stone walls, crossed by a number of iron bridges and bordered by lines of royal palms. The most famous street of the old city is the Rua do Ouvidor, running westward from the market place to the church of São Francisco de Paula, and lined with retail shops, cafés and newspaper offices. It has long been a favourite promenade, and fills an important part in the social and political life of the city. The principal business section includes a number of short and narrow streets between the Rua Primeiro de Março, once called Rua Direita, which extends from the Praça 15 de Novembro northward to São Bento hill and the Avenida Rio Branco. The widest boulevard in the city is the Avenida Presidente Vargas, which begins at the Candelaria church and, crossing the Avenida Rio Branco at right angles, extends toward the west for more than 2 mi. The streets and suburbs are served by lines of the Rio de Janeiro Tramway, Light and Power Co., Ltd., which also supplies electric power to the city from hydroelectric plants.

The public parks and gardens are numerous and include the Parque Azurem Furtado, the largest park in the central district; the botanical garden with its avenue of royal palms; the Passeio Público (dating from 1783), a small garden on the water front facing the harbour entrance; the Praça Tiradentes with its magnificent equestrian statue of Dom Pedro I; the Praça 15 de Novembro on the water front, facing the old city palace; the Quinta da Boa Vista in São Cristovão; and many smaller parks and squares.

Water Supply.—The water supply is derived from three sources: the small streams flowing down the mountainsides which serve small localities; the old Carioca aqueduct, dating from colonial times; and the modern Rio do Ouro waterworks, which bring in an abundant supply from the Serra do Tinquá, 30 mi. N.W. of the city. An extensive system of sewers was constructed and a separate system of rain-water drains.

Buildings.—There remain many public edifices and dwellings of the colonial period, severely plain in appearance, with heavy stone walls and tile roofs. The old city palace facing upon Praça 15 de Novembro, once the residence of the fugitive Portuguese sovereign Dom João VI, is a good example. The 19th century brought no important modifications until near its close, when French and Italian styles began to appear, both in exterior decoration and in architectural design. The Praça do Commercio (merchants' exchange) and post office on Rua 1° de Março and the national printing office near the Largo da Carioca are notable examples. After that time architectural styles changed radically, and apartments, hotels, office buildings and public buildings of the most advanced modern design and construction were built. At the southern end of the Avenida Rio Branco is a group of elegant state edifices, the Municipal theatre, the Monroe palace and the

National library and Academy of Fine Arts. The buildings of the ministries of finance, education and war are also among the most beautiful in the city. There are more than 200 churches in the city, including the cathedral which was built in 1761. The most noteworthy church is that of Our Lady of Candelaria, in the commercial district, with twin towers and graceful dome.

Education.—Prior to 1920 Brazil had no university system, the plans for such having crystallized into nothing more tangible than a great number of institutions of higher learning and separate faculties. When Brazil adopted the university system in 1920, the University of Brazil in Rio de Janeiro was created, in spirit at least, as a reflection of the movement toward centralization. But it was not until 1931 that the realization of this plan began to be manifested. By a presidential decree in that year the faculties of education, sciences and letters were created, and such preexisting institutions as the schools of law, medicine, pharmacy, dentistry, mines and fine arts, the Polytechnic school, the National museum, the Geological and Mineralogical institute, the Oswaldo Cruz institute (medical research), the Astronomical observatory, the Institute of Chemistry, the Botanical garden, the Institute of Legal Medicine, the Central Meteorological institute and other centres of higher learning were made integral parts of the university. Considerable progress was made in the field of teacher training, which was climaxed in Rio de Janeiro by the creation in 1935 of the University of the Federal District—comprising the teachers' college, schools of letters, sciences, economics and law and an institute of arts. This institution closed for a few years but was reopened in 1951. The school system of Brazil, and that of the Federal District, is under the administration of the ministry of education and health, with the National Council of Education acting in an advisory capacity. Private schools may be either autonomous or subject to government regulations. In addition to its two universities, Rio de Janeiro has many other institutes of learning, including preparatory schools, vocational schools and schools for the deaf and blind.

Hospitals and Asylums.—The Federal District has a number of hospitals, asylums and benevolent institutions. Chief of these is the Misericordia hospital, popularly known as the "Santa Casa," belonging to a religious brotherhood dating from 1591. Other public hospitals are a lepers' hospital in São Cristovão, the military and naval hospitals, the São Sebastião hospital and the isolation and contagious diseases hospitals in Jurujuba. The government participated in a program of remodelling and improving existing institutions and of building such new ones as the Jesus, Miguel Couto and Getulio Vargas hospitals. There are also a number of private hospitals maintained by church brotherhoods and charitable associations; among them are the Portuguese hospital in Rua de Santo Amaro and the Strangers' hospital in Botafogo. Most prominent among the asylums is the Hospicio Nacional for the insane, which was erected in 1842–52.

Harbour, Communications and Commerce.—The port and harbour of Rio de Janeiro are the largest and most important in the republic. The entrance is open to vessels of the largest draught, and there is sufficient deepwater anchorage inside for the navies of the world. The lower anchorage, where the health officers visit vessels, is below Ilha Fiscal, and the upper or commercial anchorage is in the broad part of the bay above Ilha das Cobras, the national coasting vessels occupying the shallower waters near the Saúde and Gambôa districts. The customhouse occupies a considerable part of the shore line before the old city.

The newer port works consist of an improved water front for the Saúde, Gambôa and Sacco do Alferes districts, in which the shipping interests are centred, and a continuation of the sea wall across the shallow São Cristovão bay to the Ponta do Cajú, the large reclaimed area being filled in by the removal of some small hills. The commercial quays are built in deep water and permit mooring alongside the largest vessels. The total length of the commercial quays is about 3,800 yd. Railway and streetcar connections are provided, and both electric and hydraulic power are available. Special surtaxes are levied on imports to meet the interest and redemption charges on the loans raised for the execution of these important works.

Railway communication with the interior is maintained by the Central do Brasil and the Leopoldina lines, besides which there is a short passenger line to Corcovado mountain about 2½ mi. long, an electric line to Tijuca and a narrow-gauge line running out to the Rio do Ouro waterworks. There is communication with Petrópolis by a branch line of the Leopoldina system, and also by a steamer to the head of the bay and thence by rail up the *serra*.

Rio de Janeiro is the seaport for a large area of the richest, most productive and most thickly settled parts of Brazil, including the states of Rio de Janeiro and Minas Gerais and a small part of eastern São Paulo. Its exports include coffee, sugar, hides, cabinet woods, tobacco and cigars, tapioca, gold, diamonds, iron ore, manganese and sundry small products.

The city is also a distributing centre in the coasting trade, and many imported products, such as jerked beef (*xarque*), hay, flour, wines, etc., appear among the coastwise exports, as well as domestic manufactures. The total exports for 1949 amounted to 746,487 metric tons; imports in the same year totalled 2,879,524 metric tons. Formerly Rio de Janeiro led all other ports in Brazil in the export of coffee, but the enormous increase in production in the state of São Paulo later gave Santos the lead.

Manufactures.—In spite of Rio's leading role as a commercial port, the city is not equally important as an industrial or manufacturing centre. Manufactures consist largely of consumers' goods for the domestic market, and include such items as flour (from imported wheat), biscuits, macaroni, chocolate, fruit conserves, refined sugar, confectioneries and other foodstuffs, beer, liquors, ice, mineral waters, cigars and cigarettes, soap, candles, perfumes, furniture, boots and shoes, hats, clothing, rope, matches, ink, printing type, glass, chemicals, tires, etc. In addition there are plants which manufacture finished products from processed imports, especially drugs and sundries. There are machine and repair shops, the most important of which are the shops of the Central do Brasil railway. One of the most important industrial enterprises in the city is that of the Rio de Janeiro Tramway, Light and Power Co., whose generating plants are located about 50 mi. from the city. Promotion of trade in the city is largely a function of the chamber of commerce of Rio de Janeiro and the Federation of Brazilian Chambers of Commerce.

Government.—The Federal District, including Rio de Janeiro, is governed by a prefect, who represents the national government, and a municipal council, which represents the people. The prefect is appointed by the president of the republic for a term of four years, and the appointment must be confirmed by the senate. There are seven *diretorias,* or boards, under the prefect, each one assigned to a special field of work, chief among which are education, public health and social welfare, public works and transportation, finance, police, archives and statistics, forestry, and game and fishing. The municipal council of *intendentes* is elected by direct suffrage for a term of two years and is composed of 50 members who meet in ordinary session twice a year. The Federal District is represented in congress by 3 senators elected for nine years and 17 deputies elected for three years, and is credited with the rights and privileges of citizenship. On the other hand, the city is a garrison town and under direct administration of the national executive, who controls its police force and exercises partial control over its streets, squares and water front. In the work of improving the city the national government assumed the expense of the commercial quays, the filling of the São Cristovão bay, the opening of the Mangue canal and its embellishment, the opening of the Avenida Central, the extension of the sewage system and the addition of new sources to the water supply, while the city was responsible for the Avenida Beira Mar, the opening of a new avenue from the Largo da Lapa westward to Rua Frei Caneca, the removal of the Morro do Senado, the widening of some streets crossing the Avenida Central and the opening and straightening of other streets.

History.—The discovery of the Bay of Rio de Janeiro is attributed by many writers to André Gonçalves and Amerigo Vespucci, who entered its waters on Jan. 1, 1502. Another Portuguese navigator, Martim Afonso de Souza, visited it in 1531, but passed on to São Vicente, near Santos, where he established a colony.

The first settlement in the bay was made by an expedition of French Huguenots under the command of Nicolas Durand de Villegagnon, who established his colony on the small island that bears his name. In 1560 their fort was captured and destroyed by a Portuguese expedition from Bahia under Gov. Mem de Sá, and in 1565 another expedition under Estacio de Sá, cousin of the governor, founded a Portuguese settlement in another part of the bay. Two years later the French were decisively defeated by Mem de Sá, and the Portuguese settlement was named São Sebastião do Rio de Janeiro, in honour of King Sebastian of Portugal and in honour of the saint's day (St. Sebastian the Martyr) on which the decisive battle was fought. The French had named their colony La France Antarctique, and their island fort had been called Fort Coligny. In 1710 a French expedition of five vessels and about 1,000 men under Jean François Duclerc attempted to regain possession, but was defeated; its commander was captured and later assassinated. This led to a second French expedition, under René Duguay-Trouin, who entered the bay on Sept. 12, 1711, and captured the town on Sept. 22. Duguay-Trouin released Duclerc's imprisoned followers, exacted a heavy ransom and then withdrew.

The discovery of gold in Minas Gerais at the end of the 17th century greatly increased the importance of the town. It had been made the capital of the southern captaincies in 1680, and in 1762 it became the capital of all Brazil. In 1808 the fugitive Portuguese court, under the regent Dom João VI, took refuge in Rio de Janeiro and gave a new impulse to its growth. It was thrown open to foreign commerce, foreign mercantile houses were permitted to settle there, printing was introduced, industrial restrictions were removed and a college of medicine, a military academy and a public library were founded. Dom João VI returned to Portugal in 1821, and on Sept. 7, 1822, Brazil was declared independent with Dom Pedro I as its first emperor and Rio de Janeiro as its capital. In 1839 a steamship service along the coast was opened, but direct communication with Europe was delayed until 1850 and with the United States until 1865. These services added largely to the prosperity of the port. The first section of the Dom Pedro II railway was opened in 1858, and the second or mountain section in 1864, which brought the city into closer relations with the interior. In 1874 cable communication with Europe was opened, which was soon afterward extended southward to the river Plate republics.

On Nov. 15, 1889, a military revolt in the city under the leadership of Gen. Manuel Deodoro da Fonseca led to the declaration of a republic and the expulsion of the imperial family, which was accomplished without resistance or loss of life. Disorders followed, a naval revolt in 1891 causing the resignation of President Deodoro da Fonseca and another in 1893–94 causing a blockade of the port for about six months and the loss of many lives and much property from desultory bombardments. Between 1894 and 1930 there were trifling outbreaks on the part of agitators, but at no time was the security of the government in danger. In Sept. 1930 a long-impending revolution was precipitated by the turn of events surrounding the presidential elections of that year. On Oct. 4, 1930, a group of high-ranking army officers in Rio de Janeiro seized and jailed the president (Washington Luis) and set up a military junta, which, one month later, turned over the presidency to Getulio Vargas. In 1945 Vargas was in turn overthrown by a military uprising. Under a new constitution adopted in 1945, Gen. Eurico Gasper Dutra was elected president to serve for a period of five years (1946–50). Vargas was elected president again in 1950.

BIBLIOGRAPHY.—Nearly all books relating to Brazil devote some attention to its capital city. *See also* A. Agache, *Cidade do Rio de Janeiro* (Rio de Janeiro, 1930); V. Kelsey, *Brazil in Capitals* (1942); J. Casais, *Un turista en el Brasil* (Rio de Janeiro, 1940); H. Gibson, *Rio* (1937); R. W. Moore, "Rio Panorama," *National Geographic Mag.* (Sept. 1939); Departamento de Turismo da Municipalidade, *Rio de Janeiro* (Rio de Janeiro, 1934); Pan American Union, *Rio de Janeiro,* "American City Series," No. 3-A (1940); D. Bartolotti, "La Joya de America," *Revista Geográfica Americana* (Buenos Aires, Oct. 1934); S. Zweig, *Brazil, Land of the Future* (1941).   (R. d'E.; X.)

RÍO DE ORO, the name commonly used for all of Spanish Sahara on the northwest coast of Africa, though strictly appliable only to the southern two-thirds of the territory between Capes

Bojador and Blanco (Blanc). Its length is about 425 mi. and it extends inland about 150 mi. from Cape Bojador in the north and about 250 mi. along its southern boundary. North of Cape Bojador are the other parts of Spanish Sahara, the so-called Free Zone of Occupation or Sekia el Hamara (Sp. Saguia del Hamra), extending from Cape Bojador to Cape Juby, and the southern zone of the Southern protectorate of Morocco, between Cape Juby and the Wad Draa (Dra). The three districts are surrounded by French territory. Sekia el Hamara and Río de Oro proper are administered together as the colony of Spanish Sahara. The seat of the governor is at Villa Cisneros, on the peninsula of Río de Oro; in 1947 the town was estimated to have 1,091 inhabitants, including 334 Europeans. The peninsula projects about 23 mi. into the sea and is 1¼ to 2 mi. broad. Río de Oro bay, between it and the mainland, is about 5 mi. broad and affords a good anchorage. The southern zone of Morocco is administered with the northern from Tetuán.

The territory of Río de Oro proper has an area of 73,362 sq.mi., and its population was estimated (1947) at 1,100 settled inhabitants and about 25,000 nomadic tribesmen, the latter consisting largely of Berbers, more or less arabized, with some Negro admixture. Most of Río de Oro is desert and there is hardly any agriculture. Camels, goats, sheep and zebus are reared; their meat and milk afford sustenance and there is some exportation of their skins. Villa Cisneros is connected with the rest of Spanish Sahara and the outside world by air, and there are tracks north to Cabo Juby, and south to Tichlá and La Güera (on Cape Blanco), as well as several caravan routes. A shipping service links Villa Cisneros with La Güera, Tantan and the Canaries. The total population of the Spanish Sahara colony (area 105,409 sq.mi.) is estimated at 40,000.

Río de Oro takes its name from the bay enclosed by the promontory on which Villa Cisneros stands. It was discovered by the Portuguese in the mid-15th century, mistaken for a river and named Rio de Ouro (Port. "river of gold"; Sp. Río de Oro) on account of gold dust obtained from the natives. The Spaniards had already begun the colonization of the Canary Islands and in 1476 established the fort of Santa Cruz de Mar Pequeña on the mainland in the northern part of the territory: it was abandoned in 1524, and the territory remained independent until the 19th century. In 1878 a British trading port was established by Donald Mackenzie on Cape Juby, but it was surrendered to the ruler of Morocco in 1895. Meanwhile French travellers had visited Sekia el Hamara: the Spaniard Benitez and others explored the coast in 1882, and Bonelli signed treaties with the natives on behalf of the Sociedad Española de Africanistas. In 1884 a Spanish protectorate was declared over the coastal zone from Cape Bojador to Cape Blanco and nominally subordinated to the captain-general of the Canaries. A factory was established at Villa Cisneros in 1885, but abandoned in the face of native attacks. Spanish claims were challenged by the French, who claimed a protectorate over the Sahara, and a Franco-Spanish convention of June 27, 1900, established the landward frontier of Río de Oro proper, awarding the salt deposits of Vjil to the French. Other agreements between the two powers resulted in French recognition of Spanish rule between Capes Bojador and Juby (1906 and 1912), and between Cape Juby and the Wad Draa. By the convention of 1912 Spain bound itself not to alienate its rights in these zones. It was only in 1916 that Colonel Bens took effective possession of Cape Juby. In 1920 La Güera was founded as an outpost facing Port Étienne. Other centres of Spanish influence are Tichlá and Bir Gandus.

See Foreign Office, London, *Spanish Sahara* (H.M.S.O., London, 1920); A. Flores Morales, *El Sahara español* (Madrid, 1946); E. and F. Hernandez-Pechero *et al.*, *El Sahara español* (Madrid, 1949).

(H. V. L.)

RIO GRANDE, or RIO GRANDE DO SUL (rarely São Pedro do Rio Grande do Sul), Brazil; a city and port of the state of Rio Grande do Sul, on the western side of the Rio Grande (as the outlet of the Lagoa dos Patos is called), about 6 mi. from its mouth and nearly 780 mi. S.W. of Rio de Janeiro, in lat. 32° 7′ S., long. 52° 8′ W. Pop. (1950) of Rio Grande 64,241; including the *município*, 78,941. The principal streets are served by tramways, and the Rio Grande do Sul railway has an extension to its shipping wharf called "Estação Maritima" (1½ mi.), a branch to the old port on the north side of the city (1½ mi.), and a branch to Sequeira, near the sea coast (8 mi.). The city is a port of call

for several steamship lines, and has direct communication with European ports. Vessels of 28 ft. draught have entered the port, and those of 26 ft. draught may enter with safety.

The city is built on a low sandy peninsula, barely 5 ft. above sea level, formed by two arms of the Rio Grande projecting westward from the main channel, the peninsula being part of a large sandy plain extending southward along the coast to Lagoa Mirim. The level of the plain is broken by ranges of sand dunes, some of which rise not far from the city on the south and southeast. The openness of the surrounding country and the proximity of the sea give to Rio Grande unusually healthy conditions, which, however, are partially counteracted by defective sanitary arrangements. In pleasing contrast to the drifting sands which surround the city is the fertile Ilha dos Marinheiros (Sailors' island) lying to the northwest of the city; it is highly cultivated and supplies the market with fruit and vegetables. The water front has been improved by substantial stone walls, which permit the mooring of ocean-going vessels alongside. Rio Grande is wholly a commercial and industrial city. Its exports include salted jerked beef (*carne secca* or *xarque*), preserved meats, tongues, hides, horns, hoofs, woollen fabrics, Paraguay tea, beans, onions, fruit, flour, *farinha de mandioca* (cassava flour), candles and leather. The pioneer woollen factory in Brazil, and one of the largest in the country, is in Rio Grande. Rio Grande was founded in 1737 by José da Silva Paes, who built a fort on the river near the site of the present city and called it Estreito. In 1745 the garrison and settlement was removed by Gomes Freire d'Andrade to its present site, which became a *vila* in 1751, with the name of São Pedro do Rio Grande, and a *cidade* (city) in 1807. It was the capital of the captaincy down to 1763, when it was captured by a Spanish force from Buenos Aires under the command of its governor, Don Pedro Zeballos, the seat of government being removed to Viamão at the northern end of the Lagoa dos Patos. The city was occupied by the national forces in the ten years' war which began in 1835, and in 1894 it was unsuccessfully besieged by a small insurgent force that had attempted to overthrow the government at Rio de Janeiro.

RIO GRANDE, a North American river, which rises in the San Juan mountains of southern Colorado, flows southeast and south in Colorado, south by west and southeast through New Mexico and southeast between Texas and Mexico to the Gulf of Mexico. Its length is approximately 1,800 mi. and for about 1,300 mi. it forms the international boundary between the United States and Mexico. It presents many features of a complex physiographic type, being first a river of the Rocky mountains, then of the interior deserts and then of the gulf coastal plain. The Mexicans call it the Río del Norte in its upper course, the Río Bravo in the middle section and the Río Grande only in its course through the coastal plain. From its headwaters, 12,000 ft. above the sea, it rushes rapidly down a mountain canyon to San Luis valley, in Colorado. It flows with moderate speed through this broad valley, enters a long canyon with a maximum depth of 400 ft., about 4 mi. above the boundary between Colorado and New Mexico, and is hemmed in between canyon walls or the sides of narrow mountain valleys throughout its course in New Mexico. It passes through a series of picturesque canyons, some of them 1,750 ft. in depth, in the "Big Bend," and becomes a silt-laden stream with a shifting channel in its passage through the coastal plain. In its course through the plain its channel is so much obstructed by sand bars that it is of no importance for navigation. As the increasing diversion of the water of the upper Rio Grande for irrigation in Colorado and New Mexico resulted in a scarcity of water for this purpose in Mexico, that country complained, and to remedy the evil the reclamation service of the United States proposed the construction by the United States of a storage dam across the river, near Engle, New Mexico. Mexico agreed to this proposal and a treaty covering the matter was proclaimed in Jan. 1907. Mexico receives 60,000 ac.ft. of water annually from the Elephant Butte reservoir in New Mexico. Since 1910 the delta of the Rio Grande, known as the Lower Rio Grande valley, has been developed by water diverted from the river. The irrigated districts, over 200,000 ac. in area, extend from the town Rio Grande to the gulf, a distance of about 100 mi. The semitropical climate of the region makes it ideal for citrus fruit and vegetables for the winter market.

The principal cities on the river are: Brownsville, Tex.; Matamoras, Mex.; Laredo, Tex.; Del Rio, Tex.; El Paso, Tex.; Ciudad Juárez, Mex.; and Albuquerque, N.M.

RIO GRANDE DO SUL, a southern frontier state of Brazil, bounded on the north by the state of Santa Catarina, on the east by the Atlantic, on the south by Uruguay and on the west by Uruguay and Argentina—the Uruguay river forming the boundary line with the latter. Area, 105,088 sq.mi. The northern part of the state lies on the southern slopes of the elevated plateau extending southward from São Paulo across the states of Paraná and Santa Catarina, and is much broken by low mountain ranges whose general direction across the trend of the slope gives them the appearance of escarpments.

A range of low mountains extends southward from the Serra do Mar of Santa Catarina and crosses the state into Uruguay. West of this range is a vast grassy rolling upland devoted principally to stock raising—the southwestern part being suitable in pasturage and climate for sheep and cattle. East of it is a wide coastal zone only slightly elevated above the sea; within it are two great tidewater lakes—Lagôa dos Patos and Lagôa Mirim—which are separated from the ocean by two sandy, barren peninsulas.

In addition to the Lagôa dos Patos and Lagôa Mirim, there are a number of small lakes on the sandy, swampy peninsulas that lie between the coast and these two. The largest lake is the Lagôa dos Patos (Lake of the Patos—an Indian tribe inhabiting its shores at the time of the discovery). The lake is comparatively shallow and filled with sand banks, making its navigable channels tortuous and difficult. The Lagôa Mirim occupies a similar position farther south on the Uruguayan frontier. Rio Grande lies within the south temperate zone and has a mild, temperate climate, except in the coastal zone, where it is semitropical.

There are two well-marked seasons, though the transition periods between them (about two months each) are sometimes described as spring and autumn. The winter months, June to September, are characterized by heavy rains and by cold westerly winds, called *minuanos*, which sometimes lower the temperature to the freezing point, especially in the mountainous districts. Snow is rare, but ice frequently forms on inland waters during cold winter nights, only to disappear with the first rays of the sun. In summer, which is nominally a dry season, light rains are common, northerly and easterly winds prevail and the temperature rises to 95° in the shade.

The principal industry of the state is stock raising, especially on the southern plains, where there are large *estancias* (ranches). This industry originated with the Jesuit missions on the Uruguay early in the 17th century, and its development here has been much the same as in Argentina and Uruguay. No general effort was made before the 20th century to improve the herds by the importation of better breeds, and the industry was practically in a state of decay until higher tariff rates were imposed on imported *carne secca* (jerked beef) toward the end of the 19th century. The export of livestock is insignificant, the practice being to sell the cattle to the *xarqueadas*, or modern packing plants, where they are slaughtered for *xarque*, *charqui* or *carne secca*, which is usually prepared by salting and drying in the sun, or for frozen meats for southern Europe. The jerked beef is largely exported to other Brazilian states for consumption, while the hides and other by-products are exported to Europe and the U.S. Horses, sheep and swine are also raised, the raising of sheep being fostered by the building of woollen factories, and that of swine by the duties on imported pork and lard. In some parts of the state agriculture claims much attention, especially in the forested districts of the north, where colonies of foreign immigrants are established.

The forest products include *erva-mate* or Paraguay tea (*Ilex paraguariensis*), timbers and lumber and vegetable fibre (*crina vegetal*).

Coal of an inferior quality is mined at São Jerônimo, on a small tributary (Arroio dos Ratos) of the Jacuí river, and has been discovered in other localities. Lime is burned at Caçapava, and at

some other places. Gold, copper and iron are said to exist, but are not mined. Considerable progress has been made in manufacturing.

The total length of railway lines in the state was 2,165 mi. in 1949. The main lines include the one from Rio Grande to Uruguaiana; from Livramento, on the Uruguayan border, through the central part of the state to the northern border; and one from Pôrto Alegre to Santa Maria. The Quaraí to Itaquí line belongs to an English company and runs from the Uruguayan frontier, where it connects with the North-Western of Uruguay, northward to Uruguaiana and the naval station of Itaquí.

The population of the state in 1950 was 4,213,316. There is a large foreign element, the largest single group being German. The first German colony was founded in 1824 and settled in 1825 in the rich forested country north of Pôrto Alegre, and many large and prosperous communities were established thereafter in spite of the wars and political agitations in the state. Several of these colonies, such as São Leopoldo, Novo Hamburgo and Conde d'Eu (now Garibaldi), became important towns.

Italian colonies were subsequently established, also with good results, but an Irish colony founded at Monte Bonito, near Pelotas, about 1851, failed completely. The capital of Rio Grande do Sul is Pôrto Alegre (pop., 1950, 381,964), at the northern extremity of Lagôa dos Patos, and its two next most important cities are Rio Grande and Pelotas, both at the southern extremity of the same lake.

Other important cities and towns, with populations (1950) of the *municípios* in which they are located, are Alegrete (44,796), in the western part of the state on the Pôrto Alegre to Uruguaiana railway; Bagé (66,172), about 173 mi. by rail northwest of Rio Grande in a mountainous region, 702 ft. above sea level; Cachoeira (95,067) and Rio Pardo (40,438), both on the Rio Jacuí; Passo Fundo (103,704), on the plateau in the north central part of the state; Uruguaiana (49,785), a frontier town and cattle centre; Caçapava (33,392), centre of a fine grazing district in the central part of the state; and Quaraí (15,792), a town of considerable commercial importance on the Quaraí river opposite the Uruguayan town of Artigas.

History.—The territory was settled along the Uruguay by the Jesuits when they were compelled to abandon their missions on the upper Paraná. Between 1632 and 1707 they founded on the east side of the Uruguay seven missions—all under Spanish jurisdiction—which became highly prosperous, and at the time of their transfer from Spanish to Portuguese rule by a treaty of 1750 had an aggregate population of about 14,000, living in villages and possessing large herds of cattle and many horses. A joint effort of the two powers in 1753 to enforce the treaty, remove the Indians to Spanish territory and mark the boundary line led to resistance and a three years' war, which ended in the capture and partial destruction of the missions.

On the coast the first recognized settlement—a military post at Estreito, near the modern city of Rio Grande—was made in 1737. Before this, and as early as 1680, according to some chroniclers, the region south of Santa Catarina was occupied by settlements or penal colonies of *degradados* (banished men) and immoral women from Santos, São Vicente and São Paulo, and was known as the Continente de São Pedro.

In 1738 the territory (which included the present state of Santa Catarina) became the Capitania d'El Rei and was made a dependency of Rio de Janeiro.

Territorial disputes between Spain and Portugal led to the occupation by the Spanish of the town of Rio Grande (then the capital of the *capitania*) and neighbouring districts from 1763 to 1776, when they reverted to the Portuguese. The capture of Rio Grande in 1763 caused the removal of the seat of government to Viamão at the head of Lagôa dos Patos; in 1773 Pôrto dos Cazaes, renamed Pôrto Alegre, became the capital. In 1801 news of war between Spain and Portugal led the inhabitants of Rio Grande to attack and capture the seven missions and some frontier posts held by the Spaniards since 1763; after 1801 the boundary lines established by treaty in 1777 remained unchanged.

The districts of Santa Catarina and Rio Grande had been separated in 1760 for military convenience, and in 1807 the latter was elevated to the category of a *capitania-geral,* with the designation of São Pedro do Rio Grande, independent of Rio de Janeiro, and with Santa Catarina as a dependency. In 1812 Rio Grande and Santa Catarina were organized into two distinct *comarcas,* the latter becoming an independent province in 1822 when the empire was organized.

In 1835 a separatist revolution broke out in the province and lasted ten years. It was reduced more through the use of money and favours than by force of arms; but the province had suffered terribly in the struggle and did not recover its losses for many years. An incident in this contest was the enlistment of Giuseppe Garibaldi for a short time with the forces of the separatists. In 1865 a Paraguayan army invaded the state and on Aug. 5 occupied the town of Uruguaiana. On Sept. 18 following, the Paraguayan general (Estigarribia) surrendered without a fight—an unusual occurrence in the remarkable war that followed. Political agitations became frequent in Rio Grande do Sul, whose people had acquired something of the temperament of their Spanish neighbours, but no important revolution occurred after the "ten years' war" (1835–45) until the presidency at Rio de Janeiro of Gen. Floriano Peixoto, whose ill-considered interference with the state governments led to the revolt of 1892–94, under Gumersindo Saraiva. In this struggle the revolutionists occupied Santa Catarina and Paraná, capturing Curitiba, but were eventually overthrown through lack of munitions.

RIOJA, LA, an Andean province of Argentina, bounded north by Catamarca, east by Catamarca and Córdoba, south by San Luis and San Juan and west by San Juan and Chile. Area, 35,649 sq.mi. Pop. (1947 est.) 109,776. It is traversed north to south by eastern ranges of the Andes and is separated from Chile by the Cordillera. The west part of the province is drained by the Bermejo, which flows south into the closed lacustrine basin of Mendoza. The east side of the province is arid. In the extreme north some small streams flow north into Catamarca. The scanty waters of these streams are used for irrigation purposes.

The principal industry of the province is mining, its mineral resources including gold, silver, copper, nickel, tin, cobalt, coal, alum and salt. Its best-known mines are those of the Sierra de Famatina, 16,400 ft. above sea level, where an aerial wire line is used for transportation to Chilecito in the valley. Development of mining industries has been seriously hindered by a lack of water and, for the same reason agricultural activity has been restricted in volume and area.

The climate is very hot and dry, and there is no cultivation of the soil except in the valleys of the Cordillera range and in a few other places where irrigation is possible. Under these conditions there are grown wheat in some quantity, grapes, oranges, olives and tobacco. Alfalfa is grown to a considerable extent and is used for feeding the herds of cattle driven across country to Chile.

The capital of the province is La Rioja (pop., 1941 est., 15,312), on the eastern flank of the Sierra de Velasco, about 1,770 ft. above sea level and near the gorge of Sanagasta, through which a small stream, also called Rioja, flows northward and affords water for the gardens, vineyards and orchards that surround it. The wines of Rioja are an important source of income for the district.

The town is connected by rail with Córdoba and Catamarca. It was founded in 1591 by Juan Ramírez de Velasco, governor of Tucumán, and named Ciudad Rioja la Nueva de Todos los Santos. After being destroyed by earthquake in 1894 the city was rebuilt along modern lines.

Chilecito (pop., 1941 est., 6,372) is the second largest town in the province.

RIOM, a town of central France, capital of an *arrondissement* in the department of Puy-de-Dôme, 8 mi. N. by E. of Clermont-Ferrand by rail. Pop. (1946) 12,975. Riom (*Ricomagus* or *Ricomum* of the Romans) was, along with Auvergne, seized for the crown by Philip Augustus, and was the capital of this province under the dukes of Berry and Bourbon.

Riom stands on the left bank of the Ambène, on a height above the fertile plain of Limagne. The houses, some of the 15th and 16th centuries, being built of black lava, have a sombre appearance.

The church of St. Amable, restored, of Romanesque and early Gothic architecture, dates from the 12th century. The church of Notre-Dame du Marthuret (15th century) has a well-known statue of the Virgin at its western entrance. The Sainte-Chapelle of the 14th and 15th centuries is a relic of the palace of Jean de Berry, duke of Auvergne. The rest of the site of the palace is occupied by the law courts. The 16th-century belfry and a mansion of the same period known as the Maison des Consuls are notable. Riom is the seat of a subprefect and tribunal of commerce.

RÍO NEGRO, a national territory of Argentina lying between 37° 35′ and 42° S. lat. and 62° 50′ and 72° 15′ W. long., within the geographical area formerly known as Patagonia. It is bounded north by the territories of Neuquén and La Pampa, east by the province of Buenos Aires and the Atlantic, south by the territory of Chubut and west by Chile and Neuquén. The area is 78,383 sq.mi.; pop. (1914) 42,242; (1947 est.) 133,164. That part of it lying between the Colorado and Negro rivers has much of the formation and characteristics of the "sterile pampas," but with irrigation the greater part of it can be utilized for agriculture and grazing.

South of the Negro the country is arid, barren and lies in a series of sloping tablelands. Lake Nahuel Huapí (216 sq.mi. in area), lying partly in the territory of Neuquén (*q.v.*), is the principal lake of the region. However, there are several chains of lakes in the valleys of the Andes that are considered as rivals to Swiss scenery.

The Atlantic coast line of the territory has one deep indentation—the Gulf of San Matías—in the north bend of which is the port of San Antonio Oeste. Agriculture and stock raising are the chief sources of wealth. Río Negro usually ranks about fifth among the states and territories in the production of sheep. The capital is Viedma (pop., 1947 est. 9,000), on the right bank of the Río Negro, 24 mi. from its mouth and opposite Carmen de Patagones, a port of Buenos Aires province. There are numerous small settlements along the Río Negro and the railway extending inland from San Antonio Oeste, but the only other town of importance is San Carlos de Bariloche, on the shore of Lake Nahuel Huapí, one of the two western terminals of the railway from San Antonio Oeste. Other transportation facilities are furnished by the railway which crosses the northern part of the territory.

RIO PARDO (formerly Vila do Rio Pardo), a town of Brazil in the state of Rio Grande do Sul, on the left bank of the Jacuí at its confluence with the Pardo. Pop. (1950) of the municipality, 40,438. The town is about 80 mi. due west of Pôrto Alegre, with which it is connected by rail and steamer. The Jacuí is navigable by small steamers.

The town had its origin in a frontier fort built at this point by the Portuguese in 1751.

RÍO PIEDRAS, a former city of Puerto Rico, situated on the northern coast of the island, consolidated with the capital city, San Juan, by referendum on June 4, 1951. The population was 132,369 in 1950; 19,935 in 1940; and it was 13,408 in 1930. The population of the municipal district in 1950 was 143,897; in 1940 it was 68,290; in 1930, 40,853.

RIOT, the gravest kind of breach of the peace, short of treason, known to the English law. It consists in a tumultuous disturbance of the peace by an assemblage of three or more persons who, with intent to help one another against any one who opposes them in the execution of some enterprise, actually execute that enterprise in a violent and turbulent manner, to the terror of the people.

It is not necessary that violence should be used to any person or damage done to any property. Whether the enterprise itself is lawful or unlawful is not material, the gist of the offense lying in the mode in which the enterprise is carried out (*Reg.* v. *Cunningham, Grahame, and Burns,* 1888, 16 Cox. C.C. 420). Nor is it material whether the enterprise is of a private or a public nature, though in the latter case the rioters may also be guilty of sedition or treason. An assembly in its inception perfectly lawful may become a riot if the persons assembled proceed to form and execute a common purpose in the manner above stated, although they had no such purpose when they first assembled. Riot differs from "affray" in the number of persons necessary to constitute the offence, from an "unlawful assembly" in that actual tumult or violence is an essential element, and from "rout" which is an unlawful assembly that has moved towards the execution of a common purpose.

According to the decisions in *Field* v. *Receiver of Metropolitan Police* (1907 2. K.B. 853) and *Ford* v. *Receiver of Metropolitan Police* (1921 2 K.B. 344) five elements are necessary to constitute a riot:—(1) the presence of three persons at least; (2) a common purpose; (3) the execution or inception of the common purpose; (4) an intent to help one another by force if necessary against any person who may oppose them in the execution of their common purpose; (5) force or violence not merely used in demolishing, but displayed in such a manner as to alarm at least one person of reasonable firmness and courage.

It is an indictable misdemeanor at common law, but the Riot Act (1714), creates certain statutory offences for riot attended by circumstances of aggravation. That act makes it the duty of a justice, sheriff, mayor or other authority, wherever 12 persons or more are unlawfully, riotously and tumultuously assembled together, to the disturbance of the public peace, to resort to the place of such assembly and read the following proclamation: "Our Sovereign Lord the King chargeth and commandeth all persons being assembled immediately to disperse themselves, and peaceably to depart to their habitations or to their lawful business, upon the pains contained in the act made in the first year of King George for preventing tumultuous and riotous assemblies. God save the King." It is a felony to obstruct the reading of the proclamation or to remain or continue together unlawfully, riotously and tumultuously for one hour after the proclamation was made or for one hour after it would have been made but for being hindered. The act requires the justices to seize and apprehend all persons continuing after the hour, and indemnifies them and those who act under their authority from liability for injuries caused thereby. The punishment for the felony is penal servitude for life.

By s. 11 of the Malicious Damage Act 1861 (which is a re-enactment of a similar provision made in 1827 in consequence of the frame-breaking riots), it is a felony for persons riotously and tumultuously assembled together to the disturbance of the public peace to unlawfully and with force demolish or begin to demolish or pull down or destroy any building, public building, machinery or mining plant. The punishment is the same as for a felony under the Riot Act. By s. 12 it is a misdemeanour to injure or damage such building, etc. The punishment is penal servitude for seven years, or imprisonment as in the case of the two felonies above described. Under the Shipping Offences Act (1793) a riotous assemblage of three or more seamen, ship's carpenters and other persons, unlawfully and with force preventing and hindering or obstructing the loading or unloading or the sailing or navigation of any vessel, or unlawfully and with force boarding any vessel with intent to prevent, etc., is punishable on a first conviction as a misdemeanour by imprisonment for 12 months, and on a second conviction as a felony by penal servitude for 14 years.

It is the duty of a magistrate at the time of a riot to assemble subjects of the realm, whether civil or military, for the purpose of quelling the riot. In this duty he is aided by the common law, and a statute of 1414 (Henry V.), under which all subjects of the realm are bound to assist on reasonable warning, and by various enactments enabling the authorities to call out the forces for the suppression of riot, and to close public-houses where a riot is apprehended. It is his duty to keep the peace; if the peace be broken, honesty of intention will not avail him if he has been guilty of neglect of duty. The question is whether he did all that he knew was in his power and which could be expected from a man of ordinary prudence, firmness and activity. The law as thus stated is gathered from the opinions of the judges on the trials of

the lord mayor of London and the mayor of Bristol on indictments for neglect of duty at the time of the Gordon riots of 1780 and the Bristol riots in 1831.

A matter of interest is the extent of the protection afforded at common law and by the Riot Act to soldiers and others acting under the commands of their officers, and in this regard it must always be borne in mind that "a soldier for the purpose of establishing civil order is only a citizen armed in a particular manner." The question was dealt with by Lord Bowen and his fellow-commissioners in the report on the Featherstone riots (Parl. Paper, 1893-1894, c. 7234). The substance of their views is as follows:—

By the law of England every one is bound to aid in the suppression of riotous assemblages. The degree of force, however, which may be lawfully employed in their suppression depends on the nature of each riot, for the force used must always be moderated and proportioned to the circumstances of the case and to the end to be attained. The taking of life can only be justified by the necessity for protecting persons or property against various forms of violent crime, or by the necessity of dispersing a riotous crowd which is dangerous unless dispersed, or in the case of persons whose conduct has become felonious through disobedience to the provisions of the Riot Act, and who resist the attempt to disperse or apprehend them. The necessary prevention of such outrage on person or property justifies the guardians of the peace in the employment against a crowd of even deadly weapons. Officers and soldiers are under no special privileges and subject to no special responsibilities as regards the principle of the law. The whole action of the military if once called in, ought from first to last to be based on the principle of doing, and doing without fear, only that which is absolutely necessary to prevent serious crime, and of exercising care and skill with regard to what is done. No set of rules exists which governs every instance or defines beforehand any contingency that may arise. The presence of a magistrate is not essential, but is usual, and of the highest value to aid the commander of the troops by local knowledge. But his presence or absence has no legal effect on the duties or responsibilities of the military to use their arms when it becomes necessary to do so, and without recklessness or negligence and with reasonable care and caution; and where they have so acted the killing of a rioter is justifiable homicide, and the killing of an innocent bystander is homicide by misadventure. It is not usual to resort to extremities with rioters until after reading the proclamation under the Riot Act (1714), but this preliminary is by no means a condition precedent to the exercise of the common-law powers of suppressing riots.

It was decided in *Reg.* v. *Glamorganshire County Council, ex parte Miller* (1899 2 Q.B. 536) that there is no duty upon the county council to pay out of the county funds the expenses of the maintenance of troops which have upon the application of the county justices been brought into the county for the purpose of preserving peace and order in the county.

Until 1886 persons whose property was damaged by riot had a civil remedy of an exceptional character by action against the hundred in which the riot took place. But the old statutes were repealed and replaced by the Riot Damage Act 1886. Under this act compensation is payable where rioters have injured or destroyed houses, shops, buildings, fixed or movable machinery and appliances prepared or used for or in connection with manufactures or agriculture, or for mines or quarries, or have injured, stolen, or destroyed property in houses, shops or buildings. The compensation is payable out of the police rate for the district in which the damage is done. The remedy is available in the case of stranded ships plundered by rioters (s. 515 of the Merchant Shipping Act 1894). (X.; W. DE B. H.)

United States.—Most States have enacted statutes which, though conforming generally to the outlines of the English law, have nevertheless common differences. *See* 94 Am. Dec. 36 *et seq.* In a few States only two people are required. Ga. Penal Code, 1926, sec. 360; Calif. Penal Code, 1923, sec. 404. Some States require that the acts committed be independently unlawful. Page, Ann. Ohio Code, 1926, sec. 12,809. In many others independent illegality is not essential. Cahill's Ill. Rev. Sta. 1927, ch.

38, sec. 518. There is a tendency to abolish the distinction between unlawful assembly, rout and riot by requiring merely threats of, or assembly with intent to do, such acts. Comp. Sts. Neb., 1922, sec. 9,744; Calif. Penal Code, *loc. cit. supra*. Reading of the riot act is still frequently a condition. Conn. Rev. Sts., 1918, sec. 6,336. As an additional deterrent, many statutes hold municipalities responsible to those injured by mobs or riots. Gen. Mun. Law, N.Y., Dec. 71. Diligence of municipal officers is no defence. *Arnold* v. *City of Centralia* (1915), 197 Ill. App. 73, 13 A.L.R. 765. The punishment for riot is generally comparatively mild. Burns Ann. Ind. Sts., 1926, sec. 2,529 (maximum fine of $500 and/or imprisonment for maximum of three months).

Although the courts, in interpreting these statutes, still require that there be "concert of action," a defendant, who was one of the crowd, may be convicted even though he committed none of the prohibited acts. The burden of proving no participation is on him. *Commonwealth* v. *Merrick* (1917), 65 Pa. Super. 482. Concert of action will be "implied" from the facts. *Commonwealth* v. *Frishman* (1920), 235 Mass. 449, 126 N.E. 838. Similarly, "common intent," also said to be essential, is not necessarily lacking because of a failure to prove a previously existing specific agreement. It also will be "implied." *Grier* v. *State* (1912), 11 Ga. App. 767, 76 S.E. 70. To hold otherwise in any or all of these instances would make it extremely difficult to convict. The courts, for practical purposes, consider the objective realities, apply their own gauge of social desirability in a particular case, and then by the useful tool of "inference" find the elements previously said to be necessary. (L. A. Tu.)

BIBLIOGRAPHY.—B. M. Rich, *The Presidents and Civil Disorder* (1941); S. A. Wood, *Riot Control* (1946).

RIOT AND CIVIL COMMOTION INSURANCE.
These policies cover all that is provided for by explosion insurance and in addition protect against losses due to riot, insurrection, civil commotion and strike. The rates are low, but in the case of strike, for example, they are trebled if the policy is taken out after the strike has been declared.

RÍO TINTO (MINAS DE RÍO TINTO),
a mining town of southwestern Spain, in the province of Huelva; near the source of the river Tinto, and at the terminus of a light railway from the port of Huelva. Pop. (1940), 2,727 (mun., 9,060). Río Tinto is one of the greatest copper-mining centres in the world. Its modern importance dates from 1872, when a syndicate of London and Bremen capitalists purchased the mines from Spain.

RIOUW-LINGGA ARCHIPELAGO,
five groups of islands off the east coast of Sumatra, extending from the Straits of Singapore in the north, to the Straits of Berhala in the south. They comprise the Karimon group, the Batam group, the Bintang group, the Lingga group, and the Singkep group, with territory on the mainland opposite known as Indragiri, and collectively they form a residency of the Netherlands Indies known as Riouw and Dependencies. The islands vary in height and area, from rocky crags and small coral reefs, to Bintang, or Riouw, the largest island, area 440 sq.mi., with a height of 1,235 ft.; Lingga and Singkep are almost as large, and the former attains a height of 3,500 ft. above sea level and has the largest alluvial plain of the archipelago. Coral reefs and currents make navigation difficult. The total area of the residency is 12,506 sq.mi. and its pop. (1930) was 298,225 (613 Europeans and Eurasians and 39,084 Chinese). On the mainland territory of Indragiri, a triangular-shaped wedge of land between the government of Sumatra East Coast and Jambi residency, which is mainly the valley of the river Kuantan and its tributaries, the people are Malays; the people of the islands are Malays, Buginese and Chinese, with a few aboriginals, about 1,000, known as Benua. The chief products of the islands are gambir, rubber, pepper and rice. The agriculture, shipping and finance of the islands are largely in Chinese hands, the Malays and Buginese selling their produce to the Chinese, who are also cultivators. There are large deposits of bauxite, of which those on Bintang were mined after 1935. In 1940, 275,000 tons were produced. The archipelago was occupied by Japan in 1942. The capital of the residency is Tandjung Pinang, opposite Singapore, also known as Riouw, or Bintang, pop. (1930) 5,789.

RIPLEY,
market town and urban district of Derbyshire, England, 10 mi. N. of Derby on the L.M.S.R. Pop. (est. 1938) 17,520. Area, 8.6 sq.mi. The charter for the market, held on Saturdays, was granted by Henry III. Iron working and coal mining are the principal industries. The adjoining urban district of Heage was transferred to Ripley in 1934.

RIPON, GEORGE FREDERICK SAMUEL ROBINSON,
1ST MARQUESS OF (1827–1909), British statesman, only son of the 1st earl of Ripon and his wife Lady Sarah, daughter of Robert Hobart, 4th earl of Buckinghamshire, was born in London on Sept. 24, 1827.

Ripon began his political life as *attaché* to a special mission to Brussels in 1849. In 1851 he married Henrietta Vyner (d. 1907), and their eldest son, afterwards known as Earl de Grey, was born in 1852. Under his courtesy title of Viscount Goderich he was returned to the House of Commons for Hull in 1852 as an advanced Liberal. In 1853 he was elected for Huddersfield, and in 1857 for the West Riding of Yorkshire. In Jan. 1859 he succeeded to his father's title, and in November of the same year to that of his uncle, Earl de Grey. A few months after entering the Upper House he was appointed under-secretary for war, and in Feb. 1861 under-secretary for India. Upon the death of Sir George Cornewall Lewis in April 1863 he became secretary for war, with a seat in the cabinet. In 1866 he was appointed secretary of State for India. On the formation of the Gladstone administration in Dec. 1868, Lord Ripon was appointed lord president of the council, and held that office until within a few months of the fall of the Government in 1873, when he resigned on purely private grounds. In 1871 Lord Ripon was appointed chairman of the High Joint-Commission on the Alabama claims, which arranged the Treaty of Washington. In recognition of his services he was elevated to a marquessate (1871). In 1874 he became a convert to Roman Catholicism.

On the return of Gladstone to power in 1880 Lord Ripon was appointed viceroy of India, the appointment exciting a storm of controversy, the marquess being the first Roman Catholic to hold the viceregal office. He went out to reverse the Afghan policy of Lord Lytton, and Kandahar was given up, the whole of Afghanistan being secured to Abdur Rahman. The new viceroy extended the rights of the natives, and in certain directions curtailed the privileges of Europeans. For the Ilbert bill of 1883—so named after its author Sir Courtenay Ilbert, *see* INDIA: *History*.

In 1886 he became first lord of the admiralty in the third Gladstone ministry; and on the return of the Liberals to power in 1892 he was appointed colonial secretary, which post he continued to hold until the resignation of the Government in 1895. He was included in Sir Henry Campbell-Bannerman's cabinet at the close of 1905 as lord privy seal, an office which he retained in 1908 when Asquith formed his new ministry, but which he resigned later in the same year. He died at his seat, Studley Royal, near Ripon, on July 9, 1909, when his only son, Earl de Grey, treasurer of the queen's household since 1901, became the 2nd marquess.

RIPON,
a cathedral city and municipal borough in the West Riding of Yorkshire, England, 214 mi. N.N.W. from London, 30 mi. N. of Leeds, on the L.N.E.R. Pop. (1938) 8,474. Area 2.8 sq.mi. It is a foot-hill town of the Pennines, at the confluence of the Ure with its tributaries the Laver and the Skell.

Ripon (*In Rhypum, Ad Ripam*) owed its origin to the monastery founded in 661, of which St. Wilfred became the first abbot. Tradition says that Ripon was made a royal borough by Alfred the Great and that King Aethelstan in 937 gave the borough to the Archbishop of York, and granted him privileges, as lord of the manor, of holding a market and fair. Henry I. certainly granted, or confirmed, these privileges to the Archbishops of York, who retained them until they were handed over to the Bishop of Ripon in 1837. In 1857, they were transferred to the ecclesiastical commissioners from whom they were purchased by the Corporation of Ripon in 1880. About the year 950 the monastery and town were destroyed by King Edred during an expedition against the Danes, but the monastery was rebuilt by the Archbishops of York and about the time of the Conquest it became a collegiate church. In 1318, when the Scots invaded

England, Ripon escaped being burned a second time only by the payment of 1,000 marks.

The streets of Ripon are for the most part narrow and irregular, and although most of the houses are comparatively modern, some of them retain the picturesque gables characteristic of earlier times.

The town is popular as a holiday resort. The cathedral, with a large square central tower and two western towers, is celebrated for its fine proportions and contains various styles of architecture. It was founded on the ruins of St. Wilfred's abbey of the 7th century, but of this Saxon building nothing now remains except the crypt which is known as St. Wilfred's Needle. Apart from the crypt, the oldest part is a portion of the chapter house and vestry adjoining the south side of the choir, and ending eastward in an apse. This is pure Norman work and beneath is a crypt of that period. The present building was begun about 1154 and to this transitional period belong the transepts and parts of the choir. The west front and twin towers are fine specimens of Early English architecture and were completed about 1255. The eastern portion of the choir was rebuilt in Decorated style about the close of the 13th century. The nave and parts of the central tower and two bays of the choir are Perpendicular and were rebuilt toward the end of the 15th century.

The diocese of Ripon was created in 1836 and comprises most of the West Riding and part of the North Riding of Yorkshire and a small part of Lancashire. The episcopal palace, a modern building in Tudor style, is 1 mi. N.W. of the city. To the southwest lies Studley Royal, a former seat of the marquess of Ripon, which contains the celebrated ruins of Fountains abbey. Several old charities include the hospital of St. John the Baptist, founded in 1109, and the hospital of St. Mary Magdalene, founded by the Archbishop of York early in the 12th century as a secular community whose special duty was to administer to lepers. In the 13th century a master and chaplain took the place of the lay brethren and a chantry was founded in 1334. The chapel survives with interesting Norman work and a rare example of a pre-Reformation altar of stone.

From before the conquest until the incorporation charter of 1604, Ripon was governed by a wakeman and 12 elders, but in 1604 the title of wakeman was changed to mayor, and 12 aldermen and 24 councillors were appointed. Ripon sent two members to parliament in 1295, and at intervals from then until 1328–29. The privilege was revived in 1553, and continued until 1867, from when until 1885 one member was returned. Ripon is in the parliamentary division of the same name.

RISDON: *see* HOBART.

RISHANGER, WILLIAM (*c.* 1250–*c.* 1312), English chronicler, made his profession as a Benedictine at St. Alban's abbey in 1271, of which he perhaps became the official chronicler. The most important of his writings is the *Narratio de bellis apud Lewes et Evesham*. Though written many years afterward and drawn from other sources, it is a spirited account of the barons' war. He is so great an admirer of Simon de Montfort that this work has been called a hagiography. He is credited with the authorship of a chronicle covering the period 1259–1306; this has been disputed, but the work is printed under his name by Riley.

BIBLIOGRAPHY.—*Wilhelmi Rishanger chronica et annales*, Rolls Series, Introduction ed. H. T. Riley; the *Narratio de bellis apud Lewes et Evesham*, ed. J. O. Halliwell, Camden Society, 1840.

RISK, hazard, chance of danger or loss, especially the chance of loss to property or goods which an insurance company undertakes to make good to the insurer in return for the recurrent payment of a sum called the premium (*see* INSURANCE, ARTICLES ON).

RISTIĆ, JOVAN (1831–1899), Serbian statesman, was born at Kragugevaz in 1831. He was educated at Belgrade, Heidelberg, Berlin and Paris. In 1861 he became Serbian diplomatic agent at Constantinople, and secured the withdrawal of the Turkish troops from the Serbian fortresses in 1867. On his return from Constantinople he became the recognized leader of the Liberal party. After the assassination of Prince Michael in 1868, he sat on the council of regency, and the first Serbian constitution

(Jan. 2, 1869), was mainly his creation. When Prince Milan attained his majority in 1872, Ristić became foreign minister, and then prime minister, but resigned in the following autumn (1873). He again became prime minister in April 1876, and conducted the two wars against Turkey (July 1876–March 1877 and Dec. 1877–March 1878). Owing to the failure to realize Serb aspirations at the Congress of Berlin, the Ristić government became unpopular, and resigned in 1880. In 1887 Milan recalled Ristić; a new constitution was granted in 1888, and in 1889 Ristić became head of the council of regency for the young king Alexander. On April 13, 1893, King Alexander, by a successful stratagem, imprisoned the regents and ministers in the palace, and, declaring himself of age, recalled the Radicals to office. Ristić died at Belgrade on Sept. 4, 1899.

RISTORI (*rĭst'ō-rē*), **ADELAIDE** (1822–1906), Italian actress, born at Cividale del Friuli Jan. 30, 1822, daughter of strolling players. As a child she appeared upon the stage, and at 14 made her first success as Francesca da Rimini in Silvio Pellico's tragedy. She was 18 when for the first time she played Mary Stuart in an Italian version of Schiller's play. She had been a member of the Sardinian company and also of the ducal company at Parma for some years before her marriage (1846) to the marchese Giuliano Capranica del Grillo (d. 1861); and after a short retirement she returned to the stage and played regularly in Turin and the provinces. In 1855 she took Paris by storm in the rôle of Alfieri's *Myrrha*. Furious partisanship was aroused by the appearance of a rival to the great Rachel. In 1857 she visited Madrid, playing in Spanish to enthusiastic audiences, and in 1866 she paid the first of four visits to the United States, where she had great success in Giacometti's *Elizabeth*, an Italian study of the English sovereign. She retired from professional life in 1885, and died on Oct. 9, 1906, in Rome. Her *Studies and Memoirs* (1888) contain valuable studies in the psychological explanation of the characters of Mary Stuart, Elizabeth, Myrrha, Phaedra and Lady Macbeth, in her interpretation of which Ristori combined high dramatic instinct with the keenest intellectual study.

BIBLIOGRAPHY.—E. P. Hingston, *Adelaide Ristori: A Sketch of her Life* (1856); K. Field, *Adelaide Ristori: A Biography* (1867); Adelaide Ristori, *Studies and Memoirs* (1888), new rev. ed., trans. by G. Mantellini, *Memoirs and Artistic Studies* (1907).

RITCHIE, CHARLES THOMSON RITCHIE, 1ST BARON (1838–1906), English politician, was born at Dundee on Nov. 19, 1838, and educated at the City of London school. He went into business, and in 1874 was returned to parliament as Conservative member for the working-class constituency of Tower Hamlets. In 1885 he was made secretary to the Admiralty, and from 1886 to 1892 president of the Local Government board, in Lord Salisbury's administration with a seat in the cabinet after 1887, sitting as member for St. George's-in-the-East. He was responsible for the Local Government Act of 1888, instituting the county councils; and a large section of the Conservative party always owed him a grudge for having originated the London County council. In Lord Salisbury's later ministries, as member for Croydon, he was president of the Board of Trade (1895–1900), and home secretary (1895–1900); and when Sir Michael Hicks-Beach retired in 1902, he became chancellor of the exchequer in Balfour's cabinet. Though in his earlier years he had been a "fair-trader," he was strongly opposed to Chamberlain's movement for a preferential tariff (*see* the articles on BALFOUR, ARTHUR JAMES BALFOUR, and CHAMBERLAIN, JOSEPH), and he resigned office in Sept. 1903. In Dec. 1905 he was created a peer, but he was in ill health, and he died at Biarritz on Jan. 9, 1906.

See the article in the *Dict. Nat. Biog.* Suppl. 1901–21.

RITSCHL, ALBRECHT (1822–1889), German theologian, was born in Berlin on March 25, 1822. His father, Benjamin Ritschl (1783–1858), was from 1827 to 1854 general superintendent and evangelical bishop of Pomerania. Albrecht studied at Bonn, Halle, Heidelberg and Tübingen. At Halle he came under Hegelian influences. In 1845 he was entirely captivated by the Tübingen school, and in *Das Evangelium Marcions und das kanonische Evangelium des Lukas* (1846) he appears as a disciple of F. C. Baur. But the second edition (1857) of his most important work, on the origin of the old Catholic Church (*Die Entstehung der alt-kathol. Kirche*), shows considerable divergence from the first edition (1850), and reveals an entire emancipation from Baur's method. Ritschl was professor of theology at Bonn (extraordinarius 1852; ordinarius 1859) and Göttingen (1864; *Consistorialrath* also in 1874), his addresses on religion delivered at the latter university showing the impression made upon his mind by his study of Kant and Schleiermacher. Finally, in 1864, came the influence of Rudolf Lotze. He wrote *Die Christliche Lehre von der Rechtfertigung und Versöhnung* (1870–74), and *Die Geschichte des Pietismus* (1880–86). He died at Göttingen on March 20, 1889.

Ritschl claims to carry on the work of Luther and Schleiermacher. He criticizes especially the use of Aristotelianism and speculative philosophy in scholastic and Protestant theology. He holds that such philosophy is too shallow for theology. Hegelianism attempts to squeeze all life into the categories of logic: Aristotelianism deals with "things in general" and ignores the radical distinction between nature and spirit. Neither Hegelianism nor Aristotelianism is "vital" enough to sound the depths of religious life. Neither conceives "God" as correlative to human "trust" (cf. *Theologie und Metaphysik*, esp. p. 8 *seq.*). But Ritschl's recoil carries him so far that he is left alone with merely "practical" experience. "Faith" knows God in His active relation to the "kingdom," but not at all as "self-existent."

Ritschl's school, in which J. G. W. Herrmann, Julius Kaftan and Adolf Harnack were the chief names, diverged from his teaching in many directions; *e.g.*, Kaftan appreciated the mystical side of religion and Harnack's criticism was very different from Ritschl's arbitrary exegesis. They were united on the value of faith-knowledge as opposed to "metaphysic."

See H. Schoen, *Les Origines historiques de la théologie de Ritschl* (1893); G. Ecke, *Die theologische Schule, A. Ritschl's und die evangelische Kirche der Gegenwart* (1897); J. Orr, *The Ritschlian Theology and the Evangelical Faith* (1898) and *Ritschlianism: expository and critical essays* (1903); A. E. Gavire, *The Ritschlian Theology* (1899); E. A. Edghill, *Faith and Fact, a study of Ritschlianism* (1910); R. Mackintosh, *Ritschl* (1915). The chief authority for his biography is *Albrecht Ritschls Leben* (2 vols., Leipzig, 1896) by his son Otto Ritschl.

RITSCHL, FRIEDRICH WILHELM (1806–1876), German scholar, was born in 1806 in Thuringia. He was well taught in youth by Spitzner, a pupil of Gottfried Hermann, spent a year at Leipzig, and in 1826 went to Halle. He went to Bonn in 1839, where he controlled a philological seminary. The names of Georg Curtius, Ihne, Schleicher, Bernays, Ribbeck, Lorenz, Vahlen, Hübner, Bücheler, Helbig, Benndorf, Riese, Windisch, who were his pupils either at Bonn or at Leipzig, attest his fame and power as a teacher. In 1865 a violent quarrel arose between him and Otto Jahn, now his colleague; he resigned, went to Leipzig, and died there in 1876. His great faculty for organization is shown by his administration of the university library at Bonn, and by the eight years of labour which carried to success a work of infinite complexity, the famous *Priscae Latinitatis Monumenta Epigraphica* (Bonn, 1862). This volume presents in admirable facsimile, with prefatory notices and indexes, the Latin inscriptions from the earliest times to the end of the republic.

To the world in general Ritschl was best known as a student of Plautus. Ritschl's examination of the Plautine mss. was both laborious and brilliant, and greatly extended the knowledge of Plautus: for example, by the aid of the Ambrosian palimpsest he recovered the name T. Maccius Plautus, for the vulgate M. Accius, and proved it correct by strong extraneous arguments.

In spite of the incompleteness, on many sides, of his work Ritschl must be assigned a place in the history of learning among a very select few. His studies are presented principally in his *Opuscula* collected partly before and partly since his death. The *Trinummus* (twice edited) was the only specimen of his contemplated edition of Plautus which he completed.

The facts of Ritschl's life may be best learned from the elaborate biography by Otto Ribbeck (Leipzig, 1879). An interesting estimate of Ritschl's work is that by Lucian Müller (1877).

RITTENHOUSE, DAVID (1732–1796), American astronomer, was born at Germantown, Pa., on April 8, 1732. First a watchmaker and mechanician, he afterwards became treasurer of Pennsylvania (1777–89), and from 1792 to 1795 director of the U.S. mint (Philadelphia). He was a fellow of the Royal Society of London, and a member, and in 1791 president, of the American Philosophical Society. As an astronomer, Rittenhouse's principal merit is that he introduced in 1786 the use of spider lines in the focus of a transit instrument. His researches were published in the *Transactions of the American Philosophical Society* (1785–1799). He died at Philadelphia June 26, 1796.

See *Memoir* (1813) by William Barton.

RITTER, HEINRICH (1791–1869), German historian of philosophy, was born at Zerbst on Nov. 21, 1791, and died on Feb. 3, 1869, at Göttingen, where he had been professor of philosophy for nearly 30 years. Of his numerous works the most important are the *Geschichte der Philosophie* (Hamburg, 12 vols., 1829–53), and, written with Preller, the *Historia philosophiae Graeco-Romanae* (1838, 7th ed. 1888).

RITTER, KARL (1779–1859), German geographer, born at Quedlinburg on Aug. 7, 1779, had already travelled much when in 1817–18 he wrote *Die Erdkunde im Verhältnis zur Natur und zur Geschichte des Menschen* (Berlin, 2 vols., 1817–1818). In 1819 he became professor of history at Frankfort, and in 1820 professor extraordinarius of history at Berlin, where he remained till his death. The second edition of his *Erdkunde* (1822–58) was on a much larger scale than the first, but he completed only the sections on Africa and the various countries of Asia. Ritter brought to his work a new conception of the subject. Geography was, to use his own expression, a kind of physiology and comparative anatomy of the earth: rivers, mountains, etc., were so many distinct organs, each with its own functions; and the structure of each country is a leading element in the historic progress of the nation. His death occurred in Berlin on Sept. 28, 1859.

See G. Kramer, *Karl Ritter, ein Lebensbild* (Halle, 1864 and 1870; 2nd ed., 1875); W. L. Gage, *The Life of Karl Ritter* (1867); F. Marthe, "Was bedeutet Karl Ritter für die Geographie," in *Zeitsch. der Ges. f. Erdk.* (Berlin, 1879).

RITUAL [Lat. *ritus*, a custom], a term of religion, which may be defined as the routine of worship. This is a "minimum definition"; "ritual" at least means so much, but may stand for more. Without some sort of ritual there could be no organized method in religious worship. Indeed, viewed in this aspect, ritual is to religion what habit is to life and its function is similar; namely, by bringing subordinate functions under an effortless rule, to permit undivided attention in regard to vital issues. The chief task of routine in religion is to organize the activities necessary to its stability and continuance as a social institution, in order that all available spontaneity and initiative may be directed into spiritual channels.

But, whilst ritual at least represents routine, it tends, historically speaking, to have a far deeper significance for the religious consciousness. A recurrent feature of religion, which many students of its phenomena would even consider constant and typical, is the attribution of a more or less self-contained and automatic efficacy to the ritual procedure as such. Before proceeding to considerations of genesis, it will be convenient briefly to analyse the notion as it appears in the higher religions.

Two constituent lines of thought may be distinguished. Firstly, there is the tendency to pass beyond the purely petitionary attitude which as such can imply no more than the desire, hope or expectation of divine favour, and to take for granted the consummation sought, a deity that answers, a grace and blessing that are communicated. When such accomplishment of its end is assumed, efficacy can readily be held to attach to the act of worship as such. Secondly, there is the tendency to identify such a self-accomplishing act of worship with its objective expression in the ritual that for purposes of mutual understanding makes the body of worshippers one.

The Formal Element in Ritual.—Exactly similar tendencies—to impute efficacy, and to treat the ritual procedure as the source of that efficacy—are typically characteristic of black magic, and their reappearance in religion can hardly be treated as a coincidence, seeing that magic and religion would appear to have much in common, at any rate during the earlier stages of their development. In magic a suggestion is made orally, or by dramatic action, or most often in both ways together, that is held *ipso facto* to bring about its own accomplishment. A certain conditionality attaches to the magical operation, inasmuch as each magician is subject to interference on the part of other magicians who may neutralize his spell by a counter-spell of equal or greater power; nevertheless, the intrinsic tone is that of a categorical assertion of binding force and efficacy. Again, in magic the self-realizing force is apt to seem to reside in the suggestional machinery rather than in the spiritual qualifications of the magician, though this is by no means invariably the case. On the whole, however, spells and ceremonies are wont to be regarded as an inheritable and transferable property containing efficacy in themselves. What is true of magic is true of much primitive religion.

Sir J. G. Frazer has pronounced the following to be marks of a primitive ritual: negatively, that there are no priests, no temples and no gods (though he holds that departmental, non-individual "spirits" are recognized); positively, that the rites are magical rather than propitiatory (*The Golden Bough*, 2nd ed. ii. 191). If we leave it an open question whether, instead of "spirits," it would not be safer to speak of "powers" to which there is attributed not a soul-like nature, but simply a capacity for acting with *mana* (q.v.) (which roughly is what Frazer means by "magical"), this characterization may be accepted as applying to many, if not to all, the rites of primitive religion.

As Lang well puts it, "Ritual is preserved because it preserves luck." Given an intrinsic sacredness, it is but a step to associate definite gods with the origin or purpose of a rite, whose interest it thereupon becomes to punish omissions or innovations by the removal of their blessing (which is little more than to say that the rite loses its efficacy), or by the active infliction of disaster on the community. In the primitive society it is hard to point to any custom to which sacredness does not in some degree attach, but, naturally, the more important and solemn the usage, the more rigid the religious conservatism. Thus there are indications that in Australia, at the highly sacred ceremony of circumcision, the fire-stick was employed after stone implements were known; and we have an exact parallel at a higher level of culture, the stone implement serving for the same operation when iron is already in common use. (*See* B. Spencer and F. Gillen, *The Native Tribes of Australia*, 401; *cf.* E. B. Tylor, *Early History of Mankind*, 3rd ed. 217.)

The Interpretation of Ritual.—A valuable truth insisted on by the late W. Robertson Smith (*Religion of the Semites*, 17 et sqq.) is that in primitive religion it is ritual that generates and sustains myth, and not the other way about. Sacred lore of course cannot be dispensed with; even Australian aboriginal society, which has hardly reached the stage of having priests, needs its *Oknirabata* or "great instructor" (Spencer and Gillen, *ibid.*, 303). The function of such an expert, however, is chiefly to hand on mere rules for the performance of religious acts. If his lore include sacred histories, it is largely, we may suspect, because the description and dramatization of the doings of divine persons enter into ritual as a means of suggestional control. Similarly, the sacred books of the religions of middle grade teem with minute prescriptions as to ritual, but are almost destitute of doctrine. Even in the highest religions, where orthodoxy is the main requirement, and ritual is held merely to symbolize dogma, there is a remarkable rigidity about the dogma that is doubtless in large part due to its association with ritual forms, many of them bearing the most primeval stamp.

As regards the symbolic interpretation of ritual, this is usually held not to be primitive; and it is doubtless true that an unreflective age is hardly aware of the difference between "outward sign" and "inward meaning," and thinks as it were by means of its eyes. Nevertheless, it is easier to define fetishism (q.v.) (a fetish "differing from an idol in that it is worshipped in its own character, not as the symbol, image or occasional residence of a deity,"

New Oxford Dictionary, Oxford, 1901) than it is to bring such a fetishism home to any savage people, the West African negroes not excluded (*cf.* A. B. Ellis, *The Tshi-speaking Peoples of the Gold Coast of W. Africa*, 192). It is the intrinsic *mana*, virtue or grace residing in, and proceeding from, the material object—a power the communicability of which constitutes the whole working hypothesis of the magico-religious performance—that is valued in those cases where native opinion can be tested. Moreover, it must be remembered that in the act of magic a symbolic method is consciously pursued, as witness the very formulas employed: "As I burn this image, so may the man be consumed," or the even more explicit, "It is not wax I am scorching; it is the liver, heart and spleen of So-and-so that I scorch" (W. W. Skeat, *Malay Magic*, 570), where appearance and reality are distinguished in order to be mystically reunited.

Now it is important to observe that from the symbol as embodying an imperative to the symbol as expressing an optative is a transition of meaning that involves no change of form whatever; and, much as theorists love to contrast the suggestional and the petitionary attitudes, it is doubtful if the savage does not move quite indifferently to and fro across the supposed frontier-line between magic and religion, interspersing "bluff" with blandishment, spell with genuine prayer. Meanwhile the particular meanings of the detailed acts composing a complicated piece of ritual soon tend to lose themselves in a general sense of the efficacy of the rite, as a whole, to bring blessing and avert evil. Nay, unintelligibility is so far from invalidating a sacred practice that it positively supports it by deepening the characteristic atmosphere of mystery. Even the higher religions show a lingering predilection for cabalistic formulas.

Changes in Ritual.—Whilst ritual displays an extraordinary stability, its nature is of course not absolutely rigid; it grows, alters and decays. As regards its growth, there is hardly a known tribe without its elaborate body of magico-religious rites. In the exceptional instances where this feature is relatively absent (the Masai of East Africa offer a case in point), we may suspect a disturbance of tradition due to migration or some similar cause. Thus there is always a pre-existing pattern in accordance with which such evolution or invention as occurs proceeds. Unconscious evolution is perhaps the more active factor in primitive times; imitation is never exact, and small variations amount in time to considerable changes.

On the other hand, there is also deliberate innovation. In Australia councils of the older men are held day by day during the performance of their ceremonies, at which traditions are repeated and procedure determined, the effect being mainly to preserve custom but undoubtedly in part also to alter it. Moreover, the individual religious genius exercises no small influence. A man of a more original turn of mind than his fellows will claim to have had a new ceremony imparted to him in a vision, and such a ceremony will even be adopted by another tribe which has no notion of its meaning (Spencer and Gillen, *ibid.*, 272, 278, 281). Meanwhile, since little is dropped whilst so much is being added, the result is an endless complication and elaboration of ritual. Side by side with elaboration goes systematization, more especially when local cults come to be merged in a wider unity. Thereupon assimilation is likely to take place to one or another leading type of rite—for instance, sacrifice or prayer. At these higher stages there is more need than ever for the expert in the shape of the priest, in whose hands ritual procedure becomes more and more of a conscious and studied discipline, the naïve popular elements being steadily eliminated, or rather transformed. Not but what the transference of ritualistic duties to a professional class is often the signal for slack and mechanical performance, with consequent decay of ceremonial. The trouble and worry of having to comply with the endless rules of a too complex system is apt to operate more widely—namely, in the religious society at large —and to produce an endless crop of evasions.

Good examples of these on the part alike of priests and people are afforded by Toda religion, the degenerate condition of which is expressly attributed by Dr. W. H. R. Rivers to "the overdevelopment of the ritual aspect of religion" (*The Todas*, 454–5).

It is interesting to observe that a religion thus atrophied tends to revert to purely magical practices, the use of the word of power, and so on (*ibid.*, ch. x.). It is to be noted, however, that what are known as ritual substitutions, though they lend themselves to purposes of evasion (as in the case of the Chinese use of paper money at funerals), rest ultimately on a principle that is absolutely fundamental in magico-religious theory; namely, that what suggests a thing because it is like it or a part of it becomes that thing when the mystic power is there to carry the suggestion through.

The Classification of Rites.—More than one basis of division has suggested itself. From the sociological point of view perhaps the most important distinction in use is that between public and private rites. Whilst the former essentially belong to religion as existing to further the common weal, the latter have from the earliest times an ambiguous character and tend to split into those which are licit—"sacraments," as they may be termed—and those which are considered anti-social in tendency, and are consequently put beyond the pale of religion and assigned to the "black art" of magic. Or the sociologist may prefer to correlate rites with the forms of social organization—the tribe, the phratry, the clan, the family and so on.

Another interesting contrast (seeing how primary a function of religion it is to establish a calendar of sacred seasons) is that between periodic and occasional rites—one that to a certain extent falls into line with the previous dichotomy. A less fruitful method of classing rites is that which arranges them according to their inner meaning. As we have seen, such meaning is usually acquired *ex post facto,* and typical forms of rite are used for many different purposes; so that attempts to differentiate are likely to beget more equivocations than they clear up. The fact is that comparative religion must be content to regard all its classifications alike as pieces of mere scaffolding serving temporary purposes of construction.

Negative Rites.—A word must be added on a subject dealt with elsewhere (*see* TABU), but strictly germane to the matter in hand. Ritual interdictions have the best, if not the sole, right to rank as taboos (*see* M. Mauss in *L'Année sociologique*, ix. 249). Taboo, as understood in Polynesia, the home of the word, is as wide as, and no wider than, religion, representing one side or aspect of the sacred (*see* RELIGION). The very power that can help can also blast if approached improperly and without due precautions. Taboos are such precautions, abstinences prompted, not by simple dread or dislike, but always by some sort of respect as felt towards that which in other circumstances or in other form has healing virtue. Thus the negative attitude of the observer of taboo involves a positive attitude of reverence from which it becomes in practice scarcely distinguishable. To keep a fast, for instance, is looked upon as a direct act of worship. It must be noted, too, that, whereas taboo as at first conceived belongs to the magico-religious circle of ideas, implying a quasi-physical transference of sacredness from that having it to one not fit to receive it, it is very easily reinterpreted as an obligation imposed by the deity on his worshippers.

The law observed by a primitive religious community abounds in negative precepts, and if early religion tends to be a religion of fear it is because the taboo-breaker provides the most palpable objective for human and divine sanctions. In the higher religions, to be pure remains amongst the most laudable of aspirations, and, even though the ceremonial aversion of a former age has become moralized, and a purity of heart set up as the ideal, it is on "virtues of omission" that stress is apt to be laid, so that a timorous propriety is too often preferred to a forceful grappling with the problems of life. There are signs, however, that the religious consciousness has at length come to appreciate the fact that the function of routine in religion as elsewhere is to clear the way for action.

BIBLIOGRAPHY.—For leading ideas *see* E. B. Tylor, *Primitive Culture,* ch. 18 (1903); and A. Lang, *Myth, Ritual and Religion* (1899); Sir J. G. Frazer's *The Golden Bough* (1900); W. Robertson Smith, *Lectures on the Religion of the Semites* (1889); H. Hubert and M. Mauss, "Essai sur la nature et la fonction du sacrifice," in *L'Année sociologique*, ii.; S. Levi, *La Doctrine du sacrifice dans les Brâhmanas* (1899); W. Caland and V. Henry, *L'Agnistoma, description complète de la forme normale du sacrifice de Soma dans le culte védique* (1906); H. Oldenberg, *Die Religion des Veda* (1894); A. Hillebrant, *Ritual Litteratur: Vedische Opfer und Zauber* (1896). For descriptions of Australian ritual *see* Sir B. Spencer and F. J. Gillen, *The Native Tribes of Central Australia* (1899) and *The Northern Tribes of Central Australia* (1904). For North American rituals *see* A. C. Fletcher, "The Hako: A Pawnee Ceremony," in *22nd Report of Bureau of American Ethnology;* various papers in *Peabody Reports;* J. W. Fewkes, "Tusayan Katchinas," in *15th Rep. of B. of A. Eth.;* "Hopi Katchinas," in *21st Rep.;* M. C. Stevenson, "The Zuñi Indians," in *23rd Rep.;* cf. F. H. Cushing, "Zuñi Fetiches," in *2nd Rep.* Also *see* L. R. Farnell, *The Cults of the Greek States* (1896–1907); A. Moret, *Le Rituel du culte divin journalier en Égypte* (1902); A. de Marchi, *Il culto privato di Roma antica* (1902); A. N. Whitehead, *Religion in the Making* (1926). *See also* SPELL, MANA.

RITUAL MURDER, a general term for human sacrifice in connection with religious ceremonies. False accusations as to the practice of ritual murder by various bodies have often been made. Justin Martyr in his second apology (cap. xii.) vigorously defends the Christian community against the charge: Octavius, Minutius Felix, Tertullian, Origen, and other Church Fathers all refer to the subject and indignantly repudiate the atrocious libel that the Eucharist involved human sacrifice. The myth was revived against the Montanists, and in the later middle ages against various dissenting sects of Christians. In modern times the accusation has been again levelled against "foreigners" during the disturbances in China. The chief sufferers from the libel were however the Jews. The earliest form of it (the first instance is the case of William of Norwich, 1144) was that they immolated a Christian child at Easter in mockery of the Passion. In the course of the next century there came about the elaboration that the blood was used in the manufacture of the unleavened bread for Passover (which generally coincided with Easter) or for other purposes. Ultimately, it was actually alleged that "the Jews of every province annually decide by lot" which congregation or town was to be the scene of the mythical murder. Almost invariably, the accusations were followed by spoliation and persecution. Among the classical instances are the "martyrdoms" of Hugh of Lincoln (1255) and Simon of Trent (1475), the Damascus affair (1840), and the Beilis case (1911–13). It is easy to understand how in ages when the Jews were everywhere regarded with suspicious awe such stories would find ready credence; but the revival of the myth by the anti-Semite in modern times is a deplorable instance of degeneration. That there is no foundation whatsoever for the belief is proved in the classical treatise on the subject by Hermann L. Strack, regius professor of theology at the University of Berlin. Many proselytes to Christianity have strenuously defended the Jews from the charge. Several of the popes have issued bulls exonerating them, and temporal princes have often taken a similar step. Many Christian scholars and ecclesiastics have felt it their duty to utter protests against the libel, including the most eminent Gentile students of Rabbinism of modern times. Indeed, the vast majority of the literature refuting the charge comes from non-Jewish pens. That on the other side is entirely anti-Semitic, and in no case has it survived the ordeal of criticism.

See G. A. Zaviziano, *Un Raggio di Luce* (Corfu, 1891); H. L. Strack, *Das Blut im Glauben und Aberglauben* (8th ed., Munich, 1900), Eng. trans., *The Jew and Human Sacrifice* (1909); D. Chwolson, *Blutanklage* (1901); F. Frank, *Der Ritualmord vor den Gerichtshöfen der Wahrheit und der Gerechtigkeit* (1901, 1902). A list of some of the most important cases is given by J. Jacobs in the *Jewish Encyclopaedia*, iii. 266–267.

RIVAROL, ANTOINE DE (1753–1801), French writer and epigrammatist, was born at Bagnols in Languedoc on June 26, 1753, and died at Berlin on April 11, 1801. It seems that his father was an innkeeper of cultivated tastes. The son assumed the title of comte de Rivarol, and asserted his connection with a noble Italian family. After various vicissitudes he appeared in Paris in 1777. In his *Petit Almanach de nos grands hommes pour 1788,* in which he had the assistance of Richebourg de Champcenetz, he ridiculed contemporary authors. Rivarol wrote in the Royalist press, in the *Journal politique* of Sabatier de Castres (1742–1817) and the *Actes des Apôtres* of Peltier (1770–1825). He emigrated in 1792, and established himself at Brussels, whence he removed successively to London, Hamburg and Berlin. Rivarol has had no rival in France in brilliant epigrams except Piron. His works include *Isman, ou le fatalisme* (1795), a novel; *Le Véridique* (1827), comedy; *Essai sur les causes de la révolution française* (1827).

BIBLIOGRAPHY.—*Oeuvres* (2nd ed., 1880) ed. M. de Lescure; M. de Lescure, *Rivarol et la société française pendant la révolution et l'émigration* (1882); Le Breton, *Rivarol, sa vie, ses idées* (1895); G. W. Harris, *Antoine Rivarol, Journalist of the French Revolution* (Oxford, 1940); *Moralistes du xviiie Siècle-Vauvenargues* (Paris, 1940).

RIVAS, ANGEL DE SAAVEDRA, DUKE OF (1791–1865), Spanish poet and politician, born at Cordova, March 19, 1791. He fought in the War of Independence, was a prominent member of the advanced Liberal party (1820–23) and in the latter year was condemned to death. He escaped to London and lived successively in Italy, Malta and France, until the amnesty of 1834, when he returned to Spain, shortly afterward succeeding his brother as duke of Rivas. In 1835 he became minister of the interior under Istúriz, and along with his chief had again to leave the country. Returning in 1837, he joined the Moderate party, became prime minister, and was subsequently ambassador at Paris and Naples. He died June 22, 1865. In 1813 he published *Ensayos poéticos*, and between that date and his first exile several of his tragedies (the most notable being *Alatar*, 1814, and *Lanuza*, 1822) were put upon the stage. Traces of foreign influence are observable in *El Moro Expósito* (1834), a narrative poem dedicated to John Hookham Frere; these are still more marked in *Don Alvaro ó La Fuerza del sino* (first played March 22, 1835), a drama of historical importance inasmuch as it established the new French romanticism in Spain.

BIBLIOGRAPHY.—*Obras completas del Duque de Rivas* (Madrid, 1894–1904, 7 vols.); M. Cañete, *Escritores españoles é hispano-americanos* (Madrid, 1884); E. Allison Peers, *Angel de Saavedra, Duque de Rivas . . .* in *Revue Hispanique*, lviii (1923), p. 1–600; G. Boussagol, *Angel de Saavedra, duc de Rivas* (Paris, 1926); N. Gonzalez Ruiz, *El duque de Rivas* (Madrid, 1944).

RIVER AND RIVER ENGINEERING. A river is any natural stream of fresh water, larger than a brook or creek, which flows in a well-defined channel. Usually it discharges into another and larger body of water, the ocean, a lake, or another river. In rare instances in regions of porous soil it soaks into the ground, or, in excessively arid regions, evaporates, in which case it becomes a "lost river." In other regions of favourable rock conditions it may also run underground for certain distances, disappearing and reappearing one or more times. A river with a well-cut channel and a graded bed, usually reaching base level at its mouth, is an adolescent river. Rivers as they grow older usually widen their valleys accordingly unless prevented by certain geological formations or occurrences. A river whose upper waters sometime in the past suddenly found a new outlet, diminishing the volume and force of the original river and also its length, is known as a beheaded river. For other facts relating to the origin and subsequent development of rivers and their valleys *see* GEOLOGY. The river works which the engineer may be called upon to execute vary widely in their character and object. The more important of these which are described in the present article may be grouped under the following heads:—(1) The prevention of river inundations and the mitigation of their effects; (2) the improvement for navigation of the non-tidal portions of rivers; and (3) works for the improvement of navigation in the tidal compartments of rivers, in their estuaries, and at the outlets of rivers flowing into tideless seas. Other river engineering works are dealt with under separate headings, for instance, the utilization of river waters for power production (*see* ELECTRIC POWER GENERATION: *Layout of Hydroelectric Stations;* etc.); works for water storage and supply for various purposes including irrigation (*q.v.*); works connected with fisheries (*q.v.*); and reclamation of land (*see* COAST PROTECTION AND LAND RECLAMATION). *See* also the articles on HYDRAULICS, CANALS AND CANALIZED RIVERS, WEIR, and particular rivers, *e.g.*, MISSISSIPPI and DANUBE.

PHYSICAL CHARACTERISTICS OF RIVERS

River Basins.—In general the size of rivers above any tidal limit and their average fresh-water discharge are proportionate to the extent of their basins, and the amount of rain over those basins.

They vary in extent according to the configuration of the country, ranging from the insignificant drainage areas of streams rising on high ground near the coast and flowing straight down to the sea, to immense parts of continents, where rivers rising on the slopes of mountain ranges far inland have to traverse vast stretches of valleys and plains before reaching the ocean.

The comparative size of the principal river systems of the world is shown in the following table:

River	Drainage basin in square miles	Length in miles
Nile	1,100,000	4,160
Missouri-Mississippi	1,243,700	3,891
Amazon	2,722,000	3,900
Ob	1,150,000	3,200
Yangtze	689,000	3,100
Congo	1,425,000	2,900
Amur-Kerulen	787,000	2,900
Lena	1,000,000	2,800
Yenisei	792,300	2,800
Hwang-ho	205,000	2,700
Niger	580,000	2,600
Mackenzie	682,000	2,514
Río de la Plata	1,198,000	2,330
Murray	250,000	2,310
Volga	563,300	2,300
St. Lawrence	565,200	1,900
Danube	320,300	1,725
Indus	372,000	1,700
Orinoco	350,000	1,700
Brahmaputra	361,000	1,680
Zambezi	513,500	1,600

Available Rainfall.—The rainfall varies considerably in different localities, both in its total yearly amount and in its distribution throughout the year; also its volume fluctuates from year to year.

Even in small river basins the variations may be considerable according to differences in elevation or distance from the sea, ranging, for instance, in the Severn basin in England and Wales, with an area of only 4,350 sq.mi., from an average of less than 30 in. in the year to more than 80 in. The proportion, moreover, of the rain falling on a river basin which actually reaches the river, or the available rainfall in respect to its flow, depends very largely on the nature of the surface strata, the slope of the ground and the extent to which it is covered with vegetation, and varies greatly with the season of the year. The available rainfall has, indeed, been found to vary from 75% of the actual rainfall on impermeable, bare, sloping, rocky strata, down to about 15% on flat, permeable soils.

Fall of Rivers.—The rate of flow of rivers depends mainly upon their fall, though where two rivers of different sizes have the same fall, the larger river has the quicker flow, as its retardation by friction against its bed and banks is less in proportion to its volume than that of the smaller river. The fall of a river corresponds approximately to the slope of the country it traverses. As rivers rise close to the highest part of their basins, generally in hilly regions, their fall is rapid near their source and gradually diminishes, with occasional irregularities, until, in traversing plains along the latter part of their course, their fall usually becomes quite gentle. Accordingly, in large basins, rivers in most cases begin as torrents with a very variable flow, and end as gently flowing rivers with a comparatively regular discharge.

Variations in the Discharge of Rivers.—In tropical countries, subject to periodical rains, the rivers are in flood during the rainy season and have hardly any flow during the rest of the year; while in temperate regions, where the rainfall is more evenly distributed throughout the year, evaporation causes the available rainfall to be much less in hot summer weather than in the winter months, so that the rivers fall to their low stage in the summer and are liable to be in flood in the winter. In fact, with a temperate climate, the year may be divided into a warm and a cold season, extending, in the northern hemisphere, from May to October and from November to April respectively. The rivers are low and moderate floods are of rare occurrence during the first period, and they are high and subject to occasional heavy floods after a considerable rainfall during the second period. The only exceptions are rivers which have their sources amongst mountains clad with snow, and are fed by glaciers; their floods occur in the spring and summer from the melting of the snows and ice, as exemplified by the Rhone above the Lake of Geneva, and the Arve which joins it below. But even these rivers are liable to have their flow modified by the influx of tributaries subject to different conditions, so that the Rhone below Lyons has a more uniform discharge than most rivers, as the summer floods of the Arve are counteracted to a great extent by the low stage of the Saone flowing into the Rhone at Lyons, which has its floods in the winter when the Arve on the contrary is low.

Transportation of Materials by Rivers.—In flood-time rivers bring down a large quantity of detritus, derived mainly from the disintegration of the surface-layers of the hills and slopes in the upper parts of the valleys by glaciers, frost and rain. The power of a current to transport materials varies approximately as the square of its velocity, so that torrents with a rapid fall near the sources of rivers can carry down rocks, boulders and large stones. These are by degrees ground by attrition in their onward course into shingle, gravel, sand and silt which are carried forward by the main river towards the sea, or partially strewn over flat alluvial plains during floods. The size of the materials forming the bed of the river or borne along by the stream becomes less as the reduction of velocity diminishes the transporting power of the current. In the Po, for instance, pebbles and gravel are found for about 140 m. below Turin, sand along the next 100 m., and silt and mud in the last 110 m. When, however, the fall is largely and abruptly reduced, as in the case of rivers emerging straight from mountainous slopes upon flat plains, deposit necessarily occurs owing to the sudden reduction of velocity. If the impeded river is unable to spread its detritus over the plains, its bed becomes raised by deposit, causing the river in flood-time to rise to a higher level. The materials, moreover, which are carried in suspension or rolled along the bed of the river tend to deposit when the flow of the river slackens and is finally brought to rest on encountering the great inert mass of the sea. This is the cause of the formation of the bars and, especially in the absence of a tide and any littoral current, of the deltas with their shallow outlets which occur at the mouths of many rivers.

Influence of Lakes on Rivers.—A depression along part of a valley, with a rocky barrier at its lower end, causes the formation of a lake in the course of the river flowing down the valley. The intervention of a lake makes the river, on entering at the upper end, deposit all the materials with which it is charged in the still waters of the lake. The river issues at the lower end as a perfectly clear stream with a regular discharge, because the floods, in flowing into the lake, are spread over a large surface, and so produce only a very slight raising of the level. This effect is illustrated by the river Rhone, which enters the lake of Geneva as a turbid, torrential, glacier stream, and emerges at Geneva as a sparkling, limpid river with uniform flow, though in this particular case the improvement is not long maintained, owing to the confluence a short distance below Geneva of the large, rapid, glacial river, the Arve.

The influence of lakes on rivers is, indeed, wholly beneficial, in consequence of the removal of their burden of detritus and the regulation of their flow. Thus the Swine outlet channel of the Oder into the Baltic is freed from sediment by the river having to pass through the Stettiner Haff before reaching its mouth. The St. Lawrence, again, deriving most of its supply from the chain of the Great Lakes possesses a very uniform flow.

River Channels.—The discharge of the rainfall erodes the beds of rivers along the lowest parts of the valleys; but floods occur too intermittently to form and maintain a channel large enough to contain the augmented flow. A river channel, indeed, generally suffices to carry off the average flow of the river, which, whilst comprising considerable fluctuations in volume, furnishes a sufficiently constant erosive action to maintain a fairly regular channel. But rivers having soft beds and carrying down sediment erode their beds during floods and deposit alluvium in dry weather. As the velocity of a stream increases with its fall, the size of a channel conveying a definite average flow varies inversely

with the fall, and the depth inversely with the width. A river channel, accordingly, often presents considerable irregularities in section, forming shallow rapids when the river flows over a rocky barrier with a considerable fall, and a succession of pools and shoals when the bed varies in compactness and there are differences in width, or when the river flows round a succession of bends along opposite banks alternately.

A river flowing through a flat alluvial plain has its current readily deflected by any chance obstruction or by any difference in hardness of the banks, and generally follows a winding course, which tends to be intensified by the erosion of the concave banks in the bends from the current impinging against them in altering its direction round the curves. (For Prof. James Thomson's theory of the concave banks of rivers *see* his *Collected Papers* [1912], also the article HYDRAULICS and Hunter's *Rivers and Estuaries*.) Large rivers bringing down a considerable amount of detritus shift their courses from time to time, owing to the obstructions produced by banks of deposit.

Floods of Rivers.—The rise of rivers in flood-time depends not merely on the amount of the rainfall, but also on its distribution and the nature of the strata on which it falls. The upper hilly part of a river basin often consists of impermeable strata, sometimes almost bare of vegetation. Consequently the rain flowing quickly down the impervious, sloping ground into the watercourses and tributaries feeding the main river produces rapidly rising and high floods in these streams, which soon pass down on the cessation of the rain. The river Marne, draining an impermeable part of the upper Seine basin, is subject to these sudden torrential floods in the cold season. On the contrary, rain falling on permeable strata takes longer in reaching the rivers, and the floods rise more gradually, are less high, continue longer and subside more slowly. A river fed by several tributaries, some from impermeable and others from permeable strata, experiences floods of a mixed character. An example is the Seine at Paris, below the confluence of the torrential Marne and Yonne, where the floods of the gently flowing Upper Seine and other tributaries with permeable basins also contribute to the rise of the river.

High floods are caused by a heavy rainfall on land already sodden by recent rains at a period of the year when evaporation is inactive, and especially by rain falling on melting snow. A fairly simultaneous rainfall over the greater part of a moderate-sized river basin is a tolerably common occurrence; and under such conditions, the floods coming from the torrential tributaries reach their maximum height and begin to subside before the floods from the gently flowing tributaries attain their greatest rise.

THE REGULATION OF NON-TIDAL RIVERS

Mitigation of Floods and Protection from Inundations.—As the size of the channel of a river is generally inadequate to carry down the discharge of floods, the river overflows its banks in flood-time and inundates adjacent low-lying lands. An enlargement of the river bed, principally by deepening it, in order to increase its discharging capacity, is precluded by the cost, and also, in rivers bringing down sediment, by the large deposit that would take place in the enlarged channel from the reduction in the velocity of the current when the flood begins to subside. Where, however, the depth of a tidal river has been considerably increased by dredging, the enlargement of its channel and the lowering of its low-water line facilitate the passage of the land water and consequently reduce the danger of flooding. The Glasgow quays, for instance, along the deepened Clyde are no longer subject to inundation, and the lands and quays bordering the Tyne have been relieved from flooding for 10 m. above Newcastle by the deepening of the river from Newburn to the sea. (*See* fig. 6.)

In certain cases it is important to restrict or to prevent the inundation of some riparian districts by embankments; and occasionally low-lying lands are so unfavourably situated that pumping has to be employed.

The flow of water off the slopes of a valley can be retarded by planting trees on mountain slopes, which have too often been denuded by the reckless clearing of forests.

Proposals have sometimes been made to reduce the height of floods in rivers and restrict the resulting inundations by impounding some of the flood discharge by the construction of one or more dams across the upper valley of a river, and letting it out when the flood has passed down. This arrangement, however, is open to the objection that in the event of a second flood following rapidly on the first, there might not be time to empty the reservoir for its reception. When this provision against floods can be combined with the storage of water for economic use it becomes financially practicable. A number of dams were constructed with flood control as their primary or secondary function. This was particularly true in the United States where during the 25-year period ending in 1952, 300 projects had been constructed in the interest of flood control, 77 of which were dams, while the remainder were local protection projects. The flood control project in the lower Mississippi river valley included five reservoirs, four of which had been completed.

Methods of Increasing the Discharging Efficiency of River Channels.—The discharging efficiency of a river within the limits of its bed depends on the fall and the cross section of the channel. The only way of increasing the fall is to reduce the length of the channel by substituting shorter cuts for a winding course. This involves some loss of capacity in the channel as a whole; and in the case of a large river with a considerable flow it is very difficult to maintain a straight cut, owing to the tendency of the current to erode the banks and form again a sinuous channel. Cuts therefore should be in the form of one or more flat curves. Nevertheless, where the available fall is exceptionally small, as in lands originally reclaimed from the sea, such as the English fen districts, and where, in consequence, the drainage is in a great measure artificial, straight channels have been formed for the rivers and "drains."

The removal of obstructions, whether natural or artificial, from the bed of a river furnishes a simple and efficient means of increasing the discharging capacity of its channel, and, consequently, of lowering the height of floods. Every impediment to the flow, in proportion to its extent, raises the level of the river above it so as to produce the additional fall necessary to convey the flow through the restricted channel, thereby reducing the total available fall. In the absence of legal enactments for the conservancy of rivers, numerous obstructions have in many cases been placed in their channels, such as mining refuse, sluice gates for mills, fish traps, unduly wide piers for bridges and solid weirs, which impede the flow and raise the flood level.

Prediction of Floods.—The rise of floods in the tributaries of a river, and the periods they take in passing down to stations on the main river, are ascertained by means of gauges at suitable points. With the help of these records, and full information of the rainfall over the basin area, the time of arrival and height of the top of the flood at any station can be predicted with remarkable accuracy. By telegraphing warnings to places on the river, weir keepers are enabled to open fully beforehand the movable weirs for the passage of the flood, and the riparian inhabitants receive timely warning. On some rivers, as for example the Mississippi, the Danube and the Po, the flood-prediction services serve also for the dissemination of information as to conditions of navigation, as for instance on the river Danube.

Embankments.—Where it is important to protect land from inundations, the overflow of the river must be confined within continuous embankments. By placing these embankments somewhat back from the margin of the river bed, a wide flood channel is provided for the discharge of the river directly it overflows its banks. Low embankments may be sufficient where only exceptional summer floods have to be excluded from meadows. Occasionally the embankments are raised high enough to retain the floods during most years, while provision is made for the escape of the rare exceptionally high floods at special places in the embankments, where the scour of the issuing current is guarded against, and the inundation of the neighbouring land is least injurious. Both the above methods afford the advantage of relieving the embanked channel of some of the sediment deposited in it by the confined floodwaters, when the surplus flow passes over the embankments.

When complete protection from inundations is required, the embankments have to be raised well above the highest flood level, after allowing for the additional rise resulting from the confinement of the flood within the embankments. The system has been adopted where tracts of fertile alluvial land below flood level stretch for long distances away from the river. Thus the fens of Lincolnshire, Cambridgeshire and Norfolk in England are protected from inundations by embankments along their rivers and drains; a great portion of the Netherlands is similarly protected; and the plains of Lombardy are shut off from the floods of the Po by embankments along each side of the river for a distance of about 265 mi.

When towns like New Orleans on the Mississippi, and Szegedin on the Theiss in Hungary, have been established below the flood level of an adjoining river, the channel of the river should be improved to facilitate the passage of floods past the town. The town also should be enclosed within embankments raised above the highest possible flood level to obviate the contingency of an exceptional flood, or a gradually raised flood level leading to a catastrophe such as overwhelmed the greater part of Szegedin in March 1879 and threatened New Orleans in 1927.

The Mississippi.—A system of levee embankments has been extensively developed along the Mississippi river in its alluvial valley extending from Cape Girardeau, Mo., to the Head of Passes in the delta, a distance of 1,014 mi. by river channel. The alluvial valley has a length in latitude of 600 mi. and ranges from 20 mi. to 80 mi. in width with a total area of 30,000 sq.mi. It comprises the St. Francis, the Yazoo, the Tensas, the Lafourche, the Atchafalaya and portions of the White and Arkansas basins, as well as the alluvial lands around Lake Pontchartrain (fig. 1).

These levees, begun by the French settlers in Louisiana in the early 18th century, were in 1735 about 3 ft. high and had been constructed from 30 mi. above New Orleans to 12 mi. below. From this beginning the system has been extended, until by 1951 the system included 2,780 mi. of levees having an average height of 24 ft. and a content of about 1,310,000,000 cu.yd. of earth. The levees above Baton Rouge, La., are roughly parallel to the river but have a width between them of from ¾ mi. to 15 mi. thereby greatly increasing the cross-section area of the river in times of flood. Below Baton Rouge the levees follow the bends in the river but are set back from the river bank sufficiently to prevent undercutting by the current during floods. In some parts the spacing is much greater. The low-water discharge, measured at New Orleans, 123 mi. from the mouth of the Southwest pass, has been as low as 49,200 cu.ft. per second. At Vicksburg, Miss., a discharge of 1,806,000 sec.-ft. was recorded in 1927 (estimated 2,278,000 sec.-ft. if flood had been confined to leveed river) which compares with the minimum of record of 93,800 sec.-ft. at that place. The levees had not been adequate during certain floods to withstand the water pressure which had (before the record flood of 1927) a maximum rise at Vicksburg of 61⅓ ft. above the lowest stage of record at that point. In 1927 the river at Vicksburg rose 2⅔ ft. higher and 65.2 ft. above the low stage of 1940. The floods tend to increase in height due to the confinement of the river between levees. Breaches, or crevasses as they are termed in the United States, have occurred during extraordinary flood, but no crevasses have occurred since 1928 in the lower Mississippi river valley. They produce a sudden rush of the flood waters through the opening, which is damaging to the land in the immediate vicinity of the breach but the general inundation is gradual and benefits the lands with a fertilizing deposit. The velocity of the outflowing water is rapid only immediately in front of a crevasse and the water creeps over the delta lands generally, aided by the sloping down of the land on the alluvial plains for some distance away from the river.

The great floods of the Mississippi and its tributary rivers in April–June 1927, were the most serious which had occurred since records of these rivers have been kept. They were due to the extraordinary coincidence of flood conditions in all the chief tributaries of the river. Normally the eastern floods usually culmi-

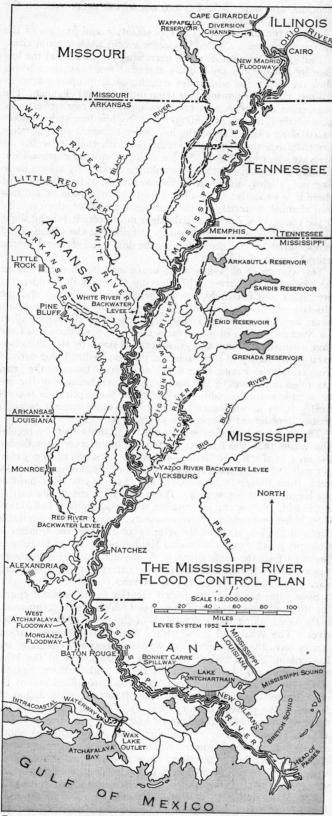

FIG. 1.—MAP OF MISSISSIPPI RIVER SHOWING AREAS SUBJECT TO OVER-FLOW AND REQUIRING PROTECTIVE ENGINEERING

homes. Apprehension was averted at the city of New Orleans by cutting a gap in the levees at Poydras, a few miles below the city, thus permitting a part of the floodwaters to take a short course of about 5 mi. to an arm of the sea instead of following the normal course of the river through the delta.

In Jan.–Feb. 1937 while the greatest flood of record was developing in the Ohio river, the conditions in the Mississippi river were favourable for receiving and disposing of this unprecedented discharge. The lower Mississippi was called on to carry a flood of more than 2,000,000 sec.-ft. The improved levee system successfully held the water within bounds, except in backwater areas of the tributaries. The Bonnet Carre spillway, 23 mi. above New Orleans, was put into operation late in January when it became apparent that the oncoming floodwaters would raise the stage at New Orleans above 20 ft. The floodway diverted a maximum of about 200,000 sec.-ft. into Lake Pontchartrain and held the crest at New Orleans to 19.3 ft. Without the relief afforded by the spillway, it is estimated that the stage at New Orleans would have been about 3 ft. higher. The Bonnet Carre floodway was also operated successfully in 1945 and in 1950. The 1950 flood, which produced the third highest stage of record at Cairo, Ill., was safely carried to the Gulf of Mexico within the levee system and control works.

In the early 1930s a system of channel cutoffs was inaugurated on the lower Mississippi river. By 1941, they had demonstrated their worth by lowering river stages more than 12 ft. at Arkansas City, Ark., and 6 ft. at Vicksburg. Sixteen such cutoffs reduced the river distance from Memphis, Tenn., to Baton Rouge by 170 mi.

Effect of Embankments upon the River Levels and Bed.—The confinement of a river to a flood channel of restricted width necessarily produces an increase in the elevation of the high-water surface. It has also been frequently asserted that this confinement by the construction of embankments is accompanied by a progressive and consequential rising of the river bed, but there does not appear to be sufficient evidence to bear out this conten-

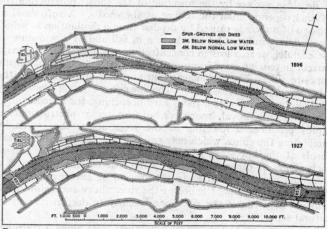

FIG. 2.—RIVER WAAL AT TIEL, HOLLAND, SHOWING THE CONDITION OF THE TIEL REACH IN 1896 AND 1927
The regulation works completed in this reach in 1911 have effected a permanent deepening of the channel and no dredging has been necessary since

tion. That river beds in those reaches where the steeper slope of hill valleys changes to the lesser slope in the plain become raised by deposit has already been mentioned. The river Po and the Hwang-Ho or Yellow river in China are frequently adduced as affording evidence of the raising of river beds in consequence of embanking; but where elevation, not attributable to the natural deposit, has taken place it seems to have been due to changes in the locus of the bed or to be local in character and accompanied by a corresponding deepening elsewhere. This question is discussed at length by John Lane Van Ornum, Curtis McDonald Townsend and John Ripley Freeman (*Trans. Am. Soc. of C.E.* 1928) and other authorities who are unable to accept the theory of consequential raising of the river bed.

Local Protection Projects.—The above discussions are pertinent to the protection of extended continuous areas along a river.

nate between January and April, while the crests of the Missouri river floods usually enter the Mississippi in June. In 1927 the levees were breached in many places and the floodwaters overflowed throughout the alluvial valley. An area of more than 23,000 sq.mi. was inundated and 700,000 people were driven from their

Levees and flood walls are also utilized for localized protection of municipal areas. After 1930 the United States especially developed many local protection projects of the latter type, designed to provide a higher degree of protection for highly developed industrial and residential areas than had been customary for the continuous embankment type of protection. A good example of a local protection project is that for the protection of Kansas City, Kan., and Kansas City, Mo., located at the junction of the Missouri and the Kansas rivers which provides for construction of a combination levee and flood wall; construction of pumping plants; construction of a river cutoff and a highway bridge across the cutoff; and alteration of 14 bridges across the Kansas river and 2 across the Missouri river.

REGULATION OF THE NONTIDAL PORTIONS OF RIVERS FOR NAVIGATION

As a river flows onward toward the sea, the current becomes more gentle and the discharge larger in volume and less subject to abrupt variations. Large rivers, therefore, often furnish important natural highways for inland navigation in the lower portions of their courses, as, for instance, the Rhine, the Danube and the Mississippi. Works are, however, often required in such rivers for preventing changes in the course of the stream, for regulating its depth, and especially for fixing the low-water channel and concentrating the flow in it, in order to increase as far as practicable the navigable depth at the lowest stage of the water level. Regulation works for increasing the navigable capabilities of rivers can be advantageously undertaken only in large rivers with a moderate fall and a fair discharge at their lowest stage; for with a large fall the current presents a great impediment to upstream navigation, and there are generally great variations in water level. Consequently, when the discharge becomes very small in the dry season it is impossible to maintain a sufficient depth of water in the low-water channel.

Removal of Shoals.—The possibility of securing uniformity of depth in a river by the lowering of the shoals obstructing the channel depends upon the nature of the shoals. A soft shoal in the bed of a river is caused by deposit from a diminution in velocity of flow, produced by a reduction in fall and by a widening of the channel, or to a loss in concentration of the scour of the main current in passing over from one concave bank to the next on the opposite side. These changes from one side of the river to the other are called "crossings." The lowering of such a shoal by dredging merely effects a temporary deepening, for it soon forms again. The removal, moreover, of the rocky obstructions at rapids produces a lowering of the river above the rapids by facilitating the efflux, which may result in the appearance of fresh shoals at the low stage of the river. Where, however, narrow rocky reefs or other hard shoals stretch across the bottom of a river and present obstacles to the erosion by the current of the soft materials forming the bed of the river above and below, their removal may enable the river permanently to deepen its bed by natural scour.

The deepening of the bed of a nontidal river along a considerable length by dredging merely lowers the water level of the river during the low stage; and though this deepening facilitates the passage of floods in the first instance, it does not constitute a permanent improvement even in this respect, for the deposit of the detritus brought down by the river as the floods abate soon restores the river to its original condition. Nevertheless, where sandbanks obstruct and divert the channel of a river at its low stage, as in parts of the Mississippi below Cairo, it has been found possible before the river has fallen to its lowest level to form a channel through these sandbanks with a depth of 9 ft. and 300 ft. wide. The project provided for an ultimate depth of 12 ft. to be secured by a program of bank stabilization (*see* DREDGERS AND DREDGING). Sand is discharged through floating pipe lines into a part of the river away from the channel; and the navigation can thus be maintained through the low stage at a reasonable cost. Though, however, these channels across the shoals, connecting the deeper parts of the river, can be easily kept open on the Mississippi till the return of the floods, they are obliterated by the currents in

floodtime, and have to be dredged out afresh every year on the abatement of the floods.

Low-water Channel.—The concentration and fixation of the low-water channel is effected by closing subsidiary low-water channels with dikes across them, and narrowing the channel at the low stage by low-dipping cross dikes extended from the river banks down the slope, and sometimes pointing slightly upstream so as to direct the water flowing over them into a central channel. The contraction of the channel can occasionally be more effectually accomplished, though at a greater cost, by low longitudinal dikes placed along either side of the low-water channel, some distance forward from the banks but connected with them generally at intervals by cross dikes at the back to prevent the current from scouring out a channel behind them during floods. By raising these dikes only slightly above the surface of the bed of the river, except where it is expedient to produce accretion for closing an old disused channel or rectifying the course of the river, the capacity of the channel for discharging floods is not affected; for the slight obstruction to the flow produced by the dikes at the sides is fully compensated by the deepening of the low-water channel in the central course of the river.

This system of obtaining a moderate increase in depth during the low stage of a river, while leaving the river quite open for navigation, has been adopted on the Rhône, the Rhine and the Mississippi. In the case of the Rhône below Lyons regulation works were preferred to canalization, in spite of the rapid fall of the river amounting in some places to 1 in 250, on account of the large quantities of sand and gravel carried down by it. The comparative regularity of the discharge, due to the flow being derived from tributaries having their floods at different times of the year, has aided the effects of the works. However, because of the unfavourable natural condition of the river, the depth does not exceed 5 ft. at lowest water level; and the rapid current forms a serious impediment to upstream navigation.

The Rhine is much better adapted for improvement by regulation works than the Rhône, for it has a basin more than double the area of the Rhône basin, and its fall does not exceed 3.1 ft. per mile at Strasbourg, Fr., and 2.5 ft. per mile through the rocky defile from Bingen to Kaub, Ger., and is much less along most of the length below Strasbourg. These works systematically carried out in wide shallow reaches between the Dutch frontier and Mainz, Ger., aided by dredging where necessary, have secured a navigable depth at the low stage of the river of 10 ft. from the frontier to Cologne, $8\frac{1}{2}$ ft. from Cologne to Kaub, and $6\frac{1}{2}$ ft. up to Bingen, beyond which the same depth is maintained up to Philippsburg, $22\frac{1}{2}$ mi. above Mannheim, and is being extended up to Strasbourg. (*See* also CANALS AND CANALIZED RIVERS.)

Soon after reaching the Dutch frontier in its seaward course the Rhine divides into three branches of which the most important is the Waal taking about two-thirds of the water of the undivided river. The Waal and its westward continuations under various names form the main navigable waterway between Germany and Rotterdam, Neth., and the sea. The improvement of the Waal was commenced about the middle of the 19th century, but the works carried out in it between 1909 and 1916 afford one of the most interesting and successful examples of river regulation effected in the present century (fig. 2). The channel at its low stage was deepened, throughout its length of 53 mi. from $7\frac{1}{2}$ ft. to $11\frac{1}{2}$ ft. almost entirely by training works, regulation of width, and its reformation in curved reaches, so that nowhere is there a straight section left in the river. Low spur groynes or cross dikes were largely employed and very little dredging work was necessary. After 1916 no dredging was required to maintain the depths.

The Mississippi also, with its extensive basin and its moderate fall in most parts, is well suited for having its navigable depth increased by regulation works. Locks and dams were built from St. Paul, Minn., to the mouth of the Missouri river just above St. Louis, Mo., furnishing a navigable depth of 9 ft. except when the river is closed by ice conditions. Project depths in the early 1950s were as follows: St. Louis to Cairo, 9 ft. or better; Cairo to Baton Rouge, 12 ft.; Baton Rouge to New Orleans, 35 ft.; and New Orleans to the Gulf through Southwest pass, 40 ft.

On the Rhône below Lyons with its rapid current, the dikes are constructed of rubble, consolidated above low water with concrete. The dikes on the Rhine consist for the most part of earthwork mounds protected by a layer of rubble or pitching on the face, with a rubble mound forming the toe exposed to the current; but occasionally fascines are employed in conjunction with the stone or simple rubble mounds. On the Waal the newer cross dikes have a core of sand protected by a mattress weighted with stone. The dams closing subsidiary channels on the Mississippi are almost always constructed of fascine mattresses weighted with stone; but whereas the regulating dikes on the upper river are usually similar in construction, a common form for dikes in the United States consists of two parallel rows of piles filled in between with brushwood or other materials not affected by water, and protected at the sides from scour by an apron of fascines and stone.

Protecting and Easing Bends.—Unless the concave banks of a river winding through wide, alluvial plains are protected from the scour of the current, the increasing curvature presents serious impediments to navigation, sometimes eventually becoming so intensified that the river at last makes a short cut for itself across the narrow strip of land at the base of the loop it has formed. This, however, produces considerable changes in the channel below, and disturbances in the navigable depth. Protection, accordingly, of concave banks is necessary to prevent excessive curvature of the channel and changes in the course of a river. On the Mississippi the very easily eroded banks are protected along their upper, steeper part by stone pitching or a layer of concrete, and below low-water level by flexible articulated concrete revetment or by fascine willow mattresses weighted with stone, extended a short distance out on the bed to prevent erosion at the toe. Dikes, also, projecting into the channel from the banks reduce the curvature of the navigable channel by pushing the main current into a more central course; while curved longitudinal dikes placed in the channel in front of concave banks are also effective in keeping the current away from the banks, which is sometimes still further promoted by dipping cross dikes in front.

Regulation of Depth.—Regulation works at bends, besides arresting erosion, also reduce the differences in depth at the bends and the crossings. The excessive depth round the concave banks is diminished and the channel along the crossings deepened by giving a straighter course to the current and concentrating it by a reduction in width of the channel between the bends. Where there are deep pools at intervals in a river, shoals are always found above them, because of the increased fall which occurs in the water line on approaching the pool, to compensate for its very slight inclination where it crosses the pool, whose ample cross section serves for the discharge of the river through this part of the river bed. These variable depths can be regulated to some extent by submerged rubble dikes or fascine-mattress sills deposited across the bed of the pool, so as to reduce its excessive depth, but not raised high enough to interfere at all with the navigable depth. These obstructions in the pool raise the water line toward its upper end, in order to provide the additional fall needed to effect the discharge through the pool with its diminished cross section.

Protection of Vessels During Floods.—On large rivers, where vessels during high floods are exposed to injury from floating debris and ice floes, shelter can be provided for them in refuge ports, formed in a recess at the side under the protection of a solid jetty or embankment constructed in the river parallel to the bank. These ports are closed against floods at their upper end and have their entrance at the lower end facing downstream. There are numerous examples of such river harbours on the Danube, the Rhine and other European rivers and in the rivers of North America. Many of them, made in the vicinity of towns, as at Düsseldorf, Ger., are inland ports of considerable size.

Many rivers have been improved, for the purpose of navigation, by canalization; and in some cases lateral canals have been constructed alongside portions of rivers to avoid rapids, falls or other serious obstructions. (*See* CANALS AND CANALIZED RIVERS.)

SMALL RIVER OUTLETS EXPOSED TO LITTORAL DRIFT

Rivers with a small discharge flowing into the sea on an exposed coast are more or less obstructed at their outlet by drift of shingle or sand along the coast. When the flow falls very low in dry weather, the outlet of a river is sometimes completely closed by a continuous line of beach, any inland or tidal waters merely trickling through the obstruction; and it is only on the descent of floods that the outlet is opened out. In rivers which always have a fair fresh-water discharge, or a small fresh-water flow combined with a tidal flow and ebb, the channel sometimes has its direct outlet closed, and is deflected parallel to the shore till it reaches a weak place in the line of beach, through which a new outlet is formed; or, where the current keeps the outlet open, a bar is formed across the entrance by the littoral drift, reducing the navigable depth. (*See* HARBOURS; JETTY. The bar formed across the outlet

Jetties at River Outlets.—The bar formed across the outlet of a river not heavily charged with sediment and flowing into a tideless sea can be lowered by carrying out solid jetties on each side of the outlet across the foreshore, so as to scour the bar by concentrating the issuing current over it. Thus by means of jetties slightly curved in plan, aided by dredging, the depth at the entrance to the Swine mouth of the Oder has been increased from 7 ft. to 27 ft.; the approach channels to the river Pernau and other rivers flowing into the Baltic have been deepened by jetties, and the outlet channels of some of the rivers flowing into the Great Lakes of North America have been improved by permanent jetties and dredging.

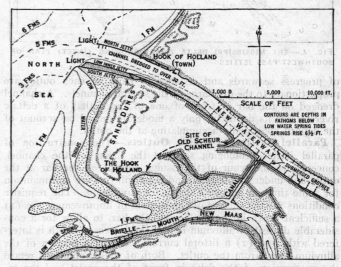

FIG. 3.—JETTY OUTLET OF THE RIVER MAAS INTO THE NORTH SEA. THE ARTIFICIAL CUT FOR THE RIVER MAAS THROUGH THE HOOK OF HOLLAND, BEGUN IN 1864

Where the littoral drift is powerful enough to divert the outlet of a river (as in the case of the Yare river, which at one time was driven to an outlet 4 mi. south of its direct course into the sea at Yarmouth, Eng., and the Adour river in France, whose outlet, because of the violent storms of the Bay of Biscay, was liable to be shifted 18 mi. from its proper position), it proved practicable to fix as well as to deepen the outlet by means of jetties. In such cases, however, where the rivers flow into tidal seas, it is important to place the jetties sufficiently apart to avoid any loss of tidal influx, since the tidal flow assists the fresh-water discharge in keeping the outlet open; whereas, with rivers flowing into tideless seas, a moderate restriction of the width between the jetties increases the scour. The tortuous and somewhat shifting outlet channel of the Scheur branch of the Maas (Meuse) river emerging on to a sandy coast where the rise of tide is small, and obstructed at its mouth by a bar, has been replaced by a straight cut across the Hook of Holland. The outlet across the foreshore is fixed in position by fascine-mattress jetties (*see* JETTY), the maintenance of the depth at the mouth by the tidal and fresh waters being aided by frequent dredging (fig. 3).

DELTAIC OUTLETS OF TIDELESS RIVERS

Large rivers heavily charged with sand and silt, when their current is gradually arrested on entering a tideless, or nearly tideless, sea, deposit these materials as a constantly advancing fan-shaped shoal through which comparatively shallow diverging channels, almost devoid of fall, have to force their way in order to convey the fresh-water discharge into the sea. These deltaic channels deposit their burden of sediment in front of their outlets, forming bars which advance with the delta and whose rate

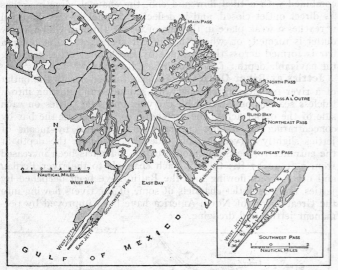

FIG. 4.—THE MISSISSIPPI DELTA (1946) SHOWING (INSET) PLAN OF SOUTHWEST PASS JETTIES

of progress seawards and distance in front of each outlet are proportionate to the discharge of the several channels. A channel dredged on the bar in front of one of the outlets of a deltaic river retains its depth for only a moderate period on account of the deposit continually accumulating at the outlet.

Parallel Jetties at Delta Outlets.—The construction of parallel jetties prolonging seaward the banks of the channel, concentrates the scour of the issuing current on the bar at the outlet and under favourable conditions will procure and maintain for some time an adequate depth for navigation. The requisite conditions for the success of this system of improvement are (1) a sufficient depth in the sea beyond the bar, to allow for a considerable deposit of alluvium before the increased depth is interfered with, and (2) a littoral current carrying a portion of the alluvium away from the outlet. Both of these conditions retard the progression of the delta in front of the outlet and the inevitable eventual formation of a new bar farther out. The rate of advance of a delta depends also on the proportion of solid matter carried in suspension by the river and on the specific gravity and size of the particles of alluvium discharged into the sea; for the heavier and coarser materials, and especially those which are rolled along the bed of the channels, come first to rest. Moreover, the larger channels of a delta bring down a larger volume of alluvium on account of their larger discharge, and their bars form farther seaward from their outlets due to the issuing current being less rapidly arrested in proportion to the volume discharged. Thus the rate of advance of the delta in front of an outlet is proportionate to the size of the channel, and the length of the jetties required is proportionate to the discharge of the channel. Consequently, the conditions are more unfavourable for the improvement of the outlets of the larger delta channels than of the smaller ones; though, on the other hand, the larger channels crossing the delta are generally more suitable for navigation on account of their size, and the natural depth over their bars is greater owing to the larger discharge.

The Rhône Outlets.—The discharge of the main branch of the Rhône, which formerly flowed into the Mediterranean at the Gulf of Foz through six mouths, was in 1852–57 concentrated in the direct eastern channel by embankments along its sides, which

closed all the lateral channels. The entire flow of the river, being thus discharged through the eastern outlet, increased for a time the depth over its bar from $4\frac{1}{2}$ ft. to $9\frac{1}{2}$ ft.; but as the great volume of alluvium brought down, including an unusually large proportion of sand rolled along the bed of the river, was also all discharged through the one outlet, the bar soon formed again farther out, and naturally advanced with the delta in front of the outlet more rapidly than formerly when the deposit was distributed through six divergent mouths. Accordingly, the very moderate deepening produced by the embankments was not long maintained, and the average depth over the bar has not exceeded 5 ft. for many years past. The St. Louis lateral canal, an artificial waterway between the Gulf of Foz and the river 4 mi. above its bar, was constructed in 1864–73 to afford a deeper navigable outlet, the entrance being $2\frac{1}{2}$ mi. north of the river outlet. The want of success of the Rhône outlet jetties was due to the selection for training of a channel opening on a sheltered, somewhat shallow bay, instead of a southern outlet discharging into deep water in the open Mediterranean and having a deep littoral current flowing across it. The closing of all the other outlets whereby the whole of the deposit, as well as all the discharge, was concentrated in front of the badly situated eastern outlet likewise contributed to the failure. The southern Roustan branch was reopened in 1893 to prevent the silting up of the outlet of the St. Louis canal.

The Delta of the Danube.—The Danube traverses its delta in three branches, the northern one of which, though conveying nearly two-thirds of the discharge of the river, is unsuitable for improvement due to its splitting up along portions of its course into several channels, and eventually flowing into the sea through twelve mouths of a small independent delta advancing about 250 ft. annually across a shallow foreshore. The central Sulina branch was selected for improvement in 1858 in preference to the southern St. George's branch, which had a more favourable outlet and a better channel through the delta. The distance of the Sulina bar from the shore was only half that of the St. George's bar due to the much smaller discharge of the Sulina branch. The jetties, begun provisionally in 1858 and subsequently consolidated and somewhat extended, were completed in 1877. They increased the depth over the bar from an average of about 9 ft. previously to 1858 up to $20\frac{1}{2}$ ft. in 1873, which was maintained for many years. In 1894, however, the increasing draught of vessels rendered a greater depth necessary; the wide inshore portion of the jetty channel was therefore narrowed by inner parallel jetties, and a powerful suction dredger was set to work in the jetty channel and outside, whereby the depth was increased to 24 ft. in 1897, and was fairly maintained up to 1907, when a second dredger became necessary to cope with the shoaling. The depth contours gradually advanced seaward while the deepest channel was deflected northward by the action of current and waves. During World War I the decrease in depth, accelerated by the interference with dredg-

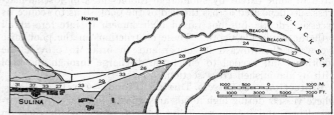

FIG. 5.—THE SULINA MOUTH OF THE DANUBE (1946)

ing which occurred, was so rapid that the navigable depth was reduced at one time to 18 ft. In 1922 the seaward extension of the jetties was commenced leaving temporary gaps, between the old heads and the new works, which were closed after the new channel had been opened for traffic (fig. 5). This extension of the jetties for about 6,000 ft. and dredging operations restored for the time being the ruling depth of 24 ft. in the direct channel. A further extension of 2,000 ft. was made. The new jetties, like the original ones, are formed of fascine mattresses covered with stone rubble.

The Mississippi Delta.—The selection of the outlet of the

South pass of the Mississippi delta for improvement by parallel jetties in 1876–79, in spite of the Southwest pass possessing a larger channel and a better depth over its bar, was due, as at the Danube, to motives of economy, as the bar of the Southwest pass was twice as far off from the shore as that of the South pass (fig. 4). Fascine-mattress jetties, 2¼ mi. and 1½ mi. long, weighted with limestone, and with large concrete blocks at their exposed ends, were constructed. The jetties, which were curved slightly southward at their outer ends to direct the sediment-bearing current more directly at right angles to the westerly littoral current, increased the depth of 8 ft. over the bar in 1875 up to 31 ft. between the jetties and out to deep water. The prolonged flow of the river produced by the jetties has, as at the Sulina outlet, carried the main portion of the heavier sediment into fairly deep water, so that the greatest advance of the foreshore in front of the South pass has occurred in the 70-ft. line of soundings, though the shallower soundings have also advanced. The shoaling, however, in the jetty channel necessitated its reduction in width by mattresses and spurs from 1,000 ft. to 600 ft., and eventually the jetties were rebuilt on lines reducing the channel width to about 650 ft. Dredging was also required to maintain the stipulated central depth of 30 ft., and 26-ft. depth for a width of 200 ft. out to deep water; while the outer channel was deflected to the east and narrowed by the alluvium carried westward by the littoral current and also deposited in front of the jetty outlet. Since 1901 suction dredging, the construction of additional sills and the increased discharge at the South pass (due to the works carried out in the Southwest pass) have widened the channel across the bar to about 600 ft., and given it a minimum depth of 30 ft.

In order to provide for the increasing requirements of seagoing vessels, the formation of a channel 35 ft. deep and 1,000 ft. wide through the larger Southwest pass and its 9-ft. bar to deep water in the gulf was begun at the end of 1903. The discharge through this pass is rather more than three times that through the South pass and the bar was double the distance seaward of the outlet. Converging jetties, about 5,600 ft. apart at their land ends, and about 3,000 ft. apart at the seaward outlet, were substituted for the parallel jetties constructed at the South pass, and suction dredging was relied upon to maintain the channel between the jetties. The channel dredging was soon found to be excessive in quantity and in 1916 the project was modified by limiting the channel to a width of 2,400 ft. between two parallel interior jetties, and the extension of the latter to the 30-ft. contour beyond the bar. In 1923 the width was still further restricted to 1,750 ft. by building spur dikes or groynes, and by 1924 a depth of 35 ft. was secured by dredging aided by the scour of the current. The jetties are formed of fascine mattresses weighted with stone and capped with rubble and concrete (see JETTY). They have been extended seaward from time to time and in 1927 the east jetty was about 4¾ mi. in length from the shore. The west jetty had a length of about 3¾ mi. The amount of dredging required to maintain the 35-ft. deep channel through the pass and over the bar has been much reduced since the contraction of the width has been effected. The artificial improvement and simultaneous maintenance of two mouths of a river is a unique experiment. The project was later modified so that the following channel dimensions were prescribed: Southwest pass from Head of Passes to the outer end of the jetties, 40 ft. deep by 800 ft. wide; Southwest pass bar, 40 ft. deep by 600 ft. wide; South pass from Head of Passes to the outer end of the jetties, 30 ft. deep by 450 ft. wide; and South pass bar, 30 ft. deep by 600 ft. wide.

The U.S. congress through the River and Harbor act of Jan. 21, 1927, assigned to the secretary of the army and to the chief of engineers, U.S. army, the duty of making surveys in accordance with house document 308, 79th congress, 1st session, with a view to the formulation of general plans for the most effective improvement of the U.S. navigable streams and their tributaries. The Flood Control act of May 15, 1928, amplified this duty with respect to the tributaries of the Mississippi river. The River and Harbor act of Aug. 30, 1935, authorized the chief of engineers to make supplemental studies as might be warranted. Under these

authorizations and subsequent acts of congress the corps of engineers investigated and reported on practically every river of any importance in the United States. Many of these surveys were published as congressional documents.

IMPROVEMENT OF TIDAL RIVERS FOR NAVIGATION

Whereas the size of tideless rivers depends wholly on their fresh-water discharge, the condition of tidal rivers is due to the configuration of their outlets, the rise of tide at their mouths, the distance the tide can penetrate inland and the space available for its reception. Accordingly, tidal rivers sometimes, even when possessing a comparatively small fresh-water discharge, have much better natural navigable channels at high tide than the largest deltaic rivers, as shown by a comparison of the Thames, the Humber and the Elbe with the Danube, the Nile and the Mis-

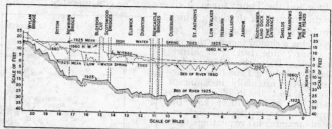

FIG. 6.—RIVER TYNE FROM THE SEA TO WYLAM: LONGITUDINAL SECTION ON THE CENTRE LINE OF THE RIVER SHOWING THE DEEPENING OF THE CHANNEL AND ALTERATION IN WATER LEVELS BETWEEN 1860 AND 1925

sissippi. Tidal water is, indeed, unlimited in volume; but, unlike the drainage waters, which must be discharged into the sea, it only flows up rivers where there is a channel and space available for its reception. Consequently, works which exclude the tide from a river may have injurious effects on the channel, as did the sluices which were erected long ago across the fen rivers of eastern Anglia to secure the low-lying lands from the inroads of the sea. The tidal influx is also liable to be reduced by the accretion which may result in an estuary from the construction of training works. The aims of all tidal river improvement should be to facilitate to the utmost the flow of the flood tide up a river, to remove all obstructions from the channel so as to increase the scouring efficiency of the flood and ebb tides, and to reduce to a minimum the period of slack tide when deposit takes place.

Tidal Flow in a River.—The progress of the flood tide up a river and the corresponding ebb are clearly shown by a diagram giving a series of tidal lines obtained from simultaneous observations of the height of the river Hooghly in India during a high spring tide in the dry season. The observations were taken at

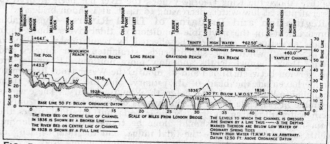

FIG. 7.—LONGITUDINAL SECTION OF THE RIVER THAMES FROM WESTMINSTER BRIDGE TO THE NORE

intervals at several stations along the river and the lines exhibit on a very distorted scale the actual water levels of the river at these periods. The steep form assumed by the foremost part of the flood tide lines from the entrance to beyond Chinsura, attaining a maximum in the neighbourhood of Konnagar and Chinsura, indicates the existence of a bore. This is caused by the sandbanks in the channel obstructing the advance of the flood tide, till it has risen sufficiently in height to rush up the river as a steep, breaking wave, overcoming all obstacles and producing a sudden reversal of the flow and abrupt rise of the water level. Such phenomena are observed on the Severn, the Seine, the Amazon and other rivers. A bore indicates defects in the tidal channel, which can be reduced only by lowering the obstructions and by the regulation of the river. No tidal river of even moderate length is ever completely filled by tidal water; for the tide begins to fall at its mouth before the flood tide has produced high water at the tidal limit. This is clearly shown in the case of a long tidal. Every improvement of the channel, however, expedites and increases the filling of the river, while the volume of water admitted at each tide is further augmented by the additional capacity provided by the greater efflux of the ebb, as indicated by the lowering of the low-water line.

Deepening Tidal Rivers by Dredging.—The improvement of tidal rivers mainly by dredging is specially applicable to small rivers which possess a width sufficient for navigation like the Clyde and the Tyne; for such rivers can be considerably deepened by an amount of dredging which would be quite inadequate for producing a similar increase in depth in a large, wide river, with shifting channels. Both the Clyde below Glasgow and the Tyne below Newcastle were originally insignificant rivers, almost dry in places at low water of spring tides; and the earliest works on both rivers consisted mainly in regulating their flow and increasing their scour by jetties and training works. They have been improved, since 1840 on the Clyde and 1861 on the Tyne, by continuous systematic dredging. The Clyde has been given a minimum depth of 27 ft. in the channel at low water of spring tides up to Port Glasgow; 25 ft. up to Rothesay Dock, and 24 ft. up to Glasgow harbour. A depth of 32 ft. at low water has been provided alongside some of the quays. The Tyne has been progressively deepened (fig. 6) until in 1929 the channel from the sea to the Northumberland dock (3½ mi.) had a minimum depth at low-water spring tides of 30 ft.; from there to Derwenthaugh, above Newcastle, 25 ft.; and about 12 ft. on to Newburn, the rise of tide at springs increasing these depths by 15 ft.

The minimum low-water depth in the Thames river below Thames Haven in its natural state was about 27 ft. (*see* HARBOURS). A channel at least 30 ft. deep at low-water spring tides now extends from the sea to the King George V dock, 37 mi. above the Nore and Shoeburyness (fig. 7). Shallow portions of the channel between Shoeburyness and Purfleet have been dredged and above Purfleet the river has been considerably deepened in recent years throughout its course to secure this depth. Above the King George V dock the river has been dredged to lesser depths at low water, decreasing to 14 ft. at London bridge.

Regulation and Dredging of Tidal Rivers.—Considerable improvements in the navigable condition of tidal rivers above their outlets or estuaries can often be effected by regulation works aided by dredging, which ease sharp bends, straighten their courses and render their channel depths and flow more uniform. Examples are the Nervion between Bilbao and its mouth, the Weser from Bremen to Bremerhaven at the head of its estuary, and the Whangpoo from Shanghai to Woosung where it enters the Yangtse estuary. These works resemble in principle the regulation works on large rivers with only a fresh-water discharge, previously described; but on tidal rivers the main low-water channel should alone be trained with an enlarging width seaward to facilitate the tidal influx, and the tidal capacity of the river above low water should be maintained unimpaired.

To secure a good and fairly uniform depth on a tidal river, it is essential that the flood and ebb tides should follow the same course in order to combine their scouring efficiency and form a single, continuous deep channel. In wide, winding reaches, however, the flood tide in ascending a river follows as direct a course as practicable; and on reaching a bend, the main flood-tide current, in being deflected from its straight course, hugs the concave bank, and, keeping close alongside the same bank beyond the bend, cuts into the shoal projecting from the convex bend of the bank higher up, forming a blind shoaling channel as clearly indicated near Brul point in fig. 8. This effect is due to the flood tide losing its guidance and consequently its concentration, at the change of curvature beyond the termination of the concave bank, where it spreads out and passes gradually over, in its direct course, to the next concave bend above along the opposite bank. The

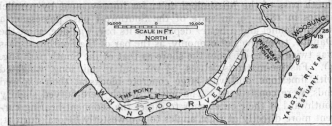

FIG. 9.—LOWER PART OF THE WHANGPOO RIVER (1946). SINCE 1907 THE CHANNEL OF THE RIVER HAS BEEN REGULATED BY BUILDING TRAINING WALLS AND GROYNES

ebb tide, on the contrary, descending the river, follows the general course of the fresh-water discharge in all rivers, its main current keeping close along the concave bank and crossing over opposite Brul point to the next concave bank below. The main currents, accordingly, of the flood and ebb tides in such reaches act quite independently between the bends, forming channels on opposite sides of the river and leaving a central intervening shoal or bar crossing.

In tidal rivers the main ebb current, being reinforced by the fresh-water discharge, generally forms the navigable channel, which is scoured out during floods. Narrowing the river between the bends to bring the two channels together would in certain cases unduly restrict the tidal flow; and, in a river such as the Hooghly, dependent on the tidal flow for the maintenance of its depth for two-thirds of the year, with channels changing with the wet and dry seasons and even shifting their position from day to day, deepening by dredging can never be permanent. Hitherto frequent redredging has been relied on for maintaining the requisite depths at the bar crossings in the Hooghly.

The training and dredging works carried out in the Whangpoo since 1906[1] have been successful in deepening the alluvial channel of the river to about 30 ft. at low water up to Shanghai including the bar crossing in a wide reach between Gough Island and Woosung where formerly the low-water depth was no more than 13 ft. to 15 ft. The problem which had to be faced differed from that of the Hooghly in that the volume of the land-water runoff is relatively small. Moreover the concave bank of the river above the crossing was being rapidly eroded, accentuating a sharp bend below it. The condition of the lower part of the river is shown in fig. 9.

The erosion of the Taylor's bank, forming the concave side of the main sea channel of the river Mersey, which threatened to intensify the bend to a dangerous degree, was countered by the revetting with stone of the concave face of the bank below low water (*see* HARBOURS).

The average rate of enlargement (of width) adopted for the trained channel of the Nervion, in proportion to its length, is 1 in 75 between Bilbao and its mouth; 1 in 71 for the Weser from Bremen to Bremerhaven; and about 1 in 73 for the Whangpoo from Shanghai to its outlet; and these ratios correspond very nearly to the enlargement of the regulated channel of the Clyde from Glasgow to Dumbarton of 1 in 83, and of the Tyne from Newcastle to its mouth of 1 in 75. Accordingly a divergence comprised between 1 in 70 and 1 in 80 for the regulated or trained channel of the lower portion of a tidal river with a fairly level bed may be expected to give satisfactory results. The divergence as originally laid down for the Seine training works,

FIG. 8.—RIVER HOOGHLY SHOWING THE MOYAPUR AND ROYAPUR BAR CROSSINGS, 1946

FIG. 10.—TRAINING WORKS IN THE SEINE ESTUARY (1946)

1 in 200, was found to be too small. (*See* fig. 10.) In rivers in which the channels are more or less in natural condition, such as the Thames, the Humber and the Scheldt, the divergence is nearly 1 in 50.

Effect of River Deepening on Tidal Levels.—The general effect of deepening and regulating the tidal section of a river by dredging and the removal of obstructions is to facilitate the propagation of the flood tide up the channel and the efflux of the ebb. Consequently such works often result in the lowering of the low-water level and the raising of the high-water level in the upper part of the improved channel and sometimes above it. Thus the deepening of the Tyne river raised the level of mean high-water spring tides at Newcastle about 1 ft. and lowered the water level by 2 ft. at Newcastle quay. In the Tyne river, the highest high water on record since 1880, 4 ft. 3 in. above high-water ordinary spring tide, occurred in Dec. 1921 and again in Feb. 1943. The lowest low water recorded on the Tyne since 1880, 3 ft. 8 in. below low-water ordinary spring tide, occurred March 13,

[1] H. von Heidenstam, *Int. Nav. Congress Papers*, 1919, and 1923.

1914. The average low-water level at Glasgow has fallen 2 ft. since 1873 and the rise in spring tides has been increased by 1 ft. 8 in.

The average high-water level in the Thames at Chelsea increased 8 in. between 1890 and 1927, a period which corresponds with the dredging carried out on a large scale in the lower reaches of the river. The maximum flood levels also increased steadily after 1874 when a tide rose 16 ft. 10 in. above O.D. at Westminster, considerably higher than any previous record. This height has been exceeded on several occasions since, the highest recorded at Westminster (up to the end of 1927) being 17 ft. 6 in. in 1881, the same level being reached again in 1882. These high levels were, however, far surpassed by the disastrous tidal flood of Jan. 6–7, 1928 (see *Report: Floods from the River Thames*, Cmd. 3045; 1928) when 18 ft. 3 in. above O.D. was reached at London bridge (equivalent to about 18 ft. 5 in. at Westminster).

The highest recorded high-tide level at London bridge between 1928 and 1951 reached 17 ft. 1½ in. and was closely approached on March 19, 1949, at a level of 16 ft. 8½ in. The lowest recorded low tide at London bridge, 10 ft. 6 in. above O.D., occurred in Feb. 1937 and was closely approached in Aug. 1951 by a low tide of 10 ft. 7 in. Both these recorded low tides are below the recorded low tides during the 1928 flood.

The level of maximum high tides and the minimum low tides in the Thames cannot be attributed entirely to the effect of deepening the river channel. The variations of tidal flow are also influenced by the extensive building of embankments and the rebuilding with enlarged waterways of several bridges which span the river.

The flood and ebb tides in navigable rivers being affected by the meteorological conditions in the Atlantic and the astronomical cycle of tidal range associated with open seas, long-period observations are necessary in comparing tidal levels. The deepening of river channels, however, is a major controlling influence in raising the high-water levels in rivers where these improvements have been carried out.

Works at the Outlet of Tidal Rivers.—Tidal rivers flowing straight into the sea, without expanding into an estuary, are subject to the obstruction of a bar formed by the heaping-up action of the waves and drift along the coast, especially when the fresh-water discharge is small. The scour of the currents is often in such cases concentrated and extended across the beach by parallel jetties for lowering the bar, as at the outlets of the Maas and the Nervion rivers. Except in the case of large rivers, the jetties have to be placed too close together, if the scour is to be adequate, to form an easily accessible entrance on an exposed coast. Accordingly, in the small bay into which the Nervion flows, a harbour has been formed by two converging breakwaters, which provide a sheltered approach to the river and protect the outlet from drift. Similar provision has been made at Sunderland, Eng., for the mouth of the Wear; while the Tynemouth piers formed part of the original design for the improvement of the Tyne, under shelter of which the bar has been removed by dredging. (See HARBOURS; JETTY.)

Training Works Through Estuaries.—Many tidal rivers flow through bays, estuaries or arms of the sea before reaching the open sea, as, for instance, the Mersey through Liverpool bay, the Tees through its enclosed bay, the Liffey through Dublin bay, the Thames, the Ribble, the Dee, the Shannon, the Seine, the Scheldt, the Weser, the Elbe and the Yangtse, through their respective estuaries, the Yorkshire Ouse and Trent through the Humber estuary, the Garonne and Dordogne through the Gironde estuary, and the Clyde, the Tay, the Severn and the St. Lawrence through friths or arms of the sea. These estuaries vary greatly in their tidal range, the distance inland of the ports to which they give access, and the facilities they offer for navigation. Some possess a very ample depth in their outer portion, though they generally become shallow towards their upper end; but dredging often suffices to remedy their deficiencies and to extend their deep-water channel. Thus the St. Lawrence, which possesses an ample depth from the Atlantic up to Quebec, has been rendered accessible for large seagoing vessels up to Montreal by a moderate amount of dredging; while dredging has been resorted to in parts of the Thames and Humber estuaries, and on the Elbe below Hamburg, to provide for the increasing draught of vessels; and the Mersey bar in Liverpool bay, about 11 mi. seaward of the actual mouth of the river, has been lowered by suction dredging from a depth of about 9 ft. down to about 26 ft. below low water of equinoctial spring tides.

The Weser from Bremen down to Bremerhaven, Ger., a distance of over 40 mi., has been regulated by constructing longitudinal training walls, cross dikes and groynes, while in the estuary between Bremerhaven and the Hoheweg light, a distance of about 18 mi., there are occasional low training walls and dikes and minor channels have been closed. These operations have secured a minimum low-water depth in the channel up to Bremerhaven of about 25 ft. and to Bremen of about 17 ft.

A remarkable improvement has been effected in the navigable condition of the upper portion of the Seine estuary by training works, begun in 1848; for in place of a shallow, intricate channel through shifting sand banks, whose dangers were at times intensified by a bore, a stable channel has been provided down to St. Sauveur, rendering access easy as far up the river as Rouen for vessels drawing up to 23 ft. at high-water neaps and up to 27 ft. at high water of spring tides. The channel itself, however, was originally made too narrow between Aizier and Berville and was subsequently enlarged, and large tracts of land were reclaimed in the upper estuary. The reduction in tidal

capacity due to the reclamations, together with the fixing and undue restriction in width of the channel, occasioned large accretions at the back of the lower portions of the training walls and at the sides of the estuary beyond them, and an extension of the sandbanks seawards.

Experience has proved that training works through sandy estuaries, by stopping the wanderings of the navigable channel, produce an increase in its depth, and, consequently, in the tidal scour for maintaining it. This scour, however, being concentrated in the trained channel, is withdrawn from the sides of the estuary, which in its natural condition is stirred up periodically by the wandering channel; and, therefore, accretion takes place in the parts of the estuary from which the tidal scour and fresh-water discharge have been permanently diverted, especially where an abundance of sand from outside, put in suspension by the action of the prevalent winds blowing into the estuary, is brought in by the flood tide, as in the cases of the estuaries of the Dee, the Ribble and the Seine. This accretion reduces the tidal capacity of the estuary, and, producing a diminution in the tidal volume passing through the outlet, promotes the extension of the sand banks seaward. To prevent as far as possible the reduction in tidal capacity, the training walls should not be raised more above low-water level than absolutely necessary to fix the channel; and the rate of enlargement of their width apart should not be less than 1 in 80 at the upper end, and increase toward the mouth of the estuary. Training works carried partially out through an estuary have the advantage of reducing the length of the shallow channel to be traversed between deep water and the entrance to the deepened river; but as the influence of these works on the channel terminates close to their seaward end, a shallow, shifting channel is always found between the end of the trained channel and deep water. Accordingly, when training works are started at the head of a sandy estuary, provision should always be made in their design for their eventual prolongation to deep water at the mouth of the estuary, to ensure the formation of a stable, continuous, navigable channel. Experiments with a model, moulded to the configuration of the estuary under consideration and reproducing in miniature the tidal ebb and flow and fresh-water discharge over a bed of very fine sand, in which various lines of training walls can be successively inserted, are capable in some cases of furnishing valuable indications of the respective effects and comparative merits of the different schemes proposed for works which have often evoked very conflicting opinions.

BIBLIOGRAPHY.—See list at the end of article CANALS AND CANALIZED RIVERS. The works by L. F. Vernon-Harcourt, D. Stevenson and B. F. Thomas and D. A. Watt mentioned therein are important. *See* also W. H. Hunter, *Rivers and Estuaries* (1913); J. L. Van Ornum, *The Regulation of Rivers* (1914), an excellent and comprehensive work dealing mainly with nontidal rivers; C. McD. Townsend, *Hydraulic Principles of River and Harbour Construction*, bibliography (1922); *Encyclopédie de Génie Civil*, two volumes by Vidal deal with rivers (1921–22); and L. Fargue, *La Forme du Lit des Rivieres* (1908). *See* River and Harbor Act, 1945 (Public Law 14, 79th U.S. Congress). The *Proceedings* Inst. Civ. Eng.; *Transactions* American Soc. C. E. and the International Navigation Congress publications contain valuable papers. The bibliographies issued by the I.N.C. bureau (Brussels) are exhaustive.   (L. F. V.-H.; N. G. G.; X.)

RIVER BRETHREN: *see* BRETHREN IN CHRIST.

RIVER HOG, a name for the African wild pig. It constitutes a genus, *Potamochoerus*, allied to the typical pigs of the genus *Sus* (*see* SWINE), from which they are distinguishable by the presence in the males of a long horny ridge below the eye, by their thick coat of bristly and often brightly coloured hair, and by tufts at the tips of the elongated ears. The red river hog,

THE RIVER HOG, A WILD HOG NATIVE OF AFRICA

P. porcus, is found in typical form in West Africa. The ear tufts are especially long and the prevailing colour is brownish red; the face and legs are marked with black, while the cheeks, a ring around the eyes, the edges of the ears, the tip of the tufts and the mane are white. It inhabits the dense tropical forests. Through a number of intergrading forms this type is connected with the brownish gray brush pig of South Africa, *P. p. koiropotamus*. A small yellowish-haired representative of the genus (*P. larvatus*) occurs in Madagascar, to which island it must have come from the mainland.

RIVERINA, an important district occupying the central south portion of New South Wales, Australia, bounded on the south by the River Murray, on the north by the Lachlan–Murrumbidgee from about Hillston down to the Murray confluence. The eastern boundary is less easy to draw. That of the administrative district runs from the Lachlan (30 mi. above Hillston) in a sinuous line curving eastwards and then westwards to the Murray at Corowa, but the lower slopes of the southern tableland—the administrative "South Western Slopes"—is perhaps to be included in the natural Riverina region. Except for these eastern and north-eastern parts, where lie the fairly open upper-middle basins of the Murrumbidgee and Murray systems, the whole area is flat. The fall of the rivers varies from 10 in. per mile in the east to 4–5 in. in the west of the area, and they meander across vast alluvial plains, periodically flooding and forming distributaries and lagoons (anabranches, billabongs) and sometimes even flowing up-stream. Higher up they are stronger, more definite, and more constant in flow and their valleys offer also sites for dams. The soil is prevailingly rich; the climate is generally mild and warm but the summers are hot and dusty and the rain, which falls in winter, is variable. (Av. ann. temps.: 75°–49° F, with extremes: 117°–20° F; av. ann. rainfall: from 12 in. in the north-west to 25 in. in the south-east.) The eastern valleys have yielded considerable quantities of gold, both alluvial and reef, and some alluvial dredging still continues (Adelong and Gundagai districts). In 1915 a deposit of soft black (Permian) sub-bituminous coal was discovered near Oaklands (area: 5 miles by 3 miles, with seams 8 ft. 6 in. to 36 ft.). It is important because of its position near the overland (Sydney–Melbourne) railway line in an otherwise fuelless area of growing population and because of the valuable kaolin deposits which overlie it.

The greater part of the western plains, which normally provide good natural fodder (including salt-bush), is used for sheep grazing, and these are still the home of the large "squatter." But improvements in wheat-growing (seed-selection, dry-farming) have enabled considerable areas to be put to the plough; and by 1922 wheat was being grown as far north-west as Hillston, and, in the south, as far west as Balranald (9.12 in. and 7.89 in. winter, April–Oct., rainfall respectively). The Riverina, indeed, ranks second amongst the wheat-growing districts of New South Wales and has also a relatively high average yield (12.3–17.8 bu. per ac.). Along the south-eastern slopes, with their cooler temperatures and more reliable rain, a good deal of arable farming and dairying is carried on, and fruits, including vines, are grown, the wines of the Albury district having an established reputation. Further west mixed wheat and sheep farming is increasingly practised. But perhaps the greatest potential wealth of the Riverina lies in its irrigation agriculture. The development of this branch is in its infancy but it is already important. Of the total 183,518 ac. under irrigated crops in New South Wales in 1938–39, c. 95,000 were included in the Murrumbidgee and Hay (Riverina) areas. The Murrumbidgee Irrigation area, supplied from the Burrinjuck reservoir below Yass, had (1938) nearly 1,400 occupied holdings (1–250 ac. each, average 15–25 ac.) occupying 314,000 ac. of the total projected area (561 sq.mi.). The principal settlements are Leeton, Yanco and Griffith. Fruit (sub-tropical and temperate climate types) is grown, dairying and pig-raising, with butter and cheese making, bacon-curing and fruit-canning carried on largely by cooperative methods. Electricity and water-supplies are provided and education and experimental research are well cared for. In Hay the area is smaller (1926, c. 1,000 ac. occupied for irrigation and 2,900 ac. non-irrigated) and is devoted mainly to dairying and pig-raising. The Murray River development scheme, with the great Hume dam above Albury as headworks, will provide further facilities. The economic and financial aspects of the irrigation projects have presented difficulties and these may still be regarded as expensive if promising experiments. A recent development is rice-growing, the hope being that Australia's needs can be satisfied from this source. Of similar importance is the great Wyangala Dam project, on the upper Lachlan river near Corowa, now (1929) being inaugurated. One million acres will be made available along the Lachlan for wheat growing and mixed (wheat and sheep) farming for 700 families at a cost of about £2,000,000. Though not an irrigation project some irrigation blocks will be provided for fodder (lucerne, etc.) growing, and the railway from Hillston is now extended to Roto.

The area of the Riverina Administrative Division (see above) is 26,600 sq.mi., its population 84,300 (3.1 per sq.mi.). (Mur-

rumbidgee Irrigation area alone: 561 sq.mi.; pop. c. 15,000=27 per sq.mi.). The chief towns are: Albury (q.v., pop. 10,543), Wagga Wagga (11,631), Junee (4,213) and Narrandera in the east, important as business centres for wheat-farming, fruit-growing, and grazing districts and also as railway junctions and river-crossing (bridge) towns with small industries; Leeton, and other irrigation centres with butter, cheese and bacon factories, electricity-supply and machine-repairing works; Jerilderie, Deniliquin, pastoral and agricultural centres with good road or rail connections; Hay, Hillston, Balranald, also pastoral centres (Hay has irrigation settlement also) and both river and rail-head importance. The rivers are still used, when seasons permit, mainly for wool transport, but railway and motor transport are increasingly opening up and serving the "back blocks." Interesting and significant is the way in which the southern borderlands—by agreement between the Victorian and New South Wales Governments—are increasingly tapped by Victorian lines, and, yielding to geographical necessity, are being drawn within the economic sphere (hinterland) of Melbourne.

Production (1938–39): Riverina (administrative division): wool: 41,765,000 lb.; wheat: 8,779,000 bu.; butter: 737,000 lb.; minerals: £28,000; manufactures: £545,000.

RIVER PLATE: see PLATA, RIO DE LA.

RIVER ROUGE, a city of Wayne county, Michigan, U.S.A., on the Detroit and the Rouge rivers, 6 m. S.W. of Detroit; served by the New York Central, Michigan Central, Detroit, Toledo and Ironton, and Detroit and Toledo Shore Line railroads and by lake steamers. Pop. (1950) 20,366 by federal census. The principal industries are shipbuilding, papermaking, blast furnaces and a gypsum products plant. It was incorporated as a village in 1899 and in 1922 was chartered as a city.

RIVERS, ANTHONY WOODVILLE, or WYDEVILLE, 2ND EARL (c. 1442–1483), statesman and patron of literature, and author of the first book printed on English soil, was born probably in 1442. He was the son of Richard de Wydeville and his wife, Jacquetta de Luxemburg, duchess of Bedford. His father was raised to the peerage in his son's infancy, and was made earl of Rivers in 1466. Anthony, who was knighted before he became of age, and fought at Towton in 1461, married the daughter of Lord Scales, and became a peer jure uxoris in 1462, two years after the death of that nobleman. Being lord of the Isle of Wight at the time, he was in 1467 appointed one of the ambassadors to treat with the duke of Burgundy, and he exalted his office by challenging Anthony, comte de la Roche, the bastard of Burgundy, to single fight in what was one of the most famous tournaments of the age. (See Bentley's Excerpta Historica, 176–182.) In 1469 Anthony was promoted to be lieutenant of Calais and captain of the king's armada, while holding other honorary posts. His father and brother were beheaded after the battle of Edgecot, and he succeeded in August of that year to the earldom. He accompanied Edward in his temporary flight to the Continent, and on his return to England had a share in the victory of Barnet and Tewkesbury and defended London from the Lancastrians. In 1473 he became guardian and governor to the young prince of Wales. In 1475 and 1476 he went on pilgrimage to the holy places of Italy.

Caxton had in 1476 rented a shop in the Sanctuary at Westminster, and here had set up a printing-press. The first book which he undertook in London was one sent to him by "the noble and puissant lord, Lord Antone, Erle of Ryvvers," consisting of a translation "into right good and fayr Englyssh" of Jean de Teonville's French version of a Latin work, "a glorious fair mirror to all good Christian people." In 1477 Caxton brought out this book, as Dictes and Sayengis of the Philosophers. (See CAXTON, WILLIAM.) To this succeeded the Moral Proverbs of Christine de Pisan, in verse, in 1478, and a Cordial, in prose, in 1479. The original productions of Lord Rivers, and, in particular, his Balades against the Seven Deadly Sins, are lost.

In 1478 a marriage was arranged between him and Margaret, sister of King James III of Scotland, but it was mysteriously broken off. He was beheaded by order of Richard III at Pontefract on June 25, 1483. His protection and encouragement of Caxton were of inestimable value to English literature, and in the preface to the *Dictes* the printer gives an account of his own relations with the statesman which illustrates the dignity and modesty of Lord Rivers in a very agreeable way. Rivers was one of the purest writers of English prose of his time.

"Memoirs of Anthony, Earl Rivers" are comprised in the *Historical Illustrations of the Reign of Edward the Fourth* (ed. W. H. B[lack]).

RIVERS, RICHARD SAVAGE, 4TH EARL (*c.* 1654–1712), the son of Thomas, 3rd earl, was styled Viscount Colchester after the death of his elder brother Thomas (*c.* 1680), until he succeeded to the peerage. Richard Savage was one of the most conspicuous rakes in the society of the period. He also had a distinguished military career from 1686 onward. He served in Ireland (1690) and Flanders (1691–92, 1695) became lieutenant general in 1697 and commander of the forces in Portugal in 1706. In 1694 he succeeded his father as the 4th Earl Rivers. He became a privy councillor in 1708 and went on missions to Hanover in 1710–11. On the fall of the Whigs, he went over to the Tories, and in 1712 was appointed master-general of the ordnance, a post hitherto held by Marlborough. In June 1712 Rivers was promoted to the rank of general, and became commander in chief in England; he died a few weeks later, on Aug. 18, 1712. River's intrigue with Lady Macclesfield was the cause of that lady's divorce from her husband in 1701.

Richard Savage (*q.v.*), the poet, claimed identity with Lady Macclesfield's son by Lord Rivers, but the evidence in its support is insufficient.

RIVERS, RICHARD WOODVILLE or **WYDEVILLE,** EARL (d. 1469), served under the duke of Bedford in France, and after his master's death married his widow Jacquetta of Luxemburg. Henry VI. created him Baron Rivers in 1448. His associations made him a strong Lancastrian. For some years he was lieutenant of Calais in Henry's interests. In 1459 he was taken prisoner, and was sent with his son Anthony to the earl of Warwick at Calais. He was, however, released in time to fight for Henry VI. at Towton. Early in the reign of Edward IV. Rivers recognized that the Lancastrian cause was lost and made his peace with the new king. The marriage of his eldest daughter, Elizabeth, widow of Sir John Grey of Groby, to Edward on May 1, 1464, secured the fortunes of his family.

Rivers was appointed treasurer in 1466, and a little later created earl. Elizabeth found great alliances for her younger brothers and sisters, and the Woodville influence became all-powerful at court. The power of this new family was very distasteful to the old baronial party, and especially so to Warwick. Early in 1468 Rivers's estates were plundered by Warwick's partisans, and the open war of the following year was aimed to destroy the Woodvilles. After the king's defeat at Edgecot, Rivers and his second son, John, were taken prisoners at Chepstow and executed at Kenilworth on Aug. 12, 1469. Rivers had a large family. His third son, Lionel (d. 1484), was bishop of Salisbury. All his daughters made great marriages: Catherine, the sixth, was wife of Henry Stafford, 2nd duke of Buckingham (*q.v.*).

BIBLIOGRAPHY.—The chief contemporary authorities are the *Paston Letters,* ed. Dr. James Gairdner, *The Chronicles of London,* ed. C. L. Kingsford (1905), and the *Chronicles* of Commines and Waurin. *See* also some notices in *Calendars of State Papers, Venetian,* ed. Rawdon Browne. For modern accounts *see* Sir James Ramsay's *Lancaster and York* (1892), *The Political History of England,* vol. iv., by Professor C. Oman, and *The Complete Peerage,* by G. E. C[okayne]. For Earl Anthony's connection with Caxton consult William Blades's *Life of Caxton* (1861–63).

RIVERS, WILLIAM HALSE RIVERS (1864–1922), British psychopathologist, was educated at Tonbridge and St. Bartholomew's hospital, London. He was made university lecturer at Cambridge in physiological and experimental psychology in Dec. 1867, and in 1907, when the two subjects were separated, lecturer in the physiology of the senses. He founded during this period the Cambridge school of experimental psychology, and was made fellow of St. John's college. In 1898, with his pupils C. S. Myers and William MacDougall, he joined the anthropological expedition to Torres Straits led by A. C. Haddon, and had charge of the psychological work. By the genealogical method of social

investigation he obtained such valuable results that whereas he joined the expedition as a pure psychologist he returned an enthusiastic ethnologist. *The Todas* (1906) records his investigation on these lines among the Todas in Southern India in 1902. His first expedition to Melanesia was in 1908. He revisited that area later, and in the *History of Melanesian Society* (2 vol., 1914) abandoned the evolutionary theory of society in favour of that of cultural migration. During World War I he obtained many valuable results as a psychopathologist (see *Instinct and the Unconscious,* 1920) and while critically interested in Freudian methods of psycho-analysis he came to very different conclusions on matters of principle and practice, holding that "though dreams are the attempted solutions of conflicts, the nature of the solution is largely determined by the affective attitude dominant before going to sleep." His *Psychology and Politics* (1923), *Medicine, Magic and Religion* (1924), *Social Organisation* (1924), were published after his death. He died at Cambridge on June 4, 1922.

RIVERSIDE, a city of southern California, U.S., on the Santa Ana river, at the base of the San Bernardino range, 53 mi. E. by S. of Los Angeles; the county seat of Riverside county. It has two commercial airports, and is served by the Santa Fe, the Southern Pacific, the Union Pacific and by motor coach and truck lines and is on federal highway 60. Pop. (1950) 46,764; it was 34,696 in 1940 by federal census. Riverside is a beautiful city, at an altitude of 800–1,000 ft., situated in the centre of the finest orange-growing district in the state. It has an area of 40 sq.mi. The climate is dry and warm, tempered by breezes from the ocean (60 mi. W.). The mean annual temperature is 63° F. and the mean annual rainfall is 11.21 in. The prevailing style of architecture is the modified Spanish type of the early missions; a noteworthy example is the Glenwood Mission inn, containing a historical museum and an art gallery. The avenues are lined with pepper and other subtropical trees. On the rock-crowned summit of Mt. Rubidoux, at the edge of the city, religious services attended by thousands are held at sunrise on Easter morning. Riverside is the seat of Sherman institute, the largest of the government nonreservation schools for Indians, with an attendance of more than 1,000; and of a liberal arts branch and the citrus experiment station of the University of California. More than $10,000,-000 worth of oranges, lemons and grapefruit are packed and shipped annually, and the poultry business is considerable. Much of the machinery used in handling citrus crops has been invented and perfected in Riverside and is manufactured there. Riverside is the home of March air force base, air defense base for southern California, and the headquarters of the fourth air district.

In 1870 the site of Riverside (called Jurupa Rancho, the name of the old Spanish grant) was bought by the Southern California Colony association, and in 1873 the cultivation of navel oranges was introduced from Brazil, laying the foundation of one of the leading industries of the state.

The city was chartered in 1883.

RIVES, WILLIAM CABELL (1793–1868), American political leader and diplomat, was born in Nelson county, Va., on May 4, 1793. He attended Hampden-Sidney and William and Mary colleges, was admitted to the bar, and practised in Nelson and Albemarle counties. A Democrat, he served in the State Constitutional convention, in the Virginia house of delegates and in the Federal House of Representatives. From 1820 to 1832 he was minister to France; in 1833 he entered the United States Senate, but resigned in the following year. From 1836 to 1845 he again served in the Senate, and in 1849–53 was again minister to France. In Feb., 1861, he was a delegate to the Peace Conference in Washington; he opposed secession, but was loyal to his State when it seceded, and was a representative in the Confederate Congress during the Civil War. He died at the country estate of Castle Hill, Albemarle county, Va., on April 25, 1868. Rives was the author of *Life and Times of James Madison* (3 vols., Boston, 1859–68), the completion of which was prevented by his death. He was the father of ALFRED LANDON RIVES (1830–1903), an engineer of some prominence, whose daughter, AMÉLIE RIVES (Princess Troubetzkoy) (1863–1945), became well known as a novelist.

RIVET is a headed pin or bolt used as a permanent fastening in metal work by forming a head on the plain end by the process of hammering or by direct pressure. Cold riveting is practicable for small sizes in copper, brass, aluminum, iron and steel, but the larger sizes have to be heated in the cases of iron and steel, in order to secure rapid and easy closing.

Machine riveting in small sizes is done either in a power press, the ram of which works a snap and closes the tail with a blow, or with a rotary rivet spinning ma-

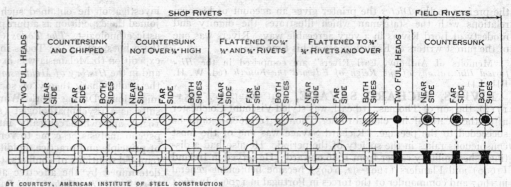

BY COURTESY, AMERICAN INSTITUTE OF STEEL CONSTRUCTION

CONVENTIONAL SIGNS FOR RIVETING SHOWING HOW THE DRAFTSMAN DRAWS RIVETS IN PLAN AND ELEVATION ON ALL STRUCTURAL DRAWINGS

chine, with hard steel rollers which spin the tail quickly and noiselessly into shape. In engineering structures, machine riveting is employed whenever practicable, portable pneumatic hammers, or fixed or portable hydraulic riveters being used.

The various shapes of rivet heads or tails include the countersunk, beaten flush into a conical recess in the plate, the cup or round head, the pan head, which has sloping sides and flat top, the conical with sloped sides ending in a point, and the thin flat head coopers' or tinmen's rivets. Bifurcated rivets for belting and harness have thin heads, but the tails are split, and opened like a paper fastener. A great deal of gas or electric welding is now substituted for riveting in the case of hollowware and other sorts of sheet metal product. Electric welding is an alternate method for the connection of structural members such as columns and beams in building construction.

(*See* also PNEUMATIC TOOLS.)

RIVIERA, the narrow coast-land between the mountains and the sea around the Gulf of Genoa in the north of Italy and in France from Nice on the west to Spezia on the east. The name is derived from *riva* (Lat. *ripa*) meaning bank. It is usually spoken of as Riviera di Ponente ("the coast of the setting sun," the portion between Nice and Genoa), and as Riviera di Levante ("the coast of the rising sun," the portion from Genoa to Spezia). All this district, being open to the south and sheltered from the north and east winds, enjoys a remarkably mild climate (winter mean, about 49° F.); the vegetation in many places partakes of a subtropical character (*e.g.*, the pomegranate, agave, prickly pear, date, palm and banana). Large numbers of flowers, especially roses, violets, hyacinths, etc., are grown near Nice, Mentone, Bordighera and other towns, for the London and Paris markets. The uncommon mildness of the climate, conjoined with the natural beauty of the coast scenery,—the steep sea-crags, the ruined towers and the range of the Maritime alps,—attracts thousands of invalids and convalescents to spend the winter there, and these resorts are frequented for sea-bathing in summer. Proceeding from west to east, the following are the places to which visitors principally resort: Nice, Monaco (an independent principality), Monte Carlo, Mentone (the last town on the French Riviera), Bordighera, Ospedaletti, San Remo, Alassio, Nervi, Santa Margherita, Rapallo, Sestri Levante, Levanto. The railway which runs close through the Riviera burrows through the many projecting headlands by means of more than 80 tunnels.

RIVIERE, BRITON (1840–1920), English artist, was born in London on Aug. 14, 1840. He was educated at Cheltenham and Oxford, and received his art training from his father, an art master. His first pictures appeared at the British Institution, and in 1857 he sent three works to the Royal Academy, becoming from 1863 a regular exhibitor. He contributed illustrations to *Punch* and other journals. He died on April 20, 1920.

RIVIÈRE-DU-LOUP, formerly Fraserville, a city and watering place in Temiscouata county, Quebec, Canada, 107 mi. (by water) N.E. of Quebec, on the St. Lawrence river, and at the mouth of the Rivière-du-Loup, on the Canadian National railways. Flour, leather, doors and furniture are produced. Pop. (1951) 9,425.

RIVINGTON, CHARLES (1688–1742), British publisher, was born at Chesterfield, Derbyshire, in 1688. He was apprenticed to a bookseller in London, and in 1711 took over the business of Richard Chiswell (1639–1711), at the sign of the Bible and the Crown in Paternoster row. His business was almost entirely theological and educational; he published one of Whitefield's earliest works, and brought out an edition of the *Imitation of Christ.*

In 1736 Rivington founded the company of booksellers called the "New Conger," in rivalry with the "Conger" which dated from about 1700. The business was handed down through the family until 1890, when it was sold to Messrs. Longmans. A business of the same character was carried on by Septimus Rivington (1846–1926) and J. G. Percival, as Percival and Co. (1889–93), and in 1897 the title of Rivington and Co. was revived.

See S. Rivington, *The House of Rivington* (1894); also *The Publishers' Circular* (Jan. 15, 1885 and June 2, 1890).

RIVINGTON, CHARLES ROBERT (1846–1928), English solicitor, was born on Dec. 7, 1846, and educated at King's college, London. He entered the old family firm of Rivington and Sons in 1869, and for 47 years held the post of clerk to the Stationers' company.

He wrote the *Records of the Stationers' Company.* He died at Appleby, on Aug. 22, 1928.

RIVINGTON'S GAZETTE (1773-1783), an American colonial newspaper, was founded in 1773 by James Rivington, the sixth son of Charles Rivington (*q.v.*), a British publisher.

James Rivington, who had emigrated to the colonies in 1760 and became a bookseller in Philadelphia, New York, Boston and again in New York, called his journal *Rivington's New-York Gazetteer, or the Connecticut, New Jersey, Hudson's River, and Quebec Weekly Advertiser;* he declared that his aim was "never to admit any Performance, calculated to injure Virtue, Religion or other public Happiness . . . or to raise a Blush in the face of Virgin Innocence." The paper was soon distributed in several colonies.

Rivington was opposed by the Sons of Liberty (*q.v.*), who in Nov. 1775 destroyed his printing plant. In 1777, however, he began to publish his paper again, having been appointed the king's printer in New York. Now an open Loyalist organ, it was published under various names until Dec. 31, 1783.

Rivington, who allegedly had secretly aided George Washington, remained in the United States after the war.

He never published a newspaper again although he continued as a bookseller.

See Isaiah Thomas, *The History of Printing in America,* 2 vol. (1874); H. R. Plomer *et al., A Dictionary of the Printers and Booksellers . . . 1726 to 1775* (1932).

RIVOLI VERONESE, a village of Venetia, Italy, in Verona, on the Adige, 13 mi. N.W. of Verona. Pop. (1951) 1,899 (commune).

Rivoli Veronese was the scene of the battle in which, on Jan. 14, 1797, Napoleon defeated the Austrians commanded by Josef Alvintzi, Baron von Barberek (1735–1810). (*See* FRENCH REVOLUTIONARY WARS.)

A famous street in Paris (rue de Rivoli) commemorates the victory, and under the empire Marshal Masséna received the title of duke of Rivoli.

The Battle of Rivoli.—This battle, fought on Jan. 14, 1797, was the climax of the repeated Austrian efforts to relieve the vital fortress of Mantua, which blocked Napoleon's advance toward Vienna. Napoleon's victory cleared the way for his advance into Austria.

RIXDORF, a suburb of Berlin, Germany. Rixdorf was a foundation of Moravian Brethren from Bohemia, who settled there in 1737. German Rixdorf was a much more ancient place, and appears as Richardsdorf in 1630 and as Riegenstorp in 1435. Before 1435 it belonged to the order of the Knights of St. John.

RIYADH, or RIYAD, a city of Nejd, Saudi Arabia, 480 mi. N.E. of Mecca. The population was estimated at 60,000 in 1951. The city is the capital of Nejd and, with Mecca, of Saudi Arabia.

The city is situated on an oasis in a hollow of the great plateau and is surrounded on all sides, except the northeast, by palm groves. The actual site is on limestone rock, forming a well marked mound on the crest of which is the royal palace. The settlement is encircled by a thick wall about 25 ft. high, pierced by many gates. The Thumairi gate on the east is the entry from the desert tracks to the north and east and south, while the Dhuhairi gate gives access to the northwestern route to Washm and the roads to Mecca. Riyadh is thus a great desert focus.

Within the walls irregular streets converge upon a central square. In the open space north of the royal palace is the market place. The great Mosque is a rectangular building about 60 by 50 yards. Architecturally it reflects the severity of the puritan Wahhabis.

In addition to the great Mosque there are a number of smaller ones. To the north of the main thoroughfare, about half way between the palace and the Thumairi gate, is the great fort built in the form of a square, but it is the royal palace that commands the whole city, and in its simplicity represents "all that is best in modern Arabian architecture." Outside the city walls stands the royal palace al-Murabba' (square) with its electric lights, telephones and elevator. The water supply of the city comes from numerous wells among the palm groves without the city, and beneath the shades of these groves there tend to grow up suburban residential quarters.

In 1951 a railway connecting Riyadh with the town of Dhahran was completed.

See H. St. J. B. Philby, *The Heart of Arabia,* vol. i.

RIZA SHAH PAHLAVI (1877–1944), shah of Persia (Iran) from 1925 to 1941, was born in Mazandaran, the son of an army officer.

Entering the army at an early age, he showed such aptitude that promotion was rapid, and he rose at length to the command of the Cossack division. In 1921, in conjunction with Zia ad-Din, he marched on Tehran with about 4,000 men and compelled the government to resign. Zia became prime minister, while Riza Khan (as he was then known) took over the ministry of war and the command of the army. In 1923 he became prime minister and virtual ruler. Two years later, after Ahmad Shah Qajar had left the country, Riza Khan was made shah and the sovereignty was vested in the Pahlavi dynasty. Riza Shah proceeded to carry out reforms on western lines, largely on the model of Kemal Atatürk in Turkey.

He broke the power of the tribes, put down brigandage and restored the authority of the central government. His greatest achievement was the construction of the Trans-Persian railway, which was completed in 1938.

Riza Shah had employed many Germans in the industrialization of his country; and when, in Aug. 1941, he rejected a joint request by Britain and the U.S.S.R. for the expulsion of these Germans, the two powers sent troops into Iran to prevent Germany from seizing control. Riza Shah thereupon abdicated in favour of his son, Mohammed Riza Pahlavi, and was sent first to Mauritius and then to South Africa. He died in Johannesburg on July 26, 1944.

(L. Lo).

RIZZIO or RICCIO, DAVID (*c.* 1533–1566), secretary of Mary (*q.v.*), queen of Scots, was a native of Turin, and came to Scotland in 1561 in the train of the Piedmontese ambassador. The queen wanted a bass singer, and he entered her service as a musician, becoming also her *valet de chambre,* and in 1564 private foreign secretary. After her marriage to Darnley in 1565 his influence with Mary became paramount. His elevation aroused the active hostility of Darnley and the other nobles, and he was suspected of being the queen's lover. On the evening of March 9, 1566, the earls of Morton and Lindsay, with armed followers, entered Mary's supper chamber at Holyrood, seized Rizzio, hacked him to death with daggers, and threw his body into the courtyard.

See Ruthven's *Narrative of Riccio's Murder* (1836); and the article on MARY, QUEEN OF SCOTS.

ROACH, JOHN (1813–1887), U.S. shipbuilder, has been called "the father of iron shipbuilding in America." Born in County Cork, Ire., on Dec. 25, 1813, the son of Patrick Roche, he emigrated to the United States at an early age.

He worked at the Howell ironworks in Howell, N.J., where he was taught the trade of iron moulding. After a short stay in Illinois, he returned to the east and, with other artisans, established an ironworks in New York city.

A manufacturer of marine engines, he acquired a number of marine-engine plants and in 1868 the Morgan ironworks in New York city. After purchasing shipyards in Chester, Pa., he built many iron ships for the government and private companies.

Although he was not the first to build such ships, he became known as "the father of iron shipbuilding in America" since he was a leading authority and builder. He also was a vigorous advocate of a strong U.S. merchant marine. He voluntarily closed his works in 1885 when the secretary of the navy, overruling the Naval advisory board, rejected the "Dolphin," a dispatch boat built by Roach, and also cancelled Roach's contract to build for the navy three cruisers—the "Atlanta," "Boston" and "Chicago"; construction of the cruisers had begun in 1883. Although an adjustment was later made, Roach retired from the business and died on Jan. 10, 1887, at New York city.

ROACH (*Rutilus rutilus*), a cyprinid fish of England, Europe and Siberia. It is a moderately deep, silvery fish. Specimens of more than 3 lb. are rare.

Although the roach provides excellent sport for the angler, it is not esteemed for the table.

In the United States the term has been applied to various members of the carp family, and the "golden shiner" minnow has been sometimes called a roach.

ROAD RUNNER (*Geococcyx californianus*), a bird characteristic of the deserts of northwest South America, Mexico and southern U.S.A. It runs with head lowered and tail horizontal,

BY COURTESY OF THE NATIONAL ASSOCIATION OF AUDUBON SOCIETIES

THE ROAD RUNNER (GEOCOCCYX CALIFORNIANUS)

stopping from time to time, when the tail assumes an almost vertical position. It belongs to the cuckoo family (*Cuculidae*).

ROADS AND STREETS. A road system implies central government over a wide area with power to command labour and with technical experts to supervise the work. The first known example of an empire larger than could be served by a single river for transport was that of Sargon, about 2600 B.C., whose rule extended from Babylonia to the Mediterranean. About this time, or even earlier, there must have been lengthy trade routes, since tombs in this area dating back to 3000 B.C. contain the blue gem lapis lazuli, mined in Afghanistan.

Any dates earlier than about 800 B.C. are usually conjectural, but there is a record of that date which claims to detail the main roads of Sargon's empire. In 800 B.C. there were in Assyria traces of a highway system of roads, built on low embankments in the valleys and with the gradients on hills eased with cuttings. Tradition assigns all such engineering feats to the reign of Semiramis, the great Assyrian princess; all that is really known is that these roads were already of great antiquity in 800 B.C. In 1928 workers for the Field Museum of Natural History, Chicago, discovered a wheeled chariot at Kish, which they dated at about 3200 B.C. There were highly skilled stonemasons at that time, so it may well be that streets in towns began to be paved with flat stones about the time that chariots came into general use, since rammed earth is too weak to carry much wheeled traffic. There is a record, dated about 2200 B.C., of Babylonian stonemasons laying two parallel rows of worked stones to take oxcarts whose wheels were about five feet apart, and remains of paved roads have been found in Crete which are believed to date back to 1500 B.C.

By 500 B.C. there were two great roads connecting the Mediterranean with the top of the Persian gulf. One began at Sardis, near Smyrna, and passed through Ankara (Angora) eastward to Nineveh (near Mosul), crossing the Euphrates, the Tigris and the Great and Little Zab to end at Susa. Herodotus, the Greek historian (484–425 B.C.), travelled this road (the ancient royal road) and describes its relay stations, fortified hostels, garrisons and toll gates. The other road ran roughly parallel to it but farther south, to reach the Mediterranean near Alexandretta. There was also a road connecting Babylon with Egypt; this was built by Cyrus after his conquest of Babylon in 539 B.C. and is the "highway" mentioned in the prophetic books of the Bible (e.g., Isaiah xl, 3–5).

By about A.D. 200 there were caravan routes linking the Roman empire with China for the importation of silks and jade and other articles of luxury. One route started at Chungking and passed through Burma and northern India to Delhi and thence to Tehran and Baghdad, or farther north to Samarkand and then west across the Caspian sea and through Tiflis to the Black sea. There are believed to have been at least two more northerly routes through Russia, since articles of jade are found in ancient barrows or tombs (dated 100 B.C. to A.D. 100) in the Crimea and in southern Siberia. These caravan routes were never safe and when navigators were skilled enough to cross the Indian ocean they were largely abandoned.

The growth in power of the Roman empire at this period led to the construction of an elaborate system of paved roads in western Europe. There was first the Via Appia from Rome to Brindisi, from which troops were shipped to Africa and the east. Then in the 2nd century B.C. the Via Egnatia was built from Durazzo, through northern Greece to Salonika, and later the Via Domitia was built across southern France and into Spain. Augustus (63 B.C. to A.D. 14) improved this road and drove it as far as Cadiz and also built two roads across the Alps. The first corresponds to the modern Petit St. Bernard and was suitable for wheeled vehicles; the second was a track for pack animals through Briançon. These two roads converged on Lyons, which was the centre of the Roman road system in France. From Lyons four main roads led respectively to the Baltic and the camps on the Rhine, the channel ports, Bordeaux and the Mediterranean sea. These and other main roads were planned for the imperial courier service and for the rapid movement of troops; they were furnished with posting stations with relays of horses about every 10 mi. and with lodging places (mansiones) about every 25 mi. These roads were the viae publicae regales. Where possible they took the direct line between towns, marshy ground being crossed by using piles and embankments, and cuttings and even tunnels being constructed in hilly country. A network of smaller roads (viae vicinales) linked up the smaller towns and there were also recognized earth tracks (viae terrenae). Drusus, the stepson of Augustus, began the building of a highway across the Alps to provide a direct route from the Adriatic to Augsburg and the Danube; it passed by Trento and over the Brenner and Reschen Scheideck passes. This road was finished by his son, the emperor Claudius, who also constructed a route over the Alps by the Great St. Bernard pass to Augst, near Basle, and from there to the permanent camps on the Rhine.

By A.D. 100 the danger of invasion from the north and east had become obvious; to meet it Trajan constructed a highway from the Rhine to the Black sea, and he and his successors built many bridges. All this was to no avail; the slow collapse of the Roman empire ushered in a thousand years of chaos and petty kingdoms whose resources were far too small for the upkeep of such roads: where dressed stone had been used in their construction they were dug up and the stones used for building. Brigandage and lawlessness prevented people from travelling, and roads and bridges fell into ruin.

Britain was a Roman colony for about 350 years (A.D. 43 to A.D. 410) and the road system was laid out to meet the strategy of the conquest, which was in stages. Thus the Fosse way (q.v.) running from Exeter to Lincoln through Ilchester, Bath, Cirencester and Leicester ran just behind the front line, which separated a lowland area that had been conquered and organized under a civil administration from a highland area still the scene of military operations. This line was fed by a series of roads radiating from the Roman base at London. The last of these front lines was the great wall between Carlisle and Newcastle. The principal road between London and the wall was Ermine street, via Lincoln and York. This stretched to the Tay river, but Scotland was never conquered. After A.D. 121 the wall with its mile-castles and forts was the northern boundary of the Roman occupation. Wales was also a turbulent military area with the occupation troops in forts. This area was served by Watling street, which ran through St. Albans to Towcester and thence to Wroxeter where it joined a road running from the Bristol channel through Kenchester to Chester. Other roads linked Manchester with Chester and with the Fosse way near Leicester.

In building their roads the Romans used any hard materials near at hand. Thus the Via Appia had for the most part a wearing surface of six inches or so of hard lava on a bed of gravel, which replaced the loose topsoil on the site of the road; on the outskirts of Rome it was paved with worked stone blocks. Stane street, from London to Chichester, was composed of a thickness of 12 in. or so of gravel, flints and pebbles, the larger aggregates at the bottom. Such roads were cambered; they had drainage ditches on either side and were about 15 ft. wide. The aggregates were sometimes mixed with lime mortar or with a lime-trass mortar to form concrete, the trass coming from Pozzuoli in Italy. The road was prevented from spreading by raised stone curbs and by wooden pegs driven into the bed at intervals. Where stone was plentiful, as on the Yorkshire moors, the roads were surfaced with stone slabs. Over marshy ground at Hartshill, Watling street consisted of a layer of oak logs laid diagonally and covered with moss and holly twigs. This raft carried 9 to 12 in. of sandstone with a covering layer of 6 in. of a black concrete. The "Iron way" between New Cross and Lewes, discovered in 1929 by air photography, is composed of iron slag and iron under concrete in the neighbourhood of the Roman iron mines in Sussex, but of flint pebbles and rammed chalk near the downs. In flat land liable to flooding the Roman road was carried on an embankment.

After the fall of the Roman empire there was no road or bridgebuilding until the custom grew up of making pilgrimages to Rome and later to the shrine of St. James of Compostella (Santiago in Spain) and to Assisi. The feudal barons levied tolls of passage on the pilgrims and some of them spent a little of this on road repairs and bridgebuilding. About 1,700 bridges were constructed in France alone between the 12th and the 16th centuries, some by bridgebuilding monks, Frères Pontifes, whose patron saint, St. Bénazet, according to tradition, built the bridge at Avignon in 1178–88. Road repairing and bridgebuilding were also works of piety in the middle ages.

With the beginning of the Industrial Revolution the state of the roads in the various countries of Europe was an indication of the strength of the central government. The roads were maintained largely by the forced labour of the householders, cottagers or other occupiers of land, who were required in England to give four days' labour every year and to provide carts and horses where they had them. By a rigorous application of forced labour Jean Baptiste Colbert greatly improved the roads in France in the reign of Louis XIV, but himself earned thereby almost universal detes-

BY COURTESY OF (TOP LEFT) U.S. BUREAU OF PUBLIC ROADS AND CATERPILLAR TRACTOR CO., (TOP RIGHT) PORTLAND CEMENT ASSN., (CENTRE LEFT, CENTRE RIGHT, BOTTOM RIGHT) BUREAU OF PUBLIC ROADS, (BOTTOM LEFT) NEW HAMPSHIRE DEPARTMENT OF PUBLIC WORKS AND HIGHWAYS

ROAD-BUILDING MACHINERY AT WORK ON GRADING AND SURFACING

Top left: Grading with a bulldozer
Top right: Portland cement concrete paving operations
Centre left: Steel reinforcing being laid, to be followed by more concrete

Centre right: Joints being cut and finished by hand from a moving bridge
Bottom left: Distributor applying bitumen through **24-ft.** spray bars
Bottom right: Bituminous paver laying asphalt

tation. In other countries such work was scamped or dodged; at that time the roads in Great Britain were among the worst in Europe. In 1716 a central administration for the upkeep of roads and bridges was formed in France and a training school for young engineers was attached to it in 1747. This was one of the beginnings of the study of the science of road construction.

In Great Britain the Jacobite rebellion had collapsed in 1715, but a nervous parliament commissioned Gen. George Wade (*q.v.*) to build a series of strategic roads in Scotland for the movement of troops. From 1726 to 1737 he built 250 mi. of road and about 40 bridges. Another pioneer in road building was John ("Blind Jack") Metcalf of Knaresborough; between 1767 and 1792 he built about 180 mi. of road which were outstandingly good. This period was the beginning of the Industrial Revolution; the need to carry goods caused many canals to be built, but the large-scale building and repairing of roads came somewhat later. This was put in hand by turnpike trusts, private companies who secured acts of parliament permitting them to close a main road with gates and charge a toll to all users, part of the money being used to repair the road; at one time there were nearly 8,000 tollgates in Great Britain. These trusts employed two great engineers. The first, Thomas Telford, was apprenticed to a stonemason. The base of his roads was formed of large blocks of stone wedged together with stone chips, giving a cambered layer 9 in. thick at the edges and 15 in. thick in the middle. This was covered with 6 in. of small broken stones followed by a wearing surface of 3 in. of gravel. Between 1802 and 1834 he built many roads, the best known being between Shrewsbury and Holyhead and between Carlisle and Glasgow. The other great engineer was John Loudon MacAdam. He made the subsoil of his roads very firm and shaped to the finished camber; side ditches were also dug for draining the road bed. His road then consisted of a layer one foot thick of small broken stones as cubical as possible, able to pass through a ring 2½ in. in diameter but not passing a 2-in. ring. No large stones, loose earth or other binding material was allowed. The wheels of the coaches ground the stones together and the dust so made filled the interstices. Most of the minor roads in Great Britain are built on this principle. They are kept in good condition by periodic surface dressings of tar or bitumen and chippings. Such roads form 58% of the total mileage of roads in Great Britain.

The delays caused by turnpikes and the burden of the tolls on merchants and travellers became so great that a mass rebellion against them broke out in Wales in 1842–43. Gates were smashed and tollhouses levelled to the ground at night by men dressed in women's nightgowns and known as Rebecca's sisters (Genesis xxiv, 60). Juries refused to convict any rioters caught and, at last, in 1864 parliament bowed to public opinion and formed a Turnpike committee to cut down the number of toll roads and bridges. A few still remain. The invention of the internal-combustion engine and the repeal of the "Red Flag" act in 1896 ushered in the modern age. (T. L.)

ADMINISTRATION: GREAT BRITAIN

Before the Highway act, 1835, responsibility for the repair of highways in England and Wales normally rested on the inhabitants of the parish in which the highway was situated. It was performed, under the supervision of the justices in special highways sessions, through the two highway surveyors appointed annually for each parish. There were two important exceptions to parochial responsibility: certain streets in towns might be the responsibility of paving commissioners under local acts; and turnpike roads were repairable by the turnpike trustees under their private acts. The act of 1835 permitted the constitution of two other bodies which might become the authority for parochial highways, namely elective highway boards and highway districts comprising two or more parishes. The act also provided that roads thereafter laid out should not become repairable by the inhabitants unless the procedure for their acceptance was complied with. This is the origin of the "private street."

The Highways and Locomotives (Amendment) act, 1878, created a new class of road called the main road, which included all roads which were no longer turnpikes after 1870 and other roads

so declared by county quarter sessions, and the county was made responsible for one-half of the cost of maintaining these roads. Under the Local Government acts of 1888 and 1894, county councils became responsible for main roads and district councils for other roads. County borough councils became sole highway authorities in their respective areas. During the 20th century the central government assumed responsibility for certain roads which are main arteries of communication, known as trunk roads, and the Local Government act, 1929, reallocated certain functions between local authorities. The highway authorities in 1955 were: (1) the minister of transport and civil aviation for trunk roads; (2) county borough councils for all roads in their areas other than trunk roads; (3) county councils for main roads, all roads in rural districts and classified roads in noncounty boroughs and urban districts; (4) noncounty borough and urban district councils for unclassified roads in their areas. The council of a noncounty borough or urban district having a population exceeding 20,000 was empowered to claim to exercise the functions of repair and maintenance of any county road in its area. The minister could arrange with a highway authority to act as his agent in relation to any trunk road. (E. J. O. G.)

BIBLIOGRAPHY.—R. Syme, *The Story of Britain's Highways* (London, 1952); A. C. Rose, *Public Roads of the Past* (Washington, D.C., 1949); W. Rees Jeffreys, *The King's Highway* (London, 1949); G. T. Salusbury Jones, *Street Life in Medieval England* (Oxford, 1948); E. B. Schieldrop, *The Highway*, vol. 2 of *The Conquest of Space and Time*, Eng. trans. (London, 1939; Philadelphia, 1941); J. W. Gregory, *The Story of the Road*, 2nd ed. rev. and enl. by C. J. Gregory (London, 1938; New York, 1939).

ROADS AND ROAD CONSTRUCTION IN THE UNITED STATES

In the mid-1950s there were approximately 3,000,000 mi. of rural roads and 350,000 mi. of municipal roads in the United States. Approximately 1,780,000 mi. or 60% of the rural mileage was surfaced and 595,000 mi. were graded and drained. Of the rural surfaced mileage about 65% was improved with low-type surfaces such as slag, sand clay, stone and gravel; 20% was improved with intermediate types of bituminous-treated or mixed-bituminous surfaces; and 15% was improved with high-type surfaces of bituminous pavements, portland cement concrete and brick or block surfaces. Highway construction, which was practically stopped during World War II, increased after the war to a rate of completion of about 60,000 mi. per year. Only a small portion of this construction resulted in an increase in highway mileage because most highway work consisted of rebuilding and modernizing existing roads. Roads are divided into three main classes—federal-aid roads, constructed with federal-aid funds and state funds under supervision of the state highway departments and the federal bureau of public roads; state roads, built with state funds under the supervision of the state highway departments; county and local roads constructed largely with county and local funds by county and local authorities.

In the various federal-aid systems there were in the mid-1950s about 665,000 mi. of road that were almost all surfaced, but additions were being made yearly. Many sections, built for a lesser and slower moving traffic, were in need of widening, straightening, resurfacing and other improvements.

The Federal-Aid Highway System.—The federal-aid highway system was designated co-operatively by the secretary of agriculture, acting through the bureau of public roads, and the officials of the several state highway departments in accordance with the Federal Highway act passed by congress, 1921. The system thus designated comprises the main interstate roads and reaches directly nearly every city of 5,000 population or greater, and the roads are so chosen that if a zone ten miles wide were marked off on each side of them, these zones would include the homes of 90% of the population.

For improvement of the federal-aid system special appropriations were made by congress for each fiscal year from 1917, with exception of the years 1934, 1935, 1944, 1945 and 1949. These funds are required generally to be matched by the states in at least equal amount. Formerly limited to $10,000 per mile and to expenditure on roads outside of cities, the federal funds may be expended without arbitrary limitation per mile and upon sections of the federal-aid system within as well as without city limits. The federal funds are appropriated from any funds in the U.S. treasury, there being no special federal tax for road construction. In addition to improvements financed with joint federal and state contributions, other improvements are made on the federal-aid system but with state funds exclusively, and the mileage improved in this way approximates that improved with federal participation.

In addition to its contribution to federal-aid roads, the federal government also assumes as a rightful obligation the duty of building those sections of the major national system which lie in the national forests and parks and other parts of the public domain. In the forest highway system in the mid-1950s were more than 75,000 mi. of road of which more than 18,000 mi. had been improved.

During the period of the depression large additional federal appropriations were made for the purpose of promoting road construction as a measure for the relief of unemployment. These appropriations were expendable upon secondary and upon feeder roads as well as upon routes of the federal-aid system, and represented the first departure by the federal government from the long-established policy of participating exclusively in the improvement of main interstate highways. Special funds were also provided for elimination of highway-railroad grade crossings. These appropriations, unlike the earlier federal grants, were not matched with state funds.

Improvement of secondary or farm-to-market roads, special urban routes and interstate highways were continued as parts of the federal-aid program. The federal government generally pays half the cost of the highway work.

State Highway Systems.—There were approximately 370,000 mi. of roads in the rural primary state highway systems in the mid-1950s. These systems include, in most states, all the roads of the federal-aid system and a number of others of important state significance. In some states the selected roads have been designated by name and description in the laws of the state; in others the designation has been left to the state highway departments.

State highway systems are constructed with state funds only and with state and county or other local funds.

Of the total state highway mileage in 1952, there were 576,918 mi. surfaced. Of the surfaced mileage, 39,131 were soil surfaced; 92,815 were of slag, gravel or stone; 150,095 were bituminous surface treated; 41,612 were of mixed bituminous (nonrigid base); 64,214 were of mixed bituminous (rigid base); 7,143 were of bituminous penetration (nonrigid base); 29,208 were of bituminous penetration (rigid base); 66,627 were of bituminous concrete and sheet asphalt; 84,093 were of portland cement concrete; 1,800 were of vitrified brick; and 180 mi. of asphalt block, wood block, stone block and miscellaneous types. The unsurfaced mileage of 59,470 included 29,974 mi. of primitive or unimproved roads and 29,496 mi. of improved roads which had been drained and had an established grade.

County and Local Roads.—There were approximately 2,320,000 mi. of county and local rural roads in the county and local road systems in the mid-1950s. All roads not included in the federal-aid and state highway systems are classified as county and local rural roads. With the exception of about 125,000 mi. transferred for administration as secondary roads by the state highway departments of six states, all local roads are built by local officials with local funds.

By far the larger part of the unimproved mileage of the country is in the county and local road system. There are hundreds of thousands of miles on which the traffic is so small that improvement is not justified. Of the local road mileage approximately 1,223,881 were surfaced; in large part these surfaces were of such low types as sand clay, topsoil, gravel and water-bound macadam. Great improvements have been made in methods of combining asphalt and tar with materials of a sandy or gravelly nature to make low-cost dustless surfaces. Such surfaces are particularly suited to secondary roads and a considerable mileage has been constructed.

Administration of Federal-Aid Road Construction.—Federal-aid roads are constructed under the immediate supervision of the several state highway departments subject to the approval of the department of commerce, which department delegates the details of administration to the commissioner, bureau of public roads. The bureau has established nine divisions throughout the United States, which groups act in consulting and advisory capacities on state highway programs and systems. Under these nine divisions are grouped all the states, each in charge of a district engineer representing the bureau of public roads.

When a state highway department desires federal aid in financing systems, it submits a complete program to the district engineer in its state. The district engineer examines the road and the plans proposed for its improvement and if he approves the state's proposal, he submits the program to Washington through his division office.

A formal agreement is made between the state and the federal government. Construction then proceeds with full authority of the government under the immediate supervision of the state highway engineers and subject to frequent inspection by federal engineers. The federal government has no official relations with city, county and local officials.

Administration of State Highways.—Control over the state roads is vested in the state highway departments. The highway department determines the order in which the roads of the state system are to be improved, prepares the plans for the improvement, supervises the construction and pays for it with state funds entirely under its own control and, after completion, maintains the roads also with state funds under its own control. The federal-aid system coincides with the more extensive state systems and, therefore, a considerable portion of state highway improvement is done with federal aid.

In four states in the mid-1950s the state highway department had full control over the construction and maintenance of all or most of the local roads. Until about 1930 the work of state highway departments extended only to city limits. Thereafter there was a strong trend toward state improvement of extensions of main routes into and through cities and by the mid-1950s every state highway department made expenditures on such sections of highway.

Early American Roads.—The first American roads were the narrow Indian foot trails which crisscrossed the wilderness. Many of these trails followed the well-worn paths originally formed by the movements of deer, elk or buffalo. The early American explorers and colonists used water routes whenever possible. In many cases, however, the narrow winding Indian trails offered the only course. These trails sought the high ground which offered a dry route generally kept free of leaves and snow by the wind. Among the more important Indian trails were the Old Connecticut path, which travelled from the upper Hudson valley near Albany to Boston; the Iroquois trail, which followed the Mohawk valley and terminated near Niagara falls after crossing the area south of Lake Ontario; Nemacolin's path, which was named after a Delaware chief and led northwest from the upper Potomac to Pittsburgh; and the Warrior's path, through the Cumberland gap and Kentucky to the falls of the Ohio river. In 1775 Daniel Boone widened the Warrior's path into the Wilderness road and as the colonists moved westward they followed the maps prepared by Lewis and Clark, Mackenzie, Frémont, Thompson and others who used the Indian trails as paths to open the west.

Virginia's first highway law was passed in 1632, and in 1639 the general court of Massachusetts passed a comprehensive act which ordered each town to appoint two or three men who would be responsible for building highways "where they may be most convenient." The early roads and streets were relatively local in character and were often seas of mud or clouds of dust, depending on what the previous day's weather had been. The Conestoga wagon was probably the most famous vehicle of this period. This wagon, later models of which became known as the western prairie schooner, was responsible for causing American traffic to move on the right. The early colonists introduced the English custom of keeping to the left and carriages and wagons were driven from the right side. The Conestoga wagon had to be guided from the left side and the drivers, in order to get a clear view of the road ahead, began to keep their vehicles to the right. Because it was much easier to follow the deep ruts formed by these heavy freight carriers, other drivers soon moved to the right, and in 1813 the state of New Jersey ordered all vehicles to keep to the right.

Toward the end of the 18th century the increased demand for better roads caused many routes to be built with private capital as turnpikes. The first United States turnpike utilized existing roads to connect settlements in the Blue Ridge mountains with Alexandria, Va. The first American macadamized road was known as the Lancaster turnpike and was initiated in 1792. It was located between Lancaster, Pa., and Philadelphia.

The federal government entered the highway construction field for the first time when it appropriated funds for the completion of a road to connect the Ohio valley with the eastern seaboard. This road, known as the Cumberland road or National road, was originally a free road. When congressional interest lagged and no additional federal funds were appropriated, the roads reverted to the states and tolls were charged. This marked the end of federal expenditures for highways until the first Federal Aid Road act was passed in 1916. In the early 1880s road-building programs declined with the expansion of the railroads. Interest in highway, road and street construction was reborn with the development of the bicycle in about 1870 and was accelerated by the development and adoption of the automobile early in the 20th century.

STATE PARTICIPATION

Development of State Highway Departments.—In 1891 New Jersey passed a law providing for a certain measure of state participation in road building. With one exception, it was the first instance in which any state had undertaken to participate directly in the construction of roads. The exception was Kentucky, which had a state highway department and a well-defined road policy from 1821 to 1837, and had completed about 340 mi. of roads.

Following New Jersey's example, laws providing for establishment of state highway departments and for granting of state aid were passed in Massachusetts in 1892, in California and Connecticut in 1895 and in Maryland, New York and Vermont in 1898.

Between 1900 and 1915, 38 other states had established highway departments and empowered them with some degree of authority. Several of these previously established departments were materially strengthened and similar agencies were created in the three remaining states when, in 1916, the Federal Aid Road act required the establishment of adequate state agencies as a condition of the granting of federal aid. The establishment of adequate state highway departments by all states was the most important immediate effect of the federal aid law. The first administrative act of the bureau of public roads under the federal aid law was to request all states to submit a five-year program map showing the system of roads upon which the state highway departments would request federal aid. The rapid and consistent improvement of the main highways of the United States is the result of concentration of authority in the state highway departments, the engineering control thus established and especially the correlating influence of the federal government. The several state systems were substantially welded into a national network by the designation in 1921 of the federal-aid highway system.

The purpose of the New Jersey law was to establish a state department, employing skilled engineers, which would act in an advisory capacity to county officials for improvement of road construction. The highway department developed plans and specifications, inspected and supervised the construction, but contracts were let by the counties and the roads were to remain county roads subject to maintenance by the county. As an inducement for counties to seek state aid, funds were appropriated by the state legislature to pay one-third of the cost of road construction.

With minor modifications, the New Jersey principle of state aid was subsequently adopted by many other states. In some states joint participation of the state and county in construction of the most important roads was made mandatory. Other variations differentiated the systems as adopted by the several states.

Organization of State Highway Departments.—In most of the states the highway departments are called state highway commissions, consisting of three to five members, appointed by the governor, with the consent of the senate in some states, for a period of from two to six years. In the majority of states the executive officer of the commission is the state highway engineer, appointed by the commission. In some states the governor serves as chairman of the commission. In some, the highway departments are bureaus or divisions of highways which are part of the department of public works. The executive officer may have the title of state highway engineer, director of highways or commissioner of highways. In other states the chief executive of the highway department is a state highway commissioner, appointed by the governor, except in one state—Michigan—where he is elected by popular vote.

Construction of practically all roads of the federal-aid and state highway systems is by contract let by the state highway departments to the lowest responsible bidder. All work is advertised. Each state highway department makes its own tests of materials either in its own laboratory or in a nearby commercial laboratory. It likewise conducts its own inspections of construction work. Federal-aid highways are subject also to federal inspection.

FINANCE

Administration of Local Roads.—County roads, in general, are built and maintained by county officials with funds raised, as a rule, by taxation of real and personal property within the county. In the mid-1950s such funds were supplemented by approximately $500,000,000 from gasoline taxes and other imposts on highway users and assigned for local road improvement. The more advanced counties employ a county engineer or an engineering organization to supervise the technical details of construction, the county governing body acting only as an administrative body. In some states the lesser roads in each county are administered, constructed and maintained by a host of township and district officials, each of whom may have charge of only a few miles of road.

Sources of Highway Revenue.—For many years the property tax and poll tax were the only sources of road revenues. They were collected and expended by the local governments. Commutation of the poll tax was permitted. As an indirect source of revenue, prison labour, while not a large factor, has been used, mainly to give employment to prisoners.

The first motor vehicle fees levied by the states were nominal and were designed merely to cover cost of registration. The rapid growth in motor vehicle registration increased the demand for improved roads with the resulting issuance of state and county bonds to secure funds to speed the improvements beyond the rate possible with limited current revenues. With improved roads, special benefits resulted to operators of motor vehicles and the motor vehicle taxes have been increased in recognition of this fact.

After 1929 all states levied a gasoline tax as a source of additional revenue. The tax had been first levied in 1919 by four states: Colorado (1 cent per gallon); New Mexico (2 cents); North Dakota ($\frac{1}{4}$ cent); and Oregon (1 cent). In 1920 Kentucky joined the four and levied a gas tax of 1 cent per gallon. In 1921, 15 states levied taxes from $\frac{1}{4}$ cent to 2 cents per gallon. In 1922, four additional states levied taxes. By 1923, 35 states levied a gasoline tax. The tax rate in the mid-1950s varied from 3 cents to 7 cents per gallon in different states. In 1952 the total state motor-fuel tax earnings, inspection fees and similar receipts amounted to $1,958,182,000 and the consumption of taxed gasoline was 40,584,530,000 gal. In that year highway users also paid $1,072,501,000 for registration of vehicles and $63,367,000 as motor carrier taxes. The total contribution of highway users was $3,094,050,000. Of the amount distributed 3% went for collection costs, 71% for state highway purposes, 21% for local roads and 5% went for nonhighway purposes.

The total income to state highway departments in 1952 was $4,651,306,000, and balances on hand brought the total funds available to $6,237,700,000. The current income from state sources was $3,278,756,000, of which motor vehicle users supplied more than 94%. Taxes on property no longer supplied significant amounts to state highway funds. The net amount of funds received from federal sources was $485,273,000. Income from sale of bonds, transfers from local units and from miscellaneous sources brought the total income from other than current state revenue sources to $1,372,550,000.

Expenditures for state-administered highways in 1952 amounted to $2,577,363,000. The states spent $1,757,349,000 for construction of highways and $563,135,000 for maintenance. These expenditures were divided as follows: $1,650,288,000 on primary state highways, $284,391,000 on secondary roads in 17 states, $358,820,000 on urban extensions of state highways and $26,985,000 on other state roads. The outlay for administration, equipment, highway police, safety and bond interest amounted to $256,879,000. In addition $103,203,000 was used for retirement of debt. The total expenditure for all purposes was $2,680,566,000. During the period 1916–52 a total of $9,010,000,000 in federal-aid funds was authorized by the federal government to aid the states in highway improvements through the fiscal year 1957. For the fiscal years 1956 and 1957 the federal-aid authorization was $315,000,000 for primary roads, $210,000,000 for secondary roads, $175,000,000 for urban roads and $175,000,000 for interstate roads.

MODERN ROAD PRACTICE

Types of Road.—Prior to 1904 the major types of surfacing were gravel and macadam, which gave entire satisfaction under the normal traffic of relatively light horse-drawn, steel-tired vehicles, with a bicycle traffic near the cities. The outpouring of motor vehicles from the cities which began about 1904 caused the macadam roads to "ravel," and maintenance under such traffic was impossible. Tars and asphalts were substituted for the weaker binders; first as dust layers and protective surface coatings, then as binders introduced into roads of the macadam type by penetration, and finally as hot admixtures according to the bituminous concrete principle. These types were entirely satisfactory for automobile traffic.

The period from 1904 to 1914 was one of bituminous construction. In 1904 there were in the entire country only 18 mi. of bituminous rural roads, all in Massachusetts and Ohio. By 1914 there were 10,500 mi., a mileage which was nearly three-quarters of the aggregate length of all roads of higher type than macadam. The decline in the surface-treated and penetration types of macadam began when motor trucks in considerable numbers began to appear on the rural highways. They brought a demand for rigid pavements of concrete and brick and bituminous concrete on a concrete base.

Although the first concrete road had been built in 1893, in Bellefontaine, O., there were no more than five miles of that type on rural highways in the entire country in 1909. The first big increase occurred in 1912 when more than 250 mi. of rural highways were paved, to be followed in 1913 with 500 mi., and in 1914 with more than 1,500 mi. At the close of 1914 there were in the entire country 2,348 mi. of concrete roads. Ten years later the mileage had increased to 31,186 and construction was proceeding at the rate of more than 6,000 mi. a year, a rate approached by no other type better than gravel.

The increase of motor trucks on the highways also caused a more extensive use of brick and the bituminous pavements of the mixed type on concrete bases. In 1914 there were approximately 1,600 mi. of brick pavement; in 1924 there were 4,319 mi. In 1914 the bituminous concrete or sheet asphalt mileage on rural highways was negligible; in 1924 there were more than 9,700 mi. of these types.

Main highways thereafter were improved with high-type surfaces such as concrete and bituminous mixtures. For moderate and light traffic water-bound macadam, gravel, sand clay, selected soil mixtures and low-cost bituminous mixtures were used. Practically all surfaces that tend to become dusty in dry weather were made dustless by applying a bituminous or chemical treatment during construction or soon thereafter. Great progress was made in learning how to combine granular materials such as sand and gravel with clay and bituminous binders to form durable surfaces that are moderate in cost.

Because the type of soil below a road surface greatly influences the ability of the pavement to carry traffic loads, the data obtained from extensive soil surveys play an important part in modern highway construction. These surveys include the use of test pits, auger borings, core drillings, resistivity methods and seismic methods to obtain samples or other information for the determination of the engineering characteristics of the materials in the various horizons or layers of the soil profile. Agriculture soil survey maps, certain types of geologic maps and aerial photographs also are utilized to obtain this type of information.

The variations in designs of pavements in use in the early 1950s on some of the several turnpikes in the United States are noteworthy from the standpoint of indicating modern trends. However, some of these designs also reflect the local influence of: (1) availability of materials of construction at very low cost; (2) prevailing soils of a granular texture; (3) low rainfall; and (4) absence of serious frost action. The highest types of highway design can be found in the multilane freeways, expressways and toll roads being built. Rigid pavements, built of portland cement concrete, are commonly eight to ten inches thick and are placed on a granular layer a few inches thick, which in turn is placed on a well compacted earth subgrade. The original sections of the Pennsylvania turnpike were constructed with a nine-inch reinforced concrete slab which was placed directly on the subgrade without a base or subbase.

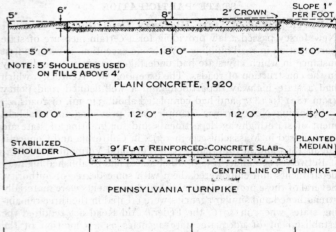

PLAIN CONCRETE, 1920

PENNSYLVANIA TURNPIKE

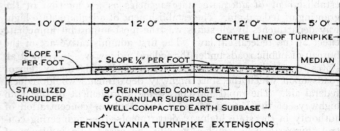

PENNSYLVANIA TURNPIKE EXTENSIONS

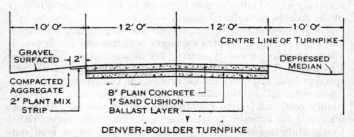

DENVER-BOULDER TURNPIKE

FIG. 1.—EXAMPLES OF BITUMINOUS PAVEMENTS IN THE UNITED STATES

Later extensions to the Pennsylvania turnpike had nine inches of reinforced concrete placed on a six-inch granular subbase while the Denver-Boulder (Colorado) turnpike, built in a dryer climate, employed eight inches of plain concrete. Construction joints and longitudinal joints are generally used but expansion joints are no longer used extensively for rigid pavements for highways. Flexible or bituminous pavements consist of several layers of different materials which serve to spread the concentrated load, imposed by the wheel on the surface, over a large area of the subgrade. The New Jersey turnpike used layers of the following materials: 4.5 in. asphaltic concrete; 7.5 in. macadam base; 6.5 in. gravel subbase; and 18 in. selected subgrade material. In the drier area crossed by the Oklahoma City-Tulsa turnpike, a five-inch layer of asphaltic concrete was placed on seven inches of rock base. Meanwhile in Maine, where frost is an important problem but where gravel is economically available in abundance, the Maine turnpike has a 2-in. asphaltic concrete surface and a 6-in. base course of sand or gravel placed on a 36-in. layer of frost-free, well-compacted granular material.

Until about 1930 road-building efforts were directed largely toward the extension of surfaced mileage. Such a policy was necessary so long as sections of unsurfaced roads remained on principal routes of travel. Most of the gaps thereafter were closed. The early objective was reached, but the amount of needed highway improvements remained greater than ever before. The great increase in volume and speed of traffic made obsolete the highways built years before when conditions were different. Existing highways were modernized by placing better and wider surfaces, eliminating sharp curves and steep grades, eliminating railroad grade crossings and placing warning and danger signs and marks. Safety of travel became an important consideration in this work.

A great many two-lane highways were built 20 or 22 ft. wide but soon there was a trend toward greater width. Many new surfaces are being built to a width of 24 ft. Provision of a third lane was resorted to where two lanes were not sufficient but because of the danger of using the middle lane it was not a satisfactory solution of traffic congestion problems. Where two lanes were not sufficient, four lanes were provided. For great volumes of traffic such as flow on main highways adjacent to large cities, the multiple-lane highway became the only satisfactory solution. Experience with four-lane highways showed that traffic flowing in opposite directions must be separated by a dividing strip of some sort if a heavy accident toll is to be avoided.

The greatest congestion, the worst traffic snarls and a large portion of the highway accidents are found on the main highways in and near cities. Only the provision of major improvements at a large cost will provide a solution.

The need for express routes into and through the centres of big cities resulted in extensive construction of such routes. Because no roads intersect at grade and parallel roads are necessary to serve abutting property, such construction cost (in the mid-1950s) more than $1,000,000 a mile. An additional special feature of these roads is the provision of two or more lanes for traffic travelling in each direction. The lanes for each direction are separated from each other by some type of dividing strip. These roads, commonly called expressways or freeways, were also built to carry heavy volumes of traffic in rural areas.

Development of the interstate system, consisting of about 40,000 mi. of the most used primary federal-aid highways, was one of the most important features of the highway program in the mid-1950s.

Toll Roads.—Although many early American roads were built with private funds as toll roads, they soon gave way to roads constructed and maintained by public funds. The Pennsylvania turnpike, opened in 1940, began a modern era of toll-road construction. As of Oct. 1954 there were 1,335.5 mi. open to traffic in 10 states, 1,256.3 mi. under construction in 11 states, 3,708 mi. authorized in 16 states and 2,640 mi. proposed in 9 states. A total of 28 states were active in various phases of toll-road development. The cost of the mileage in operation was in excess of $1,516,400,000.

CO-OPERATION OF INTERESTS

The United States Highway System.—Through the co-operation of all states and the federal government, effected initially through the agency of the Joint Board on Interstate Highways and continued by the American Association of State Highway Officials, a system of main transcontinental highways, known as the U.S. highway system, was designated in 1926. This system, which is a

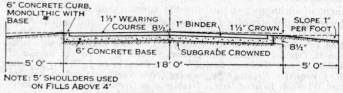
NOTE: 5' SHOULDERS USED ON FILLS ABOVE 4'
BITUMINOUS CONCRETE, 1920

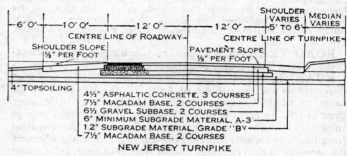
NEW JERSEY TURNPIKE

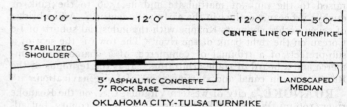
OKLAHOMA CITY-TULSA TURNPIKE

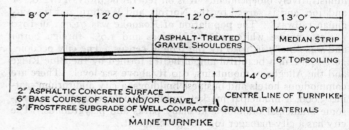
MAINE TURNPIKE

FIG. 2.—CONCRETE PAVEMENTS IN THE UNITED STATES

portion of the federal-aid system, includes approximately 186,000 mi., composing 26 through routes, many of which extend from one border of the country to the other. The various routes are designated by the distinctive numbers which are displayed upon them, on standard shield-shaped markers. The standard signs adopted are of two general classes. One group, the danger and caution signs, are of four different shapes representing as many degrees of danger. These have a red or yellow background with black letters and symbols. The other group includes the standard route marker in the form of a U.S. shield and directional and informational signs with white backgrounds and black letters.

Highway Research.—As a result of the co-operation of the bureau of public roads with state highway departments and universities in scientific research looking to the development of types of construction and methods of administration and finance adequate to meet the demands of the fast-growing traffic, there is being built up a new science of highway engineering.

The investigations conducted include studies of the characteristics of materials; determination of the forces applied to road surfaces by standing and moving vehicles; of stresses developed in the structure of roads and bridges by live loads and by temperature and other natural causes; analyses of subgrade soils and tests of methods designed for their improvement; studies of the flow of water through drainage structures; of the runoff from drainage areas; of the effect of moisture and frost on soils; analysis of human behavior as related to driver and pedestrian action; development of methods for predicting future traffic volumes; improvement of techniques to measure the adequacy of service provided by roads; and others of fundamental importance and value.

BIBLIOGRAPHY.—T. R. Agg and J. E. Brindley, *Highway Administration and Finance* (New York, 1927); Laurence I. Hewes and Clarkson H. Oglesby, *Highway Engineering* (New York, 1954); Bureau of Public Roads, *Highway Statistics, 1952* (1953); L. J. Ritter, Jr., and R. J. Paquette, *Highway Engineering* (New York, 1951); Jean Labatut and Wheaton J. Lane (eds.), *Highways in Our National Life* (Princeton, N.J., London, 1950); Public Roads Administration, *Highway Practice in the United States of America* (1949); S. Johannesson, *Highway Economics* (New York, London, 1931); J. E. Johnsen (comp.), *Financing of State Highways* (New York, 1929); 76th Congress, 1st Session, "Toll Roads and Free Roads," *House Document No. 272*; Harry Tucker and Marc C. Leager, *Highway Economics* (Scranton, Pa., 1942). (K. B. Ws.; J. E. B.)

ROAD TRANSPORT: *see* MOTOR TRANSPORT, COMMERCIAL; MOTOR TRANSPORT, MILITARY.

ROANNE, a town of east-central France, capital of an arrondissement in the department of Loire, on the left bank of the Loire, 54 mi. N.W. of Lyons on the P.L.M. railway to Moulins. Pop. (1946) 44,518. Roanne (*Rodomna* or *Roidomna*) was an ancient city of the Segusiani and a station on the Roman road from Lyons to the sea. In 1447 the lordship of Roannais became the property of the celebrated banker, Jacques Coeur, from whom it passed to the family of Gouffier. In their favour the title was raised to the rank of marquisate and in 1566 to the rank of duchy; it became extinct in the early 18th century. A fine bridge of seven arches connects Roanne with the industrial suburb of Le Côteau on the right bank of the river. The town is the seat of a sub-prefect, of a tribunal of commerce, of a chamber of commerce and a board of trade-arbitrators. It is the terminus of the Roanne-Digoin canal and starting-point of Loire navigation.

ROANOKE, a city of western Virginia, U.S., on the Roanoke river, 166 mi. W.S.W. of Richmond; in Roanoke county, but administratively independent. It is on federal highways 11, 220, 221 and 460, and is served by the Norfolk and Western and the Virginian railways. The population of Roanoke was 91,921 in 1950 (80.5% native white, 18.5% Negroes and 1.0% foreign born) and was 69,287 in 1940 by the federal census. The city occupies 26.7 sq.mi. in a beautiful amphitheatre formed by the Blue Ridge and the Allegheny mountains, 940 ft. above sea level. There are commodious hotels and business buildings, a city auditorium seating 5,000, a municipal market, public schools, churches, a handsome municipal building and many parks and playgrounds. The city has a city-manager form of government.

A few miles west is Salem, the county seat and home of Roanoke college (1842); and 6 mi. north is Hollins college for women (1842). Roanoke is an intersection point for railroads and highways, as it was formerly for Indian trails. It is headquarters of the Norfolk and Western railway.

A village called Big Lick (from the salt marshes to which the cattle and wild game came) was founded there about 1852. In 1880 it had a population of 669. In 1882, when the Shenandoah Valley railroad (now part of the Norfolk and Western) made this its southern terminus and moved its general offices there, the name was changed to Roanoke; and in 1884, with a population of 5,000, it was chartered as a city.

ROANOKE, a river of the south Atlantic slope, U.S. With the Staunton, which rises in the Appalachian valley in southwestern Virginia, it constitutes one river, and, flowing in a general southeasterly direction, crosses the boundary between Virginia and North Carolina just above the Fall line and discharges into Albemarle sound. It is 380 mi. long, with a drainage area of 9,237 sq. miles. In 1829 the Weldon canal, 12 mi. long, was opened to afford a passage around the falls, but was abandoned in 1850.

ROARING FORTIES, the belt between latitudes 40° and 50° south latitude characterized by boisterous westerly winds. In this belt the barometric gradients, both in summer and in winter, are steep, and the "planetary circulation" is but little interrupted by land; the "brave west winds" are very strong.

ROBBEN ISLAND is situated 7 mi. N.W. of Cape Town at the entrance of Table bay, and in the days of sailing ships it gave excellent anchorage during the southeasters which often drove ships out of the bay.

The island has an area of about 8 sq.mi. It was uninhabited when in 1525 it was discovered by the Portuguese. In 1615 eight English criminals were transported there. The island was used in the 17th and 18th centuries as a jail, as well as for quarrying the blue stone which was used to roof some of the houses of Cape Town, while the seals which abounded on the shore were freely hunted and gave the island its name (*robben*, Dutch for "seal"). In the 19th century it was the island jail of a succession of native chiefs. A leper colony was also established there but it was abandoned in 1928.

After World War II Robben Island was the pivot of the defense scheme of the Cape peninsula. (W. A. ML.)

ROBBER FLY. The name given to predaceous flies of the family Asilidae of the order Diptera (*q.v.*); they are also called assassin flies. They are predaceous in both the adult and larval stages. The various groups are found in a particular type of habitat. Some occur in woods, on tree trunks and foliage, some on grass and low plants or on the tips of dead twigs, some on sand or gravel and on beaches. The head is hollowed above between the eyes, which have an area of enlarged facets that gives them keen sight. A few kinds, particularly species of *Promachus*, may be serious pests of apiaries; they feed on many kinds of bees, as well as upon almost all kinds of flying insects. Their legs are long and adapted for capturing prey in flight and holding it while it is eaten. They inject a fluid into their victims which breaks down the muscular tissues so that only the skeleton remains. There are more than 4,000 species distributed through the world, most of them rather dull coloured, but some are metallic. They vary in length from ¼ in. to 1½ in. (C. H. CN.)

ROBBER SYNOD, the name given to an irregular ecclesiastical council held at Ephesus in A.D. 449. *See* EPHESUS, COUNCILS OF.

ROBBERY, a felony in English law, is the unlawful and forcible taking of goods or money from the person of another by violence or threatened violence. Robbery is larceny (*q.v.*) with violence. It is a specific offence under the Larceny Act, 1916, which provides by s. 23 that every person who (*a*) being armed with any offensive weapon or instrument, or being together with one other person or more, robs, or assaults with intent to rob, any person; (*b*) robs any person and, at the time of or immediately before or immediately after such robbery, uses any personal violence to any person; shall be guilty of felony and on conviction thereof liable to penal servitude for life, and, in addition, if a male, to be once privately whipped. Also every person who robs any person shall be guilty of felony and on conviction thereof liable to penal servitude for any term not exceeding 14 years, and every person who assaults any person with intent to rob shall be guilty of felony and on conviction thereof liable to penal servitude for any term not exceeding five years. To constitute the offense there must be violence or the placing of the prosecutor in bodily fear; the goods or money must be taken from the person or in the presence of the prosecutor; and in fact a larceny must be proved under the before mentioned circumstances. The elements of the offense are essentially the same under U.S. law.

ROBERT I (*c.* 865–923), king of France, or king of the Franks, was the younger son of Robert the Strong, count of Anjou, and the brother of Odo, or Eudes, who became king of the western Franks in 888. He did not claim the crown of France when his brother died in 898; but recognizing the supremacy of the Carolingian king, Charles III, the Simple, he continued to defend northern France from the attacks of the Normans as "duke of the Franks." About 921 Robert, supported by many of the clergy and by some of the most powerful of the Frankish nobles, took up arms, drove Charles into Lorraine, and was himself crowned king of the Franks at Reims on June 29, 922. Collecting an army, Charles marched against the usurper, and on June 15, 923, in a stubborn and sanguinary battle near Soissons, Robert was killed, according to one tradition, in single combat with his rival.

Robert left a son, Hugh the Great, duke of the Franks, and his grandson was Hugh Capet, king of France.

See F. Lot, *Les Derniers Carolingiens* (1891); and E. Lavisse, *Histoire de France*, tome ii. (1903).

ROBERT II. (*c.* 970–1031), king of France, was a son of Hugh Capet, and was born at Orleans. He was educated at Reims under Gerbert, afterwards Pope Silvester II. As the ideal of mediaeval Christianity he won his surname of "Pious" by his humility and charity, but he also possessed some of the qualities of a soldier and a statesman. His father associated him with himself in the government of France, and he was crowned in December 987, becoming sole king on Hugh's death in October 996. In 988 he had married Rosala, or Susanna, widow of Arnold II., count of Flanders. He repudiated her in 989, fixing his affections upon Bertha, daughter of Conrad the Peaceful, king of Burgundy, or Arles, and wife of Eudes I., count of Blois; and although the pair were related, and the king had been godfather to one of Bertha's children, they were married in 996, a year after the death of Eudes. Pope Gregory V. excommunicated the king, and a council at Rome imposed a seven years' penance upon him. For five years the king braved all anathemas, but about 1002 he gave up Bertha and married Constance, daughter of a certain Count William. Still attached to Bertha, Robert took this lady with him to Rome in 1010, but the pope refused to recognize their marriage, and the king was forced to return to Constance. By this wife Robert had four sons, and in 1017, the eldest of these, Hugh, (1007–1025), was crowned as his father's colleague and successor. After Hugh's death Robert's concluding days were troubled by a rising on the part of his younger sons, and after a short war, in which he was worsted, the king died at Melun on July 20, 1031.

His life was written by his chaplain, Helgaud, and this panegyric, *Epitoma vitae Roberti regis*, is published by J. P. Migne in the *Patrologia Latina*, tome cxli. (Paris, 1844). See also C. Pfister, *Études sur le règne de Robert le Pieux* (1885); and E. Lavisse, *Histoire de France*, tome ii. (1901).

ROBERT (1275–1343), king of Naples, was the son of Charles II., duke of Anjou and king of Naples. On the death of Charles in 1309 Robert succeeded to the throne, although his nephew Caroberto (Carlo Roberto), son of his elder brother Charles Martel, who had died before his father, had a prior claim. He was crowned by Pope Clement V. at Avignon, and on the descent into Italy of the emperor Henry VII. was appointed papal vicar in Romagna to resist the imperialists; thenceforth he became the recognized leader of the Guelphs or papal faction in Italy and took part in all the wars against the Ghibellines. On various occasions he obtained for himself or his sons the suzerainty over Rome, Florence and other cities, and was regarded as the most powerful Italian prince of his day. Pope John XXII. created him papal vicar in Italy against the emperor Louis the Bavarian. In 1320 Robert summoned his kinsman Philip V. of France to Italy, and he waged war against Sicily once more from 1325 to 1341, but failed to drive out the Aragonese. He died in 1343, just as he was about to lead another expedition to the island. Robert was a man of learning, devoted to literature, and a generous patron of literary men: he befriended Petrarch. Dante described Robert as a *re da sermone* (word king).

See G. Villani, *Cronache*; M. Murena, *Vita di Roberto d'Angiò, re di Napoli* (Naples, 1770); and *Archivio storico Siciliano* (1884, viii. 511 seq.)

ROBERT I., "THE BRUCE" (1274–1329), king of Scotland, the son of Robert de Bruce VII., earl of Carrick by right of his wife Marjorie, was a direct descendant of a Norman baron who accompanied William I. to England. He was probably born at Turnberry, Ayrshire, on July 11, 1274, and is said to have spent his youth at the court of Edward I., where he must have watched the progress of the suit for the crown of Scotland. After the death of Margaret, the "maid of Norway," Bruce's grandfather claimed the crown by right of his descent from David I.; but John de Balliol, grandson of Margaret, being preferred by the commissioners of Edward I., he resigned his estates to Bruce's father, who assumed the title of Lord of Annandale (1295). In 1292, Bruce became earl of Carrick, by which title he is often known. Some four years later Bruce and his father swore fealty to Edward I., but when Sir William Wallace raised his standard, Bruce followed the popular leader and harried the forces of John de Warenne, Edward's general. In July, 1297, however, he was forced to sign the capitulation of Irvine, whereby the Scottish lords were pardoned in return for their allegiance.

Bruce thus took no part in the momentary triumph and final defeat of Wallace, who continued the struggle almost unaided. Soon after Bruce again appears to have sided with his countrymen, but he was not yet regarded as an open enemy of the English, for his estates were left intact, and in 1299 he was appointed co-regent of Scotland, together with William Lamberton, bishop of St. Andrews, and John Comyn the younger. For the next four years he remained passive, and in 1304 even supported Edward I. in the capture of Stirling, but secretly he entered into a bond with Lamberton which bound him to the patriotic cause.

The second period of his life, which was occupied by the contest for the kingdom, now began. After the execution of Wallace in 1305, Edward sought to conciliate the Scottish nobles by granting a liberal constitution to Scotland. Bruce is reputed to have been one of the advisers, but his fidelity was already suspected and in 1306 he returned to Scotland secretly. In the same year he murdered his old enemy Comyn, and was thenceforward definitely committed to the Scottish cause. Collecting his adherents, Bruce marched to Scone where he was crowned on March 27, 1306, and a few days later was placed on the throne according to an ancient Celtic ceremony, by the Macduffs, earls of Fife. He then set out to win his kingdom, but after being defeated at Methven and at Dalry in Strathfillan, he fled almost alone to the island of Rathlin. Proclaimed an outlaw, excommunicated by the pope, his wife and daughter in the hands of the English, and his brother executed, Bruce's cause seemed hopeless, but on July 7, 1307, Edward I. died, and Bruce was opposed only by his incompetent son Edward II. In the winter of 1307 and in 1308, hurrying to Aberdeenshire, he harried the lands of the earl of Buchan, whom he defeated near Inverurie on May 22, 1308, while his brother Edward reduced Galloway. He then crossed to Argyllshire, took the pass of Brander (1309), captured Dunstaffnage, and in March held his first parliament at St. Andrews.

A truce having been effected by Pope Clement V. in 1309, Bruce was recognized as king by the clergy of Scotland in Feb. 1310, in spite of his excommunication; and with this backing he set out to reduce the strongholds still held by the English. Linlithgow fell towards the end of 1310, Dumbarton in Oct. 1311, Perth in Jan. 1312, two raids into the north of England were also successful in March 1313, Roxburgh and Edinburgh were captured and in May the Isle of Man was subdued. By the end of 1313, Stirling, Bothwell and Berwick alone remained English and these Edward II. made a determined effort to save. He reached Falkirk on June 22, 1314, and two days later the battle of Bannockburn was fought, in which the defeat of the English determined the independence of Scotland and confirmed the title of Bruce. On April 26, 1315, at the parliament of Ayr, the succession was unanimously settled on Bruce and his heirs.

The last part of Bruce's life, from 1315 to 1329, began with the rising of the whole Celtic race against the English. Robert Bruce declined the offer of the Irish crown, but in 1315, Edward Bruce crossed to Ireland at the invitation of the natives, and in 1317 he was joined by Robert, who defeated the English at Slane in Louth. But although they enjoyed a temporary success, Edward was finally killed at Dundalk in Oct. 1318, having previously been proclaimed king of Ireland. In 1317, Robert Bruce had been obliged to return to protect his own borders, and in 1318 he laid siege to Berwick. Refusing all offers of mediation on the part of the pope, unless his title were recognized, Bruce continued his struggle and after the capitulation of Berwick, laid waste to the English border. In Dec. 1318, he held a parliament at Scone, where the succession was settled, and legislation for the defence and administration of the kingdom was initiated.

The king's position was now so strong that foreign countries began to recognize him, and in 1323 his title was confirmed by the pope. Hostilities against England continued, however, and on May 30, 1323, Edward was forced to make a truce of 13 years. On the accession of Edward III, 1327, the treaty of York was signed, whereby "Scotland according to its ancient bounds in the days of Alexander III, should remain to Robert, king of Scots, and his heirs free and divided from England, without any subjection, servitude, claim or demand whatsoever." This was ratified by the marriage of Edward's sister, Joanna, to David, Bruce's infant son (July 12, 1328). The chief author of Scottish independence barely survived his work. In 1327 he conducted an expedition into Ireland, but on his return, he spent his remaining years at Cardross, on the Clyde, where he died from leprosy on June 7, 1329. His body was buried at Dunfermline, his heart at Melrose.

BIBLIOGRAPHY.—The chief contemporary authorities for the life of Bruce are coloured to some extent by the nationality of the writers. On the Scottish side, *The Brus,* a poem by John Barbour, ed. by W. W. Skeat (Edinburgh, 1894), and the *Chronica gentis Scotorum* of John of Fordun, ed. by W. F. Skene (Edinburgh, 1871–72), are perhaps the most valuable. The *Chronicon de Lanercost,* ed. by J. Stevenson (Edinburgh, 1839), is also important. The English chronicles which may be consulted with advantage are those of Walter of Hemingford, ed. by H. C. Hamilton (1848–49) and of Peter Langtoft, ed. by T. Wright (1866–68), and the *Scalacronica* of Thomas Gray, ed. by J. Stevenson (Edinburgh, 1836). For the documents of the time reference should be made to the *Calendar of Documents relating to Scotland,* ed. by J. Bain (Edinburgh, 1881–88), *Documents and Records Illustrating the History of Scotland,* vol. i., ed. by F. Palgrave (1837); the *Rotuli Scotiae* (1814–19), and the *Foedera* of T. Rymer, vol. i. (1704). *See* also Sir H. Maxwell, *Robert the Bruce* (1897); A. M. Mackenzie, *Robert Bruce, King of Scots* (London, 1934).

ROBERT II. (1316–1390), called "the Steward," king of Scotland, a son of Walter, the steward of Scotland (d. 1326), and Marjorie (d. 1316), daughter of King Robert the Bruce, was born on March 2, 1316. In 1318 the Scottish parliament decreed that if King Robert died without sons the crown should pass to his grandson; but the birth of a son, afterwards King David II., to Bruce in 1324 postponed the accession of Robert for nearly 42 years. Soon after the infant David became king in 1329, the Steward began to take a prominent part in the affairs of Scotland. He was one of the leaders of the Scottish army at the battle of Halidon Hill in July 1333; and together with John Randolph, 3rd earl of Moray (d. 1346), was chosen co-regent of Scotland, while David sought safety in France. The colleagues soon quarrelled; Randolph fell into the hands of the English, and Robert became sole regent until the return of David in 1341. The Steward escaped from the battle of Neville's Cross in 1346, and was again regent while the king was a captive in England.

Soon after this event some friction arose between Robert and his royal uncle. Accused, probably without truth, of desertion at Neville's Cross, the Steward as heir-apparent was chagrined by David's recognition of Edward III. as his successor.

In 1363 he rose in rebellion, and after having made his submission was seized and imprisoned together with his three sons, being only released a short time before David's death in February 1371. By the terms of the decree of 1318 Robert now succeeded to the throne, and was crowned at Scone in March 1371. His reign was unimportant; for relations with England and France *see* SCOTLAND: *History.* The king died at Dundonald on May 13, 1390, and was buried at Scone.

See Andrew of Wyntoun, *The Orygynale Cronykil of Scotland,* edited by D. Laing (Edinburgh, 1872–79); John of Fordun, *Scotichronicon,* continued by Walter Bower, ed. T. Hearne (Oxford, 1722); John Major, *Historia maioris Britanniae* translated by A. Constable (Edinburgh, 1892); and P. F. Tytler, *History of Scotland* (Edinburgh, 1841–43).

ROBERT III. (c. 1340–1406), king of Scotland, was the eldest son of King Robert II. by his mistress, Elizabeth Mure, and was legitimatized when his parents were married about 1349. In 1368 he was created earl of Carrick, and he took some part in the government of the kingdom until about 1387, when he was disabled by the kick of a horse. It was probably in consequence of this accident that his brother Robert, earl of Fife, and not the crown prince himself, was made guardian of the kingdom in 1389; but the latter succeeded to the throne on his father's death in May 1390. At this time he changed his baptismal name of John, which was unpopular owing to its connection with John de Baliol,

for that of Robert, being crowned at Scone in August 1390 as King Robert III. The new king was only the nominal ruler of Scotland, the real power being in the hands of his brother, the earl of Fife. In 1399, his elder son, David, duke of Rothesay, was appointed lieutenant of the kingdom; but this event was followed by an English invasion of Scotland, by serious differences between Rothesay and his uncle, Robert, now duke of Albany, and finally in March 1402 by Rothesay's mysterious death at Falkland. Early in 1406 the king's only surviving son, afterwards King James I., was captured by the English; and on April 4, 1406, Robert died, probably at Rothesay, and was buried at Paisley.

ROBERT, the name of two dukes of Normandy.

ROBERT I. (d. 1035), called Robert the Devil, was the younger son of Richard II., duke of Normandy (d. 1026), and father of William the Conqueror. In 1028 he succeeded his brother, Richard III., whom he was accused of poisoning, as duke of Normandy. Robert sheltered the exiled English princes, Edward, afterwards King Edward the Confessor, and his brother Alfred, and fitted out a fleet for the purpose of restoring them to their inheritance, but this was scattered by a storm. When returning from a pilgrimage to Jerusalem, he died at Nicaea on July 22, 1035. Robert is the subject of several poems and romances. (*See* ROBERT THE DEVIL.)

ROBERT II. (c. 1054–1134), called Robert Curthose, was the eldest son of William the Conquerer. Although recognized in boyhood as his father's successor in Normandy, he twice revolted against his father. (*See* WILLIAM I.) When the Conqueror died in September 1087 Robert became duke of Normandy, but not king of England; although he received offers of help, he took no serious steps to displace his younger brother, King William II. In Normandy his rule was weak and irresolute. He lost the county of Maine, which for some years had been united with Normandy, and he was soon at variance with his brothers, the younger of whom, Henry, he seized and put into prison. In 1089 his duchy was invaded by William II., who soon made peace with Robert, the two agreeing to dispossess their brother Henry of his lands in Normandy. This peace lasted until 1094, when occasions of difference again arose and another struggle began, Robert being aided by King Philip I. of France.

This warfare ended in 1096, when Robert set out on the first crusade, having raised money for this purpose by pledging his duchy to William for 10,000 marks. He returned to Normandy in September 1100.

William Rufus died while Robert was on his homeward way, and in Italy the Norman duke was greeted as king of England; but when he reached Normandy he learned that the English throne was already in the possession of Henry I. In July 1101 he crossed over to England, intending to contest his brother's title, but Henry met him near Alton, in Hampshire, and an amicable arrangement was made between them. But there was no lasting peace. In 1106 the English king crossed over to Normandy, and at the battle of Tinchebrai (Sept. 28, 1106), Henry took his brother prisoner and carried him to England. For twenty-eight years Robert was a captive, first in the Tower of London, and later in the castles of Devizes and Cardiff. He died probably at Cardiff on Feb. 10, 1134.

The chief sources for the life of Robert II. are Ordericus Vitalis, William of Malmesbury and other chroniclers of the time. *See* E. A. Freeman, *History of the Norman Conquest* (1870–76), and *The Reign of Rufus* (1882).

ROBERT, HUBERT (1733–1808), French artist, born at Paris on May 22, 1733, deserves to be remembered not so much for his skill as a painter as for the liveliness and point with which he treated his subjects. His work has a scenic character, and it was this quality which led Voltaire to entrust him with the decorations of his theatre at Ferney. Robert died of apoplexy on April 15, 1808.

See C. Blanc, *Hist. des peintres;* Villot, *Notice des tableaux du Louvre;* Julius Meyer, *Gesch. mod. fr. Malerei.*

ROBERT GUISCARD (*i.e.,* "the resourceful") (c. 1015–1085), the most remarkable of the Norman adventurers who conquered southern Italy. Those who first came in 1016 to seek their fortune in Apulia and Calabria seem to have had no political ambitions. They arrived in small groups and lacked organization and experienced leadership. They were prepared to live as mercenaries in the service of Greeks or of Lombards. It was not until 1030 that Sergius of Naples, by installing the leader Rainulf in the fortress of Aversa, gave them their first *pied-à-terre* and that they began an organized conquest of the land. Foremost in this work were the sons of Tancred de Hauteville, whose lands near Coutances were too modest to support his large family. William "Iron Arm" and Drogo were successively leaders of those Normans who from 1040 were extending their possessions in Apulia and Calabria, and among their brothers who joined them were Humphrey in 1044 and Robert Guiscard in 1046. At first, Robert was not made welcome and was forced, as were many of his compatriots, to live like a brigand, terrorizing and laying waste the countryside. Because of the distress so caused, Leo IX attempted to subdue the Normans by force; but their principal leaders, among them Robert, combined in 1053 to defeat the pope at Civitate. Thereafter Robert prospered. In 1057 he succeeded Humphrey as recognized leader of the Normans in Apulia. In 1059 Pope Nicholas II, seeking independence from the German king Henry IV and the Roman nobility, turned to the Normans as allies. On Aug. 23, 1059, Robert became a vassal of the pope, promising tribute and help when needed. In return he became "by grace of God and St. Peter duke of Calabria and Apulia and future lord of Sicily." It was a master stroke. Robert's dominion was legitimized by solemn papal investiture.

In the next 20 years Guiscard made an amazing series of conquests at the expense of Moslems, Greeks and Lombards. Invading Sicily with his brother Roger, he captured Messina (1061) and Palermo (1072). Bari was reduced (April 1071) and the Greeks were finally ousted from southern Italy. The territory of Salerno was already Robert's; in Dec. 1076 he took the city, expelling its Lombard prince Gisulf, whose sister Sicelgaeta he had married.

The Norman attacks on Benevento, a papal fief, alarmed Gregory VII but, pressed by Henry IV, he turned again to the Normans and at Ceprano (June 1080) reinvested Robert, securing him also in the southern Abruzzi, but reserving Salerno. Guiscard's last enterprise was his attack on the eastern empire, a rallying ground for his rebel vassals. He contemplated seizing the imperial throne and took up the cause of Michael VII, who had been deposed in 1078 and to whose son his daughter had been betrothed. He sailed against the empire in May 1081 and had occupied Corfu and Durazzo by Feb. 1082. He was, however, recalled to the aid of Gregory VII, who was besieged in San Angelo by Henry IV (June 1083). Marching north, he entered Rome and forced Henry to retire, but an *émeute* of the citizens led to a three days' sack of the city (May 1084), after which Guiscard escorted the pope to Salerno. His son Bohemund (*q.v.*), for a time master of Thessaly, had now lost the Greek conquests. Robert, returning to restore them, occupied Corfu and Cephalonia, but died of fever in the latter on July 17, 1085.

Guiscard was succeeded by Roger "Borsa," his son by Sicelgaeta; Bohemund, his son by an earlier Norman wife, Alberada, being set aside. At his death Robert was duke of Apulia and Calabria, prince of Salerno and suzerain of Sicily.

Robert's successes had been due not only to his great qualities but to the entente with the papal see. He created and enforced a strong ducal power which, however, was met by many baronial revolts, one being in 1078, when he demanded from the Apulian vassals an "aid" on the betrothal of his daughter. In conquering such wide territories he had little time to organize them internally. In the history of the Norman kingdom of Italy, Guiscard remains essentially the hero and founder, as his nephew Roger II is the statesman and organizer.

BIBLIOGRAPHY.—The best modern authorities are F. Chalandon, *Histoire de la domination normande en Italie et en Sicile* (Paris, 1907) and C. H. Haskins, *The Normans in European History* (1915). Contemporary authors were: Amatus, *Ystoire de li Normant,* ed. V. de Bartholomaeis (Rome, 1935); Geoffrey Malaterra, ed. L. A. Muratori in *Rerum Italicarum Scriptores,* vol. 5 (Milan, 1723–51); William of Apulia, *Gesta Roberti Wiscardi,* ed. R. Wilmans in *Mon. Ger. Hist.,* vol. 9 (Hanover, 1851). (E. Cu.; R. C. Sma.)

ROBERT OF AUXERRE

ROBERT OF AUXERRE (*c.* 1156–1212), French chronicler, was an inmate of the monastery of St. Marien at Auxerre. At the request of Milo de Trainel (1155–1202), abbot of this house, he wrote a *Chronicon,* or universal history, which covers the period between the creation of the world and 1211. Robert is an original authority for the period from 1181 to 1211. Two continuators took the work down to 1228 and it was extensively used by later chroniclers. The original manuscript is now at Auxerre.

See A. Molinier, *Les Sources de l'histoire de France,* tomes iii. and iv. (1903–04).

ROBERT OF COURTENAY

ROBERT OF COURTENAY (d. 1228), emperor of Rumania, or Constantinople, was a younger son of the emperor Peter of Courtenay, and was descended from the French king, Louis VI., while his mother, Yolande, was a sister of Baldwin and Henry of Flanders, the first and second emperors of Constantinople. When it became known in France that Peter of Courtenay was dead, his eldest son, Philip, renounced the succession in favour of his brother Robert, who set out to take possession of his distracted inheritance. Crowned emperor on March 25, 1221, Robert appealed for help to the pope and to the king of France; but meanwhile his lands were falling into the hands of the Greeks. Some little aid was sent from western Europe, but soon Robert was compelled to make peace with his chief foe, John Ducas Vatatzes, emperor of Nicaea, who was confirmed in all his conquests. Robert repudiated his affianced bride Eudoxia, daughter of Theodore Lascaris I., and married a French lady, already the fiancée of a Burgundian, by whom Robert was driven from Constantinople, and early in 1228 he died in Achaia.

See Gibbon, *Decline and Fall of the Roman Empire,* ed. Bury (1912), vol. 6, p. 449.

ROBERT OF GLOUCESTER

ROBERT OF GLOUCESTER, English chronicler, is known only through his connection with the work which bears his name. This is a vernacular history of England, from the days of the legendary Brut to the year 1270, and is written in rhymed couplets. The lines are of 14 syllables, with a break after the eighth syllable. He probably wrote about the year 1300. The earlier part of his chronicle (up to 1135) may be from another hand, since it occurs in some manuscripts in a shorter form, and with an exceedingly brief continuation by an anonymous versifier. The authorities employed for the earlier part were Geoffrey of Monmouth, Henry of Huntingdon, William of Malmesbury, the English chronicles, and some minor sources; Robert, in making his recension of it, also used the *Brut* of Layamon. From 1135 to 1256 Robert is still a compiler, although references to oral tradition become more frequent as he approaches his own time. From 1256 to 1270 he has the value of a contemporary authority. But he is more important to the philologist than to the historian. His chronicle is one of the last works written in Old English.

Robert's chronicle was first edited by T. Hearne (2 vols., Oxford, 1724); but this text is now superseded by that of W. Aldis Wright (2 vols., Rolls Series, 1887). Minor works attributed to the author are: a *Life of St. Alban* in verse (ms. Ashmole 43); a *Life of St. Patrick,* also in verse (ms. Tanner 17); a *Life of St. Bridget* (ms. C.C.C. Cambridge, 145); and a *Life of St. Alphege* (ms. Cott., Julius D. ix.). A *Martyrdom of St. Thomas Becket* and a *Life of St. Brendan,* both attributed to Robert, were printed by the Percy Society in 1845.

See T. D. Hardy's *Descriptive Catalogue of mss.* i. 25, 68, iii. 181–9, 623; K. Brossman, *Über die Quellen der Chronik des R. von Gloucester* (Striegau, 1887); W. Ellmer in *Anglia* (1888), x. 1–37, 291–322; H. Strohmeyer, *Der Stil der Reimchronik R. von Gloucester* (1891).

ROBERT OF JUMIÈGES

ROBERT OF JUMIÈGES (d. *c.* 1070), archbishop of Canterbury, was a Norman who became prior of St. Ouen at Rouen and then abbot of Jumièges. A close friend of the future king of England, Edward the Confessor, he crossed over to England with Edward in 1042, and in 1044 became bishop of London. Robert was the most trusted and the most prominent of the king's foreign friends, and was the leader of the party hostile to the influence of Earl Godwine. In 1051, although the chapter had already made an election, Edward appointed him archbishop of Canterbury. He seems to have been sent by the king on an errand to Duke William of Normandy, and on the return of Godwine from exile in 1052 he fled in great haste from England. He was outlawed and deposed, and he died at Jumièges about 1070.

See *Two Saxon Chronicles,* edited by J. Earle and C. Plummer (Oxford, 1892) ; and E. A. Freeman, *History of the Norman Conquest* (Oxford, 1870–76).

ROBERT OF TORIGNI (c. 1110–1186), mediaeval chronicler, was prior of Bec in 1149, and in 1154 became abbot of Mont St. Michel, whence he is also sometimes called Robertus de Monte. He died, according to Potthast, on May 29, 1186. He wrote additions and appendices to the chronicle of Sigebert of Gembloux, covering the period A.D. 385–1100, and a chronicle in continuation of Sigebert, extending from 1100 to 1186, of great value for Anglo-Norman history. It is for continental affairs between 1154 and 1170 that his information is valuable.

The best modern editions are the *Chronique de Robert de Torigni,* etc., edited by Léopold Delisle for the *Soc. de l'histoire de Normandie* (Rouen, 1872–1873), and *Chronicle of Robert of Torigni,* edited with an introduction, by Richard Howlett (Rolls Series, No. 82, iv. 1889).

ROBERTS, FREDERICK SLEIGH ROBERTS, EARL (1832–1914), British soldier, second son of General Sir Abraham Roberts, G.C.B., was born at Cawnpore, India, on Sept. 30, 1832. Educated at Eton, Sandhurst and Addiscombe, he obtained a commission in the Bengal Artillery on Dec. 12, 1851. In the following year he was posted to a field battery at Peshawar, where he also acted as aide-de-camp to his father, who commanded the Peshawar division. In 1856 Roberts was appointed to the quartermaster-general's department of the staff, in which he remained for 22 years, passing from one grade to another until he became quartermaster-general in India. On the outbreak of the Mutiny in 1857, Roberts, at first, was staff officer to the movable column operating against the mutineers in the Punjab, but, towards the end of June, he joined the Delhi Field Force, and was deputy assistant quartermaster-general with the artillery during the operations against Delhi. He served under Sir Colin Campbell at the second relief of Lucknow in November, at the battle of Cawnpore on Dec. 6 and the subsequent pursuit and defeat of the Gwalior contingent near Shinrajpur.

Roberts distinguished himself at the engagement of Khudaganj, on Jan. 2, 1858, and he was recommended for the Victoria Cross for acts of gallantry there. He was present at the reoccupation of Fatehgarh on Jan. 6, the storm of Mianganj in February, the siege and capture of Lucknow in March, and the action at Kursi on the 22nd of that month, after which he went home on sick leave. For his services in the Mutiny he was seven times mentioned in despatches, received the medal with three clasps, the Victoria Cross, and on his promotion to captain, in Oct. 1860, a brevet majority. On May 17, 1859 he married, at Waterford, Miss Nora Bews, and on his return to India was entrusted with the organization of the viceroy's camps during the progresses through Oudh, the North-West Provinces, the Punjab and Central India in 1860 and 1861. In Dec. 1863 he took part, under Major-General Garvock, in the Umbeyla campaign among the mountains to the north of Peshawar, and was present at the storm of Lalu, the capture of Umbeyla and the destruction of Mulka.

In 1867 Roberts was appointed assistant quartermaster-general to Sir Donald Stewart's Bengal Brigade for Abyssinia. He showed judgment in embarking each unit complete in every detail, instead of despatching camp equipage in one ship, transport in another, and so on, as was customary. He arrived at Zula, Annesley Bay, in the Red Sea, the base of the expedition, on Feb. 3, 1868, and remained there as senior base staff officer during the four months' campaign. At its close he superintended the re-embarkation of the whole army. He returned to India the following year as first assistant quartermaster-general. In the autumn of 1871 he made the arrangements for the expedition into Lushai, between southeast Bengal and Burma, fitted out two columns under Brigadier-Generals Bourchier and Brownlow, and himself accompanied the first. A road, over 100 m. long, was cut through dense gloomy forests in stifling heat, and the column was attacked by cholera; but the object of the expedition was successfully accomplished, and Roberts, who was present at the capture of the Kholel villages and the action in the Northlang range, and commanded the troops

at the burning of Taikum, was mentioned in despatches and made a Companion of the Bath. On his return in March 1872, he became deputy quartermaster-general in Bengal, and in 1875 quartermaster-general and colonel. He settled the details of the great camp of exercise at Delhi on the occasion of the visit of the prince of Wales in January 1876, and attended H.R.H. at the manoeuvres. He also superintended the arrangements for the great durbar at Delhi on Jan. 1, 1877, when Queen Victoria was proclaimed empress of India.

In 1878 Roberts was appointed to the command of the Frontier Field Force at Abbottabad, in Hazara; but in the autumn, on the repulse of the Chamberlain Mission by the Afghans, and the formation of three columns to advance into Afghanistan by the Khyber, the Bolan and the Kurram passes, he was given the command of the Kurram Field Force, with the rank of major-general. Concentrating his column at Thal, he advanced to Kurram towards the end of November, and having formed an advanced base there, moved on to Habib Kila. Under cover of preparations for a front attack on the Peiwar Kotal, he reconnoitred that formidable position, and on the night of Dec. 1, moved part of his force to attack the Spingawi Kotal, in order to turn the Afghan left flank, leaving the remainder of the force to feign a front attack on the Peiwar, and to guard the camp. After a very difficult night march the Spingawi Kotal was carried at daybreak on the 2nd, and, later, the Afghans on the Peiwar Kotal, threatened in rear, abandoned the position. The next morning Roberts occupied the Peiwar, and on the 6th advanced to Ali Khel. He reconnoitred the Shutargardan and the Sapari passes, and made a strong reconnaissance through Khost, in which some fighting took place, and at the end of January returned to Hagir Pir, in Kurram, where his force remained in occupation. In July Major Cavagnari, the British envoy to the new amir, Yakub Khan, passed through Kurram on his way to Kabul, and, shortly afterwards, Roberts left his Kurram command and went to Simla to take his seat on the army commission, where he strongly advocated the abolition of the three Presidency armies, and the substitution for them of four army corps, a measure which was carried out sixteen years later.

While Roberts was at Simla, news arrived on Sept. 5 of the murder of Cavagnari and his companions at Kabul. The Peshawar Valley Force had been broken up; Sir Donald Stewart was still at Kandahar, but most of his troops had started for India; Roberts, therefore, had the only force ready to strike rapidly at Kabul. It was hastily reinforced, and he hurried back to Kurram to take command, as a lieutenant-general, of the Kabul Field Force (7,500 men and 22 guns). By Sept. 19, a brigade was entrenched on the Shutargardan, and as Roberts advanced, the Amir Yakub Khan came into his camp. An Afghan force of 8,000 men blocked the way in a strong position on the heights beyond Charasia, and on Oct. 6, Roberts repeated the tactics that had done him such good service at the Peiwar in the previous year, and sending Brigadier-General T. D. Baker with the greater part of his force to turn the Afghan right flank, threatened the pass in front with the remainder. By the afternoon Baker had seized the position, and the enemy, severely defeated, were in full retreat. Kabul was occupied without further opposition.

The city was spared, but punishment was meted out to those convicted of complicity in the murder of the British Mission. Yakub Khan abdicated on Oct. 12, and was eventually deported to India. The troops occupied the Sherpur cantonments; but in November a religious war was proclaimed by the Mullahs, and early in December, in order to prevent a threatening combination of Afghan tribes against him, Roberts moved out two columns to attack them in detail. After considerable fighting near Kabul, the numbers of the enemy became so great that he was forced to concentrate his troops again at Sherpur, the defences of which had been greatly improved and strengthened. Sherpur was invested by the enemy, and early on Dec. 23, was attacked by over 100,000 Afghans. They were driven off with great loss; and on making a second attempt to storm the place, were met by Roberts, who moved out, attacked them in flank, and defeated them.

Roberts now recommended the political dismemberment of Afghanistan, and negotiations were carried on with the northern tribes for the appointment of an amir for the Kabul district only. On May 5, Sir Donald Stewart arrived with his column from Kandahar and assumed the supreme command in Afghanistan, Roberts retaining, under Stewart, the command of the two Kabul divisions, and organizing an efficient transport corps under Colonel R. Low, which was soon to be of inestimable value. On July 22, Abdur Rahman was proclaimed Amir of Kabul; and Roberts was preparing to withdraw his troops to India by the Kurram route, when news arrived that a British brigade had been totally defeated at Maiwand on July 27, and that Lieutenant-General Primrose was besieged in Kandahar. Roberts was ordered to proceed thither at once with a specially selected column of 10,000 troops and his new transport corps. He started on his famous march on Aug. 9, and arrived at Kandahar on the morning of the 31st, having covered 313 miles in twenty-two days. On the following day he fought the battle of Kandahar and gained a complete victory. Roberts was now created K.C.B., G.C.B. and a baronet, and was given the command of the Madras army.

Before proceeding to Madras, Roberts went home on furlough, and when the news of the disaster at Majuba Hill in South Africa arrived in London at the end of February 1881, he was appointed governor of Natal and commander-in-chief in South Africa. He arrived at Cape Town to find that peace had been made with the Boers, and that instructions were awaiting him to return home. The same year he attended the autumn manoeuvres in Hanover as the guest of the German emperor. He declined the post of quartermaster-general to the forces in succession to Sir Garnet Wolseley, and returned to India, arriving at Madras in November. The following year he visited Burma with the viceroy, and in 1885 attended the meeting between Abdur Rahman and Lord Dufferin at Rawalpindi at the time of the Panjdeh incident, in connection with which he had been nominated to the command of an army corps in case of hostilities. In July he succeeded Sir Donald Stewart as commander-in-chief in India, and during his seven years' tenure of this high position instituted many measures for the benefit of the army, and greatly assisted the development of frontier communications and defence. At the end of 1886, at the request of the viceroy, he took personal command for a time of the forces in Burma, and organized measures for the suppression of dacoity. In 1892 he was created Baron Roberts of Kandahar and Waterford. In 1893 he left India for good, and the G.C.S.I. was bestowed upon him. He was promoted to be field-marshal in 1895, and in the autumn of that year succeeded Lord Wolseley in the Irish command and was sworn a privy councillor.

After the disastrous actions in the Boer war in South Africa in December 1899 at Magersfontein, Stormberg and Colenso, where his only son was killed, Lord Roberts was sent out as commander-in-chief. He arrived at Cape Town on Jan. 10, 1900, and after organizing his force, advanced with sound strategy on Bloemfontein, the capital of the Orange Free State, and soon changed the aspect of affairs. The sieges of Kimberley and Ladysmith were raised, and the Boer general, Cronje, flying towards the capital, was overtaken at Paardeberg and, after a fine defence, compelled to surrender, with 5,000 men, on the anniversary of Majuba Day, Feb. 27, 1900. Roberts entered Bloemfontein on March 13, and after six weeks' preparation, advanced on Pretoria, the capital of the Transvaal. Mafeking was relieved on May 17, and Pretoria occupied on June 5. The two Boer states were annexed, and the war gradually assuming a guerrilla character, Roberts handed over the command to Lord Kitchener and returned to England to fill the office of commander-in-chief of the army in succession to Lord Wolseley.

On his return in 1901 he received an earldom, the thanks of both Houses of Parliament and a grant of £100,000 for his services in South Africa. In 1905 he resigned his post on the Committee of National Defence, and devoted himself to attempting to rouse his countrymen to the necessity of cultivating rifle-shooting and of adopting systematic general military training and service. As head of the National Service League, he took part in the movement in favour of compulsory military service for home defence and published in 1911, *Fallacies and Facts*, in support of

his views. On the outbreak of the World War he was a frequent visitor at the War Office, and shortly after the arrival of the two Indian divisions in France he crossed the Channel to visit them in the trenches. He was attacked by pneumonia while at the front, and he died at St. Omer on Nov. 14, 1914, the title going by special remainder to his elder daughter, Aileen Mary. He was buried in St. Paul's Cathedral, London.

Earl Roberts was the author of the following works: *The Rise of Wellington* (1895); *Forty-one years in India* (1897); *Letters written during the Indian Mutiny* (1924). See also H. Hensonan, *The Afghan War of 1879–1880* (1881); *The Anglo-Afghan War* (official account, 1881); Sir T. F. Maurice and M. H. Grant (Official), *History of the War in South Africa 1899–1902* (1906–1910); Sir G. W. Forrest, *The Life of Lord Roberts* (1914).

ROBERTSON, FREDERICK WILLIAM (1816–1853), English divine, known as Robertson of Brighton, was born in London on Feb. 3, 1816. He studied at Edinburgh university, and at Brasenose college, Oxford. He had intended to go into the army, but Oxford changed the bent of his mind, and he was ordained in 1840, and served in curacies at Winchester and Cheltenham. He entered in 1847 on his famous ministry at Trinity Chapel, Brighton, where his church was thronged with thoughtful men of all types. Robertson was not a scientific theologian; but his insight into the principles of the spiritual life was unrivalled. As his biographer says, thousands found in his sermons "a living source of impulse, a practical direction of thought, a key to many of the problems of theology, and above all a path to spiritual freedom." His closing years were full of suffering, arising mainly from the opposition aroused by his sympathy with the revolutionary ideas of the 1848 epoch. He died on Aug. 15, 1853.

Robertson's works include 5 vols. of sermons, 2 vols. of expository lectures, on Genesis and on the epistles to the Corinthians, a volume of miscellaneous addresses, and an *Analysis of "In Memoriam."* See Stopford A. Brooke, *Life and Letters* (1865).

ROBERTSON, THOMAS WILLIAM (1829–1871), English actor and dramatist, was born at Newark on Jan. 9, 1829. Robertson was familiar with the stage from his childhood; he was the eldest of a large family, the actress Margaret (Madge) Robertson (Mrs. Kendal) was the youngest. A farcical comedy by him, *A Night's Adventure,* was produced, without great success, at the Olympic, under Farren's management as early as 1851. He remained for some years longer in the provinces, varying his work as an actor with miscellaneous contributions to newspapers. In 1860 he went to London, and edited a mining journal. He was at one time prompter at the Olympic under the management of Charles Mathews. He wrote a farce entitled *A Cantab,* which was played at the Strand theatre in 1861. This brought him a reputation in a Bohemian clique, but so little practical assistance that he thought of abandoning the profession to become a tobacconist. Then, in 1864, came *David Garrick,* produced at the Haymarket with Edward Sothern in the principal character, which has kept the stage ever since.

But his name was made by the production of *Society* at the Prince of Wales Theatre in 1865, under the management of Miss Marie Wilton, afterwards Mrs. Bancroft. Play-writer and company were exactly suited one to another; the plays and the acting together—the small size of the playhouse being also in their favour—were at once recognized as a new thing. Although some critics sneered at the "cup-and-saucer comedy," voted it absurdly realistic, said there was nothing in it but commonplace life represented without a trace of Sheridanian wit and sparkle, all London flocked to the little house in Tottenham Street, and the stage was at once inundated with imitations of the new style of acting and the new kind of play. All Robertson's best known plays (except *David Garrick*) were written for the old Prince of Wales's under the Bancrofts, and that régime is now an historical incident in the progress of the English stage. *Ours* was produced in 1866, *Caste* in 1867, *Play* in 1868, *School* in 1869, *M.P.* in 1870. Robertson died in London on Feb. 3, 1871.

See *Principal Dramatic Works of Robertson; with Memoir by his son* (1889); and T. E. Pemberton, *Life and Writings of Robertson* (1893).

ROBERTSON, WILLIAM (1721–1793), Scottish historian, born at Borthwick, Midlothian, on Sept. 19, 1721, was the eldest son of the Rev. William Robertson. He was educated at the school of Dalkeith and the University of Edinburgh. In 1743 he was presented to the living of Gladsmuir in East Lothian. His services in the '45 were rewarded by his election as a member of the General Assembly, where his influence as leader of the "moderate" party was for many years nearly supreme. (*See* PRESBYTERIANISM.)

Robertson's *History of Scotland during the Reigns of Queen Mary and of James VI. until his Accession to the Crown of England* begun in 1753, was published in two volumes in 1759 (19th ed. 1812). Before the end of the author's life the book had reached its 14th edition; and it soon brought him other rewards than literary fame. In 1759 he was appointed chaplain of Stirling castle, in 1761 one of His Majesty's chaplains in ordinary, and in 1762 he was chosen principal of the University of Edinburgh. In May 1763 he was elected Moderator of the General Assembly, and in August king's historiographer. His other works were: *History of the Reign of the Emperor Charles the Fifth* (3 vols., 1769) which had a European reputation and was translated into French in 1771, German, 1770–71, Italian, 1835, and Spanish, 1846; *History of America* (2 vols., 1777); *Disquisition concerning the Knowledge which the Ancients had of India* (1791).

There are lives of Robertson by Dugald Stewart (Edinburgh, 1801 and 1802), prefixed to most of the collective editions of his works; by George Gleig, bishop of Brechin (Edinburgh, 1812); and by Lord Brougham in *Lives of Men of Letters*, etc. (1845–1846). Robertson's works were edited with a life by D. Stewart (8 vols. 1817) and were translated into French in 12 vols. (1829) by J. B. Suard and others.

ROBERTSON, SIR WILLIAM ROBERT (1860–1933),

British field marshal, was born at Welbourn, Lincs., on Sept. 14, 1860. He enlisted as a private in the 16th Lancers in 1877, and served in the ranks of that regiment until 1888, when he won a commission in the 3rd Dragoon Guards, then in India. He eagerly studied his profession in all its branches and he learned the native languages. He was railway staff officer in the Miranzai and Black Mountain operations of 1891, and in the following year joined the intelligence department at Simla; while on its staff he carried out a reconnaissance to the Pamirs, and in 1895 served with the Chitral Relief Force, being wounded and receiving the D.S.O. He passed through the Staff College in 1897–8—the first officer risen from the ranks to do so—and then, after a few months at the War Office, went out to South Africa on the Intelligence Staff; he accompanied Lord Roberts on his advance from Cape Colony into the Transvaal, and was promoted brevet lieutenant-colonel for his services. He spent the period from 1901 to 1907 at the War Office, being promoted colonel in 1903, and he then went to the staff at Aldershot, where he spent three years. In 1910 he was appointed commandant of the Staff College, was shortly afterwards promoted major-general and in 1913 became director of military training at the War Office.

On the mobilization of the army for the World War, Robertson became quartermaster-general of the Expeditionary Force, and in Jan. 1915 chief of the general staff to Sir John French. In the following December he was brought back to the War Office as chief of the imperial general staff and immediately introduced great improvements in the office organization. Convinced that the Western Front represented the decisive theatre of war, and fully aware how mischievous was dispersion of force in principle, he saw to it that, where operations in distant regions were unavoidable, the commanders on the spot were furnished with what was deemed essential to achieve success—with the result that the position of affairs in Mesopotamia, on the Suez frontier and in East Africa was completely transformed within a very few months. His services were recognized by promotion to general in 1916 and by the G.C.B. in 1917.

In the later months of 1917 he found it more and more difficult, in view of the disappointing results of Allied offensives in France and Flanders, to persuade the War Cabinet that diversion of fighting resources to other theatres of war endangered prospects of victory at the decisive point and might lead to disaster near home. His anxieties were increased by the manner in which the problem of man-power was treated. He moreover foresaw that the Su-

preme War Council, introduced towards the end of the year, would not provide effective means for combining the operations of the Allies. In Feb. 1918 he was transferred by the Government to the charge of the eastern command in England—just one month before the success that attended the great German offensive of March proved how correct had been his appreciation of the situation. Three months later he succeeded French as commander-in-chief in Great Britain. After the War he received a baronetcy, a grant of £10,000, and in 1919, the G.C.M.G. From April 1919 to March 1920 he commanded the British troops on the Rhine, and, after relinquishing that appointment on the force being reduced, was promoted field-marshal. Robertson received many English and foreign honours, including the G.C.V.O. (1931).

See his *From Private to Field-marshal* (1921); and *Soldiers and Statesmen 1914–1918* (1926).

ROBERT THE DEVIL,

hero of romance. He was the son of a duke and duchess of Normandy, and by the time he was 20 was a prodigy of strength, which he used, however, only for outrage and crime. At last he learnt from his mother, in explanation of his wicked impulses, that he was born in answer to prayers addressed to the devil. He was directed by the pope to a hermit, who imposed on him by way of penance that he should maintain absolute silence, feign madness, take his food from the mouth of a dog, and provoke ill-treatment from the common people without retaliating. He became court fool to the emperor at Rome, and delivered the city from Saracen invasions in three successive years in the guise of an unknown knight, having each time been bidden to fight by a celestial messenger. The emperor's dumb daughter recovered speech to declare the identity of the court fool with the deliverer of the city, but Robert refused the hand of the princess and the imperial inheritance and ended his days in the hermitage of his old confessor. The French romance of *Robert le Diable* is one of the oldest versions of the legend. The story had undergone much change before it was used by E. Scribe and C. Delavigne in the libretto of Meyerbeer's opera of *Robert le Diable*.

See *Robert le Diable*, ed. E. Löseth (Soc. des anc. textes fr., 1903); *Sir Gowther*, ed. K. Breul (Oppeln, 1886); M. Tardel, *Die Sage v. Robert d. Teufel in neueren deutschen Dichtungen* (1900); L. A. Hibbard, *Medieval Romance in England* (1924).

ROBERT THE STRONG (le Fort) (d. 866),

count of Anjou and of Blois, appears as rector of the abbey of Marmoutier in 852, and as one of Charles the Bald's *missi dominici*, in 853; but soon afterwards he was among those who rebelled against Charles, and invited the king's half-brother, Louis the German, to invade West Francia. In 860 Robert came to terms with Charles, who made him count of Anjou and of Blois, and entrusted him with the defence of that part of his kingdom which lay between the Seine and the Loire, a district which had suffered greatly from the ravages of the Normans and the Bretons. He was killed in battle at Brissarthe in October 866, leaving two sons, Odo, or Eudes, and Robert, both of whom became kings of the Franks. Robert was the ancestor of the Capetian kings of France.

See K. von Kalekstein, *Robert der Tapfere* (1871); and E. Favre, *Eudes, comte de Paris et roi de France* (1893).

ROBERVAL, GILLES PERSONNE (or PERSONIER) DE (1602–1675),

French mathematician, was born at Roberval, near Beauvais, on Aug. 8, 1602. In 1632 he became professor of mathematics in the Collège de France. He died in Paris on Oct. 27, 1675. Roberval studied the quadrature of surfaces and the cubature of solids, which he accomplished, in some of the simpler cases, by an original method which he called the "Method of Indivisibles." He discovered a general method of drawing tangents, by considering a curve as described by a moving point whose motion is the resultant of several simpler motions. He also discovered a method of deriving one curve from another, by means of which finite areas can be obtained equal to the areas between certain curves and their asymptotes. To these curves, which were also applied to effect some quadratures, Evangelista Torricelli gave the name of "Robervallian lines."

Gilles Personne de Roberval invented the balance which goes

by his name.

His works were published in 1693 by the Abbé Gallois, in the *Recueil* of the *Mémoires de l'Académie des Sciences.*

ROBES, the name generally given to a class of official costume, especially as worn by certain persons or classes on occasions of particular solemnity. The word robe was earliest used, in the sense of a garment, of those given by popes and princes to the members of their household or their great officers. It would be going too far to assume that, *e.g.*, peers' robes were originally the king's livery, but in most early cases where robes are mentioned, if not of cloth of gold, etc., they are of scarlet, furred. A robe is properly a long garment, and the term "robes" is now applied only in those cases where a long garment forms part of the official costume, though in ordinary usage it is taken to include all the other articles of dress proper to the costume in question. The term "robes," moreover, connotes a certain degree of dignity or honour in the wearer. We speak of the king's robes of State, of peers' robes, of the robes of the clergy, of academic robes, judicial robes, municipal or civic robes; we should not speak of the robes of a cathedral verger, though he too wears a long gown of ceremony, and it is even only by somewhat stretching the term "robes" that we can include under it the ordinary academical dress of the universities. In the case of the official costume of the clergy, too, a distinction must be drawn. The sacerdotal vestments are not spoken of as "robes"; a priest is not "robed" but "vested" for Mass; yet the rochet and chimere of an English bishop, even in church, are more properly referred to as robes than as vestments, and while the cope he wears in church is a vestment rather than a robe, the scarlet cope which is part of his parliamentary full dress is a robe, not a vestment. The official, non-liturgical costume of the clergy is dealt with under the general heading VESTMENTS and the subsidiary articles.

The coronation robes of emperors and kings, representing as they do the sacerdotal significance of Christian kingship, are essentially vestments rather than robes. Apart from these, however, are the royal robes of State; in the case of the king of England a crimson velvet surcoat and long mantle, fastened in front of the neck, ermine lined, with a deep cape or tippet of ermine. The sovereign's coronation robes are described in "The King's Coronation Ornaments," by W. St. John Hope, in *The Ancestor*, vols. i. and ii., also by L. Wickham Legg, *English Coronation Records* (1901).

All countries, East and West, which boast an ancient civilization have some sort of official robes, and the tendency in modern times has been to multiply rather than to diminish their number. In the United States few save Federal judges wear robes. The scarlet judicial robes were discarded at the Revolution. Those of black silk now worn are slightly modified academic gowns. John Jay, first chief justice of the Supreme Court (1789), set the fashion by sitting in the LL.D. gown granted him by Columbia university. The present article does not attempt to deal with any but British robes, under the headings of (1) peers' robes, (2) robes in the House of Commons, (3) robes of the Orders of Knighthood, (4) judicial and forensic robes, (5) municipal and civic robes, (6) academic costume.

Peers' Robes.—As early as the end of the 14th century peers seem to have worn at their creation some kind of robe of honour. An illumination on the foundation charter of King's college, Cambridge, represents the peers in 1446 wearing gowns, mantles and hoods of scarlet, furred with miniver, the mantle opening on the right shoulder and guarded with two, three or four bars of miniver, in the form of short stripes high up on the shoulder. The origin of these is as yet unknown, and it is not certain precisely when the peers' velvet robe of estate was first used. During the reign of Henry VIII., references are found to the "parliament robes" of peers. By the time of James II.'s coronation, the baron and viscount had the velvet robes of estate. The colour of these seems to have been crimson at first, sometimes varying to purple. They consisted of a long gown or surcoat with girdle, a mantle lined with ermine, a hood and a tippet of ermine, the rows being as follows: for a duke 4, a marquess $3\frac{1}{2}$, an earl 3, a viscount $2\frac{1}{2}$ and a baron 2.

Till late in the 18th century peers continued to attend the House of Lords in parliamentary robes, with the stars and ribbons of their orders, but robes are now only worn in the House of Lords, *e.g.*, at the opening of parliament, on occasions when the sovereign gives his assent to bills by "royal commission" (when five or six peers on the Government side appear in robes, and the lord chancellor also wears his peer's robe of scarlet ermine), and at the introduction of a newly created peer, when the new peer and his two introducers wear their parliamentary robes (over morning dress) during the ceremony of introduction only. The mover and seconder of the Address no longer wear robes, but uniform. On all the above occasions, and when the peers as a body attend church or some other ceremony, the parliamentary robe of scarlet cloth is worn; in the present day it takes the form of a mantle opening on the right shoulder, with a collar of ermine, and guarded with rows of ermine and gold lace round the right shoulder, varying in number according to the rank of the wearer. The modern coronation robes consist of a crimson velvet surcoat and a mantle with a tippet of ermine and with rows of ermine as in the parliamentary robes. The surcoat is no longer a gown, but a short sleeveless garment.

As regards peeresses' robes, the order of the earl-marshal for the regulation of these at the coronation of James II. shows that by then all peeresses wore the robes of state of crimson velvet, and minutely regulates all details, such as shape, powderings, length of train and width of the fur edging of the mantle. They have changed very little up to the present day.

House of Commons.—The speaker of the House of Commons wears on state occasions a black damask robe with gold lace and a full-bottomed wig; in the House itself he wears a black silk robe with train and a full-bottomed wig. The clerks at the table wear barristers' gowns and wigs.

Robes of the Orders of Knighthood.—The robes of the Garter were originally of blue woollen stuff, the surcoat and hood being powdered with garters embroidered in silk and gold. The surcoat varied in colour from year to year; the hood was made of the same material as the surcoat and, when hats began to be worn, was carried hanging over the shoulder. Robes were sometimes granted to ladies in the early days. The last lady to receive the robes was Margaret, countess of Richmond, in 1488. At the present day the mantle is of dark blue velvet, of the same colour as the ribbon, lined with taffeta, and with the star embroidered on the left shoulder, the hood and surcoat of crimson velvet lined with white taffeta, and with these are worn a doublet and trunk-hose of white satin and a plumed hat.

The robes worn by the knights of the Bath created at the coronation of Henry IV. were green with furred hoods, and a white silk cord hanging from the left shoulder. The mantle in the present day is of crimson velvet lined with white over a white satin under-coat and trunk-hose, and a plumed hat and white boots with red tops are worn. The mantle of the Thistle is of dark green velvet over surcoat, etc., of cloth of silver; that of St. Patrick azure, with doublet and trunk-hose of white satin; that of St. Michael and St. George of Saxon blue satin lined with scarlet; and that of the Star of India of light blue satin lined with white.

Judicial and Forensic Robes.—It is frequently stated that judicial robes had their origin in the dress of ecclesiastics. But though ecclesiastics in early days frequently acted as judges, and though, as Fortescue says, the serjeant's long robe was "after the fashion of a priest," judicial robes more probably arose from the ordinary civilian dress of the early 14th century. The chief argument for the ecclesiastical origin has been found in the coif, a cap of white linen or silk, tied under the chin, and described by Fortescue as "the principal or chief insignment and habit wherewith serjeants-at-law at their creation are decked," which is said to have been used by ecclesiastics to hide the tonsure when in court. More probably the coif was a head-dress in common use in the 13th century, which survived as the distinguishing mark of men of law.

About the time of Queen Elizabeth the square cap, otherwise known as the cornered, black or sentence cap (the last from the fact of its being put on by the judge when pronouncing sentence of death), began to appear. Sometimes it was worn over the coif only, sometimes over the coif and skullcap. Sometimes it had ear flaps, sometimes, as in its present form, it had not.

Toward the end of the 17th century the judges took to wearing wigs, and they have continued to wear them ever since. The wearing of wigs naturally concealed the coif and velvet skullcap, so a device had to be invented by which they could still be displayed. The expedient was hit upon of putting a round patch of white stuff, with a black spot in the middle of it, on the crown of the wig of certain of the judges, to represent the coif and skullcap. Serjeant being appointed no longer, this round patch has now disappeared, the only trace of it left being the circular depression on the crown of the wig. Minute details of court and levee dress, judicial and legal, of the present day, will be found in *Dress Worn at Court* (pp. 60-61), issued with the authority of the lord chamberlain—also details of mourning costume.

Municipal and Civic Robes.—The word "livery," the use of which is now practically confined to the costume of the "livery companies," the dress of menservants, etc., originally meant an allowance of food or clothing granted to certain persons. It is still used of the allowances of food made to the fellows of certain colleges. As early as the 13th century, the citizens of London used to assume a uniform dress to do honour to some great occasion, as when 600 citizens rode out to meet Queen Margaret, wife of Edward I, "in one livery of red and white, with the cognizances of their misteries embroidered upon their sleeves." By the 14th century there is evidence of the adoption of liveries by the trades and fraternities, and when the livery companies were incorporated they took care to have their liveries authorized by their charters. As to the costume of the mayor, aldermen, sheriffs, etc., the scarlet, violet and black robes, still worn by them, were early in use. The provincial mayors and aldermen at quite an early date followed the fashion of London. An account of the robes of modern provincial mayors will be found in St. John Hope's *Corporation Plate and Insignia*.

At the present day the lord mayor has several sets of robes; a special coronation robe, a crimson velvet robe of state like that of an earl, worn with the chain and jewel, *e.g.*, in the presence of the sovereign when in the city; a black robe of state trimmed with gold, which is worn with the chain and jewel, *e.g.*, at the Guildhall on lord mayor's day; the scarlet robes, which are worn, with or without the chain, on most public occasions, such as the service at St. Paul's on the first day of the Easter law term, audiences of the sovereign, the election of the lord mayor, the opening of the central criminal court, etc.; a violet gown, which is worn, *e.g.*, when the lord mayor elect is presented to the king, when he is sworn in, at the election of sheriffs, etc., and a black gown worn in church on Good Friday, etc. The aldermen wear scarlet on most occasions of ceremony, former mayors "having the Cap of Dignity attached to their gown, and being entitled to introduce a sword and mace into their badges." Violet robes are also worn on certain occasions marked in the almanac of the *Alderman's Pocket-Book,* and black gowns when the lord mayor wears his. The sheriffs and recorders have scarlet, violet and black gowns, and the members of the common council have deep mazarine blue gowns, which seem to have been first prescribed in 1761. **(X.)**

Academical Dress.—Like judicial robes, academical dress has been considered to be of ecclesiastical origin. The mediaeval scholar was, of course, a clerk and had to wear the clerkly gown and the tonsure. The ecclesiastical dress that he wore had itself probably developed out of the ordinary civilian costume at an earlier period. The robes worn in the earliest times at Oxford and Cambridge, at least in part, were monastic or ecclesiastical in origin, but the hood was certainly derived from a lay garment, at one time common to all classes and both sexes, as Herbert Norris has pointed out. This lay hood was adopted by monks, clergy and all university students, and eventually was retained in a specialized form by the various faculties, as an academical distinction. The statutes of certain colleges required of the scholars as early as the 14th century the tonsure and a "decent habit" suitable to a clerk; *i.e.*, a long gown, which it is stipulated in some cases must be closed in front like the Benedictine habit.[1] Some colleges had liveries, prescribed perhaps by the founder of the college and laid down by the statutes.[2] The differences of colour and shape in the undergraduate gowns of most of the Cambridge colleges are supposed to be a survival of this, but in fact the Cambridge college undergraduate gowns all date from the period 1805-40; *i.e.*, are late Guelphic (that is, Hanoverian) in origin, and thus quite modern.

The gown was worn by all grades as befitting clerks. It is hard to determine whether there was at first any difference between the gowns of the senior nongraduates and the bachelors of arts and that of the masters and doctors and the bachelors in the superior faculties, but it seems improbable. It was frequently fur-lined, or at least trimmed with fur, but the use of the more costly furs was forbidden, especially in the period between 1350-1500, as the *Statuta Antiqua Univ. Oxon.* (ed. S. Gibson) clearly show, to all below the degree of master, except sons of noblemen, or those possessing a certain income, bachelors using

budge (common fur or black lamb's wool); students and even doctors in theology were also, at one time, restricted to budge, lamb's wool and to sombre habits. The robes of masters had to be flowing and reach to the ankles, and it was the masters who had the earliest distinctive dress that could be called truly academical.

The cope (*i.e.*, the *capa* or *cappa clausa*, the closed and essentially ecclesiastical cope or cape, not to be confused with the open and purely decorative cope of the clergy) probably originated in the ordinary everyday mantle of the clergy. Its wear in England was made obligatory by Cardinal Archbishop Stephen Langton, 1222, at the provincial synod held at Oseney abbey, near Oxford. All bishops, deans, archdeacons, rural deans, priests and all church dignitaries were ordered to wear it.[3] This kind of cope, closed in front, was originally black; it sometimes, for the sake of convenience, had a slit in front to allow of the passage of the hands, this type of opening being the form or variation adopted by the doctors in theology and retained by them until the present day, although later on the slit was extended to the ground. Another variation was to make two side slits, one for each arm, a variation (the pallium or *chimaera*) adopted by the doctors in law and in physic and by the superior bachelors; *i.e.*, the bachelors in canon law, physic and possibly in theology. This type is the forerunner of the "convocation habit" and "ecclesiastico-academical chimere."

About 1330-40 doctors began to adopt scarlet for their hoods, and later for their robes; at any rate by about 1500, probably long before, all doctors wore scarlet and had discarded their black *cappae clausae* for scarlet ones, the original sombre, black form being retained by the M.A.'s and B.D.'s. The wearing of robes of scarlet, violet or murrey, and also the "sleveless cote" (*i.e.*, convocation habits and chimeres), *super tunica*, of these colours, was formally ratified by an act of 24 Henry VIII (1533) entitled "an Act for the Reformation of Excess in Apparel." The cope still survives at Cambridge as the dress worn by the vice-chancellor and by regius professors of divinity, law and medicine when presenting for degrees; it is lined with white fur.

The hood was originally worn by all scholars, as by everybody, and had evidently no academical significance. Sometimes a cap was also worn, the hood being thrown back. There were evidently hoods of two kinds for masters from about 1432, when masters and doctors were allowed to use silk in their linings during the summer months, so that there were silk-lined and miniver-lined hoods. These two types of hood survived, at least in Oxford, until as late as 1657, or even a little later, in the time of John Fell, dean of Christ Church and vicechancellor, and Anthony à Wood, M.A., antiquary. Eventually (from about 1674-75, in the time of George Edwards and David Loggan) the silk-lined hood was the type principally retained by masters and doctors, the miniver-lined hood being preserved as a proctorial insignia only. At a later date, at Cambridge, a distinction was made between the hoods of nonregent masters, which were lined with silk, and those of regents which were lined with miniver. Later again, the regents wore their hoods in such a way as to show the white lining, while the nonregents wore theirs "squared," so that the white did not show. Hence the name "white hoods" and "black hoods" given to the upper and lower houses of the old senate respectively. It is not settled when the modern colouring of hoods arose; they probably followed those of the robes of the faculties, but about these there is equal uncertainty. The Oxford proctor still wears a miniver hood. The modern Cambridge hood has preserved the original shape more closely than the Oxford M.A. type, being a hood and cape combined, the cape having, incorrectly, square corners.

There seem to have been in Tudor times at least three varieties of academical headdress, one, the round cap of velvet for graduates in the secular faculties, survives as part of the full dress of doctors (except doctors in theology) to the present day. The square cap was adopted at the universities, according to N. F. Robinson, after 1520, in imitation of the University of Paris. In this connection should be mentioned the term "tufthunting" (*i.e.*, attempting to thrust oneself into the society of one's social superiors), derived from the gold tufts or tassel worn by noblemen and fellow commoners on their college caps. Originally, in the two ancient English universities, no one wore a cap except doctors in the superior faculties of theology, canon law and physic. The type of cap they wore was a tight round skullcap type, with a little point at the crown: it was called the "pileus," and was thus a cap of dignity. All other graduates and nongraduates had their hoods, which were thus a shoulder cape and a covering for the head. It appears that in Paris caps were made by sewing four pieces of cloth together, and the seams produced little raised ridges, and had a squaring effect. From this particular cap (squarish in effect), two types of cap evolved: (1) the biretta or priest's cap, simply a stiffened, rather taller pileus, made of the four pieces of cloth, and (2) the academical or doctor's cap (*pileus quadratus*), a velvet cap of dignity for doctors in theology. Doctors in the secular faculties adopted in the early Tudor period a soft round lay cap of velvet (*pileus rotundus*). Foundation choristers and scholars were permitted square caps in 1549. Between 1549 and 1580 there were frequent rulings and fresh statutes issued on the subject of caps. B.A.'s and other junior graduates were not authorized to wear caps until between 1575 and 1580, and then only "humbly and submissively in the Schools." By 1580 a cap had been established for all members of the two ancient English universities,

---

[1] *E.g.*, King's college, Cambridge, 1344, statutes nos. xxiii and xxxv, quoted by E. T. Beaumont in his *Academical Habit*, p. 4 (Oxford, 1928).

[2] *E.g.*, Merton 1270, Queen's 1340 and All Souls 1445; *ibid.*, p. 3.

[3] The 28th canon.

and the restriction to doctors and senior graduates had broken down. The beautiful series of illustrations of the academical dress at Oxford, by George Edwards and by David Loggan, 1674 and 1675, show the caps then in use.

Academical dress underwent much inquiry and some revision at the time of the Reformation, chiefly in the direction of sobriety, uniformity and laicization, "excess of apparel" being repressed as severely as ever, but not with much more effect. There have been few far-reaching changes since the Laudian code of 1636. Cambridge in the 20th century inquired into and revised its regulations as to dress, and in the *Ordinances* (latest ed. 1908, statute A, ch. vii, p. 303) clear rules are laid down, again revised and systematized on Feb. 28, 1934 (*Ordinances of the Univ.*); the Oxford regulations (see *Statuta et Decreta Univ. Oxon.* for 1909, Tit. xiv, *de vestitu et habitu*, pp. 327-328) have not been revised in modern times, not in fact since 1770, and have now fallen into chaos. Some of them are dead letters: at Oxford one hood (the pale blue B.Litt. hood of 1895) by 1946 had come to be worn for four degrees, B.C.L., B.M., B.Sc. and B.Litt. The dark blue hood, lined with white fur, proper to the B.C.L. and B.M. degrees, was no longer to be seen at Oxford. The modern robe makers sell the pale blue silk B.Litt. hood, lined with white fur, for all four degrees and for the B.Phil.

Doctors of both universities have three sets of robes: first, the full-dress robe of scarlet cloth; second, the scarlet, murrey or violet convocation habit[1] and hood of scarlet (now at Cambridge a cope, at Oxford the so-called *cappa clausa*); third, the black gown or undress. The first is worn by all doctors except the doctor in music, and is accompanied by the round cap of velvet except in the case of the D.D., who continues to wear the square cap (or ecclesiastical cap) with all three forms of dress; strictly, the D.D. square cap should be soft, of black velvet and with a tuft or plain without tuft or tassel. The Oxford D.D. also wears a cassock, sash and scarf. The scarlet robe is of a different, somewhat more of a Tudor lay (or civic) shape than the M.A. and B.A. gowns. As now worn, it is faced with silk of the same colour as the hood silk lining of the faculty. The second or Cambridge cope, has now gone almost out of use, but is still worn when presenting for degrees, etc., but only actually in Cambridge. It is sometimes worn over the black gown. There are several types of black gown, but the tufted gown of David Loggan's day has now gone out of use. The M.D. and Mus.D. black gowns at Cambridge are now made after the pattern of the LL.D. gown, with a square-ended sleeve and flap collar, trimmed with black lace, but the D.D., Sc.D. and Litt.D. wear the M.A. silk gown, the former with the scarf, the two latter with lace on the sleeve, placed horizontally for Sc.D. and vertically for Litt.D. Some doctors in divinity wear the full-sleeved gown with scarf. At Cambridge the headdress of a D.D. is the square cap, of secular doctors the velvet bonnet with gold cords. The doctors in music wear, as they have done since about 1600,[2] a full-dress robe of white or cream damask brocaded silk, lined with pink satin at Oxford and with cherry-coloured satin at Cambridge. Formerly (1550 period) doctors in music at Cambridge wore the M.D. robes.

The Oxford sleeveless commoner's gown, though still by statute *toga talaris*, now reaches little below the waist, the full-sleeved or bell-sleeved scholar's gown to the knee. The tufted silk gown of the gentleman commoner and the nobleman's gold-lace gown are not yet abolished by statute, but have fallen into disuse. The University of Oxford act, 1854, brought in and passed by Gladstone, abolished these class distinctions at Oxford, although they lingered on until about 1869 at Christ Church, so that King Edward VII, then prince of Wales, wore a gentleman commoner's bell-shaped sleeved gown when up in 1860-62. Vice-chancellors have no official costume, but wear the robes of their degree. The chancellors of the older universities wear a black damask silk robe with gold lace and a black velvet square cap with gold tassel and band; those of the newer universities have had robes "created" by the robe makers, who are nowadays to a large extent the arbiters of academical dress, but based on Oxford and Cambridge customs largely.

United States.—An intercollegiate commission in 1893 drafted a uniform code for academical caps, gowns and hoods which has since been accepted by 700 to 800 colleges and universities in the United States. Three types of gown and three types of hood have been devised for bachelors, masters and doctors, respectively. The square caps remain the same except that the doctor's may be made of velvet and have a tassel of gold. The bachelor's gown is made of black worsted material and may be distinguished by its pointed sleeves of the B.A. Oxford type, though hanging only to the knee. The master's gown, made of silk, has closed sleeves of M.A. type (the arm coming through a slit at the elbow), which are square at the end and extend well below the knee. The doctor's gown is also made of silk, and, like a judge's robe, has full round open bell-shaped sleeves, is faced with velvet and has three bars of velvet on each sleeve. The hoods are lined with silk with the colour or colours of the college or university granting the degree and trimmed with velvet of the colour that represents the department of learning in which the degree was obtained. The velvet trimming of the doctor's gown may also be of the departmental colour or it may be black if preferred. Colours of the more common departments of learning are as follows: arts and letters, white; theology and

divinity, scarlet; laws, purple; philosophy, blue; science, golden yellow; medicine, green; dentistry, lilac; music, pink; engineering, orange. A few institutions, notably Harvard, retain an individual code for their hoods. The U.S. system of hoods is, therefore, progressive and enables anyone conversant with the system to pick out the university (by the colour or colours in the lining), the faculty (by the edging on the cowl or hood portion proper) and the grade (by the size and shape, bachelors and masters having silk hoods of Oxford M.A. shape, masters' being made considerably longer than bachelors', doctors' being of cloth of the Cambridge M.A. type but with, correctly enough, rounded corners to the cape portion). Obviously, only a very few universities, such as Harvard, Yale and Princeton, can have a single distinguishing colour as a hood lining; other universities and colleges have to have two colours, the second or subsidiary colour being sewn inside as a chevron. This system, although distinctive and advantageous in some respects, produces a somewhat patchy result in effect. But it would obviously be impossible to distinguish the degree hoods of 700 to 800 degree-granting colleges or universities without some such device.

The U.S. intercollegiate code has also devised a similar set of hoods for holders of continental and other foreign degrees.

BIBLIOGRAPHY.—George Edwards, *Ordinum habituumque Academicorum exemplaria* (Oxford, 1674); David Loggan, *Oxonia illustrata* (1675); *Documents Relating to the University and Colleges of Cambridge*, 3 vol. (1852); *Statutes of the Colleges of Oxford*, 3 vol. (1853); J. Griffiths (ed.), *Laudian Code* (1888); Charles A. H. Franklyn, "University Hoods and Robes," a set of 25 large cards, illustrated by A. V. Wheeler-Holohan (Oxford, Jan. 1925); "Academical Dress, a Brief Sketch from the 12th to the 20th Century, with especial reference to Doctors," *Oxford*, vol. 9, no. 2 (Oxford, 1947); Strickland Gibson (ed.), *Statuta antiqua univ. oxon.* (1931); Herbert Norris, *Costume and Fashion*, 3 vol. (1924-39); *Statuta Univ. Oxon.* (current); *Ordinances of the University of Cambridge* (current, and especially Feb. 28, 1934, *University Reporter*).
(C. A. H. F.)

ROBESON, PAUL (1898-   ), U.S. Negro actor and singer, was born at Princeton, N.J., on April 9, 1898. He graduated from Rutgers college with the highest scholastic average in the college's history, in addition to being a five-letter man in athletics and All-American football end for two successive years. In 1923 he completed the law course at Columbia university. His first stage appearance was in *Taboo* (1922), but he made his reputation with his creation of the role of Jim Harris in *All God's Chillun's Got Wings* and his playing of the title roles in *The Emperor Jones* (1923) and *Black Boy* (1926). He played a short time in *Show Boat* in New York and in 1928 played in it in London. Turning then to the concert stage with recitals of Negro spirituals, he made successful tours of the U.S., Europe and the U.S.S.R. He also sang on the radio and in motion pictures. In 1950 the U.S. state department voided the passport of Robeson, who had supported various Communist causes and "peace" movements.

ROBESPIERRE, MAXIMILIEN FRANÇOIS MARIE ISIDORE DE (1758-1794), French revolutionist, the son of an advocate, was born at Arras on May 6, 1758. His family, according to tradition, was of Irish descent. Maximilien was one of four orphan children who were left in the care of relatives when their father left Arras. His direct ancestors in the male line had been notaries at the village of Carvin near Arras from the beginning of the 17th century. His grandfather, being more ambitious, established himself at Arras as an advocate, and his father followed the same profession, marrying Jacqueline Marguerite Carraut, daughter of a brewer in the same city, in 1757. Of this marriage four children were born, two sons and two daughters, of whom Maximilien was the eldest; but in 1767 Madame Derobespierre, as the name was then spelled, died, and the disconsolate widower at once left Arras and wandered about Europe until his death at Munich in 1769. Maximilien was sent to the college of Arras and the college of Louis-le-Grand at Paris. Here he had for fellow pupils Camille Desmoulins and Stanislas Fréron. Admitted an advocate in 1781, Robespierre returned to his native city to seek for practice. His reputation had already preceded him, and the bishop of Arras, De Conzié, appointed him criminal judge in the diocese of Arras in March 1782. This appointment, which he soon resigned to avoid pronouncing a sentence of death, did not prevent his practising at the bar, and he speedily became a successful advocate. He now turned to literature and society, and came to be esteemed as one of the best writers and most popular dandies of Arras. He was a member of an Arras literary and musical society known as the "Rosati," of which L. N. M. Carnot was a member. The sympathetic quality of his voice won for his

---

[1]Confirmed by act of parliament, 24 Henry VIII, ch. 13, and authorized for all doctors and for B.D.'s.
[2]Confirmed in the Laudian code, 1636.

verses recited before this society applause not justified by their merits. In 1788 he took part in the discussion as to the way in which the states-general should be elected, showing clearly and forcibly in his *Adresse à la nation artésienne* that, if the former mode of election by the members of the provincial estates were again adopted, the new states-general would not represent the people of France. By the *Avis aux habitants de campagne* (Arras, 1789), which is almost certainly by him, he secured the support of the country electors, and, though but 30 years of age, poor and without influence, he was elected fifth deputy of the *tiers état* of Artois to the states-general. This election opened the way to his public career.

The Constituent Assembly.—When the states-general met at Versailles on May 5, 1789, the young deputy of Artois already possessed the one faculty which was to lead him to supremacy: he was a fanatic. Robespierre believed in the doctrines of Rousseau with all his heart, and would have gone to death for them; and in the belief that they would eventually succeed and regenerate France and mankind, he was ready to work with unwearied patience. While the constituent assembly occupied itself in drawing up a constitution, Robespierre turned from the assembly of provincial lawyers and wealthy *bourgeois* to the people of Paris. However, he spoke frequently in the constituent assembly, and often with great success, and was eventually recognized as second only to Jerôme Pétion de Villeneuve—if second to him—as a leader of the small body of the extreme left—the 30 voices, as Mirabeau contemptuously called them. When he instinctively felt that his doctrines would have no success in the assembly, he turned to the Society of the Friends of the Constitution, known later as the Jacobin club. The death of Mirabeau strengthened Robespierre's influence in the assembly, but on May 15, 1791, he showed his jealous suspicion of his colleagues by proposing and carrying the motion that no deputies who sat in the constituent could sit in the succeeding assembly. The flight of the king on June 20 and his arrest at Varennes made Robespierre declare himself at the Jacobin club to be *ni monarchiste ni républicain*. After the "massacre" of the Champ de Mars (on July 17, 1791) he established himself, in order to be nearer to the assembly and the Jacobins, in the house of Duplay, a cabinetmaker in the Rue St. Honoré and an ardent admirer of his, where he lived (with but two short intervals) till his death. At last came his day of triumph, when on Sept. 30, on the dissolution of the constituent assembly, the people of Paris crowned Pétion and himself as the two incorruptible patriots.

On the dissolution of the assembly he returned for a short visit to Arras, where he met with a triumphant reception. In November he returned to Paris and on Dec. 18 made a speech which marks a new epoch in his life. Jacques Pierre Brissot, the *âme politique* of the Girondin party which had been formed in the legislative assembly, urged vehemently that war should be declared against Austria, and the queen was equally urgent, in the hope that a victorious army might restore the old absolutism of the Bourbons. Two men opposed the projects of the queen and the Girondins—Jean Paul Marat and Robespierre. Robespierre feared a development of militarism, which might be turned to the advantage of the reaction. From that moment began the struggle which ended in the coups d'état of May 31 and June 2, 1793. Robespierre persisted in his opposition to the war; the Girondins, especially Brissot, attacked him violently, and in April 1792 he resigned the post of public prosecutor at the tribunal of Paris, which he had held since February, and started a journal, *Le Défenseur de la Constitution,* in his own defense. It is noteworthy that during the summer months of 1792 in which the fate of the Bourbon dynasty was being sealed, neither the Girondins in the legislative assembly nor Robespierre took any active part in overthrowing it. But Robespierre, though shocked at the shedding of blood, was willing to take his seat on the commune of Paris, which had overthrown Louis XVI, and might check the Girondins. The strong men of the commune were glad to have Robespierre's assistance, not because they cared for him or believed in him but because of the help got from his popularity, his reputation for virtue which had won for him the surname of "the Incorruptible,"

and his influence over the Jacobin club and its branches, which spread all over France. He therefore presented the petition of the commune of Paris on Aug. 16 to the legislative assembly, demanding the establishment of a revolutionary tribunal and the summoning of a convention. The massacres of September in the prisons, which Robespierre in vain attempted to stop, showed that the commune had more confidence in J. N. Billaud-Varenne than in him. Yet, as a proof of his personal popularity, he was a few days later elected first deputy for Paris to the national convention.

The Convention.—On the meeting of the convention the Girondins immediately attacked Robespierre; they were jealous of his influence in Paris, and knew that his single-hearted fanaticism would never forgive their intrigues with the king at the end of July. All personal disputes, however, gave way in December 1792 before the question of the king's trial, and here Robespierre took up a position which is at least easily understood. These are his words spoken on Dec. 3:

This is no trial; Louis is not a prisoner at the bar; you are not judges; you are—you cannot but be—statesmen, and the representatives of the nation. You have not to pass sentence for or against a single man, but you have to take a resolution on a question of the public safety, and to decide a question of national foresight. It is with regret that I pronounce the fatal truth: Louis ought to perish rather than a hundred thousand virtuous citizens; Louis must die, that the country may live.

This great question settled by the king's execution, the impracticable plans of the Girondins drove G. J. Danton, Carnot, Robert Lindet and even Billaud-Varenne to the side of Robespierre, whom, it is apparent, they thoroughly understood. In the month of May 1793 Camille Desmoulins, acting under the inspiration of Robespierre and Danton, published his *Histoire des Brissotins* and *Brissot démasqué;* Maximin Isnard declared that Paris must be destroyed if it pronounced itself against the provincial deputies; Robespierre preached insurrection at the Jacobin club; and on May 31 and June 2 the commune of Paris destroyed the Girondin party.

Committee of Public Safety.—On July 27, 1793, when the struggle was practically decided, the convention elected Robespierre to the new Committee of Public Safety. Robespierre was always in a minority in the committee of 12, at least 7 of whom, Carnot, Billaud-Varenne, J. M. Collot d'Herbois, Comte Prieur-Duvernois, Prieur de la Marne, A. J. Saint André and Lindet, were men of action and not under his personal influence. Robespierre was not the inventor of the Terror or its machinery, the revolutionary tribunal and the representatives of the committee on mission in the provinces. He served it by his gift of eloquence. He had a fanatical following among the Jacobins and was one of the most popular orators in the convention, on which his carefully prepared addresses made a deep impression. His panegyrics on the system of revolutionary government and his praise of virtue led his hearers to believe that the system of the Terror, instead of being monstrous, was absolutely laudable; his pure life and admitted incorruptibility threw a lustre on the committee of which he was a member; and his colleagues were glad to avail themselves of these advantages so long as he did not interfere with their work. Moreover, he alone never left Paris, while all the others, except Bertrand Barère de Vieuzac, were constantly engaged on missions to the armies, the navy and the provinces. It has been asserted that Robespierre, Georges Couthon and Saint-Just took upon themselves the direction of "la haute politique," while the other members acted only in subordinate capacities; undoubtedly it would have suited Robespierre to have had this believed, but as a matter of fact he was in no way especially trusted in matters of supreme importance.

It is clear, therefore, that Robespierre was not the sole author of the overthrow of the Dantonists and the Hébertists, though he thoroughly agreed with the majority and had no desire to save them, the Hébertist principle of decentralization and the Dantonist moderatism being equally obnoxious to him.

Fall of Danton.—Both parties must be crushed. Before the blows at the leaders of those two parties were struck, Robespierre retired for a month (Feb. 13–March 13, 1794) from active business in the convention and the committee, apparently to consider his position; but he came to the conclusion that the cessation of the Reign of Terror would mean the loss of that supremacy by which he hoped to establish the ideal of Rousseau; for Danton, he knew, was essentially a practical statesman and laughed at his ideas and especially his politico-religious projects. He must have considered, too, that the result of his siding with Danton would probably have been fatal to himself. The result of his deliberations was that he abandoned Danton and co-operated in the attacks of the committee on the two parties. On March 15 he reappeared in the convention; on March 19 J. R. Hébert and his friends were arrested, and on March 24 they were guillotined. On March 30 Danton, Camille Desmoulins and their friends were arrested, and on April 5 they, too, were guillotined.

It was not until after the execution of Danton that Robespierre began to develop a policy distinct from that of his colleagues in the committee, an opposition which ended in his downfall. He began by using his influence over the Jacobin club to dominate the commune of Paris through his devoted adherents, two of whom, J. B. E. Fleuriot-Lescot and C. F. de Payan, were elected respectively mayor and *procureur* of the commune. He also attempted to usurp the influence of the other members of the committee over the armies by getting his young adherent, Saint-Just, sent on a mission to the frontier. In Paris Robespierre determined to increase the pressure of the Terror: no one should accuse him of moderatism; through the increased efficiency of the revolutionary tribunal Paris should tremble before him as the chief member of the committee, and the convention should pass whatever measures he might dictate. To secure his aims, Couthon, his other ally in the committee, proposed and carried on June 10 the outrageous law of 22nd Prairial, by which even the appearance of justice was taken from the tribunal, which, as no witnesses were allowed, became a simple court of condemnation. The result of this law was that between June 12 and July 28, the day of Robespierre's death, no fewer than 1,285 victims perished by the guillotine in Paris. It was the bloodiest and the least justifiable period of the Terror. But before this there had taken place in Robespierre's life an episode of supreme importance, as illustrating his character and his political aims: on May 7 he secured a decree from the convention recognizing the existence of the Supreme Being. This worship of the Supreme Being was based upon the ideas of Rousseau in the *Social Contract*, and was opposed by Robespierre to Catholicism on the one hand and the Hébertist atheism on the other. In honour of the Supreme Being a great fete was held on June 8; Robespierre, as president of the convention, walked first and delivered his harangue, and as he looked around him he may well have believed that his position was secured and that he was at last within reach of a supreme power which should enable him to impose his belief on all France, and so ensure its happiness. The devotion of Robespierre's adherents was further excited by the news that a half-witted girl, named Cécile Renault, had been found wandering near his house with a knife in her possession, intending to play the part of Charlotte Corday. She was executed on June 17, on the very day that M. G. A. Vadier raised a laugh at Robespierre's expense in the convention by his report on the conspiracy of Catherine Théot, a madwoman, who had asserted that Robespierre was a divinity.

The 9th Thermidor.—Robespierre felt that he must strike his blow now or never. Yet he was not sufficiently audacious to strike at once, as Payan and Jean Baptiste Coffinhal, the ablest of his adherents, would have had him do, but retired from the convention for several weeks, as he had done before the overthrow of the Hébertists and the Dantonists, to prepare his plan of action. These weeks, the last of his life, Robespierre passed very peacefully. He continued to live with the Duplays, with whose daughter Éléonore he had fallen in love, and used to wander with her in the Champs Élysées during the long summer evenings. At last, on July 26, Robespierre appeared, for the first time for more than four weeks, in the convention and delivered a carefully studied harangue, which lasted for more than four hours, in which he declared that the Terror ought to be ended, that certain deputies who had acted unjustly and exceeded their powers ought to be punished and that the Committees of Public Safety and General Security ought to be renewed. The majority of the Committee of Public Safety determined to act promptly. The convention, moved by Robespierre's eloquence, at first passed his motions; but he was replied to by Joseph Cambon the financier, Billaud-Varenne, J. B. A. Amar and Vadier, and the convention rescinded their decrees and referred Robespierre's question to their committees. On the following day, July 27, or in the revolutionary calendar the 9th Thermidor, Saint-Just began to speak on behalf of the motions of Robespierre, when violent interruptions showed the temper of the convention. Jean Lambert Tallien, Billaud-Varenne and Vadier again attacked Robespierre; cries of "Down with the tyrant!" were raised; and, when Robespierre hesitated in his speech in answer to these attacks, the words "C'est le sang de Danton qui t'étouffe" showed what was uppermost in the minds of the Mountain. Robespierre tried in vain to gain a hearing, the excitement increased and at five in the afternoon Robespierre, Couthon and Saint-Just, with two young deputies, Augustin Robespierre (younger brother of Maximilien) and Philippe François Joseph Lebas, the only men in all the convention who supported them, were ordered to be arrested. Robespierre was speedily rescued from his prison, with the other deputies, by the troops of the commune and brought to the *hôtel de ville*. There he was surrounded by his faithful adherents, led by Payan and

Coffinhal. But the day was past when the commune could overawe the convention, for now the men of action were hostile to the commune and its chief was not a master of coups d'état. On the news of the release of Robespierre, the convention had again met and declared the members of the commune and the released deputies outlawed. The national guards under the command of vicomte de Barras made their way to the *hôtel de ville*; Robespierre was shot in the lower jaw by a young gendarme named Meda while signing an appeal to one of the sections of Paris to take up arms for him, though the wound was afterward believed to have been inflicted by himself; and all the released deputies were again arrested. After a night of agony, Robespierre was the next day taken before the tribunal, where his identity as an outlaw was proved, and without further trial he was executed with Couthon and Saint-Just and 19 others of his adherents on the Place de la Révolution on the 10th Thermidor (July 28), 1794.

Character.—The character of Robespierre, when looked upon simply in the light of his actions and his authenticated speeches, and apart from the innumerable legends which have grown up about it, is comparatively simple. A well-educated and accomplished young lawyer, he might have acquired a good provincial practice and lived a happy provincial life had it not been for the Revolution. Like thousands of other young Frenchmen, he had read the works of Rousseau and taken them as gospel. Just at the very time in life when this illusion had not been destroyed by the realities of life, and without the experience which might have taught the futility of idle dreams and theories, he was elected to the states-general. At Paris he was not understood till he met with his audience of fellow disciples of Rousseau at the Jacobin club. His fanaticism won him supporters; his singularly sweet and sympathetic voice gained him hearers; and his upright life attracted the admiration of all. As matters approached nearer and nearer to the terrible crisis, he failed, except in the two instances of the question of war and of the king's trial, to show himself a statesman, for he had not the liberal views and practical instincts which made Mirabeau and Danton great men. His admission to the Committee of Public Safety gave him power, which he hoped to use for the establishment of his favourite theories, and for the same purpose he acquiesced in and even heightened the horrors of the Reign of Terror. It is here that the fatal mistake of allowing a theorist to have power appeared: Billaud-Varenne systematized the Terror because he believed it necessary for the safety of the country; Robespierre intensified it in order to carry out his own ideas and theories. Robespierre's private life was always respectable; he was always emphatically a gentleman and man of culture, and even a little bit of a dandy, scrupulously honest, truthful and charitable. In his habits and manner of life he was simple and laborious; he was not a man gifted with flashes of genius, but one who had to think much before he could come to a decision, and he worked hard all his life.

On the family of Robespierre *see* A. J. Paris in the *Mémoires,* 2nd series, vol. iii, of the Academy of Arras; the *Oeuvres de Maximilien Robespierre,* 3 vol. (1840), published by Laponneraye with preface by Armand Carrel, contain some of his speeches and the memoirs of Charlotte Robespierre on her brothers. An edition of the *Oeuvres,* 2 vol. (1913) was edited by A. Lesueur. The standard work on Robespierre's career is Ernest Hamel, *Histoire de Robespierre d'après des papiers de famille, les sources originales et des documents entièrement inédits,* 3 vol. (1865–67). After the appearance of the first volume, the publisher refused to proceed for fear of prosecution until compelled to do so by the author. Another edition with a different title appeared in 1878. *See* also C. d'Hericault, *La Révolution de Thermidor,* 2nd ed. (1878); Karl Brunnemann, *Maximilien Robespierre* (Leipzig, 1880); F. A. Aulard, *Les Orateurs de l'Assemblée Constituante* (1882); M. de Lescure, "Le Roman de Robespierre," in *La Société française pendant la Terreur* (1882); E. Hamel, *La Maison de Robespierre* (1895); Hilaire Belloc, *Robespierre* (1901); C. F. Warwick, *Robespierre and the French Revolution* (1909); A. Mathiez, *Études Robespierristes,* 2 vol. (1897, 1918), and *Autour de Robespierre* (1925). Many of the books which have been written about Robespierre are most untrustworthy, and the picture of him given by Thomas Carlyle in his *French Revolution* is unjust.

THE AMERICAN ROBIN (TURDUS MIGRATORIUS), ALSO CALLED ROBIN REDBREAST IN NEW ENGLAND

ROBIN, the name applied to a number of familiar birds; in England to *Erithacus rubecula* (*see* REDBREAST); in North America to *Turdus migratorius* and *P. confinis,* which are thrushes with a loud cheery song, reddish breast and dark slate back and wings. *T. migratorius* breeds north to Alaska, wintering from the northern United States southward. The western robin (*T. m. propinquus*) is found from the eastern base of the Rocky mountains to the Pacific coast.

ROBIN HOOD, English legendary hero. The oldest datable mention of Robin Hood at present known occurs in the second edition of *Piers Plowman,* the date of which is about 1377. In that poem the figure of Sloth is represented as saying:

> "I can nou3te perfitly my pater-noster, as
> the prest it syngeth:
> But I can rymes of Robyn Hood and Randolf
> Erle of Chestre."

He is next mentioned by Andrew of Wyntoun in his *Original Chronicle of Scotland,* written about 1420. Of his popularity in the latter half of the 15th and in the 16th centuries there are many signs. In the Elizabethan era and afterward mentions abound. Of the ballads themselves, *Robin Hood and the Monk* is possibly as old as the reign of Edward II (see Thomas Wright's *Essays on England in the Middle Ages,* ii, 174); *Robin Hood and the Potter* and *Robyn and Gandelyn* are certainly not later than the 15th century. Most important of all is *A Lytell Geste of Robyn Hode,* which was first printed about 1510 (see A. W. Pollard's *Fifteenth Century Prose and Verse* [1903]). This is evidently founded on older ballads; we read in *The Seconde Fytte,* 11, 176 and 177:

> "He wente hym forthe full mery syngynge,
> As men have told in tale."

In fact, it does for the Robin Hood cycle what a few years before Sir Thomas Malory had done for the Arthurian romances.

These are the facts about him and his balladry. Of conjectures there is no end. He has been represented as the last of the Saxons—as a Saxon holding out against the Norman conquerors as late as the end of the 12th century (see Augustin Thierry's *Norman Conquest,* and compare Sir Walter Scott's *Ivanhoe*). J. M. Gutch maintains that he was a follower of Simon de Montfort. The Robin Hood story has probably some historical basis. Sloth in Langland's poem couples him with Randle, earl of Chester, whom we believe to have been the third Randle (see Bishop Thomas Percy's folio manuscript, ed. Hales and Furnivall, i, 260 [1867-68]); and, possibly enough, Hood was contemporary with that earl, who flourished in the reigns of Richard I, John and Henry III. His myth was, as is evident from what we have already said, full grown in the first half of the 14th century.

That the Robin Hood story attracted to it and appropriated other elements is illustrated by its subsequent history. Thus later on we find it connected with the Morris dance; but the Morris dance was not known in England before the 16th century or late in the 15th. The Maid Marian (*q.v.*) element has been thought to have been introduced for the purpose of these performances, which were held on May day and were immensely popular (see Hugh Latimer's *Frutefull Sermons* [1571], p. 75; also *Paston Letters,* ed. J. Gairdner, iii, 89). After 1615, the date of the pageant prepared for the mayoralty of Sir John Jolles, draper, by Anthony Munday and entitled *Metropolis Coronata,* the yeoman of the older version was metamorphosed into the earl of Huntingdon, for whom in the following century William Stukeley discovered a satisfactory pedigree. The earl of Huntingdon was probably a nickname for a hunter. The rise, development and decay of the myth deserve thorough study.

What perhaps is its greatest interest is its expression of the popular mind about the close of the middle ages. Robin Hood was at that time the people's ideal, as Arthur is that of the upper classes. He is the ideal yeoman, as Arthur is the ideal knight. He readjusts the distribution of property; he robs the rich and endows the poor. He is an earnest worshipper of the Virgin, but a vigorous hater of monks and abbots. He is the great sportsman, the incomparable archer, the lover of the greenwood and of a free life, brave, adventurous, jocular, open-handed, a protector of women. The story is localized in Barnsdale and Sherwood; *i.e.,* between Doncaster and Nottingham. In Yorkshire, Nottinghamshire and Lincolnshire a host of place names testify to the popularity of the Robin Hood legend—Robin Hood's Bay, Robin Hood's cave, Robin Hood's chase, Robin Hood's cup (a well), Robin Hood's chair and many more.

The best collections of Robin Hood poems are those of J. Ritson (1795), F. J. Child in the 5th volume of his *English and Scotch Popular Ballads* (1888); and F. Jackson, *Popular Ballads of the Olden Time,* 4th series (1912). *See also* F. B. Gummere, *Old English Ballads* (1894). The versions in the Percy folio, ed. by Hales and Furnivall, vol. i (1867), are unhappily mutilated; but they should be consulted, for some are of a unique character, and that on "Robin Hoode his death" is of singular interest. The earliest "Garland" was printed in 1670, and in 1678 appeared a prose version which was reprinted by W. J. Thomas in his *Early English Prose Romances,* vol. ii (1858). Sir S. Lee's memoir in the *Dictionary of National Biography* is extremely erudite, and two valuable articles, contributed by Sir E. Brabrook to the *Antiquary* (June and July 1906) might be consulted. *See also* W. Stukeley, *Paleographia Britannica,* no. i, 115 (1795); A. Thierry, *Conquête de l'Angleterre* (1830); J. Hunter, *Great Hero of the Ancient Minstrelsy of England, Robin Hood* (1852).

ROBIN HOOD'S BAY, a fishing town and seaside resort in the parish of Fylingdales, North Riding of Yorkshire, Eng., 6½ mi. S.E. of Whitby by the North-Eastern Region railway. The bay is a shallow indentation of the coast, fringed with a line of high cliffs which is broken in places by steep-sided gullies. On the adjoining moor are prehistoric British tumuli popularly called Robin Hood's Butts.

ROBINIA or Locust, a genus of about 15 species natives of North America and Central America, belonging to the family Leguminosae. The best-known species (*R. pseudoacacia*) was introduced into Europe in 1636. This tree, the black locust, often erroneously called acacia, is now widely cultivated as an ornamental tree in Europe. It grows from 30 to 60 ft. high, and bears long, graceful compound leaves with 9 to 17 bright-green oblong leaflets, and white fragrant flowers in loose pendulous racemes, recalling the laburnum. There are many varieties varying in the method of growth, the presence or absence of thorns (persistent spinose stipules) on the branches and the colour of the flower.

FROM HARRAR, "GUIDE TO SOUTHERN TREES"
(McGRAW-HILL BOOK COMPANY, INC.)

BLACK LOCUST
1. Leaf. 2. Cluster of flowers. 3. Individual flower, enlarged. 4. Twig. 5. Fruit. 6. Seed

In the eastern United States, where it is native, it grows from 70 to 80 ft. high with a trunk 3 or 4 ft. in diameter. It is a valuable timber tree; the wood is heavy, hard, strong, close-grained and durable.

The clammy locust (*R. viscosa*), a tree sometimes 40 ft. high, with pinkish flowers, and the rose or moss locust (*R. hispida*), a small shrub, with showy rose-coloured flowers and hispid twigs, both native to the southeastern United States, are also cultivated for ornament.

The shipmast locust, a natural variety of black locust, is being used extensively by American foresters in reforestation projects, particularly in the shelter belt regions of the midwest.

ROBINSON, EDWARD (1794-1863), U.S. biblical scholar, was born in Southington, Conn., on April 10, 1794. In 1837 he became professor of biblical literature in Union Theological seminary, and left the U.S. for three years of study in Palestine and Germany, the fruit of which, his *Biblical Researches* (published simultaneously in England, Germany and the U.S. in 1841), brought him the gold medal of the Royal Geographical society in 1842.

Later Biblical Researches appeared in 1856. His plans to sum up his important topographical studies in a work on biblical geography were cut short by cataract in 1861 and by his death in New York city on Jan. 27, 1863. A great biblical scholar and exegete, Robinson must be considered the pioneer and father of biblical geography. His *Biblical Researches,* supplemented by the *Physical Geography of the Holy Land* (1865), were based on careful personal exploration and tempered by a thoroughly critical spirit, which was possibly at times too sceptical of local tradition.

Of scarcely less value in their day were Robinson's *Greek Har-*

mony of the Gospels (1845) and his *Greek and English Lexicon of the New Testament* (1836).

See H. B. Smith and R. D. Hitchcock, *The Life, Writings and Character of Edward Robinson* (1863); a biography of Mrs. Robinson was published, with a collection of her stories, in Leipzig (1874).

ROBINSON, EDWIN ARLINGTON (1869–1935), U.S. poet, was born at Head Tide, Me., Dec. 22, 1869. From the public schools of Gardiner, Me., he proceeded in 1891 to Harvard, but withdrew after two years. Most of his later life was spent in New York city, where he was for a time a subway inspector and, through Pres. Theodore Roosevelt's recognition of his merit, a clerical worker in the customs house. He received several awards of the Pulitzer prize for poetry.

His verse includes *The Torrent and the Night Before* (1896), *The Children of the Night* (1897), *Captain Craig* (1902), *The Town Down the River* (1910), *The Man against the Sky* (1916), *Merlin* (1917), *Lancelot* (1920), *The Three Taverns* (1920), *Avon's Harvest* (1921), *Collected Poems* (1921), *Roman Bartholow* (1923), *The Man Who Died Twice* (1924), *Dionysus in Doubt* (1925), *Tristram* (1927) and *Cavender's House* (1929). Experiments in a different medium are the prose plays *Van Zorn* (1914) and *The Porcupine* (1915). Robinson's work, of singularly uniform poetic excellence and of penetrating insight, gives him a foremost place among modern writers.

See biographical and critical monographs by Lloyd Morris (with a bibliography by W. Van R. Whitall, 1923), by B. R. Redman (1926) and by Mark Van Doren (1927).

ROBINSON, HENRY CRABB (1775–1867), English journalist and diarist, the son of a tanner, was born at Bury St. Edmunds on March 13, 1775. He travelled much on the continent of Europe, and acted as special war correspondent for the *Times* in 1807–08. From 1813 to 1828 he practised at the bar. He is remembered chiefly as the friend of Lamb, Coleridge, Wordsworth and Southey.

Robinson was a great conversationalist, and his breakfast parties rivalled those of Samuel Rogers. He died in London on Feb. 5, 1867.

His *Diary* of 35 vol., his *Journals* of 30 vol. and his *Letters and Reminiscences* in 36 vol. contain vivid pictures, drawn by an acute and sympathetic observer who had exceptional opportunities of studying contemporary celebrities. They are preserved at Dr. Williams' library in Gordon Square, London. Crabb Robinson seems to have intended to edit these for publication, but except for a selection edited by Thomas Sadler and entitled *The Diary, Reminiscences, and Correspondence of H. Crabb Robinson*, 3 vol. (1869) and the *Correspondence of Henry Crabb Robinson with the Wordsworth Circle* ed. by E. J. Morley, 2 vol. (1927) they have never been reprinted. Crabb Robinson was one of the founders of the Athenaeum club and of University college, London.

ROBINSON, JOHN (1575–1625), English nonconformist divine. Robinson settled in Amsterdam in 1608, but in the following year removed, with a large contingent, to Leyden, where he ministered to a community whose numbers gradually grew from 100 to 300. In 1620 a considerable minority of these sailed for England in the "Speedwell," and ultimately crossed the Atlantic in the "Mayflower"; it was Robinson's intention to follow as soon as practicable, with the rest of his flock, but he died before the plan could be carried out, on March 1, 1625.

Among his publications may be mentioned *Justification of Separation from the Church* (1610), *Apologia Brownistarum* (1619), *A Defence of the Doctrine Propounded by the Synod of Dort* (1624) and a volume of *Essays, or Observations Divine and Moral,* printed in 1625. His *Works* (with one exception, *A Manumission to a Manduction,* since published by the Massachusetts Historical Society, series iv, vol. i), including a memoir, were reprinted by R. Ashton in 3 vol. in 1851. A summary of their contents is given in G. Punchard, *History of Congregationalism,* iii, 300–344 (1867). *See* further CONGREGATIONALISM, and the literature there cited; also O. S. Davis, *John Robinson* (1897).

ROBINSON, JOSEPH TAYLOR (1872–1937), U.S. politician, was born at Lonoke, Ark., on Aug. 26, 1872. After graduating from the University of Arkansas and receiving his law degree at the University of Virginia, he returned to Lonoke in 1895 to practise. He became interested in politics at once, was elected a member of the state legislature, 1895–97, and served as delegate to the Democratic national convention in 1900. In 1902 he was elected U.S. representative, in which office he was continued until he was elected governor of Arkansas in 1912. He was governor but a few weeks when he was elected by the state legislature to fill the position of U.S. senator left vacant by the death of Sen. Jefferson Davis.

Robinson was re-elected senator in 1918 and in 1924. In 1923 he was chosen to succeed Sen. O. W. Underwood as chairman of the minority conference and Democratic floor leader. He possessed an unusual knowledge of parliamentary procedure, was a ready debater and was influential in securing much-needed legislation.

Robinson served as permanent chairman of the Democratic convention of 1928, and received the nomination of his party for the office of vice-president.

ROBINSON, LENNOX (1886–   ), Irish dramatist and author, was born at Douglas, County Cork, on Oct. 4, 1886, and educated at Bandon Grammar school. His first play, *The Clancy Name,* was produced in 1908 at the Abbey theatre, Dublin, of which he was manager from 1910 to 1914. In 1915 he was appointed organizing librarian to the Carnegie trust, a post which he held until 1925. From 1919 to 1923 he was again manager of the Abbey theatre, and in 1923 became director.

Robinson's plays *The Lost Leader* (1918) and *The White-headed Boy* (1916) were both produced in London and in the United States. In addition to numerous plays, he wrote a novel, *A Young Man from the South* (1917), and several volumes of short stories.

His plays include *The Cross Roads* (1909); *Two Plays* (1910); *Patriots* (1912); *The Dreamers* (1915); *The Round Table* (1924); *Crabbed Youth and Age* (1924); *Birds' Nest* (1938); *Pictures in a Theatre* (1947); and *The Lucky Finger* (1949).

ROBOT. This term has long been in use in many languages. It is derived from the Czech word *robit* (work). It passed into popular use after 1923 to describe either mechanical devices so ingenious as to be almost human, or workers whom mechanical and repetitive work was making almost into machines. Its popular usage is based on the play *R.U.R.* (Rossum's Universal Robots), written by the Czechoslovakian writer, Karel Capek, in which society is described as depending on mechanical workers, called robots, which can do any kind of mental or physical work and which when worn out are scrapped and replaced by new. In the play the robots develop intelligence and a spirit of revolt, turn upon their employers and exterminate their creators.

The construction of a mechanical man has captivated the imagination of men since antiquity and early literature contains many schemes for the construction of some device that would require no human effort. It is not improbable that this idea has had a marked influence upon the development of mechanics and other branches of physics. In the Icelandic saga, Frithiof's ship needed no helmsman; she understood what was said to her and obeyed. In 1927 a steamship made a run of 21 days from San Francisco to Auckland, N.Z., during which no human hand touched her steering apparatus. A modern robot had held her true to her compass course. (*see* GYROSCOPE; NAVIGATION.)

In the *Arabian Nights'* tale of the "Forty Thieves," Ali Baba stood before the cave and said "Open Sesame." The portal swung open without the aid of human hands. A robot controlling the door of an industrial plant in the U.S. actually opens when addressed in precisely the same words; addressed in any other manner the door remains immovable. In a mediaeval romance a great brazen head in the castle of a giant would tell those who inquired whatever they wished to know about the past, present or future.

In Washington, D.C., is a robot, known as the "Great Brass Brain" and to it are put questions about future ocean tides, which are promptly answered. It predicts the tides (*q.v.*) for every port in the world for years ahead with great precision. (See MATHEMATICAL INSTRUMENTS: *Harmonic Analyzers.*)

Mythical manlike monsters permeate the folklore of all peoples. Albertus Magnus in the middle ages, Roger Bacon, Descartes and other philosophers built androids or automatons in human form, which could open doors and play musical instruments. Anthropoid figures which apparently perform actions which call for independent thought are still to be seen and are often accepted with credulity by the public. On the other hand modern mechanical men have been constructed and placed at the disposal of industry, that have sensitive fingers and ears, talk with a predetermined conversation, that are able to test by "a sense of taste" chemicals, and with some equivalent of the sense of smell and balance. By the use of photo-electric cells, the partial equivalent of the sense of sight has been accomplished. (*See* the articles SELENIUM CELLS, PHOTOELECTRICITY, AUTOMATIC MACHINES.)

Perhaps the most valuable outcome of these endeavours will be the development of mechanisms capable of taking over those tasks that men and women find too monotonous or otherwise burdensome. One such device is the Televox, invented in 1927 by R. J. Wensley of the Westinghouse Electric and Manufacturing Co. This device permits the use of the network of the telephone system for the distant control of an electrical mechanism by means of certain sounds. The mechanism is arranged to answer the telephone and execute orders in a manner peculiarly similar to that of a human being. It was developed for the use of public utility companies to supplement the use of supervisory control systems of electrical sub-stations, reservoir systems, gas regulators, etc.

The Televox can transmit electric meter readings, heights of water, gas pressures, position of valves and switches, and can execute actual mechanical operations at the direction of a distant operator. In using the Televox a call is put through exactly as though there were a human operator on the other end of the phone. The person making the call uses certain tones of the desired pitch to transmit the message. It is essential that a consistency of pitch be maintained. These tones are ordinarily delivered by electrically driven tuning forks. The telephone transmitter converts the tones into electrical vibrations, which at the distant station are caused to actuate steel reeds, which in turn actuate the selecting and operating relays. The responses are obtained from an instrument placed near the transmitter which sounds certain combinations of long and short notes, to form a code understandable by the operator at the other phone. The machine "hangs up" the receiver when the order has been executed, thereby ending the "conversation."

There are a number of processing machines which control all processes in a given industry, including temperature and humidity control during the process, starting, stopping, and varying the different materials which enter into the process in accordance with a time schedule, and independent of an outlet. If anything goes wrong, the machine stops and shows a red light until the operator has made the necessary changes. At the conclusion of the operation the machine shows a green light until the operator has removed the material in process. The Tagliabue Automatic Flue-Gas Analyzing Machine which makes an analysis for CO_2 and for CO every minute, and records the results, is such a robot.

The Product Integraph is a robot which solves almost any second-order differential equation. It performs, by a combination of electrical and mechanical means, certain computations which are actually beyond the power of the human brain, so far demonstrated. Other processes, which if performed by mathematics would require from a week to a year to solve, are solved by the integraph in a few minutes or hours.

(For New York City traffic control system *see* TRAFFIC AND TRAFFIC REGULATION.)

ROB ROY (1671–1734), the designation of a Highland outlaw whose prowess is the theme of one of Sir Walter Scott's novels, and who was by descent a Macgregor. He received the name Roy from his red hair, and latterly adopted Campbell as his surname on account of the acts proscribing the name of his own clan. At first he devoted himself to rearing cattle on his estates on the Braes of Balquhidder, but having formed a band of clansmen, he obtained, after the accession of William III, a commission from James II to levy war on all who refused to acknowledge him as king. Shortly afterwards he married Helen Mary, daughter of Macgregor of Comar. On the death of Gregor Macgregor, the chief of the clan, in 1693 he was acknowledged chief, obtaining control of the lands stretching from the Braes of Balquhidder to the shores of Loch Lomond, and situated between the possessions of Argyll and those of Montrose. To assist in carrying on his trade as cattle-dealer he borrowed money from the

1st duke of Montrose, and, being unable to repay it, was in 1712 evicted and declared an outlaw. Taking refuge in the Highlands, Rob Roy supported himself by depredations on the duke and his tenants, all attempts to capture him being unsuccessful. During the rebellion of 1715, though nominally siding with the Pretender, he took no part in the battle of Sheriffmuir except in plundering the dead on both sides. He was included in the Act of Attainder; but through the influence of the duke of Argyll, he obtained, on making his submission at Inveraray, a promise of protection. He established his residence at Craigroyston, near Loch Lomond, whence he levied blackmail as formerly upon Montrose. Through the mediation of Argyll, he was reconciled to Montrose, and in 1722 he made submission to General Wade; he was carried off, and imprisoned in Newgate, and in 1727 was pardoned just as he was to be transported to Barbados. He died at Balquhidder on Dec. 28, 1734, and was buried in Balquhidder churchyard.

The best lives are K. Macleay, *Historical Memoirs of Rob Roy* (1818; new ed., 1881); A. H. Millar, *Story of Rob Roy* (1883). *See* also Sir W. Scott's introduction to the novel *Rob Roy*. An early account, *The Highland Rogue, etc.* (1723), is ascribed to Defoe.

ROBSART, AMY, first name of LADY AMY DUDLEY (1532–1560), wife of Lord Robert Dudley, afterwards earl of Leicester. She was the daughter of Sir John Robsart of Norfolk, and was married to Lord Robert on June 4, 1550. When Elizabeth became queen in 1559 Lord Robert was soon known to be her favourite, and it was believed that she would marry him if he were free. His wife never came to court and was never in his company. In 1560 she went by her husband's directions to Cumnor Place, a house near Oxford, rented by his agent Anthony Forster or Forrester, member of parliament for Abingdon. Here she was found lying dead on the floor of the hall on Sept. 8, 1560, by her servants. The circumstances of her death were never cleared up.

See G. Adlard, *Amy Robsart and Leycester* (London, 1870), and W. Rye, *The Murder of Amy Robsart* (London, 1885); Sir B. H. T. Frere, *Amy Robsart of Wymondham; the Story of her Life and the Mystery of her Death* (Norwich, 1937).

ROC, or more correctly RUKH, a fabulous bird of enormous size which carries off elephants to feed its young. The legend of the roc, familiar from the *Arabian Nights,* was widely spread in the east; and later the home of the monster was sought in Madagascar, when gigantic fronds of the *Raphia* palm very like a quill in form appear to have been brought under the name of roc's feathers (*see* Yule's *Marco Polo,* bk. iii, ch. 33). Such a feather was brought to the Great Khan, and we read also of a gigantic stump of a roc's quill being brought to Spain by a merchant from the China seas.

The roc is hardly different from the Arabian ʿankā (*see* PHOENIX); it is also identified with the Persian sīmurgh.

BIBLIOGRAPHY.—For a collection of legends about the roc, *see* E. W. Lane, *Arabian Nights* (1839), chap. xx, notes 22, 62; H. Yule, *The Book of Ser Marco Polo* (1871). *See* also S. Bochart, *Hierozoicon* (1663), bk. vi, ch. 14; Al Kazwīnī, *Kosmographie* (1847–48), i, 419 *et seq.*; Ibn Batūta, *Voyages* (1853), iv, 305 *et seq.*; Ad Damīrī, *Hayat al-Hay-awan,* trans. A. S. G. Jayakar (1906).

ROCAILLE, in architecture, a form of ornament much used in the rococo styles, based originally on the grotesque, artificial rockeries and shells of the Louis XV period. (*See* LOUIS STYLES; ROCOCO.)

ROCAMADOUR, a village of southwestern France, in the department of Lot, 36 mi. N.N.E. of Cahors by road. Pop. (1946) 185. Rocamadour owes its origin to St. Amadour or Amateur, who, according to tradition, chose the place as a hermitage for his devotions to the Virgin Mary. The renown of Rocamadour as a place of pilgrimage dates from the early middle ages. Rocamadour is most strikingly situated. Its buildings rise in stages up the side of a cliff on the right slope of the gorge of the Alzou. Flights of steps ascend from the lower town to the churches halfway up the cliff. The chief of them is the church of Notre-Dame (1479), containing the wooden figure of the Madonna reputed to have been carved by St. Amadour. The interior walls of the church of St. Sauveur are covered with paintings and inscriptions recalling the pilgrimages of celebrated persons. The subterranean church of St. Amadour (1166) extends beneath St. Sauveur and contains relics of the saint. On the summit of the

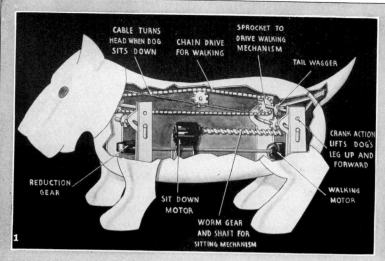

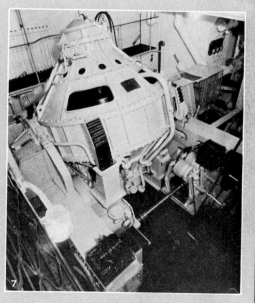

BY COURTESY OF (1) THE WESTINGHOUSE ELECTRIC AND MANUFACTURING COMPANY, (2, 7) THE SPERRY GYROSCOPE COMPANY, (3) THE WILSON-MAUELEN COMPANY, (4) THE C. J. TAGLIABUE MANUFACTURING COMPANY, (5) THE U.S. COAST AND GEODETIC SURVEY, THE U.S. DEPARTMENT OF COMMERCE, (6) THE DAILY MAIL, LONDON

ROBOTS AND THEIR FUNCTIONS IN VARIOUS INDUSTRIES

1. Cut-away drawing of "Sparko," a robot dog that walks, sits down or barks at his master's command; companion to "Elektro," mechanical man at the New York World's Fair, 1940. 2. Automatic direction finder for aeroplanes. When tuned to a radio station, it points continuously and automatically to that station without requiring the pilot's attention. 3. A single robot used in pyrometry. 4. An automatic cycle controller, used in industry for the regulation of the various steps in a manufacturing process, in this case for controlling all the operations in the curing of rubber. 5. American Coast and Geodetic Survey tide-predicting machine. 6. "Eric," a novel theatrical adaptation of the robot, which moves and talks by means of concealed apparatus. 7. The Sperry ship stabilizer by means of which freedom from undue rolling is obtained

cliff stands the mediaeval château built to defend the sanctuaries.

ROCAMBOLE (*Allium scorodoprasum*; family Liliaceae), a hardy bulbous perennial occurring in a wild state in sandy pastures and waste places throughout Europe and Asia Minor (often called giant garlic) but not common in the south; in Great Britain it is rare, and found only in the north of England and the south of Scotland. The plant is grown for its bulbs, which are smaller and milder than those of garlic, and consist of several cloves chiefly produced at the roots. The cloves are planted about the end of February or in March, and treated like shallot. It is practically unknown in the United States.

ROCH, ST. (Lat. Rochus; Ital. Rocco; Span. Roque; Fr. Roch) (d. 1327), a confessor whose death is commemorated on Aug. 16; he is specially invoked against the plague. According to his *Acta*, he was born at Montpellier, Fr., about 1295. On the death of his parents in his 20th year he gave all his substance to the poor. During an epidemic of plague in Italy, he tended the sick at Aquapendente, Cesena and Rome, and effected miraculous cures by prayer and simple contact. After similar ministries at Piacenza he himself fell ill. He was expelled from the town and withdrew into the forest, where he would have perished had not a dog belonging to a nobleman named Gothardus supplied him with bread. On his return to Montpellier he was arrested as a spy and thrown into prison, where he died Aug. 16, 1327, having previously obtained from God this favour—that all plague-stricken persons invoking him be healed. His cult spread through Spain, France, Germany, Belgium and Italy. A magnificent temple was raised to him at Venice.

See *Acta sanctorum*, August iii, 380–415; Charles Cahier, *Les Caractéristiques des saints*, pp. 216–217 (Paris, 1867).   (H. De.)

ROCHAMBEAU, JEAN BAPTISTE DONATIEN DE VIMEUR, Comte de (1725–1807), French soldier, was born at Vendôme (Loir-et-Cher) on July 1, 1725. He was brought up at the Jesuit college at Blois, but entered a cavalry regiment. He served in Bohemia and Bavaria and on the Rhine, and in 1747 had attained the rank of colonel. He became governor of Vendôme in 1749, and after distinguishing himself in 1756 in the Minorca expedition was promoted brigadier of infantry. In 1757 and 1758 he fought in Germany, notably at Crefeld, received several wounds in the battle of Clostercamp (1760), and was appointed *maréchal de camp* in 1761 and inspector of cavalry. In 1780 he was sent, with the rank of lieutenant general, in command of 6,000 French troops to help the American colonists under Washington against the English. He landed at Newport, R.I., on July 10, but was held there inactive for a year, because of his reluctance to abandon the French fleet, blockaded by the British in Narragansett bay. At last, in July 1781, Rochambeau's force was able to leave Rhode Island and joined Washington on the Hudson. Then followed the celebrated march of the combined forces to Yorktown, where on Sept. 22 they joined the troops of Lafayette; Cornwallis was forced to surrender on Oct. 19. Congress voted Rochambeau and his troops the thanks of the nation and presented him with two cannon taken from the English. These guns, which Rochambeau took back to Vendôme, were requisitioned in 1792. On his return to France he was loaded with favours by Louis XVI and was made governor of Picardy. During the Revolution he commanded the army of the north in 1790, but resigned in 1792. He was arrested during the Terror, and narrowly escaped the guillotine. He was subsequently pensioned by Bonaparte, and died at Thoré (Loir-et-Cher) on May 10, 1807.

A statue of Rochambeau by Ferdinand Hamar, the gift of France to the United States, was unveiled in Lafayette square, Washington, by Pres. Theodore Roosevelt on May 26, 1902.

BIBLIOGRAPHY.—The *Mémoires militaires, historiques et politiques, de Rochambeau* were published by Luce de Lancival in 1809. Of the first volume a part, translated into English by M. W. E. Wright, was published in 1838 under the title of *Memoirs of the Marshal Count de R. Relative to the War of Independence in the United States*. Rochambeau's correspondence during the American campaign is published in H. Doniol, *Histoire de la participation de la France à l'établissement des États Unis d'Amérique*, vol. v (1892). See Duchesne, "Autour de Rochambeau," in the *Revue des facultés catholiques de l'ouest* (1898–1900); E. Gachot, "Rochambeau," in the *Nouvelle revue* (1902); H. de Ganniers, "La Dernière Campagne du maréchal de Rochambeau," in the *Revue des questions historiques* (1901); and J. J. Jusserand, "Rochambeau and the French in America," in *With Americans of Past and Present Days* (1916).

ROCHDALE, a county and parliamentary borough, Lancashire, Eng., 11 mi. N.N.E. of Manchester by road. Pop. (1951) 88,429. Area 14.9 sq.mi. The town lies at the foot of a western spur of the Pennines and at the junction of the Spodden with the Roch, which latter flows through the town (the central part has been covered in). The moribund Rochdale canal also passes through the town. The manufacture of cotton, woollen and rayon materials are the main industries, and there are engineering, asbestos, rubber, electrical and other works. Rochdale has an art gallery, a museum, a repertory theatre and five parks in addition to Hollingworth lake (117 ac.) 3½ mi. N.E.

Rochdale was the birthplace of the co-operative movement, the Rochdale Pioneers' Equitable society having been founded there in 1844. The first shop, in Toad lane, has been restored to its original appearance. A statue of John Bright (1811–89) recalls the connection of the statesman's family with Rochdale.

Rochdale was incorporated in 1856, but the parliamentary borough has returned one member since 1832. The county borough was created in 1888 and extended in 1933.

Rochdale (Recedham, Rachedam, Rachedal) takes its name from the river on which it stands. A Roman road passed the site, and a Saxon castle stood in Castleton. During Edward the Confessor's reign most of the land was held by Gamel the Thane, but after the Conquest the manor came into the hands of Roger de Poictou, from whom it passed to the Lacys and became merged in the duchy of Lancaster. From 1462 to 1625 the crown leased it to the Byron family. In 1625 Charles I conveyed the manor in trust, and in 1638 it was sold to Sir John Byron, afterward Baron Byron of Rochdale, whose descendants held it till 1823 when it was sold to the Deardens. Henry III (1240–41) granted to Edmund de Lacy the right to hold a weekly market on Wednesday and an annual fair on the feast of SS. Simon and Jude (Oct. 28).

ROCHDALE PIONEERS: see Co-operation.

ROCHEFORT, HENRI, Marquis de Rochefort-Luçay (1830–1913), French politician, was born in Paris on Jan. 30, 1830. He was already known as a successful journalist and writer of vaudevilles when he started a paper of his own, *La Lanterne*. The paper was seized on its 11th appearance, and in Aug. 1868 Rochefort was fined 10,000 fr., with a year's imprisonment. He then published his paper in Brussels, whence it was smuggled into France. Printed in French, English, Spanish, Italian and German, it went the round of Europe. After a second prosecution he fled to Belgium. A series of duels, of which the most famous was one fought with Paul de Cassagnac apropos of an article on Joan of Arc, kept Rochefort in the public eye. In 1869 he was returned to the chamber of deputies by the first *circonscription* of Paris. He renewed his onslaught on the empire, starting a new paper, the *Marseillaise*, as the organ of political meetings arranged by himself at La Villette. The staff was appointed on the votes of the members, and included Victor Noir and Pascal Grousset. The violent articles in this paper led to the duel which resulted in Victor Noir's death at the hands of Prince Pierre Bonaparte. The paper was seized, and Rochefort and Grousset were sent to prison for six months. The revolution of September was the signal for his release. He became a member of the government of national defense, but he openly expressed sympathy with the Communards, and on May 11, 1871, he fled in disguise from Paris. A week earlier he had resigned with a handful of other deputies from the national assembly rather than countenance the dismemberment of France.

Condemned under military law to imprisonment for life, he was transported to New Caledonia. In 1874 he escaped to San Francisco. He lived in London and Geneva until the general amnesty permitted his return to France in 1880. He then founded *L'Intransigeant* in the radical interest. He was condemned to detention in a fortress in Aug. 1889 at the same time as General Boulanger, whom he had followed into exile. After his return (1895) to Paris he became a leader of the anti-Dreyfusards. Subsequently he was editor of *La Patrie*. Rochefort died at Aix-les-

Bains in 1913.

Besides his plays and articles in the journals he published several separate works, among them being: *Les Petits mystères de l'Hôtel des Ventes* (1862), a collection of his art criticisms; *Les Dépravés* (Geneva, 1882); *Les Naufrageurs* (1876); *L'Evadé* (1883); *Napoléon dernier*, 3 vol. (1884); and *Les Aventures de ma vie*, 5 vol. (1896).

ROCHEFORT, a small town of Belgium, on the Lomme, a tributary of the Lesse, in the southeast of the province of Namur close to the Ardenne. Resident pop. (1939) 3,492, doubles in July and August. It has ruins of the old castle, which gave the place its name and a title to a long line of counts who had the right of coining their own money. This castle underwent many sieges and suffered much in the earlier wars, especially at the hands of Marshal de Chatillon in 1636. Rochefort is noted for its healthfulness, and is a favourite place of residence and resort.

There are many grottoes, one of which, in the town itself, contains six halls or chambers; the largest, called the Sabbat, is remarkable for its great height. But the most famous are the grottoes of Han, 3 mi. from Rochefort where the river Lesse passes by a subterranean and undiscovered passage under the hill called Boëme or Boine. The endeavour to trace the course of the river led to the discovery of the grottoes, which consist of 15 separate halls, connected by passages more or less short and emerging on the river in a dark and extensive cavern forming a sort of side creek or bay. Near Rochefort are the famous red marble quarries of St. Remy, and the old Cistercian abbey of that name is now a Trappist seminary.

ROCHEFORT, a town of western France, capital of an *arrondissement* in the department of Charente-Maritime, 20 mi. S.S.E. of La Rochelle on the state railway from Nantes to Bordeaux. Pop. (1946) 29,472.

The lordship of Rochefort, held by powerful nobles in the 11th century, was united to the French crown by Philip the Fair early in the 14th century; but it was alternately seized during the Hundred Years' War by the English and the French and in the Wars of Religion by the Catholics and Protestants. Colbert in 1665 chose Rochefort as the seat of a repairing port between Brest and the Gironde, so the town rapidly increased in importance, and the Dutch admiral Cornelius Tromp with his fleet failed to destroy the new arsenal. The naval school, afterward transferred to Brest, was originally founded at Rochefort. Its fleet, under Admiral la Gallissonnière, a native of the place, defeated Admiral Byng in 1755 and did good service in the wars of the republic. But the destruction of the French fleet by the English in 1809 in the roadstead of Ile d'Aix and the preference accorded to Brest and Toulon and the unhealthfulness of its climate diminished its prosperity.

It was from the Ile d'Aix that Napoleon embarked on the "Bellerophon" in 1815.

Rochefort is capital of the fourth maritime *arrondissement*. The commercial harbour, higher up the river than the naval harbour, has two small basins, a third basin with a depth at neap tide of 24 ft. and at spring tide of 30 ft., and a dry dock. Trade is in wood, cereals, salt and coal.

ROCHESTER, JOHN WILMOT, 2ND EARL OF (1647–1680), English poet and wit, the son of Henry Wilmot, the 1st earl, was born at Ditchley in Oxfordshire on April 10, 1647, and succeeded his father as 2nd earl in 1658. He was educated at Wadham college, Oxford, and in 1661, although he was only 14 years of age, received the degree of M.A. On leaving Oxford he travelled in France and Italy with a tutor. He returned in 1664, and at once made his way to Charles II's court, where his youth, good looks and wit assured him of a welcome. In 1665 he joined the fleet serving against the Dutch as a volunteer. He became gentleman of the bedchamber to Charles II. John Dryden had dedicated to Rochester his *Marriage-à-la-Mode* (1672); but Dryden's *Aurengzebe* (1675) was dedicated to Lord Mulgrave, who was Rochester's enemy. Consequently Rochester thwarted Dryden at every turn, and in 1679 a band of roughs set on the poet in Rose alley, Covent Garden, and beat him. Rochester obviously felt no shame for this infamous attack, for in his "Imitation of the First Satire of Juvenal" he says, "Who'd be a wit in Dryden's

cudgelled skin?" His health was already undermined, and in the spring of 1680 he retired to High lodge, Woodstock park. He began to show signs of a more serious temper, and at his own request was visited (July 20 to July 24) by Bishop Burnet, who attested the sincerity of his repentance. He died, however, two days after the bishop left him.

When his son Charles, the 3rd earl, died on Nov. 12, 1681, Rochester's titles became extinct.

As a poet Rochester was a follower of Abraham Cowley and of Boileau, to both of whom he was considerably indebted. His love lyrics are often happy, but his real vigour and ability is best shown in his critical poems and satires.

The political satires are notable for their fierce exposure of Charles II's weakness.

BIBLIOGRAPHY.—*Poems on Several Occasions by the Right Honourable the Earl of Rochester* . . . (Antwerp, 1680) was really printed in London. Other issues, slightly varying in title and contents, appeared in 1685, 1691 and 1696. *Valentinian, A Tragedy*, adapted from Beaumont and Fletcher, was printed in 1685; a scurrilous attack on Charles II in the shape of a play in heroic couplets, *Sodom*, was printed in 1684, and is supposed, in spite of Rochester's denial, to have been chiefly his work. No copy of this is known, but there are two manuscripts extant. The completest edition of his works is *The Poetical Works of the Earl of Rochester* (1731–32). Expurgated collections are to be found in Johnson's, Anderson's and Chalmers' editions of the *British Poets*. His *Familiar Letters* were printed in 1686, 1697 and 1699. His political satires are available, with those of Sir John Denham and Andrew Marvell, in the *Bibliotheca Curiosa, Some Political Satires of the Seventeenth Century*, vol. i (Edinburgh, 1885).

ROCHESTER, LAWRENCE HYDE, EARL OF (1642–1711), English statesman, second son of Edward Hyde, earl of Clarendon, was born in March 1642. After the restoration of Charles II he sat as member of parliament, first for Newport in Cornwall and afterward for the University of Oxford, from 1660 to 1679. In 1661 he was sent on a complimentary embassy to Louis XIV of France, while he held the court post of master of the robes from 1662 to 1675. In 1665 he married Henrietta (d. 1687), daughter of Richard Boyle, earl of Burlington and Cork. When his father was impeached in 1667, Lawrence joined with his elder brother, Henry, in defending him in parliament, but the fall of Clarendon did not injuriously affect the fortunes of his sons. They were connected with the royal family through the marriage of their sister, Anne, with the duke of York, afterward James II, and were both able and zealous royalists. In 1681 Lawrence Hyde, who had been made first lord of the treasury and a privy councillor in 1679, was made Viscount Hyde of Kenilworth, and in November following earl of Rochester. He was compelled to join in arranging the treaty of 1681, by which Louis XIV agreed to pay a subsidy to Charles, at the very moment when he was imploring William, prince of Orange, to save Europe from the ambitions of the French monarch. In Aug. 1684 he was removed from the treasury to the post of lord president of the council. He was still president of the council when James II became king in Feb. 1685, and he was at once appointed lord treasurer. But in spite of their family relationship and their long friendship, James and his treasurer did not agree. In Jan. 1687 he was removed from his office of treasurer.

After the revolution of 1688 Rochester, after a brief protest, accepted the new regime. From Dec. 1700 until Feb. 1703 he was lord lieutenant of Ireland, and in 1710 he was again made lord president of the council.

Rochester died on May 2, 1711, and was succeeded by his only son, Henry (1672–1753), who in 1723 inherited the earldom of Clarendon. When Henry died without issue on Dec. 10, 1753, all his titles became extinct.

The correspondence of Rochester with his brother the earl of Clarendon, together with other letters written by him, was published with notes by S. W. Singer, 2 vol. (London, 1828).

ROCHESTER, a city and municipal and parliamentary borough of Kent, Eng., on the river Medway, 33 mi. E.S.E. of London. Pop. (1951) 43,934. Area, 5.8 sq.mi. Its situation on the Roman way from the Kentish ports to London, as well as at a Medway crossing, gave Rochester (Durobrivae, Hrofescester or Hrobicester, Roffa) an early importance. It was a walled Romano-British town, and the original bridge across the Medway probably dated from that period. The church of St.

Andrew was founded by King Aethelbert, who also made Rochester a bishop's see. Rochester was a royal borough in the time of William I, who raised a castle there, probably on Boley hill. Richard I granted the citizens quittance of *passagium* from crusaders in the town of Rochester. In 1227 Henry III granted them the city at a fee farm rent of £25; he also granted them a guild merchant, the right to be impleaded only within the city walls and other liberties. These charters were confirmed by subsequent sovereigns down to Henry VI, who in 1446 incorporated the city, and granted it the power of admiralty and many privileges. Charters were granted in later reigns down to Charles I, whose charter of 1629 remained the governing charter until 1835. Rochester returned two members to parliament from Edward I's time until 1885, one from then until 1918, and two from then on.

The cathedral church of St. Andrew was originally founded by Augustine in 604, for whom Aethelbert built the church. It was partially destroyed by the Danes, but was rebuilt by Bishop Gundulph, the second Norman bishop (1077–1108). Gundulph at the same time (1089) established an order of Benedictine monks there. Bishop Ernulf (1115–24) completed and also renovated the church, lengthening it by two bays eastward; the old chapter house remains. The Norman west front was built about 1125–30, and in 1130 the new cathedral was consecrated. The work included an extended choir by William de Hoo (1227), enlargement of the main transepts, the building of piers for a central tower and treatment of the nave to the third bay. About 1352 a low central tower was built, to which a spire was added in the next century. Toward the end of the 15th century St. Mary's chapel was added.

The ruins of Gundulph's tower stand detached from and are earlier than the church; it was built by Bishop Gundulph probably as a defensive work for the eastern boundary of the city. The crypt beneath the choir is Early Norman in the western part. The remainder is Early English, and there are traces of mural painting. The library attached to the modern chapter house contains, among various relics, the *Textus Roffensis*, being records of the cathedral compiled in the time of Bishop Ernulf.

On the eminence overlooking the right bank of the river and commanding a wide view of the surrounding country are the remains of the Norman castle, part of which was built by Bishop Gundulph at the order of William Rufus in the 11th century. The castle was besieged by King John, by Simon de Montfort in the reign of Henry III and by the followers of Wat Tyler. It was repaired by Edward IV, but soon afterward fell into decay, although the massive keep still stands. This is the work of William de Corbeil, archbishop of Canterbury, to whom the castle was granted in 1126. It is a quadrangular four-storied structure, flanked by turrets, with a height of 120 ft. Remains of the 13th-century walls which once surrounded the city also exist. Charles Dickens lived at Gad's hill, above Strood, to the northwest. At Borstal, southwest of Rochester, was a large convict prison where early experiments on the educational treatment of delinquent boys between the ages of 16 and 21 were carried out, which resulted in the Borstal system (*q.v.*).

Among the principal buildings in the city are the town hall (1687), the Richard Watt's almshouses (1579) and the almshouse of St. Catherine, which originated in 1316 as a lepers' hospital. An Elizabethan mansion was acquired by the corporation for a museum as a memorial of Queen Victoria's diamond jubilee. The principal schools are the cathedral grammar school or King's school, founded in 1544, and the Williamson mathematical school (1704), formerly for sons of freemen but now open to all. St. Bartholomew's hospital (1078) occupies modern buildings, though the ancient chapel remains. A municipal airport has been provided by the corporation.

ROCHESTER, a city of southeastern Minnesota, U.S., on the Zumbro river, at an altitude of 1,180 ft.; the county seat of Olmsted county and the home of the world-famous Mayo clinic. It is on federal highways 14, 52 and 63, and is served by the Chicago Great Western and the Chicago and North Western railways and by motorbus lines in all directions. Mid-Continent, Northwest, Western and Mid-West air lines provide the city with air transportation. Pop. (1950) 29,634; (1940) 26,312 by the

federal census. The transient population was estimated in 1950 at 300,000 annually. There are wholesale groceries and commission houses, large creameries, a canning factory, a phonograph factory and several other manufacturing industries. The Mayo Civic auditorium is municipally owned. The city also owns and operates a hydroelectric plant, as well as its electric plant and water system. Just east of the city is the Rochester state hospital for the mentally ill, in a tract of 1,424 ac., with accommodations for 1,400 patients. On Aug. 21, 1883, a severe tornado devastated the northern part of the city, killing 26 persons and injuring 41. A direct consequence of this disaster was the founding of St. Mary's hospital by the Sisters of Saint Francis, who had opened a convent there in 1877. The hospital was opened to patients in 1889, with W. W. Mayo as consulting surgeon and his sons, William J. and Charles H. Mayo, as attending surgeons. There are two other hospitals and one hotel-hospital, together with St. Mary's, accommodating 2,000 patients. About 550 graduates of medical schools were studying at mid-20th century in the clinic and hospitals, under the Mayo Foundation for Medical Education and Research, incorporated in 1915 by the Mayos and endowed by them (through the University of Minnesota) with $2,000,000.

The first settler in Rochester built his log cabin in 1854 and laid out the main street by dragging a log through the brush. He called it Rochester because the falls near by reminded him of those at Rochester, N.Y. By 1858 there was a population of 1,500, and the settlement was incorporated as a city.

ROCHESTER, a city of Strafford county, N.H., U.S., on the Cochecho and the Salmon Falls rivers, 22 mi. N.W. of Portsmouth. It is served by four lines of the Boston and Maine railroad. Pop. (1950) 13,776; (1940) 12,012; (1920) 9,673 (85% native white) by the federal census. The town of Rochester (named for Lawrence Hyde, earl of Rochester) was incorporated by royal charter in 1722, but no settlement was made until 1728. It was chartered as a city in 1891.

ROCHESTER, a city of northwestern New York, U.S., located on the Genesee river, the State Barge canal and Lake Ontario; a port of entry and the county seat of Monroe county. It has a municipal airport and is served by the Baltimore and Ohio, the Erie, the Lehigh Valley, the New York Central, the Pennsylvania and the West Shore railways, interurban buses, motorbus and truck lines, lake steamers and canal barges. Pop. (1950) 331,252; (1940) 324,975; (1930) 328,132 by federal census.

The city occupies 34 sq.mi. on a broad plateau, ranging from 500 to 697 ft. above sea level. Through the centre runs the Genesee river, in a deep gorge with banks 50 to 200 ft. high, and within the city limits are three of its many cataracts, with a combined fall of 267 ft. At the mouth of the river is the port of Rochester.

In the abandoned bed of the Erie canal a subway was constructed to accommodate local passenger and freight service and for a belt line connecting all the railways, with a boulevard (Broad street) for vehicular traffic at the street level above. The city's 1,300 streets have a total mileage of 526 (476 mi. paved). Its park system, planned by Frederick Law Olmsted, embraces 6 large and 20 small parks and provides generous facilities for outdoor play and recreation in 49 city playgrounds. Durand-Eastman park (484 ac.) has 4 mi. of frontage on Lake Ontario, and Genesee Valley park (600 ac.) contains some of the most picturesque stretches of the river. A city-planning bureau has been in existence since 1917, and zoning ordinances are in effect.

Rochester is an important educational centre, seat of the University of Rochester; Colgate-Rochester Divinity school (Baptist; 1850); St. Bernard's seminary (Roman Catholic; 1893); the Rochester School of Optometry; and the Rochester Institute of Technology (1829). The University of Rochester (founded 1850) consists of a college of arts and sciences, the Eastman school of music (established in 1918 by various gifts from George Eastman) and the school of medicine and dentistry (established in 1920 through gifts from George Eastman, the General Education board and others). The public-school system adopted by the people of the city (comprising 39 grammar, 9 junior-senior high schools and 1 trade school) led in developing the junior high school, in using the school buildings as community centres and in various other improvements. There are 38 parochial schools and more than 20 other schools under private auspices. The charitable organizations of the city are jointly financed through a community chest, which had its origin during World War I. The daily papers include the *Times-Union* (Independent; 1826), the *Democrat and Chronicle*, the German *Abendpost* (1851) and the *Daily Record*, a legal paper. Italian, German, Catholic, Polish and Jewish weeklies are published. On Jan. 1, 1928, the city adopted a commission-manager form of government. The assessed valuation for 1949 was $565,601,849. The falls of the Genesee provide water power, which has been utilized for manufacturing throughout the city's history. There were 910 manufacturing establishments in the Rochester metropolitan district in 1947, employing 104,997 people to whom was paid $307,821,-000. The factory output was valued at $510,225,000. Rochester leads the world in the manufacture of photographic film, cameras, mail chutes, optical goods, check protectors, thermometers, dental equipment, office equipment and systems, enamelled steel tanks and horticultural products. The city is represented in 15 of the 16 major classifications into which the bureau of the census subdivides U.S. industries. There are several nurseries in the city and around it, shipping seeds, bulbs and plants to all parts of the country. The city has an extensive wholesale and retail trade.

When first visited by Europeans the region about Rochester was the home of the Seneca Indians. The Jesuit missionaries Pierre Chaumonot and Frémin worked among them in the 17th century. In 1687 the marquis de Denonville fought a battle with the Iroquois near the falls, and there was a French post on Irondequoit bay in 1710. The district was included in the Phelps-Gorham purchase in 1788. In 1789 Ebenezer ("Indian") Allan built a sawmill and a gristmill at the falls; in 1802 the site of the present city passed into the hands of three men from Maryland, among them Nathaniel Rochester (1752–1831), who established a settlement, largely of New Englanders, at the falls in 1810–12; and in 1817 the village of Rochesterville was incorporated. During the early years it grew slowly, since it was not on the direct route from Albany to Buffalo and the region was malarial. There were only 1,502 inhabitants in 1820. Monroe county was established in 1821, with Rochester as its judicial seat; the Rochester and Lockport section of the Erie canal was opened in 1823; in the next two years the population doubled, and in 1834, with a population of 12,252, the village was chartered as a city. Rochester was the centre (1828–30) of the anti-Masonic political movement, and there Thurlow Weed published his *Anti-Masonic Enquirer*. Later it became an active abolitionist centre, and for many years before the Civil War was a busy station on the "underground railroad." Myron Holley began the publication of the *Freeman* there in 1839, and in 1847 Frederick Douglass established the *North Star*. It was the home of Susan B. Anthony after 1846, and a gathering place for the advocates of women's rights. About 1850 it was the scene of the spiritualistic demonstrations (the "Rochester Rappings") of Margaret and Katharine Fox. Rochester has had a series of sobriquets. For many years, while the Genesee valley was the principal wheat field of the country, it was the leading flour-milling centre of the United States, and was known as the "Flour City." When the milling industry declined and the horticultural interests (introduced in 1840) assumed greater importance, "Flower" was substituted for "Flour"; later, with the development of the Eastman Kodak company, it was called also the "Kodak City." The population of the city was 36,403 in 1850; 89,366 in 1880; 162,608 in 1900.

ROCHESTER, a borough of Beaver county, Pa., U.S., on the Ohio river at its northernmost point and at the mouth of the Beaver, 25 mi. N.W. of Pittsburgh; served by the Pennsylvania railroad. Pop. (1950) 7,197. Rochester is a busy unit in the Beaver valley industrial district. (*See* BEAVER FALLS.) The borough was settled about 1799 and incorporated in 1849.

ROCHFORD, a town in southeastern Essex, Eng., 39 mi. E. by N. from London by the Southend branch of the Eastern Region railway. Pop. (1951) 6,049. It lies on the small river Roche near the head of a long estuary. The town has a Perpendicular church (St. Andrew), a corn exchange and some agricultural trade. Rochford hall, a gabled mansion of various dates, now a farmhouse, belonged once to the Boleyns; Anne Boleyn, the queen of Henry VIII, was born there. Near Rochford is Ashingdon, the scene of the fight of Assandun in 1016 between Canute and Edmund Ironside, in which the English were defeated.

ROCK, in geology a mass of the mineral matter of which the crust of the earth is composed (*see* GEOLOGY; PETROLOGY).

ROCKEFELLER, JOHN DAVISON (1839–1937), U.S. industrialist and philanthropist, was born at Richford, Tioga county, N.Y., July 8, 1839, oldest son of William Avery and Eliza (Davison) Rockefeller.

In 1853 the family settled at Cleveland, O., and he entered the local high school. About that time he joined the Erie Street (modern Euclid Avenue) Baptist church, and became so active in its affairs that before he was of age he was placed on its board of trustees, serving on it for many years. In 1855 he took a brief course in a commercial college in Cleveland. After six weeks' search, he got employment as assistant bookkeeper in the commission house of Hewitt and Tuttle, at less than $4 a week, and within a few months became cashier and bookkeeper.

In 1859, with $1,000 he had saved and $1,000 borrowed from his father, he formed a partnership with Maurice B. Clark in the produce commission business. The first oil well was drilled that summer, at Titusville, Pa., and in 1863 the partners Clark and Rockefeller formed the firm of Andrews, Clark and Co., petroleum refiners, with capital in part from their reserve in the commission business. The partners agreed in 1865 to put the business up at auction. Rockefeller bid it in at $72,500, formed the firm of Rockefeller and Andrews and sold out his other interests. The next year he joined his brother, William, and Samuel Andrews in forming the firm of William Rockefeller and company, as well as the firm of Rockefeller and Company of New York, which represented William Rockefeller and company in the export trade.

All these interests, in 1867, were merged in a new firm, Rockefeller, Andrews and Flagler, taking in Henry M. Flagler as a general partner and S. V. Harkness as a special partner. The enterprise was incorporated in 1870 as the Standard Oil Company of Ohio, in which other investors joined, with a capital of $1,000,000. The National Refiners' association, organized in the same year, chose Rockefeller as president.

By 1872 nearly all the refining firms in Cleveland had joined the Standard Oil company, and its capital was increased to $2,500,-000. The company was soon refining 29,000 bbl. of crude oil a day. It made 9,000 oil barrels a day in its cooper shop, owned several hundred thousand barrels of oil tankage, warehouses for storing refined oil and works for the manufacture of paints and glue.

The capital was increased in 1873 to $3,500,000 to include other refining concerns, and trustees were appointed to hold properties which could not be held under the Ohio charter, all of which properties were merged in 1882 in the Standard Oil trust with a capital of $70,000,000, subsequently increased to $95,000,000.

This trust was dissolved in 1892, and the constituent companies were later joined in the Standard Oil Company of New Jersey. Rockefeller retired from active business about 1896, but retained the title of president of the Standard Oil company until it was dissolved in 1911, and the constituent companies were separated. It was estimated that the Standard Oil company owned three-fourths of the oil business of the United States in the 1890s. Besides his oil interests Rockefeller owned iron mines, large lumber tracts, and had capital invested in manufacture, transportation and other interests.

During the first 30 years of his business life, Rockefeller's donations were largely to and through organizations of the Baptist Church, in which he was long an officer. In most instances he gave money on condition that he would supply half the sum needed if the others interested would give the other half.

When the American Baptist Education society, at its anniversary in Chicago, in May 1889, resolved to found a "well equipped college" in that city, Rockefeller offered to give $600,000 of the first $1,000,000 for endowment, provided the remaining $400,000 would be pledged by others within 90 days. Thus begun, The University of Chicago was incorporated in 1890. In the next year, Rockefeller offered $1,000,000 more on condition that the Baptist Theological seminary be removed from Morgan Park to become the divinity school of the university. This was done. He gave $2,000,000 more in 1892, and up to 1896 had made gifts and pledges of more than $6,000,000, always on condition that others should join in the support of the institution.

Rockefeller, in Dec. 1910, made a final gift of $10,000,000 to The University of Chicago, which brought his total contributions up to about $35,000,000, and withdrew from further activity in its affairs.

From the time of his retirement from active business, Rockefeller devoted his time to giving away the bulk of his fortune in such form as to do the most good, so far as careful study, years of experience and the advice of able assistants could guide him. Recognizing the difficulties in the wise application of great funds to human welfare, he adopted a method and established principles which became models in the field of philanthropy. The title to great funds was vested in charitable corporations governed objectively by trustees, and served by officers of specialized training and experience devoted to the continuous study of opportunities for service. (See ROCKEFELLER BENEFACTIONS.) Rockefeller's gifts for public benevolence amounted to more than $530,000,000.

Rockefeller was married Sept. 8, 1864, to Laura C., daughter of Harvey B. Spelman, merchant, representative in the legislature and a leader in antislavery, temperance and church work in Cleveland, Brooklyn and New York city. Mrs. Rockefeller died March 12, 1915.

Four daughters, one of whom died in infancy, and a son, John D., Jr. (q.v.), were born to them. Their oldest daughter, Bessie, was married to Charles A. Strong, professor of psychology in The University of Chicago. Edith was married to Harold F. McCormick of Chicago. Alta married E. Parmalee Prentice, a lawyer of New York city.

Rockefeller died on May 23, 1937, at the Casements, his home in Ormond Beach, Fla. He was buried in Lakeview cemetery, Cleveland, O.

BIBLIOGRAPHY.—A. Nevins, *Study in Power* (New York, 1953); G. H. Montague, *Rise and Progress of the Standard Oil Company* (New York, 1903), and I. M. Tarbell, *History of the Standard Oil Company* (New York, 1904), containing opposing views of his methods, the former sympathetic, the latter hostile; J. T. Flynn, *God's Gold* (New York, 1932; London, 1933); B. J. Hendrick, *The Age of Big Business* (New Haven, 1920); M. Sullivan, *Our Times, America Finding Herself* (New York, 1927). For his philanthropies, *see* R. B. Fosdick, *The Story of The Rockefeller Foundation* (New York, 1952); M. DeHowe, *Causes and Their Champions* (Boston, 1926). *See* also J. D. Rockefeller, *Random Reminiscences of Men and Events* (New York, 1909).

ROCKEFELLER, JOHN DAVISON, JR. (1874–   ), was born in Cleveland, O., Jan. 29, 1874, the only son of John Davison Rockefeller and Laura Spelman Rockefeller. After his graduation from Brown university, Providence, R.I. (A.B., 1897), he entered his father's office, working closely with his father in the then existing business, philanthropic and civic undertakings of the family as well as in the development of new ones. His life was devoted primarily to the philanthropic and civic activities of the Rockefeller family, particularly those designed to advance human welfare and those furthering international, interfaith and interracial concepts. He was associated with his father in the creation and development of the Rockefeller Institute for Medical Research, the General Education board, the Rockefeller foundation and the Laura Spelman Rockefeller memorial. In 1923 he founded the International Education board which operated in the fields of the natural sciences, the humanities and agriculture until it was terminated in 1937, its capital fund of more than $21,000,000 having been expended.

Deeply interested in conserving natural resources and preserving historic places, Rockefeller made many contributions for these purposes, including the restoration of colonial Williamsburg in Virginia. Other gifts were directed to international causes, such as the $8,500,000 contributed in 1946 to the United Nations for the purchase of a site for its permanent headquarters. He also furthered better housing conditions in New York city and financed many scientific undertakings.

Contributions from Jan. 1, 1917, to Dec. 31, 1953, made by John D. Rockefeller, Jr., amounted to more than $346,000,000. Of this, educational organizations received $64,300,000; religious causes, $31,947,000; public parks, roads, etc., $30,926,000; charitable organizations, social welfare agencies, relief committees, etc., $79,826,000; museums, laboratories, libraries, etc., $34,669,000; and restoration and preservation of historic structures, antiquities, etc., $44,922,000.

Rockefeller was married in 1901 to Abby Greene Aldrich, who died in 1948. To them were born a daughter, Mrs. Abby Rockefeller Mauzé, and five sons, John D. 3rd, Nelson A., Laurance S., Winthrop and David. In 1951 he married Martha Baird Allen, widow of a classmate at Brown university.

ROCKEFELLER BENEFACTIONS. When John D. Rockefeller died in May 1937, it was announced that he had given more than $530,000,000 for various philanthropic and charitable purposes, the largest group of charitable and educational gifts made up to that time. Nearly four-fifths of his gifts went to four great benevolent corporations which he created: the Rockefeller foundation, the General Education board, the Rockefeller Institute for Medical Research and the Laura Spelman Rockefeller memorial, which was united in 1929 with the Rockefeller foundation.

The Spelman Fund of New York, later liquidated, was established to carry on certain specialized functions which did not fit into the program of the Rockefeller foundation when the Laura Spelman Rockefeller memorial was consolidated with it. The China Medical board, established in 1915 as a division of the Rockefeller foundation, was incorporated as a separate entity in New York state in 1928, and at that time the foundation transferred to the board ownership of the land and buildings occupied by the Peiping Union Medical college, which was one of the chief instruments in bringing the benefits of modern medicine to China. Including a final contribution of $10,000,000 to the China Medical board in 1947 the foundation made available for the Peiping Union Medical college, directly and through the board, approximately $45,000,000.

Rockefeller aimed at stimulating others to give, in addition to securing the most effective utilization of the bulk of his own fortune. Quite as significant as the magnitude of these gifts was the fact that they were, in effect, free from all restrictions, having been given outright for the purposes of the respective corporations so that the trustees of these agencies have power to dispose of the principal as well as the income. The General Education board, for example, terminated its active program in 1952, after expending almost all of its resources. Thus, with broad corporate purposes and with the gifts free from restrictions, the agencies proved to be adaptable to changing needs as their founder intended. His son, John D. Rockefeller, Jr. (q.v.), helped initiate and carry on the foundations and other eleemosynary organizations which he brought into being and heavily endowed. Rockefeller, Jr., also established a number of philanthropic agencies, including the International Education board, formed to operate in the field of the natural sciences, the humanities and agriculture, the Bureau of Social Hygiene, which made intensive studies in the field of delinquency and crime, the Institute of Social and Religious Research and the Sealantic fund, to which he contributed $20,000,000 in 1955 to strengthen and develop Protestant theological education in the United States. Many other gifts by Rockefeller, Sr., and Rockefeller, Jr., were made for a wide range of purposes to already existing institutions and agencies. The five sons of John D. Rockefeller, Jr., followed the same pattern of philanthropic, charitable and civic endeavour to promote the well-being of mankind throughout the world.

The General Education Board was founded in 1902 by John D. Rockefeller, Sr., and was chartered the following year by act of congress for "the promotion of education in the United States of America without distinction of race, sex or creed." Gifts from the founder totalled $129,209,167. In Dec. 1952, having expended almost all of its resources, the board terminated its active program. Its remaining funds were used to meet outstanding obligations and to bring to appropriate termination some of its longstanding interests in the field of education. During the 50-year period from 1902 to 1952, inclusive, the board appropriated a total of $315,965,984. These funds went to both public and private colleges and universities, to medical schools, to state departments of education, to projects in educational research and experimentation and to support fellowships and scholarships.

Rockefeller Foundation.—This foundation was endowed by John D. Rockefeller, Sr., and chartered by the state of New York in 1913 "to promote the well-being of mankind throughout the world." Prior to 1929 its activities were concerned chiefly with: (1) research and co-operation with governments in the control of hookworm disease, malaria and yellow fever; (2) aid in the improvement and development of general public health organization; and (3) aid in developing medical, public health and nursing education in this country and abroad through grants to institutions and through fellowships, surveys and the dissemination of information on new administrative and teaching methods. On Jan. 3, 1929, the Rockefeller foundation was consolidated with the Laura Spelman Rockefeller memorial, a fund which had been established by Rockefeller in 1918 in memory of his wife and which had been concerned largely with advancement of the social sciences and with support of studies in child growth and parent education. The consolidated organization retained the name of the Rockefeller foundation.

After 1929 the foundation's activities, international in scope, were concerned with the advancement and application of knowledge in the medical sciences, public health, the natural sciences, agriculture, the social sciences and the humanities. Within these areas the program came to be concerned especially with the following: in medicine and public health—professional education, medical care, basic research in virus diseases and the development of the health sciences; in the natural sciences—experimental biology and the development of basic food resources through aid to agriculture; in the social sciences—support of studies of social and economic behaviour and of social values and philosophy and exploration of ways in which knowledge gained from the social sciences may be applied to social and political problems; in the humanities—encouragement of work in history, philosophy, linguistics and, within certain limitations, in the creative arts. Except in certain phases of public health work, virus research and agriculture, the foundation does not itself engage in research or operation but seeks to advance knowledge through grants to universities, research institutions and other qualified agencies.

The resources and policies of the Rockefeller foundation are controlled by a board of 21 trustees. Its program is administered by the president and a group of officers and specialized staff who are elected or appointed by the trustees. Capital funds received from the founder totalled $241,608,359.74. The market value of unappropriated principal funds as of Jan. 1, 1955, was $442,955,745. Both income and principal are available for appropriation. From the time of its organization in 1913 to Jan. 1, 1955, the foundation has appropriated from income and principal a total of $519,591,308.

The Rockefeller Institute for Medical Research of New York was founded by John D. Rockefeller in 1901. The purposes of the institute, as set forth in its charter, are "to conduct, assist and encourage investigations in the sciences and arts of hygiene, medicine and surgery, and allied subjects, in the nature and causes of disease and the methods of its prevention and treatment, and to make knowledge relating to these various subjects available for the protection of the health of the public."

In 1908 the legislature by special act extended the charter to confer upon the institute special and broad privileges which would enable it, among other things, "to carry on such educational work along the lines of its corporate purposes as it may deem wise." In 1954, in order to make explicit the intent and purpose of this latter privilege, the charter was amended to provide that the Rockefeller institute should become a part of the University of the State of New York under the jurisdiction and visitation of the regents and, as such, should have the power to grant the advanced degrees of doctor of philosophy, doctor of medical science and the degrees *honoris causa:* doctor of science and doctor of laws. The institute was thus transformed into a university devoted to graduate education and research in the biological and medical sciences. Fellowships are available for well-qualified students who wish to train for a career in scientific research.

Six buildings located on spacious grounds in the city of New York provide extraordinary facilities for experimental research. One of these houses a 55-bed hospital which serves as a laboratory for the study of diseases and pathological processes in man; a library of more than 36,000 volumes is located in another of these buildings; the total floor area for scientific purposes exceeds 400,000 sq.ft. Facilities for research in those phases of biology and medicine for which marine organisms are especially suitable are provided for in the Jacques Loeb laboratories of the institute which are housed in the Marine Biological laboratory at Woods Hole, Mass.

In 1955 construction was started on an auditorium, a faculty house for the social uses of the staff and visiting scientists and an executive office building.

The scientific staff of the institute represents most fields of biology, medicine, chemistry and certain phases of the physical sciences. The senior members of the staff direct the several laboratories for work in these various fields. It is the policy of the institute to keep the structure of its scientific organization flexible and unrestricted by rigid departmental boundaries.

The completed researches of the institute are published in scientific journals, reprints from which are periodically assembled into volumes of *Studies.* The institute also publishes the *Journal of Experimental Medicine,* the *Journal of General Physiology* and the *Journal of Biophysical and Biochemical Cytology.* Conferences extending over a period of several months are held from time to time to evaluate and synthesize significant researches for publication in *Monographs* and for guiding future research throughout the scientific world.

The value of the institute's endowment in 1955 was somewhat more than $130,000,000. These resources and the general control of the institute are vested in a board of trustees, numbering 15, of whom approximately one-half are scientists.

ROCKETS. The extensive use of rockets in World War II by all the major nations involved again focused the attention of the public on this subject. The employment of rockets for military purposes has been revived from time to time. This last revival was brought about by extensive research and development by thousands of scientists engaged in this work for several years. Modern rockets are vastly different from the old military rockets. Their successful use in World War II makes it highly improbable that they will ever again be abandoned.

History of Rockets.—The rocket owes its existence to war pyrotechnics. Long before the modern era the Chinese, Persians, Arabians and Greeks used rockets for giving signals and for communication between the separately encamped parts of the army as well as between these and the home territory. Even in combat actions the military pyrotechnists took their part at an early date, producing fire or incendiary balls and rockets and throwing them into the hostile ranks of the combatants, but mostly into the fortresses and besieged camps, posts and buildings, in order to set them on fire.

The origin of the rocket is lost in time, and the inventor of the rocket is as yet unknown. Only this much is certain—he must have lived long before the beginning of the Christian era. It has also been known from the earliest times that a powderlike mixture was used to drive arrows forward or accelerate their flight. The so-called firebolt is referred to in the old literary sources of almost all peoples. To the Chinese belongs the credit of discovering saltpetre and its application in fireworks. They mixed this substance for the first time with sulphur and charcoal, and recognized the motive power arising from the combustion of this mixture, and made use of it in the preparation of their firebolts (incendiary arrows). At first they made use of these saltpetre mixtures for all sorts of pyrotechnical arts. Later they applied the mixture for making incendiary arrows, and in this manner created a dangerous implement of war.

The freely rising rocket as an instrument of war was apparently first developed by the Chinese about the year A.D. 1225. From China the rocket came by way of India, Arabia and Greece and gradually reached Byzantium, from which place the rest of the western world came into contact with the pyrotechnic arts. The rocket then arrived in Italy where it was adopted with special alacrity. The rocket also found its way to lower Germany, Flanders, France and England where it was frequently used in wars, from the second half of the 13th century. In Italy the rocket is mentioned for the first time in 1281 in Forli (Emilia). Almost simultaneously the rocket made its appearance in the Low Countries. In the Ghent accounts of 1314 it is reported that the Flemish burghers had made use of it in the defense against pirates raiding their coastal cities. One of the first westerners to make a detailed report on rockets and to describe them fully was the mysterious Marcus Graecus, who about the middle of the 13th century made an extract from the works of Albertus Magnus and the English "powder-monk," Roger Bacon. This work appeared in the Greek language, but it is now available only in the Latin translation under the title *Liber ignium ad comburendum hostes.*

Rockets were used as early as 1258 at the old city of Cologne on the Rhine, at Metz in 1324 and in England in 1327 in the Scottish War. Their use in warfare continued for about one century. Gradually as guns came into use, rocket development became confined to types suitable for display purposes. Use for military purposes, however, continued in the orient. The British military probably came in contact with rockets in India and attempts again were made to develop them for war purposes. The early work was unsuccessful. But in 1804 Sir William Congreve resumed the experiments and by 1806 had developed a product so satisfactory that in October of that year he sought, and obtained, permission to assail the city of Boulogne with rockets fired from small boats of the British fleet. The results were encouraging, the missiles effecting considerable property damage and starting numerous fires. From then on, rockets had an established place as an auxiliary to, and sometimes in lieu of, field artillery and ships' guns of moderate calibre. They distinguished themselves at Copenhagen (1807) and at Walcherin (same year), also in the passage of the Adour and at the battle of Leipzig (1813). But perhaps the most far-reaching achievement of the war rocket during this period was at the battle of Bladensburg, Aug. 24, 1814, during the Anglo-American War of 1812. There an intensive fire of rockets directed against Stanbury's U.S. brigade caused the regiments of Schutz and Regan to break and flee. This, when quickly followed by the arrival of British reinforcements, led to an almost general rout, which left the city of Washington unprotected, and led to its immediate capture and burning by the British forces. Likewise in the following month, when the capture of Ft. McHenry in Baltimore harbour was attempted, the rockets, whose "red glare" is so vividly recorded in "The Star-Spangled Banner," were not signal flares, but carried warheads loaded with substantial amounts of explosive—"bombs bursting in air." This time, however, they failed to gain success for their users and of several vessels which had been specially fitted for use as rocket ships on this particular mission, one was sunk with all hands by the fire of a hidden battery, and the rest were forced to withdraw without having gained their objectives.

Congreve's rockets were first made with a tail stick tangentially attached, as in the ordinary skyrocket. But these were hopelessly inaccurate, and were replaced by others with the stick centrally located, with much better results. William Hale, an American, made a further improvement in the Congreve rocket. It was stickless, being stabilized by spin in its flight by an auxiliary combustion chamber, the gases involved in which were liberated from tangential ports (pinwheel effect). The rocket enjoyed no small popularity for many decades. It was used by the Americans in the Mexican War, but periodic tests of rockets left from that war revealed that large numbers of them blew up. Eventually by military order they were all removed from storage and destroyed.

The modern rocket has its origin in the research work carried out by Dr. Robert H. Goddard, head of the physics department of Clark university. Dr. Goddard was interested in reaching extremely high altitudes and showed that this could not be done with a projectile fired from a gun and that the rocket furnished an ideal means of accomplishing the objectives. He first experimented with powder as a propellent and showed that, by adding a tapered nozzle and making the rocket motor strong enough to withstand higher pressures, the efficiency could be greatly increased. During World War I he was granted government funds under the control of the Smithsonian institution to develop long-range rockets for military purposes. The research work was started at Worcester Polytechnic institute but later moved to Pasadena, Calif., the shops of the Mt. Wilson observatory being made available to Goddard for the work. Single-charge rockets propelled by double-base powder (40% nitroglycerin and 60% nitrocellulose) developed there by Goddard and C. N. Hickman were demonstrated at the Aberdeen proving ground, Md., in Nov. 1918. These rockets were fired from lightweight launchers held by hand. The types demonstrated weighed from $1\frac{1}{2}$ to 17 lb. Designs of a 4-in. rocket for firing from planes were also disclosed. The armistice was signed while these demonstrations were in progress. The development work was dropped but Goddard continued his research work on high-altitude rockets with funds donated by the Guggenheim foundation. He dropped the idea of using solid fuels and experimented with liquid oxygen and gasoline as a fuel. He proposed and had patents granted on a number of essential features which were later used by the Germans in their V-2 rockets.

The Germans, the Russians and the English secretly began to develop rocket weapons several years before World War II started. The investigations in England were begun in 1934 (see *Rocket Developments in Great Britain for World War II*). The liquid fuel V-2 rockets developed by the Germans were massive and were capable of travelling more than 300 mi. Some of these rockets weighed more than 12 tons and were 46 ft. long and about 5 ft. in diameter. The fuel consisted of 7,600 lb. of alcohol and 11,000 lb. of liquid oxygen. The warhead weighed 2,100 lb. For a range of 200 mi., they reached a maximum height of 60 to 70 mi. They were launched vertically and the fuel burned for about 65 sec. and produced a thrust of about 68,000 lb. Since they travelled faster than sound, their impact took place before the sound produced by their travel through the air could reach the unfortunate victims. When Goddard proposed rockets of this kind during the years 1914 to 1940, his suggestions were not taken seriously. The Germans also developed assisted shell-type rockets. The shell after being fired from a gun was given still further range by an attached rocket motor.

Rocket Fundamentals.—Contrary to the general belief, the propulsion of a rocket is not caused by the reaction of the gases against the air. Its principle is based on one of Newton's laws, that to every action on any object there is an equal and opposite reaction on some other object. Thus, if M is the mass of a rocket and V its velocity and if m is the mass of the propellent and v its velocity then it can be shown that $V = v \log_e (1 + \frac{m}{M})$ or $V = \frac{mv}{M + m/2}$. The latter equation is reasonably accurate for rockets where m is not more than 50% of M. The velocity of the gas, v, may be appreciably increased by using a tapered nozzle.

The old black-powder rocket was made by packing the powder tightly in a thick paper tube. The burning took place from one end. Most of the World War II rockets used powder in such a form that it burned from all surfaces. In these rockets it was necessary to use powder traps to prevent the stick powder from being ejected. The "Bazooka" rocket had five $\frac{3}{8}$-in. powder sticks about 5 in. long, which rested against a mushroom-shaped stool trap. The U.S. army $4\frac{1}{2}$-in. rocket had 30 sticks of $\frac{7}{8}$-in. powder strung on a steel cage trap. The English $3\frac{1}{4}$-in. rocket and the navy 5-in. rocket for use on planes had single sticks which fitted the inside of the motor and had cross sections in the form of a cross (cruciform). These sticks rested against a grid trap.

Many of the German and Russian rockets had seven sticks of powder symmetrically placed, one being in the centre. The sticks were held in place by a suitable grid trap. These rockets, like U.S. and British counterparts, were spin stabilized, the spin being obtained by several canted outlet nozzles.

Rocket Developments in the United States for World War II.—Developments in the United States did not begin until July 1940. The work was started by the National Defense Research committee (NDRC) and placed under the direction of C. N. Hickman, a Bell Telephone laboratories' engineer. His first laboratory was located at Indian Head, Md., and was staffed chiefly by naval employees. Capt. L. A. Skinner had been appointed by the U.S. army ordnance department as a liaison officer with NDRC and spent most of his time in that laboratory. He had read the Goddard and Hickman reports at the army's Aberdeen proving ground and, becoming interested in the subject, had experimented with rockets from 1933 to 1940. Under the direction of Skinner and Hickman, the "Bazooka" rocket was developed by Capt. E. G. Uhl at Indian Head. It was 2.36 in. in diameter, 21.6 in. in length and weighed 3.4 lb. The warhead weighed 1.57 lb. and was of the hollow-charge type, being capable of penetrating 3–5 in. of steel. The rocket was fired from a 4½-ft. launcher which weighed 13.3 lb. The soldier held it on his shoulder and fired it by pulling a trigger. It was extensively used against tanks.

In 1941 the work was expanded by NDRC contracts with the California Institute of Technology, George Washington university, the Budd Wheel company and the Bell Telephone laboratories. Engineers were hired by the George Washington university to work at the Indian Head laboratory, and another rocket research laboratory was established at the California Institute of Technology (C.I.T.) under the direction of C. C. Lauritsen. The "Mousetrap," an antisubmarine rocket, was developed by this group. This rocket was fired from a four-rail launcher on ships ranging from destroyer escorts to small harbour-patrol vessels. They were equipped with hydrostatically armed contact fuzes and were fired forward in patterns similar to the manner in which the British "Hedgehog" bombs were used. The advantage of the "Mousetrap" was the lack of recoil which permitted it to be fired from small boats.

Forward-firing 3¼-in. British rockets were redesigned at C.I.T. for use with U.S. ballastite[1] and were effectively used by planes against ground targets, surface vessels and submarines. The request for a larger-calibre rocket brought forth a 5-in. rocket. It had a velocity of 1,375 ft. per second and weighed 140 lb. It was used for the first time against railroad yards in Paris.

The C.I.T. group also developed a 4½-in. barrage rocket propelled by a 3¼-in. motor having a range of 1,100 yd. A 12-round gravity-fed automatic projector was developed for launching these rockets. The request for a larger and longer-range rocket having more accuracy brought the development of the 5-in. spinner. This rocket had a velocity of 800 ft. per second. The development was completed in the fall of 1944 and went into use on LSM-R boats in the Pacific in the spring of 1945. These rockets were fired from these boats at the rate of 500 per minute. They were about 32 in. long and weighed about 50 lb.

The largest rocket developed by this group was "Tiny Tim," a 1,284-lb. rocket launched from planes. The propellent charge weighed 146 lb.

The army ordnance department set up a rocket research laboratory and ranges for proof firing in Oct. 1942 at the Aberdeen proving ground under the direction of H. B. Lemon, professor of physics from The University of Chicago. The ordnance department also developed many rocket launchers. One of these, the 60-tube "Calliope," was mounted on General Sherman tanks and used in the push into Germany. The army 4½-in. rockets which had been developed jointly by the army ordnance and NDRC,

were fired from these launchers at the rate of 120 rounds per minute. After discharging the 60 rockets the launcher could be jettisoned. Similar launchers mounted on trucks were developed for 7.2-n. incendiary and chemical rockets. Many types of rockets were developed by the ordnance department including a 4½-in. which was stabilized by spin. Under contracts with the war department, factories were built to make rocket powders, and high priorities were given to the manufacture of rockets of all types.

Special and improved powders were developed by other NDRC groups. As the work expanded, the Indian Head group of the NDRC was moved to Cumberland, Md., where the Allegany Ballistic laboratory was established and operated by the George Washington university under contract with the NDRC. This laboratory, under the direction of R. E. Gibson, developed a 100-lb. 115-mm. rocket for forward firing from planes. It had a velocity of 1,000 ft. per second and used a special solvent extruded powder developed by that laboratory. Jet-assisted take-off rockets, recoilless guns, mine-clearing devices and powder-pressurizing units for flame throwers were also developed by that laboratory.

Rocket motors for use in assisted take-off of planes, using both powder and liquid fuels, were developed at the Guggenheim Aeronautical laboratory at the California Institute of Technology (GALCIT). That laboratory was under the direction of Theodore Von Karman and Frank J. Malina. The navy department also operated a similar laboratory at Annapolis, Md., with which R. H. Goddard was associated.

So great had been the development of rockets in the United States that on V-J day they were being manufactured at the rate of more than 1,000,000,000 per year. The weights of these rockets ranged from 3 lb. to 1,300 lb., their diameters from 2 in. to 12 in., their lengths from 1 ft. to 10 ft., their velocities from 65 ft. to 1,500 ft. per second, their burning time from .01 sec. to 2 sec. and their maximum ranges in ground firing from 40 yd. to 10,000 yd. Their accuracies, in terms of probable angular dispersion, varied from $\frac{1}{16}$° to 3°. They were being fired from the shoulder, from tanks, small boats, planes, trucks and tripods. Rockets having very large fins were also being used as targets for training antiaircraft gunners.

                              (C. N. H.)

Rocket Developments in Great Britain for World War II.—In Dec. 1934 Sir Hugh Elles, master general of ordnance, called a meeting at the war office to "review our present knowledge of rockets in general." The organized development of modern war rockets in Great Britain dates from July 1936, when it was decided that the potentialities of rockets should be investigated for: (1) anti-aircraft defense; (2) long-range offense; (3) as recoilless armament in aircraft; (4) for assisted take off of aircraft.

After a formative period in the research department of the royal arsenal, the research work was entrusted to A. D. Crow (later Sir Alwyn Crow), at that time the director of ballistics research. For security reasons the investigations were referred to as "Projectile Development" and rockets were known as "U.P.'s," abbreviated from unrotated projectiles. A relatively small but technically powerful team of research workers in the ministry of supply was organized by Crow in two interdependent units, working secretly in remote parts of the country. The firing range section under William Blackman, responsible for rocket-firing experiments, built up an elaborate observational and recording system over a 20-mi. stretch of the west coast of Wales, and progressively installed firing batteries, ammunition magazines, engineering workshops, scientific laboratories and administrative offices at the projectile development establishment, Aberporth, Cardiganshire. The planning and development section, responsible for all phases of the investigations leading up to the range work, was housed, at first, in cottages and huts adjacent to Fort Halstead, built during the Napoleonic Wars on the top of Pol hill, near Sevenoaks, Kent, against the threat of French invasion. The underground casemates of the disused fort served as magazines for the storage of explosive materials and, though less conveniently, as assembly and testing rooms for the experimental rockets whose evolution was most vigorously proceeding. New buildings of all sorts, needed to enable rocket development to proceed on an adequate scale,

---

[1]The term "ballastite" refers to a mixture of nitroglycerine and nitrocellulose with sufficient plasticizer and stabilizer to render it workable and safe. The actual percentage of nitroglycerine was about 40 and the percentage of nitrocellulose about 60. This is known to be a "hot" powder. British cordite may have as much nitroglycerine but it has a considerable amount of centralite added which slows down and renders the powder less hazardous to extrude.

were planned and put under construction in the woods surrounding the old fort, but they were never used by the rocket group. The cumulative weight of inconvenience and upset from the activities of hundreds of workmen, added to the threat of German aerial attack, forced the temporary abandonment of the site near London and the whole team was concentrated at Aberporth. But this phase was short; the need for close and continuous contact between the new organization and the older armament and ordnance establishments and with the policy-making departments of the war office and the admiralty forced an early regrouping.

Within four months new arrangements had been settled and implemented and although from time to time they were modified in detail, in principle they were maintained throughout the succeeding six years, including more than five years of World War II. The rocket organization which stood through the war years thus comprised a planning and policy section at headquarters in London, and a self-contained projectile development establishment at Aberporth with scientists, engineers, draughtsmen, mechanics and administrative staff covering applied research, development, experimental manufacture and range firings of rockets. The whole undertaking was under the charge of Sir Alwyn Crow as director of projectile development, whose responsibility was briefly defined as "research, development and production of rockets." The headquarters section comprised a military adviser, a naval adviser and four assistant directors of projectile development; planning and ballistics, propellents and explosives, co-ordination of design and preproduction and production. The establishment at Aberporth was under the local charge of a chief superintendent, William Blackman.

It adds something in perspective to recall the degree of interest which rocket development had attracted by 1940, and which was sustained thereafter. It was typified by the attendance of Prime Minister Winston Churchill at several rocket-firing trials; and his insistence, for more than a year, on a personal weekly report of progress in rocket development. In this he was encouraged by his scientific adviser, Frederick A. Lindemann, later Lord Cherwell, who maintained the closest touch with every new phase of the developments and was the sponsor of several weapon applications of rockets, notably the rocket-propelled aerial mine.

An attempt may now be made to trace the progress in development of actual rocket weapons. Although four main objectives had been laid down originally, it transpired that for a time the whole of the limited resources available for rocket research was directed toward the successful development of rockets to supplement anti-aircraft guns.

The smallest propellent charge which it was thought would produce an efficient rocket had an outside diameter of 2 in. and the largest charges which existing cordite presses could extrude had a diameter of 3 in. These two calibres were chosen for trial and their selection was to influence the whole wartime future of rocket development.

The arrangement of the propellent charge in these early rockets was one to which postwar work reverted, although it was temporarily discarded in the successfully developed wartime rockets. It was at first believed impossible that the thin steel tube could survive the period of burning of the charge if the propellent gases, at a temperature of about 2,500° C., were allowed to come in contact with it. To avoid this, it was decided to burn the propellent on its inside surface only, and this involved the problem of inhibiting burning on the outside surface without seriously reducing the density of loading. Development was therefore put in hand of a suitable material having plastic properties to fill the narrow annulus between the propellent and the motor body, the intention being that the plastic should adhere strongly enough to the surfaces to exclude propellent gases, and at the same time be capable of flowing under the stresses caused by temperature changes, while retaining its shape and position under the stress caused by the weight of the filling. By making the internal contour of the charge of star section it was possible to obtain an almost constant burning surface, and also to adjust the time of burning within limits.

Preliminary static firing experiments were carried on by firing a rocket firmly held in a thrust-measuring block, hence without forward motion. With the onset of colder weather in the latter half of 1937 it became apparent that the development of a satisfactory material for the "plastic surround" had by no means been achieved. One of the chief difficulties was the effect of nitroglycerine which it absorbed from the propellent, and which altered the plastic properties on storage. Before starting on what might be a long research, it was decided to see what would be the effect of firing a plain charge loose in an unprotected tube, and at the same time to work out possible processes for applying a heat-insulating coating. The first 2-in. rounds were fired in Feb. 1938, using a plain cylindrical tube of propellent supported on a fabricated steel cross, which acted as the grid (powder trap). Given sufficient clearance between the propellent and the steel tube, this arrangement was unexpectedly successful, and a few experiments showed that malleable cast-iron grids could be made to stand up to the most severe conditions.

The problem of the insulating coating was overcome, after a tedious series of experiments, by spraying the inside of the tube with a suspension of finely ground alumina in a solution of sodium silicate. This process was industrialized and the refractory coating was successfully applied to several millions of 3-in. rockets. Although the thickness of the coating was only 0.008 in., the reduction in wall temperature at the end of burning was found to be of the order of 300° C., resulting not only in prevention of burning-out of the tubes but in the achievement of a significant improvement in accuracy.

Toward the end of 1938 sufficient progress had been made to justify a comprehensive series of firings designed to provide statistical data on performance and dispersion and fuze-scale data. The impending English winter, with low clouds making observation of positions of burst impossible for most of the time, led to the decision that these firings should be carried out in Jamaica, and during the first few months of 1939 about 2,500 3-in. rockets were fired in an extensive series of ballistic trials.

The results failed to satisfy the general staff. The performance and accuracy of the 3-in. rocket compared badly with those of the recently developed 3.7-in. A.A. (anti-aircraft) gun. The staff wished the development work to proceed in the hope that accuracy approaching that of the gun would be achieved, but they did not propose to adopt rockets in the service. Even after World War II started, the war office felt that it would be premature to introduce the new weapon. Contrary to expectations, there was practically no hostile air activity over England during the first few months of the war, and the provision of 3.7-in. A.A. guns was proceeding well.

However, by early 1940 a new situation had arisen. It became apparent, soon after the war started in Sept. 1939, that the German dive bomber constituted a serious menace on sea and land. By the end of September the admiralty was sufficiently impressed with the need for testing every possible counter that it demanded the speedy development of a rocket-propelled aerial mine for the protection of ships and harbours. A parachute and wire device, intended for dropping from fighters in the path of oncoming bombers, was in course of development by the air force. This was modified to withstand the setback shock imposed during rocket acceleration and the shock of unspooling at high speed, and a new 3-in. calibre rocket was developed to project it to the required height. On the whole the project was not especially successful or important, but it demonstrated the potentialities of the rocket as a carrier of relatively bulky and fragile devices and the possibility of firing large salvoes without large recoil forces. It was also the forerunner of several other wire devices, projected by rockets.

A second development, also directed against the dive bomber, assumed considerable importance at this time. Much thought had been given to the idea of a proximity fuze and there was promise of success with a device which comprised a photoelectric cell coupled to a thermionic amplifier. The arrangement was such that the image of a nearby aeroplane, projected on the cell by means of a lens, caused a sufficient change in emission from the cell to produce a pulse capable of amplification to trigger a thyratron, or gas-relay, in circuit with the high-tension battery and the detonating train of the shell. Switches were included to keep the devices inert until after it had been subjected to rocket acceleration and it could therefore be fired at an approaching aeroplane in the knowledge that the shell would detonate at the instant when it passed sufficiently close to "see" it. The optical system was so designed that this instant coincided with the most favourable position of the shell to cause lethal damage, whatever its distance or orientation from the aeroplane. Firing at a dive bomber, approaching along the line of sight, should have produced an almost certain kill with such a fuze. The projector could be simple; there would be no recoil forces and laying need take account only of wind deviation. The delicate construction of the fuze, and its bulk, precluded the use of conventional artillery but the 3-in. rocket seemed an ideal vehicle.

By the spring of 1940 many of the technical difficulties had been overcome and the weapon was sponsored jointly by the army and the navy. A period of intensive design and production followed. A design was put forward for a projector so cheap and simple that it could be built in large numbers with no elaborate facilities, and used by personnel with little or no military training. The result was the Projector, Rocket, 3-in., No. 1, Mark I, of which several thousand were made during 1940 and 1941. The design was basically simple and presented no difficulty, but a good deal of experimental work was needed to provide adequate shielding of the crew from blast reflected from the ground when firing at high angles of elevation, and also to produce simple and reliable electrical-firing contacts. In Nov. 1940, the manpower situation led to the design of a twin projector on similar lines (3-in., No. 2, Mark I) incorporating a number of improvements which experience with the single version showed to be desirable.

Meanwhile, the photoelectric (P.E.) fuze was completed, and manufacture on a considerable scale was initiated. Using fuzes from production, by this time reduced in size to a diameter of $3\frac{1}{4}$ in. and a total weight, including batteries and detonating train of less than 10 lb., a final clearance trial was carried out, firing at glider targets suspended from barrage balloons. The results of the trial were satisfactory but new factors intervened. The menace of the dive bomber had already begun to decline and certain limitations on its more general use, inherent in the nature of the fuze, were increasingly recognized. Chief among them were its inability to function at night or at dawn and dusk, and its susceptibility to direct sunlight when fired in certain directions in relation to the sun. Reluctantly, the fuze was abandoned, but the phase of its development had been one of such intense activity and interest in the rocket field that the services were, by now, thoroughly rocket-conscious and proximity fuzes of one type or another had come to stay. The radar fuze, initiated at Aberporth at the same time as the P.E. fuze and developed to a successful conclusion in the United States, was the postwar version of the device.

The 3-in. rocket then reverted to the role originally intended for it, that of supplementing the heavy gun defenses. Thus was the 3-in. rocket, through the vicissitudes of 18 months of war, finally established as a service weapon. During the same period the 2-in. rocket had established itself in the navy. It was used in several different roles: with high explosive (H.E.) heads, fired from three different types of projectors of which the 20-barrelled "Pillar Box" was the best; with flare or star heads, fired from projectors mounted on gun-shields to permit continuous illumination concurrently with continuous lethal fire; with parachute and wire devices to project new and improved types of aerial mine as a counter to low-level bombing. In all these applications it was used in merchant vessels as well as royal naval craft.

The original 5-in. rocket had also completed its development, initiated in Nov. 1939, to meet a demand for a weapon suitable for handling in slit trenches but capable of projecting a 30-lb. light-cased bomb to a range of 2 to 4 mi. with reasonable accuracy. To meet the handling requirement, the projector could not exceed 6 ft. in length. This restriction permitted only a short travel for the round; the demand for accuracy required a fairly high velocity, and therefore high acceleration, to ensure stability at launch, and precautions were required against ejection of unburned slivers of cordite which would produce equivalent variations in range.

These factors, combined with the modest ballistic performance required, account for the rather unorthodox design of the round. The propellent charge was composed of 11 tubular sticks of cordite, giving a large burning surface with consequent high thrust, disposed in the annular space between the rocket body tube and an internal axial tube, perforated to allow free flow of gas but preventing loss of cordite. Although, by present-day standards, the dispersion of this rocket is not particularly good, it does seem that the charge design has the desired effect, for the performance index[1] is high, and the unknown factor of dispersion is low. The rocket was never used for its original purpose, but it provided the basis upon which the naval beach-barrage weapon was developed in 1944.

The difficulties of production during World War II imposed such restrictions on the supply of high-grade rocket tubing as to preclude the development of calibres other than those already described. As a result, every new rocket requirement had to be met by the adaptation of 2-in., 3-in. or 5-in. rocket motors. In all, about 22 different rocket weapons were approved for the British services during the war, but it would be tedious to describe them all and more profitable to refer to such types and uses as emphasize best the characteristics peculiar to rockets.

The 3-in. anti-aircraft rocket has been described. It owed its adoption to two main features: the fact that the projectors could be manufactured cheaply, in large numbers, by engineering firms inexperienced in armaments and employing a large proportion of unskilled labour; and the fact that it was a suitable vehicle for the projection of delicate and bulky apparatus, although in the event this characteristic was only applied to the shell, containing more than 25% by weight of high explosive, and not to the fuze. The rocket ammunition cost about the same in man hours and skill as equivalent gun ammunition.

The use of rockets from aircraft had been contemplated in 1936 when the first organized attempt at rocket development was initiated. The outstanding characteristic involved in this usage was the absence of recoil forces in rocket firing. Whereas with gun armament in aircraft the maximum calibre is strictly limited by the recoil stresses which must be absorbed in the aircraft structure, with rocket armament the calibre is limited only by convenience in stowage and the avoidance of damage from blast. In Oct. 1941, the Ordnance board pressed the suggestion that rockets might be fired from aircraft against tanks. It was decided to start trials using the 3-in. anti-aircraft rocket motor, fitted with an armour-piercing head, fired from beneath the wing of a Hurricane aircraft. A variety of applications developed from this starting point and many different types of aircraft, both British and U.S., were equipped with rocket-launching apparatus for firing 3-in. rockets, adapted for the purpose from the original anti-aircraft model. Armour-piercing and high-explosive shells were employed, of calibres varying up to 6 in. To emphasize the main feature of this application, it may be observed that the regular equipment of a rocket-armed single-seat fighter aircraft enabled it to deliver a salvo equal in hitting power to that from a contemporary light cruiser.

The various wire-barrage weapons relied upon two main rocket characteristics. The first project, known as the Naval Wire Barrage or Apparatus, Aerial Defence Type B, depended on the capability of rockets for conveying fragile and bulky apparatus, without the imposition of damaging setback and centrifugal forces inescapable in gun ballistics. A more advanced development of the same principle is typified by A.A.D., Type K, in which the parachute and wire device were reduced to the same calibre as the 3-in. rocket, and fitted to the standard anti-aircraft rocket motor, for laying the barrage at greater heights, up to 20,000 ft.

Two other wire-barrage weapons, A.A.D., Type J, and A.A.D., Type L, operated in a different manner. The requirement here was that the barrage should be fully effective in the shortest possible time. It must be completely erected in about five seconds,

---

[1]Performance index $= \dfrac{\text{thrust} \times \text{time (lb. sec.)}}{\text{charge weight (lb.)}}$

A measure of the efficiency of the charge and nozzle combination, sometimes called "specific impulse."

but only modest heights need be catered for. The object was to counter low-level bombing, and machine-gunning of merchant ships. Fire was to be withheld until the enemy had committed himself to his bombing run, which involved a low level passage over, or very near to, the ship. The barrage was to be erected quite close to the ship. If the attacking aircraft saw it in time to take effective avoiding action, he must necessarily abandon the attempt to bomb; and if he persisted, he was in great danger of suffering lethal damage.

In one type, both the parachutes and the cables were contained in a canister fixed to the projector in the ship. The rocket, towing the top half of the canister containing the support parachute, and unspooling the cable behind it, attained the requisite height in a few seconds, at which point the support parachute was ejected and opened, and the mine floated slowly down. In the other type the support parachute was carried ahead of the rocket but the cable was again unspooled from the fixed canister. The rocket characteristics employed in these devices were the low starting velocity and steady acceleration, permitting the wire to be picked up without snatch and unspooled without damage. The ease of manufacture of the projection apparatus, as compared with guns, and the absence of recoil, were also influential.

Later in the war, when invasion of enemy-occupied territory was contemplated, the potentialities of rockets for laying a mass barrage were investigated. In Sept. 1942 a meeting had been held at combined operations headquarters to discuss the lessons of the Dieppe raid. The main conclusion of that meeting was that the beaches and the land overlooking the beaches must be drenched with the maximum amount of H.E. shell that could be made available immediately before the landing took place. Experience had shown that, in spite of the greatest care and preparation in the identification of enemy batteries and machine guns, and in the organization of aimed fire from naval guns or aircraft, many of the enemy's weapons would be unlocated. The dust and smoke of battle would make it difficult to engage these targets after the attack had been launched. The proposal was made that special craft should be fitted out with a large number of 5-in. rocket projectors capable of drenching an area with medium-weight H.E. shell during the period immediately before the landing took place.

Work was started at once, using the army 5-in. rocket weapon as the starting point. A new high-capacity shell was designed to give the best possible fragmentation effect by taking advantage of the low setback forces from the rocket. A sensitive impact fuze was provided, to ensure the least possible cratering, and the rocket motor was altered and improved in several respects. Sextuple projectors, made for the army from the original single-barrel light-weight projector, were adapted and fitted in large banks in the selected craft. The rockets were fired automatically in rapidly successive groups, to reduce the chance of mutual interference, and in the form eventually used a single rocket ship was able to disgorge highly lethal ammunition on the chosen target area at a rate of half a ton a second for nearly a minute at a time. The craft were first used in 1943 at the landings in Sicily and Italy, and they were conspicuously successful.

The rocket characteristics so outstandingly demonstrated in this application are the simplicity, lightness and cheapness of the projectors and the absence of recoil. A later counterpart of this weapon for land service, and known as the "Land Mattress," exemplified the same features. Each projector mounted 30 barrels and had an all-up weight of little more than 1 ton. They could be towed easily by a three-ton ammunition truck and, for short distances into action, could be towed fully loaded. This weapon was used with great success by the Canadians in crossing the Scheldt river and later by the 2nd army in crossing the Rhine. The projectors can be lightened and decreased in size so that they can be towed by a light motor vehicle and can be carried by aircraft without dismantling.

Mention has been made of star and flare heads, used with rockets, and of the naval practice of attaching light rocket projectors to a gunshield so that the gun is continuously available for lethal fire. Another aspect is worth noting; namely, that a flare for projection by a rocket can be constructed much more lightly than its gun counterpart because of the absence of setback and spin, with the result that, for equal weights projected, a brighter and longer-burning flare can be provided. Flares have also been made for rocket projection from aircraft. They are used for the detection of submarines and surface craft by night and, so that the pilot may not be blinded by the light from his own flare, they have to be fired with an upward lift to the trajectory, a problem which took some time to solve.

A variety of other uses have been made of rockets, mostly employing characteristics which have already been described. Ropes, ladders, grapnels, stores and depth charges are among the items for which rocket projection has been used, and bombs required for very deep penetration have been accelerated by rocket action. By varying the shape, and therefore the burning surface, of the charge, and the pressure at which it is burned, the time of burning can be altered over a wide range to procure the conditions most appropriate to the problem in hand, even with the restricted tube diameters imposed by war conditions. To illustrate this feature, the case of the 5-in. rocket may be quoted. As originally designed for high acceleration, with a charge composed of a number of small diameter tubes of cordite, burning freely on their whole surface, a thrust of about 20 tons is developed and burning is completed in about $\frac{1}{3}$ sec. At the other extreme, by encasing a solid stick of cordite in an inert material so that burning takes place cigarwise from the end face only, a thrust of the order of 50 lb. can be obtained for periods, governed by the length of charge employed, of 60 sec. or more. It will immediately be obvious that this possibility opens up an entirely new set of applications in which liquid propellents compete with, and sometimes supersede, the solid type. The propulsion of gliders, torpedoes and small boats has been achieved in this way and, in appropriate circumstances, the assisted take off of aeroplanes. It is well to observe, however, that in these applications, where the velocity attained is very low compared with the efflux velocity of the rocket gases, the efficiency of the unit is low on a fuel consumption or horsepower basis. The attraction of the method lies in its potentiality of providing a substantial propulsive force for a limited period, at very little expense in weight carried. An obvious application is the use of rocket motors to boost the speed of aircraft for short periods and, if desired, the spent rocket can be jettisoned after use.

It is necessary to distinguish between rocket propulsion proper, where the fuel and oxidant are both carried with the motor, and the Turbojet or propulsive duct systems where only the fuel is carried and entrained air is employed as the oxidant. In these cases a much higher fuel economy can be achieved, but there are many other factors to be taken into account in the choice of a system for any particular application. (W. H. WH.)

Other Rocket Developments for World War II.

The Germans, the Russians and the Japanese developed and used many rocket weapons. The German jet-propelled V-1 plane and the liquid-fuel V-2 rocket inflicted great punishment on the British.

At the close of the war, thousands of engineers were working on rockets in the respective countries. The Japanese had developd a large powder-driven rocket to increase the velocity of their suicide dive-bomber glider plane. The Russians reportedly saved Stalingrad by the terrific rocket barrages used against the Germans.

The rocket principle was widely used during the war for other purposes than hurling high-explosive heads. The thrust caused by jets was used to assist heavily loaded planes in getting off the ground and to propel aeroplanes. The German V-1, while not a true rocket, was a small gyroscopically guided plane, propelled by successive ejections of gas from a combustion chamber. The fuel consisted of alcohol carried in tanks, combined with air admitted through flap valves in the front of the combustion chamber. The burning of powder gases was utilized to pressurize flame throwers and fire extinguishers.

The rocket principle was used to make guns recoilless, the breech end being fitted with a nozzle so that the escaping gases gave a forward thrust to the gun which was equal and opposite to its recoil. Utilizing this principle, guns, firing 25-lb. shells, were reduced in weight to a point where they could be mounted on 30-calibre machine-gun tripods. One type of recoilless gun could be broken into 3 pieces each weighing 60 lb. or less so that, disassembled, it could readily be carried by 3 men. It required less than two minutes to put it in operation.

Although the propulsion efficiency of rockets is low, they were extensively used, their advantages being that the absence of recoil makes it possible to fire large-calibre shells from relatively light-weight launchers. Such launchers may be mounted on small boats, vehicles and planes or may be carried by one or more soldiers. The relatively low acceleration of rockets permits them to carry special fragile fuzes, cables, etc. They may be manufactured in shops which are not suited for making guns. (C. N. H.)

Lifesaving Rockets.—The use of rockets for carrying lines from ship to shore and vice versa, on the occasion of marine disaster, appears to date from 1821 when Trengrove's British apparatus—a simple 8-oz. skyrocket, was advanced for the purpose. It met little success, however, and was succeeded in 1832 by Dennet's—a much more substantial contrivance weighing about 23 lb. Made with an iron case instead of the conventional paper shell, and guided by a stick 8 ft. long, it had a range of 250 yd. Commencing in 1834 the British board of customs undertook the issue of these to many lifesaving stations. Later, 1842, the Carte rocket, an adaptation of the Congreve war variety, had a brief vogue. The next development was an improvement by Dennet on his original design. This involved the mounting, side by side, of two rockets attached to the same stick. The range was thus increased to 400 yd., but the impossibility of achieving an equal burning rate on the part of the two constituents led to its final abandonment. About this time Henri Gustave Delvigne, famous for his improvements to rifled small arms, produced a "life-arrow" to be fired from an ordinary musket. This was capable of hurling an 18-oz. mahogany stick, with a mackerel line attached, to a distance of 80 yd. But all earlier forms were superseded by one devised by Colonel Boxer of the British Royal laboratory. His rocket consisted of two separate units incorporated in a single tube—one behind the other. The case was of wrought iron, the head of hardwood; and a partition in the body separated the two charges. When the energy of one had been expended, the other became automatically ignited, the resultant maximum range materially exceeding that achieved when two separate rockets were lashed side by side (Dennet fashion) or when the double load was fired in the form of a single charge. Though favourably received and employed, in England and on the continent, none of these devices ever gained much favour in the U.S., where line-firing mortars were generally preferred for lifesaving purposes.

Special Types.—Rockets designed to attain tremendous altitudes in connection with meteorological studies, etc., have long been, and continue to be, the object of experimentation by many physicists. Motor cars and aeroplanes propelled on the rocket principle have also received consideration. (See also FIREWORKS.)

BIBLIOGRAPHY.—Albert Hausenstein, published serially in the *Zeitschrift für das gesamte Schiess- und Sprengstoffwesen* (beginning May 1939); Robert Esnault Pelterie, *L'astronautique*, TL 790.E8 (Paris, 1930); Robert H. Goddard, "A Method of Reaching Extreme Altitudes," *Smithsonian Misc. Collections*, vol. 71, no. 2 (1919), "Liquid-Propellant Rocket Development," *Smithsonian Misc. Collections*, Vol. 95, no. 3 (1936); Nikolai Alekseevich Rynin, *Mezhplanetnye soobshchenya* (Interplanetary travel) (Leningrad, 1928–32); Eugen Saenger, *Raketen Flugtchnik* (Munchen, 1933); F. J. Malina, "Characteristics of Rocket Motor Unit Based on Theory of Perfect Gases," *Journ. Franklin Inst.*, Vol. 230 (1940); "U.S. Rocket Ordnance—Development and use in World War II," a release to public by the Rocket Panel of the Joint Board on Scientific Information Policy; J. Bem, *Erfahrungen über die Congrevschen Brand-Racketen* (1820); C. Dupin, *Voyages dans la Grande-Bretagne (entrepris relativement aux services publiques de la guerre, etc.)* (1820); Sir W. Congreve, *The Congreve Rocket System* (1827); J. Frost, *The Book of the Army of the United States* (1845); J. Scoffern, *Projectile Weapons of War* (1859); E. S. Farrow, *Military Encyclopaedia* (1885); H. W. L. Hime, *Gunpowder and Ammunition* (1904); C. Rougeron, "The Rocket-Bomb and the Planing Bomb" in the *Royal Air Force Quarterly* (England, 1928); M. P. Andrews, *History of Maryland* (1929); J. R. Randolph, "What Can We Expect of Rockets?" in *Army Ordnance, U.S.A.* (1939); C. Goddard, "Rockets," in three parts, in *Army Ordnance, U.S.A.* (1939).

ROCKFORD, a city of northern Illinois, U.S., on the Rock river, 17 mi. S. of the Wisconsin line and midway between the east and west boundaries of the state; the county seat of Winnebago county. It is on federal highways 20 and 51, has a public airport and is served by the Burlington route, the Chicago and North Western, the Chicago, Milwaukee, St. Paul and Pacific and the Illinois Central railways, and by motorbus lines in all directions. Pop. (1950) 92,927; it was 84,637 in 1940 by the federal census. The city occupies 14 sq.mi. on both sides of the river, and has 1,490 ac. in parks and playgrounds. On a wooded bluff, in a beautiful campus of ten acres, stands Rockford college, one of the oldest standard colleges for women in the United States, opened as a seminary in 1847. Enrolment is limited to about 650. The public schools have an enrolment of more than 14,000,

and the parochial schools 2,000. There are many churches in the city, and a Roman Catholic procathedral. Rockford has been an important manufacturing centre since its earliest days. Water power is supplied by a dam 800 ft. long, built in 1844. There were more than 400 manufacturing establishments at mid-20th century; important products are machine tools and dies, machinery, furniture, textiles, automobile parts, stoves, hardware, hosiery, leather and paint. Bank deposits and postal savings on June 30, 1950, totalled $129,251,745.73.

Rockford was founded by New Englanders in 1834 and was chartered as a city in 1852. Rockford is a great machine-tool manufacturing centre. A million men passed through Camp Grant 4 mi. S. of the city during World War I. Again in World War II the camp was a huge reception centre for conscripted men and a large medical replacement centre.

ROCKHAMPTON, a seaport on the east coast of Queensland, Austr., situated on both banks of the Fitzroy river at the head of ocean navigation 35–40 mi. from the sea. The Fitzroy and its tributaries (Dawson, Mackenzie, etc.; maximum length 520 mi.) drain a basin of 50,000 sq.mi. of great diversity and economic value. The hinterland of Rockhampton thus includes extensive high-class pastoral areas extending at least as far west as Longreach (428 mi. by rail); rich agricultural and dairying lands which include the Dawson river irrigation area (total projected area: 200,000 ac.), besides large mineral resources including coal fields (e.g., Blair Athol mines). Around Rockhampton itself is a fertile agricultural area producing tropical fruits, maize and dairy products. The climate is hot and humid but not unhealthful (average annual temperatures, 82°–62° F.; average annual rainfall, 110 in. falling within about 44 days of the summer). The town, pop. (1947 census) 34,988, is well designed, has wide streets, many substantial buildings (including two cathedrals) and possesses good water, gas, electricity and tram services besides fine public parks and gardens. The harbour (wharfage 2,000 ft. with 8–20 ft. alongside) has been improved at considerable expense and is kept open by dredging for vessels of 18–20 ft. draught. Difficulties are the shifting sand and mud banks caused by severe floods which are liable to occur during summer. Rockhampton is the base of a branching inland railway system which taps the widely separated Longreach (428 mi.), Welford (520 mi.), Blair Athol (240 mi.), Springsure (206 mi.), and other centres, and which is being continually extended. Along the coast the Great Northern line links Rockhampton with other coastal towns, with Brisbane, with various seaside resorts (Emu Park, Yeppoon), and the ports of Gladstone (c. 80 mi.) and nearer by Port Alma, to which ocean vessels resort. Railway repairing and other industries are carried on in the town and near by are large meat-preserving and freezing works. In value of its trade Rockhampton is the second port of Queensland.

Mount Morgan, 24 mi. S.S.W., became one of the richest gold mines in Australia after 1885.

Wowan, in the same district, is the centre of the cotton region of Australia.

ROCK HILL, a city of York county, South Carolina, U.S., 27 mi. S. of Charlotte, N.C., on federal highway 21 and two lines of the Southern railway. The population in 1950 was 24,502; 15,009 in 1940 by the federal census, with an additional 5,000 in the immediate suburbs. The city lies at an altitude of 670 ft. The major industry is textile manufacturing. In 1948 there were 14 industrial establishments which manufactured products valued at more than $80,000,000. Winthrop, the state college for women (founded in 1886 by David Bancroft Johnson, who remained its president until his death in 1929, and chartered in 1891 as a state institution), has an enrolment of 1,600 and a plant valued at more than $6,000,000. Rock Hill was incorporated as a village in 1870, as a city in 1892. It has a commission-manager government.

ROCKINGHAM, CHARLES WATSON WENTWORTH, 2ND MARQUESS OF (1730–1782), twice prime minister of England, was the son of Thomas Watson Wentworth (c. 1690–1750), who was created earl of Melton in 1733 and marquess of Rockingham in 1746. The family of Watson was descended from

ROCKETS

PLATE I

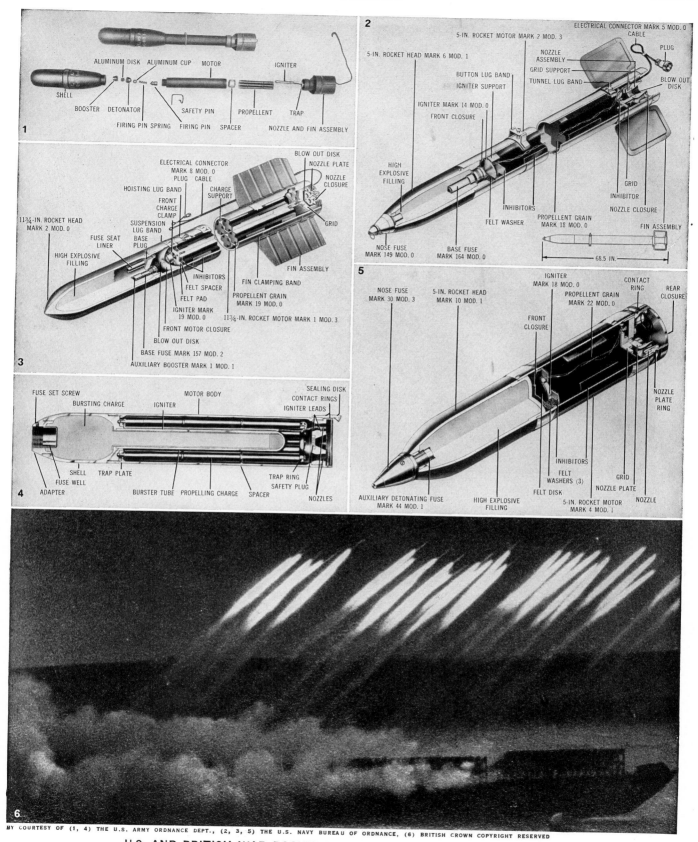

BY COURTESY OF (1, 4) THE U.S. ARMY ORDNANCE DEPT., (2, 3, 5) THE U.S. NAVY BUREAU OF ORDNANCE, (6) BRITISH CROWN COPYRIGHT RESERVED

U.S. AND BRITISH WAR ROCKETS DEVELOPED DURING WORLD WAR II

1. Bazooka rocket. The figure represents a standardized bazooka rocket shell assembled and disassembled

2. U.S. 5-in. fin stabilized aircraft rocket (Holy Moses). A sectioned view showing the component parts of the rocket

3. U.S. 12-in. fin stabilized aircraft rocket (Tiny Tim). A sectioned view showing the component parts of the rocket

4. U.S. 4½-in. spin stabilized rocket. Sectional view of the rocket showing the component parts

5. U.S. 5-in. spin stabilized rocket. A sectioned view showing the component parts of the rocket

6. Rocket ship in action

PLATE II   ROCKETS

U.S. AND BRITISH WAR ROCKETS DEVELOPED DURING WORLD WAR II

1. 9-Barrel projector for 3-in. A.A. rockets in action. The picture shows rockets in flight just after leaving the projector. Normal procedure with this type of projector is to fire rippled salvoes of three rounds each

2. Aircraft rocket installation in Coastal command Beaufighter. The 3-in. rockets shown are fitted with solid armour-piercing heads. Each projector consists of a pair of parallel rails, close together, and each rocket is provided with two saddles which act as supports and guides. Four rockets are carried under each wing and they can be fired in salvoes of 2, 4 or 8

3. Twin projector for 3-in. A.A. rockets. The photograph shows the elevating hand wheel on the right-hand side of the projector and the traversing handle on the left. The blast shields are fitted with armoured glass graticules. The double elliptical ring at the rear end of the projector rails serves as a balance weight as well as a structural member

Sir Lewis Watson (1584–1653), son and heir of Sir Edward Watson (d. 1616) of Rockingham castle in Northamptonshire. For his services to the king during the Civil War, Sir Lewis was created Baron Rockingham in 1645. His grandson Lewis, the 3rd baron (1655–1724), was created earl of Rockingham in 1714, and was succeeded by his grandson Lewis (c. 1709–45), whose brother Thomas, the 3rd earl, died unmarried in Feb. 1746, when the earldom became extinct. The barony of Rockingham, however, descended to a cousin, Thomas, father of the prime minister, a grandson of Edward, the 2nd baron (1630–89), who had married Anne, daughter and heiress of Thomas Wentworth, 1st earl of Strafford. The estates of the Wentworths had passed to Edward's son, Thomas, who took the additional name Wentworth, and then to his son, 1st marquess of Rockingham.

Charles Watson Wentworth received his education at Westminster school and St. John's college, Cambridge. In 1751 he became lord-lieutenant of the North and East Ridings of Yorkshire and a lord of the bedchamber, and in 1760 was made a knight of the Garter. In May 1762 the king's favourite, the earl of Bute, became first lord of the treasury, and the marquess of Rockingham was amongst those who in the following year were dismissed from their lord-lieutenancies. In July 1765 Lord Rockingham formed his first administration with Gen. Henry Seymour Conway and Augustus Henry Fitzroy, duke of Grafton, as secretaries of state. The cabinet seemed stronger than it really was, for it was divided by intestine quarrels, and the earl of Chatham refused to have anything to do with it. In May 1766 the duke of Grafton, a far abler man than Rockingham, though neither so conciliatory in his manners nor so generally popular, seceded from the government, and in Aug. 1766 he succeeded his former chief as first lord of the treasury and prime minister. Lord Rockingham again became prime minister in 1782, with Charles Fox and Lord Shelburne (afterwards marquess of Lansdowne) as secretaries of state. This time he enjoyed office for but a few weeks, for he died on July 1, 1782. He left no issue, and his titles became extinct.

According to his epitaph, written by Edmund Burke, Lord Rockingham was "A man worthy to be held in esteem, because he did not live for himself... He far exceeded all other statesmen in the art of drawing together, without the seduction of self-interest, the concurrence and co-operation of various dispositions and abilities of men, whom he assimilated to his character and associated in his labours."

See *Memoirs of the Marquis of Rockingham and his Contemporaries,* by George Thomas, earl of Albemarle (2 vols., 1852); Horace Walpole's *Memoirs* of the reign of George III, edited by G. F. R. Barker (1894); and the other letters, papers and diaries of the time.

ROCK ISLAND, a city of western Illinois, U.S., on the Mississippi river, 180 mi. W. by S. of Chicago, adjoining Moline and opposite Davenport, Ia.; the county seat of Rock Island county. It is 2 mi. above the mouth of the Rock river and the Hennepin canal (connecting the Mississippi and the Rock rivers with the Illinois), is on federal highways 67 and 150, and is served by the Burlington Route, the Chicago, Milwaukee, St. Paul and Pacific, the Davenport, Rock Island and Northwestern, the Rock Island and the Rock Island Southern railways, and by air lines, river steamers and barges, ferries and motorbus and truck lines. The population in 1950 was 48,710; (1940) 42,775; (1930) 37,953 by the federal census. The island from which the city takes its name, one of the largest (990 ac.) and most beautiful in the Mississippi, is owned by the U.S. and occupied as a manufacturing arsenal and ordnance depot. Government bridges connect it with all three cities. Rock Island (the city) has an area of 10 sq.mi. It is the seat of Augustana college (Evangelical Lutheran; 1860) and of the home offices of the Modern Woodmen of America and the Royal Neighbors of America (large fraternal orders) and Bituminous Casualty corporation (a coal mine and industrial insurance firm). The manufacturing industries are important and diversified, employing 15,000 workers and producing goods valued at $100,000,000 annually. On the tree-covered site of Rock Island there were villages (dating from as early as 1730) of the Sauk and Fox Indians, who helped the British in the War of 1812. The island was fortified by the British, and engagements took place in the vicinity in July and October 1814. In 1816 the United

States built Fort Armstrong (abandoned 1836) on the west end of the island. It became one of the important frontier military posts, and was the headquarters of operations in the Black Hawk War and the scene of the signing of the treaty on Sept. 21, 1832. Black Hawk was born in one of the villages on the Rock river, and a bluff near its mouth is called Black Hawk's Watchtower. The first white settlement on the mainland was made in 1826. The town was incorporated in 1837 and was chartered as a city in 1841.

The arsenal was established on Rock Island by act of congress in 1862. During the Civil War 12,000 Confederate soldiers were confined on the island, of whom 2,000 died during imprisonment.

ROCKLAND, a city of Maine, U.S., the county seat of Knox county; on Penobscot bay, 81 mi. E.N.E. of Portland. It is on federal highway 1, and is served by the Maine Central railroad, Northeast Airlines and motorbuses. Pop. (1950) 9,234; in 1940 it was 8,899 by the federal census. Rockland is the gateway to the numerous summer resorts on the shores and islands of Penobscot bay. The principal fishing port of Maine, it produces frozen fish fillets, sardines, lobsters and fish by-products. There are also clothing, machine-tool, lime and shipbuilding industries. The city is the centre of Knox county's poultry-raising and packing industry. Rockland was settled in 1769, and began to grow with the establishment of the lime industry in 1795. It was set off from Thomaston and incorporated as the town of East Thomaston in 1848; adopted its present name in 1850; and in 1852 was chartered as a city.

ROCKLAND, an inland town of Plymouth county, Mass., U.S., land area 10.2 sq.mi.; 20 mi. S. by E. of Boston, on the New York, New Haven and Hartford railroad. Pop. (1950) 8,960; (1940) 8,087. The town was set off from Abington and incorporated in 1874.

ROCK SPRINGS, a city of Sweetwater county, Wyo., U.S., in the southwestern part of the state, on Bitter creek, at an altitude of 6,271 ft. It is on the main line of the Union Pacific railroad, and is a station on United Air Lines route. Pop. (1950) 10,857. Rock Springs (named from a large saline spring issuing from the base of a bluff) is the largest bituminous coal area west of the Mississippi river and the trading point for a wide region covered with sheep ranches. The city was incorporated in 1888.

ROCKVILLE, a city of Tolland county, Conn., U.S., on the Hockanum river, 15 mi. N.E. of Hartford. It is served by the New York, New Haven and Hartford railroad. Pop. (1950) 8,016; 1940 it was 7,572. At Rockville, in 1841, fancy cassimeres were first made in the United States, and in 1870 the Hockanum mills (established 1809) produced the first American-made worsted for men's clothing. Settlement there began about 1726, and Rockville was chartered as a city in 1889.

ROCKVILLE CENTRE, a village of Nassau county, New York, U.S., on the southern shore of Long Island, 22 mi. E. of Brooklyn; served by the Long Island railroad. Pop. (1950) 22,362 (federal census). The village, settled about 1827, was incorporated in 1893.

ROCKY FORD, a city of Otero county, Colorado, U.S., on the Arkansas river, federal highway 50, and the Santa Fe railway, in the southeastern part of the state (alt. 4,177 ft.). Pop. (1950), 4,087. Rocky Ford produces the most delicious cantaloupes in the country, and is noted also for its honeydews, casabas, watermelons and Valencia onions. The first Thursday in September is Watermelon day, when thousands of melons are given to visitors. The cantaloupe industry had its origin there (about 1888). There is also a green pea industry. The city was founded in 1883 and incorporated in 1887.

ROCKY MOUNT, a city of North Carolina, U.S., in Nash and Edgecombe counties; 56 mi. E.N.E. of Raleigh, on the Tar river and federal highways 64 and 301. It is served by the Atlantic Coast Line railroad, Capital Airlines and by motorbus. Population (1950) was 27,697 by federal census.

It is an important bright leaf tobacco, cotton, peanut and livestock market. Rocky Mount has the oldest cotton mill in the state (established in 1813) and various other manufacturing plants. It operates under a council-manager form of government and owns its power plant, gas plant and water plant.

Rocky Mount was incorporated as a town in 1867 and as a city in 1907.

ROCKY MOUNTAIN GOAT (*Oreamnos montanus*), a North American hollow-horned ruminant of the family Bovidae, distinguished by its whiteness. It is the only ruminant, with the exception of the white Alaskan wild sheep, which is entirely white at all seasons of the year. In the winter coat, the hair is long and pendent, especially on the neck and chest, and elongated into a short beard on the sides of the lower jaw behind the chin; at the base of the long hair is a thick, woolly underfur. In summer the coat becomes comparatively short. The muzzle is hairy, the ears are of moderate size, and the tail is short. There is a large globular gland at the base of each horn. The black horns, ringed in their basal portion, are comparatively short and not unlike those of the Asiatic serows, in being subcylindrical and curving slightly backward. The lateral hoofs are well developed. The cannon bones are remarkably short and wide. The shape of the animal is ungainly, owing to a huge hump on the withers, at which point the height is about three feet. The affinities of the white goat are with the goat antelopes, the group which includes also the chamois and the Asiatic serows (*qq.v.*).

BY COURTESY OF THE AMERICAN MUSEUM OF NATURAL HISTORY

ROCKY MOUNTAIN GOAT (OREAMNOS MONTANUS)

See Madison Grant, "The Rocky Mountain Goat," published in the 9th *Annual Report of the New York Zoological Society* (1905).

ROCKY MOUNTAINS, THE, are the principal division of that vast system of highlands occupying the western third of the United States and a narrower belt in western Canada. Standing between the great continental plains on the east and the region of elevated basins and plateaus stretching from Nevada to central British Columbia on the west, they constitute the backbone of the continent, as well as a major topographical feature of the entire globe.

At the south, the Rockies first become prominent in northern New Mexico where there are elevations above 13,000 ft. Thence they sweep for 2,200 mi. through the United States and Canada to the Yukon. In Canada, for 450 mi. they form the boundary between Alberta and British Columbia, where they are known as the Canadian Rockies. Their greatest width and elevation are attained in Utah and Colorado. There the system of ranges is 300 mi. across. In Colorado there are 46 summits surpassing 14,000 ft., Mt. Elbert (14,431 ft.) being the highest of the system and the second highest peak in the United States. Colorado contains about 254 mountains between 13,000 and 14,000 ft. Northwest of Colorado breadth and elevation diminish, until at the Canadian boundary the ranges are less than 100 mi. wide, with few elevations exceeding 9,500 ft. From Colorado almost to the Peace river in British Columbia, the Rockies carry the watershed of the continent—the continental divide. But this does not mean that they present a continuous chain of great peaks. On the contrary the zone of uplift is rather a vast complex of separate ranges, interrupted at places by wide gaps of lofty rolling plateaus.

In the United States, the crestline of the Rocky mountains definitely breaks down at two places—the plateaus of Yellowstone park and Great Divide basin in southern Wyoming (60 mi. by 100 mi.). The three divisions thus produced—north, central and southern—may be taken as a convenient basis of description. They correspond approximately with the states of Montana, Wyoming and Colorado (with which Utah is associated). The elevations of these major breaks or passes are as follows: in

southern Arizona, 4,615 ft. (Southern Pacific railroad); in New Mexico, Campbell's pass, 7,250 ft. (Santa Fe railroad); in Great Divide basin, 7,102 ft. (at Creston, Union Pacific railroad); in Yellowstone park plateaus, about 8,300 ft.

The Southern Rockies.—The Rockies of Colorado are dealt with elsewhere. (*See* COLORADO; NATIONAL PARK SYSTEM, THE.) The most magnificent groups are probably the Sawatch range (80 mi. by 20 mi.) and the Sangre de Cristo range (40 mi. by 10 mi.) in the central part of the state. In the southwestern corner the Elk, San Miguel (with the spectacular Lizard Head, 13,156 ft.), Needle and other groups, form a wild and rugged mass of peaks.

The Wasatch mountains of central Utah, overlooking the great basin for 100 mi., present abrupt ranges, of which Mt. Delano (12,240 ft.) is the highest. Associated with the Wasatch mountains is the Uinta group (150 mi. by 25 mi.), of which Kings peak (13,498 ft.) is loftiest. Five others exceed 13,000 ft.

The Central Rockies.—The ranges just mentioned connect with the main axis of elevation of the Rockies in the region of Yellowstone park through a belt of rather indefinite uplands running north and south along the western boundary of Wyoming. There are the Crawford mountains, the Wyoming range, the Gros Ventre mountains, the Snake River range and the Teton range. The Teton range presents perhaps the most splendid spectacle of all the Rocky mountain ranges. It is 40 mi. long and 10 mi. wide, rugged and precipitous. Granite spires rise abruptly 6,000 to 7,000 ft. above the flats of Jackson's Hole. The principal peaks are the Three Tetons (Grand Teton, 13,747 ft.) and Mt. Moran (12,800 ft.) at the northerly extremity.

Reverting to the continental divide of the western part of Wyoming, the important uplift of the Wind River range is next in order, northwest of Great Divide basin. It is about 100 mi. long, the core being upward of 13,000 ft. in elevation and sending out long lateral ridges between which remarkable canyons occur. Its most prominent summits are Fremont peak (13,730 ft.), ascended in 1842 by John C. Frémont; Gannett peak (13,785 ft.), the highest in Wyoming, and Chimney Rock (13,340 ft.). Numerous small glaciers are on the northeast slopes. The largest, Dinwoody, covers several square miles. The scenery and mountains are distinctly alpine in character, with many fine waterfalls and lakes.

Northeast of the Wind River range, across the Big Horn basin, lie the Big Horn mountains, a prodigious offshoot of the main range towards the great plains, 120 mi. long and 30 to 50 mi. wide. The axis averages from 11,000 to 13,000 ft. in elevation, rising some 9,000 ft. above the neighbouring prairies. A few of the peaks surpass 13,000 ft. and bear small glaciers in their rugged amphitheatres. The highest is Cloud peak (13,165 ft.).

The Northern Rockies.—Between the northern boundary of Yellowstone park and the Yellowstone river, the Beartooth and neighbouring ranges display what are probably the principal mountain masses of this division. In the vicinity of Mt. Cowen (11,190 ft.) and Emigrant peak (10,969 ft.) the relief becomes as great as 6,400 ft., and Granite peak (12,850 ft.), the highest mountain in Montana, is situated there, as are Grasshopper glacier and other small ice bodies. The Beartooth range has a score of summits of 12,000 ft. or more.

The continental divide, however, leaves Yellowstone park in a northwesterly direction. At the 114th meridian it swings off abruptly to the northeast through the Butte and Helena districts. Beyond this swing, the western axis of elevation continues northwestward as the Bitterroot mountains to within 125 mi. of the Canadian border. They form the boundary between Idaho and Montana, the average elevation being between 7,000 and 8,000 ft. The highest peaks occur on projecting lateral spurs—El Capitan (9,936 ft.) and St. Mary (9,333 ft.). This 125-mi. interval is filled by the Coeur d'Alene (6,000 ft.) and Cabinet ranges, the latter boasting of a glacier on Bear peak (about 9,000 ft.). West of the Bitterroots in central Idaho lies a labyrinth of peaks and ridges (11,000 to 12,000 ft.), Mt. Hyndman (12,078 ft.) being the highest in that state.

In the region of Butte and Helena, the continental divide is generally featureless, the passes around Butte averaging 6,000 ft.

BY COURTESY OF (1) THE DENVER AND RIO GRANDE WESTERN RAILROAD COMPANY. (2) THE CANADIAN NATIONAL RAILWAYS

THE ROCKIES IN THE UNITED STATES AND CANADA

1. The Rocky Mountains in the United States: view showing Mount Elbert near Leadville, Colorado, the second peak in the United States in height—Mt. Whitney in California being the highest. The altitude of Mount Elbert is 14,431 feet

2. The Rocky Mountains in Canada: Mount Robson, British Columbia, having an altitude of 12,972 feet

or less. Mullan pass near Helena is 5,870 ft. The Anaconda range contains Mt. Haggin (10,598 ft.) and Mt. Evans (10,635 ft.). Beyond Helena, the divide veers to the north-northwest and follows the Lewis range, which is so wild and rugged that no wagon roads cross it for 200 mi. Opposite the Lewis range, the westerly margin of the Rockies is defined by the White Fish range (west of the north fork of Flathead river) and the Mission range (60 mi. long, southeast of Flathead lake). The latter culminates in the glacier-bearing Mt. MacDonald (9,800 ft.). Between the Mission and Lewis ranges is the Swan range (Mt. Holland, 10,400 ft.). The principal continental pass thereabouts is Marias pass (8,500 ft.), crossed by the Great Northern railroad.

The finest scenery in this quarter is within Glacier National park (see NATIONAL PARK SYSTEM, THE) with 20 peaks between 9,000 and 10,000 ft. and six between 10,000 and 10,438 ft. Mt. Cleveland is the loftiest summit. The park contains about 40 small glaciers and several large ones (from two to five square miles apiece), besides a myriad of attractive lakes.

The Canadian Rockies.—In Canada the axis of the Rockies is continuous for 1,000 mi. It is simpler, straighter and more sharply defined.

The Rockies proper, a belt averaging about 70 mi. across, are there considered as dissociated from the adjoining groups of the Purcells, Selkirks, Columbia and Pacific coast mountains. Prominent passes of the divide are: Crows Nest pass (Canadian Pacific railway), 4,450 ft.; Vermillion pass (motor road), 5,376 ft.; Kicking Horse pass (Canadian Pacific railway), 5,332 ft., and Yellowhead pass (Canadian Pacific railway), 3,711 ft. Proceeding northwesterly from the U.S. boundary, there are no glaciers for 100 mi., the peaks being mostly below 9,000 ft. A little farther on is Mt. Joffre (11,316 ft.), the first real glacier-hung peak. From there to beyond Mt. Robson (12,972 ft., the highest of all) the system is continuously alpine for about 275 mi. Two hundred miles from the boundary the Canadian Pacific railway crosses the chain near the famous Lake Louise. Halfway between this and Mt. Joffre stands the handsome Mt. Assiniboine (11,870 ft.). In the 150-mi. gap between the Canadian Pacific and the Canadian National railways at Jasper, are situated Mt. Forbes (11,902 ft.) and Mt. Columbia (12,294 ft.), the fifth and second in rank in the Canadian Rockies respectively. In these mountains about 50 peaks surpass 11,000 ft. Glaciers and snow fields abound, and with the neighbouring groups just mentioned there is presented the best sweep of truly alpine territory to be found in America short of Alaska. The northwesterly 500 mi. of the range are imperfectly known, although the mountains are lower. (See MOUNTAINEERING.)   (H. PAL.)

See W. W. Atwood, *The Rocky Mountains* (1945).

ROCKY MOUNTAIN SPOTTED FEVER AND OTHER SPOTTED FEVERS.

Rocky mountain spotted fever is a typhuslike fever (see TYPHUS FEVER), first described in the Rocky mountain section of the U.S., caused by a specific species of rickettsia (*Rickettsia rickettsii*) and transmitted to man by ticks. It was found to be identical with a disease known as Sao Paulo fever in Brazil and with the spotted fever of Colombia. A closely related disease, but distinct aetiologically, is *fièvre boutonneuse* caused by *Rickettsia conorii*, transmitted by ticks and occurring in the countries bordering on the Mediterranean sea and scattered localities of eastern and southern Africa.

History and Distribution.—Rocky mountain spotted fever was known along the Snake river in Idaho as early as 1873 but the first clinical description of the disease in a medical journal was given by E. E. Maxey in 1899. It was characteristically a disease of the open range and was noted to occur most frequently among hunters, trappers, fishermen, cattlemen and sheepherders. Up to 1930, it was thought to be confined to 11 states of the northwest, although one case was reported in Indiana. In connection with field investigations of endemic typhus in the southeastern U.S., it was noted that cases living in rural districts in the more northern states and urban dwellers vacationing in the country suffered from a very severe disease which did not exactly correspond to the clinical picture of endemic typhus. A high proportion of these cases gave histories of tick bites within a short time preceding the onset period. In 1931 L. F. Badger, R. E. Dyer and A. S. Rumreich recovered the causative agent from three patients who were residents of northern Virginia, and proved that it was identical with that of Rocky mountain spotted fever. After that time, the disease was shown to be widely distributed in the U.S., present in two provinces of western Canada, in two states of Brazil and in Colombia, S.A.

Epidemiology.—The selection of the disease in the western U.S. for persons exposed to the open range and the seasonal limitation to late spring and early summer months was explained when the tick vector species was identified as *Dermacentor andersoni*. This is a wood tick found widely distributed in the adult form upon the large mammals, particularly cattle and sheep, in the western range country from the eastern portion of the Pacific coast states to the western, North and South Dakota and Nevada, and from New Mexico on the south to Alberta, Saskatchewan and British Columbia on the north. Adult ticks live two to four years or more. Engorged females deposit their eggs in the soil. The winter is passed in the adult, nymphal or egg stage. Larvae, or seed ticks, emerge in the late spring and seek a blood meal on small animals. If successful, they moult to the nymphal stage, which may not become active until the following spring. Many small animals, especially rodents, are susceptible to infection with the rickettsia of Rocky mountain spotted fever and after having been bitten by an infected tick develop an inapparent form of the disease. During the period of time that the causative agent is in the peripheral circulation these animals serve as a source of infection for the uninfected larval, nymphal or adult ticks which chance to feed upon them. The rickettsiae pass through the stage-to-stage development in the tick and are carried to successive generations in decreasing numbers by transovarial passage. The infection is thus maintained in nature by the alternation of the small animal and tick hosts. Among the rodent hosts should be mentioned particularly the jack and the cottontail rabbits. The rabbit tick *Haemaphysalis leporis-palustris* is one of the principal vectors in maintaining continuous passage in small animals, although it does not attack man.

The occurrence of the human disease in the eastern and southern U.S. was explained when it was discovered that another tick species which attacks man, the common dog tick *Dermacentor variabilis*, also acts as a vector. There is some evidence to indicate that dogs may contract the infection in an inapparent form. In the southwestern U.S. human cases were also traced to the lone star tick *Amblyomma americanum*. In Brazil the common vector is *Amblyomma cajennense*. Many other tick species were found to be experimentally infectable but were epidemiologically unimportant.

Clinical and Pathological Features.—The clinical course of the disease is essentially similar to that described for typhus fever. In severe cases of spotted fever the rash tends to be more haemorrhagic and to be accentuated on the extremities, particularly about the wrists and ankles. Occasionally, a lesion may be detected at the site of the tick bite, but a typical primary eschar is lacking. Nervous and mental symptoms are common; restlessness, insomnia, disorientation and delirium are common manifestations of involvement of the central nervous system. Prostration may be extremely marked from the beginning, merging into coma with death as early as the sixth or seventh day. Convalescence is apt to be slow and may be complicated by visual disturbances, deafness and mental confusion. Although recovery may be delayed, it is usually complete in the end. The case-fatality rates, as in typhus, vary directly with age. The crude rate for reported cases in the U.S. is about 18%. The underlying pathology is essentially the same as that of typhus fever. The causative agent (*R. rickettsii*) proliferates in the endothelial cells lining the smaller blood vessels, causing damage to the vessel walls with haemorrhage, infiltration with round cells and thrombosis. Lesions are widely distributed in the tissues of the body but are characteristically frequent in the central nervous system and skin. Occasionally, there may be large areas of subcutaneous haemorrhage, particularly in the scrotum. Confirmation of the diagnosis is afforded by the Weil-Felix reaction, which becomes positive with *Bacillus proteus* X 19 and usually with X 2 and negative with *B. proteus*

X K during the second week of the illness. The complement-fixation test becomes positive about the same time. The causative agent may be recovered and identified by inoculation of guinea pigs with blood obtained from a patient early in the course of the illness. Reports at mid-20th century indicated that early institution of treatment with antibiotics—chloramphenicol (chloromycetin) and aureomycin—greatly shorten the disease and decrease the risk of death.

Prevention.—Prevention depends primarily upon exercise of personal care in protection against tick bites. Persons exposed to known infected areas should frequently examine the clothing and body for ticks. Usually the tick does not become attached to its host immediately but crawls about for several hours. It has been shown that the chance of receiving infection from the bite of a tick is directly proportional to the length of time that the tick has fed. Ticks should be removed from the person or from a pet with a small forceps or with a piece of paper. The skin area involved should be swabbed with tincture of iodine and the forceps disinfected with heat or chemicals. Hands should be washed with soap and water after such an operation. There is a satisfactory vaccination procedure against Rocky mountain spotted fever; it should be administered in the spring or early summer before the beginning of the tick season, and should be repeated each year, as the maximum degree of protection conferred is for less than a year. The degree of immunity afforded is relative, but the chance for subsequent infection is lessened and the risk of death is greatly reduced.

Fièvre Boutonneuse (Fièvre Exanthématique).—A. Connor and A. Bruch in 1910 described a mild typhuslike fever which they believed to be an endemic disease of Tunisia, North Africa, and proposed the name boutonneuse fever. It was subsequently observed to occur in Marseilles, Fr., and still later was discovered to have a wide geographic distribution. It was reported from most of the Mediterranean countries and the Crimea. Available evidence suggests that the diseases described as Kenya typhus and South African tick-bite fever are probably identical with boutonneuse fever, although conveyed by a different species of tick. One review indicated the widespread distribution of this human tick-borne rickettsiosis in Africa. Primarily, the vector was found to be a brown dog-tick, *Rhipicephalus sanguineus;* subsequently, other ticks were incriminated. The causative agent is *Rickettsia conorii.* The reservoir probably exists in nature in the lower animals, but the dog is apparently an important source of infection. The course of the disease is somewhat similar to Rocky mountain spotted fever, but it is milder. The case-fatality rate is less than 3%. A primary lesion, called by the French *tache noire* ("black spot") is frequently found. It is somewhat similar in appearance to the primary eschar characteristically seen in tsutsugamushi disease. It is, of course, located at the site of the infecting tick bite and, therefore, may be found on any part of the body, but usually on a part covered by clothing. The Weil-Felix reaction with X 19 strain of *B. proteus* becomes positive late in the disease. Experimental evidence suggests that both chloramphenicol (chloromycetin) and aureomycin would be found highly effective in the treatment of boutonneuse fever. Prevention depends upon protection from tick bites as outlined above.

BIBLIOGRAPHY.—S. Ross, E. B. Schoenbach, F. G. Burke, M. S. Bryer, E. C. Rice and J. A. Washington, "Aureomycin Therapy of Rocky Mountain Spotted Fever," *J.A.M.A.* 138:1213 (1948); M. C. Pincoffs, E. J. Guy, L. M. Lister, T. E. Woodward and J. E. Smadel, "The Treatment of Rocky Mountain Spotted Fever with Chloromycetin," *Ann. Int. Med.,* vol. xxix, p. 656 (1948).   (K. F. M.)

ROCOCO, a term used to describe a phase of European art originating in France and commencing in the first quarter of the 18th century. Its name is derived from the French word *Rocailles* which was used to designate the artificial grottoes and fantastic arrangements of rocks in the gardens of Versailles; and it indicates one of the features of the rococo style in its typical form—its absolute freedom and irregularity of rhythm, the twisted curves of a shell being as it were the standard of the whole system of design. Historically, it was an extreme development of the ideas of individual imagination and love of broken curves which

characterized baroque (*q.v.*) art. For the grave and pompous dignity of the style of Louis XIV, the rococo substitutes playfulness and exquisite gracefulness and charm. Up to about the middle of the 18th century, rococo art remained gay and freakish and showed much exotic influence as, for instance, the influence of Chinese art. Then a renewal of interest in classical art and archaeology which had meanwhile taken place in Italy began to make itself felt in French art. During the later phase of the rococo, much of the playfulness disappeared, and a greater calm and balance were introduced into the style; but it retained gracefulness and charm, till eventually, between 1780 and 1790, the severe neo-classical movement superseded it. This later phase of the rococo must be regarded as a stage of transition from the rococo proper to the neo-classical art or Louis XVI. (*See* LOUIS STYLES.)

BIBLIOGRAPHY.—C. Gurlitt, *Geschichte des Barockstiles, des Rococo und des Klassicismus in Belgien, Holland, Frankreich, England* (Stuttgart, 1888); S. Sitwell, *Southern Baroque Art* (1924) and *German Baroque Art* (1927); A. K. McComb, *The Baroque Painters of Italy* (1934); S. F. Kimball, *The Creation of the Rococo* (1943).

ROCROI, a town of northern France, in the department of Ardennes, 22 mi. N.N.W. of Charleville by rail, and within 2 mi. of the Belgian frontier. Pop. (1946) 751. Originally called Croix-de-Rau or Rau Croix, it was fortified in the 16th century and besieged by imperialists in 1555. Invested by the Spaniards in 1643, it was relieved by Louis II, the duke of Enghien (afterward the great Condé). Captured in 1658 by the same duke for Spain, it was not restored to France till the Treaty of the Pyrénées in 1659. In 1815 Rocroi was besieged by the Allies. As a fortified place Rocroi commands the Ardennes plateau between the valley of the Meuse and headwaters of the Oise. The fortifications, constructed by Vauban, form a pentagon and close in the town.

Battle of Rocroi.—In 1643 (*see* THIRTY YEARS' WAR) the Spaniards, under Francisco de Mello, invading France through the Ardennes, laid siege to Rocroi. The town lay in a small plain surrounded by woods and marshes, and could only be approached through a narrow defile. Contrary to the advice of his cautious lieutenant, Marshal de l'Hôpital, the young duc d'Enghien, later known as prince de Condé (*see* CONDÉ, LOUIS II DE BOURBON), though his army was inferior, decided to attack the Spaniards before the town. Either taken by surprise or deliberately courting battle, Mello omitted to block the defile and Enghien, covered by a vigorous display of cavalry under the dashing Gassion, led his army through it in safety and formed up on a low ridge facing the Spanish lines. His infantry, commanded by Espenan, was in the centre, cavalry under Gassion on the right, cavalry under la Ferté on the left, a small reserve under Sirot in rear—altogether 16,000 infantry and 7,000 cavalry, with 12 guns. The Spanish army, now concentrated on a parallel ridge facing the French, was similarly organized, 18,000 infantry in the centre under the veteran Fontaine, cavalry on the right under Isembourg, on the left under Albuquerque—27,000 men and 18 guns. Mello also expected a reinforcement of 6,000 men under Beck. Evening was approaching when la Ferté, wishing to outshine the more favoured Gassion, suddenly led his wing forward without orders, designing, perhaps, to throw a relief into Rocroi. Enghien instantly ordered him back, and Mello surprisingly allowed him to return untouched. Night fell without further action.

On May 19 the French army stood to arms at 3 A.M., Enghien, like Henry of Navarre, donning a hat adorned with white plumes instead of an armoured helmet. A deserter had reported that a battalion of musketeers was in ambush in a wood on the French right. Enghien sent a regiment of infantry to dislodge them, while cavalry, moving round behind the wood, caught them as they retired and cut them to pieces. Relieved of this danger, Enghien set himself to his main task. He himself led eight squadrons against Albuquerque's front, while Gassion with a similar force attacked his left flank. Albuquerque's force melted away before the simultaneous onslaught, and Enghien, ordering Gassion to pursue, swung his own squadrons against the left of the Spanish infantry. Meanwhile la Ferté, though ordered not to commit himself till the right attack had developed favourably, had again disobeyed. He led a ragged attack against Isembourg, was completely defeated, himself and his guns captured, while his men fled, hotly pursued by the Spaniards. Fortunately Sirot's reserve stood firm and threw off Isembourg's attack. Espenan also had advanced against the Spanish infantry, but seeing la Ferté's disaster, drew off. At this critical moment Enghien with his cavalry struck the second line of Spanish infantry in the rear and, dispersing them, swept on to attack Isembourg's victorious cavalry. Taken completely by surprise, Isembourg's men fled, leaving their own and la Ferté's captured guns in Enghien's hands. There now remained only the front line of the Spanish infantry, the famous *tercios viejos,* standing in square upon the ridge. Beck, however, was approaching and the battle might yet be lost; collecting horse and foot Enghien led them to the attack. The Spaniards stood motionless till the French were within 50 paces; then the front face of the square opened and 18 guns belched death at the oncoming French; crashing musketry joined their roar and the attackers fell back with terrible loss. Twice Enghien renewed the attack, only to be beaten off, but the Spanish ammunition was running low, their losses were heavy, the recaptured French guns were brought into action, Sirot came up with his reserve and Gassion from his pursuit. Realizing that further resistance was hopeless, the Spanish officers signalled their desire for quarter; Enghien stepped forward to receive their surrender, but the Spanish infantry, misunderstanding his intention, opened fire upon him. Infuriated at this apparent treachery, the French hurled themselves upon the square and, overwhelming it, massacred the gallant Spaniards almost to a man. Beck, warned of his danger, retreated and the victory was complete. The price of it was 2,000 Frenchmen killed and as many wounded, but 8,000 Spaniards lay dead upon the field, and 7,000 more, nearly all wounded, were prisoners in the hands of the French. Rocroi marked the beginning of the long period of French military glory which was ended only by Marlborough and Eugene.

ROD, EDOUARD (1857–1910), French-Swiss novelist, was born at Nyon, in Switzerland, on March 31, 1857. He studied at Lausanne and Berlin, and in 1878 found his way to Paris. In 1881 he dedicated his novel, *Palmyre Veulard,* to Zola, of whom he was at this period a disciple. A series of novels of similar tendency followed. In *La Course à la mort* (1885) he turned to the analysis of moral motives. He is at his best in presenting cases of conscience, the struggle between passion and duty, and the virtues of renunciation. *Le Sens de la vie* (1889), one of his most famous books, is in the nature of a complement to *La Course à la mort.* Of his many later works, *La Vie privée de Michel Teissier* (1893), translated as *The Private Life of an Eminent Politician* (1893) is justly famous. He was an ardent student of Rousseau, and his play *Le Réformateur* (1906), is based on an episode in Rousseau's life. He died in January 1910.

RODBERTUS, KARL JOHANN (1805–1875), German socialist, was born at Griefswald on Aug. 12, 1805, where his father was professor at the university. He studied law at Göttingen and Berlin, was employed in legal offices in Prussia, and, after travelling for some time, bought the estate of Jagetzow in Pomerania (whence his name of Rodbertus-Jagetzow), and settled there in 1836. Henceforward he devoted himself chiefly to economic studies and to local and provincial affairs. In 1847 he was elected a member of the provincial diet, and in the following year he supported German unity and advocated the independence of the popular assembly. As a member of the Prussian national assembly in 1848, he was made Minister of public worship and education, and he sat for Berlin in the second chamber of 1849. He died on Dec. 8, 1875.

The general position of Rodbertus was "social, monarchical and national." He held the purely economic part of the creed of the German social-democratic party, but disagreed with their methods, and with those of the Arbeiterverein which he refused to join. While regarding the establishment of a socialist state as eventually possible, he accepted existing institutions as the result of past development and looked to the ruler of a united Germany to solve all social problems. The basis of the economic teaching of Rodbertus is the principle laid down by Adam Smith and Ricardo, and insisted on by all the later socialists, that labour is the source and measure of value. In connection with this he developed the position that rent, profit and wages are all parts of a national income produced by the united organic labour of the workers of the community. Consequently wages of labour cannot be paid out of capital; for they are only that part of the national income which is received by the workmen, of a national income which they have themselves produced.

Among his works are: *Die Forderungen der arbeitenden Klassen* (1831); *Zur Erkenntniss unserer staatswirtschaftlichen Zustände* (1842); *Creditnot des Grundbesitzes* (2nd ed., 1876). See E. C. Gonner, *Social Philosophy of Rodbertus* (1899); G. Mayer, *Rodbertus und Lassalle* (1924); H. Sultan, *Rodbertus und der agrarische Social Konservatismus* (1927).

RODENT, a member of the Rodentia (*q.v.*), order of gnawing mammals, more numerous than any other order and containing about 2,000 species. More widely distributed than any other group, they are found on all but the most desert oceanic islands. Most are small to medium-sized, but the pygmy mice are among the smallest of mammals, while the capybara (*q.v.*) may attain a length of 4 ft. and a weight of 100 lb. Rodents are largely terrestrial, many burrowing, many tree-living, a few gliding by skinfolds and some partly aquatic.

Rodents are noted for destroying or injuring crops and food stores, many small species eat quantities of insects and their eggs. Most rodents are eaten in primitive societies, while rabbits, hares, and squirrels (*qq.v.*) are eaten by civilized people. Beavers, chinchillas, muskrats and squirrels (*qq.v.*) produce valuable furs. Plague (*q.v.*) is transmitted by rats and ground squirrels, tularaemia (*q.v.*) by rabbits.   (J. E. Hl.)

RODENTIA, an order of placental mammals characterized by their front or incisor teeth, which are reduced to a single functional pair in each jaw, chisellike and growing throughout life. Rodents are small or medium in size, plantigrade or partly so and generally five-toed. Canine teeth are absent; the cheek teeth, $\frac{2}{2}$ to $\frac{6}{6}$ in number, may be rooted or ever-growing and are arranged in an unbroken series. (*See* Teeth.) The orbits are not surrounded by bone except in the aberrant maned rat, *Lophiomys.*

FROM HAMILTON, "MAMMALS OF EASTERN UNITED STATES" (COMSTOCK PUBLISHING CO.)
House Mouse (MUS MUSCULUS)

The skull is characterized by large premaxillae, completely separating the nasals from the maxillae; by the wide space between incisors and cheek teeth and (except in the Duplicidentata) by the anteroposteriorly elongated groove for the articulation of the lower jaw. Rodents feed chiefly on vegetable matter, but most species eat also insects and other animal matter, while a few are fishers or predators.

A wide difference of opinion exists as to the classification of this order; the scheme here followed being that of T. Tullberg (1899), with modifications.

SUBORDER SIMPLICIDENTATA

The Simplicidentata have only one pair of incisors, above and below; these have enamel only on the front surface, and in chewing the movement is obliquely backward and forward. True rodents may be divided into two sections or infraorders: the angle of the lower jaw arises from the underside of the incisor socket in the Sciurognathi; in the Hystricognathi the angle arises from the outer side. Rodents are an ancient group; and the earliest members are quite as distinct from other mammals as are the recent types, and almost as different from each other. Adaptations to similar habits occur in unrelated groups, leading to superficial similarities of structure and appearance that are frequently very detailed.

SCIUROGNATHI

This section contains nine superfamilies, some of which may be more closely related than this classification indicates.

Aplodontioidea.—The skull is characterized by a small or moderate infraorbital foramen; the masseter muscle does not pass through this, nor does it extend in front of the zygomatic arch on the rostrum. Postorbital processes are absent or poorly marked. The tibia and fibula are free.

Family Ischyromyidae is known from the Lower Eocene to the Upper Oligocene. These rodents had marmotlike skulls and primitively cusped, rooted molars, which in later forms became crested. The dentition included $\frac{2}{1}$ premolars.

Family Aplodontiidae has as its sole existing representative the sewellel or mountain beaver of the Pacific United States. It is about the size of a marmot, with short tail, small rounded ears and small eyes. *Aplodontia* is burrowing in habit, living in damp woods. The cheek teeth are rootless and early lose the pattern; the premolars are $\frac{2}{1}$.

Family Mylagaulidae includes the strange horned rodents of the Miocene and Pliocene. In habits these animals were much like pocket gophers of the present, living in burrows on the plains. The male had a pair of horns on the nose, while the female was hornless.

Family Protoptychidae contains a few forms from the Eocene, characterized by an inflated mastoid bulla. *Eomys* of the European Upper Eocene is type of another primitive family, often referred to the Muroidea or Dipodoidea, from its generalized structure.

Sciuroidea.—Only the family Sciuridae can be placed here. The infraorbital foramen is small, while the masseter muscle arises in front of the zygomatic arch from the rostrum. Postorbital processes are present. The premolars are $\frac{2-1}{1}$. This group is a successful one, represented all over the world, except the Australian region and the oceanic islands.

Subfamily Sciurinae includes the tree and ground squirrels; it may be divided into six tribes.

Sciurini, the typical squirrels (*see* Squirrel) of Eurasia and America, includes numerous species. A number of genera have been allowed by authors; most of these are better considered subgenera. *Sciurus*, the typical genus, is complex and is most widespread. The European red squirrel (*S. vulgaris*) is found from Great Britain to Japan and eastern Siberia; it varies from reddish to dark gray and black in different parts of that range. The gray squirrel of the eastern United States, the Pacific gray squirrel and numerous other American species are closely related. Seven or eight subgeneric groups occur in the Neotropical region, exhibiting a great variety of colour and size. The pygmy squirrels of Central and South America, *Microsciurus*, are the smallest of the American species, hardly larger than mice, with delicate skull and narrow rostrum. *Rheithrosciurus*, the tufted-eared ground squirrel of Borneo, has many grooves on the front of the upper incisors (*see* Groove-toothed Squirrel). It is doubtfully referred to the typical tribe.

Tamiasciurini, the common North American red squirrels, *Tamiasciurus*, differ from all other squirrels in the reproductive system of the male; the baculum (*os penis*) is absent and the accessory glands are unique.

Funambulini includes the tree squirrels of Africa and several oriental genera. The Indian palm squirrels, *Funambulus*, are striped blackish, white and olive. *Ratufa*, the largest of the tree squirrels, includes black, red or yellowish forms, with white or yellowish undersides; they are found in India and the Malay region as far as Bali and Borneo. The African giant squirrels, *Protoxerus*, are characteristic of the tropical forest area. These squirrels are about 11 in. long, with scantily haired underparts. The red-faced giant squirrels, *Epixerus*, resemble the preceding genus but have an elongated skull. The African side-striped squirrels, *Funisciurus*, have cheek teeth $\frac{5}{4}$, the lower molars basined. The brush squirrels, *Paraxerus*, are found in the scrub of the hill country of central Africa; most are olive-gray but several striped species are known and several mountain species are handsomely coloured. *Heliosciurus* is a common squirrel from Rhodesia to Gambia; the forms vary from gray and olive to rich reddish brown. *Myosciurus*, the African pygmy squirrel, with head and body about two and one-half inches, is restricted to the Cameroons and Gabun.

Callosciurini contains mostly oriental species. *Callosciurus*, the common oriental squirrel, is represented by several species in Burma, China, the Malay region, the Philippines and Celebes. A great variety of coloration is exhibited in this genus; white, gray, buff, olive and reddish species or races are known, while one group, often separated as *Tamiops*, is striped. *Menetes*, a long-nosed ground squirrel from Burma, Siam and the Malay peninsula, is distinguished by well-marked flank stripes. Red-cheeked ground squirrels, *Dremomys*, characterized by long-nosed skulls, are found from S. China and Burma to the Malay peninsula and Borneo. The oriental pygmy squirrels, *Nanosciurus*, occur from Malaya to the Philippines and Celebes. Striped ground squirrels, *Lariscus*, of Borneo, Java, Sumatra and the Malay peninsula, are distinguished by short tails and three dark dorsal stripes. *Rhinosciurus*, the long-nosed ground squirrel of the Malay region, including Sumatra and Borneo, is largely insectivorous. It has weak, tweezerlike incisors and extensile tongue. The Celebes long-nosed ground squirrel, *Hyosciurus*, has long front claws and normal incisors. The pygmy ground squirrel of North Borneo has broad incisors and black and white flank stripes.

Xerini, the spiny squirrels (*q.v.*) of Africa, are represented in North Africa by *Atlantoxerus*, and throughout the plains country and grasslands south of the Sahara by *Xerus*. *X. rutilus*, the typical form, occurs in Ethiopia, Somaliland and Kenya; it is yellowish-brown without stripes, the skull with convex profile. *X. (Euxerus) erythropus* of Equatorial Africa has a long narrow skull and white flank mark; its colour is reddish. *X. (Geosciurus) inauris* of South Africa is pale yellowish-brown, with a well-marked white lateral stripe.

Marmotini, containing the marmots and typical ground squirrels, is best represented in Asia and North America. The chipmunks (*q.v.*), *Tamias* and *Eutamias*, have cheek pouches, are light in build and climb well. *Eutamias* is found in eastern Asia and in western North America, while *Tamias* is restricted to eastern North America. The spermophiles, sousliks or ground squirrels (*qq.v.*), *Citellus*, are found from Hungary through Asia and North America south to Mexico. The tail is usually short and flattened and the claws enlarged; the size varies from about five inches to more than one foot, excluding the tail. *Cynomys*, the prairie dog (*q.v.*) is confined to western North America. The tail is short and the body heavy. Marmots (*q.v.*), *Marmota*, are found in the Alps and eastward from Poland through Asia and in North America as far south as Alabama and New Mexico. Cheek pouches are absent. *Spermophilopsis*, the sand marmot of southern Siberia, may belong here. It is golden in colour, the pelage silky. The single species is a little smaller than the marmots. Cheek pouches are present and the cheek teeth are simplified in pattern.

Subfamily Petauristinae. The flying squirrels (*q.v.*) of the northern hemisphere are found from Scandinavia and northern Asia to the Malay region and throughout the forested parts of North America. The fore- and hindlimbs are connected by a broad skin fold, supported by a cartilaginous spur arising from the wrist, by means of which they glide from tree to tree. About 11 genera are recognized. *Petaurista*, the giant flying squirrel of southern Asia, occurs from India and Japan to Java and Palawan; the various forms are red or black, sometimes spotted with white. The woolly flying squirrel, *Eupetaurus* of the Himalayan region, is about the same size (head and body about 24 in.; tail 18 in.); its cheek teeth are high-crowned, unlike those of other Sciuridae. *Sciuropterus*, a smaller type, is found in northern Europe and Asia, east to Japan. Closely related species, usually recognized as generically distinct (*Glaucomys*), are found in North America as far south as Honduras. In the Malay region a number of other genera occur, varying in size from that of a mouse to that of a rat; they are distinguished by dental and cranial characters.

Castoroidea.—Two families are included here, one of which is extinct. The masseter muscle is similar in its attachment to that in the Sciuridae, but postorbital processes are absent; the cheek teeth are complicated in pattern and rootless in Recent forms, although originally four-cusped and rooted.

Family Castoridae is represented by two living species of beaver (*q.v.*), although formerly it was a large and varied group. Fossil forms carry the beavers back to the Middle Oligocene but, except for differences in tooth pattern, the earlier forms are much like the later ones. Subfamily Castoroidinae includes giant forms almost as large as a bear, with cheek teeth of a different pattern. These were characteristic of the Pleistocene of North America and Europe. Older types were smaller, the earliest appearing in the Lower Miocene.

Family Eutypomyidae includes a few Middle Oligocene castoroids, with two upper premolars. The cheek teeth have numerous small enamel islands.

Geomyoidea.—Two families of American rodents are referred to this superfamily. They combine characters of the squirrel, beaver and mouse groups; the masseter muscle and structure of the infraorbital canal agree with that of the squirrels. Postorbital processes are absent and all have external fur-lined cheek pouches.

Family Geomyidae. The pocket gophers (q.v.) are stout-bodied, burrowing rodents with small eyes and ears and large front claws. The skull is massive and flat. The fossil subfamily, Entoptychinae of the Oligocene and Miocene, had rooted teeth but otherwise resembled Recent gophers. The Geomyinae contains forms with simple, ever-growing cheek teeth.

Family Heteromyidae includes three subfamilies. The pocket mice (q.v.), Perognathinae, are known from Oligocene times on. The cheek teeth are rooted, the cusps of the lower premolars form a quatrefoil pattern, those of the other teeth form cross-crests. The kangaroo rats (q.v.), Dipodomyinae, have rootless teeth without pattern when worn; the enamel is restricted to bands. The spiny pocket rats, Heteromyinae, have rootless teeth, which when worn form a C-pattern, narrow anteroposteriorly. *Heteromys*, the typical genus, occurs in Central America and northern South America, also in Trinidad.

Anomaluroidea.—Part of the masseter muscle passes through the infraorbital canal, while the lateral masseter is restricted to the zygomatic arch, differing in these respects from other rodents except the Dipodoidea and Hystricoidea.

Family Anomaluridae are arboreal rodents without postorbital processes, cheek teeth $\frac{4}{4}$, and large auditory bullae. On the underside of the tail is a series of imbricated scales. A skin membrane extends between fore- and hindlimbs, supported by a cartilaginous spur from the elbow, except in *Zenkerella*. *Anomalurus* includes various species which are confined to Equatorial Africa as far south as Northern Rhodesia. The subfamily Idiurinae contains two genera: *Idiurus*, with a flying membrane, and *Zenkerella*, which is without this membrane. These are found in the West African forest area.

Family Pseudosciuridae may belong here; it agrees in the attachment of the masseter. The cheek teeth are cusped or crested, with low crowns, while the skull is long and flattened. The several genera are found in the Eocene and Oligocene of Europe.

Family Theridomyidae is also extinct, known only from the Middle Eocene to the Oligocene of Europe. The earliest forms had teeth somewhat squirrellike in pattern, while in later types the pattern was reduced to enamel islands.

Family Pedetidae. *Pedetes*, the jumping-hare (q.v.) of eastern and southern Africa, is a kangaroolike rodent about the size of a fox, buffy brown in colour with white hip stripe. *Parapedetes*, a similar form, occurs in the Miocene of Africa.

Ctenodactyloidea.—The African family Ctenodactylidae includes three genera. Part of the masseter muscle passes through the infraorbital foramen, which is large. The mandible lacks a coronoid process, the teeth are prismatic and the auditory and mastoid bullae are inflated. *Ctenodactylus*, the gundi of North Africa (Morocco to Tripoli) is about the size of a squirrel, with short tail and pale buffy coloration. *Massoutiera* is the long-tailed gundi of the Sahara desert and Senegal. *Pectinator* of Somaliland and Eritrea has a long bushy tail and $\frac{5}{5}$ cheek teeth, more than in any rodent except certain Bathyergidae. *Pectinator* is known from the Miocene of India, while other representatives of the family are reported from the Pliocene of the Mediterranean region.

Gliroidea.—This subfamily includes the dormice and their relatives. They resemble squirrels in habit and general appearance. The tail is bipennate or bushy. The cheek teeth are usually $\frac{4}{4}$ but may be $\frac{3}{3}$, with transverse crests. The lower leg bones are fused. The caecum is absent in most species.

Family Gliridae, the true dormice. The typical genus, *Glis*, includes the large edible dormouse (q.v.) found from France and Spain to Asia Minor. *Muscardinus*, the common dormouse, ranges from England to the Mediterranean and near east; it is much smaller than *Glis*, about as long as a house mouse but with heavier body. Several other types occur in Europe and Asia. The African dormice are often given subfamily rank (Graphiurinae), differing from the typical group in having a more primitive attachment of the lateral masseter muscle, and the teeth have only poorly marked cross-crests. *Graphiurus*, a large gray dormouse, is restricted to South Africa. *Claviglis* is smaller, with more rounded skull; it contains a number of species in various parts of Africa south of the Sahara. Subfamily Platycanthomyinae is characterized by cheek teeth $\frac{4}{4}$ in number; the crowns wear flat. The pelage is mixed with flat spines, while the tail is tufted. *Platycanthomys* is found in India and is arboreal. *Typhlomys* of China is apparently fossorial, with reduced eyes; it has a small caecum. Subfamily Seleviniinae contains only the Recent *Selevinia*, described in 1938 from central Asia. It differs from typical dormice in its mouselike tail, vestigial basin-crowned molar teeth and large incisive foramina.

Dipodoidea.—The jerboas and jumping mice (qq.v.) are included here. Cranially, they have a large infraorbital canal through which the medial masseter muscle passes, as in the Anomaluridae and Ctenodactylidae. The cheek teeth are typically $\frac{4}{3}$, the first upper one small.

Family Zapodidae. These mouselike rodents differ from the true mice chiefly in the characters of the superfamily. Subfamily Sicistinae, found in Europe and Asia, includes only *Sicista*, the birch mouse. This yellowish-brown rodent is marked by a single black dorsal stripe; it climbs readily, living in birch forest and feeds on seeds. The North American jumping mice (q.v.), subfamily Zapodinae, are long-tailed, long-legged rodents, found also in China.

Family Dipodidae includes jumping rodents resembling kangaroo rats but with even longer feet. The three middle metatarsal bones are usually fused into a cannon bone. Cheek teeth are $\frac{4-3}{3}$. The lateral toes are reduced or lost. The bullae are large and the mastoid inflated. *Euchoreutes* of central Asia is type of a subfamily; it is characterized by ungrooved incisor teeth, cheek teeth $\frac{4}{3}$, the zygomatic arch slanting gradually upward to the lachrymal, and enormous ears. *Cardiocranius* and *Salpingotus* of Mongolia and central Asia form a third subfamily characterized by unfused metatarsal bones and less angular zygomatic arch than in the Dipodinae.

Muroidea.—The mice and their allies are characterized by the slitlike infraorbital foramen, through which the medial masseter muscle passes and which is compressed by the development of the zygomatic plate, the flattened area from which part of the lateral masseter arises. The cheek teeth are $\frac{3}{3}$. The cardiac part of the stomach is lined by a cornified layer; the colon forms a spiral loop.

Family Cricetidae is characterized by the upper molars, the cusps of which are arranged in two rows. This pattern is frequently obscured, the cusps wearing down to form zigzag crests. Cricetids, only slightly different from modern types, are known from the Oligocene of America and Asia. Subfamily Cricetinae includes the native American muroids with the exception of the Holarctic voles and their allies. *Cricetus* and several related hamsters (q.v.) are found in Europe and Asia; they are heavy-bodied, short-tailed burrowing rodents. *Oryzomys*, found from Patagonia to New Jersey, is represented by numerous species, one group of which extends to the Galapagos Islands. The American harvest mice, *Reithrodontomys*, vary from small to large mice characterized by grooved incisors, while the white-footed or deer mice, *Peromyscus*, with internal cheek pouches, are the dominant North American forms from Alaska to Panamá. *Onychomys*, the grasshopper mouse, resembles the old world hamsters in appearance but lives chiefly on insects and other mice. *Neotoma*, the pack rat, is quite ratlike in appearance but its teeth are more like the Microtinae in their zigzag pattern. A great variety of tropical American genera are known.

Subfamily Myospalacinae includes a gopherlike genus from Siberia and northern China. The cheek teeth are ever-growing and prismatic, resembling the Microtinae. Subfamily Nesomyinae includes a few genera from Madagascar. *Nesomys* has teeth much like *Oryzomys*. *Hypogeomys*, a burrowing form, has prismatic teeth suggestive of those of *Neotoma*, as has also *Macrotarsomys*. *Eliurus* differs from these in having cross-crested teeth.

Lophiomys, the maned rat of eastern Africa, is given subfamily or even family rank because of its odd skull; the temporal fossa is completely roofed over by bone, the surface of which is granulated; the teeth, however, are cricetid. The tail is bushy. The feet are specialized for an arboreal life, with a partly opposable hallux.

Subfamily Microtinae includes the voles and lemmings (*qq.v.*) found in the northern hemisphere south to Guatemala and Burma. The cheek teeth are high-crowned and prismatic, forming a complex zigzag pattern. The skull is angular, marked with muscle ridges. As a rule, voles are heavy-bodied, short-tailed rodents, more or less modified for burrowing. *Ondatra*, the muskrat (*q.v.*), is the largest of the group, with a long dorso-ventrally flattened tail and partly webbed hind feet. This is connected with the following forms by intermediates like *Arvicola*, the Eurasian water vole, and *Neofiber*, the round-tailed muskrat of Florida. *Microtus*, the voles or meadow mice, are usually small. The lemmings, *Lemnus* and allies, have ever-growing cheek teeth with short lower incisor (the root ending in the lower jaw opposite the molars): they are chiefly arctic and northern forms. A few genera have rooted cheek teeth: *Ellobius* and *Prometheomys*, the subterranean voles of southern and central Asia; *Clethrionomys*, the red-backed bank vole of northern Europe, Asia and America; *Phenacomys*, including the red tree mouse and other North American voles. *Brachytarsomys* of Madagascar shows many similarities to the voles but it has probably developed independently from the primitive Cricetidae, probably the Nesomyinae.

Subfamily Gerbillinae contains a number of jumping rodents, with broad brain case, inflated mastoid and auditory bullae and prismatic cheek teeth, the transverse crests developed from paired cusps both above and below. The upper incisors are grooved in all but a few species. Gerbils (*q.v.*) are widespread in Africa and southern Asia. The typical genus *Gerbillus* occurs in both regions. The mastoids are not highly inflated, nor prominently bulging when the skull is viewed from above. *Tatera* is found throughout the range of the subfamily; it is more ratlike. *Ammodillus*, a dwarf form from Somaliland, lacks a coronoid on the mandible. *Pachyuromys* of North Africa, has extremely inflated bullae and mastoids and a short clublike tail in which fat is stored, while *Desmodillus* is a fat-tailed gerbil from the deserts of South Africa. *Meriones*, found in Africa and Asia, has molars which are laminated throughout life and rootless. *Psammomys* has high-crowned but rooted molars; it is found in North Africa and Palestine.

Family Spalacidae contains several burrowing rodents of the old world, resembling the American pocket gophers in general appearance but with cheek teeth of a different pattern, and the zygomasseteric structures are derived from a primitive muroid type. *Spalax*, the blind mole rat of southern Europe, Egypt and western Asia, forms a subfamily by itself. Rhizomyinae contains the bamboo rats, *Rhizomys*, of India, China and the Malay region, large rodents with soft, silky gray fur and short tail. The east African mole rats, *Tachyoryctes*, are smaller, about eight inches head and body length, with soft reddish-brown fur.

Family Muridae is an old world group, although some species have accompanied man to almost all parts of the globe. The upper molars have three rows of cusps, which often unite to form cross-crests. Subfamily Murinae contain the typical rats and mice, with a few aberrant forms. About 400 species are recognized. *Mus*, the house mouse and closely allied species, is almost world-wide. *Rattus*, containing the well-known black and brown rats and many other species native to Asia and Africa, is especially varied in the Austro-Malayan region; several species have been carried all over the world on ships and even on primitive native boats. The bandicoot-rats (*q.v.*), *Nesokia* and *Bandicota*, are burrowers, found from Egypt to China and the Malay region. African giant rats, *Cricetomys*, measure 30 in. in total length, the tail long with a white tip. The spiny mice, *Acomys*, are widely distributed in east Africa, southwestern Asia, Cyprus and Crete; these are almost as spiny as hedgehogs. The field rats of Africa, *Arvicanthis* and its relatives, are volelike but coarse-haired, some with stripes. Genera of various relationships have become arboreal, often becoming quite similar in appearance. Several shrew rats (*Mycteromys*, *Echiothrix* and *Melasmothrix*), with long wedge-shaped head and shrewlike appearance, are found in Java, Sumatra and Celebes. The Philippine shrew rat (*Rhynchomys*) has minute cheek teeth and short white incisors; it may feed on insects and worms. Two bushy-tailed rats (*Phlaeomys* and *Crateromys*) occur in the northern Philippines. The Australian native mice and rats form a varied group, some rabbitlike, others with saltatorial or leaping adaptations. Several giant rats occur in Celebes, New Guinea and the Solomons, heavy-bodied and as large as the African species. Subfamily Hydromyinae contains the water rats of Australia and New Guinea and several genera in the Philippines. Most species have only two molars, characterized by basined crowns, and the infraorbital foramen is wide. Large feet and the otterlike pelage fit them for a life in the water. Subfamily Dendromurinae contains the African tree mice, characterized by reduced number of cusps on the molars.

The tree mice (*Dendromus*) have opposable first toes, often with nails; the yellowish brown upper parts often have a single black stripe. The West African bush mouse (*Prionomys*) is pale chocolate in colour. Spiny tree rats (*Deomys*) from West Africa and the Congo, are remarkable for their long tails. The fat mice (*Steatomys*), widely distributed in Africa, are hamsterlike, short-tailed members, while *Saccostomys* of the savannas is coloured a handsome pale gray and possesses internal cheek pouches. The mouse gerbils of South-West Africa (*Malacothrix*) also belong here. Subfamily Otomyinae contains several African swamp rats, resembling large voles but with laminated teeth and long soft fur.

HYSTRICOGNATHI

These rodents are characterized by the angle of the lower jaw, arising from the side of the root of the incisor. Except in the Bathyergidae, the medial masseter muscle passes through the infraorbital foramen, which is large.

Bathyergoidea.—This superfamily includes only the burrowing molerats of south and tropical Africa. The tibia and fibula are fused. *Heliophobius* is remarkable in having $\frac{6}{6}$ cheek teeth, some of which may be deciduous. *Bathyergus* has normal incisors and large claws; the other genera have long-rooted incisors, the upper incisor roots extending to the back of the palate or into the pterygoids. *Georychus* has cheek teeth $\frac{4}{4}$; it is widespread in tropical and southern Africa. *Heterocephalus*, the naked mole-rat of Kenya, Ethiopia and Somaliland, has only $\frac{3}{3}$ cheek teeth. The Bathyergidae is represented by two genera in the Oligocene of Mongolia, one of these a large form. The cranial characters of the family were even then well established.

Hystricoidea.—The porcupines (*q.v.*) of both the old and new worlds are included here, although some doubt exists as to their relationships. Quite possibly most of their similarities may be convergence. Both families have a covering of quills and the teeth are complex, wearing flat at an early age.

Family Hystricidae includes the old world porcupines. They are ground-living rodents and their long quills are firmly attached to the skin. *Hystrix* contains the larger forms, two feet or more in length, with short tails and inflated skulls, and is found in southern Europe, Africa and southern Asia. *Thecurus* is smaller, with a flattened skull profile and nasals opening opposite the infraorbital canal; it is restricted to Borneo, Sumatra and Palawan, in the Philippines. *Atherurus* is widespread in Africa and Asia, extending south to Sumatra. It is smaller, like a large rat, with a tail about half the length of the body, ending in a brush of hollow quills, each of which resembles a string of flat beads. The long-tailed porcupine (*Trichys*) has short spines and the skull has postorbital processes.

Family Erethizontidae contains the American tree porcupines, characterized by less complex patterns on the cheek teeth, short paroccipital processes on the skull. The hind feet are modified for an arboreal life, the first toe being replaced in function by a movable pad. *Erethizon*, the North American porcupine, is a large, heavy-bodied rodent, the quills of the body nearly hidden by long hairs. *Coendou*, from South and Central America, is smaller and has a long prehensile tail. *Echinoprocta*, found in Colombia, has a short tail, only a little longer than the foot and not prehensile, but it resembles *Coendou* cranially. *Chaetomys* deserves subfamily rank; its teeth are more simple, the skull has well-developed postorbital processes and the spiny covering is restricted to the head and forelimbs. The tail is long and scaly.

Cavioidea.—The mandible differs from that in the Hystricoidea in that the angle is not distorted laterally. The coronoid is small and a deep groove indicates the insertion of the deep masseter.

Family Caviidae includes the guinea pigs, cavies and capybara (*qq.v.*). The cheek teeth are ever-growing and prismatic. The clavicles are absent, the lateral toes of the hind foot are lost and the tail is much reduced. Subfamily Caviinae is characterized by two- or three-lobed teeth. *Cavia* is represented by a number of South American species related to the well-known guinea pig and rather similar to it. *Kerodon rupestris* of Brazil is characterized by blunt nails on the toes. *Dolichotis*, containing two distinct species, is restricted to Argentina; it is rabbitlike in appearance and habits, especially *D. patagonica*, the mara.

Several rodent families described from the Santa Cruz Miocene of South America are related to the Caviidae and others are referable to this family.

Subfamily Hydrochoerinae, *Hydrochoerus*, the aquatic capybara, with complicated posterior molars, is found from Panamá to Paraguay. It is the largest existing rodent, with a body length of four feet and heavy build. Fossil rodents closely allied to the capybara are known from the Pleistocene of both South and North America.

Family Dinomyidae includes only one living species, with mandible more like that of the Hystricoidea. The tail is longer than the broad feet. The skull is broad and porcupinelike; the molars consist of four transverse plates. The family is known from the Miocene of South America and the West Indies.

Family Heptaxodontidae contains a number of extinct forms of the Pliocene, among them rodents even larger than the capybara.

Family Dasyproctidae includes the pacas and agoutis (*qq.v.*) of tropical America. The agoutis, subfamily Dasyproctinae, are the size of rabbits, with short tail and three toes on the hind foot. The pacas, subfamily Cuniculinae, have an enormous cheek plate developed from the zygomatic arch. The teeth are lobate, the crowns wearing flat and the lobes becoming enamel lakes. The hind foot has five toes.

Chinchilloidea.—The cheek teeth are ever-growing, consisting of two or three transverse plates. The skull has large bullae and inflated mastoid. The angle of the mandible is narrow and produced posteriorly, while the coronoid is minute. The fibula is small. The lateral toes of the hind foot are vestigial or lost. Only the family Chinchillidae is included here; it has been distinct since the Oligocene and is unknown outside of South America, the plains of Argentina and the Andes from Ecuador south. *Chinchilla lavigera* and *C. brevicauda* are soft-furred rodents, about the size of a large squirrel (*see* CHINCHILLA). Almost equally soft-furred are the rabbit-eared species of *Lagidium*, found from Peru and Chile to southern Argentina.

The larger viscachas (*Lagostomus*) of the Argentine pampas are the size of a hare (head and body 20 in., tail 8 in.), with large head and robust body. They live in colonies like prairie dogs but are nocturnal. The viscacha (*q.v.*) is gray, with blackish and white facial markings and a white stripe on the hind leg.

Octodontoidea.—The zygomasseteric structure resembles that in the Hystricoidea. The cheek teeth usually have an E-pattern, the branches of which may become islands on wear; in some forms there are four branches instead of three.

Family Capromyidae includes two groups. The hutias (*Capromys*) of the Greater Antilles and Venezuela are harsh-haired, robust rodents, with ever-growing cheek teeth of the E-pattern. The coypu (*q.v.*) or nutria rat (*Myocastor*) is a large beaverlike rodent found from Brazil and Argentina to Chile.

Family Octodontidae contains a number of rodents, chiefly Chilean or Argentine in distribution, with simplified kidney-shaped or bilobed cheek teeth. Subfamily Ctenomyinae includes the fossorial tuco tucos (*Ctenomys*), which resemble burrowing rodents of other groups. The cheek teeth are kidney-shaped. Subfamily Octodontinae contains ratlike or mouselike forms with tufted tails, chiefly found in the southern Andes. *Spalacopus* and *Aconaemys* of this group are fossorial types, resembling *Ctenomys* but with cheek teeth of the figure-eight pattern.

Family Abrocomidae includes only a single Recent genus *Abrocoma*, characterized by ratlike appearance, short hairy tail and inflated bullae. The cheek teeth are ever-growing, prismatic, the upper ones like a distorted figure eight, the lower ones somewhat E-shaped, with a single re-entrant angle on the cheek side. The incisive foramina are large.

Family Echimyidae contains many rodents of ratlike appearance, with pelage coarse or spiny and rooted cheek teeth. These have a distorted E-pattern, both above and below, wearing down to produce transverse enamel islands. Subfamily Echimyinae includes genera with narrow cheek teeth. Subfamily Dactylomyinae is characterized by broad upper cheek teeth with four lateral lobes and by soft fur. The third and fourth digits of the feet are usually elongated.

Family Thryonomyidae is represented by the cane rats of Africa, *Thryonomys*. The incisors are broad and powerful, the upper ones three-grooved. The cheek teeth show a modified E-pattern.

Family Petromyidae. The rock rat of South-West Africa (*Petromys*) resembles a large, bushy-tailed rat. The cheek teeth have a distorted eight-pattern.

SUBORDER DUPLICIDENTATA

Two pairs of upper incisors are present, the second pair small and situated behind the first; the enamel extends completely around the incisors. This group is often considered a distinct order, the Lagomorpha.

Family Ochotonidae includes the pikas or mouse hares; these have no external tail, the ears are short and the hind legs not modified for leaping. Pikas (*q.v.*) are widely distributed from southeastern Europe through Asia to western North America.

Family Leporidae contains the hares and rabbits (*qq.v.*); the hind limbs are elongated, the tail short and recurved and the ears are long. The cheek teeth number $\frac{6}{5}$. *Lepus*, the hare genus, occurs throughout the northern hemisphere and in Africa, represented by numerous species. *Caprolagus* of Assam and adjacent areas has harsh pelage, a brown tail and ears shorter than the head. *Nesolagus* of Sumatra is striped with black, while the rump is mahogany brown. *Pentalagus*, found in the Liu Kiu Islands, has only five upper cheek teeth; it has a black dorsal stripe. *Romerolagus*, which occurs in high mountains of southern Mexico, is tailless and is otherwise primitive. The cottontails (*q.v.*) of North and South America, *Sylvilagus*, have short ears but dig little. The red hares of South Africa (*Pronolagus*) are heavily built types with brown or red tails. The true rabbit, *Oryctolagus*, originally distributed over North Africa and southern Europe, is distinguished from *Lepus* by its short ears and limbs, its digging habits and the young, which are born blind and helpless.

BIBLIOGRAPHY.—O. Thomas, *Proc. Zool. Soc. London* (1896); G. S. Miller, *Cat. Mammals Western Europe Brit. Mus.* (1912); T. Tullberg, *Nova Acta Reg. Soc. Sci. Upsala* 1897, Ser. III (1898); M. Weber, *Die Saugetiere*, vol. 2 (2nd ed., 1928); J. R. Ellerman, *Families and Genera of Living Rodents*, 2 vols. (Brit. Mus., 1940, 1941).

(J. E. HL.)

RODEO, a series of cowboy contests stemming from the days of the early cattle industry of the southwestern plains of the United States when men, forced to spend months and even years on the range, would gather together in the "cowtowns" at the end of the trails and vie for the unofficial title of best bucking horse rider, roper, etc., the contests being accompanied by heavy betting. As the cowboy was curtailed in scope by the railroads and fencing, the contests became regular, formal programs of entertainment in the communities.

Many towns and areas claim the distinction of being the first place to hold a rodeo in the United States, among them being Cheyenne, Wyo., in 1872 and Winfield, Kans., in 1882, but at best such early contests were merely exhibitions of riding and roping skill and not the highly organized shows that modern rodeo became. The oldest continual annual rodeo on record is the Prescott, Ariz., show, first held on July 4, 1888; the first known commercial rodeo was held at Lander, Wyo., in 1893.

Formerly, as now, various titles were given to these shows, such as stampede, frontier day, roundup or fiesta. The word "rodeo," which is of Spanish origin, did not come into general use until the 1920s. It is pronounced both as, rō'dê-ō and rŏ-dā'ō, the latter being preferred by those in the industry.

Originally an outdoor sport, rodeo moved indoors in 1917 at the Stockyards coliseum in Fort Worth, Tex., thus becoming a year-round sport with a season extending from the second week in January until the middle of December.

Both professional and amateur rodeo programs are built around the six major contests—saddle bronc riding, bareback riding, calf roping, bull riding, steer wrestling and team roping. Other events such as steer roping, steer decorating, wild cow milking, barrel bending and a variety of races are added as facilities and funds permit. The specialty numbers, such as trick riding, fancy roping and the dog, horse and steer acts (known as contract acts) are spaced in the program to permit officials to prepare chutes, equipment, etc., for following contests. Integral parts of every rodeo are the queen and clown, the latter serving a useful purpose in distracting the attention of the contest animals while the dismounted or thrown rider has a chance to leave the ring. Other features may be presented such as mounted quadrilles and allied western classes, and often a popular motion-picture or television star entertains.

Organized on Nov. 1, 1936, and originally called the Cowboy's Turtle association, the Rodeo Cowboy's association (R.C.A.) raised the standards of rodeo. The R.C.A., a kind of union representing the contestants' interests and regulating their personal behaviour and the types of shows entered, established a system of fines and black lists to regulate managers' and contestants' activities. In 1929 the Rodeo Association of America, an organization of rodeo managers and producers, was founded to standardize events, rules, judging and arena conditions and to work out mutual problems pertaining to the production of professional rodeos. In 1946 the group was renamed the International Rodeo association (I.R.A.).

Both the R.C.A. and the I.R.A. established their own point-award systems, naming champions each year. In the 1950s the I.R.A.'s system was based on one point for each dollar won exclusive of entry fees; the R.C.A.'s system was the same except that entry fees were included. This double point-award system thus created two sets of champions in each event, as well as two all-around champions, which proved confusing.

Originally the working cowhand of the west, the rodeo contestants of today come from all parts of the country. This highly specialized field demands a great degree of skill and stamina of the professional contestants, who are required to compete in about 35 shows during the year; participation, however, does not guarantee a living since events must be won, and the contestant is continually faced with the hazards of accidents and injury.

Rodeo stock is valuable and the horses and steers are well cared for to the point of being pampered. Good bucking horses are not from wild herds or killers but are usually halter-broken and gentle until mounted. They are encouraged in their dislike of being mounted and further annoyed by the flank strap, which is placed around the hind quarters; any foreign object on the rear of a horse has a tendency to make him buck.

After the end of World War II, rodeo became an important amateur sport, with regular contests being held by small saddle clubs, high schools, colleges and even prisons.

Rodeo spread all over the world, becoming especially popular in Canada and Australia. The growth of the sport may be indicated by a comparison of the first rodeos, which were one-day events with total prizes not amounting to more than $100, with the Madison Square Garden show, in New York city, which gave 29 performances with prize money totalling $74,400 in 1954. (L. Sr.)

RODERICK or RUADRI (d. 1198), king of Connaught and high king of Ireland, was the son of Turlough (Tordelbach) O'Connor, king of Connaught, who had obtained the overkingship in 1151, but had lost it again in 1154 through the rise of Muirchertach O'Lochlainn in Ulster. Roderick succeeded to Connaught in 1156, and after ten years' fighting won back the title of high king. His ill-advised persecution of Dermot (Diarmait MacMurchada), king of Leinster, furnished the pretext for the Anglo-Norman invasion of Ireland. Roderick endeavoured to expel the invaders, but was driven behind the Shannon.

He delayed his submission to Henry II until 1175, when a treaty was concluded at Windsor. Roderick, under this agreement, held Connaught as the vassal of England, and exercised lordship over all the native kings and chiefs of Ireland; in return he undertook to pay an annual tribute. The treaty did not put an end to the wars of the Norman adventurers against Connaught and Roderick's dependants.

He held out till 1191; but then, weary of strife, retired to the cloister. He died in 1198, the last of the high kings of Ireland.

See Giraldus Cambrensis, *Opera*, vol. v (Rolls Series); G. Orpen's *Song of Dermot and the Earl* (1892); W. Stubbs's edition of *Benedictus Abbas* (Rolls Series); Miss K. Norgate's *England under the Angevin Kings*, vol. ii (1887).

RODEZ, a town of southern France, capital of the department of Aveyron, 51 mi. N.N.E. of Albi by rail. Pop. (1946) 20,437. Rodez, *Segodunum* under the Gauls, *Ruthena* under the Romans, was the capital of the *Rutheni*, a tribe allied to the Arverni, and was afterward the chief town in the district of Rouergue. In the 4th century it became Christian, and St. Amans, its first bishop, was elected in 401. In the middle ages the bishops held temporal power in the "cité," and the counts in the "bourg." The Albigenses were defeated near Rodez in 1210. The countship of Rodez, detached from that of Rouergue at the end of the 11th century, belonged first to the viscounts of Carlat, and from the early 14th century to the counts of Armagnac. From 1360 to 1368 the English held the town. After the confiscation of the estates of the Armagnacs in 1475 the countship passed to the dukes of Alençon and then to the D'Albrets. Henry IV finally annexed it to the crown of France.

Rodez is situated on the southern border of the Causse of Rodez, on an isolated plateau bordered on the east and south by the river Aveyron. The cathedral (1277–1535) has a great Flamboyant rose window in the principal façade, which is flanked by two square towers and has no portal. Each transept has a fine Gothic doorway. On the north side of the building rises a 16th century tower. The episcopal palace (17th and 19th centuries) is flanked by a massive tower, relic of an older palace.

The town was made the seat of a bishop, a prefect and a court of assizes with tribunals of first instance and commerce, and a chamber of commerce. The industries include wool spinning, and the weaving of woollen goods.

RODGERS, JOHN (1773–1838), U.S. naval officer, was born in 1773 on a farm in Harford county, Md., the son of a Scottish immigrant, Col. John Rodgers, who founded the family noted for its naval officers.

After service from an early age on merchant ships, John Rodgers entered the U.S. navy when it was organized in 1798. He was second in command to Commodore James Barron (1769–1851) in the expedition against the Barbary pirates and succeeded him in the command in 1805. In that year he brought both Tunis and Tripoli to terms, and later returned to the United States.

In 1811 he was in command as commodore of the U.S. frigate "President" off Annapolis when he heard that a U.S. seaman had been "pressed" by a British frigate off Sandy Hook. Commodore Rodgers was ordered to sea "to protect American commerce." On May 16, 1811, he sighted and followed the British sloop "Little Belt," and after some hailing and counterhailing, of which very different versions were given by both sides, a gun was fired. Each side accused the other of aggression, and an action ensued in which the "Little Belt" was cut to pieces.

The action was one of the incidents leading up to the War of 1812. As mentioned previously, there were discrepancies between Rodgers' report and the British accounts of the fight. A U.S. court of inquiry, however, later confirmed Rodgers' version of the encounter, and he was acclaimed by the United States government for his conduct.

When hostilities broke out, Rodgers commanded a squadron and was wounded by the bursting of one of his guns while pursuing the British frigate "Belvidera."

He was subsequently president of the board of navy commissioners from 1815 to 1824 and from 1827 to 1837. He died in Philadelphia, Pa., on Aug. 1, 1838.

His brother GEORGE WASHINGTON RODGERS (1787–1832) served in the War of 1812 and in the war with Algiers (1815). He was commander of the "Peacock" in the Mediterranean squadron from 1816 until 1819.

Rear Admiral JOHN RODGERS (1812–1882), a son of Commodore John Rodgers, served in the Union navy during the Civil War and from 1877 to 1882 was superintendent of the Naval observatory at Washington, D.C.

G. W. Rodgers had two sons who were naval officers, CHRISTOPHER RAYMOND PERRY RODGERS (1819–1892) and GEORGE WASHINGTON RODGERS (1822–1863). The former served as commandant of midshipmen at the U.S. naval academy, 1860–61, and as superintendent, 1874–78. The latter succeeded his brother as commandant of midshipmen in Sept. 1861, but the following year he went on active duty with the West India squadron. He was killed on Aug. 17, 1863, while attacking Charleston, S.C., as commander of the "Catskill."

RODIN, AUGUSTE (1840–1917), French sculptor, was born in 1840 in Paris. He began by attending A. L. Barye's classes, but did not yield too completely to his influence. From 1864 to 1870, under pressure of necessity, he was employed in the studio of Carrier-Belleuse, where he learned to deal with the mechanical difficulties of a sculptor.

Even so early as 1864 his individuality was manifested in his "Man with a Broken Nose." After the war of 1870 finding nothing to do in Paris, Rodin went to Brussels, Belg., where from 1871 to 1877 he worked, as the colleague of the Belgian artist Van Rasbourg, on the sculpture for the outside and the caryatids for the interior of the Bourse, besides exhibiting in 1875 a "Portrait of Garnier." In 1877 he contributed to the salon "The Bronze Age," which was cast in bronze for the salon of 1880 and was later moved to the Luxembourg. Between 1882 and 1885 he sent to the salons busts of "Jean-Paul Laurens" and "Carrier-Belleuse" (1882), "Victor Hugo" and "Dalou" (1884) and "Antonin Proust" (1885).

From about this time he chiefly devoted himself to a great decorative composition six metres high, which was not finished for twenty years. This is the "Portal of Hell," the most elaborate perhaps of all Rodin's works, executed to order for the Musée des arts décoratifs. It is inspired mainly by Dante's *Inferno*, the poet himself being seated at the top, while at his feet, in undercut relief, we see the writhing crowd of the damned, torn by the frenzy of passion and the anguish of despair. The lower part consists of two bas-reliefs, in their midst two masks of tormented faces. Round these run figures of women and centaurs. Above the door three men cling to one another in an attitude of despair. After beginning this titanic undertaking, and while continuing to work on it, Rodin executed for the town of Damvillers a statue of "Bastien-Lepage"; for Nancy a "Monument to Claude de Lorrain," representing the Chariot of the Sun drawn by horses; and for Calais "The Burgesses of Calais" surrendering the keys of the town and imploring mercy. In this Rodin, throwing over all school tradition, represents the citizens not as grouped on a square or circular plinth, but walking in file. This work was exhibited at the Petit Gallery in 1889. A replica of it is now placed on the embankment at Westminster.

At the time of the secession of the National Society of Fine Arts, or New Salon, in 1890, Rodin withdrew from the old Society of French Artists, and exhibited in the New Salon the bust of his friend "Puvis de Chavannes" (1892), "Contemplation" and a "Caryatid," both in marble, and the "Monument to Victor Hugo" (1897), intended for the gardens of the Luxembourg. In this the poet is represented nude, as a powerful old man extending his right arm with a sovereign gesture, the Muses standing behind him. In 1898 Rodin exhibited two very dissimilar works, "The Kiss," exhibited again in 1900, a marble group representing Paolo Malatesta and Francesca da Rimini, and the sketch in plaster for a "Statue of Balzac." This statue, a commission from the Society of Men of Letters, had long been expected, and was received with vehement dissensions. The society who had ordered it "refused to recognize Rodin's rough sketch as a statue of Balzac," and withdrew the commission, giving it to the sculptor Falguière. Falguière exhibited his model in 1899. In the same Salon, Rodin, to prove that the conduct of the society had made no change in his friendship with Falguière, exhibited a bust in bronze of his rival, as well as one of "Henri Rochefort."

In 1900, the city of Paris, to do honour to Rodin, erected at its own expense a building close to one of the entrances to the Great Exhibition, in which almost all of the works of the artist were to be seen, more especially the great "Portal of Hell," still quite incomplete, the "Balzac," and a host of other works, many of them unfinished or mere rough sketches. Here, too, were to be seen some of Rodin's designs, studies and water-colour drawings. He has also executed a great many etchings and *sgraffiti* on porcelain for the manufactory at Sèvres. His best-known etching is the portrait of Victor Hugo. Rodin's "Hand of God" was exhibited in the New Gallery, London, in 1905. In 1904 Mr. Ernest Beckett (Lord Grimthorpe) presented the British nation with the sculptor's "Le Penseur." In the same year Rodin became president of the International Society of Sculptors, Painters and Engravers, in succession to James McNeill Whistler.

He died on Nov. 17, 1917, and was buried at Meudon.

Many of Rodin's works are in private collections. At the Luxembourg he is represented by a "Danaïd" (marble), "Saint Jean" (bronze, 1880), "She who made the helmet" (bronze statuette), busts of "J. P. Laurens," and "A Lady." A statue of Victor Hugo is in the Musée Galliera. The fine collection of Rodin's sculpture at South Kensington, a gift by the artist, includes "St. John the Baptist," "Age of Bronze," "L'Enfant prodigue," "Cybele," "The Muse," "Fallen Angel" (group), "Torso of Woman," "France" (head), "Figure of Woman," "Head," "Balzac" (bust), busts of Mlle. C. C., Miss E. Fairfax, la duchesse de C. C. (two), George Wyndham, Mr. Ryan (all the above in bronze); "Cupid and Psyche" (marble group); "Dante" (mask, terra-cotta). The Metropolitan Museum, New York, has several sculptures and drawings. A Rodin Museum was opened in Philadelphia in 1929.

See SCULPTURE: *French;* also Gustave Geffroy, *La Vie artistique* (Paris, 1892, 1893, 1899, 1900); L. Maillard, *Rodin* (Paris, 1899); *La Plume, Rodin et son oeuvre* (Paris, 1900); Arsène P. Alexandre, *Le Balzac de Rodin* (Paris, 1898); H. Boutet, *Dix dessins choisis de Auguste Rodin* (1904); R. Dircks, *Auguste Rodin* (1904); H. Duhem, *Auguste Rodin* (1903); C. Black, *Auguste Rodin: the Man, his Ideas and his Works* (1905); J. Cladel, *Auguste Rodin, l'oeuvre et l'homme* (1908; Eng. trans., 1917); Gustave Kahn, *Rodin* (illustr., 1909); G. Coquid, *Le vrai Rodin* (illustr., 1913); H. Lechat, *Sculptures de Rodin* (1919); C. J. Burckhardt, *Rodin und das plastische Problem* (1921); *Siva: Sculptures Civaïstes de l'Inde,* by A. Rodin, A. Coomaraswamy, E. B. Hawell and V. Goloubew (1921); *L'Art: entretiens réunis par Paul Gsell* (Paris, 1919); M. Tirel, *Rodin intime* (1923, Eng. trans. "Last Years of Rodin" 1925); A. M. Ludovici, *Personal reminiscences of Rodin* (1926); L. Benedite, *Rodin* (illustr., 1926).

RODNEY, GEORGE BRYDGES RODNEY, BARON (1718–1792), English admiral, second son of Henry Rodney of Walton-on-Thames, was born in February 1718. George was sent to Harrow, being appointed, on leaving, by warrant dated June 21, 1732, a volunteer on board the "Sunderland." While serving on the Mediterranean station he was made lieutenant (1739) on the "Dolphin." In 1742 he attained the rank of post-captain, having been appointed to the "Plymouth." After serving in home waters, he obtained command of the "Eagle" (60), and in this ship took part in Hawke's victory off Ushant (Oct. 14, 1747) over the French fleet. On that day Rodney gained his first laurels for gallantry, under a chief to whom he was in a measure indebted for subsequent success. In 1749 he was appointed governor and commander-in-chief of Newfoundland, with the rank of commodore, it being usual at that time to appoint a naval officer, chiefly on account of the fishery interests. He was elected M.P. for Saltash in 1751, and married his first wife, Jane Compton (1730–1757), sister of the 7th earl of Northampton, in 1753. During the Seven Years' War Rodney rendered important services. In 1757 he had a share in the expedition against Rochefort, commanding the "Dublin" (74). Next year, in the same ship, he served under Boscawen at the taking of Louisburg (Cape Breton). In 1759 and again in 1760 he inflicted great loss on the French transports collected on the Normandy coast for an attack on Great Britain. Elected M.P. for Penryn in 1761, he was in October of that year appointed commander-in-chief of the Leeward Islands station, and within the first three months of 1762 had reduced the important island of Martinique, while both St. Lucia and Grenada had surrendered to his squadron. At the peace of 1763 Admiral Rodney returned home, having been during his absence made vice-admiral of the Blue and having received the thanks of both houses of parliament.

In 1764 Rodney was created a baronet, and the same year he married Henrietta, daughter of John Clies of Lisbon. From 1765 to 1770 he was governor of Greenwich Hospital. In 1771 he was appointed rear-admiral of Great Britain, and in 1778 admiral of the White. From 1771 to 1774 he held the Jamaica command, and during a period of quiet was active in improving the naval yards on his station. Election expenses and losses at play in fashionable circles had shattered his fortune; he could not secure payment of the salary as rear-admiral of Great Britain; and he lived for some time in Paris until the generosity of a friend enabled him to meet his debts.

Sir George was appointed once more commander-in-chief of the Leeward Islands late in 1779. His orders were to relieve Gibraltar on his way to the West Indies. He captured a Spanish convoy off Cape Finisterre on Jan. 8, 1780, and eight days later defeated the Spanish admiral Don Juan de Langara off Cape St. Vincent, taking or destroying seven ships. On April 17 an action, which, owing to the carelessness of some of Rodney's captains, was indecisive, was fought off Martinique with the French admiral Guichen. Rodney, acting under orders, captured the valuable Dutch island of St. Eustatius on Feb. 3, 1781. It had been a great *entrepôt* of neutral trade, and was full of booty, which Rodney confiscated. As large quantities belonged to English merchants, he was entangled in a series of costly lawsuits.

After a few months in England, recruiting his health and defending himself in parliament, Rodney returned to his command in Feb. 1782, and a running engagement with the French fleet on April 9 led up to his crowning victory off Dominica, when with thirty-five sail of the line he defeated the comte de Grasse, who had thirty-three sail (April 12). The French inferiority in numbers was more than counterbalanced by the greater size and superior sailing qualities of their ships, yet five were taken and one sunk, after eleven hours' fighting. This important battle saved Jamaica and ruined French naval prestige, while it enabled Rodney to write: "Within two little years I have taken two Spanish, one French and one Dutch admiral."

On his return to England Rodney received a barony and a pension of £2,000 a year. From this time he led a quiet country life till his death (May 24, 1792), in London.

Rodney was unquestionably a most able officer, but he was also vain, selfish and unscrupulous, both in seeking prize money, and in using his position to push the fortunes of his family. He made his son a post-captain at fifteen. He was accused by his second-in-command, Hood, of sacrificing the interest of the service to his own profit, and of showing want of energy in pursuit of the French on April 12, 1782. It must be remembered that he was then prematurely old and racked by disease.

See General Mundy, *Life and Correspondence of Admiral Lord*

Rodney (2 vols., 1830); David Hannay, *Life of Rodney;* Rodney letters in 9th *Report* of Hist. mss. Com., pt. iii.; "Memoirs," in *Naval Chronicle,* i. 353–393; and Charnock, *Biographia Navalis,* v. 204–228. Lord Rodney published in his lifetime (probably 1789) *Letters to His Majesty's Ministers, etc., relative to St. Eustatius, etc.,* of which there is a copy in the British Museum. Most of these letters are printed in Mundy's *Life,* vol. ii., though with many variant readings.

RODÓ, JOSÉ ENRIQUE (1872–1917), Uruguayan philosopher, author and politician, was born in Montevideo on July 15, 1872. He was educated in a free lay school and at the University of Montevideo, where he showed extraordinary aptitude for history, literature and philosophy. In 1895 he was one of the founders of the *National Review of Literature and Social Sciences,* in which, in the following year he published an essay on literary criticism, "El que vendrá," which brought him immediate recognition as a writer and critic. In 1898 he was made professor of literature in the university, and two years later was appointed director of the National library, but in 1901 he gave up both positions to enter congress, to which he was elected in 1902 and 1908 and where he took an earnest part in initiating social legislation; he was not, however, a radical, and in a pamphlet, *Liberalismo y jacobismo* (1907), he strenuously opposed government anti-church legislation. In 1910 he represented Uruguay at the centenary of Chilean independence. Rodó's influence, however, as a rallying point of Latin-American youth was due to his authority as exponent of optimism, as stylist and as advocate of unity in Spanish-American literature and culture. His first important philosophical work, *Ariel,* based on Renan's eclecticism, appeared in 1900 in defence of Latin-American culture against the utilitarianism of the United States. In 1909 he published *Motivos de Proteo,* an assertion of the inevitability of change and the possibility of self-improvement, which represents Rodó's highest attainment as thinker and master of the Spanish language, and caused him to be hailed by Spanish-Americans as their philosopher *par excellence.* His essays on Rubén Darío (1899), Bolívar and Montalvo won him a similarly unique place in Spanish-American letters, to which, in those on Bolívar and Montalvo, included in *El Mirador de Próspero* (1913), he gave models of historical and critical essays. He died at Palermo in May 1917.

See H. D. Barbagelata, Introduction to *Cinco Ensayos* (Madrid, 1915); M. H. Ureña, "José Enrique Rodó," *Cuba Contemporánea* (Aug. 1918); Andrés González-Blanco, *Escritores representativos de América* (Madrid, 1917); V. G. Calderón, *Semblanzas de América* (Madrid, 1919); I. Goldberg, *Studies in Spanish-American Literature* (New York, 1920). (W. B. P.)

RODOSTO: *see* TEKIRDAG.

RODRIGUEZ (officially RODRIGUES), an island in the Indian ocean in 19° 41′ S., 63° 23′ E.; a dependency of the British colony of Mauritius, from which it is 350 mi. distant. With a length from east to west of 9½ mi., it is 4¼ mi. broad. It is surrounded by a fringing reef of coral, studded with islets. This reef, only 100 yd. wide on the east, extends 3 mi. west, and both north and south forms a flat area partly dry at low water. Two passages through the reef are available for large vessels—these passages leading respectively to Port Mathurin on the north coast and to Port South East.

The island is a mass of volcanic rock, mainly a doleritic lava, rich in olivine. The land is hilly and the main ridge rises abruptly on the east, but more gradually on the west, where there is a wide plain of coral limestone, studded with caves. Of several peaks on the main ridge the highest is Mt. Limon (1,290 ft.). The ridge is deeply cut by ravines, the upper parts of which show successive belts of lava separated by thin beds of ashes, agglomerate and ochre-coloured clays. In places the cliffs rise 300 ft. and exhibit 12 distinct lava flows. The climate is like that of Mauritius, but Rodriguez is more subject than Mauritius to cyclones during the northwest monsoon (November to April).

Flora and Fauna.—When discovered, Rodriguez was clothed with fine timber trees; but goats, cattle and bush fires have combined to destroy the greater bulk, and the indigenous plants have in many cases been ousted by intrusive foreigners. Parts are still well wooded, and elsewhere there is excellent pasturage. The sweet potato, manioc, maize, millet, the sugar cane, cotton, coffee, rice

and tobacco are cultivated. Wheat is seldom seen, but Sieva beans (*Phaseolus lunatus*), lentils, gram (*Cicer arietinum*), dhal (*Cajanus indicus*) and peanuts are all grown. Mangoes, bananas, guavas, pineapples, custard apples, and especially oranges, citrons and limes flourish.

At present the only indigenous mammal is a species of fruit-eating bat (*Pteropus rodericensis*), and the introduced species are familiar creatures such as deer, pig, rabbit, rat, mouse, etc. Until recently there occurred a large land tortoise (*Testudo vosmaeri*). The island's limestone caves have yielded a large number of skeletons of the now extinct bird, the solitaire (*Pezophaps solitarius*). Of indigenous birds 13 species have been registered. The guinea fowl (introduced) has become exceedingly abundant, partly owing to a protective game law; and a francolin (*Francolinus ponticerianus*) is also common. The marine fish-fauna does not differ from that of Mauritius, and the fresh-water species, with the exception of *Mugil rodericensis* and *Myxus caecuticus,* are common to all the Mascarenes. The insects comprise at least 60 species of Coleoptera, 15 Hymenoptera, 21 Lepidoptera, 15 Orthoptera, and 20 Hemiptera. Forty-nine species of coral have been collected, showing a close affinity to those of Mauritius, Madagascar and the Seychelles.

History.—Rodriguez or Diego Ruy's island was discovered by the Portuguese in 1645. In 1690 the Dutch government sent a body of French Huguenots under François Leguat to the Island of Bourbon, but they, finding the French authorities in possession, proceeded to Rodriguez where eight of their number were landed on April 30, 1691, with a promise that they should be visited within two years. Though the two years passed without misadventure, the colonists, instead of awaiting the arrival of their friends, left the island on May 8, 1693, and made their way to Mauritius where they were treated with great cruelty by the governor. From the Dutch the island passed to the French, who colonized it from Mauritius. Large estates were cultivated and the islanders enjoyed considerable prosperity. In 1809–10 Rodriguez was seized by the British, in whose possession it has since remained. The abolition of slavery proved disastrous to the prosperity of the island and in 1843 the population had sunk to about 250. Thereafter there was a gradual recovery in the economic condition and a steady increase in population.

Population.—By 1953 there were about 15,000 inhabitants, most of them fishermen and small cultivators, and mainly of African origin, being descendants of slaves introduced by the French, and Negro immigrants direct from Africa. There are a few families of European descent and a small colony of Indians and Chinese. The bulk of the people are French-speaking and Roman Catholic. There are two small settlements, Port Mathurin, the capital, and Gabriel, in the centre of the island.

Administration.—The island is under the charge of a civil commissioner aided by officers of the police, health and agricultural departments of Mauritius. The civil commissioner, a magistrate, administers justice. The prison is a lockup and any prisoner with a sentence of 12 months and over is sent to Mauritius. Four schools ordinarily cater for more than 2,000 children.

BIBLIOGRAPHY.—F. Leguat, *Voyages et aventures* (1708), ed. by Capt. P. Oliver, in vol. lxxxii and lxxxiii of the Hakluyt society publications (London, 1891). *See also* C. Grant, *Hist. of Mauritius and the Neighbouring Islands* (London, 1801); Higgin, in *Jour. R.G. Soc.* (1849); the *Reports* of the Transit of Venus Expedition, 1874–75, published as an extra volume of the *Philosophical Transactions,* clxviii (Botany, by I. B. Balfour; Petrology, by N. S. Maskelyne, etc. 1879); E. Behm (ed.) in *Petermann's Mittheilungen* (1880); A. J. Bertuchi, *The Island of Rodriguez* (London, 1923); and the annual reports and works on Mauritius. (W. H. Is.)

RODZIANKO, MIKHAIL VLADIMIROVITCH (1859–1923), Russian politician, was born in 1859, of a family of great landowners. In 1906 and 1907 he was a member of the council of the empire for the zemstvo of the province of Ekaterinoslav. He was a member of the third and fourth dumas. He joined the right wing of the Octobrist (moderate Liberal party) and with the support of the conservatives was elected president of the third duma. As president of the fourth duma he took part in the struggle for constitutional changes in the government opposing the reactionary policy of the government and defending the rights of the duma.

During World War I he took an important part in the unifying of the Russian industries. As president of the provisional committee of the state duma, at the moment of the revolution, he sent a telegram to the tsar, pointing out the necessity of his abdication.

After the revolution he took part in the civil war as one of the managers of the Russian Red Cross and was forced to emigrate to Yugoslavia, where he died Jan. 24, 1923.

RODZINSKI, ARTUR (1894–), U.S. conductor, was born of Polish parents at Split (Spalato), in the former kingdom of Dalmatia (Yugoslavia), on Jan. 2, 1894. He took a degree in law at the University of Vienna and also studied at the Vienna Academy of Music. After World War I he became a choral director and opera conductor in Lwów (Lvov), Pol., and later conducted opera and the Philharmonic orchestra in Warsaw.

Rodzinski, who was naturalized as a U.S. citizen in 1933, served as assistant to Leopold Stokowski, conductor of the Philadelphia (Pa.) orchestra, from 1926–29. He conducted the Los Angeles Philharmonic orchestra, 1929–33, and the Cleveland Symphony orchestra from 1933. In 1943 he became musical director and conductor of the New York Philharmonic-Symphony. He was director and conductor of the Chicago Symphony orchestra, 1947–48, and thereafter was guest conductor of various orchestras in the United States, Europe and South America.

Rodzinski conducted the premier performance of Sergei Prokofiev's *War and Peace* at the May Music festival in Florence, It., in 1953.

ROE, HUMPHREY VERDON (1878–1949), British aeronautic engineer, was born on April 18, 1878. He served in the South African War and joined the royal air force during World Wars I and II. In 1918 he married Marie Carmichael Stopes and with her founded at Holloway the first birth control clinic (1921). He died in London, July 25, 1949.

ROE, SIR THOMAS (*c.* 1581–1644), English diplomatist, was born at Low Leyton, Essex, and was educated at Magdalen college, Oxford. He was appointed esquire of the body to Queen Elizabeth I, was knighted in 1605 and in 1610 was sent by Henry, prince of Wales, to the West Indies and South America to discover gold. Elected M.P. for Tamworth (1614) and Cirencester (1621), his reputation was secured by his successful mission (1615–19) to the court of the great Mogul, Jahangir, at Agra, where he obtained protection for an English factory at Surat. Appointed ambassador to the Ottoman Porte in 1621, Roe secured further privileges for English merchants, concluded a treaty with Algiers in 1624 and gained some support from the Transylvanian prince Gabriel Bethlen for the European Protestant alliance and the cause of the Palatinate.

Through his friendship with the patriarch of the Greek church the *Codex Alexandrinus* was presented to James I, and Roe himself collected several valuable manuscripts, which he gave to the Bodleian library. In 1629 he mediated successfully between the kings of Sweden and Poland and in 1630 negotiated treaties with Danzig and Denmark. In 1637 he was appointed chancellor of the order of the Garter. Subsequently he took part in the peace conferences at Hamburg, Regensburg and Vienna. In June 1640 he was made a privy councillor and in October he became member of parliament for the University of Oxford. He died on Nov. 6, 1644.

His *Journal* of the mission to the Mogul, several times printed, was re-edited, with an introduction by W. Foster, for the Hakluyt society, 2 vol. (London, 1899). Of his correspondence, *Negotiations in His Embassy to the Ottoman Porte (1621–28)*, vol. i, was published in 1740, but the work was not continued. Letters relating to his mission to Gustavus Adolphus (1629–30) were edited by S. R. Gardiner for the Camden Society Miscellany, vol. vii (London, 1875), and his correspondence with Lord Carew in 1615 and 1617 by Sir John Maclean for the same society in 1860. Roe published a *True and Faithful Relation . . . Concerning the Death of Sultan Osman . . . 1622;* a translation from the anonymous work once attributed to Paolo Sarpi, *A Discourse Upon the Reasons of the Resolution Taken in the Valteline . . .* (1628); and in 1614 T. Wright published *Quatuor Colloquia,* consisting of theological disputations between himself and Roe. Several of his speeches, chiefly on currency and financial questions, were also published. Two other works in manuscript are mentioned by Anthony à Wood: *Compendious Relation of the Proceedings . . .*

of the Imperial Dyet Held at Ratisbon in 1640 and 1641 and *Journal of Several Proceedings of the Knights of the Order of the Garter.* For Roe's missions to Vienna (1641–42) and Hamburg (1638–40), see *Eng. Hist. Rev.,* vol. xxv, xli (London, 1910, 1926).

ROEBLING, JOHN AUGUSTUS (1806–1869), U.S. civil engineer, was born at Mühlhausen, Prussia, on June 12, 1806. Soon after his graduation from the polytechnic school at Berlin he moved to the United States, and in 1831 began to practise his profession in western Pennsylvania. He established near Pittsburgh, Pa. a wire rope factory, and in May 1845 completed his first important structure, a suspended aqueduct across the Allegheny river. This was followed by the Monongahela suspension bridge at Pittsburgh and several suspended aqueducts on the Delaware and Hudson canal. Removing his wire factory to Trenton, N.J., he began in 1851 the erection at Niagara falls of a long-span wire suspension bridge with double roadway, for railway and vehicular use (*see* BRIDGES), which was completed in 1855. Because of the novelty of its design, the most eminent engineers regarded this bridge as foredoomed to failure; but, with its complete success, demonstrated by long use, the number of suspension bridges rapidly multiplied, the use of wire ropes instead of chain cables becoming virtually universal. The completion, in 1867, of the still more remarkable suspension bridge over the Ohio river at Cincinnati, O., with a clear span of 1,057 ft., added to Roebling's reputation, and his design for the great bridge spanning the East river between Manhattan and Brooklyn, New York city, was accepted. While personally engaged in laying out the towers for the bridge, Roebling received an accidental injury, which resulted in his death, at Brooklyn, from tetanus, on July 22, 1869. The bridge was completed under the direction of his son, Washington Augustus Roebling (1837–1926).

See H. Schuyler, *The Roeblings; A Century of Engineers, Bridgebuilders and Industrialists* (Princeton, N.J., London, 1931); D. B. Steinman, *The Builders of the Bridge* (New York, 1945).

ROEBOURNE, a settlement of the Northwest division of Western Australia, 8 mi. from the northwest coast, about lat. 20° 40' S., long. 117° E., 920 mi. north of Perth. It is a centre for the West Pilbara Goldfield district. It has an unusually hot climate with a low and very variable rainfall. There were extensive pearl fisheries off its port at Cossack bay.

ROEBUCK, JOHN (1718–1794), English inventor, was born in 1718 at Sheffield; after attending the grammar school there and Doddridge's academy at Northampton, he studied medicine at Edinburgh, where he was imbued with a taste for chemistry by W. Cullen and J. Black, and he finally graduated M.D. at Leyden in 1742. He started practice at Birmingham, but devoted much of his time to chemistry, especially in its practical applications. Among the most important of his early achievements in this field was the introduction, in 1746, of leaden condensing chambers for use in the manufacture of sulphuric acid. Together with Samuel Garbett he erected a factory at Prestonpans, near Edinburgh, for the production of the acid in 1749, and for several years enjoyed a monopoly. He engaged next in the manufacture of iron and in 1760 established ironworks at Carron, in Stirlingshire. There he introduced various improvements in the methods of production, including the conversion (patented in 1762) of cast iron into malleable iron "by the action of a hollow pit-coal fire" urged by a powerful artificial blast. He became interested in James Watt's engine, and in return for a two-thirds share in the invention assisted in perfecting its details, but financial troubles caused him to part with his share to Matthew Boulton in return for the cancellation of a debt of £1,200. He died July 17, 1794.

ROEBUCK, JOHN ARTHUR (1801–1879), British politician, was born at Madras on Dec. 28, 1801, and brought up in Canada. He was called to the English bar in 1824, and became M.P. for Bath in 1832. In 1838 he appeared at the bar of the commons to protest, in the name of the Canadian assembly, against the suspension of the Canadian constitution. In 1855, having overthrown Lord Aberdeen's ministry by carrying a resolution for the appointment of a committee of inquiry into the mismanagement in the Crimean War, he presided over the proceedings of the committee. For nearly 30 years he was M.P. for Sheffield. He died on Nov. 30, 1879, in London.

ROEBUCK, the smallest European deer (a full-grown buck standing 27 in. at the shoulder), the typical representative of a genus (*Capreolus*) in which the antlers lack a brow-tine and belong to the forked type, while the tail is rudimentary (*see* DEER). The antlers are short, upright, and deeply furrowed, the beam forking at about two-thirds of its length and the upper prong again dividing, thus making three points. The coat in summer is foxy red above and white below; in winter this changes to a grayish fawn, with a white rump-patch. The roebuck or roedeer (*C. capreolus*) inhabits southern and temperate Europe and Asia, represented by various races in Sweden, Scotland, Armenia, Spain and parts of Asia. They frequent woods, preferring those that have underwood and are in the neighbourhood of cultivated ground where they visit in the evening in search of food. Before pairing, the bucks pursue the does round specially trodden circular or octagonal runs. Pairing takes place in August, but the fawns are not born till the following May. Roe were formerly abundant in all the wooded parts of Great Britain, but are now restricted to the Highlands of Scotland and a few localities farther south. They take readily to water. The Siberian roe (*C. c. pygargus*), common in the Altai, is larger and paler, with shorter and more hairy ears and small irregular snags on the inner border of the antlers. The Manchurian roe (*C. c. bedfordi*) is about the size of the European species, with antlers of the type of those of the Siberian roe, but more slender.

ROEDERER, PIERRE LOUIS, COMTE (1754–1835), French politician and economist, was born at Metz on Feb. 15, 1754, the son of a magistrate. He became councillor at the parlement of Metz, and was commissioned in 1787 to draw up a list of remonstrances. His work advocating the suppression of internal customs houses (*Suppression des douanes intérieures,* 1787) is a treatise on the laws of commerce and on the theory of customs imposts. In the Constituent assembly he was a member of the committee of taxes, prepared a new system of taxation, drew up a law on patents, occupied himself with the laws relating to stamps and *assignats,* and successfully opposed the introduction of an income tax. After the close of the Constituent assembly he was elected, on Nov. 11, 1791, *procureur général syndic* of the department of Paris. When he saw the perilous drift of things, he had tried to get into touch with the king; and it was on his advice that Louis, on the fatal 10th, took refuge in the assembly. Roederer was in hiding until after Robespierre's fall. Under the empire, Roederer, whose public influence was considerable, was Joseph Bonaparte's minister of finance at Naples (1806), administrator of the grand duchy of Berg (1810), and imperial commissary in the south of France. During the Hundred Days he was created a peer of France. The Restoration government stripped him of his offices and dignities, but he recovered the title of peer of France in 1832.

Roederer died on Dec. 17, 1835.

His writings include: *Louis XII* (1820); *François I* (1825); *Comédies historiques* (1827–30); *L'Esprit de la révolution de 1789* (1831); *La Première et la deuxième année du consulat de Bonaparte* (1802); *Chronique des cinquante jours* (1832); *Mémoire pour servir à l'histoire de la société polie en France* (1835).

See his *Oeuvres,* edited by his son (1853 *seq.*); Sainte-Beuve, *Causeries du lundi,* vol. viii; M. Mignet, *Notices historiques* (1853).

ROEMER, FRIEDRICH ADOLPH (1809–1869), German geologist, was born at Hildesheim, in Prussia, on April 14, 1809. In 1845 he became professor of mineralogy and geology at Clausthal, and in 1862 director of the School of Mines. He first described the Cretaceous and Jurassic strata of Germany in *Die Versteinerungen des Norddeutschen Oolithen-gebirges* (1836–39), *Die Versteinerungen des Norddeutschen Kreidegebirges* (1840–41) and *Die Versteinerungen des Harzgebirges* (1843). He died at Clausthal on Nov. 25, 1869.

His brother, CARL FERDINAND VON ROEMER (1818–1891), educated for the legal profession at Göttingen, also became interested in geology, and abandoning law in 1840, studied science at the University of Berlin. Two years later he published his first work, *Das Rheinische Übergangsgebirge* (1844), in which he dealt with the older rocks and fossils. In 1845 he visited the U.S., the results of his work being published in *Texas* (1849), and *Die*

Kreidebildungen von Texas und ihre organische Einschlüsse (1852). From 1847 to 1855 *privatdozent* at Bonn, he was then appointed professor of geology, palaeontology and mineralogy in the University of Breslau, a post which he held until his death on Dec. 14, 1891.

He prepared, with H. G. Bronn, the third edition of *Lethaea geognostica,* and later published one section, *Lethaea palaeozoica,* of an enlarged and revised edition. In 1862 he superintended the preparation of a geological map of upper Silesia, and the results of his researches are embodied in his *Geologie von Oberschlesien.*

ROEMER, OLE (Latinized OLAUS) (1644–1710), Danish astronomer, was born at Aarhuus, Jutland, on Sept. 25, 1644. He became in 1662 the pupil and amanuensis of Erasmus Bartholinus at Copenhagen. In 1671 he assisted J. Picard to determine the position of Tycho Brahe's observatory (Uraniborg, on the island of Hveen). In 1672 he went to Paris with Picard, and spent nine years on observations at the new royal observatory and hydraulic works at Versailles and Marly. After a scientific mission to England (1679), on which he met Newton, Halley and Flamsteed, he returned to Copenhagen in 1681 as royal mathematician and professor of astronomy in the university. He also held several public offices, including that of mayor (1705). He died at Copenhagen on Sept. 23, 1710.

Roemer is remembered as the discoverer of the finite velocity of light, which was suggested to him by his observations on the eclipses of Jupiter's moons. The first noteworthy transit instrument was in 1690 erected at his house. He also set up at the university observatory an instrument with altitude and azimuth circles, and an equatorial telescope. He also built and equipped the "Tusculan" observatory at Vridlösemagle, near Copenhagen. His observations perished in the great fire of Oct. 21, 1728, except those discussed by J. G. Galle in *O. Roemeri triduum observationum astronomicarum a. 1706 institutarum* (Berlin, 1845).

BIBLIOGRAPHY.—E. Philipsen, *Nordisk Universities Tidskrift,* v, 11 (1860); P. Horrebrow, *Basis Astronomiae* (Copenhagen, 1735); J. B. J. Delambre, *Hist. de l'astr. moderne,* ii, 632; J. F. Montucla, *Hist. des mathématiques,* ii, 487, 579; R. Grant, *Hist. of Phys. Astronomy,* p. 461; R. Wolf, *Gesch. der Astronomie,* pp. 452, 489, 576; J. F. Weidler, *Historia Astronomiae,* p. 538; W. Doberck, *Nature,* xvii, 105; C. Huygens, *Oeuvres complètes,* t. viii, pp. 30–58; L. Ambronn, *Handbuch der astr. Instrumentenkunde,* ii, 552, 966; T. J. J. See, *Pop. Astronomy,* no. 105 (May 1903).

ROERICH, NIKOLAI KONSTANTINOVICH (1874–1947), Russian painter of Scandinavian origin, established his reputation with pictures of Russian prehistoric life and the wanderings of Vikings. After beginning with realistic pictures, his manner evolved under the influence of the Byzantine icon and of oriental art, toward a purely decorative and monumental style. He studied the technique of ancient Russian frescoes and his wall paintings for the Kazan railway station at Moscow, representing combats between Russians and Tatars, are his most important work. He executed a number of works for the theatre: for the Russian ballet he painted the scenery in *Prince Igor;* for Stanislavsky the setting of *Peer Gynt.* He wrote the libretto for, and designed the scenery and the costumes of, *The Rite of Spring,* for which Igor Stravinsky composed the music. After the Russian revolution of 1917 he settled successively in the U.S. and in India. More than 1,000 of his works are in the Roerich museum, New York, established in 1923, and in other famous galleries. He died Dec. 13, 1947, in Kulu, East Punjab.

ROERMOND, a town in the province of Limburg, the Netherlands, on the right bank of the Maas at the confluence of the Roer, and a junction station 28 mi. by rail N.N.E. of Maastricht. Pop. (1947) 21,428. The old fortifications were dismantled and partly converted into fine promenades. A bridge across the Roer, dating from 1771, connected Roermond with the suburb of St. Jacob. Roermond was made the seat of a Roman Catholic episcopal see. The Romanesque minster church dates from the first quarter of the 13th century. In the middle of the nave is the tomb of Gerhard III, count of Gelderland, and his wife Margaret of Brabant. It was formerly the church of a Cistercian nunnery, and in modern times was elaborately restored. The cathedral of St. Christopher is also of note; on top of the tower (246 ft.) a copper statue of the saint was erected. The interior was adorned with paintings by Rubens, Jacob de Wit (1695–1754) and others. The old bishop's palace became the courthouse, and the old Jesuits' monastery a higher-burgher school. Woollen, cotton, silk and mixed stuffs, paper, flour and beer are manufactured there. Roermond suffered damage during World War II.

ROGATION DAYS, in the Calendar of the Christian Church, the three days before Ascension Day. Their observance, by fasting and chanting litanies in procession, was introduced by St. Mamertus, bishop of Vienne (d. *c.* 475), and was ordered throughout France by the first Council of Orleans in 511. Leo III. (pope 795–816) introduced rogation days, but without fasting, at Rome. The custom had spread earlier into the English Church, where it was confirmed in 747 by the Council of Clovesho. After the Reformation the processions gradually ceased to be ecclesiastical in England, and now survive only in the perambulation of the parish boundaries on or about Ascension Day.

See also Procession and Litany.

ROGER (d. 1181), archbishop of York, known as Roger of Pont l'Evêque, was a member of the household of Theobald, archbishop of Canterbury, where he quarrelled violently with another future archbishop, Thomas Becket. In 1148 he was appointed archdeacon of Canterbury, and soon afterwards chaplain to King Stephen, who sent him on an errand to Rome in 1152; then in Oct. 1154 he was consecrated archbishop of York in Westminster abbey. When Henry II. entered upon his struggle with Becket he secured the support of Roger, and having been appointed papal legate in England, the archbishop visited Pope Alexander III. and the French king, Louis VII., in his master's interests. In June 1170 he crowned the king's son Henry, in spite of prohibitions from the pope and from Becket, and for this act he was suspended. He quarrelled with Richard, the new archbishop of Canterbury, about the respective rights of the two archiepiscopal sees, until 1176, when the king arranged a truce; and he was constantly endeavouring to assert his supremacy over the Scottish church. He died at York on Nov. 21, 1181.

ROGER (d. 1139), bishop of Salisbury, was originally priest of a small chapel near Caen. The future King Henry I., who happened to hear mass there one day, was impressed by the speed with which Roger read the service, and enrolled him in his own service. Roger, though uneducated, showed great talent for business, and Henry, on coming to the throne, almost immediately made him chancellor (1101). Soon after Roger received the bishopric of Salisbury. In the Investitures controversy he skilfully managed to keep the favour of both the king and Anselm. Roger devoted himself to administrative business, and remodelled it completely. He created the exchequer system, which was managed by him and his family for more than a century, and he used his position to heap up power and riches. He became the first man in England after the king, and was in office, if not in title, justiciar. He ruled England, while Henry was in Normandy, and succeeded in obtaining the see of Canterbury for his nominee, William of Corbeil. Duke Robert seems to have been put into his custody after Tinchebrai. Though Roger had sworn allegiance to Matilda, he disliked the Angevin connection, and went over to Stephen, carrying with him the royal treasure and administrative system (1135). Stephen placed great reliance on him, on his nephews, both bishops and on his son Roger, who was treasurer.

Roger himself had built at Devizes a splendid castle. He and his nephews seem to have secured a number of castles outside their own dioceses, and the old bishop behaved as if he were an equal of the king. At a council held in June 1139, Stephen found a pretext for demanding a surrender of their castles, and on their refusal they were arrested. After a short struggle all Roger's great castles were sequestrated. This quarrel with the church, which immediately preceded the landing of the empress, had a serious effect on Stephen's fortunes. Roger died at Salisbury in December 1139. He was a great bureaucrat, and a builder whose taste was in advance of his age. But his contemporaries were probably justified in regarding him as worldly, ambitious, avaricious, unfettered by any high standard of personal morality.

See Sir J. Ramsay's *Foundations of England,* vol. ii., and J. H. Round's *Geoffrey de Mandeville.*

ROGER I. (1031–1101), ruler of Sicily, was the youngest son of Tancred of Hauteville. Arriving in Southern Italy soon after 1057, he shared with Robert Guiscard the conquest of Calabria, and in a treaty of 1062 the brothers apparently made a kind of "condominium" by which each was to have half of every castle and town in Calabria. Robert now commissioned Roger to reduce Sicily, which contained, besides the Muslims, numerous Greek Christians subject to Arab princes who had become all but independent of the sultan of Tunis. In May 1061 the brothers crossed from Reggio and captured Messina. After Palermo had been taken in January 1072 Robert Guiscard, as suzerain, invested Roger as count of Sicily, but retained Palermo, half of Messina and the north-east portion of the island. Not till 1085, however, was Roger able to undertake a systematic crusade. In March 1086 Syracuse surrendered, and when in February 1091 Noto yielded the conquest was complete. Much of Robert's success had been due to Roger's support. Similarly the latter supported Duke Roger, his nephew, against Bohemund and other rebels, in return for which the duke surrendered to his uncle in 1085 his share in the castles of Calabria, and in 1091 the half of Palermo.

At the enfeoffments of 1072 and 1092 no great undivided fiefs were created, and the mixed Norman, French and Italian vassals owed their benefices to the count. No feudal revolt of importance therefore troubled Roger. Politically supreme, the count became master of the insular Church. While he gave full toleration to the Greek Churches, he created new Latin bishoprics at Syracuse and Girgenti and elsewhere, nominating the bishops personally, while he turned the archbishopric of Palermo into a Catholic see. The Papacy granted to him and his heirs in 1098 the Apostolic Legateship in the island. Roger was tolerant towards Arabs and Greeks, allowing to each race the expansion of its own civilization. In the cities the Muslims, who had generally secured such terms of surrender, retained their mosques, their kadis, and freedom of trade; in the country, however, they became serfs. He drew from the Muslims the mass of his infantry, but the Latin element began to prevail with the Lombards and other Italians who flocked into the island in the wake of the conquest, and the conquest of Sicily was decisive in the steady decline of Mohammedan power in the western Mediterranean. Roger, the "Great Count of Sicily," died on June 22, 1101, and was buried in S. Trinità of Mileto. His third wife, Adelaide, niece of Boniface, lord of Savona, gave him two sons, Simon and Roger, of whom the latter succeeded him.

See E. Caspar, *Roger II. und die Gründung der normannisch-sicilischen Monarchie* (Innsbruck, 1904).　　　　(E. Cu.)

ROGER II. (1093–1154), king of Sicily, son of the preceding, began to rule as count in 1112, and from the first aimed at uniting the whole of the Norman conquests in Italy. In 1127, Roger claimed the Hauteville possessions, and the overlordship of Capua, for which Richard II. in 1098 had sworn homage to Duke Roger, in virtue of a promise made by William, the late duke of Apulia. The union of Sicily and Apulia, however, was resisted by the subjects of the duchy itself, and by the pope at Capua (Dec. 1127) who preached a crusade against the claimant, setting against him Robert II. of Capua and Ranulf of Alife, or Avellino, brother-in-law of Roger. The coalition, however, failed, and in August 1128 Honorius invested Roger at Benevento as duke of Apulia. The baronial resistance, backed by Naples, Bari, Salerno and other cities, whose aim was civic freedom, also gave way, and at Melfi (Sept. 1129) Roger was recognized as duke by Naples, Capua and the rest. He at once began to enforce order in the Hauteville possessions, where the ducal power had long been falling to pieces. For the binding together of his states the royal name seemed essential, and the death of Honorius in February 1130, followed by a double election, seemed the decisive moment. While Innocent II. fled to France, Roger supported Anacletus II. The price was a crown, and on Sept. 27, 1130, a bull of Anacletus made Roger king of Sicily. He was crowned in Palermo on Dec. 25, 1130.

This plunged Roger into a ten years' war. Bernard of Clairvaux, Innocent's champion, built up against Anacletus and his "half heathen king," a coalition joined by Louis VI. of France, Henry I. of England and the emperor Lothar. Meanwhile the forces of revolt in South Italy drew to a head again, and on June 24, 1132, the king was defeated at Nocera by Ranulf. Nevertheless, by July 1134, he forced Ranulf, Sergius, duke of Naples, and the rebels to submit, while Robert was expelled from Capua. Meanwhile Lothar's contemplated attack upon Roger had gained the backing of Pisa, Genoa and the Greek emperor, all of whom feared the growth of a powerful Norman kingdom. In February 1137 Lothar moved south and was joined by Ranulf and the rebels; in June he besieged and took Bari. At San Severino, after a victorious campaign, he and the pope jointly invested Ranulf as duke of Apulia (Aug. 1137), and the emperor then retired to Germany. Roger, freed from the utmost danger, recovered ground, sacked Capua and forced Sergius to acknowledge him as overlord of Naples. At Rignano the indomitable Ranulf again utterly defeated the king, but died in April 1139, leaving none to oppose Roger, who subdued the rebels pitilessly.

The death of Anacletus (Jan. 25, 1138) determined Roger to seek the confirmation of his title from Innocent. The latter, invading the kingdom with a large army, was skilfully ambushed at Galuccio on the Garigliano (July 22, 1139), and on July 25 the pope invested him as "Rex Siciliae ducatus Apuliae et principatus Capuae."

Roger, now become one of the greatest kings in Europe, made Sicily the leading maritime power in the Mediterranean. A powerful fleet was built up under several "admirals," or "emirs," of whom the greatest was George of Antioch, formerly in the service of the Muslim prince of El Mehdia. Mainly by him a series of conquests were made on the African coast (1135–53) which reached from Tripoli to Cape Bona. The second crusade (1147–48) gave Roger an opportunity to revive Robert Guiscard's designs on the Greek Empire. George was sent to Corinth at the end of 1147 and despatched an army inland which plundered Thebes. In June 1149 the admiral appeared before Constantinople and defied the Basileus by firing arrows against the palace windows. The attack on the empire had, however, no abiding results. The king died at Palermo on Feb. 26, 1154, and was succeeded by his fourth son William.

Personally Roger was of tall and powerful body, with long fair hair and full beard. With little of Robert Guiscard's personal valour, he yet showed to the full his uncle's audacity, diplomatic skill and determination. It is Roger II.'s distinction to have united all the Norman conquests into one kingdom and to have subjected them to a government scientific, personal and centralized. The principles of this are found in the Assizes of the kingdom of Sicily, promulgated at Ariano in 1140, which enforced an almost absolute royal power. At Palermo Roger drew round him distinguished men of various races, such as the famous Arab geographer Idrisi and the historian Nilus Doxopatrius. He maintained a complete toleration for the several creeds, races and languages of his realm; he was served by men of the most diverse nationalities.

Contemporary authors are: Falco of Benevento, Alexander of Telese, Romuald of Salerno and Hugo Falcandus, all in the *Scrittori e cronisti napoletani*, ed. Del Re, vol. i. *See* also E. Caspar, *Roger II. und die Gründung der normannisch-sicilischen Monarchie* (Innsbruck, 1904). (E. Cu.; X.)

ROGER OF HOVEDEN or HOWDEN (*fl.* 1174–1201), English chronicler, was, to judge from his name and the internal evidence of his work, a native of Howden in the East Riding of Yorkshire. But nothing is known of him before the year 1174. He was then in attendance upon Henry II., by whom he was sent from France on a secret misson to the lords of Galloway. In 1175 he again appears as a negotiator between the king and a number of English religious houses. In 1189, he was a justice of the forests in the shires of Yorkshire, Cumberland and Northumberland. About the year 1192 he began to compile his *Chronica*, a general history of England from 732 to his own time. Up to the year 1192 his narrative adds little to our knowledge. From that time, however, Hoveden is an independent and copious authority. Both on foreign affairs and on questions of domestic policy he is unusually well informed. He is particularly useful

on points of constitutional history. His work breaks off abruptly in 1201. Probably his death should be placed in that year.

See W. Stubbs's edition of the *Chronica* (Rolls Series) and the introductions to vols. i. and iv. This edition supersedes that of Sir H. Savile in his *Scriptores post Bedam* (1596).

ROGER OF WENDOVER (d. 1236), English chronicler, was probably a native of Wendover in Buckinghamshire. At some uncertain date he became a monk of St. Albans; afterwards he was appointed prior of the cell of Belvoir, but he forfeited this dignity in the early years of Henry III., having been found guilty of wasting the endowments. His latter years were passed at St. Albans, where he died on May 6, 1236. He is the first of the important chroniclers who worked in the scriptorium of this house. His great work, the *Flores Historiarum*, begins at the creation and extends to 1235. It is of original value from 1202. Some critics have supposed, but on inconclusive evidence, that Wendover copied, up to 1189, an earlier compilation, the work of John de Cella, the twenty-first abbot of St. Albans (1195–1214).

A 13th-century manuscript is in the Bodleian library (Douce mss. 207), a mutilated 14th-century copy in the British Museum (Cotton ms. Otho B. v.). Matthew Paris prepared an edition which forms the first part of that writer's *Chronica Majora* (ed. H. R. Luard, Rolls Series, 7 vols.). The best edition of Wendover is that of H. O. Coxe (4 vols., 1841–42); there is another (from 1154) in the Rolls Series by H. G. Hewlett (3 vols., 1886–89). *See* Luard's prefaces to vols. i., ii., iii. and vii. of the *Chronica Majora;* and the *Monumenta Germaniae Historica, Scriptores*, Band xxviii., pp. 3–20.

ROGERS, HENRY DARWIN (1808–1866), American geologist, was born at Philadelphia on Aug. 1, 1808. At the age of 21 he was chosen professor of chemistry and natural philosophy at Dickinson college, Pennsylvania. After holding this post for three years, he went to Europe and took up the study of geology. Subsequently he was engaged for 22 years in the State surveys of Pennsylvania and New Jersey, his reports on which were published during the years 1836–41. In 1842 he and his brother WILLIAM BARTON ROGERS (1805–82), who had been similarly occupied in Virginia, brought before the Association of American Geologists and Naturalists their conclusions on the physical structure of the Appalachian chains, and on the elevation of great mountain chains. The researches of H. D. Rogers were elaborated in his final *Report on Pennsylvania* (1858), in which he included a general account of the geology of the United States and of the coal-fields of North America and Great Britain. In 1857 he was appointed professor of natural history and geology at Glasgow. One of his later essays (1861) was on the parallel roads of Lochaber (Glen Roy), the origin of which he attributed to a vast inundation. He died at Glasgow on May 29, 1866.

ROGERS, JAMES EDWIN THOROLD (1823–1890), English economist, was born at West Meon, Hampshire, in 1823, and educated at King's college, London, and Magdalen Hall, Oxford. After taking a first-class degree in 1846, he was ordained and was for a few years a curate in Oxford. Subsequently he resigned his orders. He was a classical scholar and published in 1865 an edition of Aristotle's *Ethics;* but his friendship with Richard Cobden (*q.v.*) led him to study economics, with the result that in 1859 he became professor of statistics and economic science at King's college, London, a post which he filled till his death. From 1862 he was also Drummond professor of political economy at Oxford. During that period he published (in 1866) the first two volumes of his *History of Agriculture and Prices in England*, dealing with the period 1259–1400, a masterly record upon which his reputation mainly rests. Two more volumes (1401–1582) were published in 1882, a fifth and sixth (1583–1702) in 1887, and he left at his death copious materials for a seventh and eighth. An acquaintance with Cobden and John Bright (*q.v.*) led Rogers to take an active part in politics: he represented Southwark in parliament from 1880 to 1885, and Bermondsey in 1885–86, as an advanced Liberal. In 1888, on the death of Prof. Bonamy Price, who had succeeded him at Oxford as professor of political economy, he was re-elected to the post. Previously (in 1883) he had been appointed lecturer in political economy at Worcester college, Oxford. His latter years were mainly spent at Oxford, where he died on Oct. 12, 1890. Thorold Rogers did much to promote the historical study of economics to which he made a solid contribution in his *Six Centuries of Work and Wages* (1885).

His most important publications are:—*Manual of Political Economy* (1868); an edition of Adam Smith's *Wealth of Nations* (1869); *Cobden and Public Opinion* (1873); *The Speeches of J. Bright* (edited) (1868); and *The First Nine Years of the Bank of England* (1887).

See also W. J. Ashley, in *The Political Science Quarterly* (1889); and E. Castelot, in *Nouveau Dictionnaire d'Economie Politique,* supplément.

ROGERS, JOHN (*c.* 1500–1555), English Protestant martyr, born at Aston, near Birmingham, was educated at Pembroke Hall, Cambridge, where he graduated B.A. in 1526. Six years later he was rector of Holy Trinity, Queenhithe, London, and in 1534 went to Antwerp as chaplain to the English merchants. Here he met William Tyndale, under whose influence he abandoned the Roman Catholic faith, and married an Antwerp lady. After Tyndale's death Rogers pushed on with his predecessor's English version of the Old Testament, which he used as far as 2 Chronicles, employing Coverdale's translation (1535) for the remainder and for the Apocrypha. Tyndale's New Testament had been published in 1526. The complete Bible was put out under the pseudonym of Thomas Matthew in 1537; it was printed in Antwerp, and Richard Grafton published the sheets and got leave to sell the edition (1,500 copies) in England. Rogers had little to do with the translation, but he contributed some valuable prefaces and marginal notes. His work was largely used by those who prepared the Great Bible (1539–40), out of which in turn came the Bishop's Bible (1568) and the Authorized Version of 1611. After taking charge of a Protestant congregation in Wittenberg for some years, Rogers returned to England in 1548, where he published a translation of Melanchthon's *Considerations of the Augsburg Interim.* In 1550 he was presented to the crown livings of St. Margaret Moyses and St. Sepulchre in London, and in 1551 was made a prebendary of St. Paul's, where the dean and chapter soon appointed him divinity lecturer.

On the accession of Mary, Rogers preached at Paul's Cross commending the "true doctrine taught in King Edward's days," and warning his hearers against "pestilent Popery, idolatry and superstition." Ten days after (16th August 1553), he was summoned before the council and bidden to keep within his own house. In January 1554 Bonner, the new bishop of London, sent him to Newgate, where he lay with John Hooper, Laurence Saunders, John Bradford and others for a year. On January 22, 1555, Rogers with ten others came before the council at Gardiner's house in Southwark, and held his own in the examination that took place. On the 28th and 29th he came before the commission appointed by Cardinal Pole, and was sentenced to death by Gardiner for heretically denying the Christian character of the Church of Rome and the real presence in the sacrament. He met his death on the 4th of February 1555 at Smithfield. He was the first Protestant martyr of Mary's reign, and his friend Bradford wrote that "he broke the ice valiantly."

ROGERS, JOHN (1627–1665?), English preacher, a Fifth Monarchy man, second son of Nehemiah Rogers, a royalist and Anglican clergyman, was born at Messing, Essex; he studied medicine at King's college, Cambridge. In the quarrel between the army and the parliament Rogers sided with the army, and he was one of the first to join the Fifth Monarchy movement. He approved of the expulsion of the Long Parliament, but the establishment of the Protectorate at once threw the Fifth Monarchy men into antagonism. Rogers addressed a warning letter to Cromwell, and attacked him from the pulpit on Jan. 9, 1654. His house was searched and his papers seized, and Rogers then issued another denunciation against Cromwell, *Mene, Tekel, Perez: a Letter lamenting over Oliver Lord Cromwell.* On March 28, on which day he had proclaimed a fast for the sins of the rulers, he preached a violent sermon against the protector. He was arrested in July. He confronted Cromwell with great courage when brought before him on Feb. 5, 1655, and was imprisoned successively at Windsor and in the Isle of Wight, being released in Jan. 1657. He returned

to London, and, being suspected of conspiracy, was again imprisoned by Cromwell in the Tower (Feb. 3–April 16, 1658). On the protector's death and the downfall of Richard Cromwell, the ideals of the Fifth Monarchy men seemed nearer realization. but Rogers was engaged in political controversy with Prynne and became a source of embarrassment to his own faction, which endeavoured to get rid of him by appointing him "to preach the gospel" in Ireland. On the outbreak of Sir George Booth's royalist insurrection, however, he became chaplain in Charles Fairfax's regiment, and served throughout the campaign. He was imprisoned in Dublin in Jan. 1660 by order of the army faction and released subsequently by the parliament. At the Restoration he withdrew to Holland, studied medicine at Leyden and Utrecht, where he obtained his M.D. in 1662. He was admitted to the degree of M.D. at Oxford in 1664, and is supposed to have died soon afterwards.

Besides the above pamphlet, Rogers wrote in 1653 *Ohel or Beth-shemesh, a Tabernacle for the Sun,* in which he attacked the Presbyterians; *Sagrir, or Doomesday drawing nigh,* from his new standpoint as a Fifth Monarchy man, *Challah, the Heavenly Nymph* (1653); *Dod, or Chathan; the Beloved or the Bridegroom going forth for his Bride* . . . (1653); *Prison-born Morning Beams* (1654); *Jegar Sahadutha* . . . (1657); *Mr. Prynne's Good Old Cause stated and stunted 10 Year ago* . . . (1609); *Διαπολιτεία a Christian Concertation* (1659); *Mr. Harrington's Parallel Unparalleled* (1659); *A Vindication of Sir H. Vane* (1659); *Disputatio Medica Inauguralis* (1662).

AUTHORITIES.—Ed. Rogers, *Life and Opinions of a Fifth Monarchy Man* (1867), compiled from Rogers's own works; Wood, *Athenae Oxonienses and Fasti; Calendars of State Papers (Domestic). See also* "English Ancestry of Washington," *Harper's Magazine,* xxi. (1891); "John Rogers of Purleigh," *The Nation,* vol. 53 (1891).

ROGERS, JOHN (1829–1904), American sculptor, was born at Salem, Mass., on Oct. 30, 1829. He wanted to become a sculptor, and spent eight months in study at Rome and Paris in 1858–59. Becoming discouraged, he returned to America and obtained employment as a draughtsman in the office of the city surveyor of Chicago; but soon afterwards, owing to the favourable reception of his group of small figures, "The Checker Players," he resumed sculptural work, confining himself to these small figures, known as "Rogers Groups," which had an enormous popular success and were extensively reproduced. In 1863 he became a National Academician. He died at New Haven, Conn., on July 27, 1904.

ROGERS, ROBERT (1731–1795), American frontier soldier, was born at Methuen, Mass., and in 1739 removed to Starktown (now Dunbarton), N.H. During the Seven Years' War he raised and commanded a force of militia, known as Rogers's Rangers, which won wide reputation for its courage and endurance in the campaigns about Lake George. He took part in Wolfe's expedition against Quebec and in the Montreal campaign of 1760. Afterwards he was sent by Gen. Amherst to take possession of the north-western posts, including Detroit. He was again in the West in 1763 during the Pontiac uprising, accompanying Dalyell's expedition and participating in the battle of Bloody Bridge. Soon after he went to England and in 1765 published in London a *Concise Account of North America* and his *Journals* of service in the Seven Years' War. In 1766 was published *Ponteach: A Tragedy,* one of the first American dramas, supposedly also written by Rogers. He further laid before the king a memorial proposing to lead an overland expedition from the Mississippi river to the Pacific ocean. This was refused him but instead he was given command of the north-west post of Michilimackinac. From here in 1766 he sent out on his own initiative, under Captains Tute and Carver, the first English expedition to explore the upper Mississippi and Great Lakes region, but it failed to penetrate to the Pacific as intended. Rogers's ambitions caused him to be tried for treason but he was acquitted. He again went to England to retrieve his fortune but was unsuccessful. During the Revolutionary War he came to America but was regarded as a loyalist spy. He then openly joined the British and organized and commanded the Queen's Rangers which saw service in operations around New York city. Later he organized the King's Rangers, but the command was taken by his brother, James Rogers, and Robert Rogers returned to England, where he lived in obscurity until his death in 1795.

There is a scholarly biography by Allan Nevins of 172 pages in the Caxton Club edition of *Ponteach* (Chicago, 1914). *See* also F. Parkman, *Montcalm and Wolfe* (Boston, 1884).

ROGERS, SAMUEL (1763–1855), English poet, was born at Newington Green, London, on July 30, 1763. His father, Thomas Rogers, was the son of a Stourbridge glass manufacturer, who was also a merchant in Cheapside. Thomas Rogers had a place in the London business, and married Mary Radford, daughter of his father's partner, becoming himself a partner shortly afterwards. On his mother's side Samuel Rogers was connected with the Noncomformist divines Philip and Matthew Henry, and it was in Nonconformist circles at Stoke Newington that he was brought up. He was educated at private schools at Hackney and Stoke Newington. Samuel Rogers entered the banking business in Cornhill, but his delicate health necessitated long holidays, during which he met the literary society of the day in Edinburgh as well as in London. He had already published a volume of verse when his *Pleasures of Memory* was printed in 1792. This poem may be regarded as the last embodiment of the poetic diction of the 18th century. Here is carried to the extremest pitch the theory of elevating and refining familiar themes by abstract treatment and lofty imagery.

In 1793 his father's death gave Rogers the principal share in the banking house in Cornhill, and a considerable income. He left Newington Green in the same year and established himself in chambers in the Temple. In his circle of friends at this time were "Conversation" Sharp and the artists Flaxman, Opie, Martin Shee and Fuseli. He also made the acquaintance of Charles James Fox, with whom he visited the galleries in Paris in 1802, and whose friendship introduced him to Holland House. In 1803 he moved to 22 St. James's Place, where for 50 years he entertained all the celebrities of London. Flaxman and Stothard had a share in the decorations of the house, which Rogers had almost rebuilt, and now proceeded to fill with pictures and other works of art. His collections at his death realized £50,000. An invitation to one of Rogers's breakfasts was a formal entry into literary society, and his dinners were even more select. His social success was due less to his literary position than to his powers as a conversationalist, his educated taste in all matters of art, and no doubt to his sarcastic and bitter wit, for which he excused himself by saying that he had such a small voice that no one listened if he said pleasant things. Above all, he seems to have had a genius for benevolence. "He certainly had the kindest heart and unkindest tongue of any one I ever knew," said Fanny Kemble. He helped the poet Robert Bloomfield, he reconciled Moore with Jeffrey and with Byron, and he relieved Sheridan's difficulties in the last days of his life. Moore, who refused help from all his friends, and would only be under obligations to his publishers, found it possible to accept assistance from Rogers. He procured a pension for H. F. Cary, the translator of Dante, and obtained for Wordsworth his sinecure as distributor of stamps.

Rogers played the part of literary dictator in England over a long period. He made his reputation by *The Pleasures of Memory* when Cowper's fame was still in the making. He became the friend of Wordsworth, Scott and Byron, and lived long enough to give an opinion as to the fitness of Alfred Tennyson for the post of poet laureate. Alexander Dyce, from the time of his first introduction to Rogers, was in the habit of writing down the anecdotes with which his conversation abounded. From the mass of material thus accumulated he made a selection which he arranged under various headings and published in 1856 as *Recollections of the Table-Talk of Samuel Rogers, to which is added Porsoniana*. Rogers himself kept a notebook, in which he entered impressions of the conversation of many of his friends—Charles James Fox, Edmund Burke, Henry Grattan, Richard Porson, John Horne Tooke, Talleyrand, Lord Erskine, Sir Walter Scott, Lord Grenville and the duke of Wellington. They were published by his nephew William Sharpe in 1859 as *Recollections by Samuel Rogers*; and *Reminiscences and Table-Talk of Samuel Rogers, Banker, Poet, and Patron of the Arts, 1763–1855* (1903), by G. H. Powell, is an amalgamation of these two authorities. Rogers held various honorary positions: he was one of the trustees of the National Gallery; and he served on a commission to inquire into the management of the British Museum, and on another for the rebuilding of the houses of parliament.

Rogers's later works are *An Epistle to a Friend* (Richard Sharp) (1798); *The Voyage of Columbus* (1810); *Jacqueline* (1814), a narrative poem; *Human Life* (1819) and *Italy* (1822–28). Rogers was in Italy in 1814 and again in 1820, when he visited Byron and Shelley at Pisa. The 1828 edition of *Italy* was not a success. But in an enlarged form the poem was republished in 1830, and in 1838 a sumptuous edition of *Poems* was brought out. Rogers declined the laureateship in 1850 when upon the death of Wordsworth it was offered him. He died in London on Dec. 18, 1855.

See P. W. Clayden, *The Early Life of Samuel Rogers* (1887) and *Rogers and his Contemporaries* (2 vols., 1889); Dyce, *Reminiscences and Table-talk of Samuel Rogers* (1856, ed. Powell, 1903); Roberts, *Samuel Rogers and his Circle* (1910).

ROGERS, WILL (1879–1935), popular American humourist and motion picture actor, was born Nov. 4, 1879 at Oolagh, Indian Territory (now Oklahoma). He began his career in the humble rôle of a rope-throwing cowboy on the vaudeville stage but rose to wealth and world fame as a humourist and political commentator in the cherished home-spun tradition of the old frontier. He was flying over Alaska with Wiley Post in the latter's plane when on Aug. 15, 1935 they crashed and both were killed.

ROGERS, WILLIAM (1819–1896), English clergyman and educational reformer, was born in London on Nov. 24, 1819, and died there on Jan. 19, 1896. Educated at Eton and at Balliol college, Oxford, he entered Durham university in 1842, to study theology, and was ordained in 1843. In 1845 he was appointed to St. Thomas Charterhouse, where he remained for 18 years, throwing himself passionately into the work of education of his poor, degraded and often criminal parishioners. He began by establishing a school for ragamuffins in a blacksmith's abandoned shed, and he gradually extended its scope until schools were provided throughout the parish. In 1863 he became rector of St. Botolph Bishopsgate, a prebendary of St. Paul's, and in 1857 chaplain in ordinary to the Queen. At Bishopsgate Rogers tackled the middle-class schools. He believed in secular education, leaving doctrinal training to parents and clergy. To the cry against "godless education," Rogers replied, "Hang theology; let us begin"; and his nickname of "Hang-theology Rogers" stuck to him for the rest of his life. Rogers reconstructed Edward Alleyn's charity at Dulwich. He founded the Bishopsgate Institute.

ROGIER, CHARLES LATOUR (1800–1885), Belgian statesman, descended from a Belgian family settled in the department of the Nord in France, was born at St. Quentin on Aug. 17, 1800. His father, an officer in the French army, perished in the Russian campaign of 1812; and the family moved to Liége, where the eldest son, Firmin, held a professorship. Charles, after being called to the bar, founded, in collaboration with his lifelong friends, Paul Devaux and Joseph Lebeau, the journal *Mathieu Laensberg* (afterwards *Le Politique*), which by its ardent patriotism and its attacks on the Dutch administration soon acquired a widespread influence. When the insurrection of 1830 broke out at Brussels, Rogier put himself at the head of 150 Liégeois, and inscribing on his banner the motto, "Vaincre ou mourir pour Bruxelles," he obtained arms from a local factory, and marched upon the capital. Here he took his place at once among the leaders of the revolutionary party. His influence saved the town hall from pillage on Sept. 19.

On the 24th a *commission administrative* was formed, of which Rogier became president. The energetic measures of this body and of its successor, the *gouvernement provisoire*, soon freed the greater part of the country from the Dutch troops. Rogier was sent in October to suppress an outbreak among the colliers of Hainaut, and then as delegate of the provisional government to Antwerp, where the citadel still held out for Holland. He arranged an armistice, and reorganized the entire administration of the city. He sat for Liége in the National Congress, voted for the establishment of an hereditary monarchy, and induced the congress to adopt the principle of an elective second chamber. In the long-drawn debates on the bestowal of the crown he ranged himself on the side of Louis Philippe: but when Louis Philippe declined the crown on behalf of his son, Rogier voted with the majority for Leopold of Saxe-Coburg.

In June 1831 he was appointed governor of the province of Antwerp, a post rendered exceptionally difficult by the continued presence of Dutch troops in the citadel. In October 1832 he was made minister of the interior in the Goblet-Devaux cabinet. During his office he carried, in the teeth of opposition, a law that established in Belgium the first railways on the continent of Europe, and thus laid the foundation of her industrial development. Owing to dissensions in the cabinet, he retired in 1834, together with Lebeau, and resumed the governorship of Antwerp. On Lebeau's return to power in 1840, Rogier became minister of public works and education. His education proposals were defeated by the Clerical party, and on the resignation of the ministry in 1841, Rogier gave his support to a compromise measure, which passed into law in 1842. He led the Liberal party in Opposition till 1847, when he formed a cabinet in which he held the ministry of the interior. He carried out a liberal policy which enabled Belgium to escape the general revolutionary movement of 1848.

Rogier retired in Oct. 1852, but was brought back into office by the liberal reaction of 1857. He again became president of the council and minister of the interior in a cabinet of which Frère-Orban was the most conspicuous member. The first important measure passed by the ministry was one for the fortification of Antwerp. In 1860 the fear of French designs on the independence of Belgium led to a movement of reconciliation with Holland, and inspired Rogier to write his poem "La Nouvelle Brabançonne." In 1861 Rogier exchanged the ministry of the interior for that of foreign affairs. He achieved a diplomatic triumph in freeing the navigation of the Scheldt, and thus enabling Antwerp to become the second port on the mainland of Europe. Defeated at Dinant, he sat for Tournai from 1863 till his death. In 1868 Rogier finally retired from power. He continued, however, to take part in public life, and was elected president of the extraordinary session of the chamber of representatives in 1878. From this time his age, his devoted patriotism and the unassuming simplicity of his life made him the idol of all classes. He died at Brussels on May 27, 1885, and was accorded a public funeral.

See T. Juste, *Charles Rogier, 1800-1885, d'après des documents inédits* (Verviers, 1885).

ROHAN, the name of one of the most illustrious of the feudal families of France, derived from that of a small town in Morbihan, Brittany, and claimed connection with the ancient sovereigns of Brittany. Hercule de Rohan, duc de Montbazon (1568-1654) served Henry III. and Henry IV. against the League, and was made by Henry IV. governor of Paris and the Isle of France, and master of the hounds. His grandson, Louis de Rohan-Guéménée, the chevalier de Rohan, conspired with the Dutch against Louis XIV. and was beheaded in Paris in 1674. In the 18th century the Soubise branch of the family furnished several prelates, cardinals and bishops of Strasbourg, among others the famous cardinal de Rohan, the hero of the affair of the diamond necklace. René de Rohan, seigneur of Pontivy and Frontenay, of the Gié branch, commanded the Calvinist army in 1570, and defended Lusignan with great valour when it was besieged by the Catholics (1574-75). His son Henry, the first duke of Rohan (q.v.), had an only child, Marguerite de Rohan, married in 1645 to Henri Chabot. The property and titles of Henry de Rohan thus passed to the Chabot family, which under the name of Rohan-Chabot produced some distinguished soldiers and a cardinal archbishop of Besançon.

ROHAN, HENRI, Duc de (1579-1638), French soldier, writer and leader of the Huguenots, was born at the château of Blain, in Brittany, in 1579. His father was René II., count of Rohan (1550-86). Henri appeared at court and in the army at the age of sixteen, and was a special favourite with Henry IV., after whom, failing the house of Condé, he might be said to be the natural chief of the French Protestants. Having served till the peace of Vervins, he travelled for some time. On his return to France he was made duke and peer at the age of twenty-four, and two years later (1603) married Marguerite de Béthune, the

duc de Sully's daughter. He fought from time to time in the royal army, and it was not till the decree for the restitution of church property in the south threw the Bearnese and Gascons into open revolt that Rohan appeared as a rebel. His ability and constancy contributed to the happy issue of the war for the Huguenots, and brought about the treaty of Montpellier (1623). Rohan renewed the war when the compact of Montpellier was broken. Again a hollow peace was patched up, but it lasted but a short time, and Rohan undertook a third war (1627-29), the first events of which are recounted in his celebrated *Memoirs*. After the peace he made his way to Venice, where his hosts wished to make him their general-in-chief, a design not executed owing to the peace of Cherasco (1631). At Venice he wrote his *Memoirs;* at Padua, *Le Parfait Capitaine.* Rohan returned to the French service, and was entrusted with the war in the Valtelline (1633). But Rohan was still considered dangerous to France, and was soon again in retirement. At this time he wrote his *Traité du gouvernement des treize cantons.* Rohan fought another Valtelline campaign, but without the success of the first, for the motives of France were now held in suspicion. The unfortunate commander retired to Geneva and thence went to the army of Bernhard of Saxe-Weimar. He received a mortal wound at the battle of Rheinfelden on Feb. 28, 1638, and died at the abbey of Königsfeld, canton Berne, on April 13.

Rohan's *Mémoires sur les choses qui se sont passées en France*, etc., rank amongst the best memoirs of the 16th and 17th centuries. The first three books which deal with the civil wars appeared in 1644; the fourth, containing the narrative of the Valtelline campaigns, not till 1758. His famous book on the history and art of war, *Le Parfait Capitaine,* appeared in 1631 and subsequently in 1637 and 1693 (*see also* Quincy, *Art de la guerre,* Paris, 1741). The *Memoirs* may be conveniently found in the collection of Michaud and Poujoulat, vol. 19.

See Fauvelet de Foix, *Histoire du Duc Henri de Rohan* (1667); Schybergson, *Le Duc de Rohan et la charte du parti protestant en France* (1880); Bühring, *Venedig, Gustaf Adolf, und Rohan* (Halle, 1885); Laugel, *Henri de Rohan, son rôle politique et militaire* (1889); Veraguth, *Herzog Rohan und seine Mission in Graubünden* (Berne, 1894); and Shadwell, *Mountain Warfare.*

ROHAN, LOUIS RENÉ EDOUARD, Cardinal de (1734-1803), prince de Rohan-Guéménée, archbishop of Strasbourg, a cadet of the great family of Rohan, was born at Paris on Sept. 25, 1734. After taking orders, in 1760, he was nominated coadjutor to his uncle, Constantine de Rohan-Rochefort, archbishop of Strasbourg, and he was also consecrated bishop of Canopus. But he preferred the gaiety of Paris to his clerical duties, and had political ambitions. He joined the party opposed to the Austrian alliance, which had been cemented by the marriage of the archduchess Marie Antoinette to the dauphin. This party was headed by the duc d'Aiguillon, who in 1771 sent Prince Louis on a special embassy to Vienna to find out what was being done there with regard to the partition of Poland. Rohan arrived at Vienna in Jan. 1772, and made a great noise with his lavish fêtes. But the empress Maria Theresa was implacably hostile to him; not only did he attempt to thwart her policy, but he spread scandals about her daughter Marie Antoinette, laughed at Theresa, and shocked her ideas of propriety. On the death of Louis XV. in 1774, Rohan was recalled from Vienna, and coldly received at Paris; but in 1777 he was made grand almoner, and in 1778 abbot of St. Vaast. In 1778 he was made a cardinal on the nomination of Stanislaus Poniatowski, king of Poland, and in the following year succeeded his uncle as archbishop of Strasbourg and became abbot of Noirmoutiers and Chaise-Dieu.

In an attempt to procure his reinstatement at court he fell into the hands of the comtesse de Lamotte, the notorious Cagliostro and others, whose actions form part of the "affair of the diamond necklace" (see DIAMOND NECKLACE). Rohan certainly was led to believe that his attentions to the queen were welcomed, and that his arrangement by which she received the famous necklace was approved. He was the dupe of others, and at the trial in 1786 his acquittal was received with universal enthusiasm, and regarded as a victory over the court and the queen. He was deprived, however, of his office as grand almoner and exiled to his abbey of Chaise-Dieu. He was soon allowed to return to Strasbourg, and was elected to the states-general. As a prince of the church in Jan. 1791 he refused to take the oath to the constitution, and went to Ettenheim, in the German part of his diocese. He spent what wealth remained to him in providing for the poor clergy of his diocese who had been obliged to leave France; and in 1801 he resigned his nominal rank as archbishop of Strasbourg. On Feb. 17, 1803, he died at Ettenheim.

BIBLIOGRAPHY.—The *Mémoires* of his secretary, the abbé Georgel, of the Baroness d'Oberkirch, of Beugnot and of Madame Campan; also J. Munier-Jolain, *Le Cardinal Collier; lettres à . . . de Marie Thérèse* (1918); J. D. Chamier, *The Dubious Tale of the Diamond Necklace* (London, 1939).

ROHILKHAND, a tract in Uttar Pradesh, republic of India. The name is associated with the Rohilla tribe, but historically refers to an area almost coincident with the modern division of Bareilly (*q.v.*), for which it is now the official title. This division has an area of 11,705 sq.mi. and a population (1951) of 7,217,666. It comprises the districts of Bareilly, Bijnor, Budaun, Moradabad, Shahjahanpur and Pilibhit, and the district of Rampur (*q.v.*), formerly a princely state politically controlled by the divisional commissioner, but fully absorbed into Uttar Pradesh in 1950. The Rohillas trace their ancestry to Sardar Daud Khan, an Afghan adventurer, whose adopted son annexed a large area north of the Ganges and was created a nawab by the Delhi emperor. He died in 1749, and the family split up into a number of petty chiefs. In 1774 (*see* BIJNOR) the Rohilla power was broken by a confederacy of the British and the nawab of Oudh. The state of Rampur was left under the sovereignty of Nawab Faizullah Khan and the rest of Rohilkhand was annexed to Oudh. The division was ceded to the East India company in 1801.

ROHTAK, a town and district of Punjab state, republic of India. The town, which is of great antiquity, became the headquarters of a British district in 1824. Viewed from the sand hills to the south, Rohtak, with its white mosque in the centre and a fort standing out boldly to the east, is picturesque. It has a station on the Northern railway, 44 mi. N.W. of Delhi. Pop. (1951) 71,902. It is an important trade centre, with factories for ginning and pressing cotton and a specialty in muslin turbans.

The DISTRICT OF ROHTAK has an area of 2,329 sq.mi. It is situated on the level tableland between the Jumna and Sutlej rivers, and the northern areas are watered by the Rohtak and Butana branches of the Western Jumna canal; but the greater part of the central plain is entirely dependent upon the uncertain rainfall. The population in 1951 was 1,122,046.

ROKITANSKY, KARL, FREIHERR VON (1804–1878), Austrian pathologist and pioneer in the science of pathological anatomy, was born at Königgrätz, Bohemia, on Feb. 19, 1804. He studied medicine at Prague and Vienna, where he was appointed professor extraordinary of pathological anatomy in 1834. He became president of the Vienna Academy of Sciences in 1869 and was named freiherr in 1874.

His *Handbuch der pathologischen Anatomie* (1842–46, Eng. trans. 1849–52) was an important work. Other books include *Über das Auswachsen der Bindegewebssubstanzen* (1854) and *Über Bindegewebswucherung im Nervensystem* (1857).

Rokitansky was the first to detect bacteria in the lesions of malignant endocarditis and to differentiate between lobar and lobular pneumonia. He first described acute dilatation of the stomach (1842) and left a classic account of the pathologic appearance in acute yellow atrophy of the liver (1843), which became known as Rokitansky's disease. He described and defined the bronchial and pulmonary complications of typhoid as bronchotyphus and pneumotyphus and completed Rene Laënnec's picture of emphysema of the lungs by describing the microscopic appearances. In obstetrics and orthopedics he is credited as the first to describe spondylolisthetic deformities (1839).

Rokitansky, who made more than 30,000 post-mortems during his life, was one of the chief founders of the Vienna school of pathological anatomy. He was also active in the legislature, where he favoured the Liberal party and became speaker of the house.

He died in Vienna, July 23, 1878.

ROLAND [ROLAND DE LA PLATIÈRE], **JEAN MARIE** (1734–1793), French statesman, was born at Thizy on Feb. 18,

1734. Intending to seek his fortune abroad, he went on foot to Nantes, but illness obliged him to give up his project. After working as a clerk, he joined a relative who was inspector of manufactures at Amiens, and himself rose to the position of inspector.

In 1780 he married Jeanne Manon Phlipon (1754–93), famous in history as Madame Roland. She was the daughter of Gratien Phlipon, a Paris engraver. About the year 1785 the Rolands moved to Lyons. A correspondence sprang up with J. P. Brissot and other friends of the revolution in Paris, and in 1791 the Rolands settled there.

Jean Roland became a member of the Jacobin club. Madame Roland's salon soon became the rendezvous of Brissot, Jerôme Pétion de Villeneuve, Robespierre and other leaders of the popular movement, above all of F. N. L. Buzot, whom she loved with platonic enthusiasm. In person Madame Roland was attractive though not beautiful; her ideas were clear and far-reaching, her manner calm and her power of observation extremely acute.

On March 23, 1792, Roland was appointed minister of the interior. As a minister of the crown Roland exhibited a bourgeois brusqueness of manner and a remarkable combination of political prejudice with administrative ability. The decrees against the emigrants and the nonjuring clergy still remained under the veto of the king. A letter was penned by Madame Roland and addressed by her husband to Louis. It remained unanswered. Thereupon, in full council and in the king's presence, Roland read his letter aloud. It contained many and terrible truths as to the royal refusal to sanction the decrees and as to the king's position in the state; but it was inconsistent with a minister's position, disrespectful if not insolent in tone. Roland's dismissal followed. He then read the letter to the assembly; it was ordered to be printed, became the manifesto of disaffection and was circulated everywhere.

After the insurrection of Aug. 10, Roland was recalled to power, one of his colleagues being G. J. Danton, but he was dismayed by the progress of the revolution. He was above all a provincial, and was soon in opposition to the party of the Mountain. He was hostile to the insurrectional commune of Paris, and proposed transferring the government to Blois; he attacked Robespierre and his friends. His neglect to seal the iron chest discovered in the Tuileries, which contained the proofs of Louis XVI's relations with the enemies of France, led to the accusation that he had destroyed a part of these documents. Finally, in the trial of the king he demanded, with the Girondists, that the sentence should be pronounced by a vote of the whole people, and not simply by the convention. He resigned office on Jan. 23, 1793, two days after the king's execution.

The Rolands remained in Paris. Once Madame Roland appeared personally in the assembly to repel the falsehoods of an accuser, and secured acquittal. But violence succeeded violence, and early on the morning of June 1, she was arrested and imprisoned in the Abbaye. Roland himself escaped secretly to Rouen. Released for an hour from the Abbaye, Madame Roland was again arrested and thrown among the horrors of Sainte-Pélagie. Finally, she was transferred to the Conciergerie. In prison she won the affections of the guards, and was allowed the privilege of writing materials and the occasional visits of devoted friends. She there wrote her *Appel à l'impartiale postérité*, those memoirs which display a strange alternation between self-laudation and patriotism, between the trivial and the sublime. On Nov. 8, 1793, she was guillotined. Before her execution, she bowed before the clay statue of Liberty erected in the Place de la Révolution, uttering her famous apostrophe—"O Liberty! what crimes are committed in thy name!" When Roland heard of his wife's condemnation, he wandered several miles from his refuge in Rouen; maddened by despair and grief, he wrote a few words expressive of his horror at those massacres which could be inspired only by the enemies of France, protesting that "from the moment when I learned that they had murdered my wife I would no longer remain in a world stained with enemies." He affixed the paper to his breast, and unsheathing a sword-stick fell upon the weapon, which pierced his heart, on Nov. 10, 1793.

Madame Roland's *Mémoires,* first printed in 1820, have been edited among others by P. Faugère (1864), by C. A. Dauban (1864), by J. Claretie (1884), and by C. Perroud (1905). Some of her *Lettres inédites* have been published by C. A. Dauban (1867); C. Perroud published a critical edition of her *Lettres* (1900-02), and a new series (1767-80) in 1913-15. See also C. A. Dauban, *Étude sur Madame Roland et son temps* (1864); V. Lamy, *Deux femmes célèbres, Madame Roland et Charlotte Corday* (1884); C. Bader, *Madame Roland, d'après des lettres et des manuscrits inédits* (1892); A. J. Lambert, *Le mariage de Madame Roland, trois années de correspondance amoureuse* (1896); Austin Dobson, *Four Frenchwomen* (1890); articles by C. Perroud in the review *La Révolution française* (1896-99); U. Birch, *Madame Roland, a Study in Revolution* (1917).

ROLAND, LEGEND OF. The legend of the French epic hero Roland (transferred to Italian romance as Orlando) is based on authentic history. Charlemagne invaded Spain in 778, and had captured Pamplona, but failed before Saragossa, when the news of a Saxon revolt recalled him to the banks of the Rhine. On his retreat to France through the defiles of the Pyrenees, part of his army was cut off from the main body by the Basques and entirely destroyed. The incident is related in Einhard's *Vita Karoli* (cap. ix.; Pertz. ii. 448), where the names of the leaders are given. "In this battle were slain Eggihard *praepositus* of the royal table; Anselm, count of the palace; and Hruodland, praefect of the Breton march. . . ." The scene of the disaster is fixed by tradition at Roncevaux, on the road from Pamplona to St. Jean Pied de Port. The fiction of the 12 peers may possibly arise from a still earlier tradition. In 636-637, according to the *Chronicles of Fredegarius* (ed. Krusch, p. 159), 12 chiefs, whose names are given, were sent by Dagobert against the Basques. The expedition was successful, but in the valley of Subola, identified with Mauléon, near Roncevaux, the Duke Harembert, with other Frankish chiefs, was slain. Later fights in the same neighbourhood and under similar circumstances are related in 813 (*Vita Hludowici*; Pertz ii. 616), and especially in 824 (Einhard's *Annales*; Pertz. i. 213). These incidents no doubt served to strengthen the tradition of the disaster to Charlemagne's rearguard in 778, the importance of which was certainly magnified in popular story.

The choice of Roland or Hruodland as the hero probably points to the borders of French Brittany as the home of the legend. The exaggeration of a rear-guard action into a national defeat; the substitution of a vast army of Saracens for the border tribe mentioned by Einhard; and the vengeance inflicted by Charlemagne, where in fact the enemy escaped with complete impunity—all are in keeping with the general laws of romance. Charlemagne himself appears as the ancient epic monarch, not as the young man he really was in 778. There is evidence of a continuous tradition dating from the original event and, as Roncevaux lay on the route to Compostella, the many pilgrims who must have passed the site, from the middle of the 9th century onwards, may have helped to spread the story. Whether the actual *cantilena Rollandi* chanted by Taillefer at the battle of Hastings (William of Malmesbury, *De gestis regum angl.* iii. 242, and Wace, *Brut.* ii. 11, 8035 *seq.*) was any part of the existing *Chanson de Roland* cannot be stated, but the choice of the legend on this occasion by the trouvère is proof of its popularity.

The oldest extant forms of the legend are: (*a*) chapters xix.-xxx. of the Latin chronicle, known as the *Pseudo-Turpin*, which purports to be the work of Turpin, archbishop of Reims, who died about 800, but probably dates from the 12th century; (*b*) *Carmen de proditione Guenonis*, a poem in Latin distichs; and (*c*) the *Chanson de Roland*, a French *chanson de geste* of about 4,000 lines, the oldest recension of which is in the Bodleian library, Oxford (ms. Digby, 23). It is in assonanced *tirades*, of unequal length, many of them terminated with the refrain *Aoi*. This ms. was written by an Anglo-Norman scribe about the end of the 12th century, and is a corrupt copy of a text by a French trouvère of the middle of the 11th century. The poem, which was first printed by Francisque Michel (Oxford, 1837) is the finest monument of the heroic age of French epic.

The *Pseudo-Turpin* represents a different recension of the story and is throughout clerical in tone. It was the trouvère of the *Chanson de Roland* who developed the characters into epic types; he invented the heroic friendship of Roland and Oliver, the motives of Ganelon's treachery, and many other details.

The famous fight between Roland and the giant Ferragus appears in the *Pseudo-Turpin* (ch. xviii.), but not in the poem. The *Chanson de Roland* contains allusions to many events outside the narrative, some of which refer to *chansons* which are lost. Roland was variously represented by the romancers as the son of Charlemagne's sister Gilles or Berte and the knight Milon d'Anglers. The romantic episode of the reconciliation of the pair with Charlemagne through Roland's childish prattle (*Berte et Milon*) is probably foreign to the original legend. His *enfances*, or youthful exploits, were, according to *Aspremont*, performed in Italy against the giant Eaumont, but in *Girais de Viane* his first taste of battle is under the walls of Vienne, where Oliver, at first his adversary, becomes his brother-in-arms.

In the 12th century the *Chanson de Roland* was modernized by replacing the assonance by rhyme. Several mss. of this rhymed recension, sometimes known as *Roncevaux*, are preserved. The English romances of Charlemagne (*q.v.*) are mostly derived from late and inferior sources. It was in Italy that the Roland legend had its greatest fortune; Charlemagne and Roland appear in the *Paradiso* (canto xviii.) of Dante; the statues of Roland and Oliver appear on the doorway of the cathedral of Verona; and the French *chansons de geste* regularly appeared in a corrupt Italianized French.

BIBLIOGRAPHY.—For a complete bibliography of the editions of the various mss. of the *Chanson de Roland,* of the foreign versions, and of the enormous literature of the subject, *see* Léon Gautier, *Les Epopées françaises* (2nd vol. iii. 1880) and the same author's *Bibliographie des chansons de geste* (1897). See also P. Boissonade, *Du Nouveau sur le Chanson de Roland* (1923). Among critical editions of the *Chanson* are those by Wendelin Foerster in the *Altfranz. Bibliotek,* vols. vi. and vii. (Heilbronn, 1883-86), and by E. Stengel *Das altfranzösische Rolandslied* (Leipzig, 1900, etc.). The most popular edition is *La Chanson de Roland* (Tours, 1872, and numerous subsequent editions), by Léon Gautier. L. Petit de Julleville published in 1878 an edition with the old French text, and a modern French translation in assonanced verse. There are English translations in prose by I. Butler (Boston, Mass., 1904); in verse by A. Way and F. Spencer (1895); and "in the original measure" by C. S. Moncrieff (1919). Consult further G. Paris, *Hist. poét. de Charlemagne* (reprint, 1905), and *De Pseudo Turpino* (Paris, 1865); P. Rajna, *Le Origini dell 'epopea francese* (Florence, 1884) and *Le Fonti dell' Orlando Furioso* (2nd ed. Florence, 1900); F. Picco, *Rolando nella storia e nella poesia* (Turin, 1901); G. Paris, "Roncevaux," in *Légendes du moyen âge* (1903), on the topography of the battlefield.

ROLANDSECK, a village in the Prussian Rhine province, Germany, situated on the left bank of the Rhine, 8 mi. above Bonn, with a station on the railway Cologne-Coblenz. The place consists almost entirely of villas and is a favourite summer resort. Behind it lie the ruins of the castle.

ROLL. Primarily the word "roll" is used of a piece of writing material, such as parchment or paper, which is rolled up for the purpose of convenient storage or handling, in which form it represents an early stage in the evolution of the book, an example being the Rotulus or Rodl of Joshua of *c.* 700 in the Vatican library. By extension it became the name for any document kept in this form as an official record, and hence for any register, record, catalogue or official list. "The Rolls" was the name of the building where the records of the chancery court, a division of the English high court of justice, were kept, the keeper of which was the Master of the Rolls (*q.v.*), now the title of the third member of the English supreme court of judicature. The word is used in this sense for the list of those admitted as qualified solicitors, whence the phrase "to strike off the rolls" of removal by the court of a solicitor for offences or delinquencies.

In architecture, a "roll" or "scroll" moulding is one resembling a section of a roll or scroll of parchment with the end overlapping; a "roll and fillet" moulding is a section of a cylindrical moulding with a square fillet running along the centre of the face (*see* LABEL).

ROLLAND, JOHN (*fl.* 1560), Scottish poet, appears to have been a priest of the diocese of Glasgow, and to have been known in Dalkeith in 1555. He is the author of two poems, the *Court of Venus* and a translation of the *Seven Sages.* The former, which was printed by John Ros in 1575, may have been written before 1560. The latter was translated from a Scots prose version.

The *Court of Venus* was edited by Walter Gregor (1884). The *Seven*

Sages was printed in 1578, and reprinted by David Laing (1837).

ROLLAND, ROMAIN (1866–1944), French man of letters, was born at Clamecy, Nièvre, on Jan. 29, 1866. He was educated at Clamecy, and later in Paris, where he had a distinguished academic career. From 1889–91 he was a member of the French School in Rome, and in 1895 became professor of art history at the Ecole Normale Supérieure. Later he was appointed professor at the Sorbonne, where he introduced the study of the history of music. He produced many critical and historical works, among them *Les origines du théâtre lyrique moderne, Histoire de l'opéra en Europe avant Lulli et Scarlatti* (1895); *Des causes de la décadence de la peinture italienne* (1895); *Le théâtre du peuple* (1901); besides studies on *Millet* (1902); *Beethoven* (1903) and *Michel-Ange* (1906), *Les Tragédies de la foi, Saint Louis, Aërt, Le Triomphe de la raison* (1913). His most famous work, however, is the romance of *Jean-Christophe* (1904–12), the biography of a German musician. It is in three series, *Jean-Christophe, Jean-Christophe à Paris* and *La Fin du Voyage,* and appeared in 10 volumes, the first *L'aube,* in 1904, and the last *La Nouvelle Journée,* in 1912.

When World War I broke out Rolland was in Switzerland, and although his open letter to Hauptmann expressed his horror of the burning of Louvain, he became extremely unpopular in France owing to a series of articles published in the *Journal de Genève* during Sept. and Oct. 1914. These articles were subsequently published in book form under the title *Au-dessus de la mêlée.* Although his reputation in France suffered from his political views, it increased abroad, and the performances of *Danton* and *Le 14 juillet,* which with *Les Loups* and *Le Jeu de l'amour et de la mort* belong to his *Théâtre de la Revolution* (1909), caused a furore in Berlin. His work *Mahatma Gandhi* (1924) is an impassioned defense of the Indian leader. His later works include: *Colas Breugnon* (1918); *Les précurseurs* (1919); *Clerambault, Pierre et Luce* (1919); *Voyage musical aux pays du passé* (1919); *Liluli* (1919). In 1922 appeared the first volume of a series entitled *L'Ame Enchantée.* To this series belong *Annette et Sylvie* (1922), *L'Été* (1924), *Mère et Fils* (1927), *Beethoven the Creator* (1929). Rolland received the Nobel prize for literature in 1915. He died in Vezelay, France, Dec. 30, 1944.

See Jan Romein, *Romain Rolland* (1918); 1. Debran, *M. R. Rolland, initiateur de défaitisme* (1918); W. Kuechler, *Romain Rolland* (1919).

ROLLE DE HAMPOLE, RICHARD (d. 1349), English hermit and author, was born near the end of the 13th century, at Thornton (now Thornton Dale), near Pickering, Yorkshire. His father, William Rolle, was perhaps a dependant of the Neville family. Richard was sent to Oxford at the expense of Thomas de Neville, afterwards archdeacon of Durham. At Oxford he gave himself to the study of religion rather than to the subtleties of scholastic philosophy, for which he professed a strong distaste. At the age of 19 he returned to his father's house, and, making a rough attempt at a hermit's dress, he ran away to follow the religious vocation. At Dalton, near Rotherham, he was recognized by John de Dalton, who had been at Oxford with him. After satisfying himself of Rolle's sanity, Dalton's father provided him with food and shelter and a hermit's dress. Rolle then entered on the contemplative life, passing through the preliminary stages of purification and illumination, which lasted for nearly three years, and then entering the stage of sight, the full revelation of the divine vision. He is very exact in his dates, and attained, he says, the highest stage of his ecstasy four years and three months after the beginning of his conversion.

Richard belonged to no order, though he seems to have desired to form a rule of hermits, but met with much opposition. He finally contented himself with advising those who sought him out. He began also to write the songs and treatises by which he was to exert his widest influence. He settled in Richmondshire, 12 miles from the recluse Margaret Kirkby, whom he had cured of a violent seizure. To her some of his works are dedicated. Finally he removed to Hampole, near Doncaster, where he died on Sept. 29, 1349.

Richard Rolle had a great influence on his own and the next generation. In his exaltation of the spiritual side of religion over its forms, his enthusiastic celebration of the love of Christ, and his assertion of the individualist principle, he represented the best side of the influences that led to the Lollard movement. He was himself a faithful son of the church, and the political activity of the Lollards was quite foreign to his teaching. The popularity of his devotional writings is attested by the numerous existing editions and by the many close imitations of them.

A very full list of his Latin and English works is given (pp. 36–43) in Dr. Carl Horstmann's edition (1895–96) of his works in the Library of Early English Writers.

Richard Rolle's Latin treatises, *De emendatione vitae* and *De incendio amoris,* the latter one of the most interesting of his works, because it is obviously largely autobiographical, were translated (1434–35) by Richard Misyn (ed. R. Harvey, Early English Text Soc., 1896 and by F. M. M. Comper in 1914). The *De emendatione de vitae* was also edited with an introduction, by D. Harford (1913). The *Pricke of Conscience* was edited (1863) by Richard Morris for the Philological Society. His *Commentary on the Psalms* was edited by the Rev. H. R. Bramley (Oxford, 1884). Ten prose treatises by Richard Rolle were edited by G. Perry for the Early English Text Society in 1866, rev. ed. 1921. Partial ed. of his Latin works are Paris (1510), Antwerp (1533), Cologne (1535–36), Paris (1618); and in vol. xxvi. of the "Bibliotheca Patrum Maxima" (Lyons, 1677). The office, which forms the chief authority for Rolle's life, was printed in the *York Breviary,* vol. ii. (Surtees Soc., 1882), and in Canon Perry's edition referred to above. The *Meditatis de passione Domini* was edited in 1917, with introduction, by H. Lindkvist, and the *Officium et Miracula* by R. M. Woolley in 1919. See *Richard Rolle's Version of the Penitential Psalms, with his Commentary* (1928); *The Mirror of Gifts: from the works of Richard Rolle* (ed. H. R. Cross, 1928).

See also Percy Andreae, who collated 18 mss. in the British Museum in his *Handschriften des Pricke of Conscience* (Berlin, 1888); *Studien über Richard Rolle von Hampole unter besonderer Berücksichtigung seiner Psalmencommentare,* by H. Middendorff (Magdeburg, 1888), with a list of mss., sources, etc.; J. Zupitza in *Englische Studien* (Heilbronn, vols. vii. and xii.); A. Hahn, *Quellenuntersuchungen zu Richard Rolle's englischen Schriften* (Halle, 1900); and for his prosody, G. Saintsbury, *Hist. of English Prosody,* vol. i.

ROLLER, one of several birds, especially the common roller (*Coracias garrulus*), so called from its way of occasionally rolling in its flight, after the fashion of a tumbler pigeon. It is widely though not numerously spread over Europe and western Asia in summer, breeding as far N. as the middle of Sweden, but retiring to winter in Africa. It occurs almost every year as a straggler in the British islands. Except the back, scapulars and tertials, which are bright reddish-brown, the plumage of both sexes is blue (of various shades, from pale turquoise to dark ultramarine) tinted in parts with green.

The bird is purely insectivorous. *Coracias* forms the type of the family *Coraciidae,* allied to the bee-eaters (*Meropidae*) and kingfishers (*q.v.*) (*Alcedinidae*). A number of other species exist in Asia and Africa.

ROLLER: *see* Tillage Machinery.

ROLLER SKATING, a pastime which, by the use of small wheels instead of a blade on the skate, has provided some of the pleasures of skating on ice without having ice as the surface (*see* Skating).

Wheeled skates were used on the roads of Holland as far back as the 18th century, but it was the invention of the four-wheeled skate, working on rubber pads, by J. L. Plimpton of New York, in 1863, that made the amusement popular. Still greater advance was made by the Raymond skate with ball and cone bearings.

The wheels of rollers were first of turned boxwood, but the wearing of the edges was a fault which was surmounted by making them of a hard composition or of steel. The floor of the rink on which the skating takes place is either of asphalt or of wood; the latter became the most popular material, the best floors being made of long narrow strips of maple.

ROLLESTON, THOMAS WILLIAM HAZEN (1857–1920), Irish scholar and author, was born in King's Co., Ireland, in 1857, and died at Hampstead in 1920. He was educated at St. Columba's college and at Trinity college, Dublin. He founded the *Dublin University Review* (1885–86). His works include a *Life of Lessing* (1889); *Lessing and Modern German Literature* (1900); *Sea Spray,* a book of verse (Dublin, 1909); *Parallel*

Paths, a Study in Biology, Ethics and Art (1908); and two books on Gaelic literature, *The High Deeds of Finn* (1910) and *Myths and Legends of Celtic Race* (1911).

See C. H. Rolleston, *Portrait of an Irishman* (London, 1939).

ROLLING MILL, an establishment where metal, especially iron and steel is rolled into plates and bars of various sections. (See IRON AND STEEL: *Rolling Mills;* SHEETS, IRON AND STEEL; TIN PLATE AND TERNEPLATE.)

ROLLOCK, ROBERT (*c.* 1555–1599), the first principal of the University of Edinburgh, son of David Rollock of Powis, near Stirling, received his early education at the school of Stirling from Thomas Buchanan, a nephew of George Buchanan, and, after graduating at St. Andrews, became a regent there in 1580. In 1583 he was appointed by the Edinburgh town council sole regent of the "town's college" ("Academia Jacobi Sexti," afterward the University of Edinburgh). In 1598 he was translated to the parish church of the Upper Tolbooth, Edinburgh, and then to that of the Grey Friars (then known as the Magdalen church). He died at Edinburgh on Feb. 8, 1599. His *Select Works* were edited by W. Gunn for the Wodrow society (1844–49).

A *Life* by George Robertson and Henry Charteris was reprinted by the Bannatyne club in 1826. *See* also the introduction to the *Select Works,* and Sir Alexander Grant's *History of the University of Edinburgh.*

ROLLS-ROYCE LIMITED, a firm of motorcar manufacturers. A car designed by Henry Royce of the Manchester firm of Royce Ltd. was brought to the notice of C. S. Rolls of C. S. Rolls & Co., London, in the latter half of 1904. The success of this car led, in March 1906, to the merging of the Rolls and Royce interests into one company and, in Dec. 1906, a public company was floated with £200,000 capital, under the style of Rolls-Royce Ltd. In that year Royce designed the 40–50 h.p. side-valve engined chassis—known as the Silver Ghost—which was developed from that date until May 1925, when the first of the Phantom overhead-valve engine types was introduced. In 1915 Royce devoted himself to aero-engine design and produced three types of engine, known as the Hawk, Falcon and Eagle. At the end of World War I there were Rolls-Royce aero engines in service of an aggregate of more than 2,000,000 h.p. Some of the outstanding events in the Rolls-Royce post-World War I history were J. W. Alcock and A. W. Brown's nonstop transatlantic flight in a 360-h.p. Rolls-Royce Eagle engined Vickers Vimy bomber in June 1919 (this was the first direct flight across the Atlantic); the first flights to Australia and South Africa, the winning outright of the Schneider trophy in 1931, the introduction of the Kestrel, Merlin and Peregrine aero engines and the 25–30 h.p. Rolls-Royce chassis.

During World War II the firm produced the Merlin engine for fighter aircraft. It later developed a 635-h.p. Meteor engine for the Centurion, a 52-ton British tank.   (M. BU.; X.)

See H. Nockolds, *The Magic of a Name* (London, 1945).

ROMA, a town of southeast Queensland, Austr.; pop. (1947) 3,894; on the main Western railway line 318 mi. W. of Brisbane. The town's water supplies are drawn from artesian wells (depth 1,300 ft., yield *c.* 200,000 gal. daily). Natural gas and traces of petroleum have at times appeared in bores near Roma.

ROMAINS, JULES (1885–   ), French poet and novelist, was born on Aug. 26, 1885, at St.-Julien-Chapteuil in the Ardèche. He went early to Paris and spent his childhood and adolescence in Montmartre. He entered the École Normale Supérieure in 1906, and graduated in philosophy in 1909. For ten years he taught philosophy in Paris and in the provinces, notably at Nice. His claim to fame is principally based on his position as one of the heads of the unanimist school of writers (Arcos, Vildrac, Duhamel, Chennevière and others). Romains's work falls into three categories: poems, novels and plays. The most important of his books of verse, *La Vie unanime* (1908), deals with what may be called the spiritual life inherent in the various groups of humanity. The *Odes et Prières* (1913) and *L'Ode génoise* (1925) should also be mentioned. Some of his novels, such as *Les Copains* (1913), owe their merit to a sort of Rabelaisian verve and truculent jollity. Others are in a loftier style. *Mort de quelqu'un*

(1910) traces the brief survival of a dead man in the society in which he had lived, and how he gradually fades out of memory. The dramatic works of Jules Romains include farces, the best of which is probably *Knock* (1925), dramatic prose poems, such as *L'Armée dans la ville* (1911) and *Cromedeyre-le-Vieil* (1920), and the tragedies *Le Dictateur* (1926) and *Jean le Maufranc* (1927). He went to the U.S. in 1940 and returned to France in 1945. He wrote an epic work in 27 volumes, *Les Hommes de bonne volonté* (Eng. trans. in 14 vol., 1932–46).   (G. ML.; X.)

ROMAN, capital of the department of Roman, Rum., on the main line from Czernowitz to Galatz, and on the left bank of the river Moldava, 2¼ mi. W. of its junction with the Sereth. Pop. (1930) 28,948, about one-third being Jews. Roman has been the seat of a bishop since 1401. Its seminary dates from 1402. There are old churches, including a cathedral, built in 1541.

ROMAN ARCHITECTURE. Like the rest of Roman civilization, Roman architecture is a manifestation of the essentially direct and practical Roman mind. It is concerned not with the search for any ideal of beauty but with the solution of everyday problems. Consequently while the elements of Roman architecture are derivative, being Greek and Etruscan or rather Italic in origin, they are adapted and transformed by the Roman genius in the light of increased technical knowledge to fit altered conditions of life. The influence exerted on Roman architectural forms by the materials and methods of construction used, cannot be overestimated, and the enduring stability of Roman buildings may legitimately be held to be a result of the presence of good and durable building material. The discovery of concrete in particular gave to the Roman builders an almost imperishable material which could be moulded into a homogeneous mass exerting no thrust when set, and which thus enabled them to attack and to solve entirely new problems in spatial planning.

Building Materials.—The material employed by the Romans in their earliest buildings was *tufa,* a volcanic rock of varying hardness, some soft enough to be worked with bronze tools. Later other harder volcanic stones were used; *e.g.,* peperino, and the stone from the Alban hills. Under the later republic and the empire the most important stone for building was *travertine,* which was quarried mainly at Tibur (Tivoli). This becomes very hard after exposure to air and weathers to a rich golden tone. An example of the use of travertine is the exterior of the Colosseum.

For their concrete the Romans used *pozzolana,* of which there are extensive beds at Pozzuoli, near Naples, and also round Rome. This is a fine chocolate-red volcanic earth, which when mixed with lime forms an excellent natural hydraulic cement which will set well even under water. With this cement was mixed an aggregate of broken tufa, travertine, brick or even marble, pumice stone being used in vaults after the 1st century A.D. to lighten the weight. Besides its extreme durability this concrete is practically indestructible by fire. It is used in all the great imperial buildings; *e.g.,* Pantheon, baths of Caracalla and basilica of Maxentius. The new forms of architecture which were developed by the use of this material spread all over the Roman empire.

Unburnt bricks faced with stucco were used especially for private houses under the republic. It is to these bricks that reference is made in Augustus' famous saying "that he found Rome of brick and left it of marble." Of these, naturally, very few remain. Under the empire *kiln-baked bricks and tiles* were the most common facing for concrete. They are never used to build a whole wall in the modern manner but merely as a protective skin. These bricks or tiles are almost always used in triangular shapes. Large tiles about 2 ft. square called *bipedales* were employed as bonding courses.

The use made by the Romans of *marble* was mainly decorative. It was applied in slabs to brick and concrete walls, and set in cement. It was used for pavements either in slabs cut and arranged in patterns, or as mosaic. Under the empire a great demand arose for coloured marbles and such stones as porphyry, granite and alabaster, which were imported from various parts of the empire. The abundant use of these marbles is well illustrated by the remains of the Flavian palace on the Palatine and of

Hadrian's villa at Tivoli.

The use of *stucco* over unbaked brick and over coarse stone was prevalent from the earliest times in Greece, Sicily and Italy. It served as a protection from the weather and also as a finish. Later it was used over brick and concrete. It was made of lime, sand and fine marble dust and would take a high polish. Thus it became the usual ground for decoration especially in the interiors of houses. Examples of its use abound at Pompeii, and in Rome in the House of Livia, in Nero's Golden House, etc. Another material the use of which was mainly decorative is *bronze*. Doors, grills, panels of ceilings, etc., were made of it.

Construction.—Walls were built in two ways, either of ordinary masonry or of concrete (faced or unfaced). While there are several examples of early stone walling without courses (cyclopean and polygonal) especially in some of the towns, *e.g.*, Norba, Praeneste, near Rome, most of the stone walls existing are built of squared blocks laid in regular courses as headers and stretchers (*opus quadratum*). The earliest of these walls are of tufa. Later come those of peperino and travertine. The blocks of stone in these walls are fairly large, 2 ft. x 4 ft. or more, and were often held together by iron cramps fixed in lead.

Concrete walls, except below ground, were always faced. They are divided into types according to the kind of facing used. (a) *Opus quadratum, i.e.*, ordinary stone walling, is used as a facing for concrete, especially for important public buildings under the earlier empire, *e.g.*, exterior of the Colosseum. (b) *Opus incertum* is the most common facing for ordinary concrete walls of the 2nd and 1st centuries B.C. The face of the concrete is studded with 3 in. to 4 in. irregularly shaped pieces of stone, usually tufa. (c) *Opus reticulatum* came into vogue in the 1st century B.C. and remained in use until the time of Hadrian. The construction is like that of *opus incertum* but the pieces of stone were pyramid shaped with square bases set diagonally and wedged into the concrete wall. Quoins 9 in. x 3 in. of the same material or of brick were used at the angles. (d) Brick and tile faced concrete (so called *opus testaceum*) is by far the most common material for walling under the empire. Triangular tiles were used with their points turned into the concrete and their long sides showing, thus giving the appearance of a wall built of thin bricks. Bonding courses of *bipedales* were employed at intervals of 2 or 3 feet. (e) Mixed brick and stone facing (so called *opus mixtum*) was popular under the later empire and especially under Diocletian.

The stone arch occurs frequently in Italy from the middle of the 2nd century B.C. onwards, usually in city gates, bridges and aqueducts. The discovery of concrete, however, enormously facilitated the spread of arch construction. Concrete arches were faced with stone or tile voussoirs, and with the latter *bipedales* were used at every 6th or 7th voussoir.

The vaults used by the Romans were simpler geometrical forms, *i.e.*, the barrel vault, the intersecting (groined) barrel vault and the segmental vault. By the 1st century B.C. quite extensive systems of barrel vaulting were employed as in the substructions of the Tabularium in Rome, the temple of Hercules at Tivoli, etc. The later vaults were built up on brick rings about 2 in. apart, joined by brick bonders, forming rectangular compartments which were filled with concrete. Additional layers of concrete were laid above. When set the concrete vault exerted no thrust. The surfaces of the vaults were tile faced or covered with stucco. A fine example of Roman vaulting is the basilica of Maxentius.

The construction of domes naturally follows that of vaults. Here again the fact that the concrete dome was a dead weight without thrust was of the greatest importance in simplifying the problem. Tie ribs of brick were used and sometimes relieving arches as in the case of the Pantheon where the facing bricks are laid horizontally. At the crown of the dome was a brick ring.

The Orders.—There are five Orders of Roman Architecture, Tuscan, Doric, Ionic, Corinthian and Composite, Tuscan and Composite being modifications of Doric and Corinthian respectively. The rules followed by the Roman builders were elastic; few examples are of the same proportion and there was much licence allowed in execution. It has, however, been usually supposed that some system in which form and detail were definitely

standardized was essential for the construction of Roman buildings, built as they were at a high speed by ordinary workmen. Marcus Vitruvius Pollio, the Roman writer on architecture, would at any rate have us believe that imperial architecture was brought under some such rules. But the greater part of Roman architecture is later than Vitruvius, an architect and engineer who lived, and wrote in the time of Augustus. His book (*De Architectura*) is our great authority for the earlier Roman building and construction, but was primarily a handbook for architects and is based for the most part on the works of Greeks of the late 4th century B.C. and the Hellenistic period. The Renaissance exalted Vitruvius to the supreme authority on classical building; but it is none the less certain that there were no hard and fast rules, certain general proportions only being observed. It would be impossible here to treat of the details of the Roman Orders (*see* ORDER). In general the proportion is slenderer than that of the corresponding Greek Order, and there is a tendency towards greater elaboration combined with a decline in the quality of the execution. Columns are often unfluted, but the faces of the entablature left plain in Greek work are covered with decoration.

The Doric Order has almost invariably a base moulding probably taken from the Etruscan Doric or Tuscan column. Examples of Roman Doric are to be found in the Tabularium (78 B.C.) and in the lowest order of the Colosseum (A.D. 79) where it is used in conjunction with the arch. The temple of Hercules at Cori (*c.* 80 B.C.) is the only known Roman Doric temple.

The Ionic Order is used to a limited extent in temples and public buildings, though the number of isolated capitals found suggests that it had a certain vogue in private houses. The Romans seldom used the canted angle volute though in the temple of Saturn the capitals have four canted volutes. Other examples of this Order are the temple of Fortuna Virilis, the second orders of the theatre of Marcellus and the Colosseum, Trajan's forum at Rome and various buildings at Pompeii.

The Corinthian Order was by far the most popular with the Roman builder. It attracted by its richness and by the ease with which it could be used in any position owing to the identity of the four faces of the capital. The columns removed (by Sulla) from the temple of Zeus Olympios at Athens became the model, but the whole Order shows a progressive elaboration in detail with an elimination of plain surfaces combined with inferior workmanship. Examples of this Order are the temples of Mars Ultor and of Castor and Pollux (the latter one of the most beautiful examples in Roman architecture) in Rome, the temple of Vesta at Tivoli, Agrippa's portico to the Pantheon, etc.

The Composite capital is really a Corinthian capital with the tendril at the corner replaced by an Ionic volute. Alternatively it may be regarded as a four-voluted Ionic capital enriched with an acanthus necking. Examples of this capital are to be found on the triumphal arches of Titus and Septimius Severus, the baths of Diocletian, etc.

While the Romans did not abandon the original structural use of the column, its employment as a purely decorative feature became common. It was used in conjunction with the arch; and the skilful combination of these two opposing elements not only exerted a great influence on subsequent architecture but remains the great contribution of Rome to the history of architectural design. The Roman architects themselves never abandoned the traditional idea of supremacy of the Order but its use in the simpler manner of the Greek façade was insufficient to meet the demands of Roman buildings. With the help of the arch the spacing of columns was no longer governed by the load to be carried. This opened up new possibilities in design, and all over Italy and the provinces we see the monumental use of column and arch for triumphal arches from the time of Augustus to that of Constantine, as well as in such buildings as the baths of Caracalla and Diocletian, and the basilica of Maxentius. This naturally led to the development of new details in the shape of pedestals, niches, keystones, etc. Eventually we find arcaded walls without piers, the arch being taken direct on to the column and the entablature run over the arch as an archivolt. Examples of this are in the great Propylaea at Baalbek and in the palace of Diocle-

ROMAN ARCHITECTURE

BY COURTESY OF (10, 11) PROFESSORS CALZA AND GISMONDI; PHOTOGRAPHS, (1, 2) ANDERSON, (4) VERNACCI, (5) THE ROYAL ACADEMY OF ARTS, (6) ALINARI, (7, 9) EWING GALLOWAY

ARCHITECTURE OF ANCIENT ROME

1. View of the Roman Forum, looking toward the Capitol. At the upper right is the Arch of Septimius Severus; to its left, at a right angle are the remaining columns of the Temple of Saturn and in front of this the ruins of the Basilica Iulia, built by Julius Caesar, of which only the column bases remain. Three columns of the Temple of Castor and Pollux remain standing near the centre of the Forum, and in front of these are the ruins of the House of the Vestals. At the left of the picture is a part of the Palatine Hill with remains of buildings of Imperial Rome. 2. The so-called Temple of Fortuna Virilis, in the ancient Forum Boarium, Rome (end of 2nd century B.C.). 3. Drawing attributed to Piranesi of a detail of the interior of the Pantheon, originally built by Agrippa in A.D. 27 and re-erected under Hadrian, 120–124. 4. Roman bridge across the Tagus at Alcántara, Spain. 5. Restoration of the interior of a Roman Basilica by C. R. Cockerell (1788–1863), in the Royal Academy of Arts. 6. Arch of Trajan at Ancona. 7. Interior of the Baths of Caracalla, Rome. 8. Restoration of the interior of the Baths of Caracalla (see fig. 7), by William Walcot. 9. Roman Temple of Venus at Baalbek, Syria. 10. View of Ostia, the commercial port of ancient Rome. At the lower left are ruins of the ancient Forum and commercial buildings (horrea), and beyond these, with a curved wall, the theatre. 11. A street in Ostia

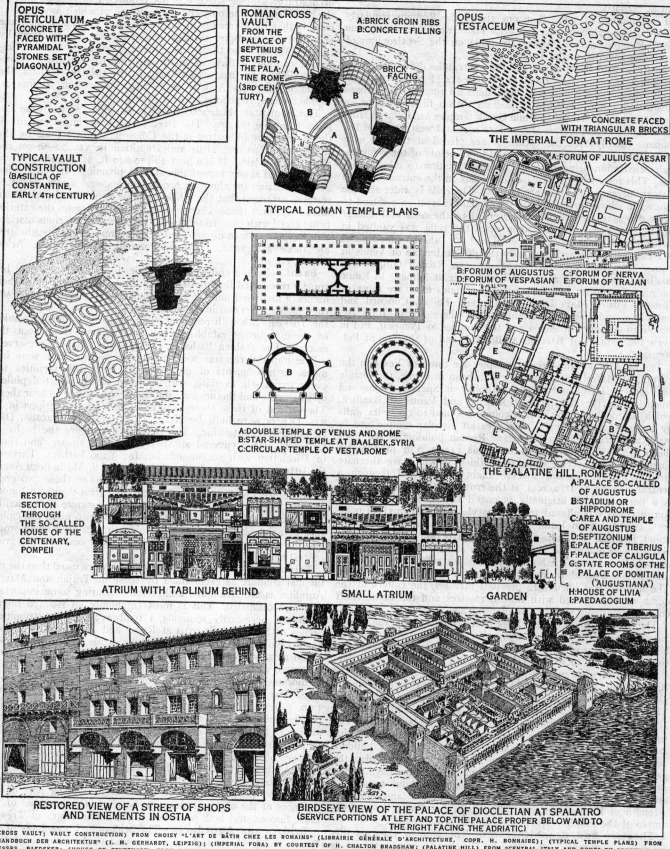

OPUS RETICULATUM (CONCRETE FACED WITH PYRAMIDAL STONES SET DIAGONALLY)

ROMAN CROSS VAULT FROM THE PALACE OF SEPTIMIUS SEVERUS, THE PALATINE ROME (3RD CENTURY)
A:BRICK GROIN RIBS
B:CONCRETE FILLING
BRICK FACING

OPUS TESTACEUM
CONCRETE FACED WITH TRIANGULAR BRICKS

THE IMPERIAL FORA AT ROME
A:FORUM OF JULIUS CAESAR
B:FORUM OF AUGUSTUS C:FORUM OF NERVA
D:FORUM OF VESPASIAN E:FORUM OF TRAJAN

TYPICAL VAULT CONSTRUCTION (BASILICA OF CONSTANTINE, EARLY 4TH CENTURY)

TYPICAL ROMAN TEMPLE PLANS
A:DOUBLE TEMPLE OF VENUS AND ROME
B:STAR-SHAPED TEMPLE AT BAALBEK, SYRIA
C:CIRCULAR TEMPLE OF VESTA, ROME

THE PALATINE HILL, ROME
A:PALACE SO-CALLED OF AUGUSTUS
B:STADIUM OR HIPPODROME
C:AREA AND TEMPLE OF AUGUSTUS
D:SEPTIZONIUM
E:PALACE OF TIBERIUS
F:PALACE OF CALIGULA
G:STATE ROOMS OF THE PALACE OF DOMITIAN ("AUGUSTIANA")
H:HOUSE OF LIVIA
I:PAEDAGOGIUM

RESTORED SECTION THROUGH THE SO-CALLED HOUSE OF THE CENTENARY, POMPEII
ATRIUM WITH TABLINUM BEHIND SMALL ATRIUM GARDEN

RESTORED VIEW OF A STREET OF SHOPS AND TENEMENTS IN OSTIA

BIRDSEYE VIEW OF THE PALACE OF DIOCLETIAN AT SPALATRO (SERVICE PORTIONS AT LEFT AND TOP. THE PALACE PROPER BELOW AND TO THE RIGHT FACING THE ADRIATIC)

(CROSS VAULT; VAULT CONSTRUCTION) FROM CHOISY "L'ART DE BÂTIR CHEZ LES ROMAINS" (LIBRAIRIE GÉNÉRALE D'ARCHITECTURE. COPR. H. BONNAIRE); (TYPICAL TEMPLE PLANS) FROM "HANDBUCH DER ARCHITEKTUR" (I. M. GERHARDT, LEIPZIG); (IMPERIAL FORA) BY COURTESY OF H. CHALTON BRADSHAW; (PALATINE HILL) FROM MESSRS. BAEDEKER; (HOUSE OF CENTENARY) FROM D'ESPOUY "FRAGMENTS D'ARCHITECTURE ANTIQUE" COPR. H. BONNAIRE; (STREET IN OSTIA) FROM "CENTRAL ITALY AND ROME" BY COURTESY OF GISMONDI; (PALACE OF DIOCLETIAN) FROM HEBRARD & ZEILLER "SPALATO" (MESSRS. MARSIN. COPR. H. BONNAIRE); BY COURTESY OF PROFESSORS CALZA AND

ROMAN INGENUITY IN THE USE OF LOCAL MATERIALS IS SHOWN BY VARIOUS WAYS OF FACING ROUGH WALLS OF RUBBLE FACED WITH STONE OR BRICK. CONCRETE, BRICK AND TILE WERE SKILLFULLY COMBINED IN VAULTING. THE IMPERIAL FORA, THE PALATINE HILL AND THE PALACE OF DIOCLETIAN ARE INGENIOUSLY COMPOSED. HOUSES AT POMPEII AND TENEMENTS AT OSTIA SHOW THE ADVANCED LIVING CONDITIONS

tian at Spalato.

For buildings of more than one storey the Romans regularly used the Orders above one another. There were four storeys on the Colosseum and seven (we are told) on the Septizonium of Septimius Severus on the Palatine.

Temples and Basilicas.—The Roman temples differed in many important respects from those of the Greeks. For the comparatively low stylobate with its three steps all round, the Romans substituted a high platform or podium with a flight of steps on the entrance façade. Again while Greek temples are isolated from other buildings and almost always face east and west, those of the Romans usually face the forum or are placed at the end of a street to close a vista, and are turned to all points of the compass, their orientation being governed by their relation to other buildings. This results in an increased emphasis on the entrance façade with an increased depth to the portico. The *cella* is wider and the colonnade which surrounds the Greek temple is often reduced to a row of engaged columns or pilasters along the cella walls except on the entrance front. In some cases the cella was vaulted in concrete and might have an apsidal end, *e.g.*, the so called baths of Diana at Nîmes and especially the double temple of Venus in Rome. The best preserved example of a Roman temple now existing is that known as the Maison Carrée at Nîmes. In Rome the most important temples of which remains exist are those of Fortuna Virilis, Mars Ultor, Castor and Pollux, Concord and Antoninus and Faustina. Besides these there are in Italy the temple of Minerva at Assisi and the temples at Pompeii, and in Syria the temples of Bacchus at Baalbek and of the Sun at Palmyra, etc.

The most important circular temples are those of Vesta in the Forum, of Mater Matuta and the Pantheon in Rome, the temple of Vesta at Tivoli and those of Jupiter at Spalato, Rome and Augustus on the Acropolis at Athens, and Venus at Baalbek, which has detached Corinthian columns joined to the cella walls by a segmental architrave. The greatest circular temple and in many respects the most important Roman building is the Pantheon (*q.v.*). This consists of a rotunda 142 ft. 6 in. in diameter surrounded by concrete walls 20 ft. thick, in which are alternate circular and rectangular niches. Light is admitted through a central opening 28 ft. across, at the crown of the dome. In front is a portico which originally belonged to the temple built by Agrippa and was altered from decastyle (ten columns) to octastyle (eight columns) and re-erected when the rotunda was built under Hadrian, A.D. 120–124. The construction of the rotunda and dome is one of the finest examples of Roman concrete work, the whole being strengthened by immense relieving arches and piers of brick set above one another in the thickness of the walls. The interior was lined with precious marbles, the coffers of the dome were decorated with bronze rosettes and the dome itself covered externally with bronze plates. (*See* TEMPLE.)

The Roman basilicas were large covered halls facing the forum, affording protection from the weather and giving space for the holding of courts of justice and for banking and other commercial transactions—all of which activities had in earlier days been carried on in the open market-place. On the forum in Rome are the Basilica Julia on the south side and the Basilica Aemilia on the north side—both of which had a central hall and side aisles. The Basilica Ulpia in Trajan's forum was similar in plan, but had at either end semicircular halls which served as law courts. The fourth and greatest of the basilicas is that begun by Maxentius and finished by Constantine, A.D. 306–310. This huge building covered 7,000 sq.yd. and followed in construction and plan the great hall of the Roman baths. The vaults over the bays on the north side are still to be seen overhanging without support, a striking testimony to the marvellous cohesion and enduring strength of Roman concrete. The basilica at Pompeii is an example of the simpler type general in the provinces.

Theatres and Amphitheatres.—The Roman theatres differed in several respects from the Greek. The auditorium was not excavated and the walls surrounding stage and seating were continuous, the entrance to the orchestra being by vaulted passages. As the chorus played no part in the Roman theatre the orchestra or dancing space was not required and became part of the auditorium. The only theatre in Rome of which any remains exist is that of Marcellus built by Augustus (13 B.C.) but there are numerous examples throughout the Roman empire especially in Asia Minor. The theatre at Orange, France, is the best preserved example. Others of importance are the theatre at Taormina, Sicily, two theatres at Pompeii, the theatre at Ostia, the Odeon of Herodes Atticus at Athens, theatres at Telmessus, Alinde, Aizani, Aspendus in Asia Minor, etc.

The Roman amphitheatre (*q.v.*) is in origin, as its name implies, a double theatre. The largest and most important of all the Roman amphitheatres is the Colosseum (*q.v.*) built by the Emperors Vespasian, Titus and Domitian in A.D. 72–80 on the site of Nero's lake. It is a huge ellipse 620 ft. × 513 ft. covering six acres and shows remarkable skill in planning. It had seating accommodation for about 45,000 spectators, and its 80 entrances were so arranged that the whole building could be cleared in an incredibly short time. The whole is built of concrete, the exterior being faced with travertine and the interior with precious marbles that have long since disappeared. Other important amphitheatres are those at Capua, Pompeii, Pozzuoli, Verona, Pola, Arles, Nîmes, etc.

Baths.—By the end of the republic, baths (*balneae*) had become a recognized feature of Roman life. Under the empire their numbers increased until at the beginning of the 4th century A.D. they numbered 1,000 in Rome alone. They were of the type of the Turkish bath with rooms at different temperatures. Remains of these ordinary establishments are common throughout the empire. The Stabian baths at Pompeii are the best preserved.

The imperial *thermae* were more than baths. They were immense establishments of great magnificence with facilities for every gymnastic exercise, with halls to which resorted philosophers, poets and rhetoricians and those who wished to hear them. The earliest of these *thermae* were those built by Agrippa in 21 B.C. Others were built by Nero, Titus, Trajan, Caracalla, Diocletian and Constantine. The best preserved are the baths of Caracalla, which covered an area of 110 yd. square, and those of Diocletian with accommodation for 3,200 bathers. Parts of the latter are now occupied by the church of S. Maria degli Angeli and by the Museo delle Terme. The remains of these two great establishments with their massive walls and great vaults are among the most impressive examples of Roman concrete construction. The planning of the *thermae* is governed by two main principles, that of axial planning, a distinctive feature in all Roman work, and the grouping of all subsidiary halls and rooms round a great central hall. (*See* BATHS.)

Triumphal Arches and Gateways.—More usual than the triumphal column, as exemplified by those of Trajan and Marcus Aurelius, is the triumphal arch commemorating some important event or campaign. This is most commonly an isolated monument not necessarily spanning a roadway; *e.g.*, the triumphal arches of Septimius Severus at Rome and of Trajan at Ancona are accessible only by flights of steps, while the archway itself is too narrow for ordinary use. The triumphal arch was usually decorated with columns and bas-reliefs of the chief events it commemorated and was frequently surmounted by a group of sculpture. The most important of these arches are the arch of Titus (A.D. 82) commemorating the capture of Jerusalem, the arches of Septimius Severus and Constantine in Rome, and Trajan's arches at Beneventum and Ancona. There are several other triumphal arches in the provinces, notably those of Tiberius at Orange, of Augustus at Susa and Caracalla at Tebesa. Others exist at Rheims, Pola, Timgad, Maktar, etc.

The monumental city gate while sometimes serving a commemorative purpose differs from the arch in being part of the defences of the city and meant to be used. Of these one of the most famous and best preserved is the Porta Nigra at Trèves.

Bridges and Aqueducts.—The bridges and aqueducts of the Romans may be treated as monumental works in spite of their utilitarian character. The most famous examples of Roman aqueducts are the Pont du Gard, Nîmes, and the aqueducts at Tarragona and Segovia in Spain. Those which crossed the Campagna bringing water to Rome from the hills are also well known and impressive in their decay.

There are not many of the larger Roman bridges now remaining. The best preserved is that built by Augustus and Tiberius at Rimini. The finest is that across the Tagus at Alcantara in Spain.

Tombs.—The larger Roman tombs consisted of an earth mound or tumulus surrounded by a ring of masonry rising usually to a considerable height. Few of these now exist, the most notable being the tomb of Cecilia Metella on the Via Appia and the mausoleum of Hadrian, now the castle of St. Angelo. The smaller tombs, in particular those known as *columbaria* (*see* COLUMBARIUM), are usually underground, though there is sometimes an upper storey, often in the shape of a small temple *in antis,* built of cut brick from which steps lead down to the tomb proper. There is a line of such tombs just outside Rome along the Via Appia and also along the Via Latina. Examples of Roman funeral monuments of various kinds exist along the Street of Tombs at Pompeii and in the provinces, in Syria at Palmyra, Jerusalem and Petra.

Palaces.—By the end of the republican period the Palatine hill had become by far the most desirable residential quarter of Rome. It was therefore natural that the Roman emperors from Augustus onwards should choose to live on it, gradually acquiring further property until the whole hill, except that part hallowed by tradition or by the presence of temples, became the imperial residence. Augustus himself bought and enlarged the house known as the House of Livia which still exists. Tiberius built a palace on the north-west side of the hill. Another palace was built on the south-east corner of the hill by Claudius or more probably by Nero. Some rooms of this palace have recently been discovered, though both it and the palace of Tiberius were partially destroyed by fire. The central space was covered by the palace of the Flavians, Domitian with his architect Rabirius being responsible for a magnificent suite of State apartments and for the sunken garden called the *hippodromus.* Hadrian extended the palace towards the forum and the House of the Vestals and finally Septimius Severus raised a huge structure overlooking the Circus Maximus, partly on the top of Hadrian's work and partly on an artificial platform supported on arches and finishing with his Septizonium. Remains of these buildings, often one above the other, cover the Palatine. Of the famous Golden House of Nero on the site now covered by the baths of Titus, the Colosseum and the basilica of Maxentius, very little remains.

The Villa of Hadrian (*q.v.*) at Tivoli, begun about A.D. 123, was another sumptuous imperial residence with parks and gardens on a large scale. There are remains of great brick and concrete structures and the unevenness of the site necessitated large terraces and flights of steps. All the buildings are Roman in style and method of construction, though with Greek names.

The palace of Diocletian at Spalato (Split), to which he retired on his abdication in A.D. 305, combines a palace with a fortress. It consists of an immense rectangle surrounded by walls guarded by towers on three sides and on the fourth to the south protected by the sea. The palace itself is on the south side with a great gallery 520 ft. long with 51 windows overlooking the sea. (*See* PALACE.)

Private Houses.—In the Roman world there were two types of houses, the *domus* and the *insula.* The word *villa* is used to describe an estate complete with house, grounds and subsidiary buildings. Of Roman villas there are very few remains and our chief authority is Pliny who gives a detailed description of his Laurentine villa. Hadrian's villa at Tivoli, an imperial residence, cannot be treated as typical. The *domus* type of house as exemplified at Pompeii (*q.v.*) has long been regarded as the typical Roman house, though in Rome itself very few remains of the *domus* have come to light, the chief examples being the House of the Vestal Virgins on the forum and that of Livia on the Palatine. The *domus* consisted of suites of rooms grouped round a central hall or *atrium,* to which were often added further suites behind grouped round a colonnaded court or *peristyle.* There are few windows on the street, light being obtained from the *atrium* or *peristyle.* The amount of ground required for such a house

while perfectly feasible in a country town such as Pompeii, would have made them beyond the means of all but the richest in a crowded city like Rome. From Latin writers we have long known that there were in Rome great blocks of flats or tenements to which the term *insulae* was applied. Recent excavations at Ostia (*q.v.*) have now revealed the design of these blocks. Planned on three or four floors with strict regard to economy of space they depended for light from the exterior, unlike the *domus* with its central court. Independent apartments had separate entrances with direct access to the street. Since Ostia is a typical town of the 1st and 2nd centuries A.D. and is almost a suburb of Rome itself, it is natural to suppose that *insulae* at Rome would present similar features. (*See* HOUSE.)

Town Planning.—While the Romans have become justly famous for the skilful planning of their towns all over the empire, Rome itself presents a strong contrast with its complete lack of any systematic scheme. For this the natural topography of the site is mainly responsible together with the conditions under which Rome grew into a great city.

The Forum (*q.v.*), the original market place, remained always irregular in plan and was soon far too small for the amount of business transacted in it. The congestion was to some extent relieved by the forums built by Julius Caesar, Augustus, Nero, Vespasian and Trajan. These were all planned on axial lines. Attempts were made to improve the street communications, the most notable being Julius Caesar's widening of the Via Lata, and colonnades and porticoes were built to protect passers-by from the sun and rain. Various emperors also laid down regulations governing the construction and height of buildings. None the less the planning of Rome was a series of expedients without any system, and after each of the fires which successively devastated great parts of the city, Rome grew up again on its old lines, and the evils of its narrow streets, poor drainage and general overcrowding became increasingly difficult to remedy.

The Roman town in the provinces on the other hand is normally planned round a central forum, close to, but separated from, the crossing of the two main roads which ran usually east to west and north to south. Less important roads run at right angles to the main roads. The forum itself is surrounded by a colonnade and facing it are the principal buildings, temples, basilica, senate-house and covered market. The whole is planned in a logical way. The forum at Pompeii may be taken as a typical example.

The layout of a whole town can be most easily seen in some of the towns in north Africa, *e.g.,* Timgad, Tebesa, Thuburbo, where there has been little or no subsequent building to modify the original lines of the plan. (*See* TOWN AND CITY PLANNING. See also ARCHITECTURE; PERIODS OF ART.)

BIBLIOGRAPHY.—A. Désgodetz, *Les Édifices antiques de Rome* (1682; new enlarged ed., 1843); J. Fergusson, *A History of Architecture* (3 vols., 1865—2nd and 3rd ed., by R. P. Spiers, 1893); A. Choisy, *L'Art de bâtir chez les Romains* (1873), and *Histoire de l'Architecture* (2 vols., 1899); Sir B. Fletcher, *A History of Architecture on the Comparative Method* (1896; 8th ed., rev. and enlarged, 1928); J. Durm, *Die Baukunst der Etrusker und der Römer* (Stuttgart, 1905); F. Noack, *Die Baukunst des Altertums* (1910; 2nd ed., 1912); F. Kimball and G. H. Edgell, *A History of Architecture* (with a bibl., 1917); G. T. Rivoira, *Architettura romana* (Milan, 1917; Eng. trans. by G. McN. Rushforth, 1925); W. J. Anderson and R. P. Spiers, *The Architecture of Ancient Rome* (with a valuable bibl., 1927). (H. C. BR.; M. BRA.)

ROMAN ARMY. In the long life of the ancient Roman army, the most effective and long-lived military institution known to history, we may distinguish four principal stages. (1) In the earliest age of Rome the army was a national or citizen levy such as we find in the beginnings of all states. (2) This grew into the Republican army of conquest, which gradually subdued Italy and the Mediterranean world. A citizen army of infantry, varying in size with the needs of each year, it eventually developed into a mercenary force with long service and professional organization. This became (3) the Imperial army of defence, which developed from a strictly citizen army into one which represented the provinces as well as Italy, and was a garrison rather than a field army. Lastly, (4) the assaults of the Barbarian horsemen compelled both the creation of a field force distinct from the frontier garrisons and the inclusion of a large mounted element, which soon counted for much more than the infantry. The Roman army had been one of foot soldiers; in its latest phase it was marked by that predominance of the horseman which characterized the earlier centuries of the middle ages.

So far as we can follow this long development in its details, it was continuous. So unbroken, indeed, is the growth that many of the military technical terms survived in use from epoch to epoch, unchanged in form though deeply modified in meaning, and ordinary readers often miss the diversity which underlies this seemingly unchanged system. The term *legio,* for example, occurs in all the four stages above outlined. But in each its significance varies. Throughout, it denoted citizen-soldiers; throughout, it denoted also a force which was chiefly, if not wholly, heavy infantry. But the setting of these two constant features varies from age to age. In the first period *legio* was the "levy," the whole host summoned to take the field. In the second period it was not the whole levy, but one of the principal units into which developing organization had divided that levy; the "legion" was now a body of some 5,000 men—the number of "legions" varied with the circumstances, and the army included other troops besides citizens, though they were for the most part unimportant. In the third or Imperial age there were many legions (indeed, a fixed number) quartered in fixed fortresses; there were also other troops, numerous and important, if not yet so formidable as the legionaries. Finally, the legions became smaller units, and the other troops of the army, notably the cavalry, became the real fighting-line of Rome. (*See* LEGION.)

First Stage.—The history of the earliest Roman army is, as one might expect, both ill-recorded and contaminated with much legend and legal fiction. We read of a primitive force of 300 riders and 3,000 foot soldiers, in which the horseman counted for almost everything. But the numbers are clearly artificial and invented, while the pre-eminence accorded to the cavalry has no sequel in later Roman history. We reach firmer ground with the organization ascribed to Servius Tullius. In this system the army included all citizens from 17 to 60 years of age, those under 47 for service in the field, the older men for garrison duty in Rome. The soldiers were grouped at first by their wealth—that is, their ability to provide their own horses, armour, etc.—into cavalry, heavy infantry, a remainder which it would be polite to call light infantry, and some artificers. The heavy infantry counted for most. Armed with long spears and divided into the three orders of *hastati, principes* and *triarii* (the origins and real senses of these names are lost), they formed a phalanx, and charged in a mass, while the cavalry protected the wings. The men were enrolled for a year—that is, for the summer campaign; in the autumn, like all primitive armies, they went home.

Second Stage.—From this Servian army a series of changes which we cannot trace in detail produced the Republican army of conquest. Our ancient authorities ascribe the chief reforms to the half-legendary Camillus (*q.v.*), who introduced the beginnings of pay and long service, improved the armour and weapons, abolished the phalanx and substituted for it an open order based on small subdivisions (maniples), each containing two centuries.

Whatever the truth about Camillus, some such reforms must at some time have been carried through, to convert the Servian system into the army which was engaged for nearly three centuries (from 350 B.C.) in conquering Italy and the world. This army broke in succession the stout native soldiers of Italy and the mountaineers of Spain and overthrew the trained Macedonian phalanx. Once only did it fail—against Hannibal. (*See* PUNIC WARS.) But not even Hannibal could oust it from entrenchments, and not even his victories could permanently break its *moral.* Much of its strength lay in the same qualities which made the Puritan soldiers of Cromwell terrible—the excellent character of the common soldiers, the rigid discipline, the high training. Credit, too, must be given to the genius of Scipio Africanus and to the more commonplace capacities of many fairly able generals. But the organism itself deserves attention, and, as it chances, we know much about it, mainly from Polybius. Its elements were three:—

(A) The principal unit was the legion, generally a division of

4,500 men—3,000 heavy infantry, 1,200 lighter-armed (*velites*), 300 horse—though sometimes including as many as 6,000 men. The heavy infantry were the backbone of the legion. They were levied from the whole body of Roman citizens who had some private means and who had not already served 16 campaigns, and in effect formed a yeoman force. For battle they were divided into 1,200 *hastati*, 1,200 *principes* and 600 *triarii*: all had a large shield, metal helmet, leather cuirass, short Spanish thrusting and cutting sword, and in addition the *hastati* and *principes* each carried two short heavy throwing spears (*pila*), while the *triarii* had ordinary long spears. They were drawn up in three lines: (1) *hastati*, (2) *principes*, (3) *triarii*; the first two were divided into ten maniples each (of 120 men, when the legion only counted 4,500), the third into ten maniples of half the strength. According to the ordinary interpretation of our ancient authorities, the maniples were arranged in a chess-board fashion (*quincunx*), the idea being that the front row of maniples could retire through the intervals in the second row without disordering it, and the second row could similarly advance. The procedure in fighting seems to have been simple: the front line discharged a volley of *pila* and rushed in with the short sword—a sequence much like the volley and bayonet charge of the 18th century—and if this failed, the second line went in turn through the same process; the third line of *triarii*, armed with spear instead of *pilum*, formed a reserve. The *velites*, armed with javelins, came to be used as skirmishers. The cavalry seem to have been of little account—a natural result if, as we have reason to think, the horses were small and stirrups were not used. Scipio Africanus alone developed his cavalry into a decisive instrument.

The officers of the legion consisted of: (*a*) Six tribunes, in part elected by the comitia, in part appointed by the consuls, and holding command in rotation. They were either veteran officers, sometimes even ex-magistrates, or young noblemen beginning their career. (*b*) Sixty centurions, each commanding one century, or, rather, a pair commanding each maniple. They were chosen by the tribunes from among the veteran soldiers serving at the time and were arranged in a complicated hierarchy, by means of which a centurion might move upwards till he became *primus pilus*, senior centurion of the first maniple of *triarii*, the chief officer of that rank in the legion. (*c*) There were also standard-bearers and other under-officers, for whom reference must be made to specialist publications.

(B) Besides the legions, composed of citizens, the Roman army included contingents from the Italian "allies" (*socii*), subjects of Rome. These contingents appear to have been large; in many armies we find as many *socii* as legionaries, but we are ignorant of details. The men were armed and drilled like the legionaries, but they served not in legions but in cohorts, smaller units of 400–500 men, and their conventional positions seem to have been on the wings of the legions. They were principally infantry, but included also a fairly large proportion of cavalry.

(C) Besides legionaries and *socii*, the Roman army included non-Italian troops of special kinds, Balearic slingers, Numidian horsemen, Rhodians, Celtiberians and others: at Trasimene, for example (217 B.C.), the Roman army included 600 Cretan archers. The numbers of these *auxilia* varied; probably they were not numerous till the later days of the Republic.

Composition and Size of Armies in the Second Stage.—According to the general practice, each of the two consuls, if he took the field alone, commanded an army of two legions with appropriate *socii*. If the two consuls combined their forces, commanding the joint force in rotation (as often occurred), the total would be—according to our authorities—four legions, each of 4,200 infantry, the same number of "allied" infantry (in all 33,600 infantry), 1,200 legionary cavalry and about 3,600 "allied" cavalry = 38,400 men. Such, for example, was the Roman army at Trebia (218 B.C.), where (says Polybius) there fought 16,000 legionaries and 20,000 allied infantry. The total number of men in the field could be increased; we even hear of 23 legions serving at one time in the Second Punic War. Just before this war, in 225 B.C., the total man-power of Rome was reckoned at three-quarters of a million, of which about 65,000 were in the field and 55,000 were in a reserve at Rome; of the total, 325,000 were Roman citizens and 443,000 (apparently a rough estimate) were allies. The battle order in normal circumstances was simple. In the centre stood the legionary infantry: on each side of that was the allied infantry: on the wings the cavalry. But sometimes the legions were held in reserve and the brunt (and honour) of the fight was left to the allies. Frequently the attack was begun by one wing, as by Caesar at Pharsalus. At Ilipa in Spain Scipio surprised his enemy by a last hour variation of the accustomed order. Putting his Spanish auxiliaries in the centre, his Roman troops on the wings, he "re-fused" his centre and attacked with both wings.

Development from the Second Stage to the Third.—Towards the end of the Republic many changes began to work themselves out in the Roman army. If Camillus began the system of pay and long service, it was effectually developed by long foreign wars in Spain and in the East. Moreover, the growth of Rome as a wealthy state tended to wreck the old theory that every citizen was a soldier, and favoured a division of labour between, *e.g.*, the merchant and the military, while the increasing complexity of war required a longer training and a more professional soldier. In consequence, the old restriction of legionary service to men with some sort of private property was abolished by Marius about 104 B.C. and the legionaries now became wholly proletariate and professionals. By a second change, also connected with the name of Marius, the legion was reorganized as a body of 6,000 men in 60 centuries, divided into ten cohorts instead of (as hitherto) into 30 maniples; the unit of tactical action thus became a body of 600 instead of 120. This was probably an adaptation within the legion of the system of cohorts already in use for the contingents of the *socii*. Soon after, the extension of the Roman franchise to all Italians converted allies and subjects into citizens, and the *socii* into legionaries. A fourth change abolished the legionary cavalry and greatly increased the *auxilia* (C., p. 396).

Third Stage.—*The Imperial Army of Defence.*—The evils of the Civil Wars (49–31 B.C.) furnished the first emperor, Augustus with both the opportunity and the necessity for reforming the army. Disorganization had reigned for 20 years. It was needful to restore loyalty and system alike. Augustus did this, as he did all his work, by adapting the past: yet there is some truth in the view that his army reforms were his greatest and most original work. The main lines of his work are simple. The Imperial army consisted henceforward of two classes or grades of troops, about equal in numbers if unequal in importance. The first grade was the legions, recruited from Roman citizens, whether resident in Italy or in the provinces. The second grade was formed by the *auxilia*, recruited from the subjects (not the citizens) of the Empire in the provinces, organized in cohorts and *alae* and corresponding somewhat to both the *socii* and the auxiliaries (B, C, above) of the Republican army. There were also in Rome special "household" troops (see PRAETORIANS), and a large body of *vigiles* who were both fire brigade and police.

Details of Troops.—(A) The legion of the Empire was what Marius had left it—6,000 heavy infantry divided into ten cohorts: Augustus added only 120 horsemen to serve as despatch-riders and the like. The supreme command was no longer in the hands of the six tribunes. According to a practice which had sprung up in the latest Republic it was in the hands of a *legatus legionis*, deputy of the general (now of the emperor, commander-in-chief of the whole army) and a man usually of senatorial rank and position. The six tribunes assisted him in theory; in practice they were now little more than young men of good birth learning their business or wasting their time. The real officers of the legion were the 60 centurions, men who (at least in the early Empire) generally rose from the ranks, and who knew their work. The senior centurion, *primus pilus*, was an especially important officer, and on retirement frequently became *praefectus castrorum*, "camp adjutant," or obtained other promotion. Below the centurions were under-officers, standard-bearers, *optiones*, clerks and the like: The men themselves were recruited from the body of Roman citizens (though we may believe that birth-certificates were not always demanded). During the 1st century Italy, and particularly north Italy, provided the bulk of the recruits. After A.D. 70, recruiting in Italy for

the legions practically ceased and men were drawn from the Romanized towns of the provinces. After Hadrian, each province seems to have supplied most of the men for the legion (if any) stationed in it, and so many sons of soldiers born during service (*castrenses*) flocked to the army that a military caste almost grew up. The term of service was, in full, 20 years, at least in theory, but recruiting was voluntary and when men were short discharges were often withheld. On discharge the ex-legionary received a bounty or land: many *coloniae* (municipalities) were established in the provinces by certain emperors for the special purpose of taking discharged veterans—according to a custom of which the first instances occur in the late Republican age. On the whole, the legionary was still the typical "Roman" soldier. If he was no longer Italian, he was generally of citizen birth, and always of citizen rank, and his connection with the Empire and the Government was real. Each legion bore a number and a title (*e.g.*, II. Augusta, III. Gallica). The custom of using such titles and numbers can be detected sporadically in the late Republic, and many titles and numbers then borne by legions passed on into the Empire with the legions themselves. As Augustus gradually became master of the world, he found himself with three armies, his own and those of Lepidus and Antony; from the three he chose certain legions to form his new standing army, and he left these with the titles and numbers which they had previously borne, although that concession resulted in three legions numbered III. and two numbered IV., V., VI. and X. respectively. Similar titles and numbers were given to legions raised afterwards either to fill up gaps caused by disaster or to increase the army.

(B) Besides the legions Augustus developed a new order of *auxilia*. Auxiliaries (as is said above) had served occasionally in the Republican armies since about 250 B.C., and in the later Republic large bodies of them had been enlisted in the armies of contending generals. Thus Caesar in Gaul enrolled a division of native Gauls, free men but not citizens of Rome, which ranked from the first in all but legal status as a legion, the "Alaudae," and in due course was formally admitted to the legionary list (legio V.). But this use of non-citizens had been limited in extent and confined in normal circumstances to special troops such as slingers or bowmen. This casual practice Augustus reduced, or rather extended, to system, following in many details the scheme of the Republican *socii* and veiling the novelty under old titles. Henceforward, regiments of infantry (*cohortes*) or cavalry (*alae*), 500 or 1,000 strong, were regularly raised (apparently, by voluntary recruiting) from the non-citizen populations of the provinces and formed a force almost equal in numbers (and ultimately much more than equal) to the legions. The men who served in these units were less well paid and served longer than the legionaries; on their discharge they received a bounty and the Roman franchise for themselves, their wives and children. They were commanded by Roman *praefecti* or *tribuni*, and were no doubt required to understand Roman orders; they must have generally become Romanized and fit for the citizenship, but they were occasionally (at least in the 1st century A.D.) permitted to retain tribal weapons and methods of fighting and to serve under the command of tribal leaders, who were at once their chiefs and Roman officers. These auxiliaries provided both the whole of the archers, etc., and nearly the whole of the cavalry of the army; they also included many foot regiments. A peculiar arrangement (to which no exact parallel seems to occur in any other army) was that a cohort of 500 men might include 380 foot and 120 horse and a cohort of 1,000 men or 760 foot and 240 horse (*cohors equitata*), and an *ala* might similarly include a proportion of foot (*ala peditata*). Each regiment bore a number and a title, the latter often derived from the officer who had raised the corps (*ala Indiana*, raised by one Julius Indus), or, still more often, from the tribe which supplied the first recruits (*cohors VII. Gallorum, cohors II. Hispanorum* and the like). To what extent recruiting remained territorial is uncertain: after the 1st century, probably, the territorial names meant in most cases very little.

Composition of Armies and Distribution of Troops in the Third Stage.—If the system of legions and *auxilia* in the early Empire was novel, the use made of them was no less so. The later Republic offers to the student the spectacle of large field armies, and though it also reveals a counter tendency to assign special legions to special provinces, that tendency is very feeble. Augustus ended the era of large field armies: he could not afford to leave such weapons for future pretenders to the throne. By keeping the Empire within set frontiers, he developed the counter tendency. That policy exactly suited the military position in his time. The early Roman empire had not to face—like modern empires—the danger of a war with an equal enemy, needing the mobilization of all its national forces. From Augustus till A.D. 250 Rome had no conterminous foe from whom to fear invasion. Parthia, her one and dangerous equal, was far away in the East and little able to strike home. Elsewhere, her frontiers bordered more or less wild barbarians, who might often harass, but could not do serious harm. To meet this there was need, not of a strong army concentrated in one or two cantonments, but of many small garrisons scattered along each frontier, with a few stronger fortresses to act as military centres adjacent to these garrisons.

Accordingly, a system grew up under Augustus and his immediate successors whereby the whole army was distributed along the frontiers or in specially disorderly districts (such as north-west Spain) in permanent garrisons. On the actual frontiers and on the chief roads leading to them were numerous cohorts and *alae* of auxiliaries, garrisoning each its own *castellum* of 3–7 acres in extent. Close behind the frontiers, or even on them, were the 25 legions, each (with a few exceptions of early date) holding its own fortress (*castra stativa* or *hiberna*) of 50–60 acres. Details varied at different times. Sometimes, where no Rhine or Danube helped, and where outside enemies were many, the frontier was fortified by a wall of wooden palisades (as in part of Germany; *see* LIMES GERMANICUS) or of earth or stone (as in Britain, *see* BRITAIN: *Roman*), or the boundary might be guarded by a road patrolled from forts planted along it (as in part of Roman Africa). The result was a long frontier guard covering Britain and Europe from the German ocean to the Black sea, and the upper Euphrates valley, and the edge of the Sahara south of Tunis and Algeria and Morocco, while the wide Empire within saw little of its soldiers.

The following table shows the disposition of the legions about A.D. 120 and for many decades subsequently. It would be impossible, even if space allowed, to add the auxiliaries, as the details of their distribution are too little known. But as the number of auxiliaries in any province was probably rather greater than the number of legionaries, the sizes of the various provincial armies can be calculated roughly. Thus Britain was held probably by 35,000–40,000 men. Each provincial army was commanded either by the governor of the province or (in a few exceptional cases) by the senior *legatus* of the legions stationed there:—

Britain	II.	Augusta (*Isca Silurum*, now Caerleon).
„	VI.	Victrix (*Eburacum*, York).
„	XX.	Valeria Victrix (*Deva*, Chester).
Lower Germany (=lower Rhine)	I.	Minervia (*Bonna*, Bonn).
„	XXX.	Ulpia Victrix (*Vetera*, Xanten).
Upper Germany	XXII.	Primigenia (*Moguntiācum*, Mainz).
„	VIII.	Augusta (*Argentorate*, Strassburg).
Pannonia (Danube to Semlin)	X.	Gemina (*Vindobona*, Vienna).
„	XIV.	Gemina (*Carnuntum*, Petronell).
„	I.	Adiutrix (*Brigetio*, near Komorn).
„	II.	Adiutrix (*Aquincum*, near Budapest).
Upper Moesia (Middle Danube)	IV.	Flavia (*Singidūnum*, Belgrade).
„	VII.	Claudia (*Viminacium*, Kostolac).
Dacia (now Transylvania)	XIII.	Gemina (*Apulum*, Karlsburg).
Lower Moesia (Lower Danube)	I.	Italica (*Novae*, Sistov).
„	XI.	Claudia (*Durostorum*, Silistria).
„	V.	Macedonica (*Troesmis*, Iglitza).
Asia Minor (Cappadocia)	XV.	Apollinaris (*Satala*, Armenian frontier).
„	XII.	Fulminata (*Melitene*, on upper Euphrates).
Syria	XVI.	Flavia (*Samosata*, on upper Euphrates).
Syria	IV.	Scythica ⎫
„	VI.	Ferrata ⎬ near Antioch (?).
„	III.	Gallica ⎭
Judaea	X.	Fretensis (Jerusalem).
Arabia	III.	Cyrenaica (*Bostra*).
Egypt	II.	Trajana (near Alexandria—a disorderly city).
Africa	III.	Augusta (*Lambaesis*).
Spain	VII.	Gemina (*Legio*, Leon, in north-west Spain).

The total of legionaries may be put at about 180,000 men, the auxiliaries at about 200,000. If we exclude the "household" troops at Rome, the police fleets on the Mediterranean and the local militia in some districts, we may put the regular army of the Empire at about 400,000 men. This army, as will be plain, was framed on much the same ideas as the British army of the 19th century. It was meant not to fight against a first-class foreign power, but to keep the peace and guard the frontiers of dominions threatened by scattered barbarian raids and risings. Field army there was none, nor any need. If special danger threatened or some special area was to be conquered—such as southern Britain (A.D. 43)—detachments (*vexillationes*) were sent by legions and sometimes also by auxiliaries in adjacent provinces, and a field force was formed sufficient for the moment and the work.

Change from the Third Period to the Fourth.—Two principal causes brought gradual change to the Augustan army. In the first place, the *pax Romana* brought such prosperity to many districts that they ceased to provide sufficient recruits. The Romans, like the British in India, had more and more to look to uncivilized regions and even beyond their borders. Hence comes, in the 2nd century and after, a new class of *numeri* or *cunei* or *vexillationes* who used (like the earlier auxiliaries) their national arms and tactics and imported into the army a more and more non-Roman element. This tendency became very marked in the 3rd century and bore serious fruit at its close. And, secondly, the old days of mere frontier defence were over. The barbarians began to beat on the walls of the Empire as early as A.D. 160: about A.D. 250 they here and there got through, and they came henceforward in ever-growing numbers. Moreover, they came on horseback, bringing new tactics for the Roman infantry to face, and they came in masses. We may doubt if any military system could have permanently stayed this series of human tides. But the Empire did what it could. It enlisted barbarians to fight barbarians, and added freely to the non-Roman elements of the army. It increased the relative strength of its cavalry and began to organize a distinct field force.

Fourth Period.—The results are seen in the reforms of Diocletian and Constantine the Great (A.D. 284–*circa* 320). New frontier guards, styled *limitanei* or *riparienses*, were established, and the old army was reorganized in field forces which accompanied or might accompany the emperors in war (*comitatenses*, *palatini*). The importance of the legions dwindled; the chief soldiers were the mercenaries, mostly Germans, enlisted from among the barbarians. New titles now appear, and it becomes plain that in many points the new order is not the old. The details of the system are as complicated as all the administrative machinery of that age. Here it is enough to point out that the significance of such officers and titles as the *dux* and the *comes* (duke, count) lies ahead in the history of the middle ages, and not in the past, the history of the Roman army itself.

War Office, General Staff.—Under the Republic we do not find, and indeed should not expect to find, any central body which was especially entrusted with the development of the army system or military finance or military policy in wars. Even under the Empire, however, there was no such organization. The emperor, as commander-in-chief, and his more or less unofficial advisers doubtless decided questions of policy. But the army was so much a group of provincial armies that much was left to the chief officers in each province. Here, as elsewhere in the Empire, we trace a love if not for Home Rule, at least for Devolution. There was, however, a central finance office in Rome for the special purpose of meeting the bounties (or equivalent) due to discharged soldiers. This was established by Augustus in A.D. 6 with the title *aerarium* *militare,* and had, for receipts, the yield of two taxes, a 5% legacy duty and a 1% on sales (or perhaps only on auction-sales). The legacy duty did not touch legacies to near relations or legacies of small amount.

BIBLIOGRAPHY.—Liebenam, "Exercitus," in Pauly-Wissowa, *Realencyklopädie;* Domaszewski, in Mommsen-Marquardt's *Handbuch der römischen Altertümer* (2nd ed., Leipzig, 1884), vol. v., pp. 319–612; H. Delbrück, *Geschichte der Kriegskunst,* vol. i., 2nd ed. (Berlin, 1907); E. Lammert, "Die Entwicklung der römischen Taktik," in *Neue Jahrbücher für das klassische Altertum,* ix. 100–128, 169–187; Cagnat's article "Legio" in Daremberg and Saglio, *Dictionnaire des antiquités grecques et romaines;* E. G. Hardy, *Studies in Roman History* (London, 1906–09); Th. Mommsen, "Das römische Militärwesen seit Diocletian," in *Hermes,* xxiv. 195–279; P. Coussin, *Les Armes Romaines* (Paris, 1926), the articles "Legio" and "Exercitus" in Pauly-Wissowa, *Realencyklopädie;* Macartney's article "The Military Indebtedness of Ancient Rome to Etruria" in *Memoirs of the American Academy in Rome* i., 121 (1917). (F. J. H.)

ROMAN ART. Modern archaeology has fully vindicated the significance of the Roman output in the field of art; yet the Romans do not, at the outset, present themselves as belonging to that small group of peoples endowed, as it were, with a spontaneous capacity for art, and the impulse to artistic creation latent in their character hardly began to develop before the 4th century B.C. Up to that time such works of art as were produced in, or imported into, Rome were apparently in the main Etruscan or Graeco-Etruscan; and in Rome, as in Latium, Etruscan artists were commissioned to decorate the temples of wood and terra-cotta which preceded the more sumptuous marble structures of the late republic and the empire. The discovery at Veii in 1917 of a magnificent Apollo in terra-cotta (*see* ETRURIA) of early 5th century style, satisfactorily confirms the tradition that Volca, an artist from Veii, made the cultus statue of the god for the temple of Jupiter Capitolinus and executed statuary for other Roman temples as well, while from considerations of style and technique the celebrated Capitoline Wolf is now assigned to the same cycle of Veientine art. Etruscan art, though originally dependent for many of its motives and for its technique on Greek models, developed an art of portraiture in which we can from the first trace that naturalism and close attention to detail which afterwards blossomed into the realism characteristic of Rome. The same desire for making permanent the memory of their dead, which led the Etruscans to decorate their funeral urns with a lid in the form of the human head, prompted the Romans to produce waxen masks, or *imagines,* which were preserved in the houses of the Roman aristocracy and were carried in funeral processions of members of the family. The Barberini statue illustrates the custom.

In architecture, too, Roman builders learnt much from their Etruscan neighbours, from whom they borrowed the characteristic form of their temples, and perhaps also the prominent use of the arch and vault. But the stream of Etruscan influence was met by a counter-current from the south, where the Greek colonies in Campania provided a natural channel by which Hellenic ideas reached the Latin race, and, at an early date, Roman architects modified the purely Etruscan type of temple under the influence of western Greek models. Greek modellers in terra-cotta came to Rome (first in 496 B.C., to decorate the temple of Ceres Liber and Libera) and worked by the side of the Etruscans. The conquests of the later republic, however, brought the Romans into more direct contact with the art of Greece proper; victorious generals adorned their triumphs with masterpieces of Greek art, and, when Philhellenism became the ruling fashion at Rome, wealthy connoisseurs formed private collections drawn from the Greek provinces, while Greek craftsmen were employed in the decoration of the palaces of the Roman nobles and capitalists. Every empire-builder—Sulla, Pompey, Caesar—dreamed in turn of modelling Rome on the plan of an Hellenistic city. Even portraiture borrowed an Hellenic character in the time of Caesar and Cicero. Yet this period also saw the beginning of the historical, or, more properly, the commemorative method to whose development the empire gave so powerful an impulse. An early example is afforded by the reliefs representing a Roman sacrifice and other episodes from the life of the army, which adorn the front face of an altar believed to have been set up by Cn. Domitius Aheno-

barbus shortly before 30 B.C. (Plate II., fig. 11).

Augustus enlisted art, as he did literature, in the service of the new order. The technical dexterity which characterizes all forms of art in this period—silver plate and stucco decoration, as well as sculpture in the round or in relief—is largely due to Greek influence; but the form is filled with a new content, the result of a determination on the part of Augustus to shift the centre of artistic activity from Greece to Rome by associating it with new religious and political ideals. But the Roman spirit, after producing in harmony with that of Greece such brilliant results, triumphed once more under Trajan in that novel "epic in stone" with which the column that bears his name is adorned. Along the path thus marked out, Roman art continued to progress, scarcely disturbed by a brief renaissance of classicism under Hadrian. The historical reliefs which survive from the Antonine period, and more especially the sarcophagi, show that the new leaven was at work, though it soon mingled with new influences which brought about radical changes in the whole domain of plastic art. Colour, rather than form, began to take the highest place in the gamut of artistic values. Painting, as recent discoveries show, continued to be practised with conspicuous success; the sister art of mosaic was carried to a high degree of technical perfection; and in sculpture new conventions, such as the plastic rendering of the iris and pupil of the eye, were dictated by the ever-growing need for contrasts of light and shadow. By the close of the 3rd century a further transformation had taken place, which coincided with the political revolution whereby the absolute monarchy of Diocletian succeeded the principate of Augustus. The portraits of Constantine and his house have dropped all traces of naturalism; they are monumental, both in scale and in conception, and their rigid "frontality" carries us back to the primitive art of the East.

Architecture.—For this branch of the subject *see* ARCHITECTURE; CAPITAL; COLUMN; ORDER; TRIUMPHAL ARCH; here it suffices to note traits which persisted in later Western art. The Etruscans, by modifying the type of the Greek temple, profoundly influenced Roman construction; the Etrusco-Roman temple was not, like the Greek, approached on all sides by a low flight of steps, but raised on a high platform (*podium*) with a staircase in the front; in many instances the cella was square in order to house the divine Etruscan triads (Jupiter, Juno, Minerva; Ceres, Liber, Libera, etc.); and this cella was faced by a deep portico, which often occupied half the platform and thus restored to the outer structure the canonical length of the classic temple. This high *podium* is a first step in the development of building in a vertical direction, whereby, as H. B. Walters remarks, the Romans "paved the way for mediaeval and more particularly Gothic architecture."

The round temple, which originated in the primitive Latin hut, was adopted for the house of the king and for the ancient cults of Vesta and of Hercules. The theme was repeated, with many variations, from the circular temple by the Tiber to those fantastic structures at Baalbek and at Petra which anticipate the innovations of Borromini and the Baroque. For the irregular temple-precincts of the Greeks, the Roman substituted the colonnaded courts, in which—as in the Imperial Fora—the temple was often set against the rear wall (Fora of Augustus, Nerva, Trajan, etc.). This type of enclosure was imitated throughout the Graeco-Roman world—Baalbek (*q.v.*) is a well known instance; from it are derived the forecourts of Christian churches and basilicas, and its inspiration is visible in Bernini's colonnade at St. Peter's.

Another specific achievement of the Roman architect was the application of the arch, the vault and the dome. The rectilinear buildings of the Greeks, with their direct vertical supports, gave place to vaulted structures in which lateral thrust was called into play, a constructional device which was a paramount influence in the Roman architecture of the 17th century. The aesthetic effect of curves was well understood by the Romans; and they were the inventors of those decorative combinations of the Greek orders with the arcade, of which the more famous—the Triumphal Arch and the Arcade order (*see* ORDER) had a far-reaching influence. It is impossible, as Rushforth points out, to overlook the analogy between the Arch of Constantine (to take a typical example) and the decorative portals of mediaeval cathedrals, while, at a later date, the triumphal arch influenced Baroque façades (fountains of Moses and of Trevi) besides being directly imitated in more modern times. Likewise, the superposed arcades adorned with columns or pilasters of a different order on each tier, formed a system of façade decoration which became almost as popular in the Renaissance as it had been in antiquity.

Republican Sculpture.—The art of the republican period may best be studied in its portraiture, where the simple naturalism of the Etruscans gradually makes way for the careful if uncompromising realism of the Romans. Of republican portraiture we have many fine examples, such as the magnificent head—probably of Brutus—which competent authorities now date back to the 4th century, an early date which would account for its partially Etruscan character (Plate I, fig. 1). Somewhat later are the statue of an orator (*Arringatore*) in Florence, in which the Etruscan manner is beginning to yield to the Roman, and the lovely head of a young man wearing the athlete's cap, in the British museum (Plate I, fig. 9). The bronze bust of the actor, Norbanus Sorix, in Naples, is an example of the first quality attributable to the age of the dictator Sulla. Numerous examples in stone or marble are provided by the funeral *stelae*, within which busts, clearly imitated from the wax *imagines*, are stiffly aligned (Plate II, fig. 3); while the more purely Hellenic manner fashionable in the 1st century B.C. may be studied in the well-known heads of Pompey and of Cicero. Apart from portraiture, examples of republican sculpture, both in the round and in relief, are now slowly emerging from oblivion; we may quote the sepulchral urn, lately acquired by the British museum, showing a company of knights, preceded by musicians, riding toward a small temple, in front of which a boy leads a sheep to sacrifice (Plate II, fig. 2). Though the relief retains something of the Etruscan style, subject and spirit are distinctly Roman. The fragment at Ny Carlsberg (Plate I, fig. 10), with a group of women looking on at a mule race, is still more highly Romanized—a crowd being suggested by three or four figures, as in Julio-Claudian art. The well-known slab, in the Museo Mussolini, of Mettius Curtius leaping into the chasm, is presumably copied from an original of republican date, and akin to it is the fine fragment in Munich, recently claimed as republican by C. Weickert, which represents a group of trumpeters and gladiators, one of whom is shown, fallen and crouching, in three-quarters view from the back (Plate I, fig. 11). Again, a circular altar in the Villa Borghese, representing a Roman sacrifice in the presence of Hercules and of Venus Genetrix—ancestress of the Julian house—is, according to the same authority, of republican date and commemorates the *ludi Caesaris* of the year 46 B.C. Another notable example of a Roman altar is the altar of Domitius Ahenobarbus, already referred to (Plate II, fig. 11), in which the historical scene of one face is naïvely juxtaposed with the "marriage-procession of Poseidon and Amphitrite" represented on the sides; we thus have here the actual event with all its accessories, told in Roman style, while the naval victories and triumphs of the donor are given in the allegorical Greek manner. The same blend of realism and allegory recurs under Augustus in the *Ara Pacis Augustae*, executed between 13 and 9 B.C. in commemoration of the emperor's pacification of the west. This altar stood in a walled enclosure with two entrances, measuring 11½ by 10½ metres. The walls, with their plinth, were about 6 metres in height, and were decorated internally with a frieze of garlands and bucrania, treated with the utmost truth to nature, and externally with two bands of relief, the lower consisting of scrolls of acanthus varied with other floral motives, the upper showing processions passing across the field from east to west; on the south wall Augustus himself with the great officers of state, the flamens and the imperial family; on the north the senators and a crowd of citizens with their children. On the western face, toward which the processions are directed, the "Sacrifice of Aeneas on his arrival in Latium" (Plate II, fig. 9) symbolizes the link between Rome and the ancient Troy. To the east front (apparently) belongs the beautiful group of the earth goddess (Tellus) and the spirits of air and water, allegorical of prosperity and of the fertility of nature under the new rule. The babes that cling to the Earth Mother and the children that accompany their

elders in the processional friezes introduce a human note which enhances the imperial beneficence. The glorification of empire is the keynote of all Augustan decoration.

Imperial Sculpture.—In the portraiture of Augustus and his successors the Hellenistic manner of the late republic is modified by a return to Etruscan naturalism. This portraiture is well represented by the Prima Porta statue of Augustus, in which he is shown in the attitude of a general addressing his army. Here again we find that the ideal mingles with the real; the emperor is not only bareheaded but barefoot, and the decoration on his corselet symbolizes what his rule has done for Rome and the world, while the tiny Cupid at his side, riding a dolphin, indicates the descent of the Julian house from Venus. The colossal bronze head in the British museum (Plate I, fig. 3), found in 1911 at Meroe, in the Sudan, belongs doubtless to another notable presentment of the emperor in armour, though we have no clue as to the style of the statue. The Augustus of Via Labicana, on the other hand, discovered in 1909, represents the emperor as pontifex maximus heavily draped, with head veiled, and in the act of sacrificing. The head (Plate I, fig. 2) has a poetic quality which we also find in certain portraits of women, as in the admirable head at Ny Carlsberg (Plate I, fig. 4), but which was unknown to earlier art. The portraiture of private individuals also had interesting developments, and not less so that of women; the charming statue from Ostia of a young girl represented as Artemis, is a good example (Plate II, fig. 4).

The art of the Julio-Claudian period, like that of the republic, is slowly emerging into the light. Among notable Julio-Claudian fragments are the relief from Nola, at Budapest, showing a trumpeter giving the signal for a naval attack (Actium?); certain processional and sacrificial scenes in the Villa Medici, of similar character to those of the Ara Pacis, but later in style, and two reliefs discovered in the Corso only three years ago and removed to the Museo Mussolini, which are attributed to the arch erected to commemorate the conquest of Britain by Claudius in A.D. 44. The more organic relation now attempted between the scenes represented and the background, leads gradually to that pictorial Flavian style best exemplified in the reliefs of the Arch of Titus, which represent the triumph of Titus and the spoils of Jerusalem (Plate III, fig. 2). These are eminently pictorial compositions in respect of depth of focus, and, so far as relief is concerned, the problem of representing form bathed in air and light is here solved. The same effects may be noted in Flavian ornament, as for example in the pilaster from the monument of the Haterii upon which is carved a tall vase, twined with roses that seem swayed by a light breeze. The delicate transitions and the subtle play of light bestow upon the best Flavian portraits the same "illusionistic" quality. New and notable effects were attained by the formal wire-mounted *toupets* of the ladies; these were used to set off the face, which appears as within a niche—a characteristically Roman effect (Plate I, fig. 6).

But even in the Flavian period we find by the side of the pictorial a more architectonic style, as in the friezes of the Flavian Forum Transitorium, which forms, as it were, the link between Flavian and Trajanic art. To the principate of Trajan belong, it is thought, four slabs of a long battle scene, later walled into the Arch of Constantine (central passage and shorter sides of attics). The composition is fine, the heads of the barbarians full of character, but the atmospheric effects sought by the Flavians are abandoned in these crowded scenes (Plate II, fig. 8). The various episodes were linked together to suggest a continuous whole, a method of composition of which the reliefs of the spiral column put up in Trajan's Forum offer another example. These reliefs, which enfold the column like a strip of embroidery, tell the story of both of Trajan's wars with the Dacians, a formal division between the two narratives being made by a figure of Victory setting up a trophy. Uniform excellence can not be claimed for the reliefs, yet, considering that the column contains 2,500 figures (arranged, it is said, on 400 slabs), the high level maintained is amazing (Plate III, fig. 4). The sacrificial pageants; Trajan's reception of troops; the opening of the bridge over the Danube; the dramatic scene of "the last water ration within the

ANCIENT ROMAN PORTRAIT SCULPTURE

1. Bronze head of Brutus. An example of the sculpture of the Republican period, dating probably from the 4th century, B.C. In the museum of the Palazzo dei Conservatori, Rome

2. Head of the statue of Augustus found in the Via Labicana, Rome, representing the Emperor Augustus as *pontifex maximus*. In the Museo delle Terme, Rome

3. Colossal bronze head of the Emperor Augustus found in 1911 at Meroe in the Sudan. In the British Museum

4. Sculpture of a lady of the Julio-Claudian period. At Ny Carlsberg, Copenhagen

5. Bronze figure of Hadrian found in the Thames. In the British Museum

6. Lady with a high coiffure, characteristic of portraits of women in the Flavian period (latter half of 1st century A.D.). In the Capitoline Museum, Rome

7. Head of Septimius Severus. In the Stettiner Collection, Rome

8. Head of a statue in armour at Barletta. It has been called a portrait of Theodosius, and also of Heraclius, but is more probably that of Valentinian I. (latter half, 4th century)

9. Head of a young man wearing the athlete's cap. Republican period. In the British Museum

10. Fragment of a Roman-Etruscan relief, representing a group of women looking on at a horse-race. At Ny Carlsberg, Copenhagen

11. Relief representing a group of trumpeters and gladiators. Attributed to the Republican period. In the Glyptothek, Munich

12. Head of Constantine the Great. In the museum of the Palazzo dei Conservatori, Rome

PLATE II

ROMAN ART

ANCIENT ROMAN RELIEFS AND OTHER SCULPTURES

1. Tombstone of late republican date. In the British Museum. 2. Relief from a sepulchral urn, showing a company of knights preceded by musicians, riding toward a small temple. Republican period. In the British Museum. 3. Funeral stele of the republican period. In the British Museum. 4. Statue from Ostia of a young girl represented as Artemis. Imperial period. In the Museo delle Terme, Rome. 5. Mourning woman, a tomb statue of the Antonine period. In the Museo delle Terme, Rome. 6. Roman carrying his ancestral busts. In the Palazzo Barberini, Rome. 7. Antinous as Silvanus. Period of Hadrian (A.D. 117–38). In the Villa Albani, Rome.

8. Relief representing a battle scene, from the Arch of Constantine, Rome; thought to have belonged to the principate of Trajan and later walled into the arch. 9. Relief from the *Ara Pacis Augustae* (altar of peace) erected by the senate 13–9 B.C. in commemoration of the pacification of the West by Augustus. In the Museo delle Terme, Rome. 10. Relief, probably of the period of Trajan, from one of the balustrades. In the Roman Forum. 11. Relief from an altar believed to have been set up by the Consul Domitius Ahenobarbus (about 30 B.C.). In the Louvre

ROMAN FRESCOES AND RELIEFS

1. Relief representing an augur taking the auspices. Detail from a frieze

2. Detail of a relief from the Arch of Titus, in the Roman Forum, showing the emperor in the triumphal car returning from Jerusalem

3. Detail of the column of Marcus Aurelius, Rome

4. Detail from the column of Trajan, Rome, dedicated in A.D. 113. The various episodes in the emperor's life are linked together in a spiral of 22 turns, to represent a continuous whole

5. Sarcophagus at Melfi, in Apulia, Antonine period (2nd century A.D.). A full-length portrait of the deceased girl is on the lid, and the sides are ornamented with figures symbolic of the soul's destiny

6. Wall-painting from the Roman house discovered in the grounds of the Villa Farnesina, Rome; thought to be possibly as early as the middle of the 1st century B.C. In the Museo delle Terme, Rome

7. Fresco from the series representing a Dionysiac initiation, discovered in 1911 in the so-called "Villa of the Mysteries" at Pompeii

8. Septimius Severus and Julia Domna sacrificing. Relief from the gateway of the Silversmiths (Argentarii), Rome

9. Fresco painting of a farm scene; period of the Severi (about A.D. 200). From the Hypogeum (underground chamber) of the Aurelii discovered in 1919 near the Viale Manzoni, Rome

10. Ivory diptych with double portrait of Honorius, about A.D. 406. In the Treasury of the Cathedral, Aosta

PLATE IV

ROMAN ART

MINOR ARTS OF ANCIENT ROME

1 and 3. Two silver goblets found in 1922 near Copenhagen, probably the work of the 1st century. They are ornamented with scenes from the Homeric cycle. In Copenhagen

2. Stucco reliefs combined with paintings, from one of the tombs on the Latin Way, Rome. From the 1st or 2nd century

4. Portrait medallion on glass, representing two ladies and a boy, now identified as Alexander Severus at the age of 16 (A.D. 221), with his mother and his grandmother. The medallion was later inserted as the centrepiece of a cross. Now at Brescia

5. Cameo of Claudius. In the Royal Collection at Windsor Castle

6. Fresco of the head of a shepherd piping, said to have been found in a tomb near Rome. In the British Museum

7. Detail of a large mosaic pavement, showing a view of the Nile and its surroundings; perhaps of the 1st century B.C. In the Palazzo Barberini, Palestrina

8. Mosaic of Silvanus, of a fountain niche at Ostia. In the Lateran Museum, Rome

9. The Good Shepherd; fresco of the period of the Severi. From the Hypogeum of the Viale Manzoni, Rome (Plate III., fig. 9)

10. Wall-painting in a room of the Roman house discovered under the Church of SS. John and Paul, Rome. The subject is the meeting of two divinities (Dionysos and Thetis?) on a sea-girt rock, surrounded by tiny love-gods. One of the largest and best preserved ancient paintings so far discovered in Rome, probably not later than the period of Marcus Aurelius (A.D. 161–180)

11. An example of *opus sectile*, a marble intarsia of various colours, from the basilica of the Consul Junius Bassus, Rome. The subject is the consul riding into the circus surrounded by mounted attendants. About A.D. 331

walls of the enemy's capital, Sarmizegetusa," are spirited compositions by a great imaginative artist. The principal character is always the Roman army, and the artist's first intention is to extol its warlike prowess, its courage, its endurance. But the figure of the emperor stands out from the whole and controls the action throughout, thus making manifest in the chief, as in his army, the right of the Roman people.

In the Trajan Column pictorial relief received its death blow; on a carved spiral that mounts in 21 windings up a column of 100 ft. high, precision of outline was imperative and perspectival or atmospheric effects out of the question. We may, however, suppose that the whole was coloured in local tints (brown for the earth, green for the trees, etc.) and that details of armour and horse trappings were added in metal. The column was dedicated in A.D. 113. On the top was a statue of the emperor in gilt bronze, and within the high pedestal, were deposited the golden urns containing Trajan's ashes and those of his consort, Plotina.

In striking contrast to the continuous spiral of the column are the fine reliefs of the arch put up at Benevento (see TRIUMPHAL ARCH), in honour of Trajan. The inscription bears the date A.D. 114, but the prominence given in the attica to Hadrian, as well as Hellenizing traits in certain of the sculptures, have led to the supposition that the arch was not finished till after Hadrian's accession. The arrangement of the panels, which summarize Trajan's achievements at home and abroad, is carefully calculated; on the side facing the city the subjects refer to Trajan's policy in Rome; on the side facing the country, to his settlement of the empire. In significance, this arch is the most important monument of Roman commemorative art; each scene, though rounded off and complete in itself, contributing to one dominating idea—the apotheosis of empire. This is consistently worked out from the picturesque relief of the passage way where the beneficent emperor is seen in the midst of grateful citizens, many of whom carry their children shoulder-high, to the grandiose panel of the attica facing towards Rome, where Jupiter offers the thunder-bolt to Trajan as supreme symbol of power, acclaiming him by this act as the *princeps optimus* of the inscription.

With the accession of Hadrian—the "Greekling," as he was called by writers hostile to his policy—a short-lived renaissance of classicism set in, restricted, however, to certain eclectic modifications of Greek statuary which do not fall within our province, and to a change in the relation of background to figures in relief-sculpture. The return to a background, either neutral or with the character of a drop-scene that has no organic connection with the figures, was doubtless responsible for the fact that the historical monuments of this and the following reign often lack the pregnancy of meaning, and vigour of execution, which distinguish those of the Flavio-Trajanic period; mention may be made of three reliefs in the Palazzo dei Conservatori, one of which represents the apotheosis of an empress.

On the other hand, the famous hunting medallions, which were later transferred to the Arch of Constantine are vigorous and interesting compositions, full of the rich and varied incident characteristic of Rome. In portraiture the most important work of this period was the idealized type of Antinous, here represented by the most exquisite of his effigies, which shows him as Silvanus (Plate II., fig. 7) and thus invests the favourite of Hadrian with a divinity expressed in the terms of Roman art, as well as a pathos which belongs to his own time. The inscription on the altar gives us the name of Antonianus of Aphrodisias in Caria, one of a family of sculptors domiciled in Rome since the time of Trajan.

The Antonine Period.—This produced in the Marcus Aurelius of the Capitol a type of equestrian statue which has served as model for all subsequent figures of the kind. The poise must have been more perfect in antiquity before the loss of the barbarian that crouched under the horse's right fore-hoof. Here we may note the different manner in which the Trajanic age and that of Hadrian, and his successor, Antoninus Pius, conceived the figures symbolic of the subject-peoples of the empire. Under Trajan, Roman sculptors had produced the finely realistic statues of Dacian captives which now adorn the Arch of Constantine, while to the period of Antoninus Pius belong the idealized figures,

classical in pose and motive, which adorn the Hadrianeum or temple of the deified Hadrian, and of which several are in the Palazzo dei Conservatori.

Under Marcus Aurelius and Commodus, Roman art underwent further transformation. The earliest monument of the time is the base (in the Vatican) of the column (now destroyed) erected in honour of Antoninus Pius and Faustina. The contrast is remarkable between the classicistic representation of the apotheosis of the imperial pair, witnessed by the ideal figures of Roma and the Campus Martius (holding an obelisk), and the vigorous realism of the *decursio*, a ceremony performed by detachments of the praetorian guard on horse and foot, in which, with total disregard of perspective as tending only to obscure the action, the artist brings all the figures into the same plane and disposes them on a few projecting ledges of equal size, a device that reappears on the column of Marcus Aurelius. The reliefs of the Aurelian column hardly suffer by comparison with the column of Trajan. We cannot, it is true, trace, as in the earlier instance, the march of events towards a dramatic climax, nor does the artist attempt to produce an impression of a chronological series of happenings. The figures are smaller and more crowded than those of the earlier column, and there is even less regard for perspective than in Trajanic art. Yet a deeper psychology informs the whole; the note of *humanitas* rings clear in the groups of barbarians with their women and children; or in those scenes which centre in the person of the good and philosophic emperor; the monotony of incident is relieved by the sculptor's power of repeating the same idea in a surprising variety of ways. Many episodes are vividly treated, *e.g.*, the famous scene of the fall of rain, ascribed in Christian tradition to the prayers of the "Thundering" Legion, the strong realism of which is in contrast to the idealism of the Hellenistic Jupiter Pluvius in a scene of the Trajan Column.

Contemporary portraiture also shows the invasion of new principles and a tendency to emphasize the contrast between hair and flesh, the face often showing signs of high polish. In the latter half of the 2nd century the contrast is heightened by a new method of treating the hair, which is rendered as a mass of curls deeply undercut and honey-combed with drill-holes; a fine example is the Commodus of the Palazzo dei Conservatori. The aim of the sculptor is to obtain an ornamental effect by the violent contrast of light and dark. This pictorial influence may be seen at work in all branches of sculpture. The sarcophagi of the Antonine and later periods, with their crowded compositions and deep shadows, attain the same effect. A tendency to isolate figures and groups also makes its appearance in Antonine relief, and is strikingly exemplified in the famous *sarcofagi a colonette*, found both in Italy and in Asia Minor, and decorated with figures placed like statues within niches between columns. We may quote as conspicuous examples the sarcophagus of "Homer and the Muses" at Constantinople (from Sidamaria); the fragment of a similar example in the British Museum (Cat. 3,312); the marriage sarcophagus at Florence in the Riccardi Palace, and the grand sarcophagus at Melfi in Apulia. The Melfi example is adorned by figures symbolic of the soul's ultra-mundane destiny and has a full-length portrait of the deceased girl on the lid (Plate III., fig. 5). Many of the statues inserted into the niches of these sarcophagi are considerable works of art and exhibit the same quality of pathos that informs the remarkable tomb-statue, also of the Antonine period, recently discovered near Rome (Plate II., fig. 5). It represents a mourning woman, closely draped and veiled, with strongly individualized features; the splendid movement of the drapery, with the broken rhythm between the hands, preannounces Gothic sculpture and has little or nothing in common with its Greek prototypes.

Later Sculpture.—Under Septimius Severus and his successors, Roman art drifts steadily in its new direction. The reliefs of his arch at the entrance to the Forum represent the emperor's campaigns in the East in a compromise between bird's-eye perspective and the "continuous" style, which, though in sharp opposition to plastic and perspectical laws, has the magnificently decorative effect of Flemish tapestry. Other examples of the art of the period are the reliefs of the little gateway of the

Argentarii in the Velabrum (Plate III., fig. 8) and the relief now in the Palazzo Sacchetti, on which is carved the presentation of Caracalla to the senate as the destined successor of his father.

The political troubles of the 3rd century, the threatened inroads of barbarism, the imminence of economic ruin did not affect the production of art as seriously as might be supposed, nor did they check the continued "progress along the ascending line" of certain of its manifestations. In the portraiture we first become aware of two different currents: the naturalistic in most imperial effigies, e.g., the bronze statue of Severus in Brussels, and the more monumental which invests with a new spiritual dignity the masterly portrait in the Stettiner collection (Plate I., fig. 7). It is conceived in accordance with the laws of frontality, which are still more operative in the grandiose head of an imperial personage (unidentified) from the middle of the 3rd century, found at Ostia (Terme). If we turn to technical methods, we note that the busts of the second quarter of the 3rd century A.D. are distinguished by the treatment of the hair and beard, which seem to have been closely clipped, and are indicated by a multitude of fine chisel strokes on a roughened surface, a technique practised with wonderful effect in the heads of Maximinus the Thracian (A.D. 235–238) in Berlin; of the emperors Pupienus (A.D. 238) and Philip the Arabian (A.D. 244–249) both in the Vatican; in the remarkable bronze, Balbinus (A.D. 238) of the Vatican library; and in a head of the Capitol (Strong, *Rom. Sc.*, Pl. 127). In these heads the expressiveness is astonishing, the Capitoline head being justly noted for its sly look of craft and cunning. Under Gallienus (A.D. 253–268) there is a momentary return to a greater naturalism, evident in the treatment of hair and beard, and in the emotional look; but in the so-called Probus (A.D. 276–282) of the Capitol, and the Carinus (A.D. 283–285) of the Palazzo dei Conservatori, frontality gets the better of naturalism till it prevails in the portraiture of Constantine (Plate I., fig. 12) and his successors. Organic has been transformed into architectonic structure; the bust (or statue) is no longer a true portrait—a block of marble made to pulsate with the life of the subject represented—but a monument.

In the togate statues of the Constantinian and later period, the deep cutting of the rigid folds contributes to the monumental effect of the figure. Among the finer examples are the two celebrated statues of consuls, in the Conservatori, attributable to the 5th century. By the side of these togate examples a place must be accorded to the statue in armour at Barletta (it has also been called Theodosius and Heraclius, but is more probably Valentinian I.), whose powerful head (Plate I., fig. 8) and splendidly poised body show post-Constantinian art at its best. The narrow bands of relief on the Arch of Constantine, some of which may even date back to the reign of Diocletian, partake of the same monumental character as the single statues of the time. Where the subject permits, as in the reliefs showing Constantine in the Forum and Constantine distributing a dole, the frontality of the central figure and the strict symmetry of the grouping, which imparts an almost geometrical regularity to the main lines of the composition, show that Constantinian reliefs, like the portraits, are calculated for architectonic rather than for plastic effect.

Roman Painting.—The arts whose proper medium is colour enjoyed a popularity with the ancients—Romans and Greeks alike—at least as great as that of sculpture, though, owing to the perishable nature of the material, the record is even more fragmentary. Etruscan painting in Italy reflected, throughout its early history, the phases through which the art passed in Greece. Thus the frescoes which adorn the walls of Etruscan chamber-tombs show an unmistakable analogy with Attic vase-paintings in their neutral background, in the use of conventional flesh-tones, and in the predominant interest shown in line as opposed to colour. This probably was the style of those early wall-paintings at Ardea and Lanuvium, which existed "before the foundation of Rome" (Pliny, *N.H.*, xxxv. 18). It is probably also to an early date that we should refer those wall-paintings "in famous temples," of which Quintilian copied the archaic inscriptions, but the first definite mention of painting in Rome is from the close of the 4th century B.C., when we hear of one Fabius

Pictor, who earned his cognomen by decorating the temple of Salus on the Quirinal (302 B.C.). The chief works of specifically Roman painting in republican times (other than the frescoes which adorned the walls of temples) were those exhibited by successful generals on the occasion of a triumph; some idea of these paintings is afforded by the fragment of a fresco in the Museo dei Conservatori, discovered in a sepulchral vault on the Esquiline in 1889, which appears to date from the 3rd century B.C. It represents scenes from a war between the Romans and an enemy who may almost certainly (from their equipment) be identified as Samnites.

We pass from the meagre remains of early Roman painting to the decorative frescoes of Rome, Herculaneum and Pompeii, which introduce us to an art influenced like the contemporary sculpture by Hellenistic models. The scheme of colour is no longer conventional but naturalistic; the picture is concentrated in space, *i.e.*, figures are no longer isolated on a neutral background; difficult effects of linear and aerial perspective are attempted and the modelling of figures is often excellent. It must be premised that this style of wall-decoration was a new thing in the Augustan period. In the Hellenistic age the walls of palaces were veneered with slabs of many-coloured marble (*crustae*); and in humbler dwellings these were imitated in fresco. This "incrustation" style is found in a few houses at Pompeii, such as the Casa di Sallustio, built in the 2nd century B.C.; but before the fall of the republic it had given place to what is known as the "architectural" style, in which columns and other architectural features are introduced in order to give the illusion of outer space, and this illusion is heightened by the landscape backgrounds, which are often enlivened by figures. An example of such decoration is afforded by the "Odyssey landscapes," discovered on the Esquiline in 1849, amongst the remains of a large private house, attributable at the latest to the period of Claudius. The walls of one room were decorated in their upper portion by pilasters treated in perspective, through which the spectator appears to look out on a continuous background of land and sea, diversified by scenes from the voyage of Odysseus. The artist, it appears, has been mainly interested in the landscape which is sketched with great freedom, but he shows no scientific knowledge of perspective, and commits the natural error of placing the horizon too high. It is clearly to such works as these that Vitruvius refers (vii. 5) when describing paintings which "unfold mythical tales in due order, as well as the battles of Troy or the wanderings of Odysseus through landscapes (*topia*)." We should doubtless reckon within the same class those "small scenes from the Homeric cycle within a framework in which blue and gold are predominant" in a room of the beautiful house on the Palatine, identified by Ashby as the *domus transitoria* of Nero, and the numerous examples from the Homeric cycle at Pompeii (*cf.* especially the series in the "House of the Cryptoporticus" in Insula 6, near the newly-explored Via dell' Abbondanza).

The use of landscape in decoration is stated by Pliny (*N.H.*, xxxv., 116) to have become fashionable in Rome in the time of Augustus. He attributes this to a painter named Studius, who decorated walls with "villas, harbours, landscape gardens, groves, woods, hills, fishponds, canals, rivers, shores," and so forth, diversified with figures of "persons on foot or in boats, approaching the villas by land on donkeys or in carriages, as well as fishers and fowlers, hunters and even vintagers," a description which exactly fits the continuous landscape of the yellow frieze in one room of the house of Augustus (the so-called "house of Livia") on the Palatine. Vitruvius, too, in the passage above quoted, speaks of "harbours, capes, shores, springs, straits, temples, groves, mountains, cattle and herdsmen. . . ." Existing paintings—those, for instance, of a columbarium in Villa Doria-Pamfili, recently transferred to the Terme—fully confirm the statements of ancient writers. In the villa of Livia at Prima Porta the walls of a room are painted in imitation of a park; from the villa of Fannius Synhistor at Boscoreale we have a variety of landscapes and perspectives; and in the house discovered at Rome in the grounds of the Villa Farnesina by the Tiber—the paintings of which are in the Museo delle Terme—we find a room decorated with black panels, upon which landscapes are sketched in with brush-strokes of white.

Figure Painting.—In the architectural style figure-painting on a large scale makes a first appearance. Occasionally it forms an integral part of the design. In the larger "Triclinium" at Boscoreale, for instance, groups and single figures—possibly family portraits—are painted in the wall-spaces between pilasters and columns, while in one room of the "Villa of the Mysteries" at Pompeii, a continuous figure-composition is painted against a panelled background. This wall-painting, which represents a Dionysiac initiation, was discovered in 1911, and may be said to surpass in beauty of colouring and composition anything previously known (Plate III., fig. 7). But figures so arranged as to appear to be moving within the room tend to confine the space. This is contrary to the principles of Roman and Pompeian wall-painting, and a commoner method, therefore, is to concentrate the figure-subject, which is usually of a mythological character, into a central panel clearly marked off from the rest of the wall and intended to be seen as through an opening in the wall. In the architectural style these subjects are usually framed in a species of pavilion or *aedicula*, sometimes painted in perspective, which allows a vista of the landscape beyond (Plate III., fig. 6, from the house of the Farnesina in Rome), but this motive gradually loses its importance in the third style and becomes a purely conventional scheme of decoration, though in the fourth or intricate style, which again reverts to true architectural forms, however fantastic and bewildering in their complexity, the figure subjects are plainly conceived as pictures and framed with a simple band of colour. In the later styles figure-subjects without landscape are extremely common, but it has been shown that, *e.g.*, in the triclinium of the Casa dei Vettii, which is decorated with a cycle of mythological paintings, the lighting is carefully calculated with regard to local conditions, so that the conception of an outlook into external space is not given up. Among Pompeian paintings effects of lighting are at times attempted with great success; for instance the groups of a striking composition—a ceremony of benediction—are executed in bold dashes of colour, especially white, according to the principles of modern impressionism. The subjects of these Pompeian frescoes are for the most part taken from Greek mythology, but this only proves that that source of inspiration was as freely drawn upon in the art as in the literature of imperial Rome. Owing to the total loss of Greek originals, the question how far these were imitated in Pompeii (or Rome) is difficult to determine. The well known Medea, possibly influenced by the painting of Timomachus, may equally well be the contemporary version of an older theme. It would probably be correct to say of such a figure, as of the mourning woman (Plate II., fig. 5), that if the framework is still Greek the spirit is Roman. Figure-subjects are also introduced within frames, directly imitated from actual pictures, and placed on stands, or shuttered like triptychs as in the houses of Livia and of the Farnesina at Rome, and in Pompeii. Examples of ancient painting in Rome are still scarce, partly because much that has been discovered of late years still awaits publication. But the magnificent series of paintings from the house of the Farnesina, which may be as early as Caesar, since they were found on or near the site of his gardens; the paintings of the house of Livia (architectural style); the famous scene of a ritual marriage known, from its former possessor, as the "Nozze Aldobrandini" (library of Vatican); the decorative ceiling panels from the newly-excavated parts of the Golden House; the lovely head of a shepherd piping, in the British Museum (Plate IV., fig. 6), found, it is said, in a tomb near Rome, show that the art of the capital equalled, or even surpassed that of the buried Campanian cities.

Mention must also be made of the combination of ornamental work in plaster with painting which is found at Pompeii and at Rome, and is a feature of tombs of the 2nd century A.D. In the Augustan period we find exquisitely modelled stucco, used to ornament vaulted ceilings in the "Farnesina" house. An example of Julio-Claudian date is provided by the famous hypogeum of a Pythagorean cult, discovered outside the Porta Maggiore in 1917,

the ceilings and wall of which are entirely covered with reliefs in stucco; and from the principate of Domitian we have the fine stucco work in the cryptoporticus of this emperor's villa at Castel Gandolfo. Painter and modeller also worked in conjunction, with admirable effect; the results are best seen in the tombs on the Latin Way (Plate IV., fig. 2).

Painting continued to flourish under the later emperors. In a room of the Roman house, under the church of SS. John and Paul, may still be seen what is the largest and best preserved ancient painting so far found in Rome (Plate IV., fig. 10); the picture—remarkable for the freshness of colouring, and the beauty of the flesh-tints—can scarcely be later than the period of Marcus Aurelius. The subject is the meeting of the two divinities (Dionysos and Thetis?) on a sea-girt rock amid a joyous escort of tiny love gods, who guide their light craft over sunlit waters. Another room of the same house has decorative paintings of a mystical and religious character. To the period of the Severi may be referred the paintings, discovered near the Monte Mario, in the tomb of the little girl, Otacilia, which represent a "children's paradise," and those wall-paintings in the hypogeum of the Aurelii, discovered in 1919 near the new Viale Manzoni, which apparently reflect the tenets of an heretical Christian sect. Among the Viale Manzoni pictures the one of a farmhouse and its dependencies (Plate III., fig. 9) shows the persistence of the Roman landscape style; that of the Good Shepherd (Plate IV., fig. 9) and the 12 sheep (symbolic of the Sermon on the Mount) is a pastoral in Virgilian vein, while the heads of the 12 figures identified as the Apostles, recall heads on the column of Marcus Aurelius. Sound Roman traditions were still operative under Aurelian, as we see from the tomb of Trebius Justus, with its picture of the building of a city-wall, and the portraits of the occupant of the tomb and his family, treated in a style of art which persists in the Christian catacombs. The fact that painting was still vigorous in Rome under Constantine is evident from the magnificent figure of Roma found on the site of the old Lateran palace and assigned by Wilpert to a group of the imperial family attended by allegorical figures and divinities.

Portrait Painting.—From the few examples still extant we may assume that portrait-painting was of the same excellence as portrait-sculpture: the group of Terentius Neo (long mistaken for Paquius Proculus) and his wife at Naples, from Pompeii, is characteristic of the Augustan period, to which we may doubtless likewise refer the original of the fine mosaic representing the poet Virgil between two muses. Portraits of poets were a common feature of book-illustration, and the poet Martial (XIV. 186) mentions a portrait of Virgil prefixed to an edition of the *Aeneid*. The celebrated portraits in "encaustic" from the Fayum, give us a series of examples from the Flavian period to the 3rd century. These paintings were executed in wax—the usual technique of portrait painting, in which the colours were mixed with liquefied wax and fixed by heat, whether in a molten state or not is uncertain, though it seems more likely that the pigments were laid on cold and a hot instrument used afterwards. These tablets have been found exclusively in Egypt, where they were inserted into the mummy-case in place of the older plastic masks. Excellent examples of portrait-painting are provided by the medallions on gold glass, which have something of the value of our modern miniatures. One of the finest is in the Museum of Arezzo; it may be attributed to the period of Marcus Aurelius, and represents a bearded man whose delicate features are drawn with the utmost subtlety on a blue ground (flesh on gold, with details in black, drapery silver with violet streaks). Another little masterpiece, later inserted as centrepiece of a cross now at Brescia (Plate IV., fig. 4) represents two ladies and a boy, now identified as Alexander Severus, in the year of his accession (A.D. 221) when he was only 16, with his mother, Mammaea, and his grandmother, Naesa.

Roman Book-illustration.—*See* ILLUMINATED MANUSCRIPTS. This was a highly-developed branch of art in Rome, as appears from the description of Varro's 15 books of *Imagines*, illustrated with 700 pictures, and from the passage in Martial already referred to. The extant material, however, is mostly later than the period we are concerned with. But the famous illustrations to a 4th century codex of the *Iliad*, in the Ambrosiana at Milan, reflect, according to Wickhoff, the Romano-Pompeian style, while the illustrations of the Vatican Virgil, No. 3,235, seem to be 4th century copies of pictures of Augustan date. On the other hand, the pictures in the 4th century Virgil (Vat. 3,867), notably the "Assembly of the Gods," are in the contemporary "frontal" style here illustrated by the Junius Bassus panel in *opus sectile* (Plate IV., fig. 11). Roman influence inspires the celebrated Dioscorides of Vienna of the year 512, the style of which is closely akin to that of the Vienna Genesis, and is still vital in the 10th century in the Joshua rotulus of the Vatican, many of whose pictures clearly depend upon Roman historic relief.

MOSAIC

The gaps in the available knowledge of Roman painting can be filled up to a certain extent by what we learn from the remains of the sister art of mosaic, which, being less easily destroyed, have survived in thousands to the present day (*see* MOSAIC). The Roman artists were, generally speaking, alive to the essential differences of principle between the arts, and did not seek to produce the impression of painting, executed with a liquid medium, by the use of solid materials. Amongst the mosaics of Roman date which employ a large number of exceedingly minute cubes, an illusion akin to that of painting seems, it is true, to be the aim, though even here the Roman mosaicist never entirely transcends the limits imposed by his material. The most conspicuous examples of this more naturalistic manner are the pavement in the Lateran museum signed by the Greek Heraclitus, which appears to reproduce the "unswept hall" of Sosos of Pergamum (*see* MOSAIC), and the mosaic of the doves from Hadrian's villa, preserved in the Capitoline museum, inspired by the "Drinking Dove" of the same artist. The former of these contains about 120, the latter as many as 160 cubes to the square inch.

A distinction must be drawn between *opus tessellatum*, consisting of cubes regularly disposed in geometrical patterns, and *opus vermiculatum* in which a picture is produced by means of cubes irregularly placed. The two methods were commonly used in conjunction by the Romans, who recognized that a pavement should emphasize the form of the room to which it belonged by means of a geometrical border, while figure-subjects should be reserved for the central space. The celebrated pavement at Palestrina (Plate IV., fig. 7), with an extensive view of the Nile and its surroundings, is possibly the earliest known Roman picture in mosaic. Though it can scarcely be dated to Sulla's restoration of the Praenestine temple, it cannot be later than the second half of the 1st century, and seems early Augustan both in its Egyptianizing subject and in its landscape motives. Small mosaic-pictures isolated in geometrical pavements were called *emblemata*, and were often transported from the great centres of production to distant provinces, where pavements were prepared for their reception. The subjects of these *emblemata*, like those of the wall-paintings of Pompeii, were taken frequently from Greek mythology, and it is not easy to determine what degree of originality is to be assigned to Roman artists. We note a certain interest in the great figures of literature and philosophy. A subject commonly known as "The Academy of Plato" shows us a group of Greek philosophers engaged in discussion. In provincial pavements it is not uncommon to find portraits of poets or philosophers used to fill ornamental schemes of decoration, as in the famous mosaic at Trier signed by Monnus. The portrait mosaic of Virgil, mentioned on p. 401 discovered in a villa at Sousse in Tunisia (ancient Hadrumetum) shows a marked new interest in Roman literature, while it has also been shown that the mythological scenes depicted by the mosaic-workers of the later imperial period are frequently inspired, not by Greek poetry or even Greek artistic tradition, but by the works of Ovid; and the popularity of the legend of Cupid and Psyche is, doubtless, to be traced to its literary treatment by Apuleius. Besides a well-chosen repertory of geometrical patterns, the mosaic-workers make use of vegetable motives taken from the vine, the olive, the acanthus or the ivy, as well as traditional figures, such as the seasons, the winds, the months and

allegorical figures of all kinds, forming elements in a scheme of decoration which, though often of great richness, is never lacking in symmetry and sobriety. Mosaic pavements were a common luxury in the provinces, those of Gaul and of Roman Africa being specially celebrated; and there are fine examples from both Africa and Roman Britain in the British Museum.

Wall and ceiling mosaics from the classical period are rare. What appears to be the earliest example in Italy was identified in 1928 by G. Lugli at the villa of Hadrian. It is a floral-geometric design in black on a white ground of marble tesserae veined with a vitreous blue paste, which adorned the vaulted ceiling of a house of republican date, afterwards transformed by Hadrian into the imperial residence. Another example of the 2nd century A.D., first noted by Ashby (*P.B.S.R.*, iii., 1906, p. 104) is afforded by a circular domed nymphaeum near the Via Tiburtina, which is entirely covered with a mosaic of plain white tesserae. But the destruction, partial or complete, of the imperial thermae and palaces has deprived us of the more elaborate means of passing judgment on the systems of *opus musivum* proper (*see* MOSAIC), *i.e.*, the decoration of vaults and wall-surfaces with mosaics in glass, enamel or precious materials. We can, however, form some idea of these from the decoration of fountains at Pompeii and elsewhere, as well as from the compositions which adorn the walls and apses of early Christian basilicas. The mosaic on blue ground of the god Silvanus, on a fountain niche from Ostia at the Lateran (Plate IV., fig. 8), shows a type of decoration whence derive the apsidal compositions of S. Pudenziana or of SS. Cosma and Damiano. On the other hand, the celebrated groups of Justinian and Theodora with their courts, in S. Vitale at Ravenna, continue the series of those imperial groups of which the families of Maximian and of Constantine Chlorus, painted in a hall of the palace of Aquileia, afforded a noted and celebrated example. The "Roma Barberini" comes, as we have seen, from a similar group in Rome, and the Theodosius, with his sons and officers of State, on the silver plate in Madrid probably reproduced yet another. Further fine and instructive examples of *opus musivum* may be studied at S. Costanza in Rome, built by Constantine early in the 4th century A.D. The mosaics of the cupola were destroyed in the 16th century, but those of the annular vault which surrounds the baptistry, though much restored, show that the decorative schemes of Erotes, vine-patterns, medallions, etc., commonly found in pavements were also used by the *musivarii*.

When employed in the service of Christianity the old pagan themes were invested with a new spiritual meaning, and mosaic became the chief channel through which motives invented by paganism were transmitted to Christian art. The acanthus decoration in green and gold on blue ground in the baptistry of S. John Lateran continues the floral arabesques of the Ara Pacis, and similar scrolls form the background of the *arbor vitae* at St. Clemente (time of Pope Paschal II., 1099–1118), and frame the central group of the apse mosaic at S. Maria Maggiore (time of Nicholas IV., 1288–92). In other mosaics we find the pagan river motive, with pleasure boats floating down stream and boys angling from the bank, to symbolize the river Jordan or the rivers of paradise.

Opus sectile, a marble intarsia of various colours, also deserves to be noted. An interesting example in Palazzo Colonna, possibly as early as the 1st century, represents the "Infancy of Romulus and Remus"; another, attributable to the 4th century, is provided by the magnificent, though sadly scattered remains of the revetments in marble and mosaic of the basilica of Junius Bassus (consul, A.D. 331) on the Esquiline. They are remarkable for brilliancy of colouring and for the magnificent frontal composition of certain of the panels; the one chosen for illustration (Plate IV., fig. 11), which represents the consul himself riding into the circus surrounded by mounted attendants, has the same pictorial quality (the same absence, for instance, of ground line), as the Ravenna mosaics of Justinian and Theodora.

PRECIOUS METALS AND BRONZE FURNITURE

For the history of plate *see* SILVERSMITHS' AND GOLDSMITHS' WORK. Pliny's lament (*N.H.* xxxiii., 154 *sqq.*) that silver chasing was, in his time, a lost art, is mere rhetoric and is disposed of by the list he gives in an earlier chapter (xxxiii, 139) of the principal ateliers in which such work was produced in his time, as well as by the numerous surviving examples of Roman plate. Of the utmost significance is the treasury discovered at Boscoreale (now in the Louvre), which contains pieces ranging from the age of Caesar to that of the Flavians. Many of the subjects are specifically Roman, like those of the pair of cups representing the triumphs of Augustus and Tiberius. A Julio-Claudian cup in Vienna, from Aquileia, shows in the same way as the corselet of the Augustus of Prima Porta, the benefits ensuing from the imperial rule. Other notable 1st century examples may be seen in Naples. Roman plate travelled far and wide and excellent examples have been found at Berthouville in Normandy, at Hildesheim in Germany, and even in Denmark. The two goblets found in 1922 near Copenhagen (Plate IV, figs. 1 and 3), reproduce scenes from the Homeric cycle (ransoming of Hector and myth of Philoctetes) so popular among the Romans. The artist, who signs himself Cheirisophos, was probably a Campanian Greek in the service of Roman employers. The gold patera with Dionysiac subjects (from Rennes, in the Cabinet des Médailles) shows the vitality of the art under Septimius Severus, and that it continued to flourish long after is attested by the silver disc of Theodosius at Madrid, and of Valentinian at Geneva.

Bronze furniture, too, was often of great beauty, and among pieces that deserve at least a mention are the *lectica* or litter of Augustan date in the Museo dei Conservatori; the couch with silver inlay in the same collection; the graceful tripod-stand at Naples, the tray of which is wrought with garlands in the style of the Ara Pacis; while the so-called Tensa Capitolina, with its rich bands of decoration and portrait medallions, is a notable example from the 3rd century A.D.

ENGRAVING AND MINOR ARTS

By far the greater part of the ancient gems which exist in the modern collections belong to the Roman period, and the great popularity of gem-engraving amongst the Romans is shown by the enormous number of imitative works, cast in coloured glass paste, which reproduce the subjects represented in more precious materials. In the Roman *intagli* we can trace the various phases of Roman plastic art. A black agate in the Hague museum (Fürtwangler, *Die Antiken Gemmen,* pl. xlvii. 13), supplies a characteristic portrait of the Ciceronian age. The splendid cornelian which has passed from the Tyszkiewicz collection at Boston (inscribed ΠΟΠΙΛ [for Popilius], ΑΛΒΑΝ [for Albanius], the names of two Roman families), which portrays Augustus, in the guise of Poseidon, in a chariot drawn by four hippocamps, should, doubtless, be referred to the victory of Actium. A sardonyx in Florence (Fürtwangler, *op. cit.,* pl. lix. 11) portrays an empress of the Julio-Claudian line as Hera. Flavian portraiture is seen at its best in the aquamarine in the Cabinet des Médailles signed by Euhodos, which represents Julia, the daughter of Titus. Amongst later gems one of the finest is the "Hunt of Commodus" in the Cabinet des Médailles, engraved in a stone popular with Roman artists—the "nicolo," a sardonyx with a bluish-grey upper layer used as background, and a dark brown under layer in which the design is cut. But the masterpieces of Roman gem-cutting are to be found in the great cameos, cut in various materials, including single coloured stones such as amethyst or chalcedony, though the stone most fitted by nature for this branch of art was the sardonyx in its two chief varieties—the Indian, distinguished by the warmth and lustre of its tones, and the Arabian, with a more subdued scale of colour. Two masterpieces survive in the "Grand Camée de France" (cab. des Antiques, Paris), a magnificent Indian sardonyx in five layers representing the apotheosis of the Julio-Claudian house, and the "Gemma Augustea," an Arabian sardonyx which shows Augustus and Roma enthroned, receiving a victorious prince, while in a lower zone are groups of captives and Roman soldiers. Other examples of the first order are the cameo of Augustus from the Strozzi and Blacas collections, now in the British Museum, the cameo of Claudius in the collection at Windsor (Plate IV., fig. 5); the busts of the same emperor and of three members of his family set on cornucopiae, at Vienna.

Engraved gems are not the only examples of Roman work in precious metals. Amongst the portraits of the first dynasty none are finer than the small head of Agrippina the younger in the British Museum in *plasma* (root-of-emerald), and the lovely head of Tiberius in turquoise, acquired by the British Museum during the World War, from a soldier, who found it in Egypt. Vases, again, were carved in precious stones, such as the famous onyx vase at Brunswick (Fürtwangler, *op. cit.,* figs. 185–88) with reliefs relating to the mysteries of Eleusis, and the smaller, but finer, onyx vase in the Berlin museum (Fürtwangler, *op. cit.,* figs. 183–184), representing the lustration or baptism of a prince of the Julian line—a rock surmounted by a small temple recalls one slab of the Ara Pacis, and the work seems of Augustan date.

As mentioned before, coloured glass was used as a substitute for gems, and it is to the school which produced the cameos of the early empire that we owe the vases in white and blue glass of which the Portland vase in the British Museum is a famous example. Pompeii furnishes a second in the amphora, decorated with vintage scenes, in the Naples museum.

We must also class amongst the fine arts that of the die-sinker. Not only are the imperial portraits found on coins worthy of a place beside the works of the sculptor, but in the medallions of the 2nd century A.D. we find figure-subjects, often recalling those of contemporary reliefs, treated with the utmost delicacy and finish. Later lead medals often reproduce landscape motives and actual views; *e.g.,* medal of Diocletian, in Paris, with view of a city, its river and bridge; medal of Constantius Chlorus, found in 1922 near Arras, with the Thames and the port of London; medal of Constantine with the famous gate of Trier. The fine bronze medallion of Valens and Valentinian, enthroned side by side in frontal pose, shows that the art of the medallist was still vital in the 4th century A.D.

Ivory was a favourite material with the Romans, as it had been with the Etruscans. It was worked both in the round and in relief and often used for the adornment of furniture. A head of 1st century date—probably Augustus—in the Stroganoff collection, and another representing a personage of mid 3rd century date, in the British Museum, rank with the best Roman portraiture. The series of consular and other diptychs are discussed in a special article (DIPTYCH). Among them are masterpieces like the magnificent Symmachorum-Nicomachorum diptych, one leaf of which is in the Victoria and Albert Museum and the other in the Cluny Museum at Paris. Diptychs also largely helped to keep portraiture alive; fine examples of this type are the diptych of Probus at Aosta with the double portrait of Honorius (Plate III., fig. 10); that of Felix, of the year A.D. 428, in Paris and that of Boethius, consul in A.D. 487, in the museum of Brescia.

Of the purely industrial arts it is unnecessary to speak at length In the last century of the republic a flourishing manufacture of red-glazed pottery was established, with its chief centre at Arretium (Arezzo); the signatures of the vases enable us to distinguish a number of workshops owned by Romans who employed Greek or oriental workmen. The repertory of decorative types reflects the cross-currents of classicism and naturalism which were contending in later Hellenistic art. In the 1st century A.D. the Italian fabrics were gradually driven out of the market by those of Gaul, where the industry took root in the Cevennes and the valleys of the Rhône and the Allier; and before long north-eastern Gaul and the Rhineland became centres of production in the various minor arts, which continued to flourish until the breakdown of the imperial system in the 3rd and 4th centuries A.D. Glass, though made in quantities for the Roman market, was usually of foreign manufacture, probably Syrian. The subject is fully treated in Kisa, *Das Glas im Altertum.*

With only limited space at our disposal, we have confined ourselves in the above section to monuments in Rome, only going outside the capital for examples of exceptional importance. The products of local or provincial art and the special problems which they raise cannot be treated here, though some clue to the literature of the subject will be found in the bibliography. The Museo del Impero Romano affords a well-arranged survey of Roman provincial art; it contains, along with much that is new, most of the objects from the Exhibition of the Roman Provinces held in the Baths of Diocletian in 1911, an account of which by E. Strong appeared in the 1st volume of the *Journal of Roman Studies*.

SUMMARY

It may be said that as the establishment of the Roman empire gave a political unity to the ancient world, and acceptance of Christianity by its rulers assured the triumph of a universal religion, so the growth of a Graeco-Roman nationality, due to the freedom of intercourse between the subjects of the emperors, led to a unity of culture which found expression in the art of the time. Yet no sooner was the fusion of the elements which contributed to the new culture complete than the process of disruption began, which issued in the final separation of the Eastern from the Western empire. In the first, the oriental factors, which produced a gradual transformation in Graeco-Roman art, definitely triumphed; and the result is seen in Byzantine art. But in the West it was otherwise. The realism native to Italy remained alive in spite of the conventions imposed upon it; the human interest asserted itself against the decorative. Therefore, the Christian art of the West is the true heir of the Roman, and, through the Roman, of the classical tradition. As we have seen, Roman art in its specific aspect was an historical art; and it was for this reason eminently fitted for the service of an historical religion. The earliest Christian art whose remains are preserved is that of the catacombs; but though not devoid of technical merit (on this point *see* A. della Seta, *Religion and Art*, p. 331 *seq.*) this art is dominated by the single idea of deliverance from the grave and its terrors, whether this be conveyed by scriptural types or by representations of paradise and its dwellers. Not until the Church's triumph was complete could she command the services of the highest art and unfold her sacred story on the walls of her basilicas; but, when the time came, the monumental art created by the demands of imperial majesty was ready to pass into the service of Christianity.

It remains to note that the scientific study of ancient Roman art dates from a comparatively recent period. The great artists of the Renaissance, headed by Raphael and Michelangelo, showed no lack of appreciation for such models as the reliefs of Trajan's Column; and Mantegna's "Triumph of Caesar" vividly suggests how great was the influence exerted by Roman historical sculpture upon their choice and treatment of monumental subjects; but their eyes were already fixed on the Greek ideal, however imperfectly represented by the monuments then available. In the 18th century the supremacy of this standard seemed established beyond challenge, and even the vision of the *Magnificenza Romana*, evoked by Piranesi, failed to arouse any response in Winckelmann and the apologists of Greece. The Greek antique, till then only dimly divined behind the copies that filled the palaces and galleries of Italy, was soon to be made more vivid by the recovery of the buried treasures of Herculaneum and Pompeii and the systematic excavation of the extant remains of Hellenic art, which began early in the 19th century and still continues, not unnaturally absorbed the attention of the majority of classical archaeologists. Nevertheless, towards the close of the 19th century, when the main lines of Greek artistic development had been traced and interest aroused in its later offshoots, critics were led to examine more closely the products of the Roman period. In 1893, Alois Riegl entered the lists on behalf of Roman Art with his *Stilfragen*, a series of essays on the history of ornament, in one of which he expressed the opinion that "there was in the antique art of the Roman empire a development along the ascending line and not merely a decadence, as is universally believed." This thesis was taken up two years later by Franz Wickhoff in a preface to the reproduction in facsimile of the illustrated ms. of Genesis in the imperial library at Vienna.

In the year following the English translation (by E. Strong) of Wickhoff's work, Riegl published the first (which, by reason of his untimely death, remained the only) volume of his *Late Roman Industrial Art* (new ed., 1927) in which he endeavoured to show that the later transformations of Roman art in the 2nd and succeeding centuries after Christ continue to mark a definite advance. The fecundity of the leading ideas put forward by Wickhoff and Riegl remains unimpaired, as Koch points out, in spite of the attacks of Josef Strzygowski, who for 30 years and more has never ceased to dispute the originality of Roman art and to insist that Roman artistic achievement, whether of the imperial or early Christian period, was at all times dependant on the Hellenistic East. By thus shifting the ground of controversy from the Mediterranean to the oriental area, Strzygowski, again to quote Koch, has immeasurably broadened the archaeological horizon; but the net result of the long conflict, so far as our enquiry is concerned, has been to bring out more clearly the essential characteristics of Roman art in the pre-Christian period, and its high significance in the formation of the art of the Christian West. The case for Roman art is stated anew by G. McN. Rushforth in the chapter "Roman Art and Architecture," contributed to the *Legacy of Rome* (1923) and by Herbert Koch in the admirable monograph, *Römische Kunst* (1925), already quoted. It will be seen from what has been said above that there is a new and growing interest in the post-Constantinian periods of Roman art, down to Justinian and later. Of this we have the proof, not only in Riegl's book quoted above, but also in Delbrueck's magnificent publication of late Roman monuments—done by care of the German Institute—and in all the newer histories of ancient art—Rodenwaldt's for instance.

BIBLIOGRAPHY.—I. General: F. Wickhoff, *Roman Art* (trans. E. Strong, 1900); P. Gusman, *L'art décoratif de Rome* (1908); A. Michaelis, *A Century of Archaeological Discovery* (1908); H. B. Walters, *The Art of the Romans* (1911); H. Stuart Jones, *Companion to Roman History* (1912); E. Baumgarten, F. Poland and R. Wagner, *Hellenistisch-Römische Kultur* (1913); A. della Seta, *Religion and Art* (trans. 1914, *Etruria and Rome*, pp. 245–291), *Italia Antica* (2nd ed., 1928), *I Monumenti dell' antichità classica* (*Italia*, p. 17 *seq.* and 123, etc.); E. Strong, *Apotheosis and After Life* (1915), for the religious element in later Roman Art; R. Cagnat and V. Chapot, *Manuel d'archéologie romaine* (2 vols., 1916, 1920); H. Koch, *Römische Kunst* (1923); A. Springer, *Die Kunst des Altertums* (12th ed., 1923); A. Riegl, *Die Spätrömische Kunstindustrie* (new ed., 1927); G. Rodenwaldt, *Die Kunst der Antike* (*Hellas und Rom*) (1927).

II. Architecture: A. Choisy, *L'art de bâtir chez les Romains* (1876), *Histoire de l'architecture*, vol. i. (1899); H. Wölfflin, "Die antiken Triumphbogen in Italien" in *Repertorium f. Kunstwissenschaft* (1893); J. Durm, *Die Baukunst der Etrusker u. Römer* (2nd ed., 1905); F. Haverfield, *Ancient Town Planning* (1913); K. Swoboda, *Römische u. romanische Paläste* (1919); F. Toebelmann, *Römische Gebälke*, vol. i. (1923); G. Giovannoni, "Building and Engineering," in *Legacy of Rome* (1923); A. von Gerkan, *Antiker Städtebau* (1924); F. Noack, *Die Baukunst des Altertums* (Berlin), *Triumph und Triumphbogen* (1925–26); G. T. Rivoira, *Roman Architecture* (1926).

III. Sculpture: W. Froehner, *La Colonne Trajane* (1872–74); C. Roberts, *Die Antiken Sarkophagreliefs* (1890–1904); T. Schreiber, *Hellenistische Reliefbilder* (1894), for Roman reliefs; E. Petersen, *Die Marcussäule* (1896); C. Cichorius, *Die Relief der Trajanssäule* (1890); E. Corbaud, *Le bas-relief romain à représentations historiques* (1899); E. Petersen, *Ara Pacis Augustae* (1902), *Trajan's Dakische Kriege* (1899–1903); W. Amelung, *Die Sculpturen der Vaticanischen Museen* (2 vols., 1903 and 1908); W. Altmann, *Die römischen Grabaltäre der Kaiserzeit* (1905); E. Ferrero, *L'Arc d'Auguste à Suse* (1910); F. Studniczka, *Zur Ara Pacis* (1909); British School at Rome, ed. H. S. Jones, *Catalogue of Sculptures in the Museo Capitolino* (1912), *Sculptures in the Museo dei Conservatori* (1926); E. Schmidt, *Archäistische Kunst in Griechenland und Rom* (1922); G. Lippold, *Kopien u. Umbildungen griechischer Statuen* (1923); K. Lehmann-Hartleben, *Die Trajanssäule* (2 vols., 1925), *Grossbronzen der römischer Kaiserzeit* (3 vols., 1927); E. Strong, *Roman Sculpture from Augustus to Constantine* (1907), Italian trans. *Scultura Romana* (2 vols., 1923 and 1926); J. Sieveking, "Das römische Relief," in *P. Arndt Festschrift* (1925); C. Weickert, "Gladiatoren-Relief der Münchner Glyptothek" in *Münchner Jahrbuch* (2nd series, 1925), *Römisches Relief der Zeit Caesars* in *P. Arndt Festschrift* (1925); R. Delbrueck, *Deukmäler der spätantiker Kunst* (1927).

IV. Portraiture: J. Bernoulli, *Römische Ikonographir* (4 vols., 1882–94); H. Brunn and F. Bruckmann, *Denkmäler griechisch-römischer Skulptur* (1888–1906); P. Arndt and F. Bruckmann, *Griechische und römische Porträts* (1891, etc.); A. Hekler, *Greek and Roman Portraits* (1912); R. Delbrueck, *Antike Porträts* (1912); *Bildnisse römischer Kaiser* (1914); C. Albizzatti, *Rassegna d'arte* (1918), for late portraiture; G. Kaschnitz-Weinberg in *Römische Mitteilungen* (1926), for Etrusco-Roman portraiture and in *Die Antike*, vol. ii. (1926) for Constantine portraiture.

V. Painting and Stuccoes: D. Raoul-Rochette, *Peintures antiques médites* (1836); W. Helbig, *Campaniens Wandgemälde* (1868),

Untersuchungen über die campanische Wandmalerei (1873); K. Woermann, *Die Landschaft in der Kunst der alten Völker* (1876); A. Soglian, *Le pitture murali campane* (1879); A. Mau, *Geschichte der Wandmalerei in Pompeii* (1882); W. F. Petrie, *Hawara* (1889), chap. vii., for Fayoum portraits; G. Ebers, *Antike Porträts* (1893), for Fayoum portraits; B. Nogara, *Le Nozze Aldobrandine* (1907), for ancient pictures in Vatican; P. Hermann ed. F. Bruckmann, *Denkmäler der alten Malerei des Altertums* (1907); G. Rodenwaldt, *Die Komposition der pompejanischen Wandgemälde* (1909); M. Rostovtzeff, *Die hellenistisch-römische Architekturlandschaft* (1911); *Mystic Italy* (1927); P. Buberl, *Die griechisch-ägyptischen Mumienbildnisse der Sammlung Th. Graf* (1922); E. Pfuhl, *Malerei u. Zeichnung der Griechen* (3 vols., 1923); E. Strong and N. Jolliffe, "Basilica of Porta Maggiore" in *Journal of Hellenic Studies* (1924); C. Cecchelli in *Roma* (1926), for hypogeum of Viale Manzoni; V. Macchioro, *La Villa dei Misteri* (trans. H. Bosco, 1926); A. Eibner, *Entwicklung und Werkstoffe der Wandmalerei* (1926); J. Carcopino, *Basilique Pythagoricienne de la Porte Majeure* (1926); G. Bendinelli, in *Monumenti dei Lincei* (1927), for basilica of Porta Maggiore.

VI. Minor Arts: P. Gauckler, "Musivum opus," in Saglio and Pottier, *Dictionnaire des antiquités* (1877–1919); A. Furtwängler, *Die antiken Gemmen* (3 vols., 1900); H. Graeven, *Elfenbeinwerke aus Sammlungen in Italien* (1900); J. G. de Pachtère and P. Gauckler, *Inventaire des mosaïques de Gaule et d'Afrique* (1909–11); W. R. Lethaby, "Late Ivories," in *Proc. Soc. Antiquaries* (1912); C. Albizzatti in *Römische Mitteilungen* (1914), for glass medallions; K. Regling, *Die Antike Münze als Kunstwerk* (1924); M. Bernhardt, *Handbuch zur Münzkunde der Römischer Kaiserzeit* (1926); H. Mattingly and E. Sydenham, *Roman Imperial Coinage* (2 vols., 1926); R. Delbrueck, *Antike Elfenbein-Reliefs*, part i. (1927); Hayford Peirce on medallion of Brescia in *Aréthuse* (No. 14, Jan. 1927).

VII. Provinces: G. Q. Giglioli, *Catalogo del Museo dell' Impero Romano* (1927), (a) Britain: R. G. Collingwood, *Roman Britain* (1923); F. Haverfield, *Romanization of Britain* (4th ed., 1924). (b) Gaul and Belgium: J. Déchelette, *Les Vases ornés de la Gaule romaine* (1904); E. Espérandieu, *Recueil général des bas-reliefs de la Gaule romaine* (1907–25); F. Cumont, *Comment la Belgique fut romanisée* (2nd ed., 1918); C. Jullian, *Histoire de la Gaule* (8 vols., 1928). (c) Germany: F. Koepp, *Die Römer in Deutschland* (2nd ed., 1912); H. Dragendorff, *Westdeutschland zur Römerzeit* (2nd ed., 1919); K. Schumacher, *Siedelungs- und Kulturgeschichte der Rheinlände* (1923); J. Colin, *Les Antiquités romaines de la Rhénanie* (1927). (d) Spain: E. S. Bouchier, *Spain under the Roman Empire* (1914); A. Schulten, *Hispania* (1921). (e) Italy and Eastern Europe: F. Studniczka, *Tropaeum Trajani* (Leipzig, 1904); E. Majonica, *Führer durch das Staatsmuseum von Aquileia* (1911); E. Hébard and J. Zeiller, *Spalato, le palais de Dioclétien* (1912); J. Weiss, *Die Dobrudscha im Altertum* (1912); C. Diehl, *Salonique* (1920); V. Parvan, "I primordi della civiltà romana alle foci del Danubio," in *Ausonia* (vol. x., 1921); C. Patsch, *Die Herzegowina ein und jetzt* (1922); E. Nischer, *Die Römer im Gebiete des ehemal Oesterreich-Ungarn* (1923). (f) Asia: V. Chapot, *La province romaine d'Asie* (1904); W. Libbey, *The Jordan Valley and Petra* (1905); G. Dalman, *Petra* (1908); A. Jaussen and R. Savignac, *Mission archéologique en Arabie* (1908); T. Wiegand, *Baalbek* (2 vols., 1921–25); Honigmann, "Baalbek" (1924) in Pauly-Wissowa's *Realenzyklopädie* (g) Africa: A. Schulten, *Das römische Afrika* (1899); G. Boissier, *L'Afrique romaine* (1901). (h) Egypt: C. Edgar, *Catalogue des antiquités du musée du Caire* (1903–11); E. Breccia, *Alexandrea ad Aegyptum* (Eng. ed., 1922); Société Archéologique d'Alexandrie, *Monuments de l'Égypte gréco-romaine* (1926). (i) Italian Africa: R. M. Smith and E. A. Porcher, *History of Recent Discoveries in Cyrenaica* (1864); E. Michon, *Statues antiques de la Cyrénaïque* (1915); *Notiziario Archeologico del Ministero delle Colonie* (1915, etc.); "Libya," *Rivista della Tripolitania* (1924); P. Romanelli, *Leptis Magna* (1925); S. Aurigenma, *Tripoli e le sue opere d'arte* (Milan, n.d.), *I Mosaici di Zliten* (1926); R. Bartocini, *Le antichità della Tripolitania* (1926), *Guida di Leptis* (Leptis Magna) (1927); *Africa italiana* (1927, etc.). (j) French Africa and Morocco: R. Cagnat and A. Ballu, *Timgad* (1892–1905); G. Boissier, *Monographies des musées et collections d'Algérie et de Tunisie* (1896); J. Toutain, *Les cités romaines de la Tunisie* (1896); S. Gsell, *Les monuments antiques d'Algérie* (1901); H. Ballu, *Guide illustré de Timgad* (1903), *Les Ruines de Djemila* (1921); R. Cagnat, *Carthage, Timgad, Tebessa* (1909); *Bulletin de la Commission des travaux historiques archéologique de l'Afrique du Nord; Revue Africaine* (1856, etc.).

Important papers treating the subject of Roman art may be found in the *Journal of Roman Studies* (founded in 1911 in response to the new interest in Roman subjects); the *Papers of the British School at Rome* (1902, etc.); the *American Journal of Archaeology* (1856, etc.); the *Revue Archéologique* (1844, etc.); the *Bollettino della Commissione Archeologica di Roma* (1872, etc.); the *Bollettino d'Arte del Ministero della Pubblica Istruzione* (1907, etc.); *Dedalo* (1920, etc.); *Jahrbuch des Archäolog. Instituts* (with its *Denkmäler*). (H. S.-J.; E. Sꜰ.)

ROMAN CATHOLIC CHURCH.

The word "ecclesia" appears in the New Testament 106 times: twice in its ordinary Greek sense of the assembly of the city-state of Ephesus, once of the community of the Israelites at Sinai and on all other occasions of the society or Church of Christ, whose members were called Christians first at Antioch. St. Paul uses the word both of local societies, "churches" of Judaea, Asia, Galatia, Macedonia, the Thessalonians or in Philemon's house (as he speaks of "them of Laodicea"), and also of the "whole Church of God." In Matt. xvi, 18, Christ answers St. Peter's confession, "Thou art Christ, the Son of the living God," by saying, "Thou art Peter; and upon this rock I will build my church." In Matt. xviii, 15-20, He defines what may be called ecclesiastical jurisdiction: "If thy brother shall offend against thee . . . tell the church. And if he will not hear the church, let him be to thee as the heathen and publican. . . . Whatsoever you shall bind upon earth, shall be bound also in heaven: and whatsoever you shall loose upon earth, shall be loosed also in heaven. Again I say to you, that if two of you shall consent upon earth, concerning anything whatsoever they shall ask, it shall be done to them by my Father who is in Heaven. For where there are two or three gathered together in my name, there am I in the midst of them." The most mature and conscious definition of the Apostolic Church is contained in the Epistles to the Ephesians and Colossians: ". . . the Kingdom of the Son of His love; in whom we have our redemption, the forgiveness of our sins; who is the image of the invisible God, the firstborn of all creation; for in Him were all things created in the heavens and upon the earth . . . all things have been created through Him and unto Him; and He is before all things and in Him all things consist. And He is the head of the Body, the Church." (Col. i, 13-18). "To sum up all things in Christ . . . and He put all things in subjection under His feet and gave Him to be head over all things to the Church which is His Body, the fullness of Him that filleth all in all" (Eph. i, 10, 22-23).

This organic unity of Christ, "the fulness of the godhead bodily," with the church "which is his body" is the essence of Catholic ecclesiology. In Christ, the godhead assumed human nature: the nature of man is united in Christ with the nature of God, and the church is therefore the divine organism. But the nature of man implies a historical and instituted existence on earth. "By the very fact of being a body," said Leo XIII, "the church is visible." Its existence, institution and operation are therefore sacramental. It is the mystery of the incarnate godhead perpetually realized and available in all time and for all the purpose of the divine incarnation. There can be but one such church and, as it is historical and instituted on earth, there can be but one church visible on earth. As it is divine as well as human, it contains and consummates the whole divine creation, "the Church triumphant, the Church suffering and the Church militant, and is the fullness [*pleroma*] of Him that filleth all in all." Hence it is holy and catholic. Its institution is simultaneously divine and human. Historically and therefore upon the authority of its divine Founder, this church is the church of His apostles. It is apostolic and its apostolicity is its perpetual attribute. Within the compass of its sacramental purpose it is infallible, in the sphere of faith (*i.e.*, man's apprehension of God) and in the sphere of morals (*i.e.*, man's essential relation with God and man). This infallible authority is not to be confounded in any sense with "power": it is the infallible authority of knowledge which is of the essence of the union of man with God—knowledge not achieved as in the natural sciences externally by observation, hypothesis and experiment, but inherent and essential as God knows Himself and His creature and the nature of the unity which He wills and accomplishes. The effectual operation of this entire sacrament, the vital activity of the divine organism, is known as grace.

Grace is the universal operation of the church. It is the initiation, process and fulfilment of the divine activity of redemption by which God unites His creatures organically with Himself and endows them thus with His own vitality. This universal grace or sacrament is effectually realized and defined in seven sacraments, acts of God in and through the divine organism by which the divine life is bestowed and the organic union is accomplished and sustained. In the Eucharist "under the appearances of bread and wine, Jesus Christ Himself is contained, offered and received." It is the whole act of redemption, the sacrifice—that is, the making holy—of the whole universe in the person of Christ, "the most divine gift emanating from the depth of the heart of the Redeemer 'with desire desiring' this wonderful union with men which was especially designed to spread everywhere the life-giving fruit of His redemptive work" (Leo XIII, encyclical *Mirae caritatis*, 1902). Baptism is the initial reception of the human being into the body of Christ. Confirmation given to members of an age to recognize and will their membership is the sacrament of moral maturity. Marriage is the sacrament which sustains in Christ human generation and family life. Penance restores the union with God when it has been injured or broken by sin. Order creates and sustains the whole institution of priesthood and episcopacy by which the divine organism lives and functions on earth. Thus the penitent confesses his sin to Christ, who hears, judges and absolves him by means of the human priest, and the sacrifice of Calvary is contemporary with all times as the same sacrifice is offered by the same High Priest employing successive generations of men ordained by Him for that purpose. The passage or expectation of death is sanctified by the sacrament or extreme unction. Thus the whole earthly life of every human being is organized in the body of Christ, and the whole organization of the church exists to realize that divine-human community. The history of the church cannot be understood unless its nature and function as the divine-human organism, wholly divine and wholly human and indissolubly one, is first recognized.

St. Luke ends his account of St. Paul's apostolate at Rome with the words "This salvation of God is sent unto the Gentiles." St. Paul himself explains the significance of that climax in the Epistle to the Galatians. As a Jew turning to the Gentiles he must claim that the old dispensation has been superseded and that to be "in Christ" (a phrase repeated six times in this Epistle and constantly used thereafter by St. Paul) is to belong to "the Jerusalem that is above" in which "there can be neither Jew nor Greek." It was only by the act of God that the sanctities and exclusions of the old law could be at once fulfilled and superseded, and hence the same authority which united Jew and Gentile realized the purpose of history. "If ye are Christ's then are ye Abraham's seed, heirs according to promise." In the Epistle to the Ephesians written probably from Rome this doctrine of divine consummation becomes explicit, "a dispensation of the fullness [*pleroma*] of the times, to sum up all things in Christ. . . . for he is our peace who made both one and brake down the middle wall of partition . . . that he might create in himself of the twain one new man, so making peace, and might reconcile them both in one body unto God through the Cross." "So then ye are no more strangers and sojourners but ye are fellow citizens with the saints and of the household of God, being built upon the foundation of the apostles and prophets, Christ Jesus himself being the chief corner stone: in whom every building fitly framed together groweth into a holy temple in the Lord." (T. S. GY.)

ORGANIZATION

The Catholic Church is governed by a hierarchy of bishops with the pope as bishop of Rome at the head. Under him patriarchs, archbishops and other greater prelates are possessed of various local jurisdictions over the bishops of their respective provinces. The church teaches that the origin of all this varied jurisdiction must be sought in the authority given by our Lord Himself, and recorded for us in the Gospels. Just as no man, not even an apostle or the chief of the apostles, could institute a sacrament, so it was not in the power of man alone to originate the fundamental organization of the church. Christ Himself before He ascended into heaven left the church an organized body, with a system of rule that could indeed be developed indefinitely to meet the constant changes which must inevitably occur as the centuries passed, but which in its fundamental principles must remain unchanged to the end of the world.

The bishop of Rome, who as head of the whole church acquired later on the exclusive title of "pope," was also the sole patriarch of the west, while Alexandria and Antioch governed most of the east. In the 5th century two other bishops attained to the patriarchal rank, Constantinople as being the seat of the empire and civil capital of the world, and Jerusalem as the cradle of the church. Under these was a complicated and ever-varying system of jurisdictions of exarchs, metropolitans and archbishops, but the principle by which alone the whole system of subordination of one bishop to another can be justified, in view of the essential equality of all, can be found only in the special grant by our Lord of the primacy to St. Peter and the delegation of some share in that primacy to the rest of the hierarchy.

This principle, which was recognized even at Nicaea, is symbolized and expressed by the practice of sending the pallium by the pope to every archbishop in possession of jurisdiction. The pallium comes from the tomb of St. Peter, where a supply is kept in readiness, and symbolizes and conveys such share in the Petrine primacy as belongs to the particular office. Till an archbishop has received his pallium from the pope, he cannot exercise any archiepiscopal jurisdiction, though he is possessed as soon as he is fully appointed of all the jurisdiction which belongs to him as bishop of his own diocese.

In 1950 the number of Catholics in the world was estimated at more than 400,000,000, governed by about 1,500 archbishops and bishops, each in his own diocese.

The Curia.—As the pope has the care of the whole church (that is, of many million Catholics spread throughout the world), there is need for an extensive and detailed organization at Rome adequate to cope with the varied questions that arise. This organization is called the Curia. (*See* the special article CURIA ROMANA for details.)

Cardinals.—At the head of the Curia is the College of Cardinals, numbering 70 in all when complete, whose members form the supreme senate of the church and the pope's immediate advisers. Historically the cardinals are the occupants of the six "suburban" sees, known as cardinal bishops; the incumbents of the principal parishes of Rome, known as cardinal priests; and seven who are the successors of the seven deacons responsible in early times for the more secular details of administration and who are known as cardinal deacons. But these ranks are distinct from the orders of the church and the cardinal priests are always bishops, and half their number being the occupants of various important sees and nonresident in Rome; while the cardinal deacons are nowadays always priests.

The cardinal secretary is, so to speak, the prime minister of the pope. It is his office to deal with all political affairs, and especially all diplomatic relations with the separate countries and governments. From his department depend the nunciatures and delegations which represent the Holy See abroad, and it is with him that the ambassadors from foreign countries to the Holy See do their business.

Congregations.—The work of the Curia is done by 11 permanent departments, called congregations, each with a cardinal at its head. These comprise: (1) the Holy Office; (2) the Congregation of Ceremonies; (3) the Consistorial Congregation, dealing with the appointment of bishops and other dignitaries, with the erection and division of dioceses and with episcopal administration; (4) the Congregation of the Eastern Church, dealing with the Uniates (*see* below); (5) the Congregation of Rites; (6) the Congregation of Seminaries and Universities; (7) the Congregation of Sacramental Discipline; (8) the Congregation for Religious, dealing with the affairs of regular orders; (9) the Congregation of the Council, dealing with the summoning and management of councils and also regulating parish priests, benefices and property; (10) the *Congregatio de Propaganda Fide*, for missionary organization; and (11) the Congregation for Extraordinary Affairs. The Congregation for the Fabric of St. Peter's is supernumerary.

Offices.—The ordinary routine business of the church is carried on by the offices; these, however, are not of so great importance as previously. They are: (1) the Chancery, which has little to do apart from the sending out of papal bulls; (2) the Dataria, dealing with those benefices the appointment to which is reserved to the Holy See; (3) the Apostolic Camera, which once controlled the affairs of the papal states and now has the care of the property of the Holy See; and (4) the Office of Briefs (sent to princes) and of Latin Letters.

Tribunals.—The tribunals, which control the judicial functions of the Curia, are: (1) the Sacred Penitentiary, handling matters of conscience; (2) the Sacred Rota, formerly the chief court of the papal states, now the court of appeals from bishops' courts to the Holy See, consisting of ten judges who sit generally in threes but for very important cases in greater numbers; (3) the Apostolic Signatura, the supreme court of appeal, consisting of six cardinals and their assistants, to which an appeal lies from the Sacred Rota.

THE LATIN RITE

The great majority of Catholics are those of the Latin rite; *i.e.,* those who use the Roman liturgy and generally have used it without interruption since the establishment of a Christian church in their country; there are local variations of little significance. The following paragraphs describe the hierarchical system of the Latin rite.

Archbishops.—Besides their own episcopal jurisdiction over their own dioceses, these greater prelates, whatever their title, have a provincial jurisdiction over their "suffragan" bishops. This jurisdiction is one strictly limited by law, the presumption being always in favour of the bishop and against the archbishop. It is attached to the office and therefore is "ordinary" jurisdiction and affects the suffragan bishops immediately and the faithful of their dioceses through them. The extent of this jurisdiction varies considerably in different localities and is everywhere less extensive than in former years. It is the archbishop's duty to summon his comprovincials to the provincial synod, which need be done only once every 20 years, and in that synod he presides of right, though his vote counts for no more than that of any other bishop. If the suffragan bishop has neglected to carry out the canonical visitation of his diocese, the archbishop may visit, after obtaining permission from Rome, and has full power of redressing abuses. When any one of the suffragan sees becomes vacant it is generally the duty of the archbishop to see that the cathedral chapter elects a vicar capitular to carry on the administration of the diocese during the vacancy. An appeal lies from the court of any one of the suffragan bishops to that of the archbishop, and where the rights of the bishop are involved he may hear cases from that bishop's diocese as a court of first instance. Appeals from his own diocesan court, which formerly had to be taken to the Holy See, are heard by some one bishop selected by the archbishop for that purpose once for all and approved by the Holy See. The archbishop has always the right of pontificating in any church in his province and may bless the people, grant 100 days' indulgence and have the cross carried before him in the church. He may not, however, except when he holds a visitation, perform any other acts which imply jurisdiction.

Bishops and Dioceses.—The bishop and the diocese form the most essential part of the church's organization, being of divine institution under the primacy of the pope.

Bishops.—A bishop is nominated under different conditions in different parts of the world, but even after he has been thus canonically nominated he has no power until that nomination has been confirmed by the Holy See. Once this confirmation has been given and has been communicated to his cathedral chapter he has full possession of all episcopal jurisdiction, though he can do no acts involving the power of order, such as ordaining clergy or confirming children, until he has been consecrated. His jurisdiction is ordinary, limited by restrictions imposed by the Holy See, but independent of his people and even of his clergy. In certain important matters he is bound to seek the advice of his cathedral chapter, though he is not usually bound to follow it. He is bound to make a visit *ad limina* to the Holy See at stated intervals to report on the state of his diocese. His authority over his diocese is fourfold: (1) *teaching,* with authority over all schools, and the right of superintending all the publications of the faithful and especially of the clergy within his diocese; (2) *legislative,* in which his power is strictly limited by the *jus commune* and by all existing laws which have wider scope than the bounds of his own diocese, though he can dispense from all diocesan laws; (3) *judicial,* whereby he is judge of first instance in all cases that be-

long to the ecclesiastical tribunal, can *in foro interno* reserve to himself the absolution from certain sins and can enforce his sentences of ecclesiastics by suspending them from their functions; (4) *administrative,* whereby he can nominate, subject to any local rights of patronage, to all benefices in his diocese, can oblige ecclesiastics to undertake special work (though he cannot force the cure of souls upon them if they are unwilling) and has authority over all ecclesiastical property, so that none can be alienated or sold without his consent. But in nothing is his power unlimited: he is always subject to the precepts of canon law.

The Cathedral Chapter.—In the general regulations of his diocese the bishop must conform to the general laws of the church and must not do anything which would impair the general unity of church government. He has as his constitutional council, to assist him in the work of government, the canons of his cathedral chapter. The cathedral itself is the church in which he has his seat (καθέδρα), and this he cannot choose at will, the pope reserving to himself the right of erecting a church to be a cathedral, as well as that of instituting a chapter. Generally, of course, the bishop finds both already established and in existence. The appointment of individual canons is generally in the hands of the bishop, though the appointment of dignitaries in the chapter is often reserved to the Holy See. As the chapter constitutes the diocesan senate, the bishop is bound to convene it and to ask its consent or advice in important matters. In some matters which touch diocesan rights or affect diocesan property, its consent is necessary and the bishop cannot validly act without it. In other matters, though the advice of the chapter must be asked, the bishop is not bound to act upon the counsel tendered. When the see is vacant by the death or resignation of the bishop, the chapter succeeds to his ordinary jurisdiction, but not to any jurisdiction that was personal to himself. Within eight days after the vacancy the chapter must elect a vicar capitular, to whom the whole administration of the diocese immediately passes. In the United States and elsewhere, where cathedral chapters have not as yet been constituted, a body of diocesan consultors has generally to be appointed by the bishop, and he is bound to ask the advice of these consultors on important matters, though they have not the power of vetoing his action.

The Vicar-General.—The bishop generally appoints one or more priests to assist him, deputing to them with a certain universality of power all his own jurisdiction within the diocese, so that the vicar-general is his alter ego, and no appeal lies from the one to the other. By virtue of this general mandate the vicar-general exercises ordinary jurisdiction throughout the diocese in the bishop's name. This jurisdiction however, being dependent on that of the bishop, ceases at the bishop's death, or with the cessation of the bishop's own jurisdiction. The office of a vicar-general ceases also with his own death or resignation, or with the withdrawal of his vicarial mandate, which last, however, can be taken from him only for a grave cause, allowing of an appeal to the Holy See.

The Diocesan Chancery.—This is the office through which the ordinary and routine work of the diocese is carried on. At its head is the chancellor. His duties are to carry on the official correspondence of the diocese and to see that records are duly kept. He can be removed by the bishop, but by the vicar capitular during a vacancy only with the consent of the whole chapter.

The Parish.—Where the full organization of the church is in force, the diocese is subdivided into parishes covering the whole ground. Each parish should have its own church and be under its own pastor, having care of souls and irremovable except for grave cause. But where the full organization is not in force, there are quasi parishes, with pastors who do not possess the full rights of parish priests. The full parish system has not yet been introduced either in England or the United States, though certain mission districts or quasi parishes have pastors who are not removable at the will of the bishop. The bishop can alter the boundaries of parishes, erect new ones or join two together where there is just cause for so doing. He is bound, however, first to ask the counsel of the chapter, though he is not bound to follow it.

The pastor of a properly constituted parish has ordinary jurisdiction. His rights within the parish are regulated by canon law and include the faculties of preaching, celebrating Mass, hearing confessions and administering the sacraments, though he can delegate this authority. Where the parish is too large to be administered by one priest, assistant priests are sent by the bishop to help him. These assistants are appointed by the bishop (though in some places the parish priest has the right of nomination) and are removable by him, but only for just cause. Their jurisdiction is delegated and they receive their faculties from the bishop.

If the parish priest is ill or incapacitated for any reason, the bishop must send a coadjutor to fill his place and in like manner will appoint an administrator of the parish during a vacancy.

Vicars Apostolic.—In districts where the ordinary hierarchy of the church has not yet been established and there are no proper dioceses erected, the Holy See governs directly by means of a delegate who has received episcopal consecration to a titular see and who has the title of vicar apostolic or prefect apostolic. The main difference between the two is that the vicar apostolic is bound to make the visit *ad limina* at certain intervals, while the prefect apostolic is not. They are not diocesan bishops and therefore have no cathedral and no chapter, and all their powers are delegated and not ordinary. Otherwise they enjoy as a rule all the powers that bishops have by canon law in their own dioceses. They have no vicar-general, though they can give special faculties to individual priests to enable them to assist in the rule of the district, and as they have no chapters they are bound to nominate three or more of their leading priests to act as counsellors. There are vicariates apostolic, prefectures apostolic and "missions."

THE UNIATE RITES

All that has been written so far about the local organization of the Catholic Church applies only to the western church and the Latin rite, which include the vast majority of Catholics. But there are also a number of so-called Uniate churches in full communion with the Holy See but organized separately. These do not represent, as is often thought, any sort of compromise or intermediate position between western Catholicism and the various schismatic or heretical churches of the east. All the Uniate churches accept the full Catholic faith and are in matters of doctrine absolutely at one with Rome. They all accept the full primacy of the Holy See and are subject to its supreme jurisdiction. Each Uniate church retains its old privileges and represents the church of its district or country as that church would have been had the schism never occurred. In no case, however, has the succession from the ancient hierarchy been preserved, but a new hierarchy has been instituted from Rome, with the old titles and privileges and with the preservation of the ancient rite. The object aimed at by Rome in instituting a Uniate church is not the latinizing of the ancient rites but the union of hearts in the one faith and under the one primacy of the Holy See.

Religion in the east has always been far more a matter of nationality than it has in the west. It has been found impossible, therefore, to carry out the strict system of territorial jurisdiction which obtains everywhere in the west. In the east the churches are distinguished rather by nationality, by languages and by rite than by locality, and in consequence there is a system of interpenetrating jurisdictions. There are, for instance, seven patriarchs of Antioch. Of these, three are schismatic, but four are in communion with the Holy See: the Latin patriarch, whose position is merely titular (originating during the crusades) and who resides in Rome; the Melchite patriarch, the Maronite patriarch and the Syrian patriarch. These last three have jurisdiction over the Catholics of their own rite only.

The Uniates in Europe are more or less directly subject to the general system of the Catholic Church. Those in Asia and Africa, however, since the rights of the patriarchates have been preserved, enjoy greater autonomy, being ruled by the Holy See mainly through their respective patriarchs. (A. S. Ba.; X.)

The Byzantine (Greek Catholic or Graeco-Slavonic Rite).—Uniates of this rite represent churches that maintain, in their various languages, the liturgy of Constantinople while acknowledging the doctrinal and hierarchical supremacy of the Holy See. The most important of these churches is the Ruthenian: this includes an archbishopric of Lwow (with suffragan bishoprics at Przemysl and Stanislawow) and bishoprics of Uzhorod, of Presov (under the Holy See), of Hajdudorog (under the Latin archbishop of Esztergom) and of Krizevci (under the Latin archbishop of Zagreb). The important dates for its union with Rome are those of the synod of Brest-Litovsk (Brzesc; 1596) and of the submission of Lwow (1700). In Poland persecutions were organized by the Russian government in 1795, 1839 and 1875 and after World War II.

The Rumanian Uniates have an archbishopric (Alba Iulia and Fagaras, established in 1701) with four suffragan bishoprics. The Russian Uniate archbishopric (Mogilev, with four suffragans) was subjected to a compulsory latinization under the tsar Alexander II. There are Catholics of Byzantine rite, however, in Greece, Bulgaria and Turkey. The Italo-Greek (Albanian) Church in Calabria and Sicily has the bishoprics of Lungro (founded in 1919) and Piana, both under Latin archbishoprics.

Of the Byzantine rite also are the Melchites (or, more properly, Melkites) of Syria, Lebanon, Jordan and Egypt, whose liturgy is in Arabic. They are so much to be distinguished from the Europeans of the Byzantine rite, however, that the term "of the Melchite rite" is now used of them. Their name, meaning "king's men," was originally a term of disparagement bestowed by their Monophysite fellow countrymen on those oriental Christians who remained loyal to Constantinople and therefore to the eastern Roman emperor's ("king's") religion after the council of Chalcedon (451). Their change from the Byzantine allegiance to the Roman is generally dated at 1724, when the patriarch Athanasius Dabbas acknowledged the Holy See on his deathbed; but his Catholic successor, Cyril VI Tanas, was deposed, and it was not until 1834, after the Egyptian invasion of Syria, that a Catholic patriarch was returned in the person of Maximus III Mazlum (confirmed by Rome in 1836). The Melchite patriarch of Antioch resides at Ain Traz in Lebanon. There are archbishops of Aleppo, of Beirut and Jebeil, of Bostra and Hauran, of Damascus (two suffragans), of Emesa, of Tyre (four suffragans) and of Jordan.

The Armenian Rite.—Uniates of this rite use a liturgy adapted from that of the Gregorian (Monophysite) Armenian Church. Their connection with Rome is sometimes dated from 1198; but a stronger movement of union began with the Dominican missions in the 14th century, although the specifically Armenian hierarchy was not established till the middle of the 18th. The patriarch of Cilicia resides at Bzommar near Beirut. There are archbishoprics of Mardin, of Sebaste (Sivas) and Tokat, of Aleppo, of Constantinople and of Lwow; bishoprics of Isfahan, of Beirut and of Alexandria, as well as 12 bishoprics in Turkey; and also churches in Greece and in Rumania. The Mechitarists (*q.v.*) of Venice are Armenian Uniates.

The Coptic Rite.—The Uniate church of this rite, in Egypt, in Ethiopia and in Eritrea, is of course drawn from the Coptic Church of the Egyptian Monophysites and has a liturgy in the Coptic language. The Catholic Coptic patriarchate of Alexandria was founded in 1895. There are suffragan bishoprics of Hermopolis Magna and of Thebes.

Syriac Liturgies.—Whereas the provenance of the Byzantine, the Armenian and the Coptic rites of Uniates is easily understood, that of the various Syriac rites may require some preliminary explanation. Historically, there are two sources: the East Syrian, Assyrian or Nestorian *Liturgy of the Apostles Addai and Mari;* and the West Syrian, Jacobite or Monophysite *Liturgy of St. James.* The former gave rise to two Uniate rites, the Chaldaean and the Syro-Malabarese; the latter to three, the Syrian, the Maronite and the Syro-Malankarese. However, a classification here by East Syrian and West Syrian groups would involve difficulties of nomenclature and a misleading fusion of distinct bodies. The rites will therefore be introduced separately.

The Chaldaean Rite.—The Uniates of this rite, mainly in Mesopotamia and Kurdistan, use the *Liturgy of Addai and Mari* and have also a Syriac vernacular. Union with Rome is dated at 1551, when John Sulaka led the first group of converts from Nestorianism, and at 1680, when Joseph of Amida (Diarbekr) led the second. The patriarch of Babylon resides at Mosul, and there are archbishoprics of Keruk and of Urmia and eight suffragan bishoprics.

The Syro-Malabarese Rite.—Catholics of this rite represent those Christians of St. Thomas (*see* THOMAS, SAINT) who were converted to the Roman allegiance by the Portuguese at the synod of Diamper (Udayamperur, in Cochin) in 1599. They use a form of the *Liturgy of Addai and Mari,* as their antecedents were Nestorian. The archbishopric of Ernakulam has suffragan bishoprics of Changanacheri, of Kottayam and of Trichur.

The Syrian Rite.—The term "of the Syrian rite," though in a general sense applicable to several churches, is used specifically to designate Uniates using the Syriac *Liturgy of St. James,* with certain formulas in Carshuni (Arabic written in Syriac), and representing Christians formerly of the Jacobite persuasion who were united with Rome in 1646. Their patriarch of Antioch resides at Mardin in Turkey, and there are archbishops of Damascus, of Emesa, of Baghdad and of Mosul, as well as four diocesan bishoprics.

The Maronite Rite.—The Maronites (*q.v.*) of Lebanon represent a community which was probably at first Monothelite, originating after the council of Constantinople in 680–681. Though they renounced Monothelitism in 1182 and were united with Rome till the end of the Latin kingdom of Jerusalem, the connection was subsequently broken and not permanently resumed till 1736. As the Syrian Uniates, they use principally the *Liturgy of St. James* and formulas in Carshuni. Their patriarch of Antioch has authority over bishops of Aleppo, of Beirut, of Cyprus, of Damascus, of Heliopolis, of Jebeil and Batrun (Botrys), of Sidon, of Tripoli and of Tyre.

The Syro-Malankarese Rite.—When the Dutch in 1663 put an end to the Portuguese domination of Malabar, numbers of the Malabarese abandoned the Roman connection (*see* above, *The Syro-Malabarese Rite*) but, instead of reverting to Nestorianism, accepted in 1665 a Monophysite bishop from the Jacobite patriarch at Mardin. In 1930, therefore, when some of these Jacobites were united with Rome again, the *Liturgy of St. James* was retained. The archbishopric of Trivandrum (established in 1932) has a suffragan bishopric at Tiruvalla. (X.)

HISTORY

The human institution that is the fullness of the godhead bodily was to be governed on earth by a sacramental sovereign as agent or representative, the apostle or "vicar" of Christ. That this "vicar of Christ" should be the bishop of Rome belongs to the "logic of history"; and, in the faith that "the Word which is God became flesh and dwelt among us," history assumed a validity not realized before or elsewhere. If, in "the fullness of time, God sent forth His Son born of a woman," He selected the Roman imperium as the historical circumstance of that incarnation. Rome was not merely the metropolis of that humanity but the seat of an actual and formative sovereignty beyond comparison more effective and significant than that of any other imperial city. Here if anywhere the City of God must encounter the "fullness of manhood bodily." Within a generation of the death of the apostles, Roman legions had destroyed the temple at Jerusalem. Less than a century later the tradition of St. Peter's presence in Rome was, as Louis Duchesne stated, "precise and universal." Duchesne further declared that Dionysius of Corinth in Greece, Irenaeus in Gaul, Clement and Origen in Alexandria and Tertullian in Africa all referred to it, that in Rome itself Caius, about 200, pointed out the tomb of the apostles, that by the 3rd century popes built on their title of successors of St. Peter and that their right to this title is nowhere denied. Clement (*c.* 97) thinks it natural for the church in Rome to address a letter of advice to the church in Corinth upon the outbreak of an "execrable and godless schism." Ignatius of Antioch apostrophizes the Roman Church with a series of titles such as he addresses to no other. It is above all "a church presiding in charity, maintaining the law of Christ,

and bearer of the Father's name." At his martyrdom he asks for the prayers of the Roman Church for the church in Syria since "Jesus Christ alone will be their bishop, together with your charity." (*Ancient Christian Writers,* vol. i, tr. J. A. Kleist, Newman Press, Westminster, Md.; 1946.) Irenaeus, who came from Asia Minor and wrote Greek in southern Gaul, and whose work found an immediate public in Egypt, was world-conscious and belonged to a world community not only as a theologian but as a subject of the Roman empire.

The city of the Caesars and of the senate and people of Rome was the seat of the apostles; it was also the city of martyrs and heretics. Persecution and heresy contributed to the mature self-consciousness of the church. The offense of Christianity as defined by Trajan (*c.* 112) was of the nature of treason—otherwise harmless. The greatest persecutions, those under Decius (250–253), Valerian (257–260) and Diocletian (303–311), were virtual acts of war against an *imperium in imperio* which seemed to threaten the empire. The danger would have been as real as it seemed but for the peculiar combination of faith and morals which enabled Christians to "dwell on earth as citizens of heaven" (*Epistle to Diognetus*). They could thus pray for the emperor's welfare while they denied his divine title (Cyprian). "They obey the established laws, yet their conduct goes beyond those laws"; and "Exposed to the wild beasts to make them renounce the Lord, are they not seen to remain invincible?" (*Epistle to Diognetus*). Origen's confidence that Christ is stronger than the emperor, the army and the senate and people of Rome were inevitably and essentially Christian. The organic unity, the κοινὴ ἕνωσις, of the church was vigorous and visible in ceaseless missionary activity at every level of society and in every province. Christians nursed the sick, visited the prisoners, found employment for the idle and cared for the poor, orphans, widows and slaves. All this, inspired and confirmed by a naïf sense of divine presence, omnipotence and justice, gave the church not only authority over the whole life of its rapidly multiplying membership but an independence of imperial sanctions. Half the interval between Nero and Constantine was persecution, and Diocletian had reason to complain that Christians did not fear death. The martyrs were not only the army of the church: they made explicit what the Christian faith had always implied, a totally new conception of the majesty of the human being as such and of human institutions. Constantine may have been a mystic, but he was certainly a political realist. Paganism died of its unreality. Julian's attempt to revive it in revolt against a corrupt and heretical Christianity (361–362) was no more than an adventure of sentiment and ideology.

Meanwhile the church defined its faith and established an orthodoxy. Definition is not, in the Catholic view, identical with the faith, but it is the means by which the faith becomes incarnate and available in the world and, as such, is implied in and authorized by the incarnation of God. It is thus conditioned by the "fullness of time" and is given to the church by the same authority that created the church, when and as the purpose of redemption and the existence of the church require it. So given it is infallible and final; but it is also the conclusion of a stage in the history of the church on earth, and its enunciation is prepared by a period of questions and uncertain or inadequate or controversial answers. The New Testament, whose canon was fixed *c.* 120, and the formulary known as the Apostles' Creed, used for the instruction of catechumens at the beginning of the 3rd century, both reveal the doubts and questions which assailed the primitive Christian. The Gospels and the Acts were historical documents; the creed is a catalogue of facts. As against the Jews, the apostolic church proclaimed an eschatology which was no longer a promise but a present reality. As against the docetism and gnosticism which represent the perennial reluctance to accept the faith as a fact, the New Testament and the creeds emphasized the event and the institution. Gnostic theories—those of Cerinthus, Valentinus, Basilides, Carpocrates and others—were not and did not claim to be histories. They were cosmological myths and speculations, ingenious and sometimes profound metaphysical guesses, against which the primitive church affirmed the supernatural history and, in doing so, realized its own divinely appointed form and existence. Fact implied revelation; revelation implied authority and tradition; and all implied the presence on earth of God in the person of Christ and in the Holy Spirit who informed the Holy Catholic Church. Irenaeus (c. 186) finds the authority in "the tradition of the great and ancient church known to all men which was founded and constituted by the most glorious apostles Peter and Paul: by its traditions and its faith announced to all men and descended through the succession of its bishops to us, we confound all those who gather where they ought not" (*Adversus haereses*, iii, 381). Irenaeus, who wrote against the Valentinians, gave also an account of all the principal heresies down to his time. Justin wrote, besides his *Apology*, a *Syntagma* against all heresies, which is lost. Hippolytus in his *Syntagma* attacked 32 heresies. Epiphanius in the 4th century catalogued 80 heresies in the *Panarion*. "The Jewish strain in Christianity with its abomination of the Gentile worships and its assumption that they connoted immorality; the links of community to community which prevented unfettered development; the hierarchic system; the principle of apostolic authority and apostolic tradition; the numerical preponderance of folk with the *foi du charbonnier* prevented what would in effect have been the absorption of Christianity in Graeco-Roman culture." (A. D. Nock, *Cambridge Ancient History*, vol. xii, p. 446.)

FROM CONSTANTINE TO CHARLEMAGNE

Imperial conversion brought into the church all the problems of the empire. Of these the most urgent was the pagan habit of toleration expressed in the Edict of Milan (313), issued in the name of Licinius and Constantine, that "everyone may have licence to worship whatever he pleases." Such toleration came to the Christians as relief, but imperial protection raised the old question of Christ and Caesar in a new, subtle and dangerous form. It not only threatened to confound the church with imperial administration but exposed the faith to the speculative ingenuity and dispute endemic in paganism. These two secular problems coalesced to make theology the subject of party strife. The teaching of Arius, according to whom the Logos was a creature not divine but free, mutable and adopted as Son of God in prevision of his merits, revived the ancient reluctance of the philosophical pagan to accept the incarnation as a fact and relieved the Arian of the revelation and authority which faith in the supreme mystery demanded and presupposed. It was a rationalization not apostolic or holy or catholic, and the Christians who adopted it ceased to be Christian. At the council of Nicaea (325) the word *homoousios* ("consubstantial"), accepted to affirm the deity of Christ against the Arians, was probably suggested by Roman legates. Eusebius, bishop of Nicomedia, who had learned his theology from Lucian of Antioch, used the heresy of his fellow-student Arius as an occasion of intrigue. Without disputing the decrees of the council of Nicaea he devised an imperial formula to comprehend Arians and Catholics and gained the support of Constantine and Flavius Julius Constantius (337–361) for a policy which seemed to promise imperial peace and actually promoted ecclesiastical dissension. This policy not only raised Arian bishops to most of the eastern sees but meant also constant interference *a latere* by bishops in the jurisdiction of their brother bishops, the employment of imperial prefects and police in the enforcement of partisan decrees and the habit of using theological formulas not to define the faith but as instruments of ecclesiastical diplomacy. Thus by the carefully packed council of Tyre (335) Athanasius was deposed on frivolous charges and an Arian, George of Cappadocia, raised with the aid of imperial police to the see of Alexandria. At Antioch in 341 an assembly of 100 bishops issued an ambiguous formulary denying that they were followers of Arius but evading the Nicene Creed. Finally, in 359, imperial pressure enforced a similar evasion on the whole episcopate, both western and eastern, at the councils of Ariminum and Selencia. In 360 the formula was accepted which "with a little complaisance Athanasius and Aetius might have repeated together"; and in 361 Constantius was succeeded by Julian, and Arian victory by pagan reaction.

Rome and the west remained comparatively free from the heresy and policy of the east. No longer head of the empire, Rome was still head of the church; the decline from its imperial status emphasized its ecclesiastical independence. The bishop's residence was established on the Caelian hill in the ancient house of the Laterani, owned by Fausta, the emperor's wife; and there Pope Miltiades held a council in 313. A basilica was raised, the existing church of the Lateran. Athanasius, exiled from Alexandria, visited Rome in 339. His news of Antony, Pachomius and the desert fathers kindled among wealthy Romans an interest in ascetic and monastic life which bore fruit in the next generation; and before Pope Julius and a council of 50 western bishops he was acquitted of the charges which had led to his deposition at the council of Tyre. The eastern bishops, who had asked to be invited to this council in Rome, nevertheless declined the invitation when it came. To their ultimatum requiring him to choose between Athanasius and themselves, Pope Julius replied that it was natural to hear complaints of bishops who said that they had been unjustly deposed; that in the absence of accusers he had examined the only available evidence, which they had themselves supplied at the council of Tyre; and that he was concerned not with trifling stories but with the unity of the church (340).

Roman theology had not generated the controversial and speculative subtleties which divided the east. A schism left by persecution, between those who had endured and those who compromised with the pagans, had occasioned some disorder which was soon overcome. A greater schism, that of the Donatists, rent the diocese of Carthage. To the historian its main interest lies in its effect upon Augustine, who during 16 years of controversy matured his conception of the Catholic Church. From 413 to 426 he was writing *The City of God*. He was baptized by Ambrose in 387. Two years earlier Jerome (c. 340–420) had retired to Bethlehem to complete his translation of the Bible (Vulgate). Ambrose, born at Trier about 340, son of the prefect of Gaul, became prefect of Upper Italy in 369 and, on the death of Auxentius (who had accepted the confession of Ariminum), was appointed bishop of Milan. So complete was the popular acclaim that the bishops accepted it as a sign of divine will, as it was certainly human prudence. One of the best of Roman governors thus became one of the greatest of Christian bishops. His most significant task was to resist the inclination of the empire to control the church. A little younger than Ambrose, his friend Theodosius was made Augustus in 379 and in 380 was baptized a Catholic. In 381 he summoned a council to Constantinople (the second general council). Ambrose at the same time presided over a council at Aquileia. Both condemned Arianism; Theodosius decreed that "all beliefs contrary to the faith clearly taught by the pontiff Damasus and by Peter, bishop of Alexandria, were heresy." He ordered all church property to be restored to the orthodox and named the bishops who were to be so accounted. The council also declared that "the bishop of Constantinople shall have the pre-eminence of honour after the bishop of Rome, for this city is the new Rome," thus founding ecclesiastical dignity on imperial status. Rome rejected this principle. In 383 Theodosius convoked a meeting of Catholic and Arian leaders, and upon its failure issued another edict, never strictly enforced, forbidding heretical worship public and private. So in Milan, Ambrose refused to allow a single Arian church even for Justina. The murder of Gratian and the advance of Maximus through Gaul and Italy called Theodosius to the west, where, after the defeat and death of Maximus, he resided for nearly three years at Milan. Valentinian II also lived there, likewise under the personal influence of Ambrose. The bishop proclaimed and maintained the principle that "the emperor is within the church, not over the church," a principle repeated by Pope Leo I (the Great) after the council of Chalcedon (451): *"Alia tamen ratio est rerum secularium, alia divinarum; nam praeter illam petram quam Dominus in fundamento posuit, stabilis erit nulla constructio."* Such was the principle also of Augustine's doctrine of the two cities, and such from the 5th century to the 10th was the fact demonstrated by the rise and fall of innumerable "powers" with the consistent spread and development of the one catholic Christendom.

Pope Leo was called upon to state once more and in uncompromising terms the fact in which and by which the Catholic Church exists. The heresy at Chalcedon was that of the Monophysites, who declared that there was but one nature in Christ, the divine—another form of the perennial desire to evade the central Christian dogma. The pope's definition, acclaimed by the council as "the voice of Peter," was an uncompromising statement of the fact:

Following, then, in the footsteps of the holy fathers, we all teach in harmony that the Son and our Lord Jesus Christ are one and the same, one and the same perfect in godhead, the same perfect in human nature, true God and true man, the same made of a rational soul and body, consubstantial with the Father according to His godhead, consubstantial with us according to His human nature, made in all things like us without sin: according to His godhead begotten of His Father before all ages; the same in these last days for us and for our salvation born according to human nature of the Virgin Mary, the Mother of God; one and the same to be acknowledged as Christ the Son, the Lord, the only begotten, in two natures not removed by reason of their union, but rather the characteristics of each preserved united together in one person and subsistence, not divided nor shared among two persons but one and the same: Son, Only-begotten, God, Word, Lord, Jesus, Christ, as the prophets before had said of Him, as He Himself taught us and as the creed of the fathers has handed down to us.

In that statement, there is obviously no attempt to placate human reason and no appeal to human experience. Words are used to command a rational submission of faith to a fact which transcends reason. It is the voice of original authority, not a resultant explanation; foundation, not superstructure—"the stone which the Lord laid as a foundation." Man is whole, is perfectly and eternally human in Christ who is Very God. Nothing can violate the distinction between God and man. The incarnation does not violate but transcends it, and it is thus not an evolution but the consummate act of transcendent godhead which the church announces and embodies. It purports to be a statement of the atonement and sacrifice in which human nature is restored to perfect unity with divine or absolute being. It is announced and accepted as fact by the Roman bishop, "the voice of Peter," at the council of Chalcedon. Thus by the 5th century the church is fully conscious of itself as the issue of that supernatural union, wholly human, wholly divine. From that position there could be no retreat.

The fall of the western empire (476) completed the isolation of the Roman see. Arianism, expelled from the empire, had been established meanwhile among the Goths of the Danube by Ulphilas (Wulfila; d. 383), appointed their bishop by Eusebius of Nicomedia. He taught a Gothic Christianity in the Gothic language, inventing an alphabet and translating the Scriptures. Untrammelled by orthodoxy, this faith needed no apostolic see and was adopted by Goths, Suebi, Burgundians, Vandals and Lombards as a kind of national religion. Gradually the west had been subdued by conquest and infiltration to these races: Africa to the Vandals, Spain to the Suebi and Visigoths, Gaul to the Visigoths and Burgundians. The Avars wasted Pannonia, the Slovenes Styria, Carinthia and Carniola. The Croats and Serbs established themselves south of the Save. Italy was defended by a barbarian army under the Herulian Odoacer, a Catholic, until his defeat and death in 493 at the hands of Theodoric the Ostrogoth, an Arian, who ruled Italy from Ravenna with conspicuous ability and tolerance with the advice of the Catholics Boethius (480–524) and Cassiodorus (c. 490–c. 585). After Theodoric's death (526) Italy was conquered by the Catholic emperor Justinian's armies (535–554) under Belisarius and was till the 8th century officially a province of the Byzantine empire under the exarch of Ravenna. The Lombards conquered northern Italy and established themselves at Pavia. At once subject to repeated attacks from the Franks and extending their own conquests in Italy, the Lombards, unlike the Goths, had neither genius nor opportunity for peace. Thus when Gregory I the Great became pope he succeeded to what might be described as "the grave of the deceased Roman empire." He had been praetor and then monk and had lived three years in Constantinople as the nuncio of Pelagius II seeking imperial aid against the Lombards. As Roman and as pope, he saw the world as a whole. Lawyer and judge by training, monk, bishop and apostle by vocation, he realized the creative and redemptive possibilities of the papacy and of the Catholic Church at the moment when outside it and apart from its supernatural certainty all civilization in the west was dead beyond hope of resurrection.

During the next six centuries the function of the church was to create Christendom, and its chief instruments in this work were episcopacy and monasticism. During Gregory's pontificate the Arian rulers of the Lombards in Italy and of the Visigoths in Spain were baptized Catholics. In 597 his mission of 40 monks landed in Kent under Augustine, "their abbot made bishop, with my permission, by the bishops of Germany and with their assistance conducted to that nation at the limit of the world." A century earlier (496) Clovis with 3,000 Franks had been baptized by Remigius, bishop of Reims, and was exhorted by Avitus, bishop of Vienne, to spread the faith among the barbarians "corrupted by heretical doctrines." Clovis had respected the property, person and advice of bishops even as a pagan, and he owed his conversion partly to the prudence which recognized in them the virtual rulers of Gaul. He broke the power of the Visigoths at Vouillé near Poitiers and extended his dominion to the Pyrenees, everywhere requiring Arians to become orthodox and restoring their churches after their reconsecration. In Paris, the seat of his government, he built and dedicated a basilica to the Holy Apostles. In the 5th century the monk St. Severinus, a friend of Odoacer, established the authority of personal sanctity over the peoples of the upper Danube. During the 7th, 8th and 9th centuries the Croats were Christianized by Roman missionaries; the Bavarians of Upper Austria by St. Rupert of Worms, who founded a see and a monastery at Salzburg (c. 700) that Charlemagne made an archbishopric (798); Moravia by the Greek monks Methodius and Cyril (Constantine); and Bohemia by its prince, whom St. Methodius baptized (871). Prague became a see in 973. The Magyars, who had withstood a succession of missions from east and west, were at length converted under Stephen I, who established the metropolitan see of Esztergom (Gran) and founded the monastery of Pannonhalma near Gyor Szent Marton (Martinsberg) with five other houses and was crowned with the golden crown sent by Pope Silvester II on the Feast of the Assumption, 1001.

Monasticism was the Christian equivalent of the imperial army, the means by which the church subdued and enlisted, colonized and administered the new peoples and revived or defended the old. The first western monk, St. Martin of Tours (c. 316–c. 400), was a Pannonian, born of pagan parents and bred a soldier; he secured his discharge in order to renounce the world. Under St. Hilary of Poitiers (c. 300–c. 368), himself a convert, Martin established a monastery at Ligugé and another at Marmoutier on the banks of the Loire. As monk and bishop of Tours he devoted himself to an ascetic discipline and to the conversion of pagans. Other monastic communities gathered at Marseilles (St. Victor) and at Lérins (St. Honoratus or Honoré) whence another St. Hilary was appointed bishop of Arles (426). St. Patrick visited Lérins and Marmoutier before setting out on his mission to Ireland, for which he was consecrated by Germanus, bishop of Auxerre. About 480 was born St. Benedict of Nursia (q.v.), whose *Regula monachorum* or Rule (c. 515) became the pattern of all western monasticism. "For thee, therefore, whosoever thou be, my words are intended who, giving up thy own will, dost take the all-powerful and excellent arms of obedience to fight under the Lord Christ, the true King." In that conception of service and society lay the seeds of the rivalry between natural and supernatural sovereignty which appeared full-grown in the 11th and 12th centuries. (*See also* BENEDICTINES.)

A few years older than the *Digest* of Justinian (who was certainly acquainted with it), the Rule established a discipline and constitution and regulated a liturgical society with impersonal precision. It represented the religious as the *Institutes* represented the civil society. The Rule required self-surrender rather than self-abnegation. Based on long monastic experience and devotion to the person of Christ (who is to be seen and served in the abbot and in all the brethren, in strangers who visit the monastery and in all its life and work), it was the perfect instrument for creating centres of Christian society above all in rural and pagan territory and for reforming the religious communities of the west. Thus a rational economy, moral training and education in the arts of peace developed about the altars of the church and were available to transform the secular barbarity of war and heroic solitude into Christian civilization. The Irish monk St. Columban, whose rule followed the older pattern of extreme austerity, established four houses for men and two for women in Gaul. His disciple Gallus founded St. Gall on the shores of Lake Constance. Columban died at Bobbio, which he founded as a mission to the Arian Lombards and equipped with books, the nucleus of the most famous of mediaeval libraries. Cassiodorus, Theodoric's minister, attempted in 535 to found a Christian academy in Rome and, failing this, established a house at Squillace in Calabria (Vivarium) with a library for which he composed his two handbooks on divine and liberal learning. "But for the existence of such a sanction for literary culture, it is quite possible that, with the exception of Virgil, no Latin classic would have reached us in a complete form" (Montague James, *Cambridge Medieval History*, vol. iii, p. 486).

The greatest single achievement of monastic missions was the conversion of Britain. Thanks to Gregory I and Augustine, English monasticism was Benedictine. The Benedictine abbey at Canterbury was the metropolitan church. The influence of this type of mission was apparent at once. It created a culture, introduced the Roman alphabet and inspired a literature first in Latin and then in the vernacular. It acquired lands and rights which were recorded in documents and, as its teaching influenced custom, it codified the laws, as Bede says, "*justa exempla Romanorum.*" The fact that England, unlike Gaul, Italy and the lands of the continental barbarians, had nothing but pagan custom and a rudimentary civilization gave the monks a more complete victory.

The attachment of English Christianity to the Roman see was the stronger as Gregory I was the apostle of the English; and Christianity without imperial tradition and Roman law was free to develop with and through indigenous custom. Benedict Biscop is said to have made seven pilgrimages to the tomb of the apostles. He visited Lérins. On the third journey he brought with him Theodore of Tarsus and Abbot Adrian of Naples, both monks who brought a knowledge of Greek and an infectious love of learning (668). Aldhelm (*c.* 640–709), trained at Malmesbury and Canterbury, abbot of Malmesbury and bishop of Sherborne, architect, Latin scholar and English poet, represents the first fruits of this English culture, whose greatest figure is Bede (*c.* 673–735). His contemporary St. Boniface or Wynfrith (d. 754), a monk of Exeter, carried the mission with the sanction of Pope Gregory II and the help of Charles Martel into Bavaria, Thuringia, Friesland, Hesse and Saxony. He established eight bishoprics and founded many monasteries, above all Fulda, where he hoped to die. He reformed the work of Irish monks with Roman and Benedictine discipline. In 747 he was appointed primate of his great province of Mainz. In 751 he consecrated Pippin, who with the authority of Pope Zacharias had been elected king of the Franks and in imitation of the English kings wished to be anointed. St. Boniface finally resigned his see and went to preach the faith to the Frisians, by whom he was martyred (754).

Meanwhile, in the civilized east the Christological discussion continued. The pope, though a subject of the (Byzantine) emperor, was head of the church, and the east, always divided in faith, had always been uncertain in ecclesiastical submission. The churches of Egypt and Syria, strongholds of Monophysite theology and jealous for the dignity of Alexandria, had refused the decision of the council of Chalcedon. The emperor Zeno tried an accommodation, the *Henoticon* (481). Justinian, a Macedonian Catholic, in the controversy of the "Three Chapters" (553), forced the aged Pope Vigilius to attend the fifth general council at Constantinople and to assent to the condemnation of Theodore of Mopsuestia, Theodoret and Ibas, three writers who had been accused and acquitted of Nestorian heresy at Chalcedon. The emperor Heraclius tried the formula known as Monothelitism, which ascribed one "active energy" to the Saviour, translated by the Latin bishop as "one will"; and Pope Honorius, mistaking the

question, professed himself willing to assent. Pope Martin I (649–653) refused this concession and was exiled by the emperor Constans II (641–668) to the Crimea. The sixth general council (680) vindicated Martin I, condemned Monothelitism and criticized Honorius. Nevertheless, in 692 the council *in Trullo* (Quinisext) was deliberately anti-Roman, and Pope Sergius, arrested at the orders of Justinian II, was saved only by force from the imperial officer. Finally the emperor Leo III the Isaurian (717–740) had initiated his campaign of iconoclasm in 725, the most unpopular and unnecessary of reforms, enforced by persecution and confirmed by the council of Hieria in 753. The schism endured till 843.

But the emperor, if he was willing to force the Roman bishop to submit in matters of doctrine, was quite unable to defend his Roman subjects from their enemies in the flesh. It was out of long Roman experience that Pope Zacharias (741–752) answered Pippin's question concerning kingship that the king should be he who really has power to rule. Neither Roman nor Byzantine sovereignty had been bound by a doctrine of legitimacy: the prince was the guardian of *jus* and *pax*. In Rome the bishop and the people were bound together by ties of faith, history and administration. The walls, defenses, aqueducts, food, hospitals, finance, justice and religion were in the bishop's charge. Not only the city but the west as a whole was in need of defense. In 711 Spain and Sardinia had fallen to the Arabs. Sicily was frequently raided by Saracens, who exacted tribute from Syracuse. In 732, at Poitiers, Charles Martel broke the Moslem invasion, saved Aquitaine and established his title as defender of Christendom. Thus, when, in 751, the Lombard Aistulf seized Ravenna, threatened Rome and meditated the conquest of Italy, Pope Stephen II (752–757), having appealed in vain for help to the emperor, turned to Pippin. He journeyed into Francia, crowned Pippin at St. Denis and, returning to Italy with the army of the Franks, received Ravenna from Pippin, who destroyed the Lombard forces (756). Charles the Great completed the conquest by capturing Pavia (772–774).

Thus the pope became a sovereign prince. His "temporal power" was the consequence of an inevitable severance of west from east, of the barbarian and Moslem invasion and of his apostolic function to maintain the faith as against the heresies and schisms which were endemic in the eastern imperial system and to evangelize the pagans of the west. Gregory I, reminding bishops that they were the salt of the earth and that, above all else, men expected of them the salvation of souls, said that "nevertheless even now there are no worldly affairs which priests do not administer" (*Liber regulae pastoralis*, 595). Pippin, son of Charles Martel, brought up by the monks of St. Denis and consecrated by St. Boniface, held much the same conception of episcopacy.

Charles the Great, after 800, was not only Augustus but "crowned of God, great and peace-bringing emperor who rules the Roman empire and who by the grace of God is king of the Franks and Lombards." He read St. Augustine's *De civitate Dei* and, admitting that the old Roman empire was the *civitas terrena*, regarded himself as governor under the Emperor of Heaven of the City of God. For 30 years (772–804) he made holy war on the pagan Saxons, and when he died in 814 his empire, extending from the Elbe to the Pyrenees, from the English sea to the Tiber, was united in so far as it was Christian. His school under Alcuin of York (735–804) was the cultural centre of this empire. Louis I the Pious, crowned at Reims by Stephen IV (816), co-operated with Pope Paschal I in his desire to convert the Danes. The archbishop of Reims, the bishop of Cambrai and a mission of monks under Anskar spread the faith about the mouth of the Elbe. A monastery was founded at Korvey (822) and a bishopric at Hamburg (831). In 826 the Danish prince Harold with many hundred followers was baptized at Mainz. Meanwhile, St. Benedict of Aniane, having reformed the monasteries of Aquitaine, was brought to advise Louis on the moral reform of the kingdom and was established in a monastery at Aachen. Under his influence the rule of St. Benedict was imposed on all monastic houses in the Frankish kingdom.

THE FORMATION OF CHRISTENDOM

At the death of Louis the Pious (840) the natural divisions of the empire and local needs, attachments and traditions were re-asserted. The idea of empire derived from Rome, taught by Alcuin of York and realized by the genius of Charlemagne, receded. The invasion of the Normans or Northmen intensified the confusion of dynastic war. Based in Flanders, they ravaged Saxony, the Rhineland and France, burned Cologne, Rouen, Paris and Aachen, captured Trier, besieged Orléans, seized Bordeaux and advanced to Toulouse. They sacked the monasteries and completed the destruction of towns and communes surviving from Roman times. The Edict of Mersen (847) commanding every man to serve a lord only defined the actual situation; feudal organization was partly, if not mostly, a defense against the anarchy the Normans left behind. In 876 they settled in Normandy. Two centuries of war thus isolated and established the church in the west as the one continuous, unifying and civilizing institution and (as it were) defined its double function of evangelizing and civilizing mankind.

This isolation of the west was emphasized by the schism of Photius in Constantinople during the pontificate of Nicholas I (858–867). The elevation of Photius, a layman, to the patriarchate and the deposition of Ignatius, his predecessor, were uncanonical. On the other hand, the interference of the Roman legates in the newly founded Bulgarian church was perhaps unlawful. The *Filioque* question (the double procession of the Holy Ghost) was used mainly as an occasion, though the theological difference between east and west is implied in the dispute. As always, the west was more simply and uncompromisingly Trinitarian and laid greater emphasis on the incarnation with its consequent exaltation of the church. Nicholas I, a canonist and political realist, advanced from the traditional Gelasian doctrine of "two swords" to that which foreshadowed the papal doctrine of Hildebrand. To the emperor Michael III he wrote that, whereas the emperor needed the pope in religion, the pope had no need of the emperor in temporal matters. At the same time (865) he demanded obedience from Charles the Bald and even quashed a judgment of the great archbishop Hincmar of Reims and declared that what the pope decides all must observe. For a century, however, the Roman see, lacking temporal protection, suffered from its temporal status. The Roman nobles, the house of Spoleto, the counts of Tusculum and the kings of Germany made and unmade popes in a succession down to John XII, deposed by Otto the Great in 963.

Weakness at the centre encouraged and exaggerated the centrifugal tendencies revealed in the wide, half-civilized rural areas that were exposed to waves of pagan and barbarian invasion. The urban organization of the church in the Roman empire was not suited to this scattered and insecure continent. The church needed an imperial idea and the co-operation of temporal powers. During the 10th century the house of Saxony laid the foundations of the mediaeval empire, Cluny revived monasticism and the canon law was gradually developed; and these three factors, together with intensified theological controversy, prepared the great reform of the 11th century, which was initiated by a reformed papacy.

1. Otto the Great (912–973), occupied during the first 25 years of his reign in uniting the German peoples and defending them against Hungarians, Slavs and Normans, was crowned emperor in 962 by Pope John XII in Rome and thereafter employed in restoring order in Italy. He founded a metropolitan see at Magdeburg, whose first archbishop, Adalbert, monk of Trier and abbot of Weissenburg, had been missionary to the Russians. Bishoprics were founded also at Oldenburg and Havelberg (946), at Prague (976), at Olomouc (Olmütz; for Moravia) and at Odense (for Denmark; 980). In 936 St. Unni of Bremen undertook a mission to Scandinavia, where he died. The second bishop of Prague, St. Adalbert, who baptized St. Stephen of Hungary, left his see in defiance of papal and imperial injunction to preach the Gospel to the Poles and Russians, by whom he was martyred in 997. The frontier churches of Bohemia, Hungary and Poland looked to Rome rather than to Germany; and Pope Gregory V (996–999),

cousin and chaplain of Otto III, revived the missionary tradition of the Holy See but fell a victim of city faction prompted by local nobles. At his death, Otto III appointed the Frenchman Gerbert of Aurillac (Silvester II, 999–1003). Silvester dreamed of an empire independent of the German kings which should embody a world faith and a world culture. Like other learned men he underestimated local ties and traditions, and like other Frenchmen he failed to realize the needs of German administration. Simony he counted the greatest evil in the church. But it was much more than the "sin of Simon Magus": in France it was, indeed, a corruption which was the result of generations of insecurity strengthening the hands of unscrupulous lords; in Germany it was rooted in Teutonic and feudal custom and continued by social and economic necessity.

The spread of Christianity among remote and barbarous peoples implied local autonomy and the adaptation of ancient pagan administrative custom. Churches were built, maintained and possessed by their chiefs. The mission church was virtually autonomous; its priest was the vassal and servant, often the kinsman, of the local landowner and protected by the local saint. Clovis, the champion of orthodoxy, accepted this arrangement. In 794 the council of Frankfurt allowed churches to be given or sold so long as they were maintained. Hincmar of Reims (c. 805–882), monk, canonist and archbishop, approved the principle and wished only to reform the abuses. Bishops were imperial and royal ministers, often viceroys. The most pious of emperors, St. Henry II, employed them in every function of government and insisted on his right to appoint bishops and to control or approve episcopal elections. Bishops trained in the imperial chancery were indispensable in the administration of the empire. Pope Leo IX (1048–54) was related to Henry III and had been employed as soldier and diplomat in the imperial service. The Holy See was constantly subject to imperial interference and protection, and the great reformer, though elected at Rome, was Henry III's nominee. Thus at every level—parochial, episcopal, papal—the question awaited decision whether the church was in effect a holy, catholic and supernatural institution appointing its own bishops and priests upon its own authority or (in the language of a later age) part of the body politic.

The system evolved by nature was subject to natural corruption. The emperor Conrad II and King Philip I of France made a traffic of bishoprics. But deeper than these abuses was the question presupposed in all movements of reform of the true function of Christian priest and bishop. Councils repeatedly forbade lay interference in parochial benefices (Ingelheim, 948; Augsburg, 952; Seligenstadt, 1023; Bourges, 1031). Linked with this question was that of clerical celibacy, since a married clergy was tied by natural duties and interests to the *civitas terrena*. Marriage implied inheritance and tended to absorb the clergy in local and feudal tenancies and obligations. At the council of Pavia (1018) Benedict VIII (1012–24) denounced clerical marriage mainly on the ground that church property should not be exploited for priests' families. But there was also the question of sexual morality and the traditional attitude of the church to virginity. Celibacy was admired by Tertullian, recommended by Eusebius, required by Cyril of Jerusalem and said to be the general practice by Jerome. Epiphanius said that the church "does not admit even sub-deacons to live in marriage and beget children." Two popes, Siricius (384–399) and Innocent I (402–417), had condemned clerical marriage. Six councils in Carthage, Spain and Gaul required continence of married clergy. The Theodosian code pronounced the children of priests illegitimate. Celibacy was a tribute to the supernatural and sacramental vocation and as such was bound up with the supernatural and sacramental body which the confusion and expansion of the 9th and 10th centuries tended to obscure.

2. Monks were the exemplars and instruments of the supernatural society. It was their business to live in "the course of these declining times" as in and for the "solid estate of eternity." Monasticism (q.v.) was in essence a lay movement, and the multiplication of monasteries and the constant succession of monastic reforms was evidence of the hold of the Catholic faith on the lay

population. In 910 William I the Pious, count of Auvergne and duke of Aquitaine, founded Cluny. Odo of Cluny reformed Fleury and then, invited to Rome by Alberic, reformed the monasteries in and about the city and Monte Cassino. The reform spread through northern Italy and France. Cluny became the head of an order whose 300 houses, subject to the abbot of Cluny and exempt from all other authority but that of the pope, were organized in ten provinces extending from Spain to Poland. Cluny, "a spiritual field where earth and heaven meet" (Pietro Damiani), trained Urban II and Paschal II. It not only revived liturgical discipline and the Benedictine rule but realized on a world scale the practical order and common prudence of Benedictine monasticism. At the same time, Gerard of Brogne in Flanders and Dunstan of Glastonbury (d. 988) in England initiated monastic reform. In Italy St. Romuald founded the order of Camaldoli (c. 1012). In Normandy Herluin founded Bec (c. 1040), which under Lanfranc and St. Anselm became one of the great schools of Europe. There Pope Alexander II, Ivo of Chartres and Theobald of Canterbury received their training. The last wave of monastic reformation produced the Carthusian order founded by St. Bruno (1084) and the Cistercian founded by Robert of Molesme (1098). St. Bernard with the 30 companions entered Cîteaux in 1112 and with 12 monks founded Clairvaux in 1115. He was the "greatest of the monks" and one of the greatest preachers of the middle ages.

3. Canon law (q.v.) derives from the Scriptures, conciliar canons, papal decrees and traditions and customs of the church. In the west it developed later and more slowly than in the east. In 774 Charlemagne received from Pope Adrian I a collection of canons and decretals accepted at the council of Aachen (802) by the Frankish church. Under the see of Toledo the Spanish church possessed a larger collection including canons of Greek, African, Gallic and Spanish councils and papal decretals. In the 9th century also appeared the collection of "false decretals" whose forgery was not detected until the 15th. This collection, containing both real and spurious decretals, circulated in Spain, Italy, France and even England but was not much used in Rome till the 11th century. Collections made by Burchard of Worms (1012–23) and Ivo of Chartres (c. 1040–1116), Lanfranc's pupil at Bec, prepared the way for Franciscus Gratianus' great work. Gratianus, or Gratian, a Camaldulian monk of Bologna, produced the Decretum (1139–41), a systematic treatise (Concordia discordantium canonum) in three parts dealing with (1) sources of law and ecclesiastical persons; (2) jurisdiction, procedure, property and marriage; and (3) consecration, sacrament and liturgy. During the 12th and 13th centuries five compilations were added. Gregory IX added the decretals of popes since the Decretum which were compiled by the Dominican Raymond of Peñafort. Later decretals were collected by Boniface VIII (1298) and Clement V (1314); and the Extravagantes (decretals not included in previous compilations) brought the law down to Sixtus IV (1484). These together formed the Corpus juris canonici, of which a definitive edition was issued by Gregory XIII in 1582.

4. St. Augustine developed his doctrine of the church against the Donatists and his doctrine of grace against Pelagius, but both doctrines were already full-grown, and the fundamental reason for his exposition lay in the need of the man Augustine, a sinner in need of grace and the citizen of a dying civilization in need of the City of God. In other words, the power and permanence of Augustinian theology was the result of his factual presentation of man as man in relation to his Maker and Saviour. The west, untroubled by the complicated disputes and theological parties of the east, developed its theology in simple and universal terms, not as a theory so much as a faith. At the council of Orange (529) under Pope Boniface II the Semi-Pelagians were condemned: "If anyone shall say that by the prevarication of Adam it was not the whole man . . . that was changed for the worse but that, while his soul's free will remained untouched, his body alone became the victim of corruption, such a man is misled by the errors of Pelagius." The question of predestination and depravity was raised in the 9th century by Gottschalk, a monk of Fulda, whose doctrine of a double predestination was condemned by Hrabanus

Maurus of Mainz and Hincmar of Reims. But the doctrine of grace developed more surely and continuously as the doctrine of the Eucharist, and here also the church insisted on the reality of the sacrifice. For Ambrose it is Christ Himself who offers the sacrifice and changes the elements into His body and blood. For Augustine the church presents itself as a whole and living sacrifice. Gregory says that the daily offering of Christ's body and blood avail for salvation and that by this means "the lowest things are united to the highest, things earthly are joined to things divine and the visible and invisible become one." In the 9th century Paschasius Radbertus, monk and abbot of Corbie, wrote a treatise De corpore et sanguine Domini, which in 844 he presented to Charles the Bald, emphasizing the fact of the real change into the body and blood of Christ and equating the daily sacrifice with daily redemption. Another monk of Corbie, Ratramnus, at the same time described the sacrifice as "spiritual" and discussed the relation of "figure" and "truth" in a work afterward attributed to Johannes Scotus Erigena and condemned during the Berengarian controversy at Vercelli in 1050. Berengarius, scholasticus and archdeacon of Tours (d. 1088), outlined his doctrine in a letter to Lanfranc, and in 1080 Lanfranc set forth the orthodox doctrine in his book De corpore et sanguine Domini.

The Christology of the western church was settled at Chalcedon. The Adoptionist heresy of Felix, bishop of Urgel (c. 783–799), and Elipandus of Toledo (d. 808) was condemned at Narbonne (791) and Regensburg (792) and answered by Alcuin of York, who said that the sonship of Christ is not of nature but of person: the divine and human natures are united in the person of the Son. During these centuries the west developed the devotion to the Virgin Mary defined at the council of Ephesus (431) and at Constantinople (553): "If anyone shall say that the holy, glorious and ever-virgin Mary was only in a certain sense and not most truly the Mother of God, or that she was so in some merely relative way as though it were simply a man that was born and not the Word of God that became incarnate and was born of her, or shall refer, as some do, the birth of the man to God the Word only in the sense that the Word was with the man when he was born . . . let him be anathema." In the 4th century St. Gregory of Nazianzus had written that "if anyone does not believe that Holy Mary is the Mother of God, such an one is a stranger to the godhead"; and in the early 8th century St. John of Damascus (c. 676–c. 754) eloquently proclaimed the doctrine of her bodily assumption. Pope Sergius I decreed that the litanies be held on the four feasts of Our Lady, and Pope Leo IV gave the feast of her "Falling Asleep" a vigil and octave. It is mentioned in Adrian I's sacramentary and commanded in the laws of Alfred. The devotion to the Mother of God became articulate and instituted as the doctrine of the incarnation was defined. The same uncompromising refusal to adapt the central mysteries of the faith or to modify them in the interests of rationalization appears through all the centuries of Christological dispute and social chaos. The sacrifice is a real sacrifice, the Saviour really present, the incarnation the real fullness of the godhead bodily, the church the really divine-human community and its head the real and effective sovereign, vicar of Christ.

This realism, the mark of Christian orthodoxy, is the heart of the work of St. Anselm (1033?–1109). His use of the ontological argument is thus the opposite in emphasis of the Cartesian: its essence is the emphasis on existence. His Cur Deus homo starts from divine justice, and his argument presupposes its absoluteness. Faith is the foundation of reason. The same unyielding realism of faith was expressed in the papal reform initiated by Leo IX (1048–54): "The head of the entire discipline of the church is in that place where Peter, the summit and cardinal member of the apostles, waits for the blessed resurrection of his flesh in the last day." Leo IX had learned administrative method in the imperial service and his episcopal duty in a poor diocese. During the first two years of his pontificate he held 12 councils. He travelled to Reims, to Mainz and as far as Hungary, organized the papal chancery to sustain a large correspondence, employed legates like Adalbert of Bremen and Humbert of Moyenmoûtier and created a college of cardinals. He dreamed of the reunion of east and west. He brought to Rome young Hildebrand (Gregory VII), who had known the city's disorders as a boy and who devoted the remaining 40 years of his life to the reform. Stephen IX (Frederick of Lorraine) was already dying when he left Monte Cassino for the chair of Peter, but in his few months he consecrated the monk St. Pietro Damiani (Peter Damian) cardinal bishop of Ostia, secured the co-operation of cardinals and Roman burghers to ensure the canonical and independent election of his successor and enjoined upon them to await the return of Cardinal Hildebrand, then in Germany. Stephen was no sooner buried than the Roman nobles proved his wisdom by electing an antipope whom the cardinals excommunicated, appointing the Burgundian bishop of Florence, Nicholas II. At his death (1061) the struggle came to a head between the reforming cardinals and the bishops of Lombardy led by Milan. The cardinals elected Anselm of Lucca, Lanfranc's pupil at Bec, as Pope Alexander II. But it was only after bloodshed and an appeal to the German court at Augsburg, and even then at the risk of his life, that Alexander began his pontificate. Nevertheless, the reform was already visibly changing the relations between church and state.

Gregory VII (1073–85), who as monk, deacon, cardinal and pope served this cause for 40 years, was perhaps alone in his vision of all its meaning as, after 1072 (when Pietro Damiani and Adalbert of Bremen died), he was the sole survivor of Leo IX's circle of reformers. For him the battle was no longer limited to simony and celibacy. Likened by his contemporaries to the prophet Elijah, he was disinterestedly certain that the pope is the voice and speaks with the authority of Peter and claimed absolute authority over the souls of Christians without misgiving and without arrogance. Italian, not German, a monk trained in the service of the papacy, elected by cardinals and acclaimed by the people of Rome, he had never been a bishop until he was made pope. As legate he had seen the church in France and Germany with the eyes of central authority. The arch-chancellor of the empire, who was also archbishop of Mainz, complained that Pope Alexander II had dealt directly with his suffragans of Prague and Olomouc instead of dealing through their archbishop. Liemar of Bremen refused to act at the orders of papal legates without consulting the German episcopate. Secular clergy revolted against a decree of celibacy. Only the Saxon bishops supported the pope, and that because they were opposed to the emperor. In 1075 Gregory revealed his determination: he suspended the archbishop of Bremen and the bishops of Bamberg, Speyer, Strasbourg and three Italian sees and threatened five imperial councillors with excommunication. Henry IV, the German king, having subdued the Saxons, was free to attack the pope. In 1076, at a council of German bishops held at Worms, he declared Gregory deposed and the north Italian bishops declared their agreement. Gregory then deposed and excommunicated the German and Lombard bishops who had signed Henry's letter, declared Henry deposed and excommunicate and his subjects absolved of their allegiance. The effect of this open clash was Henry's defeat and isolation, which he saved from complete disaster by submitting to Gregory at Canossa. There he did penance and awaited absolution, which Gregory gave in duty as a priest. The absolution disconcerted the papal party in Germany which had elected Rudolph of Swabia king in Henry's room. But now Gregory, who was not a partisan, remained neutral. Three years of civil war ended with the victory and death of Rudolph and the excommunication of Henry, who marched on Rome and was crowned by Guibert of Ravenna (the antipope Clement III). Gregory, "having loved righteousness and hated iniquity died in exile" at Salerno, the guest or prisoner of Robert Guiscard, the Norman king of southern Italy. In France, his campaign against simony and clerical marriage had been more successful. In England, Lanfranc carried out his policy but with a characteristic independence. "Our island," he said in a letter refusing to side with the emperor, "has not yet disavowed Gregory VII nor given judgment whether it ought to obey Clement III." In Spain, Gregory claimed temporal as well as spiritual authority and induced the Spanish church to institute the *Ordo Romanus*. He sent legates to Poland and claimed Hungary as the gift of St. Stephen to St. Peter.

Urban II (1088–99) inherited Gregory's exile and carried on his work. A monk of Cluny and a canonist, he had been employed as legate in Germany to organize the papal party. More firmly than Gregory he maintained the opposition to lay investiture and required free and lawful election of bishops. Deprived at first of his centre at Rome, he held a number of councils. At Clermont (1095) he forbade clergy to do homage to laymen and proclaimed the first crusade (*see* CRUSADES), which, apart from its particular occasion and important results, inspired the first great movement of popular preaching. Urban employed permanent legates, encouraged appeals to Rome, graded the hierarchy and confirmed the privileges of monastic houses, exempting many of them from episcopal control. At the same time the emergence of an international school at Paris recovered scientific theology for western Christendom. William of Champeaux (c. 1070–1121) established the reputation of the cathedral school. Peter Abélard (1079–1142), who had studied under William, made it the most famous school in Europe and, using the *Organon* of Aristotle, laid the foundation of its tradition as a school of logic and philosophy. The university was the peculiar care and favoured nursling of Innocent III, who secured its independence, finally established by Gregory IX in 1231. At Paris the study of civil law was forbidden (1219) by Honorius III, perhaps in favour of Bologna, where it was well established (in succession to Ravenna and Rome) in the 11th century, and perhaps to ensure the study of theology at Paris. By the middle of the 13th century the schoolmen of Paris had access to original translations from the Greek of nearly all Aristotle's extant works. Forbidden by the legate, Robert de Courçon, in 1215 and again in 1231 and 1263, the physical and metaphysical works of Aristotle, together with the commentaries of Averroes, were nevertheless read and studied especially by the Dominicans Albertus Magnus and Thomas Aquinas, whose Aristotelian method was to become the orthodoxy of Catholic exposition. (*See* SCHOLASTICISM.)

At the fourth Lateran council (1215) Innocent III (1198–1216) published a definition of the faith which, after affirming the doctrine of the Trinity, the Incarnation and the Judgment, says:

There is moreover one universal Church of the faithful, outside which no man at all is saved, in which the same Jesus Christ is both the priest and the sacrifice, whose body and blood are truly contained in the sacrament of the altar under the species of bread and wine, the bread being transubstantiated into the body and the wine into the blood by the divine power, in order that, to accomplish the mystery of unity, we ourselves may receive of His that which He received of ours. And this thing, the sacrament to wit, no one can make (*conficere*) but a priest, who has been duly ordained, according to the keys of the Church, which Jesus Christ Himself granted to the apostles and their successors.

But the sacrament of baptism, which is consecrated in water at the invocation of God and of the undivided Trinity, that is of the Father, and of the Son and Holy Spirit, being duly conferred in the form of the Church by any person, whether upon children or adults, is profitable to salvation. And if anyone, after receiving baptism, has fallen into sin, he can always be restored (*reparari*) by true penitence.

Not only virgins and the continent, but also married persons, deserve, by right faith and good works pleasing God, to come to eternal blessedness (cited by Alexander Hamilton Thompson, *Cambridge Medieval History*, vol. vi, p. 635).

The last article of the definition quoted above refers to the Catharist or Albigensian heresy, which in the 12th and 13th centuries threatened large areas of Hungary, Germany, Italy and France. It rejected infant baptism, purgatory, the communion of saints, the use of images and the doctrine of the Trinity. Above all, the Cathars attacked the institution of marriage, which was the basis of all social custom and law, sacred and secular, in the west. Catharism was anarchy and heresy at once. It implied the complete subversion of the social structure and the complete denial of the Christian faith. Its leaders, *perfecti,* admitted no obligation, moral or material. In Languedoc the crusades inaugurated by Innocent III against the heresy were eagerly supported by the French nobility (1209–44). At the same time the Inquisition was organized. Proposed at the council of Verona (1184) and established early in the 13th century, this court was designed to combine judicial procedure with propaganda. Under Gregory IX it was organized with specialist judges and advisers. Its activity varied with time and place. In England and Portugal it was unknown. In Spain it was obsolescent during the 15th century but revived under Ferdinand and Isabella. In Germany its vigour waned between 1250 and 1350. It was most vigorous in France. As a rule its methods were laboriously and punctiliously just, though it could be misled and sometimes, as under Ferdinand and Isabella, was used for political ends. In an age whose most important industry was definition, in which social discipline and civilized living had still to be won, there could be no question of indifference. The enemies of faith were the enemies of man.

The 13th century was the age of an apostolate at every level of human life. The leaders of the movement were friars, orders initiated by laity (St. Francis) and the lower ranks of clergy (St. Dominic) under the immediate protection of the pope. In 1210 Innocent III sanctioned the Franciscan rule. In 1216 his successor, Honorius III (1216–27), took under his government and protection "the order of Master Dominic and Friars Preachers." The Franciscan movement was popular and spontaneous and as such reflected the social movement, the learning and the spirituality which developed in centres of population. The Dominicans, a learned order from the beginning, where Augustinian canons called to preach by the spread of heresy and the demand for instruction in the faith. In Raymond of Peñafort, their third master general (1238–40) and confessor to Gregory IX, they produced the greatest canonist and constitutional lawyer of the age. The Swabian Albertus Magnus (c. 1200–1280), their regent master in Paris, "strove to make Aristotle intelligible to the Latins" and shares with his contemporary, Robert Grosseteste (1175–1253), bishop of Lincoln, the title of "father of modern science." His pupil Thomas Aquinas is still the "common doctor," the greatest teacher of the Roman Catholic Church. Leo XIII in the encyclical *Aeterni Patris* (1879) required bishops "to restore the wisdom of St. Thomas and to spread it as far as possible for the safety and glory of the Catholic faith, for the good of society and for the increase of all sciences." It was the work not only of St. Thomas but of the 13th century as a whole to synthesize those three purposes.

In Paris, the metropolis of theological and philosophical controversy, and at the moment of the full recovery of Aristotelian method, St. Thomas (*see* AQUINAS, THOMAS) represents the arrival of scientific intelligence and the discovery by Christendom of the nature of man. His work is the first clear articulation of the full human confidence in human nature which in patristic and conciliar definitions, as in the earlier scholasticism of St. Anselm and in the preaching of St. Bernard, was still overshadowed by theological, controversial and ecclesiastical purpose. St. Thomas realized what neither pagan philosophy nor Christian theology had as yet clearly discerned, the naturalism of supernature, the divine right of man.

The last end of man is the contemplation of truth. This alone is distinctive of his nature, and no other corporeal being shares it with him. Nor is there any end beyond it, for the contemplation of truth is an end in itself. Hereby man is united in likeness with superior spirits, because this alone of human activities is an activity of God and the angels as well. . . . And to this end all other activities seem to be directed. For perfect contemplation we require bodily health, which is secured by all such arts as are necessary to life. We require freedom from perturbation of the passions, a goal obtained by the moral virtues and by prudence. We require freedom from external perturbations, a freedom at which the entire organization of civil government aims. So, if you look at the matter rightly, all human occupations appear to be directed to the needs of those who contemplate the truth. (Reprinted from the *Summa Theologica* with the permission of Benziger Brothers, Inc., publishers and copyright owners.)

This coherence of economy, morals and politics in the contemplation of truth is the pattern of Catholic humanism, derived from Catholic faith in the union of human nature with the divine, by which the trial and error of subsequent history of Christendom is judged and to which man progresses and from which he falls.

Whether the claim of Nicholas I, Gregory VII and Innocent III to an effective sovereignty of Christendom was theoretically sound or not, the civilization of the west did in fact cohere in the church which cohered in the papacy. The papal victory of the 11th century, the development of law, theology and ecclesiastical order, had made the Holy See the centre of a judicial and adminis-

trative system not only more efficient than any other government but the basis of all government. It was the final court of appeal in international dealing, the source and standard of ministerial and judicial competence. The pope's authority was also popular and moral. Innocent III (*q.v.*), feudal suzerain of a large part of Europe, exercised also as head of the church a direct and real authority over its chief administrative officers, the bishops, and over the real religion of its people. He and his successors created the universities which trained public servants and presided over an international court in which every sovereign in Europe was prepared to plead. The distance between the papal and the imperial conceptions of government is illustrated in the 12th century by comparing the practical genius and personal ascendancy of Frederick I Barbarossa on the imperial side with the almost impersonal patience and judicial science of Alexander III on the papal. Both were just men, but, whereas Frederick conceived his office in terms of Otto the Great and Charles the Great, imposing peace on his vassals, making war for the dream of a Roman empire and doing personal justice which made offenders tremble at his coming, Alexander III made decisions, worthy of Gratianus' pupil, which became part of the permanent system of canon law. The third Lateran council, with its successor under Innocent III, defined a conception of life and society which still endures. Frederick's use of the civil law and comparison of himself with Constantine and Justinian as lord of the world at the diet of Roncaglia (1158) was a soldier's romance which never became even plausible and was finally shattered by the Lombard cities at the battle of Legnano (1176). But even the Angevin Henry II of England was compelled like his Norman predecessors to submit to the authority of an order which needed no armament because it was inherent in the social structure.

THE CHURCH AND THE NATIONS

The converse was also true. The papacy reflected Christendom and reacted to the national, social and cultural revolution of the 13th and 14th centuries. Frederick II of Hohenstaufen was the first secular sovereign of the modern kind. He ignored without resenting the papal excommunication and was equally prepared to hand Germany over to the church (by the *privilegium in favorem principum ecclesiasticorum* of 1220), to make friends with the sultan of Egypt (1229) and to crown himself king in Jerusalem which he had sworn to protect. Having shocked German opinion with his harem and his Saracen bodyguard, he established a central court of justice (diet of Mainz, 1235) and attended the translation of the bones of St. Elizabeth of Hungary (canonized 1234) to Marburg. His greatest achievement, the constitution of Melfi (1231), drawn up in defiance of the pope, established an enlightened despotism in the Sicilian kingdom. His University of Naples, too, was a despotism governed by a royal chancellor. His friend and fellow-heretic Hermann of Salza used the Teutonic order to found the military state of Brandenburg (1230) which developed into the modern kingdom of Prussia.

France enjoyed peace and consolidation under Louis IX, who valued his throne as a means of making Christians. Provence was united to France in 1246 and the English expelled from all France save Gascony in 1259. The military adventures of the English Edward III and Henry V, picturesque rather than political, served, as did the wars of Burgundy and Armagnac, to confirm the French nationality which Louis XI (1461–83) centralized in the throne. By the 14th century the vernaculars of Italy, France, Spain, Germany and England were mature, their legal systems organized. They were aware of commercial rivalries and of national ambitions. Feudalism was dying. The Italian cities of Venice, Florence and Milan were independent powers. The age of the crusades was passing; that of national states had arrived.

The Holy See reflected this revolution. It became the centre of Italian politics and international diplomacy, subject to international intrigue. Its judicial business was extended. From increasingly secular states it demanded increasing revenues. Nicholas III (1277–80) was a political realist; he accepted the situation in which every cardinal was the agent of a political interest, and he exalted his own family, the Orsini. His successor, Martin IV, a Frenchman, was the creature of Charles of Anjou. Honorius IV (Savelli) raised his family against the Orsini. Nicholas IV (Colonna) balanced the other two. Then the cardinals sought to remedy the corruption and forced a hermit unacquainted with the world into the chair of Peter; Celestine V survived five months, was persuaded to abdicate and died in prison. His incompetence was less disastrous than the ability and ambition of his successor. When Boniface VIII, pursuing the logic of contemporary politics and Roman law to an extreme, forbade clergy to pay taxes to the secular government (*Clericis laicos*, 1296), Philip the Fair forbade the export of money from France. When Boniface claimed Scotland as a fief of the pope, Edward I annexed it to England. Both kings relied on their national assemblies, Edward I on the parliament of Lincoln (1301), Philip the Fair on the states-general (1302). Finally French troops seized and imprisoned the pope, who died in 1303. His successor Benedict XI denounced the outrage and died in a few weeks—of poison, it was said.

The next election took ten months and the next pope, Clement V, archbishop of Bordeaux, transferred his court to Avignon in 1309. The "Babylonish captivity" had begun (*see* PAPACY). Perhaps the most dramatic as it was the most shameful sign of the changed time was the suppression by Philip IV and Clement V of the Knights Templars (whose constitution had been drawn up by St. Bernard) after a trial of extorted confessions in which the slanders were dictated by Philip's agents and then confirmed by his victims under torture. The real offense of the Templars was that with the decline of the crusades they had taken to banking; a form of usury which evoked the resentment of their noble debtors and the greed of the king. The "Great Schism" which started in 1378 with the election of Robert of Geneva as Clement VII in opposition to the reigning Urban VI was the final tribute of the papacy to national rivalry. Nations bargained with one side or the other.

The doctrine which accompanied, explained and defended the new order was nominalism, which denied the reality of universals and declared it an "error to believe that there is something in reality besides the singular entity." Thus there is no such thing as the nature of man which could be defined and must be obeyed and which might be united to the divine nature in the person of Christ; there were only individual men, and the definition of human right and duty was promulgated and enforced by the prince. Nature and supernature, reason and revelation thus parted company. Natural science, whether legal, empirical or mathematical, could thus be rid of metaphysical assumptions and set free to handle facts and concepts each on its own terms. The prince was the source of rights and obligations and, in the words of John Wycliffe (*De officio regis*, 1379), was above human laws. The doctrine was expounded by those Franciscans who supported Louis the Bavarian (1314–47) in his claim to the empire as Louis IV. Marsilius of Padua and John of Jandun affirmed the absolute authority of the civil power (*Defensor pacis*, 1324). The papacy was a human institution which had usurped power. Henry of Langenstein and Conrad of Gelnhausen (1380) thought that a council is above the pope. Wycliffe's opinions, condemned in England, found a home at Prague and a more attractive apostle in John Huss, whose preaching in the Bethlehem chapel kindled the national imagination. Huss proclaimed the doctrine of Germany for the Germans, France for the French, Bohemia for the Bohemians. The council of Constance which condemned him adopted this principle at the suggestion of the bishop of Salisbury as the basis of voting and thereby defeated John XXIII's Italian majority. The conciliar movement (Pisa, 1409; Constance, 1414–18; Basle, 1431–38) represents an attempt to establish a parliament of Christendom or perhaps a league of nations. The decree *Frequens* declared that councils ought to be held every five years. At Basle the intention was even more explicit to make the pope the constitutional sovereign or nominal head of a Christendom whose national sovereigns were absolute.

The assembled doctors were not in a position to admit what was clear to the governments represented, that their authority was without foundation.

REFORM AND DEFINITION

Meanwhile the humanism of the Renaissance and a wide and increasing practice of mysticism intensified individual religion and magnified the individual person. At length the revolution broke. It is symbolized in three events. In 1517 Martin Luther nailed his theses on the door of the church at Wittenberg. In 1534 the Act of Supremacy proclaimed Henry VIII supreme head on earth of the Church of England, which he described as "part of the body politic"; in 1535 John Fisher, Thomas More and the London Carthusians were martyred. In 1543 was published the treatise *De revolutionibus orbium coelestium* of Nicolaus Copernicus. All three events in their several kinds were acts of revolt and signs of exodus into the unknown from the given and created world which Christianity presupposed. "It is not necessary," said Copernicus, "that hypotheses should be true or even probable. It suffices that they lead to calculations which agree with observations." "By reformation," said Luther, "I do not mean the reform of this human teaching and spirituality; I mean its complete and absolute abrogation." "The true significance of the Copernican revolution consisted not so much in displacing the world's centre from the earth to the sun as in implicitly denying that the world has a centre at all." (R. G. Collingwood, *The Idea of Nature* [Oxford, 1945]). In like manner the princes denied the organic unity of Christendom. The doctrine *Cujus regio, ejus religio* (first announced at the Recess of Speyer, 1526) was adopted throughout Germany by the diet of Augsburg (1555) and then throughout Europe, Catholic and Protestant. In 1572 Catherine de Médicis answered the English protest against the St. Bartholomew massacre by proposing that Elizabeth should use the same method with Catholics. In 1593 Henry of Navarre "bought Paris with a Mass." The supreme artist in this secular statecraft is Cardinal Richelieu.

Reform of the church began under Leo X (1513–21). In Italy the Theatines (1524) were founded to reform parochial clergy. In 1526 Matteo de' Bassi founded the Capuchin branch of the Franciscans, and in 1530 the Barnabites were founded by St. Antonio Zaccaria. Paul III (1534–49) began the Counter-Reformation by appointing reformers—Giovanni Pietro Caraffa, Gasparo Contarini, Jacopo Sadoleto, Reginald Pole—to the sacred college. In 1536 they served with five others on a commission which urged the need for reform and did not spare the abuses. In 1534 St. Ignatius of Loyola and six others initiated the Society of Jesus (*q.v.*), established in 1540 by the bull *Regimini militantis ecclesiae*. In 1542, by the bull *Licet initio*, Paul III established the papal Inquisition under Caraffa's influence to supervise the whole church. Pius IV and Pius V enlarged its powers, and Sixtus V (1585–90) reorganized it as one of the Roman congregations. In 1545 a general council met at Trent, which was postponed indefinitely in 1547. It reassembled (1551–52) under Julius III and met again, finally, in 1563.

Trent was nothing that Constance had been, everything that Constance was not. Constance had seen the triumph of nationalism; Trent ignored it. Constance made no definition of the faith; Trent made nothing else. Constance had deposed the pope; Trent left everything in his hands. Convoked at the will of Paul III and interrupted by war, Trent made no pretense of gathering or expressing the will of Europe. It reformed the church and accepted the world. It recovered the centre which the movement and confusion of powers had displaced and obscured. Its answer to the theology of the Reformation was an affirmation of the divine-human unity: "In justification a person receives infused through Jesus Christ the remission of his sins, faith, hope and charity. For faith, unless there is added to it hope and charity, does not perfectly unite a person with Christ; nor does it make him a living member of His body; whence it is most truly said that faith without works is dead and unprofitable." (*See* TRENT, COUNCIL OF.)

The works were not lacking. The Counter-Reformation inaugurated above all an age of sanctity: the cardinal archbishop of Milan, St. Carlo Borromeo (1538–84); the Florentine priest St. Philip Neri (1515–95), whose Oratory founded in 1564 in Rome transformed the city; St. Francis of Sales (1567–1622), the most lovable of the doctors of the church, whose devout humanism and humane devotion influenced not only the Catholics of his century but Catholic and Protestant Christianity thereafter; St. Theresa of Avila (1515–82); St. John of the Cross (1542–91), the greatest of the mystics; and St. Vincent de Paul (1576–1660).

Nothing like the apostolate of the Jesuits had yet dawned on the Christian imagination. Within two years of the society's foundation, St. Francis Xavier under the patronage of John III of Portugal established a mission at Goa and during his ten remaining years of life made thousands of converts in India, Malacca, Amboina, the Moluccas and Ceylon (where the king of Kandy and many of his subjects were baptized); he founded a mission in Japan and was on the point of entering China when he died. At the same time Alfonso Salmeron, afterward the colleague of Peter Canisius at Ingolstadt (1549), was sent to Ireland with orders from Paul III "to be all things to all men, constant in good deeds, and to win souls by kindness." In 1542 the Jesuits were established in Bavaria. They were invited to Salzburg, to Mainz and to Osnabrück. Having carried the Counter-Reformation down the Danube and the Rhine, they were called to assist at Trent. They invaded Poland in 1570, England in 1580, Switzerland in 1586. In 1609 they took over the government of Paraguay and turned it into a perfect, almost too perfect, model of Christian social organization. In 1611 they arrived in Canada. Their Roman college, founded in 1551, was the mother of the greatest educational enterprise Christendom had ever known. In 1565 their College of Clermont was already disputing with the University of Paris, whose Gallican doctors had reason to fear their democratic and ultramontane doctrines. They were among the pioneers of patristic study. They quickly became and for two centuries remained the schoolmasters *par excellence* of Catholic Europe: their *ratio studiorum* laid down in 1585 and revised in 1599 survived till 1832, and among their pupils they number men who attained every variety of fame—Ferdinand II and Leopold I, Tilly and Wallenstein, St. Francis of Sales and St. John of the Cross, René Descartes and Molière, Pierre Huet and Jacques Bossuet, Pierre Bayle and Mazarin, Voltaire, Giovanni Vico and Denis Diderot. Placed under the direct command of the pope, they were the natural foes of national autocracy. At Trent they supported the doctrine of episcopacy *lege ecclesiastica*, which placed national bishops under the see of Rome as against episcopacy *jure divino*, which would have established their national independence. Hence they stood opposed to the Gallican ambition represented by the Paris *parlement*, the university and the Bourbons. Confessors of popes and princes, they were exponents of the "rights of man"; Juan de Mariana's treatise *De rege et regis institutione* (1599), dedicated to the future Philip III of Spain, lays its stress not on the legitimacy but on the justice of the king. It offended public opinion above all in France by defending tyrannicide. The church is the perfect society.

The splendour of French culture in the 17th century was the fruit of Catholic humanism and national self-consciousness. Gallicanism (*q.v.*) was another consequence of the union of church and nation. The relations of the Gallican church with the Holy See were defined by the concordat of 1516. The same principles of Gallican independence were affirmed in Bossuet's articles in 1681 and spread in the 18th century to the rest of Catholic Europe. The Jansenists, whose doctrines were condemned in 1713 by Clement XI in the bull *Unigenitus*, joined the Gallican cause against the "ultramontane" influence of the Jesuits. In 1763, when the French Jesuits were being suppressed, Febronius (J. N. von Hontheim), auxiliary bishop of Trier and pupil of the Jansenist canonist Z. B. van Espen of Louvain, published his treatise *De statu ecclesiae et legitima potestate Romani pontificis* maintaining the subordination of the pope to general councils and the independence of bishops. Condemned in 1764, the book circulated throughout Catholic Europe. In 1769 the ecclesiastical electors jointly protested against "papal usurpation." Joseph II (on the death of Maria Theresa, 1780) carried out a Febronian policy in the Habsburg empire. In 1773 Clement XIV was forced by the governments of Portugal, France, Spain and Naples to suppress the Society of Jesus. By 1793 the French monarchy was dead, the aristocracy abolished and an egalitarian republic was preparing to establish the rights of man starting from the year I. The *Constitution civile du clergé* (1790) was a Gallican measure. The concordat of 1801 restored the terms of 1516.

During this century of anticlerical princes and antipapal bishops was founded the Feast of the Sacred Heart (1765), the order of Passionists by St. Paul of the Cross (1694–1775) and the Redemptorists by Alfonso Maria dei Liguori (1696–1787).

THE MODERN WORLD

Napoleon passed like a storm and left Europe in ruins. Industrial revolution and economic determinism created a new absolute of natural necessity. The philosophers of reconstruction, idealist or utilitarian, were alike determinist. J. G. Fichte deified the state; G. W. F. Hegel identified God with history; T. R. Malthus and David Ricardo regarded man as the slave of natural forces. Determinism was presupposed in theories of *laissez faire* and of the absolute state, materialism loudly proclaimed by the apostles of revolution and unconsciously generated by the preoccupations of scientific industry and efficiency. Such were the elements and climate of liberalism. Joseph de Maistre opposed it; H. F. R. de Lamennais tried to capture it. In 1834, while Giuseppe Mazzini was founding Young Europe in the name of God and the people, J. B. H. Lacordaire drew crowds of young men to his *conférences* in Notre Dame with a similar message. In 1837 a German ultramontane movement under Joseph von Görres sprang to life when the Prussian king imprisoned the archbishop of Cologne and other bishops for refusing to compromise on mixed marriages. Louis Veuillot founded *L'Univers religieux* as the organ of French ultramontanism in 1843. In 1843 also Vincenzo Gioberti's book *Del primato morale e civile degli Italiani* attempted to claim national sentiment for the church: he proposed that the pope should head a confederation of Italian states.

It was not through such political enmities and affinities that the Catholic revival took place. The attitude of the church puzzled its friends and enemies alike so long as they thought of it as a party or a policy, one among many contending for authority to solve political problems. The return of Pius VII from Fontainebleau to Rome was a triumph. Whole towns came out to do him honour; kneeling crowds lined the roads. It was a spontaneous gesture and expressed a piety deeper and older than the policies and theories which transformed European government. In 1848, when Europe was in revolution, Pius IX at Gaeta was visited by a priest who had begged his way from Subiaco whither he had walked a few months earlier from Pontigny, his purpose to ask the pope's approval (willingly bestowed) on the foundation of a religious house. Then he walked back to France and, in the forest near Sens, built a hut with chapel, kitchen and dormitory where, with two companions, he lived in extreme poverty according to the Benedictine rule. Four years later he died. The community, which had become the mother of seven others in France, Palestine and America, was driven from France in 1882, took over the ruins of Buckfast and erected one of the most renowned of modern abbeys. This Jean Baptiste Muard was a child of peasants reared in poverty. So was Giovanni Bosco, whose work among the youth of Turin, begun in 1841, elicited the respect and won the support of the government and who founded the Salesian order which was approved in 1874. So was Jean Baptiste Vianney, who became the *curé* of Ars in 1818, and so was Giuseppe Sarto, who became Pope Pius X. In the fall of the monarchies, the decay of aristocracies and the advance of secularism among the intellectuals, the revival of the church sprang from the devotion, the family life and the personal sanctity of the poor. Theirs was the mind which Pius IX, an indifferent politician and a great bishop, represented and understood. Poverty, chastity and obedience, the ancient prescription for the Christian life, were also the condition of social vitality and the answer of the Catholic people to the proletarian or capitalist theories of the secularist doctrinaires. They presuppose a universal humanity. But except as functions of a dismembered humanity, the politics and economics of power were meaningless, while for deity they substituted a religion of individual, national and class emancipation and enlargement. In 1848 this ancient adversary of the church appeared in Rome and demanded a liberal pope to lead a nationalist cause, Catholic Italy against Catholic Austria; the pope fled to Gaeta. The movement carried on these secularist assumptions mastered European politics, and the pope became the prisoner of the Vatican. In 1854 he defined the Immaculate Conception, the consummate affirmation of faith in human nature. Another statement of the same faith, sorely needed in the age of Nietzsche, appeared in the Vatican constitutions (1870): "The holy Church, our mother, holds and teaches that by the natural light of human reason, God, the principle and end of all that is, may be known with certainty through the medium of created things. . . . If anyone shall say that the only and true God, our Creator and Lord, cannot be known with certainty by the natural light of human reason, let him be anathema." At the moment of Bismarck's victory the pope defined the dogma of papal infallibility. Together with the dogma of the Immaculate Conception and the Dogmatic constitutions it defined the structure of Catholic humanity against the drift and scepticism of progress and power condemned in the syllabus of 1864. Forty years later Pius X began his pontificate, "taking courage in Him who strengtheneth us to proclaim that we have no other aim but that of restoring all things in Christ, so that Christ may be all in all" (*E Supremi apostolatus*, 1903).

The word "ultramontane" belongs to an age of territorial dominion. With the loss of the papal states it passed into history. The war of ideologies began. In 1872 Bismarck launched his *Kulturkampf*. In 1873 the May laws inaugurated a policy of nationalization. The Catholic bureau in the ministry of education was abolished, schools placed under state inspectors, seminaries under state control and, as the war proceeded, many of the bishops imprisoned. Rudolf Virchow, the radical, invented the name *Kulturkampf* to mark the real conflict not between church and state but between two civilizations fundamentally opposed. Resisted not only by Catholics and the centre but by the court, the conservatives and the Lutherans, the policy failed. By 1887 the *Kulturkampf* was over in Germany. It was beginning in France. The Italian governments of left and right, unable to cope with economic distress, suffered continual disorder, and the forces of communism and socialism increased. Leo XIII, who succeeded Pius IX in 1878, issued a series of encyclicals on social and political questions which were accepted through the whole church as a classical statement of its principles: *Inscrutabile Dei* (1878), on social evils caused by rejecting the church; *Quod Apostolici muneris* (1878), on socialism, communism, nihilism; *Arcanum divinae sapientiae* (1880), on marriage; *Diuturnum illud* (1881), on civil power; *Immortale Dei* (1885), on church and state; *Libertas* (1888), on liberty; *Sapientiae Christianae* (1890), on citizenship; *Rerum novarum* (1891), on the social order.

The French attack on the church, restrained after 1870, was brought to a head in 1900 in reaction to the ultramontanism of the army and in response to an intelligentsia of liberals and Freemasons. In 1901 the Law of Associations dissolved two-thirds of the religious houses in France. By 1904, 13,000 schools had been suppressed. In 1905 the government, having broken off relations with the Holy See, confronted the church with the alternatives of wholesale confiscation or subordination to the civil authorities. Pius X decided against subordination and himself consecrated 14 bishops in St. Peter's. Persecution united the "disestablished" church more firmly to the Holy See. The secularist and anticlerical policy of the French government continued to World War I. "There are now no parties," said the president, "there is only immortal France." The government conceded to war what it denied to Christianity.

During the same period Austria was the scene of similar hostilities. *Los von Rom* and *Drang nach Osten* together marked the drift of the Habsburg dominions from their ancient and central position in Catholic Europe. Catholics, suffering from the weakness of a large traditional majority, were divided. Josephism was still alive among the clergy and at court. The Germanic myth whose centre was neither Rome nor Vienna but Berlin was propagated among the German, liberal and anti-Catholic minority. The universities of Innsbruck, Vienna, Graz and Prague were agitated by the ideological war. A campaign of slander against the clergy raised a union of priests and lawyers in their defense (*Rechtschützverein*). A Catholic university at Salzburg was projected (1902). The *Piusverein* (1905) united the Catholic press, and at the Vienna congress (1905) it was declared that the "Catholic faith is the spiritual bond which unites the peoples of Austria." Pan-German deputies in the chamber demanded that the German provinces should join the empire of the Hohenzollerns as Lajos Kossuth and others in the 19th century had demanded separation for Hungary. With the outbreak of war in 1914 and the death of Francis Joseph in 1916 the Habsburg empire fell to pieces. The church and the Catholic faith remained.

Between World Wars I and II the logic of determinism and power politics ceased to be national and became universal. The patriotism of the materialists perished and was succeeded by a materialism without frontiers or citizenship, which denied all obligations but those imposed by force and exacted by cruelty. The last acts of Benedict XV had been devoted to relief. Pius XI (1922–39), still urging relief, especially for Russia, instituted the Feast of Christ the King (1925). In 1931 he took up the theme of *Rerum novarum* in the encyclical *Quadragesimo anno* and against the fascist government reaffirmed moral freedom. Fascism, he said, was a "regime based on an ideology which amounts to a really pagan worship, the state." Two years later the struggle in Spain revealed the extent of the Russian revolution—"hatred of the Lord and His church nourished by groups subversive to any religious and social order as we have seen in Mexico and Russia." In 1937 he addressed his letter *Mit brennender Sorge* to the German bishops, denouncing the nazi regime; and in the encyclical *Divini Redemptoris* he denounced "the most persistent enemies of the church who from Moscow are directing the struggle against Christian civilization." In 1939 the next pope, Pius XII, broadcasted his five peace points, demanding the right to life and independence for all nations great and small, progressive disarmament, provision for revising treaties, the protection of minorities and the spirit of good faith. He broadcasted five points of a "new order based on moral principles" two years later and never ceased to confront the tide of racial degradation and massacre with pleas for justice and charity.

In the hemisphere dominated by the U.S.S.R. his voice could not be heard. The "iron curtain," a war frontier devised without consideration of human rights or needs by victorious powers, left eastern Europe and a great part of Asia at the mercy of a naïf necessitarianism, without faith in man or morals, to which "progress of science," in the words of *Pravda*, "all religions stand in direct contradiction." The 50,000,000 Catholics subject to this "progress" lived in a process of martyrdom. Their bishops were systematically deported, their schools controlled by Communists, their property confiscated and the unsubmissive "liquidated."

In 1949 the Congregation of the Holy Office decreed that it is unlawful for Catholics to enlist in or show favour to the Communist party, or to publish, write or read anything in support of the Communist doctrine and that any Catholic doing so must be denied the sacraments as an apostate from the Catholic faith.

The effect within the church of this consummate apostasy not only from God but from man was to realize the organic unity of the church as the body of Christ the God-Man with a unanimity and clearness which it had not known since its first generation. In 1870 the pope had become the sovereign vicar of Christ the King, exercising a type of sovereignty that the world had never seen before, rooted in the devotion of 350,000,000 subjects. He defined the Mystical Body of Christ in an encyclical in 1943 and the dogma of the Bodily Assumption into Heaven of the Blessed Virgin Mary in 1950.

In contrast with the destruction and unrest of secularized Europe, in which innumerable conflicts tended toward world war, the church was defined, consolidated and extended. Leo XIII commended Thomas Aquinas to all the bishops as the "master and prince of scholastic doctors" (*Aeterni Patris*, 1879), founded the Academy of St. Thomas in Rome (1880) and authorized a new edition of his works based on the edition of the Dominican pope, St. Pius V (1570). By 1906 the edition was complete. Pius X began the codification of canon law completed under Benedict XV in 1917. The study of philosophy and theology was ordered "to be carried on in seminaries according to the arguments, doctrines and principles of St. Thomas which they are inviolately to hold." In 1902 Leo XIII appointed a commission for biblical studies under four cardinals. Pius X imposed the study of Scripture on all seminaries (1906) and ruled (1907) that the commission should examine all important controversies relating to the Bible. He revived (1907) the work of correcting the text of the Vulgate started under Pius IX by the Barnabite Fr. Vercollone; and in 1909 he founded the Biblical institute in Rome. In 1907 (*Pascendi dominici gregis*) and again in 1910 (*Editae saepe*) he condemned "modernism," the "meeting place of all heresies." It is impossible to summarize the missionary activity of an apostolic church. Dominicans entered China in the 13th century; the Jesuits in the 16th were followed by Franciscans, Dominicans and Vincentians. The mission established by St. Francis Xavier in Japan (1549) had grown in 50 years to 300,000 members and then seemed by 1640 to be extinguished by a massacre. Yet in 1865 Catholic missionaries discovered a surviving church of 30,000 who without priests or sacraments had maintained acknowledgment of the pope and devotion to Our Lady. In 1862 Pius IX canonized the Japanese martyrs. African missions started on the coast by Jesuits and Dominicans (1596, 1614) were revived in the 19th century by the Holy Ghost Fathers (1842), the Society for African Missions (1859), the White Fathers (1868) and the Society of St. Joseph (1866).

In England the emancipation of 1829 followed by N. P. S. (later Cardinal) Wiseman's visit in 1835 began a rapid expansion. William George Ward and J. H. Newman, received in 1845, started a movement of Anglicans and intellectuals into the church. The Irish immigration, which began in 1841 and reached its highest figure in 1861, not only trebled the Catholic population but changed the character and work of the church in England: "I have given up working for the people of England," said Manning, "to work for the Irish occupation in England." The immigrants, poor and often destitute, brought their traditional Catholicism, neither English nor European, and in due course provided the bulk of the Catholic working population and a majority of parish priests. Religious orders revived. The Jesuits were at Stonyhurst in 1794, the Benedictines at Ampleforth in 1802 and at Downside in 1814. In 1840 through the work of the Downside monk Bernard Ullathorne the hierarchy was established in Australia. The Jesuit church at Farm street, London, was opened in 1849. In 1843 the Redemptorists, in 1842 the Passionists, in 1835 the Rosminians and in 1847 the Oratorians (Newman's foundation) were established. Irish Cistercians settled in 1837 at St. Bernard's in Leicestershire. In 1850 a revival of the Dominican province began at Woodchester. The Franciscans (Capuchins) returned in 1850 to work heroically among the poor, especially of South Wales, and Friars Minor started an English province in 1873. In 1850 Pius IX restored the English hierarchy. Women's orders multiplied their houses and above all their schools. The Institute of the Blessed Virgin founded by Mary Ward (1585–1645) already possessed a convent in York, and by mid-20th century the order in two branches numbered more than 5,000 sisters. Cornelia Conelly, a convert, founded the Order of the Holy Child. In 1854 Frances Lescher founded the first and greatest training college for Catholic teachers at Liverpool. Margaret Hallahan began the educational work of the Dominican Tertiaries. Carmelites with a tradition going back to St. Theresa were established at Wells (1864) and at Chichester (1892).

BIBLIOGRAPHY.—*Cambridge Ancient History*, vol. xii (Cambridge, 1939); *Cambridge Medieval History* (Cambridge, 1936); *Cambridge Modern History*, vol. i–v and relevant chapters thereafter, with bibliographies (Cambridge, 1928); J. P. Migne, *Patrologiae Latinae cursus completus*, 217 vol. (1844–55), and *Patrologiae Graecae cursus completus*, 247 vol. (1856–66); G. D. Mansi, *Sacrorum conciliorum nova et amplissima collectio*, 31 vol. (1758–98); *Corpus juris canonici*; *Liber pontificalis*; J. B. Lightfoot, *Apostolic Fathers*, 2nd ed. (1889); Irenaeus (tr. Keble and Roberts and Rabaut); L. M. O. Duchesne, *Histoire ancienne de l'Eglise* (1906), Eng. trans. (1909–24); Adolf von Harnack, *History of Dogma*; H. M. Gwatkin, *Early Church History to A.D. 313*, 2 vol., 2nd ed. (1909); B. J. Kidd, *History of the Church to A.D. 461*, 3 vol. (Oxford, 1922); F. H. Dudden, *Gregory the Great*, 2 vol. (1905); *Rule of St. Benedict*, tr. by Francis Aidan Cardinal Gasquet (1925); C. G. Herbermann et al. (eds.), *The Catholic Encyclopedia* (1907); Bede, *Ecclesiastical History*; W. R. W. Stephens and William Hunt (eds.), *History of the English Church*, vol. i–iv; R. W. Chambers, *The Saga and the Myth of Sir Thomas More* (Oxford, 1927); L. von Pastor, *History of the Popes from the Close of the Middle Ages*, 14 vol. (1915); H. K. Mann, *Lives of the Popes in the Middle Ages*, 18 vol. (1925–32); P. Hughes, *History of the Church*, vol. i–iv (1945–   ); St. Thomas Aquinas, *Summa theologica, Summa contra Gentiles*; E. H. Gilson, *La Philosophie au moyen age* and *The Spirit of Mediaeval Philosophy*, Eng. trans. by A. H. C. Downes (1936); De Lagarde, *La Naissance de l'Esprit laïque au declin du moyen age* (1934); Thomas à Kempis, *Imitation of Christ*; St. Ignatius, *Spiritual Exercises*; St. Francis of Sales, *La Vie dévote*; *Complete Works* of St. Theresa and of St. John of the Cross, ed. and trans. by E. A. Peers (1946); Henri Bremond, *L'Histoire littéraire du sentiment religieux en France*, 6 vol. (1916–24); K. E. Kirk, *The Vision of God* (1931); C. A. Ste.-Beuve, *Port-Royal*; R. A. Knox, *Enthusiasm* (1950); Jervis, *History of the Gallican Church*; Joseph Maistre, *Du pape* (1819); encyclicals, Catholic Truth Society; the best English account of contemporary history of the Catholic Church is contained in the *Tablet*.
(T. S. Gy.)

UNITED STATES

Whatever may be the final verdict of history in regard to the very ancient and fascinating Celtic tales of ocean wanderings in which St. Brendan and his companions figure so prominently, many historians of the Catholic Church in the new world have accepted some of these legends as an initial page in their chronicles. A well-documented study of the *Navigatio Brendani* and the land of promise with an exhaustive bibliography was published in the *Catholic Historical Review*, pp. 395–477 (Jan. 1921), by Joseph Dunn, head of the Celtic department of the Catholic University of America. The historical link between the alleged pre-Columbian discoveries of the new world and the mediaeval church in Greenland is found in the Norse sagas. The Norse church in mediaeval America attracted the attention of scholars as a result of the publication (1893) of the documents from the Vatican archives pertaining to the diocese of Gardar in Greenland. This first Catholic diocese in the new world was established about 1125 and had resident bishops until 1377. After this date until 1492, few of the incumbents of the see resided in Greenland. The letter of Pope Alexander VI (1493) appointing the last bishop says that "on account of the freezing of the sea no ship is supposed to have touched there during the past eighty years" (*cf.* "The Norse Church in Medieval America," in the *Catholic Historical Review*; bibliography [July 1925]).

Of the three principal colonizing nations—Spain, France and England—the two former were Catholic and the third began its voyages of discovery under a Catholic king, Henry VII. The first attempt to set up church organization in the newly discovered continent was the appointment in 1493 of Bernard Boyl, or Buil, as vicar apostolic of the "Indies." Bishop-Elect Boyl accompanied Columbus on his second voyage. His labours were of short duration and of no permanent value. In 1504 Pope Julius II appointed three bishops to Hispaniola (Haiti), but the Spanish crown refused to confirm their election and the sees were suppressed. Seven years later the permanent dioceses of San Domingo and Conception (Haiti) and San Juan (Puerto Rico) were established. The see of Santiago de Cuba, erected in 1522, was the ecclesiastical centre of the Spanish missions on the mainland until 1545, when the three provinces or archbishoprics—Lima, Mexico City and San Domingo—were erected by Pope Paul III. In 1565 the parish of St. Augustine, the first within the confines of the present United States, was founded as part of the diocese of Santiago. Thus, three-quarters of a century after the discovery by Columbus, the regular canonical life of the church was well established. Out of the archdiocese of Mexico City grew later the suffragan Mexican sees of Guadalajara, Durango, Linares and Sonora, which ruled the southwestern portion of the United States until the middle of the 19th century. One of the heroic chapters in American history is that on the Franciscan, Dominican and Jesuit missions of the southwest and in California.

The French explorers and colonizers of the 16th and 17th centuries were, with few exceptions, Catholics and were ably supported by missionary groups; among them were the Récollets, Jesuits, Sulpicians, Capuchins and the secular clergy. New

France was erected into a vicariate apostolic in 1658, with Bishop François de Montmorency Laval at its head. The see of Quebec (1674) had spiritual jurisdiction over all the vast province of France in North America, including the wide-spreading valley of the Mississippi, together with Louisiana.

In the English colonies along the Atlantic coast, Catholicism was generally legally proscribed. The exceptions were: Maryland, from its foundation by the Catholic Calverts in 1634 until the Puritan uprising of 1650; Rhode Island, presumably from its settlement by Roger Williams in 1636 and historically from the charter of 1663; and Pennsylvania, founded by William Penn in 1682, where there is evidence of Catholics from its earliest settlement. Thus, according to Catholic historians, Maryland has the distinction of being the first English settlement where religious freedom was part of the common law (cf. Russell, *Maryland, Land of Sanctuary* [1907]). From 1634 to 1773 Jesuits of English and American origin ministered to the Catholics in Maryland, Pennsylvania and northern Virginia. After the suppression of the Society of Jesus (1773), the legal Corporation of the Roman Catholic Clergy continued to carry on missionary work, with Father John Lewis as superior. In 1784 Father John Carroll, who had won national reputation through his part in the commission to Canada (1776), was appointed prefect apostolic of the church in the United States. Six years later he became the first bishop of Baltimore, with jurisdiction over the entire church in the new republic. There were at this time (1790) 25 priests and about 30,000 Catholics in the United States. In 1808 Baltimore became a province or archdiocese with suffragan sees at Boston, New York, Philadelphia and Bardstown, Ky. Ten years later, Archbishop Ambrose Maréchal reported to the Holy See that there were 52 priests and about 100,000 Catholics in the United States.

There is hardly any parallel in the history of Catholicism to the rapid growth of the church in the United States during the 100 years following the death of Archbishop Maréchal (1828)—from about 300,000 to about 20,000,000. By mid-20th century this number had increased to approximately 27,000,000. The growth of the Catholic Church in the United States was the result of immigration, natural increase and conversions.

Racial Composition.—Racially, the church in the United States is made up of groups from every nation in the world, with the English-speaking peoples in the majority. Up to the middle of the 19th century, the Irish and the Germans furnished the greater quota of its adherents. Later the French-Canadians, Italians, Mexicans, Poles, Lithuanians, Slovaks, Hungarians and others added notably to the number. There is also an appreciable percentage of oriental Catholics—Greeks (Uniates), Syrians, Armenians, etc.

External Relations.—This almost unprecedented growth of a religious organization which had been subject to legal and political disabilities since the 16th century was bound to give rise to misunderstandings in a country so largely composed of Protestants. After the rise of the American republic several organized politico-religious movements were instituted for the purpose either of hindering the exercise of the franchise on the part of U.S. Catholic citizens or of keeping Catholic Americans out of offices of public trust. Chief among these were the American Protestant association (1829), the Native-American party (1837–44), the Know Nothings (1855–61), the American Protective association (1896) and later the Ku Klux Klan. Being under the protection of the constitution, and enjoying the advantages of the common law, Catholicism did not meet with any official governmental opposition. All such political or religious anti-Catholicism was temporary or local and did not represent the more general attitude of U.S. citizens. These movements never became national and were the result of conditions in which political, social and industrial problems were closely intermingled. The political theory of an inherent antagonism between Catholicism and Americanism gave rise to many interesting studies. Many writers on the alleged incompatibility between Catholicism and republican institutions failed to give due allowance to the racial and economic adjustments involved in these sectional antagonisms to the church.

Internal Development.—The internal development of the church in the United States was of a uniform nature. Its doctrinal history offers little of importance. The church discipline in vogue is similar to that of the other churches of Catholicism. Unity of doctrine, of moral law and of liturgical observance is preserved by an intimate union with the see of Rome. The universal canonical legislation of the church as reorganized in the New Code of Canon Law (1918), the legislation by papal rescript, the decisions in contentious cases by the apostolic delegation at Washington, D.C., and a certain number of customs and practices which grew up in the U.S. church formed the basis for its domestic relations. Every five years each U.S. bishop is expected to pay a visit to Rome (*ad limina Apostolorum*) and to make a report of the spiritual condition of his diocese. A system of diocesan synods provides for local unity among the bishops, clergy and laity. Each province is convened into provincial councils from time to time, and at greater intervals a national or plenary council is held. Three such councils were held (1852, 1866, 1884) at Baltimore. A graduate school of canon law was established at the Catholic University of America, Washington, D.C.

Education.—An outstanding factor in the internal development of the church in the United States was in the field of education. According to the *Official Catholic Directory* for 1952, there were 8,358 parochial or elementary schools in which 2,692,706 boys and girls received secular and religious instruction. The outlay involved in the parochial school system was estimated at $205,000,000 annually. Catholics at the same time continued to contribute their proportionate share to the maintenance of the public schools.

There were also 1,623 diocesan high schools and 233 colleges and universities. This system of secondary and higher education was crowned by establishment of the Catholic University of America at Washington, D.C., in 1887 by Pope Leo XIII and the U.S. hierarchy and its endowment with the privileges of the old pontifical universities of Europe. The purpose of the founders of this central institution was to carry the graduates of the Catholic colleges into higher scholarship and thus prepare teachers for the entire Catholic educational system as well as leaders in the world of science and literature. The Catholic Sisters college, founded as an integral part of the Catholic University of America (1914), gave to the religious women teaching in the Catholic schools equal opportunities for higher training.

There were 17 Catholic universities in charge of the Society of Jesus at mid-20th century, three under the Vincentians, two under the Holy Cross Fathers and the Brothers of Mary and one under the Holy Ghost Fathers.

The education of the clergy was provided for by 424 seminaries, in which there were more than 30,900 students. A *Directory of Catholic Schools and Colleges* for the United States and a *Directory of Catholic Charities* were established. There were 351 institutions caring for 40,718 children and 20,543 in foster homes in 1952. For care of physically handicapped children there were 24 institutions and for the mentally handicapped 14. There were 152 protective institutions with a population of 15,029. Catholic homes for the aged totalled 271 and cared for more than 24,000 aged persons.

Administration.—The actual government of the church in the United States was represented in 1952 by the apostolic delegate at Washington, 3 cardinals (Chicago, Detroit and New York), 27 archbishops (Baltimore, Boston, Cincinnati, Denver, Dubuque (2), Indianapolis, Los Angeles, Louisville, Milwaukee, Newark, New Orleans, Omaha, Philadelphia, Portland, Ore., St. Louis, St. Paul, San Antonio, San Francisco, Santa Fe, Washington, D.C., Seattle, Brooklyn, Cleveland, Fargo, St. Augustine, Savannah-Atlanta), 158 bishops and 44,459 priests. There were 15,653 parishes, 4,790 missions and 6,953 chapels. Several hundred daily, weekly, biweekly and monthly publications were printed in English and foreign languages. There were also several literary and academic reviews, published monthly and quarterly, of a high order of merit.

National Development.—Students of the social and intellectual forces of Catholicism in the United States gave considerable attention to the development of the church along national lines. Changes in the immigration policy of the country rendered this development possible, since it permitted the racial elements to be more easily assimilated to national ideals. Many agencies helped effect this general evolution, among them the Catholic Educational association, the National Conference of Catholic Charities, the Catholic Hospital association, the International Catholic Guild of Nurses, the Catholic Near East Welfare association, the Central Bureau of the Central-Verein, the American Catholic Philosophical association and the American Catholic Historical association. All these organizations were aided by the central bureaus of the National Catholic Welfare conference at Washington. National organization was also effected through such societies as the Holy Name society, the Knights of Columbus, the Daughters of Isabella and the Catholic Daughters of America, the National Federation of Catholic College Students and the International Federation of Catholic Alumnae. An annual meeting of the U.S. hierarchy is held in November at the Catholic University of America for the discussion of mooted points in church discipline and progress. The National Catholic Welfare conference is directed by an administrative committee of bishops, reporting annually at the aforesaid meeting. The National Catholic Rural Life conference also meets annually.

Mission Work.—Missionary work was undertaken by U.S. priests and sisters in foreign fields. The Catholic Foreign Mission Society of America (Maryknoll, N.Y.) and the Dominicans and the Foreign Mission Sisters of St. Dominic established stations in China. The Holy Cross Fathers set up missions in India, the Passionists in China, the Redemptorists in Latin America, the Jesuits in China, India, the Philippines, Iraq and Latin America. A bureau for Catholic Indian missions was established at Washington and a national board for mission work among nonwhite people with headquarters in New York city. In social and welfare work the Knights of Columbus, with a membership approaching 1,000,000 men, assumed a position of leadership.

BIBLIOGRAPHY.—The chief foreign source collections for the history of the church in the United States are in Rome (Vatican archives and archives of propaganda), Paris, London (Westminster archives), Seville (Archívo General de Indias), Mexico City (national archives) and Quebec (archiepiscopal archives). Transcripts of these documents were deposited in the Shea collection at Georgetown university, in the archives of the Dominican House of Studies (Washington) and in the Guilday transcripts at the Catholic University of America. Every episcopal see has its own archives, and considerable material exists at the headquarters of the religious orders and congregations, particularly in Rome. The Catholic Archives of America at Notre Dame university are particularly rich in unpublished material. Printed sources will be found in the quarterly Records and Reviews of the Catholic historical societies in the United States and in Official Catholic Year Books. The Catholic Historical Review contains bibliographical references for all phases of U.S. Catholic history. Ecclesiastical legislation will be found in the Acta et Decreta of the Third Plenary Council of Baltimore.

The literature of American Catholic history of general and special nature is large in extent. J. D. G. Shea's four volumes on the History of the Catholic Church in the United States (1886–92) is still the standard work. The Catholic Encyclopedia contains articles on practically every noteworthy aspect of American Catholic history prior to 1918 and is especially valuable for biographical sketches. R. F. Clarke, The Lives of the Deceased Bishops, 2 vol. (1872), is generally trustworthy, though inadequate. Statistics are given annually in the Official Catholic Directory. The extended bibliographies of American church history, found in Peter Guilday's Life of Archbishop Carroll (1922) and his Life and Times of John England, First Bishop of Charleston (1786–1842) (1927), as well as in V. F. O'Daniel's Right Rev. Edward Dominic Fenwick (1920), give a list of provincial, diocesan and corporative histories. See also T. O'Gorman, A History of the Roman Catholic Church in the United States (1895); Theodore Maynard, Story of American Catholicism (1941); Peter Guilday, History of the Councils of Baltimore (1791–1884) (1932); American Catholic Historical Researches; Jesuit Relations, 73 vol. (1896–1901), edited by R. G. Thwaites, and the condensation in two volumes by Edna Kenton (1925). See also the article in the Catholic Historical Review, 7:470–477 (1927) on "Catholic Historical Scholarship in the United States"; J. P. Cadden, Historiography of the American Catholic Church: 1785–1943 (1944); J. T. Ellis (comp.), Select Bibliography of the History of the Catholic Church in the United States (1947); T. Maynard, Story of American Catholicism (1948); D. Shearer, Pontificia Americana: A Documentary History of the Catholic Church in the United States (1784–1884) (1933); L. Palladino, Indian and White in the Northwest (1894); P. J. de Smet, Western Missions and Missionaries (1863); Chittenden and Richardson, Life, Letters and Travels of Pierre de Smet, 4 vol. (1905).   (P. Gu.; J. LaF.)

ROMANCE, originally a composition written in "Romance" language; i.e., in one of the phases on which the Latin tongue entered after or during the dark ages. For some centuries by far the larger number of these compositions were narrative fictions in prose or verse; and since the special "Romance" language of France—the earliest so-called—was the original vehicle of nearly all such fictions, the use of the term for them became more and more accepted in a limited sense. Yet for a long time there was no definite connotation of fiction attached to it, but only of narrative story; and the French version of William of Tyre's History of the Crusades, a very serious chronicle written towards the close of the 12th century, bears the name of Roman d'Éracle simply because the name of the emperor Heraclius occurs in the first line. But if the explanation of the name "Romance" is quite simple, certain and authentic, the same is by no means the case with its definition, or even with the origin of the thing to which that name came mostly to be applied. For some centuries an abstraction has been formed from the concrete examples. "Romance," "romanticism," "the romantic character," "the romantic spirit," have been used to express sometimes a quality regarded in itself, but much more frequently a difference from the supposed "classical" character and spirit. The following article will deal chiefly with the matter of Romance, excluding or merely referring to accounts of such individual romances as are noticed elsewhere. But it will not be possible to conclude without some reference to the vaguer and more contentious signification.

Romance in antiquity.—Speculations on the origin of the peculiar kind of story which we recognize rather than define under the name of romance have been numerous and sometimes confident; but a wary and well-informed criticism will be slow to accept most of them. It is certain that many of its characteristics are present in the Odyssey; and it is a most remarkable fact that these characteristics are singled out for reprehension—or at least for comparative disapproval—by the author of the treatise On the Sublime. The absence of central plot, and the prolongation rather than evolution of the story; the intermixture of the supernatural; the presence and indeed prominence of love-affairs; the juxtaposition of tragic and almost farcical incident; the variety of adventure arranged rather in the fashion of a panorama than otherwise: all these things are in the Odyssey, and they are all, in varying degrees and measures, characteristic of romance. Nor are they absent from the few specimens of ancient prose fiction which we possess. If the Satyricon of Petronius was ever more than a mass of fragments, it was certainly a romance, though one much mixed with satire, criticism and other things; and the various Greek survivals from Longus to Eustathius always and rightly receive the name. But two things were still wanting which were to be all-powerful in the romances proper—chivalry and religion. They could not yet be included, for chivalry did not exist and such religion as did exist lent itself but ill to the purpose except by providing myths for ornament and perhaps pattern.

The "Saint's Life."—A possible origin of the new romance into which these elements entered (though it was some time before that of chivalry definitely emerged) has been seen by one of the least hazardous of the speculations above referred to in the hagiology or "Saint's Life," which arose at an early though uncertain period, developed itself pretty rapidly, and spreading over all Christendom (which by degrees meant all Europe and parts of Asia) provided centuries with their chief supply of what may be called interesting literature. If the author of On the Sublime was actually Longinus, the minister of Zenobia, there is no doubt that examples both sacred and profane of the kind of "fiction" ("imitation" or "representation") which he deprecated were mustering and multiplying close to, perhaps in, his own time. The Alexander legend of the pseudo-Callisthenes is supposed to have seen the light in Egypt as early as A.D. 200, and the first Greek version of that "Vision of Saint Paul," which is the ancestor of all the large family of legends of the life after death, is pretty certainly as old as the 4th century and may be as old as the 3rd. The development of the Alexandreid was to some extent checked or confined to narrow channels as long as something like traditional and continuous study of the classics was kept up. But hagiology was entirely free from criticism; its subjects were immensely numerous; and in the very nature of the case it allowed the tendencies and the folklore of three continents and of most of their countries to mingle with it. Especially the comparative sobriety of classical literature became affected with the Eastern appetite for marvel and unhesitating acceptation of it; and the extraordinary beauty of many of the central stories invited and necessitated embroidery, continuation, episode. Later, no doubt, the adult romance directly reacted on the original saint's life, as in the legends of St. Mary Magdalene most of all, of St. Eustace, and of many others. But there can be very little doubt that if the romance itself did not spring from the saint's life it was fostered thereby.

The Gathering of Matter.—Proceeding a little further in the cautious quest—not for the definite origins which are usually delusive, but for the tendencies which avail themselves of opportunities and the opportunities which lend themselves to tendencies —we may notice two things very important to the subject. The one is that as Graeco-Roman civilization began to spread north and east it met, to appearance which approaches certainty, matter which lent itself gladly to "romantic" treatment. That such matter was abundant in the literature and folk-lore of the East we know: that it was even more abundant in the literatures and folk-lore of the North, if we cannot strictly be said to *know,* we may be reasonably sure. On the other hand, as the various barbarian nations (using the word in the wide Greek sense), at least those of the North, became educated to literature, to "grammar," by classical examples, they found not a few passages in these examples which were either almost romances already or which lent themselves, with readiness that was almost insistence, to romantic treatment. Apollonius Rhodius had made almost a complete romance of the story of Jason and Medea. Virgil had imitated him by making almost a complete romance of the story of Aeneas and Dido: and Ovid, who for that very reason was to become the most popular author of the middle ages early and late, had gone some way towards romancing a great body of mythology. We do not know exactly who first applied to the legendary tale of Troy the methods which the pseudo-Callisthenes and "Julius Valerius" applied to the historical wars of Alexander, but there is every reason to believe that it was done fairly early. In short, during the late classical or semi-classical times and the whole of the dark ages, things were making for romance in almost every direction.

It would and did follow from this that the thing evolved itself in so many different places and in so many different forms that only a person of extraordinary temerity would put his finger on any given work and say, "This is the first romance," even putting aside the extreme chronological uncertainty of most of the documents that could be selected for such a position. Except by the most meteoric flights of "higher" criticism we cannot attain to any opinion as to the age and first developed form of such a story as that of Weland and Beadohild (referred to in the *Complaint of Deor*), which has strong romantic possibilities and must be almost of the oldest. The much more complicated Volsung and Nibelung story, though we may explore to some extent the existence backwards of its Norse and German forms, baffles us beyond certain points in each case; yet this, with the exception of the religious element, is romance almost achieved. And the origin of the great type of the romance that *is* achieved—that has all elements present and brings them to absolute perfection—the Arthurian legend, despite the immense labours that have been spent upon it and the valuable additions to particular knowledge which have resulted from some of them, is, still more than its own Grail, a quest unachieved, probably a thing unachievable. The longest and the widest inquiries, provided only that they be conducted in any spirit save that which determines to attain certainty and therefore concludes that certainty has been attained, will probably acquiesce most resignedly in the dictum that romance "grew"—that its birthplace is as unknown as the grave of its greatest representative figure.

But when it has "grown" to a certain stage we can find it, and in a way localize it, and more definitely still analyse and comprehend its characteristics from their concrete expressions.

CLASSES OF SOURCE

Approaching these concrete expressions, then, without at first putting forward excessively hard and fast requirements in regard to the validation of the claims, we find existing in Europe about the 11th century (the time is designedly left loose) divers classes of what we should now call imaginative or fictitious literature, nearly all (the exceptions are Scandinavian and Old English) in verse. These are: (i.) The saints' lives; (ii.) the Norse sagas, roughly so-called; (iii.) the French *chansons de geste;* (iv.) the Old English and Old German stories of various kinds; (v.) perhaps the beginning of the Arthurian cycle; (vi.) various stories more or less based on classical legend or history from the tales of Alexander and of Troy down to things like *Apollonius of Tyre,* which have no classical authority of either kind, but strongly resemble the Greek romances, and which were, as in the case named, pretty certainly derived from members of the class; (vii.) certain fragments of Eastern story making their way first, it may be, through Spain by pilgrimages, latterly by the crusades.

Now, without attempting to fence off too rigidly the classical from the romantic, it may be laid down that these various classes possess that romantic character, to which we are, by a process of netting and tracking, slowly making our way, in rather different degrees, and a short examination of the difference will forward us not a little in the hunt.

With i. (the saints' lives) we have least to do: because by the time that romance in the full sense comes largely and clearly into view, it has for the most part separated itself off—the legend of St. Eustace has become the romance of Sir Isumbras, and so forth. But the influence which it may, as has been said, have originally given must have been continually re-exerted; the romantic-dynamic suggestion of such stories as those of St. Mary of Egypt, of St. Margaret and the Dragon, of St. Dorothea, and of scores of others, is quite unmistakable. Still, in actual result, it works rather more on drama than on narrative romance, and produces the miracle plays.

In ii. (the sagas), while a large part of their matter and even not a little of their form are strongly romantic, differences of handling and still more of temper have made some demur to their inclusion under romance, while their final ousting in their own literatures by versions of the all-conquering French romance itself is an argument on the same side. But the Volsung story, for instance, is full of what may be called "undistilled" romance —the wine is there, but it has to be passed through the still— and even in the most domestic sagas proper this characteristic is largely present.

It is somewhat less so in iii. (the *chansons de geste*), at least in the apparently older ones, though here again the comparative absence of romantic characteristics has been rather exaggerated, in consequence of the habit of paying disproportionate and even exclusive attention to the *Chanson de Roland.* There is more, that is, of romance in *Aliscans* and others of the older class, while *Amis and Amiles,* which must be of this class in time, is almost a complete romance, blending war, love and religion—*salus, venus, virtus*—in full degree.

The other four classes, the miscellaneous stories from classical, Eastern and European sources, having less corporate or national character, lend themselves with greater ease to the conditions of romantic development; but even so in different degrees. The classical stories have to drop most of their original character and allow something very different to be superinduced before they become thoroughly romantic. The greatest success of all in this way is the story of *Troilus and Cressida.* For before its development through the successive hands of Benoît de Sainte-More, Boccaccio (for we may drop Guido of the Columns as a mere middleman between Benoît and Boccaccio) and Chaucer, it has next to no classical authority of any kind except the mere names. In the various Alexandreids the element of the marvellous—the Eastern element, that is to say—similarly overpowers the classical. As for the Eastern stories themselves, they are particularly difficult of certain unravelment. The large moral division—such as *Barlaam and Josaphat,* the *Seven Wise Masters* in its various forms, etc., comes short of the strictly romantic. We do not know how much of East and how much of West there is in such things as *Flore et Blanchefleur* or even in *Huon of Bordeaux* itself. Contrariwise we ought to know, more certainly than apparently is known yet, what is the date and history of such a thing as that story of Zumurrud and Ali Shahr, which may be found partly in Lane and fully in the complete translations of the *Arabian Nights,* though not in the commoner editions, and which is evidently either copied from, or capable of serving as model to, a Western *roman d'aventures* itself.

We come, however, much closer to the actual norm itself—closer, in fact, than in any other place save one—in the various stories, English, French, and to a less extent German,[1] which gradually received in a loose kind of way the technical French term just used, a term not to be translated without danger. Nearly all these stories were drawn, by the astonishing centripetal tendency which made France the home of all romance between the 11th and the 13th centuries, into French forms; and in most cases no older ones survive. But it is hardly possible to doubt that in such a case, for instance, as *Havelok,* an original story of English or Scandinavian origin got itself into existence before, and perhaps long before, the French version was retransferred to English, and so in other cases. If, once more, we take our existing English *Havelok* and its sister *King Horn,* we see that the latter is a *more* romanced form than the former. *Havelok* is more like a *chanson de geste*—the love interest in it is very slight; while in *King Horn* it is much stronger, and the increased strength is shown by the heroine being in some forms promoted into the title. If these two be studied side by side the process of transforming the mere story into the full romance is to no small extent seen in actual operation. But neither exhibits in any considerable degree the element of the marvellous, or the religious element, and the love interest itself is, even in *Horn,* simple and not very dramatically or passionately worked out. In the later *roman d'aventures,* of which the 13th century was so prolific (such as, to give one example out of many, *Amadas and Idoine*), these elements appear fully, and so they do in the great Auchinleck collection in English, which, though dating well within the 14th century, evidently represents the meditation and adaptation of French examples for many years earlier.

The last of our divisions, however, exhibits the whole body of romantic elements as nothing else does. It is not our business in this place to deal with the Arthurian legend generally as regards origin, contents, etc., nor, in the present division of this actual article, to look at it except for a special purpose and in connection with and contradistinctive to the other groups just surveyed. Here, however, we at last find all the elements of romance, thoroughly mixed and thoroughly at home, with the result not merely that the actual story becomes immensely popular and widely spread; not only that it receives the greatest actual development of any romantic theme; but that, in a curious fashion, it attracts to itself great numbers of practically independent stories—in not a few cases probably quite independent at first—which seem afraid to present themselves without some tacking on (it may be of the loosest and most accidental description) to the great *polycentric* cycle, the stages of which gather round Merlin, the Round Table, the Grail and the Guinevere-Lancelot-Mordred catastrophe. All the elements, let it be repeated, are here present: war, love and religion; the characteristic extension of subject in desultory adventure-chronicles; the typical rather than individual character (though the strong individuality of some of the unknown or half-known contributors sometimes surmounts this); the admixture of the marvellous, not merely though mainly as part of the religious element; the presence of the chivalrous ideal.

[1]Italian romance seems to have modelled itself early on French, and it is doubtful, rich as is the late crop of Spanish romances, whether we have any that deserve the name strictly and are really early.

The strong dramatic interest of the central story is rather superadded to than definitely evolved from these elements; but they are still present, just as, though more powerfully than, in the weakest of miscellaneous *romans d'aventures.*

TYPES OF STORY, INCIDENT AND PERSONAGES

A further step in the logical and historical exploration of romance may be taken by regarding the character-and-story classes round which it groups itself, and which from the intense community of mediaeval literature—the habit of mediaeval writers not so much to plagiarize from one another as to take up each after each the materials and the instruments which were not the property of any—is here especially observable. Prominent above everything is the world-old motive of the quest; which, world-old as it is, here acquires a predominance that it has never held before or since. The object takes pretty various, though not quite infinitely various, forms, from the rights of the disinherited heir and the hand or the favour of the heroine, to individual things which may themselves vary from the Holy Grail to so many hairs of a sultan's beard. It may be a friendly knight who is lost in adventure, or a felon knight who has to be punished for his trespasses; a spell of some kind to be laid; a monster to be exterminated; an injured virgin or lady, or an infirm potentate, to be succoured or avenged; an evil custom to be put an end to; or simply some definite adventure or exploit to be achieved. But quest of some sort there must certainly be if (as in *Sir Launfal,* for instance) it is but the recovery of a love forfeited by misbehaviour or mishap. It is almost a *sine qua non*—the present writer, thinking over scores, nay hundreds, of romances, cannot at the moment remember one where it is wanting in some form or another.

It will be observed that this at once provides the amplest opportunity for the desultory concatenation or congregation of incident and episode which is of the very essence of romance. Often, nay generally, the conditions, localities and other circumstances of the quest are half known, or all but unknown, to the knight, and he is sometimes intentionally led astray, always liable to be incidentally called off by interim adventures. In many (perhaps most) cases the love interest is directly connected with the quest, though it may be in the way of hindrance as well as of furtherance or reward. The war interest always is so connected; and the religious interest commonly—almost universally in fact—is an inseparable accident. But everything leads up to, involves, eventuates in the fighting. The quest, if not always a directly warlike one, always involves war; and the endless battles have at all times, since they ceased to be the great attraction, continued to be the great obloquy of romance. It is possible no doubt that reports of tournaments and single combats with lance and sword, mace and battle-axe, may be as tedious to some people as reports of football matches certainly are to others. It is certain that the former were as satisfactory in former times to their own admirers as the latter are now. In fact the variety of incident is almost as remarkable as the sameness. And the same may be said, with even greater confidence, of the adventures between the fights in castle and church and monastery, in homestead or hermitage. The actual stories are not much more alike than those who have read large numbers of modern novels critically know to be the case with them. But the absence, save in rare cases, of the element of character, and the very small presence of that of conversation, show up the sameness that exists in the earlier case.

The same deficiency in individual character-drawing, and in the conversation which is one of its principal instruments, brings out in somewhat unfair relief some other cases of apparent sameness—the "common forms" of story and of character itself. The disinherited heir, the unfaithful or wronged wife, the wicked stepmother, the jealous or wrongly suspected lover, are just as universal in modern fiction as they are in mediaeval—for the simple reason that they are common if not universal in nature. But the skeleton is more obvious because it is less clothed with flesh and garments over the flesh; the texture of the canvas shows more because it is less worked upon. Some of these common forms, however, are more peculiar to mediaeval times; and some, though not many, allow excursions into abnormalities which, until recently, were tabooed to the modern novelist. Among the former the wickedness of the steward is remarkable, and of course not difficult to account for. The steward or seneschal of romance, with some honourable exceptions, is as wicked as the baronet of a novel, but here the explanation is not metaphysical. He was constantly left in charge in the absence of his lord and so was exposed to temptation. The extreme and almost Ephesian consolableness of the romance widow can be equally rationalized—and in fact is so in the stories themselves—by the danger of the fief being resumed or usurped in the absence of a male tenant who can maintain authority and discharge duties. While such themes as the usually ignorant incest of son with mother or the more deliberate passion of father for daughter come mostly from very popular early examples—the legend of St. Gregory of the Rock or the story of Apollonius of Tyre.

Characters of Romance Proper.—The last point brings us naturally to another of considerable importance—the singular *purity* of the romances as a whole, if not entirely in atmosphere and situation, yet in language and in external treatment. It suited the purposes of the Protestant controversialists of the Renaissance, such as our own Ascham, to throw discredit upon work so intimately connected with Catholic ceremony and belief as the *Morte d'Arthur;* and it is certain that the knights of romance did not even take the benefit of that liberal doctrine of the *Cursor Mundi* which regards even illicit love as not mortal unless it be "with spouse or *sib.*" But if in the romances such love is portrayed freely, and with a certain sympathy, it is never spoken of lightly and is always punished; nor are the pictures of it ever coarsely drawn. In a very wide reading of romance the present writer does not remember more than two or three passages of romance proper (that is to say before the latter part of the 15th century) which could be called obscene by any fair judge. And the term would have to be somewhat strained in reference even to these.

The contrast with the companion divisions of *fabliaux* and farces is quite extraordinary; and nearly as sharp as that between Greek tragedy on the one hand and Greek comedy or satiric play on the other. It is brought out for the merely English reader in Chaucer of course, but in him it might have been studied. In the immense *corpus* of known or unknown French and English writers (the Germans are not quite so particular) it comes out with no possibility of deliberation and with unmistakable force.

The history of the forms in which romance presents itself follows a sufficiently normal and probable course. The oldest are always—save in the single case of part of the Arthurian division, in which we probably possess none of the *actually* oldest, and in some of the division of Antiquity which had a long line of predecessors in the learned languages—the shortest. They become lengthened in a way continued and exemplified to the present moment by the tendency of writers to add sequels and episodes to their own stories, and made still more natural by the fact that these poems were in all or almost all cases *recited.* "Go on" is the most natural and not the least common as well as the most complimentary form of "Bravo!" and the reciter never seems to have said "no" to the compliment. In not a few cases—*Huon of Bordeaux, Ogier the Dane, Guy of Warwick,* are conspicuous examples—we possess the same story in various stages; and can see how poems, perhaps originally like *King Horn* of not more than a couple of thousand lines or even shorter in the 13th century, grew to thirty, forty, fifty thousand in the 15th. The transference of the story itself from verse to prose is also—save in some particular and still controverted instances—regularly traceable and part of a larger and natural literary movement. While, also naturally enough, the pieces become in time fuller of conversation (though not as yet often of conversation that advances the story or heightens its interest), of descriptive detail, etc. And in some groups (notably that of the remarkable *Amadis* division) a very great enlargement of the proportion and degradation of the character of the marvellous element appears—the wonders being no longer mystical, and indeed being magical only in the lower sense.

CHARACTERISTIC EXAMPLES

And so we come to the particular characteristics of the kind or kinds demonstrated in individual examples. Of these the English reader possesses a matchless although a late instance in the *Morte d'Arthur* of Malory, a book which is at once a *corpus* and a pattern of romance in gross and in detail. The fact that it is not, as has been too often hastily or ignorantly asserted, a mere compilation, but the last of a singular series of rehandlings and redactions—conducted with extraordinary though for the most part indistinctly traceable instinct of genius—makes it to some extent transcend any single example of older date and more isolated composition. But it displays all the best as well as some of the less good characteristics of most if not all. Of the commonest kind—the almost pure *roman d'aventures* itself—the Gareth-Beaumains episode (for which we have no direct original, French or English, though *Lybius Disconus* and *Ipomedon* come near to it in different ways) will give a fair example; while its presentation of the later chapters of the Grail story, and the intertwisted plot and continuing catastrophe of the love of Lancelot and Guinevere, altogether transcend the usual scope of romance pure and simple, and introduce almost the highest possibilities of the romantic novel. The way in which Malory or his immediate authorities have extruded the tedious wars round the "Rock of the Saxons," have dropped the awkward episode of the false Guinevere, and have restrained the uninteresting exuberance of the continental wars and the preliminary struggles with the minor kings, keeps the reader from contact with the duller sides of romance only. Of the real variety which rewards a persistent reader of the class at large it would be impossible to present even a miniature hand-index here; but something may be done by sample, which will not be *mere* sample, but an integral part of the exposition. No arbitrary separation need be made between French and English; because of the intimate connection between the two. As specially and symptomatically noteworthy the famous pair—perhaps the most famous of all—*Guy of Warwick* and *Bevis of Hampton,* should *not* be taken. For, with the exception of the separation of Guy and Felise in the first, and some things in the character of Josiane in the second, both are somewhat spiritless concoctions of stock matter. Far more striking than anything in either, though not consummately supported by their context, are the bold opening of *Blancandin et l'orgueilleuse d'amour,* where the hero begins by kissing a specially proud and prudish lady; and the fine scenes of fight with a supernatural foe at a grave to be found in *Amadas et Idoine.* Reputation and value coincide more nearly in the charming fairy story of *Parthenopex de Blois* and the Christian-Saracen love romance of *Flore* (Florice and other forms) *et Blanchefleur.* Few romances in either language, or in German, exhibit the pure adventure story better than Chrestien de Troyes's *Chevalier au Lyon,* especially in its English form of *Ywain and Gawain;* while the above-mentioned *Lybius Disconus* (*Le Beau Déconnu*) makes a good pair with this. For originality of form and phrase as well as of spirit, if not exactly of incident, *Gawain and the Green Knight* stands alone; but another Gawain story (in French this time), *Le Chevalieur aux deux épées,* though of much less force and fire, exceeds it in length without sameness of adventure. Only the poorest romances—those ridiculed by Chaucer in *Sir Thopas*—which form a small minority, lack striking individual touches, such as the picture of the tree covered with torches and carrying on its summit a heavenly child, which illuminates the huge expanse of *Durmart le Gallois.* The various forms of the *Seven Wise Masters* in different European languages show the attitude of the Western to the Eastern fiction interestingly. The beautiful romance of *Emarè* is about the best of several treatments of one of the exceptional subjects classed above—the unnatural love of father for daughter, while if we turn to German stories we find not merely in the German variants of Arthurian themes, but in others a double portion of the mystical element. French themes are constantly worked up afresh—as indeed they are all over Europe—but the Germans have the advantage of drawing upon not merely Scandinavian traditions like those which they wrought into the *Nibelungen Lied* and

Gudrun, but others of their own. And both in these and in their dealings with French they sometimes show an amount of story-telling power which is rare in French and English. No handling of the Tristan and Iseult story can compare with Gottfried's; while the famous *Der arme Heinrich* of Hartmann von Aue (the original of Longfellow's *Golden Legend*) is one of the greatest triumphs and most charming examples of romance, displaying in almost the highest degree possible for a story of little complexity all the best characteristics of the thing.

What, then, are these characteristics? The account has now been brought to a point where a reasoned résumé of it will give as definite an answer as can be given.

Even yet we may with advantage interpose a consideration of the answer that was given to this question universally (with a few dissidents) from the Renaissance to nearly the end of the 18th century and not infrequently since; while it is not impossible that, in the well-attested revolutions of critical thought and taste, it may be given again. This is that romance on the whole, and with some flashes of better things at times, is a jumble of incoherent and mostly ill-told stories, combining sameness with extravagance, outraging probability and the laws of imitative form, childish as a rule in its appeal to adventure and to the supernatural, immoral in its ethics, barbarous in its aesthetics, destitute of any philosophy, representing at its very best (though the ages of its lowest appreciation were hardly able even to consider this) a necessary stage in the education of half-civilized peoples, and embodying some interesting legends, much curious folklore and a certain amount of distorted historical evidence. On the other hand, for the last hundred years and more, there have been some who have seen in romance almost the highest and certainly the most charming form of fictitious creation, the link between poetry and religion, the literary embodiment of men's dreams and desires, the appointed nepenthe of more sophisticated ages as it was the appointed pastime of the less sophisticated. Between these opposites there is of course room for many middle positions, but few of these will be occupied safely and inexpugnably by those who do not take heed of the following conclusions.

Romance, beyond all question, enmeshes and retains for us a vast amount of story material to which we find little corresponding in ancient literature. It lays the foundation of modern prose fiction in such a fashion that the mere working out and building up of certain features leads to, and in fact involves the whole structure of the modern novel (*q.v.*). It antiquates (by a sort of gradual "taking for granted") the classical assumption that love is an inferior motive, and that women, though they "may be good sometimes" are scarcely fit for the position of principal personages. It helps to institute and ensure a new unity—the unity of interest. It admits of the most extensive variety. It gives a scope to the imagination which exceeds that of any known older literary form. At its best it embodies the new or Christian morality, if not in a Pharisaic yet in a Christian fashion, and it establishes a concordat between religion and art in more ways than this. Incapable of exacter definition, inclining (a danger doubtless as well as an advantage) toward the vague, it is nevertheless comprehensible for all its vagueness, and, informal as it is, possesses its own form of beauty—and that a precious one. These characteristics were, if perceived at all by its enemies in the period above referred to, taken at their worst; they were perceived by its champions at the turn of the tide and perhaps exaggerated. From both attitudes emerged that distinction between the "classic" and the "romantic" which was referred to at the beginning of this article as requiring notice before we conclude. The crudest, but it must be remembered the most intentionally crude (for Goethe knew the limitations of his saying), is that "Classicism is health; Romanticism is disease." In a less question-begging proposition of single terms, classicism might be said to be method and romanticism energy. But in fact sharp distinctions of the kind do much more harm than good. It is true that the one tends to order, lucidity, proportion; the other to freedom, to fancy, to caprice. But the attempt to reimpose these qualities as absolutely distinguishing marks and labels on particular works is almost certain to lead to mistake and disaster,

and there is more than mere irony in the person who defines romance as "Something which was written between an unknown period of the Dark Ages and the Renaissance, and which has been imitated since the later part of the 18th century." What that something really is, is not to be known well except by reading more or less considerable sections of it—by exploring it like one of its own forbidden countries. But something of a sketch map of that country has been attempted here.

See also articles on the different national literatures, especially French and Icelandic; and the following:—

Classical or Pseudo-Classical Subjects.—Apollonius of Tyre; Longus; Heliodorus; Apuleius, Lucius; Troy and Troad; Thebes; Caesar, Gaius Julius; Alexander III (the Great); Hercules; Jason; Oedipus; Virgil.

Arthurian Romance.—Arthurian Legend; Chretien de Troyes; Gottfried von Strassburg; Malory, Sir Thomas; Wolfram von Eschenbach; etc.

French Romance.—Charles the Great; Guillaume d'Orange; Doon de Mayence; Ogier the Dane; Roland, Legend of; Renaud de Montauban (*Quatre fils Aymon*); Huon of Bordeaux; Girart de Roussillon; Macaire; Partonopeus de Blois; Robert the Devil; Flore and Blanchefleur; Raoul de Cambrai; Guillaume de Palerne; Benoît de Sainte-More, etc.

Anglo-Norman, Anglo-Danish, English Romance.—Bevis of Hampton; Horn; Havelok the Dane; Guy of Warwick; Robin Hood; Maid Marian.

German.—Nibelungenlied; Ortnit; Dietrich of Berne; Wolf-Dietrich; Heldenbuch; Waltharius; Gudrun; Hildebrand, Lay of; Ruodlieb.

Northern.—Sigurd; Wayland the Smith; Hamlet; Edda.

Spanish.—Amadis de Gaula.

Various.—Reynard the Fox; Roman de la Rose; Griselda and kindred stories; Genevieve of Brabant; Gesta Romanorum; Barlaam and Josaphat; Seven Wise Masters; Maelduin, Voyage of.

Bibliography.—The first modern composition of importance on romance (putting aside the dealings of Italian critics in the 16th century with the question of romantic *v.* classical unity) is the very remarkable dialogue *De la Lecture des vieux romans* written by Chapelain in mid-17th century (ed. Feillet, 1870), which is a surprising and thoroughgoing defense of its subjects. But for long afterward there was little save unintelligent and mostly quite ignorant depreciation. The sequence of really important serious works almost begins with Hurd's *Letters on Chivalry and Romance* (1762). In succession to this may be consulted on the *general* subject (which alone can be here regarded) the dissertations of Percy, Warton and Ritson; Sir Walter Scott, "Essay on Romance" in the supplement to the *Encyclopædia Britannica* (1816–24); Dunlop, *History of Fiction* (1816, usefully supplemented and completed by its 4th edition, 1888, with very large additions by H. Wilson); C. L. B. Wolff, *Allgemeine Geschichte des Romans* (Jena, 1841–50); H. L. D. Ward, *Catalogue of Romances in the British Museum* (vol. i, 1883, vol. ii, 1893) (the most valuable single contribution to the knowledge of the subject); G. Saintsbury, *The Flourishing of Romance and the Rise of Allegory* (1897), and its companion volumes in *Periods of European Literature* [W. P. Ker, *The Dark Ages* (1904); F. J. Snell, *The Fourteenth Century* (1899); G. Gregory Smith, *The Transition Period* (1900); D. Hannay, *The Later Renaissance* (1898)]; W. P. Ker, *Epic and Romance* (1897).

(G. Sa.)

ROMANCE LANGUAGES. The name given to the seven groups of languages, viz., Portuguese, Spanish, Provençal (including Catalan), French, Italian, the Rhaeto-Romanic idioms and Rumanian.

They are called "romance" (from post-classical Latin *romanice,* derived from Latin *romanus*) because their basis is the Latin which was spoken in the Imperium Romanum. They are sometimes called "daughter languages" (*langues filles*) of Latin, though in no sense daughters, but Latin itself in the transformed state it has reached in the various countries in which it was spoken. The word Neo-Latin has been used for "Romance" by some scholars.

The comparative method systematically used by F. Diez (1794–1876) in his *Grammatik der romanischen Sprachen,* of which the first volume appeared in 1836, demonstrated conclusively that each of the above-mentioned languages was directly evolved from Vulgar or Popular Latin.

Within a few years of the appearance of Diez's studies new tendencies began to be felt, tendencies which Diez had himself approved but for lack of opportunity had not embodied. First, chiefly under the impulse of Paul Meyer (1840–1917) the documents preserved in the archives were taken into account; next came the study of the *patois* instigated by Gaston Paris (1839–1903) keenly pursued by investigators such as abbé Rousselot (1846–1924) and Gilliéron (1854–1926), and yielding fresh materials for phonetic and lexicographical research; finally, the study of semantics began simultaneously in different countries.

W. Meyer-Luebke, availing himself of the philological material now accessible in recorded dialect and patois, completely revised Diez's grammar and compiled a new *Grammatik der romanischen Sprachen* (4 vols. 1890–1902) on a much broader basis. This achievement marks the close of this period of romance philology.

The opening of the latest period is distinguished by the use of "linguistic geography" initiated by the appearance of the *Atlas historique de la France* by Gilliéron and Edmont, containing 2,319 maps, 1,920 for France proper (1902–1910) and 399 for Corsica (1914). Similar surveys have been attempted in other countries, but few have attained successful completion. Alone worthy of mention as regards romance languages are Weigand, *Linguisticher Atlas des dacorumänischen Sprachgebietes* (Leipzig, 1909), containing 67 maps only and none of the Bánat; Ch. Guerlin de Guer, *Atlas dialectologique de la Normandie* (1903), comprising 123 maps but unfinished; Griera, *Atlas linguistique de Catalunya,* which is to form 10 volumes (2,000 maps) vols. i., ii., and iii., with 586 maps having so far appeared (Barcelona, 1923–24).

POPULAR LATIN

With Latin, as with all languages, there existed from the outset divergences between the written and spoken idioms affecting the vocabulary and various portions of the grammar.

The name Popular Latin, especially applied to the spoken language with all its individual and dialectical idiosyncrasies, was also termed *inconditus, cotidianus, usualis, vulgaris, plebeius, proletarius* and *rusticus,* as opposed to the written language from which it was progressively differentiated by the operation of social influences and the growth of literature. Thus the contact of Latin with Greek, and particularly Greek philosophy, science and art, resulted in the coinage of learned terms, *e.g., epistola, grammatica, schola, stylus, poeta, poesis, poema, papyrus, paragraphus, heros, aer, aether, encaustum, podagra, sarcophagus, horologium.* These were Greek words with Latin endings. In formation they were contrary to the genius of the native Latin which enriched its word-stock by its traditional system of composition and derivation, especially by means of suffixes, destined to play such an important rôle in the romance languages. Till the end of the 1st century A.D. however, the classical language withstood the assaults of Popular Latin which it dominated in some degree by the prestige of its literary masterpieces, by the exigencies of the administration which compelled all officials to employ the higher language, and by the influence of the schools in which teaching was given in the *sermo urbanus.* But, with the passing of the golden age, the written language became even more artificial. When in A.D. 212 Caracalla conferred by edict the dignity of Roman citizenship upon all free-born inhabitants of the Empire, he introduced into Rome, according to the picturesque phrase of Isidore of Seville (Origines, ii. 31) *"vitia et verborum et morum"* (sins of speech and morality) and thenceforth the evolution of Popular Latin in all provinces, as far as we can trace, proceeded to all intents unchecked conformably with its inherent character. Two fresh historical factors next intervened, hastening the downfall of classical Latin, the religious revolution and the invasions of the Barbarians. Of the Christian propagandists the vast majority belonged to the lower classes; among the most zealous were many slaves and women, the language they used was essentially popular and even the educated among them found that to carry out their evangelisation efficiently they must resort to the vulgar tongue. The greatest of the Fathers of the Church, notwithstanding he had been a professor of rhetoric, wrote without hesitating: "Non timemus ferulas grammaticorum, dum tamen ad veritatem solidam et certiorem perveniamus. Melius est quod reprehendant nos grammatici quam non intelligant populi." (S. Augustinus, *Enarrationes in Psalmos,* 138, 20.) "We don't fear the schoolmaster's cane if only we can arrive at a sure and more weighty truth. It were better to be reproved by the pedants than to be not understood by the people." Pope Gregory the Great appeals to Almighty God against the tyranny of the declensions: "Casus servare con-

temno quia indignum vehementer esistimo ut verba coelestis oraculi restringam sub regulis Donati." (*Praefatio,* Job, 1. 6.) "I refuse the slavery of the declensions because I think strongly that it is not fitting that I should force the words of the Divine Message into the rules of Donatus."

The anarchy which ensued when the Roman empire was overthrown proved eminently favourable to the growth of dialects and special idioms. Vulgar Latin and pre-literary Romance was a spoken language, but can in some measure be reconstituted from the information derived from the treatises composed by grammarians, the Latin Bible, the early Latin manuscripts, inscriptions, collection of formulae of the laws of the Barbarians, divers glossaries, literary, historical and technical texts ranging from the 4th to the 8th century, and the coins and charters of the Merovingian and Carolingian epochs. Thus the *Appendix Probi* (most probably of the 3rd century) contains remarks on declension, conjugation, orthography and the meaning of words. It is a kind of manual of "don'ts," interesting from the philological standpoint precisely on account of the forms quoted as mistakes to be avoided. The mention *porphireticum marmor* ñ *purpureticum marmur* attests the popular pronunciation of *ph,* in which Vulgar Latin dropped the aspiration, and the confusion of *ō* and *ŭ; speculum* ñ *speclum* shows the dropping in popular pronunciation of the posttonic vowel in proparoxytones; *pecten* ñ *pectinis* instances a nominative formed by popular analogy. *The Glossary of Reichenau* (the ms. dates from the 8th century) translates certain words of the Vulgate no longer understood by words which, although given Latin case or verb inflexions, belonged in fact to a dialect of Northwestern France. Thus in the sentence "Sed et serpens erat callidior" (Genesis iii., 1) *callidior* is rendered by *vitiosior.* This means that *callidus* had ceased to be intelligible (*callidus* has in fact totally vanished from the romance languages), and that *vitiosus* had taken its place in Vulgar Latin (*vitiosus* survives indeed in Italian *vezzoso,* Spanish and Portuguese *vicioso,* and is represented in Old French by *voisos*).

The material is both scarce and scanty, despite the richness and variety of the dialects spoken in all parts of the Roman empire. Reconstruction must in many cases resort to the comparative method. Thus, take the name for "finch" in various romance languages, *pincione* in Tuscan, *pintsuni* in Sicilian, *pinson* in French, *pinsó* in Catalan, *pinsón* in Spanish; comparison of these differing forms shows that all are derived from a common prototype which can be reconstituted as *pincionem.* Again if we take the words for "to advance," *avanzare* in Italian, *avaunzer* in the Engadine dialect, *vantsá* in Frioulan, *avansar* in Provençal and Catalan, *avancer* in French, there can be no doubt as to the legitimacy of our reconstituting a prototype verb *abantiare* formed from the Latin *ante.*

General Characteristics of the Romance Languages. —After an evolutionary process occupying some three centuries Popular Latin had taken on an individual character according to the different regions of the Romanic world in which it was spoken, and the dawn of "romance" may be regarded as coincident with the 8th century.

1. Vocabulary.—The Romance languages retained only negligible traces of the idioms originally spoken in their various territories before the advent of Latin. In French not more than fifty words can be traced back to Celtic; in Spanish the number of Iberian terms is no greater; in Northern Italian there are but infinitesimal relics of Osco-Umbrian and Celtic; in Southern Italian and Sicilian a few traces of Greek. As regards the Rhetic and Rumanian words which are ascribed to the primitive tongues of the Dacians, Thracians and Illyrians, the identification rests on practically indemonstrable hypotheses. The most important additions to the vocabularies of the romance languages come, for the occidental portion, from Germanic, Greek and Arabic, and, for the oriental portion, from Slavonic. The Germanic contribution embraces terms dealing with war, military art, costume, rural life and parts of the body, a few abstract terms and a great quantity of proper names. It is peculiarly important in French by reason of the Frankish invasion of Gaul and the influence exerted by the Merovingian and Carolingian kings who were of Germanic origin. The Greek element during the middle ages, was of only slight importance, and was restricted to terms' brought back by the Crusaders in the 11th and 12th centuries, or incorporated as a result of the commercial relations between Orient and Occident. The influx of Greek words was accelerated in the 14th century and with the 19th century became very abundant. The Arabic element is particularly important in Spanish, Portuguese and Provençal; many terms have percolated into Italian, and about three hundred are extant in Modern French. Finally at various periods other languages have supplied contributions, and there has been a continuous interpenetration between the different romance languages themselves. All romance languages contain (*a*) popular words, *i.e.*, derived by slow evolution from Popular Latin: (*b*) words of learned formation, *i.e.*, borrowed direct from ancient or modern languages. In some cases the same original word has yielded two derivatives belonging to *a* or *b* respectively.

2. Phonetics.—The general law applying to all romance languages is that the incidence of the tonic accent remains as in Popular Latin. All popular words are therefore stressed at the same point as they were eighteen centuries ago; as in some romance languages the vowels have persisted much as they were during the imperial epoch, a modern Italian or Spaniard pronounces some words almost exactly as did a subject of Marcus Aurelius or Commodus. The atonic or intertonic vowels have weakened, or in some of the romance languages disappeared (except *a*). Proparoxytones have tended to become paroxytones, but many have survived in Italian and Rumanian, a few in Spanish; a small number existing in Old French were gradually eliminated during the middle ages. French and Portuguese have evolved nasal vowels unknown in Latin; the *ü* sound, also unknown in Latin, is found in French, Provençal, and the Northern Italian and Engadine dialects. Initial consonants have, in general, suffered no change. In Spanish, however, *b* has developed into an intermediary sound between *b* and *v*, whilst *c* + *e* or *i* is pronounced like English voiceless *th* and *j* has become a velar fricative. In French *c* + *a* has given rise to the sound *ch*, (*e.g.*, campum > champ) and *g* + *a* to the sound *j* (*e.g.*, gaudia > joie); *h* has totally disappeared. The intervocalic consonants have proved less resistant; *b* has passed to *v* in all romance languages (even when orthographed *b* as in Spanish and Gascon, it is pronounced with the intermediary sound). Final *m* and *n* have disappeared apart from some rare exceptions (Sp. *quien*, F. *rien*) and *ns* has been reduced to *s*, processes of which signs are already visible in classical Latin. (Rumanian offers many peculiarities: *see* RUMANIAN LANGUAGE AND LITERATURE.)

3. Morphology.—The following features set forth the double character which prevailed in the evolution of the romance languages (*a*) the modification of the declension and conjugation system, (*b*) the development of the analytical tendencies of romance as opposed to the synthetic character of classical Latin.

The neuter has disappeared from all romance languages; a few relics of it still survived in the mediaeval period. The term "neuter" used in Rumanian to designate the third declension applies to substantives conforming to the masculine declension in the singular and to the feminine declension in the plural, *e.g.*, *un cutit* (a knife), *niste cutite* (knives). The two-case system of declension (nominative and accusative) characterising the early period of some romance languages (French, Provençal and perhaps Rhaeto-Romanic) has disappeared (*see* RUMANIAN LANGUAGE AND LITERATURE); substantives and adjectives now possess only a single case in the singular and in the plural. More numerous traces of declension are preserved by the personal and relative pronouns. The definite article and personal pronoun of the third person are in all romance languages derived from *ille* (or *illi*), *illa*. The cardinal numbers 1 to 10 correspond in all romance languages to the Latin cardinals, but from 11 onwards there are varied divergences. A noteworthy feature of French is the use of 20 as multiplier. The synthetic comparatives and superlatives have mostly been ousted by *magis* or *plus* preceding the positive, *e.g.*, *grandior*, *grandissimus*, replaced by *magis* or *plus grandis*. The tense paradigms have been profoundly modified; the future and conditional

of occidental romance languages are derived from new Vulgar Latin creations which substitute for the synthetic classical *amabo*, *amarem*, forms made up of infinitive + (*h*)*abeo* (*amare* + [*h*]*abeo*) for the future, and of infinitive + (*h*)*abebam* (*amare* + [*h*]*abebam*) for the conditional. In Italian, however, the prototype of the conditional was infinitive + (*h*)*abui* (*amare* + [*h*]*abui*). In Rumanian and the Rhetic idioms the future and conditional are periphrastic. Romance languages have further evolved a new perfect and pluperfect based on Latin (*h*)*abui* and (*h*)*abebam* + past participle: (*h*)*abui* + *amatum* and (*h*)*abebam* + *amatum*. The imperative either perpetuates the Latin forms (somewhat curtailed), as in Italian, or replaces the plural by indicative or subjunctive forms. The infinitives in –*are* and –*ire* have evolved regularly; but those in –*ēre* and –*ĕre* have suffered varying fates in the different romance languages. As to past participles, most striking is the extension of forms in –*ūtus* at the expense of those in –*itus* and –*ŭtus*. In the personal flexions of the various tenses analogy has worked many changes; *e.g.*, in Italian and Rumanian the second person singular of all tenses ends in –*i*. Romance retains no vestige of the deponent verbs, all of which have been assimilated to active verbs, *e.g.*, *nasci* has become *nascere*. Romance has substituted for the synthetic tenses of the passive voice, a periphrasis compounded from the different forms of *essère* (Vulgar Latin for *esse*) or of *stare* + past participle.

4. Syntax.—Evolution has been towards a more rational and logical word-order and stricter connection both of clauses and of words. Many new syntactical features are closely correlated with the modifications mentioned in **2** and **3**. There has been constant action and reaction between phonetics, morphology and syntax. If the structure of the Romance sentence is compared with that of the Latin sentence the salient innovations observable are (*a*) the normal constructional order subject, verb, complement, replacing the elaborate artifices of classical Latin which had gradually disappeared in Vulgar Latin; (*b*) the substitution of the relative clause of the Vulgar Latin type, *credo quod* (or *quem* or *quatenus*) for the infinitive construction *e.g.*, *credo quod illum verum est* for *credo illud verum esse;* (*c*) increase in use and number of prepositions which in Vulgar Latin perform the functions of the lost genitive, dative and ablative cases; (*d*) creation of a definite article (from *ille, illa*) and an indefinite article (from *unus, una*); (*e*) increase in number of tenses permitting greater precision in expression of the past (past anterior, past imperfect and past conditional); (*f*) ingenious devices for formation of adverbs and prepositions more adequately expressing the shades of abstract thought, *e.g.*, French, *en, ens, dans, dedans*, corresponding respectively to *in, intus, de* + *intus, de* + *de* + *intus;* (*g*) complexity of certain interrogative forms best exemplified by the French equivalent for the Latin *Quid est?*: *Qu'est-ce que c'est que cela?* the etymological counterpart of which would be: *Quid est eccehoc quod eccehoc est quod ecce illac?* (Example quoted from the *Dictionnaire Général*).

BIBLIOGRAPHY.—G. Gröber, *Grundriss der romanischen Philologie*, vol. i. (2nd ed.). (1904–1906), vol. ii. (1897–1902); W. Meyer-Luebke, *Romanisches Etymologisches Wörterbuch* (1911); P. Savj-Lopez, *Le origini neolatine* (1920); W. Meyer-Luebke, *Die romanische Sprachwissenschaft der letzten zwölf Jahre* in *Revue de linguistique romance* p. 9–34 (1925). The ensemble of these gives a full bibliography. *Mélanges de philologie et d'histoire offerts à Monsieur Antoine Thomas*, 1927 (containing a complete list of the contributions to romance philology by the eminent French philologist).   (L. B.)

ROMAN DE LA ROSE, a French poem of which the first part was written about 1230 by Guillaume de Lorris (*q.v.*), and which was completed about 40 years later by Jean de Meun (*q.v.*). Guillaume de Lorris wrote an allegory, which is an artistic presentment of the love philosophy of the troubadours. In a dream the Lover visits a park to which he is admitted by Idleness. In the park he finds Pleasure, Delight, Cupid and other personages, and at length the Rose. Welcome grants him permission to kiss the Rose, but he is driven away by Danger, Shame, Scandal, and especially by Jealousy, who entrenches the Rose and imprisons Welcome, leaving the Lover disconsolate. The story, thus left incomplete, was finished in 19,000 lines by Jean de Meun, who allows the Lover to win the Rose, but only after a long siege and much discourse from Reason, the Friend, Nature and Genius. In the second part, however, the story is entirely subsidiary to picturesque and poetic digressions, and to violent satire in the manner of the fabliaux against the abuse of power, against women, against popular superstition, and against the celibacy of the clergy. The length of the work and its heterogeneous character proved no bar to its enormous popularity in the middle ages, attested by the 200 mss. of it which have survived.

The *Romaunt of the Rose* was translated into English by Chaucer (*see* the prologue to the *Legende of Good Women*), but the version which has come down to us (*see* an edition by Dr. Max Kaluza, Chaucer Society, 1891), is generally admitted to be by another hand. For a list of books on the authorship of the English translation *see* G. Körting, *Grundriss der engl. Lit.* (Münster, 1905, 4th ed. p. 184). Three editions of the *Roman de la Rose* were printed at Lyons between 1473 and 1490; two by Antoine Verard (Paris, 1490? and 1496?), by Jean du Pré (Paris, 1493?), by Nicholas Desprez for Jean Petit (Paris), by Michel le Noir (Paris, 1509 and 1519). In 1503 Jean Molinet produced a prose version. Marot modernized the text (1526), and his corrections were followed in subsequent editions. There is a modern English version by F. S. Ellis (3 vols., 1900).

ROMAN-DUTCH LAW.

The term Roman-Dutch law describes the system of law which existed in the province of Holland (*see* HOLLAND) from the 15th to the 19th centuries. This system, introduced by the Dutch into their colonies, was retained in those of them which passed to the British Crown at the end of the 18th and the beginning of the 19th centuries. These were the maritime districts of Ceylon, the Cape of Good Hope, and the settlements upon the coast of South America now comprised within the colony of British Guiana. In a secondary sense therefore Roman-Dutch law is the original common law of these countries. In Ceylon this system has been extended to the Kandyan Provinces (annexed in 1815), while in South Africa it was carried forward with the expanding range of white settlement into the Republics and Natal. To-day it is in force in the whole of British Africa south of the Zambesi, as well as in the Mandated Territory, known as the Protectorate of South-West Africa.

In British Guiana on the other hand the Roman-Dutch law having been found unsuited to the existing conditions of the colony has by the local Civil Law of British Guiana Ordinance 1916, taking effect from Jan. 1, 1917, been to a very great extent replaced by the common law of England. When it is said that Roman-Dutch law forms the common law of British South Africa and Ceylon, this must be understood with a reservation in favour of native law and custom, so far as these are recognized, and with the qualification that the general law of these countries, as will be seen, has in many respects departed from its original type.

Historical Development.—It does not fall within the scope of this article to investigate the historical sources of the old Dutch law. It is enough to say that in the 15th and 16th centuries the Roman law was "received" *in subsidium* in the province of Holland, as it was sooner or later in the Netherlands generally, as well as in Germany. General and local customs, based ultimately upon Germanic tribal law (Frankish, Frisian, Saxon), afforced by privileges and by-laws (*keuren*), and affected, doubtless, by an earlier "infiltration" of Roman law, held their ground. Hence resulted the mixed system for which Simon van Leeuwen in 1652 invented the term "Roman-Dutch law." This remained in force until superseded in 1809 by the Code Napoléon, which in 1838 gave place to the existing Dutch civil code. The old law was abrogated in the Dutch colonies also, so that to-day the Roman-Dutch law is no longer in force outside the British empire. (*See* ROMAN LAW.)

We have spoken of two elements in the Roman-Dutch system, Roman law and Germanic custom. To these must be added a third, viz., legislative acts of the Burgundian and Spanish periods. Such were the Great Privilege of Mary of Burgundy of 1476; the Placaat of the emperor Charles V. of 1529, requiring immovable property to be transferred before the local court; the Perpetual Edict of the same monarch of 1540, relating to clandestine marriages and other matters; the Maritime Laws of Charles V. of 1551 and of Philip II. of 1563; the Codes of Criminal and Civil

Procedure of Philip II. of 1570 and 1580; the Political Ordinance of the States of Holland of 1580; the Placaat on Intestate Succession of 1599. There was much legislation in the 17th and 18th centuries, but it had little effect upon the general character of the legal system. Apart from legislation we derive our knowledge of the Roman-Dutch law from collections of decided cases, from collections of opinions, commonly termed *consultatien* or *advijsen*, and from a rich juristic literature.

Systematization.—The first attempt to reduce the Roman-Dutch civil law to system was made by Hugo de Groot (Grotius) in his *Introduction to the Jurisprudence of Holland* (*Inleiding tot de Hollandsche Rechts-geleertheyd*), written while he was a prisoner in Loevestein in 1619-20, published in 1631. This short treatise, a masterpiece of condensed exposition, remains to this day a legal classic. But after Grotius honor must be assigned to Johannes Voet (1647-1713), professor at Utrecht and Leyden, whose *Commentarius ad Pandectas* (1698-1704) more than any work of the old law is in use to-day. In the 18th century the most famous name is Cornelis van Bijnkershoek, for 20 years president of the Supreme Court (1673-1743). Towards the end of the century Dionysius Godefridus Van der Keessel, professor at Leyden, lectured on the *jus hodiernum*, of which he published a summary in *Theses selectae juris Hollandici et Zelandici* (1800). Copies of the lectures themselves, commonly known as Van der Keessel's *Dictata*, circulate in ms., and these have been cited in judgments of the South African Courts. A younger contemporary of Van der Keessel was Joannes van der Linden, the author of a popular textbook, *Regtsgeleerd, Practicaal en Koopmans Handboek*. These two names conclude the list of the contemporary writers on the old Dutch law.

The Dutch carried to their colonies the law of the home country, just as the English took with them their common law, and subject to the same necessary adaptation to local conditions. In practice the law of the province of Holland was followed. Hence the extension to the colonial empire of the Roman-Dutch system of law. This was supplemented by local ordinances of the governors in council, and in the East Indies by laws made by the governor-general in council established at Batavia. These were collected by Van Diemen in 1642 and by Van der Parra in 1766. The supreme direction of the East India company was exercised by the Council of XVII. and of the West India company by the Council of X. The ultimate legislative authority was vested in the States General.

In the British Empire.—When the Dutch colonies passed to the British Crown, the old law was in principle retained, but during the century and more which has since elapsed it has undergone profound modifications due partly to changed social and economic conditions, partly to the incursion of rules and institutions derived from English law. In commercial matters, in particular, English influences have been predominant. This was so even in the South African republics, and after annexation their law was brought into closer harmony with that of the neighbouring colonies.

The South Africa Act 1909 provided (sec. 135) for the continuance of all laws in force in the several colonies at the establishment of the Union until repealed by the Union parliament, or by the provincial councils within the sphere assigned to them. But since this Act took effect on May 31, 1910, the Union parliament and the appellate division of the Supreme Court of South Africa (which hears appeals not only from the Union, but also from Southern Rhodesia and the Mandated Territory) have been active in consolidating, amending and explaining the law, and will continue to introduce uniformity in place of diversity. Many of the rules of the old law have already been pronounced to be obsolete by disuse.

But, except where the field is occupied by statute or invaded by English law, the law of South Africa (and in a less degree the law of Ceylon) retains the character of a Roman law system. In many departments of the law the texts of the *Corpus Juris* are still cited as authoritative. The approach to them is through the writings of the Dutch jurists, Grotius, van Leeuwen, Voet, van der Keessel, van der Linden and the rest. The influence of English law has been profound, most of all in British Guiana, where its victory has been complete, less in Ceylon, least in South Africa. But at some points the Roman-Dutch law has offered a stubborn resistance. Thus, it is now settled for both South Africa and Ceylon that "consideration" is not necessary to the validity of a contract. South Africa (but not Ceylon) retains almost unchanged the old law of community of goods with its consequences in the proprietary relations of the spouses.

Upon a general view it must be said that a system of law, which can draw at the same time upon the treasures of the Roman and of the English law has great elements of strength, particularly in a virile and progressive community. But the need to resort to law-books of by-gone centuries is a serious inconvenience.

BIBLIOGRAPHY.—Hugo de Groot, *Inleiding tot de Hollandsche Rechtsgeleerdheid*, with notes by Groenewegen and Schorer (1767); the same edit. by S. J. Fockema Andreae (3rd ed., revised by L. J. van Apeldoorn, 1926); Engl. trans. by Herbert (1845), Maasdorp (3rd ed., 1903), Lee (1926); Simon van Leeuwen, *Het Roomsch Hollandsch Recht*, with commentary by Decker (1780; Eng. trans. and commentary by Sir J. G. Kotzé, 2nd ed., 1921); Johannes Voet, *Commentarius ad Pandectas* (best ed., 4 vols., Paris, 1827–29); D. G. van der Keessel, *Theses Selectae Juris Hollandici et Zelandici* (1800; Eng. trans. by Lorenz, 2nd ed., 1901); Joannes van der Linden, *Regtsgeleerd, Practicaal, en Koopmans Handboek* (1806), Eng. trans. by Henry (1828), Sir H. Juta (4th ed. 1904), Morice (2nd ed. 1922); A. S. Fockema Andreae, *Het Oud-Nederlandsch Burgerlijk Recht* (Haarlem, 1906) and *Bijdragen tot de Nederlandsche Rechtsgeschiedenis* (1888–1900); A. S. de Blecourt, *Kort Begrip van het Oud-Vaderlandsch Burgerlijk Recht* (2nd ed., 1924); R. W. Lee, *Introduction to Roman-Dutch Law* (2nd ed., 1925); Sir A. F. S. Maasdorp, *The Institutes of Cape Law* (4th and 3rd ed., 1922–26); Hon. J. W. Wessels, *History of the Roman-Dutch Law* (1908); Hon. W. Pereira, *The Laws of Ceylon* (2nd ed., 1913); Hon. Ll. C. Dalton, *The Civil Law of British Guiana* (Georgetown, 1921). *See* also the *Cape Law Journal* and the *South African Law Journal*.   (R. W. L.)

ROMAN EMPIRE, LATER. The reign of Constantine the Great forms the most deep-reaching division in the history of Europe. The external continuity is not broken, but the principles which guided society in the Greek and Roman world are replaced by a new order of ideas. Emperor-worship, which expressed a belief in the ideal of the earthly empire of Rome, gives way to Christianity; this is the outward sign that a mental transformation, which we can trace for 300 years before in visible processes of decay and growth, had reached a crisis.

Besides the adoption of Christianity, Constantine's reign is marked by an event only second in importance, the shifting of the centre of gravity of the empire from the west to the east by making Byzantium a second capital, a second Rome. The foundation of Constantinople (*q.v.*) determined the subsequent history of the State; it established permanently the division between the eastern and western parts of the empire—a principle already introduced—and soon exhibited, though not immediately, the preponderance of the eastern half. The eastern provinces were the richest and most resourceful, and only needed a Rome in their midst to proclaim this fact; and further, it was eastward that the empire fronted, for here was the one great civilized State with which it was in constant antagonism. Byzantium was refounded on the model of Rome, had its own senate, and presently a *praefectus urbi*. But its character was different in two ways: it was Christian and it was Greek. From its foundation New Rome had a Christian stamp; it had no history as the capital of a pagan empire. There was, however, no intention of depressing Rome to a secondary rank in political importance; this was brought about by the force of circumstances.

The Christian Roman empire, from the first to the last Constantine, endured for 1,130 years, and during that long period, which witnessed the births of all the great modern nations of Europe, experienced many vicissitudes of decline and revival. In the 5th century it lost all its western provinces through the expansion of the Teutons; but in the 6th asserted something of its ancient power and won back some of its losses. In the 7th it was brought very low through the expansion of the Saracens and of the Slavs, but in consequence of internal reforms and prudent government in the 8th century was able before the end of the 9th to initiate a new brilliant period of power and conquest. From

the middle of the 11th century a decline began; besides the perpetual dangers on the eastern and northern frontiers, the empire was menaced by the political aggression of the Normans and the commercial aggression of Venice; then its capital was taken and its dominions dismembered by Franks and Venetians in 1204. It survived the blow for 250 years, as a shadow of its former self.

During this long life its chief political rôle was that of acting as a defender of Europe against the great Powers of western Asia. While it had to resist a continuous succession of dangerous enemies on its northern frontier in Europe—German, Slavonic, Finnic and Tatar peoples—it always considered that its front was towards the east, and that its gravest task was to face the Powers which successively inherited the dominion of Cyrus and Darius. From this point of view we might divide the external history of the empire into four great periods, each marked by a struggle with a different Asiatic power: (1) with Persia, ending *c.* 630 with the triumph of Rome; (2) with the Saracens, who ceased to be formidable in the 11th century; (3) with the Seljuk Turks, in the 11th and 12th centuries; (4) with the Ottoman Turks, in which the Roman power went down.

Mediaeval historians, concentrating their interest on the rising States of western Europe, often fail to recognize the position held by the later empire and its European prestige. Up to the middle of the 11th century it was in actual strength the first Power in Europe, except in the lifetime of Charles the Great, and under the Comneni it was still a power of the first rank. But its political strength does not express the fullness of its importance. As the heir of antiquity it was confessedly superior in civilization, and it was supreme in commerce. Throughout the whole period (to 1204) Constantinople was the first city in the world. The influence which the empire exerted upon its neighbours, especially the Slavonic peoples, is the second great rôle which it fulfilled for Europe—a rôle on which perhaps the most speaking commentary is the doctrine that the Russian Tsar was the heir of the Roman Caesar.

HISTORICAL SKETCH

Diocletian's artificial experiment of two Augusti and two Caesars had been proved a failure, leading to 20 years of disastrous civil wars; and when Constantine the Great (*q.v.*) destroyed his last rival and restored domestic peace, he ruled for the rest of his life with undivided sway. But he had three sons, and this led to a new partition of the empire after his death, and to more domestic wars, Constans first annexing the share of Constantine II. (340) and becoming sole ruler of the west, to be in turn destroyed by Constantius II., who in 350 remained sole sovereign of the empire. Having no children, he was succeeded by his cousin, Julian the Apostate (*q.v.*). This period was marked by wars against the Germans, who were pressing on the Rhine and Danish frontiers, and against Persia. Julian lost his life in the eastern struggle, which was then terminated by a disadvantageous peace. But the German danger grew graver, and the battle of Adrianople, in which the Visigoths, who had crossed the Danube in consequence of the coming of the Huns (*see* GOTHS and HUNS), won a great victory, and the emperor Valens perished (378), announced that the question between Roman and Teuton had entered on a new stage. Theodosius the Great saved the situation for the time by his Gothic pacification. The efforts of a series of exceptionally able and hard-working rulers preserved the empire intact throughout the 4th century, but the dangers which they weathered were fatal to their weaker successors. On the death of Theodosius the decisive moment came for the expansion of the Germans, and they took the tide at the flood. There were three elements in the situation. Besides the Teutonic peoples beyond the frontier there were dependent people who had settled within the empire (as Visigoths in Moesia, Vandals in Pannonia), and further there were the semi-Romanized Germans in the service of the empire, some of whom had risen to leading positions (like Merobaudes and Stilicho). A Germanization of the empire, or part of it, in some shape was inevitable, but, if the rulers of the 5th century had been men of the same stamp as the rulers of the 4th, the process might have assumed a different form. The sons of Theodosius were both incapable; and in their reigns the future of the State which was divided between them was decided. The dualism between the east (under Arcadius) and the west (under Honorius) developed under the rule of these brothers into antagonism verging on hostility. The German danger was averted in the east, but it led in a few years to the loss of many of the western provinces, and at the end of 90 years the immediate authority of the Roman emperor did not extend west of the Adriatic. The reign of Honorius saw the abandonment of Britain, the establishment of the Visigothic kingdom in Aquitaine, the occupation of a great part of Spain by Vandals and Sueves (Suebi). Under Valentinian III. the Vandals founded their kingdom in north Africa, the Visigoths shared Spain with the Sueves, the Burgundian kingdom was founded in south-east Gaul. The last Roman possession in Gaul passed to the Franks in 486 (see GOTHS; VANDALS; FRANKS). It is significant that the chief defenders of the empire against the Germans who were dismembering it were men of German race, Stilicho, who defended Italy against Alaric, Aëtius, whose great work was to protect the imperial possessions in Gaul, and Ricimer. It was also a German, Fravitta, who played a decisive part in suppressing a formidable Gothic movement which menaced the throne of Arcadius in 399–400. It was characteristic of this transformation of Europe that the Germans, who were imbued with a profound reverence for the empire and its prestige, founded their kingdoms on Roman soil in the first instance as "federates" of the emperor, on the basis of formal contracts, defining their relations to the native provincials; they seized their dominions not as conquerors, but as subjects. The double position of Alaric himself, as both king of the Visigoths and a *magister militum* of the empire, is significant of the situation.

The development of events was complicated by the sudden growth of the transient empire of the Huns (q.v.) in central Europe, forming a third great power, which, reaching from the Rhine to the Caucasus, from the Danube to the Baltic, might be compared in the extent of its nominal supremacy, but in nothing else, to the empires of Rome and Persia. The Huns, whose first appearance had precipitated the Germans on the empire, now retarded for some years the process of German expansion, while they failed in their own attacks upon the empire. On Attila's death (453) his realm collapsed, and his German vassals (Ostrogoths, etc.) founded important kingdoms on its ruins.

After the death of Valentinian III., the worst of his house, the Theodosian dynasty expired in the west, and the authority of the western emperors who succeeded him in rapid succession reached little beyond Italy. For most of this period of 20 years the general Ricimer, of German birth, held the scales of power in that peninsula, setting up and pulling down emperors. After his death the western throne was no longer tenable. First there was a usurpation; the general Orestes set up his child-son Romulus Augustulus against the legitimate Augustus, Julius Nepos, who was acknowledged by the eastern emperor; but this temporary Government was overthrown (476) by a Germanic military revolution headed by Odoacer, who appropriated part of the soil to his German soldiers and founded an Italian kingdom under the nominal supremacy of the emperor at Constantinople, who, however unwilling, recognized his position (after the death of Nepos).

The escape of the eastern provinces from the fate of the western illustrates the fact that the strength of the empire lay in the east. These provinces were more populous and presented greater obstacles to the invaders, who followed the line of least resistance. But it was of immense importance that throughout this period the empire was able to preserve a practically unbroken peace with its great eastern rival. The struggle with Persia, terminated in 364 by the peace of Jovian, was not renewed till the beginning of the 6th century. It was of greater importance that the rulers pursued a discreet and moderate policy, both in financial administration and in foreign affairs; and the result was that at the end of 100 years the diminished empire was strong and consolidated. Theodosius II. was a weak prince, but his Government was ably conducted by Anthemius, by his sister Pulcheria and by the eunuch Chrysaphius. His reign was important for the Armenian ques-

tion. Theodosius I. had committed the error of consenting to a division of this buffer State in the Roman and Persian spheres of influence, Persia having much the larger. The Sassanid Government tried to suppress the use of the Greek language. But the Government of Theodosius II. officially supported the enterprise of translating the Bible into Armenian (Mesrob had just invented the Armenian alphabet), and this initiated the production of an abundant literature of translations from the Greek, which secured the perpetual connection of Armenia with European culture, and not with Oriental. This reign is also distinguished by the building of the great land walls of Constantinople, by the foundation of a university there and by the collection of the imperial laws in the Codex Theodosianus, which is a mine of material for the social condition of the empire. It reveals to us the decline of municipal liberty, the decay of the middle classes in the West, the evils of the oppressive fiscal system and an appalling paralysis of Roman administration which had once been so efficient; it shows how the best-intentioned emperors were unable to control the governors and check their corruption; and discloses a disorganization which facilitated the dismemberment of the empire by the barbarians.

In the reign of Zeno it seemed probable that an Ostrogothic kingdom would be established in the Balkan peninsula, but the danger was diverted to Italy (see GOTHS). The kingdom which Theodoric founded there was, in its constitutional aspect, a continuation of Odoacer's régime. He, like Odoacer and Alaric, held the double position of a German king and a Roman official. He was *magister militum* as well as *rex*. His powers were defined by capitulations which were arranged with the emperor Anastasius and loyally observed. The right of legislation was reserved to the emperor, and Theodoric never claimed it; but for all practical purposes he was independent.

Justinian.—In the 6th century the emperor Justinian, whose talents were equal to his ambitions, found himself, through the financial prudence of his predecessors, in a position to undertake the reconquest of some of the lost western provinces. The Vandal power had declined, and Africa was won back in one campaign by Belisarius in 533. The conquest of Italy was far more difficult. Begun by Belisarius in 535, it was not completed till 554, by Narses. A portion of southern Spain was also won from the Visigoths, so that the Romans again commanded the western straits. Justinian, possessed by large ideas and intoxicated with the majesty of Rome, aspired to be a great conqueror, a great lawgiver, a great pontiff, a great diplomatist, a great builder, and in each of these spheres his reign holds a conspicuous place in the annals of the empire. His legal work alone, or the building of Santa Sophia, was enough to ensure him immortal fame. But deep shadows balance the splendour. The reconquest of Africa was thoroughly justified and advantageous, but Italy was bought at a ruinous cost. In the first place, the Persian empire was at this time ruled by one of its greatest kings, Chosroes I. (q.v.), who was far from peacefully inclined. Justinian was engaged in a long Persian and a long Gothic war at the same time, and the State was unequal to the strain. In the second place, it was all-important for his western policy to secure the goodwill of the Italian provincials and the Roman bishop, and for this purpose he involved himself in an ecclesiastical policy (see below) which caused the final alienation of the Syrian and Egyptian provinces. The reconquest of the West was purchased by the disunion of the East. Thirdly, the enormous expenses of the Italian and Persian wars, augmented by architectural undertakings, caused a policy of financial oppression which hung as a cloud over all the brilliance of his reign, and led to the decline which ensued upon his death. Nor is it to be forgotten that he had at the same time to fulfil the task of protecting the Danube against the Germans, Slavs and Bulgarians, who constantly threatened the Illyrian provinces. He spared no expense in building forts and walls. Justinian's name will always be associated with that of the gifted Theodora, an actress of doubtful fame in her early life, who shared his throne. Their mosaic portraits are preserved in the contemporary church of San Vitale at Ravenna. She possessed great political influence, and the fact that she was a heretic (monophysite), while Justinian was devoted to orthodoxy, did not mar their harmony, but only facilitated the policy of extending secret favour to the heretics who were publicly condemned, and enabled the left hand to act without the knowledge of the right. The events of the half-century after Justinian's death exhibited the weakness to which his grandiose policy had reduced the empire. It was attacked on the west, on the north and on the east, and at all points was unequal to coping with its enemies. (1) Italy fell a victim to the Lombards (q.v.), and in a few years more than half of the peninsula had passed under their sway. (2) The Avars, a Hunnic people who had advanced from the Caspian, took possession of Pannonia and Dacia, and formed an empire, consisting of Slavonic and Bulgarian subjects, which endured for about 60 years. Their chief occupation was to invade the Illyrian peninsula and extort tribute and ransoms from the emperors. So far as the Avars themselves were concerned, these incursions had no permanent significance, but the Slavs who overran the provinces did more than devastate. These years saw the beginning of the Slavonic settlements which changed the ethnical character of the peninsula, and thus mark the commencement of a new period. Slavs occupied Moesia and a large part of Macedonia, even close to Thessalonica, which they besieged; they penetrated southward into Greece and made large settlements in the Peloponnesus (see GREECE, History, "Roman period," ad fin.). They occupied the north-western provinces, which became Croatia and Servia, as well as Dalmatia (except some of the coast towns). In the northern part of the peninsula the Slavonic element remained dominant, but in Greece it was assimilated to the Greek (after the 9th century) and has left little record of itself except in place names. (3) The empire was simultaneously engaged in the perennial strife with Persia. A short interval of peace was secured when the emperor Maurice assisted Chosroes II. to dethrone a usurper, but after Maurice's death (602) the final and mortal struggle began (see PERSIA: History: History of the Sassanian Empire). Throughout the incompetent reign of Phocas the eastern provinces were overrun by the Persians, as the Illyrian were overrun by the Slavs. The unpopular rule of this cruel usurper was terminated in 610 by the intervention of the governor of Africa, whose son Heraclius sailed to Constantinople and, welcomed by an influential party, met with little resistance. Phocas, murderer of Maurice, was murdered by the people, and the victor was crowned emperor to find himself in presence of a desperate situation. Antioch, Damascus and many other great cities were captured by the Persians; and in 614 Jerusalem was destroyed and the Holy Cross, along with the patriarch, carried off to Ctesiphon. This event produced a profound sensation in Christendom. In 616 Egypt was conquered. The army had fallen into utter disorder under Phocas, and Heraclius so deeply despaired of saving Constantinople that he thought of transferring the imperial capital to Carthage. But the extreme gravity of the situation seems to have wrought a moral change among his subjects; the patriarch Sergius was the mouthpiece of a widespread patriotic feeling, and it was largely through his influence that Heraclius performed the task of creating a capable army. His efforts were rewarded in a series of brilliant campaigns (622–628), which, in the emphasis laid on the contrast between Christianity and fire-worship and on the object of recovering the Cross, had the character of crusades. Heraclius recovered his provinces and held Persia at his mercy (decisive battle at Nineveh, end of 627).

This war is remarkable for the attempt of the Persians to take Constantinople (626) in conjunction with the Avars and Slavs. Soon afterwards the Avar power began to decay, and the Slavs and Bulgarians shook off their yoke. It seemed as if the Roman Government would now be able to regain the control in the Illyrian lands which it had almost entirely lost. It seems probable that Heraclius came to terms with the Slavs—Croatians and Servians—in the north-west; their position was regularized, as vassals of the empire. But fate allowed no breathing-time to do more; the darkest hour had hardly passed when a new storm-cloud, from an unexpected quarter, overspread the heavens.

At this point we have to note that the Hellenic element in the State had definitely gained the upper hand before the end of the 6th century, so that henceforward the empire might be described as Greek. Justinian's mother-tongue was Latin, and he was devoted to the Latin traditions of Rome, but even he found it necessary to publish his later laws in Greek and from his reign Greek was the official language.

Rise of Islam.—With the rise of Islam (see CALIPHATE; MOHAMMED) two universal religions, for the first time, stood face to face, each aspiring to win the universe. The struggle, therefore, which then began was not only a new phase of the strife between Europe and Asia, but was one in which the religious element was fundamental. Fire-worship was only a national religion and did not present the danger of Islam. The creation of the political power of the Mohammedans was so sudden that it took the world by surprise. Bostra, the fortress of Roman Arabia, fell into their hands in 634, and before the death of Heraclius in 641 they had conquered Syria and all Egypt, except Alexandria, which opened its gates to them in 643. The religious alienation of the Syrian and Egyptian peoples from Constantinople, expressing as it did a national sentiment antagonistic to the Greeks, was an important political factor in the Mohammedan (as in the previous Persian) conquest. Thus the Mohammedans definitely cut the empire short in the East, as the Germans had cut it short in the West; Egypt was never recovered, Syria only for short periods and partially, while the integrity of Asia Minor was constantly menaced and Cilicia occupied for many generations. By their conquest of Persia the Caliphs succeeded to the position of the Sassanids; this led to the conquest of Armenia (c. 654); while, in the West, Africa was occupied in 647 (though the conquest was not completed till the capture of Carthage and other strong places in 698). Thus within 20 years from the first attack the empire was girt about by the new aggressive power from the precincts of the Caucasus to the western Mediterranean.

Fortunately Constans II., grandson of Heraclius, was a man of eminent ability and firmness. The State owed to him the preservation of Asia Minor, and the creation of a powerful fleet (see below) which protected the Aegean coasts and islands against the naval power which the Mohammedans created. He was responsible for completing a new, efficient military organization, which determined the lines of the administrative reforms of Leo III. (see below). In his last years he turned his eyes to Italy and Africa. He dreamed of restoring Old Rome as the centre of the empire. But he did not succeed in recovering south Italy from the Lombards (Duchy of Beneventum), and having visited Rome he took up his residence in Syracuse, where he was assassinated, having lost two fleets which he sent against the Arabs of Africa. The strain lasted for another 50 years. Constantinople sustained two great sieges (673–677 and 717–718) which stand out as crises, for, if in either case the enemy had been successful, the empire was doomed.

The Heraclian dynasty, which had fallen on evil times and rendered inestimable services to the empire, came to an end in anarchy, which was terminated by the elevation of the Syrian (commonly called Isaurian) Leo III., whose reign opens a new period. His reforming hand was active in every sphere of government, but the ill-fame which he won by his iconoclastic policy obscured in the memory of posterity the capital importance of his work. His provincial organization was revolutionary, and his legislation departed from the Roman tradition (see below). From his reign to the middle of the 10th century the continuous warfare by land with the Caliphs consisted of marauding expeditions of each power into the other's territory, captures of fortresses, guerilla fighting, but no great conquests or decisive battles. The efficiency of the army was carefully maintained, but the neglect of the navy led to the losses of Crete (conquered by Muslim adventurers from Spain 826) and Sicily (conquered by the Saracens of Africa). Panormus was taken in 832, Syracuse in 878 (see SICILY). The Africans also made temporary conquests, including Bari, in south Italy. This period saw the loss of the exarchate of Ravenna to the Lombards (750), the expansion of the Frankish power under Pippin and Charlemagne in Italy, and in close connection therewith the loss of Old Rome.

The iconoclast emperors pursued a moderate foreign policy, consolidating the empire within its contracted limits; but under the "Macedonian" dynasty, which was of Armenian descent, it again expanded and became the strongest power in Europe. The 9th century also witnessed a revival of learning and culture which had been in eclipse for 200 years. The reign of Basil I. was marked by an energetic policy in south Italy, where his forces co-operated with the western emperor Louis II. The Saracens were expelled from their strongholds, Bari was recovered, Calabria saved, and the new province (Theme) of Longibardia formed. This secured the entrance to the Adriatic, and the increase of dominion here at the expense of the Lombards was a compensation for the loss of Sicily. Leo VI. did much for reorganizing the navy, but his reign was not fortunate; Saracen pirates plundered freely in the Aegean and, under the able renegade Leo of Tripolis, captured Thessalonica and carried off countless captives (904). But a great tide of success began 50 years later. Nicephorus Phocas won back Crete (961) as general of Romanus II., and then as emperor recovered Cilicia and North Syria (with Antioch) 968. Cyprus was also recovered. The tide flowed on under his equally able successor, John Zimisces (of Armenian race) and under Basil II.; these reigns mark the decisive victory of the empire in the long struggle with the Saracens, whose empire had been broken up into separate States. The eastern frontier was strengthened by the active policy of Basil II. in Armenia, which was more fully incorporated in the empire under Constantine IX.

Basil II.—The reign of Basil II. marks the culmination of the power of the Eastern empire, for it also witnessed the triumphant conclusion of another conflict which had lasted almost as long. In the reign of Constantine IV. the Bulgarians (*see* BULGARIA) had founded a kingdom in Lower Moesia, reducing the Slavonic tribes who had occupied the country, but less than two centuries sufficed to assimilate the conquerors to the conquered, and to give Bulgaria the character of a Slavonic State. The reign of Constantine V. was marked by continuous war with this enemy, and Nicephorus I. lost his life in a Bulgarian campaign. This disaster was followed up by Prince Krum, who besieged Constantinople in 815. His death was followed by a long peace. Prince Boris was converted to Christianity (reign of Michael III.); a metropolitan see of Bulgaria was founded, dependent on the patriarch of Constantinople; and the civilization of the Bulgarians, and beginnings of their literature, were entirely under Byzantine influence. The conversion was contemporary with the work of the two missionaries Cyril and Methodius, who (while the field of their personal activity was in Great Moravia and Pannonia) laid the south-eastern Slavs under a deep debt by inventing the Glagolitic (*q.v.*), *not* the so-called "Cyrillic" alphabet (based on Greek cursive) and translating parts of the Scriptures into Slavonic (the dialect of the Slavs of Macedonia). The most brilliant period of the old Bulgarian kingdom was the reign of Simeon (893–927), who extended the realm westward to the shores of the Adriatic and took the title "Tsar (*ie.*, Caesar) of Bulgaria and autocrator of the Romans." The aggression against the empire which marked his ambitious reign ceased under his successor Peter, who married a daughter of Romanus I., and the Bulgarian Patriarchate founded by Simeon was recognized at Byzantium. But the Byzantine rulers only waited for a favourable time to reduce this formidable Slavonic State. At length Zimisces subjugated eastern Bulgaria and recovered the Danube frontier. But while Basil II. was engaged in contending with rivals, the heroic Samuel (of the Shishmanid family) restored the Bulgarian power and reduced the Servians. After a long and arduous war of 14 years Basil (called the "Bulgar-slayer") subdued all Bulgaria western and eastern (1018). He treated the conquered people with moderation, leaving them their political institutions and their autonomous church, and to the nobility their privileges. Some Bulgarian noble families and members of the royal house were incorporated in the Greek nobility; there was Shishmanid blood in the families of Comnenus and Ducas. Greek domination was now established in the peninsula for more than 150 years. The Slavs of Greece had in the middle of the 9th century been brought under the control of the Government.

In the reign of Basil II. the Russian question also was settled. The Dnieper and Dniester gave the Russians access to the Euxine,

and the empire was exposed to their maritime attacks (Constantinople was in extreme danger in 860 and 941). In 945 a commercial treaty was concluded, and the visit of the princess Olga to Byzantium (towards the end of the reign of the learned emperor Constantine VII., Porphyrogennetos) and her baptism seemed a pledge of peace. But Olga's conversion had no results. Sviatoslav occupied Bulgaria and threatened the empire, but was decisively defeated by Zimisces (971), and this was virtually the end of the struggle. In 988 Prince Vladimir captured Cherson, but restored it to the emperor Basil, who gave him his sister Anna in marriage, and he accepted Christianity for himself and his people. After this conversion and alliance, Byzantium had little to fear from Kiev, which came under its influence. One hostile expedition (1043) indeed is recorded, but it was a failure. Much about the same time that the Russians had founded their State, the Magyars (*see* HUNGARY; the Greeks called them Turks) migrated westward and occupied the regions between the Dnieper and the Danube, while beyond them, pressing on their heels, were another new people, the Petchenegs (*q.v.*). The policy of Byzantium was to make use of the Magyars as a check on the Bulgarians, and so we find the Romans (under Leo. VI.) and the Magyars co-operating against the tsar Simeon. But Simeon played the same game more effectively by using the Petchenegs against the Magyars, and the result was that the Magyars before the end of the 9th century were forced to move westward into their present country, and their place was taken by the Petchenegs. From their new seats the Magyars could invade the empire and threatened the coast towns of Dalmatia. The conquest of Bulgaria made the Petchenegs immediate neighbours of the empire, and during the 11th century the depredations of these irreclaimable savages, who filtered into the Balkan peninsula, constantly preoccupied the Government. In 1064 they were driven from the Dniester regions into Little Walachia by the Cumans, a people of the same ethnical group as themselves. They were crushingly defeated by Alexius Comnenus in 1091, and disappear from history.

The Seljuk Turks.—In the Macedonian period a grave domestic question troubled the Government. This was the growth of the large estates of the rich nobles of Asia Minor, at the expense of small properties, to an excess which was politically and economically dangerous. The legislation against the evil began under Romanus I. and was directed to the defence of the poor against the rich, and to protecting the military organization which was based on holdings of land to which the obligation of military service was attached. There was also danger in the excessive influence of rich and powerful families, from which the great military officers were drawn, and which were extensively related by alliances among themselves. The danger was realized in the struggle which Basil II. had to sustain with the families of Sclerus and Phocas. Various kinds of legislation were attempted. Under Romanus I. alienation of property to the large landowners was forbidden. Nicephorus Phocas, whose sympathies were with the aristocracy to which he belonged, holding that there had been enough legislation in favour of the poor, sought to meet the difficulty of maintaining a supply of military lands in the future by forbidding further acquisitions of estates by the church. Basil II. returned to the policy of Romanus, but with much greater severity, resorting to confiscation of some of the immense private estates; and he endeavoured to keep down the aristocrats of Asia Minor by very heavy taxation. Through the recovery of the Balkan provinces he gained in Europe a certain political counterpoise to the influence of Asia Minor, which had been preponderant since the 7th century. Asia Minor meant the army, and opposition to its influence expressed itself in the 11th century in a fatal antimilitary policy, which is largely responsible for the conquests of a new enemy, the Seljuk Turks, who now entered into the inheritance of the Caliphs (*see* CALIPHATE *ad fin.* and SELJUKS). Constantinople was haunted by the dread of a military usurpation. An attempt of the military hero George Maniaces (who had made a remarkable effort to recover Sicily) to wrest the crown from Constantine IX. had failed; and when Isaac Comnenus, who represented the military aristocrats of Asia Minor, ascended the throne, he found himself soon compelled to abdicate, in face of the opposition. The reign of Constantine X., of the rival family of Ducas, marked the culmination of this antagonism. The senate was filled with men of the lower classes, and the military budget was ruthlessly cut down. This policy reduced the army and stopped the supply of officers, since there was no longer hope of a profitable career. The emperor thought to meet dangers from external enemies by diplomacy. The successes of the Seljuks (after the fall of the great Armenian fortress of Ani in 1064) at length awoke the Government from its dream of security. The general Romanus Diogenes was proclaimed emperor. He had to create an army and to train it; he did not spare himself, but it was too late. He was defeated and captured by Alp Arslan on the decisive field of Manzikert (1071). Released by the sultan, who honoured his bravery, he was deposed in favour of Michael Ducas, and falling into the hands of his enemies, was blinded. The east and centre of Asia Minor were thus lost; the Seljuk kingdom of Rūm was founded; Nicaea was captured by the Turks in 1080. The provinces which escaped the Seljuk occupation were thoroughly disorganized, a prey to foreign and native adventurers and usurpers (see SELJUKS).

Thus in the '70s of the 11th century the empire seemed through incompetence and frivolity to have been brought to the verge of dissolution. The disorder was terminated by the accession of the extraordinarily able statesman Alexius Comnenus (1081), who effected a reconciliation with the rival family of Ducas, established a strong Government and founded a dynasty. He had to deal with three great dangers—the Seljuks, the Petchenegs (see above), and in the west the Normans. The Normans had wrested from East Rome its possessions in south Italy (1041–71)—succeeding where German emperors had failed—and throughout the Comnenian period the empire was threatened by their projects of conquest beyond the Adriatic, projects which aimed at Constantinople itself.

Four great attempts against the empire were made by the Normans; they were unsuccessful, but they heralded the Western conquest of 1204. (1) Expedition of Robert Guiscard, 1081–85, repelled by Alexius with help of Venice; (2) Bohemond's expedition, 1105–07, foiled by the able strategy of Alexius; (3) the invasion of Greece by Roger of Sicily, 1147; Venice supported Manuel Comnenus, and the Normans were driven from Corfù, 1149; (4) the expedition of William II. of Sicily, 1185, who succeeded in capturing Thessalonica; the invaders were defeated at Demetritsa, but they gained the islands of Cephallenia and Zacynthus.

The First Crusade.—The two most important events in the reign of Alexius were the prices which he paid for help against his enemies. (1) He was obliged (1084) to grant to Venice (q.v.) in return for her naval aid against the Normans, commercial privileges which practically made the empire commercially dependent on the republic. (2) He sought auxiliary forces in western Europe to help him against the Seljuks; the answer of the pope and Latin Christendom was the First Crusade—a succour very different from that which he desired. Through his tact and discretion, the State was safely steered through the dangers with which the disorderly hosts of barbarous allies menaced it, and the immediate results were salutary; large parts of Asia Minor, including Nicaea, were restored to the empire, which was thus greatly strengthened in the East while the Turks were weakened (see CRUSADES). But for this help Byzantium might not have recovered the transient strength and brilliance which it displayed under Manuel. In Asia Minor the crusaders kept the terms of their agreement to restore to the emperor what had belonged to him; but on capturing Antioch (1098) they permitted the Norman Bohemond to retain it, in flagrant violation of their oaths; for to Antioch if to any place the emperor had a right, as it had been his a few years before. This was in itself sufficient to cause a breach between Byzantium and the Latin kingdom of Jerusalem (founded 1099). But otherwise the new political situation created by the Crusade was dangerous, ultimately fatal, to the empire. For its lands and seas became a highway from western Europe to the Latin colonies in Syria; the Byzantine Government was forced to take precautions to protect itself against the crusading expeditions which travelled to the Holy Land; and these precautions were regarded by the western Powers as a hindrance to the sacred objects of the crusades. The bitter religious antagonism between the Greek and Latin Christians increased the mutual distrust and the danger.

The history of the new relations between East and West dating from the First Crusade is closely connected with the history of the futile attempts at bringing about a reunion between the Greek and Latin Churches, which had severed communion in 1054. To heal the hurtful schism and bring the Greek Church again under the domination of Rome was a principal object of papal policy from Gregory VII. forward. The popes alternated between two methods for attaining this, as circumstances dictated: namely, a peaceful agreement—the policy of union; or an armed occupation of the empire by some western power (the Normans)—the policy of conquest. Their views varied according to the vicissitudes of their political situation and their struggles with the western emperors. The eastern emperors were also constantly preoccupied with the idea of reconciliation, constantly negotiating with a view to union; but they did not care about it for its own sake, but only for political advantages which it might bring, and their subjects were bitterly opposed to it. Manuel Comnenus during the first part of his reign was the close friend and ally of the western emperor Conrad III., but after Conrad's death he formed the ambitious plan of realizing in Europe a sovereignty like that of Justinian, and hoped to compass it in conjunction with Rome, the enemy of the Hohenstaufen. His forward policy carried war into Italy; he seized Ancona. But his strength was unequal to such designs. His Latin sympathies, no less than his financial extravagance, made him highly unpopular at home; and the national lack of sympathy with his Western policy was exhibited—after the revolution which overthrew his son Alexius and raised his cousin Andronicus I. to the throne—by the awful massacre of the Latin residents at Constantinople in 1182, for which the expedition of William of Sicily (see above) and the massacre of the people of Thessalonica was the revenge. The short reign of the wicked and brilliant Andronicus was in all respects a reaction, prudent, economical and popular. His fall was due to the aristocracy against whom his policy was directed, and the reign of Isaac Angelus undid his efforts and completed the ruin of the State. Oppressive taxation caused a revolt of the Bulgarian and Walachian population in the European provinces; the work of Zimisces and Basil was undone, and a new Bulgarian kingdom was founded by John Asen—a decisive blow to the Greek predominance which the Macedonian emperors seemed to have established.

Dismemberment of the Empire.—In the fatal year 1204 the perils with which the eastward expansion of western Christendom (the Crusades and the commercial predominance and ambitions of Venice) had long menaced the empire, culminated in its conquest and partition. It was due to a series of accidents that the cloud burst at this moment, but the conditions of such a catastrophe had long been present. Isaac Angelus was dethroned by his brother Alexius III., and his son escaped (1201) to the west, where arrangements were being made for a new crusade, which Venice undertook to transport to the Holy Land. The prince persuaded Philip of Swabia (who had married his sister) and Boniface of Montferrat to divert the expedition to Byzantium, in order to restore his father and himself to the throne, promising to furnish help to the Crusade and to reconcile the Greek Church with Rome; Venice agreed to the plan; but Pope Innocent III., the enemy of Philip, forbade it. Isaac and his son, Alexius IV., were restored without difficulty in 1203, and the crusading forces were prepared to proceed to Palestine, if Alexius had performed his promises. But the manner of this restoration, under Latin auspices, was intensely unpopular; he was not unwilling, but he was unable, to fulfil his pledges; and a few months later he was overthrown in favour of one who, if an upstart, was a patriot, Alexius V. Then the Crusaders, who were waiting encamped outside the city, resolved to carry out the design which the Normans had repeatedly attempted, and put an end to the Greek empire. The leaders of the Fourth Crusade must be acquitted of having formed this plan deliberately before they started; it was not conceived before 1204. They first arranged how they would divide the empire amongst themselves (March); then they captured the city, which had to endure the worst barbarities of war. In partitioning the empire, which was now to become the spoil of the conquerors, the guiding mind was the Venetian leader, the blind doge, Henry Dandolo. He looked to the interests of Venice from the narrowest point of view, and in founding the new Latin empire, which was to replace the Greek, it was his aim that it should be feeble, so as to present no obstacles to Venetian policy. The Latin empire of Romania was a feudal State like the kingdom of Jerusalem; the emperor was suzerain of all the princes who established themselves on Greek territory; under his own immediate rule were Constantinople, southern Thrace, the Bithynian coast, and some islands in the Aegean. But he was hampered from the beginning by dependence on Venice, want of financial resources, and want of a fleet; the feudal princes, occupied with their separate interests, gave him little support in his conflict with Greeks and Bulgarians; at the end of ten years the worthless fabric began rapidly to decline, and the efforts of the popes, for whom it was the means of realizing Roman supremacy in the East, were unavailing to save it from the extinction to which it was doomed in its cradle.

Three Greek States emerged from the ruin of the Roman empire. A member of the Comnenian house had founded an independent State at Trebizond, and this empire survived till 1461, when it was conquered by the Ottomans. A relation of the Angeli maintained in Europe an independent Greek State known as the Despotate of Epirus. But the true representative of the imperial line was Theodore Lascaris, who collected the Byzantine aristocracy at Nicaea and was elected emperor in 1206. He and his successors advanced surely and rapidly against the Latin empire, both in Europe and Asia. It was a question whether Constantinople would fall to the Walacho-Bulgarians or to the Greeks. But an astute diplomat and general, the emperor Michael Palaeologus, captured it in 1261. His object was to recover all the lost territory from the Latins, but he was menaced by a great danger through Charles of Anjou, who had overthrown the rule of the Hohenstaufen in the two Sicilies, and determined to restore the Latin kingdom of Romania. To avert this peril, Michael negotiated with Pope Gregory X.; he was ready to make every concession, and a formal union of the Churches was actually brought about at the Council of Lyons in 1274. The emperor had the utmost difficulty in carrying through this policy in face of clerical opposition; it aroused disgust and bitterness among his subjects; and it was undone by his successor. Meanwhile the pope had with difficulty bridled Charles of Anjou; but in Martin IV. he found a more pliable instrument, and in 1282 he made vast preparations for an expedition against the Greek empire. It was saved by the Sicilian Vespers (see SICILY), to be the prey of other Powers.

The Ottoman Turks.—The end of the 13th century saw the rise of the Ottoman power in Asia and the Servian in Europe. The empire was assisted by a band of Spanish mercenaries (the Catalan Grand Company; see GREECE: *History: Byzantine Period*) against the advance of the Ottoman Turks in Asia Minor; they distinguished themselves by saving Philadelphia (1304). In 1326 Brusa (Prusa) became the Ottoman capital, while on the other side the Servians (crushing the Bulgarians in 1330) were gradually closing in on Byzantium. Under Stephen Dušan (1331–55) Servia attained the height of her power. The enemies were strengthened by the domestic struggles within the empire, first between Andronicus II. and his son, then between John VI. and the usurper Cantacuzenus. But before the fate of Byzantium was settled the two enemies on its flanks came face to face. In 1389 the Servian power was crushed on the field of Kossovo by the Ottomans (who had crossed the Hellespont in 1360 and taken Philippopolis in 1363). Sultan Bayezid I. won Philadelphia, the last Asiatic possession of the empire, and conquered Trnovo, the Bulgarian capital, in 1393. Constantinople was now surrounded. The Ottoman power was momentarily eclipsed, and the career of conquest checked, by the Mongol invasion of Timur and the great defeat which it sustained in the battle of Angora (1402). Moham-

med I. found it necessary to ally himself with the emperor Manuel. But the pause was brief. Murad II. took Adrianople, and tried (1422) to take Constantinople.

It was small compensation that during this time the Palaeologi had been successful against the Franks in Greece. The situation was desperate. The Turks were in possession of the Balkan peninsula, threatening Hungary; there was no chance of rescue, except from western Europe. John VI. and Manuel had both visited the West in search of help. The jeopardy of the empire was the opportunity of Rome, and the union of the Churches became the pressing question. It was taken up earnestly by Pope Eugenius IV., and the result was the Decree of Union at the Council of Florence in 1439. The emperor and the higher clergy were really in earnest, but the people and the monks did not accept it, and the last agony of Byzantium was marked by ecclesiastical quarrels. Eugenius IV. preached a crusade for the rescue of the empire, and in 1443 an army of Hungarians and Poles, led by the Hungarian king, won a victory over Murad, which was more than avenged in the next year on the memorable field of Varna. The end came nine years later under Murad's successor, Mohammed II. An army of about 150,000 blockaded the city by land and sea, and Mohammed began the siege on the 7th of April. The emperor Constantine XI., Palaeologus, on whom the task of the forlorn defence devolved (and whose position was all the more difficult because he was alienated from his subjects, having embraced the Latin rite), can have had little more than 8,000 men at his disposal; he received no help from the Western powers; but an experienced Genoese soldier of fortune, John Justiniani, arrived with two vessels and 400 cuirassiers and aided the emperor with his courage and advice. The resident foreigners, both Venetians and Genoese, loyally shared in the labours of the defence. The final storm of the land walls took place on the night of the 29th of May. All looked to Justiniani for salvation, and when he, severely wounded, retired from the wall to have his wound looked to, a panic ensued. The enemy seized the moment, and the Janissaries in a final charge rushed the stockade which had been constructed to replace a portion of the wall destroyed by the Turkish cannon. This decided the fate of the city. Constantine fell fighting heroically. Soon after sunrise (May 30) the Mohammedan army entered Constantinople (Stambul = 's τὴν πόλιν, "the city"), which was in their eyes the capital of Christendom.

The ultimate responsibility for this disaster is generally imputed to the political adventurers who dismembered the empire in 1204. It may indeed be said that at that time the Byzantine State seemed already stricken with paralysis and verging on dissolution, and it was menaced by the re-arisen power of Bulgaria. But more than once before (in the 7th century and in the 11th) it had recovered its strength when it was weak and in dire peril; and, considering what the emperors of Nicaea and Michael VIII. accomplished, it seems probable that, if there had been no Fourth Crusade, it might have so revived and consolidated its forces in the course of the 13th century, as to be able to cope successfully with the first advances of the Ottomans. The true statement is that the Fourth Crusade was only an incident (not in itself decisive) in a world-movement which doomed the Eastern empire to extinction—namely, the eastward movement of western Europe which began in the 11th century with the rise of the Normans and the First Crusade. Henceforward the empire was a middle State, pressed between expanding forces on the east and on the west, and its ultimate disappearance was inevitable.

CHURCH AND STATE

In making the State Christian, Constantine made the Church a State institution, and therefore under imperial control. Caesaropapism was the logical consequence. The *sacerdotium* was united with the *imperium* in the person of the monarch as in the pagan State. The Church acquiesced, and yet did not acquiesce, in this theory. When a heretical emperor sought to impose his views, champions of ecclesiastical freedom never failed to come forward. At the very beginning Athanasius fought for the independence of the Church against the emperor Constantius. But the political principle which Constantine had taken for granted, and which was an indispensable condition of his adoption of Christianity, was fully recognized under Theodosius I., and, notwithstanding protests from time to time, was permanent. It is significant that Constantinople, which had become a second Rome politically, with its senate and capitol, became then a second Rome ecclesiastically, and that the elevation of the see of Constantinople to patriarchal rank next to the Roman see was due to Theodosius (381), who gave a permanent form to the dualism of the empire. The patriarch became a State minister for religion. The character of the Church as a State institution is expressed above all in the synods. The general councils are not only summoned by the emperor, but are presided over by him or by his lay deputies. The order of the proceedings is modelled on that of the senate. The emperor or his representative not only keeps order but conducts the deliberations and intervenes in the theological debates. It has been erroneously thought that at the Council of Chalcedon (451) the legate of Pope Leo presided; but the acts of that assembly teach us otherwise; the privilege which the Roman legates possessed was that of voting first (the right of the *princeps senatus*). The first general council at which a churchman presided was the seventh (at Nicaea, 787), at which the emperor (or empress) deputed, not a layman, but the patriarch Tarasius to preside. The resolutions of these ecclesiastical State-councils did not become the law of the empire till they were confirmed by imperial edicts.

The emperors, in their capacity as heads of the Church, did not confine themselves to controlling it by controlling the councils. They soon began to issue edicts dealing with theology, by virtue of their own authority. It has been said that the council of Chalcedon closed an epoch of "parliamentary constitutionalism"; a general council was not summoned again for more than 100 years, though the empire during that period was seething with religious disunion and unrest. The usurper Basiliscus in his short reign set an example which his successors were not slow to follow. He issued an edict quashing the decision of Chalcedon. Zeno's *Henōtikon* issued a few years later was the second and more famous example of a method which Justinian largely used, and of which the *Ecthesis* of Heraclius, the *Type* of Constans II. and the iconoclastic edicts of Leo III. are well-known instances. It was a question of political expediency (determined by the circumstances, the intensity and nature of the opposition, etc.) whether an emperor supported his policy or not by an ecclesiastical council.

The emperor was always able to control the election of the patriarch, and through him he directed the Church. Sometimes emperor and patriarch collided; but in general the patriarchs were docile instruments, and when they were refractory they could be deposed. There were several means of resistance open to a patriarch, though he rarely availed himself of them. His participation in the ceremony of coronation was indispensable, and he could refuse to crown a new emperor except on certain conditions, and thus dictate a policy (instances in 812, Michael I.; 969, John Zimisces). There was the power of excommunication (Leo VI. was excommunicated on account of his fourth marriage). Another means of resistance for the Church was to invoke the support of the bishop of Rome, who embodied the principle of ecclesiastical independence and whose see admittedly enjoyed precedence and primacy over all the sees in Christendom. Up to the end of the 8th century he was a subject of the emperor, and some emperors exerted their ecclesiastical control over Rome by drastic measures (Justinian and Constans II.). But after the conquest of Italy by Charles the Great, the pope was outside the Byzantine domination; after the coronation of Charles in 800 he was associated with a rival empire; and when ecclesiastical controversies arose in the East, the party in opposition was always ready to appeal to him as the highest authority in Christendom. Under the iconoclastic emperors the image-worshippers looked to him as the guardian of orthodoxy.

Theological Controversies.—As to the ecclesiastical controversies which form a leading feature of Byzantine history, their political significance alone concerns us. After the determination of the Arian controversy in 381 new questions (as to the union of the divine and human elements in the person of Christ: one or two natures?) arose, and it may seem surprising that such points

of abstruse theology should have awakened universal interest and led to serious consequences. The secret was that they masked national feelings; hence their political importance and the attention which the Government was forced to bestow on them. The reviving sense of nationality (anti-Greek) in Syria and in Egypt found expression in the 5th century in passionate monophysitism (the doctrine of one nature): theology was the only sphere in which such feelings could be uttered. The alienation and dissension which thus began had fatal consequences, smoothing the way for the Saracen conquests of those lands; the inhabitants were not unwilling to be severed politically from the empire. This ultimate danger was at first hardly visible. What immediately troubled the emperors in the first half of the 5th century was the preponderant position which the see of Alexandria occupied, threatening the higher authority of Constantinople. The Council of Chalcedon, called by Marcian, an able statesman, was as much for the purpose of ending the domination of Alexandria as of settling the theological question. The former object was effected, but the theological decision of the council was fatal; it only sealed and promoted the disunion. The recalcitrant spirit of Syria and Egypt forced Zeno, 30 years later, to issue his Henōtikon, affirming the decisions of previous councils but pointedly ignoring Chalcedon. This statesman-like document secured peace in the East for a generation. Rome refused to accept the Henōtikon, and when Justinian resolved to restore imperial supremacy in the Western kingdoms, conciliation with Rome became a matter of political importance. For the sake of this project, the unity of the East was sacrificed. The doctrine of Chalcedon was reasserted, the Henōtikon set aside; New Rome and Old Rome were again hand in hand. This meant the final alienation of Egypt and Syria. The national instinct which had been alive in the 5th century grew into strong national sentiment in the 6th. One of the chief anxieties of Justinian's long and busy reign was to repair the mischief. Deeply interested himself in matters of dogma, and prepared to assert to its fullest extent his authority as head of the church, he has been called "the passionate theologian on the throne"; but in his chief ecclesiastical measures political considerations were predominant. His wife Theodora was a monophysite, and he permitted her to extend her protection to the heretics. He sought new formulae for the purpose of reconciliation, but nothing short of repudiation of the Chalcedon acts would have been enough. The last great efforts for union were made when the Saracens invaded and conquered the dissident provinces. A new formula of union was discovered (One Will and One Energy). This doctrine of monotheletism would never have been heard of but for political exigencies. The Egyptians and Syrians would perhaps have accepted this compromise; but it was repudiated by the fanatical adherents of Chalcedon. Heraclius sought to impose the doctrine by an edict (Ecthesis, 638), but the storm, especially in Italy and Africa, was so great that ten years later an edict known as the Type was issued by Constans forbidding all disputation about the number of wills and energies. Constans was a strong ruler, and maintained the Type in spite of orthodox opposition throughout his reign. But the expediency of this policy passed when the Saracens were inexpugnably settled in their conquests, and in his successor's reign it was more worth while to effect a reconciliation with Rome and the West. This was the cause of the 6th Ecumenical Council which condemned monotheletism (680–681).

Image-worship.—In the Hellenic parts of the empire devotion to orthodoxy served as a chrysalis for the national sentiment which was to burst its shell in the 10th century. For the Greeks Christianity had been in a certain way continuous with paganism. It might be said that the old deities and heroes who had protected their cities were still their guardians, under the new form of saints (sometimes imaginary) and archangels, and performed for them the same kind of miracles. Pagan idolatry was replaced by Christian image-worship, which by the Christians of many parts of Asia Minor, as well as by the Mohammedans, was regarded as simply polytheism. Thus in the great iconoclastic controversy, which distracted the empire for nearly 120 years, was involved, as in the monophysitic, the antagonism between different racial elements and geographical sections. Leo III., whose services as a great deliverer and reformer were obscured in the memory of posterity by the ill-fame which he won as an iconoclast, was a native of Commagene. His first edict against the veneration of pictures evoked riots in the capital and a revolt in Greece. The opposition was everywhere voiced by the monks, and it is not to be overlooked that for many monks the painting of sacred pictures was their means of existence. Leo's son Constantine V. pursued the same policy with greater rigour, meeting the monastic resistance by systematic persecution, and in his reign a general council condemned image-worship (753). Iconoclasm was supported by the army, i.e., Asia Minor, and a considerable portion of the episcopate, but it was not destined to triumph. When the Athenian Irene, wife of Leo IV., came to power after her husband's death, as regent for her son, Constantine VI., she secured the restoration of the worship of icons. The Iconoclastic Council was reversed by the 7th Ecumenical Council of 787. The iconoclastic party, however, was not yet defeated, and (after the neutral reign of Nicephorus I.) came again to the helm in the reigns of the Armenian Leo V. and the first two Phrygian emperors, Michael II. and Theophilus. But the empire was weary of the struggle, and on the death of Theophilus, who had been rigorous in enforcing his policy, icon-worship was finally restored by his widow Theodora (843), and the question was never reopened. This was a triumph for the Greek element in the empire; the "Sunday of orthodoxy" on which iconoclasm was formally condemned is still a great day in the Greek Church.

The ablest champions who wielded their pens for the cause of icons, defending by theological arguments practices which really had their roots in polytheism, were in the early stage John of Damascus and in the later Theodore (abbot of the monastery of Studium at Constantinople). The writings of the iconoclasts were destroyed by the triumphant party, so that we know their case only from the works of their antagonists.

Schism Between the Greek and Latin Churches.—In this struggle the Greeks and Latins were of one mind; the image-worshippers had the support of the Roman see. When the pope resisted him, Leo III. confiscated the papal estates in Sicily and Calabria; and the diocese of Illyricum was withdrawn from the control of Rome and submitted to the patriarch of Constantinople. But when iconoclasm was defeated, there was no question of restoring Illyricum, nor could there be, for political reasons; since the iconoclastic schism had, with other causes, led to the detachment of the papacy from the empire and its association with the Frankish power. By the foundation of the rival Roman empire in 800 the pope had definitely become a subject of another State. No sooner had the iconoclastic struggle terminated than differences and disputes arose between the Greek and Latin Churches which finally led to an abiding schism, and helped to foster the national self-consciousness of the Greeks. A strife over the patriarchal chair between Ignatius (deposed by Michael III. and supported by Rome) and Photius, the learned statesman who succeeded him, strained the relations with Rome; but a graver cause of discord was the papal attempt to win Bulgaria, whose sovereign, Boris, had been baptized under the auspices of Michael III. (c. 865), and was inclined to play Old Rome against New Rome. Photius stood out as the champion of the Greeks against the claim of the Roman see, and his patriarchate, though it did not lead to a final breach, marks the definite emancipation of the Greeks from the spiritual headship of Rome. This is the significance of his encyclic letter (867), which formulated a number of differences in rite and doctrine between the Greek and Latin Churches, differences so small that they need never have proved a barrier to union, if on one side there had been no question of papal supremacy, and if the Greek attitude had not been the expression of a tenacious nationality. There was a reconciliation about 900, but the Churches were really estranged, and the open and ultimate breach which came in 1054, when the influence of the Cluny movement was dominant at Rome (Leo IX. was pope and Michael Cerularius patriarch), sealed a disunion which had long existed. Subsequent plans of reunion were entertained by the emperors merely for political reasons, to obtain Western support against their foes, or to avert (through papal influence) the aggressive designs of Western princes. They were doomed to futility because they were not seriously meant, and the Greek population was entirely out of sympathy with these political machinations of their emperors. The Union of Lyons (1274) was soon repudiated, and the last attempt, the Union of Florence in 1439, was equally hollow (though it permanently secured the union of the Rumanians and of the Ruthenians). Part of the historical significance of the relations between the Greek and Latin Churches lies in the fact that they illustrated and promoted by way of challenge the persistence of Greek national self-consciousness.

The emperors legislated against paganism and against heresy, not merely under ecclesiastical pressure, but because they thought religious uniformity politically desirable. Theodosius the Great, a Spaniard, with no sympathy for Hellenic culture, set himself the task of systematically eradicating pagan institutions and customs. Though his persecution accomplished much, paganism was far from being extinct either in the East or in the West in the 5th century. Not only did heathen cults survive in many remote districts, but the old gods had many worshippers among the higher classes at Rome, Constantinople, Antioch, Alexandria and Athens. The most distinguished Greek literati of that period were non-Christian. Justinian, who united theological enthusiasm with belief in the ideal of uniformity and, like Theodosius, was out of sympathy with Hellenism ("Hellene" now came to mean "pagan"), persecuted polytheism more earnestly and severely than his predecessors. His measures created a panic among the higher classes at Byzantium, of whom many, as he suspected, were addicted to the ancient religion. He instituted a regular inquisition, exacted oaths of orthodoxy from all officials and teachers, and closed the philosophical schools of Athens. Missionaries (and it is remarkable that he employed monophysite heretics) were sent to abolish the old heathen worship which survived in many parts of Asia Minor where Christianity had hardly penetrated. By the end of the 6th century formal paganism had practically disappeared.

In Asia Minor, especially in the east, there were many dissident communities which asserted independence of the Church of Constantinople and of all ecclesiastical traditions, founding their doctrines directly on the Bible. Most important of these heretics were the Paulicians (q.v.), a dualistic sect whom the Church regarded as Manichaeans.

THE MACHINERY OF GOVERNMENT

The Autocracy and Its Constitutional Forms.—With Diocletian the Principate of Augustus had become undisguisedly an absolute monarchy, and this constitution prevailed to the end. There is virtually no constitutional history in the proper sense of the term in the later Roman empire, for there was neither evolution nor revolution. The monarchical system remained in all its essential points unchanged, and presents a remarkable example of an autocracy of immense duration which perfectly satisfied the ideas of its subjects. No attempt was made to alter it—to introduce, for instance, a limited monarchy or a republican Government; all revolts and conspiracies were aimed at the policies of particular autocrats, not at autocracy itself; generally they only represented sectional antagonisms and personal ambitions. The emperors inherited a deeply rooted instinct of legality as a tradition from Old Rome; and this respect for law which marked their acts, along with the generally good administration of justice, was a palladium of the monarchy. They were supreme in legislation, as well as in the administrative and judicial spheres; but they were on the whole moderate in wielding legislation as an instrument of policy.

There were, however, recognized constitutional principles which it would have been impossible for the emperor to override.

(1) The elective principle, inherited from the republic, was never changed. A new emperor had to be elected by the senate and acclaimed by the people. The succession never became automatic. But even Augustus had indirectly introduced the dynastic principle. Theodosius the Great, by causing his two sons, Arcadius and Honorius, to be elected Augusti in their infancy, practically elevated the dynastic idea into a constitutional principle; hence-

forward it was regarded as in the regular course that the son born to a reigning sovereign should in his infancy be elected Augustus. Thus the election, though always an indispensable form, was only a reality when a dynasty came to an end.

(2) When the position of Christianity was assured by the failure of Julian's reaction, it was evident that profession of that religion would henceforward be a necessary qualification for election to the throne. This was formally and constitutionally recognized when the coronation of the emperor by the patriarch was introduced in 457, or perhaps in 450.

(3) The sovereignty of the emperor was personal and *not territorial*. In this respect it always retained the character which it had inherited as the offspring of a Roman magistracy. Hence no Roman territory could be granted by the emperor to another power. For instance, the Western emperor Conrad III. could promise to hand over Italy to Manuel Comnenus as the dowry of his wife, but it would have been constitutionally illegal for Manuel to have made such a promise to any foreign prince; an Eastern emperor had no right to dispose of the territory of the State. Tendencies towards a territorial conception begin indeed to appear (partly under Western influence) in the time of the Palaeologi, especially in the custom of bestowing appanages on imperial princes.

(4) While the senate of Rome generally lost its importance and at last became a mere municipal body, the new senate of Constantine preserved its position as an organ of the State till the fall of Constantinople. For the imperial elections it was constitutionally indispensable, and it was able sometimes to play a decisive part when the throne was vacant—its only opportunity for independent action. The abolition, under Diocletian's system, of the senatorial provinces deprived the senate of the chief administrative function which it exercised under the Principate; it had no legislative powers; and it lost most of its judicial functions. It was, however, still a judicial court; it tried, for instance, political crimes. In composition it differed from the senate of the Principate. The senators in the 4th century were chiefly functionaries in the public service, divided into the three ascending ranks of *clarissimi, spectabiles, illustres*. The majority of the members of the senatorial order lived in the provinces, forming a provincial aristocracy, and did not sit in the senate. Then the two lower ranks ceased to have a right to sit in the senate, which was confined to the *illustres* and men of higher rank (patricians). The senatorial order must therefore be distinguished from the senate in a narrower sense; the latter finally consisted mainly of high ministers of State and the chief officials of the palace. It would be a grave mistake to underrate the importance of this body, through an irrelevant contrast with the senate of the republic or even of the Principate. Its composition ensured to it great influence as a consultative assembly; and its political weight was increased by the fact that the inner council of imperial advisers was practically a committee of the senate. The importance of the senate is illustrated by the fact that in the 11th century Constantine X., in order to carry out a revolutionary, anti-military policy, found it necessary to alter the composition of the senate by introducing a number of new men from the lower classes.

(5) The memory of the power which had once belonged to the *populus Romanus* lingered in the part which the inhabitants of New Rome, and their representatives, played in acclaiming newly elected emperors, and in such ceremonies as coronations. In the 6th century the factions ("demes") of the circus, Blues and Greens, appear as political parties, distract the city by their quarrels, and break out in serious riots. On one occasion they shook the throne ("Nika" revolt, 532). The emperors finally quelled this element of disturbance by giving the factions a new organization, under "demarchs" and "democrats," and assigning them a definite quasi-political *locus standi* in the public ceremonies in the palace and the capital. The duty of providing *panem et circenses* was inherited from Old Rome; but the free distribution of bread cannot be traced beyond the 6th century (had the loss of the Egyptian granary to do with its cessation?), while the spectacles of the hippodrome lasted till the end   Outside

the capital the people took little interest in politics, except when theology was concerned; and it may be said generally that it was mainly in the ecclesiastical sphere that public opinion among the masses, voiced by the clergy and monks, was an influence which made itself felt.

The court ceremonial of Constantinople, which forms such a marked contrast to the ostentatiously simple establishments of Augustus and the Antonines, had in its origin a certain constitutional significance. It was introduced by Aurelian and Diocletian, not, we must suppose, from any personal love of display, but rather to dissociate the emperor from the army, at a time when the State had been shaken to its foundations by the predominance of the military element and the dependence of the emperor on the soldiers. It was the object of Diocletian to make him independent of all, with no more particular relation to the army than to any other element in the State; the royal court and the inaccessibility of the ruler were calculated to promote this object. The etiquette and ceremonies were greatly elaborated by Justinian, and were diligently maintained and developed. The public functions, which included processions through the streets to various sanctuaries of the city on the great feast-days of the Church, supplied entertainment of which the populace never wearied; and it did not escape the wit of the rulers that the splendid functions and solemn etiquette of the court were an effective means of impressing the imagination of foreigners, who constantly resorted to Constantinople from neighbouring kingdoms and dependencies, with the majesty and power of the Basileus.

The imperial *dignity* was collegial. There could be two or more emperors (*imperatores, βασιλεῖς*) at the same time; edicts were issued, public acts performed, in their joint names. Through the period of dualism, in the 4th and 5th centuries, when the administration of the Eastern provinces was generally separate from that of the Western, the imperial *authority* was also collegial. But after this period the system of divided authority came to an end and was never renewed. There was frequently more than one emperor, not only in the case of a father and his sons, or of two brothers, but also in the case of a minority, when a regent is elected emperor (Romanus I.; *cf.* Nicephorus II. and John Zimisces). But one colleague always exercised the sole authority, was the real monarch, the "great" or the "first" Basileus; the other or others were only sleeping partners. Under the Comneni a new nomenclature was introduced; a brother, *e.g.*, who before could have become the formal colleague of the ruler, received the title of *Sebastocrator* (Sebastos was the Greek equivalent of Augustus).

Legislation.—The history of the legislation of the Eastern empire is distinguished by three epochs associated with the names of (1) Justinian, (2) Leo III., (3) Basil I. and Leo VI.

For (1) the Justinianean legislation, *see* JUSTINIAN I.

(2) Justinian's reign was followed by a period in which juristic studies decayed. The 7th century, in which social order was profoundly disturbed, is a blank in legal history, and it would seem that the law of Justinian, though it had been rendered into Greek, almost ceased to be studied or understood. Practice at least was modified by principles in accord with the public opinion of Christian society and influenced by ecclesiastical canons. In a synod held at Constantinople in the reign of Justinian II. numerous rules were enacted, differing from the existing laws and based on ecclesiastical doctrine and Mosaic principles, and these were sanctioned as laws of the realm by the emperor. Thus Church influence and the decline of Roman tradition, in a State which had become predominantly Greek, determined the character of the ensuing legislative epoch under the auspices of Leo III., whose law book (A.D. 740), written in Greek, marks a new era and reflects the changed ideas of the community. Entitled a "Brief Selection of Laws" and generally known as the *Ecloga,* it may be described as a Christian law book. In regard to the *patria potestas* increased facilities are given for emancipation from paternal control when the son comes to years of discretion, and the paternal is to a certain extent replaced by a *parental* control over minors. The law of guardianship is considerably modified. The laws of marriage are transformed under the influence of the Christian

conception of matrimony; the institution of *concubinatus* is abolished. Impediments to marriage on account of consanguinity and of spiritual relationship are multiplied. While Justinian regarded marriage as a contract, and therefore, like any other contract, dissoluble at the pleasure of the parties, Leo III. accepted the Church view that it was an indissoluble bond. Ecclesiastical influence is written large in the criminal law, of which a prominent feature is the substitution of mutilation of various kinds for the capital penalty. Death is retained for some crimes, such as murder and high treason; other offences were punished by amputation (of hand, nose, etc.). This system (justified by the passage in the New Testament, "If thine eye offend thee," etc.), though to modern notions barbaric, seemed a step in the direction of leniency; and it may be observed that the tendency to avoid capital punishment increased, and we are told that in the reign of John Comnenus it was never inflicted. (The same spirit, it may be noted, is apparent in the usual, though by no means invariable, practice of Byzantine emperors to render dethroned rivals or members of a deposed dynasty innocuous by depriving them of eyesight or forcing them to take monastic orders, instead of putting them to death.) The Church, which had its own system of penalties, exercised a great influence on the actual operation of criminal law, especially through the privilege of asylum (recognized by Justinian, but with many reserves and restrictions), which was granted to Christian churches and is admitted without exceptions in the *Ecloga*.

(3) The last period of legislative activity under Basil I. and Leo VI. represents a reaction, in a certain measure, against the *Ecloga* and a return to Justinian. The *Ecloga* had met practical needs, but the Isaurian and Phrygian emperors had done nothing to revive legal study. To do so was the aim of Basil, and the revival could only be based on Justinianean law books or their Greek representatives. These books were now treated somewhat as Justinian and his lawyers had treated their own predecessors. A handbook of extracts from the Institutes, Digest and Code was issued in 879 (ὁ πρόχειρος νόμος, "the law as it is"), to fulfil somewhat the same function as the Institutes. Then a collection of all the laws of the empire was prepared by means of two commissions, and completed under Leo VI. It was entitled the *Basilika*. In many points (in civil, but not in criminal, law) the principles of the *Ecloga* are set aside in favour of the older jurisprudence. Thus the Justinianean ordinances on the subject of divorce were revived, and there remained henceforward a contradiction between the civil and the canon law.

After this there was no legislation on a grand scale; but there was a great revival of legal study under Constantine IX., who founded a new law-school, and there were many learned specialists who wrote important commentaries, such as John Xiphilin (11th century), Theodore Balsamon (12th century), Harmenopulos (14th century). The civil code of Moldavia (published 1816-17) is a codification of Byzantine law; and modern Greece, although in framing its code it took the Napoleonic for its model, professes theoretically to base its civic law on the edicts of the emperors as contained in the *Hexabiblos* of Harmenopulos.

Administration.—Three principles underlay the administrative reform of Diocletian: the separation of civil from military functions; the formation of small provincial units; and the scalar structure which depended on the interposition of the vicar of a diocese and the praetorian prefect between the provincial governor and the emperor. This system lasted unchanged for three and a half centuries. The few unimportant alterations that were made were in harmony with its spirit, until the reign of Justinian, who introduced certain reforms that pointed in a new direction. We find him combining some of the small provinces into large units, undermining the scalar system by doing away with some of the dioceses and vicars, and placing in some cases military and civil authority in the same hands. The chief aim of Diocletian in his general reform had been to secure central control over the provincial Governments; the object of Justinian in these particular reforms was to remedy corruption and oppression. These changes, some of which were soon cancelled, would hardly in themselves have led to a radical change; but they prepared the way for an administrative revolution, brought about by stress of external necessities. In the 7th century all the energies of the empire, girt about by active enemies, were centred on war and defence; everything had to give way to military exigencies; and a new system was gradually introduced which led ultimately to the abolition of the old. The change began in Italy and Africa, at the end of the 6th century, where operations against the Lombards and the Berbers were impeded by the friction between the two co-ordinate military and civil authorities (masters of soldiers, and praetorian prefects). The military governors were made supreme with the title of *exarchs*, "viceroys"; the civil authority was subordinated to them in case of collision, otherwise remaining unaltered. The change is an index of the dangerous crisis through which these provinces were passing. In the East similar circumstances led to similar results. The Saracen danger hanging imminent over Asia Minor imposed a policy of the same kind. And so before the end of the 7th century we find the empire divided into six great military provinces, three in Europe and three in Asia: (1) Exarchate of *Africa*, (2) Exarchate of *Italy*, (3) Strategia of *Thrace*, (4) County of *Opsikion* (=*obsequium*), including Bithynia, Honorias, Paphlagonia, parts of Hellespontus and Phrygia, (5) Strategia of the *Anatolikoi*, most of west and central Asia Minor, (6) Strategia of the *Armeniakoi*, eastern Asia Minor. In addition to these there was a naval circumscription, (7) the Strategia of the *Karabisianoi* (from κάραβος, a vessel), including the southern coastland of Asia Minor, and the Aegean (*see* below under *Navy*).

The lands of the old prefecture of Illyricum were not included in the system, because this part of the empire was then regarded as a lost position. On the contrary, here military powers were committed to the prefect of Illyricum, whose actual sphere extended little beyond Thessalonica, which was surrounded by Slavonic tribes.

The Eastern changes, perhaps initiated by Heraclius, but probably due mainly to Constans II., did not interfere with the civil administration, except in so far as its heads were subordinated to the military commanders. But Leo III., who as a great administrative reformer ranks with Augustus and Diocletian, did away with the old system altogether. (1) Reversing Diocletian's principle, he combined military and civil powers in the same hands. The *strategos* or military commander became also a civil governor; his higher officers (turmarchs) were likewise civil functionaries. (2) The scalar principle disappeared, including both the vicars and the praetorian prefect of the East (some of whose functions were merged in those of the prefect of the city); no authority interposed between the strategoi and the emperor. (3) The new provinces, which were called *themes* (the name marks their military origin: *thēma*=corps), resembled in size the provinces of Augustus, each including several of the Diocletian divisions. This third and last provincial reform has, like its predecessors, its own history. The list of themes in the 11th century is very different from that of the 8th. The changes were in one direction—the reduction of large provinces by cutting off parts to form smaller themes, a repetition of the process which reduced the provinces of Augustus. Hence the themes came to vary greatly in size and importance. Leo himself began the process by breaking up the Anatolic command into two themes (Anatolic and Thracesian). The principle of splitting up was carried out systematically by Leo VI. (who was also responsible for a new ecclesiastical division of the empire).

Imperial Officials.—In the central administration, the general principles seem to have remained unchanged; the heads of the great administrative bureaux in Constantinople retain the *palatine* character which belonged to most of them from the beginning. But there were many changes in these offices, in their nomenclature and the delimitation of their functions. There are great differences between the administrative corps in the 5th, in the 10th and in the 15th centuries. We can hardly be wrong in conjecturing that, along with his provincial reform, Leo III. made a rearrangement of the central bureaux; the abolition of the praetorian prefecture of the East entailed, in itself, modifications. But minor changes were continually being made, and we may note the following tendencies: (1) Increase in the number of ministers directly responsible to the emperor, (a) subordinate offices in the bureaux being raised to the rank of independent ministries; (b) new offices being created and old ones becoming merely titular. (2) Changes in nomenclature; substitution of Greek for Latin titles. (3) Changes in the relative importance and rank of the high officials, both civil and military.

The prefect of the city (ἔπαρχος) controlled the police organization and administration of justice in the capital; he was vice-president of the imperial court of justice, and, when the office of prefect of the East was abolished, he inherited the functions of that dignitary as judge of appeals from the provinces. But the *praefectus vigilum*, commander of the city guards, who was subordinate to him, became an independent officer, entitled drungary of the watch, and in the 11th century superseded him as vice-president of the imperial court. We are told that in the last years of the empire the prefect of the city had no functions at all; but his office survives in the *Shehr-imaneti*, "city prefecture," of the Ottomans, in whose organization there are many traces of Byzantine influence.

Instead of the quaestor of the sacred palace, whose duty was to draft the imperial laws and rescripts, we find in the 9th century a quaestor who possesses certain judicial and police functions and is far lower in the hierarchy of rank. It has been supposed that the later quaestor really inherited the duties of another officer, the *quaesitor*, who was instituted by Justinian. In the latest period the quaestor, if he still existed as a name, had no functions.

The master of offices, who supervised the bureaux in the palace and was master of court ceremonies, also performed many functions of a minister of foreign affairs, was head of the imperial post (*cursus*), and of the corps of *agentes in rebus* or imperial messengers. This ministry disappeared, probably in the 8th century, but the title was retained as a dignity at all events till the end of the 9th. The most important functions, pertaining to foreign affairs, were henceforward performed by the logothete of the post (λογοθέτης τοῦ δρόμου). In the 12th century this minister was virtually the chancellor of the empire; his title was changed to that of great logothete by Andronicus II.

The two financial ministers, *comes sacrarum largitionum* and *comes rei privatae*, continued to the end under the titles λογοθέσητ τοῦ γενικοῦ (general logothete) and ὁ ἐπὶ τοῦ ἰδικοῦ (Anastasius added a third, the count of the sacred patrimony, but he was afterwards suppressed). But in the 9th century we find both these ministers inferior in rank to the *sacellarius*, or private purse-keeper of the emperor. Besides these there was a fourth important financial department, that of the military treasury, under a logothete.

The employment of eunuchs as high ministers of State was a feature of the Byzantine empire from the end of the 4th century. It is laid down as a principle (A.D. 900) that all offices are open to them, except the prefecture of the city, the quaestorship, and the military posts which were held by "domestics." There were then eight high posts which could only be held by eunuchs, of which the chief were the *parakoimōmenos* and the *protovestiarios* (master of the wardrobe).

An emperor who had not the brains or energy to direct the affairs of the State himself, necessarily committed the task of guiding the helm to some particular minister or court dignitary who had gained his confidence. Such a position of power was outside the constitution, and was not associated with any particular office; it might be held by an ecclesiastic or a eunuch; it had been held by the eunuchs Eutropius and Chrysaphius in the reigns of Arcadius and Theodosius II. respectively. In later times, such a first minister came to be denoted by a technical term, ὁ παραδυναστεύων. This was the position, for instance, of Stylianus, the father-in-law of Leo VI. Most of the emperors between Basil II. and Alexius Comnenus were under the influence of such ministers.

The orders of rank (which must be distinguished from titles of office) were considerably increased in later times. In the 4th and 7th centuries there were the three great classes of the *illustres*, *spectabiles* and *clarissimi*; and above the *illustres* a small, higher class of patricians. In the 9th century we find an entirely different system; the number of classes being largely augmented, and the nomenclature different. Instead of epithets, like *illustres*, the names are titles which had designated offices; "patrician" alone survives. The highest rank is now (1) the *magistroi;* then come the patricians in two classes: (2) proconsular patricians, (3) respectable patricians; below these (4) *protospatharioi*, (5) *dishypatoi* (=*bis consules*), (6) *spatharokandidatoi*, (7) *spatharioi*, and other lower ranks. Particular ranks do not seem now to have been inalienably attached to particular offices. The *strategos* of the Anatolic theme, *e.g.*, might be a patrician or only a protospathar. Whoever was promoted to one of these ranks received its insignia from the emperor's hand, and had to pay fixed fees to various officials, especially to the palace eunuchs.

In the provinces ordinary justice was administered by judges (κριταί) who were distinct from the governors of the themes, and inherited their functions from the old provincial governors of Diocletian's system. In Constantinople higher and lower courts of justice sat regularly and frequently. The higher tribunals were those of the prefect and the quaestor, before whom different kinds of cases came. Appeals reached the emperor through the bureau of petitions (τῶν δεησέων); he might deal with the case immediately; or might refer it to the imperial court of appeal, of which he was president; or else to the special court of the Twelve Divine Judges (θεῖοι δικασταί), which was instituted by Justinian.

Fiscal System.—While the administration of justice was one of the best features of the Eastern empire, its fiscal system, likewise inherited from the early empire, was one of its worst. If the Government had been acquainted with the principles of public economy, which have not been studied till comparatively recent times, a larger revenue might have been raised without injuring the prosperity of the inhabitants. Taxes were injudiciously imposed and oppressively collected. The commerce of the empire was one of its great sources of strength, but the Government looked on the merchants as a class from which the utmost should be extorted. The chief source of revenue was the land. The main burdens which fell upon the landed proprietors throughout the whole period were the land tax proper and the *annona*. The land tax (*capitatio terrena*=the old *tributum* of the imperial, *stipendium* of the senatorial provinces) was based, not on the yearly produce, but on the capital of the proprietor, the character and value of the land being taken into account. In later times this seems to have become the καπνικόν, or hearth tax. The *annona* was an additional impost for supporting the army and imperial officials; it was originally paid in produce. The province was divided into fiscal districts, and the total revenue to be derived from each was entered in a book of assessment. The assessment was in early times revised every 15 years (the "indiction" period), but subsequently such revisions seem to have been very irregular. The collection of the taxes was managed through the curial system, while it lasted (till 7th century?). The decurions, or municipal councillors, of the chief town in each district were responsible for collecting and delivering the whole amount, and had to make good the sums owed by defaulters. This system of collective responsibility pressed very heavily on the decurions, and helped to cause their decay in the Western provinces. After the abolition of the curial organization, the principle of collective responsibility remained in the form of the ἐπιβολή or additional charge; that is, if a property was left without an owner, the taxes for which it was liable became an extra charge on the other members of the district. The taxes were collected by *praktores*, who were under the general logothete. The peasant proprietors were also liable to burdens of other kinds, of which the most important was the furnishing of horses, vehicles, postboys, etc., for the State post (see ANGARIA).

The history of landed property and agrarian conditions in the Eastern empire still awaits a thorough examination. It may be noted that individual hereditary proprietorship was always the rule (on Crown and monastic lands as well as in other cases), and that the commonly supposed extensive existence of communities possessing land in common is based on erroneous interpretation of documents. When imperial lands were granted to monasteries or as fiefs to individuals, the position and rights of the peasant proprietors on the estates were not changed, but in many cases the imposts were paid to the new master instead of to the fisc. In the 4th, 5th and 6th centuries the cultivators were attached to the soil (*coloni, ascripticii; see* SERFDOM), in the interests of the fiscus; it has been supposed, on insufficient grounds, that this serfdom was abolished for a time by Leo III., though it is probable that the condition of the peasants was largely changed by the invasions of the 7th century. In any case the system of compulsory attachment of peasants to their lands remained in force, and the class of *adscripticii* (ἐναπόγραφοι) existed till the latest times. The chief sources for agrarian conditions are, besides the imperial laws, monastic records, among which may be mentioned as specially valuable those of the monastery of Lemboi near Smyrna.

MEANS OF DEFENCE

The general principle of the military defence of the empire in the 4th century consisted in large forces stationary on the frontiers, and reserve forces, stationed in the interior provinces, which could be moved to any point that was in danger. Thus the army was composed of (1) the *limitanei*, frontier-troops (under *duces*), and (2) reserve forces (under *magistri militum*) of two denominations, (*a*) *palatini* and (*b*) *comitatenses*. The *limitanei* were the more numerous; it has been estimated that if they numbered about 350,000, the *comitatenses* and *palatini* together amounted to less than 200,000. It is to be noted that for the old legion of 6,000 men a smaller legion of 1,000 had been substituted, and that the proportion of cavalry to infantry was small. In the 6th century the fundamental principles of the system were the same; but the cavalry had become a much more important branch of the service, and in the wars of Belisarius the *foederati*, barbarian mercenaries of various races, commanded by their own chiefs, played a great rôle. The peasants of Illyria and Thrace, the mountaineers of southern Asia Minor still supply an important part of the army, but the number of barbarians (Heruli, Vandals, Goths, Slavs, Arabs, etc.) is much larger. Solidity and a corresponding want of mobility characterized at this time both cavalry and infantry; their great merit was straight and rapid shooting: Belisarius ascribed his success in Italy to the excellence of the archery. It is remarkable with what small forces (not more than 25,000) the first conquest of Italy was achieved, though Belisarius was far from being a military genius and the discipline in his army was flagrantly defective.

Justinian carried out on the frontiers and in the exposed provinces a carefully devised and expensive system of defensive works. Fortified towns along the *limes* were connected by intervening forts, and at some distance behind was a second line of more important fortresses more strongly garrisoned, which furnished both a second barrier and places of refuge for the inhabitants of the open country. There was an elaborate system of signals by which the garrisons of the front stations could announce not only the imminence of a hostile invasion, but the number and character of the enemy. In North Africa there are abundant remains of the forts of the 6th and 7th centuries, displaying the military architecture of the period and the general frontier system. The typical fortress had three defences: the wall flanked by square towers of three storeys; at a few yards' distance a second wall of stone; and outside a deep foss about 20yd. wide, with vertical sides, filled with water, and along its edge a rampart of earth.

The Army.—We have already seen how the disasters and losses of the 7th century led to a radical change in the military organization, and how the empire was divided into themes. The preponderant influence which Asia Minor won and retained till the 11th century is reflected in the military establishment, which mainly depended on the Asiatic provinces. The *strategos* of a large theme commanded a corps of 10,000 and the scheme of the divisions and subordinate commands has a remarkable resemblance to the organization of some of the armies of modern Europe.

The recorded scheme was probably not uniform in all the themes, and varied at different periods. The *Thēma* (corps) consisted of 2 *turmai* (brigades) under *turmarchai;* the *turma* of 5 *banda* (regiments), each under a *drungarios* (colonel); the *bandon* of 5 *pentarkhiai* (companies) under a *komētes* (captain). The *pentarkhia*, containing 200 men had 5 subdivisions under *pentekontarkhai* (lieutenants); and there was a smaller unit of ten men under the *dekarkhes* (corporal). The total strength in the 9th century was 120,000; in Justinian's time it was reckoned at 150,000.

Distinct from the military forces (θέματα) of the provinces were the forces (τάγματα) stationed in or near the capital. The most important of these were the *scholae* and the *excubitores*. The scholarian troops were in early times under the master of offices, but subsequently their chief officer, the domestic of the schools, became the highest military commander in the empire next to the *strategos* of the Anatolic theme. In war, when the emperor did not assume the chief command himself, he might entrust it to any commander, and he often entrusted it to the domestic. In the 11th century, after the conquest of Bulgaria, there were two domestics, one for the East and one for the West, and under Alexius Comnenus the domestic of the West received the title great domestic. Under the Palaeologi the great domestic was superior in rank to all other ministers.

Besides the scholarians and the *excubitores* (who had been organized in the 5th century), there were the regiments of the *hikanatoi*, the *arithmos* and the *numeroi*. The *numeroi* were foot-soldiers. The *optimatoi*, also infantry, properly belonged to the same category, though they were constituted as a theme. It is to be observed that the demes or corporations of Constantinople were partly organized as militia, and were available for purposes of defence.

The great difference between this Byzantine army and that of the earlier empire is that its strength (like that of the feudal armies of the West) lay entirely in cavalry, which the successors of Heraclius and the Isaurian emperors developed to great perfection. The few contingents of foot were subsidiary. The army was free from the want of discipline which was so notable in the 6th century; it was maintained in Asia Minor, which was the great recruiting ground, by a system of military holdings of land (an extension of the old Roman system of assigning lands in the frontier districts to federate barbarians and to veterans). The conditions of the marauding expeditions and guerilla warfare, continuously carried on against and by the Saracens in the 8th, 9th and 10th centuries, were carefully studied by generals and tacticians, and we possess the theory of the Byzantine methods in a treatise composed by the emperor Nicephorus Phocas, and edited by one of his pupils. Every detail of an inroad into Saracen territory is regulated.

In the 8th and 9th centuries there was a system of signals by which an approaching Saracen incursion was announced to Constantinople from the Cilician frontier. The news was flashed across Asia Minor by eight beacon fires. The first beacon was at Lulon (which commanded the pass between Tyana and the Cilician Gates), the last on Mt. Auxentius in Bithynia. When this fire appeared, a light was kindled in the pharos of the imperial palace at Constantinople. The system was discontinued in the reign of Michael III., probably after the capture of Lulon by the enemy in 860, and was not renewed, though Lulon was recovered in 877.

The loss of a great part of Asia Minor to the Seljuks, and the disorganization of the provinces which they did not acquire, seriously weakened the army, and the emperors had recourse more and more to foreign mercenaries and barbarian auxiliaries. The employment of Scandinavians had begun in the 10th century, and in 988 was formed the Varangian guard. In the arsenal of Venice are two lions, which were transported from the Peiraeus, inscribed with obscure Runic characters, carved perhaps by Scandinavians in the army of Basil II. Under Michael IV. the famous Norwegian prince Harald Hardrada (described by a Greek writer as "Araltes, son of the king of Varangia") fought for the empire in Sicily and in Bulgaria. But in the latter part of the 11th century foreign mercenaries greatly increased in numbers and importance.

The note of the Byzantine army was efficiency, and nowhere is the immeasurable superiority of the civilization of the Eastern empire to the contemporary States of Europe more apparent. The theory of military science was always studied and taught; constant practice, interpreting and correcting theories, safeguarded it against pedantry; and a class of magnificent staff officers were trained, who in the 10th century were the terror of the enemy. The particular tactics of the various foes whom they had to face were critically studied. We have a series of military text-books, from the time of Anastasius I. to that of Basil II., in which we can learn their principles and methods. In this army there was plenty of courage, and distinct professional pride, but no love of fighting for fighting's sake, nor the spirit which in western Europe developed into chivalry. The Byzantines despised such ideas as characteristic of barbarians who had physical strength and no brains. The object of a good general, as Leo VI. shows in his important treatise on Tactics, was in their opinion not to win a great battle, but to attain success without the risks and losses of a great battle. The same author criticizes the military character of the Franks. Paying a tribute to their fearlessness, he points out their want of discipline, the haphazard nature of their array and order of battle, their eagerness to attack before the word was given, their want of faculty for strategy or tactical combinations, their incapacity for operations on difficult ground, the ease with which they could be deceived by simple artifices, their careless-ness in pitching camps, and their lack of a proper intelligence department. These criticisms, borne out by all we know of feudal warfare, illustrate the contrast between a Western host, with its three great "battles," rushing headlong at the foe, and the Byzan-tine army, with its large number of small units, co-operating in perfect harmony, under a commander who had been trained in military science, had a definite plan in his head, and could rely on all his subordinates for strict and intelligent obedience.

The Navy.—Under the early empire, as Rome had no rival in the Mediterranean, it was natural that the navy and naval theory should be neglected. When Constantine the Great decided to be-siege Byzantium by sea, both he and his opponent Licinius had to create fleets for the struggle. Even when the Vandals in Africa made transmarine conquests and became a naval power, the Romans did not seriously address themselves to building an effi-cient navy. The Vandals harried their coasts; their expeditions against Africa failed. And even when the Vandal power was in its decline and Belisarius set forth on his successful expedition of con-quest, his fears for the safety of his squadron in case he should be attacked at sea allow us to suspect that the fleet of the enemy was superior to the Roman. The conquest of Africa secured for Jus-tinian the undisputed command of the Mediterranean, but he did nothing for the naval establishment. It was not till the Saracens, aspiring to conquer all the Mediterranean coastlands, became a naval power that the Roman empire was forced, in a struggle for its being, to organize an efficient fleet. This, as we saw, was the work of Constans II., and we saw what it achieved. In this first period (c. 650-720) the naval forces, designated as the *Karabisi-anoi,* were placed under the command of an admiral, with title of *strategos.* They consisted of two geographical divisions, each under a *drungarios*: the province of the Cibyrrhaeots (probably named from the smaller Cibyra in Pamphylia) which included the southern coast districts of Asia Minor, and the Aegean province, which embraced the islands and part of the west coast of Asia Minor. The former was the more important; the marines of this province were the hardy descendants of the pirates, whose subju-gation had taxed the resources of the Roman Government in the last years of the republic. It was a new principle to impose the burden of naval defence on the coast and island districts. Distinct from these fleets, and probably organized on a different principle, was the naval contingent stationed at Constantinople. Leo III. changed the naval administration, abolishing the supreme com-mand, and making the Cibyrrhaeot and Aegean provinces separate independent themes under *strategoi.* The change was due to two motives. There was a danger lest a commander of the whole navy should become over powerful (indicated by the political rôle played by the navy before Leo's accession); but apart from this,

the general reform of Leo, which united civil and military powers in the same hands, naturally placed the commanders of the two branches of the navy on a new footing, by making them provincial governors. In this and the following reigns, the tendency was to neglect the fleet; the interest of the Government was concen-trated on the army. For a time this policy was prosecuted with impunity, since the Omayyad dynasty was growing weak, and then under the Abbasids, who transferred the capital from Damascus to Baghdad, the sea-power of the caliphate declined. But the neglect of the fleet was avenged in the 9th century, when Crete and Sicily were wrested from the empire, the loss of south Italy was immi-nent, and Muslim squadrons sailed in the Adriatic—losses and dangers which led to a reorganization of the navy under Basil I. and Leo VI. After this reform we find the navy consisting of two main contingents: the imperial fleet (stationed at Constantinople), and the provincial fleets, three in number, of (a) Cibyrrhaeot theme, (b) Aegean theme, (c) theme of Samos. A small distinct contingent was supplied by the Mardaites who, natives of Mt. Lebanon, had been transplanted (partly to Pamphylia, partly to Epirus, the Ionian islands and Peloponnesus). The imperial fleet seems to have consisted of about 100 warships manned by 23,000 marines (the same men fought and rowed); the provincial fleets of 77 warships manned by 17,000. When the fleets acted together, the admiral in supreme command for the time was called the "drungary of the naval forces." The warships (δρόμωνες, "drom-onds") were mainly biremes, but there were also uniremes, built for speed, called "galleys" (γαλαῖαι). Pyrotechnic was an impor-tant department in the naval establishment; the manufacture of the terrible explosive known as *liquid* or *marine fire* (see GREEK FIRE) was carefully guarded as a State secret.

The navy, active and efficient in the 10th century, is described by a military and therefore unprejudiced officer of the 11th as the glory of Romania. But towards the end of the 11th century it declined, the main cause being the disorganization of the naval provinces of Asia Minor, which, as we saw, was a result of the Seljuk conquest of the interior. This decline had important indi-rect consequences; it led to the dependence of the empire on the Venetian navy in the struggle with the Norman power, and for this help Venice exacted commercial privileges which injured Byzantine commerce and opened the door to the preponderant influences of the Venetians in eastern trade. In the period of the Palaeologi the imperial navy, though small, was active; and the importance which it possessed for the State is illustrated by the high rank at court which the admiral (who in the 11th century had received the title of great duke, μέγας δούξ) then occupied; the only minister who was superior to him was the great domestic.

Diplomacy.—In protecting the State against the barbarians who surrounded it, diplomacy was a weapon as important in the eyes of the Byzantine Government as soldiers or fortifications. The peace on the frontiers was maintained not only by strong mili-tary defences, but by more or less skilful management of the fron-tier peoples. In the later empire this kind of diplomacy, which we may define as the *science of managing the barbarians,* was prac-tised as a fine art; its full development was due to Justinian. Its methods fall under three general heads. (1) One people was kept in check by means of another. The imperial Government fo-mented rivalry and hatred among them. Thus Justinian kept the Gepidae in check by the Lombards, the Kuturgurs by the Utigurs, the Huns by the Avars. (2) Subsidies were given to the peoples on the frontiers, in return for which they undertook to defend the frontier adjacent to them, and to supply fighting men when called upon to do so. The chiefs received honours and decorations. Thus the Berber chiefs on the African border received a staff of silver, encrusted with gold, a silver diadem, white cloak, embroidered tunic, etc. More important potentates were invested with a cost-lier dress. In these investitures precedence was carefully observed. The chiefs thus received a definite position in the empire, and the rich robes, with the ceremony, appealed to their vanity. In some cases they were admitted to posts in the official hierarchy,—being created patricians, masters of soldiers, etc. They were extremely fond of such honours, and considered themselves half-Romans. Another mode of winning influence was to marry barbarian princes to Roman wives, and rear their sons in the luxury of the palace. Dissatisfied pretenders, defeated candidates for kingship, were welcomed at Constantinople. Thus there were generally some princes, thoroughly under Byzantine influence, who at a favourable opportunity could be imposed on their compatriots. Throughout Justinian's reign there was a constant influx of foreign potentates to Constantinople, and he overwhelmed them with attentions, pompous ceremonies and valuable presents. (3) Both these methods were already familiar to the Roman Government, although Justinian employed them far more extensively and systematically than any of his predecessors. The third method was new and characteristic. The close connection of religion and politics at Constantinople prepares us to find that Christian propaganda should go hand-in-hand with conquest, and that the missionary should co-operate with the soldier. The missionary proved an excellent agent. The typical procedure is as follows. In the land which he undertakes to convert, the missionary endeavours to gain the confidence of the king and influential persons, and makes it a special object to enlist the sympathies of the women. If the king hesitates, it is suggested that he should visit New Rome. The attraction of this idea is irresistible, and when he comes to the capital, the pomp of his reception, the honours shown him by the emperor, and the splendour of the religious ceremonies overcome his last scruples. Thenceforward imperial influence is predominant in his dominion; priests become his advisers; a bishop is consecrated, dependent on the patriarch of Constantinople; and the barbarians are transformed by the penetration of Byzantine ideas. By the application of these various means, Justinian established Roman influence in Nubia, Ethiopia and south Arabia, in the Caucasian regions, and on the coast of the Euxine. The conversion of the Lazi (of Colchis) was specially notable, and that of the Sabiri, who were politically important because they commanded the eastern pass of the Caucasus known as the Caspian Gates. It will be observed that the great prestige of the empire was one of the conditions of the success of this policy.

The policy had, of course, its dangers, and was severely criticized by one of Justinian's contemporaries, the historian Procopius. Concessions encouraged greater demands; the riches of the empire were revealed. It was a system, of course, which could not be permanently successful without military power behind it, and of course it was not infallible; but in principle it was well-founded, and proved of immeasurable value.

In the 10th century we have again the means of observing how the Government conducted its foreign policy on carefully thought out principles. The empire was then exposed to constant danger from Bulgaria, to inroads of the Magyars, and to attacks of the Russians. The key to the diplomatic system, designed to meet these dangers, was the cultivation of friendly relations with the Petchenegs, who did not menace the provinces either by land or sea and could be incited to act against Russians, Bulgarians or Magyars. The system is explained in the treatise (known as *De administrando imperio*) composed by the emperor Constantine Porphyrogenitus (c. 950). The series of these northern States was completed by the kingdom of the Khazars (between the Caucasus and the Don), with which the empire had been in relation since the time of Heraclius, who, to win its co-operation against Persia, promised his daughter in marriage to the king. Afterwards the Khazars gave two empresses to New Rome (the wives of Justinian II. and Constantine V.). Their almost civilized State steered skilfully between the contending influences of Islam and Christianity, and its kings adopted the curious means of avoiding suspicion of partiality for either creed by embracing the neutral religion of the Jews. Commercial and political relations with the Khazars were maintained through the important outpost of the empire at Cherson in the Crimea, which had been allowed to retain its republican constitution under a president ($\pi\rho\omega\tau\epsilon\acute{\nu}\omega\nu$) and a municipal board ($\H{\alpha}\rho\chi o\nu\tau\epsilon\varsigma$), though this freedom was limited by the appointment of a *strategos* in 833, a moment at which the Khazars were seriously threatened by the Petchenegs. The danger to be feared from the Khazars was an attack upon Cherson, and it seems probable that this was a leading consideration with Leo III. when he wedded his son Constantine V. to a Khazar princess. In the 9th

century it was an object of the Government to maintain the Khazars (whose army consisted mainly of mercenaries) against the Petchenegs; and hence, if it should become necessary to hold the Khazars in check, the principle was to incite against them not the Petchenegs, but other less powerful neighbours, the Alans of the Caucasus, and the people of "Black Bulgaria" on the middle Volga (a State which survived till the Mongol conquest).

For this systematic diplomacy it was necessary to collect information about the peoples whom it concerned. The ambassadors sent to the homes of barbarous peoples reported everything of interest they could discover. We owe to Priscus a famous graphic account of the embassy which he accompanied to the court of Attila. We possess an account of an embassy sent to the Turks in central Asia in the second half of the 6th century, derived from an official report. Peter the Patrician in Justinian's reign drew up careful reports of his embassies to the Persian court. When foreign envoys came to Constantinople, information was elicited from them as to the history and domestic politics of their own countries. It can be shown that some of the accounts of the history and customs of neighbouring peoples, stored in the treatise of Constantine Porphyrogenitus referred to above (furnishing numerous facts not to be found anywhere else), were derived from barbarian ambassadors who visited Constantinople, and recorded by the imperial secretaries. We may conjecture with some probability that the famous system of the *Relazioni,* which the Venetian Government required from its ambassadors, goes back originally to Byzantine influence.

BIBLIOGRAPHY.—1. General works: Gibbon's *Decline and Fall of the Roman Empire;* Finlay's *History of Greece* (ed., Tozer; vols. i.–iv., 1877); C. W. C. Oman, *The Byzantine Empire* (1892) (a popular sketch). 2. Works dealing with special periods, or branches of the subject: T. Hodgkin, *Italy and her Invaders* (8 vols., 1879–99) (to A.D. 800); J. B. Bury, *History of the Later Roman Empire,* A.D. 395–800 (2 vols., 1889); E. Pears, *The Fall of Constantinople, being the Story of the Fourth Crusade* (1885), and *The Destruction of the Greek Empire* (1903). *See* bibliographies in the *Cambridge Mediaeval History,* vol. iv. (J. B. B.)

ROMANES, GEORGE JOHN (1848–1894), British biologist, was born at Kingston, Canada, on May 20, 1848. He was educated at Gonville and Caius college, Cambridge, and early formed an intimate friendship with Charles Darwin, whose theories he did much during his life to popularize and support. When studying under Sir J. Burdon Sanderson at University college, London, in 1874–76, he began a series of researches on the nervous and locomotor systems of the Medusae and Echinodermata. The results were published in *Jelly-fish, Star-fish, and Sea-urchins* (1885). In 1879 Romanes was elected F.R.S. Meantime he had been also devoting his attention to broader problems of biology. In 1881 he published *Animal Intelligence,* and in 1883 *Mental Evolution in Animals,* in which he traced the parallel development of intelligence in the animal world and in man. He followed up this line of argument in 1888 with *Mental Evolution in Man,* in which he maintained the essential similarity of the reasoning processes in the higher animals and in man, applying Darwin's theory of evolution to the development of the mind. From 1886–90 Romanes delivered a course of lectures on "The Philosophy of Natural History" at Edinburgh, and was Fullerian professor of physiology at the Royal Institution from 1888 to 1891. In 1892 he brought out an *Examination of Weismannism,* in which he upheld the theory of the hereditability of acquired characters. In 1890 he settled at Oxford, where he founded a lectureship to be delivered annually on a scientific or literary topic. In 1893 he published the first part of *Darwin and after Darwin,* a work dealing with the development of the theory of organic evolution, and physiological selection, first propounded in a paper contributed to the Linnean Society in 1886, which provoked much controversy; a second part appeared in 1895 after his death, which occurred at Oxford on May 23, 1894; the third part is still unpublished.

His *Life and Letters,* by his widow, appeared in 1896; his essays were edited by C. L. Morgan (1897). He was also the author of a number of poems, a selection from which was published in 1896.

ROMANESQUE ARCHITECTURE: *see* BYZANTINE AND ROMANESQUE ARCHITECTURE.

ROMANESQUE ART. The term Romanesque is used in widely varying senses by different authorities. In general, it denotes the art and culture of Europe exclusive of the eastern empire and Russia, from the time of the fall of Rome (476) down to the development of Gothic art which occurred at various dates in different countries, but entirely between 1100 and 1300; in portions of Italy art remained dominantly Romanesque well into the 14th century. The attempt is sometimes made to limit the use of the word to the era following the Carolingian empire (800–987); this, however, causes undue difficulties of chronology and complexities in the identification of much work, so that the broader sense is both more true and more simple.

The dominant element in all Romanesque art is the attempt, increasingly successful with the passage of time, of peoples originally barbaric, brought gradually into touch with the ruins of a magnificent culture, and at the same time under the inclusive and unifying influence of an enthusiastic Christianity, to develop, for themselves, art forms which they could, with their own skill, create and which would satisfy their own emotional demands, so different both from those of the Roman empire and those of the cultivated and Christianized earlier Roman provinces. At first, this attempt was most evidently influenced by Roman art forms and produced caricatures of them; only in such long Christianized provinces as Gaul did some traces of the traditional, technical skill persist through the much troubled pre-Carolingian times. As time went on, however, not only did the fast growing skill of the former barbarians and the conquered peoples under them lead to an increasing freedom from the Roman models, but other influences crept in. Thus, by the beginning of the 12th century, there is evident in all Romanesque work throughout Europe a combination of differing tendencies and traditions whose varying proportions in different localities gave rise to the individual characteristics of different schools of art. These commingled influences may be briefly listed. The first, and still the most important, is Roman art; the fact that Rome was the centre of the Christian church at the time added to its power. The second element was Byzantine, for in Constantinople, throughout the dark ages, the manufacture of all sorts of objects of great beauty continued unabated; with the growing culture of the west, Byzantine and Syrian artists and craftsmen were in great demand and apparently large numbers of them were at work, at least in France. The third element is that which comes directly from the near east, especially Persia and Mesopotamia, through the medium of textiles which were among the most prized church decorations of the time and whose ornamental forms were copied alike in stone carvings and on manuscripts. The last element, which is the most difficult to analyze and evaluate, is the influence of the northern background of Lombard, Goth, Teuton and Celt. The intense vigour of Romanesque art, however crude, is evidence of the power of this influence; to it are also probably due the obvious love of beasts and some of the grotesque element.

This young and vigorous art found expression in many fields. In architecture new forms were developed which eventually gave birth to the Gothic style. (*See* Byzantine and Romanesque Architecture.) The sculpture of the period is so largely architectural that separate treatment of it can only consider part of its purpose and effect. Up to the 12th century it is crude but tremendously alive. Unable to render the polished graciousness of classic forms, the early sculptor turned first to shallow imitations of Byzantine ornaments, and later naïve interpretations in stone of manuscript decorations and miniatures. Only in Italy, where some remnants of earlier skill seem to have persisted, there developed in the latter part of the 11th century any adequate sculptural technique. In Tuscany this seems to have been largely based on classic tradition, but in Lombardy there appears a mixture of Byzantine elements absorbed from Venetia and more vivid and naturalistic elements, at times strongly impregnated with grotesque feeling, more like the Romanesque across the Alps. Meanwhile, farther north, sculptural technique was rudimentary. Anglo-Saxon sculpture consisted of hardly more than scratchings on stone, and the earliest Norman work, both in France and England, is hardly more advanced. In Scandinavia

and countries in which a Scandinavian culture was imposed upon a Celtic background, as in Ireland, the Scottish islands and western England, a much greater skill appears; traditional Scandinavian and Celtic forms, such as the intricate interlaces, frequently based on dragon or snake forms, and much simplified human figures, often themselves worked into geometrical forms, are carved with brilliant decorative effect; the old Norse, pagan shapes merging with the new Christian symbolism, as in the famous stone crosses of England and Ireland.

During the 12th century there was an enormous change throughout Europe, as if, almost suddenly, latent decorative imagination and technical skill had come to maturity. Twelfth century sculpture, alike in France, Italy, Germany, Spain and England was accomplished, and at times, almost sophisticated. A blend of conventionalism and naturalism makes the porches of hundreds of churches beautiful examples of architectural sculpture.

In painting and mural decoration the influences at work were largely Byzantine. (*See* Byzantine Art.) Crude attempts to imitate Byzantine mosaic are found in much early Italian Romanesque work, and from manuscript accounts it would appear that similar attempts were once common in Romanesque churches farther west and north. Decorative painting shows also the dominance of Byzantine tradition into the 12th century; here, however, various local schools of illuminated manuscripts (*q.v.*) modified and freed mural decoration. Nevertheless, the chief aim was decorative rather than pictorial. Architectural members were richly patterned and wainscots painted with imitations of stone joints and hanging textiles, with little attempt at realism. Figures were painted flat, with little or no desire for light and shade, and arranged according to a purely decorative pattern; their size was frequently determined by relative importance or decorative necessity rather than any endeavour to achieve realism.

The Romanesque genius found one of its most congenial outlets in the decoration and illustration of books. As early as the 7th century, a vivid school of manuscript design had developed in Ireland and from there spread to the Scotch islands. The works of the school are marked by rich capitals, borders made of geometric interlaces, which often also cover the field of the page, and an occasional use of dragon's heads, birds and grotesque human figures. The complex beauty of these pages exerted a strong influence on later Romanesque work in many parts of Europe and Carolingian manuscripts show a combination of Celtic interlaces with classic motives and drawings inspired by late Roman manuscripts. Later, the intricate Celtic forms passed out of use, the Roman traditions were modified and naturalistic treatment appeared. By the beginning of the 12th century manuscripts in all the countries north of the Alps tended to resemble each other, and the figures show many of the characteristics of 12th century sculpture; the same dignity, decorative design and convincing emotional quality. Borders and ornamental initials had lost the intricate geometric shapes of the earlier period and the stylized leaves and flowers which were later to develop into the glories of Gothic illumination were beginning to appear.

South of the Alps manuscript decoration was following different lines. There, the influence of Byzantine manuscripts, with occasional reminiscences of classic work, remained dominant.

Romanesque metal work followed many of the same lines of development as Romanesque sculpture. In early work that of the Celtic countries was outstanding and magnificent silver-ware and jewellery were produced. Filigree (*q.v.*) was peculiarly congenial to the northern love of interlaces and complexities and was frequently applied, with excellent decorative effect, in small areas, to large, simple cups and chalices. (*See* Drinking Vessels.) Meanwhile, Byzantine church silver-ware and goldsmith's work was widely imported into Europe and exerted a strong influence upon the metal work of the later Romanesque times. (*See* Silversmiths' and Goldsmiths' Work.) Particularly important was the development in France of a famous school of enamel workers, who worked both in *cloisonné* and *champlevé*. (*See* Enamel.) Little of the early wrought iron remains, but the exquisite workmanship and powerful design of many 12th century grilles, door hinges, etc., give evidence of a tradition which must have existed

ARCHITECTURAL DETAILS OF THE ROMANESQUE PERIOD

1. Celtic cross of limestone from Monasterboice, Ireland (900–923?)

2. Church of the Madeleine (restored) at Vézelay, in central France. Built about 1130 by the Benedictine order. Central door of the narthex (enclosed porch) looking into the nave. The circular doorway, richly carved, with columns of varied design and recessed arches, is characteristic of the French Romanesque style

3. Columns and spring of the arches of a doorway in the Abbey of St. Denis, near Paris, begun 1137. The carving of the shafts as well as of the capitals of the columns, and the use of sculptured figures in the recesses of the arches, are features typical of the Romanesque and early Gothic periods

4. A side door of the narthex in the Church of the Madeleine, Vézelay (see fig. 2)

Plate II   ROMANESQUE ART

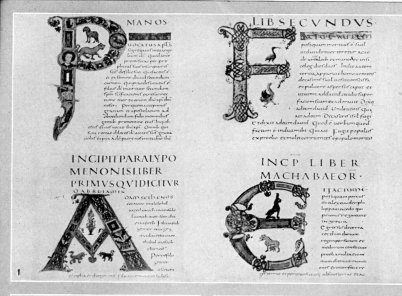

APPLIED ARTS OF THE ROMANESQUE PERIOD

1. A portion of the illuminated manuscript of the Alcuin Bible. English, 9th century. 2. An illuminated page from the "Lindisfarne Gospels" or the "Gospel of St. Cuthbert." English, about 700. 3. Reproduction of a Sicilian brocade of the Norman period (12th century). The design is in buff on a green ground, with the details in silver thread. 4. Processional cross of silver repoussé work and parcel-gilt on a wood core. Designed by Sanccia Guidisalvi, 12th century. 5. The (reputed) sword of Charlemagne in the Vienna Museum. 6. The chalice of Ardagh, of gold, 7" high; believed to be not later than the 10th century. 7. Reliquary or chasse of Limoges enamel (champlevé on copper). French, 12th or 13th century

for some time. In these 12th century examples the chief beauty comes from the expression of structure and the harmony of the decorative forms with their material. (*See* BRONZE AND BRASS.)

The popularity of Byzantine and Persian textiles in Romanesque Europe was a distinct hindrance to the formation of native schools of vital decorative textile design; in most cases products of Romanesque looms were the plainest and simplest materials for practical use. There was, on the other hand, a great deal of rich embroidery produced, of which the Bayeux tapestry (11th century) is the best known example. There are also, in many church sacristies, altar frontals and occasional vestments which reveal a similar skill in the medium and an even greater richness and decorative imagination. (*See* TEXTILES AND EMBROIDERIES; TAPESTRY.)   (T. F. H.)

ROMAN LAW. The term "Roman law" is one of somewhat indefinite meaning. It denotes first of all the law of the city of Rome and of the Roman empire. This in itself is an enormously wide subject, for it includes, in the west, the law in force at any period from the foundation of the city (traditional date 753 B.C.) until the fall of the Western empire in the 5th century A.D., and in the east, can be taken to include the law of the Eastern empire, until it too fell with the capture of Constantinople by the Turks in 1453; for the law even of the later Eastern empire remained, in spite of changes, more Roman in character than most other branches of its civilization.

But "Roman law" does not mean merely the law of those political societies to which the name Roman may in some sense be applied, for the legal institutions evolved by the Romans have had, not merely influence on those of other peoples, but in many cases actual application, in times long after the disappearance of the Roman empire as a political entity, and even in countries which were never subject to Roman rule. Thus, to take the most striking example, in a large part of Germany until the adoption of a common code for the whole empire in 1900, the Roman law was in force as "subsidiary law," *i.e.*, it was applied unless excluded by contrary local provisions. This law, however, which was in force in parts of Europe long after the fall of the Roman empire, was not the Roman law in its original form. Its basis was indeed always the *Corpus iuris civilis, i.e.*, the codifying legislation of the Emperor Justinian (A.D. 527–565, *see* below), but from the eleventh century onwards (*see* GLOSS; IRNERIUS, ACCURSIUS) this legislation was interpreted, developed and adapted to later conditions by generations of jurists, and necessarily received additions from non-Roman sources. All the forms which it assumed in different countries and at different epochs can also claim to be included under the title "Roman law."[1]

The importance of Roman law is, however, not confined to the actual application of its rules as such either in the Roman empire or elsewhere, for its influence on the development of law in general has been immense. Even to-day, if we look at the legal systems of peoples with a Western civilization, we can say that they fall (with some exceptions, especially the Scandinavian countries) into two groups—an' English group, and a group in which the main elements are of Roman origin. To the English group belong England, nearly all the United States of America, and most of the British dominions and colonies; to the Roman group belong the rest. The nations of the Continent are, nearly all of them, living to-day under Codes which, though they contain much that is not Roman, are Roman in their structure, their fundamental categories and their general method of thought. Within the British empire there is Scotland with a system fundamentally Roman, Quebec with its French law, built largely with Roman materials, and South Africa which, like Ceylon, has a system known as "Roman-Dutch," that is to say based on the Roman law as developed by the jurists of the Netherlands. Even English law itself, though owing less to Roman law than any other system, has at different times and in different ways received considerable accessions from Roman sources. (*See* ENGLISH LAW; and *e.g.*, Pollock and Maitland, *History of English Law* I. 88 *seq.*,

Holdsworth *History of English Law* II. 145–149, 176–178 IV. 228 *seq.*)

These developments however lie outside the scope of the article which is confined to the history of private law within the empire up to the death of Justinian.

Periods in the History of the Law.—Considerations of space make it impossible to discuss separately the different stages through which Roman law passed during the 13 centuries which elapsed between the foundation of the city and the death of Justinian, but some idea of the chief periods and their characteristics is essential for the understanding of what follows, and we may perhaps divide as follows:—

(*a*) *The Period of Conjecture.*—This includes the monarchy (753–510 B.C. according to tradition) and the republic up to the passing of the XII. Tables (451–450). For this period we have really no evidence but unreliable tradition and inference from later institutions.

(*b*) *The Mid-Republican Period, from the XII. Tables Until About the Middle of the Second Century B.C.*—Apart from fragments of the Tables and from the historians, who are of course chiefly of use for constitutional law, our evidence is not a great deal better than for the previous period when it comes to detail, and the history of law, like the rest of Roman history, suffers still from the destruction of records when Rome was burnt by the Gauls in or about 387 B.C. However we know of some laws passed, of the existence of certain legal institutions and the names of some famous lawyers, though no professedly legal work has survived, and indeed few were written. The period is pre-eminently one of the *ius civile,* as opposed both to the *ius honorarium* or magisterial law and to the *ius gentium,* in the sense to be explained below.

(*c*) *The Late Republican Period.*—For the last century and a half of the republic the position as regards evidence is already different. A few quotations from legal writers of the time survive in Justinian's digest; we have Cicero, in all of whose works there are numerous references to legal matters, and we have other non-legal literature from which information on law can be deduced. We have too the text of a few laws in inscriptions. The period is that in which magisterial edict comes to be the chief reforming factor in Roman law and it may thus be described as the period of the earlier *ius honorarium.* It was also the period in which the *ius gentium* began to be of importance, and these two facts are not unconnected, for it was probably through the medium of the Edicts that a large part of the *ius gentium* found its way into the law as administered between citizens.

Ius gentium is a difficult phrase to explain, because it has two distinct, though related, meanings, the one practical, the other theoretical. In the practical sense it means that part of the Roman law which was applied by the Romans both to themselves and to foreigners, while *ius civile,* as opposed to it, means that part which the Romans applied only to themselves. This dichotomy can only be explained historically. Roman law like other ancient systems, adopted originally the principle of personality, *i.e.* that the law of the state applied only to its citizens. The foreigner was strictly rightless, and unless protected by some treaty between his state and Rome could be seized, like an ownerless piece of property, by any Roman. But from early times there were treaties with foreign states guaranteeing mutual protection, and even where there was no treaty, the increasing commercial interests of Rome made it necessary for her to protect, by some form of justice, the foreigners who came within her borders. Now a magistrate charged with the administration of such justice could not simply apply Roman law, because that was the privilege of citizens, and even had there not been this difficulty, the foreigners, especially those coming from Greek cities and used to a more developed and freer system, would probably have objected to the cumbrous formalism which characterized the early *ius civile.*

What the magistrate in fact did, was to apply a system composed of the already existing "law merchant" of the Mediterranean peoples and a strong Roman flavouring, the Roman element being, however, purged to a large extent of its formalist elements. This system was also adopted when Rome began to have

[1]The term "civil law" is frequently used, in England at least, to denote the Roman system in this sense, as opposed to the native "common law."

provinces and her governors administered justice to the provincial *peregrini* (foreigners), a word which came to mean, not so much persons living under another government (of which, with the expansion of Roman power, there came to be fewer and fewer) as Roman subjects who were not citizens. The general principle adopted seems to have been to allow disputes between members of the same (subject) state to be settled by their own courts according to their own law, while the governor's courts applied *ius gentium* to disputes between the provincials of different states or between provincials and Romans. The law thus developed in its turn reacted on the law as administered between Romans, especially by way of making it less formal, with the result that to a considerable extent the two systems were identical, and this is true particularly of the law of contract. When therefore a Roman lawyer says that the contract of sale, for instance, is *iuris gentium,* he means that it is formed in the same way and has the same legal results whether the parties to it are citizens or not. This is the practical sense of *ius gentium,* but the idea is closely interwoven with a theoretical sense, that of a law common to all peoples and dictated by Nature which the Romans took from Greek philosophy.

Aristotle had already divided law into that which is natural (φυσικόν) and that which is man-made (νομικόν) and had asserted that the natural part was in force everywhere. This conception fitted well with the Stoic ideal of a life "according to nature," and became a commonplace which was borrowed by the Roman jurists, who, like other educated Romans, were much under the influence of the Stoic system. In their works this theoretical law of nature, "common to all mankind," then becomes identified with the really practical law which the Romans administered to all free men, irrespective of citizenship, simply on the basis of their freedom.

(d) *The Early Empire and the Classical Period.*—The change from republic to empire did not make any immediate difference to private law, except in so far as, bringing peace after a century of turmoil, it was favourable to legal progress. Legal literature, too, increased in volume and a number of quotations from authors of the first century survive in the Digest. This age in fact merges insensibly into the classical period, which is generally taken to include the second century A.D. and the early third century, and is thus considerably later than the classical period of Latin literature. It falls roughly into two divisions, an earlier one covered by the reigns of Hadrian (A.D. 117–138) and the Antonine emperors (death of Commodus A.D. 193) and a later one under the Severi (accession of Septimius Severus A.D. 193—death of Severus Alexander A.D. 235). Not that there is any break in the continuity of development, but the work of the earlier period was of a more creative character, while the later represents the working out of existing principles over the whole field of law. In the Digest there are quotations from all the authors of the classical age, but those taken from three writers of the later period (Papinian, Paul, Ulpian) alone comprise over half the work.

(e) *The Post-classical Period.*—With the era of confusion that followed the murder of Severus Alexander, there came a rather sudden falling off in the value of the legal work done, and the restoration of order by Diocletian (A.D. 284–305) did not revive legal literature. The law, of course, did not stand still. New ideas were introduced, especially from Greek sources, through the establishment of the Eastern empire with its capital at Constantinople, and through the growth of Christianity, while the great social and political changes of the sinking empire necessarily had their repercussions on private law. But it was not until the age just preceding Justinian that there was something of an intellectual revival in legal matters, and this revival Justinian was able to use for his great purpose.

SOURCES OF LAW

The Romans themselves divided their law into *ius scriptum* and *ius non scriptum;* by "unwritten law" they meant custom, by "written law," not only that derived from legislation, but, literally, that which was based on any source which was in writing and the list of written sources comprises *leges, plebiscita, senatus con-* *sulta, edicta magistratuum, responsa prudentium* and *constitutiones principum.* This list is repeated in Justinian's Institutes though ever since the close of the classical period the only source of new law (apart from custom) had been the emperor's constitutions.

A. **Ius Non Scriptum or Custom.**—Custom (*mos maiorum, consuetudo*) was recognized by the Romans not only as having been the original source of their law, but as a source from which new law could spring. The theory given by the jurists is that the people, by adopting a custom, show tacitly what they wish to be law, just as they might do expressly by voting in the assembly. In the developed law it would seem, however, that custom as an independent source was not very fruitful, and that it exercised its influence rather through the medium of juristic opinion and the practice of the courts.

B. **Ius Scriptum.**—(1) *Leges and Plebiscita.*—*Lex* is properly an enactment of one of the assemblies of the whole Roman people, the *comitia centuriata, tributa* or *curiata* (see COMITIA), but the most ancient of these, the *comitia curiata,* ceased, before the beginning of reliable history, to have any real political functions, though it continued right up to classical times to exist for certain formal purposes. The validity of *plebiscita, i.e.,* resolutions of the purely plebeian assembly, was one of the chief matters of contention between the patricians and plebeians, and the struggle between the orders may be said to come to an end in 287 B.C. when, by the *lex Hortensia, plebiscita* were given the force of *leges.* Thereafter enactments which were strictly *plebiscita* were often loosely referred to as *leges.*

Roman assemblies, like those of the Greek city states, were primary, *i.e.,* the citizen came and voted himself and did not send a delegate, but their power was restricted by the rule that only a magistrate could put a proposal before them and by the absence of any opportunity for amendment or debate. The only function of the people was to answer "yes" or "no" to the magistrate's "asking" (*rogatio*), and constitutional practice further required that the magistrate should consult the senate before putting a proposal to the assembly. In the later republic, at any rate, rejection of a bill was practically unknown and the real power lay with the senate and the magistrates.

Leges Regiae.—The historians have a good deal to say of *leges* passed in the time of the kings, but legislation at so early a date is unlikely. What they took for laws were probably statements of ancient custom from pontifical sources.

The XII. Tables.—Of greater importance are the XII. Tables, said to have been passed in 451–450 B.C., some 60 years after the expulsion of the kings. The accounts given by the historians of their compilation (*see* ROME: *Ancient History: The Republic*) are inconsistent and mainly mythical, but tradition is no doubt right in representing it as an incident in the struggle of the plebeians for political equality. The moving cause was a desire to obtain a written and public code which patrician magistrates could not wrest at their will against plebeian litigants. What weight should be given to that part of the story which tells of a preliminary embassy sent to Athens to study the laws of Solon, has been much debated. That the embassy itself is legendary can hardly be doubted, but on the other hand, that there was some Greek influence is clear. (See, *e.g.,* Tab. VII. 2–D. 10.1.13.) In the main, however, the materials of the code were taken from native customary sources. The authenticity of the whole compilation has been attacked in recent times, but the most authoritative modern opinion holds, in spite of all scepticism as to details, that the XII. Tables really were an enacted code of law, and that tradition is not far wrong in ascribing them to the middle of the fifth century B.C.

The text of the code has not survived, a remarkable fact, for copies (probably in more or less modernized language) must have been abundant in Cicero's time if, as he says (De Leg. 2, 23, 59) it was still customary in his youth for boys to learn it by heart. All that we have is a number of "fragments" which have had to be collected from allusions and quotations in the works of various authors, *e.g.,* Cicero. (Modern collections are to be found in Bruns' *Fontes iuris Romani antiqui,* 7th ed., 1919, Girard's *Textes de droit Romain,* 5th ed., Paris, 1923, and Riccobono's

Fontes iuris Romani anteiustiniani.)

On the establishment of the empire by Augustus, the assemblies did not immediately cease to function, but their assent to any proposal was a mere formal ratification of the emperor's wishes. The last *lex* known to have been passed was a *lex agraria* under Nerva (A.D. 96–98).

Senatus Consulta.—The senate acquired legislative power in early imperial times though this was never conferred on it by any imperial enactment. The resolution of the senate preceding the placing of a bill before the people had always been practically decisive, and with the decay of the *comitia* their assent evidently came to be regarded as a formality which might be omitted. Actually, the senate nearly always, if not always, legislated at the instigation of the emperor, latterly, indeed, simply embodying his *oratio* or proposal in a resolution, and not long after the classical period, the emperors ceased to use the senate as a vehicle of their legislation.

Edicta Magistratuum.—An edict is a proclamation, originally no doubt oral, later in writing, and any superior magistrate might find it necessary to issue such edicts regarding matters which came within his competence. A peculiarity of Roman law, however, is that the magistrates entrusted with jurisdiction made particular use of this power and that their edicts became one of the most important sources of law. Originally the duty of *iurisdictio*, which means supervising the administration of justice rather than actually deciding cases (*see* p. 454, "Procedure") had presumably lain with the king, from whom it descended to the consuls. With the growth of business it became impossible for the consuls to discharge this duty in addition to their other functions and in 367 B.C. a new magistrate, the *praetor,* was appointed for the purpose. About the year 242 B.C. the increase of foreigners at Rome made it necessary to separate the conduct of suits in which they were concerned from those to which citizens alone were parties, and a second praetor, *praetor peregrinus,* was appointed to deal with cases in which a foreigner was involved. In contradistinction to him, the original praetor, now confined to suits between citizens, came to bear the title *urbanus*[1].

Other judicial officers at Rome whose edicts were of importance were the curule aediles, whose duties included the supervision of the market place. In the provinces supreme judicial power lay with the governors, and quaestors carried out functions analogous to those of the aediles at Rome. The law derived from the edicts of all these magistrates was called *ius honorarium,* as opposed to *ius civile* in the sense of law based on legislation or custom, but owing to the pre-eminent position of the praetors, the phrase is often used simply as equivalent to *ius praetorium.* The nature of this magisterial law is peculiar. The praetor was not a legislator, and he could not therefore make law directly as could the sovereign people, but the Roman system of procedure (especially the formulary system, *see* p. 454) gave him a great power over the provision or refusal of remedies as well as over the form which remedies were to take, and consequently the edict which he issued at the beginning of his term of office setting out what he intended to do was a document of the greatest importance. In it he could say, for instance, "If one man makes such and such an allegation against another, *I will give an action,"* even though the circumstances alleged would not give any right at civil law. The edict called *perpetuum* (continuous) because it was intended to announce the principles by which the praetor would be governed throughout his year of office, necessarily ceased to have any validity when that term expired, but it became the practice for each succeeding praetor to take over and reissue as his own much of his predecessor's edict, and by the end of the republic, the part which was thus carried on from year to year (*tralaticium*) must have been considerable, for jurists were just beginning to write commentaries on the edict, a practice which would not have been worth while if the greater part of it had been liable to annual alteration.

[1]This is the usual story, but the historians in an endeavour to reconcile discordant tradition may have read back into early times the institutions of their own day. *See* E. Pais, *Ricerche sulla Storia,* etc. Serie iv. (1921), 265 *seq.*

The change from republic to empire did not immediately make any difference, and the praetors continued to issue their edicts (though we may doubt whether they ever made changes without imperial or senatorial authority), but in the long run their wide powers were evidently felt to be inconsistent with the emperor's supremacy. Hadrian consequently, in or about A.D. 131, instructed the famous jurist Salvius Iulianus to revise and settle the praetorian and aedilician edicts. The changes in substance do not appear to have been of a far-reaching character, but the edict as revised was henceforward made unalterable except by the emperor himself.

The relationship between *ius honorarium* and *ius civile* has often been compared with that existing in England between common law and equity. In both cases we find, as Maine put it (*Ancient Law,* p. 25) a "body of rules existing by the side of the original civil law, founded on distinct principles, and claiming incidentally to supersede the civil law in virtue of a superior sanctity inherent in these principles," and in both cases the resulting duality enormously complicates the law, but, of course, when we come to detail the comparison no longer holds.

Responsa Prudentium.—The force attributed to professional opinions of a certain type was another peculiar feature of the Roman system, and one which contributed in no small measure to its success, for it was the "learned lawyers" (*prudentes*) to whom the moulding of the law into a coherent system was really due.

Originally, according to an entirely credible tradition, law was considered the special province of the *pontifices* (see PONTIFEX), who seem to have regarded it as a mystery to be exploited in the interests of their order. Their monopoly was however broken down, according to legend, in 304 B.C., by Gn. Flavius, a clerk of Appius Claudius Caecus, who is said to have stolen from his master and made public, a list of *legis actiones* (*i.e.,* forms of words which had to be followed exactly in the conduct of lawsuits), thereafter known as the *ius Flavianum.* The first known legal treatise, called the "cradle of the law" by Pomponius, is the *Tripertita* of Sextus Aelius Paetus Catus (consul 198 B.C.) which contained the text of the XII. Tables, the *interpretatio* put upon it by the jurists and the *legis actiones.* Probably the last part was identical with the *ius Aelianum* which, according to Pomponius, was a collection of *legis actiones* like the earlier *ius Flavianum.*

It is plain in any case that from about 300 B.C. onwards there came into existence a class of men who made the study of the law their special interest. These *iuris consulti* or *iuris prudentes* were not professional lawyers in the modern sense, but men of rank who sought by giving free legal advice to obtain popularity and advancement in a public career. The *responsa* (answers) which they delivered to those who consulted them were of greater weight than are our modern "opinions of counsel" because the person who actually decided a case under the Roman system of procedure was not, as with us, a trained lawyer, but a lay *iudex,* who did not, like our jurymen, have a judge to direct him on points of law. Augustus empowered certain jurists to give *responsa* with the emperor's authority, and this practice led, perhaps by insensible degrees, to the view that the *iudex* was bound to abide by the *responsum* of a jurist who had received this *ius respondendi.* Gaius at any rate mentions a rescript of Hadrian which laid down that *responsa* were binding if they agreed, and that if they disagreed, the *iudex* could decide for himself which to follow. (*See* Wlassak, *Die klassische Prozessformel,* p. 45.)

The practice of conferring the *ius respondendi* appears to have fallen into disuse about the end of the third century A.D. when the classical period was over, but in the meanwhile, *responsa* had certainly come to be regarded as binding not only for the case for which they were originally given, but also as precedents for future cases, and, further, authority gradually came to be attached to the other writings of those jurists who had the emperor's patent. The "law of citations," an imperial enactment of 426, ultimately laid down that only the works of five jurists, Papinian, Paul, Gaius, Ulpian and Modestinus, might be cited and, subject to some provisos which are obscure, the works of authors quoted by these five. If the authorities cited disagreed, the majority was to be followed; if numbers were equal, the side on which Papinian stood was to prevail; if he was silent, the *iudex* might please himself.

For the long succession of jurists reference must be made to the individual articles, but mention must be made here of the two "schools," the Sabinians (or Cassians) and the Proculians, into which they were divided in the early empire. Labeo (died between A.D. 10 and A.D. 22), one of the greatest figures in the history of jurisprudence, was the founder of the Proculians (who, however, took their name from a successor, Proculus); Capito, that of the Sabinians (so called from Massurius Sabinus, who was given the *ius respondendi* by Tiberius). What principles, if any, divided these schools, is unknown, though a number of controversies on particular points are preserved, especially in Gaius' Institutes. It is probable, though by no means certain, that there were teaching establishments or societies of some sort in connection with the "schools," for otherwise the list of "heads" given by Pomponius would be difficult to explain. The distinction does not seem to have survived the Antonine age; for Gaius, a Sabinian, is the last jurist of whom we know that he belonged to one or other of the schools.

Constitutiones Principum.—Neither Augustus nor his immediate successors expressly assumed legislative power, and yet Gaius, writing about A.D. 160, can say "there has never been any doubt that what the emperor lays down has the force of law." Ulpian, indeed, refers the validity of constitutions to the so-called *lex regia,* passed at the beginning of each emperor's reign; and there is indeed in the only surviving example of such a *lex* (the *lex de imperio Vespasiani* line 17 seq., see Bruns *Fontes* p. 202) a clause conferring such wide powers on the emperor that legislation might be deemed to be included. Nevertheless it is now generally held that this was not the original meaning of the clause and that the emperor's legislative power is a gradual growth. The chief forms of imperial legislation were:—(*a*) *Edicta, i.e.,* proclamations which the emperor, like other magistrates, might issue; but whereas the other magistrates were confined to their own spheres, the sphere of the emperor was in fact unlimited. (*b*) *Mandata, i.e.,* instructions to subordinates, especially provincial governors. (*c*) *Rescripta,* written answers to officials or others who have consulted the emperor, in particular on a point of law. In such cases the rescript lays down the point of law applicable and, since the emperor is supreme, the rule may be a new one. (*d*) *Decreta, i.e.,* decisions of the emperor sitting as a judge. Here too the emperor may lay down a new rule.

The Earlier Collections of Constitutions and the Legislation of Justinian.—The growth of legal literature and especially of imperial constitutions created a need for works of reference which made itself felt long before Justinian, and a beginning was made, almost certainly in Diocletian's day, by a collection of constitutions known as the *codex Gregorianus,* which was followed by the *codex Hermogenianus,* perhaps also dating in its original form from Diocletian. Both collections were unofficial, but their compilers must have had official countenance, for they clearly had access to the imperial archives. The *Gregorianus* contained constitutions from Hadrian to Diocletian, the *Hermogenianus* almost exclusively those of Diocletian's time; later constitutions attributed to it were probably only added in subsequent editions. It was clearly intended to supplement the *Gregorianus.* Unlike these two, the *codex Theodosianus* was an official work compiled by a commission appointed under Theodosius II. and Valentinian III., it was given the force of law as from Jan. 1, 439. Constitutions from the time of Constantine the Great onwards were, with very few exceptions, not to be valid unless contained in it. For the earlier imperial legislation the older *codices* still had to serve. Nearly the whole of the *codex Theodosianus* has been preserved, whereas we only have fragments of the others. Theodosius had also planned a collection which would include juristic literature as well as imperial legislation, but this never came to fruition until it was taken up again by Justinian.

Justinian's Legislation.—(*See* also JUSTINIAN I.) Justinian's main object was, as he himself expresses it, to clear the path of legal authorities of the tangles with which it had become overgrown during the course of centuries, and he set about the task almost immediately on ascending the throne. It must be noted however that he was no mere codifier, but also the author of much new legislation, some of which was of the utmost importance for the later development of law. The emperor was no doubt largely responsible himself for the work undertaken, but it would probably not have been possible to carry it through but for the genius of his chief minister, Tribonian, who was clearly the leading spirit throughout the work. The course of legislation was as follows:—

(1) *The Old Codex.*—In Feb. 528, a commission of ten members including Tribonian (who, however, was not president) was appointed to compile a new collection of imperial constitutions which was to supersede the older ones entirely and, of course, to include legislation subsequent to the Theodosian. The commissioners were to cut out repetitions and contradictions and had large powers of alteration for this purpose. The work was rapidly done and published in April 529, with the force of law as from the 16th. It has not survived as it was later superseded.

(2) *The "Fifty Decisions."*—Justinian, probably partly with a view to facilitating the work of compiling the Digest, issued a number of constitutions settling matters on which the writings of the classical jurists disagreed and abolishing finally some institutions and distinctions which had ceased to be of practical importance. Some 90 constitutions of this character are known to us, but a collection of 50 seems to have been made and published separately. Its exact date cannot be determined.

(3) *The Digest.* (*Digesta or Pandectae*).—Instructions were given on Dec. 15, 530, to Tribonian to form a commission to collect excerpts from the works of the jurists. The collection was to serve practical purposes and consequently everything obsolete or superfluous was to be cut out and, where necessary to bring the matter up to date, alterations were to be made in the text. The excerpts were to be arranged in fifty books and the books into titles according to the subject matter, and the whole was to include all that it was necessary to know of juristic as opposed to imperial law. The compilers were definitely instructed not to adopt the summary methods of the "law of citations" but where the authorities disagreed, to choose what they thought best for themselves. The commission, consisting of 16 members in addition to Tribonian, rapidly completed their task and the Digest was published on Dec. 16, 533, with the force of law as from Dec. 30. Thenceforth no reference might be made to any other text for juristic law. Justinian gives us some idea of the work involved when he says that 2,000 books consisting of 3,000,000 lines were read and that this number was then reduced to 150,000 lines. The Digest is the most important of Justinian's works, for in it are preserved the writings of the classical jurists who were really responsible for the greatness of Roman law, and the "inscription" at the head of each quotation enables us to see from which jurist and from which work it is taken. But of course as evidence for the classical law quotations must be used with care, for the compilers made considerable use of their powers of alteration; much ingenuity, especially within the last 50 years, has gone to the discovery of their "interpolations."

The Institutes.—The revision of the law by Justinian was accompanied by a detailed scheme for the reform of legal education in the universities of Constantinople and Berytus, and one of the requirements of this scheme was a new book to be used for elementary instruction instead of the Institutes of Gaius which had for centuries been the standard work. While the Digest was still unpublished therefore orders were given to Tribonian and two professors to compile a manual for this purpose, and the Institutes were published on Nov. 21, 533, and given the force of law. The work is based on Gaius' Institutes, from which a great part is copied literally, as well as on other elementary works of the classical period; occasional references to imperial legislation are added. It is in fact almost as much a compilation as the Digest, but the references to the authors quoted are omitted and the whole made to read like a lecture delivered by the emperor to his students.

The New Code (Codex Repetitae Praelectionis).—The 50 decisions and the many other new constitutions promulgated since 529 necessitated a revision of the old codex and Tribonian, together with four others, was instructed shortly after the publication of the Digest, to prepare a new edition. This was published on Nov. 16, 534, and given the force of law as from Dec. 29.

The Novels.—Although the new code completed Justinian's scheme for providing a collection of authoritative legal texts, he did not cease to introduce new legislation. In all 175 laws published after 534 are known and these are called *Novellae Constitutiones* or Novels. Nearly all are in Greek, which was becoming more and more the official as well as the spoken language of the Byzantine Empire. Justinian never made any official compilation of them, but three private collections have come down to us, and the Novels, together with the Institutes, the Digest and the (new) Code together form what is known as the *Corpus Iuris Civilis*.

THE LAW OF PERSONS

I. Slavery.—"The main distinction in the law of persons," says Gaius, "is that all men are either free or slaves." The slave according to Roman law was in principle a human chattel who could be owned and dealt with like any other piece of property. As a piece of property the slave was not only at the mercy of his owner, but rightless, and (apart from criminal law) dutyless. This is the principle, but if the slave was, in law, a thing, he was, in fact, a man, and this fact produced modifications of the principle. In particular, a slave might be manumitted and would then become in most cases not only free but a citizen.

II. Citizenship.—This was of importance for the purposes of private law, because certain parts of private law applied only to citizens (*ius civile*). The general rule was that, if the status of the parents differed, the child followed that of the father, if the union was one recognized as marriage by Roman law; otherwise that of its mother, but a *lex Minicia* of republican times enacted that in cases of unrecognized unions between citizens and foreigners the child should always follow the inferior parent. The great extension of the citizenship by Caracalla in A.D. 212 reduced the importance of this part of the law.

III. Family.—(a) *Patria potestas*. The chief characteristic of the Roman family is the famous *patria potestas* which the father exercised over his children and over his more remote descendants in the male line, whatever their age might be, as well as over those brought into the family by adoption—a very common practice at Rome. This meant originally not only that he had control over the persons of his children, amounting even to a right to inflict capital punishment, but that he alone had any rights in private laws. Thus any acquisitions made by a child under power became the property of the father. The father might indeed allow a child (as he might a slave) certain property (*peculium*) to treat as his own, but in the eye of the law it continued to belong to the father. In classical times there were already modifications of the system; the father's power of life and death had shrunk to that of slight chastisement, and the son could bind his father by contract with a third party within the same strict limits as applied to slaves and their masters. Sons too could keep as their own what they earned as soldiers (*peculium castrense*) and even make wills of it. In Justinian's day the position as regards property had changed considerably; what the father gave to the son still remained in law the father's property, but the rules of *peculium castrense* had been extended to many sorts of professional earnings (*pec. quasi castrense*) and in all other sorts of acquisitions (*e.g.*, property inherited from the mother) the father's rights were reduced to a life-interest (usufruct). At all times *Patria potestas* ceased normally only with the death of the father, but the father might voluntarily free the child by *emancipation*, and a daughter ceased to be under her father's *potestas* if she was married in such a way as to come under the *manus* of her husband.

(b) *Marriage*.—There were two types of marriage known to the law, one with *manus* and one without, but the former was rare already in the late republic and had disappeared long before Justinian's day. *Manus* was the autocratic power of the husband over the wife, corresponding to *patria potestas* over the sons, and

it might result in any of three ways:—

(1) by *confarreatio*, a religious ceremony confined to patricians.

(2) by *coemptio*, a type of *mancipation* (*see* below) which was originally no doubt the Roman form of marriage by purchase; it was purely secular.

(3) *usus;* if a woman lived with a man as his wife for a year, he acquired *manus* over her by a kind of prescription. The XII. Tables had already provided that this might be prevented if the woman absented herself for a space of three nights during the year (*usurpatio trinoctii*). *Usus* was already quite obsolete in classical times.

It may be that at one time marriage with *manus* was the only form of union recognized as marriage at all, but by the time of the XII. Tables this was apparently no longer the case, for it is clear that the *usurpatio trinoctii*, though it prevented *manus*, left the marriage subsisting, so that it was possible to be married without *manus*.

In any case marriage without *manus* was by far the more common in all periods of which we have any real knowledge. It was formed (provided the parties were above the age of puberty and if under *potestas* had their fathers' consent) simply by the beginning of conjugal life with the intention of being married, and this was normally evidenced by the bringing of the bride to the bridegroom's house. It was however legally independent of all ceremonies whether pagan or Christian which might accompany it, and of consummation. The wife remained under her father's *potestas* if he were still alive, if he were dead, she continued (so long as guardianship of women continued) to have the same guardian as before marriage. It was necessary that both spouses should be citizens, or if one was not, that he or she should have *conubium*, the right given to some non-Romans of contracting a Roman marriage. The chief importance of this was that if a Roman contracted a union with a foreign woman, the children would not be in his *potestas* unless she had *conubium*. In marriage without *manus* the property of the spouses remained entirely distinct, and even gifts between husband and wife were invalid. It was usual however for a dowry to be given to the husband on the marriage by the woman or her father; this originally became the indefeasible property of the husband, but in classical times already the wife could recover it if the marriage ended by divorce or by the husband's death, and by Justinian's legislation it had always to be returned to the wife or her heirs.

Divorce was always possible at the instance of the husband in cases of marriage with *manus*, and in marriage without *manus* it was free to either party to put an end to the relationship at will; a letter of *repudium* was usual, but any manifestation of intention to end the relationship made clear to the other party and accompanied by actual parting was all that was legally necessary (*see* E. Levy, *Der Hergang bei der römischen Ehescheidung*). The Christian emperors imposed penalties on those who divorced without good reason, but the power of the parties to end the marriage by their own act was not taken away. *Concubinatus* was recognized in the empire as a sort of morganatic marriage, differing from marriage only by the different intentions of the parties, and excluding marriage, for a man could not have both a wife and a concubine. Constantine first enacted that the children of such unions might be legitimated by the subsequent marriage of their parents, a rule which the mediaeval civil law extended to all illegitimate children.

(c) *Guardianship*.—(1) Of children. Persons under the age of puberty (14 for males, 12 for females) needed *tutores* if they were not under *patria potestas*. Such tutors could be appointed under the will of the *pater familias;* failing such appointment the guardianship went to the nearest agnates (*see* p. 453 "Succession") until Justinian gave it to the next of kin whether agnatic or cognatic; if there were no qualified relation the magistrates made an appointment.

(2) Of women. Originally all women not under *patria potestas* or *manus* needed *tutores*, who were appointed in the same way as those for children. In classical times already this *perpetua tutela mulierum* was little more than a burdensome technicality and it had long disappeared from Justinian's law.

(3) Of lunatics and spendthrifts. Originally such persons were placed under the *cura* of their agnates; later, magistrates appointed curators.

(4) Of minors. Originally children were considered adult when of the age of puberty, but, by a long development, it became usual for those above puberty and under 25 to have *curatores* who were always magisterially appointed.

PROPERTY AND POSSESSION

The most striking thing to an English lawyer accustomed to the complexities of English real property law is the absence of any fundamental distinction between the treatment of land and the treatment of movables. Both can, in the law as we know it, be owned absolutely by individuals, though there may have been a time at Rome as elsewhere when land was subject to communal ownership of some sort. This conception of absolute ownership (*dominium*) is also characteristically Roman, as opposed to the relative idea of ownership as the better right to possession which underlies the Germanic systems, which also, originally, underlay that of Rome. This can be seen by comparing the form of a *vindicatio* (the claim of an owner out of possession) under the *legis actio* system of procedure with that which it later assumed under the formulary system. In the earlier system the plaintiff first makes his assertion of ownership ("I say that this thing is mine") and then the defendant makes a similar assertion. Finally, the thing goes to the one whose assertion is based on the better right. Under the later system there is no assertion by the defendant at all; the *iudex* is instructed to condemn the defendant if it appears to him that the thing belongs to the plaintiff, otherwise to absolve the defendant. Hence, unless the plaintiff makes good his title absolutely, the defendant, though he may have no title at all, remains in possession.

A great part of what the jurists have to say on the subject of property comes under the heading "methods of acquiring ownership." These were divided into two classes according as they fell under the *ius civile* or the *ius gentium*.

I. **Methods of the Ius Civile** (a) *Mancipatio.*—This was a ceremonial conveyance needing for its accomplishment the presence of the tranferor and transferee, five witnesses (Roman citizens of full age) a pair of scales, a man to hold them (*libripens*) and an ingot of copper. The transferee grasped the thing and said: "I assert that this thing is mine by Quiritarian law; and be it bought to me with this piece of copper and these copper scales." He then struck the scales with the ingot which he handed to the transferor "by way of price." Clearly this was, as Gaius says, a "symbolical sale," and the relic of a real sale. Originally, when money was unknown, the price in uncoined copper had been really weighed out to the vendor. When this became unnecessary there was still a pretence of weighing, but the price was paid separately, and the form could be used as a conveyance where it was not intended that a price should be paid at all, *e.g.*, because the transferor was making a gift to the transferee.

(b) *In Iure Cessio.*—This was a conveyance in the form of a lawsuit. The transferee claims before the magistrate that the thing is his, and the transferor who is the defendant, admits the claim. The magistrate then adjudges the thing to the transferee.

(c) *Usucapio.*—According to the XII. Tables, two years' continuous possession gave title in the case of land, one year in the case of movables. In the developed law, possession must have begun in good faith, the thing must not be one which has been stolen (even though the possessor himself is quite innocent of the theft) or occupied by violence (this applies especially to land, which could not be stolen) and the possession must have had a justifiable beginning (*iustus titulus*). Usucapio, being an institution of the *ius civile* was possible only to citizens, but Justinian fused it with a similar institution (*praescriptio longi temporis*) which had grown up in the provinces. Under his system, three years were required for movables, 10 or 20 for land.

II. **Methods of the Ius Gentium** (a) *Occupatio.*—Ownerless things, provided they are capable of private ownership (not, *e.g.*, *res sacrae*, such as temples) became the property of the first person to take possession of them. This applies *e.g.*, to game, and to articles which have been abandoned or left unattended by their owners.

(b) *Accessio.*—If an accessory thing belonging to A was joined to a principal one belonging to B, the ownership in the whole went to B, *e.g.*, if A's purple be used to dye B's cloth, the dyed cloth belongs wholly to B. By far the most important application of this rule is expressed by the maxim *superficies solo cedit, i.e.*, whatever is built on land becomes part of the land and cannot be separately owned.

(c) *Specificatio.*—If A made a thing out of material belonging to B the Proculians held that ownership went to A, the Sabinians, that it remained in B. Justinian adopted a famous "middle opinion," according to which B retained ownership if reconversion to the original condition was possible (a bronze vase can be melted down), A obtained ownership if it was not (wine cannot be reconverted into grapes).

(d) *Thesauri Inventio.*—The final rule as regards treasure trove was that if it were found by a man on his own land, it went to him; if on that of another, half went to the finder, half to the landowner.

(e) *Traditio, i.e.*, simple delivery of possession with the intention of passing ownership. This was the method of conveyance of the *ius gentium*. It sufficed to pass full Quiritarian ownership of *res nec mancipi*, but not of *res mancipi* (land in Italy, slaves, beasts of draft and burden, and certain rustic servitudes) for which either *mancipatio* or *in iure cessio* was necessary. If therefore A sold and merely delivered a slave to B, A remained at civil law owner of the slave until usucapion had taken place. The praetor however devised methods of protecting B's possession in such a way that A's title became valueless, and B was said to have the thing *in bonis*. From this phrase later writers coined the expression "bonitarian" ownership. Already before Justinian's day *mancipatio* and *in iure cessio* had become obsolete and Justinian took the final step of abolishing the theoretical distinction between Quiritarian and "bonitarian" ownership.

Forms of Property in Land Other Than Ownership.—The ordinary leaseholder according to Roman law had no protection beyond a contractual right against his landlord, and he could not assign his tenancy, but there were two kinds of tenure which, under the praetorian system, obtained protection against third parties as well, and became assignable. These were *superficies* and *emphyteusis;* the former resulting from building leases granted for a long term or in perpetuity, the latter from similar agricultural leases. Both appear to have first originated in grants by the State, or municipalities. Under *emphyteusis* the grantee did not become owner, though he enjoyed a *jus in re aliena* hardly distinguishable from ownership.

Servitudes.—(a) *Praedial servitudes* (*i.e.*, easements or *profits à prendre*) were divided into two categories, rustic and urban, according as they served the need of agricultural land or of buildings. Thus rights of way and of water are usually classed as rustic, while rights to light, to view or to support were urban. Praedial servitudes could only be appurtenant, *i.e.*, they could not exist except as additional advantages attached to the ownership of a piece of land (the "dominant tenement").

(b) *Personal Servitudes.*—The law of Justinian's day brought under the heading of servitudes also the rights of *usufructus* and *usus*. Usufruct was the right to use and take the fruits (*e.g.*, crops) of a thing and corresponded to our life-interest. *Usus* was a more restricted right, also not extending beyond the life of the holder, merely to the use of a thing; thus the usuary of a house could live in it himself but could not let it, as that would be equivalent to taking the fruits.

Possession.—Implied in the absolute conception of ownership is a sharp distinction between ownership and possession. The civil law did not protect possession as such, but one of the most important parts of the praetorian system was constituted by the *interdicta* (special types of remedy) which protected an existing possession irrespective of its rightfulness, *i.e.*, anyone wishing to interfere with it must bring an action and prove his title. If he interfered on his own authority, the praetor would see that the original state of affairs was restored.

OBLIGATIONS

Obligations were classified by the jurists into two main categories, according as they arose from delict (tort) or contract: the remaining obligations the Byzantines placed under the headings of quasi-contract and quasi-delict.

I. Delict.—The XII. Tables already show the law in a state of transition from the system of private vengeance to that in which the state insists on the acceptance of compensation instead of vengeance by the person wronged and fixes its amount. Thus in the case of assault (*iniuria*) if one man broke another's limb, talion was still permitted, *i.e.*, the person wronged could inflict the same injury as he had received, but in other cases there were fixed money penalties, *e.g.*, 25 *asses* for a blow. Theft involved a penalty of twice the value of the thing stolen, unless the thief was caught in the act (*furtum manifestum*) in which case he was flogged and "adjudged" to the person wronged.

In classical times, praetorian reforms had substituted a four-fold penalty in the case of *furtum manifestum* and penalties for *iniuria* (which now included defamation and insulting behaviour) were assessed in each case by the court. The law of damage to property was regulated by a statute (*lex Aquilia*) dating from the republic, but later than the XII. Tables, much extended by interpretation and by the praetor, and praetorian actions lay for a number of new delicts of varying importance.

II. Contract.—At the time of the XII. Tables a law of contract can hardly be said to have existed, though we know of an institution called *nexum* of which hardly anything can be said with certainty except that it was a kind of loan so oppressive in character that it might result in the debtor's complete subjection to the creditor. It was obsolete long before classical times. The contracts of classical law were divided into four classes, literal, verbal, real and consensual. The literal contract was a type of fictitious loan formed by an entry in the creditor's account book; it was comparatively unimportant, and obsolete in Justinian's day. The verbal contract or *stipulatio* was of great importance, for it provided a form in which any agreement (provided it was lawful and possible) might be made binding by the simple method of reducing it to question and answer, *e.g.*, "do you promise to pay me ten thousand sesterces?"—"I promise." Originally it was absolutely necessary that the words should be spoken, but it may be said (technicalities apart) that by Justinian's day a written memorandum of such a contract would be binding, even though in fact there had been no speaking at all. If an agreement was not clothed in the form of a stipulation, it must, to be valid, fall, according to its content, under one of the types of real, or consensual contracts. A real contract is one which needs for its conclusion (in addition to the consent of the parties) that some thing should be transferred from one party to the other and that the obligation arising should be for the return of the thing transferred. The real contracts are *mutuum* (loan, *e.g.*, of money), *commodatium* (loan, *e.g.*, of a horse), deposit and pledge. Consensual contracts need no element for their formation except agreement—whether expressed in words or otherwise—between the parties, and though there were only four such known to the law, these were the most important in ordinary life—*emptio venditio* (sale), *locatio conductio* (hire of things or services and also giving out jobs to be done), *societas* (partnership) and *mandatum* (agency). In Justinian's day it was further a principle that in any case of reciprocal agreement, *e.g.*, an agreement for exchange (which was not sale), if one party had performed, he could bring an action to enforce performance by the other ("innominate contract").

SUCCESSION AT DEATH

I. Testamentary Succession.—That wills existed already at the time of the XII. Tables is certain, and it is highly probable that the form used was still that mentioned by Gaius as the oldest, the will made publicly in the assembly of the *curiae* (*testamentum comitiis calatis*), with the will made before the people drawn up for battle (*testamentum in procinctuas*) as a variant. It may be however that the mancipatory will (*testamentum per aes et libram*) had already been invented. This began as an expedient for effecting the purposes of a will in an emergency, when the other forms were impossible, and consisted in the use of mancipation to convey the estate of the dying man to a kind of trustee (*familiae emptor*) who then distributed it in accordance with the testator's instructions. By the end of the republic, however, the older forms had disappeared, the mancipation had become a mere formality and the instructions of the testator, which were now contained in a written document, constituted a true will, operative only at death and revocable at any time during the testator's lifetime by the making of a new will. In post-classical times the mancipation had ceased to be necessary and the commonest form of will was the *testamentum tripertitum*, needing for its completion the seals of seven witnesses and the signatures of the witnesses and of the testator. In classical times the praetor had already given effect in most cases to a document sealed by seven witnesses.

The first requirement of any Roman will of historical times was the appointment of one or more *heredes*. A *heres* is a universal successor, *i.e.*, he takes over the rights and duties of the deceased (in so far as they are transmissible at all) as a whole. On acceptance, the heir becomes owner where the deceased was owner, creditor where he was creditor and debtor where he was debtor, even though the assets were insufficient to pay the debts. It was thus possible for an inheritance to be *damnosa*, *i.e.*, to involve the heir in loss. Until Justinian's day this consequence could only be avoided by not accepting the inheritance, but Justinian made one of his most famous reforms by introducing the *beneficium inventarii*, *i.e.*, the heir who, within a certain time after the acceptance made an inventory of the deceased's assets, need not pay out more than he had received. In addition to appointing an heir, the testator might also leave legacies, *i.e.*, particular gifts which are a burden on the heir. Freedom of testation was, however, not complete, a man being obliged to leave a certain proportion of his property to his children and, in some cases, to ascendants, and brothers and sisters.

II. Intestate Succession.—The history of intestate succession consists broadly in the gradual supersession of a purely agnatic system (*i.e.*, one which takes account of relationship through males exclusively) by a cognatic system (in which relationship is traced indifferently through males or females). The agents in the change were first the praetors and afterwards imperial legislation.

By the XII. Tables those first entitled were the *sui heredes* of the deceased, *i.e.*, those who were in his *potestas* or *manus* when he died and became free from power at his death. Failing these, the nearest agnatic relation (or relations, if there were several of the same degree) succeeded, and, if there were no agnates, the members of the *gens* (clan) of the deceased. Praetorian reforms placed emancipated children on an equality with *sui* and gave to the nearest cognates, or failing such, to the surviving spouse (in marriage without *manus*) rights of succession in the absence of agnates; gentile succession became obsolete probably in the first century A.D. Even under this system it will be seen that a woman would not succeed to a child of hers if any agnate (*e.g.*, a paternal uncle) were alive, nor a child to its mother if there were any agnate of hers. Both these cases were dealt with before the end of the classical period, the former by the *Sc. Tertullianum* (under Hadrian) which gave certain rights of succession to mothers who had the *ius liberorum* (*i.e.*, had borne three children) and the latter by the *Sc. Orphitianum* of A.D. 178, which gave to children the first right to succeed to their mothers. Succeeding emperors made many changes but it was not until Justinian's day that the cognatic system completely triumphed. By Novel 118, completed by Novel 127, a new system was introduced, the principal features of which were the following: Descendants had the first claim, and failing these, a composite class consisting of ascendants, brothers and sisters of the full blood, and children of deceased brothers and sisters. Next came brothers and sisters of the half blood and finally the nearest cognate or cognates if there were several in the same degree.

Husband and wife were not mentioned, but their old (praetorian) rights were kept alive in the absence of any of the above categories. Justinian also gave to the poor widow a right to one quarter of her husband's estate unless there were more than three children, in which case she shared equally with them. If, however, the heirs were her own children by the deceased, she only received the usufruct (life interest) in what she took.

PROCEDURE

The earliest form of procedure known to have existed is that of the *legis actiones;* this was superseded by the formulary system, which in its turn, gave way to *cognitio extraordinaria.* Characteristic of both the earlier systems is the division into two stages, a preliminary one before the jurisdictional magistrate (*in iure*) and the actual trial before the *iudex.* The object of the first stage is to arrive at an issue, which under the *legis actio* system has to be achieved by the speaking of set forms of words by the parties and sometimes, at least, by the magistrate. Thus in a *vindicatio* (*v. supra*) each party, when making his assertion of ownership grasps the thing in dispute and lays a wand on it, after which the magistrate intervenes and says "Let go both of you." So formal was the procedure that a plaintiff who made the slightest mistake lost his case. For this state of affairs the formulary system provided a remedy. It superseded the older system, so Gaius tells us, as a result of the *lex Aebutia* (date much disputed, perhaps between 149 and 126 B.C.), and two *leges Iuliae* (of Augustus). Between the *lex Aebutia* and the *leges Iuliae* the two systems were both in use.

Under the new procedure the issue was formulated in written instructions (*formula*) to the *iudex,* couched in the form of an alternative, *e.g.,* "If it appear that the defendant owes the plaintiff ten thousand sesterces the *iudex* is to condemn the defendant to pay the Plaintiff ten thousand sesterces; if it does not so appear, he is to absolve him." A draft of the *formula* was probably prepared by the plaintiff before he came into court, but there could be no trial until it was accepted by the defendant; for there was always a contractual element about a lawsuit under both older systems. Pressure could, however, be exercised by the magistrate on a defendant who refused to accept a *formula* of which the magistrate approved, just as a plaintiff could be forced to alter a *formula* of which the magistrate disapproved, by the magistrate's refusal to give his order to the *iudex* to decide the case unless the alteration were made.

The process by which the *cognitio extraordinaria* took its place was gradual, and was accomplished in the provinces earlier than in Rome. Briefly, the new system meant that the magistrate used his administrative powers, always large, for the purpose of settling disputes. He could command, and thus if one man brought a complaint against another before him, he could investigate the matter and give the order he thought fit. As imperially appointed officers who had no *iurisdictio* in the old sense, superseded republican magistrates, so this administrative process became more common. The result is that the old contractual element in procedure disappears, as well as the old division into two stages. Justice is now imposed from above by the state, not, as originally, a kind of voluntary arbitration supervised by the state.

BIBLIOGRAPHY.—Among the chief modern text-books are:—W. W. Buckland, *A Text-book of Roman Law from Augustus to Justinian* (Cambridge, 1921), and (shorter) *A Manual of Roman Law* (Cambridge, 1925); P. F. Girard, *Manuel élémentaire de droit romain* (7th ed., Paris, 1924); R. Sohm, *Institutionen des römischen Rechts* (17th ed., Munich and Leipzig, 1926) (English translation of 9th edition by Ledlie, Oxford, 1901). For Sources and History see *e.g.,* P. Krüger, *Geschichte der Quellen und Literatur des röm. Rechts* (2nd ed., Munich and Leipsic, 1912); T. Kipp, *Geschichte der Quellen des röm. Rechts* (4th ed., Leipsic, 1919); B. Kübler, *Geschichte des röm. Rechts* (Leipsic, 1925); G. Cornil, *Droit romain, aperçu historique sommaire* (Brussels, 1921); E. Costa, *Storia del diritto romano privato* (2nd ed., Turin, 1925); J. Muirhead, *Historical Introduction to the Private Law of Rome,* 3rd ed., London, 1916. In Holtzendorff's *Enzyklopädie der Rechtswissenschaft,* Vol. 1 (2nd ed. of revised version, Munich and Leipsic, 1915); O. Lenel's article on history and sources (*Geschichte u. Quellen des röm. Rechts*) and E. Rabel's on the private law of classical times (*Grundzüge des röm. Privatrechts*) are both authoritative and contain full references to modern literature.

(H. F. J.)

ROMANOFF DYNASTY, the rulers of Russia from 1613 to 1917. The last direct descendant of the earlier dynasty of Rurik, Tsar Theodor, son of Ivan (John) the Terrible, died in 1598. After him the throne was occupied first by his brother-in-law, Boris Godunov, then by an adventurer claiming to be a son of Ivan the Terrible (usually known as the false Demetrius). After his murder, in 1606, Prince Basil Shuiski was proclaimed tsar, but was dethroned four years later. The faction which was in power offered the crown to Vladislas, son of the king of Poland. A Polish army advanced to support his claim. Another faction brought in a Swedish army to fight the Poles. In the meantime two more men sprang up in succession, both pretending to be Demetrius, miraculously saved from death. The country was in confusion and civil war till Minin, a tradesman from Nijni-Novgorod, joined hands with Prince Pojarski, one of the generals who had proved himself an efficient soldier. They formed an army and took Moscow in Oct. 1612; they then sent messengers all over the country urging the people to choose representatives who would assemble in Moscow to elect a new ruler. On Feb. 21, 1613, Michael Romanoff was unanimously proclaimed tsar.

The Romanoffs were not of Rurik's stock, nor were they even of very ancient lineage. They descended from a German nobleman who had emigrated to Moscow early in the 14th century. His fifth son, nicknamed Koshka (the Cat), became head of the family of Koshkins, many of whom were prominent at the court of Moscow in the 14th and 15th centuries. Early in the 16th century one of them, whose first name was Roman, called himself Romanoff. His daughter, Anastasia, was Ivan the Terrible's first wife; it was her son, Theodor, who was the last tsar of the Rurik dynasty. As Ivan the Terrible had no high opinion of his son's mental powers, he appointed a council of noblemen to transact business for his successor, and Anastasia's brother, Nikita, was chairman of this council. He made himself very popular by his constant defence of common people's rights, and one of his sons, Theodor, was celebrated for his learning and refined manners. Boris Godunov, fearing the popularity of the Romanoffs, had obliged Theodor and his wife to divorce and to become monk and nun. It was their son, Michael, who was elected tsar in 1613.

Theodor's monastic name was Philarete. After Boris Godunov's death Philarete became metropolitan of Rostov. At the time of his son's election to the throne, he was a prisoner in Poland. Michael was only 16 years old, and was living with his mother in a convent. His personal reputation played a minor part with those who chose him, as in their eyes he was the lawful heir, being nephew to the last tsar descending from Rurik. His name had been often mentioned in those years of civil war as the only one on which all shades of opinion might meet. A popular rumour asserted that when Tsar Theodor was dying, he appointed his cousin Theodor Romanoff (now the monk Philarete) as his successor, but Godunov stepped in and prevented the tsar's will being fulfilled. As Philarete had taken monastic vows, he could not ascend the throne; besides the *boyars* thought Michael, a mere boy, would be a more manageable sovereign. His election was no doubt due to the general striving after legitimacy, which was satisfied by his close relationship to the extinct dynasty. Three years later his father returned to Moscow and was made patriarch; he then reigned jointly with his son and up to his death in 1633 all State documents bore Philarete's signature on a par with Michael's.

The main work of the Romanoff dynasty was to extend Russia up to her natural geographical limits, and to turn her into a European State from the semi-Asiatic one she had become after being under Tatar rule. Though this policy is usually connected with the name of Peter the Great, it was actually started by his grandfather and unswervingly pursued by his successors down to the 20th century. But though the general trend of Russia's internal and international development progressed along the same lines for three centuries, various undercurrents predominated at certain times and are characteristic of definite epochs. Those epochs, into which the history of the Romanoff dynasty may be divided for purposes of study, correspond fairly exactly with the customary division by centuries. The first epoch, when Moscow was the only important centre and when the general intercourse with western Europe was nearly as limited as in previous days, corresponds to the 17th century, as it lasted not only till 1689, when Peter the Great became sole ruler, but more exactly till the end of 1698, when, after his first journey abroad, he began transacting State business himself. The second period, down to the death of Paul I., corresponds to the whole of the 18th century, during which Russia, with St. Petersburg as principal centre, gradually became a European country and reached the shores of all the seas bordering on the Russian plain. The third period, from the accession of Alexander I., in 1801, down to the overthrow of the dynasty in 1917, marks the highest point of Russia's activity as a European Power. Whatever territorial enlargements were acquired in this period were in Asia and mostly due to the necessity of reaching a natural and easily defensible frontier on the Asiatic continent, whereas most of the Government's energies were devoted to the work of internal progress, both economic and educational.

I. THE 17TH CENTURY

The state of chaos to which the country had been reduced in the first years of the 17th century, set a hard task to the new dynasty. The pervading poverty, insecurity and disorder required protracted and patient labours before the country could overcome its weakness and disorganization. All the first tsars of the Romanoff house came to the throne at such an early age that no personal guidance could be expected from any one of them for a long time. Michael, and his son Alexis, were both tsars at 16; Alexis's eldest son Theodor, at 14; Peter the Great at 10. Therefore the actual work of government was always in the hands of a council. The first three tsars never took any decision without its having been discussed by this council, but favouritism and intrigue naturally influenced the choice of its members, and all through the century continual popular risings aimed at the exclusion of one *boyar* or another, to whose predominance or to whose cupidity common gossip attributed the calamities of the day. In order to disarm public opinion the Government was constantly convening assemblies of deputies from the whole land—sometimes to discuss a special question, sometimes for submitting all pending business to their decisions. In those assemblies, called *zemski sobor*, the permanent *boyar* council represented the nobles; in addition came deputies from the clergy and from "all the land," both towns and villages. The first nine years of Michael's reign *sobors* sat in Moscow almost uninterruptedly; three more were called together in 1632, 1637 and 1642; in the first eight years of Tsar Alexis's reign there were five *sobors*. Those of later days, between 1653 and 1682 became mere commissions for elaborating points of law and had no positive authority. The Government had become stronger and had built up an efficient staff of agents of its own. On the other hand the *sobor* of 1648–49 had promulgated a code of laws, which was commonly followed and did not require further commissions to enforce universality.

Wars of the New Dynasty.—A great part of the country's strength was wasted in attempts to counteract the encroachments effected by the neighbouring powers on its territory during the period of anarchy. Out of the first 70 years of the new dynasty's rule, 30 were spent in wars against Poland and Sweden. Russia got back Smolensk and Seversk, which had been seized by the Poles, and annexed Kief and part of Little Russia, east of the Dnieper, owing to a rising against Poland of the Cossack hetman, Bogdan Khmelnitski, whom Moscow after long hesitations decided to back. But the effort required for obtaining those advantages did not allow of an equal amount being spent in the direction of the Baltic, where Sweden had put Russia's weakness to profit and had annexed a large area of land. The wars against Sweden led to no result in the 17th century, and Russia had to wait for Peter the Great in order to regain what she had lost in the north-west.

Down south, where since the 15th century a separate State, the khanate of Crimea, had arisen under Turkey's protectorate, the first Romanoffs waged no regular wars; but the danger of Tatar incursions demanded the building up of defences which

slowly advanced into the Steppe, for when outposts gradually became prosperous towns, they required in turn a new line of forts to protect them. At the end of the 16th century the Crimean Tatars had twice raided the country up to the very walls of Moscow; 100 years later the fortified line of defence was already 400 m. south of the capital. But the farther Russia spread down in that direction the clearer it became that no peaceful agreement was possible so long as the Black sea was not reached, and that would have meant war with Turkey, a much too formidable opponent at that stage. A cossack hetman, Doroshenko, went to war with the Turks, applied to Moscow for help and was eventually supported; but this adventure merely led to a disastrous peace (1681) by which Western Ukraine had to be surrendered to Turkey. It took 100 years more, and all the energy of Catherine II. and of Potemkin to reverse the situation.

Taxation Reforms.—The finances of the country at the beginning of the new dynasty's rule were perhaps in a still more disastrous condition than any other branch of public service. The main spring of former revenue, taxation of cultivated land, was no more adequate owing to so many fields having been abandoned during the years of anarchy. Besides, those peasants who returned to their devastated villages were often successful in defrauding the State of their taxes. The Government was obliged gradually to work out a new system, that of taxing no more the land, but the landowner, not the "field," but the "house," as owing to the vast expanse of Russia and Siberia, where runaways could always escape with ease from official supervision, taxation of communal land laid too heavy and too iniquitous a burden on the thrifty agriculturists, whereas the lazy ones paid nothing. The same occurred with large landowners; they were responsible for the taxes due from peasants who were settled on their land, besides being obliged to come forward with a fixed number of soldiers in case of war. In order that they should be able to fulfil their obligations the peasants were gradually attached to the soil; and thus a serfdom arose which lasted up to 1861 and practically transformed the peasants into slaves.

Religious Matters.—The administration of the Church was at first entirely in the hands of Philarete, who was elected patriarch in 1616. Till his death, in 1633, he was the actual sovereign, and in ecclesiastical matters his power was absolute. In 1652 the patriarchal see was again occupied by a strong personality, Nikon. Tsar Alexis called him his "particular friend" and gave him a free hand in the reforms he undertook. He revised and corrected the texts of prayer books, the mss. of which had been disfigured by ignorant scribes, and abolished ceremonial practices for which no authority existed. But his activity met with strong opposition, due in most part to Nikon's tactlessness, and led to a schism, *Raskol*. Its followers, *Raskolniki*, are still numerous. Nikon's opposition to secular legislation about monastic property, and his efforts to place his own authority above that of the tsar, eventually made Alexis alter his attitude towards him. He then retired to a convent and refused to perform his duties. For nearly ten years the tsar ruled the Church in his stead, till a council was convened which deposed Nikon and appointed a new patriarch. The danger of having a man next to himself who might succeed in usurping such a measure of power, made Peter the Great abolish the Russian patriarchate.

A curious feature of the first Romanoffs is that notwithstanding their efforts to rule in accordance with the people's wishes, and though each of them in turn manifested a total lack of personal ambition, circumstances so imperiously demanded a strong hand that autocracy was evolved and imposed upon a succession of totally ungrasping autocrats. This general leaning of the country towards a firm rule prepared the way for Peter the Great's activities.

II. THE 18TH CENTURY

The salient figures among the Romanoffs of the 18th century are those of Peter the Great and of Catherine II. With Peter, Russia reached the Baltic sea after 20 years' war against Sweden; with Catherine, her southern frontier, after two wars against Turkey, came down to the Black sea, whereas, on the west, owing to the partition of Poland, and the annexation of Courland, she came in contact with the Germanic confederation. Two brilliant episodic wars; that of the empress Elizabeth against Frederick the Great, when Russian troops occupied Berlin, and that of Paul I., against the French in Italy and Switzerland, were brought on by political alliances and led to no tangible results. Sweden's two attempts (1741 and 1788) to regain by a sudden attack some of her lost advantages nearly led to Russia spreading further over south-east Finland. Though the conquest of Finland was based neither on historical nor on ethnographical considerations, it became necessary for the security of St. Petersburg, which was founded early in the 18th century and gradually became the seat of government. Two attempts at advance in Central Asia remained fruitless; Peter the Great's conquest of the southern border of the Caspian in 1723 was annulled by the empress Ann in 1732 when the annexed provinces of Mazanderan and Ghilan were handed back to Persia. As for Peter the Great's attempt to seize Khiva and liberate the Russians who were there in bondage, the whole of his army perished in the desert.

Reforms of Peter the Great.—Peter the Great's decision to turn Russia into a Western Power demanded a complete upheaval of existing conditions. The emperor (he assumed this title in 1721 at the close of the Swedish war) carried through his reforms against a stubborn resistance of the greater part of the nation, with hardly any efficient supporters to back him. The whole of his tremendous energy was aimed at making Russia strong, and at opening her to the influence of Western science and art. He started alone in the field, and the motto he chose for his seal during his journey abroad in 1697 is most characteristic; "I am of those who must be taught and am seeking for teachers." The work he performed between 1699 and his death in 1725 is astounding. He created an army and a fleet, transformed the country's culture by putting it on a secular instead of a religious basis, made the acquisition of riches and honour dependent upon services to the State instead of birthright, and enforced justice and legality independently of the persons concerned; he developed the natural resources of the country by encouraging industries, and opened schools and obliged his subjects to travel abroad so as to learn from other nations; he fought against ancient customs and costumes, which kept the people tied up in an atmosphere where any innovation was deemed impure, manifested absolute religious tolerance and encouraged the building of Roman Catholic and Protestant churches for the foreigners whom he invited to Russia, and dragged Russian women out of oriental seclusion; he tried every branch of knowledge himself and strove to impart all he knew to his subjects; he instituted a senate, supreme court of law and highest organ of administration and offices for all branches of public service; he founded a newspaper, opened a theatre, bought works of art, made some himself, ordered geographical maps, and sent naturalists to explore Siberia. Three weeks before his death, and already in ill-health and pain, he wrote instructions for Captain Behring, commissioning him to find out whether Asia and America were separated by a sea. He composed a multitude of laws, taught people how to build houses, erect stoves, extinguish fires, bridle horses, shave beards, pray in church, and generally how to behave under every probable circumstance. Catherine II. was wont to say that whenever she saw the necessity of a new regulation she first ordered a search to be made in Peter the Great's archives, where she invariably found a draft of what she had been pondering over. He not only set a marvellous example of what personal energy can accomplish, but he was also the first to put forward the idea of "citizen" or "servant of his country," as being the highest aim of a man's activity. The real motto of his reign is contained in the order of the day he addressed to his soldiers on the eve of the battle of Poltava, the turning point in his struggle against Charles XII. of Sweden: "As for Peter, remember that life is of no value to him unless Russia lives in happiness and glory," and this formula became the leading principle of all the most representative members of his dynasty. He never hesitated to sacrifice even his only son when he saw he would undo his father's work and lead a life of ignorant self-indulgence. Later in the century Catherine II.

also seized every opportunity of showing that all her life and energies were devoted to the service of the country. Her grandsons, Alexander I. and Nicholas I., and her great grandson, Alexander II., proclaimed the same rule and symbolized it by always sleeping on camp-beds, with a soldier's great coat for a blanket, so as not to forget that they were ever ready to go where their duties might claim them. In this respect Peter the Great was ahead of his times, not only in Russia, but in Europe, since the first Western sovereign who prided himself on being the servant of his people was Frederick II., nearly half a century later. Peter's daughter, Elizabeth (1741–61) was also a pioneer in her way when she abolished capital punishment (1744), which from then on was not practised in Russia except in retribution for attempts to overthrow the existing order of government. She also opened a fine arts academy. The short reigns of Peter the Great's immediate successors, his widow and his grandson, during which favourites ruled in their stead, prompted a group of political men to offer the throne in 1730 to Ann, a niece of the great reformer's, but on the condition that she signed a promise to take no steps without the approval of a council of eight men (themselves) and this council would recruit its members by free election. Ann signed the paper and then, backed by the guards, destroyed it as soon as she reached Moscow for her coronation. That was the only attempt made in the 18th century for limiting autocracy in Russia.

The two 18th century sovereigns of the Romanoff dynasty whose political activity was not regulated by their sense of duty, but merely by their personal whims, Peter III. and Paul I. rapidly became so unpopular, that conspiracies at once arose which did away with them, the first after six months, the second after four years rule. The one law of Peter III.'s which it was not possible to abrogate was that which freed the members of the nobility from being obliged to serve the country, an obligation which was the only justification of the privileges they enjoyed.

Liberalism Under Catherine II.—The 34 years of Catherine II.'s reign produced a fundamental change in all paths of life. Liberal ideas, those of the French encyclopaedists, became the foundation of her reforms. She convened a commission for preparing a new code of laws and composed instructions to guide this assembly in its labours. The fundamental principles she propounded were mostly taken from the works of Montesquieu and Beccaria, but though the author of this treatise was an empress, Louis XV.'s Government forbade the sale of the French edition as being too liberal. Catherine accomplished a vast number of reforms tending to economic prosperity and encouraging certain manifestations of local self-government. She did a great deal for art, protected artists and formed the nucleus of a collection which, under the name of the "Hermitage museum," is well known all over the world, and has been a powerful instrument of culture in Russia.

III. THE 19TH CENTURY

The beginning of the century saw the last of Russia's expansion in Europe, as the annexation of the Swedish province of Finland took place in 1809. The changes which occurred in the redistribution of parts of Poland and of Bessarabia, in the first half of the century, partook more of the character of frontier rectifications than conquest. Russia's territorial acquisitions of the century were mostly in Asia. In 1801 the kingdom of Georgia was annexed to Russia, and that led to a gradual absorption of Transcaucasia, the last part of which was pacified in 1864. Central Asia (or Russian Turkistan with Bokhara and Khiva), that perpetual hotbed of raids and stronghold of the slave trade, was conquered between 1830 and 1876, with the addition of the Turkoman steppe in 1831. But Russia's advance to the Black sea had opened up a new question, that of the Straits (Dardanelles and Bosphorus), for, without a free passage into the Mediterranean, the Black sea was of small commercial value. Catherine II. had obtained from Turkey the right of protection over Turkish subjects of the Orthodox faith. This new principle, akin to the more modern idea of "spheres of influence," originated the efforts of the Romanoffs for the liberation of Slav nationalities from Turk-

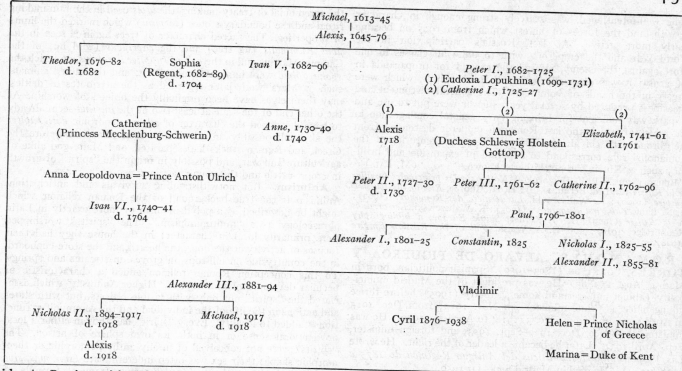

Michael, 1613–45

Alexis, 1645–76

Theodor, 1676–82
d. 1682

Sophia
(Regent, 1682–89)
d. 1704

Ivan V., 1682–96

Peter I., 1682–1725
(1) Eudoxia Lopukhina (1699–1731)
(2) *Catherine I., 1725–27*

Catherine
(Princess Mecklenburg-Schwerin)

Anne, 1730–40
d. 1740

(1)
Alexis
1718

(2)
Anne
(Duchess Schleswig Holstein
Gottorp)

(2)
Elizabeth, 1741–61
d. 1761

Anna Leopoldovna = Prince Anton Ulrich

Peter II., 1727–30
d. 1730

Peter III., 1761–62

Catherine II., 1762–96

Ivan VI., 1740–41
d. 1764

Paul, 1796–1801

Alexander I., 1801–25

Constantin, 1825

Nicholas I., 1825–55

Alexander II., 1855–81

Alexander III., 1881–94

Vladimir

Nicholas II., 1894–1917
d. 1918

Michael, 1917
d. 1918

Cyril 1876–1938

Helen = Prince Nicholas
of Greece

Alexis
d. 1918

Marina = Duke of Kent

ish rule; Russia participated in the war for the independence of Greece and bore the greater part of the burden in those which eventually led to the creation of Rumania, Bulgaria, Serbia and Montenegro. The same policy brought on the Crimean War, which was disastrous for Russia and bared her weakness, even in military matters, before the eyes of the world. For ever since the Napoleonic wars Russian military prestige had been on a high level. Paul I.'s admiration for Prussian discipline and uniforms was inherited by his sons, and under their personal guidance the art of military parades reached such perfection that it often concealed important drawbacks of organization. The staunch qualities of the Russian soldier had left a durable impression in Europe from the time of the Napoleonic wars, but the Crimean War led to a general revaluation of Russian methods, both inside the country and abroad.

Conservatism of Later Romanoffs.—However, the main characteristics of the Romanoffs' rule in the 19th and early 20th century is undoubtedly the opposition to the principles of revolution which had triumphed in France. When Alexander I. was confronted with them, as personified by Napoleon, he was beaten, then pretended to yield till his forces were ready for a second and triumphant struggle. He realized so well the true meaning of his victory that, though the halo of "liberator of Europe" put him in a situation in which he would hardly have met with a refusal on any point, he never turned Napoleon's downfall to any merely material advantage for Russia. All he had gone through; the disasters of Jena and Austerlitz, the humiliations of Tilsit and Erfurt, the fire of Moscow, the entry into Paris, the Congress of Vienna, he used all that to enhance Russia's prestige and to create a situation where his own voice would carry most weight against revolutionary propaganda. The Holy Alliance was the only harvest he sought to reap for having led his army from Moscow to Paris.

Growth of Revolutionary Sentiment.—But this moral comfort was of short duration, and the emperor very soon perceived that he and his allies were unable to cope with the tide. Moreover, in his own country a vast conspiracy was formed, of which he was aware in the last weeks of his life, though he took no steps against it. A military revolt was organized the very moment his brother and successor came to the throne (Dec. 1825), and though it was suppressed in the course of one day, the danger he had undergone left its imprint on the whole of Nicholas I.'s

mind and behaviour. After 1848, when most European Governments gave way to political reform, the emperor of Russia remained almost the sole bulwark of legitimacy. His son, Alexander II., understood that however well the principles of his ancestors might have been adapted to the requirements of his country, they had to be exercised in conformity with the spirit of the times, and he effected a number of important reforms, such as abolition of serfdom, new courts of law with participation of a jury, local self-government (*zemstvo*) conscription for the army, education for the masses, etc. But the enemies of tsardom used these liberal measures merely as a broader basis for revolutionary propaganda, and this at once became so strong that it led to the murder of the emperor (1881).

His son, Alexander III., proclaimed his allegiance to reaction; the Constitution his father had elaborated and would have granted had he lived a few days longer, was forgotten, and a police régime was instituted which appeared to stifle a recrudescence of revolutionary activities but in reality drove them into underground channels. Outwardly, the country was quiet and prosperous. The political alliance with France, which was the personal achievement of the emperor, created an era of peace and permitted the whole force of the nation to be devoted to economic development. The building of railroads, without which no modern State can live, was bound in Russia, owing to her vast expanse, to be protracted over a much longer period than in other European countries; this work was, however, pushed on in gigantic strides; the trans-Siberian railway (due to the emperor's personal initiative) being the most notable achievement in this branch.

The last Romanoff emperor, Nicolas II., came to the throne at the age of 26, and strove to continue his father's work along the same lines. He succeeded in creating a wonderful economic prosperity. His desire to obtain a strong footing on the Pacific, and thereby to prompt the development of Eastern Siberia, led to a war with Japan (1904), which ended in disaster. A revolution broke out, and though it was suppressed by rapid and forceful measures, the emperor attempted to pacify the land by granting constitutional rights (Oct. 1905). This, however, was done but half-heartedly, and led to incessant misunderstandings between the Government and the people's representatives.

Final Success of Revolution.—Propaganda was already strong, and every liberal concession, instead of quieting public opinion, gave fresh opportunities of carrying it on. The emperor, while well-intentioned, was scarcely strong enough in character to withstand the forces of unrest which from 1905 on became yearly more active. At last, Russia's participation in the World War and the emperor's wish to unite all classes in one effort against the enemy, cleared the ground for propaganda in the army; it was especially active in the hospitals, which were largely in the hands of volunteers. The general discontent and uneasiness produced by several years of war were put to use and a spark was sufficient for bringing on a general conflagration in the midst of which the last Romanoff emperor descended from the throne with chivalrous dignity. The three centuries of the Romanoffs' rule correspond to a period of expansion and brilliancy such as Russia had not hitherto known.   (M. Pal.)

Bibliography.—P. V. Dolgorukov, *Notice sur les principales familles de la Russie* (2nd ed. Berlin, 1858); H. H. Munroe, *Rise of the Russian Empire* (1900); K. Waliszewski, *La derniere des Romanovs* (1902); R. N. Bain, *The First Romanovs* (1905); K. Waliszewski, *Les origines de la Russie* (1909); R. J. Kerner, *Slavic Europe, a bibliography* (Cambridge, 1918); and E. A. Walsh, *Fall of the Russian Empire* (1928).

ROMANONES, ALVARO DE FIGUEROA Y TORRES, Count de (1863–1950), Spanish politician, born in Madrid, Aug. 1, 1863. He was president of the Madrid municipality, cabinet minister and home secretary (1905), before thrice taking office as prime minister—in Nov. 1912; from Dec. 1915 to April 1917, and from Dec. 3, 1918, to April 15, 1919. He was minister of justice, Dec. 1922–Sept. 1923, and foreign minister, Feb.–April 1931. Later he became a leader of the right. He wrote *Las Responsibilidades Políticas del Antiguo Régimen de 1875 a 1922* (1924). He died in Madrid Sept. 11, 1950.

ROMANOS, called ὁ μελῳδός, Greek hymn-writer, was born at Emesa (Homs) in Syria. He resided in Constantinople during the reign of the emperor Anastasius, probably the first emperor of that name (491–518). Having officiated as a deacon in the church of the Resurrection at Berytus, he removed to Constantinople. According to the legend, when he was asleep in the church of Cyrus, the Virgin appeared to him and commanded him to eat a scroll. On awaking (it was Christmas Day), he immediately mounted the pulpit, and gave forth his famous hymn on the Nativity. Romanos is said to have composed more than 1,000 similar hymns or *contakia* (Gr. κοντάκιον, "scroll"). The MS. of the hymns, written by his own hand, was said to have been preserved in the church of Cyrus, in which he was buried and celebrated as a saint on the 1st of October.

Editions: J. B. Pitra, *Analecta Sacra*, i. (1876), containing 29 poems, and *Sanctus Romanus Veterum Melodorum Princeps* (1888), with three additional hymns from the monastery of St. John in Patmos. *See* also Pitra's *Hymnographie de l'Église grècque* (1867); C. Krumbacher, *Geschichte der byzantinischen Literatur* (1897); and Hymns.

ROMAN RELIGION. The Roman people were in origin a small community of agricultural settlers, which gradually won its way to the headship first of Latium, then of Italy and finally of a European empire. Its religion, which was always marked by an absence of dogmatism and a readiness to adopt foreign ideas, has therefore a shifting and ever widening character, which tends to obscure the original essentials; the genuine Roman religion becomes gradually buried or fossilized in formal observance. The careful analysis of survivals in literature and monumental remains, and in particular of the extant calendars, has enabled scholars, using the comparative method, to make good progress in separating the elements due to different periods and influences.

Survivals.—Broadly speaking, the religion of the early agriculture settlement was arrested at the stage of Animism. It had passed beyond the primitive stages of magic and Fetishism or "Animatism," which regards natural objects as themselves divine and the source of power, and had not yet entered the stage of Anthropomorphism, which recognizes "gods" (*dei*) as personal and independent beings; it is in essence a worship of "spirits" (*numina*) which are thought of as dwelling in external objects or localities. But it is in a state of transition. There are still traces of the earlier attitude in the recognition of the sacredness of stones, such as the *silex* (flint) which played a prominent part in

the ceremonial of treaty-making, the *lapis* used in the rain-making ritual and the boundary-stones (*termini*) which marked the limits of properties. The sacred character of trees again is seen in the *ficus Ruminalis* (fig tree) and the *caprificus* (wild fig) of the Campus Martius and in the oak of *Iuppiter Feretrius,* on which the *spolia opima* were hung after a victory; and the sacred animals, such as Mars' wolf, later regarded as the attributes of deities, may themselves have been originally the objects of worship. At the other end of the scale at least two of the *numina* seem already to have developed the character of anthropomorphic *dei: Jupiter* the sky-god, possibly an inheritance from the time before the Greek and Roman stocks had separated, and Mars, god alike of agriculture and war, and possibly in origin the "spirit" of growth in crops, cattle and the young warriors.

Animism.—But notwithstanding survivals and anticipation, Animism is the true background of the Roman religion, which might be described as a polydemonism or more exactly in Latin phraseology as a "multinuminism." The "spirits" worshipped were primarily local in character: in the house they had their focuses of activity at the door, the hearth and the store-cupboard, in the countryside on hill-tops, in groves, in streams and springs. To this conception Roman religion added a characteristic or peculiar development in a kind of "Higher Animism" which associated the "spirit" not only with visible objects, but with states and actions in the life of the individual and the community: function is added to locality. Every "spirit" had thus in either a local or temporal sense or in both, its own sphere of action. The "spirits" were not conceived of in any anthropomorphic or theomorphic shape: their sex was often indeterminate (*sive mas, sive femina*, "whether male or female" was a frequent formula of prayer), they had no form of sensuous representation, nor did they need a home to dwell in: statue and temple were alien to the spirit of Roman religion. Nor could they have a personal history or relation to one another: there was no Roman mythology. But in their individual spheres they could influence the fortunes of men, and men could enter into relations with them. The primary attitude of men to the spirits was one of fear, expressed in the conception of *religio*, the sense of awe or "anxiety" in the presence of a superhuman power. But the practical mind of the Roman soon gave this relation a legal turn, and later the *ius divinum*, which regulated the dealings of men with the divine powers became a department of the *ius publicum*, the general body of civil law. The act of worship was a kind of contract: the "spirits," if they were given their due, were bound to make a return to man, and the object of worship and festival was to place them under this obligation and so to secure the *pax deum* (a state of peace between gods and men).

Ritual.—In such a religion exactness of ritual must play a large part—so large, indeed, that many modern critics have been misled into regarding the Roman religion as a mere network of formalities without any background of genuine religious feeling. This formalism shows itself in many ways. It was necessary in the first place to make quite certain that the right deity was being addressed: hence it was well to invoke all the spirits who might be concerned, and even to add a general formula to cover omissions. Place, again, was an essential element even in the conception of the *numen*, and was therefore all-important in ritual. So, too, was the character of the offering: male victims must be sacrificed to male deities; female victims to goddesses; white animals were the due of the *di superi*, the gods of the upper world, black animals of the gods below; the more rustic *numina*, such as Pales (*q.v.*), should be given milk and millet cakes rather than a blood-offering. All-important, too, was the order of ceremonial and the formula of prayer: a mistake or omission or an unpropitious interruption might vitiate the whole ritual, and though such misfortunes might occasionally be expiated by the additional offering of a *piaculum*, in more serious cases the whole ceremony had to be recommenced from the beginning.

Household Worship.—In the original agricultural community, the unit both from the legal and religious point of view was not the individual but the household. The household was thus at once the logical starting-point of religious cult, and throughout

Roman history the centre of its most real and vital activity. The head of the house (*paterfamilias*) was the natural priest and had control of the domestic worship: he was assisted by his sons as acolytes (*camilli*) and deputed certain portions of the ritual to his wife and daughters and even to his bailiff (*vilicus*) and his bailiff's wife. The worship was offered to the spirits indwelling in the sacred places of the round hut in which the family lived. Janus, the god of the door, came first in the prayer-formulae, though unfortunately we know but little of his worship in the household, except that it was the concern of the men. To the women was committed the cult of the "blazing hearth," Vesta, the natural centre of the family life, and it is noticeable that even Ovid (*Fast.*, vi. 291–92) describes Vesta as "nought but the living flame." The Penates (q.v.) were the *numina* of the store-cupboard, at first vague and animistic, but later on, as the *deus*-notion was developed, individualized by selection from the other divinities of household or state religion.

Lar and Genius.—To these *numina* of the sacred places must be added two other important conceptions, that of the *lar familiaris* and the *genius*. The *lar familiaris* has sometimes been regarded as the embodiment of all the family dead and his cult as a consummation of ancestor-worship, but a more probable explanation regards him as one of the *lares* (q.v.; *numina* of the fields worshipped at the *compita*, the places where properties marched) who had special charge of the house or possibly of the household servants (*familia*); for it is significant that his worship was committed to the charge of the *vilica*. The *genius* was originally the "spirit of developed manhood," the *numen* which is attached to every man and represented the sum total of his powers and faculties as the *iuno* does of the woman; each individual worshipped his own *genius* on his birthday, but the household-cult was concerned with the *genius* of the *paterfamilias*. In the ordinary religious life of the family there was a more direct connection with morality and a truer religious sense than in any other part of the Roman cult. The family meal was sanctified by the offering of a portion of the food to the household *numina*: the chief events in the individual life, birth, infancy, puberty, marriage, were all marked by religious ceremonial in some cases of a distinctively primitive character. The dead, too, though it is doubtful whether in early times they were actually worshipped, at any rate had a religious commemoration as in some sense members still of the family.

From the life of the household we may pass to the outdoor occupations of the fields, where the early Roman settler met with his neighbours to celebrate in religious ceremonies the various stages of the agricultural year. Here we have a series of celebrations representing the occupations of the successive seasons, addressed sometimes to *numina* who developed later on into the great gods of the State, such as Jupiter, Mars or Ceres, sometimes to vaguer divinities who remained always indefinite and rustic in character, such as Pales and Consus. Sometimes again, as in the Lupercalia (q.v.) the attribution was so indefinite that it is hard to discover who was the special deity concerned; at other festivals, such as those of the Robigalia and the Meditrinalia, the worship seems at first to have been addressed generally to any interested *numina* and only later to have developed a specific deity of its own. Roughly we may distinguish three main divisions of the calendar year, the festivals of spring, of the harvest and of winter. (1) In the spring (it must be remembered that the old Roman calendar began the year with March) we have ceremonials of anticipation and prayer for the crops to come: prominent among them were the *Fordicidia*, with its symbolic slaughter of pregnant cows, addressed to Tellus, the *Cerealia*, a prayer-service to Ceres for the corn-crop, and the most important of the rustic celebrations of lustration and propitiation, the *Parilia*, the festival of Pales. To these must be added the *Ambarvalia* (q.v.), the lustration of the fields, a movable feast (and therefore not found in the calendars) addressed at first to Mars in his agricultural character (*see* MARS). (2) Of the harvest festivals the most significant were the twin celebrations on Aug. 21 and 25 to the divinity-pair Consus and Ops, who were both concerned with the storing of the year's produce, and two vintage festivals, the

Vinalia Rustica and the *Meditrinalia*, connected with Jupiter. (3) The winter festivals were less homogeneous in character, but we may distinguish among them certain undoubtedly agricultural celebrations, the *Saturnalia* (connected with the sowing of the next year's crop), and a curious repetition of the harvest festivals to Consus and Ops.

State Religion.—In passing to the religion of the State we enter on a later period and a more developed form of society. The loose aggregation of agricultural households gives place to the organized community with new needs and new ideals. Thus we find two prominent notes of the State influence, firstly, the adaptation of the old ideas of the household and agricultural cults to the broader needs of the city-community, especially to the new necessities of internal justice and war against external enemies; and secondly the organization of informal worship into a consistent system. Adaptation proceeded at first naturally enough on the lines of analogy. As Janus was in the household the *numen* of the door, so in the State he was associated with the great gate near the corner of the forum: the Penates had their analogy in the *Di Penates populi Romani Quiritium* by whom the magistrates took their oath on entering office, the *lar familiaris* in the *Lares Praestites* of the community, and the *genius* in the new notion of the *Genius populi Romani* or *Genius urbis Romae*. But the closest and most striking analogy is seen in the cult of Vesta. The Vesta of the State was in fact the king's hearth, standing in close proximity to the *Regia*, the king's palace; the Vestal Virgins, who had charge of the sacred fire, were the "king's daughters," and as such even in republican times were in the legal power of the *pontifex maximus*. But adaptation meant also the widening of old conceptions under the influence of reflexion. Thus, since the door is used for the double purpose of entrance and exit, the Janus of the State was represented as *bifrons* ("two-faced"): the thought of the door as the first part of the house to which one comes produces the more abstract idea of Janus as the "god of beginnings," in which character he had special charge of the first hour of the day, the calends of the month and the first month of the year in the later calendar. But development proceeded also on broader lines. Jupiter in the rustic-cult was a sky-god concerned mainly with the wine festivals and associated with the sacred oak on the Capitol. Now he developed a twofold character: as the receiver of the *spolia opima* he became associated with war, especially in the double character of the stayer of rout (*Stator*) and the giver of victory (*Victor*). As the sky-god again he was appealed to as the witness of oaths in the special capacity of *Dius Fidius*. In these two conceptions, justice and war, lie the germs of the later idea of Jupiter as the embodiment of the life of the Roman people, both in their internal organization and in their external relations. In much the same manner the agricultural character of Mars became submerged by his functions as war-god. Finally, we must notice, as the sign of the union of two settlements, the inclusion of the Colline deity, Quirinus, apparently the Mars of the originally rival community. In these three deities, Jupiter, Mars, Quirinus, we have the great triad of the earliest stage of the State religion.

Organization showed itself in the fixing of the annual calendar of festivals, the development of the character and functions of the priesthood and in a new conception of the legal relation of the gods of the State. The State now approached the gods through its duly appointed representatives, the magistrates and priests, and the private citizen was required to do no more on festival days than observe a ceremonial abstinence from work. The State religion had thus a less direct connection with morality and the religious sense than the worship of the household, but it had its ethical value in a sense of discipline and a consecration of the spirit of patriotism.

External Influences.—The later stages represent not the spontaneous development of the genuine Roman religion, but its alteration and supersession by new cults and ideas introduced from foreign sources. Three periods may be recognized: (1) from the end of the regal epoch to the second Punic War—the period of contact with the peoples of Italy; (2) from the second Punic War to the end of the Republic—the period of contact with

Greece and the Orient; (3) the imperial epoch, opening with a revival of old religious notions and later marked by the official worship of the deified emperors and the wide influence of oriental cults.

Italian Influence.—By the end of the regal period Rome was a really developed city-state. There was a large artisan class, excluded from the old patrician *gentes* and therefore from the State cult. At the same time the beginnings of commerce had opened relations with neighbouring peoples. The consequence was the introduction of certain new deities, the *di novensides*, from external sources, and the birth of new conceptions of the gods and their worship. We may distinguish three main influences:—

(*a*) *Etruria.*—The last three kings of Rome were Etruscans and Etruscan influence under their rule was strong. From Etruria came Minerva, who, as the goddess of handicraft and protectress of the artisan guilds, was established in a temple on the Aventine. Soon a new Etruscan triad, Jupiter, Juno and Minerva, was enshrined on the Capitol in a magnificent new temple built by Etruscan workmen and decorated in the Etruscan manner. In this temple the deities were represented by images.

(*b*) *Latium.*—Secondly, in war and peace Rome formed relations with her neighbours of Latium, and, as a sign of the Latin league which resulted, the cult of Diana was brought from Aricia and established on the Aventine in the *commune Latinorum Dianae templum;* about the same time the temple of *Iuppiter Latiaris* was built on the Alban mount, its resemblance in style to the Capitoline temple pointing to Rome's hegemony. Latin cults were introduced even inside the *pomoerium*, the old city limits, the worship of Hercules, which came from Tibur in connection with commerce, was established at the Great Altar in the *forum boarium*, and the Tusculan cult of Castor as the patron of cavalry found a home close to the *forum Romanum*.

(*c*) *Magna Graecia.*—Later on contact with the cities of Magna Graecia brought about the wide-reaching introduction of the Sibylline books. They came from Cumae and were placed in the Capitoline temple under the care of a special commission; their "oracles," which were referred to in time of great national stress, recommended the introduction of foreign cults. In this way were brought to Rome the Greek triad Demeter, Dionysus and Persephone, who were identified with the old Roman divinities Ceres, Liber and Libera, Apollo, Mercury, and Aesculapius Dis and Proserpina, with their strange chthonic associations and night ritual. With new deities came new modes of worship: the "Greek ritual" in which, contrary to Roman usage, the worshipper's head was unveiled, the *lectisternium* (q.v.), an elaborate form of the "banquet of the gods" and the *supplicatio*, an appeal to the gods in which the whole people took part. In this period, then, we find first a legitimate extension of cults corresponding to the needs of the growing community and secondly a religious restlessness and a consequent tendency to more dramatic forms of worship.

Foreign Influence.—The two chief notes of the next period were superstition and scepticism: both the populace and the educated classes lost faith in the old religion, but they supplied its place in different ways. The disasters of the early part of the second Punic War revealed an unparalleled religious nervousness: portents and prodigies were announced from all quarters, it was felt that the divine anger was on the State, yet there was no belief in the efficacy of the old methods for restoring the *pax deum*. Accordingly recourse was had, under the direction of the Sibylline books, to new forms of appeal for the divine help, the general vowing of the first fruits (*Ver sacrum*) and the elaborate Greek *lectisternium* after Trasimene in 217 B.C., and the human sacrifice in the forum after Cannae in the following year. The same spirit continues to show itself in the introduction of Greek deities and their ready identification with gods of the old religion. Thus we hear of temples dedicated to Iuventas = Hebe (191 B.C.), Diana = Artemis (179 B.C.), Mars = Ares (138 B.C.), and find even the Bona Dea (q.v.) identified with a Greek goddess of women, Damia. At the same time cult statues are made in which the identified Greek type is usually adopted without change, with

such curious results as the representation of the *Lares* under the form of the Dioscuri. But more far-reaching still was the order of the Sibylline books in 206 B.C. for the introduction of the worship of the *Magna Mater* (*see* GREAT MOTHER OF THE GODS) from Pessinus and her installation on the Palatine in 191 B.C.: the door was thus opened to the wilder and more orgiastic cults of Greece and the Orient.

Oriental Deities.—After *Magna Mater* came the secret cult of Bacchus, which had to be suppressed by decree of the senate in 186 B.C., and later on the cults of Ma of Phrygia, and the Egyptian Isis were established. In all these more emotional rituals, the populace sought expression for religious feelings which were not satisfied by the formal worship of the older deities. Meanwhile a corresponding change was taking place in the attitude of the educated classes owing to the spread of Greek literature. The knowledge of Greek legends set poets and antiquarians at work on the task of creating a Roman anthropomorphic mythology. In this way grew up the "religion of the poets," whose falseness and shallowness was patent even to contemporary thinkers. But more important was the influence of philosophy, which led soon enough to a general scepticism among the upper classes.

Scepticism.—In the last century of the Republic the two later Greek schools of Epicureanism and Stoicism laid hold on Roman society. The influence of Epicureanism was wholly destructive to religion, but not perhaps very widespread: Stoicism became the creed of the educated classes and produced attempts at a reconciliation of popular religion with philosophy. Since, however, the former was regarded as untrue in itself, but a presentation of truth suited to the popular mind, the way was opened for statecraft to use religion as its tool.

The result was twofold. Worship passed into formalism and formalism into disuse. Some of the old cults passed away altogether, others survived in name but were wholly devoid of inner meaning. The old priesthoods came to be regarded as tiresome restrictions on political life and were neglected: from 87 to 11 B.C. the office of *flamen Dialis* was vacant. On the other hand religion passed into the hands of the politicians: cults were encouraged or suppressed from political motives, the membership of the colleges of pontifices and augurs was sought for its social and political advantages, and augury was debased till it became the mere tool of the politician. Little survived but the household cult, protected by its own genuineness and vitality.

Imperial Religion.—The Augustan revival was largely political, a part of his plan for the general renaissance of Roman life focused no longer on the abstract notion of the State, but on the persons of an imperial house. He saw, however, that no revival could be effective which did not appeal to the religious sentiments of the populace. It was thus his business to revitalize the old forms with a new and more vigorous content. His new palace on the Palatine was to be the centre of the new popular religion. With this object he consecrated there his new temple of Apollo (28 B.C.), whom he had adopted as his special patron at Actium, and transferred to its keeping the Sibylline books, thus marking the new headquarters of the Graeco-Roman religion. Similar in purpose was his institution of the Secular Games (*ludi saeculares*) in 17 B.C. Horace's hymn written for the festival is a good epitome of Augustus's religious intentions. Further he established a new shrine of Vesta Augusta within the palace. Still more marked was the building of a great temple at the end of his new forum to Mars Ultor—Mars, the ancestor of the Julian family now to be worshipped as the avenger of Caesar's murderers. He also erected on the spot where Caesar's body had been cremated in the Forum a permanent temple to his adopted father, under the definitely religious title of *divus Iulius*. No doubt he also did much generally to revive the ancient cults; he rebuilt, as he tells us himself, 82 temples which had fallen into disrepair, he re-established the old priesthoods and filled once more the office of *flamen Dialis*. But religious feeling was now to be mainly diverted to the reigning house, and this project was aided by the natural prominence in the palace of the cult of the *genius* of the emperor himself. As the palace cults became national, the worship of the *genius* was bound to spread, and ultimately Augustus sanctioned its celebration at the *compita* (crossways) together with the worship of the old *lares*. But here he and the wiser of his successors drew the line, and though under oriental influence divine honours were paid to the living emperor outside Italy, they were never permitted officially in Rome.

With this last period the story of the genuine Roman religion draws to a close. For, though the form of the old cults was long preserved, the vital spirit was almost gone. In the popular mind the many exciting oriental cults held undisputed sway; and with the more educated a semi-religious philosophy gave men a clearer monotheistic conception and an idea of individual relations with the divine in prayer. It was with these elements (fiercely antagonistic because so closely allied in character) that the battle of Christianity was really fought, and though, after its official adoption, the old religion lingered on as "paganism" and died hard at the end, it was really doomed from the moment when the Augustan revival had taken its irrecoverable bias in the direction of the emperor-worship.

BIBLIOGRAPHY.—W. Warde Fowler, *The Roman Festivals of the Period of the Republic* (1899); *The Religious Experience of the Roman People* (1911); *Roman Ideas of Deity* (1914); *Roman Essays and Interpretations* (1920); W. R. Halliday, *Lectures on the History of Roman Religion* (1922); H. J. Rose, *Primitive Culture in Italy* (1926); A. de Marchi, *Il Culto privato di Roma Antica* (Milan 1903); G. Boissier, *La Religion romaine d'Auguste aux Antonins* (1891); *La fin du Paganisme* (1891). F. Cumont, *Oriental Religions in Roman Paganism* (English translation); J. Toutain, *Les Cultes Païens dans l'Empire romain* (1907). *See* further: GREEK RELIGION; ETRURIA; RELIGION, and articles on the deities, festivals and priestly colleges.

(C. B.)

ROMANS, EPISTLE TO THE.

The occasion of this New Testament epistle is revealed in i.8f, xv. 14f. St. Paul had finished his mission in Greece and was on his way to Jerusalem with the proceeds of the collection made by his churches for the poor Christians in Judaea. Casting about for a new sphere, he turns to the extreme West of the Mediterranean, to Spain, where evidently no one had preached the gospel. On his way to Spain, after settling the business at Jerusalem, he proposes to visit the Christians at Rome. This corresponds to the situation outlined in Acts xx. 2f; it is probable, though not certain, that the apostle wrote the epistle from Corinth or on his way from Corinth eastward, *i.e.*, after the Corinthian epistles. What is certain is that he takes this opportunity of stating his gospel in its width and range of appeal. In the light of his experience and in view of the fresh propaganda which he contemplated in the Western Empire, his aim is to reiterate the principles of the Christian religion as he preached it. There was an appropriate note in such an epistle being sent to Christians at the capital of the Empire. Besides, the apostle was not confronted here as, *e.g.*, in Galatia, with any attacks upon himself by the Jewish Christian party in the Church. Hence the breadth of view and the comparative absence of controversial references. He sets himself to put forward what he regards as vital Christianity rather than to counteract any policy of his opponents at Rome, and this vital Christianity is stated in its relations to the older Jewish religion, with the object of persuading the Roman Christians, most of whom seem to have been Gentile converts, that the hopes and promises of God as revealed in the Christian gospel rest upon His previous revelation to Israel, although they go far beyond that. The two main errors before his mind seem to have been a tendency to throw over the earlier revelation and a tendency on the part of Jews to depreciate Christianity as morally inferior to Judaism. The epistle therefore is more of a treatise than any other; it does not ignore the Roman Christians, but it is not written with them constantly in view, since their local situation offered no particular problems. But, while it is a tract, it does not contain any compendium of Christianity; topics like the sacraments, eschatology, and the resurrection, for example, are not discussed as they are in the First Epistle to the Corinthians. The predominating motive of the epistle is the desire to propound the faith as a faith for all men, which has its roots in the earlier revelation of God to the Jews and yet goes far beyond that. He pours out his very soul in expounding the glory of the gospel as the final and all-embracing revelation of God for mankind; every now and then the argument glows with passion, and the exposition thrills with the writer's joy in expressing convictions which had become for him living powers and hopes.

The outline of the epistle is as follows. After apologizing for his inability to visit the Roman Christians before now, he promises to visit them, bringing "some spiritual gift" to this world-famous church of the capital. Meantime he explains the gospel of which he is so proud, endeavouring to stir up his readers to a sense of its wonder and strength. Such is the theme of the first five chapters, God's "righteousness" or salvation for faith offered in Jesus Christ to all men, apart from national restrictions. To be right with God, to enjoy His fellowship and favour, is a position which is His gift. Both pagans and Jews have hitherto missed it, but in Jesus Christ (iii. 21f) it is now brought within reach of all men, as they believe. Not that faith and revelation had been absent from the earlier history of God's people; the apostle shows that this was implicit in the religious experience of Abraham (iv.). Only, it required the divine revelation in Christ to overcome the sin of man, which had weakened the race hitherto (v. 1f). From a philosophy of history he is now passing to the deeper experience of religion, and the magnificent sweep of the next passage (vi.–viii.) shows how this faith embodies the power of receiving and realising the gift of God, since it invests man with the divine Spirit, which is the sole guarantee of a sound life in the present and of a secure life in the future.

Reverting to history, he now (ix.–xi.) faces the problem of the Jewish nation's antipathy to the gospel, seeking to reconcile this with the justice and promises of God in the Old Testament. God is not to blame for such unbelief, he argues. And, with patriotic pathos, he hopes it will not be final; the rejection of Christ by the Jews, he contends, is merely partial and temporary. But part of his interest is to prevent Gentile Christians from depreciating their relation to God's earlier revelation in Israel and from disparaging the historical link between themselves and the saving purpose of God in the world. All men are equally under the sweep of God's marvellous mercy, he concludes, in an impassioned outburst (xi. 25–36).

Such an experience of the divine mercy brings obligations in its train, however, and these are now outlined (xii.–xiii.) as they bear upon the conduct of Christians as members of the Church, of society, and of the State; love is the supreme law, and as the Day of the Lord is near, there is no time for indulgence in vice. "It is high time to wake up." But, instead of dwelling on this motive, he proceeds to apply the law of Christian love to one special problem of contemporary ethic, viz., the strain set up between the narrower and the more liberal parties over total abstinence and vegetarianism (xiv.–xv. 13), pleading for consideration on the part of the liberal majority, and finally calling on all alike to glorify God for His mercy to them in Jesus Christ.

Such is the outline of the epistle as a whole. It is not unfair to suggest that faith dominates the first part (i.–v.), hope the second (vi.–viii., ix.–xi.), and love the third (xii.–xv.), though none of the three is ever isolated entirely from the others. The epilogue (xv. 14–33) reverts to the situation noted in the opening paragraph; the apostle tells them of his plans and asks for their prayers.

The sixteenth chapter seems to contain a note intended for a different audience. It is possible that the apostle may have known a number of Christians who had found their way to Rome, but the probability is that the first part of this chapter (1–16, 1–20, or 1–23), represents a letter of commendation for Phoebe, addressed to the church at Ephesus. The number of personal references and the unusual wealth of detail point to some community with which St. Paul was more familiar than he could be with the Roman church. Ephesus answers this requirement better than almost any other sphere; besides, the sharp warning against errorists in verses 17–20 applies to Ephesus at this period (1 Cor. xvi. 8–9, Acts xx. 29f) better than to what we know of the Roman church, for it is improbable that the apostle meant the words to be a vague warning against something that might happen in the future. For these reasons many editors and critics detach xvi from the original Roman epistle.

The tone and style of xvi. 25–27 suggest also that it is an editorial addition, later than St. Paul. Indeed in some early copies of the epistle during the second century it is found after xiv. 23, perhaps in editions drawn up for reading in worship. This is merely one of a number of textual phenomena, which are discussed fully in Lake's *The Earlier Epistles of St. Paul* (pp. 335f), in Lightfoot's *Biblical Essays*, in Zahn's *Einleitung in das Neue Testament* (section 22), in Westcott and Hort's *Greek New Testament* (appendix), and in the present writer's *Introduction to the Literature of the New Testament* (pp. 134f), as well as by the critical editors. Some early editions of Romans seem to have omitted the words "in Rome" at i. 7 and 15. Unless this was due to a desire to make the epistle a catholic document, or to Marcion's revision, it may point to the fact that there were more than one edition of the epistle. Lake, for example, argues on textual grounds that Paul himself wrote an edition, without "in Rome," consisting of i. 1.–xiv. 23, xvi. 25–27, as a companion letter to Galatians, and that later he edited the epistle as we have it for the special purpose of instructing the Roman church. Others, like Renan (*St. Paul*, pp. 461f), think of two editions, the first (i.–xiv., xvi. 1–20) intended for Asia or Ephesus, the second for Rome—a hypothesis which assumes a variety of forms. But it is not easy to suppose that the apostle ever left xiv. 23 with xvi. 25–27 as a self-contained letter, even if the doxology be accepted as Pauline. It is fairly clear that the canonical epistle represents an edited form of the original, and one natural hypothesis is that the original ended with xv., whilst xvi. if contains an addition. As Deissmann points out, the papyri supply numerous analogies for a "letter of commendation plunging at once *in medias res* and beginning with 'I commend'" (*Light from the Ancient East*, p. 235); and if Tertius wrote both, the smaller letter might be put in the wake of the larger, as the canonical editors drew upon the copybook in which both were preserved. The mechanical conditions for such a practice are discussed in Gregory's *Canon and Text of the New Testament* (pp. 319f).

It is no longer necessary to discuss theories that the whole epistle is a later forgery: Schmiedel's examination of this aberration (in *Hibbert Journal* i. 532f) sufficiently indicates the impossibility of taking such views seriously. Nor is it needful to criticize the theories which attribute xv.–xvi. in whole or part to some later hand, much less the idea, voiced recently by H. Delafosse (*L'épître aux Romains, traduction nouvelle, avec introduction, notes et commentaire*, Paris, 1926), that the canonical Romans represents an originally Pauline letter which was first edited by Marcion and then catholicized. The epistle as it stands was known early to writers of the second century like Justin and Polycarp, possibly even to Ignatius; indeed traces of it are to be found in the epistle of Clemens Romanus, which lies within the last decade of the first century, at the very latest (*see* for an even earlier date, G. Edmundson's *The Church of Rome in the first Century*, 1913, pp. 14f, etc).

BIBLIOGRAPHY.—The ablest editions of modern days are those by B. Weiss in Meyer's *Commentary* (9th edition, 1899), R. A. Lipsius in the *Handcommentar* (1892), Sanday and Headlam (*International Critical Commentary*, 5th ed. 1905), Denney (*Expositor's Greek Testament*, 1901), Lietzmann in his own *Handbuch* (1906), Parry (*Cambridge Greek Testament*, 1912), E. Kühl (1913), P. Lagrange (Paris, 1916), and Hauck in Zahn's *Commentar* (1925), although the older work of men like Godet (1879, Eng. Tr. 1888) and E. H. Gifford (in the *Speaker's Commentary*, 1881) deserves attention still for its delicate exegesis. Lightfoot's posthumously published notes do not go beyond vii. 25 (*Notes on Epistles of St. Paul*, 1895), but we have Hort's invaluable *Romans and Ephesians* (1895) for a study of the general data of the epistle, as well as the chapters in Kirsopp Lake's *The Earlier Epistles of St. Paul*, Liddon's *Explanatory Analysis* (1893), Pfleiderer's *Primitive Christianity* (vol. i. pp. 211f), G. Semeria's *Il pensiero di S. Paolo nella lettera ai Romani* (Rome, 1903), and J. Drummond's article in the *Hibbert Journal* (1913, pp. 787f). The critical movements are chronicled by C. Clemen in his *Paulus* (i. pp. 85f, ii. 238f), and by A. Robertson (Hastings' *Dictionary of the Bible*, iv. 295f) and C. W. Emmett (*Dictionary of the Apostolic Age*, ii. 408f). The first chapter of Matthew Arnold's *St. Paul and Protestantism* discusses Romans, and Sievers has just published an edition in rhythmical form, in the first volume of his *Paulinische Briefe, klanglich untersucht und herausgegeben* (Leipzig, 1926).   (J. Mof.)

ROMANSHORN, an important commercial town in the Swiss canton of Thurgau, on the west shore of the lake of Constance. By rail it is 51½ mi. N.E. of Zürich. In 1950 its population was 6,648, mostly German-speaking. In 1930 there were 4,535 Protestants and 1,898 Roman Catholics. Originally a small fishing village, it belonged to the abbot of St. Gall from 1432 to 1798, when it became part of the canton of Thurgau. In 1856 the railway from Romanshorn to Zürich was opened, and this vastly increased the commercial importance of Romanshorn. It is the centre of a great transit trade, chiefly in corn and timber, and has many industrial establishments.

ROMANS-SUR-ISÈRE, a town of southeastern France, in the department of Drôme, 12½ mi. N.E. of Valence on the railway to Grenoble. Pop. (1946) 22,171. Romans stands on a height on the right bank of the Isère, a bridge uniting it with Bourg-de-Péage (pop. 6,018) on the other side of the river. The present parish church belonged to an abbey founded in 837 by St. Bernard, bishop of Vienne. Romans has a tribunal of commerce. Its industries include tanning, leather dressing and shoemaking, distilling and oil refining.

ROMANUS, pope for about four months in the latter half of the year 897, was born at Gallese, near Città Castellana. He was cardinal of St. Peter ad Vincula before his election as successor to Stephen VI (VII). It has been suggested that he began the reaction in favour of the memory of Formosus (*q.v.*), whom Stephen had done so much to discredit.

ROMANUS, the name of four East Roman emperors.

ROMANUS I (Lecapenus), who shared the imperial throne with Constantine VII (*q.v.*) and exercised all the real power from 919 to 944, was admiral of the Byzantine fleet on the Danube when, hearing of the defeat of the army at Achelous (917), he resolved to sail for Constantinople. Soon after the marriage of his daughter Helena to Constantine he was crowned colleague of his son-in-law. His reign was terminated by his own sons, Stephen and Constantine, who in 944 compelled him to become a monk. He died in 948.

ROMANUS II succeeded his father Constantine VII in 959 at the age of 21, and died—poisoned, it was believed, by his wife, Theophano—in 963. He was a pleasure-loving sovereign, but showed judgment in the selection of his ministers. The great event of his reign was the conquest of Crete by Nicephorus Phocas.

ROMANUS III (Argyrus), emperor 1028–1034, was an undistinguished Byzantine patrician, who was compelled by the dying emperor, Constantine VIII, to marry his daughter Zoe and to become his successor. He showed great eagerness to make his mark as a ruler, but was mostly unfortunate in his enterprises, and in his endeavour to relieve the pressure of taxation disorganized the finances of the state. In 1030 he resolved to retaliate upon the incursions of the Moslems on the eastern frontier by leading a large army against Aleppo, but was defeated at Azaz near Antioch. His early death was supposed to have been due to poison administered by his wife.

See J. B. Bury in the *English Historical Review* (1889), pp. 53–57; G. Schlumberger, *L'Épopée byzantine* (Paris, 1905), iii, pp. 56–158.

ROMANUS IV (Diogenes), emperor 1068–1071, had risen to distinction in the army, when he was convicted of treason against the sons of Constantine X. He was pardoned, however, by the empress Eudocia, whom he subsequently married. After his coronation he carried on three successful campaigns against the Saracens and Seljuk Turks; in a fourth he was defeated by Alp Arslan on the banks of the Araxes and taken prisoner. After releasing himself by the promise of a large ransom and the conclusion of a peace, he turned his arms against the pretender Michael VII, but was compelled after a defeat to resign the empire and retire to the island of Prote, where he soon died in great misery. It was during this reign that, by the surrender of Bari (1071), the Byzantine empire lost its last hold upon Italy.

See J. J. C. Anderson in the *Journal of Hellenic Studies* (1897), pp. 36–39. On all the above *see* also J. B. Bury's edition of Edward Gibbon, *Decline and Fall of the Roman Empire*.

ROMANY LANGUAGE. The strongest proof that the gypsies came originally from India is found in their language

For all its dialects are clearly Indo-Aryan, that is to say, modifications of the language from which have sprung all the Aryan languages of modern India and Ceylon, and of which Sanskrit, with its oldest document the R̥gveda, is the literary expression. Moreover, gypsy is not only derived from the same original source as the other Aryan languages of India, but must for many centuries after the Vedic age have shared their development within or near the borders of India. For in general it shows the phonetic and grammatical changes which the Indian languages as a whole did not reach long before the beginning of the Christian era.

Dialectical Position.—The question in which dialect-group of these languages gypsy had its origin has been much discussed. One school holds that it belongs to the north-western and especially to the Dardic, which comprises certain dialects of the Hindu Kush and includes also the more important Kashmiri. These languages, in some respects more conservative than those further in India, have kept certain features of the old Sanskrit sound-system unchanged, e.g., the preservation of two or more sibilants (ś, ṣ, s) or of an r preceded by a consonant. The gypsy dialects also show some of these peculiarities. But the preservation by descendants of characteristics that existed in the parent language is not proof that they have any specially close relationship (other than common origin). The existence of the same early innovations in both is proffered by those who hold that gypsy belonged originally to a more central group of dialects, of which a typical modern representative in India is Hindi. It is with these it shares its earliest sound-changes. Gypsy does not, however, share other later innovations of the central group which had set in or were setting in at the time of Aśoka (c. 250 B.C.). They must, therefore, have severed their relations with this group before that date. The word rom, "Gypsy man," south-east European ṛom, Armenian Gy. lom, Palestinian Gy. dōm, is the same word as the Skt. ḍomba-, "a low caste of dancers and singers," from whom the Ḍōms of India also derive their name. It is probable that wandering tribes, perhaps of the same character as some of the criminal tribes of modern India, speaking a central dialect, made their way to the north-west (probably western Panjab or Peshawar district) before the middle of the 3rd century B.C. There, among speakers of the north-western dialect-group, they stayed until, at some time before the 9th century A.D., they left India behind them in a migration which spread them all over western Asia, Europe and even America.

Dialects.—It is not known whether the gypsies left India in one or several separate migrations or whether there were even at that time marked dialectical variations in the language they spoke. But at the present day there are at least three distinct groups of dialects, the Asiatic, the Armenian, and the European. One of the most noticeable differences lies in the treatment of the original voiced aspirates of Sanskrit. The Asiatic dialects have either preserved these or, losing the aspiration, have reduced them to simple voiced sounds; the European and Armenian dialects, on the other hand, have changed them to surd aspirates: Skt. bh, dh, gh become Asiatic b, d, g, but Armenian and European ph, th, kh (pʻ, tʻ, kʻ). Thus we find Skt. bhrátā "brother," dhūmáḥ "smoke," ghr̥tám "melted butter" in Eur. Gy. pʻral, tʻuv, kʻil, in Pal. Gy. bar, dif, gir.

To-day there is considerable dialectical variation even within a single group such as the European, dating probably from the time of separation within Europe itself. These dialects differ according to locality and to the degree in which they have been influenced by surrounding languages. In this respect they may vary from the comparatively pure Indian idiom of, for example, some of the Balkan gypsies or even of the gypsies of Wales, to mere jargons consisting of a framework of the local language, for example, English, in which a certain portion of the vocabulary is replaced by gypsy words.

Sounds.—The vowel-system rests on that of Sanskrit. As in all Middle Indian dialects Skt. ai and au have become ē and ō (e.g., Arm. Gy. tel, "oil," from tailám; mol, "price," from maulyam). In the European dialect Skt. a in an open syllable appears as e, but in an originally closed syllable as a, which is also the representative of Skt. ā: merel, "dies," rakʻel, "keeps," manuš, "man", from márate, rákṣati, mānuṣáḥ.

In the consonant-system, the chief innovation is the change of the voiced aspirates already mentioned. Of the surd aspirates, ph appears to remain (pʻal, "board" from Skt. phálaḥ); ch loses its aspiration in west European gypsy (W. Eur. čin-, "to cut," S. E. Eur. čʻin- from Skt. chinná-); kh perhaps becomes a spirant χ (χanro, "sword" from Skt. khaṇḍakaḥ). Intervocalic consonants, as in all other descendants of Sanskrit, are weakened. The gutturals and palatals disappear altogether; the cerebrals remain as r (S. E. Eur. r̥), the labials partly as v, the dentals as l in the European and Armenian dialects and as r in the Asiatic.

Sanskrit	Gypsy	Sanskrit	Gypsy
yūkā "louse"	ǰuv id.	ágataḥ "came"	alo id.
sūcī "needle"	suv id.	vijanati "bears young"	benel id.
kīṭáḥ "insect"	kiri "ant"	biḍālaḥ "cat"	blári (Syr.) id
sthāpáyati "places"	tʻovel id.	píbati "drinks"	piel id.
yuvatíḥ "young woman"	ǰuvel id.	hr̥dayam "heart"	yilo id.
	ǰuăr (Syr.)		ḷri (Syr.)

Assimilation of consonant-groups has occurred generally, with the exception of r preceded by a stop and of sibilants followed by dental or cerebral stops (except in the Armenian dialect). Thus

Sanskrit	Gypsy
dugdhám "milk"	tʻud (from duddhaṁ), Arm. lutʻ.
bhrátā "brother"	pʻral id., Arm. pʻal, Syr. bar.
hástaḥ "hand"	vast, Syr. ḫăst, Arm. atʻ.

Grammar.—In grammar, too, the main structure of the better preserved dialects rests upon its Sanskrit original. The declension of the noun is based on two cases—a direct (descended from the Sanskrit nominative and accusative) and an oblique (descended from the Sanskrit genitive) to which various postpositions can be added.

	Sanskrit	Prakrit	Gypsy
Sing. nom.	córáḥ (-ō)	córō	čor
acc.	córám	córaṁ	
gen.	córásya	córassa (-asa)	čores
Plur. nom.	córáḥ	córā	čor
gen.	córáṇām	córáṇaṁ	čoren

The verb is built up of the old present stem, of which the indicative, the imperative and the participle still survive, and of the past participle, which alone or combined with auxiliaries forms past tenses.

		Sanskrit	Gypsy
Present indicative:	Sing.	rákṣāmi	rakʻav
		rákṣasi	rakʻes
		rákṣati	rakʻel
	Plur.	rákṣāmasi	rakʻas
		rákṣathana	rakʻen
		rákṣanti	rakʻen

The opposition between present stem and past participle, though in most cases the latter has been remodelled on the former, still survives in a few verbs:

Skt. márate "dies" : mr̥táḥ "dead" =Gy. merel : mulo.
„ yáti "goes" : gatáḥ "gone" = „ ǰal : gelo.

Gypsy has preserved the Sanskrit numerals 1 to 6, 10, 20, 100. But 7, 8, 9 and higher numbers are borrowed—by Asiatic generally from Persian, by European from Greek—or are formed by various methods of addition or multiplication from existing numerals.

The borrowing of vocabulary has been extensive. The first examples can be dated back to the time when, leaving the central group of dialects in India, the gypsies sojourned among the speakers of the north-western group. Indeed, the borrowed words of a gypsy dialect disclose the itinerary of its migrations. When in the dialect of the gypsies of Wales we find borrowed words from Persian, Armenian, Greek, Rumanian, Bulgarian, Serbian, Czech, German, French and English, we may assume that at some time or other the ancestors of this particular group passed through the countries where these languages were spoken. The form in which the words appear may give some clue as to the date when they were borrowed. The most numerous source for the European dialects is Greek, a fact which accords with the long stay the gypsies appear to have made in the Eastern empire.

BIBLIOGRAPHY.—G. F. Black, *A Gypsy Bibliography* (1913, bibl.); *Journal of the Gypsy Lore Society* (from 1888); J. Sampson, *The Dialect of the Gypsies of Wales* (1925, bibl.), invaluable for the study of any gypsy dialect; R. L. Turner, *Position of Romani in Indo-Aryan* (1927); R. A. S. Macalister, *Language of the Nawar* (1914); F. N. Finck, *Sprache der armenischen Zigeuner* (1907); A. G. Paspati, *Les Tchinghianés de l'empire ottoman* (1870); R. von Sowa, *Die Mundart der slovakischen Zigeuner* (1887), *Wörterbuch des Dialekts der deutschen Zigeuner* (1898); B. C. Smart and H. J. Crofton, *The Dialect of the English Gypsies* (1875); F. Miklosich, *Mundarten der Zigeuner Europa's* (1872–80); Albert Thomas Sinclair, "An American Romani Vocabulary," comp. and ed. by George F. Black, *New York Pub. Lib. Bull.*, vol. xix., pp. 727–738 (1915).　(R. L. T.)

ROMBLON, a municipality, capital and port of the province and island of Romblon, Philippine Islands, about 187 mi. from Manila. It has a deep well sheltered harbour which makes it one of the best ports south of Luzon. Pop. (1939) 14,309; 13 were white. The exportation of copra is extensive. Ornamental buri mats are made there. Cebuano is the vernacular. Of the inhabitants aged 6 to 19 inclusive, 32.4% attended school in 1939, while 42.2% of the population 10 years old and over was literate.

ROME, a province of modern Italy, forming a part of the district of Latium (Lazio) (*q.v.*).

ROME, the capital of the kingdom of Italy, lies on the Tiber river, 17m. north-east from its mouth on the Mediterranean. It was the capital of the ancient Roman republic and of the Roman empire and became very early the headquarters of the Christian Church. With a longer record of continuous political and religious importance than any other city it is unique for its antiquarian interest. In the following account the general subject of Rome is treated broadly under two aspects, themselves subdivided. These are: (1) the topography and growth of the city of Rome, the evolution of which is traced from the earliest times to the present, and (2) Roman history, *i.e.*, the political and social history of the Roman republic, empire, the mediaeval commune, and briefly the modern Rome.

THE ANCIENT CITY

The primitive city of Rome stood not in the Tiber valley, but on the ridges—so-called hills—of the Latin plain that jut unevenly into the valley. During the empire the city encroached more and more on the lower level till it covered the whole of the Campus Martius that lay in the wide bend of the river opposite the Vatican hill. These ridges, like the whole Latin plain, consisted of volcanic ash, partly cemented into hard tuff, which had, during a long series of eruptions in the Alban hills, filled an inland lake and built up an uneven plateau. In drilling wells outside of Rome's gates the following strata, enumerated from top to bottom, are usually pierced: several layers of brownish ash or tuff, a stratum of cappellaccio or friable grey tufa mixed with alluvial sediment, sand and gravel of the former lake bottom, and finally pliocene clay. Where erosion has not been very active the volcanic deposit near Rome rises to about 100 feet. Nearer the Alban hills it is far deeper. Here and there drilling also encounters hardened streams of lava that flowed from the craters from time to time. The Appian way lies partly upon a tongue of hard lava that flowed northwards during one of the last eruptions, not long before historic times.

The First Settlements.—On the part of Latium covered by the ash deposits we have as yet no convincing proofs of human settlements prior to the early iron age (about 1000 B.C.), whereas on the calcareous areas of Latium—on the Sabine and Volscian hills—which this ash did not reach, numerous remains even of Neolithic settlements have been found. It would seem that the site of Rome (and its neighbourhood on the south and east) was not an attractive place for settlement until about 1,000 years before our era, and the cause may well have been the activity of the Alban volcanoes. The first settlers coming from north of the Tiber seem to have taken possession first of the Alban hills and then of the Roman "hills." They were apparently shepherd and agricultural peoples of the "Italic" branch of the Indo-European race, related to the Villanovans (*q.v.*) who were settling in southern Etruria at the end of the second millennium B.C. The highest and

safest points (the Palatine hill, probably the Capitoline and the outjutting spurs of the Esquiline) seem to have been chosen for the first communities. The graves of these early people that have been found in the Sepulcretum at the edge of the Forum show that they were a cremating folk that possessed the same kind of utensils and pottery that have been found in the Alban cemeteries. About the 8th century a related people, which however buried their dead, came in from the older settlements of the Sabine hills and built their straw huts on the Esquiline and Quirinal ridges. In the 6th century Etruscan princes seem to have conquered the whole of Latium. They soon organized these communities (which had apparently coalesced to some extent) into a city, and, bringing it into connection with the rapidly growing Etruscan cities north of the river, laid the foundations of a flourishing principality. Before they were driven out, about 500 B.C., a large temple had been built to Jupiter, Juno and Minerva on the Capitoline, a stone wall had been raised enclosing all the hill communities, and the forum valley had been drained so that the area could be used as a common market place.

In early Rome ordinary dwellings were straw huts or straw-thatched adobe huts, while temples and public buildings were erected in the Etruscan manner to suit the materials of the vicinity. The Capitoline temple, for instance, had walls of volcanic tuff well coated with stucco to hide the ugliness of the material. The ceiling beams which supported a tile roof were probably held up by a cantilever brace. The roof of the portico rested on four tuscan columns of wood or stuccoed tufa. The wooden architraves were covered with figured terra-cotta slabs that provided some adornment and protection for the beams. The pediment figures were also of terra-cotta. Because of the absence of good building stone the Etruscans early developed for architectural adornment a dignified plastic art in terra-cotta, and its artistic qualities can now be appreciated in the splendid Apollo-figure recently discovered in Veii, a few miles north of Rome. This Etruscan method of building sufficed for the city till Greek artists were brought to Rome in the second century B.C. The building of stone bridges and aqueducts during the 2nd century popularized the use of the stone arch. The concrete dome which became so striking an element in later Roman construction was not used to good effect till the latter part of the 1st century of the empire when the art of making reliable concrete had been fully developed.

Materials.—Since public buildings were frequently rebuilt and enlarged it is difficult to assign the present remains to their proper epoch, and the accounts of early Roman architecture do not by any means agree as to dates. It is only by careful observation of the materials[1] used that we can assign the remains of the republican period to their approximate periods. Before the Gallic fire in 387 B.C. practically the only stone used was the soft grey volcanic tufa called cappellaccio, the principal source of which was the quarry at the foot of the Capitoline where the Mamertine prison now stands. This is a very poor weathering stone so that it was regularly protected by a coat of stucco when used above ground. After the Gallic fire, when Rome had gained possession of the Veientian quarries of Grotta Oscura near the Tiber some 10m. north of the city, the yellowish grey tufa of that region came into popular use. This stone was as easily worked as the native one, and being more uniform in texture was cut into larger blocks of 2×2 feet. The massive fortification walls of Rome were largely rebuilt of this material during the 4th century, as were many of the public structures that had been destroyed by the Gauls. For rough work some very ugly volcanic stone, full of inclusions of black scoria, was also used for a while. This was also found in southern Etruria, and the blocks that were used at Rome and Ostia may have come from the abandoned walls of Fidenae, north of Rome. The grey tufa of Grotta Oscura was the favourite building stone of the city for over 200 years, while the scoria-filled stone was soon abandoned.

These materials also weathered poorly and proved too weak for

[1]Middleton, *The Remains of Ancient Rome* (1892); Lanciani, *Ruins and Excavations* (1897); Delbrück, *Hellenistische Bauten* (1907); Van Deman, *The Date of Concrete Monuments* (1912); Frank, *Roman Buildings of the Republic* (1924).

heavy loads. Hence in the 3rd century architects went to the Alban hills for the stronger dark grey tufa (*Lapis Albanus, peperino*) when in search for architrave beams and heavy column drums. The Tullianum, Rome's first prison, which required a very hard stone, seems to be the first structure built of this material. It probably was constructed about 250 B.C., certainly not in the regal period as has been supposed. All the large temples built during the 2nd century B.C. used peperino for points of great stress and weight. At the Gabine lake, an old volcanic crater which was nearer Rome, a tufa somewhat rougher than peperino, but equally strong, was then brought into use. This Gabine stone (*Lapis Gabinus, sperone*) was freely employed in massive walls for a century or more, but its use was limited by the fact that it would not yield to ornamental cutting. Both of these stones were costly because of the heavy transportation charges. Hence during the 2nd century experiments were made with the brown tufas nearer Rome. As can still be seen, the hills of Rome had an abundant supply of this brown tufa lying above the cappellaccio, but these hills were now so well covered with buildings that quarrying inside the city was impracticable. South of the Janiculum, on Mt. Verde, a quarry was opened and used for several buildings of the second century and of the early decades of the first. The Mt. Verde stone is hard, close-grained, but too brittle for heavy burdens, and was seldom used after Sulla's day. The brown tufa from the Anio river just above Rome proved to be very strong and uniform, in fact an excellent material except for its ugly appearance. After the fine arches of the Aqua Marcia were built of it in 144 B.C., it remained because of its durability and cheapness the favourite stone for ordinary ashlar masonry for two centuries. This Anio tufa is now to be found in the ruins of more than half of the buildings of the forum. During the 2nd century B.C. two very important discoveries of materials were made. The travertine deposits at Bagni on the road to Tivoli were found. This is a limestone of recent formation caused by the deposit of the carbonate of lime from the hot springs that arise at that point. Since the ground was level and covered with vegetation the splendid deposit had for centuries lain unobserved. The stone being rather soft when at first exposed is easily sawed and worked. It soon hardens under exposure. The Romans used it at first with some hesitation, but by Caesar's day they had learned to appreciate its good qualities. During the early empire it was freely used, as may be seen in the massive walls of the Colosseum. Recently this stone has been exported in large quantities to America.

Unfortunately for the aesthetic qualities of Roman architecture the process of making a cheap and durable, though ugly, concrete was discovered at about the same time. Since good sand is difficult to find near Rome, volcanic ash (*pozzolana*), which lies in abundance everywhere in Latium, was substituted. This ash is of course a crushed dehydrated slag, and it was eventually found that if the ash was taken from deep pits where rain-water had not destroyed its qualities it would mix with lime into a very firm hydraulic cement. By adding a filler of tufa fragments a very cheap and durable concrete could thus be made. Concrete was first used freely in the foundations and podia of the temple of Concord in 120 B.C. and the temple of Castor in 117 B.C., but it is found even earlier in a part of the platform that was constructed in front of Castor several years before. This platform probably belongs to the Gracchan period. Concrete however came into free use in superstructures only in the age of Caesar, when marble was imported in such abundance that it could be used as a veneer for ugly concrete walls. The great importance of concrete for Roman architecture lay in the fact that during the empire, when Rome required very extensive structures, domes and vaults of immense span could be built of this material. During the empire most of the heavy walls were constructed of concrete because of its cheapness and durability. They were usually faced with brick or with marble slabs. The bricks when used were generally triangular with one angle stuck into the concrete; the marble slab veneering was usually held in place by iron clamps.

Though the art of making good terra-cotta ware was known in primitive Rome, and roof-tiles of terra-cotta of excellent quality had freely been used for six centuries before Augustus' day, bricks were not burned at Rome for use in wall-construction during the republic. Immense heaps of fragments of broken roof-tiles had however accumulated, and the Augustan architects began to use these fragments in facing concrete walls. When this supply gave out, triangular bricks were made for the same purpose—during the reign of Claudius—and when, after the great fire of Nero's day, a vast programme of rebuilding followed, brick yards turned out an immense quantity of material for the facing of concrete walls. This material continued to be used freely through imperial times.

Marble was very expensive and relatively few buildings were made of solid marble; but for veneering, for columns, entablatures and decorative members large quantities of marble were imported. A few wealthy nobles had imported marble columns for their porticoes before Caesar's day. While Caesar was governor of Cisalpine Gaul his architects and engineers began to import to Rome Carrara marble, found in that province. The architects of Augustus developed the Numidian quarries of Simitthu, which yielded a variety of yellow and cream coloured marbles of great beauty (giallo antico). The transportation costs were very heavy since it had to be brought 100m. over land before it was loaded on ships. Its use was largely confined to decorative purposes. The pavonazzetto of Synnada, 200m. inland from Smyrna in Asia Minor, also came into use, as well as the greenish cipollino of Euboea, the marbles of Pentelicon, Hymettus and Paros, and the red granites of Aswan in Egypt. During the empire architects vied with each other in attaining new colour effects with contrasting veneers, and the Christian basilicas and churches of Rome which are decorated with the marbles stripped from Roman buildings are rich with stones that the emperors had imported from all parts of the world. Besides those mentioned we may name the products of quarries of Chios (called *Africano*), Thasos (*porta santa*), Laconia (*rosso antico* and *nero antico*), Thessaly (*verde antico*), and the alabasters and porphyries of Egypt.

Early Town Walls.—Tradition speaks of very early fortifications around the Palatine and Capitoline hills. These may have been earthen mounds bearing a fence of stakes. There is no doubt that a stone wall was constructed of cappellaccio blocks around the whole city at the time of the Etruscan kings. This wall was almost wholly rebuilt after the Gallic fire (387 B.C.) with the stronger Grotta Oscura stone, and later strengthened and improved from time to time with better materials. This so-called Servian wall (at first not including the Aventine) was nearly 6km. long. It began at the Tiber near the present Ponte Rotto, had two gates between the Tiber and the Capitoline hill, skirted the Capitoline on its west side (where a few blocks of the 4th-century wall are visible), then proceeded across the valley to the edge of the Quirinal hill. A small gate (perhaps an embrasure for artillery) is still visible inside the Palazzo Antonielli, but this consists of Anio tufa and must date from about the time of the first civil war. The fragment of wall seen in the via Nazionale just above is of Grotta Oscura stone belonging to the 4th century. From this point the wall followed the edge of the Quirinal hill north-eastwards for over a mile to the porta Collina. At the via Finanze may be seen a well preserved portion in cappellaccio. Because of the material this part has usually been assigned to the 6th century, but the fine workmanship and battering would rather indicate a 4th century reconstruction. From the Porta Collina the wall turned southwards across the level plateau to the porta Esquilina, a distance of about a mile. Here the city was especially exposed to attack and the wall was not only made with special care in the 4th century but was later frequently strengthened and repaired. In constructing this portion a moat 30ft. deep and 100ft. wide was dug and the earth of this excavation was used for an agger about 40ft. thick. The stone wall itself that stood behind the moat and supported the mound was about 10ft. thick and more than 30ft. high and was made of Grotta Oscura stone. The inner side of the agger was supported by a lower cappellaccio wall. The numerous quarry marks found in the section near the railway station are probably those of the Etruscan workmen of the 4th century, while those found at Piazza Fanti seem to belong to the repairs of the second Punic War. The Gabine and Monte Verde stones of the reconstructed

Viminal gate may belong to the time of the Social War, while the concrete work and Anio stone at Piazza Macao seem to be a part of the repairs made during the Catilinarian Rebellion or the civil war.

The original wall skirted the Palatine hill on the south side and ran directly to the river. Here several portions of the 4th-century wall, built in Grotta Oscura tufa and the scoriated Fidenae stone, have been found, but at the south-west corner of the hill a fragment of the original 6th-century wall in cappellaccio blocks may still be seen. During the 4th century the Aventine was also included in the fortifications. The large wall on the Via di porta S. Paulo, however, was repaired with Anio stone and a concrete backing during the Sullan period, and near the gateway arched openings for the placement of defensive artillery were neatly constructed.

Streets.—It is doubtful whether Rome had paved streets before the 2nd century B.C. The earliest pavement that has been found is that of the street which ascends the Capitoline hill from the forum. It was laid in 174 B.C. The few remains of it still visible at the side of the temple of Saturn are hard rough lava blocks full of leucitic crystals. This lava was brought from beyond Civita Castellana and was preferred to the native lava of the Appian Way because the crystals furnish a rough surface which is essential on a steep roadway. During the 1st century B.C. most of the streets were paved with large polygonal lava blocks neatly fitted and (at times) set in a concrete bedding and curbed with travertine. Outside of the city some of these pavements are still in use after 2,000 years of wear.

Bridges and Drains.—The first bridges of Rome were laid on wooden piles. In 179, stone piers were built for the Aemilian bridge (the *ponte rotto*). In the period between Gracchus and Sulla, architects had learned to make strong arches and then the Aemilian and the Mulvian bridges were constructed of splendid stone arches. The Fabrician bridge, contracted for apparently during Cicero's consulship, with two vast arches, is still in use. The first large sewer which drained the forum and cattle market seems to have been an open channel lined with cappellaccio masonry. It was covered over early in the republic. The magnificent Cloaca Maxima which opens out near the Palatine bridge and was in use until the beginning of the 20th century was, to judge from its free use of Gabine stone, not constructed till the latter part of the 2nd century B.C. During the empire the whole city was as thoroughly drained with well-built sewers as any modern city.

Aqueducts.—Before 312 B.C. the city depended upon wells and springs for its water supply. In that year Appius Claudius, the censor, constructed an underground aqueduct 7m. in length to supply water to the poor of the crowded sections of the city. Forty years later the Anio Vetus was added. In 144 the Aqua Marcia was laid bringing an abundant supply of excellent water from high in the Sabine hills 44m. away. Where it crossed the lower plain outside of Rome the conduit was raised on splendid arches so as to bring the water to the top of the Capitoline hill. Some of these arches are still standing near Porta Furba; and the city of Rome is still using the springs that supplied the Aqua Marcia. Augustus, Claudius and later emperors enlarged the water supply, laid an extensive system of leaden pipes in the streets and built numerous fountains, till in Trajan's day the city was generously supplied with pure water.

THE FORUM[1]

In the early days the valley between the Palatine hill and the Capitoline was marshy ground with an open pool, the Lacus Curtius, near the centre, another near the west end, the Lacus Servilius, which caught the spring waters of the Capitoline hill, and another, the Lacus Juturnae at the base of the Palatine. On the lower slope of the Capitoline hill, on a protruding ledge of rock, were altars to Saturn and to Vulcan, and between them a speaker's platform. On the corresponding lower slope of the Palatine was the shrine of Vesta with the house of the vestals near by and the

office of the pontifex maximus. Below the Esquiline was an extensive burial ground. When the marsh was drained and the three springs walled in the central part became an open market place—*forum*—which was soon lined with two rows of shops (*tabernae*), while the north-west corner was laid off for open-air town-meetings (the *comitium*), and a speaker's platform was early constructed between the *comitium* and the forum. Without regard for chronology we shall briefly mention the more important buildings of the forum of which there are remains, beginning at the Tullianum on the north-west corner.

The *Tullianum*[2] ("Mamertine prison") took the place, as death-chamber, of the older quarry caverns that here ran deep into the Capitoline hill. It was apparently built in the 3rd century B.C. Alban stone—the hardest material available—was used. The chamber was a truncated cone, about 12ft. high. It originally had a ceiling of oak beams, and could be entered only from a trap-door above. In the 2nd century an arc of the circle was cut away to make room for the road in front, and a straight wall of Grotta Oscura stone was built in its place. About 100 B.C. an upper vaulted chamber of Mt. Verde and Anio stone was constructed above the Tullianum, and later the lower chamber was given a horizontal stone vault. Finally, in the reign of Tiberius, a massive façade of travertine was built on the forum front. This is the chamber where noted prisoners like Jugurtha, the Catilinarian conspirators and Vercingetorix were kept before execution. It could never have been a well-house, as has been supposed, since the floor is actually above the republican level of the *comitium*. The present floor is about 6ft. above the original, if Sallust's measure of its depth is correct.

On the south of the Tullianum are the remains of the *Temple of Concordia*.[3] The original temple was erected to the deified abstraction of Concord in 366 to mark the temporary peace in the class conflict between the patricians and plebeians. The temple was rebuilt, partly with the earlier materials, and enlarged by the aristocratic consul Opimius in 120 B.C., to mark the end of the Gracchan class contests. The rededication to Concord was however considered an insult by the defeated Gracchans. Here Cicero delivered two of his Catilinarian speeches, using the temple for his addresses not only because he wished to remind the people of his programme of *concordia ordinum* but also because of the suggestive proximity of the place to the death-chamber. Tiberius rebuilt the temple in marble to commemorate the Concord of the Augustan régime. This new temple had a large portico and entrance on the forum side and the concrete base of this comes forward nearly to the Vulcanal. Portions of the elaborately carved cornice and of some of the capitals and bases are still to be seen in the corridor of the Tabularium. The temple was one of the most richly decorated at Rome and became a veritable museum of precious works of art. The corner of the podium nearest the prison originally belonged to the *senaculum*—a gathering place of senators—but was incorporated in the enlarged portico of this later temple.

Below the steps of the temple of Concord may be seen the remains of a very old *Altar of Vulcan* cut in the native cappellaccio, and near by several cuttings in the rock which give evidence of an early cemetery here. Passing the *Arch of Septimius Severus*, a work of pleasing proportions though covered with confused reliefs of a decadent and boastful art, we reach the remains of the old *Rostra*, the scene of Rome's legislative struggles from the time of the *Twelve Tables* till Caesar. It is the birthplace of modern democracy. In the centre of the mass may be seen a few of the old steps that may belong to the platform of the decemviral times. The name rostra derived from the iron rams taken as trophies from the warships of Antium (338 B.C.) and fastened on the back of the platform (on the forum side). The outer steps of Mt. Verde stone on the side of the Comitium and the circular rear wall of concrete lined with reticulate blocks belong to a rebuilding of the Sullan period.

Between the rostra and the Arch lies a *black stone* pavement that marks a sacred area uncovered in the excavations of 1899.

[1]Jordan, *Topographie*, i.; Lanciani, *Ruins and Excavations;* Huelsen (Carter, tr.), *The Roman Forum*, with references to the reports of the excavators: Carlo Fea, Rosa, Fiorelli, Lanciani, Boni, et al.; Thédenat. *Le Forum Romain;* Lugli, *La Zona Archeologica di Roma.*

[2]Frank, *Roman Buildings of the Republic*, 39 ff.

[3]Rebert and Marceau, in *Memoirs of Amer. Acad. in Rome*, v. 53.

The layer of gravel which covered this area as well as the pre-Sullan rostra shows that the sacred area was abandoned and covered up when the Sullan rostra were built. The objects found beneath the black stone are a 6th-century inscription of very great importance, though so much damaged that no line is complete, a truncated cone which probably supported a statue, a double base which, according to Varro, supported two figures of lions, presumably such as Etruscans placed in front of important tombs, and a great many votive objects of different periods—now to be seen in the forum museum. Some of these objects were found in their original setting, others had been removed here and buried as being too sacred to destroy at the time when the rostra were rebuilt.

The inscription is cut on stone imported from Etruscan territory, and since the lettering is too archaic for the 4th century, when Rome captured the region from which it came, we must assume that it was brought here during the Etruscan period, i.e., before 509 B.C. The "black stone" was supposed by the Romans to mark the tomb of Romulus, of Faustulus or of Hostilius. The riddle has not yet been solved.

The *Curia* or senate chamber, which stands in the comitium, is the debased structure of Diocletian's day, much altered and converted into a church. The first senate house (attributed to the king Hostilius) stood farther back, leaving room for a large comitium between the Curia and the rostra. The original bronze doors of Diocletian's Curia may now be seen at the end of the nave of the Lateran basilica.

Crossing the narrow street, the *Argiletum*, which led into the Forum from the north, we come to the extensive remains of the *Basilica Aemilia*. This was a covered hall in which court could be held when the weather was too inclement for sessions in the open forum. When building it in 179 B.C. Aemilius Lepidus and Fulvius Nobilior also rebuilt the row of public shops (*tabernae novae*) and included these under the same roof with a covered arcade in front. There was a hasty reconstruction by Aemilius Lepidus in 79. About the year 54 when Caesar planned his basilica along the opposite side of the forum at a higher level he lent large sums to Aemilius Paullus to reconstruct the Aemilian basilica at a corresponding level and in an appropriate style. This rebuilding, frequently interrupted, was not completed for 20 years. The foundations now visible are chiefly of this period, though the shop walls reveal materials of all three periods. Augustus later provided money for lavish repairs and decorations after the structure had been damaged by fire. Most of the splendid marble decorations now to be seen date from the Augustan period, deriving partly from the Doric façade, partly from the interior porticoes decorated with Ionic and Corinthian columns.

East of this basilica stands the temple which Antoninus Pius built in honor of his deified wife *Faustina*. After the emperor's death his name was added to the inscription. The columns are of the expensive and garish Carystian stone (*cipollino*) from Euboea, the walls are of peperino, a good fire-proof material, and were of course faced with marble slabs. The frieze has a charming design of griffins grouped in pairs around a candelabrum.

In front of this temple are the remains of the *Regia*, one of the oldest buildings of Rome. It may have been the office of the early kings, and certainly was of the pontifex maximus throughout the republic. The cappellaccio podium of the main quadrangle may well date from the fifth century. Professor Huelsen, who excavated the site, has drawings of a decorated terracotta slab from its frieze which belonged to the 5th-century structure. The rear wall, however, contains materials of a reconstruction, probably made in 148 B.C., when the place was damaged by fire. In this building were kept the important pontifical records and lists of magistrates which provided the skeleton of facts that historians eventually used in writing the story of the early republic. And because of this historical association, Domitius Calvinus, when rebuilding the house in 36 B.C. in marble, had a complete list of magistrates and of triumphs inscribed on its walls. Some remains of these inscriptions, called Capitoline Fasti, are now preserved in the Capitoline museum. The few architectural remains that lie near by reveal the fact that even as late as 36 B.C. marble cutting

was still very crude.[1] The pontifex himself had his home in the *domus publica*, the foundations of which, as it was when Caesar lived there, may still be seen a few yards to the south-east of the regia.

The extensive *House of the Vestals*,[2] as it appeared in the late empire, has many of its walls intact. They date from several rebuildings and additions made at various times during the empire. A few of the Vestal statues and honorary inscriptions remain, but not on their original locations, since all were found in a confused heap ready for the limekiln. Of the small republican structure there are few remains except the simple mosaic floor visible at a low level near the entrance. The foundation of the round shrine of Vesta is visible between this Atrium and the Regia, and near by are remains of the marble entablature cut in the decadent workmanship of Septimius' day.

Between the Regia and the open space of the forum stands the podium of the *Temple of Divus Iulius* which Augustus erected to the deified Caesar (dedicated 29 B.C.). This site was chosen because Caesar's body was burned upon a speaker's platform at this place (probably the *tribunal Aurelianum*). The spot had first been marked by an altar, the foundations of which may still be seen.

Augustus in building the temple respected the altar, indenting the portico so that the steps of the temple rose at the sides of the altar. Hence the strange ground-plan. This temple was the first striking proof at Rome of the acceptance of the theory of "Divine rights" of Rome's princes. Foundation walls of heavy masonry built outside of the concrete mass now visible supported the walls of the temple. The temple itself was an Ionic hexastyle building of marble, the columns being about ten and a half metres high. The interior was very richly decorated with imported works of art, but the architectural decoration of the entablature, fragments of which are still to be seen on the south side, was rather crude, as was all such work at Rome during the period. A few feet south of this temple there still exist the foundations of the *Arch of Augustus* erected only ten years later. Fragments of the marble decoration of this arch may be seen lying at the nearby corner of the Regia. Though somewhat too graceful and delicate for the purpose of a triumphal arch those carvings are done with a care which shows a remarkable advance in such work during the ten years after the construction of the temple of Divus Iulius.

The famous *temple of Castor and Pollux*,[3] which still has three Pentelic columns erect with a part of the entablature, is the most prominent ruin of the Forum. The first temple on the site was built in the Tuscan style early in the republic (484 B.C.) to the divinities of the Greek cavalry who aided the Romans at the battle of Lake Regillus. Since these gods were adopted as the patron-deities of the Roman knights, the temple became the official meeting place of the knights and wealthy business men of Rome, and these took some interest in maintaining it. They used its coffers for safety deposits, and its basement offices for the protection of standard weights and measures and for an assay-laboratory for the testing of coins and metals. It thus came to be Rome's "Bureau of Standards." The cappellaccio blocks which may be seen in the podium remain from the first structure, while those found in a small room under the front stairway belonged to an early speaker's platform not directly connected with the first temple. Much of the inner core of concrete belongs to a reconstruction made by Caecilius Metellus in 117 B.C., while the rest of the concrete, as well as the heavy masonry, are a part of the reconstructed temple built by Tiberius in A.D. 6. The splendid Pentelic columns seem, however, to belong to a reconstruction of Hadrian's day, though of this we are not yet certain. This last temple was Corinthian, octostyle and peripteral, with 11 columns on each side, the whole measuring about 30x50 metres. No temple at Rome reveals finer decorative workmanship.

Along the west side of this temple runs the vicus Tuscus which leads to a very large brick structure behind Castor. This has long been called the *temple of Augustus*, though the brick-work belongs chiefly to the Flavian period and no traces of an earlier temple

[1] Töbelmann-Fiechter, *Römische Gebälke*; p. 8 (1923).
[2] Van Deman, *Atrium Vestae* (1909).
[3] *Memoirs Amer. Acad. in Rome*, v. p. 79.

have been found. The suggestion has also been made that it was intended as an audience chamber by Domitian.[1] There are serious objections to both hypotheses. East of this massive structure one enters the remains of the mediaeval church, S. Maria Antica, directly from the area of the Lacus Iuturnae. It contains frescoes—interesting to students of early Christian art, from the 7th, 8th and 9th centuries.[2] What the building was before Christian times is still a matter of dispute: older authorities assumed that it was a library, though it has not the usual form of a Roman library. A more recent suggestion is that it was the Atrium Minervae where the records of honourable dismissal of legionaries were kept. The impluvium, part of which is visible, belonged to the palace which Caligula had built here as an extension of his Palatine residence.

West of the vicus Tuscus, in the forum, are the confused remains of the Basilica Iulia. Caesar first built this on the site of the small basilica Sempronia, dedicating it in 46 B.C. To gain the necessary space he removed the shops which lined the Via Sacra of the Forum, and built in their place a row of shops all along the rear colonnade of his basilica. The whole was a vast structure designed to serve as a set for the four lower civil courts as well as for a market place. After a fire Augustus rebuilt it with lavish adornments of Oriental marbles, but later rebuildings after fires in the 3rd and 4th centuries left little of these structures to be seen. The modern excavators attempted to outline the ground plan by erecting bases of brick and marble fragments, but succeeded only in confusing the evidence of the structure found. An accurate reconstruction is no longer possible. The old praetor's tribunal, which stood in the forum in front of the Basilica Iulia, has now quite disappeared, but the remains of an inscription in honour of Naevius Surdinus, praetor, cut into the pavement blocks of the forum reveals the location. It was merely a low platform large enough to seat judges and jury, and was unprotected except for a canopy over the praetor's seat. The place was seldom used after the larger basilicas were built to house the courts, but it was here that the principles of Roman law were first formulated.

West of the Basilica Iulia, beyond the narrow street that was called the vicus Iugarius, stands a large part of the old temple of Saturn. The ugly granite columns with a portion of the entablature belong in part to a hasty reconstruction of the 4th century A.D.[3] (a part of one column is even inverted). The inscription recording the final restoration avoids mention of the pagan god, and the building was then in secular use. Some fragments of the cornice are remains of the republican temple of 42 B.C.—from the period of crude stone-carving—while others are later work done on the same design. On the interior facing of the frieze may be seen some good decorative slabs that were actually filched from Trajan's forum for this hasty patchwork. The podium has not a little of the splendid travertine masonry of Plancus' temple of 42 B.C. The only remains of the original temple of the early republic (497 B.C.) are the few cappellaccio blocks visible in the podium (at the very base of the east side), and in the crude wall in front of the temple—remains apparently of the original altar. The low drain-vault that appears near the latter—also early work—carries a shelf on which was found a shallow trough, apparently the runnel constructed to carry away the blood of the victims sacrificed on the altar. Saturn was an early agrarian divinity, but since his temple stood not far from the senate house, the senators—who knew that temples alone might escape looting in times of war—began to store State moneys in this temple. It thus became the official Aerarium or State treasury at Rome.

West of the temple of Saturn stands the colonnade of the Dei Consentes, the 12 chief gods whose images were represented at public festivals, according to an imported Greek rite. The older parts of the structure belong to the 3rd century B.C., when the rite was introduced at Rome. The cult never received much attention. Between this and the temple of Concord is seen the podium of the Vespasian Temple, on which three fine Corinthian columns

still stand. Titus began to build this temple to his deified father and after his death it was completed by Domitian. The well carved frieze and cornice are good examples of Flavian workmanship.

Finally at the very head of the market place are the remains of the Rostra built by Caesar and Augustus. What we see is a semicircular approach in travertine steps from the area of Concord to the platform, and, on the forum side, the front foundation in tufa blocks (partly restored). The timber platform extending from the one to the other was at first supported by travertine posts standing upright, a few of which are still visible. When these proved too weak brick piers were added. The fragment of a fine wall of tile seen on the inside seems to be Augustan, and is one of the earliest instances of brick (broken-tile) masonry of Rome. It was removed in large part during the empire and the foundation which it lined was cut back into a semicircle to make room for a small chamber. The tufa wall on the forum side was originally faced with marble and to this wall were attached the beaks of ships (rostra) brought from the old platform of the comitium. The platform held numerous statues, and in the older concrete mass of Caesar's period we may discern separate concrete bases which probably supported such statues. The interesting marble balustrades that now stand near the centre of the forum, decorated with excellent representations of political and sacrificial scenes, were probably made for this platform in Trajan's day.

East of the forum along the Via Sacra in its course over the Velia the excavations have left many problems unsolved. Between the street and the Palatine there are remains of many residences of the republican period. The foundations of old shops along the street—it was the jeweller's street—are probably of the Gracchan era. After Nero's fire the emperor covered the whole area with one vast commercial hall with an imposing portico of travertine arches along the street.[4] Owing to faulty construction this building had to be strengthened later with brick-lined concrete piers which are now seen everywhere throughout the building. North of the Via Sacra, beyond Faustina's temple, stands the church of Cosmas and Damianus, which seems to have been the temple of the Penates.[5] In front of this, later used as entrance to it, is an ugly round temple not yet identified with certainty.

Beyond the narrow street is the massive Basilica of Constantine (almost completed by Maxentius) which Michelangelo and Bramante studied for their plans of Saint Peter's, and which has influenced the architects of more than one structure in England and America. This basilica first had its entrance at the east end with its apse at the west. Constantine's architect built a portico at the centre of the south wall on the street, and made a tribunal against the north wall opposite this new entrance. Of the immense marble monolith columns (brought from the sea of Marmora) one is still standing in the piazza in front of S. Maria Maggiore. The plan is that which had been developed for the central halls of Roman baths rather than for the earlier basilicas. The four enormous piers, for instance, bear the weight on the interior, whereas in the Basilica Iulia, which is only a third as large, 74 pillars are used. The material of this immense basilica was sumptuous to a degree, but the decorative carving reveals the tasteless exaggerations and lack of practised artistry of Constantine's day.

At the top of the Velia stands the tasteful arch of Titus, as restored by Valadier more than a century ago. It commemorates the capture of Jerusalem, A.D. 70, and is decorated with two of the best reliefs that Roman art produced; the triumphal quadriga with the Dea Roma entering the city, and the floats that bore the chief objects of booty.

PALATINE HILL

The Palatine hill,[6] according to tradition, was the site of the earliest settlement at Rome. Since the "hut of Romulus" stood

[1]Delbrück, Jahrbuch des Instituts (1921).
[2]Rushforth, Papers of the British School at Rome, i. (1902); Wilpert, Mosaiken und Malerien; M. Avery, in Art Bulletin (1925).
[3]Töbelmann-Fiechter, Röm. Gebälke, p. 65 (1923)

[4]Van Deman, in Memoirs Am. Acad. vol. v.
[5]Whitehead, "The Church of S.S. Cosma e Damiano," Am. Jour. Arch., 1927.
[6]Haugwitz, Der Palatin (1901); Jordan-Huelsen, Topographie (1907); Lugli, La Zona Archeologica di Roma (1924); Platner, Topography and Monuments of Ancient Rome (1911); Huelsen, The Forum and the Palatine (with bibliography and illustrations, 1928).

ST. PETER'S AND THE VATICAN

1. Front view of St. Peter's and the Piazza San Pietro, enclosed by a quadruple colonnade designed by Bernini and constructed in 1656–67. The obelisk in the centre was brought from Heliopolis by Caligula in the 1st century A.D. and was moved to the Piazza San Pietro in 1586

2. Airview of the Vatican City state. The tiny area, less than $\frac{1}{6}$ sq.mi. in extent, is surrounded by a wall. The rectangular structures to the left of St. Peter's are the Vatican palace and the Vatican gardens

PLATE II ROME

PHOTOGRAPHS, (1) FRITZ HENLE FROM EUROPEAN, (2, 3, 6) FRITZ HENLE, (4, 7) FRITZ HENLE FROM BLACK STAR, (5) TOPICAL PRESS AGENCY

MONUMENTS AND BUILDINGS OF ANCIENT AND MODERN ROME

1. The Colosseum, begun by Vespasian and completed in A.D. 80

2. The monument of Victor Emmanuel II, designed by Giuseppe Sacconi, begun in 1885 and dedicated in 1911

3. Stairway of the Piazza di Spagna

4. The ancient walls of Rome

5. The Pantheon, built by Hadrian and consecrated as a Christian church in 609

6. The Appian Way

7. Bridge and Castle of S. Angelo, begun by Hadrian as a mausoleum for himself and his successors. It later became the mediaeval citadel of Rome

on the southern brow of the hill above the *Scalae Caci,* farthest removed from the forum, that side was presumably the aristocratic quarter in the early day. Fragments of good terra-cotta revetments of temples and palaces of the 5th and 6th centuries B.C. have been found in this area, two large cisterns of early workmanship, and cappellaccio blocks of an early town wall. After the second Punic War many of the nobles are incidentally mentioned as living on the Palatine, especially on the northern brow of the hill, which overlooks the forum. In Cicero's day the Clivus Victoriae, the street which ran near the crest of the hill above the house of the vestals, was lined with palaces of important men, *e.g.,* Cicero, Catullus, Crassus, Metellus Celer, Scaurus and several members of the Claudian family. During the empire a large part of the hill was gradually covered by the expanding imperial palace. Augustus' first palace arose south of the centre on property confiscated from republican nobles. The Claudian emperors, especially Tiberius and Caligula, built extensively on the old properties of the family at the north-west corner. Nero enlarged the Augustan palace, connecting it with the Tiberian structure. Vespasian abandoned the Palatine palace for more modest quarters, but Domitian moved into the Augustan structure, enlarging it with magnificent State apartments and public halls. Septimius Severus finally threw out on massive substructures a vast complex of wings toward the south-east corner of the hills with a lofty façade on the Appian Way. As early as Augustus' day the word *palatium* began to be used to designate the imperial palace.

We begin the topographical survey at the very south-west corner of the hill, where there may be seen a portion of the regal fortifications in grey tufa, as well as a large section of the 4th century town wall built in Grotta Oscura and Fidenae stone. Turning eastwards we pass apartments of the Antonine period, perhaps those of the imperial guard. Ascending the hill by the old *Scalae Caci* we reach the confusion of walls that mark one of Rome's most venerated sites. From the area of Cybele's temple a few steps, made of brown tufa (2nd century B.C.), lead down to the stone platform on which the rethatched *hut of Romulus* apparently stood in Cicero's day. The stone water-trough around the platform indicates that the building above was incapable of bearing its own water-gutter. South of this, and at a lower level, the native rock of the hill has borings that seem to mark the position of poles that supported an early straw hut. Then are found a few stones of the 4th-century fortification, and immediately beyond an early inhumation grave. This is probably a grave of the very early period, since its position proves that it was there before the wall was built. The 4th-century urn found in it may have been placed there for expiation when the grave was disturbed by the builders of the wall. Here then we have actual remnants of the primitive settlement though much confused by later builders. The two cisterns near by probably belong to the same community. The one near the house of Livia has an interesting corbelled vault.

The concrete foundation overgrown with ilexes near by is a part of the *temple of Cybele* or *Magna Mater,* first built soon after the second Punic War. Here the first oriental cult gained entrance to Rome, and the orgiastic rites practised here probably inspired Catullus' remarkable poem, the *Attis.* The concrete podium and the peperino fragments from its stuccoed entablature date from a rebuilding in III B.C. Augustus' architects who reconstructed it in A.D. 3 seem to have used much of the old material, which they restuccoed in a new design. This temple became very important in the empire, being considered the "mother church" of a widely extended cult.

East of this temple area is the *house of Livia,* the wife of Augustus. Its very low level is due to the desire of later emperors to preserve this house intact when the other palaces about it were being raised on lofty substructures. It was built about 50 B.C., and contains excellent wall paintings (now badly faded) which correspond to the "second style" of decoration at Pompeii. The house is the best preserved of Roman houses of its period. South of this house is a level platform laid over the ruins of republican houses not yet excavated. On this platform, according to a plausible conjecture,[1] may have stood Augustus' first palace. The house at any

rate was connected with Livia's.

The temple foundation that projects into this platform at the southern corner has recently been identified with plausible arguments as that of the great *temple of Apollo* erected by Augustus in 28 B.C.[2] (*cf.* Horace *Odes I.* 28 and Propertius' description in Bk. II. 31). The final proofs have not yet appeared. The temple, octostyle and peripteral, was of Luna marble, with Numidian columns. The acroterion represented the sun-god in his chariot, the pediment group Apollo with Artemis and Leto; the doors were covered with ivory reliefs of the defeat of the Gauls at Delphi and the death of the Niobids—two themes reminding of Apollo's power. This too became a museum of splendid works of art. Adjoining the temple area—in the space on the south-east of the temple, if the identification is correct, was the extensive portico of the Danaids into which Augustus built the first great public library of Rome.

The centre of the Palatine is occupied by the ruins of *Domitian's palace* (usually called the *domus Augustiana*) which faces northwards. At the front are the audience and public chambers: (1) a "basilica" with an apse in the rear for the emperor's tribunal, used when he acted as judge in political cases; (2) on the east of this room, the *aula* or large audience room where foreign legations were heard and meetings of the senate were held; (3) farther to the right a smaller room which is incorrectly called the *lararium.* The centre of the palace was occupied by an extensive peristyle containing a garden with an elaborate fountain. In the rear was the large dining room flanked on both sides with curious fountain-chambers. The emperor's table apparently stood on a dais at the end. All of these rooms were decorated with coloured marbles and floor mosaics, and the architectural carving reveals the exquisite designing of the Flavian architects. The large central audience chamber was roofed with concrete vaulting, the earliest example of such a vault employed on a large scale.

Under this vast palace there are buried many houses of earlier periods which have recently been excavated in part but not yet described.[3] Under the basilica one enters the segments of a large room that has not only wall paintings of the second style but also stuccoed reliefs of bold design. The masonry is not unlike that of the house of Livia. If this is not a part of Octavian's first palace it must have belonged to one of his powerful friends. The room was later abandoned for the construction of a large reservoir and finally cut through by a solid curved wall which must be a part of the foundations of Nero's palace. Deep under the lararium are five rooms of an even earlier period; the oldest frescoes and mosaics of this house point to a period of about 75 B.C. Some important family of Cicero's time lived here. Under the dining room there are remains of two previous periods of the palace, the lower rooms pertaining apparently to the reign of Claudius. The delicate decorations of a fountain-house and the very charming wall-decorations in coloured stucco plaques that resemble those of the "golden house" of Nero are as successful as anything in their kind at Rome.

Of the *Domus Tiberiana* which occupied a large part of the north-west corner of the Palatine and which is now covered with pleasing gardens very little remains but the substructures with their dark rooms. Many of these rooms have not even been excavated, and since they must have been used for servant quarters it is not likely that things of importance would be found here. Tiberius' palace did not extend to the Clivus Victoriae on the brow of the hill because this street still retained several of its republican mansions when the palace was built. Caligula seems to have connected this corner of the palace with a new wing on the forum level behind the temple of Castor. The magnificent ramp that zigzags down to the forum seems to belong to the Flavian period. The splendid arches thrown over the Clivus Victoriae to carry the palace grounds forward to the very edge of the hill above the forum are attributed to the architects of Trajan and Hadrian. These lend much to the picturesqueness of the Palatine as seen from the forum and to the long vistas over Rome when viewed

[1]Richmond, *Jour. Roman Studies* (1914).

[2]Pinza, *Bull. Com.* (1910 and 1913); Richmond, *Jour. Rom. Stud* (1914).

[3]Lugli, *La Zona Archeologica di Roma,* pp. 202 ff.

from the platform laid over these piers.

The north-east quarter of the Palatine is still occupied by S. Sebastian and S. Bonaventura. What buildings stood there in antiquity we do not know. The south-east quarter is occupied chiefly by the so-called "hippodrome" and the substructures of Septimius' additions to the palace. The "hippodrome" (the word was sometimes used for gardens of the long oval type) seems to have been a large garden which was surrounded by high retaining walls to keep the higher portions of ground from caving in. It certainly contained fountains, trees and walks, with a portico circling the whole within the wall. Perhaps the portico roof had hanging gardens. The masonry is of the Flavian period with additions and changes of a century later. The substructures of Septimius' palace spread in several directions. The central portion contained very luxurious baths. The lofty ruins that extend along the brow of the hill were apparently substructures that supported apartments from which the emperor could view the games of the circus below, while farther south-east stood the Septizonium with its lavishly decorated façade which was to remind the African friends of Septimius on approaching Rome that one of their countrymen occupied the imperial palace. A large part of the Septizonium stood till the 16th century, when it fell a prey to the greed of Sixtus V. (1588).

THE CAPITOLINE HILL

The Capitoline hill,[1] which in ancient times could be approached only from the forum, had in the regal period a fort (*arx*) on the northern height, an area sacred to Jupiter on the southern height and a wooded asylum on the depression that lay between these two. In the area sacred to Jupiter the last of the kings built a magnificent Etruscan temple with three cellas to the triad Jupiter, Juno and Minerva, and this, officially called the temple of Jupiter Optimus Maximus, was ready for dedication the first year of the republic, 509 B.C. The foundations of this temple have long been known, and when in 1919 the German embassy, which stood upon it, was torn down to make place for an enlargement of the Capitoline museum the old walls were excavated and measured. (*Notizie degli Scavi*, 1919.) These foundations, built of the native cappellaccio, are now visible at two corners, and prove that though masonry was still fairly crude in technique, the original temple was built on the magnificent scale that it had in imperial restorations, about 60x50 metres. Since it was the largest temple in existence in Italy in that day we may conclude that the tradition was not far from correct which held that Rome was a large and wealthy city under the Etruscan princes. The first temple was probably, like the foundations, built of native tufa and covered with a white stucco. The porch was probably supported in four wooden columns set wide apart, and the wooden architraves were in Tuscan fashion covered with painted terra-cotta slabs. A few fragments which may possibly belong to the early temple have been found and placed in the museum near by. On the roof was placed a quadriga of Jupiter in terra-cotta made by the artists of Veii, probably by the same school of artists which created the splendid Apollo now to be seen in the Villa Giulia museum. This old temple, with its decorations renewed from time to time, stood until it was burned in 83 B.C. After various rebuildings it was reconstructed in marble with Pentelic columns by Domitian, and the surviving marble fragments of the entablatures that are in the museum give some idea of the magnificence of this Flavian temple. This marble structure was hexastyle with three rows of columns across the front and a row on each side.

Of the Arx and the temple of Juno Moneta later built thereon all traces have been hidden by the church of Ara Coeli and the recent monument to Victor Emmanuel II. The *Tabularium*, the gaunt walls of which command the view of the forum, has so frequently been altered in rebuilding the rooms of the modern council chamber of Rome that little but the rear remains intact. It was erected after the Sullan fire, which destroyed the Capitoline temple, to serve as a fireproof hall of records for the State. Gabine stone was employed for the exterior walls because it was known not to suffer

from fire. The ceilings of the rooms were domed with concrete and an arcade of round and flat arches was developed far beyond the usual architectural customs of the day to avoid the use of inflammable material. It is probably the first attempt at a hall of records that was to be absolutely impervious to the accidents of the elements, and the attempt was successful as the present condition of the store-chambers proves.

THE IMPERIAL FORA[2]

The Julian Forum.—Julius Caesar set aside a large part of the moneys which he derived from Gallic booty for the relief of the overcrowded forum. Thus he moved the comitium to the new *saepta* farther north, and built in the forum the large basilica mentioned above. His most extensive building, however, was a new forum enclosure with high walls and numerous shops lining the walls north of the old forum. In the via delle Marmorelle there are remains of the portico and walls ingeniously constructed of the three varieties of stone best adapted to the requirements. This wall was veneered with marble. Beneath, not now visible, are the remains of several of the shops built of tufa and vaulted with concrete. In the centre of the forum Caesar erected a marble temple to Venus Genetrix, the "ancestress" of the Gens Iulia. This temple he vowed at the battle of Pharsalus, doubtless intending that it should be a visible reminder of his own exalted claims. The forum itself was planned in 54 B.C. but not yet fully completed at Caesar's death in 44.

Forum Augusti.—Augustus completed the forum of his predecessor and built a larger one on adjacent ground chiefly for the purpose of enclosing a *temple to Mars Ultor* which he vowed at Philippi, 42 B.C. To protect the temple from fire he raised a massive wall of Gabine and Alban stone about the area. This wall, one of the most imposing now at Rome, rises 100ft. high. On the outside the great blocks were left rustic, while on the inside, where it was faced with marble, two rows of niches were cut to hold statues and honorary tablets to the noted heroes of Roman history. The statues have disappeared but many fragments of the tablets have been found. The area in front of the temple and on its north side was excavated in 1925–27 and revealed fragments enough of the entablature to ensure complete drawings of the whole structure. The marble decoration was of the best that the Augustan age could produce. The temple proves to be octostyle with a row of columns on each side while the rear of the cella stands solidly against the massive enclosure wall.

Forum Vespasiani.—The next imperial forum to be built was that of Vespasian, through the area of which the Via Cavour now runs. In its centre he constructed a magnificent temple to Peace, which is frequently mentioned for its library and its large collection of works of art—among them statues of Phidias and Lysippus. No part of this structure is now visible. Between the forum of Augustus and that of Vespasian lay the long and narrow area of the lower Argiletum about forty metres wide in which Domitian began to build a forum to contain a small *temple of Minerva*. Since Nerva completed and dedicated it, the structure bore his name, but the decorative work is all of the luxurious style of the Flavian period. Two of the columns of the handsome colonnade still remain with a part of the entablature. Its frieze is in bold relief representing the story of Arachne and other themes suitable for the adornment of a precinct sacred to the goddess of arts and crafts. No portion of the temple of Minerva is now visible but the whole area will probably soon be excavated.

Forum Traiani.—The *forum of Trajan*, north-west of the Augustan group, was a large complex of open areas and buildings, including the spacious forum proper enclosed with a portico, the basilica Ulpia, the two library buildings, the column of Trajan, and, an addition of Hadrian, the massive temple of Trajan. Since the valley was too narrow for all these structures the opposing slopes of the Capitoline and Quirinal hills were cut back, and when necessary heavy retaining walls of concrete and brick erected, a part of which still remain. The forum proper had its stately entrance in the form of a triumphal arch near the forum

[1]Rodocanachi, *Le Capitole romain*, 1904; Platner, *Ancient Rome*, p. 291.

[2]Platner, *Ancient Rome*, p. 274 (1911), with earlier bibliography.

of Augustus. Its area is rectangular, 116 metres wide and 95 metres long. The large hemicycle against the Quirinal which is now being excavated served as a retaining wall of the Forum. The corresponding one on the opposite side has disappeared. The forum was of course open to the sky, but was surrounded by a very beautiful marble portico backed by a masonry wall. Many fragments of this portico may be seen lying about in the area. Next to the forum proper stood the basilica, which far surpassed the earlier ones in magnificence. A double row of 96 Corinthian columns supported the upper arcade that bore the roof. The nave was 25 metres wide; the apses at the end have been destroyed. North of this judgment hall were the two wings of the library, a rendezvous of literary men and students. In the area between these was built the column of Trajan[1] which is still standing. This column is 100ft. high and is covered with reliefs arranged in a spiral band representing the events of Trajan's two campaigns in Dacia. This is apparently the first column which was decorated in this manner, and the reliefs are made with such fidelity to fact as to be our best document for the history of the wars. Since the porticoes of the library rose on both sides, the reliefs could then be seen from near at hand. Nothing now remains of the great temple of Trajan which Hadrian erected north of the column.

FORUM BOARIUM AND CAMPUS MARTIUS

Between the Capitoline and the well known church of S. Maria in Cosmedin is an area which in early Rome was used as a cattle market, though during the empire it was as thickly populated as it is now. In this area, near the river, are found two republican temples for which the original names have not yet been discovered. The rectangular temple, usually called the *Temple of Fortuna,* was freed from mediaeval additions in 1923 and conservatively restored. It is exceedingly interesting as showing the type of building used at Rome in the late republic before Caesar and Augustus began to reconstruct Rome's temples in marble. It is an Ionic tetrastyle pseudo-peripteral temple of pleasing proportions, though small, measuring only 20x12 metres. The walls are of Anio tufa as are also the imbedded columns except those at the corners. These latter, as well as the free columns of the portico, all the capitals, the entablature of the porch and the facing of the podium are of travertine. The whole was covered with white stucco and the stucco of the frieze was neatly moulded into low reliefs of ox-skulls and garlands. The careful distribution of these materials points to the period of about 70–50 B.C. The round temple near by stands on a foundation of the 3rd or 4th century B.C., but the marble temple itself seems to belong to the Augustan period. It would be a graceful temple if the entablature and roof could be restored as well as several of the capitals which have apparently been replaced by alien material. It is of course not a temple of Vesta, but its true name is not known. Huelsen has suggested "Portunus."

The double-arched *Ianus quadrifrons* which stands over the Cloaca Maxima, is of late date and of ugly proportions. The extensive remains that are found in and under S. Maria in Cosmedin apparently belong to the public granary as it was in Cicero's day. Under the church of *S. Nicola in Carcere* near the Piazza Montanara are seen the foundations of three temples that stood beside the vegetable market outside the ancient Porta Carmentalis. These seem to be—from north to south—the temples of Janus, Juno Sospita, and Spes, originally built respectively in 260, 194 and 258 B.C. Most of the materials now visible belong to the rebuildings of *c.* 90 B.C. (Janus), 90 B.C. (Juno Sospita) and 31 B.C. (Spes). For the architectural history of the republic they are very important. Farther north on the site of S. Maria in Campitelli stood the famous old *temple of Apollo* where the sibylline books were kept and near which, on the slope of the Capitoline, Rome's early plays were given at the games of Apollo. The temple was first built in the early republic (431 B.C.) but the extensive remains now to be seen under the church seem to belong

to the reconstruction of 179 B.C.[2] Because of the association of this district with early dramatic performances Augustus constructed a very large theatre near by (first used, when still incomplete, in 17 B.C.) which he named in honour of his nephew Marcellus. A large part of the semicircular façade is still standing and when it has been cleared of its ugly shops and superstructure —excavations are in progress—it will be one of the most imposing ruins of ancient Rome. The exterior consisted of three series of open arcades, the lower one being decorated with engaged columns of the Doric order, the middle with Ionic ones, the third with Corinthian pilasters. The theatre seated about 10,000 spectators and had a stage of the enormous proportion of 80x20 metres.

North of this theatre may be seen the portal of the extensive Porticus of Octavia (originally the Porticus of Metellus) which enclosed large temples of Juno and Jupiter. The whole was originally built in the 2nd century B.C., but all the remains now visible belong to the debased art of the Septimian period. Within may be seen, rising above shabby walls, a column and capital of one of the great temples. North-east of this lay the extensive *Circus Flaminius* built before the second Punic war as a place to hold the plebeian games. Fragments of the supporting walls may be seen in the basements of several houses on the Via d. Bottege Oscure, but these all belong to a rebuilding of about 50–30 B.C. A few hundred feet to the north-west of this circus, Pompey built his massive theatre in 55 B.C., the first permanent theatre of Rome. This was about the same size as the Marcellus theatre and its stage was even longer. Considerable remains of it are to be found under the shops east of the Campo dei Fiori.

Farther north, in the old Campus Martius is the Pantheon,[3] a structure which Hadrian built to replace the earlier temple of Agrippa and Domitian. This round temple was one of the boldest of old Roman structures, having a brick and concrete dome with a diameter of 43½ metres without support except on the walls of the temple. The dome itself was built of narrowing circles of brick on which were laid several layers of concrete which hardened into one firm mass so that there is no lateral thrust on the walls. The walls of the rotunda are also of brick-faced concrete with solid brick arches running through the mass to aid in carrying the weight over the niches while the mass was solidifying. The portico is a rectangular structure, most of whose columns belong to Hadrian's time. Some of the repairs of its entablature seem to be of a later period. The large inscription on its front generously credits the building to Agrippa while the smaller one mentions the repairs of Septimius. Nothing is said of the actual builder, but the brick stamps and the style of work prove that Hadrian should have the chief credit. The exterior was of course faced with marble slabs, and the sumptuous decoration of the interior— originally even more elaborate—will give some idea of how lavish the whole building must have been. The temple was dedicated by Agrippa to the divinities of the Julian house, and the name was intended to convey the idea of "all-holy." Of other notable buildings in this region we may mention the *temple of Hadrian,* the walls of which have been incorporated in the Borsa, or stock exchange; the *Mausoleum of Augustus* which has till recently served as a concert hall, called the Augusteo, and the *tomb of Hadrian,* on the right bank of the Tiber, rebuilt during the middle ages into a fort called the Castel Sant' Angelo.[4]

The *Colosseum,*[5] or more correctly, the *Amphitheatrum Flavium,* was begun by Vespasian on the low ground that Nero had used for a lake in the centre of his imperial villa. It was used for hunts, sham battles, gladiatorial shows and races, and the arena could be flooded for sham naval battles. The façade consists of three series of 80 arches decorated in the three orders as were the theatres of Pompey and Marcellus, and rises 48½ metres. Stone masonry in travertine lined with tufa supports the heavier outer portion, while the vaulting of the arcades and the inner bowl consist of concrete. The seats were of marble and could hold about 50,000 spectators. The building which is elliptical measures

---

[1]Cichorius, *Die Trajans-Säule* (1896); Lehmann-Hartleben, *Die Trajans-Säule* (1926).
[2]Frank, *Roman Buildings of the Republic,* p. 133.
[3]Ashby's revision of Anderson and Spiers, *Architecture of Rome* p. 78.
[4]Pierce in *Journal Rom. Studies* (1925).
[5]Ashby, *The Architecture of Ancient Rome,* p. 93.

188 metres in length and 156 metres in width, while the arena measures 86x54 metres. It was apparently the largest amphitheatre in the Roman world.

Near by stands the well proportioned *Arch of Constantine* which however is largely constructed of materials taken from previous arches. The only sculpture upon it that belongs to Constantine's day is the very narrow frieze rudely carved in a band about its centre. The other reliefs were taken from structures of the second century and in the use of these the imperial portraits were rechiselled to represent Constantine. North-east of the Colosseum one may enter several rooms of the *golden house* of Nero,[1] or rather the private apartments of that emperor. The rooms have been to some extent preserved because the walls were later used as substructions for a part of Trajan's baths built at a higher level. Many of the rooms of the palace have recently been excavated and reveal much damaged frescoes and stucco reliefs which represent the best work of its kind at Rome for the period of Nero. It was here, as graffiti on the walls indicate, that several of the Renaissance painters borrowed themes and designs for the arabesque and "grotesque" decoration so popular when the loggia of the Vatican was decorated.

Several of the massive *Thermae* (Baths) of ancient Rome are still among the most conspicuous ruins of the city. The first large structure of this type was the one built by Agrippa in 20 B.C. south of the Pantheon. Little now remains of this. More may be seen of the ruins of those constructed by Titus and Trajan (on the grounds of Nero's *Domus Aurea*), by Caracalla on the edge of the Aventine and by Diocletian (part of which is now used for the national museum). Since these buildings contained, besides the baths, playgrounds, gymnasia, clubrooms and auditoria for immense crowds, the architects who constructed them had to employ all the arts and sciences at their disposal. The central building of Caracalla's baths covers an area of 270,000sq.ft.; and the central hall has a clear space of 183x79ft. It is roofed with a solid concrete intersecting barrel vault that rests chiefly on four massive piers and rises 108ft. from the pavement. It was while solving the problems of such construction that the Roman architects made those contributions to their art which have been most frequently studied by recent architects. The baths of Diocletian have suffered more from time, but the church of S. Maria degli Angeli has preserved two of its great halls. Here may be seen in their most advanced use at Rome good examples of flying and rectangular buttresses, a careful system of thrusts and counter thrusts and of ribbed quadripartite vaulting. A large number of the smaller rooms are used by the Museo delle Terme.

Finally the *Subterranean Basilica*[2] discovered near Porta Maggiore in 1917 has proved to be not only one of the best preserved of ancient buildings but one of the most important for the interpretation of Roman life. Though it seems to have been built before the middle of the 1st century A.D. it has the regular basilican form with nave, apse and two aisles. It was built wholly underground apparently for the purposes of a secret religious sect. The ceilings of the nave, the apse and the aisles are richly adorned with excellent stucco reliefs, the interpretation of which has proved as difficult as would be the explanation of the biblical illustrations of a mediaeval cathedral if we had no copies of the Bible. The most generally accepted view is the one proposed by Cumont, that this basilica was the temple of a Neo-Pythagorean congregation which practised mystic rites of initiation that were not approved of by the imperial authorities, and that the reliefs in question pertain to myths and rites which had been given a symbolic interpretation in the Neo-Pythagorean ritual. But quite apart from their meaning, they now give us the best conception possible of the beauty of Roman interior decoration for the 1st century of the empire. (*See* Rivoira, *Roman Architecture*, p. 204.)

(T. F.)

THE MODERN CITY

In the middle ages the population of Rome had dwindled to twenty or thirty thousand inhabitants, who lived huddled together

[1]Weege, *Das Goldene Haus, Jahrb. des Arch. Inst.* p. 127 (1913).
[2]Carcopino, *La Basilique Pythagoricienne* (1927); for illustrations see *Memoirs Amer. Acad.* iv. (1924).

about the strongholds of the barons, and the modern city grew slowly upon the exiguous foundation of a mediaeval town. The first plan for modernizing and improving Rome was that of Pope Julius II., who aimed at the enlargement of the lower city on both sides of the Tiber. Following him, Sixtus V. did his best to develop the upper part of the city by laying out the Via Sistina, from the Trinità dei Monti to S. Maria Maggiore and Porta S.

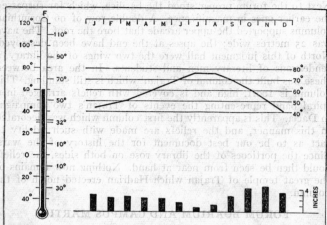

WEATHER GRAPH OF ROME. THE THERMOMETER INDICATES THE ANNUAL MEAN TEMPERATURE. THE CURVE SHOWS THE MONTHLY MEAN TEMPERATURE AND THE COLUMNS, THE MONTHLY PRECIPITATION

Giovanni. A plan of improvements was made, under the direction of Mgr. de Merode, during the reign of Pius IX.; and, although only very partially executed, has served as a basis for later efforts.

Great changes in the municipal and social conditions followed the occupation of the city by the Italians (Sept. 20, 1870), and the rapid increase of population due to immigration from other parts of Italy. In a rush of land-speculation, trees and fine villas were unfortunately destroyed. As soon as political circumstances admitted, the municipality set to work.

Two principal problems presented themselves. The more important was the confinement of the Tiber in such a manner as to render impossible the serious floods which had from time to time inundated the city, often causing great damage to property and rendering the lower streets more or less impassable. There were floods which almost reached the level of the first storey near San Carlo in the Corso, and it was common to see the great Piazza Navona and the neighbourhood of the Pantheon full of water for days together during the winter. The interruption of traffic can be imagined, and the damage to property was serious. The other urgent matter was one of which the government of Pius IX. had been partially aware, namely, the necessity for opening better thoroughfares between different parts of the city.

It is necessary to distinguish between the work carried out by the municipality, and that which was done in the way of private speculation. The first was on the whole good, and has proved enduring; the second was in many cases bad, and resulted in great loss. As soon as the opening of such streets as the Via Nazionale and the Via Cavour, the widening and straightening of the Via dell' Angelo Custode, now the Via del Tritone Nuovo, and similar improvements, such as the construction of new bridges over the Tiber, had demonstrated that the value of property could be doubled and quadrupled in a short time, and as soon as the increase of population had caused a general rise in rents, owners of property awoke to the situation of affairs, and became as anxious as they had at first been disinclined to improve their estates by wholesale building.

The most important work executed by the government with the assistance of the municipality was the construction of the embankments along the Tiber. Though damaged by the great flood of December 1900, their truly Roman solidity saved the city from the disastrous consequences of a wide inundation. It is impossible not to admire them, and not to feel respect for a people able to carry out such a plan in such a manner and in so short a time, in

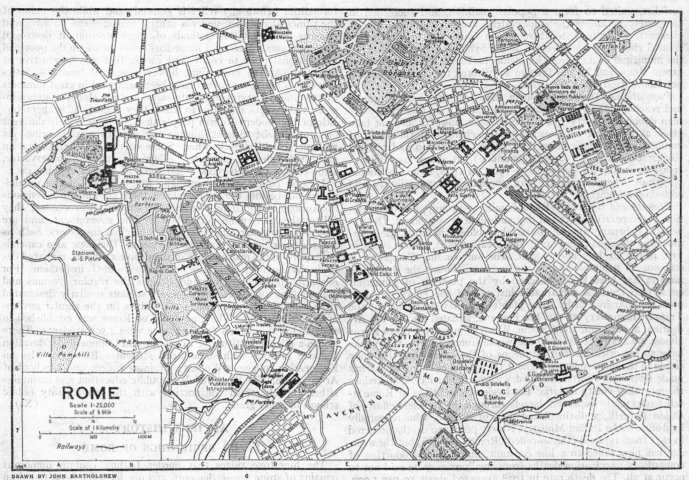

ROME

Scale 1:25,000

Scale of ½ Mile

0   ¼   ½

Scale of 1 Kilometre

0   500   1000 M

Railways

DRAWN BY JOHN BARTHOLOMEW

the face of such great difficulties. But so far as the life of the city was concerned, the cutting of new streets and the widening of old ones produced a more apparent immediate result. The opening of such a thoroughfare as the Via Nazionale now named in part Via Cesare Battisti, and in part Via Quattro Novembre could not but prove to be of the greatest value. It begins at the Piazza delle Terme, in which the principal railway station is situated, and connects the upper part of the city by a broad straight road, and then, by easy gradients, with the Forum of Trajan, the Piazza dei Santi Apostoli and the Piazza di Venezia, whence, as the Corso Vittorio Emanuele, it runs through the heart of the old city, being designed to reach St. Peter's by a new bridge of the same name opened in 1911 near the bridge of S. Angelo. It is true that, in order to accomplish this, the Villa Aldobrandini had to be partially destroyed but this is almost the only point which lovers of beauty can regret, and in compensation it opened to full view the famous palace of the Massimo family, the imposing church of S. Andrea della Valle, and the noble pile of the Cancelleria, one of the best pieces of architecture in Rome. Another great artery is the Via Cavour, which was intended to connect the railway station with the south-western part of Rome, descending to the Forum, and thence turning northwards to reach the Piazza di Venezia on the east side of the monument to Victor Emanuel II. It was proposed again (1928) to extend the Via Cavour to the Piazza. Rome is now divided clearly into two parts, the old and the new, of which the old is incomparably the more artistic and the more beautiful, as it will always remain the more interesting. A tunnel under the Quirinal Hill connects the north end of the old city, the Corso, Babuino, etc., and the upper part of modern Rome, including the former Via Nazionale and the Esquiline. A causeway and bridge unites the Pincio with the Villa Borghese, or, as it is now called, the Villa Umberto Primo. In 1911 zoological gardens were arranged in the grounds of the Villa and a fine collection of modern Italian art was opened in the Palazzo delle Belle Arti, to the west of the Villa.

The Policlinico, on the Macas, is one of the finest hospitals in Europe. It is on part of the large site, east and south of the Castro Pretorio, requisitioned by the Government for building a new University, and bringing together various institutions scattered about the city. Of this scheme the hospital forms part. The military hospital is on the Coelian. In 1910 in honour of the jubilee of the unity of Italy, the formation of an archaeological park, extending from the Via Appia to the foot of the Aventine and almost to the Aurelian Wall, was approved by the Parliament. It contains the Baths of Caracalla. Among the important modern buildings are the Cassa del Risparmio, in the Corso; the Palazzo Negroni, near the Piazza Nicotia, the Chamber of Deputies, with its principal front on the new Piazza del Parlamento and the Palace of Justice, near the castle of St. Angelo. It was proposed in 1922 to make the barracks and storerooms of the Castle of St. Angelo into a topographical museum. In the same year a museum of antiquities from the Forum was arranged in a building adjoining the church of Santa Francesca Romana; and the Museo Petriano, containing objects connected with the foundation and development of St. Peter's was opened in 1925.

Municipal Administration.—After 1870, those who remained loyal to Pius IX. took no part whatever in public affairs, and the municipal administration was entirely in the hands of the liberals. The expression "nè eletti nè elettori," meaning that Catholics are to be neither voters nor candidates, which came to be regarded as a sort of rule of the party, was invented at that time by an epigrammatic journalist, and it seems at first to have been applied also to municipal matters, whereas it was later understood to refer only to parliamentary elections. Leo XIII encouraged the formation of a Catholic party in the municipal administration, and the municipal government then drifted largely into the hands of Catholics. In the year preceding the fascist régime the three democratic parties, known as the liberal, republican and socialist, united to form a popular coalition, and succeeded in completely excluding the conservative, aristocratic and Catholic elements. Prior to 1926 there was a municipal or Communal council chosen by the electors and a Syndic (mayor) drawn by the municipal council from its members. In all Italian communes except Rome and Naples fascism substituted for these a *Podestà*, but Rome itself has a governor.

Population.—The population in 1870 was 226,022, by 1901 it had reached 462,743 (communal population). It therefore more than doubled in thirty years. The increase, however, did not take place at a regular rate, owing to the changes in the rates of immigration and emigration. In 1936 the population had reached 1,094,710 (town), 1,150,589 (commune), an almost as rapid increase as during the period 1870–1901. In 1938, it was estimated 1,279,748. There are in the city population many military and ecclesiastical officials.

Climate and Hygiene.—Rome is mild and sunny, but the variation in temperature between day and night is very great. December to February appear to be the coldest months, the thermometer then averaging 47°; the greatest heat, which averages 75°, is felt in July and August. The surrounding Campagna is still not all habitable during the summer, though the dangerous malaria has been much checked by the planting of numerous eucalyptus trees. A remarkable instance of the effect produced upon the marshy soil by these plantations may be studied at the Trappist monastery of the Tre Fontane, situated on the Via Ardeatina, about 4 mi. from Rome. Whereas in former times it was almost always fatal to spend the whole summer there, the monks have so far dried the soil by means of the eucalyptus that they reside in the monastery throughout the year. The municipality has made strenuous efforts, attended with marked success, to reduce the mortality due to malaria. The hygienic conditions of Rome itself have greatly improved, largely through the ceaseless efforts of Guido Baccelli, a distinguished man of science, who repeatedly held office in the Italian Ministry. Ninety per 1,000 deaths occurred in 1871 from typhoid (the so-called "Roman fever"), but the average has now fallen to a low constant. Since the introduction of compulsory vaccination deaths from smallpox may be said not to occur at all. The death rate in 1928 averaged about 19 per 1,000.

Charities and Education.—A great number of small charitable institutions for children and old people have been founded, which are organized on the most modern principles, and in many of these charitable persons of the upper classes give their individual assistance to the poor. There are also private hospitals for diseases of the eye, in which poor patients are lodged and treated without payment. There are two hospitals entirely maintained by private resources, where infants are treated whose mothers fear to send them to a public hospital, or in cases refused by the latter as not being serious enough for admission. Of course, the numbers of the poor greatly increased with the growth of population, especially after the failure of building speculations between 1888 and 1890, though great efforts were made by the municipality to send all persons then thrown out of employment back to their homes. One of the difficulties under which Rome labours is that while it attracts the population of the country, as other capitals do, it possesses no great mechanical industries in which the newcomers can be employed. Efforts to create small industries in the populous quarters of the poor met with little success. Before 1870 a society was formed, which has since greatly developed as an intelligent private enterprise, to provide the poor with sanitary tenements; but its success is much hampered by the absence of employment, which again is partly due to the heavy taxation of small industries. A number of trade schools are also maintained by private funds, such as the Instituto degli Artigianelli, managed by the Fratelli della Dottrina Cristiana, and the Ricovero pei Fanciulli Abbandonati (home for friendless children), which is under lay management and has flourishing work shops. The character of official charities has certainly improved in principle, so far as their educational and moral scope are concerned, for whereas in former times the limited number of the poor made individual and almost paternal relief possible, that form of charity had a pauperizing influence. If anything, the present tendency is to go too far in the opposite direction, and to require too many

formalities before any relief is granted; and while the union of the principal charities under a central management on advanced theories improved the methods of administration, it destroyed numerous small sources of immediate relief on which the poor had a traditional right to count, and was in that way productive of hardship. At the same time, however, mutual benefit societies (*società di mutuo soccorso*) have been organized in great numbers by the different crafts and professions, and are chiefly distinguishable by the political parties to which they belong. It is characteristic of the modern Roman people that the most widely different elements subsist without showing any signs of amalgamating, yet without attacking each other. Some of these societies have an exclusively clerical character, others are merely conservative, some consist of monarchists, and some of avowed republicans.

Popular education is principally in the hands of the municipality, but besides the public schools there are numerous religious institutions attended by the children of the lower classes; they follow the curriculum prescribed by the government, and are under the constant supervision of municipal inspectors, both as regards their teaching and their hygiene. The pope also expends large sums in the maintenance of the people's schools, managed entirely by laymen, and also under government inspection. For education of the higher grade, besides the regular lyceums and gymnasiums, there are many private schools similarly designated from which pupils can present themselves for the regular government examinations. The University of Rome was established in 1265 and in the session 1924–25 there were 4,500 students. There is also a Higher Institute of Economic and Commercial Education founded in 1906 with some 2,000 students. Rome has also an Engineering college, a Women's Training college and a School of Architecture. The State regulates public education and maintains either entirely or in conjunction with the municipality public schools of every grade.   (X.)

ANCIENT HISTORY

I. THE BEGINNINGS OF ROME

The limestone ridges that border Latium contain numerous remains of stone age settlements, and one has even been found on Monte Mario within 3m. of the Vatican in the old volcanic stratum that borders the right bank of the Tiber. On the left bank, however, within the area that was in prehistoric times subject to rains of volcanic ash from the Alban craters there are very few traces of human habitation before the iron age.[1] Perhaps the activity of the volcanoes kept migrants from settling there during the bronze age. The oldest settlements so far discovered within this peculiar region seem to be those of the Alban hills, between Grotta Ferrata and Albano. Here several groups of cremating people belonging apparently to the so-called Villanova[2] (*q.v.*) branch of the Indo-Europeans came down from Tuscany and settled, about the end of the 2nd millennium B.C. In the early part of the 1st millennium they spread here and there over the Latin plain as far at least as Antium on the sea and the Palatine hill on the Tiber. In the primitive cemetery of the Forum 40 graves have so far been excavated. The deepest and earliest were cremation burials containing the same kind of pottery and personal ornaments as those of the Alban hills. Later, possibly in the 8th century, the rite of inhumation began to take the place of cremation here as on the Alban hills, at Antium, at Veii and at Falerii north of the Tiber. It is generally assumed that Sabine people from the central mountains were at this time pressing into Latium in large enough groups to become in several towns the dominating element. Whether further excavations will prove that this rite replaced cremation in all the primitive burial places at Rome is very doubtful. The fact that cremation again became the orthodox rite during the Roman republic would incline us to assume that cremation survived in some cemeteries that have not yet been discovered.

Early Institutions.—By the 7th century we may assume that

[1]Von Duhn, *Italische Gräberkunde*, 392 (1924); Antonielli, in *Bull. Palet. Ital.*, 161 (1924).
[2]Randall-MacIver, *Villanovans and Early Etruscans* (1925); *Iron Age in Italy* (1927).

the Palatine, the Capitoline, the Esquiline and the Quirinal hills had compact settlements of "Villanovan" and Sabine farmers and shepherds. These two groups were closely related in culture, language and religion. Philology proves that the bearers of the Latin language (probably the cremating group) and those who spoke the Sabellic dialects had not been separated very many centuries, and that they had been one people before entering Italy over the Alps. Several of their deities—Jupiter, Mars, Juno, Minerva and others—were also a common inheritance, and were worshipped by both peoples with rites that knew nothing of anthropomorphism. That it was a religion peculiarly adapted to an agricultural people we learn from the oldest calendar of festivals, which was drawn up before the Etruscans came to Rome. (W. Warde-Fowler, *The Religious Experience of the Roman People* [1911], 92.) Their political and social organizations were also of the same kind. The property-owning males constituted the "town-meeting" and the army. They elected the annual leaders (usually two "praetors" or "consuls") who summoned and conducted the meetings, held the elections and directed the army. The consuls must consult a smaller group of elders (senators), heads of important families, in all matters of public interest. Without the approval of the elders no proposal was put before the commons. For purposes of transacting business the commons of a town were usually divided into ten wards called *curiae*. That Rome had 30 instead of ten seems therefore to indicate that Rome was a union of three settlements already organized into regular polities before the city government was formed. In taking possession of the country, these people had settled in village groups, usually upon some hill which could be defended, and which gave access to a good spring of water or a stream. Most of the land near each village was apparently divided into private holdings, though it also seems probable that some land was left undivided for community grazing. Sacred land, used for the support of the cult, was also set apart at a very early period. These villages were independent and autonomous within the tribe. A tribal organization, however, existed, which supported a tribal cult on the Alban mount. This tribal organization was kept alive by an annual religious festival, and it had a presiding officer whose duty it was in time of danger to summon the forces of the different communities to common action. Since both the Villanovan and the Sabine communities shared in these democratic customs they coalesced readily in such a large tribal organization.

Finally both peoples long retained the institutions of a very strong patriarchal organization. Women, children and slaves were subject to the *potestas* of the family patriarch. He gave the members of his household in marriage, assigned the properties—there are but shadowy traces of clan-ownership, and testamentary rights are highly developed—and he, with his family council, meted out punishment for crimes committed within the family, and in the earlier day at least, directed the vendetta of the family against those who had committed a wrong against him or his. While the villages were still small, there were few opportunities for community action, whether judicial or legislative, so long as the patriarchal customs were respected.

City States.—At an early day these numerous communities belonging to a wide-spread tribe began to aggregate to a few favoured centres where cities grew up. Such cities soon overshadowed the villages and endangered the existence of the Latin tribal organizations. It is likely that raids from across the Tiber and from the Sabine and Volscian hills emptied the more exposed villages that could not well be fortified, drove the populace to more defensible villages, and in the case of places like Praeneste, strongly situated near the natural road between Etruria and Campania, trade of a lucrative kind also attracted settlers. It was in this way that some six city-states gradually grew up in Latium to take the place in each case of several villages. The growth of such cities in these circumstances naturally required stronger and more efficient governments, a better army organization, the building of walls or at least defensible earthen mounds with protecting pickets.

Kings.—At Rome the coalescing of three villages with their 30 curiae may date from the 8th century B.C. And here since the

threats of Etruscan raiders from Veii and Caere added much to the difficulty of governing communities that are not wholly homogeneous, elective princes holding office for life seem for a while to have displaced the customary annual magistrates. Tradition held that of these early princes Romulus (*q.v.*), Hostilius and Ancus Marcius were Latins, but that Titus Tatius (the prince of a Sabine group) and Numa Pompilius (*q.v.*) were Sabine in origin, while Tarquinius Priscus was said to be the son of a Corinthian adventurer who had first settled in Tarquinium and married an Etruscan woman, and Servius Tullius was an Etruscan chief by the name of Mastarna.

There is nothing unreasonable in this tradition, and since the art of writing was already known, the names may well have survived from early times on inscriptions of public buildings, treaties and tombs. The tradition regarding Servius Tullius was at least derived from Etruscan documents of an early date. (*See* the speech of the Emperor Claudius, Dessau, *Ins. Lat. Sel.*, 212.) History, however, need not take seriously the numerous legends preserved by Livy regarding the wars and deeds of these kings. Villages near Rome which naturally dwindled to insignificance under the attractive power of a neighbouring city left traces of themselves in abandoned walls; and picturesque legends grew up to account for their annihilation, but most of them had decayed several centuries before history was written.

Etruscan Kings.—The Etruscan (*see* ETRURIA) house of the Tarquins seems to be more tangible. Tradition places their rule in the latter half of the 6th century B.C., at a time in fact when we know that Etruscan princes were making conquests southward as far as Capua, when Etruscan art and Greek objects of art carried by Etruscans came into Rome as they did into Praeneste, Velitrae, Ardea, Satricum[1] and other Latin towns, when Rome received a stone ring-wall enclosing a remarkably large area and ceased to use the Forum cemetery for burial—since that now was included within the ring—and when Rome's rulers began to reach out for the control of the larger part of Latium.

The Etruscan adventurers, employing methods like those of the Normans who ruled the Sicilian cities in the 12th century, had come by sea to govern and exploit the unorganized communities of the Villanovans some two centuries before. Different families had secured control of most of the districts of Tuscany, had fortified their various cities, trained their subjects into effective armies as well as into obedient tenants and serfs, had developed farming by improved methods of planting, draining and irrigation, had exploited the copper and iron mines of Etruria and organized a flourishing industry in metal work with which they attracted Phoenician and Greek traders and had even entered actively into maritime commerce.[2]

Whether the Tarquins actually seized Rome by force or migrated to Rome and secured control by political devices we do not know. Under them Rome and Latium underwent very remarkable changes. An extensive wall[3] of almost 6m. was built to enclose an area that would readily house 200,000 inhabitants living in low small houses. There could hardly have been so many inhabitants when the enclosure was made; and indeed the walls, in order to make use of natural escarpments and to include outlying shrines, probably took in many undeveloped tracts. We cannot be sure that the regal wall extended as far out as the so-called Servian wall, despite the existence of very old remains in the gardens of the "Villa Spithoever." Tombs of the 4th century within the area seem to prove at least that the sacred *pomerium* did not extend so far, even if the fortifications did. Nevertheless the regal city was remarkably large when compared with other Italian cities, and its size points to a builder who was intent upon extensive projects of development. The Tarquins certainly opened the city to the currents of Mediterranean commerce now being attracted westward by Etruscan prosperity. Tradition plausibly holds that a port was used at the mouth of the Tiber as early as the 6th century; Greek and Etruscan articles came

[1]Della Seta, *Museo di Villa Giulia*, i., 235 (1918).
[2]D. Randall-MacIver, *The Etruscans* (1927).
[3]*Papers of the American Academy in Rome*, iii., 112 (1924).

to the city, Greek and Etruscan artisans were at work on the public buildings, and it is not unlikely that some of the industries that prospered in Etruria were enticed to Rome.

A strong army was also organized. Tradition attributes the regal army of nearly 20,000 men to Servius, who came from Etruria and doubtless employed the same methods as other Etruscan princes. Of these, 9,800 belonged to the "first class" of property holders, the rest to the other four classes; that is to say, all of the "first class" men were liable to army service, but

INVASIONS
OF
ANCIENT ITALY

CELTS
C.500

LIGURIANS

TERRAMARA
C.2000-1000

VILLANOVA

UMBRIANS

ETRUSCANS

SABINES

LATINS

SAMNITES

LUCANIANS

ETRUSCANS C.600

GREEKS

GREEKS

CARTHAGINIANS

C.730

GREEKS

PHOENICIANS C.800

James Darling

FROM FRANK, "HISTORY OF ROME" (CAPE)
MAP SHOWING INVASIONS OF ANCIENT ITALY, WITH APPROXIMATE DATES

only a diminishing proportion of the lower classes. In any modern industrial city where 10,000 males of military age constitute the highest 20% of taxpayers one would have to assume a population of at least 500,000 souls, or 100,000 male citizens; and that would be a very large population for a city with a rural territory of only about 500sq.m. (320,000ac.). It must, however, be remembered that in early Latium the proportion of property owners was large, that the Latin communities had consisted chiefly of farmers practising hoe-culture to whom 5–10ac. would not only suffice for a family but would require all its energies for cultivation. In the rural area, at least, property was more evenly divided than would be the case in an industrial community to-day, so that the 9,800 soldiers of the first class need not imply as large a population as it might to-day. Considering the extent of the city walls and the intensive cultivation of the Latin soil, we may accept for the last years of the regal period the tradition of the army of 193 centuries (19,300 men), and conjecture an urban population of about 200,000 and a rural population of about the same size. That the Latin country was at that time intensively cultivated we may well believe, when we recall the long underground drainage channels which were driven through the tufa on the Alban slopes to carry off torrential rain waters in order to save the surface soil from erosion. Such expensive work of salvage would not have been undertaken unless

land had been very much in demand and the population much more dense than in historical times.

The Etruscan princes were also vigorous conquerors, bent on extending their power throughout Latium. Tradition, reported by Livy and Dionysius, dwells long on their wars of conquest with Veii, Latin towns like Gabii, Aricia, Ardea and the Volscians as far as Tarracina. That this tradition happens to be fairly correct we may conclude from the facts that the region below Velitrae was particularly submitted to agricultural development (Frank, *Economic History of Rome*, 8 and 35, 2nd ed. 1927), that the colony of Cora existed at the founding of the first Latin league, and that the terms of the first treaty between Carthage and Rome, signed in 509, prove that the principality developed by Tarquin extended as far as Tarracina. This famous treaty recorded by Polybius (III. 22–3) is our oldest genuine document of Roman history. It was signed with the new republic of Rome immediately after the Etruscans had been banished and doubtless to a large extent reiterated the provisions of the previous treaty which the Tarquins had signed when in control of Rome. In the first sections it assumes that the free Romans would continue commerce on the seas to the extent that the Tarquins had, and it therefore makes an effort to safeguard the Punic trade monopoly at Punic ports. That proved to be a needless precaution, for the Romans abandoned the seas soon after they fell out of touch with Etruscan enterprise. A paragraph of the second part of the treaty reveals how far the ambitions of Etruscan Rome had advanced. It reads, "The Carthaginians shall do no injury to the people of Ardea, Antium, Laurentum, Circeii, Tarracina, nor any other people of the Latins that are subject to Rome. From those townships of Latium which are not subject to Rome they shall hold their hands; and if they shall take one they shall deliver it unharmed to the Romans." If, as seems to be the case, these clauses remain standing from Tarquin's last treaty with Carthage, they indicate that Tarquin had conquered at least the towns named, and that such towns as Pometia and Satricum, which are not mentioned, are considered within the sphere of Rome's natural interests, so that even if Carthage in some dispute should attack them she must deliver them to Rome. Needless to say the Roman republic which signed this treaty could not long entertain such ambitions, inherited for the time from Tarquin. Rome discovered within a few years that she had to release the Latins from subjection in order to win their support in her struggle with the returning Etruscans.

The terms of this treaty reveal how powerful Rome had become under the Tarquins and explain to us the resources that could pay for the building of a wall of 6m. and the power that could muster and employ an army of 20,000 men. They also help us to picture the resources that were expended in a very aggressive building programme. The temple to Jupiter which Tarquin nearly completed on the Capitoline hill stood on a lofty stylobate more than 20ft. high and measured about 200ft. x 185ft. None of the flourishing Etruscan cities with all their commercial prosperity had any temple comparable to this. Tarquin also moved the Diana cult from Aricia to Rome so as to make Rome the religious centre of the Latin communities of the Alban hills, and to Diana he built a famous temple on the Aventine. To the Etruscan period are also attributed several Fortuna temples—since soothsaying was particularly in favour with the Etruscans. Then in the first years of the republic there were built several temples begun by the Tarquins or vowed in the vigorous spirit of enterprise that the Tarquins had instilled; the large temple of Saturn below the Capitoline, the temple of Mercury—the god of commerce—behind the Palatine, the temple of Ceres nearby, and the splendid temple of Castor in the Forum. Not till two centuries later did the republic spend so much energy and money in public buildings, for with the expulsion of the Etruscans Rome became again a rural market place.

The effects of the Etruscan régime were widespread, though it apparently did not last more than about a century—if we are right in dating the last of the Forum burials about 600 B.C. In the Etruscan Government the senate had been retained, though virtually stripped of power, and the assembly was probably never summoned by the last Tarquin. A large industrial class must have come into existence in the city in the regal period, for even though the walls were raised by forced citizen-labour as tradition held, the increase in trade at the Roman market, the manufacture of the elaborate decorations for the new buildings, the service of a luxurious court, the provisioning and equipping of a large army would require much skilled labour. In some of the regions of Latium taken by force it is probable that the natives were reduced to serfdom as had been the custom in various parts of Etruria. The long and expensive drainage canals that are found between the Alban hills and the sea are not explicable in a system of small free farmers. In that region at least there must have been one or more strong lords who commanded much labour and capital. Whether the prince retained the land as a royal domain or assigned it as fiefs to favourites we have no means of knowing, and we must also admit that no conclusive evidence survived in Roman custom of the servile system which is frequently posited for this period.

This foreign régime also accounts for certain changes in rites, customs and institutions that were more or less lasting. The Etruscans had usually accepted the Italic deities from their subjects, but having come from the East and imbued with anthropomorphic conceptions they made representations of these deities in bronze or terra-cotta and built temples for them. Since such representations were usually derived from figures of Greek gods this process not only localized and gave human form to the Italic deities, but syncretized them with definite Greek gods regarding whom there existed a mythology. In this respect therefore the intervention of the Etruscans completely revolutionized the ideas of the younger generation of Romans. The Etruscans also lent their influence to the growing custom of inhuming the dead, and, for a while at least, to the interment of costly adornments with the body. Since the Etruscan burial rites—brought from Asia—were definitely connected with beliefs of the survival of the *genius* in a state of happiness or suffering, the Italic ideas of future existence were thus permanently altered, even though the Republican Government when restored tried to abolish funeral adornments and encourage a return to the Italic burial customs. That the Latin language was not displaced at Rome even in official regal inscriptions is proved by the survival of the famous "stele" of the forum, which is written in Latin though on an Etruscan stone and containing a reference to the king.

Expulsion of the King.—Near the end of the 6th century the Etruscan usurpers were ejected and a republican government formed with a restoration of annual elective magistrates, an advisory senate of nobles and a timocratic popular assembly. The traditional date is 509 B.C., but since the chronology adopted by later writers is a reconstruction from consular lists and from the marks made every year on the doorposts of the Capitoline temple, and since a discrepancy of a few years existed between these two records, we must not insist upon exact dates. Livy attributes the revolt against the Tarquins to a general objection to forced labour on public buildings and in the last instance to the wrong done to Lucretia by a son of the king. That tradition should have kept an accurate and adequate explanation of causes for several hundred years is not plausible, but in view of the evidence of archaeology and of institutional survivals we cannot doubt that Etruscan princes held Rome for a while and that they were ejected with a restoration of native rule.

II. THE REPUBLIC

Period A: 509–265 B.C.—(*a*) **The Struggle Between the Orders.**—The Tarquins apparently did not at once acquiesce in the results of the revolution. Securing the aid of friends in Etruscan cities and also in some Latin towns like Tusculum, still held by friendly princes, they attacked Rome again and again. An Etruscan tradition mentions a temporary victory by Lars Porsenna of Clusium by which he was able to disarm Rome for a while; and as late as 499 there was a famous battle at Lake Regillus in which the Romans won a decisive victory over Etruscan and some Latin forces, and the general on that occasion vowed the temple to Castor in recognition of aid received from

Greek cavalry. Rome also had trouble with the Latin cities, for the new Government attempted to take over the hegemony of the Latin towns that had been subjected by the Tarquins, while these Latin towns also wished a restoration of independence. Rome's wars with the Etruscans made it impossible to enforce her claims over the Latins, and consequently she had to come to terms with them. The independent league of Latin towns[1] consisting of Tibur, Tusculum, Aricia, Lanuvium, Ardea, Pometia and Cora, formed in order to resist Rome's pretensions, soon (*c.* 493) entered into a defensive alliance with her (the *foedus Cassianum*), and this new league made enough progress at once so that Signia and Norba were settled as common Latin colonies. But the Volscian towns of Antium, Satricum, Velitrae and Tarracina fell away from Latin connections.

The Government.—The new Government of Rome was more nearly an aristocracy than the old native Italic Governments. During the regal period with its great prosperity, its immigration of labourers, its partial imposition of serfdom, and grants of fiefs and privileges, class distinctions had come into existence. The favoured elders, selected by position, influence and favour for seats in the senate, were now considered a caste apart from the rest and they and their descendants were called patricians (*q.v.*). Since this group seems to have led the revolution and formed the new Government it is not strange that they imposed the requirements that patricians alone could hold the magistracies and priesthoods and interpret the laws, and that no resolution of the popular assembly should be binding unless ratified by the patrician senators. And when the more influential of the plebeians were enrolled as senators these *conscripti* apparently were not allowed to participate in the ratification of laws. Economic changes added to the disagreement between the classes. With the departure of the king and his court Rome fell out of the current of sea-going commerce, if we may judge from the evidence of excavations. For a while also trade relations with Etruria were cut off. Building construction which had flourished also soon came to an end. Furthermore when Rome had to surrender her hegemony not only over the Volscians of southern Latium but also over all the towns of central Latium, the profits that had flowed into the city from those regions ceased. There must have been much poverty and a large number of unemployed. And since the laws still permitted imprisonment and under certain conditions enslavement for debts, there arose among the poorer plebeians a demand for political rights with which to win some relief from economic distress. There were still in the vicinity several primitive Latin villages with their old town meetings which reminded the Romans of the old democratic government that had existed before the Etruscan invasion.

In the domain of external politics the 5th century was largely devoted to a reconquest by the league of the parts of Latium which were lost to the Volsci and Aequi during the distressing years of warfare with the Etruscans. In internal politics the plebeians made some progress during the century in their battle for recognition. What the plebeians first asked for was the right to elect advocates (tribunes of the people) who should have the right to prevent arbitrary arrest, and to speak for them in court when arrested. This seems to have been an attempt to find a remedy against harsh debtor-laws, and a substitute for the king who had listened to such appeals. The historians say that the plebeians were not granted this request until they had seceded to Mons Sacer when called upon for service against the Volsci. The fact that the privilege was granted by a sacred agreement which also invoked a curse upon any who impeded a tribune in the performance of his duty gives evidence that the measure rested upon a solemnly sworn compact between the orders. The story of the political strike is therefore plausible. There may at first have been four tribunes, one for each city tribe; but before the time of the decemvirs there were ten, and this remained henceforth the standing number.

It would be difficult to find a parallel to the tribunate anywhere. The tribune never became, strictly speaking, a magistrate of the Roman people. His one prerogative in the early day was

[1]Rosenberg, in *Hermes*, 159 (1919).

to protect individual plebeians against summary arrest by patrician officials and he must exercise this function in person and within the city. That he was sacrosanct and absolutely protected in the performance of his duty clearly points to the intention that in this one function he was to be as efficient a protector of the oppressed individual as the absolute monarch had been. Such powers could hardly be kept from abuse, and in time the tribunes became powerful individuals who could intervene in almost any department of state.

Since the tribunes were elected annually by the plebeians it was only natural that the plebeian assembly—which met by local groups or tribes—might remain to discuss policies and instruct the tribunes by resolution. In 471, if Livy is correct, a law was passed (the lex Publilia) which recognized the plebeian tribal assemblies as lawful, and authorized the tribunes to propose and carry resolutions in such assemblies. These resolutions (plebiscites) had of course only such force as plebeian influence gave them, but the time was to come when the plebeians were the most powerful element of the state, and when the law-making body dared not long resist the demands of plebiscites.

The Twelve Tables.—The plebeians now had advocates in court, but the tribunes were hampered by the fact that court judgments were rendered according to unwritten custom preserved from father to son within a narrow group of learned patricians. It therefore became apparent that the customary law must be codified and posted. After many years of discussion a law was passed substituting for the while a board of ten patricians in place of the two consuls and authorizing this board of ten to frame and publish a code of laws to be binding upon all. The *decemviri* worked on this code in 451 and 450, when it was inscribed and posted in the Forum. These "XII. tables" were in no sense a reform or a liberalizing of old custom. They recognized the prerogatives of the patrician caste and of the patriarchal family, the validity of enslavement for unpaid debt and the interference of religious custom in civil cases. That they reveal a remarkable liberality for their time in respect to testamentary rights and to contracts is probably not due to any alteration brought in by the *decemviri*, but rather to the progress that had been made in commercial customs in the Roman Forum in the days of prosperity and vigorous trade. The gist of this code has survived in quotations and is now the historian's safest index of the state of Rome's culture in the 5th century.   (T. F.)

Constitutional Changes.—The *decemviri*, who had incurred much opposition because of their autocratic administration of Rome, were deposed at the demand of the plebeians who seceded to the Janiculan Hill and made a formal demand that the former Government be restored. The assemblies accordingly met and elected consuls and tribunes again. But the plebeian assembly went farther and demanded certain reforms in the constitution. These demands were embodied in the very important Valeric-Horatian laws passed by the popular (centuriate) assembly in 449. These laws granted or reaffirmed the inviolability of the tribunes, the right of every citizen to carry his appeal to the assembly in cases of death sentences, and finally enacted that plebiscites passed by the plebeian assembly should be placed before the senate and if ratified by the *patres* should be recognized as law. Only a few years after the Valerio-Horatian legislation came the lex Canuleia, itself a *plebiscitum* (445 B.C.), by which mixed marriages between patricians and plebeians were declared lawful, and the social exclusiveness of the patriciate broken down. In the same year with this measure, and like it in the interests primarily of the wealthier plebeians, a vigorous attack commenced on the patrician monopoly of the consulate, and round this stronghold of patrician ascendancy the conflict raged until the passing of the Licinian laws in 367. The original proposal of the tribune Gaius Canuleius, in 445, that the people should be allowed to elect a plebeian consul was evaded by a compromise. The senate resolved that for the next year, in the stead of consuls, six military tribunes with consular powers should be elected, and that the new office should be open to patricians and plebeians alike. The consulship was thus for the time saved from pollution, as the patricians phrased it, but the growing

strength of the *plebs* is shown by the fact that in 50 years out of the 78 between 444 and 366 they succeeded in obtaining the election of consular tribunes rather than of consuls. Despite, however, these discouragements, the patricians fought on. Each year they strove to secure the creation of consuls rather than consular tribunes, and failing this strained every nerve to secure for their own order at least a majority among the latter. Even the institution of the censorship (435), though rendered desirable by the increasing importance and complexity of the census, was, it is probable, due in part to their desire to discount beforehand the threatened loss of the consulship by diminishing its powers. Other causes, too, helped to protract the struggle. Between the wealthier plebeians, who were ambitious of high office and the poorer, whose minds were set rather on allotments of land recently taken from Veii, there was a division of interest of which the patricians were not slow to take advantage, and to this must be added the pressure of war. The death struggle with Veii and the sack of Rome by the Gauls absorbed for the time all the energies of the community. In 377, however, two of the tribunes, G. Licinius Stolo and L. Sextius, came forward with proposals which united all sections of the *plebs* in their support. Their proposals were as follows: (1) that consuls and not consular tribunes be elected; (2) that one consul at least should be a plebeian; (3) that the priestly college, which had the charge of the Sibylline books, should consist of ten members instead of two, and that of these half should be plebeians; (4) that no single citizen should hold in occupation more than 500 ac. of the common lands, or pasture upon them more than 100 head of cattle and 500 sheep; (5) that interest already paid on debts should be deducted from the principal, and the remainder paid off in three years. The last two proposals were obviously intended to meet the demands of the poorer plebeians, and to secure their support for the first half of the scheme. Ten years of bitter conflict followed, but at last, in 367 B.C., the Licinian rogations became law, and one of their authors, L. Sextius, was created the first plebeian consul. For the moment it was some consolation to the patricians that they not only succeeded in detaching from the consulship the administration of civil law, which was entrusted to a separate officer, *praetor urbanus*, to be elected by the *comitia* of the centuries, with an understanding apparently that he should be a patrician, but also obtained the institution of two additional aediles (*aediles curules*), who were in like manner to be members of their own order. With the opening of the consulship, however, the issue of the long contest was virtually decided, and the next 80 years witnessed a rapid succession of plebeian victories. Now that a plebeian consul might preside at the elections, the main difficulty in the way of the nomination and election of plebeian candidates was removed. The proposed patrician monopoly of the new curule aedileship was almost instantly abandoned. In 356 the first plebeian was made dictator; in 350 the censorship, and in 337 the praetorship was filled for the first time by plebeians; and lastly, in 300, by the lex Ogulnia, even the sacred colleges of the pontiffs and augurs, the old strongholds of patrician supremacy, were thrown open to the *plebs*. The patricians lost also the control they had exercised so long over the action of the people in assembly. The *patrum auctoritas*, the sanction given or refused by the patrician senators to laws and to elections, had hitherto been a powerful weapon in their hands. But in 339 a law of Q. Publilius Philo, a plebeian dictator, enacted that this sanction should be given beforehand to laws enacted in the *comitia centuriata*, and a lex Maenia of uncertain date extended the rule to elections in the same assembly. Henceforward the *patrum auctoritas* sank into a meaningless form, though as such it still survived in the time of Livy. From 287 onwards it is certain that measures passed by the *plebs*, voting by their tribes, had the full force of laws without any further conditions whatsoever. The legislative independence of the plebeian assembly was secured, and with this crowning victory ended the long struggle between the orders.

(b) **Conquest of Italy.**—Twelve years after the passing of the lex Hortensia, King Pyrrhus, beaten at Beneventum, withdrew from Italy, and Rome was left mistress of the peninsula.

The steps by which this supremacy had been won have now to be traced.

The expulsion of the Tarquins from Rome, followed as it seems to have been by the emancipation from Etruscan supremacy of all the country between the Tiber and the Liris, entirely altered the aspect of affairs. North of the Tiber the powerful Etruscan city of Veii, after a vain attempt to restore the Tarquins, relapsed into an attitude of sullen hostility towards Rome, which, down to the outbreak of the final struggle in 407, found vent in constant and harassing border forays. The Sabines recommenced their raids across the Anio; from their hills to the south-east the Aequi pressed forward as far as the eastern spurs of the Alban range, and ravaged the low country between that range and the Sabine mountains; the Volsci overran the coast-lands as far as Antium, established themselves at Velitrae and even wasted the fields within a few miles of Rome. But the good fortune of Rome did not leave her to face these foes single-handed, and it is a significant fact that the history of the Roman advance begins, not with a brilliant victory, but with a timely alliance. According to Livy, it was in 493, only a few years after the defeat of the prince of Tusculum at Lake Regillus, that a treaty was concluded between Rome and the Latin communities of the Campagna. The alliance was in every respect natural. The Latins were the near neighbours

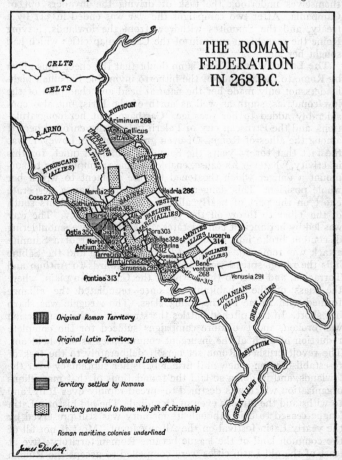

THE ROMAN FEDERATION IN 268 B.C.

Original Roman Territory

Original Latin Territory

Date & order of Foundation of Latin Colonies

Territory settled by Romans

Territory annexed to Rome with gift of citizenship

Roman maritime colonies underlined

James Darling.

FROM FRANK, "HISTORY OF ROME" (CAPE)

MAP SHOWING GROWTH OF THE ROMAN FEDERATION UP TO 268 B.C.

and kinsmen of the Romans, and both Romans and Latins were just freed from Etruscan rule to find themselves as lowlanders and dwellers in towns face to face with a common foe in the ruder hill tribes on their borders. The exact terms of the treaty cannot, any more than the precise circumstances under which it was concluded, be stated with certainty (*see* LATIUM), but two points seem clear. There was at first a genuine equality in the relations between the allies; Romans and Latins, though combining for defence and offence, did so without sacrificing their separate freedom of action, even in the matter of waging wars

independently of each other. But, secondly, Rome enjoyed from the first one inestimable advantage. The Latins lay between her and the most active of her foes, the Aequi and Volsci, and served to protect her territories at the expense of their own. Behind this barrier Rome grew strong, and the close of the Aequian and Volscian wars left the Latins her dependents rather than her allies. Beyond the limits of the Campagna Rome found a second ally, hardly less useful than the Latins, in the tribe of the Hernici, in the valley of the Trerus, who had equal reason with the Romans and Latins to dread the Volsci and Aequi, while their position midway between the two latter peoples made them valuable auxiliaries to the lowlanders of the Campagna.

Capture of Veii.—During the period 449–390 there is an unmistakable development of Roman power on all sides. In southern Etruria the capture of Veii (396) virtually gave Rome the mastery as far as the Ciminian forest. Sutrium and Nepete, "the gates of Etruria," became her allies and guarded her interests against any attack from the Etruscan communities to the north, while along the Tiber valley her suzerainty was acknowledged as far as Capena and Falerii. On the Anio frontier we hear of no disturbances from 449 until some ten years after the sack of Rome by the Gauls. In 446 the Aequi appear for the last time before the gates of Rome. After 418 they disappear from Mt. Algidus, and in the same year the communications of Rome and Latium with the Hernici in the Trerus valley were secured by the capture and colonization of Labicum. Successive invasions, too, broke the strength of the Volsci, and in 393 a Latin colony was founded as far south as Circeii. In part, no doubt, these Roman successes were due to the improved condition of affairs in Rome itself, consequent upon the great reforms carried between 450 and 442; but it is equally certain that now, as often afterwards, fortune befriended Rome by weakening, or by diverting the attention of, her opponents. In particular, her rapid advance in southern Etruria was facilitated by the heavy blows inflicted upon the Etruscans during the 5th century B.C. by Celts, Greeks and Samnites. By the close of this century the Celts had expelled them from the rich plains of what was afterwards known as Cisalpine Gaul, and were even threatening to advance across the Apennines into Etruria proper. The Sicilian Greeks, headed by the tyrants of Syracuse, wrested from them their mastery of the seas, and finally, on the capture of Capua by the Samnites in 423, they lost their possessions in the fertile Campanian plain. These conquests of the Samnites were part of a great southward movement of the highland Sabellian peoples.

Sack of Rome by the Gauls.—But in 390, or more probably 389, the Roman advance was for a moment checked by a disaster which threatened to alter the course of history in Italy, and which left a lasting impress on the Roman mind. In 391 a Celtic horde left their newly won lands on the Adriatic, and, crossing the Apennines into Etruria, laid siege to the Etruscan city of Clusium (Chiusi). Thence, provoked, it is said, by the conduct of the Roman ambassadors, who, forgetting their sacred character, had fought in the ranks of Clusium and slain a Celtic chief, the barbarians marched upon Rome. On July 18, 390 B.C., only a few miles from Rome, was fought the disastrous battle of the Allia. The defeat of the Romans was complete, and Rome lay at the mercy of her foe. But in characteristic fashion the Celts halted three days to enjoy the fruits of victory, and time was thus given to put the Capitol at least in a state of defence. The arrival of the barbarians was followed by the sack of the city, but the Capitol remained impregnable. For seven months they besieged it, and then in as sudden a fashion as they had come they disappeared. The Roman chroniclers explain their retreat in their own way, by the fortunate appearance of M. Furius Camillus with the troops which he had collected, at the very moment when famine had forced the garrison on the Capitol to accept terms. More probably the news that their lands across the Apennines were threatened by the Veneti, coupled with the unaccustomed tedium of a long siege and the difficulty of obtaining supplies, inclined the Celts to accept readily a heavy ransom as the price of their withdrawal. But, whatever the reason, it is certain that they retreated, and, though during the next 50 years marauding bands appeared at intervals in the neighbourhood of Rome, and even once penetrated as far south as Campania (361–360), the Celts never obtained any footing in Italy outside the plains in the north which they had made their own.

Annexation of Southern Etruria.—Nor, in spite of the defeat on the Allia and the sack of the city, was Rome weakened except for the moment by the Celtic attack. The storm passed away as rapidly as it had come on. The city was hastily rebuilt, and Rome dismayed the enemies who hastened to take advantage of her misfortunes by her undiminished vigour. Her conquests in southern Etruria were successfully defended against repeated attacks from the Etruscans to the north. The creation in 387 of four new tribes (Stellatina, Sabatina, Tromentina and Arnensis) marked the final annexation of the territory of Veii and of the lands lying along the Tiber valley. The addition of these tribes, containing Roman settlers as well as Veientines, increased the number and influence of the plebeian group. A few years later Latin colonies were established at Sutrium and Nepete for the more effectual defence of the frontier, and finally, in 353, Caere (*q.v.*) signed a treaty of peace for 100 years[1].

Next to the settlement of southern Etruria, the most important of the successes gained by Rome between 390 B.C. and 343 B.C. were those won against her old foes the Aequi and Volsci, and her old allies the Latins and Hernicans. The Aequi indeed, already weakened by their long feud with Rome, and hard pressed by the Sabellian tribes in their rear, were easily dealt with, and after the campaign of 389 we have no further mention of an Aequian war until the last Aequian rising in 304. The Volsci, who in 389 had advanced to Lanuvium, were met and utterly defeated by Camillus, the conqueror of Veii, and this victory was followed up by the gradual subjugation to Rome of all the lowland country lying between the hills and the sea as far south as Tarracina. Latin colonies were established at Satricum (385), at Setia (382), and at Antium and Tarracina some time before 348. In 358 two fresh Roman tribes (Pomptina and Publilia) were formed in the same district.

Reorganization of the Latin League.—Rome had now nothing more to fear from the foes who a century ago had threatened her very existence. The lowland country, of which she was the natural centre, from the Ciminian forest to Tarracina, was quiet, and within its limits Rome was by far the strongest power. But she had now to reckon with the old and faithful allies to whose loyal aid her present position was largely due. The Latini and Hernici had suffered severely in the Aequian and Volscian wars; it is probable that not a few of the smaller communities included in the league had either been destroyed or been absorbed by larger states, and the independence of all alike was threatened by the growing power of Rome. The sack of Rome by the Celts gave them an opportunity of reasserting their independence, and we are consequently told that this disaster was immediately followed by the temporary dissolution of the confederacy, and this again a few years later by a series of actual conflicts between Rome and her former allies. Between 383 and 358 we hear of wars with Tibur, Praeneste, Tusculum, Lanuvium, Circeii and the Hernici. But in all Rome was successful. In 382 Tusculum was fully incorporated with the Roman state by the bestowal of the full franchise; in 358, according to Livy and Polybius, the old alliance was formally renewed with the Latini and the Hernici. We cannot, however, be wrong in assuming that the position of the allies under the new league was far inferior to that accorded them by the treaty of Spurius Cassius. Henceforth they were the subjects rather than the equals of Rome, a position which it is evident that they accepted much against their will, and from which they were yet to make one last effort to escape.

First Samnite War.—Rome had won her supremacy from the Ciminian forest to the Liris as the champion of the comparatively civilized communities of the lowlands against the rude highland tribes which threatened to overrun them, and so, when her legions first crossed the Liris, it was in answer to an appeal from a lowland city against invaders from the hills. While she was engaged in clearing Latium of Volsci and Aequi, the Sabellian

[1]For the status of Caere, see *Klio* xi., 377.

tribes of the central Apennines had rapidly spread over the southern half of the peninsula. Foremost among these tribes were the Samnites, a portion of whom had captured the Etruscan city of Capua in 423, the Greek Cumae in 420, and had since then ruled as masters over the fertile Campanian territory. But in their new homes the conquerors soon lost all sense of relationship and sympathy with their highland brethren. They dwelt in cities, amassed wealth, and inherited the civilization of the Greeks and Etruscans whom they had dispossessed; above all, they had before long to defend themselves in their turn against the attacks of their ruder kinsmen from the hills, and it was for aid against these that the Samnites of Campania appealed to the rising state which had already made herself known as the bulwark of the lowlands north of the Liris, and which with her Latin and Hernican allies had scarcely less interest than the Campanian cities themselves in checking the raids of the highland Samnite tribes.

The Campanian appeal was listened to. Rome with her confederates entered into alliance with Capua and the neighbouring Campanian towns, and war was formally declared (343) against the Samnites. While to the Latins and Hernicans was entrusted apparently the defence of Latium and the Hernican valley against the northerly members of the Samnite confederacy; the Romans themselves undertook the task of driving the invaders out of Campania. After two campaigns the war was ended in 341 by a treaty, and the Samnites withdrew from the lowlands, leaving Rome the recognized suzerain of the Campanian cities which had sought her aid.

The Latin War.—There is no doubt that the check thus given by Rome to the advance of the hitherto invincible Sabellian highlanders not only made her the natural head and champion of the low countries, south as well as north of the Liris, but also considerably added to her prestige. Carthage sent her congratulations, and the Etruscan city of Falerii voluntarily enrolled herself among the allies of Rome. Of even greater service, however, was the fact that for 15 years the Samnites remained quiet, for this inactivity, whatever its cause, enabled Rome triumphantly to surmount a danger which theatened for the moment to wreck her whole position. This danger was nothing less than a desperate effort on the part of nearly all her allies and dependents south of the Tiber to throw off the yoke of her supremacy. The way was led by her ancient confederates the Latini, whose smouldering discontent broke into open flame directly the fear of a Samnite attack was removed. From the Latin Campagna and the Sabine hills the revolt spread westwards and southwards to Antium and Tarracina, and even to the towns of the Campanian plain, where the mass of the inhabitants at once repudiated the alliance formed with Rome by the ruling class. The struggle was sharp but short. In two pitched battles the strength of the insurrection was broken, and two more campaigns sufficed for the complete reduction of such of the insurgent communities as still held out. The revolt crushed, Rome set herself deliberately to the task of re-establishing on a new and firmer basis her supremacy over the lowlands, and in doing so laid the foundations of that marvellous organization which was destined to spread rapidly over Italy, and to withstand the attacks even of Hannibal. The old historic Latin league ceased to exist, though its memory was still preserved by the yearly Latin festival on the Alban Mount. Most if not all of the common land of the league became Roman territory; five at least of the old Latin cities were compelled to accept the Roman franchise (Livy viii. 14; Lanuvium, Aricia, Nomentum, Pedum and Tusculum) and enter the pale of the Roman State. The rest, with the Latin colonies, were ranked as Latin allies of Rome, but on terms which secured their complete dependence upon the sovereign city. The policy of isolation, which became so cardinal a principle of Roman rule, was now first systematically applied. No rights of *conubium* or *commercium* were any longer to exist between these communities. Their federal councils were prohibited, and all federal action independent of Rome forbidden.

In Campania and the coast-lands connecting Campania with Rome, a policy of annexation was considered safer than that of alliance. Of the two frontier posts of the Volsci, Antium and

Velitrae, the former was constituted a Roman colony, its long galleys burnt and their prows set up in the Forum at Rome, while the walls of Velitrae were razed to the ground, its leading men banished beyond the Tiber, and their lands given to Roman settlers. Farther south on the route to Campania, Fundi and Formiae were, after the precedent set in the case of Caere, declared Roman and granted the civil rights of Roman citizenship, while lastly in Campania itself the same status was given to Capua, Cumae and the smaller communities dependent upon them[1]. During the ten years from 338 to 328 the work of settlement was steadily continued. Tarracina, like Antium, was made a Roman colony. Privernum, the last Volscian town to offer resistance to Rome, was subdued in 330, part of its territory allotted to Roman citizens, and the state itself forced to accept the Roman franchise. Lastly, to strengthen the lines of defence against the Sabellian tribes, two colonies with the rights of Latin allies were established at Cales (334) and at Fregellae (328). The settlement of the lowlands was accomplished. As a single powerful and compact state with an outer circle of closely dependent allies, Rome now stood in sharp contrast with the disunited and degenerate cities of northern Etruria, the loosely organized tribes of the Apennines, and the decaying and disorderly Greek towns of the south.

Second Samnite War.—The strength of this system was now to be tried by a struggle with the one Italian people who were still ready and able to contest with Rome the supremacy of the peninsula. The passive attitude of the Samnites between 342 and 327 was no doubt largely due to the dangers which had suddenly threatened them in South Italy. But the death of Alexander of Epirus, in 332, removed their only formidable opponent there, and left them free to turn their attention to the necessity of checking the steady advance of Rome. In 327, the year after the ominous foundation of a Roman colony at Fregellae, a pretext for renewing the struggle was offered them. The Cumaean colony of Palaepolis had incurred the wrath of Rome by its raids into her territory in Campania. The Samnites sent a force to defend it, and Rome replied by a declaration of war. The two opponents were not at first sight unequally matched, and had the Sabellian tribes held firmly together the issue of the struggle might have been different. As it was, however, the Lucanians to the south actually joined Rome from the first, while the northern clans, Marsi, Vestini, Paeligni and Frentani, after a feeble and lukewarm resistance, subsided into a neutrality which was exchanged in 304 for a formal alliance with Rome. An even greater advantage to Rome from the outset was the enmity existing between the Samnites and the Apulians, the latter of whom from the first joined Rome and thus gave her a position in the rear of her enemy and in a country eminently well fitted for maintaining a large military force. These weaknesses on the Samnite side were amply illustrated by the events of the war.

After several years of partial success, the Romans were thoroughly defeated at Caudine Forks (321) and, in order to save their captured army, were compelled to sign a dishonourable treaty of peace. Rome, however, continued to strengthen her connections with the Lucanians and Apulians, settling a Latin colony at Luceria (314), and to draw the net of alliances more closely by winning over the Vestini and Frentani, north and east of Samnium. The Samnites accordingly, finding that peace was more dangerous than war, renewed hostilities in 316, by making a series of desperate efforts to break through the lines of defence which protected Latium and Campania. Sora and Fregellae on the upper Liris were captured by a sudden attack; the Ausones in the low country near the mouth of the same river were encouraged to revolt by the appearance of the Samnite army; and in Campania another army, attracted by rumours of disturbance, all but defeated the Roman consuls under the very walls of Capua. But these efforts were unavailing. Sora and Fregellae were recovered as quickly as they had been lost, and the frontier there

[1]For the controversy as to the precise status of Capua and the "equites Campani" (Livy viii. 14), *see* Beloch, *Ital. Bund,* 122 seq.; *idem, Campanien,* 317; Mommsen, *Staatsr.* iii. 574; Frank, *Roman Imperialism* 41.

was strengthened by the establishment of a colony at Interamna. The Ausones were punished by the confiscation of their territory, and Roman supremacy further secured by the two colonies of Suessa and Pontiae (313). The construction of the famous Via Appia, the work of the censor Appius Claudius Caecus, opened a safe and direct route to Campania, while the capture of Nola deprived the Samnites of their last important stronghold in the Campanian lowlands. The failure of these attempts broke the courage even of the Samnites. Their hopes were indeed raised for a moment by the news that Etruria had risen against Rome (310), but their daring scheme of effecting a union with the Etruscans was frustrated by the energy of the Roman generals. Five years later (305) the Romans revenged a Samnite raid into Campania by an invasion of Samnium itself. Arpinum on the frontier was taken, and at last, after a 22 years' struggle, the second Samnite War was closed by a renewal of the ancient treaty with Rome (304).

The six years of peace which followed (304–298) were employed by Rome in still further strengthening her position. Already, two years before the peace, a rash revolt of the Hernici had given Rome a pretext for finally annexing the territory of her ancient allies. The tribal confederacy was broken up, and all the Hernican communities, with the exception of three which had not joined the revolt, were incorporated with the Roman State as municipia, with the civil rights of the Roman franchise. Between the Hernican valley and the frontiers of the nearest Sabellian tribes lay what remained of the once formidable people of the Aequi. In their case, too, a revolt (304) was followed by the annexation of their territory, which was marked in this case by the formation there (301) of two Roman tribes (Aniensis and Teretina). Not content with thus carrying the borders of their own territory up to the very frontiers of the Sabellian country, Rome succeeded (304) in finally detaching from the Sabellian confederacy all the tribes lying between the north-east frontier of Latium and the Adriatic sea. Henceforward the Marsi, Paeligni, Vestini, Marrucini and Frentani were enrolled among the allies of Rome, and not only swelled her forces in the field but interposed a useful barrier between her enemies to the north in Etruria and Umbria and those to the south in Samnium, while they connected her directly with the friendly Apulians. Lastly, as a security for the fidelity at least of the nearest of these allies, colonies were planted in the Marsian territories at Alba Fucentia (303) and at Carsioli (298). A significant indication of the widening range of Rome's influence in Italy, and of the new responsibilities rapidly pressing upon her, is the fact that when in 302 the Spartan Cleonymus landed in the territory of the Sallentini, far away in the south-east, he was met and repulsed by an Italic and Roman force.

Third Samnite War.—Six years after the conclusion of the treaty which ended the second Samnite War, news arrived that the Samnites were harassing the Lucanians. Rome at once interfered to protect her allies. Samnium was invaded in force, the country ravaged and one stronghold after another captured. Unable any longer to hold their own in a position where they were hedged round by enemies, the Samnite leaders turned as a last hope to the communities of northern Etruria, to the free tribes of Umbria and to the once dreaded Celts. With a splendid daring they formed the scheme of uniting all these people with themselves in a last desperate effort to break the power of Rome.

For some 40 years after the final annexation of southern Etruria (351 B.C.) matters had remained unchanged in that quarter. Sutrium and Nepete still guarded the Roman frontier; the natural boundary of the Ciminian forest was still intact; and up the valley of the Tiber, Rome had not advanced beyond Falerii, a few miles short of the most southerly Umbrian town Ocriculum. But in 311, on the expiry, apparently, of the long truce with Rome, concluded in 351, the northern Etruscans, alarmed no doubt by the rapid advances which Rome was making farther south, rose in arms and attacked Sutrium. The attack, however, recoiled disastrously upon the heads of the assailants. A Roman force promptly relieved Sutrium, and its leader, Q. Fabius Rullianus, without awaiting orders from home, boldly plunged into the wilds of the Ciminian forest, and crossing them safely swept with fire and sword over the rich lands to the north. Then turning southwards he met and utterly defeated the forces which the Etruscans had hastily raised in the hopes of intercepting him at the Vadimonian lake. This decisive victory ended the war. The Etruscan cities, disunited among themselves, and enervated by long years of peace, abandoned the struggle for the time, paid a heavy indemnity and concluded a truce with Rome (309–08). In the same year the promptitude of Fabius easily averted a threatened attack by the Umbrians, but Rome proceeded nevertheless to fortify herself in her invariable fashion against future dangers on this side, by an alliance with Ocriculum, which was followed ten years later (299) by a colony at Narnia, and an alliance with the Picenes, whose position in the rear of Umbria rendered them as valuable to Rome as the Apulians had proved farther south.

Fourteen years had passed since the battle on the Vadimonian lake, when the Samnites appeared on the borders of Etruria and called on the peoples of northern Italy to rise against the common enemy. Their appeal, backed by the presence of their troops, was successful. The Etruscans found courage to face the Roman legions once more; a few of the Umbrians joined them; but the most valuable allies to the Samnites were the Celts, who had for some time threatened a raid across the Apennines, and who now marched eagerly into Umbria and joined the coalition. The news that the Celts were in motion produced a startling effect at Rome, and every nerve was strained to meet this new danger. While two armies were left in southern Etruria as reserves, the two consuls, Q. Fabius Maximus Rullianus and P. Decius Mus the younger, both tried soldiers, marched northwards up the valley of the Tiber and into Umbria at the head of four Roman legions and a still larger force of Italian allies. At Sentinum, on the farther side of the Apennines, they encountered the united forces of the Celts and Samnites, the Etruscans and Umbrians having, it is said, been withdrawn for the defence of their own homes. The battle that followed was desperate, and the Romans lost one of their consuls, Decius, and more than 8,000 men. But the Roman victory was decisive. The Celts were annihilated, and the fear of a second Celtic attack on Rome removed. All danger from the coalition was over. The Etruscan communities gladly purchased peace by the payment of indemnities. The rising in Umbria, never formidable, died away, and the Samnites were left single-handed to bear the whole weight of the wrath of Rome. During four years more, however, they desperately defended their highland homes, and twice at least, in 293 and 292, they managed to place in the field a force sufficient to meet the Roman legions on equal terms. At last, in 290, the consul M. Curius Dentatus finally exhausted their power of resistance. Peace was concluded, and it is significant of the respect inspired at Rome by their indomitable courage that they were allowed to become the allies of Rome, on equal terms and without any sacrifice of independence.

Between the close of the third Samnite War and the landing of Pyrrhus in 281 B.C. we find Rome engaged, as was her wont, in quietly extending and consolidating her power. In southern Italy she strengthened her hold on Apulia by planting on the borders of Apulia and Lucania the strong colony of Venusia. In central Italy the annexation of the Sabine country (290) carried her frontiers eastwards to the borders of her Picentine allies on the Adriatic. Farther east, in the territory of the Picentes themselves, she established colonies on the Adriatic coast at Hadria and Castrum (286–283). North of the Picentes lay the territories of the Celtic Senones stretching inland to the north-east borders of Etruria, and these too now fell into her hands. Ten years after their defeat at Sentinum (285–284) a Celtic force descended into Etruria, besieged Arretium and defeated the relieving force despatched by Rome. In 283 the consul L. Cornelius Dolabella was sent to avenge the insult. He completely routed the Senones. Their lands were annexed by Rome, and a colony established at Sena on the coast. This success, followed as it was by the decisive defeat of the neighbouring tribe of the Boii, who had invaded Etruria and penetrated as far south as the Vadimonian lake,

awed the Celts into quiet, and for more than 40 years there was comparative tranquillity in northern Italy.

Pyrrhus.—In the south, however, the claims of Rome to supremacy were now to be disputed by a new and formidable foe. At the close of the third Samnite War the Greek cities on the southern coast of Italy found themselves once more harassed by the Sabellian tribes on their borders, whose energies, no longer absorbed by the long struggles in central Italy, now found an attractive opening southwards.

The city of Thurii appealed to Rome for protection, and the plebeian assembly at Rome—recently given full legislative powers by the Hortensian law—voted to send the consul Fabricius to aid the Greeks. The consul easily routed the barbarians and established a garrison in the city. Thurii thus accepted Rome's suzerainty. The Tarentines, who claimed to be the protectors of the Greeks in Italy, were offended at the course taken by Thurii, and rightly feared that Rome's advance to the sea would soon compel all the cities of Magna Graecia to acknowledge the dominance of Rome's influence. While the Tarentines were debating whether to protest, several Roman ships (presumably of the *socii navales*), bound for the Adriatic colonies of Rome, appeared off the harbour of Tarentum. Since the Romans had long before signed a treaty that no Roman ships of war should sail east of the Lacinian cape, the Tarentines regarded the appearance of this squadron as a hostile act, attacked it, killed the admiral and sank most of the ships. Rome, desiring peace, asked for reparations without making a hostile demonstration, but the democratic party in Tarentum, bent upon asserting the independence and power of their city, engaged King Pyrrhus of Epirus to come to their aid and, in reliance upon his forces, declared war upon Rome (281).

King Pyrrhus (*see* PYRRHUS), whose timely appearance seemed for the moment to have saved the independence of Tarentum, was the most brilliant of the military adventurers whom the disturbed times following the death of Alexander the Great had brought into prominence. High-spirited, generous and ambitious, he had formed the scheme of rivalling Alexander's achievements in the East, by winning for himself an empire in the West. He aspired not only to unite under his rule the Greek communities of Italy and Sicily, but to overthrow the great Phoenician state of Carthage—the natural enemy of Greeks in the West, as Persia had been in the East. Of Rome it is clear that he knew little or nothing; the task of ridding the Greek seaports of their barbarian foes he no doubt regarded as an easy one; and the splendid force he brought with him was intended rather for the conquest of the West than for the preliminary work of chastising a few Italian tribes, or securing the submission of the unwarlike Italian Greeks. He defeated the Roman consul, M. Valerius Laevinus, on the banks of the Siris (280), and gained the support of the Greek cities as well as that of numerous bands of Samnites, Lucanians and Bruttians. But, to the disappointment of his new allies, Pyrrhus showed no anxiety to follow up his advantage. His heart was set on Sicily and Africa, and his immediate object was to come to terms with Rome. But though he advanced as near Rome as Anagnia (279), nothing could shake the resolution of the senate, and in the next year (278) he again routed the legions at Asculum (Ascoli), but only to find that the indomitable resolution of the enemy was strengthened by defeat. He now crossed into Sicily, where, though at first successful, he was unable to achieve any lasting result. Soured and disappointed, Pyrrhus returned to Italy (276) to find the Roman legions steadily moving southwards, and his Italian allies disgusted by his desertion of their cause. In 275 the decisive battle of the war was fought at Beneventum. The consul M. Curius Dentatus, the conqueror of Samnium, gained a complete victory and Pyrrhus, unable any longer to face his opponents in the field, and disappointed of all assistance from his allies, retreated in disgust to Tarentum and thence crossed into Greece.

A few years later (272) Tarentum was surrendered to Rome by its Epirot garrison; it was granted a treaty of alliance, but its walls were razed and its fleet handed over to Rome. In 270 Rhegium also entered the ranks of Roman allies, and finally in 269 a single campaign crushed the last efforts at resistance in Samnium. Rome was now at leisure to consolidate the position she had won. Between 273 and 263 three new colonies were founded in Samnium and Lucania—Paestum in 273, Beneventum in 268, Aesernia in 263. In central Italy the area of Roman territory was increased by the full enfranchisement (268) of the Sabines, and of their neighbours to the east, the people of Picenum. To guard the Adriatic coast, colonies were established at Ariminum (268), at Firmum and at Castrum Novum (264), while to the already numerous maritime colonies was added that of Cosa in Etruria.

Rome the Mistress of Italy.—Rome was now the undisputed mistress of Italy. The limits of her supremacy to the north were represented roughly by a line drawn across the peninsula from the mouth of the Arnus on the west to that of the Aesis on the east. Beyond this line lay the Ligurians and the Celts; all south of it was now united as "Italy" under the rule of Rome.

But the rule of Rome over Italy, like her wider rule over the Mediterranean coasts, was not an absolute dominion over conquered subjects. It was in form at least a confederacy under Roman protection and guidance; and the Italians, like the provincials, were not the subjects, but the "allies and friends" of the Roman people. In the treatment of these allies Rome consistently followed the maxim, *divide et impera*. In every possible way she strove to isolate them from each other, while binding them closely to herself. The old federal groups were in most cases broken up, and each of the members united with Rome by a special treaty of alliance. In Etruria, Latium, Campania and Magna Graecia the city was taken as the unit; in central Italy where urban life was non-existent, the unit was the tribe. The northern Sabellian peoples, for instance—the Marsi, Paeligni, Vestini, Marrucini and Frentani—were now constituted as separate communities in alliance with Rome. In many cases, too, no freedom of trade or intermarriage was allowed between the allies themselves. Nor were all these numerous allied communities placed on the same footing as regarded their relations with Rome herself. To begin with, a sharp distinction was drawn between the "Latini" and the general mass of Italian allies. The "Latins" of this period had little more than the name in common with the old 30 Latin peoples of the days of Spurius Cassius. With a few exceptions, such as Tibur and Praeneste, the latter had either disappeared or had been incorporated with the Roman State, and the Latins of 268 B.C. were almost exclusively the "Latin colonies," that is to say, communities founded by Rome, composed partly of allies but chiefly of men of Roman blood, and whose only claim to the title "Latin" lay in the fact that Rome granted to them some portion of the rights and privileges formerly enjoyed by the old Latin cities under the Cassian treaty. Though nominally allies, they were in fact offshoots of Rome herself, bound to her by community of race, language and interest, and planted as Roman garrisons among alien and conquered peoples. The Roman citizen who joined a Latin colony lost his citizenship—to have allowed him to retain it would no doubt have been regarded as enlarging too rapidly the limits of the citizen body; but he received in exchange the status of a favoured ally. The member of a Latin colony had the right of *commercium* and down to 268 of *conubium* also with Roman citizens. Provided they left sons and property to represent them at home, they were free to migrate to Rome and acquire the Roman franchise. In war-time they not only shared in the booty, but claimed a portion of any land confiscated by Rome and declared "public." These privileges, coupled with their close natural affinities with Rome, successfully secured the fidelity of the Latin colonies, which became not only the most efficient props of Roman supremacy, but powerful agents in the work of Romanizing Italy. Below the privileged Latins stood the Italian allies; and here again we know generally that there were considerable differences of status, determined in each case by the terms of their respective treaties with Rome. We are told that the Greek cities of Neapolis and Heraclea were among the most favoured; the Bruttii, on the other hand, seem, even before the Hannibalic War, to have been less generously treated. But beyond this we have no detailed information.

Rome, however, did not rely only on this policy. Her allies were attached as closely to herself as they were clearly separated from each other, and from the first she took every security for the maintenance of her own paramount authority. Within its own borders, each ally was left to manage its own affairs as an independent State. The badges which marked subjection to Rome in the provinces—the resident magistrate and the tribute—were unknown in Italy. But in all points affecting the relations of one ally with another, in all questions of the general interests of Italy and of foreign policy, the decision rested solely with Rome. The place of a federal constitution, of a federal council, of federal officers, was filled by the Roman senate, assembly and magistrates. The maintenance of peace and order in Italy, the defence of the coasts and frontiers, the making of war or peace with foreign Powers, were matters the settlement of which Rome kept entirely in her own hands. Each allied State, in time of war, was called upon for a certain contingent of men, but, though its contingent usually formed a distinct corps under officers of its own, its numerical strength was fixed by Rome, it was brigaded with the Roman legions, and was under the orders of the Roman consul.

The Roman State.—This paramount authority of Rome throughout the peninsula was confirmed and justified by the fact that Rome herself was now infinitely more powerful than any one of her numerous allies. Her territory, as distinct from that of the allied States, covered something like one-third of the peninsula south of the Aesis. Along the west coast it stretched from Caere to the southern borders of Campania. Inland, it included the former territories of the Aequi and Hernici, the Sabine country, and even extended eastwards into Picenum, while beyond these limits were outlying districts, such as the lands of the Senonian Celts, with the Roman colony of Sena, and others elsewhere in Italy, which had been confiscated by Rome and given over to Roman settlers. Since the first important annexation of territory after the capture of Veii (396), 12 new tribes had been formed, and the number of male citizens registered at the census had risen from 152,000 to 290,000. Within this enlarged Roman State were now included numerous communities with local institutions and government. At their head stood the Roman colonies (*coloniae civium Romanorum*), founded to guard especially the coasts of Latium and Campania. Next to these eldest children of Rome came those communities which had been invested with the full Roman franchise, such, for instance, as the old Latin towns of Aricia, Lanuvium, Tusculum, Nomentum and Pedum. Lowest in the scale were those which had not been considered ripe for the full franchise, but had, like Caere, received instead the *civitas sine suffragio*, the civil without the political rights. Their members, though Roman citizens, were not enrolled in the tribes, and in time of war served not in the ranks of the Roman legions but in separate contingents. In addition to these organized town communities, there were also the groups of Roman settlers on the public lands, and the dwellers in the village communities of the enfranchised highland districts in central Italy.

The administrative needs of this enlarged Rome were obviously such as could not be adequately satisfied by the system which had done well enough for a small city State with a few square miles of territory. The old centralization of all government in Rome itself had become an impossibility, and the Roman statesmen did their best to meet the altered requirements of the time. The urban communities within the Roman pale, colonies and *municipia*, were allowed a large measure of local self-government. In all we find local assemblies, senates and magistrates, to whose hands the ordinary routine of local administration was confided, and, in spite of differences in detail, *e.g.*, in the titles and numbers of the magistrates, the same type of constitution prevailed throughout. But these local authorities were carefully subordinated to the higher powers in Rome. The local constitution could be modified or revoked by the Roman senate and assembly, and the local magistrates, no less than the ordinary members of the community, were subject to the paramount authority of the Roman consuls, praetors and censors. In particular, care was taken to keep the administration of justice well under central control. The Roman citizen in a colony or *municipium* enjoyed, of course, the right of appeal of the Roman people in a capital case. We may also assume that from the first some limit was placed to the jurisdiction of the local magistrate, and that cases falling outside it came before the central authorities. But an additional safeguard for the equitable and uniform administration of Roman law, in communities to many of which the Roman code was new and unfamiliar, was provided by the institution of prefects (*praefecti iuri dicundo*), who were sent out annually, as representatives of the Roman praetor, to administer justice in the colonies and *municipia*. To prefects, moreover, were assigned the charge of those districts within the Roman pale where no urban communities, and consequently no organized local government, existed. In these two institutions, that of municipal government and that of prefectures, we have already two of the cardinal points of the later imperial system of government.

Lastly, the changes which the altered position and increased responsibilities of Rome had effected in her military system tended to weaken the intimate connection between the Roman army in the field and the Roman people at home, and thus prepared the way for that complete breach between the two which in the end proved fatal to the republic. It is true that service in the legion was still the first duty and the highest privilege of the fully qualified citizen. But this service was gradually altering in character. Though new legions were still raised each year for the summer campaigns, this was by no means always accompanied, as formerly, by the disbandment of those already on foot, and this increase in the length of time during which the citizen was kept with the standards had, as early as the siege of Veii, necessitated a further deviation from the old theory of military service—the introduction of pay. Moreover, while in the early days of the republic the same divisions served for the soldier in the legion and the citizen in the assembly, in the new manipular system, with its three lines, no regard was paid to civic distinctions, but only to length of service and military efficiency, while at the same time the more open order of fighting which it involved demanded of each soldier greater skill, and therefore a more thorough training in arms than the old phalanx. One other change resulted from the new military necessities of the time, which was as fruitful of results as the incipient separation between the citizen and the soldier. Under the early republic, the chief command of the legions rested with the consuls of the year. But, as Rome's military operations increased in area and in distance from Rome, a larger staff became necessary, and the inconvenience of summoning home a consul in the field from an unfinished campaign became intolerable. The remedy found, that of prolonging for a further period the imperium of the consul, was first applied in 327 B.C. in the case of Q. Publilius Philo, and between 327 and 264 instances of this *prorogatio imperii* became increasingly common. This proconsular authority, originally an occasional and subordinate one, was destined to become first of all the strongest force in the Republic, and ultimately the chief prop of the power of the Caesars.

Period B: Rome and the Mediterranean States, 265–146 B.C.—(*a*) *Conquest of the West.*—Though marked out by her geographical position as the natural centre of the Mediterranean, Italy had hitherto played no active part in the Mediterranean politics, but, now that she was for the first time united, it was felt throughout the Mediterranean world that a new Power had arisen, and Rome, as the head and representative of Italy, found herself irresistibly drawn into the vortex of Mediterranean affairs. Egypt sought her alliance, and Greek scholars began to interest themselves keenly in the history, constitution and character of the Latin republic which had so suddenly become famous. But Rome looked naturally westwards rather than eastwards. The western coasts of the peninsula were the most fertile and populous and wealthy; and it was in this direction that the natural openings for Italian commerce were to be found. It was, however, precisely on this side that Rome had serious ground for anxiety. Carthage was now at the height of her power. Her outposts were threateningly near to Italy in Sardinia and in Sicily, while her fleets swept the seas and jealously guarded for the benefit of Carthage alone the hidden treasures of the West. In the east of Sicily, Syracuse still upheld the cause of Greek independence against

the hereditary foe of the Greek race; but Syracuse stood alone, and her resources were comparatively small. What Rome had to fear was the establishment, and that at no distant date, of an absolute Carthaginian domination over the western seas—a domination which would not only be fatal to Italian commerce, but would be a standing menace to the safety of the Italian coasts.

First Punic War, 265–241.—It was above all things essential for Rome that the Carthaginians should advance no farther eastwards. But in 265 Rome was threatened with the establishment of Carthaginian rule at Messana, within sight of the Italian coast. The intervention of both powers in a quarrel between the Mamertines, a body of Campanian mercenaries who had occupied Messana, and Hieron II. of Syracuse, led to the outbreak of war between Rome and Carthage in 264 B.C. The military history of the struggle which followed is treated in the article PUNIC WARS; it will suffice to note here that the war lasted until 241 B.C., when the Carthaginians were compelled to cede Sicily and the Lipari islands to Rome, and to pay an indemnity of 3,200 talents (about £800,000).

The struggle was one in which both Rome and Carthage were serving an apprenticeship in a warfare the conditions of which were unfamiliar to both. The Roman legions were foes very unlike any against which the Carthaginian leaders had ever led their motley array of mercenaries, while Rome was called upon for the first time to fight a war across the sea, and to fight with ships against the greatest naval power of the age. The chief dangers for Carthage lay obviously in the jealousy exhibited at home of her officers abroad, in the difficulty of controlling her mercenary troops, and in the ever-present possibility of disaffection among her subjects in Libya—dangers which even the genius of Hannibal failed finally to surmount. Rome, on the other hand, was strong in the public spirit of her citizens, the fidelity of her allies, the valour and discipline of her legions. What she needed was a system which would make a better use of her splendid materials than one under which her plans were shaped from day to day by a divided senate, and executed by officers who were changed every year, and by soldiers most of whom returned home at the close of each summer's campaign.

The interval between the first and second Punic Wars was employed by both Rome and Carthage in strengthening their respective positions. The eastern end of Sicily was still left under the rule of Hieron as the ally of Rome, but the larger western portion of the island became directly subject to Rome, and a temporary arrangement seems to have been made for its government, either by one of the two praetors, or possibly by a quaestor. Sardinia and Corsica had not been surrendered to Rome by the treaty of 241, but three years later (239), on the invitation of the Carthaginian mercenaries stationed in the islands, a Roman force occupied them; Carthage protested, but, on the Romans threatening war, she gave way, and Sardinia and Corsica were formally ceded to Rome, though it was some seven or eight years before all resistance on the part of the natives themselves was crushed. In 227, however, the senate considered matters ripe for the establishment of a separate administration in her oversea possessions. In that year two additional praetors were elected; to one was assigned the charge of western Sicily, to the other that of Sardinia and Corsica, and thus the first stones of the Roman provincial system were laid. Of at least equal importance for the security of the peninsula was the subjugation of the Celtic tribes in the valley of the Po. These, headed by the Boii and Insubres and assisted by levies from the Celts to the westward, had in 225 alarmed the whole of Italy by invading Etruria and penetrating to Clusium, only three days' journey from Rome. Here, however, their courage seems to have failed them. They retreated northwards along the Etruscan coast, until at Telamon their way was barred by the Roman legions returning from Sardinia to the defence of Rome, while a second consular army hung upon their rear. Thus hemmed in, the Celts fought desperately, but were completely defeated and the flower of their tribesmen slain. The Romans followed up their success by invading the Celtic territory. The Boii were easily reduced to submission. The Insubres, north of the Po, resisted more obstinately, but by 222 the war was over,

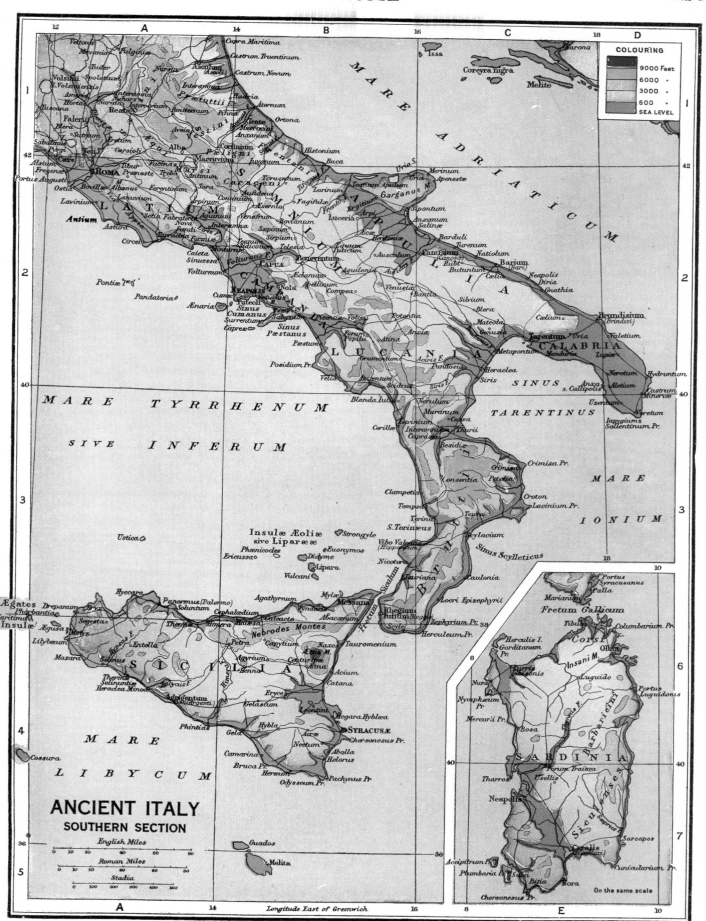

ANCIENT ITALY
SOUTHERN SECTION

MAP II   ROME

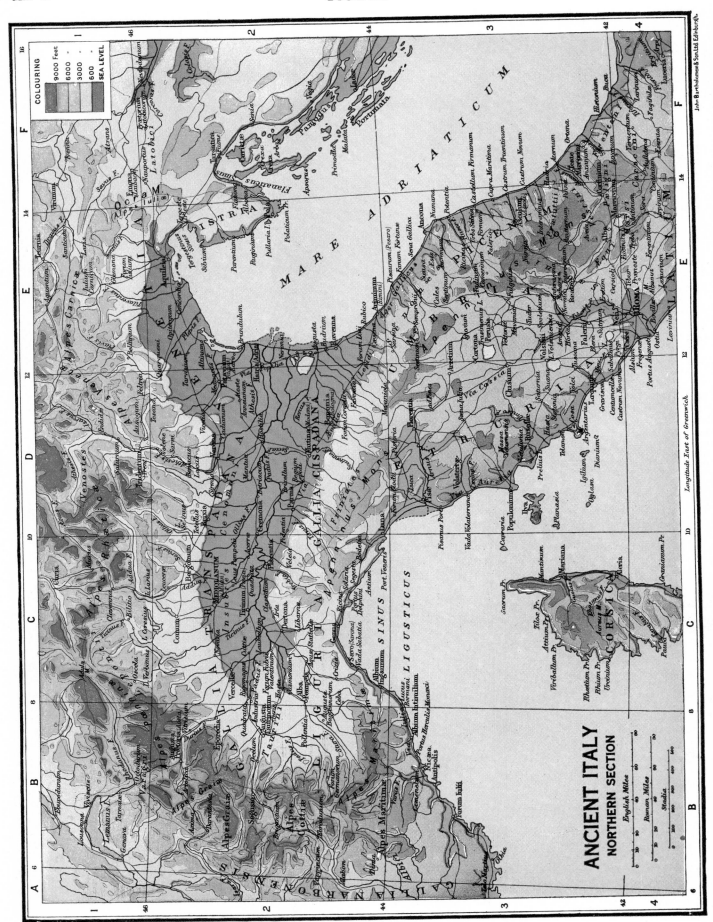

ANCIENT ITALY
NORTHERN SECTION

COLOURING

9000 Feet
6000 „
3000 „
600 „
SEA LEVEL

English Miles

Roman Miles

Stadia

Longitude East of Greenwich

John Bartholomew & Son, Ltd. Edinburgh.

and all the tribes in the rich Po valley acknowledged the supremacy of Rome. The conquered Celts were not enrolled among the Italian allies of Rome, but were treated as subjects beyond the frontier. Two colonies were founded to hold them in check— Placentia (218) and Cremona in the territory of the Insubres— and the great northern road (Via Flaminia) was completed as far as the Celtic border at Ariminum.

On the Adriatic coast the immediate interests of Rome were limited to rendering the sea safe for Italian trade. It was with this object that, in 229, the first Roman expedition crossed the Adriatic, and inflicted severe chastisement on the Illyrian pirates of the opposite coast. This expedition was the means of establishing for the first time direct political relations between Rome and the states of Greece proper, to many of which the suppression of piracy in the Adriatic was of as much importance as to Italy. Alliances were concluded with Corcyra, Epidamnus and Apollonia; and embassies explaining the reasons which had brought Roman troops into Greece were sent to the Aetolians, the Achaeans and even to Athens and Corinth. Everywhere they were well received, and the admission of the Romans to the Isthmian games (228) formally acknowledged them as the natural allies of the free Greek states against both barbarian tribes and foreign despots. Meanwhile Carthage had acquired a possession which promised to compensate her for the loss of Sicily, Sardinia and Corsica. The genius of her greatest citizen and soldier, Hamilcar Barca, had appreciated the enormous value of the Spanish peninsula, and conceived the scheme of founding there a Carthaginian dominion which should not only add to the wealth of Carthage, but supply her with a base of operations for a war of revenge with Rome. The conquest of southern and eastern Spain, begun by Hamilcar (236–228) and carried on by his kinsman Hasdrubal (228–221), was completed by his son Hannibal, who, with all his father's genius, inherited also his father's hatred of Rome, and by 219 the authority of Carthage had been extended as far as the Ebro (*see* SPAIN, *History*). Rome's ancient ally Massilia (mod. Marseilles) was especially disturbed by these advances, for she had trading posts on the coast of Spain which would become unprofitable if Carthage conquered the whole of the interior and drew the commerce of the peninsula southwards to the Punic ports. Furthermore, since Carthage forbade Massiliot traders to make use of the straits of Gibraltar, Massiliot trade in British tin would be endangered if Carthage succeeded in reaching southern Gaul. From the fact that Marseilles lent her whole navy to Rome when the war broke out we may assume that her envoys were active in reporting the advance of Carthage in Spain and in interpreting that advance as aimed at Rome. Rome finally was induced to act. A defensive alliance was signed with Saguntum, a seaport of Spain which was still independent, and Hasdrubal was asked to promise that Carthage should not carry her arms beyond the Ebro river (226).

Second Punic War, 218–211.—But these precautions were of no avail against the resolute determination of Hannibal, with whom the conquest of Spain was only preliminary to an attack upon Italy, and who could not afford to leave behind him in Spain a state allied to Rome. In 219, therefore, disregarding the protests of a Roman embassy, he attacked and took Saguntum, an act which, as he had foreseen, rendered a rupture with Rome inevitable, while it set his own hands free for a further advance.

For the details of the war which followed, *see* the articles PUNIC WARS; HANNIBAL; and SCIPIO, PUBLIUS CORNELIUS. From the outbreak of hostilities until the crowning victory of Cannae in 216 Hannibal's career of success was unchecked; and the annihilation of the Roman army in that battle was followed by the defection of almost the whole of southern Italy, with the exception of the Latin colonies and the Greek coast towns. In 215, moreover, Philip V. of Macedon formed an alliance with Hannibal and threatened to invade Italy; in 214 Syracuse revolted, and in 212 the Greek cities in northern Italy went over to Hannibal. But the indomitable spirit of the Romans asserted itself in the face of these crushing misfortunes. In 212 Syracuse was recovered; in 211 Capua fell after a long siege which Hannibal failed to raise, even by his famous march up to the gates of

Rome, and in the same year a coalition was formed in Greece against Philip V. of Macedon, which effectually paralysed his offensive action. Hannibal was now confined to Lucania and Bruttium; and his brother Hasdrubal, marching from Spain to join him, was defeated and slain on the river Metaurus (207). The war in Italy was now virtually ended, for, though during four years more Hannibal stood at bay in a corner of Bruttium, he was powerless to prevent the restoration of Roman authority throughout the peninsula. Sicily was once more secure; and finally in 206, the year after the victory on the Metaurus, the successes of the young P. Scipio in Spain (211–206) were crowned by the complete expulsion of the Carthaginians from the peninsula. On his return from Spain Scipio eagerly urged an immediate invasion of Africa. The senate hesitated; but Scipio gained the day. He was elected consul for 205, and given the province of Sicily, with permission to cross into Africa if he thought fit. Voluntary contributions of men, money and supplies poured in to the support of the popular hero; and by the end of 205 Scipio had collected in Sicily a sufficient force for his purpose. In 204 he crossed to Africa, where he was welcomed by the Numidian prince Massinissa, whose friendship he had made in Spain. In 203 he twice defeated the Carthaginian forces, and a large party at Carthage were anxious to accept his offer of negotiations. But the advocates of resistance triumphed.

Hannibal was recalled from Italy, and returned to fight his last battle against Rome at Zama, where Scipio, who had been continued in command as proconsul for 202 by a special vote of the people, won a complete victory. The war was over. The Roman assembly voted that the Carthaginian request for peace should be granted, and entrusted the settlement of the terms to Scipio and a commission of ten senators. Carthage was allowed to retain her territory in Africa; but she undertook to wage no wars outside Africa, and none inside without the consent of Rome. She surrendered all her ships but ten triremes, her elephants, and all prisoners of war, and agreed to pay an indemnity of 10,000 talents in 50 years. The Numidian Massinissa (*q.v.*) was rewarded by an increase of territory, and was enrolled among the "allies" and "friends" of the Roman people.

The West Under Roman Rule.—The battle of Zama decided the fate of the West. The power of Carthage was broken and her supremacy passed to Rome. Henceforth Rome had no rival to fear westward of Italy, and it rested with herself to settle within what limits her supremacy should be confined and what form it should take. In Sicily the former dominions of Hieron were at once united with the western half of the island as a single province, and in Spain, after nine years of a provisional Government (206–197), two provinces were in 197 definitely established, and each, like Sicily, assigned to one of the praetors for the year, two additional praetors being elected for the purpose. But here the resemblance between the two cases ends. From 201 down to the outbreak of the Slave War in 136 there was unbroken peace in Sicily, and its part in the history is limited to its important functions in supplying Rome with corn and in provisioning and clothing the Roman legions. The governors of the two Spains had very different work to do from that which fell to the lot of the Sicilian praetors. The condition of Spain required that year after year the praetors should be armed with the consular authority, and backed by a standing force of four legions, while more than once the presence of the consuls themselves was found necessary. Still, in spite of all difficulties, the work of pacification proceeded. To M. Porcius Cato (consul, 195) and to Tiberius Sempronius Gracchus (praetor and pro-praetor, 180–179), father of the two tribunes, is mainly due the credit of quieting the Celtiberian tribes of central Spain, and the government of Gracchus was followed by 30 years of comparative tranquillity. The insurrection headed by Viriathus in 149 was largely caused by exactions of the Roman magistrates themselves, while its obstinate continuance down to the capture of Numantia, in 133, was almost as much the result of the incapacity of the Roman commanders. But the re-settlement of the country by Scipio Africanus the younger in that year left all Spain, with the exception of the highland Astures and Cantabri in the north-west, finally and tranquilly subject to

Rome.

Third Punic War, 153–146.—In Africa there was no question at first of the introduction of Roman government by the formation of a province (*see* AFRICA, ROMAN). Carthage, bound hand and foot by the treaty of 201, was placed under the jealous watch of the loyal prince of Numidia, who himself willingly acknowledged the suzerainty of Rome. But it was impossible for this arrangement to be permanent. Every symptom of reviving prosperity at Carthage was regarded at Rome with feverish anxiety, and neither the expulsion of Hannibal in 195 nor his death in 183 did much to check the growing conviction that Rome would never be secure while her rival existed. It was therefore with grim satisfaction that many in the Roman senate watched the increasing irritation of the Carthaginians under the harassing raids and encroachments of their favoured neighbor Massinissa, and waited for the moment when Carthage should, by some breach of the conditions imposed upon her, supply Rome with a pretext for interference. At last in 151 came the news that Carthage, in defiance of treaty obligations, was actually at war with Massinissa. The anti-Carthaginian party in the senate, headed by M. Porcius Cato, eagerly seized the opportunity, and war was declared, and nothing short of the destruction of their city itself was demanded from the despairing Carthaginians. The demand was refused and in 149 the siege of Carthage begun. During the next two years little progress was made, but in 147 P. Cornelius Scipio Aemilianus, grandson by adoption of the conqueror of Hannibal, was, at the age of 37, and though only a candidate for the aedileship, elected consul and given the command in Africa. In the next year (146) Carthage was taken and razed to the ground. Its territory became the Roman province of Africa, while Numidia, now ruled by the three sons of Massinissa, remained as an allied state under Roman suzerainty, and served to protect the new province against the raids of the desert tribes (*see* CARTHAGE).

In Italy itself the Hannibalic War had been followed by important changes. In the north the Celtic tribes paid for their sympathy with Hannibal by the final loss of all separate political existence. Cispadane Gaul, studded with colonies and flooded with Roman settlers, was rapidly Romanized. Beyond the Padus (Po) in Polybius's time Roman civilization was already widely spread. In the extreme north-east the Latin colony of Aquileia, the last of its kind, was founded in 181, to control the Alpine tribes, while in the north-west the Ligurians were held in check by the colony of Luna (180), and by the extensive settlements of Roman citizens and Latins made on Ligurian territory in 173. In southern Italy the depression of the Greek cities on the coast, begun by the raids of the Sabellian tribes, was completed by the repeated blows inflicted upon them during the Hannibalic struggle. Some of them lost territory[1]; all suffered from a decline of population and loss of trade; and their place was taken by such new Roman settlements as Brundisium (Brindisi) and Puteoli (Pozzuoli). In the interior the southern Sabellian tribes suffered scarcely less severely. The Bruttii were struck off the list of Roman allies, and nearly all their territory was confiscated. To the Apulians and Lucanians no such hard measure was meted out; but their strength had been broken by the war, and their numbers dwindled; large tracts of land in their territories were seized by Rome, and allotted to Roman settlers, or occupied by Roman speculators. That Etruria also suffered from declining energy, a dwindling population, and the spread of large estates is clear from the state of things existing there in 133. It was indeed in central Italy, the home of the Latins and their nearest kinsmen, and in the new Latin and Roman settlements throughout the peninsula, that progress and activity were henceforth concentrated.

(*b*) **Rome in the East, 200–133.**—Ever since the repulse of Pyrrhus from Italy, Rome had been slowly drifting into closer contact with the eastern states. With one of the three great powers which had divided between them the empire of Alexander, with Egypt, she had friendly relations since 273, and the friendship had been cemented by the growth of commercial intercourse

between the two countries. In 228 her chastisement of the Illyrian pirates had led naturally enough to the establishment of friendly relations with some of the states of Greece proper. In 214 the alliance between Philip V. and Hannibal, and the former's threatened attack on Italy, forced her into war with Macedon, at the head of a coalition of the Greek states against him, which effectually frustrated his designs against herself; at the first opportunity, however (205), she ended the war by a peace which left the position unchanged. The results of the war were not only to draw closer the ties which bound Rome to the Greek states, but to inspire the senate with a genuine dread of Philip's restless ambition, and with a bitter resentment against him for his union with Hannibal. The events of the next four years served to deepen both these feelings. In 205 Philip entered into a compact with Antiochus III. of Syria for the partition between them of the dominions of Egypt, now left by the death of Ptolemy Philopator to the rule of a boy-king. Antiochus was to take Coele-Syria and Phoenicia, while Philip claimed for his share the districts subject to Egypt on the coasts of the Aegean and the Greek islands. Philip no doubt hoped to be able to secure these unlawful acquisitions before the close of the second Punic War should set Rome free to interfere with his plans. But the obstinate resistance offered by Attalus of Pergamum and the Rhodians upset his calculations. In 201 Rome made peace with Carthage, and the senate had leisure to listen to the urgent appeal for assistance which reached her from her Eastern allies. With Antiochus indeed the senate was not yet prepared to quarrel; but with Philip the senate was ready to have a serious discussion despite the depletion of all resources. Philip had compelled Rome to give way to him in Illyricum, and he had proved by his attack on Egypt that he would prove to be a dangerous neighbour in time of peril. Furthermore philhellenism had grown very strong at Rome since Livius, Naevius and Ennius had translated scores of Greek plays for production at the Roman festivals. To the nobles who were now eagerly reading Homer, Plato and Euripides, the appeal of the old Greek cities for protection of independence, democracy and culture in Greece came to open ears. The people, to be sure, remembering all too well what they had suffered in the last war, at first rejected the senate's proposal to aid the Greeks, but the nobles, insisting that postponement would only result in a Macedonian invasion of Italy, finally secured a declaration of war (200).

Second Macedonian War, 200–197.—The war began in the summer of 200 B.C. and, though the landing of the Roman legions in Epirus was not followed, as had been hoped, by any general rising against Philip, yet the latter made no progress south of Boeotia. The fleets of Pergamum and Rhodes, now the zealous allies of Rome, protected Attica and watched the eastern coasts. The Achaeans and Nabis of Sparta were obstinately neutral, while nearer home in the north the Epirots and Aetolians threatened Thessaly and Macedonia. His own resources both in men and in money had been severely strained by his constant wars, and the only ally who could have given him effective assistance, Antiochus, was fully occupied with the conquest of Coele-Syria. It is no wonder then that, in spite of his dashing generalship and high courage, he made but a brief stand. T. Quinctius Flamininus (consul, 198), in his first year of command, defeated him on the Aous, drove him back to the pass of Tempe, and in the next year utterly routed him at Cynoscephalae. Almost at the same moment the Achaeans, who had now joined Rome, took Corinth, and the Rhodians defeated his troops in Caria. Further resistance was impossible; Philip submitted, and early the next year a Roman commission reached Greece with instructions to arrange terms of peace. These were such as effectually secured Rome's main object in the war, the removal of all danger to herself and her allies from Macedonian aggression. Philip was left in possession of his kingdom, but was degraded to the rank of a second-rate Power, deprived of all possessions in Greece, Thrace and Asia Minor, and forbidden, as Carthage had been in 201, to wage war without the consent of Rome, whose ally and friend he now became.

The second point in the settlement now effected by Rome was the liberation of the Greeks. The "freedom of Greece" was

---

[1] *E.g.*, Tarentum, Livy, xliv. 16. A Roman colony was established at Croton in 194, and a Latin colony (Copia) at Thurii in 193 (Livy, xxxiv. 45, 53).

proclaimed at the Isthmian games amid a scene of wild enthusiasm, which reached its height when two years later (194) Flamininus withdrew his troops even from the "three fetters of Greece"— Chalcis, Demetrias and Corinth. There is no reason to doubt that, in acting thus, not only Flamininus himself, but the senate and people at home were influenced, partly at any rate, by feelings of genuine sympathy with the Greeks and reverence for their past. It is equally clear that no other course was open to them. For Rome to have annexed Greece, as she had annexed Sicily and Spain, would have been a flagrant violation of the pledges she had repeatedly given both before and during the war; the attempt would have excited the fiercest opposition, and would probably have thrown the Asiatic as well as the European Greeks into the arms of Antiochus. But a friendly and independent Greece would be at once a check on Macedon and a barrier against aggression from the East. Nor while liberating the Greeks did Rome abstain from such arrangements as seemed necessary to secure the predominance of her own influence. In the Peloponnese, for instance, the Achaeans were rewarded by considerable accessions of territory; and it is possible that the Greek states, as allies of Rome, were expected to refrain from war upon each other without her consent.

War with Antiochus, 192–189.—Antiochus III. of Syria, Philip's accomplice in the proposed partition of the dominions of their common rival, Egypt, returned from the conquest of Coele-Syria (198) to learn first of all that Philip was hard pressed by the Romans, and shortly afterwards that he had been decisively beaten at Cynoscephalae. It was already too late to assist his former ally, but Antiochus resolved at any rate to lose no time in securing for himself the possessions of the Ptolemies in Asia Minor and in eastern Thrace, which Philip had claimed, and which Rome now pronounced free and independent. In 197–196 he overran Asia Minor and crossed into Thrace. But Antiochus was pleasure-loving, irresolute, and no general, and it was not until 192 that the urgent entreaties of the Aetolians, and the withdrawal of the Roman troops from Greece, nerved him to the decisive step of crossing the Aegean; even then the force he took with him was so small as to show that he completely failed to appreciate the nature of the task before him. At Rome the prospect of a conflict with Antiochus excited great anxiety, and it was not until every resource of diplomacy had been exhausted that war was declared, and the real weakness which lay behind the once magnificent pretensions of the "king of kings" was revealed.

Had Antiochus acted with energy when in 192 he landed in Greece, he might have won the day before the Roman legions appeared. As it was, in spite of the warnings of Hannibal, who was now in his camp, and of the Aetolians, he frittered away valuable time between his pleasures at Chalcis and useless attacks on petty Thessalian towns. In 191 Acilius Glabrio landed at the head of an imposing force; and a single battle at Thermopylae broke the courage of Antiochus, who hastily recrossed the sea to Ephesus, leaving his Aetolian allies to their fate. But Rome could not pause here. The safety of her faithful allies, the Pergamenes and Rhodians, and of the Greek cities in Asia Minor, as well as the necessity of chastising Antiochus, demanded an invasion of Asia. A Roman fleet had already (191) crossed the Aegean, and in concert with the fleets of Pergamum and Rhodes worsted the navy of Antiochus. In 190 the new consul L. Scipio, accompanied by his famous brother, the conqueror of Africa, led the Roman legion for the first time into Asia. At Magnesia ad Sipylum, in Lydia, he met and defeated the motley and ill-disciplined hosts of the great king. For the first time the West, under Roman leadership, successfully encountered the forces of the East, and the struggle began which lasted far on into the days of the emperors. The terms of the peace which followed the victory at Magnesia tell their own story clearly enough. There is no question, any more than in Greece, of annexation; the main object in view is that of securing the predominance of Roman interests and influence throughout the peninsula of Asia Minor, and removing to a safe distance the only eastern Power which could be considered dangerous. The line of the Halys and the Taurus range, the natural boundary of the peninsula eastwards, was established as the boundary between Antiochus and the kingdoms, cities and peoples now enrolled as the allies and friends of Rome. This line Antiochus was forbidden to cross; nor was he to send ships of war farther west than Cape Sarpedon in Cilicia. Immediately to the west of this frontier lay Bithynia, Paphlagonia and the immigrant Celtic Galatae, and these frontier states, now the allies of Rome, served as a second line of defence against attacks from the east. The area lying between these "buffer states" and the Aegean was organized by Rome in such a way as should at once reward the fidelity of her allies and secure both her own paramount authority and safety from foreign attack. Pergamum and Rhodes were so strengthened—the former by the gift of the Chersonese, Lycaonia, Phrygia, Mysia and Lydia, the latter by that of Lycia and Caria—as not only amply to reward their loyalty, but to constitute them effective props of Roman interests and effective barriers alike against Thracian and Celtic raids in the north and Syrian aggression in the south. Lastly, the Greek cities on the coast, except those already tributary to Pergamum, were declared free, and established as independent allies of Rome.

In a space of little over 11 years (200–189) Rome had broken the power of Alexander's successors and established throughout the eastern Mediterranean a Roman protectorate.

Third Macedonian War, 171–168.—It was in the western half of this protectorate that the first steps in the direction of annexation were taken. The enthusiasm provoked by the liberation of the Greeks had died away, and its place had been taken by feelings of dissatisfied ambition or sullen resentment. Internecine feuds and economic distress had brought many parts of Greece to the verge of anarchy, and, above all, the very foundations of the settlement effected in 197 were threatened by the reviving power and aspirations of Macedon. Loyally as Philip had aided Rome in the war with Antiochus, the peace of Magnesia brought him nothing but fresh humiliation. He was forced to abandon all hopes of recovering Thessaly, and he had the mortification to see the hated king of Pergamum installed almost on his borders as master of the Thracian Chersonese. Resistance at the time was unavailing, but from 189 until his death (179) he laboured patiently and quietly to increase the internal resources of his own kingdom, and to foment, by dexterous intrigue, feelings of hostility to Rome among his Greek and barbarian neighbours. His successor, Perseus, his son by a left-handed alliance, continued his father's work. He made friends among the Illyrian and Thracian princes, connected himself by marriage with Antiochus IV. of Syria and with Prusias of Bithynia, and, among the Greek peoples, strove, not without success, to revive the memories of the past glories of Greece under the Macedonian leadership of the Great Alexander. The senate could no longer hesitate. They were well aware of the restlessness and discontent in Greece; and after hearing from Eumenes of Pergamum and from their own officers, all details of Perseus's intrigues and preparations, they declared war. The struggle, in spite of Perseus's courage and the incapacity at the outset of the Roman commanders, was short and decisive. The sympathy of the Greeks with Perseus, which had been encouraged by the hitherto passive attitude assumed by Rome, instantly evaporated on the news that the Roman legions were on their way to Greece. No assistance came from Prusias or Antiochus, and Perseus's only allies were the Thracian king Cotys and the Illyrian Genthius. The victory gained by L. Aemilius Paulus at Pydna (168) ended the war. Perseus became the prisoner of Rome, and as such died in Italy a few years later. Rome had begun the war with the fixed resolution no longer of crippling but of destroying the Macedonian State. Perseus's repeated proposals for peace during the war had been rejected; and his defeat was followed by the final extinction of the kingdom of Philip and Alexander. Macedonia, though it ceased to exist as a single State, was not, however, definitely constituted a Roman province. On the contrary, the mistake was made of introducing some of the main principles of the provincial system—taxation, disarmament and the isolation of the separate communities—without the addition of the element most essential for the maintenance of order—that of a resident Roman governor. The four petty republics now created were each autonomous, and each separated from the rest by the prohibition of *commercium* and *conubium*, but no central controlling authority was substituted for that of the Macedonian king. The inevitable result was confusion and disorder, resulting finally (149-48) in the attempt of a pretender, Andriscus, who claimed to be a son of Perseus, to resuscitate the ancient monarchy. On his defeat in 148 the senate declared Macedonia a Roman province, and placed a Roman magistrate at its head.

From 189 to the defeat of Perseus in 168 no formal change of importance in the status of the Greek states had been made by Rome. The senate, though forced year after year to listen to the mutual recriminations and complaints of rival communities and factions, contented itself as a rule with intervening just enough to remind the Greeks that their freedom was limited by its own paramount authority, and to prevent any single state or confederacy from raising itself too far above the level of general weakness which it was the interest of Rome to maintain. After the victory at Pydna, however, the sympathy shown for Perseus, exaggerated as it seems to have been by the interested representations of the romanizing factions in the various states, was made the pretext for a more emphatic assertion of Roman ascendancy. All those suspected of Macedonian leanings were removed to Italy, as hostages for the loyalty of their several communities, and the real motive for the step was made clear by the exceptionally severe treatment of the Achaeans, whose loyalty was not really doubtful, but whose growing power in the Peloponnese and independence of language had awakened alarm at Rome. A thousand of their leading men, among them the historian Polybius, were carried off to Italy (*see* POLYBIUS). In Aetolia the Romans connived at the massacre by their so-called friends of 500 of the opposite party. Acarnania was weakened by the loss of Leucas, while Athens was rewarded for her unambitious loyalty by the gift of Delos and Samos.

But this somewhat violent experiment only answered for a time. In 148 the Achaeans rashly persisted, in spite of warnings, in attempting to compel Sparta by force of arms to submit to the league. When threatened by Rome with the loss of all that they had gained since Cynoscephalae, they madly rushed into war. They were easily defeated, and a "commission of ten," under the presidency of L. Mummius, was appointed by the senate thoroughly to resettle the affairs of Greece. Corinth, by orders of the senate, was burnt to the ground and its territory confiscated. Thebes and Chalcis were destroyed, and the walls of all towns which had shared in the last desperate outbreak were razed to the ground. All the existing confederacies were dissolved; no *commercium* was allowed between one community and another. Everywhere an aristocratic type of constitution was established, and the payment of a tribute was apparently imposed. Into Greece, as into Macedonia in 167, the now familiar features of the provincial system were introduced—disarmament, isolation and taxation. The Greeks were still nominally free, and no separate province with a governor of its own was established, but the needed central control was provided by assigning to the neighbouring governor of Macedonia a general supervision over the affairs of Greece. From the Adriatic to the Aegean, and as far north as the river Drilo and Mt. Scardus, the whole peninsula was now under direct Roman rule.

The Roman Protectorate in Asia.—Beyond the Aegean the Roman protectorate worked no better than in Macedonia and Greece, and the quarrels and disorders which flourished under its shadow were aggravated by its longer duration and by the still more selfish view taken by Rome of her responsibilities. At one period indeed, after the battle of Pydna, it seemed as if the more vigorous, if harsh, system then initiated in Macedon and Greece was to be adopted farther east also. The levelling policy pursued towards Macedon and the Achaeans was applied with less justice to Rome's two faithful and favoured allies, Rhodes and Pergamum. The former had rendered themselves obnoxious to Rome by their independent tone. On a charge of complicity with Perseus they were threatened with war, and though this danger was averted they were forced to exchange their equal alliance **with** Rome for one which placed them in close dependence upon

her, and to resign the lucrative possessions in Lycia and Caria given them in 189. Finally, their commercial prosperity was ruined by the establishment of a free port at Delos. With Eumenes of Pergamum no other fault could be found than that he was strong and successful; but this was enough. His brother Attalus was invited, but in vain, to become his rival. His turbulent neighbours, the Galatae, were allowed to harass him by raids. Pamphylia was declared independent, and favours were heaped upon Prusias of Bithynia. These and other annoyances and humiliations had the desired effect. Eumenes and his two successors—his brother and son, Attalus II. and Attalus III.—contrived indeed by studious humility and dexterous flattery to retain their thrones, but Pergamum (*q.v.*) ceased to be a powerful State, and its weakness, added to that of Rhodes, increased the prevalent disorder in Asia Minor. During the same period we have other indications of a temporary activity on the part of Rome. The frontier of the protectorate was pushed forward to the confines of Armenia by alliances with the kings of Pontus and Cappadocia beyond the Halys. In Syria, on the death of Antiochus Epiphanes (164), Rome intervened to place a minor, Antiochus Eupator, on the throne, under Roman guardianship. In 168 Egypt formally acknowledged the suzerainty of Rome, and in 163 the senate, in the exercise of this new authority, restored Ptolemy Philometor to his throne, but at the same time weakened his position by handing over Cyrene and Cyprus to his brother Euergetes.

But this display of energy was short-lived. From the death of Eumenes in 159 down to 133 Rome, secure in the absence of any formidable power in the East, and busy with affairs in Macedonia, Africa and Spain, relapsed into an inactivity the disastrous results of which revealed themselves in the next period, in the rise of Mithridates of Pontus, the spread of Cretan and Cilician piracy, and the advance of Parthia.

Both the western and eastern Mediterranean now acknowledged the suzerainty of Rome, but her relations with the two were from the first different. The West fell to her as the prize of victory over Carthage, and, the Carthaginian power broken, there was no hindrance to the immediate establishment in Sicily, Sardinia, Spain, and finally in Africa, of direct Roman rule. To the majority, moreover, of her western subjects she brought a civilization as well as a government of a higher type than any before known to them. And so in the West she not only formed provinces but created a new and wider Roman world. To the East, on the contrary, she came as the liberator of the Greeks; and it was only slowly that in this part of the empire her provincial system made way. In the East, moreover, the older civilization she found there obstinately held its ground. Her proconsuls governed and her legions protected the Greek communities, but to the last the East remained in language, manners and thought Greek and not Roman.

(c) **The Period of the Revolution (146–49 B.C.).**— In the course of little more than a century, Rome had become the supreme power in the civilized world. Although in its outward form her old constitution had undergone little change during the age of war and conquest from 265 to 146, the causes, both internal and external, which brought about its fall had been silently at work throughout. Its form was in strictness that of a moderate democracy. The patriciate had ceased to exist as a privileged caste, and there was no longer any order of nobility recognized by the constitution. The senate and the offices of state were in law open to all, and the will of the people in assembly had been in the most explicit and unqualified manner declared to be supreme alike in the election of magistrates, in the passing of laws, and in all matters touching the *caput* of a Roman citizen. But in practice the constitution had become an oligarchy. The senate, not the assembly, ruled Rome, and both the senate and the magistracies were in the hands of a class which, in defiance of the law, arrogated to itself the title and the privileges of a nobility. The ascendancy of the senate is too obvious and familiar a fact to need much illustration here. It was but rarely that the assembly was called upon to decide questions of policy, and then the proposal was usually made by the magistrate in obedience to the express directions of the senate. In the enormous majority of cases the matter was settled by a *senatus consultum*, without any reference to the people at all. The assembly decides for war or peace, but the conduct of the war and the conditions of peace are matters left to the senate (*q.v.*). Now and then the assembly confers a command upon the man of its choice, or prolongs the *imperium* of a magistrate, but, as a rule, these and all questions connected with foreign affairs are settled within the walls of the senate-house. It is the senate which year after year assigns the commands and fixes the number and disposition of the military forces, directs the organization of a new province, conducts negotiations and forms alliances. Within Italy, though its control of affairs was less exclusive, we find that, besides supervising the ordinary current business of administration, the senate decides questions connected with the Italian allies, sends out colonies, allots lands, and directs the suppression of disorders. Lastly, both in Italy and abroad it managed the finances. Inseparably connected with this monopoly of affairs to the exclusion of the assembly was the control which in practice, if not in theory, the senate exercised over the magistrates. The latter had become what Cicero wrongly declares they were always meant to be, merely the subordinate ministers of the supreme council, which assigned them their departments, provided them with the necessary equipment, claimed to direct their conduct, prolonged their commands, and rewarded them with triumphs. It was now at once the duty and the interest of a magistrate to be *in auctoritate senatus*, "subject to the authority of the senate," and even the once formidable *tribuni plebis* are found during this period actively and loyally supporting the senate, and acting as its spokesmen in the assembly.

The Senatorial Government.—Behind both senate and magistrates, lay the whole power and influence of the new nobility. These *nobiles* were essentially distinct from the older and more legitimate patrician aristocracy. Every patrician was of course noble, but the majority of the "noble families" in 146 were not patrician but plebeian. The title had been gradually appropriated, since the opening of the magistracies, by those families whose members had held the consulship. It was thus in theory within the reach of any citizen who could win this office, and, moreover, it carried with it no legal privileges whatsoever. Gradually, however, the ennobled plebeian families drew together, and combined with the older patrician *gentes* to form a distinct order. Office brought wealth and prestige, and both wealth and prestige were liberally employed in securing for this select circle a monopoly of political power, and excluding new men. Already by the close of the period it was rare for anyone but a noble to find his way into high office or into the senate. The senate and magistrates were the mouthpieces of this order, and identified with it in policy and interest. Lastly, it must be allowed that both the senate and the nobility had to some extent justified their power by the use they made of it. It was their tenacity of purpose and devoted patriotism which had carried Rome through the dark days of the Hannibalic War. The heroes of the struggle with Carthage belonged to the leading families; the disasters at the Trasimene lake and at Cannae were associated with the blunders of popular favourites.

From the first, however, there was an inherent weakness in this senatorial government. It had no sound constitutional basis, and with the removal of its accidental supports it fell to the ground. Legally the senate had no positive authority. It could merely advise the magistrate when asked to do so, and its decrees were strictly only suggestions to the magistrate, which he was at liberty to accept or reject as he chose. It had, it is true, become customary for the magistrate not only to ask the senate's advice on all important points, but to follow it when given. But it was obvious that if this custom were weakened, and the magistrates chose to act independently, the senate was powerless. It might indeed anathematize the refractory official, or hamper him if it could by setting in motion against him a colleague or the tribunes, but it could do no more, and these measures failed just where the senate's control was most needed and most difficult to maintain—in its relations with the generals and governors of provinces abroad. The virtual independence of the proconsul

was before 146 already exciting the jealousy of the senate and endangering its supremacy. Nor again had the senate any legal hold over the assembly. Except in certain specified cases, it rested with the magistrate to decide whether any question should be settled by a decree of the senate or a vote of the assembly. If he decided to make a proposal to the assembly, he was not bound except by custom to obtain the previous approval of the senate, and the constitution set no limits to the power of the assembly to decide any question whatsoever that was laid before it.

From 150, at least, onwards, there were increasing indications that both the acquiescence of the people in senatorial government and the loyalty of the magistrates to the senate were failing. The rich landowners were not only taking possession of the public lands but were buying out the small farmers. And since the Government took little interest in commerce and industry, the poor were drifting idly to the cities or migrating to the Po valley. Slaves were being brought in to do the work of citizens, and the levies for the wars, which never ceased, fell more and more upon a decreasing citizenry. Between 165 and 135 the number of citizens, which should have increased by at least 100,000, actually dropped 20,000. The populace began to object to the constant levies and to criticize the régime which seemed only to be interested in foreign policies.

It is possible that these constitutional and administrative difficulties would not have proved so rapidly fatal to the republic had not its very foundations been sapped by the changes which followed more or less directly on the conquests of the 3rd and 2nd centuries B.C. For the opening of the world to Rome, and of Rome to the world, produced a radical change in the structure of Roman society. The subjugation of the Mediterranean countries, by placing at the disposal of Rome the vast natural resources of the West and the accumulated treasures of the East, caused a rapid rise in the standard of wealth and a marked change in its distribution. The Roman State was enabled to dispense with the direct taxation of its citizens, since it derived all the revenue which it needed from the subject countries. But this wealth enticed the Romans away from a beneficial development of their own resources into a dangerous parasitism. In time generals and soldiers learned to depend upon the profits of wars, governors to provide for their estates out of illegitimate perquisites of office far away from the vigilant eyes of magistrates at home. Speculators learned to place mortgages in the provinces where interest rates were high, to profit by the protection of Rome's armies, and secure the high return of their investments from lenient governors. Roman nobles, engaged all their lives in the expensive civil and military service, unable to devote any attention to developing their own properties for a livelihood, excused their own and their fellows' exploitation of the subjects. Compelled to find leisure from financial concerns, they disregarded the needs of industry and commerce that might have employed citizens and developed the resources of Italy. Instead they acquiesced in the slave-driven culture of large estates which yielded meagre returns and begot out of war captives a body of citizens bred in servility, ignorance and hatred. Surely the great successes of the 2nd century had come too speedily.

The New Learning.—It was not only the structure and composition of Roman society that underwent a transformation. The victory of Rome in her struggle for supremacy in the Mediterranean basin had been largely due to the powerful conservative forces by which her institutions were preserved from decay. Respect for the *mos maiorum*, or ancestral custom, imposed an effective check on the desire for innovation. Though personal religion, in the deeper sense, was foreign to the Roman temperament, there was a genuine belief in the gods whose favour had made Rome great in the past and would uphold her in the future so long as she trod in the old paths of loyalty and devotion. Above all, the healthy moral traditions of early Rome were maintained by the discipline of the family, resting on the supreme authority of the father—the *patria potestas*—and the powerful influence of the mother, to whom the early training of the child was entrusted. Finally, the institution of the censorship, backed as it was by the mighty force of public opinion, provided a deterrent which prevented any flagrant deviation from the accepted standard of morals. All this was changed by the influence of Greek civilization, with which Rome was first brought face to face in the 3rd century B.C. owing to her relations with Magna Graecia. At first the results of contact with the older and more brilliant culture of Hellas were on the whole good. In the 2nd century B.C., when constant intercourse was established with the communities of Greece proper and of Asia Minor, "philhellenism" became a passion, which was strongest in the best minds of the day and resulted in a quickened intellectual activity, wider sympathies and a more humane life. But at the same time the "new learning" was a disturbing and unsettling force. The Roman citizen was confronted with new doctrines in politics and religion, and initiated into the speculations of critical philosophy. Under the influence of this powerful solvent the fabric of tradition embodied in the *mos maiorum* fell to pieces; a revolt set in against Roman discipline and Roman traditions of self-effacement, and the craving for individual distinction asserted itself with irresistible vehemence. As it had been in the days of the "sophistic" movement at Athens, so it was now with Rome; a higher education, which, owing to its expense, was necessarily confined to the wealthier classes, interposed between the upper and lower ranks of society a barrier even more effectual than that set up by differences of material condition, and by releasing the individual from the trammels of traditional morality, gave his ambition free course. The effect on private morals may be gauged by the vehemence with which the reactionary opposition, headed by M. Porcius Cato (consul, 195 B.C.; censor, 184 B.C.), inveighed against the new fashions, and by the list of measures passed to check the growth of luxury and licence, and to exclude the foreign teachers of the new learning. It was all in vain. The art of rhetoric, which was studied through the medium of Greek treatises and Greek models, furnished the Roman noble with weapons of attack and defence of which he was not slow to avail himself in the forum and the senate-house. In the science of money-making which had been elaborated under the Hellenistic monarchies, the Roman capitalists proved apt pupils of their Greek teachers. Among the lower classes, contact with foreign slaves and freedmen, with foreign worships and foreign vices, produced a love of novelty which no legislation could check. Even amongst women there were symptoms of revolt against the old order, which showed itself in a growing freedom of manners and impatience of control, the marriage tie was relaxed, and the respect for mother and wife which had been so powerful a factor in the maintenance of the Roman standard of morals, was grievously diminished. Thus Rome was at length brought face to face with a moral and economic crisis which a modern historian has described in the words: "Italy was living through the fever of moral disintegration and incoherence which assails all civilized societies that are rich in the manifold resources of culture and enjoyment, but tolerate few or no restraints on the feverish struggle of contending appetites." In this struggle the Roman republic perished, and personal government took its place. The world had outgrown the city-state and its political machinery, and as representative government, tried in Thessaly and Macedonia, was out of the question in a heterogeneous empire, no solution of the problem was possible save that of absolutism. But a far stronger resistance would have been opposed to political revolution by the republican system had not public morals been sapped by the influences above described. Political corruption was reduced to a science for the benefit of individuals who were often faced with the alternatives of ruin or revolution; there was no longer any body of sound public opinion to which, in the last resort, appeal could be made; and, long before the final catastrophe took place, Roman society itself had become, in structure and temper, thoroughly unrepublican.

The Gracchi, 133–121.—The first systematic attack upon the senatorial government is connected with the names of Tiberius and Gaius Gracchus (*qq.v.*) and its immediate occasion was an attempt to deal with no less a danger than the threatened disappearance of the class to which of all others Rome owed most in the past. The small landholders throughout the greater part of Italy were sinking deeper into ruin under the pressure of accumulated difficulties. The Hannibalic war had laid waste their fields and thinned their numbers, nor when peace returned to Italy did it bring with it any revival of prosperity. The heavy burden of military service still pressed ruinously upon them, and in addition they were called upon to compete with the foreign corn imported from beyond the sea, and with the foreign slave-labour purchased by the capital of wealthier men. Farming became unprofitable, and the hard laborious life with its scanty returns was thrown into still darker relief when compared with the stirring life of the camps with its opportunities of booty, or with the cheap provisions, frequent largesses and gay spectacles to be had in the large towns. The small-holders went off to follow the eagles to try fortune in some province, or swell the proletariat of the cities, and their holdings were left to run waste or merged in the vineyards, olive-yards and above all in the great cattle farms of the rich, and their own place was taken by slaves. The evil was worst in Etruria and in southern Italy; but everywhere it was serious enough to demand the earnest attention of Roman statesmen. Of its existence the Government had received plenty of warning in the declining numbers of able-bodied males returned at the census, in the increasing difficulties of recruiting for the legions, in servile outbreaks in Etruria and Apulia, and between 200 and 160 a good deal was attempted by way of remedy. In addition to the foundation of 20 colonies, there were frequent allotments of land to veteran soldiers, especially in Apulia and Samnium. In 180, 40,-000 Ligurians were removed from their homes and settled on vacant lands once the property of a Samnite tribe, and in 160 the Pomptine marshes were drained for the purpose of cultivation. But these efforts were only partially successful. The colonies planted in Cisalpine Gaul and in Picenum flourished, but of the others the majority slowly dwindled away, and two required recolonizing only eight years after their foundation. The veterans who received land were unfitted to make good farmers; and large numbers, on the first opportunity, gladly returned as volunteers to a soldier's life. Moreover, after 160 even these efforts ceased, and with the single exception of the colony of Auximum in Picenum (157) nothing was done to check the spread of the evil, until in 133 Tiberius Gracchus, on his election to the tribunate, set his hand to the work.

The remedy proposed by Gracchus amounted in effect to the resumption by the State of as much of the "common land" as was not held in occupation by authorized persons and conformably to the provisions of the Licinian law, and the distribution in allotments of the land thus rescued for the community from the monopoly of a few. It was a scheme which could quote in its favour ancient precedent as well as urgent necessity. Of the causes which led to its ultimate failure something will be said later on; for the present we must turn to the constitutional conflict which it provoked. The senate from the first identified itself with the interests of the wealthy occupiers, and Tiberius found himself forced into a struggle with that body, which had been no part of his original plan. He fell back on the legislative sovereignty of the assembly; he resuscitated the half-forgotten powers of interference vested in the tribunate in order to paralyse the action of the senatorial magistrates, and finally lost his life in an attempt to make good one of the weak points in the tribune's position by securing his own re-election for a second year. But the conflict did not end with his death. It was renewed on a wider scale and with a more deliberate aim by his brother Gaius, who on his election to the tribunate (123) at once came forward with a vast programme of legislation. He shrewdly began by weakening the influence of the senate. Since his followers had every reason to dread the *senatus consultum ultimum*, the senate's chief weapon of attack against opponents, his first plebiscite reasserted the "right of appeal." He then destroyed the senate's prerogative to assign the provinces to its partisans, took away the jury panels from the senators, and also claimed for the assembly the right to assign public contracts and to control the budget so far as it desired. Thus the senate lost control of the gifts by which it cajoled and the lashes by which it compelled obedience. Very early also he gave doles of grain to the poor. This later led to great evils, but it must have been instituted as a temporary measure since he intended soon to distribute the needy in colonies. The evils of the dole must be accredited to the senate which stopped the colonization and did not have the courage to stop the dole. The jury panels he now made up of knights instead of senators. Gracchus wished, it seems, to give official recognition through civil service to men of business, in whom he had great faith. He would thus widen the group interested in public concerns and build up an influential order as a balance to the old nobility. Later it proved a disadvantage that publicans could sit in judgment over provincial governors who had to hold the publicans in check, but this difficulty could hardly have been foreseen since publicans did not yet have provincial contracts. In order to secure larger returns from the Asiatic province recently inherited by Rome, Gracchus permitted the knights to form corporations of limited liability (such corporations were otherwise prohibited) with the privilege of taking contracts to gather and dispose of the Asiatic tithe. The advantages would be that the State would receive in advance the sums bid, would not have to build up a large taxing bureau in order to get all that was due, and the taxpayers could pay the tithe in kind according to the yield of each year. Since this system had not been tried before by Rome, its inherent evils were probably not yet known. In time it led not only to harsh exactions because of collusion between governors and publicans, but also to costly exploitation, because the publicans lent money to delinquents at high rates and engaged generally in unseemly speculation. Gracchus used the money in such public works as the assembly at his bidding authorized. The colonies which Gracchus founded—it was only the beginning of a large project—were well selected. Two were planted in southern Italy where many allotments had recently been made to small farmers—at Tarentum and Scylacium. For these, men specially selected for their capacity were chosen. Then 6,000 hardy farmers were sent to the province of Africa which had been lying desolate for a generation, and which had had to depend upon the Punic city of Utica for its harbour and its praetorian residence. Not even then did the senate comprehend its duty to its provincials, but cancelled the colonial charter, though it dared not cancel the allotments. And now though Gracchus lost his re-election to the tribunate he attempted his last great reform of giving the franchise to the Latins in order that the democracy might rest on a wider and sounder basis. Since Caesar, who took many suggestions from Gracchus, later proposed to extend balloting through Italy by local polls, it is not unlikely that Gracchus had that in view. That would finally have removed democratic legislation from the control of the urban crowd. Be that as it may, the attempt to broaden the franchise failed, not this time because of senatorial opposition but because of the selfishness of the voters who did not wish to diminish their own prerogatives. Gracchus lost his influence, and soon after when a riot arose the senate declared martial law and summoned Gracchus to the bar of the senate. He refused to recognize a procedure which the assembly had outlawed the year before. The senate insisting on the legality of its course ordered his arrest and in the riot which ensued he was slain.

The agrarian reforms of the two Gracchi had little permanent effect. Even in the lifetime of Gaius the clause in his brother's law rendering the new holdings inalienable was repealed, and the process of absorption recommenced. In 118 a stop was put to further allotment of occupied lands, and finally, in 111, the whole position of the agrarian question was altered by a law which converted all land still held in occupation into private land. The old controversy as to the proper use of the lands of the community was closed by this act of alienation. The controversy in future turns, not on the right of the poor citizens to the State lands, but on the expediency of purchasing other lands for distribution at the cost of the treasury.

But, though the agrarian reform failed, the political conflict it had provoked continued, and the lines on which it was waged were in the main those laid down by Gaius Gracchus. The sovereignty of the assembly continued to be the watchword of the popular party, and a free use of the tribunician powers of interference and of legislation remained the most effective means of accomplishing their aims.

Marius, 118–100.—Ten years after the death of Gaius the *populares* once more summoned up courage to challenge the supremacy of the senate; but it was on a question of foreign administration that the conflict was renewed. The course of affairs in the client state of Numidia since Micipsa's death in 118 had been such as to discredit a stronger government than that of the senate. In defiance of Roman authority, and relying on the influence of his own well-spent gold, Jugurtha had murdered both his legitimate rivals, Hiempsal and Adherbal, and made himself master of Numidia. The declaration of war wrung from the senate (112) by popular indignation had been followed by the corruption of a consul (111) and the crushing defeat of the proconsul Albinus. On the news of this crowning disgrace the storm burst, and on the proposal of the tribunes a commission of enquiry into the conduct of the war was appointed. But the popular leaders did not stop here. Q. Caecilius Metellus, who as consul (109) had succeeded to the command in Numidia, was an able soldier but a rigid aristocrat; and they now resolved to improve their success by entrusting the command instead to a genuine son of the people. Their choice fell on Gaius Marius (see MARIUS), an experienced officer and administrator, but a man of humble birth, wholly illiterate, and one who, though no politician, was by temperament and training a hater of the polished and effeminate nobles who filled the senate. He was triumphantly elected, and, in spite of a decree of the senate continuing Metellus as proconsul, he was entrusted by a vote of the assembly with the charge of the war against Jugurtha (*q.v.*).

Jugurtha was vanquished; and Marius, who had been a second time elected consul in his absence, arrived at Rome in Jan. 104, bringing the captive prince with him in chains. But further triumphs awaited the popular hero. The Cimbri and Teutones were at the gates of Italy; they had four times defeated the senatorial generals, and Marius was called upon to save Rome from a second invasion of the barbarians. After two years of suspense the victory at Aquae Sextiae (102), followed by that on the Raudine plain (101), put an end to the danger by the annihilation of the invading hordes; and Marius, now consul for the fifth time, returned to Rome in triumph. There the popular party welcomed him as a leader with all the prestige of a successful general. Once more, however, they were destined to a brief success followed by disastrous defeat. Marius became for the sixth time consul; of the two popular leaders Glaucia became praetor and Saturninus tribune. But Marius and his allies were not statesmen of the stamp of the Gracchi; and the laws proposed by Saturninus had evidently no serious aim in view other than that of harassing the senate. His corn law merely reduced the price fixed in 123 for the monthly dole of corn, and the main point of his agrarian law lay in the clause appended to it requiring all senators to swear to observe its provisions[1]. The laws were carried, but the triumph of the popular leaders was short-lived. Their period of office was drawing to a close. At the elections fresh rioting took place, and Marius as consul was called upon by the senate to protect the State against his own partisans. Saturninus and Glaucia surrendered, but while the senate was discussing their fate they were surrounded and murdered by their opponents.

The popular party had been worsted once more in their struggle with the senate, but none the less their alliance with Marius, and the position in which their votes placed him, marked an epoch in the history of the revolution. The transference of the political leadership to a consul who was nothing if not a soldier was at once a confession of the insufficiency of the purely civil authority of the tribunate and a dangerous encouragement of military interference in political controversies. The consequences were already foreshadowed by the special provisions made by Saturninus for Marius's veterans, and in the active part taken by them in the passing of his laws. Indirectly, too, Marius, though no politician, played an important part in this new departure. His military reforms at once democratized the army and attached it more closely to its leader for the time being. He swept away

[1] For the *leges Appuleiae*, see SATURNINUS, LUCIUS APPULEIUS, and authorities there quoted.

the last traces of civil distinctions of rank or wealth within the legion, admitted to its ranks all classes, and substituted voluntary enlistment under a popular general for the old-fashioned compulsory levy. The efficiency of the legion was increased at the cost of a complete severance of the ties which bound it to the civil community and to the civil authorities.

The Social War.—The next important crisis was due partly to the rivalry which had been growing more bitter each year between the senate and the commercial class, and partly to the long-impending question of the enfranchisement of the Italian allies. The *publicani*, *negotiatores* and others, who constituted what was now becoming known as the equestrian order (*see* EQUITES), had made unscrupulous use of their control of the courts and especially of the *quaestio de repetundis* against their natural rivals, the official class in the provinces. The threat of prosecution before a hostile jury was held over the head of every governor, legate and quaestor who ventured to interfere with their operations in the provinces. The average official preferred to connive at their exactions; the bolder ones paid with fines and even exile for their courage. In 92 the necessity for a reform was proved beyond a doubt by the scandalous condemnation of P. Rutilius Rufus, ostensibly on a charge of extortion, in reality as the reward of his efforts to check the extortions of the Roman equites in Asia. The difficulties of the Italian question were more serious. That the Italian allies were discontented was notorious. After nearly two centuries of close alliance, of common dangers and victories, they now eagerly coveted as a boon that complete amalgamation with Rome which they had at first resented as a dishonour. But, unfortunately, Rome had grown more exclusive in proportion as the value set upon Roman citizenship increased. During the last 40 years feelings of hope and disappointment had rapidly succeeded each other; Marcus Fulvius Flaccus, Gaius Gracchus, Saturninus, had all held out promises of relief—and nothing had yet been done. On each occasion they had crowded to Rome, full of eager expectation, only to be harshly ejected from the city by the consul's orders. The justice of their claims could hardly be denied, the danger of continuing to ignore them was obvious—yet the difficulties in the way of granting them were formidable in the extreme, and from a higher than a merely selfish point of view there was much to be said against the revolution involved in so sudden and enormous an enlargement of the citizen body.

Marcus Livius Drusus (*q.v.*), who as tribune gallantly took up the task of reform, is claimed by Cicero as a member of that party of the centre to which he belonged himself. Noble, wealthy and popular, he seems to have hoped to be able by the weight of his position and character to rescue the burning questions of the day from the grasp of extreme partisans and to settle them peacefully and equitably. But he, like Cicero after him, had to find to his cost that there was no room in the fierce strife of Roman politics for moderate counsels. His proposal to reform the law courts excited the equestrian order and their friends in the senate to fury. The agrarian and corn laws which he coupled with it alienated many more in the senate, and roused the old antipopular party feeling; finally, his known negotiations with the Italians were eagerly misrepresented to the jealous and excited people as evidence of complicity with a widespread conspiracy against Rome. His laws were carried, but the senate pronounced them null and void. Drusus was denounced in the senate house as a traitor, and on his way home was struck down by the hand of an unknown assassin. His assassination was the signal for an outbreak which had been secretly prepared for some time before. Throughout the highlands of central and southern Italy the flower of the Italian peoples rose as one man. Etruria and Umbria held aloof; the isolated Latin colonies stood firm; but the Sabellian clans, north and south, the Latinized Marsi and Paeligni, as well as the Oscan-speaking Samnites and Lucanians, rushed to arms. No time was lost in proclaiming their plans for the future. A new Italian State was to be formed. The Paelignian town of Corfinium was selected as its capital and re-christened with the proud name of Italica. All Italians were to be citizens of this new metropolis, and here were to be the place of assembly and

the senate house. A senate of 500 members and a magistracy resembling that of Rome completed a constitution which adhered closely to the very political traditions which its authors had most reason to abjure.

Now, as always in the face of serious danger, the action of Rome was prompt and resolute. Both consuls took the field; with each were five legates, among them the veteran Marius and his destined rival L. Cornelius Sulla, and even freedmen were pressed into service with the legions. But the first year's campaign opened disastrously. In central Italy the northern Sabellians, and in the south the Samnites, defeated the forces opposed to them. And though before the end of the year Marius and Sulla in the north, and the consul Caesar himself in Campania, succeeded in inflicting severe blows on the enemy, and on the Marsi especially, it is not surprising that, with an empty treasury, with the insurgents' strength still unbroken, and with rumours of disaffection in the loyal districts, opinion in Rome should have turned in the direction of the more liberal policy which had been so often scornfully rejected and in favour of some compromise which should check the spread of the revolt, and possibly sow discord among their enemies. Towards the close of the year 90 the consul L. Julius Caesar (killed by Fimbria in 87) carried the *lex Iulia*, by which the Roman franchise was offered to all communities which had not as yet revolted; early in the next year (89) the Julian law was supplemented by the *lex Plautia Papiria*, introduced by two of the tribunes, M. Plautius Silvanus and C. Papirius Carbo Arvina, which enacted that any citizen of an allied community then domiciled in Italy might obtain the franchise by giving in his name to a praetor in Rome within 60 days. A third law (*lex Calpurnia*), apparently passed at the same time, empowered Roman magistrates in the field to bestow the franchise there and then upon all who were willing to receive it. This sudden opening of the closed gates of Roman citizenship was completely successful, and its effects were at once visible in the diminished vigour of the insurgents. By the end of 89 the Samnites and Lucanians were left alone in their obstinate hostility to Rome, and neither, thanks to Sulla's brilliant campaign in Samnium, had for the moment any strength left for active aggression.

The termination of the Social War brought with it no peace in Rome. The old quarrels were renewed with increased bitterness, and the newly enfranchised Italians themselves complained as bitterly of the restriction which robbed them of their due share of political influence by allowing them to vote only in a specified number of tribes. The senate itself was distracted by violent personal rivalries—and all these feuds, animosities and grievances were aggravated by the widespread economic distress and ruin which affected all classes. Lastly, war with Mithridates VI. had been declared; it was notorious that the privilege of commanding the force to be sent against him would be keenly contested, and that the contest would lie between the veteran Marius and L. Cornelius Sulla.

Sulla.—It was in an atmosphere charged with the elements of disturbance that P. Sulpicius Rufus as tribune brought forward his laws. (*See* SULPICIUS RUFUS, PUBLIUS.) He proposed: (1) that the command of the Mithridatic War should be given to Marius, though it had legally been assigned to the consul Sulla; (2) that the new citizens should be distributed through all the tribes; (3) that the freedmen should no longer be confined to the four city tribes; (4) that any senator owing more than 2,000 denarii should lose his seat; (5) that those exiled on suspicion of complicity with the Italian revolt should be recalled. These proposals provoked a storm, and both sides were ready for violent measures. The consuls, in order to prevent legislation, proclaimed a public holiday. Sulpicius armed his followers and drove the consuls from the forum. The proclamation was withdrawn and the laws carried, but Sulpicius's triumph was short-lived. From Nola in Campania, where lay the legions commanded by him in the Social War, Sulla advanced on Rome, and for the first time a Roman consul entered the city at the head of the legions of the republic. Resistance was hopeless. Marius and Sulpicius fled, and Sulla, summoning the assembly of the centuries, proposed the measures he considered necessary for the public security, the most important being a provision that the sanction of the senate should be necessary before any proposal was introduced to the assembly. Then, after waiting in Rome long enough to hold the consular elections, he left for Asia early in 87.

Sulla had conquered, but his victory cost the republic dear. He had first taught political partisans to look for final success, not to a majority of votes in the forum or campus, but to the swords of the soldiery. The lesson was well learnt. Shortly after his departure L. Cornelius Cinna as consul revived the proposals of Sulpicius; his colleague, Gnaeus Octavius, at the head of an armed force, fell upon the new citizens who had collected in crowds to vote, and the forum was heaped high with the bodies of the slain. Cinna fled, but fled, like Sulla, to the legions. When the senate declared him deposed from his consulship, he replied by invoking the aid of the soldiers in Campania in behalf of the violated rights of the people and the injured dignity of the consulship, and, like Sulla, found them ready to follow where he led. The neighbouring Italian communities, who had lost many citizens in the recent massacre, sent their new champion men and money; while from Africa, whither he had escaped after Sulla's entry into Rome, came Marius with 1,000 Numidian horsemen. The senate had prepared for a desperate defence, but fortune was adverse, and after a brief resistance they gave way. Cinna was acknowledged as consul, the sentence of outlawry passed on Marius was revoked and Cinna and Marius entered Rome with their troops. Marius's thirst for revenge was gratified by a frightful massacre, and he lived long enough to be nominated consul for the seventh time. But he held his consulship only a few weeks. Early in 86 he died, and for the next three years Cinna ruled Rome. Constitutional government was virtually suspended. For 85 and 84 Cinna nominated himself and a trusted colleague as consuls. The state was, as Cicero says, without lawful authority. A partial registration of the newly enfranchised Italians was made, but beyond this little was done. The attention of Cinna and his friends was in truth engrossed by the ever-present dread of Sulla's return from Asia. The consul of 86, L. Valerius Flaccus (who had been consul with Marius in 100 B.C.), sent out to supersede him, was murdered by his own soldiers at Nicomedia. In 85 Sulla, though disowned by his Government, concluded a peace with Mithridates. In 84, after settling affairs in Asia and crushing Flaccus's successor, C. Flavius Fimbria, he crossed into Greece, and in the spring of 83 landed at Brundusium with 40,000 soldiers and a large following of *émigré* nobles. Cinna was dead, murdered like Flaccus by his mutinous soldiers; his most trusted colleague, Cn. Papirius Carbo, was commanding as proconsul in Cisalpine Gaul; and the resistance offered to Sulla's advance was slight. At Capua, Sulla routed the forces of one consul, Gaius Norbanus; at Teanum the troops of the other went over in a body to the side of the outlawed proconsul. After a winter spent in Campania he pressed forward to Rome, defeated the younger Marius (consul, 82) near Praeneste, and entered the city without further opposition. In north Italy the success of his lieutenants, Q. Caecilius Metellus Pius (son of Metellus Numidicus), Cn. Pompeius and Marcus Crassus, had been fully as decisive. Cisalpine Gaul, Umbria and Etruria had all been won for Sulla, and the two principal leaders on the other side, Carbo and Norbanus, had each fled, one to Rhodes, the other to Africa. Only one foe remained to be conquered. The Samnites and Lucanians whom Cinna had conciliated, and who saw in Sulla their bitterest foe, were for the last time in arms, and had already joined forces with the remains of the Marian army close to Rome. The decisive battle was fought under the walls of the city, and ended in the complete defeat of the Marians and Italians (battle of the Colline gate).

For a period of nearly ten years Rome and Italy had been distracted by civil war. Sulla (*q.v.*) was now called upon to heal the divisions which rent the State asunder, to set in working again the machinery of civil government, and above all so to modify it as to meet the altered conditions, and to fortify it against the dangers which visibly threatened it in the future. The real charge against Sulla is not that he failed to accomplish all this, for to do so was beyond the powers even of a man so able, resolute and self-confident as Sulla, armed though he was with absolute authority and backed by overwhelming military strength and the prestige of unbroken success. He stands convicted rather of deliberately aggravating some and culpably ignoring others of the evils he should have tried to cure, and of contenting himself with a party triumph when he should have aimed at the regeneration and confirmation of the whole State. His victory was instantly followed, not by any measures of conciliation, but by a series of massacres, proscriptions and confiscations, of which almost the least serious consequence was the immediate loss of life which they entailed. From this time forward the fear of proscription and confiscation recurred as a possible consequence of every political crisis, and it was with difficulty that Caesar himself dissipated the belief that his victory would be followed by a Sullan reign of terror. The legacy of hatred and discontent which Sulla left behind him was a constant source of disquiet and danger. In the children of the proscribed, whom he excluded from holding office, and the dispossessed owners of the confiscated lands, every agitator found ready and willing allies. The moneyed men of the equestrian order were more than ever hostile to the senatorial government, which they now identified with the man who cherished towards them a peculiar hatred, and whose creatures had hunted them down like dogs. The attachment which the new Italian citizens might in time have learnt to feel for the old republican constitution was nipped in the bud by the massacres at Praeneste and Norba, by the harsh treatment of the ancient towns of Etruria, and by the ruthless desolation of Samnium and Lucania. Quite as fatal were the results to the economic prosperity of the peninsula. Sulla's confiscations, following on the civil and social wars, opened the doors wide for a long train of evils. The veterans whom he planted on the lands he had seized did nothing for agriculture, and swelled the growing numbers of the turbulent and discontented. The "Sullan men" became as great an object of fear and dislike as the "Sullan reign." The *latifundia* increased with startling rapidity—whole territories passing into the hands of greedy partisans. Wide tracts of land, confiscated but never allotted, ran to waste. In many districts of Italy the free population finally and completely disappeared from the open country; and life and property were rendered insecure by the brigandage which now developed unchecked, and in which the herdsmen slaves played a prominent part. The outbreaks of Spartacus in 73, and of Catiline ten years later, were significant commentaries on this part of Sulla's work. His constitutional legislation, while it included many useful administrative reforms, is marked by as violent a spirit of partisanship, and as apparently wilful a blindness to the future. The re-establishment on a legal basis of the ascendancy which custom had so long accorded the senate was his main object. With this purpose he had already, when consul in 88, made the *senatus auctoritas* legally necessary for proposals to the assembly. He now as dictator followed this up by crippling the power of the magistracy, which had been the most effective weapon in the hands of the senate's opponents. The legislative freedom of the tribunes was already hampered by the necessity of obtaining the senate's sanction; in addition, Sulla restricted their wide powers of interference (*intercessio*) to their original purpose of protecting individual plebeians, and discredited the office by prohibiting a tribune from holding any subsequent office in the State. The control of the courts (*quaestiones perpetuae*) was taken from the equestrian order and restored to the senate. To prevent the people from suddenly installing and keeping in high office a second Marius, he re-enacted the old law against re-election, and made legally binding the custom which required a man to mount up gradually to the consulship through the lower offices. His increase of the number of praetors from six to eight, and of quaestors to 20, though required by administrative necessities, tended, by enlarging the numbers and further dividing the authority of the magistrates, to render them still more dependent upon the central direction of the senate. Lastly, he replaced the pontifical and augural colleges in the hands of the senatorial nobles, by enacting that vacancies in them should, as before the *lex Domitia* (104), be filled up by co-optation. It cannot be said that Sulla was successful in fortifying the republican system against the dangers which menaced it from without. He accepted as an accomplished fact the enfranchisement of the Italians, but he made no provision to guard against the consequent reduction of the *comitia* to an absurdity, and with them of the civic government which rested upon them, or to organize an effective administrative system for the Italian communities. In fact he prevented the further registration of the new citizens by abolishing the censorship. Of all men, too, Sulla had the best reason to appreciate the dangers to be feared from the growing independence of governors and generals in the provinces and from the transformation of the old civic militia into a group of professional armies, devoted only to a successful leader, and with the weakest possible sense of allegiance to the State. He had himself, as proconsul of Asia, contemptuously and successfully defied the home Government, and he, more than any other Roman general, had taught his soldiers to look only to their leader, and to think only of booty. Yet, beyond a few inadequate regulations, there is no evidence that Sulla dealt with these burning questions, the settlement of which was among the greatest of the achievements of Augustus. One administrative reform of real importance must, lastly, be set down to his credit. The judicial procedure first established in 149 for the trial of cases of magisterial extortion in the provinces, and applied between 149 and 81 to cases of treason and bribery, Sulla extended so as to bring under it the chief criminal offences, and thus laid the foundation of the Roman criminal law.

Overthrow of the Sullan Constitution.—The Sullan system stood for nine years, and was then overthrown—as it had been established—by a successful soldier. It was the fortune of Cn. Pompey, a favourite officer of Sulla, first of all to violate in his own person the fundamental principles of the constitution reestablished by his old chief, and then to overturn it. In Spain the Marian governor Q. Sertorius (*see* SERTORIUS, QUINTUS) had defeated one after another of the proconsuls sent out by the senate and was in 77 master of all Hither Spain. To meet the crisis, Pompey (*q.v.*), who was not yet 30 and had never held even the quaestorship, was sent out to Spain with proconsular authority. Sertorius held out, until in 73 he was foully murdered by his own officers. The native tribes who had loyally stood by him submitted, and Pompey early in 71 returned with his troops to Italy, where, during his absence in Spain, an event had occurred which had shown Roman society with startling plainness how near it stood to revolution. In 73 Spartacus (*q.v.*), a Thracian slave, escaped with 70 others from a gladiators' training school at Capua. In a startlingly short time he found himself at the head of 70,000 runaway slaves, outlaws, brigands and impoverished peasants, and for two years terrorized Italy, routed the legions sent against him, and even threatened Rome. He was at length defeated and slain by the praetor, M. Licinius Crassus, in Apulia. In Rome itself the various classes and parties hostile to the Sullan system had, ever since Sulla's death in 78, been incessantly agitating for the repeal of his most obnoxious laws, and needed only a leader in order successfully to attack a Government discredited by failure at home and abroad. With the return of Pompey from Spain their opportunity came. Pompey, who understood politics as little as Marius, was anxious to obtain a triumph, the consulship for the next year (70), and as the natural consequence of this an important command in the East. The opposition wanted his name and support, and a bargain was soon struck. Pompey and with him Marcus Licinius Crassus, the real conqueror of Spartacus, were elected consuls, almost in the presence of their troops, which lay encamped outside the gates in readiness to assist at the triumph and ovation granted to their respective leaders. Pompey lost no time in performing his part of the agreement. The tribunes regained their prerogatives. The "perpetual courts" (*quaestiones perpetuae*) were taken out of the hands of the senatorial *iudices*, who had outdone the equestrian order in scandalous corruption, and finally the censors, the first since 86 B.C., purged the senate of the more worthless and disreputable of Sulla's partisans. The victory was complete; but for the future its chief significance lay in the clearness with which it showed that the final decision in matters political lay with neither of the two great parties in Rome, but with the holder of the military authority. The tribunes ceased to be political leaders and became lieutenants of the military commanders, and the change was fatal to the dignity of politics in the city. Men became conscious of the unreality of the old constitutional controversies, indifferent to the questions which agitated the forum and the curia, and contemptuously ready to alter or disregard the constitution itself when it stood in the way of interests nearer to their hearts.

Pompey, Caesar and Cicero.—When his consulship ended, Pompey impatiently awaited at the hands of the politicians he had befriended the further gift of a foreign command. He declined an ordinary province, and from the end of 70 to 67 he remained at Rome in a somewhat affectedly dignified seclusion. But in 67 and 66 the laws of Gabinius and Manilius gave him all and more than all that he expected (*see* POMPEY). By the former he obtained the sole command for three years against the Mediterranean pirates. He was to have supreme authority over all Roman magistrates in the provinces throughout the Mediterranean and over the coasts for 50m. inland. Fifteen *legati*, all of praetorian rank, were assigned to him, with 200 ships, and as many troops as he thought desirable. The Manilian law transferred from Lucullus and Glabrio to Pompey the conduct of the Mithridatic War in Asia, and with it the entire control of Roman policy and interests in the East. The unrepublican character of the position thus granted to Pompey, and the dangers of the precedent established, were clearly enough pointed out by such moderate men as Q. Lutatius Catulus, the "father of the senate," and by the orator Hortensius—but in vain. Both laws were supported, not only by the tribunes and the populace, but by the whole influence of the *publicani* and *negotiatores*, whose interests in the East were at stake.

Pompey left Rome in 67. In a marvellously short space of time he freed the Mediterranean from the Cilician pirates and established Roman authority in Cilicia itself. He then crushed Mithradates (*q.v.*), added Syria to the list of Roman provinces, and led the Roman legions to the Euphrates and the Caspian, leaving no power capable of disputing with Rome the sovereignty of western Asia. He did not return to Italy till towards the end of 62. The interval was marked in Rome by the rise to political importance of Caesar (*q.v.*) and Cicero, and by Catiline's attempt at revolution. As the nephew of Marius and the son-in-law of Cinna, Caesar possessed a strong hereditary claim to the leadership of the popular and Marian party. He had already taken part in the agitation for the restoration of the tribunate; he had supported the Manilian law; and, when Pompey's withdrawal left the field clear for other competitors, he stepped at once into the front rank on the popular side. He took upon himself, as their nearest representative, the task of clearing the memory and avenging the wrongs of the great popular leaders, Marius, Cinna and Saturninus. He publicly reminded the people of Marius's services, and set up again upon the Capitol the trophies of the Cimbric War. He endeavoured to bring to justice, not only the ringleaders in Sulla's bloody work of proscription, but even the murderers of Saturninus, and vehemently pleaded the cause of the children of the proscribed. While thus carrying on in genuine Roman fashion the feud of his family, he attracted the sympathies of the Italians by his efforts to procure the Roman franchise for the Latin communities beyond the Po, and won the affections of the populace in Rome and its immediate neighbourhood by the splendour of the games which he gave as curule aedile (65), and by his lavish expenditure upon the improvement of the Appian Way. But these measures were with him only means to the further end of creating for himself a position such as that which Pompey had already won; and this ulterior aim he pursued with an audacious indifference to constitutional forms and usages. His coalition with Crassus, soon after Pompey's departure, secured him an ally whose colossal wealth and wide financial connections were of inestimable value, and whose vanity and inferiority of intellect rendered him a willing tool. The story of his attempted *coup d'état* in Jan. 65 is probably false, but it is evident that by the beginning of 63 he was bent on reaping the reward of his exertions by obtaining from the people an extraordinary command abroad, which should secure his position before Pompey's return; and the agrarian law proposed early that year by the tribune P. Servilius Rullus had for its object the creation, in favour of Caesar and Crassus, of a commission with powers so wide as to place its members almost on a level with Pompey himself. It was at this moment when all seemed going well, that Caesar's hopes were dashed to the ground by Catiline's desperate outbreak, which not only discredited every one connected with the popular party, but directed the suspicions of the well-to-do classes against Caesar himself, as a possible accomplice in Catiline's revolutionary schemes.

The same wave of indignation and suspicion which for the moment checked Caesar's rise carried Marcus Tullius Cicero to the height of his fortunes. Cicero (*q.v.*), as a politician, has been equally misjudged by friends and foes. That he was deficient in courage, that he was vain, and that he attempted the impossible, may be admitted at once. But he was neither a brilliant and unscrupulous adventurer nor an aimless trimmer, nor yet a devoted champion merely of senatorial ascendancy[1]. He was a representative man, with a numerous following, and a policy which was naturally suggested to him by the circumstances of his birth, connections and profession, and which, impracticable as it proved to be, was yet consistent, intelligible and high-minded. Born at Arpinum, he cherished like all Arpinates the memory of his great fellow-townsman Marius, the friend of the Italians, the saviour of Italy and the irreconcilable foe of Sulla and the nobles. A "municipal" himself, his chosen friends and his warmest supporters were found among the well-to-do classes in the Italian towns. Unpopular with the Roman aristocracy, who despised him as a *peregrinus,* and with the Roman populace, he was the trusted leader of the Italian middle class, "the true Roman people," as he proudly styles them. It was they who carried his election for the consulship (63), who in 58 insisted on his recall from exile, and it was his influence with them which made Caesar so anxious to win him over in 49. He represented their antipathy alike to socialistic schemes and to aristocratic exclusiveness, and their old-fashioned simplicity of life in contrast with the cosmopolitan luxury of the capital. By birth, too, he belonged to the equestrian order, the foremost representatives of which were indeed still the *publicani* and *negotiatores,* but which since the enfranchisement of Italy included also the substantial burgesses of the Italian towns and the smaller "squires" of the country districts. With them, too, Cicero was at one in their dread of democratic excesses and their social and political jealousy of the *nobiles*. Lastly, as a lawyer and a scholar, he was passionately attached to the ancient constitution. His political ideal was the natural outcome of these circumstances. He advocated the maintenance of the old constitution, but not as it was understood by the extreme politicians of the right and left. The senate was to be the supreme directing council, but the senate of Cicero's dreams was not an oligarchic assemblage of nobles, but a body freely open to all citizens, and representing the worth of the community. The magistrates, while deferring to the senate's authority, were to be at once vigorous and public-spirited; and the assembly itself which elected the magistrates and passed the laws was to consist, not of the "mob of the forum," but of the true Roman people throughout Italy. For the realization of this ideal he looked, above all things, to the establishment of cordial relations between the senate and nobles in Rome and the great middle-class of Italy represented by the equestrian order, between the capital and the country towns and districts. This was the *concordia ordinum,* the *consensus Italiae,* for which he laboured.

Cicero's election to the consulship for 63 over the heads of Caesar's nominees, Antonius and Catiline, was mainly the work of the Italian middle-class, already rendered uneasy both by the rumours which were rife of revolutionary schemes and of Caesar's boundless ambition, and by the numerous disquieting signs of disturbance noticeable in Italy. The new consul vigorously set himself to discharge the trust placed in him. He defeated the insidious

proposals of Rullus for Caesar's aggrandizement and assisted in quashing the prosecution of Gaius Rabirius (*q.v.*). But with the consular elections in the autumn of 63 a fresh danger arose from a different quarter. The "conspiracy of Catiline" (*see* CATILINE) was not the work of the popular party, and still less was it an unselfish attempt at reform; Catiline himself was a patrician, who had held high office, and possessed considerable ability and courage; but he was bankrupt in character and in purse, and two successive defeats in the consular elections had rendered him desperate. To retrieve his broken fortunes by violence was a course which was only too readily suggested by the history of the last 40 years, and materials for a conflagration abounded on all sides. The danger to be feared from his intrigues lay in the state of Italy, which made a revolt against society and the established Government only too likely if once a leader presented himself, and it was such a revolt that Catiline endeavoured to organize. Bankrupt nobles like himself, Sullan veterans and the starving peasants whom they had dispossessed of their holdings, outlaws of every description, the slave population of Rome, and the wilder herdsmen-slaves of the Apulian pastures, were all enlisted under his banner, and attempts were even made to excite disaffection among the newly conquered people of southern Gaul and the warlike tribes who still cherished the memory of Sertorius in Spain. In Etruria, the seat and centre of agrarian distress and discontent, a rising actually took place headed by a Sullan centurion, but the spread of the revolt was checked by Cicero's vigorous measures. Catiline fled from Rome, and died fighting with desperate courage at the head of his motley force of old soldiers, peasants and slaves. His accomplices in Rome were arrested, and, after an unavailing protest from Caesar, the senate authorized the consuls summarily to put them to death.

Coalition of Pompey, Caesar and Crassus.—The Catilinarian outbreak had been a blow to Caesar, whose schemes it interrupted, but to Cicero it brought not only popularity and honour, but, as he believed, the realization of his political ideal. But Pompey was now on his way home[2], and again as in 70 the political future seemed to depend on the attitude which the successful general would assume; Pompey himself looked simply to the attainment by the help of one political party or another of his immediate aims, which at present were the ratification of his arrangements in Asia and a grant of land for his troops. It was the impracticable jealousy of his personal rivals in the senate, aided by the versatility of Caesar who presented himself not as his rival but as his ally, which drove Pompey once more, in spite of Cicero's efforts, into the camp of what was still nominally the popular party. In 60, on Caesar's return from his propraetorship in Spain, the coalition was formed which is known by the somewhat misleading title of the First Triumvirate. Pompey was ostensibly the head of this new alliance, and in return for the satisfaction of his own demands he undertook to support Caesar's candidature for the consulship. The wealth and influence of Crassus were enlisted in the same cause, and the *publicani* were secured by a promise of release from their bargain for collecting the taxes of Asia. Cicero was under no illusions as to the significance of this coalition. It scattered to the winds his dreams of a stable and conservative republic. The year 59 saw the republic powerless in the hands of three citizens. Caesar as consul procured the ratification of Pompey's acts in Asia, granted to the *publicani* the relief refused by the senate, and carried an agrarian law of the new type, which provided for the purchase of lands for allotment at the cost of the treasury and for the assignment of the rich *ager Campanus*. But Caesar aimed at more than the carrying of laws in the teeth of the senate or any party victory in the forum. An important military command was essential to him. An obedient tribune, P. Vatinius, was found, and by the *lex Vatinia* he was given for five years the command of Cisalpine Gaul and Illyricum, to which was added by a decree of the senate Transalpine Gaul also. This command not only opened to him a great military career, but enabled him, as the master of the valley of the Po, to keep an effective watch on the course of affairs in Italy.

---

[1] Mommsen is throughout unfair to Cicero. The best estimates of Cicero are those given by Strachan-Davidson in his *Cicero* (1894), by Prof. Tyrrell in his Introductions to his edition of Cicero's *Letters,* and by Petersson, *Cicero, a Biography* (1920).

[2] For the history of the next 18 years, the most important ancient authority is Cicero in his letters and speeches.

Early the next year the attack upon himself which Cicero had foreseen was made. P. Clodius (*q.v.*) as tribune brought forward a law enacting that anyone who had put a Roman citizen to death without trial by the people should be interdicted from fire and water. Cicero, finding himself deserted even by Pompey, left Rome in a panic, and by a second Clodian law he was declared to be outlawed. With Caesar away in his province and Cicero banished, Clodius was for the time master in Rome. But, absolute as he was in the streets, and recklessly as he parodied the policy of the Gracchi by violent attacks on the senate, his tribunate merely illustrated the anarchy which now inevitably followed the withdrawal of a strong controlling hand. A reaction speedily followed. Pompey, bewildered and alarmed by Clodius's violence, at last bestirred himself. Cicero's recall was decreed by the senate, and early in Aug. 57 in the *comitia centuriata,* to which his Italian supporters flocked in crowds, a law was passed revoking the sentence of outlawry passed upon him.

Break-up of the Coalition.—Intoxicated by the acclamations which greeted him, and encouraged by Pompey's support, and by the salutary effects of Clodius's excesses, Cicero's hopes rose high. With indefatigable energy he strove to reconstruct a solid constitutional party, but only to fail once more. Pompey was irritated by the hostility of a powerful section in the senate, who thwarted his desires for a fresh command and even encouraged Clodius in insulting the conqueror of the East. Caesar became alarmed at the reports which reached him that the repeal of his agrarian law was threatened and that the feeling against the coalition was growing in strength; above all, he was anxious for a renewal of his five years' command. He acted at once, and in the celebrated conference at Luca (56) the alliance of the three self-constituted rulers of Rome was renewed. Cicero succumbed to the inevitable and withdrew in despair from public life. Pompey and Crassus became consuls for 55. Caesar's command was renewed for another five years, and to each of his two allies important provinces were assigned for a similar period—Pompey receiving the two Spains and Africa, and Crassus Syria. The coalition now divided between them the control of the empire. For the future the question was, how long the coalition itself would last. Its duration proved to be short. In 53 Crassus was defeated and slain by the Parthians at Carrhae, and in Rome the course of events slowly forced Pompey into an attitude of hostility to Caesar. The year 54 brought with it a renewal of the riotous anarchy which had disgraced Rome in 58–57. Conscious of its own helplessness, the senate, with the eager assent of all respectable citizens, dissuaded Pompey from leaving Italy; and he accordingly left his provinces to be governed by his legates. But the anarchy and confusion only grew worse, and even strict constitutionalists like Cicero talked of the necessity of investing Pompey with some extraordinary powers for the preservation of order[1]. At last in 52 he was elected sole consul, and not only so, but his provincial command was prolonged for five years more, and fresh troops were assigned him. The rôle of "saviour of society" thus thrust upon Pompey was one which flattered his vanity, but it entailed consequences which it is probable he did not foresee, for it brought him into close alliance with the senate. In the senate there was a powerful party which was resolved to force him into heading the attack upon Caesar that otherwise they could not successfully make. It was known that Caesar, whose command expired in March 49, but who in the ordinary course of things would not have been replaced by his successor until Jan. 48, was anxious to be allowed to stand for his second consulship in the autumn of 49 without coming in person to Rome. His opponents in the senate were equally bent on bringing his command to an end at the legal time, and so obliging him to disband his troops and stand for the consulship as a private person, or, if he kept his command, on preventing his standing for the consulship. Through 51 and 50 the discussions in the senate and the negotiations with Caesar continued, but with no result. On Jan. 1, 49, Caesar made a last offer of compromise. The senate

[1]Cicero himself anticipated Augustus in his picture of a *princeps civitatis* sketched in a lost book of the *De republica,* written about this time, which was based upon his hopes of what Pompey might prove to be; *Ad Att.* viii. 11; August *De civ. Dei,* v. 13

replied by requiring him on pain of outlawry to disband his legions. Two tribunes who supported him were ejected from the senate house, and the magistrates with Pompey were authorized to take measures to protect the republic. Caesar hesitated no longer; he crossed the Rubicon and invaded Italy. The rapidity of his advance astounded and bewildered his foes. Pompey, followed by the consuls, by the majority of the senate and a long train of nobles, abandoned Italy as untenable, and crossed into Greece. At the end of March Caesar entered Rome as the master of Italy. Four years later, after the final victory of Munda (45), he became the undisputed master of the Roman world[2].

Dictatorship of Caesar, 48–44.—From the very first moment when Pompey's ignominious retreat left him master of Italy, Caesar made it clear that he was neither a second Sulla nor even the reckless anarchist which many believed him to be. The Roman and Italian public were first startled by the masterly rapidity and energy of his movements, and then agreeably surprised by his lenity and moderation. No proscriptions or confiscations followed his victories, and all his acts evinced an unmistakable desire to effect a sober and reasonable settlement of the pressing questions of the hour; of this, and of his almost superhuman energy, the long list of measures he carried out or planned is sufficient proof. The "children of the proscribed" were at length restored to their rights, and with them many of the refugees who had found shelter in Caesar's camp during the two or three years immediately preceding the war; but the extreme men among his supporters soon realized that their hopes of *novae tabulae* and grants of land were illusory. In allotting lands to his veterans, Caesar carefully avoided any disturbance of existing owners and occupiers, and the mode in which he dealt with the economic crisis produced by the war seems to have satisfied all reasonable men. It had been a common charge against Caesar in former days that he paid excessive court to the populace of Rome, and now that he was master he still dazzled and delighted them by the splendour of the spectacles he provided, and by the liberality of his largesses. But he was no indiscriminate flatterer of the mob. The popular clubs and gilds which had helped to organize the anarchy of the last few years were dissolved. A strict enquiry was made into the distribution of the monthly doles of corn, and the number of recipients was reduced by one-half; finally, the position of the courts of justice was raised by the abolition of the popular element among the indices. Nor did Caesar shrink from the attempt, in which so many had failed before him, to mitigate the twin evils which were ruining the prosperity of Italy—the concentration of a pauper population in the towns and the denudation and desolation of the country districts. His strong hand carried out the scheme so often proposed by the popular leaders since the days of Gaius Gracchus, the colonization of Carthage and Corinth. Allotments of land on a large scale were made in Italy; decaying towns were reinforced by fresh drafts of settlers; on the large estates and cattle farms the owners were required to find employment for a certain amount of free labour; and a slight and temporary stimulus was given to Italian industry by the reimposition of harbour dues upon foreign goods.

The reform of the calendar (*q.v.*) completes a record of administrative reform which entitles Caesar to the praise of having governed well, whatever may be thought of the validity of his title to govern at all. But how did Caesar deal with what was after all the greatest problem which he was called upon to solve, the establishment of a satisfactory government for the empire? One point indeed was already settled. Some centralization of the executive authority was indispensable, and this part of his work Caesar thoroughly performed. From the moment when he seized the moneys in the treasury on his first entry into Rome down to the day of his death, he recognized no other authority but his throughout the empire. He alone directed the policy of Rome in foreign affairs; the legions were led, and the provinces governed, not by independent magistrates, but by his legates; and the title *imperator* which he adopted was intended to express the absolute and unlimited nature of the *imperium* he claimed, as distinct

[2]For the Civil Wars, *see* CAESAR, GAIUS JULIUS; CICERO; POMPEY.

from the limited spheres of authority possessed by republican magistrates. In so centralizing the executive authority over the empire at large, Caesar was but developing the policy implied in the Gabinian and Manilian laws, and the precedent he established was closely followed by his successors. It was otherwise with the more difficult question of the form under which this new executive authority should be exercised and the relation it should hold to the republican constitution.

Caesar did not explain to the public what shape he intended ultimately to give to the new system. It could hardly have been the "perpetual dictatorship," which was decreed him by the senate after his victory at Munda (45). The dictatorship was associated with those very Sullan traditions from which Caesar was most anxious to sever himself, and the name had no value in the empire at large. It was rumoured that he intended to follow Alexander's example and at least in the eastern provinces adopt the title of king with the theocratic associations which the title bore in the East. Roman proconsuls who had served in Asia and had seen the ease with which kings ruled when not hampered by constitutions and privileged to utter decrees that were considered sacred, would well have comprehended the advantages of such divine absolutism. Caesar might readily remain in the East for some years after his Parthian campaign, and while busy reorganizing the provinces there he would inure his court and the senators in his train to accept the new *rex*. When the time was ripe he might proclaim the title at Rome, and then, being recognized as more than human and above legal restrictions, he could carry whatever reforms he desired by decree. That these rumours deserve some credit we may believe, not only because Caesar before his death accepted several "divine" honours from the senate, but also because Mark Antony, who knew Caesar's plans, pursued such a course after Caesar's death. It is not unlikely that Caesar intended some day to accept for himself the position of an absolute monarch like Alexander or Ptolemy Philadelphus[1]. But he was well aware that it would require many years of training to prepare the senate for the announcement.

The old constitution was not formally abrogated. The senate met and deliberated; the assembly passed laws and elected magistrates; there were still consuls, praetors, aediles, quaestors and tribunes; and Caesar himself, like his successors, professed to hold his authority by the will of the people. But senate, assembly and magistrates were all alike subordinated to the paramount authority of the dictator; and this subordination was, in appearance at least, more direct and complete under the rule of Caesar than under that of Augustus. For months together Rome was left without any regular magistrates, and was governed like a subject town by Caesar's prefects. At another time a tribune was seen exercising authority outside the city bounds and invested with the *imperium* of a praetor. At the elections, candidates appeared before the people backed by a written recommendation from the dictator, which was equivalent to a command. Finally, the senate itself was transformed out of all likeness to its former self by the raising of its numbers to 900, and by the admission of old soldiers, sons of freedmen and even "semi-barbarous Gauls." But, though Caesar's high-handed conduct in this respect was not imitated by his immediate successors, yet the main lines of their policy were laid down by him. These were: (1) the municipalization of the old republican constitution, and (2) its subordination to the paramount authority of the master of the legions and the provinces. In the first case he only carried farther a change already in progress. Of late years the senate had been rapidly losing its hold over the empire at large. Even the ordinary proconsuls were virtually independent potentates, ruling their provinces as they chose, and disposing absolutely of legions which recognized no authority but theirs. The consuls and praetors of each year had since 81 been stationed in Rome, and immersed in purely municipal business; and, lastly, since the enfranchisement of Italy, the *comitia*, though still recognized as the ultimate source of all authority, had become little more than assemblies of the city populace, and their claim to represent the true Roman people was indignantly questioned, even by republicans like

[1]E. Meyer, *Kleine Schriften* (2nd ed. i. 449).

Cicero. The concentration in Caesar's hands of all authority outside Rome completely and finally severed all real connection between the old institutions of the republic of Rome and the Government of the Roman empire. But the institutions of the republic not merely became, what they had originally been, the local institutions of the city of Rome; they were also subordinated even within these narrow limits to the paramount authority of the man who held in his hands the army and the provinces Autocratic abroad, at home he was the chief magistrate of the commonwealth; and this position was marked, in his case as in that of those who followed him, by a combination in his person of various powers, and by a general right of precedence which left no limits to his authority but such as he chose to impose upon himself. During the greater part of his reign he was consul as well as dictator. In 48, after his victory at Pharsalia, he was given the *tribunicia potestas* for life, and after his second success at Thapsus the *praefectura morum* for three years. As chief magistrate he convenes and presides in the senate, nominates candidates, conducts elections, carries laws in the assembly and administers justice in court. Finally, as a reminder that the chief magistrate of Rome was also the autocratic ruler of the empire, he wore even in Rome the laurel wreath and triumphal dress, and carried the sceptre of the victorious imperator.

Nor are we without some clue as to the policy which Caesar had sketched out for himself in the administration of the empire, the government of which he had centralized in his own hands. The much needed work of rectifying the frontiers he was forced, by his premature death, to leave to other hands, but within the frontiers he anticipated Augustus in lightening the financial burdens of the provincials, and in establishing a stricter control over the provincial governors, while he went beyond him in his desire to consolidate the empire by extending the Roman franchise and admitting provincials to a share in the Government. He completed the Romanization of Italy by his enfranchisement of the Transpadane Gauls, and by establishing throughout the peninsula a uniform system of municipal government, which under his successors was gradually extended to the provinces.

The Second Triumvirate, 43–28.—On the eve of his departure for the East, to avenge the death of Crassus and humble the power of Parthia, Caesar fell a victim to the republican nobles; and between the day of his death (March 15, 44) and that on which Octavian defeated Antony at Actium (Sept. 2, 31) lies a dreary period of anarchy and bloodshed.

For a moment, in spite of the menacing attitude of Caesar's self-constituted representative Marcus Antonius (Mark Antony), it seemed to one man at least as if the restoration of republican government was possible. With indefatigable energy Cicero strove to enlist the senate, the people, and above all the provincial governors in support of the old constitution. But, though his eloquence now and again carried all before it in senate house and forum, it was powerless to alter the course of events. By the beginning of 43 civil war had recommenced; in the autumn Antony was already threatening an invasion of Italy at the head of 17 legions. Towards the end of October Antony and his ally M. Aemilius Lepidus coalesced with the young Octavian, who had been recently elected consul at the age of 20, in spite of senatorial opposition; and the coalition was legalized by the creation of the extraordinary commission for the "reorganization of the commonwealth" known as the Second Triumvirate. It was appointed for a period of five years, and was continued in 37 for five years more. The rule of the triumvirs was inaugurated in the Sullan fashion by a proscription, foremost among the victims of which was Cicero himself. In the next year the defeat of M. Iunius Brutus and C. Cassius Longinus at Philippi, by the combined forces of Octavian and Antony, destroyed the last hopes of the republican party. In 40 a threatened rupture between the two victors was avoided by the treaty concluded at Brundisium. Antony married Octavian's sister Octavia, and took command of the eastern half of the empire; Octavian appropriated Italy and the West; while Lepidus was forced to content himself with Africa. For the next 12 years, while Antony was indulging in dreams of founding for himself and Cleopatra an empire in the East, and shocking Roman feeling by his wild excesses and his affectation of Oriental magnificence, Octavian was patiently consolidating his power. Lepidus, his fellow-triumvir, was in 36 ejected from Africa and banished to Circeii, while Sextus Pompeius, who had since his defeat at Munda maintained a semi-piratical ascendancy in the western Mediterranean, was decisively defeated in the same year, and his death in 35 left Octavian sole master of the West. The inevitable trial of strength between himself and Antony was not long delayed. In 32 Antony openly challenged the hostility of Octavian by divorcing Octavia in favour of the beautiful and daring Egyptian princess, with whom, as the heiress of the Ptolemies, he aspired to share the empire of the eastern world. By a decree of the senate Antony was declared deposed from his command, and war was declared against Queen Cleopatra. On Sept. 2, 31, was fought the battle of Actium. Octavian's victory was complete. Antony and Cleopatra committed suicide (30), and the eastern provinces submitted in 29. Octavian returned to Rome to celebrate his triumph and mark the end of the long-continued anarchy by closing the temple of Janus; at the end of the next year he formally laid down the extraordinary powers which he had held since 43, and a regular Government was established.

III. THE EMPIRE

Period I.: The Principate, 27 B.C.–A.D. 284—The Constitution of the Principate.—The conqueror of Antonius at Actium, the great-nephew and heir of the dictator Caesar, was now summoned, by the general consent of a world wearied out with 20 years of war and anarchy, to the task of establishing a Government which should as far as possible respect the forms and traditions of the republic, without sacrificing that centralization of authority which experience had shown to be necessary for the integrity and stability of the empire.

The new system which was formally inaugurated by Octavian in 28–27 B.C. assumed the shape of a restoration of the republic under the leadership of a *princeps*. Octavian voluntarily resigned the extraordinary powers which he had held since 43, and, to quote his own words, "handed over the republic to the control of the senate and people of Rome." The old constitutional machinery was once more set in motion; the senate, assembly and magistrates resumed their functions; and Octavian himself was hailed as the "restorer of the commonwealth and the champion of freedom." But his abdication, in any real sense of the word, would have simply thrown everything back into confusion. Any revival of the kingly title was out of the question, and Octavian himself expressly refused the dictatorship. Nor was any new office created or any new official title invented for his benefit. But by senate and people he was invested according to the old constitutional forms with certain powers, as many citizens had been before him, and so took his place by the side of the lawfully appointed magistrates of the republic—only, to mark his pre-eminent dignity, as the first of them all, the senate decreed that he should take as an additional cognomen that of "Augustus," while in common parlance he was henceforth styled *princeps*, a simple title of courtesy, familiar to republican usage, and conveying no other idea than that of a recognized primacy and precedence over his fellow-citizens. The ideal sketched by Cicero in his *De Republica*, of a constitutional president of a free republic, was apparently realized; but it was only in appearance. For in fact the special prerogatives conferred upon Octavian gave him back in substance the autocratic authority he had resigned, and as between the restored republic and its new *princeps* the balance of power was overwhelmingly on the side of the latter.

Octavian had held the *imperium* since 43; in 33, it is true, the powers of the triumvirate had legally expired, but he had continued to wield his authority, as he himself puts it, "by universal consent." In 27 he received a formal grant of the *imperium* from the senate and people for the term of ten years, and his *provincia* was defined as including all the provinces in which military authority was required and legions were stationed. He was declared commander-in-chief of the Roman army, and granted the

exclusive right of levying troops, of making war and peace, and of concluding treaties. As consul, moreover, he not only continued to be the chief magistrate of the State at home, but took precedence in virtue of his *maius imperium*, over the governors of the "unarmed provinces," which were still nominally under the control of the senate. Thus the so-called "restoration of the republic" was in essence the recognition by law of the personal supremacy of Octavian, or Augustus, as he must henceforth be called.

In 23 an important change was made in the formal basis of Augustus's authority. In that year he laid down the consulship which he had held each year since 31, and could therefore only exert his *imperium pro consule*, like the ordinary governor of a province. He lost his authority as chief magistrate in Rome and his precedence over the governors of senatorial provinces. To remedy these defects a series of extraordinary offices were pressed upon his acceptance; but he refused them all, and caused a number of enactments to be passed which determined the character of the principate for the next three centuries. First, he was exempted from the disability attaching to the tenure of the *imperium* by one who was not an actual magistrate, and permitted to retain and exercise it in Rome. Secondly, his *imperium* was declared to be equal with that of the consuls, and therefore superior to that of all other holders of that power. Thirdly, he was granted equal rights with the consuls of convening the senate and introducing business, of nominating candidates at elections, and of issuing edicts. Lastly, he was placed on a level with the consuls in outward rank. Twelve lictors were assigned to him and an official seat between those of the consuls themselves.

Tribunicia Potestas.—Thus the proconsular authority was for the time admitted within the walls of Rome; but Augustus was too cautious a statesman to proclaim openly the fact that the power which he wielded in the city was the same as that exercised in camps and provinces by a Roman military commander. Hence he sought for a title which should disguise the nature of his authority, and found it in the "tribunician power," which had been conferred upon him for life in 36, and was well suited, from its urban and democratic traditions, to serve in Rome as "a term to express his supreme position." From 23 onwards the *tribunicia potestas* appears after his name in official inscriptions, together with the number indicating the period during which it had been held (also reckoned from 23); it was in virtue of this power that Augustus introduced the social reforms which the times demanded; and, though far inferior to the *imperium* in actual importance, it ranked with or even above it as a distinctive prerogative of the emperor or his chosen colleague.

The *imperium* and the *tribunicia potestas* were the two pillars upon which the authority of Augustus rested, and the other offices and privileges conferred upon him were of secondary importance. After 23 he never held the consulship save in 5 and 2 B.C., when he became the colleague of his grandsons on their introduction to public life. He permitted the triumvir Lepidus to retain the chief pontificate until his death, when Augustus naturally became *pontifex maximus* (12 B.C.). He proceeded with the like caution in reorganizing the chief departments of the public service in Rome and Italy. The *cura annonae*, i.e., the supervision of the corn supply of Rome, was entrusted to him in 22 B.C., and this important branch of administration thus came under his personal control; but the other boards (*curae*), created during his reign to take charge of the roads, the water-supply, the regulation of the Tiber and the public buildings, were composed of senators of high rank, and regarded in theory as deriving their authority from the senate.

Such was the ingenious compromise by which room was found for the master of the legions within the narrow limits of the old Roman constitution. Augustus could say with truth that he had accepted no office which was "contrary to the usage of our ancestors," and that it was only in *auctoritas*[1] that he took precedence of his colleagues. Nevertheless, as every thinking man must have realized, the compromise was unreal, and its signif-

[1]*See* Ramsay and Primerstein. *Mon. Antioch.* iv. 3 (1927).

icance was ambiguous. It was an arrangement avowedly of an exceptional and temporary character, yet no one could suppose that it would in effect be otherwise than permanent. The powers voted to Augustus were (like those conferred upon Pompey in 67 B.C.) voted only to him, and (save the *tribunicia potestas*) voted only for a limited time; in 27 he received the *imperium* for ten years, and it was afterwards renewed for successive periods of five, five, ten and ten years. In this way the powers of the principate were made coextensive in time with the life of Augustus, but there was absolutely no provision for hereditary or any other form of succession, and various expedients were devised in order to indicate the destined successor of the *princeps* and to bridge the gap created by his death. Ultimately Augustus associated his stepson Tiberius with himself as co-regent. The *imperium* and the *tribunicia potestas* were conferred upon him, and he was thus marked out as the person upon whom the remaining powers of the principate would naturally be bestowed after the death of his stepfather. But succeeding emperors did not always indicate their successors so clearly, and, in direct contrast to the maxim that "the king never dies," it has been well said that the Roman principate died with the death of the *princeps*.

Changes in the Constitution of the Principate.—In theory, at least, the Roman world was governed according to the "maxims of Augustus" (Suet. *Ner.* 10), down to the time of Diocletian. Even in the 3rd century there is still in name at least a republic, of which the emperor is in strictness only the chief magistrate, deriving his authority from the senate and people, and with prerogatives limited and defined by law. The case is quite different when we turn from theory to practice. The division of authority between the republic and its chief magistrate became increasingly unequal. Over the provinces the *princeps* from the first ruled autocratically; and this autocracy reacted upon his position in Rome, so that it became every year more difficult for a ruler so absolute abroad to maintain even the fiction of republican government at home. The republican ·institutions, with the partial exception of the senate, lose all semblance of authority outside Rome, and even as the municipal institutions of the chief city of the empire they retain but little actual power. The real government even of Rome passes gradually into the hands of imperial prefects and commissioners, and the old magistracies become merely decorations which the emperor bestows at his pleasure. At the same time the rule of the *princeps* assumes an increasingly personal character, and the whole work of government is silently concentrated in his hands and in those of his own subordinates. Closely connected with this change is the different aspect presented by the history of the empire in Rome and Italy on the one hand and in the provinces on the other. Rome and Italy share in the decline of the republic. Political independence and activity die out; their old pre-eminence and exclusive privileges gradually disappear; and at the same time the weight of the overwhelming power of the *princeps,* and the abuses of their power by individual *principes,* press most heavily upon them. On the other hand, in the provinces and on the frontiers, where the imperial system was most needed, and where from the first it had full play, it is seen at its best as developing or protecting an orderly civilization and maintaining the peace of the world.

The decay of the republican institutions had commenced before the revolutionary crisis of 49. It was accelerated by the virtual suspension of regular government between 49 and 28; and not even the diplomatic deference towards ancient forms which Augustus displayed availed to conceal the unreality of his work of restoration. The *comitia* received back from him "their ancient rights" (Suet. *Aug.* 40), and during his lifetime they continued to pass laws and to elect magistrates. But after the end of the reign of Tiberius we have only two instances of legislation by the assembly in the ordinary way[1], and the law-making of the empire is performed either by decrees of the senate or by imperial edicts and constitutions. Their prerogative of electing magistrates was, even under Augustus, robbed of most of its importance by the control which the *princeps* exercised

over their choice by means of his rights of nomination and commendation, which effectually secured the election of his own nominees. By Tiberius this restricted prerogative was still further curtailed. The candidates for all magistracies except the consulship were thenceforward nominated and voted for in the senate house and by the senators, and only the formal return of the result (*renuntiatio*) took place in the assembly (Dio lviii. 20). The *princeps* himself as long as the principate lasted, continued to receive the *tribunicia potestas* by a vote of the assembly, and was thus held to derive his authority from the people.

This almost complete effacement of the *comitia* was largely due to the fact that they had ceased to represent anything but the populace of Rome, and the comparatively greater vitality shown by the old magistracies is mainly attributable to the value they continued to possess in the eyes of the Roman upper class. But, though they were eagerly sought (Plin. *Epp.* ii. 9, vi. 6), and conferred on their holders considerable social distinction, the magistrates ceased, except in name, to be the popularly choser. executive officers of the Roman State. In the administration of the empire at large they had no share, if we except the subordinate duties still assigned to the quaestor in a province. In Rome, to which their sphere of work was limited, they were overshadowed by the dominant authority of the *princeps,* while their range of duties was increasingly circumscribed by the gradual transference of administrative authority, even within the city, to the emperor and his subordinate officials.

The senate alone among republican institutions retained some importance and influence, and it thus came to be regarded as sharing the government of the empire with the *princeps* himself. It nominally controlled the administration of Italy and of the "public provinces," whose governors it appointed. It is to the senate, in theory, that the supreme power reverts in the absence of a *princeps*. It is by decree of the senate that the new *princeps* immediately receives his powers and privileges, though he is still supposed to derive them ultimately from the people. After the cessation of all legislation by the *comitia*, the only law-making authority, other than that of the *princeps* by his edicts, was that of the senate by its decrees. Its judicial authority was co-ordinate with that of the emperor, and at the close of the 1st century we find the senators claiming, as the emperor's "peers," to be exempt from his jurisdiction. But in spite of the outward dignity of its position, and of the deference with which it was frequently treated, the senate became gradually almost as powerless in reality as the *comitia* and the magistracies. The senators continued indeed to be taken as a rule from the ranks of the wealthy, and a high property qualification was established by Augustus as a condition of membership; but this merely enabled the emperors to secure their own ascendancy by subsidizing those whose property fell short of the required standard, and who thus became simply the paid creatures of their imperial patrons. Admission to the senate was possible only by favour of the emperor, both as controlling the elections to the magistracies, which still gave entrance to the curia, and as invested with the power of directly creating senators by *adlectio,* a power which from the time of Vespasian onwards was freely used. As the result, the composition of the senate rapidly altered. Under Augustus and Tiberius it still contained many representatives of the old republican families, whose prestige and ancestral traditions were some guarantee for their independence. But this element soon disappeared. The ranks of the old nobility were thinned by natural decay and by the jealous fears of the last three Claudian emperors. Vespasian flooded the senate with new men from the municipal towns of Italy and the Latinized provinces of the West. Trajan and Hadrian, both provincials themselves, carried on the same policy, and by the close of the 2nd century even the Greek provinces of the East had their representatives in the senate. Some, no doubt, of these provincials, who constituted the great majority of the senate in the 3rd century, were men of wealth and mark, but many more were of low birth; on some rested the stain of a servile descent, and all owed alike their present position and their chances of further promotion to the emperor. The procedure of the senate was as completely

[1]The *plebiscita* of Claudius, Tac. *Ann.* xi. 13, 14, and the *lex agraria* of Nerva; *Digest,* xlvii. 21, 3; Dio lxviii. 2; Plin. *Epp.* vii. 31.

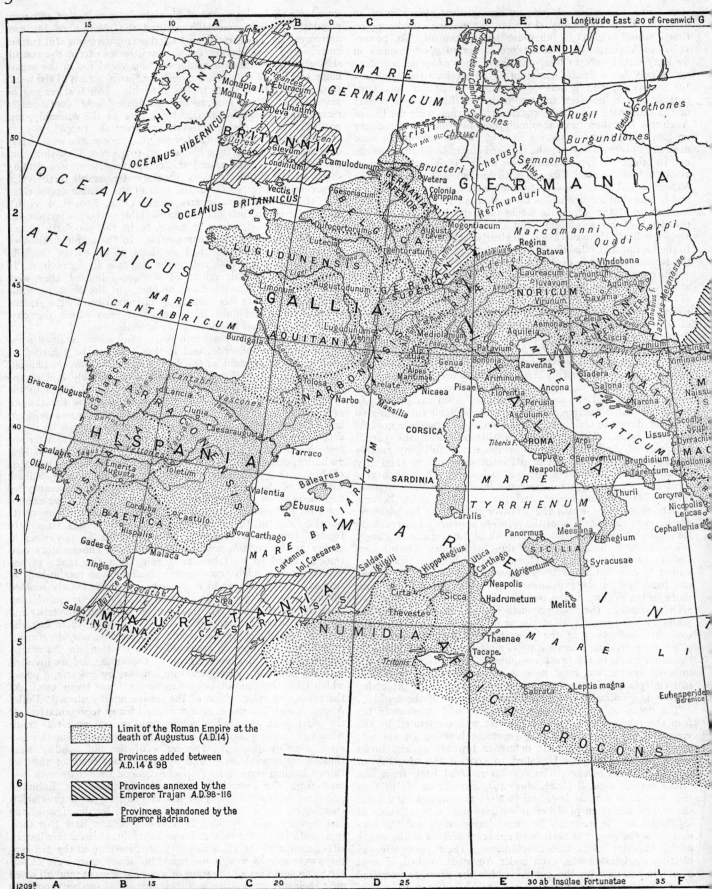

Limit of the Roman Empire at the death of Augustus (A.D.14)

Provinces added between A.D.14 & 98

Provinces annexed by the Emperor Trajan A.D.98-116

Provinces abandoned by the Emperor Hadrian

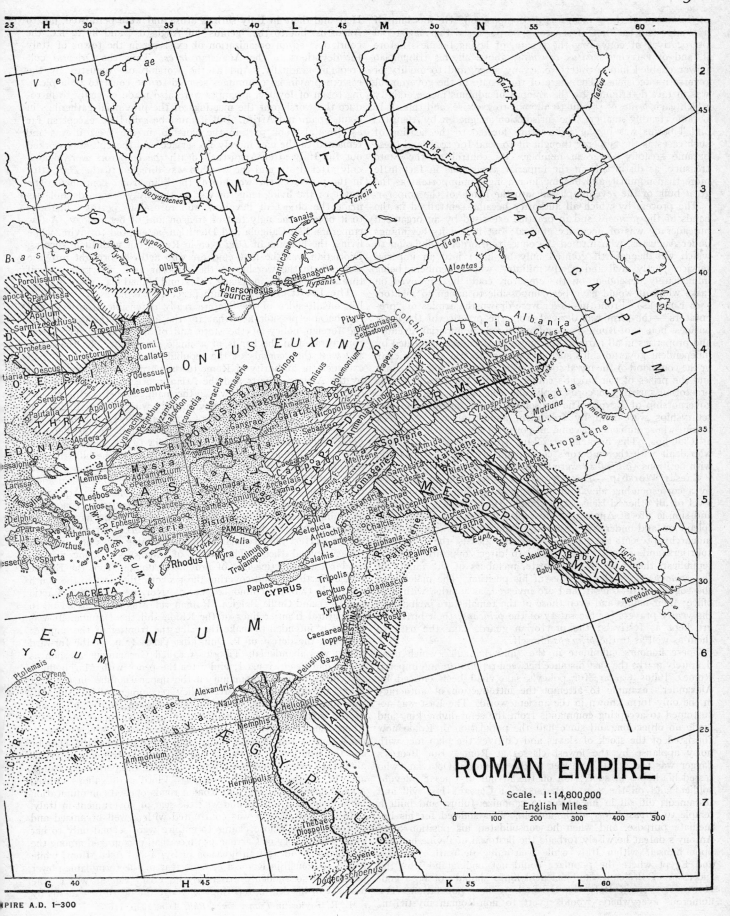

ROMAN EMPIRE

Scale. 1:14,800,000
English Miles
0   100   200   300   400   500

at the mercy of the *princeps* as its composition. He was himself a senator and the first of senators; he possessed the magisterial prerogatives of convening the senate, of laying business before it, and of carrying *senatus consulta;* above all, his tribunician power enabled him to interfere at any stage, and to modify or reverse its decisions. The share of the senate in the government was in fact determined by the amount of administrative activity which each *princeps* saw fit to allow it to exercise, and this share became steadily smaller. The jurisdiction assigned it by Augustus and Tiberius was in the 3rd century limited to the hearing of such cases as the emperor thought fit to send for trial, and these became steadily fewer in number. Its control of the State treasury, as distinct from the imperial *fiscus,* was in fact little more than nominal, and became increasingly unimportant as the great bulk of the revenue passed into the hands of the emperor.

The process by which all authority became centralized in the hands of the *princeps* and in practice exercised by an organized bureaucracy was of necessity gradual; but it had its beginnings under Augustus, who formed the equestrian order (admission to which was henceforth granted only by him) into an imperial service, partly civil and partly military, whose members, being immediately dependent on the emperor, could be employed on tasks which it would have been impossible to assign to senators (*see* EQUITES). From this order were drawn the armies of "procurators"—the term was derived from the practice of the great business houses of Rome—who administered the imperial revenues and properties in all parts of the empire. Merit was rewarded by independent governorships such as those of Raetia and Noricum, or the command of the naval squadrons at Misenum and Ravenna; and the prizes of the knight's career were the prefectures of the praetorian guard, the corn-supply and the city police, and the governorship of Egypt. The household offices and imperial secretaryships were held by freedmen, almost always of Greek origin, whose influence became all-powerful under such emperors as Claudius. The financial secretary (*a rationibus*) and those who dealt with the emperor's correspondence (*ab epistulis*) and with petitions (*a libellis*) were the most important of these.

Caesar Worship.—This increase of power was accompanied by a corresponding elevation of the *princeps* himself above the level of all other citizens. The comparatively modest household and simple life of Augustus were replaced by a more than regal splendour, and under Nero we find all the outward accessories of monarchy present, the palace, the palace guards, the crowds of courtiers and a court ceremonial. In direct opposition to the republican theory of the principate, members of the family of the *princeps* share the dignities of his position. The males bear the cognomen of Caesar, and are invested, as youths, with high office; their names and even those of the females are included in the yearly prayers for the safety of the *princeps;* their birthdays are kept as festivals; the praetorian guards take the oath to them as well as to the *princeps* himself.

These honours culminate in the "imperial cult" which most definitely marks the vast distance between republican and imperial Rome. Julius Caesar, for policy's sake, had been enticed by Alexander's example to attempt the introduction of autocracy in the only form known in the ancient world. The East was accustomed to accepting commands from the semi-divine king and made no objection, and since half the population of Rome now consisted of the stock of slaves and captives the plan met with noisy applause by the lowest classes at Rome. But Brutus's dagger was the senate's answer to the proposal. Octavian, who rested his hopes of succession on the favour of Caesar's devout soldiers and on the sacred character of Caesar's last will and testament, did all in his power to canonize Julius, and built a temple to *Divus Iulius* in the Forum. This sufficed for his immediate purpose, and when he consolidated his position after Antony's defeat he wisely forbade the bestowal of divine honours upon himself within Italy while welcoming deification in Asia and Egypt where the populace could not understand why the successor of Ptolemies and Seleucid kings should not be a god. However, even in Italy the Oriental ex-slave population, very numerous everywhere, would revert to non-Roman mysticism.

Here and there in Italy shrines arose and were permitted, not to Augustus, but to the "genius" of Augustus[1], and in 12 B.C. the court devised an organization of ex-slaves in the towns of Italy for devotions to the Augustan *lares.* Thus the Oriental cult crept in gradually. And as the worship of Augustus by the eastern provincial communes seemed to the court to be a pleasing token of loyalty, attempts were also made officially to introduce the worship at the meetings of the provincial gatherings in Gaul, Spain and Africa. But it must be said that, except so far as Orientals took part in the worship, in the West it was and remained to the end merely lip service. As the cult was worked out for Italy after Augustus's death the emperors were deified only after death and the worship was directed to the *Divi.* But in the provinces the worship of the living ruler continued. The image of the living emperor was on the army standards and was made the object of devotion, and refusal to perform libations to it became the ugly test of treason and of heterodoxy. A few emperors, like Caligula and Domitian, attempted to invite, while living, the honours of *Divi* even in Rome, but with little success. Diocletian was the first emperor who actually brought into the very senate the worship of the emperor as it was practised all through the empire in Asiatic cities, and he had his capital in Asia.

The Frontiers.—To secure peace it was necessary to establish on all sides of the empire really defensible frontiers; and this became possible now that for the first time the direction of the foreign policy of the state and of its military forces was concentrated in the hands of a single magistrate. To the south and west the generals of the republic, and Caesar himself, had extended the authority of Rome to the natural boundaries formed by the African deserts and the Atlantic ocean, and in these two directions Augustus's task was in the main confined to the organization of a settled Roman government within these limits. In Africa the client state of Egypt was ruled by Augustus as the successor of the Ptolemies, and administered by his deputies (*praefecti*), and the kingdom of Numidia (25 B.C.) was incorporated with the old province of Africa. In Spain the hill-tribes of the north-west were finally subdued and a third province, Lusitania, established. In Gaul Augustus (27 B.C.) established in addition to the "old province" the three new ones of Aquitania, Lugdunensis and Belgica, which included the territories conquered by Julius Caesar. Towards the north the republic had left the civilized countries bordering on the Mediterranean with only a very imperfect defence against the threatening mass of barbarian tribes beyond them. The result of Augustus's policy was to establish a protecting line of provinces running from the Euxine to the North sea, and covering the peaceful districts to the south —Moesia (A.D. 6), Pannonia (A.D. 9), Noricum (15 B.C.), Raetia (15 B.C.) and Gallia Belgica. Roman rule was thus carried up to the natural frontier lines of the Rhine and the Danube. It was originally intended to make the Elbe the frontier of the empire; but after the defeat of P. Quintilius Varus (A.D. 9) the forward policy was abandoned. Tiberius recalled Germanicus as soon as Varus had been avenged; and after the peace with Maroboduus, the chief of the Marcomanni on the upper Danube, in the next year (A.D. 17), the defensive policy recommended by Augustus was adopted along the whole of the northern frontier. The line of the great rivers was held by an imposing mass of troops. Along the Rhine lay the armies of Upper and Lower Germany, consisting of four legions each; eight more guarded the Danube and the frontiers of Pannonia and Moesia. At frequent intervals along the frontier were the military colonies, the permanent camps and the smaller intervening *castella.* Flotillas of galleys cruised up and down the rivers, and Roman roads opened communication both along the frontiers and with the seat of government in Italy.

In the East, Rome was confronted with a well organized and powerful State whose claims to empire were second only to her own. The victory of Carrhae (53 B.C.) had encouraged among the Parthians the idea of an invasion of Syria and Asia Minor, while it had awakened in Rome a genuine fear of the formidable power which had so suddenly arisen in the East. Caesar was at the moment of his death preparing to avenge the death of Crassus by

[1]L. R. Taylor, in *Trans. Amer. Phil. Assn. 1920,* 116.

an invasion of Parthia, and Antony's schemes of founding an Eastern empire which should rival that of Alexander included the conquest of the kingdom beyond the Euphrates. Augustus, however, adhered to the policy which he recommended to his successors of "keeping the empire within its bounds"; and the Parthians, weakened by internal feuds and dynastic quarrels, were in no mood for vigorous action. Roman pride was satisfied by the restoration of the standards taken at Carrhae. Four legions guarded the line of the Euphrates, and, beyond the frontiers of Pontus and Cappadocia, Armenia was established as a "friendly and independent ally."

The Provinces.—Next in importance to the rectification and defence of the frontiers was the reformation of the administration, and the restoration of prosperity to the distracted and exhausted provinces. The most serious defect of the republican system had been the absence of any effective control over the Roman officials outside Italy. This was now supplied by the general proconsular authority vested in the emperor. The provinces were for the first time treated as departments of a single State, while their governors, from being independent and virtually irresponsible rulers, became the subordinate officials of a higher authority. Over the *legati* of the imperial provinces the control of the emperor was as complete as that of the republican proconsul over his staff in his own province. They were appointed by him, held office at his good pleasure, and were directly responsible to him for their conduct. The proconsuls of the senatorial provinces were in law magistrates equally with the *princeps,* though inferior to him in rank; it was to the senate that they were, as of old, responsible; they were still selected by lot from among the senators of consular and praetorian rank. But the distinction did not seriously interfere with the paramount authority of the emperor. The provinces left nominally to the senate were the more peaceful and settled districts in the heart of the empire, where only the routine work of civil administration was needed, and where the local municipal governments were as yet comparatively vigorous. The senatorial proconsuls themselves were indirectly nominated by the emperor through his control of the praetorship and consulship. They wielded no military and only a strictly subordinate financial authority, and, though Augustus and Tiberius, at any rate, encouraged the fiction of the responsibility of the senatorial governors to the senate, it was in reality to the emperor that they looked for direction and advice, and to him that they were held accountable. Moreover, in the case of all governors this accountability became under the empire a reality. Prosecutions for extortion (*de pecuniis repetundis*), which were now transferred to the hearing of the senate, were tolerably frequent during the first century of the empire; but a more effective check on maladministration lay in the appeal to Caesar from the decisions of any governor, which was open to every provincial, and in the right of petition. Finally, the authority both of the legate and the proconsul was weakened by the presence of the imperial procurator, to whom was entrusted the administration of the fiscal revenues; while both legate and proconsul were deprived of that right of requisitioning supplies which, in spite of a long series of restrictive laws, had been the most powerful instrument of oppression in the hands of republican governors. The financial reforms of Augustus are marked by the same desire to establish an equitable, orderly and economical system, and by the same centralization of authority in the emperor's hands. The institution of an imperial census or valuation of all land throughout the empire, and the assessment upon this basis of a uniform land tax, in place of the heterogeneous and irregular payments made under the republic, were the work of Augustus, though the system was developed and perfected by the emperors of the 2nd century and by Diocletian. The land tax itself was directly collected, either by imperial officials or by local authorities responsible to them, and the old wasteful plan of selling the privilege of collection to *publicani* was henceforward applied only to such indirect taxes as the customs duties. The rate of the land tax was fixed by the emperor, and with him rested the power of remission even in senatorial provinces. The effect of these reforms is clearly visible in the improved financial condition of the empire. Under the republic the treasury had been nearly always in difficulties, and the provinces exhausted and impoverished. Under the emperors, at least throughout the 1st century, in spite of a largely increased expenditure on the army, on public works, on shows and largesses, and on the machinery of government itself, the better emperors, such as Tiberius and Vespasian, were able to accumulate large sums, while the provinces showed but few signs of distress. Moreover, while the republic had almost entirely neglected to develop the internal resources of the provinces, Augustus set the example of a liberal expenditure on public works, in the construction of harbours, roads and bridges, the reclamation of waste lands and the erection of public buildings.

The Julio-Claudian Line.—Augustus founded a dynasty which occupied the throne for more than half a century after his death. The first and by far the ablest of its members was Tiberius (A.D. 14–37). He was undoubtedly a capable and vigorous ruler, who enforced justice in the government of the provinces, maintained the integrity of the frontiers and husbanded the finances of the empire, but he became intensely unpopular in Roman society, and was painted as a cruel and odious tyrant. His successor, Gaius (A.D. 37–41), generally known as Caligula, was the slave of his wild caprices and uncontrolled passions, which issued in manifest insanity. He was followed by his uncle, Claudius (A.D. 41–54), whose personal uncouthness made him an object of derision to his contemporaries, but who was by no means devoid of statesmanlike faculties. His reign left an abiding mark on the history of the empire, for he carried forward its development on the lines intended by Augustus. Client-states were absorbed, southern Britain was conquered, the romanization of the West received a powerful impulse, public works were executed in Rome and Italy, and the organization of the imperial bureaucracy made rapid strides. Nero (A.D. 54–68), the last of the Julio-Claudian line, has been handed down to posterity as the incarnation of monstrous vice and fantastic luxury. But his wild excesses scarcely affected the prosperity of the empire at large; the provinces were well governed, and the war with Parthia led to a compromise in the matter of Armenia which secured peace for half a century.

The Antonine Empire.—The fall of Nero and the extinction of the "progeny of the Caesars" was followed by a war of succession which revealed the military basis of the principate and the weakness of the tie connecting the emperor with Rome. Galba, Otho, Vitellius and Vespasian represented in turn the legions of Spain, the household troops, the army of the Rhine, and a coalition of the armies of the Danube and the Euphrates; and all except Otho were already *de facto* emperors when they entered Rome. The final survivor in the struggle, Vespasian (A.D. 70–79), was a man of comparatively humble origin, and as the principate ceased to possess the prestige of high descent it became imperatively necessary to remove, as far as possible, the anomalies of the office and to give it a legitimate and permanent form. Thus we find an elaborate and formal system of titles substituted for the personal names of the Julio-Claudian emperors, an increasing tendency to insist on the inherent prerogatives of the principate (such as the censorial power), and an attempt to invest Caesarism with an hereditary character, either by natural descent or by adoption, while the worship of the *Divi,* or deified Caesars, was made the symbol of its continuity and legitimacy. The dynasty of Vespasian and his sons (Titus, A.D. 79–81, Domitian, A.D. 81–96) became extinct on the murder of the last named, whose high-handed treatment of the senate earned him the name of a tyrant; his successor, Nerva (A.D. 96–98), opened the series of "adoptive" emperors (Trajan, A.D. 98–117, Hadrian, 117–138, Antoninus Pius, 138–161, Marcus Aurelius 161–180) under whose rule the empire enjoyed a period of internal tranquillity and good government. Its boundaries were extended by the subjugation of northern Britain by Agricola, A.D. 78–84 (*see* BRITAIN: *Roman*), by the annexation of the districts included in the angle of the Rhine and Danube under the Flavian emperors, and by the conquest of Dacia (the modern Transylvania) under Trajan (completed in A.D. 106). Trajan also annexed Arabia

Petraea and in his closing years invaded Parthia and formed provinces of Armenia, Mesopotamia and Assyria; but these conquests were surrendered by his successor, Hadrian, who set himself to the task of consolidating the empire and perfecting its defences. To him is due the system of permanent *limites* or frontier fortifications, such as the wall which protected northern Britain and the palisade which replaced the chain of forts established by the Flavian emperors from the Rhine to the Danube. The construction of these defences showed that the limit of expansion had been reached, and under M. Aurelius the tide began to turn. A great part of his reign was occupied with wars against the Marcomanni, Quadi, Sarmatians, etc., whose irruptions seriously threatened the security of Italy. Henceforth Rome never ceased to be on the defensive.

Within the frontiers the levelling and unifying process commenced by Augustus had steadily proceeded. A tolerably uniform provincial system covered the whole area of the empire. The client-states had one by one been reconstituted as provinces, and even the government of Italy had been in many respects assimilated to the provincial type. The municipal system had spread widely; the period from Vespasian to Aurelius witnessed the elevation to municipal rank of an immense number of communities, not only in the old provinces of the West, in Africa, Spain and Gaul, but in the newer provinces of the North, and along the line of the northern frontier; and everywhere under the influence of the central imperial authority there was an increasing uniformity in the form of the local constitutions, framed and granted as they all were by imperial edict. Throughout the empire again the extension of the Roman franchise was preparing the way for the final act by which Caracalla assimilated the legal status of all free-born inhabitants of the empire, and in the west and north this was preceded and accompanied by the complete romanizing of the people in language and civilization. Yet, in spite of the internal tranquillity and the good government which have made the age of the Antonines famous, we can detect signs of weakness. It was in this period that the centralization of authority in the hands of the *princeps* was completed; the "dual control" established by Augustus, which had been unreal enough in the 1st century, was now, though not formally abolished, systematically ignored in practice. The senate ceased to be an instrument of government, and became an imperial peerage, largely composed of men not qualified by election to the quaestorship but directly ennobled by the emperor. The restricted sphere of administration left by Augustus to the old magistracies was still further narrowed; their jurisdiction, for example, tended to pass into the hands of the Greek officers appointed by Caesar—the prefect of the city and the prefect of the guards. The complete organization of Caesar's own administrative service, and its recognition as a state bureaucracy, was chiefly the work of Hadrian, who took the secretaryships out of the hands of freedmen and entrusted them to procurators of equestrian rank. All these changes, inevitable, and in some degree beneficial, as they were, brought with them the attendant evils of excessive centralization. Though these were hardly felt while the central authority was wielded by vigorous rulers, yet even under Trajan, Hadrian and the Antonines we notice a failure of strength in the empire as a whole, and a corresponding increase of pressure on the imperial Government itself. The reforms of Augustus had given free play to powers still fresh and vigorous. The ceaseless labours of Hadrian were directed mainly to the careful husbanding of such strength as still remained, or to attempts at reviving it by the sheer force of imperial authority. Among the symptoms of incipient decline were the growing depopulation, especially of the central districts of the empire, the constant financial difficulties, the deterioration in character of the local governments in the provincial communities, and the increasing reluctance exhibited by all classes to undertake the now onerous burden of municipal office.

It is to such facts as these that we must look in passing a final judgment on the imperial Government, which is admittedly seen in its best and most perfect form in the Antonine period. In our review of the conditions which brought about the fall of the Roman republic, we saw that the collapse of the city-state made

Caesarism inevitable, since the extension of federal and representative institutions to a heterogeneous world-empire was out of the question. The benefits which Caesarism conferred upon mankind are plain. In the first place, the Roman world, which had hitherto not been governed in the true sense of the word, but exploited in the interests of a dominant clique, now received an orderly and efficient government, under which the frightful ravages of misrule and civil strife were repaired. The financial resources of the empire were husbanded by skilled and, above all *trained* administrators, to whom the imperial service offered a *carrière ouverte aux talents;* many of these were Greeks, or half-Greek Orientals, whose business capacity formed an invaluable asset hitherto neglected. Augustus caused an official survey of the empire to be made, and a scientific census of its resources was gradually carried out and from time to time revised; thus the balance of revenue and expenditure could be accurately estimated and adjusted, and financial stability was established. The system of tax-farming was gradually abolished and direct collection substituted; commerce was freed from vexatious restrictions, and large customs-districts were formed, on whose borders duties were levied for revenue only. The Government took even more direct measures for the encouragement of industry and especially of agriculture. The most remarkable of these were the "alimentary" institutions, originally due to Nerva and developed by succeeding emperors. Capital was advanced at moderate rates of interest to Italian landowners on the security of their estates, and the profits of this system of land banks were devoted to the maintenance and education of poor children. The foundation of colonies for time-expired soldiers, who received grants of land on their discharge, contributed something to the formation of a well-to-do agricultural class; and although the system was not successful in lower Italy, where economic decline could not be arrested, there can be no doubt that central and northern Italy, where the vine and olive were largely cultivated, and manufacturing industries sprang up, enjoyed a considerable measure of prosperity. The extension of the Roman municipal system to the provinces, and the watchful care exercised by the imperial Government over the communities, together with the profuse liberality of the emperors, which was imitated by the wealthier citizens of the towns, led to the creation of a flourishing municipal life still evidenced by the remains which in districts such as Asia Minor or Tunis stand in significant contrast with the desolation which was brought about by centuries of barbaric rule. Mommsen[1] has, indeed, expressed the opinion that "if an angel of the Lord were to strike the balance whether the domain ruled by Antoninus were governed with the greater intelligence and the greater humanity at that time or in the present day, whether civilization and national prosperity generally had since that time advanced or retrograded, it is very doubtful whether the decision would prove in favour of the present."

But there is another side to the picture. During the last two centuries of the republic Rome, by introducing slaves and captives to perform the hard labour of Italy while the free population spent itself in war or lost itself in the provinces, had thoroughly changed the Italian stock. Had the change come gradually and had Rome received the newcomers into schools that might have trained them into a consistent tradition this introduction of a varied stock might perhaps have enriched the spirit of Rome. But this was not to be. Such an amalgam requires time to eliminate the products of incongruous physical mixture,[2] to unify the peoples of a dozen languages until they can comprehend each other and effectually shape common ideals, to distil and throw off the hatred, servility and unsocial hostility to the community bred by years of suffering in slavery, and in a word to create a new people homogeneous enough to act together. The invasion was so rapid and the time so short that such a process of unification never completed itself at Rome. And when Rome, which was the heart of the empire, lost its rhythm and balance, when Rome no longer had a definite culture, a certain inspiration to impart to the provinces, when Rome's religion suc-

[1]*Provinces*, i. p. 5.
[2]M. P. Nilsson, in *Hereditas* (1921), 370.

cumbed to the several mystical cults brought in by her slaves, when her moral standards yielded before a dozen incongruous traditions, and her literature lost itself in blind gropings after a bygone tradition of a freer day, the provincials in despair abandoned her guidance.

Furthermore, the empire brought into being in the provinces a new nationality, due to the partial fusion of Roman ideas with Hellenic culture, beside which other elements, saving only, as we shall see, those contributed by the Oriental religions, were insignificant. This new nationality grew in definition through the gradual disappearance of distinctions of language and manners, the assimilating influence of commercial and social intercourse, and the extinction of national jealousies and aspirations. But the cosmopolitan society thus formed was compacted of so many disparate elements that a common patriotism was hard to foster, and doubly hard when the autocratic system of government prevented men from aspiring to that true political distinction which is attainable only in a self-governing community. It is true that there was much good work to be done, and that much good work was done, in the service of the emperors; true, also, that the *carrière ouverte aux talents* was in large measure realized. Distinctions of race were slowly but steadily effaced by the grant of citizen rights to provincials and by the manumission of slaves; and the career open to the romanized provincial or the liberated slave might culminate in the highest distinctions which the emperor could bestow. In the hierarchy of social orders—senate, *equites* and *plebs*—ascent was easy and regular from the lower grade to the higher; and the more enlightened of the emperors—especially Hadrian—made a genuine endeavour to give a due share in the work of government to the various subject races. But nothing could compensate for the lack of self-determination, and although during the first century and a half of imperial rule a flourishing local patriotism in some degree filled the place of the wider sentiment, this gradually sank into decay and became a pretext under cover of which the lower classes in the several communities took toll of their wealthier fellow-citizens in the shape of public works, largesses, amusements, etc., until the resources at the disposal of the rich ran dry, the communities themselves in many cases became insolvent, and the inexorable claims of the central Government were satisfied only by the surrender of financial control to an imperial commissioner. Then the organs of civic life became atrophied, political interest died out, and the whole burden of administration, as well as that of defence, fell upon the shoulders of the bureaucracy, which proved unequal to the task.

The Empire, 180–284.—Marcus Aurelius died in 180, and the reign of his worthless son, Commodus (A.D. 180–192), was followed by a century of war and disorder, during which nothing but the stern rule of soldier emperors saved the empire from dissolution. The first and ablest of these was Septimius Severus (193–211), whose claims were disputed by Clodius Albinus in the West, and by Pescennius Niger in the East; in these struggles rival Roman forces, for the first time since the accession of Vespasian, exhausted each other in civil war. Severus emphasized strongly the military character of the principate; he abstained from seeking confirmation for his authority from the senate, and deprived that body of most of the share in the government which it still retained; he assumed the title of proconsul in Rome itself, made the prefect of the guard the vicegerent of his authority, and heaped privileges upon the army, which, although they secured its entire devotion to his family, impaired its efficiency as a fighting force and thus weakened Rome in face of the barbarian invader. He succeeded in founding a short-lived dynasty, which ended with the attempt of the virtuous but weak Alexander (222–235) to restore the independence of the senate. This led to a military reaction, and the elevation of the brutal Maximinus, a Thracian peasant, to the throne. The disintegration of the empire was the natural result; for the various provincial armies put forward their commanders as claimants to the purple. These "tyrants," as they were called when unsuccessful, sprang up in ever-increasing numbers, and weakened Rome's power of resistance to the new enemies who were threatening her frontiers—

the Alamanni and Franks, who broke through the German *limes* in 236; the Goths, who crossed the Danube in 247, raided the Balkan provinces, and defeated and slew the emperor, Decius, in 251, and the restored Persian kingdom of the Sassanidae (*see* PERSIA), whose rulers laid claim to all the Asiatic possessions of Rome and in 260 captured Antioch and made the emperor, Valerian, a prisoner. During the reign of Gallienus, the son of Valerian (260–268), the evil reached its height. The central authority was paralysed; the romanized districts beyond the Rhine were irrevocably lost; the Persians were threatening to overrun the eastern provinces; the Goths had formed a fleet of 500 sail which harried Asia Minor and even Greece itself, where Athens, Corinth, Sparta and Argos were sacked; and the legions on the frontiers were left to repel the enemies of Rome as best they could. A provincial empire was established by M. Cassianius Latinius Postumus in Gaul and maintained by his successors, M. Piavonius Victorinus and C. Pius Esuvius Tetricus. Their authority was acknowledged, not only in Gaul and by the troops on the Rhine, but by the legions of Britain and Spain; and under Postumus at any rate (259–269) the existence of the Gallic empire was justified by the repulse of the barbarians and by the restoration of peace and security to the provinces of Gaul. On the Danube, in Greece and in Asia Minor none of the "pretenders" enjoyed more than a passing success. In the Far East, the Syrian Odaenathus, prince of Palmyra (*q.v.*), though officially only the governor of the East (*dux Orientis*) under Gallienus, drove the Persians out of Asia Minor and Syria, recovered Mesopotamia, and ruled Syria, Arabia, Armenia, Cappadocia and Cilicia with all the independence of a sovereign. Odaenathus was murdered in 266. His young son Vaballathus (Wahab-allath) succeeded him in his titles, but the real power was vested in his widow Zenobia, under whom not only the greater part of Asia Minor but even the province of Egypt was forcibly added to the dominions governed by the Palmyrene prince, who ceased to acknowledge the supremacy of Rome.

Gallienus was murdered at Milan in 268, and after the brief reign of Claudius II. (A.D. 268–270), who checked the advance of the Goths, Aurelian (270–275) restored unity to the distracted empire. Palmyra was destroyed and Zenobia led a prisoner to Rome (273) and in the next year the Gallic empire came to an end by the surrender of Tetricus. Aurelian, it is true, abandoned the province of Dacia, but the defences of the Danube were strengthened, and in 276 Probus repulsed the Franks and Alamanni, who had been pressing on the Rhine frontier for some 40 years. Finally, Carus (282) recovered Armenia and Mesopotamia from the Persians and restored the frontier fixed by Septimius Severus.

The Empire at the Close of the 3rd Century.—Although any serious loss of territory had been avoided, the storms of the 3rd century had told with fatal effect upon the general condition of the empire. The "Roman peace" had vanished; not only the frontier territories, but the central districts of Greece, Asia Minor, and even Italy itself, had suffered from the ravages of war, and the fortification of Rome by Aurelian was a significant testimony to the altered condition of affairs. War, plague and famine had thinned the population and crippled the resources of the provinces. On all sides land was running waste, cities and towns were decaying and commerce was paralysed. Only with the greatest difficulty were sufficient funds squeezed from the exhausted taxpayers to meet the increasing cost of the defence of the frontiers. The old established culture and civilization of the Mediterranean world rapidly declined, and the mixture of barbaric rudeness with Oriental pomp and luxury which marked the court, even of the better emperors, such as Aurelian, was typical of the general deterioration, which was accelerated by the growing practice of settling barbarians on lands within the empire and of admitting them freely to service in the Roman army.

Period II.: The Dominate, A.D. 284–476. (a) From the Accession of Diocletian to the Death of Theodosius (A.D. 284–395).—The work of fortifying the empire alike against internal sedition and foreign invasion, begun by Aurelian and Probus, was completed by Diocletian and Constantine the Great, whose system of government, novel as it appears at first sight, was in reality the natural and inevitable outcome of the history of the previous century. Its object was two-fold, to give increased stability to the imperial authority itself and to organize efficient administrative machinery throughout the empire. In the second year of his reign Diocletian associated Maximian with himself as colleague, and six years later (293) the hands of the two "Augusti" were further strengthened by the proclamation of Constantius and Galerius as "Caesares." Precedents for such an arrangement were to be found in the earlier history of the principate; and it divided the burdens and responsibilities of government without sacrificing the unity of the empire; for, although to each of the Augusti and Caesars a separate sphere was assigned, the Caesars were subordinate to the higher authority of the Augusti, and over all his three colleagues Diocletian claimed to exercise a paramount control. It also reduced the risk of a disputed succession by establishing in the two Caesars the natural successors to the Augusti, and it satisfied the jealous pride of the rival armies by giving them *imperatores* of their own. The distribution of power between Diocletian and his colleagues followed those lines of division which the feuds of the previous century had marked out. The armies of the Rhine, the Danube and of Syria fell to the lot respectively of Constantius, Galerius and Diocletian, the central districts of Italy and Africa to Maximian.

Diocletian's Reforms.—In the new system the imperial authority was finally emancipated from all constitutional limitation and control and the last traces of its republican origin disappeared. The emperors from Diocletian onwards were autocrats in theory as well as in practice. This avowed despotism Diocletian, following in the steps of Aurelian, hedged round with all the pomp and majesty of Oriental monarchy. The final adoption of the title *dominus,* the diadem on the head, the robes of silk and gold, the replacement of the republican salutation of a fellow-citizen by the adoring prostration even of the highest in rank before their lord and master, were all significant marks of the new régime. In the hands of this absolute ruler was placed the entire control of an elaborate administrative machinery. Most of the old local and national distinctions, privileges and liberties which had once flourished within the empire had already disappeared under the levelling influence of imperial rule, and the process was now completed. Roman citizenship had, since the edict of Caracalla, ceased to be the privilege of a minority. Diocletian finally reduced Italy and Rome to the level of the provinces: the provincial land-tax and provincial government were introduced into Italy, while Rome ceased to be even in name the seat of imperial authority.[1] Throughout the whole area of the empire a uniform system of administration was established, the control of which was centred in the imperial palace. Between the civil and military departments the separation was complete. At the head of the former were the praetorian prefects, next below them the *vicarii,* who had charge of the *dioceses;* below these again the governors of the separate provinces (*praesides, correctores, consulares*), under each of whom was a host of minor officials. Parallel with this civil hierarchy was the series of military officers, from the *magistri militum,* the *duces* and *comites* downwards. In both there is the utmost possible subordination and division of authority. The subdivision of provinces, begun by the emperors of the 2nd century, was systematically carried out by Diocletian, and each official, civil or military, was placed directly under the orders of a superior; thus a continuous chain of authority connected the emperor with the meanest official in his service. Finally, the various grades in these two imperial services were carefully marked by the appropriation to each of distinctive titles, the highest being that of *illustris,* which was confined to the prefects and to the military *magistri* and *comites,* and to the chief ministers.

There can be little doubt that on the whole these reforms prolonged the existence of the empire, by creating a machinery which enabled the stronger emperors to utilize effectively all its available resources, and which even to some extent made good the deficiencies of weaker rulers. But in many points they failed to attain their object. Diocletian's division of the imperial authority among colleagues, subject to the general control of the senior Augustus, was effectually discredited by the 20 years of almost constant conflict which followed his own abdication (305-323). Constantine's partition of the empire among his three sons was not more successful in ensuring tranquillity, and in the final division of the East and West between Valens and Valentinian (364) the essential principle of Diocletian's scheme, the maintenance of a single central authority, was abandoned. The "tyrants," the curse of the 3rd century, were far from unknown in the 4th. The system, moreover, while it failed altogether to remove some of the existing evils, aggravated others. The already overburdened financial resources of the empire were strained still further by the increased expenditure necessitated by the substitution of four imperial courts for one, and by the multiplication in every direction of paid officials. The gigantic bureaucracy of the 4th century proved, in spite of its undoubted services, an intolerable weight upon the energies of the empire.

The Division of the Empire.—Diocletian and Maximian formally abdicated their high office in 305. Nineteen years later Constantine I. the Great, the sole survivor of six rival emperors, united the whole empire under his own rule. His reign of 14 years was marked by two events of first-rate importance—the recognition of Christianity as the religion of the empire and the building of the new capital at Byzantium. The alliance which Constantine inaugurated between the Christian Church and the imperial Government, while it enlisted on the side of the State one of the most powerful of the new forces with which it had to reckon, imposed a check, which was in time to become a powerful one, on the imperial authority. The establishment of the new "City of Constantine" as a second Rome paved the way for the final separation of East and West by providing the former for the first time with a suitable seat of government on the Bosporus. The death of Constantine in 337 was followed, as the abdication of Diocletian had been, by the outbreak of quarrels among rival Caesars. Of the three sons of Constantine who in 337 divided the empire between them, Constantine the eldest fell in civil war against his brother Constans; Constans himself was, ten years afterwards, defeated and slain by Magnentius; and the latter in his turn was in 353 vanquished by Constantine's only surviving son Constantius. Thus for the second time the whole empire was united under the rule of a member of the house of Constantine. But in 355 Constantius granted the title of Caesar to his cousin Julian and placed him in charge of Gaul, where the momentary elevation of a tyrant, Silvanus, and still more the inroads of Franks and Alamanni, had excited alarm. But Julian's successes during the next five years were such as to arouse the jealous fears of Constantius. In order to weaken his suspected rival the legions under Julian in Gaul were suddenly ordered to march eastward against the Persians (360). They refused; and when the order was repeated, replied by proclaiming Julian himself emperor and Augustus. Julian, with probably sincere reluctance, accepted the position, but the death of Constantius in 361 saved the empire from the threatened civil war. Julian's attempted restoration of pagan and in especial of Hellenic worships had no more permanent effect than the war which he courageously waged against the multitudinous abuses which had grown up in the luxurious court of Constantius. But his vigorous administration in Gaul undoubtedly checked the barbarian advance across the Rhine, and postponed the loss of the western provinces; on the contrary, his campaign in Persia, brilliantly successful at first, ended in his own death (363), and his successor, Jovian, immediately surrendered the territories beyond the Tigris won by Diocletian 70 years before. Jovian died on Feb. 17, 364; and on Feb. 26, Valentinian was acknowledged as emperor of the army at Nicaea. In obedience to the wish of the soldiers that he should associate a colleague with himself, he conferred the title of Augustus upon his brother Valens, and the division of the empire was at last effected—Valentinian became emperor of the West, Valens of the East. Valentinian maintained the integrity of the empire until his death (in 375), which deprived the weaker Valens of a trusted

[1] The seats of government for Diocletian and his three colleagues were Nicomedia, Mediolanum, Augusta Trevirorum, and Sirmium.

counsellor and ally, and was followed by a serious crisis on the Danube. In 376 the Goths, hard pressed by their new foes from the eastward, the Huns, sought and obtained the protection of the Roman empire. They were transported across the Danube and settled in Moesia, but, indignant at the treatment they received, they rose in arms against their protectors. In 378 at Adrianople Valens was defeated and killed, and the victorious Goths advanced eastwards to the very walls of Constantinople. Once more, however, the danger passed away. The skill and tact of Theodosius, who had been proclaimed emperor of the East by Gratian, conciliated the Goths; they were granted an allowance, and in large numbers entered the service of the Roman emperor. The remaining years of Theodosius's reign (382–395) were mainly engrossed by the duty of upholding the increasingly feeble authority of his western colleague against the attacks of pretenders. Maximus, the murderer of Gratian (383), was at first recognized by Theodosius as Caesar, and left in undisturbed command of Gaul, Spain and Britain; but, when in 386 he proceeded to oust Valentinian II. from Italy and Africa, Theodosius marched westwards, crushed him and installed Valentinian as emperor of the West. In the very next year, however, the murder of Valentinian (392) by Arbogast, a Frank, was followed by the appearance of a fresh tyrant in the person of Eugenius, a domestic officer and nominee of Arbogast himself. Once more Theodosius marched westwards, and near Aquileia decisively defeated his opponents. But his victory was quickly followed by his own illness and death (395), and the fortunes of East and West passed into the care of his two sons Arcadius and Honorius.

(b) From the Death of Theodosius to the Extinction of the Western Empire (395–476).—Through more than a century from the accession of Diocletian the Roman empire had succeeded in holding at bay the swarming hordes of barbarians. But, though no province had yet been lost, as Dacia had been lost in the century before, and though the frontier lines of the Rhine and the Danube were still guarded by Roman forts and troops, there were signs in plenty that a catastrophe was at hand.

From all the writers who deal with the 4th century we have one long series of laments over the depression and misery of the provinces.[1] To meet the increased expenditure necessary to maintain the legions, to pay the hosts of officials and to keep up the luxurious splendour of the imperial courts, not only were the taxes raised in amount but the most oppressive and inquisitorial methods were adopted in order to secure for the imperial treasury every penny that could be wrung from the wretched taxpayer. The results are seen in such pictures as that which the panegyrist Eumenius draws of the state of Gaul (306–312) under Constantine, in the accounts of the same province under Julian 50 years later, in those given by Zosimus early in the 5th century, and in the stringent regulations of the Theodosian code, dealing with the assessment and collection of the taxes. Among the graver symptoms of economic ruin were the decrease of population, which seriously diminished not only the number of taxpayers, but the supply of soldiers for the legions; the spread of infanticide; the increase of waste lands whose owners and cultivators had fled to escape the tax collector; the declining prosperity of the towns; and the constantly recurring riots and insurrections, both among starving peasants, as in Gaul, and in populous cities like Antioch. The distress was aggravated by the civil wars, by the rapacity of tyrants, such as Maxentius and Maximus, but above all by the raids of the barbarians, who seized every opportunity afforded by the dissensions or incapacity of the emperors to cross the frontiers and harry the lands of the provincials. Constantine (306–312), Julian (356–360) and Valentinian I. (364–375) had each to give a temporary breathing-space to Gaul by repelling the Franks and Alamanni. Britain was harassed by Picts and Scots from the north (367–370), while the Saxon pirates swept the northern seas and the coasts both of Britain and Gaul. On the Danube the Quadi, Sarmatae, and above all the Goths, poured at intervals into the provinces of Pannonia and Moesia, and penetrated to Macedon and Thrace. In the East, in addition to the

[1]Rostovtzeff, *Social and Economic History of Rome*, ch. 12.

constant border feud with Persia, we hear of ravages by the Isaurian mountaineers, and by a new enemy, the Saracens.

Even more ominous of coming danger was the extent to which the European half of the empire was becoming barbarized. The policy which had been inaugurated by Augustus himself of settling barbarians within the frontiers had been taken up on a larger scale and in a more systematic way by the Illyrian emperors of the 3rd century, and was continued by their successors in the 4th. In Gaul, in the provinces south of the Danube, even in Macedon and Italy, large barbarian settlements had been made—Theodosius in particular distinguishing himself by his liberality in this respect. Nor did the barbarians admitted during the 4th century merely swell the class of half-servile *coloni*. On the contrary, they not only constituted to an increasing extent the strength of the imperial forces, but won their way in ever-growing numbers to posts of dignity and importance in the imperial service. Under Constantine the palace was crowded with Franks. Julian led Gothic troops against Persia, and the army with which Theodosius defeated the tyrant Maximus (388) contained large numbers of Huns and Alans, as well as of Goths. The names of Arbogast, Stilicho and Rufinus are sufficient proof of the place held by barbarians near the emperor's person and in the control of the provinces and legions of Rome; and the relations of Arbogast to his nominee for the purple, Eugenius, were an anticipation of those which existed between Ricimer and the emperors of the latter half of the 5th century.

Barbaric Invasions.—It was by barbarians already settled within the empire that the first of the series of attacks which finally separated the western provinces from the empire and set up a barbaric ruler in Italy was made, and it was in men of barbarian birth that Rome found her ablest and most successful defenders. The Visigoths whom Alaric led into Italy had been settled south of the Danube as the allies of the empire since the accession of Theodosius. But, like the Germans of the days of Caesar, they wanted land for their own, and Alaric aspired to raise himself to the heights which had been reached before him by the Vandal Stilicho at Ravenna and the Goth Rufinus at Constantinople. The jealousy which existed between the rulers of the western and eastern empires furthered his plans. In the name of Arcadius, the emperor of the East, or at least with the connivance of Arcadius's minister Rufinus, he occupied the province of Illyricum, and from thence ravaged Greece, which, according to the existing division of provinces, belonged to the western empire. Thence in 396 he retreated before Stilicho to Illyricum, with the command of which he was now formally invested by Arcadius; he thus gained a base of operations against Italy. In 400 he led his people, with their wives and families, their wagons and treasure, to seek lands for themselves south of the Alps. But in this first invasion he penetrated no farther than the plains of Lombardy, and after the desperate battle of Pollentia (402 or 403) he slowly withdrew from Italy, his retreat being hastened by the promises of gold freely made to him by the imperial Government. Not until the autumn of 408 did Alaric again cross the Alps. Stilicho was dead; the barbarian troops in Honorius's service had been provoked into joining Alaric by the anti-Teutonic policy of Honorius and his ministers, and Alaric marched unopposed to Rome. The payment of a heavy ransom, however, saved the city. Negotiations followed between Alaric and the court of Ravenna. Alaric's demands were moderate, but Honorius would grant neither lands for his people nor the honourable post in the imperial service which he asked for himself. Once more Alaric sat down before Rome, and the citizens were forced to agree to his terms. Attalus, a Greek, the prefect of the city, was declared Augustus, and Alaric accepted the post of commander-in-chief. But after a few months Alaric formally deposed Attalus, on account of his incapacity, and renewed his offers to Honorius. Again they were declined, and Alaric marched to the siege and sack of Rome (410). His death followed hard on his capture of Rome. Two years later (412) his successor Ataulf led the Visigoths to find in Gaul the lands which Alaric had sought in Italy. It is characteristic of the anarchical condition of the West that Ataulf and his Goths should have fought for Honorius in Gaul against the tyrants and in Spain against the Vandals, Suebi and Alani; and it was with the consent of Honorius that in 419 Wallia, who had followed Ataulf as king of the Visigoths, finally settled with his people in south-western Gaul and founded the Visigothic monarchy.

It was about the same period that the accomplished fact of the division of Spain between the three barbarian tribes of Vandals, Suebi and Alani was in a similar manner recognized by the paramount authority of the emperor of the West. These peoples had crossed the Rhine at the time when Alaric was making his first attempt on Italy. A portion of the host led by Radagaisus actually invaded Italy, but was cut to pieces by Stilicho near Florence (405); the rest pressed on through Gaul, crossed the Pyrenees, and entered the as yet untouched province of Spain.

Honorius died in 423. With the single exception of Britain,[1] no province had yet formally broken loose from the empire. But over a great part of the West the authority of the emperors was now little more than nominal; throughout the major part of Gaul and in Spain the barbarians had settled, and barbarian states were growing up which recognized the supremacy of the emperor, but were in all essentials independent of his control.

The long reign of Valentinian III. (423–455) is marked by two events of first-rate importance—the conquest of Africa by the Vandals[2] and the invasion of Gaul and Italy by Attila. The Vandal settlement in Africa was closely akin in its origin and results to those of the Visigoths and of the Vandals themselves in Gaul and Spain. Here, as there, the occasion was given by the jealous quarrels of powerful imperial ministers. The feud between Boniface, count of Africa, and Aëtius, the "master-general" or "count of Italy," opened the way to Africa for the Vandal king Gaiseric (Genseric), as that between Stilicho and Rufinus had before set Alaric in motion westwards, and as the quarrel between the tyrant Constantine and the ministers of Honorius had paved the way for the Vandals, Suebi and Alani into Spain. In this case, too, land-hunger was the impelling motive with the barbarian invader, and in Africa, as in Gaul and Spain, the invaders' acquisitions were confirmed by the imperial authority which they still professed to recognize. In 429 Gaiseric, king of the Vandals, crossed with his warriors, their families and goods, to the province of Africa, hitherto almost untouched by the ravages of war. Thanks to the quarrels of Boniface and Aëtius, their task was an easy one. The province was quickly overrun. In 435 a formal treaty secured them in the possession of a large portion of the rich lands which were the granary of Rome, in exchange for a payment probably of corn and oil. Carthage was taken in 439, and in the following year the Vandal kingdom was firmly established over a wide area in the ancient Roman realm.

Eleven years later (451) Attila invaded Gaul, but this Hunnish movement was in a variety of ways different from those of the Visigoths and Vandals. Nearly a century had passed since the Huns first appeared in Europe and drove the Goths to seek shelter within the Roman lines. Attila was now the ruler of a great empire in central and northern Europe and, in addition to his own Huns, the German tribes along the Rhine and Danube and far away to the north owned him as king. He confronted the Roman power as an equal; and, unlike the Gothic and Vandal chieftains, he treated with the emperors of East and West as an independent sovereign. His advance on Gaul and Italy threatened, not the establishment of one more barbaric chieftain on Roman soil, but the subjugation of the civilized and Christian West to the rule of a heathen and semi-barbarous conqueror. But the Visigoths in Gaul, Christian and already half romanized, rallied to the aid of the empire against a common foe. Attila, defeated at Châlons by Aëtius, withdrew into Pannonia (451). In the next year he overran Lombardy, but penetrated no farther south, and in 453 he died. With the murder of Valentinian III. (455) the western branch of the house of Theodosius came to an end, and

the next 20 years witnessed the accession and deposition of nine emperors.

The End.—Under the three months' rule of Maximus, the Vandals under Gaiseric invaded Italy and sacked Rome. From 456–472 the actual ruler of Italy was Ricimer, the Suebe. Of the four emperors whom he placed on the throne, Majorian (457–461) alone played any imperial part outside Italy. Ricimer died in 472, and two years later a Pannonian, Orestes, attempted to fill his place. He deposed Julius Nepos and proclaimed as Augustus his own son Romulus. But the barbarian mercenaries in Italy determined to secure for themselves a position there such as that which their kinsfolk had won in Gaul and Spain and Africa. Their demand for a third of the lands of Italy was refused by Orestes, and they instantly rose in revolt. On the defeat and death of Orestes they proclaimed their leader, Odoacer the Rugian, king of Italy. Romulus Augustulus laid down his imperial dignity, and the court at Constantinople was informed that there was no longer an emperor of the West.

The installation of a barbarian king in Italy was the natural climax of the changes which had been taking place in the West throughout the 5th century. In Spain, Gaul and Africa barbarian chieftains were already established as kings. In Italy, for the last 20 years, the real power had been wielded by a barbarian officer. Odoacer, when he decided to dispense with the nominal authority of an emperor of the West, placed Italy on the same level of independence with the neighbouring provinces. But the old ties with Rome were not severed. The new king of Italy formally recognized the supremacy of the one Roman emperor at Constantinople, and was invested in return with the rank of "patrician," which had been held before him by Aëtius and Ricimer. In Italy too, as in Spain and Gaul, the laws, the administrative system and the language remained Roman. But the emancipation of Italy and the western provinces from direct imperial control, which is signalized by Odoacer's accession, has rightly been regarded as marking the opening of a new epoch. It made possible in the West the development of a Romano-German civilization; it facilitated the growth of new and distinct states and nationalities; it gave a new impulse to the influence of the Christian Church and laid the foundations of the power of the bishops of Rome.

Chronological Table of the Roman Emperors

B.C.	A.D.
27. Augustus.	244. Philip.
A.D.	249. Decius.
14. Tiberius.	251. Gallus.
37. Gaius.	253. Aemilianus.
41. Claudius.	260. { Valerian. Gallienus.
54. Nero.	268. Claudius.
68, 69. { Galba. Otho. Vitellius.	270. { Quintillus. Aurelian.
69. Vespasian.	275. Tacitus.
79. Titus.	276. Probus.
81. Domitian.	282. Carus.
96. Nerva.	283. Carinus and Numerian.
98. Trajan.	284. { Diocletian (Maximian associated with him, 286).
117. Hadrian.	
138. Antoninus Pius.	
161. Marcus Aurelius.	
180. Commodus.	305. Constantius and Galerius.
193. { Pertinax. Didius Iulianus. Septimius Severus.	311. { Licinius. Constantine I.
211. Caracalla.	324. Constantine I.
217. Macrinus.	337. { Constantine II. Constantius II. Constans.
218. Elagabalus.	
222. Alexander Severus.	
235. Maximinus.	350. Constantius II., sole emperor.
238. { The two Gordiani. Pupienus and Balbinus. Gordian III.	361. Julian.
	363. Jovian.

[1] The Roman troops were withdrawn from Britain by Constantine in 407; Mommsen, *Chron. min.* i, 465.
[2] Hodgkin vol. ii. bk. iii., chap. ii.; Gibbon ii. 400 *sqq.*; Jung, 183. The leading ancient authority is Procopius. *See* Ranke iv. (2) 285; Papencordt, *Gesch. d. Vandal. Herrschaft in Africa.*

Division of the Empire

West	East
A.D.	A.D.
364. Valentinian I.	364. Valens.
375. Gratian and Valentinian II.	379. Theodosius I.
383. Valentinian II.	
	392. Theodosius I.
395. Honorius.	395. Arcadius.
423. Valentinian III.	408. Theodosius II.
455. Maximus.	450. Marcian.
455. Avitus.	
457. Majorian.	457. **Leo I.**
461. Severus.	
467. Anthemius.	
472. Olybrius.	
473. Glycerius.	
474. Julius Nepos.	474. **Leo II.**
475. Romulus Augustulus.	

For subsequent events *see* ROMAN EMPIRE, LATER.

BIBLIOGRAPHY.—I. REPUBLICAN PERIOD: *Ancient Sources.* No history of Rome was written till Fabius Pictor issued his Annals about 200 B.C. His sources were inscribed laws, treaties and *senatus consulta,* a great many of which had been preserved, the annual priestly records of important events requiring thank-offerings and atonements—tablets that contained the lists of magistrates from the early republic—family records that did not go far back, some inscriptions on public buildings, some records of early colonies and oral tradition. Recent excavations indicate that the substructure of history which he gave from the early republic is fairly sound. But the traditional account of the regal period must be considered legendary, as indeed the Roman historians assumed that it was. The early historians, Fabius, Cincius, Acilius and Postumius, were all statesmen who seem to have written with a keen sense of responsibility. Those who followed, Cato the Elder, Calpurnius Piso, Cassius Hemina, Tuditanus and Fannius (who wrote of the Gracchan period), were also well informed, and wrote chiefly regarding contemporary events. At the same time the Greek statesman, Polybius, wrote an accurate history from the time of the first Punic War, valuable portions of which have survived. After the Gracchi, historians like Gnaeus Gellius began to insert family legends into the dry annals of the early period and he was followed by diffuse and rhetorical writers like Claudius Quadrigarius and Valerius Antias who composed popular accounts with little regard for accuracy. During the same period numerous apologetic autobiographies, memoirs and political pamphlets appeared which unduly coloured later accounts of Rome. Of all that we have mentioned (except Polybius) only brief fragments are extant, but the substance of all these books went into later histories that have survived. We have two valuable pamphlets of the amateur historian Sallust, the excellent commentaries of Julius Caesar (*q.v.*), the exceedingly important correspondence of Cicero (*q.v.*) as well as many of his speeches. In the Ciceronian period much valuable antiquarian work was done by men like Varro, Pomponius Atticus, and others which aided later writers to correct the mistakes of their predecessors.

In the Augustan age the materials accumulated by previous generations were worked up by compilers whose works are in some cases preserved. The work of Livy (*q.v.*) covered the history of Rome from its foundation to 9 B.C. in 142 books; of these only 35 are preserved in their entirety, while the contents of the rest are known in outline from an epitome (*periochae*) and from the compendia of Florus and later authors. Diodorus Siculus (*q.v.*) of Agyrium in Sicily followed the earlier annalists in the sections of his *Universal History* (down to Caesar) which dealt with Roman affairs; Dionysius Halicarnassensis (*q.v.*), in his *Roman Archaeology* (published in 7 B.C.), treated early Roman history in a more ambitious and rhetorical style, with greater fullness than Livy, whose work he seems to have used. Universal histories were also written in the Augustan age by Trogus Pompeius, whose work is known to us from the epitome of Justin (2nd century A.D.), and Juba, the learned king of Mauretania. Strabo (*q.v.*), whose *Geography* is extant, was the author of a continuation of Polybius's history (to 27 B.C.). The learning of the time was enshrined in the encyclopaedia of Verrius Flaccus, of which we possess part of Festus's abridgement (2nd century A.D.), together with an epitome of Festus by Paulus Diaconus (*temp.* Charlemagne). An official list of the consuls and other chief magistrates of the republic was inscribed on the walls of the Regia (rebuilt 36 B.C.), followed somewhat later by a similar list of *triumphatores;* the former of these is known as the *Fasti Capitolini* (C.I.L.I.², I. sqq.), since the fragments which have been recovered are preserved in the palace of the Conservatori on the Capitol.

Among writers of the imperial period who dealt with republican history the most important are Velleius Paterculus, whose compendium of Roman history was published in A.D. 30; Plutarch (*c.* A.D. 45-125), in whose biographies much contemporary material was

worked up; Appian, who wrote under the Antonines and described the wars of the republic under geographical headings (partly preserved) and the civil wars in five books, and Dio Cassius (*v. infra*), of whose history only that portion which deals with events from 69 B.C. onwards is extant.

The evidence of inscriptions (*q.v.*) and coins (*see* NUMISMATICS) begins to be of value during the last 150 years of the republic. A series of laws and *Senatus consulta* (beginning with the *Senatus consultum de Bacchanalibus,* 189 B.C.) throws light on constitutional questions, while the coins struck from about 150 B.C. onwards bear types illustrative of the traditions preserved by the families to which the masters of the mint (*triumviri monetales*) belonged.

MODERN AUTHORITIES.—The criticism of early Roman history begins with Giambattista Vico, 1725, and Louis de Beaufort, 1738, Niebuhr (1811-12) and Schwegler (1853-58) laid a sound foundation for the historical reconstruction of Theodore Mommsen, whose great history appeared in 1854-56. In Roman constitutional history Mommsen's *Staatsrecht* (1st ed. 1872-75) has not been superseded, though Lange's *Römische Alterthümer* (1856-71) is still serviceable. The soundest modern history of republican Rome (incomplete) is De Sanctis, *Storia dei Romani* (1907-   ). Heitland's *Roman Republic* (3 vols., 1909) is a fresh and independent work. Groebe's recent revision of Drumann is of value for its accumulation of references for the later period. Other briefer histories devoted to special topics are Greenidge, *History of Rome* vol. i. (for the Gracchan period); several volumes of Pais chiefly concerned with criticism; E. Meyer, *Caesars Monarchie und der Principat des Pompeius;* Homo, *L'Italie Primitive;* Holleaux, *Rome, la Grèce;* Beloch, *Römische Geschichte;* Holmes, *The Roman Republic* (chiefly military history of the late republic); Rostovtzeff, *Rome;* Frank, *Roman Imperialism* and *An Economic History of Rome;* and finally the chapters devoted to Rome in volumes vii.-ix. of the *Cambridge Ancient History.* (See VICO, GIOVANNI BATTISTA.)

II. IMPERIAL PERIOD: *Ancient Sources.*—The memoirs of Augustus as well as those of his contemporaries (Messalla, Agrippa, Maecenas, etc.) and successors (Tiberius, Agrippina the younger, etc.) have perished, but we possess the *Res gestae divi Augusti* inscribed on the walls of his temple at Ancyra (ed. Mommsen, 1883, Ramsay and Premerstein's *Mon. Antiochenum,* 1927, includes the fragments recently found at Antioch). Aufidius Bassus wrote the history of the civil wars and early empire, perhaps to A.D. 49, and this was continued by Pliny the Elder (*q.v.*) in 31 books, probably to the accession of Vespasian. These works and others were used by Cornelius Tacitus (*q.v.*), whose *Annals* (properly called *ab excessu divi Augusti*) and *Histories,* carried the story of the empire down to A.D. 96. Pliny's correspondence with Trajan about the affairs of Bithynia, which he administered in A.D. 111-113, is of great historical value. Suetonius (*q.v.*), who was for some time secretary of state to Hadrian, wrote biographies of the emperors from Julius Caesar to Domitian. Arrian, a Bithynian Greek, wrote on Rome's policy and wars in the East. Appian (*v. supra*) dealt with the wars waged under the early empire in the closing books of his work, which have not been preserved. Dio Cassius, a Bithynian, wrote a history of Rome to the death of Elagabalus in 80 books. We possess only epitomes and excerpts of the portion dealing with events from A.D. 46 onwards, except for parts of the 78th and 79th books, in which Dio's narrative of contemporary events is especially valuable. Herodian, a Syrian, wrote a history of the emperors from Commodus to Gordian III., which as the work of a contemporary is not without value. The *Historia Augusta* (see AUGUSTAN HISTORY), upon which we are obliged to rely for the history of the 3rd century A.D., consists in a series of lives of the emperors (including most of the pretenders to that title) from Hadrian to Carinus, professedly written by six authors, under Diocletian and Constantine. Modern criticism has shown that (at least in its present form) it is an unreliable compilation made in the latter half of the 4th century. The fragments of Dexippus, an Athenian who successfully defended his native town against Goths, throw much light on the barbaric invasions of the 3rd century. The most important historian of the 4th century was Ammianus Marcellinus, a native of Antioch and an officer in the imperial guard, who continued the work of Tacitus (in Latin) to the death of Valens. We possess the last 18 books of his history which cover the years A.D. 353-378. Two compendia of imperial history pass under the name of Aurelius Victor, the *Caesares,* or lives of the emperors from Augustus to Julian, and the *Epitome de Caesaribus* (not by the same author) which goes down to Theodosius I. Similar works are the *Breviarum* of Eutropius (secretary of state under Valens) and the still more brief epitome of Festus. The writings of the Emperor Julian and of the rhetoricians Libanius, Themistius and Eunapius—the last-named continued the history of Dexippus to A.D. 404—are of great value for the latter part of the 4th century A.D. They wrote as pagans, while the Christian version of events is given by the three orthodox historians Socrates, Sozomen and Theodoret, and the Arian Philostorgius, all of whom wrote in the 5th century. An imperial official, Zosimus, writing in the latter half of that century, gave a sketch of imperial history to A.D. 410; the latter part is valuable, being based on contemporary writings. The bishops Synesius and Palladius, who lived under Arcadius and Theodosius II., furnish valuable information as to their own times;

while the fragments of Priscus tell us much of Attila and the Hunnish invasions. Mention must also be made of the poets and letter-writers of the 4th and 5th centuries—Ausonius, Claudian, Symmachus, Paulinus of Nola, Sidonius Apollinaris, Prudentius, Merobaudes and others—from whose writings much historical information is derived. Cassiodorus, the minister of Theodoric, wrote a history of the Goths, transmitted to us in the *Historia Gothorum* of Jordanes (*c.* A.D. 550), which gives an account of the earlier barbaric invasions. Several chronological works were compiled in the 4th and 5th centuries. It will suffice to name the *Chronology of Eusebius* (to A.D. 324), translated by Jerome and carried down to A.D. 378, and the *Chronography of A.D. 354,* an illustrated calendar containing miscellaneous information.

The codes of law, especially the *Codex Theodosianus* (A.D. 438) and the code of Justinian, as well as the army list of the early 5th century, known as the *Notitia Dignitatum,* possess great historical value. For the inscriptions of the empire, which are of incalculable importance as showing the working of the imperial system in its details, *see* INSCRIPTIONS; the coins (*see* NUMISMATICS) also throw much light on the dark places of history in the lack of other authorities. Egyptian papyri are not only instructive as to legal, economic and administrative history, but also contribute to our general knowledge of events. (*See* especially Mitteis-Wilcken, *Chrestomatie,* 1912, and bibliography in Rostovtzeff, *Social and Economic History of Rome,* 1926.) The *Zeitschrift für Papyrusforschung,* ed. by U. Wilcken, gives an account of progress in this branch of study.

MODERN AUTHORITIES.—Tillemont's *Histoire des empereurs* (6 vols., 1690–1738), supplemented by his *Mémoires,* furnished Gibbon with material for his *Decline and Fall of the Roman Empire* (1776–78), which has never been superseded as a history of the entire imperial period, and has been rendered adequate for the purposes of the modern reader by Prof. J. B. Bury's edition (1897–1900). The history of the empire has yet to be written in the light of recent discoveries. Mommsen's fifth volume (Eng. trans., as *Provinces of the Roman Empire,* 1886) is not a narrative, but an account of Roman culture in the various provinces. H. Schiller's *Geschichte der römischen Kaiserzeit* (1883–88) is a useful handbook. Rostovtzeff's *Social and Economic History of Rome* (1926) is very valuable for its thorough sifting of inscriptions and papyri, while Dessau's *Gesch. der römischen Kaiserzeit* (1924), two volumes of which have appeared, promises to give a good survey of political history. H. S. Jones, *The Roman Empire* (1908) and Chapot, *Le Monde romain* (1927) are brief but sound and independent. For the later period we have Seeck, *Gesch. des Untergangs der antiken Welt* (6 vols., 1897–1920), Bury's *History of the Later Roman Empire* (1889), beginning from A.D. 395, and *Constitution of the Later Empire* (1910), and T. Hodgkin's *Italy and her Invaders* (8 vols., 1880–99), which tells the story of the barbaric invasions at great length. The imperial constitution is described by Mommsen in the second volume of his *Staatsrecht* (*v. supra*); divergent views will be found in Herzog's *Geschichte und System der römischen Staatsverfassung* (1884–91); the working of the imperial bureaucracy is treated by O. Hirschfeld, *Die römischen Verwaltungsbeamten* (1905). The *Prosopographia Imperii Romani,* compiled by Dessau and Klebs (1897–98), is a mine of information, as is the new edition of Pauly's *Realencyklopädie der classischen Alterthumswissenschaft* (in progress). Other useful books are: Greenidge, *Roman Public Life* (1901); Abbott and Johnson, *Municipal Administration in the Roman Empire* (1926); Dill, *Roman Society in the Last Century* (1906), Paribeni, *Trajano* (1927); Mattingly, *Roman Coins* (1928). (H. F. P.; H. S.-J.; T. F.)

MEDIAEVAL HISTORY

The history of the city of Rome during the middle ages was overshadowed by the history of the papacy. The latter has left many documents; for the city there are very few, especially for the period before the 13th century. As the foundations were so ill-defined there was opportunity for historians to theorize on what the superstructure had been; and the theories were influenced by the ideas, patriotic or otherwise biased, held in the 19th century. One favourite theory was the existence of an aristocratic republic contending against the popes until overthrown by the popular revolution in 1143, when the commune arose. Of this aristocratic republic the consuls were thought to have been the heads, and the existence and functions of the senate were much discussed. This theory was held by some of the leading historians: Hegel, Gregorovius and Villari.

These views are no longer held. Some important documents have been discovered and made accessible by publication. Halphen and others whose works are cited in the bibliography have done much to elucidate the early history. Much still remains to be done, but it is probable that the analogies drawn in the past between the history of Rome and that of the other cities in Italy are misleading. The deserted Campagna surrounding the city

checked any notable increase of trade or industry and prevented the establishment of gilds on the footing that elsewhere made them the basis and support of a commune. Moreover, the Campagna was unhealthy and ill-fitted for agriculture. The population of the city was very small. There was no strong middle class among its citizens, whose leaders were usually rude, illiterate nobles. Only slowly did the forces which were at work elsewhere in Italy penetrate into the city and cause the rise of a belated commune. What part was played by the memory of the traditions of republican Rome is a mooted question. The city was styled *respublica;* the titles senator, consul, prefect, occur repeatedly; but it is necessary to be on one's guard against drawing inferences from the long-continued or revived use of old terms.

Gothic and Byzantine Rule.—The removal of the seat of empire to Constantinople effected a radical change in the political situation of Rome, but the civil administration remained unaltered. The Gothic rule merely superimposed upon the Roman social order a Teutonic stratum that never penetrated beneath its surface. The senate, the principal magistrates, both provincial and municipal, the prefect of the city, and the Roman judges enforcing the enactments of the Roman law, were all preserved. Hence there was no visible change in the constitution of the city. The wars of Belisarius and Narses against the Goths (A.D. 535–555) caused terrible slaughter and devastation in Italy, and finally subjected her to Constantinople. In place of a Gothic king she was ruled at first by a pretorian prefect and later by an exarch (first mentioned in 584), who had his seat of government at Ravenna. The pragmatic sanction (554), promulgating the Justinian code, separated the civil from the military power, and, by conferring on the bishops the authority over the provincial and municipal government, soon led to the increase of the power of the Church.

Roman institutions were altered; but their original features were still to be traced, and no heterogeneous element had been introduced. The dawn of a new epoch can be dated from the invasion of the Lombards (568–572). Their conquest of a large portion of Italy reduced the inhabitants almost to slavery. But, in the unsubdued parts of the country—namely, in Ravenna, Rome and the maritime cities—a very different state of things prevailed. The necessity for self-defence and the distance of the empire, now too weak to render any assistance, compelled the inhabitants to depend solely on their own strength. In Rome we behold the rapid growth of the papal power and the continual increase of its political influence. Not only the superintendence but often the nomination of public functionaries and judges was in the hands of the popes. And the accession to St. Peter's chair of a man of real genius in the person of Gregory I., surnamed the Great, marked the beginning of a new era. By force of individual character this pope was the true representative of the city, the born defender of Church and State. His ecclesiastical authority, already great throughout Italy, was specially great in the Roman diocese and in southern Italy. The offerings of the faithful had endowed the Church with enormous possessions in the province of Rome, in Sicily, Sardinia, and other parts. The administration of this property assumed the shape of a small government council in Rome. The use made by the pope of his revenues greatly contributed to the increase of his moral and political authority. When the city was besieged by the Lombards and the emperor left his army unpaid, Gregory supplied the required funds and thus made resistance possible. And when the defence could be no longer maintained he alone, by the weight of his personal influence and the payment of large sums, induced the Lombards to raise the siege. He negotiated in person with Agilulf and was recognized by him as the true representative of the city.

A prefect of Rome is not mentioned between 599 and 772, and then again there is silence until the time of the Ottos. It is impossible to say whether the office was discontinued. In the later days the prefect was an official of the pope, who had taken over the care of the aqueducts and the preservation of the city walls. There is also much doubt about the existence of a senate. We know that many senators had lost their lives in the long war. The pragmatic sanction of 554 did mention the senate, but this was the last formal recognition of it as a governing body; and, if we may trust a despairing cry of Gregory the Great, it had disappeared, or at least was reduced to a shadow.

The popes now make common cause with the people against the Lombards on the one hand and the emperor on the other. This alliance was cemented by the religious disputes of the East and the West; for Pope Gregory II. (715–731) opposed the celebrated edict of the iconoclastic emperor Leo the Isaurian, and Venice, Ravenna, the Pentapolis and Rome took up arms against the emperor and elected dukes of their own.

Duchy of Rome.—In the midst of these warlike tumults a new constitution was being set up in Rome. In 711 the *Liber Pontificalis* makes the first mention of the duchy of Rome, and we find the people struggling to elect a duke of their own. In the early days of the Byzantine rule the territory appertaining to the city was no greater than under the Roman empire; but, partly through the weakness of the government of Constantinople, and above all through the decomposition of the provinces under the Lombards, this dukedom was widely extended; its limits were always changing in accordance with the course of events. At the beginning of the 8th century it had almost the same extent, except on the north, that the papal states had in 1860–70.

In the provinces, the administrators of church lands were important personages, and exercised both judicial and political functions. It was very natural that the heads of this vast administration resident in Rome should have a still higher standing and, in fact, from the 6th century, their power increased to such an extent that in the times of the Franks they already formed a species of papal cabinet with a share and sometimes a predominance in the affairs of the republic. The pope was thus at the head of a large administrative body and, in addition, was possessed of enormous revenues. He considered himself the real representative of the Roman republic. Gregory II. (715–731) accepted in the name of the republic the submission of other cities and protested against the conquest by the Lombards of those already belonging to Rome. The empire was now powerless in Italy, while the advance of the Lombards was becoming more and more threatening; they seized Ravenna in 751, thus putting an end to the exarchate, and next marched towards Rome, which had only its own forces and the aid of neighbouring cities to rely upon. To avoid being conquered Stephen II. (752–757) appealed to Pippin, king of the Franks, and concluded an alliance with him. The pope consecrated Pippin king of the Franks and named him *patricius Romanorum.* This title was given to Pippin as defender of the Church, for the pope styled him at the same time *defensor* or *protector ecclesiae.* And the king pledged himself not only to defend the Church but also to wrest the exarchate and the Pentapolis from the Lombards and give them to the pope. Pippin brought an army (754–755) and fulfilled his promise. The pope accepted the donation in the name of St. Peter and as the visible head of the Church. Thus in 755 central Italy broke its connection with the empire; thus was inaugurated the temporal power of the papacy.

Charles the Great.—In the years immediately succeeding the popes vacillated in their policy but it was soon apparent that their hopes must be placed on renewed aid from the Franks in order to check the constantly threatened danger from the Lombards, who were seeking to recover the territory which they had lost and also to seize Rome. Adrian I. (772–795) besought the assistance of Charlemagne, who made a descent into Italy in 773, destroyed the Lombard kingdom, and seized the iron crown. Entering Rome in 774, he confirmed the donation of Pippin. The pope was now regarded and regarded himself as master of Rome; he always spoke of Rome and the Romans as "our city," "our republic," "our people." It is true that Charlemagne held the supreme power, but this power was only occasionally exercised in Rome. The pope was most tenacious of his own authority, made vigorous protest whenever rebels fled to Charlemagne or appealed to that monarch's arbitration, and contested the supremacy of the imperial officials in Rome. Yet the pope was no absolute sovereign, nor, in the modern sense of the term, did any then exist. The Roman nobles were different from other aristocratic bodies elsewhere. Their power was chiefly derived from the high offices and large grants of money and land conferred on them by the popes. Every pope aggrandized his own kindred and friends, and these were the natural and often open adversaries of the next pontiff and his favourites. Thus the Roman nobility was powerful, divided, restless, and turbulent; the pope needed the support of an effective force for his own preservation; hence the necessity of creating an empire of the West.

Leo III. (795–816) further strengthened the ties between Charlemagne and the Church by sending the former the keys of the grave of St. Peter and the banner of Rome. Charlemagne had already joined to his office of patrician the function of high justice. The pope urged him to despatch an envoy to receive the oath of fealty from the Romans. Leo had antagonized the Romans, and during a procession had been attacked and barbarously maltreated (799). He fled to Charlemagne and returned guarded by his envoys; Charlemagne himself went to Rome in Nov. 800. As there was no one authorized to try a pope, Leo was permitted to clear himself of the charges against him by taking an oath on three altars. Then, on Christmas day, in St. Peter's, before an assemblage of Roman and Frankish lords, clergy, and people, the pontiff placed the imperial crown on Charlemagne's head and all proclaimed him emperor. Thus the new emperor was accepted by the Romans and consecrated by the pope. Yet Charlemagne was not sovereign of Rome; he possessed scarcely any regalia there, and was not in command of the army.

The death of Charlemagne in 814 was the signal for a further conspiracy of the nobles against the pope, who instantly put the ringleaders to death. He was severely blamed by the new emperor Louis for this violation of the imperial prerogative, as the emperor was determined to have his power recognized in Rome, and especially to insure that his assent must be secured for the election of a pope. To assure this he sent his son Lothair to be king of Italy, and the latter was crowned co-emperor in 823. In the following year Lothair promulgated a new constitution, to which Pope Eugenius II. (824–827) had to give his oath of adherence. The more direct power was to appertain to the pope—the supreme authority, presidency of the tribunals, and final judgment on appeal to the emperor. The new constitution also established the right of contending parties to select either the Roman or a Teutonic code for settlement of their disputes.

This is a convenient point to attempt a summary of the relations of the papacy with the City of Rome. By the donations and aid of the Franks it had become legal as well as actual ruler of the city. Charles the Great as emperor was the sovereign, but he never wished to take the place of the pope as chief of the Roman administration. The imperial *missus* of the constitution of 824 had as an associate a papal *missus,* and the two were ordered to refer all matters first to the pope; the emperor reserved a right of appeal to himself. But the power of the pope was secure only when he had outside support. At other times there was always danger that the nobles in the city would either revolt against him or, and more frequently, put in their own pope and use him for their own advantage. It must be noted, however, that the nobility as such never, before the middle of the 12th century, played a constitutional rôle in the administration of the city.

The City Officials.—The principal official was the prefect, who was the chief of police and judge in criminal matters. In civil cases he presided over the court and announced the decision, but was not himself a judge. He held his power from the pope except during periods of strife between an emperor and a pope, when the former sometimes usurped the right of appointment. Next in rank were the consuls of the Romans, or the dukes. They were nobles employed by the popes for special duties such as presiding over tribunals. Apparently the titles were applied to the same office, "duke" being used before the 11th century and "consul of the Romans" later, although in the period of transition the same man was sometimes styled both "duke" and "consul." Then there were "the seven judges," the *primicerius* and the *secundicerius,* who may be roughly described as first and under secretaries of state; the *arcarius,* or papal receiver; the *sacellarius,* or cashier;

the *protoscriniarius,* who was at the head of the papal chancery; the *primus defensor,* who was the advocate of the Church and administered its possessions; and the *nomenclator,* who pleaded the cause of widows, orphans and paupers. These men were called judges, a term then used generally for officials. (For example, the *judices de militia* were military officials and not judges at all.) These seven officials had apparently been created as need arose; the *primicerius* is mentioned in the 4th century, the *protoscriniarius* not until the ninth. They gradually ceased to be chiefs of administration and by the middle of the 11th century were thought of only as civil judges. For example, the *camerarius,* or treasurer, had taken over the duties of both the *arcarius* and *sacellarius.* In addition there were other civil judges, the *judices dativi,* who assisted the seven, but could not give judgment without the consent of some of "the seven ordinary judges." The latter were always members of the clergy; the *judices dativi* were not. For administrative purposes the city was divided into 12 districts. These 12 had succeeded the division of the city in the 6th century into 14 districts for civil administration and seven for ecclesiastical. Just when the change was made is uncertain, but Duchesne thinks it goes back to the time of the Byzantine rule. Finally it may be noted that "senator" was merely a title of honour carrying no power except when a usurping aristocrat bore the title. These statements as to the officials are based mainly on Halphen's study, which has done so much to correct former erroneous notions. Many details are still in doubt, but in general this outline applies to the period before the rise of the commune.

The fall of the Frankish empire left all Italy a prey to anarchy and torn by faction fights. The Saracens were advancing from the south, the Hungarians from the north. Anarchy was at its climax in Rome. The aristocracy gained strength and wrested fresh privileges from the pontiffs. Early in the 10th century Theophylact, who had been an official of the Sacred palace, was the chief of the Roman nobles. He was a senator, and his wife Theodora was styled "senatrix." She and her daughter Marozia were influential, and tradition has assigned to them both greater influence and more vice than can be proved by historical data. Marozia's husband was Alberic, the marquis of Spoleto. After Theophylact, Theodora and Alberic were all dead Marozia became the leader of the noble faction, and added to her power by marrying Guy, marquis of Tuscany. The pope was imprisoned by her and soon died, possibly murdered. Marozia was supreme, and raised her son to the papacy as John XI. When on Guy's death she married King Hugh of Italy (932), a revolt against her and her new husband was led by Alberic, her son; he was successful and became the ruler of the city. Of Marozia no more is heard.

Otto the Great.—Alberic, as "prince and senator of all the Romans," ruled Rome and the duchy until his death in 954. "His yoke was heavy on the Romans and on the Holy Apostolic See"; but the popes were docile and the nobles were kept in order by a stern hand. Alberic was so completely master of Rome that he may have dreamed of creating an hereditary dynasty. He gave his son the name of Octavian, and on his deathbed he made the nobles swear to elect Octavian pope at the next vacancy. The lad was then 16 years old, and the following year was elected pope with the name of John XII. His palace was the scene of scandalous licence, while his public acts were those of a tyrant. He desired to be both pope and prince, but utterly failed to be either. In 960, realizing the impossibility of maintaining his power without outside aid, he sought help from Otto I. and promised him the imperial crown. Otto vowed to defend the Church, to restore her territories, to refrain from usurping the power of the pope or the republic, and was crowned on Feb. 2, 962. Otto confirmed to the pope the territories granted by the Carolingians and even enlarged them, but he also revived the constitution of 824, by which the election of a pope required the imperial confirmation, and he reserved for himself the suzerainty over the papal territory as the Carolingians had done. John XII., finding a master in the protector he had invoked, joined the discontented nobles who were conspiring against the emperor. But the latter hastened to Rome in Nov. 963, assembled the clergy, nobles and heads of the people, and made them take an oath never again to elect a pope without his consent and that of his son. He also convoked a synod presided over by himself in St. Peter's, which judged, condemned and deposed Pope John and elected Leo VIII. (963–965), a Roman noble, in his stead. All this was done at the direct bidding of the emperor, who thus deprived the Romans of their most valued privilege, the right of choosing the pope. Moreover, Otto was hated as a foreign ruler and the clergy were resentful at the uncanonical deposition of a pope and the equally uncanonical election of a layman. On Jan. 3, 964, the Romans attacked the Vatican, where the emperor was lodged. The German knights repulsed them with much slaughter, but Otto departed in February, and John XII. returned with an army of followers and compelled the defenceless Leo VIII. to seek safety in flight. Soon afterwards Leo was deposed and excommunicated by a new synod, and many of his adherents were cruelly murdered. When on May 14, 964, John suddenly died, the Romans, amid violent struggles and tumults, elected Benedict V., and procured his consecration in spite of the emperor's veto. Otto appeared at the head of an army, besieged the city, reduced it by famine and, after holding a council which deposed Benedict, restored Leo VIII. to the papal throne.

The emperor's arbitrary exercise of power roused a long and obstinate resistance. When Leo VIII. died in 965, the imperial party elected John XIII. (965–972), who tried to create a party of nobles to offset the power of the party of Alberic. Upon this there was a general revolt. The nobles were led by Peter, prefect of Rome. The leaders of the people were 12 *decarconi,* a term of unknown derivation but probably indicating chiefs of the 12 regions. The new pope was seized and imprisoned; but the emperor quickly marched against Rome, and this was sufficient to produce a reaction which recalled the pope (Nov. 966), sent the prefect into exile and put several of the rebellious nobles to death. Shortly after the emperor sacked the city; many Romans were exiled, some tortured, others, including the 12 *decarconi,* killed.

The Crescentii.—Pope John XIII. was succeeded by Benedict VI. (973–974) and Otto I. by his son Otto II., a youth of 18. Thereupon the Romans, who had supported the election of another pope, and were in no awe of the new emperor, rose to arms under the command of Crescentius, a rich and powerful noble. They not only seized Benedict VI. by force, but strangled him in the castle of St. Angelo. The factions then successively elected popes who were either exiled or persecuted, and one of them is said to have been murdered. During this turmoil the anti-imperial party, led by Crescentius II., son of the Crescentius mentioned above, had taken possession of the government. Crescentius assumed the title of patrician and sought to imitate Alberic. Fortunately for him, the reigning pope was a detested tyrant, and the emperor Otto III. a child entirely guided by his mother. But the emperor was backed by a powerful party, and on coming to Rome in 996 was able, although only aged 15, to quell the rebellion, oust Crescentius from public life, and elect as successor to John XV. his own cousin, Gregory V. (996–999). This first German pope surrounded himself with compatriots, and by raising them to lofty posts even in the tribunals excited a revolt that drove him from the throne (Sept. 29, 996). Crescentius, being master of the castle of St. Angelo, resumed the title of patrician, expelled the German judges, reconstituted the government and created a new pope. The following year Otto III. came to Rome, and his party opened the gates to him. Although deserted by nearly all his adherents, Crescentius held the castle valiantly against its besiegers, until, on April 29, 998, he was forced to make terms, and the imperialists, violating their pledges, first put him to torture and then hurled him from the battlements.

Thus Otto III. was enabled to establish his mastery of Rome. He wished to reconstitute a Romano-Byzantine empire with Rome for his capital. Nevertheless he was German, and during his reign Germanic institutions made progress in Rome and many families of feudal barons arose. The Church made grants of lands, cities and provinces in the feudal manner, while the bishops, like feudal barons, became actual counts. Meanwhile the Roman barons were growing more and more powerful, and were neither submissive nor faithful to the emperor. On the contrary, they resented his attitude as a master of Rome, and, when he subjected Tivoli to the Holy See, attacked both him and the pope with so much vigour as to put both to flight (Feb. 16, 1001).

By the emperor's death in Jan. 1002 the family of the Ottos became extinct; the papacy then began to decline, and the nobles, divided into an imperial and an anti-imperial party, were again predominant. They reserved to themselves the office of patrician, and, electing popes from their own ranks, obtained enlarged privileges and power. John Crescentius was elected patrician; one of his kinsmen was invested with the office of prefect, and the new pope John XVIII. (1003–09) was one of his creatures. His power lasted for ten years, until his death in 1012. Pope Sergius IV. having died the same year, the count of Tusculum compassed the election of Benedict VIII. (1012–24), one of his own kin. This pope expelled the Crescentii, changed the prefect and reserved the title of patrician for Henry II. whom he consecrated emperor on Feb. 14, 1014. He also succeeded in placing his own brother, Romano, at the head of the republic with the title of "Senator of all the Romans." The prefect still retained his authority, and the emperor was by right supreme judge; but when a violent revolt broke out the emperor only stayed to suppress it and then went to Germany in disgust. The pope, aided by his brother, conducted the government with energy; he awed the party of Crescentius and waged war against the Saracens in the south. When he died in 1024 there was a repetition of the same events that had followed the death of Alberic, and with no less fatal consequences. Benedict's brother, Romano, head of the republic, was, although a layman, elected pope. He took the name of John XIX. (1024–33), and in 1027 conferred the imperial crown on Conrad the Salic. The latter abolished the Lotharian edict of 824 and decreed that throughout Rome and its territory justice should be administered solely by the Justinian code.

The Three Rival Popes.—John XIX. was succeeded by his nephew, Benedict IX. (1033–45), whose brother became head of the republic. Thus Church and State assumed the aspect of hereditary possessions in the powerful house of the counts of Tusculum. The vices and excesses of Benedict were so monstrous that he was driven from the city and Sylvester III. elected by his opponents. Benedict still had some support and succeeded in driving out Sylvester; then, finding his position untenable, he sold the papacy to a reformer who took the name of Gregory VI. Benedict soon attempted to regain his office, and in 1045 three popes were struggling for the tiara in the midst of scandal and anarchy. The streets and neighbourhood of Rome swarmed with thieves and assassins; pilgrims were plundered; citizens trembled for their lives, and petty barons threatened the rival popes, who were obliged to defend themselves by force. This state of things lasted until Henry III. came to re-establish order. He summoned a synod which deposed the three popes, and then, with the consent of the Romans, assuming the right of election, proposed a German, Clement II., who was consecrated at Christmas 1046. Henry III. was then crowned, and also took the title of patrician.

Henry III. procured the election of four German popes in succession. But the fourth German pope, Victor II., died in 1057, and Henry III. had been succeeded in 1056 by the young Henry IV. under the regency of a weak woman, the empress Agnes. The nobles by violence and bribery brought about the election of Benedict X. The cardinals were opposed to him and, fleeing from the city, elected Nicholas II. (1059–61). This pope could only enter Rome when escorted by the troops of Godfrey of Tuscany. When Nicholas died the nobles, assisted by some Lombard bishops, elected Honorius II. and sought aid from the German king, while the cardinals chose Alexander II. (1061–73). Although supported by an armed force of Normans, the latter had to fight his way into Rome, whither Honorius II. soon followed and won a battle against the forces of Alexander II. with much slaughter. Both candidates were compelled to withdraw from the city until their claims were settled by the German court. Strife continued, but Alexander II. finally was recognized as pope and attempted to reform the church, though he had little power in the city.

At Alexander's funeral Hildebrand was seized by the crowd and acclaimed as pope. The cardinals who were favourable to him, hastened to go through the form of an election in order to give a legal warrant to what had been done by popular violence; he chose the name of Gregory VII. (1073–85) and secured recognition from Henry IV. Gregory confirmed his predecessor's decrees against simoniacal and non-celibate priests and forbade the clergy to receive investiture at the hands of laymen. As the high ecclesiastical dignitaries held much territory and were also high officials of the empire, this decree was certain to cause a fierce contest between the emperor and the pope. Some of the nobles had already shown their hostility to Gregory; at Christmas 1075 the prefect Cencius and other nobles seized Gregory while he was celebrating mass in Santa Maria Maggiore and dragged him away to imprisonment. The people were incensed at this outrage and fear of popular wrath compelled Cencius to release Gregory. About the same time Henry IV., exasperated by a letter in which Gregory had sharply rebuked him for his sins, declared Gregory deposed from the papacy, and Gregory in turn decreed the excommunication and deposition of the emperor. That monarch afterwards made submission to Gregory at Canossa (1077), then again turned against him and was again excommunicated. In 1081, with his anti-pope Clement III., he besieged Rome in vain. He was equally unsuccessful in each of the two following years, but at last forced his way into the city (March 1084) and compelled Gregory to seek refuge in the castle of St. Angelo. The emperor, as master of Rome, procured the consecration of Clement III., by whom he was crowned in turn. He then attacked and seized the capitol and assaulted the castle of St. Angelo in the hope of capturing the pope. But Robert Guiscard brought his Norman army to the rescue. Emperor and anti-pope fled; the city was taken, the pope liberated, and Rome was brutally sacked for three days by the Normans. After this Gregory, broken with grief and hated by the Romans, had to go away with the Normans and died at Salerno on May 25, 1085.

Victor III. was elected only after an interval of a year and reigned only a short time. He was consecrated in St. Peter's but was unable to maintain his position in Rome. Urban II. (1088–99), the next pope elected, also had little power in Rome, as the city was usually in the hands of the supporters of the anti-pope. It was not until 1096, when he had won prestige by preaching the crusade, that he could enter the city as its master, and even then the castle of St. Angelo was held by the followers of the anti-pope, until 1098.

Revolt Under Paschal II.—Pope Paschal II. (1099–1118) tried to rule the city through the faction of nobles who favoured him, but with little success, as the imperial party frequently had the upper hand. When Henry V. seized the pope in 1111 the people rose in his defence and forced Henry to leave the city; but under ordinary circumstances Paschal could not count on any hearty support. In 1116, when he wished to make one of the Pierleoni prefect, there was a bloody revolt and a rival was put in as prefect by the imperial partisans. Soon after this Henry V. came to Rome and Paschal had to flee. Later he returned with Norman troops but could not put down the revolt, and the opposition still held the capitol when Paschal died.

The cardinals met in haste and secretly elected Gelasius II. The election had scarcely been completed when Cencius Frangipani broke into the assembly, seized the pope and carried him bleeding to one of the Frangipani towers. As they had done when another Cencius had seized Gregory VII., the people of the 12 districts rose in their wrath and, led by the prefect (whose election Paschal had opposed), forced the Frangipani to give up their prisoner. The Frangipani fled to the emperor and he came to Rome. Gelasius had to flee to his native city of Gaeta, where he was safe under Norman protection. An anti-pope was chosen by the imperial party; but when Henry left Rome Gelasius was able to return, although the anti-pope was also in Rome and a new revolt threatened the life of Gelasius. Consequently he fled to France, where he died in 1119, having been pope a year and a few days.

Calixtus was next chosen and restored peace. The Frangipani succeeded in electing his successor Honorius II. (1124–30), who was quietly accepted by the Roman people. At his death some of the cardinals chose Innocent II.; others, and the more numerous part, elected one of the Pierleoni, who took the name of Anaclete II. The greater part of the people now favoured the Pierleoni, and his rival, who was supported by the Frangipani, had to flee. He secured support in France and Germany, especially through the aid of Bernard of Clairvaux, and was finally recognized as pope almost everywhere except in Rome and among the Normans in Italy. Anaclete II. retained the upper hand in the city almost until the time of his death in 1138. In the following year Innocent attempted a military campaign against Roger of Sicily, but was captured by him and compelled to acknowledge his kingship, with which he had been invested by Anaclete. Humiliated, Innocent returned to Rome and there he was to suffer further humiliation.

Rise of the Commune.—Throughout upper and central Italy the cities were being organized as free and independent communes on a democratic basis. Their example was followed in the ancient duchy of Rome and almost in the immediate neighbourhood of the city. The same tendencies were at work in Rome. Gradually in the troubled times when the factions of the nobles were contending together and the papal rule was so weak, a lesser nobility had grown into power in the city, in alliance with the people, with whose interests they had much in common. They were irritated against the pope by his submission to the Normans and this irritation was greatly increased by his attitude toward Tivoli. In 1142 this city openly rebelled against the mother city, and the pope sent the Romans to subdue it. They were not only repulsed, but ignominiously pursued to their own gates. Afterwards, returning to the assault in greater numbers, they conquered the hostile town. Its defenders surrendered to the pope, and he immediately concluded a treaty of peace without consulting the people. The soldiery, still flushed with victory, were furious at this slight. They demanded the submission of Tivoli to the Roman people, as well as permission to demolish its walls and dwellings and expel its population. Innocent II. refused his consent and a revolution ensued. In 1143 the rebellious people rushed to the capitol, proclaimed the republic, reconstituted the senate, with the almost entire exclusion of the nobles, and declared the abolition of the temporal power. Just after this Innocent died.

The pontificates of the next two popes, together, lasted less than 17 months. The second, Lucius II. (1144–45), tried to withstand the revolution by seeking Norman aid and throwing himself into the arms of the feudal party, but this only precipitated the course of events. The people, after having excluded nearly all aristocrats from the senate, now placed at its head the noble Jordan Pierleoni, who had joined the revolutionary party. They named him patrician, and also conferred on him the judicial powers appertaining to the aristocratic and imperial office of prefect. The pope was requested to resign the temporal power, the regalia and every other possession and content himself with the tithes and offerings of the faithful. He indignantly refused, marched at the head of the nobles against the capitol, but was repulsed, and received a blow on the head from a stone, which is supposed to have caused his speedy death, Feb. 15, 1145. Eugenius III. was then elected (1145–53), but soon had to flee to Viterbo in quest of armed assistance, in consequence of the senate's resolve to prevent by force his consecration until he recognized the new state of things in the Eternal City.

It was at this time that Arnold of Brescia (q.v.) was absolved by the pope and ordered to make a pilgrimage to Rome. An arch-revolutionist, he began to preach and his eloquence brought him fame. But his influence on events has been greatly exaggerated in most accounts. The people had already formed an equestrian order, which was probably a mounted force of the lesser nobility, and also were fortifying the capitol. The revolution spread beyond the walls, several cities of the state proclaimed their independence, and the barons of the Campagna profited by the opportunity to act as independent sovereigns. Thus the whole domain of the Church was threatened with dissolution. The pope marched towards Rome with an army, but hoped to come to terms. The Romans in fact recognized his authority, and he in his turn recognized the republic. The office of patrician was abolished, and the prefect was revived. The senators received investiture from the pope, who returned to Rome at Christmas 1145.

The Commune Fully Constituted.—The commune now seems to have been fully constituted, so a short sketch will be given here of its more important features. The senate was drawn, at least in part, from the lower classes and the petty nobility, and this was the special characteristic of the new revolution. In 1144 there were 56 senators, but the number often varied. In 1151 there were 50; in 1163 only 25; in 1181 again 56, and still more in 1191. After that it was more usual to have only one or two senators and these were generally chosen from the aristocracy. From the few existing documents of the period we learn that the senators were divided into *senatores consiliarii* and ordinary senators. The former constituted a smaller council, which consulted with the head or heads of the republic on the more urgent and secret affairs of the State. The senate exercised its powers under the control of the council and parliament. The former was a deliberative assembly called together by the senate to discuss important affairs such as treaties or declarations of war. The councillors varied in number—at times nine, once as many as 84. Their advice was taken but not necessarily followed by the senate. The parliament was an assemblage of all the citizens. In it there was no discussion of the matters brought before it by the senate, but each matter was accepted or rejected by the people. Senators held office for only one year. They were elected usually by the whole people; but at times the pope was allowed to appoint an elector or electors to choose the senator or senators; in this latter case, however, the choice apparently had to be submitted to the popular assembly for ratification. The pope also was compelled to pay salaries to the senators and their officials.

The senate had usurped the right of coinage; and although by a treaty of 1188 it agreed to restore this right to the pope on condition that one-third of the money coined should be given to the senate, the pope did not take advantage of the retrocession and all the money was coined by the senate; Innocent III. even decreed that only senatorial coins should be used in the whole of the Campagna. The senate also seized for its own advantage the right of levying taxes on merchandise brought into the city. It also took over the appointment of judges, but in place of seven appointed a single Palatine judge for a term of three months. He was assisted by a *judex dativus*. Thus it is seen that while the pope still exercised certain rights he had actually lost control of the city.

The agreement with Pope Eugenius was of short duration. The revolution could not be checked; the Romans desired independence, and their spiritual lord fled to France, whence, in 1147, he proclaimed a new crusade, while the Romans were employed in demolishing Tivoli, banishing its inhabitants and waging war on other cities. Jordan Pierleoni was head of the republic, and Arnold, supported by the popular favour and the enthusiasm of the lower clergy, was preaching with even greater fervour than before. The new pope now re-entered Italy, proclaimed Arnold a schismatic, and advancing to Tusculum assembled an army in order to attack Rome. In this emergency the Romans applied to Conrad III., the first emperor of the house of Hohenstaufen; and their letters are expressive of Arnold's theories and his medley of ancient and modern, sacred and profane, ideas. "Rome," so they said, "is the fountain of the empire confided to you by the Almighty, and we seek to restore to Rome the power possessed by her under Constantine and Justinian. For this end we conquered and destroyed the strongholds of the barons who, together with the pope and the Normans, sought to resist us. These are now attacking us on all sides. Haste to Rome, the capital of the world, thus to establish thy imperial sway over the Italian and German lands." After long delay the king of the Romans replied to these appeals, stating that he would come "to re-establish order, reward the faithful and punish the rebellious." These words promised ill. In fact, Conrad had already arranged terms with the pope; but his life came to an end on Feb. 15, 1152.

Frederick Barbarossa.—He was succeeded by Frederick I., surnamed Barbarossa, who took no notice of letters urging him to come and receive the empire from the Roman people. In accordance with his design of subduing all the independent cities, he made an agreement with the pope, in which he vowed to give no truce to the Romans, but subject them to their spiritual lord, whose temporal power should be restored. The pope, on his side, promised to crown him emperor. Thereupon the people again rose to arms and broke off all negotiations with Eugenius III. Frederick was in command of a powerful army, and was no friend of half measures. To increase the gravity of the situation, an English pope, Adrian IV., was elected (1154-59), who was also a man of strong and resolute temper. In fact, even before he was able to take possession of the Lateran, he requested the Romans to banish Arnold, who was directing his thunders against the papacy. These utterances increased the wrath of Adrian, who, encouraged by the knowledge that Frederick and his host were already in Italy, at last launched an interdict against Rome. It was the first time that a pope had laid an interdict on the Eternal City. This put a summary stop to the religious life of the inhabitants and men's minds were seized with terror; a fierce tumult broke out. Thereupon the senators implored pardon; but Adrian demanded the expulsion of Arnold before consenting to raise the interdict. Arnold was therefore obliged to leave Rome, and, abandoned by all, was forced to wander from castle to castle, until given up to Frederick Barbarossa and then consigned by the latter to the papal legates. The pope in his turn gave the reformer into the hands of the prefect, who hanged his prisoner, burnt his body at the stake, and cast his ashes into the Tiber.

But the Romans would not give up their commune. Their envoys went to meet Frederick near Sutri, and made an address in the usual fantastic style on the privileges of the Roman people and its sole right to confer the imperial crown. Frederick indignantly cut short their harangue, and they had to depart full of rage. He then continued his march, and, entering Rome on June 18, 1155, was forthwith crowned in St. Peter's by the pope. Thereupon the Romans rushed to arms and made a furious attack on the Leonine city and the imperial camp. A desperate battle went on throughout the day; many Romans perished by the sword or by drowning, but their fellow-citizens made such determined preparations to continue the struggle that Frederick, on June 19, hastily retreated, or rather fled, together with the pope and the cardinals. The commune still survived. Its existence was in truth favourable rather than injurious to Frederick, but he had not yet discerned that his best policy would be to support the commune against the pope. The latter, with keener acumen, made alliance with the communes of Lombardy and encouraged them in their resistance to the emperor. Adrian IV. died in 1159, and the anti-imperial party elected Alexander III. (1159-81), who energetically opposed the pretensions of Frederick, but, having to struggle with three anti-popes successively raised against him by the imperial party, was repeatedly driven into exile. During these schisms the senate quietly carried on the government, administered justice and made war on some neighbouring cities and barons. An army comprising many nobles marched against Tusculum, but found it defended by several valiant officers and a strong band of German soldiery, who, on May 29, 1167, inflicted on the Romans so severe a defeat that it is styled by Gregorovius "the Cannae of the middle ages." Shortly afterwards the emperor arrived in Rome with his anti-pope Paschal III., and Alexander had to flee. Then, at last, Frederick came to terms with the commune, recognized the senate, which accepted investiture at his hands, re-established the prefecture as an imperial office, and bestowed it on John, son of Peter di Vico. He departed hastily, as a deadly fever broke out and decimated his army.

Concord between Pope and Commune.—Meanwhile Pope Alexander continued Adrian's policy with better success, however, for the Lombard cities had now formed a league and inflicted a signal defeat on the emperor at Legnano on May 29, 1176. One of the results of this battle was the conclusion of an agreement between the pope and the emperor, the latter resigning his pretensions on Rome and yielding all that he had denied to Adrian. By the Treaty of Venice (Aug. 1, 1177), the anti-pope was forsaken, Alexander III. recognized and hailed as the legitimate pontiff and the prefect of Rome was again to be nominated by the pope, to whom the emperor restored the temporal power, acknowledging him the independent sovereign of Rome and of the ecclesiastical State. Frederick's troops accompanied the pope to Rome, where the commune was forced to make submission to him. But, proudly conscious as it still was of its strength, its surrender wore the aspect of a voluntary concession, and its terms began with these words: "It has been decreed by the council and deliberation of the whole Roman people," etc. The senators, elected yearly in November, had to swear fealty to the pope. On his return to Rome Alexander received a solemn welcome from all. He died on Aug. 30, 1181. The fact that between 1181 and 1187 there were three popes always living in exile proves that the commune was by no means crushed. On Dec. 20, 1187, Clement III. (1187-91) made a solemn agreement with the government of the capitol before coming to Rome. And this peace or *concordia* had the air of a treaty between potentates of equal importance. Rome confronted the pope from the same standpoint from which the Lombard cities had confronted the emperor after Legnano. This treaty was confirmed on the last day of May 1188 (*Anno XLIV.* of the senate). The pope was recognized as supreme lord, and invested the senators with their dignity. Almost all the old pontifical rights and prerogatives were restored to him. The pope might employ the Roman militia for the defence of his patrimony, but was to furnish its pay. The rights of the Church over Tivoli and Tusculum were confirmed; but the commune reserved to itself the right of making war on those cities, and declared its resolve to dismantle and destroy the walls and castle of Tusculum. In this undertaking the pope was to co-operate with the Romans, even should the unhappy city make surrender to him alone.

From all this it is clear that the Church had been made independent of the empire, and that the commune, despite its numerous concessions, was by no means subject to the Church. The republic had no patrician nor any other imperial magistrate and preserved its independence even as regarded the pope, who merely granted investiture to magistrates freely chosen by the people and had no legislative nor administrative power in the city. His temporal dominion was limited to his great possessions, to his regalia, to a supreme authority that was very indefinite, and to a feudal authority over the barons of the Campagna and many cities of a State that seemed ever on the point of dissolution. The senate continued to frame laws, to govern, and to administer justice. The army carried on the wars of the commune, as we see by the tragic fate of Tusculum, which was razed to the ground on April 19, 1191. In consequence, the nobles, seeing that the commune remained firmly established, began to adhere to it and succeeded in obtaining admission to the senate. In fact, whereas since 1143 plebeians and petty nobles had prevailed in its ranks, nobles of ancient descent are now found outnumbering the knights and burghers. In 1191 this state of things caused a sudden popular outbreak which abolished the aristocratic senate and gave the headship of the commune to a single senator, of unknown origin. During the two years he remained in office this personage stripped the pope of his revenues, despatched *justitiarii* even to the provinces, and with the aid of the parliament and council promulgated laws and statutes. He was overthrown by a counter-revolution; John Capoccio of the party of the nobles became senator for two years, and had been succeeded by one of the Pierleoni when, in 1197, a fresh revolution re-established a senate of 56 members, chiefly consisting of feudal barons in high favour with Henry VI., who had revived the imperial faction in Rome. But this emperor's life ended the same year, and the pope's in 1198, and the new pontiff, Innocent III. (1198-1216), began to make war on the nobles, who were again masters of the commune. Their leader was the prefect Peter di Vico. Owing to the revolution of 1143, most of the prefectorial attributes were now vested in the senate; nevertheless, Peter still retained a tribunal of police both within and without the city, and derived great strength from the vast possessions of the Vico family, in which the office of prefect now became hereditary. Very soon after this, however, the independent municipal office lost its true character. Then the popes made a point of according great pomp and dignity to this nominal prefect, in order to overshadow the senator, who still represented the independence of the republic.

Innocent III., dissatisfied with this state of things, contrived by bribing the people to arrogate to himself the right of appointing a commissioner to elect the senator, who had to swear fealty and submission to the pope, and also that of nominating the provincial *justitiarii,* formerly chosen by the government of the capitol. This was a deadly blow to the commune, for the principal rights of the people—*i.e.,* the election of pope, prefect, and senate—were now lost. The general discontent provoked fresh revolutions, and the people made a loud outcry for a senate of 56 members; the pope, making a virtue of necessity, caused that number to be chosen by 12 *mediani* specially named by him for the purpose. Even this did not calm the popular discontent, and when, six months later, the pope again had a single senator elected the Romans rose to arms and in 1204 formed a government of "Good Men" (*Buoni Uomini*) in opposition to that created by the pope. But an amicable arrangement being concluded, the pope once more had 56 senators nominated; and when, soon after, he again reduced them to one, the people were too weary to resist (1205).

Pretensions of the Commune.—On Nov. 22, 1220, Honorius III. (1216–27) conferred the imperial crown on Frederick II., who confirmed to the Church the possession of her former States, of those bequeathed to her by Countess Matilda, and even of the March of Ancona. But it was soon seen that he sought to dominate all Italy, and was therefore a foe to be dreaded. The successor of Honorius, Pope Gregory IX. (1227–41), was speedily insulted and put to flight by the Ghibelline nobles, whose courage had revived, and the republic began to subdue the Latian cities on its own account. Peace was several times made and unmade by pope and people; but no enduring harmony was possible between them, since the former wished to subject the entire State to the Church, and the latter to escape from the rule of the Church and hold sway over "the universal land from Ceprano to Radicofani" formerly belonging to the duchy. Accordingly, the Roman people appointed judges, imposed taxes, issued coin, and made the clergy amenable to secular tribunals. In 1234 the senator Luca Savelli published an edict declaring Tuscia and Campania territories of the republic, and sent judges thither to exact an oath of obedience. He also despatched the militia to the coast, where it occupied several cities and erected fortresses; and columns were raised everywhere inscribed with the initials S.P.Q.R. The pope, unable to prevent but equally unable to tolerate these acts, fled from Rome, hurling his anathema against Savelli and his associates. The Romans sacked the Lateran and the houses of many cardinals and marched on Viterbo, but were driven back by the papal troops. The people had to make peace and submission in 1235, and were obliged to give up their pretensions of subjecting the clergy to ordinary tribunals and the urban territory to the commune. Thus matters were virtually settled on the footing established by Innocent III., thanks to the aid given to the pope by Frederick II., who had previously aided the rebellion.

Meanwhile the struggle between Frederick II. and the pope was once more renewed. The nobility was again split into a Guelph party headed by the Orsini and a Ghibelline party under the Colonna. In 1238 it was deemed advisable to elect two senators instead of one, in the hope of conciliating both factions by simultaneously raising them to power. Afterwards one only was elected, alternately an Orsini and a Colonna, then again two, and so on. But all these changes failed in their aims, since the struggle between emperor and pope exasperated party feeling in Rome. Frederick desired to emancipate the State from the Church, but he was opposed to the communal democracy, which was then the chief strength of the secular State in Italy. Thus, although he had a strong party in Rome, it seemed to dissolve at his approach, inasmuch as all feared that he might abolish the statutes and liberties of the commune. In fact, when he advanced towards Rome on the death of Gregory IX. in 1241, he was energetically repulsed by the people, and later even by Viterbo, a city that had always been faithful to him. After he had withdrawn, his adherents gained strength and put to flight his oppo-

nent, Innocent IV. (1243–54), the newly elected pope, who then from Lyons hurled an excommunication against him. On Frederick's death in Dec. 1250 the pope instantly returned to Rome with the set purpose of destroying the power of the Hohenstaufens.

Brancaleone.—The commune meanwhile being harassed by the factiousness of the nobility in 1252 decided on the election of an alien senator armed with ample powers, precisely as other communes gave the government into the hands of a podesta. Accordingly a Bolognese noble, Brancaleone degli Andalo, count of Casalecchio, and a Ghibelline, was invited to Rome. Before accepting office he insisted on making definite terms; he desired to hold the government for three years; and this although contrary to the statutes, was granted. Further, to insure his personal safety, he demanded that many scions of the noblest Roman houses should be sent as hostages to Bologna; and to this also the commune consented. Then, in Aug. 1252, he came with his judges and notaries, made oath to observe justice and the laws, and began to govern. He was head of the republic in peace and in war, supreme judge and captain in chief. He nominated the podestas of subject territories, despatched ambassadors, issued coin, concluded treaties, and received oaths of obedience. He convoked the council as seldom as was possible, although he frequently assembled the people in parliament. The chief complaint made against him was of undue severity in the administration of justice. He rendered the clergy amenable to secular tribunals, subdued the neighbouring cities of Tivoli, Palestrina, etc., and commanded in person the attacking force. But his greatest energy was directed to the repression of the more turbulent nobles, hanging some and banishing others. He recognized the expediency of winning the popular favour and was the first senator to add to his title that of "captain of the people." He befriended the people by promoting the organization of gilds, 13 in all. The admission of their heads into the councils of the commune in 1267 shows how far their interests had been promoted by Brancaleone.

When, on the expiration of his three years' term of office, Brancaleone's re-election was proposed, his enemies rose against him, accused him, threw him into prison, and vehemently protested against the continuance of "foreign tyranny." His life was spared only on account of the hostages sent to Bologna. The next senator chosen was a Brescian Guelph, Emanuele de Madio, a tool of the nobles, who were masters of the situation. But soon afterwards, in 1257, the people rose in revolt, drove the nobles from power, put the pope to flight, and recalled Brancaleone for another three years' term. He ruled more sternly than before, hung several nobles, and made alliance with Manfred, the representative of the Swabian party in Italy. This rendered him increasingly odious to the pope and procured his excommunication. But, disregarding the thunders of the Church, he marched against Anagni, the pope's birthplace, and Alexander was quickly obliged to humiliate himself before the senator of Rome. Brancaleone next set to work to destroy the fortified towers of the nobility, and in razing them to the ground ruined many of the adjacent dwellings. In 1258 Brancaleone died. Thus ended the career of a truly remarkable statesman. He was succeeded by his uncle, Castellano degli Andalo, who only retained office until the following spring (1259). Then the people, being bribed by the pope, joined with the nobles and overthrew him. His life too was saved by having followed his nephew's shrewd plan of sending hostages to Bologna. Two senators of Roman birth were next elected.

Charles of Anjou Senator.—At this period the fall of the empire had induced many Italian republics to seek strength by placing their governments in the hands of some prince willing to swear respect for their laws and to undertake their defence. In Rome the Guelphs and Ghibellines proposed various candidates for this office, and after many fierce quarrels ended by electing a committee of *boni homines,* charged with the revision of the statutes, reorganization of the city, and choice of a senator. This committee sat for more than a year without nominating anyone; then, the Guelph party being predominant, the majority agreed on the election as senator of Charles of Anjou, who after a long delay became senator, but held office for less than a year. Two Romans were elected in his stead, but soon fell out with the pope, because the Guelph nobles again tried to exercise tyranny. The people, however, profited by these disturbances to rise on their own account, and formed a democratic government of 26 *boni homines* with Angelo Capocci, a Ghibelline, as its captain. By this government Don Henry, son of Ferdinand III., of Castile, was elected senator (1267). The rule of the new senator was very energetic, for he kept down the clergy, subdued the Campagna, persecuted the Guelph nobles, made alliance with the Tuscan Ghibellines, forcibly drove back the troops of King Charles, who was advancing towards Rome, and gave a splendid reception to Conradin. But the battle of Tagliacozzo (Aug. 23, 1268), followed by the murder of Conradin, proved fatal to the Ghibelline party. Charles was re-elected senator immediately after the battle, and the pope confirmed his powers for a term of ten years.

In 1278, the ten years' term having expired, the pope, after declaring that he left to the people the right of electing the senator, promulgated a new constitution (July 18, 1278), which, while confirming the rights of the Church over the city, prohibited the election of any foreign emperor, prince, marquis, count or baron as senator of Rome. Thus the Colonna, Savelli, Orsini, Annibaldi and other Roman nobles again rose to power, and the republic was again endangered and plunged into disorder. The Romans then gave the reconstitution of the city into the pope's hands by yielding to him the right of nominating senators. So Nicholas proceeded to name senators, alternating a Colonna with an Orsini, or simultaneously choosing one of each faction. The same power over the senate was granted with the same restriction to Martin IV. (1281–85), and he at once re-elected Charles of Anjou. Thus, greatly to the disgust of the Romans, the capitol was again invaded by French vicars, notaries, judges and soldiery. But the terrible blow dealt at Charles's power by the Sicilian Vespers (March 31, 1282) resounded even in Rome. The Orsini, backed by the people, rose in arms, massacred the French garrison, and quickly re-established a popular government. John Cencio, a kinsman of the Orsini, was elected captain and defender of the people, and ruled the city with the co-operation of the senator and a council of priors of the gilds. This government was of brief duration, for, although the pope had professed his willingness to tolerate experiment, he quickly arranged fresh terms, and, forsaking Charles of Anjou, again nominated two Roman senators. Pope and king both died in 1285, and Nicholas IV. (1288–92), also holding sway over the senate, favoured the Colonna in order to curb the growing mastery of the Orsini. But thus there were two powerful houses instead of one. In fact, John Colonna, when elected senator, ruled from the capitol as an independent sovereign, conducted in person the campaign against Viterbo, and subjected that city to the republic on May 3, 1291.

Boniface VIII. (1294-1303) tried to reduce the power of the Colonna family and succeeded for a time in exercising more power in Rome than any of the recent popes. This was due largely to the Jubilee which brought thousands of pilgrims to Rome. The citizens wished to profit by the gold which the pilgrims brought and for that reason were ready to postpone their rivalries.

Removal of the Popes to Avignon.—When the popes removed to Avignon the city was left almost entirely to govern itself. There was the same strife between the "ins" and the "outs," who persisted in using the names Guelphs and Ghibellines, although these names had lost their old meaning since the fall of the Hohenstaufens. The commune employed its freedom in trying to hold its own against the nobles, whose power was much lessened by the absence of the pope, and endeavoured to gain fresh strength by organizing the 13 regions. Accordingly, in 1305, a captain of the people was elected with 13 elders and a senator, Paganino della Torre, who governed for one year. The pope was opposed to these changes at first, but in 1310 he issued a brief granting Rome full permission to select its own form of government. Thus, the first pope in Avignon restored the rights of the Romans. The latter still considered Rome the Eternal City, the source of all law, and the only natural seat of the spiritual and temporal government of the world. To their republic, they thought, appertained a new and lofty destiny. In 1312, in spite

of the opposition of the nobles, they insisted upon the coronation of the emperor Henry VII. In the same year, after a brief interval of rule by the nobles, the popular party again got the upper hand, only to be overthrown the following year.

Then the pope appointed King Robert of Naples as senator. Affairs took a fresh turn under Pope John XXII. (1316–34). Rome was still ruled by the vicars of King Robert; but, owing to the continued absence of the pope, matters grew daily worse. Trade and industry declined, revenue diminished, the impoverished nobles were exceedingly turbulent, deeds of murder and violence occurred on all sides; even by day the streets of the city were unsafe. Hence there was universal discontent. Accordingly the Italian Ghibellines hailed Louis the Bavarian as they had previously hailed Henry. The Roman people were roused to action, and, driving out the representatives and partisans of King Robert, in the spring of 1327 seized on the castle of St. Angelo and again established a democratic government. Regardless of the reproofs of the pope, they elected a haughty Ghibelline, Sciarra Colonna, captain of the people and general of the militia, with a council of 52 *popolani,* four to each region. Then ranged under the standards of the militia, the Romans gave chase to the foes of the republic, and Sciarra, returning victorious, ascended to the capitol, and invited Louis the Bavarian to Rome.

Encircled by a crowd of heretics, reformers and Minorite brethren, Louis convoked a parliament on the capitol, asking that the imperial crown might be conferred upon him by the people, from whom alone he wished to receive it. And the people proclaimed him their captain, senator and emperor. On Jan. 17, his coronation took place in St. Peter's. But, as he had neither money nor practical sense, his method of taxation and the excesses committed by himself and his over-excited philosophers speedily aroused the popular discontent. His ecclesiastical vicar, Marsilius of Padua, and John Janduno placarded the walls with insulting manifestos against the pope, whom the Minorites stigmatized as a heretic and wished to depose. The emperor decreed that henceforth the popes must reside in Rome—that if, when invited, they should fail to come they would be thereby held deposed from the throne. As a logical consequence, proceedings were immediately begun for the election of a new pope, Nicholas V., who on May 12 was proclaimed by the popular voice in St. Peter's square, and received the imperial sanction. But this ephemeral drama came to an end when the emperor departed with his anti-pope on Aug. 4. This caused the immediate downfall of the democratic government. A new parliament cancelled the emperor's edicts, and had them burnt by the public executioner. Meanwhile King Robert was again supreme in Rome, and being re-elected senator appointed vicars there as before. Anarchy reigned.

After the election of Benedict XII. (1334–42) confusion reached so great a pitch that, on the expiration of Robert's senatorial term, the Romans named 13 heads of regions to carry on the government with two senators, while the king still sent vicars as before. The people, for the sake of peace, once more granted the supremacy of the senate to the pope, and he nominated two senators. But in 1339 the Romans attacked the capitol, named two senators of their own choice, re-established a democratic government, and sent ambassadors to Florence to ask for the ordinances of justice by which that city had broken the power of the nobles, and also that a few skilled citizens should lend their help in the reconstitution of Rome. Accordingly some Florentines came with the *ordinamenti,* some portions of which may be recognized in the Roman statutes, and, after first rearranging the taxes, elected 13 priors of the gilds, a gonfalonier of justice, and a captain of the people after the Florentine manner. But there was a dissimilarity in the conditions of the two cities. The gilds having little influence in Rome, the projected reform failed, and the pope, who was opposed to it, re-elected the senators. Thereupon public discontent swelled. Another revolution in Rome re-established the government of the 13 elders and the two senators.

Cola di Rienzi.—The people, anxious to show their intention of respecting the papal authority, had despatched to Avignon as ambassador of the republic, in 1343, Cola di Rienzi (*q.v.*), who begged the pope to return to Rome, to allow the city to celebrate a jubilee every 50 years, and then, as a personal request, asked to be nominated notary to the urban chamber. The pope consented to everything, and Rienzi communicated this good news to Rome in an emphatically worded epistle. After Easter, in 1344, he returned to Rome and found that the city was a prey to the nobles. He secretly built up a party of conspirators and in May 1347 convoked a parliament of the people and obtained its sanction for the following proposals: that all pending lawsuits should be at once decided; that justice should be equally administered to all; that every region should equip 100 foot soldiers and 25 horse; that the dues and taxes should be rearranged; that the forts, bridges, and gates of the city should be held by the rector of the people instead of by the nobility; and that granaries should be opened for public use. On the same day, amid general homage and applause, Rienzi was proclaimed head of the republic, with the title of tribune and liberator of the Holy Roman Republic, "by authority of the most merciful Lord Jesus Christ." The nobles withdrew scoffing but alarmed. Rienzi engaged a body-guard of 100 men, and assumed the command of the 1,300 infantry and 390 light horse; he abolished the office of senator, retained the Thirteen and the general and special councils, and set the administration on a new footing. These measures and the prompt submission of the other cities of the State brought an instant increase of revenue to Rome.

The pope, willingly or unwillingly, accorded his approval to Rienzi's deeds. The provincial cities did homage to Rome and her tribune, and almost all the rest of Italy gave him its enthusiastic adherence. Great men like Petrarch were transported with joy. But on the convocation of a national parliament few representatives obeyed the summons and the scheme was a failure. Nevertheless, on Aug. 15, Rienzi caused himself to be crowned tribune with great pomp, and confirmed the rights of Roman citizenship to all natives of Italy. The nobles remained steadily hostile; conflict was unavoidable. At first Rienzi succeeded in vanquishing the Gaetani by means of John Colonna; he next endeavoured to suppress the Guelph and Ghibelline factions, and to restore Italy to "holy union."

The pope, however, was weary of toleration, and, coming to terms with the nobles, incited them to war. A battle took place in which 80 nobles, chiefly of the Colonna clan, were left dead; the aristocracy never again achieved the rule of the republic. Rienzi's head was turned by this sudden success, and in his great need of money he began to play the tyrant by levying taxes and exacting instant obedience. The papal legate saw his opportunity and seized it, by threatening to bring a charge of heresy against the tribune. Rienzi was dismayed. He declared himself friendly to the pope and willing to respect his authority; and he even sought to conciliate the nobles. At this moment certain Neapolitan and Hungarian captains, after levying soldiers with the tribune's consent, joined the nobles and broke out in revolt. On their proving victorious in a preliminary encounter with some of Rienzi's guards, the tribune suddenly lost heart, resigned the power he had held for seven months, and fled to Naples.

Meanwhile the Romans remained tranquil, intent on making money by the jubilee; but no sooner was this over than disorders broke out and the tyranny of the baronage recommenced. To remedy this state of things, application was made to the pope. He consulted with a committee of cardinals, who sought the advice of Petrarch, and the poet suggested a popular government, to the complete exclusion of the nobles, since these, he said, were strangers who ruined the city. The people had already elected the Thirteen, and now, encouraged by these counsels, on Dec. 26, 1351, chose John Perrone as head of the commune. But the new leader was unable to withstand the hostilities of the nobles; and in Sept. 1353 Francis Baroncelli was elected tribune. He was a follower of Rienzi, and did little beyond imitating his mode of government and smoothing the way for his return.

Rienzi, after various adventures, was at Avignon in confinement. Innocent VI. (1352–62) decided to send Cardinal Albornoz to Italy, in order to bring the State into subjection to the Church; and he further decided that Rienzi should accompany him to give him the support of his own popularity in Rome. In fact, directly the pair arrived Baroncelli was overthrown, the supremacy of the senate granted to the pope, and the government confided to Albornoz, who, without concerning himself with Rienzi, nominated a senator. Rienzi, profiting by his prestige and the apparent favour of the pope, was able to collect a band of 500 soldiers of mixed nationalities and on Aug. 1, 1354, took possession of the government. But his money ran short, and he resorted to violence to fill his purse. The result was a sudden revolt on Oct. 8, when the people stormed the capitol with cries of "Death to the traitor." Rienzi was killed.

Foreign Senators and the Banderesi.—Rome submitted to the pontiff, and the pope, instead of two senators, hastened to name a single one of foreign birth. This was a shrewd device of Albornoz and another blow to the nobles, with whom he was still at war. Thus was inaugurated, in 1358, a series of foreign senators, fulfilling the functions of a podesta, and changed every six months together with their staff of judges, notaries, and knights. The people approved of this reform as being inimical to the nobles and favourable to the preservation of liberty.

Hitherto the senators had been assisted, or rather kept in check, by the 13 representatives of the regions. In 1360 these were replaced by seven reformers, who soon became the veritable chiefs of the republic and were elected by ballot every three months, and the nobles, already shut out from power, were also excluded from the militia, which had been reorganized on the democratic system. Three thousand men, mostly archers, were enrolled under the command of two *banderesi*, with four *antepositi*, or lieutenants, constituting a supreme council of war. And the whole body was styled the *"Felix societas balestrariorum et pavesatorum."* It was instituted to support the reformers and re-establish order in the city and Campagna, to keep down the nobles and defend the republic. It fulfilled these duties with much severity. *Banderesi* and *antepositi* had seats in the special council beside those of the reformers, the gonfaloniers of the companies were seated beside the priors. Later these officials constituted the so-called *signoria dei banderesi.* When in 1362 the nobles made a riot in Rome, the *banderesi* drove them all from the city. The fight became so furious that all Rome was in arms, and even mercenaries were hired. Finally renewed submission was made to the pope.

On the death of Innocent VI. in 1362, an agreement was concluded with his successor, Urban V. (1362–70), who was obliged to give his sanction to the government of the reformers and *banderesi.* And then, Albornoz being recalled in disgrace to Avignon and afterwards sent as legate to Naples, these Roman magistrates were able, with or without the co-operation of the foreign senator, to rule in their own way. They did justice to the nobles by hanging a few more; and they defended the city from the threatening attacks of the mercenaries, who had become Italy's worst foes. It was at this period that the Roman statutes were revised and rearranged in the compilation which has come down to us supplemented by alterations of a later date.

Urban V. Begins to Destroy the Republic.—Urban V. (1362–70), no longer in safety at Avignon, decided to return to Italy. The Romans implored him to do so, and he was urged to it by the Italian *literati,* with Petrarch at their head. In April 1367 he left Avignon, and, entering Rome on Oct. 16, was given the lordship of the city. He showed much acumen in profiting by the first burst of popular enthusiasm to effect quick and dexterous changes in the constitution of the republic. After naming a senator, he abolished the posts of reformers and *banderesi,* substituting three conservators, or rather a species of municipal council, alone charged with judicial and administrative powers. The 13 leaders of the regions and the consuls of the gilds still sat in the councils, which were left unsuppressed. But all real power was in the hands of the pope, who, in Rome as in his other cities, nominated the principal magistrates. Thus, by transforming political into civil institutions, and concentrating the supreme authority in his own grasp, Urban V. dealt a mortal blow to the liberties of Rome. Yet he felt no sense of security among a people who, after the first rejoicings over the return of the Holy See, were always on the brink of revolt. Besides, he felt himself a stranger in Italy, and was so regarded. Accordingly, in 1370 he decided to return to France, and died there on Dec. 19.

The Romans retained the conservators, conferring on them the political power of the reformers; they re-established the *banderesi* and the four *antepositi*. The new French pope, Gregory XI. (1370–78), had to be content with obtaining supremacy over the senate and the possession of the castle of St. Angelo. In Feb. 1376 the Romans nominated John Cenci captain of the people and gave him uncontrolled power over the towns of the patrimony and the Sabine land. The two councils were preserved, and a new magistracy was created, the "Three Governors of the Peace and Liberty of Rome."

Gregory XI. decided in 1376 to return to Rome and entered into a treaty with the republic, which, anxious for his return, promised him the same powers that Urban V. had had. He returned early in 1377, but was not able to get control of the government before his death in the following year. The next pope, Urban VI. (1378–89), whose election and acts provoked the Great Schism (1378–1417), had much trouble, but finally got himself recognized as supreme in Rome by promising a jubilee in 1389. He died before it could take place, and was succeeded by Boniface IX. (1389–1404). The latter was very shrewd. He crowned Ladislaus and by a skilful use of jubilees, of which he celebrated two, succeeded in bringing the city wholly under his power; he also reduced the Colonna to submission.

The next pope, Innocent VII. (1404–6), aided by Ladislaus of Naples, put down a revolt of the people, but had to make a concession that they might elect "seven governors of the liberty of the Roman republic." After Innocent's death King Ladislaus seized Rome, sacked it brutally and held sway over it until his death in 1414. Then the Romans revolted against the Neapolitans, and with the aid of the papal legate established a new government of 13 conservators.

Martin V. Supreme.—When after the Schism Martin V. was elected pope he made peace with Joanna, queen of Naples, who yielded Rome to him. Martin V. reduced the remains of the free Roman government to a mere civil municipality. Following the method of the other despots of Italy, he allowed the old republican institutions to retain their names and forms, their administrative and some of their judicial attributes, while all their political functions were transferred to the new government. Order was re-established and justice rigidly observed. Rome was in ruins; nobility and burghers were equally disorganized, the people unable to bear arms and careless of their rights, while the battered walls of the capitol recorded the fall of two republics.

Eugenius IV. (1431–47) was forced by a revolt to flee from Rome, and then the people re-established the "Seven Governors of Liberty." Later Eugenius recovered control over Rome. Under Nicholas V. (1447–55) there were conspiracies to restore the republic, headed by Stephen Porcari, who attempted to play the part of a Rienzi. He was pardoned the first time, but was executed after a second attempt. After that the Popes ruled Rome. Under Paul II. some scholars were seized on the charge of desiring to re-establish paganism in the republic. Under Sixtus IV. (1471–84) the Colonna were either put to death or made powerless, and the Orsini met the same fate under Alexander VI. (1492–1503). There was still a senator of Rome, whose nomination was entirely in the hands of the pope, still three conservators, and an elected council of 26 citizens. Now and then also a shadowy semblance of a popular assembly was held to cast dust in the eyes of the public, but even this was not for long. All these officials, together with the judges of the capitol, retained various attributes of different kinds. They administered justice and gave sentence. There were numerous tribunals, all with undefined modes of procedure, so that it was very difficult for the citizens to ascertain in which court justice should be sought. But in last resort there was always the supreme decision of the pope. Thus matters remained up to 1789. For Modern City *see* p. 472.

BIBLIOGRAPHY.—There is a good bibliography for mediaeval Rome in E. Calvi, *Bibliografia generale di Roma* (1906). The more important sources for the history of Rome in the middle ages, as far as they have been edited, are found in the *Liber Pontificalis*, edit. by Duchesne (1886–92) and by Mommsen, in the *Monumenta Germaniae Historica* (1896); in Baronius, *Annales Ecclesiastici* (best ed. Paris, 1864–82); and in the *Archivio della Reale Società Romana di Storia Patria*. *See* also Watterich, *Pontificum romanorum*, etc. (1862); Kehr, *Regesta pontificum*, etc. (1896). For the period 568–751 there is a good bibliography in C. Diehl, *Études sur l'administration byzantine* (1888); for 751–1252, in L. Halphen, *Études sur l'administration de Rome au moyen âge* (1907); for 1354–1471, in E. Rodocanachi, *Histoire de Rome* (1922). Each of these three books also has a bibliography of secondary works. Duchesne's *Les premiers temps de l'état pontifical, 754–1073* (1898) has corrected many errors formerly held. Older books which are still valuable are: Savigny, *Geschichte des römischen Rechts im Mittelalter*; J. Ficker, *Forschungen zur Reichs- und Rechtsgeschichte Italiens* (Innsbruck, 1868–74); F. Papencordt, *Geschichte der Stadt Rom.* (Paderborn, 1857); A. von Reumont, *Geschichte der Stadt Rom.* (1867–68). F. Gregorovius, *Geschichte der Stadt Rom* is a standard work and very interesting. It was finished in 1872 and consequently needs correction on many points. There is a fifth edition in German (Stuttgart, 1903 *seq.*) and an English translation, from the fourth edition, by Annie Hamilton (1894 *seq.*). P. Villari, *Il comune di Roma nel medio evo*, in his *Saggi storici e critici* (Bologna, 1890) is a "brilliant essay"; *cf.* also his *Mediaeval Italy from Charlemagne to Henry VII.* (1910). Camillo Re, *Statuti della città di Roma* (1880) prints the statutes, with a long introduction; *cf.* G. Gatti, *Statuti dei mercanti di Roma* (1885). For the time of Innocent III., A. Luchaire, *Innocent III.; Rome et Italie* (1904); *cf.* his article in *Revue Historique*, vol. 81 (1903). For Brancaleone, M. Rovere, *Brancaleone degli Andalò* (Udine, 1895). For the 14th and 15th centuries, the work of Rodocanachi, cited above, and also his *Les institutions communales de Rome* (1901), which is better for this later period than for the earlier ages. Hartmann Grisar S.J. announced a very elaborate work on the history of Rome and the popes in the middle ages, only the first volume, in German, was published (1899–1901, Eng. trans. 1911 *seq.*). O. Rössler, *Grundriss einer Geschichte Roms im Mittelalter* (1909) is useful. *See* also the two series *Storia politica d'Italia*, one written by a *Società di professori* and the other by a *Società d'amici*, in which appeared the following useful volumes: G. Romano, *Dominazioni barbariche 395–1024* (1909); F. Bertolini, *Dominazioni germaniche* (1872); F. Lanzani, *Comuni* (1881); C. Cipolla, *Signorie italiane* (1881) (all published at Milan). Some material is to be found in M. Creighton, *History of the Papacy* (2nd. ed., 1897) and in L. Pastor, *Geschichte der Päpste* (Leipzig, 1884 *seq.*), of which there is an English translation (St. Louis, 1898 *seq.*). A brief account is W. Miller's *Mediaeval Rome* (1902) in the Story of the Nations series.

(D. C. M.; X.)

ROME, a city of Georgia, U.S., the county seat of Floyd county; 70 mi. N.W. of Atlanta, at the confluence of the Etowah and the Oostanaula rivers to form the Coosa. It is served by the Central of Georgia and the Southern railways and by air and bus lines. Population 29,617 in 1950 and 26,282 in 1940 by the federal census. The city has a beautiful location (650 to 1,500 ft. above sea level) on hills and surrounded by pine-clad ridges and cultivated valleys. Rome is an important cotton market and an industrial centre producing a wide variety of products. Shorter college (for women) is located there, and the Berry schools and colleges (industrial, for boys and girls). The city has a commission-manager form of government. Ferdinando de Soto camped for a month on the site of Rome in 1540. It was in the territory of the Cherokee nation, and there Gen. John Sevier in Oct. 1793 defeated a band of marauding Indians. The city was founded in 1834 and chartered in 1847. Its name was chosen by lot from several proposed by the four founders. In 1863 there were brilliant cavalry manoeuvres in the vicinity, resulting in the capture (on May 3) of 1,600 Union soldiers by Gen. Nathan B. Forrest with only 410 Confederates. On May 19, 1864, the city was taken by a detachment of Gen. W. T. Sherman's army. Before the Civil War Rome was an important river port.

ROME, a city of Oneida county, N.Y., U.S., 15 mi. N.W. of Utica, on the Mohawk river, Wood creek and the State Barge canal; served by the New York Central and the New York, Ontario and Western railways. Pop. (1950) 41,379; 1940 federal census 34,214. The city lies at an altitude of 450 ft., on a level stretch between the river and the creek, which flow respectively into the Hudson river and through Oneida lake and the Oswego river into Lake Ontario. It is an important manufacturing city, with great brass and copper mills which employ three-fifths of the workmen of the city. About one-tenth of all the copper fabricated in the United States is made there. The retail district of Rome stands on the old portage between the Mohawk river and Wood creek (about 1 mi. apart), which was used from time immemorial by the Indians and for nearly two centuries by the Dutch and English traders. To protect it Fort Bull was built on Wood creek and Fort Williams on the Mohawk by the British in 1755. The former was taken by French and Indians in March 1756, and the latter was destroyed by British Gen. Daniel Webb after the reduction of Oswego by the French in August of the same year. In 1758 Fort Stanwix was erected by British Gen. John Stanwix at a cost of £60,000. There in Oct.-Nov. 1768 Sir William Johnson and representatives of Virginia and Pennsylvania met with 3,200 Indians of the Six Nations and made a treaty with them, under which, for £10,460 in money and goods, they surrendered to the crown their claims to what is now Kentucky, West Virginia and western Pennsylvania. The fort was dismantled immediately afterward. In 1776 it was rebuilt and renamed in honour of Gen. Philip Schuyler, but the old name clung to it in popular usage. On Aug. 2, 1777, Fort Schuyler, containing about 750 continental troops, under Col. Peter Gansevoort and Lieut. Col. Marinus Willett, was besieged by Col. Barry St. Leger's British forces coming from the west. On Aug. 6 Gen. Nicholas Herkimer, with about 800 patriot militia, on his way to the relief of the fort, was ambushed by St. Leger's Tories and Indians in the forest near Oriskany (q.v.), 6 mi. E. During the action Willett, with 250 men and a small cannon, made a sortie from the fort, drew off a part of the enemy from Herkimer (so that he, though mortally wounded, was able to conduct the remnant of his force in orderly retreat down the valley) and brought back much booty. On Aug. 23 St. Leger, hearing exaggerated reports of enforcements approaching under Gen. Benedict Arnold, withdrew from the siege. The successful resistance to St. Leger contributed greatly to the American success at Saratoga. It was during the investment of Fort Schuyler (or Stanwix) on this occasion that the Stars and Stripes was first raised (early Sunday morning on Aug. 3, 1777) in the face of an enemy. The making of it (from bits of clothing of members of the garrison) "taxed the invention of the garrison," Colonel Willett records, but "a decent one was soon contrived." In 1779 Fort Schuyler was the headquarters of Col. Gozen van Schaick when he destroyed the Onondaga villages; and on Oct. 22, 1784, a treaty was concluded there by three commissioners representing the U.S. and the chiefs of the Six Nations. In 1796 the township of Rome was organized, receiving its name "from the heroic defense of the republic made here." In 1817 the first earth was turned at Rome for the Erie canal. The village of Rome was incorporated in 1819 and in 1870 it was chartered as a city.

ROMFORD, a market town, municipal borough and residential centre in the Romford parliamentary division of Essex, England, 12½ mi. E.N.E. from London by the L.N.E.R., also served by the L.M.S.R. Pop. (1938) 54,600. Area, 14.6 sq.mi. Romford was in the liberty of Havering-atte-Bower which until 1892 had a jurisdiction of its own distinct from that of the county. Romford has ironworks and electrical engineering works. It was incorporated in 1937. Gidea Park, which includes Hare Street village, was developed as a garden suburb.

ROMILLY, SIR SAMUEL (1757–1818), English legal reformer, second son of Peter Romilly, came of a Huguenot family that migrated to England. Samuel Romilly was born in Frith street, Soho, on March 1, 1757. He entered at Gray's Inn in 1778 and was called to the bar in 1783; his practice was mainly on the chancery side. In 1784 he became friendly with Mirabeau, and later supplied him with an account of house of commons procedure for use in France. As a result of a visit to France he published in 1790 *Thoughts on the Probable Influence of the Late Revolution.* He married in 1798. In 1800 he became a K.C., and in 1806 he was solicitor-general in the Ministry of All the Talents, sitting as M.P. for Queenborough. Sir Samuel Romilly then commenced his attempt to reform the criminal law of England, then cruel and illogical. He had already published *Observations* on the subject. By statute law innumerable offenses were punishable by death, but, as wholesale executions would be impossible, the larger number of those convicted and sentenced to death at every assizes were respited, after having heard the sentence of death solemnly passed upon them. This led to many acts of

injustice, as the lives of the convicts depended on the caprice of the judges, while at the same time it made the whole system of punishments and of the criminal law ridiculous. In 1808 Romilly managed to repeal the Elizabethan statute, which made it a capital offense to steal from the person. This success, however, raised opposition, and in the following year three bills repealing equally sanguinary statutes were thrown out by the house of lords under the influence of Lord Ellenborough. Year after year the same influence prevailed, and Romilly saw his bills rejected; but his patient efforts and his eloquence ensured victory eventually for his cause by opening the eyes of Englishmen to the barbarity of their criminal law. The only success he had was in securing the repeal, in 1812, of a statute of Elizabeth making it a capital offense for a soldier or a mariner to beg without a pass from a magistrate or his commanding officer. Lady Romilly died on Oct. 29, 1818, and Sir Samuel committed suicide on Nov. 2.

See the Memoirs of the Life of Sir Samuel Romilly written by himself, with a selection from his Correspondence, edited by his Sons (3 vols., 1840); *The Speeches of Sir Samuel Romilly in the House of Commons* (2 vols., 1820); "Life and Work of Sir Samuel Romilly," by Sir W. J. Collins, in *Trans. of the Huguenot Society* (1908).

ROMMEL, ERWIN (1891–1944), general field marshal of the German army during World War II, was born in Swabia in 1891 and was educated for military service at Stuttgart. During World War I, at that time a lieutenant, he served in the German army, taking part in numerous battles and campaigns and winning the Prussian Ordre pour le Mérite for distinguished service in the first battle of Champagne. After the war he attended the University of Tübingen for a time, but with Hitler's rise to power became a member of the National Socialist party and, according to some authorities, was at one time head of the S.S., Hitler's elite guard. During Hitler's invasions of central Europe he was ordered from his teaching position at the Potsdam war college to serve successively as commandant of field headquarters in Austria, the Sudetenland and Poland. In 1940, the tank divisions under his command played a substantial part in the German victory in France, and in 1941 he was placed in charge of the German Afrika Korps, then fighting in Libya. By the middle of 1942 he had retaken from the British the strategically important seaport town of Tobruk and driven the British 8th army back to El Alamein, Egypt. The British counter-attacked in Nov. 1942, and Rommel's army was driven back to Tunisia and eventual surrender (May 1943). Rommel returned to Germany in March 1943, was made inspector-general of Germany's defenses, Jan. 1944, and was in command of the mechanized army which opposed the Allied invasion in Normandy. His death was announced Oct. 14.

ROMNEY, GEORGE (1734–1802), English historical and portrait painter, was born at Dalton-in-Furness, Lancashire, on Dec. 26, 1734. His father was a builder and cabinet-maker, and the son, having manifested a turn for mechanics, was instructed in the latter craft, executing carvings of figures in wood, and constructing a violin, which he spent much time in playing. He was also busy with his pencil; and some of his sketches having attracted attention, his father apprenticed the boy, at the age of 19, to Steele, an itinerant painter of portraits and domestic subjects who had studied in Paris under Vanloo. In 1756 Romney married a young woman who had nursed him through a fever, and started as a portrait painter on his own account, travelling through the northern counties, executing likenesses at a couple of guineas, and producing a series of some 20 figure compositions, which were exhibited in Kendal, and afterwards disposed of by a lottery.

Having, at the age of 27, saved about £100, he left a portion of the sum with his wife and family, and started to seek his fortune in London, never returning, except for brief visits, till he came, a broken-down and aged man, to die. In London he rapidly rose into popular favour. His "Death of General Wolfe" was judged worthy of the second prize at the Society of Arts, but a word from Reynolds in praise of Mortimer's "Edward the Confessor" led to the premium being awarded to that painter, while Romney had to content himself with a donation of £50, an incident which led to the subsequent coldness between him and the president and prevented him from exhibiting at the academy or presenting himself for its honours.

In 1764 he paid a brief visit to Paris, where he was befriended by Joseph Vernet; and his portrait of Sir Joseph Yates, painted on his return, bears distinct traces of his study of the works of Rubens then in the Luxembourg palace. In 1766 he became a member of the Incorporated Society of Artists, and three years later he seems to have studied in their schools. He removed to Great Newport street, near the residence of Sir Joshua, whose fame in portraiture he began to rival in such works as "Sir George and Lady Warren" and "Mrs. Yates as the Tragic Muse"; and his professional income rose to £1,200 a year. But this marked increase in his popularity had the effect of enlarging his ambitions. Realizing the need for more thorough knowledge, he was seized with a longing to study in Italy; and in the beginning of 1773 he started for Rome with Ozias Humphrey, the miniature painter. On his arrival he devoted himself to study, raising a scaffold to examine the paintings in the Vatican, and giving much time to work from the undraped model, of which his painting of a "Wood Nymph" was a result. At Parma he studied Correggio.

In 1775 Romney returned to London, establishing himself in Cavendish square, and resuming his work as a portrait painter. The admiration of the town was divided between him and Reynolds. Romney became acquainted with Hayley, his future biographer, then in the zenith of his popularity as a poet. His influence on the painter seems to have been far from salutary. He encouraged Romney's excessive and morbid sensibility, and tempted him to expend his talents on ill-considered, seldom-completed paintings of ideal and poetical subjects. About 1783 Romney was introduced to Emma Hart, afterwards celebrated as Lady Hamilton, and she became the model from whom he worked incessantly. He painted her as a Magdalene and as a Joan of Arc, as a Circe, a Bacchante, a Cassandra; and he confessed that she was the inspirer of what was most beautiful in his art. But her fascinations had their share in aggravating that nervous restlessness and instability, inherent in his nature, which finally ruined both health and mind.

In 1786 Alderman Boydell started his great scheme of the Shakespeare gallery, apparently at the suggestion of Romney. The painter entered heartily into the plan, and contributed his scene from the *Tempest*, and his "Infant Shakespeare attended by the Passions," the latter characterized by the Redgraves as one of the best of his subject pictures. Gradually he began to withdraw from portrait painting, to limit the hours devoted to sitters, and to turn his thoughts to mighty schemes of the ideal subjects which he would execute. Already, in 1792, he had painted "Milton and his Daughters," which was followed by "Newton making Experiments with the Prism." He was to paint the Seven Ages, Visions of Adam with the Angel, "six other subjects from Milton—three where Satan is the hero, and three from Adam and Eve—perhaps six of each." Having planned and erected a large studio in Hampstead, he removed thither in 1797, with the fine collection of casts from the antique which his friend Flaxman had gathered for him in Italy. But his health was now irremediably shattered. In the summer of 1799, suffering from great weakness of body and depression of mind, he returned to Kendal, where his faithful and long-suffering wife received and tended him. He died on Nov. 15, 1802.

See the *Memoirs* by William Hayley (1809) and by the artist's son, the Rev. John Romney (1830). In the fully illustrated *George Romney*, by Lord Ronald Sutherland Gower (1904), pictures, mainly studies, are reproduced not elsewhere to be found. But the great work upon the artist is *Romney*, by Humphry Ward and W. Roberts (1904), containing 70 illustrations, a biographical and critical essay, and a *catalogue raisonné* of the painter's works. *See* also Arthur B. Chamberlain, *Romney* (1910).

ROMNEY, HENRY SIDNEY, EARL OF (1641–1704), fourth son of Robert, 2nd earl of Leicester, was born in Paris in 1641. Sidney's handsome face helped his advancement at court, but the favour in which he was held by the duchess of York, to whom he was master of the robes, led to his temporary disgrace. In 1672 he was sent on a mission of congratulations to Louis XIV, and in 1677 became master of the robes to Charles II. He entered parliament in 1679, and became a close political ally of his nephew Sunderland, with whose wife he carried on an intrigue which caused scandal. Sunderland used this intimacy to further his political ends. Sidney was sent by Sunderland and others in 1679 on a special mission to urge William of Orange to visit England, a task which he discharged while acting as the official envoy of Charles II at The Hague. He was recalled in 1682, but was again sent to Holland in 1685. He returned to England in the spring of 1688, and sought support for the prince of Orange in the event of his landing. He was allowed to leave England on giving his word not to visit The Hague, but he broke his promise on getting clear of England, and conveyed to William a duplicate of the invitation addressed to him by the English nobility, together with intelligence of affairs of state obtained through the countess of Sunderland.

He landed with William at Torbay, and received substantial rewards for his undoubted services, including the titles of Baron Milton and Viscount Sidney of Sheppey. William made him secretary of state in 1690, and in 1692, lord-lieutenant of Ireland. His inability to cope with the difficulties of this position led to his recall in the next year, when he became master-general of the ordnance. He was created earl of Romney in May 1694. On Anne's accession he was dismissed from his various offices. His titles became extinct on his death on April 8, 1704.

ROMNEY (Kent, England): *see* NEW ROMNEY.

ROMORANTIN, a town of central France, in the department of Loir-et-Cher, 31 mi. S.E. of Blois by rail. Pop. (1936) 7,130. In 1560 Romorantin gave its name to an edict which prevented the introduction of the Inquisition into France. The town stands on the Sauldre at its confluence with the Morantin, whence its name (*Rivus Morantini*).

ROMSDAL, the valley of the river Rauma, in Norway. The Rauma is a torrent with several waterfalls (Mongefos, Vaermofos and Slettafos) which descends from Lake Lesjekogan to the Romsdal fjord on the west coast (62° 30′ N.). The nearest port is Molde, from which steamers run to Veblungsnaes (30 mi.) at the foot of the valley. A good road traverses the valley, which is one of the finest in southern Norway, flanked by steep mountains terminating in abrupt peaks—Vengetinder (5,960 ft.), Romsdalshorn (5,105), Troldtinder ("witch-peaks," 6,010) and others. Lake Lesjekogan also drains from the opposite end by the Laagen or Lougen river to the Glommen, and so to the Skagerrak, and the road follows its valley, the Gudbrandsdal.

ROMSEY (rŭm′zĭ), market town and municipal borough in the New Forest and Christchurch parliamentary division of Hampshire, England, 7 mi. N.W. of Southampton by the S.R. Pop. (est. 1938) 5,730. Area, 1.9 sq.mi. The abbey church of SS. Mary and Elfleda is a fine Norman church little altered by later builders. A house founded there by Edward the Elder (c. 910) became a Benedictine nunnery. The church, which is the only important relic of the foundation, is cruciform, with a low central tower. Building began in the first half of the 12th century, and continued through it, as the western part of the nave shows the transition to the Early English style, which appears in the west front. Decorated windows occur in the east end, beyond which a chapel formerly extended. Perpendicular insertions are insignificant. The nave and choir have aisles, triforium and clerestory. The transepts have eastern apsidal chapels, as have the choir aisles, though the walls of these last are square without. Foundations of the apse of a large pre-Norman church have been discovered below the present building. At the time of the Domesday Survey Romsey (Romesyg, Romeseie) was owned by the abbey, which continued to be the overlord until the dissolution. Romsey was incorporated by James I in 1608. In mediaeval times the town had a considerable share of the woollen trade of Hampshire, but it declined in the late 17th century.

ROMULUS, the son of Mars by the Vestal Rhea Silvia or Ilia, daughter of Numitor, who had been dispossessed of the throne of Alba by his younger brother Amulius. Romulus and Rĕmus, the twin sons of Silvia, were placed in a trough and cast into the Tiber by their grand-uncle. The trough grounded in the marshes where Rome afterwards stood, under the wild fig tree (*Ficus ruminalis*), which was still holy in later days. The babes were suckled by a she-wolf and fed by a woodpecker, and then fostered by Acca Larentia, wife of the shepherd Faustulus. They became leaders of a warlike band of shepherds on the Palatine, and in course of time were recognized by their grandfather, whom they restored to his throne, slaying Amulius. They now founded a city on the site where they had been nurtured; later a quarrel broke out and Remus was slain. Romulus strengthened his band by offering an "asylum" to outcasts and fugitives, found wives for them by capture and waged war with their kinsmen. His most formidable foe was Titus Tatius (*q.v.*), king of the Sabines, but after an obstinate struggle he and Romulus united their forces and reigned side by side till Tatius was slain at Lavinium in the course of a blood-feud with Laurentum. Romulus then reigned alone till he suddenly disappeared in a storm. He was thereafter worshipped as a god under the name of Quirinus. Various rationalizing accounts also exist of the legend.

The whole story, probably first given by the annalists Fabius Pictor and Cincius Alimentus, is artificial and shows strong Greek influence. The birth, exposure, rescue, and subsequent adventures of the twins are a Greek tale of familiar type. Mars and his sacred beast, the wolf, are introduced on account of the great importance of this cult. The localities described are ancient sacred places; the Lupercal, near the *ficus ruminalis*, was naturally explained as the she-wolf's den. (*See* ROME: *The Ancient City.*) The *asylum* is pure Greek, both name and institution. The story was probably invented to give an explanation of the sacred spot named *inter duos lucos* between the arx and the Capitol. Another Greek touch is the deification of an eponymous hero. The rape of the Sabine women is clearly aetiological, invented to account for the custom of simulated capture in marriage; these women and also Titus Tatius represent the Sabine element in the Roman population. The name Romulus (=*Romanus*, cp. the forms *Siculus* and *Sicanus*) means simply "Roman," the derivation of Remus is obscure.

Romulus is regarded as the founder of the military and political institutions (*see* ROME), as Numa and his counterpart Ancus Marcius are of the religious institutions, of Rome.

BIBLIOGRAPHY.—Schwegler, *Römische Geschichte*, bks. viii.–x.; Sir George Cornewall Lewis, *Credibility of early Roman History*, chap. 11; W. Ihne, *History of Rome*, i.; Sir J. Seeley, Introduction to his edition of Livy, bk. i.; E. Pais, *Storia di Roma* (1898), i. pt. 1, and *Ancient Legends of Roman History* (Eng. trans., 1906); J. B. Carter in Roscher's *Lexikon*, art. Romulus.

ROMULUS AUGUSTULUS, last Roman emperor of the West (Oct. 31, A.D. 475, to Sept. 4, 476), was elevated to the throne by his father, Orestes, "master of the soldiery" (Jordanes), who drove the emperor Julius (Nepos) to Dalmatia in the summer of 475. Romulus, who was then probably about 14 years old, owed his first name to an uncle, a *canes* of Patavio in Noricum; his nickname he probably owed to the barbarian soldiery; and by these two chances the last emperor successor of a Julius Caesar bore the names both of the first emperor and the first king. The reins of power were naturally held for him by his father, Orestes, nor is there any event of his reign worthy of record except the conclusion of peace with Gaiseric the Vandal. Shortly after his elevation to the throne, the barbarian mercenaries in the service of Rome presented to Romulus's father, Orestes, a demand that they should be allotted one-third of the lands of all Italy. With a last flicker of Roman courage and pride, Orestes refused: the mercenaries revolted under their leader and instigator, Odoacer (Aug. 23, 476), and in a very short while Orestes was defeated and beheaded and the Western empire came to an end. The victorious Odoacer was touched by the beauty and helplessness of Romulus, and spared his life, ordering him to retire to the villa built by Lucullus four centuries before, near Naples. Here he died at a date unknown to us.

RONALDSHAY, LAWRENCE JOHN LUMLEY DUNDAS, EARL OF (1876–), British administrator, was born June 11, 1876, the eldest surviving son of the 1st Marquess of Zetland and was educated at Harrow and Trinity College, Cambridge. From 1898–1907 he travelled extensively in Ceylon, India, Persia, Asiatic Turkey, Central Asia, Siberia, Japan, China and Burma. In 1900 he was appointed aide-de-camp to the staff of the viceroy, Earl Curzon, in India. He sat in the House of

Commons as Conservative member for the Hornsey division from 1907 to 1916. He was a member of the royal commission on the public services in India, 1912–14, and governor of Bengal, 1916–22, when he was created G.C.S.I. He succeeded to the marquisate of Zetland in 1929. Ronaldshay was secretary of state for India, 1935–40, and, in addition, for Burma, 1937–40.

Lord Ronaldshay published *Sport and Politics under an Eastern Sky* (1902); *On the Outskirts of Empire in Asia* (1904); *A Wandering Student in the Far East* (1908); *An Eastern Miscellany* (1911); *Lands of the Thunderbolt: Sikhim, Chumbi and Bhutan* (1923); *The Heart of Aryavarta* (1925); *Life of Lord Curzon of Kedleston,* 3 vol. (1927–28); *Steps Towards Indian Home Rule* (1935).

RONCESVALLES (Fr. *Roncevaux*), a village of northern Spain, in the province of Navarre; situated on the small river Urrobi, at an altitude of 3,220 ft. among the Pyrenees, and within 5 mi. from the French frontier. Pop. (1940) 149. Roncesvalles is famous in history and legend for the defeat of Charlemagne and the death of Roland in 778. The small collegiate church contains several relics associated with Roland, and is a favourite place of pilgrimage. The battle is said to have been fought in the picturesque valley known as Valcarlos, which is now occupied by a hamlet (pop. in 1940, 303; mun., 970) bearing the same name, and in the adjoining defile of Ibaneta. Both of these are traversed by the main road leading north from Roncesvalles to St. Jean Pied de Port, in France.

RONDA, a town of southern Spain, in the province of Málaga; on the river Guadiaro and on the Algeciras-Bobadilla

A RONDA MILKMAN MILKING HIS GOAT FOR A CUSTOMER

railway. Pop. (1940) 15,813 (mun., 26,170). Ronda is built on a high rock nearly surrounded by the Guadiaro or Guadalevín, which flows through an abrupt chasm 530 ft. deep and 300 ft. wide, by which the old town is separated from the new. The stream was probably bridged by the Romans. Ronda has a considerable trade in leather, saddlery, horses, soap, flour, chocolate, wine and hats. The poet Vicente Espinel was born here in 1551.

Some remains of an aqueduct and theatre, about 7 mi. N. of Ronda, are supposed to represent the *Acinipo* or *Arunda* of ancient geographers. Ronda gives its name to the Sierra or Serrania de Ronda, one of the main sections of the coast mountains which rise between the great plain of Andalusia and the Mediterranean.

RONDEAU, a structural form in poetry and (in the form of "rondo") in music. In poetry the rondeau is a short metrical structure which in its perfect form consists of 13 eight- or ten-syllabled verses divided into three strophes of unequal length, and knit together by two rhymes and a refrain. In Clement Marot's time the laws of the rondeau were laid down, and, according to Voiture, in the 17th century, the following was the type of the approved form of the rondeau:—

"Ma foy, c'est fait de moy, car Isabeau
M'a conjuré de luy faire un Rondeau:
    Cela me met en une peine extrême.
    Quoy treize vers, huit en *eau*, cinq en *ème*.
Je luy ferois aussi-tôt un bateau!

En voilà cinq pourtant en un monceau:
Faisons en huict, en invoquant Brodeau,
    En puis mettons, par quelque stratagème,
    Ma foy, c'est fait!

Si je pouvois encore de mon cerveau
Tirer cinq vers, l'ouvrage seroit beau;
    Mais cependant, je suis dedahs l'onzième;
    Et si je croy que je fais le douzième,
En voilà treize ajustez au niveau.
    Ma foy, c'est fait!"

All forms of the rondeau are alike in this, that the distinguishing metrical emphasis is achieved by a peculiar use of the refrain. Though we have a set of rondeaux in the *Rolliad* (written by Dr. Lawrence the friend of Burke, according to Gosse), it was not till modern times that the form had any real vogue in England.

Considerable attention, however, has lately been given in England to the form. Some English rondeaux are as bright and graceful as Voiture's own. Swinburne, who in his *Century of Roundels* was perhaps the first to make the refrain rhyme with the second verse of the first strophe, has brought the form into high poetry. In German, rondeaux have been composed with perfect correctness by Weckherlin, and with certain divergences from the French type by Götz and Fischart; the German name for the form is *rundum* or *ringel-gedicht*.

Although the origin of the refrain in all poetry was no doubt the improvisatore's need of a rest, a time in which to focus his forces and recover breath for future flights, the refrain has a distinct metrical value of its own; it knits the structure together, and so intensifies the emotional energy, as we see in the Border ballads, in the *Oriana* of Lord Tennyson, and in the *Sister Helen* of Rossetti. The suggestion of extreme artificiality—of "difficulty overcome"—which is one great fault of the rondeau as a vehicle for deep emotion, does not therefore spring from the use of the refrain, but from the too frequent recurrence of the rhymes in the strophes—for which there is no metrical necessity as in the case of the Petrarchan sonnet. The rondeau is, however, an inimitable instrument of gaiety, delicacy, colour and grace.

RONDEL, a form of verse closely allied to the rondeau (*q.v.*) but distinguished from it by containing 14 instead of 13 lines, and by demanding a slightly different arrangement of rhymes. The initial couplet is repeated in the middle and again at the close. The arrangement of rhymes is as follows: a, b b, a; a b, a b; a, b, b, a, a, b. This form, which was invented in the 14th century, was largely used in later mediaeval French poetry, but particularly by Charles d'Orléans (1391–1465), the very best of whose graceful creations are all rondels. The rondel, in French, may begin with either a masculine or a feminine rhyme, but its solitary other rhyme must be of the opposite kind.

One of the Prince d'Orleans' rondels may be given here as a type:—

> Le temps a laissié son manteau
> De vent, de froidure et de pluye,
> Et s'est vestu de brouderie
> De souleil luisant, cler et beau.
> Il n'y a beste ne oyseau
> Qu'en son jargon ne chante ou crie;
> Le temps a laissié son manteau
> De vent, de froidure et de pluye.
> Rivière, fontaine et ruisseau
> Portent, en livrée jolie,
> Gouttes d'argent d'or faverie;
> Chascun s'abille de nouveau;
> Le temps a laissié son manteau
> De vent, de froidure et de pluye.

Rondels existed in English from the 15th century, but the early specimens of it are very clumsy. It was revived in the 19th century. Correct examples are found in the poems of Robert Bridges, Dobson, Gosse and Henley. The following, by Austin Dobson, is a good example of what an English rondel should be in all technical respects.

> Love comes back to his vacant dwelling,—
> The old, old Love that we knew of yore!
> We see him stand by the open door,
> With his great eyes sad, and his bosom swelling.
> He makes as though in our arms repelling
> He fain would lie as he lay before;—
> Love comes back to his vacant dwelling,—
> The old, old Love that we knew of yore!
> Ah! who shall help us from over-spelling
> That sweet, forgotten, forbidden lore?
> E'en as we doubt, in our hearts once more,
> With a rush of tears to our eyelids welling,
> Love comes back to his vacant dwelling,
> The old, old Love that we knew of yore!

Théodore de Banville remarks that the art of the rondel consists in the gay and natural reintroduction of the refrain, which should always seem inevitable, while slightly changing the point of view of the reader. If this is not successfully achieved, "on ne fera que de la marqueterie et du placage, c'est-à-dire, en fait de poésie,—rien!" In Germany, the rondel was introduced, in the 18th century, under the name of *ringel-gedicht* by Johann Nikolaus Götz (1731–81).

RONDO, a musical form originally derived from the rondel in verse; as may be seen, long before the development of instrumental forms, in some of the *chansons* of Orlando di Lasso. The *rondeau en couplets* of Couperin and his contemporaries shows the same connection with verse. It consists of a single neatly rounded phrase alternating with several episodes (the *couplets*) without any important change of key. Ex. 1 shows Bach's handling of this early form. The later rondo is an important member of the sonata forms (*q.v.*), chiefly found in finales; but rondo-form sometimes occurs in slow movements. Ex. 2 is not more elaborate than the adagio of Beethoven's 4th symphony. Philipp Emanuel Bach invented an extraordinary kind of rondo, not part of a sonata, but on a voluminous scale with wildly incoherent episodes and modulations.

The later sonata-style rondo forms may be divided into two main classes:

(i.) *Sectional rondos; i.e.,* with little or no development or transition between the episodes and the main theme; very characteristic of Haydn, who, however, may run away with it in unexpected developments. The name rondo implies at least two episodes, and a sectional rondo may have more. Beethoven in his early works shows the influence of Haydn in this type of rondo; *e.g.,* the finales of sonatas, opp. 10, No. 3, and 14, Nos. 1 and 2; and the slow movements of the sonatas, opp. 2, No. 2, and 13 (*Pathétique*). The sectional rondo last appears on a gigantic scale in the finale of Brahms's G minor pianoforte quartet, op. 25; and it lends itself, like the cognate idea of a dance with several "trios" to Schumann's pianoforte pieces and to some of his finales.

(ii.) *Rondos influenced by the form of a first movement* (for which *see* SONATA FORMS). In the normal scheme for this, which is Mozart's favourite rondo-form, the rondo-theme (which may contain several clauses) is followed by a well-organized transition to the key of the first episode, which key is chosen as if for the "complementary key" of a first movement. The return to the rondo-theme may be elaborate or abrupt, and the theme itself may be reduced to its first complete clause (but not to a mere fragment, without loss of the rondo effect). The second episode will be in a new key and may be followed by wide modulations, or itself be widely modulatory, or it may even be entirely a development of the previous material, as in the rondo of Beethoven's Sonata Op. 90, given on p. 525. When the rondo-theme returns again it is followed by a recapitulation of the first episode (perhaps preceded by the transitional passage suitably modified) in the tonic; after which the coda may contain a final return of the rondo-theme. When the second episode is concentrated on development the only difference between the rondo and a first movement is the slender fact that the whole first theme returns immediately after the first episode. Yet the rondo style can be recognised from the outset by the tunelike character of the main theme, and also by the fact that, unlike the most tuneful openings of first movements, it comes to a definite close instead of swinging continuously into the transition passage. A rondo with a development in its middle episode may return to the tonic with an immediate recapitulation of the first episode, omitting the expected second return of the main theme, thus: A, B (new key), A, C (development), B (tonic), A, Coda (where A is the rondo-theme and B and C the episodes). Mozart, Schubert and Brahms have a form, always worked on a very large scale, which consists only of A, B (new key), A, B (tonic), Coda; where a certain amount of development is edged in *à propos* of the transition-passage on its recapitulation. Only the style of the main theme can distinguish this from a first movement that omits its normal development-section.

In the rondos of classical concertos (*q.v.*) the orchestra (especially in Mozart) finds its opportunity in a series of accessory themes announced as soon as the solo instrument has given out the rondo-theme. These accessories are then held in reserve for the coda.

Two examples of rondo-forms are given on pp. 524–6:—

RONDO

EX. I.

Gavotte en Rondeau (Rondeau en Couplets) from Bach's Sixth Violin Solo.

Fine

Couplet I

Dal 𝄋 e poi

Couplet II

Dal 𝄋 e poi

Couplet III

Dal 𝄋 e poi

Couplet IV

Dal 𝄋 e Fine

RONDO

RONSARD

RONSARD, PIERRE DE (1524–1585), French poet and "prince of poets" (as his own generation in France called him), was born at the Château de la Poissonnière, near the village of Couture in the province of Vendômois (department of Loir-et-Cher), on Sept. 11, 1524. His family is said to have come from the Slav provinces to the south of the Danube (provinces with which the crusades had given France much intercourse) in the first half of the 14th century. Pierre was the youngest son of Loys de Ronsard, *maître d'hôtel du roi* to Francis I. Pierre was sent to the Collège de Navarre at Paris when he was nine years old. It is said that the rough life of a mediaeval school did not suit him. He was quickly appointed page, first to the king's eldest son François, and then to his brother the duke of Orleans. When Madeleine of France was married to James V. of Scotland, Ronsard was attached to the king's service, and he spent three years in Great Britain. The latter part of this time seems to have been passed in England, though he had, strictly speaking, no business there. On returning to France in 1540 he was again taken into the service of the duke of Orleans, and travelled to Flanders and again to Scotland. After a time he was attached as secretary to the suite of Lazare de Baïf, the father of his future colleague in the Pléiade and his companion on this occasion, Antoine de Baïf, at the diet of Spires. Afterwards he was attached in the same way to the suite of the cardinal du Bellay-Langey. His diplomatic career was cut short by an attack of deafness which no physician could cure, and he devoted himself to study at the Collège Coqueret, the principal of which was Daurat—afterwards the "dark star" (as from his silence he has been called in France) of the Pléiade, and already an acquaintance of Ronsard's from his having held the office of tutor in the Baïf household. Antoine de Baïf, Daurat's pupil, accompanied Ronsard; Belleau shortly followed; Joachim du Bellay, the second of the seven, joined not much later. Muretus (Marc Antoine Muret), a great scholar and by means of his Latin plays a great influence in the creation of French tragedy, was also a student here.

The Pléiade.—Ronsard's period of study occupied seven years, and the first manifesto of the new literary movement, which was to apply to the vernacular the principles of criticism and scholarship learnt from the classics, came not from him but from Joachim du Bellay (*q.v.*). The *Défense et illustration de la langue française* of the latter appeared in 1549, and the Pléiade (or *Brigade*, as it was first called) may be said to have been then launched. The orthodox canon is beyond doubt composed of Ronsard, Du Bellay, Baïf, Belleau, Pontus de Tyard, Jodelle the dramatist, and Daurat. Some single and minor pieces, an epithalamium on Antoine de Bourbon and Jeanne de Navarre (1550), a "Hymne de la France" (1549), an "Ode à la Paix," preceded the publication in 1550 of the first four books of the *Odes* of Ronsard. This was followed in 1552 by his *Amours de Cassandre* with the fifth book of *Odes*. These books excited a violent literary quarrel. Marot was dead, but he left a numerous school, some of whom saw in the stricter literary critique of the Pléiade, in its outspoken contempt of merely vernacular and mediaeval forms, in its strenuous advice to French poetry to "follow the ancients," and so forth, an insult to Marot and his followers. An acute rivalry ensued between the followers of Clément Marot, the

"École Marotique," and the new school. The Pléiade found a powerful supporter at court in Marguerite de Valois. Ronsard published his *Hymns*, dedicated to Marguerite de Savoie, in 1555; the conclusion of the *Amours*, addressed to another heroine, in 1556; and then a collection of *Oeuvres complètes*, said to be due to the invitation of Mary Stuart, queen of Francis II., in 1560; with *Elégies, mascarades et bergeries* in 1565. To this same year belongs his most important and interesting *Abrégé de l'art poétique français*.

Charles IX. gave him rooms in the palace; he bestowed upon him divers abbacies and priories; and he called him and regarded him constantly as his master in poetry. Neither was Charles IX. a bad poet. This royal patronage excited violent dislike to Ronsard on the part of the Huguenots, who wrote constant pasquinades against him, strove (by a ridiculous exaggeration of the Dionysiac festival at Arcueil, in which the friends had indulged to celebrate the success of the first French tragedy, Jodelle's *Cléopatre*) to represent him as a libertine and an atheist, and (which seems to have annoyed him more than anything else) set up his follower Du Bartas as his rival. According to some words of his own, which are quite credible considering the ways of the time, they were not contented with this variety of argument, but attempted to have him assassinated.

During this period Ronsard's work was considerable but mostly occasional, and the one work of magnitude upon which Charles put him, the *Franciade* (1572), has never been ranked, even by his most devoted admirers, as a chief title to fame. The metre (the decasyllable) which the king chose could not but contrast unfavourably with the magnificent alexandrines which Du Bartas and Agrippa d'Aubigné were shortly to produce; the general plan is feebly classical, and the very language has little or nothing of that racy mixture of scholarliness and love of natural beauty which distinguishes the best work of the Pléiade. Moreover it had the singular bad luck almost to coincide with the massacre of St. Bartholomew, which had occurred about a fortnight before its publication. The death of Charles made little difference in the court favour which Ronsard enjoyed, but, combined with his increasing infirmities, it seems to have determined him to quit court life. During his last days he lived chiefly at his house in Vendôme, the capital of his native province, at his abbey at Croix-Val in the same neighbourhood, or else at Paris, where he was usually the guest of Jean Galland, well known as a scholar, at the Collège de Boncourt. It seems also that he had a town house of his own in the Faubourg Saint-Marcel. He received gifts and endowments from foreign patrons, including Elizabeth of England. Mary, queen of Scots, who had known him earlier, addressed him from her prison; and Tasso consulted him on the *Gerusalemme*. He died at his priory of Saint-Cosme at Tours, and he was buried in the church of that name on Dec. 27, 1585.

After Ronsard's death the classical reaction set in under the auspices of Malherbe. After Malherbe the rising glory of Corneille and his contemporaries obscured the tentative and unequal work of the Pléiade, which was, moreover, directly attacked by Boileau himself, the dictator of French criticism in the last half of the 17th century. Then Ronsard was, except by a few men of taste, like La Bruyère and Fénelon, forgotten when he was not sneered at. In this condition he remained during the whole 18th century and the first quarter of the 19th. The Romantic revival, seeing in him a victim of its special *bête noire* Boileau and attracted by his splendid diction, rich metrical faculty and combination of classical and mediaeval peculiarities, adopted his name as a kind of battle cry, and for the moment exaggerated his merits somewhat. The critical work, however, of Sainte-Beuve in his *Tableau de la littérature française au 16ème siècle* established his place in French literature.

Generally speaking, Ronsard is best in his amatory verse (the long series of sonnets and odes to Cassandre, Marie, Genèvre, Hélène—Hélène de Surgères, a later and mainly "literary" love—etc.), and in his descriptions of the country (the famous "Mignonne allons voir si la rose," the "Fontaine Bellerie," the "Forêt de Gastine," and so forth) which have an extraordinary grace and freshness. No one used with more art than he the graceful diminutives which his school set in fashion. He also knew well how to manage the gorgeous adjectives ("marbrine," "cinabrine," "ivoirine" and the like) which were another fancy of the Pléiade, and in his hands they rarely become stiff or cumbrous. In short, Ronsard shows eminently the two great attractions of French 16th-century poetry as compared with that of the two following ages—magnificence of language and imagery and graceful variety of metre.

BIBLIOGRAPHY.—Of editions of his *Oeuvres complètes* he himself published seven—the first in 1560, the last in 1584. Between his death and 1630 ten more complete editions were published, the most famous of which is the folio of 1609. From 1630 Ronsard was not again reprinted for more than two centuries. Just before the close of the second, however, Sainte-Beuve printed a selection of his poems to accompany the above-mentioned *Tableau* (1828). There are also selections by M. Noel (in the *Collection Didot*) and Becq de Fouquières. M. Prosper Blanchemain, who had previously published a volume of *Oeuvres inédites de Ronsard*, undertook a complete edition of 8 vol. (1857–67) for the *Bibliothèque Elzévirienne*. Later editions are by Marty-Laveaux (1887–93), and B. Pifteau (1891); and by P. Laumonier, 2 vol. (1914). C. H. Page published a translation of his *Songs and Sonnets* with introductory essay and notes (1924). As for criticism, Sainte-Beuve followed up his early work by articles in the *Causeries du lundi*, and the chief later critics have dealt with him in their collected works. In English A. Tilley's *Literature of the French Renaissance* (1904) and Saintsbury's *History of Criticism*, vol. ii may be consulted. *See* also P. Champion, *Ronsard et son temps* (1905); P. de Nolhac, *Ronsard et l'humanisme* (1921); H. Franchet, *Le Poète et son oeuvre d'après Ronsard* (1923); P. Laumonier, *Ronsard* (1923); S. de Ricci, *Catalogue d'une collection unique des éditions originales de Ronsard* (1925); H. Wolfe, *Ronsard and French Romantic Poetry* (1935); and D. B. W. Lewis, *Ronsard* (1944).

RÖNTGEN, DAVID (1743–1807), German cabinetmaker, eldest son of Abraham Röntgen, was born at Herrnhag on Aug. 11, 1743, and died at Wiesbaden on Feb. 12, 1807. In 1750 his father migrated to Neuwied, near Coblenz, where he produced furniture of outstanding quality often decorated with inlay work of ivory and other material, much of it for the courts of German princes. David learned his trade in his father's workshop and succeeded to the paternal business in 1772 while his father continued as a partner until 1784. His father's firm having already achieved renown in Germany, the son won European reputation after he had displayed his furniture in Paris in 1779 and secured King Louis XVI, Queen Marie Antoinette and other members of the court as customers. Röntgen was appointed cabinetmaker to the queen and in 1780 was granted admission as master (*maître ébéniste*) to the trade corporation of Paris cabinet-makers, a fact which made it possible for him to keep in Paris a stock of the furniture manufactured at Neuwied. In this fashion Röntgen was able to compete with the great French cabinetmakers of the period such as Jean Henri Riesener and others. King Frederick the Great of Prussia and Empress Catherine II of Russia were also customers of Röntgen. The latter, after Röntgen's first visit to St. Petersburg in 1783, bought great quantities of his furniture. When in 1795 the French Revolutionary armies threatened to cross the Rhine, Röntgen evacuated his establishment and moved his stock of furniture farther inland. While he never succeeded in starting production again, former apprentices of his whom he had helped to establish in Berlin (David Hacker) and in Brunswick (Christian Härder) were successful in their enterprises. Röntgen had begun his career by continuing and developing the style of furniture his father had introduced. There is his so-called "French" style with furniture of curved outline sometimes decorated with rich carvings, and there is his "English" cabinet-work based on elements dating from the early years of George III and occasionally influenced by Thomas Chippendale. Both types of furniture are frequently decorated with rich inlay work of outstanding charm and elegance made up of a variety of woods, some tinted and composed to form figural and floral compositions, often in the *chinoiserie* manner. Between 1775 and 1780 Röntgen's previous style is altogether abandoned and rigid, classical forms are introduced, the effect of which is often based on the contrast of mahogany with

rich bronze appliques. The Röntgen workshop indulged in mechanical devices which made appear or disappear drawers, mirrors, etc., by pressing on hidden releases. Peter Kinzing was the mechanical genius who invented many of these tricks and provided clockworks. Furniture by Röntgen is in most large museums in Europe, at the Metropolitan museum in New York and the Art Institute of Chicago.

See Hans Huth, *Abraham and David Röntgen und ihre Neuwieder Werkstatt* (1938). (Hs. H.)

RÖNTGEN, WILHELM KONRAD (1845–1923), German physicist, was born at Lennep on March 27, 1845. He received his early education in Holland, and then went to study at Zürich. He then became assistant to August Kundt at Würzburg and afterward at Strasbourg, becoming *privatdozent* at the latter university in 1874. Next year he was appointed professor of mathematics and physics at the Agricultural academy of Hohenheim, and in 1876 he returned to Strasbourg as extraordinary professor. In 1879 he was chosen ordinary professor of physics and director of the Physical institute at Giessen, and in 1885 he went to Würzburg in the same capacity. It was at the latter place that he made the discovery for which his name is chiefly known, the Röntgen rays. In 1895, while experimenting with a highly exhausted vacuum tube on the conduction of electricity through gases, he observed the fluorescence of a barium platinocyanide screen which happened to be lying near. Further investigation showed that this radiation had the power of passing through various substances which are opaque to ordinary light, and also of affecting a photographic plate. Its behaviour being curious in several respects, particularly in regard to reflection and refraction, he doubted whether it was to be looked upon as light or not, and put forward the hypothesis that it was due to longitudinal vibrations in the ether, not to transverse ones like ordinary light; in view of the uncertainty existing as to its nature, he called it X-rays. For this discovery he received the Rumford medal of the Royal society in 1896, jointly with Philip Lenard, who had already shown, as also had Heinrich Hertz, that a portion of the cathode rays could pass through a thin film of a metal such as aluminum. Röntgen also conducted researches in various other branches of physics, including elasticity, capillarity, the ratio of the specific heats of gases, the conduction of heat in crystals, the absorption of heat rays by different gases, piezo-electricity, the electromagnetic rotation of polarized light, etc. Röntgen received the Nobel prize for physics in 1901. He died at Munich on Feb. 10, 1923.

See also X-RAYS, NATURE OF.

ROOFS. A roof is the covering of a structure. Its chief purpose is to enclose the upper parts of a building as a protection against wind, rain and snow; in communities of dwellings, domestic buildings, industrial and commercial structures, fire-resistance is a necessary property of roofing.

Roofs may be flat, or may be inclined at an angle to suit the roof covering. Covering materials are selected for pitched roofs according to their resistance to rain and snow, durability in changes of temperature and in acid atmospheres, and for their artistic qualities in relation to architectural design. Modern buildings erected in concrete usually have flat roofs, consisting of concrete slabs surfaced with asphalt or with waterproofed cement coatings. Sufficient fall must be given to drain water off quickly and adequate gutters formed in the concrete to discharge the water in heavy storms.

For buildings erected in steel framework flat concrete roofs may be adopted, but in order to keep the eaves of a building at a lower level, while providing additional storeys in the accommodation, it is more usual in cities to adopt a Mansard type of roof, having the general form shown in fig. 5, but constructed in steel. Cross members are avoided as much as possible—except where required as floor girders—and the frame is made rigid by strong steel gussets at the changes of direction of the slopes. Two storeys in the roof—or more—can be obtained in this way.

While timber framework continues to be used for supporting roof coverings of lead, copper, zinc, special felts, asbestos sheets, slates and tiles—both for flat and pitched roofs—steel has largely replaced timber for the main supports and for many transverse members in the larger buildings, and even for semipermanent

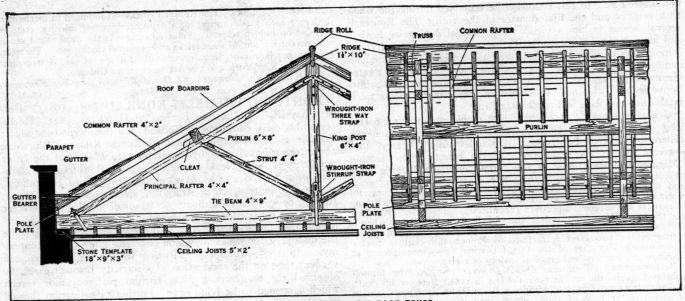

FIGS. 1 & 2.—KING-POST ROOF TRUSS

industrial buildings and stores, because of the rapidity with which materials can be prepared, assembled and erected. Steel is also economically justified for use in roof framing except for dwellings and small buildings, or for dye-works and bleach-works where rapid oxidation renders steel unsuitable. Roofs are often made with considerable projection at the eaves. This serves to protect the upper portion of the external walls and also possesses aesthetic value in design.

Forms of Roofs.—The simplest form is the "flat roof" consisting of horizontal wood joists laid from wall to wall as in floors. The roof must have sufficient fall to allow water to drain away into gutters placed at convenient points. The joists are covered with boards followed by a waterproof material such as asphalt, lead, zinc or copper. These flat roofs cannot be economically constructed for cold climates with heavy snowfalls; they are difficult to maintain weathertight under such conditions.

"Lean-to," "shed," or "pent" roofs are developments of the same form of construction as the flat roof, one end of the joists (now called "rafters") being lifted to form a decided slope, which enables slates, tiles, asbestos sheets and other materials to be employed in small units.

Simple roofs in general use with a double slope are called "coupled rafter roofs," the rafters meeting at the highest point upon a horizontal ridge-piece which stiffens the framework and gives a level ridge-line. In some old roofs the rafters are connected without any intervening ridge-plate, with the result that after a time the ridge instead of remaining level takes on a wavy outline, due to the fact that some of the timbers have settled slightly owing to decay or other causes, whilst others have remained firm. The lower ends of the rafters should rest upon a wood plate bedded on the top of the wall; this assists in spreading the weight over the wall, and provides fixing for the timbers. The simple "couple roof" consists merely of two sets of rafters pitched from plates on the walls on either side of the building and sloping upwards to rest against a common ridge-piece. There are no ties between the feet of the rafters, which therefore exert a considerable thrust against the supporting walls; this form of roof is only suitable for spans of 10 to 12 feet. Where the ends of the rafters are connected by ceiling joists which form a level ceiling the joists act as ties and prevent any outward thrust on the supports. Such roofs are termed "couple close roofs." When used for spans between 12 ft. and 18 ft. a binder supported by an iron or wood "king" tie every 5 or 6 ft. should be run along across the centres of the ceiling joists and the latter spiked to it. When ties are fixed about half-way up the rafters the roof is called a "collar roof," and may be used for spans up to 16 ft. This type of roof is commonly used in dwelling-houses where the

fir framing is generally hidden from view by the ceilings. Where required extra support is obtained from partitions and cross walls. If the span is above 20 ft. without intermediate support, it is necessary to employ "principals" and "purlins." American usage sanctions much greater spans than English for simple raftered roofs. Frequently spans as great as 30 ft. or more are roofed without trusses or interior supports, provided that the feet of the rafters are adequately tied by means of ceiling or floor joists at or near the plate level. Principals are strong trusses of timber rigidly framed together and placed at intervals of about 10 ft. to support the weight of the roof covering. Purlins—stout timbers running longitudinally—are supported on the principal rafters at intervals of 6 to 8 ft., and on these the common rafters are fastened. Principals, or "roof trusses" as they are more often called, are framed together in various ways; they may be of timber members with iron fastenings, or entirely of steel, or again a combination of steel and timber. In the latter case they are called "composite trusses" and the use of steel is confined to tension members.

The "king-post truss" may be used for spans up to 30 ft. and is constructed as shown in figs. 1 and 2. It has a central post sustaining the "tie-beam" in the centre with struts projecting from its base to support the principal rafters at a point where the weight from the purlins renders strutting necessary. The members are connected by wrought-iron straps and bolts; a strap connects the king-post and tie-beam and is often fitted with a gib-and-cotter arrangement (iron folding wedges) which allows the whole truss to be tightened up should any settlement or shrinkage occur. "Queen-post trusses" have two queen-posts supporting the tie beam (fig. 3). Trusses of this type are suitable for spans up to 45 ft. The joints between the members are made in a similar manner to those of the king-post principal with wrought-iron straps. There are two purlins on each slope, one supported at the top of each "queen," the other about half-way down the principal rafter. A stout straining beam connects the heads of the queens. In fig. 4, a and b are details at the foot of the queen-post, and c at the head. In roofs of larger span, up to 60 ft., the tie-beam requires to be upheld at more than two points, and additional posts called "princesses" are introduced for this purpose. This also entails extra struts and purlins. In such large spans the straining beam often becomes of such a length as to require support and this is effected by continuing the principal rafters up to the ridge and introducing a short king-post to sustain the beam in the middle of its length.

Open Timber Roofs.—Open timber roofs of various types but principally of "hammer-beam" construction were used in the middle ages where stone vaulting was not employed. Many of

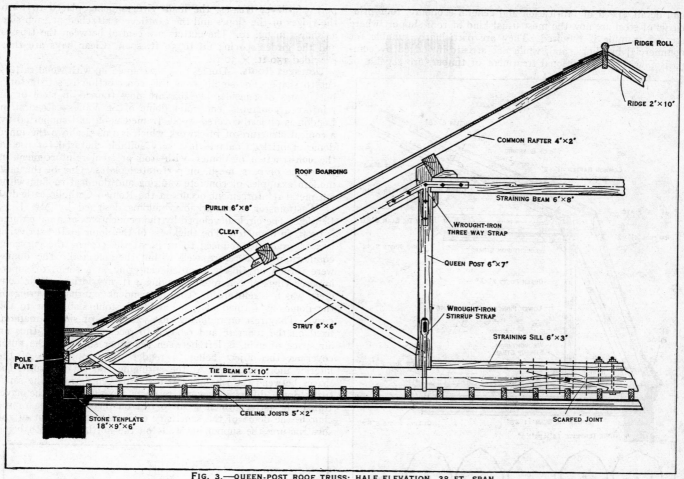

FIG. 3.—QUEEN-POST ROOF TRUSS: HALF ELEVATION, 38 FT. SPAN

these old roofs still exist in good preservation and exhibit the great skill of the mediaeval carpenters who designed and erected them. Such forms are still used, chiefly for ecclesiastical buildings and the roofs over large halls. In the best periods of Gothic architecture the pitch of these roofs was made very steep, sometimes as much as 60° with the horizon. In the hammer-beam

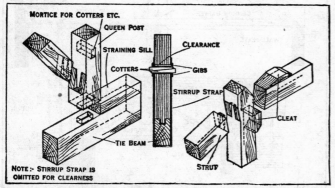

FIG. 4.—(A) DETAIL OF QUEEN-POST TRUSS AT B. (B) VERTICAL SECTION THROUGH QUEEN-POST. (C) DETAIL OF QUEEN-POST TRUSS AT HEAD; PURLIN AND WROUGHT-IRON STRAPS ARE OMITTED FOR THE SAKE OF CLEARNESS

type of roof the tie-beam at the foot of the rafters is omitted, a collar connecting the principal rafters at a point about half-way in their length, and the lower portion of the rafters consisting of struts and braces rigidly connected to relieve thrust upon the walls serving as abutments. There are two kinds of hammer-beam, the arched and the bracketed. The "hammer-beam" projects from the top of the wall and is bracketed from a corbel projecting from the wall some distance below. This form

of roof has a style and dignity appropriate to the period in which it was developed.

The Mansard Roof (fig. 5) is a useful form of construction which obtains its name from François Mansart (*q.v.*). This kind of roof has been largely used in France and other European countries, and in America in the old colonial days. It is well adapted to some styles of architecture, but requires careful proportioning of the slopes for a satisfactory effect. In America the term "Mansard Roof" (*q.v.*) is reserved for roofs of double pitch sloping up from all 4 sides of building; the term "gambrel roof" (*q.v.*) being applied to double pitched roofs ending in gables. By the use of a Mansard roof extra rooms can be obtained without adding an additional storey to the building. Fig. 5, A, B, C, D and E show various sectional forms. A similar type of curb roof is often used having a flat lead or zinc-covered top in place of the pitched slate or tile-covered top of the ordinary Mansard roof.

Composite Roof Trusses of wood and iron are frequently used for all classes of buildings, and have proved very satisfactory. They are built upon the same principles as wooden roof trusses. The struts—that is, those members subjected to compressional stress—are of wood, and iron bars or rods are used for the ties, which have to withstand tensile forces. When shrinkage occurs, as usually happens in large trusses, the joints of the framing are tightened up by the bolts attached to the tie-rods. Figs. 6, 7 and 8 are the sections and plan of a simple method of constructing the roof for a small domestic building with plaster ceilings to the top rooms. It is a couple close roof with the addition of a collar and struts, and king-rod to every fourth rafter. Trimming is necessary for openings and where portions of the structure, such as chimney stacks, cut into the roof. A dragon tie is framed to the wall-plates at the hipped angles to receive the thrust from the hip rafters.

Steel Roof Trusses.—Because of their adaptability in form and detail, speed of fabrication and general economy, roof principals of steel are now the most usual kind of roof support where trussed framing is required. They are particularly suitable for commercial buildings, and, while not artistic if judged by comparison with the traditional treatment of timber, are capable of

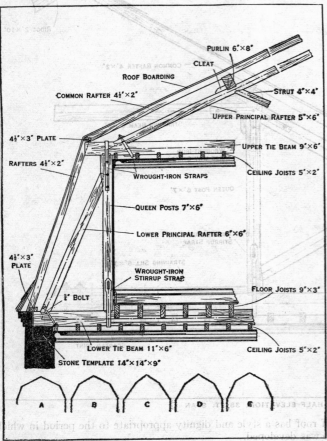

FIG. 5.—MANSARD ROOF TRUSS: DETAIL OF OUTLINE AS A; OTHER OUTLINES AT B, C, D AND E

acceptable aesthetic form based on the economic suitability for their particular purpose.

In the early days of steel trusses, T sections for rafters and struts were usually employed, with rounds and flats for the tie bars. Modern methods of fabrication have gradually developed the use of the L (angle) section for nearly all structural members in roof trusses of moderate span, double angles being used for rafters and ties, single gusset plates riveted between the angles, and ties and struts of either single or double angle section riveted to the faces of the gussets.

The guiding principle is simplicity of form and of detail, and efficiency for service. Often more material is employed in a member than is strictly necessary—and a more economical use of material might be arranged—but usually economy of material means a loss in fabrication costs or the necessity of carrying stocks of many and variable sections of steel.

Double channels are very convenient and largely used for compression members in large span roofs and in unusual structures.

The types of trusses in modern use are given in fig. 9. These include the "queen rod," having vertical ties and inclined struts, the "trussed rafter," in which the struts are at 90° to the rafter, and variations of these forms. Perfect triangulation of steel frames is easy to arrange and the dimensions of the members can be suitably arranged by selection from a large number of standard sections of rolled steel.

Where large areas of uninterrupted floor space are required in textile sheds, garages, etc., a form of roof is often adopted in which main girders of the parallel type, up to 150 ft. span, sup-

port cantilever trusses, the main girders being placed to form the ridges of the slopes and the cantilevers attached at each side as shown in fig. 10. The gutters are central between the trusses and the girder spacing up to 30 ft. span. Clear bays are thus provided 150 ft. × 30 ft.

Domical Roofs.—Domes may be framed up with wood rafters cut to shape. For small spans this construction is satisfactory, but domes of considerable size are now framed in steel or in reinforced concrete. The outer dome of St. Paul's cathedral in London is of lead-covered wood, framed upon and supported by a conical structure of brickwork which is raised above the inner dome of brick. Concrete is a very suitable material for use in the construction of domes, with iron or steel reinforcement in the shape of bars, mesh, or perforated plates. One of the best modern examples of concrete vaulting and domical roofing without metal reinforcement occurs in the Roman Catholic cathedral at Westminster, a remarkable building designed by Mr. J. F. Bentley. The circle developed by the pendentives of a nave dome is 60 ft. in diameter. The thickness of the dome at the springing is 3 ft. gradually reduced to 13 in. at the crown; the curve of equilibrium is therefore well within the material. The domes were turned on closely boarded centering in a series of superimposed rings of concrete, averaging 4 ft. in width, and the concrete was not reinforced. The independent external covering of the domes is formed of 3 in. artificial stone slabs cast to the curve. They rest on radiating ribs 5 in. deep of similar material fixed on the concrete and rebated to receive the slabs; thus an air space of 2 in. is left between the inner shell and the outer covering, the object being to render the temperature of the interior more uniform. At the springing and at the crown the spaces between the ribs are left open for ventilation. The sanctuary dome differs in several respects from those of the nave. Unlike the latter, which seem to rest on the flat roofing of the church, the dome of the sanctuary emerges gradually out of the substructure, the supporting walls on the north and south being

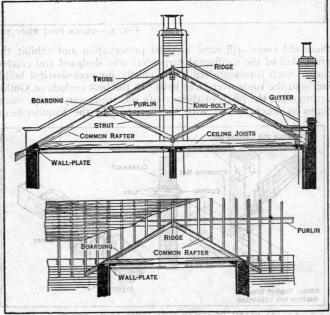

FIGS. 6 & 7.—ROOF FOR DOMESTIC BUILDING

kept down so as to give greater elegance to the eastern turrets. The apsidal termination of the choir in the east is covered in with a concrete vault surmounted by a timber roof, in striking contrast to the domes covering the other portions of the structure. Fig. 11 is a section through the nave showing how the domes are buttressed, fig. 12 is a section through the sanctuary dome, and figs. 13 and 14 a section and part plan of the vaulting of the choir with its wood span roof above the concrete vault.

Covering Materials for Roofs.—There are many different roof-covering materials in common use, of which the principal

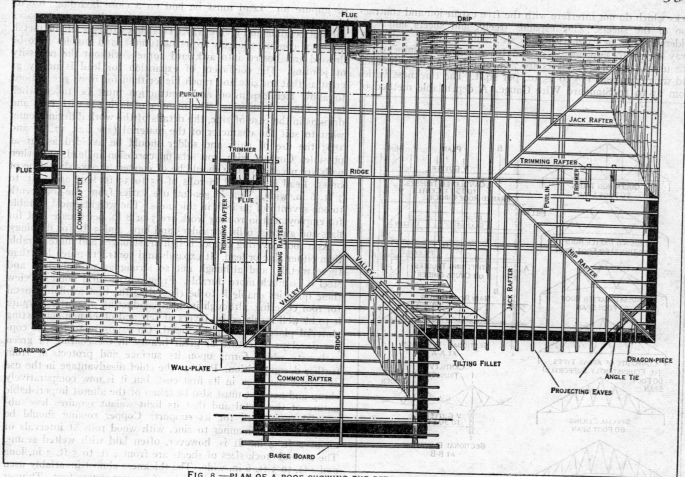

FIG. 8.—PLAN OF A ROOF SHOWING THE DETAILS OF CONSTRUCTION

characteristics are given. The nature of the outer covering affects the details of roof construction in many respects. A light covering such as felt or corrugated iron can be safely laid upon a much lighter timber framing than is necessary for a heavy covering of tiles or slates.

Roofing felt is an inexpensive fabric of animal or vegetable fibre treated with bituminous preparations to make it capable of resisting the weather. It is used as a roofing material for temporary buildings. When exposed to the weather it should be treated with a compound of tar and slaked lime well boiled and applied hot, the surface being sprinkled with sand before it becomes hard. Bituminous felt is employed as a non-conducting and safeguarding under-cover to slates and tiles, used only for the roofs of important buildings. The felt is supplied in rolls containing from 25 to 35 yd. by 30 in. wide. The sheets should be laid with a lap of at least 2 in. at the joints and secured to the boarding beneath by large-headed clout-nails driven in about 2 in. apart.

Corrugated iron is supplied either black or galvanized. It is especially suited for the roofs of out-buildings and buildings of a temporary or semi-permanent character. Being to a large extent self-supporting, it requires a specially designed roof framework of light construction. If, as is usually the case, the sheets are laid with the corrugations running with the slope of the roof, they can be fixed directly on purlins spaced 5 ft. to 10 ft. apart according to the stiffness and length of the sheets. In pure air zinc coating of the galvanized sheets is durable for many years, but in large cities and manufacturing towns its life is short unless protected by painting. In such districts it has often been found that plain ungalvanized sheets well coated with paint will last longer than those galvanized, for the latter are attacked by corrosive influences through minute flaws in the zinc coating developed in the process of corrugation or transit or resulting from

some defect in the coating. The stock sizes of corrugated sheets vary from 5 ft. to 10 ft. long, and from 2 ft. to 2 ft. 9 in. wide with corrugations measuring 3 in. to 5 in. from centre to centre. For roofing purposes the sheets are supplied in several thicknesses ranging from No. 16 to No. 22 Standard Wire Gauge. No. 16 is for exceptionally strong work, No. 18 and No. 20 are used for good-class work, and No. 22 for the roofs of temporary buildings. The sheets when laid should lap one full corrugation at their sides and from 3 in. to 6 in. at the ends. Riveting is the best method of connecting the sheets, although galvanized bolts, which are not so satisfactory, are frequently employed. The joints should be made along the crowns of the corrugations to avoid leakage. Holes can be punched during the erection of the roof. For attachment to timber framework, galvanized screws or nails with domed washers are used. Fixing to a steel framework is effected by galvanized hook bolts which clip the purlins and pass through the sheet. Sheets corrugated in the Italian pattern have raised half-rounds every 15 in. or so, the portions between being flat. Such sheets have a very neat appearance and give a better effect in some positions than the ordinary corrugations.

Zinc in sheets is a material largely used as a roof covering, and if care be taken to ensure metal of good quality, it is strong and durable, as well as light and inexpensive. Zinc is stronger weight for weight than lead, slate, tile or glass, but weaker than copper, wrought-iron or steel, although with the exception of the latter two it is not so durable under normal roofing conditions. It is not liable to easy breakage as are slates, tiles and glass. It is usually supplied in flat sheets, although it can also be had in the corrugated form similar to corrugated sheet-iron. When exposed to air, a thin coating of oxide is formed on the surface which protects the metal beneath from any further change, and obviates the necessity of painting. In laying the sheets, the use of solder and nails should be avoided entirely except for fixing clips and tacks which do not interfere with the free expansion and contraction of the sheets. Zinc expands freely, and sheets laid with soldered seams or fixed with nails are liable to buckle and break away owing to movements caused by changes of temperature. The usual sizes of zinc sheets are 7 ft. or 8 ft. long by 3 ft. wide and weighing from 11½ to 25 oz. per sq.ft. The thickness varies from 25 to 19 Standard Wire Gauge. A dependable method of

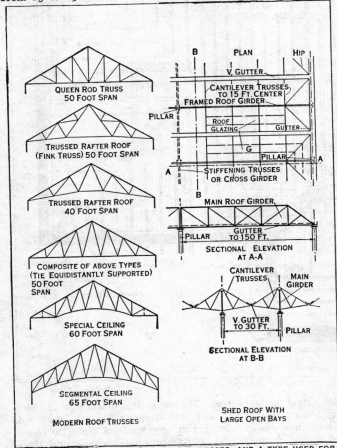

FIGS. 9 & 10.—TYPES OF MODERN ROOF TRUSSES, AND A TYPE USED FOR LARGE UNINTERRUPTED FLOOR AREAS

laying zinc on flat roofs is with the aid of wood "rolls," about 2 in. × 2 in. in section, splayed at the sides, spaced 2 ft. 8 in. apart and fixed to the roof boarding with zinc nails. Iron nails should not be used as this metal affects the zinc. The sheets of zinc are laid between the rolls with their sides bent up 1½ in. or 2 in. against them, and held firmly in position by clips of zinc attached to the rolls. A cap of the same metal is then slipped over each roll and fastened down by tacks about 3 in. long soldered inside it so as to hook under the same clips that anchor the sheet. Drips of about 2½ in. are made in the slope at intervals of 6 ft. or 7 ft.—that is, the length of a sheet—and care must be taken at these points to keep the work waterproof. The lower sheet is bent up the face of the drip and under the projecting portion of the upper sheet, which is finished with a roll edge to turn off the water. The end of the roll has a specially folded cap which also finishes with a curved or beaded water check, and this in conjunction with the saddle piece of the roll beneath forms a weather-proof joint (figs. 15 and 16). The fall between the drips is usually about 1½ in. deep, but where necessary it may be less, the least permissible fall being about 1 in 80. Felt laid beneath zinc has the effect of lengthening the life of the roof and should always be used, as the edges of the boarding upon which it is laid are, when the latter warps, apt to cut the sheets. It also forms a cushion protecting the zinc if there is traffic across the roof.

Sheet-lead forms a much heavier roof covering than zinc, but it lasts a great deal longer and more easily withstands the attacks

of impure air. Lead must be laid on a close boarding, for its great ductility prevents it from spanning even the smallest spaces without bending and giving way. This characteristic of the metal, however, conduces largely to its usefulness, and enables it to be dressed and bossed into awkward corners without the necessity of jointing. The coefficient of expansion for lead is nearly as great as that for zinc and much higher than for iron; precautions to allow free expansion and contraction must be taken when laying the lead covering. The manner of laying is with rolls and drips as in the case of zinc, the details of the work differing somewhat to suit the character of the material (see figs. 17, 18 and 19); the use of nails and solder should be avoided as far as possible. Contact with iron sets up corrosion in lead, and when nails are necessary they should be of copper; screws should be of brass. Lead is supplied in rolls of 25 to 35 ft. long and 6 ft. to 7 ft. 6 in. wide. That in general use varies from one-fourteenth to one-seventh of an inch in thickness. The weights most suitable for employment in roofing work are 7 or 8 lb. per square foot for flats and gutters, 6 lb. for ridges and hips, and 5 lb. for flashings.

As a roof covering copper is lighter, stronger and more durable than either zinc or lead. It expands and contracts much less than these metals, and although not so strong as wrought-iron and steel it is much more durable. From a structural point of view these qualities enable it to be classed as the best available metal for roof covering, although its heat-conducting properties require it to be well insulated by layers of felt and other non-conducting material placed beneath the metal. On exposure to the air copper develops a feature of great beauty in the coating of green carbonate which forms upon its surface and protects it from further decomposition. Perhaps the chief disadvantage in the use of copper has been in its first cost, but it is now comparatively cheap and account must also be taken of the almost imperishable nature of the metal and that its light weight requires less substantial framework for its support. Copper roofing should be laid in a similar manner to zinc, with wood rolls at intervals of about 2 ft. 4 in. It is, however, often laid with welted seams. The general stock sizes of sheets are from 4 ft. to 5 ft. 3 in. long and 2 ft. to 3 ft. 6 in. wide. The thickness almost invariably used is known as 24 S.W.G. and weighs 16 oz. per square foot. Thinner metal would suffice, but owing to the increased cost of rolling very little would be gained by adopting the thinner gauges.

In the United States of America "tin" roofs are quite commonly used. Sheets of wrought-iron coated either with tin or zinc are used of a size usually 14 in. by 20 in., though they may be had double this size. Preparation for laying is made by fixing an insulating foundation of somewhat stout paper or felt; this must be dry, else it is apt to spoil the impermeable covering laid upon it by causing it to rust. Junctions between the sheets are made by welted seams in which the four edges of the sheets are turned over so as to lock together, thus forming one large sheet of tin covering the roof. In high-class work of a permanent nature the seams in addition are soldered, rosin only being used as a flux. Each sheet also is secured to the roof with two or three tin cleats. The life of such a roof may be practically doubled by the application of a coat of good paint, which, however, adds considerably to the cost.

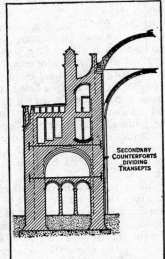

FIG. 11.—WESTMINSTER CATHEDRAL: SECTION THROUGH NAVE

The greatest use of bituminous materials in modern roof coverings is in the form of tar and gravel or tar and slag roofs. These consist of three or more layers or plies glued to each other and covered by heavy coats of coal tar pitch. Onto the upper layer of pitch, before it has hardened, there is sprinkled a bed of gravel or slag, which is held in place by the pitch, and at the same time protects it. Flat tile roofs, terraces or promenades are frequently built in a somewhat similar manner, with an under layer of several plies of pitch and felt, covered with an inch thick bed of cement, on which the tile is laid. Adequate expansion joints, filled with some elastic cement, are usually installed in the tiled surface. Such roofs, either tile covered or gravel and slag covered, are perfectly watertight, do not crack under extremes of heat and cold, and have become the most common type for the better class of flat roof, such as those of large modern office and apartment buildings, etc. If adequately flashed at the intersections with walls and parapets, they can be built perfectly level without fall or slope.

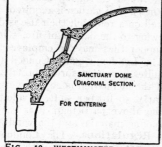

FIG. 12—WESTMINSTER CATHEDRAL: DIAGONAL SECTION THROUGH SANCTUARY DOME

Slate (q.v.) is a strong and very impermeable material, and these qualities and the fact that it is easily split into thin plates suitable for laying, as well as its low cost, for many years caused it to be by far the most generally used of all materials for roof covering.

Slates are cut to many different sizes varying in length from 10 in. to 36 in. and in width from 5 in. to 24 in. There are perhaps thirty or more recognized sizes, each distinguished by a different name. In common practice those generally used are "large ladies," 16 in. by 8 in.; "countesses," 20 in. by 10 in.; and "duchesses," 24 in. by 12 in. Generally speaking, the rule governing the use of the different sizes is that the steeper the pitch the smaller the slate, and vice versa. Buildings in very exposed positions naturally require steeply pitched roofs, if they are to be covered and rendered weather-tight by small lapped units of covering.

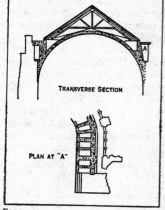

FIGS. 13 & 14.—WESTMINSTER CATHEDRAL: CHOIR-VAULTING

Slates may be fixed by nailing at the head or at about the middle. The latter method is the stronger, as the levering effect of the wind cannot attain so great a strength. There is a small economy effected by centre nailing, as the margin is slightly larger and fewer slates are required to cover a given space; longer nails, however, are required, for as slates are laid at an angle with the pitch of the roof their centres cannot be made to approach so

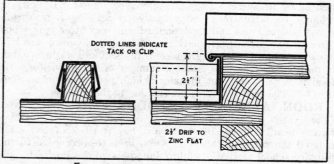

FIGS. 15 & 16.—DETAILS OF ZINC FLATS

near to the slating battens or boarding as the head, which lies close on the surface to which it is fixed. Another important point is that the nail-holes in the centre-nailed slating are only covered by 3 in. of the tail (the amount of the "lap") of the course of slates above, and rain is very liable to be forced under by the wind and cause the wood battens or other woodwork to rot. Head-nailed slates, on the other hand, have their holes covered by two layers of slate, and are removed from exposure by the length of the gauge plus the lap, which in the case of "countess" slating equals 11 in.

A point in favour of centre-nailing is that the slates are more securely held to the battens or boards and offer much more resistance to being lifted by the wind.

"Open slating" is an economical method of laying slates that is often adopted for the roofs of sheds, foundries and temporary buildings. The slates in the same course are not laid edge to edge as in close slating, but at a distance of two or more inches apart. This forms a roof covering light in weight and inexpensive, which, although not strictly weather-proof, is sufficiently so for the buildings upon which it is used.

Slates are laid upon open battens fixed upon the rafters or upon close boarding or upon battens fixed upon boarding. The battens are ¾ in. or 1 in. thick and 1½ in. to 3 in. wide, and are spaced to suit the gauge of the slates. When close boarding is used it is

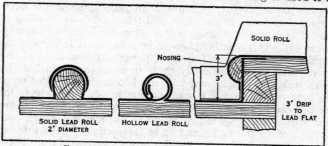

FIGS. 17, 18 & 19.—DETAILS OF LEAD FLATS

often covered with inodorous asphalted felt, and to allow of ventilation of the materials, under-battens are sometimes fixed vertically, ridge ventilators introduced and air inlets arranged at the eaves. The beds of slates laid without provision for the admission of air have been found occasionally to have rotted so as to scale and crumble easily.

The nails used in slating are important and the durability of the work depends on a good selection. They should have large flat heads. The most satisfactory are those made of a composition of copper and zinc, but others of copper, zinc, galvanized iron and plain iron are used. Those of copper are most durable, but are soft and expensive while zinc nails are soft and not very durable; they will last for about twenty years. Iron nails even if galvanized are only employed in cheap and temporary work; they may be preserved by being heated and plunged in boiled linseed oil. The pitch of a roof intended for slating should not incline less than 25° with the horizontal, while for the smaller sizes 30° is a safer angle to adopt.

Modern slate roofs are frequently laid with varying courses and of varying thicknesses, usually with the heavier slate from three-quarters to an inch and a half thick at the eaves, with thinner and smaller slate in the upper part of the roof. Marked variation of colour is often sought by combining green and purple slate, or fading and unfading slate.

Tiles for roofing purposes are made from clay and baked in a kiln, like bricks. The clay from which they are made is, however, of a specially tenacious nature and prepared with great care so as to obtain a strong and non-porous covering. Tiles are obtainable in many colours, some having a beautiful effect when fixed and many improving with age. They comprise tints from yellowish red, red and brown to dark blue. As with bricks the quality depends to a large extent upon the burning; underburnt tiles are weak and porous, liable to early decay, while overburning, though improving the tiles as regards durability, will cause warping and variation of colour. Variation of colour is now deliberately obtained, and artistic effects are secured by sand facing, artificial rustication and by burning to metallic surfaces. The usual shape is the "plain tile," but they are made in various other shapes with a view both to easier fixing and lighter weight, and to ornamental effect. There are also several patented forms on the market for which the makers claim special advantages. The ordinary tiles are slightly curved in the direction of length to enable them to lie closely at their lower edges. Some of them have small "nibs" at the head by which they may be hung upon the battens without nails. Nail-holes are provided, and it is advisable to nail every 4th or 5th course, at least. Others are made without the nibs, and are fixed either by nailing to the battens or boarding or hung by means of oaken pegs wedged in the holes to the battens, the pegs in the latter case acting in the same way as the above-mentioned nibs. Plain tiles are of rectangular form, the standard dimensions are 10½ in. long by 6½ in. wide. They are usually ½ in. thick and weigh about 2½ lb. each.

There are many forms of ornamental tiles, which are plain tiles having their tails cut to various shapes instead of moulded square. A number of patented forms of tiles also are on the market, some of which possess considerable merit. *Pantiles* are suitable for temporary and inferior buildings, if laid dry and on flat slopes, but if laid upon boards and felt and bedded and pointed in mortar, pantiles may prove an excellent covering. They are laid on a different principle from plain tiles, merely overlapping each other at the edges, and this necessitates bedding in mortar and pointing inside and sometimes outside with mortar or cement. This pointing plays an important part in keeping the interior of the building free from the penetration of wind and water. Pantiles are generally made to measure 13½ in. long by 9½ in. wide, and weigh from 5 lb. to 5½ lb. each. Moulded on at the head of each tile is a small projecting nib which serves for the purpose of hanging the tile to the lath or batten. They are laid with a lap of 3½ in., 2½ in. or 1½ in., giving a gauge (and margin) of 10 in., 11 in. and 12 in., respectively. The side lap is generally 1½ in., leaving a width of 8 in. exposed face. There are many other forms based upon the shape of the pantile, some of which are patented and claim to have advantages which the original form does not possess. Among such are "corrugated tiles," of the ordinary shape or with angular flutes, and also the Italian pattern "double roll tiles," "Foster's lock-wing tiles." Poole's bonding roll tiles are a development of the Italian pattern tile. French and Belgian tiles of the "Marseille" pattern are economical and therefore popular for housing schemes and cheap building.

Wood shingles are common roofing materials throughout the United States and Canada, and were at one time in general use in Europe. The present customary usage is to make them either of cedar or cypress, varying from 18 to 24 inches long, and from 6 inches to a foot or more wide. The butts at the thick end are from a half to three-quarters of an inch thick; the upper end tapers to not over one-eighth of an inch. They are usually laid from four and one-half to five and one-half inches to the weather. Owing to the fire risk, wood shingle roofs are gradually passing out of use, and in many localities are prohibited.

The 20th century has seen the development of many specialized roof materials, either with an asbestos or a bituminous felt base, designed for sloping roofs and intended to give an aesthetic effect similar to that of either shingles or slate. In the better and heavier types the units come separately as individual shingles; in the lighter and cheaper classes, the shingle shapes are cut upon strips.

Glass as a roof covering and the different methods of fixing it are dealt with in the article GLAZING.

There are many other materials used for roof covering besides those already described, many of them of considerable value. Some have in the past enjoyed considerable vogue, but have practically died out of use owing to the development and cheapening of other forms of roofing. Among these may be included thatch and wood shingles, the use of which in these days is practically reduced to special cases. Other roofing materials are those of recent invention, some of which may have a great future, depending upon the development, reliability and aesthetic value of the products. Sheets of asbestos-cement used as slates or tiles make a light, strong and fireproof covering. Large terra-cotta tiles or slabs are much used in the United States of America. A good form of flat roof is that in which concrete is used as a foundation for a waterproof layer of asphalt, laid to falls to allow the water to run off easily. This is the usual method adopted when a roof garden is required. Shingles or thatch look extremely well on a roof, but their use is debarred in a great many districts owing to the danger of fire. Galvanized iron tiles, zinc tiles and copper tiles may be employed on small areas with good effect. The London County Council (General Powers) Act, 1909, requires provision for a normal wind pressure of 28 lb. per sq.ft. if the inclination is 20° or more. Flat roofs must be designed to carry 56 lb. per sq.ft. in addition to their own weight. From the above particulars it is easy to calculate the weight of the roofing material and the wind pressure on the roof.

Regulations.—The London Building Act of 1894 and its amendments set forth with regard to roofs erected in the London district that every structure on a roof is to be covered with slate, tile, metal or other incombustible material, except wooden cornices and barge boards to dormers not exceeding 12 in. in depth, and doors and windows and their frames. Every dwelling-house or factory above 30 ft. in height and having a parapet must have means of access to the roof. The pitch of the roofs of warehouse buildings must not exceed 47°, and those of other buildings 75°, but towers, turrets and spires are excepted. In domestic buildings not more than two storeys are to be formed in the roof, and if the floor is more than 60 ft. above the street level fireproof materials must be used throughout and a sufficient means of escape provided.

The Building and Health Laws and Regulations and Amendments affecting the city of New York are similar to those of London. They give very full working details as to the strengths of materials required to be used and the wind pressure to be provided against. They provide that where a building exceeds three storeys or 40 ft. in height and the roof has a pitch of over 60°, it shall be constructed of iron rafters and be lathed with iron or steel inside and plastered or filled in with fireproof material not less than 3 in. thick and covered with metal, slate or tile.

LITERATURE—The principal reference books on this subject are the following:—G. L. Sutcliffe, *The Modern Carpenter, Joiner and Cabinet Maker*; J. Gwilt, *Encyclopaedia of Architecture*; F. E. Kidder, *Trussed Roofs and Roof Trusses*; J. Brandon, *Analysis of Gothic Architecture*; A. Pugin, *Ornamental Gables*; M. Emy, *L'Art de la charpenterie*; Viollet le Duc, *Dictionnaire*; J. K. Colling, *Details of Gothic Architecture*; G. Ellis, *Modern Practical Carpentry*; Jaggard & Drury, *Architectural Building Construction*; Blake, *Roofs & Roof Coverings*; J. W. Riley, *Carpentry & Joinery*; C. F. Mitchell, *Building Construction*; Rivington, *Building Construction*.

ROOK (*Corvus frugilegus*), throughout a great part of Europe, the commonest of the crow tribe. Besides its gregarious habits, which are distinctive, the rook is distinguished from the rest of the *Corvidae* by losing at an early age the feathers from its face, leaving a bare, scabrous and greyish-white skin visible at some distance. In the rare cases in which these feathers persist, the rook may be known from the crow (*q.v.*) by the rich purple gloss of its black plumage, especially on the head and neck, as well as by its voice. The sexes are very similar. It nests in colonies on large trees (occasionally on buildings), making a strong nest of twigs and earth and using it year after year. The three to five green eggs, marked with grey and brown, are laid in early April. In Britain the rook is resident and stationary, but in most of Europe it is either a summer or winter visitor. Its food is very varied, but includes a high percentage of noxious insects. The bird is thus of great value to the farmer.

ROON, ALBRECHT THEODOR EMIL, COUNT VON (1803–1879), Prussian general field-marshal, was born at Pleushagen, near Colberg, in Pomerania, on April 30, 1803. He entered the corps of cadets at Kulm in 1816, proceeded to the military school at Berlin, and in Jan. 1821 joined the 14th (3rd Pomeranian) regiment. In 1826 he was appointed an instructor in the Berlin cadet school, and in 1832 published his *Grundzüge der Erd-, Völker- und Staaten-Kunde* (3 vols.), gaining a great reputation. This was followed by *Anfangsgründe der Erdkunde* (1834), *Militärische Länderbeschreibung von Europa* (1837) and *Die iberische Halbinsel* (1839).

In 1832, he rejoined his regiment, and became alive to the inefficient state of the army; in 1842 he was promoted to be major and attached to the staff of the VII. Corps. In 1848 he was appointed chief of the staff of the VIII. Army Corps, and during the disturbances of that year served under the Crown Prince William (afterwards emperor), distinguishing himself in the suppression of the insurrection at Baden. At that time he broached the subject of his schemes of army reform. In 1850 came the revelation of defective organization; next year Roon was made a full colonel and began active work as reorganizer.

Prince William became regent in 1857, and in 1859 he appointed Roon (now lieutenant-general) a member of a commission to report on military reorganization. Supported by Manteuffel and Moltke, Roon was able to get his plans to create an armed nation, to extend Scharnhorst's system and to adapt it to Prussia's altered circumstances generally adopted. To attain this he proposed a universal three years' service, and a reserve (*Landwehr*) for the defense of the country when the army was actively engaged. During the Italian War he was charged with the mobilization of a division. At the end of 1859, though the junior lieutenant-general in the army, he succeeded von Bonin as war minister, and two years later the ministry of marine was also entrusted to him. His proposals of army reorganization met with the bitterest opposition, and it was not until after long fighting against a hostile majority in the chambers that, with Bismarck's aid, he carried the day. Even the Danish campaign of 1864 did not wholly convince the country of the necessity of his measures, and it required the war with Austria of 1866 (when he was promoted general of infantry) to convert obstinate opposition into enthusiastic support. After that von Roon became the most popular man in Prussia, and his reforms were ultimately copied throughout continental Europe. His system, adopted after 1866 by the whole North German Confederation, produced its inevitable result in the war with France 1870–71. He was created a count, and in Dec. 1871, succeeded Bismarck as president of the Prussian ministry. Ill-health compelled him to resign in the following year. He was promoted field-marshal on Jan. 1, 1873, and died at Berlin on Feb. 23, 1879.

After his death his son published the valuable *Denkwürdigkeiten aus dem Leben des Generalfeldmarschalls Kriegsministers Grafen Roon* (2 vols., Breslau, 1892), and *Kriegsminister von Roon als Redner politisch und militärisch erläutert* (Breslau, 1895). His correspondence with his friend Professor Cl. Perthes, 1864–67, was also published at Breslau in 1895.

ROORKEE, a town of British India, in the Saharanpur district of the United Provinces. Pop. (1941) 23,329, including the cantonment. It is the headquarters of the workshops of the Ganges canal, and also of the Bengal Sappers and Miners. The Thomason Civil Engineering college, founded in 1848, was instituted in order to train Indians in engineering, and students originally received stipends. The college works in co-operation with the workshops and foundry of the canal, and also trains in surveying, photography and other subjects, having chemical, physical, electrical and mechanical laboratories and workshops.

ROOSEVELT, FRANKLIN DELANO (1882–1945), thirty-second President of the United States, was born at Hyde Park, N. Y., Jan. 30, 1882. His father, James Roosevelt a wealthy landowner, vice-president of the Delaware & Hudson Railroad, and Democratic politician, held several minor diplomatic offices under President Cleveland; his mother, Sara Delano, had sprung from a family of New York merchants and shippers. The upper Hudson Valley community in which Franklin D. Roosevelt was reared was devoted to sports, and he early learned to hunt to hounds, shoot, play polo and tennis, and manage an ice-boat. In summers at Campobello on the New Brunswick coast he made long cruises by catboat and yacht. European travel began when the boy was three and he learned to speak German and French fluently. Passing through Groton School, he entered Harvard in 1900 and on graduation went to the Columbia University Law School in 1904. In March, 1905, he married Anna Eleanor Roosevelt of New York, a sixth cousin, the wedding being attended by President Theodore Roosevelt, who was uncle of the bride and fifth cousin of the groom. Thereafter the couple frequently saw President Roosevelt in Washington or at Oyster Bay. In 1907 Franklin D. Roosevelt completed his course at Columbia, was admitted to the bar, and began practice in New York City. His father had meanwhile died, and he combined his legal work with frequent visits to Hyde Park where he took an important position in business, philanthropic and social activities.

Contact with Theodore Roosevelt inspired the young man with an interest in politics; the Democratic leaders in Dutchess County saw in him a promising recruit. In 1910 they gave him the nomination for State Senator. Though only one Democrat had been elected to that post since 1856, by virtue of a pleasing personality, a strenuous automobile campaign, and a schism in the Republican party, he obtained a narrow majority. In his first year in Albany he attained prominence by leading a small band of Democratic legislators who refused to accept the Tammany Hall candidate for election to the U. S. Senate, William F. Sheehan. Declaring Sheehan unfit for the place by his character and close association with predatory traction corporations, Roosevelt held his fellow-insurgents firm against the party caucus till a better candidate was substituted. The reputation for progressivism and independence which he thus obtained was extended by his championship of reform legislation. In 1911 he was prominent in the New York movement for nominating Woodrow Wilson to the Presidency, and in June, 1912, led an unofficial delegation of 150 men to the Democratic Convention in Baltimore, where he did effective work. Reëlected that fall to the State Senate, he introduced some notable bills for protecting the farmers against unfair commission merchants and stimulating rural co-operation. The incoming Wilson Administration offered him a choice of several minor posts; he accepted the Assistant Secretaryship of the Navy.

Spending the years 1913–1921 in the Navy Department, Mr. Roosevelt was the principal lieutenant of Secretary Josephus Daniels in administering naval affairs. During 1913–1916 he was an unwearying advocate of greater naval preparedness, producing many speeches and articles; he set about converting useless navy yards into industrial plants for making naval supplies; and he and Mr. Daniels broke up an alleged combination of armour plate manufacturers. Before war broke out he had built up a small Naval Reserve on the basis of systematic civilian training. During the conflict he gave much attention to the submarine problem. He was one of the earliest and most enthusiastic advocates of the mine barrage between Norway and the Orkneys, refusing to heed American and British experts who pronounced it impossible; and he was also largely responsible for the 110-foot submarine chasers, of which about 400 were built. In the summer of 1918 he had charge of the inspection of American naval forces in European waters and did much to promote co-operation with the British Admiralty. After the armistice he took charge of demobilization in Europe and helped dispose of naval supplies stored there. He returned to the United States on the same ship with Wilson (February, 1919) and began speaking for the League of Nations. The following year he received the Democratic nomination for Vice President, made approximately a thousand speeches, and after the Democratic defeat returned to New York to practise law.

In August, 1921, Mr. Roosevelt was stricken with infantile paralysis and emerged with the muscles of his legs and lower abdomen paralyzed. By careful exercises and winter treatments at Warm Springs, Ga., he gradually recovered. Meanwhile he continued legal work, establishing the firm of Roosevelt & O'Connor in 1924, and kept up much of his business and civic activity. As head of the Boy Scouts Foundation in New York City he raised large sums, and at Warm Springs he established an important hydrotherapeutic centre on a non-profitmaking basis. In 1924 he placed Alfred E. Smith in nomination at the Democratic National Convention. After the Democratic defeat of that year he made efforts to bring the Bryan-McAdoo and Smith-Raskob factions together on a progressive basis. These failed, but he succeeded in softening much of the Southern opposition to Smith. In 1927 he urged acceptance of Smith and in 1928 nominated him again at the Houston Convention. At Smith's insistence, though protesting that two more years of private life were necessary to his health, he allowed himself to be drafted as Democratic candidate for governor of New York. Carrying the State by about 25,000 votes while Smith lost it by more than 100,000, he was inaugurated in January, 1929. He furnished a conciliatory administration, and in 1930 was reëlected by the unprecedented plurality of 725,000, economic depression and the quarrel over prohibition cutting down the Republican vote. His principal achievements in his two terms as governor were partial settlement of the hydroelectric question on the basis of public development of the St. Lawrence waterpower; a strengthening of the Public Service Commission; and passage of various pieces of social welfare legislation, including an old-age pension law.

With the approach of the election of 1932, it became evident that Mr. Roosevelt was in a happy position to unite the discordant Democratic elements. At the Chicago Convention in July the rival candidates proved unable to unite, and on the third ballot a change by the California and Texas delegations gave Mr. Roosevelt the nomination. He at once began a campaign which took him into every section, travelling 12,500 miles and delivering some 200 speeches. Making effective use of demands for tariff reduction, farm relief, and greater attention to the "forgotten man," he enlisted the support of many influential Progressive Republicans. The economic depression caused an enormous defection of Republican voters, and in November Roosevelt received 472 electoral votes against 59 for Hoover, carrying all but six states with a popular plurality of over seven million.

Mr. Roosevelt took office, March 4, 1933, amid the throes of a crisis unprecedented in time of peace. Between his election and inauguration he had realized its imminence and had prepared the broad outlines of a programme. Details of his plans, in a fast-changing situation, had to be worked out in the heat of the moment. His first task, as the nation seemingly stood on the brink of an abyss, was to restore its morale. An eloquent inaugural address caught the popular imagination. It was at once followed by a proclamation closing banks, embargoing gold, and proving the government's power to cope with the financial crisis. From that point he moved swiftly toward three objectives already outlined: restoration of prosperity "by re-establishing the purchasing power of half the people"; a better balance between farm, factory, and trade; and reshaping the American economic system to eliminate abuses and excesses.

The 99-day session of the 73rd Congress which began March 9, 1933, witnessed the most daring Presidential leadership in American history. Congress, dazed and planless, found itself subjected to a carefully timed bombardment of bills. Mr. Roosevelt sent a rapid succession of presidential messages, sufficiently spaced to avoid confusion; followed each message by a bill to implement it; and thus dealt with the agricultural crisis, banking crisis, relief crisis, and a dozen other problems with amazing speed. The fact that Congress was passing laws to order was never concealed; never before had the American Government so closely approached the British system of Ministerial leadership. In his first month Mr. Roosevelt used this unprecedented authority (1) to reopen banks; (2) to restore Federal credit by temporarily abolishing some of the worst forms of waste; (3) to relieve distress by Federal grants, creation of the Civilian Conservation Corps, and stoppage of foreclosures; (4) to reform the handling of investments and securities; and (5) to begin a system of public works. These emergency measures were at once followed by four steps of the most far-reaching character: (1) a farm relief law; (2) creation of the Tennessee Valley Authority to plan the development of a 640,000-sq. mi. region; (3) passage of the National Recovery Act; and (4) the decision to abandon the gold standard and move toward revaluation of the dollar. His programme had a scope never before approached in time of peace. When Congress adjourned June 16, after heeding all his principal recommendations, the nation had been placed squarely upon a new path.

Mr. Roosevelt's administration then entered upon a different phase. His primary task for the next three years was to administer the legislation already obtained. Since his genius was for originating rather than executing, his record was uneven. The Agricultural Adjustment Administration under Secretary Henry A. Wallace proved highly efficient. Its crop restriction plans, together with two great droughts, relieved the farmer of the incubus of crop surpluses and restored prices. When the Supreme Court struck down the A. A. A., Mr. Roosevelt and Mr. Wallace had a substitute scheme ready for immediate operation. Mr. Roosevelt was less fortunate when he placed the National Recov-

ery Administration under General Hugh Johnson, whose attempt to carry the code system into all industries and to resort to moral coercion brought the law into discredit. When the Supreme Court held the Recovery Act unconstitutional (May 27, 1935), Mr. Roosevelt expressed bitter disappointment and indicated a temporary disposition to seek an amendment to the Constitution conferring enlarged power in social and economic spheres upon Congress. But public opinion was chilly and he abandoned the idea. He made excellent appointments for administering the Tennessee Valley Authority (Dr. Arthur Morgan) and the Securities Commission (Mr. Joseph P. Kennedy); his choice of Mr. Harry Hopkins as principal agent in charge of relief was also sound, though he was not able to prevent costly bickering between Mr. Hopkins and Secretary Harold L. Ickes. His administration at first moved too rapidly for the civil service merit system, but the attacks on its alleged subserviency to spoilsmen were grossly exaggerated.

While busy with administration Mr. Roosevelt continued to demand new measures of social and economic reconstruction. One of the most important was the Gold Reserve Act of January 1934, under which he devalued the dollar to 59.06 cents in terms of its former gold parity. A measure close to Mr. Roosevelt's heart, the Utilities Act, designed to end abuses in the organization of huge holding companies, became law Aug. 26, 1935. It was essentially an attack upon one of the most complicated and mischievous forms of quasi-monopoly in the postwar period. Still more important was the Social Security Act, passed in August 1935. Setting up two great Federal-State systems for unemployment compensation and contributory old-age insurance, it obviously required amendment in the light of future experience, but held great social possibilities. Meanwhile Mr. Roosevelt on June 19, 1935, urged legislation to effect a wider distribution of wealth, calling for two sets of measures: one (inheritance taxes, high income surtaxes, abolition of tax-exempt securities) to halt the accumulation and transmission of great fortunes; the other (graduated corporation income taxes, holding-company taxes, and taxes on unwieldy corporate surpluses) to limit the concentration of power in big business. A highly controversial tax law shortly embodied some of these proposals.

Mr. Roosevelt's views on national policy were never left in doubt. He was an earnest advocate of national planning; but by this he meant not the regimentation of society, but only a constant use of foresight in dealing with national problems. He was hostile to great accumulations of wealth; suspicious of efforts by large-scale business to manipulate the government; eager to give better treatment to the farmer as against urban industry, and to labour as against capital; a believer in constant experimentation in government; certain that a more co-operative, less individualistic society must come into existence. In a time when conflict of opinion was violent, his way of zigzagging between "right" and "left" perhaps gave him a maximum of public support. His method of pushing reform, as the Securities and Exchange Act and other laws showed, was to ask for maximum remedies, then accept modifications as experience showed them necessary.

The Democratic national convention renominated Mr. Roosevelt by acclamation June 27, 1936, and the balloting on Nov. 3 resulted in what was probably the most sweeping victory in all American elections, a popular plurality of 11,069,785 votes, and an electoral vote of 523 to 8 for Alfred M. Landon, governor of Kansas.

A political precedent as old as the republic was broken July 18, 1940, when Mr. Roosevelt was nominated by the Democrats for a third term. He was elected the following November 5 by 27,241,-939 votes to 22,327,226 for Wendell L. Willkie. In 1944 he was elected to a fourth term, defeating Gov. Thomas E. Dewey of New York. Although Roosevelt's plurality was only slightly more than 3,000,000 votes, he won 432 electoral votes to Dewey's 99. Franklin D. Roosevelt died on April 12, 1945, at Warm Springs, Ga. (For events of the second and third Roosevelt administrations, *see* UNITED STATES.) (A. N.; X.)

ROOSEVELT, THEODORE (1858–1919), 26th president of the United States, was born in New York city on Oct. 27, 1858. His father, Theodore Roosevelt, was of a Dutch family conspicuous for centuries in the affairs of the city of his birth; his mother, Martha Bulloch, came of Scotch-Irish and Huguenot stock, which had given men of distinguished quality to the service of Georgia and the South. Young Roosevelt's ill-health necessitated tutors and withheld him from the rough-and-tumble companionship of boys his own age; but deliberately and with great persistence, he built up his frail body. He was graduated from Harvard in 1880 and the same year married Alice Hathaway Lee, of Boston. At the Columbia Law school, and in the office of his uncle, Robert B. Roosevelt, he prepared himself for the bar. But the law did not attract him. His interest lay rather in literature, in natural history and in the prospect of useful and strenuous activity, which the world of politics presented. Against the counsel of his friends who urged that politics was a "dirty business" Roosevelt joined a local political club. His associates there were his first political mentors, they guided him (1881) through his initial campaign for the State legislature. Within six weeks of the opening of the session, Roosevelt made his mark at Albany when he offered a motion to impeach a certain highly respectable judge who had proved over-lenient to a group of notorious financiers. He was sharply and at last successfully opposed, but his characterization of the sinister forces behind a corrupt legislature as "the wealthy criminal class" stuck in the public mind. Roosevelt was in the New York assembly three years; and in 1884 his party's candidate for speaker. He became the acknowledged leader of a small but potent group of young men who felt keenly the need of a new spirit in political life and were willing to fight both in the legislature and within the Republican party to keep the corrupting influences in check. As chairman of the New York delegation to the Republican convention in Chicago in 1884, Roosevelt supported the candidacy of Sen. George F. Edmunds, and with vigour and courage opposed the nomination of James G. Blaine. But when Blaine was chosen Roosevelt refused to desert the party, contending that Blaine, having been fairly nominated, had a right to the support of all loyal Republicans. It became clear to him that, for the moment at least, his political career was ended. The death of his wife early in 1884, following the birth of a daughter, had been followed 12 hours later by the death of his mother. When the campaign was over, therefore, he betook himself to the ranch which he had established the previous autumn in Western Dakota. For three years he lived a ranchman's life, and at odd moments wrote biographies of Thomas H. Benton and Gouverneur Morris. Within six months of his coming, he virtually took the leadership of the forces of law and order in the region, organized a protective association to check the cattle-thieves and did active duty as deputy-sheriff. A call from the Republicans in New York city to be their candidate for mayor brought Roosevelt back into politics in 1886. The widespread fear on the part of the propertied classes that Henry George, the candidate of the United Labor party, might be elected caused many Republicans, however, to vote for Abram S. Hewitt, the Democratic nominee, who was chosen, Roosevelt running third.

Official Appointments.—Immediately after the election, Roosevelt married Edith Kermit Carow, a friend of his childhood, and thereafter made his home at Sagamore Hill, near Oyster Bay, L.I. It was his intention to devote himself to literature; but his interest in public affairs drew him again into political life. In 1889, President Harrison appointed him a member of the U. S. Civil Service commission in Washington, and for six years he directed the battle against the entrenched defenders of the "spoils system." He left the Civil Service commission in 1895 to become president of the police board of New York city. On the force money ruled, politics ruled; merit was only incidentally a consideration in appointments. Roosevelt built up the *morale* of the force by substituting a system of appointment and promotion by merit; by rewarding bravery and devotion, by swiftly punishing negligence and venality and by enforcing the laws regardless of "pressure." The politicians of both parties opposed him; all the sensational, and most of the "respectable" newspapers derided or scolded him.

The election of William McKinley to the presidency brought Roosevelt back to Washington as assistant secretary of the navy. He had since his first entrance on the political scene been an ardent advocate of preparedness. He frankly favoured a strong foreign policy and looked forward, in fact, to the ultimate withdrawal of the European powers from the Western Hemisphere. The conditions in Cuba had long convinced him that war with Spain was inevitable. With vigour, he set to work to make the navy ready. He reorganized the system of rank and promotion among naval officers; he adjusted the differences between the "line" and the "engineers." When the United States battleship *Maine* was blown up in Havana harbour on Feb. 15, 1898, Roosevelt sharpened his efforts. During a temporary absence of his chief, John D. Long, he took it upon himself to instigate the preparations which he had in vain asked the secretary of the navy to make. He ordered great quantities of coal and ammunition, directed the assembling of the American fleet, stirred the arsenals and navy yards to activity and, finally, cabled Commodore George Dewey what would be expected of him in case war came.

The Spanish War.—On the outbreak of hostilities, in April, Roosevelt resigned from the Navy Department and joined with his friend, Leonard Wood, a young army surgeon, to organize the 1st U. S. Volunteer Cavalry. The history of the Santiago campaign on the Spanish side is a history of incredibly inept generalship, and, on the American side, of inefficiency and blundering. Roosevelt, who succeeded to the command of the regiment on the promotion of Wood after the first fight, established himself in the affection of his men by his solicitous care for their welfare, and his insistence on sharing their occasional privations on equal terms. In the battle of San Juan hill Roosevelt personally led the cavalry division in the assault of the Spanish outpost known as Kettle Hill and from that position, at the head of his brigade, charged across an intervening valley and up the slopes of the ridge which was the enemy's main line of defence. The advance of the Rough Riders, as they were popularly known, lacked military form and was called "the school-boy charge" by officers of the regular army who led the orderly advance of the regiments of regular infantry which captured the San Juan blockhouse. But the impetuous rush of Roosevelt and his men—joined by the 1st and 10th (coloured) cavalry, all dismounted—had a reckless and exultant sweep which contributed notably to breaking the Spanish spirit.

Governor of New York.—The Rough Riders were mustered out of service on Sept. 15, 1898. Two weeks later, the Republican party of New York State nominated Roosevelt as its candidate for governor. The party owing to scandals connected with the administration of the Erie canal had come into bad odour; and Thomas C. Platt, the Republican "boss," who distrusted Roosevelt as a radical of "altruistic" views, reluctantly agreed to his nomination. Roosevelt was elected by a scant majority, and instantly a struggle began between himself and Platt, but to fight him meant to accomplish absolutely nothing; for the State legislature was in the main in the hands of the astute Platt. Roosevelt solved the dilemma by yielding on points not involving fundamental principles and insisting on going his own way on all issues of real importance. Roosevelt remained governor for two years. He reformed the administration of the canals, making the canal commission non-partisan; he introduced the merit system into many of the subordinate offices of the State; he secured extensive legislation to provide better protection for the workers of the State, and laws in behalf of forest preservation, the protection of wild life, and the purity of food products. When, in matters of economic legislation, Platt proved obdurate, Roosevelt went to the public for support.

By this means he was able to secure (1899) from Platt's own legislature, against his plaintive protests and the angry opposition of the conservative press, the important Ford Franchise Act, taxing corporation franchises. His administration as governor remains significant in American political history because it marks the beginning of an effort on his part to secure the subservience to government and law of great business combinations. It became clear to Platt that his first apprehensions regarding Roosevelt had been only too accurate. He decided, therefore, to resist Roosevelt's desire to succeed himself as governor by lifting him into the honourable seclusion of the vice-presidency. Neither President McKinley nor Senator Hanna, his astute political guide, approved the idea; Roosevelt and his Eastern friends laboured hard to prevent his nomination, but his friends in the West, out of a real enthusiasm, played into the hands of the man who was plotting their hero's political demise. The combination proved irresistible, McKinley refused to intervene and Roosevelt was nominated. He spoke a little ruefully of having "taken the veil," and made plans to beguile the dreary boredom of the vice-presidency with the study of law.

ROOSEVELT AS PRESIDENT

President McKinley was shot in Buffalo on Sept. 6, 1901, and died Sept. 14. On the same day Theodore Roosevelt took the oath as president of the United States. His sudden accession to power caused a flutter of apprehension in the ranks of what was known as "Big Business." The new president was, as a matter of fact, by nature a conservative, but he wore his conservatism with a difference, standing as far removed from the reactionary position of men like Platt and Hanna, as he was from the radicalism of Bryan. He recognized what many of the spokesmen of capital refused to recognize, that true conservatism demanded a just re-appraisal of industrial and economic conditions and prompt, far-reaching remedial action. On Feb. 18, 1902, he threw what was in effect a bomb into the financial world, when he announced through his attorney general, Philander C. Knox, that he had brought suit in behalf of the United States for the dissolution of a holding corporation known as the Northern Securities Company. The announcement caused consternation among such financiers as J. P. Morgan, Edward H. Harriman and James J. Hill. The holding company was a device designed by shrewd legal minds to evade the restrictions of the Sherman anti-Trust act of 1890, and was generally regarded as impregnable. In the Knight case (1895) involving the American Sugar Refining Company, the Supreme Court had, in fact, held that Congress was without constitutional power to forbid it.

Campaign Against Financial Interests.—When Roosevelt came to the presidency, the average American was moving rapidly toward the cynical conclusion that there was one law for the corporations and another for the individual; one law for the rich, another for the poor. The corporations carried on their existence in a kind of "twilight zone" between State and Federal authority, where neither seemed able to reach them; and when finally a body so revered and so obviously incorruptible as the Supreme Court admitted that Congress was powerless to check the growth and extension of the power of organized wealth, the common man began to wonder whether he would have to seek a corrective which other peoples had found effective. "The United States," said the New York *World* years later, "was never closer to a social revolution than at the time Roosevelt became president." Roosevelt, made aware of the danger first by the campaign of 1896, recognized that the fundamental principles of democratic government—equal justice and national solidarity—were being undermined and that on the outcome of the struggle between the financial powers and the government depended the future vitality of American Government. His vision and courage were vindicated by the courts which he had invoked. On April 9, 1903, the U.S. circuit court, sitting at St. Louis, ordered the dissolution of the Northern Securities Company; and on March 14, 1904, the Supreme Court affirmed the decree.

The anthracite coal strike in 1902 brought the menace of popular unrest to the surface. The miners, under the leadership of John Mitchell, were insistent in their demands; the operators led by J. P. Morgan and George F. Baer, president of the Philadelphia and Reading Railway, were obdurate. Roosevelt for the first time asserted the right of the President to act as representative of the public in an industrial dispute. The miners agreed to arbitrate, but the operators were indignant at the President's "interference" in what they regarded as their private concern. Roosevelt saw clearly what the operators failed to see, that the labour problem had entered upon a new phase; that the growth of industry necessitated a new approach to the questions affecting it: that

the public was in no mood to suffer for the inability of the operators to recognize the parity of human rights with the rights of property, and that in a winter of coal famine lay the possible beginnings of irreparable discontent. After a long-drawn struggle he succeeded in impressing these views upon the operators.

The initiation of the Government's suit against the Northern Securities Company marked the beginning of a conflict between Roosevelt and the large financial interests which continued unabated throughout his administration and for years thereafter, until the outbreak of the World War (1914) brought a shift of issues and a truce. The business leaders were convinced that the President was a destroyer, and was shaking the foundations of the social structure and undermining the institution of private property. His objection, in regard to corporations, as he frequently pointed out, was not to size but to wrongdoing. In swift succession, the President ordered suits brought against the United States Steel Corporation, the Standard Oil Company, the American Sugar Refining Company and other powerful combinations. Meanwhile, he inspired important legislation involving the regulation of railroads. The Elkins law (Feb. 19, 1903) forbade rebates; the Hepburn rate bill (June 29, 1906) granted the interstate commerce commission the right to fix railroad rates. A Pure Food bill, forbidding the manufacture, sale or transportation of adulterated foods, drugs, medicines and liquors, became law on June 30, 1906; the following day another act, providing for the inspection of stockyards and packing-houses, was signed by the President. An Employers' Liability act was adopted. A department of commerce and labour, including a bureau of corporations, was established by congressional action on Feb. 14, 1903. President Roosevelt strengthened his position in reference to the excesses and transgressions of corporations by setting himself with equal firmness against the violence of labour agitation. He noted that the hunger for special privilege was not limited to the ranks of capital. He was by nature sympathetic to the labouring man and scrupulously fair to his interests, but struck at him fearlessly when he thought he was wrong, linking two advocates of violence in the ranks of labour on one occasion with a law-dodging railroad magnate, as "undesirable citizens."

Conservation.—Early in his administration, with the purpose of breaking the strangle-hold of a small minority on the sources of wealth which should be open to the honest endeavours of all the people, the President—under the guidance of Gifford Pinchot—embraced the policy of conservation. The established theory in regard to the national resources was that the general prosperity of the country could best be advanced by the development of these resources by private capital, and upon this theory land was either given away or sold for a trifle. Under this policy, over wide areas, the timber-lands had been stripped bare with reckless waste; the control of the nation's water power had to a dangerous extent passed into private hands; and the public grazing lands and the wealth in minerals and oil in the public domain were bringing enormous dividends to a few, but no returns whatsoever to the people as a whole to whom these natural resources belonged.

Under Roosevelt's administration the area of the national forests was increased from 43 to 194 million acres, the water power resources of those areas were put under government control to prevent speculation and monopoly, and cattle-raisers grazing their herds on the reserves were forced to pay for what they got. In March 1907 Roosevelt created the Inland Waterways commission, and in May 1908 held a conference of State governors at the White House in behalf of conservation. As a result of this conference he appointed a national conservation commission to prepare an inventory, the first ever made for any nation, of all the natural resources within the territory of the United States. A joint Conservation Congress held in Dec. 1908 was followed by a North American Conservation conference in Feb. 1909. The movement for the reclamation of land either excessively or insufficiently watered was essentially a part of the effort in behalf of conservation. It received congressional sanction in the Reclamation Act (June 17, 1902) and achieved its most noteworthy result in the building of the Roosevelt dam in

Arizona, which, by impounding the waters of the Salt river, turned a desert into one of the most fertile farming districts in the world. No policy of Roosevelt's administration excited deeper public interest or sharper opposition than his efforts in behalf of conservation. His official acts and the influence of his speeches and messages led to the adoption by both citizens and government of a new theory regarding natural resources. It is that the Government, acting for the people who are the real owners of public property, shall permanently retain the fee in public lands, leaving their products to be developed by private capital under leases which are limited in their duration and which give the Government complete power to regulate the industrial operations of the lessees.

Re-election.—The popularity which Roosevelt enjoyed at the end of his first term found emphatic expression in the election of 1904. By the largest majority which, up to that time, had been accorded any candidate, Roosevelt was chosen to succeed himself in the White House, receiving 7,623,486 popular votes and 336 electoral votes, against 5,177,971 popular votes and 140 electoral votes cast for Alton B. Parker, the Democratic nominee.

Foreign Policy.—Roosevelt's warfare with the forces popularly symbolized as "Wall Street" was punctuated at intervals during his administration by actions in the realm of international relations which greatly stimulated national pride. The President was brilliantly assisted in his conduct of foreign affairs, first by John Hay and then by Elihu Root, but he was in reality his own Secretary of State. His policy in regard to the army and navy was a highly important part of his foreign policy. He believed in the virtue of being ready as a preventive of war, pointing out the results of unpreparedness in the preface to his first book, *The History of the Naval War of 1812* (1882), and urging an effective army and navy in many of his later writings. He increased greatly the general efficiency of the army. His promotion of officers for merit in defiance of the rules of seniority and his order directing officers to demonstrate their ability to ride 90 m. in three successive days caused some criticism, especially in the more conservative element in the army. Roosevelt's services as Assistant Secretary of the Navy contributed vitally to the distinguished success of the American fleets during the Spanish War. As President he sought with great persistence to build up the navy's power and to make it as effective as possible, giving younger and more progressive officers the prestige of his support in their struggles within the service. When in 1907 he sent the battleship fleet around the world—against the advice of experts in naval construction—he did so partly to call the attention of the great powers, notably Japan, to the fighting strength of the United States, and partly to dramatize the navy and its needs to the American people. The voyage was brilliantly successful.

The attitude of Roosevelt in foreign affairs as in domestic was frank, clear-cut and firm. He knew the involutions of international politics in the Old World as no American president before him had known them, and he countered and checked his subtle opponents in diplomacy with skill and relish. He was bold—startlingly bold at times—but never reckless, calculating costs in advance, saying unambiguously what he had to say and taking account of the human equation. His handling of the German emperor in the matter of Venezuela in 1902 was so firm and so courteous that the emperor became his devoted admirer even though he recalled the ambassador who had failed to warn him that the President meant what he said. His action in regard to an old dispute with Great Britain over the boundary of Alaska was equally friendly and effective.

Swift and vigorous was his action (1903) in sending a cruiser to Panama immediately following its secession from Colombia. He was one of the first Americans to apprehend the part which the Pacific was destined to play, both commercially and politically, in world history. The long delay, moreover, during the Spanish War, in bringing one of the navy's greatest battleships, the *Oregon,* from the Pacific coast of the United States to the Atlantic, had convinced Roosevelt of the urgent need, if only for strategic reasons in the event of war, of a canal across the Isthmus of Panama. When, therefore, after years of fruitless negotiations, the opportunity came to him to acquire for the United States the right to build the canal, he acted promptly, convinced that to do otherwise was to invite a new and dangerous succession of postponements.

The charge was made that President Roosevelt had encouraged or even fomented the revolution in Panama; but no evidence has been produced to give the accusation the slightest support. Roosevelt's boast (1911) "I took Panama," must, moreover, be considered in conjunction with a phrase he added at the semi-jocose request of a French engineer who himself claimed the credit and the responsibility for the insurrection—"when Bunau-Varilla handed it to me on a silver platter." Roosevelt's leadership in the actual construction of the canal was of vital significance. When private engineers failed in the task, he appointed an army engineer, Col. George W. Goethals, as head of the Canal commission with autocratic powers. He broke the precedent which was supposed to prevent an American president from leaving the territory of the United States during his term of office in order to inspect the work and encourage the workers.

Roosevelt approved and eloquently defended the policy of national expansion adopted by the Government under President McKinley. Aside from the acquisition of the Canal Zone, however, he made no move to acquire further territory for the United States. To the surprise of Europe, he carried out the provisions of the American pledge not to annex Cuba, and launched that long-oppressed people as an independent republic under the protection of the United States but not under its Government. By assuming supervision of the finances of San Domingo, he put an end to controversies in that unstable republic which threatened to disturb the peace of Europe.

Roosevelt's action in bringing about peace between Japan and Russia in 1905 added greatly to his prestige at home and abroad. Portions of Roosevelt's papers, published since his death, reveal the extent to which international politics on the Continent were involved in a struggle which appeared to be localized in the Orient and indicate that it was Roosevelt's intervention which prevented in 1904 and again in 1906, during the Algeciras Conference, the outbreak of the World War which actually came in 1914. The Nobel Prize committee recognized his services in ending the Russo-Japanese War by conferring upon him in 1906 its award for the promotion of international peace. In accepting the honour in an address at Christiania in 1910, he suggested the possibility of a League of Nations for the prevention of war. He was the first to send an international controversy for settlement to the International Court of Arbitration at The Hague and was instrumental in having the Second Hague Conference called. He was opposed, however, to peace treaties which promised more than human nature could be counted upon to fulfil, and had no patience with any policy remotely resembling "peace at any price."

His administration had a profound effect on the national prestige of his country. He found the Government of the United States, when he took up the reins, in the position among world powers of a new boy in school; he left it firmly established in the first rank, admired and feared, its favour sought after, its citizenship respected in the remotest corners of the globe.

Home Affairs.—In domestic affairs his influence was even more far-reaching. His success in drawing the leaders on both sides of the social and economic struggle back from the danger zone where extremes meet in violent disturbance was possible only because he had to an unprecedented degree the support of the public, regardless of party. His vigour, his courage, his abounding vitality, his lack of presidential pomposity, his familiarity with all manner of men, even his loudness of action or utterance, and his undisguised delight in driving the "band wagon," all endeared him to "plain folks." He entered into men's lives, kindled fires in them, impelled them to scorn ease and safety and rejoice to do the fine, the difficult thing. His power to inspire his followers to take a pride in their country and her welfare brought to his side hundreds of young men of ability, who asked no greater privilege than to serve under him in an enterprise which in its details was prosaic enough but which he had somehow invested with the spirit of high adventure. The President gave them work to do in the Federal departments and in the island possessions. Their high quality impelled the British ambassador, James Bryce, an acute observer of governments, to remark to Roosevelt that he had "never in any country seen a more eager, high-minded and efficient set of public servants, men more useful and creditable to their country, than the men then doing the work of the American Government in Washington and in the field." Roosevelt had, indeed, the gift of stimulating men to raise themselves for the moment above the ordinary level of their abilities and their desires.

SCIENTIFIC EXPEDITIONS AND TRAVELS

In March, 1909, Roosevelt retired from the Presidency. He adhered to a pledge which he had made after his election in 1904 not to accept the nomination for the Presidency in 1908, and gave his support to the candidacy of William H. Taft, his Secretary of War. Taft was nominated and elected. On April 23, 1909, Roosevelt, accompanied by his son Kermit, sailed for Africa on a scientific expedition under the auspices of the Smithsonian Institution in Washington.

Africa.—Roosevelt entered Africa at Mombasa, and for ten months, moving slowly northward, he hunted big game and collected specimens. He was a keen naturalist, accepted by scientists in his field as a trustworthy observer who had added substantially to the study of American fauna. He had a memory which all who came in contact with him agreed was astonishing in its tenacity and accuracy; and for one who had given only the off-hours of a busy life to scientific study, his knowledge was wide and thorough; but he recognized its limitations and humbly yielded to instruction.

Roosevelt emerged from the wilderness at Gondokoro at the end of Feb. 1910. Nothing showed better the fascination which he exercised over the imaginations of men the world over than the interest which his reappearance created. An address at Khartum on orderly government created a mild stir, but another address, delivered before the students of the University of Cairo, denouncing the assassination by nationalists of the pro-British premier, Boutros Pasha, brought him threats of assassination.

Europe.—Roosevelt's journey northward was in the nature of a triumphal procession. An official at the Vatican precipitated an unpleasant situation by stipulating certain conditions for an interview with the Pope, but Roosevelt's refusal to permit any limitation on his freedom of action was direct and emphatic. In Paris he made a public address at the Sorbonne on "Citizenship in a Republic," in Berlin he spoke at the University on "The World Movement," and, at the emperor's side, reviewed the Imperial Guard, the first civilian who had ever reviewed German troops.

Before he reached England, the king, Edward VII., died, and when Roosevelt arrived in London it was as President Taft's special ambassador to the funeral. His Romanes lecture at Oxford on "Biological Analogies in History" was widely praised, but a speech at the Guildhall in London in which he criticized what appeared to him as the timid ineptitude of the British Government in Egypt brought sharp rebukes from both sides of the Atlantic, but had the endorsement of the new king and of his Foreign Secretary. The address had certain momentous consequences in the appointment of Lord Kitchener as consul general to Egypt (in effect, governor) and the strengthening of a British position which, through its control of the Suez canal and the road to India, became of vital importance to the British Empire on the outbreak of the World War four years later. What remained to Englishmen, however, as the most striking memory of Roosevelt's stay in England, was the walk he took through the New Forest with Sir Edward Grey, when he proved that, though he had spent less than a month altogether in England since his boyhood, he could identify every bird which he saw or heard.

THE RETURN TO POLITICS

Roosevelt returned to the United States on June 18, 1910, disembarking at New York, and received a tumultuous welcome. He had already been put in touch with the political situation.

The struggle between the conservative and the progressive elements in the Republican party, which under Roosevelt had remained under the surface, had, under President Taft, developed into what threatened to become a definite schism. A new tariff law, the dismissal of certain commissions which Roosevelt had appointed, the President's position in a bitter controversy regarding western lands, and the general mood of the Administration led Roosevelt to believe that Taft, instead of carrying forward the policies of the former administration, was definitely aligned with their opponents.

Security for Roosevelt and his fame lay in his retirement to his home acres as a kind of national sage; but at the request of the governor of New York, Charles Evans Hughes, he plunged into a factional fight within the Republican Party in the State (1910) and was sharply defeated. In numerous addresses in many parts of the country, however, and in the columns of the *Outlook,* a weekly periodical of which he was "contributing editor," Roosevelt carried forward his fight for what he called the new nationalism; a struggle for "social justice and popular rule," the control by the people of their political instruments and their government for the purpose of providing a condition approximating equality of opportunity. "The new nationalism" was denounced as revolutionary; it was, in fact, essentially conservative, seeking, as it did, merely a reinvigoration of established American institutions. Certain mildly radical expedients which it proposed were: the recall of elective officers by popular vote, the referendum, intended to make the legislatures more directly responsive to the popular will, and the direct primary. The recall of judicial decisions, advocated by Roosevelt as a check on the reactionary tendency of the judiciary in its function as the interpreter of the constitution, frightened the conservatives. As the struggle between the two factions in the Republican Party became increasingly bitter, pressure was brought to bear upon Roosevelt to declare himself a candidate for the presidency; and on Feb. 25, 1912, to use his own phrase, he "threw his hat in the ring."

It was not in Roosevelt's nature, once he had entered a struggle of any sort, to strike with cushioned gloves. The quarrel between Roosevelt and Taft, brought into the open by the contest for delegates, proved distressing alike to the friends of the protagonists and to the general public. In the 13 States where presidential primaries were held, the result, however, gave evidence that the majority of the Republican voters wanted him as their candidate; for of 362 delegates thus selected, 278 favoured Roosevelt and 48 Taft. The President's strength, in fact, came largely from States which cast a very small Republican vote and in which the control of the political machinery was in the hands of the office-holders. In many cases, the progressive voters named protesting delegations who appeared before the Republican National Committee in Chicago before the convention met (June 22, 1912) to claim the seats which they declared had been fraudulently assigned to their rivals. By a margin of 15 votes—which were offered to Roosevelt, but on terms which he felt he could not accept—the convention was organized by his opponents.

In the stirring events of the convention—though not in the hall itself—Roosevelt played the dominant part. He was ready to agree on a compromise candidate, but only on condition that the rolls of the convention be purged of those delegates who, he insisted, had been fraudulently seated. The convention nominated Taft, and the defeated elements, under the leadership of Roosevelt, formed the Progressive Party. Its first convention, held in Chicago early in August, proved unique in American political history in the fact that women were admitted as delegates. Roosevelt announced the principles of his party, demanding what he had fought for throughout his presidency—the control of the government and the resources of the United States by the people rather than by the professional politicians and financiers; asking, in effect, for a return to fundamental principles. On Aug. 7, the convention nominated Roosevelt for president and Hiram Johnson of California, for vice-president. The Democrats, meanwhile, meeting in Baltimore, had nominated Woodrow Wilson for president. During the campaign, both Wilson and Taft concentrated their artillery on Roosevelt. At the height of the campaign, on Oct. 14, Roosevelt was shot by a maniac in Milwaukee as he was getting into the automobile which was to take him to the hall where he was to speak; he insisted, however, on making his address and it was an hour and a half before he consented to be taken to a hospital. In the election, Wilson received 435 electoral votes, Roosevelt 88 and Taft 8. The popular vote was 6,293,097 for Wilson; 4,119,507 for Roosevelt; 3,484,956 for Taft, and 901,873 for the Socialist candidate, Eugene V. Debs.

RETIREMENT

Roosevelt had expected defeat and it brought no bitterness. He returned to his editorial work on the *Outlook,* wrote his *Autobiography* and only interrupted the life of a country gentleman to move upon a little town in Michigan with a score of "character witnesses" in May, 1913, to confound the editor of a magazine called *Iron Ore* who had rashly put in print a charge widely current, that the ex-president was occasionally or, in fact, frequently, drunk. The defendant admitted that he had combed the country in vain for witnesses to substantiate his charge, acknowledged his error and paid the six cents in damages which was all Roosevelt would accept.

In the autumn of 1913, Roosevelt went to South America to address numerous learned bodies and to secure specimens in the jungles of Brazil for the American Museum of Natural History. His journey from capital to capital—a repetition of his triumphal progress through Europe—belied the theory that his action as President regarding Panama had angered the South American peoples. At the suggestion of the Brazilian government and accompanied by a gallant Brazilian explorer, Col. Candido Rondon, he set out to determine the course of a hitherto unknown river, vaguely indicated on existing maps as the River of Doubt. The journey of 900 m. through primeval wilderness was arduous and full of peril, with death by starvation awaiting the expedition if it went too slow; and death in the rapids waiting if it went too fast. Canoes were crushed in the treacherous waters; supplies were lost; fever made sharp inroads. Finally Roosevelt himself was taken desperately ill, but he struggled forward, until at last, when disaster seemed inevitable, the party reached civilization at the confluence of the river they had charted with the Madeira, a tributary of the Amazon. In honour of the exploit the Brazilian government christened the stream the Rio Roosevelt.

The World War.—He returned to the United States in May 1914. Early August brought the catastrophe in Europe which, as President, he had foreseen and postponed. His sympathies were with France and England, for he distrusted the German emperor whose imperious and unstable mind had during his presidency caused him frequent irritation and anxiety; but he maintained for a few weeks a neutrality in utterance if not "in thought," which he later regretted. But before September was over, he was once more in the centre of public discussion and debate. He saw earlier than the leaders of the administration in power that America could not remain untouched by the gigantic struggle, since any disturbance of the existing balance of power would have a profound effect not only on the foreign relations of the United States but on the personal lives of the American people. America could afford to see England, France and their allies win, but she could not afford to see Germany win, for a German victory implied an aggressive neighbour in Canada and in the Caribbean and the adoption by the United States of the European condition of an "armed peace." He wanted America to enter the war on the side of the Allies because he was convinced that if she did not accept the gage of battle at that time, she would have to accept it later under less favourable conditions. He pleaded for preparedness, but he went beyond the immediate need to what he was convinced was the ultimate necessity—an international tribunal backed by force to execute its decrees. He attacked the divided allegiance—"fifty-fifty Americanism" was his phrase—which permitted certain Americans of German origin to praise all things German at the expense of the American institutions under which they lived; but at the same time he pleaded for justice for the German-American who kept his head and was loyal.

The destruction of the *Lusitania* by a German submarine brought from Roosevelt a scathing denunciation of German methods of warfare, and successive attacks on what seemed to him the timid and inept statesmanship of the Wilson administration. There was a kind of berserker fury in these attacks. Between himself and his opponents in power he knew no middle ground of compromise and party truce; the issues that divided him from them were to his mind not political but moral. It seemed to him that Wilson was deliberately lulling the public into a sense of false security, permitting it to dissipate its spiritual energies in an orgy of acquisition while their president set about with gestures and phrases to exorcise an opponent both aggressive and armed. Once more Roosevelt appealed to the public conscience, and stirred it as never before.

In this last struggle of a stormy life, he rose to what seemed to many of his countrymen new heights of devotion, as he pleaded for the defence of those institutions which he had as president himself revitalized. "Let us pay with our bodies for our souls' desire!" The shift of issues had brought to Roosevelt's support many of the men who had been his bitterest enemies, and early in 1916 he was put forward as a candidate for the Republican nomination for president. He warned the public that he must not be nominated unless the nation were in an "heroic mood." An effort was made by the Progressives to persuade the Republicans to join them in nominating Roosevelt, but the majority of the Republican delegates were not ready to forgive the schism of 1912, and his suggestion that Gen. Wood be named as a compromise candidate never reached the convention. Roosevelt refused the nomination of the Progressive Party, and gave the Republican nominee, Charles Evans Hughes, his support.

When the United States entered the war in April 1917, "the Colonel," as he was affectionately known, offered to raise a division of volunteers from among the ranks of the "outdoor men" of the country who would be almost immediately ready for service; 250,000 men recorded their desire to go under his leadership to France and Congress passed a bill authorizing the creation of two divisions of volunteers, but the President refused his consent. "This is a very exclusive war," Roosevelt remarked, "and I have been blackballed by the committee on admissions." His four sons all went to the front; two were wounded, one Quentin, the youngest, a lieutenant in the Air Service, was killed in combat over the German lines. Roosevelt, forbidden to fight in the field, grimly and in bitter disappointment flung himself into the work that lay at hand. Here and there over the country he spoke for the Liberty Loan campaign, for the Red Cross and other relief agencies, and in the pages of the Kansas City *Star* and the *Metropolitan Magazine* fought week after week for speed in military preparation, for an honest facing of facts and for whole-hearted and unreserved participation in the war by the side of the allies, greeting the Administration's satisfaction over the "happy confusion" of the war preparations with words of stinging realism.

The fever he had contracted in Brazil returned now and again. For weeks he travelled and made public addresses in spite of it. In Feb. 1918, however, he became dangerously ill; was operated upon, recovered, returned to his full activity and was again laid low. His illness scarcely abated his ceaseless activity and in nowise seemed to weaken the force of his fighting spirit. At no previous period in his career was his following so large or so devoted. It seemed as though, in the intensity and grief of the war-years, his countrymen turned to him with new understanding and affection. While scholars talked of this or that notable act of an administration which was already acquiring a kind of glamour in the perspective of a decade, the common man called him "the great American" and let others analyse why. He died in his sleep on Jan. 6, 1919.

Character and Influence.—It can be said of Washington that he founded the American nation, and of Lincoln that he preserved it; it can be said of Roosevelt that he revitalized it. Twice, at critical times, through his vision, his ardour, his effective anger, his faith in American institutions and his peculiar understanding of all sections of the American people, he cleansed the body of the nation of treacherous poisons, and set its soul to work on labours higher than the acquisition of physical comforts. He dreamed nobly for his country and impelled millions of his countrymen to dream nobly. Roosevelt was one of the most versatile presidents of the United States. In addition to his talents as a politician, statesman and popular leader, he was eminent as naturalist, soldier, orator, historian; and was one of the most widely-read men of his time. *The Winning of the West* has faults of hasty composition inevitable in a book written in the off-hours of a crowded life, but it maintains its authority; his *Naval History of the War of 1812* has not been supplanted as the leading work on the subject. He was an assiduous and occasionally a brilliant writer. His narratives are lucid and swift, his descriptions full of colour and significant detail, his literary criticism straightforward and free from the jargon of the craft. His letters have taken a high place in epistolary literature; his volume of *Letters to his Children* is already a classic. His political writings, moreover, are direct and clear, open to the most untutored intelligence, and flashing at intervals with arresting epithets. Under the stress of emotion, in some of the prefaces of his hunting books, in a descriptive passage here and there—in his appeal, for instance for imagination in the writing of history—his prose became transmuted into the gold of poetry.

"A man who could do so much could not do everything perfectly, though few have ever done so many things so well," wrote his friend Albert Bushnell Hart (*Encyclopædia Britannica,* 12th edition). "It was more true of him than of most men that his defects were inherent in his virtues. There were few half-tones in Roosevelt's moral perceptions and fewer in his vocabulary; he saw things as either black or white, and he forgot sometimes that he had not previously seen them as he saw them at the moment. . . . The very intensity of his convictions sometimes blinded him to the sincerity and even to the justice of other points of view. Nevertheless, this intensity, this moral fervour, gave his ideas a momentum and a success which they could never have acquired had they proceeded from a more judicial mind. He scorned 'weasel words,' and on occasion he did not hesitate to describe his enemies as thieves and liars. His remarkable energy reminded observers of some great elemental force which, like any natural phenomenon, is controlled by its own necessary laws."

Writings.—Theodore Roosevelt's published works, including books, pamphlets, addresses, campaign speeches, contributions to the books of others, translations and periodical articles, number between two and three thousand titles and date from 1877 to his death. During his life Theodore Roosevelt wrote not less than 150,000 letters, most of which were included with the Roosevelt papers in the Library of Congress in Washington, and there are a great number of published works dealing with his colourful life. There have been many collections of Roosevelt's works, including the Memorial edition, 24 vol. (1923–26); and the National edition, 20 vol. (1926).

Roosevelt's principal works are: *Naval War of 1812* (1882); *Hunting Trips of a Ranchman* (1885); *Thomas Hart Benton* (1887); *Gouverneur Morris* (1888); *Ranch Life and the Hunting Trail* (1888); *Winning of the West,* 4 vol. (1889–96); *New York* (1891); *Wilderness Hunter* (1893); *Hero Tales from American History* (with Henry Cabot Lodge) (1895); *American Ideals* (1897); *Rough Riders* (1899); *Oliver Cromwell* (1900); *Outdoor Pastimes of an American Hunter* (1905); *African and European Addresses* (1910); *African Game Trails* (1910); *New Nationalism* (1910); *Realizable Ideals* (1912); *History as Literature* (1913); *Progressive Principles* (1913); *Autobiography* (1913); *Through the Brazilian Wilderness* (1914); *Life Histories of African Game Animals* (with Edmund Heller) 2 vol. (1914); *America and the World War* (1915); *Book-lover's Holidays in the Open* (1916); *Fear God and Take Your Own Part* (1916); *Foes of our Own Household* (1917); *Great Adventure* (1918); *Theodore Roosevelt's Letters to his Children* (1919); *Theodore Roosevelt and his Time Shown in his Own Letters,* Ed. by J. B. Bishop, 2 vol. (1920); *Roosevelt in the Kansas City Star* (1921); *Letters to Anna Roosevelt Cowles* (1924); *Selections from Correspondence of Theodore Roosevelt and Henry Cabot Lodge* (1925).

BIBLIOGRAPHY.—The more important biographical studies are: L. F. Abbott, *Impressions of Theodore Roosevelt* (1920); Corinne Roosevelt Robinson, *My Brother Theodore Roosevelt* (1921); H. A. Beers, *Four Americans* (1920); Joseph Bucklin Bishop, *Theodore Roosevelt and His Times* (1920); Archie, Butt, *Letters* (1924); Lord Charnwood, *Theodore Roosevelt* (1924); Tyler Dennett, *Roosevelt and the Russo-Japanese War* (1925); Bradley Gilman, *Roosevelt the Happy Warrior* (1921); H. F. Gosnell, *Boss Platt and His New York Machine* (1924); William Hard, *Theodore Roosevelt: a Tribute* (1919); Henry L. Stoddard, *As I Knew Them—from Grant to Coolidge* (1927); W. D. Lewis, *Life of Roosevelt* (1919); J. F. Rhodes, *McKinley and Roosevelt Administrations* (1922); Kermit Roosevelt, *Happy Hunting Grounds* (1920); Theodore Roosevelt, Jr., *Average Americans* (1919); Albert Shaw, *Cartoon History of Roosevelt's Career* (1910); Julian Street, *The Most Interesting American* (1920); Mark Sullivan, *Our Times* (1926–28); F. S. Wood, *Roosevelt as We Knew Him* (1927); C. B. Whittlesey, *Roosevelt Genealogy* (1902); J. E. Amos, *Theodore Roosevelt, a Hero to His Valet* (1927); Hermann Hagedorn, *Boy's Life of Roosevelt* (1918), and *Roosevelt in the Bad Lands* (1921); O. K. Davis, *Released for Publication* (1924); H. F. Pringle, *Theodore Roosevelt. A Biography* (1931). For fuller record of Roosevelt's writings *see* R. W. G. Vail, *Roosevelt Bibliography* (1929). (H. HAG.)

ROOT, ELIHU (1845–1937), American lawyer and political leader, was born at Clinton (N.Y.), on Feb. 15, 1845. He graduated at Hamilton college where his father was a professor in 1864, taught at the Rome (N.Y.) academy in 1865, and graduated at the University Law school, New York city, in 1867. As a corporation lawyer he soon attained high rank and was counsel in many famous cases. Politically, he became identified with the reform element of the Republican Party. He was U.S. attorney for the Southern District of New York (1883–85), and a delegate to the State Constitutional Convention of 1894, acting as chairman of its judiciary committee. From Aug. 1899 until Feb. 1904 he was secretary of war in the cabinets of Presidents McKinley and Roosevelt, and in this position reorganized the army and created a general staff, and in general administered his department with great ability during a period marked by the Boxer uprising in China, whither troops were sent under Gen. A. R. Chaffee, the insurrection of the Filipinos, the withdrawal of U.S. troops from Cuba and the establishment of a government for the Philippines under a Philippine Commission, for which he drew up the "instructions," in reality comprising a constitution, a judicial code and a system of laws. In 1903 he was a member of the Alaskan Boundary Tribunal. In July 1905 he re-entered President Roosevelt's cabinet as secretary of State, where he considerably improved the consular service. In the summer of 1906, while attending the Pan-American Conference at Rio de Janeiro, he was elected its honorary president, and during a tour through the Latin-American republics, brought about a better understanding between the United States and these republics. In general he did much to further the cause of international peace, and he concluded treaties of arbitration with Japan, Great Britain, France, Italy, Spain, Portugal, Austria-Hungary, Switzerland, Norway, Sweden, Denmark, Holland and other countries. Upon his resignation from the cabinet he was elected, in Jan. 1909, as U.S. senator from New York. In 1910 he was chief counsel for the United States before The Hague Tribunal for the arbitration of the long-standing dispute concerning fisheries between his country and Great Britain. Upon his return, he was appointed by President Taft a member of the Permanent Court of Arbitration. In the same year he was elected president of the Carnegie Endowment for International Peace. Root thus took up again the work which he had initiated when secretary of State, and became the recognized leader of the peace movement in the United States. In 1912 he was awarded the Nobel Peace Prize. He strongly supported in the Senate the treaty of obligatory arbitration concluded between the United States and Great Britain in 1912, but failed to prevent amendments to the treaty being inserted by the Senate which prevented an exchange of ratifications.

He took a leading part in the passage of the Federal Reserve bill of 1913, providing for a Federal Bank under Federal control, in order to stabilize the finance of the country. In matters of foreign policy also his opinion had great weight. In 1915 a treaty negotiated by Secretary of State Bryan with Colombia provided for payment by the United States of $25,000,000 to Colombia in settlement of all outstanding claims between the two countries arising out of the independence of Panama; Mr. Root opposed ratification, principally because a statement of regret on the part of the United States had been inserted in the preamble, though he also considered the sum too much. His opinion prevailed, and later on, in 1922, when the Senate finally ratified the treaty, the clause in question was omitted.

On March 4, 1915, his term as senator expired and he declined to be a candidate for re-election. That summer he was president of the New York State Constitutional Convention, and advocated, among other measures, the short ballot, means for remedying the law's delays, the reduction of costs involved in the administration of justice and measures which would facilitate the impeachment of unworthy public officials. After the declaration of war by the United States, on April 6, 1917, he gave his whole support to the Government. He was asked by President Wilson to head the mission which was sent to Russia shortly thereafter with a view to encouraging the Revolutionary Government under Kerensky to carry on the war with vigour. He accepted, but while in Russia the overthrow of the Moderates there by the Bolsheviks under Lenin frustrated the purposes of his mission.

At the conclusion of the war, though not a member of the U.S. Mission to Paris to conclude peace, his advice was requested in the matter of the Covenant of the League of Nations and his views prevailed to a certain extent. To the Covenant as actually drafted, however, he was opposed. He was, nevertheless, of the opinion that the Covenant and the Treaty of Versailles should be accepted with reservations, to secure the interests of the United States, inasmuch as the President's re-election in 1916 and his presence as negotiator at Paris had led the other plenipotentiaries, however erroneously, to believe that he represented the opinion of his fellow countrymen. In Mr. Root's opinion it would be better to accept the Covenant with reservations, and by subsequent amendments to remove the obstacles which had originally stood in the way of its acceptance.

He accepted an invitation from the League of Nations to become a member of the Advisory Committee of Jurists which met at The Hague in 1920 for the purpose of devising a plan for a permanent court of international justice, in accordance with Art. 14 of the Covenant. His presence enabled the committee to frame a plan acceptable to all by which the judges were to be elected by the separate and concurrent action of the Council (in which the Great Powers had a preponderance) and the Assembly (in which the Small Powers were in a majority), each interest, real or alleged, having thus a veto upon the abuse of power by the other. The plan was accepted with modifications by the Council and Assembly on Dec. 14, 1920, and became the statute of the court. It functioned perfectly when the judges were elected in 1921.

Root was appointed by President Harding one of the U.S. delegates to the International Conference on Armament Limitation, which met at Washington in Nov. 1921. There he secured the adoption of the convention subjecting submarines to the requirements of surface vessels and prohibiting the use of noxious gases in warfare. He devised the Pacific agreements which resulted in the cancellation of the Anglo-Japanese alliance, and drafted the Four Power Pacific Treaty, which took its place. In Jan., 1929, he accepted an invitation to be a member of a committee of jurists meeting at Geneva to test and revise the original statutes of the Permanent Court of International Justice in the light of eight years' experience. He participated in every session held for this purpose and offered valuable suggestions. His main work, however, was the working out of a formula upon which the United States might see its way clear to become a member of the court. This Root protocol, as redrafted by Sir Cecil Hurst, was unanimously accepted by the committee of jurists, and was intended to replace the protocol of Sept. 23, 1926 drawn up in answer to the American Senate reservations. The changes made were only in the article on advisory opinions and were held to be favourable to the United States. The hope was general that the United States Senate would act favourably after the report of the committee had been formally accepted by the League Council, but the Senate rejected it. Mr. Root died Feb. 7, 1937.

A collection of Root's public addresses has been edited by Robert Bacon and James Brown Scott in eight volumes. He also published *Experiments in Government and the Essentials of the Constitution* (Princeton Lectures, 1913) and *American Ideals During the Past Half Century* (International Conciliation, no. 210, 1925).

ROOT, in popular usage, the part of the plant which is normally below the surface of the earth. Botanically its application is more restricted, for many plants develop subterranean structures that are in reality specialized stems (rhizomes, tubers,

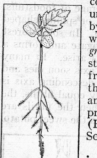

corms). The root is distinguished from such underground stems by not bearing leaves and by having its apex enclosed by a cap (*root-cap*) which protects the actively dividing cells of the *growing point* or *meristem*. There are also structural differences which distinguish roots from stems. The most important of these are the manner in which lateral members originate and the arrangement and development of the primary vascular tissues (xylem and phloem). (For internal structure see PLANTS AND PLANT SCIENCE: *Anatomy*.)

FROM STRASBURGER'S "LEHRBUCH DER BOTANIK" (GUSTAV FISCHER)
FIG. 1. — SEEDLING (ULTIMATE ROOT-BRANCHES)

Not all plants have true roots; they are lacking in Thallophytes (algae and fungi) and Bryophytes (mosses and liverworts), although some of these lower plants develop organs, *rhizoids*, which perform some of the functions of roots. In phylogeny the root is associated with the evolution of the sporophytic generation in the higher plants and with the development of the land habit. They occur in Pteridophytes (ferns and their allies) and Spermatophytes (seed plants). The primary function of the root is absorption of water and inorganic salts in solution and the conduction of these to the stem, but it also affords anchorage and support and frequently serves for storage of reserve foods. In some instances it may function in vegetative reproduction and in special cases (some aerial and aquatic roots) may carry on photosynthesis. The root usually develops *root-hairs*, slender unicellular outgrowths formed by the lateral extension of cells of the outer layer, *epidermis*. These serve to increase the absorbing surface of the root and bring it into intimate relationship with the soil particles. The older root hairs generally die; rarely some are persistent, so that the active zone of root-hairs usually lies just back of the apex of the root.

When the seed germinates, the *primary root* or *radicle* is the first organ to appear. It grows downward through the soil, anchoring the seedling and establishing contact with the soil. Secondary roots, which often repeat the form and structure of the main root, are developed in regular succession from above downwards (acropetal), and owing to the fact that they originate in a definite position in the interior of the root (generally opposite the xylem masses) they develop in longitudinal rows and have to break through the overlying tissue of the parent root. True forking of the root (dichotomy) occurs in the Lycopodiaceae (the shoots of which also branch dichotomously), but not in the higher plants.

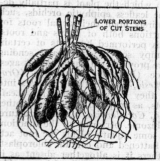

LOWER PORTIONS OF CUT STEMS

FROM STRASBURGER'S "LEHRBUCH DER BOTANIK" (GUSTAV FISCHER)
FIG. 2.—FLESHY ROOTS OF DAHLIA VARIABILIS

Roots which originate elsewhere than as acropetal outgrowths of a main root are known as *adventitious*, and may arise on any part of a plant. They are especially numerous on underground stems, such as the under side of rhizomes, and also develop from stems under favourable conditions, such as moisture and absence of light; a young shoot or a cutting placed in moist soil may quickly form adventitious roots.

The potentiality of many plants to develop adventitious roots from stems is widely used in horticulture and floriculture as a means of vegetative propagation. This insures the production of plants that resemble the parent stock and avoids the possibility of undesirable variation that may result from propagation by means of seed. It is also a rapid method of propagation in the case of slow-growing woody plants. Adventitious roots may also arise from leaves under similar conditions, as, for instance, from begonia leaves when planted in soil.

The forms of roots depend on their shape and mode of branching. When the central axis goes deep into the ground in a tapering manner without dividing, a *taproot* is produced. This kind of root is sometimes short, and becomes swollen by storage of foodstuffs, as in the *conical* root of carrot, or the *fusiform* or spindle-shaped root of radish, or the *napiform* root of turnip. In some forest trees the first root protruded continues to elongate and forms a long primary root-axis, whence secondary axes arise. In many plants, especially monocotyledons, the primary axis soon dies and the secondary axes take its place. When the descending axis is very short, and at once divides into thin, nearly equal fibrils, the root is called *fibrous*, as in many grasses; when the fibrils are thick and succulent, the root is *fasciculated*, as in the sweet potato, dahlia, *Ranunculus ficaria*, and *Oenanthe crocata*. Some so-called roots are formed of a stem and root combined, as in *Orchis*, where the tuber consists of a fleshy swollen root bearing at the apex a stem bud. As in the stem, growth in length occurs only for a short distance behind the apex, but in long lived roots increase in diameter occurs continually in a similar manner to growth in thickness in the stem.

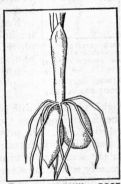

FIG. 3.—FLESHY ROOT OF ORCHIS

Roots are usually underground and may be white or variously coloured as in the beet or carrot. In some cases where they arise from the stem they pass for some distance through the air before reaching the soil. Such roots are called *aerial*. They are well seen in maize (*Zea*), the screw-pine (*Pandanus*), the Banyan (*Ficus indica*), and many other species of *Ficus*, where they eventually assist in supporting the stem and branches. In the mangrove they often form the entire support of the stem, which has decayed at its lower part. In tree-ferns they form a dense coating around, and completely conceal the stem; such is also the case in some Dracaenas and palms. In *epiphytes*, or plants growing in the air, attached to the trunks of trees, such as orchids of warm climates, the aerial roots produced do not reach the soil; they continue always aerial and greenish, and they possess stomata. Delicate hairs are often seen on these epiphytic roots, as well as a peculiar spongy investment formed by the cells of the epidermis which have lost their succulent contents and are filled with air. This layer is called the *velamen*, and serves to absorb the moisture contained in the air, on which the plant is partially dependent for its water supply. Some leafless epiphytic orchids, such as species of *Angraecum*, depend entirely upon their aerial roots for nourishment; these perform the functions both of leaves and roots. A respiratory or aerating function is performed by roots of certain mangroves (*q.v.*), growing in swampy soil or water and sending vertical roots up into the air which are provided with aerating passages.

Parasitic plants, as the mistletoe (*Viscum*), broomrape (*Orobanche*), dodder (*Cuscuta*) and *Rafflesia*, send rootlike processes into the substance of the plants whence they derive nourishment. Leaf-buds are sometimes formed on roots, as in plum, cherry and other fruit trees. In the coral-root orchid, *Corallorhiza*, a stem structure, the shortly branched underground rhizome, performs all the functions of a true root, which is absent. In some aquatic plants the root acts merely as a holdfast or it may be flattened and contain chloroplasts for the manufacture of food; in others it is altogether absent as in *Salvinia* and *Utricularia*. The well-known epiphyte *Tillandsia usneoides* (Spanish moss) is rootless.   (H. E. Hd.)

ROOT. Arab writers of the 9th century spoke of one of the equal factors of a number as a root, and their mediaeval translators used the Latin *radix* (root) for the same concept. The adjective is radical.

If a is a positive real number and n is a positive integer, there exists a unique positive real number x such that $x^n = a$. This number is called the (principal) nth root of a, and is written $\sqrt[n]{a}$. The integer n is called the index of the root. For $n=2$, the root is called the square root and is written $\sqrt{a}$. The root $\sqrt[3]{a}$ is called the cube root of a. If a is negative and n is odd, the unique negative nth root of a is termed principal.

The practical determination of square and higher roots of positive numbers is discussed in the article on ARITHMETIC.

If a rational integer (whole number) has a rational nth root, *i.e.*, one which can be written as a common fraction, then this root must be an integer. Thus 5 has no rational square root since $2^2 < 5$ while $3^2 > 5$.

There are exactly n complex numbers which satisfy the equation $x^n = 1$, called the complex nth roots of unity. If a regular polygon of n sides is inscribed in a unit circle with centre at the origin so that one vertex lies on the positive half of the x-axis, the radii to the vertices are the vectors representing the n complex nth roots of unity. If the root whose vector makes the smallest positive angle with the positive direction of the x-axis is denoted by ω, then $\omega, \omega^2, \omega^3, \ldots \omega^n = 1$ constitute all of the nth roots of unity. Thus $\omega = -\frac{1}{2} + \frac{1}{2}\sqrt{-3}, \omega^2 = -\frac{1}{2} - \frac{1}{2}\sqrt{-3}, \omega^3 = 1$ are the cube roots of unity.

Any root ϵ which has the property that $\epsilon, \epsilon^2, \ldots \epsilon^n = 1$ give all of the nth roots of unity is called primitive.

Evidently the problem of finding the nth roots of unity is equivalent to the problem of inscribing a regular polygon of n sides in a circle. For every integer n, the nth roots of unity can be determined in terms of the rational numbers by means of rational operations and radicals; but they can be constructed by ruler and compasses (*i.e.*, determined in terms of the rational operations and square roots) only if n is a product of distinct prime numbers of the form $2^h + 1$, or 2^k times such a product, or is of the form 2^k.

If a is a complex number not 0, the equation $x^n = a$ has exactly n roots. (*See* COMPLEX NUMBERS.) All of the nth roots of a are the products of any one of these roots by the nth roots of unity.

The term root has been carried over from the equation $x^n = a$ to all polynomial equations. Thus a solution of the equation

$$f(x) = a_0 x^n + a_1 x^{n-1} + \ldots + a_{n-1} x + a_n = 0, \ a_0 \neq 0$$

is called a root of the equation. If the coefficients lie in the complex field, an equation of the nth degree has exactly n not necessarily distinct complex roots. If the coefficients are real and n is odd, there is a real root. But an equation does not always have a root in its coefficient field. Thus $x^2 - 5 = 0$ has no rational root.

If $f(x) = 0$ is an equation with coefficients in a field F, there exists a unique field F^* obtained by adjoining to F all of the roots of $f(x) = 0$. This field is called the root field of $f(x) = 0$. In F^* the polynomial $f(x)$ can be factored into linear factors. (*See* EQUATIONS, THEORY OF.)

A rigorous proof of the existence of the root field F^* can be made along the following lines. Let $f_1(x)$ be a factor of $f(x)$ which is irreducible in F. The set of all polynomials in x with coefficients in F, taken modulo $f_1(x)$, constitute a field F' containing F in which $f_1(x)$ has a linear factor. A continuation of this process leads to the root field F^*.   (C. C. M.)

BIBLIOGRAPHY.—On the Greek theory, *see* Sir T. L. Heath, *A History of Greek Mathematics* (Cambridge, 1921); on the general history, L. E. Dickson, *History of the Theory of Numbers* (1919-23); on the algebraic theory, G. Chrystal, *Algebra*, 2nd ed. (Edinburgh, 1889); on the history of terms and methods, D. E. Smith, *History of Mathematics,* especially vol. 2 (1923-25).

ROOT CROPS. Many kinds of roots are cultivated for human use, some such as carrots, parsnips, etc., being grown extensively on a commercial scale. But what are commonly termed root crops are those which are grown on farms in rotation with other field crops (*see* ROTATION OF CROPS; also BEET; MANGEL; TURNIP). In a broad sense, however, all roots grown for human food are called root crops, as are many grown for other useful purposes. The root crops most commonly produced for human food include the beet, carrot, onion, parsnip, potato, radish, sugar beet, sweet potato and turnip. Representative minor root crops are the chufa (*Cyperus esculentus*), cultivated by the Negroes of the southern U.S., and the so-called tule-potato (tubers of *Sagittaria latifolia*), cultivated by the Chinese in central California.

Many roots grown for other economic purposes assume local importance as crops, as the liquorice, which is grown in southern Europe.

ROOT CUTTER: *see* PROCESSING MACHINERY.

ROOZEBOOM, HENDRIK WILLEM BAKHUIS

(1854–1907), Dutch physical chemist, was born on Oct. 24, 1854; he was at first (1878) assistant in the Chemistry institute at Leyden, then lecturer (1890), and finally (1896) professor of inorganic and physical chemistry at Amsterdam. He died on Feb. 8, 1907. Roozeboom is best known for the introduction into chemistry of the "phase rule" (*see* CHEMISTRY: *Physical*), which had been deduced previously by J. Willard Gibbs on thermodynamical grounds. With his students he made a large number of investigations of melting points and solubilities in studying the equilibria between solid and liquid phases in various systems. He started in 1904 to publish a compilation under the title of *Die heterogene Gleichgewichte vom Standpunkt der Phasenlehre*, which was completed in 1918, after his death, by his pupils.

See *Recueil Trav. Chim. Pays-Bas* (1908); *Ber. d. Deutsch Chem. Ges.* (1907).

ROPE AND ROPEMAKING.

Rope is made of animal or vegetable fibres and of metallic wires. Fibre rope alone will be considered here. (*See* WIRE ROPE.) "Cordage" is a term applied generally to yarns, twines, ropes and cables but refers specifically to "rope" in the industry.

Fibre rope is cordage of "stranded" construction, *i.e.*, fibres or hairs laid parallel and twisted together making a yarn; two or more of these yarns twisted together "forming" the strand and three or more of these strands twisted together "laying" the rope. Three or more ropes laid together make a "cable-laid" rope, sometimes referred to colloquially as "hawser-laid." The smallest fibre ropes made are approximately $\frac{1}{2}$ in. in circumference or $\frac{3}{16}$ in. in diameter so that any similar products of less than these dimensions are not rope in the usual acceptation of the term.

Two or more yarns twisted together, either plain twisted or laid, are twine regardless of the form of put-up; laid twine is sometimes referred to as "corded." Single yarns are known as yarns except binder twine, which is a single yarn product. This group of products is known as "ply and yarn goods" in the hard fibre cordage industry and as yarns, twines or cords in the soft fibre industry. Braided construction of yarns, such as sash cords, is sometimes referred to as "rope." (X.)

Early History of Ropemaking.—Rope is already represented in use in southwest Asia (Elam) in the chalcolithic period (4th millennium B.C., *v.* Lasso), but this was probably made of plaited thongs, a type which has persisted down to modern times, especially in arrested cultures, *e.g.*, among the Rodiyas of Ceylon, a retarded, outcast group. But probably almost, if not quite, as ancient is that of bark fibre, represented in more evolved forms by the coir types of southeast Asia, where one kind is still made in the very primitive technique of rolling the fibres together with the palm of the hand on the bare thigh, *e.g.*, among the Nayadis of Malabar, the nucleus of whose culture remains epipalaeolithic in character. The thong-plaiting is the simplest and quite likely the first stage of plaiting out of which grew, before the end of the palaeolithic period, mat- and basketmaking, which in turn engendered, in the neolithic, true weaving. The primitive coir-ropemaking method, on the other hand, is the most rudimentary, and almost certainly the initial way of spinning, still used, *e.g.*, well down into historical times in Egypt. Thus ropemaking is the technical ancestor of both the *two* fundamental textile processes.

Cord (the primary element of rope, and incorporating its essential principle) must have been used very early, probably in the upper palaeolithic period at least, to attach tools to handles; and the same need for rope implies its common currency in the 4th millennium, when numerous bone handles are sometimes found with the blade or point missing (E. Schmidt, *Tepe Hissar*, Phil., 1937, p. 59). In the middle of the 3rd millennium B.C., patterns impressed with spun cords are the definitive feature of a southeastern European pottery; and by the middle of the 2nd millennium heavy rope must have been a commonplace in the east Mediterranean, given the development there of shipping and hence ships, which even when propelled by oars require rope equipment. Moreover, at about this same time a number of terms for "rope" are found in Akkadian, *e.g.*, though they are not yet more specifically translatable, while actual examples of papyrus rope of about this period have been found in Egyptian tombs. Late in the millennium heavy cables are reproduced in bronze as handles of vessels in China, whither the technique had probably been conveyed by the bronze casters, most likely from the eastern Asia Minor-Adharbayjan region, and heavy cable mouldings appear about the same time on pottery from Luristan whose bronze art can be traced to the same source.

When Xerxes (480 B.C.) built the bridge of boats across the Hellespont "the Phoenicians constructed one line with cables of white flax, the Egyptians in the other used ropes made of papyrus (Herod., Hist., vii, 34). In India in the 4th century B.C., ropemaking was so specialized that one class of experts made ropes just for horses, another for elephants (*Arthasastra*); and in China, in the Han period if not earlier, the emperor's carriage in time of mourning was equipped with silk ropes (*Li Ki*, Bk. iii, sect. iii). The craft was carried, along with various textile and other techniques such as pottery making and metallurgy, into the early American cultures. (P. An.)

Ropemaking had been going on for centuries with little change up to the time of the introduction of machinery about the middle of the 19th century. In the early days all the yarn was spun by hand. The hemp was first hackled by combing it straight over a board studded with sharp steel teeth. A bunch or "head" of this hackled hemp was placed around the spinner's waist, who attached a few fibres to a hook on the spinning wheel and, as the hook was revolved by means of a large wheel turned by hand, walked backwards away from the wheel feeding the fibre from the supply around his waist, preserving the uniformity and proper size of the yarn. Several yarns were twisted together by use of a hand wheel and several hooks, forming the "strand" and three or more strands twisted together "laying" the rope. Horsepower was used in old times for forming and laying rope which was too large to be made by hand. The term "ropewalk" came from the long low buildings used and the walking back and forth of the spinners and ropemakers. In the early days every community of any size had its ropewalk, there being 173 in the United States in the year 1810. These walks were often 900 ft. or more in length. Many were in the open air.

The crude methods of ropemaking of centuries ago are still used in many parts of the world today. Improved ropewalk methods are used extensively today for making extra large ropes and all but the smaller sizes of tarred hemp ropes; it is also an economical and quick method of making ropes to special order for immediate delivery.

Raw Materials.—In the United States and European countries soft fibres, principally hemp (coming mostly from Russia, Italy and the United States) and flax were used for rope until the second quarter of the 19th century. Hemp is still used for tarred hemp rope and fittings for marine purposes. Abaca commonly referred to as Manila fibre, because it is grown almost exclusively in the Philippine Islands and exported principally from the port of Manila, has established itself as the best material for ropemaking where strength and durability are the prime requirements. Henequen, sometimes misnamed sisal, is next in importance as a rope fibre, and comes from Yucatan, Mexico and Cuba. Sisals are important rope fibres and come principally from Java, Africa and the Bahamas. Other fibres used are New Zealand, Mauritius, Maguey and Istle fibres. Jute and cotton are used to a limited extent in the manufacture of ropes of stranded construction. Cotton is used to a greater extent in the manufacture of braided cords.

Present Manufacturing Processes.—The primary object of twisting fibres together in a rope is that, by mutual friction, they may be held together when a strain is applied to the whole. Hard twisting has the further advantage of compacting the fibres and preventing, to some extent, the penetration of moisture when the ropes are exposed to water; but the yield of rope from a given length of yarn diminishes in proportion to the increase of twist.

The ropemaking process is essentially the same, no matter what kind of fibre is used. The process divides itself into five

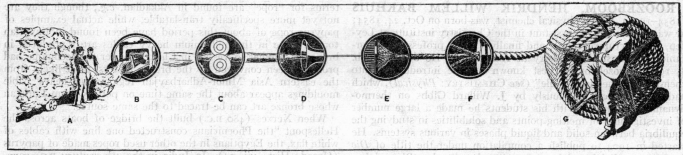

PROCESSES THROUGH WHICH FIBRE PASSES IN THE MANUFACTURE OF ROPE: (A) FIBRE FROM BALES WITH TANGLES SHAKEN OUT; (B) THE BREAKER WHERE THE FIBRE IS COMBED; (C) SLIVER (FIBRE AFTER IT IS COMBED) COMPRESSED INTO COMPACT FORM; (D) FIBRE TWISTED INTO YARN; (E) YARN DRAWN THROUGH A GUIDE AND TWISTED INTO A READY OR STRAND; (F) STRANDS LAID UP INTO ROPE; (G) FINISHED ROPE COILED AND READY FOR SHIPPING

operations. First, selection of fibre; second, preparing the sliver; third, spinning the yarn; fourth, forming the strands; fifth, laying the strands into rope. With cable-laid ropes there is another operation, laying the strands of the cable, which are in fact completed ropes, into the finished cable.

At the start of the manufacturing process the bales of fibre are opened and heads of fibre shaken out. The fibre is put through several processes of combing and straightening. These operations are, in general, all of the same kind. The fibre is slowly carried along on a series of bars connected by endless chains, the bars being studded with sharp steel pins, like combs, that stand upright as the fibre passes along with them. A similar set of combs, moving very much faster, pulls the fibre rapidly away from the first set, combing it out at the same time. Fine jets of lubricant are sprayed on the fibre as it enters the first machine.

The fibre is delivered from the machine in a heavy, continuous stream or sliver which is coiled by hand or machine into a receptacle, or on the floor. Several of these slivers are then fed into a similar machine, and the kinks and unevenness further removed by a repetition of the same process. This preparation or combing is repeated from 8 to 12 times on five different machines, each operation combing the fibre and producing a smaller and more even sliver, until finally it comes out of the finisher in a continuous stream as water flows from a hose. The thoroughness with which these operations are carried out—the care taken in preparing the fibre—is largely responsible for the uniformity and excellence of the finished product.

In the preparation of the sliver, the object has been merely to eliminate all sorts of dirt and foreign matter and to lay these fine, threadlike strands parallel with one another so that they can be more easily spun together. As the sliver enters the spinning machine it is taken from the rollers by another series of fine combs. From the combs it passes through a funnel-shaped tube and is then wound about a little capstan. It is between the tube and the capstan that the yarn comes into being. The friction on the revolving capstans draws the yarn through the machine. From the capstans it is automatically wound on a large spool about 12 in. long, named a bobbin. The capstans and the bobbin whirl very fast, and the combination of this whirling motion and the drawing forward of the revolving capstans, spins the heretofore parallel fibres into what is known as a yarn. For different sizes of yarn and for yarns designed for various purposes, a varying number of twists per foot are imparted to the yarn. This yarn is the first merchantable product of the cordage mill and may be sold in this original form or used as the basis of other cordage products.

A rope is usually formed of three or four strands, each strand composed of a number of yarns laid parallel and slightly twisted together. Making these strands is "forming." As the strand is twisted it is wound on a large reel and appears as a smooth, round strand composed of a number of individual yarns. This is known as the "ready." The yarn has a tendency to untwist; to overcome this the twist of the ready or strand is made in the opposite direction. The result is that the tendency of the yarn to untwist in one direction, and the tendency of the ready to untwist in the other direction balance

each other.

The ropemaking operation is "laying." In laying the rope, three or four of the reels containing the readies or strands are put on the laying machine, and the strands are led through a "block," wound around the capstan, and reeled on the finishing end of the laying machine. In laying there is a different twisting problem, for the ready is neutral—that is, it has no tendency to untwist—and if the readies were twisted together without altering this neutral condition the rope would continually untwist. So an extra twist is added to the ready as it is passed into the machine, this twist being computed so that it will be just sufficient to counteract the tendency of the three strands to untwist when they are formed into a rope. All good rope is absolutely neutral; if cut off in 5-ft. to 10-ft. lengths and laid on the ground, it will not untwist of its own accord.

Cable-laid rope consists of three completed ropes, nine of the simple strands which form an ordinary rope. The same method of balancing the twisting strands is used, an additional twist or foreturn being given to the three-strand ropes just before they are laid up, so that their tendency to untwist in one direction shall exactly counterbalance the tendency of the cable to untwist in the opposite direction.

Uses and Care of Rope.—The uses of rope are many and varied. The marine and fishing industries consume more than half of the rope produced. Cable-laid rope is also used extensively for the drilling of oil, water and gas wells. Ropes are used in the transmission of motive power. (*See* POWER TRANSMISSION: *Mechanical.*) Small cotton ropes are used extensively in textile mills for small machine drives. Rope is used on the farms for hoisting, hauling, harness and many other uses. Rope is used in building and engineering projects construction. In the home also it has many applications.

The useful life of rope depends on the quality of the rope, and on the care and treatment it receives. To give the best service, it must be made of high-grade raw material, selected with a thorough knowledge of what the rope is to do. It must be so made that every strand will be of even tension. It must be properly treated with a lubricant which will at once preserve and lubricate. There are three general sources of damage which will shorten the life of rope: first, mechanical injury, such as bending over too sharp a pulley; second, damage from chemicals, such as acids; and third, damage from climatic or other conditions of storage, such as moisture or dry rot. It should be stored in a cool dry place with air circulation.   (J. S. McD.)

In addition to the heavy rope there are many varieties of cord and twine made by means of the preparing, spinning and doubling machines. The fishing industry takes many different types for lines and nets, while the variety of cord and twine for other industrial and for household purposes is almost unlimited. All yarn from long vegetable fibre is more or less rough as it leaves the spinning frame, even after two or more threads have been twisted together. It is therefore necessary, for many uses, to impart a polish to the cord or twine. Special machines are used for this purpose. Bobbins of yarn, equal to the number required, and depending upon the capacity of the machine, are placed in a bank or creel, and the ends are collected and passed under a roller which is immersed in hot starch. The yarns become saturated with this starch, but, as they emerge from the starch-box, the superfluous starch is removed by passing the yarns between two rollers. The yarns now pass over a series of drying cylinders and polishing rollers, and are finally rewound by the same machine on to other bobbins. This machine is termed a bobbin-to-bobbin polishing machine. In some cases the hot drying cylinders are replaced by a system of hot-air drying. The finished yarns are now made up by machinery into hanks, balls or cheeses, according to which happens to be the best state for future use and for transport.

Driving Ropes.—It has already been stated that cotton driving ropes are extensively applied in the transmission of motive power. Although the mechanical efficiency of transmission by ropes is less than that obtained by wheel gearing, rope driving has several compensating advantages:—

1. It is practically noiseless.

2. It occupies less space than belt driving, and the slip is not so great.

3. The turning movement is better; machines therefore run more steadily and production is increased.

4. Shafts may be run at higher speeds.

5. Greater range of drives; anything from 10 ft. to over 80 ft., and much greater distances when carrier pulleys are used.

6. The drive is usually obtained by a number of ropes; if one should break, the rope may be removed and the machinery run in most cases, until stopping-time.

The number of ropes to be used depends upon the power to be transmitted; upon the sectional area of the ropes, and upon the surface speed of the driving pulley. The speed of the rope may vary from 2,000 ft. to 6,000 ft. or over per minute. In some few exceptional cases 60 ropes have been used on one pulley; the number usually varies between 15 and 40. (See POWER TRANSMISSION: *Mechanical.*)

The foregoing refers exclusively to ropes made from fibrous yarns; metallic ropes appear under the heading WIRE ROPE.

See T. Woodhouse and P. Kilgour, *Cordage and Cordage Hemp and Fibres* (1919); Robert Chapman, *A Treatise on Rope-making* (1868); H. R. Carter, *Modern Flax, Hemp and Jute Spinning and Twisting* (1925); P. J. Stopford, *Cordage and Cables* (1925); "U.S. Government Master Specifications for Rope Cotton," *Bureau of Standards Cir.* 326, (1927).

ROPE MOULDING, in architecture and the decorative arts, a convex half or quarter round moulding, spirally channelled, so that it resembles a rope; also called cable moulding (*q.v.*).

ROPES, JOHN CODMAN (1836–1899), American military historian and lawyer, was born at St. Petersburg on April 28, 1836. He graduated at Harvard in 1857, was admitted to the bar in 1861 and became a successful lawyer. He founded in 1876 the Military Historical Society of Massachusetts for the collection and discussion of evidence relating to the Civil War. To it he presented his military library and his collection of prints and medals. He died at Boston on Oct. 28, 1899. His principal work is an unfinished *Story of the Civil War,* to which he devoted most of his later years; this covers the years 1861–62 (1894–98). It was completed in five volumes in 1913 by W. R. Livermore. *The Army under Pope* (in "Campaigns of the Civil War," vol. iv., 1881) is a detailed narration of the Virginia campaign of Aug.–Sept., 1862, which played a great part in reversing contemporary judgment on the events of those operations, notably the condemnation of Gen. Fitz John Porter's conduct. His *Campaign of Waterloo* (1892) is a standard work.

ROPE-WALKING, the art of walking, dancing and performing tricks on a rope or wire stretched between two supports.

ROPEWAYS AND CABLEWAYS. The aerial ropeway is essentially an intermittent handling device and may be defined as that method of handling materials which consist of drawing receptacles—such as buckets or skips—suspended from ropes and by means of ropes, from place to place, such receptacles being manually or automatically filled and discharged. There is no limit to the length of a ropeway installation, since it may consist of any number of units, while the length of a single unit may be as much as 4½ miles.

Historical.—At what period of history ropeways were first used it is impossible to say, but the fact that ropes and pulley blocks—which are the essential parts of a ropeway—were known to the ancients, seems to render a pedigree of at least 2,000 years possible. An old engraving shows a ropeway in use in the City of Danzig in 1644. This was the work of Adam Wybe, a Dutch engineer, and is a single ropeway in its simplest form, consisting of an endless rope passing over pulleys suspended on posts; to the rope were attached a number of small buckets which carried earth from a hill outside the city to the rampart inside the moat. The rope was probably of hemp.

In modern ropeways wire ropes are exclusively used, which date back from about 1860, when a ropeway was erected in the Harz mountains. Since then several systems have been evolved, but space does not permit of entering into details of all the possible applications of a ropeway; it must suffice, therefore, to mention the two principal types, which are known as single and double ropeways. In the former, one endless travelling rope both supports and conveys the load, while in the latter the load carriers are supported by a stationary rail rope on which they are hauled along by an independent endless hauling rope. The systems are also termed, respectively, mono-cableway and bi-cableway, but since a cableway is generally understood to be a different type of aerial transport altogether the names single and double ropeway are preferable.

Such aerial transport resembles in substance vehicular rail transport; in this case, however, the rolling stock is suspended from a rope which serves as a rail, instead of running on the permanent way of a light railway. It is obvious that a single overhead rope as a track, has enormous advantages over a pair of rails laid on the ground, as in the orthodox rail-track with its sleepers, the cost of preparation of the ground has to be considered, which may involve the construction of embankments, bridges, etc. When building a ropeway the overhead rope should run in a bee-line from place to place—say from an undeveloped area to the nearest available point where main transport is available, whereas in the case of a light railway, owing to limitations of grade, usually about 3%, the permanent way has to traverse a tortuous route, three or four times as long possibly, as the bee-line of the rope-track, which, moreover, may be negotiated with safety on a grade of 40%. For example, a ropeway may be cited, which has a total length of 5,400 ft. with a total difference in altitude of 2,000 ft., the ground which it covers could not have been negotiated by a rail track of less than 15 m. in length, graded at 1 in 42. It is essential to take as straight a line as possible when laying out a ropeway because curves generally necessitate angle-stations, which entail expenditure of more capital and increase in working cost. On the other hand, ground that would be difficult for the railway engineer, such as steep hills, deep valleys and turbulent streams, has no terrors for the ropeway erector.

The Single Ropeway.—The single ropeway consists essentially of an endless running rope from which the carriers are suspended and with which they move in the following way:—The receptacles are fitted with simple curved hangers pivoted from a ∧-shaped saddle, which holds sufficiently tight by frictional contact to the rope and therefore travels with the same. The suspended frame of the load carrier is also fitted by the side of the ∧-shaped saddle with the small grooved pulley which engages at the terminals with shunt rails and thus disengages itself from the running rope; the frame of the load carrier becomes stationary on these shunt rails for filling or emptying, after which it is pushed on to the returning rope again. Or the carriers may be permanently fixed to this rope and move with it. The ropeway itself consists of an endless rope running between two terminal drums, one of 6 to 10 ft. diameter, known as the driving drum, being provided with power receiving and transmitting gear, while the drum at the opposite terminal is fitted with tightening gear. The endless rope is supported on suitable pulleys which are, in turn, supported on standards or trestles spaced at intervals, varying with the nature of the ground. The rope runs at an average speed of 4 m. per hour, at which speed the bucket or skip can be arranged to load and unload itself automatically. Generally speaking, the single ropeway is not so suitable for heavy loads and long distances as the double. The work of Ropeways Ltd. favours the single-rope system. The founder of that firm, J. Pearce Roe, introduced multiple sheaves for supporting the rope at each standard. The maximum load carried on such a ropeway is 150 tons per hour. Another installation on the same system serves an iron mine in Spain and spans 6,500 yd. of very rough country so steep that in many places even the sure-footed mule cannot keep on the track. This ropeway can deal with 85 tons per hour. The greatest distance covered on any one section of the single ropeway is 7,100 yd., or about 4 miles. The Dorada ropeway which is the longest in the world—47 m. in length—is built on the single-rope system. It has 15 units and a capacity of 20 tons per hour. In addition to the conveyance of merchandise, principally coffee, it is also occasionally used for passenger traffic.

The Double Ropeway.—This consists, as already stated, of an independent rail rope and a separate continuous hauling rope disposed parallel to one another. The carrier runs on the stationary rope which is fitted with running heads having grooved steel wheels. The load is borne by a hanger pivoted from the carrier and conveyed along the rail rope by the endless hauling rope at an average speed of 4 to 6 m. per hour. A great variety of clips have been introduced for the purpose of coupling the carriers to the hauling rope, but these are automatically connected and disconnected at the shunt rails of the terminals. The hauling is operated by driving gear at one end and controlled at the other by tightening gear, just as in the single rope system. The rail ropes of a double ropeway are sectionalized every 2 or 3 m., whilst the longest section for a hauling rope is about 9 miles. Such ropeways will support single loads of 6 cwt. to a ton or more.

Motive Power.—The power required for a ropeway will vary according to conditions but is relatively moderate. If the aggregate down gradients exceed the up gradients the power consumption may be nil or the ropeway may even produce power which may be harnessed to drive other machines; or it may have to be absorbed by some form of brake device. In a Japanese ropeway 1,800 yd. in length, which runs mostly at an incline of 1 in 1½, the force generated is absorbed by a hydraulic brake, the revolving fan of which drives the water against fixed vanes which repel and heat it. In this way 50 h.p. is absorbed and the speed brought under the control of a hand brake.

The initial outlay for a ropeway is usually moderate, though of course it varies according to topographical conditions.

Ropeways are largely independent of weather conditions and their working need not be interrupted even by heavy snowfalls. Their construction is very simple and there is little to get out of order. Sound workmanship and good material will ensure a relatively long life. The ground space occupied by ropeway installations, beyond that occupied by the terminals is exceedingly small and is confined to the emplacements of the standards which, in modern ropeways are few and far between.

Aerial Cableways.—The aerial cableway is a development of the ropeway and is a conveyor capable of hoisting and dumping at any desired point. The load is carried along a track consisting of a single span of suspended cable which covers a comparatively short distance as rope haulage goes. The trackway may either run in a more or less horizontal direction, *i.e.*, the terminals may be on the same level, or it may be inclined at such an angle that the load will descend by gravity. The trackway or rail rope rests upon saddles of hard wood or iron on the tops of terminal supports usually known as towers, which may likewise be constructed of wood or iron, and if the exigencies of the work render it desirable they can be mounted on trolleys and rails, in which case the cableway is rendered portable and can be moved about, which is sometimes a great advantage in connection with dock and harbour work. The motive power may be either steam, gas, or electricity. The motor is situated in what is termed the head tower, which is occasionally a little higher than the tail tower. The span between the two towers sometimes extends to 2,000 ft., but this is exceptional. Objects weighing as much as 8 tons are handled by such devices. The load, which may be carried in a skip or tray, is borne by an apparatus called the carrier, which is a modification of a running head, consisting of pulleys and blocks and running along the main cable or trackway. This carrier is also fitted with pulleys or guides for the dump line, and is drawn along the main cable by an endless hauling rope which passes from the carrier over the head tower and is wound several times around the drum of the winding engine to secure frictional hold, then back over the head tower to the tail tower, returning to the rear end of the carrier. The hoisting rope passes from the engine to the fall-block for raising the load. The dump line comes from the other side of the winding engine drum and passes to a smaller block attached to the rear end of the skip or tray. The whole weight of the skip is borne by the hoisting rope, while the dump line comes in slack but at the same rate of speed. Whenever it is desired to dump the load the dump line is shifted to a section of the drum having a slightly larger diameter, and being thus drawn in at a higher rate of speed the load is discharged. The engine is then reversed and the carriage brought back for the next load.

This is, in outline, the mode of operating all cableways. These appliances have rendered great service as labour-savers in navvying, mining and quarrying work; for instance in placer-mining cableways have been found very useful when fitted with a self-filling drag-bucket which will take the place of a great number of

hands. Cableways can be worked at a great speed; a good mean speed, however, would be 500 to 750 ft. per min. for conveying, and 200 to 300 ft. per min. for hoisting.

BIBLIOGRAPHY.—G. F. Zimmer, *Mechanical Handling and Storing of Material* (1916); H. Blyth, *Modern Telpherage and Ropeways* (1926).

(G. F. Z.)

ROPS, FÉLICIEN (1833–1898), Belgian painter, designer and engraver, was born at Namur, in Belgium, on July 7, 1833; he spent his childhood in that town, and afterwards in Brussels, where he composed in 1856, for his friends at the university, the *Almanach Crocodilien*, his first piece of work. He also brought out two *Salons Illustrés,* and collaborated on the *Crocodile,* a magazine produced by the students. The humour shown in his contributions attracted the attention of publishers. He designed, among other things, frontispieces for Poulet-Malassis, and afterwards for Gay and Doucé. In 1859–60 he contributed some of his finest lithographs to a satirical journal in Brussels called *Uylenspiegel.* About 1862 he went to Paris and worked at Jacquemart's. He subsequently returned to Brussels, where he founded the short-lived International Society of Etchers. In 1865 he brought out his famous "Buveuse d'Absinthe," which placed him in the foremost rank of Belgian engravers; and in 1871 the "Dame au Pantin." After 1874 Rops resided in Paris. His talent was stimulated by travels in Hungary, Holland and Norway. He executed 600 original engravings enumerated in Ramiro's *Catalogue of Rops' Engraved Work* (Paris, Conquet, 1887), and 180 from lithographs (Ramiro's *Catalogue of Rops' Lithographs,* Paris, Conquet, 1891), besides a large number of oil-paintings in the manner of Courbet, and of pencil or pen-and-ink drawings, several very remarkable water-colour pictures, among which are "Le Scandale," 1876; "Une Attrapade," 1877 (now in the Brussels Museum); a "Tentation de St. Antoine," 1878; and "Pornocrates," 1878. From 1880 to 1890 Rops devoted himself principally to illustrating books: *Les Rimes de joie,* by Théo Hannon; *Le Vice suprême* and *Curieuse,* by J. Péladan; and *Les Diaboliques,* by Barbey d'Aurévilly; *L'Amante du Christ,* by R. Darzens; and *Zadig,* by Voltaire; and the poems of Stéphane Mallarmé have frontispieces due to his fertile and powerful imagination. Before this he had illustrated the *Légendes Flamandes,* by Ch. de Coster; *Jeune France,* by Th. Gautier; and brought out a volume of *Cent Croquis pour réjouir les Honnêtes Gens.* His last piece of work, an advertisement of an exhibition, was done in November 1896. Rops died on Aug. 23, 1898, at Essonnes, Seine-et-Oise, on his estate, where he lived in complete retirement with his family. Rops joined the Art Society of the "XX.," formed at Brussels in 1884, as their revolutionary views were in harmony with the independence of his spirit. After his death, in 1899, the Libre Esthétique, which in 1894 had succeeded the "XX.," arranged a retrospective exhibition, which included about fifty paintings and drawings by Rops. His engraved work is the most important, both as to mastery of technique and originality of ideas. Hardly any artist of the 19th century equalled him in the use of the dry-point and soft varnish.

In 1896 *La Plume* (Paris) devoted a special number to this artist, fully illustrated. E. Deman, Brussels, brought out a volume in 1897 entitled *Félicien Rops et son oeuvre*—papers by various writers. We may also mention a study of *Félicien Rops,* by Eugène Demolder (Paris, 1894), and another by the same writer in *Trois Contemporains* (1901); *Les Ropsiaques,* by Pierre Gaume (London, 1898), and the notice by T. K. Huysmans in this volume called *Certains. See also* E. Romiro, *Félicien Rops* (1905).

RORIDULA, a genus of the Droseraceae, of which there are two species peculiar to the mountains of South Africa. In both species the leaves are armed with numerous stalked glands, resembling closely but superficially the tentacles of *Drosera* (see SUNDEW) and secreting a sticky material which catches insects. These characters led to the belief that the plants are carnivorous. It was, however, shown that the secretion is not mucilaginous but resinous, which at once excludes the possibility of carnivory, since enzymes work in a watery medium. Moreover, the tentacular glands in *Roridula* are of entirely different structure from that in *Drosera,* having resin glands opening by ducts at the apex of the gland. R. Marloth, having in earlier years regarded *Rori-*

dula as carnivorous, later took the opposite view. He pointed out that the secretion contains a caoutchouc, and this was later confirmed to the extent that the substance is at least caoutchouc-like. Marloth pointed out also that branches of the plants, which are both shrubby, can be used as fly-paper, as *Drosophyllum* is said to have been used in Portugal. *See* R. Marloth, "Some Recent Observations on the Biology of Roridula," *Annals of Botany*, vol. 17, p. 151 (1903); F. E. Lloyd, "Is Roridula a Carnivorous Plant?" *Canadian Journal of Research*, vol. 10, p. 557 (1934). (F. E. L.)

RORQUAL, a name for a species of *Balaenoptera*, large whales of elongated shape, with a small back fin and longitudinal folds on the throat (*see* CETACEA). The flippers are small, the head small and flat, the whalebone coarse and short, the tail much compressed. There are probably four species. Sibbald's rorqual or blue whale (*Sibbaldus musculus*) is the largest of all animals, reaching lengths of over 100 ft. The common rorqual (*Balaenoptera physalus*) is some 20 ft. shorter, slate colour above and white beneath. (For illustration *see* CETACEA.)

RORSCHACH, a busy commercial town in the Swiss canton of St. Gall, situated on the south-west shore of the Lake of Constance, and by rail 62 mi. N.E. of Zürich. In 1941 its population was 10,536, mostly German-speaking. From 1408 to 1798 it belonged to the abbot of St. Gall, and then to the canton Säntis (named canton of St. Gall in 1803) of the Helvetic republic.

ROS, SIR RICHARD (b. 1429), English poet, son of Sir Thomas Ros, lord of Hamlake (Helmsley) in Yorkshire and of Belvoir in Leicestershire, was born on March 8, 1429. In Harl. ms. 372 the poem of "La Belle Dame sanz Mercy," first printed in W. Thynne's *Chaucer* (1532), has the ascription "Translatid out of Frenche by Sir Richard Ros." "La Belle Dame sanz Mercy" is a long and rather dull poem from the French of Alain Chartier, and dates from about the middle of the 15th century. It is written in the Midland dialect and is surprisingly modern in diction. The opening lines—

> Half in a dreme, not fully wel awaked,
> The golden sleep me wrapped under his wing,

have often been quoted, but the dialogue between the long-suffering lover and his lady does not maintain this level.

See W. W. Skeat, *Chaucerian and Other Pieces* (1897); and Dr. H. Gröhler, *Ueber Richard Ros' mittelenglische Uebersetzung* . . . (Breslau, 1886).

ROSA, CARL AUGUST NICHOLAS (1842-1889), English musical impresario, was born at Hamburg on March 22, 1842, his family name (which he subsequently changed) being Rose. He started as a solo violinist, studying at Leipzig and Paris. In 1867 he met and married the famous operatic soprano Madame Parepa (1836-74). In 1875 he started the Carl Rosa Opera company. He died in Paris on April 30, 1889.

ROSA, SALVATOR (1615-1673), Italian painter of the Neapolitan school, was born in Arenella, in the outskirts of Naples, on July 21, 1615, according to Passeri. His father, Vito Antonio de Rosa, an architect, sent him to study in the convent of the Somaschi fathers. Salvator went to his uncle Paolo Greco to learn painting, then to his brother-in-law Francesco Fracanzaro, a pupil of Ribera, and afterward to Ribera himself. He obtained some instruction under the battle-painter Aniello Falcone. Encouraged by Lanfranco, he went to Rome in 1635 to study, but catching fever, he returned to Naples and Falcone, and for a while painted nothing but battle-pieces. He went on to the landscape art peculiarly characteristic of him—wild scenes peopled with shepherds, seamen or, especially, soldiers. He then revisited Rome and was housed by Cardinal Brancaccio. In 1646 he took part in the insurrection of Masaniello against the Spaniards but on the approach of Don John of Austria he escaped to Rome. He was an actor, poet and musician as well as a painter. It was about this time that Rosa wrote his satire named *Babylon*, under which name Rome was indicated.

Cardinal Giancarlo de' Medici now invited the painter to Florence. Salvator remained in the Tuscan capital for the better part of nine years, introducing there the new style of landscape; he had no pupils, but various imitators. Lorenzo Lippi the painter poet, and other *beaux esprits* shared with Rosa the hospitalities

of the cardinal, and they formed an academy named *I Percossi* (the Stricken). He was well acquainted also with Ugo and Giulio Maffei and housed with them more than once in Volterra, where he wrote four other satires—*Music, Poetry, Painting* and *War*. Finally he returned once more to Rome. To confute his detractors he wrote the last of the series, entitled *Envy*. Among the pictures of his closing years were the "Battlepiece" now in the Louvre; "Pythagoras and the Fishermen"; the "Oath of Catiline" (Pitti Gallery); and "Saul and the Witch of Endor" (Louvre), almost his latest work. He died on March 15, 1673.

His etchings reflect his sympathy with the rough and ready life of the soldier and peasant. He also produced a number of large mythological and historical plates.

See G. B. Passeri, *Vite dei Pittori, Scultori ed Architetti* (Rome, 1772); F. Baldinucci, *La Vita di S. Rosa* (Venice, 1830); Lady Morgan, *Life and Times of S. R.* (1824); G. A. Cesareo, *Poesie e lettere di S. R.* (Naples, 1892); Leandro Ozzola, *Vita e Opere di Salvator Rosa* (Strasbourg, 1908); E. W. Manwaring, *Italian Landscape in 18th Century England* (New York, 1925).

ROSA, MONTE, the name of a great glacier-clad mountain mass (Aostan patois word *roëse*, a glacier) which rises southeast of Zermatt and on the frontier between Switzerland and Italy. Ten summits in this huge mass are distinguished by name, of which four (Nordend, 15,132 ft., Zumsteinspitze, 15,004 ft., Signalkuppe or Punta Gnifetti, 14,965 ft., and Parrotspitze, 14,-643 ft.) rise on the frontier. The five lower summits are on the Italian slope, but the highest of all, the Dufourspitze, 15,217 ft. (named by the Swiss government in honour of General Dufour, the head of the survey which first accurately fixed the position of these points), rises west of the frontier ridge, on a buttress, and being entirely in Switzerland, is its highest peak (not, as often stated, the Dom, 14,942 ft., in the Mischabel group). The summit of the Dufourspitze was first attained in 1855 by a large English party, including G. and C. Smyth and C. Hudson. The Zumsteinspitze was first climbed in 1820, the Signalkuppe (on top of which there is now a club hut) in 1842, the Nordend in 1861 and the Parrotspitze in 1863.

ROSACEAE, a large cosmopolitan family of seed-bearing plants which belong to the series Rosales of dicotyledons and contain about 100 genera with about 2,000 species. The plants vary widely in manner of growth. Many are herbaceous, growing erect, as *Geum*, or with slender creeping stem, as in species of *Potentilla*, sometimes sending out long runners, as in strawberry; others are shrubby, as raspberry, often associated with a scrambling habit, as in the brambles and roses, while apple, cherry, pear, plum and other British fruit trees represent the arborescent habit. Vegetative propagation takes place by means of runners, which root at the apex and form a new plant, as in strawberry; by suckers springing from the base of the shoot and rising to form new leafy shoots after running for some distance beneath the soil, as in raspberry; or by shoots produced from the roots, as in cherry or plum. The scrambling of the brambles and roses is effected by means of prickles on the branches and leaf-stalks.

The leaves, which are arranged alternately, are simple, as in apple, cherry, etc., but more often compound, with leaflets palmately arranged, as in strawberry and species of *Potentilla*, or pinnately arranged, as in the brambles, roses, mountain ash, etc. In warm climates the leaves are often leathery and evergreen. The leaves are stipulate, the stipules being sometimes small and short-lived, as in *Pyrus, Malus* and *Prunus* (cherry, plum, etc.), or more important structures adnate to the base of the leaf-stalk, as in roses, brambles, etc. The flowers, which are regular,

COTYLEDON

STONY LAYER OF CARPEL

A

TESTA OF SEED

B

VENTRAL SUTURE

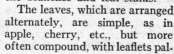

CHERRY (PRUNUS CERASUS)

A. Vertical section of the 'drupe of Cherry, cut vertically through the ventral and dorsal suture; B. fruit cut vertically in a plane at right angles to preceding one

generally bisexual and often showy, are sometimes borne singly, as in some species of rose, or of the cloudberry (*Rubus chamaemorus*), or few or more together in a corymbose manner, as in some roses, hawthorn and others. The inflorescence in agrimony is a raceme, in *Poterium* a dense-flowered spike, in *Spiraea*, a number of cymes arranged in a corymb. The parts of the flowers are arranged on a pentamerous plan, with generally considerable increase in the number of stamens and carpels. The shape of the thalamus or floral receptacle, and the relative position and number of the stamens and carpels and the character of the fruit, vary widely and form distinguishing features of the different suborders, six of which may be recognized.

Suborder I. Spiraeoideae is characterized by a flat or slightly concave receptacle on which the carpels, frequently two to five in number, form a central whorl; each ovary contains several ovules, and the fruit is a follicle except in *Holodiscus*. The plants are generally shrubs with simple or compound leaves and racemes or panicles of numerous small white, rose or purple flowers. This suborder is nearly allied to the family Saxifragaceae, chiefly north temperate in distribution. The largest is *Spiraea*, numerous species of which are cultivated in gardens; *S. salicifolia* occurs in Britain apparently wild in plantations, but is not indigenous. The native British meadowsweet is *S. ulmaria;* dropwort is *S. filipendula,* but some botanists now place the last two in a separate genus, *Filipendula*.

Suborder II. Pomoideae is characterized by a deep cup-shaped receptacle with the inner wall of which the two to five carpels are united; the carpels are also united with each other, and each contains generally two ovules. The fruit is made up of the large fleshy receptacle surrounding the ripe ovaries, the endocarp of which is leathery or stony and contains one seed. The plants are shrubs or trees with simple or pinnately compound leaves and white or rose-coloured often showy flowers. The genera are distributed through the north temperate zone, extending southward in the new world to the Andes of Peru and Chile.

While some botanists still continue to include the pears and the apples and even the mountain ash in *Pyrus* as a collective genus, most now recognize three genera, *Malus* to take the apples, a genus of about 25 species, the common apple being *Malus pumila*, formerly known as *Pyrus malus;* *Pyrus* to take the pears, a genus of about 20 species, the common pear being *Pyrus communis;* and *Sorbus*, a genus of about 80 species to take the rowan or mountain ash (*S. aucuparia*), wild service (*S. torminalis*), American mountain ash (*S. americana*), and white beam (*S. aria*). *Mespilus* (medlar), with a single species, and *Cotoneaster,* with about 50 species, are also included. All of these genera are confined to the north temperate zone.

Suborder III. Rosoideae is characterized by the receptacle being convex and swollen, as in strawberry, or cup-shaped, as in rose, and bearing numerous carpels, each of which contains one or two ovules, while the fruit is one-seeded and indehiscent. The genera are grouped in tribes according to the form of the receptacle and of the fruit. The Potentilleae bear the carpels on a large, rounded or convex outgrowth of the receptacle. In the large genus *Rubus* the ripe ovaries form drupels upon the dry receptacles; the genus is almost cosmopolitan, but the majority of species occur in the forest region of the north temperate zone and in the mountains of tropical America. *R. fruticosus* is blackberry, *R. idaeus,*

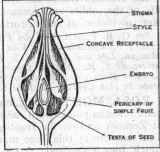

FROM GROOM, "ELEMENTARY BOTANY" (G. BELL & SONS)

DOG ROSE (ROSA CANINA), SHOWING VERTICAL SECTION OF COMPOUND FRUIT

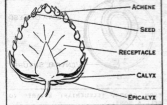

FROM GROOM, "ELEMENTARY BOTANY" (G. BELL & SONS)

STRAWBERRY (FRAGARIA VESCA), SHOWING VERTICAL SECTION OF COMPOUND FRUIT

raspberry and *R. chamaemorus,* cloudberry. In the flower of *Potentilla, Fragaria* (strawberry) and a few allied genera an epicalyx is formed by stipular structures arising at the base of the sepals. The fruits consist of numerous dry achenes borne in *Fragaria* on the much-enlarged succulent torus, which in the other genera is dry. In *Geum* (avens) and *Dryas* (an arctic and alpine genus) the style is persistent in the fruit, forming a feathery appendage (*Dryas*) or a barbed awn (avens), either of which is of service in distributing the fruit. The Potentilleae are chiefly north temperate, arctic and alpine plants.

The Roseae comprise the large genus *Rosa* (150 species), characterized by a more or less urn-shaped torus enclosing the numerous carpels which form dry one-seeded fruits enveloped in the bright-coloured fleshy torus. The plants are shrubs bearing prickles on the stems and leaves; many species have a scrambling habit resembling the brambles. The species of *Rosa*, like those of

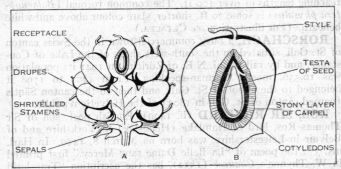

FROM GROOM, "ELEMENTARY BOTANY" (G. BELL & SONS)

BLACKBERRY (RUBUS FRUTICOSUS); SHOWING (A) VERTICAL SECTION OF COMPOUND FRUIT, (B) VERTICAL SECTION OF SINGLE DRUPE (ENLARGED)

Rubus, are extremely variable, and a great number of subspecies, varieties and forms have been described. Petals are often wanting, as in *Alchemilla* (lady's mantle) and *Poterium,* and the flowers are often unisexual and frequently wind-pollinated, as in salad burnet (*Sanguisorba minor*), where the small flowers are crowded in heads, the upper pistillate, with protruding feathery stigmas, and the lower staminate (or bisexual), with exserted stamens. *Agrimonia* (agrimony) has a long spike of small honeyless flowers with yellow petals; in the fruit the torus becomes hard and crowned by hooked bristles, which ensure the distribution of the enclosed achenes.

Suborder IV. Neuradoideae contains only two genera of desert-inhabiting herbs with yellow flowers; and the five to ten carpels are united together and with the base of the cup-shaped torus, which enlarges to form a dry covering round the one-seeded fruits.

Suborder V. Prunoideae is characterized by a free solitary carpel with a terminal style and two pendulous ovules, and the fruit a one-seeded drupe. The torus forms a cup from the edge of which spring the other parts of the flower. The plants are deciduous or evergreen trees or shrubs with simple leaves, often with small caducous stipules, and racemes or umbels of generally showy, white or pink flowers. There are five genera, the chief of which is *Prunus*, to which belong the plum (*Prunus communis*), with several well-marked subspecies—*P. spinosa* (sloe or blackthorn), *P. insititia* (bullace), *P. domestica* (wild plum), the almond (*P. amygdalus*) with the nearly allied peach (*P. persica*), cherry (*P. cerasus*), birdcherry (*P. padus*) and cherry laurel (*P. laurocerasus*). The tribe is distributed through the north temperate zone, passing into the tropics.

Suborder VI. Chrysobalanoideae resembles the last in having a single free carpel and the fruit a drupe, but differs in having the style basal, not terminal, and the ovules ascending, not pendulous;

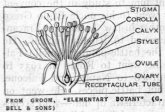

FROM GROOM, "ELEMENTARY BOTANY" (G. BELL & SONS)

VERTICAL SECTION OF FLOWER OF CHERRY

the flowers are also frequently zygomorphic. The genera are tropical evergreen trees or shrubs, the great majority being South American.

In North America the family is represented by about 40 genera, the largest being *Crataegus* (hawthorn) with about 70

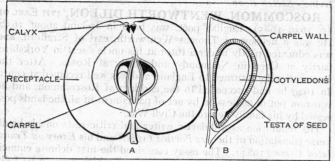

FROM GROOM, "ELEMENTARY BOTANY" (G. BELL & SONS)

APPLE (MALUS PUMILA): SHOWING (A) VERTICAL SECTION THROUGH FRUIT, (B) ONE OF THE PARCHMENT-LIKE CHAMBERS, REMOVED FROM THE FRUIT CONTAINING A SEED

species, *Rubus* (bramble) with 40 species, *Potentilla* (cinquefoil, five-finger) with about 40 species, *Prunus* (plum, cherry, etc.) with 20 species, and *Rosa* with 15 species. *Potentilla* is the most generally distributed genus in the United States.

The family is characteristically typical of temperate and sub-temperate regions, but some genera, such as *Rubus*, are of world-wide distribution. The strictly tropical groups are mostly trees and shrubs in such genera as *Chrysobalanus*, *Hirtella*, *Coupeia*, *Parinarium*, etc.

ROSAMOND, known as "The Fair" (d. *c.* 1176), mistress of Henry II, king of England, is believed to have been the daughter of Walter de Clifford of the family of Fitz-Ponce. Rosamond is said to have been Henry's mistress secretly for several years, but was openly acknowledged by him only when he imprisoned his wife Eleanor of Acquitaine as a punishment for her encouragement of her sons in the rebellion of 1173–74. Rosamond died in 1176, and was buried in the nunnery church of God-stow before the high altar. The body was removed by order of St. Hugh, bishop of Lincoln, in 1191, and was, seemingly, re-interred in the chapter house. The story that she was poisoned by Queen Eleanor first appears in the French Chronicle of London in the 14th century. The romantic details of the labyrinth at Woodstock, and the clue which guided King Henry II to her bower, were the inventions of story-writers of later times. There is no evidence for the belief that she was the mother of Henry's natural son William Longsword, earl of Salisbury.

ROSARIO, a city and river port of Argentina, in the province of Santa Fé, on the west bank of the Paraná, 186 mi. by rail N.W. of Buenos Aires. Pop. (1943 estimate) 521,210. It ranks next to Buenos Aires in size and in trade. It is accessible to ocean-going steamers of 26 ft. draught. The city stands on the eastern margin of the great pampean plain, 65 to 75 ft. above the wide river-bed washed out by the Paraná. It extends back a consider-able distance from the river. The city is laid out with chessboard regularity, with wide streets and spacious parks. The Boulevard El Santafecino is an attractive residence street with double drive-ways separated by a strip of garden and bordered by fine shade trees. The chief edifices of an official character are the custom-house, post office, municipal hall and law courts. Industries in-clude sugar refining, flour milling, brewing, printing and the manu-facture of bricks, leather, furniture and various kinds of food. The city is chiefly commercial, being the shipping port for a large part of northern Argentina. Among its exports are wheat, flour, baled hay, linseed, Indian corn, sugar, rum, cattle, hides, meats, wool, quebracho extract, etc. The railway connections are good in all directions except to the east across the Paraná river. A ferry service, however, connects the city with Victoria in the province of Entre Rios to the east. The port of Rosario is well equipped with modern appliances for handling freight.

Rosario was founded in 1725 by Francisco Godoy, but it grew so slowly that it was still a small village up to the middle of the 19th century.

In 1854 Gen. Justo José de Urquiza, then at the head of the Argentine confederation, made it the port of the ten upper prov-inces then at war with Buenos Aires, and in 1857 imposed differ-ential duties on the cargoes of vessels first breaking bulk at the southern port.

ROSARY, a popular devotion of the Roman Catholic Church, consisting of 15 Pater Nosters and Glorias and 150 Aves. The word also denotes the chaplet of beads for counting the prayers. It is divided into three parts, each containing five decades, a decade comprising one Pater, ten Aves and a Gloria, in addition to a subject for meditation selected from the "mysteries" of the life of Christ and of the Blessed Virgin. The Christian prac-tice of repeating prayers is traceable to early times: Sozo-men mentions (*H.E.*, v, 29) the hermit Paul of the 4th century who threw away a pebble as he recited each of his 300 daily prayers. It is not known precisely when the mechanical de-vice of the rosary was first used. William of Malmesbury (*De gest. pont. Angl.*, iv, 4) says that Godiva, who founded a re-ligious house at Coventry in 1043, left a string of jewels, on which she had told her prayers, that it might be hung on the statue of the Blessed Virgin. Thomas of Cantimpré, who wrote about the middle of the 13th century, first mentions the word "rosary" (*De apibus*, ii, 13), using it in a mystical sense as Mary's rose garden. Jacob Sprenger, a Dominican, founded the first confraternity of the Rosary at Cologne in 1474. The feast of the Rosary of the Blessed Virgin Mary was ordered to be observed on the first Sunday in October in such churches as main-tained an altar in honour of the Rosary. Clement XI, by bull of Oct. 3, 1716, directed the observance of the feast by all Chris-tendom.

BIBLIOGRAPHY.—See the critical dissertation in the *Acta sanctorum*, *Aug.* 1, 422 *et seq.*; Quétif and Échard, *Script. Ord. Praed.* i, 411 *et seq.*; Benedict XIV olim Prospero de Lambertini, *De festis B.V.M.*, i, 170 *et seq.*; H. Holzapfel, O.F.M., *St. Dominikus u. der Rosenkranz* (Mu-nich, 1903); Pradel, *Rosenkranz-Büchel* (Trier, 1885); D. Dahm, *Die Brüderschaft vom hl. Rosenkranz* (Trier, 1902); *Acta S. Sedis . . . pro Societate SS. Rosarii*, 4 vol. (Lyons, 1891); F. D. Joret, *Le rosaire* (Juvisy, 1931); M. Gorce, *Le rosaire et ses antécédents his-toriques* (Paris, 1931); H. Thurston, in *Catholic Encycl.*, art. "Rosary," and in *The Month*, Oct. 1900 to April 1901 (vol. 96–97), Sept. 1902 (vol. 100), July 1903 (vol. 102), May, June 1908 (vol. 111). For the indulgences attached to the devotion consult Beringer-Steinen, *Die Ablässe*, 15th ed., i, n. 880–910, ii, n. 236–38 (Paderborn, 1921–22), and *The Raccolta* (London, 1930) n. 360 *ff*. See also art. "Rosen-kranz." by Zöckler in Herzog-Hauck, *Realencyklopädie*, 3rd ed., and art. "Rosary" in Hastings, *Encyclopedia of Religion and Ethics*.

ROSAS, JUAN MANUEL DE (1793–1877), tyrant of Buenos Aires and outstanding figure in the history of Argentina, was born on March 30, 1793, in the city of Buenos Aires.

His father, Leon Ortiz de Rosas, was an owner of cattle runs (*estancias*) and a trader in hides who took an active part in defeat-ing the English attack on Buenos Aires in 1807. Juan Rosas re-ceived so little education that he had to learn to read and write when he was already a married man and a successful cattle breeder. From an early age he was left in charge of one of his father's es-tablishments. When he was 18 years of age he was married to Maria de la Encarnacion Escurra. He left his parents and for some time subsisted by working as a *vaquero*, or cowboy, and then as overseer on the estates of other owners; but he accumulated money, and by the help of a loan from a friend he became the owner of a cattle run of his own, Los Cerrillos.

The anarchical state of the country since winning its independ-ence enabled him to obtain leave to arm his cowboys, who became the most efficient fighting force in the country. By adroit use of this weapon, and by strict attention to his own interest, he rapidly became the dominant figure in the province of Buenos Aires. As governor of the province from 1829 to 1832, he gave it the first peace it had known in 20 years, so that in 1835, after a brilliant Indian campaign, he was unanimously elected dictator of Buenos Aires, and held that position until 1852. Throughout his regime, he waged a war of extermination against the leaders of the interior provinces who sought to combine against him or to set up for themselves as independent rulers. In spite of the continual combinations, domestic and foreign, in which this policy embroiled him, and of wars with Paraguay, Chile, Peru, Brazil, Uruguay, France and England, from which he had scarcely a moment's freedom, he broke the powers of the *caudillos* and upheld the supremacy of Buenos Aires in the country. In 1852 he was finally overthrown by a coalition of his neighbours and disaffected generals. He took refuge in England, at Swaythling, near Southampton, where he lived in poverty until his death on March 17, 1877.

(W. B. P.; X.)

ROSCELLINUS (RUCELINUS or ROUSSELIN) (*c.* 1050–*c.* 1122), often called the founder of Nominalism (*see* SCHOLASTICISM), was born at Compiègne (Compendium). He studied at Soissons and Reims, was afterwards attached to the cathedral of Chartres, and became canon of Compiègne. It seems most probable that Roscellinus was not strictly the first to promulgate nominalistic doctrines; but in his exposition they received more definite expression, and, being applied to the dogma of the Trinity, attracted universal attention. Roscellinus maintained that it is merely a habit of speech which prevents our speaking of the three persons as three substances or three Gods. If it were otherwise, and the three persons were really one substance or thing (*una res*), we should be forced to admit that the Father and the Holy Spirit became incarnate along with the Son. Roscellinus seems to have put forward this doctrine in perfect good faith, and to have claimed for it at first the authority of Lanfranc and Anselm. In 1092, however, a council convoked by the archbishop of Reims condemned his interpretation, and Roscellinus, who was in danger of being stoned to death by the orthodox populace, recanted his error. He fled to England, but having made himself unpopular by an attack on the doctrines of Anselm, he left the country and repaired to Rome, where he was well received and became reconciled to the Church. He then returned to France, taught at Tours and Loc-menach (Loches) in Brittany (where he had Abelard as a pupil), and finally became canon of Besançon. He is heard of as late as 1121, when he came forward to oppose Abelard's views on the Trinity.

Of the writings of Roscellinus, nothing is preserved except a letter to Abelard, mainly concerned with the doctrine of the Trinity (ed. J. A. Schmeller, Munich, 1850). *See* F. Picaret, *Rosselin, philosophe et théologien* (1896), and authorities quoted under SCHOLASTICISM.

ROSCIUS GALLUS, QUINTUS (*c.* 126–62 B.C.), Roman actor, was born, a slave, at Solonium, near Lanuvium. He studied the delivery and gestures of the most distinguished advocates in the Forum, especially Q. Hortensius, and won universal praise for his grace and elegance on the stage. He especially excelled in comedy. Cicero took lessons from him. The two often engaged in friendly rivalry to try whether the orator or the actor could express a thought or emotion with the greater effect, and Roscius wrote a treatise in which he compared acting and oratory. Q. Lutatius Catulus composed a quatrain in his honour, and the dictator Sulla presented him with a gold ring, the badge of the equestrian order, a remarkable distinction for an actor in Rome, where the profession was held in contempt. Like his contemporary Aesopus, Roscius amassed a large fortune, and he appears to have retired from the stage some time before his death. In 76 B.C. he was sued by C. Fannius Chaerea for 50,000 sesterces (about £400), and was defended by Cicero in a famous speech.

See H. H. Pflüger, *Cicero's Rede pro Q. Roscio Comoedo* (1904).

ROSCOE, WILLIAM (1753–1831), English historian and miscellaneous writer, was born on March 8, 1753, at Liverpool, the son of a market gardener and publican. In 1769 he was articled to a solicitor and in 1774 he commenced business as an attorney. Roscoe was also a political pamphleteer and like many other Liberals of the day hailed the promise of liberty in the French Revolution. The commercial crisis of 1816 brought to Roscoe great difficulties and forced him to sell his great collection of books and pictures. Some of these were secured by friends and placed in the library of the Liverpool Athenaeum. Roscoe now found a pleasant task in arranging the library of his friend Coke of Holkham. He died on June 30, 1831.

The first edition of his *Poetical Works* was published in 1857 and is sadly incomplete, omitting, with other verses known to be from his pen, the *Butterfly's Ball*, a fantasy, which has charmed thousands of children since it appeared in 1807. Other verses are in *Poems for Youth, by a Family Circle* (1820).

The *Life* by his son Henry Roscoe, 2 vol. (1833), contains full details of Roscoe's career, and there are references to him in the *Autobiographical Sketches* of Thomas de Quincey and in Washington Irving's *Sketch Book*.

ROSCOMMON, WENTWORTH DILLON, 4TH EARL OF (*c.* 1630–1685), English poet, was born in Ireland about 1630. He was a nephew of Thomas Wentworth, earl of Strafford, and was educated partly under a tutor at his uncle's seat in Yorkshire, partly at Caen in Normandy and partly at Rome. After the Restoration he returned to England and was well received at court. In 1649 he had succeeded to the earldom of Roscommon, and he was now put in possession by act of parliament of all the lands possessed by his family before the Civil War.

His reputation as a didactic writer and critic rests on his blank verse translation of the *Ars Poetica* (1680) and his *Essay on Translated Verse* (1684). The essay contained the first definite enunciation of the principles of "poetic diction," which were to be fully developed in the reign of Queen Anne. Roscommon, who was fastidious in his notions of "dignified writing," was himself a very correct writer and quite free from the indecencies of his contemporaries. He thought that a low code of morals was necessarily followed by a corresponding degradation in literature, and he insisted that sincerity and sympathy with the subject in hand were essential qualities in the poet. He was buried in Westminster abbey on Jan. 21, 1685.

Roscommon's poems were collected in 1701 and were printed in a composite volume in 1717. They are included in R. Anderson, *A Complete Edition of the Poets of Great Britain,* vol. vi (London and Edinburgh, 1793), and other collections.

ROSCOMMON, a county of Ireland in the province of Connaught, bounded northeast by Leitrim, northwest by Sligo, west by Mayo, east by Longford and east and south by Galway, east by Longford and east and south by Westmeath and Offaly counties. The area is 608,540 ac. or 951 sq.mi. Pop. (1951) 68,102. Most of the county belongs to the great limestone plain of central Ireland. The land is generally poor and used for grazing, with oats as the principal crop; there are a few small market towns and villages. In the northeast, on the Leitrim border, the Bralieve mountains, consisting of flat-topped ridges, attain an elevation in Cashel mountain of 1,377 ft.; and in the northwest the Curlew hills, of similar formation, between Roscommon and Sligo, rise abruptly to a height of more than 800 ft. In the east the Slieve Bawn range, formed of sandstone, has a similar elevation. The Shannon forms nearly the whole eastern boundary of the county, and on the west the Suck from Mayo forms for more than 50 mi. the boundary with Galway till it unites with the Shannon at Shannon Bridge. The other tributaries of the Shannon within the county are the Arigna, the Feorish and the Boyle. The lakes formed by expansions of the Shannon are Loughs Allen, Boderg, Boffin, Forbes and Ree. Other lakes are Lough Key in the north and Lough Gara (mostly in County Sligo) in the northwest. The county town, Roscommon, has a population of (1951) 2,013.

The district was granted by Henry III to Richard de Burgh, but remained almost wholly in the possession of the native septs. Until the time of Elizabeth I Connaught was included in the two districts of Roscommon and Clare and when these were subdivided, Roscommon was assigned its present limits. All the old proprietors were dispossessed at the Cromwellian settlement, except the O'Connor family headed by the O'Connor Don. Within the county are the ruins of Croghan, the palace of the kings of Connaught. The principal ancient castles are the stronghold of the M'Dermotts on Castle Island, Lough Key, the dismantled castle of the M'Donoughs at Ballinafad and the extensive fortress at Roscommon rebuilt by John d'Ufford, justiciary of Ireland in 1268. The abbey of Boyle, which is in good preservation, has Norman arches. The Irish bard Carolan, who died in 1738, is buried by the ruined church of Kilronan. The Protestant bishopric of Elphin was united with Kilmore and Ardagh in 1833. The Roman Catholic diocese of Achonry has its seat at Ballaghaderreen, but some parts of the county are included in the dioceses of Clonfert and Elphin.

The administrative county of Roscommon returns four members to *dail eireann*.

ROSE, JOHN HOLLAND (1855–1942), English historian, was born at Bedford and educated at Owens college, Manchester. He was reader in modern history, 1911–19, and Vere-Harmsworth professor of naval history, 1919–33, at Cambridge university. His researches were directed to the French Revolutionary and Napoleonic era on which he became a recognized authority.

His numerous historical works include *The Life of Napoleon I* (1902); *The Development of the European Nations, 1870–1900* (1905); *William Pitt and the Great War* (1911); *The Personality of Napoleon* (1912); *The Origin of the War* (1914); *Nationality as a Factor in Modern History* (1916); *Man and the Sea* (1935); and many articles and papers.

ROSE (*Rosa*). The rose has been closely associated with the culture of many civilizations. Not only is it a favourite flower but it serves as a symbol of perfection, elegance, romance and love. The Greek poetess Sappho in her "Ode to the Rose" first called it "the queen of flowers." No other flower is so universally known and even the name is easily recognized in most languages of Latin or Germanic origin. It is prominent in painting, architecture, music and literature and figures in legends, customs, heraldry and religion. Roses have been used in medicines and during World War II rose hips or fruits were a source of vitamin C. Rose petals can be used in cookery, particularly for confections, and extracts containing the essential oil which gives the fragrance are used for flavouring desserts or for scent in cosmetics and perfume. From the horticultural point of view roses are an important crop. Large

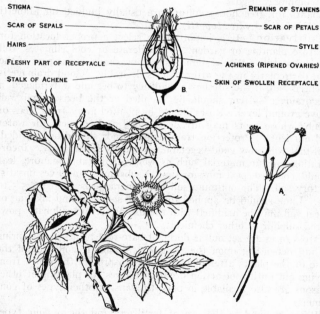

DOG ROSE (ROSA CANINA), SHOWING SPRAY WITH FLOWERS, LEAVES AND THORNS
(A) Rose hips. (B) One hip cut vertically to show achenes or true fruits inside the ripened receptacle

acreages are devoted to the production of rose plants for garden and greenhouse culture in the leading countries of the world. In the Balkans, France and India large quantities of blooms are grown for the production of attar of roses. The great variation in habit of growth makes them useful in almost any landscape situation.

As a garden flower they possess many admirable qualities. The colour ranges from white through various tones of yellow, pink and dark crimson and maroon. Many varieties with beautiful blends of colour including apricot and salmon tones exist. The form of the rose bloom varies from the delicate primitive charm of the species roses to the fully double, high-centred, beautifully sculptured blooms of the modern hybrid. Size ranges from the tiny miniatures not more than one-half inch in diameter to exhibition flowers seven inches or more across. Few persons fail to enjoy the delightful fragrance of most roses, which varies according to the

variety and climatic conditions. While the typical rose odour is that produced by the damask and similar roses known as attar of roses, the scent of other kinds may suggest spices, fruits, hay, other flowers or, as in the case of the tea rose, fresh green tea leaves. Many species and varieties have brilliantly coloured hips which are ornamental during the fall and winter. Because of the history and romance associated with them and the scientific challenge of their culture, rose study is an absorbing hobby. There are national amateur and professional rose organizations in several countries.

The rose gives its name to the botanical family Rosaceae, of which it may be considered the type. Most botanists agree that the genus consists of from 100 to 200 species, although thousands of botanical names have been applied. Roses, even from widely separated regions, hybridize readily, giving rise to types which overlap the parental forms and thus make it difficult to determine basic species. Rose species are distributed primarily in the temperate part of the northern hemisphere, but some are found above the Arctic circle and a few at the higher elevations in the tropics.

Roses are erect, climbing or trailing shrubs, never herbs or trees, generally more or less copiously armed with prickles of various shapes and sizes popularly called thorns. The leaves are invariably alternate, provided with stipules which are often aromatic gladular, and unequally pinnate, the leaflets varying in number from 1 to 11 or more, the odd leaflet always being at the apex, the others in pairs. The flowers are solitary or in loose corymbs or panicles produced at the ends of the shoots. The flower stalk expands into a fleshy vase- or urn-shaped hypanthium, called the receptacle or receptacular tube or hip which ultimately contains the numerous achenes (seeds).

From the edge of the hypanthium proceed five sepals, often more or less compound like the leaves and overlapping in the bud. Within the sepals are five petals, generally broad or roundish in outline, with a very short stalk or none at all, and of various shades of white, yellow or red. The numerous stamens originate slightly above the sepals and petals; each has a slender filament and a small two-celled anther. The carpels are numerous, covered with hairs, and each is provided with a long style and buttonlike stigma. The carpels are concealed within the hypanthium and only the stigmas as a rule protrude from its mouth. Each carpel contains one ovule.

The hips are usually brightly coloured as an attraction to birds, which devour them and thus bring about the dispersion of the seed. The stamens are in whorls and, according to Payer, originate in pairs, one on each side of the base of each petal so that there are ten in each row; a second row of ten alternates with the first, a third with the second, and so on. By repeated radial and tangential branching a vast number of stamens are ultimately produced. These stamens may become petaloid, giving rise to double flowers so much admired by gardeners. Under natural circumstances rose flowers do not secrete nectar, the attraction for insects being provided by the colour and perfume and the abundance of pollen for food. The stigmas and anthers come to maturity at the same time; consequently, while cross-pollination by insects is common, self-fertilization is not prevented.

The large number of roses described as European may be included under about 12 generally accepted species. *R. spinosissima*, the Scotch rose, is a low bush densely provided with slender prickles and producing white, pale pink or yellowish flowers one and one-half to two inches across. *R. eglanteria*, the eglantine or sweetbrier, is a stiff, erect, branching bush with pink blooms and sweet-smelling foliage. The dog rose, *R. canina*, including numerous subspecies and varieties, is common along the lanes and hedgerows of England and bears white or pinkish single flowers one to two inches across. The large-fruited apple rose, *R. pomifera*, is prized because of its large scarlet hips which may be one inch or more in diameter. *R. arvensis*, the parent of the Ayrshire rose, is a very thorny shrub with more or less decumbent or creeping branches. The French rose, *R. gallica*, a small shrub three to four feet high, is a variable old and familiar garden rose. The damask rose, *R. damascena*, possibly of hybrid origin, is similar to *R. gallica* but larger. The cabbage rose, *R. centifolia*, has been cultivated since ancient times for its double fragrant flowers. The moss rose, which has a "mossy" pedicel and calyx, is a variant of this species. *R. rubrifolia* is an unusual shrub because of its reddish glaucous stems and foliage. The cinnamon rose, *R. cinnamomea,* is a hardy old garden species common along fences and roadsides and has double fragrant blooms in shades of red, two inches or more across.

The numerous roses native to North America belong to about 35 species. The smooth rose (*R. blanda*), usually lacking prickles, with flowers about three inches broad, occurs abundantly from Newfoundland to Saskatchewan and southward to New Jersey and Missouri. The prickly rose (*R. acicularis*), with spiny stems, leaves composed of from five to nine leaflets and solitary flowers two and one-half inches broad, ranges from Quebec to Alaska and south to Colorado. The pasture rose (*R. virginiana*), from one-half to six feet high, with few or solitary flowers two to three inches across, sometimes double, occurs from Newfoundland to Wisconsin and south to Georgia. This is the most common wild rose of the eastern states and Canada. The prairie rose (*R. setigera*), a large shrub with a tendency to climb, the leaves usually with three leaflets, bears rose-pink flowers which turn white with age. This handsome rose, which grows wild from Ontario to Wisconsin and south to Florida and Texas, has become naturalized eastward to New England. The California rose (*R. californica*), a sparsely prickly shrub three to nine feet high, flowering nearly the year round, sometimes forms thickets along streams.

Many species important as cultivated plants and for the hybrids produced with European and North American species are of Asiatic origin. The tea rose (*R. odorata*) from western China is nearly evergreen, has five to seven leaflets and blooms more or less continuously through the year. The fragrant tea-scented flowers are one to three inches across, white, light pink or salmon yellow. The China or Bengal rose (*R. chinensis*) is similar to *R. odorata* but the plants are smaller and the flowers odourless. The Austrian briar (*R. foetida*) is a three- to five-foot shrub with deep yellow flowers two to three inches in diameter, usually solitary. *R. multiflora* is an attractive shrub with long, arching branches. The flowers are one-half to three-fourths inches across and borne 25 to 100 in dense panicles. The memorial rose (*R. Wichuraiana*) produces long prostrate stems and fine glossy foliage; the slightly fragrant white flowers are one inch across, borne in clusters. *R. rugosa* is a remarkable species because of its bold rugose foliage, its large red, pink or white flowers and its conspicuous fruits. *R. Moyesii* is an attractive ten-foot shrub with two and one-half inch deep red flowers. *R. Hugonis* is a handsome, hardy shrub producing an abundance of light yellow flowers in early spring. The Macartney rose (*R. bracteata*), introduced into England from China, is a stout evergreen shrub producing lopping shoots 10 to 20 ft. long. The Cherokee rose (*R. laevigata*) is a rampant plant climbing over fences and trees. It is widely planted in southern United States, where it has run wild and appears to be indigenous; in fact, the species was first described botanically from American plants. The Lady Banks rose (*R. Banksiae*) is a high-climbing evergreen with few or no prickles and smooth slender twigs. The flowers are about one inch across, single or double, white or yellow, somewhat fragrant and borne in umbellike clusters.

Roses have been cultivated for so many centuries and have been hybridized so extensively that it is difficult to refer the cultivated forms to wild prototypes. It is generally agreed, however, that the present-day garden varieties of bush roses have been evolved through the repeated intercrossing of *R. gallica*, *R. damascena*, *R. centifolia*, *R. chinensis*, *R. odorata* and *R. foetida*. Certain traits such as continuous blooming and certain fragrances characteristic of modern roses are traceable to the influence of *R. chinensis* and *R. odorata*. The influence of *R. foetida* is shown through the strong yellow hues of many garden hybrids. Vigour, hardiness and other growth, flower and odour characteristics are apparently derived from *R. gallica*, *R. damascena* and *R. centifolia*. Many climbing roses resulted from crosses between hybrids of bush types with *R. Wichuraiana*, *R. multiflora* or other species.

The number of cultivated clones is very large and about 100 are introduced into commerce each year. To facilitate grouping varieties (clones) with similar characteristics, a horticultural classification has evolved which is complicated and often inconsistent. In some cases it is based upon origin from wild species, in others upon habit of growth or manner of flowering. There is considerable overlapping and mergence of classes as the result of relentless interbreeding. Among bush roses the main classes include hybrid perpetuals, teas, hybrid teas, polyanthas, floribundas or hybrid polyanthas and grandifloras. Climbing roses are classed as ramblers, large-flowered climbers, everblooming hardy climbers, climbing forms of hybrid teas, floribundas and other bush types and trailing varieties. A comprehensive list is given in J. H. McFarland's *Modern Roses IV* (1952), which includes 6,150 names. Of these 300 are classed as species or botanical varieties; 3,264 as hybrid teas; 215, hybrid perpetuals; 617, polyanthas and floribundas; 325, climbing hybrid teas; 249, ramblers; and 173, large-flowered climbers. The list, however, represents only a small proportion of the roses hybridized and named during the preceding 250 years.

Propagation.—Roses are propagated by seeds, cutting, layering, grafting and budding. Most rose seed requires a stratification treatment to hasten germination. Commercially, rose plants are produced largely by budding the desired clone onto an understock. In Europe forms of *R. canina* are used extensively while in the U.S. forms of *R. multiflora* are commonly used although in some areas Ragged Robbin, Dr. Huey and forms of *R. odorata* are employed. Tree or standard roses are budded from two to six feet above ground level on a tall, straight cane of the understock. For this purpose forms of *R. canina*, *R. multiflora*, *R. rugosa* and I.X.L. are commonly used.

Plants for greenhouse culture are usually budded on Manetti (*R. Noisettiana* var. *Manetti*).

Cultivation.—It is important to select a proper location for the rose planting or garden. In moderate or cool climates, full sun is desirable. Where summers are hot, shade during part of the day, particularly in the afternoon, is desirable. Good drainage is essential and, if the site has a tendency to become waterlogged, a tile drainage system should be installed or the beds raised well above ground level. Roses should be planted away from trees or shrubs whose roots may invade the bed and compete for water and nutrients. Protection from strong winds should be provided. Soil that will grow good vegetables is usually satisfactory. Incorporating organic material such as well-rotted stable manure, leaf mould, compost, peat moss or similar substances improves unsatisfactory soil. The optimum soil reaction range is from pH 5.5 to 6.5. Lime should be applied to acid or sour soil and alkaline or sweet soil may be acidified with the use of ferrous sulphate, powdered sulphur or other chemicals.

Most roses are set out as dormant bare-root plants in the spring or fall depending upon the climate. Mounding soil around the base of the plants after planting helps to protect the canes from drying out until root action occurs. Bushes for planting at other seasons are also available in pots, tin cans or other types of containers.

Roses respond to the use of fertilizers and the organic types are preferred, although inorganic mixed fertilizers are satisfactory when properly used. Top-dressing with rotted manure or using liquid manure is advantageous. Watering the beds immediately after fertilizer is applied is recommended.

Watering during dry periods is important for successful rose culture. A great deal of water is given off by the leaves and experiments have shown that an average-sized hybrid tea bush may transpire as much as 30 gal. of water during a single growing season. Thorough watering is essential; this means soaking the soil to a depth of from six to eight inches.

Cultivating the beds to eliminate weeds and keeping the surface loose and well aerated is recommended but it should not be so deep as to destroy roots. Mulching with grass clippings, peat moss, buckwheat hulls, ground corncobs, rice hulls and comparable materials helps to conserve moisture, keep down soil temperature and eliminate weeds.

Pruning is practised to keep the plants in vigorous condition and to improve their appearance and productivity. The different classes and even different varieties in the same class may respond to different pruning treatment, but in general the practice for bush roses involves cutting out all dead or injured wood in the spring, removing weak, twiggy growth and cutting back the strong canes to a moderate height to give the plant a symmetrical, well-balanced appearance.

The climbers that bloom only once during the season are best pruned immediately after flowering. Withered blooms should be removed promptly from everblooming climbers so that new flowering shoots will be produced.

In cold climates where the temperature normally goes below 5° F., protection during the winter is necessary. This is accomplished by mounding soil around the base of the plants just before the surface freezes and later covering with evergreen boughs, marsh hay, straw or other coarse material. Where climbing roses are likely to freeze they may be removed from their supports, laid on the ground and covered with soil. In the spring the canes are again tied back on the supports.

Caused mostly by fungi, a number of diseases infect roses. Powdery mildew is widespread wherever roses are grown and is observed as a grayish-white mouldlike growth on the surface of young leaves, stems and buds. Copper and sulphur fungicides are effective for control when applied either as a spray or dust. Black spot may be troublesome in humid climates if precautions are not taken.

Conspicuous black spots appear on the leaves, which soon drop, defoliating the plants. The spores are formed in the spots on the leaves and are washed from one plant to another by rain or overhead sprinkling. If the surface of the leaf remains wet for a period of about six hours, the spores can germinate and cause infection unless the surface of the leaf is protected by a thin film of fungicide. Fixed or insoluble copper fungicides, finely powdered, or wettable sulphur are standard control materials. There are also a number of organic fungicides such as Ferbam and Captan that are highly effective if applications are timely and thorough. Removing infected leaves as soon as a spot is detected and keeping all fallen leaves removed from the surface of the bed is recommended. Rust appears on both cultivated and wild roses in the spring, bursting through the bark in the form of masses of orange powder consisting of the spores of the fungus. The spores infect the leaves and produce on them in the summer small orange dots and later groups of spores that are able to live through the winter.

It is important that all the affected leaves should be destroyed in the autumn and the bush sprayed with a copper, sulphur or Ferbam fungicide in the spring to prevent infection of leaves by spores brought from a distance.

Other diseases that are sometimes troublesome are canker, crown or root gall and anthracnose.

There are a number of insects which may prove troublesome. Aphids are common but are easily controlled by nicotine spray or dust and many other insecticides. Various caterpillars, sawfly larvae and similar insects feed on the leaves and young shoots. These are easily controlled, however, by stomach poisons such as arsenate of lead, DDT and other materials. Red spider mites which multiply in great numbers, largely on the undersides of the leaves, are sometimes serious pests because they are difficult to see and may cause damage before being discovered. A number of materials such as Malathion, Aramite and Ovatran are available for their control.

Other insects that may be troublesome are thrips, earwigs, midge and scale insects.

BIBLIOGRAPHY.—George M. Taylor, *The Book of the Rose* (London, Toronto, 1949), (ed.), *Pearson's Encyclopaedia of Roses* (London, Toronto, 1948); Bertram Park, *Roses* (London, 1949); A. S. Thomas, *Better Roses* (Sydney, 1950; New York, 1952); N. P. Harvey, *The Rose in Britain* (New York, London, 1951); J. Horace McFarland, *Modern Roses IV*, ed, by C. E. Meikle and G. H. M. Lawrence (Harrisburg, Pa., 1952); Jean Gordon, *Pageant of the Rose* (New York, 1953); Cynthia Westcott, *Anyone Can Grow Roses*, 2nd ed. (New York, London, 1954); Roy E. Shepherd, *History of the Rose* (New York, 1954); R. C. Allen, *Roses for Every Garden* (New York, 1948). See also publications of the National Rose Society of Great Britain, the American Rose Society and the Australian and New Zealand Rose Societies.
(R. C. AL.)

ROSEBERY, ARCHIBALD PHILIP PRIMROSE, 5TH

EARL OF (1847–1929), British statesman, born in London on May 7, 1847, was the son of Archibald, Lord Dalmeny (1809–1851) and Catherine, daughter of the 4th earl Stanhope. Lady Dalmeny married, after her husband's death, the duke of Cleveland. Young Dalmeny was educated at Brighton and at Eton, where he had as slightly junior contemporaries A. J. Balfour and Randolph Churchill. In 1866 he matriculated at Christ Church, Oxford, but went down in 1868, by the request of the dean, rather than abandon the possession of a small racing stud. In the same year he succeeded his grandfather, the 4th earl, in the earldom and the family estates. After some time spent in travel he acquired an English country house called The Durdans, Epsom, which he largely rebuilt and adorned with some of the finest turf portraits of George Stubbs. He had a famous stable, and, later, won the Derby three times, in 1894, 1895 and 1905. In 1878 he married Hannah, only child of Baron Meyer Amschel de Rothschild.

Though impeded in his political career by his exclusion from the House of Commons, Lord Rosebery's reputation as a social reformer and orator was steadily growing. In 1878 he was elected Lord Rector of Aberdeen and in 1880 of Edinburgh University, where he gave an eloquent address upon Patriotism. In 1880 he entertained Gladstone at Dalmeny, and during the "Mid Lothian campaign" he arranged the demonstrations. In August 1881 he became under-secretary at the home office, his immediate chief being William Harcourt. His work was practically confined to the direction of the Scottish department of the office, and he resigned in 1883. He resumed office (1884) as first commissioner of works with a seat in the cabinet.

In the brief Gladstonian government of 1886 Lord Rosebery threw in his lot with the old leader, and was foreign secretary. His views on foreign policy differed materially from those of Granville and Gladstone. His mind was dwelling constantly upon the political legacy of the two Pitts; he was a reader of John Seeley; he had himself visited the colonies; had predicted that a war would not, as was commonly said, disintegrate the empire, but rather the reverse; had magnified the importance of taking colonial opinion, and had always been a convinced advocate of some form of Imperial Federation. He was already taunted with being an Imperialist, but his independent attitude won public approval. In January 1889 he was elected a member of the first county council of London, and on Feb. 12, chairman of that body by 104 votes to 17. With a view to the impending political campaign he found it necessary to resign the chairmanship of the county council in June. In November of this year, however, Lady Rosebery died, and he withdrew for a period from public business. In January 1892 he again for a few months became chairman of the county council. In October he received the Garter.

In August 1892, upon the return of Gladstone to power, he was induced with some difficulty (for he was suffering at the time from insomnia) to resume his position as foreign minister. He strongly opposed the evacuation of Egypt; he insisted upon the exclusive control by Great Britain of the Upper Nile Valley, and also upon the retention of Uganda. In 1893 the question of Siam came near to causing serious trouble with France, but the crisis was averted, and the lines were laid down for preserving Siam, if possible, as a buffer state between the English and French frontiers in Indo-China. In the spring of 1895 he was clear-sighted enough to refuse to join the anti-Japanese league of Russia, France and Germany at the end of the China-Japan War.

Lord Rosebery's personal popularity had been increased at home by his successful intervention in the coal strike of December 1893, and when in March 1894 the resignation of Gladstone was announced, his selection by Queen Victoria for the premiership was generally welcomed, but the malcontents in his own party, who considered that William Harcourt should have been the prime minister, or who were perpetually intriguing against a leader who did not satisfy their idea of radicalism, made Lord Rosebery's personal position no easy one. The support of the Irish Nationalists was endangered by his insistence that the goodwill of England, the "predominant partner," was essential to the success of Home Rule. On June 24, 1895, the government fell.

For the state of disorganization and discontent in the Liberal Party during the next ten years of opposition see LIBERAL PARTY. The breach between William Harcourt and Rosebery had never been healed, and Rosebery found himself also, to his great grief, at variance with Gladstone. He declined to support Gladstone's demand for intervention on behalf of the Armenians at the risk of a European war, and on Oct. 8, 1896, he announced to the Liberal whip, Thomas Ellis, his resignation of the Liberal leadership. For some time he held aloof from party politics, "ploughing his furrow alone," as he afterwards phrased it.

In 1898, on the death of Gladstone, he paid a noble and eloquent tribute in the House of Lords to the life and public services of his old leader. He gave a general support to the policy of the Salisbury government on the South African War. But the war had brought to the front a section antagonistic to the war and known in the jargon of the day as pro-Boers. These had won the qualified support of Campbell-Bannerman, the leader in the House of Commons. Lord Rosebery maintained for the most part a sphinx-like seclusion, but in July 1901 he at last came forward strongly as the champion of the Liberal Imperialist section of the party, which included Asquith, Grey and Haldane. At a meeting at Chesterfield (Dec. 1901), he spoke of "cleaning the slate" of the old party cries, and eventually spoke of his separation from the "tabernacle" of Campbell-Bannerman. But the main body of the party stood by Campbell-Bannerman, and a partial reconciliation was effected. Chamberlain's tariff reform campaign helped to bring the Liberal Imperialists nearer to the rest of the party. Rosebery's own pronouncements on the tariff issue were hesitating, and to some extent contradictory. But though he eventually came into line with his colleagues on tariff reform, he finally broke with Campbell-Bannerman on the question of Home Rule for Ireland. On the fall of the Conservative government in Dec. 1905, Campbell-Bannerman was invited to form a cabinet, and Rosebery retired from party politics, though he encouraged his immediate associates to join the new government.

Rosebery continued eloquent and witty addresses on miscellaneous subjects. No public man of his time was more fitted to act as unofficial national orator; none more happy in the touches with which he could adorn a social or literary topic and charm a non-political audience; and on occasion he wrote as well as he spoke. His *Pitt* (1891) was already a classic; his *Appreciations and Addresses* and his *Peel* (containing a remarkable comment on the position of an English prime minister) were published in 1899; his *Napoleon: the Last Phase*—an ingenious, if paradoxical attempt to justify Napoleon's conduct in exile at St. Helena—in 1900; his *Cromwell* in the same year.

Lord Rosebery took an active part in the constitutional crisis in 1910 and 1911. He treated the Parliament Bill as a revolutionary measure, which in effect constituted single-chamber government, and did his utmost to arouse the nation to its danger. In 1914, as lord-lieutenant of Midlothian and Linlithgowshire he promoted recruiting and other war-like activities among his own people. He was chancellor of Glasgow university in 1908, as he had long been chancellor of London university, and he was chosen lord rector of St. Andrew's university for the year of its quincentenary celebration in 1911.

Lord Rosebery had two sons and two daughters. His eldest son, Lord Dalmeny (b. Jan. 1882), entered parliament in 1906 as Liberal member for Midlothian, but retired in 1910. The younger son, Neil Primrose (1882–1917) was undersecretary for the Foreign Office in 1915 and parliamentary secretary for munitions in 1916. He died of wounds received in action in Palestine on Nov. 18, 1917. The elder daughter, Lady Sybil, in 1903 married Captain Charles Grant; the younger, Lady Margaret, in 1899 married the 1st earl of Crewe. Lord Rosebery died at Epsom, Surrey, May 21, 1929.

ROSEBURG, a city of western Oregon, U.S., 196 mi. S. of Portland; county seat of Douglas county; it is located on federal highway 99 and the Southern Pacific railroad. Pop. (1950) 8,390. Timber resources of the area have been estimated as 70,000,000,-000 bd.ft. The city was founded in 1852 and incorporated in 1872.

ROSECRANS, WILLIAM STARKE (1819–1898), American soldier, was born in Kingston (O.), on Sept. 6, 1819, and graduated in 1842 from the U.S. Military Academy. After serving (1843–47) as assistant professor at West Point, he resigned (April 1854) and went into business in Cincinnati. On the outbreak of the Civil War he volunteered for service under McClellan and helped raise the Ohio "Home Guards," with which he served in the West Virginian operations of 1861 as brigadier general. He was second in command to McClellan during this campaign, and succeeded to the command when that officer was called to Washington. In the latter part of 1861 he conducted further successful operations in the same region, and early in 1862 was transferred to the West as a major general of volunteers. He took part in the operations against Corinth, and when Gen. John Pope was ordered to Virginia, Rosecrans took over command of the army of the Mississippi, with which he fought the successful battles of Iuka and Corinth. Soon afterwards he replaced D. C. Buell in command of the forces. In December he advanced against Gen. Braxton Bragg, and on Dec. 31 to Jan. 3 fought the bloody, indecisive battle of Stone river (Murfreesboro), after which Bragg withdrew his army to the southward. In 1863 Rosecrans, refusing to advance until the isolation of Vicksburg was assured, did not take the offensive until late in June. The operations thus begun were most skilfully conducted and Bragg was forced back to Chattanooga, whence he had to retire. But Rosecrans sustained a great defeat at the battle of Chickamauga (q.v.), and was soon besieged in Chattanooga. He was then relieved from his command. Later he did good service in Missouri, and in March 1865 was made brevet-major general U.S.A. He resigned in 1867, and in 1868 became minister to Mexico. He was a representative in Congress from California, 1881–85, and register of the treasury, 1885–93. Under an act of Congress he was, on March 2, 1889, restored to the rank of brigadier general and retired. He died near Redondo (Calif.), March 11, 1898. On May 17, 1902 his body was reinterred with military honours in the National Cemetery at Arlington.

See Edward Channing, *History*, vol. vi.; J. B. McMaster, *History of the People During Abraham Lincoln's Administration* (1927).

ROSEGGER, PETER (1843–1918), Austrian poet and novelist, known down to 1894 under the pseudonym *Petri Kettenfeier*, was born at Alpl near Krieglach in Upper Styria, on July 31, 1843, the son of a peasant. His work includes novels, poems, religious writings and autobiographical volumes, notably *Waldheimat* (1873) and *Mein Weltleben* (1898).

ROSELLE AND ROSELLE PARK, two contiguous boroughs of Union county, New Jersey, U.S.A., adjoining Elizabeth on the west; served by the Central of New Jersey, the Lehigh Valley and (for freight) the Rahway Valley railways. The population of the borough of Roselle in the year 1950 was 17,646 and of Roselle Park in the same year 11,521.

ROSELLINI, IPPOLITO (1800–1843), Italian Egyptologist, was born at Pisa. He studied under Mezzofanti at Bologna, and in 1824 became professor of oriental languages at Pisa. He was the associate of J. F. Champollion (q.v.) in his Egyptian explorations (1828), the account of which he published as *Monumenti dell' Egitto e della Nubia* (Florence, 1832–40, 10 vols. fol.).

ROSEMARY, botanically *Rosmarinus officinalis*, a plant of the mint family (Labiatae), the only representative of the genus and a native of the Mediterranean region. It is a low shrub with linear leaves, dark green above, white beneath, and with margins rolled back on to the under face. The flowers are in small axillary clusters. Each has a two-lipped calyx, from which projects a bluish two-lipped corolla enclosing two stamens. The fruit consists of four smooth nutlets. Rosemary was highly esteemed by the ancients for its aromatic quality and medicinal uses. In modern times it is valued mainly for its perfume; the oil is obtained by distillation. Rosemary plays an important part in literature and folk-lore, being an emblem of remembrance.

ROSENHEIM, German town and watering-place in Upper Bavaria, at the confluence of the Mangfall and the Inn, 40 m. by rail S.E. of Munich. Pop. (1939) 21,340. Rosenheim is frequented for its saline and sulphur baths, and there are saltworks.

ROSENKRANZ, KARL (1805–1879), German philosopher of the Hegelian school, was born at Magdeburg on April 23, 1805. He was professor of philosophy at Königsberg from 1833 until his death on July 14, 1879. Rosenkranz was a loyal Hegelian. In the great division of the school, he, in company with Michelet and others, formed the "centre," midway between Erdmann and Gabler on the one hand, and the "extreme left" of Strauss, Feuerbach and Bruno Bauer. With F. W. Schubert he edited Kant's *Sämtliche Werke* (Leipzig, 12 vols., 1838–42), the last vol. of which contains his *Geschichte der kantischen Philosophie*.

ROSENWALD, JULIUS (1862–1932), American merchant and philanthropist, was born in Springfield, Ill., on August 12, 1862, the son of Samuel Rosenwald and Augusta (Hammerslough) Rosenwald. His father came to the United States about 1854 from Germany and finally established himself as one of the leading clothing merchants of Springfield, Ill. Julius Rosenwald was educated in the public schools of Springfield. At the age of sixteen he went to New York City to learn the clothing business. In 1885, together with his brother, Morris S. Rosenwald, and his cousin, Julius Weil, he established the clothing business of Rosenwald & Weil in Chicago. In 1897, he became active as vice-president of Sears, Roebuck & Company. The mail-order business prospered enormously, and the gross sales of Sears, Roebuck & Company increased from $3,020,557 in 1897 to $443,476,176 in 1929. In 1909 Richard W. Sears retired as president of Sears, Roebuck & Company, and Julius Rosenwald succeeded him in that office and held the position until 1924, when he became chairman of the board and remained in that position until his death.

In 1916 Rosenwald, with Albert H. Loeb, treasurer of the company, was instrumental in establishing an employees' savings and profit-sharing pension fund. Provision was thus made for the old age of employees, and by voluntary contributions of employees and contributions of the company, both invested in the stock of Sears, Roebuck & Company, a profit-sharing pension fund was set up, which in the twenty years between its inception in 1916 and 1936 had paid 65,000 former employees the sum of $45,-203,989 on deposits of their own of $10,042,304. In Dec. 1921, Rosenwald pledged from his personal fortune the sum of $21,000,-000 to safeguard the interests of Sears, Roebuck & Company during the critical period of business readjustment after the war.

In December 1916, at the request of President Wilson, Julius Rosenwald began his service as a member of the Advisory Commission of the Council of National Defense, and he served as chairman of the Committee on Supplies of that body until the summer of 1918. During the period of America's participation in the war he made huge purchases of equipment and materials for the Army and Navy and for the Allies of the United States.

As soon as he began to acquire a large personal fortune, Rosenwald started to engage in charitable and philanthropic activities on a great scale. He was active in Jewish charities in Chicago from the early nineteen hundreds until the time of his death. He became actively interested in the welfare of the Negro in 1911 and maintained that interest throughout his lifetime. The Julius Rosenwald Fund, established in 1917, is dedicated to "the well-being of mankind." Rosenwald, who was firmly opposed to perpetual endowments, provided that the entire fund, which in 1928 was worth $40,000,000, must be expended within twenty-five years after his death. His propaganda against perpetual endowments exercised a creative influence on philanthropy throughout the world.

The chief effort at first of the Julius Rosenwald Fund was to better the condition of Negroes through education. The Fund has contributed to the construction of more than 5,000 schools for Negroes in fifteen southern states, with contributions from the Rosenwald Fund, local tax funds, Negroes themselves and other white friends interested in Negro education. It was always one of Rosenwald's principles of public giving to inspire others to give by the example of his own gifts, and frequently he made his offers, large and small, in such form that they had to be matched by other gifts before they were gained.

In addition to his work for Negro education through the Julius Rosenwald Fund, Rosenwald served as a trustee of Tuskegee Normal and Industrial Institute, founded by Booker T. Washington

in 1881, from 1912 until the time of his death, and he donated approximately $200,000 to the activities of that institution.

During the war Julius Rosenwald donated $1,000,000 to the Jewish War Relief Fund. After the war, he pledged $6,000,000 for the effort of the Joint Distribution Committee to settle the Jews of Russia in agricultural colonies in that country. He contributed $100,000 in 1920 for the relief of German children.

Rosenwald made gifts of more than $4,000,000 to the University of Chicago, and he gave approximately $6,600,000 for a Museum of Science and Industry in Chicago. He also founded dental infirmaries in the Chicago public schools. He was a large contributor to the work of the Y.M.C.A. in Chicago and elsewhere, and he contributed $25,000 towards the cost of erecting each Y.M.C.A. building for Negroes in 21 cities of the United States. Rosenwald's gifts during his lifetime exceeded $22,000,000 exclusive of the Rosenwald Fund, which had assets worth $40,000,000 in 1928.

Rosenwald took an active interest in the civic affairs of Chicago for many years, and he was deeply interested in the improvement of municipal and national government. For many years he was chairman of the Bureau of Public Efficiency of Chicago.

In recognition of his work for the Negro, Julius Rosenwald received the William E. Harmon award of a gold medal for distinguished achievement in race relations in 1928. In that same year he was awarded a medal by the Austrian Republic for his encouragement of science and art. In 1929 he received the Gottheil medal for the most distinguished service to Jewry during the year 1928. In 1930 President Paul von Hindenburg of Germany presented Rosenwald with a porcelain vase of German artisanship in recognition of his "many magnanimous gifts" to German war widows and orphans. He was a trustee of the University of Chicago, of the Rockefeller Foundation, of the Baron de Hirsch Fund and of other organizations. Julius Rosenwald died in Chicago January 6, 1932.   (M. R. W.)

ROSES, WARS OF THE, a name given to a series of civil wars in England during the reigns of Henry VI., Edward IV. and Richard III. Their importance in the general history of England is dealt with elsewhere, and their significance in the history of the art and practice of war is small. They were marked by a ferocity and brutality practically unknown in the history of English wars before and since. The honest yeoman of Edward III.'s time had evolved into a professional soldier of fortune, and had been demoralized by the prolonged and dismal Hundred Years' War, at the close of which many thousands of ruffians, whose occupation had gone, had been let loose in England. At the same time the power of feudalism had become concentrated in the hands of a few great lords, who were wealthy enough and powerful enough to become king-makers. The disbanded mercenaries enlisted indifferently on either side, corrupting the ordinary feudal tenantry with the evil habits of the French wars, and pillaged the countryside, with accompaniments of murder and violence, wherever they went. It is true that the sympathies of the people at large were to some extent enlisted: London and, generally, the trading towns being Yorkist, the country people Lancastrian—a division of factions which roughly corresponded to that of the early part of the Great Rebellion, two centuries later, and similarly in a measure indicative of the opposition of hereditary loyalty and desire for sound and effective government. But there was this difference, that in the 15th century the feeling of loyalty was to a great extent focussed upon the great lords.

It is from the Wars of the Roses that there originated the deep-rooted dislike of the professional soldier which was for nearly four centuries a conspicuous feature of the English social and governmental system, and it is therefore in their results rather than their incidents that they have affected the evolution of war. They withdrew the English army system from European battlefields precisely at the moment of transition when the regimental and technical organization of armies was becoming a science and seeking models, and the all-powerful English longbow at the moment when the early, scarcely effective firearms were, so to speak, struggling for recognition as army weapons. On the other hand, they destroyed the British military organization, which remained for 150 years an aggregation of county levies armed with bills and bows.

The first campaign, or rather episode, of these wars[1] began with an armed demand of the Yorkist lords for the dismissal of the Lancastrian element in the king's council, Henry VI. himself being incapable of governing. The Lancastrians, and the king with them, marched out of London to meet them, and the two small armies (3,000 Yorkists, 2,000 Lancastrians) met at St. Albans (May 22, 1455). The encounter ended with the dispersion of the weaker force, and the king fell into the hands of the Yorkists. Four years passed before the next important battle, Blore Heath, was fought (Sept. 23, 1459). In this the earl of Salisbury trapped a Lancastrian army in unfavourable ground near Market Drayton, and destroyed it; but new political combinations rendered the Yorkist victory useless and sent the leaders of the party into exile. They made a fresh attempt in 1460, and, thanks partly to treason in the Lancastrian camp, partly to the generalship of Warwick, won an important success and for the second time seized the king at Northampton (July 10, 1460). Shortly afterwards, after a period of negotiation and threats, there was a fresh conflict. Richard duke of York went north to fight the hostile army which gathered at York and consisted of Lancashire and Midland Royalists, while his son Edward, earl of March, went into the west. The father was ambushed and killed at Wakefield (Dec. 30, 1460), and the Lancastrians, inspired as always by Queen Margaret of Anjou, moved south on London, defeated Warwick at St. Albans (Feb. 17, 1461), and regained possession of the king's person. But the young earl of March, now duke of York, having raised an army in the west, defeated the earl of Pembroke (Feb. 2, 1461) at Mortimer's Cross (5m. west of Leominster). This was the first battle of the war which was characterized by the massacre of the common folk and beheading of the captive gentlemen—invariable accompaniments of Edward's victories, and notably absent in Warwick's. Edward then pressed on, joined Warwick, and entered London, the army of Margaret retreating before them. The excesses of the northern Lancastrians in their advance produced bitter fruit on the retreat, for men flocked to Edward's standard. Marching north in pursuit, the Yorkists brought their enemy to bay at Towton (q.v.), 3m. south of Tadcaster, and utterly destroyed them (March 29, 1461). For three years after Towton the war consisted merely of desultory local struggles of small bodies of Lancastrians against the inevitable. The duke of York had become King Edward IV., and had established himself firmly. But in 1464, in the far north of England, the Red Rose was again in the field. Edward acted with his usual decision. His lieutenant Montagu (Warwick's brother) defeated and slew Sir Ralph Percy at Hedgley Moor, near Wooler (April 25, 1464), and immediately afterwards destroyed another Lancastrian army, with which were both Henry VI. and Queen Margaret, at Hexham (May 15, 1464). The massacres and executions which followed effectively crushed the revolt. For some years thereafter Edward reigned peacefully, but Warwick the king-maker and all the Neville following having turned against him (1470), he was driven into exile. But at a favourable moment he sailed from Flushing with 1,500 retainers and Burgundian mercenaries, and eluding the Lancastrian fleet and the coast defence troops, landed at Ravenspur (Spurn Head) in Yorkshire in March 1471. His force was hardly more than a bodyguard; the gates of the towns were shut against him, and the country people fled. But by his personal charm, diplomacy, fair promises and an oath of allegiance to King Henry VI., sworn solemnly at York, he disarmed hostility and, eluding Montagu's army, reached his own estates in the Wakefield district, where many of his old retainers joined him. As he advanced south, a few Yorkist nobles with their following rallied to him, but it was far more the disunion of the Warwick and the real Lancastrian parties than his own strength which

enabled him to meet Warwick's forces in a pitched battle. At Barnet, on Easter Eve, April 14, 1471, the decisive engagement was fought. But in the midst of the battle reinforcements coming up under the earl of Oxford to join Warwick came into conflict with their own party, the badge of the Vere star being mistaken for Edward's *Rose-en-soleil*. From that point all the mutually distrustful elements of Warwick's army fell apart, and Warwick himself, with his brother Montagu, was slain. For the last time the unhappy Henry VI. fell into the hands of his enemies. He was relegated to the Tower, and Edward, disbanding his army, reoccupied the throne. But Margaret of Anjou, his untiring opponent, who had been in France while her cause and Warwick's was being lost, had landed in the west shortly after Barnet, and Edward had to take the field at once. Assembling a fresh army at Windsor, whence he could march to interpose between Margaret and her north Welsh allies, or directly bar her road to London, he marched into the west on April 24. On the 29th he was at Cirencester, and Margaret, engaged in recruiting an army, was near Bath. Edward hurried on, but Margaret eluded him and marched for Gloucester. At that place the governor refused the Lancastrians admittance, and seeking to cross the Severn out of reach of the Yorkists, they pushed on by forced marches to Tewkesbury. But Edward too knew how to march, and caught them up. The battle of Tewkesbury (May 4, 1471) ended with the destruction of Margaret's force, the captivity of Margaret, the death of her son Edward (who, it is sometimes said, was stabbed by Edward IV. himself after the battle) and the execution of 16 of the principal Lancastrians.

This was Edward's last battle. The rest of his eventful reign was similar in many ways to that of his contemporary Louis XI., being devoted to the consolidation of his power, by fair means and foul, at the expense of the great feudatories. But the Wars of the Roses were not yet at an end. For 14 years, except for local outbreaks, the land had peace, and then Richard III.'s crown, struck from his head on Bosworth Field (Aug. 22, 1485), was presented to Henry earl of Richmond, who, as Henry VII., established the kingship on a secure foundation. A last feeble attempt to renew the war, made by an army gathered to uphold the pretender Lambert Simnel, was crushed by Henry VII. at Stoke Field (4m. south-west of Newark) on June 16, 1487.

ROSETTA (Coptic *Rashit*, Arabic *Rashīd*), a town situated at the western or "Rosetta" mouth of the Nile on the west bank, and called Bolbitine by the Greeks. When the other branches and the Alexandria canal silted up, Rosetta prospered like its sister port of Damietta on the eastern branch; the main trade of the overland route to India passed through it until Mehemet Ali cut a new canal joining Alexandria to the Nile. Rosetta is now much decayed. A railway joins it to Alexandria. The celebrated Rosetta Stone which supplied Champollion with the key for the decipherment of the ancient monuments of Egypt was found near Fort St. Julien, 4 m. N. of the town, in 1799, by Boussard, a French officer. It is a basalt stele inscribed in hieroglyphic, demotic and Greek with a decree of the priests assembled at Memphis in favour of Ptolemy V. Epiphanes. It was ceded to the English at the capitulation of Alexandria (1801) and is now in the British Museum.

ROSETTE, an ornament, usually circular, oval or polygonal, formed by a series of petals or leaves radiating from the centre and symmetrically disposed. The form undoubtedly originated as an attempt to represent, systematically, the corolla of an open flower. Egyptian rosettes were thus, probably, representations of the open lotus. In Assyrian ornament, and in the Persian work based upon it, rosettes are one of the most common ornaments and are used, by continuous repetition, to form decorative bands. Although common in archaic pottery of the Greek islands, they were little used in the developed art of Greece itself. The Romans, on the other hand, used the form lavishly and gave it great richness by employing the complex acanthus leaf as the basic radiating form. It was used not only at the centre of each face of the Corinthian capital, but also to decorate the little panels between the modillions (q.v.) or scrolled brackets of the Corinthian order and as a decoration for the centre of the coffers or sunk panels of

---

[1]The name, as is well known, comes from the "white rose of York" and the "red rose of Lancaster"; but these badges, though more or less recognized as party distinctions, by no means superseded the private devices of the various great lords, such as the "falcon and fetterlock" of Richard duke of York, the "rose in sun" of Edward IV., the "crowned swan" of Margaret, the Vere star, and even the revived "white hart" of Richard II.

a coffered vault or ceiling. The rosette almost went out of use in the mediaeval period save as it sometimes occurred as an individual flower in Gothic naturalistic ornament. In the Perpendicular period in England, the popularity of the heraldic Tudor rose gave a new importance to the rosette idea, and rosettes were frequently employed, repeated at regular intervals, to decorate hollow mouldings. Renaissance rosettes in design are based upon those of Rome, but were used even more lavishly, owing to the immense development of wooden coffered and panelled ceilings.

In metalwork the idea of the rosette was probably developed independently, owing to the ease with which little drops of metal could be soldered or fastened in a circle, to a basic utensil. Such rosettes, formed either of a simple circle of nearly hemispherical shape, or of one large hemisphere surrounded by several smaller ones, are favourite late Bronze and early Iron age decorations in the metalwork of the Celts, Scandinavians and the people of northern Europe generally.

(T. F. H.)

ROSEVILLE, a city of Placer county, Calif., U.S., 18 mi. N.E. of Sacramento. Pop. (1950) 8,723; (1940) 6,425. It is at the junction of federal highways 40 and 99 and on the main lines of the Southern Pacific railroad. The railroad maintains an immense railroad construction and repair shop and there is a large diesel terminal. The freight classification yards are the largest west of Chicago, Ill. The Pacific Fruit Express company maintains a large ice-manufacturing and storage plant for the refrigeration of fruit and vegetable cars.

ROSE WINDOW or WHEEL WINDOW, in architecture, a term applied to any decorated circular window. Undecorated circular windows are found in certain imperial Roman structures, used especially in the upper portions of rooms or pierced through vaults, as in the tomb of the time of Hadrian known as the Casale dei Pazzi, near Rome, but structural decoration of such forms was apparently not attempted until the Byzantine and Romanesque periods.

One of the earliest decorated circular windows extant is that of the Italian Romanesque church of S. Maria in Pomposa, possibly as early as the 10th century, in which the decoration consists of a pierced marble slab of great richness, with a design of interlaces and birds purely Byzantine. In French Romanesque work circular windows also appear, but in the earlier work, such as the late 11th century apse of S. Sernin at Toulouse, they are undecorated, like those of the Roman empire. Meanwhile, in Mohammedan work, the cusped circle had been a common form, usually, however, not as a window, but as the outer boundary of a sunk hemisphere, as in the mosque of Ibn Touloun at Cairo, Egy. (876–78).

The crusaders probably saw many examples of such forms; in any case it is only after the earlier crusades and especially toward the middle of the 12th century that the idea of making a rich decorative motive out of a round window appeared. From then on the simple rose window became more and more common, and was, in fact, a distinguishing characteristic of many transitional and early Gothic cathedrals. It was particularly used at the west end of the nave and the ends of the transepts. An exceptional early use is the round window which lighted the triforium roof space from the nave in the original form of Notre Dame at Paris (before 1177). In the west front of Laon cathedral (completed prior to 1200) there is an enormous rose window with 12 semicircles around the edge and the central foiled and cusped circle separated from the apexes of these semicircles by a considerable distance, the connection between being made by little radiating colonnettes like spokes. This window is remarkably advanced for its date, as the filling, like that of the Paris triforium, is essentially bar tracery. The rose window of the west front of Chartres cathedral (1194–1212) consists, on the other hand, of plate tracery, the circle being filled with a thin plate of stone, through which are pierced many small foiled or cusped holes. A similar form of plate tracery within a circle is used to cap the twin windows of the clerestorey bays.

The introduction of developed bar tracery gave a compelling impetus to rose window design. The general scheme consisted of a series of radiating forms, each of which was tipped by a pointed arch at the outside of the circle. The bars between these forms were joined at the centre by a pierced circle of stone and the forms themselves frequently treated like little traceried windows with subsidiary, subdividing bars, arches and foiled circles. The most beautiful examples of this type are those of the west front of Rheims cathedral (end of the 13th century) and the transepts of Rheims, Amiens and Notre Dame at Paris (all of the last half of the 13th century). The introduction of the wavy lines of flamboyant tracery completely changed the character of French rose windows, but they continued basically radiating in design. The radiating elements consisted of an intricate network of wavy, double curved bars, creating all sorts of interesting circles and flame shapes and, incidentally, furnishing a diagonal bracing to the whole composition which added materially to its structural strength. The rose at the end of the transept at Beauvais (early 16th

century) is characteristic.

The influence of the French rose windows was widespread from an early period. Variations of the form appear in a multitude of late Italian Romanesque churches, as in the widely varying type in the late 12th century west front of S. Pietro in Toscanella, and the more normal example in S. Zeno at Verona (late 12th century). In England the rose window has never been so popular as in France. Those in the transepts of Westminster abbey are more characteristically French than English. The most typically English examples are in the transepts of Lincoln cathedral; that on the north from the Early English period is a remarkably delicate example of plate tracery; that on the south from the Curvilinear period of the early 14th century is striking because it is not radiating in design, and therefore completely at odds with the French prototypes. (*See* TRACERY.) (T. F. H.)

ROSEWOOD, the name given to several distinct kinds of ornamental timber. That, however, so called in the United Kingdom is Brazilian rosewood, the *palissandre* of the French, the finest qualities of which, coming from the provinces of Rio de Janeiro and Bahia, are believed to be the produce principally of *Dalbergia nigra,* a leguminous tree of large dimensions, called *cabiuna* and *jacaranda* by the Brazilians. The same name, jacaranda, is applied to several species of *Machaerium,* also trees belonging to the family Leguminosae; and there can be no doubt that a certain proportion of the rosewood of commerce is drawn from these sources.

Rosewood is exported in large quantities from Rio de Janerio, Bahia, Jamaica and Honduras. The heartwood attains large dimensions, but as it begins to decay before the tree arrives at maturity it is always faulty and hollow in the centre. On this account squared logs or planks of rosewood are never seen, the wood being imported in half-round flitches 10 to 20 ft. in length and from 5 to 12 in. in the thickest part. Rosewood has a deep ruddy brown colour, richly streaked and grained with black resinous layers. It takes a fine polish, but, on account of its resinous nature, it is somewhat difficult to work. The wood is very much in demand by cabinetmakers and piano makers.

ROSICRUCIANISM. There are Rosicrucian societies, fraternities, orders, fellowships or lodges in most countries of the modern world. Some of them are very active; others are obscure and highly secret; some seem to be primarily religious in their emphasis, and some categorically deny that Rosicrucianism is a religion, holding rather that it is a philosophy, making use of the most modern scientific methods and techniques, as well as methods of the occultist, the mystic and the seer, in the quest for truth.

But, while Rosicrucianism is sectarian in character and the various branches are sometimes bitterly critical of each other, they do have common features, the central one being the purported possession of certain secret wisdom handed down from ancient times, through a secret brotherhood, an esoteric wisdom that can only be imparted to the initiated. Their teachings so far as known seem to combine something of Egyptian Hermetism, Christian Gnosticism, Jewish Kabbalism, alchemy and a variety of other occult beliefs and practices. While alchemy seems to have been prominent in the movement, modern Rosicrucians affirm that their language must be taken symbolically rather than literally and that they have no interest in such things as the transmutation of metals.

Whether all Rosicrucian organizations can trace their origins back to the main historic stream of Rosicrucianism is a matter of grave doubt. But after all, what is the true Rosicrucianism?

The earliest extant writing which unequivocally mentions a Rosicrucian order appeared in the early 17th century. But even here the actual existence of such an order cannot be affirmed absolutely. Indeed, not a few scholars believe rather that the order had its rise from the publication of this document and that it was written with this definite purpose in mind.

The document was the famous *Fama Fraternitatis,* first published in 1614 but probably circulated in manuscript form somewhat earlier than this. Seven editions appeared during the years 1614–17. It recounts the journey of the reputed founder of the movement, Christian Rosenkreuz, to Damascus, Damcar in Arabia, Egypt and Fez, where he was well received and came into possession of much secret wisdom. He returned finally to Germany, where he chose three others to whom he imparted this wisdom and thus founded the order. Later the number was increased to eight who separated, each going to a separate country.

One of the six articles of agreement they adopted was that the fraternity should remain secret for 100 years. At the end of 120 years the secret burial place and the perfectly preserved body of the founder were discovered by one of the then members of the order, along with certain documents and symbols held in very high esteem by Rosicrucians. The sacred vault was re-covered, the members of the order dispersed, and no one knows its location. The *Fama* ends with an invitation to "some few" to join the fraternity.

According to the *Confessio*, which is bound up with the *Fama* in some of the editions, Christian Rosenkreuz was born in 1378 and lived 106 years, or until 1484. His tomb was then hidden for 120 years, making its discovery fall in 1604. If this is a true account of the founding of the order, it must have come into being sometime in the 15th century.

Some regard the story as a statement of fact, and hold Christian Rosenkreuz to have been the founder of the order. More generally it is held to be a mythical explanation of the order, and Christian Rosenkreuz not a real person at all, but rather a symbolic character. R. Swinburne Clymer saw in the travels of Christian Rosenkreuz in the *Fama* an obvious parallel to the travels of Paracelsus, whom he regarded as the real founder of the movement. H. Spencer Lewis held that it marks only a revival of the order which began in remote antiquity in Egypt, where the great Akhnaton made significant contributions to it. He listed numerous persons of antiquity, including Solomon, Jesus, Plato, Philo, Plotinus and others, as well as movements such as the Essenes of Jesus' day, the young Christian movement itself, and later movements such as Jewish Kabbalism, as related to the ancient order. These he identified as truly Rosicrucian because he was able to find among their reported teachings ideas which he regarded as Rosicrucian. His conclusions do not seem convincing to objective students. There can be no doubt that there were in ancient times persons whose outlook and thought were similar to that of the Rosicrucians. That there was a continuing order in existence previous to the 15th century, or even the 17th, is impossible to prove beyond question, on the basis of any sources available to non-Rosicrucian research.

With the publication of the *Fama*, international interest in the order was aroused and it was not long before there were Rosicrucian orders in several European countries. Michael Maier, a learned alchemist, became its chief exponent in Germany. Robert Fludd is thought to have introduced it into England. Thomas Vaughan translated the *Fama* into English in 1652, and though he knew of no existing order in England at that time, he remarked that he was not unacquainted with Rosicrucian doctrine and had no doubt concerning the existence of the order.

That it is not always possible to prove the existence of the order in a given country at any particular moment does not disturb the Rosicrucians, for it seems to be recognized that there occur periods when the order is deliberately "in sleep." H. Spencer Lewis reduced these periods to a definite rhythm of 108 years of activity followed by 108 years of silence, in a given country. It was in accordance with this cyclic theory, he said, that he was led at the proper time to seek out the leaders of the order in France in the early years of the 20th century and under their authority to inaugurate a new cycle of activity in the United States in 1915, under the name Ancient Mystical Order Rosae Crucis, usually abbreviated to A.M.O.R.C. It became affiliated with the Fédération Universelle des Ordres et Sociétés Initiatiques, established in Europe in 1934.

R. Swinburne Clymer, head of a rival U.S. order with headquarters at Quakertown, Pa., who as early as 1902 published *The Rosicrucians: Their Teachings*, spoke of the periods of silence, but these were determined by specific conditions rather than by the passage of time. His organization, traced through a definite line of Rosicrucian adepts in the U.S. from revolutionary times, with Paschal Beverly Randolph and Freeman B. Dowd as his more immediate predecessors, is known as the Fraternitas Rosae Crucis. Its foreign affiliation was with La Fédération Universelle des Ordres, Sociétés et Fraternités des Initiés.

Rosicrucianism and Freemasonry have not a little in common. Indeed, there is a degree in masonry known as the Rose Croix degree. Likewise, the *Societas Rosicruciana in Anglia* and its affiliates are held to be more masonic than Rosicrucian.

The symbol of Rosicrucianism is a combination of the cross and the rose, from which the order takes its name. The origin of the symbol is variously given, but there seems to be no one explanation which is completely satisfactory.

BIBLIOGRAPHY.—Eugenius Philalethes (Thomas Vaughan), tr., *The Fame and Confession of the Fraternity of R: C: . . .*, originally printed in London in 1652 (Margate, 1923); A. E. Waite, *History of the Rose Cross Order* (London, 1887); A. E. Waite, *The Brotherhood of the Rosy Cross* (London, 1924); Hargrave Jennings, *The Rosicrucians, Their Rites and Mysteries* (London, 1887); J. F. Sachse, *The German Pietists of Pennsylvania*; Will Erich Peuckert, *Die Rosenkreuzer; Zur Geschichte einer Reformation* (Jena, 1928); H. Spencer Lewis, *Rosicrucian Questions and Answers with Complete History of the Rosicrucian Order*, 3rd ed. (1941); R. Swinburne Clymer, *The Book of Rosicruciae*, 3 vol. (1946–48).   (C. S. B.)

ROSIN or COLOPHONY, the resinous constituent of the oleoresin exuded by various species of pine, known in commerce as crude turpentine. The separation of the oleoresin into the essential oil spirit of turpentine and common rosin is effected by distillation in large stills. Rosin (a later variant of "resin," *q.v.*), varies in colour, according to the age of the tree from which the turpentine is drawn and the amount of heat applied in distillation, from an opaque almost pitchy black substance through grades of brown and yellow to an almost perfectly transparent colourless glassy mass. The commercial grades are numerous, ranging by letters from A, the darkest, to N, extra pale, and X, most pale, W (window glass) and WW (water white) varieties, the latter having about three times the value of the common qualities.

Rosin is a brittle and friable resin, with a faint pine-like odour; the melting point varies with different specimens, some being semifluid at the temperature of boiling water, while others do not melt till 220° F. or 250° F. It is soluble in alcohol, ether, benzene and chloroform. In addition to its extensive use in soapmaking, rosin is largely employed in making inferior varnishes, sealing wax, various cements and as a sizing agent in the manufacture of paper. It is also used for preparing shoemakers' wax, as a flux for soldering metals, for pitching lager beer casks, for rosining the bows of musical instruments, etc. In pharmacy it forms an ingredient in several plasters and ointments.

The chief region of rosin production is the south Atlantic and eastern gulf states of the United States. American rosin is obtained from the turpentine of the swamp pine, *Pinus palustris*, and of the loblolly pine, *P. Taeda*. The main source of supply in Europe is the "landes" of the departments of Gironde and Landes in France, where the cluster pine, *P. Pinaster*, is extensively cultivated. In the north of Europe rosin is obtained from the Scotch fir, *P. sylvestris*, and throughout European countries local supplies are obtained from other species of pine.

ROSKILDE, or ROESKILDE, a town of Denmark in the *amt* (county) of Kjøbenhavn (Copenhagen), 20 mi. by rail W. of Copenhagen, on the great lagoon-like inlet named Roskilde fjord. Pop. (1950) 26,355. Its chief interest is historical. It was the capital of the kingdom until 1443, and the residence of the bishops of Zealand until the Reformation. The cathedral was consecrated in 1084, but of this early building only foundation walls remain; the present structure of brick was begun in 1215, and enlarged and restored at various later dates. It contains the tombs of most of the Danish kings from Harold I (987).

ROSMEAD, HERCULES GEORGE ROBERT ROBINSON, 1ST BARON (1824–1897), British colonial administrator, was born on Dec. 19, 1824. He was of Irish descent on both sides; his father was Admiral Hercules Robinson, his mother a Miss Wood of Rosmead, County Westmeath, from which he afterward took his title. Passing from Sandhurst into the 87th Foot, he attained the rank of captain; but in 1846, through the influence of Lord Naas, he obtained a post in the board of public works in Ireland, and subsequently became chief commissioner of fairs and markets. His energy in these positions, notably during the famine of 1848, and the clearness and vigour of his reports, secured for him at the age of 30 the office of president of the island of Montserrat. He was governor of St. Christopher from 1855 to 1859, when he was knighted in recognition of his services in introducing coolie labour into the island. Subsequently he was governor of Hong Kong, of Ceylon (K.C.M.G. in 1869), and, in 1872, of New South Wales. It fell to his lot to annex the Fiji Islands to the British empire, and his services were rewarded in 1875 by promotion to G.C.M.G. In 1879 he was transferred to New Zealand, and in 1880 he succeeded Sir Bartle Frere as high commissioner of South Africa. He arrived in South Africa shortly before the disaster of Majuba, and was one of the commissioners for negotiating a peace which was personally distasteful to him. It left him with the task of conciliating on the one hand a Dutch party elated with victory, and on the other hand a British party almost ready to despair of the British connection. He was called home in 1883 to advise the government on the terms of the new convention concluded with the Transvaal Boers in Feb. 1884. On his return to South Africa he found that a critical situation had arisen in Bechuanaland, where Boer commandoes had seized large tracts of territory and proclaimed the "republics" of Stella and Goshen (*see* KRUGER, STEPHANUS JOHANNES PAULUS). They refused to retire within the limits of the Transvaal as defined by the new convention, and Robinson, alive to the necessity of preserving this country—the main road to the north —for Great Britain, took action which led to the expedition of Sir Charles Warren and the annexation of Bechuanaland early in 1885. Robinson won Kruger's confidence by his fair-mindedness, while he seconded Rhodes's efforts to unite the British and Dutch parties in Cape Colony. His mind, however, was that of the administrator as distinguished from the statesman, and he was content to settle difficulties as they arose. In 1887 Robinson was induced by Rhodes to give his consent to the conclusion of a treaty with Lobengula which secured British rights in Matabele and Mashona lands. In May 1889 Robinson retired. In his farewell speech he declared that there was no permanent place in South Africa for direct imperial rule. This was interpreted to mean that South Africa must ultimately become independent—an idea repugnant to him. He explained in a letter to *The Times* in 1895 that he had referred to the "direct rule of Downing Street over the Crown colonies, as contrasted with responsible colonial Government." He was made a baronet in 1891.

Early in 1895, when he had entered his 71st year and was not in robust health, he yielded to Lord Rosebery's entreaties, and went out again to South Africa, in succession to Sir H. Loch. The Jameson raid produced a permanent estrangement between him and Cecil Rhodes, and he was out of sympathy with the new colonial secretary, Joseph Chamberlain, who had criticized his appointment, and now desired Robinson to take this opportunity of settling the whole question of the position of the Uitlanders in the Transvaal. Robinson answered that the moment was inopportune, and that he must be left to choose his own time. Alarmed at the imminent danger of war, he confined his efforts to inducing the Johannesburgers to lay down their arms on condition that the raiders' lives were spared, not knowing that these terms had already been granted to Jameson. He came home to confer with the Government, and was raised to the peerage as Baron Rosmead. He returned to South Africa later in the year, but was compelled by ill-health, in April 1897, to quit his post, and died in London on Oct. 28, 1897.

ROSMINI-SERBATI, ANTONIO (1797–1855), Italian

philosopher, was born at Rovereto, Italian Tirol, on March 25, 1797. In 1828 he founded a new religious order, the Institute of the Brethren of Charity, known in Italy generally as the Rosminians. The members might be priests or laymen, who devoted themselves to preaching, the education of youth, and works of charity—material, moral and intellectual. They have branches in Italy, England, Ireland, France and America. In London they are attached to the church of St. Etheldreda, Ely Place, Holborn. Rosmini's *The Five Wounds of the Holy Church* and *The Constitution of Social Justice* were placed (1849) upon the Index. Rosmini at once declared his submission and retired to Stresa on Lago Maggiore, where he died on July 1, 1855. Before his death he had the satisfaction of learning that the works in question were dismissed, that is, proclaimed free from censure by the Congregation of the Index. Twenty years later, the word "dismissed" (*dimittantur*) became the subject of controversy, some maintaining that it amounted to a direct approval, others that it was purely negative and did not imply that the books were free from error. The controversy continued till 1887, when Leo XIII. finally condemned 40 of his propositions and forbade their being taught.

The most comprehensive view of Rosmini's philosophical standpoint is to be found in his *Sistema filosofico,* in which he set forth the conception of a complete encyclopaedia of the human knowable, synthetically conjoined, according to the order of ideas, in a perfectly harmonious whole. Rosmini laid down ideal being as the fundamental principle of all philosophy and the supreme criterion of truth and certainty.

Of his numerous works—collected ed. (17 vols., Milan, 1842–44) supplemented by *Opere postume* (5 vols., Turin, 1859–74)—the most important are the *New Essay on the Origin of Ideas* (Eng. trans., 1883); *The Principles of Moral Science* (1831); *The Restoration of Philosophy in Italy* (1836); *The Philosophy of Right* (1841–45). The following have also been translated into English: *A Catholic Catechism,* by W. S. Agar (1849); *The Five Wounds of the Holy Church* (abridged trans. with introd. by H. P. Liddon. 1883); *Maxims of Christian Perfection,* by W. A. Johnson (1889); *Psychology* (Anonymous) (1884–88); *Sketch of Modern Philosophy,* by Lockhart (1882); *The Ruling Principle of Method Applied to Education,* by Mrs. W. Grey (Boston, Mass., 1887); *Select Letters,* by D. Gazzola. Rosmini's *Sistema filosofico* was translated by Thos. Davidson (*Rosmini's Philosophical System,* 1882, with a biographical sketch and complete bibliography); *see also Lives* by G. S. Macwalter (1883) and G. B. Pagani (1907); C. Werner, *Die italienische Philosophie des 19. Jahrhunderts* (1884); F. X. Kraus, "Antonio Rosmini: sein Leben, seine Schriften," in *Deutsche Rundschau,* liv. lv. (1888);

"Church Reformation in Italy" in the *Edinburgh Review,* cxiv. (July 1861); and numerous recent Italian works, for which Baldwin's *Dictionary of Philosophy* or Pagliani's *Catalogo Generale* (Milan, 1905) should be consulted.

ROSNY, JOSEPH HENRY, a pseudonym covering the

collaboration of the French novelists, Joseph Henri Honoré Boëx (1856–1940), and his brother Séraphin Justin François Boëx (1859–1948). The novels of J. H. Rosny are full of scientific knowledge, of astronomy, anthropology, zoology and, above all, sociology. The stories are approached from the point of view of society rather than of the individual, but the characters, strongly individualized and intensely real, are only incidentally typical. The elder Rosny was the sole author of the earlier novels, and began novel-writing as an avowed disciple of Zola. Among these earlier works may be mentioned *Le Bilatéral* (1886), and the "prehistoric" novel, *Vamireh* (1891), a masterpiece of its kind. MM. Rosny were among the writers who in 1887 entered a formal protest in the *Figaro* against Zola's *La Terre,* and they were designated by Edmond de Goncourt as original members of his academy. Among their other novels the more famous are: *Daniel Valgraive* (1891); *L'Indomptée* (1895), the history of a girl medical student in Paris; *Le Serment* (1896, dramatized 1897); *Les Ames perdues* (1899), an anarchist novel; *La Charpente* (1900); *Thérèse Degaudy* (1902); *Le Crime du docteur* (1903); *Le Docteur Harambur* (1904); *Le Millionaire* (1905); *Sous le fardeau* (1906); *La Guerre de feu* (1911) and *La Carapace* (1914).

ROSS, BETSY (1752–1836), heroine of one of the most

picturesque legends which has grown up around the origin of the American flag, was born in Philadelphia, Pa., on Jan. 1, 1752. She married John Ross, whose uncle, George Ross, was one of the signers of the Declaration of Independence.

The versions of the flag story as told by her descendants, agree in the following main points: Washington, accompanied by Robert Morris and Gen. George Ross, called at the little upholstery shop in Arch street, where she was carrying on the business in which she and her husband had been engaged, and asked if she could make a flag. She said she never had made one, but that she could try. They thereupon produced a design, rather roughly drawn. She examined it and, noticing that the stars were six-pointed, suggested that they should be made with five points. The gentlemen agreed with her that five points would look better, but that the six-pointed stars would be easier to make. She then showed them how a five-pointed star could be made with a single clip of the scissors. Washington then and there changed the sketch and the three gentlemen left. Soon after a new design was sent to her, coloured by William Barrett, a painter of some note. She thereupon set to work to make the famous flag, which was soon completed and approved.

This story was first presented by William J. Canby, grandson of Betsy Ross, in a paper read in 1870 before the Historical Society of Pennsylvania, and it was verified by other descendants of the family who remembered the story as frequently told to them. No contemporary documentary evidence has ever been found to support the story, nor has any, on the other hand, been found which gives the honour to anyone else. All that has been verified is that there was a Mrs. Ross living in Philadelphia at the time of the flag's adoption, and that she was an upholsterer and flagmaker by trade. She died at Philadelphia on Jan. 30, 1836.

Canby's claims are ably presented by L. Balderston in *The Evolution of the American Flag* (1909). *See also* P. D. Harrison, *The Stars and Stripes* (1914); G. H. Preble, *Origin and History of the American Flag* (new ed., 1917); S. Abbott, *Dramatic Story of Old Glory* (1919).

ROSS, SIR JAMES CLARK (1800–1862), British rear-

admiral and Polar explorer, was born in London on April 15, 1800. He entered the navy in 1812 accompanying his uncle, Captain (afterwards Sir) John Ross, on his first Arctic voyage in search of a North-West passage (1818). Between 1819 and 1827 he made four Arctic expeditions under Parry, and in 1829–33 again under his uncle, and determined (1831) the position of the North Magnetic Pole. In 1834 he was promoted captain, and in 1835–38 worked on the magnetic survey of Great Britain. In 1839–43 he commanded the Antarctic expedition of the "Erebus" and "Terror." (*See* ANTARCTIC REGIONS.) He wrote *A Voyage of Discovery and Research to Southern and Antarctic Regions* (1847). He was elected to the Royal Society in 1848, and was captain of the "Enterprise," in the first Franklin search expedition. He died at Aylesbury on April 3, 1862.

ROSS, JANET ANNE (1842–1927), English writer, daughter of Sir Alexander Cornewall Duff Gordon, was born in London on Feb. 24, 1842. She is the original of Rose Jocelyn in Meredith's *Evan Harrington*. She married in 1860 Henry Ross, a banker in Egypt and a great traveller, and her life in Egypt, where she spent six years, is described very vividly in her *Fourth Generation: Reminiscences* (1912). From 1863 to 1867 she was a correspondent of *The Times*. In 1867 she and her husband settled in Italy, where her house was a centre for the lovers of Italian culture. She died in Florence on Aug. 23, 1927. Her publications include: *Three Generations of English Women* (2 vols., 1888); *The Land of Manfred* (1889); *Old Florence and Modern Tuscany* (1904); *Lives of the Early Medici* (1910); *Letters of Principal J. M. Lindsay to Janet Ross* (1922).

ROSS, SIR JOHN (1777–1856), British rear-admiral and Arctic explorer, son of the Rev. Andrew Ross, entered the Royal Navy in 1786. In 1808 he captained the Swedish Fleet, and in 1812 was promoted commander. In 1818 he commanded an Arctic expedition fitted out by the Admiralty, but failed to discover much that was new; but in 1829–33 he made a second Arctic expedition, which achieved important geographical and scientific results. In 1850 he undertook a third voyage in search of Sir John Franklin, and in the following year he attained flag-rank.

His publications include—*Voyage of Discovery for the Purpose of Exploring Baffin's Bay* (1819); *Narrative of a Second Voyage in Search of a North-West Passage, including the Discovery of the North Magnetic Pole* (1835); *Memoirs and Correspondence of Lord De Saumerez* (1838).

ROSS, JOHN, or KOOESKOOWE (1790–1866), chief of the Cherokee Indian nation, was of Scottish-Indian descent, born among the Cherokees in Georgia in 1790. He was principal chief from 1828 until his death. In 1830–31 he applied to the Supreme Court of the U.S. for an injunction restraining the State of Georgia from executing its laws within the Cherokee territory, but the court dismissed his suit on the ground that it had no jurisdiction. A small party among the Cherokees under the leadership of John Ridge, a subchief, were disposed to treat with the U.S. for the removal of their nation west of the Mississippi, and in Feb. 1835, while Ridge was negotiating at Washington, Ross proposed to cede the Cherokee lands to the U.S. for $20,000,000. The U.S. Senate resolved that $5,000,000 was sufficient. Both the Ridge treaty and the $5,000,000 proposal were rejected in a full council of the Cherokees Oct. 1835. The council authorized Ross to renew negotiations, but before leaving for Washington he was arrested by the Georgia authorities on the ground that he was a white man residing in the Indian country contrary to law. He was soon released, but in December of this year a few hundred Cherokees concluded a treaty of removal with the U.S. Indian commissioner at New Echota. When Ross learned this he called a council in Feb. 1836, and at this meeting the treaty was declared null and void and a protest against the proceedings at New Echota was signed by more than 12,000 Cherokees. Notwithstanding Ross's opposition, the Senate in the following May ratified the treaty and in Dec. 1838, Ross, with the last party of Cherokees, left for the West (*see* GEORGIA). During the Civil War, Ross signed a treaty with the Confederate States in Oct. 1861, but in the summer of 1862 was forced (by Union sympathizers in the nation) to proclaim neutrality and soon afterwards went over to the Union lines. He was in Washington treating with the Federal Government in Feb. 1863 when the treaty with the Confederate States was abrogated by the Cherokees. He died at Washington on Aug. 1, 1866.

See C. C. Royce, "The Cherokee Nation of Indians" in the *Fifth Annual Report of the Bureau of Ethnology* (1887), and T. V. Parker, *The Cherokee Indians* (New York, 1907).

ROSS, SIR RONALD (1857–1932), British physician and bacteriologist, was born at Almora, India, on May 13, 1857. He studied medicine at St. Bartholomew's hospital, London, and in 1881 entered the Indian medical service. In 1892 he commenced a series of special investigations on the subject of malaria, in 1895 undertook the experimental verification of the theory that the micro-organisms of this disease are spread by mosquitoes, and in 1897–98 investigated the life history of the parasites. In 1899 he retired from the Indian medical service, and, after a journey to west Africa in 1899 for the study of malaria-bearing mosquitoes, devoted himself to research and teaching, joining the Liverpool school of tropical medicine as lecturer and subsequently becoming professor of tropical medicine at Liverpool university. In 1913 he became physician for tropical disease at King's college, London, and later, director-in-chief of the Ross Institute and Hospital for Tropical Diseases. During World War I, Ross was appointed to the R.A.M.C. and became War Office consultant in malaria. After the War he was consultant in malaria for the Ministry of Pensions. In 1902 he received the Nobel Prize for medicine, in 1911 a K.C.B. and in 1918 a K.C.M.G. He received the Royal Medal of the Royal Society, of which he was a fellow, in 1901. He was editor of *Science Progress*, and his other publications include *The Prevention of Malaria* (1910), *Philosophies* (1910), *Psychologies* (1919), *The Revels of Orsera*, a romance (1920), and *Memoirs* (1923), as well as mathematical and medical works. (*See* MALARIA.) Ross died Sept. 16, 1932.

ROSS (ROSS-ON-WYE), a market town and urban district in Herefordshire, England; 133 mi. W. from London and 12 mi. S.E. from Hereford by the G.W.R. Pop. (1938) 4,607. Area, 1.6 sq.mi. There are manufactures of machinery and agricultural implements, and cider and malt are produced. The church of St. Mary the Virgin, surmounted by a lofty spire, shows good Decorated and Perpendicular work. The market house (1670) is a picturesque building supported on columns, the upper portion serving as a town hall. The town owes much to John Kyrle (d. 1724), eulogized by Pope (*Moral Epistle*, 1732). Wilton castle, near the town, was burned by the Royalists during the Civil War. The inhabited portion is modern. Ross was granted to the see of Hereford by Edmund Ironside, but became crown property in 1559.

ROSS AND CROMARTY, northern county, Scotland. The mainland portion is bounded north by Sutherland and Dornoch firth, east by the North sea and Moray firth, south by Beauly firth and Inverness-shire and west by the strait of the Minch. The island portion (for details *see* HEBRIDES) consists of the northern part of Lewis-with-Harris, and many smaller islands, all but eleven uninhabited, are scattered principally off the west coasts of Lewis and the mainland. The land area of the mainland is 1,572,294 ac., of the islands 404,413 ac., a total of 1,977,248 ac. or 3,089.5 sq.mi. The inhabited islands belonging to the mainland are all situated off the west coast. They are Bernera, Gillean (lighthouse), Horrisdale, Dry, Ewe, Martin and Flannen (lighthouse). On the North sea front the chief indentations are Beauly firth and Inner Moray firth, marking off the Black Isle from Inverness-shire; Cromarty firth, bounding the districts of Easter Ross and the Black Isle; Moray firth, separating Easter Ross from Nairnshire; and Dornoch firth, dividing northeast Ross from Sutherlandshire. On the Atlantic face, the principal sea lochs and bays, from S. to N., are Loch Duich, Loch Alsh, Loch Carron, Loch Kishorn, Loch Torridon, Loch Shieldaig, Upper Loch Torridon, Gairloch, Loch Ewe, Gruinard bay, Little Loch Broom and Enard bay. Almost all the southern boundary with Inverness-shire is guarded by a rampart of peaks, ranging from 3,400 to nearly 3,900 ft. To the north of Glen Torridon rise the masses of the Liatach, with summits of 3,456 and 3,358 ft. On the northeastern shore of Loch Maree rises Ben Slioch (3,217), while the Fannich group contains at least six peaks of more than 3,000 ft. The isolated mass of Ben Wyvis (3,429) is the most noteworthy feature in the northeast, and the Challich hills in the northwest with peaks of 3,483 and 3,474 ft. are equally conspicuous, though less solitary. Only a small fraction of western and southern Ross is under 1,000 ft. in height. Easter Ross and the peninsula of the Black Isle are comparatively level. The longest stream is the Orrin, which rises in An Sithean and flows mainly east by north to its confluence with the Conon after a run of about 26 mi. during a small part of which it forms the boundary with Inverness-shire. At Aultgowrie the stream forms the falls of Orrin in a narrow gorge. From its source in the mountains in Strathvaich the Blackwater flows southeast for 19 mi. until it joins the Conon, forming soon after it leaves Loch Garve the picturesque falls of Rogie. Within a short distance of its exit from Loch Luichart the Conon pours over a series of graceful cascades and rapids and then pursues a winding course of 12 mi., mainly E. to the head of Cromarty firth. The falls of Glomach, in the southwest, are the deepest in Britain (370 ft. sheer). Twelve miles south by east of Ullapool are the three falls of Measach, close to the gorge of Corriehalloch. The Oykell, throughout its course, forms the boundary with Sutherlandshire, to which it properly belongs. The largest and most beautiful of the many fresh-water lakes is Loch Maree (*q.v.*). Of the straths or valleys the more important run from the centre eastward, such as Strathconon (12 mi.), Strathbran (10 mi.), Strathgarve (8 mi.), Strathpeffer (6 mi.) and Strathcarron (14 mi.). Excepting Glen Orrin (13 mi.), in the east central district, the longer glens lie in the south and toward the west. In the extreme south Glen Shiel (9 mi.) runs between fine mountains to its mouth on Loch Duich. General Wade's road passes down the glen. Farther north are Glen Elchaig (9 mi.), Glen Carron (12 mi.), in the latter of which the track of the Dingwall and Skye railway is laid, and Glen Torridon (6 mi.).

Geology.—The central portion of the county is occupied by the younger highland schists or Dalradian series. On the eastern side of the county the Dalradian schists are covered unconformably by the Old Red Sandstone. The western boundary of the younger schist is formed by the great pre-Cambrian dislocation line which traverses the county from Elphin on the north by Ullapool to Glen Carron. Most of the area west of the line of disturbance is covered by Torridonian Sandstone, mainly dark reddish sandstones, grits and shales, resting unconformably on the ancient Lewisian gneiss. Within the Torridonian tract the gneiss occupies large areas north of Coigach, on the east of Enard bay, between Gruinard bay and Loch Maree. The Lewisian gneiss is everywhere penetrated by basic dikes, generally with a N.W.-S.E. direction; some of these are of great breadth. The Torridonian rocks are succeeded unconformably by a series of Cambrian strata which is confined to a narrow belt west of the line of main thrusting. Glacial striae are found upon the mountains up to heights of 3,000 ft., and much boulder clay is found in the valleys and spread over large areas in the eastern districts. Raised beaches occur at 100, 50 and 25 ft. above the present sea level; they are well seen in Loch Carron. (*See*, further, HEBRIDES.)

Agriculture and Industries.—The most fertile tracts lie on the eastern coast, especially in Easter Ross and the Black Isle, where the soil varies from a light sandy gravel to a rich deep loam. Among grain crops, oats is that most generally cultivated, and occupied 28,946 ac. in 1938, but barley and wheat are also raised, though together they occupied only 6,214 ac. Turnips and swedes, and potatoes are the chief green crops, the former, at 11,334 ac., having more than twice the acreage of the latter. On the higher grounds there is a large extent of good pasturage which carries heavy flocks of sheep (355,979 animals in 1938), Blackfaced being the principal breed. Most of the horses are maintained for the purposes of agriculture. The herds of cattle, mainly native Highland or crosses, are large. Owing partly to the unkindly nature of the bulk of the surface—which offers no opportunity for other than patchwork tillage—the number of small holdings is enormous, 56% of the 7,295 in 1938 being of 5 ac. and less, and the average size 18½ ac. More than 800,000 ac. is devoted to deer forests, a greater area than in any other county in Scotland. The natural woodland has largely disappeared, but afforestation has been undertaken. Apart from agriculture, the salmon fisheries in the bays and river mouths, and the herring, cod and ling fisheries are the only considerable industry. There are distilleries near Dingwall, Tain and Invergordon.

The L.M.S. railway entering the county to the north of Beauly runs northward to Dingwall, and then strikes off to the northeast by Invergordon and Tain, where it bends to the west by north, leaving the shire at Culrain, having largely followed the coast throughout. At Muir of Ord it sends off the Black Isle branch and at Dingwall a branch to Strathpeffer, as well as a line to Strome Ferry and Kyle of Loch Alsh on the southwestern shore.

Population and Administration.—Pop. (est. 1938) 62,846. In 1931 there were 37,534 on the mainland and 25,265 on the islands. Ross and Cromarty, though the third largest in size, is the fourteenth county in population. In 1931 there were 3,333 who spoke Gaelic only and 31,058 speaking Gaelic and English. Of the six small burghs, the chief are Stornoway (est. 1938 pop., 4,557), Dingwall (2,828), Invergordon (1,490) and Tain (1,421). Ullapool is a fishing port near the mouth of Loch Broom. There are 12 county districts and the county returns one of the Inverness members to parliament. Dingwall, Tain and Fortrose are royal burghs, and Dingwall is the county town. Ross and Cromarty form a sheriffdom, and there are resident sheriffs-substitute at Dingwall and Stornoway, the former also sitting at Tain and Cromarty.

The shire is under school board control and there are academies at Dingwall and Fortrose.

History and Antiquities.—It may be doubted whether the Romans ever effected even a temporary settlement in the area of the modern county. At that period, and for long afterward, the land was occupied by Gaelic Picts, who, in the 6th and 7th centuries, were converted to Christianity by followers of St. Columba. Throughout the next three centuries the natives were continually harassed by Norse pirates, of whose presence tokens have survived in several place names (Dingwall, Tain, etc.). At this time the county formed part of the great province of Moray. When the rule of the Celtic *mormaors* or earls ceased in the 12th century, consequent on the plantation of the district with settlers from other parts (including a body of Flemings), by order of David I, who was anxious to break the power of the Celts, the bounds of Moravia were contracted and the earldom of Ross arose. At first Ross proper only included the territory adjoining Moray and Dornoch firths. The first earl was Malcolm MacHeth, who received the title from Malcolm IV. After his rebellion in 1179 chronic insurrection ensued, which was quelled by Alexander II, who bestowed the earldom on Farquhar Macintaggart, then abbot of Applecross, and in that capacity lord of the western district. William, 4th earl, was present with his clan at the battle of Bannockburn (1314), and almost a century later (1412) the castle of Dingwall, the chief seat on the mainland of Donald, lord of the Isles, was captured after the disastrous fight at Harlaw in Aberdeenshire, which Donald had provoked when his claim to the earldom was rejected. The earldom reverted to the crown in 1424, but James I soon afterward restored it to the heiress of the line, the mother of Alexander MacDonald, 3rd lord of the Isles, who thus became 11th earl. In consequence, however, of the treason of John MacDonald, 4th and last lord of the Isles and 12th earl of Ross, the earldom was again vested in the crown (1476). Five years later James III bestowed it on his second son, James Stewart, whom he also created duke of Ross in 1488. By the 16th century the whole area of the county was occupied by different clans, the Rosses, Munroes, Macleods, Macdonalds and Mackenzies. The county of Ross was constituted in 1661, and Cromarty in 1685 and 1698, both being consolidated into the present county in 1889. (*See* CROMARTY.) Apart from occasional conflicts between rival clans, the only battles in the shire were those of Invercarron (1650), when Montrose was crushed by Colonel Strachan, and Glenshiel (1719), when the Jacobites, under the earl of Seaforth, aided by Spaniards, were defeated, near Bridge of Shiel, by General Wightman.

Stone circles, cairns and forts are found in the eastern district. A vitrified fort crowns the hill of Knockfarrel in the parish of Fodderty, and there is a circular dun near the village of Lochcarron. Some fine examples of sculptured stones occur, the finest being at Shandwick. Among old castles are those of Lochslin, in the parish of Fearn, said to date from the 13th century, which, though ruinous, possesses two square towers in good preservation; Balone, in the parish of Tarbat, once a stronghold of the earls of Ross; the remains of Dingwall castle, their original seat; and Eilean Donain in Loch Alsh, which was blown up by English warships during the abortive Jacobite rising in 1719.

ROSSANO, a city of Calabria, Italy, in the province of Cosenza, 24 mi. N.N.E. from that town direct, with a station 4 mi. distant on the line from Metaponto to Reggio. Pop. (1936) 8,763 (town), 15,393 (commune). It is on a spur of Sila mountain, overlooking the Gulf of Taranto, the highest part of the town being 975 ft. above sea-level. Rossano is the seat of an archbishop, and in the cathedral is preserved the *Codex Rossanensis,* an uncial ms. of the Gospels of Matthew and Mark in silver characters on purple vellum, with twelve miniatures, of great interest in the history of Byzantine art, belonging to the 6th century A.D.

Rossano (*Roscianum*) was one of the important fortresses of Calabria. Totila took it in 548. In the 14th century Rossano was made a principality for the great family of De Baux. Passing to the Sforza, and thus to Sigismund of Poland, it was united in 1558 to the crown of Naples by Philip II. of Spain. During World War II it was bombed by the Allies.

ROSSBACH, a village in the *Land* of Saxony, Germany, in the district of Merseburg, 8 mi. S.W. of that place and N.W. of Weissenfels, famous as the scene of Frederick the Great's victory over the allied French and the army of the Empire on Nov. 5, 1757. For the preceding events *see* SEVEN YEARS' WAR. The Prussian camp on the morning of the 5th lay between Rossbach (left) and Bedra (right), facing the Allies, who, commanded by the French general, Charles de Rohan, prince de Soubise, and Joseph Frederick William, duke of Saxe-Hildburghausen, General Feldzeugmeister of the Empire, had manoeuvred in the preceding days without giving Frederick an opportunity to bring them to action, and now lay to the westward, with their right near Branderoda and their left at Mücheln (*see* sketch). The advanced posts of the Prussians were in the villages immediately west of their camp, those of the Allies on the Schortau hill and the Galgenberg.

The Allies possessed a numerical superiority of two to one in the battle itself, irrespective of detachments,[1] and their advanced post overlooked all parts of Frederick's camp. They had had the best of it in the manoeuvres of the previous days, and Hildburghausen determined to take the offensive. He had some difficulty, however, in inducing Soubise to risk a battle, and the Allies did not begin to move off their camping-ground until after eleven on the 5th, Soubise's intention being probably to engage as late in the day as possible, with the idea of gaining what advantages he could in a partial action. The plan was to march the Allied army by Zeuchfeld, round Frederick's left (which was covered by no serious natural obstacle), and to deploy in battle array, facing north, between Reichardtswerben (right) and Pettstädt (left). The duke's proposed battle and the more limited aim of Soubise were equally likely to be attained by taking this position, which threatened to cut off Frederick from the towns on the Saale. This position, equally, could only be gained by marching round the Prussian flank, *i.e.,* by a flank march before the enemy. The obvious risk of interference on the exposed flank was provided against by a considerable flank guard, and in fact it was not in the execution of their original design but in hastily modifying it to suit unfounded assumptions that the Allies met with disaster.

Frederick spent the morning watching them from a house-top in Rossbach. The initial stages of their movement convinced him that the Allies were retreating southward towards their magazines, and about noon he went to dinner, leaving Captain von Gaudi on the watch. This officer formed a different impression of the Allies' intentions, for the columns which from time to time became visible in the undulations of the ground were seen to turn eastwards from Zeuchfeld. Gaudi's excited report at first served only to confirm Frederick in his error. But when the king saw for himself that hostile cavalry and infantry were already near Pettstädt, he realized the enemy's intentions. The battle for which he had manoeuvred in vain was offered to him, and he took it without

[1] V. der Goltz (*Rossbach bis Jena,* 1906 edition) gives 41,000 Allies and 21,600 Prussians as the combatant strengths. Berndt's statistical work, *Zahl im Kriege,* gives the respective forces engaged as Allies 43,000, Prussians 21,000. Other accounts give the Allies' total strength as 64,000 and the Prussians' as 24,000.

hesitation. Leaving a handful of light troops to oppose the French advanced post (or flank guard) on the Schortau hill, the Prussian army broke camp and moved—half an hour after the king gave the order—to attack the enemy. The latter were marching in the normal order in two main columns, the first line on the left, the second line on the right; farther to the right was a column consisting of the reserve of foot, and between the first and second lines

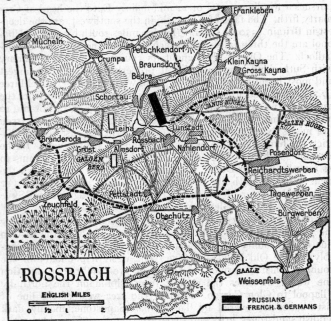

PLAN OF THE BATTLE OF ROSSBACH, NOV. 5, 1757

was the reserve artillery on the road. The right-wing cavalry was of course at the head, the left-wing cavalry at the tail of the two main columns. At first the regulation distances were preserved, but when wheeling eastward at Zeuchfeld there was much confusion, part of the reserve infantry getting in between the two main columns and hampering the movements of the reserve artillery, and the rest, on the outer flank of the wheel, being unable to keep up with the over-rapid movement of the wheeling pivot. A weak flank guard was thrown out towards Rossbach. When it was seen that the Prussians were moving, as far as could be judged, eastward, it was presumed that they were about to retreat in order to avoid being taken in flank and rear; and the Allied generals thereupon hurried the march, sending the cavalry on ahead.

Frederick had no intention either of forming up parallel to the enemy or of retreating. As his army could move as a unit twice as fast as the enemy's, he intended to make a détour, screened by the Janus Hügel and the Pölzen Hügel, and to fall upon them suddenly from the east. If at the moment of contact the Allies had already formed their line of battle facing north, the attack would strike their right flank; if they were still on the move in column eastwards or north-eastwards, the heads of their columns would be crushed before the rest could deploy in the new direction—deployment in those days being a lengthy affair. To this end General von Seydlitz, with every available squadron, hurried eastward from Rossbach, behind the Janus Hügel, to the Pölzen Hügel; Colonel von Moller, with eighteen heavy guns, came into action on the Janus Hügel at 3.15 against the advancing columns of the Allied cavalry; and the infantry followed as fast as possible. When they came under the fire of Moller's guns, the Allied squadrons, which were now north of Reichardtswerben and well ahead of their own infantry, suffered somewhat heavily; but it was usual to employ heavy guns to protect a retreat, and they contented themselves with bringing some field-guns into action. They were, however, amazed when Seydlitz's thirty-eight squadrons suddenly rode down upon the head and right flank of their columns from the Pölzen Hügel *"avec une incroyable vitesse."* Gallantly as the leading German regiments deployed to meet him, the result was scarcely in doubt for a moment. Seydlitz threw in his last squadron, and then himself fought like a trooper, receiving a severe wound. The mêlée drifted rapidly southward, past the Allied infantry, and Seydlitz finally rallied his horsemen in a hollow near Tagewerben, ready for fresh service. This first episode was over in half an hour, and by that time the Prussian infantry, in échelon from the left, was descending the Janus Hügel to meet the already confused and disheartened infantry of the Allies. The latter, as their cavalry had done, managed to deploy some regiments on the head of the column, and the French in particular formed one or two columns of attack—then peculiar to the French army—and rushed forward with the bayonet. But Moller's guns, which had advanced with the infantry, tore gaps in the close masses, and, when it arrived within effective musketry range, the attack died out before the rapid and methodical volleys of the Prussian line. Meanwhile the Allies were trying in vain to form a line of battle. The two main columns had got too close together in the advance from Pettstädt, part of the reserve which had become entangled between the main columns was extricating itself by degrees and endeavouring to catch up with the rest of the reserve column away to the right, and the reserve artillery was useless in the middle of the infantry. The Prussian infantry was still in échelon from the left, and the leftmost battalions that had repulsed the French columns were quickly within musket-shot of this helpless mass. A few volleys directed against the head and left flank of the column sufficed to create disorder, and then from the Tagewerben hollow Seydlitz's rallied squadrons charged, wholly unexpectedly, upon its right flank. The Allied infantry thereupon broke and fled. Soubise and the duke, who was wounded, succeeded in keeping one or two regiments together, but the rest scattered over the countryside. The battle had lasted less than an hour and a half, and the last episode of the infantry fight no more than fifteen minutes. Seven Prussian battalions only were engaged, and these expended five to fifteen rounds per man. Seydlitz and Prince Henry of Prussia, the cavalry and the infantry leaders engaged, were both wounded, but the total loss of the king's army was under 550 officers and men as compared with 7,700 on the part of the Allies. (C. F. A.)

ROSSE, WILLIAM PARSONS, 3RD EARL OF (1800–1867), Irish astronomer and telescope constructor, was born at York on June 17, 1800, a son of the 2nd earl, Lawrence. Until his father's death he was known as Lord Oxmantown. Entered at Trinity college, Dublin, in 1818, he proceeded to Magdalen college, Oxford, in 1821, and in the same year he was returned as M.P. for King's County, a seat which he resigned in 1834. He was Irish representative peer from 1845, president of the British Association in 1843, president of the Royal Society from 1849 to 1854, being awarded the Royal Medal in 1851, and chancellor of the University of Dublin from 1862. He died at Monkstown on Oct. 31, 1867.

The first constructor of reflecting telescopes on a large scale, William Herschel, never published anything about his methods of casting and polishing specula, and Lord Rosse had no help towards his brilliant results. His speculum metal is composed of four atoms of copper (126·4 parts) and one of tin (58·9 parts), a brilliant alloy. Chiefly owing to the brittleness of this material, Lord Rosse's first larger specula were composed of a number of thin plates of speculum metal (16 for a 3-foot mirror) soldered on the back of a strong but light framework made of a brass (2·75 of copper to 1 of zinc), which has the same expansion as his speculum metal. In Brewster's *Edinburgh Journal of Science* for 1828 he described his machine for polishing the speculum, which in all essential points remained unaltered afterwards. In Sept. 1839 a 3-foot speculum was finished and mounted, but, though the definition of the images was good, its skeleton form allowed the speculum to follow atmospheric changes of temperature very quickly, so Lord Rosse decided to cast a solid 3-foot speculum. Hitherto a great difficulty in casting specula was the fact that they generally cracked while cooling. Rosse experimented, ingeniously overcame this difficulty, and successfully cast a solid 3-foot speculum in 1840. In 1842 he began a speculum of 6 ft. diameter, and in 1845 this great reflector was mounted and ready for work.

From 1848 to 1878 it was but with few interruptions employed for observations of nebulae (*see* NEBULA); and many previously unknown features in these objects were revealed by it, especially the similarity of "annular" and "planetary" nebulae, and the remarkable "spiral" configuration in many of the nebulae. A special study was made of the nebula of Orion, and the resulting large drawing gives an extremely good representation of this complicated object. (*See* TELESCOPE.)

See Ball, *Great Astronomers* (London, 1895).

ROSSELLINO, ANTONIO (1427–c. 1479), Florentine sculptor, was the son of Mateo Gamberelli, and had four brothers. The Gamberelli were a family of stonecutters of Settignano. Antonio's works are full of religious sentiment, and executed with the utmost delicacy of touch and technical skill. The style of Antonio and his brother Bernardo is a development of that of Donatello and Ghiberti; it possesses all the refinement and sweetness of the earlier masters, but is not equal to them in vigour or originality. Antonio's chief work, still in perfect preservation, is the lovely tomb of a young cardinal prince of Portugal, who died in 1459. It occupies one side of a small chapel, also built by Rossellino, on the north of the nave of San Miniato al Monte. The recumbent effigy of the cardinal rests on a handsome sarcophagus, and over it, under the arch which frames the whole, is a beautiful relief of the Madonna between two flying angels. The tomb was begun in 1461 and finished in 1466.

ROSSELLINO, BERNARDO (1409–1464), sculptor, the eldest brother of Antonio. In Sept. 1439 he acquired a house in the Via Proconsolo, Florence, and opened a botega with his four brothers. His finest piece of sculpture is the tomb, in the Florentine Santa Croce, of Leonardo Bruni of Arezzo, the historian of Florence, executed in 1443. In the church of S. Stefano at Empoli is an annunciation dated 1447. The tomb of Beata Villana at S. Maria Novella, Florence, was ordered in 1451. Bernardo's works as an architect were numerous and important. He was probably associated with Alberti in the construction of the Rucellai palace, Florence, and in extensive restorations and reconstructions of churches under Nicholas V. in Rome. Between the years 1461 and 1464 (when he died while engaged on the Lazzari monument at Pistoia) he occupied the important post of *capo-maestro* to the Florentine duomo.

See Wilhelm Bode, *Die Italienische Plastik* (1902).

ROSSETTI, CHRISTINA GEORGINA (1830–1894), English poet, was the youngest of the four children of Gabriele Rossetti. (*See* article on her brother DANTE GABRIEL ROSSETTI.) She was born at 38 Charlotte Street, Portland Place, London, on Dec. 5, 1830. She enjoyed the advantages and disadvantages of the strange society of Italian exiles and English eccentrics which her father gathered about him, and she shared the studies of her gifted elder brother and sister. As early as 1847 her grandfather, Gaetano Polidori, printed privately a volume of her *Verses,* in which the richness of her vision was already faintly prefigured. In 1850 she contributed to *The Germ* seven pieces, including some of the finest of her lyrics. In her girlhood she had a grave, religious beauty of feature, and sat as a model not only to her brother Gabriel, but to Holman Hunt, to Madox Brown and to Millais. In 1853–54 Christina Rossetti for nearly a year helped her mother to keep a day-school at Frome-Selwood, in Somerset. Early in 1854 the Rossettis returned to London, and the father died.

In poverty, in ill-health, in extreme quietness, she was now performing her life-work. She was twice sought in marriage, but each time, from religious scruples (she was a strong high-church Anglican), she refused her suitor; on the former of these occasions she sorrowed greatly, and her suffering is reflected in much of her early song. In 1861 she saw foreign countries for the first time, paying a six weeks' visit to Normandy and Paris. In 1862 she published what was practically her earliest book, *Goblin Market,* and took her place at once among the poets of her age. In this volume, indeed, is still to be found a majority of her finest writings. *The Prince's Progress* followed in 1866. In 1867 she, with her family, moved to 56 Euston Square, which became their home for many years. Christina's prose work *Commonplace* appeared in 1870. In April 1871 her whole life was changed by a terrible affliction, known as "Graves's disease"; for two years her life was in constant danger. She had already composed her book of children's poems, entitled *Sing-Song,* which appeared in 1872.

After a long convalescence, she published in 1874 two works of minor importance, *Annus Domini* and *Speaking Likenesses.* The former is the earliest of a series of theological works in prose, of which the second was *Seek and Find* in 1879. In 1881 she published a third collection of poems, *A Pageant,* in which there was evidence of slackening lyrical power. She now gave herself almost entirely to religious disquisition. The most interesting and personal of her prose publications (but it contained verse also) was *Time Flies* (1885)—a sort of symbolic diary or collection of brief homilies. In 1890 the S.P.C.K. published a volume of her religious verse. She collected her poetical writings in 1891. In 1892 she was led to publish a very bulky commentary on the Apocalypse, entitled *The Face of the Deep.* After this she wrote little. Her last years were spent in retirement at 30 Torrington Square, Bloomsbury, which was her home from 1876 to her death. In 1892 her health broke down finally, and she had to endure terrible suffering. From this she was released on Dec. 29, 1894. Her *New Poems* were published posthumously in 1896.

In spite of her manifest limitations of sympathy and experience, Christina Rossetti takes rank among the foremost poets of her time. In the purity and solidity of her finest lyrics, the glow and music in which she robes her moods of melancholy reverie, her extraordinary mixture of austerity with sweetness and of sanctity of tone with sensuousness of colour, Christina Rossetti, in her best pieces, may challenge comparison with the most admirable of our poets. The union of fixed religious faith with a hold upon physical beauty and the richer parts of nature has been pointed to as the most original feature of her poetry. Hers was a cloistered spirit, timid, nun-like, bowed down by suffering and humility; her character was so retiring as to be almost invisible. All that we really need to know about her, save that she was a great saint, was that she was a great poet.   (E. G.)

See the *Poetical Works* of C.G.R., with Memoir by W. M. Rossetti (1903); Edmund Gosse, *Critical Kit-Kats* (1896); an article by Ford Madox Hueffer in the *Fortnightly Review* (March, 1904); and another in *The Christian Society* (Oct. 1904). The *Family Letters of Christina Rossetti* were edited by W. M. Rossetti in 1908; *Selected Poems of Christina G. Rossetti,* edited by C. B. Burke (1913); T. Watts-Dunton, *Old Familiar Faces* (1916); Marjorie A. Bald, *Women Writers of the Nineteenth Century* (1923).

ROSSETTI, DANTE GABRIEL (1828–1882), English poet and painter, was born on May 12, 1828, at 38 Charlotte Street, London. He was the second of the four children of Gabriele Rossetti (1783–1854), Italian poet and liberal, a political refugee from Naples, who came to England about 1824, and married in 1826 Frances Mary (d. 1886), sister of Byron's physician, Dr. John Polidori. The elder Rossetti became professor of Italian at King's College, London, and was a subtle and original, if eccentric, commentator on Dante. His other children were Maria Francesca (1827–76), who eventually entered an Anglican sisterhood, and is known to scholars by her valuable *Shadow of Dante;* William Michael (*q.v.*); and Christina (*q.v.*) the poet.

Dante Gabriel Rossetti was educated at King's College School, London. On leaving school he went (1843) to Cary's Art academy (known as Sass's), near Bedford Square, and then (about 1846) to the Royal Academy Antique school. He did not find the instruction he desired in the Royal Academy schools, and asked Ford Madox Brown to take him as a pupil. Brown remained his friend even after Rossetti had transferred his admiration to Holman Hunt.

Pre-Raphaelite Brotherhood.—The point of Pre-Raphaelite crystallization which had so great though brief an influence upon Rossetti's life and art was found at a chance meeting, in 1848, between Rossetti, Millais and Holman Hunt in Millais's house in Gower Street, where certain prints from early Italian frescoes were studied. Rossetti proposed the formation of a "Brotherhood" with lofty aims, and they were joined by J. Collinson, F. G. Stephens, T. Woolner and W. M. Rossetti. Brown, though invited, declined to become a P.-R.B. Rossetti's first effort was "The Girl-hood of Mary, Virgin," which in March 1849 was exhibited at the "Free Exhibition," at Hyde Park Corner. The style of this famous picture was jejune, its handling was timid, while its coloration and tonality were dry, not to say thin. Its technique owed something to Brown, but its mysticism was Rossetti's own. Such was his advent in art under the Pre-Raphaelite banner. "Ecce Ancilla Domini!" the smaller picture which is now in the Tate Gallery, London, was his one perfect expression of the original motive of the "Brotherhood." He chose virginal white and its harmonies as its aptest coloration, and the intense light of morning sufficed for its tonality. There is real grace and sweetness in the figure of the Virgin, for which his sister Christina was the model. This picture was exhibited at the Portland Gallery in 1850 and was violently attacked by the critics at the time.

In December 1850 appeared the first of the four numbers of *The Germ,* the organ of the "Brotherhood," in which Rossetti had a leading place in verse and prose. He contributed to it some of his most famous poems—*The Blessed Damozel,* six sonnets and four lyrics.

The attack on the Pre-Raphaelites by the critics prejudiced their sales, and Rossetti turned to water-colours. His first considerable effort in this medium, which proved well-suited to his talent, was the illustration to Browning's poem "The Laboratory," depicting a lady's visit to an old poison-monger to obtain a fatal potion for her rival in love. This wonderful gem of colour marked the opening of the artist's second period, and his departure from that phase of Pre-Raphaelitism of which "Ecce Ancilla Domini!" was the crowning achievement. Other water-colours followed including the original (pen and ink) of "Hesterna Rosa," a gambling scene (1852), and "Dante drawing the Angel" (1852). "Found" was begun in 1853; but this piece of pictorial moralizing (the analogue of the poet's *Jenny*), vigorous and intensely pathetic as it is, was never really finished.

Marriage to Elizabeth Siddal.—Rossetti had now become acquainted with the beautiful Elizabeth Siddal, whose sumptuous and individual type moved Hunt, Millais and Rossetti to paint her. Rossetti painted her innumerable times, and they became engaged to be married about 1851. The friends called her "Lizzy" and "Guggums," though the names ill suited her tragic temperament and ominous beauty. By 1854 the Brotherhood, championed by John Ruskin, was respectable, but at the moment of success the group was broken up. Ruskin became Rossetti's patron and friend; it was rather a onesided friendship, for Rossetti was not prepared to accept Ruskin's pretensions. In May 1860 Rossetti and Elizabeth Siddal were married, but the two years of their marriage were painful years, for she was dying of tuberculosis. She gave birth to a still-born child, and on Feb. 11, 1862, she died of an overdose of laudanum, which she took from time to time to allay her sufferings. In the meantime Rossetti had met William Morris and Burne-Jones, both of them his enthusiastic disciples. To these new friendships are due Rossetti's part in the luckless decorations of the Oxford Union (1857–8). To the exhibition of the Pre-Raphaelites in 1857 he sent many works, including the "Wedding of St. George and Princess Sabra" and "Arthur's Tomb" (both in the Tate Gallery, London). "Bocca Baciata," the portrait (in oils) of a woman, a work of wonderful fire, and the pictures on the pulpit at Llandaff Cathedral, marked the close of the second epoch in Rossetti's art and the beginning of the third, last and most powerful of all the phases of his career. The picture "Dr. Johnson at the Mitre" (Tate Gallery), when the "pretty fools" consulted the lexicographer on Methodism, is a good example of his humour. In 1861 Rossetti published the exquisite translations in *The Early Italian Poets,* later revised as *Dante and his Circle* (1874).

Achievements in Painting.—With Morris he began to take a keen interest in decorative art. He produced several fine designs for stained glass, and had a large share in the revival of stained-glass painting as an art. The practice of designing on a large scale, and employing masses of splendid deep-toned colours, was probably largely responsible for the development of his powers in painting at this period (1862–63). He produced at this time a striking and highly imaginative triptych (Tate Gallery), representing three events in the careers of Paolo and Francesca. The composition of the group of figures with the circular window behind them, is as fine as it was comparatively novel in Rossetti's practice. Other outstanding works are "Beata Beatrix" (Elizabeth Siddal as the blessed Beatrice contemplating the eternal) (1865), now in the Tate Gallery; "Proserpina in Hades" (1874), perhaps the most original, if not the most poetical and powerful of all his output; "Sibylla Palmifera" (1870); "Venus Verticordia," "Lilith," the better of the two versions is now referred to (1873); "Monna Vanna," in the Tate Gallery (1866); "Aurea Catena" (Janey Morris) (c. 1869); "La Ghirlandata" (1878); "Pandora," another study of Mrs. Morris (1871); "The Blessed Damozel" (1877); and the famous "Dante's Dream," now in the Walker Art Gallery at Liverpool. Nearly all Rossetti's last work was exhibited by the Royal Academy and at the Burlington Fine Art Club in 1883, after his death.

Development As a Poet.—The literary side of Rossetti developed *pari passu* with his achievements as a painter. After his wife's death he moved from Blackfriars to 16, Cheyne Walk, (The Queen's House), Chelsea, where for a short time A. C. Swinburne, W. M. Rossetti and Theodore Watts-Dunton lived with him. Rossetti had felt his wife's death—and perhaps his own remorse for having so frequently betrayed her—so acutely that in the first paroxysm of his grief he insisted upon his poems (then in manuscript) being buried in her coffin. But in 1869 they were disinterred and published in 1870. The volume contained the poems printed in *The Germ*, the sonnet-sequence *The House of Life*, very much enlarged at a later date. From this time to his death he continued to write poems and produce pictures—in the latter relying more and more upon his manipulative skill and less and less upon his inventive faculty. He depended also to some extent on the assistance of an artist whose name was Treffry Dunn.

In 1871 Robert Buchanan, in an unsigned article in the *Contemporary Review* on "The Fleshly School of Poetry," made a fierce attack on Rossetti's poems from a moral point of view, to which he answered by one on the "Stealthy School of Criticism." The attack was deeply felt by him, and his tendency towards gloomy brooding was further increased about 1868, by persistent insomnia. The result of this malady was a nervous shrinking from personal contact with any save a few intimate friends, which was aggravated by the use of narcotics, and at one time he saw scarcely anyone save his own family and Theodore Watts-Dunton. Fears were felt for his sanity, and in 1872 he was under medical care. He was frequently away with William Morris at Kelmscott, in Oxfordshire; indeed he was for some time (1872–74) a co-tenant of Kelmscott. This friendship was broken by the disputes arising out of the reorganization of the Morris firm, but Mrs. Morris was still an occasional visitor at Cheyne Walk.

While his *Ballads and Sonnets* was being printed (1881) his health began to give way and he died on April 9, 1882. His *Ballads and Sonnets* contained much of his best work, including the completed *House of Life*, and the fine ballads, *Rose Mary, The White Ship*, and *The King's Tragedy*.

BIBLIOGRAPHY.—See W. M. Rossetti—*Dante Gabriel Rossetti as Designer and Writer* (1889); *Ruskin, Rossetti, Pre-Raphaelitism* (1899); *Some Reminiscences* (1906) and *Rossetti, Classified Lists of his Writings with the Dates* (1906). Memoir by W. M. Rossetti prefixed to the *Collected Works* (1886, Revised edition 1911). Lady Burne-Jones's *Memorials of Edward Burne-Jones* (1904) is full of interesting sidelights. *See* also F. G. Stephens, *D. G. Rossetti;* "Portfolio" monograph (1894); H. C. Marillier, *D. G. Rossetti* (1899 and 1901); W. Sharp, *Dante Gabriel Rossetti: A Record and a Study* (1882); T. Hall Caine, *Recollections of Dante Gabriel Rossetti* (1882, revised and enlarged edition, 1928); W. Allingham, *Letters of Dante Gabriel Rossetti to William Allingham, 1854-70* (1807); A. C. Benson, *Rossetti*, in the "English Men of Letters" series (1904); E. Waugh, *Rossetti, his Life and Works* (1928); R. L. Mégroz, *Dante Gabriel Rossetti* (1929).

ROSSETTI, WILLIAM MICHAEL (1829–1919), English author and critic, born in London, second son of Gabriele and Frances Rossetti. In 1845, owing to pressure of family circumstances, he entered the Excise Office, afterwards the Inland Revenue Office, where he remained till 1894, retiring with the rank of under-secretary. He was a founder of the Pre-Raphaelite Brotherhood, and edited its organ *The Germ*, to which he contributed several papers of criticism and some verse. From 1850 onward, he wrote on matters of art and literature for *The Spectator* and other papers, defending the Pre-Raphaelite cause.

W. M. Rossetti is best remembered for his work in connection with Shelley (1869), Blake and Walt Whitman. His edition and memoir of Shelley (1869), with a carefully emended text and a dispassionate study of the poet's life, was invaluable at the time of its publication.

In 1874 he married Lucy (1843–1894), daughter of Ford Madox Brown, by whom he had five children.

W. M. Rossetti's most important works are: Blank verse translation of Dante's *Inferno* (1865); *Fine Art, Chiefly Contemporary* (1867); *Aldine Edition of Blake's Poems* (1874); *Lives of Famous Poets* (1878); *Collected Works of D. G. Rossetti* (1886–1904); *Life of Keats* (1887); *D. G. Rossetti: His Family Letters with Memoir* (1895); Memoir of D. G. Rossetti prefixed to *New Poems* (1896); *Ruskin, Rossetti, Pre-Raphaelitism* (1899), the first of a series of Family records; *Gabriele Rossetti—A Versified Autobiography* translated and supplemented (1901); *Some Reminiscences* (1906); *Democratic Sonnets* (1907).

ROSSI, PELLEGRINO LUIGI EDOARDO, COUNT (1787–1848), Italian economist, and statesman, was born at Carrara on July 13, 1787. He was educated at Pavia and Bologna. In 1815 he supported Joachim Murat, and on his fall left the country and went to Geneva, where he lectured on Roman law. He was made a citizen of Geneva, and as member of the extraordinary diet of 1832, was employed to draw up a revised Constitution, the *Pacte Rossi*. This was rejected, and Rossi went to France, where he was professor of political economy in the College de France, and in 1834 professor of constitutional law at Paris university. In 1839 he was given a peerage and in 1845 sent to Rome, where he became French ambassador. After the revolution of 1848 he stayed in Rome, and became minister of the interior under Pius IX. He was assassinated on the steps of the House of Assembly on Nov. 15, 1848.

As a statesman, Rossi was a man of signal ability and intrepid character, but it is as an economist that his name will be best remembered. His *Cours d'économie politique* (1838–54) gave in classic form an exposition of the doctrines of Say, Malthus and Ricardo. His other works were *Traité de droit pénal* (1829); *Cours de droit constitutionnel* (1866–67); and *Mélanges d'économie politique, d'histoire et de philosophie* (2 vols., 1857).

See le Comte Fleury d'Ideville, *Le Comte Pellegrino Rossi, sa vie, ses oeuvres, sa mort* (1887).

ROSSINI, GIOACHINO ANTONIO (1792–1868), Italian operatic composer, was born at Pesaro on Feb. 29, 1792. His father was town trumpeter and inspector of slaughter-houses, his mother a baker's daughter. The elder Rossini was imprisoned by the Austrians in 1796, and the mother took Gioachino to Bologna, earning her living as a *prima donna buffa* at various theatres of the Romagna, where she was ultimately rejoined by her husband. Gioachino remained at Bologna in the care of a pork butcher, while his father played the horn in the bands of the theatres at which his mother sang. The boy learned singing and the pianoforte, and at thirteen appeared at the theatre of the Commune in Paër's *Camilla*—his only appearance as a public singer (1805). He was also able to play the horn. In 1807 he was admitted to the Conservatorio of Bologna, but his insight into orchestral resources was gained rather by scoring the quartets and symphonies of Haydn and Mozart, than from his teachers. At Bologna he was known as "il Tedeschino" on account of his devotion to Mozart. His first opera, *La Cambiale di Matrimonio*, was produced at Venice when he was eighteen. Two years before he had received the prize at the Conservatorio of Bologna for his cantata *Il pianto d'armonia per la morte d'Orfeo*. Between 1810 and 1813, at Bologna, Rome, Venice and Milan, Rossini produced operas of which the successes were varying. *Tancredi*, produced at the Fenice, Venice (1813) made him famous. The libretto was an arrangement of Voltaire's tragedy by J. A. Rossi. Traces of Paër and Paisiello were undeniably present in fragments of the music. But the sweetness and clarity of such melodies as "Mi rivedrai, ti rivèdrò" and "Di tanti palpiti," conquered Venice. Italians would sing "Mi rivedrai" in the law courts until called upon by the judge to desist. Rossini continued to write operas for Venice and Milan during the next few years, but without repeating the success of *Tancredi.*

In 1815 he retired to Bologna, where Barbaja, the impresario of the Naples theatre, engaged him as musical director of the Teatro San Carlo and the Teatro Del Fondo at Naples, on the understanding that he compose for each of them one opera a year. His payment was to be 200 ducats (about £35 or $175) per month; he was also to receive a share in the gaming-tables, also owned by Barbaja, amounting to about 1,000 ducats (£175 or $875) per annum. General enthusiasm greeted the court performance of his *Elisabetta regina d' Inghilterra,* in which Isabella Colbran, whom Rossini afterwards married, took a leading part. The opera was the first in which Rossini wrote the ornaments of the airs instead of leaving them to the fancy of the singers, and also the first in which the *recitativo secco* was replaced by a recitative accompanied by a quartet of strings. In *Almaviva* (Rome, 1816) the libretto, a version of Beaumarchais' *Barbier de Séville* by Sterbini, was the same as that already used by Paisiello in his *Barbiere,* an opera which had enjoyed European popularity for more than a quarter of a century. But Rossini had created such a masterpiece of musical comedy that the title of *Il Barbiere di Siviglia* passed inevitably to his opera.

Between 1815 and 1823 Rossini produced twenty operas. Of these *Otello* formed the climax, contrasting interestingly with the treatment of the same subject at a similar point of artistic development by Verdi. In deference to the taste of the day the story was made to end happily! The opera *Cenerentola* (1817) is to be ranked with the *Barbiere,* as a masterpiece in comedy. *Mose in Egitto* was produced at Naples in 1818. In 1821, Rossini married Isabella Colbran. In 1822 he directed his *Cenerentola* in Vienna, where *Zelmira* was also performed. After this he returned to Bologna; but an invitation from Prince Metternich to "assist in the general re-establishment of harmony" brought him to Verona at the opening of the Congress on Oct. 20, 1822. Here he made friends with Chateaubriand and Madame de Lieven.

In 1823, at the suggestion of the manager of the King's Theatre, London, he came to England, being much fêted on his way through Paris. In England he was given a generous welcome, which included an introduction to King George IV. and the receipt of £7,000 after a residence of five months.

In 1824 he became musical director of the Théâtre Italien in Paris at a salary of £800 per annum, and when the agreement came to an end he was appointed chief composer to the king and inspector-general of singing in France. The production of *Guillaume Tell* in 1829 brought his career as a writer of opera to a close. The libretto was by Étienne Jouy and Hippolyte Bis, but their version was revised by Armand Marrast. The music is free from the conventions discovered and utilized by Rossini in his earlier works, and marks a transitional stage in the history of opera. In 1829 he returned to Bologna on family business. His return to Paris was delayed by the July Revolution of 1830 until November 1830. Six movements of his *Stabat Mater* were written in 1832 and the rest in 1839, the year of his father's death, and the success of the work bears comparison with his achievements in opera; but his comparative silence during the period from 1832 to 1868 makes his biography appear almost like the narrative of two lives—the life of swift triumph, and the long life of seclusion, of which the biographers give us pictures in stories of the composer's cynical wit, his speculations in fish culture, his mask of humility and indifference. His first wife died in 1845, and political disturbances in the Romagna compelled him to leave Bologna in 1847, the year of his second marriage with Olympe Pelissier, who had sat to Vernet for his picture of "Judith and Holofernes." After living for a time in Florence he settled in Paris in 1855, where his house was a centre of artistic society. He died at Passy on Nov. 13, 1868.

See Stendhal, *Vie de Rossini* (1823); A. Azevedo, *G. Rossini, sa vie et ses oeuvres* (1865); H. de Curzon, *Rossini* (1920).

ROSSLYN, ALEXANDER WEDDERBURN, 1st Earl of (1733-1805), Lord Chancellor of Great Britain, was the eldest son of Peter Wedderburn (a lord of session as Lord Chesterhall), and was born in East Lothian on Feb. 13, 1733. He was educated at Edinburgh university and entered the Inner Temple in 1753. It was always his intention to practise at the English bar, but in deference to his father's wishes he qualified as an advocate in Edinburgh in 1754, and practised there for three years. In 1757, following a quarrel with Lockhart, then dean of faculty, he left the Scottish bar, and was called at the Inner Temple. He engaged Thomas Sheridan and Macklin to teach him oratory and to eliminate his native accent. His countrymen, Lords Bute and Mansfield, were also useful to him, and it was he who suggested to Bute a pension for Dr. Johnson. Bute's influence got him into parliament in 1761, and he took silk in 1763. In 1767 he married an heiress. His political career after this is complicated in the extreme. In 1768 he was a Tory, but next year he resigned his seat over the Wilkes business, thereby winning enormous popularity in the country, and getting a pocket-borough from Clive in 1770. His new associates, however, distrusted him, and with reason; in January 1771 he deserted to the North ministry and was made solicitor-general. As Junius said "there is something about him which even treachery cannot trust." Throughout the American war he savagely attacked the colonies, and in 1778 he was made attorney-general. In 1780 he became Chief Justice of the Common Pleas with the title of Baron Loughborough. During North and Fox's coalition he was a commissioner of the great seal, and appears as leader of the Whigs in the Lords, with full expectations of the Woolsack. The King's recovery, however, blighted their hopes, and in 1792 Loughborough seceded from Fox, and became Lord Chancellor in Pitt's Tory cabinet. In 1801, Pitt's resignation was the end of him; Addington had no room for him, but he received the earldom of Rosslyn, and retired. He died at his country house near Windsor on Jan. 2, 1805, and was buried in St. Paul's.

At the bar Wedderburn was the most elegant speaker of his time, and, although his knowledge of the principles and precedents of law was deficient, his skill in marshalling facts and his clearness of diction were marvellous; on the bench his judgments were remarkable for their perspicuity, particularly in the appeal cases to the House of Lords. For cool and sustained declamation he stood unrivalled in parliament, and his readiness in debate was universally acknowledged. In social life, in the company of the wits and writers of his day, his faculties seemed to desert him. He was not only dull, but the cause of dulness in others.

See Brougham's *Statesmen of the Reign of George III.;* Foss's *Judges;* Campbell's *Lives of Lord Chancellors.*

ROSTAND, EDMOND (1869-1918), French dramatist, was born on April 1, 1869, the son of a prominent Marseilles journalist and economist. His first play, a burlesque, *Les romanesques,* was produced on the 21st of May 1894 at the Théâtre Français. He took the motive of his second piece, *La Princesse lointaine* (Théâtre de la Renaissance, 5th April 1895), from the story of the troubadour Rudel and the Lady of Tripoli. The part of Mélisande was created by Sarah Bernhardt, who also was the original Photine of *La Samaritaine* (Théâtre de la Renaissance, 14th April 1897), a Biblical drama in three scenes taken from the gospel story of the woman of Samaria. The production of his "heroic comedy" of *Cyrano de Bergerac* (28th December 1897, Théâtre de la Porte Saint-Martin), with Coquelin in the title rôle, was a triumph. No such enthusiasm for a drama in verse had been known since the days of Hugo's *Hernani.* The play was quickly translated into English, German, Russian and other European languages. For his hero he had drawn on French 17th-century history; in *L'Aiglon* he chose for his theme the unhappy life of the duke of Reichstadt, son of Napoleon I. and Marie Louise, under the surveillance of Metternich at the palace of Schönbrunn. *L'Aiglon,* in six acts and in verse, was produced (March 15, 1900) by Sarah Bernhardt at her own theatre, she herself playing the part of the duke of Reichstadt, one of her most famous later roles. In 1902 Rostand was elected to the French academy. *Chantecler,* produced in February 1910, had Lucien Guitry in the title role. During

World War I he wrote chiefly patriotic verse. He died in Paris on Dec. 2, 1918.

His son, MAURICE ROSTAND, author of plays, made a sensation in 1928 by the production of *Napoléon IV*, in which it was sought to ascribe responsibility for the death of the prince imperial to Queen Victoria.

The following works by Edmond Rostand were published posthumously: *La dernière nuit de Don Juan* (1921); *Le cantique de l'aile* (1922); *Le Vol de la Marseillaise* (1922). See G. Haraszti, *Edmond Rostand* (1913); J. Suiberville, *Le Théâtre d'Edmond Rostand* (1919).

ROSTOCK, a town of Germany, situated in the *Land* of Mecklenburg, one of the most important commercial cities on the Baltic. It is situated on the estuary of the Warnow, 8 mi. from the port of Warnemünde on the Baltic, 177 mi. N.W. of Berlin by rail, 80 mi. E.N.E. of Lübeck and 106 mi. S. of Copenhagen. Pop. (1939) 122,374. It is probable that the site was occupied by a village from very early times but the first definite mention of the settlement occurs in the 12th century. The town received its municipal charter in 1218. The earliest signs of commercial prosperity date from about 1260. In the 14th century it joined the Hanseatic league, and was one of the original members of the powerful Wendish Hansa, in which it exercised an influence second only to that of Lübeck. The most prosperous epoch of its commercial history began in the latter half of the 15th century. Rostock never entirely lost the independence which it enjoyed as a Hanse town. In the suburbs was located, after Hitler came to power, the Heinkel aircraft factory, one of the largest in Germany. As a result, the population of Rostock increased by 35,000 between 1933 and 1939. On April 28, 1942, a large British bombing squadron blasted Rostock and the Heinkel works with terrific results. Three more raids followed within a week. The aircraft factory was badly damaged, two large areas of Rostock were laid in ruins, and thousands of frightened citizens fled to the open country.

Rostock had five old churches: St. Mary's dating from 1398 to 1472, one of the most imposing Gothic buildings in Mecklenburg, with two Romanesque towers and containing a magnificent bronze font and a curious clock; St. Nicholas', begun about 1250 and restored in 1450 and again in 1890–94; St. Peter's, with a lofty tower built in 1400, which serves as a landmark to ships at sea; St. James's, completed in 1588; and the church of the Holy Rood, begun in 1270. St. Mary's church contains a monument marking the original tomb of Hugo Grotius, who died in Rostock in 1645, though his remains were afterward removed to Delft. Among other buildings are the curious 14th-century Gothic town hall, the façade of which is concealed by a Renaissance addition; the former palace of the grand dukes, built in 1702; and the university buildings, erected in 1867–70. The University of Rostock was founded in 1418. From 1437 till 1443 it had its seat at Greifswald in consequence of commotions at Rostock, and in 1760 it was again removed, on this occasion to Bützow. The professors appointed by the city, however, still taught at Rostock, so that there were practically two universities in the duchy until 1789 when they were reunited at the original seat.

Rostock has a considerable trade, being the chief commercial town of Mecklenburg, and vessels drawing 19 ft. of water are able to get up to the wharves. By far the most important export is grain, but bricks, sugar and salt are also shipped. The chief imports are ordinarily coal, herrings, timber, wine and colonial goods. A train-ferry service to Denmark runs from Warnemünde, the outpost of Rostock.

ROSTOPTSCHIN, COUNT FEODOR VASSILIE-VICH (1763–1826), Russian general, was born on March 23, 1763, in the government of Orel. The tsar Paul made him in 1796 adjutant general, grand marshal of the court, then minister of the interior. He was disgraced in 1801 for his opposition to the French alliance, but was restored to favour in 1810, and was appointed military governor of Moscow. He was charged with its defense against Napoleon. He is alleged to have instigated the burning of Moscow the day after the French had made their entry; it is certain that the prisons were opened by his order, and that he took no means to stop the outbreak. He defended himself against the charge of incendiarism in a pamphlet printed in Paris in 1823, *La Vérité sur l'incendie de Moscou*, but he subsequently made grave admissions. Shortly after the Congress of Vienna, to which he had accompanied the tsar Alexander, he was disgraced. He returned to Russia in 1825, and died at Moscow on Feb. 12, 1826. His *Mémoires écrits en dix minutes* were posthumously published at St. Petersburg in 1853, his *Oeuvres inédites* in Paris in 1894.

ROSTOV-ON-DON, a seaport of the Russian S.F.S.R., in the North Caucasian area, in 47° 15′ N., 39° 40′ E., on the Sea of Azov, 25 mi. from the point where the Don river reaches that sea by a number of mouths, only two of which are used, one for shipping and one for rafts. A channel through the former has been dredged with a minimum depth of 14 ft. The river is frost-bound for 100 days per annum on an average. Trade consists of transit from rail or river vessels to lighters or local steamers on which cargoes are carried to Taganrog roads, there to be loaded for foreign voyages. Very few vessels from foreign ports reach Rostov itself. Imports and exports are thus practically the same as those of Taganrog (*q.v.*). Rostov is an industrial centre with shipbuilding yards, a dyeing industry, zinc, tobacco, boot and shoe factories and other enterprises. There is a fishing industry. It is linked by rail with the north and west, with the Volga river and with the Caspian sea. Pop. (1939) 510,253, much swollen in summer by seasonal hands coming in for the grain shipping industry.

During World War II Rostov-on-Don played a considerable role in the Russo-German campaign, being one of the main centres of the Ukrainian front. It changed hands many times and was definitely liberated only after the German retreat of 1943.

ROSTOV VELIKI, a town of the Russian S.F.S.R. in the region of Yaroslavl, in 57° 14′ N., 39° 15′ E., near Lake Rostov or Nero. Rostov was founded by the Slavs about 862, and played a great part in early Russian history as the centre of the Rostov principality. Its pink washed Kreml (or citadel) walls have iron doors with quaint legends and paintings in each square; *e.g.*, a crow on a branch with the legend, "I sing only to relieve my sorrow." Its ancient cathedral, with the famous peal of bells, its numerous church domes, its 12th-century shrines and relics, the alleys and closes of its market, give a wonderful picture of mediaeval Russian life. After the Mongol invasion of 1239–42, it rapidly declined and in 1474 was purchased by Ivan III and annexed to Moscow. It was repeatedly plundered by Tatars, Lithuanians and Poles in the 15th, 16th and 17th centuries. The population (23,305) is mainly employed in the drying of vegetables and medicinal herbs, in coffee and chicory preparation and in flour milling. There is fishing in the lake. The district was once famous for its enamelled icons.

ROSTRA (beaks), in Roman antiquities, the orators' platform which stood in Rome between the Comitium and the Forum, opposite the Curia. In 338 B.C. it was decorated by Gaius Maenius with the prows of ships captured from the people of Antium. From that time it was called *Rostra*, having previously been known as *templum* (literally consecrated place), since it had been consecrated by the augurs. Here were exhibited the statues of famous Romans, and state documents and memorials (the laws of the Twelve Tables, etc.). Caesar had it pulled down, intending that it should be rebuilt on the west side of the Forum, but it was left for Augustus to carry out his plan. The use of the term *Rostra Vetera* by classical authors makes it doubtful whether the old platform was entirely demolished, unless the name was simply transferred to the new rostra of Augustus to distinguish it from the *Rostra Iulia*. This consisted of a rectangular platform, 78 ft. long, 11 ft. above the level of the Forum, reached by steps from the back; in front there was a marble balustrade with an opening in the centre where the speaker stood. In the existing remains, the holes in which the beaks of the ships were fastened are visible. See ROME: *The Forum*.

BIBLIOGRAPHY.—For results of the excavations *see* C. Huelsen, *Das Forum Romanum*, Eng. trans. by J. B. Carter (Rome, 1906); *see also* O. Richter, "Topographie der Stadt Rom," in I. von Mueller, *Handbuch der klassischen Altertumswissenschaft* (1901); H. Thédenat, *Le Forum Romain*, 3rd ed. (1904); J. E. Sandys, *Companion to Latin Studies* (1921).

ROSWELL, a city of southeastern New Mexico, U.S., the county seat of Chaves county; 200 mi. N.E. of El Paso, Tex., at an altitude of 3,570 ft., 8 mi. from the Pecos river, on federal highways 70, 380 and 285 and served by the Santa Fe railway and by Continental and Pioneer air lines. Pop. (1950) 25,738; 13,482 in 1940 by federal census. It is a trade centre for fertile farm lands and an extensive stock-raising region; the seat of the New Mexico military institute and Walker Air Force base; and the gateway to the Lincoln National forest of 1,500,000 ac. in the Gallina, Capitan, White, Sacramento and Guadalupe mountains. There are oil fields in the vicinity. • Roswell was founded in 1885 as a cattle-trading point. The railway reached it from the south in 1894 and from the east in 1898. The city was incorporated in 1890.

ROSYTH, a town and naval base of Fife, Scot., on the north shore of the Firth of Forth, 2½ mi. S.E. of Dunfermline (with which it was incorporated in 1911). Plans for the establishment of a large naval base there were drawn up in 1903; 285 ac. of foreshore and 1,184 ac. of land behind were purchased and work was begun in 1909. The scheme included a high-level main basin covering an area of 55 ac., a dry dock, a submarine tidal basin and an entrance channel. A great sea wall was built to form the southern boundary of the three docks. During World War I Rosyth was used as a secondary base to Scapa Flow, particularly for battle cruisers. In 1925 the dockyard was reduced to the basis of a care and maintenance establishment, but on the outbreak of World War II it recovered its former importance. After the end of that war, it continued to function as one of the main dockyards of the United Kingdom and to provide employment for about 7,000 people.

Rosyth has been built as a "garden city" and the number of its inhabitants in 1955 was estimated to be 13,000.

ROTA, COURT OF, one of the departments of the mediaeval papal organization in the Vatican. The Rota was the supreme court of appeal of Christendom. It declined in importance when a special court of appeal for Italy was set above it, and more so as the geographical jurisdiction of the pope was gradually lessened.

After the Council of Trent the old arrangements were replaced by the congregations, permanent committees of cardinals which deal with definite branches of business. The Rota, however, was restored to its functions as supreme court of appeal by Pope Pius X in 1908.

See Curia Romana; and art. "Rota" in *The Catholic Encyclopedia.*

ROTARY CLUB, an organization of business and professional men founded for the purpose of furthering the object of service to others in all relationships. The first Rotary club was founded in Chicago, Ill., on Feb. 23, 1905, by a lawyer, Paul P. Harris. The members met in rotation at the offices or places of business of the various members. This method suggested the name, Rotary club. Similar clubs were organized in other cities of the U.S. and in Aug. 1910, at Chicago, the 16 clubs then in existence formed the National Association of Rotary clubs. In 1912, after the formation of clubs in Winnipeg, Can.; Dublin, Ire.; and London, Eng., the organization became the International Association of Rotary clubs. In 1922 the name was changed to Rotary International.

The object of Rotary is: to encourage and foster the ideal of service as a basis of worthy enterprise and, in particular, to encourage and foster (1) the development of acquaintance as an opportunity for service; (2) high ethical standards in business and professions; the recognition of the worthiness of all useful occupations and the dignifying by each Rotarian of his occupation as an opportunity to serve society; (3) the application of the ideal of service by every Rotarian to his personal, business and community life; and (4) the advancement of international understanding, good will and peace through a world fellowship of business and professional men united in the ideal of service.

The program of Rotary based on this object brings together in an atmosphere of personal friendship men of diverse occupations without reference to religion or politics. Some clubs (such as those in Cairo, Egy.; Singapore; Hong Kong; Jerusalem) have a membership composed of many different nationalities and races.

Membership in a Rotary club is based upon activity in a business, profession or institution. Basically, there may be one representative of each classification of business, professional or institutional activity in a community. An additional active member from the same concern or establishment as an active member may be elected to membership in the same classification. Men who distinguish themselves by meritorious service in the furtherance of Rotary ideals may be elected to honorary membership. The affairs of each club are administered by a board of directors assisted by various standing committees. The officers (president, vice-president, secretary and treasurer) are elected annually. Clubs hold weekly luncheon or dinner meetings. Membership in the club is forfeited if the required standards of attendance are not maintained. Clubs are grouped in districts for administrative purposes. The club presidents and secretaries in each district meet together each year. Delegates and members of the clubs of each district meet in annual district conferences. The administrative officer of Rotary International in a district is a district governor, nominated by the clubs in the district and elected by delegates of all Rotary clubs at the annual international convention. The annual international convention elects a president and members of the board of directors, who form the administrative body of Rotary International. The Rotary constitution provides that of the fourteen directors, at least seven must be from countries other than the United States.

A permanent secretariat, consisting of the secretary and his staff, is maintained with offices at Evanston, Ill.; and Zürich, Switz. An office in London serves Rotary clubs in Great Britain and Ireland. The official publications are *The Rotarian* (English) and *Revista Rotaria* (Spanish), published at Evanston. Other Rotary magazines are published in various languages by districts or groups of districts. In the mid-1950s there were about 8,700 Rotary clubs with a membership of 414,000 business and professional executives in 92 countries and regions.

The Rotary movement in Great Britain and Ireland was started in 1911 with the organization of a Rotary club in Dublin by an Irishman who, while in the U.S., had been a member of the San Francisco Rotary club. About the same time a club was organized in London by Rotarians from Chicago and Boston who had business connections in London. The club in Manchester was formed by London Rotarians and subsequently clubs were formed in Belfast, Glasgow, Edinburgh, Liverpool and Birmingham. In 1914 the clubs in Great Britain and Ireland organized into an association called Rotary International in Great Britain and Ireland. The association is administered by a general council, consisting of a president, immediate past president, vice-president, treasurer, secretary and the Rotary International representatives in the several districts. In the mid-1950s there were almost 800 clubs in Great Britain and Ireland with a membership of 35,000. Each year one member of the board of directors of Rotary International comes from this region. Rotary International in Great Britain and Ireland has a secretariat at London, a number of committees, an annual conference of delegates and members from all clubs in the region, and issues a monthly publication (*Rotary Service*). The Rotary movement in Great Britain and Ireland differs in no essential way from the movement in other parts of the world. Clubs meet weekly for luncheon or dinner and have a speaker on a topic of general interest, preferably one reflecting in a general way the Rotary ideal of service to others.   (G. R. M.; C. R. P.)

ROTARY ENGINE. A type of engine in which the use of reciprocating parts is avoided with the object of saving the energy wasted in converting reciprocal or to-and-fro movement into rotary movement. The rotary principle never had any practical success in competing with the smaller reciprocating engines, but steam turbines (which are really a class of rotary engine) furnished the first solution of the problem for moderate and large size installations. Many rotary mechanisms have been tried. Some have comprised a flap piston rotating within a cylinder, the pressure of the steam causing rotation. Sometimes the flap has a sliding action within the piston, the shaft of the latter being mounted eccentrically in relation to the bore. More or less complicated arrangements of levers and of gears were also patented, with multiple pistons. James Watt's famous attempt was really a semirotary engine, with a radial piston which swung to and fro and actuated a pinion and rack device for working the rods of pit pumps.

In the earlier periods of aeroplane construction rotary engines were much employed, notably the Gnôme and the Le Rhône, but the radial engine later formed the equivalent of these types. Weaknesses of the rotary aero engine, in use during World War I, were the fact that it could be lubricated with only castor oil and the objectionable gyroscopic action produced by its rotating mass. Yet the rotary principal found great success in certain other directions, such as pumps, blowers and gas-exhausters. The latter are in principle blowers reversed. In a well-known type the piston or drum is set with its axis eccentrically in the cylinder, and radial blades slide in its slots, making a gas-tight fit against the bore. The drum rotates and pumps the gas from the inlet which is at one side of the cylinder to the outlet at the other side.

After World War II there was a continuous development of the gas turbine. In a gas turbine an atomized oil-air mixture burns and produces an expanding gas that serves the same function as steam. Great difficulties were overcome in developing materials that operate under the extremely high temperatures of the gas turbine. Gas turbines are used for stationary power installations particularly where there is a shortage of water for operating a steam plant. (*See* Aero Engines; Turbine: Steam.)

ROTARY TILLER: *see* Tillage Machinery.

ROTATION OF CROPS refers to the repeated growing of different kinds of crops in a specific order, on the same land, in contrast to a one-crop system or to haphazard crop successions. The time required to complete a growing cycle will depend upon the number of crops and whether the changes are seasonal, annual, biennial or perennial. For field crops, the successions are usually repeated in periods ranging from two to eight years. Rotations may classify as both good and bad. The basis for judgment rests in the changes brought about in the soil and in production economy. The beneficial effects of well-planned cropping systems are such, however, that few farmers can afford to neglect them.

On many farms, the cropping systems are confined chiefly to crops that tend to give the highest immediate cash returns. This usually means the intensive use of row crops like corn, cotton and soybeans that require annual plowing for seedbed preparation, as well as cultivation during the growing season. If continued too long such systems bring about unfavourable changes in the soil: (1) sizable reductions in organic matter and nitrogen; (2) development of less desirable physical conditions; (3) accelerated loss of soil and water by surface runoff; and (4) lowered nutrient-supplying powers. Such changes are often accompanied with greater damage to the crop from insects, diseases and weeds. The end results are declining yields, loss of crop quality and reduced incomes. Cropping practices need to be considered, not only from the immediate point of view, but from their long-time effects as well. Good crop rotations will not prevent all of the unfavourable effects of crop production on the soil, but they will do much to ensure the continued efficient use of the soil.

Rotation planning consists essentially in fitting soils and crops together in such ways as to be desirable and suitable for livestock, grain, truck garden or other type of farming. The harmonious balances developed between soil, water and vegetation in the natural landscape, suggest some of the underlying principles. The soil is rarely devoid of vegetation and sod-forming crops are much in evidence. In field crop production, carefully selected row crops should be balanced with equally well-selected close-growing grain and sod-forming crops, the latter of which may be legumes, nonlegume grasses or combinations of these. The acreage devoted to the sod-forming crops should be expanded at the expense of the row crops on soils of increasing slope and declining fertility. This will provide better vegetative covering to protect sloping lands from excessive erosion and supply organic matter for improving soil productivity on both sloping and level lands. With lessening slope and increasing fertility the row crops may be expanded, but this should not be done with too much reduction in the sod-forming crops.

The differing effects of crops on soils, on each other and in behaviours to insect pests, crop diseases and weeds, require carefully planned crop sequences. Often the less desirable of these effects can be offset by the order in which crops follow each other. If, for instance, corn, a high nitrogen requiring crop, fol-

lows a small grain, it may suffer seriously from nitrogen starvation, in some seasons. If the preceding crop were a satisfactory legume, this difficulty would not arise and higher yields would be obtained.

Rotation planning should also include a consideration of the crop handling practices. Sufficient legume residues should be returned to the soil, either directly or indirectly through animal manure, to supply all or much of the nitrogen required by the rotation. Sufficient nonlegume residues (stover and straw) should be associated with the legume residues to obtain the greatest benefits from the legume crops. Experiments show that association increases the yields of succeeding crops more than the combined yields obtained from the two types of residues used separately. These benefits cannot be secured if these residue materials are destroyed or removed from the land.

Broadly speaking, cropping systems should be built around the use of deep-rooted legumes. If too little use is made of these crops, productivity will decline; if too much land is devoted to them, wastes may occur and other useful crops will be displaced. Rotations depending wholly on green manure legumes should be confined to the more fertile and level lands. It will be desirable to include legumes alone or in mixtures with nonlegume sod-forming crops, as a regular crop in most field rotations. In general, this should occur about once in every four years.

Satisfactory rotations may be planned for time periods ranging upward from two years. Rotations for short periods, however, are not likely to provide the best crop balances, while longer rotations may become too complicated. Four-field rotations, generally, provide adequately for the requirements of good cropping. One-fourth of the land can be kept in sod crops and three-fourths in the row and the close-growing grain crops. Additional flexibility can be obtained by employing split cropping on one or more fields.

If the sod crop is a perennial legume like alfalfa, additional advantages can be secured by bringing these crops in two successive rotations together in one two-year period. With this modification the perennial legume will be seeded only every other year. This will permit the seeding of a green manure crop like sweet clover, in the alternate years when the perennial legume is not seeded. The original four-field rotation will be in evidence each year, but it will take eight years to complete the cycle. The sequences on one field for the four-crop rotation of (1) corn, (2) soybeans, (3) oats, (4) alfalfa, under the above modification will be as follows: (1) corn, (2) soybeans, (3) oats (sweet clover), (4) corn, (5) soybeans, (6) oats, (7) alfalfa, (8) alfalfa. Practical farmers will discover in this plan advantages other than those mentioned.

In addition to the many beneficial effects on soils and crops, well-planned crop rotations also provide the business aspects of farming with advantages. Labour, power and equipment can be handled with more efficiency; weather and market risks can be reduced; livestock production requirements can be met more easily; the farm can be made a more effective year-round enterprise. In other words, good crop rotations are indispensable to a smooth running and effective farm organization. Using a well-designed cropping system is a major farm problem. (*See* also Soil.)

(F. C. Br.)

ROTHAMSTED EXPERIMENTAL STATION, Harpenden, Eng., is the oldest agricultural experiment station in the world and one of the largest in the British Commonwealth. It was founded in 1843 as a private enterprise. John Bennet Lawes (1814–1900), coming into possession of his ancestral estate of Rothamsted at a difficult time, realized that he must increase the output from his land, and from 1838 onward tried the effect of various soil "amendments." Bones had little action: he realized that their phosphate was insoluble and tried therefore the effect of treating them with acid. The results were successful. At the same time mineral phosphates were being discovered but no use for them was known. Lawes found them ineffective as fertilizer but highly effective after treatment with acid which produced what was then known as superphosphate. He patented the process in 1842, set up a factory and thus founded the artificial fertilizer industry. He proved also the great fertilizer value of sulphate of ammonia and of the "alkalis" as indicated by J. von Liebig. Wishing to see whether these fertilizers would have any deleterious effects, he invited a young chemist, Joseph Henry Gilbert (1817–1901), to join him in 1843, and together they inaugurated the continuous field experiments on wheat, barley, roots (turnips at first, then mangolds) and grass, in which the same crop is grown year after year on the same land, receiving each year the same fertilizer or manurial treatment. The 100th successive crop of wheat was reaped in 1943 and of barley in 1952. Records of crop weights and of meteorological data are taken, and many chemical analyses of crops and soils have been made. Nowhere else do such full records exist. Lawes and Gilbert also made pioneering investigations on the nutrition of animals. For most of the time Gilbert had no scientific staff, but he trained village boys to make routine analyses and observations which they did remarkably well. In 1878 another chemist, Robert Warington, was brought in by Lawes; Warington started the study of soil micro-organisms, particularly those causing nitrification.

Lawes died in 1900 but in 1889 he had set up a trust endowed with £100,000 to continue his work in perpetuity. Gilbert's successor in 1901, A. D. Hall, realizing that chemistry alone could not solve the problems of agricultural science, appointed a botanist in 1906 and a bacteriologist and a soil chemist in 1907. In 1911 the newly established development fund, the first government provision for agricultural research in Great Britain, supplied the means for continuing expansion and Hall was called to administer the fund in 1912. E. John Russell was appointed director at Rothamsted; he held the post till 1943 and was succeeded by W. G. Ogg. Among the earliest problems studied by the 1907 group was the population of micro-organisms in the soil. Methods of estimating numbers were devised and the complex interactions of the various groups studied.

There was also a notable development of soil physics with a view to elucidating the physical structure of the soil and the factors relating to tilth. The water relations of soil, crop and atmosphere have been studied in order to provide useful guides for irrigation practice. On the chemical side much has been done toward the solution of the old problem of discovering by analysis the kind and amount of nutrients to be added to the soil to ensure optimum crop production. In 1929 a new and highly important development was started by R. A. Fisher: the science of mathematical statistics was applied to agricultural problems. This led to a complete refashioning of the designs of field and other experiments with variable material so that a valid estimate of the experimental error could be made, and also to the devising of ways of studying relationships between different observations such as rainfall at stated periods and crop yields. Methods of sampling have also been studied in detail.

In 1919 investigations in plant pathology were started. Notable studies have been made on the causes of variation in insect populations, statistical treatment being adopted wherever possible. Special departments deal with bees and with nematodes. Diseases of wheat and potatoes caused by soil fungi have been extensively investigated. There has been much joint work by chemists and entomologists on insecticides. Much attention has been given to the virus diseases of plants and their mode of transmission; the properties of the different viruses have been studied chemically and by use of the electron microscope.

Important physiological studies of growing crops have been made by special methods suitable for field work. The investigations have included studies of weeds of arable crops, mixed herbage of grassland and trace elements. Since 1943 the National Soil Survey has been centred at Rothamsted. The library at Rothamsted station is rich in old agricultural books and prints.   (E. J. R.)

ROTHE, RICHARD (1799–1867), Lutheran theologian, was born at Posen on Jan. 28, 1799. He studied theology in the universities of Heidelberg and Berlin (1817–20) under Karl Daub (1765–1836), Schleiermacher and Neander. In the autumn of 1823 he was appointed chaplain to the Prussian embassy in Rome, of which Baron Bunsen was the head. This post he exchanged in 1828 for a professorship in the Wittenberg theological seminary,

of which in 1832 he became also second director and *ephorus*. In 1837 he became professor and director of a new clerical seminary at Heidelberg; in 1849 he was professor and university preacher at Bonn, but in 1854 he returned to Heidelberg as professor of theology, and afterward became member of the Oberkirchenrath, a position he held until his death on Aug. 20, 1867. His removal to Heidelberg and the publication of his *Die Anfänge der christlichen Kirche und ihrer Verfassung* (1837), coincide with the attainment of the principal theological positions with which his name is associated. Rothe's most important work is his *Theologische Ethik* (3 vols., 1845–1848; 2nd ed., 5 vols. 1867–71).

See F. Nippold, *Richard Rothe, ein christliches Lebensbild* (2 vols., Wittenberg, 1873–74); W. Hönig, *Richard Rothe, sein Charakter, Leben und Denken* (1898); Adolf Hausrath, *Richard Rothe und seine Freunde* (1902).

ROTHENBURG-OB-DER-TAUBER, a Bavarian town of Germany, in Middle Franconia, 49 mi. by rail W. of Nuremberg. Pop. (1950) 11,214. Rothenburg-ob-der-Tauber, mentioned in the chronicles in 804 as *Rotinbure,* first appears as a town in 942 and in 1108 passed to the family of Hohenstaufen. In 1172 it became a free imperial city and it attained the zenith of its prosperity under the famous burgomaster Heinrich Toppler (1350–1408). It is probably the finest surviving example of a mediaeval town, flanked by mediaeval walls, towers and gates. Perhaps the most interesting building is the town hall, one part of which dates from 1240 and the other from 1572. The latter is a beautiful Renaissance structure and contains a grand hall in which every Whit Monday a play, *Der Meistertrunk,* which commemorates the capture of the town by Tilly in 1631, is performed. It has manufactures of toys, soap and agricultural machinery, and breweries, linen weaving establishments, sandstone and limestone quarries.

ROTHENSTEIN, SIR WILLIAM (1872–1945), English artist, born at Bradford, Yorks., on Jan. 29, 1872, was educated at Bradford. In 1888 he studied in the Slade school under Legros, and afterwards worked in Paris. In 1893 he began exhibiting at the New English Art club. From 1917 to 1926 he was professor of civic art at the University of Sheffield, and was principal of the Royal College of Art 1920–35. His paintings include "The Browning Readers" (1900), "The Dolls' House" (1900), and "Jews Mourning" (1905), Tate gallery; "Aliens at Prayer" (1904), Melbourne art gallery; "Carrying the Law" (1910), "Morning at Benares" (1911), "Bourlon Church" (1919) and "The Last Phase: on the Rhine" (1919). Among his portraits may be mentioned those of Augustus John, Walker art gallery, Liverpool; Sir Francis Darwin (1905), Mr. Charles Booth (1908), Liverpool university; Prof. Alfred Marshall (1908), Cambridge; Mr. Bernhard Berenson (1910) and Sir Rabindranath Tagore (1912), besides a portrait of himself (1900), Metropolitan museum, New York. His portrait drawings are notable for their sound draughtsmanship. He was one of the artists who decorated St. Stephen's hall, Westminster. He was knighted in 1931. Rothenstein died on Feb. 14, 1945.

His published works include *Oxford Characters* (1896); *English Portraits* (1898); *The French Set, and Portraits of Verlaine* (1898); *Manchester Portraits* (1899); *Liber Juniorum* (1899); a *Life of Goya* (1900); *Plea for a Wider Use of Artists and Craftsmen* (1918); *Twenty-four Portraits* (first series 1920, second series 1923); *Ancient India* (1925); *Men and Memories* (3 vols., 1931–39).

ROTHERHAM, a county and parliamentary borough in the West Riding of Yorkshire, England, 5 mi. N.E. of Sheffield. Pop. (1951) 82,341. Area 14.5 sq.mi.

Rotherham lies at the confluence of the Don with its tributary the Rother, which affords a notable north-to-south route on the east side of the Pennine upland, and for more than 40 years a branch from Rotherham along the Don valley was Sheffield's only link with the main railway line. Rotherham is connected by the Don canal with Goole and the Humber and is an important railway and road junction. It is a small counterpart of Sheffield, possessing iron, steel and brass works, railway wagon works, potteries, glassworks, breweries, sawmills and ropeyards. Ironworks were established at Masborough on the opposite bank of the Don in 1746. Rotherham came into some prominence as a city of mediaeval life and education. Rotherham was taken by the royalists in 1643, but after the battle of Marston moor, it was surrendered to a detachment of parliamentary forces. It was incorporated in 1871 and became a county borough in 1902. The town developed rapidly, and a large planning scheme came into operation. A technical college and art school and a central public library were opened in 1931. In 1943 there were four large parks and 250 ac. of playing fields. The parliamentary borough returns one member. Nearby is Wentworth Woodhouse, seat of earl Fitzwilliam.

ROTHERMERE, HAROLD SIDNEY HARMSWORTH, 1ST VISCOUNT (1868–1940), British newspaper proprietor, was the second son of Alfred Harmsworth, and brother of Viscount Northcliffe. He was born on April 26, 1868, London, was created a baronet in 1910, Baron Rothermere in 1914 and Viscount Rothermere of Hemsted, after his services as air minister, in 1918. He married in 1893 Mary Lilian, daughter of George Wade Share.

At the age of 21 he entered the publishing firm of which his brother, Alfred, was the principal, soon after the date when *Answers* was launched. He assisted in developing the business on sound and economic lines, and for the next 20 years was the close associate of his brother in all his great undertakings. He took an important part in the reorganization of *The Evening News*, London, was one of the three principals in the establishment of *The Daily Mail* (1896) and was largely responsible for developing its methods of distribution. He founded *The Daily Record* (1895), bought *The Leeds Mercury* and shared in the purchase of *The Times* (1908). He became known also as a most generous benefactor of charities. By the gift of a large sum he enabled the Union Jack club to provide worthy accommodations for sailors and soldiers in London; and he gave £10,000 to the Territorial Force County of London association. In 1910 he founded the King Edward chair of English literature at Cambridge, and in 1910 he ceased his connection with *The Times*, *The Daily Mail* and *The Evening News*. In 1914 he acquired *The Daily Mirror* from Lord Northcliffe and in 1915 he founded *The Sunday Pictorial*, the first fully illustrated Sunday newspaper in London. On the death of Lord Northcliffe, in Aug. 1922, Lord Rothermere by purchase acquired control of *The Daily Mail* and Associated Newspapers Ltd.; subsequently he bought large newspaper properties owned by E. Hulton & Co. Ltd. He was air minister in 1917–18. He retired from active business in 1938 but accepted a wartime mission to Canada in 1940. His health broke, and he died at Hamilton, Bermuda, Nov. 26, 1940.

(H. W. W.; X.)

ROTHES, EARLS OF. The first earl of Rothes was George Leslie, son of Norman Leslie of Rothes in Moray and of Ballinbreich in Fife. In 1445 he was created Baron Leslie of Leven, and about 1458 earl of Rothes in the peerage of Scotland. His grandson GEORGE, the 4th earl (d. 1558), whose father, William, the 3rd earl, was killed at Flodden, was accused, but acquitted in 1546, on complicity in the murder of Cardinal Beaton, in which his brother and his two sons were undoubtedly implicated; he was one of the Scottish commissioners who witnessed the marriage of Mary Queen of Scots with Francis, the dauphin of France.

His son ANDREW, 5th earl of Rothes (d. 1611), took an active part with the lords of the congregation, first against the queen-mother, Mary of Guise, when regent of Scotland, and afterward against Mary Queen of Scots in opposing her marriage with Darnley, and in devising the murder of David Rizzio. He was, however, one of the peers who acquitted Bothwell of Darnley's murder; and going over to the side of the queen, he fought for her at Langside. He continued to occupy a position of some prominence in Scottish affairs until his death in 1611.

His great-grandson, JOHN, 7th earl of Rothes (1630–1681), held a command in the Royalist army at the battle of Worcester in 1651, and accompanied Charles II to England at the Restoration, when he became lord president of the council in Scotland. He was lord treasurer of Scotland from 1663 till 1667, when he was made lord chancellor of Scotland for life. His estates having been sequestrated by the parliament in 1651, he received a re-grant in 1663 of the earldom of Rothes.

See Sir R. Douglas, *The Peerage of Scotland*, ed. Sir J. B. Paul; and G. E. C., *Complete Peerage*.

ROTHESAY, a royal and small burgh, and the chief town of the county and island of Bute, Scotland. Pop. (est. 1938) 8,161. It is situated on a beautiful bay, 40 mi. S.W. of Glasgow, with which there is regular communication by steamers from Wemyss Bay, Gourock, Greenock, Craigendoran, Adrishaig, Inveraray, Glasgow, etc. It is a popular watering place with a promenade 4 mi. long. The sheltered bay affords excellent anchorage, and is the headquarters of the Royal Northern Yacht club. Rothesay is a centre for the herring fisheries, and the head of a fishery district. The town is under the jurisdiction of a provost and council. Owing to its mild and equable climate it is a resort of invalids. There is a tramway to Port Bannatyne, on the east horn of Kames bay (now practically part of Rothesay), and to Ettrick bay; and Craigmore, about 1 mi. west of Rothesay, is a suburb. Ardbeg Point, Loch Fad, Loch Ascog and Barone hill (530 ft.) are all within a mile and a half of the town, and the Kyles of Bute within a short sail.

In the centre of the town are the ruins of a castle erected in 1098 either by Magnus Barefoot, king of Norway, or by the Scots as a defense against the Norwegians, with whom during the 13th century, and earlier, there was constant strife. The village which grew up round the castle was made a royal burgh by Robert III, who, in 1398, created his eldest son David duke of Rothesay, a title which became the highest Scottish title of the heir-apparent to the crown of the United Kingdom. During the Commonwealth the castle was garrisoned by Oliver Cromwell's troops. It was burned by the followers of Argyll in 1685, and remained neglected till the rubbish was cleared away by the second marquess of Bute in 1816. It was repaired by the third marquess.

ROTHSCHILD, the name of a Jewish family which has acquired an unexampled position from the magnitude of its financial transactions. The name was derived from a red (*rot*) shield on the house in which the family lived, in the ghetto of Frankfurt-on-Main, during the early period of its history. Setting up as a moneylender, Mayer Anselm (1744–1812), born on Feb. 23, 1744, became agent in 1801 to the wealthy prince William, 9th landgrave, later elector of Hesse-Cassel. In his first large loan (1802) to the Danish government, Mayer Anselm acted as the front for his prince.

By the time Mayer Anselm died, leaving five sons and five daughters, his third son, Nathan Mayer (1777–1836), born on Sept. 16, 1777, was well established in England, where he had gone about 1798 to seek advantageous textile connections. Nathan Mayer came to be regarded as the financial genius of the family. His bold and brilliant innovations, together with his firm belief in Napoleon's defeat, won him the gratitude of the English government. After he had successfully negotiated some of Wellington's drafts which the English government was unable to meet, Rothschild became the chief representative of the Allied powers in their loan arrangements. He helped to popularize foreign loans in Britain by issuing them in sterling and making the interest payable in London.

Anselm Mayer (1773–1855), born on June 12, 1773, Mayer Anselm's eldest son, took over the Frankfurt house, became a member of the Prussian privy council of commerce and in 1820 Bavarian consul and court banker. Solomon (1774–1855), born on Sept. 9, 1774, settled in Vienna, where his intimate relations with Metternich served as the continental link between the firm and the Allied powers. The Naples branch was established by Karl (1788–1855), born on April 24, 1788, and although originally significant, it was discontinued after the annexation of Naples to Italy in 1860. Jacob (1792–1868), born on May 15, 1792, also known as James, was the youngest brother. He started a business in Paris after the restoration of the Bourbons, for whom he negotiated large loans.

One of Nathan Mayer's few examples of shortsightedness was his failure to foresee the future of railways in England. Family co-operativeness, however, turned his mistake into an advantage for Jacob and Solomon, who sponsored the construction of the first railways in France and Austria.

Legends surrounding the early generations of the family have it that Mayer Anselm guarded the elector's wealth during the Napoleonic invasion by burying it and that Nathan Mayer had direct carrier-pigeon information about the battle of Waterloo. Another tale says that Nathan Mayer was himself a spectator of the battle.

All the sons of Mayer Anselm received the right to use *von* before their names in 1817 and were made Austrian barons in 1822. But not until 1842 did Solomon, as a Jew, receive special dispensation to own real property in Austria.

The important London house, after Nathan Mayer's death on July 28, 1836, was managed by his son Lionel (1808–1879), born on Nov. 22, 1808. Lionel was elected a member of parliament for the City of London in 1847, but his fidelity to the Jewish faith barred him from the customary Christian oath, and he could not take his seat. Returned by his constituency in 1849, 1852 and 1857, he remained unseated until 1858, when an act of parliament and a resolution of the house of commons made a variation of the oath possible. Lionel remained in commons until 1874.

Lionel's son, Nathaniel Mayer (1840–1915), born on Nov. 8, 1840, inherited a baronetcy from his uncle Anthony (1810–1876), born on May 29, 1810, and was made a peer in 1885 by W. E. Gladstone—the first Jew to be raised to the peerage. From 1865 until 1885 he was Liberal M.P. from Aylesbury. The second baron, Lionel Walter (1868–1937), born on Feb. 8, 1868, was a naturalist. Some 280,000 skins from his bird museum in Tring park were bought by the American Museum of Natural History in New York in 1932. After his death the British museum acquired most of the 1,500,000 butterflies and moths in the collection.

On the continent the French and Austrian houses retained their importance, although the Frankfurt house remained open until 1902. The interests of the houses did not notably cross over to the western hemisphere.

Mayer Anselm's Jewish piety was transmuted in his descendants to interest in the welfare of their co-religionists everywhere. Solomon won Clemens Metternich's support for emancipatory measures for the Jews of Europe. In England the head of the Rothschild family has been considered the lay head of British Jewry; the Balfour declaration of Nov. 2, 1917, stating that the government viewed with favour "the establishment of a national home for the Jewish people" in Palestine, was addressed to Lionel Walter. Edmond James (1845–1934), born on Aug. 19, 1845, of the French branch of the family, invested more than 70,000,000 gold francs in helping to establish Jewish communities in Palestine.

Political interests have absorbed some members of the family. Lionel Nathan (1882–1942), born on Jan. 25, 1882, was a member of the house of commons from 1910 to 1923. James Armand (1878–   ), born on Dec. 1, 1878, entered the house of commons in 1929. Maurice (1881–   ), born on May 19, 1881, of the French house, was a member of the French senate.

When the nazi reich and its anti-Semitic doctrines overran Austria in 1938, Louis (1882–   ), born on March 5, 1882, was held prisoner in Vienna for more than a year. Among the many members of the family in France who left the country as the result of the nazi invasion in 1940 were Édouard (1868–1949), born on Feb. 24, 1868, who was president of the Chemin de fer du Nord, and Henri (1872–1947), born on July 26, 1872, a physician and playwright.

See *Das Haus Rothschild* (1858); Picciotto, *Sketches of Anglo-Jewish History* (1875); Francis, *Chronicles and Characters of the Stock Exchange* (1853); Treskow, *Biographische Notizen Über Nathan Meyer Rothschild nebst seinem Testament* (1837); Roqueplan, *Le Baron James de Rothschild* (1868); Corti, *The Rise of the House of Rothschild* and *The Reign of the House of Rothschild* (Eng. trans. by Brian and Beatrix Lunn, 1928); C. Roth, *The Magnificent Rothschilds* (1939).   (L. Bt.)

ROTHWELL, urban district, West Riding of Yorkshire, England, 4 mi. S.E. of Leeds. Pop. (est. 1938) 24,440. Area, 16.7 sq.mi. Soon after the Conquest, Rothwell was a dependency of the castle of Pontefract, and a baronial residence, of which there are slight remains, was erected here. Coal and stone are obtained here and the town has match works and rope and twine factories.

Methley urban and Hunslet rural districts were added to Rothwell in 1937.

ROTIFERA (or Rotatoria), a well-defined class of aquatic animals of microscopic size, remarkable for the astonishing diversity of their forms, the vivacity and variety of their movements and the high level of their structural development. Being extremely transparent, the largest can hardly be detected by the unaided eye. In length they rarely exceed 1.7 mm. or $\frac{1}{15}$ in., ranging downward to .08 mm., and they probably average under .25 mm., with breadth and thickness very considerably less. In general rotifers are compact in body and symmetrical in structure. They are plentiful in most weedy ponds and boggy pools, and are also to be found in lakes and reservoirs, canals and rivers, ditches and runnels,—in short, in any collection of water containing suitable food. The great majority live in fresh water, yet many are seldom met with except in water either brackish or alkaline, and some are restricted to sea water. Many flourish in places only intermittently wet, such as among the stems of land-growing mosses and liverworts. Some are parasitic within the cells of water plants, or the bodies of other larger water animals, living even in the gill-chambers of fresh-water crabs and cray-fish. Others are literally "hangers-on" to the leaves and stems of water weeds for the sake of a favourable position, or to the exte-

FIG. 1.—A BDELLOID ROTIFER (PHILODINA ACUTICORNIS)

riors of water animals for the benefit of constant change of surroundings as their hosts move about. While they mostly live in waters of moderate temperature, they have been found established in hot springs. They can endure intense cold, being capable of reviving after being frozen in thick ice. Some appear only in the spring and summer, others carry on through the winter as well.

The duration of their individual lives has been little studied, but some species are known to live a few days only, while others survive for at least three months. They are greatly dependent upon their immediate environment and the quality, no less than the quantity, of the water inhabited. Sudden changes of temperature, or in the density of the water, or, perhaps, a decrease in the proportion of oxygen held in solution, are quickly fatal to them.

Whatever the variations of their outward form, an arched back and a flattened ventral surface, two similar sides and a division of the body into head, trunk and foot, by shallow constrictions, can in general be readily distinguished, though the head is often merged into the trunk, and there is frequently no foot. The whole may be maggot-shaped, slender or elongate, ovoid or squat. Especially diversified in form are those species in which the skin is hardened to become an armourlike covering (lorica) which may be much flattened or laterally compressed. While mostly smooth and hyaline, the surface may be shagreened, faceted, grooved or otherwise obscured. It may carry defensive spines, supplemented by numerous prickles. It may consist of one or of several pieces connected by yielding skin. In species without a lorica, the skin is generally smooth and flexible, but is sometimes tough and leathery, and may carry spines. The head, trunk and foot are often subdivided into smaller areas, segments or joints, by annular infoldings of the skin, frequently permitting the telescoping of one segment into that next to it.

Corona.—The collection of food and the swimming and gliding movements of rotifers are effected by the lashing action of numerous cilia crowded upon a particular area of delicate skin close to or encircling the mouth, or fringing several fleshy lobes or discs protrusible from it. The whole area, including the mouth itself, as seen when the cilia are active, is called the corona, and there are many varieties of the organ, differing widely in the arrangement of the cilia, etc. All these may be assigned to two leading types, the external and the evertile. In the main, the external type is characteristic of the hunting rotifers, which go about,

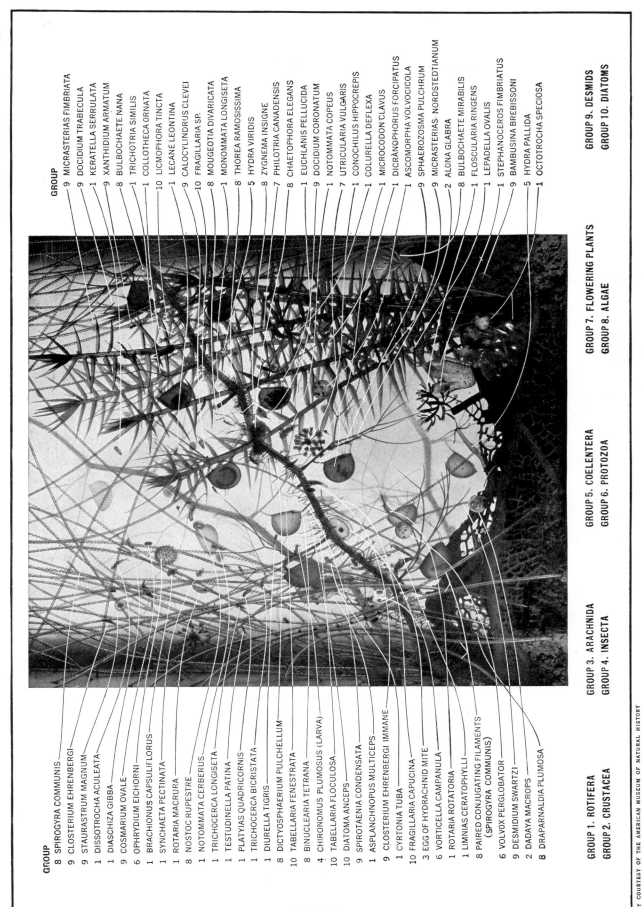

GROUP

8 SPIROGYRA COMMUNIS
9 CLOSTERIUM EHRENBERGI
9 STAURASTRUM MAGNUM
1 DISSOTROCHA ACULEATA
1 DIASCHIZA GIBBA
9 COSMARIUM OVALE
6 OPHRYDIUM EICHORNI
1 BRACHIONUS CAPSULIFLORUS
1 SYNCHAETA PECTINATA
1 ROTARIA MACRURA
8 NOSTOC RUPESTRE
1 NOTOMMATA CERBERUS
1 TRICHOCERCA LONGISETA
1 TESTUDINELLA PATINA
1 PLATYIAS QUADRICORNIS
1 TRICHOCERCA BICRISTATA
1 DIURELLA TIGRIS
8 DICTYOSPHAERIUM PULCHELLUM
10 TABELLARIA FENESTRATA
1 BINUCLEARIA TETRANA
4 CHIRONOMUS PLUMOSUS (LARVA)
10 TABELLARIA FLOCULOSA
10 DIATOMA ANCEPS
9 SPIROTAENIA CONDENSATA
1 ASPLANCHNOPUS MULTICEPS
9 CLOSTERIUM EHRENBERGI IMMANE
1 CYRTONIA TUBA
10 FRAGILLARIA CAPUCINA
3 EGG OF HYDRACHNID MITE
6 VORTICELLA CAMPANULA
1 ROTARIA ROTATORIA
1 LIMNIAS CERATOPHYLLI
8 PAIRED CONJUGATING FILAMENTS
   (SPIROGYRA COMMUNIS)
6 VOLVOX PERGLOBATOR
9 DESMIDIUM SWARTZI
2 DADAYA MACROPS
8 DRAPARNALDIA PLUMOSA

GROUP

9 MICRASTERIAS FIMBRIATA
9 DOCIDIUM TRABECULA
1 KERATELLA SERRULATA
9 XANTHIDIUM ARMATUM
8 BULBOCHAETE NANA
1 TRICHOTRIA SIMILIS
1 COLLOTHECA ORNATA
10 LICMOPHORA TINCTA
1 LECANE LEONTINA
9 CALOCYLINDRUS CLEVEI
10 FRAGILLARIA SP.
8 MOUGEOTIA DIVARICATA
1 MONOMMATA LONGISETA
8 THOREA RAMOSISSIMA
5 HYDRA VIRIDIS
8 ZYGNEMA INSIGNE
7 PHILOTRIA CANADENSIS
8 CHAETOPHORA ELEGANS
1 EUCHLANIS PELLUCIDA
9 DOCIDIUM CORONATUM
1 NOTOMMATA COPEUS
7 UTRICULARIA VULGARIS
1 CONOCHILUS HIPPOCREPIS
1 COLURELLA DEFLEXA
1 MICRODODON CLAVUS
1 DICRANOPHORUS FORCIPATUS
1 ASCOMORPHA VOLVOCICOLA
9 SPHAEROZOSMA PULCHRUM
9 MICRASTERIAS NORDSTEDTIANUM
2 ALONA GLABRA
8 BULBOCHAETE MIRABILIS
1 FLOSCULARIA RINGENS
1 LEPADELLA OVALIS
1 STEPHANOCEROS FIMBRIATUS
9 BAMBUSINA BREBISSONI
5 HYDRA PALLIDA
1 OCTOTROCHA SPECIOSA

GROUP 1. ROTIFERA   GROUP 3. ARACHNIDA   GROUP 5. COELENTERA   GROUP 7. FLOWERING PLANTS   GROUP 9. DESMIDS
GROUP 2. CRUSTACEA   GROUP 4. INSECTA   GROUP 6. PROTOZOA   GROUP 8. ALGAE   GROUP 10. DIATOMS

ROTIFER GROUP SEEN THROUGH A MICROSCOPE

General view of the marine inhabitants found in one-half inch of pond-bottom. Rotifers are invisible to the human eye and the group represented is magnified one hundred diameters, or, cubically one million times. In the centre of the group is a spray of the bladder-wort (*Utricularia vulgaris*), a flesh-eating water plant which ensnares tiny rotifers and other creatures by means of its bladder-shaped traps spread diagonally across the field of vision

Plate II ROTIFERA

ROTIFER GROUP SHOWING MINUTE INHABITANTS OF A POND

Detail of microscopic life found in ½ in. of pond-bottom. The bladderwort (*Utricularia vulgaris*), a water plant, is seen on the right, showing a single "utricle" about the size of a pin head in the living plant. At its upper right margin is a trap door with a captured rotifer visible inside. The stem is covered with tiny algae. At the top, approximately in the centre, is shown a spherical colony of rotifers (*Conochilus hippocrepis*) which cling together by their stems, and below it, centre bottom, is a crescent-shaped desmid (*Closterium*)

swimming or gliding, in search of their food. The mouth is generally a little below the centre of the convex front of the head and the ciliated area, sometimes extending over various prominences, may be mainly before or mostly behind it. In certain species which only swim feebly by their ordinary cilia, these are often supplemented by auricles, small evertile pouches, one on each side of the head, lined with more powerful cilia. When the pouches are everted, these stronger cilia drive the rotifer along at greatly augmented speed. Other species rely almost entirely on their auricles. Certain footless species possess, besides the corona, from 2 to 12 leaping spines, attached to the "shoulders," which enable them, in emergencies, to spring suddenly several times their own length. In *Pedalia*, these spines are replaced by six limbs, having flattened ends fringed with stiff bristles.

FIG. 2.—A PELLET MAKING BDELLOID ROTIFER (HABROTROCHA LATA)

The corona is much more complicated in the evertile type, characteristic of the stationary or sessile, and of the bdelloid rotifers, two groups very different otherwise, but alike in that they do not sally forth to seek their food, but wait for it to be brought to them by external currents or by those set up by themselves. The sessile rotifers are unique among the class in having an immature stage, lasting some days. When hatched, the young animals, little resembling their parents, and having a very simple corona, swim about for a while. Having chosen a position they affix themselves (for life) by the foot, and as they grow, develop the evertile corona proper to the adult. They are mostly independent, but certain of them form communities by affixing themselves, when young, close to others. Sometimes such communities are attached to plant stems, sometimes they are free, the animals radiating from a common centre, and the community swimming through the water as a revolving sphere.

The ciliated area is mostly disposed as a band fringing a shallow disclike expansion, rounded, elliptic, heart-shaped, or two-, four-, or eight-lobed, into which the head opens as the corona unfolds. In one family the whole head opens out as a cup whose rim is drawn out into lobes beset with long hairlike setae arranged to form a living net, wherein the animals can draw their prey by the influence of cilia hidden in the depth of the cup. In one of the most beautiful of such forms, the "crown animalcule" (*Stephanoceros fimbriatus*), the rim is drawn out into erect arms with approximating tips and furnished with regularly placed tufts of cilia, closing the gaps between the arms and so forming a trap.

Among the bdelloids the corona consists mainly of two discs usually distinct, surmounting short pedicels arising from the back of the gaping mouth. The discs can be employed for swimming and for feeding while swimming, but most species feed when anchored by the foot, and when they desire to travel usually creep in leechlike manner; some exceptional species however, swim continuously, and some can not swim at all.

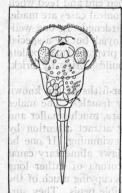

FIG. 3.—A HUNTING ROTIFER (MICROCODON CLAVUS)

In the typical form of the evertile corona, the cilia of the band fringing the upper surface of the lobes or discs are conspicuous and constitute the *trochus*. Almost parallel with it is another band, of much shorter cilia, the *cingulum*. Among the sessile species it passes round the under edge of the lobes or discs, and in the Bdelloida, round the bases of the pedicels and so to and around the lower lip on the inside, merging into the cilia of the mouth. Particles floating within reach of the trochus-cilia are struck by them within range of those of the cingulum, which in turn impel them to the mouth to be swallowed.

A curious illusory appearance of cogged wheels in rapid revolution, which greatly puzzled the early microscopists, is caused by the trochus-cilia. It happened that species showing this appearance were among the first rotifers discovered and that a long period elapsed before it was satisfactorily explained. Meanwhile it had led to all the known species being called "wheel animalcules" and thus to the later name of Rotifera (wheel-bearers) here employed. It is now believed that a succession of nerve-impulses, following each other at short and regular intervals, travel along the protoplasmic bases of the cilia, causing each of them, when reached, to lash violently downward.

Among the many-segmented bdelloids, the first two segments form the rostrum, a structure peculiar to the group; the rostral tip, specially adapted, is employed to affix the body when creeping, the mouth, on the third or oral segment, being then closed with the corona hidden within. When it is desired to feed or to swim, the mouth is opened, the corona pushed forth, and the rostrum, in a collapsed condition, is thrust to the back and kept there while the corona continues active.

Mastax.—The food of rotifers consists in most cases of floating particles, excessively minute fragments of plant or animal tissues, bacteria, etc., but there are numerous exceptions. Many of the hunting rotifers will pounce upon weaker forms and gulp them down, tear them to shreds or suck out the soft interiors. Others successfully attack small Cladocera, such as *Chydorus*, and test-dwelling rhizopods are sometimes invaded and eaten. The contents of a water-snail's egg or of confervoid cells are obtained by piercing the investing shell or cell-wall. Diatoms, swallowed whole, are a favourite food of many forms and the smaller flagellates are also in request. Among the sessile rotifers the trap-making species prey upon the lesser animalcules and also upon flagellates. When secured, the food is passed down a short, distensible gullet to the mastax, or jaws.

Important as are the functions of the mastax, they are by no means identical throughout the Rotifera, and the general plan of the organ has been very greatly modified in the various series of species according to the requirements of their respective habits of life. In itself the mastax is a complicated arrangement of seven principal hardened parts (adapted for biting, cutting, holding and crushing), of powerful muscles, of controlling nerves and tiny glands, all enclosed in a stout-walled chamber, into whose upper cavity the food is carried. Each hardened part varies greatly in size, shape and relative prominence in the combination, and the parts that are dominant in the mastaces of one series of species may be of secondary importance or even suppressed, in those of another series. The different forms of the mastax have been grouped under six leading types.

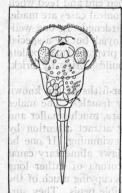

FIG. 4.—A SESSILE ROTIFER (PTYGURA STYGIS)

In the malleate type, figured in ventral aspect (fig. 5), the seven hardened parts are all present and of average development. In the centre is the *incus*, or anvil, comprising the *fulcrum*, or base (now viewed edgewise), to whose upper portion are hinged two *rami*, or branches, flattened parts whose free ends, mostly directed upward, open and shut like shears. In lateral view, the fulcrum appears as a moderately wide plate. It is secured strongly to the mastax wall and has no independent motion. Outside the rami, to right and left and further dorsalward, are two *mallei*, or hammers, each comprising a *manubrium*, or handle, nearly perpendicular, and an *uncus*, or striker, bent sharply inward toward its fellow, and often ending in fingerlike teeth. The two rami move in unison, as do also the two mallei, but generally independently of the rami. Only the two unci and the two rami come in contact with the food. This type of mastax obtains among numerous species of the hunting rotifers.

The other types can only be briefly indicated. In the virgate type, adapted for pumping, the manubria and the fulcrum are both elongate; the canal being distended, and its wall being supported by the hardened parts, a piston is supplied by a muscle. In the incudate, or seizing type, the whole incus (but especially the rami), is extremely developed; in the ramate, or bruising type, the unci are divided into several teeth and the fulcrum is reduced. The uncinate, or tearing type, has both manubria and fulcrum greatly reduced, while in the forcipate type, having somewhat elongate jaws, the mastax can be thrust forth from the mouth for at least half its length.

FROM HUDSON IN THE "QUARTERLY JOURNAL OF MICROSCOPICAL SCIENCE"
FIG. 5.—MALLEATE JAWS OF HUNTING ROTIFERA (BRACHIONUS SP.)

Stomach.—From the mastax the food passes next by a usually short oesophagus to the stomach, a fairly capacious organ, occupying in general a large part of the body cavity. It has a stout wall lined with cuticle, mostly ciliated, and on the outside a strong elastic covering. Between these is a dense layer of granular tissue, often divided into conspicuous cells and containing many oil globules. The interior of the stomach is mostly baglike, but in the bdelloid group it is generally narrowly tubular with a very thick wall and is baglike only in certain species, known as pellet makers, because, in their case, while the food passes through the oesophagus, it is agglutinated into small pellets before entry into the stomach. Though fairly numerous, such species are mostly small and dwell in mosses.

In one small group of hunting rotifers the stomach is blind and the undigested residue of food is returned to the mouth for ejectment. In others the stomach is divided into two portions, the lower of which functions as intestine, but usually that organ is a separate dilation of the food canal, following closely behind the stomach, and much smaller, with thinner walls. Thence the residue passes through a short cloaca to the dorsally placed anus, whose position marks generally the hinder limit of the trunk. A pair, or more, of small glands, which secrete digestive juices, are linked to the food canal near its entrance into the stomach.

Foot.—The foot has mostly a secondary role and many species get on very well without one. In others it is highly important and is frequently longer than the remainder of the body, serving for some as a rudder, for others as a balancer, or as a highly contractile stalk. In loricated species and in some others, its cuticle is mostly hardened and divided off into several segments, sometimes telescopically retractile. In certain species the skin covering the muscular and very flexible core of the foot falls into numerous annular wrinkles.

Among the sessile group the foot commonly ends in a blunt point by which the rotifer can attach itself in any selected position. Among other forms the extremity most frequently carries one, two, or more processes, known as toes, having great variety of form and diversity of function. There are two distinct types, one having a single piece, the other having two, the lower retractile within the upper. The latter type is normal among bdelloid species, which have two, three or four toes, but in some they are replaced by a kind of sucking disc. Among the hunting rotifers, the toes are always of one piece, sometimes furnished with somewhat clawlike tips. While many have but one, there are generally two, which may be alike in size and form, or very dissimilar. They may be straight, decurved or recurved, short or exceedingly long, slender or stout. Both types are hollow, with perforate tips, from which exudes a viscid secretion brought by tiny ducts from two glands in the upper foot, or lower trunk. By this secretion, the toes, or the sucking disc, or the blunt point of the sessile foot, are attached to any surface touched, but can be freed at will. Among the bdelloids, the second last segment has two dorsal processes resembling the toes of the hunting rotifers and called spurs to distinguish them. They are mostly short yet vary much in shape and pose.

Nervous System.—A nervous system is well developed. Within the head lies a large ganglion, or brain, which is mostly of flattened form. From thence nerve-threads pass down each side and to the eyes, the antennae and other sense-organs. The bdelloids and many of the hunting rotifers have a single antenna behind the head, sometimes of conspicuous length, but frequently very

minute. Others of the latter group and many of the sessile forms have two antennae on the head, and certain loricated species have one antenna on the head, and two more to right and left further to the rear. Finally, several largish species are furnished with four distinct antennae. There are often two eyes, either in front of the head or behind the brain, but a single eye is more usual, and while there are occasionally three, many species have none. When examined the eyes show mostly a crystalline particle backed by ruby-red pigment. Among secondary sense-organs frequently present may be mentioned the trochal setae of the bdelloids, and the tactile setae of the Synchaetidae and allied forms. In many species, notably in the great family Notommatidae, there is conspicuous in close contact with the brain, the so-called retro-cerebral organ, of three principal parts, viz.—a central pendulous sac stretching some way behind the ganglion, having its interior filled with coarsely granular matter usually somewhat opaque, and flanked by two glands, sometimes larger, sometimes smaller, than the central sac. In many of the swimming species the organ has not been detected, and its function is not yet certain.

Excretion and Secretion.—An excretory system is represented by a very slender, much convoluted tube, which passes down each side of the body from the head rearward. To the tubes are attached at intervals by short stalks a series of minute "flame-cells," taglike in form, hollow and closed at the free end and enclosing a pulsating bunch of cilia. The tags, which usually number five to each tube, but in certain Asplanchnae are greatly in excess of this, are believed to draw out from the body the effete fluids, which are carried either to the cloaca or to a collapsible bladder near, whence they are discharged at short intervals.

Besides the special muscles, which operate the motions of the mastax, there are numerous sinews, which pass freely through the body, each having its own course and office, and operate the movements of the several parts of the rotifer, apart altogether from those arising from ciliary action. The illoricated species, bdelloids and others, have also an exceptionally interesting system of muscles, nestling close under the skin, and somewhat difficult to see, but controlling the skin tension.

When there is no lorica, the skin-pores of the trunk exude a secretion, frequently so viscid that debris, etc., readily adhere to it. Sometimes this becomes a close-fitting coat, but it may be made into a loose case, often of flasklike shape, enclosing the rotifer, which can protrude its head from the open end and feed when it pleases. Among the sessile forms slightly conical cases are made, often of gelatinous substance, sometimes hardened. In one well-known species the skin secretion is not employed, but by a special organ connected with the corona, the rotifer prepares small pellets of unswallowed particles, and with these builds, brick by brick, a more permanent dwelling.

Reproductive Organs.—More than four-fifths of the known species of Rotifera are represented only by females. The males of the others are in most cases extremely rare, much smaller and somewhat unlike their own females. They attract attention by their restless, rapid and seemingly aimless swimming. If one be examined, it will generally be found minus jaws, alimentary canal or bladder, but having a very simplified corona of rather long cilia, and as sex organs, a great sperm-sac, occupying much of the body, a seminal duct and mostly a protrusible penis. They survive a very few days. No male has yet been found among Bdelloida. As sex organs the females have only the two-fold ovary, usually conspicuous in the trunk. The larger part, the yolk-mass, contains generally eight large nuclei and produces yolk material; the smaller and separated part, the germ-mass, containing germ-cells. Among the bdelloids and a small series of marine parasitic forms, there are two such ovaries; in all others one only. The combined organ is usually of ovoid shape, rarely elongate and bandlike. From the ovary a long, collapsible tube leads to the cloaca.

Reproduction is in general oviparous, sometimes ovoviviparous, the eggs being retained until the embryos are well advanced. Three kinds of eggs are produced, always by different females, (1) unfertilized or parthenogenetic, hatching in a few days, having a thin shell, and producing females (see PARTHENOGENESIS); (2)

male, much smaller, also thin-shelled and parthenogenetic, hatching promptly and producing males; (3) resting, as large as the unfertilized eggs but having a stouter shell, requiring fertilization and not hatching for a protracted period and then producing females, which later develop the ordinary unfertilized eggs. By means of the resting eggs, the species is carried over a danger period. Fertilization is internal; the males of certain species possess intromittent organs, but in other cases, the body-wall of the female is penetrated. The spermatozoa may be very large and in some species superficially resemble trypanosomes. (W. T. C.)

Ecology and Distribution.—The rotifers are among the most common fresh-water animals, living in almost any type of fresh-water habitat from hot springs with temperatures as high as 46°C. to arctic and antarctic pools where they are frozen for the greater part of the year. Certain types of bdelloids can withstand extreme desiccation lasting for weeks or months. On drying, they contract into the smallest possible volume and lose all but a minute trace of water, but there is no secretion of a protective cyst.

Most species of rotifers are cosmopolitan, but some probably have a limited distribution determined by the chemical and physical properties of the habitat.

The fresh-water rotifers are divisible into benthic, limnetic and sessile types. The benthic types, mostly of moderately elongated form with normal foot, crawl or swim about near the bottom or among aquatic plants, feeding on small organisms, or algae, diatoms and detritus. The limnetic rotifers, characteristic of the open waters of ponds and lakes throughout the world, exhibit certain common features as transparency; stout or sacciform shape; loss, reduction, or ventral displacement of the foot; carnivorous habits with grasping type of mastax; and occurrence of spines or other projections to lend buoyancy. Many limnetic rotifers, as species of *Keratella, Brachionus, Notholca* and *Asplanchna*, occur in a number of form varieties, with regard to length of spines and to body and head shape, and these may show cyclic recurrence in relation to seasonal conditions. The sessile rotifers such as *Floscularia, Collotheca, Stephanoceros*, etc., live attached throughout adult life to water plants and other objects. Their elegant trumpet form, with long stalklike foot and anterior end expanded into a circular, oval or lobed disc or cup, makes them among the most admired of microscopic objects (fig. 4). They feed on minute particles brought in by ciliary currents or on animals trapped in the cup. Besides these main ecological types, there are also commensal rotifers that habitually live in or on specific animals or plants and a few endoparasites with reduced corona inhabiting the intestine of annelid worms and slugs.

(L. H. H.)

SYSTEMATIC AFFINITIES

The systematic affinities of the Rotifera have been much discussed without any general measure of agreement being arrived at. Since C. G. Ehrenberg in 1838 distinguished them from the ciliate Protozoa they have been approximated in turn to nearly every one of the major divisions of the animal kingdom except the Chordata. In 1851 Huxley compared them with the free-swimming ciliated larvae of Annelids and, more particularly, of Echinoderms. In 1858, Semper's discovery of *Trochosphaera* gave fresh support to the comparison with the larvae of Annelids and for a long time the view that the Rotifera were persistent trochophores may be said to have held the field. In 1871 *Pedalion* was described by Hudson, and this remarkable form with its three pairs of hollow limbs moved by muscles, giving it a superficial resemblance to a crustacean Nauplius larva, revived an older view that the Rotifera were in some way related to the Arthropoda. E. R. Lankester included them with the Annelida and Arthropoda in his phylum Appendiculata. But the resemblances between *Trochosphaera* and the trochophore larva break down when examined in detail until little more is left than the common possession of a preoral ciliary wreath which they share with the Peritrichous Infusoria; and on the other hand the fact that two of the appendages of *Pedalion* are median and unpaired seems to preclude any close comparison with the other "Appendiculata." More recently C. Wesenberg-Lund and P. de Beauchamp have argued that the ciliary wreath is a secondary development and that the most primitive Rotifers are those like *Notommata* in which there is a ventral uniformly ciliated field surrounding the mouth. From these it is easy to pass to the ventrally ciliated Gastrotricha and to imagine the derivation of both from a uniformly ciliated Turbellarianlike stock.

With organisms like the Rotifera, however, where palaeontology can give no help, phylogeny must remain a matter of speculation. All that we can be sure of is that they are unsegmented Metazoa without definite mesoderm or coelom, with branching excretory canals furnished

with flame-cells and having a single pre-oral nerve-ganglion. They are, therefore, on the same grade of organization as the Platyhelminths and the early larvae of several groups of higher Metazoa. It is likely that the exact arrangement of the locomotive appendages, whether ciliary or appendicular, is without any important phylogenetic significance.

(W. T. C.)

CLASS ROTIFERA

Order 1. Seisonacea.—Rotifers of peculiar form, slender with long necks, inhabiting the marine crustacean *Nebalia*; sexes of equal size and like form; ovaries paired. Example, *Seison*.

Order 2. Ploima.—Free-swimming rotifers of normal form, with undivided terminal or ventral corona, not consisting of trochal and cingular circlets; foot with usually two toes; ovary single; males more or less reduced in size and structure; mastax various. Examples, *Notommata, Proales, Synchaeta, Trichocerca, Euchlanis, Brachionus, Lecane, Asplanchna*, etc.

Order 3. Flosculariacea.—Sessile or swimming rotifers, with more or less lobed corona of trochal and cingular circlets; toes lacking; mastax malleoramate; ovary single; males free-swimming, greatly reduced. Examples, *Floscularia (=Melicerta), Conochilus, Limnias, Pedalia, Filinia (=Triarthra), Trochosphaera*.

Order 4. Collothecacea.—Mostly sessile rotifers with large funnel-like corona, often lobed, lacking a ciliary border in some forms; mastax uncinate; toes wanting; ovary single; males free-swimming, greatly reduced. Examples, *Collotheca (=Floscularia), Stephanoceros, Cupelopagis (=Apsilus)*.

Order 5. Bdelloida.—Benthonic rotifers with jointed cuticle; both ends retractile into the trunk joints; corona of two trochal discs, set on pedicels, their bases encircled by the cingulum; two ovaries; mastax ramate; toes often present; males wanting. Examples, *Philodina, Rotifer, Callidina, Habrotrocha*.

BIBLIOGRAPHY.—P. de Beauchamp, "Morphologie et variations de l'appareil rotateur dans la serie des Rotifères," *Arch. Zool. Exp. Gén.*, 36 (1907); idem, "Recherches sur les Rotifères: les formations tégumentaires et l'appareil digestif," *Arch. Zool. Exp. Gén.*, 40 (1909); H. K. Harring, "Synopsis of the Rotatoria," *Bull. U.S. Natl. Mus.*, no. 71 (1913); H. K. Harring, and F. J. Myers, "The Rotifer fauna of Wisconsin," *Trans. Wis. Acad. Sci.*, 20, 21, 22, 23 (1924–1930); L. M. Hickernell, "A study of desiccation in the rotifer *Philodina roseola*," *Biol. Bull.*, 32 (1917); C. T. Hudson and P. H. Gosse, *The Rotifera or Wheel-animalcules*, London (1886–1889); F. J. Myers, "The Rotifer fauna of Wisconsin," *Trans. Wis. Acad. Sci.*, 25 (1930); A. Remane, "Rotatoria" in H. G. Bronn (ed.), *Klassen und Ordnungen des Tier-Reichs*, Band IV, Abt. I, Buch 1 (1929); C. Wesenberg-Lund, "Contributions to the biology of the Rotifera, I and II," *Danske Vidensk. Selsk. Skrifter, Natur. Math. Afd.*, 8, R. 4, Bind 4 (1923) and 9, R. 2, Bind 1 (1930); "Rotatoria" in W. Kükenthal and T. Krumbach (eds.), *Handbuch der Zoologie*, Band 2, Hälfte 1. (L. H. H.)

ROTOGRAVURE: *see* PHOTOGRAVURE (MACHINE).

ROTOR SHIP. Wind propulsion for navigational purposes, in the commonly accepted sense, although suited for some particular trades, is practically obsolete for cargo carrying; and the sailing ship, pure and simple, cannot be said to have a definite future. Many sailing vessels are fitted with auxiliary propelling machinery, but, excluding fishing craft, these vessels have not proved an unqualified success.

Anton Flettner, the inventor of the rotor ship, originally intended to construct ships with metal sails, being convinced that the effect of metal sails is much greater than that of canvas sails. The idea was to build the metal sails with sections similar to those used in the construction of aircraft planes. It was intended that the sails should revolve freely around a pivot mast, and then be put by a special rudder blade in such a position that the wind would drive the ship ahead.

Experiments were carried out at the University of Göttingen, Germany, with canvas sails, metal sails and model ships. The result of these experiments showed that the effect of metal sails could be made approximately double that of canvas sails, a necessary condition being, however, that a third part of the sail area should be turnable. Designs were got out, but the plans did not materialize.

In the case of the rotor ship the inventor states that it is not intended to drive ships solely by wind rotors, but that they shall serve as an auxiliary power upon steam and motor vessels. In the vessel under discussion, the power of the wind is not made use of by sails, but by means of large metal cylinders.

Revolving Cylinders.—In 1922 experiments were carried out at Göttingen with revolving cylinders, and it was then discovered that the pressure exerted upon a cylinder revolving in an air current was considerably greater than had been supposed. Actually, the power exerted on a normal cylinder was about four or five times as large as that on a normal sail. When, however, discs of a larger diameter were provided at the ends of the cylinders, it was found possible to increase the effect to nine or ten times the amount of wind effect in the normal sail. One condition for this, however, is that the revolving speed of the cylinders is about 3 to 4½ times as great as that of the wind. An ordinary sailing vessel requires to take down all her canvas in a hurricane, but the rotor ship could continue sailing, with more stability for manoeuvring.

The vessel selected for the first tests was the three-masted schooner "Buckau." She had a displacement of 960 tons, and was fitted with an auxiliary motor of some 200 horse-power. The canvas rig of the vessel was dismantled, and in place of the fore and third masts, two very strong masts were erected. The new masts were shorter, being 42ft. in height. These masts were provided with bearings at the upper and lower ends to allow for the free rotation of the cylinders, which were placed over the masts. The cylinders were fitted with discs at either end, the discs being of greater diameter than the cylinders, but built as a part of them. In this particular case the cylinders are of sheet steel of 0·04in. thickness.

Naturally, the whole structure is suitably stiffened. The cylinders are rotated by means of electromotors, which will give the towers a speed of 125rev. per minute. Circumferential speed is approximately 60ft. per sec., and the power required to rotate the towers is nine horse-power. For working the plant one man only at the switch-board is required. By altering the circumferential speed of one or other of the cylinders the operator can correspondingly change the pressure exerted by the wind upon this, and so alter the vessel's course. When cruising, changing the wind side can be effected solely by the towers, when the ship can be stopped and driven astern.

The Magnus-effect.—The explanation of the phenomenon of the rotor ship may be traced to the so-called *Magnus-effect*, explained in 1853 by Prof. Magnus of Berlin, who found that a special power is exerted by an air current upon a revolving cylinder. The explanation of the reason for this effect was found, after more than 20 years of investigation, to be briefly as follows: When a cylinder revolves, the nearest stratum of air revolves with the cylinder, owing to the friction of the cylinder being much greater than the friction of the air molecules against each other. The nearest stratum induces the next one also to revolve, but, naturally, this is done at a much slower speed. In the same manner the strata lying more distantly from the cylinder are moved more and more slowly, until at a certain distance the influence stops. If such a rotating cylinder is impinged upon by an air current, the speed of which is slower than the circumferential speed of the cylinder, the streamlines are directed, so that at one side the air is rarefied by the frictional effect of the cylinder, and at the other side it is compressed. These changes of pressure are the causes of the *Magnus-effect*, and they create a power in a direction away from the side of the rarefied air, and through the centre of the densest air patch, or side in which the streamlines are compressed. Actually the real direction of the power is not always at right angles to the wind direction, but diverges in a measure which is dependent on the speed ratio of the wind current to that of the circumferential speed of the cylinder.

The sea-going trial of the rotor ship "Buckau," from Germany to the Forth, was claimed to be successful, but little has since been heard of the subject.

See *Marine Engineer Officers' Magazine* (Jan. 1925).

(F. J. D.)

ROTORUA, a town of Rotorua county, North Island, New Zealand. It lies in the midst of a remarkable volcanic district generally known as the Hot Spring district, which covers an area of 660 sq.m. and extends 160 m. from north-east to south-west from White Island, an active volcanic cone in the Bay of Plenty to the mountains of Tongariro, Ngaruhoe and Ruapehu in the interior of the island, S.W. of lake Taupo. Rotorua attracts many visitors on account of the beauty and scientific interest of the

locality and the bathing in its various medicinal springs. It is a scattered township lying on the south-western shore of lake Rotorua, amid hills reaching 2,600 ft. in the immediate neighbourhood, with a rich growth of forest. Pop. (1936) 6,531.

The springs are principally alkaline, alkaline and siliceous, acidic, or acidic and hepatic (sulphurous). The township includes the Maori village of Ohinemutu, an interesting collection of native dwellings. In the vicinity, on the lake-shore, is the government sanatorium. One mile south of the Rotorua is another native village, Whakarewarewa, where there are geysers as well as hot springs. Four miles from Rotorua, near the centre of the lake, the island of Mokoia rises to 1,518 ft. A short channel connects lake Rotorua with lake Rotoiti to the N.E. Both this lake and the smaller ones to the east, Rotoehu and Rotoma, have deeply indented shores, and are set in exquisite scenery. The waters of Rotoma are of a particularly vivid blue. To the south of Rotoiti is Tikitere, a sombre valley abounding in mud volcanoes, springs and other active volcanic phenomena. Mount Tarawera (16 m. S.E. of Rotorua) is noted for the eruption of June 1886, which changed the outline of several lakes, destroyed the famous Pink and White terraces on the adjoining lake Rotomahana.

ROTROU, JEAN DE (1609–1650), French tragic poet, born at Dreux on Aug. 19 or 20, 1609, became in 1632 playwright to the Hôtel de Bourgogne company. He was three years younger than Corneille, but began writing plays earlier than his great contemporary, for his first play *L'Hypochondriaque*, was printed in 1631. Most of his earlier plays were adaptations from the Spanish of Lope de Vega and by 1634 he is said to have produced 34 pieces. The importance of Rotrou in French dramatic literature lies in the fact that he sought to naturalize the romantic English and Spanish comedy in France, where the tragedies of Seneca and the comedies of Terence were still the only accepted models. *Diane* (acted 1630; pr. 1633), *Les Occasions perdues* (acted 1631; pr. 1635), praised by Richelieu; and *L'Heureuse Constance* (acted 1631; pr. 1635); praised by Anne of Austria, were all in the Spanish manner, but in *Les Menechines* (pr. 1636), and in *Hercule Mourant* (pr. 1636) he followed the Latin authors Plautus and Seneca. In 1639 Rotrou bought the post of *lieutenant particulier au bailliage* at Dreux, where he married and settled. His four masterpieces were written after that date; they are: *Le Véritable Saint Genest* (acted 1646; pr. 1648), a story of Christian martyrdom containing some amusing by-play, one noble speech and a good deal of dignified action; *Don Bertrand de Cabrère* (1647), a tragi-comedy; *Venceslas* (1647; pr. 1648); *Cosroès* (1649), a play with an oriental setting, claimed as the only absolutely original piece of Rotrou. He died of the plague and was buried at Dreux on June 28, 1650.

A complete edition of Rotrou was edited in five volumes by Viollet le Duc in 1822. In 1882 M. de Ronchaud published a handsome edition of six plays—*Saint Genest, Venceslas, Don Bertrand de Cabrère Antigone, Hercule Mourant* and *Cosroès. See further J. Jarry, Essai sur les oeuvres dramatiques de Jean Rotrou* (Paris and Lille, 1868); Léonce Person, *Hist. du Venceslas de Rotrou, suivie de notes critiques et biographiques* (1882), in which many legends about Rotrou are discredited; *Hist. du véritable Saint Genest de Rotrou* (1882), *Les Papiers de Pierre Rotrou de Saudreville* (1883); Henri Chardon, *La Vie de Rotrou mieux connue* (1884); and Georg Steffens, *Jean de Rotrou als Nachahmer Lope de Vega's* (1891).

ROTTERDAM, a city of the Netherlands in the province of South Holland, on both banks of the New Maas, at the confluence of the canalized Rotte, and a junction station 14½ mi. by rail S.S.E. of The Hague. The population of the city, the principal Dutch port, was about 20,000 in 1632; 53,212 in 1796; 105,858 in 1860; 379,017 in 1905 and 612,372 in 1940.

Rotterdam probably owes its existence to two castles, which existed in feudal times. In 1299 John I, count of Holland, granted to the people of Rotterdam the same rights as were enjoyed by the burghers of Beverwijk, which were identical with those of Haarlem (K. Hegel, *Städte und Gilden*, 1891, Bd. ii). This privilege marks the origin of the town. It continued to increase in size, various extensions of its boundaries being made, and its trading importance is to a large extent the result of its commercial intercourse with England. Its shipping facilities made it the first commercial city of Holland, and the third largest port on the continent. By means of the New Waterway (1869–90) to the Hook of Holland it is accessible for the largest ships. Ships drawing 24 ft. can come up at any time, and those drawing 24 to 33 ft. at high water. The length of the quays is about 16 mi. The river is spanned by a road bridge (1878) and a railway bridge (1877) passing from the Boompjes to the North Island, whence they are continued to the farther shore by swing-bridges through which the largest ships can pass to the upper river. These bridges prove useful in breaking up the ice which forms above them in winter. On the south side of the river are numerous large docks and wharves, which were enlarged after World War I, while the city proper on the north side consists of a labyrinth of basins and canals with tree-bordered quays. These were bombed systematically by the Germans during the invasion of May 10–14, 1940, and later by the Allied air forces.

In the centre of the town is the Beursplein or Exchange square. Behind the exchange is the great market-place, built on vaulting over a canal, and containing a bronze statue of Erasmus, who was born in Rotterdam in 1467. The statue is the work of Hendrik de Keyser, and was erected in 1622 to replace an older one. Beyond the market-place is the High street, which runs along the top of the Maas dyke. On the west of the city a pretty road leads from the zoological gardens (1857), on the north to a small park, which contains a statue of the popular poet Hendrik Tollens (d. 1856), a native of the city. Among the churches of Rotterdam is an English church, originally built by the 1st duke of Marlborough, whose arms may be seen with the royal arms over the entrance. The Groote Kerk, or Laurens Kerk (end of the 15th century), contains a fine brass screen (1715), a celebrated organ with nearly 5,000 pipes, and the monuments of Admiral Witte de Witte (d. 1658), and other Dutch naval heroes. In the new market adjoining is a fountain adorned with sculptures erected in 1874 to commemorate the jubilee of the restoration of Dutch independence (1813). The museums of the city comprise an ethnographical museum, the maritime museum established by the yacht club in 1874, and the Boymans museum (1867) containing pictures, drawings and engravings, as well as the town library. Of the original collection of pictures bequeathed by F. J. O. Boymans in 1847, more than half was destroyed by fire in 1864; but the collection has been enlarged since and is representative of both ancient and modern artists. In 1935 the Boymans museum was erected outside the business centre of the city. It contains some of the most famous masterpieces of Dutch art and an extremely fine collection of old delft china. Close to the museum is a statue of the statesman Gysbert Karel van Hogendorp (1762–1834), a native of the city. Among the remaining buildings must be mentioned the old town hall (17th century; restored 1823), the new town hall, the concert-hall of the "Harmonic" club, the record office (1900), the *leeskabinet,* or subscription library and reading-rooms, and the ten-storied *Witte Huis* (1897), which is used for offices and is one of the highest private buildings on the continent.

On May 14, 1940, shortly after the Dutch had ceased resistance to the German invaders, enemy bombers completely destroyed the business centre of Rotterdam. An estimated 25,000–30,000 people were killed in the raid.

The industries comprise the manufacture of tobacco, cigars, margarine, rope, leather, etc., and there are breweries, distilleries and sugar refineries. Shipbuilding yards extend above and below the city, one of the earliest being that of the Netherlands Steamboat company (1825). It is, however, as a commercial rather than as a manufacturing city that Rotterdam became distinguished, its progress in this respect having been very striking. Between 1850 and 1902 the area of the port was increased from 96 to more than 300 acres.

Rotterdam ordinarily has a great transit trade of goods in bulk, and, besides its maritime trade, it has an extensive river traffic. Its overseas trade is principally with the Dutch colonies, New York, La Plata and the east and west coasts of Africa. The great harbour works on the south side of the river required to accommodate this growing trade were planned by Stieltjes (d. 1878).

ROTTWEIL, German town, in the Swabian Alps of Württemberg, on the Neckar, 46 mi. S.W. of Tübingen by rail. Pop. (1939) 12,977. In the 13th century Rottweil became a free imperial city and was subsequently the seat of an imperial court of law, the jurisdiction of which extended over Swabia, the Rhineland and Alsace. The functions of this tribunal came to an end in 1784. In 1803 Rottweil passed into the possession of Württemberg. It is partly surrounded by walls, and has a mediaeval town hall. The Gothic Heilige-Kreuz-kirche, built in the 14th century, was restored in 1840, and the Capellen-kirche has a Gothic spire.

ROTUMA: *see* PACIFIC ISLANDS: *Tonga.*

ROUBAIX, a manufacturing town of northern France, in the department of Nord, 6 mi. N.E. of Lille on the railway to Ghent. Pop. (1947) 100,978. Roubaix is about 1 mi. from the Belgian frontier on the Roubaix canal, which connects the lower Deule with the Scheldt by way of the Marcq and the Espierre. It unites with Wattrelos (pop. 28,796) to form a great industrial centre. The prosperity of Roubaix had its origin in the first factory franchise granted in 1469 by Charles the Bold, duke of Burgundy, to Peter, lord of Roubaix, a descendant of the royal house of Brittany. In the 18th century Roubaix suffered from the jealousy of Lille, of which it was a dependency, and not till the 19th century did its industries acquire importance. During World War I Roubaix was in the hands of the Germans, and the factories were emptied. As the mills were largely spared, work was started again with government help and bank credits in 1919.

The chief business is the woollen manufacture, but cotton, silk and other materials are also produced. The chief of these are fancy and figured stuffs for garments, velvet and upholstering fabrics. There are wool-combing and wool-dressing works, spinning and weaving mills, dyehouses and printing works, rubber-works, metal foundries and machinery works in the town.

ROUBILIAC (more correctly ROUBILLAC), **LOUIS FRANÇOIS** (1695–1762), French sculptor, was born at Lyons and became a pupil of Balthasar of Dresden and of N. Coustou. It is generally stated that he settled in London about 1720, but as he took the second grand prize for sculpture in 1730, while still a pupil of Coustou, it is unlikely that he visited England at an earlier date. The date 1744, as given by Dussieux, is incorrect. He was at once patronized by Walpole and soon became the most popular sculptor in England, superseding the success of the Fleming Rysbraeck and even of Scheemakers. He died on the 11th of January 1762, and was buried in the church of St. Martin-in-the-Fields. Roubiliac was largely employed for portrait statues and busts, and especially for sepulchral monuments. His chief works in Westminster abbey are the monuments of Handel, Admiral Warren, Marshal Wade, Mrs. Nightingale and notably that of the duke of Argyll, which established his fame. He possessed skill in portraiture and was technically a master, but lived at a time when his art had sunk to a low ebb. His figures are frequently uneasy, devoid of dignity and sculpturesque breadth, and his draperies treated in a manner more suited to painting than sculpture. There are, however, noteworthy exceptions, his bust of Pope, for example, reaching a high standard.

His most celebrated work, the Nightingale monument, in Westminster abbey, a marvel of technical skill, is saved from being ludicrous by its ghastly and even impressive hideousness. The celebrated bust of Shakespeare, known as the Davenant bust, in the possession of the Garrick Club, London, is his.

See Le Roy de Sainte-Croix, *Vie et ouvrages de L. F. Roubillac, sculpteur lyonnais (1695–1762)* (Paris, 1882). (An extremely rare work, of which a copy is in the National Art library, Victoria and Albert museum, South Kensington, London.) Allan Cunningham, *The Lives of the Most Eminent British Painters, Sculptors, and Architects,* vol. 3, pp. 31–67 (London, 1830)—the fount of information of later biographies. (M. H. S.)

ROUBLE. The rouble is the monetary unit of Russia (U.S.S.R.). It is divided into 100 kopecks, and is either gold, silver or paper. Kopecks are either silver, bronze or copper. The par of exchange with sterling before World War I was: R.10=21s. 2d. The main currency in circulation between 1863 and 1921 was credit notes issued by the state bank. Towards the end of the

19th century, these depreciated sharply in relation to gold. A law of 1897 stabilized the paper rouble at 66⅔ kopecks in gold. The credit note was maintained at this ratio until World War I. On July 1, 1914, there were 500,000,000 gold roubles, 230,000,000 silver roubles and 1,630,000,000 roubles in credit notes in circulation. The gold cover was higher than 100%, and under normal conditions the monetary system would have been stable. But Russia, like certain other countries, faced with huge expenditures in connection with financing the war, resorted to the issue of paper money. The resultant inflation ruined the stability of the monetary system. By the end of 1915, 9,097,000,000 roubles were in circulation, and on Nov. 1, 1917, some 19,000,000,000 roubles (paper money) with a gold cover of one-fifth of their value.

Under the influence of war and revolution, followed by economic chaos, inflation developed at a terrific pace, and the value of the paper rouble fell catastrophically. By Jan. 1, 1921, the total issue of paper money had reached 1,168,000,000,000 roubles and on Oct. 1, 1921, 4,529,428,000,000 roubles. In 1921, the soviet government introduced the "new economic policy," one of the most important achievements of which was the creation of a stable monetary system and the restoration of the state bank. The monetary reform was accomplished in two stages. On Oct. 11, 1922, the state bank created a new currency—the *chervonetz*. The chervonetz was equal to ten prewar roubles, and its fine gold content was established at 7.74234 grams. The notes were issued in denominations of 1, 3, 5, 10, 25 and 50 chervontsi. The obligatory cover was established at 25% gold, platinum or stable foreign currency, and 75% in easily realizable commodities, short-term bills and other short-term bonds. Simultaneously, the old paper currency was maintained in circulation. As compared with the chervonetz, its value fell steadily. On March 10, 1924, the rate of redemption was defined at 50,000,000,000 roubles of the old denomination in one rouble in gold, *i.e.*, one chervonetz rouble. The depreciation of the old rouble created instability in the budget and in the entire economy. Between February and June 1924, a series of decrees was passed constituting the second phase of the monetary reform. The old soviet rouble was withdrawn from circulation by means of an exchange on fixed rates against the new treasury roubles, issued in denominations of 1, 3 and 5 roubles. The new rouble was made legal tender. The volume of issue of the treasury roubles was limited to no higher than 50% of the chervontsi in circulation.

Towards the end of 1924, a ratio of ten new roubles to the chervonetz was established, and after that the monetary system consisted of chervontsi (bank notes), paper roubles (treasury notes) and various coins. On Oct. 1, 1924, the currency in circulation totalled 49,000,000 roubles in silver, 346,000,000 in bank notes and 202,000,000 in treasury notes. This made a total circulation, including various small coinage, of 622,000,000 roubles.

After the reform of 1924, the monetary system in the soviet union acquired a stable character. Although on several occasions (1926, 1928, 1930, 1933) the stepping-up in the issuing of notes for financing industrialization, collectivization and defense industry caused inflationary fluctuations of the rouble, on the whole, the monetary system remained unshaken and the soviet government, through relatively speedy control measures, maintained the rate of the rouble. After the monetary reform, there was further established in the U.S.S.R. a system of stable deficitless budget. On April 1, 1936, after the devaluation of world currencies (the dollar and the pound), the soviet government established the fine gold content of the rouble at 0.1776 grams, instead of 0.77423 grams as theretofore. The total amount of money in circulation on Jan. 1, 1937, was 11,255,000,000 roubles, including 8,020,000,000 roubles in state bank notes, 2,801,000,000 roubles in treasury notes and 435,000,000 in coin. The strengthening of the economic system (monopoly of foreign trade, prohibition upon the export of currency, stabilization of the budget system, introduction of domestic checking accounts, strict regulation of the volume of merchandise and money in circulation), and, to a certain extent, the rapid growth of gold production, all contributed to the strengthening of the soviet monetary system. Although the soviet rouble is not quoted on the world stock exchange, its stability at home made it possible to finance the five-year plans of industrial-

ization and to increase the soviet union's defensive capacity. The commissariat of finance periodically publishes the official foreign exchange rates, according to which it conducts payments on foreign trade. In order to arrest inflation which had developed in the U.S.S.R. during World War II, the Soviet government on Dec. 14, 1947, established a new currency; one new rouble was exchanged for ten roubles of the old currency. Under the revaluation of the rouble of Feb. 28, 1950, the rate of exchange was set at 11.20 to the pound sterling and 4.00 to the U.S. dollar. (*See also* RUSSIA: *Economic and Financial Conditions*.)   (A. A. Y.; X.)

ROUEN, a city of France, capital of the department of Seine-Inférieure and the ancient capital of the province of Normandy, on the Seine, 87 mi. N.W. of Paris by rail. Pop. (1946) 107,739.

History.—*Ratuma* or *Ratumacos,* the Celtic name of Rouen, was modified by the Romans into *Rotomagus,* and by the writers of mediaeval Latin into *Rodomum,* of which the present name is a corruption. Under Caesar and the early emperors the town was the capital of the Veliocasses, and it did not attain to any eminence till it was made the centre of Lugdunensis Secunda at the close of the 3rd century, and later the seat of an archbishop. Rouen owed much to its first bishops—from St. Mello, the apostle of the region, who flourished about 260, to St. Remigius, who died in 772.

Under Louis le Débonnaire and his successors, the Normans several times sacked the city, but after the treaty of St. Clair-sur-Epte in 912, Rouen became the capital of Normandy and the principal residence of the dukes. In 1087 William the Conqueror, mortally wounded at Mantes, died at Rouen. The succeeding Norman kings of England tended to neglect Rouen in favour of Caen and afterwards of Poitiers, Le Mans and Angers; but it maintained an importance during the 12th century indicated by the building of churches, notably that of St. Ouen. In 1203 Rouen was the scene of the murder of Arthur of Brittany at the hands of King John of England. Ostensibly to avenge the crime, Philip Augustus invaded Normandy and entered the capital unopposed. Philip confirmed its communal privileges and built a new castle.

A convention between the merchants of Rouen and those of Paris relating to the navigation of the Seine was followed by treaties with London, with the Hanseatic towns and with Flanders and Champagne. In 1302 the seat of the exchequer or sovereign court, afterward the parlement, of Normandy was definitely fixed at Rouen. A stubborn resistance was offered to Henry V of England, who after a long siege occupied the town in 1419. The prosperity of Rouen continued under the English domination, and during this period the greater part of the church of St. Ouen was constructed. In 1431 Joan of Arc was tried and burned in the city. From that year the French began attempts to recapture the town, which they did in 1449. During the close of the 15th century and the first half of the 16th, Rouen was a metropolis of art and taste. In 1562 the town was sacked by the Protestants. This did not prevent the league from gaining so firm a footing there that Henry IV besieged it unsuccessfully, and only obtained entrance after his abjuration. The revocation of the edict of Nantes in 1685 greatly affected Rouen. During the Franco-German War the city was occupied by the invaders from Dec. 1870 till July 1871. In World War I Rouen played a great part in the supporting organization of the British army in France.

Monuments.—The old city lies on the north bank of the river in an amphitheatre formed by the hills which border the Seine valley. It is surrounded by the suburbs of Martainville, St. Hilaire, Beauvoisine, Bouvreuil and Cauchoise; 2½ mi. east is the industrial town of Darnétal (pop. 1946, 7,604), and on the opposite bank of the Seine is the manufacturing suburb of St. Sever with the industrial towns of Sotteville (pop. 18,469) and Le Petit Quevilly (pop. 19,953) in its immediate neighbourhood. Finally in the centre of the river, northeast of St. Sever, is the Ile Lacroix, which also forms part of Rouen. Communication across the Seine is maintained by three bridges, including a *pont transbordeur,* or moving platform, slung between two lofty columns and propelled by electricity. The central point of the old town is the *Place de l'Hôtel de Ville,* occupied by the church of St. Ouen and the *hôtel de ville.*

The cathedral was built on the site of a previous cathedral

burned in 1200, and its construction lasted from the beginning of the 13th century (lateral doors of the west portal), to the beginning of the 16th century (Tour de Beurre). The western façade belongs, as a whole, to the Flamboyant style. But the northern tower, the Tour St. Romain, is in the main of the 12th century, its upper stage having been added later. The southern tower, the Tour de Beurre, so named because funds for its building were given in return for the permission to eat butter in Lent, is of a type essentially Norman, and consists of a square tower pierced by high mullioned windows and surmounted by a low, octagonal structure, with a balustrade and pinnacles. These contrasted towers are the most striking feature of the wide façade. The portals of the transept are each flanked by two towers. The most remarkable part of the interior is the Lady Chapel (1302–20) behind the choir with the tombs (1518–25) of Cardinal Georges d'Amboise and his nephew, the statuary of which is of the finest Renaissance workmanship. Behind the cathedral is the archiepiscopal palace, a building of the 14th and 15th centuries.

St. Ouen was formerly the church of an abbey dating to the Roman period and reorganized by Archbishop St. Ouen in the 7th century. It was founded in 1318 in place of a Romanesque church which previously occupied the site and of which the only relic is the chapel in the south transept. The choir alone was built in the 14th century. The nave of the church belongs to the 15th century, by the end of which the central tower with its octagonal lantern and four flanking turrets had been erected. The western façade dates from 1846. The large stained glass windows are of the 14th, 15th and 16th centuries. The Portail des Marmousets, the entrance to the south transept, has a projecting porch, behind and above which rises a magnificent rose window. The north façade has no entrance.

The church of St. Maclou, behind the cathedral, begun in 1437 and finished early in the 16th century, is a rich example of the Flamboyant style, and has a rich portal with five arched openings. It is celebrated for carving attributed to Jean Goujon.

The church of St. Vincent, near the Seine, is a building of the 16th century and contains very fine stained-glass windows at the end of the north aisle, by Engrand and Jean le Prince, artists of Beauvais. The stained glass in the churches of St. Patrice (16th century) and St. Godar (late 15th century) is inferior only to that of St. Vincent.

The most important secular building in Rouen is the Palais de Justice, once the seat of the exchequer and, later, of the *parlement* of Normandy. It is in the late Gothic style and consists of a main building flanked by two wings. The left wing, known as the Salle des Procureurs, was built in 1493 and has a lofty barrel-roof of timber. South of the Palais de Justice is the Porte de la Grosse Horloge, an arcade spanning the street and surmounted by a large clock of the 15th century with two dials. The Tour de la Grosse Horloge, which rises beside the arcade, was built in 1389. The tower known as the Tour de Jeanne d'Arc was the scene of her trial, and is all that remains of the castle built by Philip Augustus early in the 13th century. The Porte Guillaume-Lion, opening on to the Quai de Paris, is a handsome gateway built in 1749.

Rouen is the seat of an archbishop, a prefect, a court of appeal and a court of assizes, and headquarters of the III. army corps. Its public institutions also include a tribunal of first instance, tribunals of commerce and of maritime commerce, a board of trade-arbitrators and a chamber of commerce. All the more important nations have consulates in the city.

Rouen is an important centre for trade in wines, spirits, grain and cattle. Grain, wine, coal, timber and petroleum are leading imports. Besides its manufactures it exports plaster and sand. The principal industries of Rouen and its district are the spinning and weaving of cotton, notably the manufacture of *rouenneries* (cotton fabric woven with dyed yarn), the printing and dyeing of the manufactured material and the spinning of other fibres; shipbuilding and the making of various articles of clothing are also carried on, and there are distilleries, petroleum-refineries and manufactories of chemicals, soap, machinery, carding-combs and brushes. The port of Rouen comprises the marine docks below the Boïeldieu bridge, and the river dock, the timber dock and the

petroleum dock above it. There is also a repairing dock. The Seine is tidal beyond Rouen. The port is accessible for ships drawing 19½ to 25 ft. of water, and its quays have a superficial area of about 194 acres. It is served by the lines of the Orléans, the Ouest-État and the Northern railways and these, in addition to the waterways connected with the Seine, make Rouen a convenient centre for the distribution of merchandise.

See A. Chervel, *Histoire de Rouen pendant l'époque communale* (Rouen, 1843); *id., Sous la domination anglaise* (Rouen, 1840); C. Enlart, *Rouen* (Paris, 1904); J. Levainville, *Rouen.*

ROUERGUE, formerly a French province, derives its name from the Gallic tribe of the *Rutheni.* It was bounded on the north by Auvergne, on the south and south-west by Languedoc, on the east by Gévaudan and the Cévennes and on the west by Quercy. It included (1) the county of Rodez, (2) Haute and Basse Marche; and it was divided between the dioceses of Rodez and Vabres (province d'Alby after this province had been separated from that of Bourges in 1678). Administratively it formed first a *sénéchaussée*, dependent on Languedoc (capital Villefranche, in the Basse Marche), and later it was attached to the military governments of Guienne and Gascony. It was then part of the departments of Aveyron and of Tarn-et-Garonne.

ROUGE, a French name applied to various colouring substances of a brilliant carmine tint, especially when used as cosmetics. The best of these preparations have for their basis carthamine, obtained from the safflower (*q.v.*), *Carthamus tinctorius.* (*See* COLCOTHAR; PAINTS, CHEMISTRY OF; COSMETICS.)

ROUGET DE LISLE, CLAUDE JOSEPH (1760–1836), French author, was born on May 10, 1760, at Lons-le-Saunier (Jura). He entered the army as an engineer, and attained the rank of captain. The song which has immortalized him, the *Marseillaise,* was composed at Strasbourg, where Rouget de Lisle was quartered in April 1792. He wrote both words and music in a fit of patriotic excitement after a public dinner. The piece was at first called *Chant de guerre de l'armée du Rhin,* and only received its name of *Marseillaise* from its adoption by the Provençal volunteers whom Barbaroux introduced into Paris, and who were prominent in the storming of the Tuileries. The author was a moderate republican, and was cashiered and thrown into prison; but the counter-revolution set him at liberty. He died at Choisy-le-Roi (Seine et Oise) on June 26, 1836. Rouget de Lisle published *Chants français* (1825), in which he set to music fifty songs by various authors. His *Essais en vers et en prose* (1797) contains the *Marseillaise,* a prose tale of the sentimental kind called *Adélaïde et Monville,* and some occasional poems.

See J. Tiersot, *Histoire de la Marseillaise: oeuvres musicales de Rouget de Lisle* (1915).

ROUGH CAST, in architecture, a term used in England for any stucco or mortar combined with gravel and sand, employed as the finishing coat of covering plaster over a rough structure of masonry, and frequently decorated by the addition of pebbles of different colours, or even small pieces of glass. In American usage the term is limited to the rougher textures of a stucco surface, obtained either by throwing on the finished coat in unequal masses or by sprinkling over the finished surface, while still wet, a coating of coloured pebbles, tile or brick fragments, marble chips, etc.

ROUHER, EUGÈNE (1814–1884), French statesman, was born at Riom (Puy-de-Dôme) on Nov. 30, 1814. He entered the Chamber in his native department in 1848, and held office from 1849, with short intervals, until 1852. Napoleon entrusted him (1851) with the redaction of the new Constitution, and made him (1852) vice-president of the Council of State. As minister of agriculture, commerce and public works, from 1855 onwards, he greatly improved the economic situation of France, and in 1863 became minister president. He resigned in 1867, but shortly afterwards resumed office as finance minister. After the fall of the Empire he fled to England, but returned to France in 1872 to work for the interests of the Prince Imperial. He returned to the Chamber as deputy of Ajaccio, and, later, sat for Riom. After the death of the Prince Imperial, Rouher supported the claims of Prince Napoleon, son of the ex-king Jerome. He died on Feb. 3, 1884. (*See* the references under NAPOLEON III.)

ROULERS, a town in the province of West Flanders, Belgium, 13 mi. N.W. of Courtrai, on the Mandel. Its Flemish name is Roesselaere. Pop. (1947) 31,839. Its weavers were already famous in the 11th–12th centuries and the neighbourhood cultivates flax. Lace, carpets and linen are manufactured.

ROULETTE, a gambling game of French origin, is played in nearly all gambling casinos of Europe and America. It is principally identified with the gaming rooms at Monte Carlo, but elsewhere it has been superseded by other games (in the U.S., principally craps; see DICE) among those who gamble for large sums. Countless systems have been devised for winning at roulette, but none is of demonstrable mathematical efficacy and in fact all can be proved fallacious.

The original French terminology of roulette has been replaced in English-speaking countries by equivalent English terms, and both will be used in this description.

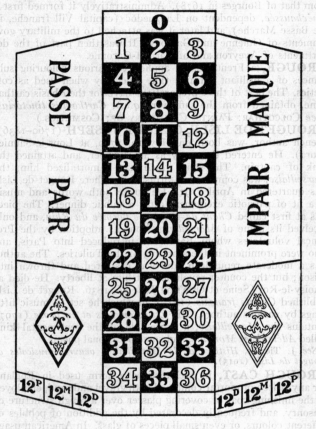

ROULETTE CLOTH, OR LAYOUT

Equipment for roulette consists of a table in which is mounted a compartmented wheel and one or two layouts, usually enameled on green cloth. Any number of persons may play, betting only against the bank (proprietor of the game). The *tourneur,* one of the croupiers in attendance, calls, "Make your bets, gentlemen" (*faites vos jeux, messieurs*), whereupon players indicate on the layout their bets on the number, or classification of number, they hope will win. The *tourneur* then spins the wheel in one direction and in contrarotation spins a small ivory ball which, when the wheel slows down sufficiently, falls into one of the numbered compartments and thus designates the winning number. When it appears to the *tourneur* that the ball will soon come to rest, he calls, "The betting is closed" (*rien ne va plus*). No bet may be placed thereafter.

When the ball rests, the *tourneur* announces the winning number and whether it is red or black, odd or even, low (1 to 18) or high (19 to 36). The bank pays winning bets at the established rates (*see* below) and collects losing bets, which a croupier gathers in with a rake.

For a winning bet on red (*rouge*), black (*noir*), high (*passe*), low (*manque*), even (*pair*) or odd (*impair*), the bank pays "even money"—the amount of the bet. For a winning bet on the dozen (1 to 12, 13 to 24 or 25 to 36) in which the number falls, the bank pays 2 to 1; these bets are indicated on the layout as 12ᵖ, 12ᵐ and 12ᵈ (respectively, *première, milieu* and *dernière douzaine*). Likewise, the bank pays 2 to 1 for a winning bet on the column in which the number lies.

ROULETTE WHEEL. NUMBERS ABOVE BLACK PANELS ARE BLACK, OTHER NUMBERS RED, EXCEPT ZERO, WHICH IS GREEN

Other bets, and the rate of payment when they win, are: (1) on a single number (*en plein*), 35 to 1; (2) on two numbers (*à cheval*), if either wins, 17 to 1. Such a bet is placed on the line between the two numbers. A bet may be made *à cheval* on two adjacent columns, or two adjacent dozens, and pays ½ to 1. (3) On three numbers (*transversale pleine*), if any wins, 11 to 1. A bet on 4, 5 or 6 would be indicated by placing a coin on the line between 4 and *passe,* or between 6 and *manque.* (4) On four numbers (*en carré*), if any wins, 8 to 1. A bet on the point of intersection between 14, 15, 17 and 18 would be a bet on those four numbers. (5) On six numbers (*transversale six*), if any wins, 5 to 1. A bet on the point of intersection between 15, 18 and *impair* would be a bet on 13, 14, 15, 16, 17 and 18.

The zero may be played *à cheval* with any adjoining number; or *en carré* (but called *quatre premiers*) with 1, 2 and 3; or in combination with 1 and 2, or with 2 and 3.

The advantage of the bank arises when the zero shows. Only bets on the zero *en plein* or in combination with 1, 2 and 3 are paid; all other bets are collected. Thus the bank should win one part in 37, or 2.7%, of all bets made against it.

At Monte Carlo, and in a few other casinos, this advantage is reduced by almost one-half in the case of the even-money bets. When the zero occurs, the player who placed such a bet may let the bank take half his bet (*partager*) or may have the bet put "in prison," to be decided on the next roll; whereon if the player wins he may withdraw his bet but is not paid in any case.

In distinction to this practice, many American gambling houses have roulette wheels with 38 compartments including both a zero and a double zero (oo) and if either of them occurs all bets are taken except those involving the winning zero. The bank's advantage is thus increased to 5.26%. Finally, some wheels (seldom seen except in the smaller U.S. gambling houses and in Mexico) have o, oo and an eagle bird (equivalent to a third zero), giving the bank an advantage of 3 parts in 39, or 7.7%.

There is little possibility of the exercise of skill in roulette, though a certain judgment is advisable in betting; it would, for example, be unwise to place a bet on red and also on the number 17, which is black, for if one bet wins the other must lose.

Many books have been published on roulette, most of them being devoted to demonstration that no system of betting can be expected to win against the bank in the long run.   (A. H. MD.)

ROUNDERS, an old English ball game played in Tudor times but not attaining any popularity before 1800. According to some, it was the immediate ancestor of baseball (*q.v.*), but there are several differences, the most radical being that the ball can be hit in any direction. Rounders in its primitive form was more of a romp than a regular game, but it experienced a big revival in Scotland and England in 1889 when two governing bodies were formed, the National Rounders association of Liverpool and vicinity and the Scottish Rounders association, and later with the Gloucester and Ling Physical Education association when rules similar to the modern ones were drawn up. The National Rounders association was formed in 1943.

A hard ball weighing 2½ oz. to 3 oz. and measuring 7½ in. in circumference is used; the rule by which a runner could be put out by hitting him with a thrown ball was abandoned. A round wooden stick is used measuring not more than 6¾ in. round the thickest part, not more than

18 in. in length and not more than 13 oz. in weight. The field is marked in an elongated diamond, the home base being at one end and first, second and third post at the other points, while fourth post is situated on the line of third post toward home and 28 ft. from the former, the sides of the diamond being 39½ ft. The bowler stands in a square in the centre of the diamond and tosses the ball to the batsman who must take a good ball, i.e., one that passes over the batting square and is below the head and above the knee; three consecutive bad bowls scores half a rounder for the batsman. The batsman must run to first and second post and so on to home base and scores one rounder if he does so after hitting the ball or half a rounder if he does so without hitting the ball and without having an opposing player touch the post to which he is running. He can be put out if: the ball is caught on the fly; the post to which he is running is stumped or he is touched with the ball while it is in the possession of the fielder. If the ball is hit behind the home base, he can run only to first post until the ball has been thrown across the front line of the batting square or a continuation of it.

Nine players constitute a side and two innings apiece are played in each match. The back stop is placed directly behind the batsman; first, second, third and fourth basemen are stationed at the posts and there are three deep fielders. Two umpires preside over the game: (1) a batter's umpire who attends to balls that are too high or too low, first and fourth post catchers and to the bowler who must have both feet in the square during the bowling action and (2) a bowler's umpire who attends to balls that are too near or too wide and to second and third posts.

ROUNDHEAD, a term applied to the adherents of the parliamentary party in England during the great Civil War. Some of the Puritans, but by no means all, wore the hair closely cropped round the head, and there was thus an obvious contrast between them and the men of fashion with their long ringlets. "Round-head" appears to have been first used as a term of derision toward the end of 1641 when the debates in parliament on the Bishops Exclusion Bill were causing riots at Westminster. John Rushworth (*Historical Collections*) is more precise. According to him the word was first used on Dec. 27, 1641, by a disbanded officer named David Hide, who during a riot is reported to have drawn his sword and said he would "cut the throats of those round-headed dogs that bawled against bishops." Baxter ascribes the origin of the term to a remark made by Queen Henrietta Maria at the trial of Strafford; referring to Pym, she asked who the round-headed man was. The name remained in use until after the revolution of 1688.

ROUNDSMAN SYSTEM (sometimes termed the billet, or ticket, or item system), in the English poor law, a plan by which the parish paid the occupiers of property to employ the applicants for relief at a rate of wages fixed by the parish. It depended not on the services, but on the wants of the applicants, the employer being repaid out of the poor rate all that he advanced in wages beyond a certain sum. According to this plan the parish in general made some agreement with a farmer to sell to him the labour of one or more paupers at a certain price, paying to the pauper out of the parish funds the difference between that price and the allowance which the scale, according to the price of bread and the number of his family, awarded to him.

It received the local name of billet or ticket system, from the ticket signed by the overseer which the pauper in general carried to the farmer as a warrant for his being employed, and afterwards took back to the overseer, signed by the farmer, as a proof that he had fulfilled the conditions of relief. In other cases the parish contracted with a person to have some work performed for him by the paupers at a given price, the parish paying the paupers. The system disappeared in 1834.

ROUND TABLE, the celebrated board of King Arthur (*q.v.*) around which he and his knights sat. The origin of the myth is obscure, and certainly cannot be said to have been yet settled; it has been traced by various scholars to Welsh, Irish and Breton sources. The story was at first independent of the Arthurian saga. The first known trace of it in an Arthurian connection is in the *Brut* of Wace (*q.v.*) in the reign of Henry II. Here the allusion is brief. Arthur made a round table at which, because of its shape, none of the "barons" could claim precedence over others. The size is left indefinite. Wace adds that the "Bretons" told many stories about the table, and this seems to indicate that there was a mass of Breton (or British) tradition about it known to Wace— a probability strengthened by the fact that elsewhere Wace shows

signs of knowing many stories unknown to his main authority, Geoffrey of Monmouth (*q.v.*).

Half a century later, Layamon adds considerably to our information, and it would seem almost certain that he was drawing on Welsh tradition. There had been a great slaughter of the knights through disputes as to who should be greatest; and a Cornish carpenter, hearing of it, told Arthur he would make him a table at which more than 1,600 men could sit, so that there would be no more quarrels for the place of honour. Yet Arthur would be able to carry it about with him. It was finished in four weeks. "This," added Layamon, repeating Wace's words, "was the table about which the Britons told many tales." There is no reason to think that the poet was inventing; he makes more than 30 additions to Wace, some of which are certainly not original; nor does he show anywhere a trace of inventive capacity.

Addition to the Legend.—Later romancists added many details. For example, the "Diot" *Perceval* (see PERCEVAL) tells that just after Arthur's coronation Merlin related past history. A round table, said the seer, had been made for Joseph of Arimathaea (*q.v.*) and a new one for Arthur's father, Uther Pendragon; let the king use it for his knights; without it the Romans could not be overcome. The table was also brought into connection with the Holy Grail (see GRAIL, THE HOLY) and with the "Siege Perilous" which is so prominent a feature in the Percival legend, and became ultimately an inseparable adjunct of the Arthurian cycle.

Whether the tale reached Wace and Layamon directly from Wales or from Brittany, it is certainly of ancient Celtic origin. A round table seems to have been a feature of primitive Celtic life; a circular form was the rule in primitive Irish architecture, and the primitive Celtic watch house, both in Gaul and in Ireland, was circular. To what this in its turn is to be traced is more doubtful; it is not unlikely that it arose from sun worship or possibly (*cf.* the "four weeks") from the moon. The magical character of the table seems, again, to be of a peculiarly Celtic cast; it resembles that of the enchanted bowls, bushels and horns so often found in Irish and Welsh saga; and it was inevitable that when the attractive force of the Arthurian legend was felt, such a magical table should be assigned to the king along with his enchanted sword, boat, lance and shield.

The Table at Winchester.—The famous round table fixed in the wall of the great hall at Winchester is certainly of considerable antiquity. It is a tabletop 18 ft. in diameter, divided into 25 sectors, one for the king and one for each of the knights (whose number had long been reduced from the 1,600 of Layamon). The present colouring of the sections (green and white successively) is due to Henry VIII. Hardying, in his *Chronicle* (*c.* 1436), differing slightly from *Perceval*, says that it is the very table made by Joseph of Arimathea for the brethren of the Grail, which was transferred to Winchester by Uther to comfort Ygerne. He speaks in a manner that implies a great age for this table.

A good summary of the story is given by A. C. L. Brown in *Harvard Studies in Philology and Literature,* vol. vii, where other authorities are referred to. Incidental references will be found in the various works on different aspects of the Arthurian saga.   (E. E. K.)

ROUNDWORM, the common name for the parasitic worms of the genus *Ascaris,* and especially for *A. lumbricoides,* which occurs in the intestine of man. Closely allied species inhabit the pig and the horse. The name roundworm is often extended to include all members of the class Nematoda (*q.v.*).

ROUS, FRANCIS (1579–1659), English Puritan, was born at Dittisham, in Devon, in 1579, and educated at Oxford (Broadgates hall, afterward Pembroke college) and at Leyden. For several years he lived in seclusion in Cornwall and occupied himself with theological studies, producing among other books *The Arte of Happines* (1619) and *Testis Veritatis,* a reply to Richard Montagu's *Appello Caesarem.* He entered parliament in 1625 as member for Truro, and continued to represent that or some neighbouring west country constituency in such parliaments as were summoned till his death. He obtained many offices under the Commonwealth, among them that of provost of Eton college. At first a presbyterian, he afterward joined the independents. In 1657 he was made a lord of parliament. He died at Acton in Jan. 1658–59. The subjective cast of his piety is reflected in his *Mystical Marriage . . . Betweene a Soule and Her Saviour* (1635), but he is best known by his metrical version of the Psalms (1643), which was approved by the Westminster assembly and (in a revised form) is still used in the Scottish Presbyterian churches.

ROUSSEAU, HENRI JULIEN FÉLIX, called LE DOUA-

NIER (1844–1911), French painter, born at Laval (Mayenne), May 20, 1844, was the son of a tinware dealer. A soldier in Mexico in 1862–66, he served intermittently till 1871 when he entered the customs service, but retired in 1885 to adopt professionally his hobby of painting. He then began to exhibit his now famous pictures—at first portraits, still life and views of Paris and its people such as "Un Soir de Carnaval" (1886; L. E. Stern collection, U.S.), "Myself: Portrait-Landscape" (1890; Prague) and "The Centenary of Independence" (1892). These are deceptively simple and arranged frontally with clear contours separating fields of even, solid, often brilliant colour; but their strength lies in their whole-hearted regard for the occasion they represent. Between 1886 and 1890 Rousseau exhibited 20 works at the Paris Salon des Indépendants and was attacked by critics both "advanced" and orthodox. But he was defended by Edgar Degas and Henri de Toulouse-Lautrec and later knew A. Jarry the author and Pablo Picasso. After 1890 his work becomes less static and includes jungle and animal scenes. Some landscape studies are unexpectedly tentative and atmospheric; large works such as the "Sleeping Gipsy" (1897; Musem of Modern Art, New York city) have an imaginative, remote lyricism which later recommended them to Jean Cocteau and Guillaume Apollinaire. Some of Rousseau's best work dates from 1900 on; it includes "Jungle With a Lion" (1904–06; Museum of Modern Art) and "The Cart of Père Juniet" (1908; Mme. Paul Guillaume's collection, Paris). He died in Paris, Sept. 4, 1910.

See Editions Cahiers d'Art, *Rousseau* (Paris, 1920); D. C. Rich, *Henri Rousseau*, 2nd ed. (New York, 1946), with bibliography; M. Garçon, *Le Douanier Rousseau accusé naïf* (Paris, 1953). (D. C. T. T.)

ROUSSEAU, JEAN BAPTISTE (1671–1741), French poet, was born at Paris on April 6, 1671. His earlier comedies, *Le Café* (1694), *Le Flatteur* (1696), and *Le Capricieux*, and the opera of *Venus et Adonis* (1697) were not successful. He was turned out of the Café Laurent, which was much frequented by literary men, on account of the libellous verse written by or attributed to him, but in 1701 he was made a member of the Académie des inscriptions, and in 1710 he presented himself as a candidate for the Académie française. But in 1712 he was prosecuted for defamation of character and, on his non-appearance in court, was condemned to perpetual exile. He spent the rest of his life abroad, refusing to accept permission to return in 1716, because it was not accompanied by complete rehabilitation. He died at Brussels on March 17, 1741.

ROUSSEAU, JEAN JACQUES (1712–1778), French philosopher, was born at Geneva on June 28, 1712. His family had established themselves in that city at the time of the religious wars, but they were of pure French origin. Rousseau's father Isaac was a watchmaker; his mother, Suzanne Bernard, was the daughter of a minister; she died in childbirth, and Rousseau, who was the second son, was brought up in a haphazard fashion. When the boy was ten years old his father got entangled in a dispute with a fellow-citizen, and being condemned to a short term of imprisonment abandoned Geneva and took refuge at Lyons. Rousseau was taken charge of by his mother's relations and was committed to the tutorship of M. Lambercier, pastor at Boissy. In 1724 he was taken into the house of his uncle Bernard, by whom he was shortly afterwards apprenticed to a notary. His master, however, found or thought him incapable and sent him back. After a short time (April 25, 1725) he was apprenticed afresh, this time to an engraver. He did not dislike the work, but was or thought himself cruelly treated, and in 1728 he ran away. Then began an extraordinary series of wanderings and adventures, for much of which there is no authority but his own *Confessions*. He first fell in with some proselytizers of the Roman faith at Confignon in Savoy, and by them he was sent to Madame de Warens (or Vuarrens) at Annecy, a young and pretty widow who was herself a convert. Her influence, however, was not immediately exercised, and he was passed on to Turin, where there was an institution specially devoted to the reception of neophytes. His experiences here were unsatisfactory, but he abjured duly and was rewarded by being presented with 20 francs and sent about his business. He wandered about in Turin for some time, and at last established himself as footman to a Madame de

Vercellis. Here occurred the famous incident of the theft of a ribbon, of which he accused a girl fellow-servant. Madame de Vercellis died not long afterwards, but he found another place with the Comte de Gouvon. This he soon lost; he then resolved to return to Madame de Warens at Annecy. The chronology of all these events, as narrated by himself, is somewhat obscure, but they seem to have occupied about three years.

Even then Rousseau did not settle at once in the anomalous position of domestic lover to this lady, who, nominally a converted Protestant, was in reality a kind of deist, with a theory of noble sentiment and a practice of libertinism tempered by good nature. She thought it necessary to complete his education, and he was sent to the seminarists of St. Lazare to be improved in classics, and also to a music master. In one of his incomprehensible freaks he set off for Lyons, and, after abandoning his companion in an epileptic fit, returned to Annecy to find Madame de Warens gone. Then for some months he relapsed into the life of vagabondage, varied by improbable adventures, which (according to his own statement) he so often pursued. Hardly knowing anything of music, he attempted to give lessons and a concert at Lausanne; and he actually taught at Neuchâtel. Then he became, or says he became, secretary to a Greek archimandrite who was travelling in Switzerland to collect subscriptions for the rebuilding of the Holy Sepulchre; then he went to Paris, and, with recommendations from the French ambassador at Soleure, saw something of good society; then he returned on foot through Lyons to Savoy, hearing that Madame de Warens was at Chambéry. This was in 1732, and Rousseau, who for a time had unimportant employments in the service of the Sardinian Crown, was shortly installed by Madame de Warens, whom he still called Maman, as *amant en titre* in her singular household, wherein she diverted herself with him, with music and with chemistry. In 1736 Madame de Warens, partly for Rousseau's health, took a country house, Les Charmettes, a short distance from Chambéry. Here in summer, and in the town during winter, Rousseau led a delightful life, which he has delightfully described. In a desultory way he did a good deal of reading, but in 1738 his health again became bad, and he was recommended to go to Montpellier. By his own account this journey to Montpellier was in reality a *voyage à Cythère* in company with a certain Madame de Larnage. This being so, he could hardly complain when on returning he found that his official position in Madame de Waren's household had been taken by a person named Vintzenried. In 1740 he became tutor at Lyons to the children of M. de Mably, not the well-known writer of that name, but his and Condillac's elder brother. But Rousseau did not like teaching and was a bad teacher, and after a visit to Les Charmettes, finding that his place there was finally occupied, he once more went to Paris in 1741. He was not without recommendations. But a new system of musical notation which he thought he had discovered was unfavourably received by the Académie des sciences, where it was read in Aug. 1742, and he was unable to obtain pupils, though the paper was published in 1743 under the title of *Dissertation sur la musique moderne*. Madame Dupin, however, to whose house he had obtained the entry, procured him the honourable if not very lucrative post of secretary to M. de Montaigu, ambassador at Venice. With him he stayed for about 18 months, and had as usual infinite complaints to make of his employer and some strange stories to tell. At length he threw up his situation and returned to Paris (1745).

His Literary Triumphs.—Up to this time—that is to say, till his 33rd year—Rousseau's life, though continuously described by himself, was of the kind called subterranean, and the account of it must be taken with considerable allowances. From this time, however, his general history can be checked and followed with reasonable confidence. On his return to Paris he renewed his relations with the Dupin family and with the literary group of Diderot, to which he had already been introduced by M. de Mably's letters. He had an opera, *Les Muses galantes*, privately represented; he copied music for money, and received from Madame Dupin and her son-in-law M. de Francueil a small but regular salary as secretary. He lived at the Hotel St. Quentin for a time, and once more arranged for himself an equivocal domestic establishment. His mistress, whom towards the close of his life he married after a fashion, was Thérèse le Vasseur, a servant at the inn, whom he first met in 1743. She had little beauty, no education or understanding, and few charms that his friends could discover, besides which she had a detestable mother, who was the bane of Rousseau's life. But he made himself happy with her, and (according to Rousseau's account, the accuracy of which has been questioned [see F. Macdonald, *J. J. Rousseau*, 1906]) five children were born to them, who were all consigned to the foundling hospital. This disregard of responsibility was partly punished by the use his critics made of it when he became celebrated as a writer on education and a preacher of the domestic affections. Diderot, with whom from 1741 onwards he became more and more familiar, admitted him as a contributor to the *Encyclopédie*, for which he wrote the articles on music and political economy. He formed new musical projects, and he was introduced by degrees to many people of rank and influence, among them Madame d'Epinay, to whom in 1747 he was introduced by her lover M. de Francueil.

It was not, however, till 1749 that Rousseau made his mark as a writer. The academy of Dijon offered a prize for an essay on the effect of the progress of civilization on morals. Rousseau took up the subject, developed his famous paradox of the superiority of the savage state, won the prize, and, publishing his essay (*Discours sur les arts et sciences*) next year, became famous. The anecdotage as to the origin of this famous essay is voluminous. It is agreed that the idea was suggested when Rousseau went to pay a visit to Diderot, who was in prison at Vincennes for his *Lettre sur les aveugles*. Rousseau says he thought of the paradox on his way down; Morellet and others say that he thought of treating the subject in the ordinary fashion and was laughed at by Diderot, who showed him the advantages of the less obvious treatment. Diderot himself, who in such matters is trustworthy, does not claim the suggestion, but uses words which imply that it was at least partly his. It is very like him. The essay, however, took the artificial and crotchety society of the day by storm. Francueil gave Rousseau a valuable post as cashier in the receiver-general's office. But he resigned it either from conscientiousness, or crotchet, or nervousness at responsibility, or indolence, or more probably from a mixture of all four. He went back to his music-copying, but the salons of the day were determined to have his society, and for a time they had it. In 1752 he brought out at Fontainebleau an operetta, the *Devin du village*, which was successful. He received 100 louis for it, and he was ordered to come to court next day. This meant the certainty of a pension. But Rousseau's shyness or his perversity (as before, probably both) made him disobey the command. His comedy, *Narcisse*, written long before, was also acted, but unsuccessfully. In the same year, however, a letter *Sur la musique française*, in which he indulged in a violent tirade against French music, again had a great vogue. Finally, for this was an important year with him, the Dijon academy, which had founded his fame, announced the subject of "The Origin of Inequality," on which he wrote a discourse which was unsuccessful, but at least equal to the former in merit. During a visit to Geneva in 1754 he abjured his abjuration of Protestantism and was enabled to take up his freedom as citizen, to which his birth entitled him and of which he was proud. Shortly afterwards, returning to Paris, he accepted a cottage near Montmorency (the celebrated Hermitage) which Madame d'Epinay had fitted up for him, and established himself there in April 1756. Here he wrote *La Nouvelle Héloïse*; here he indulged in the passion which that novel partly represents, his love for Madame d'Houdetot, sister-in-law of Madame d'Epinay. Here too arose the obscure triangular quarrel between Diderot, Rousseau and Frederick Melchior Grimm, which ended Rousseau's sojourn at the Hermitage. The supposition least favourable to Rousseau is that it was due to one of his numerous fits of half-insane petulance and indignation at the obligations which he was nevertheless always ready to incur. That most favourable to him is that he was expected to lend himself in a more or less complaisant manner to assist and cover Madame

d'Epinay's passion for Grimm. At any rate, Rousseau quitted the Hermitage in the winter of 1757–58, and established himself at Montlouis in the neighbourhood.

Hitherto Rousseau's behaviour had frequently made him enemies, but his writings had for the most part made him friends. The quarrel with Madame d'Epinay, with Diderot, and through them with the *philosophe* party reversed this. In 1758 appeared his *Lettre à d'Alembert sur les spectacles*, written in the winter of the previous year at Montlouis. This was at once an attack on Voltaire, who was giving theatrical representations at Les Délices, on D'Alembert, who had condemned the prejudice against the stage in the *Encyclopédie*, and on one of the favourite amusements of the society of the day, and Rousseau was henceforward as obnoxious to the *philosophe* coterie as to the orthodox party. He still, however, had no lack of patrons—he never had—though his perversity made him quarrel with all in turn. The duke and duchess of Luxembourg made his acquaintance, and he was industrious in his literary work—indeed, most of his best books were produced during his stay in the neighbourhood of Montmorency. A letter to Voltaire on his poem about the Lisbon earthquake embittered the dislike between the two, being surreptitiously published. *La Nouvelle Héloïse* appeared in the same year (1760), and it was immensely popular. In 1762 appeared the *Contrat social* at Amsterdam, and *Émile*, which was published both in the Low Countries and at Paris. For the latter the author received 6,000 livres, for the *Contrat* 1,000.

Julie, ou La Nouvelle Héloïse, is a novel written in letters describing the loves of a man of low position and a girl of rank, her subsequent marriage to a respectable freethinker of her own station, the mental agonies of her lover, and the partial appeasing of the distresses of the lovers by the influence of noble sentiment and the good offices of a philanthropic Englishman. It is too long, the sentiment is overstrained; but it is full of pathos and knowledge of the human heart. The *Contrat social*, as its title implies, endeavours to base all government on the consent, direct or implied, of the governed, and indulges in much ingenious argument to get rid of the practical inconveniences of the theory. *Émile*, the second title of which is *De l'Éducation*, is much more of a treatise than of a novel.

Exile from France.—Rousseau's reputation was now higher than ever, but the term of the comparative prosperity which he had enjoyed for nearly ten years was at hand. The *Contrat social* was obviously anti-monarchic; the *Nouvelle Héloïse* was said to be immoral; the sentimental deism of the "Profession du vicaire Savoyard" in *Émile* irritated equally the *philosophe* party and the church. On June 11, 1762, *Émile* was condemned by the parlement of Paris, and two days previously Madame de Luxembourg and the prince de Conti gave the author information that he would be arrested if he did not fly. They also furnished him with means of flight, and he made for Yverdon in the territory of Berne, whence he transferred himself to Motiers in Neuchâtel, which then belonged to Prussia. Frederick II. was not indisposed to protect the persecuted when it cost him nothing and might bring him fame, and in Marshal Keith, the governor of Neuchâtel, Rousseau found a true and firm friend. He was, however, unable to be quiet or to practise any of those more or less pious frauds which were customary at the time with the unorthodox. The archbishop of Paris had published a pastoral against him, and Rousseau did not let the year pass without a *Lettre à M. de Beaumont*. The council of Geneva had joined in the condemnation of *Émile*, and Rousseau first solemnly renounced his citizenship, and then, in the *Lettres de la montagne* (1763), attacked the council and the Genevan constitution unsparingly. All this excited public opinion against him, and his unpopularity is said, on uncertain authority, to have culminated in a nocturnal attack on his house. At any rate he thought he was menaced if he was not, and migrated to the Île St. Pierre in the Lake of Bienne, where he once more for a short, and the last, time enjoyed that idyllic existence which he loved. But the Bernese Government ordered him to quit its territory.

David Hume offered him, late in 1765, an asylum in England, and he accepted. He passed through Paris, where his presence was tolerated for a time, and landed in England on Jan. 13, 1766. Thérèse travelled separately, and was entrusted to the charge of James Boswell, who had already made Rousseau's acquaintance. Here he had once more a chance of settling peaceably. Severe English moralists like Johnson thought but ill of him, but the public generally was not unwilling to testify against French intolerance, and regarded his sentimentalism with favour. He was lionized in London to his heart's content and discontent, for it may truly be said of Rousseau that he was equally indignant at neglect and intolerant of attention. When, after not a few displays of his strange humour, he professed himself tired of the capital, Hume procured him a country abode in the house of Mr. Davenport at Wootton in Derbyshire. Here, though the place was bleak and lonely, he might have been happy enough, and he actually employed himself in writing the greater part of his *Confessions*. But his habit of self-tormenting and tormenting others never left him. His own caprices interposed some delay in the conferring of a pension which George III. was induced to grant him, and he took this as a crime of Hume's. The publication of a spiteful letter (really by Horace Walpole) in the name of the king of Prussia made Rousseau believe that plots of the most terrible kind were on foot against him. Finally he quarrelled with Hume because the latter would not acknowledge all his own friends and Rousseau's supposed enemies of the *philosophe* circle to be rascals. He remained, however, at Wootton during the year and through the winter. In May 1767 he fled to France, addressing letters to the lord chancellor and to General Conway, which show an unbalanced mind. He was received in France by the marquis de Mirabeau (father of the great Mirabeau), of whom he soon had enough, then by the prince de Conti at Trye. From this place he again fled and wandered about for some time in a wretched fashion, still writing the *Confessions*, constantly receiving generous help, and always quarrelling with, or at least suspecting, the helpers. In the summer of 1770 he returned to Paris, resumed music-copying, and was on the whole happier than he had been since he had to leave Montlouis.

Many of the best-known stories of Rousseau's life date from this last time, when he was tolerably accessible to visitors. He finished his *Confessions*, wrote his *Dialogues* (the interest of which is not quite equal to the promise of their curious sub-title, *Rousseau juge de Jean Jacques*), and began his *Rêveries du promeneur solitaire*, intended as a sequel and complement to the *Confessions*, and one of the best of all his books. It should be said that besides these, which complete the list of his principal works, he has left a very large number of minor works, the fragments of another opera, *Daphnis et Chloé* (printed in 1780), and a considerable correspondence. During this time he lived in the Rue Platière, which is now named after him. But his suspicions of secret enemies grew stronger, and at the beginning of 1778 he was glad to accept the offer of M. de Girardin, a rich financier, and occupy a cottage at Ermenonville. The country was beautiful; but his old terrors revived, and his woes were complicated by the alleged inclination of Thérèse for one of M. de Girardin's stable-boys. On July 2 he died in a manner which has been much discussed, suspicions of suicide being circulated at the time by Grimm and others, though there is no reason to doubt the original verdict of apoplexy.

His Character and Influence.—There is little doubt that for the last 10 or 15 years of his life Rousseau was not wholly sane —the combined influence of late and unexpected literary fame and of constant solitude and discomfort acting upon his excitable temperament so as to overthrow the balance, never very stable, of his fine and acute but unrobust intellect. His moral character was undoubtedly weak, but it is fair to remember that but for his astounding *Confessions* the more disgusting parts of it would not have been known, and that these *Confessions* were written, if not under hallucination, at any rate in circumstances entitling the self-condemned criminal to the benefit of considerable doubt. If Rousseau had held his tongue, he might have stood lower as a man of letters; he would pretty certainly have stood higher as a man. He was, moreover, really sinned against, if still more sinning. Like other men of letters of his time he had to submit to something like persecution. The conduct of Grimm to him was certainly bad; and, though Walpole was not his personal friend, a worse action than his famous letter, considering the well-known idiosyncrasy of the subject, would be difficult to find. Only excuses can be made for him; but the excuses for a man born, as Hume after the quarrel said of him, "without a skin" are numerous and strong.

His peculiar reputation increased after his death, when the paradox of Rousseauism, the belief in the superiority of "the noble savage" to civilized man, became more and more fashionable. The men of the Revolution regarded him with something like idolatry, and his literary merits conciliated many who were far from idolizing him as a revolutionist. His style was taken up by Bernardin de Saint Pierre and by Chateaubriand. Byron's fervid panegyric enlisted on his side all who admired Byron—that is to say, the majority of the younger men and women of Europe between 1820 and 1850—and thus different sides of his tradition were continued for a full century after the publication of his chief books. His religious unorthodoxy was condoned because he never scoffed; his political heresies, after their first effect was over, seemed harmless from the very want of logic and practical spirit in them, while part at least of his literary secret was the common property of almost every one who attempted literature.

In religion Rousseau was undoubtedly what he has been called above—a sentimental deist; but sentimentalism was the essence, deism the accident of his creed. In his time orthodoxy at once generous and intelligent hardly existed in France. There were ignorant persons who were sincerely orthodox; there were intelligent persons who pretended to be so. But between the time of Massillon and D'Aguesseau and the time of Lamennais and Joseph de Maistre the class of men of whom in England Berkeley, Butler and Johnson were representatives did not exist in France. Little inclined by nature to any but the emotional side of religion, and utterly undisciplined in any other by education, course of life, or the general tendency of public opinion, Rousseau took refuge in the nebulous kind of natural religion which was at once fashionable and convenient.

In politics Rousseau was a sincere and, as far as in him lay, a convinced republican. He had no great tincture of learning, he was by no means a profound logician, and he was impulsive and emotional in the extreme—characteristics which in political matters predispose the subject to the preference of equality above all political requisites. He saw that under the French monarchy the actual result was the greatest misery of the greatest number, and he did not look much further. The *Contrat social* is for the political student one of the most curious and interesting books existing. Historically it is null; logically it is full of gaping flaws, practically its manipulations of the *volonté de tous* and the *volonté générale* are clearly insufficient to obviate anarchy. But its mixture of real eloquence and apparent cogency is exactly what always carries a multitude with it, if only for a time. Moreover, in some minor branches of politics and economics Rousseau was a real reformer. Visionary as his educational schemes (chiefly promulgated in *Émile*) are in parts, they are admirable in others, and his protest against mothers refusing to nurse their children hit a blot in French life which is not removed yet, and has always been a source of weakness to the nation.

But it is as a literary man pure and simple—that is to say, as an exponent rather than as an originator of ideas—that Rousseau is most noteworthy, and that he has exercised most influence. The first thing noticeable about him is that he defies all customary and mechanical classification. He is not a dramatist—his work as such is insignificant—nor a novelist, for, though his two chief works except the *Confessions* are called novels, *Émile* is one only in name, and *La Nouvelle Héloïse* is as a story diffuse, prosy and awkward to a degree. He was without command of poetic form, and he could only be called a philosopher in an age when the term was used with such meaningless laxity as was customary in the 18th century. If he must be classed, he was before all things a describer—a describer of the passions of the human heart and of the beauties of nature. In the first part of his vocation the novelists of his own youth, such as Marivaux, Richardson and Prévost, may be said to have shown him the way; in the second he was almost a creator. In combining the two and expressing the effect of nature on the feelings and of the feelings on the aspect of nature he was absolutely without a forerunner or a model. And, as literature since his time has been chiefly differentiated from literature before it by the colour and tone resulting from this combination, Rousseau may be said to hold, as an influence, a place almost unrivalled in literary history. The defects of all sentimental writing are noticeable in him, but they are palliated by his wonderful feeling, and by the passionate sincerity even of his insincere passages.

BIBLIOGRAPHY.—The first complete edition of Rousseau's works appeared at Geneva in 1782–83 in 47 small volumes. There have been many since, the most important of them being that of Musset-Pathay (1823). Some unpublished works, chiefly letters, were added by Bosscha (1858) and Streckeisen Moulton (1861). *See* also the latter's *Rousseau et ses amis* (1865), and the edition of Rousseau's *Correspondance Générale* by Dufour and Plan (1924 *et seq.*). The chief biographies are: in French that of Saint Marc Girardin (1874), in English the *Life* by Viscount Morley (1873; new ed. 1915). But the materials for his biography are so controversial and so personal that the correct historical view can hardly be said yet to be standardized. Mrs. Frederika Macdonald, in her *Jean Jacques Rousseau* (1906), makes out a good case for regarding Mme. d'Epinay's *Memoirs* as coloured, if not actually dictated, by the malevolent attitude of Grimm and Diderot; and her study of the documents undoubtedly qualifies a good many of the assumptions that had previously been made. *See* also E. Ritter, *Famille et jeunesse de Rousseau* (1896); A. Houssaye, *Les Charmettes* (2nd ed., 1864); L. Ducros, *J. J. Rousseau de Genève à l'Hermitage, 1712–57* (1908). The *Annales de la Société J. J. Rousseau* began to appear in 1905; Albert Schinz, *La Pensée de J. J. Rousseau* (1929).

ROUSSEAU, PIERRE ÉTIENNE THÉODORE (1812–1867),

French painter of the Barbizon school, was born in Paris on April 15, 1812, the son of a tailor. At the age of 15 he began his artistic education under the landscapist Charles Rémond and then under Guillon-Lethière. But his style was formed chiefly by his own efforts in working direct from nature in various parts of France. Théodore Rousseau shared the difficulties of the romantic painters of 1830 in securing for their pictures a place in the annual Paris exhibition. The influence of the classically trained artists was against them. He exhibited one or two unimportant works in the Salon of 1831 and 1834, but in 1836 his great work "La Descente des vaches" was rejected; and from then until 1848 he was persistently refused. He was not without champions in the press, and under the title of "le grand refusé" he became known through the writings of Thoré, the critic who afterwards resided in England and wrote under the name of Bürger. During these years of artistic exile Rousseau produced some of his finest pictures: "The Chestnut Avenue," "The Marsh in the Landes" (Louvre), "Hoar-Frost" (now in America); and in 1851, after the reorganization of the Salon in 1848, he exhibited his masterpiece, "The Edge of the Forest" (Louvre), a picture similar in treatment to the composition called "A Glade in the Forest of Fontainebleau," in the Wallace collection.

Up to this period Rousseau had lived only occasionally at Barbizon, but in 1848 he took up his residence in the forest village. At the Exposition Universelle of 1855, where all Rousseau's rejected pictures of the previous 20 years were gathered together, his works were acknowledged to form one of the finest groups. However, his struggles continued and his health began to give way. He was elected president of the fine art jury for the 1867 Exposition. Finally he began to sink, and he died, in the presence of his friend, J. F. Millet, on Dec. 22, 1867.

Rousseau's pictures are always grave in character, with an air of exquisite melancholy. He left a number of sketches and watercolour drawings. His pen work is rare; it is particularly searching in quality, he also executed four etchings and two heliogravures. There are a number of fine pictures by him in the Louvre, and the Wallace collection contains one of his most important Barbizon pictures. There is also an example in the Ionides collection at the Victoria and Albert museum.

See A. Sensier, *Souvenirs sur Th. Rousseau* (1872); E. Michel, *Les Artistes célèbres: Th. Rousseau* (1891); J. W. Mollett, *Rousseau and Diaz* (1890); D. Croal Thomson, *The Barbizon School of Painters: Th. Rousseau* (1892); E. Chesneau, *Peintres romantiques: Th. Rousseau* (1880); P. Burty, *Maîtres et petit-maîtres: Th. Rousseau*

(1877); W. Gensel, *Millet und Rousseau* (Bielefeld, 1902); L. Delteil, *Le Peintre-Graveur* (1906); E. Michel, *La Forêt de Fontainebleau* (1909).

ROUSSEAU DE LA ROTTIÈRE, JEAN SIMÉON (b. 1747),

French decorative painter, was the youngest son of Jules Antoine Rousseau, "sculpteur du Roi." He studied at the Académie Royale in 1768 winning the medal given to the best painter of the quarter. He appears, with his brother Jules Hugues, to have been employed by his father for the decorative work executed by the family at Versailles. Many of the attributions are fairly determined by dates, Jules Antoine Rousseau having been at work at Versailles for years before the birth of his famous son. There can be little doubt that the "Bains du Roi," the "Salon de la Méridienne," part of the bedchamber of Madame Adelaïde, and the "Garde-robe of Louis XVI" were shared in by Rousseau de la Rottière. His most individual and most famous undertaking was, however, the decoration of the lovely "Boudoir de Madame de Sévilly," purchased for the Victoria and Albert museum in 1869. There is no information as to Rousseau's later life. The last known mention of him is in 1792.

ROUSSEL, ALBERT (1869–1937),

French composer, was born at Tourcoing on April 5, 1869. He left the navy in 1894 to study music in Paris, and in 1902 became professor at the Schola Cantorum. The delightful *Rustiques* (1904–06), the first symphony *Le Poème de la Forêt* (1904–06) and the charming ballet *Le Festin de l'Araignée* (1912) were all manifestly the work of a gifted composer. The *Divertissement* (piano and wind instruments, 1906), *Evocations,* three symphonic poems, one with chorus (1910–11), the orchestral prelude *Pour une Fête de Printemps* (1920), the second symphony (op. 23, 1919–20) and the opera-ballet *Padmâvati* (1923) are among his other works.

ROUSSILLON,

a former province of France, corresponding geographically to the fertile plain bounded by the eastern Pyrenees, the Corbières and the Mediterranean and to the modern department of Pyrénées-Orientales (*q.v.*). It derives its name from a Roman town, Ruscino, near Perpignan, the later capital. It formed part of the Roman province of Narbonensis and, in the 5th century, of the Visigothic kingdom that extended over Spain and Aquitaine. Even after the defeat of Alaric II at Vouillé (507) and the loss of Aquitaine, Roussillon long remained in Visigothic hands, as did the rest of Septimania (from the lower Rhone to the Pyrenees). Only after being overrun by the Arabs, from 719 to 759, was it occupied by the Franks. Under Charlemagne it was incorporated in the Marca Hispanica, but in 865 Charles the Bald detached the districts around Narbonne. Henceforth Roussillon was closely linked with Catalonia and looked mostly southward to Barcelona. In 873 Joffre the Hairy, count of Barcelona, killed the Frankish count, occupied the country and gave it to his brother Miron, who was the head of a line of hereditary counts that lasted until 1172, when Gerard II left his inheritance to the count of Barcelona, King Alphonso II of Aragon. Yet it remained legally part of the French kingdom till 1258, when, by the treaty of Corbeil, Louis IX surrendered it with the countship of Barcelona to James I of Aragon. Under Aragonese rule the province was prosperous; Collioure, the port of Perpignan, became a centre of Mediterranean trade. From 1276 to 1344 Roussillon was part of the ephemeral kingdom of Majorca created by James I in favour of his younger son, James, and the new state had Perpignan as its capital. But in the 15th century the French king became interested in Roussillon, and in 1462, by the treaty of Bayonne, Louis XI promised to help John II of Aragon against the rebellious Catalans and was to occupy the castles of Perpignan and Collioure as a security for the reimbursement of his expenses. In fact he had the whole of Roussillon and Cerdagne occupied and annexed to France in 1463. French rule was most unpopular, and Roussillon revolted in 1472, but after two sieges (1473 and 1475) Perpignan was retaken by the French and the country subdued. Still, in 1493 by the treaty of Barcelona, Charles VIII gave it back to Ferdinand of Aragon to win his good will for the Italian campaign. However, in 1639 and in 1641 (when Catalonia revolted against Spain) the French invaded Roussillon; Perpignan was taken after a long siege (Jan.-Sept. 1642), and the treaty of the Pyrenees (1659) secured Roussillon and half of Cerdagne to the French crown. During the revolutionary wars, Roussillon was for a short time invaded by a Spanish army (1793–94). The 19th century was marked by the steady growth of left-wing opinion and by a complete transformation of agriculture which made the country a rich producer of early vegetables and fruits, as well as of wines.

BIBLIOGRAPHY.—E. Brutails, *Etude sur la condition des populations rurales du Roussillon au moyen âge* (Paris, 1891); J. Calmette, *Le Roussillon* (Paris, 1912), *La Question des Pyrénées et la Marche d'Espagne au moyen-âge* (Paris, 1947) and, with P. Vidal, *Histoire de Roussillon* (Paris, 1923). (F. Ct.)

ROUTLEDGE, GEORGE (1812–1888), English publisher, was born at Brampton in Cumberland on Sept. 23, 1812. He started in business for himself as a bookseller in London in 1836, and as a publisher in 1843. He was a pioneer of cheap classics; the shilling volumes called the "Railway Library" were a success, including as they did *Uncle Tom's Cabin.* He also published in popular form writings of Washington Irving, James Fenimore Cooper, Edward Bulwer-Lytton and Benjamin Disraeli. A branch of Routledge's publishing business was established in New York in 1854. Routledge died in London on Dec. 13, 1888.

ROUVIER, MAURICE (1842–1911), French statesman, was born at Aix on April 17, 1842. He supported Léon Gambetta's candidature at Marseilles in 1867, and in 1870 he founded an anti-imperial journal, *L'Egalité.* In July 1871 he was returned to the national assembly for Marseilles at a by-election. He became a recognized authority on finance, and repeatedly served on the budget commission as reporter or president. In 1881 he joined Gambetta's cabinet as minister of commerce and the colonies, and in the 1883–85 cabinet of Jules Ferry he held the same office. He became premier and minister of finance on May 31, 1887, with the support of the moderate republican groups, the Radicals holding aloof in support of Gen. Georges Boulanger, who began a violent agitation against the government. Then came the scandal of the decorations in which Pres. François Grévy's son-in-law Daniel Wilson figured, and the Rouvier cabinet fell. Rouvier was minister of finance in a succession of ministries between 1889 and 1893.

He was driven out of office by the Panamá scandals; in 1902, after nearly ten years of exclusion from office, he joined the Radical cabinet of Combes; and on the fall of the Combes ministry in Jan. 1905 he became premier, with Theophile Delcassé at the head of the foreign office. Delcassé, reproached with imprudence in the Morocco affair (*see* EUROPE: *History*), resigned, and the prime minister took over foreign affairs and came to an agreement with the German government. His ministry fell in 1906 over questions connected with the Separation law. Rouvier died at Neuilly on June 7, 1911.

ROUX, PIERRE PAUL EMILE (1853–1933), French bacteriologist, was born at Confolens, Charente, on Dec. 17, 1853. He studied medicine, and obtained an appointment to the faculty of medicine in Paris, which he held from 1874 to 1878. He then worked for ten years in Louis Pasteur's laboratory, before being appointed to a post in the Pasteur institute. He was director of the institute from 1904 to 1918.

Roux did a great deal of research in collaboration with Pasteur, and studied the treatment of infectious diseases, including hydrophobia. He studied anthrax in conjunction with Pasteur and Charles Edouard Chamberland, and produced vaccines against this disease. He was associated with the Swiss bacteriologist Alexandre Yersin in the study of the diphtheria bacillus and its toxins. With Emil von Behring he introduced the use of an antitoxin in diphtheria. He made a famous communication on this subject to the International Congress of Medicine at Budapest, Hung., in 1894. He claimed antitoxin as of value prophylactically and as a remedy. *Figaro* opened a public subscription and in a few weeks more than 1,000,000 fr. rolled in. The money was devoted to the preparation and distribution of diphtheria antitoxin by the Pasteur institute.

See *Lancet*, vol. 225, p. 1124 (1933).

ROUYN, a mining city in northwest Quebec, Can., on Lake Osisko, on the Canadian National and Nipissing Central railways, 340 mi. N.W. of Montreal and 320 mi. N. of Toronto. Pop. (1951) 14,633; with its twin city of Noranda (immediately adjoining but under separate administration) the 1951 population totalled 24,305, compared with 13,346 in 1941. The rapid expansion from raw bush in 1925 to modern urban development was a result of the discovery of minerals and the completion in 1927 of a branch of the Canadian National railway. Rouyn lies east, and is on the continuation of the mineral-bearing rocks of the Porcupine gold district and the Cobalt silver district of Ontario. Its chief industry is copper-gold production, and the Noranda mine (with capital expenditure of more than $12,000,000 by mid-century

on smelter and concentrator equipment) is the most important in the Rouyn area. It ships copper anodes to Montreal for refining.

(C. Cy.)

ROVERETO, a town of the province of Trento, Italy, 15 mi. by rail southwest of the town of that name. Pop. (1951) 22,642 (commune). Built on the left bank of the Adige, in the widest portion of the valley, it is divided into two parts by the Leno torrent. Save in the newer quarter of the town, the streets are narrow and crooked, one being named after the most distinguished native of the place, Antonio Rosmini-Serbati (*q.v.*). The finest church is that of Sta. Maria del Carmine, the old 14th-century church now serving as a sacristy to that built from 1678 to 1750. The church of San Marco dates from the 15th century, and so do the municipal palace and the savings bank. The town is dominated by the castle (containing a war museum), which was reconstructed in 1492 by the Venetians, after it had been burned in 1487 by the count of Tirol. It was very much damaged in World War I, but its industries (silk, cotton, gloves, paper, metals, etc.) later revived.

In 1132 the emperor Lothair found the passage of the gorge above the site of the town barred by a castle, which he took and gave to one of his Teutonic followers, the ancestor of the Castelbarco family. The first record of the town dates from 1154. In 1411 it was taken by the Venetians. In 1509 the town gave itself voluntarily to the emperor Maximilian, to whom it was ceded formally by Venice in 1517, and next year incorporated with Tirol.

ROVIGNO, a seaport of Italy, in Istria, 23 mi. N.N.W. of Pola by rail. Pop. (1936) 9,035 (town), 10,028 (commune). It is on the west coast of Istria, and possesses a cathedral, built on the summit of Monte di Sant' Eufemia. Its campanile, built after the model of the famous campanile in Venice, is crowned with a bronze statue of St. Eufemia, the patron saint of the town, whose remains are preserved in the church. In the neighbourhood are vineyards and olive gardens. Rovigno is the principal centre of the local sardine fishery and cannery.

Rovigno is the ancient Arupenum or Rubinum. It became Venetian in 1283.

ROVIGO, town of Venetia, It., capital of the province of Rovigo. It stands between the lower Adige and the lower Po, 50 mi. S.W. of Venice by rail and 27 mi. S.S.W. of Padua, and on the Adigetto canal, 17 ft. above sea level. Pop. (1936) 14,561 (town), 39,954 (commune). It is a station on the line between Bologna and Padua, with branches to Legnago and Chioggia. The architecture of the town bears the stamp both of Venetian and of Ferrarese influence. The finest church is the Madonna del Soccorso, an octagon with a lofty campanile, begun in 1594 by Francesco Zamberlan of Bassano, a pupil of Andrea Palladio. The town hall contains a library including some rare early editions and a fair picture gallery. The Palazzo Roncale is a fine Renaissance building by Sanmicheli (1555). Two towers of the mediaeval castle remain (920). Rovigo (Neo-Latin *Rhodigium*) is mentioned as Rodigo in 838.

ROVNO (Pol. ROWNE), a city of the Ukrainian S.S.R., capital of Rovno oblast, on a tributary of the Goryn; formerly in Volhynia province, Poland. Pop. (1931) 40,788. Though it never had the political importance of Luck or Ostrog, Rovno grew to be a larger town than either of these. It is an important railway junction, the centre of an agricultural district, near the Volhynian forests and in a region famous for its horses and cattle. It is on the famous route west from Kiev along which many Russian conquerors, Tatar raiders and foreign armies have passed. It is first mentioned in 1282, and formerly possessed a royal palace. It was taken by the U.S.S.R. in 1939 and by Germany in 1941, and was ceded to the U.S.S.R. in 1945.

ROVUMA, a river, about 500 mi. long, forming the boundary between Tanganyika territory and Portuguese East Africa. The lower Rovuma is formed by the junction of two branches of nearly equal importance, the longer, the Lujenda, coming from the southwest; the other, the Rovuma, from the west. Its source lies on a plateau of Archaean rocks 3,000 ft. high, east of Lake Nyasa. In its eastward course the Rovuma flows near the base of the escarpment of an arid plateau to the north, from which direction the streams, which have cut themselves deep channels in the plateau edge, have almost all short courses. On the opposite bank the Rovuma receives, besides the Lujenda, the Msenga and Luchulingo, flowing in broad valleys running from south to north. The Lujenda rises near Lake Chilwa, in the small Lake Chiuta (1,700 ft.), the swamps to the south of this being separated from Chilwa only by a narrow wooded ridge. The river, at its mouth about 1 mi. wide, is fordable in many places in the dry season.

ROWE, NICHOLAS (1674–1718), English dramatist and miscellaneous writer, son of John Rowe (d. 1692), barrister and serjeant-at-law, was baptized at Little Barford in Bedfordshire on June 30, 1674. Nicholas Rowe was educated at Westminster school under Dr. Busby. He became in 1688 a King's scholar, and entered the Middle Temple in 1691. On his father's death he became the master of an independent fortune. His first play, *The Ambitious Stepmother,* the scene of which is laid in Persepolis, was produced in 1700, and was followed in 1702 by *Tamerlane.* In this play the conqueror represented William III, and Louis XIV is denounced as Bajazet. It was for many years regularly acted on the anniversary of William's landing at Torbay. In *The Fair Penitent* (1703), an adaptation of Massinger and Field's *Fatal Dowry,* occurs the character of Lotghario, whose name passed into current use as the equivalent of a rake. Calista is said to have suggested to Samuel Richardson the character of Clarissa Harlowe, as Lothario suggested Lovelace. Other plays are: *The Biter* (1704), *Ulysses* (1706), *The Royal Convert* (1707), *The Tragedy of Jane Shore* (1714) and *The Tragedy of Lady Jane Grey* (1715).

In 1715 Rowe succeeded Nahum Tate as poet laureate. He died on Dec. 6, 1718, and was buried in Westminster abbey.

Rowe was the first modern editor of Shakespeare. It is unfortunate that he based his text (6 vols., 1709) on the corrupt Fourth Folio, a course in which he was followed by later editors. We owe to him the preservation of a number of Shakespearian traditions, collected for him at Stratford by Thomas Betterton. These materials he used with considerable judgment in the memoir prefixed to the *Works.* He divided the play into acts and scenes on a reasonable method, noted the entrances and exits of the players, and prefixed a list of the *dramatis personae* to each play.

Rowe's *Works* were printed in 1727, and in 1736, 1747, 1756, 1766 and 1792; his occasional poems are included in Anderson's and other collections of the British poets.

ROWELL, NEWTON WESLEY (1867–1941), Canadian jurist, was born on Nov. 1, 1867, in Middlesex county, Ontario. He was called to the bar in 1891, and became head of a law firm in Toronto. He was elected to the Ontario legislative assembly for North Oxford in 1911, and from that year to 1917 was leader of the liberal opposition in the Ontario legislature. In Oct. 1917 he entered the federal government as president of the council and vice-chairman of the war committee of the cabinet, and was a member of the dominion lower house 1917–21. He was a member of the Imperial war cabinet and Imperial War conference, 1918; Canadian representative at the International Labour conference at Washington, 1919; and a Canadian delegate to the first assembly of the League of Nations at Geneva, 1920, subsequently becoming vice-president of the League of Nations society in Canada. He wrote *The British Empire and World Peace* (1922), and *Canada, a Nation* (1923). He became a K.C. in 1902, and was chief justice of Ontario, 1936–38. He died Nov. 22, 1941.

ROWING, the propulsion of a boat by means of oars in a succession of strokes. An oar is a shaft of wood with a rounded handle at one end and a blade at the other. The blade, a thin broadened surface is either flat or slightly curved to offer increased resistance to the water (spoon-oar). The loom or middle portion rests in a notch or row-lock or between thole-pins on the gunwale or outrigger of the boat.

Racing oars are provided with leather buttons to prevent the oar from slipping outward. An oar may be regarded as a lever of the first order, the weight to be moved being the water and the fulcrum being at the lock or thole-pin; or as a lever of the second order, the weight to be moved being the boat, and the ful-

crum the water pressing against the blade. Theoretically an oar functions at one and the same time in both capacities (see G. C. Bourne, *A Text-Book of Oarsmanship,* chapter 11, Oxford, 1925), but practically the lock or pin is the fulcrum, and the point at which the oar is buttoned determines the leverage and is a fundamental factor in the mechanics of rowing.

Rowing a boat and paddling a canoe (*q.v.*) have in common the propulsion of a floating craft through the water by muscular power applied to a lever, oar or paddle, in a succession of strokes. But in rowing, the oarsman, seated on a thwart, faces toward the stern and pulls the oar handle toward his body with the tholepin or oarlock as a fixed fulcrum, while in paddling a canoe the canoeist, generally in a kneeling position, faces toward the bow and throws forward the weight of his body, using one arm as a moving fulcrum. In nautical use sculling is the propulsion of a boat by a single long oar worked to and fro from a notch in the stern transom, the blade being turned under water so as to give both projection and direction and acting like the tail of a fish. "Sweeps" and "sculls" are traditional terms for long and short oars.

As rowing developed into a form of competitive sport new terms were introduced and traditional terms acquired special meanings. Technically a stroke includes all the motions of an oarsman from the time he dips his oar for the catch to the time when it is again in the same position. The recovery is the part of the stroke during which the blade is in the air. Feathering is turning the blade by a wrist motion as it is lifted from the water and carrying it toward the bow in a nearly horizontal position until it is squared or bevelled (*i.e.,* the upper edge inclined slightly to the stern) for the next stroke. If the oarsman fails to clear the water with his blade on the recovery, because he has feathered too soon or too much or too little or because the boat has lurched down on his side, he "catches a crab."

Sculling as distinguished from its nautical sense is propelling a light racing craft with an oar in each hand. Oars so used are called sculls. "Singles" and "doubles" are popular entries in all regattas, and champion scullers have won wide acclaim. Rowing in the specialized sense is the art of propelling a racing craft by two or more oarsmen, each of whom handles a single oar, called a sweep. Paddling in boat racing parlance is rowing at reduced speed and at a leisurely pace. Sweep oarsmen row in pairs, fours, sixes (obsolete) and eights, the latter achieving the greatest speed and requiring the most complete co-ordination of skill. Eights are numbered from the bow, and number eight is known as stroke.

The coxswain (cock, a small boat; swain as in boatswain) not only steers but gives the necessary commands and in a race calls for spurts and in a stern chase informs the captain or the stroke of the position of the competing boats. The coxswain is the quarterback of the rowing team and with the stroke should plan and determine the strategy and rowing of each race.

A well-trained and finished eight-oared crew and a single sculler represent the highest developments of the art of rowing, and to produce a winning eight is the ambition of every club or school or college that fosters rowing as a form of competitive sport.

History.—Rowing is now confined almost entirely to small boats and racing shells, but in ancient times it was the chief means of propelling vessels of war. As the size of vessels increased, sails gradually displaced oars, in both warships and merchant ships, but large galleys (*q.v.*) continued to be rowed in the Mediterranean until the 18th century. The oarsmen, generally captives of war or criminals, were chained to the benches, whence the term "galley slaves." Ancient galleys were rated according to the number of rowing banks or tiers of oars. The first recorded Roman fleet consisted of triremes. The earliest amateur oarsmen of whom there is record were the islanders who hospitably entertained Ulysses on his return to Ithaca. Their epithet in the Odyssey is "the oar-loving Phaeacians" (Φαίηκες φιλήρετμοι). Boat races probably formed part of the Panathenaic and Isthmian festivals (*see* BOAT).

Virgil, in his account of the funeral games instituted by Aeneas for his father Anchises, gives a vivid description of a boat race (*Aeneid,* v, 114–285):

The waiting crews are crowned with poplar wreaths;
Their naked shoulders glisten, moist with oil.
Ranged in a row, their arms stretched to the oars,
All tense the starting signal they await.
Together at the trumpet's thrilling blast
Their bent arms churn the water into foam;
The sea gapes open by the oars up-torn;
With shouts and cheers of eager partisans
The woodlands ring, the sheltered beach rolls up
The sound, the hills re-echo with the din.

The earliest invasions of England were effected with the help of oars. The Britons, paddling wicker coracles, were no match for the legions that Caesar landed on their beachheads from his Roman triremes. Later the Anglo-Saxons, rowing and sailing across the North sea, and after them the Danes, entered the estuaries of the east coast. Sails are mentioned oftener than oars in Old English literature, and rowing had not yet become a sport that could be described in Shakespeare's words:

There are some sports are painful, and their labour
Delight in them sets off.

William of Malmesbury (c. 1080–c. 1143) records that Edgar the Peaceful was rowed in state on the river Dee by tributary kings, himself acting as coxswain.

Boat Racing in England.—The Thames may fairly be called the cradle of rowing as a pastime and competitive sport in modern times. The nobility and gentry who had mansions on the banks of the river relied almost entirely on their elaborately fitted barges as a means of conveyance. As early as 1454 Sir John Norman, mayor of London, "built a noble barge, and was rowed by watermen with silver oars." The lord mayor's procession by water to Westminster was an annual event until 1856. From the 15th century on, a considerable body of men lived by "the trade of rowing" as the statutes define the occupation of the watermen. In Queen Anne's time the river was still the highway of London, and there were about 10,000 licensed watermen on the tidal reaches of the Thames above London bridge. There were undoubtedly competitions between these in the 16th and 17th centuries, but the first race of which there is record is that for the "Doggett's Coat and Badge." Thomas Doggett, an Irish comedian, in 1715 offered an "orange livery with a badge representing Liberty to be rowed for by six watermen from London Bridge to Chelsea, annually on the same day, August 1, forever." Except during World Wars I and II, the race was rowed regularly under the administration of the Fishmongers' company.

The first English regatta (Italian *regata,* originally a gondola race in Venice) took place on the Thames in 1775. Though there are numerous instances of professional matches at the beginning of the 19th century, the increased participation in boat racing by amateur oarsmen, after the Napoleonic wars, overshadowed professional rowing, which never had the vogue in England which it attained in the United States (*see* below). Eton had a ten-oared boat, the "Monarch," and three eight-oars as early as 1811, but there is no record of any formal racing between amateur crews until 1817, the date of the founding of the Leander club, which rapidly gained the prestige it maintained from that time, as the oldest and most distinguished rowing club, whose eights, composed mainly of Oxford and Cambridge varsity oarsmen, upheld the highest standards of English rowing and sportsmanship.

The first race between Oxford and Cambridge was rowed in 1829 over a 2-mi. course at Henley, but it was not renewed until 1836. In 1845 the race was rowed over a 4¼-mi. course from Putney to Mortlake, and in 1856 became an annual event except during World Wars I and II, attracting huge crowds along the banks of the river.

The Henley Royal Regatta.—The reaches of the Thames at Henley are not only the most beautiful along the river, but, because of a straight stretch of more than a mile immediately below the town, offer an ideal course for racing shells.

The Henley Royal regatta, established in 1839, has brought together not only the pick of English crews but, in the open events, has attracted competitors from Europe, America and Australia. Like other comparable events, it was interrupted by World Wars I and II. The course is 1 mi. 550 yd. with its finish near the town bridge in sheltered water, with sunny meadows and the shaded lawns of country houses on each side of the river. The races are rowed in the first week of July and furnish three days of continuous excitement to the spectators that throng the towpath and the enclosures at the finish. Owing to the narrowness of the river and the many entries, the races are now rowed in heats of two or more entries. The course is protected by booms on each side, behind which spectators in punts and on houseboats moored along the banks obtain an unobstructed and close view of the competing oarsmen. There have for many years been eight events, four of which are open to all amateurs; viz., the Grand Challenge cup for eight oars (the oldest, established in 1839), the Stewards' cup for fours, the Silver Goblets for pair-oars and the Diamond Sculls for single scullers. In 1939 a ninth event, the Double Sculls, was added. The Grand Challenge cup and the Diamond Sculls have long been the most coveted trophies in the rowing world.

Australia and Canada.—Rowing as a sport began in Tasmania about 1830, and by 1880 eight-oared races between crews representing the various states had become annual fixtures, held alternately in the six capital cities. Interuniversity rowing originated in 1870. In 1893 Old Blues from Oxford and Cambridge presented the magnificent Oxford and Cambridge cup, which thereafter was contested for by the six state universities and like the interstate contest is rowed in each capital city by rotation.

In Canada, the 1870s were the heyday of the professional scullers. Purses ran from $50 upward to $1,000 and in international matches from £500 to £2,000. The outstanding world champion was Edward Hanlan of Toronto, who defeated the best scullers of Canada, the U.S., England and Australia. As the distinction between professional and amateur rowing became more sharply drawn, following the lead of England, Canada developed numerous amateur rowing clubs, among them the famous Argonauts of Toronto. There is a Royal Canadian Henley regatta held annually at Port Dalhousie, Ont.

United States.—In the United States, as in England, rowing as a competitive sport originated in contests between "occupational" oarsmen. In 1811 and 1823 the ferrymen of Whitehall in New York city defeated their Long Island and Staten Island rivals on the Hudson. In 1824 they outrowed a crew of Thames watermen from the visiting British frigate "Hussar," in a four-mile race finishing at the Battery. This international race aroused tremendous local interest and the betting far exceeded the original stake of $1,000 offered by the captain of the "Hussar." Light keelless racing shells soon displaced the service boats of the early contests. The cleavage between amateur and professional, following the organization of the National Association of Amateur Oarsmen (N.A.A.O.) in 1872, inaugurated the golden age of professional sculling. Among the scullers who won national and international fame were James Hamill, J. A. Ten Eyck, Wallace Ross, George Hosmer, Fred A. Plaisted, Walter Brown and Joshua Ward. The four Ward brothers had won an international race at Saratoga, N.Y., in 1871. Charles Courtney, who had begun as an amateur, turned professional and became the leading rival of the great Canadian Hanlan for championship honours and rewards. He was defeated by Hanlan in an exciting race at Lachine, Ont., in 1878. A return match for a purse of $6,000 at Lake Chautauqua was never rowed because Courtney's shell was found hacked in two on the morning of the race. This fiasco and the suspicion that betting and shady "deals" influenced the results of races were responsible for the decline of professional sculling in the United States. Courtney's later reputation was based on his success as coach of the Cornell crews, as was Ten Eyck's as coach of the Syracuse university crews for 35 years.

Amateur Clubs.—The first organization of amateur clubs was the Castle Garden Boat Club association of New York (1834); pleasure boating rather than racing was the main interest of these early clubs, their membership being based on social rather than aquatic prestige. The Detroit Boat club, 1839, the oldest survivor of these early clubs, is today one of the most important members of the N.A.A.O. and has entered crews in many regattas. In 1858 the boat clubs along the Schuylkill river, Philadelphia, Pa., were organized as the Schuylkill Navy. The boathouses of the

Navy stretch for nearly a quarter-mile along the banks of the river in Fairmount park, and until the silting up of the river, the Schuylkill course was one of the most popular and picturesque in the U.S., during the years when Philadelphia was a centre of the two great English sports of cricket and rowing. The first regatta to which only amateur oarsmen were admitted followed the organization of the N.A.A.O. in 1872 and was rowed on the Schuylkill under the auspices of the Schuylkill Navy. The N.A.A.O. thereafter was the chief promoter of rowing among the amateur clubs, holding annual regattas for the championship of the United States in singles, doubles, quadruples, fours and eights.

Intercollegiate Rowing.—The first formal intercollegiate boat race was rowed between Harvard and Yale in 1852 on Lake Winnipesaukee. In 1944, because of the use of the New London course by the United States navy, the race was shortened to two miles and rowed on the Housatonic river. The Yale-Harvard boat race is the oldest college contest in the United States and antedates football by 17 years.

In the 1870s rowing became popular at a number of eastern colleges. In 1875 there was a regatta on Saratoga lake in which 13 colleges participated. When Yale and Harvard in 1878 went to New London for their dual race, Lake George became the scene of college races in fours in which Cornell or Pennsylvania generally won, Wesleyan, Bowdoin, Columbia and Princeton affording good competition. In 1887 eights took the place of fours, and, until the establishment of the Poughkeepsie regatta in 1895, these races were rowed at New London, Cayuga lake, Lake Minnetonka and one on the Delaware at Torresdale (1894). From the inauguration of the four-mile race at New London, Harvard and Yale regarded this as the culmination of their rowing season. Though the record of the Cornell crews in the 1890s, the defeats of Yale and Harvard by Cornell and Princeton crews in the decade 1911–21, and the appearance of California and Washington and the U.S. Naval academy at Poughkeepsie challenged the leadership in college rowing that formerly could fairly be claimed by Harvard and Yale, the picturesqueness of the New London course, the tradition of the race and the prestige of Yale and Harvard among U.S. universities continued to surround the Harvard-Yale boat race with an interest analogous to that surrounding the Oxford-Cambridge race in England, the one rowed on the English Thames at London and the other on the United States Thames at New London. In 1895 Cornell, Columbia, Syracuse and Pennsylvania joined in a rowing association with annual regattas open to invited crews at Poughkeepsie. The Poughkeepsie regatta continued not only to attract the foremost eastern college crews; it also brought to the Hudson winning eights from the universities of California, Washington and Wisconsin and the United States Naval academy. Because of unsatisfactory water conditions and lack of interest, the Intercollegiate Rowing association (I.R.A.) regatta was moved to Marietta, O., for 1950 and 1951. Bad water conditions there caused its removal to Lake Onondaga, Syracuse, N.Y., where a satisfactory regatta, the 50th anniversary of the I.R.A., was held in 1952.

In contrast to the dual race at New London, Poughkeepsie has had as many as nine starters in the interuniversity race. From 1895 to 1915 Cornell led in number of victories. Since the entrance of the U.S. Naval academy, Washington and California, these have been the most frequent winners.

Rowing was established on the Pacific coast in 1899. The first race, in fours, was between Washington and California. In 1907 eights displaced fours, and the Washington-California race, alternating between Lake Washington and the estuary at Oakland, Calif., became the rowing feature in the far west, and these crews soon began winning laurels at Poughkeepsie and in Olympic competitions. The favourable climatic conditions of the far west, permitting rowing in the open the year round, the abundance of material in the great state universities and the program of rowing developed in the western universities all contributed to the enviable record of the western crews.

Princeton had abandoned rowing in 1884, but, as a result of Andrew Carnegie's gift of a lake formed by the damming of two streams and affording 3½ mi. of rowing water, resumed the sport in 1910. At this time the only races that college crews trained for were the long-distance contests at New London and Poughkeepsie. Princeton's revival of rowing was responsible for the inauguration of a series of short-distance races, 1⅞ to 2 mi., rowed on college waters and during term time, generally participated in by three crews and called triangular races. In 1912 the Childs cup race, next to the Yale and Harvard race the oldest intercollegiate fixture, was revived. This trophy had been given in 1879 by George W. Childs, the publisher of the *Philadelphia Ledger,* to be competed for by Columbia, Princeton and Pennsylvania, but the race had lapsed after 1884. In 1911 Princeton inaugurated intercollegiate rowing on Lake Carnegie with a triangular race between Yale, Cornell and Princeton, in which Princeton defeated Yale and came in as a close second to a fast Cornell crew that later won at Poughkeepsie. The Carnegie cup offered for this race in 1921 came into annual competition. Later a race between Yale, Columbia and Pennsylvania for the Blackwell cup and between the U.S. Naval academy, Pennsylvania and Harvard for the Adams cup became annual fixtures. All these races are alternately rowed on college waters, on Lake Cayuga, Lake Carnegie, the Charles river, the Housatonic river, the Schuylkill river and the Severn river at Annapolis, and before the close of the spring term. Later, Syracuse university and Massachusetts Institute of Technology also participated.

An annual regatta conducted by a group of smaller colleges under the name of the Dad Vail Rowing association, in honour of a former coach of Wisconsin, is participated in by Amherst college, Boston university, Dartmouth college, Florida Southern college, La Salle college, Marietta college, Rollins college, Rutgers university and the University of Tampa.

The increased interest in rowing at the colleges led to the organization of lightweight crews averaging 150 lb. per man. Some of these crews made up in skill and speed for lack of weight, and in competing at the Royal Henley for the Thames Challenge cup defeated in trial heats some of the best English college crews.

Rowing became a highly popular sport among both public and private schools. U.S. schoolboy crews have won the Thames cup at Henley. There are various regattas especially for school crews and attracting numerous entries.

In 1902 the American Rowing association was formed to increase intercollegiate competition by means of short-distance races in the early season, concluding with an annual regatta at the Henley distance of 1 mi. 550 yd. Thus this regatta became popularly known as the American Henley. This association, with the introduction of short-distance races, did a great deal to stimulate college rowing. It likewise had events at its annual regatta open for club crews who thereby matched their skill against college crews.

U.S. College Crews in Europe.—In 1869 Harvard challenged Oxford and Cambridge to a four-oared race on the Thames from Putney to Mortlake; Oxford accepted and won.

In the only other interuniversity race between English and Americans, Cambridge in 1906 defeated Harvard by about two lengths. There have been many U.S. entries at Henley. In 1878 a four from Columbia university won the Visitors' cup. In 1881 a Cornell four was defeated for the Stewards' cup, and in 1895 a Cornell eight lost to Trinity hall, Cambridge. In 1896 Leander beat a Yale crew coached by Bob Cook. In 1901 a University of Pennsylvania eight lost by a few seconds to Leander in the finals for the Grand Challenge cup. In 1914 the survivors in the finals for the Grand Challenge cup were Harvard and the Union Boat club of Boston, composed of former Harvard oarsmen; Harvard won, bringing the cup to the United States for the first time. Princeton in 1934 was defeated by Leander in the finals of the Grand Challenge; both crews broke the Henley record established in 1891. In 1939 and 1950 Harvard again brought the Grand Challenge cup to the U.S. Princeton in 1930 and 1934 and Yale and Harvard in 1938 entered 150-lb. crews for the Thames cup, which was won by Kent school in 1933, 1938, 1947 and 1950, by Tabor academy in 1936, 1937 and 1939 (both schoolboy crews) and by the University of Pennsylvania in 1951 and 1952.

Strokes, Styles and Coaches.—Sweep rowing was early differentiated from sculling in England. The so-called "English stroke" was developed by Oxford and Cambridge oarsmen. As exemplified by the best Leander crews and described by Edmond Warre, provost of Eton (*A Grammar of Rowing*, Oxford, 1909), and R. C. Lehman of Cambridge (*The Complete Oarsman*, London, 1924), this stroke was based on early fixed-seat rowing, when body swing was the main source of power and the arms were used chiefly as connecting rods to transfer the weight of the body to the oar. When the sliding seat, an American invention, was introduced, the leg drive was added but the main stress was still on the body swing with shoulders carried well beyond the perpendicular at the finish. This required muscles which only years of practice could develop. The first challenge to this "orthodox" stroke came from a Cambridge student, Stephen Fairbairn, who had entered Jesus college from Australia in 1881 and as a member and coach of his college crews upset tradition by winning races in a style taboo to the "rigidly righteous" of the old school. Fairbairn (*Rowing Notes; Chats on Rowing*, Cambridge, 1934) emphasized leg drive and arm pull and considered smooth bladework more important than what he called the "showy style" of body work. If the proponents of the traditional stroke sometimes laid more emphasis on form than on speed, Fairbairn's stroke sacrificed form for speed.

The success of his and foreign crews was responsible for the adoption of innovations from abroad, such as the lengthened slide, the use of the swivel lock in place of tholepins and the seating of crews amidships in straight alignment instead of in the staggered order formerly used to increase leverage.

The British have devoted much time to the technical and theoretic aspects of rowing. A good exposition of the British system is G. C. Bourne's *A Text-Book of Oarsmanship*. R. C. Lehman, a leading exponent of the British system, was in 1896 invited to coach the Harvard crews. To Yale in 1914 went Guy Nickalls as head coach, and to Pennsylvania his brother Vivian. Though all these men had brilliant records as oarsmen and coaches in England and stimulated interest in rowing at the universities they visited, the English system did not permanently strike root in the U.S. Many of the dons in the English universities assist in coaching their college crews. Sir Leslie Stephen was an enthusiastic coach in his Oxford days. At Henley may frequently be seen on the towpath coaches who are equally at home among books and boats and who combine reading as a vocation with rowing as an avocation.

In the United States as in England the colleges first popularized rowing as a competitive amateur sport. The first college coaches were former professional scullers. Charles Courtney at Cornell, Ellis Ward at Pennsylvania, Edward Hanlan Ten Eyck at Syracuse, Richard Glendon at Annapolis, William Haines at Harvard and M.I.T. were types of "professionals" who instilled into their charges principles of honour, loyalty and courage, besides rowing technique and strict conformity to training rules.

The stroke they taught was essentially a sculling stroke adapted to sweep rowing. The first attempt to introduce a stroke differentiated from sculling and based on the scientific principles of the "English" stroke was made by Robert Cook of Yale, who, as an undergraduate in 1881, when captain of his crew, went to England and studied the system prevailing at Oxford and Cambridge. The Yale crews of the next 20 years coached by him were noted both for speed and form. The "Bob Cook" stroke was characterized by a hard catch with squared shoulders, straight back, straight arms, quick hand shoot and slow slide on the recovery, length in the water and lower beat than the prevailing "sculling" strokes. After the Cornell experience at Henley in 1895, Courtney, always ready to experiment and improve both rigging and rowing, modified the short sculling stroke his crew had previously rowed, and in the Poughkeepsie regatta of 1896, in which both Yale and Harvard participated, it was difficult to distinguish Cornell from Yale.

In later years Courtney modified the hard catch, shortened the swing at the finish and developed the slow slide and run between strokes that enabled Cornell to defeat crews rowing a much higher stroke. The advocates of the lower stroke say, "If men were machines, the crew rowing the highest stroke would always win, but men are not machines and a lower stroke and smooth form conserve power." Richard Glendon at the U.S. Naval academy taught a stroke with exaggerated swing of the body at the finish. The fine physique of the midshipmen, combined with their finished watermanship, brought victories to this stroke at Poughkeepsie and in the Olympics. The nearest approach to what may be called an "American stroke" was made by Hiram Connibear and his pupils at the University of Washington. Connibear, himself not an oarsman, when appointed rowing coach at Washington in 1907, studied Yale, Cornell and Syracuse methods, and on his return became an expert technician as well as an inspiring leader. He developed at the University of Washington, aided by the Pocock brothers, expert builders and riggers of racing shells, a system that by the 1940s dominated college rowing east and west. Edward Leader at Yale, Thomas Bolles at Harvard, Fred Spuhn at Princeton, Russell Callow at Pennsylvania, Harrison Sanford at Cornell, Alvin Ulbrickson at Washington, Carroll Ebright at California, Robert Mock at Massachusetts Institute of Technology and Charles Logg at Rutgers were all products of the University of Washington and as coaches belonged to what fairly may be called the "Washington school" of rowing. As a matter of fact, there were only a few universities whose coaches were not former Washington oarsmen; viz., Edward Hanlan Ten Eyck of Syracuse, Charles S. Walsh of the U.S. Naval academy, Hubert Glendon of Columbia and Allen W. Walz of Wisconsin.

While in England college coaches are "invited" by the captains of crews or boat clubs, in the United States intercollegiate athletics became increasingly subject to faculty control, and coaches of major sports such as football and rowing are appointed by college authorities and considered part of the salaried staff of the institution. They are usually college graduates who have as amateurs been active in the sport they direct. A similar departure from the earlier system of professional coaching took place in the boat clubs.

Robert F. Herrick at Harvard, Averell Harriman and Mather Abbott at Yale, J. Duncan Spaeth and Gordon Sikes at Princeton and Father Sill at Kent acted as volunteer amateur coaches at their institutions; similar examples among the rowing clubs could be noted. However, the system of salaried but otherwise nonprofessional coaches described above became prevalent in the United States.

Governing Bodies and the Olympic Games.—The first duty of the governing bodies for rowing in each nation is to establish an amateur rule specifying the qualifications necessary for anyone to engage in amateur rowing competition. The governing body's authority and rulings must be respected by the organizations and individuals participating in the sport, and it must have power to disqualify and suspend those who violate the amateur status or other rules prescribed for rowing competition.

It is also the responsibility of the national governing body in each nation to hold a championship regatta each year which shall be open to all classes that are eligible under the amateur rule.

Winners of Singles and Eights in Olympic Regattas

Year*	Place	Singles		Eights	
		Winner	Country	Winner	Country
1900	Paris	Barreleti	France	Vesper Boat club	U.S.
1904	St. Louis	F. B. Greer	U.S.	Vesper Boat club	U.S.
1908	London	H. T. Blackstaffe	England	Leander	England
1912	Stockholm	W. D. Kinnear	England	Leander	England
1920	Antwerp	J. B. Kelly	U.S.	U.S. Naval academy	U.S.
1924	Paris	J. Beresford, Jr.	England	Yale university	U.S.
1928	Amsterdam	H. R. Pearce	Australia	University of California	U.S.
1932	Los Angeles	H. R. Pearce	Australia	University of California	U.S.
1936	Berlin	G. Schaeffer	Germany	University of Washington	U.S.
1948	London	M. Wood	Australia	University of California	U.S.
1952	Helsinki	J. Tjukalov	U.S.S.R.	U.S. Naval academy	U.S.

*In 1916, 1940 and 1944 there were no Olympic games.

It is also the duty of the governing body, which in the U.S. is the Olympic Rowing committee, to conduct tryouts every four years to select those who are to compete in the international Olympic regatta.

The National Association of Amateur Oarsmen is the governing body in the U.S. for the clubs. For college rowing the Intercollegiate Rowing association and the Eastern Association of Rowing Colleges are the governing bodies in all regattas. In Canada it is the Canadian Association of Amateur Oarsmen, and in Great Britain it is the British Amateur Rowing association.

For international competition, the International Rowing federation, whose exact name is the Fédération International Sociétés d'Aviron (F.I.S.A.), is composed of the recognized national rowing organization in each nation. The International Rowing federation is the only organization that is recognized by the International Olympic committee; it is given charge of organizing and conducting the rowing competition in the Olympic games which are held every four years. In addition to this the international federation conducts a European championship regatta every year. At this regatta entries are accepted only from the nations whose governing bodies are members of the international federation. For the Olympic regatta, entries from any nation are acceptable providing that the amateur status of the oarsman entered is in accordance with the Olympic rules.

There are seven events on the Olympic program; viz., single sculls, double sculls, pair-oared shells without coxswain, pair-oared shells with coxswain, four-oared shells without coxswain, four-oared shells with coxswain and eight-oared shells. The distance at the Olympic regatta is 2,000 m., or 13 yd. less than $1\frac{1}{4}$ mi. As in most regattas, the two principal events are the single sculls and the eight-oared shells.

Thirty-three nations competed in the XVth Olympiad rowing events at Helsinki, Fin., in 1952. There were 114 entries in the seven events.

The National Association of Amateur Oarsmen was organized in 1872 in order to make a necessary distinction between amateur and professional competition. There was much professional rowing up to that time; amateurs and professionals were competing together and it was necessary that some means be found to meet this situation. The same condition in other sports prompted similar governing organizations for the same purpose. The association is composed of clubs and rowing organizations throughout the United States. Actual administration of the association is vested in an executive committee of 19.

Outstanding Oarsmen.—Records indicate that the three most outstanding English oarsmen were Guy Nickalls, Sr., who won the Diamonds five times and stroked pairs, fours and eights to victory many times at Henley; F. S. Kelly, a great sculler who won the Diamonds three times; and J. Beresford, Jr., who won the Diamonds four times and competed in five Olympic regattas, being a victor in three and second in two.

Among the oarsmen of the United States, perhaps the most outstanding have been Edward Hanlan Ten Eyck, John B. Kelly, Paul Costello, Walter M. Hoover, Joseph W. Burk and Joseph Angyal. Kelly was the most versatile. In addition to winning three Olympic championships, he stroked pairs, fours and eights to victory many times. Burk made a most remarkable record in single sculling. In four years, 1937–40 inclusive, he won a total of 46 races in single sculls. These included the United States national championship four times, the Canadian championship four times, the Diamond Sculls twice and the Philadelphia Gold Challenge cup. He was voted the most outstanding athlete in the United States in 1939 when he was awarded the James E. Sullivan trophy.

In Canada, the dean of rowing and the most outstanding was Joseph Wright, Sr., of the Argonaut Rowing club, who won many races as stroke of pairs, fours and eights and as such competed at Henley five times. Other outstanding Canadian oarsmen were Lou Scholes, first Canadian to win the Diamonds, Robert Dibble, Joseph Wright, Jr., and later H. R. Pearce; the last represented Australia in his first Olympic competition in 1928 and thereby under the rules was required to represent Australia in 1932, although he had in the meantime transferred his residence to Canada.

Australia produced many good crews and scullers. An Australian crew won the Grand Challenge cup at Henley and the Diamond Sculls. In single sculling, the most outstanding was H. R. Pearce, who won the Olympic single sculls championship in 1928 and 1932, and Mervyn Wood, who was world champion single sculler for nearly a decade until his defeat at the XVth Olympiad in 1952 by J. Tjukalov of the U.S.S.R.

BIBLIOGRAPHY.—R. C. Lehman, *The Complete Oarsman*, 3rd ed. (1924); G. C. Bourne, *A Text-Book of Oarsmanship* (Oxford, 1925); R. A. Glendon and R. J. Glendon, *Rowing* (1923); Robert F. Kelley, *American Rowing* (1932); C. V. P. Young, *Courtney and Cornell Rowing* (1923); George Pocock, "Technique and History of Shell Building," *N.A.A.O. Official Guide* (1940); Henry Penn Burke, *N.A.A.O. Year Books*.
(J. D. S.; H. P. B.; C. Gs.)

ROWLAND, HENRY AUGUSTUS (1848–1901), U.S. physicist, was born at Honesdale, Pa., on Nov. 27, 1848. He graduated as a civil engineer at Rensselaer Polytechnic institute at Troy in 1870, and two years later returned there as instructor in physics, becoming assistant professor in 1877. While at Troy he made investigations on magnetic induction, permeability and distribution, which established fundamental results. In 1875 he was chosen to occupy the chair of physics in the newly founded Johns Hopkins university, a position which he held until his death, at Baltimore, on April 16, 1901. Before beginning his work at Johns Hopkins he went to Europe, to visit the various physics research centres of the continent, and to purchase laboratory apparatus. He studied under Helmholtz in Berlin, where he carried out experiments proving that an electrostatic charge carried at a high rate of speed had the same magnetic action as an electric current. At Johns Hopkins he carried on a long series of experiments in which he computed the accepted value of the mechanical equivalent of heat, experiments which necessitated more careful thermometric and calorimetric methods than had ever been used before. Similar refined apparatus and technique enabled him to make a more nearly accurate determination of the value of the ohm, than had been calculated before. Becoming interested in the study of spectrum analysis, he realized the importance of securing more accurate diffraction gratings, and to this end constructed a dividing engine which allowed from 14,000 to 20,000 grating lines to be ruled to the inch on a plane surface of either glass or speculum metal. He next investigated the action of a grating ruled on a spherical concave surface, and, discovering the advantages proceeded to rule them. These gratings came to be used in physics laboratories the world over, and the modern study of spectroscopy as an exact science dates from this work. With these gratings Rowland studied and photographically mapped the solar spectrum for the first time. He then undertook the systematic study of the arc-spectra of all the elements so far as possible, and published his results between 1895 and 1900. In his last years he became interested in alternating currents and their practical application to motors, measuring instruments, etc. He devised a system of multiplex telegraphy depending upon synchronous motors which received a grand medal at the Paris Exposition of 1900. He was the recipient of many honours, including the Rumford and Draper medals.

See H. A. Rowland, *Physical Papers* (1902), which contains a bibliography of his writings.

ROWLANDSON, THOMAS (1756–1827), English caricaturist, was born in Old Jewry, London, in July 1756, the son of a tradesman or city merchant. On leaving school he became a student in the Royal academy, but at the age of 16 he went to study in Paris, and afterwards made frequent tours on the continent. In 1775 he exhibited at the Royal academy a drawing of "Delilah Visiting Samson in Prison." He took to drawing caricatures as a means of livelihood. His academy drawing of Vauxhall (1784) had been engraved by Pollard, and the print was a success. Rowlandson was largely employed by Rudolph Ackermann, the art publisher, who in 1809–11 issued in his *Poetical Magazine* "The Schoolmaster's Tour"—a series of plates with verses by Dr. William Coombe which became very popular. Again engraved by Rowlandson himself in 1812, and issued under the title of the "Tour of Dr. Syntax in Search of the Picturesque," they had reached a fifth edition by 1813, and were followed (1820) by "Dr. Syntax in Search of Consolation," and (1821) by the "Third Tour of Dr. Syntax in Search of a Wife." The same collaboration of designer, author and publisher resulted in the English "Dance of Death" (1814–16), and the "Dance of Life" (1822). Rowlandson also illustrated Smollett, Goldsmith and Sterne. Other designs are in *The Spirit of the Public Journals* (1825), *The English Spy* (1825), and *The Humourist* (1831). He died in London on April 22, 1827.

Rowlandson's designs were usually executed in outline with the reed-pen, and delicately washed with colour. They were then etched by the artist on the copper, and afterwards aqua-tinted—usually by a professional engraver, the impressions being finally coloured by hand. As a designer the quality of his work suffered from haste and over-production.

See J. Grego, *Rowlandson the Caricaturist, a Selection From his Works*, etc., 2 vol. (1880).

ROWLEY, WILLIAM (c. 1585–c. 1642), English actor and dramatist, collaborator with several of the dramatists of the Elizabethan period, especially with Thomas Middleton (q.v.). He is not to be identified with the "Master Rowley" whom Francis Meres described in his *Palladis Tamia*. William Rowley is described as the chief comedian in the Prince of Wales's company. He joined the King's Servants in 1623 and retired from the stage about four years later. He is supposed to have died about 1642. The following plays attributed to his sole authorship are extant: *A New Wonder, A Woman Never Vext* (printed 1632), *A Match at Midnight* (1633) and a *Shoomaker a Gentleman With the Life and Death of the Cripple That Stole the Weathercock at Paules* (1637). They are distinguished by effectiveness of situation and ingenuity of plot. It is recorded by Langbaine that he "was beloved of those great men Shakespeare, Fletcher and Jonson." With George Wilkins and John Day he wrote *The Travailes of the Three English Brothers* (1607); with Thomas Heywood he produced *Fortune by Land and Sea* (printed 1655); he was associated with Thomas Dekker and John Ford in *The Witch of Edmonton* (printed 1658); *A Cure for a Cuckold* (printed 1661) and *The Thracian Wonder* (printed 1661) are assigned to the joint authorship of Webster and Rowley; while Shakespeare's name was unjustifiably coupled with his on the title page of *The Birth of Merlin: or, The Childe Hath Found His Father* (1662). Rowley also wrote an elegy on Hugh Attwell, the actor, and a satirical pamphlet describing contemporary London, entitled *A Search for Money* (1609).

SAMUEL ROWLEY, the dramatist, described without apparent reason by J. P. Collier as William Rowley's brother, was employed by Henslowe as a reader of plays. He wrote some scriptural plays now lost, with William Borne (or Bird, or Boyle) and Edward Juby. His only extant pieces are: *When You See Me, You Know Me, or the Famous Chronicle Historie of King Henry the Eighth, With the Birth and Vertuous Life of Edward Prince of Wales* (1605), of interest because of its possible connection with the Shakespearean play of *Henry VIII*, and *The Noble Souldier, or, A Contract Broken, Justly Reveng'd* (1634), which was entered, however, in the Stationers' Register as the work of Thomas Dekker, to whom the major share is probably assignable.

ROWLEY REGIS, a municipal borough (since 1933) in the Rowley Regis and Tipton parliamentary division of Staffordshire, Eng., in a hilly district 7 mi. W. of Birmingham. Pop. (1951) 49,402. Area 6 sq.mi. The word Regis was added to Rowley (Roughlea) in 1140. Dud Dudley at Cradley forge first used coal instead of charcoal for smelting iron (patented 1620). The oldest and biggest industries are nail making (17th century) and chain making. By 1820 "Rowley rag," a basaltic stone, was being quarried extensively for roads and Rowley was thoroughly industrialized. Heavy engineering, enamelled hollow ware, brickworks at Blackheath and clay mines at Netherton are other industries. Haden Hill park was given to the council in 1921 and the Elizabethan house is used as a restaurant.

ROWLOCK (pronounced in England *rollock*), a device, on the gunwale of a boat, in or on which an oar rests, forming a fulcrum for the oar in rowing. The word is a corruption due to "row" of the earlier "oarlock," O.E. *ārlōc*, a lock or enclosed place for an oar. The simplest form of rowlock is a notch, square or rounded, on the gunwale, in which the oar rests; other kinds are formed by two pins or pegs, tholepins ("thole" being ultimately the same word as Norw. *toll*, a young fir tree), and by a swivel with two horns of metal, pivoted in the gunwale or on an outrigger. (*See* ROWING.)

ROWTON, MONTAGUE WILLIAM LOWRY-CORRY, BARON (1838–1903), son of the Right Hon. Henry Corry and Harriet, daughter of the 6th earl of Shaftesbury, was born in London on Oct. 8, 1838, educated at Harrow and at Trinity college, Cambridge, and called to the bar in 1863. His father, a son of the 2nd earl of Belmore, represented County Tyrone in parliament continuously from 1826 to 1873, and was a member of Lord Derby's cabinet (1866–68) as vice-president of the council and afterward as first lord of the admiralty. In 1866 Corry became private secretary to Disraeli, with whom he maintained close relations until the statesman's death in 1881. When Disraeli resigned office in 1868 Corry declined various offers of public employment in order to be free to continue his services, now given gratuitously, to the Conservative leader; and when the latter returned to power in 1874, Corry resumed his position as official private secretary to the prime minister. He accompanied Disraeli (then earl of Beaconsfield) to the congress of Berlin in 1878, where he acted as one of the secretaries of the special embassy of Great Britain. On the defeat of the Conservatives in 1880, Corry was raised to the peerage with the title of Baron Rowton, of Rowton Castle, Shropshire. After Beaconsfield's removal to the house of lords, Rowton assisted him in keeping in touch with the rank and file of the party, and on Beaconsfield's death he was put in charge of his correspondence and papers.

Lord Rowton will long be remembered as the originator of the scheme known as the Rowton houses. Consulted by Sir Edward Guinness (afterward Lord Iveagh) with regard to the latter's projected gift of £200,000 for endowment of a trust for the improvement of the dwellings of the working classes, Rowton made himself personally familiar with the conditions of the poorest inhabitants of London, and determined to establish "a poor man's hotel," which should offer better accommodation than the common lodginghouses at similar prices. The first Rowton house was opened at Vauxhall in Dec. 1892, the cost (£30,000) being defrayed by Lord Rowton, and it proved so successful that in 1894 a company, Rowton Houses (Limited), was incorporated to extend the scheme which was subsequently imitated throughout Great Britain, Europe and America. Lord Rowton also devoted himself to the business of the Guinness trust, of which he was a trustee. As he was unmarried the title became extinct on Lord Rowton's death on Nov. 9, 1903, at London.

See *Reports of the Rowton Houses, Ltd.*, 1895–1903; E. R. Dewsnup, *The Housing Problem in England* (1907); R. H. Vebch, *General Sir Andrew Clarke* (1905).

ROXANA or ROXANE, daughter of the Bactrian king Oxyartes and wife of Alexander the Great. After the latter's death she gave birth at Babylon to a son (Alexander IV), who was accepted by the generals as joint king with Arrhidaeus. Having crossed over to Macedonia and thrown in her lot with Olympias, mother of Alexander the Great, she was imprisoned by Cassander in the fortress of Amphipolis and put to death (310 or 309 B.C.). The marriage of Alexander and Roxana was the subject of a famous painting by Aëtion.

See Plutarch, *Alexander*, 47, 77; Arrian, *Anab.*, iv, 18, vii, 27; Diod. Sic. xviii, 3, 38, xix, 11, 52, 105; Strabo xi, p. 517, xvii, p. 794.

ROXAS CITY (formerly CAPIZ), in the province of Capiz, Phil., is an important town and port on the north side of Panay Island, at the mouth of the Panay river. The town is 11° 35′ N. and 122° 45′ E.; the port, 2½ mi. away, is 11° 36′ N. and 122° 43′ E. The town is the terminus of a railway from Iloilo and has an aeroplane field. The population of the municipality steadily increased for several decades and was 32,353 in 1948. The town is on the border of a region of rich tropical agricultural products—principally rice, sugar cane and coconuts on the plain, abacá in the mountains.

The harbour, in Capiz bay, protected from the open water of Jintotolo channel by Culasi hill on the north and strong moles on the west and south, can accommodate vessels of a draught of ten feet. Typhoons occur from time to time and do considerable damage. The villages of Culasi and Libas are on the harbour, the landward vicinity of which has dense growths of nipa and other swamp vegetation. The port does a coasting trade with Manila, Iloilo and other Philippine ports and has a fishing industry and fish canneries. Two roads connect the port with the town of Roxas City.

The town is celebrated for weaving abacá and pineapple fibre.

With the province of Capiz, Roxas City suffered heavily during World War II, but later recovered considerably. It was named after Manuel Roxas y Acuna, first president of the Philippine republic. (J. W. CR.)

ROXAS Y ACUNA, MANUEL (1892–1948), first president of the Republic of the Philippines, was born at Cadiz, Panay Island, P.I., on Jan. 1, 1892. He studied law at the University of the Philippines, entered politics, and in 1917 was appointed to the municipal council of Capiz (now Roxas City). He was governor of Capiz from 1919 to 1921, when he was elected to the house of representatives in the Philippines, later becoming speaker of the house. He was a member of the Philippine constitutional convention in 1934 and secretary of finance from 1938 to 1940.

During World War II he served as a colonel under Gen. Douglas MacArthur and later was captured by the Japanese. He helped to co-ordinate underground resistance to the invaders for three years, however. In 1945 he was president of the senate when, as a Liberal candidate, he was elected president of the Philippine commonwealth. When the country achieved its independence, July 4, 1946, Roxas became the first president of the new republic. He died at Clark field, Pampagna, on April 15, 1948.

ROXBURGHE, EARLS AND DUKES OF. ROBERT KER, 1st earl of Roxburghe (c. 1570–1650), was the eldest son of William Ker of Cessford (d. 1606) and the grandson of Sir Walter Ker (d. c. 1584), who fought against Mary queen of Scots both at Carberry hill and at Langside. He was descended from Sir Andrew Ker of Cessford (d. 1526), who fought at Flodden and was killed near Melrose in Jan. 1526 by the Scotts of Buccleuch. After a turbulent life on the border Robert Ker became a Scottish privy councillor in 1599 and was made Lord Roxburghe about the same time; he accompanied King James to London in 1603 and was created earl of Roxburghe in 1616. He was lord privy seal for Scotland from 1637 to 1649, and in the Scottish parliament he showed his sympathy with Charles I; but he took no part in the Civil War, although he signed the "engagement" for the king's release in 1648. His titles and estates passed by special arrangement to his grandson, WILLIAM DRUMMOND (d. 1675), the youngest son of his daughter Jean and her husband John Drummond, 2nd earl of Perth. William took the name of Ker, became 2nd earl of Roxburghe, and married his cousin Lord Ker's daughter Jean.

JOHN, 5th earl and 1st duke of Roxburghe (c. 1680–1741), received the dukedom in 1707 for his services in connection with the union. This was the last creation in the Scottish peerage. The duke was a representative peer for Scotland in four parliaments; George I made him a privy councillor and keeper of the privy seal of Scotland, and he was loyal to the king during the Jacobite rising in 1715. He was again a secretary of state from 1716 to 1725.

His grandson JOHN, 3rd duke of Roxburghe (1740–1804), was a famous bibliophile. The duke's library, including a unique collection of books from Caxton's press and three rare volumes of broadside ballads, was sold in 1812, when the Roxburghe club was founded to commemorate the sale of Valdarfer's edition of Boccaccio. Roxburghe's cousin William, 7th Lord Bellenden (c. 1728–1805), who succeeded to the Scottish titles and estates, died childless in Oct. 1805, and for seven years the titles were dormant.

Then in 1812 SIR JAMES INNES, Bart. (1736–1823), a descendant of the 1st earl, established his claim to them, and, taking the name of Innes-Ker, became 5th duke of Roxburghe. In his family the dukedom remained. Its holder has a seat in the house of lords as Earl Innes in the peerage of the United Kingdom.

ROXBURGHSHIRE, a border county, Scotland, bounded north by Berwickshire, east and southeast by Northumberland, south by Cumberland, southwest by Dumfriesshire and northwest by Selkirkshire and Midlothian. It has an area of 425,564 ac. or 664.9 sq.mi. The only low ground is in the north and in the valleys of the larger rivers, and the whole of the south is markedly hilly, though the Cheviots, forming for a considerable distance the natural boundary with England, mostly belong to Northumberland. The Tweed flows through the north of the shire for 26 out of its total run of 97 mi., though for about 2 mi. (near Abbotsford) it is the boundary stream with Selkirkshire, and for 10 mi. lower down with Berwickshire. On the right its affluent is the Teviot with its tributaries, and on the left the Allan and the Eden. The Teviot is the principal river entirely in Roxburghshire. From its source near Causeway Grain Head on the Dumfriesshire border, it follows mainly a northeasterly direction of 37 mi. to its confluence with the Tweed at Kelso. The Liddel is the main stream in the south. The Kershope and Liddel, during part of their run, serve as boundaries with Cumberland. Excepting the Liddel, which drains to the Esk, much the greater portion of the surface is drained, by the Tweed, to the North sea. Teviotdale, Liddesdale, Tweedside and Jedvale are the principal valleys. The county contains a considerable range of sedimentary rocks from the Ordovician to the Carboniferous systems, and with these are associated large tracts of volcanic rocks. The Ordovician and Silurian rocks occupy the northwest and west part of the county. Two divisions of the Old Red Sandstone occur; the lower is confined to the Cheviots; the strata are unconformable upon the upturned Silurian beds. The upper division, which in its turn is unconformable upon the lower, occupies about one-third of the county, being well developed in the north, where volcanic rocks come in. An interesting section about half a mile south of Jedburgh exposes the meeting of the Old Red Sandstone with the Greywacke. Carboniferous rocks are represented by the Calciferous sandstone series in the southwest in Liddesdale and on the uplands of Carter Fell, etc. An interesting series of volcanic "necks" belonging to the Carboniferous period is exemplified in Dunain Law, Black Law, Maiden Paps, Ruberslaw and other hills. Glacial deposits are represented by boulder clay and beds of sand and gravel.

History and Antiquities.—Among the more important remains of the original inhabitants are the standing stones and circles at Plenderleath between the Kale and Oxnam; on Hownam Steeple, a few miles to the northwest; and at Midshiels on the Teviot. The stones on Ninestane Rig, near Hermitage castle, and on Whisgill are supposed to commemorate the Britons of Strathclyde who, under Aidan, were defeated with great slaughter by Aethelfrith of Bernicia, king of Northumbria, at the battle of Daegsastan in 603. There are hill forts in Liddesdale on the Allan, in the parish of Oxnam, and on the most easterly of the three Eildons. This last is said to be the largest example of its kind in Scotland. One of the most important and most mysterious of British remains is the Catrail, or Picts' Work Dyke. In its original condition it is supposed to have consisted of a line of double mounds or ramparts, with an intervening ditch 6 ft. broad. It is now far from perfect and in places has disappeared for miles. Beginning at Torwoodlee, northwest of Galashiels, it ran southwest to Yarrow church, where it turned first south and then southeast, following a meandering course to Peel Fell in the Cheviots, a distance of 48 mi. Roman remains are also of interest. Dere street crossed the border north of Brownhart Law in the Cheviots, then took a mainly northwestern direction across the Kale, Oxnam, Jed and Teviot to Newstead, near Melrose, where it is conjectured to have crossed the Tweed and run up Lauderdale into East Lothian. Another so-called Roman road is the Wheel Causeway or Causey, a supposed continuation of the Maiden way which ran from Overburgh in Lancashire to Bewcastle in Cumberland, and so to the Border. It entered Roxburghshire north of Deadwater and went (roughly) north as far as Wolflee, where its direction becomes a matter of surmise. Of Roman camps the principal appear to have been situated at Cappuck, to the southeast of Jedburgh, and near Newstead, at the base of the Eildons, the alleged site of Trimontium. After the retreat of the Romans the country was occupied by the Britons of Strathclyde in the west and the Bernicians in the east. It was then annexed to Northumbria for more than four centuries until it was ceded, along with Lothian, to Scotland in 1018.

David I constituted it a shire, its ancient county town of Roxburgh (see KELSO) forming one of the Court of Four Burghs. The castle of Roxburgh, after changing hands more than once, was captured from the English in 1460 and dismantled. Other towns were repeatedly burned down, and the abbeys of Dryburgh, Jedburgh, Kelso and Melrose ultimately ruined in the expedition of the earl of Hertford (the Protector Somerset) in 1544–45. The Border freebooters—of whom the Armstrongs and Elliots were the chief—conducted bloody frays on their own account. Of the ancient castles, that of Hermitage, though now only a shell, is still the most striking. Dating from the 13th century, it is one of the oldest baronial buildings in Scotland.

Agriculture and Industries.—The soil is chiefly loam in the level tracts along the banks of the larger streams, where it is also very fertile. In other districts a mixture of clay and gravel is mostly found, but there is besides a considerable extent of mossy land. Many districts on the Tweed and Teviot are beautifully wooded.

More than half the county is under rough grazings carrying flocks of the smaller south country Cheviots and, to a less extent, the hardier and thriftier Blackface Highlands. On the intermediate ground, where there is some cropping, the larger north country Cheviot is crossed with the Border Leicester to produce half-bred lambs. On the lower-lying fertile farms half-bred ewes crossed with Oxford or Suffolk rams produce large quick-fattening Down cross lambs. In September the largest outdoor ram sales in Scotland are held at Kelso and are attended by buyers from all parts of the country and from overseas. Great numbers of sheep are sold at the autumn sales at Hawick. Arable farming is important in the rich low-lying areas around Kelso, where wheat, barley and some sugar beets are grown in addition to oats and roots, which are the common crops on upland stock farms.

On the hills herds of Galloway cows are increasingly common. On arable farms Blue Grey cows are much favoured. Dairying, however, is not an important feature. The arable farms are highly mechanized. In some parts of Tweedside and Jedvale several kinds of fruit are successfully grown.

The "Common Ridings," celebrated each year with much pageantry at Hawick, Selkirk, etc., date from the time when the community grazed their stock on common land which had to be held against encroachment.

The county is a principal seat of the tweed and hosiery manufactures in Scotland. Ironfounding and dyeing are also carried on at Hawick and tanning at Jedburgh, and agricultural implements, chemical manures and fishing tackle are made at Kelso. The salmon fisheries on the Tweed are of considerable value.

Population and Administration.—The population in 1951 was 45,557 and there were 92 persons who spoke Gaelic and English, but none Gaelic only. The small burghs are Hawick (1951 pop. 16,717), Kelso (4,119), Jedburgh (4,083), the only royal burgh and the county town, and Melrose (2,146). The four county districts have the same names.

The county returns one member to parliament with Selkirkshire and Peeblesshire. The shires of Roxburgh, Berwick and Selkirk form a sheriffdom, and a resident sheriff-substitute sits at Jedburgh and Hawick. The county offices are at Newton St. Boswells. There are secondary schools at Hawick and Jedburgh.

ROXBURY, formerly a city of Norfolk county, Mass., U.S., situated between Boston and Dorchester, but since 1868 a part of Boston. It is primarily a residential district. The town of Roxbury (at first usually spelled Rocksbury) was founded in 1630 by some of the Puritan immigrants who came with Gov. John Winthrop; the settlers were led by William Pynchon, who in 1636 led a party from there and founded Springfield, Mass. At the home of Thomas Welde (d. c. 1662), the first minister, Anne Hutchinson (q.v.) was held in custody during the winter of 1637–38. Associated as teacher with Welde and his successors, Samuel Danforth and Nehemiah Walter, was John Eliot, the apostle to the Indians, who moved to Roxbury in 1632 and died there in 1690. Roxbury was the home also of Thomas Dudley, of his son Joseph and of his grandson Paul; of Robert Calef (d. 1719), the leader of the opposition to the witchcraft craze; of Gen. Joseph Warren and of William Eustis (1753–1825), who was U.S. secretary of war (1809–12) and governor of Massachusetts (1823–25); and from 1837 to 1845 Theodore Parker was the pastor of the Unitarian church of West Roxbury.

Of special interest in the old Roxbury burial ground is the Minister's tomb, containing the remains of John Eliot, and the tomb of the Dudleys. West Roxbury was the scene of the Brook farm (q.v.) experiment.

The Roxbury Latin school was founded in 1645 by a group of town fathers, among them John Eliot, and was known as the Free School of Roxburie.

After several hazardous years the school progressed and grew steadily thereafter.

See F. S. Drake, *The Town of Roxbury, Its Memorable Persons and Places* (Boston, 1878 and 1905).

ROY, WILLIAM (*fl.* 1527), English friar, studied at Cambridge university and later joined the Franciscan order at Greenwich as a friar observant.

As secretary to William Tyndale (*c.* 1492–1536), Roy assisted him in the translation of the New Testament at Cologne and later at Worms, 1625–26.

Roy's works included *A lytle treatous or dialoge very necessary for all Christen men to learne and to knowe* (1526; 1527–28; reprinted at Vienna, 1874); *Rede me and be nott wrothe, for I say no thynge but trothe* (Worms, 1526; Strasbourg, 1528; London, 1546); *An exhortation to the diligent studye of scripture, made by Erasmus Roterodamus, and translated into English, to which is appended an exposition unto the seaventh chapter of the first epistle to the Corinthians* (Marburg, 1529); *A proper dyaloge betwene a gentillman and a husbandman, eche complaynynge to other their miserable calamitie through the ambicion of the clergy* (Marburg, 1530; London, 1863); and *A compendious olde treatyse howe that we ought to have ye Scripture in Englysshe* (Marburg, 1530; Bristol, 1863).

ROYAL AGRICULTURAL SOCIETY: see AGRICULTURE: *Agricultural Organizations.*

ROYAL FERN, the common name for the fern *Osmunda regalis,* native to Asia, Europe (including Great Britain), North America, Mexico and South America, growing usually in bogs and marshy woods. It is a handsome plant with bipinnate fronds 2 to 6 ft. long and 1 ft. or more broad; the tops of the fronds are fertile, the fertile pinnae being cylindrical and densely covered with the spore cases, giving the appearance of a dense panicle of flowers, whence the plant is known as the flowering fern. There are various cultivated forms—*cristata* has the ends of the fronds and the pinnae finely crested, and *corymbifera* has curiously forked and crested fronds.

Two related species, *O. cinnamomea* and *O. claytoniana,* natives of North America, are known in Great Britain as handsome greenhouse ferns.

ROYAL OAK, a suburb of Detroit, Mich., U.S., located on Woodward avenue (U.S. federal highway 10). It is the shopping centre of South Oakland county and is served by the Grand Trunk railway commuter trains. Pop. (1950) 46,898; (1940) 25,087.

ROYAL PALM (*Roystonea*), a small genus of tropical American palms, formerly known as *Oreodoxa.* They occur in southern Florida and the West Indies. *Roystonea regia* is much planted as an ornamental, especially in avenues.

(*See* PALM.)

ROYAL SOCIETY, THE, the oldest scientific society in Great Britain and one of the oldest in Europe. The Royal society (more fully, The Royal Society of London for Improving Natural Knowledge) is usually considered to have been founded in 1660, but a nucleus had been in existence for several years before that date. As early as the year 1645 weekly meetings were held in London of "divers worthy persons, inquisitive into natural philosophy and other parts of human learning, and particularly of what hath been called the *New Philosophy* or *Experimental Philosophy,*" and there can be little doubt that this gathering of philosophers is identical with the "Invisible college" of which Robert Boyle speaks in sundry letters written in 1646 and 1647.

Some of these "Philosophers," resident in Oxford about 1648, formed an association there under the title of the Philosophical Society of Oxford, and used to meet, most usually in the rooms of John Wilkins, warden of Wadham college. A close intercommunication was maintained between the Oxford and London philosophers; but ultimately the activity of the society was concentrated in the London meetings, which were held principally at Gresham college.

On Nov. 28, 1660, the first journal book of the society was opened with a "memorandum," from which the following is an extract: "Memorandum that Novemb. 28, 1660, These persons following, according to the usuall custom of most of them, mett together at Gresham Colledge to heare Mr. Wren's lecture, viz.,

ROYAL SOCIETY

The Lord Brouncker, Mr. Boyle, Mr. Bruce, Sir Robert Moray, Sir Paul Neile, Dr. Wilkins, Dr. Goddard, Dr. Petty, Mr. Ball, Mr. Rooke, Mr. Wren, Mr. Hill. And after the lecture was ended, they did, according to the usuall manner, withdrawe for mutuall converse. Where amongst other matters that were discoursed of, something was offered about a designe of founding a Colledge for the promoting of Physico-Mathematicall Experimentall Learning." It was agreed at this meeting that the company should continue to assemble on Wednesdays at three o'clock; an admission fee of 10s. with a subscription of 1s. a week was instituted; Wilkins was appointed chairman; and a list of 41 persons judged likely and fit to join the design was drawn up. On the following Wednesday Sir Robert Moray (or Murray) brought word that the king (Charles II) approved the design of the meetings; a form of obligation was framed, and was signed by all the persons enumerated in the memorandum of Nov. 28 and by 73 others. On Dec. 12 another meeting was held at which 55 was fixed as the number of the society—persons of the degree of baron, fellows of the College of Physicians and public professors of mathematics, physics and natural philosophy of both universities being supernumeraries.

Gresham college was now appointed to be the regular meeting place of the society. Sir Robert Moray was chosen president (March 6, 1661) and continued from time to time to occupy the chair until the incorporation of the society, when Lord Brouncker was appointed the first president under the charter. In Oct. 1661 the king offered to be entered one of the society, and next year the society was incorporated under its present title. The name "Royal society" appears to have been first applied to the "Philosophers" by John Evelyn, in the dedication of his translation of a book by Gabriel Naudé, published in 1661.

The charter of incorporation passed the great seal on July 15, 1662, to be modified, however, by a second charter in the following year, repeating the incorporating clauses of the first charter but conferring further privileges on the society. The second charter passed the great seal on April 22, 1663, and was followed in 1669 by a third, confirming the powers granted by the second charter, with some modifications of detail, and granting certain lands in Chelsea to the society. The council of the Royal society met for the first time on May 13, 1663.

At this early stage of its history the "correspondence" which was actively maintained with continental philosophers formed an important part of the society's labours, and selections from this correspondence furnished the beginnings of the *Philosophical Transactions* (a publication now of world-wide celebrity). At first the publication of the *Transactions* was entirely "the act of the respective secretaries." The first number, consisting of 16 quarto pages, appeared on Monday, March 6, 1664–65, under the title of *Philosophical Transactions: giving some Accompt of the present undertakings, studies and labours of the Ingenious in many considerable parts of the world*, with a dedication to the Royal society signed by Henry Oldenburg, the first secretary of the Royal society. The society also from its earliest years published, or directed the publication of, separate treatises and books on matters of philosophy, most notable among these being the *Philosophiae naturalis principia mathematica Autore Is. Newton. Imprimatur: S. Pepys, Reg. Soc. Praeses. Julii 5, 1686, 4to Londini 1687.*

In 1887 the *Philosophical Transactions* were divided into two series, labelled A and B, respectively, the former containing papers of a mathematical or physical character and the latter papers of a biological character. More than 480 quarto volumes had been published by 1955. In 1832 appeared the first volume of *Abstracts of papers, printed in the Philosophical Transactions from the year 1800*. This publication developed in the course of a few years into the *Proceedings of the Royal Society*, which has been continued up to the present time.

It is, however, certain that one of the most important functions of the society at its inception was the performance of experiments before the members. In the royal warrant of 1663 ordering the mace which the king presented to the society, it is described as "The Royal Society for the improving of Natural Knowledge by experiments"; and during its earlier years the time of the meetings was principally occupied by the performance and discussion of experiments. The society early exercised the power granted by charter to appoint two "curators of experiments," the first holder of that office being Robert Hooke, who was afterward elected a secretary of the society.

Another matter to which the society gave attention was the formation of a museum, the nucleus being "the collection of rarities formerly belonging to Mr. Hubbard," which, by a resolution of council passed in 1666, was purchased for the sum of £100. This museum, at one time the most famous in London, was presented to the trustees of the British Museum in 1781, upon the removal of the society to Somerset house. A certain number, however, of instruments and models of historical interest have remained in the possession of the society, and some of them, more peculiarly associated with its earlier years, are still preserved at Burlington house. The remainder have been deposited in the Victoria and Albert museum, South Kensington.

After the Great Fire of London in Sept. 1666 the apartments of the Royal society in Gresham college were required for the use of the city authorities, and the society was invited by Henry Howard (later duke of Norfolk) to meet in Arundel house. At the same time he presented them with the library purchased by his grandfather Thomas, earl of Arundel, and thus the foundation was laid of the important collection of scientific works, exceeding 140,000 volumes, which the society possesses. Of the Arundel manuscripts the bulk was sold to the trustees of the British Museum in 1830 for the sum of £3,559, the proceeds being devoted to the purchase of scientific books. These manuscripts are still kept in the British Museum as a separate collection. The society, however, still possesses a valuable collection of scientific correspondence, official records and other manuscripts, including the original manuscript, with Newton's autograph corrections, from which the first edition of the *Principia* was printed.

Under date Dec. 21, 1671, the journal book records that "the lord bishop of Sarum proposed for candidate Mr. Isaac Newton, professor of the mathematicks at Cambridge." Newton was elected a fellow Jan. 11, 1671–72, and in 1703 he was appointed president, a post which he held till his death in 1727. During his presidency the society moved to Crane court, its first meeting in the new quarters being held on Nov. 8, 1710. In the same year they were appointed visitors and directors of the Royal observatory at Greenwich, a function which they continued to perform until the accession of William IV, when by the new warrant then issued the president and six of the fellows of the Royal Astronomical society were added to the list of visitors.

In 1780, under the presidency of Sir Joseph Banks, the Royal society removed from Crane court to the apartments assigned to it by the government in the new Somerset house, where it remained until its removal to Burlington house in 1857. The policy of Sir Joseph Banks was to raise the status of the fellowship. A step in pursuance of the same policy was taken in the year 1847, when the number of candidates recommended for election by the council was limited to 15, and the election was made annual. This was augmented to 20 in 1938, and seven years later the number was raised to 25. Concurrent with the gradual restriction of the fellowship was the successive establishment of other scientific bodies. The founding of the Linnean society in 1788 under the auspices of several fellows of the Royal society was the first instance of the establishment of a distinct scientific association under royal charter; and this has been followed by the formation of the large number of societies now active in the promotion of special branches of science.

From the time of its royal founder onward the Royal society has constantly been appealed to by the government for advice in connection with scientific undertakings of national importance. The following are some of the principal matters of this character upon which the society has been consulted by, or which it has successfully urged upon the attention of, the government: the improvement and equipment of the Royal observatory, Greenwich, in 1710, when it was placed in the sole charge of the society; the change of the calendar in 1752; ventilation of prisons; protection of buildings and ships from lightning; measurement of a degree of latitude; determination of the length of a pendulum vibrating seconds; comparison of the British and French standards of length;

the Geodetic survey in 1784, and the General Trigonometrical survey begun in 1791; expeditions to observe the transits of Venus in 1761, 1769 (commanded by Capt. James Cook), 1874 and 1882; the antarctic expeditions of 1772 (under Captain Cook, whose voyage extended to the circumnavigation of the globe), 1839 (under Sir James Clark Ross) and 1900; help with the reports of the British Antarctic expedition of 1910–13; observations for determining the density of the earth; arctic expeditions of 1817 (in search of the northwest passage), of 1819 (under Sir William Parry), of 1827 (Parry and Ross), of 1845 (under Sir John Franklin), of 1875 (under Sir George Nares); numerous expeditions for observing eclipses of the sun; 1822, use of coal tar in vessels of war; best manner of measuring tonnage of ships; 1823, corrosion of copper sheathing by sea water; Charles Babbage's calculating machine; lightning conductors for vessels of war; 1825, supervision of gasworks; 1832, tidal observations; 1835, instruments and tables for testing the strength of spirits; magnetic observatories in the colonies; 1862, the great Melbourne telegraph; 1865, pendulum observations in India; 1866, reorganization of the meteorological department; 1868, deep-sea research; 1872, "Challenger" expedition; 1879, prevention of accidents in mines; 1881, pendulum observations; cruise of the "Triton" in Faeroe channel; 1883, borings in delta of Nile; 1884, Bureau des Poids et Mesures; international conference on a prime meridian; 1888, inquiry into lighthouse illuminants; 1890, the investigation of colour blindness; 1895, examination of the structure of a coral reef by boring; 1896, inquiry into cylinders for compressed gases; the establishment of an International Geodetic bureau; 1897, determination of the relations between the metric and imperial units of weights and measures; an inquiry into the volcanic eruptions in the West Indies; international seismological investigation; international exploration of the upper atmosphere; measurement of an arc of the meridian across Africa. During 1913–17 the society completed a magnetic survey of the British Isles. In 1920 it sent two expeditions to observe the total solar eclipse of May 29, and to note any deflection of rays of light by the sun's gravitational field, as required by Albert Einstein's general theory of relativity. In later years also the society, acting at the request of the government, has taken the leading part in investigations, in the course of which important discoveries have been made, in relation to various tropical diseases, beginning with the tsetse-fly disease of cattle in Africa, followed by investigations into malaria, Mediterranean fever and sleeping sickness. In 1924 the society received a bequest of £10,000 for medical research on tropical diseases, etc., and sent an expedition to study kala azar in north China. The society has also shown an active interest in problems of respiration and circulation in high altitudes (Peru expedition, 1921), and in investigations into glassworkers' cataract. It has taken a leading part in the promotion of the *International Catalogue of Scientific Literature* and of the International Association of Academies.

In addition to the occasional services enumerated above, the Royal society has exercised, and still exercises, a variety of important public functions of a more permanent nature. It still provides seven of the board of visitors of the Royal observatory, has 11 representatives on the Joint Permanent Eclipse committee and has a Solar Research committee of its own. From 1877 until the reconstitution of the meteorological office in 1906 the society nominated the meteorological council, which had the control of that office. The Gassiot and other committees of the society continued to co-operate with the meteorological office. Since 1919, when the meteorological office was attached to the air ministry, the society has two representatives on the Meteorological committee. The society has the custody of standard copies of the imperial standard yard and pound. The president and council have the scientific control of the National Physical laboratory, an institution established in 1900 in pursuance of the recommendations of a treasury committee appointed by H.M. government in response to representations from the Royal society (the financial control was transferred to the Department of Scientific and Industrial Research in 1918). It also appoints the British delegates to the meetings of the International Research council.

One of the most important duties which the Royal society performs on behalf of the government is the administration of an annual grant of (in 1955) nearly £60,000 for the promotion of scientific research and the assistance of scientific publications. This grant originated in a proposal by Lord John Russell in 1849 that at the close of the year the president and council should point out to the first lord of the treasury a limited number of persons to whom the grant of a reward or of a sum to defray the cost of experiments might be of essential service. The majority of these grants are utilized to provide apparatus, and they are made with the advice of nine scientific boards of eight experts each.

A proposal for bursaries to assist investigators of proved ability to work in other parts of the commonwealth for short periods when this would augment their capacity to advance knowledge was put forward by Sir Edward Salisbury in 1953. This was implemented as the Royal Society and Nuffield Foundation Bursaries scheme, and is mainly financed by the Nuffield foundation and contributions from various countries of the commonwealth.

A statement of the trust funds administered by the Royal society will be found in the *Year Book* published annually, and the origin and history of these funds will be found in the *Record of the Royal Society*.

Five medals (the Copley medal, two royal, the Davy and the Hughes) are awarded by the society every year, the Rumford and the Darwin medals biennially, the Sylvester triennially and the Buchanan quinquennially. The first of these originated in a bequest by Sir Godfrey Copley (1709), and is awarded "to the living author of such philosophical research, either published or communicated to the society, as may appear to the council to be deserving of that honour"; the author may be an Englishman or a foreigner. The Rumford medal originated in a gift from Count Rumford in 1796 of 1,000 3% consols, for the most important discoveries in heat or light made during the preceding two years. The royal medals were instituted by George IV and are awarded annually for the two most important contributions to science published in the British dominions not more than ten years nor less than one year before the date of the award. The Davy medal was founded by the will of John Davy, F.R.S., the brother of Sir Humphry Davy, and is given annually for the most important discovery in chemistry made in Europe or Anglo-America. An enumeration of the awards of each of the medals and the conditions of the awards are published in the *Year Book*. In 1953 the Royal society and the Nuffield foundation jointly provided funds for a scheme of commonwealth bursaries.

Six special lectures endowed by the benefactors named are delivered to the society, namely the Croonian (William Croone, 1684), the Bakerian (Henry Baker, 1775) and the Ferrier (Sir David Ferrier, 1928), to be delivered triennially, on the advances in knowledge of the structure and function of the brain; the Wilkins (J. D. Griffith Davis, 1947) on the history of science; the Leeuwenhoek (George Gabb, 1948) on some microbiological subject; and, in 1952, lectures in memory of Lord Rutherford.

Under the existing statutes of the Royal society every candidate for election into the society must be recommended by a certificate in writing signed by six or more fellows, of whom three at least must sign from personal knowledge. From the candidates so recommended the council annually selects 25, and the names so selected are submitted to the society for election by ballot. Princes of the blood, however, and not more than two persons selected by the council on special grounds once in two years, may be elected by a more summary procedure. Foreign members, not exceeding 50, may be selected by the council from among men of the greatest scientific eminence abroad, and proposed to the society for election.

The anniversary meeting for the election of the council and officers is held on St. Andrew's day. The council for the ensuing year, which includes the president, treasurer, two scientific secretaries (one for the biological and one for the physical sciences) and a foreign secretary, must consist of 11 members of the existing council and ten fellows who are not members of the existing council. These are nominated by the president and council previously to the anniversary meeting. The president and foreign secretary normally hold office for five years, the two scientific secretaries and the treasurer for ten years. There is also a permanent assistant secretary who is not usually a fellow. The session of the society is from November to June; the ordinary meetings are held on Thursdays during the session, at 4:30 P.M. The selection for publication from the papers read before the society is made by the Committee of Papers, which consists of the members of the council for the time being aided by committees appointed for the purpose. The papers so selected are published either in the society's *Philosophical Transactions* (quarto) or *Proceedings* (octavo).

BIBLIOGRAPHY.—T. Sprat, *The History of the Royal Society of London* (London, 1667; 4th ed., London, 1734); T. Thomson, *History of the Royal Society* (London, 1812); A. B. Granville, *The Royal Society in the 19th Century* (London, 1836); C. R. Weld, *A History of the Royal Society*, 2 vol. (London, 1848); H. B. Wheatley, *The Early History of the Royal Society* (London, 1905); Sir W. Huggins, *The Royal Society* (London, 1906); A. H. Church, *The Royal Society: Some Account of the Classified Papers in the Archives* (Oxford, 1907, etc.); *Signatures in the First Journal Book and the Charter Book of the Royal Society*, 3rd ed. (London, 1950); T. G. Bonney, *Annals of the Philosophical Club of the Royal Society* (London, 1919); D. Stimson, *Scientists and Amateurs* (New York, 1949); see also *The Record of the Royal Society of London*, 4th ed. (London, 1940) and *Year Book of the Royal Society* (annual).

(R. W. F. H.; A. Wo.; E. J. S.)

ROYALTIES. Payment by royalties based on a percentage of the published price has now become the customary method of sharing receipts between publisher and author from sales of a book. The amount of royalty agreed upon depends on the cost (including advertising) and the estimated sale of the book, as well as on the respective bargaining powers of publisher and author. British publishers are accustomed to contracts calling for payment to the author of 10% of the original published price —usually 7/6d.—of a novel by a new author, with provision that the royalty shall rise by agreed-upon stages to 15 or 20%. The successful British author whose sales are already established ordinarily gets a percentage beginning at 15 or 20, and rising to 25 after a sale of from 10,000 to 20,000 at the original price. The royalties on non-fiction books published at higher prices are as a rule somewhat higher than the royalties on novels.

Most British contracts for fiction now contain a provision for publication in cheaper form after the sales at the original published price have ceased. Royalties on these cheap editions range from a farthing a copy on sixpenny editions to 10% on 2/6d. editions.

Another phase of royalties is the advance. When it became apparent that the royalty system was fairer to publisher and author than the old system of payment outright for all rights, the author was prompt to point out that he might starve while waiting for his money—hence the publishers' custom of paying an advance on account of royalties on the day of publication. Authors whose previous sales had been large commanded proportionately large advances.

In the United States, where costs of distribution and advertising are greater than in the British Isles, royalties are lower. Whereas 20% was not uncommon for a successful writer, 15% is now the rule, though 20% after a sale of 10,000 at the original price in America is not unknown, despite the declaration of most of the American publishers that they cannot now go above 15%. The tendency is to begin at 10% of the advertised price, rising to 12½% or 15% after a sale of 5,000 copies at the original price.

When advances are paid to the author before any royalties are earned they are customarily made (a) upon the signing of the agreement, (b) upon delivery of the complete manuscript ready for publication and (c) on the publication date.

It is not the general custom of American publishers to bring out cheap editions of their own novels, though more publishers are bringing out these cheaper editions than ever before. The more usual practice is to sell the cheap edition rights, when possible, to firms who specialize in such editions, the original publisher providing the plates and giving the author half of the royalties, which usually yields to the author a royalty of 5% of the published price of the cheap edition.

As regards royalties on the Continent, it is only within recent years that this system of payment has been generally adopted, and even yet in some of the central European countries and in Holland it is only for particularly important books that royalties can be obtained. As a rule the percentages are lower than those prevailing in England. In Germany and Austria the royalty is not paid on the retail published price but on the "Broschiert," that is to say, on the retail price to the bookseller of the stitched and unbound copy.

A compromise between the percentage royalty on the retail price of every copy sold and the outright payment for the copyright has now been extensively adopted by foreign publishers; the system being the payment of an outright sum for every 1,000 copies printed. The advance on such payment usually covers the number of copies printed in the first edition.

Recent Developments.—The royalty system has undergone a notable change since the beginning of the twentieth century. It was formerly customary for the publisher to contract for the world rights of his author, reselling on a basis of half receipts to himself and half to the author such rights as he could not use— *e.g.*, foreign rights, serial rights, dramatic rights and, at first, moving-picture rights. But such contracts are now rare, the author selling each right separately.

The same tendency is observable in play sales. Here the normal royalty in England and America has become fixed at approximately 5% of the gross weekly receipts up to £500 or $2,500; 7½% on the next £200 (or $1,000) and 10% on all gross weekly receipts above £1,000 or $5,000, with an advance on account of these royalties, payable on the signing of the contract, of from £100 to £200. If the play is sold first in England, the English manager claims a share in the American rights and the film rights —and vice versa if the play is sold in America. If the author is in a strong position he claims and gets a separate royalty in each country for each right, with somewhat lower royalties for translation rights on account of the cost of translation and possibly adaptation. He even reserves the royalties obtainable on his amateur rights, broadcasting rights, and book publication rights.

When moving pictures first presented themselves to the authors as a possible source of suddenly augmented income, an attempt was made to apply the royalty system to payment per foot of film for what soon came to be known as "film rights": but the difficulties of collection and checking became such that the system has been practically abandoned for outright payment. However, the preference for profit-sharing has brought forth a new form of royalty payment that may presently prevail—*i.e.*, payment on signature of contract of an advance on account of a royalty of usually from 5 to 10% on the "bookings," *i.e.*, the purchases of exhibitors of the rights to show the film for varying periods.

A normal agreement for publication of music is 10% per copy of the retail selling price; half royalty on copies sold for export; half of any broadcasting fees, and half of the moneys received by the publishers as royalties on mechanical reproduction rights. These royalties on mechanical contrivances for the performance of musical works were altered in Great Britain in 1928 by order of the Board of Trade from 5% to 6¼%.

Earlier Systems.—The royalty system became general only in the last century, although before that authors were occasionally paid a stipulated sum for the first impression of a book, and a further sum if a further impression were called for. Samuel Simmonds paid Milton £5 for *Paradise Lost* and agreed to pay a further £5 at the end of the sale of each of the first three impressions. Richard Baxter records that he arranged with Thomas Underhill and Francis Tyton to publish his *Saints' Everlasting Rest*, a quarto of nearly 1,000 pages, for a payment of £10 for the first impression and £20 for every subsequent impression up to 1665.

Sidney Lee records that the highest price known to be paid before 1599 to an author for a play by the manager of an acting company was £11. "A small additional gratuity, rarely exceeding 10s., was bestowed on a dramatist whose piece on its first production was especially well received, and the author was customarily awarded, by way of benefit, a certain proportion of the receipts of the theatre on the production of a play for the second time. The 19 plays which may be set to Shakespeare's credit between 1591 and 1599 combined with such revising work as fell to his lot during those nine years cannot consequently have brought him less than £200 or some £20 a year. Between 1599 and 1611 his remuneration as both actor and dramatist was on the upward grade. The fees paid dramatists rose rapidly. The exceptional popularity of Shakespeare's work after 1599 gave him the full advantage of the higher rates of pecuniary reward in all directions. The 17 plays that were produced by him between that time and the close of his professional career could not have brought him less on an average than £25 each, or some £400 in all." But the pound of that day had over five times its present value. Later on prices improved and Fielding, for example, received £1,000 from Andrew Miller for *Amelia,* while Gibbon received two-thirds of the proceeds on his history.

Edward Chapman, of Chapman and Hall, in a letter to Forster (1837) said: "There was no agreement about *Pickwick* except a verbal one. Each number was to consist of a sheet and a half, for which we were to pay 15 guineas, and we paid him for the first two numbers at once, as he required the money to go and get married with. We were also to pay more according to the sale, and I think *Pickwick* cost us altogether £3,000." Forster adds: "I had always pressed so strongly the importance to him of some share in the copyright that this at last was conceded in the deed above mentioned (though five years were to elapse before the rights should accrue) and it was only yielded as part consideration for a further agreement entered into on the same date (Nov. 19, 1837) whereby Dickens engaged to write a new work (*Nickleby*) the first number of which was to be delivered on the 15th of the following March and each of the numbers on the same day of each of the successive 19 months, which was also to be the date of the payment to him by Chapman and Hall, and 20 several sums of £150 each for five years' use of the copyright, the entire ownership in which was then to revert to Dickens."

On July 2, 1840, Dickens wrote to Chapman and Hall: "Your purchase of *Barnaby Rudge* is made upon the following terms: It is to consist of matter sufficient for ten monthly numbers of the size of *Pickwick* and *Nickleby,* which you are, however, at liberty to divide and publish in 15 smaller numbers if you think fit. The terms for the purchase of this edition in numbers and for the copyright of the whole book for six months after the publication of the last number are £3,000. At the expiration of six months, the whole copyright reverts to me."   (C. Bn.)

See Copinger's *Law of Copyright* (6th ed., 1927); Michael Joseph, *The Commercial Side of Literature* (1925); Stanley Unwin, *The Truth about Publishing* (1926).

ROYALTIES, IN MINING.

In some countries (*e.g.* France) minerals are owned by the State which may grant concessions to private individuals or corporations. In others (*e.g.* the United States) they belong to the landowner.

Until the coming into force of the Coal Mines Act of 1938 all minerals in Great Britain—apart from special customs and excepting mines of gold and silver, which are the property of the Crown (*i.e.* "Royal" metals, hence the term "royalty")—were privately owned. But under the Coal Mines Act alluded to the coal and associated mineral substances (fireclays, stratified ironstone) pass to the State under a system of compulsory purchase, the total amount of the compensation payable being £66,450,000. A Central Valuation Board was appointed in Sept. 1938 to divide this amount as between the coal "regions" in accordance with the terms of the Act, which specified that the amount allocated to each "valuation region" should bear the same proportion to the global figure as the value of all the principal coal hereditaments in the said region bears to the value of all such hereditaments in Great Britain.

The valuation of the individual ownerships, region by region, commenced in Jan. 1, 1939, the date determined by the Act, from which date the coal is held as if all existing owners had entered into a contract for the sale of the coal to the Coal Commission (a body set up by Parliament to control the nationalized coal property, and clothed with certain other powers), the contract being completed on the "vesting date", July 1, 1942.

Presumably the transfer of the ownership of the coal and allied minerals will not materially affect the terms upon which it is leased to the colliery proprietors. These terms are such as include the right to work the coal on the payment of a "fixed," "certain" or "dead" rent per annum, which merges in the royalty rent. When in any year the tonnage worked at this rent exceeds in royalty value the certain rent, the surplus is paid as "overworkings"; when it falls short, the deficiency is carried forward as "short workings" to the next year's account.

The royalty rent is payable either (1) as a tonnage rate pure and simple, (2) a sum per acre per foot thick of coal in the seam, (3) simply a sum per acre as a proportion of the value of the mineral raised, or (4) by way of a sliding scale. The first two are the methods most commonly adopted. The average royalty per ton inclusive of way-leave (*i.e.* the right of passage through another's land—surface or underground) of all coal raised in Great Britain, is usually taken at 5⅝d. per ton. The total gross revenue derivable from ownership of coal (royalties and way-leaves) was, in 1918, £5,960,365. The average taken by government for purposes of compensation under the Act was £4,430,000, being the average for the years 1928–34 inclusive. In the case of metalliferous ores, both in Great Britain and in other countries, the royalty is assessed as a proportion of the "dressed" ore (*i.e.* as ready for smelting): *e.g.* 1/20th to 1/30th. China clay, ganister, and other "clays," oil shale, slate, building stone, and stratified ironstone are also subject to royalty.

In the United States the royalty payable on coal is usually based upon a fixed rate per ton, which in the case of bituminous coal would be a uniform rate for all coal sold; but in the case of anthracite the rate per ton frequently varies with the size, a higher royalty being paid upon larger sizes; and, in some instances, the royalty is a sliding scale varying with the sale price. Royalties vary from a few cents per ton in the case of bituminous, to as much as $1.00 per ton for the highest grades and largest sizes of anthracite.

Natural petroleum does not occur in commercial quantity in Great Britain, but in the United States, where it is produced in vast quantities, oil lands are usually leased on a royalty basis, the royalty being paid to the owner of the land on a percentage of the oil produced. In the case of natural gas, royalties are rarely paid on a percentage basis, but usually as a stipulated amount for the right to pipe and sell the gas.

In Canada the royalty is 10% of the crude oil; in British India 5%; France and Algeria 20%; Rumania from 8% when the output per well per day averages 10 metric tons up to 35% when it exceeds 150 metric tons, payable to the State which allows 20% of the receipts to the surface owner; in Colombia and Peru, from 10 to 6 per cent; in Argentina and Venezuela, 10 per cent. Crude oil for royalty purposes usually means crude oil after deduction of water, foreign substances, and oil consumed in production.

See J. H. Cockburn, *The Law of Coal and Minerals* (1902); R. A. S. Redmayne and G. Stone, *The Ownership and Valuation of Mineral Property* (1920); E. R. Willey, *The Oil Industry* (1926).   (R. R.)

ROYAN,

a town of W. France, in the department of Charente-Inférieure, on the right bank of the Gironde at its mouth 63 mi. below and N.N.W. of Bordeaux. Pop. (1936) 10,193. It belonged to the family of Trémoille, in whose favour it was made first a marquisate and then a duchy. During the first half of the 15th century it was held by the English. During the wars of religion it was the centre of Calvinism and in 1622 was besieged by Louis XIII. At the end of the 18th century it had about 1,000 inhabitants and was noticeable only for its priory. Its prosperity dates from the Restoration, when steamboat communication was established with Bordeaux.

ROYCE, JOSIAH

(1855–1916), American philosopher and teacher, was born at Grass Valley, a California mining town, on Nov. 20, 1855. At 16 he entered the newly-opened University of California, inclined to the study of engineering. But the teaching of Joseph LeConte, the geologist, and of Edward Rowland Sill, the poet, roused his extraordinary speculative power; and on receiving his baccalaureate degree, 1875, he gave himself to the study of philosophy, first in Leipzig and Göttingen (under Lotze) and then, as one of the first fellows of Johns Hopkins university, with William James and Charles Peirce. Here he received the degree of Ph.D., 1878. After teaching English for four years in the University of California he was called to Harvard university as lecturer in philosophy, becoming assistant professor in 1885, professor in 1892 and succeeding George Herbert Palmer as Alford professor in 1914. He received various honorary degrees and was made in 1916 Honorary Fellow of the British Academy. He died at Cambridge, Mass., Sept. 14, 1916.

His effect as teacher and writer was profound: no previous American thinker had so united moral energy with wide historical learning, command of scientific method and intense interest in logical technique. His versatile mind concerned itself effectively with a wide range of subjects; he contributed to mathematical logic, psychology, social ethics, literary criticism and history as well as to metaphysics. His thought was massive and intimately human; yet it was sustained with a dialectical skill of such evident virtuosity as, on the one hand, to excite the critical opposition first of pragmatic and then of realistic schools, and, on the other hand, to set a new standard in the systematic treatment of philosophy. In this latter respect, Royce did for American philosophy what his older contemporary, F. H. Bradley, did for British philosophy: in many ways the views of these thinkers are akin. Like Bradley, Royce teaches a monistic idealism. Scientific laws he describes—anticipating certain developments of recent physics— as statistical formulae of average behaviour. His absolute idealism is supplemented, not corrected, by the ethical and social teachings of his later years and, in particular, by the conception of the world of human selves as the Great Community, the literally personal object of moral loyalty.

BIBLIOGRAPHY.—Among his more important publications (selected from a far greater number) are: *The Religious Aspect of Philosophy* (1885); *The Spirit of Modern Philosophy* (1892); *The Conception of God* (1895), with Supplementary Essay (1897); *Studies of Good and Evil* (1898); *The World and the Individual* (Gifford Lectures), vols. i., ii. (1900-01); *The Conception of Immortality* (1900); *Outlines of Psychology* (1908); "The Relation of the Principles of Logic to the Foundations of Geometry," in *Transactions of the American Mathematical Soc.*, vi., 3 (1905); *The Philosophy of Loyalty* (1908); *The Sources of Religious Insight* (1912); "Prinzipien der Logik," *Enzyklopädie der Philosophischen Wissenschaften*, Bd. i. (1912), English translation in *Encyclopaedia of the Philosophical Sciences*, vol. i. (1913); *The Problem of Christianity* (lectures delivered at the Lowell Institute, Boston, and at Manchester college, Oxford), vols. i., ii. (1913); "The Mechanical, the Historical and the Statistical," *Science*, n.s. xxxix. (1914); *Lectures on Modern Idealism* (1919). For a bibliography (exclusive of posthumous publications) *see* B. Rand, *Philosophical Rev.*, xxv. (1916). (M. W. C.; W. E. H.)

ROYDEN, AGNES MAUDE (1876–   ), British social worker and preacher, youngest daughter of Sir Thomas Royden, 1st bart. of Frankby hall, Cheshire. Until 1914 she edited *The Common Cause,* the organ of the National Union of Women's Suffrage societies. She was assistant preacher at the City temple, London, from 1917 until 1920, when she founded, with Percy Dearmer, the Fellowship services at Kensington, later transferred to Great Ormond street, London. She was created C.H. in 1930.

Her numerous books and pamphlets include *Women and the Sovereign State* (1917); *Sex and Common-sense* (1922; rev. ed. 1947); *Prayer as a Force* (1922); *Political Christianity* (1922); *The Church and Woman* (1924); *Here—and Hereafter* (1934); and *A Threefold Cord* (1947).

ROYER-COLLARD, PIERRE PAUL (1763-1845), French statesman and philosopher, was born on June 21, 1763, at Sompuis, near Vitry le Français (Marne), the son of Antoine Royer, a small proprietor. He was sent to the college of Chaumont of which his uncle, Father Paul Collard, was director. He followed his uncle to Saint-Omer, where he studied mathematics. At the outbreak of the Revolution he was practising at the Parisian bar. He was returned by the Island of Saint Louis to the Commune, of which he was secretary from 1790 to 1792. After the revolution of Aug. 10, 1792, he was replaced by J. L. Tallien. His sympathies were now with the Gironde, and after the insurrection of the 12th Prairial (May 31, 1793) he was in danger of his life.

He returned to Sompuis, and was saved from arrest possibly by the protection of Danton. In 1797 he was returned by his department (Marne) to the Council of the Five Hundred. He made one great speech in the council in defence of the principles of religious liberty, but retired into private life at the *coup d'état* of Fructidor (Sept. 4, 1797).

From that time until the Restoration Royer-Collard devoted himself to the study of philosophy. His opposition to the philosophy of Condillac arose from the study of Descartes and his followers, and from his early veneration for the fathers of Port-Royal. He desired to establish a system which should provide a moral and political education consonant with his view of the needs of France. From 1811 to 1814 he lectured at the Sorbonne.

Royer-Collard was the moving spirit of the "Doctrinaires," led by Guizot, P. F. H. Serre, Camille Jordan and Charles de Rémusat, who met at the house of the comte de Ste. Aulaire and in the salon of the duchesse de Broglie. In 1820 Royer-Collard was excluded from the council of State by a decree signed by his former ally Serre. In 1827 he was again elected; in 1828 he became president of the chamber, and fought against the reactionary policy which precipitated the Revolution of July. In March 1830 he presented the address of the 221. From that time he took no active part in politics, although he retained his seat in the chamber until 1839.

He died at his estate of Châteauvieux, near Vitry, on Sept. 2, 1845. He had been a member of the Academy since 1827.

Fragments of Royer-Collard's philosophical work are included in Jouffroy's translation of the works of Thomas Reid. The standard life of Royer-Collard is by his friend Prosper de Barante, *Vie politique de M. Royer Collard, ses discours et ses écrits* (2 vols., 1861). There are also biographies by M. A. Philippe (1857), L. Vingtain (1858), E. Spuller (1895), in *Grands écrivains français*. See E. Faguet, *Politique et morale du xixe siècle* (1891); H. Taine, *Les Philosophes français du xixe siècle* (1857); L. Séché, *Les Derniers Jansénistes* (1891); and Lady Blennerhasset, "The Doctrinaires" in the *Cambridge Modern History* (vol. x. chap. ii., 1907).

ROYSTON, a market town and urban district in Hertfordshire, England, near the border of Cambridgeshire, 48 mi. N. of London. Pop. (1951) 4,663. Area, 2.5 sq.mi.

The town lies on the Roman Ermine street. Roman relics have been found, and several barrows and earth-mounds occur on the neighbouring hills. A monastery of Augustinian canons was founded here about 1180. The church of St. John the Baptist is mainly Early English.

ROYTON, urban district, Lancashire, England, on L.M.S.R. Pop. (1951) 14,772. Area, 3.4 sq.mi. It lies next to Oldham and owes its rise to the cotton manufacture.

ROZAS, JUAN MARTINEZ DE (1759–1813), the earliest leader in the Chilean struggle for independence, was born at Mendoza in 1759. In early life he was a professor of law, and of theology and philosophy at Santiago.

He was acting governor of Concepción at one time, and was also colonel in a militia regiment. In 1808 he became secretary to the last Spanish governor, Francisco Antonio Carrasco, and used his position to prepare the nationalist movement that began in 1809. After resigning as secretary, Rozas was mainly responsible for the resignation of the Spanish governor, and the formation of a national Junta on Sept. 18, 1810, of which he was the real leader. Under his influence many reforms were initiated, freedom of trade was established, an army was organized and a national congress was called in July 1811. Rozas died at Mendoza March 3, 1813.

RUANDA-URUNDI, United Nations trust territory in East Africa, administered by Belgium. It lies between 1° and 4° S. latitude and 29° to 31° E. longitude and is bound on the north by Uganda, on the east and south by Tanganyika territory (boundary adjusted by treaty, Nov. 22, 1934), on the west by the Belgian Congo. Area: 20,115 sq.mi. Pop. (1950) 3,904,779, including 3,733 Europeans (2,605 Belgians) and 1,896 Asiatics.

After World War I Belgium assumed administration under a mandate of the League of Nations, which was formally accepted by the Belgian parliament on Oct. 20, 1924, after concurrence of the United States had been secured by treaty, April 18, 1923. It had previously been a portion of German East Africa.

In Dec. 1946 the United Nations placed it under U.N. trusteeship. Under the law of Aug. 21, 1925, Ruanda-Urundi was organized as an integral part of the Belgian Congo but with a separate budget. A vice-governor general, under the direction of the governor general of the Belgian Congo, was named the administrator.

The residency of Ruanda is comprised of the territories of Kigali, Nyanza, Astrida, Shangugu, Kisenyi, Ruhengeri, Byumba and Kibungu; the residency of Urundi is comprised of Kitega, Muramvya, Ngozi, Muhinga, Ruyigi, Rutana, Bururi, Usumbura and Bubanza.

The greater part of the country is mountainous and lies at a high altitude. The bulk of the people are of Bantu stock, but the ruling caste, about one-tenth of the total population, are of the pastoral Wahima race, as in Uganda, Bunyoro and Ankole. The wealth of the country consists in its flocks and herds.

Early in 1928 there was a revolt against Musinga, the king of Ruanda. The movement was also antiwhite and spread across the border into the southwest corner of Uganda. Belgian and British forces restored order.

As a result of its distance from the sea and the lack of cheap transport, the trade of the country developed slowly.

In 1950 the value of exports was 1,082,979,340 fr. and the value of imports 1,174,854,788 fr. Roads totalled 4,803 mi., including 216 mi. of principal roads. There were no railways.

BIBLIOGRAPHY.—*Rapports sur L'Administration Belge du Ruanda-Urundi* (annual); R. De Rouck, *Atlas géographique et historique du Congo Belge et des territoires sous mandat du Ruanda-Urundi* (1938).
(P. W. I.; X.)

RUBBER: BOTANY, CULTIVATION AND CHEMISTRY.

During his second visit to South America, Columbus was astonished to see the native Indians amusing themselves with a black, heavy ball made from a vegetable gum. Later explorers were equally impressed by these balls, and an historian of the time remarked that they rebounded so much that they appeared alive. Three centuries elapsed before the material was brought into commercial use in Europe, and it was then marketed not for

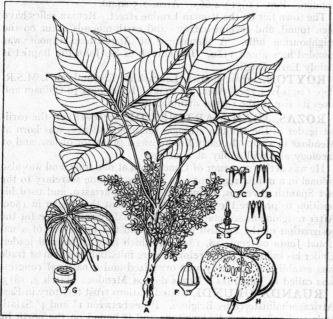

FROM "MEDIZINAL PFLANZEN" (KOEHLER)
FIG. 1.—HEVEA BRASILIENSIS
(A) Sprig bearing trifoliate leaves and several inflorescences, (B, C, D) detached naked unisexual flowers, (E) androecium, (F) gynaecium, (G) section through the trilocular ovary, (H) ripe, (I) dehiscent capsule, showing the large oleaginous seeds

its elastic properties but to rub out lead pencil marks—hence the name indiarubber or rubber. Since then the principal constituent (caoutchouc) of this material has been found as a vegetable product in many parts of the world, sometimes mixed with as little as one twentieth and sometimes with eight times its own weight of other substances. Some of these mixtures are strong and elastic, others are weak and brittle, but they are all classified as rubber. In addition, the term has been broadened by common use to include a wide range of vulcanised products derived from rubber by heating with sulphur, generally after mixing with large propor-

tions of powders and plastic solids.

Although raw rubber is a coherent, elastic solid, it is obtained from a milky liquid known as *latex,* which occurs in special tubes in the roots, stem, branches, leaves and fruit of a wide variety of trees growing for the most part in the tropics. Rubber latex consists of a watery solution (serum), in which float small globules of rubber visible under a microscope. Although neither the rubber nor the serum is definitely opaque in thin layers, the many reflecting surfaces presented by these globules cause the latex to have the appearance of cows' milk, but whereas cows' milk contains only about 12% solid matter, rubber milk contains 30–40%. When rubber milk is suitably treated the globules unite (coagulate) and float in the serum as a soft, doughy mass (coagulum), which can be easily rolled to a sheet or other convenient form. On drying the coagulum loses its doughy character and becomes the firm, elastic solid known as raw or crude rubber.

Sources of Supply.—The numerous varieties of trees which contain rubber latex belong to many different botanical families, but nearly the whole of the world's rubber supply is obtained from a tree known as *Hevea brasiliensis* belonging to the family Euphorbiaceae. The rubber obtained from the latex of this tree usually contains over 90% caoutchouc of excellent quality. Few other trees furnish rubber of a purity and quality approaching this. In some cases the latex yields a product which consists chiefly of resin. Jelutong rubber, for example, obtained from *Dyera costulata,* a large tree growing in the East Indies, is very resinous, as also is the rubber produced from shrubby species of *Euphorbia* indigenous to South Africa.

Certain tropical African plants yield rubber of good quality, but the methods of preparation employed by the natives are crude and tend to degrade the product. The most important are *Funtumia elastica,* a tall and stately tree, and various species of *Landolphia,* which are big woody climbers.

A tree which is well known because it is cultivated in Europe as an ornamental plant under the name of the indiarubber tree is *Ficus elastica,* indigenous to Assam and Burma, where it grows to a considerable size. It yields moderately resinous rubber.

Guayule rubber from *Parthenium argentatum*—a silvery-leafed shrub found in north Mexico and is also moderately resinous.

The tropical American rubbers include Ceara rubber from *Manihot Glaziovii,* a tree of moderate size growing in Brazil, and Caucho rubber from *Castilloa elastica,* a large tree found in Central America and portions of Brazil. In both cases the rubber is of fairly good quality. The purest and best, however, is undoubtedly the Para rubber obtained chiefly from *Hevea brasiliensis* and to a lesser extent from *Hevea Benthamiana.* Both these trees are found in the Amazon valley, the former around the southern and the latter around the northern tributaries. *Hevea Benthamiana* is not so widely distributed as *Hevea brasiliensis,* but both yield rubber which is classed as "hard fine para"—the highest grade on the market.

Origin of Plantations.—In spite of huge natural resources the demand for Para rubber is far in excess of the quantity which the Amazon can supply. At one time there was no other source of *Hevea* rubber, but as long ago as 1834 Thomas Hancock, the English discoverer of vulcanisation and a rubber manufacturer, called attention to the high price of rubber and the possibility of growing it in the East. The requisite climate conditions appeared to be a heavy, well-distributed rainfall (about 100ins. per annum) and a temperature of 70°–90° F. These conditions are obtained over wide areas in the East. Eventually Sir Joseph Hooker, Director of the Royal Botanical Gardens, Kew, London, interested himself in the problem, and in 1873 2,000 Hevea seeds from the Amazon were delivered to Kew by a Mr. Farris. Only a dozen germinated, and six sent to the Royal Botanical Gardens, Calcutta, did not thrive. Arrangements were then made for further supplies of seeds. The most successful collector was H. A. Wickham (now Sir Henry Wickham) who displayed much enterprise and care in successfully bringing to Kew a consignment of 70,000 seeds of *Hevea brasiliensis.* Hot houses were summarily emptied, and within two weeks of the arrival of the seeds in England there were over 2,000 young plants, nearly all of which were despatched to Ceylon, where they proved very successful.

After the establishment of Hevea trees in Ceylon steps were taken to distribute plants and seeds to other countries. Difficulties were experienced in exporting seeds in a sound condition, and the problem was studied by H. N. Ridley in the Botanical Gardens at Singapore. He found that seeds packed in moist, powdered charcoal retained their fertility for a long time, and when shortly after the beginning of the twentieth century planters began to take an increasing interest in rubber, large quantities of seeds were distributed by this means from Malaya.

The countries producing the largest quantities of plantation rubber are Malaya, the Dutch East Indies, and Ceylon. Smaller amounts are also obtained from India, Sarawak, Borneo, French Indo-China, Siam and various parts of Africa. Owing chiefly to the demands of the motor car industry the production of plantation rubber has made phenomenal progress. The first occasion on which a considerable amount of plantation rubber was offered on the market was in 1910, when the output reached 11,000 tons. By 1920 it was nearly 317,000 tons and in 1927 it amounted to 567,000 tons. In this period there were wide fluctuations in price, ranging from 12s. od. per lb. in 1910 to 7½d. per lb. in 1921.

While the production of plantation rubber has continued to increase that of wild rubber has decreased until in 1927 the world's production of all grades of wild rubber was only 6% of that produced on plantations. The reason for this is that not only is plantation rubber of good quality, comparable with that from the Amazon, but it is put on the market in a clean, dry condition.

Description of Principal Rubber Tree.—*Hevea brasiliensis* is a large tree which on occasions grows to a height of over 100ft. with a well developed trunk more than 12ft. in circumference. The usual height on plantations is from 60 to 80ft. The leaves are three-lobed, the segments being long and narrow and tapering at each end. The flowers are usually pale green and inconspicuous, separate male and female flowers being borne on the same tree. The fruit is a capsule containing three seeds which are oval and have a mottled brown, smooth coat. When ripe the

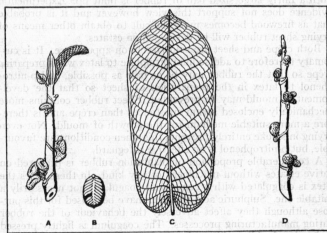

FIG. 2.—CASTILLOA ELASTICA
(A) Sprig bearing male flowers, (B) a seed, (C) a leaf, (D) twig bearing female flowers

capsules explode violently and eject the seeds to a distance of 20yd. or more, well beyond the shadow cast by the parent tree.

The structure of what is popularly known as the bark is of considerable importance in *Hevea brasiliensis*, because, as already indicated, the latex vessels in this part of the tree are the chief source of the world's rubber supply. The trunk of a tree may be divided roughly into an inner portion of wood and an outer portion of bark. At the junction of the bark and the wood is a layer of cells about the thickness of a sheet of paper, known as the cambium, which appears as a slimy layer when the bark is torn away from the tree. This layer is the seat of growth, on the one hand adding new cells to the wood and on the other new cells to

the bark. Next to the cambium and in the soft portion of the bark are found the latex tubes. Outside the soft bark is a hard portion where there are comparatively few latex tubes. The whole is protected by an external layer of cork. The diameter of the latex tubes is considered to be about 0·0015 inch.

Cultivation.—*Hevea brasiliensis* is planted on many types of soil and thrives remarkably well as long as reasonable precautions are taken to avoid swampy, undrained or exposed lands. It is sometimes grown at an altitude of over 2,000ft., but the trees do not flourish so well at this altitude as at a lower level.

In opening up a new plantation the land is cleared of all growth as soon as possible not only to make room for the rubber trees but also to avoid the possibility of disease from rotting timber.

At one time it was the practice on rubber plantations to remove all weeds and leave bare the ground between the trees, but this is no longer regarded as an attribute of a well-kept estate. It is still the practice to remove the weeds, but heavy tropical rains have caused such loss of top-soil, particularly on sloping land, that many estates find it necessary to plant cover crops. Shrubby types of plants such as species of *Crotalaria* and *Tephrosia* which are periodically lopped and mulched into the soil, or herbaceous types such as *Centrosema pubescens* and *Vigna oligosperma* are among those used.

On sloping land cover crops are not sufficient to prevent the loss of valuable top-soil. In Ceylon for example stone walls are sometimes built across the hills. As a general rule however it is considered better to level the land in a series of contours about 15 to 20ft. apart, cutting into the side of the hill at a slight gradient to a depth of about six feet.

The loss of top-soil can also be reduced by drains which prevent the accumulation of a continuous stream of water during heavy rain. In Ceylon a series of lateral drains empty into main drains (herring-bone drains) which carry the water away, but in Malaya and Sumatra the water is trapped in blind drains (silt pits) from which it ultimately percolates into the soil.

Where considerable erosion has taken place or the soil has been impoverished by previous cultivation it is sometimes possible to effect great improvement in the health of the trees by the addition of manures, particularly those containing nitrogen and phosphorus. This increased health is reflected in a more vigorous canopy of leaves, better replacement of bark removed for collection of latex, and a greater yield of latex.

The number of trees planted per acre on estates is largely dictated by local conditions, such as the quality of the soil and the contour of the land. Most estates plant out more trees than will eventually be required and thin them out, removing weak ones or those which prove low yielders, leaving about 90 trees per acre.

The rubber tree is by no means free from disease but a careful watch is kept by scientific officers, and nowhere in the East have the diseases assumed serious proportions. The most troublesome are an abnormal leaf-fall (not to be confused with that which occurs while the trees are wintering) and a pathological condition of the bark often associated with heavy tapping. Measures have been devised to counteract both, but they still occur.

Selection of Planting Material.—Most trees on estates yield 4 to 5lb. of rubber per annum, but there are a few which yield as much as 30lb. growing by the side of others which yield only 2-lb. As yield capacity is partly hereditary, it seems probable that the yield per acre may be greatly increased by propagating from high-yielding trees only. For this purpose two methods of propagation have received considerable attention. In one the plants are raised from seeds from carefully selected high yielding mother-trees. In the other a bud from a high yielding mother-tree is grafted on to a vigorous young plant grown from seed. Unless special care is taken a high yielding mother tree is liable to be fertilised by pollen from neighbouring low yielders, so that the daughter trees grown from seed may not be particularly good yielders. On the other hand it is to be expected that the budded material will have the vegetative characteristics of the mother tree.

Tapping.—The trees are ready for tapping for latex when about five years old, but the yield of latex and the quality of rubber obtained are not so good as when the trees are a few years older. Tapping is a very delicate and important operation, consisting in the removal of a shaving of bark with a sharp knife. The cut passes through the latex tubes and there is a flow of latex in consequence. If the cut is too deep, it penetrates into the cambium and bark renewal is hindered, but if it is not deep enough only a portion of the latex tubes are pierced and the yield of latex is reduced. For perfect tapping it is necessary to cut within $\frac{1}{25}$ in. of the wood, an operation requiring practice and skill.

The only tapping tools in general use on the plantations are a gouge (straight or bent) and the ordinary farrier's knife (or its modification).

It is the usual practice to make the first cut at between two and four feet from the ground. A shaving is then taken at definite intervals of time from the lower edge of the exposed bark. The thickness of the shaving removed is so arranged that the consumption of bark is between half an inch and one inch per month, some districts, such as Ceylon, preferring thin shavings while others, such as Malaya, prefer thicker shavings.

The length of the shaving varies from one-half to one-quarter of the circumference, some estates employing a single spiral cut at an angle of about 30° to the horizontal and some a V cut. In Ceylon it is the practice to change the tapping panel every six or twelve

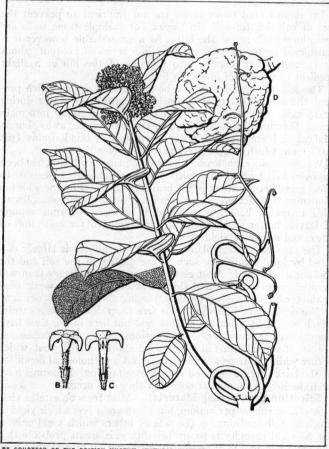

FIG. 3.—LANDOLPHIA COMORENSIS
(A) Sprig bearing leaves and inflorescence, (B) detached flower, (C) vertical section through flower, (D) fruit

months, but elsewhere it is customary to continue tapping on one panel down to the ground before commencing a fresh panel. Tapping is generally carried out every alternate day, one portion of an estate being rested while the other is tapped.

After the bark has been cut away, it is regenerated complete with latex vessels in a few years. With the most conservative system it is eventually necessary to tap on renewed bark. As the replacement of bark becomes more difficult each time a panel is tapped, there is a limit to the economic life of the tree, but the industry is too young for definite information on this point.

Tapping operations are always carried out in the early morning when the flow of latex is greatest. The latex from each tree is collected in a cup, transferred to a pail and taken to the factory as quickly as possible. Sometimes sodium sulphite is added to prevent premature coagulation. When the latex has ceased to drip there remains on the bark a thin film which dries in the sun leaving a strip of rubber. This is collected, washed in the factory and sold as "tree scrap"—an inferior grade.

Preparation.—The details of the methods employed in the preparation of plantation rubber depend upon the shape and appearance of the product to be put on the market, but in nearly all cases the outlines of the procedure adopted are the same. The sieved and diluted latex containing 15–25% rubber is treated with a coagulant such as acetic or formic acid or sodium silicofluoride. This causes the rubber to rise to the surface as a wet, white, doughy coagulum leaving in solution a small quantity of mineral and organic matter. The coagulum is then pressed between rollers until it is the required consistency, thickness and shape. After that it is hung to dry and eventually packed in wooden cases and shipped to its destination.

The two most important forms of plantation rubber are sheet and crêpe. Sheet is generally dark brown in colour because it is dried in smoke, whilst crêpe is a straw colour and is dried in air.

Sheet is obtained from latex coagulated in shallow tanks divided into compartments of suitable dimensions, each piece of coagulum being pressed by light machinery to the required thickness.

In the preparation of crêpe the coagulum is machined much more drastically, heavy rollers being necessary. During this process the coagulum is torn and pressed until it is sufficiently thin to dry in air without artificial heat. The rubber is dried by hanging on racks in well ventilated sheds for about a week.

Sheet is thicker than crêpe and requires artificial heat to dry it in a reasonable time. It is therefore exposed to the smoke of a wood fire for about 14 days. It was at one time presumed that smoking had a beneficial effect on quality because the highest grade rubber was obtained from the Amazon where the latex is coagulated with smoke, a wooden paddle being repeatedly dipped into the latex and exposed to the smoke of burning Urucuri nuts until a fairly large sized ball of rubber is built up. Experimental evidence does not support this view however and it is probable that as firewood becomes more difficult to obtain other means of drying sheet rubber will be developed on estates.

Both crêpe and sheet are sold largely on appearance. It is customary therefore to add sodium bisulphite to latex when preparing crêpe so that the rubber may be as pale as possible, and p-nitrophenol to latex in the preparation of sheet so that the development of mould may be prevented. Sheet rubber contains more mechanically enclosed serum substances than crêpe and is therefore a more suitable medium for the growth of mould. Not even drying in smoke entirely prevents this when conditions are favourable, but p-nitrophenol is an effective safeguard.

A considerable proportion of plantation rubber is prepared on native estates without machinery of any kind. In these cases the latex is coagulated with a convenient coagulant, not necessarily a suitable one. Sulphuric acid and alum have been used for this purpose although they affect adversely the behaviour of the rubber during manufacturing processes. The coagulum is lightly pressed by hand and whilst still wet is sent to a central factory where it is milled to crêpe and sold as an inferior grade of rubber.

Chemistry.—The microscope has been particularly useful in yielding information concerning the structure of rubber latex. The array of globules dancing here and there (Brownian movement) are easily seen at moderate magnifications, and it is possible to measure them and show that they vary in shape and size. In Hevea latex the globules are shaped like a pear and vary in length from 0·00002in. to six times that size. In spite of their minute size the expert has been able to ascertain that the globules in Hevea latex consist of an outer skin of non-rubber material, enclosing a viscous rubber shell surrounding semifluid rubber.

When Hevea latex is treated with any but very weak acids, the Brownian movement of the globules ceases, and they unite to form a coherent coagulum. Dehydrating agents such as alcohol and protein precipitants such as tannic acid also cause Hevea latex to coagulate.

In the presence of suitable proportions of an alkali such as ammonia or caustic soda, Hevea latex retains its liquid condition for many years, but in the absence of such additions bacterial action occurs, acids are developed and the latex quickly coagulates. Disinfectants also have a preserving effect on latex.

As already indicated, undiluted Hevea latex usually contains 30–40% of rubber. There are also present a number of other substances, amongst which by a remarkable chance are small quantities of compounds essential to the commercial applications of the product. When latex is coagulated with an acid only a portion of the accessory substances are coagulated with the rubber. The rest remains in the serum. The active non-rubber substances still mixed with the rubber are ample, however, to satisfy commercial requirements. For this reason methods of preparing rubber by evaporating latex have not met with general approval. In such cases the pure rubber may only amount to 85% of the solid material, whereas commercial crêpe and sheet prepared by acid coagulation may contain as much as 95%.

The following table shows the average percentage of the different non-rubber substances in dried Hevea latex in comparison with the amounts present in crêpe and sheet.

| Non-rubber constituent | Amount present in | |
	Dried latex per cent	Crêpe and Sheet per cent
Protein and nitrogenous matter	4–5	2
Constituents soluble in acetone	4–5	3
Mineral matter (ash)	1½	0·3
l-methyl inositol	1½	traces
Sugars	½	traces

Some of the constituents of the accessory substances are particularly active in accelerating vulcanisations and are therefore of great importance to the rubber manufacturer. A similar effect may also be produced by another of the accessory substances, viz., the ash which consists chiefly of potassium compounds.

Constituents soluble in acetone (a solvent which does not affect the rubber portion of the product) contain an appreciable amount of fatty acids such as oleic and stearic which dissolve and disperse some of the mineral powders mixed with rubber during commercial operations. The acetone-soluble material also contains a substance (allied in chemical composition to the sterols) which is particularly useful in preserving vulcanized rubber goods against the effects of atmospheric oxidation, so that they remain supple and elastic for a longer period than they otherwise would.

Pure rubber (caoutchouc) is a compound containing carbon and hydrogen only, in the proportion corresponding to five atoms of carbon and eight of hydrogen (C_5H_8). It belongs to the class of bodies known as terpenes and is related in chemical composition to the constituents of turpentine.

The specific gravity of rubber is a little less than that of water. It decreases regularly with increase of temperature except between 30 and 35° C when the decrease is greatly accelerated. At the temperature of liquid air rubber is transparent and brittle like glass. At 0–10° C it is hard and opaque, but quickly reverts to a soft and translucent condition above 20° C. As the temperature increases the rubber becomes softer, stickier, weaker and less elastic. These changes are greatly accelerated at temperatures of 50–60° C. At a little below 200° C rubber decomposes yielding liquid hydrocarbons of the terpene series.

When rubber is repeatedly pressed between rollers it becomes more plastic and sticky and less elastic. While in this condition large quantities of powders and plastic solids may be mixed with the rubber merely by repeatedly passing through rollers.

Rubber is insoluble in water and is unaffected by alkalis or moderately strong acids, but these substances may react with the non-rubber accessory substances present. Rubber is dissolved by benzol, petrol, carbon disulphide, chlorinated hydrocarbons, etc. It forms compounds with halogens, halogen acids, ozone, certain oxides of nitrogen, chromyl chloride and certain metallic halides. It is oxidised by nitric acid, potassium permanganate and hydrogen peroxide. It is also slowly affected by atmospheric oxygen, par-

ticularly in the presence of copper salts. It is reduced by hydrogen in the presence of a catalyst.

When rubber is heated at 120–160° C with sulphur it forms a product known as vulcanized rubber, which is stronger, more elastic and less affected by changes of temperature than the raw material. It is also insoluble in all the usual solvents. These changes are considerably modified by the amount of sulphur and heat applied and also (although to a lesser extent) by powders and other substances which may have been mixed with the rubber. With suitable adjustments it is possible to obtain from the raw materials a product which is as soft and elastic as an inner tube or as hard and brittle as a piece of vulcanite.

BIBLIOGRAPHY.—H. Brown, *Rubber, its sources, cultivation and preparation* (1914); O. de Vries, *Estate rubber, its preparation, properties and testing* (1920); G. Stafford Whitby, *Plantation rubber and testing of rubber* (1920), full information concerning chemistry of non-rubber accessory substances, physical tests, technical; T. Petch, *The diseases and pests of the rubber tree* (1921), technical; Sydney Morgan and Henry P. Stevens, *The preparation of plantation rubber* (1922), a practical account written for the planter; W. Bobilioff, *Anatomy and physiology of Hevea brasiliensis* (Zurich, 1923) suitable for non-technical as well as advanced readers; C. W. Bedford and H. A. Winkelmann, *Systematic survey of rubber chemistry* (1923), complete bibliography; S. P. Schotz, *Synthetic rubber* (1926), optimistic review of methods of preparation. (G. MAR.)

RUBBER: PRODUCTION AND MANUFACTURE.

Spanish explorers to the new world 400 years ago found the natives playing games with a ball made from latex, the fluid exudate of a tree. The first written reference to this gum was by Gonzalo Fernandez De Oviedo y Valdes in *La historia natural y general de las Indias,* published in Seville, 1535–57. The natives of tropical America referred to rubber by the names *Hevea,* "Olli" ("Ule"), "kik" and "cauchuc" (Spanish adaptation). In ancient Peru "cauchos" was regarded as one of three substances with magical properties. Charles Marie de la Condamine, who was dispatched by the French government in 1731 on an expedition to study the shape of the earth, sent back from the Amazon a dark-coloured resinous material from *Hevea* trees called "caoutchouc," and reported: "Linen is covered with this material and used like oil-cloth at home; the natives make shoes of it which are waterproof. They also cover molds of earth, in the shape of bottles, with this material and when the resin is dry they smash the mold, take the pieces of earth out through the bottle neck, and have an unbreakable bottle which is useful for preserving all kinds of liquids." Some of the crude rubber found its way to England, where Joseph Priestley, discoverer of oxygen, observed that it rubbed out pencil marks and gave it the name "rubber." By 1825 "gum boots" of native make were imported into the United States. These were soon to be made on wooden lasts supplied by Yankee traders. This business reached a volume of 462,230 pairs in 1842. In 1831 similar shoes, made in a factory in the United States by coating fabric with a solution of rubber in turpentine, proved unsatisfactory as the rubber became soft in summer and stiff in winter and was degraded by turpentine. People in Europe and America, who had taken an interest in rubber, became disgusted with its limitations. The German F. Ludersdorff, 1832, and the American Nathaniel Hayward had found sulphur effective in lowering the tendency of rubber to grow sticky. Yet, it was Charles Goodyear's experiment (Jan. 1839) in cooking a mixture of rubber, white lead and sulphur on a kitchen stove that pointed the way to the commercial use of rubber. Thomas Hancock in England, working on the same problem, was shown samples made by Goodyear. The sulphur bloom on these samples prompted him to heat raw rubber in molten sulphur which effectively "vulcanized" the rubber as his friend William Brockedon termed the operation. Hancock patented his discovery in England in 1843, while Goodyear's U.S. patent was issued in 1844.

The discovery of hot vulcanization led to great activity in the manufacture of rubber in Europe and the U.S. In the United States, rubber footwear, waterproofed clothing, bumpers for railway cars, rubber balls and other articles were made until, by 1858, 10,000 workers, located mainly in New England and New

Jersey, were engaged in making rubber goods valued at nearly $5,000,000. In 1870 rubber manufacturing was started in Akron, O., by B. F. Goodrich. By 1910 Akron had become the greatest centre of rubber manufacture in the world. The manufacture of rubber articles at mid-20th century was being conducted on every continent and in all parts of the world, but most extensively in the United States, United Kingdom, France, Canada and Germany. Important commercial developments in the production and manufacture of rubber goods comprise transportation items (used in the assembly of automobiles, aeroplanes, farm machinery, bicycles and other vehicles; see TYRE); the industrial products (belting, hose, packing, jar rings, typewriter platens, shock absorbers, sponge rubber and a host of other items); footwear and clothing; sports items (rubber balls, shoes and wearing apparel); druggists' sundries (hot-water bottles, bulbs, syringes and gloves); and novelty items (toys, balloons, aprons, stationers' bands, etc.).

Rubber Consumption.—The world consumption of natural rubber in long tons was 100,000 in 1910, 297,500 in 1920, 710,000 in 1930 and 1,110,000 in 1940. The increased rate of consumption was caused mainly by the development of automotive transportation. In each of years 1910 to 1949 (except 1944) 40% to 75% of the crude rubber used was consumed in the United States. The importance of synthetic rubber for general-purpose uses began to be recognized after 1940.

Two basic developments anticipated the growth of the modern rubber industry—the discovery of the hot vulcanization of rubber by Charles Goodyear of New Haven, Conn., 1839, and the noteworthy contributions of Thomas Hancock, England, 1820–56, who invented processes and machines the basic principles of which have continued to find widespread use in the industry. Hancock invented the masticator for kneading tough natural rubber into soft masses, the calender, a set of squeeze rolls to sheet rubber or coat it on fabrics, and he used moulds, 1846, to form rubber articles under heat and pressure. Hancock was also among the first to recognize the advantages of forming articles from natural rubber latex. Both these pioneer inventors were unusually productive of new ideas. Between them they anticipated the use of rubber in making hundreds of new articles and laid the groundwork for almost every important development made by the industry. Contemporary with these two men were Charles Macintosh of London who introduced the practice of spreading fabrics with rubber solutions and doubling the plies to give the mackintosh raincoat fabric, and Edwin M. Chaffee of Massachusetts who introduced the smooth roll mill for mixing rubber batches in 1835, and the first set of calender rolls, 1836, for the frictioning of rubber masses onto fabric.

Other prominent technical advances in the rubber industry were the development of the applied science of compounding; the introduction of reclaimed rubber made from discarded rubber articles by a number of methods; the development of reinforcing pigments like the fine particle size carbon blacks which impart to cured rubber marked improvement in tear and abrasive wear; the advantageous use of rubber in composite structures with materials such as textiles, metals, wood, glass, asbestos and other components; the invention of many ingenious machines for use in the assembly of rubber articles; and the development and extensive use of synthetic rubber. The discovery of organic accelerators by George Oenslager of Akron, O., in 1906, benefited the industry by speeding up the vulcanization step and by making possible products of better quality and higher uniformity. The

discovery of age resisters, chemicals which retard the deterioration of rubber goods without affecting the state of vulcanization, was announced by Herbert Winkelmann and Harold Gray in 1923, and by Sidney Cadwell in 1924.

Crude Rubber.—(*See* RUBBER: BOTANY, CULTIVATION AND CHEMISTRY.) The source of natural rubber is the latex of certain plants, mainly the tree *Hevea brasiliensis*. In plantation practice coagulated latex may either be washed and air dried to make "pale crepe," or sheeted and cured to form "smoked sheets." These two grades are the standard types of commercial rubber. Commercial grades include various types of ribbed smoked sheets, latex crepes, brown crepes, remilled crepes, flat bark crepes, fine Para, central scrap, Congo and guayule rubbers. Crude rubber is usually shipped in rectangular bales wrapped in sheets of similar rubber. The weight of a bale is about 224 lb. Originally, rubber came from wild trees and vines and was collected by natives of the region where these grew. Great variability and scores of different grades prevailed even for some time after the advent of plantation rubber, c. 1910. Washing and drying operations formerly widespread in the manufacturing industry are most extensively practised near the source of the rubber. A great deal of the rubber used by the factories is cleaned by straining in a screw-fed machine in the head of which is mounted a screen to retain foreign matter.

Synthetic Rubber.—After 1941 the use of synthetic rubber was necessary in the manufacture of rubber articles; first, because Japan captured Malaya, Indo-China and Indonesia—source of more than 90% of the world's rubber—and withheld crude rubber from world markets until its defeat in 1945; and, second, because the world production of crude rubber was inadequate to supply the demand after World War II. Scientists from mid-19th century had envisaged the possibility of getting from chemical reactions a product like rubber. The idea started when Michael Faraday, at the request of Hancock, made a chemical analysis of natural rubber and reported, 1826, the empirical formula C_5H_8; the German, C. Himly, in 1838 named the volatile distillate which he derived from rubber "Faradayine," a tribute to the pioneer chemist in the field of rubber; the French chemists, A. Bouchardat, 1837, and G. Bouchardat, 1875, starting from this type of distillate, made resinous products from it. C. Greville Williams in England, 1860, found that isoprene, key to the puzzle, was the probable main component in Faradayine and that rubbery masses could be made from isoprene. His countryman, W. Tilden, 1892, reported that isoprene from turpentine gave rubberlike yellowish masses on standing. But none of these products was rubber, the molecule that has never been created except in the latex cells of growing plants. Intense nationalism and bickering marred the progress of scientific discovery in the search for synthetic rubber after 1900. Contention increased as the need came for more and more rubber in world trade, and thus promised large rewards in prestige and profit. Three Rus-

TABLE I.—*Consumption by Countries of Natural and Synthetic Rubbers*
(In long tons)

	U.S.	U.K.	France	Germany	Total Europe*	Canada	India	South Africa	Grand total
Natural rubber									
1940	648,500	147,056	35,000	26,500	137,500	36,996	11,047	10,000	1,110,000
1941	775,000	156,549	14,883	22,000	97,500	53,232	13,249	12,500	1,240,000
1942	376,791	97,056	10,193	26,000	85,000	42,144	14,398	10,000	765,000
1943	317,634	74,391	1,126	4,000	35,000	9,588	12,110	10,021	387,500
1944	144,113	45,195	250	2,500*	32,500	5,892	15,233	8,578	262,500
1945	105,429	27,275	3,553	1,000*	32,500	9,580	14,037	10,528	555,000
1946	277,597	96,647	29,767	1,668	70,000	32,274	17,000	15,000	1,110,000
1947	562,661	153,626	61,190	8,090	210,000	41,567	19,719	15,000	1,420,000
1948	627,332	103,731	86,471	45,555	375,000	38,299	19,662	17,000*	1,437,000*
1949	574,522	184,255	91,163	65,948	432,500				
Synthetic rubber									
1940	2,560			40,000	40,000				42,500
1941	6,259			50,500	65,000				72,500
1942	17,651		6,060	69,000	95,000				112,500
1943	170,891	3,339	10,247	88,500	115,000	3,688			292,500
1944	566,670	41,782	5,426	80,000*	100,000	24,722	2	3	737,500
1945	693,580	63,772	17,419	22,500*	55,000	35,944	2	2,600	865,000
1946	761,699	30,123	28,705	11,852	75,000	29,616	7	2,732	912,500
1947	559,666	2,773	12,556	7,852	32,500	29,178		165	625,000
1948	442,072	2,555	7,401	4,422	15,000	20,554	1	120	480,000
1949	414,381	2,367	8,303	2,230	14,000*	18,063	1	120*	450,000*

*Estimated or partly estimated.

sian scientists made significant early discoveries. I. Kondakow in 1900 made leatherlike plastic masses from 2,3-dimethyl butadiene-1,3, the substance which about 1910 was to serve as the basis of the earliest chemical rubber made independently both in the United States and in Germany. S. V. Lebedev in 1910 converted butadiene-1,3 to a rubberlike product, which later became the most important molecule with which to start in the making of chemical rubbers; Lebedev also originated one of the simplest methods for obtaining butadiene from alcohol. A third Russian scientist, I. Ostromislensky, not only contributed valuable information on the source of butadiene, 1915, but also worked on the polymers of vinyl chloride, 1916, new giant molecules which by 1940 had proved of great industrial importance in supplementing rubber.

The German attempts to make synthetic rubber from dimethyl butadiene, 1910–18, led to a production of only 2,350 tons of the "methyl" rubbers—grades "W" for use in soft rubber goods and "H" in hard rubbers—but these rubbers were not competitive with natural rubber. Parallel with this early German effort, L. P. Kyrides (Kyriakides) and Richard Earle, 1910–13, worked out three processes for synthetic rubber for the Hood Rubber company near Boston, Mass. The most promising of these depended upon dimethyl butadiene from acetone and gave rubber from which satisfactory footwear was made at a high cost. C. Harries in Germany and F. E. Mathews and E. H. Strange in England independently in Oct. 1910 found metallic sodium an excellent catalyst for polymerization of butadiene and isoprene. This type of rubber was to be made commercially in the U.S.S.R. after 1928 under the designation SKB (based on alcohol) or SKA (based on petroleum).

The first commercially important and successful synthetic rubber, neoprene, was announced in 1931 for sale by E. I. du Pont de Nemours and company. Neoprene (first called Duprene) stemmed from the work of the Rev. Julius Arthur Niewland, S.J., and was perfected by the work of du Pont chemists, Wallace Carothers, Elmer K. Bolton and others, which started about 1925. Neoprene, made from 2-chlorobutadiene-1,3 (chloroprene), resembles natural rubber chemically more closely than any of the other chemical rubbers. Its finished products resist oil, sunlight and ozone, and are used widely. Consumption of neoprene annually averaged 43,000 long tons over the period 1944–48.

Buna Rubbers.—German chemists of I. G. Farben A. G. began an intensive search for a commercial synthesis of rubber about 1925. The numbered Buna rubbers, such as Buna 85 and Buna 115, were made by Lebedev's method from *Bu*tadiene and sodium (*Na*trium) whence the name "Buna," but these rubbers which ranged from a rubbery to a pitchy consistency were not of good enough quality to replace crude rubber in general use. Hence, the search was continued and led to the emulsion copolymerization of butadiene and styrene, two chemicals which the German industry could provide abundantly from grain alcohol and coal, respectively. The copolymer Buna S was made by charging the butadiene and styrene into a pressure vessel with soap, water and minor ingredients. The emulsion thus formed was transformed overnight into a suspension of rubbery particles, an opaque latex from which Buna S rubber was derived by coagulation with salts and acids. When washed and dried Buna S resembled crude rubber. By a similar method Buna N was formed from the reactants butadiene and acrylonitrile. The first large factory, capacity 24,000 metric tons, for the synthesis of these "lettered" Buna rubbers by the emulsion process was subsidized by the nazi government and began operation about 1939. Those who were required to use Buna S to make rubber goods complained that it took two to three times as much milling capacity as natural rubber, but reports indicated that tires made from it gave good mileages. During the shortage of neoprene in 1937, Buna N from Germany was sold in the United States under the name "perbunan." Manufactured articles made from it gave good service in withstanding oil exposure.

After 1925 several polymers other than neoprene with properties akin to rubber were perfected and produced mainly in the United States. Some of these, such as the plasticized polyvinyl esters (Koroseal, Vinylite, Geon), are of the nonvulcanizing type and are often listed as plastics, but their performance in uses once rendered only by cured rubber entitles them to rate as rubbery materials. The noncuring polyisobutylene and polyethylene were also used commercially to supplement rubber. Thiokol, 1928, a polyalkylene polysulphide, had a limited use, mainly for articles required to withstand lacquer solvents.

Perbunan, Hycar, Chemigum and Butaprene, all nitrile-butadiene rubbers of the oil-resistant type, not only replaced natural rubber in parts exposed to various oils but were used extensively in new fields such as compounding with synthetic resins to replace plasticizer (Polyblends) in making films for food packaging or as latex in paper impregnation. Silicone and Silastic rubbers, organic polymers containing silicon, support loads at temperatures in the range from −50° F. to 550° F. without loss of shape or insulating properties. At temperatures somewhat lower than 500° F. the sun-resistant Hycar P.A. (acrylate type) rubbers impart good elasticity under both compression and elongation.

In June 1940 the B. F. Goodrich company announced the Ameripol tire in which more than 50% of the rubber consisted of a butadiene copolymer, and the Standard Oil Development company announced butyl rubber for inner tubes. Butyl rubber was a polymer made at temperatures about −100° F. from isobutylene with only about 2%–5% of a diene such as isoprene.

GR-S.—In 1940 the United States began to recognize the threat of war to the world's supply of rubber. The Rubber Reserve company of the Reconstruction Finance corporation was created June 28, 1940, to build up domestic stocks of crude rubber from the alarmingly low level of 125,000 long tons at the end of 1939. The National Defense Advisory committee in Aug. 1940 held meetings with informed men in the rubber industry and drew up a program for 100,000 long tons a year capacity of synthetic rubber since private companies appeared unwilling to risk the capital needed to go ahead on this scale. Even the government at that time was reluctant to approve such a large operation, and in May 1941 scaled it down to about 40,000 long tons with plans for four plants, each of 10,000 tons capacity. Meantime, privately financed plants of 30,000-ton capacity were in prospect by 1942. After the attack by Japan on Pearl Harbor this government program was increased tenfold, and again doubled after the fall of Singapore. With relatively slight alterations these programs when completed had a capacity of 1,000,000 long tons a year of synthetic rubber. Even after their authorization the public was not convinced that they could be completed in time to supply the needs of the United Nations in a global war. Hence, on Aug. 6, 1942, Pres. Franklin D. Roosevelt appointed the Rubber Survey committee to study the rubber situation and make recommendations, with Bernard M. Baruch as chairman. The specific recommendations of the committee, Sept. 1942, were quickly enforced. These were rationing of motor fuel and tires, limiting driving speeds to 35 m.p.h., and for "bulling through" the gigantic synthetic program with the reorganization and consolidation of the government agencies then dealing with rubber. The president in Sept. 1942 created the Office of Rubber Director under the War Production board. Among the chemicals required each year to effect this synthetic program were 600,000 tons of butadiene, 220,000 tons from alcohol and the balance from petroleum feed stocks; 187,500 tons of styrene; about 100,000,-000 pounds of soap, and smaller amounts of auxiliary chemicals, catalysts and solvents. Besides the plants to make these starting materials there were polymerization plants for GR-S (government rubber, styrene type, the general purpose rubber) and plants of entirely different design for the manufacture of butyl (GR-I) and neoprene (GR-M). Fifty-one plants were designed, built and operated by 49 rubber, chemical and industrial companies under the supervision of Rubber Reserve company. The estimated plant investment exceeded $700,000,000. These operations involved full co-operation of the industry with the pooling of patents and the exchange of technical information under an agreement which extended from Dec. 19, 1941, to March 31, 1949. Plants were located mainly in Connecticut, Pennsylvania, Ohio, West Virginia, Kentucky, Louisiana, Texas,

Arkansas and California. The Canadian plant at Sarnia, Ont., under the dominion government, had a designed yearly capacity of 30,000 long tons of GR-S and 7,000 tons of butyl, with facilities for butadiene, styrene and isobutylene manufacture.

From 1945 on disposal of government-owned plants was actively studied by government agencies and by industry. U.S. public law 469 (1948) prescribed a minimum consumption of GR-S of 200,000 long tons a year with stand-by plant capacity up to 600,000 long tons to ensure national security, and with 65,000 long tons capacity for specialty rubbers, including those suitable for inner tube manufacture. The president of the United States, Jan. 1950, recommended the policy of selling government-owned plants to the industry under conditions that would ensure adequate supplies of the needed rubbers, encourage developments designed to improve their quality and restrain the ownership of the plants by a monopoly.

TABLE II.—*Production of Synthetic Rubbers*
(In long tons)

| Year | United States | | | | Germany | World total |
	GR-S	Neoprene	Butyl	Nitrile type	Buna S	
1939		1,738		12	20,251	23,748
1940		2,469		91	36,550	42,386
1941	227	5,423	0	2,464	65,075	77,475
1942	3,721	8,998	23	9,734	96,399	120,161
1943	182,259	33,648	1,373	14,487	108,822	350,043
1944	670,268	58,102	18,890	16,812	95,953	900,525
1945	719,404	45,651	47,426	7,871	—	866,069†
1946	613,408	47,766	73,114	5,738	14,945	806,564
1947	407,769	31,495	62,820	6,618	7,835	559,324
1948	393,880	34,848	52,603	7,012	3,388*	532,186
1949	295,166	35,215	52,337	11,072	‡	440,332†

*Total of all types.
†Excluding German production.
‡Not available.

The year 1948 marked the introduction of "cold" rubber made from the same basic ingredients as GR-S in an activated recipe at 41° F. compared with the temperature 122° F. ordinarily used. The road wear of tires made from cold rubber was improved over those from crude rubber by 10% to 25%. At the end of 1949 GR-S plants had been equipped to make up to 180,000 long tons a year of cold rubber.

MATERIALS USED IN THE INDUSTRY

Rubber Materials.—The new rubbers consumed by the industry, including natural and synthetic, comprise the largest tonnage of any material used.

Reclaimed Rubber.—Vulcanized rubber scraps (tires, tubes, footwear, etc.) are plasticized and are available for reprocessing by the ordinary methods of rubber goods manufacture. The process of scrap treatment is known as reclaiming and the product as reclaimed rubber, reclaim or shoddy. The two methods most extensively used are the alkali process, patented by A. H. Marks, 1899, and the heater process, in which pans of scrap rubber, softeners and caustic are exposed to steam at about 350° F. Reclaim originates in at least 23 countries with an aggregate reclaiming capacity estimated as of 1945 at 530,000 long tons. Reclaim blends readily with crude rubber and GR-S to give compositions which process smoothly and is of great economic importance as a supplement to the new rubber consumed by the industry. In 1948 the tonnage of reclaim consumed by the U.S. manufacturing industry was 25% of the total new rubber consumption. Proportionate consumption in 1939 was 29% and in 1942 was 65%.

Scrap.—Unvulcanized trimmings containing no fabric or other materials are not waste. They may be blended with fresh stocks of the same composition and utilized with no loss of material value. Unvulcanized waste containing fabric may be treated to pulverize the fabric and utilized in rubber compositions with some reduction in value. Even vulcanized waste is incorporated in certain goods.

Dry Pigments.—*Reinforcing and Filling Pigments.*—Powdered materials are blended with rubber materials in order to modify the stiffness, strength and resistance to abrasion or chemical action of the vulcanized rubber. Reinforcing pigments possess the property of stiffening and strengthening rubber com-

positions so that the total energy necessary to extend a strip of the compound to its breaking point is greater than that necessary to stretch a similar mix containing only rubber, sulphur and accelerator. Fillers, though they may stiffen the vulcanized compound, do not increase the total energy of rupture. Carbon blacks of two types (impingement and furnace), zinc oxide, certain clays, calcium silicate and magnesium carbonate are common reinforcing pigments. Whiting and barytes are extensively used as fillers.

Colours.—Most of the colours for rubber goods are useful in powdered form, and few colours soluble in rubber are used. For white goods, zinc oxide, lithopone, titanium oxide and zinc sulphide are used. Reds, blues, yellows and other colours and shades are secured with pigments such as ferric oxide, ultramarine blue and zinc chromate. The utilization of certain organic dyestuffs (phthalocyanine colours) and certain salts of azo dyes has enhanced the aesthetic appeal of rubber articles.

Other Compounding Ingredients.—*Softeners.*—For modifying the characteristics of the vulcanized rubber mixtures and for improving their properties for ease in processing, many kinds of softening materials are incorporated in rubber stocks. Petroleum products from oils to paraffin wax, tars, oxidized petroleum residues (mineral rubber), rosin, pine tar, fatty acids or their zinc salts, and many others are common to the industry. For use with the synthetic rubbers, resins derived from coal by distillation and by ensuing chemical treatments of distillates have been highly regarded.

Vulcanizing Agents.—By far the commonest vulcanizing agent is sulphur, used in the form of ground brimstone. The proportion used depends upon the character of the product required. Soft rubber goods carry from 2 to 10 parts of sulphur, but in most compounds not more than 3½ parts per 100 of rubber are used. Synthetic rubber articles in general require about four-fifths as much sulphur as those made from crude rubber. Compositions unusually resistant to natural deterioration are produced containing less than 1% of sulphur. Hard rubber compositions carry 20% to 50%. Some organic sulphur compounds which liberate sulphur at vulcanizing temperatures have been used in special cases without addition of sulphur itself. Selenium and tellurium will produce vulcanization also, and have been used to some extent, usually, however, with some sulphur. Benzoyl peroxide, dinitro- and trinitro-aromatic compounds, dioximes, diisocyanates and dinitroso-compounds also vulcanize rubber.

Accelerators of Vulcanization.—Vulcanization of rubber by sulphur alone proceeds at a slow rate and almost invariably suitable materials, called accelerators, are added to the rubber mixes to hasten the process. From the time of Goodyear's experiment, in which he used white lead, until 1906, the only accelerators used were inorganic oxides or hydroxides—litharge, white lead, quick or slaked lime, magnesia. Organic accelerators shortened the time of vulcanization and enhanced the tensile and other properties of the vulcanizate. The early accelerators (1906)—thiocarbanilid and para-amino dimethyl aniline—gave way to diphenyl guanidine, mercaptobenzothiazole, the aldehyde-amines, thiuram sulphides and many newer chemicals. The activity of accelerators is improved by secondary ingredients such as zinc oxide, litharge or magnesia, and even by other organic accelerators. They are often further assisted by acid materials, such as oleic or stearic acids or pine tar. Pneumatic tires, formerly requiring three hours for vulcanization without accelerators, are vulcanized by the action of organic accelerators in less than an hour. Deterioration of rubber may be greatly retarded by the use of certain accelerators.

Age Resisters.—Deterioration of vulcanized rubber in storage or in service may be retarded also by incorporating in the mixture, before vulcanization, 0.5% to 6% of certain organic chemicals which have practically no effect on the vulcanization rate but greatly retard the rate of oxidation or change in properties of the vulcanized product. Some age resisters also impart to rubber compounds resistance to deterioration by heat and resistance to cracking under repeated flexure. The age resisters used in largest volume are secondary amino compounds. The term "antioxidant" is widely used in referring to the behaviour of chemicals which retard the deterioration of rubbers. While crude rubber from most sources contains a natural antioxidant, it is necessary to stabilize synthetic rubbers by the incorporation of 1% to 2% antioxidant in their manufacture to keep these rubbers fresh during storage. Usually, additional antioxidant is used in compounding these rubbers.

Other Materials.—Factice is made either by the action of sulphur chloride on vegetable oils—white substitute—or by heating these oils with sulphur—brown substitute. White substitute is used in cold vulcanized articles (*see* below) and brown substitute in hot vulcanized goods.

TECHNOLOGY

"Compounding" is that branch of technology concerned with systematic study of the composition and physical properties of natural and synthetic rubbers and their vulcanizates in relation to the performance of rubber articles. Compounding, as an applied science, has contributed to the growth of the industry by testing and specifying those compositions which perform best under severe service. As a result of these technical advances by anonymous compounders, rubber has come to be properly regarded as a state of matter rather than the specific hydrocarbon analyzed by Faraday in 1826. In the United States during World War II the consumption of new rubber changed from 96% natural in 1942 to 80% synthetic in 1944. The fact that the performance of rubber products remained without interruption at a very high level during this period is a tribute to the compounders. (The term "compounding" is also used to refer to the weighing of the various ingredients in preparation for the factory mixing of rubber batches, but in this article "compounding" will be used only in the technological sense.) Certain physical properties of compositions based upon natural and synthetic rubbers are shown in Table III and Table IV.

TABLE III.—*Properties of Widely Used Rubbers*
(Not loaded with pigment)

Property	Unit	Natural rubber (Hevea)		Synthetic rubber vulcanizates		
		Unvulcanized	Vulcanized	GR-S*	Butyl	Neoprene GN
Tensile	Kg./cm.²	20-40	275-350	22-24	220-240	350-400
Elongation	%	800-1,200	675-850	400-500	950	850-1,050
Hardness	Shore durometer A	20-30	40-45	37-40	35	38-42
Permanent set	After 200% elongation 24 hr.	75-125	3-5	2-4	3-5	8-12
Modulus of elasticity at 300% elongation	Kg./cm.²	5-10	11-24	14-16	12	10-20
Specific gravity at 20° C.		0.914	0.96	1.00	0.92	1.24
Permeability for H_2	Cm.³-atm. per cm.² per atm./cm. per sec.	—	40-50	—	5.5	11
Thermal properties						
Coefficient of linear expansion	10^{-5}/° C.	15-20	16-19	—	—	—
Specific heat	Cal./g./° C.	0.55	0.5	0.35	0.44	0.49
Brittle point	° C.	-62 -58	-58 -53	-60	-50 -45	-39
Electrical properties						
Volume resistivity	Ohm × cm.	10^{16}	10^{16}	10^{15}†	10^{16}	c.10^{10}
Dielectric strength	K.V./mm.	10-20	—	—	20	14
Dielectric constant × 10^{-3}	1,000 cycles	2.5	—	—	2.1-2.6	6.7-8
Power factor × 10^{-3}	1,000 cycles	2-3	—	—	4-5	18-20

*The corresponding values for Buna S are as follows: Tensile 30-60, elongation 300-450, hardness 50-55, permanent set 5-10, modulus of elasticity at 300% elongation 10-50, specific gravity at 20° C. 1.00, permeability for H_2 30, brittle point —58, volume resistivity 10^{14}, dielectric strength 20-25², dielectric constant × 10^{-3} 3-4, power factor × 10^{-3} 7-8.
†Special insulating mix.

Properties of Vulcanized Rubber.—Typical uses of rubber in the unvulcanized state are for cements, surgical adhesive tape, insulating tape and crepe soling. Nearly all rubber depends upon vulcanization and compounding for the properties which make it useful. The primary properties which lead to the wide use of rubber comprise high elongation with rapid recovery over a wide range of temperatures, the cohesive strength with flexibility needed

TABLE IV.—*Properties of Widely Used Rubbers*
(Loaded with carbon black and vulcanized)

Property	Unit	Natural rubber	Buna S	GR-S	Nitrile rubber Hycar O.R.-15	Neoprene GN
Formulation		*	†	‡	§	‖
Physical properties						
Tensile	Kg./cm.²	275-350	200-250	170-250	250-290	250-310
Elongation	%	550-650	400-750	600-650	500-550	500-750
Hardness	Shore durometer A	62-67	65-70	60-65	60-70	62-67
Permanent set	After 200% elongation 24 hr.	8-12	5-15	5-10	3-6	4-8
Modulus of elasticity at 300% elongation	Kg./cm.²	50-90	30-115	85	60-130	45-75
Specific gravity at 20° C.		1.13	1.2	1.2	1.15-1.25	1.4
Thermal properties						
Coefficient of linear expansion	10^{-5}/° C.	12-15	21-23	—	—	20-22
Specific heat	Cal./g./° C.	0.4	0.35	0.35	—	0.42
Brittle point	° C.	-58 -56	-58	-60	-34	-40

*C. 30% carbon black + 10% softener.
†C. 30% carbon black + 25% softener.
‡C. 30% carbon black + 10% softener.
§C. 30% carbon black + 20% softener.
‖C. 20% carbon black.

to cushion shocks and impacts, impermeability to gases and to water, and low specific gravity. Moreover, rubber compositions are relatively unaffected by oxygen, acids, bases, many organic solvents and other chemicals, and show good electrical properties. Outstanding among other materials is the performance of rubber against abrasive wear which accounts for many of its applications such as in transportation, conveyor belts, chutes, linings and air hose. Among the various rubbers, natural rubber compounds have relatively the lowest hysteresis and the best resistance to cutting, chipping and crack growth. Of the compounded synthetic rubbers, butyl has the lowest permeability by gases, GR-S (cold rubber) shows the best tread wear, the nitrile rubbers show the least swelling in oils and most solvents, the acrylate rubbers (consisting mainly of polyethyl acrylate) are remarkably resistant to dry heat and sunlight, and neoprene is notably unaffected by ozone.

Laboratory Controls and Specifications.—Incessant technological changes within the industry have been made possible only by vigilant control over quality at every step in manufacture. Chemical and physical tests on the raw materials, the rubber mixtures in process and on the end products of manufacture have become routine. For example, tread mixings are tested for specific gravity, for plasticity and for cured hardness to ensure uniform performance on the road. More accurate testing methods have led to rigorous specifications governing the selection of materials, the operations of processing and assembly and the performance of finished products.

Cleaning and Straining.—*See* section on *Crude Rubber* above.

Washing and Drying.—*See* section on *Crude Rubber* above.

Mastication.—Unvulcanized rubbers are softened by the influence of temperature, oxidation and mastication. Crude rubber breaks down, loses toughness when masticated, and most effectively when the mill rolls are chilled. This type of softening is due to oxidation under the electrical stresses generated by friction. Both crude and synthetic rubbers are more quickly masticated for large production operations at temperatures c. 350° F. in which process temperature is the important variable. Chemical softeners usually of the thio-aromatic type may be incorporated in amounts customarily under 1% to facilitate mastication, but these are not used in most batches. Rubber is often plasticized on two-roll mills and in internal mixers, but by far the largest tonnages are passed through powerful extrusion type (Gordon) plasticators in preparation for the subsequent steps.

Mixing.—The mixing operation is the most important of all through which the rubber compositions pass in the fabrication of goods. In fact, proper running in all subsequent operations depends upon the mixing operation having been properly performed.

Mixing mills vary in size from 24 in. to 84 in. in width. The 84-in. mills are the largest in common use. They consist of two parallel, horizontal rolls set close together side by side and revolving in opposite directions. The back roll is fixed in position and geared directly to a drive shaft; the front roll is floating. The clearance between the rolls is adjustable by means of set screws near the ends of the front roll. Rolls are made of cast iron with chilled surface. The rolls of 84-in. mills are 24 in. or 26 in. in diameter, cast hollow and fitted for service with internal perforated pipes for the introduction of cooling water. The procedures for mixing batches containing crude rubber, reclaim or one of the chemical rubbers will differ somewhat from each other. It is essential, however, in all cases, that all parts of the batch be uniformly blended. This blending is secured by cutting the sheet on the mill roll with a sharp knife, beginning at one end and rolling it on itself until the sheet has been cut almost entirely across. The roll thus formed is permitted to sheet out again on the mill and the process repeated in the opposite direction. This is repeated six or seven times to secure uniform mixtures. Mills of 84-in. width will mix batches from 150 lb. to 300 lb. in 25 min. to 40 min. Internal (Banbury) mixers have been used extensively since c. 1927 for nearly all large tonnage formulations. These closed mixers handle batches weighing up to 1,000 lb., operate at higher temperatures than roll mills and may do the mixing in a time interval as short as five minutes to eight minutes. A typical large Banbury mixer, three stories in height, is provided with a hydraulic ram which is lifted as soon as the rubber is sufficiently softened and jammed home after the charge of carefully weighed pigments has been added. Two irregularly shaped opposing rotors knead the contents together by a powerful smearing action. The energy is supplied at such a rate that much heat is generated. To avoid precure the sulphur and vulcanizing ingredients are often added later on 84-in. mills, three of which serve the Banbury, and sheet out the finished batch stock.

Calendering.—The calendering operation produces sheeted stock by pressing the rubber between rolls to form sheets of predetermined size and thickness. Calenders of various types and sizes are used in the industry. The usual type, a three-roll calender, consists of a heavy vertical frame holding adjustable horizontal rolls. The rolls can be driven either at even speed or at odd speed, and heated or cooled by internal circulation. Sheeting calenders are usually operated with the rolls at even speed and at 10 yd. to 30 yd. per minute. Calenders 100 in. wide with rolls 30 in. in diameter are the largest used in the industry. Sheets varying in thickness from point to point and sheets with embossed surfaces are also run on calenders equipped with special rolls. Footwear calenders are four-roll machines with engraved or embossed rolls so mounted that they are quickly detachable. Frictioning calenders for rubberizing fabrics are run so as to squeeze the rubber into the meshes of the fabric. The driven middle roll bears the rubber and delivers the sheet at a slightly faster speed than the bottom roll which supports the fabric. The frictioning process may be repeated on the opposite face of the fabric. Coating calenders of the three-roll type operate with the lower two rolls at even speed. The rubber sheet is firmly pressed against the prepared fabric as it passes through the calender but is not forced through the meshes as in frictioning. Successive operations of frictioning and coating are frequently employed. The use of the four-roll calender to coat both faces of the prepared fabric simultaneously has found wide acceptance, particularly in the tire industry. In a typical operation, parallel cords delivered from a creel are treated with latex, dried and fed between the squeeze rolls of the coating calender where uniform coats of rubber from the second and third rolls are compressed so as to join and surround the cords, thus forming a single ply of cord tire fabric. Coating calenders are run at speeds of 10 yd. to 40 yd. per minute.

Tubing Operations.—Tubing machines, or extruding machines, are devices for forcing continuous strips of rubber from a die. These strips may be tubular, rectangular or any one of a great variety of irregular cross-sectional shapes. The tubing machine consists of a horizontal cylinder in which a power-driven screw

rotates, forcing the rubber stock through a die inserted at the end of the machine. They are used for the production of tubing, hose tubes, pneumatic tire treads, solid tire treads, inner tubes for pneumatic tires, channel rubber slides for the windows of automobiles and many other articles.

Cements.—Among the oldest of all operations in the industry is the preparation of solutions of rubber in organic solvents (cements). For each rubber variety the solvent must be properly chosen. Cements are usually prepared in enclosed churns with stirring. The relative importance of cements to dry mixing operations and to latex applications has lessened since c. 1930.

Spreading.—The fabric is drawn over a roller under a spreader knife, which can be set at varying distances from the roll, carrying from a cement feed a thin layer of the cement, and then over steam-heated pipes to evaporate the solvent. This process is repeated until the required thickness of rubber coating is built up. By this method the rubber surfacing is applied to shoe cover and backing cloth, balloon fabrics, printers' blankets for offset work and similar products. Thin coatings similarly applied are used to improve the adhesion to fabric of rubber layers later applied on a calender. Cements applied by brushing are extensively used in the manufacture of rubber articles, notably footwear.

Vulcanization (Curing).—Before vulcanization, rubber is weak, softened by moderate heat, rendered stiff by cold, soluble in gasoline or other solvents and easily plasticized and sheeted between warm rolls. After vulcanizing it is strong, not greatly softened by heat nor stiffened by cold, insoluble in gasoline, and will crumble if run between rolls. Unvulcanized rubber is easily deformed to assume new shapes permanently; vulcanized rubber returns to its original form after deformation. Hot vulcanization, the process most generally used, is conducted in a number of ways.

Mould Cures.—Many articles are given their final form and vulcanized at the same time by application of heat and pressure to the rubber material in metal moulds. A typical mould for large tonnage production in the industry is the dome-type tire vulcanizer in which the two halves of the steel mould with faces engraved with the design of the tire and tread are heated internally with steam. Uncured tires in the closed mould are inflated by a heated fluid in a heavy-walled rubber inner tube (bag), forcing the tire against the mould and thus curing it, usually at temperatures under 300° F. for less than an hour. Closely akin to this equipment is the watch-case type of vulcanizer in which inner tubes are cured in an even simpler cycle involving air inflation.

Press Curing in Moulds.—Presses consist of parallel-faced, steam-heated plates between which are placed metal moulds in which the articles are formed. Pressure between the plates (platens) is secured hydraulically with the article receiving its heat only by conduction through the plates and mould faces, not by contact with steam. Most presses in production are provided with more than two platens to accommodate the work scheduled for them. Hollow articles like syringe bulbs, tennis or toy balls are vulcanized in moulds under inflation either by air or by nitrogen generated by the action of heat upon such a mixture as sodium nitrite and ammonium chloride in pelleted form. Special presses are made for curing long flat belts, a section of 20 ft. to 36 ft. being cured at one time. Heavy conveyor belts, made in this fashion, may weigh 30,000 lb.

Lead Coating for Curing.—Garden hose made in long lengths is run through a lead press and covered with a lead sheath. A 500-ft. length thus covered is wound on a drum and water connections leading outside the heater are made at both ends. A number of the drums are placed side by side in a horizontal, cylindrical vulcanizer and hot water under pressure run through the hose, while steam is admitted to the vulcanizer. In this manner, heat is applied simultaneously from both sides of the rubber structure and the internal water compacts the hose against the lead sheath. The lead covering is stripped, melted and used again for covering.

Open Steam Curing.—Articles which require no further forming than is produced in building operations may be vulcanized without enclosure in moulds. Steam is permitted to come into contact either with the bare goods or with wet fabric wrappings around them. Air brake hose is built on mandrels, wrapped tightly with wet cloth and vulcanized by steam directly surrounding the wrapped hose. Pressure may be applied during vulcanization in open steam to articles built on hollow forms. Boots and shoes, for example, built on hollow, perforated lasts, each of which is connected in the vulcanizer with a vent to the atmosphere, receive from the steam around them not only the heat necessary for vulcanization, but also mechanical pressure which forces out the air between the shoes and the forms and between the separate pieces composing the goods.

Continuous Curing of Insulated Wire.—Wire covered with a rubber insulation compound which cures rapidly is passed continuously through superheated steam in long steel pipes to effect vulcanization of the rubber in about one minute. The nipples for passing the wire in and out of the vulcanizer are sealed by a slip fit between the rubber cover of the wire and the wall of the nipple.

Water Curing.—Some rubber goods are cured immersed in hot water

BY COURTESY OF (1) GOODYEAR TIRE AND RUBBER CO.; (2-4) THE B. F. GOODRICH CO.; PHOTOGRAPHS, (5, 6) EWING GALLOWAY

PREPARING RUBBER FOR COMMERCIAL USES

1. Native tapping a rubber tree for latex

2. The latex, after being sieved and diluted, is placed in tanks containing acetic acid or other coagulant. The rubber rises to the surface in the form of white coagulum

3. The coagulum is passed through a series of sheeting rolls which press out most of the moisture. Following this operation, the sheets are cut to length and sent to the smokehouse

4. A plantation smokehouse, where the rubber sheets are hung on long racks. A fire is kept burning continuously in the lower part of the building. The smoke passes over baffles into the upper chamber, where it comes into contact with the sheets before it passes out through vents in the top. The smoking process takes from one to two weeks

5. Making crêpe rubber from coagulum. The rolls rotate at different speeds, thus giving the typical crêping action

6. Crêpe rubber is air-dried in sheds in order to preserve the natural light colour. This drying process takes from four to five weeks

PLATE II   RUBBER: PRODUCTION AND MANUFACTURE

BY COURTESY OF (1) GRANITE ROCK CO., WATSONVILLE, CALIF., (2) U.S. OFFICE OF RUBBER RESERVE AND THE B. F. GOODRICH CHEMICAL CO., (3-5) THE B. F. GOODRICH CO., (6) U.S. OFFICE OF RUBBER RESERVE AND THE NECHES BUTANE PRODUCTS CO.

RUBBER MANUFACTURE AND PRODUCTS

1. Rubber conveyor belt elevator, 14 stories high, lifts 100 tons of rock every hour
2. GR-S polymerizers in a U.S. government rubber plant, Port Neches, Tex.
3. Two-roll mixing mill. The batch shown is white sidewall stock for passenger-car tires
4. Mould curing. Dome-type vulcanizers are hinged like waffle irons. The tire is shown before (right) and after cure. Internal curing bags transmit both heat and pressure
5. The creel starts about 3,000 parallel cords on their way to form the sandwich between sheets of rubber at the coating calender. Such a sandwich makes up one ply in a passenger-car tire
6. Butadiene row, in Port Neches, Tex. Still columns which separate butadiene from cracked petroleum feed stock

under pressure. The pressure may be equal to or greater than that of saturated steam at the same temperature. Rubber sheet to be cut into thread is wrapped with wet cloths on drums, covered with a vulcanized rubber sheet and cured under water. To secure a smooth surface on sheets of hard rubber the unvulcanized stock is rolled on sheeted tin, a number of these slabs piled together and vulcanized under water.

Air Curing.—Varnished footwear and shoes containing wool fabrics are cured by heating in air, which is used most effectively under pressure and circulated by pumps.

Sulphur Chloride Curing.—The process of cold vulcanization was discovered in 1846 by Alexander Parkes in England. It is conducted by exposing rubber surfaces to sulphur chloride as vapour or in solution. Cold curing was practised extensively in the "dipped goods" industry to make thin articles like surgeon's gloves and finger cots on forms by repeated dipping in rubber cements. The curing of the thin rubber tissues in the vapour of sulphur chloride was followed by a neutralizing exposure to ammonia gas. Dental dam, a calendered sheet, is cured by this process, but most of the articles formerly made by dipping and cold curing have more recently been made from compounded latex and in some instances from prevulcanized latex.

Hard Rubber Vulcanization.—The commercial heating of rubber with large proportions of sulphur was first actively studied by Nelson Goodyear, who patented in 1851 a process for making hard rubber (ebonite). Articles of hard rubber are ordinarily formulated with 30% to 50% sulphur on the weight of the rubber, often with numerous other ingredients. Typical cures for these articles are carried out at higher temperatures and over longer periods than for soft rubber articles. Extensive heat evolution, and volume shrinkage and the generation of some hydrogen sulphide gas accompany ebonite vulcanization. Hence, cures are most frequently conducted in steam or water. Small masses of hard rubber can be cured in moulds.

Assembly Operations.—Primitive fabrication, c. 1820, of rubber hand stripped from fine Para biscuits was by cutting these sheets into patterns, forming articles from the pieces and joining the seams by compression or the use of rubber cement. The evolution of the industry has progressed through cement dipping and spreading, through mastication, mixing and calendering, through the use of pressure moulding and vulcanization, away from the handicraft arts toward mass production methods in which machines continue to replace human labour. In the industry the principle of flat-built assembly was in 1950 widely prevalent. Films of rubber from cement or latex were flowed by machine onto hundreds of rotated can ends a minute to form gaskets for pressure sealing; conveyor and transmission belts were built on tables from plies of frictioned and coated fabrics and cured in flat presses. Rubber footwear starts with plies of rubberized fabric and sheeted rubber to be punched out into pieces of many sizes and shapes on toggle presses. These parts are placed in flat books ready for the building assembly on shoe or boot lasts. Passenger car tires (*see* TYRE) start with coated cord fabric plies and tubed-out tread sections. The final assembly, including the rubber insulated wire bead, is made on a steel drum. The industry consistently favoured machine assembly operations and conveyor installations which reduced drudgery, enhanced uniformity and quality of products and markedly lowered costs to the consumers.

Latex.—*Hevea* latex from far eastern and Liberian plantations usually reaches the market in concentrated form of about 60% total solids with ammonia as the preservative. Various synthetic rubbers, mainly of U.S. production, including the nitrile rubbers, are also available as latices. Suitably compounded with ingredients in finely divided aqueous dispersions, these latices find extensive use commercially in the treatment of tire cord for improved adhesion and in numerous novel applications whereby articles are formed by coating, dipping, casting inside or outside of porous forms, by ionic coagulation and by electrodeposition. The latter process, and a type of ionic coagulation, are covered by patents of the American Anode company.

TABLE V.—*Consumption of Natural Rubber Latex*
(In long tons—dry solids content)

Year	U.S.	U.K.	France	Canada	Others	Total (est.)
1943	9,578	1,638	—	345	—	11,750
1944	6,085	885	—	150*	67	7,250
1945	3,886	673	—	96	42	4,750
1946	5,724	2,123	—	186	792	8,825
1947	13,909	5,705	601	516	4,174	24,905
1948	28,489	9,263	2,652	1,002	5,684	47,090
1949	36,117	10,679	2,757	1,439	†	†

*Estimated.
†Not available.

TABLE VI.—*Production of GR-S and Neoprene Latices in the U.S.*

Year	GR-S	Neoprene	Total
1945			22,253
1946	24,810	13,603	38,413
1947	22,474	6,089	28,563
1948	21,018	5,022	26,040
1949	19,761	*	*

*Not available after 1948.

Prevulcanized latex compounds are available in most countries made by a process originated by Philip Schidrowitz, of London, Eng. Latex compounds have been made available both to the industry and to artists and craftsmen by the latex suppliers who are usually the large manufacturers of rubber. Those latices which require vulcanization give sheets of tensile strengths in excess of 5,500 psi. while sheets made from prevulcanized latex test over 4,000 psi.

BIBLIOGRAPHY.—U.S. Department of Commerce, Bureau of the Census, *Census of Manufactures 1947, Rubber Products* (1949); R. Houwink (ed.), *Elastomers and Plastomers*, Part III, *Their Chemistry, Physics and Technology* (1948); U.S. Department of Commerce, *Rubber Industry Report*, bimonthly; Secretariat of the Rubber Study Group, *Rubber Statistical Bulletin*, monthly (London).

(H. L. TL.)

RUBBER ACCELERATORS are substances which increase the rate or lower the temperature of the vulcanization of rubber (*see* RUBBER: PRODUCTION AND MANUFACTURE).

RUBBLE, broken stone, of irregular size and shape. This word is closely connected in derivation with "rubbish," which was formerly also applied to what we now call "rubble."

"Rubble-work" is a name applied to several species of masonry (*q.v.*). One kind, where the stones are loosely thrown together in a wall between boards and grouted with mortar almost like concrete, is called in Italian *muraglia di getto* and in French *bocage.*

RUBELLITE, a red variety of tourmaline (*q.v.*) used as a gem-stone. It generally occurs crystallized on the walls of cavities in coarse granitic rocks, where it is often associated with a pink lithia-mica (lepidolite). The most valued kinds are deep red; the colour being probably due to the presence of manganese. Some of the finest rubellite is found in Siberia. The mills at Ekaterinburg, where it is cut and polished, draw most of their supplies from the Urals—chiefly from Mursinka, Sarapulskaya and Shaitanka—but specimens are occasionally found at Nerchinsk in Transbaikalia. Burma is famous for rubellite; the pits which yield it are dug in alluvial deposits in the Mönglong valley, some miles to the S.E. of Mogok, the centre of the ruby country. Very fine rubellite is found in the United States, notably at Mount Mica, near Paris, Oxford Co., Maine, where the crystals are often red at one end and green at the other. Mount Rubellite, near Hebron, and Mount Apatite at Auburn, are other localities in the same State from which fine specimens are obtained. Chesterfield and Goshen, Mass., also yield red tourmaline, frequently associated with green in the same crystal. Pink tourmaline also occurs, with lepidolite and kunzite, in San Diego Co., California. In Europe rubellite occurs sparingly at a few localities, as at San Piero in Elba and at Penig in Saxony.

RUBENS, PETER PAUL (1577–1640), Flemish painter, was born at Siegen, in Westphalia, on June 29, 1577. His father, Johannes Rubens, a druggist, although of humble descent, was a man of learning, and councillor and alderman in his native town (1562). A Roman Catholic by birth, he adopted the Reformed faith, and we find him spoken of as *le plus docte Calviniste qui fust pour lors au Bas Pays.* After the plundering of the Antwerp churches in 1566, Johannes Rubens hastily quitted Spanish soil, ultimately settling at Cologne (October 1568) with his wife and four children.

Here he became legal adviser to Anne of Saxony, the second wife of the prince of Orange, William the Silent. Before long it was discovered that their relations were not purely of a business kind. Rubens was imprisoned at Dillenburg for two years, and after that he was confined to the small town of Siegen. Here he lived with his family from 1573 to 1578, and here Maria Pypelincx gave birth to Peter Paul. A year after (May 1578) he returned to Cologne, where he died on March 18, 1587.

Rubens went to Antwerp with his mother when he was scarcely ten years of age. He was an excellent Latin scholar. Part of his boyhood he spent as a page in the household of the countess of Lalaing at Audenarde but soon his mother allowed him to follow his proper vocation, choosing as his master Tobias Verhaecht, a landscape painter. From 1592–96 he worked under Adam Van Noort, whose aspect of energy is well known through Van Dyck's beautiful etching, the highly esteemed master of numerous painters—among them Jordaens, later his son-in-law. Rubens thereafter studied under Otto Vaenius of Van Veen, a gentleman by birth and a court painter to archduke Albrecht, sovereign of the Spanish Netherlands. In 1598, Adam Van Noort acting as dean of the Antwerp gild of painters, Rubens was officially recognized as "master." His style at this early period may be judged from the "Annunciation" in the Vienna Museum.

Italian Period.—From 1600 to the latter part of 1608 Rubens belonged to the household of Vincenzo Gonzaga, duke of Mantua. The duke, who spent some time at Venice in July 1600, had his attention drawn by one of his courtiers to Rubens's genius, and induced him to enter his service. The influence of the master's stay at Mantua was of extreme importance to his artistic development. Sent to Rome in 1601, to take copies from Raphael for his master, he was also commissioned to paint several pictures for the church of Santa Croce, by archduke Albrecht. "St. Helena with the Cross," "The Crowning with Thorns" and "The Crucifixion" are to be found in the hospital at Grasse in Provence.

At the beginning of 1603, "The Fleming," as he was termed at Mantua, was sent to Spain with a variety of presents for Philip III. and his minister the duke of Lerma, and thus had opportunity to spend a whole year at Madrid and become acquainted with some of Titian's masterpieces. Among his own works, known to belong to the same period, in the Madrid Gallery, are "Heraclitus" and "Democritus." Of Rubens's abilities so far back as 1604 we get a more complete idea from an immense picture now in the Antwerp Gallery, the "Baptism of Our Lord," originally painted for the Jesuits at Mantua. Here may be seen the influence of Italian surroundings on the painter. Vigorous in design, he reminds us of Michelangelo, while in decorative skill he seems to be descended from Titian and in colouring from Giulio Romano. Executed simultaneously with this picture, were "The Transfiguration," now in the museum at Nancy, and the portraits of "Vincenzo and his Consort, kneeling before the Trinity," in the library at Mantua. To 1606 belong a large altar-piece of "The Circumcision" at St. Ambrogio at Genoa, the "Virgin in a Glory of Angels," and two groups of Saints, painted on the wall, at both sides of the high altar in the church of Santa Maria in Valicella in Rome.

Return to Antwerp.—While employed at Rome in 1608, Rubens received alarming news of his mother's health. He at once set out for the Netherlands. When he arrived in Antwerp, Maria Pypelincx was no more. His wish to return to Italy was overruled by the express desire of his sovereigns, Albrecht and Isabella, to see him take up a permanent residence in the Belgian provinces. On Sept. 23, 1609, Rubens was named painter in ordinary to their Highnesses, with a salary of 500 livres, and "the rights, honours, privileges, exemptions," etc., belonging to persons of the royal household, not to speak of the gift of a gold chain. Not least in importance for the painter was his complete exemption from all the regulations of the gild of St. Luke, entitling him to engage any pupils or fellow-workers without being obliged to have them enrolled—a favour which has been of considerable trouble to the historians of Flemish art. By order of the municipality he painted the first among the numerous repetitions of the "Adoration of the Magi," a picture in the Madrid Gallery, measuring 12 ft. by 17, and containing 28 life-size figures, many in gorgeous attire, warriors in armour, horsemen, slaves, camels, etc.

Apart from his success, another powerful motive had helped to detain the master in Antwerp—his marriage with Isabella Brant (Oct. 13, 1609). Many pictures have made us familiar with Isabella. We meet her at The Hague, Leningrad, Berlin, Florence, but more especially at Munich, where Rubens and his wife are depicted at full length on the same canvas. "His wife is very handsome," observes Sir Joshua Reynolds, "and has an agreeable countenance"; but the picture, he adds, "is rather hard in manner." This, it must be noted, is the case with all those pictures known to have immediately followed Rubens's return, when he was still dependent on the assistance of painters trained by others than himself. Even in the "Raising of the Cross," now in the Antwerp cathedral, and painted for the church of St. Walburga in 1610, the dryness in outline is striking. The picture is tripartite, but the wings only serve to develop the central composition, and add to the general effect. In Witdoeck's beautiful engraving the

partitions disappear. Thus, from the first, we see Rubens quite determined upon having his own way, and it is recorded that when he painted the "Descent from the Cross," "St. Christopher," the subject chosen by the Arquebusiers, was altered so as to bring the artistic expressions into better accordance with his views. Although the subject was frequently repeated by the great painter, this first "Descent from the Cross" has not ceased to be looked upon as his masterpiece. Begun in 1611, the celebrated work was placed in 1614. Rubens received 2,400 florins for this picture. In many respects, Italian influence remains conspicuous in the "Descent from the Cross." Rubens had seen Ricciarelli's fresco at the Trinità de' Monti, and was also acquainted with the grandiose picture of Baroccio in the cathedral of Perugia. But in Rubens strength of personality could not be overpowered by reminiscence; and the "Descent from the Cross" may be termed thoroughly Flemish.

If Sir Dudley Carleton could speak of Antwerp in 1616 as *Magna civitas, magna solitudo,* there was no place nevertheless which could give a wider scope to artistic enterprise. Spain and the United Provinces were for a time at peace; almost all the churches had been stripped of their adornments; monastic orders were powerful, and corporations eager to show the fervour of their Catholic faith, now that the "monster of heresy" seemed for ever quelled. Gothic churches began to be decorated according to the new fashion adopted in Italy. Altars magnified to monuments, sometimes reaching the full height of the vaulted roof, displayed, between their twisted columns, pictures of a size hitherto unknown. No master seemed better fitted to be associated with this kind of painting than Rubens. The church of St. Charles, erected by the reverend fathers in Antwerp, was almost entirely the painter's work, and if he did not, as we often find asserted, design the front, he certainly was the inspirer of the whole building. Hitherto no Fleming had undertaken to paint ceilings with foreshortened figures, and blend the religious with the decorative art after the style of those Italian buildings which owe their decorations to masters like Titian, Veronese and Tintoretto. Thirty-nine ceiling-panels were composed by Rubens, and painted under his direction in the space of two years. All were destroyed by fire in 1718.

Rubens delighted in undertakings of the vastest kind. "The large size of a picture," he writes to W. Trumbull in 1621, "gives us painters more courage to represent our ideas with the utmost freedom and semblance of reality. . . . I confess myself to be, by a natural instinct, better fitted to execute works of the largest size." The correctness of this appreciation he demonstrated by a series of twenty-four pictures, illustrating the life of Marie de' Medici, queen-mother of France. The gallery at the Luxembourg Palace, which these paintings once adorned, has long since disappeared, and the complete work is now exhibited in the Louvre. The sketches of all these paintings—now in the Munich Gallery—were painted in Antwerp, a numerous staff of distinguished collaborators being entrusted with the final execution. But the master himself spent much time in Paris, retouching the whole work, which was completed within less than four years. On May 13, 1625, Rubens writes from Paris to his friend Peiresc that both the queen and her son are highly satisfied with his paintings, and that Louis XIII. came on purpose to the Luxembourg, "where he never has set foot since the palace was begun sixteen or eighteen years ago." We also gather from this letter that the picture representing the "Felicity of the Regency" was painted to replace another, the "Departure of the Queen," which had caused some offence. Richelieu gave himself some trouble to get part of the work, intended to represent the life of Henry IV., bestowed upon Cavalier d'Arpina, but did not succeed. The queen's exile, however, prevented the undertaking from going beyond a few sketches, and two or three panels, one of which the "Triumph of Henry IV.," now in the Uffizi Gallery, is one of the noblest works of Rubens or of any master.

Rubens's comprehension of religious decorative art is disclosed in the "Assumption of the Virgin" at the high altar of Antwerp cathedral, finished in 1626. Every outline is bathed in light, so that the Virgin is elevated to dazzling glory. Rubens penetrates into the spirit of his subjects more deeply than, at first sight, seems consistent with his prodigious facility in execution. The "Massacre of the Innocents," in the Munich Gallery, is a composition that can leave no one unmoved.

Diplomatic Activity.—In the midst of his activity as a painter, Rubens was now engaged on diplomatic business. The truce concluded between Spain and the Netherlands in 1609 ended in 1621; Archduke Albrecht died the same year. His widow wished to prolong the arrangement, still hoping to see the United Provinces return to the Spanish dominion, and in her eyes Rubens was the fittest person to bring about this conclusion. The French ambassador writes from Brussels in 1624—"Rubens is here to take the likeness of the prince of Poland, by order of the infanta. I am persuaded he will succeed better in this than in his negotiations for the truce." But, if Rubens failed to bring about an arrangement with the Netherlands, other events enabled him to render service to the state.

Rubens and Buckingham met in Paris in 1625; a correspondence of some importance had been going on between the painter and the Brussels court, and before long it was proposed that he should endeavour to bring about a final arrangement between the Crowns of England and Spain. The infanta willingly consented, and King Philip acceded on hearing that the negotiator on the English side, Sir Balthasar Gerbier—a Fleming by birth—was likewise a painter. Rubens and Gerbier met in Holland, and Rubens volunteered to go to Spain and lay before the council the result of his negotiations (1628). The nine months then spent at Madrid rank among the most important in Rubens's career. He had brought with him eight pictures as presents from the infanta, and he was also commissioned to paint several portraits of the king and royal family. Philip delighted to see Rubens at work in the studio prepared for him in the palace, where he not only left many original pictures, but copied for his own pleasure and profit the best of Titian's. In Spain Rubens and Velazquez met, to the delight and advantage of both.

The king now commissioned Rubens to go to London as bearer of his views to Charles I., and the painter, honoured with the title of secretary of the king's privy council in the Netherlands, arrived in London just as peace had been concluded with France. He induced Charles to engage in no undertakings against Spain so long as the negotiations remained unconcluded, and he remained immovable in this resolution. The tardiness of the Spanish court in sending a regular ambassador involved the unfortunate painter in distressing anxieties, and the tone of his despatches is very bitter. But he speaks with the greatest admiration of England. On September 23, 1629, the University of Cambridge conferred upon him the honorary degree of master of arts, and on February 21, 1630, he was knighted. During his stay in England Rubens, besides his sketches for the decoration of the Banqueting Hall at Whitehall, painted the admirable picture of "The Blessings of Peace" now in the National Gallery.

Rubens was now fifty-three years of age, he had been four years a widower, and in December 1630 he contracted a second marriage with a beautiful girl of sixteen, named Helena Fourment. She was an admirable model, and often appears in his works.

Later Works.—Rubens's return was followed by an almost incredible activity. Inspired more than ever by the glorious works of Titian, he now produced some of his best paintings. Brightness in colouring, breadth of touch and pictorial conception, are specially striking in these later works. Could anything give a higher idea of Rubens's genius than, for example, the "Feast of Venus," the portrait of "Helena Fourment ready to enter the Bath," or the "St. Ildefonso" in the Vienna gallery?

Isabella died in 1633, and we know that to the end Rubens remained in high favour with her, alike as an artist and as a political agent. The painter was one of the gentlemen she deputed to meet Marie de' Medici at the frontier in 1631, after her escape from France.

Ferdinand of Austria, the cardinal-infant of Spain, the new governor of the Netherlands, arrived at Antwerp in May 1635. The streets had been decorated with triumphal arches and "spectacula," arranged by Rubens. Several of the paintings detached from the arches were offered as presents to the new governor-general, which accounts for the presence of many of these works in public galleries (Vienna, Dresden, Brussels, etc.). The painter was confirmed in his official standing. The last years of his life, however, were employed in working much more for the king than for his brother. About a hundred and twenty paintings of considerable size left Antwerp for Madrid in 1637, 1638 and 1639; they were intended to decorate the pavilion erected at the Pardo, and known under the name of Torre de la Parada. Another series had been begun, when Ferdinand wrote to Madrid that the painter was no more, and Jordaens would finish the work. Rubens breathed his last on May 30, 1640.

Rubens left the world in the midst of his glory. Not the slightest failing of mind or skill can be detected even in his latest works, such as the "Martyrdom of St. Peter" at Cologne, the "Martyrdom of St. Thomas" at Prague, or the "Judgment of Paris" at Madrid, where his young wife appears for the last time.

Rubens was a Fleming throughout, notwithstanding his frequent recollections of those Italian masters whom he most admired. But it must be borne in mind how completely his predecessors were frozen into stiffness through italianization, and how necessary it was to bring back the Flemish school to life and nature. In no other school do we find these animated hunts of lions, tigers, and even the hippopotamus and the crocodile, in which life and nature are displayed with the utmost power. "His horses are perfect in their kind," says Reynolds; his dogs are of the strong Flemish breed, and his landscapes the most charming pictures of Brabantine scenery, in the midst of which lay his seat of Steen. As a portrait painter, he shows Van Dyck the way; and his pure fancy subjects, as the "Garden of Love" (Madrid and Dresden) and the "Village Feast" (Louvre), have never been equalled.

Paintings by Rubens are found in all the principal galleries in Europe.

In America, the Metropolitan Museum of Art contains his "Return of the Holy Family from Egypt," "The Holy Family," and others; the Frick Collection, also in New York City, has his "Ambrose Spinola." The Cleveland Museum of Art contains his "Triumph of the Holy Sacrament over Folly"; the Joseph Widener Collection, Philadelphia, his "Rape of the Sabine Women"; the Detroit Institute of Arts, his "Abigail Meeting David with Presents"; and the Gardner Museum, Boston, his "Thomas Howard, Earl of Arundel."

LITERATURE.—E. Gachet, *Lettres inédites de P. P. Rubens* (Brussels, 1840); W. Noel Sainsbury, *Original Unpublished Papers concerning Rubens in the State Paper Office* (1859); A. Michiels, *Rubens et l'école d'Anvers* (1877); Gachard, *Histoire politique et diplomatique de P. P. Rubens* (Brussels, 1877); Max Rooses, *Titres et portraits gravés d'après P. P. Rubens, pour l'imprimerie plantinienne* (Antwerp); *L'oeuvre de P. P. Rubens* (5 vols. Antwerp, 1886–92); *Rubens* (English trans. 1904); Max Rooses and Rubens, *Codex Diplomaticus Rubenianus* (Antwerp, 1887); J. Smith, *Catalogue raisonné of the Works of the most eminent Dutch and Flemish Painters* (1842); Waagen, *Peter Paul Rubens* (trans. by R. Noel, 1840); H. Hymans, *Histoire de la gravure dans l'école de Rubens* (Brussels, 1879); C. G. Voorhelm Schneevoogt, *Catalogue des estampes gravées d'après Rubens* (Haarlem, 1873); R. A. M. Stevenson, *P. P. Rubens* (Portofolio Monograph, 1898); Émile Michel, *Rubens: his Life, his Work and his Time* (1899); H. Knackfuss, *Rubens* (English trans. 1904) and E. Dillon, *Rubens* (1909); R. Oldenbourg, *P. P. Rubens, Abhandlungen, etc.* (1922). For illustrations of his paintings *see* A. Rosenberg, *P. P. Rubens* (Klassiker der Kunst, Leipzig, 1906); and of his drawings G. Glück and F. M. Haberditzl, *Die Handzeichnungen von U. Rubens* (1928).

(H. Hy.; X.)

RUBIACEAE, a large family of seed plants, belonging to the series Rubiales of the subclass Sympetalae (Gamopetalae) of dicotyledons, and containing about 450 genera with about 5,500 species. It is mainly a tropical family of trees, shrubs and herbs, but some of the tribes, especially Galieae, to which the British representatives belong and which contains only herbs, are more strongly developed in temperate regions; some species of *Galium* reach the Arctic zone.

The most striking characteristic of the family are the opposite, decussate, generally entire, stipulate leaves. The stipules are very varied in form; they generally stand between the petiols of a pair of leaves (interpetiolar). The two stipules of adjacent leaves are usually united, and in the Galieae, as well shown in the British species, are enlarged and leaflike, forming with the two leaves an apparent whorl; by fusion or branching of the stipules the number of leaves in the whorl varies from four to eight or more. The flowers are mostly arranged in cymes or panicles or crowded into heads, and are frequently showy. The flowers are hermaphrodite and regular with parts in fours or fives; the four or five sepals, petals and stamens are placed above the ovary, which consists of two carpels and is crowned by a simple style usually ending in a head or in two lobes. The sepals are often small, sometimes reduced to a narrow ring encircling the top of the ovary or altogether absent. The united petals form a corolla which varies widely in form in the different genera; it is often funnel- or salver-shaped. The stamens are fixed to the corolla-tube and alternate in position with its segments; the flowers are often dimorphic (or heterostyled) with short-styled and long-styled forms.

The fruit also varies widely in form and is dry or fleshy. When dry it forms a capsule with septicidal or loculicidal dehiscence or is a schizocarp separating when dry into two one-seeded mericarps which, as in the British cleavers (*Galium aparine*), sometimes bear hooked appendages which aid their dispersal.

The family is divided into a large number of tribes based on the number of ovules in each ovary chamber, the character of the fruit seed and ovule, and the aestivation of the corolla. These may be arranged in two classes as follows:

Cinchonoideae, often woody plants with scalelike stipules, and numerous ovules in each ovary chamber; the fruit is generally a capsule. To this belong *Cinchona* (*q.v.*), a genus of large trees with handsome flowers containing about 40 species in the Andes of South America; it is well known as a source of quinine. An allied genus, *Bouvardia* (*q.v.*), is cultivated for its flowers.

Coffeoideae, often woody or shrubby plants with scalelike stipules; each ovary chamber contains only a single ovule. *Coffea*, a genus of shrubs with about 45 species in the old world tropics, includes the coffee plant (*C. arabica* and *C. liberica*); the fruit is a two-seeded drupe, the seed is the coffee bean. The thickened root of *Uragoga ipecacuanha* yields ipecacuanha. In this class is the tribe *Stellateae*, herbaceous plants with leaflike stipules; each ovary chamber contains one ovule only. It includes the four British genera: *Rubia*, one species of which, *R. tinctorum*, is madder; *Galium*, including *G. verum* (lady's bedstraw), *G. aparine* (goosegrass or cleavers) and other British species; *Asperula*, including *A. odorata* (woodruff) and *Sherardia*.

The commonest representatives in eastern North America are *Galium* (cleavers, goosegrass, wild licorice, etc.), *Houstonia* (bluets, innocence) and *Mitchella* (partridge berry). In western North America, in addition to a few species of *Galium*, the genus *Kelloggia* is very characteristic.

RUBICON, a small stream of ancient Italy, which flowed into the Adriatic between Ariminum and Caesena and formed the boundary between Italy and the province of Cisalpine Gaul in republican times, while Augustus adopted the Marecchia, a few miles farther south. Hence Caesar's crossing of it in 49 B.C. meant a declaration of war against Pompey and the senate. The historic importance of this event gave rise to the phrase "crossing the Rubicon" for a step which definitely commits a person to a given course of action.

Its upper course is represented by that of the Pisciatello (called Rubigone in the 11th or 12th century and now Rugone or Urgone), and its lower portion by the Fiumicino, which the Urgone once joined. The point was marked by a station on the Via Aemilia below their confluence, 12 mi. N.W. of Ariminum, bearing the name *ad Confluentes*; and there is still preserved a three-arched bridge.

RUBIDIUM, a rare metallic element belonging to the group of alkali metals (symbol Rb, atomic number 37, atomic weight 85.48, isotopes 85 [72.8%], 87 [27.2%]) was discovered by Robert Bunsen and Gustav Kirchhoff in 1861. While studying the alkalies extracted from lepidolite, they noticed that the chloroplatinate precipitate contained a salt whose flame spectrum had two especially prominent red lines so they suggested, for the new element, the name rubidium (Lat. *rubidus*, red).

No definite rubidium minerals are known. Lepidolite (lithium mica) is the richest rubidium-bearing mineral; European and American deposits containing from 0.5% to 1% and some African deposits containing as high as 3% rubidium oxide (Rb_2O) have readily met the rather limited demands for raw materials. Rubidium is also found in very small quantities in a number of minerals such as feldspars, micas and carnallite.

Rubidium salts are generally prepared from rubidium-bearing lepidolite by direct treatment of the finely powdered, calcined mineral with sulphuric acid followed by fractional crystallization of the alums. The lithium values together with the sodium and potassium alums are quite soluble and are readily separated from the more insoluble rubidium and caesium alums. The latter are not easily fractionated but by converting them into chlorides and adjusting to 3N-HCl concentration, pure fractions of rubidium chloride can be obtained by the addition of successive portions of ethyl alcohol to the hot solution. Since there are no truly specific reagents for potassium, rubidium or caesium ions in the presence of one another, probably the simplest way to determine rubidium is to compare the spectrum with that of known standards.

Metallic rubidium can be prepared by heating the hydroxide or carbonate in an atmosphere of hydrogen with an excess of magnesium. It is a silvery white metal with the melting point at 38.7° C., boiling point at 700° and a specific gravity of 1.52. It oxidizes rapidly on exposure to air, developing enough heat to ignite spontaneously. It dissolves in cold water with great energy, evolving hydrogen and forming rubidium hydroxide (RbOH), an exceedingly strong base. Next to caesium, rubidium is the most electropositive of all the metals and unlike caesium it shows a slight natural radioactivity. The ordinary salts of rubidium such as the carbonate, chloride and nitrate are colorless, relatively soluble in water and similar to the corresponding potassium salts. The chloroplatinate, perchlorate and acid tartrate are all very sparingly soluble in water.

Metallic rubidium has been employed in the manufacture of photoelectric cells being especially suitable because an extremely thin layer can be applied to the metal electrode and the photoemission of the molecular layer of metal is greater than that of the massive metal. Rubidium compounds are employed as reagents in microchemistry since their ability to form well defined crystalline compounds makes them of great value in this important and rapidly developing field.

See L. Gmelin, *Handbuch der anorganischen Chemie*, 8th ed. (1937). (J. J. Ky.)

RUBINSTEIN, ANTON GRIGORIEVICH (1829–1894), Russian pianist, was born of Jewish parentage on Nov. 28, 1829, at Vykhovatinets, Volhynia. Besides his mother Anton had but one teacher, the piano master Alexander Villoing, of whom he declared at the end of his own career that he had never met a better. In July 1839 Rubinstein appeared in the theatre of the Petrovsky park at Moscow; and in the following years in the principal centres of Europe, including London. He then studied in Berlin and Vienna. The years 1848 to 1854 were spent in St. Petersburg in performing and composing. His opera *Dmitry Donskoy* was produced there in 1852, and *Tom the Fool* in 1853. The *Siberian Huntsmen*, written about the same time, was produced at Weimar in 1854. In 1857 he paid his second visit to London where, at a Philharmonic concert he introduced his own concerto in G. In 1858 he was appointed concert director of the Imperial Russian Musical society and in 1862, in collaboration with Carl Schuberth, he founded the St. Petersburg conservatory, of which he was director until 1867, and again from 1887 to 1890. For 20 years from 1868 he made prolonged concert tours in Europe and the United States, enjoying prodigious success wherever he went and being accounted by some the superior even of Liszt. He died on Nov. 20, 1894. Rubinstein left compositions in almost every known form, but it is as one of the greatest of all pianists that he will be remembered. His autobiography was published in an English translation in 1890.

His brother NIKOLAY GRIGORIEVICH RUBINSTEIN (1835–1881) was also a fine pianist and teacher. He founded the Russian Musical society in 1859 and the Moscow conservatory in 1864, and was the latter's director until his death. Tschaikovsky wrote his pianoforte *Trio in A minor* in memory of him, although he had quarrelled with him on the B-flat minor concerto.

RUBRUQUIS (or RUBROUCK), **WILLIAM OF** (c. 1215-1270; fl. 1253-55), Franciscan friar, one of the chief mediaeval travellers and travel-writers. Nothing is known of him save what can be gathered from his own narrative, and from Roger Bacon, his contemporary and brother Franciscan. The name of Rubruquis ("Fratris Willielmi de Rubruquis," probably meaning "of Rubrouck," Flanders) is found in the imperfect ms. printed by Hakluyt in his collection, and followed in his English translation, as well as in the completer issue of the English by Purchas. (Itinerarium fratris Willielmi de Rubruquis de ordine fratrum Minorum, Galli, Anno gratiae 1253, ad partes Orientales.)

Friar William went to Tartary under orders from Louis IX. (St. Louis). That king, at an earlier date, viz., December 1248, when in Cyprus, had been visited by alleged envoys from Elchigaday (Ilchikadai, Ilchikdai), who commanded the Mongol hosts in Armenia and Persia. The king then despatched a return mission consisting of Friar Andrew of Longjumeau or Lonjumel and other ecclesiastics, who carried presents and letters for both Ilchikadai and the Great Khan. They reached the court of the latter in the winter of 1249-50, when there was no actual khan on the throne; and they returned, along with Tatar envoys, bearing a letter to Louis from the Mongol regent-mother which was couched in terms so arrogant that the king repented sorely of having sent such a mission. The envoys reached the king at Caesarea, between March 1251 and May 1252. But not long after the king, hearing that the Tatar prince Sartak, son of Batu, was a "baptized Christian," felt moved to open communication with him, and for this purpose deputed Friar William of Rubrouck. The former rebuff had made the king chary of sending formal embassies, and Friar William on every occasion, beginning with a sermon delivered in St. Sophia's on Palm Sunday (i.e., April 13) 1253, disclaimed that character.

Friar William apparently received his commission at Acre, but he travelled by way of Constantinople and there received letters to some of the Tatar chiefs from the emperor, Baldwin de Courtenay, the last of the Latin dynasty.

Rubrouck and his party landed at Soldaia, or Sudak, on the Crimean coast, then a centre of intercourse between the Mediterranean world and what is now S. Russia. Equipped with horses and carts for the steppe, they travelled successively to the courts (i.e., the nomad camps) of Scacatai (Kadan?), Sartak and Batu, thus crossing the Don and arriving at the Volga: of both these rivers Friar William gives vivid and interesting sketches. Batu Khan (q.v.) kept the travellers for some time in suspense, and then referred them to the Great Khan himself, an order involving the enormous journey to Mongolia. The actual travelling of the party from the Crimea to the khan's court near Karakorum cannot have been, on a rough calculation, less than 5,000 m., and the return journey to Lajazzo in Cilicia would be longer by 500 to 700 m. The envoys embarked on the "Euxine" on May 7, 1253. They were at the camp of the Great Khan from Dec. 27, 1253, to about July 10, 1254. They reached Tripoli on the way home on Aug. 15, 1255.

Roger Bacon, in the geographical section of the Opus Maius (c. 1262), cites the traveller repeatedly and copiously, describing him as "frater Wilhelmus quem dominus rex Franciae misit ad Tartaros, Anno Domini 1253 . . . qui perlustravit regiones orientis et aquilonis et loca in medio his annexa, et scripsit haec praedicta illustri regi; quem librum diligenter vidi et cum eius auctore contuli." (See Opus Maius, Oxford edition of 1897, i. 353-66.) Add to this William's own incidental particulars as to his being—like his precursor, Friar John de Plano Carpini—a very heavy man (ponderosus valde), and we know no more of his personality, except the abundant indications of character afforded by the story itself. These paint for us an honest, pious, stout-hearted, acute and most intelligent observer, keen in the acquisition of knowledge, the author of one of the best narratives of travel in existence. His language indeed is dog-Latin of the most un-Ciceronian quality; but it is in his hands a pithy and transparent medium of expression. In spite of all the difficulties of communication, and of the badness of his turgemannus or dragoman, he gathered a mass of particulars, wonderfully true or near the truth, not only as to Asiatic nature, geography, ethnography and manners, but as to religion and language.

The narrative of Rubrouck, after Roger Bacon's copious use of it, seems to have dropped out of sight, though five mss. are still known to exist: the chief of these are (1) Corp. Chr. Coll., Cambridge, No. 66, fols. 67 v.–110 v. of about 1320; (2) No. 181 of the same library, fols. 321-98, of about 1270-90; (3) Leiden Univ. Libr., No. 77 (formerly 104), fols. 160 r.–190 r. of about 1290. It has no place in the famous collections of the 14th century. It first appeared imperfectly in Hakluyt (1598 and 1599), as we have mentioned. See the two editions in the Hakluyt Society's publications, (i.) William of Rubrouck . . . John of Pian de Carpine, trans. and edited by William W. Rockhill (London, 1900); (ii.) Texts and Versions of . . . Carpini and . . . Rubruquis . . ., edited by C. Raymond Beazley (London, 1903). See also Beazley, Dawn of Modern Geography, ii. 266, 278-79, 281, 298-99, 303, 320-82, 421, 449-52; iii. 17-18, 31-32, 46, 69, 84-85, 88, 98, 101, 105, 188, 336-37, 544.

RUBY, the most valued of all gem-stones, a red transparent variety of corundum, or crystallized alumina (Lat. rubeus, red). It is sometimes termed "oriental ruby" to distinguish it from the spinel ruby, which is a stone of inferior hardness, density and value. (See SPINEL.)

The ruby crystallizes in the rhombohedral system (see CORUNDUM); the crystals have no true cleavage, but tend to break along certain gliding planes. The colour varies from deep cochineal to pale rose-red, in some cases, with a tinge of purple, the most valued tint being that called by experts pigeon's-blood colour. The oriental ruby is a mineral of very limited distribution. It most famous localities are in Upper Burma, principally in the neighbourhood of Mogok, 90 m. N.N.E. of Mandalay. It occurs in bands of a crystalline limestone, associated with granitic and gneissose rocks, some of which are highly basic; the limestone also contains spinel, garnet, graphite, wollastonite, scapolite, felspar, mica, pyrrhotite and other minerals. The ruby, like other kinds of corundum, suffers alteration under certain conditions, and passes by hydration into gibbsite and diaspore, which by further alteration and union with silica, etc., may yield margarite, vermiculite, chlorite and other hydrous silicates.

Rubies have been produced artificially (see GEMS, SYNTHETIC) with much success. It was once the practice to make "reconstructed rubies" by fusing together small fragments of the natural stone; but this process has given way to Prof. A. Verneuil's method of forming artificial ruby from purified ammonia-alum with a certain proportion of chrome-alum. The finely powdered material is caused to fall periodically into an oxyhydrogen flame, the heat of which decomposes the alum, and the alumina thus set free forms liquid drops which collect and solidify as a pear-shaped mass. When of the characteristic pigeon's-blood colour, the synthetical ruby contains about 2·5% of chromic oxide. The manufactured ruby possesses the physical characters of corundum, but may generally be distinguished by microscopic bubbles and striae. The manufacture of synthetic rubies is carried out commercially.

RÜCKER, SIR ARTHUR (1848–1915), English physicist, was born at Clapham on Oct. 23, 1848, and educated at Clapham grammar school and Brasenose college, Oxford. He became professor of mathematics and physics at the Yorkshire college, Leeds, in 1874, and professor of physics at the Royal College of Science in 1886. In 1901 he was appointed principal of the University of London. He was a secretary of the Royal Society from 1896 to 1901, receiving its Royal medal in 1891, and was knighted in 1902. He died at Newbury, Berks., on Nov. 1, 1915. Rücker's most important work in physics was a magnetic survey of the British Isles carried out in conjunction with Professor T. E. Thorpe; the results were published in a series of papers between 1883 and 1890. In conjunction with Professor Reinold he carried out investigations on thin liquid films; their work was published between 1877 and 1893. Rücker also made contributions to the theory of direct current dynamos and motors.

RŪDAGĪ (d. 954). Farīd-eddīn Mohammed 'Abdallāh, the first great literary genius of modern Persia, was born in Rūdag, a village in Transoxiana, about 870–900. Most of his biographers assert that he was totally blind, but the accurate knowledge of colours shown in his poems makes this very doubtful. The fame of his accomplishments reached the ear of the Sāmānid Nasr II. bin Ahmad, the ruler of Khurāsān and Transoxiana (913–42), who invited the poet to his court. Of the 1,300,000 verses attributed to Rūdagī, there remain only 52 kasīdas, ghazals and rabā'īs; of his epic masterpieces we have nothing beyond a few stray lines in native dictionaries. But the most serious loss is that of his translation of Ibn Mokaffa's Arabic version of the old Indian fable book *Kalilah and Dimnah*. Fragments are preserved in the Persian lexicon of Asadī of Tus (ed. P. Horn, Göttingen, 1897).

There is a complete edition of all the extant poems of Rūdagī, in Persian text and metrical German translation in H. Ethé's "Rūdagī der Sāmānidendichter" (*Göttinger Nachrichten*, 1873); *see also* his "Neupersische Literatur" in Geiger's *Grundriss der iranischen Philologie* (ii.); P. Horn, *Gesch. der persischen Literatur* (1901), p. 73; E. G. Browne, *Literary History of Persia*, i. (1902); C. J. Pickering, "A Persian Chaucer" in *National Review* (May 1890).

RUDD (*Scardinius erythrophthalmus*), a Cyprinid fish of Europe and western and northern Asia, deep-bodied, with reddish fins, and with the dorsal fin farther back than in the roach. It reaches a length of 18 in. and a weight of $3\frac{1}{2}$ lb. It is called pearl roach in the United States where it has been introduced.

RUDDER, that part of the steering apparatus of a ship which is fastened to the stern outside, and on which the water acts directly (O.E. *Rother, i.e.*, rower). The word may be found to be used as if it were synonymous with "helm." But the helm (A.S. *Hillf*, a handle) is the handle by which the rudder is worked. The tiller, which is perhaps derived from a provincial English name for the handle of a spade, has the same meaning as the helm. In the earliest times a single oar, at the stern, was used to row the vessel round. In later times oars with large blades were fixed on the sides, near the stern. In Greek and Roman vessels two sets were sometimes employed, so that if the pitching of the ship lifted the after pair out of the water, the foremost pair could still act. As these ancient ships were, at least in some cases, sharp at both ends and could sail either way, steer (or steering) oars were fixed both fore and aft. The steer oar in this form passed through a ring on the side and was supported on a crutch, and was turned by a helm, or tiller. Norse and mediaeval vessels had, as far as we can judge, one steer oar only placed on the right side near the stern—hence the name "starboard," *i.e.*, steerside, for the right side of the ship looking forward. In the case of small vessels the steer oar possesses an advantage over the rudder, for it can bring the stern round quickly. Therefore it is still used in whaling boats and rowing boats which have to work against wind and tide, and in surf when the rudder will not act. The side rudder was generally displaced by the stern rudder in the 14th century. (*See* SHIPBUILDING.)

RÜDESHEIM, a town in the Prussian province of Hesse-Nassau, Germany, 19 mi. S.W. of Wiesbaden. Pop. (1933) 4,740. It lies at the lower end of the vineyard district of the Rheingau, opposite Bingen and just above the gorge of the Rhine, and is a popular tourist centre. Rüdesheim has some interesting towers: the Brömserburg, or Niederburg (13th century), formerly belonging to the archbishops of Mainz; the Boosenburg, or Oberburg; the Adlerturm, a relic of the fortifications of the town; and the Vorderburg, the remains of an old castle.

RUDINÌ, ANTONIO STARABBA, MARQUIS DI (1839–1908), Italian statesman, born at Palermo on April 6, 1839, joined the revolutionary committee in 1859. After spending a short time at Turin as attaché to the Italian foreign office he was elected mayor of Palermo. In 1866 he quelled a separatist insurrection. He was then appointed prefect of Palermo, and put down brigandage throughout the province; in 1868 he was prefect of Naples. In October 1869 he became minister of the interior in the short-lived Menabrea cabinet. On the death of Minghetti in 1886, he became leader of the Right. Early in 1891 he succeeded Crispi as premier and minister of foreign affairs by forming a coalition cabinet with a part of the Left under Nicotera; his administration initiated the economies by which Italian finances were put on a sound basis, and also renewed the Triple Alliance. He was overthrown in May 1892 by a vote of the Chamber and succeeded by Giolitti. Upon the return of his rival, Crispi, to power in December 1893, he

resumed political activity, allying himself with the Radical leader, Cavallotti. The crisis consequent upon the disaster of Adowa (March 1, 1896) brought Rudinì back to power as premier and minister of the interior in a cabinet formed by the veteran Conservative, General Ricotti. He concluded peace with Abyssinia, but endangered relations with Great Britain by the unauthorized publication of confidential diplomatic correspondence in a Greenbook on Abyssinian affairs. To satisfy the anti-colonial party he ceded Kassala to Great Britain, provoking thereby much indignation in Italy. He was overthrown in June 1898. His conduct of affairs had gravely divided his party. He died on Aug. 6, 1908, leaving a son, Carlo, who married a daughter of Henry Labouchere.

RUDOLF (otherwise known as BASSO NOROK and GALLOP), a large lake of eastern equatorial Africa, forming the centre of an inland drainage system, occupying the south of the Abyssinian highlands and a portion of the great equatorial plateau. The lake itself lies towards the north of the great East African rift valley, between 2° 26' and 5° N., while the meridian of 36° E. passes through the lake. The lake is in part in Uganda, in Kenya, in Abyssinia and in Anglo-Egyptian Sudan. The length along the curved axis is 185 m., the maximum width 37 m. Its altitude is 1,250 ft. Towards the south it is deep, but comparatively shallow in the north. Its water is brackish, but drinkable. The country bordering the lake on almost every side is composed of Archaean metamorphic rock and is sterile and forbidding. The southern end is shut in by high cliffs—the escarpments of a rugged lava-strewn country, which shows abundant signs of volcanic activity. In particular, the great Teleki volcano stands at the southern end of the lake. The highest point of the south-east side of the lake is Mt. Kulal, 7,812 ft., while the culminating height within the basin of the lake is Mt. Sil, 9,280 ft., which lies about 20 m. south of Lubburua. Farther north, on the west side, sandy plains alternate with lines of low hills. Lagoons cut off from the lake are the haunt of great numbers of water-birds. In 3° 8' N. the dry bed of the Turkwell approaches the lake. Near the northern end mountains again approach the shores, the most prominent being Mt. Lubur (5,200 ft.), an extinct volcano with a well-preserved crater. At the extreme north-west a bay some 35 mi. long (Sanderson gulf) is almost separated from the rest of the lake by two long points of land. On the east side, open arid plains, with few trees, occupy most of the north country. One hill, in 3° 20' N., has a height of 3,470 ft., and at the north-east end, separating the lake from Lake Stefanie, is a hilly country, the highest point between the lakes being 3,524 ft. Immediately north of these hills rises the Hummurr range, with one peak exceeding 7,000 ft. Near the south end is the volcanic island of Elmolo, 10 mi. long, and there are a few small islets. Just north of 4° N. is a small volcanic island with highest point 2,100 ft. At the north end of the lake a level swampy plain is traversed by various arms of the lake and by the Nianam river (identical with the Omo). Lake Rudolf was discovered in 1888 by Count Samuel Teleki and Lieutenant Ludwig von Höhnel.

BIBLIOGRAPHY.—Ludwig von Höhnel, *Discovery of Lakes Rudolf and Stefanie* (London, 1894); A. Donaldson Smith, *Through Unknown African Countries* (London, 1897); L. Vannutelli and C. Citerni, *L'Omo* (Milan, 1899); M. S. Wellby, *'Twixt Sirdar and Menelik* (London, 1901); H. H. Austin, *Among Swamps and Giants in Equatorial Africa* (1902); C. H. Stigand, *To Abyssinia through an Unknown Land* (1910); and the reports of the Colonial office (annual).

RUDOLPH II. (1552–1612), Roman emperor, son of the emperor Maximilian II. by his wife Maria, daughter of the emperor Charles V., was born in Vienna on July 18, 1552. In 1563 he was sent to Spain, where he was educated. In 1572 he was crowned king of Hungary, in 1575 king of Bohemia; and in Oct. 1575 he was chosen German king, at Regensburg, becoming emperor on his father's death in Oct. 1576.

The more active part of the emperor's life was the period from his accession to about 1597. During that time he attended the infrequent imperial diets, and took an interest in the struggle in the Netherlands and the defence of the empire against the Turks. He was at times suspicious of the papal policy, while his relations with Spain were somewhat inharmonious. He forwarded the progress of the counter-reformation, and in general the tolerant policy of Maximilian II. was reversed. Political as well as religious privileges were attacked; and discontent became very pronounced about the opening of the 17th century. Meanwhile Rudolph had become increasingly subject to attacks of depression, which bordered on insanity. In 1604, after a war with Turkey had been in progress since 1593, many of the Hungarians rebelled against Rudolph and chose Stephen Bocskay as their prince. In April 1606 the Habsburg family declared Rudolph incapable of ruling, and recognized one of his younger brothers, the archduke Matthias, afterwards emperor, as their head; and in the following June Matthias, having taken over the conduct of affairs, made peace by granting extensive concessions to the rebellious Hungarians, and concluded a treaty with the sultan in November of the same year. Then shaking off his lethargy Rudolph prepared to renew the war with the Turks, a move which Matthias met by throwing himself upon the support of the national party in Hungary. Matthias also found adherents in other parts of his brother's dominions, with the result that in June 1608 the emperor was compelled to cede to him the kingdom of Hungary together with the government of Austria and Moravia. Rudolph now sought the aid of the princes of the empire, and even of the Protestants; but he had met with no success in this direction when trouble arose in Bohemia. Having at first rejected the demand of the Bohemians for greater religious liberty, the emperor was soon obliged to yield to superior force, and in 1609 he acceded to the popular wishes by issuing the Letter of Majesty (*Majestätsbrief*), and then made similar concessions to his subjects in Silesia and elsewhere. A short reconciliation with Matthias was followed by further disorder in Bohemia, which was invaded by Rudolph's cousin, the archduke Leopold (1586–1632). The Bohemians invoked the aid of Matthias, who gathered an army; and in 1611 the emperor, practically a prisoner at Prague, was again forced to cede a kingdom to his brother. Rudolph died at Prague, his usual place of residence, on Jan. 20, 1612, and was succeeded as emperor by Matthias.

Rudolph was greatly interested in chemistry, alchemy, astronomy and astrology; he was a patron of Tycho Brahe and Kepler, and was himself something of a scholar and an artist. He was the greatest collector of his age, his agents ransacking Europe to fill his museums with rare works of art. His education at the Spanish court and an hereditary tendency to insanity, however, made him haughty, suspicious and consequently very unpopular.

The sources for the life and times of Rudolph II. are somewhat scanty, as many of the official documents of the reign, which were kept at Prague and not at Vienna, were destroyed, probably during the Thirty Years' War. The best authorities, however, are: *Rudolphi II. epistolae ineditae*, edited by B. Comte de Pace (Vienna, 1771); M. Ritter, *Quellenbeiträge zur Geschichte des Kaisers Rudolf II.* (Munich, 1872); and *Deutsche Geschichte im Zeitalter der Gegenreformation und des dreissigjährigen Krieges* (Stuttgart, 1887 fol.); L. von Ranke, *Zur deutschen Geschichte: Vom Religionsfrieden bis zum 30-jährigen Kriege* (Leipzig, 1868); A. Gindely, *Rudolf II. und seine Zeit* (Prague, 1862–68); F. Strieve, *Die Verhandlungen über die Nachfolge Kaiser Rudolfs II.* (Munich, 1880); in the *Allgemeine Deutsche Biographie*, Band xxix. (Leipzig, 1889); and *Der Ursprung des dreissigjährigen Krieges* (Munich, 1875); F. von Bezold, *Kaiser Rudolf II. und die heilige Liga* (Munich, 1886); J. Janssen, *Geschichte des Deutschen Volks seit dem Ausgang des Mittelalters* (Freiburg, 1878 fol.), of which there is an English translation by M. A. Mitchell and A. M. Christie (1896 fol.); and H. Moritz, *Die Wahl Rudolfs II.* (Marburg, 1895).

RUDOLPH or RAOUL (d. 936), king of the Franks and duke of Burgundy, was a son of Richard duke of Burgundy, and was probably a member of the Carolingian family. He succeeded his father in 921, married Emma, daughter of Robert duke of the Franks, and assisted his father-in-law to drive the Frankish king, Charles III. (the Simple), from his throne. Robert then became king of the Franks, but was killed in battle in June 923 and was succeeded by Rudolph. At Limoges Rudolph defeated the Normans, the Aquitanians and Herbert of Vermandois. Rudolph died at Auxerre, leaving no sons, on Jan. 14, 936.

See W. Lippert, *König Rudolf von Frankreich* (Leipzig, 1886).

RUDOLPH (d. 1080), German king, and duke of Swabia, was a son of Kuno, count of Rheinfelden, who possessed estates in both Burgundy and Swabia. He received the duchy of Swabia

from Agnes, regent and mother of the young king, Henry IV., in 1057, and two years later married the king's sister Matilda, and was made administrator of the kingdom of Burgundy. When Henry was excommunicated and deposed by Pope Gregory VII., the princes met at Forchheim, and elected Rudolph as German king. He renounced the right of investiture, disclaimed any intention of making the crown hereditary in his family, and was crowned at Mainz, on March 27, 1077. He found no support in Swabia, but, uniting with the Saxons, won two victories over Henry's troops, and in 1080, was recognized by the pope. On Oct. 15, 1080, Rudolph was severely wounded at Hohenmölsen, and died the next day. He was buried at Merseburg, where his beautiful bronze tomb is still to be seen.

See O. Grund, *Die Wahl Rudolfs von Rheinfelden zum Gegenkönig* (Leipzig, 1880).

RUDOLPH I. (1218–1291), German king, son of Albert IV. count of Habsburg, and Hedwig, daughter of Ulrich count of Kyburg, was born at Limburg, on May 1, 1218. At his father's death in 1239 Rudolph inherited the family estates in Alsace, and in 1245 married Gertrude, daughter of Burkhard III. count of Hohenberg. A partisan of the emperor Frederick II. and his son Conrad IV., he was richly rewarded by them, but in 1254 was excommunicated by Pope Innocent IV. In the general disorder after the fall of the Hohenstaufen, he increased his estates largely at the expense of his uncle, Hartmann of Kyburg, and the bishops of Strassburg and Basle, becoming the most powerful prince in south-western Germany. His election as German king at Frankfurt (Sept. 29, 1273) was largely due to the efforts of his brother-in-law, Frederick III. of Hohenzollern, burgrave of Nuremberg. The support of Albert duke of Saxe-Lauenburg, and of Louis II. count palatine of the Rhine and duke of upper Bavaria, had been purchased by betrothing them to two of Rudolph's daughters; so that Ottakar II. king of Bohemia, a candidate for the throne, was almost alone in his opposition. Rudolph was crowned at Aix-la-Chapelle on Oct. 24, 1273. To win the approbation of the pope Rudolph renounced all imperial rights in Rome, the papal territory and Sicily, and promised to lead a new crusade; and Pope Gregory X., in spite of Ottakar's protests, not only recognized Rudolph himself, but persuaded Alphonso X. king of Castile, who had been chosen German king in 1257, to do the same. From 1274–78 Rudolph was engaged in an intermittent struggle with Ottakar, which ended with the latter's death. (*See* AUSTRIA, EMPIRE OF.) Rudolph then set about consolidating his authority in Austria and the adjacent countries, where he met much opposition. At length in Dec. 1282 Rudolph invested his sons Albert and Rudolph with the duchies of Austria and Styria at Augsburg, and so laid the foundations of the greatness of the house of Habsburg.

In 1281 Rudolph compelled Philip I. count of upper Burgundy to cede some districts to him, forced the citizens of Berne to pay tribute, and in 1289 marched against Philip's successor, Otto IV., and compelled him to do homage. He was much less successful, however, in maintaining order in Germany, although in 1289 he led an expedition into Thuringia and destroyed some robber castles. In 1281 his first wife died, and on Feb. 5, 1284 he married Isabella, daughter of Hugh IV. duke of Burgundy. In 1291 he attempted to secure the election of his son Albert as German king; but without success, although Albert, the only son who survived him, was crowned German king after Rudolph's death. Rudolph died at Spires on July 15, 1291 and was buried in the cathedral of that city. His reign is memorable rather for the house of Habsburg than for the kingdom of Germany.

See K. Hagen, *Deutsche Geschichte von Rudolf von Habsburg bis auf die neueste Zeit* (Frankfort, 1854–57); O. Lorenz, *Geschichte Rudolfs von Habsburg und Adolfs von Nassau* (Vienna, 1863–67); A. Huber, *Rudolf von Habsburg vor seiner Thronbesteigung* (Vienna, 1873); J. Hirn, *Rudolf von Habsburg* (Vienna, 1874); H. von Zeissberg, *Ueber das Rechtsverfahren Rudolf von Habsburg gegen Ottokar von Böhmen* (Vienna, 1882); H. Otto, *Die Beziehungen Rudolfs von Habsburg zu Papst Gregor X.* (Erlangen, 1893); A. Busson, *Der Krieg von 1278 und die Schlacht bei Dürnkrut* (Vienna, 1880); and O. Redlich, *Rudolf von Habsburg* (Innsbruck, 1903). *See also* GERMANY; AUSTRIA, EMPIRE OF; HABSBURG.

RUDOLPH or RAOUL, known as RUDOLPH GLABER (Rudolph the Bald) (d. c. 1050), French chronicler, was born in Burgundy about 985, and was in turn an inmate of the monasteries of St. Leger at Champeaux and St. Bénigne at Dijon, afterward entering the abbey of Cluny, and becoming a monk at St. Germain at Auxerre before 1039. He also appears to have visited Italy. His *Historiarum sui temporis libri V*, dedicated to St. Odilon, abbot of Cluny, purports to be a universal history from 900 to 1044; but is an irregular narration of events in France and Burgundy.

The *Historiarum* was first printed in 1596, and published by A. Duchesne in the *Historiae Francorum Scriptores*, tome iv (1639-49). Extracts are printed in the *Monumenta Germaniae historica*, Band vii; but perhaps the best edition of the work is the one edited by M. Prou in the *Collection de textes pour servir à l'étude et l'enseignement de l'histoire* (1886). Rudolph also wrote a *Vita S. Gulielmi, abbatis S. Benigni*, published by J. Mabillon in the *Acta Sanctorum*, tome vi (1668).

See A. Molinier, *Les Sources de l'histoire de France*, tome ii (Paris, 1902); and A. Potthast, *Bibliotheca historica* (Berlin, 1896).

RUDOLPH OF HABSBURG (1858–1889), crown prince of Austria, was born on Aug. 21, 1858, the only son of the emperor Francis Joseph I of Austria (*q.v.*) and his wife Elizabeth. Great hopes centred on the boy, who possessed unusual talents. Although his father was chiefly intent on his military education, Rudolph's own chief interests were natural history and literature. The monumental description of the Austro-Hungarian monarchy, *Oesterreich-Ungarn in Wort und Bild*, was truly his conception and in part his work; he also wrote some minor works of his own. He early developed an interest in modern literature and thought; became known as a freethinker, and even a revolutionary, and made no secret of his anticlerical views. He thus drifted into increasing opposition to his father, which was accentuated by his notoriously easy morality. His marriage with Stephanie, daughter of the king of the Belgians, took place on May 10, 1881, and was at first happy, although its only fruit—unfortunately for the Austrian succession—was one daughter, Elizabeth (afterward Princess Windischgrätz). Later he developed a deep passion for the young and beautiful Baroness Marie Vetsera, and on Jan. 30, 1889, the sudden and appalling news reached Vienna that the bodies of the two lovers had been found in Rudolph's hunting lodge of Mayerling, near Vienna. It was at once officially announced that the pair had committed suicide. All persons in any way connected with the story were sworn to secrecy, and the official dossier was excluded from the state archives. Numerous extraordinary rumours naturally arose, connecting the death with the Jesuits, the Hungarian nobles, or an injured husband; but it is generally accepted that the crown prince actually shot his lover, and afterward committed suicide in a fit of despair, partly due to his father's order to break off the liaison. (C. A. M.)

RUDOLSTADT, a town of Germany, in the *Land* of Thuringia, on the left bank of the Saale, 18 mi. S.W. of Jena, by the railway to Saalfeld. Pop. (1939) 19,471. The name of Rudolstadt occurs in an inventory of the possessions of the abbey of Hersfeld in the year 800. After passing under various rulers, it came into the hands of the counts of Schwarzburg in 1335. Its civic rights were confirmed in 1404, and from 1599 it was the residence of the ruling house of Schwarzburg-Rudolstadt. The town is a favourite tourist resort. The former residence of the prince is the Heidecksburg, a palace which was rebuilt after a fire in 1735 on an eminence 200 ft. above the Saale. The Ludwigsburg is another palace in the town built in 1742. The town also has a hydropathic establishment. The industries of the place include the manufacture of porcelain, chemicals, machinery, dyestuffs and thermos flasks.

RUDRA, a minor god in Vedic India who doubtless personified lightning (the "red" one, probably), but also protected cattle against it. In the *Rig Veda* he is identified with Agni (*q.v.*), but in the later *Vedas* he is called an archer and his malevolence emphasized. Best known as father of the storm-gods (Maruts, *q.v.*), in the Epic period he becomes many Rudras and in modern Hinduism is identified with Siva (*q.v.*).

RUE, the name of a woody or bushy herb, belonging to the genus *Ruta* (family Rutaceae), especially *R. graveolens*, the "common rue," a plant with bluish green spotted leaves and greenish yellow flowers, native to Europe and sparingly naturalized in eastern North America. It has a strong pungent smell and the leaves have a bitter taste. The plant was much used in mediaeval and later medicine as a stimulative and irritant drug. It was commonly supposed to be much used by witches. From its association with "rue" (sorrow, repentance), the plant was also known as "herb of grace," and was taken as the symbol of repentance.

RUEDA, LOPE DE (1510?–1565), Spanish dramatist, was born at Seville, where, according to Cervantes, he worked as a metal beater. His name first occurs in 1554 as acting at Benavente, and between 1558 and 1561 he was manager of a strolling company. Rueda's more ambitious plays, such as *Eufemia*, *Armelina* and *Los Engañados*, are mostly adapted from the Italian. They follow the original so closely that they give no idea of his talent; but in his *pasos* or prose interludes he displays an abundance of riotous humour, great knowledge of low life, and a most happy gift of dialogue. Rueda, with his strollers, created a taste for the drama which he was able to gratify, and he is admitted by both Cervantes and Lope de Vega to be the true founder of the national theatre.

RUEIL-MALMAISON, a town of north France, in the department of Seine-et-Oise, at the west foot of Mt. Valérien, 6 mi. W. of Paris. Pop. (1936) 18,565. Rueil has a church rebuilt by Napoleon III in the original Renaissance style and containing the tombs of the Empress Josephine and her daughter Hortense de Beauharnais. Rueil has important photographic works and manufactures of lime and cement, etc. Close to the town is the 18th century château of Malmaison, the residence of the Empress Josephine.

RUFA'A: *see* ARABS.

RUFF, a limicoline bird, taking its name from the frill of elongated feathers round the neck of the breeding male, to which the name is properly confined; the female, a much smaller bird, is termed the reeve. The plumage of the male is extremely variable, but the same markings are reproduced after every moult in each individual bird. The ruff (*Machetes pugnax*) no longer breeds in Britain, but its range extends across the whole of N. Europe and Asia, and it migrates south to India, Ceylon and Africa in winter. Except for its remarkable frill and its polygamous habit, the ruff does not differ in any marked manner from the ordinary sandpipers.

The extraordinary courtship antics of the cock bird are described in Montagu's *Ornithological Dictionary*, Stevenson's *Birds of Norfolk*, Selous' *Realities of Bird Life* (Constable & Co., London, 1926), and elsewhere.

The nest is made on the ground and, as in almost all polygamous animals, the male takes no interest in his offspring.

RUFFO, FABRIZIO (1744–1827), Neapolitan cardinal and politician, was born at San Lucido, Calabria, on Sept. 16, 1744. His father, Litterio Ruffo, was duke of Baranello, and his mother, Giustiniana, was a Colonna. Ruffo was placed by pope Pius VI among the *chierici di camera*—the clerks who formed the papal civil and financial service. He was later promoted to be treasurer-general, a post which carried with it the ministry of war. In 1791 he was removed from the treasurership, but was created cardinal on Sept. 29, though he was not in orders. He never became a priest. Ruffo went to Naples, and, when in Dec. 1798 the French troops advanced on Naples, he accompanied the royal family to Palermo. He was chosen to head a royalist movement in Calabria, where his family exercised large feudal powers. He was named vicar-general on Jan. 25, 1799. On Feb. 8, he landed at La Cortona with a small following, and began to raise the so-called "army of the faith" in association with Fra Diavolo.

Ruffo had no difficulty in upsetting the republican government established by the French and by June had advanced to Naples. (*See* NAPLES, KINGDOM OF and NELSON, HORATIO NELSON.) But he lost favour with the king by showing a tendency to spare the republicans. He resigned his vicar-generalship to the prince of Cassero, and during the second French conquest and the reigns of Joseph Bonaparte and Joachim Murat he lived quietly in Naples. During the revolutionary troubles of 1822 he was consulted by the king, and was even in office for a very short time as a "loyalist" minister. He died on Dec. 13, 1827.

The account of Ruffo given in Colletta's *History of Naples* (English trans., Edinburgh, 1860) is biased. *Cf.* the duca de Lauria, *Intorno alla storia del Reame di Napoli di Pietro Colletta* (Naples, 1877). Ruffo's own side of the question is stated in *Memorie Storiche sulla vita del Cardinale Fabrizio Ruffo*, by Domenico Sacchinelli (Naples, 1836). *See also* Baron von Helfert, *Fabrizio Ruffo: Revolution and Gegen-Revolution von Neapel* (Vienna, 1882).

RUFIJI, a large river of Tanganyika Territory, East Africa, entering the sea by a delta, between 7° 45′ and 8° 13′ S. Its upper basin is drained by three main branches, of which the two southern, the Luwegu and the Ulanga, though shorter than the northernmost (the Ruaha), carry more water, as they come from a more rainy region, and by their junction in 8″ 35′ S., 37° 25′ E., the Rufiji proper may be said to be formed.

The Luwegu rises 10° 50′ S., 35° 50′ E., and flows in a narrow wooded valley and in its lower course it is 100 to 150 yd. wide. The Ulanga is formed by a number of streams descending from the escarpment which runs north-east from Lake Nyasa and in Uhehe becomes broken up in ranges of mountains. The most important head-stream is the Ruhuje. As a whole, the Ulanga valley is broad, level and swampy, the meandering river sending off many diverging arms. It is navigable throughout the greater part of its course, having in the dry season a general depth of 3 to 12 ft., with a width of 40 to 120 yd. In April and May nearly all the streams overflow their banks. Below the junction of the Luwegu and Ulanga, the Rufiji flows through a narrow pass by the Shuguli falls, and continues to the junction of the Ruaha, in 7° 55′ S., 37° 52′ E. The most remote branches of the Ruaha rise in the Livingstone Mountains. The united stream sweeps round the N. of the Uhehe Mountains, finally flowing to the Rufiji. Below the junction the Rufiji is broken by the Pangani falls, but is thence navigable by small steamers to its delta, receiving no large tributaries but sending out divergent channels The country on either side is a generally level plain, inundated, on the south, in the rains, and the river varies in width from 100 to 400 yd. The main mouth of the river is that known as Simba Uranga, the bar of which can be crossed by ocean vessels at high water, but all the branches are very shallow as the apex of the delta is approached. Much of the delta is suited for rice-growing. (For geology *see* TANGANYIKA TERRITORY.)

RUFINUS, TYRANNIUS, presbyter and theologian, was born at or near Aquileia at the head of the Adriatic, probably between 340 and 345. In early manhood he entered the cloister as a catechumen, receiving baptism about 370. About the same time a visit of Jerome to Aquileia led to a close friendship between the two, and shortly after Jerome's departure for the East Rufinus also was drawn thither (in 372 or 373) by his interest in its theology and monasticism. He first settled in Egypt. There, if not even before leaving Italy, he had become intimately acquainted with Melania, a wealthy and devout Roman widow; and when she removed to Palestine, taking with her a number of clergy and monks on whom the persecutions of the Arian Valens had borne heavily, Rufinus (about 378) followed her. While his patroness lived in a convent of her own in Jerusalem, Rufinus, at her expense, gathered together a number of monks in a monastery on the Mount of Olives, devoting himself at the same time to the study of Greek theology. When Jerome came to Bethlehem in 386, the friendship formed at Aquileia was renewed. Another of the intimates of Rufinus was John, bishop of Jerusalem, and formerly a Nitrian monk, by whom he was ordained to the priesthood in 390. In 394, in consequence of the attack upon the doctrines of Origen made by Epiphanius of Salamis during a visit to Jerusalem, a fierce quarrel broke out, which found Rufinus and Jerome on different sides; and, though three years afterwards Jerome and John were reconciled, the breach between Jerome and Rufinus remained unhealed.

In the autumn of 397 Rufinus embarked for Rome, where he published a Latin translation of the *Apology* of Pamphilus for Origen, and also (398–99) a somewhat free rendering of the περὶ ὑρχῶν (or *De Principiis*) of that author himself. In the preface to the latter work he referred to Jerome as an admirer of Origen, and as having already translated some of his works with modifications of ambiguous doctrinal expressions. This led to a bitter dispute between Jerome and Rufinus. At the instigation of Theophilus of Alexandria, Anastasius (pope 398–402) summoned Rufinus from Aquileia to Rome to vindicate his orthodoxy; but he excused himself from a personal attendance in a written *Apologia pro fide sua*. The pope in his reply expressly condemned Origen, but left the question of Rufinus's orthodoxy to his own conscience. He was, however, regarded with suspicion in orthodox circles (*cf.* the *Decretum Gelassii*, § 20) in spite of his services to Christian literature. In 408 we find Rufinus at the monastery of Pinetum (in the Campagna?); thence he was driven by the arrival of Alaric to Sicily, being accompanied by Melania in his flight. In Sicily he was engaged in translating the *Homilies* of Origen when he died in 410.

The original works of Rufinus are—(1) *De Adulteratione Librorum Origenis*—an appendix to his translation of the *Apology* of Pamphilus, and intended to show that many of the features in Origen's teaching which were then held to be objectionable arise from interpolations and falsifications of the genuine text; (2) *De Benedictionibus XII. Patriarcharum Libri II.*—an exposition of Gen. xlix.; (3) *Apologia s. Invectivarum in Hieronymum Libri II.*; (4) *Apologia pro Fide Sua ad Anastasium Pontificem*; (5) *Historia Eremitica*—consisting of the lives of thirty-three monks of the Nitrian desert[1]; (6) *Expositio Symboli*, a commentary on the creed of Aquileia comparing it with that of Rome, which is valuable for its evidence as to church teaching in the 4th century. The *Historiae Ecclesiasticae Libri XI.* of Rufinus consist partly of a free translation of Eusebius (10 books in 9) and partly of a continuation (bks. x. and xi.) down to the death of Theodosius the Great.

See W. H. Freemantle in *Dict. Chr. Biog.* iv. 555–60; A. Ebert, *Allg. Gesch. d. Litt. d. Mittelalters im Abendlande*, i. 321–27 (Leipzig, 1889); G. Krüger in Herzog-Hauck's *Realencyk. für prot. Theol.*, where there is a full bibliography.

RUFUS, LUCIUS VARIUS (*c.* 74–14 B.C.), Roman poet of the Augustan age. He was the friend of Virgil, after whose death he and Plotius Tucca prepared the *Aeneid* for publication, and of Horace, for whom he and Virgil obtained an introduction to Maecenas. Horace and Virgil speak highly of his epic poetry. From Macrobius (*Saturnalia*, vi. 1, 39; 2, 19) we learn that Varius composed an epic poem *De Morte*, some lines of which are quoted as having been imitated or appropriated by Virgil. But his most famous literary production was the tragedy *Thyestes*, which Quintilian (*Inst. Orat.* x. 1. 98) declares equal to any of the Greek tragedies. It was presented at the games of 29 B.C.

Fragments in E. Bährens, *Frag. Poetarum Romanorum* (1886); monographs by A. Weichert (1836) and R. Unger (1870, 1878, 1898); M. Schanz, *Geschichte der römischen Literatur* (1899), ii. 1; Teuffel, *Hist. of Roman Literature* (Eng. trans., 1900), 223.

RUGBY, a municipal borough in the Rugby parliamentary division of Warwickshire, England, on a tableland rising from the south bank of the Avon, near the Oxford canal. Pop. (1938) 38,130. Area, 11 sq.mi. It is 82½ mi. N.W. from London by the L.M.S.R., and is also served by the L.N.E.R. Rugby (Rocheberie, Rokeby) was originally a hamlet of the adjoining parish of Clifton-upon-Dunsmore, and is separately treated as such in Domesday. In the reign of Henry III it became a separate parish, and the same king granted the town a weekly market and a yearly fair. Cromwell was quartered there in 1645, and William III passed through on his way to Ireland. The town was not of great importance until the 19th century, its rise being mainly due to the advent of railways. It is an important junction on the L.M.S.R. and has large engineering and electrical works. From 1894 to 1932, when it was incorporated, Rugby was governed by an urban district council. The boys' school, ranking as one of the first public schools in England, was founded and endowed under the will (1567) of Laurence Sheriff of Rugby. The endowment consisted of the parsonage of Brownsover, Sheriff's mansion house in Rugby and one-third (8 ac.) of his estate in Middlesex, which, being let on building leases, gradually increased to about £5,000 a year. The full endowment was obtained in 1653. The school originally stood opposite the parish church, and was removed to its present site on the south side of the town between 1740 and 1750. In 1809 it was rebuilt from designs by Henry Hakewill (1771–1830); the chapel, dedicated to St. Lawrence, was added in 1820. The chapel was rebuilt and reconsecrated in 1872, and additions were

[1]On this work *see* Dom Butler in *Texts and Studies*, vi. i. pp. 10 ff.

made in 1898. The Temple observatory, containing a fine equatorial refractor by Alvan Clark, was built in 1877, and the Temple reading-room with the art museum in 1878. The workshops underneath the gymnasium were opened in 1880, and a new big school and class-rooms were erected in 1885. Later additions include the science school (1914), enlarged in 1940.

RUGE, ARNOLD (1802–1880), German philosopher and political writer, was born at Bergen, on the island of Rügen, on Sept. 13, 1802. He studied at Halle, Jena and Heidelberg, and became an adherent of the party which sought to create a free and united Germany. For his zeal he was confined for five years in the fortress of Kolberg, where he studied Plato and the Greek poets. On his release in 1830 he published *Schill und die Seinen*, a tragedy, and a translation of *Oedipus in Colonus*. Ruge settled in Halle, where in 1837 with E. T. Echtermeyer he founded the *Hallesche Jahrbücher für deutsche Kunst und Wissenschaft*. In this periodical he discussed the questions of the time from the point of view of the Hegelian philosophy. The *Jahrbücher* was detested by the orthodox party in Prussia; and was finally suppressed by the Saxon government in 1843. In Paris Ruge tried to act with Karl Marx as co-editor of the *Deutsch-Französische Jahrbücher*, but had little sympathy with Marx's socialistic theories, and soon left him.

In the revolutionary movement of 1848 he organized the Extreme Left in the Frankfurt parliament, and for some time lived in Berlin as the editor of *Die Reform*. The Prussian government intervened and Ruge soon afterwards left for Paris, hoping, through his friend Alexandre Ledru-Rollin, to establish relations between German and French republicans; but in 1849 both Ledru-Rollin and Ruge had to take refuge in London. Here, in company with Giuseppe Mazzini and other advanced politicians, they formed a "European Democratic Committee." From this Ruge soon withdrew, and in 1850 went to Brighton, where he supported himself by teaching and writing. In 1866 and 1870 he vigorously supported Prussia against Austria, and Germany against France. In his last years he received from the German government a pension of 1,000 marks. He died on Dec. 31, 1880. After the publication of his *Gesammelte Schriften* (10 vols., 1846–48) he wrote, among other books, *Unser System, Revolutionsnovellen, Die Loge des Humanismus*, and *Aus früherer Zeit* (his memoirs). His *Letters and Diary* (1825–80) were published by Paul Nerrlich (1885–87).

RUGELEY, market town, urban district, Lichfield parliamentary division of Staffordshire, England, in the Trent valley 123¼ mi. N.W. of London on the L.M.S.R. and on the Grand Trunk canal. Pop. (1938) 7,504; area 4.5 sq.mi. To the S.W. is Cannock Chase. A grammar school was founded in 1611. There are iron foundries, corn-mills and tanneries; the parish has several collieries. The urban district included Brereton after 1934.

RÜGEN, an island of Germany, in the Baltic, immediately opposite Stralsund, 1½ mi. off the northwest coast of Pomerania in Prussia, from which it is separated by the narrow Strelasund, or Bodden. Its shape is exceedingly irregular, and its coast line is broken by numerous bays and peninsulas, sometimes of considerable size. The general name is applied by the natives only to the roughly triangular main trunk of the island, while the larger peninsulas, the landward extremities of which taper to narrow necks of land, are considered to be as distinct from Rügen as the various adjacent smaller islands which are also included for statistical purposes under the name. The chief peninsulas are those of Jasmund and Wittow on the north, and Mönchgut, at one time the property of the monastery of Eldena, on the southeast; and the chief neighbouring islands are Ummanz and Hiddensöe, both off the northwest coast. Rügen is the largest island in Germany. Its greatest length from north to south is 32 mi.; its greatest breadth is 25½ mi.; and its area is 377 sq.mi. The surface gradually rises towards the west to Rugard (335 ft.) —the "eye of Rügen"—near Bergen, but the highest point is the Hertaburg (505 ft.) in Jasmund. Erratic blocks are scattered throughout the island, and the roads are made with granite. The most beautiful and attractive part of the island is the peninsula of Jasmund, which terminates to the north in the Stubbenkammer

(Slavonic for "rock steps"), a sheer chalk cliff, the summit of which, the Königsstuhl, is 420 ft. above the sea. The east of Jasmund is clothed with an extensive beech wood called the Stubbenitz, in which lies the Borg, or Hertha lake. Connected with Jasmund by the narrow isthmus of Schabe to the west is the peninsula of Wittow, the most fertile part of the island. At its northwest extremity rises the height of Arcona, with a lighthouse.

A ferry connects the island with Stralsund, and from the landing stage at Altefähr a railway traverses the island, passing the capital Bergen to Sassnitz, on the northeast coast. The other chief places are Garz, Sagard, Gingst and Putbus, the last being the old capital of a barony of the princes of Putbus. Sassnitz, Göhren, Sellin, Binz and Lauterbach-Putbus are favourite bathing resorts. Schoritz was the birthplace of the patriot and poet, Ernst Moritz Arndt. The inhabitants of Rügen are distinguished from those of the mainland by peculiarities of dialect, costume and habits; and even the various peninsulas differ from each other in these particulars. The inhabitants raise some cattle, and Rügen has long been famous for its geese; but the chief industry is the herring fishery.

The original Germanic inhabitants of Rügen were dispossessed by Slavs; and there are still various relics of the long reign of paganism that ensued. In the Stubbenitz and elsewhere Huns' or giants' graves are common; and near the Hertha lake are the ruins of an ancient edifice which some have sought to identify with the shrine of the heathen deity Hertha or Nerthus, referred to by Tacitus. On Arcona in Wittow are the remains of an ancient fortress, enclosing a temple which was destroyed in 1168 by the Danish king, Waldemar I, when he made himself master of the island. Rügen was ruled then by a succession of native princes, under Danish supremacy, until 1218. After being for a century and a half in the possession of a branch of the ruling family in Pomerania, it was finally united with that duchy in 1478, and passed with it into the possession of Sweden in 1648. With the rest of western Pomerania Rügen has belonged to Prussia since 1815.

See Fock, *Rügensch-pommersche Geschichten* (6 vols., Leipzig, 1861–72); R. Baier, *Die Insel Rügen nach ihrer archäologischen Bedeutung* (Stralsund, 1886); R. Credner, *Rügen, Eine Inselstudie* (Stuttgart, 1893); Edwin Müller, *Die Insel Rügen* (17th ed., Berlin, 1900); Schuster, *Führer durch die Insel Rügen* (7th ed., Stettin, 1901); Boll, *Die Insel Rügen* (Schwerin, 1858); O. Wendler, *Geschichte Rügens seit der ältesten Zeit* (Bergen, 1895); A. Haas, *Rügensche Sagen und Märchen* (Greifswald, 1891); U. John, *Volkssagen aus Rügen* (Stettin, 1886); and E. M. Arndt, *Fairy Tales from the Isle of Rügen* (London, 1896).

RUGS AND CARPETS. "Carpet" (M.E. *carpete* or *carpette*, from O. Fr. *carpite* or direct from Med. Lat. *carpita*) was used until the 19th century for any cover made of a thick material, especially a table cover, but now it means almost exclusively a floor covering. This may be of felt, tapestry, a shuttle-woven material or a pile fabric, but the last is the most frequent and typical. Some kind of covering for the floor is indispensable for comfort, especially for the beaten-earth floors in the ancient and primitive orient. Even in the west the advantages of a fabric underfoot are so obvious and even imperative that carpets of some kind have been an almost universal adjunct of civilization, and in both the east and west their manufacture finally developed into a prodigious industry. Such floor coverings offer most interesting opportunities for ornamentation, and in the orient, where both the craft and the art originated, carpet-weaving and design attained, over a period of at least 2,500 years, a remarkable degree of excellence which warrants ranking the finest specimens with man's most notable artistic achievements.

Felt (*q.v.*) is almost certainly the most ancient of the carpet techniques for it probably originated as bark felt, even as early as the Upper Palaeolithic period, about 25,000–30,000 years ago. It is noteworthy that the earliest existing specimen (4th or 3rd century B.C.) which might be classed as a carpet is felt: a rectangle of black wool or hair felt, about 3½ x 5 ft., with a white border along one side, to which are appliquéd with split-stitch silhouettes of feline heads about 6 in. high, cut from red or blue felt and evenly spaced in a straight row. This piece, now in the

SPANISH AND TURKISH RUGS, 15TH-16TH CENTURY

1. Spanish rug, 15th or 16th century. Wool; principal colours: red, yellow, blue
2. Cairene carpet, 16th century. About 10 ft. x 9 ft. 6 in. Wool; the colours are: ground tone, a deep cherry red with patterns in sky-blue and yellowish green

PLATE II

RUGS AND CARPETS

TURKISH CARPETS, 16TH CENTURY

1. Ushak, with Buccleuch armorial escutcheon and dated 1584. Made in Turkey to British order
2. Ushak carpet, c. 1600. 15 ft. 9 in. x 8 ft. The pattern shows red panels and flattened hexagons, with serrated borders, and floral forms and arabesques. The colours used are red, l ght blue, dark blue, yellow, black (brown in places), white and rose

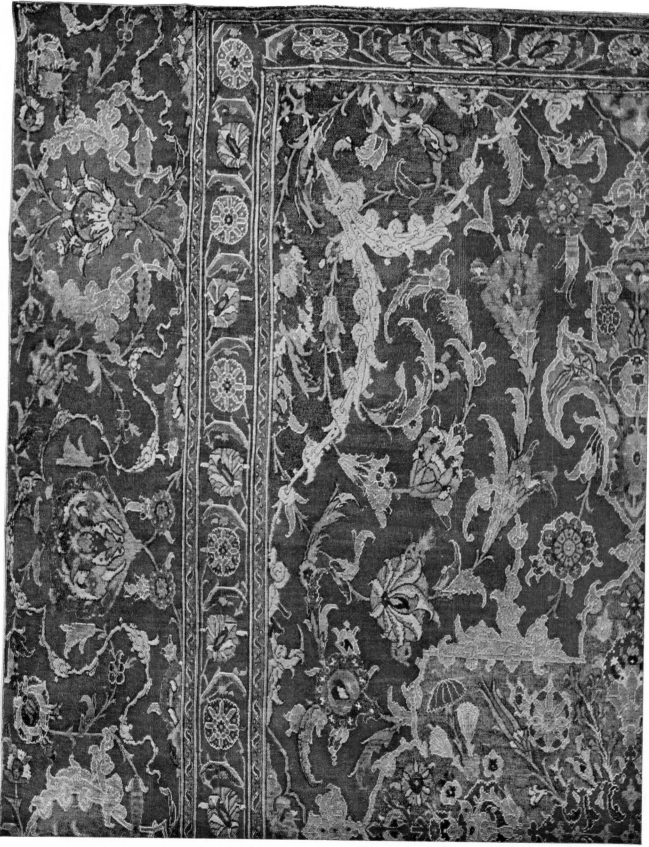

TURKISH COURT CARPET, 16TH CENTURY

Section of Turkish carpet, court manufactory, 16th century. Dimensions of whole, about 18 ft. x 10 ft. The warp is of yellow silk, the weft of dyed red silk, the pile and cotton in seven colours. The pattern, of cartouches and conventionalized flowers and leaves and Chinese cloud bands, gives the effect of graceful movement

PERSIAN AND TURKISH RUGS, 16TH CENTURY

1. Silk rug, showing animal combat, probably Kashan, 2nd half of 16th century. The colour of the inner field is a deep rose-red. The central border is blue-green. The patterns are in yellow, green and tan

2. Turkish rug, court manufactory, 2nd half of 16th century. The foundation colour is a soft red, with green, blue and yellow prevailing in the design, with accents in cotton white

PERSIAN VASE CARPET, EARLY 17TH CENTURY

Vase carpet, so-called because of the vases of flowers in the
pattern. Court looms of Shah Abbas, probably Joshaghan Ghali

PLATE VI   RUGS AND CARPETS

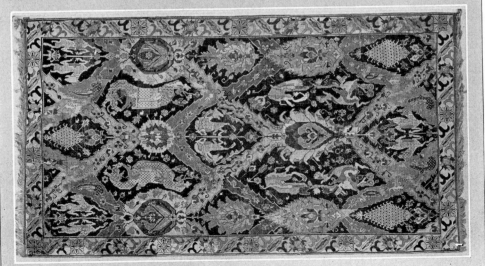

THREE CARPETS

1. South Caucasian Dragon carpet, probably woven at Kuba, 17th century. 11 ft. x 6 ft. 4 in., with diamond-shaped compartments in the field, and conventionalized representations of the dragon and phoenix. The colours are brown, white, blue, yellow, red and purple

2. Indian carpet, late 16th or early 17th century. 4 ft. 8 in. x 2 ft. 11 in. This shows a type of pattern exclusive in Indian carpets with the field divided into ogee compartments, each containing naturalistic flowers or floral patterns. The colours are: crimson ground, with the design in yellow; the floral forms are in red, white, rose, blue, green, yellow and purple

3. Spanish carpet, with design derived from Asia Minor models, with Spanish armorial escutcheon for medallion, 18th century

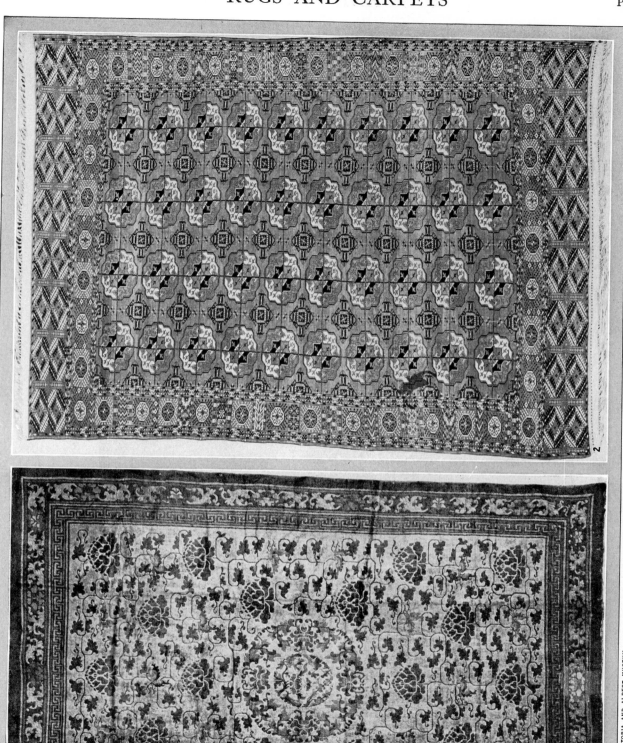

ORIENTAL CARPETS, 18TH AND 19TH CENTURIES

1. Chinese carpet, late 18th century. The colour of the inner field is ivory, with the pattern in blue. The outer border is a deep blue, with the design in ivory and yellow. 11 ft. 8 in. x 8 ft. 4 in. Knotted in woollen pile on a cotton warp

2. Tekke-Turcoman carpet, 19th century, 9 ft. 7 in. x 7 ft. 2 in., made of silky wool. Sometimes erroneously called Bokhara, the carpets are often very finely woven; the principal colour is a deep, glowing crimson

PLATE VIII   RUGS AND CARPETS

CAUCASIAN CARPET, 17TH CENTURY

So-called Armenian carpet, Caucasus region, end of 17th century. About 11 ft. 6 in. x 6 ft. 6 in. The ten colours are strong in tone; the ground colours, deep-blue, white and red. The warp and weft of white cotton, the knotting is of sheep's wool, with the pile slightly to the right. The pattern of large stems and cartouches includes floral motives angularly conventionalized. The border, narrow in relation to the field, shows leaf-motives and blossoms

BY COURTESY OF (1-4) W. AND J. SLOANE, (5, 6) THE KENT-COSTIKYAN TRADING CO., INC.

PREPARATION OF WOOL FOR CARPETS IN INDIA AND CHINA

1. Old process of clipping wool from the sheep with shears, still practised in India. This scene is in Amritaar, India

2. Carding wool with a bow string, showing how an ancient weapon of war is used for a peaceful purpose, Amritsar

3. The *charkha* or spinning-wheel still used to-day by millions of Indian home workers. The spinning-wheel has become a symbol of the principle of the encouragement of home industry preached by Gandhi

4. Dyers dyeing wool for carpets, Amritsar

5. Dye-vats of a large carpet plant, Tientsin, China

6. Drying the dyed wools in large drying-space, Tientsin

PLATE X

RUGS AND CARPETS

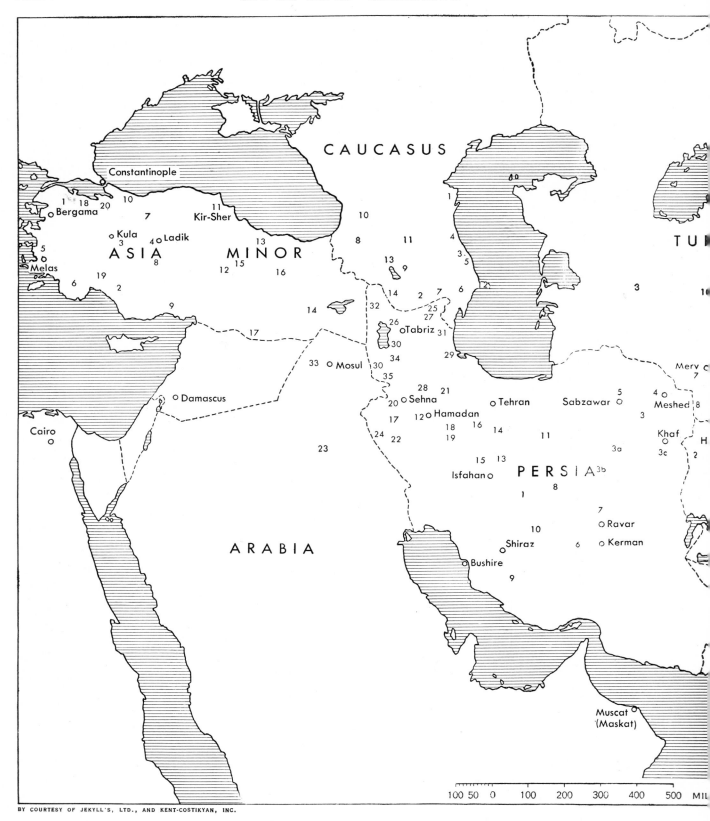

CAUCASUS

Constantinople

ASIA MINOR

TU

1 18 20
Bergama
Kula
3
4 Ladik
8
Melas
5
19
6
2
9
Kir-Sher
10
7
11
13
15
12
16
14
14
17
33 Mosul
Damascus
Cairo

ARABIA

10
8
11
13
9
14
2 7 6
25
27
26 Tabriz 31
30
34
30
35
28 21
20 Sehna
17 12 Hamadan
24 18 16
22 19
23
15 13
Isfahan
1
3
5
4
3
29

PERSIA

Merv
4
Meshed 8
Khaf
3a
3c
3b
8
7
Ravar
10
6 Kerman
Shiraz
Bushire
9
Sabzawar 5
Tehran
14

Muscat
(Maskat)

100 50 0   100   200   300   400   500 MIL

BY COURTESY OF JEKYLL'S, LTD., AND KENT-COSTIKYAN, INC.

MAP OF THE PRINCIPAL RUG-WEAVING CENTRES

TURKISH OR ASIA MINOR CARPETS: 1. Bergama. **2.** Ghiordes. **3.** Kulah. **4.** Ladik. **5.** Melas. **6.** Makri. **7.** Ushak. **8.** Konia. **9.** Karaman. **10.** Héreké. **11.** Kir-Sher. **12.** Mujur. **13.** Sivas. **14.** Yuruk. **15.** Tuzla. **16.** Kaisariya. **17.** Anatolian. **18.** Ak-Hissar. **19.** Sparta. **20.** Brusa.

CAUCASIAN CARPETS: 1. Daghestan. **2.** Shirvan. **3.** Kabistan. **4.** Derbent.

5. Kuba. **6.** Soumak (pileless). **7.** Shemakha. **8.** Leshgian. **9.** Chichi (Tchechen). **10.** Cherkess. **11.** Kazak. **12.** Baku or Khila. **13.** Ghenga. **14.** Karabagh

PERSIAN CARPETS: 1. Isfahan. **2.** Herat. **3.** Khurasan (a) Kain (b) Birjand (c) Khaf. **4.** Meshed. **5.** Sabzawar. **6.** Kerman. **7.** Ravar.

100 0   200   400   600   KILOMETERS

8. Yezd. 9. Shiraz. 10. Niriz. 11. Ferghana. 12. Hamadan. 13.
Sarouk. 14. Kashan. 15. Joshagan. 16. Saraband. 17. Burujird.
18. Sultanabad. 19. Muskabad. 20. Sehna. 21. Bijar. 22. Kermanshah.
23. Western Kurdistan. 24. Persian Kurdistan. 25. Karaja. 26. Tabriz.
27. Bakshais. 28. Gorevan. 29. Serapi. 30. Sauj Bulakh. 31. Herez.
32. Kara Dagh. 33. Mosul. 34. Kultuk. 35. Mianeh

TURCOMAN CARPETS: **1.** Tekke. 2. Bukhara. 3. Yomud. 4. Ersari.

5. Afghan. 6. Beshir. 7. Salor. 8. Saryks. 9. Pinde'. 10. Khiva.
11. Adraskand. 12. Baluchi

CHINESE TURKISTAN CARPETS, Middle Asian (Mongolian): 1. Khotan.
2. Yarkand. 3. Samarkand. 4. Kashgar. 5. Tibetan

INDIAN CARPETS: 1. Agra. 2. Lahore. 3. Amritsar. 4. Srinagar.
5. Kandahar. 6. Jaipur

PLATE XII

RUGS AND CARPETS

CARPET-WEAVING

Indian workers at a loom in one of the factories for the manufacture of hand-made carpets at Jaipur, Rajputana, in northern India. Between the two rollers which, with the supporting framework, constitute the loom, are stretched the vertical warp threads. The coloured wools (or silks) are knotted in horizontal rows on the warp threads, the knots being cut to form the pile of the carpet. The weft threads are passed alternately

Hermitage museum, Leningrad, together with saddle (cushion) covers in the same technique and style, was found in a tomb at Pasyryk in the Altai mountains.

Floor coverings of plaited rushes were also very ancient. Evidences of basket plaiting also appear in the Upper Palaeolithic period, and archaeological finds in Iraq indicate by the 5th or 4th millennium floor coverings of plaited rushes, such as grew in the

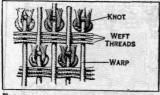

FIG. 1.—SPANISH OR SINGLE-WARP KNOT

Mesopotamian swamps. These made stout, durable, portable mats, and even at an early period they were probably handsomely ornamented, judging from the competence in decorative pattern shown on contemporary painted pottery and on the decorated walls of the Chalcolithic village at Persepolis. The weaving of rush mats has continued to the present in the near east, which had reached a high degree of artistic perfection and prestige by mediaeval times.

Rug design, however, in western Asia at least, had long since evolved beyond the rudimentary scheme of the appliqué felt or

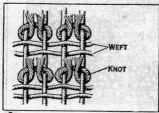

FIG. 2.—TURKISH OR GHIORDES KNOT, ONE OF THE TWO TYPES OF KNOTS USED IN ORIENTAL CARPETS

the hypothetical iconographic geometry of plaited mats, for a threshold rug, represented in stone carving (now in the Musee du Louvre), from the Assyrian palace of Khursabad (8th century B.C.) has an all-over field pattern of quatrefoils, framed by a lotus border, completed by guard stripes. Other Assyrian stones of the period also show rich and handsome patterns that have survived in the repertoire of carpets ever since.

The general layout of the Assyrian type is more or less followed in the next oldest surviving carpets, embroidered felts found by Kozlov at Noin Ula in northern Mongolia, preserved by the frozen subsoil in chieftains' tombs (C. Trever, *Excavations in Northern Mongolia* [Leningrad, 1932]; W. P. Yetts, in *The Burlington Magazine*, 1926), likewise now in the Hermitage museum. One, *e.g.* (originally *c.* 6 ft. 5 in. by 8 ft. 6 in.), had the field filled with a spiral meander; a broad border with animal-combat groups (alternately tiger and yak, and griffon and elk), alternating with a tree; an inner guard stripe of geometrical units; and a wide margin of Chinese lozenge-patterned silk. The patterns were executed with quilting (field), and couched cord

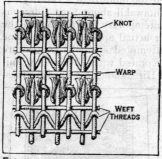

FIG. 3.—PERSIAN OR SEHNA KNOT, THE OTHER TYPE OF KNOT USED IN ORIENTAL CARPETS

on a quilted ground (main border; inner guard stripe solid couched cord), and the colours as reconstituted by chemical tests (V. Komonov, Moscow-Leningrad, 1937) were vivid; yellow quilting on a red field; a red border with blue and green figures outlined with white; and green, red, yellow and blue in varying succession in the guard stripes.

Another piece embroidered in wool on wool in stem-and-satin stitches, was still more complex in organization: on the field, a diagonal lattice defined by scrolling stems, with a cross-treflé at each intersection and a tortoise alternating with a fish in each unit, in blue, purple and tans on a red ground; a diagonally-hatched field margin; beyond, an inner border system, with double guard stripes on both sides; then the main wide border filled with a concentric-lozenge diaper, with an inner guard stripe; and an outer binding of red and brown checked flax and wool material. These pieces are datable by a lacquer bowl found with them which is inscribed with the equivalent of A.D. 3. Some of them

are of genuine beauty; their intricate patterns are clearly delineated and well co-ordinated.

Among these fragments and technically the most interesting are the earliest extant specimens of pile carpets. They are woven of fine, lustrous, still-elastic wool, of deep indigo blue. The pile is very thick and dense, the knots or loops having been firmly compacted, though the strands are merely wrapped round one

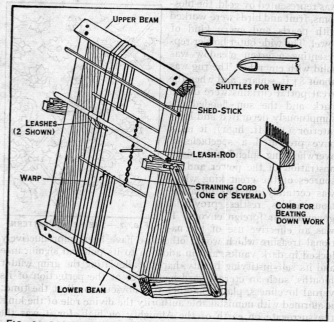

FIG. 4.—LOOM WITH FIXED BEAMS: SUITABLE FOR SMALL WORK AND ILLUSTRATES CHIEF PARTS OF LARGER LOOMS

warp thread, a simple technique that later made its way to Spain. (A. U. Pope, in Pope [ed.], *A Survey of Persian Art*, Oxford, 1938, III, pp. 2272–73.) This same technique is also used in a number of fragments found by Sir Aurel Stein in Loulan, Niya and Tun-Huang in Chinese Turkistan, assignable to the first three centuries of our era (*see* Stein, *Serindia* [1921], Pls. 3, 7, 8; and *Innermost Asia* [1928]), and was continued in this region at least into the 7th or 8th century, as is proven by a fragment discovered by A. von LeCoq at Kizil.

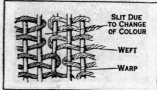

FIG. 5.—TAPESTRY WEAVING

By historic times the carpets of the near east had attained fame and great magnificence. Classical authors speak with admiration of the luxurious Babylonian carpets (*see* A. U. Dilley, *Rugs and Carpets*, p. 11), and in the tomb of Cyrus, Alexander the Great found the gold funeral couch resting on carpets of very fine fabric. Both Athenaeus and Xenophon indicate that some of these were thick and resilient, but whether pile woven or embroidered felt we cannot be sure, though some were evidently gold-enriched. Moreover certain types were reserved for court use, and so costly that they were important items in the royal treasury. Carpet weaving was always a kingly concern in near eastern lands.

By late Sassanian times (6th–7th century A.D.) carpet weaving in Persia had won international prestige, and according to the Sui annals woollen rugs were being exported to distant China (*Sui-šu*, chap. 83; Berthold Laufer, *Sino-Iranica*, p. 493). The carpets of this period were of several kinds: woollen or silk, either pile or tapestry woven, embroidered, or even of shuttle-woven silk (*dibaj*) (Pope, *A Survey of Persian Art*, III, p. 2273).

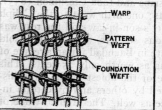

FIG. 6.—SHEMAKA WEAVING, A MODIFIED FORM OF THE TAPESTRY METHOD

Carpets made for the royal palace exceeded in cost and magnificence anything created or imagined either before or since. Surpassing them all was the so-called Spring or Winter carpet of Khusraw, made for the vast audience hall of the palace at Ctesiphon. It represented a formal garden with its water courses, paths, rectangular beds filled with flowers and blossoming shrubs and fruit trees. The body of the rug was silk, the yellow gravel was represented by gold, the blossoms, fruit and birds were worked with pearls and every kind of jewel. The wide outer border representing a green meadow was solid with emeralds. The rug was about 84 ft. square, and when the great portal curtains were drawn back and the sun flooded the sumptuously decorated and lofty interior (121 ft. high), it must have presented a spectacle of overwhelming splendour, a demonstration of the power and resources of the great king which was certainly not lost on ambitious nobles, restless provincial governors or foreign envoys. It was an effective use of the na-

FIG. 7.—THE HERATI PATTERN

tional treasure which would otherwise have been unproductively locked in dark vaults, and in addition to its political significance and its self-justifying beauty, happily alleviating the grim winter months, such an eternal garden, forever at the perfection of its vernal loveliness, played another role obvious to all at the time; it affirmed with unmistakable authority the divine role of the king, the surrogate on earth of the Almighty on high, for it was the king's primal task to regulate the seasons, to guarantee and compel the return of the spring, thus renewing the earth's fertility and assuring the livelihood and prosperity of his subjects. This gorgeous carpet was the sympathetic call to nature to conceive and deliver the longed-for spring. Moreover the carpet had still further religious significance: it prefigured paradise, was a foretaste of the glory that is to come and the substance of things hoped for. For paradise is a Persian word meaning "walled park," and for the Persians, with its flowers, birds and water, so happily con-

FIG. 8.—THE MINA KHANI PATTERN

trasting with the asperities of the desert, it was the abode of all felicity, the reward for struggle and suffering, the symbol of the perfect eternal moment. The whole notion of paradise seems to have entered into Jewish and Christian theology via the Babylonian captivity, and the Persian restoration of the Jews to Palestine.

The carpet was part of the fabulous booty of the Arabs, captured when they defeated the Persians and took Ctesiphon (635). It was cut up into small fragments; one-fifth went to the Caliph Omar, one piece to Ali, the prophet's son-in-law and the rest was distributed to the 60,000 victorious soldiers, who in turn sold their pieces to a jeweller's syndicate in Baghdad for an average of $3,000 each, counting the drachma as worth only 25 cents. This is on the authority of Tabari, one of the ablest of the Arab historians, whose account is confirmed by others and by certain internal and supplementary evidence as well. The original value of the carpet was thus certainly in excess of $200,000,000.

This most sumptuous of all fabrics made a profound impression on all, especially the Persians. It entered as a living, legendary power into history, poetry and art; and for centuries it served to sustain Persian morale. For more than 1,000 years it furnished the model and inspiration for subsequent carpets, though the most ambitious attempts of later years could no more than hint at the general design of this fabulous creation. Of the subsequent

renderings of the garden scheme the oldest is a printed cotton panel to be dated between the 9th and 11th century (O. Wulff-W. F. Volbach, *Spätantike und koptische Stoffe,* Berlin, 1926, pl. 130) which shows in miniature essentially the same scheme, and this has persisted down to the present as one of the best defined carpet designs (fig. 9). The carpets for another of the

FIG. 9.—GARDEN CARPET, NORTHERN PERSIA, 18TH CENTURY

royal palaces depicted the four seasons, also still a theme of carpet designing down to recent times.

The carpets of the Abbasid caliphate at Baghdad (Haroun al-Rashid and his successors) seem almost to have rivalled the carpet of Khusraw. Caliph Hashim, who died in 743, had a silk, gold-enriched carpet that was approximately 150 x 300 ft. The history of this carpet can be traced for more than a century. It was finally inherited by Caliph Mutawakil about 850. Gorgeous carpets are mentioned in all the contemporary descriptions of the period. We know little about their actual appearance, but some had inscriptions; some actually attempted symbolic portraiture of the Sassanian kings; carpets decorated with all kinds of animals were made in Numaniya and Hira, showing a growing mastery of pictorial effects. Dark blue was probably the commonest colour, but the Caliph El Mahdi owned a rose coloured carpet.

Whether these Sassanian and early Islamic carpets were pile-knotted or tapestry-woven is impossible to say. There is no evidence to support the usual assumption that they were all done in some kind of flat stitch, but tapestry (*q.v.*) [Lat. *tapes*—covering for floors, walls, etc.; Gr. τάπες —carpet, rug; Fr. *tapisserie,* and also *tapis*—carpet, cover] was already by that time a much used technique as well as an old one, for it was well developed by 1500 B.C. (Ackerman, *Tapestry,* p. 12, New York, 1933.)

FIG. 10.—HAMADAN

Fragmentary examples, dating from the 7th to the 14th century, have been found on the rubbish heaps of Fustat (ancient Cairo), including some so stiff and heavy that they could only have been floor coverings. Many of these pieces are of genuine beauty, with rich and harmonious colours and ingenious but rational patterns.

Various of the Arabic geographers give valuable though meagre information about carpet weaving in the near east from the 8th to the 14th century. Armenia was certainly one of the most productive districts. Here were found good wool, clear water and fine dyes, especially a fine scarlet

FIG. 11.—SARABAND PATTERN

made from the *Coccus ilicis* called *kermez* and widely exported. Armenian rugs were famous in the 8th century, and we know that by the 10th such cities as Devin, Van, Kalikala (Ezerum), Bitlis, Vartan, Aklat and Tiflis, all produced famous rugs. Marco Polo credited the Armenians and Greeks in the towns of central Asia Minor (Konia, Sivas and Caesarea) with weaving the most beautiful carpets in the world (*Marco Polo,* Yule trans. p. xxx). But unfortunately we have no description of these carpets.

In northwest Persia, the towns of Khoi, Bargari, Arjig, Nachshirvan and Mukhan are all credited with rug production. The south Caspian coast, Gilan and Mazanderan, evidently supported an immense industry. Its prayer carpets were exported everywhere, and in the 8th century 600 rugs were sent at one time as tribute to the Caliph Mamun.

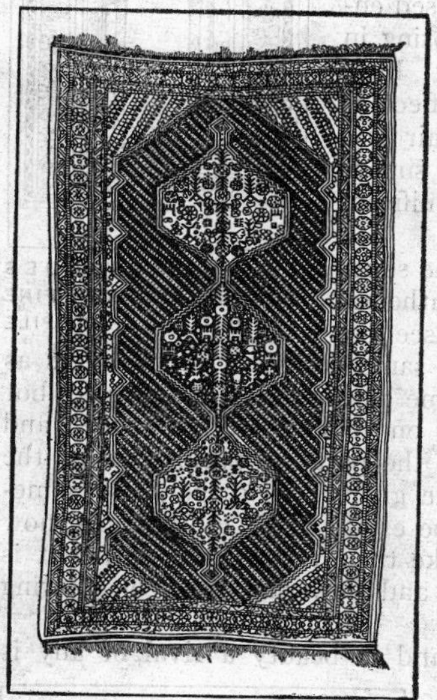

FIG. 12.—SHIRAZ RUG WITH PATTERN OF HEXAGONAL PANELS, LATE 19TH CENTURY

Rugs were an important part of the equipment of palaces and homes in northeast Persia and in Afghanistan. It is probable that there was local production, but we have no real knowledge of it. In the 8th and 9th centuries, Turkistan, according to contemporary literature, was famous for its carpets which were exported all over the world, particularly to China. Bukhara, Tashkent and Darzangi are all mentioned as producing fine rugs. Darzangi was especially noted for its tapestry rugs. The designs were probably all geometrical, as in the so-called Bukhara rugs of the day. Wall paintings from the Turfan oasis, from Kizil, and fragments of Manichaean book illustration depict floor coverings with hexagonal and other simple geometric designs.

Southern Persia, Khuzistan and Fars were also noted for carpet weaving. Basinna and Shustar were active centres of production. Gundigan, Fass, Darabjird, Jahrarn, all produced rugs, and the kilims are specially mentioned as of precious quality.

In the 13th, 14th and 15th centuries Asia Minor and the Caucasus were producing rugs, rather coarse in weave, of strong colour and simple geometric design—stars, polygons, entrelacs, often with border patterns of stylized Kufic writing, and a special group of rugs with simple, highly conventionalized animal forms. The most important of these are

FIG. 13.—MESHED CARPET, 19TH CENTURY, PATTERN BASED ON THE "CLASSICAL" MEDALLION CARPETS

a group of three somewhat fragmentary carpets of strong, repeating geometric patterns in somewhat harsh colours, red, yellow and blue, which were found in the mosque of Ala-ud-Din in Konia and are now treasured in the Ewfkaf museum at Istanbul. Local tradition assigns them, reasonably enough, to the period of the Seljuks of Rum, cousins of the Persian Seljuks, who maintained their authority in Asia Minor through the 13th century. In the Berlin museum and in the National museum at Stockholm are a pair of rugs of very primitive design, the former a highly conventionalized dragon-and-phoenix combat, the latter stylized birds in a tree, both patterns that were later richly developed in

FIG. 14.—SO-CALLED "HOLBEIN" RUG, BLUE, RED, GREEN AND WHITE. ASIA MINOR, 16TH CENTURY

the Caucasus, which warrants attributing them to the Caucasus of the early 15th century.

A little later there began to appear in Europe, coming from the same as yet unspecified region, a considerable number of rugs of finer weave, more delicate patterns and richer colours. These also are almost wholly geometrical in pattern. They were depicted by the Flemish painters such as Hans Memlinc, Van Eyck, Petrus Cristus, with such skill and loving care that the separate knots are sometimes visible, and the full artistic character of the rugs, which was considerable, is adequately presented. The designs of many of these rugs have been quite faithfully repeated in the later weavings from the Bergamo district in Asia Minor and from the southern Caucasus almost to the present day—an impressive evidence of the conservatism of rug design which so complicates the problem of dating.

CLASSIFICATION

Because of the difficulty of classification it has been customary to name the great court carpets of the 16th century in accordance with their presumed themes, and we read of "Hunting carpets," "Garden carpets," "Medallion carpets," "Compartment carpets," "Vase carpets" (so-called because of the presence of a vase in the design), "Prayer carpets," "Animal carpets." This classification is hardly more than a temporary convenience, and really evades the problem. These various themes were embodied in the carpets of many different regions and over long periods. A more serious classification attempts to connect a given carpet style with some dominant cultural unit; the court of a great monarch; the locality in which the patterns were developed; the actual place where the carpet was fabricated, including the sources of design elements. This method is difficult because of the dearth of contemporary documents, and because in a court-supervised art, material was often gathered in one place and shipped to some court-subsidized loom, while court-approved cartoons also were apparently supplied to the various weaving centres, and the provinces also copied the cosmopolitan styles in vogue at the capital. On the other hand, we know from an actual document of Shah Abbas that even at his time when the imperial dominion was formally established, in all matters cultural as well as political and economic, the integrity of the local weaving centres was not only respected but the officers of the crown were charged to see that they were preserved. The majority of the more important carpets of the 16th century, in colour, pattern, materials and

FIG. 15.—SO-CALLED "LOTTO" RUG. CONVENTIONALIZED ARABESQUES IN YELLOW ON RED GROUND. ASIA MINOR, 16TH-17TH CENTURIES

technique fall into groups of such marked individuality and integrity that we can be sure that in most cases we are in the presence of a real school. The finest of them are almost all now in museum collections. The complex designs are thought out with perfect lucidity controlled by a rigorous decorative logic, with imagination and frequently with deep feeling for a genuinely noble effect. They are in the proper sense a monumental art. Their very size is impressive. The more important of them may be from 20 to 40 ft. long, and in the 17th century, more than 50 ft., though such a size somewhat exceeds the power of unified comprehension.

FIG. 16.—SO-CALLED "BIRD" RUG, ASIA MINOR, 17TH CENTURY

The materials, both dyes and wool, were of the finest that the unlimited power and wealth of the shah could command. Sheep were specially bred and tended; dye plantations cultivated like flower gardens; aspiring designers and weavers, could by submitting cartoons or finished work win a court appointment which conferred prestige and privileges which were greatly prized. The 15th and 16th centuries were the heirs to the slowly accumulated artistic tradition of a deeply artistic people. The ambition was there; the material and means were present; and a passion for perfection, which was a special attribute of the Timurid period, where "artists had no other thought than to make their work the most perfect possible," brought about just that unique combination of favourable circumstances which alone supports supreme artistic achievement.

FIG. 17.—TURKISH COPY OF A CAIRENE RUG, 17TH CENTURY

The rugs of this period can with a certain confidence be divided into six well defined groups.

The stately Medallion carpets of northwest Persia, judging by the tonality, the materials and the subsequent history of the type seem to have been done in the vicinity of Karabagh in northern Azerbaijan. At the same time a special court atelier, possibly located at Sultaniya, as an elusive contemporary document hints, translated into carpets the most gorgeous and varied creations that the illuminators could devise. A dozen or more pieces of this group have survived. Each one is a separate masterpiece, and if they do form a class, it is first of all on the basis of outstanding artistic quality, superb design, majestic size, colours of great purity and depth, and perfection of detail. They all use a fine, crisp, very white wool, probably from Ahar in the extreme northwest, which today furnishes the most brilliant wool found in Persia, a wool which takes dyes most beautifully.

This group includes the world's most famous carpets. The great pair of carpets from the mosque

FIG. 18.—SO-CALLED "TRANSYLVANIAN" RUG, ASIA MINOR, 17TH CENTURY

at Ardabil, dated 1539 (one owned by Paul Getty, the other by the Victoria and Albert museum, London), are the best known carpets of the period.

The ornamentation consists of an extremely rich and intricate system of stems and blossoms on a velvety glowing indigo field, which in turn is dominated by a complex golden star medallion. (The colour-quality designations belong only to the Getty piece, as the Victoria and Albert piece was still [1944] in grievous need of cleaning.)

The Ardabil weaving has a near rival in the Anhalt carpet, named for the duke of Anhalt who once owned it, now also owned by Duveen. An intricate star medallion dominates a brilliant yellow field covered with an ingenious system of scrolling arabesques and fluttering cloud bands, framed by a scarlet border. Another pair of carpets from the same region has a scarlet medallion on a white field, which is interspersed with lively animal forms and framed by a dark blue arabesque border. One belongs to the Berlin museum and the other to Paul Getty, the American collector. An impressive pair, one in the Musée des Tissus at Lyons, and the other in the Metropolitan museum in New York (the Lyons piece sadly wrecked, and the New York piece mutilated by reduction) is composed entirely of cartouche patterns enclosing in their irregular spaces brilliant little arabesque compositions. The effect is somewhat incoherent but the pair rise to greatness by virtue of the superb finesse of detail and the magnificent colour.

FIG. 19.—GHIORDES PRAYER RUG OF FINE TEXTURE AND SHORT PILE

One of the most beautiful in the series is the animal carpet half in the cathedral of Cracow and half in the Musee des Arts Decoratifs in Paris, by the same designers and weavers as the Anhalt carpet. It has the same glowing scarlet and gold, but with more subtle halftones (buff on yellow, gray on taupe) and a more pictorial presentation of the paradise park. One of the most striking of the series is the great Tree carpet, also somewhat reduced, that belongs to the estate of C. F. Williams, now in the Philadelphia museum. Like the Cracow-Paris carpet it is a garden scene, with cypresses and flowering trees of glowing vernal splendor.

Historically more important and in beauty a rival of any is the great Hunting carpet in the Poldi-Pezzoli museum in Milan, which carries the precious historical inscription: "It is by the efforts of Giyath-ud-din 'Jami that this renowned carpet was brought to such perfection in the year 1522–23." Again a rich scarlet and gold medallion dominates a field of deep blue, covered with an angular network of blossoming stems, across which in every direction hunters dash after their prey.

This small group, in the opinion of many, represents the supremest achievement in the whole field of carpet designing. None the less, other ateliers under royal direction were also producing many beautiful specimens. One type, also under the domination of the court and possibly done at Tabriz (possibly also at a little town near Hamadan, called Derguzin, in western Persia) reflects even more precisely the art of the illuminator. Some of these are in small size, all with medallions dominating the field which is covered with very intricate systems of two-toned arabesques beautifully co-ordinated and subordinated one with another, with inscription cartouches in the border. More than a score of these have survived and they are like pages from a 16th century manuscript. A few beautiful prayer rugs discreetly illuminated with silver and gold belong to the same group. Most of these rugs have come out of Istanbul

FIG. 20.—KULAH PRAYER RUG

and may be part of a famous gift of rugs that Shah Tahmasp made in 1665 to the sultan of Turkey. The largest and best-known single example is a beautiful multiple-medallion carpet in the Victoria and Albert museum (London) which Dr. Bode was inclined to ascribe to the end of the 15th century and to rank as the finest carpet extant.

But rug weaving was also the concern of other parts of Persia. In Kashan, in the second half of the 16th century, superlative silk animal rugs were woven, of which three large specimens

FIG. 21.—LADIK PRAYER RUG

survive. The finest—some think the finest of all known carpets—is the silk, gold and silver enriched Hunting carpet which is one of the principal treasures in the Austrian state collection. It is a *tour de force* of both designing and weave. The cartoon was obviously the work of a master painter. Another large piece from the same looms is owned by the king of Sweden and a similar one belongs to the government of Poland. About a dozen smaller pieces of the type are known, each worth many times its weight in gold. The famous so-called Isfahan carpets, which were not from Isfahan at all, were made in east Persia in the vicinity of Herat and Sabzawar. They are the most abundant and most familiar of the so-called classical carpets. The typical field is a very rich claret or dark *rose du Barry*, covered with a delicious pattern of tendrils and graceful lanceolate leaves, framed by a broad border either in deep emerald green or dark blue, carrying magnificently constructed palmettes alternating with lotus or peony blossoms.

North of Isfahan in the picturesque hill town of Joshaghan a strikingly beautiful and highly individual class of carpets was produced that has been called Vase carpets. The pattern structure is generally a series of ogival latticelike systems which carry a profusion of blossoms interspersed with foliage. Only a few of these whole carpets have survived, of which the pair divided between Lady Baillie and the Berlin museum is typical. The glowing blue of the background and the very finely divided clear colours are scarcely to be caught on a colour plate. There are a scant 20 whole pieces of this splendid type, though many very fine fragments still exist. These rugs were apparently not exported from Persia but used almost exclusively for court and mosque. They are woven on a solid double warp, which gives them a boardlike stiffness that holds them flat to the floor—a desirable feature for a carpet. They are still called in Persia "Shah Abbas carpets." The style (which

FIG. 22.—BERGAMO SQUARE RUG

was indigenous, very ancient and characteristically Persian), reinforced by the prestige of the court, exercised a wide influence, and derivatives show up in Kurdistan, the Caucasus and even in the embroideries of Bukhara, as well as in the court carpets of India.

There are other beautiful carpets of the 16th and early 17th centuries for which the provenance is still doubtful. Magnificent rugs were, we know, woven in Kerman, Yazd and Fars, and perhaps Khuzistan, but just what they were like we can only guess, as we have no extant example that can with any surety be assigned to any of these places.

From time immemorial, the rugs of Persia had been enriched by gold and silver thread, a device that was discreetly used in some of the 16th century carpets from east Persia, but by the time of that mighty monarch, Shah Abbas, the scheme was carried to a most sumptuous perfection and many carpets of sheer opulence made of silk with great masses of interwoven silver and

FIG. 23.—KUBA CARPET

FIG. 24.—SHIRVAN RUG

gold were made to delight the monarch and to dazzle the astonished ambassadors and travellers from Europe. The most gorgeous of these carpets is the so-called "coronation carpet," still preserved in its pristine splendor in the Rosenborg castle in Copenhagen. The gold background gleams as brightly as the day it was woven and the velvetlike pile, with its accurately drawn arabesques is no less perfect.

As the 17th century wore on, both the demand for more luxury and the increasing wealth that sustained it, multiplied the manufacture of these carpets until they were not only available for purchase to ordinary civilians in the bazaars, but were exported in great numbers to Europe, where more than 200 of them have been found. They are closer to the European Renaissance and baroque idiom, with their high-keyed fresh colours and demonstrative opulence, and the finest of them are indeed beautiful. A large number of these pieces were found in possession of some of the great families in Poland, for Poland had very close relations with Persia in the 17th century, and Polish royalty and nobility ordered gold-threaded rugs of this type from the looms in Kashan. There had been a rug-weaving industry in Poland in the 18th century and a silk-weaving industry also which used

FIG. 25.—BAKU OR KHILA CARPET

gold thread. So when these Polish rugs were first exhibited at the Paris exposition in 1878 it was natural to think that they were really Polish, for nothing quite like them had at the time been found in Persia. They were accordingly labelled *Tapis Polonais*, and the name has stuck to the type ever since. Actually, they were primarily a product of the looms of Kashan but were probably also woven in the royal shops in Isfahan. The style degenerated rather rapidly. By the second half of the 17th century materials were cheapened, weaving coarser and more careless, the designs clumsy and confused.

Similarly the east Persian Herat carpets which came into the European market by way of India and the gulf export trade, partly in Portuguese control, partly in English, became known in Europe as the typical Persian carpet. The demand was furious and the competition among the great of the land to acquire them even had international political consequences, as when the duke of Buckingham delayed signing a treaty with Spain until the Spanish ambassador could procure some of these carpets for his new palace, Hampton Court. Many of the European artists of the period owned them, and Van Dyke and "Velvet" Breughel, particularly, rendered them with such complete fidelity in dated paintings that we can with a little care and stylistic analysis date these so-called Isfahan carpets to within a couple of decades.

FIG. 26.—DAGHESTAN PRAYER RUG

FIG. 27.—KAZAK PRAYER RUG

The Indian princes also were enamoured of them and acquired them by plunder and purchase alike. The result was mass production with the inevitable consequence of a rapidly deteriorating art. Designers were no longer employed, cartoons were wearily repeated *ad infinitum*, the weavers had little interest or pride in their work, the pressure for speed and for economy deteriorated every process, and the style finally expired in a repulsive mediocrity, painful proof of how and why a great art can be brought to ruin.

During the 17th century there was an increasing emphasis, where the court could afford it, on refinement and luxury, but on the whole a steadily slackening inspiration. Routine increasingly displaced invention. But in 1666, a set of silk carpets was woven to surround the sarcophagus of Shah Abbas II in the shrine at Qum, of such finesse that even orientalists have mistaken them for velvet. The drawing is beautiful, the colour varied, clear, brilliant and harmonious, and the set has the important merit of being dated and signed by a master artist, Nimat'ulla of Joshaghan. This set marks the last really high achievement in Persian rug weaving, although handsome carpets were woven throughout the century and even in the 19th century, and these, despite the increasing poverty of the time and the decline of all the arts, still surpass any floor covering ever conceived or rendered in the western world.

The carpets so far described were all specially made for the court or for the great nobles. They could afford to concentrate on perfection and disregard expense, which was often considerable. Indeed, a carpet like the Ardabil or the Austrian Hunting carpet cost as much as a small palace. Such rugs could be of silk, gold and silver, almost too fragile for anything but contemplation or the most lavish ostentation. They were cared for by special custodians, brought out only as actually needed, often for state occasions only, and even

FIG. 28.—KAZAK CARPET

when the king sat on them they were generally partly covered with a lighter fabric for completest protection. The mosque carpets had severer and more continuous use. Carpets that reached Europe were for the most part treasured with equal solicitude. They were precious items in royal treasuries like the Austrian

Hunting carpet, which Peter the Great gave to the emperor of Austria, the Danish Coronation carpet or the Anhalt carpet, which are all almost as fresh and perfect as the day they were taken off the loom.

Persia.—Little is known of carpet weaving of the 13th and 14th centuries in Persia, but by the 15th the art was rapidly moving toward an artistic climax. The horrors and devastation of the Mongol invasion certainly depressed the artistic life of most of the 13th century, which was only partly restored by the magnificence of the architecture and miniature painting of the Ilkhan renaissance (1290–1355). The bloody conquests of Tamerlane were disastrous to Persia, but he spared and favoured artisans, who were removed in large numbers to work on his great palaces in Turkistan, particularly at Samarkand and Bukhara, where they were chiefly responsible for a new school of painting and decorative design.

Out of this, under the enlightened and cultivated rule of Tamerlane's successors, particularly Shah Rukh (1377–1447) and Baizangur (1396–1433), literature and art in all its branches were brought to magnificent floriation. Out of this matrix came the supreme achievement of the carpets of the 16th century.

FIG. 29.—KARABAGH CARPET, BLUE AND MAGENTA

These great carpets of Persia, like most of the finest art of the times, were produced in the palace ateliers or on court-subsidized looms and this made for unity and integrity of style, while a sensitive and exacting clientele imposed the highest standards, and the lavish royal support guaranteed supreme technical proficiency, the most perfect materials and the utmost in skill. All these conditions obtained under the Timurids through the 15th century and under the Safavids (1501–1723).

Authoritative at court and generally supervising all artistic enterprises were the miniature painters, illuminators and book binders, for the art of the book had long been considered the supreme accomplishment and a genuinely great calligrapher outranked weaver, architect or even poet. The art of the book in the 15th century, which already had behind it centuries of superb achievement, reached a degree of elegance and sophistication that it has never known either before or since. Bindings, frontispieces, chapter headings, and in the miniatures themselves, canopies, panels, brocades and carpets, furnished the spaces, mostly rectangular, which by the taste of the time, called for the richest and most elegant patterning.

The beautiful designs thus conceived were in various degrees appropriated by the other arts and the illuminators were given authority over the weavers whom they tended to regard as mere assistants—at best only colleagues.

FIG. 30. — TEKKE — SO-CALLED KHATCHLI (CROSS) DESIGN

This domination of outstanding artists accounts in no small measure for the special character of the court carpets of the period, the variety of colour, the ingenuity and imaginative range of pattern schemes, the superlative draftsmanship which is both lucid and expressive, as well as the intensity of artistic perception which raised these products to the rank of great painting. Indeed, John Sargent and Sir Charles Holmes, both independently used almost the same words referring to two different 16th century carpets: "There is more art in a really great carpet than

FIG. 31.—TEKKE RUG, FIELD PATTERN

FIG. 32.—YOMUD TENT BAG OF MEDIUM FINENESS

in any picture ever painted." (*See* Pope, *A Survey of Persian Art*, vol. I, p. 2.)

India.—Very little is known of early and indigenous carpet weaving in India where it was apparently a late development, for in a tropical country carpets are not so necessary as in northern climates where their warmth is an asset. As an art it was brought in from Persia by the Mogul princes in the 16th and 17th centuries. Akbar set up royal looms that were thought to surpass Persia's finest although, as his biographer Abul Fazl tells us, rugs were still imported from various centres in Persia. The Herat carpet-weaving establishments that made the so-called Isfahans, being nearest, furnished models and apparently weavers were brought thence to continue the style in India, where it was rapidly crystallized, with the elements reduced and formalized, the drawing rigid and meagre. Colours and wool also deteriorated and there were few compensating additions from Indian sources.

The carpets made for the courts of the Grand Moguls, however, were of extravagant and luxurious beauty. Shah Jehan, for example, had made for the palace of Amber a set of rugs from the most precious wool, imported from Kashmir and from remote Himalayan valleys. With the Mogul princes, expense was never

FIG. 33.—ERSARI PATTERN, CHIEFLY A BROWN RED

FIG. 34.—AFGHAN RUG, FIELD PATTERN

any object. The cost of fine weaving was quite ignored and a series of carpets turned out with 800 to 1,200 knots to an inch, which provided a luscious velvety texture. Special carpets were of even finer weave and a fragment of a prayer rug has survived (Metropolitan museum) which has the incredible fineness of nearly 2,400 knots to an inch. Master draftsmen, designers and dyers were, of course, employed and no obvious beauty neglected.

But the art was young and its sources were in imitation, not deep in the life roots of the people. The standards of taste were too recent and too personal, and despite the magnificent models they worked from, despite the limitless subsidies which they could command, these wonderful fabrics never reached the artistic height that characterized many periods of Persian weaving. Their beauty is too obvious, there is no deep and significant organization of pattern, there is a want of imagination and a want of feeling for the possible and the appropriate. The aim was too

pictorial, the stately palmettes and curving leaves of Persian carpets which were in themselves noble and significant compositions, are reduced in Indian carpets to a meticulous botany, faultless in

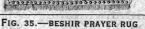

FIG. 35.—BESHIR PRAYER RUG

FIG. 36.—BELUCHI PRAYER RUG

detail but lacking in meaning, much too photographic to sustain any poetic fancy.

The rug industry, once established, continued down to the present. It became a jail industry, particularly in the Punjab. The designs were increasingly meagre and the art could not longer sustain comparison with the Persian weaving.

The later Indian carpets are mostly very inferior, largely on account of the difficulty of obtaining good wool. Many still have the designs of Persia and of other countries but purely Indian patterns are also common. From time to time better carpets have been made in the factories and during the 19th century the government established a fairly successful manufacture in the jails, but it is rarely that in both design and quality they rival the better products of Persia. The best come from Agra and Warangal, the latter producing some good silk rugs. Carpets from Masulipatam, Mirzapore and Tanjore are very cheap and very

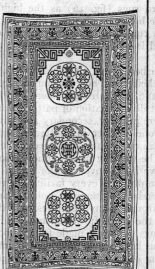

FIG. 37.—CHINESE TURKISTAN CARPET WITH THREE MEDALLIONS

substantial but the wool is so harsh and the colours so dull and gray that they are quite unattractive. Cotton rugs are made in Multan, and tapestry-woven ones, called *daris*, in many places. During the 20th century carpets of good quality, with any desired pattern, are being made in Kashmir, where some handsome reproductions of famous classical carpets have been made.

Turkey.—Turkish rugs, after the 16th century, were of two markedly contrasting types, those made on court looms following Persian designs and possibly the work of imported Persian and Egyptian weavers. Exquisite cloud bands, feathery lanceolate leaves in white on grounds of pale rose relieved by blue and a deep emerald green, carry the rug-weaving art to a special type of perfection. These rugs are somewhat like Persian poetry which was so much admired and copied by the upper classes. The more indigenous Turkish styles are embodied in large and handsome carpets made for a clientele of mosques and nobles; styles best illustrated in the Oushak carpets, ornamented complex star medallions in gold and yellow and dark blue centring on a field of rich red. The so-called Holbein carpets (fig. 14) with Caucasus-like polygon on a ground of deep red often with green borders and a conventionalized interlacing Kufic such as is shown in Holbein's famous portrait of George Gyscze. A handsome carpet of interlacing yellow arabesques on a ground of deep red appears so often in the paintings of Lorenzo Lotto that the rugs are now designated

FIG. 38.—KHOTAN CARPET WITH "FIVE BLOSSOM" PATTERN

as "Lotto" rugs (fig. 15). From some unidentified region, perhaps Bergamo, come rugs again on a ground of deep muffled red of wonderful depth and intensity, also focused on small medallions. This type developed in the 17th century into carpets known as Transylvanian (fig. 18), because so many of them have been found in the churches of Transylvania. But they are purely Turkish in feeling and have the Turkish merits of rich and quiet colour and placid designs, aside from prayer panels, vases and conventionalized foliage, ultimately of Persian derivation. Many of these are prayer rugs. The majority are dominated by a fine red but a few use a wool that is now approximately the colour of old parchment.

The 17th century saw the development of another characteristic type, erroneously called Bird rugs (fig. 16) as the highly conventionalized pair of arabesque blossoms on stems enclosing a leaf does suggest a bird. The few rugs that have survived are of serene and quiet beauty, the field is of soft ivory white and all the colours discreet and modest.

The Turkish rugs are distinguished above all things by their rich and harmonious colours and their broad and spacious designs. They have none of the lively and intricate movement of the Persian carpets, none of the adroit differentiation of pattern, none of the fuguelike counterpoint where primary, secondary and tertiary patterns are played against one another in subtle rhythms, dissonances and resolutions, Persian qualities unsurpassed and unapproached in these respects by the weaving of any other region.

The Caucasus.—Fine rugs have been woven in the Caucasus from earliest times, for this region provides every facility for the art. The enormous prestige of Persia, the dominant political and cultural power in this region through many centuries and the magnificent carpets produced at the court furnished models for the more serious Caucasus weavings that were made for the local nobles or khans. But the Caucasus has its own individual character and while it took motives from other sources, like the dragon and phoenix fighting (so common in Persian illuminations), sunburst medallions, latticelike field divisions derived from the Vase carpets and other sources, or repeating lotus forms often in huge scale, all these contributory elements were completely transformed, and were used only as indications or design material to be refashioned. The Caucasus rugs, perhaps because of questions of expense (for the little Caucasus kingdoms could never compete in luxury with sultans or shahs) were of coarser weave, the famous Kuba Dragon carpets being not infrequently less than 80 knots to the square inch, and hence the designs were much simplified; but the taste that controlled these virile and powerful

designs was genuine and original and warrants classifying the rugs of this region as one of the principal types.

One of the most famous of the Caucasus weavings, the Dragon carpets, concerning which there has been a heated controversy, seems to have come from the town of Kuba, which was one of the great weaving centres. These carpets are of a prodigious scale and furious vigour of design that has no rival in the textile world.

(A. U. P.)

Central Asia.—As the carpets of western Turkistan are made by nomadic Turcoman tribes living in tents and constantly moving about, it is not to be expected that very old ones can still exist. Probably in fact few go back more than 100 years, though it is almost certain that similar rugs have been made for centuries. Turcoman rugs are easily identified, for they all, excepting the Beluchis, have a dark red colouring and geometric designs. Many of the older pieces are not in reality rugs at all though those intended for hanging in tent doorways have that appearance. Many are just bags used for storage in the tents or on the pack animals. Those called camel bags measure about five by three feet, and the tent or wall bags three by one or more. Saddle bags consist of two squares of about two feet, joined together. There are also long bands about a foot wide and perhaps 60 yards long, which are for wrapping round the large tents. The small squarish rugs and larger ones of about ten by seven feet seem to be later in date and were perhaps made chiefly for sale. The Turcoman carpets (wrongly called Bukhara) have woollen warp, weft and pile, two lines of weft and nearly always the Sehna knot. They are surprisingly well woven for nomads with none but the most primitive appliances. After the predominant red, the chief colours are blue, white and a natural black that tones to a very pleasant brown. The characteristic design is the octagon—or so-called elephant's foot—arranged in rows and columns, often with diamond-shaped figures in between. The doorway hangings—called Tekkes (see fig. 30)—have cross shaped panelling and the smaller pieces often have a rectangular diaper. Woven end webs and tassels are freely used as embellishments.

The best classification is on a tribal basis.

Tekke.—These are often very finely woven, sometimes with 400 knots to the square inch. The principal colour is a deep muffled red (fig. 31).

Yomud.—Of medium fineness, mostly with the Ghiordes knot. The chief colour is a purple red, and there is a good deal of white, especially in the border. In the pattern diamonds often displace the usual octagon (see fig. 32). The long tent bands, which have the pattern in pile on a woven ground, belong to this group.

Saryk.—Like the Tekkes but with an almost black-purple or very deep crimson colouring, together with some very prominent white. Not very common.

FIG. 39.—PILLAR CARPET, DRAGON DESIGN

Ersari.—These are rarely large pieces. The chief colour is a brown-red; dark green and a little bright yellow are characteristic. The patterns are very varied, with a tendency to zigzags, diagonal lines and spotted effects (see fig. 33).

Afghan.—Mostly large rugs with long pile and a pattern of large octagons almost touching in columns (see fig. 34), and akin to the Ersaris.

Beshir.—A rare type apparently made near Bukhara, with rich colouring including a lot of yellow, and patterns apparently based on the Persian. Many are prayer rugs with a characteristic pointed arch (see fig. 35). Large carpets are more common.

Beluchi.—These differ from the other Turcomans in that they have a black weft, and dark purple and red colouring, sometimes with natural camel-colour and very staring white. The patterns are almost geometrical but the prayer rugs often have tree forms (see fig. 36). Most of them come from eastern Persia in the vicinity of Khaf near the Afghan border.

Chinese Turkistan.—The earliest rugs of Chinese Turkistan date from the 17th century and mostly have a silk pile and some metal and gilded thread. The patterns are formal floral ones, based on the Persian but with unmistakable Chinese treatment of the detail. The later carpets are loosely woven with the Sehna knot, wool, or more rarely silk pile, and a cotton warp. The 18th century examples have rich but dark colouring, which during the 19th century gets gradually more vivid until at last it becomes excessively crude. There are two important types of design.

Medallion.—These usually have three medallions suggesting in shape a square with well-rounded corners (see fig. 37). One border almost invariably has a conventional Chinese pattern of foam-crested waves. This pattern is mostly called Samarkand in the trade, but the rugs themselves come from Kashgar and Yarkand.

Five Blossom.—These have a floral diaper with characteristic groups of five blossoms (see fig. 38). The colouring is often richly red and orange with a little clear blue.

China.—The rugs of China proper are easily recognized by their characteristic Chinese ornament. They are of coarse texture and are woven with the Sehna knot on a cotton warp: the pile is thick with a very smooth surface. A peculiar feature is the clipping of the pile so as to form a furrow at the contours of the pattern. The prevailing colour is yellow, sometimes intentional but often resulting from the fading of shades of red and orange. Blue and white are also freely used but there is little true red, brown or green.

Some of the carpets have repeating scrolling plant forms. Others have, scattered about, flowers, medallions of frets and the countless symbols that are so familiar in Chinese art. Frets of the Greek type are very common in the border. Pillar carpets are peculiar to China. They are designed (see fig. 39) so that when wrapped round a pillar the edges will fit together and give a continuous pattern, which mostly is a coiling dragon. Many small mats, seat covers and the like are found. The dating of Chinese rugs is an almost impossible task, as patterns have varied very little with time, and internal evidence is almost nonexistent. During the 20th century numbers of large carpets have been made for export.

Morocco.—Large carpets, twice as long as wide, are made in Morocco. They are loosely woven with very bright but mostly faded colours. The field is often cut up into rectangular panels filled with ornament taken directly from Turkish carpets.

Spain.—Carpets seem to have been made in Spain as early as the 14th century. They are made entirely of wool. The knot is tied, or rather twisted, on one warp thread instead of on two, and the weft passes several times after each row of knots. The colours are bright and few in number, little being used but yellow, blue, red and green. The designs fall into two groups, being based either upon oriental models, such as the geometrical Turkish one or upon purely Spanish ornament. The latter type of carpet frequently introduces heraldry. One early type of long rug has shields of arms on a field with a honeycomb pattern introducing plant forms and birds. A common design is a succession of foliated wreaths; another is a diaper of ogee compartments containing the floral device known as the "artichoke." Few knotted pile carpets seem to have been made after the 17th century, but small rugs woven in narrow breadths with a looped pile were common until very recently. They come principally from Alpujarras in the Pyrenees.

England.—The art of making hand-woven carpets in England soon followed their importation from Turkey, though actual specimens of the 16th and 17th centuries are so rare that only about a dozen complete rugs are known. They have a hempen warp and weft and a woollen pile of medium fineness, tied with the Ghiordes knot. The ground is usually green and there are so many shades of the other colours that the whole number of tints is greater than in oriental carpets. The designs may be divided

into two groups. In the first are found typical English patterns resembling contemporary embroidery, and often introducing heraldic devices and, fortunately, dates. The earliest known carpet of this type belongs to the earl of Verulam and is dated 1570. Large numbers of pieces of carpet knotting—called at the time "Turkey-work"—were made for covering chairs and stools. As the demand for carpets increased in the 18th century small factories were started at Paddington, Fulham, Moorfields, Exeter and Axminster; and the home production was stimulated by premiums offered by the Society of Arts in 1756. The designers continued to adopt the decoration of the time or to copy eastern carpets. The famous Axminster factory worked on well into the 19th century and then became merged into the Wilton factory, which is still in operation. With the advent of machinery the industry dwindled and almost disappeared until, about 1880, the craft was revived by William Morris. Quite late in the century a successful factory was opened in Donegal and during the 20th century many small rugs have been knotted by handicraft societies, though their products can scarcely compete commercially with the machine or with the oriental rug. (C. E. Ta.)

THE UNITED STATES

The first carpet factory in the United States was established in 1791 by W. P. Sprague at Philadelphia. From that time the development of carpet-weaving machinery has progressed rapidly, especially in the line of broadlooms. One of Sprague's earliest Axminster carpet designs represented the arms and achievements of the United States. This attracted the attention of Alexander Hamilton, who recommended the imposition of a small duty on imported carpeting, thus initiating the policy of a protective tariff. While in the early days of carpet manufacturing in the United States, looms were imported from Great Britain and the continent, it was not long before looms were invented and constructed in the different carpet mills which had come into existence in several cities in the United States. The Jacquard pattern device was put into use in the United States shortly after its introduction in Europe. At Medway, Mass., in 1825, a small ingrain carpet mill, owned by Henry S. Burdett and managed by Alexander Wright, was started with hand looms brought from Scotland. In 1839 Erastus B. Bigelow began experimental work at Lowell, Mass., which resulted in the perfection of the first power loom ever made for weaving carpets. This wove an ingrain type, and was followed by Mr. Bigelow's development of the Brussels power loom in 1848. John Johnson of Halifax, England, undertook tapestry and velvet weaving (q.v.) in Newark, N.J., producing the pattern by printing the dyestuff on the individual strands of yarn. In 1876, after several years of research, Halcyon Skinner invented the moquette or spool Axminster at West Farms, N.Y. James Dunlap, in Philadelphia, developed a method of printing tapestry and velvet carpeting in the finished fabric. Imitation Smyrna rugs were made in considerable quantity by many factories during the latter part of the 19th century, the process being of the chenille Axminster type, but double faced. The three-quarter width or 27 in. was the limit of weave in the several types for long periods after invention, but in the closing years of the 19th century a movement to widen the looms began in the United States. The ingrain carpet and Smyrna rugs gradually lost favour, while the tapestry, velvet, Axminster, Wilton and chenille rapidly grew in demand as the processes were perfected and the looms widened. Rugs were first formed by sewing carpet strips together. Later the corners of a border pattern strip were mitred to form the framed design effect. Slowly the necessary changes were made to allow weaving the border patterns in the straight strips and avoid the mitred corners. (See CARPET MANUFACTURE.) To eliminate the seam through the centre of rugs and in the medallion designs, popular at the time, required a wider strip and loom to weave it. Looms nine feet in width followed this trend in tapestry, velvet and Axminster in the early years of the 20th century and Wilton broadlooms followed after many years of experimental work and became popular about 1926. All these weaves are commonly woven up to 15 ft. in width and even wider looms were developed. The chenille weave, developed in Great Britain in 1839, was not introduced into the United States until 1909 and was not produced in quantity until 1916. It has had a steady growth since because it is the only woven floor covering that can be woven to special order up to 30 ft. in width, any reasonable length, any shape, design or colour arrangement and an inch or better in thickness.   (X.)

France.—There are early records of carpet weavers in France, but nothing is known of their work until the foundation of the famous Savonnerie factory near Paris in 1626. There many large carpets were made, mostly with flaxen warp and weft and a woollen pile tied with the Ghiordes knot. The designs accord with contemporary French decoration and few if any were based on oriental carpets. In 1825 the factory was closed and the manufacture transferred to the Gobelins tapestry factory. During the 18th century and afterwards many tapestry-woven carpets were made at Aubusson and in other tapestry factories.

Other Countries.—A few carpets are still in existence that were made in Poland in the 17th century, with floral patterns in light colouring. Loosely woven rugs have been much made by the peasants of Finland. They often have human figures and dates and seem mostly to have formed part of the bridal dowries. Kilims are made in the Balkan states and in southern Russia; they resemble the Turkish pieces but have, especially the Russian, more naturalistic floral patterns. Those from Rumania generally include birds in the design.

PRACTICAL CONSIDERATIONS

It is perhaps more important that a carpet for use should be soundly made than beautiful, and certainly better that it should be beautiful than that it should accord with any particular scheme of decoration. Oriental carpets, on account of their depth of tone, rarely go badly with other objects. Accordingly when buying, the first thing to ascertain is that the foundation threads are sound and strong and that the pile is not unduly worn away. If a rug is held up to the light, holes and thin places are often revealed that were quite unnoticed when it lay on the floor. Holes that have been properly repaired are of little consequence. It should be noticed whether it is of good shape and whether it lies flat on the floor. Few rugs have the sides perfectly parallel but an excessive distortion is unsightly. A rug that is not flat tends to wear badly in the baggy places, but certain good rugs, such as the Shiraz, are rarely quite free from this defect. A guarantee should be asked that the rug has not been chemically treated, as is too often done with the object of effecting a supposed improvement in colour. Such treatment usually results in a hopeless deterioration of the yarns. Undesirable though less destructive, is the process of hot rolling, which gives to inferior wool a silky gloss that is only transitory.

The Care of Carpets.—Carpets will give remarkably long service if treated with proper consideration. Their two great enemies, apart from the inevitable destructive effect of wear, are moth and damp. The former is best kept at bay by frequent moving or handling and by regular exposure to light and air. If rugs must be stored, then inspection at intervals is essential. A carpet in use is rarely in danger. There seems to be a great future for certain chemical applications that render the wool uneatable by moth, but the method appears not fully established. Damp will in time rot the threads and destroy the fabric, but it can be avoided by obvious means. If any mechanical injury is suffered, such as a cut or burn, the damage should be dealt with as soon as possible by a competent repairer, for such lesions get worse very quickly. In ordinary use, quite apart from accident, the ends and sides often tend to wear and fray out, in which case the parts should be re-overcast—a very simple operation if done in time. Places in the middle locally worn or damaged can have new knots inserted and even large holes can be restored so as to be almost as good as new, though such work is rather expensive. In carpets of lesser value, instead of new knotting, patches cut from a suitable rug can often be inserted at less cost, and sometimes a serviceable small rug can be made from a larger worn one by cutting away the bad parts.

From time to time but not more often than necessary carpets should be cleaned and the improvement in their appearance is often astonishing. If there is any doubt as to the stability of the dyes of the carpet, it should be entrusted to one of the many firms who specialize in this kind of work. In many cases, however, surface washing with a limited supply of hot water and carpet soap applied with a stiff brush may be done at home, though drying the fabric afterwards is often a difficulty, as a clean and airy place must be available for some days at least. It is most important to wash out all traces of soap. Some of the new cleaning compounds using irium as a base are superior to soap. In ordinary use carpets are properly kept free from dust by brushing, or by means of a vacuum cleaner, but in all cases where a brush is employed it is *most important* that it is not used against the lie of the pile. (*See* also TEXTILES AND EMBROIDERIES; TAPESTRY; INTERIOR DECORATION.)   (C. E. TA.)

Uses of Carpets.—The carpets so far mentioned have been practically all special productions for a wealthy clientele but at the same time, although few have survived, the common people also had their rugs.

Throughout the near east rugs have from the beginning been for commonest use and an affair of the whole population. This very universality was one of the reasons for their excellence. The traveller Herbert from England, writing in the 17th century, said there was no house too poor but what it was furnished with carpets. From immemorial time they covered the floors of house and tent as well as mosque and palace, and served many other uses besides. They made handsome portieres and were sometimes hung on the wall like tapestries. They were a convenient, portable and durable form of wealth, served as tribute money, and were frequently gifts of one state to another. They were used as blankets, canopies and tomb covers. In past times they were also handy for committing and concealing murder. The last caliph of Baghdad (1357) made his tragic exit via a carpet in which he was rolled up and beaten to death, a not uncommon mode of execution, quite the reverse of Cleopatra's dramatic entrance to the presence of a Caesar (Mark Antony) when she stepped out of an unrolled rug. Woven with an apex that could be pointed to Mecca, they served as prayer rugs for an individual, or, given sufficient size and reduplicate prayer panels, they could serve simultaneously for a whole family or some religious fraternity. They made excellent saddle covers and carryall bags as well. These modest rugs had their own merits. They were closer to the life of the people; the best of them have an air of genuineness and respect for the limits of the craft. On them were lavished loving care, into them were woven life-protecting symbols which in early times people understood and took seriously—even now the meanings of the more obvious patterns are dimly remembered.

Size and Shape.—Rugs—a term understood to include all carpets for use on the floor—are mostly rectangular, though occasionally pieces are seen made to fit into irregular spaces, and a few round carpets are known, probably woven for tents. The rectangle may vary from a square to a strip at least six times as long as it is wide. A very usual ratio is about three to two. The strips, called runners or *kanara,* made in pairs to go along the sides of a Persian room, are very useful in corridors. A very common size for small rugs is about 6½ ft. by 4½ ft., while large ones may reach 25 ft. in length or occasionally more.

A very common room size for modern carpets is 10 ft. by 14 ft. but not for old carpets which are much narrower in proportion to length, owing primarily to their use in combinations in the oriental house. Some old carpets are nearly three times as long as wide, for example, the famous McCormick Vase carpet now in the Metropolitan museum is 10 ft. by 29 ft. Some of the palace carpets woven in the early 17th century (especially of the Herat type) are 50 ft. long. There are recently woven fine quality hall carpets in the ministry of foreign affairs in Tehran that are approximately 6 ft. by 125 ft.

The Low School Rugs of Persia.—By the end of the 17th century the summit of the rug-weaving art was past. The impoverishment of the court and the general slackening of cultural energy throughout the near east are clearly reflected in the steady decline of the court art. None the less the conditions out of which this art arose continued to operate in more humble circumstances throughout most of western Asia. The wandering nomads and the settled town dwellers alike continued to design and weave carpets which if increasingly stereotyped and of steadily diminishing artistic vigour, none the less maintained genuine artistic character until within a few generations ago. They used dye methods that had been developed and tested through centuries. Each group stuck to its own characteristic pattern content to maintain the artistic tradition intact with little addition or embellishment. These carpets were not made for a greedy impatient western market and could with oriental respect for time and perfection continue to embody traditional merits of high quality. Most of the indigenous rug weaving centres have been corrupted by western demand and the commercial organization of weaving centres, but these various humble rugs, the so-called Low School type, are frequently of a very high artistic character, beautiful in colour, design, of fine material and excellent technique. They are worthy of the collectors' enthusiasm of the last 50 years and deserve a more serious study as works of art than they have received.

The identification of the localities in which these humble rugs were woven is by no means certain. Russian investigators have identified about 40 or 50 weaving centres in the Caucasus but the results are not yet published. Names are attached to rugs frequently in the international markets at Istanbul, Smyrna and Tabriz, and do not fully correspond to the actualities. Different and contrasting rugs are often woven in closely related districts, such as Bijar and Sehna, where similar appearing rugs may be woven in districts far apart. The nomadic wanderings, the forcible transfer of populations several times in the 18th century, tribal intermarriages and many other factors have tended to confuse the type and conceal their true origins. A few of the better known types may be briefly designated.

Kashan was noted for its fine textiles as early as the 12th century, and by the 16th it was producing the sumptuous velvets rivalled by even more sumptuous silks and in the 17th by the silver and gold-threaded rugs called "Polonaise" carpets. The skill and tradition survived and Kashan has produced the finest woven, most elaborately designed, richly coloured rugs of recent times. Their high cost restricted the output and the best of them were finally crowded out of the market.

Joshaghan, 60 mi. northwest of Isfahan, wove the great Vase carpets of the Sefavid period and like Kashan and Tabriz continued fine weaving down to the present day. During the 19th century the most characteristic Joshaghans were distinguished by flower sprays, very precisely drawn, on a field of soft red.

The finest rugs made today come from special looms in Meshed and Birjand which have been especially favoured by court orders. The materials are excellent, the weaving leaves nothing to be desired, the colours are beautifully toned and need no chemical washing as do most contemporary eastern carpets, though the designs still lack the spaciousness, the originality and expressive power of earlier days.

These less pretentious rugs, the product of tribal nomads or of sedentary townfolks, maintained their standards down to the latter half of the 19th century when their near ruin as art was completed by western commercialism with its insatiable demand for quantity, cheapness and speed.

Western taste also intruded destructively, and European importers began to supply designs with confused or meaningless patterns, and to order shapes and colours that were in conflict with the oriental tradition. Competition was intensified and the weaver reduced to an animated machine. Aniline dyes, harsh and fugitive, displaced the older, far more costly dyeing processes. Poor wool was cheaper than good, and various processes of chemical washing temporarily concealed the deficiencies and imparted an enticing sheen to the carpet which the unsophisticated thought charming.

However, the more intelligent European importers were aware of the destructiveness of such practices and made real efforts to arrest the deterioration of the craft and to restore something

of the old quality, though the factory system was now too well established ever to be displaced. The Persian government made several sporadic attempts to contest commercialization, imposed severe penalties for the use of aniline dyes, but the commercial tide was not so easily checked. In recent years the government, however, has made a much more systematic effort to revive the art, with considerable success. A school of design, under Taherzadeh Behzad in Tehran based its work on faithfully studied 15th and 16th century models. Sound methods of dyeing, wool selection and testing are taught and the school graduates go into the various rug producing districts to improve their standards. In various places the original, indigenous methods have been maintained, and particularly in Meshed and Birjand, carpets are woven which for technical competence and in beauty of colour stand comparison with the 17th century weavings. The art of designing great carpets, however, is not so quickly recovered. The tendency to over-elaboration needs to be curbed by a more sympathetic study of the early models with their aristocratic restraint and the fundamental strength of their designs.

The principal weaving centres in the 19th century were Tabriz in the northwest, Joshaghan in central Persia, Kerman and Ravar in the southeast and Meshed in the northeast. These centres have all woven large carpets, Meshed, Kerman and Tabriz utilizing the medallion schemes of early classical time, Joshaghan and some Kerman carpets repeating various interpretations of the garden motive.

The province of Azerbaijan in the extreme northwest of Persia is ideally fitted for rug weaving. Excellent wool, water and dye plants are readily available, and hence it is natural that the region has produced some of the finest rug types. Among the more important are those from Karadar and Karajar, where the weavers remained faithful to the highest ideals until they were no longer producing. The region around Ardabil produced many handsome nomadic rugs difficult to identify. South of Ardabil the principal types have been the so-called Heriz, Gorevan and Serapi carpets that make liberal use of tan and blue and hold to bold and simple patterns.

The Kurdish region in northwest Persia produced many fine medium-sized rugs in thick lustrous wool of fine colours, repeating the designs of other parts of Persia. Curiously enough, in the heart of the Kurdish district from the immediate vicinity of the town of Sehna (now Senandaj) have come finely woven carpets and kilims. The patterns are exquisitely rendered medallions or the bouté (the so-called pear or palm leaf motive), with imbrications.

A great rug industry was developed in western Persia in the Sultanabad district. From individual towns come beautifully woven rugs like the Sarouks, with their ancient medallion pattern; the Sarabandes, with their repeating bouté patterns on a ground of silvery rose, the Ferraghan, with their so-called Herati pattern—an all-over, rather dense design with a light green border on a mordant dye that leaves the pattern in relief. The earlier Ferraghans (two are known, dated at the end of the 18th century) are on fields of dark lustrous blue and a pattern delicately drawn and clear and open. Later, toward the end of the 19th century, Ferraghans degenerated in colour and material; the pattern became clumsy and crowded.

The Kerman rugs were made of brilliant wool, finely and skilfully woven, and beginning about 1870, they became the most favoured of all the Persian weavings. They are lighter in tone, thanks to the discreet use of light ivory and pale rose, and were particularly adapted to western drawing rooms in the late 19th century, with their over-emphasis on elegance.

From the province of Fars come a large number of semi-nomadic rugs and a few large-scale carpets, reflecting ancient models. The Bahtiari region west of Isfahan turned out a few large double-warp stoutly woven carpets and a few smaller rugs that occasionally attained very great merit. Northeastern Persia from Meshed down to Birjand and Ghayian produced large carpets predominantly violet or purplish in tone with wide multiple borders and very soft and not too durable wool.

Throughout Persia in the 18th and 19th centuries, probably

about 50 to 100 different types of rugs were woven. Occasionally large carpets of quite individual design, but all with their roots in the classical past, appear to baffle the students seeking for precise classification. Extensive studies are required for their identification and interpretation.

Caucasus—Low School.—The Low School rugs of the Caucasus region are among the most individual and satisfactory. Their patterns are practically all geometrical densely juxtaposed generally without organic connection and without implied movement, but they are clear, ingenious, logical and entirely suitable for floor decoration. The more recent examples seem a little dry in colour but many of them, like the rugs woven by the Kazaks, Suruks and other nomads, are sometimes of flaming brilliance, and the older rugs from Daghestan, Kuba and Shirvan are done in beautifully clear, discreet and well balanced tones.

Kilim or tapestry rugs were woven all over the near east, but the most artistic come from the Caucasus. The Shirvan kilims, with their broad horizontal stripes, have bold and clearly defined motives that are harmoniously assembled by virtue of their perfect colour balance.

A more important type of flat-stitch carpet, embroidered and with a mass of loose threads at the back, which comes from the region of the ancient fortified city of Shemakha, has been improperly called cashmere because of its superficial resemblance to cashmere shawls. The design is most often composed of large, beautifully articulated mosaic tile patterns in rich and sober colour. In design they are descendants of the carpets that so delighted Memlinc and the Van Eycks.

Turkish—Low School.—The Low School rugs of Asia Minor of the 18th and 19th centuries continue the earlier qualities of quiet and sober patterns and luxurious colour. Some of the 18th century weavings still faithfully follow the simple geometrical patterns of the 15th century. But the chief output of the Turkish weavers are prayer rugs, with which the Turks were more lavishly supplied than any other of the faithful. Melas, Konia, Ladik, Kirsher and Sivas all wove handsome carpets, those of Ladik being the most brilliant, both in pattern and colour. The most famous prayer rugs came from the towns of Ghiordes and Kula, mostly of the 18th and 19th centuries, and in the United States, the first passion of the collector. Regions like Smyrna produced a great many utility carpets for the western world.

Knotted-Pile Technique.—The technique used in the earliest extant pile fragments is logically also the most primitive, for the pile yarn is wrapped round only a single warp, the warps being held together by two or more wefts woven the full width in ordinary cloth binding (alternately over and under), after each line of knots. Such a technique was most probably invented among the nomads of the central Asiatic steppes and may well have evolved out of a still more rudimentary weave still practised in the Kerghiz tribes whereby a simulated fleece is made on a straw mat by catching in bits of wool in the course of the plaiting (A. U. Dilley, *Rugs and Carpets*, p. 1).

The simple pile looping around a single warp had travelled, by the early middle ages, to the east Mediterranean for it is found in pile carpet fragments recovered from the Fustat refuse heaps. A fine example (Musée Arabe, Cairo) bears on a dark blue ground an inscription in white Kufic letters which makes it datable in the late 9th or early 10th century. Not long thereafter the technique was carried into Europe and was used in Germany, at Quedlinburg, at the end of the 12th century, for a hanging illustrating an allegory centred on Mortian's *Marriage of Mercury and Philologia* (Ackerman, *Tapestry*, p. 33). Moreover, by the beginning of the 14th century *tapisserie sarrazinoise* is discussed in industrial statutes, and clearly differentiated from both *tapisserie nostre* and *haute-lisse* (true tapestry). Evidently looped-pile weaving continued in Europe (*ibid.*, pp. 312–313). The same technique was still in use in Spain in the 17th century.

Meanwhile in Egypt and probably other east Mediterranean centres also, two other forms of looped weaving were being developed which made either a potential pile (uncut pile) or actual long-ended pile surface. One of these practised in two variants, was a forerunner of velvet. In this a supplementary weft for the pile is carried on top of regularly spaced foundation wefts (from the fifth to the ninth in general) and passes under a certain number of warps to hold it firm (from three to six overpassed warps, as a rule), then is deeply looped over a single warp, and so repeated; or alternatively, it is deeply looped between two warps. But the second of these loop weaves contains the germ of the development of true rug-knotting form. This, the supplementary weft after passing under a certain number of overpassed warps in the same way (*e.g.*, two), is then floated over a certain number of them (*e.g.*, two or three), and is carried back under the same number of warps. This leaves a cut end at the beginning of the unit (of say seven warps in all), and another in the middle thereof—a coarse version of the knot which came to be known as the Persian knot. The two techniques were used equally for garments and wall hangings but the latter was used also for carpets as is shown by a good-sized specimen in the Metropolitan museum from Antinoe, datable c. A.D. 500–600, with a broad conventional polychrome design (M. Dimand, in *Metropolitan Museum Studies*, iv, pp. 159–61 [1932–33]).

But the earliest true knotted pile carpets are not in the knot related to this form of looped weaving, but the alternative, so-called Turkish knot, which had been developed by the 14th century at least, as the Ala-ud-Din carpets show. Moreover by the end of the 15th it had penetrated Europe for a fragment of an Annunciation, probably Flemish, possibly French, is in this technique (E. B. Saxe, in *Metropolitan Museum Studies*, I).

In these fully evolved forms of the technique the pile yarn, instead of being wrapped round a single warp (fig. 1), is knotted round two. These warp threads—most often cotton, but in both Spanish and near eastern nomad rugs sometimes wool, or in some finer qualities, silk—are stretched vertically on a loom (fig. 4), and a length of the pile yarn is tied on every two threads the full width of the loom; then two or more weft threads likewise of any of the materials cited, or of a combination thereof, are cloth woven (alternately over and under), back and forth across the full width, two or more times, and the process is repeated. There are thus three sets of threads involved, each with its specific function: warp, weft, pile. The pile is usually wool but may be silk or cotton, though the last is not desirable except for very small areas where the crisp accent of an unfadeable white is wanted. In the Turkish pile knot (fig. 2) the yarn is passed under one warp, back over two, and back again under the second so that both ends come up together between the two warps on the same side of the overpass loop. In the other type (fig. 3) the yarn passes under one warp, over and back under the next, so that the two ends stand on the surface with one warp between them. The pattern is obtained by changing the colour of the pile yarn. When a row of knots is tied it is beaten down with a heavy malletlike comb against the preceding rows, so that the pile completely conceals on the front both the warp and weft; and when a certain area is woven the pile ends are sheared to an even height, which varies according to the character of the rug from very close to, on some nomad rugs, a depth of about an inch, which produces a shaggy effect.

The fineness of the weave depends on the number of knots to the square inch which varies according to the weight and spacing of the warps and also, though to a lesser extent, of the wefts, and the thickness of the pile yarn. The permissible range is from about 80 to the square inch, used for instance in some of the Kuba Dragon carpets of the late 16th or 17th century, to more than 2,400, found in a fragment of a Mughal (Indian) prayer carpet of the 17th century, obviously an emperor's property (Altman collection, Metropolitan museum, N.Y.). But the most finely woven carpets are not by any means those of greatest artistic or historic importance. Thus, *e.g.*, the beautiful and famous pair of carpets from the mosque of Ardabil, dated by an inscription 1539, have only about 325 to the square inch.

In certain types of pile rugs, both wool and silk, some areas are brocaded with gold or silver thread, usually cloth woven but with a surface float over several warps (basket-weave) to obtain the maximum richness. In these the weft is carried forward over four of the warp threads and then backwards behind two (*see* fig. 6). This gives a kind of herringbone texture at the front and a series of ribs at the back of the fabric. Because a weft looped round the warp threads as described has much less than the usual binding effect, alternate wefts are cloth-woven, but these are concealed in compacting the loop-woven wefts, which are changed in colour according to pattern as in straight tapestry weaving.

Dyes.—Red is most often obtained from madder root (*rubia tinctorum*). Thus the red of the Noin Ula carpets is madder with the usual alum mordant. The shade which runs through the gamut of reds and pinks to reddish brown and orange varies with the age of the plant, and also other components, including the mordant, the density of the solution and the duration of the immersion. Some reds, however, are obtained from the *coccus ilicis* which breeds on oaks in the near east, related to but not identical with, the cochineal (*q.v.*) (*coccus cacti*) of Mexico. Blues are made from indigo. The yellow of the Noin Ula carpet is rhamnetin, the dye obtained from unripe berries of various bushes of the Rhamus family. The famous saffron (*q.v.*) dye, made from the dried stigmas and part of the style of a crocus (*Crocus sativus*) is too expensive to use to any extent. Greens are usually blue plus yellow; violets (only rarely used), red plus blue. Black, when not the natural wool, is done with iron filings in citric acid, a corrosive dye whose destructive effect on wool especially is often conspicuous in old rugs. White is the natural wool, but occasionally when a sharper white is desired, a little cotton is introduced.

The time required for weaving rugs has been very greatly exaggerated. They are often spoken of as having required lifetimes, but a careful check made by Heinrich Jacoby (*A Survey of Persian Art*, vol. III, p. 2464) shows that the finest carpets would hardly have taken three years. Even the huge Ardabil carpet, with its 33,000,000 knots, could have been woven, from the preparation of the cartoon through all the processes to its completion, within four years. Great carpets like the Milan Hunting carpet probably only required a year and a half.

Another common fallacy concerning rugs is that they were designed to be seen on the floor. This is only partly true; most of them were worked on vertical elements and the designs are traditional and derivative and not very often planned in relation to the destined environment of the carpet. Moreover, the great court carpets of the 16th century, for example, were the work of illuminators who were accustomed to think of the book page and a vertical design. The designs of the great carpets, when seen on the floor from a normal eye height, are compressed and distorted. Their full effect comes only when hung where they can be viewed so that the eye is nearly equidistant from all points.

Carpets in museums are almost all underlighted. Oriental fabrics were all woven and used in regions of high illumination and their colours are only at their maximum and in proper relation to one another when the illumination is strong.

Design.—Both the pile carpet technique and the flat techniques, whether straight tapestry or the looped Shemakha weaving, permit unlimited variation within the design—in sharp contrast to all shuttle weaving which necessitates regularly recurring repeats. But while the rug designer thus has unrestricted liberty, needs of the eye and the mind, further defined by habits of tradition and discipline, guide invention. A division into field and border is the basis of all rug design. The border serves, like the cornice on a building or the frame on a picture, to emphasize the limits, isolate the field, concentrate attention on it, and sometimes control the implied movements of the interior pattern. The value of a border had already been recognized by pottery painters in 4000 B.C. and is fully developed in rug patterns from Assyrian times on. Its function is so fundamental, logically and psychologically, that it cannot be successfully omitted.

The field may be decorated with an all-over pattern, a panel composition, or a medallion system. The all-over pattern may be of identical repeats, either juxtaposed or evenly spaced, though the latter, while common on textiles, is rare on carpets; or it may be of varied motives in a unified system, *e.g.*, different plant forms of about the same size and in the same relation to each other, but even in this freest type of design it almost invariably

includes bilaterally balanced repetitions which agreeably, almost necessarily reflect the human bilateral equilibrium. The latter type of design is found most typically in formalized representations of the paradise parks or woods which are a feature of Persian palace plans. Another type of allover design appears entirely free but is actually organized on systems of scrolling stems, notably on the east Persian carpets of the 16th–17th centuries.

The value of panel subdivisions for controlling patterns had been discovered by the Upper Palaeolithic period (*c.* 25,000 B.C.) in a simple rectangular version, and panel systems have been a basic form of design since 4000 B.C., when pottery painters were already devising varied systems. On carpets the lattice provides the simplest division of the field, often a diagonal lattice as on the embroidered carpet from Noin Ula, a scheme that appears on Sassanian capitals and in Coptic tapestries. But a characteristic field design of the court carpets of the Shah Abbas period, the so-called Vase carpet, is constructed from the ogee, a motive that becomes prominent in near eastern textile design in the 14th century. Simple rectangular panelling—really a large-scale check— is typical of one style of Spanish rugs of the 15th–16th centuries.

The most frequent medallion composition consists of a central panel of more or less elaborate construction in the centre of the field superimposed on an allover design, but this is also often complemented with corner pieces, which are typically quadrants of the central medallion.

But multiple medallion systems also are developed, either a succession or a chain of medallions on the vertical axis; or two or more forms of medallions alternating in bands, a scheme typical of the Turkish ("Ushak") carpets of the 16th–17th centuries; or systematically spotted medallions which may or may not be interconnected, or may interlock when the scheme logically becomes an elaborate lattice.

Persian carpets of the great period (15th–17th centuries) commonly have multiple design schemes, that is, composition systems on two or more "levels." The simplest is the medallion superimposed on an allover design, but more typical are subtler inventions such as two or three spiral stem systems, sometimes overlarded with large-scale cloud bands, the whole intertwining and mutually supplementary, but each independently conceived and individually carried to completion. The finer Vase carpets have double or triple ogival lattices set at different intervals ("staggered"), each with its own centre and tangent motives which also serve other functions in the other systems. What at first sight appears to be a great multiplicity of independent motives thus proves on careful exploration to be firmly controlled and logically distributed.

Occasionally stripe systems are used, either vertical or diagonal, but this conception is more natural to shuttle-woven fabrics, and probably, when employed in the free techniques of rug weaving, are imitations of textiles.

The border invariably consists of a minimum of three members: the main band, which can vary greatly in width in accordance with both the size of the rug and the elaborateness of the field design, and the guard stripes, a decidedly subordinate band on either side, really the borders of the border. These may be the same on both sides or different. But multiple border systems also are quite common, as on one of the Noin Ula carpets, very elaborate schemes having been developed in mosaic floors of the Roman period. Some of the greatest carpets, however, have the simplest border arrangements, while on certain types of commercially produced carpets of the late 19th and early 20th centuries meaninglessly multiple and complex compositions were developed. The court designers of the 16th century developed many beautiful correlations of rhythm and accent between border and field.

Patterns.—Four main classes of motives are used: geometrical, conventional, plant and illustrative. The geometrical repertoire is built up from variations and combinations of meanders, polygons, crosses and stars. Meanders, chiefly for borders, range from the simple serration which is ageless (actually already much used in the Upper Palaeolithic) to fairly complex hooked forms, characteristically the angular "running-wave" or "Greek-key," which is also very ancient. Such meanders typically constitute reciprocals, *i.e.*, designs which form the identical shape in the positive and negative areas, and so when executed in contrasted colours can be alternatively interpreted; or differentiated reciprocals, the negative space created by the main motive having a different but destructive form, a type of narrow border well developed in early mediaeval textile design. Little trefoil reciprocals are used for guard stripes in the Caucasus, central Persia (so-called Polonaise) and in India. Chief among the polygons employed are the lozenge and the octagon. The Maltese cross is frequent, and the gamma cross (or swastika) is frequent. The purely geometrical stars are usually based on the cross or the octagon. Many of these motives, which are rudimentary and very ancient, may have originated in basket-weaving and the related reed-mat plaiting, for they are natural to both techniques; but in rug weaving they have survived chiefly in the work of central Asia, Asia Minor and the Caucasus, pile-knotted and flat-woven, whether tapestry or of the Shemakha type.

One of the principal motives in the 16th and 17th century Persian carpets is the so-called arabesque, an ambiguous term that generally implies an intricate scrolling vine system that in Persian ornamental schemes (12th to 18th centuries) usually terminates in a lilylike blossom of two uneven and asymmetrical members meeting at a narrow acute angle, generally with a rounded lobe on one side underneath, and describing two curves in opposite directions which continue readily into further scroll systems. This highly individual form was well begun in China in the late Chou period (*c.* 600 B.C.), notably on a few bronze mirrors, and is beautifully developed during the Han dynasty (220 B.C.–A.D. 220). It does not appear in Persia, however, until the 12th century (on pottery and architectural stucco ornament), and its intermediate history has not been traced in either country, yet when it does emerge in Persian design the essential forms are so close to those that had been current in the far east more than 1,200 years before, a hiatus and reinvention seem improbable.

Directly traceable to China, on the other hand, are the cloud knot (or *'tchi*) and cloud band or ribbon—both begun by the Han period at least and with a continuous history thereafter. The cloud ribbon first appeared in western Asia in Syrian silk design of the 7th century but was sporadic until the 13th century when it was reintroduced as an aftermath of the Mongol invasion and at this time it became associated with the three-ball motive, an astral symbol that goes back to Babylonia of the second millennium B.C. and referred to the sun, moon and planet Venus, decisive astral bodies in the west Asiatic cults. The combination moved from Syrian textile design into Asia Minor textile design with the Ottoman Turkish conquest in the 15th century and became typical of one group of 16th–17th century Turkish carpets.

The cloud band or ribbon, already skilfully used on book covers, manuscript illumination and in architectural faïence, became important on 16th century carpets and was employed with especial elegance and skill by the Persian designers, and perhaps most beautifully in the Turkish court carpets which owed much to Persian inspiration, while the cloud knot or *'tchi*, a feature of the court carpets of the time of Shah Abbas, was continued to the end of the 18th century.

A second major class of conventional motives dominant in a considerable range of carpet designs from Asia Minor to India, the palmettes, are of plant derivation, and are justifiably named in that they originated in Assyrian design as stylizations of the palm, a symbol of the vitalistic power, often, if not always, in relation to the moon. Moreover, many of the almost uncountable variations that developed through the centuries continued to refer directly to the palm. Others, however, also beginning early in the first millennium B.C., derived from the lotus blossom, a complementary figure since it was connected primarily with the fertility repertoire in relation to sun symbolism. Still others involved the symbolically closely related pomegranate, utilizing primarily the fruit while still others presented the general vitalistic emblem, the vine, this last built on the single leaf. The forms of all these four main types of palmettes found in the rug designs are directly descended from styles current in textile designs from

the 4th century, and are more or less modified by Chinese influences. These patterns in the 16th and early 17th centuries were beautifully and realistically elaborated, and blossoms like the Chinese peony sometimes compete with the more conventional lotus. The lanceolate leaf often associated with palmettes especially in east Persian designs, is also largely conventional.

Outstanding among the more naturalistic plants are the cypress and blossoming fruit tree, typically shown thus combined in Persian designs, still suggesting the ancient meaning of life eternal and resurrection. Willows are especially favoured in the Shah Abbas Vase carpet, as are jasmine flowers, and in Turkish court carpets, tulips. Many minor foliate and floral forms had no specific botanical identification though they give a realistic effect. Naturalistic red or pink roses, as on Karabagh and Kerman rugs from the 18th–19th centuries, are imitated from French patterns or English chintz and had no place in the old Persian repertoire, despite the importance of the rose in Persian poetry, life and even economy, and its ancient symbolic importance throughout western Asia as an alternative to the lotus blossom.

In one widely distributed class of design some of the plant forms grow out of a vase, a residue of an old symbolic complex, a cosmological tree, usually the Tree of Life, sustained by the Water of Life as implied by the "cloud-jar," a design already well developed in Babylon.

Of the illustrated motives, in addition to the naturalistic plants, the most important are those connected with the garden and the hunt: many small songbirds of which the nightingale meant most to the Persian; the *feng huang* (pheasant) taken over from China and much favoured in the 16th century and occasionally the peacock, which further west in Asia had had considerable symbolic value; the great felines—lions and the semiconventional lion-mask, sometimes used as the centre of a palmette; tigers; cheetahs; bear; fox; deer of numerous species; goats, sometimes picturesquely prancing; or the wild ass, a fleet prey; ferocious looking Chinese dragons and the gentle *kilim*, a fantastic equine likewise imported from China. Fish sometimes swim in pools or streams, or are conventionally paired to suggest an escutcheon in the borders of one type. Huntsmen, usually mounted, are the major human figures, though musicians and angels also occur (Austrian State Hunting carpet).

In the utilization of the conventional and illustrative vocabularies the underlying theme is nearly always fertility or abundance. These principles are magnificently embodied in the great carpet of Ardabil. A huge golden stellate medallion, the ultimate fulfillment of the multiple-pointed rosette that from immemorial time symbolized the sun, has at its very centre a little gray-blue pool on which are floating four lotuses, obviously representing the old notion of the atmosphere pool located in the depths of the heavens, from which comes the rain; the whole figure thus standing for the two basic vitalizing elements—sun and water. Out of this medallion, proof of its magical potencies, issues a complex system of tendrils and blossoms. The vitalistic power, the moon and sun as its fulfillment are assembled as a petition for, and recognition of the earth's generosity.

The Mughal (Indian) carpets were derived from Persian styles but show a marked tendency to greater naturalism. The Chinese knotted rugs are decorated with motives of native origin and development including characteristic meanders, conventional plant motives among which the peony is important, good-luck symbols, and such traditional themes as the kilims.

The carpets from the Caucasus region are primarily geometrical in design. In the early pieces they reflect the Persian court styles with foliation and even animal forms but all reduced to a very precise and rich geometry but very bold in scale. The principal design elements of the later Caucasus rugs are the lattice system (fig. 26), enclosing conventionalized flowers and foliage (figs. 23, 25), complex polygons (fig. 24) and radial rosettes (fig. 28), a cross pattern with foliation on the diagonal, also derived from early 16th century Persian carpets, a design that was developed from Assyrian times.

The finest of the Caucasus weavings are varied in colour, of clear and resonant tones, colours which tended to meagreness as the art degenerated toward the end of the 19th century.

BIBLIOGRAPHY.—F. R. Martin, *A History of Oriental Carpets Before 1800* (Vienna, 1908); F. Sarre, *Altorientalische Teppiche* (Leipzig, 1908); W. Bode and E. Kühnel, *Vorderasiatische Knüpfteppiche aus älterer Zeit* (Leipzig, 1922; English translation by R. M. Riefstahl, New York, 1922); A. F. Kendrick and C. E. C. Tattersall, *Handwoven Carpets, Oriental and European* (London, 1922); F. Sarre and H. Trenkwald, *Altorientalische Teppiche* (Leipzig-Vienna, 1926–29; English transl. by A. F. Kendrick entitled *Old Oriental Carpets*, Vienna-Leipzig, 1926–29); W. Grote Hasenbalg, *Der Orientteppich, seine Geschichte und seine Kultur* (Berlin, 1922); R. Neugebauer and S. Troll,

Handbuch der orientalischen Teppichkunde (Leipzig, 1930); A. U. Dilley, *Rugs and Carpets* (1931); John Kimberley Mumford, *Oriental Rugs* (1902); Walter A. Hawley, *Oriental Rugs* (1913). Collections: A. F. Kendrick and C. E. C. Tattersall, *Guide to the Collection of Carpets, in Victoria and Albert Museum* (London, 1931); K. Erdmann, *Orientteppiche, Islamische Abteilung d. Staatlichen Museum* (Berlin, 1935); A. Riegl, "Altere Orientalische Teppiche aus dem Besitz des allerhöchsten Kaiserhauses," in *Jahrbuch der Kunsthistorischen Sammlungen*, xiii, p. 267 sqq. (Vienna, 1892); J. K. Mumford, *The Yerkes Collection of Oriental Carpets* (London, 1910); J. Breck and F. Morris, *The James F. Ballard Collection of Oriental Rugs* (New York, 1923); Heinrich Jacoby, *Eine Sammlung Orientalischer Teppiche* (Berlin, 1922); J. Arthur MacLean, *Catalogue of Oriental Rugs in the Collection of James F. Ballard* (Indianapolis, 1924). Exhibitions of Carpets: F. Sarre and F. R. Martin, *Die Ausstellung von Meisterwerken muhammedanischer Kunst in München*, 1910, i (Munich, 1912); W. R. Valentiner, *Catalogue of a Loan Exhibition of Early Oriental Rugs, Metropolitan Museum of Art* (New York, 1910); A. U. Pope, *Catalogue of a Loan Exhibition of Early Oriental Carpets, Arts Club of Chicago* (Chicago, 1926); M. S. Dimand, *A Guide to an Exhibition of Oriental Rugs and Textiles, Metropolitan Museum of Art* (New York, 1935). Miscellaneous: J. Lessing, *Altorientalische Teppiche nach Bildern und Originalen des XV bis XVI Jahrhunderts* (Berlin, 1877); (English edition: London, 1879; French edition: Paris, 1879). Special works: M. S. Dimand, "An Early Cut-Pile Rug from Egypt," in *Metropolitan Mus. Studies*, iv, p. 151–162 (1933); F. Sarre, "Die ägyptische Herkunft der sogenannten Damaskus-Teppiche," in *Zeitschrift für Bildende Kunst*, i, p. 75 sqq. (1921); F. Sarre, "Die ägyptischen Teppiche," in *Jahrbuch der Asiatischen Kunst*, i, p. 19 sqq. (1924); F. Sarre, "Mittelalterliche Knüpteppiche kleinasiatischer und spanischer Herkunft," in *Kunst und Kunsthandwerk*, x, p. 503 sqq. (1907); R. M. Riefstahl, "Primitive Rugs of the 'Konya' Type in the Mosque of Beyesehir," in *Art Bulletin*, xiii, p. 177–220 (1931); K. Erdmann, "Orientalische Tierteppiche auf Bildern des XIV und XV Jahrhunderts," in *Jahrbuch der Preussischen Kunstsammlungen*, l, p. 261–298 (1929); A. U. Pope, "The Myth of the Armenian Dragon Carpets," in *Jahrbuch der Asiatischen Kunst*, ii, p. 147 sqq. (1925); A. Sakisian, "Les tapis à dragons et leur origine arménienne," in *Syria*, ix, p. 238–256 (1928); K. Erdmann, "Later Caucasian Dragon Carpets," in *Apollo*, xxii, p. 21–25 (1935); E. Schmutzler, *Altorientalische Teppiche in Siebenbürgen* (Leipzig, 1933); A. U. Pope, "History of Persian Carpets," in *A Survey of Persian Art; idem*, "Un tappeto persiano del 1521 nel Museo Poldi-Pezzoli," in *Dedalo*, vii, p. 82 sqq. (1927); K. Erdmann, "Tappeti Persiani," in *Dedalo*, xii, p. 707–738 (1932); M. S. Dimand, *Loan Exhibition of Rugs of the So-called Polish Type in the Metropolitan Museum* (New York, 1930); V. Slomann, "The Coronation Carpet of the King of Denmark," in *Bull. of the Amer. Institute for Persian Art*, no. 7, p. 13–18 (1934); T. H. Hendley, *Asian Carpets, XVIth and XVIIth Century Designs, from the Jaypur Palaces* (London, 1905); F. Sarre, "Some Fifteenth Century Spanish Carpets," in *Burlington Magazine*, xx, p. 46 sqq. (1911); A. van de Put, "Some Fifteenth Century Spanish Carpets," in *Burlington Magazine*, xix, p. 344 (1911); E. Kühnel, "Maurische Teppiche aus Alcaraz," in *Pantheon*, vi, p. 416–420 (1930); P. Ricard, "Tapis de Rabat," in *Hespéris, Archives Berbères et Bulletin de l'Institut des Hautes Études Marocaines*, iii, p. 125 sqq. (1923); P. Ricard, "Corpus des tapis marocains," i, *Tapis de Rabat* (Paris, 1923); A Bogoloubov, *Tapis de l'Asie centrale* (St. Petersburg, 1908); R. Ettinghausen, "Kali" in *The Encyclopaedia of Islam*, Supplement no. 2 (1936); A. U. Pope, "Oriental Rugs as Fine Art," in *International Studio* (New York, Nov. 1922–April 1923); A. U. Pope, "Values in Oriental Rugs," in *Arts and Decoration* (New York, June, Aug., Oct. 1922); J. deVégh and Charles Layer, *Tapis Turcs* (Paris, 1925); A. U. Pope, "The Art of Carpet Weaving (Persian)," *Survey of Persian Art*, vol. iii, pp. 2257–2465 (1938); *ibid.*, vol. vi, Pls. 1107–1275 (64 in colour).

(A. U. P.)

RUHLA, a town of Germany, in the *Land* of Thuringia. Pop. (1933) 8,212. It stretches along the valley of the Erb 8 mi. S. of Eisenach, and attracts a number of visitors owing to its surroundings and its mineral springs. Its staple industry is the making of wooden and meerschaum pipes; it also manufactures electrical apparatus, amber ware, watches and toys.

RUHNKEN, DAVID (1723–1798), one of the most illustrious scholars of the Netherlands, was of German origin, having been born in Pomerania in 1723. His parents had him educated for the church, but after two years at the University of Wittenberg he determined to live the life of a scholar. At Wittenberg Ruhnken lived in close intimacy with the two most distinguished professors, Ritter and Berger. To them he owed a thorough grounding in ancient history and Roman antiquities and literature; and from them he learned a pure and vivid Latin style. But neither at Wittenberg nor at any German university was Greek seriously studied, so Ruhnken went to Leyden, where, stimulated by the influence of Bentley, the great scholar Tiberius Hemsterhuis had founded the only real school of Greek learning which had existed on the Continent since the days of Joseph Scaliger and Isaac Casaubon. At Leyden he became a close friend of Hemsterhuis, and when Hemsterhuis died in 1766 Ruhnken and his fellow-pupil Valckenaer carried on the tradition. With the exception of a fruitful year (1755) spent in the libraries of Paris, he spent the rest of his life at Leyden where he died in 1798.

Ruhnken's principal works are editions of (1) Timaeus's *Lexicon of Platonic Words*, (2) Thalelaeus and other Greek commentators on Roman law, (3) Rutilius Lupus and other grammarians, (4) Velleius Paterculus, (5) the works of Muretus. He also occupied himself much with the history of Greek literature, particularly the oratorical literature, with the Homeric hymns, the scholia on Plato and the Greek and Roman grammarians and rhetoricians. A discovery famous in its time was that in the text of the work of Apsines on rhetoric a large piece of a work by Longinus was embedded.

See Wyttenbach, *Vita Ruhnkenii* (Leyden, 1799).

RUHR, a river of Germany, 142 mi. long, an important right-bank tributary of the lower Rhine. It rises on the side of the Winterberg in the Sauerland, at about 2,000 ft. above the sea. It flows north and then west in a deep, well-wooded valley past the town of Arnsberg. Shortly after reaching Neheim it bends south-west, and courses through the important mining district of the Ruhr coalfield around Hagen. Hence in a tortuous course it passes Witten, Steele, Kettwig and Mülheim, and joins the Rhine at Ruhrort. The river is navigable from Witten downwards, by the aid of eleven locks. Its chief affluents are the Mähne (right) and Lenne (left).

French Occupation.—Though the occupation of the left bank of the Rhine arranged for in the Treaty of Versailles included the bridgehead at Cologne, and thus practically touched the Ruhr district, the French were not satisfied from a military point of view, as the "Westphalian basin" was the hub of the German iron and steel industry. In March 1921 the French extended the occupation to Duisburg, Ruhrort and Düsseldorf, containing 5,000 sq.km. and 877,000 inhabitants, as a sanction for Germany's refusing the Paris reparation proposals; another 37,700 sq.km. with 3,191,000 inhabitants were occupied during 1923–24, when they controlled almost the entire Ruhr district.

Before World War I most of the Lorraine iron and steel works were owned by or closely affiliated with concerns in the Ruhr. The low grade iron ore of Lorraine, apart from the quantities used on the spot went to the blast furnaces of the Ruhr. Of 21,100,000 tons mined, 3,100,000 tons went to the Ruhr. On the other hand the coke of the Ruhr was needed for the smelting of Lorraine ores, while the finished iron and steel goods of Lorraine found their market in southwestern Germany.

The re-annexation of Alsace-Lorraine and the retirement of Luxembourg from the German customs union reduced Germany's home supply of iron ore to about 20% of its former size. At the same time France became the greatest iron ore producing country of Europe; moreover she controlled the well equipped iron and steel mills in Lorraine, expropriating the German iron and steel-masters. She also temporarily annexed the Saar mines, partly in the hope of getting coke for her iron industries. As the Saar coal did not coke well, special clauses were inserted in the Treaty of Peace, guaranteeing to France (and to the other Allies) a regular supply of the Ruhr coal and coke at statutory prices.

Political pressure apart, however, the German coalmasters held the winning hand. Compensation from the German government enabled them to erect new iron and steel works on the Ruhr, which could easily be run with high-grade Swedish or Spanish ore or with the enormous quantities of scrap available after the war. The low grade Lorraine ore, on the other hand, had either to be smelted locally or sent to the Ruhr. Smelting in Lorraine depended on the regular supply of Ruhr coke. And the export of finished products depended mainly on German markets which were open to France without duty for five years only (within the limits of Alsace-Lorraine's prewar sales to Germany). Thus those who controlled the Ruhr coal really controlled the Lorraine iron and steel industry.

As early as the Conference of Spa (1920) when Germany had

fallen short on coal deliveries, the Allies presented her with an ultimatum, which threatened the occupation of the Ruhr in case of non-acceptance. Though this extension of the area of occupation was an arbitrary act, the German Government gave way. From this moment the French began to use this threat of an extension of the occupation as a weapon in the struggle about reparation. When the German Government refused the proposals of the Paris Conference (Jan. 29, 1921) they occupied Düsseldorf, Ruhrort and Duisburg, and continued the occupation after Germany had accepted the London ultimatum of May 5, 1921.

On Dec. 26, 1922, the Reparation Commission under French pressure announced that Germany had fallen short on the delivery of 20,000 cu.m. of boards and of 130,000 telegraph poles, the total averaging but a few million marks; a few days later a similar shortcoming in coal-deliveries variously estimated at 11 to 15·6%, was declared. Against the vote of the British delegates the Reparation Commission came to the conclusion that Germany's short-comings had been "intentional" (*manquement volontaire*), constituting a case under Annex 11 § 18, which permitted the Allied and Associated Powers to take "such other measures as the respective Governments may determine to be necessary in the circumstances." The French and Belgian Governments decided to send a commission of engineers into the Ruhr, to control the activities of the Coal Syndicate and the carrying out of the deliveries as, in their opinion the coal mine owners were trying to sabotage the Treaty. This technical mission, in which Italy was to participate, but not Great Britain, was accompanied by a military force, though military occupation was not intended.

When the French and Belgian troops entered the Ruhr on Jan. 11, 1923, the Coal Syndicate had transferred their seat and their papers to Hamburg. The German Government issued a protest (Jan. 12, 1923); all reparation payments especially the delivery of coke and coal to France and Belgium ceased. Civil servants and railway officials were forbidden to obey orders from the occupying powers. The French tried to get hold of the proceeds of taxes and of government property. They controlled the distribution of coal and insisted on cutting timber. They expelled the German officials, railway servants and leading citizens and heavily fined or imprisoned recalcitrants. They erected a customs frontier, dividing the occupied district from the rest of Germany, thus controlling and stopping exports and imports into unoccupied Germany. The aim of the German resistance was to prevent the French from getting coal and coke, whilst the French tried to cut the connection with unoccupied Germany and to paralyse the district's economic life.

The struggle for the Ruhr completely destroyed German finance and with it German currency. Passive resistance in the long run meant the withdrawal of all workers, starting with the railway men, from such productive and distributive processes as might help the army of occupation. This involved the maintenance of all persons out of work at the public expense. The Ruhr occupation was the deciding factor in the collapse of the mark.

Germany's various proposals for a settlement were not accepted by the French, nor were the various suggestions of the British. At last the new German Government, presided over by Stresemann, gave up passive resistance on Sept. 26. The French Government continued to refuse negotiations and strongly supported the separatist movement all over the left bank of the Rhine.

In Nov., 1923, the industrial concerns in the occupied districts negotiated an agreement with the *Mission Interalliée de Contrôle des Usines et des Mines* (called Micum) with the object of freeing the huge iron and coal stocks which had accumulated, as the French Government would not negotiate with the German Government. It demanded the payments of the German coal tax and the coal on the dumps, whilst the new output could be sold by the works against payment of a duty; the delivery of reparation coal and coke was to be resumed on a percentage basis of the total output. Iron and steel might be sold by the works against payments. The German Government (by letters of Nov. 1 and 21) acknowledged their obligation to refund the cost of payments of delivery to the industries concerned. They did so later on by paying the iron and coal firms 700,000,000 marks.

These provisional arrangements paved the way for peace, after British and American pressure had induced the French government to agree to the appointment of the Dawes committee by the Reparation Commission. The total payments realized from the Ruhr were 490,000,000 gold marks in cash and the value of 491,-900,000 gold marks in goods, leaving a total balance—after deduction of 184,000,000 marks expenses—of 798,000,000 gold marks—or not a third of the minimum payment expected under the London ultimatum.

The new French Government was willing to accept the Dawes plan, to free the prisoners and to leave the Ruhr. The plan was formally signed on Aug. 30. Within the next two months administration, railways and government property were handed back to Germany. The evacuation of the Ruhr ended on July 31, 1925 when the French troops left Essen and Mülheim. On Aug. 25 the old occupied areas of Düsseldorf, Duisburg and Ruhrort were given back.

After political pressure ceased, the mere compulsory economic co-operation of the Treaty of Versailles came to an end. But the German industrialists had realized that France had held the winning cards in the political game, whilst the French Government began to understand the limits of military pressure in the economic field. The result was the Franco-German commercial treaty, and the Franco-German (international) iron-and-steel pact. The former secured French iron and steel goods a limited sale in German territory, to be effected through the German Steel Syndicate, whilst the ore and coal supplies were left to more or less private agreements. The latter combined French and German and Belgian steel works in an international syndicate, giving each country a fixed percentage of the total output.

The economic unity which the Treaty of Peace had destroyed, was thus being restored by extremely complicated measures, after a six years' struggle between governments and industrial groups, which cost much money and bloodshed. After Germany's entry into the League of Nations and the Locarno treaties the plan of using the Ruhr as an additional security became obsolete.

BIBLIOGRAPHY.—*Survey of international affairs*, 1925 Supplement (London, 1928); C. Bergmann, *Der Wag der Reparationen* (Frankfurt-am-Main, 1926); *see* also German official publications.   (M. Bo.)

RUHRORT, after 1905 a part of Duisburg, in the Prussian Rhine province, Germany, at the junction of the Ruhr and the Rhine, in the midst of a productive coal district, 15 mi. N. of Düsseldorf and 12 mi. E. of Crefeld by rail. Ruhrort is first mentioned in 1379 and obtained civic rights in 1551. Having been in the possession of the counts of La Marck, it passed into that of Brandenburg in 1614. Ruhrort has one of the largest river harbours in the world, and it is the principal shipping port for the coal of the Westphalian coalfield, which is dispatched in the fleet of steamtugs and barges belonging to the port. The coal is sent ordinarily to south Germany and the Netherlands. Grain and timber are also exported and iron ore is imported. The industries of the former town include large iron and steel works, shipbuilding yards and tanneries. The area was heavily bombed during World War II.

RUIZ, JUAN (*c.* 1283–*c.* 1350), Spanish poet, became archpriest of Hita. It may be inferred from his writings that he was not an exemplary priest, and one of the manuscript copies of his poems states that he was imprisoned by order of Gil Albornoz, archbishop of Toledo. It is not known whether he was sentenced for his irregularities of conduct, or on account of his satirical reflections on his ecclesiastical superiors. What seems established is that he finished his *Libro de buen amor* in 1343, while in gaol, and that he was no longer arch-priest of Hita in Jan. 1351; it is assumed that he died shortly before the latter date.

Ruiz is by far the most eminent poet of mediaeval Spain. His natural gifts were supplemented by his varied culture; he clearly had a considerable knowledge of colloquial (and perhaps of literary) Arabic; his classical reading was apparently not extensive, but he knew by heart the *Disticha* of Dionysius Cato, and admits his indebtedness to Ovid and to the *De Amore* ascribed to Pamphilus; his references to Blanchefleur, to Tristan and to Yseult, indicate an acquaintance with French literature, and he utilizes the *fabliaux* with remarkable deftness; lastly, he adapts fables and apologues from Aesop, from Pedro Alfonso's *Disciplina clericalis,* and from mediaeval bestiaries. All these heterogeneous materials are fused in the substance of his versified autobiography, into which he intercalates devout songs, parodies of epic or forensic formulae, and lyrical digressions on every aspect of life. Ruiz, in fact, offers a complete picture of picaresque society in Spain during the early 14th century. From his Don Furón is derived the hungry gentleman in *Lazarillo de Tormes,* in Don Melón and Doña Endrina he anticipates Calisto and Melibea in the *Celestina,* and Celestina herself is developed from Ruiz' Trotaconventos. Moreover, Ruiz was justly proud of his metrical innovations. The *Libro de buen amor* is mainly written in the *cuaderna via* modelled on the French alexandrine, but he imparts to the measure a variety and rapidity previously unknown in Spanish.

See J. Puyol y Alonso, *El Arcipreste de Hita* (1906).   (J. F.-K.)

RUIZ ZORRILLA, MANUEL (1834–1895), Spanish politician, born at Burgo de Osma. Deputy in 1856, he soon attracted notice among the most advanced Progressists and Democrats. After the military movement in Madrid of June 22, 1866, he had to flee to France, returning only at the revolution of 1868. In 1869 he became minister of grace and justice under Serrano: elected president of the House of Deputies in 1870, he seconded Prim in offering the throne to Amadeus of Savoy. In 1871 he formed a cabinet, and continued to be the king's chief councillor until his abdication (Feb. 1873), when Ruiz Zorrilla advocated a republic. On the restoration of Alphonso XII (1875), he went to France, where for nearly 18 years he was the soul of the republican conspiracies. He was eventually allowed to return to Spain and died at Burgos on June 13, 1895.

RUKWA (sometimes also Rikwa and Hikwa), a shallow lake in Tanganyika Territory, lying 2,650 ft. above the sea in a north-west continuation of the rift valley which contains Lake Nyasa. The sides of the valley here run in steep parallel walls 30 to 40 mi. apart, from south-east to north-west, leaving between them a level plain extending from about $7\frac{1}{2}°$ to $8\frac{1}{2}°$ S. This whole area was once covered by the lake, but this has shrunk so that the permanent water occupies only a space of 30 by 12 mi., immediately under the east escarpment. In the rains it extends about 40 mi. farther north, and the north of the plain is likewise then covered with water to a depth of about 4 ft. The rest of the plain is a bare expanse intensely heated by the sun in the dry season, and forming a tract of foul mud near the lake shores. The lake has two large feeders. The one from the west, the Saisi, or Momba, rises in 8° 50′ S., 31° 30′ E., and traverses a winding valley cut out of the high plateau between lakes Nyasa and Tanganyika. The other chief feeder, the Songwe, rises in 9° 8′ S., 33° 30′ E. on the same plateau as the Saisi and flows north-west. The Songwe is joined by the Rupa. The maximum depth of the lake is about $10\frac{1}{2}$ ft. Its water is very brackish and of a milky colour from the mud stirred up by the wind. It contains many fish.

RULED SURFACE: *see* SURFACE; MATHEMATICAL MODELS.

RULE OF ST. BENEDICT: *see* BENEDICT OF NURSIA, SAINT.

RULE OF THE ROAD. In the United States the term "rule of the road" customarily applies to the entire composite of regulations governing the movement of vehicles on public highways. Basic to this body of law is the rule that, unless otherwise posted, travel is on the right half of the highway except when overtaking and passing other vehicles. By posting, a highway may become entirely one-way, or the centre portion of three-lane highways may be reserved for certain movements. Vehicles meeting each other pass on the right, each driver yielding at least half the highway. Upon overtaking another vehicle travelling in the same direction, passing is accomplished on the overtaken vehicle's left, with a duty upon the passing driver to clear the passed vehicle by a safe distance before returning to the right-hand lane. Overtaking and passing on the right are permissible only when (1) the overtaken vehicle is making a left turn; (2) two or more lines of vehicles are moving in the same direction; or (3) upon one-way streets. Self-evidently, highway safety requires that driving to the left of the centre line be prohibited upon a curve or when approaching the crest of a hill, a railroad crossing or a structure preventing normal visibility.

Fundamental to all right-of-way rules is the principle that no one is authorized to take the right of way regardless of consequences, but rather, under certain circumstances one must yield the right of way to others. At intersections right of way must be yielded to vehicles already in the intersection, or where two vehicles approach from different directions at the same time, the vehicle on the left must yield to the one on the right. Drivers intending to turn left at an intersection yield right of way to vehicles coming from the opposite direction already in the intersection.

Special stops are customarily required for all vehicles at railroad crossings having frequent service, limited view or difficult approaches; and for certain types of vehicles (*i.e.,* school buses, vehicles carrying passengers for hire and trucks hauling explosives or inflammables) at all railroad crossings. Similarly, all vehicles must stop at designated through highways and before emerging from alleys and driveways. Vehicles overtaking or approaching a school bus loading or discharging passengers must stop short of the bus until signalled to proceed by the bus driver. Parking restrictions in municipalities are largely matters of local determination. On open highways, however, state laws prohibit the parking of vehicles whenever they may possibly be moved off the highway.

Pedestrians' rights and duties include crossing streets in obedience to traffic control devices at marked crosswalks. When crossing at other than authorized crosswalks, pedestrians yield right of way to vehicles. Notwithstanding statutory duties, drivers must exercise due care toward pedestrians at all times since young children, aged and infirm persons and persons of little experience with traffic rules constantly create unforeseeable situations. Pedestrians walking along highways are required to walk on the left side facing oncoming traffic.

Although many states define speed limits in terms of fixed maximums, the most approved rule provides a basic prohibition against driving at a speed more than reasonable and prudent under existing traffic conditions, together with prima-facie limits beyond which the driver is presumed in law to be in violation of the limit and must prove that he was driving safely. Prima-facie limits vary for residential and business districts, school zones and open highways, and for day and night driving. Minimum limits are frequently established for areas where slow speeds create traffic safety hazards.

The rule of the road requires drivers to signal their intention to turn and stop. Although considerable variation exists in state laws, the favoured method of signalling specifies that the hand and arm be extended horizontally for a left turn, upward for a right turn and downward for stopping or decreased speed. Traffic laws also require that at night headlights be dimmed when approaching other vehicles and that all vehicles, parked or moving, carry front and rear identifying lights.

After 1945 increasing attention was given to legislation permitting use of lights instead of hand signals. Also, increased average traffic speeds led to upward revision of prima-facie speed limits and use of the right lane of multiple-lane highways for slow-moving vehicles. Heavy concentrations of vehicles in urban areas has led to increasing experimentation with one-way streets and limited access throughways as means of facilitating traffic flow. The need for uniformity of traffic rules was recognized by the National Conference on Street and Highway Safety in 1924. As an outgrowth of this conference, the National Committee on Uniform Traffic Laws and Ordinances drafted the Uniform Vehicle code (1926) and Model Traffic ordinance (1928). This code and ordinance, revised quadrennially from 1926, provided models for uniform state and municipal legislation. By 1952 the Uniform Vehicle code rules of the road were recognized in 28 states. Uniform design and location of traffic signs and control devices are based on the *Manual on Uniform Traffic Control Devices* developed by a joint committee of the American Association of State Highway Officials, Institute of Traffic Engineering and National Committee on Uniform Traffic Laws and Ordinances.

BIBLIOGRAPHY.—National Committee on Uniform Traffic Laws and Ordinances, *Uniform Vehicle Code,* ch. 11 (1954), *Model Traffic*

Ordinance (1953); American Automobile Association, *Sportsmanlike Driving*, ch. 12 (1955), *Digest of Motor Laws*, 22nd ed. (1955).
(R. D. N.)

GREAT BRITAIN

The rule in Great Britain and Ireland that vehicles should keep to the left was formerly a custom which the courts would enforce; in other words, it was a matter of common law, and its origin is too remote for anything but conjecture. It acquired the force of statute under s. 78 of the Highways act of 1835, which laid down that all vehicle drivers must keep to the left side of the road when encountering other traffic. Those seeking for a reason for the original choice have surmised that the left side was adopted because drivers needed to have their whip hand free, which would not have been possible on the narrow tracks and roads then existing if the right side had been selected. A more fanciful explanation was that it was thought wise, in turbulent times, for horsemen to keep to that side of the road which would admit of the sword arm being free in case of attack. But, while plausible, both these theories leave unexplained why most other nations reversed the order, their traffic flowing along the right side of the road. On the continent of Europe the right is the correct side for wheeled traffic in nearly every country. In North and South America, too, the right is the correct order of the road for wheeled traffic.

The rule of the road acquired new importance with the advent of the motorcar, and the Motor Car order of 1904 directed that drivers of motor vehicles, when meeting other traffic, must keep to the left or near side of the road and when passing any traffic proceeding in the same direction must keep to the off or right side of it. The greatly increased use of the roads for motor traffic after World War I brought about a new approach to problems of road traffic and s. 45 of the Road Traffic act, 1930, laid upon the minister of transport the duty of preparing a code, comprising such directions as appeared to him to be proper for the guidance of persons using roads, and empowered him from time to time to revise this code as he thought fit. This code was referred to in the section and is generally known as the highway code.

The highway code is designed to prescribe a code of behaviour for all road users. There is nothing in the Road Traffic act, 1930, which repeals or amends s. 78 of the Highways act, 1835; and the rule referred to above is repeated in the highway code in the words "keep well to the left unless you are about to overtake or turn right," but the driver is told to overtake only on the right except when the driver in front has signalled that he is going to turn right. This direction is qualified by a note that it does not necessarily apply at roundabouts and in one-way roads or when overtaking streetcars. Nor does the rule apply to pedestrians, who are advised by the code to use a footpath where there is one but that, if there is no footpath, it is generally better to walk on the right so as to face oncoming traffic. In 1955 the future of the highway code was a matter of some controversy since a new edition was in preparation. But any change did not seem likely to affect the rule of the road, although the application of this was necessarily modified on roads where there was one-way traffic and on trunk roads.

The highway code removed one doubt in relation to led horses, namely, whether the horseman should ride with the led horse on the off or the near side. The code states unequivocally "When leading an animal, always place yourself between it and the traffic and keep the animal to the edge of the road."

The question of assimilating the rule of the road in all countries has been frequently discussed but by the mid-1950s it had aroused little interest and no action was in view. (W. T. Ws.)

RULE OF THE ROAD AT SEA. The present article is a summary of the regulations that came into force on Jan. 1, 1954, following the International Conference on Safety of Life at Sea, 1948. The regulations apply to all vessels on the high seas. A "power-driven" vessel means any vessel propelled by machinery. When under sail only she is considered a sailing vessel and under sail and power is considered a power-driven vessel. The rules for seaplanes apply when they are water-borne. Vessels and seaplanes are "under way" when not at anchor, moored or aground.

Lights and Shapes.—The word "visible" when applied to lights means visible on a dark night with a clear atmosphere. The rules concerning lights must be complied with in all weathers from sunset to sunrise. No other lights which might be mistaken for the prescribed lights, impair their visibility or interfere with the keeping of a proper lookout must be exhibited. Shapes shall be not less than two feet in diameter.

Power-Driven Vessels Under Way.—(1) *Masthead light:* in the fore part of the vessel a white light visible over an arc of 225°, *i.e.*, from right ahead to 22½° abaft the beam on either side for five miles; (2) a second white light of similar character either forward or abaft the above light (not compulsory for vessels less than 150 ft. in length or when towing). These two lights must be in line with the keel, one 15 ft. higher than the other. The horizontal distance between them must be at least three times the vertical distance. The lower light shall not be less than 20 ft. above the hull. (3) *Side lights:* (a) on the starboard side a green light clearly visible over an arc of 112½°, *i.e.*, from right ahead to 22½° abaft the beam for two miles; (b) on the port side a similar red light. These side lights must be fitted with screens projecting three feet forward of the light. (4) *Seaplanes:* (a) in the fore part amidships a white light visible over an arc of 220°, *i.e.*, from right ahead to 20° abaft the beam on either side for three miles; (b) on the starboard wing tip a green light visible from right ahead to 20° abaft the beam for two miles; (c) on the port wing tip a similar red light. (5) *Stern light:* (a) vessels under way shall carry at their stern a white light visible over an arc of 135°, *i.e.*, from right astern to 67½° on each side for two miles; (b) small vessels unable to carry this light must have ready an electric torch or lighted lantern to show to an overtaking vessel; (c) a seaplane shall carry a white light on her tail visible over an arc of 140°, *i.e.*, from right astern to 70° on each side for two miles.

Towing Lights.—(1) (a) A power-driven vessel towing or pushing another or seaplane shall carry in addition to her side lights two white masthead lights vertically, not less than six feet apart; if the tow exceeds 600 ft. an additional white light to be carried six feet above or below them; (b) a stern light or a white light abaft the funnel or aftermast for the tow to steer by. (2) A seaplane towing, in addition to her under way lights, shall show a second white light six feet above or below the forward white light.

Not Under Control.—(1) A power-driven vessel shall carry in lieu of the masthead lights, where best seen, two red lights vertically, not less than six feet apart and visible all round for two miles. By day, the red lights shall be replaced by two black balls. (2) A seaplane may carry, where best seen, two red lights vertically, not less than three feet apart, visible all round for two miles. (3) A vessel working telegraph cables, navigation marks, surveying or on underwater operations and unable to manœuvre shall carry in lieu of masthead lights three lights vertically, thus—red, white, red—visible all round for two miles. By day, similarly placed, she shall carry three shapes vertically, the highest and lowest globular in shape and red in colour, the middle diamond in shape and white. (4) Vessels and seaplanes not under control shall only carry side lights when making way through the water.

Sailing vessels under way, vessels and seaplanes towed shall carry the same lights as prescribed for a power-driven vessel or seaplane but not the masthead lights. *Small vessels unable to fix the side lights* must have them ready for immediate display on nearing another vessel.

Power-Driven Vessels of Less Than 40 Tons.—(1) In the fore part, not less than nine feet above the gunwale, a white light constructed and screened as a masthead light visible for three miles. (2) Side lights constructed and screened as described above visible for one mile, or a combined lantern showing green and red lights from ahead to 22½° abaft the beam on their respective sides. Small power-driven boats may carry the white light lower than nine feet but it must be higher than the side lights.

Vessels of less than 20 tons under oars or sails if without side lights shall carry a lantern fitted with a green and red light visible for one mile. *Rowing boats under oars or sails* shall show a white light from an electric torch or lantern in time to prevent collision.

Pilot Vessels.—(1) Sailing pilot vessels under way on station shall carry a white all-round light at the masthead visible for three miles and exhibit a flare-up light at intervals not exceeding ten minutes, and also show their side lights on the approach of or to other vessels. (2) Power-driven vessels on station duty under way shall carry the above lights and flares and eight feet below the white masthead light a red light visible all round for three miles and side lights. (3) When on station duty at anchor, pilot vessels will exhibit the above lights and anchor lights but not side lights. (4) When not on station duty, they shall carry the same lights as other vessels of their class and tonnage.

Anchor Lights and Shapes.—(1) Vessels less than 150 ft. in length shall carry forward a white light showing all round for two miles. (2) If 150 ft. or more, the above light not less than 20 ft. above the hull, and at the stern at least 15 ft. lower than the forward light, another such light, both to be visible all round for three miles. (3) Between sunrise and sunset every vessel at anchor shall carry forward one black ball. (4) Working telegraph cables, navigation marks, surveying or on underwater operations, a vessel at anchor shall carry the lights and shapes previously described for such vessels and also anchor lights. (5) A vessel aground shall carry by night anchor lights and the two red lights prescribed for a vessel not under control; by day three black balls, vertically not less than six feet apart. (6) Seaplanes less than 150 ft. long, a white light visible all round for two miles. If more than 150 ft., a white light forward and one aft, each visible all round for three miles. If more than 150 ft. in span, a white light on each side to indicate the maximum span, visible all round for one mile. If aground, they shall carry anchor lights and may carry two red lights vertically three feet apart, visible all round.

Fishing Vessels.—(1) When not fishing they shall show the lights and shapes for similar vessels of their tonnage. When fishing only the prescribed lights and shapes must be shown visible for two miles. (2) With trolling (towing) lines: as for a power-driven or sailing vessel under way. (3) With nets or lines (not trolling) extending less than 500 ft. into the seaway, an all-round white light and on the approach of or to another vessel, another white light six feet below it and at least ten feet horizontally from it in the direction of their gear. By day, display a basket, which must, if at anchor, be shown in the direction from the anchor ball toward the gear. If the gear extends more than 500 ft., three white lights in a vertical triangle, three feet apart, visible all round. Side lights must be shown only when making way through the water. By day, a basket must be shown close to the stern not less than ten feet above the rail; also, conspicuously, one black conical shape apex upward. At anchor with gear out they shall show the basket to approaching vessels in the direction from the anchor ball toward the gear. (4) (a) A power-driven vessel trawling shall carry in lieu of the masthead light, a tricoloured lantern showing a white light from right ahead to 22½° on each bow and green and red lights showing from 22½° on each bow to 22½° abaft the beam on the starboard and port sides respectively, and not less than 6 nor more than 12 ft. below the lantern a white all-round light and also a stern light; (b) sailing vessels trawling shall carry a white light showing all round and on approach of or to another vessel show a white flare-up light; (c) by day, vessels trawling shall display a basket in a conspicuous position. (5) Fishing vessels may in addition to the above lights show a flare-up light in order to attract attention, and use working lights. (6) Vessels fishing at anchor shall show anchor lights and shapes and an additional white light six feet below the forward anchor light and ten feet horizontally from it, in the direction of the gear. (7) (a) If a vessel when fishing becomes fast by her gear to an obstruction, she shall in daytime haul down the basket and show the shape required for a vessel at anchor, by night show anchor lights; (b) in bad visibility whether by day or night sound the signal for a vessel not under control which signal shall also be used on the approach of another vessel in good visibility.

Special Lights and Signals.—(1) Vessels and seaplanes may, to attract attention, show a flare-up light or use detonating sound signals which cannot be mistaken for any signal authorized elsewhere. (2) Ships of war, convoys and merchant ships may operate station or signal lights or recognition signals adopted by shipowners, duly authorized by their respective governments.

Vessels under sail and power in daytime shall display one black conical shape, point upward, carried forward.

Fog signals by whistle, siren, foghorn and bell. A "short blast" means one of one second; a "prolonged blast", one of four to six seconds. Signals prescribed shall be given by vessels, if power-driven, on the whistle; if sailing vessels, on the fog horn; if towed, on the whistle or fog horn.

In fog and restricted visibility, by day or night, the following signals shall be used. (1) Power-driven vessel making way: every two minutes a prolonged blast. (2) Stopped and not making way: every two minutes two prolonged blasts with one second between them. (3) Sailing vessel under way: every minute, on the starboard tack one blast; port tack two blasts; wind abaft the beam, three blasts. (4) A vessel anchored shall ring her bell rapidly for five seconds every minute. If more than 350 ft. in length: sound the bell forward, and aft sound a gong or similar instrument. She may also sound to approaching vessels, one short, one prolonged and one short in succession. (5) Towing or unable to manoeuvre: one prolonged and two short in succession every minute. (6) The last vessel of a tow: one prolonged and three short in succession every minute, after the towing vessels signal. (7) Vessel aground: three separate strokes on the bell immediately before and after ringing the bell as prescribed in (4). (8) Vessels less than 20 tons, rowing boats and seaplanes: an efficient sound signal every minute. (9) Vessels fishing of 20 tons upward: a blast followed by ringing the bell every minute.

Speed in Fog.—(1) Every vessel or seaplane shall in conditions of restricted visibility go at a moderate speed. (2) A power-driven vessel hearing, apparently forward of her beam, the fog signal of a vessel the position of which is not ascertained shall, circumstances permitting, stop her engines and then navigate with caution until danger of collision is over.

Steering and Sailing Rules.—*Sailing vessels* approaching one another with risk of collision shall take action as follows. (1) A vessel running free shall keep out of the way of the vessel close-hauled. (2) A vessel close-hauled on the port tack shall give way to the vessel close-hauled on the starboard tack. (3) When both are running free with the wind on different sides, the vessel with the wind on the port side shall keep clear of the other. (4) When both are running free with the wind on the same side, the vessel to windward shall keep clear of the one to leeward. (5) The vessel with the wind aft shall keep clear of the other vessel.

Power-Driven Vessels.—(1) When meeting end on or nearly end on with risk of collision, each shall alter course to starboard so that they pass port to port. This applies only to cases when by day each vessel sees the masts of the other in a line or nearly so with her own and by night to cases in which each vessel is in such a position as to see both the side lights of the other. For these purposes a seaplane shall be included as a power-driven vessel. (2) When two power-driven vessels are crossing so as to involve risk of collision, the vessel which has the other on her own starboard side shall keep out of the way of the other.

Power-Driven and Sailing Vessels.—(1) When risk of collision is involved the power-driven vessel shall keep out of the way of the sailing vessel. (2) A seaplane shall in general keep well clear of all vessels and avoid impeding their navigation. However, where risk of collision exists she shall comply with these rules.

General.—(1) Where by these rules one of two vessels is to keep out of the way of the other, the other shall keep her course and speed. When from any cause the latter vessel finds herself so close that collision cannot be avoided by the action of the giving-way vessel alone, she also shall take action as will best aid to avert collision. (2) Every vessel which is directed by these rules to keep out of the way of another vessel shall, if the circumstances of the case admit, avoid crossing ahead of the other. (3) Every power-driven vessel shall, on approaching another vessel which she is directed by these rules to keep clear of, if necessary slacken her speed, stop or reverse.

Vessels overtaking shall keep out of the way of the overtaken vessel. An overtaking vessel is one coming up with another from any direction more than 22½° abaft her beam, *i.e.*, a position from which by night she would be unable to see the side lights of the vessel she is overtaking and no subsequent alteration of the bearing between them shall make the overtaking vessel a crossing vessel within the meaning of these rules or relieve her of the duty of keeping clear until she is finally past and clear. If the overtaking vessel is doubtful whether she is forward or abaft this direction from the other vessel, she shall assume that she is an overtaking vessel and keep clear.

Narrow Channels.—(1) Every power-driven vessel proceeding along the course of the channel shall, when it is safe and practicable, keep to that side of the fairway or mid-channel which lies on the starboard side of such vessel. (2) A power-driven vessel nearing a bend in a channel when another vessel approaching from the other direction cannot be seen shall give a prolonged blast when within one-half mile of the bend, which signal shall be answered by a similar blast by any approaching power-driven vessel within hearing around the bend. The bend shall be rounded with alertness and caution.

All vessels not engaged in fishing shall keep out of the way of vessels fishing with nets, lines or trawls. This rule shall not give to any vessel engaged in fishing the right of obstructing a fairway used by vessels other than fishing vessels.

Navigational Dangers and Proper Precautions.—Due regard shall be had to all dangers of navigation and collision and special circumstances, including the limitations of the craft involved, which may render a departure from the rules necessary in order to avoid immediate danger. Nothing in these rules shall exonerate any vessel, owner, master or crew thereof from the consequences of any neglect to carry lights or signals or to keep a proper lookout or of the neglect of any precaution required by the ordinary practice of seamen or by the special circumstances of the case.

Sound Signals for Vessels in Sight of One Another.—(1) When vessels are in sight of one another, a power-driven vessel in taking any course authorized or required by these rules shall indicate that course by the following signals: one short blast to mean "I am altering my course to starboard"; two short blasts, "I am altering my course to port"; three short blasts, "My engines are going astern." (2) A power-driven vessel which is the stand-on vessel finding herself in doubt through the keep-out vessel not taking sufficient action to avert collision may indicate such doubt by giving at least five short and rapid blasts on the whistle, but this does not relieve her of any obligations under these rules or of her duty to indicate any action taken under them of giving the appropriate sound signals laid down under (1).

Reservation of Rules for Harbours and Inland Navigation.—Nothing in these rules shall interfere with the operation of a special rule duly made by local authority relative to the navigation of any harbour, river or inland water, including a reserved seaplane area.

Distress Signals.—Vessels and seaplanes in distress and requiring assistance from other vessels or the shore shall use or display the following signals either together or separately: (1) a gun or other explosion signal fired at intervals of about a minute; (2) a continuous sounding with any fog-signal apparatus; (3) rockets or shells throwing red stars fired one at a time at short intervals; (4) a signal made by radiotelegraphy or by any other signalling method consisting of the group SOS in the Morse code; (5) a signal sent by radiotelegraphy consisting of the spoken word "Mayday"; (6) the international code signal of distress NC; (7) a square flag having above or below it a ball or anything resembling a ball; (8) flames on the vessel (as from a burning tar barrel, etc.); (9) a rocket parachute flare showing a red light. (L. F. H.)

RULES OF ORDER, as the term is ordinarily used in the United States, embodies the generally accepted rules, precedents and practices commonly employed in the government of deliberative assemblies. Its function is to maintain decorum, ascertain the will of the majority, preserve the rights of the minority and facilitate the orderly and harmonious transaction of the business of the assembly. While it had its origin in the early British parliaments, the modern system of general parliamentary law is, in many respects, at wide variance with the current systems of procedure of both the English parliament and the U.S. congress. These legislative systems are designed for bicameral bodies, generally with paid memberships, meeting in continuous session, requiring a majority for a quorum and delegating their duties largely to committees. Their special requirements and the constantly increasing pressure of their business have produced highly complex and remarkably efficient systems peculiar to their respective bodies but which are as a whole unsuited to the needs of the ordinary assembly. As a result there has been simultaneously developed through years of experiment and practice a simpler system of procedure adapted to the wants of deliberative assemblies generally and which, though variously interpreted in minor details by different writers, is now in the main standardized and authoritatively established.

Organization.—Assemblies convene with the implied under-

standing that they will be conducted and governed in accordance with these fundamental principles. The routine ordinarily followed in the preliminary organization of an assembly includes the call to order by any of those present with a request for nominations for temporary chairman. The temporary chairman having been elected and having taken the chair, a temporary secretary is chosen and those addressing the chairman are recognized to explain and discuss the purposes of the meeting. If the assembly has convened for a single session only or is in the nature of a mass meeting a presiding officer and recording officer will suffice. If permanent organization is contemplated a committee is usually appointed to draft a constitution and bylaws and on the adoption of its report, with or without amendments, the assembly proceeds to the election of the permanent officers thus authorized. In a permanent organization such officers commonly consist of a presiding officer known as the president, chairman, speaker or moderator; a vice-presiding officer; a recording officer, known as the secretary or clerk, who keeps the records, attends to the clerical work of the organization and in the absence of the presiding officers calls for the selection of a temporary president; a treasurer or bursar who receives and disburses its funds; and a sergeant at arms who preserves order and carries out the wishes of the assembly through the presiding officer.

It is the duty of the presiding officer to call the assembly to order at the appointed time, cause the journal or minutes of the preceding meeting to be read, call up the business of the assembly in the order provided by its rules and conduct its proceedings in accordance with parliamentary law. He is especially charged with the responsibility of ascertaining the presence of a quorum, the minimum number of members prescribed by the rules of the assembly as competent to transact business. In legislative assemblies a quorum is presumed to be present unless the question is raised, but where the bylaws of an ordinary assembly require a quorum it devolves upon the presiding officer to ascertain that a quorum is present before proceeding with business.

Motions.—The will of an assembly is determined and expressed by its action on proposals submitted for its consideration in the form of motions or resolutions offered by members recognized for that purpose. In order to make a motion a member must rise and address the chair and secure recognition. If the motion is in order and is seconded by another member it is "stated" by the presiding officer and is then subject to the action of the assembly. A second is not required in legislative assemblies but is requisite under general parliamentary law. Motions may be classified as main or principal motions, introducing a proposition; and secondary or ancillary motions, designed to affect the pending main motion or its consideration. A main motion is in order only when there is no other business before the assembly, and yields in precedence to all other questions. Secondary motions may be subdivided into subsidiary, incidental and privileged.

Subsidiary motions are applicable to other motions for the purpose of modifying the main question or affecting its consideration and disposition. They have precedence of the motion to which applied but yield to privileged and incidental motions. They take precedence among themselves in the following order: to lay on the table; for the previous question; to close or extend debate; to postpone to a day certain; to commit, recommit and refer; to amend; and to postpone indefinitely.

Motion to Lay on the Table.—The motion to lay on the table is in effect a motion to suspend consideration of the question and, if agreed to, also suspends consideration of all pending questions relating to the motion to which applied until such time as the assembly may determine to take it from the table for further consideration. The motion is not debatable and may not be amended, postponed, committed, divided or reconsidered.

Motion for the Previous Question.—The purpose of the motion for the previous question is to close debate peremptorily and bring the assembly to an immediate vote on the pending question. It may be ordered on a single question, a group of questions or any part of a pending question, as on an amendment. It precludes both debate and amendment and requires a majority vote only for passage. It yields to the motion to table, to the question of consideration and to privileged and incidental motions and may be reconsidered, but takes precedence of motions to postpone, amend and commit.

Motion to Close or Extend Debate.—The motion is not admitted in either house of the U.S. congress when not sitting as committee of the whole but is in order under general parliamentary law and insofar as applicable is subject to the rules governing the previous question.

Motion to Postpone to a Day Certain.—This applies to the main motion and its pending amendments and is debatable only as to the advisability of the postponement proposed, and does not open to debate the subject matter of the motion to which applied. It is subject to amendment and reconsideration, to privileged and incidental motions, to motions for the previous question and to lay on the table but has precedence of all other subsidiary motions.

Motion to Commit, Recommit and Refer.—The motions to commit, recommit and refer are practically equivalent and provide for reference of the pending proposition to a committee. While the motion to recommit ordinarily applies to the whole subject including pending amendments, it may apply to certain features only. It may be amended as by adding instructions to the committee as to time and manner of report. Debate on the motion is limited to the question of reference and instructions. It takes precedence of motions to amend and indefinitely postpone but yields to other subsidiary motions and to all incidental and privileged motions. It may be tabled or postponed with the main question but no subsidiary motions except the motions to amend and for the previous question may be applied separately. It is subject to reconsideration at any time before the committee begins consideration of the question submitted to it but after that time the subject matter may only be reclaimed by a motion to discharge the committee.

Motion to Amend.—Changes in the text or terms of the proposition require a second and must be reduced to writing if requested by the chairman. There is no limit to the number of amendments which may be proposed and new amendments may be offered as rapidly as the pending amendment is disposed of. Amendments in the second degree, that is, amendments to amendments, are admissible but amendments in the third degree, that is amendments to amendments to amendments, are not in order. Only four amendments in the first and second degrees may be pending simultaneously, as follows: (1) amendment; (2) amendment to the amendment; (3) substitute for the amendment (*i.e.,* when it is desired to replace the entire pending amendment); and (4) amendment to the substitute. The amendment must, of course, be offered first and the substitute before the amendment to the substitute, but otherwise there is no rule governing the order in which the four amendments may be presented. They must, however, be voted on in the following order: first, amendments to the amendment; second, amendments to the substitute; third, the substitute; and last, the amendment. Debate on an amendment is in order only when the main motion is debatable, and is then limited to the proposed modification. An amendment which has been rejected may not be offered the second time in identical form, and no amendment may be proposed reversing the operation of an amendment previously adopted. Motions to amend will not be entertained unless germane or relevant to the main question, and no proposition different from that under consideration will be admitted under guise of amendment. This motion yields to all privileged, incidental and subsidiary motions except indefinite postponement. It is subject to amendment, to the operation of the previous question and to reconsideration, and when laid on the table carries with it the proposition proposed to be amended. Likewise, when the main question is laid on the table, postponed or recommitted, all pending amendments accompany it. The motion to amend is not applicable to the motion to lay on the table or for the previous question, to adjourn or to suspend the rules.

Motion to Postpone Indefinitely.—The motion to postpone indefinitely provides for final adverse disposition for the session and amounts to summary rejection. It is debatable and opens to debate the question to which applied but is subject to no subsidiary motion except the motion for the previous question.

Incidental Motions.—Incidental motions include questions arising incidentally in the consideration of other questions and decided before disposition of the one to which they are incident. They have no relative rank and merely take precedence of the pending question in the consideration of which they have arisen. All are undebatable with the exception of appeal. They comprise motions to suspend the rules, withdraw motions, read papers, raise the question of consideration, questions of order and appeal, reconsider, take up out of order, determine method of procedure, divide pending questions and questions relating to nominations.

The motion temporarily to suspend the rules may not be debated or reconsidered and is not subject to the application of any subsidiary motion. The vote required to pass the motion is ordinarily fixed by the rules of the assembly and in the absence of such provision is two-thirds of those present and voting.

Withdrawal or modification of a motion after it has been "stated" by the presiding officer is usually effected by unanimous consent but in event of objection by any member must be submitted to the assembly. Consent of the seconder is not required but if modified the seconder may withdraw the second. When applied to the main motion it includes all adhering motions, but when applied to amendments or adhering motions the main question is not affected. The reading of papers on which a vote is to be taken may be demanded by any member as a matter of right. Papers on which a vote is not required are usually read by unanimous consent but if objection is made the question must be submitted to the assembly.

The question of whether the assembly desires to take up a proposition regularly presented for its consideration may be tested by raising the question of consideration, which may be moved at any time before actual consideration commences and does not require a second. It is not in order after debate begins or after a subsidiary motion has been applied. When the question is properly raised the assembly may by a two-thirds adverse vote decline to take up any business it prefers not to consider.

Points of Order may be made while another has the floor, and when the question concerns the use of unparliamentary language the member so called to order must be seated pending disposition of the matter. The question must be raised at the time the proceeding giving rise to the objection occurs and will not be entertained after the assembly has passed to other business. If the point of order is overruled the member resumes the floor but if the objection is sustained he may proceed only by consent of the assembly. Debate on questions of order is for the information of the chair and may be closed by the presiding officer at any time. Any member may appeal from a decision by the chair and such appeal is debatable unless arising out of an undebatable question.

The motion to reconsider must be made by one who voted with the prevailing side but may be seconded by any member. It is only in order on the day or the next calendar day after the vote proposed to be reconsidered is taken. The motion is of the highest privilege and may be entered for record on the minutes while another has the floor, but cannot be called up for consideration until the pending question is disposed of, when it takes precedence of all new business. If applied to a debatable question it reopens the entire subject to debate. The motion may not be amended, committed or indefinitely postponed and requires a majority vote for passage. If agreed to, the motion reopens the entire question for further action as if there had been no final decision. The motion to take up out of order is merely another form of the motion to suspend the rules and requires a two-thirds vote for enactment. It is not amendable and debate is limited to the specific question presented.

A motion to divide the question is in order where the pending question includes propositions so distinct that, one being taken away, a substantive proposition will remain. Such motions are applicable to main questions and their amendments only and no subsidiary motion except the motion to amend is admitted. The rules of the U.S. house of representatives provide that any member may demand the division of a question as a matter of right, but under general parliamentary procedure the question must be submitted to the vote of the assembly.

Nominations do not require a second. Where the rules of an assembly fail to provide a method of nomination a motion for such provision is in order. The motion to close nominations is subject to none of the subsidiary motions save the motion to amend, and is decided by a two-thirds vote.

Privileged Motions relate to the needs and interests of the assembly and its members in matters of such urgent importance as to supersede temporarily pending business. They take precedence of all other motions and may be offered while other questions are pending. In this class of motions is the motion to fix the time to which to adjourn, to adjourn, to take a recess, raising questions of privilege and the call for the orders of the day, all of which are undebatable.

Other motions variously referred to as supplementary, miscellaneous and unclassified are the motions to take from the table, to discharge a committee, to accept the report of a committee, to rescind, to repeal, to annul, to expunge and to permit a member to resume the floor after having been called to order for words spoken in debate.

Rules for Debate.—In order to debate a question, a member must rise and address the chair and be recognized by the presiding officer for that purpose. The presiding officer should first recognize the mover of a proposition or the member of a committee presenting a report and should endeavour to alternate recognitions between those favouring and those opposing a question. It is also customary, though not necessarily incumbent upon the chair, to permit the proponent of a proposition to close debate. A member may speak but once on the same question at the same stage of the proceedings if others desire recognition, but is entitled to speak on the main question and on each amendment as presented. Under general parliamentary procedure a member securing the floor may speak without limit and this practice still obtains in the U.S. senate, but the house of representatives by rule limits speakers to one hour in the house and to five minutes in the committee of the whole. Most assemblies and all legislative bodies provide a limit for debate and in conventions it is customary to adopt a rule at the opening session limiting debate to a specified number of minutes. In debate a member must confine himself to the question under consideration, must avoid personalities and must not arraign motives. Members should be silent and respectful while another has the floor and in questioning the speaker should first address the chair, who will in turn inquire if the speaker desires to yield. Where the presiding officer is a member of the assembly he has the right to debate and to participate in the proceedings but should call another to the chair before taking the floor and should not resume it again until the pending question has been decided.

Voting.—Voting may be by ballot; by division, that is a rising vote; viva voce, that is by acclamation, the presiding officer deciding by the volume of voices; by show of hands; by tellers, the members passing between tellers appointed from opposite sides to count them as they pass through; and by yeas and nays, the clerk calling the roll and recording each vote as given. If there is doubt as to the result of a viva voce vote any member may request a division and the presiding officer thereupon proceeds to take a rising vote. A member may change his vote at any time prior to announcement of the result. Only members in attendance may vote and voting by proxy is never permissible unless by operation of law.

A tie vote defeats an affirmative motion. The presiding officer if a member of the assembly votes to break a tie but not to make one.

Committees.—Much of the work of assemblies and especially of legislative bodies is transacted by committees. The committee system provides for a better division of labour and for a more detailed consideration than the assembly as a whole is ordinarily prepared to give. Committees are classified as standing committees with fixed terms of office and rendering continuous service; and special committees serving temporarily and assigned to limited service. In the absence of a rule making other provision, committees are selected by the assembly. Frequently the chair is authorized to appoint committees. Or selection may be made by ballot, by resolution or by designation in motions of reference. If no

chairman is designated the member first named acts as chairman until the committee elects a chairman. As far as applicable the rules of the assembly govern its committees. The chairman of the committee submits its report to the assembly and unless it is of elementary character is required to present it in writing. Members who do not concur in the report may submit minority views over their signatures. When called up for consideration in the assembly such minority report is read in connection with the majority report unless there is objection, in which event the question of reading the minority views is submitted without debate to the vote of the assembly.

The committee of the whole consists of the entire assembly acting as a general committee. In legislative assemblies it affords greater freedom of consideration but in nonlegal bodies is rarely used.

Parliamentary Practice.—Use of motions to effect a purpose in the assembly or its committees when applicable may be summarized as follows: The body may protect itself against business which it does not wish to consider by invoking the motion to lay on the table, by raising the question of consideration or by voting to postpone indefinitely. If it is desired to suppress debate, the motion to limit debate and the demand for the previous question are available. Modification of a proposition may be secured through amendment or reference to a committee with or without instructions. Action may be deferred by postponement to a day certain, by providing a special order or by the motion to table. A question may be brought up a second time for consideration in the assembly by voting to take from the table, by reconsideration or by the motion to rescind, repeal or annul.

(C. CA.)

RULHIÈRE (or RULHIÈRES), **CLAUDE CARLOMAN DE** (1735–1791), French poet and historian, was born at Bondy, near Paris, on June 12, 1735. He served Marshal Richelieu in the Hanoverian campaign of 1757, and during his government at Bordeaux in 1758. At St. Petersburg (Leningrad) where he was sent as secretary of legation, he witnessed the revolution which seated Catherine II on the throne. In 1773 Rulhière became secretary to the future Louis XVIII; in 1787 he was admitted to the academy. He lived chiefly at Paris, where he held an appointment in the foreign office.

Rulhière died at Bondy on Jan. 30, 1791. He befriended J. J. Rousseau in his old age.

Rulhière's historical works include *Histoire de l'anarchie de Pologne* (4 vols., 1807), edit. P. C. F. Danon; and *Éclaircissements historiques sur les causes de la révocation de l'édit de Nantes* (2 vols., 1788).

RULLUS, PUBLIUS SERVILIUS, a Roman tribune of the people in 64 B.C., well known as the proposer of one of the most far-reaching agrarian laws brought forward in Roman history. This law provided for the establishment of a commission of ten, empowered to purchase land in Italy for distribution amongst the poorer citizens and for the foundation of colonies. The commission was to be invested with praetorian powers, and Pompey, then in the East, was excluded by a provision that personal attendance was necessary to election. In fact, the commission as a whole was intended to act as a counterpoise to his power. There were provisions for the purchase of further land by the sale of recently conquered territory and the use of the revenues from Pompey's provinces. The places to which colonies were to be sent were not specified, so that the commissioners would be able to sell wherever they pleased, and it was left to them to decide what was public or private property. Cicero delivered four speeches against the bill, of which three are extant. It was not greeted with enthusiasm and was dropped before the voting. The whole affair was obviously a political move, probably engineered by Caesar, his object being to make the democratic leaders the rulers of the state. Although Caesar could hardly have expected the bill to pass, the aristocratic party would be saddled with the odium of rejecting a popular measure, and the people themselves would be more ready to welcome a proposal by Caesar himself, an expectation fulfilled by the passing of the *lex Julia* in 59, whereby Caesar at least partly succeeded where Rullus had failed.

See the orations of *Cicero De lege agraria,* with the introduction in

G. Long's edition, and the same author's *Decline of the Roman Republic*, iii, p. 241; Mommsen, *Hist. of Rome*, bk. v, ch. 5; art. AGRARIAN LAWS.

RUM or ROUM, an indefinite term in use among Mohammedans at different dates for Europeans generally and for the Byzantine empire in particular; at one time for the Seljuk empire in Asia Minor, and now for Greeks inhabiting Ottoman territory (Arab. *ar-Rūm*). When the Arabs met the Byzantine Greeks, these called themselves 'Ρωμαῖοι, or Romans; so the Arabs called them "the Rūm" as a race-name (already in Qur. xxx, 1), their territory "the land of the Rūm," and the Mediterranean "the Sea of the Rūm." Later, inasmuch as Moslem contact with the Byzantine Greeks was in Asia Minor, the term Rūm became fixed there geographically and remained even after the conquest by the Seljuk Turks, so that their territory was called the land of the Seljuks of Rūm.

RUM is the potable spirit obtained by distillation of the fermented products of the sugar cane. Its source is principally the West Indies, where it originated, but there is a considerable production in the United States and it is produced in most sugar cane growing areas.

Rum (the origin of the name is uncertain) has a characteristic flavour which some people consider to be derived from the esters in the spirit but which has later been thought to be derived from the presence of a rum oil. The quantity and type of the esters and other secondary constituents vary according to the process of manufacture, of which there are numerous modifications. Thus, the raw materials may vary from fresh cane juice to skimmings and exhausted molasses, and the fermentation may be rapid or prolonged. Modern methods of manufacture with consequent closer control of fermentation and distillation produced marked improvement in the efficiency of the processes involved. The Sugar Industry commission of Jamaica, 1945, indicated that such improvements might profitably be extended in that island.

Jamaican Rum.—This spirit, made by a time-honoured process, is the product of the fermentation of the scum and washings from the boiling of cane juice together with primary molasses and "dunder," which is the residue left in the still from a previous distillation. The scum is allowed to sour, this being assisted by the addition of a small quantity of the fibrous residue (megasse) of the crushed cane. The other ingredients are added with water in proportions determined by the distiller to give a wash of specific gravity 1.072–1.096 and the whole is allowed to ferment over a period of 6 to 12 days or longer. Distillation from a pot still follows. Later practice involves the separate initial fermentation of part of the wash before its addition to the main bulk.

Jamaican rum is not produced at strengths exceeding 45° over proof and receives no additions other than caramel for colouring. There are two grades, one the usual drinking rum, the other a high ester rum for blending and the production of factitious rum.

Demarara Rum.—Practically the only raw material used in making Demarara rum is molasses, from which a slightly acid wash of specific gravity 1.065 is prepared by the addition of 1 pt. of sulphuric acid and 1 lb. of ammonium sulphate to 100 gal. of diluted molasses. The acidity checks the growth of undesired organisms and the ammonia provides yeast food, all designed to assist a rapid fermentation, which is complete in 48 hr. Both pot and patent stills are used for the distillation, the intention being to obtain a high yield of alcohol whose ester content, particularly higher esters, is low. Some Demarara spirit is subsequently flavoured.

United States Rum.—The only raw material used is blackstrap molasses from which a wash of definite acidity is prepared and fermented with pure culture yeast. Light rums of slight rum flavour are distilled at 190° American proof, broken down to just over proof and rapidly aged with oak chips. Heavier-bodied rum is distilled at 160° American proof and stored in oak barrels to age, whereby acids, esters, solids and colour are increased.

Other Rums.—Materials and methods of making rum in Cuba and Puerto Rico follow the U.S. pattern, Cuban rum being finally purified by filtration through charcoal to produce an almost neutral spirit which is subsequently flavoured.

Imitation rum is produced by flavouring a neutral spirit (obtained from grain, potatoes or beets) with high-ester Jamaican rum or with artificial essences. Originally manufactured in Europe, largely in Germany, its importation into Great Britain had practically ceased by mid-20th century. By customs order, 1891, entry was not allowed except as imitation rum, the title rum being reserved for spirits coming from ports in sugar-cane areas.

Pineapple rum, flavoured by the addition of the sliced fruit to the wash, and Negro rum made from sugar-cane refuse are potable. Bay rum is a spirituous perfumed hairwash made by dissolving oil of pimento (bay oil) in strong rum.

Rums may contain from 43% to 79% by volume of ethyl alcohol at importation. Other constituents, expressed as parts per 100,000, vary widely. (J. G. N. G.)

RUMANIA or RŎMANIA, a nation of southeast Europe to the north of the Balkan peninsula. Its area within the boundaries established after World War I covered 113,889 sq.mi., with a population of 18,025,237 at the census of 1930. In 1940 Rumania lost about a quarter of its territory. After the peace treaty of 1947 the estimated area was 91,671 sq.mi. and the population (census of 1948) 15,872,624.

RUMANIA AFTER WORLD WAR II AND THE PEACE TREATY OF 1947

PHYSICAL FEATURES

Rumania is a land of great contrasts and contains within its boundaries examples of most of the physiographical regions characteristic of the European continent. Of the total area within the 1947 boundaries, mountains occupy 26%, hills 39% and plains 35%.

The Carpathians form the predominant feature of Rumania. They run in a great arc from the junction of the Hungarian and U.S.S.R. frontiers in the north, in the districts of Maramures and Bukovina, to the junction of the Yugoslav and Bulgarian frontiers in the south. Within the arc lie the related Bihorului mountains, forming the core of Transylvania and distinguishing it from the plains of Hungary. These great ranges of alpine-fold mountains, which run in a continuous zone from the Danube river at Bratislava in Czechoslovakia to the Danube at the gorge of the Iron Gate in Rumania, form a link between the Alps proper and the Balkan ranges of Yugoslavia and Bulgaria.

In Rumania the mountains are characterized mainly by their penetrability. The rivers, which drain entirely toward the Danube, by cutting back into the numerous upland basins (*e.g.*, that of Brasov) provide routes linking the hills and plains on either side. Most of the summits are remarkably uniform in height, and the formation of what is almost a plain has resulted in gently rounded plateaus, forming the *plaiu* (way) or high alpine meadows above the deep forest-shrouded upper valleys. Sharp mountain peaks, such as those of the Fagaras mountains, are more the exception than the rule. One Danube tributary, the Olt, has, by cutting a narrow gorge, succeeded in crossing from the Transylvanian to the Walachian side of the Carpathians. Apart from the Olt, the other tributaries that drain southward to the Danube are the Jiu, the

Dambovita on which stands the capital Bucharest (Bucuresti) and the Ialomita. The eastern slopes of the Carpathians drain into the Siret (with its tributary, the Bistrita) and the Prut which join the Danube a little above its delta. The interior basins of Transylvania, together with the inner slopes of the Carpathians and the Bihorului mountains, are drained westward by a complicated network of headstreams which feed the Tisza (Tisa) and two of its major tributaries, the Somes and the Mures. One other river, the Timis, makes its way independently of the Tisza reaching the Danube at Belgrade.

Two crystalline massifs, composed mainly of granite and schist, form the northern and southern ends of the Carpathians in Rumania. They are, in the north, that of Bukovina-Maramures running northwest to southeast with summits usually reaching from 5,400 ft. to 6,400 ft. (Pietros is 7,568 ft.); in the south that of Banat-Transylvania, generally known as the Transylvanian Alps, running east-west and reaching over 7,400 ft. at many points. The highest peak in Rumania is Negoi (8,346 ft.) in the Fagaras mountains. Between these two terminal bastions, and linking them, is a somewhat lower north-south group, the Moldavian Carpathians, in which the so-called Flysch (folded and fractured sandstones, etc.) predominates. Along the inner edge of the ranges there are numerous examples of volcanic intrusions; e.g., the rocks forming the Caliman mountains in Maramures. The Bihorului mountains (about 6,000 ft.) are composed of both crystalline and volcanic rocks and show the rounded characteristic of the Rumanian ranges.

Within the arc of the Carpathians and abutting against the hard core of the Bihorului mountains lie the Tertiary rocks of the Transylvanian basin, a much-folded upland basin of sandstones and clays eroded into a country of hilly relief by the mountain-fed streams, the soft banks of which are much given to landslides. The outer edge of the mountain belt is ringed by the sub-Carpathian foothill zone bordering Moldavia and Walachia. The latter is subdivided into two smaller divisions by the Olt river, Oltenia to the west, Mutenia to the east. The foothills, composed of folded sedimentary rocks which provide the famous oil-bearing strata, afford one of the most verdant regions of the whole country.

The general accessibility of the Carpathians, which are crossed by numerous passes provided usually by low cols between the gently rounded mountain summits and often approached by upland basins, provides a contrast to the alpine-fold mountains elsewhere. In Rumania the mountains are not only crossed at many points, but actually form a well-populated region; with Transylvania they formed the cradle and refuge of the Rumanian nation above the tides of conquest that swept back and forth along the Danube plains and across the plains of northern Europe.

The most important passes—those followed by railway lines—are: (1) the Caransebes corridor leading from Timisoara to Orsova at the Iron Gate by way of the Porta Orientalis; this is an alternative to the Orient Express route; (2) the Olt gorge and the Red Tower (Turnu Rosu) pass leading from Oltenia to Transylvania; (3) the Predeal pass (3,445 ft.) linking Brasov with Ploesti and Bucharest, joining Muntenia (Greater Walachia) and Transylvania—the Orient Express route; (4) the Ghimes pass linking lower Moldavia and Transylvania and (5) the Bargau pass (3,940 ft.) linking Jassy (Iasi) in northern Moldavia and Chernovtsky (Cernauti), U.S.S.R. (a Rumanian city until 1940), with northern Transylvania.

The lowlands of Walachia and Moldavia consist in reality of plateaus of various elevations composed of horizontal or slightly tilted sedimentary strata of the Tertiary period, overlaid by a covering of recent deposits. These recent deposits, particularly in Moldavia, consist largely of the wind-borne loess, from which the rich black earth, or chernozem, soils are derived. The plateaus are crossed by the rivers descending from the Carpathian mountains. These streams are often deeply entrenched into the general level and are usually dry in the late summer when acute droughts are common. The Danube itself flows in a broad flood plain known as the Balta, characterized by numerous swamps and abandoned arms of the river, between bluffs marking the edge of the plateaus and the edge of the sub-Balkan platform of Bulgaria.

The Dobruja (Dobrogea), a unique region forming part of the sub-Balkan platform, consists of a core of folded crystalline rocks which are exposed in the northern hills (up to 1,300 ft.), but mainly concealed by a layer of chalk and recent deposits of loess. Dry valleys resembling the wadies of northern Africa dissect this hill region, which by its northward projection accounts for the diversion of the Danube in its lower course.

Climate.—Because Rumania is one of the more southerly European countries—the 45° N. parallel dissects the Danube delta—it is to be expected that it would experience high temperatures and much sunshine in summer. Atlantic influences, however, are remote (Bucharest is 26° E.). A great diurnal and seasonal range of temperature and a continental distribution of precipitation (with a marked early summer maximum) are characteristic of the whole country. The marked variations of relief have a great effect on climate; the plains of Moldavia and Walachia are essentially steppelike with less than 20 in. of rainfall a year, cold winters and hot summers, while the Carpathian foothills have enough rainfall to support verdant forests and enjoy slightly more temperate conditions. The Carpathian zone receives a much greater precipitation than the other highland districts of the country, and is much cooler. It has some of the heaviest snowfalls of Europe. Transylvania, although higher and mountain-fringed like the Hungarian basin, has a noticeably harsher climate than the other hill regions, and is not so suited to the ripening of maize and the warmer fruits.

The year is divided into three seasons—winter, summer and autumn. The winters are long, often with much snow, and unpleasant when the northeast wind (the *crivat*) brings severe conditions from the Russian steppes. Summer can be of tropical intensity; a feature of this season is the southwest wind (the *austru*) which sometimes brings oppressive weather. Late summer is occasionally accompanied, especially in the Moldavian and Walachian plains, by severe drought; if this is combined with excessively low winter temperatures it produces famine conditions like those that arose in 1947. Autumn is the most temperate and enjoyable season of the year.

Data for Bucharest taken from a representative year illustrate these general conditions: with a mean annual range of temperature between 26.6° F. (January) and 71.6° F. (July), Bucharest recorded absolute extremes of –11.2° F. and 102.2° F. There were 78 days with frost and an equal number with tropical heat; one-third of the days were cloudless, one-third partly overcast and one-third sunless.

Fauna.—In its fauna, Walachia has far more affinity to the lands lying south of the Danube than to Transylvania, although several species of *Claudilia,* once regarded as exclusively Transylvanian, are found south of the Carpathians. Moldavia and the Baragan steppe resemble the Russian prairies in their variety of molluscs and the lower kinds of mammals. More than 40 species of fresh-water mussels (Unionidae) have been observed in the Rumanian rivers. The lakes of the Dobruja likewise abound in molluscs—parent forms, in many cases, of species which reappear greatly modified, in the Black sea. Insect life is somewhat less remarkable; but besides a distinctive genus of Orthoptera (*Jaquetia hospodar*), there are several kinds of weevils (Curculionidae) said to be peculiar to Rumania. Birds are numerous, including four varieties of crows, five of warblers, seven of woodpeckers, eight of buntings, four of falcons and five of eagles, while among the hosts of waterfowl which inhabit the marshes of the Danube are nine varieties of ducks and four of rails. Roe deer, foxes and wolves find shelter in the forests, where bears are not uncommon. Chamois frequent the loftiest and most inaccessible peaks.

(G. W. S.)

HISTORY

The early history of the lands which constitute modern Rumania, down to the end of the period of Roman domination, is traced in the article DACIA. Roman rule in Dacia lasted for 163 years. The legions were finally withdrawn south of the Danube in 271 A.D. by the emperor Aurelian. From the 3rd to the 12th century wave after wave of barbarian invaders from the east passed over the undefended country—first came the Goths and

Gepidae, then Slavs, followed by the Avars (q.v.), and in the second half of the 7th century by the Bulgars. The Bulgarian domination, lasting for two centuries, allowed a rudimentary civic life to take shape, and it was the Bulgars who, after the conversion of their tsar Boris in 864, brought Christianity in its eastern form to the ancestors of the Rumanians, building on earlier Latin foundations (see *Religion* below.) At the end of the 9th century the Bulgars were overcome by the Magyars; later came a brief incursion by the now almost vanished Petchenegs and Cumans (qq.v.).

One school of historians maintains that the Daco-Roman population north of the Danube was obliterated during these invasions and that the Rumanians of today are descended from Vlach tribes south of the river who pushed northward in the early 13th century. The Rumanian view, supported by linguistic and other evidence, is that the Roman withdrawal affected only the military and official classes, while the body of the Daco-Roman inhabitants were driven by the invaders into the Carpathians, becoming the Vlachs of Transylvania. The Macedo-Romans south of the Danube, later known as Kutso-Vlachs, similarly sought shelter in the Pindus mountains. The controversy is considered in the article VLACHS.

Transylvania, regarded by Rumanians as the cradle of their nation, was conquered in the 11th century by King Stephen of Hungary, but all records of its early inhabitants were destroyed in the Mongol invasion of that country in 1241. The authentic history of the Vlachs does not begin until the end of the 13th century, when they are found establishing themselves south of the Carpathians in two distinct groups, one settling in the area later known as Walachia (called Muntenia by the chroniclers) and the other to the east in Moldavia. The incoming Vlachs fused with a population that already contained a Vlach element, but consisted mainly of Slavs and Tatars with an admixture of Petchenegs and Cumans.

The two regions thus colonized became the principalities of Walachia and Moldavia, whose annals remain distinct until 1774, but can thereafter be combined in one narrative, the Turkish administration being uniform. In 1859 the two principalities were formally united under the name of Rumania. The historical narrative which follows is therefore arranged under four headings, *Walachia, Moldavia, The Danubian Principalities* and *Rumania*.

WALACHIA

Tradition, embodied in a local chronicle of the 16th century entitled "History of the Ruman land since the arrival of the Rumans" (*Istoria tierei Românesci decându au descălicati Românii*) gives 1290 as the date of the founding of the Walachian state, asserting that in that year a voivode (prince) of Fagaras in southern Transylvania crossed the mountains with a body of followers and established himself at Campulung in the foothills, moving later to Curtea de Arges. The name given for this first leader, Radu Negru (Ralph the Black), is probably a confusion with that of a later Walachian voivode, but the southward movement at that period of Vlach peoples from the mountains to the Danubian plain can be affirmed with certainty. Walachia itself was known to its own people as Muntenia, land of the mountains, after their former home. Historians who deny the continuity of Daco-Roman (Vlach) settlement in Transylvania have to postulate a northward migration of Vlachs from across the Danube to the Carpathians at the beginning of the 13th century to account for the indisputable southward movement at its close. The seeking of a new home in the south was due to the consolidation of Hungarian feudal power in Transylvania and of the feudal system, to the arrival of German settlers and to the growing proselytizing zeal of the Hungarian kings as faithful servants of the papacy. The Vlachs, since the introduction of organized Christianity under Bulgarian influence, had belonged to the Eastern Orthodox Church, taking the Byzantine side against Rome in the schism of 1054, though later some of their leaders came under Roman influence. (*See also Religion* below.)

The new principality remained at first under the domination of Hungary, but the voivode Bassarab defeated the Hungarian king Charles Robert in 1330 and secured independence. Vladislav (c. 1360–74), although again defeating the Hungarians, accepted a form of Hungarian suzerainty in return for investiture by Louis

the Great, Charles Robert's successor, with the banat (frontier province) of Severin and the duchy of Omlas.

The early days of the principality were conditioned by the struggle against Hungary, but with the reign of Mircea the Old (1386–1418) a new period began, that of the struggle against the Turks. The first voivodes of Walachia, in search of help against Hungary, had contracted matrimonial and military alliances with the two Slav states south of the Danube, Bulgaria and Serbia, but both empires were already at the point of extinction at the hands of the Turks. Tradition recounts that a Walachian contingent helped the Serbs at the battle of Kosovo in 1389; it is a fact that the sultan followed up his victory by invading Walachia, which first appears in 1391 as a tributary of the Sublime Porte. The final overthrow of Bulgaria in 1393 left Walachia open to further Turkish advance but Mircea succeeded in holding the invaders back on the Danube marshes in 1394, and in the following year made an alliance with Hungary. The joint Christian forces, which included French and Burgundian contingents, were defeated in 1396 at the battle of Nicopolis (Nikopoli). Mircea had thrown over an earlier alliance with Poland in order to secure one with Hungary; accordingly the Poles, taking advantage of the defeat at Nicopolis, intrigued for his deposition and replaced him by his son Vlad, who accepted Polish suzerainty. Mircea later returned, re-established, and for a time increased, his power by exploiting the quarrels between the sons of the sultan Bayazid. In 1417, however, Walachia was forced to capitulate to Turkey under Sultan Mohammed II, though its dynasty, territory and Christian religion were left intact. Mircea died a year later.

Early Years of Turkish Rule.—After Mircea's death, Walachia, convulsed by internal struggles, could take no active part against the Turks, but they were for a time again driven back by the Hungarians under the brilliant John Hunyadi (q.v.), a Rumanian by race though enrolled in the Hungarian nobility. He deposed one of the weak Walachian voivodes and nominated Vlad IV—who in 1456 acknowledged Hungary as suzerain—a man whose unbelievable cruelties earned him the name of "the Impaler" (Tepes). Vlad (1455–62 and 1476–77) was able briefly to defy the Turks; with his death, resistance crumbled rapidly, Walachian voivodes succeeding one another after very short reigns.

The instability of the throne was in part due to the mixture of the hereditary and elective principles in the system of succession; the council of boyars (nobles), which came under Turkish rule to be known as the divan by analogy with the Turkish institution of that name, chose the prince from legitimate and illegitimate heirs of his dead predecessor.

The only voivode of the 16th century deserving mention is Neagu Bassarab (1512–1521), who founded cathedrals at Curtea de Arges (q.v.) and at Targoviste, which had become the Walachian capital, and endowed monasteries in Walachia, besides making noble contributions to Mount Athos. The patriarch of Constantinople honoured the dedication of the Arges monastery with his presence.

Neagu's son and successor was imprisoned by the Turks who proceeded to nominate Turkish governors in the towns and villages of Walachia. The Walachians resisted desperately. They elected Radu, a kinsman of Neagu, as voivode and defeated the Turkish commander Mahmud Bey with Hungarian help at Grumatz in 1522. The continuance and extension of Turkish control became inevitable, however, after the crushing defeat of Hungary in 1526 at the battle of Mohacs.

Walachia thereafter became a line of communication for Turkish expeditions against Hungary and Transylvania. The voivode Alexander, who succeeded in 1591, actually farmed out his possessions to his Turkish supporters, and it seemed that Walachia must succumb to direct Ottoman rule.

Michael the Brave, 1593–1601.—The Turkish advance was once more to be halted, though for the last time, under a new voivode, Michael, son of Petrusko, ban of Craiova. He secured the deposition of Alexander and his own election by raising a loan at Constantinople of 400,000 ducats to make the customary presents to the Porte and was supported by Sigismund Bathory (q.v.), prince of Transylvania, and by the English ambassador at Constantinople, Edward Barton. Michael was to prove a thorn in the flesh to the Turks, but was much criticized for making Walachia once more subject to Hungarian princes in return for their help. In concert with the Moldavian voivode Aaron, Michael organized a massacre of Turkish guards and settlers (Nov. 1594) and with the support given by Bathory in return for the acknowledgment of his suzerainty proceeded to invade Turkish territory, taking Ruschuk, Silistra and other places on the right bank of the Danube. A simultaneous invasion of Walachia by a large Turkish and Tatar host was defeated at the battle of Mantin (1595). The sultan next sent Sinan Pasha the Renegade to invade Walachia with 100,000 men. Michael withdrew to the mountains, but with aid from Bathory and a Transylvanian contingent resumed the offensive and stormed Bucharest, pursuing the main body of Sinan's forces to the Danube. In 1597 the sultan, wearied with these defeats, reinvested Michael for life.

Walachia's subjection to Hungary was not permanent. On the abdication of Sigismund Bathory, Michael, with the support of the emperor Rudolf II, attacked and defeated his successor Andreas Bathory in Oct. 1599 and had himself proclaimed prince of Transylvania, being acknowledged by the emperor as his lieutenant and having his position ratified by the diet. The Vlach peasant population of Transylvania was encouraged to revolt against the Magyars by having an overlord of their own race, but Michael, whose support in Walachia rested on the boyars, helped the Magyar nobility to suppress the peasant rising. Despite this the Magyars distrusted Michael, both as a despised Vlach and as a Habsburg agent, and he found his position in Transylvania insecure while Moldavia remained as a centre for Magyar and Polish intrigue. In May 1600 he invaded that principality, deposed the voivode and without waiting for the emperor's sanction had himself proclaimed "prince of all Ungro-Vlachia, of Transylvania and of Moldavia."

Though Rudolf confirmed Michael in his appointment he grew suspicious of his vassal's progress and determined to undermine his position. The imperial commissioner, Gen. George Basta, was instructed to give support to the disaffected Magyar element in Transylvania, and Michael was driven out by a successful revolt. At the same time the Poles invaded Moldavia, and restored the unseated voivode, while Walachia itself was also attacked. Michael appealed to the emperor, who restored him to favour, and in conjunction with Basta he defeated the Transylvanian forces at Goroslau in 1601. Basta, however, jealous of Michael's returning prosperity, procured his murder almost immediately after their joint victory.

Michael the Brave (Mihai Viteazul) is the leading Rumanian national hero, partly because it was he who made the last stand before the era of Turkish and Greek domination, but chiefly because for the first time since Dacian days he brought all the Rumanians, scattered in three principalities, under one rule, thus weaving the stuff of the national dream which was not to become reality until 1918.

The Period of Greek Penetration, 1634–1711.—After Michael's death Radu Serban of the Bassarab dynasty was appointed voivode of Walachia by the emperor's wish, but was deposed by the Turks in 1611. A succession of insignificant puppet princes followed him, the Greek element becoming increasingly apparent. There was a temporary rally in the second quarter of the 17th century under Matthias Bassarab, who succeeded in holding the throne for 22 years—warding off repeated attacks from his rival Basil the Wolf of Moldavia—and did much for the arts and the endowment of churches. He founded a printing press at the Govora monastery which issued a compendium of canon law, *Pravila cea mica*, the first Rumanian book to be printed in the principalities (Gospels in Rumanian had been printed in the preceding century by the Protestants in Transylvania).

The successor of Matthias, Constantine Serban, was the last Bassarab to rule in Walachia. On his death the Turks, who in 1698 moved the capital to Bucharest—at a safer distance from the Transylvanian frontier—began to exercise a more direct influence over the ruling families, who were now frequently of Greek origin. Serban Cantacuzino (1678–88), the first important Greek voivode, was an able man; forced to assist the Turks at the siege of Vienna,

he opened up secret communications with the emperor, who granted him a diploma creating him a count of the empire and recognizing his descent from the imperial house of Cantacuzino. In 1688, the year of Serban's death, the first Rumanian Bible was printed.

Serban's successor was his nephew Constantine Brancovan (Brancoveanu), descended on his mother's side from the Bassarabs, who pursued a policy of cautious balancing between the Porte, the emperor, Poland and the rapidly westward-thrusting Russia. Brancovan sent congratulations to Peter the Great on his victory at Poltava and asked for help for the Christian cause. Finally falling a victim to intrigues, Brancovan was deposed and executed at Constantinople in 1714.

The Phanariot Regime, 1714–1821.—At the beginning of the 18th century Turkish power was in obvious decline and the strength of Austria and Russia growing. Alarmed by the intrigues of Brancovan of Walachia and Cantemir of Moldavia with Vienna and Moscow, the Porte decided to exercise direct control over the principalities. Instead of reducing them to mere pashaliks, however, the Turks employed Greeks from the Phanar district of Constantinople as their agents. The new princes, or hospodars, insecure of tenure, had to extract the maximum from the country in the minimum of time—the average duration of a reign was only two and a half years—and thus the word Phanariot has come to stand for bribery, exaction and corruption, though the hospodars themselves were often men of culture and intelligence.

Under this oppressive regime many peasants emigrated; in 1741 there were 147,000 peasant families in Walachia, but four years later their number was reduced by half. In the face of this, the enlightened hospodar Constantine Mavrocordato decreed the abolition of serfdom in 1747, but after numerous rises and falls from favour he was finally imprisoned in 1763 after efforts at reform had proved abortive.

The tide of Ottoman domination was now ebbing fast under Russian pressure; after defeating the Turks at Hotin in 1769, Russian troops occupied both principalities, the bishops and clergy taking an oath to the empress Catherine. At Focsani in 1772 Catherine demanded that the Porte recognize the independence of Walachia and Moldavia under Russian guarantee, but she was deterred by Austrian opposition, and temporarily satiated by the partition of Poland.

MOLDAVIA

Moldavia took shape in circumstances similar to those of its sister state but somewhat later: according to chronicles, more plentiful than those dealing with Walachia, Dragos, founder of the principality, emigrated southward with his followers from Maramures in the northern Carpathians (the dates given vary from 1299 to 1342). An independent state first emerged about 1349 under Bogdan. One of the early voivodes, Peter Musat (1375–90) was a member of the Bassarab family of Walachia and, in pursuance of the interests of his kinsman, Mircea the Old, recognized the suzerainty of the king of Poland whose sister he married. From this period date Poland's ambitions to control the new state, which had hardly emancipated itself from Hungarian tutelage. The first important voivode, Alexander the Good (1401–35), acknowledged Polish overlordship and laid the foundations of organized life in the principality. Civil war reigned among Alexander's successors, but a new era in Moldavian history opened with the reign of his grandson Stephen the Great (1457–1504), who was to prove one of the greatest champions of Christendom against the Turks. Patriotic and religious, Stephen was doubly affected by the fall of Constantinople four years before his accession; the cutting of the trade route through the Bosphorus was disastrous for the commerce of the principalities and the desecration of St. Sophia was a blow to Christian feeling. Stephen's whole reign was devoted to the attempt to rally the west against the infidel; he appealed for help to Poland, Hungary and Venice as well as to the pope Sixtus IV, who gave him the title "athlete of Christ."

Stephen inflicted a crushing defeat on the Turks at Rahova in 1475, and again repelled them the following year. Poland and Hungary, however, never gave him the solid support for which he had hoped; in 1484 the Turks captured his key fortresses of Chilia and Akkerman (later Belgorod-Dnestrovski), and the following year burned the Moldavian capital Suceava. Once again Stephen rallied and defeated the Turks in 1486 at Scheia near Roman. As early as 1484, after the loss of his fortresses, he had been compelled to do public homage to King Casimir IV of Poland, but in 1499 he was able to draw up a treaty on equal terms. Poland, however, once again failed to honour its pledge to give help. On his deathbed Stephen, realizing the hopelessness of securing united action from Christendom, advised his son to submit to the Turks if they would respect the framework of church and state.

Stephen encouraged the arts, gave generous grants of monastic lands and built more than 40 stone churches, and the great monastery of Putna. Stephen's son Bogdan III, the "one-eyed" (1504–17), at feud with Poland over Pokutia, which his father had annexed, and lacking support from the already shaken Hungary, was forced in 1513 to pay annual tribute to the sultan while securing guarantees for the Christian religion and Moldavian institutions. In the anarchy following on the battle of Mohacs a strange figure ascended the Moldavian throne, Peter Rares (1527–38 and 1541–46), an illegitimate son of Stephen. Allying himself with the Turks, he made war on the imperial forces in Transylvania and on Poland, attempting to recover the lost Pokutia. Later he allied himself with the emperor against Poland and the sultan, but was defeated and deposed in 1538. In 1541 he returned to the throne with Turkish help, but concluded a secret treaty with the emperor against the Turks. His successors could no longer oppose Turkish power.

Turkish Penetration.—Peter's son actually accepted Islam; the sultan strengthened his hold on Moldavia by occupying a series of fortresses and increased the tribute. From the middle of the 16th century each aspirant to the Moldavian throne had to buy the consent of the Porte, and the way was thus open to adventurers. The most dramatic was Jacob Basiliscus Heraclides who seized Moldavia from the voivode Alexander Lapusneanu with Turkish support. A Greek by birth, he had travelled over Europe and had become the friend of Philipp Melanchthon; he attempted to found an educational system in Moldavia, but his heavy taxation led to revolt and he was assassinated in 1563. Under the restored Lapusneanu and under Bogdan IV (1568–72), Moldavia relapsed into obscurity. Bogdan's successor John the Terrible (1572–74), provoked by the Porte's demand for increased tribute, rose against the oppressor, but was defeated and slain in 1574. Moldavia did not rally until the victories of Michael the Brave at the turn of the century when it was actually incorporated for a year in Michael's Great Dacian realm. After Michael's murder, the Poles again asserted supremacy, but the Porte resumed its domination in 1618. No voivode of any importance occupied the throne until Basil the Wolf (1634–53), a brave soldier of Albanian origin. He might have achieved success against the Turks, but chose instead to attack his neighbour Walachia, coveting its throne. He married one of his daughters to Timothy, son of the celebrated Ukrainian hetman (general) Bogdan Chmielnicki and raided Walachia with the help of his son-in-law, but was routed by the veteran Matthias Bassarab. He was overthrown by a conspiracy of Moldavian boyars, and after his death Greek influence became paramount. One of the Greek hospodars, Demetrius Cantemir, attempted to exchange Turkish for Russian sovereignty, and proving unsuccessful went into exile in St. Petersburg. He was a scholar whose *Descriptio Moldaviae* is a valuable historical source.

The Phanariot regime in Moldavia is generally reckoned from the reign of Nicholas Mavrocordato, Cantemir's successor; it was similar to that in Walachia, and indeed the hospodars were frequently shifted by the Turks from one throne to the other. Moldavia was perhaps more prosperous than Walachia at this period and had a considerable export trade in timber, salt, wine and foodstuffs.

THE DANUBIAN PRINCIPALITIES

The treaty of Kuchuk Kainarji which ended the Russo-Turkish war in 1774 altered the situation in both Walachia and Moldavia. Russia restored the principalities which it had occupied, to the sultan (Moldavia, however, lost its northern tip, Bukovina, which Austria, profiting by the situation, annexed) on conditions which included provisions favourable to the territories themselves. The tribute was to be reduced, and the agents of Walachia and Moldavia at the Porte were to have diplomatic status; Russia was accorded a virtual protectorate. In view of Turkish attempts to evade fulfilment of the treaty, Russia secured a more precise definition of its rights in the convention of Ainali-Kavak (1779) and strengthened its position in 1782 by appointing a consul in Bucharest. Austria countered by dispatching an "agent" Ignaz Rajcevic, whose *Osservazioni storiche intorno la Valachia* (1788) is one of the best sources for the period. In the Russo-Turkish fighting which broke out again in 1787 the principalities once more provided battlefields, and Prince Potemkin made his headquarters at Jassy (Iasi). In 1791, when peace was imminent, a group of Walachian boyars, fearing the effects of renewed Ottoman rule, addressed an appeal to Austria and Russia which, though it achieved no results, is of interest as an early sign of the awakening of national feeling. The boyars asked for the ending of Phanariot rule, the return of native princes and the creation of a national army. By the peace of Jassy (1792) Russia had to evacuate the principalities, the Dniester (Dnestr) being recognized as its frontier, and the privileges of the principalities accorded in earlier treaties were confirmed. In defiance of treaties the Porte continued to change the hospodars almost yearly, until in 1802 the Russians obtained a fresh convention under which every prince was to hold office for at least seven years and could not be dispossessed without Russian consent.

The two new hospodars were strongly under Russian influence. Constantine Ypsilanti of Walachia, encouraged by the convention, refused some Turkish requisitions, acted as intermediary between the Serbs and Russia in the Serb revolt of 1804 and tried to embroil the French and the Porte. Napoleon's envoy at Bucharest denounced both hospodars as traitors and influenced the Porte's decision to dethrone them in 1806 without consulting Russia. Russia occupied the principalities and the Turks declared war in Dec. 1806; Moldavia and Walachia had become pawns in the intrigues between the tsar, the Porte and Napoleon. The Russian occupation, which lasted six years, reduced the country to a desert; produce was carried off, the coinage debased and labour requisitioning was enforced by the deportation of recalcitrants to Siberia. The Christian populations exchanged hope and confidence in a liberator for a profound suspicion and fear of Russia which remained rooted in Rumanian minds.

Russia's design to incorporate the principalities in its empire was frustrated by the peace of Bucharest (1812), but it secured the cession of southeastern Moldavia, known as Bessarabia (q.v.). The two hospodars who were appointed after the peace in 1812, Ion Caragea in Walachia and Scarlat Callimachi in Moldavia, were masters of extortion. The former increased the taxation eightfold, partly by creating 4,000 new boyars. Both were strongly Greek in feeling, and were supported by some of the boyars, who, disappointed in Russia, dreamed of a new Graeco-Rumanian Byzantium. Caragea was in secret relations with the Greek revolutionary movement, Philike Hetairia, which was being fostered at Odessa under Russian auspices. The way was thus prepared for the adventure of Alexander Ypsilanti, son of the Walachian hospodar Constantine and *aide-de-camp* of the tsar, who marched into Moldavia at the head of the Hetairists in 1821. He received the support of the Moldavian hospodar Michael Sutu (Sutzu), but the boyars were hostile in Moldavia and still more so in Walachia where a national popular movement led by Tudor Vladimirescu (q.v.) turned not against the Turks but against the Phanariots. Turkish troops which invaded to crush Ypsilanti were not finally withdrawn until 1824. The Turks, anxious to divide the Rumanians from the Greeks, thought it wise to heed the former's demands and the Rumanians took advantage of this to secure a number of reforms in the national interest. The reforms included the promulgation of laws in Rumanian and the appointment of native princes, the first of whom were Ion Sturdza in Moldavia and Gregory Ghica in Walachia. Ghica's family, though of Albanian extraction and settled at the Phanar, was entirely rumanized.

Both princes were anti-Greek and unacceptable to the Russians; Sturdza was accused of subversive tendencies because he cherished plans for constitutional reform, including an elected assembly.

Kiselev and the "Règlement Organique".—Russia and Turkey resumed relations in 1825 and by the convention of Akkerman signed by them in 1826 the privileges of the principalities were once more confirmed, and Russia was again allowed a voice in elections to the two thrones. On the outbreak of hostilities between Russia and Turkey again in 1828, Russia once more occupied Walachia and Moldavia. The peace of Adrianople in 1829 left them still tributary to the sultan, but wholly under Russian protection. The two hospodars were thenceforth elected for life.

Russia secured a continuation of its occupation by making evacuation conditional on the payment of an impossibly high indemnity by Turkey. The occupation, which had again been exceedingly onerous during the war, became more enlightened after the signing of the treaty, a change which was largely due to the Russian administrator, Count Pavel Kiselev. The boyars, under Kiselev's supervision, drew up a constitution known as the *Règlement organique*, promulgated in Walachia in 1831 and in Moldavia in 1832. It was wholly oligarchic in character, but was an advance in that legislative and administrative powers were vested in a native elected body. The economic provisions of the *Règlement*, however, deepened the cleavage between the boyars and the peasant class and were censured by Kiselev. The *Règlement* was ratified by the Porte in 1834, whereupon Russia withdrew its troops.

The National Movement and 1848.—The new hospodars, Alexander Ghica (1834-42) in Walachia and Michael Sturdza in Moldavia, were, however, strongly under Russian influence. Ghica's successor George Bibescu (1842-48) had been educated in Paris and was influenced by the new spirit of romantic nationalism. In agreement with Sturdza he removed the fiscal barriers between the principalities. Meanwhile a new generation of Rumanians was growing up, educated in Paris or looking to France for inspiration; these came rapidly to the front in the great crisis of 1848 which in the principalities took a form partly national and partly social. The national movements in Moldavia and Walachia were spurred on by the dramatic upsurge among the downtrodden Rumanian peasants of Transylvania, which culminated in the "field of liberty" demonstrations at Blaj in May 1848. Sturdza in Moldavia proved able to quell popular agitation; Bibescu, although he had some sympathy with the movement, lacked courage to lead it and fled, leaving in power a provisional government largely controlled by Ion C. Bratianu (q.v.), first head of the great Liberal family which for so long dominated Rumanian politics. The Turks, under Russian pressure, were forced to put down the new movement; joint Russo-Turkish military intervention restored the *Règlement organique*. The Balta-Liman convention of 1849 laid down that the hospodars should again be appointed for seven years only; the assemblies were replaced by so-called *divans ad hoc*. Gregory Alexander Ghica was appointed hospodar in Moldavia, and Barbu Stirbey, brother of George Bibescu, in Walachia.

Crimean War and Treaty of Paris.—Russian troops did not evacuate the principalities until 1851, and during the Crimean War they were occupied in turn by Russia and Austria. Although they suffered severely, the Austrian occupation brought material benefits and opportunities of contact with the west. The treaty of Paris (1856) placed the principalities with their existing privileges under the collective guarantee of the contracting powers, thus ending the Russian protectorate, though retaining the suzerainty of the Porte. The Russian frontier was withdrawn from the mouths of the Danube by the return of a strip of southern Bessarabia to Moldavia. The existing statutes were revised in 1857 by a European commission with a Turkish member meeting at Bucharest, assisted by two *divans ad hoc* called together by the Porte.

Union of the Principalities.—The divans voted unanimously for autonomy, union of the principalities under the name of Rumania, a foreign hereditary prince and neutrality. The divans were dissolved by the Porte in Jan. 1858 and in August the convention of Paris accepted their decisions with modifications. There were still to be two princes and two assemblies, but a central com-

mission at Focsani was to prepare measures of joint concern. The two assemblies, meeting at Jassy and Bucharest respectively, then elected a single prince in the person of Alexander Cuza (q.v.) on Jan. 17, 1859. The *de facto* union of Rumania was thus accomplished.

RUMANIA

A new conference met in Paris to discuss the situation and in 1861 the election of Prince Cuza was ratified by the powers and the Porte. In Feb. 1862 a single ministry and a single assembly replaced the divans and central commission. Cuza, in May 1864, promulgated by plebiscite a new constitution providing for a senate as well as an assembly and extending the franchise to all citizens, with the reservation of a cumulative voting power for property. An important agrarian law of the same year emancipated the peasantry from forced labour. Prince Cuza's agrarian and educational reforms were progressive, but his methods of enforcement were despotic. He alienated the boyars by abolishing forced labour, and the clergy by confiscating monastic estates (see *Religion* below), while the agrarian reform was not radical enough to satisfy the peasantry. In Feb. 1866 he was compelled to abdicate and the principalities by referendum elected as prince, almost unanimously, Charles (see CHARLES [Karl Eitel or Carol]), second son of Prince Charles Anthony of Hohenzollern-Sigmaringen, the candidate of Ion Bratianu, who had secured the veiled support of Napoleon III. The new prince reached Bucharest on May 22, 1866, and in July took the oath to a new constitution modelled on the Belgian charter of 1831, which provided for upper and lower houses and gave the prince an unconditional veto on all legislation. Turkish assent was secured in October; Prince Charles was recognized as hereditary ruler and was allowed to maintain an army of 30,000 men.

Internal Politics, 1866-75.—Prince Charles's policy was to avoid all political adventures and to give Rumania a sound administration. The internal situation was at first unsettled; ten governments held office in five years. The dominant figure was the Liberal leader Ion Bratianu.

In 1869 Prince Charles paid a series of state visits to consolidate his position, and married Princess Elizabeth of Neuwied, the poetess later known as Carmen Sylva, who earned great popularity in her adopted country. Prince Charles was a Roman Catholic and his wife a Protestant, but he agreed to bring up his successor in the Eastern Orthodox faith.

Tension arose between the German prince and his pro-French politicians on the outbreak of the Franco-German War in 1870 and there was an abortive attempt to overthrow him in a revolutionary outbreak at Ploesti. Anti-German feelings were increased by a scandal in the new Rumanian railways; the German contractor failed to honour the coupons of the bonds, mainly held by influential Germans, and the Prussian government attempted to coerce the Rumanian government into payment. Indignation in Rumania culminated in a mob attack on the German colony in Bucharest in March 1871, and Prince Charles contemplated abdication. A Conservative government formed under Lascar Catargiu succeeded in restoring order, however, and retained office for five years. After another crisis threatening Prince Charles, the Liberals again took office in 1876 and Bratianu became premier; he enjoyed almost absolute power for the next 12 years.

The Russo-Turkish War, 1877-78, and the Treaty of Berlin.—Domestic problems were temporarily eclipsed by the reopening of the Eastern Question in 1877. Russia rejected Rumania's offer of co-operation on equal terms against Turkey and threatened occupation. On April 16, 1877, Rumania signed a secret convention allowing free passage to the Russian armies, while the tsar promised to respect Rumanian territory. The Russians crossed the Rumanian frontier in April, and on May 11 Rumania declared war on Turkey. Rumanian troops contributed materially to the joint victory at Plevna in September, which left the Russian army free to march on Constantinople. Nonetheless Russia refused to admit Rumanian representatives to the peace negotiations at Adrianople and later at San Stefano. The Russians insisted on the handing back of southern Bessarabia which had been restored to Moldavia after the Crimean War, and despite bitter Rumanian protests this provision was incorporated in the treaty of Berlin; Rumania received an alternative outlet to the mouths of the Danube in northern Dobruja, a territory with little or no Rumanian population, the possession of which later caused discord with Bulgaria.

The treaty recognized Rumanian independence and guaranteed absolute freedom of worship without loss of political rights. The latter article (44) caused indignation in the country and could not be implemented without constitutional revision. Article 7 of the 1866 constitution stated that "only Christians can become citizens of Rumania," thus excluding Jews from civic rights. Jews had not been numerous in the principalities until the early 19th century, but their influx after the treaty of Adrianople had caused the safeguard to be put into the constitution. Under pressure from the powers, article 7 was finally repealed.

Independence of Rumania: the Kingdom.—The independence of Rumania was recognized by Italy in Dec. 1879 and by Great Britain, France and Germany in Feb. 1880. Prince Charles, having no children, regulated the succession in 1880 in favour of his nephew Prince Ferdinand of Hohenzollern, and the idea of making Rumania a kingdom was mooted. The Liberal government, accused by the Conservatives of republican tendencies, itself took the initiative in proclaiming the kingdom. This action was hastened by the general fear of revolution consequent on the assassination of Tsar Alexander II. Charles was crowned king on May 22, 1881, and secured the immediate recognition of the powers.

Internal Politics, 1878–1912.—Since 1876 Bratianu had exercised almost dictatorial power. His Liberals stood for the rapid development of a strong middle class able to control the Jews, and were mainly Francophil. The Conservatives were divided into the old boyar group, which tended to look to Russia, and the so-called Young Conservatives, the Junimists, led by Petre Carp, who had studied in Germany rather than France and favoured the Central Powers. Bratianu retired after electoral defeat in 1888, and died three years later. Thereafter various Conservative and Junimist administrations held office, the Liberals under Sturdza returning to power in 1895.

The country was in considerable financial difficulties and there was much discontent, particularly in the countryside where the peasants, though emancipated in 1864, were forced by poverty into the hands of Jewish moneylenders. A serious peasant rising in 1907, stimulated by the Russian upheaval of 1905, attacked first the Jews and then the large landowners. The Conservative ministry had to resign and it was a Liberal government which restored order. In 1909 the Liberal leader Sturdza resigned and was succeeded by Ionel Bratianu, eldest son of the great statesman, who continued to base his policy on the expansion of the urban middle class, though some of his younger colleagues concentrated on the agrarian problem. The Conservatives under Carp came to power again in 1911, but were violently attacked by the Liberals and a group of Conservative dissidents formed after the peasant rising under Take Jonescu. Under the pressure of foreign events the cabinet was reconstituted in 1912 with Titu Maiorescu as prime minister and Jonescu as minister of the interior. In Jan. 1914 Ionel Bratianu succeeded Maiorescu and formed a Liberal administration; together with the party theorist Constantine Stere, a Bessarabian boyar who had been banished to Siberia for his radical views, he worked out a program of agrarian reform.

Foreign Affairs, 1878–1912.—The foreign political situation remained comparatively calm between the treaty of Berlin and the outbreak of the Balkan wars, though Rumania's relations with its neighbours could not be cordial. Bulgaria, a traditional friend, was embittered by the loss of northern Dobruja; against Russia the Rumanians were incensed by the forced retrocession of southern Bessarabia. The resentment aroused against Austria at the end of the 18th century by its seizure of Bukovina, the first home of the Moldavian principality and repository of its chief artistic and ecclesiastical treasures, had died down, but ill feeling was aroused by the commercial treaty of 1875, which Rumania considered unfair, and was intensified by Austria's insistence on having a delegate on the Danube commission, though the commis-

sion's writ only ran from Galati (Galatz) to Orsova and did not reach Austrian soil. The oppressed Rumanians of Transylvania had been increasingly conscious of grievance against Hungary since 1848 and their feelings were shared in Rumania. With Greece there was a constantly reviving dispute in which Bulgaria was also involved, concerning the status of the Vlach (q.v.) communities in Macedonia over which Rumania claimed the rights of a protector; this caused a diplomatic rupture between Rumania and Greece from 1905 to 1911.

King Charles had a natural and pronounced preference for the Central Powers, and in this he was supported by Ion Bratianu, whose fear and dislike of Russia after the treaty of Berlin outweighed his Francophilia. It was Bratianu, with Sturdza as foreign minister, who signed the secret treaty of 1883 with Austria and Germany. The treaty, remaining a close secret, was formally renewed under a Conservative administration in 1892. It was, however, the first signatory, Sturdza, leader of the Liberals since 1893, who was most active in support of the claims of the Transylvanian Rumanians against Hungary. The Bosnian crisis of 1908 alarmed Rumania because it showed that Austria was prepared to further the fortunes of Bulgaria in order to destroy Serbia. Ionel Bratianu, however, on succeeding Sturdza in 1909, remained faithful to the secret treaty.

First Balkan War, 1912.—The outbreak of war between the Balkan league and Turkey in 1912 found the Conservatives in office. Rumania's sympathies were at first uncertain; the secret Serbo-Bulgarian military convention of March 13, 1912, had provided against a possible Rumanian attack. The rapid success of the Bulgarians caused Rumania to abandon its original profession of disinterestedness and to stake a claim. Rumania intimated to Bulgaria that in the event of a partition of European Turkey it would, in the interests of the balance of power in the Balkans, require a frontier rectification in the Dobruja. Danev, president of the Bulgarian house of deputies, returning through Bucharest from a visit to Vienna and Budapest, offered only minor frontier rectifications, excluding Silistra, which was the kernel of Rumania's claims. He did, however, consider the renunciation of Bulgaria's claim to northern Dobruja and the giving of a guarantee for the Vlachs of Macedonia. No agreement was reached in Bucharest or in London in Jan. 1913. The case was finally submitted for arbitration to the conference of St. Petersburg (May 1917) which assigned Silistra to Rumania. Bulgaria regarded the concession as excessive and Rumania no longer looked on it as a satisfactory price for neutrality.

Second Balkan War, 1913.—Bulgaria's attack on its allies in July 1913 was used by Rumania as a pretext for intervention. The Rumanian army, 500,000 strong and commanded by the crown prince, crossed the frontier (July 10), occupied southern Dobruja and advanced on Sofia. Negotiations were immediately opened at Bucharest, where an armistice was signed on July 31, 1913, between Rumania, Serbia, Greece and Bulgaria. By the treaty of Bucharest, signed on Aug. 10, Rumania obtained southern Dobruja which it had already occupied.

Rumania's position was now precarious in view of the growing tension between Vienna and St. Petersburg. The king renewed the secret treaty with the Central Powers at the beginning of 1914 and Austria made great efforts to win Rumanian friendship, but popular sentiment ran the other way. The feeling of kinship with Transylvania grew steadily among the younger generation, while Austria's continued diplomatic support of Bulgaria aroused resentment. The growing feeling of the need for a policy covering the interests of the entire Rumanian nation, within and without the national frontiers, led to a new inclination toward Russia. Though Russia held Moldavian Bessarabia, Austro-Hungary, as arbitrator of the destinies of the much more highly developed Rumanian communities in Transylvania, was the greater obstacle to the realization of dreams of unity. The visit to St. Petersburg of Prince Ferdinand, heir to the throne, in March 1914 and of the tsar to Constanta in June, did not bring about a definite change of policy, however.

Rumania and World War I.—On the outbreak of war in 1914 Ionel Bratianu and his Liberal party were in office. The politicians were divided in their views, not along party lines, and Rumania at first maintained armed neutrality, though tempted by the Central Powers with the promise of the return of Bessarabia and by the Allies with the offer of Transylvania. Grief at the country's failure to honour the secret alliance hastened King Charles's death in Oct. 1914. His successor Ferdinand had married Marie of Edinburgh, granddaughter of Queen Victoria and of Alexander II, stronger in character than her husband and a staunch lover of England and Russia. Her influence, Allied promises, and alarm at the extent of German victories finally brought Rumania into the war. By a treaty of Aug. 17, 1916, Great Britain, France, Russia and Italy guaranteed Rumania the Banat, Transylvania, the Hungarian plain up to the Tisza (Theiss) river and Bukovina as far as the Prut river. Rumania declared war on Austria-Hungary on Aug. 22; its troops at once crossed the passes into Transylvania, but were expelled by mid-November. Bucharest was occupied by the Central Powers on Dec. 6, 1916. The king and his ministers and parliament had already retired to Jassy and were followed by the army, which reorganized in Moldavia under the shelter of the Russian forces. The Russian Revolution of Feb. 1917 led to the collapse of the front and left the German Field Marshal August von Mackensen free to throw all his forces against the Rumanian army, which was rendered incapable of further resistance after a prolonged stand at Marasesti in August. After the October revolution the Russian army disintegrated into pillaging bands, hostilities were suspended and an armistice was concluded on Dec. 6, 1917.

During this period the parliament in exile at Jassy was busy with projects of agrarian and electoral reform. Bratianu had already been considering these topics in 1914, and in Dec. 1916 he made a coalition with Take Jonescu and his dissident Conservatives, who had been concerned with the peasant question since the 1907 rising. The effects of the Russian Revolution in the Ukraine and Bessarabia (q.v.), where the peasants had appropriated the land, made the question urgent. King Ferdinand was personally concerned and induced the Conservatives to agree to a project of radical expropriation, which was passed in July 1917.

The Treaty of Bucharest.—After Bratianu resigned on Feb. 9, 1918, Gen. Alexandru Averescu was charged with the peace negotiations at Buftea, near Bucharest. The Dobruja was ceded as far as the Danube, Bulgaria taking over the southern half which it had lost in 1913, while the Central Powers administered the northern half conjointly. Rumania was to have a trade route to the Black sea via Constanta. The frontier of Hungary was advanced in the Carpathians. The Central Powers secured such terms on the Danube, in the Rumanian oilfields and over the railways, as would have placed Rumania in a state of economic slavery to them for many years. Averescu's cabinet hesitated to sign and resigned on March 12 in favour of the pro-German Alexandru Marghiloman ministry, which signed the treaty at Bucharest on May 7, 1918.

Marghiloman's ministry struggled against almost unsurmountable difficulties throughout the succeeding months. The Central Powers forced the Banque Générale to issue 2,500,000,000 lei in paper money. This disorganized the finance of the kingdom, while economic ruin was ensured by the forced export of sheep and cattle, the cutting down of forests and the dismantling of factories. The population meanwhile was starving, and the morale of the working class was being perverted by revolutionary propaganda.

On Nov. 8, 1918, when the defeat of the Central Powers was assured, the king called to power General Coanda, who repealed all laws introduced by the Marghiloman ministry and decreed universal, obligatory and secret suffrage for all male voters over 21 years of age. War was declared again on Nov. 9. The king re-entered Bucharest (Nov. 30) after the German troops had evacuated Rumania under the terms of the Armistice. Bratianu again became prime minister on Dec. 14.

GREATER RUMANIA

The dream of greater Rumania was realized, but it was no easy task to unite provinces which had been under the domination of different alien states. Bessarabia (q.v.) was already incorporated in the old kingdom, having abandoned an earlier idea of autonomy. Its council voted for unconditional union on Dec. 9, 1918. The incorporation of Transylvania (q.v.) followed in virtue of a resolution passed by a Rumanian assembly at Alba Julia on Dec. 1, and that of Bukovina (q.v.) on Nov. 28. The government had to carry on difficult diplomatic negotiations for the recognition by the Allies of the new frontiers. Those fixed by the agreement of Aug. 1916 were drawn back in places to give the Hungarians a part of the hinterland of Oradea Mare, and the Yugoslavs the western half of the Banat. A line of demarcation was fixed in Hungary, and Rumanian troops occupied the country up to this line, pending final settlement by treaty. In March 1919 a further neutral zone was established and Rumania was given the right of occupying it. Bela Kun's Communist government which then came into power in Hungary started a campaign as a result of which the Rumanians advanced to the Tisza river, where they were stopped by the Allies on May 9. On July 22 Kun started a new offensive, but the Rumanian army defeated his troops, crossed the Tisza—despite the interdiction of the Allies—and occupied Budapest on Aug. 4. There they remained, in the face of numerous protests, until Nov. 14. The treaties of St. Germain and Trianon recognized as Rumanian the predominantly Rumanian territories of the old dual monarchy, and the treaty of Neuilly sanctioned Rumanian possession of southern Dobruja.

Domestic Politics, 1919–1930.—The political scene was transformed after 1918; the old Conservative party was swept away because of its pro-German policy and the impoverishment of its chief supporters, the boyars. The Liberals became the party of the business and professional classes, while the peasants, who gained new status through the land reform, founded a party of their own in the old kingdom headed by Ion Mihalache. More radical elements came in from Transylvania, notably the National Popular party headed by Iuliu Maniu and Alexandru Vaida-Voevod. The Socialists were not influential as more than 80% of the population of Rumania were peasants; in the old kingdom the Socialists were mainly Marxist and supported the Russian Revolution, but in Transylvania they looked to the west.

The new parties had their chance as early as Dec. 1919 in a coalition cabinet headed by Vaida-Voevod, the Bratianu government having resigned in protest against the minorities clause of the treaty of Trianon (article 60), but their tenure of office was short. General fear of Communist propaganda and the alarm of the landowners at the proposed expropriation led to the government's resignation in March 1920 and the return of a new People's party containing many former Conservatives, led by General Averescu, hero of two wars.

He secured the able Take Jonescu as minister of foreign affairs. The general, despite personal sympathy with the peasants, had to take strong measures to restore order. A revolutionary movement was breaking out on the Dniester and securing support among extremists in the old kingdom, and social tension reached a climax in the general strike of Oct. 1920. The failure of the strike split the Rumanian socialist movement. The more moderate leaders were imprisoned, and the Communists, who had kept underground, gained the upper hand. They voted for the affiliation of the party with the Comintern at a congress in May 1921, whereupon 70 leaders were arrested. The Social Democrats thereafter kept separate, and the Communist party was outlawed in 1924.

Meanwhile Averescu had to put through the promised land reform. The bill was introduced in the spring of 1921 by the minister of agriculture, Constantin Garoflid, himself a large landowner. After impassioned controversy, expropriation was put through on the lines agreed in July 1917, estates being limited to 500 ha. in the old kingdom, and to much smaller areas in Bessarabia and Bukovina. The peasants were not wholly satisfied; the holdings allotted were often unduly small and there was no adequate arrangement for the granting of credits for the purchase of seed and tools.

The Liberals came to power at the beginning of 1922, remaining in office with one short break until 1928. Bratianu dominated the scene until his death in 1927 and thus had the satisfaction of being in office for the coronation of King Ferdinand as sovereign of united Rumania at Alba Julia on Oct. 15, 1922.

A new constitution was adopted in March 1923 based on that of 1866 but with the addition of manhood suffrage. The Jews were given citizenship rights, but their inflow in large numbers after World War I provoked violent hostility. In the financial sphere the Liberal government pushed through the difficult policy of coupling industrialization with the exclusion as far as possible of foreign capital, which bore heavily on the peasants who had to pay for it by export duties. The chief cause of Liberal unpopularity, however, was the centralization of administration. All the new provinces, even including backward Bessarabia, had hoped for a measure of autonomy, and this feeling was strongest in Transylvania where bitter hostility was aroused by the arrival of officials from the old kingdom. The minorities problem was to prove troublesome to all Rumanian administrations in the years following World War I, and none succeeded in finding a solution.

Bratianu proceeded in 1926 to push through an electoral law giving great advantages to the party in power at election time. By this law those who secured 40% or more of the votes were given half the seats in the chamber, plus a share in the remainder in proportion to the number of votes obtained. When a ministry fell as a result of an adverse vote in the chamber, the king could call on the leader of the next largest party to form a cabinet and hold elections. Until 1937 no party in charge ever failed to secure the necessary 40%. The Liberal party's popularity was slowly waning at the end of 1925, and in the face of growing discontent King Ferdinand again called on General Averescu to form a cabinet. His party, with some peasant support, secured four-fifths of the seats in the chamber in the elections of March 1926, largely because of successful pressure at the polls. Though the Liberals only had 16 deputies it was clear that the new administration governed largely with their support. Meanwhile the opposition was greatly strengthened by the fusion, in Oct. 1926, of Maniu's National Popular party with Mihalache's Peasant group to form the National Peasant party, which was to represent the majority of the Rumanian people. Averescu resigned in June 1927 and Bratianu was again returned; the newly formed National Peasant party, despite universal popularity, polled only 20% of the votes in the obviously manipulated elections.

The political situation was complicated by the dynastic position. In Dec. 1925 Crown Prince Carol had left Rumania, renouncing all his rights in favour of his young son Michael. In view of King Ferdinand's precarious health a council of regency was formed in Jan. 1926 consisting of the patriarch Miron Cristea, the president of the supreme court Gheorghe Buzdugan, and the king's second son, Prince Nicholas.

King Ferdinand died on July 20, 1927, and Bratianu died in November of the same year. The Liberal party, thus weakened, was faced with an economic crisis and peasant demonstrations. The regency council in May 1928 entrusted Maniu with forming a cabinet and holding elections: his National Peasant party was returned with a majority of more than 75%. The new government abolished censorship and martial law, mitigated the police regime, promised concessions to the minorities and in June 1929 introduced, to the great satisfaction of the Transylvanians, an administrative reform bill aiming at extensive decentralization. The peasants were helped by the repeal of the export duties; cooperatives were encouraged and free sale of land allowed, a measure which unfortunately led to an increase of the rural proletariat rather than to a consolidation of prosperous peasant holdings as had been intended. The economic situation was greatly eased by the entry, at last allowed, of foreign capital.

Foreign Policy, 1920–1937.—Rumania's foreign policy after Trianon was necessarily based on an endeavour to maintain the *status quo* and to protect itself against aggression. Rumania was from the first a consistent member of the League of Nations, but built up a careful system of regional pacts to buttress collective security. The first such pact was concluded with Poland in March 1921, when Take Jonescu and Prince Eustachy Sapieha signed a treaty providing for mutual assistance in the event of

unprovoked attack on the eastern frontier. Both countries were threatened by the U.S.S.R., which had not recognized Rumania's right to Bessarabia and seemed little satisfied with Poland's possession of its former Ukrainian and Byelorussian territories.

Take Jonescu had hoped to form a Baltic-Aegean bloc to act as a buffer between Germany and the U.S.S.R., but had to be content with joining the little entente (*q.v.*) system. An agreement with Czechoslovakia for mutual protection against Hungary was signed in April 1921 and with Yugoslavia for similar protection against Hungary and Bulgaria in June. He sought further to cement Balkan friendships by dynastic alliances. Marriages were concluded between Crown Prince Carol and Princess Helen of Greece (March 10, 1921), between his elder sister Princess Elizabeth and the crown prince of Greece (Feb. 1921) and between Princess Marie and King Alexander of Yugoslavia (June 6, 1922).

General Averescu, in his 1926–27 administration, extended Rumania's system of pacts to include its "Latin sisters." A treaty of alliance and nonaggression was signed with France in June 1926 and another in September of that year with Italy. The Italians, after long hesitation, recognized the incorporation of Bessarabia in Rumania in March 1927. Relations with the U.S.S.R. remained in a state of tension; during 1924 the Soviet Union kept up continuous agitation and threats of war, even setting up a three-day Communist republic at Tatar Bunar in southern Bessarabia. A conference held in Vienna in April 1924 between Rumanian and Soviet representatives led to no results. The situation was eased when Nicolae Titulescu became foreign minister in 1927. In 1933 both countries signed the convention of London defining the aggressor, and with the U.S.S.R.'s entry into the League in 1934 and the exchange of letters between Titulescu and Maxim Litvinov later that year it was hoped that the Bessarabian question was settled. Rumania entered into diplomatic relations with the U.S.S.R. in 1934, but the Bessarabian question remained open and was raised again by the Russians after Titulescu had been dropped from the Rumanian cabinet in 1936.

Agreement with Bulgaria, resentful at the loss of southern Dobruja to Rumania and at the inclusion of parts of Macedonia in Yugoslavia and Greece, proved out of reach; nonetheless, the Balkan pact, signed in 1934 between Rumania, Yugoslavia, Turkey and Greece, was left open to Bulgaria.

Rumania under King Carol.—Maniu, dissatisfied with the regency, arranged for the return of Carol from exile with the agreement of all the major parties. Carol was proclaimed king on June 9, 1930, his son Michael becoming crown prince (grand voivode). Conflict soon arose between the king and Maniu, who had exacted a promise that Carol would leave his Jewish mistress Magda Lupescu abroad if he resumed the throne and would seek reconciliation with Queen Helen. On the king's breaking this promise Maniu resigned the prime ministry in Oct. 1930, though his party remained in power under Gheorghe Mironescu. King Carol was from the first determined to secure absolute power and to break up the old political parties. Maniu's resignation and the world economic crisis helped to bring down the National Peasants in 1931. After Mironescu's resignation the foreign minister Titulescu attempted to form a cabinet, and on his failure the king appointed one of his own choice headed by his former tutor Nicolae Jorga. The elections of June 1931 gave the government a majority of 291 seats out of 387, but it resigned a year later. The National Peasants had a brief return to power and it fell to Vaida-Voevod to deal with the serious Communist-inspired railway strike at Grivita in Feb. 1933, but the party, split through King Carol's intrigues, could no longer keep itself in power. The Liberal opposition was also split; the leaders Ionel Bratianu and his brother Vintila were dead and the third brother Constantin (Dinu) had not their grip over the party, while their nephew Gheorghe was on the king's side. Nevertheless the Liberals returned to power in 1933 under an anti-Carol leader Ion Duca.

Rise of the Iron Guard.—The king was helped in his disruption of the older parties by the rise of a new group of fascist type which was taking shape in Moldavia, feeding on endemic Rumanian anti-Semitism and the economic crisis. The leader, a young man named Corneliu Zelea Codreanu, first called his group the legion of the archangel Michael; later it had many names, the best known being the Iron Guard. Priests, officers and students flocked to Codreanu's standard; the party had a mystical appeal and its leaders wore the trappings of romance. Its slogan was the Christian and racial renovation of Rumania: in foreign affairs it opposed co-operation with France, the U.S.S.R. or the League of Nations and sympathized with Germany and Italy and later with Francisco Franco in Spain; at home it tempted the peasants with the slogan *omul si pogonul*—"one man, one acre."

The Iron Guard gained its first four seats in parliament in 1932; its policy of violence, which had already been demonstrated by the murder of the prefect of Jassy, was carried forward by the assassination of the prime minister Duca, on Dec. 30, 1933, a month after he had assumed office. Unlike the neighbouring Balkan states Rumania had not in modern times been prone to political murders and the country was profoundly shocked. The new Liberal premier Gheorghe Tatarescu proscribed the Iron Guard, but reappearing under another name—*Totul Pentru Tara* (everything for the fatherland)—it succeeded in securing Titulescu's removal from the foreign ministry in Aug. 1936.

In the 1937 elections, presided over by Tatarescu, the government for the first time failed to secure the necessary 40% of the votes. It was highly unpopular, and the opposition was unexpectedly consolidated by the conclusion of an electoral pact between the National Peasants and the Iron Guard, which led to much criticism of Maniu. The Guard secured 16% of the votes. King Carol, alarmed at this success and not wishing to have Codreanu as a rival dictator, dropped his earlier policy of covert support and called on the elderly Transylvanian poet Octavian Goga, leader of the right wing anti-Semitic National Christian party, to form a government. After a few weeks of violent anti-Semitic action, at which the British and French ministers protested, Goga was dismissed by King Carol, who then proclaimed a personal dictatorship. A new constitution of corporative type was published on Feb. 20, 1938, and "accepted" in a plebiscite. The patriarch Miron Cristea was made prime minister with Tatarescu as his deputy. In April Codreanu and other guardists were sentenced to ten years' imprisonment. The guard replied with a renewed terror campaign, and in November King Carol, returning from a post-Munich visit to the western capitals, had Codreanu and 13 of his followers "shot while trying to escape."

On Dec. 16 the king founded a monopoly party, the National Renaissance Front, to support his government, and announced certain concessions to the minorities, who accordingly joined the front. Miron Cristea, the patriarch and prime minister, died in March 1939 and was succeeded by Armand Calinescu, minister of the interior in the former government. Elections on a corporative basis were held in June, the electorate under the new constitution being 2,000,000 compared with 4,500,000 in 1937. The senate was designed to include old parliamentarians, and the leading political figures, Maniu and Mihalache of the National Peasant party and Dinu Bratianu, head of the National Liberals who disapproved of the Tatarescu faction, automatically became members. They refused, however, to take the oath to the new constitution, and were suspended. Women could vote and, for the first time in Rumanian history, stand as candidates, but only for the senate. The Iron Guard continued to foment unrest during the summer of 1939 with German backing and on Sept. 20 murdered the prime minister, Calinescu; after the brief premiership of Gen. Gheorghe Argesanu, who was able to secure some degree of public order, Constantin Argetoianu became prime minister for two months and was then succeeded by Tatarescu.

Foreign Policy, 1938–39.—The anschluss and the Munich agreement overthrew the whole system of Rumanian foreign policy. Relations with Italy were already embittered through Rumania's adopting sanctions at the League's bidding during the Abyssinian war, and the pact with Italy had lapsed in 1936. Rumania had been ready to fulfil its obligations under the little entente and to come to the aid of Czechoslovakia during the Munich crisis, even secretly agreeing to allow Soviet troops to cross its territory. The Polish alliance stood, even after Munich, but Rumania refused Poland's offer of a slice of Czechoslovak ter-

ritory in Ruthenia in Oct. 1938. Confidence in the west had been shaken by Munich, and in March 1939 a trade treaty was signed with Germany designed to put the whole of Rumania's economic life at German disposal. The new foreign minister, Grigore Gafencu, made a last attempt to seek support in the west, securing a Franco-British guarantee of Rumanian territorial integrity on April 13, 1939. Rumania's only real hope, however, lay in German-Soviet antagonism, and that was shattered by the Ribbentrop-Molotov pact in August.

World War II.—The invasion and dismemberment of Poland in Sept. 1939 found Rumania powerless to help its ally; Rumania declared neutrality on Sept. 4. The collapse of France in the summer of 1940 removed the last prop of Rumanian morale; nonetheless, King Carol made efforts to put the army on a war footing and announced that the country's frontiers would be defended at any cost. Under German pressure the foreign minister, Grigore Gafencu, was forced to resign and was succeeded by the strongly pro-German Ion Gigurtu. On June 21 the king agreed to turn the National Renaissance Front into a still more totalitarian national party which included Iron Guardists, under Horia Sima, released on German orders.

The first blow fell on June 27 when in agreement with Germany the U.S.S.R. occupied not only Bessarabia, but northern Bukovina, which had never been in Russian possession. Rumania was forced to accept, renounced the British guarantee on July 2 and on July 4 appointed a new pro-German cabinet with Gigurtu as prime minister and Horia Sima as minister of culture. On July 16 Germany was "invited" to send a military mission. Hungary now had to be conciliated; on Aug. 30 Germany and Italy imposed the Vienna award whereby Hungary was to be given northern Transylvania, an especially bitter blow to Rumanian patriotism. The people wished to fight and looked for a lead to Maniu, the grand old man of Transylvania. While he hesitated the Iron Guard, despite their pro-German attitude, led the national protest and demanded the abdication of King Carol, who was made the scapegoat. The king left on Sept. 6 with Magda Lupescu, leaving his 19-year-old son Michael on the throne as Mihai I. Before his departure he entrusted power to a general, Ion Antonescu, who formed a government consisting largely of Iron Guardists, with Horia Sima as vice-premier. The constitution was suspended and Antonescu given full powers. Meanwhile Bulgaria, with German support, had been agitating for the return of southern Dobruja; the agreement for its cession was signed at Craiova the day after Carol's departure. Rumania lost about 3,500,000 subjects to the U.S.S.R., 2,400,000 to Hungary and 360,000 to Bulgaria. There were rumours that Germany intended also to separate the Banat (*q.v.*) from Rumania, but in the end that territory was merely accorded semiautonomy under the large local German minority. Germany and Italy guaranteed rump Rumania. Rumania was declared a "national legionary state" on Sept. 15 and joined the Tripartite pact on Nov. 23.

German troops had been pouring into the country since September, but as the Germans had decided to reduce Rumania to complete subservience by playing off the Iron Guard against Antonescu, the *Wehrmacht* stood by when the guardists staged a St. Bartholomew's night on Nov. 28 in which 64 prominent members of the old regime were assassinated, including Jorga and the peasant leader Virgil Madgearu. Antonescu now secured German support in putting down the Guard, which staged a more serious rising at the end of Jan. 1941 under the leadership of Sima, vice-premier in Antonescu's cabinet, and Ion Codreanu, father of Corneliu. The revolt was finally suppressed with about 6,000 casualties; Sima escaped. The new administration formed at the end of January was mainly military, all guardists being excluded. Some 500,000 German troops were in the country by February, and on Feb. 10 Great Britain broke off diplomatic relations. Antonescu refused to join Adolf Hitler in smashing Rumania's ally Yugoslavia in April 1941, but the country was behind him in entering the war against the U.S.S.R. as Germany's ally on June 22. Great Britain declared war on Rumania on Dec. 7 and on Dec. 12 Rumania declared war on the United States. Rumania's recovery of Bessarabia in the summer of 1941 was highly popular in the country, but the opposition leaders underground, in particular Maniu, strongly disapproved of the army crossing the Dniestr into Soviet territory in 1942 and of the organization of a new Rumanian province beyond the river known as Transnistria. This did give outlet to national energies, however, and the war did not become thoroughly unpopular until the disastrous casualty lists came in from Stalingrad.

The Communist Regime.—Although Rumania had not had a parliamentary government since 1938, the chief political parties had kept their organizations intact; the National Peasants under Maniu and the Liberals under Dinu Bratianu were therefore able to form a rallying point for popular discontent with the fruits of Antonescu's pro-Axis policy, and undertook secret negotiations with the Allies during 1943. The traditional parties were supported in the desire for an armistice by the pro-Soviet left-wing groups, the Social Democrats under Titel Petrescu and the Communists under Lucretiu Patraşcanu. The Communists, whose organization had long been illegal, numbered only about 20,000 in 1944; they had no war record of partisan activity to give them prestige and few of the leaders were of Rumanian race, the majority being Russian-trained Jews, Ukrainians or Hungarians. The party gained powerful reinforcement in its lower ranks after 1941 from among the leaderless and disillusioned Guardists, ready for any violence. In the spring of 1944 these four parties agreed to form a national bloc to bring the country out of the war. The coup d'état of Aug. 23, 1944, which overthrew Antonescu and brought Rumania into the war against Germany, was largely the work of King Michael himself, supported by the National Peasants and Liberals, but the Social Democrats and Communists were given representation out of proportion to their numbers in the first postarmistice administration. The armistice was signed in Moscow on Sept. 12, Soviet troops having been in occupation of Rumania since the end of August. The peace treaty subsequently provided for their remaining until after the conclusion of the Austrian treaty, a period which would ensure their presence while Rumania was being remodelled on the Soviet pattern. The Russians had prepared during the war a division of indoctrinated Rumanian prisoners named after the hero of 1821, Tudor Vladimirescu; these marched into Rumania beside the Red army.

Until elections could be held, three short-lived governments of a mainly military character took office, the first two headed by Gen. Constantin Sanatescu, and the third by the chief of staff Nicolae Radescu. Radescu made no secret of his anti-Communist attitude and the Soviet deputy foreign minister, Andrei Vishinsky, came in person to Bucharest to insist on his removal and the installation as premier of Petre Groza, head of a splinter left-wing country party known as the Ploughmen's front which, though not forming part of the national bloc, had been included under Soviet pressure in the last Sanatescu administration. The Groza government, which took office in March 1945, excluded the National Peasants and Liberals and proved highly unpopular. In August of that year the Potsdam conference proposed the resumption of diplomatic relations with Rumania provided that the government was "recognized and democratic." The U.S.S.R. immediately resumed relations, but Great Britain and the United States refrained on the ground of the unrepresentative nature of the Groza administration. King Michael then appealed to the three powers, who, meeting in Moscow in Dec. 1945, advised that a government, broadened by the inclusion of a National Peasant and a Liberal member, should hold elections.

The 1923 constitution had been restored after the armistice, but before the elections a law was passed abolishing the senate. The government bloc announced that it had polled 71% of the votes in the elections held on Nov. 19, 1946. The Communists secured the key portfolios in the new government, excepting that of foreign affairs which was given to Tatarescu, and split the Social Democrats, the bulk of the party remaining aloof under its leader Petrescu, who was later imprisoned. The elections were followed by a wave of arrests of former prominent politicians and their followers, including Maniu himself (Antonescu was shot as a war criminal in 1946). The National Peasant party, which had the allegiance of the majority of Rumanians, was declared illegal

in Aug. 1947 and Maniu tried and condemned to life imprisonment. Evidence given at his trial was used as a pretext for supplanting Tatarescu at the foreign ministry by the Moscow-trained Jewess Ana Pauker. The peace treaty signed in March and ratified on Sept. 15, 1947, restored northern Transylvania to Rumania and confirmed the cession of Bessarabia and northern Bukovina to the U.S.S.R. and of southern Dobruja to Bulgaria. In December King Michael, abdicating under Communist pressure, left the country. The Rumanian Workers' party (R.W.P.) was formed in Feb. 1948 by the merger of the Communists with the rump of the Social Democrats led by Lothar Radaceanu; together with the Ploughmen's front and the Hungarian People's union, this R.W.P. made up the People's Democratic front, which claimed 405 out of 414 seats in the grand national assembly after the elections of March 28. A constitution on the Soviet model was adopted in April 1948 and Rumania proclaimed a people's republic with C. Parhon as president (chairman of the state presidium).

In 1948 private schools were abolished, banking and industry nationalized, the Uniate Church suppressed and the other churches deprived of their leadership and independence. Peasants were given additional plots of land as a preliminary to collectivization. State farms were set up on the remaining land of former owners, who were finally dispossessed entirely. The collectivization drive was launched in March 1949, with a ruthless campaign against the prosperous peasantry. The R.W.P. purged itself by 18% during 1949, Patraşcanu having been dismissed from the key ministry of justice and arrested the year before. Local boundaries were redrawn and local administration refashioned in 1950 to conform to that of the U.S.S.R. In 1952 the currency, which had undergone a drastic stabilization in 1947, was adjusted to the rouble. As scapegoats for the distress caused by this measure three leading Communists were removed: the finance minister Vasile Luca, Ana Pauker and Techari Georgescu. Gheorghe Gheorghiu-Dej, emerging supreme, became premier in June 1952, Petru Groza being relegated to the presidency of the R.P.R. vacated by Parhon. A new constitution even closer to the Soviet pattern than that of 1948 was adopted in September. Elections under a new law were held in November, about 97% of the purged electorate duly voting for the People's Democratic front. After Stalin's death, the R.P.R. copied the U.S.S.R.'s changes in party and government structure so as to emphasize collective leadership. In April 1954, Gheorghiu-Dej, remaining premier, renounced the office of secretary general of the R.W.P. In the same month Patraşcanu was tried and executed and in September Vasile Luca was sentenced to life imprisonment.

Rumania, as every other Soviet-controlled state, has no separate foreign policy. It is integrated in the Soviet system of treaties of mutual assistance.

(B. Br.)

POPULATION

The total population fluctuated with the various territorial changes which Rumania underwent. In 1914, before the addition of Transylvania and Bessarabia, the figure was 7,600,000; in 1940, before incurring the losses arising out of the Vienna award and the Soviet and Bulgarian seizures (see *History*, above) it stood at 19,900,000; the 1948 census, reflecting the eventual peace settlements, with Bessarabia and northern Bukovina remaining in Soviet hands, southern Dobruja under Bulgaria but the former Hungarian frontier restored, gave a total of 15,872,624 inhabitants. The 1948 figure represented a density of 173.1 per sq.mi., low compared with western Europe. The net reproduction rate was estimated, however, to be at a high level. The population was distributed among the various provinces as follows: Muntenia (the most densely settled region), 31.4%; Transylvania 21.6%; Moldavia, 16.4%; Oltenia, 13.8% and 16.8% shared by the small border provinces of Crisana, Banat, Maramures, Bukovina and Dobruja.

The rural character of much of Rumania's population is illustrated by the fact that according to the 1948 census only 23.4% of the total lived in urban centres. Rumania is essentially a nation of peasants. The largest town, the greatest manufacturing centre and the capital of the country, is Bucharest (pop., 1939,

684,164; 1948 census, 1,401,807). The two next largest towns, Kishinev (Chisinau) (113,000 in 1939) and Chernovtsy (Cernauti) (110,000 in 1939) became part of the U.S.S.R. Next to Bucharest in size in 1948 was Cluj (Kolozsvar) (117,915), the important route centre in Transylvania. Several other towns had reached the 100,000 mark by 1948—Brasov (renamed Stalin), Timisoara, Jassy, Braila and Galatz (Galati). The expulsions of Germans, Magyars and Jews decreased the urban population, but detailed figures of the changes are not available. The big increase in Bucharest is partly accounted for by changes in administrative boundaries.

Not only did the total population of the country decrease as a result of the territorial losses, but the ethnographic composition was considerably modified between 1920, when the previous ethnographic details were published, and 1948. In 1920, most of the peasants, shepherds and woodmen were Rumanian, but only 70% of the total population was of that nationality; according to the 1948 census, Rumanians had increased by 2,000,000 to form 85.7% of the total. In 1948, there were said to be 1,499,851 Magyars (9.4% of the total); the actual number was only slightly less than in 1920, the post-1945 expulsions from Transylvania having been suspended later. The third largest element in 1920, the Jews, had then numbered 900,000; in 1948, there were only 150,000, as they had suffered considerably under the Iron Guard and Antonescu regimes—though less severely than the Jews of Poland and Germany—and many of the survivors emigrated to Israel. The fourth largest group, the Germans, declined from 792,000 in 1920 to 343,915 in 1948; they were affected by the wartime schemes of repatriation to Germany and by deportations to the U.S.S.R. in the period immediately after 1944. The Slav group in 1920 was large and included: 792,000 Ukrainians and Russians in Bessarabia; 440,000 Poles, Czechs and Ruthenians in Bukovina and Maramures and 290,000 Bulgars in the Dobruja. The Slavs were much reduced by the Soviet and Bulgarian acquisitions of territory, and the 1948 census recorded their combined total as 200,000. Finally, smaller ethnographic groups, such as Turks, Tatars, Greeks, Albanians and gypsies, numbered about 100,000 persons in 1948. The Turks had been reduced before World War II by the exchanges carried out in the Balkans after 1922.

It is generally accepted that the Rumanians are partly the descendants of Roman merchants and veterans who settled in Dacia, even as far north as the modern Polish border, before and after the campaign of Trajan, and partly of the native Dacians. Archaeological and historical evidence shows that there was a long and thorough period of penetration of the Carpathians by Roman commerce and after the Roman withdrawal the various established Roman elements remained in the country. The very word *batran* in Rumanian, meaning "old," is derived from the Latin *veteranus* and the word *biserica* (church) indicates the western origin of Christianity in these parts (*biserica = basilica*) and so the western connections with Italy and the Roman culture. The Rumanian physical type, in many cases, seems more definitely Latin than the Italian and the language is in many respects closer to Latin than is Italian. Slavonic elements are clear in some of the prevalent types but it is by no means the preponderant influence.

The Magyars are found for the most part in the towns of Transylvania. By training, education and tradition they associate themselves more happily with the German elements than with the Rumanian and they take only a small part in the agricultural development of the land. They are industrious and honest but in the past they were regarded as politically unreliable since they were encouraged by their fellow Magyars in Hungary to oppose in every way the rule under which they lived. A branch of the Magyars known as Szeklers were military colonists planted by the kings of Hungary to guard the frontier passes at the head of the Mures and Olt rivers. Those of the Banat were later agricultural colonists.

Germans settled in Rumania from time to time for various reasons. The earliest were knights and their companies, perhaps crusaders, in the 12th century, who were persuaded by the Hungarians to settle in towns that commanded the main passes of the Carpathians and so prevent inroads of barbarians into Europe. Gradually they developed their settlements and in 1224 their position and independence were recognized. Alsatians and Saxons together with some groups from the Rhineland were settled in these early times. Until 1944 they still lived an exclusive and separate life, largely with their own institutions and local government. They are mainly of the Lutheran persuasion. It is remarkable to see in their churches the one hint of the orient, which they were brought there to combat, in the shape of fine Turkish carpets of the 16th century, survivals of the period when the Turks overran the Transylvanian plateau but left the German settlements still independent. They formed a very useful element in the state and, if rather an isolated enclave in a foreign land, yet were loyal subjects of whatever regime controlled them. The Germans of the Banat are of a different type. They colonized the waste plains of this fertile region in the 18th century and are mostly Rhinelanders and Alsatians. Their activities are almost entirely agricultural and their wealth and industry is considerable.

The Turk survivors from the days of Turkish domination, settled mainly in the 16th century. They lived in the remoter districts along the Danube, particularly on the Dobruja coast and near Silistra. They were old-fashioned and recalled the Turkey of the early 19th century; they bore little resemblance to their brethren of the new Turkish republic. The gypsies and Bulgars were the least satisfactory element in the country. The former contributed the attractive traditional Tszigan music and were at least picturesque, but the latter were a difficult element. Both were found mainly in the Moldavian and Dobruja provinces. Bulgar villages were common throughout the Dobruja, intermingled with Tatar settlements and Rumanian hamlets. But the Bulgars there were of a savage type, perhaps descendants from the original Cumans (*q.v.*), of the middle ages. (G. W. S.)

Religion.—The great majority of Rumanians belong to the Orthodox Eastern Church (*q.v.*). No firm evidence of the first coming of Christianity to their ancestors survives, but the fact that most of the basic words of church observance in the Rumanian language are of Latin origin suggests that the first missionaries belonged to the Church of Rome. Dacia was separated from the empire before the conversion of Constantine, but the Daco-Romans later had contact with their kinsmen in Moesia south of the Danube. The beginnings of Christian life were submerged in the barbarian invasions, and an organized church was not founded until the 9th century, when the Bulgarians, then masters of the former Dacia, became Christian and introduced to the province the Slavonic alphabet and liturgy that they had received from SS. Cyril and Methodius (*qq.v.*). This Slav rite, maintained in the Rumanian Church until the 17th century, helped to keep the Vlach Christians in Transylvania apart from their neighbours, so that, unlike the strongly propapal Hungarians, they followed eastern Christendom against the western in the schism of 1054. When the principalities of Moldavia and Walachia took shape in the 14th century the people were staunchly Orthodox and attached to their Slav rite, though some of the early princes, intermarrying with Poles and Hungarians, temporarily took the Roman Catholic side. Orthodox bishoprics were at once founded in the new states, depending at first on the Bulgarian Church and later on the patriarchate of Constantinople, but having a large measure of autonomy. In Transylvania Orthodoxy was oppressed, not being one of the four "received religions" and the Orthodox bishop there was dependent on the Walachian metropolitan. Hence the title of the Rumanian primate—*mitropolit Ungro-Vlahia si exarhul plaiurilor* (metropolitan of Ungro-Walachia, and exarch of the mountains [*i.e.*, the Carpathians]). The Moldavian and Walachian princes and boyars were exceptionally generous in their endowments to monasteries; in order to protect them in the unsettled conditions under Turkish rule the practice arose of dedicating them to one of the patriarchates of the east or to the holy places. This led to an infiltration of Greek monks. As the source of Slavonic teaching dried up and the village priests knew no Greek, Rumanian gradually became the liturgical language in the 17th century, particularly in the villages. The first Gospels in Rumanian were printed in Transylvania in 1561 under Protestant influence, and the first Rumanian Bible appeared in 1688. The work of Rumanian printers was helped in Moldavia by the metropolitan of Kiev, Peter Mogila, himself of Moldavian origin and one of the leading theologians of the Eastern Church. In Phanariot times, from the 18th century onward, Greek influence spread rapidly, the bishops frequently being Greek and the liturgy being celebrated in Greek in the richer churches.

With the union of the principalities in 1859 the churches of Walachia and Moldavia were united and anti-Greek reaction had full swing. In 1863 the dedicated monasteries, whose lands covered more than one-fifth of the area of the new state and most of whose revenues left the country, were expropriated, and the use of Greek in all churches and monasteries was forbidden. In 1865 an autonomous Church of Rumania was set up, which in 1872 was given an organic statute, and shortly after Rumania had been proclaimed a kingdom (1881) the Orthodox Church was declared autocephalous and arranged to consecrate its own holy chrism instead of procuring it from Constantinople. The oecumenical patriarch protested, fearing that complete ecclesiastical independence in Rumania would lead to an undue growth of Russian influence, but finally agreed.

With the formation of greater Rumania in 1918 the Orthodox Church received many new adherents. In Transylvania there was only one Orthodox bishopric, at Sibiu, which had been granted autonomy in 1869 after former dependence on the Church of Serbia. The majority of Transylvanian Orthodox, soon after the province had come under direct Habsburg rule, had signed an act of union with Rome in Oct. 1698, whereby they kept their own rite but acknowledged the Holy See's jurisdiction. The Orthodox had suffered severe disabilities under Calvinist control and looked on the union as a way of escape. In Bukovina, which had been Austrian since 1775, the people remained Orthodox and had had their own metropolitanate at Czernowitz since 1873. In Bessarabia, the majority of the people were Orthodox and had been under the jurisdiction of the Russian Holy Synod. All these churches united after 1918, and in 1925 the enlarged Church of Rumania was elevated to a patriarchate with the consent of Constantinople, the first patriarch being a Transylvanian, Miron Cristea. With the collapse of the Russian Church in the Revolution the Rumanian Church, with 13,000,000 members, became a leading force in the Orthodox world and took the initiative in many matters of general ecclesiastical interest. In 1936 it recognized Anglican orders.

The old kingdom of Rumania had been relatively homogeneous in religion, but the new provinces brought in a big influx of other denominations. More than 3,000,000 owed allegiance to Rome in 1930, half being Uniates from Transylvania, all of whom were Rumanian by race, and the other half Latin Catholics, mainly Hungarians of Transylvania and Swabians of the Banat. Many of the Hungarians were Calvinist or Unitarian, while the Saxons of Transylvania were Lutheran. In Bukovina and Bessarabia there were many Jews, and in the latter province and in Dobruja there were Mohammedan Tatars.

Under the constitution of 1923 the Orthodox Church and the Uniate Church of Transylvania were declared Rumanian churches, the former being dominant and the latter having precedence over all other denominations. Liberty of conscience was established, but the Jews, the Baptists and other sects suffered under considerable disabilities. A concordat with the Vatican was concluded in 1929. Under the Antonescu regime a decree on the recognition of cults was issued (Sept. 12, 1940) suppressing a number of sects and putting restrictions on Jewish worship.

After the armistice of Sept. 23, 1944, relations between the churches of Rumania and the U.S.S.R., interrupted since 1918, were resumed. The second patriarch of Rumania, Nicodim, died in Jan. 1948 and was succeeded in June by a young bishop, Justinian. Government nominees did not cease to vote for the patriarch or for the bishops now that the government was officially atheist. The Communist constitution of April 1948 removed the special privileges of the Orthodox Church. Laws on religion and education in Aug. 1948 ended all church control in schools and laid down that all denominations must submit a statute before being

allowed to function. Under the Orthodox Church statute, 1949, several of the old dioceses were suppressed.

In Oct. 1948 the Uniates of Transylvania were reincorporated in the Orthodox Church and their five bishops were arrested. By 1952 the Roman Catholic Church had not secured approval for a statute. The concordat with the Vatican was denounced on July 17, 1948, and the five Latin-rite bishops put under arrest. The Lutherans, Calvinists and Unitarians secured approval for their respective statutes and the Baptists formed a federation with the other neo-Protestant sects. The different Jewish sects were also amalgamated into a federation of the Mosaic cult, and the Tatar Moslems were put under the muftiate in Constanta. All these recognized religions expressed full loyalty to the Communist government. Apart from the Catholic hierarchy many priests of the Orthodox Church and of other denominations were imprisoned.

(B. Br.)

ANTIQUITIES AND EARLY SETTLEMENT

Rumania is rich in antiquities of all periods from the Neolithic to the Roman but no scientific archaeological work can be said to have been done before 1900 when G. Tocilescu published the results of his surveys of Roman Dacia. Excavation by Rumanians did not begin before 1914.

The Neolithic period is hard to distinguish from the Chalcolithic but in general it is abundantly clear that Rumania in the first half of the third millennium B.C. formed part of a homogeneous region in which Bulgaria, Thrace, Thessaly and the Ukraine as far north as Kiev were included. This culture is distinguished by a remarkable painted pottery of high artistic quality in design and shape. The people of this area and period have, for convenience, been called the people of the Black Earth region because the soil is rich and alluvial and because those living upon it at this period were largely agriculturalists.

The most important sites in Rumania hitherto examined are Cucuteni near Jassy where abundant remains were found of two periods of this culture, Erosd in Transylvania and Brasov (Kronstadt), and some sites (excavated by Germans during World War I) near Cernavoda on the Danube. The culture so revealed is one of the most remarkable that developed in Europe in the early prehistoric period. It is thought by some to have oriental affinities with regions as far afield as Turkistan and Honan in China, where remarkably similar pottery is found. In any case the Black Earth culture came to an abrupt end about 2000 B.C. and was replaced by a culture coming from the northeast, whose people had war weapons. The Bronze Age that ensued develops rapidly and concentrates mainly in the western half of Transylvania and the Hungarian plains. It is of great artistic merit and some of the finest products of the European Bronze Age in gold and bronze come from Transylvania. Inhabited sites are numerous but not large and the gold of Transylvania seems certainly to have been worked on a large scale. There was a nobility and a subordinate or serf population and the accoutrement of the nobility and their gold ornaments and plate form an outstanding feature of the civilization they represented. The *floruit* of this Bronze Age seems to have been about the 15th century B.C. and the Hungarian plain seems to have been the breeding place for movements that extended far and wide. Bronze swords of Danubian type from these regions are found during the 14th and 13th centuries B.C. penetrating, perhaps more as signs of invasion than as elements of trade, as far afield as Mycenae, Egypt, Cyprus and Crete. The makers of the swords seem to have been the peoples who were gradually pressing down southward into the Mediterranean and who subsequently were responsible for the northernization of the Minoan world. Their gold may have reached the wealthy cities of the Mycenaean mainland. Certainly they were in close touch with Troy and Anatolia.

Toward the close of the second millennium before Christ the Bronze Age culture of Rumania was modified by external influences and at the dawn of the Mediterranean Iron Age, Italy played a preponderant part in the commerce of the Carpatho-Danubian regions. Villanovan culture from north Italy sent its wares (particularly its fine bronze work), far and wide into Transylvania and western influences predominated. Rumania proper is almost out of touch with the Hallstatt Iron Age and its Bronze Age does not end until the 8th century when devastating invasions from Scythia entered from the northeast. Scythian graves are found in three large areas—in north Hungary, in south Transylvania and in Walachia. They are never rich and they indicate the intrusion of large bodies of well-armed warriors who for a time controlled the country. They were, however, soon absorbed by the native population. But the wealth and prosperity of Rumania was checked, and never really recovered until Roman times.

Hellenic penetration was marked but never very effective and the Daco-Getic peoples of Rumania were never Hellenized as were the Balkan Thracians. But of the Greek period there are many archaeological evidences. The important Milesian settlement of Histria near the Danube mouth on a lagoon island facing the modern village of Karanasuf has been well excavated. Over 150 inscriptions illustrate the life over many centuries of this remote Hellenic town. The wealth of the inhabitants, as is evident from two large and important inscriptions of the Roman period, had at all times come from the fishing in the delta, over which the Histrians had immemorial rights.

Kallatis, an old Dorian settlement on the site of the modern Mangalia in the Dobruja, was partly excavated. Inscriptions there indicate that the population was strongly Dorian and that the city, with others along that coast, was largely subject to the Thraco-Scythian kings of the interior. Kallatis was evidently one of the great grain-exporting emporiums of the Black sea. Constanta has been identified as the ancient Tomi, the place of exile of Ovid. Remains of the city walls were discovered across the promontory upon which the residential part of the town is built. A small museum which contained all local antiquities was looted by Bulgarian soldiers during 1917 and the contents dispersed. Greek objects of commerce were found as far inland as the headwaters of the Pruth and the Argesul. Wine from Thasos and the Aegean was a much valued commodity in these regions.

The country is extremely rich in Roman remains. The great wall of Trajan can be traced without difficulty between Constanta and the Danube near Cernavoda. Extensive remains of Axiopolis at its western end can be seen on the Danube, and excavations were carried out there. The most impressive of all the Roman monuments is the Tropaeum Trajani at Adamklissi. It stands in a wild and desolate region in the rolling steppeland between the Danube river and Constanta with much of its sculptured decoration still lying round the massive concrete core which survives. The Roman town of Ulmetum midway between Harsova on the Danube and the coast has also been explored and excavated. Along the Danube the traces of Trajan's campaigns are numerous. The inscription recording his construction of the road along the south bank near the Iron Gate is still visible in the cliff face near the island of Ada Kalesi. Some of the piles of the bridge he built across the Danube still survive.

In Transylvania inscriptions are found as far north as the Polish border and elements of the various fortifications built at different periods can be made out. At the village of Verespatak, near Cluj considerable traces of Roman gold mining are to be seen and a series of important inscribed wax tablets was found there, bearing record to the manner and method by which the mines were worked. Of the Dacians who opposed the Romans there is much evidence but the archaeological discoveries are not of the first importance. The site of Sarmigetusa has been identified in the mountains a little south of Deva in Hunedoara. It is a powerfully fortified hill city and was the metropolis of the Dacians.

Post-Roman remains of the time before the Rumanians came under the influence of Byzantium are rare, and little or nothing is known about the country at this time. The great gold treasure of Petroasa, however, which was transported to Moscow during World War I, is certainly of Hunnish or semioriental origin. It consists of two superb chalices of pure gold, inset with large garnets and with handles shaped like panthers, a large necklet of the same material, several large gold ewers elaborately chased

and some superb torques.

Byzantine remains are not of importance until the 14th century when the Byzantine church and monastery of Curtea de Arges was built. The frescoes there rank as the finest and oldest Byzantine works of art in the country.

A special architectural style grew up after this, particularly in Moldavia, based upon the Byzantine, but of a very marked character and of great beauty. It flourished mostly in the 16th and early 17th centuries. The Church of Trei Erarchi (Three Saints) at Jassy, founded in 1639, is one of the finest examples. The style of architecture so evolved is purely Rumanian and owes little or nothing to Greek or Slavonic tradition in matters of decoration, though the structure is in essence Byzantine. Byzantine traditions in painting dominated the artists of the churches and monasteries down to the 18th century.　　　　　　(S. Ca.)

EDUCATION

Elementary education in Rumania, both before and after World War II, was described officially as free and compulsory. The remark of the old Rumanian academician, I. Simionescu, describing pre-1939 conditions, remains apposite: "In reality, it is not so free as one would think, because the committees charge a fee for each child: it is not compulsory because the state budget never allows for the setting up of enough schools to accommodate all the children of school age."

A national educational system was a comparatively late development in Rumania, partly because of the lack of a literary form of the language; a system began to take shape in the 19th century but development was most rapid after World War I. In regard to the state-provided schools, in the year 1937–38, 120,516 children were said to be in attendance at infant schools, 2,358,059 at elementary schools, 164,603 at secondary schools; the numbers at private schools were much smaller, being respectively 8,922, 133,184 and 35,922. By 1950, the numbers attending elementary schools were 2,079,357, secondary schools 365,310.

In 1952, Rumania possessed four universities, the same number as in 1939, that at Cernauti (founded in 1875) noted as a centre of germanization, having been lost to the U.S.S.R. and replaced in 1945 by a new foundation at Timisoara. The other three are at Bucharest (founded 1864), Jassy (1860) and Cluj (1872). The university of Cluj was formerly a Magyar institution, but after its nationalization in 1919 had both Rumanian and Hungarian colleges. The superior learned society, the Academia Romana of Bucharest, was founded in 1866 by C. A. Rosetti.

The Communists paid a great deal of attention to the problem of providing an adequate elementary education for the Rumanian people. Their great interest lay in complete control of the young mind and the implantation therein of their particular political beliefs, and the exclusion of other concepts, interpretations of history and so forth that tended formerly to influence the nation in the direction of western thought. Political instruction, in fact, became compulsory at each stage of education. Education was rendered completely secular in 1948, with the abolition of private schools, of religious teaching in school hours and of all the religious orders. The other great concern of the party was the provision of skilled personnel to carry through the ambitious program of industrial development envisaged in the five-year plan. Formerly many foreign experts had been employed in specialist fields, and their place was now taken to some extent by the officials of the various Sovrom companies. Polytechnics are situated at Bucharest, Timisoara, Craiova and Jassy.

ECONOMIC CONDITIONS

Economically Rumania is probably one of the most retarded countries in Europe. The causes of this were essentially political, although Rumania has no large resources of coal and iron (wood, petroleum and water power to some extent making up for the lack of coal). In the past the Rumanian nation felt acutely the effects of the rivalry of the Austro-Hungarian, Russian and Turkish empires. The Rumanians remained penned in the forests and pastures of the Carpathian mountains, and the lower Danube plains, the pioneer fringe of Europe, were not settled permanently until the 19th century. It was not until the 18th century that the Rumanians began to filter into the borders of the Hungarian plain, in the Banat and Crisana.

The comparatively recent emergence of Rumania as a political entity together with the continuing instability of frontiers and of internal politics are factors which tended to exaggerate the lack of economic balance. Resources were exploited rather than husbanded, the more so as German economic imperialism (and to a lesser extent Italian) began to dominate the scene in the 1930s. During World War II the Rumanian oil resources and surplus grains were of supreme importance to the German war machine. After the Soviet occupation in 1944, Germany's position was taken by the U.S.S.R., and Rumanian industries, especially oil, mining, timber, textiles and heavy industries were at the disposal of the Soviet Union. The transfer to the U.S.S.R. of German assets in Rumanian industries and commerce was made law by a Rumanian decree of April 1946. Thus, for example, the largest iron and steel concern, Resita, passed to the Soviet Union and the Soviet State Insurance company took over German assets in Rumanian insurance. Other foreign assets passed to the Soviet Union; e.g., the Hungarian holdings (amounting to 62% of the total) which accounted for about three-fourths of the total Rumanian output. Special Soviet-Rumanian or "Sovrom" companies, with the Soviet Union as the controlling partner, were set up to exploit these assets, and became dominating features of the Rumanian economy; in some services, for example water transport, these companies took the monopoly. The companies set up were as follows: Sovromtransport, Sovromlemn (timber), Sovromchim (chemicals), Sovrometal (metallurgy), Sovrompetrol, Sovromgaz (oil industry), Sovromasig (insurance), Sovrombanc (domestic and foreign banking), Sovromcarbune (coal mining), Sovromconstructie, Sovromtractor, Sovromfilm and T.A.R.S. (air transport).

The Rumanian economy indeed became completely tied to that of the U.S.S.R. as the Sovrom companies naturally imported Soviet practices and personnel, and set the pace and example for the rest of industry. Under the armistice arrangements, large quantities of Rumanian products, especially petroleum and timber, were paid out to the Soviet Union as reparations—so much so that between 1945 and 1948, when reparations were reduced by 50%, there was little left for export to any other customer. It became necessary for the maintenance and development of Rumanian industry to obtain capital goods not only from the U.S.S.R., but also from the other countries forming the Soviet bloc, especially Czechoslovakia and Poland; even more necessary were the machinery, equipment and technical skills available in the west, particularly in the United Kingdom, France, Italy, Switzerland and Austria. Indeed, industrial firms and experts from these countries had, with those of Germany, played a leading part in the construction and financing of Rumanian industry in the past.

Although surplus supplies of timber, grains, oilseeds, etc., and even some oil, were then made available to the western European nations, trade negotiations were made difficult by Rumania's inability or unwillingness to supply more than a fraction of the former volume of goods, and by her continued refusal to pay compensation for the foreign assets in Rumanian industry. In 1949, Rumania joined the Moscow Committee of Mutual Economic Assistance, and the annual trade agreements signed in Moscow, as well as the first five-year plan, all contributed to the further development of the new trend in the Rumanian economy.

Statistical data concerning economic developments in Rumania have always been regarded with some reserve, because of the difficult administrative and political conditions in the country. After 1945, little detailed statistical information was published. Pronouncements by the Rumanian Communist leaders and by the Cominform bureau, which set up its headquarters in Bucharest, confirmed that the trend toward closer integration with the U.S.S.R. was continuing undiminished. An official press statement issued in 1950 announced that the Soviet bloc's share in Rumanian foreign trade had increased from 19% in 1938 to 73% in 1948 and 81% in 1949; over the same period the western countries' share decreased from 81% to 27% and 19% respec-

tively. Soviet-Rumanian trade in 1950 was to increase by a further 30%.

Planning.—Rumania followed closely the pattern of economic reform set after 1944 throughout the Soviet-dominated sphere of Europe. In Rumania's case, this pattern was set by the establishment of the Sovrom companies and by the control exerted upon the government by the Soviet representative on the Allied Control commission in Bucharest. After the signing of the peace treaty and just before the withdrawal of the bulk of the Soviet forces, communization was speeded up by the expulsion of King Michael and the final seizure of power by the Communists.

In agriculture, the road to collectivization had already been prepared by the reform of 1945, and collectivization itself put into operation fully after the 1949 reform. In industry, state control was not unfamiliar—in the Carolist period and under the nazis, it was applied to a great extent to the major industries and to transport. After 1947, privately owned industry, commerce and finance, and western types of trade-union organization, social welfare and cultural activities were gradually destroyed by communist reforms. By 1952, industry, transport and communications were the property of the state, controlled directly by it or by the various Sovrom companies. The establishment of state distributing agencies, state and municipal stores, state banks and insurance companies, the communist-controlled peasant associations, the Central Co-operative administration and General Confederation of Labour, together with state-owned information, propaganda and educational services, completed the transformation of Rumania.

In June 1948, a law was passed nationalizing the subsoil rights, industry, banking, insurance, mining, transport and telecommunication undertakings. This was followed immediately by the establishment of a supreme State Planning commission and the reorganization of the existing industrial boards into state industrial centres for each industrial group. An important survey of industry and housing was carried out in Nov. 1948. The national plans of economic rehabilitation which covered development from July 1947 to Dec. 1950 eventually culminated in the first five-year plan, for the years 1951–55. The lack of coal as a source of power to supplement the oil and wood supplies, and the existence of a considerable hydroelectric potential, encouraged the planners to undertake a special ten-year electrification plan for 1950–60, which was to include the electrification of the Stalin (Brasov)-Bucharest industrial region and to achieve an annual output of 2,600,000 kw.

TABLE I.—*Rumanian Production, 1938, and Targets, 1955*

	Production 1938	Target 1955
Crude oil (metric tons)	6,594,000	10,000,000
Electric energy (kw.hr.)	568,000,000	4,700,000,000
Aluminum (metric tons)	...	5,500
Steel (metric tons)	277,000	1,250,000
Coal (metric tons)	2,396,000	8,533,000
Sulphuric acid (metric tons)	43,000	143,000
Natural gas (cu.m.)	1,860,000,000	3,900,000,000
Bread grains (metric tons)	5,410,000	3,740,000
Maize (metric tons)	5,223,000	4,030,000
Sugar beet (metric tons)	720,000	2,125,000
Cotton (metric tons)	1,400	230,000

The cumulative effects of such planning were to be noticed in the continuing scarcity of food and other consumer goods. Rationing was carried out according to the communist interpretation of political and economic "usefulness" of various classes of consumer. The cost of living increased enormously between 1944 and 1947. The government, facing great financial difficulties after World War II, introduced a measure of currency reform in Aug. 1947 which did something to stabilize prices but which was also used as a lever in the class war. Under the reform law one new leu was exchanged for 20,000 old lei; but whereas wage earners, civil servants and salaried persons were allowed to exchange up to 8,000,000 old lei, the farming class was allowed up to 5,000,000 and all others only 1,500,000. Assets in excess of these amounts were deposited in frozen amounts with no interest.

The new rate for the leu was fixed at U.S. $1 = 150 lei. This was only a temporary measure, and the leu was finally tied to the rouble and to the Soviet economic system by a reform introduced in Jan. 1952; instead of the former rate of 37.4 lei to the rouble, a rate of 2.80 lei to the rouble, or 4 lei to the U.S. dollar was now fixed.

AGRICULTURE

Farming and forestry continue to be of great economic importance. In 1948 more than 75% of the total population was still engaged in rural pursuits. The years immediately following the Soviet occupation of 1944 were overshadowed by the aftermath of war, and what surpluses there were of Rumania's traditional exports of cereals, oilseeds and timber were earmarked for the U.S.S.R. In 1946 a serious drought reduced the maize crop (the staple food of the peasants) and relief ships carrying grain from the U.S., the U.S.S.R. and Argentina reversed the normal direction of trade. The return to stable conditions was prevented by the land reform laws of 1945 and 1949 which were but a prelude to the large-scale application of communist collectivization methods. After 1948 Rumania offered only certain restricted quantities of cereals and other foodstuffs to its former customers in the west, such as the U.K. and Italy.

The farming areas fall into several natural regions: (1) the Carpathians are given over mainly to forestry, but are noted for the old-established summer pastures—the *plaiu*—above the timber line. Under settled conditions, transhumance—the seasonal migrations of men and animals—was also practised by the peasants of the Danubian plains who sought out the hill pastures of northern Dobruja. The mountain sheep pastures are the basis of the home wool production, which is usually enough to provide for the manufacture of the coarse woollen garments worn by the Rumanian peasants. The Carpathian settlements are of the characteristic line type, often strung out, for five or six miles along the valleys; the houses have high-pitched roofs and thick carved beams. (2) Transylvania, an upland, hilly country with a harsh climate and forest, has mixed farming, producing the cooler grains, oats and rye, and much cattle and other livestock. (3) The piedmont zone of the Banat and Crisana are more akin to the Hungarian plains, the Banat producing large quantities of feeding grain for its pigs. (4) The Carpathian foothill zone in Moldavia and Walachia is a verdant country with mixed farming, vineyards, plain orchards, groves of walnut trees and market gardens. (5) The Moldavian and Walachian plains slope gradually down to the Danube, and are steppe-like and in part even semiarid. This is the region of concentrated settlement, of extensive farming, of occasional famine and outbreaks of pellagra, of large-scale wheat production, maize, sunflowers, rape, soya, tobacco, cotton and hemp. The largest areas of oilseed and industrial fibre production were lost when Bessarabia was annexed by the U.S.S.R. (6) The Danube flood plain produces a certain amount of rice. The lower Danube, in the shallows and lagoons below Giurgiu and in the delta itself, has an important fishing industry, specializing in carp, sturgeon, the black caviare from sturgeon, crayfish, etc.

TABLE II.—*Annual Production of Principal Grains*
(In thousand metric tons)

	Wheat	Maize	Barley	Oats
1921–25 average*	2,437.7	3,561.3	1,208.3	911.8
1944†	2,052.9	3,264.9	382.1	350.2
1946	1,608.7	1,004.0	233.4	282.3
1947	1,279.0	5,279.0	360.0	...
1948	2,600.0	...	...	...

*Within Jan. 1938 frontiers. †Within Jan. 1941 frontiers.

The principal categories of land utilization are as follows (in thousand hectares, 1948): arable, 9,751; forests, 6,705; pastures, 2,820; meadows, 1,696; farmyards, 618; vineyards, 227 and orchards, 221.

Agrarian Reform.—As in other countries of eastern Europe, the rapid growth of the peasant population, the survival of feudal systems of tenure and servitude, and the new demands for export foodstuffs arising from the industrialization of western Europe, combined to produce in Rumania in the latter part of the 19th century an acute agrarian problem. It was only in the remoter hill regions that there appears to have been any development of free peasant communities— the *razesi* and *mosneni*. The majority of peasants were serfs, or *rumani* as they were commonly termed, bound to the boyars, who with the churches had come by the 18th century to be the greatest landowners. The pressure placed upon the semipastoral peasants to produce larger and larger grain crops for export as the 19th century proceeded was a great cause of tension. Absenteeism increased, as did also an insidious form of speculation in large-scale tenantry and subletting. Peasant revolts in 1821, 1848 and 1907 were the outcome of these varied political, social and economic conditions.

After the emancipation of the peasants in 1864, they were granted from time to time allotments from crown lands, but such grants were never sufficient to satisfy the general land hunger. Distribution was equally unsatisfactory in the case of Bessarabia under the Russian and Transylvania under the Austro-Hungarian empire, but the Bukovinan peasants had been more fortunate in obtaining possession of a considerable share of the land. It was found expedient in 1920 to pass an expropriation law for Bessarabia, which was rapidly followed by similar laws for the old kingdom (1921) and for Transylvania and the

Bukovina (also 1921), whereby provision was made for the total expropriation of absentee landlords, foreigners, mortmain estates and for partial expropriation of large landed properties. The thousands of peasants who took over the land in the first years of the agrarian reform were unskilled in management, inadequately organized on the co-operative side and lacked both the machinery and capital required for successful farming.

Under the Communist regime, two further land reform acts were passed, that of 1945, mainly concerned with the expropriation of

TABLE III.—*Number of Holdings of a Given Area as a Percentage of Total Number**

Area (ha.)	1907	1941	1948
0–½	0.34	12.0	7.3
½–1	0.93	9.3	9.5
1–3	7.31	33.0	35.9
3–5	17.16	19.2	23.3
5–10	14.55	19.5	17.8
10–20	8.89	5.1	4.7
20–50	...	...	...
More than 50	51.02	0.7	0.4

*The 1907 figures apply to the old kingdom; the 1941 and 1948 figures exclude northern Transylvania; but although covering the same regions, the 1941 figures apply to some 2,300,000 holdings covering more than 10,000,000 ha., three-quarters of which was arable land, while the 1948 figures apply to 2,600,000 holdings covering 17,000,000 ha., less than half of which was arable. The table does, however, serve as a guide to the process of "parcellation" prior to the commencement of the collectivization drive.

private properties in excess of 50 ha. and the properties of certain categories of individuals such as Germans, war criminals, etc., and that of 1949, when the remaining property of the large landowners was confiscated. The 1945 act was followed by the distribution of land to the landless and the poorer small landholders; but the whole aim of the Communist reforms was to replace the old system by one not of peasant ownership but one of collective farming on the Stalinist model. The liquidation of the kulak (*chiabur* in Rumanian), or larger peasant farmer, went hand in hand with the development of collective farms. In 1949 there were about 50 collectives; in 1951 there were more than 1,000. The large estates of the past and the small peasant holdings still in existence were being gradually converted into the large state farms and collectives, the sovkhozes and the kolkhozes, which were the ultimate objectives of the Communist agrarian policy.

Timber Industry.—The forests of the Carpathian ranges and foothills, of the Transylvanian uplands and of the better-watered lowlands provide Rumania with one of its most valuable resources. In 1938, about 10% of the country's workers were connected with forestry, and timber exports were the third most important after oil and grain. It provides an important source of fuel, supplementing the oil supply and the scanty coal resources. Associated industries, such as furniture making, pulp and paper, and cellulose are to be found at a number of suitably located centres such as Stalin (Brasov), Busteni, Bacau and Timisoara.

The species belong mainly to the broadleaf forest types of southern Europe—oak, beech, ash, hornbeam, lime, alder and willow. Beech is most widespread in the hills and oak is the commonest tree in the lowlands. Conifers cover only one-quarter of the forest area and are found mainly in the northern and eastern ranges at higher levels, between the deciduous forests and the alpine pastures of the summits.

The forests were overcut during and immediately after World Wars I and II. In the interim period there was also some deforestation resulting from the distribution of holdings to peasants under the land reform acts. In the same period, the state owned about one-third of the forest wealth, communes and churches owned a similar proportion, and companies and private individuals owned the remainder. By 1952, exploitation was being shared by Sovromlemn and the Rumanian state. Besides annexing valuable stands in northern Bukovina, the U.S.S.R., through Sovromlemn, carried out new development work in southern Bukovina and northern Moldavia.

Oil Industry.—The oil-bearing strata are found in a crescent-shaped belt running along the edge of the Carpathian foothills zone in Muntenia and Moldavia. Even before oil became the leading industry, this belt was one of the most populous in Rumania, and many peasants supplied seasonal labour to the oil producers. The chief producing regions are Bacau, Buzau, Prahova and Dambovita. Most of the refineries are situated in Ploesti, the oil capital, from which pipe lines go to the oil ports of Constanta and Giurgiu.

Natural gasoline had been used locally, but it was not until 1854 that the extraction of petroleum began on a commercial scale. Production increased steadily, except during World War I, until a peak of 8,700,000 tons (3.5% of world production) was reached in 1936. Rumanian geologists estimated in 1937 that reserves would last for ten years, but the decline which set in after the 1936 peak was largely the result of dislocation caused by World War II. Oil technicians from western Europe and the U.S. who had been largely responsible for the development of the industry, were no longer available; and after 1945, the position in this respect did not change. Lack of technical skill and equipment held up production, although prospecting and drilling were carried out with increasing vigour especially after the five-year plan started in 1951. According to this plan, the 1936 peak was to be reached in 1952, and 10,000,000 tons of crude petroleum was the target for 1955. Statistics of production were not made available after 1942, but estimates for the years 1944–50 are as follows (in millions of tons): 1944, 3.5; 1945, 4.6; 1946, 4.1; 1947, 3.7; 1948, 4.1; 1949, 4.3 and 1950, 4.4. By 1952 Rumania was still the largest producer in Europe.

In 1938, about 60% of Rumania production was either owned or controlled by Germany, about 10% by Great Britain (Unirea company), 12% by Anglo-French interests (Steaua Romana), 10% by Rumania, 5% by Italian and 3% by various small Anglo-French-Belgian firms. Sovrompetrol took over the German share at the time of the Soviet occupation, and the rest was confiscated by the Rumanian government and placed under two state centres named Mutenia and Moldava. No compensation was paid to the owners expropriated; countercharges of sabotage, the levying of large fines and the arrest of foreign experts by the Rumanian government hindered production.

Oil had become the chief Rumanian export before 1938, replacing the export of cereals in that position. In 1938, the value of oil exports was 43% of the total exports of 21,500,000,000 lei. The almost exclusive dependence of Rumania on these two commodities—the one exploitive and relying on foreign skill and capital, the other requiring extensive farming in an area often subject to crippling droughts—gave Rumanian economy its precarious nature. Thus in 1946–47 the food position, as a result of bad weather, was so serious that much grain had to be imported, and oil production fell to the 1927 level. Oil exports in 1938 went to all the countries in Europe (Germany 700,000 tons, United Kingdom and Italy 500,000 tons each, France and Czechoslovakia 300,000 tons each), and to North Africa as well. After 1944, exports were almost exclusively to the U.S.S.R., small quantities going to the other Soviet bloc countries, especially Czechoslovakia, Poland and Hungary. After 1948, small quantities were offered to other former customers, such as Italy and Great Britain, as the need for re-equipping the industry made itself felt.

No country in Europe was, at mid-20th century, so dependent upon oil for home consumption as Rumania, a position emphasized by the shortage of coal. Fuel oils were consumed on a large scale by industry, the railways, power stations, by the shipping services and for central heating, milling and agriculture. The need to conserve this most valuable resource was evident when petrol rationing was reintroduced in 1950. The armed forces were also taking an increasing amount.

In 1947, when it was estimated that Rumania produced about 3,700,000 tons of crude petroleum, the output of natural gasoline was about 114,000 tons. In addition to this, Rumania possesses the largest source of natural gas in Europe, with a production in 1947 of about 42,000 tons. It is methane, found near Medias, Copsa Mica and Sarmasel in the Transylvanian basin, and is widely used for lighting and heating purposes.

Coal, Iron and Steel.—Rumania has no large resources of coal and iron, and heavy industry is therefore on a restricted scale, entirely dominated after 1945 by the Sovrom companies. Coal production in 1947 was given as 2,200,000 tons, and in 1948 as 2,600,000 tons. Iron ore production in 1947 was about 100,000 tons; in 1950, according to estimates, it was about 390,000 tons.

Coal production was as follows in 1947: brown coal 1,632,469 tons; lignite 439,674 tons; bituminous coal 137,173 tons and anthracite 23,404 tons. The most important field is in Oltenia, in the upper Jiu valley in the southern Carpathians centring on Petrosani, producing anthracite and lignite. The hard coal, some of which is suitable for coking, is found toward the western end of the Carpathians in the Anina-Resita area of the Banat. Other fields of brown coal are found in the foothills in Muntenia (Filipesti), Transylvania and Moldavia (Comanesti).

The deposits of iron ore, mainly limonite (47% to 54% iron) and siderite (28% to 35%) are small, and are found chiefly in the vicinity of the metallurgical centres of Resita and Hunedoara. After the severance of relations with Yugoslavia, the Rumanian iron and steel industry became almost completely dependent on Soviet ores. Imported scrap is also a vital necessity. The centres of heavy industry are Bucharest (machinery, machine tools, agricultural equipment, locomotives, railway wagons, pipes, etc.), Resita (iron and steel, armaments); Hunedoara (iron and steel) and Brasov (tractors, aircraft, armaments, machinery, locomotives, etc.). Under the five-year plan, a new steel centre was set up at Campia Turzii near Cluj.

TABLE IV.—*Iron and Steel Production*
(In metric tons)

	1938	1946	1950*
Pig iron and ferroalloys	107,000	54,000	330,000
Steel ingots and castings	326,000	155,000	549,000
Iron ore	137,000	105,000	175,000

*Estimate.

Other Minerals.—In 1948, as part of the communist plan for nationalizing industry, the mining of precious and nonferrous metals was put in charge of a state centre, with divisional headquarters at Bai Mare, northern Transylvania, and Brad, in the Bihorului moun-

tains of central Transylvania. The first district has gold, silver and lead mines as well as processing and refining plants, the second possesses gold, silver, lead, zinc, bauxite and mercury mines, with plants for processing, refining and distilling, and for the manufacture of chemicals. Rumania is normally self-sufficient in lead, but needs to supplement zinc supplies by imports from Poland. Gold production in 1947 was 71,728 fine troy ounces, Rumania ranking with Sweden as one of the leading producers in Europe. Bauxite production was never on a large scale, and aluminum production was on an experimental basis, at least until 1939. Other products are mica, chrome and manganese.

The Tertiary rocks of the Transylvanian basin and the foothills of the Carpathians in Oltenia and Moldavia contain vast reserves of salt; extraction is carried on at Ocnele Mari on the Olt Slanic in the Prahova valley, and Targu Ocna.

Communications.—Compared with those of western Europe, transport and communication standards are low. Up to the 1950s political and economic conditions had prevented a great development of roads and railways; the former were few indeed, and the oxcart and unmetalled track were a more familiar sight than the motorcar and surfaced highway; most railways were single track, with the exception of certain sections of the Orient Express route, notably from Bucharest to Stalin, and parts of the Bucharest-Braila line.

The Germans attempted during World War II to improve certain road and rail communications in order to make Rumanian resources, petroleum, minerals and timber, more easily accessible; to enlarge facilities on the Danube at minor ports to relieve congestion at the bigger centres; and to aid the flow of military traffic across the Danube into Bulgaria. In the period after 1945 similar operations were undertaken with the difference that trade was now directed not toward Germany and the western European countries but mainly toward the U.S.S.R. and the other Soviet bloc countries. The new railways were extended into the Jiu coalfield and into the forests of the Moldavian Carpathians.

The Danube.—Besides being the main artery of trade in Rumania, the Danube forms such an important through routeway that, after the treaty of Paris of 1856, it was subject to some form of international control. From Braila to Ulm (1,474 mi.) it was supervised by the International Danube commission (C.I.D.); from Braila to the sea at Sulina by the European Danube commission (C.E.D.). Both the C.I.D. and C.E.D. were reconstituted by the treaty of Versailles. The C.I.D. had representatives of the riparian states and France, the United Kingdom and Italy; the C.E.D. had representatives of Rumania, France, the U.K., and Italy (Germany was admitted in 1938). A meeting was called in 1948 by the United States government to consider the establishment of a new supervisory body; invitations were sent by the state department to the U.S.S.R., the Ukrainian S.R.R., Great Britain and France, and to the riparian states (including Austria but excluding occupied Germany). The Soviet Union and its supporters carried through a decision to set up a new Danubian commission at Galatz (Galati), from which western and Yugoslav influence was excluded. By 1952, Sovromtransport controlled the entire Danube navigation within Rumania, including the delta section, and the ports and shipbuilding yards at Turnu Severin, Giurgiu, Galatz and Braila, as well as the only Rumanian Black sea port of any size, Constanta.

The Danube is navigable throughout its whole length in Rumania, but there are two distinct sectors for traffic—seagoing vessels of 2,000-3,000 tons go upstream as far as Braila and Galatz, and river vessels ply on the rest. Heavy-draught shipping does not enter the Danube but docks at Constanta, as the Sulina bar needs constant dredging to maintain a depth of water of 22 to 23 ft. In the Iron Gate gorge, between Turnu Severin and Orsova, specially skilled pilots and smaller tows of barges are required to navigate the reefs and rapids, but below Calafat the current is slight. Ice blocks the river during about three winters out of every ten, the blockage lasting sometimes from mid-December to March; occasionally late summer droughts close the Danube for a period in the autumn. The river has a steep bank on the Bulgarian side but on the left bank below the Iron Gate gorge the flood plain, with its marshes and lagoons, is several miles wide. The railway bridge carrying the Bucharest-Constanta line across the Danube at Cernavoda is 7¼ mi. in length; the next bridge above this is in Yugoslavia, at Novi Sad. No bridges cross from the Rumanian to the Bulgarian bank; the chief road ferries are at Silistra and between Giurgiu and Ruschuk (Ruse), the latter crossing being the site of a proposed new bridge. Another project, the Danube-Black sea canal, first publicized in 1949, was reported to have been begun soon after but, like the Oder-Danube canal, appears to have been delayed by lack of equipment. This new waterway would save the long detour of the delta and the Sulina bar by linking Cernovoda to a point a short distance north of Constanta on the Black sea coast.

Traffic remained at a very low ebb between 1945 and 1948, but increased subsequently with the development of trade between the Soviet-bloc countries. The goods carried consist mainly of Soviet iron ore destined for Czechoslovakia, Hungarian bauxite and Rumanian timber, oil and cement for the U.S.S.R.

Ports.—The ports tend to specialize according to their hinterland and harbour facilities. Thus Constanta is the chief oil port, handling about three times the quantity exported through Giurgiu; both are connected with Ploesti by oil pipe lines. In addition Constanta is the maritime port of call. Braila is the chief grain port, and Galatz, besides being the main port of entry and principal naval base, handles most of the timber which is floated down the Siret or comes by rail from Bukovina and Moldavia.

The pre-1939 Rumanian shipping lines connecting with Levantine and Mediterranean ports, although reopened after World War II, were in 1952 still operating on a reduced scale.

Finance.—The economic and political conditions peculiar to Rumania have been nowhere more apparent than in the financial sphere. Although the country possesses considerable man power and natural resources, a certain lack of balance and an emphasis on exploitation rather than conservation always characterized the country's economy.

The want of settled conditions, coupled with the tendency to concentrate upon the development of a few specialized cash crops (grain, timber, oilseed) and petroleum for export, maintained the country as a whole at a very low general standard of existence. Foreign investment which was needed to bring Rumania into a more typically European level was attracted to more tangible short-term projects, and this is true not only of the later German economic penetration but also of the post-1945 Soviet attitude. The bulk of the population was peasants, and remained so in mid-20th century. In 1928, it was calculated that the capital engaged in peasant farms in Rumania, calculated in gold francs per hectare, was only one-third of that enjoyed in Poland and only one-tenth of that in Switzerland. The five-year plan paid more attention to investment in certain specialized heavy industries than to any general plan which would benefit the people as a whole.

During the 1930s, the financial situation was dominated by the sharp drop in world agricultural prices, and the mounting foreign debt which by 1935 had risen to 80% of the total national debt of 139,000,000,000 lei. A temporary improvement was more than offset by the deterioration caused by general rearmament in the late 1930s. After 1945, and before reparations payments were reduced by the U.S.S.R., a serious degree of inflation resulted. Two currency reforms ensued, the first in Aug. 1947 when 20,000 old units were made exchangeable for one new leu, and the second in Jan. 1952. The latter pegged the Rumanian currency officially to the Soviet rouble, and one new leu was exchanged for 37 old ones. In carrying out these reforms, not only was Rumanian economy made entirely dependent upon that of the U.S.S.R., but class warfare inside Rumania was furthered. Private financial power was destroyed, and the independent farmer, craftsman, manufacturer and professional man was reduced to a position of complete dependence upon the state. At the same time, the real value of wages was not increased; scarcities and rationing were the order of the day. The majority of Rumanian banks were dissolved in Aug. 1948, and a few months later the National Bank of Rumania was transformed into the Bank of the Rumanian People's Republic. Apart from certain co-operative and savings banks, which were all placed under state control, the powerful Sovrombanc was set up to conduct the business of the various Sovrom companies.

The 1951 national budget estimates were as follows (in millions of lei): revenue 433,900, expenditure 429,900.

DEFENSE

After 1945, Rumania formed an integral part of the Soviet defense system in eastern Europe. The country was occupied by a large Red army force until the signing of the peace treaty in 1947, and certain numbers were maintained there subsequently. The new Rumanian army was rebuilt around the three divisions of Rumanian prisoners of war who had been trained in the U.S.S.R. and crossed the frontier as liberators alongside the Soviet troops.

The peace treaty laid down that the Rumanian armed forces should be restricted to the following: (1) land forces (including frontier guards) of up to 120,000 men; (2) anti-aircraft artillery with 5,000 men; (3) an air force with 150 aircraft, of which not more than 100 might be for combat, and a personnel of 8,000 and (4) a navy of up to 15,000 tons and 5,000 men.

By 1952 the total numbers under arms including security police and other quasimilitary forces had, according to generally accepted estimates current in the western press, risen to more than 400,000 or more than three times the peace treaty level. In addition, Soviet forces occupied certain positions in Rumania, and formed part of the "Cominform cordon" lined up along the Yugoslav frontier.

Rumania continued to keep small naval forces in the Black sea and on the Danube. In 1951 the former were said to consist of two old destroyers, one submarine and one submarine depot ship, two old torpedo boats, two motor gunboats, two motor torpedo boats, one mine layer and one training ship; the Danube flotilla comprised four monitors and an assortment of small craft. (G. W. S.)

BIBLIOGRAPHY.—On geography, economics, etc.: E. Pittard, *La Roumanie* (Paris, 1917); F. Pax, *Pflanzengeographie von Rumänien* (Halle, 1920); M. Constantinescu, *L'Evolution de la propriété rurale . . . en Roumanie* (Bucharest, 1925); E. de Martonne, "La Roumanie," *Geographie universelle*, vol. iv, *L'Europe centrale* (Paris, 1930); D. Mitrany, *The Land and the Peasant in Rumania* (London, 1930); M. Pizanty, *Petroleum in Roumania* (Bucharest, 1930); G. Alexiano and M. Antonesco, *Roumanie* (Paris, 1933); K. Hielscher, *Rumänien* (Leipzig, 1933); N. Moricz, *The Fate of the Transylvania Soil* (Budapest, 1934); H. J. Fleure and R. A. Pelham (eds.), *Eastern Carpathian Studies: Roumania* (London, 1936); S. Mehedinti, *Le Pays et le peuple roumain* (Bucharest, 1937); R. Inst. Internat. Affairs, *South-East Europe, a Political and Economic Survey* (London, 1939); N. St. Predescu, *Die Wirtschaftsstruktur Rumäniens* (Bucharest, 1940); A. Basch, *The Danube Basin and the German Economic Sphere* (London, 1944); League of Nations, *Economic Demography of Eastern and Southern Europe* (Geneva, 1945); A. Bilic, *The Book of Agricultural Cooperation* (London, 1950); H. L. Roberts, *Rumania: Political Problems of an Agrarian State* (London, 1951).

On history, politics, etc.: E. de Hurmuzaki, *Documente privitore la Istoria Românilor* (Bucharest, 1876 *et seq.*); N. Jorga, *Geschichte des rumänischen Volkes*, 2 vol. (Bucharest, 1905); N. Jorga and G. Bals, *Histoire de l'art roumain ancien* (Paris, 1922); V. Parvan, *Tara Noastra* (Bucharest, 1934); N. Jorga, *A History of Roumania* (English trans., J. McCabe, London, 1925); A. D. Xenopol, *Istoria Românilor din Dacia Traiană*, 3rd ed., 14 vol. (Bucharest, 1925–30); abridged French trans., *Histoires des Roumains*, 2 vol., 1896); G. G. Rommenhoeller, *La Grande Roumaine* (The Hague, 1926); V. Pârvan, *Dacia* (Cambridge, 1928); C. U. Clark, *United Rumania* (1932); T. W. Riker, *The Making of Rumania* (Oxford, 1931); R. W. Seton-Watson, *History of the Roumanians from Roman Times to the Completion of Unity* (1934); J. Clark (ed.), *Politics and Political Parties in Rumania* (London, 1936); N. Jorga, *Histoire des Roumains et de la romanité orientale*, 4 vol. (Bucharest, 1937); P. Pavel, *Why Rumania Failed* (London, 1944); R. H. Markham, *Rumania under the Soviet Yoke* (1949); A. Gould Lee, *Crown against Sickle: The Story of King Michael of Rumania* (London, 1950).

RUMANIAN LANGUAGE. Rumanian represents the Latin language spoken in the eastern Roman empire, north and south of the Danube, with the changes that it acquired during the 2,000 years of development. The frequency of the Latin element in modern Rumanian amounts to 85%–90%. The non-Latin elements are: Slavonic, Albanian, Hungarian, Greek, Turkish and other oriental. These loanwords reflect the political, cultural and ethnic contacts in Rumanian history. Their numerical proportion is large; their circulation, however, is limited. The Slavonic element is more numerous because Church Slavonic was the vehicle of the Byzantine civilization. The original home of the Rumanian language is the Carpatho-Balkan region, which was Romanized before and after the conquest of Dacia (A.D. 101-107).

Rumanian has four main dialects: (1) Daco-Rumanian, spoken by about 18,000,000 in Rumania (the historical provinces of Walachia, Moldavia, Transylvania, Banat, Bukovina and Dobruja) as well as in Bessarabia (from 1940 Moldavian S.S.R.) and east of the Dniester river, south of the Danube in Bulgaria (Vidin), in Yugoslavia (Timok and Banat) and in neighbouring Hungary; (2) Macedo-Rumanian (A-Rumanian, Armân, Vlakh, Kutso-Vlah, Tsintsar), spoken in Greece (Pindus, Thessaly, Epirus), Albania (Musacchia or Myzeqe) and in Yugoslav and Bulgarian Macedonia, the number of speakers being estimated at about 500,000 (*cf.* A. J. B. Wace and M. S. Thompson, *The Nomads of the Balkans*, 1914); (3) Megleno-Rumanian (Vlasi), spoken in the isolated region of the Caragiova mountains (main villages: Cupa, Huma, Liumnitsa, Lungutsa, Nânta, Oşani, Târnareca) northwest of Salonika (*cf.* T. Capidan, *Megleno-Românii*, 1925); (4) Istro-Rumanian (Rumeri, Ĉiribiri, Vlasi), spoken by about 3,000, most of them bilinguals, in Istria. The northern group, in the province of Rijeka (Fiume), with the centre in the village of Jeiăni (Castelnuovo), is separated by Uĉka Gora (Monte Maggiore) from the southern group in the Arsa valley (Brdo, Gradinie, Grobnik, Kostrĉeani, Lettay, Noselo, Sukodru, Susnievitsa). This dialect represents the survivals of an east-west migration which reached this region in the 12th and 13th centuries, and which appear in documents also as Maurovlakhs, Uskoks, Ĉiĉi. A similar migration moved in the northwest direction, along the Carpathians, and reached the Sudeten mountains and Silesia.

Characteristic features of the phonetic system which illustrate the development of Latin into Rumanian are as follows (unidentified words are Rumanian).

1. In agreement with the other Romance languages, Latin long $\bar{e}$ and short i are reduced to close e: Lat. *crēdo* > cred, AR. cred, IR. credu, Italian *credere*; Lat. *ligo* > leg, AR. leg, IR. legu, French *lier*.

2. Diverging from the other Romance languages (and in agreement with Sardinian, Corsican and Dalmatian dialects), Rumanian differentiates between Latin long $\bar{o}$ and short $\breve{u}$; this feature is shared also by the Latin element in Albanian: Lat. *fŏcum* > R., AR., IR. foc, Portuguese *fogo*; Lat. *cōco* > R., AR., MR., IR.

coc, Spanish *cocer*; Lat. *fŭrcam* > R., AR. *furcă*, IR. *furkę*, Alb. *furkë*, Port. *forca*; Lat. *dūco* > R., AR. *duc*, IR. *ducu*, Sard. *duc*, Prov. *dozer*.

3. Lat. -*ct*-, -*cs*-, -*gn*- > R. -*pt*-, -*ps*-, -*mn*-; Albanian and Dalmatian show a similar development: Lat. *luctam* > *luptă*, Alb. *luftë*, It. *lotta*; Lat. *ŏcto* > *opt*, AR. *optu*, IR. *uopt*, Dalm. *uapto*; Lat. *coxam* > R., AR. *coapsă*, Alb. *kofshë*, Fr. *cuisse*; Lat. *cognatus* > R., AR., MR. *cumnat*, IR. *cumnǫt*, Alb. *kunat*, Veglia *comnut*, Sard. *konnadu*, It. *cognato*.

4. The same trend of development is indicated by Lat. *gu* and *qu* followed by back or front vowels: Lat. *linguam* > R., AR., MR. *limbă*, IR, *limbę*, Sard. *limba*; Lat. *aquam* > R., AR., MR. *apă*, IR. *ǫpę*, Sard. *abba*; Lat. *sanguis* > *sânge*, AR. *sândze*, MR. *sǫndzi*, IR. *sănze*, Sard.-Logod. *sambene*; Lat. *quaerere* > *cerere*, AR., MR. *tserere*, Sard. *kerrere*. In discrepancies, Rumanian agrees with Sardinian: Lat. *qualem* > *care*, Sard. *cale*; Lat. *quando* > *când*, AR. *cându*, MR. *cǫn*, Lat. *căn(d)*, Sard. *cando*.

5. Two dark back vowels (in MR. and IR. only one) have been developed: *ă* and *â* (*î*), the first in an original generally unstressed syllable, the second in front of a nasal consonant. The dark vowel *ă* appears also in Albanian and in Bulgarian, and an attempt has been made to explain it through the common substratum; the dark vowel *â* is an early development, in which the Slavonic loanwords do not participate generally: Lat. *carbōnem* > *cărbune*, AR. *cărbune*, IR. *cărbur(e)*; Lat. *calcaneum* > *călcâi*, AR. *călcânu*, MR. *călcǫnu*; Lat. *canto* > *cânt*, AR. *cântu*, MR. *cǫnt*, IR. *cănt*; Lat. *veteranus* > *bătrân*, AR. *bitârnu*, MR. *bitǫrn*, IR. *betăr*; but, Slavonic *hrana* > R. *hrană*; Sl. *rana* > R. *rană*.

6. The stressed vowels *e* and *o*, followed by a syllable containing *e* or *a* (*ă*), were diphthongized into *ęa* and *ǫa*: Lat. *nĭger*, *nĭgra* > R., MR., IR. *negru*, AR. *negru*, *negur*: R., AR. *neagră*, MR. *nęgră*, IR. *nęgrę*; Lat. *mollis* > R., AR. *moale*, MR. *moali*, IR. *mǫle*. The Slavonic element, not being an organic part of the language, does not participate regularly in this development: Sl. *kofa* > R. *cofă*: Sl. *kosa* > R. *coasă*.

7. The dental and the velar consonants followed by front vowels were palatalized: Lat. *dīem* > *zi* (*ziuă*), AR. -*dzi* (*dzuă*), MR. *zuă*, IR. *zi*; Lat. *terram* > *țeară*, *țară*, AR., MR. *tsară*; Lat. *caelum* > *cer*, AR., MR. *tser*, IR. *tșer*; Lat. *gelu* > *ger*, AR. *dzer*.

8. Intervocalic *l* (in Istro-Rumanian and dialectally also in Daco-Rumanian also intervocalic *n*) changed into *r* (rhotacism): Lat. *solem* > R., AR. *soare*, MR. *soari*, IR. *sǫre*; Lat. *bene* > R. *bine*, AR. *ģine*, MR. *bini*, IR. *bire*, Old R. *bire*.

9. Because of the falling rhythm (as in Albanian), final -*i*, -*u* were loosely articulated and disappeared, the former after palatalizing the preceding consonant: Lat. *boni* > *buni*; Lat. *lupum* > *lupŭ* > *lup*. Diverging from the other Romance languages, final -*e* is kept: Lat. *panem* > *pâne* (*pâine*), AR. *pâne*, MR. *pǫini*, IR. *păre*, Sp. *pan*, F. *pain*; Lat. *talem* > *tare*, MR. *tari*, IR. *tǫre*.

10. Intervocalic voiceless stops are not voiced, as in North Italian, French, Spanish: Lat. *casam* > *casă*: NI. *kaza*; Lat. *rotam* > *roată*: Sp. *rueda*; Lat. *ripam* > *râpă*, AR. *arâpă*, MR. *rǫpă*, IR. *ărpă*: F. *rive*, Port., Sp., Prov. *riba*. Implosive consonants are preserved: Lat. *piscem* > *pește*.

11. Among the morphological features the most characteristic is the postponed article in the nouns. The article is a demonstrative suffixed to the noun or adjective when this precedes the noun: Lat. *dōmnum* (= *dominum*) *illum bonum* > *domnulŭ bunŭ* > *domnul bun*; Lat. *solem ille* > *soarele*; *casam illam* > *casa*. The forms without article are: *domn*, *soare*, *casă*. Albanian and Bulgarian have similar suffixed articles: Alb. *vajza* = the girl, *vajzë* = girl.

12. The nouns have: (*a*) one singular and one plural form without article (*domn*, *domni* [masc.]; *soare*, *sori* [masc.]; *casă*, *case* [fem.]; *carte*, *cărți* [fem.]); (*b*) two singular and two plural forms with article (direct case: *domnul*, *soarele*, *casa*, *cartea*; *domnii*, *sorii*, *casele*, *cărțile*; oblique case: *domnului*, *soarelui*, *casei*, *cărții*; *domnilor*, *sorilor*, *caselor*, *cărților*). The Latin masculine vocative has survived: *Doamne*! *domnule*!

13. A mixed gender has been developed (*masc.* in sing., *fem.* in plur.): *câmp* (sing.), *câmpuri* (plur.); *lemn* (sing.), *lemne* (plur.).

14. The verb shortened the Latin infinitive: the long form functions as a verbal noun: Lat. *cantare* > *a cânta*, Old R. *a cântare*. Macedo-Rumanian and Megleno-Rumanian do not shorten the infinitive.

15. The future is formed by means of the auxiliary Lat. *volere* > *a voi* + the short infinitive, or by means of the auxiliary Lat. *habere* > *a avea* + *să* + subjunctive; in the last case the auxiliary may take an invariable form *o*: *voi cânta* "I shall sing," *am să cânt* "I shall sing," *o să cânt*. Similar formations occur in Albanian, Greek, Bulgarian and Serbian.

16. In the word formation, numerous Slavonic affixes have replaced the Latin ones, with which they often interchange: *ne-bun*, *ne-vinovat*; *răz-bat*, *stră-bat*, *răz-bun*, *răs-tignesc*; *tocme-ala*, *răce-ală*; *bun-ic*, *voi-nic*. These affixes are loanwords; they have not created new functions in the derivational system of the language. There are no phonetical or morphological Slavonic influences in the grammar of the Rumanian language which could not be explained by the internal development of the language.

17. The formation of the numerals from 11 to 90 is similar to that in Albanian and Slavonic according to the pattern *unus* (*su*)*per decem*, *tres decem*: *unsprezece*, *treizeci*; Alb. *nji më dhit*, *tridhit*; Sl. *jedinŭ na desete*, *tri deseti*. The ordinals are formed (as in Albanian) by adding to the cardinals, preceded by a definite article, the ending -*le*(*a*) (masc.), -*a* (fem.): *al treile*(*a*), *a treia*, Alb. *i-tre-te*.

18. Outstanding syntactic features, divergent from the other Romance languages, are: (*a*) the repetition of the personal pronoun in oblique cases (similar to Albanian, Greek, Bulgarian): *pe mine nu m'a văzut* "he hasn't seen me," *mie nu mi-a spus* "he didn't tell me"; (*b*) the replacement (not general) of the infinitive object by a subjunctive construction (common to Albanian, Greek, Bulgarian): *vreau să spun* "I wish to say"; *începe să vorbească*, *începe a vorbi* "he begins to speak"; (*c*) the replacement of the possessive pronoun (when the possessor is not emphasized) by the dative of the personal pronoun: *mi-ai luat cartea* "you took my book," this construction is more general in Macedo-Rumanian, and it is found also in Italian and Portuguese; (*d*) the use of the preposition *pe* with the direct object, when this is a person: *am văzut pe vecinul nostru* "I have seen our neighbour"; (*e*) the stress is strong, dynamic, and may stand on any syllable of the word. With the exception of a few morphological categories (conjugation, suffixal formations), it remains on the same syllable.

The oldest trace of Rumanian is that appearing in the Greek texts of Theophylact Simocatta (7th century) and of Theophanes the Confessor (8th century) taken from some source of the 6th century: *Torna* (*retorna*), *torna*, *fratre*! It represents the Balkan Latin of the 6th century, showing a Rumanian morphological form (*fratre* > *frate*) and a dialectal form (*retorna*). In the same century Latin *montem* had become Rumanian *munte*, as shown by the place name, quoted by Theophylact: *Calvomunti*. In the ensuing centuries Rumanian proper names appear; *e.g.*, the proper name *Fichur* < R. *ficior* < Lat. *fētiolum* appears in Hungarian in the 12th century. The first text in Rumanian is a letter dating from 1521.

BIBLIOGRAPHY.—O. Densusianu, *Histoire de la langue roumaine*, 2 vol. (Paris, 1901–32); A. Philippide, *Originea Românilor*, 2 vol. (Jassy, 1923–27); S. Pușcariu, *Limba română* (Bucharest, 1940), *Die rumänische Sprache* (Leipzig, 1943); *Atlasul Lingvistic Român*, 2 vol. (Cluj, 1938–42); *Istro-Românii*, 3 vol. (Bucharest, 1906–29); T. Capidan, *Les Macédo-Roumains* (Bucharest, 1943); K. Sandfeld, *Linguistique balkanique* (Paris, 1930); Academia Română, *Dicționarul Limbii Române*, 2 vol. (Bucharest, 1906–34); H. Tiktin, *Rumänisch-Deutsches Wörterbuch*, 3 vol. (Bucharest, 1903–20). (G. Ns.)

RUMANIAN LITERATURE.

The written literature in Rumanian is paralleled by a rich folklore, lyric, epic, dramatic and didactic, which has continued till modern times. The lyric poetry consists of *doine* (love songs, songs expressing an undefined longing), *bocete* (dirges), *colinde* (carols), *cântece* (lyrics). The epic genre is represented by ballads in verse (*cântece bătrânești*) and by folk tales in prose. The dramatic genre has its representatives in mystery plays, scenes of the nativity, new year plays (*Vicleim*, *Irozi*). The didactic literature shows a great richness in proverbs, riddles, satiric songs.

The geographical position of Rumania enabled its folklore to mediate the transfer of folklore themes from the Balkans to the east (Ukraine, Russia). The religious homogeneity of the region, situated between Byzantium and Kiev, favoured, on the other hand, the circulation all over this area of the literature written or printed in the Rumanian principalities. Western influence reached the Rumanian lands through Hungary, Transylvania and Poland, when the first political organizations were founded, east and south of the Carpathian range, in the 12th–14th centuries. In the next centuries the Reformation prompted the first translation of church literature from Slavonic into Rumanian (15th century). Up to the 17th century, Church Slavonic was the language of the church and of the chanceries. In 1600 Prince Michael of Walachia issued, in Alba Iulia, Transylvania, the first state paper in Rumanian. In the 18th century the autochthonous ruling princes were replaced by Greek rulers from Constantinople (in Moldavia in 1711, in Walachia in 1714), and for more than a century the culture of the principalities was mainly Greek, Rumanian and Slavonic playing a secondary role. As after the fall of Constantinople and the disappearance of the Slavonic states south of the Danube, the Rumanian principalities became the haven of the Slavo-Byzantine culture, so in the 17th and 18th centuries they became the centre of Greek Orthodox culture, which spread from there over all Orthodox countries. The French Revolution and the ideas of the romantic movement shook off the domination of the Phanariotes and, under western influences, began the national revival.

The development of Rumanian literature may be divided into four periods: (1) from the first Rumanian texts, written in the 15th century and preserved in copies of the 16th century, to the Phanariote period; the activity of this period is crowned by the translation of the whole Bible (1688); (2) the 18th century up to the national movement of Tudor Vladimirescu (1821); (3) the national renaissance under western influences, from 1820 to World War I; (4) the national unity and the literary integration.

The Old Period.—The oldest translations from Slavonic are Rumanian interlinear verses or interpolations in religious texts of the 15th century. From the same period date the so-called rhotacizing texts, preserved in copies of the 16th century, written in Maramureş (northern Transylvania), under the impetus of the Hussite movement, or according to another opinion under the influence of the Reformation. Such texts are: *The Psalter of Şcheia, The Psalter of Voroneţ, The Acts of the Apostles.* Their characteristic feature is the change of intervocalic *n* into *r* in words of Latin origin (*bire* for *bine* < Lat. *bene*).

The printing press was introduced in Walachia in the first years of the 16th century from Venice. On this press was printed in 1508, in Târgovişte, a Slavonic liturgical book. Toward the end of the century a certain Deacon Coresi moved from Târgovişte to Braşov and printed, in 1560–61, a translation of the Gospels. Of a Rumanian Lutheran catechism, printed in 1544, no copy has so far been found. Coresi, assisted by local clergy, revised, completed and printed the existing translations. Among those printed are found: the *Acts of the Apostles* (*Lucrul Apostolesc*, 1563); *Sermons and Book of Prayers* (*Tâlcul Evangheliilor şi Molitvenic*, 1564); *Psalters* (1568, 1570); *Interpretation of the Gospels* (*Evanghelie cu învăţătură*, 1581). Coresi's prints enhanced the spreading of the Rumanian language in the churches of the three principalities. Other centres which supported this movement by their printing activity were: *Sas-Sebeş* (produced probably Coresi's *Slavo-Rumanian Psalter*, 1577); Alba Iulia (*Evanghelia cu învăţătură*, 1641; *The Gospels*, 1579); Orăştie (*Palia*, printed in 1582 for the Calvinist Rumanians).

This activity, enhanced by the ferment of the Reformation in Transylvania, continued in the 17th century. In 1648 there appeared in Alba Iulia the Gospels translated by the metropolitan Simion Ştefan (*Noul Testament dela Bălgrad*), a version collated with the Greek, Latin and Slavonic texts. The first Rumanian book printed with Latin characters is a Calvinist hymnbook of 1570.

The religious literature printed in the first half of the 17th century in Walachia and Moldavia came partly as a reaction to this activity stirred up by the Reformation. South of the Carpathians, in Walachia, the most important centres in which books were printed are: Câmpulung (*Învăţături preste toate zilele*, 1642); Govora (*Pravila*, 1640; *Evanghelie învăţătoare*, 1642); Mănăstirea Dealului (*Evanghelie învăţătoare*, 1644); Târgovişte (*Mystirio sau Sacrament*, 1651; *Îndreptarea Legii*, 1652 = Nomokanon); Râmnicu-Vâlcea (*Antologhion*, 1705); Bucharest (Bucureşti) (*Cheia Înţelesului*, 1678); Buzău (*Octoih*, 1700); Snagov (*Carte sau lumină*, 1699).

In Moldavia, whose monasteries were centres of theological studies, the reaction against the Reformation found its expression in the metropolitan Varlaam's *Reply* (1645) to the Calvinist catechism printed in Alba Iulia (1642). In 1643 Varlaam published in Jassy (Iaşi) *Cartea Românească de învăţătura* ("Sermons"). In 1646 was printed in Jassy the *Pravila lui Vasile Lupu* ("Laws of Vasile Lupu, Prince of Moldavia"). The Walachian *Pravila lui Matei Basarab* (1652) incorporated in its texts also the Moldavian code of 1646. This collection of canonical and civil laws remained in force, with some additions, up to the middle of the 19th century.

The Moldavian metropolitan Dosoftei, a great scholar and theologian, published in 1673 in Uniejów (Uniev), Pol., where he was in exile, the first book of poetry, *The Rhymed Psalter*. In 1679 he translated the liturgy from the Greek. At this time the Orthodox see of Kiev was occupied by Peter Movila or Mogila (*q.v.*), a countryman of the two former hierarchs. At his request, Vasile Lupu convoked in Jassy the last pan-Orthodox synod, 1642, to counteract Roman Catholic propaganda. The *Confessio Orthodoxa*, drawn up in that synod, remained the dogmatic charter of all Orthodox churches. A Rumanian translation from Greek by Radu Greceanu (*Pravoslavnica Mărturisire*) was printed in Buzău.

Toward the end of the 17th century the monastery of Snagov, near Bucharest, became the centre of a pan-Orthodox literary activity, and on the initiative of a monk, Antim Ivireanu, books were printed not only in Rumanian but also in Greek, Slavonic and Arabic. A Rumanian printer, Mihai Ştefan, introduced the press into the Caucasus where he printed the first Georgian books: *The Gospels* (1709) and *The Georgian Liturgy* (1710).

The religious literature, common to all three principalities, reached its climax with the edition of the complete Bible (1688) translated from the Septuagint by Radu and Şerban Greceanu. This Bible was the basis for all successive translations. With the fall of the principalities under the Phanariote rule begins the downfall of Rumanian culture.

Early historiography is represented by Slavonic annals and commemorative tables of the monasteries (*Letopiseţul dela Bistriţa*, 1359–1506). It reached its climax with the humanist historiographers of 17th-century Moldavia. The Italian *Rinascimento*, through the Polish humanism, finds its expression in the slogan of Grigore Ureche, the father of Moldavian historiography: "We descend from Rome, and our language is made of Latin words." This creed will be echoed through the following centuries. Miron Costîn (1633–91), a student of Polish schools, who also wrote in Polish a chronicle of Moldavia and composed a poem on the history of his country, is the leader of this historiography. He took up the thread of the history of Moldavia where it was left by his predecessor G. Ureche (*Letopiseţul Tării Moldovei 1359–1595*), and continued its tale (1595–1661). Costîn's son, Niculae Costîn, amplified the chronicle of his father; Ion Neculce carried it forward up till 1743. He is a pioneer in folklore with his collection of legends (*Ocsamă de cuvinte*). The learned Demetrius Cantemir (*q.v.*), prince of Moldavia, wrote in Latin the history of the Rumanians (1698), which was translated into Rumanian in 1710 (*Hronicul Româno-Moldo-Vlahilor*). His Latin *Descriptio Moldaviae* (1716) was translated into Russian (1786), German (1769), Greek (1819) and Rumanian (1825). He took his place among the western historiographers, as member of the Academy of Berlin and as a knight of the Roman empire, with his *Historia incrementorum atque decrementorum aulae othomanicae* (1715–16), translated into French (1743), German (1745) and English (1734–35 and 1756) by the care of his son Antioch, Russian ambassador in London.

A special place among the Moldavian historians is occupied by the great polyglot Spatharius Niculae Milescu who wrote theological, historical and travel works. As envoy of Tsar Alexius Mikhailovich he undertook a journey across Siberia to China. (His description of this journey was published by J. F. Baddeley, *Russia, Mongolia, China*, 1919).

The Walachian chroniclers are less original and more personal. Stoica Ludescu compiled from earlier annals a *History of Walachia* up to 1688. He was chronicler of the Cantacuzinos. Radu Popescu wrote a history of the rulers of Walachia (*Cronica Tării Româneşti*) from the point of view of a boyar party headed by the Băleanu family. Radu Greceanu carried the history of Walachia up to 1714, when Constantin Brâncoveanu (Brancovan), his four sons and his son-in-law were beheaded in the market place of Constantinople. The *stolnic* (steward) Constantin Cantacuzino, a student of the University of Padua, the political mentor and the cultural patron of his country, wrote a history of Walachia (*Istoria Tării Româneşti*, c. 1710).

The profane literature is represented by numerous translations from Greek or Slavonic of historical or apocryphal books. The last category was written mainly under the influence of the Bogomils. A collection of such texts is contained in the *Codex Sturdzanus*. Many Byzantine and oriental popular books found their way into the Rumanian literature. *Fiore di virtù* was translated, in the 16th century, from Italian. The most important didactic works of this period are the *Teachings* (*Învăţăturile*) of the prince Neagoe Basarab, written in Church Slavonic in the 16th century and translated into Rumanian c. 1654. This is a treatise on policy based on Christian morals.

The 18th Century.—The Phanariotes counted among them some well-meaning rulers who patronized Christian culture in the Rumanian principalities. However, politically and economically this period presents a sad picture of social oppression and decadence. A rich profane and apocryphal literature circulated in numerous manuscripts (*Erotocritul, Fiziologul, Istoria lui Archir, Viața lui Esop, Halimaua*, etc.); the printing presses of the monastic centres continued to produce beautiful books, but there was no progress in comparison with the past. A great number of liturgical books were printed in all three principalities. In Moldavia a new cultural centre arose at Rădăuți where there appeared a *Catavasier* (1744) and a *Ceasoslov* (1745). The achievements of the century are the *Minei* ("The Lives of the Saints") (1776–80) published in Râmnicu-Vâlcea, and the *Minei* (1807–15), each in 12 volumes, published in the monastery of Neamțul. The richness and lucidity of the language, as well as their execution, put these publications alongside the Bible of 1688.

In 1700 a minority of Rumanians of Transylvania joined the Church of Rome with a view to obtaining protection from Vienna against the Hungarians. The disciples of the theological schools of Rome and Vienna amplified the ideas of the Latin origin taken from the Moldavian chroniclers and from the church books in Walachia. This ferment, however, was not favourable for literary creation. The representatives of the Latinist school of Blaj, the cultural centre of the Uniate Rumanians, were zealous scholars and great patriots.

Samuil Micu-Clain (1774–1806) wrote *Istoria . . . Românilor* (Buda, 1806) according to western standards and, in collaboration with Gheorghe Șincai (1753–1816), the author of the *Hronica Românilor* (1807), he published the first Rumanian grammar, *Elementa linguae daco-romanae sive valachicae* (1780). The third scholar of Blaj, Petru Maior (1755–1821), fought for the introduction of the Latin alphabet with his *Orthographia romana sive latino-valachica* (1819) and wrote *Istoria pentru începutul Românilor în Dachia* (1812). A collective work of this school is the *Lesicon românesc-latinesc-unguresc-nemțesc* (1825). Many religious books completed the arduous task of these apostles of Latinity. The bishop Ioan Bobb published (1812) Thomas à Kempis' *Imitatio Christi* in a translation by Samuil Clain, who also revised the Bible of 1688 and published it in Blaj (1795).

Lyric poetry was cultivated, toward the end of the century, by Anacreontic love songs of Alecu Văcărescu (1796), one of the writers of the gifted Văcărescu family. His father Ienăchiță (1720–96?) wrote the first grammar in Rumanian: *Observații sau băgări de seamă asupra regulilor și orânduielilor gramaticii românești* (1787); his son Iancu (1786–1863) overshadowed his predecessors by his poems, published only in 1848. The lyric tradition was carried on in Walachia by B. P. Mumuleanu (*Rost de poesii*, 1820; *Caracteruri*, 1825), who wrote under the influence of Alphonse de Lamartine, Edward Young and neo-Greek poetry; by Vasile Cârlova and others. In Moldavia this early versification is represented by Costachi Conachi and Enache Kogălniceanu who versifies historical events.

Epic verse was tried by Ion Budai-Deleanu who wrote a satirical epos *Țiganiada* (1812), in which the heroes are gypsies. Vasile Aaron (1770–1822) sang, in 10,000 verses, the Passion (*Patima și moartea Domnului Isus Christos*, 1805), an imitation of Milton's *Paradise Lost;* he also wrote *Piram și Tisbe* (1807), inspired by Ovid's *Metamorphoses.* I. Barac (1779–1848) produced the epic *Risipirea Ierusalimului* (1821), *Arghir și Elena* (1800) and translated from Homer and Ovid. Foreign plays were adapted and produced in Greek and in Rumanian: Molière, Corneille, Kotzebue, Metastasio (*Ahilefs la Schiro*, 1797), Schiller and also Shakespeare's *Hamlet* in a translation from German by Barac.

Anton Pann (1797–1854) popularized religious and profane folk literature and edited church service books with musical notations. His *Povestea vorbii* (1847–53) is an interpretation of proverbs connected by popular tales.

This period closes with the annexation of Bukovina (1774) by Austria and of Bessarabia (1812) by Russia. These events brought about translations of law codes in Russia and Austria. Also in the principalities law codes were compiled, in Moldavia in 1833 and in Walachia in 1780 and 1817.

The National Renaissance.—The landmark of this period was the rising of Tudor Vladimirescu (1821) and the return of national rulers. Romanticism carried forward the falling wave of the Lat-

inist movement. In the second half of the 19th century a sober literary criticism, whose origins were in German philosophy and in French culture, inaugurated modern literature.

The Transylvanian Latinism crossed the Carpathians and had some beneficial effects on the Hellenized culture of Walachia. Gheorghe Lazar (1799–1823) came as teacher to St. Sava's college in Bucharest and Rumanized the teaching. One of his pupils, I. Eliade Rădulescu (1802–72), developed a prodigious literary activity and exercised a great influence on the literary development. In 1828 he founded the political newspaper *Curierul Românesc,* followed, in 1836, by a literary supplement *Curierul de ambe sexe.* His works include translations from Byron and Lamartine, but he was a pioneer of Italian influence. He founded the Societatea Filarmonică (1833), which afterward created the National theatre in Bucharest, and was the first president of the Rumanian academy (Societatea Academică Română, 1866).

The Societatea Pentru Cultură (1862) in Bukovina called the Latinist Aron Pumnul (1818–66) from Blaj to Cernăuți (Czernowitz), where he had among his pupils the greatest Rumanian poet of the 19th century, Mihail (Michail) Eminescu (*q.v.*). He published the *Lepturariu rumînesc* (4 vol., Vienna, 1862–64). The historian Simion Bărnuțiu (1808–64), who pronounced the speech of liberation on the Field of Freedom in Blaj (1848), took refuge to Jassy, where he taught in the university and created a school of lawyers and economists.

Gheorghe Asachi (1788–1869) represented the Italian influence in Moldavia; he created the historical short story, wrote verses in Rumanian and in Italian and founded the periodical *Albina Românească* (1828), with a literary supplement, *Alăuta Românească.*

A galaxy of poets enriched the romantic heritage. The Bessarabian A. Donici, in collaboration with C. Negruzzi, translated from Russian the satires and fables of his countryman Antioch Cantemir; another Bessarabian, C. Stamate, wrote under the influence of French and Russian romantics and translated from Thomas Moore and Sir Walter Scott. Andrei Mureșanu, the author of the revolutionary hymn *Deșteaptă-te, Române,* translated from Young. The Macedo-Rumanian D. Bolintineanu versified historical legends. The outstanding literary personality among them is Grigore Alexandrescu (1812–85), who wrote *Poezii* (1832), *Meditații* (1863), fables and satires under the influence of Boileau, Lamartine and La Fontaine, and translated from Voltaire and from Byron. Western romanticism penetrated through translations from French, Italian and German. *Robinson Crusoe* was translated twice about 1830. The learned boyar D. Golescu travelled through western Europe and recorded his experiences in *Însemnare a călătoriei mele* (1826).

The national historian of this heroic period was N. Bălcescu (1819–59), the author of *Românii sub Mihai Viteazul; Puterea armată și arta militară* and of other historical and literary works. He edited the periodical *Magazinul istoric pentru Dacia* (1845–47). Modern historiography was inaugurated by Mihai Kogălniceanu (1817–91), who was the leading statesman in the newly organized monarchy under Alexander Cuza (1859–66) and Charles I (1866–1914). He produced the first edition of the old chronicles (*Letopisețele Moldovei,* 1845–52) and edited the historical review *Arhiva românească* (1840) and the literary magazine *Dacia Literară* (1840), which marks the beginning of the traditionalist trend in literature. Alecu Russo (1819–59), another leader of 1848, enriched the letters with his biblical poem in prose, *Cântarea României.*

The second half of the century was dominated by Vasile Alecsandri (1821–90) and Mihail Eminescu (1850–89). Alecsandri's rich literary heritage comprises poetry (*Doine și lăcrimioare,* 1853; *Suvenire și Mărgăritarele,* 1856), prose (*Buchetiera din Florența; Călătorie în Africa*) and plays (*Fântâna Blanduziei; Ovidiu; Despot Vodă*). Helped by A. Russo, he revealed treasures of folklore by publishing *Balade* (1852–53) and *Poezii populare* (1866).

Eminescu, the philosophical lyric poet, created modern Rumanian poetry (*Poezii,* 1884). His genius was influenced by Hindu thought and German philosophy (Schopenhauer), but he remained deeply rooted in the ancestral tradition. He raised poetry to heights not since surpassed, and remained the guiding star of the whole cultural life. His heritage includes also short stories and political and philosophical essays.

Free from any outside influence, Ion Creangă (1837–89), a peasant by origin from the eastern Carpathians, wrote folk tales and *Amintiri din copilărie* ("Recollections from Childhood"). They are a sincere reflection in the mirror of a literary genius, of unassuming artistry, of the village life and of the peasant mind.

The literary critic under whose aegis literary creation developed up into the first decade of the 20th century was the statesman and eclectic philosopher Titu Maiorescu (1840–1917). He founded in Jassy (1863) the literary circle Junimea, which represented a reaction against form without content in art, and repudiated the extremism of the Latinist school. Its periodical *Convorbiri Literare* (1867) continued to appear till World War II.

C. Negruzzi (1808–69) excelled in prose, especially with his historical short story *Alexandru Lăpușneanu* under Walter Scott's influence. The archaeologist A. Odobescu (1834–95) created the historical novel (*Mihnea Vodă*, 1858; *Doamna Chiajna*, 1860), but his artistic talent was revealed in *Pseudokinegetikos* (1874), an archaeological mosaic of high aesthetic emotions. I. Ghica (1816–97), the first Rumanian diplomatic representative in London, attempted the same genre in his *Convorbiri economice* (1879) and *Amintiri* (1890). In his short stories Ion Slavici (1848–1915) described the moral conflicts of village life. I. Popovici-Bănățeanu (1860–93) wrote about the life of the tradesmen in the Banat (*Nuvele*, 1909). N. Gane translated Dante's *Inferno* and wrote short stories (*Domnița Ruxandra*). The translation of Dante's *Divina Commedia* was undertaken by Gheorghe Coșbuc (1866–1918), the bard of rustic life (*Balade și Idile*, 1898; *Fire de tort*, 1896; *Cântece de vitejie*, 1904). Eminescu's follower in lyric pessimism, Alexandru Vlahuță (1858–1919), wrote a masterly description of the Rumanian landscape (*România pitorească*, 1903).

The greatest writer of this period is I. L. Caragiale (1852–1912) who created the social comedy (*O scrisoare pierdută; O noapte furtunoasă; D'ale Carnavalului; Conul Leonida față cu reacțiunea*); he also wrote a realistic drama (*Năpasta*), delightful *Moments and Sketches* and short stories of high aesthetic value. With caustic humour and sparkling irony he presented a society in transition from orientalism to occidentalism.

Outside the influence of Junimea, sometimes opposed to its ideology, stood: the creator of the historical national drama Barbu Delavrancea (1858–1918), with his historical trilogy *Apus de soare* ("Sunset"), *Luceafărul* ("The Evening Star"), *Viforul* ("The Storm"), and a number of short stories; the historian-philologist B. P. Hasdeu (1836–1907), with a rich literary activity (*Răzvan și Vidra*, 1867, a historical drama in verse); and the neoclassicist Duiliu Zamfirescu (1858–1922), whose cycle of novels *Neamul Comăreștilor* described the family life of the old country gentry.

The folklore and the numerous manuscripts of folk literature found their collectors and interpreters in A. M. Marienescu (1859), Urban Iarnik and Andrei Bârseanu in Transylvania; S. F. Marian in Bukovina (1873); G. D. Teodorescu in Walachia (1885); T. T. Burada in Dobruja (1880); and G. Tocilescu (1900). P. Ispirescu's fairy tales, *Basmele Românilor*, emulate those of Creangă. Moses Gaster, the pioneer in research into Rumanian folklore and folk literature, continued his activity in London. I. A. Zanne published *Proverbele Românilor* (9 vol., 1895–1901); A. Gorovei collected the riddles, *Cimiliturile Românilor* (1898).

The traditionalist movement of Dacia Literară was continued in the 20th century by a galaxy of writers whose organ was *Sămănătorul* (1901). The poets S. O. Iosif (1875–1913) and D. Anghel (1872–1914) brought the perfection of their graceful verses in their conjoint creation (*Legenda Funigeilor*, 1907). P. Cerna (1881–1913) attempted with success the philosophical lyric inaugurated by Eminescu. But the poet of this generation was the vigorous national bard of Transylvania, Octavian Goga (1879–1938), whose first volume of poems appeared in 1905.

The prose writers found their inspiration in village life and in history. E. Gârleanu (1878–1914) described the patriarchal life (*Bătrânii*); C. Hogaș (1847–1916) pictured the magic landscapes of his Moldavian mountains (*Pe drumuri de munte; In munții Neamțului*); A. Sandu-Aldea (d. 1927) described peasant life in the plain of the Bărăgan and in the Danube delta.

A parallel movement to that of *Sămănătorul*, with its romantic background, was that of the periodical *Viața Românească* (1906) of Jassy. Its ideology, labelled *poporanism* on the pattern of the Russian populism, had a social and political background. The Russian influence found its way through the literary critic C. Dobrogeanu-Gherea, a disciple of H. Taine and Karl Marx. The aesthete of the group was G. Ibrăileanu, author of the psychological novel *Adela*. The social critic was the Bessarabian C. Stere.

Western modernism penetrated under its various aspects. Symbolism found a great supporter in the learned philologist and gifted writer O. Densusianu (1873–1938), who founded the periodical *Viața Nouă* (1905). The poets I. Minulescu (1881–   ), author of *Romanțe pentru mai târziu* (1908) and of *De vorbă cu mine însumi* (1914), and G. Bacovia (1881–   ), who wrote *Plumb* (1916), compared favourably with any western symbolist. Impressionism found a worshipper in E. Lovinescu, author of a *History of Contemporary Literature* (4 vol., 1926–28). Outside these schools, N. Davidescu, after publishing a volume of poems (1910), translated Oscar Wilde's *Parables*, produced several volumes of lyric poems and an epic one, *Cântecul omului* ("The Song of the Man"). Cincinat Pavelescu (1872–   ) was the troubadour of the madrigal and romance. A. Macedonski (1854–1920) ostentatiously opposed his exotic modernism of French origin to the academic discipline of Junimea as well as to the rustic traditionalism of *Sămănătorul*; he also wrote verses in French, as did others of his generation—Julia Hasdeu and Elena Văcărescu. Carmen Sylva (Elizabeth), wife of Charles I, wrote in German and in Rumanian; in the following period Queen Marie, wife of Ferdinand, wrote in English and in Rumanian. Panait Istrati wrote also in French; A. Busuioceanu, the art historian, became a Spanish poet during World War II.

Between World Wars I and II.—In the period of national unity, the novel entered into competition with lyric poetry. Attempts at introducing the novel go back as far as 1863, when N. Filimon (1819–65) produced a social fresco of his period in *Ciocoii vechi și ciocoii noui* ("Old and New Upstarts"); but only after 1918 did the novel come into the foreground. Liviu Rebreanu described the peasant's thirst for soil and independence in his novel *Ion* (1920); he presented his suffering and his struggle for freedom in the novel of epic breadth, *Răscoala* (1932); in *Crăișorul Horia* (1929) he described the peasant revolution of 1784 in Transylvania; among his psychological novels *Ciuleandra* (1927) is a fascinating clinical description, but the most powerful novel, inspired by Rumanian participation in World War I, is *Pădurea spânzuraților* ("The Forest of the Hanged"; 1922), translated into all European languages.

World War I also inspired Cezar Petrescu (1892–   ) who wrote, among other novels, *Scrisorile unui răzeș* (1922) and *Întunecare* (1927). In his novel *Roșu, Galben și Albastru*, the symbolist I. Minulescu gave a picture of life under German occupation. The lyric novelist Ionel Teodoreanu (d. 1954) described the melancholy disappearance of the patriarchal life (*La Medeleni*, 1926–27; *Turnul Mileni*, 1928). Victor Ion Popa found the subjects of his novels in village life (*Velerim și Lerim, Doamne*, 1932; *Sfârleaza cu Fofează*); he also wrote the biography of the pioneer in aviation Aurel Vlaicu (1939) and enriched the theatre with exquisite plays (*Mușcata din fereastră*). E. Bucuța (1887–   ), in his *Fuga lui Șefki* (1926), and G. Mihăescu (1894–   ), in *Rusoaica* (1933) and *Donna Alba* (1935), described the exotic life of the borderlands. Mircea Eliade brought an Indian atmosphere into one of his novels, *Maitreyi* (1933). Matei Luca Caragiale, the son of I. L. Caragiale, in his short-lived literary career produced a refined piece of art with his *Craii de Curtea Veche*.

Gala Galaction (1879–   ) translated the Bible (1938), in collaboration with Vasile Radu, and wrote mystical prose (*Bisericuța din Răzoare*, 1914) and novels with biblical subjects (*Roxana*, 1930). Hortensia Papadat-Bengescu is a psychological analyst (*Concert din Muzică de Bach*, 1927). Life in the suburbs of Bucharest found its interpreter in the novelist G. M. Zamfirescu (d. 1939). Humorous prose found able representatives in D. D. Pătrășcanu (1872–1937) who wittily described political life (*Can-*

didat fără naroc); in Damian Stanoiu, the caricaturist of monastic life; in Gheorghe Brăescu, who found his material in military life.

The link with the older generation was assured by two prose writers. I. A. Brătescu-Voineşti (1868–1946?) was the kind-hearted representative of the landed gentry, whose stories are mainly centred round the defeated inadaptables in life. Mihail Sadoveanu (1880–   ), whose talent reached maturity between World Wars I and II, tried the historical novel under the influence of Henryk Sienkiewicz (*Şoimii, Fraţii Jderi, Zodia Cancerului*), but his art was revealed in landscape descriptions and hunting scenes. The Transylvanian writer I. Agârbiceanu (1892–   ) carried on Slavici's tradition, presenting in his novels and short stories the village and the middle class of his province against a religious background (*Dela ţară*, 1906; *Arhanghelii*, 1914; *În pragul vieţii*). He was one of the founders of the Transylvanian periodical *Luceafărul* (1902).

The scholars and philosophers took part in the literary movement of the period as critics and writers. The classical archaeologist Vasile Pârvan (d. 1927), commemorating the sacrificed generation of World War I, wrote *Parentalia*, inspired by Thucydides. The prodigious historian and cultural animator, Nicolae Iorga (Nicholas Jorga, *q.v.*; 1871–1940), edited *Sămănătorul*, founded several literary periodicals and wrote literary criticism, poetry, numerous plays and travel descriptions. The geographer S. Mehedinţi (Soveja) edited *Convorbiri Literare* and wrote village stories (*Oameni dela munte*). The philosopher I. Rădulescu-Motru exercised a great influence on intellectual life with some of his works (*Personalismul energetic*, 1927). Lucian Blaga (1895–   ) is the philosophic essayist (*Filosofia stilului*, 1924; *Etnografie şi artă*, 1926) as well as the poet of the generation. He began as a lyric poet (*Poemele luminii*, 1919) under the influence of western expressionism, and developed a philosophical system based on the traditional way of life interpreted as a cosmic mystery (*Trilogia cunoaşteril*, 1931–34). His poetic dramas express his philosophic thinking (*Meşterul Manole*, 1927; *Cruciada copiilor*, 1930; *Avram Iancu*, 1934).

Literary criticism counted among its best representatives the aesthetician M. Dragomirescu, editor of the *Convorbiri Critice*; D. Caracostea, the analyst of Eminescu; G. Bogdan-Duică, the literary historian; A. Busuioceanu, the art historian; and Paul Zarifopol (*Pentru arta literară*, 1934).

The national and the private theatres offered great opportunities for playwrights. Rumanian plays and translations, old and new plays, held the stage. A. Davila's historical drama in verse *Vlaicu Vodă* (1922), Victor Eftimiu's *Cocoşul negru* (1913), M. Sorbul's *Letopiseţii* (1914) and *Patima roşie* (1916), Caton Theodorian's *Bujoreştii*, C. Ciprian's *Omul cu mârţoaga* and Ion Sân-Giorgiu's *Masca* (1922) are among the best.

Lyric poetry was the most cultivated in modern Rumanian literature. Schools and periodicals were numerous indeed (*cf.* Mario Roques, *La poésie roumaine contemporaine*, Taylorian lecture, Oxford, 1934). Nichifor Crainic, the leader of the literary magazine *Gândirea* (1920), represented the religious traditionalist tendency (*Darurile pământului*, 1920); I. Pillat developed under the influence of the French and German lyric and sang the beauty of his native landscape (*Pe Argeş în sus; Satul meu*); V. Voiculescu was a profound mystic poet (*Întrezăriri*, 1940); Adrian Maniu produced the play *Meşterul* (1922) and wrote refined verses inspired by the rustic landscape. The poems of the mathematician I. Barbu evoke the geometric forms of the crystal (*Joc secund*, 1930). Dragoş Protopopescu, the translator of Shakespeare, is an original poet and talented essayist on English literature.

The poet who, after Eminescu, created a new lyric poetry was Tudor Arghezi (1880–   ). In his poems the language acquires an unexpected expressiveness and magic harmony. His prose (*Cartea cu jucării*, 1935; *Ochii Maicii Domnului*, 1935; *Cimitirul Buna Vestire*, 1936) and his verses (*Cuvinte potrivite*, 1927; *Flori de mucegai*, 1931; *Versuri de seară*, 1935) set a new landmark in the development of Rumanian letters.

BIBLIOGRAPHY.—I. Bianu, N. Hodoş and D. Simionescu, *Bibliografia Românească Veche*, 4 vol. (Bucharest, 1903–44); N. Cartojan, *Istoria literaturii române vechi*, 3 vol. (Bucharest, 1940–45), *Cărţile populare în literatura română*, 2 vol. (Bucharest, 1929 and 1938); L. Feraru, *The Development of Rumanian Poetry* (New York, 1929); P. Haneş, *Histoire de la littérature roumaine* (Paris, 1934); N. Iorga, *Istoria literaturii religioase a Românilor până la 1688* (Bucharest, 1904), *Istoria literaturii româneşti*, vol. i, 2nd ed. (Bucharest, 1925), vol. ii (Bucharest, 1907–09); B. Munteanu, *Modern Rumanian Literature* (London, 1939); D. Murăraşu, *Istoria literaturii române* (Bucharest, 1940).

(G. Ns.)

RUMELIA, a name used by the Turks to denote their possessions in the Balkans (Turkish *Rumili*, the land of the Romans, *i.e.*, Byzantines), particularly the ancient provinces, including Constantinople and Salonika, of Thrace and Macedonia; later particularized to denote the province composed of central Albania and western Macedonia. Eastern Rumelia (afterward southern Bulgaria) became, by the Berlin treaty of 1878, an autonomous province within the Turkish empire, but proclaimed its unity with Bulgaria on Sept. 18, 1885. (*See* BULGARIA.)

RUMEX, a genus of the buckwheat family to which belong the well-known weeds known as dock and sorrel (*qq.v.*).

RUMFORD, BENJAMIN THOMPSON, COUNT (1753–1814), British-American scientist, philanthropist and administrator, was born at Woburn (Mass.), on March 26, 1753. The Thompson family to which he belonged settled in New England about the middle of the previous century and were moderately wealthy farmers. At the age of 14 Benjamin was sufficiently advanced "in algebra, geometry, astronomy, and even the higher mathematics," to calculate a solar eclipse within four seconds of accuracy. In 1766 he was apprenticed to a storekeeper at Salem, in New England, and there occupied himself in chemical and mechanical experiments, and in engraving. At the outbreak of the American War when he was between 17 and 18 years of age he went to Boston, where he became assistant in another store. At 19 he married the widow of Col. Benjamin Rolfe, a woman possessed of considerable property, and his senior by 14 years.

This marirage was the foundation of his success. Soon after it he became acquainted with Governor Wentworth of New Hampshire, who conferred on him the majority of a local regiment of militia. As he was distrusted by friends of the American cause, it was considered prudent that he should seek an early opportunity to leave the country. On the evacuation of Boston by the royal troops, therefore, in 1776, Governor Wentworth sent him with despatches to England. On his arrival in London Lord George Germain, secretary of state, appointed him to a clerkship in his office. Within a few months he was advanced to the post of secretary of the province of Georgia, and in about four years under-secretary of state. He continued his scientific pursuits, however, and in 1779 was elected a fellow of the Royal Society. The explosive force of gunpowder, the construction of firearms, and a system of signalling at sea were subjects which particularly interested him. On the resignation of Lord North's administration, of which Lord George Germain was a member, he left the civil service, and was nominated to a cavalry command in the revolted provinces of America. But the War of Independence was practically at an end, and in 1783 he quitted active service, with the rank and half-pay of a lieutenant-colonel. He now decided to join the Austrian army, to campaign against the Turks. At Strassburg he was introduced to prince Maximilian, afterwards elector of Bavaria, and was by him invited to enter the civil and military service of that State. Having obtained leave of the British Government to accept the prince's offer, he received the honour of knighthood from George III, and remained at Munich 11 years as minister of war, minister of police, and grand chamberlain to the elector. During his stay in Bavaria he contributed a number of papers to the *Philosophical Transactions*. He reorganized the Bavarian army; he improved the condition of the industrial classes and he did much to suppress mendicity. In one day he had 2,600 beggars and depredators in Munich and its suburbs alone arrested and transferred to an industrial establishment which he prepared for them. In this institution they were housed and fed, and they not only supported themselves, but earned a surplus for the electoral revenues. The principle on which he acted is stated by him in the following words: "To make vicious and abandoned people happy, it has generally been supposed necessary first to make them virtuous. But why not reverse this order? Why not make them happy, and then virtuous?"

In 1791 he was created a count of the Holy Roman empire, and chose his title of Rumford from the name of the American township to which his wife's family belonged. In 1795 he visited England, where he lost all his private papers, including the materials for an autobiography. In London he applied himself to the discovery of methods for curing smoky chimneys and to improvements in fireplace construction. But he was quickly recalled to Bavaria, Munich being threatened at once by an Austrian and a French army. The elector fled, and it was entirely owing to Rumford that a hostile occupation of the city was prevented. It was now proposed that he should be Bavarian ambassador in London; but the fact that he was a British subject presented an insurmountable obstacle. He returned to England, however, as a private citizen. In 1798 he presented to the Royal society his "Enquiry concerning the Source of Heat which is excited by Friction," in which he combated the current view that heat was a material substance, and regarded it as a mode of motion. In 1799, he, with Sir Joseph Banks, projected the establishment of the Royal institution. It received its charter from George III in 1800, and Rumford selected Sir Humphry Davy as scientific lecturer there. He lived in London until 1804, when he went to Paris, marrying (his first wife having died in 1792) the wealthy widow of Lavoisier, the celebrated chemist. He separated from her eventually and took up his residence at Auteuil. He died there suddenly on Aug. 21, 1814, in the 62nd year of his age.

Rumford was the founder and the first recipient of the Rumford medal of the Royal society. He was also the founder of the Rumford medal of the American Academy of Arts and Sciences, and of the Rumford professorship in Harvard university. His complete works with a memoir by G. E. Ellis were published by the American Academy of Arts and Sciences in 1870-75.

RUMFORD, a town of Oxford Co., Maine, U.S., on the Androscoggin river, 60 mi. N. of Portland; served by the Maine Central railroad. The population in 1950 was 7,888. Rumford has a large hydroelectric station and large book paper mill, all under one roof. It was founded in 1893 as an industrial community, and is a ski centre.

RŪMĪ (1207-1273). Mohammed b̄. Mohammed b. Husain albalkhī, better known as Maulānā Jalāl-uddīn Rūmī (or simply Jalāl-uddīn), the greatest Sūfic poet of Persia, was born on Sept. 30, 1207 (604 A.H. 6th of Rabī' I) at Balkh, in Khorāsān. His father was invited to Iconium (or Rum), and from this place Jalāl-uddīn took his pen-name.

Jalāl-uddīn founded the order of the Maulawī (Mevlevi) dervishes, famous for their piety as well as for their garb of mourning, their music and their mystic dance (samā), which is the outward representation of the circling movement of the spheres, and the inward symbol of the circling movement of the soul caused by the vibrations of a Sūfi's fervent love to God. Most of Rūmī's matchless odes were composed in honour of the Maulawī dervishes, and even his *opus magnum*, the *Mathnawī* (*Mesnevi*), or, as it is usually called, *The Spiritual Mathnawī* (*mathnawī-i-ma'nawī*), in six books with 30,000 to 40,000 double-rhymed verses, can be traced to the same source. The idea of this immense collection of ethical and moral precepts was first suggested to the poet by his favourite disciple Hasan, better known as Husām-uddīn, who in 1258 became Jalāl-uddīn's chief assistant. Jalāl-uddīn dictated to him, with a short interruption, the whole work during the remaining years of his life. Soon after its completion Jalāl-uddīn died, on Dec. 17, 1273.

Jalāl-uddīn's life is fully described in Shams-uddīn Ahmed Aflākī's *Manāḳib-ul 'ārifīn* (written between A.D. 1318 and 1353), the most important portions of which have been translated by J. W. Redhouse in the preface to his English metrical version of *The Mesnevi, Book the First* (London, 1881); there is also an abridged translation of the *Mathnawī*, with introduction on Sufism, by E. H. Whinfield (2nd ed., 1898). Complete editions have been printed in Bombay, Lucknow, Tabriz, Constantinople and in Bulaq (with a Turkish translation, 1268 A.H.), at the end of which a seventh daftar is added, the genuineness of which is refuted by a remark of Jalāl-uddīn himself in one of the Bodleian copies of the poem, Ouseley, 294 (f. 328a seq.). A revised edition was made by 'Abd-ullatīf between 1024 and 1032 A.H., and the same author's commentary on the *Mathnawī*, *Latā'if-ulma'nawī*, and his glossary, *Latā'if-allughāt*, have been lithographed in Cawnpore (1876) and Lucknow (1877) respec-

tively, the latter under the title *Farhang-i-mathnawī*. For the other numerous commentaries and for further biographical and literary particulars of Jalāl-uddīn, see Rieu's *Cat. of the Persian MSS. of the Brit. Mus.*, vol. ii, p. 584 *seq.*; A. Sprenger's *Oudh* Cat., p. 489; Sir Gore Ouseley, *Notices of Persian Poets*, p. 112 *seq.*; H. Ethé, in *Morgenländische Studien* (Leipzig, 1870), p. 95 *seq.*, and in Geiger and Kuhn's *Grundriss der iranischen Philologie* (Stuttgart, 1896-1904), vol. ii, pp. 287-292. Selections from Jalāl-uddīn's diwan (often styled *Dīwān-i-Shams-i-Tabrīz*) are translated in German verse by V. von Rosenzweig (Vienna, 1838); into English by R. A. Nicholson (2nd ed., 1898) and W. Hastie (1903).

RUMINANTIA, a term employed by Cuvier to include all the artiodactyle ruminating ungulate mammals classed under the groups Pecora, Tylopoda and Tragulina. (*See* ARTIODACTYLA; PECORA; TYLOPODA.)

RUMMY, or RUM, RHUM, ROMME, a card game having a common origin with Coon-Can (*q.v.*). It was given its name "rum" (queer), or "rummy," in England, but attained its greatest popularity in the United States, where a survey made in 1941 showed it to be the most generally known card game.

The basic idea of rummy is the formation of structures. A standard pack of 52 playing cards, with or without one or more jokers, is used. The cards rank: king (high), queen, jack, ten, nine . . . ace (low). The player's object is to form matched sets: "groups" of three or four of a kind (as, three 9s, or four 6s); or sequences of three or more cards of consecutive rank in the same suit (as, ♠K-♠Q-♠J). When the joker is used its holder may cause it to represent any card he chooses.

Rummy has no official rules and has countless variants, but substantially the following procedure is common to them all:

Two or more play. The rotation of the deal and turn to play is clockwise, beginning with the player at the dealer's left. Each player receives seven cards (in a two-hand game, ten cards; in a five- or six-hand game only six or five cards), dealt one at a time face down. The next card is placed face up on the table to found a "talon" (waste pile) and the remaining undealt cards form a "stock" placed face down beside the talon. Each player in turn must draw the top card from either the talon or the stock, and add it to his hand; he may then "lay down" any matched set, or may "lay off" one or more matching cards on any matched set previously laid down by any player; and must then discard one card face up on the talon. A player may not lay down more than one matched set in a turn (unless, as in many variants, he can lay down his entire hand at one time, in which case he is said to be "rummy" and in most methods of settlement collects double).

The game is won by the first player who "goes out" (that is, who has laid down all his cards). He wins from each other player the total pip value of the cards remaining in that player's hand, face cards counting 10 each. In some variants the ace ranks high (as in the sequence A-K-Q) as well as low, and counts 11 points in the settlement; the joker, when used, counts 15.

A game may end when any player reaches an agreed score, as +100, or −100; or after an agreed number of deals.

The Block Game.—After the stock has been exhausted each player in turn may draw or not, as he pleases, from the talon. Then, if no one has gone out, the player with the lowest pip count wins, collecting from the others as though he had gone out. Players who tie for low divide the winnings. (As some play, the talon is shuffled, or simply turned over, and used again as the stock.)

Double Rum.—Two full packs plus one or two jokers, all mixed to form a 105- or 106-card pack, are used. Each player receives ten cards and play proceeds until someone goes out, the talon being turned as often as necessary. In laying off on a sequence containing a joker at either end, a player may change the designation of the joker provided it remains a card in sequence: thus, with joker-♥6-♥7 showing, a player may add the ♥5, ♥4, ♥8 or ♥9; but with ♥6-joker-♥8 showing, he may not add the ♥7.

In forms of double rum called variously Progressive Rummy, Liverpool, Joker Rummy, Zioncheck and by other names, each game consists of a series of five or six deals. In each deal a specified combination is required to go out, as, two groups on the first deal, one group and one sequence on the second, two sequences on the third, and so on.

500 Rum.—This is the most scientific rummy variant, and differs in principle from all others. Each player starts with ten cards and may in turn draw as many cards as he pleases from the talon, provided in the same turn he lays down some matched set including the bottom card drawn. Play ends when any player goes out, whereupon each player scores the pip count of all cards he has laid down (or laid off) minus the pip count of any cards remaining in his hand. The ace ranks high or low and counts 15; the joker, when used, counts 20. The first player to reach +500 wins the game. 500 Rum may be played with one or two packs. It is a good four-hand partnership game.

Continental Rummy.—Up to five players use two packs of cards; six to eight players, three packs; nine to twelve players, four packs; in each case with one joker per pack. Only sequences count, ace ranking high or low. Each player receives fifteen cards and must go out all at one time with (a) five three-card sequences; (b) three four-card and one three-card sequences; or (c) one five-, one four-, and two three-card sequences.

Knock Rummy.—Any player in turn may end the game by knocking (or, "going down"), whereupon the unmatched cards in every player's hand are counted and the player with the lowest pip count wins from each other player the difference between their totals. Thus, if one player knocks with a count of 9, another player holding K-K-K-6-5-5-4 would lose 11 points to him. In certain variants a player may not knock unless his own count is at most 7, or 10, or 15, depending on the custom of the game.

Gin Rummy.—An American variant originally called Gin Poker or simply Gin, was first played in 1907 and in 1941 became a fad as widely publicized as that of contract bridge (q.v.) in 1931–32. Two play, each receiving ten cards. A player may knock when the pip count of his unmatched cards, after he discards, will be 10 or less. He scores the difference between his pip count and that of his opponent (who may first lay down and lay off what he can). If the opponent has the same or a lower count he scores the difference, if any, plus 10 points. For "going gin" (knocking and laying down all ten cards in matched sets) a player scores the difference in counts, if any, plus 20 points. If only two cards remain in the stock and neither player has knocked, there is a redeal. The first player whose score reaches 100 points wins the game, and receives a 100-point bonus. Each player then adds to his score 20 points for every deal on which he was the winner. If the loser has not scored, the bonus for game is 200 points.

Partnership play is possible, with two or more players to a team, playing separate two-hand games and combining the scores of all partners to produce one winning team for each deal.

In Hollywood Gin, the two players score their results in three games at once: Each player's first winning score is credited to him in Game 1, his second winning score in Games 1 and 2, and subsequent winning scores in all three games.

See *Gin Rummy: The Official Laws*, 1943.   (A. H. Md.)

RUNCORN, market town, urban district, river port, Northwich parliamentary division, Cheshire, England, on the south of the estuary of the Mersey, 16 mi. above Liverpool. Pop. (1938) 23,340. Area, 4.5 sq.mi. It is on the L.M.S.R., and the Bridgewater canal (1773), which here descends into the Mersey by a flight of locks. Runcorn, being on the Manchester ship canal, is a subport of Manchester, and has extensive wharfage and warehouse accommodation. The chief exports are coal, salt and pitch; but there is also a large traffic in potters' materials. It is connected with Widnes by a railway and a transporter bridge. The town possesses shipbuilding yards, iron foundries, rope works, tanneries, soap and alkali and chemical works. Runcorn was in early times of considerable importance. On a rock which formerly jutted into the Mersey Aethelfleda erected a castle in 916. The ferry is noticed in a charter in the 12th century.

RUNDALE, the name of a form of occupation of land, somewhat resembling the English "common field" system. The land is divided into discontinuous plots, and cultivated and occupied by a number of tenants to whom it is leased jointly. The system was common in Ireland, especially in the western counties. In Scotland, where the system also existed, it was termed "run-rig."

RUNEBERG, JOHAN LUDVIG (1804–1877), national poet of Finland, son of a sea captain, was born at Jakobstad, on Feb. 5, 1804. He was educated at the University of Abo and after its removal to Helsingfors, Runeberg became, in 1830, amanuensis to the council of the university. In 1831 his verse romance of Finnish life, *Grafven i Perrho* (The Grave in Perrho), received the small gold medal of the Swedish academy, and the poet married Fredrika Charlotta Tengström, daughter of the archbishop of Finland. In the same year he was appointed university lecturer on Roman literature. In 1837 Runeberg accepted the chair of Latin at Borgå college, of which he was rector in 1847–50, and lived at Borgå for the rest of his life.

His two idylls, *Elgskyttarne* (The Elk-Hunters) and *Hanna* had won for him a place second only to Tegnér among the poets of Sweden. Later works are *Nadeschda* (1841); *Julqvällen* (1841); *Fänrik Ståls Sägner* (2 series, 1848 and 1860), patriotic poems on the war of independence of 1808; and *Kungarne pa Salamis* (1863), a tragedy. In 1844 he published the noble cycle of unrhymed verse romances derived from old Scandinavian legend and entitled *King Fjalar*. Runeberg died at Borgå on May 6, 1877. His writings were collected by C. R. Nyblom in six volumes in 1870, and his posthumous writings in three volumes (1878–79). The poems of Runeberg show the influence of the Greeks and of Goethe upon his mind; but he possesses a great originality. It is hardly possible to overestimate the value of his patriotic poems as a link between the Swedish and Finnish nations. He has remained one of the most popular poets writing in Swedish, although his whole life was spent in Finland.

An account of his life and works by C. R. Nyblom is prefixed to the *Samlade Skrifter* of 1870. For a minute criticism of Runeberg's principal poems, with translations, see Gosse's *Studies in the Literature of Northern Europe* (1879). A selection of his lyrical pieces was published in an English translation by Messrs. Magnusson & Palmer in 1878. There are also monographs on Runeberg by Dietrichson and Rancken (Stockholm, 1864), by Cygnäus (Helsingfors, 1873), by Ljunggren (Lund, 1882–83), Peschier (Stuttgart, 1881), and by W. Soderhjelm (Stockholm, 1904). A further edition of his *Samlade Skrifter* appeared in 1907.

RUNES, the oldest form of Germanic writing. This form of writing was in use in the Scandinavian North in the 3rd century, and in remote districts of Sweden almost down to our own times.

futharkgw   hntjêpRs   tb emlngod

FIG. 1.—THE EARLIER RUNE-STAVES

During the first centuries of their vogue runes consisted of 24 letters: the so-called older or all-Germanic runic staves (fig. 1). Their peculiar forms appear first in inscriptions found all over Europe from Rumania and western Russia to the east of France and Friesland, but in greatest number in England and Scandinavia. Runes, which at first sight seem to betray derivation from the southern European alphabets, the Greek and the Latin, differ from these radically in their arrangement, as we may see from some inscriptions which use the runic staves in their entirety, the most important being the Kylver Stone in Gothland (5th century), the Vadstena *braktea* from Östergötland, Sweden (fig. 2), the Charnay clasp from eastern France and the Thames sword from southern England. Moreover every rune had its special name which we know through the oral traditions recorded in Anglo-Saxon manuscripts. The 24 runes were divided up into three groups of eight each, each group coming later to be called in Scandinavian an *ætt*, a word which probably meant "number of eight." The runic staves, at least at a later

FROM L. F. A. WIMMER, "DIE RUNENSCHRIFT" (WEIDMANN)

FIG. 2.—THE VADSTENA BRAKTEA

period, were called *futhark*, after their initial letters.

As regards sound values, it may be mentioned that *th* was pronounced approximately as in the English *thing*; *d* like *th* in the
English *this*; *g* had a sound corresponding to a fricative *d*; *b* in
the same way, therefore corresponding to *b* in the Spanish *Habana*;
ŋg like *ng* in *England* and *R*, finally, almost like *s* in the English *is*.

The oldest extant decipherable runic writings as to the origin
of which we can speak with any certainty hail from discoveries
in the bogland in south-western Denmark, Vi-mose in Fyn, and
Torsbjaerg in Slesvig. Most archaeologists date the first-men-
tioned from the middle of the 3rd century, the second from the
4th. The inscriptions are few in number and brief. Those which
can be deciphered contain one or two names of men. These earliest
finds of runes in Denmark were supplemented by a whole series of
others from the 4th, 5th and 6th centuries—inscriptions on single
objects, arms, ornaments, and more especially gold *brakteas*.
Archaeological research establishes the fact that south-western
Denmark was really the cradle of the knowledge of runes, whence
the use of runes spread to Norway and Sweden. It has been ascertained, moreover, that from Slesvig it made its way in the
5th century along the southern coast of the North Sea to England
and the Continent.

If then Slesvig and Fyn are the original home of the runes in
northern and western Europe, our next question is: did the runes
originate in Denmark or were they imported from elsewhere?
It has been established that a number of runes which are contemporaneous with the oldest of those found in the Danish bogland have been discovered along a line of country passing through
Pomerania, Brandenburg, Volhynia and Rumania. Moreover
these discoveries include archaic objects the primary forms of
which do not hail from western Europe but are found in southeastern Europe, on the northern coast of the Black Sea and along
the lower Danube. From this fact the Swedish archaeologist,
B. Salin, drew the conclusion a quarter of a century ago that the
runes came to Scandinavia from south-eastern Europe. The eastern European runes are certainly Gothic in part, and it is certain
that runes were known and used among the Goths in the first half
of the 4th century, because Ulfilas, the Apostle of the Goths,
constructed his Gothic writing on the basis of runes. It may be
added that in the 3rd and 4th centuries there is no trace of the
existence of runes in the western Teutonic world, *i.e.*, south-west
of the line Slesvig, Berlin, Bukarest.

This signifies that the runes originated with the Goths in southeastern Europe, in a milieu, therefore, in immediate touch with
Greek and Latin culture. Greek was the prevailing language along
the lower Danube; Latin was the language of the Roman forces
and colonists. Archaeological and historical discoveries indicate,
therefore, that the runes had their source in one or other of the
classical alphabets—or in both.

It remains to consider what the runes themselves have to tell
about their origin. The Dane, L. Wimmer, has made it clear
paleographically that they are derived from classical writing. It
has been demonstrated by him that the runes have the same signs
for the vowels *a, e, o,* as the Greek and Latin alphabets, but
these letters in the Latin are the result of a Greek modification
of the Semitic guttural signs. Wimmer has demonstrated, too,
once for all, that at least the runes for *f, h,* and *r,* derive from the
Latin alphabet. As quite a number of runes like *a, i, b, t, m* and *n,*
may be traced typographically to the Greek and Latin alphabets,
and as it undoubtedly would be natural to seek the source of the
runes in a single alphabet, Wimmer seeks to trace all the runes
back to Latin. In so seeking, however, he has been forced into
assumptions and deductions which must be regarded as improbable
and irrational. In February 1928, the Norwegian, C. J. S. Marstrander, in a very weighty treatise, seeks to show that the runes
derive from a late Northern Etruscan alphabet, most of the letters of which were made up out of the Latin but which in regard
to sounds, not to be found in the Latin, preserved a number of
Northern Etruscan letters. This alphabet was in use at the beginning of our era in the region of the eastern Alps among Celtic
tribes and it was through intercourse with these that the Teutons,
probably the Marcomanni who lived in Bohemia, created the

runes. Certain runes are more easily and naturally explained
in the light of Marstrander's paper than in that of any other
interpretation that has been put forward, but on the other
hand new difficulties present themselves in regard to other
runes. Archaeological and chronological facts seem also hard to
reconcile with Marstrander's hypothesis. He has promised us a
more exhaustive treatise on certain questions bearing upon the

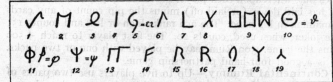

FIG. 3.—CLASSICAL LETTERS AND RUNES

problem. Until this is available, or at all events until Marstrander's hypothesis can be examined thoroughly, the theory regarding the origin of the runes put forward in 1904 by von Friesen along the following lines may be accepted.

We have just noted that certain runes may safely be said to
derive from Latin letters. On the other hand the runes possess
certain characteristic features which are in agreement with the
Greek alphabet. These are: (a) the phonetic signs in both alphabetical systems number 24, which in view of the use of the runes
for magical purposes has acquired its special significance. The
Latin alphabet consisted originally of 21 letters, afterwards, when
y and *z* were adopted from the Greek, of 23; (b) the use in the
runes of a special sign for ŋg points directly to the Greek indication of ŋg by γγ; (c) every rune has its special name, an
arrangement which seems to be inspired by the peculiar Greek
names inherited from the Semitic alphabet, *alpha, beta, gamma,*
etc. The Latin letters, on the contrary, were called in classic
times as they are now *a, be, ce, de,* etc.

In addition we come upon a question of phonetic nature. Like
the early Germanic, the Gothic language was specially notable
for its wealth in spirant sounds such as *th* in the English *thing*
and *this, ch* in the German *auch, g* in the German *tage, b* in the
Spanish *Habana*. Hardly any sounds of this kind are to be met
with in the later Latin of Imperial Rome except *f* and *s*, while
Greek at this period possessed in addition both *th* and *ch*.

A comparison between the runes and the ordinary cursive form
of the Greek alphabet gives us a number of concordances which
can scarcely be attributed to chance. The Greek cursive alphabet
has two forms of *e* (fig. 3, 1 and 2), the runes also have two
forms: a Greek form of *o* (fig. 3, 3), which accords with the runic
o. In the Greek is found a consonant *i*-sound which is written
as fig. 3, 4 or fig. 3, 5, which latter form accords with the runic
j. Also in the formation of other consonants we find the runic
letters in remarkable accord with the Greek: the runic *l* accords
with the Greek, fig. 3, 6 (compare the Latin fig. 3, 7); the
runic *g*, with the sound value *ch* and *g* (ʒ), accords with the
Greek (fig. 3, 8) *ch*; the runic (fig. 3, 9) *th* in the English *this*
with the Greek (fig. 3, 10). In other cases we find in the runes
forms which are identical with the Greek but with different sound
values: the runic form for *th* in the English *thing* accords with the
Greek, fig. 3, 11 (f); the runic form for *R* or *z* (in the English *is*)
accords with the Greek (fig. 3, 12). Finally the runic form for ŋg
clearly derives from the Greek (fig. 3, 13) except for the symmetrical stylization usual in the formation of the runes.

These numerous resemblances between the runes and the Greek
letters can scarcely be the result of chance. The concordance between the runes and the Greek cursive writing is particularly striking and, significantly, the runes which have their source in the
Latin also in many cases derive clearly from the cursive form:
the runic *f* is stylized Latin cursive (fig. 3, 14), and the runic *r* is
always open in its middle part like the Latin cursive (fig. 3, 15),
while the Latin uncial and lapidary *r* (fig. 3, 16) is closed. The
runic for *u* also seems to come from the Latin cursive *o* (fig. 3, 17).

The close relationship between the runes and the classic cursive handwriting—the ordinary handwriting used in everyday life
and also by less cultured people—indicates that the art of writing

did not come to the Goths by the way of scholarship. Some individual Goths—mercenaries, for instance—from the north-western coast of the Black Sea, in the course of visits to the Roman provinces, learnt Greek and Latin and the Greek and Latin forms of writing used in state edicts and in private life. They acquired in addition an imperfect acquaintance with the lapidary and uncial style which was the basis for the ordinary cursive handwriting, wherefore some forms of the better style occasionally appear. Such a Goth or several such Goths working together, undertook to write out the Gothic language on the basis of the knowledge of Latin and Greek writing thus acquired. The result of these efforts is the runic stave.

FROM L. F. A. WIMMER, "DIE RUNENSCHRIFT" (WEIDMANN)

FIG. 4.—THE KOVEL SPEAR-HEAD

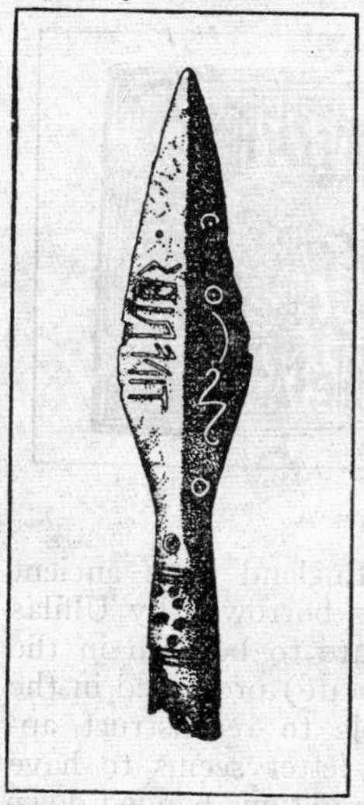

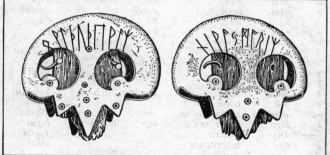

Like the letters of the classic alphabet, runes soon came to be used for purposes of magic, a use which continued for a long time. But that the chief purpose of the runes was to give the spoken language a fixed form is demonstrated at an early date by the fact that Ulfilas built up his Gothic letters upon runes, which even before his time had solved the difficult problem of representing the Gothic phonetic system by the use of classic letters.

Removed from the sphere of classical culture, the runic writing soon came to be used chiefly for inscriptions: it was carved or cut on wood, metal or stone. In the process the individual letters began to undergo a certain kind of symmetrical stylization or conventionalization which gave them a substantially different appearance from that of their classic prototypes, and, probably, in connection with this the runes came to be put in an order entirely different from that of the classic alphabets.

From the region of the Black Sea the knowledge of runes soon spread to distant corners of the great dominion which the Goths established in the 3rd and 4th centuries between the Black Sea and the Baltic, and in the middle of the 3rd century we begin to find single objects with runic inscriptions on them in Gothland, Denmark and Norway.

Between the Black Sea and the Baltic we find at the same period runic letters in the Gothic language as on the spear-head from Kovel in Volhynia (fig. 4). On this may be read *tilarids,* which is either a man's name or, more likely, the name given to the costly spear-head inlaid with silver ornamentation. The word

FROM L. F. A. WIMMER, "DIE RUNENSCHRIFT," (WEIDMANN)

FIG. 5.—THE THORSBJAERG CHAPE

means "the one which reaches the goal," and it may have some magical significance.

Of the same period are certain Scandinavian discoveries of runes, among them the Thorsbjaerg chape from Slesvig (fig. 5) which bears the inscription *owlthuthewaR niwajmariR;* this is probably the names of two men, *Wulthu-thewaR* and *NiujamariR,* both names being of the familiar old Germanic double-jointed type.

It has already been pointed out that Slesvig and Fyn constituted a cradle for the runes during the Roman iron age and the earlier portion of the transmigration era (A.D. 250–450). There are many signs that runic writing was brought hither from the Black Sea by the Heruli, a people who play an important part in the history of the transmigration period and who seem to have had their origin in Denmark. Slesvig in those early days and until well into the middle ages was of primary importance for the intercommunication and exchange of merchandise between the Baltic regions on the one side and Western and Southern Europe on the other. In particular Slesvig had been long the traffic-route from the Rhineland and England up to the Scandinavian North. Regular communication by sea round Skagen and by the Skagarack and Kattegatt into the Baltic did not begin until the 13th century.

FROM S. MÜLLER, "NORDISCHE ALTERTUMSKUNDE" (WALTER DE GRUYTER & CO.)

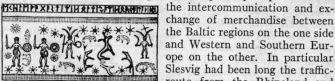

FIG. 6.—THE GALLEHUS INSCRIPTION

A remarkable runic inscription found in Slesvig is that on a golden horn from Gallehus (fig. 6), which dates from the beginning of the 5th century. It reads: *ek hlewagastiR holtijaR horna tawido*—"THlewagast from Holt made the horn." There are altogether about a dozen inscriptions on loose objects, also inscriptions of the older type as well as about 40 runic *brakteas* dating from between the 3rd and 6th centuries, which were found in Danish soil.

At a very early period—some time in the 3rd century—runic writing had spread from Denmark into Norway. Here as early as the 4th century the custom had begun of fitting stone monuments with runic inscriptions. One of the finest and longest inscriptions is that of the Tune stone from South-Eastern Norway (fig. 7). It would seem to date from the earlier half of the 5th century and reads: *(wiwa)R (?) woduride staina (satido) thrijoR dohtriR da(i)lidun arbija si(bi)josteR arbijano, ek wiwaR after woduride wita(n)-dahalaiban worahto(runoR),* which apparently may be translated: "Viv (?) raised this stone to Vodurid. Three daughters shared the inheritance as nearest of kin among his survivors. But I, Viv, engraved the runes to my master (=breadgiver, *cf.* the English *lord*) Vodurid."

FROM L. F. A. WIMMER "DIE RUNENSCHRIFT," (WEIDMANN)

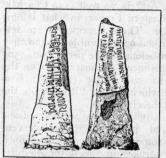

FIG. 7.—THE TUNE STONE, SOUTH-EASTERN NORWAY

In Norway the older runic staves had a relatively wide vogue: from the period A.D. 250 to A.D. 800 there are extant, in addition to 10 *brakteas* with runic inscriptions, about 50 inscriptions, mostly on erected stones or stones inserted in tumuli but also on loose objects.

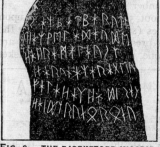

FIG. 8.—THE BJORKETORP INSCRIPTION

But the runes moved from south-western Denmark also up the Baltic. Here, as one might expect, the ancient centre for trade and intercourse in Northern Europe, the island of Gothland became also a region in which the older runic staves continued to be written throughout the entire period, though not to such an extent as in Norway. We find the runic inscriptions more sparsely on the mainland of Sweden—in Uppland, Södermanland and Östergötland. They are more frequent in Västergötland. In all about 20 runic inscriptions from the transmigration period have been found in Sweden, as well as a few runic *brakteas.* Of special note among them are the late (7th century) inscriptions from the most western parts of Blekinge which show a continuation of the

development of the runic letters which took place in south-western Norway, so rich in runes, during the early and middle periods of the transmigration era. Probably these inscriptions also came from Norwegian immigrants. The best preserved specimen is the Bjorketorp stone (fig. 8) which has its place in a fine stone setting and bears inscriptions on both its sides: *uthArAbAsbA*=ruin-bringing prophecy, and *hAid runo ronu fAlAhAk hAd(e)rA ginarunAR ArAgeu hAerAmAlAusR uti AR welAdAude sAR thAt bArutR*="This is the secret meaning of the runes; I hid here power-runes, undisturbed by evil witchcraft. In exile shall he die by means of magic art who destroys this monument." The inscription constitutes, therefore, a magical protection for the fine stone setting.

Of these Blekinge Stones the runic *k* has the form, fig. 3, 18, which about the year 500 was developed in Norway, while at the same time the form, fig. 3, 19, appears in Denmark, a form which proceeds thence to England.

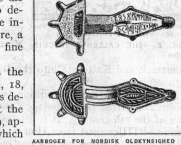

FIG. 9.—THE FREILAUBERSHEIM BROOCH

For in the 5th century the runes went to the Germanic Continent and to England from South-Western Denmark. On the continent, where the runic *k* retains its original form, there have been found inscriptions from the Rhine Province, Hesse, Nassau, Thüringen, Württemberg, Bavaria, Austria, as well as in Charnay, the old Burgundian Kingdom in Eastern France, in what is now the *département* of Saône et Loire. These inscriptions are few and, like the Danish ones, all inscribed on loose objects, and they are not long. They are all held to belong to the period A.D. 450–550. As an illustration may be instanced the inscription on the clasp from Freilaubersheim in Rhenish Hesse (fig. 9): *boso wraet run-ath(i)k dalina godd(a)*, which means: "Boso wrote the runes—to thee, Dallina, he gave (the clasp)."

If this knowledge of runes constituted merely a brief episode on the western Germanic continent, it flourished for five centuries in England. The Anglo-Saxon rune staves like the continental-Germanic, have two cross-strokes in the letter *h*, differ from it in the form of the *k*, and from the Scandinavian and Eastern-Germanic, as well as from the Continental-Germanic runes with their 24 letters, in this, that new letters are created to render the most important novelties in the rich Anglo-Friese vowel system. Later there were added also new consonant letters. The beginning of this development of the system of letters had already been effected on the southern portion of the coast of the North Sea in Friesland, where, in the Holland of to-day, may be seen inscriptions belonging to the end of the 5th century and to the 6th with new runic letters for *a*- and *o*- sounds. In England there developed a runic stave with 28 letters in it (fig. 10) and in the 9th century the number increased to 33.

In England there are extant about 50 runic inscriptions upon loose objects and upon raised stones (stone crosses). Among the most remarkable and also the best preserved are those which are carved on a casket made of whalebone, the so-called Frank's casket

FIG. 10.—THE EARLIER ANGLO-SAXON RUNES

(fig. 11). The inscriptions together with illustrations from Biblical history and from Roman and Germanic legends cover the sides of the casket and the lid and are held to be not later than about A.D. 650. The inscription on one side reads: *hronæs ban fisk flodu ahof on fergenberig warth gasrik grorn thær on greut giswom,* which means: "The whalebone (is this). The flood threw the fish on the firm rock. The monster (?) was stranded on the stone in agony."

Here may also be reproduced the younger 33 lettered Anglo-Saxon runic stave (fig. 12), out of the Cod. Cotton. Otho B. 10. in the British Museum, a manuscript which gives the runic names of oldest date.

In England the runes persisted throughout the entire Anglo-Saxon period. The most remarkable monuments from later times are the two celebrated runic crosses from Bewcastle and Ruthwell on the Anglo-Scottish border.

FIG. 11.—FRANK'S CASKET

Thanks to the tradition kept alive in England from ancient times and also to the fact that the names borrowed by Ulfilas from the runes to render Gothic letters are to be seen in the manuscript (not, indeed, in an unchanged state) preserved in the National Museum at Vienna, we are able to reconstruct approximately the name which every runic letter seems to have borne from the commencement. Younger traditions handed down in Scandinavia are also of value although the later peculiarly

FIG. 12.—THE LATER ANGLO-SAXON RUNES

Northern runic staves contained only 16 letters and the names of 8 letters therefore have been lost. In the first column below are given the Anglo-Saxon names of runic letters, in the second the Scandinavian and in the third the Gothic names reconstructed:—

f	*feh,*	money	*fé, fa*	goods	*faihu* (read fehu)
u	*úr*	aurochs	*úrr*	aurochs	*urus*
th	*thorn*	thorn	*thurs*	giant	*thauris*
a	*ós*	god	*óss*	god	*ansus*
r	*rád*	ride	*reið*	journey	*raida*
k	*cán*	torch	*kaun*	ab oil	*kaun* ?
g	*geofu*	gift			*giba*
w	*wynn*	joy			*winja*
h	*hægl*	hail	*hagl*	hail	*hagl*
n	*nied*	need	*nauð*	need	*nauths*
i	*ís*	ice	*íss*	ice	*eis*
j	*géar*	year	*aar*	year, harvest	*jer*
e	*éoh=éow*	yew-tree	*ýr*	small fir, bow	*eiws*
þ	*peorð*	?			*pairthra*
z	*eolhs*	?	*elgr*	elk	*algs*
s	*sygil*	sun	*sol*	sun	*sauil*
t	*tír*	honour	*tyr*	god	*teiws*
b	*beorc*	birch	*biarkan*	birch-seed	*bairkan*
e	*eoh*	horse			*aihos*
m	*man*	human being	*maðr*	human being	*manna*
l	*lagu*	water, sea	*legr*	liquid	*lagus*
—	*Ing*	a hero			*Iggws*
o	*éðel*	inheritance			*othal*
d	*dæg*	day			*dags*

Thus the great modification of the Germanic sound-system caused by vowel-mutation, by breaking and by other changes in sound during the transmigration period resulted in a considerable enlargement of the runic alphabet in England. In Scandinavia, it is curious to note, the same linguistic development produced a directly opposite result: the number of the runes was reduced from 24 to 16. And this, although the Scandinavian stock of sounds reached 30 or 40 during the later transmigration period. The explanation of this would seem to lie in the fact that, while the original 24 runes covered adequately the old Germanic sounds, it became the habit later, as the result of the increase in the sound-system, to represent different sounds with the same runic letter. This brought about the simplifying of the alphabet: when a single runic letter could be used to render several sounds, many of the old letters became superfluous. Simultaneously the formation of many of the runes was simplified. This twofold reduction of numbers and forms began in Scandinavia as far back as the 6th century, and at the beginning of the Viking era this had resulted in a special 16 letter Scandinavian alphabet. This alphabet appears in two distinct forms, the one

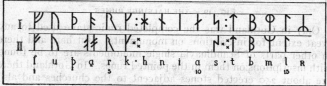

FIG. 13.—THE DANISH RUNES

Danish (fig. 13), the other Swedish-Norwegian (fig. 14). The Danish was used also in South-western Sweden.

In Denmark runes seem to have been very little used after the close of the 6th century, and the form of the runic *k*, as well as other details, indicates that it was through an impulse from Norway or Sweden that runes came into use again in Denmark at the close of the 8th century. About 200 inscriptions upon raised stones are extant, as well as a few upon loose objects. Most of these inscriptions date from between A.D. 800 and the middle of the 11th century. Despite their laconic and often stereotyped wording, they are among the most remarkable, both as regards style and matter, that have been found in Scandinavia. They give us the names of several hundred men and women who lived in Denmark during this important period, from members of the Royal house down to the lower grades of society, and they provide us with data for visualizing the life of the people and of individuals in war and peace.

The runic monuments which date from the beginning of this period are few in number. One of the oldest and most remarkable inscriptions with runes of the later period is the Helnæs stone at Fyn (fig. 15): *rhuulfR sati stain nuRa kuthi aft kuthumut bruthur sunu sin turuknathu (haliR uti) ouaiR fathi.* If it were written in a more adequate phonetic alphabet, *e.g.,* ð the Early Norwegian Icelandic alphabet which includes δ, this inscription would have run: *"HrólfR setti stein, NóRa goði, aft Guðmund broð urusunu sinn drunknaðu haliR uti. ÁveiR fáði;* which means: "Rolf raised this stone, priest and chieftain of the Helnæs dwellers, in memory of his brother's son, Gudmund. The men were drowned at sea. Aveir wrote (the runes)."

From the earlier half of the 10th century we have the smaller of the two famous Royal Stones of Jällinge in Jutland (fig. 16): *kurmR kunu(n)kR karthi ku(m)bl thusi aft thurui kunu sina tanmarkaR but;* which means: "King Gorm made this monument

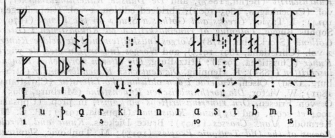

FIG. 14.—THE SWEDISH-NORWEGIAN RUNES

in memory of his wife, Tyra: he (Gorm) who improved Denmark."

The great majority of Denmark's 200 runic stones date, however, from the end of the 10th and the beginning of the 11th centuries. It was the period when the Vikings' raids on England were renewed, resulting at last in the conquest of the country by the Danish King Sven Twybeard, who is mentioned in two of the runic inscriptions, and Canute the Great. The relations between Denmark and England are reflected in the history of the

runic inscriptions inasmuch as it was probably due to influence by the Anglo-Saxon runes that the Danish alphabet now began to be enlarged by so-called pointed runes, see page 664.

From Denmark the Danish runes spread about A.D. 1000 to Sweden where runic inscriptions on raised stones became more numerous than anywhere else in the world. There are known in Sweden about 2,400 runic inscriptions, chiefly from the 11th century and the beginning of the 12th, the majority of them written in Danish runes. No fewer than half of them belong to the cen-

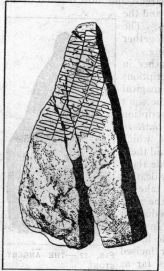

FROM L. F. A. WIMMER, "DIE RUNENSCHRIFT" (WEIDMANN)

FIG. 15.—THE HELNÆS STONE

tral region of the kingdom, Uppland. These monuments enable us to follow the upward course of the Danish runes through Sweden from Shåne and Västergötland to the southern part of Norrland, and it can be noted that the inscriptions in the south are, on an average, of earlier date than those in the north. The custom of erecting runic stones was not long-lived anywhere. Generally speaking, it was abandoned whenever a region became definitely Christianized and controlled by the Catholic Church, but it seems to have had a vigorous final revival during the missionary period. The course of the spread of Christianity throughout Sweden during the 11th century —beginning in the south and proceeding to the north—is therefore traceable in a special way in the appearance of the runic stones. From the beginning runic stones were erected for the most part in the graveyard of the villages, and one principal reason for giving up the custom of erecting them must have been that with the spread of Christianity the dead had to be buried in the cemetery adjoining the parish church, often at a distance from the home. Thereby monuments lost much of their interest for the survivors. In Uppland, more especially, the runic inscriptions were accompanied by cleverly executed ornamental design, the patterns of which were taken from wood-cuts—the art of wood-cuts having been highly developed during the transmigration and Viking periods. Not merely the runes themselves but also these ornamental designs needed craftsmanship, therefore, and we find that many runic inscriptions are executed by expert craftsmen.

The oldest and most remarkable (about A.D. 1025–1050) of these Uppland professional writers of runes was Asmund. He is probably identical with Osmundus, who is mentioned by the Bremen ecclesiastical historian, Adam. Osmundus was one of the Englishmen of Scandinavian origin who prepared the way in Sweden for the conquest of Christianity. Other talented masters of the art were Fot and Öpir. Asmund's stones record the names of a number of Swedes who took part in Canute the Great's conquest of England. On the Ängeby Stone (fig. 17), one of Asmund's inscriptions reads as follows: *rahnfrithr lit risa stain thina aftiR biurn sun thaiRa kitilmuntaR. kuth hialbi hans ant aukuths muthiR. hon fil a uirlanti. in osmuntr markathi.* This means: "Ragnfrid had this stone erected in memory of Björn, her and Kättilmund's son. God and God's Mother help his soul! He fell in Estland. But Asmund engraved (the Stone)."

When the reduction of the runic alphabet from 24 letters to

FROM L. F. A. WIMMER, "DE DANSKE RUNS-MINDESMAERKE" (GYLDENDALSKE BOGHANDEL)

FIG. 16.—THE EARLIER JÄLLINGE STONE

16 came about, the simplifying of the individual letters was carried furthest in the Swedish-Norwegian runes. These are to be found in Gothland, in eastern Götaland, in Svealand, and in Norway, dating from the beginning of the Viking era, about A.D. 800. As we have just seen, they are displaced on monuments by the Danish runes in the beginning of the 11th century in Sweden, but many circumstances indicate that even after this period they are used for more private purposes. Comparatively few runic monuments have Swedish-Norwegian runes on them but among these few must be mentioned the largest and most original of all, the Rök-Stone (fig. 18). The top and the four sides are covered with runes. The older forms of runes are also used together with different kinds of secret writing.

The stone was erected by a father in memory of his son and the inscriptions would seem to have in some degree magical purpose: to wreak vengeance on the son's slayers. The beginning of the inscription reads: *aft uamuth stonta runaR thaR in uarin fathi fathiR aft faikion sunu;* which means: "In memory of Vämod stand these runes. And Varin, the father, made them in memory of his son, overtaken by death."

The Swedish-Norwegian runes take an original form in Sweden. From the start they are characterized by a great reduction in the length of the cross strokes. In order to reduce as much as possible the length of the stroke whether written or incised also, the vertical strokes were as far as possible done away with.

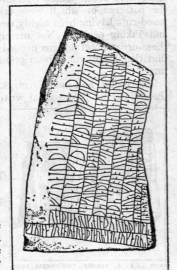

FIG. 17.—THE ÄNGEBY STONE

Thus came into existence the so-called Hälsinge Runes (fig. 19), named after the region of Hälsingland, in which they have been found inscribed on a number of rune stones dating from the 11th century. It is, however, now established that they were known and used in the central region of Sweden adjoining Lake Mälar, where very likely they were invited. The Hälsinge Runes are a kind of runic shorthand and they give us a clear indication that runes were widely used not merely on monuments but for all kinds of announcements: legal provisions, contracts, genealogies, poems, etc. The abbreviated form of the Hälsinge Runes is clearly due to the need of saving time, trouble and material.

In Norway there appeared in the 11th century a peculiar mixture of Swedish-Norwegian and Danish runes, which later led to an extension of the 16 letter alphabet to one better adapted to the northern sounds system—the pointed runes. The Danes probably got the idea from England at the close of the 10th century. The Anglo-Saxon rune for *y* was a *u* inside which an *i* was written. This rune is to be met with in Denmark before the year A.D. 1000, and after this model there was constructed out of the *i* a special letter for *e* and out of the *k* a special letter for *g*. These new letters are used generally in the Danish runes during the 11th century, although not consistently.

When the Danish and Swedish-Norwegian alphabet came to be blended during the 11th century in Norway, it would seem that towards the close of the century means were found to employ the wealth of letters thus produced to form a systematic representation of all the sounds in the language. The Latin alphabet, which had come into use with the introduction of Christianity, must have

been of service in the construction of this radical improvement of the runes as equivalent for sounds. Thus came into existence the completed pointed runic alphabet (fig. 20).

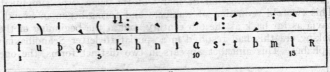

FIG. 19.—THE HÄLSINGE RUNES

Only in Gothland was the completed runic stave used to any great extent for inscriptions on monuments. But here and there in other parts of Scandinavia single monuments are to be found with inscriptions on them in the pointed runes. In Gothland there are about 250 erected stones adjacent to the churches and also out in the country parts, and the custom of raising such monuments persisted until much later. Gothland, moreover, had to begin with its own pointed runic alphabet, built up on the basis of the Danish runes alone. This was displaced later by the pointed runic alphabet in general use in Scandinavia.

The pointed runes were generally known and used in the whole of the Scandinavian North throughout the Middle Ages as the writing of cultured laymen. They were mainly used for private records. We possess a Danish legal manuscript, *Codex runicus,*

FIG. 20.—THE COMPLETED POINTED RUNIC ALPHABET

written in runes, dating from the end of the 13th century. There is extant, too, a prayer book of later date, which is evidently intended also for a layman not familiar with Latin. St. Bridget, who was a member of a Swedish family of nobles, spells Swedish, when she comes to acquire the use of the Latin alphabet, in the way in which she learnt as a child with runic letters. There is evidence of the use of runes in Gothland as late as the 17th century though they were widely reinforced by Latin letters.

Runes were kept up longer than elsewhere in outlying Swedish regions like Dalarna and Härjedalen, where they were used for making occasional notes down to our own times.　(O. v. F.)

BIBLIOGRAPHY.—Wilhelm Grimm, *Ueber deutsche Runen* (Göttingen, 1821); G. Stephens, *The Old Northern Runic Monuments of Scandinavia and England,* 4 vol. (Copenhagen, 1866–1901), and *Handbook of Runic Monuments* (1884); Cleesby and Vigfussen, *Icelandic-English Dictionary* (Oxford, 1874); Ludwig F. A. Wimmer, *Runenskriftens oprindelse og udvikling i Norden* (Copenhagen, 1874), *Die Runenschrift* (Berlin, 1887), and *De Danske Runernindesmarker,* 4 vol. (Copenhagen, 1893–1908), abridged edition, 1 vol. (Copenhagen, 1914); I. Taylor, *Greeks and Goths: a Study on the Runes* (1879); Sophus Bugge, *Tolkning of runeindskriften på Rökoåstenen i Öster-Götland* (Stockholm, 1878); *Norges Indskriften med de aeldre Runer,* 2 vol. (Christiana, 1891–1913), and *Norges Indskriften med de yngre Runer* (Christiana, 1902); Fritz Burg, *Die älteren nordischen Runeninschriften* (1885); R. Henning, *Die deutschen Runendenkmäler* (Strasburg, 1889); Olsen, *Runerae i den oldislandske Literatur* (Christiana, 1891); W. Victor, *Die northumbrischen Runensteine* (Marburg, 1895); O. von Friesen, *Orn runerindskriftens närkomst,* in prep. (Uppsala, 1904 *et seq.*), and *Upplands Runstenar* (Uppsala, 1913); P. C. M. Kermode, *Manx Crosses* (1907); Bruce Dickens, *Runic and Heroic Poems of the Old Teutonic Peoples* (1915); M. Tunkovič, *Slavische Runendenkmäler* (Starosloxan, 1915); O. Hupp, *Runen und Hakenkreuz* (Munich, 1921); A. Jóhanesson, *Grammatik der urnordischen Runeninschriften* (Heidelberg, 1923); E. Brate, *Södermanlands Runerskrifter* (Stockholm, 1924). See also Hermann Paul's *Grundriss der germanischen Philologie,* vol. i, 2nd ed. (Strasburg, 1901) for Sievers' "*Runen und Runeninschriften*" and vol. iv, 3rd ed. (Strasburg, 1913) for Norein's treatise on the grammar of Norse runes, and the *Catalogue of Runic Literature forming part of the Icelandic Collection* at Cornell University (1918).

RUNNIMEDE or RUNNYMEDE, a meadow on the south bank of the river Thames, England, in the parish of Egham, Surrey. It is celebrated as the scene of the granting of Magna Carta by King John on June 19, 1215. A tradition that the scene was Magna Carta, or Charter, island, higher up the river, probably arose about 1834, when G. S. Harcourt erected on it a castellated cottage in which he placed a stone tablet bearing an inscription to the effect that the charter was sealed there. Runnimede was presented to the nation by Lady Fairhaven in 1929.

RUNNING. The most primitive form of athletic exercise considered as a sport, running has been in vogue from the earliest times, and the simple footrace (δρόμος) run straight away from starting point to goal, or once over the course of the stadium (a little over 200 yd.), formed an event in the Greek Olympic pentathlon, or quintuple contest (*see* GAMES, CLASSICAL). There was also the race once over the course and return (δίαυλος) and the δόλιχος, a long race run many times (often as many as 12; *i.e.*, about 2¾ mi.) up and down the stadium. There was also the δρόμος ὁπλιτῶν, a short race for warriors, who wore full armour and carried sword and shield. Except in the warriors' race, the Greek runners were naked, save occasionally for a pair of light shoes. No records of the times returned have been handed down, but the contests must have been severe since the ancient Olympic chronicles preserve the memory of several men who fell dead at the end of the long course. According to Virgil (*Aen.* V. 286 *et seq.*) running was practised in circus exhibitions in ancient Italy.

The best runners in the middle ages were most often found among the couriers maintained by potentates and municipalities. The Peichs, or Persian couriers, of the Turkish sultans, often ran from Constantinople to Adrianople and back, a distance of about 220 mi., in two days and nights. In districts of India and Africa not traversed by railways, native runners are still employed to carry the mails.

In all parts of Great Britain track, road and cross-country running have been popular forms of recreation for many centuries. Today practically all the sprint records are held by Americans, while many of those for the middle distances stand to the credit of European athletes.

Modern running is divided into three classes:

Sprinting.—Sprinting consists of running over short distances with a full and continuous burst of speed, the chief distances being 100 yd., 220 yd. and 440 yd., and the corresponding metric distances. Distances up to and including 220 yd. are, in the United States, called dashes. The course for sprint races, when run in the open air, is marked off in lanes for the individual runners. In the modern style of sprinting the result depends often upon the start. The old method of dropping a handkerchief was the worst way to give the starting signal, since the muscles react slowly to the impression of sight, less so to those of touch and most quickly to those of sound, a difference of $\frac{1}{25}$ sec. in reaction amounting to more than 1 ft. in a run of 100 yd. All modern foot races are, therefore, started by the report of a pistol. Until 1887 all classes of foot runners commenced their races from a standing position. In that year Charles H. Sherrill, Jr., of Yale university, demonstrated an entirely new method known as the crouch, this method of starting becoming universal in a short time.

Experiments made with an electrical timing apparatus of his own invention by A. V. Hill, F.R.S., of the University of London brought to light many interesting points in connection with the physiological processes involved in severe muscular exercise in man. Hill's experiments indicated that 90% to 95% of the effort made by a sprinter travelling at top speed is expended in overcoming the frictional resistance of his own muscles. The force exerted by the first-class sprinter at maximum speed is equal to from 80% to 90% of his body weight, and in running 100 yd. he does sufficient work to lift himself from 240 ft. to 270 ft. into the air. He will bring into play approximately 8 h.p. and attain his maximum speed at 60 yd. or 70 yd. from the start, when he may be travelling as fast as 24 m.p.h. Approximately one second is lost in the starting process. After the 70 yd. mark is reached the runner begins to lose speed through fatigue occasioned by the rapid appearance of lactic acid in the muscles, as much as ⅛ oz. of such acid being secreted in the muscle substance every second. In the course of a 200-yd. race the speed drops as much as 15% between 70 yd. and 190 yd.

None of the sprint records at mid-20th century was older than 1936, and the outstanding feature of modern sprinting during the Olympiads of 1936 to 1952 was the success of the U.S. athletes. In 1948 Melvin Patton made a world's 100 yd. record of 9.3 sec. The world's record of 10.2 sec. for 100 m. was shared by J. C. Owens (1935), H. Davis (1941) and H. N. Ewell (1948) of the U.S., L. B. LaBeach (1948), Panamá, and E. McDonald Bailey (1951), Trinidad. Patton was world's record holder for 220 yd. and 200 m. in 20.2 sec.

Races at 400 m. and 440 yd. are almost invariably run on a circular track, each runner being provided with his own lane, to which he must keep throughout the race, the starts being so staggered that each runner may traverse the full course. Until 1924 the theory was held that quarter milers could be divided into two categories. It was held that the sprinter type of runner should endeavour to start fast enough to secure a good position rounding the first bend, and should hold his pace for perhaps 100 yd., and then get into a "float" with a long swinging stride. He would make his dash for victory about 120 yd. from the tape. The middle distance type of quarter miler, on the other hand, was advised to keep out of the first struggle for position and to husband his strength for the final dash.

In 1924 Eric Liddell, Great Britain, consciously or otherwise, set a new fashion when he won the Olympic 400 m. in 47.6 sec., by going flat out from pistol flash to finishing post in one effort, thus making a new world's record. Other athletes were quick to see the value of this innovation and have made it the practice to run the distance as a race of exhaustion from start to finish. The Olympic games, 1932, showed an extraordinary runner in William A. Carr, U.S., who made a new 400 m. Olympic record of 46.2 sec., equalled in 1948 by A. Wint, Jamaica, who beat H. H. McKenley, Jamaica, holder of the world's record for 440 yd. in 46.0 sec. V. G. Rhoden, also of Jamaica, holder of the record for 400 m. at 45.8 sec., won the 1952 Olympic event and McKenley again finished second.

Middle-Distance Running.—Ben Eastman was *facile princeps* of middle distance runners. He held records of 440 yd. (46.4 sec.), 600 yd. (1 min. 9.2 sec.) and 880 yd. (1 min. 49.8 sec.). It was, however, Thomas Hampson, Great Britain, who exploded the theory that there should be a variation of 3 sec. in the pace at which the two quarter-miles of a half mile should be run. Hampson's theory was that each of the two quarter-miles should be run in the same time, as nearly as possible. Acting on this principle he made a world's 800 m. record of 1 min. 49.8 sec.

TABLE I.—*World's Amateur Records to June 29, 1952**

Event	Time or Distance	Holder	Country	Date
100 yd.	9.3 sec.	M. E. Patton	U.S.	May 15, 1948
220 yd.	20.2 sec.	M. E. Patton	U.S.	May 7, 1949
440 yd.	46.0 sec.	H. H. McKenley	Jamaica	June 5, 1948
880 yd.	1-49.2 sec.	S. C. Wooderson	Great Britain	Aug. 20, 1938
		M. G. Whitfield	U.S.	Aug. 19, 1950
1 mi.	4-01.4 sec.	G. Haegg	Sweden	July 17, 1945
2 mi.	8-42.8 sec.	G. Haegg	Sweden	Aug. 4, 1944
3 mi.	13-32.4 sec.	G. Haegg	Sweden	Sept. 20, 1942
6 mi.	28-30.8 sec.	V. A. Heino	Finland	Sept. 1, 1949
10 mi.	48-12.0 sec.	E. Zatopek	Czechoslovakia	Sept. 29, 1951
15 mi.	1 hr. 17-28.6 sec.	M. Hietanen	Finland	May 23, 1948
100 m.	10.2 sec.	J. C. Owens	U.S.	June 20, 1936
		H. Davis	U.S.	June 6, 1941
		L. B. LaBeach	Panamá	May 15, 1948
		H. N. Ewell	U.S.	July 9, 1948
		E. McDonald Bailey	Trinidad	Aug. 25, 1951
200 m.	20.2 sec.	M. E. Patton	U.S.	May 7, 1949
400 m.	45.8 sec.	V. G. Rhoden	Jamaica	Aug. 22, 1950
800 m.	1-46.6 sec.	R. Harbig	Germany	July 15, 1939
1,000 m.	2-21.4 sec.	O. R. Gustafsson	Sweden	Sept. 4, 1946
		M. Hansenne	France	Aug. 27, 1948
1,500 m.	3-43.0 sec.	G. Haegg	Sweden	July 7, 1944
		L. Strand	Sweden	July 16, 1947
		W. Lueg	Germany	June 29, 1952
2,000 m.	5-07.0 sec.	G. Reiff	Belgium	Sept. 29, 1948
3,000 m.	7-58.8 sec.	G. Reiff	Belgium	Aug. 12, 1949
5,000 m.	13-58.2 sec.	G. Haegg	Sweden	Sept. 20, 1942
10,000 m.	29-02.6 sec.	E. Zatopek	Czechoslovakia	Aug. 4, 1950
20,000 m.	59-51.8 sec.	E. Zatopek	Czechoslovakia	Sept. 29, 1951
25,000 m.	1 hr. 20-14.0 sec.	M. Hietanen	Finland	May 23, 1948
30,000 m.	1 hr. 38-54.0 sec.	Y. Moskatchenkov	U.S.S.R.	Oct. 3, 1951
1 hr.	12 mi. 809 yd.	E. Zatopek	Czechoslovakia	Sept. 29, 1951

*The International Amateur Athletic federation decided in 1938 that records would only be passed in the events included in Tables I and II.

TABLE II.—*Relay Records to Aug. 4, 1952**

Event	Time	Holder	Country	Date
4 x 110 yd.	40.5 sec.	University of Southern California (La Fond, Anderson, Jordan, Talley)	U.S.	May 14, 1938
4 x 220 yd.	1-24.0 sec.	University of Southern California (Patton, Frazier, Pasquali, Stocks)	U.S.	May 20, 1949
4 x 440 yd.	3-09.4 sec.	University of California (Reese, Froom, Barnes, Klemmer)	U.S.	June 16, 1941
4 x 880 yd.	7-29.2 sec.	U.S. National team (W. Ashenfelter, Pearman, Barnes, Whitfield)	U.S.	Aug. 4, 1952
4 x 1 mi.	16-42.8 sec.	Gefle Idrottsförening (Bengtsson, Bergqvist, Aberg, Eriksson)	Sweden	Aug. 5, 1949
4 x 100 m.	39.8 sec.	U.S. National team (J. C. Owens, Metcalfe, Draper, F. Wykoff)	U.S.	Aug. 9, 1936
4 x 200 m.	1-24.0 sec.	University of Southern California (Patton, Frazier, Pasquali, Stocks)	U.S.	May 20, 1949
4 x 400 m.	3-03.9 sec.	Jamaican National team (Wint, Laing, McKenley, Rhoden)	Jamaica	July 27, 1952
4 x 800 m.	7-29.0 sec.	Swedish National team (Sten, Linder, Lingard, Strand)	Sweden	Sept. 13, 1946
4 x 1,500 m.	15-30.2 sec.	Gefle Idrottsförening (Bengtsson, Eriksson, Aberg, Bergqvist)	Sweden	July 3, 1949

*The International Amateur Athletic federation decided in 1938 that records would only be passed in the events included in Tables I and II.

when he won the Olympic title in 1932. Sydney C. Wooderson, England, in 1938 ran 880 yd. in the world's record time of 1 min. 49.2 sec., and in 1939 Rudolf Harbig, Germany, ran 800 m. in 1 min. 46.6 sec. Malvin Whitfield, U.S., in 1950 equalled Wooderson's record.

The other most important middle distance, which is regarded as the blue ribbon of athletics in England, is the 1 mi. At the time when Walter G. George (England) made his world's professional record of 4 min. 12¾ sec. in 1886, the theory obtained that the first lap should be fast and that the runner should rest himself as much as possible during the third quarter-mile. George's quarter-mile times were 58.5 sec., 63.25 sec., 66 sec. and 65 sec. Then, in the period 1920–31, Paavo Nurmi, Finland, evolved the theory of level-pace running and broke almost every world's record from a mile in 4–10.4 sec., to the one hour record of 11 mi. 1,648 yd. It was the opposition of the Swedish runner, E. Wide, which caused Nurmi to depart from his prearranged schedule of 62 sec. per quarter-mile when he made his world's record, referred to above, in 1923. Jules Ladoumegue, France, got nearer to the ideal when, in 1931, he reduced the record to 4 min. 9.2 sec. The year 1933 brought to light a new world's record breaker in John E. Lovelock, New Zealand, who ran a mile in 4 min. 7.6 sec., his theory being somewhat in the nature of a reversion to the principles advocated by George, except that it was Lovelock's belief that a man should train to run only one record-breaking race in any given year and to that end all training and preliminary competition should be subordinated.

The last word in the science of mile running had not, however, yet been said. In Lovelock's record-breaking race the second half-mile had been 1 sec. slower than the initial half-mile. Glenn Cunningham, U.S., when he set the world's record at 4 min. 6.8 sec. in 1934, ran the second half of the race 4.2 sec. faster than the initial half-mile. The record was lowered to 4 min. 6.4 sec. by Sydney Wooderson, Great Britain, in 1937, his second half-mile taking 1.4 sec. longer than the first. In 1936 Lovelock won the Olympic 1,500 m. title in the new world's record time of 3 min. 47.8 sec. which approximates to 4 min. 4.4 sec. for the full distance of 1 mi. He also ran the second half of the race faster than the first. The following schedule sets out the quarter-mile lap times of four of the fastest miles run compared with George's time in 1886:

Yd.	W. George (England) 1886	J. E. Lovelock (New Zealand) 1933	G. Cunningham (U.S.) 1934	S. C. Wooderson (Great Britain) 1937	G. Haegg (Sweden) 1945
	Sec.	Sec.	Sec.	Sec.	Sec.
1st 440	58.5	61.4	61.8	58.6	56.6
2nd 440	63.25	62.2	63.7	64.0	61.9
3rd 440	66.0	65.1	61.8	64.6	61.2
4th 440	65.0	58.9	59.5	59.2	61.7
1 mile	4-12.75	4-07.6	4-06.8	4-06.4	4-01.4

It is significant that nothing approaching W. G. George's performance of 1886 was produced until 1915, in which year Norman Taber, an amateur, of Brown university, U.S., by means of a specially framed handicap, beat George's record by 3/20 sec. The spell of nearly 30 years having been broken, new and progressively better performances were produced, and during the next 20 years the record for the 1 mi., or its equivalent, 1,500 m., was broken no less than seven times. Cunningham's mile in 4–06.8 sec. was almost 6 sec. better than George's record, while Lovelock's com-

parative time for 1,500 m. would be 2 sec. better than the record made by Cunningham, whom Lovelock beat when he won the Olympic title in 1936.

During and after World War II few things were more remarkable than the advance in 1 mi. performances: the 20 fastest all beat the time of 4 min. 10.4 sec. returned in 1923 by Paavo Nurmi, Finland, as the world's record. Of the world's 20 best milers in 1946, 9 were Swedish, 6 were from the United States, 2 were French and 1 was English. The best times were as follows: Haegg, Andersson, Persson, Gustavsson and Strand, Sweden, Hulse and Dodds, U.S., and Wooderson himself, had all beaten Wooderson's 1937 world record of 4 min. 6.4 sec. and Ahlsen, Sweden, had equalled it.

The 2 mi., although not a standard championship event, is popular at indoor meetings and corresponds to the 3 mi. at the U.S. Inter-Collegiate Outdoor championships and at the English Oxford and Cambridge sports. In 1944 Gunder Haegg, Sweden, established a new world's record by running 2 mi. in 8 min. 42.8 sec.

Long-Distance Running.—This includes all flat races from the 3 mi. upward, as well as steeplechasing, road and cross-country running. Great Britain was for centuries the home of long-distance running, and for many years all world's records from two to ten miles were held by Alfred Shrubb, England. Of the remaining distance records up to 30,000 m. and the 1 hr. run, the longest distances recognized by the International Amateur Athletic Federation, seven were held at mid-20th century by Finland, three by Sweden and one by Czechoslovakia. It is perhaps remarkable that none of the world's long-distance records was held by the U.S. The decline of British supremacy began with the advent of two great foreign runners, Jean Bouin, France, and Hannes Kolehmainen, Finland. Finland established a long line of world's champions. Swedish athletes showed remarkable development during the years of World War II at distances from 1,500 m. and 5,000 m., challenging even the supremacy of the Finns. The Finns, despite the rigours of two stern campaigns in World War II, produced and sustained great runners such as Taisto Mäki who in 1939 made a world's record by running 20,000 m. in 1 hr. 3 min. 1.2 sec. and Erkki Tamila, who was fourth in the Olympic marathon, 1936, and in 1939 made what remained, until beaten by M. Hietanen in 1948, the world's 25,000 m. record of 1 hr. 21 min. 27.0 sec. The record made by Paavo Nurmi in 1928 of running 11 mi. 1,648 yd. within the space of one hour was broken by Viljo Heino, also a Finn, who in 1944 also made new figures at five and six miles. Heino was the first man to get inside 50 min. for 10 mi., his time being 49 min. 41.6 sec., and he went on to complete the 1 hr. by covering 12 mi. 28 yd. He was the first man ever to beat 12 mi. for the time-running record, which E. Zatopek of Czechoslovakia has since improved.

In England the championship track distances are three and six miles. In the U.S., however, the Amateur Athletic union for a few years adopted the 5,000 and 10,000 m. events which figure in the Olympic games. There is also in each case the marathon race of 26 mi. 385 yd. A marathon race of 40,000 m. was held in the 1896 Olympic games, but the modern distance of 26 mi. 385 yd. was first held in 1908 in London and became the standard from 1924 in the Olympics. As courses vary considerably no records are recognized. This classic of the Olympic games has been won by Argentina, Finland, France and the U.S. (twice by each country), while Greece, Japan, South Africa and Czechoslovakia each have had one victory.

Steeplechasing was originally only a cross-country run over a course plentifully provided with natural obstacles; but the modern steeplechase takes place partly on the grass and mainly on the cinder track of the athletic field. A water jump must be included, in addition to which there are four flights of hurdles 3 ft. in height. The championship distance in England is 2 mi.; in the U.S. and at the Olympic games 3,000 m. The U.S. won the first two Olympic steeplechases, at 2,500 m., Great Britain taking two other races at 3,300 m. and 4,000 m., but after the distance was stabilized at 3,000 m. in 1920, when P. Hodge of Great Britain was victorious, the subsequent four Olympic titles went to Finland, Sweden winning in 1948 and the U.S. in 1952.

Cross-Country Running had its inception with the founding of the Crick run at Rugby school in 1837, followed by many other famous schools who also held annual cross-country races. About 30 years later the Thames Hare and Hounds held cross-country runs and races as a winter sport, and in a few years many other clubs were formed throughout England. Many amateur athletes use this winter sport, often formerly termed paperchasing, as a means of keeping fit and developing stamina for track athletics. English championships over the senior distance of 10 mi. were first held in 1876 and of the 64 contests held up to 1952, the famous Midlands club, Birchfield Harriers, won on 26 occasions. The number of runners in this event increased from 33 in the first race to 450 in 1949. In England races are limited for juniors (18 to under 21 years) to 6 mi. and for youths (over 16 to under 18) to 3 mi. The first international race was held in 1898 between England and France, and an international championship was instituted in 1903 between England, Ireland, Scotland and Wales. In 1907 France first competed, followed by Belgium in 1923, while Italy, Luxembourg, Spain and Switzerland also competed in 1929. From 1903 until 1949 England won 25 times, France winning on 9 occasions in this event organized by the International Cross-Country union. The sport is popular in many other countries.

In the Olympic games of 1912 an 8,000-m. race was held and won by Hannes Kolehmainen, Finland, Sweden winning the team race; in 1920 and in 1924, when the distance was increased to 10,000 m., Paavo Nurmi won, Finland also winning the team races. The event was not held thereafter as it was not considered suitable for inclusion in the summer Olympic games.

Relay Racing.—This form of competition has long been practised in the U.S. and has become popular throughout the world. Relay races are usually run by four men, each going a quarter of the distance. From 1911 to 1926 only one relay race was included in the English championships. This was really a medley race in which four men ran 880, 220, 220 and 440 yd., respectively. In 1927 the medley race was abandoned and two other relay races substituted, *i.e.*, a 440 yd. relay, in which each of the four runners goes 110 yd., and a mile relay (4 × 440 yd.).

The U.S. national championship relay distances are 440 yd., 880 yd., 1 mi. and 2 mi., four runners representing each team, and each running an equal distance.

The Olympic relay distances are 400 m. (437.45 yd.) and 1,600 m. (almost a mile).

This method of racing was started in the United States about 1890, on the model of the Massachusetts firemen's "bean-pot" race. The old method was for the men running the second quarter of the course each to take over a small flag from the first man as he arrived, before departing on their own stage of the race, at the end of which they, in their turn, handed on their flags to the awaiting next runners. The flags, however, were considered cumbersome, and for a time it was sufficient for the outgoing runner to touch or be touched by his predecessor. Nowadays a hollow cylinder of wood, constituting a baton, is carried and must be exchanged between lines drawn at right angles to the side of the track 11 yd. or 10 m. on each side of the starting line for each particular relay.

As the progenitor of relay racing, it is not surprising that the success of the U.S. has been phenomenal. Of the Olympic tests at 4 × 100 m. instituted in 1912, Great Britain won the initial contest, after which time the U.S. won the subsequent seven titles. The 4 × 400 m. Olympic relay was instituted in 1912, the U.S.

winning upon every occasion except 1920 and 1936, in which Great Britain and in 1952 Jamaica proved victorious. Of the world's records at the ten standard distances (metric and English measure) at mid-20th century, seven were held by U.S. teams, three by Sweden.

BIBLIOGRAPHY.—S. A. Mussabini and Charles Ranson, *The Complete Athletic Trainer* (1913); G. T. Bresnahan and W. W. Tuttle, *Track and Field Athletics* (1937); A. F. H. Newton, *Running* (London, 1935), *Running in Three Continents* (London, 1940); F. A. M. Webster, *Why? The Science of Athletics* (London, 1936), *Coaching and Care of Athletes* (1938), *Athletics: Teaching and Training* (London, 1948); R. L. Quercetani and D. H. Potts, *A Handbook on Olympic Games Track and Field Athletics* (London, 1948).   (F. A. M. W.)

RUNNING WATER. Water flowing down slopes contributes more than any other external agent to the sculpture of the surface forms of the land. As it flows from higher to lower levels, the potential energy it possesses because of its height above sea level is changed into energy of motion at a rate that is the greater the steeper the slope down which it flows. Most of its work is done in the channels of streams and consists principally of the transportation of weathered rock material toward the sea or toward the enclosed depressions into which the local streams of arid regions flow. Part of this rock waste is transported in solution. Although it often constitutes an appreciable fraction of the load carried by a stream, dissolved matter is mechanically a part of the water and affects its physical behaviour only by making it slightly denser and more viscous. The far larger part of the loads of streams consists of undissolved fragments, to which the water transfers a part of its momentum.

Turbulence.—Only a thin film of the water of a stream is at any time in actual contact with its bed, and so in a position to impart momentum to the material over which it flows. The momentum of the rest of the water must be conveyed through the fluid to its bed. Except for intermolecular friction through the film next to the bed, the transfer is effected by the irregular motion of water within the stream toward and away from the bed; that is, by turbulence. Under the pull of gravity, the water attains its highest speed in those parts of the cross section of the stream that are farthest from the bed; the parts that flow, so to speak, on a moving bed of other water. The more slowly moving water near the bed exerts a restraining pull upon it. The stress of the mechanical couple between the faster and the slower water in the cross section causes parcels of rapidly moving water to become detached from the interior parts of the cross section and force their way through the more slowly moving water toward the bed. A part of their momentum is expended in displacing the water through which they move, and a part in friction with the bed when they reach it.

Invasion of the passive layers of water near the bed by the active parcels from the interior of the stream forces equal volumes of the slower passive water away from the bed. Arriving in the middle parts of the cross section, the water thus displaced is speeded up, and in turn contributes active parcels that invade the slower water near the bed. The turbulent interchange of water between the central and the peripheral parts of the cross section of a stream regulates its average speed and the distribution of velocity in its cross section. With a given discharge through a uniform channel, the stream attains a constant average speed at which the energy imparted to the water by the acceleration of gravity is expended in friction with the bed and in internal friction.

Transport of Sediment: Traction and Suspension.—If the bed of a stream consists wholly or in part of rock fragments, the frictional drag exerted by the water may propel a part of the bed material downstream. This form of propulsion is called traction, and the material so propelled constitutes the bed load. The fragments that make up the bed load vary in size with the energy of the stream, from boulders to fine silt; in most streams the bed load consists of sand. Rock particles transported by streams are constantly reduced in size by mutual abrasion, so that long rivers that flow through plains in their lower courses arrive at their mouths with their bed loads reduced to fine sand or silt.

If the channel of a stream is cut in a thick accumulation of unconsolidated rock fragments, the water propels only the superficial layers of its bed. But if the layer of bed load is thin and all of it is in motion over a surface of solid rock, the load abrades the solid bed, and thus deepens it. Abrasion of the beds of streams by their loads is the mechanism by which they cut channels in consolidated rock; the cutting is greatly aided by fractures and other inhomogeneities in the rock. By itself, a stream can cut only a narrow gorge having the width of its channel. Valleys, which have cross profiles that approximate the shape of a more or less open V, are produced by a combination of downcutting by streams and retreat of the valley sides through rock weathering and movement of rock waste down slope to the stream channels. Most of the load carried by a stream is contributed by the slopes of its valley and those of its tributaries, not by abrasion of its channel. Flat bottoms of valleys are usually the result of a partial filling of the valleys by deposition of load.

In addition to their bed loads, streams carry rock fragments suspended in the water by the upward components of turbulence. A sharp distinction cannot be drawn between suspended and bed load, since particles are continually settling out and being picked up again. Both propulsion of bed load and the passage of fragments into suspension depend on the turbulent interchange of water between the interior of the stream and the vicinity of the bed. Bed load is propelled by the transfer of momentum from the active parcels. Passive water is displaced abruptly in front of an active parcel arriving at the bed, and forced away from the bed. The upward speed of the water thus forced from the bed carries into suspension fragments that are sometimes as large as fine gravel. The upward speed of the displaced water is gradually lost as it moves into the interior of the stream and the coarsest material taken into suspension soon settles back to the bottom. Finer particles, which are held in suspension by weak turbulence, are carried long distances.

In flood, a stream propels a thicker layer of bed load than at lower stages, and takes more and coarser material into suspension. As a flood subsides, sediment is deposited over all the area covered by water, including the channel itself. The bed is built up again to its low-water level, and the deeper bed material that was in motion during the flood becomes stationary again. Deposits laid down in the subsiding stages of high water are to be seen along almost all streams. In mountain torrents, they consist of boulders in or at the sides of the channel, or of bars composed of cobbles and coarse gravel. In streams having smaller gradients, they are usually bars of gravel or sand at the sides of the channel. Silt and clay settle out from quiet flood waters far from the channels in which they were taken into suspension.

Meandering.—The interaction between stream and channel, which induces a continuous turbulent displacement of masses of water within the cross section, seems to permit an approximately stable state of flow only when the current swings from side to side in a rhythm appropriate to the size of the stream. Such a pendulation is observed in all streams, and the channels are moulded to fit the pendulating current. The bed load does not travel downstream as a smooth sheet, but in the form of bars that lie alternately on opposite sides of the channel, connected by diagonal shallows. Opposite each bar is a pool or deep, in which the highest speed of water in the local cross section is observed. The thread of maximum speed swings from side to side, especially at low stages, passing from one deep to the next one downstream.

The lateral bars grow sidewise into the adjacent deeps, narrowing them and thus increasing the speed of the water through them. If the side of the channel opposite the bar consists of unconsolidated material, it is undermined and caves into the stream and the caving material becomes part of the load, some of it to be added to bars downstream. Opposite each bar the channel is shifted sidewise in the direction of the undermined bank and becomes sinuous. Smoothly curved sinuosities so produced are meanders. Some degree of meandering is seen in all streams that flow in channels cut in unconsolidated material stable enough to form channel walls but capable of being undermined and transported by the stream. Meanders are formed most readily in channels cut in material that consists of or contains fragmental material intermediate in coarseness between sand and clay. Channels cut in sand sometimes meander to a limited extent, but usually become broad and shallow, without the juxtaposition of bars and deeps that produce meanders. Channels cut in clay do not meander, since clay resists undercutting. The banks of a meandering stream are cut most rapidly in the downstream parts of its bends, and the meanders therefore migrate bodily down the valley. Variations in the resistance of channel walls to undermining induce distortions of meanders. Almost all accumulations of unconsolidated rock differ in resistance from point to point, and streams flowing through them often display distortions of meanders such as angular turns and exaggerated loops that nearly return on themselves. It is the last-named bends that are most likely to be cut off at flood stages and become, by the silting up of their ends, oxbow lakes.

Changes in Stream Gradients.—By transporting rock material and eroding their beds, streams are constantly lowering the land surfaces they drain, and so reducing their gradients. Gradients may also be increased or diminished by the action of the internal forces that lift or depress, tilt or warp the land surfaces. All changes in their gradients change the ability of streams to keep their burden of rock fragments moving and to deepen their channels. An increase in gradient enables a stream to cut its channel deeper, and so to leave the deposits outside its channel above its new level as river terraces. Meanders are cut down, even into underlying consolidated rocks. Where highlands are uplifted across the courses of rivers, they are often able to cut their channels down as fast as the land rises. They then carve gorges through the rising blocks of land. An increase in the rate of downcutting by a stream is often called rejuvenation, from a fancied analogy between the history of streams and the life of organisms. Diminution of the gradient of a stream causes it to deposit part of its load. The material deposited, by raising the floor of the valley to a wider part of its V-shaped profile, produces a flood plain. If weak and resistant rocks alternate along the course of a river, the gradient of the river and the declivity of the tributary slopes of the land become adjusted so that they are gentler in weak than in resistant rocks.

Effect of Reduction of Load.—Valleys of the regions through which flowed the melt water from the continental glaciers of the Pleistocene period display the results of overloading during that time and of a subsequent reduction of the load fed into streams. In North America, most of the drainage from the edge of the melting continental ice sheet found its way to the sea through the northern streams of the Mississippi system. The Ohio and Missouri rivers and their northerly tributaries carried enormous quantities of debris from the edge of the ice, depositing part of it in their valleys and discharging the rest into the Mississippi, which in turn built a vast depositional plain southward from near the mouth of the Ohio. Since the disappearance of the ice sheet, the rivers have cut their channels deeper, leaving the remaining rock waste as terraces.

Changes at the Mouths of Streams.—All changes in the level of the sea or of lakes affect the streams that discharge into them. A fall in sea or lake level steepens the gradients of the streams, and they deepen their channels, first near their mouths. A wave of channel-cutting progresses upstream at a rate determined by the resistance of the channels to erosion. The relative heights of land and sea have had a complicated history which is not easy to untangle. It is certain, however, that the lower courses of streams that flow into the sea have been strongly affected by the world-wide changes in sea level that resulted from the removal of water to form the glaciers of the Pleistocene period, and the subsequent return of that water to the sea as the glaciers melted. The effects of such general changes in sea level are superimposed on the changes in height of the land produced by the earth's internal forces.

Streams also change their own gradients by deposition at their mouths and hence ultimately throughout their courses. The sediment they bring to the sea is deposited promptly, since at their mouths their gradients vanish and provide no more energy to propel bed load or maintain turbulence. Sediment can be removed from the vicinity of a river mouth only by currents in the body of water into which the river flows. Where the range of the tide is large, tidal currents prevent the accumulation of stream-borne rock waste at the mouths of rivers. But where rivers flow into parts of the sea in which tidal action is weak, or into completely enclosed seas or lakes, their burden of debris accumulates to form deltas, the terminal deposits of rivers. As a delta grows forward, the length of the stream is increased, while the vertical distance from its mouth to any point upstream remains unchanged. Its gradient is therefore reduced, and with every extension of the delta sediment must be deposited along the whole length of the stream. By building a delta a stream thus induces a continuous filling of its valley. The great flood plains of the world are extensions upstream of deltaic deposits. As the delta grows forward and upward, and the flood plain is built up accordingly, more sediment is deposited in and near the channel than on the parts of the plain at a distance from the river. Hence the channel is lifted to a level higher than the more remote parts of the flood plain. The highest parts of the plain are next to the river, in the form of embankments called natural levees. From these natural dikes the surface of the plain slopes away from the river toward the sides of the valley.

Basins of Interior Drainage.—The water that runs off the land surface to the sea is the excess of precipitation over the water that evaporates. Toward the dry parts of the continents this excess becomes progressively less, and finally evaporation disposes of all the precipitation that falls. The climatic distinction between humid and arid regions produces differences in the surface forms sculptured by running water. Crustal disturbances frequently make depressions that have no outlets to the sea. In humid climates, streams may cut down outlets as fast as barriers are uplifted, or the depressions may be at first occupied by lakes. Lakes are, however, relatively short-lived, since the streams that flow into and out of them fill them with sediment and deepen the channels that drain them. Surface streams in humid climates thus act to maintain continuous slopes of the land all the way to the sea. Not all the precipitation that falls in dry regions is immediately evaporated or absorbed by the ground. Particularly in highlands, ephemeral runoff transports rock waste and excavates valleys. In the depressed parts of the surface, however, the rock waste from the neighbouring highlands accumulates to great depths, gradually filling them and lapping up against the slopes of the highlands. The water that flows out into the depressions soaks into the dry rock waste or spreads out on the surface and evaporates. All the continents possess basins of interior drainage, with their characteristic features: highlands flanked by long slopes of fragmental rock material that extend out into enclosed depressions, the lowest parts of which are occupied permanently or temporarily by shallow salt lakes. So long as their climates remain arid, these basins are exempt from the rule that land surfaces that drain to the sea are continuously lowered toward sea level. The elevations of arid basins are fixed by the primary disturbances that produced them, whether they lie below sea level or thousands of feet above it.

BIBLIOGRAPHY.—Grove Karl Gilbert, "The Transportation of Debris by Running Water," *U.S. Geol. Surv., Prof. Paper 86* (1914); A. K. Lobeck, *Geomorphology* (1939); Gerard H. Matthes, "Basic Aspects of Stream Meanders," *Trans. Amer. Geophys. Union,* pp. 632–636 (1941), "Macroturbulence in Natural Stream Flow" *ibid.* vol. 28, pp. 255–262 (1947). (J. B. L.)

RUODLIEB, a romance in Latin verse by an unknown German poet who flourished about 1030; he was almost certainly a monk of the Bavarian abbey of Tegernsee. The poem is one of the earliest German romances of knightly adventure, and its picture of feudal manners gives it value as an historical document. The best edition is by F. Seiler (Halle, 1882).

RUPEE, the standard coin of the monetary system in India and Pakistan (Hindustani *rupiya,* from Sanskrit *rupya*). A silver coin of 175 grains troy, called *tanka,* approximating to the rupee, was struck by the Mohammedan rulers of Delhi in the 13th century; but the rupee itself, of 179 grains, was introduced by Sher Shah in 1542. The English at first followed various indigenous standards; but since 1835 the rupee has uniformly weighed 180 grains, containing 165 grains of pure silver. The weight of the rupee (one *tola*) is also the unit upon which the Indian standard of weights is based.

The term "lakh" (from the Sans. *laksha,* 100,000) is colloquially used in India as signifying 100,000 rupees (written Rs.100,000). It appears constantly in trade returns. The term "crore" (from the Hindustani *karor*) is similarly used to denote 100 lakhs, or 10,000,000 rupees. Down to about 1873 the gold value of the rupee was 2s., and ten rupees were thus equal to £1; but after 1873, owing to the depreciation of silver, the rupee at one time sank as low in value as 1s. In order to provide a remedy the government of India decided in 1893 to close the mints, and in 1899 to make the rupee legal tender at 15 to £1. The government also engaged to sell council drafts on India to an unlimited amount at a price from 1s., $4\frac{1}{8}d$. to 1s. $3\frac{29}{32}d$. per rupee. This worked satisfactorily, owing to the fact that normally India exports more than it imports. Should there be a trade balance temporarily adverse to India, so that the market quotation of sterling against the rupee fell below 1s. $3\frac{29}{32}d$., the government undertook to sell reverse council drafts on London. The exchange was thus maintained at 1s. 4d., and the rupee linked to a gold currency, sterling, with the sale of council and reverse council drafts as a somewhat artificial substitute for the shipment of gold.

The success of this system depended upon two conditions. First, the bullion value of the rupee must not rise above 1s. 4d., otherwise it would pay the public to melt down rupees for their silver content. Secondly, the secretary of state must have sufficient rupees at his command to enable him to redeem such quantities of council drafts as the public wished to buy. Until the outbreak of World War I, both these conditions were fulfilled. The secretary of state had little difficulty in amassing sufficient rupees to meet his engagements, while it was only found necessary to sell reverse councils on three occasions after 1900.

The Rupee Crisis.—World War I altered the situation. India's exports increased owing to the Allies' demand for raw materials, while imports of manufactured goods were forcibly curtailed owing to the inability of belligerent countries to produce them. Also the campaign in Mesopotamia was financed in rupees. All these causes led to a greatly increased demand for rupees, and by 1916 the secretary of state was experiencing great difficulty in obtaining enough to meet in full the demand for council drafts.

At the same time, partly owing to troubles in Mexico, the price of silver rose; in short, by 1916 the two conditions on which the Indian currency was based were ceasing to operate. Radical modifications had to be introduced. The sale of council drafts was rationed, and their price gradually increased in sympathy with that of silver. All gold imported had to be sold to the government, and the private importation of silver was prohibited. Rupee notes could be issued to a certain extent, but the danger of inconvertibility had to be watched. But the quantity of silver available still fell below the country's requirements, and the convertibility of the note issue was threatened. In April 1918 the Pittman act enabled the U.S. government to sell 200,000,000 fine ounces of silver to India at a price of $1.015 per fine ounce. This shipment eased the situation and preserved the currency till the Armistice.

In May 1919 the Babington-Smith committee sat to evolve a new system, made necessary by the grave modifications caused by war measures. It recommended the fixation of the exchange at Rs. 10 to the gold sovereign; the sale by open tender of council and, if necessary, of reverse council drafts; free importation and exportation of gold and free importation of silver. Owing to unforeseen circumstances, the scheme broke down almost immediately. The report was issued at the moment when the prices of commodities, including silver, were at their highest; and the slump followed. The price of silver collapsed, and rendered unnecessary the raising of the value of the rupee. Also the 1921 trade depression had a serious effect in India. The demand for raw materials dried up, but meantime goods ordered from Europe continued to arrive up till the end of 1921. Consequently, a heavy adverse trade balance set in. The rupee began to fall, until finally it arrived at about the prewar level of 1s. 4d. The sale of reverse councils was quickly found to be too expensive a remedy, and was abandoned.

By 1923 conditions had improved, and the excess in imports of 1921 had largely been absorbed. The Babington-Smith report still remained nominally in force for a few years, but it became necessary to reconcile the official currency system with the facts of the case. The Hilton-Young committee was appointed, and presented its report in 1926. In 1927 the government published three bills embodying the recommendations of the Hilton-Young committee. The first bill was for the purpose of establishing a gold standard currency for British India and for constituting a reserve bank of India, the second amended the Imperial Bank Act of 1920 and the third amended the Coinage Act of 1906 and the Paper Currency Act of 1923, in order to empower the government in matters relating to the purchase of gold and the sale of gold exchange.

This third bill was the subject of bitter controversy but finally passed the legislature by a narrow majority and the Indian Currency bill became law on April 1, 1927.

The act established the ratio of 1s. 6d. to the rupee by enabling the government to purchase gold in unlimited quantities at the Bombay mint in the form of bars containing not less than 15 oz. at the price of 21 rupees 3 annas 10 pies per *tola* of fine gold. Holders of silver rupees and paper notes were entitled to obtain either gold or sterling for immediate delivery in London, provided the value involved was not less than 165 *tolas* of fine gold at the above rate. Sovereigns and half sovereigns ceased to be legal tender in India. Thus, the Currency Act of 1927 might be said to have established a gold bullion-sterling exchange standard.

The Reserve Bank of India act was passed by the legislative assembly in 1934 and the bank began to function on April 1, 1935. The new institution took over the management of the currency department of the government of India and the assets of the gold standard reserves were transferred to the bank to be combined with the assets of the currency department. The banking department was opened on July 1, 1935. The share capital of the reserve bank was 50,000,000 rupees fully paid up and the reserve fund of 5 crores was provided by the government in the form of rupee securities. The bank's offices were at Bombay, Calcutta, Delhi, Madras and Rangoon. The exchange value of the rupee fell to the statutory minimum point of 1s. 5 49/64 d. in June 1938, but the situation improved shortly after and the exchange rates steadily improved to 1s. 5 31/32 d. in March 1939. On the whole, the exchange rates remained steady until the outbreak of World War II in Sept. 1939.

On the declaration of war, the government delegated to the reserve bank authority to administer control of dealings in coins, bullion, securities and foreign exchange. Measures taken shortly after were designed to prevent the export of capital from India and check wartime speculation in exchange. In May 1940 a system of licensing imports in order to conserve foreign exchange was introduced by the government.

After the partition of the subcontinent in 1947, both India and Pakistan continued the rupee as their monetary unit. The exchange rate was different, however, the Indian rupee being valued at 20.87 U.S. cents and the Pakistani rupee at 30.22 cents, or at about 1s. 6d. and 2s. 2d. respectively, in the early 1950s. (*See also* CURRENCY.)   (N. E. C.; W. D. C.)

RUPERT (HRODBERT), **ST.,** according to the *Gesta Sancti Hrodberti,* which dates from the ninth century, a kinsman of the Merovingian house, and bishop of Worms under Childebert III (695–711). At the invitation of the duke of Bavaria, Theodo II, Rupert went to Regensburg (Ratisbon), where he began his apostolate. He founded the church of St. Peter near the Wallersee, and subsequently, at Salzburg, the church of St. Peter, together with a monastery and a dwelling for the clerks, as well as a convent for women "in superiori castro Iuvavensium." He died at Salzburg. He is regarded as the apostle of the Bavarians.

See *Bibliotheca hagiographica Latina* (Brussels, 1899), n. 7390–7403; W. Levison, "Die älteste Lebensbeschreibung Ruperts von Salzburg" in *Neues Archiv für aeltere deutsche Geschichtskunde,* xxviii. 283 *seq.;* Hauck, *Kirchengeschichte Deutschlands* (3rd ed.).

RUPERT (1352–1410), German king, and, as Rupert III, elector palatine of the Rhine, was a son of the elector Rupert II and Beatrice, daughter of Peter II, king of Sicily. He was born at Amberg on May 5, 1352, and succeeded to the government of the Palatinate on his father's death in 1398. On Aug. 21, 1400, having helped depose King Wenceslaus at Oberlahnstein, Rupert was elected German king at Rense, and crowned at Cologne on Jan. 6, 1401. An expedition to Italy against Gian Galleazzo Visconti, duke of Milan (1401–2), proved a failure, but he was recognized by Pope Boniface IX in Oct. 1403. After some years of struggle with the anarchy in Germany and the partisans of Wenceslaus, Rupert died at Landskron near Oppenheim on May 18, 1410. He was buried at Heidelberg. He married Elizabeth, daughter of Frederick IV of Hohenzollern, burgrave of Nuremberg, and left three sons and four daughters. Rupert, who earned the surname of *clemens,* was brave and generous, but his resources were totally inadequate to bear the strain of the German kingship.

BIBLIOGRAPHY.—C. Höfler, *Ruprecht von der Pfalz genannt Clem römischer König* (Freiberg, 1861); A. Winkelmann, *Der Romzug Ruprechts von der Pfalz* (Innsbruck, 1892); and J. Weizsäcker, *Die Urkunden der Approbation König Ruprechts* (1899).

RUPERT, PRINCE, COUNT PALATINE OF THE RHINE AND DUKE OF BAVARIA (1619–1682), third son of the elector palatine and "winter king" of Bohemia, Frederick V, and of Elizabeth, daughter of James I of England, was born at Prague late in 1619. A year later his father was defeated at the battle of the White Mountain, near Prague, and driven from Bohemia. After many wanderings the family took refuge in the Netherlands, where Rupert's boyhood was spent. In 1633 the boy was present at the siege of Rheinberg in the suite of the Prince of Orange, and in 1635 he served in this prince's bodyguard. In 1636, during his first visit to England, he was made an M.A. of Oxford and his name was entered as a member of St. John's college. He was also named as the governor of a proposed English colony in Madagascar. But this scheme did not mature, and Charles I sent his nephew back to the Netherlands, having, however, formed a high opinion of his energy, talent and resolution. In 1637 he was again serving in the wars, and in 1638, after displaying conspicuous bravery, he was taken prisoner by the imperialists at the action of Vlotho (Oct. 17) and held in a not very strict captivity for three years. In 1641 he was released, and rejoined his mother in the Netherlands. Early in 1642 he again visited England but returned immediately as escort to his aunt, Queen Henrietta Maria.

Rupert returned to England in July of the same year when the Civil War began. Charles at once made him general of the horse and independent of Lord Lindsey, the nominal commander of the whole army. From this point until the close of the first Civil War in 1646 Prince Rupert was one of the dominant figures of the war. His battles and campaigns are described in the article GREAT REBELLION. He was distinctively a cavalry leader and it was not until the battle of Marston Moor in 1644 that the Royalist cavalry was beaten. The prince's strategy was bold as well as skilful, as was shown both in the Royalist movements of 1644 which he proposed and in the two far-ranging expeditions which he carried out for the relief of Newark and of York. In Nov. 1644, in spite of the defeat at Marston Moor, he was appointed general of the king's army. But this appointment, though welcome to the army, was obnoxious to the king's counsellors, who resented the prince's independence of their control, to some of the nobility over whose titles to consideration he had ridden roughshod, and to some of the officers whose indiscipline and rapacity were likely to be repressed with a heavy hand. These dissensions culminated, after the defeat at Naseby and the prince's surrender of Bristol to Lord Fairfax (Sept. 1645), in a complete break with Charles, who dismissed him from all his offices and bade Rupert and his younger brother Maurice seek their fortunes beyond the seas.

Rupert's character had been tempered by these years of responsible command. The parliamentary party accused him not merely of ingratitude for the kindnesses which his family had received from English people in the days of the Palatinate War, but also of barbarity in his conduct of the Royalist armies in England. He had, of course, been brought up in the rough school of continental warfare. Moreover, he often had to use force to secure pay and supplies for his troops. But it is clear that he did his best to restrain their licence; and he did on occasion display notable generosity to his enemies. When, after Marston Moor, he became convinced that the king's cause was in a military sense lost, he also became an advocate of peace. In consequence he came to be suspected by Charles's more optimistic advisers, such as Lord Digby, while to Charles himself the news of Rupert's capitulation at Bristol came as a thunderbolt. "It is the greatest trial to my constancy that has yet befallen me," he wrote to the prince, "that one that is so near to me both in blood and friendship submits himself to so mean an action." Rupert was deeply wounded by the implied stain on his honour; he forced his way to the king and demanded a court-martial. The verdict of this court smoothed matters for a time, but Rupert was too far estranged from the prevailing party at court to be of any assistance, and after further misfortunes and quarrels they separated, Charles to take refuge in the camp of the Scots, Rupert to stay without command in the Oxford garrison. He received at the capitulation a pass from the parliament to leave England, as did also his comrade Maurice.

For some time after this Rupert commanded the troops formed of English exiles in the French army and received a wound at the siege of La Basse in 1647. Charles in misfortune had understood something of his nephew's devotion and wrote to him in the friendliest terms, and though the prince had by no means forgiven Digby, Lord Colepeper and others of the council, he obtained command of a Royalist fleet. The king's enemies were now no longer the Presbyterians and the majority of the English people, but the stern Independent community, with whose aims and aspirations Rupert could not have any sympathy whatever. A long and unprofitable naval campaign followed, in which Rupert's small fleet was chased by Robert Blake from Kinsale to Lisbon, Cartagena and Toulon. Driven from the Mediterranean, Rupert cruised to the Azores and to the West Indies (1651–52), returning to France in 1653 with a single ship and a few prizes. After this the prince, having again quarrelled with the council, spent six years (1654–60) in Germany. At the Restoration he settled in England again, receiving from Charles II an annuity and becoming a member of the privy council. He never again fought on land but, turning admiral, he played a prominent part in the Dutch Wars. He also took an interest in trading enterprises and was a member of the Royal African company (1663) and of the Hudson's Bay company (1670). He died at his house in Spring Gardens, Westminster, on Nov. 29, 1682.

Apart from his military renown, Prince Rupert is a distinguished figure in the history of art as one of the earliest mezzotinters. It has often been said that he was the inventor of mezzotint engraving, but this is erroneous, as he obtained the secret from a German officer, Ludwig von Siegen. One of the most beautiful and valuable of early mezzotints is his "Head of St. John the Baptist." He was also interested in science, experimented with the manufacture of gunpowder, the boring of guns and the casting of shot and invented a modified brass called Prince's metal.

Prince Rupert was created duke of Cumberland and earl of Holderness in the English peerage in 1644. He was unmarried, but left two natural children: one a daughter who married Gen. Emmanuel Scrope Howe and died in 1740, and the other a son, whose mother (who claimed that she was married to the prince) was Frances, daughter of Sir Henry Bard, Viscount Bellamont. The son was killed in 1686 at the siege of Buda.

See E. Warburton, *Memoirs of Prince Rupert and the Cavaliers including their private correspondence,* 3 vol. (London, 1849); E. Scott, *Rupert, Prince Palatine* (London, New York, 1899); J. Cleugh, *Prince Rupert* (London, 1934). (R. B. Wm.; X.)

RUPERT [Rupprecht-Maria-Luitpoldt Ferdinand von Wittelsbach] (1869–   ), German prince, the eldest son of King Louis III of Bavaria, was born on May 18, 1869, at Munich. In 1906, after extensive travels, he was appointed to the command of the 1st Bavarian army corps. At the outbreak of World War I he was commander of the Bavarian troops (the 6th German army) and led them to victory in the great battles fought in Lorraine (Aug. 20–22, 1914). In the following October he was placed in command on the German front in Artois and southern Flanders.

Having been advanced to the rank of field marshal, he was entrusted in the spring of 1917 with the chief command of the northern group of armies on the western front. In 1900 he married Marie Gabrielle, a sister of the queen of the Belgians, who died in 1912; and in 1921 he married Princess Antoinette of Luxembourg and Nassau. He renounced his rights to the Bavarian crown on Nov. 8, 1918, and was allowed to reside in his castle near Starnberg, Bavaria. Through his mother, the archduchess Marie-Thérèse of Austria-Este, Prince Rupert was the descendant of the Stuart kings of England and, according to legitimist ideas, in the succession to the British crown.

RUPERT'S LAND, a former district of Canada. The generous charter of Charles II, given in 1670 to the Hudson's Bay company (q.v.), was interpreted to include all the country which was drained into Hudson bay. As Prince Rupert was first governor of the Hudson's Bay company his name was given to the concession under the name Rupert's Land. It must be observed that Athabasca, New Caledonia and British Columbia were not included in the grant. They were held under the title of Indian territories by the Hudson's Bay company by licence terminable every 21 years, the last term closing with 1859. Rupert's Land was transferred to Canada by the imperial government in 1870, and ceased to exist as a political name. It is still used as the title of the Anglican episcopal diocese, which is in the main coincident with the province of Manitoba; and as a provincial electoral district, where it applies to the far northern section of the province.

RUPILIUS, PUBLIUS, Roman statesman, consul in 132 B.C. During the inquiry that followed the death of Tiberius Gracchus, conducted by himself and his colleague Popillius Laenas, he proceeded with the utmost severity against the supporters of Gracchus. In the same year he was dispatched to Sicily, where he suppressed the revolt of the slaves under Eunus. During 131 he remained as proconsul of the island and, with the assistance of ten commissioners appointed by the senate, drew up regulations for the organization of Sicily as a province. These regulations were known by the title of *leges Rupiliae.* Rupilius was subsequently brought to trial (123 B.C.) and condemned for his treatment of the friends of Gracchus. He died soon afterward.

See Cicero, *De Am.* 19, *Tusc. disp.* iv 17, *in Verr.* ii 13, 15; Diod. Sic. xxxiv 1, 20; Vell. Pat. ii 7.

RURAL DEPOPULATION. In all countries of the world during the first half of the 20th century there was a trend from the countryside toward the town; even in countries where the rural population was increasing, the urban population was increasing at a greater rate, so that practically everywhere the proportion of the rural to the total population was decreasing.

In the old world this tendency was very noticeable in Great Britain, where the rural population decreased not only relatively, but absolutely. In the new world, Australia showed the most striking drift from rural to urban districts; statistics showed that by mid-century about half of its population lived in the five capital cities, and only somewhat more than 20% could be classed as rural. This is an example of a new country, scarcely out of the agricultural stage of its development, with approximately the same apportionment of population as a long industrialized country, Great Britain.

It is extremely difficult to form an adequate picture of the true position, because of the different bases on which statistics are collected. In the United States the bureau of the census recorded for 1950 96,467,686 persons as urban, equivalent to 64% of the total for continental United States and 54,229,675 or 36% as rural. In contrast with the high figures of rural population, less than 10% of the working population of the country is engaged in agriculture. In Britain those who live in the administrative divisions known as rural districts are classed as rural and on this basis about 17% of the population are rural dwellers. According to the Scott report (Report of the Committee on Land Utilization in Rural Areas, cmd. 6378, 1943) the population of rural district areas of England and Wales was about 7,200,000 out of a total for the country of 41,215,000. But rural districts may include towns often purely industrial such as Didcot in Berkshire, or Greenhithe in Kent, or residential such as Horley in Surrey, so that the population living in the open countryside does not exceed 2,000,000 or 2,500,000, that in villages 3,500,000 or 4,000,000—a total of about 6,000,000. Out of these it was estimated that there were 300,000 farmers and 700,000 farm workers—a total of 1,000,000—and so, even making a liberal allowance for dependents, only about half the rural dwellers were connected with agriculture. It is clearly a serious fallacy to equate the crude figures for a rural population with those engaged in agriculture.

Ratio Between Urban and Rural Population.—From time to time many writers have attempted to assess an ideal balance between urban and rural population. One old idea was that half the nation should live in the country and the other half in towns. In general, however, it may be said that with every advance in the technology and science of agriculture, the output per worker engaged in farming is potentially increased and so a small number of primary producers is needed to supply the nation's food. On the other hand, as the standard of living rises there is an ever increasing demand for a wider and wider range of manufactured goods and a large proportion of the nation's workers are engaged in secondary production, servicing and distribution. It is thus the more backward nations, with the lower standards of living, which have the largest proportions of rural dwellers and agricultural workers. In India, two-thirds of the people are dependent on agriculture but, as the country develops, the proportion is falling rapidly.

The accompanying chart taken from the publication *Czechoslovak Republic* throws an interesting light on the conditions in five European sections as it existed in the period between World Wars I and II.

Effects of Rural Depopulation.—Many writers regard rural depopulation as a natural phenomenon consequent upon the increased efficiency of agriculture whereby a skilled minority produces the food for a town-dwelling majority. Sentiment has been allowed to enter into the assessment of the problems, and it is difficult to substantiate claims that the physical standard of the urban population deteriorates unless there is a constant infusion of country blood. While it is true that rural birth rates and rural family sizes tend to remain above those of the towns, it is difficult to prove that the country-born or their children produce more leaders of men as some have claimed. A more definite and serious consequence of rural depopulation is well seen in Britain and others of the older countries of the old world. Where population becomes thinly spread it is difficult, sometimes impossible, to maintain the social structure of the community and the social services which have been built up. This is seen with closing of village schools, churches and chapels which in turn may lead to the abandonment of land and the removal of such facilities as public transport by road and rail.

Causation.—Some of the major causes of rural depopulation which operated prior to World War II were largely removed later and their interest became largely historical. It is true, for example, that the main causes of the drift to the towns were primarily the superior economic as well as social conditions offered by town life. While the higher wage attraction was often chimerical when all pros and cons were weighed, the general rise in agricultural prices and wages during and following World War II resulted in a very different economic position. Although much rural housing remained inferior to town housing, the spread of rural electrification, piped water supplies and main drainage was breaking down the difference. Radio and motor transport removed the former isolation of the countryside. It has been shown that, on the whole, mechanization of agriculture in the older settled countries of Europe leads to an increase of output rather than a drop in labour needs while young men find a satisfaction in dealing with modern machines requiring all their care though not needing attention all seven days of the week as did horses.

Great Britain has certain causes of rural depopulation which are peculiarly its own. Perhaps the most basic is that, with the development of steam power, and with world conditions particularly favourable to British industry during the first half of the

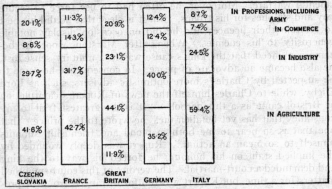

FROM CISAR & POKORNY, "CZECHOSLOVAK REPUBLIC" (BENN)

COMPARATIVE CHART SHOWING HOW THE POPULATION OF VARIOUS COUNTRIES WAS DIVIDED AMONG DIFFERENT OCCUPATIONS IN THE PERIOD BETWEEN WORLD WARS I AND II

19th century, the nation's whole attention was concentrated upon urban industry. The very future of the race was deemed to depend upon industrial development, its civilization was to be an urban civilization. This may be regarded almost as the *idée fixe* not only of economists and politicians but of the whole nation; in consequence, the rural side was neglected. Other nations, for various reasons, did not suffer to the same extent from this complex, they did not lose sight of the importance of the rural side, and they definitely endeavoured to keep a just balance between urban and rural development.

Britain suffered a rude awakening with the advent of World War II and the danger of starvation by blockade if home food products were not increased.

Remedies.—The mere enumeration of the causes of depopulation indicates the possible remedies. In Britain the remedies were studied with great care in the Scott report. The underlying principle was held to be that economic, social and educational opportunities in town and country should be made, not the same, but on a level so that there could be, as there should be in a democracy, a freedom of choice. What was needed was not settlement on the land of unemployed urban workers but encouragement to those who definitely prefer rural life and work. In particular, rural housing was then lagging behind urban.

Since agriculture is the main industry of the countryside it is essential that it should be efficiently organized. In the period between the World Wars I and II, British agriculture received some state help in the form of subsidies for certain products, but wartime experience led to the general accepted belief that prices allowing a reasonable margin of profit fixed in advance, combined with a guaranteed market such as through a state buying organization would afford the essential conditions of stability to enable the industry to organize itself efficiently. This was the basis after the agricultural act was passed in 1947 by the British parliament. It is a common fallacy to believe that Britain has natural conditions inferior to those of its continental neighbours. The reverse is the case and for many purposes climate and soils are excellent, if not unsurpassed.

Rural Depopulation and National Policy.—There is a growing appreciation all over the world that the problems raised by rural depopulation, with the consequent drift to towns and urban overcrowding, cannot be solved apart from a comprehensive policy of national planning. The demand for a central planning authority—either a department of state under a minister or a permanent commission—became so insistent in Britain that a ministry of town and country planning for England and Wales was set up in 1943 to deal with physical reconstruction and the apportionment of land. In 1951 this was merged in the ministry of housing and local government. In a small country such as England and Wales with an average of only about 1 ac. per head of population, the basal problem is to determine the optimum use in the national interest of each acre. In many cases, a multiple use, such as combining afforestation, water supply and public recreation, is possible. The thrifty use of home resources of land is in no way incompatible with the maintenance and development of international trade. Between World Wars I and II there was a great growth both in house building by public authorities and in individual home ownership but owing to lack of foresight much land, especially good agricultural land, was wasted by sprawling urban growth and ribbon development along roads. At the same time almost 30% of the urban population of Britain was suffering from malnutritional diseases caused by a lack of fresh foods which could have been produced from the neglected agricultural land.

It is recognized that for a balanced national life land must be provided for industrial development, for adequate housing—the general desire in Britain is for individual homes with gardens—for a more adequate system of modern roads and facilities for air traffic, for open spaces for recreation. This still leaves the bulk of the land for agriculture and, other things being equal, the best land should be kept inviolate for food production and efficient farmers should enjoy security of tenure of good farm units.

The execution of a national policy of rural land use planning involved much careful study of the problems of rural depopulation. Following the proposals of L. D. Stamp it became usual to divide the rural population into three groups: (1) the primary rural population of farmers, farm workers, foresters and their dependents, (2) the secondary rural population of workers who are required to support the life of the first group; i.e., village storekeepers, garage men, schoolteachers, postal workers, doctors, veterinarians, religious leaders, produce brokers, etc., and (3) the adventitious rural population of those either active or retired who live in the country by choice. In areas scenically unattractive or difficult of access the third group may be completely absent. Where this is the case S. W. E. Vince showed that the primary rural population constitutes two-thirds of the whole. Even in the intensively farmed districts of central England the primary rural population may not reach 20 persons per square mile so that official policy came to encourage the adventitious population in order to maintain the social structure of rural life. Retired people of this group are often the most active in performing the innumerable functions of local administration.

In some countries much attention was paid to the introduction of alternative employment in country areas. Factories, especially those processing agricultural products, were introduced but experience showed their location in small towns is better than in villages or open country. Various forms of dual occupation exist. For example, fruit growers find it advantageous to locate their farms near towns were casual labour is available at the time of the fruit harvest. In Germany, Britain and elsewhere it has long been the custom for factory workers to rent a small piece of land or allotment for intensive cultivation in their spare time. In later industrial developments in Italy, the workers were encouraged to continue part-time farming. In New England farms which cannot support a full time farmer are kept in cultivation on a part-time basis by those whose first occupation is in industry. The realization that town and country are interdependent is so important that all such integrations are to be encouraged.

(L. D. S.)

UNITED STATES

After the 1840s urban population in the United States grew more rapidly than rural—rural population being defined approximately as that living outside cities and other incorporated places of 2,500 or more.

In 1790 almost 95% of the population of the United States was rural and even in 1850 the rural population formed 84.7% of the total. The rural percentage declined rather rapidly from this time on, however, being 71.8% in 1880; 60.3% in 1900; 48.8%, for the first time less than half, in 1920; 43.5% in 1940; and 41.0% in 1950, using the same basis for classification as in the earlier years. Using a new definition set up in 1950, under which the rural area excludes all places of 2,500 or more and the urban fringe around the larger cities, the official figures for rural population showed an actual decline from 57,545,373 in 1940 to 54,229,675, or 36.0% of the total, in 1950. But this represented a change in the basis

of classification, not a real decline in rural population.

Nevertheless, while the rural population of the country as a whole continued to grow, there was local rural depopulation, in the strict sense of a decline in the number of persons living in rural areas. In 1920, for example, there were more than 1,000 counties, mainly rural counties, in which the census showed fewer inhabitants than in 1910. Many of these counties were in areas in which agriculture had been the principal occupation, and in which, because the land was not as good farm land as could be found elsewhere, one-time farms were being used only for pasture or even completely abandoned and permitted to revert to forest.

The acreage of land in farms continued to increase rapidly until about 1920, however; and after that date there was additional increase, or at least no appreciable decrease, either in total farm land or in the acreage of crops harvested. This means simply that agricultural activities had been transferred to areas with better soils or other advantages, or that, with increased use of farm machinery and better methods of farming, smaller numbers of workers had been necessary to operate the existing farms.

The definition of rural population, as used in the censuses of the various countries, may be such as to include considerable numbers of families having no connection whatever with farming. Because of this situation, provision was made in the 1920 census of the United States to subdivide the rural population into rural-farm, comprising only those families living on farms, and rural-nonfarm, made up largely of families living in villages and in the outskirts of cities. As an indication of the relation between agricultural activities and other economic activities, the rural-farm population figures are doubtless more significant than the total rural.

The rural-farm population of the United States numbered 31,393,262 (29.7% of the total) in 1920; 30,157,513 (24.6% of the total) in 1930; 30,216,188 (22.9% of the total) in 1940; and 23,048,350 (15.3% of the total) in 1950. The slight increase shown in 1940 was doubtless the result of the depression conditions which for the time being checked the urban trend; and the rapid decline during the subsequent decade in part made up for this temporary check, though there were unusually numerous and effective improvements in farming techniques during this period, almost forced upon farmers as a result of the high wages offered labour in war industries during World War II.

By way of justification for subdividing the rural classification, it may be noted that, in 1940, 78.5% of the workers in the rural-farm area were engaged in farm work, as compared with 6.9% of the rural-nonfarm workers (or 46.0% of the total rural workers), and 1.0% of the urban workers.

Reasons for the Changes.—The fundamental reason for the decline in the relative numbers of persons living in rural or farming areas lies in the fact that, with improvement in standard of living, the demand is for more manufactured products and more services, rather than for more farm products. The food requirements of 1,000,000 persons in 1950 were probably even less than the food requirements of the same number of persons 100 years earlier. But the nonfood items required for satisfactory living, even in the open country, were far and away greater in 1950 than the similar requirements in 1850. They include, to mention only a few, automobiles, radios and television, electric lights, hard-surface highways, sanitary plumbing, household machinery and mechanical refrigeration.

Meanwhile, the number of workers required to produce the nation's food requirements had been greatly reduced by the introduction of farm machinery (such as the tractor and the milking machine) and improved methods of farming, supplemented by new varieties of crops, improved breeds of livestock, and such incidental matters as hybrid corn (maize, not wheat) and more effective sprays and dusting materials for the control of insects and diseases.

And with greater specialization in farming, as in other industries, came an increasing production per worker. This was partly offset (as also in other lines of production) by the increased numbers of persons who must be employed in marketing and the physical distribution of the product. But these functions must be discharged largely in the cities and market towns, so that this type of employment, as well as the expanding of manufactures, contributes to the growth of the urban population, not the rural.

Tendencies and Prospects.—During the decade following 1940 the tendency among workers in the U.S. away from agricultural occupations (and especially toward trade and service occupations) was even more rapid than in earlier years. By way of background, figures are presented in Table I giving relative number of gainful workers ten years old and over in agricultural and nonagricultural occupations from 1920 to 1940, with 1950 estimates limited to employed civilian workers 14 years old and over distributed in the same way.

TABLE I.—*Gainful Workers in the United States Engaged in Agricultural and Nonagricultural Occupations: 1820–1950*

Census year	All occupations	Agricultural occupations		Nonagricultural occupations	
		Number	Per cent	Number	Per cent
1820	2,881,000	2,068,958	71.8	812,042	28.2
1830	3,931,537	2,772,453	70.5	1,159,084	29.5
1840	5,420,000	3,719,951	68.6	1,700,049	31.4
1850	7,697,196	4,901,882	63.7	2,795,314	36.3
1860	10,532,750	6,207,634	58.9	4,325,116	41.1
1870	12,924,951	6,849,772	53.0	6,075,179	47.0
1880	17,392,099	8,584,810	49.4	8,807,289	50.6
1890	23,318,183	9,938,373	42.6	13,379,810	57.4
1900	29,073,233	10,911,998	37.5	18,161,235	62.5
1910	37,370,794	11,591,767	31.0	25,779,027	69.0
1920	42,433,535	11,448,770	27.0	30,984,765	73.0
1930	48,829,920	10,471,998	21.4	38,357,922	78.6
1940	52,148,251	9,162,547	17.6	42,985,704	82.4
1950	58,668,000	7,195,000	12.2	51,473,000	87.8

The percentages for 1950 are reasonably comparable with those for earlier years, in spite of their narrower base, and indicate a decline in the relative importance of agricultural employment from 17.6% in 1940 to 12.2%, thus indicating the continuance of a series which began with 71.8% in 1820, and declined to 49.4% in 1880, to 27% in 1920, and to 21.4% in 1930.

This was the situation with regard to agricultural workers, who represent the core of the rural-farm population. (The urban-farm population, comprising persons living on farms in urban areas, is negligible, numbering usually no more than 300,000.

On the other hand, the percentage of all farm-resident members of the labour force who were engaged in agriculture was lower in 1950 than earlier, being only about 70, as compared with 78.5 in 1940. This might indicate the inclusion of larger numbers of farm families for whom the farm was primarily a place of residence, rather than a source of primary income, though special effort was made in the 1950 census to exclude from the farm-population classification those families who occupied homes physically located on a farm but had no real connection with agricultural activities.

The fundamental factors named above as responsible for the historical decline in the percentage of the population of the U.S. living in rural areas would seem to be in full operation. The proportion of city-produced goods required to support further improvements in the standard of living might well continue its rapid growth, as against very small increases in the per capita demand for farm products; and there would certainly be further improvements in the techniques of agriculture. True, the 1950 estimates indicated some increase in the numbers of workers living on farms and working elsewhere; but this certainly did not foreshadow any strong tendency toward rural or farm residence for urban workers. The tendency had been toward specialization and mechanization, even in agriculture; and this tendency was not at all consistent with the relatively inefficient production of subsistence or part-time farming.

(L. E. T.)

RURAL EDUCATION is the term given to the education of children living in the countryside.

GREAT BRITAIN

The instruction of country children is different in several ways from that given in urban schools, and is based on observation of the life and processes of the countryside. The Scott report (*Report of the Committee on Land Utilisation in Rural Areas*, H.M.S.O., London, 1942) stated that more than 80% of the population of England and Wales lived in urban areas. It may be assumed that about one-fifth to one-sixth of the school population in England and Wales, which totals about 6,367,000 (*Education in 1952*, H.M.S.O., London), attends schools in rural areas.

The infant stage of the primary school—from five to seven years of age—is basically the same everywhere, but country children learn to recognize a variety of common plants, animals and birds. Many of the stories told to them are about animals and birds, and they also learn about the changing seasons of the year. In the junior stage—from 7 to 11 years of age—the field of observation is enlarged to include insects and pond life, and a wider use is made of environment. Exercises in arithmetic are based on farm work—practical measurement takes place in the open; geography and history are taught through local surveys. More than half of the schools in which rural education is given are small, with one, two or three teachers, and have a family atmosphere which it is difficult to engender in the largest schools.

At 11 years of age, children are examined and allocated to secondary education in technical, grammar or modern schools in accordance with their aptitudes and abilities. In rural areas technical secondary education is only just beginning. It is intended in this form of education to introduce vocational bias, *e.g.*, toward agriculture and rural crafts, in the latter half of the four-year course. In the country grammar schools the usual academic subjects are taught, but the broadened basis of the syllabus for the general certificate of education at ordinary level makes it possible for grammar-school pupils to take some subjects which are particularly pertinent to life in a rural area; *e.g.*, agricultural science, elementary surveying, geology. The work of the modern schools in rural areas has shown the greatest advance in recent years. Provided with school gardens, and often equipped with science and gardening laboratories, greenhouses and room for stockkeeping, they give courses in rural science based on the observation previously encouraged in the primary schools, and on what the children learn through experiment in the garden and farm visits and observation. Cookery for girls (and sometimes for boys) is closely linked with food production and preservation; and woodwork and metalwork for boys, together with the science of everyday things (for boys and girls), are linked with the handyman and maintenance work of the village, farm and cottage. Young Farmers' clubs are found in many of the schools, and in many of them small stock—pigs, rabbits, poultry—is kept. Bird and tree competitions are conducted within and between counties. The children who remain to 15 years of age in all-standard schools, of which there are relatively more in rural than in urban areas, are handicapped by difficulties of premises and organization and can carry out only some of the work done in fully equipped modern schools. All local education authorities intend to reorganize their schools in accordance with the recommendations of the Hadow report (*The Education of the Adolescent*, H.M.S.O., London, 1926) in order that primary- and secondary-school children may be taught in separate school premises.

In most rural areas a cooked midday meal is served in the schools, and may be taken by as many as 90% of the children. Meals have been provided in rural schools for more than 30 years, since distance makes it hard for the children to return home to the midday meal, and parents find difficulty in providing an adequate packed meal. Children under eight are transported if they have farther than two miles to walk to school, and so are children over that age who have more than three miles to walk. Transport is usually by bus, but bicycles, railways, motor launches, rowing boats, private cars and ponies and traps may also be used. Grammar schools, being fewer in number than modern schools, draw pupils from areas often up to 20 mi.; modern schools draw pupils from villages up to 5 and 7 mi. away.

Rural education is designed to enable country children to understand and appreciate what is going on around them, but it is not vocational training for agriculture. The number of children who enter agricultural occupations when they leave school varies from county to county; in the North Riding of Yorkshire about 4% of the population are agricultural workers, in Somerset about 5%, in Norfolk about 11.9% and in the Holland division of Lincolnshire about 16.9% (*Ministry of Agriculture Returns, 1950*). While these boys and girls need a thorough grounding in rural science, all who live in the countryside and serve the industry of agriculture in various ways must be able to understand its problems. They need teachers who understand and love the rural way of life. Some such teachers have been brought up in the countryside; others have been brought up in urban surroundings but trained in colleges with a special bias for rural education. "As a man sows, so shall he reap"—this proverb represents a fundamental truth in rural education.

(L. R. Mn.)

UNITED STATES

The term rural education formerly referred chiefly to schools located in the open country and in villages of fewer than 2,500 population. The development of consolidated schools resulted in the concept that rural education refers to educational services for people who live in a rural environment, including farm families and their village neighbours and their children who are transported to urban schools. Important aspects of rural education include the teaching of vocational agriculture and homemaking in many high schools serving rural pupils; and 4-H clubs, many of which operate through the schools, and adult education sponsored by the co-operative extension service of the U.S. department of agriculture through the land-grant colleges and the county agents. While the ultimate aims of rural and urban education are the same, the former attempts to utilize the materials of the rural environment in the selection of curriculum materials and teaching procedures. Under an increasing emphasis on the community-centred school many rural schools not only strive to teach the three R's, but also to bring about better living in their communities. Rural education is also identified by some distinctive problems: the reorganization of school districts, the consolidation of schools, the operation of pupil transportation and special instructional organization for small schools.

In efforts to equalize educational opportunities it has been evident that the greatest need has been among certain rural groups, notably, migratory agricultural workers, people in areas of low economic resources, agricultural labourers and sharecroppers, the Negroes of the cotton belt, the Latin Americans of the southwest and many Indians.

Rural education is administered locally through five principal types of organization: (1) common-school districts; (2) community or consolidated districts; (3) town or township districts; (4) county units; and (5) the intermediate district, usually a county or a combination of two or more local districts, a unit superimposed over small-type districts to give services to pupils and teachers that the constituent districts cannot afford.

In 1950 the U.S. office of education reported that urban schools as compared with rural schools on the average paid higher salaries to teachers, spent more money per pupil and had slightly longer school terms.

By the second half of the 20th century about 44% of the school-age children, and of those enrolled in school, resided in rural areas. After 1945 the number of rural farm children remained approximately stationary. The greatest growth in numbers of school children was in the rural nonfarm areas, the increase being nearly twice as great as in cities.

During the decade 1945–55 the number of school districts and the number of one-teacher schools were reduced by nearly 50%; while the number of pupils transported by school bus daily approximately doubled.

(H. A. D.)

RURKI: *see* ROORKEE.

RUSCHUK (Bulg. *Russé*), the capital of the department of Ruschuk, Bulgaria, on the right bank of the Danube, where it receives the R. Lom. Pop. (1946) 53,420. It is connected by rail with Varna and Sofia; by boat and rail with Bucharest. It is the chief Danubian port of Bulgaria, and an important commercial centre.

It possesses sugar, tobacco and cigarette factories, soapworks, breweries, aerated water factories, dyeworks, tanneries, sawmills, brick and tile works and a celebrated pottery.

In Roman times Ruschuk was one of the fortified points along the line of the Danube. In the *Tabula Peutingeriana* it appears as Prisca, in the *Antonine Itinerary* as Serantaprista, in the *Notitia*

as Seragintaprista and in Ptolemy as Priste Polis. Destroyed by barbarian invaders in the 7th century the town recovered its importance only in comparatively modern times. It played an important part in the Russo-Turkish wars of 1810, 1828–29, 1853–54 and 1877–78. In 1877 it was nearly destroyed by Russian artillery.

RUSELLAE, an ancient town of Etruria, Italy, about 10 mi. S.E. of Vetulonia and 5 mi. N.E. of Grosseto, situated on a hill with two summits, the higher 636 ft. above sea level. It was one of the twelve cities of the Etruscan confederation, and was taken in 294 B.C. by the Romans. In 205 B.C. it contributed grain and timber for the needs of Scipio's fleet. The place was deserted in 1138, and the episcopal see was transferred to Grosseto. The walls, nearly 2 mi. in circumference, are in places well preserved. They consist of large unworked blocks of a travertine which naturally splits into roughly rectangular blocks; these are quite irregular, and often as much as 9 ft. long by 4 ft. wide; in the interstices smaller pieces are inserted.

RUSH, BENJAMIN (1745–1813), U.S. physician, was born in Byberry township, near Philadelphia, Pa. In 1760 he graduated at Princeton university. In 1768 he took his M.D. at Edinburgh, and after spending a year in the hospitals of London and Paris began practice in Philadelphia. In 1774 he founded with James Pemberton the first antislavery society in America. In 1776, as a member of congress for the state of Pennsylvania, he was one of those who signed the Declaration of Independence. In 1787 he was a member of the Pennsylvania convention which adopted the federal constitution. He became professor of the institutes of medicine and of clinical practice, succeeding in 1796 to the chair of the theory and practice of medicine, at the University of Pennsylvania. He engaged in epidemiological work and was actively interested in the investigation of yellow fever. In 1799 he was appointed treasurer of the U.S. mint in Philadelphia. He died in Philadelphia on April 19, 1813, after a five days' illness from typhus fever.

Rush's writings covered an immense range of subjects. His last work was an elaborate treatise on the *Diseases of the Mind* (1812). He is best known by the five volumes of *Medical Inquiries and Observations*, which he brought out at intervals from 1789 to 1798.

RUSH, RICHARD (1780–1859), American statesman and diplomat, son of Dr. Benjamin Rush, was born in Philadelphia, Pa., on Aug. 29, 1780. He graduated at Princeton in 1797, and was admitted to the bar in 1800. He was attorney-general of Pennsylvania in 1811; controller of the Treasury of the United States, 1811–14; attorney general in the cabinet of President James Madison, 1814–17; acting secretary of State from March to Sept., 1817; minister to Great Britain, 1817–25; secretary of the treasury in the cabinet of President J. Q. Adams, 1825–29; and candidate for vice-president on the Adams ticket in 1828. In 1818, while minister to Great Britain, he, in association with Albert Gallatin, concluded with British plenipotentiaries the important treaty which determined the boundary line between the United States and Canada from the Lake of the Woods to the Rocky mountains and provided for the joint occupation of Oregon for ten years. He also conducted the negotiations with Canning in 1823 relating to the South American policy of the Holy Alliance.

He followed the Adams-Clay faction of the Democratic-Republican party in the split of 1825–28, but returned to the Democratic party about 1834 on the bank issue. In 1835 he and Benjamin C. Howard, of Baltimore, Md., were sent by President Jackson to prevent an outbreak of hostilities in the Ohio-Michigan boundary dispute. In 1836–38 Rush was commissioner to receive the Smithson legacy (*see* SMITHSONIAN INSTITUTION), and in 1847–49 he was minister to France. He died in Philadelphia on July 30, 1859.

He published *A Narrative of a Residence at the Court of London from 1817 to 1825* (2 vols. 1833–45; all editions after the 1st ed. of the 1st vol. are entitled *Memoranda of a Residence*, etc.); *Washington in Domestic Life* (1857), compiled from letters written by Washington to his private secretary in 1790–98; and *Occasional Productions, Political, Diplomatic and Miscellaneous*

(1860); and while attorney-general he suggested the plan for the compilation, *Laws of the Nation* (5. vols., 1815), ed. by John B. Colvin.

RUSH. Under the name of rush or rushes, the stalks or hollow stem-like leaves of several plants have minor industrial applications. The common rushes (species of *Juncus; see* JUNCACEAE) are used in many parts of the world for chair bottoms, mats and basketwork, and the pith serves as wicks in open oil lamps and for tallow candles—whence rushlight. The fibrous stems and leaves of the bulrush, reed mace or cattail, *Typha angustifolia,* are used in north India for ropes, mats and baskets. *Scirpus* and other Cyperaceae are used for chair bottoms, mats and thatch; the rush mats of Madras are made from a species of *Cyperus.* The sweet rush, yielding essential oil, is a grass, *Cymbopogon citratus,* known also as lemon grass. Quantities of the horse-tail, *Equisetum hyemale,* are used under the name of Dutch or scouring rush for scouring metal and other hard surfaces on account of the large proportion of silica the plant contains. Flowering rush is *Butomus umbellatus* (*see* ALISMATACEAE); wood rush is the common name for *Luzula* (*see* JUNCACEAE).

Acorus calamus (family Araceae), sweet flag, is also known as sweet rush.

RUSHDEN, urban district, in the Wellingborough parliamentary division, Northamptonshire, Eng., 66 mi. N.W. from London by the London Midland Region railway route. Area 6 sq.mi.; pop. (1951) 16,321. The church of St. Mary, a cruciform building, is mainly Decorated with Perpendicular additions, but retains some Early English details. The population is employed in boot- and shoemaking. The town is now almost continuous with Highham Ferrers.

RUSHDI PASHA (c. 1864–1928), Egyptian statesman, was born about 1864, and educated in France. On his return to Egypt he entered the government service, becoming a minister in 1908. In April 1914 he was made prime minister, and at the outbreak of World War I he was acting as regent in the absence of the khedive. The fact that Egypt was still technically part of the Ottoman empire and that Turkey at first declared for neutrality made his position extremely difficult. He had, however, a strong cabinet and when Turkey entered the war on the side of Germany he agreed to the proclamation of a British protectorate.

After the armistice Rushdi pressed the British government for a definition of Egypt's position and asked to be received in London to discuss the question. This proposal was not accepted, and on March 1, 1919, he and his cabinet resigned. A few days later Zaghlul Pasha was arrested by the British authorities and deported to Malta. This step led to serious rioting, and he was soon released and continued his journey to Paris to champion Egypt at the peace conference. The British government had to appeal once more to Rushdi Pasha, who consented, after the release of Zaghlul, to form a ministry again. The treatment which he had received had, however, greatly diminished his prestige, and he was obliged to resign again ten days later. He retired into private life, and did not take office again until the Milner commission (1919) had made its report.

An Egyptian cabinet was required which should have sufficient support in Egypt to undertake negotiations in London toward an agreed settlement. Adly Pasha was made prime minister, and Rushdi became president of the council, being chosen to accompany him to England. He was, however, failing in health, and he died on March 13, 1928.

RUSHMORE, MOUNT, MEMORIAL: *see* BORGLUM, GUTZON.

RUSHVILLE, a city of Indiana, U.S., 39 mi. S.E. of Indianapolis, on Flat Rock creek, at an altitude of 967 ft.; the county seat of Rush county. It is on federal highway 52 and is served by the Baltimore and Ohio, the New York Central, the Erie, the Nickel Plate and the Pennsylvania railways.

The population in 1950 was 6,761 and it was 5,960 in 1940 by the federal census. It has various manufacturing industries and a large trade in grain and livestock (especially blooded hogs), and lumber. Rushville was chartered as a town in 1816 and as a city in 1883.

RUSHWORTH, JOHN (c. 1612–1690), the compiler of the *Historical Collections* commonly described by his name, was the son of Lawrence Rushworth of Acklington Park, Warkworth, Northumberland. In 1638 he was appointed solicitor to the town of Berwick. He was enrolled in Lincoln's Inn in 1641, and was called to the bar in 1647. He attended all public occasions of a political and judicial character, such as proceedings before the Star chamber or the council, and made shorthand notes of them. On April 25, 1640, he was appointed an assistant clerk to the house of commons. He became secretary to Fairfax, and then, for a short time, to Cromwell. He was afterward employed by the council of state and during the protectorate, and sat in Cromwell's parliament for Berwick.

He made his peace with the government of Charles II, and though he was threatened with trial as a regicide he was not seriously molested. During the reign of Charles II he continued to act as agent for the town of Berwick, and he sat for it in parliament. He was also for a time agent for Massachusetts. From 1684 till his death on May 12, 1690, he was a resident in the King's bench prison. At this time he had destroyed his memory by overindulgence in drink.

The collection of papers which he made was published in eight volumes folio between 1659 and 1701. The volumes from the fourth onward appeared after his death.

RUSKIN, JOHN (1819–1900), English writer and critic, was born in London, at Hunter street, Brunswick square, on Feb. 8, 1819, being the only child of John James Ruskin and Margaret Cox. They were Scots, first cousins, the grandchildren of a certain John Ruskin of Edinburgh (1732–1780). John Ruskin, the author's grandfather, was a wine merchant in Edinburgh, who ran through his fortune, and ended his days in debt. His son, John James Ruskin (1785–1864), father of the author, was sent, on leaving Edinburgh High School, to London to enter the wine trade. There, in 1809, he founded the sherry business of Ruskin, Telford and Domecq; Domecq being proprietor of a famous vineyard in Spain, Telford contributing the capital of the firm, and Ruskin having sole control of the business. Ruskin built up a great business, paid off his father's debts and formed near London a most hospitable and cultured home, where he maintained his taste for literature and art.

Margaret Ruskin, the author's mother, was a handsome, strong, stern, able, devoted woman of the old Puritan school, Calvinist in religion, unsparing of herself and others, rigid in her ideas of duty, proud, reserved and ungracious. The child was brought up under a rigid system of nursing, physical, moral and intellectual; kept without toys, not seldom whipped, watched day and night, but trained from infancy in music, drawing, reading aloud and observation of natural objects. When he was four the family removed to a house on Herne Hill, then a country village, with a garden and rural surroundings. The father, who made long tours on business, took his wife, child and nurse year after year across England as far as Cumberland and Scotland, visiting towns, cathedrals, castles, colleges, parks, mountains and lakes. At 14 the child was taken through Flanders, along the Rhine, and through the Black Forest to Switzerland, where he first imbibed his dominant passion for the Alps. His youth was largely passed in systematic travelling in search of everything beautiful in nature or in art. And to one so precocious, stimulated by a parent of much culture, ample means and great ambition, this resulted in an almost unexampled aesthetic education. In childhood also he began a systematic practice of composition, both in prose and verse. His mother trained him in reading the Bible, of which he read through every chapter of every book year by year; and to this study he justly attributes his early command of language and his pure sense of style. His father read to him Shakespeare, Scott, Don Quixote, Pope and Byron, and most of the great English classics; and his attention was especially turned to the formation of sentences and to the rhythm of prose. He began to compose both in prose and verse as soon as he had learned to read and write, both of which arts he taught himself by the eye. He wrote enormous quantities of verse, and began dramas, romances and imitations of Byron, Pope, Scott and Shelley.

His schooling was irregular and not successful. At 15 he was sent for two years to the day-school of the Rev. T. Dale of Peckham, and at 17 he attended some courses in literature at King's college, London. In painting he had lessons from Copley Fielding and afterwards from J. D. Harding. But in the incessant travelling, drawing, collecting specimens and composition in prose and verse he had gained but a very moderate classical and mathematical knowledge when he matriculated at Oxford; nor could he ever learn to write tolerable Latin. As a boy he was active, lively and docile; a good walker, but ignorant of all boyish games, as naïve and as innocent as a child; and he never could learn to dance or to ride. He was only saved by his intellect and his fine nature from turning out an arrant prig. He was regarded by his parents, and seems to have regarded himself, as a genius.

At the age of 17 he saw Adèle, the French daughter of Monsieur Domecq, Mr. Ruskin's partner, a lovely girl of fifteen. John fell rapturously in love with her; and, it seems, the two fathers seriously contemplated their marriage. The young poet wooed the girl with poems, romances, dramas and mute worship, but received nothing except chilling indifference and lively ridicule. To the gay young beauty, familiar with Parisian society, the raw and serious youth was not a possible *parti*. She was sent to an English school, and he occasionally saw her. His unspoken passion lasted about three years, when she married the Baron Duquesne. Writing as an old man, long after her death, Ruskin speaks of his early love without any sort of rapture. But it is clear that it deeply coloured his life, and led to the illness which for some two years interrupted his studies and made him a wanderer over Europe.

As the father was resolved that John should have everything that money and pains could give, and should one day be a bishop at least, he entered him at Christ Church, Oxford, as a gentleman-commoner—then an order reserved for men of wealth and rank. Ruskin's Oxford career, broken by the two years passed abroad, was not very full of incident or of usefulness. Both he and his college took kindly the amazing proceeding of his mother, who left her husband and her home to reside in Oxford, that she might watch over her son's health. The one success of his Oxford career was the winning the Newdigate Prize by his poem "Salsette and Elephanta," which he recited in the Sheldonian Theatre (June 1839). Two years of ill-health and absence from home ensued. And he did not become "a Graduate of Oxford" until 1842, in his 24th year, five years after his first entrance at the university. In fact, his desultory school and college life had been little more than an interruption and hindrance to his real education—the study of nature, of art and of literature. Long before Ruskin published books he had written for various periodicals on architectural and other subjects.

After leaving Oxford, Ruskin set to work steadily at Herne Hill on the more elaborate defence of Turner, which was to become his first work. *Modern Painters,* vol. i., by "a Graduate of Oxford," was published May 1843, when the author was little more than twenty-four. It was vehemently attacked by the critics, and coolly received by the painters. Even Turner was somewhat disconcerted; but the painter was now known to both Ruskins, and they freely bought his pictures. The family then went again to the Alps, that John might study mountain formation and "Truth" in landscape. In 1845 he was again abroad in Italy, working on his *Modern Painters,* the second volume of which appeared in 1846. He had now plunged into the study of Bellini and the Venetian school, Fra Angelico and the early Tuscans, and he visited Lucca, Pisa, Florence, Padua, Verona and Venice, passionately devoting himself to architecture, sculpture and painting in each city of north Italy. He wrote a few essays for the *Quarterly Review* and other periodicals, and in 1849 (*aet.* 30) he published *The Seven Lamps of Architecture,* with his own etchings, which greatly increased the reputation acquired by his *Modern Painters.*

On April 10, 1848, a day famous in the history of Chartism, Ruskin was married at Perth to Euphemia Chalmers Gray, a lady of great beauty, of a family long intimate with the Ruskins. The marriage, we are told, was arranged by the parents of the pair, and was a somewhat hurried act. It was evidently ill-assorted, and brought no happiness to either. They travelled, lived in Lon-don, saw society, and attended a "Drawing-room" at Buckingham Palace. But Ruskin, immersed in various studies and projects, was no husband for a brilliant woman devoted to society. No particulars of their life have been made public. In 1854 his wife left him, obtained a nullification of the marriage under Scots law, and ultimately became the wife of John Everett Millais. John Ruskin returned to his parents, with whom he resided till their death; and neither his marriage nor the annulling of it seems to have affected seriously his literary career.

Ruskin's architectural studies, of which *The Seven Lamps* was the first fruit, turned him from Turner and *Modern Painters.* He planned a book about Venice in 1845, and *The Stones of Venice* was announced in 1849 as in preparation. After intense study in Italy and at home, early in 1851 (the year of the Great Exhibition in London) the first volume of *The Stones of Venice* appeared (*aet.* 32). It was a concrete expansion of the ideas of *The Seven Lamps*—that the buildings and art of a people are the expression of their religion, their morality, their national aspirations and social habits. It was, as Carlyle wrote to the author, "a sermon in stones," "a singular sign of the times," "a new *Renaissance.*" It appeared in the same year with *The Construction of Sheepfolds* —a plea for the reunion of Christian churches—in the same year with the essay on *Pre-Raphaelitism,* the year of Turner's death (19th December). *The Stones of Venice* was illustrated with engravings by some of the most refined artists of his time. The author spent a world of pains in having these brought up to the highest perfection of the reproductive art, and began the system of exquisite illustration, and those facsimiles of his own and other sketches, which make his works rank so high in the catalogues and price-lists of collectors. This delicate art was carried even farther in the later volumes of *Modern Painters* by the school of engravers whom Ruskin inspired and gathered round him. And these now rare and coveted pieces remain to rebuke us for our modern preference for the mechanical and unnatural *chiaroscuro* of photogravure—the successor and destroyer of the graver's art.

Although Ruskin was practised in drawing from the time that he could hold a pencil, and had lessons in painting from some eminent artists, he at no time attempted to paint pictures. He said himself that he was unable to compose a picture, and he never sought to produce anything that he would call a work of original art. His drawings, of which he produced an enormous quantity, were always intended by himself to be studies or memoranda of buildings or natural objects precisely as they appeared to his eye. Clouds, mountains, landscapes, towers, churches, trees, flowers and herbs were drawn with wonderful precision, minuteness of detail and delicacy of hand, solely to recall some specific aspect of nature or art, of which he wished to retain a record. In his gift for recording the most subtle characters of architectural carvings and details, Ruskin has hardly been surpassed by the most distinguished painters.

In 1853 *The Stones of Venice* was completed at Herne Hill, and he began a series of *Letters* and *Notes* on pictures and architecture. In this year (*aet.* 34) he opened the long series of public lectures wherein he came forward as an oral teacher and preacher, not a little to the alarm of his parents and amidst a storm of controversy. The Edinburgh Lectures (November 1853) treated Architecture, Turner and Pre-Raphaelitism. The Manchester Lectures (July 1857) treated the moral and social uses of art, now embodied in *A Joy for Ever.* Some other lectures are reprinted in *On the Old Road* and *The Two Paths* (1859). These lectures did not prevent the issue of various *Notes* on the Royal Academy pictures and the Turner collections; works on the *Harbours of England* (1856); on the *Elements of Drawing* (1857); the *Elements of Perspective* (1859). At last, after prolonged labour, the fifth and final volume of *Modern Painters* was published in 1860 (*aet.* 41). This marks an epoch in the career of John Ruskin; and the year 1860 closed the series of his works on art strictly so called.

The last forty years of his life were devoted to expounding his views, or rather his doctrines, on social and industrial problems, on education, morals and religion, wherein art becomes an incidental and instrumental means to a higher and more spiritual life.

And his teaching was embodied in an enormous series of lectures, letters, articles, selections and serial pamphlets. These are now collected in upwards of thirty volumes in the final edition. The entire set of Ruskin's publications amounts to more than fifty works having distinctive titles. For some years before 1860 Ruskin had been deeply stirred by reflecting on the condition of all industrial work and the evils of modern society. His lectures on art had dealt bitterly with the mode in which buildings and other works were produced. In 1854 he joined F. D. Maurice, T. Hughes and several of the new school of painters, in teaching classes at the Working Men's College. But it was not until 1860 that he definitely began to propound a new social scheme, denouncing the dogmas of political economy. Four lectures on this topic appeared in the *Cornhill Magazine* until the public disapproval led the editor, then W. M. Thackeray, to close the series. They were published in 1862 as *Unto this Last.* In the same year he wrote four papers in the same sense in *Fraser's Magazine,* then edited by J. A. Froude; but he in turn was compelled to suspend the issue. They were completed and ultimately issued under the title *Munera Pulveris.* These two small books contain the earliest and most systematic of all Ruskin's efforts to depict a new social Utopia. They contain a vehement repudiation of the orthodox formulas of the economists; and they are for the most part written in a trenchant but simple style, in striking contrast to the florid and discursive form of his works on art.

In 1864 Ruskin's father died, at the age of 79, leaving his son a large fortune and a fine property at Denmark Hill. John still lived there with his mother, aged 83, infirm, and failing in sight, to whom came as a companion his cousin, Joanna Ruskin Agnew, afterwards Mrs. Arthur Severn. At the end of the year 1864 Ruskin delivered at Manchester a new series of lectures—not on art, but on reading, education, woman's work and social morals— the expansion of his earlier treatises on economic sophisms. This afterwards was included with a Dublin lecture of 1868 under the fantastic title of *Sesame and Lilies* (perhaps the most popular of his social essays), of which 44,000 copies were issued down to 1900. He made this, in 1871, the first volume of his collected lectures and essays, the more popular and didactic form of his new Utopia of human life. It contains, with *Fors,* the most complete sketch of his conception of the place of woman in modern society.

In the very characteristic preface to the new edition of 1871 Ruskin proposes never to reprint his earlier works on art; disclaims many of the views they contained, and much in their literary form; and specially regrets the narrow Protestantism by which they were pervaded. In the year 1866 he published a little book about girls, and written for girls, a mixture of morals, theology, economics and geology, under the title of *Ethics of the Dust;* and this was followed by a more important and popular work, *The Crown of Wild Olive.* This in its ultimate form contained lectures on "Work," "Traffic," "War" and "The Future of England." It was one of his most trenchant utterances, full of fancy, wit, eloquence and elevated thought. But a more serious volume was *Time and Tide* (1867), a series of twenty-five letters to a workman of Sunderland, upon various points in the Ruskinian Utopia. This little collection of "Thoughts," written with wonderful vivacity, ingenuity and fervour, is the best summary of the author's social and economic programme, and contains some of his wisest and finest thoughts in the purest and most masculine English that he had at his command. In 1869 he issued *The Queen of the Air,* lectures on Greek myths, a subject he now took up, with some aid from the late Sir C. Newton. It was followed by some other occasional pieces; and in the same year he was elected Slade professor of art in the University of Oxford.

He now entered on his professorial career, which continued with some intervals down to 1884, and occupied a large part of his energies. His lectures began in February 1870, and were so crowded that they had to be given in the Sheldonian Theatre, and frequently were repeated to a second audience. He was made honorary fellow of Corpus Christi, and occupied rooms in the college. In 1871 his mother died, at the age of 90, and his cousin, Miss Agnew, married Arthur Severn. In that year he bought from Linton, Brantwood, an old cottage and property on Coniston Lake,

a lovely spot facing the mountain named the Old Man. He added greatly to the house and property, and lived in it continuously until his death in 1900. In 1871, one of the most eventful years of his life, he began *Fors Clavigera,* a small serial addressed to the working men of England, and published only by George Allen, engraver, at Keston, in Kent, at 7d., and afterwards at 10d., but without discount, and not through the trade. This was a medley of social, moral and religious reflections interspersed with casual thoughts about persons, events and art. *Fors* means alternatively fate, force or chance, bearing the *Clavis,* club, key or nail, *i.e.,* power, patience and law. It was a desultory exposition of the Ruskinian ideal of life, manners and society, full of wit, play, invective and sermons on things in general. It was continued with intervals down to 1884, and contained ninety-six letters or pamphlets, partly illustrated, which originally filled eight volumes and are now reduced to four.

The early years of his Oxford professorship were occupied by severe labour, sundry travels, attacks of illness and another cruel disappointment in love. In spite of this, he lectured, founded a museum of art, to which he gave pictures and drawings and £5,000; he sought to form at Oxford a school of drawing; he started a model shop for the sale of tea, and model lodgings in Marylebone for poor tenants. At Oxford he set his pupils to work on making roads to improve the country. He now founded "St. George's Guild," himself contributing £7,000, the object of which was to form a model industrial and social movement, to buy lands, mills and factories, and to start a model industry on co-operative or Socialist lines. In connection with this was a museum for the study of art and science at Sheffield. Ruskin himself endowed the museum with works of art and money; a full account of it has been given in E. T. Cook's *Studies in Ruskin* (1890), which contains the particulars of his university lectures and of his economic and social experiments. It is unnecessary to follow out the history of these somewhat unpromising attempts. None of them came to much good, except the Sheffield museum, which is an established success, and is now transferred to the town.

In *Fors,* which was continued month by month for seven years, Ruskin poured out his thoughts, proposals and rebukes on society and persons with inexhaustible fancy, wit, eloquence and freedom, until he was attacked with a violent brain malady in the spring of 1878 (*aet.* 59); and, although he recovered in a few months sufficiently to do some occasional work, he resigned his professorship early in 1879. The next three years he spent at Brantwood, mainly in retirement, and unhappy in finding nearly all his labours interrupted by his broken health. In 1880 he was able to travel in northern France, and began the *Bible of Amiens,* finished in 1885; and he issued occasional numbers of *Fors,* the last of which appeared at Christmas 1884. In 1882 he had another serious illness, with inflammation of the brain; but he recovered sufficiently to travel to his old haunts in France and Italy—his last visit. And in the following year he was re-elected professor at Oxford and resumed his lectures, but increasing brain excitement, and indignation at the establishment of a laboratory to which vivisection was admitted, led him to resign his Oxford career, and he retired in 1884 to Brantwood, which he never left. He now suffered from frequent attacks of brain irritation and exhaustion, and had many causes of sorrow and disappointment. His lectures were published at intervals from 1870 to 1885 in *Aratra Pentelici, The Eagle's Nest, Love's Meinie, Ariadne Florentina, Val d'Arno, Proserpina, Deucalion, The Laws of Fesolé, The Bible of Amiens, The Art of England* and *The Pleasures of England,* together with a series of pamphlets, letters, articles, notes, catalogues and circulars.

In the retirement of Brantwood he began his last work, *Praeterita,* a desultory autobiography with personal anecdotes and reminiscences. He was again attacked with the same mental malady in 1885, which henceforth left him fit only for occasional letters and notes. In 1887 it was found that he had exhausted (spent, and given away) the whole of the fortune he had received from his father, amounting, it is said, to something like £200,000; and he was dependent on the vast and increasing sale of his works, which produced an average income of £4,000 a year, and at times on the sale of his pictures and realizable property. In 1872 a correspondent had remonstrated with him in vain as to taking "usury," *i.e.*, interest on capital lent to others for use. In 1874 Ruskin himself had begun to doubt its lawfulness. In 1876 he fiercely assailed the practice of receiving interest or rent, and he henceforth lived on his capital, which he gave freely to friends, dependants, public societies, charitable and social objects. The course of his opinions and his practice is fully explained in successive letters in *Fors*.

Until 1889 Ruskin continued to write chapters of *Praeterita*, which was designed to record memories of his life down to the year 1875 (*aet.* 56). It was, in fact, only completed in regular series down to 1858 (*aet.* 39), with a separate chapter as to Mrs. Arthur Severn, and a fragment called *Dilecta*, containing letters and early recollections of friends, especially of Turner. These two books were published between 1885 and 1889; and except for occasional letters, notes and prefaces, they form the last writings of the author of *Modern Painters*. His literary career thus extends over fifty years. But he has left nothing more graceful, naïve and pathetic than his early memories in *Praeterita*—a book which must rank with the most famous "Confessions" in any literature. The last ten years of his life were passed in complete retirement at Brantwood, in the loving care of the Severn family, to whom the estate was transferred, with occasional visits from friends, but with no sustained work beyond correspondence, the revision of his works, and a few notes and prefatory words to the books of others. He wished to withdraw his early art writings from circulation, but the public demand made this practically impossible.

The close of his life was one of entire peace and honour. He was loaded with the degrees of the universities and membership in numerous societies and academies. "Ruskin Societies" were founded in many parts of the kingdom. His works were translated and read abroad, and had an enormous circulation in Great Britain and the United States. He died suddenly after only two days' illness on Jan. 20, 1900. He was buried in Coniston churchyard by his own express wish, the family refusing the offer of a grave in Westminster Abbey.

Ruskin's life and writings have been the subject of many works composed by friends, disciples and admirers. The principal is the *Life*, by W. G. Collingwood, his friend, neighbour and secretary (2 vols., 1893; 2nd ed., 1900). His pupil, E. T. Cook, published his *Studies in Ruskin* in 1890, with full details of his career as professor, and a *Life of Ruskin* in 1911. J. A. Hobson, in *John Ruskin, Social Reformer* (2nd ed., 1899), has elaborately discussed his social and economic teaching, and claims him as "the greatest social teacher of his age." An analysis of his works has been written by Mrs. Meynell (1900). His art theories have been discussed by Professor Charles Waldstein of Cambridge in *The Work of John Ruskin* (1894), by Robert de la Sizeranne in *Ruskin et la religion de la beauté* (1897), and by Professor H. J. Brunhes of Fribourg in *Ruskin et la Bible* (1901). The monumental "library edition" of Ruskin's works (39 vols., 1903–12), prepared by E. T. Cook, with A. Wedderburn, is the greatest of all the tributes of literary admiration. *See* also *Centenary Addresses* (1919) ed. J. H. Whitehouse; J. R. Morley, *John Ruskin and Social Ethics* (1917); A. Williams-Ellis, *The Tragedy of John Ruskin* (1928). (F. Har.)

RUSSELL (Family). The great English Whig house of the Russells, earls and dukes of Bedford, rose under the favour of Henry VIII. Obsequious genealogists have traced their lineage from "Hugh de Rozel," *alias* "Hugh Bertrand, lord of le Rozel," a companion of the Conqueror, padding their fiction with the pedigree of certain Russells who are found holding Kingston Russell in Dorset as early as the reign of King John. But the first undoubted ancestor of the Bedford line is Henry Russell, a Weymouth merchant, returned as a burgess for that borough in four parliaments between 1425 and 1442. He may well have been the son of Stephen Russell, another Weymouth merchant, whose name is just before his in the list of those men of substance in Dorsetshire who, in 1434, under the act of parliament, were to be sworn not to maintain breakers of the peace. Stephen Russell, having served the office of bailiff of Weymouth, was returned as burgess to the parliament of 1395, and one William Russell was returned for King's Melcombe in 1340. Both Stephen and Henry were in the wine trade with Bordeaux, and in 1427 Henry

Russell was deputy to the chief butler of England for the port of Melcombe. In 1442 a pardon under the privy seal significantly describes Henry Russell of Weymouth, merchant, as *alias* Henry Gascoign, gentleman, and it is therefore probable that the ducal house of Bedford springs from a family of Gascon wine-merchants settled in a port of Dorsetshire, a county remarkable for the number of such French settlers.

Henry Russell of Weymouth made a firm footing upon the land by his marriage with Elizabeth Hering, one of the two daughters and co-heirs of John Hering of Chaldon Hering, a Dorsetshire squire of old family, heir of the Winterbournes of Winterbourne Clenston and of the Cernes of Draycot Cerne. John Russell, eldest son of this match, born before 1432, and returned to parliament for Weymouth in 1450, had his seat at Berwick in Swyre, he and his son and heir, James Russell, being buried in the parish church of Swyre.

John Russell, son and heir of James, on the accession of Henry VIII. advanced rapidly serving the crown as soldier and as diplomatic agent. He fought well at Thérouanne, saw the Field of the Cloth of Gold and the French disaster at Pavia, lost an eye by an arrow at Morlaix. In 1523 he was knight-marshal of the king's household. In 1526 he married a rich widow, Anne, daughter and co-heir of Sir Guy Sapcotes by the co-heir of Sir Guy Wolston, a match which brought to the Russells the Buckinghamshire estate of Chenies, in whose chapel many generations of them lie buried. His peerage as Lord Russell of Chenies dated from 1539, and in the same year he had the Garter. Having held many high offices, he was named by Henry VIII. as one of his executors. At the crowning of Edward VI. he was lord high steward, and after his defeat of the western rebels was raised, in 1550, to the earldom of Bedford. Queen Mary, like her brother, made him lord privy seal. He died in London in 1555, leaving to his son a vast estate of church lands. In the west he had the abbey lands of Tavistock, which give a marquess's title to his descendants. In Cambridgeshire he had the abbatial estate of Thorney, in Bedfordshire the Cistercian house of Woburn, now the chief seat of the Russells. In London he had Covent Garden with the "Long Acre."

He left an only son, Francis, second earl of Bedford, K.G. (*c.* 1527–1585), who, being concerned in Wyatt's plot, escaped to the Continent and joined those exiles at Geneva whose religious sympathies he shared. He returned in 1557, and was employed by Queen Mary before her death. Under Queen Elizabeth he governed Berwick, and was lord-lieutenant of the northern counties.

Three of his four sons died before him, the third, killed in a border fray, being father of Edward, third earl of Bedford, who died without issue in 1627. The fourth son, William, created Lord Russell of Thornhaugh in 1603, was a soldier who fought fiercely before Zutphen beside his friend Sir Philip Sidney, whom he succeeded as governor of Flushing, and was from 1594 to 1597 lord-deputy of Ireland. He died in 1613, leaving an only son, Francis, who in 1627 succeeded his cousin as fourth earl of Bedford. This earl built the square of Covent Garden, and headed the "undertakers" who began the scheme for draining the great Fen Level. He opposed the king in the House of Lords, but might have played a part as mediator between the sovereign and the popular party who accepted his leadership had he not died suddenly of the smallpox in 1641 on the day of the king's assent to the bill for Strafford's attainder. William, the eldest surviving son, succeeded as fifth earl, Edward, the youngest son, being father of Edward Russell (1653–1727), admiral of the fleet, who, having held the chief command in the victory of La Hogue, was created in 1697 earl of Orford. The fifth earl of Bedford, after fighting for the parliament at Edgehill and for the king at Newbury, surrendered to Essex and occupied himself with completing the drainage of the Bedford Level. He carried St. Edward's staff at the crowning of Charles II., but quitted political life after the execution of his son, Lord Russell, in 1683. In 1694 he was created duke of Bedford and marquess of Tavistock, titles to which his grandson, Wriothesley Russell, succeeded in 1700.

The "patriot" Lord Russell had added to the family estates by his marriage with Rachel, daughter and co-heir of Thomas Wriothesley, the fourth earl of Southampton, from whom she finally inherited the earl's property in Bloomsbury, with Southampton house, afterwards called Bedford house. Her son, the second duke of Bedford, married the daughter of a rich citizen, John Howland of Streatham, a match strangely commemorated by the barony of Howland of Streatham, created for the bridegroom's grandfather, the first duke, in 1695. The third duke, another WRIOTHESLEY RUSSELL (1708–1732), died without issue, his brother JOHN (1710–1771) succeeding him. This fourth duke, opposing Sir Robert Walpole, became, by reason of his rank and territorial importance, a recognized leader of the Whigs. In the duke of Devonshire's administration he was lord-lieutenant of Ireland, and he served as lord high constable at the coronation in 1760.

His son Francis, styled marquess of Tavistock, was killed in 1767 by a fall in the hunting field, and Lord Tavistock's son FRANCIS (1765–1802) became the fifth duke. This was the peer whom Burke, smarting from a criticism of his own pension, assailed as "the Leviathan of the creatures of the crown," enriched by grants that "outraged economy and even staggered credibility." He pulled down Bedford house, built by Inigo Jones, Russell square and Tavistock square rising on the site of its gardens and courts. Dying unmarried, he was succeeded by his brother JOHN, the sixth duke (1766–1839), whose third son was the statesman created, in 1861, Earl Russell of Kingston Russell, better known as Lord John Russell. Lord Odo Russell, a nephew of "Lord John," and ambassador at Berlin from 1871 to his death in 1884, was created Lord Ampthill in 1881. HERBRAND ARTHUR RUSSELL (1858–1940), the eleventh duke and fifteenth earl, succeeded an elder brother in 1893.   (O. B.)

RUSSELL, BERTRAND ARTHUR WILLIAM RUSSELL, 3RD EARL, F.R.S. (1872–   ), was born May 18, 1872.
His grandfathers were Lord John Russell (afterwards Earl Russell) and the second Lord Stanley of Alderley. At the age of three he was left an orphan. His father had wished him to be brought up as an agnostic; to avoid this he was made a ward of Court, and brought up by his grandmother at Pembroke lodge, in Richmond park. Instead of being sent to school he was taught by governesses and tutors, and thus acquired his perfect knowledge of French and German. In October 1890 he went into residence, as a very shy undergraduate, at Trinity college, Cambridge. After being a very high Wrangler and obtaining a First Class with distinction in philosophy he was elected a fellow of his college in the autumn of 1895. But he had already left Cambridge in the summer of 1894 and for some months was attaché at the British embassy at Paris. In Dec. 1894 he married Miss Alys Pearsall Smith. After spending some months in Berlin studying social democracy (*German Social Democracy*, 1896), they went to live near Haslemere, where he devoted his time to the study of philosophy. In 1900 he visited the Mathematical Congress at Paris with his friend Alfred Whitehead (afterwards professor of philosophy at Harvard). He was impressed with the ability of the Italian mathematician Peano and his pupils, and immediately studied Peano's works. In 1903 he wrote his first important book, *The Principles of Mathematics* and with Whitehead proceeded to develop and extend the mathematical logic of Peano and Frege. The first volume of their joint book, *Principia Mathematica*, was published in 1910. During all this period Russell lived very simply and worked very hard. From time to time, as when Joseph Chamberlain started his tariff reform campaign, he abandoned philosophy for politics. In 1910 he was appointed lecturer at his old college. After World War I broke out he took an active part in the No Conscription fellowship. He was fined £100 as the author of a leaflet criticizing a sentence of two years on a conscientious objector. His library was seized to pay the fine; it was bought in by a friend; but many valuable books were lost. His college deprived him of his lectureship. He was offered a post at Harvard university, but was refused a passport. He intended to give a course of lectures (afterwards published in America as *Political Ideals*, 1918) but was prevented by the military authorities. In 1918 he was sen-

tenced to six months' imprisonment for a pacifistic article he had written in the *Tribunal*. His excellent *Introduction to Mathematical Philosophy* (1919) was written in prison. His *Analysis of Mind* (1921) was the outcome of some lectures he gave in London which were organized by a few friends who got up a subscription for the purpose. The *Practice and Theory of Bolshevism* (1920) was written after a short visit to Russia.

In the autumn of 1920 he went to China to lecture on philosophy at the Peiping university. On his return in Sept. 1921, having been divorced by his first wife, he married Miss Dora Black and they lived for six years in a small house in Chelsea during the winter months. He earned a livelihood by lecturing, journalism and writing popular books such as *The A.B.C. of Atoms* (1923), *The A.B.C. of Relativity* (1925) and *On Education* (1926). The summers, spent near Lands End, were devoted to serious work such as the new Introduction to the second edition of the *Principia Mathematica; The Analysis of Matter* (1927); *The Outline of Philosophy* (1928); *Mysticism and Logic* (1929); *Marriage and Morals* (1929). In 1927 he and his wife started a school for young children, which they operated until 1932. He succeeded to the earldom in 1931. Russell was divorced by his second wife in 1935 and the following year married Patricia Helen Spence. In 1938 he went to the United States and during the next years taught at many of the country's leading universities. In 1940 he was involved in legal action when his right to teach philosophy at the College of the City of New York was questioned because of his views on morality. When his appointment to the college faculty was cancelled, Russell accepted a five-year contract as a lecturer for the Barnes foundation, Merion, Pa., but cancellation of this contract was announced in Jan. 1943 by Albert C. Barnes.

In 1944 Russell returned to England and was elected to a fellowship of Trinity college for the second time. He gave the first series of the Reith lectures, 1948–49, on the topic "Authority and the Individual." In Nov. 1950 he was awarded the Nobel prize for literature.

Russell's later writings include *The Conquest of Happiness* (1930); *The Scientific Outlook* (1931); *Education and the Social Order* (1932); *Freedom and Organisation, 1814–1914* (1934); *Power: A New Social Analysis* (1938); *An Inquiry into Meaning and Truth* (1940); *A History of Western Philosophy* (1946); *Authority and the Individual* (1949); *Unpopular Essays* (1950).
(C. P. SA.; X.)

Philosophy.—What is fundamental in Russell's philosophy is his logic; his views on metaphysics and ethics, on the nature and relations of matter and mind have changed profoundly in the course of his life, but these changes have all proceeded from successively deeper applications of his logical method. He, therefore, preferred to classify his philosophy not as a species of Idealism or Realism but as "Logical Atomism," since what distinguishes the whole of his work is his use of logical analysis as a method and his belief that by it we can arrive at ultimate "atomic facts" logically independent both of one another and of being known.

His first great achievement was to free logical analysis from the domination of ordinary grammar, and to realize that the grammatical form of a sentence often fails to reflect the logical form of its meaning. In his *Principles of Mathematics* (1903) he insisted that relations could not be reduced to qualities of their terms, and that relational facts were not of the subject-predicate form, but he still thought that any descriptive phrase which could be made the subject of a sentence must stand for a term which had being, even if like "the round square" it were self-contradictory. But in his article "On Denoting" (*Mind*, 1905), and in subsequent writings, he put forward his "Theory of Descriptions" which is perhaps the most important as well as the least controvertible of his discoveries. According to this theory "the present king of France" is not a name for a nonexistent entity but an "incomplete symbol" which only has meaning in connection with a context. The meaning of such a statement as that "the present king of France is bald" is firstly that there is someone who is at present both king of France and bald, and secondly that there are not at present two kings of France; and when such statements are analyzed in this way the need to believe in entities such as "the present king of France" (which are said by some philosophers to have "being" but not "existence") is altogether removed. Similarly when it is said that "unicorns are not real," this does not have the same kind of meaning as the grammatically similar statement that "lions are not versatile." For this last statement means that certain animals, namely lions, lack a certain characteristic, namely versatility; but "unicorns are not real" does not mean that certain animals, namely unicorns, lack the characteristic of reality. For there are no such animals and no such characteristic; what is meant is simply that there are no animals which have one horn but otherwise resemble horses. The destructive effect of this logical analysis on many philosophical theories of existence and reality is important.

Russell applied similar methods to propositions, classes and numbers and argued that each of these categories consists of what he called "logical constructions," and not of genuine entities. In saying, e.g., that classes are logical constructions, he did not mean that they are entities constructed by the human mind, but that when we express facts by sentences which have for subject such a phrase as "the class of men," the true analysis of the fact does not correspond to the grammatical analysis of the sentence. When, for instance, we say "the class of men includes the class of criminals," the fact we assert is really about the characteristics of being a man and being a criminal and not about any such entities as classes at all. This notion of a logical construction was much employed by Russell in his work in mathematical logic, and he also used it extensively in the philosophy of matter and mind, and even adopted as a fundamental principle that constructions (in his special sense of the word) are to be substituted for inferred entities wherever possible.

By applying this method he was led to a view of the world on which the ultimate constituents of mind and matter are of the same type, the difference between minds and bodies lying in their structure and not in the elements of which they are composed. A man's mind is composed of sensations and images, which are identified by Russell with physical events in his brain, the difference between physics and psychology lying not in the events they study but in the kind of laws about those events which they seek to establish, physics being concerned with structure and psychology with quality. This theory was worked out in connection with physics in *The Analysis of Matter* (1927).

In the theory of knowledge Russell's earlier rationalism was considerably modified in a pragmatist or behaviourist direction, and in the *Analysis of Mind* (1921) he rejected consciousness as a fundamental characteristic of mind and adopted a form of "neutral monism" about perception, which he combines with representationism in regard to memory and judgment.

Mathematics.—Russell maintained that mathematics and formal logic are one and that the whole of pure mathematics can be rigidly deduced from a small number of logical axioms. He argued this in outline in the *Principles of Mathematics* (1903) which was followed by a detailed demonstration of his thesis in *Principia Mathematica* (1911-13) written in collaboration with A. N. Whitehead. In this colossal work the deduction is actually performed according to the strictest symbolic principles and carried so far as to include all the essential parts of the theory of aggregates and real numbers. Besides this the great advances made by Russell in the analysis of logical concepts allowed the deductions to be carried not only much further forwards, but also much further backwards towards first principles. Above all he succeeded in solving the notorious Paradoxes of the Theory of Aggregates by means of the "Theory of Types." As part of this theory, it was, however, found necessary to introduce an "Axiom of Reducibility" which has never obtained general acceptance, so that Russell's work cannot be regarded as a final solution of the problem, although in the second edition of *Principia Mathematica* (1925) he found an ingenious way of overcoming the difficulties in the particular case of mathematical induction.

See also MATHEMATICS, FOUNDATIONS OF. (F. P. R.)

RUSSELL, GEORGE WILLIAM (1867-1935), Irish writer and painter, known as Æ, was born at Lurgan, Co. Armagh, April 10, 1867. Educated at Rathmines School, Dublin, he en-

tered an accountant's office, but in 1897 joined the Irish Agricultural Organisation Society, and became an organiser of agricultural societies. From 1904 to 1923 he was editor of *The Irish Homestead,* the organ of the agricultural co-operative movement. In 1923 he became editor of *The Irish Statesman.*

Russell's publications include *Homeward: Songs by the Way* (1894); *The Earth Breath* (1897); *Literary Ideals in Ireland* (1899), a collection of essays written in collaboration with W. B. Yeats, W. Larminie and John Eglinton; *Ideals in Ireland* (1901), another book of collaborative essays; *The Nuts of Knowledge* (1903), a selection of lyrics. In 1904 appeared two books of verse, the *Divine Vision* and *New Poems,* an anthology of verses by young Irish poets; and a collection of mystical tales, *The Mask of Apollo.* Other books of verse include *By Still Waters* (1906), *Collected Poems* (1913), and *Gods of War* (1915). *The Hero in Man* (1909) and *The Renewal of Youth* (1911) were imaginative musings, as was *Imaginations and Reveries* (1915). In 1906 appeared *Some Irish Essays,* and in 1907 *Deirdre,* a three-act play. *Co-operation and Nationality* and *The Rural Community,* published in 1912 and 1913 respectively, were pamphlets embodying co-operative ideals, which are further developed in his *The National Being, Thoughts on an Irish Polity* (1916). *The Candle of Vision,* an attempt to discover the element of truth in the mystical imagination, appeared in 1918. This was followed by *The Interpreters* (1920), a symposium in the Platonic fashion. A volume of poems, *Voices of the Stones,* appeared in 1925. He received the honorary degree of Litt.D. from Dublin University in July, 1929.

RUSSELL, JOHN (1745-1806), British portrait painter in pastel, was born at Guildford, Surrey, on Mar. 29, 1745. At an early age he entered the studio of Francis Cotes, R.A. In 1767 he set up his own studio, and in 1770 obtained the gold medal at the Royal Academy for figure drawing. He exhibited regularly at the Academy from its beginning down to 1805. Although he painted in oil, in water-colours and in miniature, it was by his works in crayon that he became famous. He made his own crayons, blending them on his pictures by a peculiar method termed "sweetening," which consisted in rubbing in the colours with his fingers and softening them in outline until they melted one into another. His works have survived in perfect condition. He died at Hull on April 20, 1806.

His "Child with Cherries" is in the Louvre. The J. Horace Harding Collection, New York City, contains his "Mr. and Mrs. Aigar and Children." In *The Elements of Painting in Crayon* he described his methods. *See* George C. Williamson, *John Russell* (1894).

RUSSELL, JOHN RUSSELL, 1ST EARL (1792-1878), British statesman, third son of the 6th duke of Bedford, by Georgiana Elizabeth Byng, second daughter of the 4th Viscount Torrington, was born in London on Aug. 18, 1792. After an early education desultory on account of his weak health he spent three years at Edinburgh university, living in the house of Professor John Playfair. On leaving the university, he travelled in Portugal and Spain, and in 1813 he was returned for the ducal borough of Tavistock. In domestic questions he cast in his lot with those who opposed the repressive measures of 1817, and protested that the causes of the discontent at home should be removed by remedial legislation. Failing of success, he resigned his seat for Tavistock in March 1817, and meditated permanent withdrawal from public life, but was dissuaded from this step by the arguments of his friends. In the parliament of 1818-20 he again represented the family borough in Devon, and in May 1819 began his long advocacy of parliamentary reform by moving for an inquiry into the corruption which prevailed in the Cornish constituency of Grampound. During the first parliament (1820-26) of George IV. he sat for the county of Huntingdon, and secured in 1821 the disfranchisement of Grampound, but the seats were not transferred to the constituency which he desired. Lord John Russell paid the penalty for his advocacy of Catholic emancipation with the loss in 1826 of his seat for Huntingdon county, but he found a shelter in the Irish borough of Bandon Bridge. He led the attack against the Test Acts by carrying in February 1828 with a majority of forty-four a motion for a committee to inquire into their operations, and after this decisive victory they were repealed (May 9, 1828). He warmly supported the Wellington ministry when it realized that the king's government could only be carried on by the passing of a Catholic Relief Act (April 1829). For the greater part of the short-lived parliament of 1830-31 he served his old constituency of Tavistock, having been beaten in a contest for Bedford county at the general election by one vote; and when Lord Grey's Reform ministry was formed, in November 1830, Lord John Russell became paymaster-general, without a seat in the cabinet. This exclusion was the more remarkable in that he was chosen (1st of March 1831) to explain the provisions of the Reform Bill, to which the cabinet had given formal sanction. The Whig ministry was soon defeated, but, after the general election, returned with increased strength. The Reform Bill became law (June 7, 1832), and Lord John stood justly in the mind of the people as its champion. After the passing of the Reform Bill he sat for South Devon, and was paymaster-general in the ministries of Grey and Melbourne.

Russell had visited Ireland in the autumn of 1833, and had come back with a keen conviction of the necessity for readjusting the revenues of the Irish church. To these views he gave expression in a debate on the Irish Tithe Bill (May 1834), whereupon Stanley, with the remark that "Johnny has upset the coach," resigned his place. The latter was abruptly, if not rudely, dismissed (Nov. 1834) by William IV. when the leadership of the House of Commons became vacant and Russell was proposed as leader. In Lord Melbourne's new administration of 1835 Russell became home secretary and leader of the House of Commons. In the third Melbourne administration (1839) Russell was secretary of State for the colonies and under him New Zealand became a British colony and England claimed the whole of Australia. A fine literary sense and a great love of all forms of religious and civil liberty fed his keen interest in culture for the people and resulted in a Government grant of £30,000 for education and the institution of official inspectors for schools. With Brougham he founded in 1835 the Society for Promoting the Diffusion of Useful Knowledge. At the general election of 1841 the Whigs sustained a crushing defeat; the return of Russell for the City of London was one of their few triumphs. In 1845 he committed himself for the first time to the repeal of the Corn Laws.

On Peel's resignation (1846) the task of forming an administration was entrusted to Russell, and he remained at the head of affairs from July 1846 to Feb. 1852, but, though his ministry at once set to work to adapt the Free Trade policy to all branches of British commerce, his tenure of office was not marked by any great legislative enactments. His celebrated Durham letter (Nov. 4, 1850) on the threatened assumption of ecclesiastical titles by the Roman Catholic bishops weakened the attachment of the "Peelites" and alienated his Irish supporters. The impotence of their opponents, rather than the strength of their friends, kept the Whig ministry in power, and, although beaten by a majority of nearly two to one on Locke King's County Franchise Bill in Feb. 1851, it could not divest itself of office. Lord Palmerston's unauthorized recognition of the French coup d'état was followed by his dismissal from the post of foreign secretary (Dec. 1851), but he had his revenge in the ejectment of his old colleagues in Feb. 1852. During Lord Aberdeen's administration Lord John Russell led the Lower House, at first as foreign secretary (to Feb. 21, 1853), then without portfolio, and lastly as president of the council (June 1854). In 1854 he brought in a Reform Bill, but in consequence of the war with Russia the bill was allowed to drop. His popularity was diminished by this failure, and although he resigned in Jan. 1855, on Mr. Roebuck's motion for an inquiry into the conduct of the war in the Crimea, he did not regain his old position in the country. At the Vienna conference (1855) Lord John Russell was England's representative, and immediately on his return he became secretary of the colonies (May 1855), but the errors in his negotiations at the Austrian capital followed him and forced him to retire in July of the same year.

For some years after this he was the "stormy petrel" of politics. He was the chief instrument in defeating Lord Palmerston

in 1857. He led the attack on the Tory Reform Bill of 1859. A reconciliation was then effected between the rival Whig leaders, and Russell become foreign secretary in Palmerston's ministry (1860) and accepted an earldom (July 1861). During the American War Russell exercised a powerful influence in restraining his country from taking sides in the contest, and he warmly sympathized with the efforts for the unification of Italy, but he was not equally successful in preventing the spoliation of Denmark. On Palmerston's death (Oct. 1865) Russell was once more summoned to form a cabinet, but the defeat of his ministry in the following June on the Reform Bill which they had introduced was followed by his retirement from public life. His leisure hours were spent after this event in the preparation of numberless letters and speeches, and in the composition of his *Recollections and Suggestions* (1875). He died at Pembroke Lodge, Richmond Park, on May 28, 1878.

Earl Russell was twice married—first in 1835, to Adelaide, daughter of Mr. Thomas Lister, and widow of Thomas, second Lord Ribblesdale, and secondly, in 1841, to Lady Frances Ann Maria, daughter of Gilbert, second earl of Minto.

Russell's tales, tragedies and essays (including *The Nun of Arrouca*, 1822, and *Essays and Sketches by a Gentleman who has left his Lodgings*, 1820) are forgotten, but his historical works, *Life of William Lord Russell* (1819), *Memoirs of the Affairs of Europe* (1824-29, 2 vols.), *Correspondence of John, 4th Duke of Bedford* (1842-46, 3 vols.), *Memorials and Correspondence of C. J. Fox* (1853-57, 4 vols.) and *Life and Times of C. J. Fox* (1859-66, 3 vols.) are among the chief authorities on Whig politics. He also edited the *Memoirs, Journal and Correspondence of Thomas Moore* (1853-56, 8 vols.).

The chief biography is that by Sir Spencer Walpole (1891, 2 vols.). The volume by Stuart J. Reid (1895, "Prime Ministers of Queen Victoria" Series) should also be consulted.

See also J. Russell, *The Latter Correspondence of Lord John Russell, 1840-1878* (1925, 2 vols.).

RUSSELL, THOMAS (1762-1788), English poet, was born at Beaminster, early in 1762. He was educated at Winchester under Joseph Warton, and at New college, Oxford. He died at Bristol on July 31, 1788, and was buried at Powerstock, Dorset. In 1789 was published a thin volume, containing his *Sonnets and Miscellaneous Poems,* now a very rare book. It contained 23 sonnets, of regular form, and a few paraphrases and original lyrics. The sonnets are the best, and by right of these Russell takes his place as a precursor of the romantic school. His sonnet, "Suppos'd to be written at Lemnos," is his masterpiece.

RUSSELL, LORD WILLIAM (1639-1683), English politician, was the third son of the 1st duke of Bedford and was born on Sept. 29, 1639. About 1654 he was sent to Cambridge with his elder brother Francis (on whose death in 1678 he obtained the courtesy title of Lord Russell). On leaving the university, the two brothers travelled abroad, visiting Lyons, Geneva, Augsburg, and Paris, but returned to Woburn in December 1659. At the Restoration he was elected for the family borough of Tavistock. He appears to have indulged in the follies of court life and intrigue; for both in 1663 and 1664 he was engaged in duels, in the latter of which he was wounded. In 1669 he married Rachel (1636-1723), second daughter of the 4th earl of Southampton, and widow of Lord Vaughan, thus becoming connected with Shaftesbury, who had married Southampton's niece. With his wife Russell always lived on terms of the greatest affection and confidence. She corresponded with Tillotson and other distinguished men, and a collection of her admirable letters was published in 1773.

On the formation of the "country party," in opposition to the Cabal and Charles's French-Catholic plots, Russell began to take an active part in affairs. He then joined Cavendish, Birch, Hampden, Powell, Lyttleton and others in vehement antagonism to the court. With a passionate hatred and distrust of the Catholics, and an intense love of political liberty, he united the desire for ease to Protestant Dissenters. He inveighed (Jan. 22, 1673) against the stop of the exchequer, the attack on the Smyrna fleet, the corruption of courtiers with French money, and "the ill ministers about the king"; he supported the proceedings against the duke of Buckingham, and against Danby (see LEEDS, THOMAS OSBORNE); and in March 1678 he seconded the address praying the king to declare war against France. The country party hated Danby and James more than they hated Louis. The French king formed a temporary alliance with Russell, Hollis and the opposition leaders, on terms. Russell in particular entered into close communication with the marquis de Ruvigny (Lady Russell's maternal uncle), who came over with money for distribution among members of parliament. By the testimony of Barillon, however, it is clear that Russell refused any part in the intended corruption.

By the wild alarms which culminated in the Popish Terror Russell was apparently deeply affected. He threw himself into the party which looked to Monmouth as the representative of Protestant interests, a grave political blunder, though he afterwards was in confidential communication with Orange. On Nov. 4, 1678, he moved an address to the king to remove the duke of York from his person and councils. At the dissolution of the pensionary parliament, he was, in the new elections, returned for Bedfordshire. Danby was at once overthrown, and in April 1679 Russell was one of the new privy council formed by Charles on the advice of Temple. Only six days after this we find him moving for a committee to draw up a bill to secure religion and property in case of a popish successor. He does not, however, appear to have taken part in the exclusion debates at this time. In June, on the occasion of the Covenanters' rising in Scotland, he attacked Lauderdale personally in full council.

In January 1680 Russell, along with Cavendish, Capell, Powell, Essex and Lyttleton, tendered his resignation to the king, which was received by Charles "with all my heart." On June 16, he accompanied Shaftesbury, when the latter indicted James at Westminster as a popish recusant; and on Oct. 26 he took the extreme step of moving "how to suppress popery and prevent a popish successor"; on Nov. 2, now at the height of his influence, he seconded the motion for exclusion in its most emphatic shape, and on the 19th carried the bill to the House of Lords for their concurrence. The limitation scheme he opposed, on the ground that monarchy under the conditions expressed in it would be an absurdity. On December 18 he moved to refuse supplies until the king passed the Exclusion Bill. The prince of Orange having come over at this time, there was a tendency on the part of the opposition leaders to accept his endeavours to secure a compromise on the exclusion question. Russell, however, refused to give way a hair's-breadth.

On March 26, 1681, in the parliament held at Oxford, Russell again seconded the Exclusion Bill. Upon the dissolution he retired into privacy at his country seat of Stratton in Hampshire. In the wild schemes of Shaftesbury after the election of Tory sheriffs for London in 1682 he had no share; upon the violation of the charters, however, in 1683, he began seriously to consider as to the best means of resisting the government, and on one occasion attended a meeting at which treason, or what might be construed as treason, was talked. Monmouth, Essex, Hampden, Sidney and Howard of Escrick were the principal of those who met to consult. On the breaking out of the Rye House Plot, of which neither he, Essex, nor Sidney had the slightest knowledge, he was accused by informers of promising his assistance to raise an insurrection and compass the death of the king. Refusing to attempt to escape, he was brought before the council, when his attendance at the meeting referred to was charged against him. He was sent on June 26, 1683, to the Tower. Monmouth offered to appear to take his trial, if thereby he could help Russell, and Essex refused to abscond for fear of injuring his friend's chance of escape. Before a committee of the council Russell, on June 28, acknowledged his presence at the meeting, but denied all knowledge of the proposed insurrection. He reserved his defence, however, until his trial. He would probably have saved his life but for the perjury of Lord Howard, who expressly declared that Russell had urged the entering into communications with Argyll in Scotland. Howard's perjury is clear from other witnesses, but the evidence was accepted. Russell spoke with spirit and dignity in his own defence, and, in especial, vehemently denied that he had ever been party to a design so wicked and so foolish as that of the murder of the king or of rebellion. The legality of the trial, in so far as the jurors were not properly qualified and the law of treason was shamefully strained, was denied in the act of 1 William & Mary which annulled the attainder. Hallam maintains that the only overt act of treason proved against Russell was his concurrence in the project of a rising at Taunton, which he denied, and which, Ramsay being the only witness, was not sufficient to warrant a conviction.

Russell was sentenced to die. Many attempts were made to save his life. The old earl of Bedford offered £50,000 or £100,000, and Monmouth, Legge, Lady Ranelagh, and Rochester added their intercessions. Russell himself, in petitions to Charles and James, offered to live abroad if his life were spared, and never again to meddle in the affairs of England. He refused, however, to yield to the influence of Burnet and Tillotson, who endeavoured to make him grant the unlawfulness of resistance, although it is more than probable that compliance in this would have saved his life. He drew up, with Burnet's assistance, a paper containing his apology, and he wrote to the king a letter, to be delivered after his death, in which he asked Charles's pardon for any wrong he had done him. A suggestion of escape from Lord Cavendish he refused. He behaved with his usual quiet cheerfulness during his stay in the Tower, and spent the last morning in devotion with Burnet. He was executed at Lincoln's Inn Fields on July 21, 1683.

A true and moderate summing-up of his character will be found in his *Life*, by Lord John Russell (1820).

RUSSELL, SIR WILLIAM HOWARD (1821-1907), English war correspondent, was born at Lilyvale, near Tallaght, Co. Dublin, on March 28, 1821, being one of the Russells of Limerick, whose settlement in Ireland dates from the time of Richard II. He entered Trinity college in 1838. Three years later he was thrown very much on his own resources, but a relative, R. W. Russell, who had been sent to Ireland by *The Times*, deputed him to report the Irish elections at Longford, and his success definitely turned his attention to journalism. Coming to London in 1842, he went to Cambridge, but left before taking a degree. He was special correspondent for *The Times* in Ireland in 1845, in Denmark in the war of 1849-50, and in the Crimean War. His letters written from the Crimea were published in book form as *The War, 1855-56*. The exposure made by Russell of the mismanagement in the Crimea contributed to the fall of the Aberdeen ministry. Russell also served as correspondent in India in 1858, in America in 1861-3, in the Seven Weeks' War of 1866, in the Franco-German war of 1870; and he was with Wolseley in South Africa in 1879 and in Egypt in 1882. In 1860 he founded the *Army and Navy Gazette*. Russell was knighted in May 1895, and was the recipient of numerous war medals and various foreign orders. He died on Feb. 11, 1907.

His works include: *My Diary in India in 1858-59* (1860); *My Diary, North and South, during the Civil War in America, 1862* (1862); *My Diary during the Last Great War* (the Franco-Prussian War of 1870) (1873); *Hesperothen*, a description of a tour in the United States and Canada (1882); and *The Great War with Russia* (1895).

RUSSELL OF KILLOWEN, CHARLES RUSSELL, BARON (1832-1900), lord chief justice of England, was born at Newry, county Down, on Nov. 10, 1832, the son of Arthur Russell. The family was Roman Catholic. Educated first at Belfast, afterwards in Newry, and finally at St. Vincent's College, Castleknock, Dublin, in 1849, he was articled to a firm of solicitors in Newry. In 1854 he was admitted, and began to practise his profession. In the legal proceedings arising out of Catholic and Orange disturbances young Russell distinguished himself in the cause of his co-religionists. After practising for two years, he determined to seek a wider field for his abilities. He went to London in 1856, and entered Lincoln's Inn. In 1858 he married Ellen, daughter of Dr. Mulhulland of Belfast, and in 1859 he was called to the bar, and joined the Northern Circuit. He had to rely upon himself. But the equipment was sufficient. A well-built frame; a strong, striking face, with broad forehead, keen grey eyes, and a full and sensitive mouth; a voice which, though not musical, was rich, and responded well to strong emotions, whether of indignation, or scorn, or pity; an amazing power of concentrating thought; an intellectual grasp, promptly seizing the real points of the most entangled case, and rejecting all that was secondary, or petty, or irrelevant; a faculty of lucid and forcible expression, which, without literary ornateness or grace of style, could on fit occasions rise to impassioned eloquence—all these things Russell had. But beyond and above all these was his immense personality, an embodiment of energetic will which riveted attention, dominated his audience, and bore down opposition. In his early years Russell's practice was mostly at the Passage Court at Liverpool, and he published a book on its procedure in 1862.

In 1872 Russell "took silk," and from that date for some time he divided the best leading work of the circuit with Holker, Herschell and Pope. Holker became solicitor general in 1874, Herschell in 1880, and about that time Pope left the circuit. Russell's success as a Q.C. during this period of his career was prodigious. He excelled in the conduct alike of commercial cases and of those involving, as he used to say, "a human interest," although undoubtedly it was the latter which more attracted him. He was seen to the least advantage in cases which involved technical or scientific detail. If his advocacy suffered a defeat, however, it was never an inglorious defeat. Those who were on the Northern Circuit at the time could not easily forget the case of *Dixon* v. *Plimsoll*—a libel action brought by a Liverpool shipowner against Plimsoll—in which Holker won a notable victory for the defendant; or *Nuttall* v. *Wilde*, a breach of promise action, in which Pope led brilliantly for the successful plaintiff, and Russell's speech for the defence was one of the finest in point of passion and pathos that was ever heard upon the Northern Circuit.

In 1880 Russell was returned to parliament as an independent Liberal member for Dundalk. From that time forward until 1894, he sat in the House of Commons: for Dundalk until 1885, and afterwards for South Hackney. During the whole of this epoch, in home affairs, Irish business almost monopolized the political stage; and Russell was Irish to the core. From 1880 to 1886, as a private member, and as the attorney-general in Gladstone's administrations of 1886 and 1892, he worked in and out of parliament for the Liberal policy in regard to the treatment of Ireland as few men except Russell could or would work. His position throughout was clear and consistent. Before 1886 on several occasions he supported the action of the Irish Nationalist party. He opposed coercion, voted for compensation for disturbance, advocated the release of political prisoners and voted for the Maamtrasna inquiry. But he never became a member of the Irish Home Rule or of the Parnellite party; he was elected at Dundalk as an independent Liberal, and such he remained. When, as attorney-general in the Gladstone administration, he warmly advocated the establishment of a subordinate parliament in Ireland, he did so because he sought the amelioration and not the destruction of Ireland's relations with the rest of the kingdom.

Russell rapidly became in London what he was already in Lancashire, a favourite leader in *nisi prius* actions. The list of *causes célèbres* in the period 1880–94 is really a record of Russell's cases, and, for a great part, of Russell's victories. The best known of the exceptions was the libel action *Belt* v. *Lawes* in 1882, which, after a trial lasting more than 40 days, resulted in a verdict for the plaintiff, for whom Sir Hardinge Giffard (afterwards Lord Chancellor Halsbury) appeared as leading counsel. The triumph of his client in the Colin Campbell divorce suit in 1886 afforded perhaps the most brilliant instance of Russell's forensic capacity in private litigation. More important, however, as well as more famous, than any of his successes in the ordinary courts of law during this period were his performances as an advocate in two public transactions of mark in British history. The first of these in point of date was the Parnell Commission of 1888–90, in which Sir Charles Russell appeared as leading counsel for Parnell. In April 1889, after 63 sittings of the commission, in the course of which 340 witnesses had been examined, Sir Charles Russell, who had already destroyed the chief personal charge against Parnell by a brilliant cross-examination, in which he proved it to have been based upon a forgery, made his great opening speech for the defence. It lasted several days, and concluded on April 12. This speech, besides its merit as a wonderful piece of advocacy, possesses permanent value as an historical survey

of the Irish question during the last century, from the point of view of an Irish Liberal. The second was the Bering Sea Arbitration, held in Paris in 1893. Russell, then attorney-general, with Sir Richard Webster (afterwards Lord Alverstone, L.C.J.), was the leading counsel for Great Britain. Russell maintained the proposition, which he again handled in his Saratoga address to the American Bar Association in 1896, that "international law is neither more nor less than what civilized nations have agreed shall be binding on one another as international law." The award was, substantially, in favour of Great Britain.

In 1894, on the death of Lord Bowen, Russell accepted the position of a lord of appeal. A month later he was appointed lord chief justice of England in succession to Lord Coleridge. Brief as was his tenure of the office, he proved himself well worthy of it. He was dignified without pompousness, quick without being irritable, and masterful without tyranny. In 1896 Lord Russell (Pollock and Hawkins being on this occasion his colleagues on the bench) presided at the trial at bar of the leaders of the Jameson Raid. Russell's conduct of this trial, in the midst of much popular excitement, was by itself sufficient to establish his reputation as a great judge. One other event at least in his career while lord chief justice deserves a record, namely, his share in the Venezuela Arbitration in 1899. Lord Herschell, a British representative on the Commission, died somewhat suddenly in America before the beginning of the proceedings, and Russell took his place.

Russell contributed to the reform of the law by his advocacy of improvement in the system of legal education, and in promoting measures against corruption and secret commissions, though the bills he introduced did not become law. He died on Aug. 10, 1900. Few English lawyers have ever excited the admiration abroad that Lord Russell did, both on the Continent of Europe and in America.

See R. B. O'Brien, *Life of Lord Russell of Killowen* (1909).

RUSSELL SAGE FOUNDATION, an institution established by Mrs. Russell Sage in memory of her husband. The initial endowment was $10,000,000, to which $5,000,000 was added by her will. It was incorporated by an act of the legislature of New York in April 1907, "for the improvement of social and living conditions in the United States of America." The charter further states: "It shall be within the purposes of said corporation to use any means to that end which from time to time shall seem expedient to its members or trustees, including research, publication, education, the establishment and maintenance of charitable or benevolent activities, agencies and institutions, and the aid of any such activities, agencies or institutions already established." The income only may be spent.

The management of the foundation is vested in a board of twelve trustees, which is self-perpetuating. The staff of the foundation study social conditions and methods of social work, interpret the findings, make the information available by publications, conferences and other means of public education, and seek in various ways to stimulate action for social betterment. Departments exist for dealing with charity organization, industrial relations, consumer credit, family welfare, social statistics, etc. The foundation does not relieve individual need and it avoids duplicating the work of existing agencies. In 1922 the foundation organized the Committee on Regional Plan of New York and its environs, providing the funds and office space and some staff assistance in preparing a plan for the future development of the New York region, an undertaking which took about seven years to complete.

RUSSIA is the general name given to those territories of the Eurasian continent which are comprised within the Union of Soviet Socialist Republics (U.S.S.R.) or, more shortly, the Soviet Union. The 11 republics within the union in 1939 were the Russian Soviet Federated Socialist Republic and the Ukrainian, Byelorussian, Azerbaijanian, Georgian, Armenian, Turkmen, Uzbek, Tadzhik, Kazakh and Kirghiz Soviet Socialist Republics. The first three of the above, together with the former Transcaucasian Soviet Federated Republic, were original members of the U.S.S.R.; the Uzbek and Turkmen republics were added in 1924, the Tadzhik republic in 1929; the Kazakh and Kirghiz republics were admitted in 1936, when also the Transcaucasian S.F.S.R. was split into the Azerbaijanian, Georgian and Armenian Soviet Socialist Republics. To the above 11 republics were later added the Karelo-Finnish Soviet Socialist Republic (admitted to the union by the supreme soviet in March 1940) and the Moldavian, Latvian, Lithuanian and Estonian Soviet Socialist Republics (all admitted in Aug. 1940), thus bringing the total number of the republics of the union to 16. (See Table I.)

TABLE I.—*Union of Soviet Socialist Republics after World War II*

Republic	Capital	Area (sq.mi.)	Population (1946 est.)
Russian S.F.S.R.	Moscow	6,533,600	109,905,030
Ukrainian S.S.R.	Kiiv (Kiev)	222,700	40,548,310
Byelorussian S.S.R.	Minsk	80,200	9,400,000
Uzbek S.S.R.	Tashkent	157,300	6,282,450
Kazakh S.S.R.	Alma-Ata	1,063,200	6,145,940
Georgian S.S.R.	Tbilisi (Tiflis)	29,400	3,577,290
Azerbaijanian S.S.R.	Baku	33,100	3,209,730
Lithuanian S.S.R.	Vilnius (Wilno)	25,200	3,032,000
Moldavian S.S.R.	Chisinau (Kishinev)	13,000	2,400,000
Latvian S.S.R.	Riga	24,900	1,765,320
Tadzhik S.S.R.	Stalinabad (Diushambe)	55,100	1,485,090
Kirghiz S.S.R.	Frunze	76,000	1,459,300
Armenian S.S.R.	Erivan	11,500	1,281,600
Turkmen S.S.R.	Ashkhabad	187,200	1,253,990
Estonian S.S.R.	Tallinn (Reval)	17,400	968,680
Karelo-Finnish S.S.R.	Petrozavodsk	68,900	500,000
Total		8,598,700	193,214,730

Source: Areas are taken from the *Bolshaya Sovietskaya Entsiklopedia: Soyuz Sovietskikh Sotsialisticheskikh Respublik* (Moscow, 1948). All the areas are post-World War II (that is, including territorial aggrandizements in the west and east). Population figures are from *Geographical Review* (April 1946).

By 1952 the Russian S.F.S.R. included 47 regions or *oblasti*; 12 autonomous republics (Bashkir, Buriat Mongol, Chuvash, Daghestan, Kabardinian, Komi, Marii, Mordovian, North Ossetian, Tatar, Udmurt and Yakut); 6 autonomous regions (Adigei, Cherkess, Birobidzhan, Khakass, Gorno-Altai and Tuva); 6 territories or *krai* (Altai, Khabarovsk, Krasnodar, Krasnoyarsk, Primorsky and Stavropol); and 10 small national districts or *okrughi* (Aghinsk, Chukot, Evenki, Khanty-Mansi, Komi-Permyak, Koryak, Nenets, Taimyr, Ust-Orda and Yamalo-Nenets).

The four autonomous republics outside the R.S.F.S.R. are Kara-Kalpak, Abkhazia, Adzharia and Nakhichevan, of which the first is part of Uzbekia, the last is part of Azerbaijan and the remaining two are parts of Georgia.

The three autonomous regions outside the R.S.F.S.R. are the Nagorno-Karabakh (part of Azerbaijan), the South Ossetian (part of Georgia) and Gorno-Badakhshan (Tadzhikistan).

The name "Russia" (*Rossiya*) comes from the Slavonic *Rus*, possibly derived from *Ruotsi* (a Finnish name for the Swedes), which seems to be a corruption of the Swedish *rothsmenn*, "rowers" or "seafarers."

The total area of the Soviet Union in Sept. 1939 was 8,173,666 sq.mi. This, because certain non-Russian lands had been lost after the revolution of 1917, was smaller than the area of the former Russian empire. Between 1939 and 1945 the Soviet Union annexed the following territories: Estonia, Latvia, Lithuania, the northeastern part of East Prussia (renamed the Kaliningrad region and part of the R.S.F.S.R.), the formerly Polish western Ukraine and western Byelorussia, the formerly Finnish Karelian isthmus and Pechenga region (Petsamo), the formerly Rumanian Bessarabia and northern Bukovina, the formerly Czechoslovakian Sub-Carpathian Ruthenia, the formerly Japanese Karafuto (southern Sakhalin) and Kurile (Kurilskyie) Islands and the formerly "independent" republic of Tannu Tuva. (See Table II.) The total area of the Soviet Union including these new territories was 8,598,700 sq.mi.

The Soviet Union extends over the eastern part of Europe and the northern and central parts of Asia, stretching north and south from Cape Chelyuskin (77° 43′ N. lat.) to Kushka on the Afghan frontier (35° 08′ N. lat.). East and west the country extends approximately from a point on the Gulf of Danzig near 19° 38′ E. long. to Cape Dezhnev (East cape) on the Chukchi (Chukotski) peninsula near 169° 40′ W. long. Occupying one-seventh of the land surface of the world the Soviet Union is exceeded in area only by the British Commonwealth, but while the latter is scattered, the Soviet Union forms a single geographical and political unit.

The northern frontier of the U.S.S.R. extends along the shores of the Arctic ocean, from the Rybachy peninsula on the Murman coast in the west to the Bering strait in the east. The western frontier runs from the shores of the Barents sea down to the shores of the Black sea. On the west the Soviet Union borders on Norway, Finland, Poland, Czechoslovakia, Hungary and Rumania. Since June 1940, when Rumania had to cede Bessarabia to the Soviet Union, the southern frontier runs from the Kiliya mouth of the Danube and proceeds along the shores of the Black sea. Thence it extends eastward along the southern limit of the Armenian highland to Nakhichevan, along the Araks river, south along the Talysh range and across the Caspian sea. The frontier from the eastern shore of the Caspian sea follows approximately along the crest of the Kopet-dagh range and east onto the Pamir highland. Thence it extends along the Tien-shan, the Altai, the Tannu Ola and the Trans-Baikal mountains. From the Manchurian frontier the boundary runs along the Argun river to its confluence with the Shilka and thence along the Amur river to its junction with the Ussuri, where it turns south to follow the Ussuri river to Lake Khanka whence it runs to the shore of the Sea of Japan. On the south the Soviet Union borders on Turkey, Iran, Afghanistan, China (Sinkiang), Mongolia, China again (Manchuria) and Korea. The eastern frontier is entirely a sea border.

More than two-thirds of the Soviet borders are maritime. The northern frontier on the Arctic ocean is maritime in its entire length, but apart from Murmansk, which is washed by the warm Atlantic drift, this frontier is frozen for nearly ten months of the year. The northern sea route, providing a direct connection with the far east, was considerably developed as part of the third five-year plan, and by means of icebreakers the route is kept open during much of the winter, but only with great difficulty. On the eastern coast Vladivostok, the southernmost Soviet port, also requires icebreakers to keep it open during the winter, while the Sea of Okhotsk is frequently closed to shipping by dense fogs and floating ice. The Black sea ports are ice-free but the only outlet from this sea is through the narrow straits of the Bosporus. Leningrad is the most important port on the Baltic sea and is kept open by icebreakers for much of the winter.

The island possessions of the Soviet Union are numerous, but the majority are in the Arctic ocean and are of little use. The Aleutian archipelago and Alaska were sold to the United States in 1867. The Kurile Islands,

TABLE II.—*Areas Annexed by the U.S.S.R., 1939–45*

Area	Date and form of incorporation	Area (sq.mi.)	Population (1939 est.)
In Europe:			
Estonia	Decision of the supreme soviet of the U.S.S.R. { Aug. 6, 1940	18,357	1,134,000
Latvia	{ Aug. 5, 1940	25,395	1,994,000
Lithuania (including both Klaipeda and Vilnius)	{ Aug. 3, 1940	25,173	3,032,000
From Finland (Karelia and Petsamo-Pechenga)	Soviet-Finnish treaty of March 12, 1940; Finnish-Allied armistice of Sept. 19, 1944	17,598	54,000*
From Poland (excluding the Vilnius area)	German-Soviet agreement of Sept. 28, 1939; Polish-Soviet treaty of Aug. 16, 1945	64,824	10,315,000
From Rumania (Bessarabia and northern Bukovina)	Soviet ultimatum of June 28, 1940; Paris peace treaty of Feb. 10, 1947	19,459	3,700,000
From Czechoslovakia (Sub-Carpathian Ruthenia)	Soviet-Czechoslovakian treaty of June 29, 1945	4,873	798,000
From Germany (northeast part of East Prussia)	Decision of the Potsdam conference, Aug. 2, 1945	4,247	1,075,000
Total (Europe)		179,926	22,102,000
In Asia:			
From Japan: Karafuto (southern Sakhalin)	Yalta agreement of Feb. 11, 1945	13,935	415,000
Kurile Islands	Japanese surrender of Sept. 2, 1945	3,994	4,000
Tannu Tuva People's Republic	Decision of the supreme soviet of the U.S.S.R., Oct. 10, 1944	64,000	70,000
Total (Asia)		81,929	489,000
Grand total		261,855	22,591,000

*About 423,800 Karelians left in 1944 to resettle in Finland.

ceded to Japan in 1875, were recovered by the Soviet Union in Sept. 1945. The Baltic islands, which were given up after the revolution of 1917, were recovered from Finland. The Komandorskyie Islands off Kamchatka, the Shantar Islands near the Pacific coast and, from Aug. 1945, the whole of the island of Sakhalin are Soviet possessions. The chief Soviet islands off the arctic coast are Kolguev Island, Novaya Zemlya and Vaigach Island, the Severnaya Zemlya (formerly Nicholas II Land) north of the Taimyr peninsula, the New Siberian Islands (north of Laptev sound) and Wrangel Island. Franz Josef Land is Soviet territory, but Spitsbergen and Bear Island were recognized in 1920 as being under Norwegian sovereignty. (I. Gy.; X.)

PHYSIOGRAPHY

In very general terms Russia as considered in this article may be described as a wide amphitheatre open to the arctic but bordered to the south, to the west and to the east by high mountain regions. The great inner lowland can be divided into four regions; viz., European Russia, the plain of western Siberia, the Turkistan basin and the central Siberian plateau. The first two of these regions, both plains of low relief, are similar in most of their geographical features but are separated by the Ural mountains; the former drains mainly southward to the Black and Caspian seas, the latter to the Arctic ocean. The Turkistan basin is essentially the drainage area of the Sea of Aral; between it and the Siberian plain to the north is a belt of low hills. The central Siberian region, between the Yenisei and the Lena, is an ancient, eroded plateau, much dissected by river valleys but otherwise gently undulating.

The mountain border, with its vast and lofty chains and deep valleys, is in marked contrast to the lands it encircles. Eastern Siberia has a most irregular surface. It is a complex of great blocks and rifts, of plateaus separated from one another by steep scarps as they rise in tiers toward ridges crowned with snowclad peaks. Side by side are features obviously of great age and others, such as the gorges and rapids of many of its rivers, indicative of recent changes. To the southwest rise the Altai ranges, alpine in their height and character and forming a barrier difficult to surmount between the Siberian lowland and Mongolia. Still farther south and west, across the Dzungarian Gate, are the loftier and abrupt ridges of the Tien-shan and the Trans Alai, between Turkistan and the Tarim basin. From the Pamirs the frontier with Iran is marked by lesser ranges, not much easier to cross in spite of their lower altitude. Between the Caspian and the Black seas lies the great wall of the Caucasus, with a dozen peaks higher than any in the Alps and only a few usable passes. The low Yaila mountains of the Crimea are a reminder that this vast mountain system was once continuous into the Balkans.

The great contrast of relief between the plains and the mountain border reflects a similar contrast in structure. Underlying the plains is a relatively undisturbed floor or platform of Archaean and Palaeozoic rocks. Though usually buried beneath later deposits, this platform is exposed in Karelia, the Ukraine (where it contains the iron ores of Krivoi Rog and the manganese ores of Nikopol), the Timan mountains and the central Siberian plateau. Its surface is no longer horizontal throughout the whole area of course, for it suffered warping and some dislocation as a result of Huronian and Caledonian earth movements. Still more important deformations resulted from the pressures set up by Hercynian folding. The Valdai plateau, the Volga heights, the Urals, the Altai, the Sayan mountains and the ranges east of Lake Baikal were all formed during this period. The more recent Tertiary folding, which produced such striking effects in mountain building further south, affected little more than the highland borders of Russia.

Much more important in the geological history of the country than these violent crustal movements were the alternating advances and retreats of the surrounding seas over the land. In the wide shallow basins so formed were laid down, age after age, the sedimentary rocks which now cover most of the platform. In general these surface rocks are of decreasing age from northwest to southeast, and they are still almost as horizontally disposed as when they were first laid down.

Tertiary movements in the border country had very marked effects along its whole extent from Kamchatka to the Carpathians. Old ranges, such as the Altai, were further uplifted and new ones, such as the Caucasus, formed. Under the pressures then experienced the whole of eastern and much of central Siberia was shattered by faults and rifts (e.g., the great Baikal rift).

Though the major surface features are thus seen to be of ancient origin, the minor ones are nearly everywhere the results of more recent happenings. Morainic deposits form low hills on the northern lowlands, while many of the flattest areas of the plains are covered by deposits laid down on the floors of postglacial lakes. The separation of the Aralo-Caspian depression from the Arctic has been completed only since Oligocene times. The shrinkage of the inland seas exposed wide expanses covered by Quaternary and recent deposits.

Glaciation.—Russia was profoundly affected by glaciation during the Pleistocene ice age, and the details of its topography over large areas resulted from the events of that period. These are best known and most marked in European Russia. There the ice sheets, issuing mainly from the Scandinavian highlands but also in part from areas near the northern end of the Urals, moved southeastward. Their maximum extension may be regarded as having been marked, roughly, by a line from Nijni-Novgorod (now Gorki) to Smolensk, though two great lobes pushed forward far into the Dnieper and the Don basins.

Over Finland and extending into Karelia the main effects of the glaciation were erosive, removing surface soils and leaving bare rock surfaces with many lakes in irregular, shallow hollows. Long, low, sandy ridges (eskers) cross this region, and near its margin is a great end moraine marking a pause in the final retreat of the ice. Beyond this region to the limit of the ice sheets is the accumulation belt now covered mainly with boulder clays as far as the main end moraine. There was here much interference with river drainage, and many wide valleys were eroded along the edges of the ice sheet. The two great headwaters of the Northern Dvina occupy such a channel. The most important of the moraines, marked by a belt of hilly country northeast and southwest from the Valdai hills, forms the chief watershed of European Russia. The main highways to the west follow the crests of moraines through the marshy country toward Poland. The boulder clays extend southward where the ice lobes penetrated the Dnieper and Don basins.

Beyond the edge of the last ice sheet is the zone of deposition. There much of the surface is covered by loess or *limon*, a fine-grained deposit of material carried by winds from the drying surfaces left after the retreat of the ice sheets. The northwestern belt of the zone has many sandy tracts of outwash left by streams flowing from the surface of the melting ice.

Little is known in detail of the glaciation of Asiatic Russia. Local glaciers were certainly developed (some still exist) in the mountain borders and in the far northeast. In the central Siberian plateau no drift deposits have been found. The northern portions of the lowland were certainly ice-covered, but drift deposits were largely removed or covered by the marine transgression which followed the ice age in the far north. Asiatic loess deposits follow the foothills of the central ranges but are not certainly related to the glaciation. (T. Her.)

STRUCTURAL DIVISIONS

For a more detailed description of structure the following division of the land is convenient:

1. Northward-draining areas: (a) northern European Russia; (b) the Urals; (c) the Ob lowland; and (d) the Yenisei-Lena plateau.

2. Southward-draining areas: (a) southern European Russia; (b) the Moscow basin; and (c) the Aralo-Caspian basin.

3. The mountain border: (a) eastern Siberia; (b) the central Asiatic ranges; and (c) the Caucasus.

Northward-Draining Areas.—*Northern European Russia.*—This division possesses large areas of unfolded Palaeozoic rocks lying on an ancient (Archaean) floor of granites, gneisses and syenites which emerges on the west in Finland, the Kola peninsula and Scandinavia. Along the line from the White sea to the Gulf of Finland (via lakes Ladoga and Onega) the ancient floor is covered by Palaeozoic rocks, Devonian, Carboniferous and Permian succeeding one another eastward toward the Northern Dvina. The Upper Permian beds have yielded Glossopteris and other plants characteristic of "Gondwanaland" and animal remains like those of the corresponding formation in South Africa. Beyond that river the lower levels are mainly alluvials but there are glacial Pleistocene deposits between the river lines. The basin of the Pechora is divided from the land farther west by a minor fold belt bringing up Devonian and some crystalline schist along the line of the Timan hills that may be traceable as a branching of the mid-Urals northwestward to Cape Kanin. The whole region has a very low relief and is consequently unprotected from arctic cold. Apart from the Timan hills this region is below the 600-ft. contour. Its lakes are discussed in the article on Europe (q.v.). Its chief rivers are the Pechora (1,000 mi.), the Mezen (500 mi.) and the Northern Dvina (400 mi.). The upper waters of the Pechora and the Northern Dvina interlace with those of the feeders of the Kama, a tributary of the Volga. As a consequence of the low relief the Pechora is navigable for 770 mi., the Mezen for 450 mi. and the Northern Dvina for 330 mi., while the Vychegda, a large tributary of this river, is navigable for 500 mi. The Onega river has rapids.

The Urals.—In the Urals the Palaeozoic strata are folded on the west of a longitudinal axis which exhibits crystalline rocks and is faulted on a large scale. The Devonian rocks in this area are of marine origin. Its greatest heights are chiefly in the regions of folded Palaeozoic rocks and the folds die away into the Russian platform westward in small parallel chains known as Parma. Though there is much copper in the Permian rocks on the west the main metalliferous veins of the area are in the faulted zone of crystalline rocks to the east. The greatest height reached in the Urals is 5,545 ft. in the northern Urals (at Tel Pos-iz or Muraï-Chakhl). The passes are often low, that on the way from Molotov (Perm) to Sverdlovsk being only 1,245 ft. above sea level. The range is continued to the Arctic coast, Vaigach Island and Novaya Zemlya. (*See* further NOVAYA ZEMLYA; URAL MOUNTAINS.) On the south the Urals finger out in a plateau region dissected by feeders of the Ural and a few feeders of the Volga. The Ural river drains the southern Ural mountains, turns west and then south to the Caspian sea, which it reaches after a course of 1,477 mi.

The Ob Lowland.—Eastward the Urals fall rapidly down to the Ob basin, which is one of the largest areas of unbroken lowland on the earth. The floor material is almost entirely alluvial with a little Tertiary here and there. The river rises in the westward prolongations of the Sayan mountains and is 2,260 mi. long, but its very large tributary the Irtysh comes from the Dzungarian Gate and adds enormously to the area of the basin, which is bounded southward by the Turgai and the hills of Semipalatinsk. The Tobol, another large tributary, flows to the Ob from the north of the Turgai. It is generally accepted that under the alluvial floor lies a continuation of the platform of north European Russia let down through the dislocation of the eastern border of the Urals. The lowland extends without an appreciable break to the Yenisei, and only at some places near that river do the older rocks help to form the surface.

The Yenisei Area.—East of the Yenisei the character of the land changes abruptly: a sharp edge rises rapidly to more than 600 ft. and in one place to about 3,300 ft. above sea level, and east of this edge is a great dissected plateau of ancient rocks. Archaean rocks with granites, etc., are exposed near the Yenisei and away to the northeast, but there are larger areas of Cambrian and Silurian rocks and these are covered over a vast stretch of country by Permo-Carboniferous rocks. The plateau extends eastward to the Lena along the valley of which is found evidence of an invasion of the sea in Cretaceous times. The plateau is an ancient block to which E. Suess gave the name of Angara land. Large areas on this plateau rise somewhat above the 1,600-ft. contour, and the diversities of surface are largely the result of river dissection. There is evidence in the Taimyr peninsula of a fold

axis with a general direction from west-southwest to east-northeast but apparently no heights reaching above the 1,500-ft. contour.

The Yenisei is the collecting stream beneath the western edge of this old block, and it rises in the Sayan mountains receiving nearly all its tributaries from the eastern side. Of these the Upper Tunguska or Angara comes from Lake Baikal, the Middle or Stony Tunguska and the Lower Tunguska from the block itself. The river is 2,800 mi. long.

Southward-Draining Areas.—These regions are those which drain to the enclosed seas, the Black sea, Caspian sea, Aral sea and Lake Balkash. Considered structurally they reveal on the west a succession of very slight undulations, anticlines and synclines with axes northwest to southeast from the vicinity of the Carpathians to the borders of the arctic region; on the east the subdued features result mainly from the great virgations of the Tien-shan range.

Southern European Russia.—From the Sea of Azov westnorthwestward to beyond Kiev stretches an anticlinal zone in which appear granites and gneisses, some of which are thought to be Archaean. The Dnieper from Kiev to Dnepropetrovsk (Ekaterinoslav) follows the northern border of this zone of hard rock through which the river cuts its way below the latter town. Next follows a syncline in which early Tertiary deposits are widespread, whereas farther south they only cap parts of the old rocks. The syncline is named after the river Donets which follows its axis. Toward the Sea of Azov Palaeozoic rocks are brought to the surface and the land stands somewhat higher. In this region is the Donets coal field, the coal belonging to upper Carboniferous strata as in western Europe. The next zone is the central anticline which is parallel with the two structural zones described and which is thought to die away toward the Caspian. The axis of this anticline is marked to some extent by the Don river where it flows southeastward below Pavlovsk while, much further northwest, the course of the Southern Dvina is clearly related to it. Along it in the Don region the Cretaceous deposits, capped interfluvially by early Tertiary here and there, form the most important outcrops, but on the northwest there is a great area of Devonian (*v. inf.*).

The Moscow Basin.—Northeast of this anticlinal zone is the immense "Moscow basin," floored mainly by Palaeozoic rocks mainly still horizontal, with some Triassic deposits; but there are patches of Jurassic and Cretaceous strata as, for example, around Moscow and in the great bend of the Volga and also farther north from Kostroma to Syktyvkar (Ust-Sysolsk) on a tributary of the Vychegda. There was an intrusion of the sea in Jurassic times which became much more extensive in the Cretaceous period; no upper Cretaceous is known, however, in northern Russia. Around the Moscow basin in the southwest and west the Lower Carboniferous system (with poor coal at Tula, etc.), outcrops in a great curved belt from the region of Tula almost to the White sea. Beyond this belt northwestward is the area of Devonian rocks toward Latvia and Estonia and across to the White sea. They rest unconformably on Silurian rocks which outcrop along the southern shore of the Gulf of Finland and of Lake Ladoga. The Devonian rocks are partly lacustrine (old red sandstone) and partly marine in origin, and the two types are often interstratified: a basal red sandstone is covered by a dolomitic limestone which in turn has a sandstone over it. The Timan hills (*see* above) on the northeast may be said to be an upfold bordering the Moscow basin.

The main axis of the basin is parallel to the course of the Volga above Gorki (Nijni-Novgorod), continued northwestward by the Mologa; *i.e.*, rivers running broadly parallel to the sections of the Dnieper, Donets and Don already noted. Permian rocks outcrop over large areas on the north. The dips of the strata are small, and anticlines and synclines there are really slight undulations which might be followed right across Russia from the Dniester to the Timan hills, always with lines roughly northwest to southeast (or west-northwest to east-southeast) well marked in geology and drainage, though not much indicated in relief save that there is a marked low line of the Dnieper valley above Dnepropetrovsk, the Pripet marshes or Rokitno swamps and the upper Bug, where it continues the line of the Dnieper and Pripet into Poland. This belt of lowlands is of special importance because of the great marshes just named; they form the historic barrier between Russia and peninsular Europe.

The Aralo-Caspian Basin.—Turning now to the east one notes the virgations of the Tien-shan, orographically very subdued in the Aralo-Caspian lowland. One stretches northwestward parallel to and north of the Syr-darya and apparently re-emerges from the lowland in one of the southern branches of the Urals, which are at first a plateau and rise to any considerable height only north of lat. 52° N. Another virgation stretches parallel to the first, this time just north-northeast of the Amu-darya or Oxus river, and is continued into the Mangishlak peninsula that projects into the northeast of the Caspian sea. Farther south still are the hills of the Iranian border reaching the Caspian sea between the Gulf of Kara Bogaz and the town of Krasnovodsk and continued on the west of that sea by the mighty Caucasus. In the Aralo-Caspian lowland the rocks of these virgations are masked by a Quaternary covering with Tertiary deposits south of the lower Oxus and on the Ust Urt plateau between Aral and Caspian. Between the Aralo-Caspian-Balkash area and the Arctic drainage area of the Ob and its feeders is the higher land of Karaganda, related structurally to the Altai and floored by Palaeozoic and igneous rocks. West of this the land continues to be somewhat above the level of the lowlands on either side and is floored by Tertiary deposits, but the higher land narrows down in the Turgai region, which according to general opinion until Oligocene times had a sea communication directly to the Arctic ocean on the north. The two great rivers of the region are the Amu-darya (Oxus), 1,500 mi. long, and the Syr-darya, 1,500 mi. long, both reaching the Aral sea.

Structural geologists have spread familiarity with the idea of a great sea called Tethys reaching in Mesozoic and Eocene times from the present Mediterranean area eastward through the region occupied later by the young folded ranges of Asia Minor, Armenia, the Hindu Kush and Himalaya, etc., to Malaya. Without venturing into details of advances and retreats of the sea, it may be said that the uprise of the fold mountains of Asia Minor, Armenia, the Elburz range and the Hindu Kush left the part of that sea to the north of this more or less isolated as the brackish Pontic lake, losing its former connection via the Turgai low line with the Arctic ocean probably in Oligocene times and becoming much modified by the sinking of the southern parts of the Black and Caspian seas, which are both deep. Apart from these two depressions the land shelves easily from land to sea around the northern parts of the Black and Caspian seas, while the shallow Aral sea is a shrunken part of the Pontic lake, now cut off by lowland from the northeast of the Caspian sea. Balkash is a fresh-water lake on higher land farther east—now at any rate without outlet, whatever may have been the condition of things in the past.

We thus have a series of enclosed seas and lakes of which Balkash, the Aral and the Caspian have no outlet, and the two latter are salt, while the Sea of Azov communicates with the Black sea through a break in the mountain line between the Caucasus and the Yalta mountains of the Crimea, and the Black sea has communicated with the Aegean and the Mediterranean since the sinking of the former. The rivers Dnieper (1,400 mi.) and Don (1,100 mi.) both flow southeastward for a considerable distance and then turn sharply southwestward to the Black sea, probably as a consequence of the recent dominance of flow toward the Aegean following the sinking of the latter. Before that sinking the Danube may for a time have made its way eastward across the lowland to the Caspian area via the curious Manych depression. The Volga (2,300 mi.) is the longest river of Europe, flowing broadly east-southeast parallel to the axis of the Moscow basin and meeting the Kama as it turns south below Kazan. On its course southward it has a sharp eastward loop with Kuybyshev (Samara) at the head opposite the southward bend of the Don. Below Stalingrad the Volga bends southeast, thus continuing the previous line of the Don, and so reaches its delta on the Caspian sea. The great rivers of the Aral basin, the Amu-darya and the Syr-darya, have already been mentioned.

The Mountain Border.—The fold ranges which border the Russian lands on the south were uplifted at various periods, those in the western sections being generally younger than those to the east, though in Kamchatka they are of approximately the same age as the Caucasus. In central Asia they show a characteristic arrangement: range after range runs, more or less, east and west, each successive one tending to extend farther west than that to the north of it. As these are discussed in the general article on Asia (*q.v.*) they will be mentioned only briefly here.

Eastern Siberia.—Beyond the Angara block eastward stands an important series of mountain ranges. The Stanovoi mountains and the Kolymski (Kolyma) mountains are more or less parallel to the coasts of the Sea of Okhotsk; but the former are also roughly parallel to the edge of the Angara block on the other side of the Lena and, 100 mi. or so north of Okhotsk, are linked not only with the Kolymski mountains to the east but with the Verkhoyansk mountains which go westward and northward, keeping more or less parallel to the edge of the Angara block with the Lena between them and it. Like the other great rivers mentioned above, this one is formed of a pair, the upper Lena and the Vitim. The length of the Lena is estimated at 2,860 mi. The Verkhoyansk and the Kolymski mountains thus form a great semicircle of mountains apparently determined in the west by the Angara block and in the east by the depression of the Sea of Okhotsk. Within this semicircle other ranges are disposed in more or less parallel curves.

The Tas Kistabit mountains come next to the western Kolymski. The Cherski mountains are a longer range parallel to the whole curve of the Verkhoyansk-Kolymski line and stretching from the east of the Yana river to the west of the Omolon river. Within this again is a smaller range. The Cherski mountains are named after a Russian explorer who died in this region in 1892. The river Indigirka traverses them by a winding gorge often less than a mile wide, and the tributaries of this river also make gorges in the range, in which an altitude of 10,217 ft. is reached in the Gora Chen. These high mountains are apparently almost without glaciers because of the aridity of the region. A geological traverse going northward between the Kolyma and the Indigirka shows an east-west axis of igneous material alternating with Permian and Triassic rocks.

East of the mouth of the Omolon river a great axis of crystalline rock, flanked on both sides by Permian, runs parallel to the coast as far as Cape Dezhnev (East cape). The Kolymski mountains curving from the south come northeastward as the Anadyr mountains and end in the Chukchi (Chukotski) peninsula. This latter high line is flanked on the southeast by the Penzhina and Anadyr valleys, forming an almost continuous low line from the Sea of Okhotsk across the base of the Kamchatka peninsula to the Gulf of Anadyr north of the Bering sea. (*See* KAMCHATKA.) Northward from Cape Lopatka along the east coast as far north as the curve of the Aleutian Islands is a belt of volcanoes, part of the "girdle of fire" of the Pacific. The central longitudinal range of the peninsula is continued northeastward, south of the Anadyr valley to Cape Navarin. There thus seem to be three great structural lines abutting upon the neighbourhood of the Bering strait and the northern coast of the Bering sea.

The main curve of the Stanovoi mountains, supposedly fold mountains, continues westward on the south and apparently approaches the Yablonoi mountains, really the eastern edge of the Malkan horst, at an angle. To the west-northwest lies the Vitim plateau. To the southeast is found a type of topography analogous to that of Kamchatka and extreme northeast Asia. There are successive ranges more or less parallel to the coast, imbricating to some extent and separated by lines of lowland fairly parallel with their axes. The Liao, Sungari and lower Amur valleys form a continuous lowland from the Gulf of Pohai (Pechili) to the strait between the mainland and Sakhalin. The Ussuri and lower Amur valleys form a low line from Vladivostok northward with the high range of the Sikhote Alin on its eastern flank. The Sea of Japan and the Gulf of Tatary, narrow waters separating Sakhalin from the mainland, form still another low line with the Sikhote Alin on the west and the high axis of Sakhalin, Hokkaido, etc., on the east. As in the case of Kamchatka, so also here the high axis is met on the east at a considerable angle by the Kurile Islands, of volcanic type; and south of this junction (that is, in Japan) the high axis is volcanic, just as eastern Kamchatka is volcanic south of its link with the Aleutians. The great river of this eastern region is the Amur, which has a very large tributary, the Sungari, on the south; the Amur's course is governed mainly by the mountain lines of the region; its length is 2,900 mi.

The Central Asiatic Ranges.—These mountains, extending from the Pamirs to the river Aldan, are sometimes grouped together as the Sayanid system. They are mainly the products of folding and faulting in Caledonian times but have in many places been further uplifted by later movements. Thus the Sayan ranges after heavy denudation appear to have been lifted again en masse. This is clearly shown by the relatively flat surfaces of many of the highest areas. The northern ranges of the Tien-shan and the Altai mountains show a similar history. The middle ranges of the Tien-shan are of Hercynian age. The mighty southern ranges, with their vast glaciers and peaks of more than 20,000 ft., and the equally lofty Pamirs are the products of Tertiary movements. The border ranges of Turkistan and Iran consist mainly of folded beds of Cretaceous and Tertiary age.

The Caucasus and Transcaucasia.—These regions are distinct structurally and physically, the Armenian mountain knot being separated from the Caucasus by a relatively low, narrow line occupied by the river Rion on the west and the river Kur on the east, but a long stretch of this low line is well over 1,500 ft. above sea level. This line has to the east the deep basin of the southern Caspian and westward the deep basin of the southern Black sea. (*See* CAUCASUS.) (R. M. F.; T. HER.)

CLIMATE

The climate of the U.S.S.R. has two outstanding characteristics: its uniformity and its continentality. They are results of its low relief and compact form. Its great plains present over immense distances the same monotony of climate as of level. It is possible, of course, to recognize areas whose climates differ significantly one from another, but the transition from one such province to its neighbours is, practically everywhere, accomplished by almost imperceptible gradations.

Maritime influences are extremely feeble, which is not surprising because 75% of the area is more than 250 mi. from the surrounding seas, several of which, moreover (the Baltic, the Black and the Caspian), are land-enclosed. The frozen Arctic ocean obviously can have little effect; the mountain barrier shuts out monsoonal winds from the south; and offshore winds and high coastal ranges limit Pacific influences to a narrow coastal belt on the east. Hence the Russian lands almost everywhere show to a high degree the features of a continental climate: great extremes of temperature, both diurnal and annual; abrupt change from winter to summer and vice versa; low rainfall with summer maximum and largely convectional in character; violent windstorms. The south coast of the Crimea and Transcaucasia (both sheltered by high ground on the north and with winter rains drawn from the Black sea) and the area between the lower Amur and the Pacific (feebly monsoonal in character) are the only areas to which this general description does not apply.

The climate of the U.S.S.R. is dominated by the polar continental air mass which extends over the whole land for the greater part of the year. In the summer it shrinks to a narrow belt along the arctic coasts of Asiatic Russia. It is characterized by its low temperature and low humidity. Disturbances are infrequent and local. Thus, still, dry days with clear skies, very low temperatures and slight snowfall are characteristic of the nine months or so during which it covers the land—conditions which though harsh are by no means unhealthful but do severely limit human activities.

In winter, pressures are high over the whole of Siberia, especially so near Lake Baikal where in January they exceed 30.5 in. Outblowing winds are therefore normal over Asiatic Russia. A narrow extension of this high-pressure area spreads westward, roughly along lat. 50° N., as far as central Europe. On its northern side southwest and west winds blow, while to the south the winds are generally between north and east. The feeble low pressures experienced during the brief summer give a much more irregular air circulation.

Rainfall is generally less than 20 in. except in coastal and mountainous areas and the middle and western areas of European Russia. It is almost entirely derived from Atlantic sources, being brought by cyclonic disturbances, more frequent in summer. The total precipitation decreases eastward along a middle zone from Moscow to Lake Baikal and, much more rapidly, both to the northeast and to the southwest of this zone. The arctic northeast has a rainfall as low as that of the desert Aral basin.

The summer isotherms follow the latitudinal lines with remarkable regularity. In January their direction is rather from northwest to southeast, with the pole of cold in the region of Verkhoyansk (January mean −59° F., minimum recorded near −100°). Temperature ranges thus increase toward the east, from 31° at Batum to more than 100° northeast of Yakutsk. In the Siberian arctic only 60 days, on the average, are frost-free, and even in European Russia it is only in the Ukraine that the surface is snow-covered for fewer than 100 days. Both the Sea of Azov and the northern half of the Caspian are frozen over in January.

Siberian Climates.—All the features of the Russian climate already outlined are particularly sharply shown in Siberia. Its northerly situation, its isolation from Atlantic and Pacific, the increasing altitude of the land toward the south (offsetting in part the decreasing latitude) and its openness toward the arctic all tend to bring down its temperatures. By reason of its winter high pressures, bitterly cold winds blow out from it over the surrounding lands. Its low atmospheric pressure in summer draws in warmer and more humid air from beyond its borders, thus producing its summer maximum rainfall. Snow lies long, but the depth of fall is slight—in the northeast so slight in many parts that the sledge is not usable. On the whole the weather is dry, the sky generally cloudless. Temperature ranges are unequalled in any other land. Verkhoyansk is generally credited with the lowest recorded temperature (about −100° F.), but it has also recorded 100° F. The Siberian summer, though short, is hot rather than warm.

Winter is clearly the dominant season, as much by its unchangeableness during many weeks as by its severity. The general absence of wind alone makes the cold bearable. When the buran (Siberian blizzard) blows, only shelter from its blast will save the life of the traveller. In the absence of heavy snow the soil and subsoil are deeply frozen. Over nearly all Siberia east of the Yenisei "permafrost" obtains: the subsoil is frozen all the year and the surface soil thaws only for a brief period and only to shallow depths in summer. The depth of this thaw has important effects in determining the nature of the vegetation.

Spring arrives in April. The ice on the rivers breaks up rapidly and, as the thaw begins in the south, the flowing waters cause floods over the still frozen northern channels. As the snow melts, village streets become apparently bottomless seas of mud. For several days outdoor movement of man or beast becomes almost impossible. The surface soon dries, however, and a brief period of delightful spring weather is experienced, though often interrupted by the return of severe cold for a short time. Summer follows quickly. The days are warm or hot and the hours of daylight long. Its monotony is broken by sudden storms, sometimes accompanied by hail, or there may be short burning spells with dust storms. In any case one can be sure of the return of clouds of voracious mosquitoes. By August, however, or by early September in the south, night frosts are experienced and in two or three weeks winter has returned.

Over such a vast expanse there are naturally variations in climatic conditions, and these make possible a division into climate provinces or regions.

The *polar* or *tundra province* includes a narrow belt along the Arctic shores from the Kola peninsula to the Bering strait. Its southern limit may be taken at the 50° July isotherm, which is also near the limit of tree growth. The chief characteristics are its very long winters (about ten months), short summers (temperatures as high as 80° F. have been recorded), low precipitation and strong winds. Both temperature and precipitation decrease eastward, the latter falling as low as four inches near the Lena delta. Winter temperatures are higher near the coast than in the interior.

The *far eastern province* is characterized by a monsoonal reversal of wind direction—land to sea in winter, sea to land in summer. Winter conditions are severe (even Vladivostok, in the extreme south, has 110 days of frost and a January mean temperature of 5° F.). It is sharply distinguished from other Siberian regions by its humidity. Fogs are frequent, snowfall heavy (particularly near the Sea of Okhotsk) and rainy days numerous in summer.

Eastern Siberia is notably dry and cold. Precipitation varies from 14 in. near Lake Baikal to 4 in. in the north. Days with snow are few (nine at Blagoveshchensk, none in some years and in some sections). Immense areas have mean annual temperatures below freezing point. On the other hand, the July isotherm of 68° F. does not reach so far north in any other part of the world.

Central Siberia is also very dry. The number of snowy days is higher, though the total fall is still slight. Temperatures remain very low (Irkutsk January mean —5° F.). Lake Baikal reduces temperature ranges very considerably in its immediate vicinity.

In *western Siberia* the winters are still harsh (Tomsk January mean —3° F.). Heavy snow is often brought by violent storms and piled in great drifts. Tomsk has an average of about 120 snowy days. The snow cover limits the depth to which the soil is frozen, so that it is quickly fit for cultivation after the spring thaw. Its thorough soaking at this time is also favourable to seed germination. During the warm-to-hot summer, rain falls in heavy showers, though the total precipitation is still only moderate (Tomsk 20 in., Omsk 12 in.).

Russian Climate.—The climate of European Russia is controlled by the same major influences as that of Siberia: its northerly latitude and openness toward the arctic, the absence of any barrier on the Asiatic side and the shutting out of marine influences (except to a limited degree) by the Scandinavian highlands, the Carpathians and the Balkans. It is accordingly both continental and uniform, in marked contrast to that of the rest of Europe. Nevertheless, the Baltic depression and the north German plain do permit, if only in attenuated form, the penetration of Atlantic influences.

As has been seen, the Siberian anticyclone in winter throws west across central Russia an arm of high pressure bringing cold Asiatic winds to the east, centre and south of the country. The lower pressures to the northwest permit the entry of humid and relatively mild air from the west. In summer, while the east and south still receive hot, dry continental winds, the north, northwest and centre experience cooler and moister oceanic air. Precipitation therefore decreases from northwest to southeast (Riga 22 in., Moscow 21, Saratov 15, Astrakhan 6). Snowfall, fairly heavy in the lake region, becomes quite light toward the Black sea and the lower Volga, a reminder that winter is the season of least precipitation (Moscow 16%). The summer, though it has often long periods of drought interrupted by brief but heavy rainstorms, is the season of greatest precipitation (Moscow 36%, Kaluga 40%).

Latitude has a marked effect on summer temperatures (Archangel July mean 60° F., Astrakhan 78° F.) but has less effect in winter when distance from the sea becomes a more important factor (Leningrad January mean 15°, Moscow 12°, Orenburg 3° F.). But it is the length of the seasons rather than their mean temperatures that has most influence on Russian life. In the far north at least six and one-half months of frost can be expected, Leningrad, Nijni-Novgorod (Gorki) and Orenburg (Chkalov) have from five to six, Moscow and Kuybyshev from four to five, Odessa and Kherson from one to three. Unlike the Siberian winter, however, conditions are liable to violent changes: blizzards, sudden falls in already low temperatures, or brief thaws (*ottepeli*).

Spring, coming in April or May, sets free the frozen rivers and puts an end to all outdoor movement. In a couple of months, except in the far north, summer has arrived, bringing hot days everywhere. Evaporation is then intense, the soils dry quickly and river levels fall considerably. Dry winds from the east bring dust storms that may cover and often scorch the growing crops. Harvest follows seedtime with but a brief interval for festival between. By early October the first snow showers have fallen in Moscow. From mid-November winter tightens its grip on the whole country once more.

The southern shores of the Crimea and the northeastern coast of the Black sea have a Mediterranean climate. There the winters are generally mild and rainy, the summers dry and rainless. Frosts are experienced only in a few days in January and February. High ground to the north provides shelter in each case.

Transcaucasia has a subtropical climate. The Kolkhiz lowland, open on the west to the Black sea, has a milder winter than even the Crimea and a cooler summer. Precipitation is heavy with a slight winter maximum. Winds from the Caucasus produce foehn effects.

Turkistan.—Across the lower Volga, in Kazakhstan, the climate becomes yet drier and more extreme. Wild blizzards sweep it in winter, though the total snowfall is slight. Autumn and spring are virtually nonexistent, a grilling summer (July mean 77°) following immediately on a bitterly cold winter (January mean 5°).

Further south, in the Aralo-Caspian basin, conditions are still more severe. Precipitation varies between 3 in. and 8 in. a year, except along the mountain margins (Tashkent 14 in.). Most of it falls in spring and the rest near the end of the year. Temperature ranges, both annual and diurnal, are large. Cold waves from the north sweep across the basin in winter, while the cloudless summer skies and dry air give full play to a burning sun. The Aral sea is frozen for five months; three months later eggs can be cooked in the sands near its shores.

SOILS AND THEIR INFLUENCE

The science of pedology or soil study owes much of its modern position to the work of Russian investigators. This might perhaps have been expected in a land for so long almost wholly dependent on agriculture. Uniformity of level and of climate over wide areas naturally emphasized the importance of soil variations in the choice of crops and in their productivity. The derivation of the soil from the underlying surface rocks by processes of denudation which varied with climatic conditions and the later addition of products of organic decomposition was of course widely recognized. The main value of Russian work arose from the emphasis that it placed on regarding the soil as a living, or at least an evolving, thing.

Among the first of Russian workers in this field was V. V. Dokuchayev (1846–1903), after whom was named the Institute of Soils responsible for continuing his researches and for the publication of important papers and maps on the subject. K. D. Glinka was an important early follower; it was the publication in 1928 by the department of agriculture of the United States of a translation of his classic *The Great Soil Groups of the World and Their Development* that first made the work of the Russian school known to English-speaking students.

From the standpoint of their origin, the soils of Russia fall into three main groups, each covering a wide area. Those of the north are derived from the drift left on the final recession of the ice sheets, mainly their ground moraine and the outwash from it. To the south lies the belt of loessic soils produced by wind action on the drying surface of the newly uncovered glacial deposits. Over the areas formerly covered by the Aralo-Caspian sea the surface consists of marine deposits left behind as these waters shrank. Since their formation all have been changed by the action of the weather, especially by fluctuations of temperature and by rain and soil water. The growth and decay of the vegetation that covered them and the action of burrowing animals, of cultivators and especially of bacteria all helped in varying degree to determine the nature of the present soil cover and are still controlling its development. The great importance of climate in this respect is suggested by the zoning. The rise of temperature, decrease of rainfall and increase of evaporation from northwest to southeast are evidently largely responsible for the soil changes.

The soil is clearly "alive" in the sense that it is still developing,

PHOTOGRAPHS, (1-3, 5, 6) SOVFOTO, (4) ACME

VIEWS OF THE CRIMEA AND NEWER INDUSTRIAL CENTRES

1. Harvesting barley on a collective farm in the Crimea
2. View along the Crimean coast
3. Gathering Crimean grapes in the vineyards of the Massandra winery, where white and pink Muskat and other wines are produced

4. A busy square in Stalingrad, site of the historic siege of 1942
5. A machine plant and school at Sverdlovsk in the Urals
6. The State Drama theatre and the Palace of Culture of Metal Workers in Magnitogorsk

PLATE II

RUSSIA

PHOTOGRAPHS, (1, 3, 5, 6) SOVFOTO, (2) TOPICAL PRESS AGENCY, (4) BURTON HOLMES FROM EWING GALLOWAY, (7) ACME

CITIES OF THE WESTERN U.S.S.R.

1. A winter view along the River Moskvá and the Kremlin in Moscow
2. A comprehensive view of Moscow, looking toward the Kremlin along the Moskvá with its cast-iron bridge
3. The Frunze military academy in Moscow
4. The Red Army building in Kharkov
5. Theatre square in Kiev
6. General view of Odessa on the Black sea, showing units of housing erected before the German invasion of 1941
7. A view of Leningrad taken from St. Isaac's cathedral

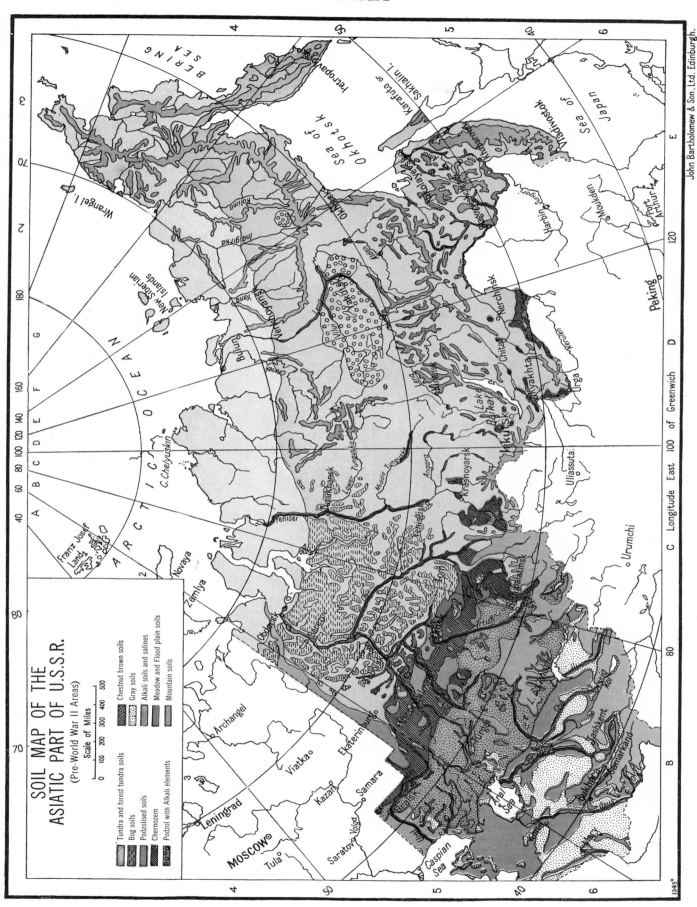

SOIL MAP OF THE ASIATIC PART OF U.S.S.R.

(Pre-World War II Areas)

Scale of Miles

0 100 200 300 400 500

Legend:
- Tundra and forest tundra soils
- Bog soils
- Podzolised soils
- Chernozem
- Podzol with Alkali elements
- Chestnut brown soils
- Gray soils
- Alkali soils and salines
- Meadow and Flood plain soils
- Mountain soils

John Bartholomew & Son. Ltd. Edinburgh.

1343°

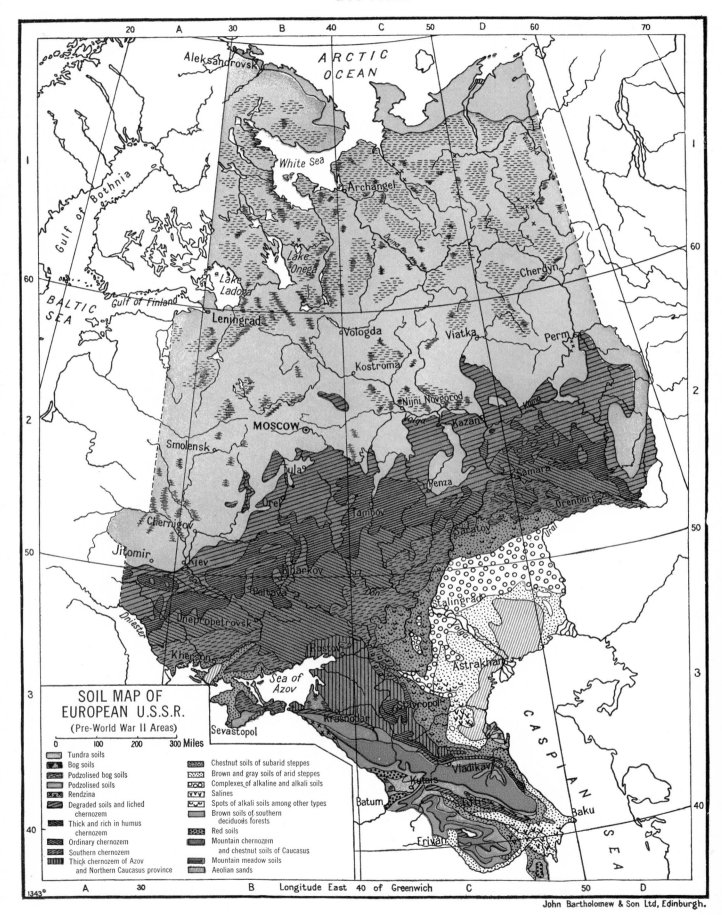

ARCTIC OCEAN

Aleksandrovsk

White Sea

Gulf of Bothnia

BALTIC SEA

Gulf of Finland

Lake Onega

Lake Ladoga

Leningrad

Vologda

Kostroma

Archangel

Viatka

Cherdyn

Perm

Nijni Novgorod

MOSCOW

Smolensk

Kazan

Samara

Tula

Penza

Orenburg

Orel

Tambov

Saratov

Chernigov

Jitomir

Kiev

Kharkov

Poltava

Don

Stalingrad

Dniester

Dnepropetrovsk

Kherson

Rostov

Astrakhan

Sea of Azov

Sevastopol

Stavropol

Krasnodar

CASPIAN SEA

Vladikavkaz

Kutais

Tiflis

Batum

Baku

Erivan

SOIL MAP OF EUROPEAN U.S.S.R.

(Pre-World War II Areas)

0   100   200   300 Miles

Legend:
- Tundra soils
- Bog soils
- Podzolised bog soils
- Podzolised soils
- Rendzina
- Degraded soils and liched chernozem
- Thick and rich in humus chernozem
- Ordinary chernozem
- Southern chernozem
- Thick chernozem of Azov and Northern Caucasus province
- Chestnut soils of subarid steppes
- Brown and gray soils of arid steppes
- Complexes of alkaline and alkali soils
- Salines
- Spots of alkali soils among other types
- Brown soils of southern deciduous forests
- Red soils
- Mountain chernozem and chestnut soils of Caucasus
- Mountain meadow soils
- Aeolian sands

Longitude East 40 of Greenwich

1343°

John Bartholomew & Son Ltd, Edinburgh.

though that development may be, and is in many districts, extremely slow. The humus produced from decaying vegetation largely determines soil colour and is of great importance because of its water-holding property. In suitable conditions of temperature and water, bacteria rapidly reduce the organic content of the soil to inorganic forms (the "mineral stage" of Russian authors), which then become available for new plant growth. These salts are normally dissolved in the soil water and so carried to the lower soil layers. In this way is produced the soil profile, which in a well-developed soil consists of three horizons: the upper or A horizon, usually loose in texture and being robbed of its mineral content by the soil water; the B horizon, more compact and containing most of the salts leached from A; and the C horizon, consisting mainly of fragments of the underlying mother rock.

In arid regions the soils contain little humus since lack of moisture limits the growth of vegetation. Excessive evaporation brings soil water to the surface where it leaves behind its dissolved mineral contents. Thus carbonates especially are found at or near the surface, sometimes forming a clearly marked layer. Frost, with the check that it places on plant growth and on bacterial activity, prevents development. The steepness of mountain slopes, producing constant downward movement of rock fragments, also checks development.

Glinka classified soils into about two dozen types, not all represented in the U.S.S.R. Only the major groups are distinguished in the following survey.

Tundra Soils.—This most northerly group of soils is found over nearly one-sixth of the total area of the U.S.S.R., extending beyond the tree line (the word "tundra" implies the absence of trees) to the shores of the Arctic ocean. The outstanding characteristics of these soils are due to the rigorous climate. In the brief summer only the upper layers are thawed, the subsoil remaining permanently frozen and therefore impervious. Neither surface water nor burrowing animals can penetrate the frozen layers. Marsh conditions are widespread over all the lower areas in the warmer period. Vegetation is shallow-rooted and scanty. Its decaying remains lie on the surface and accumulate there to form a black acid layer. This bog soil is, almost entirely, partially decomposed vegetable matter. The subsoil, on the other hand, is almost wholly inorganic. Low temperatures limit bacterial activity and the frozen subsoil prevents earthworms from carrying on their beneficent work of conveying organic material underground and bringing mineral fragments to the surface.

Where the subsoil is sandy there is some leaching from the surface soil, and tundra soils approach the podsol type. On drier mounds uplifted by the action of frost peat may develop, but this is less common than is generally believed. In the tundra of the far northeast of Siberia the very low precipitation is accompanied by an almost total absence of vegetation, and the land surfaces are often of bare rock or pebble-covered, with little soil of any kind.

Under such conditions agriculture is clearly impossible. The few inhabitants are pastoral nomads dependent on their reindeer herds, on summer fishing and on winter hunting in the forest fringe. There is some reindeer breeding to provide animals for winter haulage in the forest zone to the south. Transition from tundra to forest gives rise to a narrow belt where scattered examples of dwarf species of birch and spruce are typical. These, like the forest trees themselves, first become evident in the river valleys, where there is some shelter from winds and the subsoil ice lies at a deeper level.

Forest Soils.—Soils of this group cover more than half the U.S.S.R. All are podsols or modified podsols; that is to say, soils of an ash-gray colour (*zol* = "ash") typical of cool, humid climates. They are best developed in the taiga or coniferous forest region. There surface water can reach deeper than in the tundra, since temperatures are high enough to prevent the permanent freezing of the subsoil and, in dry periods, to cause some rise of water in the soil to replace the slight loss from the surface by evaporation. These conditions are evidently favoured by the forest cover, for it prevents heavy leaching by rain while maintaining fairly constant humidity of the soil. The shelter it gives from winds also reduces losses by evaporation. On the other hand, leaf transpiration keeps the subsoil fairly dry.

Coniferous Forest Type.—The decay of the needle leaves of the conifers proceeds very slowly by reason of their resinous nature and gives rise to a thin and rather peaty surface layer. It produces a very acid type of humus and the soil water passing through it is therefore capable of bringing about almost complete decomposition of the mineral constituents of the underlying layer. Iron and aluminum hydroxides are thus carried downward, leaving behind little but silica or fine clay. The A horizon in a typical podsol is thus frequently sandy, grayish where a proportion of humus remains but sometimes almost white where it has been removed, and strongly acid. Since almost all the plant food it contained has been removed, these soils are agriculturally of little value. This is evidently of great importance, since they cover about two-fifths of European Russia. Horizon B shows two distinct layers. The upper of these is brownish yellow or coffee coloured and contains most of the products of humus decomposition. In texture it is usually clayey, the finer mineral fragments being cemented by gummy substances resulting from this decomposition. Sometimes a hardpan layer is produced at this level. The lower section is usually rusty brown in colour and heavily impregnated with iron hydroxide. When this layer is sufficiently thick and consolidated it is often a factor in the production of the marshes common throughout the taiga belt. Red-brown patches, due either to humus or ferrous hydroxide concentrations, are sometimes seen in the subsoil below the B horizon.

Coniferous trees form the major part of the vegetation except on the northern edge of the forest; there a belt of birch occurs, at first dwarf and lichen-covered but increasing in size and number southward. Where the A horizon is sandy the Scotch pine is prevalent, on the clays some variety of spruce. In Siberia the silver fir and Siberian larch are the commonest trees. Economically the forests are important as sources of softwood timbers and of furs.

Bog and Marsh Type.—This is common north of about the 60th parallel of latitude in Europe, in the wide, ill-drained northern parts of the west Siberian lowland and in the Pripet area of western Russia. It is especially common on surfaces of glacial clay. The water table is high, and hence there is little downward movement of soil water. Decomposition of vegetation is incomplete because of lack of aeration, so that peaty surface layers are common. The remains of dwarf birch and alder and of marsh plants and mosses accumulate slowly, giving an acid surface soil. Dissolved iron is often precipitated in nodular form and, as bog iron ore, has been worked in some regions for several centuries (*e.g.*, in the Vychegda valley).

The marsh areas have been of great strategical importance in Russian history. In the earlier days of invasion from the Asiatic steppe they were often places of refuge. The great Pripet marshes formed an important barrier across the European plain, giving a natural western frontier toward Poland. Peat is worked extensively and is used for power production in some areas.

Mixed Forest Types.—From central Europe across European Russia to the Urals near Molotov (Perm) there extends a wedge of mixed forest where deciduous trees mingle with and ultimately almost replace the northern conifers. Beyond the Urals this forest occurs again in a narrow belt as far as the Ob. As has been seen, this is the area in which Atlantic influences upon the Russian climate are most effective and are particularly evident in the heavier precipitation. The soils of the region vary in character in accordance with differences in local climate and in the mother rock from which they are derived, but in general they show a transition from the podsolized soils of the coniferous forest to the black earth of the steppe.

Heavier precipitation causes a continuance of the leaching of the A horizon, but the surface layers are less acid than farther north. Higher temperatures encourage more complete decomposition with greater activity of earthworms and bacteria. The horizon is darker in colour, gray rather than white, as the humus content of the upper layer rises to from 3% to 6%. This upper layer, seven to nine inches in depth, accounts for the greater agricultural productivity of this zone as compared with the region to the north.

In texture the layer is said to be nutlike. In the lower layers of the horizon this structure becomes coarser and the colour grayer. The A horizon may be as thick as 30 in. The change is gradual to the B horizon which may reach to a depth as great as nine feet in the southern areas. The colour of this horizon is generally brown, grayish in the upper layers but reddish in the lower. Very fine clay particles and some calcareous material occur at the lower levels. The origin of these grayish soils is still disputed. Some hold that they represent a degraded form of the black earth, caused by a southward spread of tree growth over the steppe. In support of this view it is noted that where patches of woodland occur in the steppe valleys they are accompanied by gray soils. Another opinion sees in them mainly the result of forest clearing and the improvement by long-continued cultivation of a formerly podsolized soil.

The gray soils occur in a narrow but irregular band across European Russia and in the still narrower zone of the wooded steppe of western Siberia. Though still essentially forested, this country allowed its early inhabitants to maintain themselves by agriculture in the clearings. As settlement increased these could be and were extended by cutting and burning. The longer frost-free period makes possible the growth of deciduous trees except in eastern Siberia, where this type of forest is completely absent. The heavier leaf fall from this type of tree increases the supply of humus to the surface layer of soil. The richer undergrowth, which consists mainly of perennial grasses, contributes to the same result and also encourages the rearing of farm animals.

In the narrow west Siberian area the trees are mainly aspen and birch. West of the Urals the forest is much richer in species. The most important of these are the oak, especially common on the glacial clays, the lime, the maple and the ash. The last-named is most abundant in the more southerly areas. Conifers are still common, more particularly on the sandy outwash soils and alluvial areas along the rivers.

The mixed forest zone has played a great part in the history of Russia for within it the Russian nation was born. Groups fleeing from the Asiatic invaders of the steppes there found shelter. Under the influence of a settled agricultural life they were welded into groups which later coalesced to form the first Russian state. All the suitable land has long been cultivated and the hardier cereals —barley, rye and oats—grown. Flax and hemp provided fibres for early industrial use, and the potato was soon widely grown after its first introduction. Forage crops—hay and lucerne—also do well and support the growing dairying and cattle-breeding industry, especially in parts of Siberia.

Black Earth.—Soils of the black earth type (chernozems) underlie about 12% of the U.S.S.R. and form in European Russia the largest continuous area of the type anywhere. They occur south of the forest soils and north of the arid and mountain areas. Their essential characteristics are the high humus content and the presence of calcium salts, especially the carbonate. They evidently represent a modification of an earlier soil enriched by the decay of animal and plant remains. Because of their wide development in loess areas, it was at one time thought that they were simply loess with an addition of humus; this is not now accepted, as they are found to occur in quite characteristic form on mother rocks of varied kinds. At the same time there seems little reason to doubt that loess and the *limons* found over calcareous rocks are particularly favourable to their development. Sandy subsoils, too, carry thicker coverings of chernozem than do clayey subsoils. The better drainage afforded by loess and sands is probably the reason in each case.

The humus content of the black earth varies from 6% to about 16%. It is lowest in the north and west and increases to the south and east. Thus the percentage varies from 6 to 10 in the Ukraine, where it occurs over the widest area, but increases to 15 or 16 east of the Volga, where it forms but a narrow belt, and in western Siberia, where its distribution is patchy. The black earth is thickest in the Ukraine.

It is clear that the principal factor leading to the development of chernozem is climate. It occurs in regions with a long and severe winter but with summer conditions of high evaporation leading to a virtual desiccation of the surface soils. Snow accumulates during the winter, and the spring thaw provides the moisture necessary for a quick and abundant growth of grass. This water supply, however, is exhausted by late May or early June. Rain falls during the summer months but only at considerable intervals, and the total amount is small. The intervening periods of drought stop the growth of the steppe grasses, the decay of whose roots is the chief source of humus. It also prevents the growth of trees, and this also may be of some importance in the development of chernozems since tree roots encourage oxidation. The blackness of the surface layer which gives the soil its name is due to the long-accumulated products of the decomposition of grass roots. The droughts of summer and the frosts of winter both slow down the rate of decomposition. Leaching of the A horizon is largely prevented by the low summer precipitation and rapid evaporation, which moreover produce a strong upward movement of the soil water that leads to a concentration of mineral salts just below the humus level. This is another factor inimical to the growth of trees and explains their restriction to valley areas in the steppelands. Layers of gypsum and of calcium carbonate at different levels are often produced by this movement of soil water.

The typical soil profile in a black earth region shows two major horizons. The upper portion of the A horizon is normally neutral not acid. The surface soil is crumbly, granular in structure and black or deep chocolate in colour because of the high humus content. The lower portions of the horizon, which has a total thickness of 18–40 in., is grayish black to yellowish brown and has a nutlike structure. It is in this portion of the profile that calcareous concretions occur, the carbonates formed in the humus horizon being carried down by leaching.

The black earth lands practically coincide with what are sometimes called the tillable steppes. These have produced grain for many centuries without any great loss of fertility. The main handicaps to their utilization are climatic, as they require not manure so much as moisture. Recurrent drought has given rise to terrible famines. The dry soils in the summer months are particularly liable to wind erosion and to loss of topsoil in heavy rain showers. Modern cultivation by machines on a large scale, as in the United States, tended to accentuate these difficulties. Increased diversification of crops, the construction of vast tree belts as windscreens and the utilization of Volga waters for irrigation were developed to offset them. In earlier times the Slav cultivators occupied the wooded valleys and left the bare plateaus of the steppes to the nomadic pastoralists. The modern tendency has been the reverse of this, the open plateau lands being more suited to working by machines. For further information on the region *see* UKRAINE and BLACK EARTH AREA.

Arid Soils.—Beyond the black earth zone to the southeast, climatic conditions rapidly approach desert character. The decrease in total rainfall, its increasing uncertainty and the rapid rise in the evaporation rate produce marked changes in the soils and their development. The cultivation of the steppe becomes more and more risky, though it is perhaps no longer true to speak of the whole region as untillable steppe. The chestnut soils are fertile when, or where, sufficient moisture is available, the brown soils less so and the gray desert soils only occasionally and then with great difficulty. The humus content decreases rapidly and salinity increases as the chernozems are left behind. A fertile belt, however, lies along the foot of the bordering ranges.

Chestnut and Brown Soils.—These extend from the Crimean steppes across the Volga delta and through Kazakhstan and the extreme south of western Siberia. The chestnut soils are the result of extreme temperatures accompanied by a low rainfall and high summer evaporation. The grass cover is much less rich and less continuous than on the chernozem, with the result that the humus content of the surface soils falls to 5%. Increasing aridity produces the brown soils with only 3% humus. Insufficient leaching of the surface soils causes an increase of their soluble salt content, and this adds to the effect of the growing aridity in limiting vegetation. The A horizon in the chestnut soils seldom exceeds 25 in. (with a humus zone 12–18 in. thick) and in the brown soils falls to 12 or 15 in. Both types show a prismatic structure. The rising soil waters, consequent on heavy evaporation, cause the concentration of soluble salts in the upper layers. Thus, calcareous concretions often form an almost continuous layer quite near the surface. Because of the poverty of vegetation the nature of the mother rock has more influence on the soil character than is usual. On the other hand, the dryness of the surface reduces the rate of decomposition of mineral fragments.

All arid soils show a tendency toward salinity. This is particularly evident in surface depressions or where there is poor drainage or a high water table. Under such conditions the ground water is often brackish. This is most marked in soils resting on argillaceous rocks. Saline soils, lightly impregnated with soluble salts of potassium, magnesium or calcium and constituting the type known as *solonchak,* are found in these areas. Their salinity is harmful to vegetation. A white crust sometimes appears on the surface if the concentration of soluble salts is excessive. An alkaline soil known as *solonets* is produced by the leaching of *solonchak; e.g.,* if it is irrigated or if its drainage is improved in any way. The removal of most of the soluble salts leads to both chemical and physical change. Thus the flocculated clay particles of the *solonchak* are dispersed and its loose texture is replaced by a closer texture, so that the *solonets* is sticky and plastic when wet but sets into hard clods when dry. It is thus practically unworkable.

The chestnut soils are very fertile when supplied with enough water, but their irrigation must be carefully controlled. Raising of the water table is always liable to produce alkalinity at the surface and thus bring about the formation of *solonchak* or *solonets* and the deflocculation of their clay particles.

Gray Soils.—These are found chiefly in the inland drainage areas of Asiatic Russia. They underlie the shifting sands of the deserts and cover the loessic deposits of their southern mountain margins. Under desert conditions neither water nor vegetation is sufficient to play much part in soil production and the evolution of the soil has not proceeded far. In the areas where drifting sand forms the surface one can say it has not begun. Along the northern edge of the basins occur *solonets* clays, poor in carbonate and with a very low humus content. These increase in salinity southward.

The gray soils are alkaline and clayey with a humus content seldom more than 1%. Their colour results from the presence of sodium salts and their bleaching effect. Where the gray soils cover the southern loess they are rich in calcium carbonate, the content being sometimes as high as 15% at the surface and increasing to 25% at lower levels. Where they are well watered, as where mountain streams emerge, they may be very fertile. Cotton and Mediterranean fruits are important products where the problems that the gray soils present to the cultivator can be solved.

Mountain Soils.—In general these vary with altitude wherever the slopes are gentle enough to permit their development and stream or ice erosion does not remove them. As temperatures fall and humidity increases with height, the succession of soils closely parallels that seen in travelling from southeast to northwest across the plains. Thus, in the Altai, chestnut soils at the foot pass into black soils and then to podsolized forest soils at higher levels. The gray desert soils of the Turkistan lowlands similarly pass into chestnut and then into black earths on the mountain slopes. In eastern Siberia, where the soil generally is of the coniferous forest podsol type, the mountain ranges are capped with tundra-type soils.

BIBLIOGRAPHY.—P. J. Camena d'Almeida, *Etats de la Baltique, Russie,* vol. 5 of *Géographie universelle,* ed. by L. Gallois and P. Vidal de la Blache (Paris, 1932); T. Shabad, *Geography of the U.S.S.R.* (1951); W. G. Kendrew, *The Climates of the Continents,* 3rd ed. (Oxford, 1937); L. S. Berg, *Natural Regions of the U.S.S.R.* (1950); K. D. Glinka, *The Great Soil Groups of the World and Their Development* (1928); the series *Russian Pedological Investigations* (in English; Leningrad, 1927 ff.); M. and D. Haviland, *Forest, Steppe and Tundra* (Cambridge, 1926); B. A. Keller, "Distribution of Vegetation on the Plains of European Russia," *Journal of Ecology,* vol. xv, no. 2 (1927).
(T. Her.)

HISTORY

The great east European plain which was united, together with Siberia, under the Russian tsars, presents in spite of its general uniformity two contrasting geographic aspects which profoundly influenced the trend of its historical development: the northern and the southern. A primitive forest extending over the northern part of Russia reminds one of that described by Tacitus in his *Germania.* It was indeed its continuation and connected Russia with the western part of the European plain. It was comparatively late that this part of Europe was set free from its prehistoric ice cover. It is still full of lakes and great rivers which for long remained the only ways of communication for a scanty population scattered in distant glades. The primitive settlers added a few patches of cultivated land to their habitual means of livelihood—river fish, wild beehives and fur-bearing animals in the forests.

Quite different is the southern Russian landscape. It is the steppe, the prehistoric seat of nomad hordes which inhabited it from time immemorial until quite recently. These lived on horseback and in tents, used mare's milk as their food and throve on the booty taken in regular incursions against northern sedentary tribes. There the most ancient traces of aborigines are found, of the Palaeolithic stage, followed by the Neolithic, with traces of Aegean culture in its primitive form. There also we learn, by the intermediary of ancient Greek colonies on the northern Black sea shore, the names of ancient peoples of southern Russia; we are unable, however, to identify their nationality. The most ancient of them, the Cimmerians, are said to have been replaced by the Scyths (*see* SCYTHIA) and these by Sarmatians (*see* SARMATAE). Some patriotic Russian historians (I. Y. Zabelin, D. I. Ilovaisky, D. Y. Samokvasov) tried to prove that these populations were Slavs, but later research pointed to an Iranian origin; for instance, the modern representatives of the Sarmatae-Alani are found to be the Ossetes, who are not Slavs but a Caucasian people.

The original home of all Slavs is not to be sought in the steppe, but in the forest. Lubor Niederle stated that, originating in the marshy land between the Vistula and Dnieper, the southern Slavs (Serbs and Bulgarians) descended to the Danube as early as the 1st century A.D. The first federation of eastern Slav tribes (Russians) appears in the 3rd–4th centuries A.D. as a powerful and numerous people called Antae, living between the Dnieper and Dniester. They were involved in the wars of the Goths and Huns and were defeated by the Avars in the 6th–7th centuries. In the 7th century appears a new conquering nomad nationality in the steppe, the Khazars (*q.v.*) possessing a certain degree of civilization. They brought under their subjection some eastern Slav tribes whose names are given in the ancient Russian annals (Severyane, Radimichi, Vyatichi, Polyane). Khazar domination lasted until the beginning of the 10th century, when other nomads of Turkish descent and wilder habits—Hungarians (middle 9th century) and Petchenegs (end of 9th century)—overran the steppe and broke for long the connection between Slav settlements and the Black sea shore.

Origin of the Rus.—The Slav forest tribes were now obliged to adapt themselves to the new situation. As a reply to the invasion of the steppe by the Turkish hordes there appears a new organization of defense from the north. The defenders are the "Rus"—a Varangian tribe, in ancient annals considered as related to the Swedes, Angles and Northmen. Both Rus and Varangians are also known to Byzantine chroniclers ('Ρῶς, Βαραγγοι), first as Norse pirates, then as warriors serving in the imperial guard and finally (10th century) as chiefs of the caravans of traders coming yearly to Constantinople by the "Great Waterway," the *Austrvegr* of northern sagas, through the waterfalls of the Dnieper, whose names are given by the emperor Constantine Porphyrogenitus both in "Russian" (Scandinavian) and in "Slavish" ('Ρωσσιστί and Σκλαβινιστί). Arabian writers represent the original seat of the Rus as an island covered with woods and marshes; this brings us to the source of the waterway mentioned—Lake Ilmen, near the ancient town of Novgorod, and Lake Ladoga, where the river Neva has its origin. Excavations of 9th–10th century tumuli confirm the presence of Norse warriors, buried (or burned) with their horses and arms, in that very tableland where four chief waterways of Russia, the Neva basin, Volga, Dnieper and Dvina, converge and form outlets to the Baltic, the Caspian and the Black seas and thus determine the direction of ancient trade routes. Numerous finds of Arabian, Byzantine and Anglo-Saxon coins (9th–11th centuries) along all these routes testify to a flourishing trade which corresponds exactly to the period of foundation of new states by Vikings at the one end and the florescence of Arabian and Persian caliphates before the Mongol invasion at the other end of these trade routes.

KIEV

Russian legend says that the Rus were first asked to come to Novgorod by the local population to put an end to their internal feuds. Rurik (Hrörekr) was the first (semilegendary) *knyaz* (*koning*, prince) of Novgorod, but his companions wished to descend the *Austrvegr*, nearer to Byzantium, and Oleg (Helgi) settled in Kiev. The Russian annals date the arrival of Rurik in Novgorod A.D. 862. But the first reliable datum is Oleg's commercial treaty with the Byzantines (911). A subsequent treaty was concluded in A.D. 945 by Oleg's successor, Igor (Ingvar), together with his companions, whose signatures contain only 3 Slav names among 50 Norse. Constantine Porphyrogenitus gave a very picturesque description of this trade which still remained the chief business of the Rus dynasty. During winter the princes and their *gesiths*, who distributed among themselves the towns in the basin of the Dnieper, were busy making circuits among neighbouring tribes in order to force them to pay annual tribute. Their booty consisted of furs, money and slaves. As spring came they loaded their small boats "made of one single tree" (μονόξυλος) and convoyed their caravans down the Dnieper ready to ward off the attacks of nomad steppe tribes. In the treaties mentioned their rights of trading in the capital were strictly defined. The *konings* extended their power over local tribes and, to defend the land from nomad incursions, they constructed earthen walls on the frontiers of the steppe. The local aristocracy joined the ranks of their *druzhina* (*gesith*, *comitatus*) and the process of assimilation began. The term "Rus" was now used to designate the southern outpost of the whole system of defense; *i.e.*, Kiev with the surrounding country. The son of Igor and his wife Olga (Helga) had already a Slav name, Svyatoslav. However, he still remained part northern Viking as well as part southern nomad. Svyatoslav did not yet feel at home in Kiev. He wanted to come still nearer to Byzantium and chose Pereyaslavets on the Danube in the Bulgarian land, because, he said "there was the centre where all goods gather from all parts: gold, clothes, wine, fruits from the Greeks, silver and horses from the Czechs and Hungarians, furs, wax, honey and slaves from the Rus." Svyatoslav also defeated the Khazars and the Volga Bulgars, but he was defeated by the emperor John I Tzimisces and slain on his way back home by the Petchenegs (972). With him died the Scandinavian tradition of the Kiev dynasty.

From the reign of Svyatoslav's youngest son, Vladimir, the Norman dynasty was definitely settled in Kiev. It still preserved its connections with other parts of Europe, attempted distant military expeditions against its Slav neighbours and ruled the large territory from the northern lakes to the steppe and from the then uncertain Polish frontier to the river Volga and the Caucasus. This was the most brilliant period of southern Russian history, but its brilliance rested on an extremely unsafe base, as the connection between the newly built state and the country inhabitants remained very loose. The only link which unified the subdued tribes was the power of the grand duke of Kiev. The people paid their tribute to the prince's tax collectors, but otherwise they were left to themselves and preserved their ancient tribal organization and habits.

Another element of union of enormous importance was added by the acceptance of Christian faith in 988 by Vladimir the Saint. He took his religion from Byzantium, but the service was in the vernacular as the prayer books and Bible had already been translated into Slavonic by the "Slav apostles" Cyril and Methodius in the 9th century. From 1037 the Russian church was subject to the Constantinopolitan patriarchate; for two centuries nearly all metropolitans and most of the bishops were Greeks. Eventually the Slav and Russian element prevailed. After Vladimir's death (1015), his son Svyatopolk the Damned assassinated his brothers

(Boris and Gleb, canonized as saints) but was defeated by another brother, Yaroslav, elective prince of Novgorod, who reunited all territory under the grand duchy of Kiev and embellished his capital with a cathedral in Byzantine style. He also founded the monastery at Pechersk, which became a famous seat of faith and learning; he collected books and had them translated. Under Yaroslav the earliest document of Russian law was revised under the name of *Russkaya pravda* ("Russian right"). He gave refuge to two sons of Edmund of England who fled from Canute, to Olaf II of Norway and also to Harald III Haardraade, who married his daughter; he gave his other daughter to Andrew I of Hungary; his third daughter married Henry I of France. His sons married Polish, Greek and German wives.

Yaroslav died in 1054. In order to prevent feuds among his numerous descendants he introduced an order of succession to the grand duchy of Kiev which was based on the principle that all territory as a whole belonged to the family, and different parts of it were distributed among them in temporary possession according to seniority and to the profitableness of the seat of administration. The most profitable towns on the main trade route were Kiev, Pereyaslavl (on the steppe frontier), Novgorod (the first Norman residence), then Smolensk (on the upper Dnieper) and Chernigov (on its confluent, the Desna). All brothers of the first generation were considered as senior to the following generation. As soon as Kiev passed to another brother all the members of the family changed their seats and approached one step nearer to Kiev. If one died before reaching Kiev, his descendants were called *izgoi* and excluded from "mounting the scale." In the accompanying chart are numbered the successive reigns in Kiev during seven generations after Yaroslav.

The order of succession from brother to brother was kept only in the two first generations (1 to 5). Numbers 9 and 12 show preference given to nephews over uncles. And indeed, as early as 1097, at a conference held by the dukes at Lyubech it was decided that the sons should keep their fathers' heritages. The di-

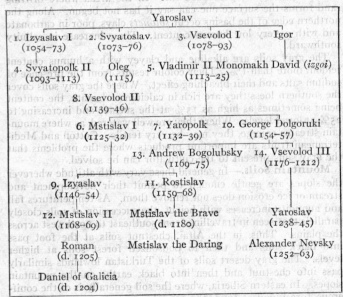

rect succession from father to son prevailed in all dukedoms. Kiev was seen to be losing its former significance. Its great importance was based on trade; but southern trade was destroyed by the appearance in the steppe (1054) of the Polovtsy (Cumans), nomads far more dangerous than the Petchenegs. It will also be seen that of all Yaroslav's sons only one line survived: that of Vsevolod and his brilliant son Vladimir Monomakh. Monomakh's line was then divided into two: the elder one (6, 9, 12) remained in Kiev and in its turn it was subdivided in two—Roman and Daniel preferred to move west from the then unsafe Kiev to Halicz (Galich; *see* GALICIA), while two Mstislavs, the Brave and the Daring, as their nicknames show, remained to the end the knights errant of the chivalrous south. The cadet branch of

Vladimir Monomakh (10, 13, 14) opened a new period of Russian history. The centre of influence changed then to northern woodland, far from the steppe. It was a far poorer but safer and, in the long run, more profitable settlement. In 1169 Andrew's troops stormed Kiev. This was the end of southern brilliance, though Kiev was not definitely destroyed till 1240 by a last and most terrible invader, the Mongol Batu, Jenghiz Khan's nephew.

The title of grand duke of Kiev thus lost its importance and with it broke down the unity of Russia. Ducal appanages became independent dukedoms; Russian territory was split in a dozen separate units which waged endless wars against each other. The old Kiev centre suffered the most from these internal dissensions and from incursions from the steppe. The frontier population was nearly exterminated and mixed with Turkish ethnic elements. However, the ancient tribes remained untouched to the west and north of the river Dnieper. In their midst, about the 14th century, appeared new branches of Russian people, speaking their separate dialects: the Little Russians and the White Russians (the old Krivichi).

NOVGOROD AND MOSCOW

By and by three distinct centres emerged from the chaos: Halicz, Novgorod and Moscow. Each was characterized by the prevalence of one of three main features of the political life of Russia during the Kiev period. These three features are: (1) the popular assembly (*veche*), which represented the ancient tribal organization and which met in towns thus consisting chiefly of townsfolk; (2) the princes; (3) the boyars and the *druzhina* (*comitatus*), a landed aristocracy, partly of ancient tribal descent, partly the military companions of the prince at the conquest. This aristocracy developed especially in Halicz, where the social structure approximated to western feudalism. On the northwestern frontier it was, on the contrary, the democratic element that prevailed. The chief city, Novgorod, became a republic. "Lord Novgorod the Great" was ruled by a popular assembly (*veche*) which elected its mayor (*posadnik*) and its commandant (*tysyatsky*) and concluded treaties with the dukes who were invited only to watch over the defense. Novgorod had a largely developed trade and large dominions extending from its gates and from the mouth of the Neva over the whole Russian north up to the White sea and the Urals. That country was rich in furs, the chief export. The higher class of citizens was here formed of capitalists and rich merchants, who were to form the aristocratic element in Novgorod.

Another element existed in the political structure of central Russia: the backwoods of the Oka and upper Volga. This country was cut off from all European connections. Its population consisted exclusively of agricultural colonists settled on ducal land. Thus, the duke appeared there as a proprietor and as the organizer of social life. Towns were scarce and the population scattered in clearings. The few *veches* in the chief towns had no influence; noble landed proprietors were completely absent. Thus, the power of the duke was there practically unlimited. Ducal psychology was framed accordingly; unlike the valiant knights of the south, they formed a dynasty of great appropriators, stingy and acquisitive, ruling their dukedoms as private estates. They thus accumulated elements of strength which as time went on aided them to become masters of the whole of Russia.

After the conquest of Kiev by Andrew Bogolubsky the title of grand duke passed from Kiev to a northern town, Suzdal, and from there to Vladimir on the Klyazma. But as early as 1147 Moscow is mentioned in the annals. Its situation was exactly at the centre of Russia between the Oka and the upper Volga. It had long been a great centre of continental river trade, far from the southern area of Tatar devastation. The line of dukes of Moscow starts from Alexander Nevsky's younger son Daniel. Their genealogy during the domination of the Golden Horde (1240–1480) is shown in the accompanying table.

All these princes had to ingratiate themselves with the khans of the Golden Horde to receive from them the *yarlyk* (investiture) as grand dukes. They regularly journeyed to Sarai, the capital of the khans at the mouth of the Volga, and underwent every kind of humiliation. But they returned as chief collectors of the Tatar tribute, which gave them power over neighbouring dukedoms. Only the dukedom of Tver competed with them very stubbornly.

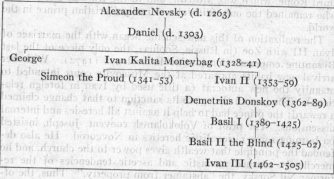

The dukes themselves involved the Tatars in their feuds and brought punitive expeditions on Russia. The khan's protection gave the Muscovite dukes the upper hand over their enemies. They soon succeeded in increasing their possessions. Ivan I extended his domains, by purchase and by violence, over the whole province of Moscow. Demetrius (Dmitry) added to it the upper Volga region (excepting Tver and Yaroslavl), Tula and Kasimov; Basil (Vasily) I the remaining part of Oka and Suzdal, Vladimir, Murom and Nijni-Novgorod; Basil II Elets in the south, Vologda and Ustyug in the north. A religious sanction was given to Muscovite unionist tendencies by the metropolitans of the Russian church who in the persons of Peter, Theognost and Alexius settled in Moscow. Accordingly, the grand dukes of Moscow added to their title: "of all Russia." Demetrius won a great name by his brilliant victory over the Tatars of the Golden Horde led by Mamai in a bloody battle on Kulikovo plain (1380). He thus appeared as a leader of all the national forces (excepting the grand duke of Ryazan) against the oppressors, and he received the blessings of the church at the hand of St. Sergius of Radonezh, the prior of the convent of the Holy Trinity. However, two years later Moscow was sacked and burned by another conqueror, Toktamish, who in his turn was defeated by Timur, his former protector. The Mongolian yoke lasted for another hundred years, although in milder forms. While Moscow was steadily growing in importance in comparison with the rival grand dukedoms of Tver and Ryazan, the boyars and other "men of service" came in crowds to serve the grand duke of all Russia. The institutions of Moscow, which up to then resembled very much those of a large private estate, began to evolve into a system of state administration.

Ivan III and Basil III.—Ivan III's acquisitions of Novgorod and Tver (1471 and 1485) enlarged Russian territory up to the limits of settlement of the Great Russian branch of the nation and brought Russia into direct contact with other countries, Livonia, Lithuania and the Tatar khanate of Crimea. The title "of all Russia" became a reality, and systematic foreign relations were started. The all-Russian potentate proffered historical claims against Lithuania, which possessed a part of formerly Russian territories. The successful wars which followed extended the western frontier to Chernigov and Novgorod Seversk, while leaving further claims for Smolensk, Kiev "and all Russian patrimony" to Ivan's successors. Ivan also built the fortress Ivangorod close to the Gulf of Finland, thus opening the chapter of Russian pretensions on the Baltic. The Crimean khan Mengli Ghirai accepted his friendship and helped him to put an end to the Golden Horde. As early as 1480 Ivan refused the Tatar tribute and threw off the yoke.

The title of grand duke seemed inadequate after all these successes; more pretentious claims were based on a new theory suggested by southern Slav and Greek divines. According to this theory the Muscovite duke was a successor of the Byzantine emperors and the only representative of the Orthodox Church in the world. Indeed, the Greek Orthodox Church had accepted the "union" with the Catholics as early as 1439, at the council of Florence, while Constantinople, "the second Rome," had been taken by the Turks in 1453. Obviously, the Greeks had been punished by God for their apostasy, and their succession had to pass to the third Rome, which was Moscow, and to the Russian grand duke, who remained the only faithful and really Christian prince in the world.

The realization of this new scheme began with the marriage of Ivan III with Zoë (in Russia, Sophia), the only niece of the last Byzantine emperor, Constantine Palaeologus (1472). With her arrival new habits appeared at the Muscovite court intended to magnify the new autocrat (a title used by Ivan in foreign relations). The church that gave its sanction to that change claimed a reward: the prince had to help it against all heresies and internal dissensions. The prior of Volokolamsk convent, Joseph, insisted on burning some rationalistic heretics in Novgorod. He also defended the principle that wealth gives power to the church, and he mercilessly crushed monastic and ascetic tendencies of the reformer Nil Sorsky, the "abstainer from property." Thus, the official theory on Russian church and state was formed as early as the end of the 15th century. Under Basil III the unification of Russian territory was consummated by the acquisition of another republic, Pskov (1510); by the final annexation of Ryazan, the last independent grand dukedom; and by a new extension at the expense of Lithuania—the acquisition of the frontier city of Smolensk (1514). The minority of Basil's son Ivan, who was three years old when his father died (1533), and subsequent disputes over the regency between rival factions, lasting 14 years, did not interrupt the growth of the Muscovite state. The reign of Ivan the Terrible marks the beginning of a new period of Russian history.

Ivan IV the Terrible (1533–84).—The reign of Ivan IV the Terrible was an epoch of great and systematic reform. It gave its final shape to the Muscovite tsardom which it preserved until the epoch of Peter the Great. At the age of 17 Ivan demanded to be crowned as tsar (shortened from Latin Caesar), and he connected this official assumption of title with a legend according to which the imperial regalia had been handed over to his predecessor Vladimir Monomakh by a Byzantine *basileus*. The Constantinopolitan patriarch was induced to confirm that legend, but he substituted Vladimir the Saint for Vladimir Monomakh in order to make good a chronological error. Popular songs preserved the memory of Ivan IV as a democratic tsar, who "ferreted out treason [*i.e.*, the boyars] from Russian land." And, indeed, he definitely deprived the "little dukes" who gathered at his court of their remaining sovereign rights and forced them to exchange their hereditary possessions for other landed estates, while their service to Moscow was made obligatory. To pass over to foreign countries was qualified as treason. The same measures were extended to boyars. Both dukes and boyars tried to recompense themselves by assuming political power in the duma of the tsar, and the most powerful of them formed a "selected rada" (a sort of privy council) through which they ruled the state. They summoned the first Russian *zemsky sobor* or "assembly of the country" in 1550, at which representatives of the people revised the criminal code of Ivan III. They also took part in a church council of 1551, where this code was signed and certain traditional rites in church and private life were sanctioned as specifically national. At two previous synods of 1547 and 1549 about 40 new Russian saints were canonized.

However, the regime of the selected rada did not last long. Ivan IV resented it as an interference with his own power, and he broke with the counsels of his youth. He grew nervous and suspicious and began systematically to extirpate ducal and boyars' families. To show his wrath against his enemies he left Moscow (1564) and settled in Alexandrovskaya Sloboda. He then divided the kingdom into two parts: his private *oprichnina* which he ruled personally, and the remaining "land" (*zemshchina*) which he handed over to a christened Tatar, Prince Simeon Bekbulatovich. Far from suspending reconstruction, this curious division helped to reorganize the Russian ruling class—the men of service—on more democratic lines. Ivan IV imitated for this purpose Byzantine patterns. He strictly regulated the connection between possession of landed estates and military obligations. His foreign policy—his long and successful war with Poland, Lithuania and Sweden in order to break through to the Baltic—also forced him to adopt reforms in the army and the financial system. Russian fusiliers (*streltsy*) and foreign mercenaries first appeared under Ivan IV. He also introduced new military taxation and ordered a first general description of taxable land (*pistsoviya knighi*) in order to make the levies proportionate to the record of lots of taxed land; here too he borrowed his system from Byzantium. At the same time he centralized the receipts of the state in a "great treasury" while separating them from his own income, which was concentrated in the "great palace." Through its four boards (the fourths) the great treasury collected taxes chiefly from the north, while the peasants of the Muscovite centre had to work for men of (military) service. The nobles received the honorary title of "courtiers" (*dvoryane*), to distinguish their upper section—the tsar's guard—from the "sons of boyars," who formed the lower section—the provincial gentry. Both courtiers and sons of boyars were yearly sent to defend the western and the southern frontiers —especially the latter, which was fortified by walls and hedgerows (*zaseki*)—against the Tatar incursions. The posts of commandants for each campaign were distributed by the central board called *razryadny prikaz*.

Theodore (1584–98).—The son and heir of Ivan IV, Theodore (Fedor, Fyodor), was a weak man whom Ivan called more fit to be a bell ringer in a convent than a tsar. The direction of affairs fell to his brother-in-law Boris Godunov, an able man who continued Ivan's policy. The Church of Russia received its independence and equality with other Orthodox churches by the granting to its head, the metropolitan Job, of the title of patriarch at the hands of Jeremiah, patriarch of Constantinople (1589). Another important measure was intended to strengthen economically the middle landlord class created by Ivan IV as against the boyars. Peasant labourers were forbidden to leave their estates or migrate to other landowners. All such fugitives who fled from their masters after 1592 (the time of the completion of government registers) were ordered back in 1597. This was the origin of legal serfdom.

Boris Godunov and Basil Shuisky.—In 1598 Theodore died; after some hesitation Boris had himself elected tsar by a *zemsky sobor*. He pursued Ivan IV's policy of weakening the boyars, but he met with opposition on their part. The only legal heir of Theodore, Demetrius, had been killed in Uglich, the place of his exile, in 1591. But the boyars with the help of the Poles opposed to Boris a "Pseudo-Demetrius," a young and well-educated man of obscure origin. Boris died (April 1605) soon after the appearance of this pretender (autumn, 1604), who was accompanied by Polish volunteers and aided by the Cossacks. On June 19, 1605, the impostor entered Moscow. On May 17, 1606, he was killed in a popular outbreak caused by the boyars, who took advantage of the popular dislike of Pseudo-Demetrius' free habits of life and the Catholic tendencies of his Polish protectors. The old dynasty was completely extinguished. The throne of the tsar passed to an influential boyar, Basil Shuisky (1606–10). He gave a formal promise to the boyars "not to repeat the policy of Ivan IV" against them; *i.e.*, not to exterminate them by capital punishment or by exile and the confiscation of estates, without resorting to their court. However, the power of the boyars could not be restored; much more influential now was the rising class of small landlords, men of service. Still more dangerous for Basil were the Cossacks and the fugitive serfs in the newly colonized south of Russia. A real social uprising was started in the south by a former serf, Bolotnikov. The ferment was rife over the south and the east. A second false Demetrius appeared and in the spring of 1608 marched on Moscow. He established his camp at Tushino, near Moscow. The boyars wavered between the tsar Basil and the "thief of Tushino"; there were many flittings. Basil turned to Sweden for help, but as soon as he received aid from Charles IX of Sweden Charles's rival, Sigismund III of Poland, also entered Russia as Basil's adversary and as pretender also to the Russian throne. In Sept. 1609 Sigismund appeared before Smolensk. In July 1610 Basil was dethroned by the boyars and the men of service. The throne remained empty through internal dissensions, and a real time of troubles set in which lasted for three more years (1610–13).

The "Time of Troubles."—The boyars preferred a Polish candidate, and together with the men of service they offered the throne to Sigismund's son Wladyslaw (Wladislaus). A delegation was sent to Smolensk, and Moscow voluntarily received Polish troops under Stanislaw Zolkiewski. A treaty was concluded with Wladyslaw which secured the rights of the duma and the privileges of the landed gentry. A Polish dynasty might have settled in Moscow but for Sigismund's desire to keep the throne for himself. Sigismund's pretension woke up the spirit of national opposition. The second Pseudo-Demetrius at once won popularity, especially among the Cossacks and the lower classes. But in Dec. 1610 the impostor was killed by a Tatar of his suite. The middle landlord class then took action on the urging of the patriarch Hermogen. The men of service under Prokopy Petrovich Lyapunov and the Cossacks under Prince Dmitry Timofeyevich Trubetskoy and the ataman Ivan Martynovich Zarutsky blockaded Moscow; inside the town a popular uprising forced the Poles to retreat to the Kremlin. But here again dissensions arose among the besiegers. Lyapunov was killed by the Cossacks, and the men of service returned to their homes. The south of Russia was in complete disorder; crowds of Cossacks and Polish marauders dispersed all over the north. This finally decided the gentry to make a new effort and to gather a new national army which would "exclude the Cossacks and stand firm until a new sovereign is elected by all the land." Prince Dmitry Mikhailovich Pozharsky was made commander in chief of the army and Kuzma Minin, a butcher from Nijni-Novgorod, the treasurer. All northern towns and districts sent their detachments and their representatives to the army as it advanced up the Volga. In April 1612 it stopped at Yaroslavl. As Novgorod had been taken by the Swedes, Pozharsky offered the throne to Charles Philip, brother of Gustavus Adolphus. In August Pozharsky's army moved southward to Moscow. On Nov. 27 the Poles capitulated in the Kremlin, and a national candidate was set free: the young Michael Romanov, whose father, the metropolitan Philaret (Theodore Nikitich Romanov), a nephew of the first wife of Ivan IV, was at that moment a prisoner in Poland. All votes were at the disposal of a national tsar, more acceptable to the gentry as he did not belong to an old princely family and was young enough (he was 17) to secure the boyars against overbearing conduct. Michael was unanimously elected by a regular *zemsky sobor* on Feb. 21, 1613.

THE ROMANOV (ROMANOFF) DYNASTY

Michael and Alexius.—The *zemsky sobor* which elected Michael (1613–45) continued its session for three years, helping the new tsar to restore the disorganized and ravaged country. A second *zemsky sobor* was then summoned, which pursued for three more years the work of pacification. The co-operation of the tsar with the representatives of different social groups was becoming a regular system. But as the third year's session began (1619), Michael's father Philaret, now patriarch, came back from Polish captivity, and until his death in 1633 he ruled Russia as the "second lord" at the side of his weak son. Peace was concluded with the Swedes, who gained the Finnish seashore, at Stolbova in 1617 and with the Poles, who gained Smolensk, at Deulino (1618). But the struggle on the western as well as on the southern frontier was far from being finished. Anticipating new conflicts the government entirely reconstructed the army; it invited foreign commanders and hired whole regiments of mercenary infantry. To cover the increased expenses it had to introduce new heavy taxation. New registers of lots of cultivated land which had survived the devastation of the troubled times were established. However, an attempt to take back Smolensk from the Poles (1632–34) proved unsuccessful and the government did not feel strong enough to wage war with the Turks to retain Azov, which had been taken by a Cossack raid in 1642. The Russian colonization at that time went no farther than the lines of Belgorod and those of Simbirsk and Zakamsk, which were fortified in the period 1636–56. To the south of the Belgorod line there developed at that very time a crosscurrent of Little Russian (Ukrainian) colonization from

the western bank of the Dnieper. The new Cossack settlers (Poltava, Kharkov) felt the more independent from the Poles the farther they went east, and in 1654 their hetman Bogdan Chmielnicki (Khmelnitsky) voluntarily surrendered the Ukraine to the protectorate of the Eastern Orthodox tsar. A large autonomy of the Ukraine was acknowledged by Alexius (Aleksey), Michael's son and successor (1645–76). A war with the Poles ensued in which the Russians finally took Smolensk, occupied Vilnius and Kaunas and forced Lublin to surrender. But before finishing with the Poles Moscow was implicated in a war with Sweden. By the peace of Kardis (1661) Russia gave Livonia to Sweden; by the peace of Andrusovo it resigned Lithuania to Poland but kept for itself Smolensk, the eastern Dnieper bank and Kiev (1667).

European Influences.—The reigns of the tsars Michael and Alexius are closely connected in home as well as foreign policy. Moral and intellectual development was steadily influenced by the increasing intercourse with western Europe. Since the time of troubles foreigners had come in crowds to Moscow. The clergy objected to too-close relations with these foreigners as having their reflection in a change of habits and even of religion. Consequently, about 1652, foreigners were relegated to a suburb called "the German suburb." However, this proved still worse for the old Russian tradition, as the European culture now formed a single and undiluted unit which strongly influenced the court and the upper social classes. Russian boyars—such as A. L. Ordyn-Nashchokin, A. S. Matveyev and Prince Vasily Vasilevich Golitsyn —began to learn foreign languages, to acquire foreign books, to wear foreign clothes and to furnish their apartments with foreign household goods. Translations of foreign books increased in number from 24 in the first half of the 17th century to 94 in the second half. Alexius was especially accessible to the allurements of foreign comfort and pastime, going so far as to enjoy in private "English comedy" in German adaptations.

The Raskol.—The national religious tradition of the 16th century appeared antiquated. The patriarch Nikon found that certain rites of the national church which distinguished it from Greek orthodoxy, far from proving Russian superiority in faith, were based on ignorant distortion of ancient Greek originals of the books of service. He asked some scholars of the theological academy of Kiev (founded by Peter Moghila about 1625) to prepare a revised edition. The majority of the clergy declared this attempt sacrilegious, as the old Russian saints had saved their souls according to the old books and rites. Nikon insisted on his corrections. He invited two patriarchs (of Alexandria and Antioch) to come to Moscow, and at a council of 1667 the schismatics were excommunicated. A long struggle began between the faith of the Old Believers and the Nikonianism, as the official church was now generally called. Masses of the people followed the schism (*raskol*), and as hopes for reconciliation passed they began to believe that the end of the world was approaching.

Peter I the Great (1682–1725).—The reign of Alexius' invalid son Theodore (1676–82) was a sort of prologue to Peter the Great's reform. The leading part fell, under Theodore as well as during the minority of Peter (1682–89), to a well-educated boyar, Prince Vasily Vasilevich Golitsyn. He was the favourite of Theodore's energetic sister Sophia, who broke the tradition of seclusion of Russian women. After Theodore's death Sophia, with the help of the *streltsy,* made her brother Ivan a second tsar as Ivan V (resigned 1689) at the side of Peter and assumed the regency. Peter (ten years old) was left to himself and amused himself in the neighbouring village of Preobrazhenskoye with technical and mechanical arts as applied to military games. He surrounded himself with boys of his age who soon became his first regular soldiers. The ill success of Golitsyn's much-vaunted expeditions to Crimea (1687 and 1689) gave Peter the chance to overthrow Sophia, to send her to a convent and to exile Golitsyn. However, as tsar, Peter continued his free life of sport. He now became a habitué of the German suburb, where he made acquaintance with many foreign specialists. A Swiss adventurer, François Lefort, initiated him into the pleasures of debauchery and became his best friend. He also encouraged Peter to extend his playing at soldiers to a real campaign against Azov. During two difficult campaigns (1695–96) Peter learned chiefly the insufficiency of his knowledge, and Lefort urged him to complete his military and naval education abroad. Peter followed the advice; he joined his embassy in the capacity of a private workingman and visited Germany, Holland and England (1697–98). He was forced to return speedily to Russia to stifle the new rebellion of the *streltsy* fostered by Sophia's agents.

He then made peace with the Porte (1699) and on the following day declared war on Sweden and invaded Livonia. This Northern War lasted until 1721, and it proved to be the chief factor in Peter's military, financial and administrative reforms. Independently from these reforms made necessary by the war, Peter directly after his return from western Europe forced his subjects to shave their beards (which was felt as an unbearable religious offense) and to dress as foreigners. The Old Believers (schismatics) especially saw in it a proof that Peter was the expected Antichrist.

Peter's army was crushed by Charles XII at Narva (1700). But while Charles was engaged in defeating Peter's allies, Denmark and Poland, Peter called up the yearly levies, created a new standing infantry, cavalry and artillery, and occupied Livonia, Estonia and the mouth of the Neva, where he founded his new capital, St. Petersburg, on May 1, 1703. The "window to Europe" was thus opened. To cover his new and enormous expenses, he acquired the habit of taking money wherever he found it. He thus completely destroyed the old system of central administration, the *prikazy;* instead, he distributed the financial resources of Russia directly among his generals by dividing Russian territory into eight "governments." Each government (*gubernia*) had to pay for the upkeep of a certain number of regiments. Russia thus received in 1708–12 its first regular division into provinces.

Charles XII made the mistake of advancing from Poland to the south of Russia, instead of proceeding straight against Moscow. The Cossack hetman Mazepa (Ivan Stepanovich Mazepa-Koledinsky) promised to help him, but was unable to raise the Ukraine. He joined Charles with an insignificant force. At Poltava (June 27, 1709) Charles was defeated by Peter and fled to Turkey. The Poltava battle produced a strong impression abroad; Russia was becoming a European state. Russian soldiers restored (Aug. 11) the Polish throne, drove the Swedes from Pomerania and appeared in the middle of Germany. The young Russian fleet won a naval victory over the Swedes at Hanko Head. Peter married his niece, Anne, to the duke of Courland (1710) and another niece, Catherine, to the duke of Mecklenburg (1716). He favoured Prussia at the expense of Denmark and Hanover. A Russian army landed near Stockholm (1719 and 1720). In 1721 peace was concluded at Nystad; Russia received Ingermanland, Estonia and Livonia, and parts of Karelia and Finland. After that Peter accepted the title "emperor" (*imperator*), which gave him a claim to equality with the Holy Roman emperor.

Peter was now free to pay more attention to internal reforms. He had to restore the central administration which he had destroyed and to bring it in harmony with his new provincial organization. In the absence of Peter, who only once a year, at Christmas, appeared in his capital (since 1715 in Petersburg), the only central institution which ruled Russia was the senate. From 1711 Peter engaged foreign advisers (Baron Johann Ludwig Luberas and Heinrich Fick) to introduce into Russia the colleges on Swedish pattern (1718–22). Three colleges managed finance: *Kammer-, Staats-* and *Revision-collegia.* Three others were to increase the productive forces of Russia: *Kommerz-, Manufactur-* and *Berg-collegia.* Three chief colleges stood above the others, on an equal footing with the senate, as they represented the tsar's prerogatives: foreign affairs, army and navy. In the provinces all the colleges were supposed to be represented, but as this proved too expensive the whole government of a *gubernia* was reduced to the single *voyevoda* of former times and to his office.

Peter was not a social reformer, but his reforms brought about great changes in the social composition of Russian society. All strata of men of service now melted definitely into one unified class of *dvoryanstvo* (gentry), which had to pass a uniform time (the 14 ranks of the "Table" of 1722) of obligatory service. Possession of landed estates lost all trace of being a remuneration for service. At the same time the different groups of land labourers, half-free and unfree, on the gentry's estates became a unified class of serfs, subject to the poll tax, introduced by Peter in 1718–22 and collected by the landlords. Peter also tried unsuccessfully to differentiate the burgesses from other classes by organizing them in merchant guilds and introducing a kind of municipal self-government under the German name of *Rathaus* and burgomaster (1699–1721).

Peter's educational reforms proved premature. There had been already founded, under Sophia, a Slavo-Greek-Latin theological academy in Moscow (1685–87), where the influence of Kiev amalgamated with the more orthodox Greek tendencies. Peter added a navigation school, led by an English mathematician, Farquharson (1701; transferred to Petersburg as the naval academy, 1715). Both academies soon became centres of two sets of lower schools, clerical and lay, in the provinces. But they were few—about 40 of each for the whole of Russia—and they had to secure their pupils almost by force. A few hundred pupils only finished their studies there. Peter also ordered the publication of useful books —mostly translations—and he introduced the Russian lay alphabet that remained in use till the Soviet reform. But Peter's books proved too specialized for Russian readers and the language of the translations was nearly unreadable; a literary language had first to be created.

Peter's reforms did not leave untouched the sphere of religion. As the clergy was mostly opposed to his reforms, he deprived the Russian church of its spiritual head—the patriarch, a second monarch. Aided by an educated bishop, Theofan Prokopovich, Peter abolished the patriarchate and put in its place the holy synod (1721). The beheaded church was thus deprived, in the opinion of adversaries of that reform, like Stepan Yavorsky, of its legislative authority in questions of dogma.

From Peter I to Catherine II (1725–62).—Peter met with opposition in his own family; his son Alexius (Aleksey Petrovich) grew up under the influence of the clergy and obviously disapproved of Peter's reform. He fled abroad from Peter's menaces, was brought back by fraud and imprisoned on suspicion of a conspiracy against his father's life and died by torture (1718). There remained only two daughters, Anne and Elizabeth, from the second marriage of Peter with a Livonian prisoner, Martha Skavronskaya, renamed Catherine. In 1722 Peter reserved for the monarch the right to designate his successor. But at the moment of death on Jan. 28, 1725, he failed to do so. Peter's creatures, like Alexander Danilovich Menshikov (*q.v.*), who had everything to fear from the survivors of old nobility, resorted to the guards and with their help proclaimed Catherine. The legitimate heir, the son of Alexius, Peter, was thus put aside. The Russian throne became "not hereditary and not elective, but *occupative.*" The period from Peter's death to Catherine II's accession (1725–62) was an eclipse. Male members of the Romanov dynasty (that is to say, Peter's grandsons Peter II and Peter III, the sons of his son Alexius and of his daughter Anne of Holstein, respectively) were frail and feeble of mind. The women—both Peter's niece Anne (Ivan V's daughter) and his daughter Elizabeth—were stronger in mind and body. But they shared their power with favourites, and their choices were not always happy. Court life flourished under these women's reigns and it became very luxurious and expensive. A special school was founded by Anne (the corps of nobles) to teach the noble guards foreign languages, dances and good manners. Balls, theatrical plays, musical entertainments—chiefly by foreign artists—became regular pastimes. The country was badly ruled; foreign policy was venal. Russia took part in European wars with little benefit for itself. From reign to reign the noble guards gained in influence, as they practically disposed of the throne. Catherine I (1725–27) was followed by the rightful heir Peter II (1727–30), thanks to a compromise between Menshikov and the representatives of the old nobility. His reign was fraught with struggle between the two. But Anne, the widowed duchess of Courland, possessed a bad title. The aristocrats offered her the throne on the condition of limiting her power by the supreme council (created under Catherine I) in questions of her marriage, succession, war and peace, taxation, military appointments, etc. Anne signed, but profiting by the guards' dissensions tore up the signed charter and reigned as an autocrat (1730–40), aided by her favourite, Ernst Johann Biren (*q.v.*). She tried to secure the succession in the lineage of her sister, the deceased Catherine of Mecklenburg, by designating as successor under the regency of Biren the baby Ivan VI, just born to her niece, Anna Leopoldovna, duchess of Brunswick. Anna Leopoldovna herself succeeded Biren as regent, but after a few months the guards showed their hatred of the rule of the "Germans" by overthrowing her regency and enthroning Elizabeth, Peter the Great's daughter, who was expected to return to Peter's national policy (1741–62). Indeed, the first fruits of Peter's reforms ripened during Elizabeth's reign: national poetry, a theatre and the first Russian university (Moscow, 1755), all auguring a deeper culture and knowledge for the next generation.

Elizabeth wished to secure the throne for the lineage of her sister Anne of Holstein, and she invited her nephew Peter, educated in the Lutheran religion and in the ideas of Prussian drill, to come to St. Petersburg to learn Orthodoxy and Russian habits. He came and was married (1745) to princess Sophia of Anhalt-Zerbst, the future Catherine II. He was no mate for her. As fast as he lost Russian sympathy by his open aversion to everything Russian, Catherine ingratiated herself by exactly opposite behaviour. After half a year of the reign of Peter III, Catherine was raised by the guards officers to the throne. The brother of her favourite Count Gregory Orlov, Alexis, assassinated Peter as soon as he was banished to Ropsha by Catherine.

For a representation of the succession to the throne of Peter the Great *see* the genealogical table in the article ROMANOFF DYNASTY. Consult also the articles on the several emperors, empresses and regents just mentioned: ANNA LEOPOLDOVNA; ANNE; BIREN, ERNST JOHANN; CATHERINE I; ELIZABETH (PETROVNA); IVAN VI; PETER II; and PETER III.

Catherine II (1762–96).—The long reign of Catherine II was a turning point in Russian history. She received the fruit of half a century's evolution since Peter the Great's reforms. A prolific writer herself, in regular correspondence with the foremost men of her age, with Voltaire, Diderot, Jean le Rond d'Alembert, Friedrich, baron von Grimm, etc., not to speak of fellow potentates such as Frederick II, Maria Theresa and Joseph II, she wished to make her reign brilliant and herself an ideal enlightened monarch. She began her reforms by compiling from Montesquieu and Cesare Bonesana, marchese de Beccaria, an instruction (*nakaz*) on the basis of which a new code of laws was to be composed. In order to discuss it she gathered an elective assembly of 564 deputies chosen from all classes except the clergy and the serfs, and from all parts of the empire. However, she met with opposition on the part of the gentry to her schemes to fix within definite limits their power over the serfs. Far from engaging in a struggle with the ruling class she yielded to their desires; their power was increased and a number of crown estates were distributed among the ranks of her favourites, thus turning their peasant population into serfs.

Catherine then began to search for glory in foreign politics. She conceived a bold scheme: (1) to recover from Poland the western provinces with an Orthodox White Russian and Little Russian population and (2) to take possession of the Black sea shore, drive the Turks from Europe and found in their place a series of new states in Moldavia and Walachia, in the Balkans and in Greece. She wished to take Constantinople and to place there her second grandson, Constantine, as the emperor of a new Greek empire. His very name was chosen to symbolize this project. Catherine was favoured in accomplishing at least a part of these designs by discords between two German states, Prussia (under Frederick II and Frederick William II) and Austria (under Joseph II, Leopold II and Francis II). In her first Turkish war (1768–74) she had Prussia on her side and Austria against her; after P. A. Rumyantsev's victories she concluded a peace at Kuchuk Kainarji, the beginning of the Eastern Question (*q.v.*), as by it Russia received the right to protect Turkish Christians. Moreover, in 1772 she took part in the first partition of Poland, pro-

posed by Frederick II in order to consolidate his territory and to compensate Russia for its war expenditure. In the second Turkish war (1787–91) Catherine had Austria on her side and Prussia against her. She had to content herself, after the victories of Suvorov (Alexander Vasilievich, Count Suvorov Rimniksky) and Prince N. V. Repnin, with the acquisition of Ochakov and the steppe between the Dniester and the Bug. But she consoled herself with new annexations from Poland (the second partition, 1793, and the third partition, 1795; *see* POLAND), while Prussia and Austria were busy fighting against the French Revolution. Catherine also annexed Courland (1795). Her numerous lovers flattered her imperial ambitions: the bold Gregory Orlov in her early years (1762–74), the ingenious Prince Grigory Potemkin in the midst of her reign (1775–91) and the young Platon Zubov, handsome but insignificant, in her declining years (1791–96).

Between her two Turkish wars (1775–85) Catherine returned to the legislative mania of her early years. Made wise by her experience with the commission of the code of 1767, she turned from Montesquieu to Blackstone and profited by the administrative knowledge of J. Sievers, a skilful adviser of German Baltic origin. She then published in 1775 her statute of provinces, a good piece of organic legislation. Here for the first time in Russian history a local unit of administration, judiciary and self-government was created. The statute introduced a regular system of courts of justice, separate financial and administrative offices and —last but not least—corporations of local gentry meeting every three years to discuss their affairs and to elect their marshals. This system lasted until the reforms of Alexander II. The reform of 1775 was completed by two charters granted in 1785 to nobility and to burgesses. The charter of nobility served to perpetuate the power of the ruling class until the liberation of the serfs in 1861, while the burgesses' charter laid the basis for real municipal self-government.

The protection extended to the gentry inevitably created a growing disaffection on the part of the serfs, who impatiently awaited their turn for emancipation. In 1773 the Yaik (Ural) Cossacks revolted under E. I. Pugachev, who called himself Peter III. He roused the Bashkirs and the serfs allotted to the factories in the Urals, assailed Kazan on the Volga and sacked it. Through the whole empire the peasants only awaited his coming to rise, but he did not feel equal to the task, nor could his bands stand against regular troops. He therefore suddenly returned to Cossack country, where he lost his army; he was extradited by his associates, tried and beheaded in Moscow.

Catherine definitely turned her back on the liberal ideas of her youth after the beginning of the French Revolution. She began to persecute representatives of the advanced opinion which she herself had helped to create. A. N. Radishchev, the author of a spirited book, *A Journey from Petersburg to Moscow,* was sentenced to death as a Jacobin in 1790, but the sentence was commuted to ten years' exile in Siberia. N. I. Novikov, a freemason who accomplished admirable educational and editorial work, was sent to Schlusselburg prison in 1792.

Paul I (1796–1801).—Catherine's son and successor, Paul, mounted the throne when he was 42, barely sane and with a bitter feeling of having been deprived by his mother of his right to succeed his assassinated father Peter III. He hated Catherine's favourites and her policy, both internal and external. He stabilized the succession of the Russian throne by his imperial family statute (1797; in force until 1917). He sent Suvorov to Italy to fight against the French Revolution, and he ended his reign while preparing with Napoleon an expedition to India against England. In social questions Paul's policy was also inconsistent: he alleviated the serf's obligatory work for his landlord by reducing it to three days in a week, but he gave away the peasants of the crown to noble proprietors as serfs in an even larger number than Catherine (120,000 yearly). This did not make him, however, popular among the nobility, as his exalted idea of the divine right of the tsars caused him to treat them in a purely oriental way. He used to say that a person could be reputed of importance only as long as he was permitted to converse with his majesty. His ill-balanced mind and tyrannical proclivities inspired fear in his associates, and in the sixth year of his reign he was assassinated by court conspirators.

Alexander I (1801–25).—Paul's son and successor began his reign, as had Catherine (whom he professed to imitate), with attempts at liberal legislation (1801–05), which gave place to active foreign policy and wars (1806–09). There followed a new attempt at a constitutional reform (1809), hampered by the nationalist opposition, which urged and approved the annexation of Finland (1809) and of Bessarabia (1812). The invasion of Napoleon (1812) brought the national feeling to extreme tension. The following years (1813–18) were devoted to the assertion of Russia's influence in Europe. The last years of the reign (1819–25) were marked by a reactionary policy, which provoked the first revolutionary movement in Russia.

Alexander received a careful education at the hand of his grandmother, who wished him to inherit the throne instead of Paul, his father. The Swiss republican F. C. de la Harpe had a strong influence on him in his early years (1784–95). But this education was interrupted by Alexander's marriage (at 16) and did not go beyond imparting to him some general ideas unsustained by exact knowledge. His sentimental feelings were cooled by the court intrigues, by the hidden enmity between his grandmother and father and finally by the harsh system of Paul's reign, which Alexander was expected to approve and obliged to share in. The consequence was that he grew up a past master in dissimulation and self-restraint. His evasiveness in face of other people's strong opinions was often taken for weakness. But he knew how to promote his own views and if impeded in his designs he was capable of violent explosions of wrath.

Initial Liberalism.—In the first year of his reign Alexander surrounded himself with a few friends of his youth—N. N. Novosiltsev, P. A. Stroganov, Prince Adam Czartoryski, Prince V. P. Kochubey—a "private committee" whom he wished to help him in drafting large schemes of reforms. He at once cancelled a series of reactionary measures of Paul and declared his desire to abolish arbitrariness and to inaugurate a reign of law. Public opinion received him with enthusiasm. But the private committee, which met regularly for about a year, found dangerous and untimely both a formal declaration limiting the autocrat's power and the abolition of serfdom. The most important fruit of these good intentions was the introduction of ministries instead of the colleges of Peter the Great, which had been practically abolished by Catherine. A new senate statute was intended to make this institution the highest legal authority (1802). A very cautious ukase of 1803 permitted noble landowners to liberate their serfs, granting them at the same time lots of land. Only 47,000 serfs were thus liberated and became "free agriculturists." Somewhat larger measures limited the power of landowners over the serfs in Livonia and Estonia (1804–05). A new and important impulse was given to public education, which was considered to be a preliminary condition to all substantial reforms. Three new universities were created.

Since 1801 Alexander had feared the consequences of Napoleon's ambition, and he took upon himself, although it had no relation to Russian national interest, to organize a new coalition against France. In 1805 and 1806 he was involved in wars which ended in crushing defeats at Austerlitz and Friedland. He then changed his policy and concluded an accord with Napoleon directed against England, whose commerce with the continent had to be forbidden in all countries which adhered to this continental system. At his personal meeting with Napoleon at Tilsit (1807) Alexander played a part which made Napoleon call him a "northern Talma" (a renowned actor) and a "Byzantine Greek." But he was in part genuinely under Napoleon's influence and was entangled into new wars: with Sweden, which finished with the annexation of Finland (1809), and with Turkey, which lasted for six full years (1806–12) and ended with the annexation of Bessarabia. A year later (1808) Alexander again met Napoleon at Erfurt, but Napoleon's intention to raise the Polish question did not please Alexander, while Napoleon was offended by the refusal of the tsar to give him his sister in marriage. Relations were very strained by the end of 1810.

Conservative opinion was very much incensed against Alexander's alliance with the "Corsican usurper," especially as at that very time another and more serious attempt was made to introduce in Russia a constitutional government. Mikhail Mikhailovich Speransky, a prominent statesman, whose views were favoured by the emperor at that time, prepared a scheme based on the introduction of self-government in four stages, beginning with electoral assemblies (dumas) in the cantons and ending at the top with the duma of the state. Each lower duma elected deputies to the upper one: cantonal dumas to district dumas, district dumas to provincial ones; these latter sent all their members to the state duma, a legislative assembly, deprived of legislative initiative but enjoying the right to make motions concerning the interest of the state, the responsibility of functionaries and the violation of fundamental laws. The senate retained only judicial power, while the newly reformed ministries remained organs of the executive. The council of state, composed of high dignitaries and presided over by the tsar, was to prepare drafts of laws. In fact nothing except the council of state and the reformed ministries was realized (1810). Conservative opinion, as represented by nobility and bureaucracy, was furious with Speransky, and the tsar did not choose to defend him. On a futile pretext Speransky was dismissed from his office of imperial secretary and sent to exile (1812). His successor was an extreme nationalist and conservative, Adm. A. S. Shishkov.

Nationalism and Reaction.—When the war of 1812 began, the nationalist feeling reached its pitch. It was to be a Scythian war—a war of retreat. Time and space were to be the chief allies of Russia, whose military forces were one-half or one-third the size of Napoleon's. And, indeed, the deeper Napoleon penetrated into Russia's endless plain the more equal the chances became. Alexander named another conservative, M. Kutusov, commander in chief in the place of M. Barclay de Tolly (Aug. 29), and a third conservative, Count Feodor Vassilievich Rostoptschin, general governor of Moscow, which was the final aim of Napoleon's strategy. After the bloody but undecided battle at Borodino (Sept. 7) Moscow surrendered to Napoleon. For five weeks of his stay in Moscow he waited in vain for a peace proposal. Moscow was burned by the inhabitants. His army was in process of dissolution, and winter was approaching. Then followed the famous retreat, during which the Grand army was nearly annihilated, and the wars of liberation of 1813 and 1814, which brought Alexander and his army to the walls of Paris. At the Congress of Vienna (1815) he figured as a saviour of Europe, and he continued to play a leading part at Aix-la-Chapelle (1818), Troppau and Laibach (1820) and Verona (1822). All these events produced an enormous impression on the sensitive temperament of Alexander. "The fire of Moscow," he said later to the German pastor R. F. Eylert, "lit up my soul, I then got to know God and became another man." Alexander now found in the Bible the proofs of his mission and proposed to his allies to establish a Holy alliance, a monarchs' league based on the precepts of the Scriptures. His intention was liberal, but Metternich made use of the idea for his policy of repressing all liberal movements in Europe.

The Revolutionary Movement.—Quite different were the impressions which the younger generation of officers who took part in the Napoleonic wars brought with them back to Russia. Many of them while abroad read political newspapers and were present at the debates of representative assemblies. They learned to quote the books of J. L. Delolme, Count Destutt de Tracy, Benjamin Constant, Gaetano Filangieri, Baron Bignon, etc. After their return to Russia they were shocked by the contrast of arbitrary rule, the abuses of bureaucracy, the venality and secrecy of the courts, the sufferings of the serfs and the indifference to popular education. Two secret political societies were formed by the most active of these officers in 1816–18: one by Pavel Ivanovich Pestel in the southern army and the second by a group of guard officers in Petersburg headed by N. M. Muraviev and Nikolay Ivanovich Turgenev. The former society—more radical—imitated the organization of the Carbonari; the latter borrowed its principles from the Tugendbund. Later on Pestel drafted a republican and strongly centralized constitution, while Muraviev composed a monarchical and federal constitution on the basis of those of Spain of 1812 and of the United States. Pestel's tactics were revolutionary, while the Petersburg group intended to help the government openly in questions of education, philanthropy, economics and improvement of justice, thus preparing Russia for a constitutional regime. They expected Alexander to sympathize with them, as in 1815 he gave a constitution to Poland and mentioned at the opening of the *sejm* that he was preparing one for Russia. He also acknowledged the old institutions of Finland. However, Alexander soon ceased to distinguish between "the holy principles of liberal institutions" and "destructive teaching which threatens a calamitous attack on the social order" (his expressions in the speech mentioned). He entirely agreed with Metternich (in 1820) that the liberal principles themselves were destructive. A period of reaction began in Russia. The transition to it was marked by an attempt to impart to Russia Alexander's religious enlightenment. The ministry of public education was united, for that purpose, with a new ministry of spiritual affairs, where all religions including the Russian Orthodox were treated equally (1817). Prince A. N. Golitsyn, the procurator of the holy synod and the president of the Russian branch of the Bible society founded in 1812, was made the chief of the united ministries. The consequence was that in 1819–21 the young universities recently opened were entirely destroyed—especially by the curators of Kazan and Petersburg circuits, M. L. Magnitsky and D. P. Runich. They removed the best professors and prohibited good textbooks on natural law, morals and logic, on the ground that the teaching must be based exclusively on Holy Scripture. For Russian church dignitaries even their mystical pietism was heresy: Golitsyn was forced to leave his office, after he had been anathematized by the archimandrite Photius, a fanatic protected by Alexander's favourite Aleksyei Andreyevich Arakcheyev. During the last part of the reign Arakcheyev, an ignorant and brutal man, enjoyed the power of prime minister.

Under these conditions secret societies changed their character. The measures of Alexander convinced them that monarchs' promises are not to be relied upon. They were also impressed by military pronunciamentos in Spain and Naples (1820). Nikolay Turgenev recorded in his diary in 1820: "We formerly asked, every time we met the readers of newspapers in the club, whether there was a new constitution. Now we ask whether there is a new revolution." One may judge of the impression produced on the officers of the guard when they learned that they had to stifle the Neapolitan uprising, by orders of the Laibach congress.

The former secret society of welfare, imitating the Tugendbund, was officially closed in 1821, as being too moderate. Two societies appeared instead: the northern and the southern constitutionalists and republicans. The constitutionalists were losing ground; radical elements even among them (like the poet K. F. Ryleyev) began to prevail. Proposals of regicide were heard from P. G. Kakhovsky and A. I. Yakubovich but were rejected or indefinitely postponed. In any case, revolutionary tactics were considered inevitable, but no definite scheme was in preparation. Suggestions were made for forcing the tsar, at some favourable opportunity, to nominate a liberal ministry under Speransky and N. S. Mordvinov, who would convoke a great council (later, Russian revolutionaries called it a constituent assembly) which should decide on the form of the government.

A favourable occasion presented itself quite unexpectedly. Alexander died in Taganrog on Nov. 19 (Dec. 1), 1825. The order of succession happened to be undecided. Constantine, the elder of Alexander's surviving brothers, had renounced the throne in 1823, but Nicholas, the younger, did not wish to acknowledge this and swore allegiance to his brother. Constantine would not accept the throne. Nicholas threatened to leave Russia. The correspondence between Warsaw and Petersburg was thus protracted for about two weeks. The Decembrists, as they were called later, decided finally to raise the guard regiments for Constantine against Nicholas and to force Nicholas—in case he survived that day—to appoint a liberal ministry which would do the rest. The rising was a failure (*see* NICHOLAS I). The last of Russian palace

revolutions was spoiled by too much idealism, but it served as an ominous prognostication of the coming democratic revolutionary movement.

Nicholas I (1825–55).—Nicholas was quite unlike Alexander. With a rough nature of limited understanding, he was conscious of his inferiority and sincerely disliked the idea of becoming tsar. But once tsar, he was sure that he would be enlightened from above for the accomplishment of his divine mission, and he conceived an exalted idea of his personal dignity and infallibility. But he was no mystic. Cold and reserved, he inspired fear and hatred and he consciously made use of these feelings as the instrument of his power. His aim was to freeze every germ of free thought and independent moral feeling, as disturbing agents of the order of things entrusted by God to his personal care.

Nicholas' reign is divided into three parts by two European sets of revolutions: those of 1830 and those of 1848. During the first five years (1825–30) he did not feel quite sure of himself and he appealed for help to advisers of Alexander's liberal period, such as Kochubey, Speransky and E. F. Kankrin (Count Georg Cancrin). He even instructed a special committee of Dec. 6 (18), 1826, to collect for him all useful hints about necessary reforms. While punishing severely the Decembrists (five of them were hanged, others sent to Siberia), he wished to make use of all their good ideas. But he reserved for himself the control over public opinion and confided to Count A. K. Benckendorff the organization of a new secret police of gendarmes controlled by the "third section" of his personal chancery. He adopted Alexander's policy of protecting the kings from their peoples, but he made an exception for Christian Turkish subjects (in the first place the Greeks). He thus carried on a war against Turkey (1827–29). By the treaty of Adrianople Greece was liberated; the hospodars of the Danubian principalities were to be appointed for life and free from Turkish interference in internal affairs. The straits and the Black sea were to be open.

Nicholas especially attended to education; he wished to clear it of everything politically dangerous and confine it to the upper class. He abolished the liberal university statutes of Alexander (1804); by the new statutes of 1835 he detached the primary education intended for the lower classes from the gymnasiums and universities, where only children of gentry and of officials were to be admitted.

The expulsion of Charles X from France and the Polish insurrection of 1830–31 determined the legitimist tendency of Nicholas' foreign policy; he wished to become a real "policeman" of Europe, and at Münchengrätz he renewed relations with Metternich. But his excessive interest in the "sick man" in Constantinople finished by rousing Europe against him. In 1833 Nicholas saved the sultan from the Egyptian rebel Mohammed Ali, and by the treaty of Unkiar-Skelessi received for that service free passage for Russian ships to the Mediterranean, while to all other powers the Dardanelles were to be closed during wartime. This concession drew the attention of the European powers, and in 1841 all the five great powers agreed that the Dardanelles should be closed to warships of all nations.

Slavophils and Westernizers.—In sharp contrast with Nicholas' educational policy, a new generation grew up which was bred by Russian universities, especially Moscow university, between 1830 and 1848. They were not politicians or liberals of a Franco-English type. They were idealists and students of the philosophy of F. W. J. von Schelling, J. G. Fichte and G. W. F. Hegel. In Moscow literary salons they did not discuss the form of the government, but dug deep into the very foundations of Russian history and the Russian national mind. Most of them declared that Russia was unlike Europe and its type of civilization potentially far higher than the European one. They thought to discover Russia's peculiarity in its old peasants' commune (mir), which, they said, revealed the socialistic soul of Russia as unlike the individualist western soul. They execrated Peter the Great's Europeanization of Russia as a fatal deviation from the genuine course of Russian history, and they wanted Russia to come back to the forsaken principles of the Eastern Church and state—to orthodoxy and autocracy. The majority of public opinion, led by A. I. Herzen, V. G. Belinsky, Mikhail Bakunin, T. N. Granovsky and others, revolted against this Slavophil doctrine. They opposed to it their own doctrine of the western origin of Russian civilization. Herzen and Bakunin emigrated from Russia on the approach of the revolutions of 1848. They became the originators of Russian socialism, which however did not frighten Nicholas so much as Russian liberalism—an applied doctrine whose dangers he had experienced at the hands of the Decembrists.

Nicholas was not insensible to the chief social question in Russia —that of serfdom. How could he be when peasants' uprisings were steadily growing in frequency? They numbered about 41 in the first four years of his reign, and there were 378 between 1830 and 1849 and 137 during the last five years. Nicholas formed a series of secret committees which, after many failures, prepared the law of 1842 on voluntary accords, which abolished personal serfdom and fixed the amount of peasant lots and payments. Through P. D. Kiselev's energy, the same changes were obligatorily introduced in Poland (1846) and in some western provinces (1847). A real persecution of intellectuals began after the revolutions of 1848. A secret committee, presided over by D. P. Buturlin, was founded to punish press offenses. S. S. Uvarov himself was found too liberal and resigned. His successor, Prince P. A. Shirinsky-Shikhmatov, wished to "base all teaching on religious truth." The university chairs of history and philosophy were closed, the number of students limited; many writers were arrested, exiled or otherwise punished. The private circle of followers of M. V. Butashevich-Petrashevsky, a young socialist, was sent to forced labour in Siberia (including Theodore Dostoievsky) for having read and discussed prohibited literature.

The Crimean War.—Nicholas also wished to dictate his will to Europe. "Submit yourselves, ye peoples, for God is with us": thus ended his manifesto published on March 27, 1848. He sent a Russian army to subdue Hungary when it had revolted against the Habsburgs. A few years later he inadvertently provoked a conflict with Turkey, because of a special question on the distribution of holy places in Jerusalem between Catholic and Orthodox priests, which he involved with the question of the general protectorate of Russia over Christian subjects of the sultan. European powers would not admit this protectorate, and Nicholas found against himself not only Napoleon III and England but also "thankless Austria." Turkish forces attacked the advanced Russian troops in the Danubian principalities on Nov. 4, 1853; France and England declared war on Russia on March 28, 1854. The courage displayed in the defense of Sevastopol proved useless, as the whole fabric of Russian bureaucratic and autocratic government appeared incapable of competing with European technique. Corruption and lack of communication, feeble development of industry and financial deficiency deprived the valiant soldiers of the most necessary means of defense. (See CRIMEAN WAR; TURKEY: *History*.) Nicholas died on March 2, 1855, feeling that all his system was doomed to destruction. A wholesale change of regime was indicated to his son and successor, Alexander II.

Alexander II (1855–81).—Alexander, a man of weak character but good-natured, possessed no steadfast views on politics. During the reign of his father he had sometimes surpassed Nicholas in reactionary intentions. But the Crimean War proved too clearly the danger of Nicholas' martinet system, and public opinion was too impetuous for Alexander to resist. He swam with the current, and this period coincides with the great reforms which made his reign a turning point in Russian history. But Alexander was always conscious of his power as unlimited monarch, and his liberalism ended as soon as his reforms brought with them a revival of political or autonomous tendencies. He then began to waver; the reforms were left unachieved or curtailed. Public opinion grew impatient, extremist tendencies won the ground, and the gap between the government and advanced opinion finally became insuperable. As a consequence, the original impulse for reform was exhausted as early as 1865. There followed a period of faltering which turned into a sheer reaction as the revolutionary movement grew.

Emancipation of the Serfs.—The greatest achievement of the era was the liberation of peasants. It paved the way for all other reforms and made them necessary. It also determined the line of future development of Russia. The chief motive which decided Alexander is clearly expressed in his words to the Moscow gentry: "The present position cannot last, and it is better to abolish serfdom from above than to wait till it begins to be abolished from below." However, Alexander met with passive opposition from the majority of the gentry; their very existence as a class was menaced. The preparatory discussion lasted from 1857 to March 1859 when the drafting commissions of the main committee were formed, composed of young officials—such as N. A. Milyutin and Y. A. Soloviev and their Slavophil friends Y. F. Samarin and Prince V. A. Cherkasski—enthusiastically devoted to the work of liberation. Y. I. Rostovtsev, an honest but unskilled negotiator enjoying the full confidence of the emperor, was mediator. The program of emancipation was very moderate at the beginning, but was gradually extended under the influence of the radical press and especially Herzen's *Bell*. But Alexander wished that the initiative should belong to the gentry and exerted his personal influence to persuade reluctant landowners to open committees in all the provinces, while promising to admit their delegates to discussion of the draft law in Petersburg. No fewer than 46 provincial committees containing 1,366 representatives of noble proprietors were at work during 18 months preparing their own drafts for emancipation. But they held to the initial program, which was in contradiction with the more developed one. The delegates from the provincial committees were only permitted—each separately—to offer their opinions before the drafting committees. Unfortunately, Rostovtsev died in Feb. 1860. Alexander, who already feared that he had gone too far in his concessions, appointed as his successor Count V. N. Panin, a reactionary. Under his influence the proposed allotments of land to peasants were diminished and the rents were increased. However, it was impossible to change the main lines of the draft. By the law of Feb. 19 (March 3), 1861, the peasant became personally free at once, without any payment, and his landlord was obliged to grant him his plot for a fixed rent with the possibility of redeeming it at a price to be mutually agreed upon. If the peasant desired to redeem his plot, the government paid at once to the landowner the whole price (in 5% bonds), which the peasant had to repay to the exchequer in 49 years. Although the government bonds fell to 77% and purchase was made voluntary, the great majority of landowners—often in debt—preferred to get the money at once and to end relations which had become insupportable. By 1880 only 15% of the peasants had not made use of the redemption scheme, and in 1881 it was declared obligatory. The landowners tried, but in vain, to keep their power in local administration. The liberated peasants were organized in village communities governed by elected elders.

Administrative Reform—After the emancipation of the peasants, the complete reform of local government was necessary. It was accomplished by the law of Jan. 1 (13), 1864, which introduced the district and provincial *zemstva* (county councils). Land proprietors had a relative majority in these assemblies. They were given (in all Russia) 6,204 seats (48%) while the peasants were entitled to choose only 5,171 delegates and the town inhabitants 1,649 (12%). The competence of *zemstva* included roads, hospitals, food, education, medical and veterinary service and public welfare in general. Before the end of the century services in provinces with *zemstvo* government were far ahead of those in provinces without.

A third capital reform touched the law courts. The law of Nov. 20 (Dec. 2), 1864, put an end to secret procedure, venality, dependence on the government, etc. Russia received an independent court and trial by jury. The judges were irremovable; trials were held in public with oral procedure and trained advocates. Appeals to the senate could take place only in case of irregularities in procedure.

A little later came the reforms of municipal self-government (1870) and of the army (1874). Gen. D. A. Milyutin (the brother of N. A. Milyutin) reduced the years of active service from 25 to 16 and made military service obligatory for all classes. The only exemptions admitted were for reasons of education. Military courts and military schools were humanized.

The Revolutionary Movements.—The only branch of public life exempted from reform was the press. The press profited indeed by the new spirit of Alexander's reign. While in the last ten years of Nicholas' reign only 6 newspapers and 19 (mostly specialist) monthlies were permitted, during the first ten years of Alexander's there were 66 newspapers and 156 monthlies. The general tendency of the press, very moderate at the beginning, soon became very radical. The leading spirits were the nihilists N. G. Chernyshevsky, N. A. Dobrolyubov and D. I. Pisarev, the last of whom preached extreme individualism. As early as 1862 temporary measures were applied against radical periodicals. Instead of a law on the liberty of the press there appeared in 1865 new temporary rules (which remained in force for fully 40 years) compiled from Napoleon III's law of 1852. They set free from "previous censure" books of more than ten sheets, but the censors continued to seize printed books before their issue.

A new wave of revolutionary movement set in. It proceeded from the young generation of university students, who expected an agrarian revolution directly after the liberation of peasants. They were busy preparing for it workingmen, soldiers and peasants through popular education. Secret circles were formed, proclamations issued and even a revolutionary movement was attempted in connection with the Polish uprising of 1863. Finally, an attempt was made by a student, D. Karakozov, to assassinate the tsar in April 1866. All these attempts were extremely naïve; a few young revolutionaries were executed or sent to Siberia and the whole movement was stifled in its primary stage. But Alexander was frightened. Gradually he dismissed his liberal advisers, and conservatives took their place. The home office was given (1861) to P. A. Valuyev, who tried to paralyze the introduction of the emancipation law and formally prosecuted its faithful adherents. University troubles brought about the removal of the liberal minister of public instruction, A. V. Golovnin, the author of a model university statute of 1863. His successor was a reactionary, Count Dmitry Andreyevich Tolstoy, who found the means of salvation in the classics. The old chief of gendarmes, Prince V. A. Dolgorukov, had to give place, after Karakozov's attack, to Count Peter Shuvalov, who became the soul of reaction. The government-general of St. Petersburg was abolished and the martinet Gen. F. F. Trepov made grand master of the police. D. N. Zamyatnin, minister of justice, under whom the reform of tribunals was carried through, fell a victim to his defense of this reform against an imperial whim; he had to yield to an ignorant reactionary, Count K. I. Pahlen (1867), who nearly annihilated the reform. The same was done for the press by A. Timashev who superseded Valuyev as home minister in 1868. Two radical monthlies, the *Contemporary* and the *Russian Word,* were closed (1866). M. N. Katkov, a former European liberal who now inclined to extreme nationalism and reaction, became the most influential journalist.

All this contributed to uphold and to increase the disaffection of educated public opinion. About 1869 a new young generation appeared which gave expression to that state of mind. Russian emigrants in Switzerland discussed at that time a new revolutionary doctrine later called populism (*narodnichestvo*). P. L. Lavrov was giving it a scientific basis, but Mikhail Bakunin found this too learned and plainly invited the youth to give up the study and go straight to the people with the aim of inducing disorder. He found this easy, since Russian peasants with their communes were born socialists. The youth of Russia, chiefly the young girls who went to study abroad as there were no female institutes of learning in Russia, listened to these discussions in Zürich and, of course, mostly preferred Bakunin's active optimism to Lavrov's learning. In 1873 they were all ordered back to Russia by the government, and they met, when at home, with many student circles which were busy distributing books and revolutionary pamphlets among their provincial branches and workingmen. N. V. Tschaikovsky, Prince P. A. Kropotkin and Sergius Stepniak (S. M. Kravchinsky) were among the leaders of that educational and (later on) revolutionary work. They decided, in the spring of 1874, to go to the people—a naïve crusade by inexperienced youth, hardly out of their teens—in order both to teach the people and to learn from

them their socialistic wisdom. Of course they were not acknowledged by the people, in spite of their peasant attire, and were easily ferreted out by the police; 770 were arrested and 215 sent to prison. They then decided to change their tactics. A regular secret society was founded in 1876 under the name of Land and Liberty (or "Will"). They still hoped to provoke a mass uprising according to the ideals of the people, but their village settlements proved useless for revolution while in the towns they soon got engaged in a lively conflict with the police. As a result the terrorist side of their activity came to the forefront. In the autumn of 1879 the terrorist group formed a separate party, the People's Will, while the remaining members led by G. V. Plekhanov—under the name of Black Partition (*i.e.,* agrarian revolution)—remained inactive. A series of terrorist acts then followed, beginning with that of Vera Ivanovna Zasulich, who fired on Trepov for his having flogged a prisoner and was acquitted by the jury (1878). In 1879 A. Solovyev fired five shots at the tsar. On Feb. 17, 1880, a workman, S. N. Khalturin, blew up the imperial dining room at the Winter palace. The police seemed powerless against the famous executive committee which directed the blows, and the government asked the loyal elements of public opinion for support. The answer was given, in the name of the Chernigov *zemstvo,* by Ivan Petrunkevich: he said that no cooperation was possible with the government as long as public opinion was stifled. The Tver *zemstvo,* led by F. I. Rodichev, asked the tsar to "give us what he gave to Bulgaria" (*i.e.,* constitution and political freedom). After the Winter palace explosion a supreme commission was appointed under the chairmanship of M. T. Loris-Melikov, who was given a sort of dictatorial power. Loris-Melikov's design was to isolate revolutionary elements by concessions to the liberals and, after exterminating the revolutionaries, to summon a sort of consultative assembly, thus renewing certain projects of aristocratic landowners in 1861–63. He submitted to the tsar, on Feb. 9, 1881, a proposal to appoint two drafting committees for administrative and financial reforms and to submit their drafts to a general commission, where experts chosen by the *zemstva* and municipalities should also be heard (two from each of them). The respective laws would be issued in the ordinary way by the council of state, but 15 delegates should be admitted to its session. It did not at all look like a constitution, but it might have served as an introduction to it. Fate decided otherwise: on the very day when Alexander signed Loris-Melikov's project, on March 1 (13), 1881, he was assassinated by revolutionaries, led by Sophia Lvovna Perovskaya, on his way back home.

Foreign Policy.—Alexander II was more successful in his foreign policy. He ascended the throne at a moment of great exhaustion and humiliation for Russia. The Paris treaty (1856) substituted European control for a Russian protectorate over Turkish Christians; the Russian fleet in the Black sea ceased to exist; the portion of Bessarabia nearest to the Black sea was given to the Danubian principalities. However, Russia did not permit Napoeon III to make an international question of the Polish uprising of 1863; Alexander then approached his relative William of Prussia and helped him against France in the foundation of the German empire. Russia made use of the Franco-German War to repudiate the provisions of the Paris treaty forbidding Russia to construct naval arsenals and to keep a fleet in the Black sea (1870). In 1872 the German, Austrian and Russian emperors met at Berlin and concluded the Three Emperors' league (without any formal treaty being signed; *see* EUROPE). However, Russia did not wish to strengthen Germany too much at the expense of France. In 1875 thanks to Russia's insistence a Franco-German conflict was averted, to the great dissatisfaction of Bismarck, who threatened the Russian foreign minister, Prince A. M. Gorchakov, with revenge. In the same year the Eastern Question was reopened by a rising of Christian Slavs in Bosnia and Hercegovina (*see* EUROPE and TURKEY). In 1876 (summer) began the Bulgarian uprising. Russia proposed co-operative action to the powers, but, meeting with hidden aid to Turkey from Disraeli, Alexander decided to act alone. When Serbia and Montenegro declared war on Turkey he met Francis Joseph at Reichstadt and on July 8, 1876, concluded an agreement in which all possibilities of defeat, victory or the collapse of Turkey were anticipated. Austria was to receive Bosnia and Hercegovina for occupation and administration; Russia was permitted to take back the lost portion of Bessarabia. A last attempt to formulate a European program of pacification of the Balkans was made by the powers at the Constantinople conference (Dec. 1876). After its failure Count Nicholas Pavlovich Ignatiev visited the European capitals to discuss the possibility of war. Austria and England put as conditions of their neutrality: no attack on Constantinople; no Russian territorial acquisitions; no thrusting Serbia into war; Bulgaria, in case of its liberation, not to be under direct Russian control. Thus, Russia was in advance deprived of possible gains in case of victory; as a matter of fact, Disraeli looked for its defeat. Nevertheless, Alexander went to war (*see* RUSSO-TURKISH WARS). Close to the walls of Constantinople the Russian army was stopped by the British fleet, and the treaty of San Stefano (March 3, 1878), favourable to the Bulgarians, was emasculated at the Congress of Berlin (*q.v.*). Russian public opinion, ignorant of the agreements concluded before the war, was much incensed against Bismarck, "the honest broker." Russia received the lost part of Bessarabia and Kars, Ardahan and Batum in Transcaucasia. Far more important were the acquisitions of Alexander in central Asia. From 1864 his generals were active against Kirghiz and Turkoman tribesmen who raided the unprotected frontier of Siberia. Russian soldiers marched up the Syr-darya, subjugated Bukhara and from there, through the desert of Khiva, reached the Caspian shore. In 1867 the territory between Issyk-Kul and the Aral sea was constituted into a province called Turkistan, and in 1874 another province under the title of Transcaspia was formed of territories between the Amu-darya and the Caspian sea. Russia reached the frontiers of Afghanistan and Chinese Turkistan, while in the far east by the treaty of Aigun (1858) it obtained from China territory running east from the rivers Amur and Ussuri to the Pacific seaboard, and the naval base of Vladivostok was founded. Japan ceded Sakhalin in 1875 in exchange for two Kurile islands. In 1867 Alaska was sold to the United States for $7,200,000.

Industrial Progress.—Under Alexander II Russia made decisive steps toward industrialization. The length of railway increased from 644 mi. (1857) to 2,260 (1867) and to 11,070 (1876). Factory production grew from 352,000,000 (1863) to 909,000,000 roubles (1879); the number of workingmen from 419,000 to 769,000; the export of grain from 52,800 bu. (1860–62) to 125,600 (1872–74). In 1850 and 1857 Russia (for the second time since 1819) tried the experiment of free trade, but as it brought with it an excess of imports—a thing unusual in Russia—M. K. Reutern, the minister of finance in 1862–78, returned to the protectionist system of Kankrin (1823–44). He also favoured the organization, for the first time in Russia, of private credit institutions. The 10 land banks which were in existence at the end of the 19th century were all founded in 1871–73; there were also 28 commercial banks (founded 1864–73), 222 municipal banks (1862–73) and 71 societies of mutual credit (1877).

Alexander III (1881–94).—Alexander III succeeded his father and was at first expected to continue his tradition. But the quasi-constitutional scheme of Loris-Melikov, discussed on March 8 in the Winter palace, met with the opposition of Constantine Petrovich Pobedonostsev, the former tutor of Alexander and his most trusted adviser. On April 29, 1881, appeared a manifesto written by Pobedonostsev without the ministers' knowledge, in which the tsar described himself as "chosen to defend" autocratic power. At the same time a promise was made to continue Alexander II's reforms. Loris-Melikov, with D. A. Milyutin, at once resigned and was replaced by N. P. Ignatiev, a friend of the Slavophils, who promised to leave untouched the powers of the *zemstva* and municipalities and to alleviate the burdens of the peasants. And indeed, in June and September 1881, Ignatiev summoned the experts selected by the government among liberal *zemstvo* men. With their help he drafted a scheme for lowering the redemption prices, abolishing the poll tax and regulating internal colonization and land rents. The new minister of finance, N. K. Bunge, assisted by opening a peasants' bank and also enacted

the first factory acts (1882) and appointed special factory inspectors to enforce their application. A special commission under M. S. Kakhanov (1881–84) prepared a reform of peasant self-government based on the principle of the equality of peasants with other social classes. In May 1882 Ignatiev proposed to Alexander to summon a *zemsky sobor* in Moscow of about 3,000 representatives from all classes, on the day of the coronation.

Here Katkov and Pobedonostsev won their victory. Ignatiev resigned; the reactionary Count Dmitri Tolstoy took his place as home minister. His tool I. D. Delyanov enacted in his former ministry a new reactionary statute for the universities (1884). He now became the mouthpiece of the nobility and gentry, a decaying class that tried to preserve as much as possible of their vanishing power and property. In 1885 a special Bank for the Nobility was opened with the aim of preserving the landed property of the gentry from final liquidation (for debt). Then Tolstoy proposed to A. D. Pazukhin—a sworn defender of noble privileges —to revise the *zemstvo* institution with the avowed aim of making the nobles' influence paramount in the countryside. As a result two important laws were published, on July 12, 1889, on land captains and on June 12, 1890, on *zemstva*. The composition of district assemblies was changed from the figures given above to 5,433 representatives of landed owners (57%), 1,273 municipal representatives (13%) and 2,817 representatives of village communities. However, the chief aim of the government was, rather than to favour the gentry, to incorporate both the land captains and the executive boards of the *zemstva* in its civil service by making them subordinate to the provincial governors and destroying their representative character.

An outstanding feature of Alexander III's reign was an increased persecution of everything dissimilar to the officially accepted national type. Dissenting sects, the Uniates and the Lutherans in the western provinces, Lamaist Kalmucks and Buriats and especially Jews suffered a systematic persecution. The press was definitely muzzled, revolutionary organizations were destroyed and revolutionary movement was stifled. Public opinion was silent until the great famine of 1891; from that year symptoms of a revival appeared. The new movement was entirely different from the populism of the '60s and '70s. The Russian socialists became Marxists. Russia, they argued, was becoming an industrial country and the numbers of the industrial proletariat were speedily increasing. In fact, I. A. Vyshnegradsky, minister of finance since 1887, not only continued Reutern's policy in developing the railway (14,900 mi. at the beginning, 24,000 mi. at the end of Alexander's reign) and in protecting industry (prohibitive tariff, 1891), but tried to influence the foreign market and to stabilize the rate of exchange of the Russian rouble. He also resorted to foreign capital. In 1889–94 its influx was 5,300,000 roubles, as compared with 1,500,000 of 37 years before (1851–88). However, the position of the Russian consumer who had to pay about 34% ad valorem for imported goods, instead of 13% as before the tariff of 1891, was much worsened. The peasants especially suffered, as the price of grain, their only article for sale, fell from 1.19 roubles per *pud* (1881) to 0.59 in 1894, while their allotments, which had been insufficient at the moment of liberation, further diminished (1861–1900) to 54.2%. As a result, their arrears of taxes increased more than five times compared with 1871–80. Vyshnegradsky tried to relieve the treasury by increasing enormously the customs and excise. In the decade 1883–92 taxation increased 29% while the population increased only 16%. Thus, elements of an agrarian crisis were increasing as the 19th century was nearing its end.

Alexander III's foreign policy was peaceful. He wished to be his own foreign minister; Gorchakov gave place to a submissive Germanophil, N. K. de Giers. Bismarck profited by this and, in spite of his alliance with Austria (1879) which was avowedly concluded against Russia, contrived to renew, as early as 1881, the Three Emperors' league of 1872. In 1884 it was renewed for three following years and in 1887, as Austria seceded, Bismarck concluded his famous "reinsurance" treaty with Russia. All these treaties fettered Russia in its Balkan policy but secured the country against the opening of the straits to England and even permitted to it, by a secret protocol, the military occupation of the straits in case of necessity. As at the same time the Triple alliance with Italy was concluded (1882), Bismarck's policy proved too complicated for his successor, and in 1890 a Russian proposal to prolong the treaty for the next six years was rejected by Count Caprivi. Thus the way was opened to a Franco-Russian *rapprochement*, while Germany was courting England, Russia's competitor in Asia (where Alexander in 1885 took Merv, thus establishing Russia on the frontiers of Afghanistan). France opened to Russia its market for loans and its factories for armaments in 1889; a French squadron was enthusiastically received in Kronstadt in 1891; and the subsequent *rapprochement* culminated in a military convention worked out in Aug. 1892 and definitely ratified by the tsar in March 1894.

Alexander III died on Nov. 1, 1894, in Livadia, 50 years old. His robust constitution had been sapped by constant fear of the revolutionaries, which made him live at Gatchina like a prisoner, surrounded by a cordon of police agents.

Nicholas II, to 1917.—There can hardly be imagined a more tragic contrast than that of the extremely complicated situation inherited by Nicholas II and the complete nullity of the man who had to solve the problem. Like his father, Nicholas was not prepared to reign; like Alexander III, he would have preferred to live as a private man in his family circle, and he hated his exalted position which clashed with his modesty and bashfulness. However, like Alexander III, he felt it a duty to bear the burden of autocratic power and, moreover, to preserve autocracy untouched for his successor. He had to wait long for this heir, as his marriage (1894) with Princess Alix of Hesse, known as the empress Alexandra Fedorovna, brought him first four daughters, and when finally a son (Alexius) was born (1904), the parents had constantly to tremble for his life, as he inherited through his mother the dangerous disease of haemophilia. In their wish to save him at any cost they put their confidence in every kind of quack, beginning with M. Philippe, the spiritist from Lyons, and ending with the famous Gregory Rasputin. Her relations with them finally brought the nervous Alexandra to a state of religious exaltation and mystic faith in her predestined mission to save the tsar and her son from evil by obeying the precepts of God's elect.

The initial hopes of the liberals that the "leaden coffin lid" of Alexander III's reign would be raised by the new tsar were soon dispelled. When messages of congratulation on his marriage were brought to the tsar by innumerable deputations at a reception (Jan. 17 [29], 1895) the delegates asked the tsar "that the voice of the people should be heard" and "that the law should henceforth be respected and obeyed not only by the nation but also by the ruling authorities." The tsar, instructed by Pobedonostsev, answered: "I am aware that in certain *zemstvo* meeting voices have been lately raised by persons carried away by senseless dreams of the participation of *zemstvo* representatives in internal government. Let all know that I intend to defend the principle of autocracy as unswervingly as did my father." The liberals answered next day in an open letter: "'Senseless dreams' concerning yourself are no longer possible. If autocracy proclaims itself identical with the omnipotence of bureaucracy, its cause is lost.... It digs its own grave.... You first began the struggle, and the struggle will come."

The struggle had come. In June 1896 St. Petersburg saw the first strike of 30,000 workingmen. The evolutionary wing of the Marxist socialists triumphed; here at last the masses had come forward with purely economic demands. In 1898 the Russian Social Democratic Labour party was formed. However, the old leaders did not approve of this peaceful and legal economism of the young generation. In their "orthodox" organ *Iskra* (*Spark*), published abroad, they defended the political and revolutionary side of Marxism. In 1903, at a conference in London, their tendency, represented by V. I. U. (Nicolai) Lenin, obtained the majority and bolshevism (*Bolsheviki*=majoritarians) was created. On the other hand, the People's Will party was revived under the name of Social Revolutionaries with a new program in 1898. They remained true to their two leading ideas, agrarian revolution and terrorism. Agrarian riots began two years later in southern Rus-

sia. In 1899 began also student disorders which were answered by the minister of public instruction, N. P. Bogolepov, by the menace of military service for delinquents. On Feb. 27, 1901, Bogolepov was killed by the student P. V. Karpovich. On April 15, 1902, the home minister, D. S. Sipyaghin, was killed by S. V. Balmashev. Pobedonostsev recommended V. K. Plehve for his successor. Plehve had to struggle not only against the agrarian uprisings but also against moderate elements—the *zemstvo* liberals and the radicals of the liberal professions (professors, lawyers, journalists, engineers, the so-called third element, officials of the *zemstva*, etc.). They formed a secret Union for Liberation and from July 1902 published their weekly, *Liberation*, abroad. The number of persons accused of political crime rose from 919 (1894) to 1,884 (1899) and 5,590 (1903). The minister of finance, Serge Julievich Witte, tried to oppose Plehve's policy but was dismissed in Aug. 1903.

The Russo-Japanese War.—Witte's removal proved especially fatal for Russian policy in the far east. William II of Germany suggested to Nicholas the idea that Russia's true mission was in Asia, not in Europe. The Trans-Siberian railway (begun 1891) presented new facilities for penetration, especially when a treaty with Li Hung-chang (May 1896) secured its extension by the East China railway; and in May 1898 a new lease was received to construct a branch through Mukden to Port Arthur, which six months before had been occupied by the Russian fleet. A chauvinistic guard officer, A. M. Bezobrasov, profited by Nicholas' confidence to cover with the tsar's protection his concession for cutting wood on the Yalu river. Many "patriotic" courtiers, grand dukes and the tsar himself acquired the bonds of the Eastern Asiatic Industrial society. Japan objected to the occupation of the left bank of the Yalu. As Prince Hirobumi Ito received no satisfaction in Petersburg, he went to London and concluded (1902) a five-year alliance with England. Russia was then obliged to withdraw its troops from Manchuria and promised to do so before Oct. 8, 1903. The promise was not fulfilled. The war party, led by Bezobrasov and Plehve, decided against Witte for war. They knew nothing of Japan's readiness for war and were stupefied by the famous night attack of Feb. 8, 1904, on the Russian fleet in Port Arthur (*see* RUSSO-JAPANESE WAR).

The Revolution of 1905.—The revolutionary movement found new substance in Russian military defeats. Patriotic feeling began to turn against the government. The war grew extremely unpopular. Plehve, who had wished to divert public attention from the internal situation by war, was blown up with his carriage in July 1904. After much wavering Nicholas appointed on Sept. 8, 1904, Prince P. D. Svyatopolk-Mirsky as successor to Plehve. Public opinion was delighted. The liberal *zemstvo* men met in Petersburg, on Nov. 19–22, 1904, in private and worked out a petition to Nicholas asking for inviolability of the person, freedom of conscience, of speech, of meeting, of press, of association and equal civil rights. The majority also asked for a regular popular representation in a separate elective body which should participate in legislation, in working out the budget and in controlling the administration. The professional groups organized banquets to support the *zemstvo* program. Nicholas still wavered. His *ukase* of Dec. 12 (25) did not go beyond general promises and kept silence over the representative assembly. The chance of peaceful compromise with moderate constitutionalists was passing by. The revolution began.

On Sunday, Jan. 9 (22), 1905, many thousand workingmen, led by the priest Georgii Gapon, marched with icons, singing religious songs, to the Winter palace to speak to "their tsar." But the tsar was absent; the troops fired on the defenseless crowd and killed about 1,000 people. Svyatopolk-Mirsky resigned. A. G. Bulyghin, a bureaucrat, was appointed his successor. As a reply, Grand Duke Sergius was blown up in the Kremlin of Moscow by the Social Revolutionary Ivan Kalyayev. The tsar still wavered. He issued a promise merely to summon "the worthiest persons" to share in the drafting and discussing of laws.

Meanwhile, public excitement was growing, fanned by the news of Tsushima (May 27–28). The constitutional and the revolutionary movements began to separate. Constitutionalists (*zemstvo* men and Liberation union) held their congresses and prepared drafts of constitutional Laws. After Tsushima they sent to Nicholas a deputation which repeated the demands of the November petition of 1904 and received (June 6 [19]) the answer that the "tsar's will was unshakable." Two weeks later Nicholas promised to another delegation of the nobility that he would keep the tradition of the past. On Aug. 6 (19) a law conceded a duma of the empire. But it was to be a consultative chamber, composed of class delegates, representing peasants (43%), landed proprietors (34%) and burgesses (23%). This duma was entitled only to prepare drafts of laws for the council of state. This, "Bulyghin's constitution," provoked general indignation. Its only result was to give the upper hand to revolutionary elements (the Socialist parties). There was now no end to meetings, workmen's and students' strikes, agrarian uprisings, which finally, on Oct. 10–14, united in one general strike all over Russia. From railway employees it spread to post and telegraph personnel, factories, shops, business offices and even children in primary schools. Communication with the provinces was interrupted; Nicholas was isolated in his summer residence at Peterhof. On Oct. 14 (27) a soviet (council) of workmen's delegates was formed whose vice-chairman was L. D. Trotsky. On Oct. 15 (28) the Constitutional Democratic (Kadet) party was founded, which included the radical wing of the *zemstvo* men and the moderate elements from the Liberation union and other professional unions. The common aim of the left wing of public opinion was a constituent assembly elected on universal suffrage and leading to parliamentary government.

Nicholas thought of abdication. But he was saved by Witte, who had just concluded (Sept. 5) peace with Japan at Portsmouth, N.H., and was generally expected to become a peacemaker inside Russia. On Oct. 17 (30) Nicholas signed the famous manifesto prepared by Witte (now a count) and published it together with Witte's report, in which the necessity of concession was laid down. The manifesto promised a real inviolability of person, freedom of thought, speech, meetings and associations. No law was to be enacted without consent of the duma. But the word "constitution" was not used; the tsar retained his title of autocrat (*samoderzhets*). He openly favoured the newly formed reactionary organization, the Union of the Russian People. Then a wave of absolutist demonstrations and Jewish pogroms organized by the police followed, in a few days, the short-lived outbreak of enthusiasm elicited by the tsar's concessions.

Witte was made prime minister of a unified cabinet. But he could not persuade liberal leaders to enter his cabinet as the situation remained extremely uncertain. His minister of the interior, P. N. Durnovo, was a reactionary. Pobedonostsev resigned (Nov. 1), but Gen. D. F. Trepov was retained in proximity to the tsar. Agrarian troubles reached their height in November, and Count Witte proposed to his minister of agriculture, N. N. Kutler, to prepare a draft of law on the basis of the expropriation of the landowners. It roused against Witte the nobility, who also founded a union. On the other hand, Witte had to fight against the revolutionary movement which found its headquarters in the Petersburg soviet of workmen's delegates. The soviet published decrees and tried to play the part of a second government. Trotsky, backed by Lenin, preached a permanent revolution. However, the policy of the Socialist parties definitely alienated the sympathy of the possessing class. On Dec. 3 (16) the soviet with all its members present was arrested. Its substitutes replied by an armed uprising in Moscow (Dec. 7 [20]). Until Dec. 13 (26) there was shooting in the streets; then the guard regiments came down from Petersburg and the rebels were dispersed. There followed the so-called punitive expeditions led by Generals G. A. Min, Paul Rennenkampf and A. N. Möller-Zakomelsky which exterminated with ruthless cruelty what remained of the revolutionary movement in Russia and Siberia.

This decisive blow at the revolution weakened also the constitutional movement. Witte was losing ground. A certain extension of electoral right, especially in the towns (Dec. 11 [24]) was his last success. The predominance of peasant deputies remained untouched as the peasantry was considered more conservative and reliable than the nobility. Witte promised to the tsar a pliant duma. He dismissed Kutler, but he refused to promise to dissolve the duma if it raised the agrarian question, a measure proposed by his competitor, the former home minister I. L. Goremykin. Nicholas was encouraged to resistance by the repression of the revolutionary movement. He assured the deputations of the Union of Russian People that "the sun of Truth will shine bright over the Russian land" (Jan. 1906) and that his "autocracy will remain unchanged as it had been of old" (March).

The First Duma.—Witte's fate was sealed when the elections, which he left comparatively free, gave the majority to the Constitutional Democrats (the Kadets) together with peasants who wanted a radical agrarian reform. The Socialists, who still hoped for a revolution resulting in a real constituent assembly, decided to boycott the elections. Witte resigned after having rendered the tsar his last service: he concluded a loan in France, which made the tsar free to deal with the duma as he liked. Just before the duma met (April 27, 1906) new fundamental laws were published which curtailed its power (*see* DUMA) while leaving to the tsar an extensive prerogative and to the council of empire equal rights in legislation and the budget. The government preserved the right of extraordinary legislation, without the duma, in emergency.

Under these conditions the struggle was unequal. The dissolution of the duma was assured when in its address to the throne it proposed its own program of embodying into laws and enlarging the liberal promises of the October manifesto. After much delay Goremykin declared the program inadmissible. He received a vote of censure, which was, however, of no consequence. There was an avalanche of questions and interpellations in order to expose and to restrain the arbitrary rule of the bureaucracy—but all in vain. The government answered by practically boycotting the duma. Then a long debate began on the agrarian project introduced by the Kadets, on the basis of partial expropriation of big landed estates. The government published a sort of counterproject and warned the country not to believe in the duma's promises. The duma replied by a declaration which was interpreted by the government as an illegal appeal to the country and served as a pretext for dissolution. On July 9 (22) the delegates found the Taurida palace locked and surrounded by army detachments and artillery. About 200 of them moved to Viipuri in Finland in order to protest and to invite the people to passive resistance should no new duma be convoked. On the other hand, the congress of the United Nobility demanded the changing for their benefit of the electoral law by the mere will of the tsar, in violation of the fundamental laws. P. A. Stolypin, who had dissolved the first duma and taken the succession of Goremykin, did not dare to do so. But he tried instead to solve the agrarian question by means of emergency legislation. His scheme was to increase the lots of the well-to-do peasants at the expense of the poorer ones by dividing the communal land at the first request of the former and thus to avert the danger of expropriating the estates of the nobles (edicts of Oct. 2 and Nov. 22). He also set up field courts-martial to pronounce death sentences against the remaining revolutionaries (Sept. 1).

The Second Duma.—The second duma, convoked Feb. 20 (March 5), 1907, in spite of all pressure on electors proved much more radical than the first. The Kadets' representation sank from 187 to 123, while the Socialists, who this time took part in the elections, rose from 26 to 83 and the Labour group (mostly peasants) rose from 85 to 97. Both extremist groups of urban and agrarian socialism thus nearly formed the majority, while on the right wing there were only 34 Octobrists (a party of landlords and rich merchants, formed soon after the Kadets with the government's connivance—they professed to be constitutionalists) and 63 nationalists and avowed autocratists. However, the new majority was not so confident as had been the first duma and shared the cautious tactics of the Kadets. The United Nobility was afraid of that moderation. They now induced Stolypin to prepare a new electoral law and only sought for a pretext to dissolve the duma. They found it in the duma's lack of desire to denounce revolutionary terrorism and in the propaganda of the Social Democratic party. On June 3 (16) the duma was dissolved and at the same time a new electoral law was published which partly disfranchised the nationalities (especially the Poles) and gave predominance to the representatives of the gentry.

The Third and Fourth Dumas.—Extreme pressure was used during the elections to the third duma (1907–12), as well as to the fourth (1912–17). However, the government did not succeed entirely in stifling the opposition groups. The party composition of the two last dumas was as shown in the accompanying table.

TABLE III.—*Party Composition of Third and Fourth Dumas*

Parties	Third	Fourth
Right wing		
Extreme right	52	65
Nationalists	93	88
Total	145	153
Centre		
New (Nationalist) centre		32
Octobrists	133	98
Total	133	130
Left wing (opposition)		
Poles and Moslems	26	21
Progressives	39	48
Constitutional Democrats (Kadets)	53	59
Labour group	14	
Social Democrats	14	9
Total	146	152

At the beginning of the decade of duma activity Stolypin worked with the leading group of Octobrists and their leader Alexander Guchkov. By that co-operation Stolypin was able to pass his agrarian laws and the nationalist bills depriving Finland of the last remains of autonomy. It was the consummation of Nicholas' policy against Finland which had cost the life of his general governor, N. I. Bobrikov, in 1904. Poland was deprived of a part of Kholm territory. Measures were taken against the Ukranian national movement and against the Jews, with the acquiescence of the duma. However, on the questions of the reconstruction of the army and navy Guchkov took a sharp line against the government and the grand dukes, which incensed the tsar and seemed an attack on his prerogative. It made Stolypin go to the side of the Nationalists—a party newly created with the pecuniary aid of the government and thus very submissive, led by Count Vladimir Bobrinsky and Pavel Krupensky. On the other hand, the Octobrists approached somewhat the Kadets and worked together on questions of foreign policy and the budget. An open conflict with Stolypin took place in 1911 over his reckless use of emergency legislation in order to break the opposition of the legislative institutions, including the upper house. As soon as Stolypin lost his credit with the duma he was no more needed by the tsar, who still cherished the hope of complete freedom from the duma. The assassination of Stolypin (Sept. 14, 1911) by a revolutionary, Dmitry Grigorevich (Mordka) Bogrov, did not elicit any expression of regret from the tsar and was ascribed by rumour to a police plot.

The elections of the fourth duma were so arranged by the government as to give an overwhelming majority of Nationalists, who would then ask for the transformation of the duma into a consultative chamber. At the court Rasputin enjoyed already a paramount influence, and the tsarina began to meddle in politics with the aim of strengthening the weak tsar against all risk of concessions to constitutionalism and also preserving autocracy unimpaired for her son. However, the results of the elections were a disappointment: the opposition increased in number and authority; the right wing of autocratists was merely equal to it; and there was no strong centre to lead the duma.

The beginning of World War I brought nearly all parties together in a patriotic cry for a sacred union. But the government did not know how to make use of this disposition of mind. It continued its exasperating internal policy and tried to do without the duma. The situation was so much the worse when the Russian retreat began and the army proved unprepared. The war minister, V. A. Sukhomlinov, and other reactionary ministers were then dismissed and the duma was summoned for Aug. 1, 1915. The duma was empowered to control the supply of munitions through its members in a special committee together with the Union of the *Zemstva* led by Prince G. E. Lvov. The duma found finally its majority, but it was the majority of a Progressive bloc which proposed to the tsar a national coalition government "pos-

sessing the confidence of the country" and a program of reforms necessary to appease the country (Aug.-Sept. 1915). Unhappily there was no Witte to advise the tsar. Goremykin was only a courtier and he made the tsar answer by a prorogation of the duma and by the expulsion of all liberal ministers who favoured the idea of a national cabinet (Sept. 16).

Thus the last chance of a peaceful solution was lost. The duma could no more lead public opinion, which turned to revolution. The chiefs of the army were this time on the side of the duma and public opinion, as they did not believe in the possibility of victory as long as the regime lasted. The universally hated Goremykin had to resign when the duma met (Feb. 2, 1916); but his successor—the old master of ceremonies of the court, B. V. Sturmer, an ignorant and comic figure, especially when he was made successor of S. D. Sazonov in foreign affairs (July)—only helped to discredit the whole system and to demonstrate its weakness. As the tsar had made himself commander in chief instead of the grand duke Nicholas and was absent at headquarters, the tsarina took the lead in Petrograd (the new wartime name of the capital). She surrounded herself with an adventurous crowd of irresponsible advisers, the friends of her great confidant Rasputin. The duma was at last summoned on Nov. 14. She poured her wrath on Sturmer, who had to go, and on A. D. Protopopov, her former vice-president, who passed through the antechamber of Rasputin to get the post of home minister. Sturmer's successor, A. F. Trepov, was hissed by the duma. Warning on warning came to the tsar even from grand dukes and foreign diplomatists, insisting on serious concessions to the people in order to prevent revolution. But the tsar, profoundly influenced by the tsarina, would not listen. On Dec. 17 (30) Rasputin was assassinated by Prince F. F. Yusupov, husband of the emperor's niece, and V. M. Purishkevich, the leader of the extreme absolutists in the duma. Not even that blow could change the obstinacy of Alexandra Fedorovna. Protopopov seemed to wish to provoke an outbreak. In certain circles a scheme for the tsarina's arrest and the tsar's abdication was being discusssed. The meeting of the duma had been postponed until Feb. 14 (27), 1917. Disorders began in Petrograd during its session, and on Feb. 26 (March 11) the duma was prorogued. The following day was the first day of the revolution.

(P. M.; X.)

THE REVOLUTION, 1917

The Russian Revolution of 1917 had two sharply contrasted phases. There were, indeed, two revolutions, those of February and of October in the old Russian calendar (which is preserved in the traditional historiography of the period), or of March and of November in the western calendar (which the Russians adopted on Feb. 1 [14], 1918). The former was the product of the discontent of the democratic forces with the conduct of war, the latter exploited war weariness in the interests of the international revolutionary doctrines of Marxism. The former revolution overthrew Russian tsardom and, through its liberalism, gave scope to those who were preparing for the latter.

The attack made by the Progressive bloc of the duma on the autocracy was in fact animated by its conviction of the double danger in which the country stood from defeat in the field and from revolution following on such defeat. It demanded the establishment of a government "invested with the people's confidence," and an underlying aim was to forestall more radical changes. Its members were indeed so opposed to any semblance of revolutionary activity on the part of the masses that again and again they refused to countenance strikes or demonstrations which had been organized with the very intention of supporting the duma's demands.

By the end of 1916 the attempt to bring down the government by constitutional means had obviously failed. This failure compelled the more active and impetuous of the liberal patriots to consider whether it was possible to realize their aims by a military coup d'état and a court revolution. The initiative in this matter was notoriously taken by prominent officers at the front who were in close touch with the headquarters staff. The propaganda in favour of a court revolution was started by Gen. A. I. Krymov, the officer who subsequently commanded the army sent by Gen.

L. G. Kornilov in Aug. 1917 to suppress the government of Alexander Feodorovich Kerensky and to establish a military dictatorship. Only a few of the Liberal leaders seem to have been personally associated with Krymov's scheme; but sufficient documentary evidence exists to prove that the Progressives in the duma were at least taken into the confidence of the conspirators and were considering the formation of a cabinet in case the plot succeeded. The complete scheme of the Krymov conspiracy was revealed by Guchkov, the war minister in the provisional government, in the evidence which he gave before the tribunal set up for investigating the criminal record of the ministers of the old regime. The idea according to Guchkov was to seize the tsar as his train was proceeding from headquarters to Tsarskoye Selo, to compel him to abdicate in favour of the tsarevich with the grand duke Michael as regent, to arrest the tsar's ministers with the help of the Preobrazhensky guards and then to proclaim the abdication simultaneously with the names of the new duma ministers. This court revolution, planned to take place in the early months of 1917, was first postponed by the strikes and unrest which prevailed at that time in the capital and was finally rendered abortive by the success of the March Revolution.

The Bolshevik party, which had been consistently against the war from the beginning, took no part in the preparations for the March Revolution. Lenin and other leaders, who were at that time abroad, were formulating views as to the possibilities of revolution which were subsequently acclaimed as prophetic. But the international antiwar conferences organized by Lenin at Zimmerwald and Kienthal had no obvious effects, and as late as Jan. 1917 Lenin, then aged 46, told a Swiss audience that it was doubtful whether "we the old would live to see the decisive battles of the coming Revolution." Anyhow, views expressed in exile could not easily be propagated in Russia, since the Bolshevik members of the duma and almost all the minor leaders had been arrested and banished to Siberia. Indeed what these statements prove is that the few Bolshevik agitators remaining in Petrograd (including G. A. Shlyapnikov, the representative of the central committee of the party) were as little aware as the Mensheviks or the Liberals that the strikes, started early in March 1917, were likely to bring about the revolution. On the contrary, as far as they could, they discouraged the idea of a revolution as premature and likely to lead to disaster and gave it their official support only after it had actually broken out.

The March Revolution and First Provisional Government.—Strikes for higher wages at some of the factories had been occurring sporadically for some time, and on March 8 no fewer than 130,000 men are said to have been out. To this number must be added a considerable figure to account for the women workers who were demonstrating on that day (the Women's day). But though the number of the strikers and of their sympathizers was large, and though several bakers' shops were demolished by the mob, neither the leaders of the duma on the one hand nor the government and the police on the other gave the matter any particular attention. The only precaution taken by the authorities was to prevent the demonstrators from reaching the centre of the city. The next day the strikers were still more numerous and probably amounted to 30% of all the workers in Petrograd. Some sections of the crowd succeeded in reaching the centre of the city and their mood soon became sinister and threatening. On that day, too, the university students joined the movement, and though the watchword of the strikers remained "bread," it is asserted that a few cries were raised denouncing the autocracy and the war.

The third day (March 10) proved the critical day. The strike became general and the strikers assumed an aggressive demeanour, raiding the police stations in the Viborg (factory) districts and disarming the police. In this quarter the police practically disappeared and the political demonstration began to assume the character of an armed rising. Meanwhile, the Cossacks, who had in the traditional way been patrolling the streets as the bulwark of the autocracy, had begun to manifest neutrality and even friendliness toward the strikers. That night Gen. S. S. Khabalov, military governor of the capital, received a telegram from the tsar, then at the front, ordering him to suppress the strike movement.

N. D. Golitsyn, the prime minister, had already decided to prorogue the duma in the hope, shared by most of the ministers, that the tsar would return to the capital, accept their resignations and form a more popular government.

The attempt to use force to put down the disorders in the capital was temporarily successful, but one regiment after another mutinied on March 11 and 12 and the situation became clearly untenable. The duma refused to disperse on March 11 when it received the prorogation order, and there were discussions among the Progressive and Labour leaders about the possibility of forming a new government. On the same day M. V. Rodzianko, the speaker of the duma, sent an urgent telegram to the tsar ending with the words "May the blame not fall on the wearer of the crown." But the tsar put it aside. Rodzianko also got into touch with the generals holding the main field commands, asking for their support.

When the tsar and his advisers at last learned that the revolt of the Petrograd troops had endangered the existence of the monarchy they immediately ordered a number of regiments from various parts of the front to proceed to the capital. The first detachments under Gen. N. Ivanov were prevented by the railwaymen from approaching Petrograd, while the picked regiments were never sent because before they could actually be moved the revolution had developed such impetus and had gained such support even at the front that the attempt to crush it by military force was recognized as hopeless. The army indeed could no longer be relied on, and it may plausibly be assumed that even if the troops had been dispatched they would probably have mutinied and fraternized with the revolutionists.

The critical day was March 12. While the city was largely in the hands of the mutinous regiments and the mob, news came to the duma that elections were in progress by show of hands for a new soviet or council of workers' delegates such as had seized power in the capital during the revolution of 1905. The leaders of the different political groups meeting in the duma building were informed that a large crowd was on its way there and that decisive action was necessary. On the initiative of V. V. Shulgin a provisional committee was set up with the leaders of all the parties presented upon it except those of the right. Kerensky largely took charge of events and improvised some kind of guard. The cabinet met during the evening and, failing to get a definite reply from the tsar to a suggestion for the appointment of a new prime minister, simply dispersed. By that night most of the ministers were in hiding. It was only on March 14, after prolonged discussions and with considerable reluctance, that the members of the duma committee made up their minds to constitute a government. It was set up on March 15. Three considerations were obviously instrumental in leading them to this decision: first, a clear consciousness of the elemental force of the revolution; second, the apprehension that the Petrograd soviet might be tempted to assume power; and, third, the hope that by constituting themselves the ruling authority they might be able to cope with the increasing anarchy and to save the monarchy and even the dynasty.

The Soviet.—Meanwhile, the revolutionary workers had succeeded in setting up a soviet. Its first session opened in the evening of March 12, with an attendance of approximately 250 members consisting of Socialist deputies of the duma, the Worker group of the munition committee, a number of prominent worker leaders representing the various shades of revolutionary opinion, and members of strike committees who had been active during the few previous days. It managed to appoint a strong executive committee which immediately took over the business of food supplies and the strategical defense of Petrograd against any possible attack from the autocracy. It also came to the decision to change its constitution by including along with worker deputies army deputies. In this way the soviet made a palpable bid for real power.

From this very moment, enlisting as it did the support of the workers and of the Petrograd garrison, the soviet executive committee was the depository of real power. It had its headquarters in the duma building, and one of its vice-presidents was Kerensky, who constituted a link with the duma committee and subsequently with the provisional government. Its members had been conscious of this power and probably overestimated rather than underestimated their authority. But they made no overt or covert attempt to constitute a revolutionary government, and when the duma committee decided at last to assume the responsibility of forming the new government its decision was unanimously welcomed by the leaders of the soviet. Why the Petrograd soviet refused immediately to proclaim itself the government of revolutionary Russia can only be a matter of surmise. Speaking in the first All-Russian Conference of Soviets, which was held early in April 1917, G. Steklov, one of the prominent members of its first executive committee, ascribed the refusal to the prevailing uncertainty as to the attitude of the army. But this explanation scarcely covers the whole of the ground. An orderly government, representing a compromise between the insurgent masses and the bourgeois classes, was obviously the sole bulwark against counterrevolution, and the desire for the establishment of such a government must undoubtedly have constituted the main factor in the unopposed assumption of power by the duma. Still, fear of the outbreak of a counterrevolution cannot be regarded as an adequate explanation of the willingness of the soviet's leaders to delegate power to the duma. Their decision to step aside and to leave the formation of a government to the *bourgeoisie*, the class determined to arrest the onrush of the revolution, would be unintelligible unless the fact is recalled that most of them accepted the Menshevik view that the aim of the revolution was solely to establish a democratic regime and that any attempt to associate the movement with socialistic experiments or the dictatorship of the proletariat would ruin it and so repeat the disastrous failure of 1905.

Among the members of the soviet's first executive committee were a few Bolsheviks who accepted Lenin's dictum that the Russian Revolution was the vanguard of the world socialist revolution. But so unprepared were they for taking action that when Lenin arrived in Petrograd three weeks later he found that his most difficult task was to inspire his own party with the necessary enthusiasm for deepening the revolution. The Bolsheviks, however, were in such an insignificant minority both in the Petrograd soviet and outside that their views could not possibly carry much weight. In fact, most members of the executive committee of the soviet expected and welcomed the advent of the world revolution and believed in the missionary character of their own. They refused to accept the national victory over the autocracy as the sole aim of the revolution, and they may have regarded it as merely the first step. What they never denied was that the *bourgeoisie* had a part to play in the revolution and a rightful claim to form the first national government. But, while they were prepared to stand aside and to delegate the power to the *bourgeoisie* they reserved to themselves the right to keep a steady watch on the activities of the new government, for they made no secret of their suspicion that, left to their own devices, these "bourgeois" ministers might be tempted to abuse their authority by favouring the interests of their own class.

The First Provisional Government.—The members of the duma committee, on the other hand, were not only willing to form a government with the consent of the soviet but insisted on the latter's issuing an open proclamation of support. The program of the provisional government published on March 16 was indeed largely dictated by the soviet leaders and was accepted in full by the members of the duma committee. The status of the government created as a result of this compromise was necessarily precarious in the extreme. Nominally invested with full powers and sovereign authority, the provisional government—whole principal figures were Prince Lvov (prime minister), P. N. Milyukov (foreign affairs), M. I. Tereshchenko (finance), Alexander Guchkov (war) and A. F. Kerensky (justice)—was in reality powerless and the mere creature of the soviet. Its position was bound to be unstable because the basis of the compromise which established it was vague and uncertain. But the revolutionary impetus of the masses and the constant changes in the constitution of the soviet and hence in the point of view of its leaders soon combined to render this basis even more unstable. Every day fresh groups joined the soviet and new leaders replaced old ones, with the con-

sequence that new adjustments had constantly to be made and even relative stability became difficult to maintain.

Arrest of the Imperial Family.—While negotiations between the soviet and the duma were still proceeding and before the provisional government formally took over the administration (March 16), the extremely delicate question of the position of the tsar and of the dynasty came up for settlement. That the tsar Nicholas could no longer remain autocrat was a foregone conclusion, but the leaders of the duma, dreading the idea of Russia's becoming a republic, were determined to save the monarchy and even the dynasty. They accordingly dispatched Guchkov and Shulgin, two Conservative members of the duma, to the tsar's headquarters at Pskov with the mission of obtaining the tsar's abdication in favour of the tsarevich and the appointment of his brother the grand duke Michael as regent. But the tsar declared that the illness of his son made it impossible for him to contemplate being separated from him and changed the instrument of abdication so as to provide for the succession of his brother as tsar. Such a solution was by now widely unacceptable, and, when the members of the duma committee visited the grand duke on March 16, Kerensky strongly appealed to him not to accept in the name of national unity. Despite Milyukov's strong pleas that he should ascend the throne on the ground that the monarchy was the only axle of the country, the grand duke refused. The Romanov dynasty that had ruled Russia for three centuries came to an end.

A few days later the question of the dynasty came up again in a dramatic fashion which incidentally demonstrated both the strength of the soviet and its determination when necessary to use it in defiance of the government. The tsar had requested the new ministers to arrange for the departure of himself and his family to Great Britain, a request which the leaders of the soviet heard of by mere accident. At once they called on the government to put the tsar and his family under arrest and gave orders to the railwaymen to stop the imperial train. The actual usurpation of power in this instance, however, proved unnecessary: the new ministers themselves proceeded to put the tsar Nicholas and his family under arrest.

The Army and the War, March–May.—The struggle for support that took place between the duma and the soviet was the paramount business of the next few weeks. The battle was fought out in the main on two planes, one the question of the new status of the army, the other the question of continuing or terminating the war. The leaders of the soviet championed the civil rights now claimed by the soldiers, while the duma appealed to them in the name of national safety. That the harsh conditions which had hitherto prevailed in the barracks had now to be modified was obvious enough, and Guchkov was preparing an official declaration to this effect. But, while he was for confining the liberties of the soldiers within the strict limits of discipline, the leaders of the soviet declared that these liberties must be vindicated unconditionally. This resolve to gain the adherence of the soldiers by supporting their claims at all costs was responsible for the issue on March 14 of the notorious *prikaz* (order) number 1[1], which helped in the disintegration of the already badly shaken Russian army.

But despite all the privileges which the Petrograd soviet had granted to the soldiers, the devotion of the army at the front and even at the capital had to be secured. At first the provisional government seemed to be the body which had won the support of the army. When the ministers proclaimed the necessity of a more vigorous prosecution of the war, the army seemed to be rallying to their support. For about a fortnight regiments stationed at Petrograd as well as delegations sent by those in the provinces and

[1]*Prikaz* number 1 was composed by a commission of the Petrograd soviet headed by N. D. Sokolov. In the name of the Soviet of Workers' and Soldiers' Deputies it ordered that committees of soldiers were to be formed in all military and naval units in Petrograd and to send one representative each to the Taurida palace next morning. In their political actions units were to be subject to their committees and to the soviet. Orders of the military commission of the duma were to be obeyed only when they did not contradict those of the soviet. Arms were to be under the control of the committees and on no account to be given up if demanded by the officers. Strict discipline was to be preserved when on duty. Salutes, etc., when off duty were abolished. Special titles used in addressing officers, "Your excellency" and references to the officer's noble birth, were abolished. Officers were forbidden to use the second person singular in addressing soldiers.

at the front marched to the duma commanded by their officers, proclaimed their readiness to serve the revolution and offered the government their allegiance and joyful support. But the army's enthusiasm for prosecuting the war soon began to cool, while the propaganda made by the soviet for the clarification of the Russian war aims as a sure promise of terminating hostilities became increasingly popular.

On March 27 the soviet issued a manifesto to the world declaring that Russia sought no gains from the war and was ready to conclude peace on the basis of no annexations and no indemnities. From this time onward the question of peace terms became the main bone of contention between the government and the soviet, the government adhering to the secret treaties made by the Allies, and the soviet insisting on the denunciation of these treaties and agreeing to continue the war only for purposes of self-defense. The pressure put on the government to identify itself with the principles laid down in the soviet's manifesto became at last so strong that ministers felt compelled to make a public declaration (April 9) in which Russia's war aims were formulated as the establishment of a permanent peace on the basis of the self-determination of the peoples. This declaration was hailed as a great victory by the soviet, which thereupon demanded that the provisional government take the next step and communicate this declaration to the Allied Powers, with a view to their adopting its principles. After some hesitation Milyukov on May 1 transmitted the text of the declaration, but in the covering letter which he dispatched to the Russian ambassadors he asked them to reassure the governments to which they were accredited by informing them that Russia's position with regard to the war remained unchanged.

Milyukov's note became known in Russia on May 3 and caused great indignation on the left. For two days Russia seemed to be on the brink of civil war, the outbreak of which was finally prevented only by the action of the soviet, which prohibited all meetings and demonstrations for three days and ordered the garrisons to remain in the barracks. The strength and discipline shown by the masses at this time finally convinced the soviet leaders that the real power was in their hands.

The Second Provisional Government.—Discredited and disheartened by this proof of ministerial impotence, Prince Lvov, the prime minister, issued a proclamation in which he expressed his conviction that a reconstruction of the government on a wider basis, with the inclusion of soviet representatives, was essential to the safety of the state. The soviet at first (May 12) refused to entertain the idea of making a coalition with the bourgeois parties; but after the resignations of Milyukov and Guchkov and when the danger of a complete breakup of the government seemed imminent, it reconsidered its decision and agreed to enter the government (May 18).

The soviet was allotted five portfolios in the reconstructed cabinet, those of justice, agriculture, labour, food supplies and post and telegraphs. The last-mentioned ministry was created specially to make room for Irakly Gheorghievich Tseretelli, a Menshevik member of the second duma who had been banished to Siberia and was now the most popular and powerful member of the soviet. To this list of Soviet and Socialist ministers must be added the name of Kerensky, who was now promoted from the ministry of justice to the all-important ministry of war. The sugar millionaire M. I. Tereshchenko, minister of finance, replaced Milyukov.

The fall of the first provisional government resulted from two main reasons. The first was its assumption of responsibility without the backing of power. The second was its equivocal foreign policy of balancing between the pledged war aims of the Allies, which seemed to involve an indefinite prolongation of the war, and the soviet's policy of limiting the war to a revolutionary defense ("No annexations. No indemnities.") with a view to an immediate peace. The new government, in which Kerensky was the dominant figure, occupied a more favourable position, for it represented both the *bourgeoisie* and the masses and thus possessed not only responsibility but actual power. It was confronted, however, by formidable difficulties; not only had the crucial question of peace or war to be settled but also the growing unrest in the

villages and the dissolution of the empire into separate national units called urgently for solutions which the government was totally unable to furnish. The consequence was that the coalition lasted only two months and was finally brought down by the resignation of four Liberal (Kadet) ministers, who adopted this method of protesting against the concessions made to the Ukrainian autonomist movement. The new government crisis coincided with the greatest crisis which the revolution had so far had to face, in the disastrous failure of the offensive in Galicia and the first Bolshevik rising in the capital.

Sound strategy demanded that, while a most determined effort should be made to increase the fighting morale of the army, it should not be submitted too early to the test of challenging the enemy on the military front. But the offensive which the Kerensky government so blindly and so enthusiastically adopted was obviously undertaken more for political than for military reasons. The effect of renewing the offensive, it was believed, would be either to prove in case of victory that Russia had still to be taken into account and so to compel the Germans to come forward with the offer of a democratic (nonannexationist) peace, or, in the event of defeat, to compel the German Socialists definitely to take their stand either in defense of the Russian Revolution or in support of German militarism.

The preparation of the offensive was equally frivolous and fantastic, based as it was on the naïve belief that the army's will to fight could be resuscitated by melodramatic speeches made by the war minister and a group of military and civil idealists. In the speeches which he made to the troops on his theatrical tour of the front, Kerensky was fatuous enough to declare that the country expected them to work a miracle. The soldiers listened, applauded and even swore to fight and to die for the revolution. But the moment the war minister left they went back to their barracks and refused to go to the trenches and relieve the first-line men. Several regiments, indeed, had to be disbanded for refusal to obey orders. In this atmosphere the offensive was launched on July 1. At first it proved remarkably successful; the Austrian lines were broken and many prisoners and guns were taken. But in less than a fortnight after operations opened not only were the Russian armies destroyed but Russia had ceased to exist as a great power.

Meanwhile, the Bolsheviks were becoming a major factor in the development of the situation. Lenin had arrived from Switzerland on April 16 via Sweden, having travelled across Germany in the famous sealed train with the connivance of the German military authorities, who had nothing to lose, it seemed, by facilitating the movements of such a declared opponent of the Russian war effort. Lenin immediately took the view that the soviet's support of the bourgeois revolution had been overtaken by events and that the time was ripe for a proletarian revolution in Russia as the signal for a world-wide socialist revolution. Whereas he had previously vacillated on the value of the soviets in such a revolution, he now came out in his "April Theses," published in *Pravda* (the Bolshevik organ) on April 20, in favour of the soviet as the "*one possible* form of Revolutionary government." He made it clear that it was first necessary for the Bolsheviks to become the dominant element in the soviet, and that as soon as this was achieved the moment to strike would have come. Although the Bolsheviks were very weak where the soviet executive committee was concerned, they now began, under the energetic leadership of Lenin, to win wide support in the soviet itself.

Soviets had by now been formed all over the country, and the first All-Russian Congress of Soviets was held in June. The Bolsheviks accounted for 105 of its 822 delegates and secured 35 seats out of the 250 on the central executive committee which it set up. At the conference the Bolsheviks made it plain that they were prepared to take power as a party.

After street demonstrations in June had shown the growing influence of the party, thanks largely to its opposition to the war, a popular rising broke out in the capital on July 16. This rising was a strange demonstration, the most marked characteristic of which was its lack of leadership. The members of the central committee of the Bolshevik party hesitated to identify themselves with it beforehand for fear it might prove unsuccessful. Ostensibly a demonstration in favour of the transference of power to the soviet, it was in essence an attempt to stampede that assembly, a fact which its leaders were prompt to recognize. For nearly two days the gunmen were in occupation of the capital, but their lack of objective and of leadership perplexed them and paralyzed their efforts. The Bolshevik leaders in the capital (Lenin did not return from a convalescence in Finland until July 17) were forced to assume some kind of control of the movement and to channel it toward bringing pressure on the Petrograd soviet and the central executive committee to take power. But the soviet did not respond to the mob's demands.

During the two days that the rising lasted the coalition government was absolutely quiescent. But Kerensky on the very first day proceeded to the front and procured picked troops, which arrived in the capital on the day after the movement had fizzled out. Meantime, any attempt to renew disturbances was rendered hopeless by the publication of documents which purported to prove that Lenin was a spy and a paid agent of the German general staff. The result of the disturbances was the practical suppression of the Bolshevik party. L. B. Kamenev was arrested. Lenin and G. E. Zinoviev went into hiding, to the considerable dismay of their friends.

Kerensky's Provisional Government.—These events coincided with the failure of the Galician offensive and made yet another change of government inevitable. Prince Lvov was presented by the soviet members of the government with an ultimatum which required him, in accordance with the decisions of the Congress of Soviets, to declare Russia a republic without waiting for the convocation of a constituent assembly, to suppress finally the duma and the council of state and to accept the congress's policy of forbidding any sale of land before the meeting of the constituent assembly. The prince refused to comply with these demands, regarding them as a usurpation of the rights of the constituent assembly, and promptly sent in his resignation. The ministry was reconstructed on July 21, Kerensky becoming prime minister as well as minister of war and Tseretelli succeeding Prince Lvov as minister of the interior. With the formation of the new ministry, not completed until Aug. 6, the Russian Revolution entered on a new phase—a phase of inaction. The record of Kerensky is indeed singularly barren. He failed to put new vigour into the prosecution of the war. He left the question of concluding peace just as he found it. He made no attempt to settle the various difficulties involved in the labour question. And he was so incapable of handling the agrarian problem that he allowed the peasants to settle it as best they could by local initiative.

In fact, the only achievements of Kerensky's administration were the declaration of Russia as a republic and the convocation in August of a spectacular state assembly representing all classes in the country and all political groups. The actual purpose which this assembly was meant to serve is obscure, but its composition and the choice of Moscow for its sittings seem to show that it was convoked with some vague hope of investing Kerensky's government with that moral authority and sanction which it had hitherto conspicuously lacked. Nothing remarkable, however, resulted from its three meetings save a series of hysterical speeches in which the prime minister announced his determination strenuously to support the revolution and ruthlessly to suppress its enemies, whether they came from the right or from the left.

After the failure of the July rising, Trotsky, who had been taking an independent line since his return to Russia on May 17, joined the Bolsheviks with his supporters. On Aug. 6 he and A. V. Lunacharsky were arrested. The Bolsheviks themselves had recast their tactics. Lenin had decided that the soviets had proved themselves unsuitable for the task allotted to them, and the slogan "All power to the soviets" was replaced at the sixth party congress (held in the second week of August) by a recognition that it was the task of the proletariat and of the poorer peasantry to liquidate the dictatorship of the counterrevolutionary *bourgeoisie*, as the provisional government was now styled by the Bolsheviks.

Meanwhile, the generals at the front and the members of the general staff in the capital began to think that their time had come. Taking stock of the anarchy prevailing in the country and of the disorganization of the army, they began to be more and more inclined to favour the creation of a military dictatorship. Kerensky, supported Gen. L. G. Kornilov, the commander in chief, in the preliminary steps for establishing one. He quarrelled with him only when he realized that the general himself was aspiring to become dictator. Suspecting Kornilov's designs, he promptly declared him a traitor and an enemy of the revolution; to which the general replied by sending on Sept. 9 picked Cossack regiments under the command of Gen. A. I. Krymov against Petrograd with the object of intimidating Kerensky and forcibly suppressing the soviet. Thereupon Kerensky, turning his back on the right, appealed to the left for support, and the central executive committee of the soviets appealed in its turn to the workers to fight the threatened counterrevolution. The Bolshevik leaders, now released from prison, took up the challenge with enthusiasm and, recognizing that their opportunity had arisen, proceeded to arm the workers, in anticipation of the arrival of Krymov's troops. Deputies from the Petrograd workers and soldiers went to meet the Cossacks and persuaded them that they had been sent on a false errand. Kornilov, A. I. Denikin (his close colleague at the front) and three other generals were arrested and imprisoned, and Krymov shot himself after being interrogated by the prime minister.

Just as the failure of the Bolshevik rising in July proved to be the opportunity of the right, so now the collapse of Kornilov's raid gave the extreme left its chance. The first result of this revival of revolutionary fervour was a renewal of the hatred of the officer class; a new wave of massacre swept over the country, taking peculiarly ugly form in Finland, where sailors killed their admirals and officers by throwing them overboard and beating them to death in the water. The central executive committee was reduced to sending emissaries to stop these outrages; another sign of the times was that these emissaries had to be chosen from the Bolshevik ranks. The moderates were speedily losing their hold on the masses. Lenin's supporters, indeed, were now rapidly increasing their forces, so much so that by the middle of September both the Petrograd and the Moscow soviets passed for the first time Bolshevik resolutions; while the moderate leaders, who had presided over them since their creation, were soon replaced by Trotsky at the new and by V. P. Nogin at the old capital. It now became possible for Lenin to revive the slogan "All power to the soviets."

For it became increasingly evident that the next Congress of Soviets, which was summoned for the end of October, was likely to elect an all-Russian central executive committee on which the Bolsheviks would have a majority and that this majority would declare in favour of assuming the supreme power in the state. Kerensky's last improvisation was a democratic conference, which met in Petrograd on Sept. 27. Unlike the state assembly, this was confined to left-wing parties and organizations. The Bolsheviks took part against Lenin's wishes; but the impunity with which they were allowed to shout Kerensky down showed the weakness of their opponents, as did the failure of the latter to agree on the continuation of a coalition including non-Socialist elements. The existing central executive committee, though it continued to support Kerensky, who formed a new cabinet including the Kadets on Oct. 6, withdrew its representatives from his government. The united front of soviet democracy, which had seemingly been reestablished by the challenge thrown out by Kornilov, was now finally broken. The Bolsheviks proceeded to declare the members of the central executive committee traitors to the revolution and at last worked openly for their overthrow and for that of the bourgeois government.

The provisional government was formally invested with full and sovereign power and was responsible neither to the Petrograd soviet nor to the recently convoked council of the republic or preparliament, which was a consultative body representing all the main parties. But actually it possessed no power at all. The real authority, then more than at another time in the revolution, was held by the soviets in the capitals and in numerous provincial towns, which openly defied the government and exercised, each in its area, legislative as well as executive powers. In many of the provincial soviets as well as in those of Petrograd and Moscow the Bolsheviks now counted on solid majorities; and in most cases the Bolshevik provincial soviets constituted themselves quasi-independent republics.

The various nationalities, which had long been clamouring for autonomy, now began openly to secede from the state and to organize their own armies by withdrawing their nationals from the army under the plea of defending their newly created frontiers and their national flags. The whole country, town and village alike, was in a state of feverish unrest which soon developed into riots and anarchy. In the towns bread riots broke out; but the most destructive of these revolts were those of the peasants, who began to solve the land problem in their own way by expropriating the land, driving off the cattle, burning down the landowners' dwellings and barns, demolishing agricultural machinery, felling wood in the forests and wantonly destroying trees in the orchards. Landowners who delayed their flight were captured, tortured and murdered. Yet the ministers were inactive and helpless. They lacked the necessary military backing to put these disturbances down by force; even the Cossacks refused to obey orders, remembering how they had been repudiated by Kerensky in the Kornilov episode. Reprisals would in any case have proved ineffective; the only measure which might possibly have tranquillized the countryside would have been the speedy convocation of the constituent assembly with a guarantee that it would be invested with full power to solve the land question. But the government repeatedly postponed the convocation of the assembly. Closely connected with the peasants' revolt and with the general anarchy prevailing everywhere were the crimes committed by bands of armed soldiers.

At the front the army still preserved on the surface a certain degree of discipline; but the mutual distrust and hatred of soldiers and officers was so profound that at any time an open clash might be expected, especially as a shortage of food and supplies, and in some cases actually famine, made the preservation of military subordination increasingly difficult. It became obvious that the army was likely to withdraw from the field either in the autumn or at any rate before the winter had passed. The soldiers discussed this possibility openly, declaring that they cared neither for freedom nor for land but only for peace. Even leading generals such as V. A. Cheremisov (who held the northern command) advised the government that the army was unreliable and might withdraw from the field at any time.

Meantime, the Germans had been penetrating further and further into the Baltic provinces. On Oct. 12, with the support of their fleet, they occupied the island of Oesel and so secured the command of the Baltic. Petrograd was now obviously menaced, and ministers declared their intention of transferring the seat of government to Moscow. To dream of continuing the war after abandoning Petrograd, the biggest arsenal in the country, was denounced as sheer treason, and the proposal furnished the Bolsheviks with an admirable lever for stirring up the masses. Another mistake which ministers made, an attempt to replace the Petrograd garrison by more reliable troops from the front, was used by their enemies as a pretext for openly organizing military forces for an attack on them. The Petrograd soviet accordingly, under Trotsky's command, promptly came forward and countermanded the movement of troops. On Oct. 26 the leaders of the soviet constituted a military revolutionary committee which declared itself the highest military authority in the capital and province of Petrograd. This step was ostensibly taken for the defense of the capital against the enemy, but actually it was a movement for the creation of a general staff for the Bolshevik revolution. Three days earlier, after much debate, the central committee of the Bolshevik party had pronounced in favour of an armed uprising. Trotsky openly organized his forces without meeting with the slightest interference from the government.

The November (Bolshevik) Revolution.—The Bolshevik revolution was inseparably connected with the convocation of the second Congress of Soviets. The central executive committee, which consisted entirely of Mensheviks and Social Revolutionaries, supporters of Kerensky, was reluctant to convene a second congress and postponed doing so from day to day. But when finally the Petrograd soviet threatened to convene the congress itself the committee fixed Nov. 7 as the date of convocation. It was obvious that the congress would have a Bolshevik majority. The convocation of the All-Russian Congress of Soviets was preceded by the holding of a number of regional congresses, all of which declared for a termination of the coalition and for the establishment of a Soviet government, the aim of which would be immediately to propose terms of peace, to give the land to the peasants, to establish a complete workers' control of the factories and to deal with the famine by expropriating the hoards of foodstuffs supposed to have been accumulated by the capitalists and landlords.

Meanwhile, ministers waited patiently on events, believing that nothing could happen till Nov. 7. But Trotsky gave battle two or three days before the appointed date. On Nov. 3 he confronted the general staff with a demand that all its orders should be countersigned by the military revolutionary committee. When the general staff refused this demand he ordered the Petrograd garrison to stand at arms in defense of the committee. On Nov. 4 a meeting attended by delegates from all the troops passed a resolution refusing obedience to commands of the general staff and recognizing the committee as the sole organ of power. This resolution was immediately circulated over the government telephones to all the regiments in the capital.

To these proceedings Kerensky replied on the following day by issuing an ultimatum to the committee requiring it to withdraw the resolution. The ultimatum was ignored by the committee, which promptly called out parts of the garrison and organized worker detachments (Red guards) for the defense of the Smolny palace, headquarters of the soviet and of the committee. Kerensky tried to counteract these measures by adopting the traditional method of defense, the raising of the bridges, to prevent communication between the left and right banks of Neva. He then proceeded to the Marinsky palace, where the preparliament was holding its sessions, and demanded that it should invest him with dictatorial powers to cope with the Bolshevik revolt. They debated all night before refusing. Meanwhile, the Bolsheviks quietly and systematically took over, without firing a shot, the telegraph, the telephone and all government offices with the exception of the Winter palace and the offices of the general staff. The same night Lenin, who had been in hiding since July, appeared at the meeting of the Petrograd soviet and in glowing language congratulated the delegates on inaugurating a new era. The new regime, which established the soviet as the embodiment of supreme power in the state, was thus established one day in advance of the meeting of that soviet congress which had been proclaimed by the Bolsheviks as the sole authority competent to make such a decision. But nobody present at the meeting of the soviet seemed to care, for Lenin announced that the first step taken by the new government would be to offer belligerents a just peace.

Early in the morning of Nov. 7 Kerensky left for the front, in order to bring back troops to crush the revolt. The other members of the government decided to await his return at the Winter palace. But when they were informed that the guns of both the cruiser "Aurora" and the Peter and Paul fortress were trained on the palace, they decided to surrender. When next day the Congress of Soviets formally opened, the non-Bolshevik members and the old executive committee registered a vigorous protest against the unconstitutional methods of the Bolsheviks and withdrew from the congress to join the committee of public defense which had its headquarters at the municipal buildings.

Kerensky meantime made frantic efforts to move the troops from the front to the capital. He succeeded only in persuading the Cossack Gen. P. N. Krasnov to move. On Nov. 11 Krasnov's troops were reported outside Gatchina, about 10 mi. from the capital. Encouraged by this news and definitely expecting a crushing defeat of Trotsky's Red guards, the committee of public defense gave orders to the cadets of the military schools to arrest the military revolutionary committee and to make a general attack on all the soviet strongholds. The attack was made in the morning; but by three o'clock in the afternoon the Bolsheviks, supported by some of the cruisers of the Kronstadt fleet, decisively repelled it and occupied the military schools. In the report of the events of the day which he sent to the Petrograd soviet Trotsky made the following declaration: "We hoped to establish a compromise without bloodshed. But now when blood has been shed there is only one way left, a ruthless fight." With these words Trotsky proclaimed the approaching civil war. The same night he proceeded to the Gatchina front. Next day he reported the repulse of Krasnov's advanced detachments, and a day later he announced that the Cossack forces had been completely defeated. Kerensky fled, and the Bolshevik regime was now for a time immune from military menace.   (M. Fa.; M. Bf.)

CIVIL WAR AND INTERVENTION, 1917–21

The Petrograd Revolution of Nov. 7 swept Russia. There were a few days of street fighting in Moscow and sporadic resistance elsewhere, but by the end of the month the soviets held power throughout the country. In the urban centres the victory was won under the red flag of class warfare, with the watchword "All power to the workers' soviets." The words "land," "bread" and "peace" gave the Bolsheviks the support of the soviets of peasants and soldiers.

The soviets were the only strong political force in a social structure whose disintegration was nearly complete. They were the organs of the proletariat, upon which the Bolsheviks, taught by the Marxist doctrine of revolution, were resolved to build their state. They challenged not only the weakened capitalism of Russia but the capitalist system throughout the world. In the first days of success they exaggerated the effect of war weariness upon the masses of western Europe and underestimated the effect of war hatred. Their dream of a new proletarian utopia and their appeals to fellow workers of the world to throw off the burdens of capital and war prepared the way for the conflict that was soon to plunge the new state into a three-year fight for life.

In an all-night session on Nov. 7–8 the Congress of Soviets in Petrograd declared the power of government to be vested in the council of people's commissars, appointed mainly from the ranks of the Bolshevik central committee, with Lenin as premier and Trotsky as commissar of foreign affairs. The first act of the Soviet government on Nov. 8 was to decree that all land belonged to those who worked it, without rent or other payment. This satisfied the peasants, who had been expropriating landlords' estates for several months, and their chief political organization, the Left Social Revolutionary party, decided to collaborate with the Bolsheviks. Vigorous measures were taken to ensure a supply of food for Petrograd and other urban and industrial centres. To reinforce the victory of the industrial proletariat a universal eight-hour day was instituted on Nov. 11, and the control of the factory soviets over industry was established by successive decrees in the next two months.

The peace campaign began on Nov. 9, when Trotsky sent out a wireless invitation to all the belligerent powers to conclude an immediate armistice. The Allied governments at once protested, and their representatives in Russia tried to enlist the commander in chief of the army, Gen. N. N. Dukhonin, against the council of commissars. Dukhonin was replaced by N. V. Krylenko, a member of the Bolshevik central committee, by a soviet decree of Nov. 22. Soon afterward, the former commander was torn to pieces by a mob of soldiers. This deed showed that Lenin had gauged the temper of the army and that the Allied insistence that Russia should go on fighting would be fruitless.

The German government accepted the armistice proposal. After brief negotiations within the German lines a ten-day truce was signed on Dec. 5, 1917. The Central Powers agreed not to transfer troops from the eastern front to the western, but they moved several divisions to France before the end of the year.

Meanwhile the Soviet government was facing serious internal difficulties. The bourgeois classes, at first stunned by the success of the revolution, began to rally. Instead of armed resistance they used the more dangerous weapon of sabotage, hoping to paralyze the Bolshevik regime. With no civil service, no personnel trained in finance, transport and the management of industry, the new government was suddenly called upon to undertake the administration.

Lenin met the bourgeois offensive with characteristic energy. Banks and some factories were nationalized, and a supreme economic council was created to manage the latter. Other decrees followed in rapid succession. Some of these were measures of immediate necessity rather than a part of the Bolsheviks' deliberate program. In a sense they were the beginnings of the later War Communism, but all the responsibility for their adoption cannot be laid upon Bolshevik shoulders. Some form of centralization was necessary to prevent economic collapse, and Lenin had previously published a pamphlet demanding nationalization of transport and state control of the means of production to save the country from chaos.

The nationalization of industries was legalized in Dec. 1917. At first it was applied haphazardly. No entire industry was nationalized until May 1918, when a department of the supreme economic council was organized to supervise the monopoly production of sugar. The following month oil production was centralized in the same way, and various other commodities were declared state monopolies. It was not until June 28, 1918, that all industrial and commercial enterprises of more than 1,000,000 roubles' capital were declared the property of the state.

The Treaty of Brest-Litovsk.—While the Soviet government was trying to cope with sabotage and weld local soviets into an administrative machine, relations with Germany were still unsettled. Peace negotiations began on Dec. 22, 1917, at Brest-Litovsk. On behalf of the soviet, Trotsky put forward the principles of no annexation or indemnity and self-determination of subject races. At first the Germans seemed willing to accept, with certain reservations. They demanded the independence from Russia of Poland, Finland and the Baltic states on Dec. 28 and the independence of the Ukraine Jan. 8, 1918. On Feb. 10 Trotsky announced the Soviet refusal to sign a "peace of annexation," but declared the war between Russia and the Central Powers at an end—the celebrated formula "No war: no peace." A week later the German general staff ordered an immediate advance.

When the Germans advanced, Lenin at once decided for peace, but acceptance of the German terms was not reached without a struggle in the central committee. Lenin still believed that a general European revolution, as the result of war exhaustion, was not far distant. His prime object, therefore, was to gain time, a breathing space, as he called it. His associates argued that to yield was to betray the revolution. It was only by a threat of resignation that Lenin beat down the adverse majority. On March 3 a new Soviet delegation accepted the German terms on behalf of the Soviet government. The so-called Independent Government of the Ukraine had already signed a separate treaty, which meant virtual German control, and this the Russians were forced to confirm. The Soviet government further agreed to pay a large indemnity or its equivalent in raw materials. Poland and the Baltic states were left in the hands of the Germans, and the armies of Count Rüdiger von der Goltz and Baron Karl Mannerheim soon crushed the revolutionaries in Finland.

Lenin had won his breathing space, but the agricultural and mineral resources of the Ukraine and the oil of the Caucasus were at the disposal of the Germans, and the German general staff was now free to concentrate its forces against the Allied front in France. Two days after the signature of the Brest-Litovsk treaty Trotsky approached Raymond Robins of the American Red Cross and the British high commissioner R. H. Bruce Lockhart as to the attitude of the Allied governments should the soviets not ratify the treaty or the German advance continue for any other reason. But nothing came of these feelers. The Congress of Soviets ratified the treaty on March 16 by a majority of 523.

Lenin used his breathing space to patch up the administrative and economic machine and to drill an army to defend the revolution. The fight against sabotage was not yet won, and the adversaries of the new regime were growing bolder. Trouble was brewing in the Cossack provinces and in Manchuria, where a hostile army was assembling on Chinese soil. The German threat against Petrograd had driven the Soviet government in flight to

Moscow. The fact that the Allied ambassadors, instead of accompanying the government, had preferred to go to Vologda, junction of the trunk lines of escape eastward to Siberia and northwest to the coast, was no good omen for future relations with the powers they represented.

In the field of foreign affairs the Soviet government had two severe handicaps. From the first the Allies suspected complicity with Germany and were inclined to regard the peace of Brest-Litovsk as a betrayal of the Allied cause. Second, neither they nor the Central Powers believed that a Soviet government in Russia could endure. The Allies declined to recognize the treaty of Brest-Litovsk, which they held responsible for Gen. Erich Ludendorff's victory in March. Their missions in Russia reported that trainloads of war supplies, leather, copper, oil and food were being shipped into Germany. Although the Bolsheviks claimed that this was part of the indemnity imposed by the treaty, the Allies saw it as aid to the enemy, to be prevented if possible. It was suspected that some of their representatives in Russia co-operated with anti-Bolshevik elements to hamper the transfer of supplies.

The Social Revolutionary Revolt.—The breach between the other political parties in Russia and the Bolsheviks had been widened by the suppression of the long-awaited constituent assembly, which met in Moscow on Jan. 18, 1918. About 62% of the votes were cast for moderate Socialists of all kinds. Most of these had gone to the Social Revolutionaries, whose lists had been made up before the Left Social Revolutionaries broke away to collaborate with the Bolsheviks in Lenin's government. The Bolsheviks had got 25% of the votes and the Kadets and other "bourgeois" parties about 13%. The election of a Right Social Revolutionary, Victor Tchernov, as president convinced the Bolsheviks that they had nothing to gain from the assembly, and it was closed by Red soldiers on Jan. 19.

The Left Social Revolutionaries continued for a time to collaborate with the Soviet government, but broke away completely after unsuccessful opposition to the ratification of the Brest-Litovsk treaty. The strength of the Social Revolutionary party was mainly drawn from the villages, which were growing increasingly restive as the Bolsheviks developed their basic program of a workers' government, class warfare and socialism. The peasants had thought that the revolution gave the land to them. They now found it was the property of the state and that its surplus produce over their needs was required for state purposes. The bourgeois groups had become more hostile still, as they realized that their very existence was menaced by the new regime.

Led by Boris Savinkov, Kerensky's former war minister, the Right Social Revolutionaries became the pivot of patriotic and anti-Bolshevik sentiment, eager to co-operate with military representatives of the Allies to nullify the effects of the treaty of Brest-Litovsk. From attempts to blow up depots of stores, railway bridges and trains carrying supplies westward, the Social Revolutionaries proceeded to the desperate coup of assassinating the German ambassador in Moscow, Count Wilhelm von Mirbach-Harff, on July 6, 1918, in the vain hope of provoking Germany to break with the Soviets. The Social Revolutionaries then tried to incite the country to rebellion.

Savinkov captured the town of Yaroslavl, 180 mi. N. of Moscow on the railway to Vologda and Archangel, with a disciplined force which he had hoped to make the nucleus of an army of insurrection. The Red troops from Moscow and Petrograd converged on Yaroslavl too swiftly, however, and retook the town after two weeks. Savinkov escaped, but the possibility of overt resistance by the Social Revolutionaries vanished.

The Czechs.—Forty-five thousand Czech deserters from the Austrian forces had been formed into an army to fight for their country's freedom beside the Russians on the Austrian front. When the Russians collapsed they remained a fighting force, and plans were made in Paris to move them round the world to the western front. In early March 1918 the Soviet government agreed to provide transport across Russia, but the Czech legionaries had continual trouble with local soviets over food supplies and right of way for their trains.

By the middle of May the entire force, moving eastward to the Pacific, was strung out in detachments across 5,000 mi. of railway from Kazan to Vladivostok, a natural prey to anxiety and rumour. On May 14 one of their detachments met a trainload of Austro-German prisoners being repatriated in accordance with the treaty of Brest-Litovsk. A fracas ensued, with bloodshed which involved the local Red forces.

Moscow at once demanded that the Czechs fulfil their pledge to surrender their arms. They refused and, on May 29, forcibly resisted attempts to carry out the disarmament order. In June they fought the Bolsheviks openly throughout Siberia, and the local soviets were powerless against their disciplined troops. At the end of the month their Vladivostok contingent overthrew the soviet there and set up an anti-Bolshevik government with the approval of the Allies. By July 31 almost all Siberia was changed from Red to White and the Czech forces were moving westward to attack the Soviet state.

Death of the Tsar.—The advance of the Czech and White Russian armies brought death to the former Tsar Nicholas II, who with his family had been held for several months at Ekaterinburg. The local soviet professed to believe that the imperial family planned to escape to Omsk, where the White Adm. A. V. Kolchak had established a counterrevolutionary government. Without a trial the soviet voted to execute "Citizen and Citizenness Romanov" and their family and did so on the night of July 16–17, 1918.

Intervention.—The month of August saw intervention in full swing. On Aug. 2 the British, who had already landed forces at Murmansk to prevent war supplies from falling into German hands, disembarked several thousand Allied troops at Archangel; they overthrew the local soviet and set up a provisional government of the north. A few days later British and French contingents landed at Vladivostok, followed by a Japanese division on Aug. 12 and by two U.S. regiments on Aug. 15 and 16. Western Siberia was already in the hands of the Czechs and a number of anti-Soviet governments. On Aug. 24 Anglo-Japanese troops crushed Red resistance in the maritime provinces in a battle on the Ussuri river. Chita was captured on Sept 6, and organized soviet government beyond the Urals disappeared. The Czechs had seized the chief cities of the northern Volga and an anti-Soviet army was marching from the Cossack provinces of the Don.

At the beginning of the autumn the tide turned. The Bolsheviks threw back the Czechs at the end of Sept. 1918 and halted the White advance from the Don. As Germany weakened on the western front, the Baltic provinces, Finland and the Ukraine lost its support. Turkey was on the verge of capitulation, and Turkish and German control over the Caucasus was vanishing. Lenin's prediction was coming true; the Central Powers and the treaty of Brest-Litovsk were crumbling together, and the European revolution appeared to be at hand. When the German sailors in Kiel raised the red flag on Nov. 9, 1918, the Soviet government saluted the event with triumph.

The Bolsheviks had still to reckon with the Allies. The autumn of 1918 saw the reinforcement of foreign forces on Russian soil. By the end of the year there were approximately 15,000 British and U.S. troops occupying a fan-shaped area in northern Russia, at least 70,000 Japanese holding the important strategic points of eastern Siberia and the maritime provinces, 7,000 Americans protecting the Trans-Siberian and Chinese Eastern railways, and about the same number of British supporting and instructing the armies of Admiral Kolchak, who had become dictator of the so-called all-Russian government of Siberia by a coup d'état at Omsk on Nov. 18. The French had occupied Odessa with a powerful fleet and a mixed force from Salonika.

The abandonment of the campaign by the Czechs, eager for home, counterbalanced the accession of foreign anti-Soviet forces, and the Whites were not yet in a position to strike an effective blow. When the new year began neither side could show much gain, except that the revolution had reached the Baltic by the establishment of a Soviet government at Riga on Dec. 26.

The Red Terror.—During these months of pressure the Bolsheviks had hardened. Troops were called up, grain and cattle requisitioned, property confiscated. In the summer of 1918 to external dangers was added a deadlier enemy in their midst. After his defeat at Yaroslavl, Boris Savinkov revived against the Soviet the Social Revolutionary terrorist centre which he had formed years before to combat tsardom by assassination. On Aug 30, 1918, one of his agents, a girl named Fanny (Anna) Kaplan, shot and wounded Lenin as he left a workers' meeting in Moscow. The following day M. S. Uritsky, chief of the Petrograd Cheka, was shot dead by Social Revolutionaries. The Bolsheviks met Savinkov's terrorism with their own Red terror. The Cheka had been organized in Dec. 1917 to deal with sabotage and other counterrevolutionary manifestations. (The word "Cheka" was formed from the initials of the Russian words meaning "extraordinary commission.") Its power grew to include summary arrest, judgment and execution. In revenge for the wounding of Lenin 500 of the most prominent figures of the old regime were shot that night in Moscow. The killing of Uritsky led to similar reprisals in Petrograd. A veritable reign of terror began.

War Communism.—The effects of this period were momentous. On the one hand it stamped deep into the minds of western countries the belief that Russia had relapsed into Mongol savagery. On the other it confirmed the Soviet leaders in their hatred of the non-Bolshevik world.

Intervention gave impetus and coherence to the work of nationalization, which had been proceeding sporadically. In some cases factories had been nationalized in order to fight sabotage by their owners or managers, in others to legalize confiscation already accomplished by the workers. Under the pressure of war the important industries were given control boards. The attempt to fix prices in a period of acute currency inflation had produced the inevitable flight of commodities from the market. As the situation grew more difficult it became necessary to control not only industry and transport but the supply and distribution of food. From that stage the step to the control of all production and distribution was not a long one for a government of Marxian Socialists.

At first, in the early summer of 1918, restrictions were not so harsh as to prevent much private trade and speculation. It happened that the beginning of the Red terror coincided with the period of greatest food shortage, before the harvest. The extraordinary powers given to the Cheka to suppress internal enemies were quickly directed against speculators seeking for profits.

From the outset an influential section of the central committee of the Bolshevik party had been advocating a full Communist program rather than Lenin's more cautious policy. Circumstances were now on their side, and by Aug. 1918 the period of War Communism which lasted nearly three years may be said to have begun. Private buying and selling were prohibited by law and offenders were severely punished. Cash wages lost their importance. Workers and other employees were given cards for food, clothing and other necessities, free lodging and free transport on trams and railways. All nonworking elements of the population were disfranchised. The peasants were subjected to requisitions of all their crops save what was needed for their households. They obtained nothing but promises in exchange, and the breakdown of distribution and the difficulties of transport in a country ravaged by war progressively diminished their return from their labour. Extreme Communists declared that money would soon be wholly abolished. This hope was perhaps a screen for the conventional motives for inflation and the unavoidable fall in the value of the currency.

Money did not become wholly worthless, and a host of bagmen and hucksters, too numerous and unimportant to be imprisoned, continued private trade. The government tried to eliminate them by entrusting distribution to the co-operatives, which had had an extensive network in Russia for many years. In spite of these efforts much of the lesser retail trade remained in private hands.

Attempts at Peace.—Representatives of every section of anti-Bolshevik Russians, from the Social Revolutionaries Kerensky and Savinkov to the grand duke Nicholas (Nikolay Nikolayevich), former commander in chief and uncle of the former tsar, went to Paris to enlist the support of the peace conference. But the Allies were chiefly concerned with Germany. They feared that circumstances might induce Germany and Russia to make common cause, and their first impulse was to neutralize the Bolshevik danger.

On Jan. 12, 1919, the commissar for foreign affairs, G. V. Chicherin, asked the U.S. state department to open peace negotiations. On Jan. 16 the representatives in Paris of Great Britain, France, Italy and the United States discussed a general truce plan for Russia put forward by David Lloyd George. Pres. Woodrow Wilson suggested that representatives of all Russian groups including the Bolsheviks should hold a meeting on the island of Prinkipo in the Sea of Marmora under the auspices of the Allies. The anti-Bolshevik governments in Russia refused to participate and the project was dropped.

In spite of continued hostility on the part of the French another attempt was made to reach a peaceful settlement. William C. Bullitt, attached to the U.S. delegation in Paris, was sent to Petrograd in March 1919. After a week's discussion he brought back peace terms which the Soviet government pledged itself to accept if the Allies agreed not later than April 10. The most important features of this document were a plan for the pacification of Russia on the basis of its several existing governments, a willingness by the said governments, including the Soviet, to recognize responsibility for the financial obligations of the former Russian empire, an exchange of official representatives between the Soviet government and the foreign powers and an immediate withdrawal of foreign troops. In spite of warm support by Col. Edward House and the approval of Lloyd George and V. E. Orlando this project also was shelved, perhaps because of the rapid advance of Kolchak's army, which once more strengthened the belief that the Soviet government was doomed to extinction.

Renewed Intervention.—The White armies of Kolchak in Siberia, of Denikin in southwestern Russia and of Gen. N. N. Yudenich in Estonia had been amply supplied by the Allies with money, equipment and instructors. Kolchak threatened Kazan and Samara, on the Volga, in May and planned to reach Moscow before the end of June, but strategic co-ordination was lacking; neither Denikin nor Yudenich was ready. Kolchak could not withstand the full weight of the Red army, which had now been welded into a competent fighting force. An attempt at diversion by the British in the north came too late to help him.

The next stage of the White campaign was more dangerous. Denikin made rapid progress northward in the summer, and in mid-October had taken Orel, within 200 mi. of Moscow, and was threatening the capital. Simultaneously Yudenich drove at Petrograd. His English tanks broke the weak resistance of the Reds, whose main forces were concentrated against Denikin. Yudenich's advance guard was within 10 mi. of Petrograd before the Soviet troops rallied. Then the tide ebbed. Yudenich was thrown back, and Denikin's offensive, heavily repulsed at Orel, fell to pieces. In December he was making a last stand at Novorossiisk in the Kuban, and by April he had fled to Constantinople. Kolchak lost his capital, Omsk, in November and he finally resigned command a month later. The Czechs betrayed him to the Red army at Irkutsk. He was put on trial as a traitor, condemned to death and shot on Feb. 7, 1920. The bewildering collapse of the White armies was caused by the hostility of the masses in the territory they controlled no less than by military defeat.

Kolchak's execution marked the end of the intervention period; nearly all the Allied troops had been withdrawn late in 1919. Japanese troops were still in occupation of Vladivostok, however, and the maritime provinces, and Gen. P. N. Wrangel was reforming the shattered army of Denikin in the Crimea. Later, during the war with Poland, Wrangel had some successes on the mainland, but the armistice released overwhelming forces against him, and in Nov. 1920 the remnants of his army were transported by the Allied fleet to Constantinople.

The Soviet army had been progressively demobilized as the enemy weakened, but the internal economy of the country was in a chaotic state. The peasants, irritated by requisitions, had reduced the production of grain, and industry, which had been harnessed everywhere to war, had to be reconstructed on a peace basis. Trotsky, the commissar of war, proposed that the army should be utilized directly for production. The "labour army" helped to reorganize transport and some sections of heavy industry, but discontent was generated among the workers.

War with Poland.—Before the situation became critical an emergency, war with Poland, settled the problem. The Soviet government proposed peace to Poland in Jan. 1920 on terms similar to those offered Finland and Estonia. The Poles at first seemed willing to agree, but their circumstances improved as supplies of war material from France and a food loan of $50,000,000 from the United States strengthened their country. At the end of March they demanded all the territory west of the Polish frontier of 1772, a large cash indemnity and the occupation of the Russian town of Smolensk as guarantee. The Bolsheviks refused, and the Polish army occupied Kiev early in May. Within a month the Bolsheviks struck back. The Soviet cavalry retook Kiev in June, while the main force advanced from Smolensk through Vilnius and along the German border. The Red armies, marching forward almost without combat, converged upon Warsaw. The Polish retreat became a rout, and by the middle of August the Russians had reached the outskirts of the city.

France and England were appalled; a sovietized Poland would mean bolshevism in the heart of Europe. The French therefore sent Gen. Maxime Weygand, with a small group of officers, to Warsaw. The counterattacks beginning on Aug. 14 were completely successful; almost overnight, with little fighting, the Red armies were in retreat. A great part of the troops on the German border gave up their arms. On Oct. 11, after Polish territory had been entirely cleared, an armistice agreement was concluded at Riga. On March 18, 1921, peace was signed on terms favourable to Poland, with a new frontier which placed 4,000,000 Ukrainians and White Russians under the Polish flag. Again the Soviet government had paid a heavy price for peace. (*See* RUSSO-POLISH CAMPAIGN.)

De Facto Recognition.—An improvement of relations with the new Baltic states followed the collapse of Denikin and Yudenich. In the autumn of 1919 Maxim Maximovich Litvinov was sent by the Soviet to Tartu (Dorpat) in Estonia to negotiate peace with Estonia and Finland. Peace treaties with both states were signed early in the following year on reasonable terms. A settlement with Latvia was delayed by the Lettish claim to the province of Lettgalen. The Letts refused to negotiate and in a three-week campaign, Jan. 3-24, 1920, drove the Red troops from the province. Peace with Latvia was signed on Aug. 11, 1920. In the previous January the Allied blockade had been lifted. Anglo-Russian negotiations began in the winter of 1919-20 but were interrupted by the Polish war, and it was not until March 16, 1921, that a trade agreement according *de facto* recognition to the Soviet was signed in London. In the same year similar agreements were made with Germany (May 6), Norway (Sept. 2), Austria (Dec. 7) and Italy (Dec. 26).

SOVIET AFFAIRS TO 1941

The new regime was faced with the constitutional problem of blending together the real authority of the council of people's commissars with the nominal sovereignty of the soviets. This was possible because of the prominence, in both council and soviets, of the Bolsheviks, who took the title of All-Russian Communist party (of Bolsheviks) in March 1918. The task of constitution making was fulfilled in the constitution of July 10, 1918, which remained the fundamental document of Soviet constitutionalism. It applied only to the Russian Socialist Federal Soviet Republic, which consisted essentially of the Great Russian core of the old empire together with Siberia; its federative form reflected the exploitation by the Communists of the national grievances of the non-Russian peoples embedded within it. In addition, the course of the civil war had finally resulted in the setting up of Soviet governments in the Ukraine and in White Russia and also in Georgia, Armenia and Azerbaijan—which were formed into a Transcaucasian federation in Dec. 1922. In form, the Ukraine, White Russia and Transcaucasia were independent states, linked with the R.S.F.S.R. only by treaties of a peculiarly intimate kind; but their governments owed their existence to the Red army and

were firmly under the control of the Communist party, which remained a single centralized unit.

Early in 1922 Joseph Vissarionovich Stalin (*q.v.*), the general secretary of the Communist party, was instructed as commissar of nationalities to draw up a plan of federation between these governments. In Dec. 1922 the first Congress of Soviets of the U.S.S.R. met at Moscow and confirmed the pact for the formation of a union. The Far Eastern Republic, a semi-independent buffer state closely affiliated to the R.S.F.S.R., had been merged with the latter in the preceding November.

The constitution of the new state, the Union of Soviet Socialist Republics, was accepted by the central executive committee on July 6, 1923, and became effective from that date. To the four allied republics two others were added in 1925 by the inclusion of two central Asian republics, Turkmenistan and Uzbekistan. These were formed partly of Turkistan (an area hitherto within the R.S.F.S.R.) and partly of the old amirates of Khiva and Bukhara (which had been gradually sovietized after their subjection to Soviet power in 1919-20).

As in other federal constitutions, the powers of government in the U.S.S.R. were nominally divided between the centre and the constituent republics. But the division of functions left to the central power not only the usual ones relating to external relations and defense but most of the major economic ones.

The centre's overriding authority was guaranteed in a number of ways. Indeed the whole process was little more than an extension of the R.S.F.S.R. constitution to cover the whole area under sovereign control. No real importance could be attached to the affirmation of the right of the republics to secede from the federation. Those states of the old empire which had successfully seceded and maintained their independence—Poland, Finland, Estonia, Latvia and Lithuania—had done so because non-Soviet regimes with foreign support had finally established themselves against Russian-backed Soviet movements.

The most important unifying force of the new state, which contained so many races, creeds and languages, was not mentioned in the constitution. The Communist party, with its rigid discipline and centralized authority, was destined to control each of the constituent states and to cement them more firmly together.

The Peasants and the Famine, 1921–22.—War Communism pressed heavily upon the peasants. Difficulties of transport and distribution prevented them from receiving manufactured goods in exchange for their requisitioned food products, and although their contribution to the national budget decreased proportionately as the currency emission to cover deficits grew greater, their position showed no corresponding improvement. Administrative confusion, red tape and contradictory instructions made the requisitions more onerous. Gradually the peasants reduced the area sown and concealed the harvested grain. The total harvest in 1921 was only about 40% of the average yearly harvest in 1909–13, while the area sown had decreased by almost one-half and the yield per *desyatina* had decreased by more than one-third. The decline was progressive from 1916 to 1921, except that the yield per *desyatina* improved slightly in 1921.

The Bolsheviks tried to counter this passive resistance by an extension of class warfare to the villages. They divided the rural population into three groups: rich peasants ("kulaks" or exploiters), middle peasants and poor peasants. The poor were their protégés, they said, the middle their friends and the rich their enemies. In 1918 "committees of village poor" were organized to supervise the grain requisitions and to take the part in village management which had hitherto belonged to the prosperous peasants. These were soon replaced by the village soviets, over which the Bolsheviks had established control. It was hoped that by this means kulak opposition would be overcome without antagonizing the middle peasants.

Events showed that the rural communities were no favourable terrain for class warfare. The ties of family and religion, a common dislike of tax collectors, towns and townsmen, and a sullen distrust of any central authority which took their young men as soldiers and requisitioned their grain and cattle proved stronger than arbitrary distinctions. Many of the middle peasants were the young relatives of kulaks, whose chief aim was to become kulaks themselves; many of the poor were dependent, ignorant and shiftless. Bolshevik orators and newspapers spoke only of kulak opposition, but the attempts to apply class warfare and communism to the villages were resented by the middle peasants also.

Peasant delegates to the eighth and ninth congresses of the Communist party in 1919 and 1920 had expressed the murmurs of the villages, and there were signs that the army, largely recruited from the middle peasant class, was growing restive. The Polish war brought a new *élan* of patriotic ardour in which this sentiment was for a time forgotten, but early in 1921 it burst forth. In February the garrison of the naval fortress of Kronstadt, near Petrograd, demanded the abolition of the grain monopoly, and a mutiny followed which was suppressed only after heavy fighting. Almost simultaneously the peasants of Tambov, one of the central provinces of Russia, refused to yield their grain to requisition. Troops sent to enforce obedience made common cause with the peasants. Resentment had become revolt.

Lenin realized the danger and induced the tenth Communist congress in March 1921 to sanction a decree substituting a graduated food tax for the system of requisitions. Commodities demanded by the peasants, kerosene, salt, tools and leather, were rushed to Tambov, to be sold or bartered on a free trading basis. Those measures quickly ended the revolt. The source of trouble had been economic discontent rather than political unrest or counterrevolutionary agitation.

It is significant that both these outbreaks occurred at the end of winter, when climatic conditions had caused a failure of the autumn-sown grain and the peasants, whose reserves were depleted by requisitions, were beginning to fear one of the famines that had devastated Russia periodically. Their anxiety was well founded. A prolonged drought in the early summer ruined the spring-sown grain throughout the black earth districts of the Volga, north Caucasus and Ukraine. By the middle of July 1,000,000 peasants were in flight from their parched fields toward the centres of urban and river transport, where they were huddled in refugee camps infested with cholera and the epidemics caused by malnutrition. The crop failure was reckoned to have affected an area inhabited by 20,000,000 to 30,000,000 people. Unless help was forthcoming, at least 10,000,000 seemed doomed to die from starvation before spring.

In July the Soviet government permitted an appeal by the writer Maxim Gorky to Herbert Hoover, then chairman of the American Relief administration (A.R.A.), which had kept alive millions of hungry children in Belgium and northern France during the war and had been at work later in central and eastern Europe. Hoover agreed to help, and a *modus operandi* was soon arranged between the A.R.A. and the Soviet authorities. This example was followed by a number of European charitable organizations, but the brunt of the work was done by the A.R.A., which at the peak of its activity, in March 1922, was giving daily rations to 10,000,000 children and adults. Altogether foreign aid fed probably 12,000,-000 persons, and the Soviet Relief administration maintained at least an equal number.

It was difficult to estimate the famine death roll because of the confusion between disease and starvation in the vital statistics. Deaths from actual hunger probably did not exceed 500,000. Foreign relief for the famine rendered two other important services. It allayed much of the xenophobia provoked by intervention and thus paved the way for a renewal of normal relations between Russia and the outer world. It also helped the Soviet cope with the problem of disease, especially cholera and typhus, which had been epidemic in Russia for centuries; after 1922 there was no widespread recurrence of either pest.

The New Economic Policy.—It is customary to regard the New Economic Policy instituted by Lenin in the spring of 1921 as a more or less temporary abandonment of communism to mollify the peasants. There is no question that an influential section of the Communist party saw it in that light. Lenin himself may not have shared this view. He was above all a realist, alive to the practical necessities of the moment. He had shown that he was well aware of the anomaly of an industrial proletarian revo-

lution in a country 85% of whose people were backward peasants. By force of circumstance and the exigencies of war he had been compelled to adopt a program of socialist centralization which many of his followers welcomed as the correct and natural policy of a socialist state.

Before the Communist party reached a new decision in its protracted discussion of agrarian policy in 1920 and 1921, Lenin found himself advocating not merely a change with regard to requisitions and the grain monopoly but also a general readjustment of the economic framework. The reform of industry for peace purposes would require effort and expenditure which the state was unable to provide, and finance and transport were also in a desperate position.

Lenin's influence and insistence won. His critics had no valid alternative to offer. The New Economic Policy (called N.E.P.) was confirmed by a decree published Aug. 9, 1921. It permitted freedom of trading within the country, sanctioned overtime and piecework payment for workers, offered encouragement to foreign capitalists and concessionaires and recognized by implication the rights of private property which had been abolished under War Communism. The state continued its monopoly of foreign trade into the N.E.P. period, but later a number of the more important trusts into which Soviet industry was divided were allowed to trade abroad directly.

During the period of civil war and War Communism the financial tools of capitalist states had been laid aside. Private banks, cheques, securities—all had gone. Money had depreciated rapidly as more and more of the national budget was covered by inflation; 85% of the 1920 budget was provided by the emission of notes.

If the New Economic Policy was to succeed it clearly had to have banking facilities and a more convenient medium of exchange. The shift of policy was quickly made. The state bank was established in the autumn of 1921 and given the authority to issue bank notes as well as to serve as a credit institution. On Nov. 16, 1921, it began credit operations. By a year from that time the essentials of currency reform had been prepared, and the bank began to issue notes. The monetary unit chosen for the new bank notes was the chervonets, with a gold value of 10 prewar roubles; that is, 119.4826 gr. of fine gold or $5.146 in United States currency. The rouble was thus given its prewar gold equivalent. The law provided that the new bank notes should be secured to 25% by precious metals and foreign currencies. For a time the chervontsi circulated side by side with the earlier sovznaki (government or "Soviet" notes), whose value was adjusted to the chervonets from day to day. In March 1924 the emission of sovznaki was stopped and in May they passed out of circulation. Henceforth the currency system of the Soviet government was on the same general basis as that of western countries.

The reform of the currency required in turn the establishment of the state budget on a solid foundation, since the government could no longer print notes to meet the deficits. Agricultural taxation, which had been substituted for requisitions early in 1921, was again revised. In May 1922 a single tax in kind was established by decree, and the peasants were permitted to pay in specified commodities the graduated taxes imposed. In May 1923 a more extensive reform was made. Cumbrous miscellaneous taxes were swept aside, a single agricultural tax was substituted and money payments gradually replaced commodity payments. Meanwhile, urban taxation had been developed by indirect taxes and income and property taxes, so that the peasants, instead of forming the principal taxpaying body of the state, came to furnish only a small fraction of the national income.

The most radical change involved in the New Economic Policy was the restoration of the whole internal economy of the country, industry, commerce, transport, housing and employment, to a straight money basis. Instead of the vague system of accounting prevalent under War Communism, every state enterprise was compelled to issue a regular balance sheet and to show profit and loss in the old-fashioned way. Employees received a regular wage paid in cash. Housing committees were entitled to charge rent on a graduated scale in accordance with the social position and earnings of the tenant. The railways and tram companies were allowed to charge fares for passengers and freight.

Communist critics of the New Economic Policy were perhaps justified in declaring it a reversion to capitalist methods. In any case, the Soviet government could not avoid the process of decentralization which was a phase of postwar reconstruction in all the belligerent countries of World War I. For them, no doubt, wartime centralization and control boards were matters of necessity rather than choice. For the Bolsheviks, choice and necessity coincided. But if centralization proved unwieldy in the advanced industrial countries of the west, it was a yet heavier burden upon the backward economy of Russia. Under the New Economic Policy a great many nationalized enterprises were released, not to former proprietors or private owners, but to face competition in the open market. The financing of such corporations was carried out by the Industrial and Commercial bank and by other new banking establishments.

As the New Economic Policy developed, industry was divided into "trusts," as they were called, such as the Oil trust, the Coal trust and the Flax trust, at first horizontal in character, but gradually becoming vertical also. With the trusts, which were organs of production, were associated syndicates, organs of sale and purchase, handling both foreign and internal trade. The trusts were later divided into sections; for example, the Oil trust subdivided into Azneft (Azerbaijan Oil), Grozneft (Grozny Oil) and Embaneft (Emba Oil). United action and governmental control were secured by an expansion of the supreme economic council to include representatives of the trust sections, so as to form a kind of industrial general staff.

The New Economic Policy stimulated the foreign trend toward commercial *rapprochement* with the Soviet, and in the spring of 1922 an international conference was held at Genoa, It., where the Soviet envoys for the first time met foreign statesmen on equal terms. The atmosphere was at first cordial and a proposal was made to provide financial assistance to the Soviet on condition that the debts of the tsarist government were recognized. A period of haggling followed, but on April 16, 1922, Germany and the Soviet government privately signed an agreement at Rapallo, It., shelving the debt question, affirming mutual friendship and re-establishing full diplomatic relations. This unexpected event revived fears of a Russo-German combination to upset the treaty of Versailles, and the Genoa conference ended without reaching a solution. There were obvious limits to Soviet-German co-operation in the political field; but there was henceforth a silent collaboration in military matters by which the Russians received help for the reorganization of the Red army and gave Germany facilities for circumventing the disarmament clauses of the Versailles treaty. Although a meeting of experts to discuss financial matters was held in the summer at The Hague, Neth., prospects of a settlement were never bright and little was accomplished.

The Soviet government took the position that the western powers had tried to enforce a humiliating abandonment of the principle of the repudiation of tsarist debts and of the monopoly of foreign trade, which it had now come to regard as one of the main pillars of its economic system. If the stability of the new currency was to be maintained, rigid control over exports and imports was imperative. But in the first years of the New Economic Policy foreign trade was somewhat hampered by the attempt to force it all through the bottleneck of an untrained bureaucratic department. With growing experience there was a tendency to transfer the placing of orders and sales abroad to the trusts directly concerned, while the foreign trade department continued to act as control. Soviet trading corporations were established in London, Berlin, New York city and other centres. French and U.S. businessmen hesitated to allow long-term credits, but the English and Germans found them possible, and the volume of trade steadily increased. Some trade was still carried on by the Russian co-operatives, which, since they were a pre-Soviet organization, had been allowed by some western countries to trade with them in the pre-N.E.P. period. But it was much less important. The policy of industrial and mining concessions to foreign businesses was unproductive and not of long duration.

The growth of exports was the most striking change after the introduction of the New Economic Policy. Total trade expanded, and imports, following the Soviet policy of rigid control, fluctuated widely; but exports were multiplied two and one-half times between 1922 and 1923 and were nearly doubled again in the newly established fiscal year ending Sept. 30, 1924.

The first years of N.E.P. showed a corresponding improvement in internal trade and production. Indications that turnover was multiplied by four between the summer of 1922 and the spring of 1924 were probably not far wrong. In the autumn of 1923 prices of agricultural products fell to 60% of the prewar level. Meanwhile, stimulated by the necessity for showing profits which the New Economic Policy required, the trusts and other industrial enterprises had raised the prices of manufactured goods to 80% above that level. The disproportion was so great that the peasants refused to sell grain or buy goods. Warehouses were glutted and industrial stagnation was threatened. Trotsky used the word "scissors" to describe the crisis which followed, because the graph illustrating the ratio of industrial and agricultural prices to the prewar average had the form of opened scissors, with industrial prices forming the upper blade.

To close the scissors was imperative. It was done in six months, by the sale of goods below cost price, which swept away most of the paper profits of the trusts but removed the danger of industrial stagnation, and by the progressive increase in the price of food products. Although this serious crisis was past, the task of keeping the scissors closed remained one of the major problems of the Soviet state.

The comparative liberty given to private trade under the New Economic Policy had produced a host of prosperous nepmen, as they were called. They were largely middlemen, retail traders and small manufacturers, for the state continued to hold the principal sources of production and wholesale business in its own hands. They doubtless served their purpose in getting the commercial machine back into running order and furnishing new accumulations of capital; but they were peculiarly repugnant to the extreme Communists and to the organized workers.

By the beginning of 1924 the New Economic Policy may be said to have justified itself as a practical measure. Currency had been restored to a gold basis, production was approaching prewar standards and agriculture had recovered from the effects of the famine and civil war. Much of the improvement had been caused by the nepmen and the kulaks. For a further discussion of the New Economic Policy see *Economic and Financial Conditions*, below.

Foreign Relations, 1924–28.—The outer world seemed ready by 1924 to believe that Russia had now entered upon an evolutionary process similar to that which followed the French Revolution under the Directory and was eager to share in the development of the country's vast resources. But it misunderstood the determination of the Soviet leaders to retain their position and their conviction that the regime could not afford to allow the growth of bourgeois elements or the survival of a landowning peasantry. Nor was the ultimate expectation of the world revolution absent at any time from the calculations of Soviet leaders of any group. Such differences of policy as emerged were concerned with means rather than ends. During Lenin's lifetime his authority served to settle most issues that arose; but already during his long last illness important fissures in the Communist party revealed themselves, and his death on Jan. 21, 1924, precipitated a struggle for the succession which lasted for several years and in the course of which the remnants of democracy in the party vanished as they had already long vanished in the organs of the state.

The effect of Lenin's death had been discounted abroad because of his long illness and absence from public affairs. The growing prosperity of the Soviet state had stimulated the interest of foreign businessmen, who were beginning to feel that trade would be improved by the establishment of regular diplomatic and consular relations with Russia. Germany had taken this step two years before. The new Labour government in England had promised to do the same as one of the means of diminishing unemployment, and the Fascist government of Italy was seeking new fields for commercial expansion. France was still preoccupied with the memory of its lost loans to the tsarist government and with its own reconstruction problems, but French hostility to the Soviet had to some extent diminished.

On Feb. 1, 1924, the British government recognized the Soviet *de jure*. Other countries followed in rapid succession, and by the beginning of 1925 all the great powers except the United States had established diplomatic relations with the Soviet Union. The order was as shown in Table IV.

TABLE IV.—*Recognition of the Soviet Government*

Country	Date	Country	Date
Great Britain	Feb. 1, 1924	Sweden	March 15, 1924
Italy	" 7, "	Denmark	June 18, "
Norway	" 13, "	Mexico	Aug. 4, "
Austria	" 20, "	Hungary	Sept. 18, "
Greece	March 8, "	France	Oct. 28, "
Danzig	" 13, "	Japan	Jan. 1, 1925

Japanese recognition had been delayed by their claim to compensation for a massacre of Japanese soldiers by Red partisans in the Siberian town of Novo-Nikolaevsk (later Novosibirsk) in May 1920. Although the Japanese had evacuated Vladivostok and the mainland in Nov. 1922, they retained northern Sakhalin until their claim should be satisfied. After two failures negotiations were resumed in Aug. 1924, and recognition was granted on Jan. 1, 1925. A supplementary agreement on Jan. 20 pledged the Japanese to withdraw from northern Sakhalin before the end of May and gave them important oil and coal concessions in the Russian half of the island.

The establishment of normal diplomatic relations led to an increase of foreign trade, but the absence of a settlement of tsarist debts, war debts and private claims prevented any extension of loans to the Soviet. Nevertheless, short-term credits were soon arranged in many countries, and the regularity with which Soviet bills were met gradually overcame distrust. A number of important English firms gave terms of credit running from three to five years. In 1925 Germany provided a state-assisted credit of 300,-000,000 marks for a period of three years. The French and Americans were more cautious, but heavy annual purchases of cotton in the United States on a short-term credit basis were made possible by longer credits elsewhere and by the general improvement of Russia's economic situation.

Another factor, however, hampered not only financial but political relations between the Soviet and the rest of the world. It was interference in the internal affairs of foreign countries by the Third or Communist International, known as the Comintern. Founded by Lenin in March 1919, the Third International was pledged to the cause of world revolution, which had, Lenin declared, been betrayed by the Second International of Amsterdam. Its establishment completed the split which had taken place in the socialist movements of most countries during World War I. The Russians insisted that the choice be made, and almost every advanced country came to have a Communist party looking to Moscow as well as a Socialist party still affiliated to the Second International.

The Comintern was an aggregation of Communist parties, and in theory, at least, the successful Communist party of Russia was no more than *primus inter pares*. The avowed purpose of the Comintern to overthrow their regimes and institutions by violence caused foreign powers to take a different point of view. Declining to regard casuistic distinctions, they considered the Comintern and the Soviet government as vassals of one lord, the Russian Communist party.

Moreover, the Comintern extended its activities to the colonies of foreign powers and to semicolonial countries or spheres of influence, such as China. This caused ill feeling between Russia and the foremost colonial power, Great Britain, and in May 1923 Lord Curzon, as foreign secretary in the Conservative government, addressed to Moscow a note on the subject so sharply worded as to be the equivalent of an ultimatum. There were a number of points at issue, but the question of Communist propaganda in Great Britain and its colonies was the principal grievance. The Soviet government acceded to the British demands, under protest; but the propaganda ghost was not laid, and it continued to trouble Anglo-Russian relations.

The British Labour government of 1924 took steps toward a friendly settlement with the Soviet Union. An agreement was reached in the autumn of 1924 whereby the Soviet promised to repay old debts over a long term of years in return for immediate financial aid. Before the accord could be signed there was a general election in England, in which no small role was played by a letter said to have been written by G. E. Zinoviev, president of the Communist International, giving instructions about the Communist attitude toward the election and Communist activities in the British army. The Labour party was decisively beaten, the Conservatives returned to power and the agreement with the Soviet was shelved. The stir caused by this incident might have been forgotten but for events in Asia and other colonial regions.

Asiatic Interests.—In 1919 Russia's influence was a negligible factor in Turkey and the near east, Persia, Afghanistan and China. England, on the contrary, had never held so strong a position and seemed on the verge of obtaining permanent control over what had formerly been the buffer states between its empire and the tsar's.

Three years later, however, the Soviet had signed treaties of friendship with Turkey, Persia and Afghanistan, as states independent of external influence, and established a virtual protectorate over Outer Mongolia. The central Asian principalities of Khiva and Bukhara were firmly under Soviet rule, and the new Russian republic was now ready to challenge Britain in China.

The Soviet government and the Comintern achieved this result jointly, under Lenin's guidance. The former disavowed unequal treaties, capitulations, treaty ports, protected areas and unilateral tariffs, while the latter devoted its energies to fostering not Communism but nationalism, by virtue of the Leninist doctrine of colonial slaves. This doctrine was Lenin's answer to the question which had long perplexed orthodox Marxists; namely, why the working masses of western Europe had failed to revolt, as Marx had predicted, against their capitalist masters. Lenin argued that the surplus profits from the exploitation of colonies and semicolonial countries such as China had enabled the European capitalists to maintain their "wage slaves" above the starvation level which would make revolution inevitable. To free such countries from capitalist exploitation would therefore be a long step toward the proletarian world revolution. Lenin thus reconciled three apparently contradictory forces, the nationalist aspirations of colonial and semicolonial countries, the spirit of Marxist Communism and the reborn desire of new Russia for expansion.

The Mongolian treaty of Nov. 1921 caused irritation in Peking and helped delay a full accord between the Soviet and Chinese governments until May 31, 1924. In a manifesto issued in July 1919 and formally repeated in Sept. 1920, the Soviet had affirmed in the most categorical manner its renunciation of previous pacts infringing Chinese sovereignty in any way, its abandonment of all claim to the Boxer indemnity and its willingness to treat with China on terms of full equality.

The treaty of 1924 put a Soviet ambassador, L. M. Karakhan, in the old tsarist embassy in the Legation Quarter of Peking. Meanwhile, the Communist International was at work in south China, where both Russian and Chinese Communists supported the Nationalist slogan, "China for the Chinese!" As the Nationalists advanced northward from Canton, the influence of their Russian advisers, Mikhail Markovich Borodin (Gruzenberg) in political affairs and B. K. Galen (Blücher) in the army, grew stronger. By March 1927 the Nationalists were masters of south China, including the Yangtze valley, and the Chinese section of the greatest treaty port, Shanghai.

At this moment Chang Tso-lin, the anti-Nationalist dictator of Peking, raided the premises of the military attaché in the Soviet embassy there, with the knowledge and permission of the foreign diplomatic corps. A mass of documents was seized and a number of arrests made, including subordinate members of the Russian staff and Chinese Communists who had sought refuge in the embassy compound.

The documents published immediately showed a financial connection between the Soviet embassy in Peking and the Comintern or unofficial activities of Borodin and Galen in south China. A rupture of relations between Moscow and Peking followed. The foreign powers, especially Great Britain, began to realize the danger of the position. Strong military and naval forces enabled the foreigners to retain the treaty ports and the Legation Quarter of Peking, but they were compelled to abandon their privileges at Hankow on the middle Yangtze, which for a time became the Nationalist headquarters.

In 1927, however, there was a break between the Nationalists and the Russians. The Communists were pressing for a more radical agrarian policy with which the Nationalist leadership had no sympathy. They were also trying to direct the whole force of the Nationalist drive against European and, particularly, British interests in China. By the end of the year, the Russian advisers had left, the Chinese Communists were being vigorously suppressed and relations between the Chinese Nationalists and the Soviet government had been severed.

Relations with the West, 1927–28.—Events in China had increased anti-Soviet feeling in Great Britain, already aggravated by Russian financial contributions to the British coal miners on strike in 1926 and in May 1927 the premises of the Soviet trading corporation in London, Arcos, were raided by the police. In this case no seized documents were made public, but the result was similar to that in Peking. Diplomatic relations between England and the Soviet were severed on May 24, 1927. This caused a reduction of English credits and imports and thus affected the internal economic situation, which had now come to depend in no small measure upon smooth relations with foreign capital and business.

The rupture with England did not, however, prevent the Soviet from taking part in international disarmament conferences at Geneva, Switz., in the autumn of 1927 and the spring of 1928. Disarmament had long been advocated by the Soviet government, which in the winter of 1922–23 had attempted to arrange a scheme of armament limitation in a conference with its neighbours, Poland, Finland and the Baltic states. At Geneva the Soviet government proposed to begin immediately the progressive reduction of land, sea and air forces. The other European powers were distrustful and unprepared for such sweeping action, and the conferences ended without result.

Although the Geneva conferences did little to improve the relations of the Soviet with the leading powers of western Europe, and although the Soviet was excluded from the number of original signatories to the Kellogg World Pact of Non-Aggression signed at Versailles in the summer of 1928, there were signs in the following autumn that the United States, which had become a reservoir of capital for European postwar reconstruction, was beginning to modify its aloof or even hostile attitude toward the Soviet.

In the autumn of 1928 a contract between the Soviet trading corporation in New York city and the General Electric company in the United States, giving the former five years' credit on purchases, was the first real breach in the "credit blockade," as it was called, which had hampered business relations between Russia and the United States.

Internal Politics, 1924–28.—Lenin's death occurred at a time when the growing prosperity of the nepmen and the new *bourgeoisie* had begun to raise fears in the minds of many Communists that the New Economic Policy might become a surrender to capitalism. It was felt, moreover, that the state business organizations were now sufficiently strong to take the place of private enterprise and that the restoration of the currency to a sound basis would permit their being financed by the newly created state banking organizations. In the first half of 1924, therefore, private trade was loaded with heavy taxes and other restrictions. The nepmen were unpopular with the masses and the measures taken against them were not unwelcome, but the reduction of private enterprise in the towns led the extremist section of the Communist party to demand a similar suppression of "capitalist elements" in the villages. The struggle between the forces of capitalism and socialism thus provoked a sharper struggle within the Communist party itself. In the first part of the controversy, 1925–26, the opposition, led by Trotsky, tried to force the social-

izing process, which was the avowed aim of the Communist party, at too swift a pace.

In the cities the state might now hope to supplant the nepmen without economic disorganization, but in the villages it was still dependent upon the kulaks, who produced the grain surplus needed for export and to feed the urban centres. When Trotsky demanded their repression the majority of the Bolshevik leaders did not yet see how they could be replaced, and the Communist party congress of April 1925 confirmed the rights of "individual peasant producers," despite a screen of antikulak phrases to cover this compromise with Marxist principles.

A good crop in the summer of 1926, however, strengthened national food resources and brought forward a demand that the village capitalist be curbed. He was becoming dangerously strong, and the state had begun to feel, as it had about the nepman two years before, that it could do without him. The opposition platform, therefore, was in accord with prevailing Communist sentiment, and by 1927 it had attracted such prominent figures of the Bolshevik regime as Zinoviev, the president of the Third International, and L. B. Kamenev, one of Lenin's closest associates. But Trotsky's adherents declared that their arguments were perverted in the official press and that they were not given proper opportunity to state their case. They had recourse to underground methods, which the majority denounced as an attempt to split the party. The adherents of Trotsky refused to abandon their tactics and, after a hot discussion at a joint meeting of the party's central committee and control commission in Nov. 1927, were expelled from the party. At the 15th party congress in December Zinoviev and Kamenev capitulated to the majority and asked to be readmitted into the party as rank-and-file members. Trotsky was sent into exile in central Asia in Jan. 1928 (he was later allowed to go abroad). Soon afterward, it became clear that the majority had adopted the opposition's program of repressing the "capitalist elements" in the villages.

The immediate reason for this step was the failure in the summer of 1927 of the state grain collections. This was the name given to the system of state purchases of grain to provide for the needs of the urban population and the army and for export. In the previous year the state had collected approximately 10,000,000 tons of cereals, of which more than 2,000,000 were exported, and it was planned to collect an equal amount in 1927–28. A renewal of the "scissors" disproportion between the prices of grain and manufactured goods caused difficulty. The peasants preferred to keep the grain for themselves and their stock, rather than sell it. Communist sentiment was already prepared for a drive against "anti-socialist forces" in the villages. During the spring and summer of 1928 vigorous measures, reminiscent of the War Communism period, were employed to extract surplus grain from the richer peasants, who were described as class enemies.

The quota was attained, but the growing needs of the towns left only a small margin for export, which fell to less than 500,000 tons. This reacted unfavourably upon the foreign trade balance, which had now become most important because in 1927 the state had embarked upon an ambitious five-year program of industrialization (that is, an attempt to build up a self-sufficient industrial production) which required heavy purchases of machines and raw materials abroad. The enforced collections of grain caused much discontent in the villages, and in July 1928 the central committee of the Communist party announced their abolition and promised that they should not be repeated. Once again Communist insistence upon class warfare in the villages had overemphasized the distinction between kulaks and the rest of the peasants.

For an account of the first five-year plan, introduced in 1928, see *Economic and Financial Conditions,* below.

(W. Dy.; M. Bf.)

The Rise of Stalin.—Joseph Vissarionovich Stalin emerged as the outstanding leader of the Soviet regime during this period. Although he held no state office until the spring of 1941, when he succeeded his faithful adherent Vyacheslav Mikhailovich Molotov as premier, after being hitherto simply general secretary of the central committee of the Communist party, his power in every field, political and economic, was absolute and unquestioned. It became almost a matter of course to ascribe every Soviet achievement, political, military, economic or social, to his genius and initiative.

Stalin's personal power was further confirmed by the political elimination and, in many cases, by the physical execution of most of the leading "Old Bolsheviks," the men who, along with Lenin and Trotsky, had played prominent roles in the first years of the revolution. Trotsky himself had first been banished to Turkistan and then sent into exile, finally taking up residence in Mexico. There he was murdered in the summer of 1940. Meanwhile, there had been three spectacular trials of prominent revolutionaries in Russia, in Aug. 1936, Jan. 1937 and March 1938. The defendants confessed various acts of treason and sabotage, and almost 50 persons were sentenced to death. Among the victims of these trials were some of the most famous names of the revolution and of the early phases of the Soviet regime. They included a former premier, A. I. Rykov; two former presidents of the Communist International, Zinoviev and Nikolay Ivanovich Bukharin; the once-dreaded chief of the O.G.P.U. (successor of the Cheka as political police), G. G. Yagoda; and many former diplomats, cabinet ministers and prominent economic executives. Marshal M. N. Tukhachevsky, one of the most gifted leaders of the Red army in the civil war, and seven generals of the Red army were shot after an alleged secret trial in June 1937. Throughout these years there were many secret executions, some of which were and others were not subsequently reported, and a far greater number of incarcerations in labour camps and administrative banishments.

The trials and the accompanying purge were a dark and debatable subject. Foreign critics emphasized the factual discrepancies in certain details of the trials which were subject to verification in foreign countries; they interpreted the whole purge as a method of ensuring Stalin's personal power and the confessions as the false self-incriminations of exhausted and broken men, who were influenced by threats against their families. Stalin's power certainly remained unshaken, and the regime stood up to the shock of war without the internal disintegration which had been predicted as a result of the purges. It is, of course, quite possible that the masses of the Russian people who were not involved in the purge viewed with relative indifference this ruthless destruction of one part of the ruling class by another.

The Constitution of 1936.—The All-Union Congress of Soviets adopted a new constitution for the U.S.S.R. on Dec. 5, 1936. This instrument provided for direct, instead of the formerly indirect, election to the new bicameral national legislature, the supreme soviet, with representation in one house based on population, in the other on nationality (there were at that time 11 soviet republics in the union).

Politically, the new constitution brought little if any change in practice. Stalin remained a dictator of unlimited powers. Only one political organization, the Communist party, remained legal, and its dominant role was for the first time given constitutional sanction. Nor was any opposition permitted to manifest itself in speech or writing after the promulgation of the constitution.

Socially, however, and in everyday life, there were considerable changes in Russia after the end of the first five-year plan. There was no reversion to private capitalism, but in the overriding interests of productivity there was toleration and even encouragement of much more material inequality than would have been found during the bleak, austere period of the first five-year plan, when the acute shortage of food and consumers' goods almost enforced a kind of equality of privation. The discrepancy between the incomes of the higher members of the bureaucracy, army and O.G.P.U. officers, industrial executives, popular authors, engineers, etc., and those of the masses of workers and peasants became greater, as also did the difference in wages between skilled and unskilled workers.

There were significant changes of emphasis in education, in literature, in cultural life. The state set the tone in all these fields; there was no tolerance for the dissenter. But the Soviet school, experimental and loosely disciplined for more than a decade after the revolution, became much stricter in its methods, with marks

and examinations, uniforms for students and more authority for teachers. Middle and higher education, formerly free, was paid for from 1940.

Up to the middle 1930s it was fashionable and, indeed, almost compulsory to deprecate the Russian past extravagantly and uncritically. But subsequently the nationalist note was often struck in newspapers and literature: tsars of outstanding personality such as Peter the Great and Ivan the Terrible were referred to with respect, instead of being indiscriminately abused.

There was an important change of attitude toward family life. Early Soviet legislation practically eliminated all restrictions on intercourse between the sexes. Divorce could be had immediately for the asking by either partner, and there was no distinction between legitimate and illegitimate children. Abortions were frequent and permitted. In the middle '30s there was a severe tightening of restrictions on divorce; the performance of abortions was made illegal and women were urged and encouraged to bear many children.

During the period from 1929 to 1933 there was a good deal of persecution of children whose class origin was suspect. Sons and daughters of priests, former aristocrats and well-to-do families were barred from universities and found it hard to get employment. After 1933 there was more social equality, more feeling that class lines within the state had been ironed out. It was perhaps not accidental that these changes of a moderate and conservative character coincided with the decimation of the ranks of the veteran revolutionaries who were identified with the more active destructive period of the revolution.

Foreign Relations, 1928-41.—Between 1928 and 1941 the U.S.S.R. passed through three fairly well-differentiated stages of foreign policy, as follows:

1. Collaboration to some extent with Germany, antagonism to Great Britain and France. This had been the general course of Soviet foreign policy after the revolution, and it continued until Adolf Hitler's rise to power in Germany in 1933. There were occasional variations in this policy, periods of coolness between Moscow and Berlin. But Soviet policy in the main was to support the German demand for disarmament, as opposed to the French thesis of security, to abstain from co-operation with the League of Nations, to depict Great Britain and France as the chief potential enemies. Soviet support of the British general strike and of the Nationalist revolutionary movement in China aggravated relations with Great Britain, and there was a suspension of British-Soviet diplomatic relations from 1927 until 1929.

2. Collective security, antifascism, united front. Hitler's rise to power on an outspokenly anticommunist program and the obviously militarist, aggressive character of the nazi regime caused a change of orientation. Karl Radek, the well-known publicist, who was often an unofficial spokesman for the government until his arrest in connection with the treason and sabotage trials, heralded this shift in the spring of 1933 when he wrote a series of articles about the undesirability of violent change in the territorial settlement. The U.S.S.R. joined the League of Nations on Sept. 18, 1934, the year when Germany left it. Military alliances were concluded with France and Czechoslovakia and pacts of nonaggression, elaborately worded so as to exclude every form of disguised aggression, were concluded with Russia's western neighbours—Poland, Latvia, Lithuania, Estonia and Finland. The regular Soviet representative at important sessions of the League of Nations, Maxim Maximovich Litvinov, repeatedly advocated the ideas that peace was indivisible and that security must be organized on a collective basis.

The Communist International, fully in the service of Soviet policy, changed strikingly the character of its propaganda. Extreme revolutionary demands were pushed into the background, and political alliances were sought not only with Socialists but with Liberal and Radical parties and in China with Chiang Kaishek. One result of this policy was the formation in 1936 of left-wing popular front governments in France and Spain. During the Spanish Civil War which broke out in 1936, the Soviet government, although represented on the "nonintervention committee" in the beginning, sent a considerable amount of aid in tanks, planes and military specialists to the Republicans.

3. Abandonment of the west, aggression. A tremendous change in foreign policy occurred on Aug. 23, 1939, when Stalin and Hitler signed a pact of nonaggression. There had been signs earlier in the year that the Soviet government, which had been rebuffed and cold-shouldered at the time of the Munich conference in Sept. 1938, was considering a change of policy. Stalin in his important speech to the 18th party congress in March 1939 had spoken of unwillingness to pull foreign chestnuts out of the fire. Litvinov, apostle of collective security, had been summarily dropped from the cabinet on May 3, 1939, and replaced by Molotov. The Soviet-German agreement broke upon the world at a time when the negotiations were still proceeding between the U.S.S.R. and Great Britain and France with the object of bringing the union into a common front against Germany. In the course of these the Soviet government had made demands concerning the Baltic states and Poland which the governments of those countries found unacceptable.

During this third phase, the Soviet government pursued a policy of independent aggression, endeavouring to strengthen its strategic position and to derive benefit from the war in which the other major European powers were involved. By a secret protocol (revised on Sept. 28) to the treaty of August, Germany had agreed not to oppose Russian action in the areas in which the Soviet government declared itself to be interested. Soviet troops crossed the Polish frontier on Sept. 17, 1939, and the partition of that country with Germany was effected. Finland was attacked on Nov. 30. The Finnish resistance was unexpectedly strong, but on March 12, 1940, a peace treaty was concluded which gave the U.S.S.R. the isthmus of Karelia, the naval base of Hangö and other concessions. The Baltic republics, Latvia, Lithuania and Estonia, which had been obliged to accept "mutual aid" treaties with the U.S.S.R. admitting Soviet garrisons in their territory in Sept.–Oct. 1939, were annexed outright and organized as soviet republics in the summer of 1940. At the same time, Rumania was forced to cede Bessarabia, a former Russian province, and northern Bukovina. With some internal reorganization the number of soviet republics was now 16. (W. H. Ch.; M. Bf.)

By the autumn of 1940 the Soviet Union was becoming anxious at the extent of Germany's successes, and Molotov was sent to Berlin in November to attempt to strike a new bargain. But he failed to get agreement to Russian demands concerning the Balkans and the straits. The Russians had taken part in the Montreux conference of 1936, which had revised the Lausanne straits convention of 1923 much in their favour; but now they wished for physical guarantees of their security in this area. Thereafter, despite various appeasing gestures, the die was cast, and on June 22, 1941, Hitler attacked without warning. Warnings from the west that such an attack was being prepared had apparently been taken lightly.

The major success of Soviet diplomacy in the period immediately before the German attack was a nonaggression treaty with Japan, signed on April 13, 1941. By aggression in Manchuria in 1931, Japan had become a neighbour of the U.S.S.R. and of its satellite Outer Mongolia on a much wider front. The Soviet government, preoccupied by the European threat, had done its best to appease Japan by selling it in 1935 the rights in the Chinese Eastern railway that the Soviet Union had recovered in 1924 and defended against China in 1929. By helping to bring about a temporary united front of the Chinese Nationalists and Communists and by signing a nonaggression treaty with the Chinese Nationalists, it had also helped to stiffen Chinese resistance toward Japan. Nevertheless, there had been some fairly severe fighting—almost an undeclared war—along parts of the Manchurian frontier in 1938 and 1939. The nonaggression pact with Germany's ally thus removed some of the Soviet fear of a war on two fronts.

WORLD WAR II

The first five months of the war were almost fatal to the Russians. The Germans advanced rapidly, encircling great Russian forces and conquering about 500,000 sq.mi. of territory. By November all southern Russia, including the Crimea except the naval base of Sevastopol, had been overrun, and Rostov had fallen. In the Ukraine Kharkov had fallen, and further north Tula was almost surrounded. The Germans were within 20 or 30 mi. of Moscow, whence much of the administration had been evacuated, with the foreign embassies, to Kuybyshev (Samara). Leningrad was virtually encircled—the beginning of a siege that was to take a heavy toll through famine and to rob Russia of historic monuments of its past.

The winter brought relief; Rostov was retaken and a counter-offensive in December relieved the pressure on Moscow. By the time the spring thaw of 1942 came, the Russians had made deep penetrations into several sections of the German front. The summer of 1942, however, was almost as disastrous as the preceding one. The new offensive in the south carried the Germans to the Don along most of its length and across it to the Volga at Stalingrad. Meanwhile Rostov, Sevastopol, Novorossiisk and the Maikop oil fields as well as the rich agricultural lands north of the Caucasus had all been lost, and the southeastward thrust of the German armies in this sector had almost reached the major oil centre of Grozny. In 15 months it was reckoned that the Red army had sustained 5,000,000 casualties.

The defense of Stalingrad marked the turning of the tide. Again winter came to the rescue of the Russians, and a great counter-offensive cut off a huge German army outside Stalingrad where it eventually surrendered in Feb. 1943. In the summer a new German offensive was defeated and the Soviet armies went over to the offensive, freeing Orel and Belgorod on the central front, liberating Kharkov and the Donets coal field, as well as Novorossiisk and the eastern shore of the Black sea. A sudden advance to the Dnieper cut off large German forces in the Crimea. By the beginning of November, the Red army was back in Smolensk, Gomel and Kiev. This offensive merged without a break into the winter offensive of 1943–44, in which, in addition to further gains in the south and centre, the Russians at last broke out in the north, clearing the Leningrad area and driving on toward the Baltic states. With the reconquest of the Crimea in May, the Russians had cleared most of the pre–1939 Soviet Union.

In the summer of 1944 a series of new offensives began. Finland agreed to an armistice in September, but the Germans refused to leave the country and fighting continued. In the far north the retreating Germans were pursued over the Norwegian border. Farther south big gains were made in the Baltic republics, White Russia and Poland. But the Russians failed in much-debated circumstances to relieve the Polish home army which had risen in Warsaw, and both there and on the Baltic front, where the Red army had suffered a reverse, the advance came to a halt in August. The most spectacular gains were obtained in the south. An offensive against Rumania led to the Rumanian government's accepting armistice terms and declaring war on Germany on Aug. 25; in September war was declared against Bulgaria (hitherto neutral as regards the war on the eastern front), and on Sept. 8 Bulgaria, too, changed sides and declared war against Germany. In their pursuit of the Germans into Yugoslavia, the Russians on Oct. 20 entered Belgrade simultaneously with Tito's (Josip Brozovich or Broz) partisans; in Hungary, Budapest was encircled by the end of the year and a rival Hungarian government was set up in Debrecen under Russian sponsorship. The Russians had also crossed into eastern Czechoslovakia.

A new winter offensive on all fronts began in Jan. 1945, and by the time of Germany's collapse in May, Russian armies were deep into the heart of the reich with Warsaw, Budapest, Vienna and (by inter-Allied agreement) Berlin and Prague among the capitals taken by the Red army.

In the far east the U.S.S.R. entered the war only on Aug. 8, 1945, on the eve of Japan's collapse, and rapidly overran Manchuria and northern Korea.

Internal Affairs, 1941–45.—The war provided the biggest test to date of the capabilities and stability of the Soviet regime. But any opportunity the Germans had to exploit political discontent in the occupied areas was soon thrown away by the ruthless exploitation of their resources and by the brutality which the Germans showed toward their populations. The ill treatment of the civilian population was completed by large deportations for slave labour in the reich and by massacres of the Jews. Hatred of the invader proved a powerful welding force in adversity.

On June 30, 1941, a new state committee of defense was set up which for the period of the war was the supreme governing body under Stalin's leadership. The general line was to stress even more strongly than in the preceding period the patriotic elements in the Soviet ideology and to call upon the people to resist in the name of Russia's heroic past rather than in that of the revolution. A new measure of toleration for the Orthodox Church was part and parcel of this process. The Communist party itself, on the contrary, was allowed to fall into the background, and its ranks were widely opened to soldiers in the field and outstanding workers in the arms factories. Its membership rose from 3,876,000 in 1941 to 5,700,000 at the end of the war, despite the heavy losses in battle. The nation's gaze was concentrated on the army, of which Stalin (now commissar for defense) was in supreme control; and after the early failures of the survivors of the old guard of Communist generals, K. E. Voroshilov, S. M. Budenny and S. K. Timoshenko, new ones came to the fore: G. K. Zhukov, I. S. Konev, R. Y. Malinovsky, K. K. Rokossovsky, F. I. Tolbukhin, A. M. Vasilevsky. Up till 1943, when illness caused his replacement by Vasilevsky, the chief of staff was the former tsarist officer B. M. Shaposhnikov.

In March 1944 the "Internationale" was replaced as the national anthem by a new patriotic song.

Stern measures were meted out after the German retreat to those minorities that had collaborated with them. The Volga German Autonomous Republic was abolished early in the war and its population deported into Siberia. The same fate now befell the Kalmuck, Chechen-Ingush and Crimean (Tatar) Autonomous Republics and the Karachay Autonomous Region. In 1944 the hitherto nominally independent republic of Tannu Tuva entered the Soviet Union as an autonomous region of the R.S.F.S.R.

By constitutional amendments of Feb. 1944, the republics of the U.S.S.R. were given the right of entering into direct relationships with foreign countries and of having their own defense formations. For this purpose they were to have the right to set up commissariats of foreign affairs and defense. The only practical consequence of these changes seems to have been the seats allotted to the Ukraine and to Byelorussia in the United Nations.

Foreign Relations, 1941–45.—Foreign policy during the war naturally gave the same overwhelming priority to the direct defense of the Soviet Union as was manifest in every other sphere of national life. The Communist parties abroad, which only yesterday had been sabotaging the "imperialist war" against Germany, were ordered to take a patriotic line in all countries fighting the axis and henceforth devoted themselves to trying to influence Allied strategy in such a way that the maximum burden should be lifted from Soviet shoulders. This was the origin of the clamour for the second front, and Soviet diplomacy was largely directed to the same end. In a further effort to reassure foreign opinion, the announcement was made on May 22, 1943, that the Communist International had been formally dissolved on May 15.

The Soviet Union signed a number of treaties with the Allied governments (including a 20-year treaty of alliance with Great Britain on May 26, 1942) and with Allied governments in exile. It entered into diplomatic relations with certain countries for the first time: Canada, South Africa, the Netherlands. But although the prior consideration was the immediate war crisis, the Soviet government was concerned from the beginning to safeguard its own postwar position. Unsuccessful efforts were made to get from Great Britain and the United States formal recognition of its recent annexations in the Baltic. With regard to Poland, the agreement signed with the Polish government in exile on July 30, 1941, recognized the abrogation of the territorial changes resulting from the Soviet-German pact and the rebirth of an independent Polish state. There followed a brief period of apparent Polish-Soviet friendliness during which the surviving Poles who had been deported into the Soviet Union were allowed to form an army. But relations were not cordial, and between March and April 1942 some of the Poles were withdrawn from Soviet territory to the middle east. The Russians also formed a Communist Polish army which took a part in the later campaigns. Relations with the London Polish government were envenomed by constant controversy over the frontier question, and relations with it were broken off after it had appealed in April 1943 to the International Red Cross to investigate German allegations that the bodies of large numbers of Polish officers who had been interned in Russia but of whom no account had hitherto been given had been found in circumstances that pointed to the Russians' having massacred them. (A subsequent Russian commission naturally retorted that the Germans were responsible for the murders.)

Poland remained the main source of difference between the Allies until the end of the war, particularly when it became clear that the Russians were determined to have the new Poland governed by a regime chosen by themselves and ready to grant the U.S.S.R. its territorial demands in return for compensation at Germany's expense. This question, however, was only part of the general planning of the postwar world carried out by negotiations with the United States and Great Britain, in particular at the tripartite conferences of Tehran (Nov.–Dec. 1943), Yalta (Feb. 1945) and Potsdam (July 1945).

The three main questions involved were the treatment of the defeated countries; the new territorial settlement; and the nature of the new United Nations organization, planned at the Dumbarton Oaks conference in Aug.–Sept. 1944 and brought into being at the San Francisco conference in May–June 1945.

In regard to the first of these, the original Russian point of view was in favour of the partition of Germany into separate states; but this was not maintained at Potsdam, when a decision to treat Germany as a single economic unit was reached despite the quadripartite nature of the occupation. The Russian insistence on the punishment of war criminals was largely met by the Allies, and the Russians co-operated in the Nuremberg trials; but it was soon made clear, both in regard to "denazification" in Germany and "democratization" in Japan, that the Russians meant far greater transformations of the social structure of these countries than had been contemplated. Under Russian occupation, eastern Germany was rapidly sovietized. Of more immediate concern was the difference in the attitude toward reparations from Germany, which manifested itself at Yalta and was bridged neither by the Potsdam agreement nor by the subsequent conference of foreign ministers held in Moscow in Dec. 1945. The Russians held that the restoration of Russia through reparations in kind from Germany should be given absolute priority, whereas the western powers considered that nothing should be done to the German economy that would make the occupation a drain on their own resources. No agreement was reached on Japanese reparations either. On the other hand, the Russian war against Japan, which began only on Aug. 8, 1945, enabled them to seize as war booty much of the industrial wealth that the Japanese had built up in Manchuria. The Soviet Union also made much use of the labour of prisoners of war for reconstruction purposes.

On the territorial side, the Russians achieved their demands in Europe, acquiring part of East Prussia, including Königsberg, as well as the Baltic states, eastern Poland, Bessarabia and Bukovina. To these acquisitions a treaty with Czechoslovakia on June 29, 1945, added Sub-Carpathian Ruthenia. All independent efforts at co-operation between the eastern European states were frowned on during and after the war. In addition, of course, the Russians acquired zones of occupation in Germany and Austria and the right to garrison troops to guard their lines of communication in Poland, Hungary and Rumania. Since Aug. 1939 the effective boundaries of Russian power had shifted about 750 mi. to the west and about 600 mi. to the southwest. Russian troops in the Thuringian forest were within 100 mi. of the Rhine. There was strong pressure against Turkey for territorial concessions and for bases on the straits.

In Asia, the negotiations for Russia's entry into the war against Japan had led to the promise of concessions in Manchuria which had the effect of replacing it in the position from which it had been ousted as a result of the Russo-Japanese war of 1904–05. Port Arthur again became a Russian naval base. By a treaty revealed Aug. 14, 1945, these positions were confirmed by the Chinese government of Chiang Kai-shek, which also accepted, subject to the formality of a plebiscite, the abandonment of claims over the Soviet satellite Outer Mongolia. Soviet influence in Sinkiang, dominant in the 1930s but relaxed in the war years, was gradually reasserted.

On the side of international organization, the Russian position was that matters should be handled in the postwar world by the continued co-operation of the three great powers, as during the war. The Soviet Union was eventually persuaded to give a formal position of equality to France, with whom a treaty of alliance had been signed on Dec. 10, 1944, and to China. The special position given to the permanent members of the Security council and the demand for their unanimity on all decisions other than purely procedural ones reflected the Soviet attitude in the drafting of the charter of the United Nations.

POLITICS FROM 1945

There was little change in the political structure of the Soviet Union in the years after World War II. The domination of Stalin and his immediate associates in the Politburo and the council of ministers was beyond question, and apart from the death in Aug. 1948 of A. A. Zhdanov (who had played an important wartime role) and the disappearance of N. Voznesensky there was little change in its composition. From the dozen leading figures, the names of Vyacheslav M. Molotov (whose appointment as vice-premier was announced on March 4, 1949, when he was replaced as foreign minister by A. Y. Vishinsky), of G. M. Malenkov and of L. P. Beria gradually became the most prominent. No new party congress had met by the early 1950s. The supreme soviet and the soviets of the republics resumed the regular elections and sessions that had been abandoned in the war years. The chief task of the former was still the ratification of the annual budget. The chairman of its presidium, the elderly Mikhail Ivanovich Kalinin, died in 1946 and was replaced by N. M. Shvernik, till then head of the trade-union organization.

There was a sharp reversal, beginning even before the end of the war, of the emphasis laid on the state and on the army at the Communist party's expense. The names of the leading Soviet marshals largely disappeared from the foreground and some of them, including Zhukov, the conqueror of Berlin, seem to have been relegated to relative obscurity. This represented, on the top level, part of the process by which the links between east and west, built up perforce during the war, were broken down again. Anxiety was shown as to the effect that contact with the higher standards of living of central Europe might have on the Soviet troops in occupation, and propaganda for their re-education was undertaken. The party itself was subjected to a purging process to get rid of persons who had entered during the war and who did not show sufficient political aptitude for its peacetime tasks; the old standards of indoctrination were demanded once more.

Another process begun during the war involved a modification of the old policy toward the problem of nationalities, with which the name of Stalin was particularly connected. A new emphasis was laid on the Great Russian element in the Soviet Union. It became official doctrine that even prerevolutionary Russia had been a progressive force in relation to the subordinate nationalities absorbed within the Russian empire, and the histories of the latter were rewritten in accordance with this. The language policy exalting the role of Russian, for which a theoretical basis was given in Stalin's attack on the philological theories connected with the name of Nikolay Marr, must also be noted in this connection.

The most effective antidote to the survivals of "bourgeois nationalism" which were regularly castigated in the Soviet press was biological rather than cultural. The policy of large-scale population movements for economic and political reasons would tend to break up the national homogeneity of all the republics and in the long run to create a single undifferentiated Soviet type.

In cultural matters, the same general trend toward Russian self-sufficiency was seen. Much emphasis was laid on the priority of Russian scientists in discoveries in all important fields.

Zhdanov began a campaign against all signs of "servility" toward western cultural models in 1946, and this continued in subsequent years. "Cosmopolitan" became a general term of abuse directed against all tendencies in literature and the arts which did not have as a direct purpose the support of the national effort. Science also was forced to conform to the dominant ideology, a high light in the process being the formal proscription in 1948 of all theories of genetics other than those of the I. V. Michurin–T. Lysenko school—the repudiation, in fact, of all the accepted views of genetics in favour of theories which gave greater scope to the influence of environment and so seemed better fitted to the Soviet attempt to "remake nature."

Foreign Policy after World War II.—The disagreements between the Soviet government and its wartime allies which had become apparent before the end of the war were soon to assume a shape that made further co-operation impossible. Although the Soviet representatives continued to take part in the work of the United Nations (except for the period Jan.–Aug. 1950 when they absented themselves as a result of the dispute over the membership of Communist China), that organization was in fact little more than a forum where the disagreements between the Soviet Union and its associates on the one hand and the rest of the world on the other could be aired. On the matter of disarmament, both conventional and atomic, no agreement was reached. Although Vishinsky had declared in Nov. 1949 that Soviet work on atomic energy was exclusively directed to peaceful purposes, the fact that the Soviet Union was experimenting with atomic bombs was admitted by Stalin in Oct. 1951.

In Europe, a conference in Paris was held in 1946 for discussion of the draft treaties with Italy, Rumania, Hungary, Bulgaria and Finland; these were finally signed in the following year. But there was no agreement either on Austria or on Germany. Continued friction with the western powers over policy in the occupied countries, particularly in Germany, culminated in the effort to dislodge them from Berlin in 1948 through an economic blockade that was frustrated by the air lift. An attempt to deal with the outstanding issues led to a long, fruitless four-power conference of foreign ministers' deputies at Paris in the spring of 1951.

The U.S. offer of support to Greece and Turkey and of economic aid to Europe in 1947, and the refusal of the Soviet Union to participate in the organization for its distribution or to allow either Poland or Czechoslovakia to do so marked the turning point of the postwar period. The success of the European Recovery program made the triumph of Communism in western Europe unthinkable without direct Soviet aid. In eastern Europe the result was to accelerate the Soviet effort (which had already gone a long way) to convert the whole area into a series of Communist-ruled satellites that would be totally dependent on the Soviet Union economically, politically and militarily as well. The last point was well brought out by the appointment in Nov. 1949 of the Soviet marshal Rokossovsky as Polish defense minister.

The symbol of the new situation was the creation in Sept. 1947 of the Communist Information bureau or Cominform, with its headquarters in Belgrade, Yugos., linking together the Communist parties of Europe and being the successor to some extent of the defunct Comintern. Its formal and overt expression was the series of treaties between the Soviet Union and the eastern European countries: Czechoslovakia, Dec. 12, 1943; Yugoslavia, June 8, 1946; Albania, July 1947; Poland, Jan. 26, 1948; Rumania, Feb. 4, 1948; Hungary, Feb. 18, 1948; Bulgaria, March 18, 1948; Finland, April 6, 1948. Treaties between many of these states were also concluded. The eastern German government set up by the Russians in Oct. 1949 belonged for many purposes to the same grouping, though there was no indication that its creation meant the abandonment of hopes for a Germany united on Russian terms.

In 1948 two crucial developments took place. Czechoslovakia, which (though less independent than Finland) had retained a democratic form of government, was forced in a crisis in February to accept Communist rule and rapidly began to travel the same Soviet path as its neighbours. In June the friction between Marshal Tito of Yugoslavia and the Russians over the methods of control adopted by the latter broke into the open. The Soviet-

Yugoslav treaty was denounced by the Soviet government and Yugoslavia was expelled from the Cominform, which moved its headquarters from Belgrade to Bucharest, Rum.

From 1948 relations with the western powers were dominated by the Soviet objections to their rearmament and to all agreements between them on defensive matters, in particular to anything that looked like the remilitarization of a revived western Germany. For the purposes of propaganda in favour of the main theses of Soviet foreign policy a new organization, the World Peace Movement, was set up in March 1950.

The Far East.—The end of World War II saw Russia entrenched in Manchuria and North Korea facing the United States as the occupying power in Japan and South Korea. Officially, as has been seen, the Soviet government fully accepted the claims of the Nationalist government of Chiang Kai-shek to rule in liberated China. But the presence of Soviet troops in Manchuria was used in such a way as to give certain advantages to the Chinese Communist forces when they advanced into it from their strongholds in the north. For a long time, as the Chinese civil war developed, the Russians gave no outward indication of a change in their formal relations with the Chinese government, perhaps calculating that they could not hope for more than that the Chinese Communists should become strong enough to force Chiang Kai-shek to abandon his alignment with the United States, the country that was increasingly regarded as the Soviet Union's main enemy in the postwar world. The picture was changed by the Communist victories in 1948–49. On Oct. 2, 1949, the U.S.S.R. broke off relations with the Chinese Nationalists and recognized the government set up at Peking by Mao Tse-tung. The Chinese leader went to Moscow in December, and on Feb. 14, 1950, a series of new agreements was signed.

Russia promised to leave the naval base of Port Arthur and agreed to lend China $300,000,000 over a period of five years. On Oct. 11, 1954, Russia agreed to give back Port Arthur by May 31, 1955, to lend China a further $230,000,000 and to hand over all its shares in the joint stock Sino-Soviet companies which had been set up in 1950.

Elsewhere in Asia the Russians showed full sympathy with all movements against restoring the prewar position of the main colonial powers and, when national independence had been wholly or largely achieved, with the Communist movements. These Communist movements had gained ground particularly in southeastern Asia and took to open violence in Indochina, Burma, the Philippines and Malaya. When North Korea attacked South Korea in June 1950, the Russians took the view that the attack had in fact been launched by the South Koreans at U.S. instigation.

After Stalin.—On March 6, 1953, the day after the official announcement of Joseph Stalin's death, a complete reorganization of the government and the Communist party key bodies was decreed. G. M. Malenkov assumed the post of chairman of the council of ministers, supported by four first deputy chairmen, L. P. Beria, V. M. Molotov, N. A. Bulganin and L. M. Kaganovich. The number of ministries had been reduced from 51 to 25, although many were redivided later: by April 26, 1954, there were 46 and by Feb. 7, 1955, again 51. (*See* Table X.) The leadership of the

Communist party was similarly concentrated (*see* below). Beria had risen to second place in the new leadership but not for long: on June 26, 1953, he was divested of all his functions, arrested and accused, *inter alia,* of acting as an agent for the western powers. He was tried *in camera* and was shot on Dec. 23, 1953.

An effect of Stalin's death was to produce a softening in the tone of the government's pronouncements on foreign policy. Nevertheless the three major objectives of the allegedly "new" Soviet foreign policy remained the consolidation of Soviet influence over the whole of eastern Europe, including eastern Germany, and over China and North Korea; and avoidance of a major armed conflict; the weakening of the non-Communist world by the encouragement of dissension between the western powers and the promotion of "anti-imperialist" movements in the colonial and dependent countries.

Malenkov resigned on Feb. 8, 1955, accusing himself of "inadequate experience" and admitting responsibility for the "unsatisfactory state of affairs in agriculture." He was succeeded as premier by Bulganin.

BIBLIOGRAPHY.—B. H. Sumner, *Survey of Russian History,* 2nd ed. rev. (London, 1948); Sir Bernard Pares, *A History of Russia,* 5th ed. rev. (1947); K. Stählin, *Geschichte Russlands von den Anfängen bis zur Gegenwart,* 4 vol. (Stuttgart, 1923–39); P. Miliukov, ed., *Histoire de Russie,* 3 vol. (Paris, 1932–33), and *Outlines of Russian Culture* (1948); A. Brückner, *Geschichte Russlands bis zum Ende des 18 Jahrhunderts,* 2 vol. (Gotha, 1896–1913), and other works; A. Rambaud and E. Haumant, *Histoire de la Russie . . . jusqu'à 1917* (Paris, 1918); R. Nisbet Bain, *Slavonic Europe: A Political History of Poland and Russia* (1908); A. Pypin, *Die geistigen Bewegungen in Russland in der ersten Hälfte des Jahrhunderts* (Berlin, 1894); F. H. B. Skrine, *Expansion of Russia, 1815–1900* (Cambridge, 1915); A. Kornilov, *Modern Russian History,* 2 vol. (London, 1916); S. Korff, *Russia's Foreign Relations during the Last Half Century* (1922); F. A. Golder (ed.), *Documents of Russian History, 1914–1917* (1927); Sir Bernard Pares, *The Fall of the Russian Monarchy* (1939); W. H. Chamberlin, *The Russian Revolution, 1917–1921,* 2 vol. (1935); E. H. Carr, *The Bolshevik Revolution* (London, 1951 ff.); D. Shub, *Lenin* (1948); J. V. Stalin, ed. anon., *Short History of the Communist Party of the Soviet Union* (Moscow, 1938; many translations) and *Leninism,* Eng. trans. (London, 1942); L. Trotsky, *The Revolution Betrayed* (1937) and *Stalin* (London, 1947); I. Deutscher, *Stalin* (Oxford, 1949); J. Towster, *Political Power in the U.S.S.R., 1917–1947* (Oxford, 1948); N. de Basily, *Russia under Soviet Rule* (London, 1938); Louis Fischer, *The Soviets in World Affairs,* 2 vol. (London, 1930); F. Borkenau, *The Communist International* (1938); M. Beloff, *The Foreign Policy of Soviet Russia, 1929–1941,* 2 vol. (London, 1947–49); Jane Degras (ed.), *Soviet Documents on Foreign Policy,* 3 vol. (London, 1951 ff.). For a fuller bibliography on the U.S.S.R. *see* Philip Grierson, *Books on Soviet Russia, 1917–1942* (1943), with regular supplements in the *Slavonic Review.* (M. Bf.; X.)

POPULATION

The population of the U.S.S.R. is shown in Table V. Although the third largest of any state in the world, it is small in comparison with the vast area over which it is spread. According to the census of 1939, two-thirds of the country was occupied by only 6% of the population, while 48% of the population was concentrated in 6% of the territory. This is partly explained by the existence of vast areas unsuitable for close settlement; the great belts of tundra and taiga in the north of Russia and the deserts of central Asia, for instance, can never be heavily populated.

TABLE V.—*Population of the U.S.S.R. according to the Census of Dec. 17, 1926, and Jan. 1939*

Republics	Rural population			Urban population			Total population			Area* 1939, up to Sept. (thousand sq.mi.)	Density of population per sq.mi.	
	1926	1939	Increase or decrease (%)	1926	1939	Increase (%)	1926	1939	Increase (%)		1926	1939
Russian S.F.S.R.	76,672,807	72,620,606	− 5.3	16,785,189	36,658,008	118.4	93,457,996	109,278,614	16.9	6,374.7	14.6	17.1
Ukrainian S.S.R.	23,669,381	19,764,601	−16.5	5,373,553	11,195,620	108.3	29,042,934	30,960,221	6.6	171.9	168.9	180.0
Byelorussian S.S.R.	4,135,410	4,195,454	1.5	847,830	1,372,522	61.9	4,983,240	5,567,976	11.7	48.9	101.8	113.7
Azerbaijanian S.S.R.	1,664,187	2,049,004	23.1	649,557	1,160,723	78.7	2,313,744	3,209,727	38.7	33.2	69.7	96.7
Georgian S.S.R.	2,083,012	2,475,729	18.9	594,221	1,066,560	79.5	2,677,233	3,542,289	32.3	26.9	99.6	131.8
Armenian S.S.R.	714,192	915,183	28.1	167,098	366,416	119.3	881,290	1,281,599	45.4	11.5	76.1	110.6
Turkmen S.S.R.	861,172	837,609	− 2.7	136,982	416,376	204.0	998,154	1,253,985	25.6	171.3	5.8	7.3
Uzbek S.S.R.	3,553,158	4,837,382	36.1	1,012,274	1,445,064	42.8	4,565,432	6,282,446	37.6	146.1	31.2	43.0
Tadzhik S.S.R.	926,213	1,233,209	33.1	106,003	251,882	137.6	1,032,216	1,485,091	43.9	55.5	18.6	26.7
Kazakh S.S.R.	5,554,905	4,439,787	−21.1	519,074	1,706,150	228.7	6,073,979	6,145,937	1.2	1,059.6	5.7	5.8
Kirghiz S.S.R.	879,364	1,188,714	35.2	122,333	270,587	121.2	1,001,697	1,459,301	45.7	75.9	13.2	19.2
Total for the U.S.S.R. . . .	120,713,801	114,557,278	− 5.1	26,314,114	55,909,908	112.5	147,027,915	170,467,186	15.9	8,175.5	17.98	20.85

*According to an official Soviet computation (1939).

It is partly explained also by the fact that the people were until recently almost wholly devoted to agriculture and, unlike the densely populated monsoon lands of southeast Asia, the Russian agricultural regions, where climatic conditions prevent all-the-year-round production, will not support a dense population. If allowance is made for these factors, however, it must still be noted that except for certain small areas in the black soil belt the Russian agricultural lands are far from having reached saturation point. The obstacles to more intensive settlement in the past were primitive methods of agriculture, uneconomic distribution of land, lack of transport facilities and backwardness in industrial development.

The reasons for Russian backwardness are primarily historical. Lack of natural frontiers encouraged invasion, and the Slav population was engaged in a long struggle with Asiatic invaders. In the 13th century the Tatar hordes overran the country and held it in subjection for nearly 300 years. This long isolation from western Europe was the most important of many factors which caused the people to fall far behind European standards. The history of Russia from this time up to the 20th century had been the history of sporadic endeavours to catch up with Europe in industrial and social development.

The Soviet government's planned resettlement, begun in 1925, led to a striking redistribution of population. But while this resettlement reduced in some small measure the concentration of population in European Russia and was accompanied by a great development of Russian industrial resources and transport facilities, the vast country remained sparsely populated and capable of supporting a far greater population.

Vital Statistics.—The first Russian census was taken in 1897 and recorded a population of 129,200,200. In 1929 the population was 146,980,460 despite the loss of densely populated areas in the west and despite the high death rate which resulted from World War I, the civil war, famine and epidemics. The census of 1939 recorded a population of 170,467,186. In the years 1939–40 Soviet annexations in Europe increased the population by 21,800,000. The official estimate of the population for 1946 was 193,000,000 (E. Davydov in *Bolshaya Sovietskaya Entsiklopedia: S.S.S.R.* [Moscow, 1948]). An estimate published in *Pravda* on Jan. 23, 1946, by G. F. Alexandrov, then propaganda chief of the All-Union Communist party, gave the same figure. This figure, if correct, implied that by 1946 Soviet losses in World War II had been made up by the natural increase in population. The only official estimate of numbers killed in fighting was 7,000,000 (A. A. Zhdanov in a speech on Nov. 6, 1946). Gen. Augustin Guillaume, chief of the French military mission to the Soviet Union during World War II, estimated the number of soldiers killed at 7,500,000, of severely wounded who died later at 3,000,000 and the number of civilians who were killed or died from hunger or exhaustion at 11,000,000.

The rate of increase of the population had been high for many years and was increasing. At the beginning of the 20th century the percentage of births over deaths in the Moscow region was 34. The percentage dropped during the civil war and the famine and epidemics that followed, but rose sharply thereafter. In 1938 there were 195 births to every 100 deaths. In the period 1926–39 the rate of growth of population increased by 15.9% in contrast with the average increase of 8.7% in the countries of western Europe during the same period. One of the results of this high birth rate's being coupled with a fairly high death rate is that the proportion of young people is large. In 1939 more than 45% of the population was under 19 years of age; in England the percentage was less than 30.

In the past the high death rate was the result of harsh living and working conditions, undernourishment, absence of medical services and ignorance of hygiene. The Soviet government effected considerable improvements, particularly through the provision of medical services and of instruction in hygiene; but the unsatisfactory living and working conditions still applying to the majority of the population contribute to making the death rate higher than is common in the countries of western Europe and of North America.

Under the Soviet regime the infant mortality rate was greatly reduced. It was calculated that in the 18th century up to 400 out of every 1,000 children born died before reaching the age of one year. The Soviet government achieved much in town and in country centres in its struggle against this high mortality rate. In Moscow the rate had been 23 per 1,000 in 1913 but was 13 per 1,000 in 1925; this figure declined mainly after 1922, having naturally been high during World War I and the revolution. The mortality rate of children in their first year of life for the whole country fell from 177 per 1,000 in 1924 to 135 per 1,000 in 1925. This was achieved despite poor housing conditions, mainly through the establishment of crèches, clinics and maternity hospitals, through campaigns of pictorial as well as written instructions in hygiene and through financial encouragement given to large families. It was claimed that from 1913 to 1934 the infant mortality rate had been reduced by 44% and that it was later reduced further, but exact figures were not available.

Ethnic Groups.—In ethnographic character the population of the U.S.S.R. is remarkably varied. The Soviet Academy of Sciences represented the country as being inhabited by 169 ethnic groups, divided into ten major divisions as follows: Indo-European 36 groups, Caucasians (Japhetic) 40, Semites 6, Finns 16, Samoyedes 1, Turks 48, Mongols 3, Tungus-Manchurian tribes 6, Palaeo-Asiatics 9 and groups of tribes from the far east with an ancient culture 4. (*See* Table VI.)

TABLE VI.—*U.S.S.R.: Population by Nationality, 1939, Compared with Population by Ethnic Group, 1926*

Designation in 1939	Number, 1926, in corresponding group	Number, 1939	Ratio of 1939 to 1926
Russian	77,791,124	99,019,929	1.273
Ukrainian	31,194,976	28,070,404	0.900
Byelorussian	4,738,923	5,267,431	1.112
Uzbek	3,954,701	4,844,021	1.225
Tatar	3,477,507	4,300,336	1.237
Kazakh	3,968,289	3,098,764	0.781
Jewish	2,672,499	3,020,141	1.130
Azerbaijanian	1,706,605	2,274,805	1.333
Georgian	1,821,184	2,248,566	1.235
Armenian	1,567,568	2,151,884	1.373
Mordvinian	1,340,415	1,451,429	1.083
German	1,246,540	1,423,534	1.142
Chuvash	1,117,419	1,367,930	1.224
Tadzhik	980,509	1,228,904	1.253
Kirghiz	762,736	884,306	1.159
Peoples of Daghestan	669,186	857,371	1.281
Bashkir	741,080	842,925	1.137
Turkmen	763,940	811,760	1.063
Polish	792,471	626,905	0.791
Udmurt (Votyak)	504,187	605,673	1.201
Marii	428,192	481,262	1.124
Komi (Zyryan, Permyak)	375,871	408,724	1.087
Chechen	318,522	407,690	1.280
Ossetian	272,272	354,547	1.302
Greek	259,740	285,896	1.101
Moldavian (Rumanian)	278,905	260,023	0.932
Karelian	248,120	252,559	1.018
Kara-Kalpak	146,317	185,775	1.270
Korean	172,000	180,417	1.049
Kabardian	139,925	164,106	1.173
Finnish	138,791	143,074	1.031
Estonian	155,903	142,465	0.913
Kalmuck	129,321	134,327	1.039
Latvian	154,239	126,900	0.823
Bulgarian	114,011	113,479	0.995
Ingush (Galga)	74,097	92,074	1.243
Adigei (Cherkess)	65,270	87,973	1.348
Karachay	55,123	75,737	1.374
Abkhazian	56,957	58,969	1.035
Khakass	45,608	52,602	1.153
Oirot (Altai)	39,062	47,717	1.222
Kurdish	54,661	45,866	0.839
Balkar	33,307	42,666	1.281
Iranian	43,971	39,037	0.888
Lithuanian	42,709	32,342	0.757
Chinese	92,030	29,620	0.322
Czech, Slovak	30,671	26,919	0.878
Arab	28,978	21,793	0.752
All other	1,221,423	1,775,545*	
Total	147,027,915	170,467,186	

*Including 948,059 not tabulated.
Source: F. Lorimer, *The Population of the Soviet Union* (1946).

According to the census of 1939, Russians form 58.4% of the population, Ukrainians 16.6%, Byelorussians 3.1%, Uzbeks 2.9%, Tatars 2.5%, Kazakhs 1.8%, Jews 1.8%, Azerbaijanis 1.34%, Georgians 1.33% and Armenians 1.27%. No other nationality numbers 1%. Thus three branches of the Slavs form 78.1% of the total population. To this figure should be added the Slav populations of the territories gained by the Soviet Union in 1939, 1940 and 1945. The Ukrainian areas increased the Ukrainian population by 5,640,000 while the Byelorussian territory brought an additional 1,458,000 Byelorussians into the Soviet Union, thus swelling the large proportion of Slavs.

The distribution of these races varies with the different regions of the country. The Slavs comprise about three-quarters of the population of the R.S.F.S.R. and are most dense in European Russia. In Asiatic Russia they have spread in a dense belt through the cultivable lands lying south of latitude 55° N. as far as the Yenisei river. East of the Yenisei Slavonic colonization has been mainly in ribbons along the rivers or concentrated in mining and industrial districts. In the 20th century Slavonic colonization of Asiatic Russia was intensified, and with the opening up of the mineral resources of this vast area the flow of Slavonic settlers was bound to increase.

After the Slavs the Turki peoples are the most numerous and important. The Turki race (Uzbeks, Turkmen, Kirghiz, Kazakhs etc.) is most continuous in the central Asiatic republics. The Mongol peoples are mainly to be found south and east of Lake Baikal; the Kalmuck (Kalmyk) region on the lower Volga represents a Mongol intrusion far to the west, separated from its original base by a wedge of Turki settlement. The Yakuts of the Lena represent a northeastern spread of the Turki element, now much intermingled with Slavonic blood.

The Finnish aboriginal population, Karelians, Mordvinians, Marii, Votyaks, Permyaks, Komi and the allied Samoyedes, were increasingly pushed outward by the Slavonic settlement. Finns are to be found mainly in the north and west and also in a belt of Finnish settlement in Asiatic Russia, lying north of the main Slavonic belt and extending to the Yenisei, again much intermingled with the incoming Slavonic population. East of the Yenisei the Finns form an insignificant element in the population. Scattered Cossack Ukrainian and trading settlements exist even in the tundra zone and in Kamchatka. These Slavonic settlers have tended to amalgamate to a marked degree with the natives in a region where the difficulties of the environment made unity of human effort essential. An interesting feature of Russian settlement is the greater density of population in high latitudes in comparison with other parts of the world.

Movements of Population.—The institution of serfdom restricted the tendency of the people to wander and to colonize, and after the abolition of serfdom in 1861 movements of the population greatly increased. The existence of large areas that were unsettled or sparsely populated encouraged colonization, but in the 19th and early 20th centuries political discontent was so great that large numbers of non-Russians emigrated abroad. In the period 1891–1900, for instance, 594,000 Russian subjects (mainly Poles and Jews) emigrated to the United States, and between 1900 and 1909 the number of these emigrants rose to 1,400,000. There was also during these years a considerable movement of people inside Russia from the more thickly populated regions of European Russia, in particular from the black earth belt and from the western and southwestern Ukraine, to the south and southeast and—beginning in the last quarter of the 19th century— to the Urals, Siberia and the far east. The government's policy of encouraging migration to the Urals, initiated at the end of the 19th century, resulted in the following increases: 300,000 in 1861–85, 450,000 in 1886–94, 1,440,000 in 1895–1905 and 3,274,000 in 1906–13. In the same period there was a greater flow of people to the towns: between 1863 and 1897 the increase of population in the towns was more than double the increase on the land.

The Soviet policy of planned resettlement, which was a part of the intensive policy of industrialization and of collectivization of agriculture, resulted in considerable movements of population. Between 1926 and 1939 more than 3,000,000 people were resettled in the Urals, Siberia and the far east. In certain areas the population increased by 33%. In the Sverdlovsk and Novosibirsk regions the increase was 53%, while in the Khabarovsk territory the population increased by 136%. World War II accelerated the movement eastward as industrial areas in the west were evacuated in the face of advancing German armies and whole factories were moved beyond the Urals.

Simultaneously with the settlement of the east there was a flow of people to the industrial regions. In the period 1926–39 about 3,500,000 moved to the Moscow region, 1,300,000 to the Leningrad region and 350,000 to the Gorki region. In the Stalino region the population increased by 91% and in the Voroshilovgrad region by 37%. The republics of central Asia received about 1,700,000 settlers, thus increasing their population by 38%.

The third migratory stream in the Soviet period flowed north. Though on a smaller scale, this settlement of the extreme north— where in the past the population had been negligible—was important. The Murmansk region up to 1917 had a population of about 10,000; in 1928 it was about 22,000 and in 1939 it was 291,200. This growth of the population in the north was accompanied by industrial development, planned as part of the first and second five-year plans.

Following World War II the continued policy of intensive industrialization in the Moscow region, the Ukraine, the Urals and the Kemerovo region undoubtedly led to further increases in the urban population and to further movements of population to industrial areas, particularly in the east. Figures were not, however, available after 1939.

Colonization of Siberia.—Furs were the prize which drew the Russians beyond the Urals and led to the conquest of Siberia. Siberian furs were in demand not only in Moscow but in Europe and provided Moscow with an important source of revenue. It was not until the 18th century that the fur trade ceased to be the dominating attraction of Siberia and the peasant settler and the miner became important. Peter the Great initiated the official policy of mining development and in particular the exploitation of the rich mineral deposits which in the 19th century gave rise to the Siberian gold rushes.

The conquest of Siberia began late in the 16th century. Kuchum, the last khan of the Siberian Tatars, challenged the Stroganov family, whose members, as the Russian lords of the Ural frontier, were encroaching on Tatar territory. The Stroganovs called on Yermak Timofeyevich, the Cossack leader, to meet this challenge. In 1581, with a small company, Yermak took Sibir, the Khan's chief settlement, from which the name of Siberia is derived. From this start the Russian advance continued rapidly, making full use of the vast web of rivers which covers Siberia. The first settlements were Tyumen (1585) on the Tura river and Tobolsk (1586) on the juncture of the Tobol and Irtysh rivers. From these two bases the Slavs advanced northward and eastward. Early in the 17th century they crossed the Yenisei river and founded Yeniseisk (1618) and Krasnoyarsk (1627). Within a few years they had reached the Lena river and by 1632 they had founded the fortified post of Yakutsk. The first Russian settlement on the Sea of Okhotsk was founded in 1639. This advance had been opposed by the Kazakhs and by the Kalmucks (Kalmyks) but had been halted only in the Amur basin, where it had come against the Chinese empire under the new Manchu Ch'ing dynasty. In 1689 the first treaty between China and Russia was signed.

The task of administering so vast an area was formidable, and for many years the government was able to provide only a rudimentary administration which left nearly all power in the hands of the corrupt local officials. The problem of populating Siberia was equally difficult. Throughout the 17th century colonists were sent beyond the Urals to settle. By the end of the century a policy of exile as a means of colonization had gained acceptance and, like the convicts transported to the British colonies in the 18th and 19th centuries, men were sent to Siberia for trifling offenses. Old Believers, after the great schism in the Russian Orthodox Church, the rebel palace guards under Peter the Great and, after the Northern War, Swedish prisoners of war were sent to Siberia. The Polish confederates under Catherine II, the Decembrists under Nicholas I, nearly 50,000 Poles after the insurrection of 1863 and whole generations of Socialists, including 45,000 political exiles after the 1905 revolution, were also exiled to Siberia. In the early days they were driven in herds from village to village and often left to die of starvation on the road. In the 19th century the conditions were slightly improved, but the hardships of the journey and of climatic and living conditions continued to cause many deaths. Between 1823 and 1898 no fewer than 700,000 exiles with 216,000 voluntary followers went to Siberia. In 1900 exile as a means of political persecution was abolished, but it was restored again in 1904 because of the increasing political unrest.

The Soviet government continued the policy of sending political and criminal prisoners to Siberia, but on a far greater scale than before. It was officially stated that "forced labour is one of the basic measures of punishment of Soviet Socialist criminal law" (*Bolshaya Sovietskaya Entsiklopedia*, vol. 47, p. 36 [Moscow, 1940]), and the Corrective Labour code of the R.S.F.S.R. of Aug. 1, 1933, provided that political opponents of the regime and "class-hostile elements" be punished by forced labour. In addition to the penal and political motives of Soviet policy there are also the economic motives. Molotov, as chairman of the council of people's commissars, stated in 1931 that forced labour was employed in "highway construction, in the building industry, in peat exploitation, in timber works, in mining, stone quarries, gravel and stone crushing, on transportation projects." These projects resulted in the organization of large forced labour camps in regions, such as the extreme north of Siberia and the Kazakh desert, where the climate is too severe for normal colonization and the work under primitive conditions is too arduous to attract voluntary labour. Evidence on the size of the population of forced labour camps in the Soviet Union is conflicting. The British undersecretary of state for foreign affairs gave on May 3, 1949, an estimate of this population on the basis of evidence in the hands of the British government as between 5,000,000 and 12,000,-000.

The notoriety of Siberia as a place of exile has tended to overshadow the role of free settlers in colonizing the vast area. The first settlers were hunters, seeking the furs of the sable, fox, ermine and squirrel. But runaway serfs and fugitives from religious persecution and from conscription, which in the reign of Peter the Great had become particularly severe, were soon the most numerous colonists. Many intermarried with the Yakuts and Buriats; their descendants were called Siberyaks. At the beginning of the 20th century these colonists were rapidly outnumbered by waves of voluntary settlers seeking their fortunes in Siberia. The completion of the Trans-Siberian railway (1891–1903) encouraged and facilitated further settlement. Between 1909 and 1913 more than 350,000 families were settled there, and of these few returned to European Russia. In 1913 the number of settlers was 234,877. During the revolution of 1917 and the civil war colonization virtually ceased, but it quickly revived. In 1925 a special commission of the Soviet government drew up a five-year plan for settling 1,200,000 colonists in Siberia; rebates from taxation and exemption from conscription were offered to encourage suitable settlers. Between 1926 and 1939 nearly 3,000,000 settlers went to Siberia, and after World War II the flow of settlers was no doubt revived, although no figures were available.

The rate of colonization of Siberia is illustrated by the growth of the towns. The population of Novosibirsk, for instance, was 5,000 in 1897 and had grown to 405,589 by 1939; Omsk increased from 37,470 to 280,716 (1939) and Vladivostok from 28,896 to 206,432 (1939). An even more striking illustration was the creation of new towns in the Kuzbas coal basin, some of which had populations of more than 100,000: Stalinsk (Kuznetsk) 169,538, Kemerovo 132,978 and Prokopyevsk 107,227. Karaganda and Magnitogorsk did not exist in 1926, but in 1939 had 165,937 and 145,870 inhabitants, respectively.

Towns and Settlements.—The census of 1926 showed that there were 30 towns with populations of more than 100,000. All these had grown considerably since the census of 1897, with the exception of Odessa, which had declined because of the diminished trade in the Black sea and the loss of Bessarabia to Rumania. Two cities had more than 1,000,000 inhabitants according to the census of 1926; these were Moscow (2,029,425) and Leningrad (1,690,065). Kiev, Baku, Odessa and Kharkov had more than 400,000 inhabitants, while Gorki (Nizhni-Novgorod), Tbilisi (Tiflis), Dniepropetrovsk, Saratov, Tashkent and Rostov-on-Don had more than 200,000 inhabitants.

The census of Jan. 17, 1939, showed that 11 cities had a popu-lation of more than 500,000. It was probable that there was considerable growth in the populations of these cities after 1939, but figures were not available. (See Table VII.)

The growth of the town population in Russia after the beginning of the 20th century was striking. Between 1897 and 1914 it increased from 15,825,600 to 24,686,600; *i.e.*, from 14.8% to 17.7% of the total population. From 1926 to 1939 it rose from 26,314,100 to 55,909,900; from 17.9% to 32.8% of the total. This leap in the rate of increase was a result of the Soviet government's policy of intensive industrialization.

The most rapid growth took place during the first two five-year plans (1928–32 and 1933–39). In this period the number of towns with 50,000 inhabitants or more increased almost four and one-half times. The number of towns with a population of 100,000 or more increased almost six times, while 10 new towns with a population of more than 100,000 and 20 with a population of more than 50,000 appeared.

The source of this new urban population between 1926 and 1939 was estimated as follows: from country to town, 18,500,000 (62.5%); natural growth of population, 5,300,000 (17.9%); villages converted into towns, 5,800,000 (19.6%).

In certain areas the growth of the town population was especially noteworthy. The Donets basin in 1926 contained a large number of small mining settlements and only eight towns, of which the largest were: Stalino (Yuzovka), 174,230; Makeyevka, 79,421; and Voroshilovgrad (Lugansk), 71,765. By 1939 the region had about 60 towns, of which 13 had more than 50,000 inhabitants and 5 more than 100,000, including Stalino with 462,-395, Makeyevka with 240,145 and Voroshilovgrad 213,007. Similarly, in the Urals the town population in 1926 was 1,251,000, concentrated in 27 towns of which only 3 had more than 50,000 and 2 had more than 100,000 inhabitants. By 1939 the town population had grown to 3,513,200, living in 47 towns of which 11 had more than 50,000 and 5 more than 100,000 inhabitants. The same rapid growth of the towns was to be found in the Kuznetsk basin; whereas in 1926 not one town there had more than 30,000 inhabitants, in 1939 there were five towns with more than 50,000, three of them having more than 100,000.

The pattern of the old Russian towns reflected something of the long struggle against invaders, particularly against Asiatic nomads. This pattern was concentric with radiating streets and at the centre a *kreml*, kremlin or fort, built originally of timber, but later of stone. Another feature of Russian towns was the low wooden house on the outskirts of the same type as the peasant *izba* or hut. The smaller towns were distinguished by a single broad main street which in spring and autumn was a sea of mud. A few of the cities in the west obtained the Magdeburg rights under Polish rule (notably Kiev in 1499), and traces of western influence still remain in some towns. The influence of Byzantium was, however, far stronger throughout European Russia, and evidence of it may be found in all the older towns. The modern Soviet towns were planned with a water supply, electricity and sanitation. In the centre, at least, of these towns roads are laid and the houses no longer follow the old Russian pattern but are of brick and are severely utilitarian in design. But in both new and old towns the overcrowding is serious and the living conditions of the people are often primitive.

Housing.—The housing shortage in the cities and towns is acute. During World War I many towns suffered damage, and in the disastrous period 1920–22 wooden houses were torn down for fuel. The climate limits the building season, and the shortage of building materials and of skilled labour as well as the greater priority given to industrial development all aggravated the housing shortage. The rapid increase in the urban population during the first two five-year plans added further complications to the already serious overcrowding. In 1939 it was estimated that in the cities the average dwelling space per person was approximately five square metres, a figure from one-third to one-fifth below the average in western Europe. Large-scale destruction of housing in European Russia during World War II added to the severity of the problem. It was officially estimated that in the areas afflicted 1,200,000 out of a total of nearly 2,600,000 dwelling units in the cities and 3,500,000 out of a total of 12,000,000 houses in the rural areas were destroyed. It was further estimated by N. A. Voznesensky that 60,000,000 sq.m. of dwelling space were required for rehabilitation in the urban areas.

Soviet policy after the first five-year plan gave absolute priority to industrial development almost to the exclusion of consumer goods, including housing. Not until the fourth, or first postwar, five-year plan was there provision for an extensive building program, calling for repairs and construction of urban dwellings to a figure of 10,350,000. The plan was reported to have been overfulfilled in urban areas, 100,000,000 sq.m. being constructed; but in rural areas only 2,700,000 houses were built, just one-fifth of the plan's figure. In 1951 there was a further advance in the provision of urban housing, although the construction of rural housing continued to be inadequate. Thus by 1951 reconstruction in urban areas had more than made up for wartime destruction; and in rural areas 90% of the destruction had been made good. The output of building materials, which had seriously slowed up the building program, was stepped up and was considerably higher than before World War II; in 1950 the output of cement was 80% greater than in 1940, of glass 90% greater, of slate 115% greater and of timber 36% greater. There remained however, the serious countereffect of obsolescence and the task of providing housing for a population rise of 5% in the period from 1940 to 1951.

GOVERNMENT AND ADMINISTRATION

The Party.—The constitution of 1936 described the All-Union Communist party as the leading core of all organizations of the working people, both public and state. Stalin referred to the

TABLE VII.—*Population of Major Cities in the U.S.S.R. by the Censuses of 1897, 1926 and 1939**

City	Population			Increase, 1926–39
	Jan. 28, 1897	Dec. 17, 1926	Jan. 17, 1939	
Moscow (Moskva)	988,614	2,029,425	4,137,018	103.9%
Leningrad (Petrograd, St. Petersburg)	1,267,023	1,690,065	3,191,304	88.8
Kiev	247,432	513,637	846,293	64.8
Kharkov	174,846	417,342	833,432	99.7
Baku	112,253	453,333	809,347	78.5
Gorki (Nizhni-Novgorod)	95,124	222,356	644,116	189.7
Odessa	405,041	420,862	604,223	43.6
Tashkent	156,414	323,613	585,005	80.8
Tbilisi (Tiflis)	160,045	294,044	519,175	76.6
Rostov-on-Don	119,889	308,103	510,253	65.6
Dnepropetrovsk (Ekaterinoslav)	121,216	236,717	500,662	111.5
Stalino (Yuzovka)		174,230	462,395	165.4
Stalingrad (Tsaritsyn)	55,967	151,490	445,476	194.1
Sverdlovsk (Ekaterinburg)	55,488	140,300	425,544	203.3
Novosibirsk (Novo-Nikolaevsk)		120,128	405,589	237.6
Kazan	131,508	179,023	401,665	124.4
Kuybyshev (Samara)	91,672	175,636	390,267	122.2
Saratov	137,109	219,547	375,860	71.2
Voronezh	84,146	121,612	326,836	168.7
Yaroslavl	70,610	114,277	298,065	160.8
Zaporozhe (Alexandrovsk)		55,744	289,188	418.8
Ivanovo (Ivanovo-Voznesensk)	53,949	111,460	285,069	155.8
Archangel (Arkhanghelsk)		76,774	281,091	266.1
Omsk	37,470	161,684	280,716	73.6
Chelyabinsk		59,307	273,127	360.5
Tula	111,048	155,005	272,403	75.7
Molotov (Perm)	45,403	119,776	255,196	113.1
Astrakhan	112,880	184,301	253,655	37.6
Ufa	49,961	98,537	245,863	149.5
Irkutsk	51,434	108,129	243,380	125.1
Makeyevka		79,421	243,380	
Minsk	91,494	131,803	240,145	202.4
Alma-Ata (Verny)		45,395	238,772	81.2
Mariupol	31,772	63,920	230,528	407.8
Kalinin (Tver)	53,477	108,413	222,427	248.0
Voroshilovgrad (Lugansk)		71,765	216,131	99.4
Vladivostok	28,896	107,980	213,007	196.8
Krasnodar (Ekaterinodar)	65,697	161,843	206,432	91.2
Erivan (Yerevan)	29,033	64,613	203,946	26.0
Khabarovsk		52,045	200,031	209.6
Krivoi Rog		38,228	199,364	283.1
Krasnoyarsk	26,600	72,261	197,621	417.0
Taganrog	51,965	86,444	189,009	162.9
Izhevsk		63,211	188,808	118.4
Chkalov (Orenburg)	72,740	123,283	175,740	178.0
Grozny		97,087	172,925	40.3
Stalinsk (Kuznetsk)		3,894	172,468	77.6
Vitebsk	65,871	98,857	169,538	4,253.8
Nikolayev	92,060	104,909	167,424	69.4
Karaganda	Nil	Nil	167,108	59.3
Nizhni-Tagil		38,820	165,937	
Penza	61,851	91,924	159,864	311.8
Smolensk	46,889	78,520	157,145	71.0
Shakhty		41,043	156,677	99.5
Barnaul	29,408	73,858	155,081	277.9
Dneprodzerzhinsk (Kamenskoye)	Nil	Nil	148,129	100.6
Magnitogorsk	33,846	86,409	147,829	332.9
Gomel			145,870	
Kirov (Vyatka)		62,097	144,160	66.8
Simferopol	48,821	87,213	143,181	130.6
Tomsk	52,430	92,274	142,678	63.6
Rybinsk	25,223	55,546	141,215	53.0
Samarkand	54,000	105,206	139,011	150.3
Kemerovo (Shcheglovsk)		21,726	134,346	27.7
Poltava	53,060	91,984	132,978	512.1
Ulan Ude (Verkhne-Udinsk)		28,918	130,305	41.7
Dzaudzhikau (Ordzhonikidze, Vladikavkaz)	43,843	78,346	129,417	347.5
Ashkhabad (Poltoratsk)		51,593	127,172	62.3
Tambov	48,134	72,256	126,580	145.3
Kostroma	41,268	73,732	121,285	67.9
Kursk	52,896	82,440	121,205	64.4
Murmansk		8,777	119,972	45.5
Sevastopol	50,710	74,551	117,054	1,233.6
Orel	69,858	75,968	111,946	50.2
Semipalatinsk	26,353	56,871	110,567	45.5
Gorlovka		23,125	109,779	93.0
Prokopyevsk		10,717	108,693	370.0
Kerch	28,982	35,690	107,227	900.5
Dzerzhinsk (Rastyapino)		8,910	104,471	192.7
Chita		61,526	103,415	1,060.7
Ulianovsk (Simbirsk)	43,298	70,130	102,555	66.7
Kirovograd (Elizavetgrad, Zinovievsk)	61,841	66,467	102,106	45.6
			100,331	50.9

*Figures for 1897 shown only for cities with more than 25,000 population in that year.
Source: S. S. Balzak, V. E. Vasyutin and Y. G. Feigin, *Economic Geography of the U.S.S.R.* (1949).

Communist party as the basic guiding force in the system of the dictatorship of the proletariat and stated that not a single important political or organizational question was decided without directions from the party. This indicated the importance of the Communist party in the U.S.S.R., where it acquired a monopoly of political power, all real and potential opposition having been exterminated since the revolution.

The party wields its powers through its central committee and through the Politburo (renamed presidium in 1952) and the secretariat. The central committee is elected at the party congress, which was formerly convened annually but after 1925 met at increasingly longer intervals. The committee meets on an average three times a year when it receives reports from the presidium on past and future work. The presidium exercises enormous power over every aspect of public policy, including foreign affairs.

The Communist party greatly increased in size, although its membership was limited. From 23,600 members in Nov. 1917 it had grown by the time of its 18th congress in March 1939 to 1,588,852 members and 888,814 candidates. The 19th congress assembled in Oct. 1952, after a 13-year delay. At that time the party had 6,013,259 members and 868,886 candidates. The name of the party was changed from the All-Union Communist party (of the bolsheviks) into the Communist Party of the Soviet Union (*Kommunisticheskaya Partia Sovietskogo Soyuza*, or K.P.S.S.). While the 1939 rules had described the party as "a section of the Third International, a shock detachment of the working class of the U.S.S.R.," the 1952 rules defined it as "a voluntary militant union of like-minded Communists consisting of people from the

TABLE VIII.—*Communist Party and Government of the U.S.S.R.**

Members of the key bodies of the central committee		Council of ministers‡
Presidium†	Secretariat	
N. A. Bulganin	N. S. Khrushchev	N. A. Bulganin, chairman
K. E. Voroshilov§	M. A. Suslov	V. M. Molotov, first deputy
L. M. Kaganovich	P. N. Pospelov	L. M. Kaganovich ″ ″
G. M. Malenkov	N. N. Shatalin	A. I. Mikoyan ″ ″
A. I. Mikoyan		M. G. Pervukhin ″ ″
V. M. Molotov		M. Z. Saburov ″ ″
M. G. Pervukhin		I. F. Tevosian, deputy premier
M. Z. Saburov		V. A. Malyshev ″ ″
N. S. Khrushchev		A. N. Kosygin ″ ″
P. K. Ponomarenko‖		G. M. Malenkov ″ ″
N. M. Shvernik‖		A. P. Zavenyaghin ″ ″
		V. A. Kukharenko ″ ″
		P. P. Lobanov ″ ″
		M. V. Khrunichev ″ ″

*As of Feb. 7, 1955.
†In Russian alphabetical order, a custom introduced in May 1954.
‡In addition there were 46 ministers, two chairmen of ministerial committees and the chairman of the board of the State Bank of the U.S.S.R.
§Also chairman of the presidium of the supreme soviet of the U.S.S.R., or nominal head of state.
‖Candidate member of the party presidium.

working class, the working peasants and working intelligentsia." The Politburo and the Orgburo were replaced by the presidium of 25 members and 11 candidates to be appointed by the central committee, composed of 125 members and 111 candidates. The secretariat, composed of 10 members, was also appointed by the central committee. This composition of the party key bodies did not last. The decree of March 6, 1953, reduced the membership of the presidium to 10 (9 from June 1953) and that of the secretariat to 5 (4 from April 1953) with Malenkov as secretary-general, but eight days later he had to resign from the secretariat and was succeeded by Nikita S. Khrushchev. (*See* Table VIII.)

The main "nursery" for the party rank and file is the All-Union Lenin League of Communist Youth (*Vsesoyuzny Leninsky Kommunistichesky Soyuz Molodezhi* or *Komsomol*) which by July 16, 1954, its 30th anniversary, had a membership of 18,825,327.

The Police.—The task of eliminating political opposition to the Communist party in the Soviet Union was originally in the hands of the All-Russian Extraordinary Commission for Repression of the Counterrevolution and Sabotage (V.Ch.K. or Cheka). On Feb. 6, 1922, the Cheka became the United General Political administration (O.G.P.U.). On July 10, 1934, the people's commissariat of internal affairs (N.K.V.D.) replaced the O.G.P.U.

The first chief of the Cheka and later of the O.G.P.U. was Felix E. Dzierzynski (Dzerzhinsky); in 1924 he was succeeded by Vyacheslav R. Menzhinsky, who died in 1934; the next chief of the N.K.V.D. was G. G. Yagoda, who was dismissed in Sept. 1936 and shot in March 1938; N. I. Yezhov was the chief of the N.K.V.D. until Dec. 1938 when he, too, was shot and L. P. Beria was appointed his successor.

On Jan. 31, 1941, the N.K.V.D. was itself divided, the N.K.V.D. to deal with internal affairs and the N.K.G.B. with state security. In March 1946 the commissariats became ministries and Beria supervised both the ministry of the interior (M.V.D., headed by Serghey N. Kruglov) and that of state security (M.G.B., headed by V. S. Abakumov). On March 6, 1953, the two ministries were reunited under Beria; in July, after Beria's arrest, Kruglov became minister of the interior. On April 26, 1954, it was revealed that the two component parts of the ministry were again separated, but this time a committee for state security was formed with Ivan A. Serov as chairman. In Dec. 1954 Abakumov was shot.

The Supreme Soviet.—The constitution of 1936 vested all legislative power in the supreme soviet of the U.S.S.R., but this power was so widely delegated that it can only be regarded as nominal. All citizens over the age of 18 years who are not insane

TABLE IX.—*Elections to the Supreme Soviet of the U.S.S.R.*

Item	1950	1954
Number of registered electors	111,116,373	120,750,816
Electors who went to the polls	111,090,010	120,727,826
Percentage of the total electorate	99.98%	99.98%
Electors who voted against the official candidates	300,146	247,897
Percentage of electors who voted	0.27%	0.21%
Number of deputies		
Council of the union	678	699
Council of nationalities	638	631

and have not been deprived of their civil rights by a responsible tribunal are entitled to vote in the elections of deputies, which take place every four years. Every citizen over the age of 23 years is eligible for election as a deputy.

The supreme soviet consists of two chambers: the council of the union and the council of nationalities. The election of deputies to the council of the union is by electoral districts on the basis of one deputy for every 300,000 citizens. The election of the council of nationalities is by republics, autonomous regions and national districts on the basis of 25 deputies from each union republic, 11 deputies from each autonomous republic, 5 deputies from each autonomous region and 1 deputy from each national district. The two chambers have equal rights and all acts must be passed by a majority in both chambers—except amendments to the constitution, which require a two-thirds majority in each chamber. The supreme soviet is convened twice yearly by the presidium of the supreme soviet. (*See* Table IX.)

The Presidium.—At a joint session of the two chambers the supreme soviet elects the presidium, which consists of a chairman, 16 vice-chairmen, a secretary and 15 members. The functions of the presidium, as defined by article 49 of the constitution, are that it

(1) convenes the sessions of the supreme soviet of the U.S.S.R.; (2) issues decrees; (3) gives interpretations of the laws of the U.S.S.R. in operation; (4) dissolves the supreme soviet of the U.S.S.R. in conformity with article 47 of the constitution of the U.S.S.R. and orders new elections; (5) conducts nation-wide referendums on its own initiative or on the demand of one of the union republics; (6) annuls decisions and orders of the soviet of ministers of the U.S.S.R. and of the soviets of ministers of the union republics if they do not conform to law; (7) in the intervals between sessions of the supreme soviet of the U.S.S.R. releases and appoints ministers of the U.S.S.R. on the recommendation of the chairman of the soviet of ministers of the U.S.S.R., subject to subsequent confirmation by the supreme soviet of the U.S.S.R.; (8) institutes orders and medals and titles of honour of the U.S.S.R.; (9) awards orders and medals and confers titles of honour of the U.S.S.R.; (10) exercises the right of pardon; (11) institutes military titles, diplomatic ranks and other special titles; (12) appoints and removes the high command of the armed forces of the U.S.S.R.; (13) in the intervals between sessions of the supreme soviet of the U.S.S.R. proclaims a state of war in the event of military attack on the U.S.S.R. or when necessary to fulfil international treaty obligations concerning mutual defense against aggression; (14) orders general or partial mobilization; (15) ratifies and denounces international treaties of the U.S.S.R.; (16) appoints and recalls plenipotentiary representatives of the U.S.S.R. to foreign states; (17) receives the letters of credence and recall of diplomatic representatives accredited to it by foreign states; (18) proclaims martial law in separate localities or throughout the U.S.S.R. in the interests of the defense of the U.S.S.R. or of the maintenance of public order and the security of the state.

The Soviet of Ministers.—At its first session after election the supreme soviet of the U.S.S.R. appoints the soviet of ministers (*Sovmin*), which consists of a chairman, a number of vice-chairmen, the ministers of the U.S.S.R. and the chairmen of a few state committees. Members appointed to the soviet need not necessarily be deputies of the supreme soviet.

The soviet of ministers is the highest executive and administrative organ in the Soviet Union and is answerable only to the supreme soviet or, when it is not in session, to its presidium. The ministries of the Soviet Union are of two types: all-union ministries and the union-republican ministries. The all-union ministries are common to all federal republics. The union-republican ministries function in Moscow and in the capitals of the federal republics. Both types are almost annually merged, divided or suppressed by decrees of the presidium of the supreme soviet, the supreme soviet approving the changes and promulgating the necessary amendments to the constitution. By Feb. 1955 there were 25 all-union ministries, 26 union-republican ministries and 3 state committees. (*See* Table X.) With few exceptions the heads of both types of ministry were Russians. In Moscow, capital of the U.S.S.R. and of the R.S.F.S.R., many union-republican ministries existed in duplicate, one Soviet and one Russian. There were, however, no Russian ministries of state security, internal affairs, war or foreign affairs.

Article 68 of the constitution defines the functions of the soviet of ministers as being that it

(1) co-ordinates and directs the work of the all-union and union-republican ministries of the U.S.S.R. and of other institutions under its

TABLE X.—*The Council of Ministers of the U.S.S.R.*

TABLE X.—*The Council of Ministers of the U.S.S.R.*

All-union (*Obshchesoyuznyie*) ministries:	Union-republican (*Soyuzno-Respublikanskyie*) ministries:
Aircraft industry	Motor transport and highways
Motor, tractor and agricultural machinery	Internal affairs
Paper and woodworking industry	Higher education
Foreign trade	Town and country building
Geology and conservation of mineral wealth	State control
Agricultural stocks	Health
Machine- and instrument-making industry	Foreign affairs
Merchant navy	Culture
Defense industry	Timber industry
Railways	Oil industry
Radio equipment industry	Defense
Inland water transport	Meat and dairy industry
Medium engineering industry	Food industry
Machine-tool and toolmaking industry	Building materials industry
Building and road-building machinery	Manufactured consumer goods
Construction of metallurgical and chemical industry works	Fishing industry
Construction of oil industry enterprises	Communications
Construction of power stations	Agriculture
Shipbuilding industry	State farms
Transport machinery industry	Construction
Transport building	Trade
Heavy engineering industry	Coal industry
Chemical industry	Finance
Power stations	Nonferrous metallurgical industry
Electrical equipment industry	Iron and steel industry
	Justice
State committees of the council of ministers:	
State planning, Construction and State security	

Source: Law of Feb. 7, 1955, revising articles 77, 78 and 83 of the constitution of the U.S.S.R.

jurisdiction; (2) adopts measures to carry out the national economic plan and the state budget and to strengthen the credit and monetary system; (3) adopts measures for the maintenance of public order, for the protection of the interests of the state and for the safeguarding of the rights of citizens; (4) exercises general guidance in the sphere of relations with foreign states; (5) fixes the annual contingent of citizens to be called up for military service and directs the general organization of the armed forces of the country; (6) sets up, whenever necessary, special committees and central administrations under the soviet of ministers of the U.S.S.R. for economic and cultural affairs and defense.

The federal republics have parallel organs of government and administration. Each republic has a supreme soviet which appoints a presidium and a soviet of ministers. The constitution reserves to each republic the right to secede from the Soviet Union (article 17), but it is doubtful that this right could be exercised. The federal republics, autonomous republics and autonomous regions prepare their own budgets, which are incorporated in the single state budget for the whole Soviet Union. But the soviet of ministers of the U.S.S.R. determines taxes and revenues for the whole union; it can also, if necessary, overrule the decisions of a republican soviet of ministers.   (I. Gy.; X.)

The Judicial System.—An early result of the revolution was the decree of Dec. 7, 1917, abolishing all existing general legal institutions and sweeping away the imperial legal system. Two new types of courts were created in their place, the ordinary courts and the revolutionary tribunals. The ordinary courts had jurisdiction in civil and criminal cases. The revolutionary tribunals had special jurisdiction in matters of counterrevolution, sabotage, abuses of officials, etc. This system proved unsatisfactory and was replaced in 1922 by a new hierarchy of courts headed by a supreme court in each republic and with the supreme court of the U.S.S.R. at the apex. Article 104 of the constitution charged the supreme court of the U.S.S.R. "with the supervision of the judicial activities of all the judicial organs of the U.S.S.R. and of the union republics."

The ordinary courts in the new hierarchy fall into four groups: (1) the people's courts; (2) the regional, provincial, territorial courts, the courts of the autonomous regions and the supreme courts of the autonomous republics; (3) the supreme courts of the union republics; (4) the supreme court of the U.S.S.R. The judges in all courts are either permanent judges or people's assessors. Judges of the people's courts are elected by all the citizens within the jurisdiction of that court. The respective soviets of the autonomous republics or other areas appoint the judges to the courts of the second group. The supreme soviets of the union republics and of the Soviet Union appoint the judges to the courts in groups 3 and 4.

Article 112 of the constitution states that "judges are independent and subject only to the law," but this does not mean that they are independent of government policy; in practice they must follow and seek to enforce that policy whether explicit in published laws or not. Judges may be relieved of their duties if recalled by their electors. An appeal lies from all courts, except from the supreme courts of the U.S.S.R. and of the union republics, to the court next above.

A judicial office of great power is that of the procurator-general, which was established in June 1933. Article 113 of the constitution states that "supreme supervisory power to ensure strict observance of the law by all ministries and institutions subordinated to them, as well as by officials and citizens of the U.S.S.R. generally, is vested in the procurator-general of the U.S.S.R." It is noteworthy that the procurator-general, who is appointed for a term of seven years by the supreme soviet of the U.S.S.R., and the procurators, appointed by him for a five-year period throughout the republics and regions of the Soviet Union, are independent of the supreme court and of other courts.

Certain special courts exist in addition to the ordinary courts referred to above. These include the military tribunals, which have jurisdiction over criminal matters in the Soviet armed forces, and the water-transport courts and railway-transport courts, which deal with crimes involving obstruction of the efficiency of the service or of labour discipline. There are also comrade's courts set up primarily in large industrial undertakings at which fellow workers sit as judges in cases of petty crimes.

EDUCATION AND RELIGION

In tsarist Russia schools were few in number and education was possible for only a small proportion of the population. Illiteracy was widespread: in 1897 about 76% of the people could neither read nor write. Successive governments had paid scant attention to the improvement of education, to the building of schools and universities and to the training of teachers. Their policy was one of inactivity, and they seem to have been content that the mass of their people should remain backward and ignorant. In 1895 there were in Russia only 9 universities with 13,976 students and 29,241 primary schools with 1,937,076 pupils.

During the period of 1895–1904 some development of educational facilities, mainly in the field of technical training, took place. These were years of industrial expansion, and the new industries created a need for technicians who could handle machinery. The plentiful unskilled peasant labour which had served Russian needs in the past was no longer adequate. In this period the numbers of medium and primary technical institutes increased from 51 to 93, of handicraft schools from 91 to 237, of communal schools from 6 to 139. But these and other developments directly concerned the technical needs of the new industries and did not greatly affect the general problem of illiteracy in Russia. The Soviet government found itself confronted with this problem and achieved in many respects remarkable success toward solving it.

By 1953 there were in the U.S.S.R. 220,000 primary and secondary schools with a total of 37,900,000 pupils and 1,250,000 teachers. In 1939, within the frontiers of 1921, there had been 31,517,000 pupils. In 1914, within the same frontiers, there had been 7,260,000 pupils in 93,311 elementary and 764,600 in 459 secondary schools. The totals for 1953 include about 3,700 secondary technical schools with 1,094,000 pupils. In 1914 there had been only 295 schools of this type with a total of 35,800 pupils.

There were, by 1953, 31 universities and 856 other institutions of higher education (V.U.Z.), including 375 teachers' colleges, with 1,356,000 students, including 467,000 taking correspondence courses. In 1938 there had been 23 universities and 727 V.U.Z. with 602,900 students. In 1914 there had been 10 universities and 81 institutions of higher education with a total of 112,000 students. A further illustration of the Soviet government's achievement is to be found in the figures for illiteracy: the percentage of illiterates had been reduced to 48.9% by 1926 and to 18.8% by 1939. This latter figure was further reduced after 1939, universal education at least to the extent of the elementary four-year school being achieved in most of the republics of the Soviet Union.

Early Soviet Measures.—The Bolshevik revolution of 1917

was followed by the destruction of all tsarist institutions and systems. The old ministry of education was replaced by two new bodies, the people's commissariat for education and the state commission for education, the latter being headed by Anatoly V. Lunacharsky. Within a week of the revolution Lunacharsky published an "exhortation to the citizens of Russia on national education" in which the tasks in the field of education were summarized as follows: abolition of illiteracy as quickly as possible; introduction of universal, compulsory and free education; establishment of institutes and seminaries for the training of "people's teachers." A fourth point might have been added concerning the association of the church with education. Militant atheism was proclaimed by the Communist leaders as part of their policy. It was therefore to be expected that the church schools would be taken over by the government and that all forms of religious instruction in schools would be forbidden. In Dec. 1917 the people's commissariat for education issued an ordinance bringing under its authority all church schools, seminaries and academies. This step was followed on Jan. 21, 1918, by a decree of the council of people's commissars disestablishing the church and introducing secular education. Another important innovation of this period was the introduction of coeducation by decree dated May 31, 1918.

A decree issued on Oct. 16, 1918, codified the educational measures introduced after the revolution. The declaration of the state commission for education attached to this decree gave the name "united labour school" to all schools under the people's commissariat for education. The new school was divided into two grades: grade I for children 8 to 13 years of age, and grade II for children 13 to 17 years of age. Education in both grades was free and compulsory, although in practice the great shortage of schools and of qualified teachers made it impossible for more than a small proportion of children to attend. Further innovations were the abolition of the old forms of discipline and punishment, of homework and of examinations. Schools were to be run by school soviets in which senior pupils took part. Teachers, whose hands were tied by these soviets, were in future to be known as school workers and were to concentrate on breaking away from the old tsarist methods and on practising Communist methods of teaching.

The "liquidation of illiteracy" was recognized by the new regime as one of its basic tasks, and on Dec. 26, 1919, the council of people's commissars passed a decree directing that "the entire population of the republic between the ages of 8 and 50, unable to read or write, be obliged to become literate in either their native or the Russian language, according to their preference." But the implementation of this decree proved most difficult, particularly in a country rent by civil war. The anxiety of the government over the slow progress made in reducing illiteracy was shown in the series of decrees and exhortations that was issued. Finally on Jan. 26, 1930, the central executive committee of the party and the council of people's commissars issued a joint ordinance setting up special local committees for the liquidation of illiteracy to be attached to each regional and district executive committee.

University education also received close attention in the postrevolutionary period. On Aug. 2, 1918, a decree of the council of people's commissars opened all higher educational establishments, as they were called, to all citizens, without respect to nationality or sex, simply on condition that they should be over the age of 16 years. In Sept. 1919 universities were directed to provide special courses, known as "worker's facilities," to prepare workers and peasants for higher education.

The Educational Reform.—It was soon found that most of these innovations were unsatisfactory. Teachers were unable to enforce discipline, and conditions in schools were chaotic. Nor were the new teaching methods found to equip the young Russian or non-Russian citizen to assist in the reform and development of the country along the lines laid down by the party. The new methods tended to produce undisciplined and untrained youths of little use in industry or otherwise.

An order of the central committee of the party issued on Sept. 5, 1931, contained the first suggestion of change. The order pointed to "certain serious defects" in soviet education and specified changes to be made in the syllabus for schools. The central committee issued a further and more important order on Aug. 25, 1932, which called for a recasting of the programs of schools and for a revision of the syllabuses. A routine was laid down to be followed in all schools. The brigade system of teaching was abandoned and teachers were directed to give individual instruction. Examinations and discipline were revived although not so strictly as was to be required by subsequent decrees. This order together with the subsequent order of May 16, 1934, abolished the innovations of the postrevolutionary period and established a system of education incorporating many of the principles and practices in force in Europe.

The order of May 16, 1934, replaced the united labour school with the general educational school, divided into three stages. The elementary school contains four classes and is known as the four-year school. Until the publication of the ordinance of the council of people's commissars on Sept. 8, 1943, compulsory education began in the four-year school at the age of eight years, but the ordinance reduced it to seven. The second stage is the seven-year school or the incomplete secondary school, containing seven classes. The third stage is the secondary school proper, known as the ten-year school and containing ten classes. The government in its attempts to achieve universal compulsory education was faced with many difficulties, particularly the shortage of teachers and of school accommodation. It was nevertheless claimed by Stalin at the 16th party congress in 1930 that universal compulsory education had been introduced throughout the U.S.S.R. It would seem, however, that only four-year education, the equivalent of European elementary education, had been introduced. The 18th party congress, held in 1939, proclaimed that the aim must be to achieve universal ten-year or complete secondary education in towns and workers' settlements and universal seven-year education in the country. World War II prevented the realization of this aim and it was made one of the tasks of the fourth five-year plan (1946–50). The Soviet government released little factual information after World War II on the success or failure of these plans, but an announcement on Aug. 17, 1949, stated that the school year 1949–50 would see in the R.S.F.S.R. "seven-year education on a very wide scale." This suggested that even in the towns of the most highly developed of the republics the ten-year school was not common, while in the less well-developed areas even the seven-year school was far from universal.

Introduction of Fees.—An important amendment to the strongly proclaimed Communist principle of free education as a right of all citizens was the introduction of fees in the senior classes of secondary schools and in higher educational establishments of the U.S.S.R. as laid down in the ordinance of Oct. 2, 1940, of the council of people's commissars. The fees are payable in the three senior classes of the complete secondary school and in higher educational establishments at rates specified by the ordinance. Free education and stipends are allowed in these grades only to students of outstanding ability. Three subsequent ordinances exempted from payment of fees students in military faculties and in national theatrical and musical studios and national groups of ballet schools in Moscow and Leningrad. Exemption was also extended to the children of noncommissioned members of the army and navy and in certain circumstances to the children of persons drawing invalid pensions. The reasons for this change in the government's policy were not clear. It has been suggested that it was due to anxiety to divert the younger generation from higher education to factory work and to military training and to meet the urgent need for medium-grade experts. It is probable that this was one of the purposes behind the introduction of fees, which must certainly have restricted the number of students able to enter higher educational establishments.

Mention should also be made of the abolition of coeducation which had been regarded in the early postrevolutionary period as an important innovation. This change was effected by the ordinance of the council of people's commissars issued on July 16, 1943, which called for separation of the sexes in secondary schools as rapidly as facilities would permit.

Higher Education.—The educational system includes the specialized secondary educational establishments and the higher educational establishments. The former serve to train technicians and specialists of the middle grade, which includes elementary school teachers. Pupils who have completed the seven-year school are eligible for these establishments, at which they receive stipends, free training and subsistence allowances.

The higher educational establishments comprise the universities and certain institutes which train top-grade specialists. These institutions are charged with the task of training intellectuals and in particular technicians whom the party can entrust with the carrying out of its policies and above all its policy of intensive industrialization. The two most important pronouncements affecting higher education were the resolution of the party central committee of July 17, 1928, on improving the training of new specialists and the joint ordinance of June 23, 1936, issued by the party central committee and the council of people's commissars on the work of the higher educational establishment. The former devoted considerable attention to the development of new cadres and specified that by 1932 the number of engineering and technical specialists in heavy industry should be doubled. The ordinance of 1936 in many respects produced a reorganization of higher education. Students to be eligible for higher educational establishments had to complete the full ten-year school and also to pass a special entrance examination. The ordinance then laid down the conditions applying to professorial staff, the examining of students and the granting of grade I and II diplomas.

A further change was made by a joint ordinance of Dec. 1935 abolishing the ban against the admission of people of undesirable social origin and of the children of parents with "limited social rights" to higher educational establishments. This reform was part of the general abolition of proletarian class privileges which came with the introduction of the new Stalin constitution of 1936.

The Content of Education.—All education in the Soviet Union is permeated by the ideology and directed by the needs of the Communist party. The following quotation from the editorial of *Pravda* of Sept. 1, 1949, illustrates the nature of this influence:

To bring up active fighters for the cause of Communism, all-round educated people, possessing thorough and firmly-based knowledge, such is the main task of our schools, such is the law of their life. All must be subordinated to this task; the process of education, extra-school occupations, propaganda among parents, the work of the Young Communist and Pioneer organizations in the schools.

Equally plain is the following injunction published in the *Literaturnaya Gazeta* of Sept. 3, 1949:

The country entrusts the school with its most treasured possession, its children, and no one should be allowed to indulge in the slightest deviation from the principles of the Communist materialistic upbringing of the new generation.

The party ideology informs all activities in the general secondary schools, and indeed the daily lives of Russian children and adults, but instruction in Marxism-Leninism and in dialectical and historical materialism is included in the curriculums only of the higher educational establishments, where a considerable amount of attention is devoted to them.

Religion.—Under the tsars the Orthodox Church was the established church to which the vast majority of the people belonged. Other religions were permitted but did not enjoy the same freedom as the established church, and adherents of certain religions, as, for example, the Uniate rite of the Roman Catholic Church, Islam and Judaism, were at times actively persecuted. At no time, however, had religion in Russia been subjected to such organized persecution as under the Soviet regime. The reason for this is that the Communist party is based on an ideology materialistic in character and militantly atheistic in action.

The first campaign of persecution lasted from 1917 to 1923. The Orthodox Church was disestablished; church property was seized and confiscated; divine service was allowed only under certain highly restrictive conditions; religious instruction was prohibited in schools and for groups of children under the age of 18 years. In an attempt to weaken the Orthodox Church the government sought to create a schism by supporting a new religious organization, the so-called "Living Church," but this collapsed through lack of popular support. In May 1922 the patriarch was imprisoned, with a large number of bishops and priests; his release in June 1923, the result of popular protests, marked the end of the first campaign. The second period of persecution lasted from 1923 to 1930. It differed from the first period in that direct attacks on the clergy more or less ceased, and the party concentrated on antireligious propaganda. A special publishing house called Bezbozhnik ("The Godless") had been set up in Feb. 1922 to print and disseminate antireligious material. An antireligious seminary was opened, and the celebration of Christmas and Easter in 1923 was marked by mock processions and services designed to hold religion up to ridicule. The foundation of the League of Militant Atheists on Feb. 7, 1925, which became the centre of violent antireligious propaganda, was the most important step in the government's campaign. In the third period the persecution took the form of a renewal of attacks on churches and on the clergy. Hundreds of priests were arrested and many were sent to the dreaded Solovetsky concentration camp in the White sea. But despite the innumerable restrictions, the imprisonment of the clergy and the wide use of antireligious propaganda, the church retained its large following, and it was apparent that the campaign for atheism had failed. The persecution seems to have been most intense in the years 1937–38, when the church leaders were denounced officially as "the implacable enemies of social reconstruction" and arrested in large numbers.

Signs of a new policy toward religion were noticeable in 1939 and developed into what has been called the government's New Religious Policy. This new policy was confirmed on Sept. 5, 1943, when Stalin received the acting patriarch Serghey and subsequently on Sept. 12, 1943, when Serghey was officially installed as patriarch of Moscow and all-Russia. From this date numerous concessions were made to the church, although its activities continued to be severely circumscribed. In 1946 Karpov, the head of the council of the Russian Orthodox Church, which had been established by the Soviet government as the liaison body between church and state, announced that the Orthodox Church had a patriarch, 3 archbishops and 67 bishops, while 22,000 churches and 89 monasteries and convents were functioning normally.

It was clear that the Soviet government's policy since 1939 had been more lenient toward the Church; at the same time it was to be noted that the party had not in any respect departed from its basic teaching that religion and communism must always be incompatible. The profession of atheism continues to be a condition of membership of the party. Religious instruction continues to be prohibited in schools, although antireligious propaganda informs much of the teaching—a situation in accordance with article 124 of the constitution; namely, "In order to ensure to citizens freedom of conscience, the church in the U.S.S.R. is separated from the state, and the school from the church. Freedom of religious worship and freedom of antireligious propaganda is recognized for all citizens."

It is noteworthy that the party continues to pay particular attention to the promotion of atheism in the Young Communist league. The party's policy is summed up in the injunction published in June 1947 in the *Komsomolskaya Pravda*, the official organ of the league: "Young Communists must be not only convinced atheists and opposed to all superstitions, but must actively combat the spread of superstitions and prejudices amongst youth."

(I. Gy.)

DEFENSE

The prerevolutionary Russian army was strong in manpower but otherwise reflected all the weaknesses of the political, social and economic order of the imperial regime. Although traditionally the Russian soldier is a hard fighter, with exceptional powers of endurance, the quality of the recruits was lowered by the fact that four in five were illiterate. Despite some progress in industrialization at the end of the 19th and at the beginning of the 20th century, the country was still backward; in 1913 it produced only 30 kg. of pig iron per head as compared with 254 kg. in Germany; the army had only 60 batteries of artillery against German's 380; the extent of the railway system in European Russia alone was

1 mi. of railway to 60 sq.mi. of territory, or one-tenth the German figure. Though there was no lack of talented generals and patriotic officers, both alike were helpless under a system undermined by corruption and nepotism. Participation in World War I against Germany and Austria-Hungary led to appalling losses and ultimately to the complete collapse of the old army. Imperial Russia had a peacetime army of 1,100,000 and 42,000 officers; from 1914 to 1917 it mobilized 12,000,000 men, of whom 1,700,000 were killed, 4,950,000 wounded and 2,500,000 taken prisoners of war.

The revolution of March 1917 in the midst of a war for survival resulted in a rapid dissolution of all fundamental institutions and notions. The minister of war in the provisional government, Alexander Guchkov, strove to stop the decline of discipline in the army but in May resigned in despair. He was succeeded by Kerensky, an eloquent speaker who assumed that by personal magnetism he would be able to counteract the progress of defeatist Communist propaganda (see *History*, above). The Communists alone were unequivocally against the continuance of the war, and this attitude greatly contributed to the success of their revolution of Nov. 1917, which ended a short-lived attempt to create a Russian democracy. The conclusion of the oppressive treaty of Brest-Litovsk with the Central Powers, on which Lenin insisted, was necessary because the appeals of the more impatient Communists and left-wing Socialists for "revolutionary war" fell on deaf ears.

Formation of the Red Army.—On Jan. 15, 1918, the council of people's commissars issued a decree creating a Workers' and Peasants' Red army on a voluntary basis. The first units distinguished themselves against the Germans at Narva and Pskov on Feb. 23, 1918, which date became the Soviet Army day. By April 22, 1918, the Soviet government felt strong enough to decree compulsory military training for workers and peasants who did not employ hired labour. This was the beginning of the Red army. Trotsky, from March 1918 people's commissar for war, was its founder and Mikhail Frunze, Mikhail Tukhachevsky and S. M. Budenny were among the most successful of its commanders in the field. It was an army based on the class principle; people who belonged to the *bourgeoisie* were ineligible for combatant service.

The problem confronting every revolutionary army, that of creating a competent and reliable officers' corps, was solved by Trotsky by mobilizing former officers of the imperial army, allowing them tolerable material conditions and warning them that their families would be held as hostages in the event of treason or desertion. Altogether about 50,000 such officers served in the Red army up to 1921 and the overwhelming majority remained loyal to the Soviet regime. To ensure the officers' reliability a political adviser, *politichesky rukovoditel* or *politruk*, was attached to every unit. These officials, who were Communists, not only kept the officers under observation but also carried out political propaganda in the ranks to stimulate morale. As the war went on, a more reliable type of young officer began to emerge from the short-term officers' training schools that were set up.

After the Riga peace treaty with Poland the Red army was demobilized and reduced to a more efficient and manageable force. At the end of 1920 it had 5,300,000 effectives; the number was reduced to 1,800,000 by Sept. 1921 and to 825,000 a year later. In 1925 the permanent strength of the Soviet armed forces was 562,000, and for nine years it remained at this level. Trotsky, losing his contest for power with Stalin, had to resign as people's commissar for war in Nov. 1924 and was succeeded by Frunze. On the latter's death Oct. 31, 1925, K. E. Voroshilov, trusted friend of Stalin, became commissar for war, remaining in this post until May 8, 1940.

Between 1925 and 1933 the percentage of All-Union Communist party members among the ranks increased from 19% to 49%; the percentage of party members among the officers was much higher. By this time only a few officers from the imperial army remained on active service. All the commanders were graduates from Soviet military academies and officers' training schools, where only candidates recommended by the Komsomol or Communist Youth league, by the Communist party and by the security services could be accepted as pupils.

The fight against all who were critical of Stalin's leadership extended also to the army, where a drastic purge took place in May 1937. On June 12 Marshal Tukhachevsky, first deputy people's commissar of war, and seven other prominent generals of the Red army were shot, having been accused of spying to betray the Soviet Union to the Japanese and Germans. Gen. Ian Gamarnik, second deputy people's commissar in charge of political education, was said to have committed suicide. Many other generals were either sent to forced labour camps or cashiered.

Gen. B. M. Shaposhnikov, a graduate of the Imperial academy of the general staff, who had served in the Red army from May 1918 and been chief of the general staff in 1929–31, was again appointed to that position in 1937. The Japanese intervention in China and the German rearmament compelled the Soviet Union to increase its peacetime armed forces; it had 940,000 men in 1934, about 1,300,000 in 1936 and about 1,600,000 under arms at the beginning of 1939. The country was then divided into 13 military areas and the army was composed of 87 infantry divisions and 32 cavalry brigades.

The Red Army in World War II.—When the German armies attacked the Soviet Union on June 22, 1941, their early successes caused general surprise. By October they had covered three-quarters of the distance separating Moscow from the German frontier and had taken more than 2,050,000 prisoners of war and a vast haul of war material. A hard winter, as well as Russian heroism, halted them at the gates of Moscow. Nevertheless, in 1942 they were able to push as far as Stalingrad. The epic resistance of Stalingrad should not hide the fact that when the Soviet armies started their counteroffensive there were 800,000 Soviet citizens, former prisoners of war, serving in the German army, the most prominent of them being Lieut. Gen. Andrey Vlasov, one of the two army commanders (the other being K. K. Rokossovsky) who had stopped the Germans before Moscow but who, defeated by the Germans east of Leningrad, had surrendered in Aug. 1942. Although for years Soviet propaganda had denounced them as "fascist beasts," the Germans were welcomed as liberators in many parts of the Soviet Union, especially in those with a non-Russian population. Without underestimating the resilience of the Soviet regime and of the Soviet army, it should be recorded as a historical fact that one cause of the German defeat in Russia was Hitler's blunder in maintaining the kolkhozes detested by the peasants, and in discouraging the non-Russian nationalisms, in particular that of the Ukrainians.

By the end of World War II the Soviet armed forces were estimated at 11,000,000 men and 360 divisions. According to Voznesensky, they had 5 times as much artillery, 15 times as many tanks and 5 times as many aircraft as in 1941. Demobilization started by the end of 1945, but by 1952 the postwar armed forces were about three times as strong in numbers as they were in 1939. On Oct. 3, 1946, the word "Red" was officially discarded from the title of the Soviet armed forces.

Allied Aid to the Soviet Union.—The Soviet government was always unready to acknowledge the extent of Allied aid in weapons, munitions of war, strategic raw materials and foodstuffs received from the United States and Great Britain during World War II. Voznesensky maintained that the Allied deliveries were only 4% of the domestic production during the war. Lend-lease to the Soviet Union amounted to $10,982,089,000 from the United States and to £428,000,000 from Great Britain. From Oct. 1941 to Aug. 1945 the United States delivered 375,883 trucks, 51,503 jeeps, 7,056 tanks, 8,075 tractors, 35,170 motorcycles, 2,328 ordnance service vehicles, 14,795 aircraft, 189,000 field telephones with 670,000 mi. of wire, considerable railway equipment (1,900 steam locomotives, 66 diesel locomotives, 9,920 flatcars, 1,000 dump cars, 120 tank cars and 35 heavy machinery cars), 4,478,116 tons of foodstuffs, 2,670,371 tons of petroleum products and quantities of boots, aluminum, copper, explosives, etc.

Great Britain likewise, between Oct. 1941 and March 1945, shipped 7,410 aircraft, 5,218 tanks, raw materials, machinery, industrial plant, foodstuffs and medical supplies, which were sent to the U.S.S.R. in 40 convoys by the northern route; despite considerable risks and hardships involved, 92.6% of the supplies arrived safely in Russian ports.

The Soviet Forces after World War II.—A British estimate of July 1951 placed the Soviet armed forces at 4,600,000 men. The army comprised 2,100,000, the forces of the interior 1,100,000, the air force and anti-aircraft defense 800,000 and the navy 600,000. There were 175 divisions, excluding 40 artillery and anti-aircraft divisions. In his report published April 2, 1952, Gen. Dwight D. Eisenhower, the North Atlantic Treaty organization supreme commander, gave a similar estimate for the Soviet divisions, and estimated the forces of the European Soviet satellite powers at 60 divisions. Speaking before the U.S. senate's foreign relations committee on March 24, 1952, Gen. Alfred M. Gruenther, chief of staff at supreme headquarters, Allied powers in Europe, added that while the size of the Soviet armed forces had remained static in the postwar years, the high command had concentrated on improving and perfecting them; 65 out of 175 divisions, for instance, had been armoured and mechanized.

The armed forces of the Soviet Union in the early 1950s were divided into the army, the air force, the anti-aircraft defense, the navy and the forces of the interior. The army was composed of four types of division: (1) the infantry division, consisting of three rifle regiments on foot, one horse-drawn artillery regiment of 72 guns and howitzers and one tank regiment (full strength, 11,000 men); (2) the motorized division, that is, an infantry division with lorry (truck)-borne infantry and motorized artillery; (3) the armoured division, designed for short-range combat in co-operation with infantry, consisting of three medium tank regiments of about 200 tanks, one mixed regiment of about 50 heavy tanks and 25 heavy self-propelled guns, and a motorized rifle regiment (full strength, 10,500 men); and (4) the mechanized division, designed for more independent action, comprising three regiments of motorized infantry, two tank regiments (medium and heavy), one howitzer regiment and rocket, anti-aircraft and reconnaissance battalions (full strength, about 13,000 men). There were also mountain and cavalry brigades. The typical Soviet artillery division (150 guns and howitzers, 10,000 men) was controlled directly by army headquarters.

The air force in the Soviet organization was not an independent arm but was divided between the army and the navy, about 90% of the first-line air strength belonging to the former. According to General Gruenther, the Soviet air force had 20,000 operational aircraft in 1952, including 4,000 jet planes. The highest formation was an air army composed of a number of divisions, each containing from three to four regiments of about 50 aircraft each. According to Asher Lee, there were two air armies, each of about 1,000 operational aircraft, attached to each of the army group headquarters of Leningrad, Minsk, Odessa, Tbilisi, Tashkent and Chita. In addition, there were air divisions in eastern Germany and an independent long-range air force. The air force also comprised a certain number of parachute brigades.

The anti-aircraft defense or P.V.O. (Protiv-Vozdushnaya Oborona) was an independent arm composed of anti-aircraft artillery divisions and fighter divisions.

The Workers' and Peasants' navy was created by a decree of the council of people's commissars on Feb. 14, 1917. Until Dec. 31, 1937, the navy was administered by the common people's commissariat for war and navy. On that date a navy commissariat was created; but on Feb. 25, 1946, it disappeared when by a decree of the presidium of the supreme soviet a people's commissariat of the armed forces was organized. (In March 1946 the name "people's commissariat" was dropped in favour of "ministry.") Although *Pravda* commented that this decision emerged from the whole experience of World War II, a navy ministry was restored on Feb. 25, 1950. Adm. I. S. Yumashev, the first minister, was succeeded on July 23, 1951, by Adm. N. G. Kuznetsov, who had been people's navy commissar from 1937 to 1946. According to Adm. William Fechteler, U.S. chief of naval operations, the Soviet navy consisted in 1951 of 3 old battleships, about 15 cruisers, 45 or 50 destroyers and about 300 submarines. Approximately 60 of the submarines were former German U-boats and about 100 were of a small coastal type.

The forces of the interior were divided into frontier guards and security troops administered by the ministry of the interior. They were not intended for the front, although equipped in every way, down to tanks, artillery and aircraft.

Military service extended for two years in the army (three years for noncommissioned officers), three years in the air force and anti-aircraft defense, four in the navy and 27 months in the forces of the interior. Conscription age was 18 for men with secondary education and 19 for all others. From 1946 about 1,200,000 men were conscripted yearly.

Up to Oct. 1946 described as "Red army man" (*krasnoarmeyets*), a Soviet soldier was afterward termed a "ranker" (*ryadovoy*). Discipline in the Soviet army was strict and punishments were severe, transgressors being sent to penal battalions, which in World War II were set almost suicidal tasks. Pay and privileges rose rapidly with rank. Thus, while in the U.S. army a general's pay was in the ratio 15 to 1 to a private's, in the Soviet army a marshal's pay was in the ratio of 114 to 1 to a private's. The officer's corps was a separate caste, and the times when a private could address a colonel simply as *tovarishch* were long forgotten; he would now say *tovarishch polkovnik* (comrade colonel) and give the once-outlawed salute not only to officers but also to noncommissioned officers.

Until Sept. 1951 there existed three organizations for premilitary training, one for the army, one for the air force and one for the navy. It was announced on Sept. 26 that the three organizations had merged into one All-Union Association for Voluntary Assistance to the Army, Air Force and Navy (D.O.S.A.A.F.); this provided military training for young men from the age of 15 years onward.

The proportion of the total estimated expenditure allocated to defense rose between 1951 and 1952 from 18.5% to 21.3%. This declared expenditure was, however, not the whole picture; a great proportion of the military expenditure was detectable under the guise of investment in national economy, while the cost of military academies and schools was included in expenditure on education.

The nominal head of the Soviet land and air forces was the minister of war. After K. E. Voroshilov had ceased to be people's commissar in May 1940, this post was occupied by Marshal S. K. Timoshenko (May 8, 1940–July 20, 1941), Marshal Joseph Stalin (July 20, 1941–March 3, 1947), Marshal N. A. Bulganin (March 3, 1947–March 24, 1949) and Marshal A. M. Vasilevsky (from March 24, 1949). The minister had under his command the chief of the general staff. After B. M. Shaposhnikov's resignation in the summer of 1940 on the ground of ill health, the post was occupied for a few months by Marshal Kiril Meretskov, then by Marshal G. K. Zhukov (Feb. 24–Oct. 31, 1941), then again by Shaposhnikov till he was replaced in Nov. 1942 by Marshal Vasilevsky (Shaposhnikov died on March 26, 1945). From Nov. 12, 1948, Gen. Sergey Shtemenko was chief of the general staff.

There were six deputy ministers of war and each was in charge of an arm or a service. The post of commander in chief of the air force was occupied during World War II by Marshal A. A. Novikov, from 1946 by Marshal K. A. Vershinin and from July 1950 by Col. Gen. P. F. Zhigarev. (K. Sm.)

COMMUNICATIONS

Russia is well endowed with navigable waterways and has throughout most of its area a flat surface which lends itself to railway construction, but the country has always lacked an adequate system of communications. The railways were unevenly distributed, being concentrated in the central and southern industrial regions of European Russia. Vast areas remained unserved. In 1913 the whole of Asiatic Russia had only 15% of the country's railways. Another difficulty was the long and uneconomic haul of freight from the south to Moscow, and before the revolution it was cheaper to import coal to St. Petersburg from abroad than to haul it from the Donets basin. The severe continental climate meant a heavy seasonal demand on the railways and other means of transport, and this invariably resulted in congestion and serious delays. Quantities of freight were hauled by wagons drawn by horses, mules or oxen, but this slow method was further handicapped by the fact that roads were virtually nonexistent. Many rivers have been constantly used to transport freight, but little attempt was made until after the revolution to make full use of the great networks of waterways. The Soviet government gave priority to the construction of railways, canals and roads, and the development of the system of transport went ahead rapidly.

Railways.—The first Russian railway—from St. Petersburg to Tsarskoye Selo—was laid down in 1837, but despite this early start the nation lagged behind in railway construction. It was not until 1851 that the first main line—from St. Petersburg to Moscow—was laid. The two great periods of expansion of the railways were 1868–74 and the 1890s; the Trans-Siberian railway was built in 1891–1903 and had been double-tracked by 1936. In 1913 the length of railways per 10,000 inhabitants was about one-fourth that of England, and in quantity and quality the engines and rolling stock were far inferior to those in use in England.

The main trunk lines were constructed before the revolution, and the Soviet government concentrated on developing and extending them, while modernizing equipment. During the period 1920–40 the total length of Soviet railways increased from 35,700 mi. to 64,200 mi. In 1937 the railways hauled almost four times as much freight as in 1913. Much was done to eliminate long and uneconomic hauls. Imports of coal from distant basins such as the Donbas, Kuzbas and Karaganda were reduced by utilizing local coal deposits near Moscow, in the Urals and in the Caucasus. The creation of a second oil base between the Volga and the Urals meant a considerable decrease in the long hauls of oil. The shipment of lumber from the forests of northern European Russia to the central and southern regions and from Siberia to central Asia also reduced costly hauls.

The construction of the Turkistan-Siberian (Turksib) railway, completed in 1930, linking Novosibirsk with Kazakhstan and central Asia, was by mid-20th century the most important achievement of Soviet railway policy; not only were great difficulties of engineering overcome but also it made possible the direct exchange of cotton from central Asia for grain and timber from western Siberia.

A South Siberian (Yuzhsib) line, branching off from the Trans-Siberian at Kinel (east of Kuybyshev), linked the steelworks of Magnitogorsk with the coal basin of Karaganda. By 1950 the line was extended farther east from Akmolinsk to Barnaul (where it crossed the Turksib), and continued eastward to Stalinsk, in the Kuzbas (already linked to the Trans-Siberian via Kemerovo). From Stalinsk the line was being extended to Abakansk, source of supply in iron ore and manganese for the Kuzbas steelworks, and was expected to join the Trans-Siberian at Tayshet, east of Krasnoyarsk. Before World War II work had been begun on a new railway across eastern Siberia, branching off the main line at Tayshet and passing north of Lake Baikal to Kirensk, Chekunda, Komsomolsk and Sovietskaya-Gavan (on the Sea of Japan). By 1950, with the exception of the link Kirensk-Chekunda, this line was believed completed.

The outlets from the Donbas were greatly increased by the laying of new lines or the double-tracking of existing lines. Action was also taken in modernizing rolling stock and equipment. L. M. Kaganovich, appointed people's commissar for transport in 1935, organized a campaign for technical improvement. More powerful engines were brought into service with rolling stock of greater capacity. About 38% of the entire network of rails was relaid to allow for this heavier traffic. In regions where hydroelectric power was available some lines were electrified; for example, Murmansk-Kandalaksha and Tbilisi-Batum. Serious losses of rolling stock were suffered in World War II, but these were later made good.

The following are the chief freight routes in the U.S.S.R.: Donbas to Krivoi Rog; Donbas and the northern Caucasus to Moscow and Leningrad; Donbas to the Volga region; Murmansk to Leningrad; Archangel to Moscow; Leningrad to the Urals; Moscow to the Urals; Moscow to central Asia; the Urals to the Kuzbas; Siberia to the far east; and Siberia to central Asia.

Waterways.—Russia is covered by a dense network of waterways, most of which are navigable. They provide an invaluable means of transport in a country of such vast distances. Before the revolution little was done to develop the waterways, but in 1913 about 48,200,000 tons of freight were hauled by this means, chiefly in the Volga basin. By 1937 this figure had risen to 66,900,000 tons.

The disadvantages of river transport are that all Russian rivers are frozen over and closed to navigation for four or five months of the year and, second, that freight must of necessity follow the natural flow of the rivers. The Soviet government planned to overcome the latter disadvantage by the construction of canals and dams, and it appeared that eventually the European and Asiatic waterways might be linked in this manner. Three canals were completed: (1) the Moscow-Volga canal, opened in 1937, connecting Moscow with the whole Volga basin; (2) the Volga-Baltic water route (Mariinsk system), allowing transport by small vessels from the Volga river to pass through a series of rivers, canals and lakes to Leningrad; (3) the White sea-Baltic canal, opened in 1933 and leading to important developments in the north and, by connecting the White sea through Lake Onega with the Mariinsk system, contributing greatly to the exchange of goods between north and south.

The importance of the Dnieper river for transport had always been reduced by the rapids just south of the great bend in its course. The construction of a dam and canals as part of the "Dneproges" (Dnieper hydroelectric station) made the rapids navigable. By 1952 much was being done to make the Don river navigable, including the construction of the Volga-Don canal. In Siberia and the far east the main rivers—the Ob, the Irtysh, the Yenisei, the Lena and the Amur—are all navigable throughout most of their courses and are chiefly utilized for moving timber. In addition to constructing dams and canals, much was done to deepen and improve the waterways so that they would allow the use of larger barges and more powerful river fleets.

Maritime Transport.—The principal ports are in the White, Barents and Black seas. Of these Murmansk in the north and the ports of the Sea of Azov and the Black sea are ice-free the year round. The southern ports handle more than half the total seaborne cargo destined for foreign or for other Soviet ports. Modern tanker fleets are in commission in the Black and Caspian seas, transporting oil from Batum in the former and from Baku to Astrakhan and Krasnovodsk in the latter sea. After the revolution maritime transport grew in importance, particularly with the development of the northern sea route, which allows the direct shipment of timber from Siberia to European Russia and the more rapid transport of machinery and manufactured goods from the White sea to Siberia and the far east.

Roads.—In Russia transport had always relied primarily on the railways and rivers and in winter on the use of sledges. Lack of stone for road construction, except in the Urals, has been one of the difficulties, and before the revolution such roads as had been built were so primitive as to be often impassable. The real demand for surfaced roads was created by the sharp increase in the number of motor vehicles manufactured in the new Soviet factories. Before the revolution there were about 9,000 motor vehicles in the whole of Russia; the number had grown to 19,000 by 1928 and to 760,000 by 1938. In 1950 the production of motor vehicles was said to amount to 65,000 cars, 6,400 buses and 428,000 trucks.

The roads constructed by the Soviet government proved their value during World War II when, making use of fleets of trucks, mainly provided by the Soviet Union's western allies, they relieved the railways of some of the heavy wartime burden. Before World War II highways were built to link many of the most important centres, as, for example, Moscow-Leningrad, Moscow-Minsk, Moscow-Kiev, Leningrad-Vitebsk-Kiev in the eastern parts of the Soviet Union; the Tashkent highway system in central Asia; and the reconstructed Georgian military highway running from Dzaudzhikau (Vladikavkaz) across the Caucasus mountains to Tbilisi and Erivan. These highways are of strategical importance.

Air Transport.—After 1923 air transport became an important part of the Soviet transport system. By 1940 more than 88,000 mi. of airways were in regular operation, carrying passengers, mail and freight to all parts of the union. The Moscow-Vladivostok arterial air line crosses the entire country and is of particular importance also for the branch lines which connect it with Magnitogorsk, Karaganda, Alma Ata, Yakutsk, Komsomolsk and Sakhalin. The arterial air lines Moscow-Kharkov-Rostov-Baku-Tbilisi and Moscow-Kuybyshev-Aktyubinsk-Tashkent are also of considerable importance. After World War II, in the vast regions where other methods of transport remained undeveloped, new air routes were established.

In 1923 the air lines carried 200 passengers, 1,800 kg. of mail and 100 kg. of freight; in 1939 they carried 307,000 passengers, 11,500 tons of mail and more than 40,000 tons of freight.

(I. Gy.)

ECONOMIC AND FINANCIAL CONDITIONS

In its economy, as in many other aspects of its life, Russia before World War I was a land of contrasts. It was predominantly agricultural, with a small class of wealthy and well-to-do landowners and a majority of peasants, who lived, with few exceptions, in poor and primitive circumstances. The industrial revolution had come late to Russia, but the country was rich in mineral and agricultural resources, in coal, iron, oil, manganese, cereals, cotton, flax and sugar beets, among other products. And, although industry played a less important part in the national economy than was the case in western Europe, about half its industrial workers were employed in large plants with more than 1,000 workers.

This was largely attributable to the fact that foreign capital, French, British, German, Belgian and U.S., in this order of importance, had been flowing into Russia rapidly since the last quarter of the 19th century. The foreign capitalist often found it profitable to put up a big factory, equipped with the latest machinery. So Russian industry was only partially the result of the slow accumulation of capital by pioneer Russian companies. It was the hothouse fruit of foreign investment. About one-third of the capital invested in Russian stock companies in 1914 was of foreign origin.

After the conclusion of the Franco-Russian alliance in 1891, Russian loans, state and municipal, found a ready market in France. French capital was strongly interested in the Russian mining and metallurgical industries. French money was heavily invested in the coal and iron industries of the Donets basin. British capitalists specialized in the Caucasian oil fields and in the textile industries which grew up in the neighbourhood of Moscow. Germans were active in the electrical industry. A number of Russian streetcar lines were built with Belgian capital. There was some British and U.S. mining and engineering development in the Ural mountains and in Siberia.

Partly because of the stimulus of an inflow of foreign capital that averaged 200,000,000 gold roubles (about $100,000,000) annually during the years before World War I, partly because Russia was a new country, from the industrial standpoint, with great possibilities of development, the pace of industrial advance during the last decades of the 19th century and especially during the first decade of the 20th was very swift.

Russian industry before World War I was located mainly in four areas, Moscow, St. Petersburg, the Donets basin and the Urals. (The Polish industrial basin of Dabrowa-Sosnowiec was a fifth area until Aug. 1914, when it was occupied by the Germans; in Nov. 1918 it became part of Poland.) St. Petersburg and Moscow, the two largest cities in Russia, were natural markets for industrial goods. St. Petersburg developed, in the main, heavy industries, of which the Putilov metalworks was one of the largest. Moscow specialized in textiles and consumers' goods. It was able to draw on the coal field southeast of Moscow for fuel. The Donets basin, with its coal deposits, and the adjacent iron ore of Krivoi Rog formed the natural basis for an iron and steel industry. The Urals possess iron, coal, copper, asbestos and other valuable minerals.

The outbreak of war in 1914 interrupted Russia's industrial progress and placed a heavy strain on its growing but inadequate economy. Russia was largely isolated from its allies, France and Great Britain, and its industries and its transport system could not measure up to the needs of the huge army that was mobilized. Production for civilian use declined and inflation began to make itself felt in the later years of the struggle. While Russia was normally self-sufficient in staple foodstuffs and exported large quantities of cereals to western Europe, the overloading of the railway system and the tendency of the peasants to hold back their products from the market as they found that they could not buy a normal equivalent in manufactured goods led to food shortage in the towns, where the population had swelled because of the growth of the munitions industry. Food riots in Petrograd were the beginning of the overthrow of the imperial regime in 1917.

The national economy deteriorated rapidly during the eight months which elapsed between the March Revolution of 1917 and the Bolshevik revolution of Nov. 7. The bases of social and economic order were shaken to their foundations. The peasants began to seize the land of the larger owners. There were continual workers' strikes and demonstrations, partly for political reasons, partly because the provisional government proved unable to check the inflationary trend and there was a continual rise in the cost of living. A good deal of class hatred entered into the strikes and in some cases unpopular employers and engineers were driven away from the factories, which the workers undertook to operate themselves. The Bolshevik revolution brought into power the most extreme group of Russian Socialists. It was immediately followed by a decree nationalizing the land and expropriating all large holders. A decree of Nov. 27 subjected industry to a system of workers' control. The banks were nationalized on Dec. 27.

War Communism.—It was not the immediate purpose of the Bolsheviks to nationalize all industry and trade. Lenin recognized Russia's technical backwardness and the difficulties of abruptly instituting full-fledged socialism in a land where the peasants constituted the great majority of the population. For a few months after the conclusion of the treaty of Brest-Litovsk with the Germans in March 1918, Lenin was inclined to emphasize the necessity for labour discipline and skilled management; he asserted that it would be profitable for the new regime to hire bourgeois specialists in order to obtain a smooth flow of production.

But as the civil war became more intense, the Soviet government found itself driven from one measure to another in the direction of establishing complete control over the industrial plant, the manpower and the labour of the country. The factory owners, as a class, were naturally hostile to the new regime; many of them fled, abandoning their enterprises. The sugar industry was nationalized on May 2 and the petroleum industry on June 17, 1918. A decree of June 28 clearly pointed the way to the expropriation of the private industrialist; it provided for the nationalization of the largest undertakings in the mining, metallurgical, metalworking, textile, electrotechnical, pottery, tanning and cement industries. A decree of Nov. 29, 1920, completed the process by declaring nationalized all enterprises that employed more than ten persons, or more than five if motor power were employed.

Foreign trade was nationalized (it practically ceased to exist during the years of civil war and blockade) and on Nov. 21, 1918, private trade within the country was forbidden. In theory, Russia was supposed to live under a gigantic rationing system, with city dwellers receiving food products and manufactured goods on ration cards and the peasants delivering up their surplus produce in exchange for manufactured goods from the towns.

In practice, this system could not and did not work out effectively, because the government lacked both the goods and the technical organization to make it function with even passable efficiency. There was a good deal of surreptitious barter between city and village, and town dwellers obtained about as much food from those theoretically illegal operations as they received on their ration cards.

New organizations came into existence to administer this new system. One of the most important of these was the supreme economic council, established on Dec. 15, 1917. Originally, it had been conceived as a body which would supervise the whole economic life of Russia, but its functions were gradually restricted to the management of industry.

The council of labour and defense (S.T.O.) assumed considerable powers; it may be described as a kind of war economic cabinet. The food commissariat, which took charge of the distribution not only of food but also of manufactured goods, occupied a key position in the scheme of War Communism. The commissariat for transportation operated the railways and waterways on semimilitary lines; the commissariat for agriculture, especially in the later phases of the War Communism period, tried to direct the peasants as to their selection of crops and their sowing.

Money tended to lose all value under this system. The rouble had declined considerably in buying power when the Bolsheviks came into power. Unchecked use of the printing press and the fact that the distribution of both food and manufactured goods was supposed to be on a rationed basis soon led to an inflation as sweepingly destructive as that of Germany. A new currency had to be built up when a new policy was adopted. Toward the end of the period of War Communism, such things as housing, transport and public services were supposed to be supplied free to all citizens.

Another feature of the period was the attempt of 1920 to use armies, under military discipline, for labour tasks. This was a pet idea of Trotsky, who believed that the terrific jam in production could be broken by the same methods that had led to the defeat of the Whites in the civil war: mobilization of labour under conditions of stern discipline, accompanied by fiery emotional appeals. The labour armies, however, proved a fiasco and were soon discarded.

Considered as an economic experiment, War Communism was a disastrous failure. There are few parallels in history for the collapse that overtook Russia's productive forces. By 1920 the big industries were producing 18%, the small industries 43%, of their prewar output. The prostration was most complete in the heavy industries. Pig iron was down to 2.4%, iron ore to 1.7%, of the prewar figure. The output of copper ceased entirely. The railways, which suffered from the depredations of both sides during the civil war, crawled along with an ever-increasing percentage of damaged and disused locomotives and freight cars. In Jan. 1917 there were 537,328 freight cars in the country, of which 4.2% were out of use; by the end of 1919 the number of freight cars had diminished to 244,443, of which 16.6% were damaged. There were 20,394 locomotives (16.5% out of commission) in Jan. 1917 and 8,955 (47.8% unfit for use) at the end of 1918.

Wages and productivity of labour declined tremendously, while a large part of the city workers dispersed to the villages in search of food. The average wage of the Russian worker during these bleak years was little more than one-third what it has been under the tsars. Productivity of labour in 1920 was only 26% of the average of 1913.

Agriculture was also hard hit by the crisis, although the peasants, until actual famine devastated a great area of the Volga valley and of the Ukraine in 1921–22 (see History, above), suffered less from hunger than did the city dwellers. The Russian harvest of cereals, which had averaged about 80,000,000 metric tons in the pre-1914 years, declined to 50,000,000 tons in 1920. The tendency of the peasants was to concentrate on food crops and to cease planting other market crops, or at least to cut down the acreage substantially. By 1920 the area under flax had declined by 50% as compared with the prewar average, that under sugar beets by 74%, that under cotton by 87% and that under tobacco by 90%.

The cities of northern and central Russia lost more than one-third of their population between 1916 and 1920. Many Russian town dwellers, especially among the labouring classes, had friends and relatives in the country, and there was a widespread impulse to go back to the villages, where, in spite of the requisitions, there was more chance of getting food.

The effect of War Communism was temporarily to frustrate the realization of almost every Communist economic ideal. Lenin and his associates believed in a state order based on the industrial proletariat as the ruling class and were eager to see Russia over-

take and surpass the leading capitalist countries in quantity and efficiency of production. They were also convinced, as Marxists, that large industrial units would supplant small and medium ones. The actual circumstances of life under War Communism tended to contradict all these ideals. The working class was dispersing and a good many of the workers who remained in the factories turned into small speculators, making little objects of daily use which could be sold or exchanged for food. The big factories in many cases stood idle or worked at a fraction of their normal capacity for lack of machinery and raw material. The Communists in theory were worshippers of modern efficiency, of the machine. But the storm of social revolution and civil war had destroyed most of what little efficiency and mechanization had formerly existed in Russia and threatened to throw the country back into extremely primitive forms of economic life.

It would be incorrect to regard War Communism as an experiment undertaken entirely for its own sake. Many of its features were almost inseparably associated with the hard exigencies of civil war. It was impossible, for instance, for the Soviet government to give the peasants any adequate supply of manufactured goods when the factories, often cut off from sources of raw material, were unable to work at normal capacity and when war needs took precedence over everything else. Requisitioning evoked much bitterness in the villages and was accompanied by many abuses. But the army and the cities could not have been given even a minimum food ration without requisitioning.

The New Economic Policy.—An uprising of sailors in the important naval base of Kronstadt in March 1921 sounded the doom of War Communism. There had already been sporadic peasant revolts in the Ukraine, in Tambov province, in Siberia. But the revolt in a fortress so close to Petrograd, a fortress which had always been considered a stronghold of Communism, was interpreted by Lenin as a definite warning that other economic methods must be tried. The tenth congress of the Communist party, which met in Moscow in March 1921 and was strongly affected by the news of the Kronstadt rebellion, adopted without opposition Lenin's proposal that a tax in kind, of about one-tenth of the peasant's produce, should be substituted for the former arbitrary requisitioning of all the peasants' surplus. This was the cornerstone of the New Economic Policy, or N.E.P., as it was generally called; a number of other changes inevitably followed.

Since the peasant was given the right to sell his produce, private trade within the country automatically became legal. A whole new class of so-called nepmen, shrewd and cunning speculators who had survived all the rigours and repressions of War Communism, emerged from hiding and commenced to play a conspicuous part in Soviet life. Small private business was again permitted. The slack accounting and financial methods of War Communism were revised, and the trusts or organs of management for the state industries were required to balance their budgets and, if possible, show a profit. Payment of rent and taxes and charges for public services were restored.

The rouble was stabilized at its old value of 51.2 cents (U.S.) and for a short time this new Soviet currency was freely interchangeable for foreign currencies. This situation soon came to an end, however; both the export and the import of roubles into Russia were forbidden and the Soviet currency remained strictly reserved for internal use. There was a vast discrepancy between the official value of the rouble and its quotation on the black market.

The adoption of the New Economic Policy, coinciding as it did with the end of the civil war, broke the many vicious circles in which Soviet economy had become entangled. The curve of industrial production, of agricultural output, of wages and of productivity turned upward. Houses were repaired and made habitable. The cities again filled up. The light industries which produced goods for everyday use were first to recover; but in time the coal and iron mines of the Donets basin and Krivoi Rog, the oil wells of Baku, the metal and machine factories of Leningrad and Kharkov and other industrial centres were again able to set their wheels in motion and to work up to normal productivity.

The chief economic organizations of this period were the trusts and the syndicates. A trust, which was entirely state-owned, administered an industry or part of an industry, and in some cases a number of trusts combined and vested selling functions in a syndicate. The supreme economic council continued to function as a general state board of direction for industry. A body that began to acquire more importance in the late '20s was the Gosplan, or State Planning commission. Originating as a commission attached to the council of labour and defense, it assumed the function of endeavouring to plot the graph of the national economic development by publishing so-called control figures, in which the output of the coming year in every branch of national economy was laid down. There were distinct limits to this planning under the N.E.P., because the peasants, the private traders and small businessmen were outside its scope. But it acquired increased significance in the third phase of Soviet economic life, that of planned economy.

It had been a part of the New Economic Policy to grant concessions to foreign capitalists and businessmen. While the Soviet government refused either to restore integrally the properties of foreign business firms which it had seized or to pay compensation for the seizures, it professed willingness to lease various mines and factories, which it lacked resources to operate itself, to foreign concessionaires. The two largest concessions which were granted were for the exploitation of gold fields in the Lena river region of Siberia and for the development of manganese mines in the region of Chiatura in Georgia. An Anglo-U.S. group obtained the first concession, the Averell Harriman interests the second. Concessions enjoyed their most flourishing period during the years of the N.E.P. They never, however, played an important role in Soviet economic development. They were practically all wound up and liquidated during the first five-year plan. Russia's industrialization was financed entirely by the sacrifices which were imposed on the Russian people.

Although the New Economic Policy was a period of industrial and agricultural progress and of a rising standard of living after the appalling depression of War Communism, it contained some features that were disquieting to the Communist party. There was a feeling that capitalism was undermining the bases of socialist economy. Elbowed out in the struggle for power that went on behind the scenes after Lenin's death, Trotsky directed criticism against the alleged compromising of socialist principles by Stalin, who emerged more and more as the outstanding leader of the Communist party and, consequently, of the Soviet regime.

While the New Economic Policy was an immense improvement, from the peasants' standpoint, over War Communism, it did not prove able to adjust satisfactorily the relations between city and village. The theoretical buying power of the peasant was considerably increased, for two reasons. With the recent memory of inflation and worthless paper money, he had little incentive or desire to save. He could not use his money, as the thrifty peasant before 1914 would have done, to buy land and enlarge his farm, for the purchase and sale of land remained forbidden. Consequently, the peasant's instinct was to spend his surplus money for consumers' goods, and the light industries were never able to satisfy his needs. Shortage of manufactured goods, high prices and poor quality became constant peasant complaints, and by 1928 there was already a tendency for the peasants to carry out a kind of slowdown strike, to raise less for the city market, which did not seem able to give them a fair equivalent in exchange.

Perhaps the basic cause of the liquidation of the N.E.P. was the fundamental incompatibility between socialist industry for the towns and small peasant proprietorship in the villages. One system or the other had to be greatly modified, and Stalin decided that it would be possible both to cut the ground from under the feet of his critics within the party and to find a way out of the economic crisis by driving toward the double goal of a highly industrialized state and an agriculture that would be mechanized and placed under strong state control. For a political account of the N.E.P. see *History* above.

First Five-Year Plan.—Industrialization and collectivization of agriculture dominated Soviet life during the first five-year plan, which was shortened to four and a quarter years and ran from Oct. 1928 until the end of 1932. The task which the government had set was a formidable one and could probably only have been realized by a regime which possessed absolute political power and the will to use that power with utter ruthlessness. Labour under the N.E.P. had been free and there were between 1,000,000 and 2,000,000 unemployed who received state and local relief. The effect of the five-year plan, with its many new factories and tremendous demand for labour, was to wipe out unemployment and to create a labour shortage. This led to a growing tendency to attach the worker or the engineer to his job, to forbid him to leave under threat of legal penalties. Forced labour on a large scale was introduced for the classes which were doomed to economic extinction under the new policy, the kulaks and the nepmen. The O.G.P.U., or political police, was constantly carrying out roundups of suspected elements in the cities, a familiar penalty being an administrative sentence to work on one of the new enterprises; and there were mass deportations of kulaks and their families from their native villages to timber camps and new industrial plants, where they were set to work at unskilled labour for bare subsistence rations.

A marked characteristic of Russia throughout the first five-year plan was the acute shortage of foodstuffs and of manufactured goods. There were several reasons. Agriculture was in a state of turmoil and upheaval. The dispossessed kulaks, being the better farmers, had produced a larger than normal share of food and other crops. Their elimination left a vacuum that was not immediately filled. Moreover, everything was subordinated to the needs of the heavy industries. Foodstuffs that were very short in Russia were shipped abroad to obtain foreign exchange to finance the purchases of machinery and equipment for the new industrial plants. Transport was under a heavy strain, and food products were often not brought from places where there was a surplus to places where there was a lack. There was a vast influx of peasants into the cities and new industrial towns, and this meant an increased demand on all sources of supply.

Rationing, unknown since the end of the civil war, was reintroduced. Money to a very considerable extent became devalued. The insufficient supplies in the state and co-operative shops were distributed on a rationed basis and a system grew up under which every institution or factory had its own shop or its own restaurant, exclusively for the use of its own employees. Private trade again became illegal, in fact if not in law, the supply of goods in the private markets diminished and prices soared. The purchasing power of the rouble in free trade shrank by 90% or more. How much money a man earned became less important for his well-being than what type of shop or restaurant he was permitted to patronize.

Some observers, both in Russia and abroad, foresaw disaster in this reversion to some practices of War Communism. But this third phase of the Soviet economy developed under much more favourable auspices than the primitive experiment of 1918–21. There was no distraction by war and all the mobilized energy of the country could find expression in new industrial construction. A younger generation had grown up under the influence of the Soviet schools and the Young Communist league, indoctrinated with the ideas of the new regime and willing to endure hardship and to smash pitilessly any opposition. The Soviet Union was no longer blockaded and cut off from the outside world. It was possible to engage the services of thousands of foreign engineers and technicians, mostly Americans and Germans, to direct the building and the first stages of operation of the factories, mines and electrical power plants which were part of the scheme of industrial development.

So, although the human and material costs of this experiment in planned economy were prodigious (there were millions of deaths from famine and related diseases in the Ukraine and in the northern Caucasus in 1932–33, and the casualties among the deported kulaks and other "class enemies" of the Soviet regime were considerable), the political structure successfully withstood the strain. By the time the plan was completed a considerable stride had been taken toward the goal of making Russia industrially self-sufficient.

Some industries that had been nonexistent or negligible before the five-year plan, such as the manufacture of tractors, automobiles and motor trucks, were put on a mass production basis. Indeed, the advance of the tractor and agricultural machinery industries was intimately bound up with the Soviet scheme for the collectivization of agriculture. Beginning in 1929, a mass drive was launched to induce the peasants to give up their individual holdings and organize themselves into collective farms (kolkhozes). It was made inconvenient not to join these collective farms; anyone who opposed the change was likely to be denounced and sometimes arrested and deported as a kulak.

Co-operative farming had not been unknown in Russia before this great change in the national agricultural system. While the overwhelming majority of the peasants farmed their allotments on an individual basis, restricted only by the prohibition against buying or selling land, there were a few communes and a somewhat larger number of artels. The members of a commune (mir) usually lived together in a common dwelling and shared equally the produce of their labour. The artel was a looser form of association, in which land and working animals were pooled, the members retained their own homes and the output was shared in proportion to the amount of labour and equipment which each member contributed. It was the artel that furnished the approved model for the collective farm. A typical collective farm included about 100 peasant families as members, with between 1,000 and 1,500 ac. of land. A small village would often be transformed into a single collective farm, while a larger village would be divided into several collective farms.

The collective farms went through several changes of organization. The type of organization that prevailed before World War II was as follows: the collective farm was an inalienable unit; its boundaries could not be changed; the members possessed the right to cultivate individual gardens and to possess cows and keep pigs, fowl, sheep and goats. Their main work, however, was supposed to be for the collective farm and they were paid, partly in kind, partly in cash, on the basis of the quantity and quality of the work performed. The president of the collective farm was elected by the members, but, as in all Soviet elections, the local Communist cell, or group, exercised a good deal of influence in the selection. The larger machines, tractors, harvesting combines, threshing machines, were not sold directly to the collective farms. They were placed in machine-tractor stations, state-controlled organizations which undertook to cultivate the land of the collective farms within a given radius of territory. Payment for this service was made in kind. Receipts from the machine-tractor stations and from the fixed quantities of grain, cotton, sugar beets and other products, which the collective farms were required to sell to the state at a price so low as to be practically nominal, assured the food supply of the cities and of the army. After deductions of the payments in kind for tax and debt obligations, the peasant might sell his share of the crop, so far as this was not required for his own needs, either individually or through a co-operative to which he might belong. He was also free to sell his vegetables, poultry, eggs and small animals.

The unfamiliarity of this system, together with the lack of trained organizers and the excesses of zeal on the part of some local officials, made its first years very difficult and led to a tremendous destruction of livestock that depleted the country's normal output of meat and dairy products for several years to come. The ravages of civil war, which had been generally more than made good by 1929, were repeated on an even larger scale during the stormy first years of collectivization. As the peasants became resigned to the inevitability of the new system, as the supply of machinery increased and managerial capacity improved, collective farming struck firmer roots in the Russian soil.

The degree of realization of the first five-year plan was mixed and spotty. Heavy industry certainly received a powerful impetus and the ground had been prepared for further progress by the erection of such large factories and hydroelectric power installations as the Magnitogorsk iron and steel works, the Kuznetsk iron and steel plant, the tractor factories at Stalingrad and Kharkov, the Moscow and Gorki automobile plants, the agricultural machinery works at Sverdlovsk, the chemical plants at Berezniki and Stalinogorsk and the Dnieper dam and power plants, which were designed to supply power to several newly built factories. On the other hand, the desired figures of agricultural production were not realized and the parts of the plan which had provided for an increased standard of living, even specifying the increased amounts of meat, eggs and butter which should be available, were entirely unfulfilled. General living conditions during the first five-year plan were bleak and hard, more suggestive of war than of peace.

(W. H. Ch.; X.)

Second and Third Five-Year Plans.—The second five-year plan, covering the years 1933–37, was followed by a third plan for 1938–42 which was interrupted by World War II. During the first five-year plan 17 new blast furnaces, 45 open-hearth furnaces and many rolling mills were built. During the second five-year plan 20 blast furnaces, 86 open-hearth furnaces and 49 rolling mills were built. Compared with the period before World War I (1913 = 100) the index number of industrial production stood at 380.5 in 1933 and rose to 908.8 in 1938. Reporting to the 18th congress of the All-Union Communist party on March 10, 1939, Stalin stated that as regards the technique of production and the rate of growth of industry the Soviet Union had already "overtaken and outstripped" the principal capitalist countries. He insisted, however, that the economic power of a country's industry was expressed not by the volume of industrial output alone but also by the volume of production per head of population. In this respect, the U.S.S.R. was still lagging behind because in 1938, the first year of the third five-year plan, the country produced only 87 kg. of pig iron per head, as compared with 145 kg. in Great Britain. In order to outstrip the United States, Stalin said, the Soviet Union should aim at a yearly pig-iron production of 50,000,-000 or 60,000,000 tons.

As to the collectivization of agriculture, by 1938 there were 242,400 kolkhozes uniting 18,843,000 peasant households, or 93.5% of the total, and holding together a crop area of 289,000,000 ac.; that is, 85.4% of the total. The total crop area, which was 259,500,000 ac. in 1913, had increased by 1938 to 338,300,000 ac., of which 253,000,000 ac. were under grain, 27,200,000 ac. under industrial crops, 23,200,000 ac. under vegetables and 34,800,000 ac. under fodder. The total number of tractors employed increased between 1933 and 1938 from 210,900 to 483,500, of which 394,000 were in 6,350 machine-tractor stations and 85,000 in sovkhozes, or state farms.

The sovkhozes, created under the first five-year plan, were worked by hired labour under a state-appointed management. Through their new techniques they were meant to have a propaganda value among the peasants unwilling to join the kolkhozes; their purpose was also to produce high-quality grain for sowing, to promote the breeding of pedigree livestock and to produce marketable foodstuffs to be sold in state-owned shops. By 1934 the sovkhozes owned a total area of 207,974,000 ac. of land, and their sown area amounted to 35,568,000 ac. In 1936 it was decided to reduce the latter area. By 1938 there were 3,961 sovkhozes with a total cultivated area of 30,628,000 ac.; they were employing 1,300,000 workers. While mixed farming was reserved to kolkhozes, the sovkhozes specialized in certain lines of production. In 1938 they were distributed as follows: grain 478; meat and dairy produce 769; pigs 659; sheep 204; horses 119; poultry 102; other livestock 62; fruit and vegetables 474; market gardening (near the larger cities) 723; industrial crops and other types 371.

World War II and the Soviet Economy.—Russian losses during World War II were staggering, for the German armies rapidly overran the most productive areas of the country. According to figures subsequently given by N. A. Voznesensky, head of the State Planning commission, about 40% of the population of the Soviet Union lived in the areas overrun by the Germans in 1941; these areas also accounted for about 66% of Soviet heavy industries, 38% of its grain and 30% of its cattle. In the following year, the loss of the Maikop area involved an important centre of high-grade fuel extraction, and in general it was estimated that the output of oil fell from 31,000,000 tons to 18,000,000 tons between 1940 and 1942. Between one-fifth and one-quarter of the capacity of the engineering industry and 40% of the capital equipment of the food industry was also reckoned as lost.

According to Voznesensky the number of workers in the occupied areas was reduced by the end of the war to a mere 17% of the former figure and the number of industrial plants to 13%. Almost two-thirds of the cattle and four-fifths of the horses had been lost. Productive resources destroyed included 31,850 factories employing 4,000,000 persons, 98,000 collective farms, 137,000 tractors, 49,000 combines, 13,000 railway bridges. In addition, the homes of perhaps 25,000,000 people, together with schools, hospitals, cultural and scientific establishments and every form of material wealth had been ground to rubble; in all, about two-thirds of the entire capital of the occupied areas.

The evacuation at high speed of much industrial plant to the eastern regions away from the war fronts was a fundamental factor in the Soviet war achievements. The population evacuated to work in the new and expanded industries, which may even have numbered more than 12,000,000 persons, suffered terrible hardships from the severe climatic conditions and from the lack of housing as well as from food shortages. Such, however, was the lot of the civil population throughout the U.S.S.R. The industrial and agricultural output in the Urals, Siberia, central Asia and the Volga area rose sharply. The coal production of the Kuzbas and at Karaganda was increased to make up for the loss of the Donbas, and, in the actual output of guns, tanks, aircraft and ammunition, Soviet industry seems to have been able to meet the demands of the great offensives of the later years of the fighting.

Postwar Five-Year Plan.—The major task of the Soviet Union in the postwar years was that of reconstructing its internal economy. The advances made in the eastern areas were not abandoned and were indeed extended, much importance being attached particularly after 1950 to new projects for hydroelectric works and irrigation. But the overrun European provinces of the Soviet Union had also to be restored. Reparations were exacted from the former enemy states, and favourable trade treaties with the Soviet Union's western neighbours brought other foreign resources to her aid; but the decision to reject aid from the European Recovery program after the Paris conference in July 1947 meant that the main basis of reconstruction was the work of the Soviet peoples themselves.

During the postwar period the methods of economic organization pursued were not substantially different from those of the 1930s. A new five-year plan (1946–50) was adopted by the supreme soviet in March 1946. Apart from electricity and coal the output targets were lower than those which were to have been reached in 1942 but for the German attack.

In a speech of Feb. 9, 1946, Stalin directed that in the shortest possible time the Soviet Union must heal the wounds inflicted by the enemy and not only recover the prewar level but even surpass this level in the near future. "We must," he said, "achieve a situation wherein our industry is able to produce annually up to 50,000,000 metric tons of pig iron, up to 60,000,000 tons of steel, up to 500,000,000 tons of coal, up to 60,000,000 tons of oil. Only under such conditions can we regard ourselves as guaranteed against any accidents. This will require perhaps three five-year plans, if not more. But this task can be accomplished, and we must accomplish it."

On the whole the published figures suggest that the 1946–50 plan was successful, many of the targets originally set being reached by the end of 1949. During the period of the plan, the output of coal rose by roughly 75%, that of oil and electricity by 100%, that of pig iron and ingot steel by more than 100% and that of rolled steel by nearly 150% (indicating the great emphasis placed on machinery). The figures all show the eastward trend in the main centres of output as regards coal, steel and oil, with obvious strategic implications for any would-be attacker of the Soviet Union's western frontiers. In estimating the effect of these achievements on the lives of the people it is necessary to bear in mind the growth in population, the relative neglect of consumer-goods industries, the lag in rehousing and certain marked failures on the agricultural side, particularly as regards livestock. An ambitious scheme of afforestation announced in 1948 and the plans for irrigation were directed clearly toward improving the position, by making more land available for cultivation and by eliminating the periodic droughts.

The war and the destruction of much agricultural machinery had forced some relaxation of agricultural collectivism—a development seemingly welcome to much of the peasant population. Measures were taken to restore the prewar system in full vigour, and in 1950 a campaign was started for amalgamating the kolkhozes into larger units and for assisting thereby in the ultimate Communist objective of assimilating rural and urban labour conditions.

By the beginning of 1950 a drive was started by N. S. Khrushchev, a member of the Politburo, for building of "agrotowns" (*agrogorody*); that is, barracks for proletarianized peasants working in the "large grain factories" of which Stalin dreamed in 1929. But by April 1951 all propaganda for the vision of agrotowns had ceased, and the project was temporarily abandoned because the building industry could not fulfil its part of the new program.

After World War II collectivization of agriculture was ruthlessly enforced upon the populations of the areas annexed to the Soviet Union. By Jan. 1950 the total number of kolkhozes had increased to 254,000 and that of sovkhozes to 4,540. Many smaller kolkhozes were merged to form bigger ones and by March 1951 their total number was reduced to 123,000. All this

TABLE XI.—*Industrial Production*
(In million metric tons; electricity, thousand million kw.hr.)

Product	1913*	1928	1932	1938	1940	1950 (plan)	1950 (actual)	1951
Coal and lignite	29.1	35.5	64.4	132.9	166.0	250.0	264.0	288.0
Crude petroleum	9.2	13.8†	21.4	32.2	31.0	35.4	37.6	42.1
Electric power	1.9	6.2†	16.3‡	39.6	48.3	82.0	86.7	104.0
Pig iron	4.2	3.3	6.2	14.7	15.0	19.5	19.2	21.9
Crude steel	4.2	4.3	5.9	18.0	18.3	28.4	27.6	31.6

*Russia before World War I in 1921 frontiers.   †1929.   ‡1933.

TABLE XII.—*Agricultural Production*
(In million metric tons)

Product	1913*	1922	1930	1932	1938	1940†	1950 (plan)	1950 (actual)	1951 (est.)
Grain‡	80.1	50.3	83.6	69.9	90.0	119.0	127.0	124.7	121.2
Sugar beets	10.9	1.5	14.0	6.6	16.7	21.8	26.0	24.7	27.0
Potatoes	23.3	...	...	...	65.6	84.2	115.3	...	...
Cotton	0.7	...	1.1	1.3	2.7	2.7	3.1	3.8	...

*Russia before World War I in 1921 frontiers.
†Including the annexed territories in the west.
‡Bread grain and coarse grain together. According to Soviet statistics in 1938, for example, 67% of all grain produced was bread grain (wheat 39.0, rye 24.5, buckwheat 1.1, millet 2.1 and rice 0.3). After 1933 the Soviet grain crops were determined in the field before the harvest. Detailed analysis by Naum Jasny (*The Socialized Agriculture of the USSR* [1949]) shows that from 1947 Soviet official estimates of the grain crops are around 25% higher than the actual crops.

TABLE XIII.—*Livestock*
(In million head)

Livestock	1916*	1922	1929	1933	1938	1940†	1950 (plan)	1950 (actual)	1951
Cattle	60.6	45.8	67.1	38.4	63.2	71.0	65.3	57.2	58.8
Pigs	20.9	12.1	20.7	12.1	30.6	36.1	31.2	24.1	25.7
Sheep and goats‡ . . .	121.2	91.1	146.8	50.2	102.5	108.5	121.5	99.0	107.5
Horses	35.8	24.1	34.6	16.6	17.5	20.6	15.5	13.7	14.6

*Russia before World War I in 1921 frontiers.
†Including the annexed territories in the west.
‡Number of goats (in million head) was 8.2 in 1916, 6.8 in 1922 and 13.5 in 1929.

was being done with a triple aim in mind: first, to crush the recalcitrant peasantry, which might undermine socialist agriculture by passive resistance; second, to release more manpower for industry; and, third, to increase agricultural production.

The insufficiency of the agricultural output remained the most striking weakness of the Soviet economy. Between 1940 and 1950 the gross output of Soviet industry was said to have increased by 73%; in the same period agricultural production was said to have increased only by 7%. In 1950 the total sown area was about 360,766,000 ac., which was only 22,485,000 ac. more than in 1938 (that is, before the 1939–45 annexations) and 30,000,000 ac. less than envisaged in the 1946–50 plan. The total grain production in 1950 allegedly amounted to 124,700,000 tons; that is to say, to 2,300,000 tons less than planned but to 5,700,000 more than in 1940. But if the Soviet statistics in general are not reliable, those concerning agricultural production are especially misleading. In 1933 the Soviet Union turned to estimating its grain yields and crops in the fields before harvest. The yields and crops thus established are called "biological." According to the analysis by Naum Jasny, the actual grain yields and crops in the years 1933–39 were thus exaggerated by 20%. After 1947 the only official estimates were those made, in general figures, by the central government; for grain crops they were about 25% higher than the actual crops.

The year 1951 was the last of a special three-year plan for the development of animal husbandry; but from a report published by the Central Statistical administration of the U.S.S.R. it was known that by the end of 1951 the Soviet Union had fewer cattle and fewer sheep than the prerevolutionary Russia, and fewer pigs than in the smaller territory of 1938.

Five major hydroelectric schemes were started in 1950 and 1951, including two power stations on the Volga, at Kuybyshev and Stalingrad, and one near Kakhovka on the Dnieper, with respective capacities of 2,000,000, 1,700,000 and 1,200,000 kw. In connection with these schemes work was begun on two big canals: the Volga-Don canal for ocean-going ships and the South Ukrainian canal which was to continue as a North Crimean canal through Dzhankoy to Kerch. The construction of the main Amu-darya-Krasnovodsk canal was calculated to alter fundamentally the situation in western Turkmenistan. A system of water reservoirs and smaller waterways would irrigate 3,700,000 ac. in the Ukraine and the Crimea; an area equal to that of England between the lower Volga and the Ural rivers; and about 20,000,000 ac. in Turkmenistan. The planting of forest shelter belts along the watershed between the Volga and Ural rivers, west of the Volga from Stalingrad to the Caucasus and across the Don and Donets was also started to protect southern Russian and the Ukraine against the desiccating power of the *sukhovey*, a hot, dry east wind.

For the development of the Soviet Union's industrial and agricultural production and for the numbers of its livestock, both as contrasted with prerevolutionary output and as affected by the five-year plans, *see* Tables XI, XII and XIII.   (K. SM.)

Fishing and Hunting.—The fishing industry was completely reorganized by state trusts after the revolution and achieved a high degree of efficiency. At all the main fishing centres there are collective stations which supply motorboats, equipment of all kinds, repair facilities and trained mechanics. On the eve of World War II the fishing industry employed about 220,000 fishermen and about 130,000 other workmen, the total annual catch being 1,600,000 metric tons of fish.

The Caspian sea provides rich fishing grounds and yields more than one-third the total annual Soviet catch. Ashtrakhan at the mouth of the Volga is the chief centre of the industry, whence pike, bream, perch, roach, herring and sturgeon are dispatched by the Volga waterways to the densely populated regions of European Russia. The sturgeon from which is obtained the renowned Russian black caviar is caught in the lower reaches and delta waters of the Volga.

The far east became the second most important centre of the industry in the union after the revolution. The main fishing grounds are near the mouth of the Amur river and off the shores of Kamchatka, and large catches of herring, salmon and other fish are landed. The development of these far eastern fisheries was at first delayed by a number of factors, chiefly by the great distance from the areas of consumption in the west, by lack of labour and by the acute shortage of salt (which had to be brought from the Black sea). Rich salt deposits were later discovered in northern Siberia near the Khatanga river, and salt is shipped from Kozhevnikovo (Nordvik), at the mouth of the Khatanga, to the far east via the Arctic and Pacific oceans. There are large canneries and refrigeration plants, and most of the catch is canned and some of it exported.

The northern fishing industry is centered on Murmansk, which has a large trawl-fishing station and also important canning and refrigeration plant. Cod and herring are the main catch. Archangel and Kandalaksha are also important centres, both possessing large canneries. The rivers and seas of the Soviet Union abound in fish, and fishing is a supplementary occupation in many regions, particularly in the Black sea, the Sea of Azov and at the mouths of the Ob, Yenisei and Lena rivers in Siberia. Breeding ponds for fresh-water fish were constructed near Moscow and Leningrad to supply the large urban markets.

Hunting and fur trading were reorganized by the government on a co-operative basis. At suitable points in the valleys of nearly all the rivers of Siberia fur-trading stations were established. Originally the native tribesmen had been the hunters and had traded their furs to Russian merchants. Gradually the Russians themselves became the main hunters, but the tribesmen were still active; in 1925 a congress of native hunters in the far east met to discuss better methods of hunting and barter. Trading in furs is closely supervised by the government as furs continue to be a valuable export. The furs of greatest importance in order of total value are squirrel, wolf, ermine, hare, fox, skunk, bear, marten, Siberian skunk, lynx, wildcat and sable. Seals and beavers are also hunted, but the sable, once so numerous and important, has been almost exterminated. Hunting normally continues from October to March, and closed seasons are enforced. In the far east and also in Siberia farms have been established for breeding fur-bearing animals, and in the north of Siberia a number of reindeer state farms operate.

Economic Divisions.—The U.S.S.R. may be considered as comprising the following economic areas:

1. *The northwestern area,* comprising the Karelo-Finnish S.S.R. and the Leningrad, Novgorod and Pskov regions, contains extensive forests and valuable mineral resources which were developed greatly after the revolution. The transport facilities include railways, the White sea-Baltic canal and the two well-equipped ports of Murmansk and Leningrad, which made this development possible. The timber industry and pulp, paper and cellulose manufacture are the most important industries of the area, three-quarters of which is covered by dense forests. More than 30% of the Soviet Union's paper is manufactured at Kondopoga, Leningrad, Kandalaksha and other towns in the area, which yields also about 20% of the entire Soviet timber export (and the quantity exported was by 1952 eight times greater than it had been in 1912). In Karelia about 60% of the population is engaged in the timber industry.

The area is studded with lakes into which flow rivers and streams suitable for generating hydroelectric power. A number of these rivers were harnessed, and of the 24 hydroelectric stations operating in 1939 in the Soviet Union seven were in the northwestern area. The development of industries and the working of the mineral resources was formerly restricted by a lack of coal, but the provision of adequate electric power removed this obstacle. Electric power is largely used by the factories of Leningrad, but peat fuel and brown coal mined near by are also used, as well as coal (*see* below). In the Kola peninsula near Lake Imandra rich deposits of apatite are worked, as also is nepheline, from which aluminum can be produced. Kirovsk, the centre of these mines, is a new town with a population approaching 50,000. Nickel, copper and iron are also mined, while in the east of the peninsula there are deposits of mica. In the southern industrial part of the area the towns of Tikhvin and Zvanka are important, the former as the centre of the valuable bauxite mines and the latter for the manufacture of aluminum from the bauxite. Pitkyaranta on the shore of Lake Ladoga was developed as a centre of the metallurgical industries. The deposits of iron ore in this area would, when fully exploited, make the industries of Leningrad independent of the supplies of iron ore which are hauled at heavy cost from the Ural mines.

Leningrad ranks as the third most important industrial centre in the Soviet Union, although it is almost completely lacking in raw materials. Coal, once imported from Great Britain, is hauled by rail or brought by barge from the Donbas and the Urals. Such long hauls are expensive and the industries of Leningrad began to make increasing use of local peat deposits and of hydroelectric power. Leningrad is not only the chief western port of the Soviet Union but also a great engineering centre, producing nearly 25% of the total Soviet industrial output. Machine tools, precision instruments, electrical equipment of all kinds, ships, textiles, paper and fertilizers are among the more important products of the Leningrad region.

Agriculture is restricted by the extreme climate, but much has been done to extend its northern limit. A large state farm near Kirovsk produces vegetables. Extensive use is made of the apatite fertilizers to increase the amount of land under cultivation. In Karelia the cultivated land amounted to no more than 3%, but in the Leningrad region it was more than 25%. Potatoes, oats, rye and flax are grown, and near Leningrad dairying has been developed as part of the policy to reduce the amount of foodstuffs brought long distances.

2. *The Baltic Republics.*—The Estonian republic has moderately fertile lands with rye and barley as the main crops. Dairying is the most important industry, and dairy products are sent to the Leningrad region and to Moscow in the central area. The oil shale industry, developed before World War II, is concentrated in the northeastern part of the republic. It was believed that by 1948 the oil production had reached 358,000 tons; that is, twice as much as before 1939. Tallinn (Reval) is the leading transit port of the republic and is kept open in winter by the use of icebreakers. Pärnu is a centre of woollen mills, and cotton mills are located at Narva. Lumbering is an important occupation and a certain amount of timber is exported through Tallinn and other ports.

The Latvian republic has a rich agriculture, oats, rye, barley and potatoes being the main crops. As in Estonia dairying is an important industry. Riga, Liepaja and Ventspils are the chief ports, being more or less ice-free in winter. It has been part of Soviet policy to develop the industries of Latvia and the production of agricultural machinery and of building materials has grown in importance.

The Lithuanian republic is primarily agricultural, industry having been little developed. The chief crops are wheat, oats, rye, potatoes and sugar beets, while cattle rearing, dairying and lumbering are important occupations. Vilnius, the capital of the republic, is at the junction of railways running from Moscow, Warsaw, Liepaja and Leningrad and is a market for wool, flax, timber and dairy produce. Kaunas and Klaipeda are also noteworthy, the latter being an ice-free port.

3. *The northeastern area* includes the lands within the Pechora basin in the east and the Northern Dvina basin in the west. The whole region suffers from long cold winters (with an average of 200 days of frost yearly) and short hot summers. Navigation on the four main rivers—the Onega, the Northern Dvina, the Mezen and the Pechora—begins in May and ends in September. It is during this period that logs are floated down to the ports whence they are exported or sent to mills for pulping or preparation for other uses. Dense forests cover 77% of the area and lumbering is the most important occupation. The region produces 15% of the total Soviet output of sawn timber and 33% of the timber for export. Archangel is, after Leningrad, the chief Soviet timber exporting port and an important centre of the woodworking industries. Other centres of these industries are Syktyvkar, Mezen, Vologda, Kotlas, Shenkursk, Ukhta and Vorkuta. The tundra zone in the northeast occupies about 20% of the region. Apart from reindeer farms, of which there are several, fishing is the main occupation, and Naryan-Mar at the mouth of the Pechora river is the chief fishing centre in the east. Only 3% of the region is under cultivation, and agriculture tends to be concentrated in the southwest where the climate is slightly less severe. The chief crops are rye, oats, flax and hay, the latter serving as fodder for dairy cattle.

The northwestern section, with Archangel as its centre, is the most important part of the area and contains 95% of the population. In addition to numerous sawmills, it contains pulp, paper and wood chemical industries. The tanning and dressing of hides and the construction of small ships are also carried on. Fish canning and salting are important, salt being obtained from plentiful deposits on the White sea coast to the west of Archangel. Electricity for these industries is generated locally. Coal is either imported by sea from Spitsbergen or transported by railway from the Vorkuta basin to Kotlas. The area is also served by the Archangel-Vologda railway and by another line running from Kotlas to Kirov (Vyatka).

4. *The western area,* bordered in the west until 1939 by Poland and Latvia and in the east by the central area, comprises Byelorussia and the Russian western regions of Smolensk, Bryansk and Velikiye Luki. Forestry is an important occupation in this region, although about two-thirds of the forest lands have been cleared for agriculture. The comparatively small forests remaining have the economic advantage of being close to markets and the even greater advantage of growing varieties of timber not found in the vast forest expanses farther to the north. Agriculture is a valuable industry in this area, and the land under cultivation was increased from 6,200,000 ac. in 1913 to 10,000,000 ac. in 1937. On the whole the soil is poor, but through the extensive use of chemical fertilizers and through the mechanization of agriculture the yield per acre was increased. Large crops of hay, grass, potatoes, oats and barley are grown as fodder for the expanding dairying and cattle and pig breeding industries. Hemp and flax are grown extensively and the area provides about 30% of the raw materials for the whole Soviet linen industry.

The industries of the area are numerous and are mainly centred on Minsk, Bryansk, Smolensk, Vitebsk and Gomel. After the revolution the industrial output of these centres increased greatly; the volume of manufactured goods produced in the Byelorussian factories, for example, was by 1939 about 20 times greater than in 1913. The industries include important linen mills as well as the production of alcohol, starch, treacle and acetone from potatoes and the manufacture of shoes, boots, matches, textiles and dairy products. The paper and cellulose mills at Bobruisk are among the largest in the Soviet Union. At Orsha, another important textile-manufacturing centre, a dam was planned to raise the level of the Dnieper river and allow river steamers to dock in Smolensk. In addition to its historical significance as one of the old Russian merchant towns, Smolensk is an important transport and textile centre with one of the largest Soviet linen mills. In the south Bryansk contains the largest locomotive and rolling stock works in the Soviet Union, as well as cement and glass works and sawmills.

The western area has no rich mineral resources, although valuable phosphate deposits are worked at several points in the eastern part. Some brown coal is mined near Sukhinichi, at the southwestern corner of the Moscow coal basin. Electricity is generated for the various industries by regional power stations which make use of the large quantities of peat found throughout the region. The power stations at Bryansk, Osinovsk, Minsk and Gomel burn peat fuel exclusively.

Western Byelorussia, annexed by the U.S.S.R. in Nov. 1939, is little developed and sparsely populated. It has a damp climate and poor soils. In the north, some rye and potatoes are grown and pig breeding is of importance. In the south, marsh and forest cover large areas and agriculture is restricted. Dairy farming is carried on where possible, and oats, rye and flax are sown. Much of the southern part of this area, extending into the western Ukraine, is covered by the Pripet marshes, broken only by sandy patches and by pine forests. Marsh and bog account for about 5,000,000 ac. of land in the Byelorussian republic.

5. *The central area* includes Moscow, Vladimir, Ivanovo, Kalinin (Tver), Yaroslavl, Kostroma, Ryazan, Kaluga, Tula, Tambov, Orel, Kursk, Voronezh and Rostov regions. It is a densely populated area with more than 28,000,000 inhabitants by 1939, and is for historical, geographical and economic reasons the heart of the Soviet Union. Moscow, the capital, is the centre of an industrial area which is responsible for one-seventh of the total Soviet industrial output. The growth of the city has been striking, its population having increased from 1,618,000 in 1917 to 4,137,018 inhabitants in 1939.

The area is divided by the river Oka into the northern part which is predominantly industrial and the southern part which is predominantly agricultural. The distribution of population illustrates this division. According to the 1939 census, 50% of the population of the Moscow region and 30% of that of the Ivanovo and Yaroslavl region was urban; in the Voronezh region 11.5% and in the Orel and Kursk regions only 8.5% of the population was urban. Agriculture is nevertheless important in the north, developed to supply vegetables and, by means of an expanding dairying industry, dairy products to the towns. Potatoes comprise more than 40% of the crop of the Rostov-Yaroslavl region and a large proportion of the crop in the Moscow region. Fodder crops for dairy cattle are widely sown. In the south, where the soils are more fertile and the climate milder, grain is a more important crop and potatoes are grown primarily as fodder for the pig-breeding industry. The Black Earth area to the south of the Oka river is extremely fertile, and the number of crops was increased to include sugar beets, hemp, potatoes, tobacco and sunflowers. A large part of this area has been devoted to fodder crops for pigs, poultry and cattle. The Kursk region became the second most important source of sugar in the Soviet Union.

Moscow and the central industrial area date from prerevolutionary Russia, when the area produced nearly half the industrial output of the whole country. The industries in this area have continued to expand, and many new ones were added, but because of the Soviet policy of developing industry throughout the country the central area no longer contributes so large a proportion of the total industrial output of the country. Few of the raw materials required are available locally, and the bulk of the raw materials has always had to be brought from other parts of the country, even coal being brought from the Donbas. Under the Soviet government the large deposits of brown coal in the Moscow basin have been mined, and by 1938 the annual output of brown coal from this area had reached 7,800,000 tons. Peat has also been extensively used as fuel, particularly in the large electric power stations at Yaroslavl, Orekhovo-Zuyevo, Ivanovo and Shatura, while brown coal is used almost exclusively by the power stations at Kashira and Stalinogorsk. By 1939 two-thirds of the fuel consumed by industry and the electric power stations of the central area were produced locally. Power for the factories of the region is largely supplied by the numerous electric power stations which are joined in a great grid system covering such centres as Tula, Kalinin, Yaroslavl, Ivanovo and Gorki (Nijni-Novgorod).

Iron ore has been mined at Tula since Peter the Great began exploiting these rich deposits early in the 18th century. Tula and also Kursk and Lipetsk have continued to be important sources of iron ore for the central industries, but large quantities of scrap iron and iron ore are still brought from the Ukraine. The heavy industries of the Moscow region produce motor vehicles and also printing, textile, agricultural, electrical and transport machinery, as well as machine tools, lathes and ball bearings. Moscow has always been important as a textile-producing centre, supplying much of the Soviet Union with cotton, woollen, silk and linen fabrics. The Soviet policy of opening new mills near to the sources of raw materials in central Asia, Siberia and Transcaucasia largely satisfied local consumption with the result that the Moscow mills are able to concentrate more on the production of special industrial fabrics and high-grade cloths. The development of the chemical industry is noteworthy in the Moscow region and also at Voskresensk, Stalinogorsk and Dzerzhinsk. Another important centre of cotton and linen mills is Ivanovo, which produces about 40% of the total Soviet cotton fabric output and has a number of supporting industries producing dyes, starch and chemicals. Kalinin is also the centre of a number of important cotton and, more particularly, linen mills, and the Kalinin region is responsible for a large proportion of the linen fabrics produced in the Soviet Union. Kalinin is further of importance as a centre of heavy industry; its plants produce 16% of the freight cars and 28% of the coaches for the Soviet railways. Another centre of heavy industry, specializing in the production of locomotives and rolling stock, is located at Kolomna. Other noteworthy industrial centres are Yaroslavl, specializing in the manufacture of synthetic rubber, machinery and motor vehicles; Rybinsk, producing printing machinery; and Voronezh, producing agricultural and textile machinery. The synthetic rubber industry, using potatoes as raw materials, has plants at Yefremov, Kursk, Tambov and Voronezh, and at Yaroslavl the plant manufacturing rubber tires for vehicles has an annual output of about 8,000,000 motor tires. The communications of the central area are the most highly developed in the Soviet Union.

6. *The upper Volga area* comprises the area to the south of the northern areas which is drained by the upper Volga and its tributaries the Sviyaga, Kama, Vyatka, Sura and Vetluga. A large part of this region is covered by forests, and logs are floated by river to the Moscow region, the treeless steppelands and the Don basin. Sawmills located at points along the rivers prepare such of the timber as is required for local industries. Near Gorki the Balakhna paper mills are of considerable importance. Paper, cellulose and woodworking plants have also been established at the mouth of the Vetluga river in the Marii A.S.S.R. and at Shumalin in the Chuvash A.S.S.R. In the southwest of the latter republic oak and other deciduous trees provide timber for the furniture industry. The climate and poor soils of the region restrict agriculture. Potatoes, flax, rye and oats are the main crops. Pigs, cattle and poultry are also reared. A number of industries dependent on materials produced in the Volga lands are carried on. At Bogorodsk, for instance, tanning and the manufacture of boots and shoes, as well as the flax and hemp industries, make use of locally produced materials. At Kirov (Vyatka) sheepskins are prepared and sheepskin coats are made. In the vicinity of Pavlovo woodwork and metalwork are carried on by handicraft artels.

Gorki, formerly Nijni-Novgorod, has been an important centre of trade and communications throughout Russia's history. After the revolution Gorki also was developed as a centre of heavy industry. Motor vehicles, tractors, diesel engines, aeroplane engines, barges and river steamers are its main manufactures. The iron ore required for these industries has had to be brought over long distances from the Donbas or from the Urals, but local deposits of iron ore are being worked near Murom on the Oka river and also to the north of Omutninsk.

7. *The Ural area* (*with Bashkir A.S.S.R.*) includes northern country, between the rivers Pechora and Ob, that naturally resembles other lands in the far north of the Soviet Union both in climate and in the occupations of the people. The long cold winters prevent utilization of the land, so that fur hunting, fishing and lumbering are the main activities. The central and southern parts, similar to the neighbouring lands of the Volga and western Siberian areas, were long undeveloped and so not of great economic importance. In the 20th century, however, with the full appreciation and exploitation of the fabulous mineral wealth of the Urals, this country became one of the most valuable of Soviet industrial areas.

The iron ore deposits are virtually inexhaustible. Whole mountains such as Mt. Vysokaya and Mt. Magnitnaya are composed of magnetite ore, the latter mountain having ore with an iron content of 60% and with total deposits amounting to 450,000,000 tons. Rich deposits of nickel, manganese, copper, zinc, wolfram, lead, silver, platinum, bauxite, dolomite and other minerals are also located in the Ural area. Some coal is mined at Kizel, Yergoshino and Chelyabinsk, but deposits are small and coal is brought from Karaganda in Kazakhstan. In fact, the Urals lack fuel resources; but oil has been found and the claim made that the new oil fields would be developed into a second Baku.

Soviet industrial policy joined the Urals in a great industrial enterprise with the Kuznetsk basin in the east (from which coking coal is exchanged for iron ore) and with Karaganda (whence coal is sent). Magnitogorsk, a new city with a population in 1939 of 145,870, was built during the first and second five-year plans and is the centre of a great industrial combine covering 27 sq.mi. It has vast machine tool and machine manufacturing works which make use of the steel supplied by the mills and blast furnaces of Mt. Magnitnaya. Chelyabinsk is another important centre of heavy industry, with an electric power station and one of the largest tractor-producing works in the Soviet Union. Other noteworthy industrial towns are Zlatoust, Bakal, Byeloretsk and Karabash.

Sverdlovsk to the north of Magnitogorsk is the centre of another area of heavy industry. Copper is mined and refined at several points, notably Krasnouralsk, Kirovograd and Revda, while high-grade steel and alloys are produced at these and other towns. Machinery of all kinds, machine tools and equipment for steel mills and blast furnaces are manufactured at Sverdlovsk and other towns, while Nizhni Tagil possesses one of the largest factories in the U.S.S.R. producing rolling stock. Under the pre-World War II five-year plans new sources of bauxite were opened up in the Urals. Kamensk is the main centre of the aluminum industry, while bauxite deposits are being exploited at Serov (Nadezhdinsk) and Alapaevsk. Another industrial area is centred on Molotov (Perm) and is important for the production of fertilizers and chemicals, making use of the salt, potassium and phosphate deposits near by.

The Bashkir Autonomous Republic has been linked with the great industrial combines of the Urals. Manganese, chrome, iron ore, copper and gold are mined, and the oil industry has been rapidly developed. Oil from Ishimbay and Tuymaza is sent to the cracking plant at Ufa, which is also a valuable industrial centre producing machinery, barges, river steamers and rolling stock.

8. *The middle Volga area* includes the Ulianovsk, Penza and Saratov regions and the Tatar A.S.S.R. It is predominantly an agricultural area, although industry has been developed considerably since the revolution. Agriculture flourishes to a greater extent in the lands on the west bank of the Volga river than in those on the east bank, thanks mainly to the Volga heights, which rise on the west bank to an altitude of between 600 and 1,200 ft. and secure a good rainfall for the area. This plateau also possesses fertile soils suitable for agriculture. The main occupations are the rearing of dairy cattle, poultry and pigs, while crops include sugar beets, potatoes, flax and hemp. The encouragement of intensive mixed farming led to great increases in the yields of food products. On the east bank the soils are poor, the rainfall inadequate and droughts frequent. Wheat is the main crop, and, as irrigation has been developed, agriculture mechanized and drought-resisting seed sown, it has been possible to increase the acreage cultivated. These lands are still, however, mainly pastoral. Sheep and cattle are reared for their wool and meat.

The industries of this area are of late growth. Paper, woodworking and wood chemical works of considerable size are located at Kondopobsk and at other points on the river and depend on the timber floated downstream from the northern forests. Leather is tanned and manufactured into boots and shoes, while wool is used in local factories to produce textiles and clothing. Kuybyshev is the chief centre of the middle Volga area and not only produces cement in great quantities but also has metal industries utilizing nickel, copper, chrome and iron brought from the Urals. Kazan, the administrative centre of the Tatar Autonomous Republic, is the other important industrial centre, producing chemicals, wood products, machinery and river steamers.

Electric power, on which the industries mainly depend, is transmitted on a grid system and supplies such industrial centres as the woollen and clothing factories at Penza and Ulianovsk and the metal industries at Kuybyshev. Deposits of combustible shale at Kashpir to the southeast of Kuybyshev and at Undori to the north of Ulianovsk provide the fuel for generating electricity. Peat as well as Donbas coal and Baku oil are also used as fuel. Two powerful hydroelectric power stations were under construction at Kuybyshev in the early 1950s, to provide power for the whole region.

9. *The Ukraine and Moldavia.*—The Ukraine is one of the richest and most densely populated areas of the Soviet Union. The population in 1939 was 30,960,221 (in 1946 it was estimated at 40,548,310),

representing 20% of the population of the Soviet Union although the republic occupied only 2% of its total area. The wealth of the Ukraine is both agricultural and industrial. By 1939 about 60% of the land (63,000,000 ac.) was devoted to agriculture, which was highly mechanized. In 1937 the Ukraine was responsible for 72% of the sugar beets, 32% of the barley, 24% of the maize and 22% of the wheat produced in the Soviet Union. The republic is also rich in mineral deposits. The most productive coal mines in the U.S.S.R. are in the Don basin, the output of which increased between 1913 and 1938 from 23,000,000 tons to 81,000,000 tons, thus yielding 62% of the total Soviet coal output in 1938. Vast deposits of iron are located at Krivoi Rog. The powerful hydroelectric station opened on the Dnieper river in 1932 supplements coal as the source of power for local industries.

In addition to its industrial and agricultural wealth the Ukraine has a highly developed system of communications. The Dnieper and its tributaries provide a useful network of waterways for local transport. The Dnieper dam, by raising the level of the water at the Zaporozhe rapids, made the river itself navigable. The object of the great Dnieper plan was to link the Dnieper with the Oka and Volga rivers so that barges of considerable size would be able to navigate these waterways. The railway network covering the Ukraine is probably the most effective in the Soviet Union and amounted in 1938 to nearly one-third of the total railways in the U.S.S.R. Sugar, coal, grain and salt are carried to various parts of the country by rail and water, principally to Moscow and to the other important industrial towns in the north.

The Ukraine falls into three natural divisions: (1) In the northern region the soil is sandy and the natural vegetation a mixture of deciduous and coniferous trees. Dairying is the main occupation, and agriculture is primarily devoted to producing fodder crops; in the northwest the cultivation of hemp is of particular importance and second only to dairying. (2) The forest steppe zone, where the climate is warmer, rainfall more plentiful and the sandy soils are replaced by black soils, has a far greater variety of crops. Sugar beets and wheat are the most important and, as elsewhere, are grown in rotation; rye, barley and oats are also cultivated. Pig breeding and intensive cattle rearing are important, and the waste products of the sugar beet are used as fodder, although some fodder crops are grown. More than 20% of the pigs in the Soviet Union were in 1937 reared in the Ukraine. On the right bank of the Dnieper fruitgrowing is one of the main occupations. (3) The southern steppe is primarily a wheat-growing region. On the left bank of the Dnieper, where rainfall is not plentiful, spring wheat, maize and sunflowers are the chief crops, while on the right bank sugar beets, wheat and pig breeding are most important. Fruit, particularly grapes and peaches, is grown in the lower Dnieper valley. The valleys of the Donets heights form a separate region of dairy farming and fruitgrowing. The area below the great Dnieper dam in the bend of the river is particularly noteworthy; by making use of the abundant hydroelectric power to pump water, a vast area which suffers from inadequate rainfall has been irrigated so as to allow intensive cultivation. Dairy farming is important and cotton, rice, fruit and vegetables are grown in large quantities.

The four chief industrial centres in the Ukraine are the Donbas basin, Krivoi Rog, the new industrial region on the Dnieper and Kharkov. In the Donbas basin the main industrial cities are Voroshilovgrad, Voroshilovsk and Stalino, specializing in the production of locomotives. Kramatorsk and Gorlovka, both towns constructed under the prewar five-year plans, specialize in the production of machinery for the metallurgical and mining industries. Slavyansk and Lubichansk are the main centres of the chemical industry which makes use of the by-products of the heavy industries.

Krivoi Rog is the centre of the iron ore district and was responsible for two-thirds of the total Soviet output of 28,000,000 tons of iron ore in 1940. The industrial region centred on the Dnieper hydroelectric station produces high-grade steels, agricultural and mining machinery, machine tools, tractors, ball bearings, steel alloys, aluminum and chemicals. These industries are carried on chiefly at Zaporozhe, a town constructed under the five-year plans, at Dnepropetrovsk and Dneprodzerzhinsk. Kharkov, lying to the north of these industrial towns, is noteworthy as a railway junction and as the third most important engineering centre in the Soviet Union. Locomotives and tractors, mining and agricultural machinery and machine tools are produced as well as certain food products and textiles. Kiev, the capital of the Ukrainian republic and the third largest city in the Soviet Union, is an important industrial centre, although less important than Kharkov. Kiev has a number of valuable light industries producing leather, footwear, textiles, some machinery and also tramcars, river steamers and barges.

The Ukraine has a number of ports on the Black sea, from which the bulk of Soviet exports are shipped. Odessa, Kherson and Nikolayev are the most important. Odessa, in addition to being the largest port on the Black sea, is an industrial centre where machinery and chemicals are manufactured and a number of light industries located.

The Moldavian S.S.R. lies to the southwest of the Ukraine, of which it forms a continuation. Wheat, maize and potatoes are the chief crops, and on the slopes of the Dniester valley various fruits, particularly grapes, as well as tobacco are cultivated. Bessarabia, which was annexed by the Soviet government from Rumania in 1940, was almost wholly incorporated in the Moldavian republic. It is a fertile area

where good crops of maize, wheat and tobacco are gathered and various fruits are grown.

The Crimean peninsula is for the most part flat steppe. The rainfall is poor and agriculture depends mainly on artesian water. Wheat, barley and tobacco are the main crops, but cotton and fruit are also grown. Oil and valuable deposits of iron ore, the second largest in the Soviet Union, are found in the Kerch peninsula and are actively exploited.

Volhynia, Podolia and eastern Galicia, annexed by the Soviet government in Sept. 1939 and incorporated in the Ukrainian republic, contain extremely fertile black soil lands. The Podolian plateau and the hilly country of Volhynia are particularly fertile. Pigs and horses are reared and wheat, sugar beets and hops grown. The borderlands between the plateau and the Carpathian mountains are forested and the timber industry is important. Some petroleum deposits are exploited in this area. Between Lvov and the Dniester the plateau land, sometimes known as the "Opolye," has rich soils, and as much as 75% of the area is cultivated, the remainder being covered by deciduous forests. Flax, rye and wheat are the chief crops and the industries are concerned with dairy products, sugar beets and timber. A further region of deciduous forests, including oak, birch and beech, which provide valuable timber, is found between the Dniester and the outliers of the Carpathians. Between the Pruth and the Dniester rivers the fertile black earth lands yield rich crops of maize, tobacco, wheat and rye, and such fruits as cherries, grapes, plums, apples and pears are cultivated. Lvov, with a population estimated at about 240,000 in the 1950s, is the largest town and an important commercial centre on the route from Cracow to Kiev. Its main occupations are mining, metallurgy, woodworking and the manufacture of textiles, chemicals and paper.

10. *The lower Volga area* includes the Saratov, Stalingrad and Astrakhan provinces and part of the east of north Caucasian lands. This area is subarid, and the soils vary from the black soils in the northwest to the salt light-brown clays and sands of the semidesert and to the salt desert near the Caspian sea. Agriculture in the region is concentrated in the northwest and in the Volga delta.

The black soils and the good rainfall in the northwest make it a very fertile district. Rye, oats, potatoes, sugar beets and vegetables are the main crops. Wheat and sunflowers are cultivated farther to the south, while near the cities dairy farming, pig breeding and market gardening are important. The steppes between Saratov and Stalingrad have rich soils, but lack rain. The greater part of this area is sown with wheat and some tobacco is grown. The Volga delta is an extremely fertile area which benefits from the spring floods of the river. Irrigation extended the area under cultivation northward, and the lands between Stalingrad and the Caspian sea form one of the most important areas of intensive cultivation in the Soviet Union. Fruits of all kinds are grown as well as cotton and sesame.

Fishing is one of the most important industries of the area, which produces more than one-third of the total annual Soviet catch. Fish is canned or salted and sent to the more densely populated parts of European Russia. Salt for the industry is obtained from lakes Baskunchak and Elton, which produce about 25% of the total Soviet requirements of salt. The canning of fruit, vegetables and meat has become an important occupation, and the lower Volga area is one of the leading food-producing areas in the Soviet Union. Phosphate deposits are worked in the Volga heights, and iron ore is mined to the north of Stalingrad. Other raw materials for local industries have to be brought to the region by rail or by river. Stalingrad is the industrial and economic centre of the whole lower Volga area, and both the city and its industries were restored after their destruction by the German armies in 1942. Stalingrad has sawmills, an oil refinery and woodworking plants and is also noteworthy for its production of heavy tractors. Saratov has become a modern industrial city producing agricultural machinery and with factories engaged in the manufacture of lathes, diesel engines, ball bearings and chemicals. At Krasnoarmeysk, a new city, railway cars, river steamers and vehicle engines are produced.

The Volga river has always been the most important waterway in Russia, carrying about 40% of the country's river traffic, but the severe floods in spring and the shallows in summer and autumn have restricted its use. By means of dams on the Kama and Volga rivers it was planned to control the spring floods and to maintain a more even flow of water in summer, thus improving the navigation conditions for river transport and also making possible the irrigation of the arid lands on the east bank of the Volga and the generation of hydroelectric power for industry.

11. *The Caucasian area* falls into three natural divisions: the plains and foothills of the Caucasus mountains, the mountain ranges and Transcaucasia. The plains to the north of the Caucasus mountains are steppelands which in the west have fertile black soils and good rainfall. The chief crop is wheat; almost 10% of the wheat grown in the Soviet Union is produced there. Maize, sunflowers, cotton, jute, tobacco, fruits and vegetables are the other crops. In the east, where conditions are drier, sheep and cattle breeding is an important occupation. The industries of this area are mainly centred on Krasnodar, Rostov and Armavir and include distilling, tanning of hides, fruit and vegetable canning, tobacco manufacturing and flour milling. Heavy industry has grown in importance with the increase in output of oil.

The oil deposits are located near Grozny and Maikop, Krasnodar and Neftegorsk and at Makhachkala. The Grozny oil wells have the second largest output in the Soviet Union, and Grozny has become an important manufacturing centre, producing machinery and chemicals. Other important industries are the mining of lead, silver, copper and zinc near Orjonikidze (Dzaudzhikau) and also the manufacture of cement near Novorossiisk.

The Caucasus mountains have valuable forests and their oak, ash and beech are used in industry. Fertile lands in the valleys grow cotton, soybeans and good crops of fruit. Sheep and cattle graze on the mountain slopes. The Sulak and other rivers were harnessed to produce hydroelectric power, and a number of new industries were established, notably at Makhachkala and in the Derbent district.

The mountainous country of Transcaucasia supports a great variety of crops, including cotton, tobacco, maize, tea, fruits and vegetables, while dairy farming and cattle and sheep rearing are important occupations. Nearly all the Soviet tea crop comes from this area, in particular from Adzharia and the subtropical districts of Azerbaijan. The area under tea has been greatly expanded; output was 6,400 tons in 1938. Adzharia also produces more than two-thirds of the Soviet citrus fruit crop. Other important crops of this district are silk and tobacco.

Hydroelectric stations, which are numerous in the Caucasus, are the main source of power both for transport and industry. In addition, coal is mined in Georgia, and the oil wells at Baku are of considerable importance.

Transcaucasia is rich in minerals. The manganese deposits at Chiatura are among the richest in the world. Armenia has valuable copper deposits (mined and refined at Allaverdy and Kafan) and also valuable deposits of magnetite iron ore (mined at Dashkezan). Iron and steel are produced at Tbilisi and supplied to local industries.

Transcaucasia has an important textile industry. Leninakan, Kirovabad and Baku are centres of cotton milling, while silks are woven at Tbilisi, Nukha and Kutais. Tbilisi is also noteworthy for clothing manufacture and for the production of chemicals, films and vegetable oils. There are throughout Transcaucasia important centres for food processing and canning and for the treating and packing of tea and tobacco. It also has a valuable timber industry based on the great variety of deciduous and coniferous trees in the Caucasian area, particularly oak, beech, maple and chestnut.

12. *Soviet Central Asia.*—The vast area of the Kazakh S.S.R. is in the main barren desert land and the home of nomadic herdsmen. The broad area of the Irtysh valley is, however, like an oasis, being extremely fertile and producing fruits and other crops. The irrigation of some areas in the southeast of Kazakhstan has resulted in an intensive cultivation which yields rich crops of rice, cotton, fruits, tobacco and sugar beets. The Tien-shan mountains contain rich deposits of silver, gold, zinc, lead, wolfram and copper.

The development of industries in the Kazakh republic followed the exploitation of its rich deposits of coal, iron ore, nonferrous metals, oil and salt. Kazakhstan possesses about 50% of the entire nonferrous metal deposits of the Soviet Union and supplies copper, zinc and lead to the industrial centres of the Urals and of the Kuznetsk basin. The Karaganda coal basin is the third most important coal field in the Soviet Union and has an annual output of more than 4,000,000 tons. Other coal mines are at Pavlodar, Mangyshlak and near Karsakpay. The great industrial development of the republic has been accompanied by considerable improvement in its communications, particularly in the railway system which links Kazakhstan with the Urals and the Kuznetsk basin.

The southern republics of central Asia are the Turkmen, Uzbek, Tadzhik and Kirghiz. They occupy a varied area of mountains, desert and steppelands. The cultivated areas are mainly in the south, where the soil is fertile but arid. Cattle and sheep are reared, but the greater part of the population is concentrated in the irrigated lands, which occupy little more than 3% of the total area but which are intensively cultivated. Rice, cotton, fruits, raw silk and grain are the chief crops in these irrigated lands. The most noteworthy irrigation scheme is that of the Ferghana canal in the Uzbek republic which waters about 12,000 ac. Plans were adopted for extending the area of irrigation there and in other districts. Hydroelectric power is supplied by a number of stations constructed to make use of the many swiftflowing rivers in the mountainous districts. A number of coal mines are worked, particularly in the Kirghiz republic, which in 1939 had an output of 1,500,000 tons. Oil deposits are being utilized in the Ferghana valley of Uzbekistan and at Nefte Dag on the shores of the Caspian sea.

13. *The southern Siberian area* is for the greater part divided into dry steppelands, mountainous regions and coniferous forests. Development may in fact be dated from the construction of the Trans-Siberian railway. The area possesses great mineral wealth and considerable agricultural resources and has been intensively developed.

To the east the Chita region, containing fertile soils, produces good crops of wheat, oats, rye, flax and hay. The dairy industry is important. Iron, brown coal, zinc, lead, molybdenum and other mineral deposits are worked between the Shelka and Amur rivers. Ferrous and nonferrous metallurgical industries have been established at Petrovsk and in the neighbourhood of Chita. The Buriat Mongol A.S.S.R. is another area which was greatly developed under the prewar five-year

plans. At Ulan Ude (Verkhne-Udinsk) a large engineering plant has been established and the mineral wealth of the republic is being exploited. In the Irkutsk region coal, manganese and iron ore are mined and there has been considerable industrial development. Irkutsk itself has become an important industrial centre where machine tools, aircraft engines and mining machinery are manufactured, and it is the largest industrial town on the route of the Trans-Siberian railway, which connects it with the Chita region and with the Kuznetsk industrial basin.

Southwestern Siberia contains the Kuznetsk coal basin, which, making use of local deposits of iron, copper and manganese and being linked with the resources of the Urals, has become the second most important area for coal and metallurgy in the Soviet Union. The mines are well equipped, and more than 25,000,000 tons of coal were being produced annually by 1940, representing about 15% of the total Soviet coal output. The great steel industry of Stalinsk makes use of iron ore from the Magnitogorsk mines of the Urals and has an output of more than 2,000,000 tons of steel a year. Iron ore deposits are worked near Stalinsk and also at Minusinsk and Kemerovo. An important chemical industry has been developed to make use of the by-products of the coking plants. Industries producing machine tools, mining equipment, locomotives and rolling stock and agricultural and textile machinery have been established throughout the area and particularly at Novosibirsk, Leninsk, Barnaul, Prokopyevsk, Omsk and Tomsk. Communications have been developed to serve these industries, and railways were constructed in the Novosibirsk area to feed the Turkistan-Siberian railway (Turksib).

14. *The central Siberian area* lies in the basin of the middle and lower reaches of the Yenisei river, which, being navigable by river steamers and barges as far as Krasnoyarsk, has facilitated development. The mineral deposits include gold, nickel and, particularly in the Lower Tunguska and Kureyka valleys, considerable resources of coal, which are mined and sent to the industrial areas southward through Krasnoyarsk and north through Igarka. The area has rich deposits of gold, platinum and copper, and nickel is mined at Norilsk, a settlement near Dudinka. The native population depends for its livelihood on hunting, fishing and the rearing of reindeer. It has been Soviet policy to organize the reindeer industry into state farms, where more economic and scientific methods can be employed, and there are several of these farms in the central Siberian area. Fur hunting is an important occupation, and marten and sable in particular constitute a valuable export. The fishing industry has been highly developed, and collectives have been established at suitable points along the rivers and along the coast to supply equipment and handle the catch. Ust Yeniseisk has a refrigeration and canning plant, and along the lower reaches of the Yenisei fish is cured for winter food and also sent to the industrial areas in the south.

Within reach of the Yenisei and its tributaries the lumber industry is important. Logs are floated down to Igarka and other points. Igarka has special importance as the main port of the northern sea route; by 1939 its population had grown to 20,000 inhabitants. It has sawmills, but in summer the timber assembled there is shipped to other centres of the timber industry. As shipping must be clear of the Arctic ocean by October, the loading must be done in September-October. This brief period is one of intense activity, and during the winter logs are sawed and stacked ready for loading in summer. Interesting experiments have been made in growing grain and vegetables in the region of Igarka and of other towns; some oats, barley, vegetables and hothouse tomatoes have been produced. Poultry, pigs and dairy cattle are reared in small numbers under special conditions. It is necessary, however, to transport flour and other supplies to Igarka by sea in summer.

Aviation has proved of great value in the development of the vast frozen expanses to the north. Aircraft regularly fly on routes linking Igarka with Krasnoyarsk, which is on the established routes to the far east and to European Russia.

15. *The northern Siberian area*, bitterly cold, has neither roads nor railways and is almost uninhabited. The greater part of the region lies in the basin of the Ob river, which is navigable only by small boats. The lack of mineral wealth and the difficulties of lumbering in the swampy land restrict the small native population to hunting, fishing and reindeer rearing for a livelihood.

16. *The Yakut A.S.S.R. and the northeastern Siberian area* consist of vast plateau lands including the basins of the Lena, Yana, Indigirka and Kolyma rivers. The rivers are of particular importance; in an area lacking railways and roads they provide the only means of communication. Except in the tundra zone of the far north the whole region is covered with dense forests predominantly of pine (although in the south the variety of trees is greater and includes alder, aspen and larch). The whole area is sparsely populated and the main occupations are fishing, fur hunting and reindeer breeding. At the mouth of the Lena there are deposits of silver, lead and coal; in the Yana valley silver and lead mines are worked; and in the mountains of the upper Kolyma a gold-mining industry has been developed. Verkhoyansk, on the right bank of the Yana, is the chief trading post of the area; the furs and mammoth ivory collected there are sent by sledge to Yakutsk in winter.

The plains and valleys of the middle reaches of the Lena and its tributaries are cultivated in parts; more than 250,000 ac. were sown to barley, oats, rye and wheat in 1936. A certain industrial development has been achieved in the Lena coal basin, although the output of coal is small. Iron ore deposits are worked in the Vilyuy and Lena valleys, and gold is also mined. Plans were made to develop the lumbering industry, and the utilization of the enormous timber resources of the area was attempted on a small scale.

17. *The far eastern area*, comprising the basins of the Amur, Ussuri and Sungari rivers, has, in the Trans-Siberian railway and local lines and in its numerous waterways, good communications with southern Siberia and with the Pacific coast, where it is served by Vladivostok, the main Soviet port on the Pacific ocean. Much of the area is cultivated, and the rich mineral and timber resources have been greatly developed. Coal and lead are mined in the Zeya valley and in the Bureya valley, while the plateau between the two valleys has valuable deposits of gold. At Khabarovsk oil and gasoline refineries and also an iron and steel industry have been established. Blagoveshchensk, a highly industrialized town, has important engineering works. The population of the region is in the main concentrated in agricultural and industrial areas where the main occupations are coal mining, lumbering and woodworking, metallurgy, leather tanning and dairying. The far eastern fisheries are extremely important to the economy of the area and of the Soviet Union itself, for they produce nearly 25% of the total Soviet catch. Vladivostok and Nikolayevsk-na-Amure, the two chief centres of the industry, have large canning factories from which fish is exported or sent to the more densely populated areas in the west. (I. Gy.)

Foreign Trade.—The management of foreign trade, a state monopoly, is in the hands of the Soviet government. Not yet a fully developed country, the Soviet Union has little to export. Early in the 1930s, when it was necessary to pay for machinery and heavy equipment imported from the United States and from Germany and other industrialized countries of Europe, the Soviet Union exported oil and oil products, but with the progress of industrialization the home consumption of oil increased and the exportable surplus was negligible. Other main items of export were timber, grain, furs, flax and caviar. From its great forest wealth the Soviet Union theoretically could export any quantity of timber, but in fact the home market was acutely in need of timber, the shortage being caused by a lack of essential machinery, of skilled lumberjacks and of transport. Even in 1930, when they reached their highest level, the value of Soviet exports amounted only to 3.5% of that of the total Soviet production; in 1938 the proportion fell to 0.8%.

Soviet imports were strictly limited to raw materials and machinery necessary to equip expanding industry. Items described as machinery, apparatus and parts, nonferrous metals and goods, iron and steel goods and electrical equipment formed 34.7% of imports in 1929, then 66.1% in 1933 and 57.0% in 1938.

Among the trading partners of the U.S.S.R., Germany held the predominant part up to 1933; in that year it supplied 42.5% of Soviet imports and took 17.3% of Soviet exports. In 1938 the chief suppliers were the United States (28.5%) and Great Britain (16.9%). Great Britain was also the best customer, taking 17.6% of Soviet exports in 1933, then 32.7% in 1937 and 28.2% in 1938. (*See* Table XIV.)

TABLE XIV.—*Foreign Trade, 1909–13 and between World Wars I and II*
(In million roubles)

Item	1909–13	1921	1924	1930	1938
Export	6,514	89	1,476	4,539	1,332
Import	4,994	923	1,139	4,637	1,423

The average for 1909–13 and the figures for 1921 and 1924 in 1913 prices; figures for 1930 and 1938 in current roubles.
Source: I. Zhlobin in *The Finances of the U.S.S.R. in the Years 1917–1947* (Moscow, 1947).

After World War II the Soviet Union was able to exploit the economic resources of its satellites, buying from them at much cheaper rates and selling to them at much higher rates than the world market prices. The Soviet government declared the statistics of foreign trade a state secret, presumably because publication of the value and weight of foreign trade would inform the world at large about Soviet home shortages and would bring to the knowledge of the Soviet people the sales of grain to foreign markets, when they themselves were short of food, and of timber in spite of acute domestic need for housing; as also such data would expose to the satellite nations the fact that their economies were being exploited. (*See* Table XV.)

A. I. Mikoyan, deputy prime minister and the member of the Politburo in charge of foreign trade, wrote in *Pravda* on Dec. 21, 1949, that the volume of Soviet trade with the capitalist countries had decreased to one-third of the prewar total; on the other hand, trade

TABLE XVI.—*Budgets*
(In thousand million roubles)

with the people's democracies had grown, on an unprecedented scale, to two-thirds of that total. In 1938 the United States and ten countries of western Europe took 64% of Soviet exports and supplied

TABLE XV.—*Foreign Trade with Western Europe, 1938 and 1948–51**
(In million U.S. dollars)

Item	1938	1948	1949	1950	1951
Imports from the U.S.S.R.	265	223	120	138	224
Exports to the U.S.S.R.	174	113	140	110	87

*Austria, Belgium-Luxembourg, Denmark, France, western Germany, Italy, Norway, the Netherlands, Sweden, Switzerland, Turkey and the United Kingdom.
Source: *Economic Bulletin for Europe*, vol. 3, no. 2 (Geneva, Oct. 1951).

67% of Soviet imports; Soviet trade with the countries of eastern Europe was negligible. In 1949 the Soviet Union took only 0.6% of British exports and supplied 0.7% of British imports; in the same year 0.66% of U.S. imports came from the Soviet Union, which received only 0.07% of U.S. exports. (K. Sm.)

Finances.—The completely different economic organization of the Soviet Union makes the national budget distinct in character and far wider in scope than the budgets of countries where private enterprise prevails. The financing of industry, transport, commerce and agriculture, which is arranged mainly through private channels in noncommunist countries, is an item in the Soviet budget. The character of revenue is equally distinctive and unusual by comparison with the revenue of western countries. (*See* Table XVI.)

Revenue in 1950, for example, derived from the following sources: turnover tax, 236,069,000,000 roubles; profit tax, 40,374,000,000 roubles; direct taxes, 35,771,000,000 roubles; state loans, 31,013,000,000 roubles; unspecified income, 78,867,000,000 roubles. It will be noted that the biggest item of revenue, accounting for nearly 55% of the total revenue, was the turnover tax, levied on the proceeds of retail trade in grain, alcohol, oil, sugar, meat, cotton tissues, petroleum and other commodities.

Expenditure in 1950 was grouped under the following headings: grants to national economy, 157,312,000,000 roubles; social and cultural, 116,818,000,000 roubles; defense, 82,867,000,000 roubles; state administration, 13,848,000,000 roubles; unspecified, 41,820,000,000 roubles. Defense expenditure in 1950 amounted allegedly to about 21% of the total expenditure, which may be compared with 32.5% expended on defense in the war budget of 1940. It is not possible, however, to estimate even approximately what percentage of the Soviet national income this represents, since real Soviet expenditure on defense is not confined to the ministries of war and navy but is distributed among the budgets of many other ministries.

Inflation developed in the Soviet Union during World War II but was drastically arrested by a decree of Dec. 14, 1947, whereby 10 roubles of the old currency in cash were exchanged for 1 new rouble. Control of consumer prices and of wages together with the application of the turnover tax can be counted upon to regulate actual demands in accordance with the availability of consumer goods. The practically compulsory state loans serve to absorb surplus purchasing power. A further weapon against inflation was the policy of distributing the benefits of increased productivity by lower prices rather than by higher wages.

The official rate of exchange of the rouble was revised by a decree of March 1, 1950. This decree "raised" the value of the rouble to the high and fictitious rate of 4.00 to the U.S. dollar and of 11.20 to the pound sterling.

The Statistical office of the United Nations calculated that the national income in the Soviet Union on a per capita basis amounted in 1949 to $308 as compared with $1,453 in the United States and $778 in the United Kingdom. (I. Gy.)

BIBLIOGRAPHY.—W. Leimbach, *Die Sowjetunion: Natur, Volk und Wirtschaft* (Stuttgart, 1950). On population: F. Lorimer, *The Population of the Soviet Union: History and Prospects* (1946); F. W. Notestein and others, *The Future Population of Europe and the Soviet Union: Population Projections, 1940–1970* (1944). On government and administration: Barrington Moore, Jr., *Soviet Politics—The Dilemma of Power* (1950); W. Duranty, *Stalin & Co.: The Politburo* (1949); H. J. Berman, *Justice in Russia* (Oxford, 1951); I. Deutscher, *Soviet Trade Unions* (London, 1950). On religion: G. R. Timasheff, *Religion in Soviet Union 1917–1942* (London, 1943); N. Yarushevich and others, *The Truth about Religion in Russia* (Moscow, 1942). On defense: D. Fedotoff White, *The Growth of the Red Army* (1944); A. Guillaume, *La Guerre germano-soviétique* (Paris, 1949); M. Mitchell, *The Maritime History of Russia, 848–1948* (1949); Asher Lee, *The Soviet Air Force* (1952). On economics and finance: H. Schwartz, *Russia's Soviet Economy* (1950); S. S. Balzak, V. E. Vasyutin and Y. G. Feigin, *Economic Geography of the U.S.S.R.* (1949); Sir John Maynard, *The Russian Peasant, and Other Studies* (London, 1942); M. H. Dobb, *Soviet Economic Development since 1917* (1948); W. H. Chamberlin, *Russia's Iron Age* (1934); N. A. Voznesensky, *Soviet Economy during the Second World War* (1949).

TABLE XVI.—*Budgets*
(In thousand million roubles)

Item	1928	1933	1938	1940	1946	1947	1948	1949	1950	1951	1952*
Revenue	8.8	46.4	127.5	180.2	322.7	385.2	408.4	436.9	422.8	468.0	508.8
Expenditure	8.7	42.1	124.0	174.4	304.1	361.2	368.8	412.3	413.3	441.3	476.9

*Estimate.

RUSSIA, CAMPAIGN IN NORTH. The campaign in north Russia must not be regarded as an isolated incident of World War I, but as a definite part of the Allies' plan for the defeat of the Central Powers.

Allied Expeditionary Force.—The original force consisted of 150 British marines who landed at Murmansk in April 1918. They were followed by 370 more at the end of May, with a further reinforcement of infantry and machine-gunners to the number of 600 on June 23. The strength of the forces gradually grew till the maximum strengths reached were: White Russians, 20,000; British, 18,400; U.S., 5,100; French, 1,800; Italian, 1,200; Serbian, 1,000. Maj. Gen. F. C. Poole, commander in chief of the Allied forces in north Russia, arrived at Murmansk on May 24, 1918, and found that the Allies were holding the Kola peninsula with detachments at Kandalaksha. He pushed southward down the Petrograd railway, and by the end of June had secured Kem and Soroka, the point where the road to Archangel via Onega branched eastward. The ice-free port of Murmansk was thus fully protected against any possible raid by German forces in Finland. On Aug. 3 Poole occupied Archangel with a force of 1,500 men, supported by British and French warships and a force of Serbs and Russians under Col. Thornhill moving overland via Soroka and Onega. Early in Oct. 1918 Gen. Poole proceeded to England, and in November Maj. Gen. W. E. Ironside, formerly chief general staff officer in north Russia, succeeded him. The commands of Archangel and Murmansk were then made independent of one another. The question of the maintenance of the Allied forces in north Russia had been early considered by the authorities. Murmansk, being an ice-free port, could be used all year round, and the troops based upon it could be withdrawn at any time. But with Archangel the case was different. The port becomes frozen from early November till late April. It was of the utmost importance to prevent the resources of Russia becoming available to the Germans, should they be able to continue fighting throughout 1919. The decision was therefore made to remain at Archangel during the winter.

The expedition to north Russia in the summer and autumn of 1918 undoubtedly did much to complicate the plans of the Germans. There is definite evidence that the German military authorities were unable to continue the transference of troops from east to west in the final stages of the World War of 1914–18, despite the urgent demands of Hindenburg and Ludendorff. The original object of the expedition was therefore fully achieved.

Peculiar Difficulties of the Campaign.—The armistice in Europe came just at the closing of the White sea with ice. For the north Russian force a new campaign was beginning, and all knew that relief could not come for at least six months. The feeling that demobilization was being carried out on all other fronts had a demoralizing effect upon all ranks of the force. Furthermore, the object of the campaign was obviously no longer the same. Germany as an enemy had disappeared from the scene, and the Allied troops were never again quite clear as to the reasons for the continuance of the fighting. In their efforts to reconstruct the Eastern Front, the Allies had espoused the cause of the White Russians and had called upon the Czech ex-prisoner of war units in Siberia to march westwards to join them. It was thus that the Bolsheviks became the new adversaries of the Allies.

For the British authorities the campaign was a serious responsibility. Food, clothing and munitions had to be unified so far as possible for the simplifying of supply. The town of Archangel contained at least three times its normal population owing to the influx of refugees, and it was impossible to let the population starve. Large supplies had to be imported for this purpose.

Winter of 1918–19.—The transition stage from summer to winter proved a difficult period for the Allies. The freezing of the Dvina came unusually late in Nov. 1918 and the Allied gunboats were withdrawn too soon for wintering in Archangel. The Bolshevik gunboats were thus enabled to descend the river from their more closely situated winter quarters and bombarded the Allied positions with their long-range guns. The situation was at one time critical, British and Americans, supported by Canadian artillery, fighting desperately to maintain their positions.

At Archangel during the winter the attitude of the Allies was purely defensive, covering the mobilization and training of the new troops of the north Russian provisional government. In the Murmansk area their task was to maintain a perpetual threat towards Petrograd and to divert as much of the Bolshevik forces as possible from Archangel. Fighting continued throughout the winter in both areas at irregular intervals, the Bolsheviks growing more efficient and exerting greater and greater pressure on the Allied columns. Nevertheless all the main Archangel positions were maintained intact against the repeated attacks of a superior enemy. In the Murmansk area, Gen. Maynard's troops succeeded in seizing the northern end of Lake Onega, thus making their threat against Petrograd an effective one, and containing a considerable force of active Bolshevik forces.

Arrival of Relieving Force.—The general thaw commenced in the first week of May, and by the 12th the river was free of ice. Two relief brigades under Brig.-Gens. Grogan and Sadlier-Jackson arrived at Archangel on May 26 and June 10 respectively, and evacuation of all troops which had spent the winter in north Russia commenced at once. The old contingents were embarked in turn, the British being the last to leave. Then followed those elements of the population which had elected to leave the country. In all, some 17,000 persons were transported from north Russia in British ships. By the end of July nothing remained but the fighting troops of the relief force and a few necessary administrative services.

A gradual substitution of Russian for British troops and administration was commenced, the process being accompanied by several outbreaks of mutiny amongst the new troops. The fronts of the various columns were cleared by vigorous action on the part of Brig.-Gens. Graham and Sadlier-Jackson, ably supported by the naval flotilla under Capt. Altham. By August 10 the withdrawal of the British troops to the inner defences of Archangel commenced.

Gen. Lord Rawlinson arrived at Archangel on August 12 and approved of the plans already arranged. Withdrawal continued without a hitch, and on September 27 the last 5,000 men were embarked simultaneously from 13 different points and the evacuation of Archangel was complete. The long withdrawal in the Murmansk area was then completed under the direction of Brig.-Gen. H. C. Jackson, who had replaced Gen. Maynard on September 20 owing to the latter's illness, the last man leaving the port on October 12.

BIBLIOGRAPHY.—B. Heroys, *Lenin's Fighting Force* (1919); J. Pollock, *The Bolshevik Adventure, 1917–19* (1919); British Parliamentary Papers No. 2,246, *The Evacuation of North Russia, 1919* (1920); A. F. Kerensky, *Soviet Russia in 1919* (1920); J. Ward, *With the Die-Hards in Siberia, 1918* (1920). (W. E. I.; X.)

RUSSIAN ARCHITECTURE. Historically, Russian architecture may be divided into two principal periods: the first, from the 10th to the end of the 17th century; the second, from about 1700 to the present. This chronological division is a consequence of the revolutionary activities of Peter the Great (1689–1725), whose drastic political and social reforms, intended to bring Russia into close contact with western Europe and its civilization, broke with the traditional conservative tendencies of Russian life and in architecture caused a shift from a deeply national style to the forms of western Europe. The architecture of the pre-Christian period was almost exclusively wooden, and, mainly due to the unlimited supply of lumber, the majority of buildings remained of timber during the era immediately following Russia's conversion to Christianity in 988. Typical peculiarities of this early wooden architecture are a horizontal disposition of wall logs and steeply pitched roofs.

Christianity found a fertile soil among the tribes inhabiting the widespread territories of what was to become the Russian empire, and an intensive building of churches set in after the acceptance of the new faith. The rulers of the various feudal principalities into which Russia was divided became defenders and champions of the church, and the building of a church became the central event in the reign of each of the numerous princes who, apart from religious considerations, wished to demonstrate

BELL TOWER OF IVAN THE GREAT, MOSCOW

This graceful belfry in the Kremlin was begun in 1600 at the direction of Boris Godunov. In front is the Tsar Kolokol, largest bell in the world, broken during the fire of 1737

PLATE II

RUSSIAN ARCHITECTURE

RUSSIAN CHURCHES, 12TH–17TH CENTURY

1. Church of the Ascension, 1532, at Kolomenskoie, near Moscow
2. Church of the Intercession of the Holy Virgin, 1165, on the river Nerl near Vladimir
3. ... ment of Archangel
4. Cathedral of the Saviour of the Transfiguration, in Mirozh Monastery, 1156, at Pskov

BY COURTESY OF IGOR GRABAR

RUSSIAN SECULAR ARCHITECTURE, 18TH AND 19TH CENTURIES

1. Exchange Building, 1806–16, Leningrad
2. Pavilion of the Admiralty Building, 1806–15, Leningrad. This building was severely damaged in World War II
3. Mining Institute Building, 1806–11, Leningrad
4. Former Imperial Rumyantzev Museum, 1787, later Lenin State Public Library, Moscow
5. Colonnade and portal of the Sheremetiev Hospital, 1806, Moscow
6. Riding school of the Horse Guards, 1800–04, Leningrad
7. House of Prince V. N. Gagarin, 1817, Moscow
8. Stable on the estate of Prince Golitzin, "Kusminki," 1823, near Moscow

their power and wealth with splendour eclipsing that of predecessors and neighbours. Russian life centred in these churches; there new leaders were installed; the most important public questions were decided there; the prince kept his treasury in the church; the church was the last haven of refuge from invaders. Until the 17th century religion dominated Russian architecture which, nevertheless, was also closely connected with the fates of rulers and the geographical locations of the centres of political power. During this first period the most important schools of architecture were those of Kiev, Novgorod-Pskov, Vladimir-Suzdal and Moscow.

Early Centres.—The beginning of organized political life found Russia somewhat unified under the rule of the princes of Kiev, a city on the Dnieper river, the first capital of Christianized Russia. The Christian missionaries from the Eastern Church had brought their Byzantine culture with them, and this transplanted Byzantine art (*see* BYZANTINE AND ROMANESQUE ARCHITECTURE; BYZANTINE ART) was the starting point for the development of the new national architecture. In the different parts of Russia, Byzantine art, interpreted in different ways, developed into distinct forms. Sometimes, as in the neighbourhood of Novgorod-Pskoff (in north-western Russia), Byzantine influence is scarcely perceptible; at others it flowered into exquisite forms representing a happy combination of the two cultures, as in the Vladimir district.

The oldest church in Kiev, still existing in part, is the Dessiatinnaya church, begun in 991; it was the reproduction of a Byzantine church, rectangular in plan, with three altar-apsides. The cathedral of St. Sophia in Kiev (1017), with five apsides and crowned by 13 cupolas, is the next in age and the largest built during the first two centuries after conversion; the principal parts of this cathedral are still extant, but later additions have considerably changed its exterior.

The erection of churches in the Novgorod-Pskov district, which was to play an important part in the development of a national Russian architecture, began only a few decades later. An independent and distinctive school of architecture appeared there in the 12th century. Here Byzantine art lost its influence much quicker than in Kiev, where it was applied with only insignificant structural changes. The influence most responsible for the appearance of this deeply national art was that of the thoroughly original local wooden architecture which affected both design and construction. The two-storey cross-shaped church appeared with one-storey lateral additions. The church with only one apsis replaced the church with three apsides. In conformity with climatic conditions, the arched roof became one that sloped. The spherical cupola gave way first to the helmet-shape; then it assumed the characteristic bulb-shape, a form similar to that which had developed centuries before and spread over Asia with the influence of Buddhism. The entrance took the form of a kind of porch; the belfry appeared, first as only an opening for bells on top of the wall, but later as an independent, high tower in which bells were hung in several tiers. The Byzantine cubic form of the church was broken up into a picturesque group of buildings, reflecting, like most of the innovations, national tastes that had been educated on wooden architecture. The rich Byzantine ornamentation either disappeared completely from the austere and simple walls of Novgorod churches, or else gave way to a plainly modelled geometric pattern, accentuating here and there the picturesque smoothness of the walls. The treatment of the stucco shows a characteristic feature. The lines and contours of the architectural forms were finished freehand, and are uneven, as is the surface of the walls, which lends the buildings a singular and effective charm.

In the principalities of Vladimir and Suzdal in the Central part of Russia we find, in the 13th century, not only Byzantine influences but partly Romanesque (*see* BYZANTINE AND ROMANESQUE ARCHITECTURE) brought there from Italy. The former manifests itself in the general form of the churches, the latter mainly in their decoration. The Romanesque arched gallery on the level of the second storey of the church was introduced as a decorative element in the form of an ornament of arches. In general the archi-

tecture of Vladimir is characterized by a love for ornamentation that accentuates architectural masses. The walls of St. George in Youryev, wholly covered with ornaments of Romanesque origin, but strongly influenced by motifs of the native wood-sculpture for which Vladimir was famous, are typical. In the native wooden architecture projecting beams were carved, and the whole length of the crest of a building was sometimes ornamented by such beams projecting through. When stone became common in buildings designers drew inspiration from these forms.

Moscow.—The dominance of Moscow's architecture increased gradually with its political ascendancy. Masters from Novgorod and Pskov worked there, and the Russian national architecture reached its highest development in Moscow during the 14th and 15th centuries. The application of the motifs of the wooden architecture to stone building found its best expression in the tented church. As in the wooden, the square plan of the stone church was transformed by a system of little arches of peculiar form (*kokoshniki*) into an octagon, the basis of the tent. This turret-shaped church was frequently used during the 16th and 17th centuries; the tent was also widely applied to the roofs of belfries and towers. The basic elements of the Moscow church architecture took final form in the 16th century, and thereafter attention centred on structural ornamentation, some of which is comparable in richness to the best examples of the Florentine Renaissance. A reaction followed, characterized by pettiness of form and excessive flourishes, and sometimes erroneously regarded as the typical Russian style. One typical feature, however, is evident even in this period of decadence: the grouping of buildings in ensembles in whose composition as well as that of the individual buildings picturesque effects were produced. Many of the old monasteries, which, being surrounded by towered and crenellated walls, frequently resemble little fortresses, are interesting specimens of such ensembles.

In the majority of Russian cities of the period their central part was surrounded by strong walls with towers and battlements and sometimes by embankments and water-filled moats. This was called the Kremlin. It contained the ducal palace, government buildings, houses for the dignitaries and ducal guard and the principal cathedrals and churches. The Kremlin was really a fortress and was usually located on an elevation dominating the surrounding territory. Beginning with the austere lines of the fortress wall and ending with a group of majestic cathedrals whose golden cupolas sparkled in the sun, it generally made an extremely picturesque composition. The Moscow Kremlin is probably the best preserved. Although rebuilt many times it nevertheless presents a true picture of an ancient Kremlin; at the same time having a considerable number of Italian details, it is a good example of the Russianizing of foreign architectural forms.

St. Petersburg.—At the beginning of the 18th century, while Moscow and the rest of Russia continued to live according to tradition, Peter the Great (1689–1725) undertook to build a new capital, St. Petersburg, in the far north of his empire—a move which at once involved extensive and imposing building and a radical change from an isolated political existence to closer contact with western Europe. A new epoch in Russian architecture began. Being an innovator in everything, Peter strove from the first to create a new architecture. Instead of employing Moscow masters, he enlisted an army of architects, engineers and craftsmen from all parts of Europe. Their work resulted in the erection of incongruous buildings in western European forms. A degree of order came into this architectural chaos only after Peter's death, when Russian architects became educated in western European art, and Russian architecture, although it could look back on nearly eight centuries of national traditions, turned toward classicism. Thereafter its evolution was divided into two currents, one characteristic of the new capital, St. Petersburg, the other of Moscow, the old. All subsequent architectural periods and fashions were perceived and developed differently in each. In St. Petersburg, the official capital, which grew rapidly, building progressed on a large scale. Architectural ensembles grew up along whole tracts of streets and quays and around vast squares. Most of the new buildings erected by the Government, its officials and the aristocracy were palatial, solemn and somewhat haughty. In Moscow, which had then dropped out of political life but where the charm of the traditions of a great past still existed, the buildings were simple, noble and showed a certain intimate affability.

The influence of the Renaissance (*see* RENAISSANCE ARCHITECTURE) scarcely reached Russia, but an outgrowth of it, the Baroque (*see* BAROQUE ARCHITECTURE), made a strong and lasting impression on Russian architecture, leaving numerous examples, which were, however, sometimes considerably affected by peculiar local conditions. In Moscow a wonderful specimen in this style is the church of Our Lady in Fili, representing a further evolution of the tented church. Here the tent loses its continuity and consists of several tiers of octagonals diminishing in size and put one above the other. In St. Petersburg and in the provinces the Baroque was widely used by the court architect, Count V. V. Rastrelli, one of the greatest architects of the time, whose talent created an epoch for the development of the Baroque. One of the principal reasons for the great success of the Baroque in Russia was its picturesqueness, a quality after which Russian architecture had always striven.

Catherine the Great.—In all Europe, the middle of the 18th century was a period of reaction against the pretentious forms of the Baroque and of reawakening interest in the austere and noble forms of classic architecture. In Russia, the brilliant reign of Catherine the Great (1762–96) was favourable for the development of this movement and it found an immediate response. A multitude of architects, both Russian and foreign, invited by the court, carried on the beautifying of the new capital, surrounding its vast squares with rows of classic columns, with elegant porticoes and with majestic façades. Catherine's interest in architecture was exceptional. Peter influenced the direction of Russian architecture; she assisted the development of the new school itself. With an energy equal to Peter's, she continued to create the capital, not only personally examining the designs but also, according to contemporaries, giving instructions and even supplying sketches for proposed buildings. During her reign the classic style was so intimately mixed with the creative genius of Russia that it occupied almost the same position as the traditional Russian style prior to the 17th century. An inexhaustible supply of serf labour allowed ambitious building programmes to be carried out. The ruling class, the aristocracy and gentry, living on estates scattered throughout the vast country, kept in close touch with the capital and, anxious to keep abreast of its fashions, built many mansions in the fashionable classic style whose solemnity and austerity fitted the epoch to perfection. Considering the numerous and diverse structures built in the classic style, it would be no exaggeration to call Russia of the 18th and 19th centuries a country of classic architecture.

19th and 20th Centuries.—The beginning of the 19th century inclined to even more austere forms, the Corinthian column gave way to the Doric, Rome seemed not simple and severe enough and early Hellenic forms came into favour. The Temple of Paestum became an ideal for the artist and the so-called Russian Empire style, very different from the dry and formal designs of Persier and Fontaine, appeared. Its characteristic traits are a Paestum-like archaism combined with great flat planes, here and there accentuated by severe but pithy ornamentation. The architecture of this period may be regarded as the climax of the Russian classic style. Under Nicholas I. (1825–55) the character of the building activity in St. Petersburg changed and from the erection of grandiose palaces, turned to more practical and commonplace problems. Porticoes and great wall surfaces with few window-openings which did not respond to the practical requirements gradually lost favour. Petty, unnecessary details were frequently applied with the intention to conceal by their display the shortcomings of a weak composition. Russian architecture, with frequently changing artistic tastes, declined steadily during almost the whole second half of the 19th century. At one time designers turned to the old Russian national style, but inspiration was sought from its most decadent period, the end of the 17th century; fortunately this tendency was of short duration and

left no deep traces.

With the end of the 19th and the beginning of the present century the advent of industry introduced a new and rapidly growing factor. A period of active building began and symptoms of a renascence of the best of the old Russian architecture appeared. Aside from current buildings a number of large factories were constructed. Residences no less splendid than the old palaces of the dignitaries of Catherine were built for the new kings of industry. At this time when the modernistic style prevailed in Europe, two more architectural currents were evident— one purely national, traditionally Russian, founded on the early and best sources of Russian art; the other classical, suggested by the severe and elegant architectural forms of Palladio. These two logically reflected the main traditions and the historical development of Russian architecture as though representing its two main courses of development. The World War and the subsequent revolution interrupted building for a whole decade.

(W. O.-J.)

Post Revolutionary.—Since the World War, many attempts have been made to create a national architecture from existing European styles, but these have been found unsuitable to represent the revolutionary ideas of the nation. All modern fads have been tried—"cubism," "futurism," "new art," "the heroic," but these have gone their way. The form of architecture in favour in 1929 and employed in all the new government buildings is based entirely on what the Russians call "mechanical technical" facts. The aeroplane, motor car and modern battleship are their inspiration, and all decoration other than the "scythe and hammer" the Bolshevik coat of arms, is eliminated. As Ladovski, the professor of the department of "modern architecture" at the Moscow academy has stated, "The future belongs to those who have remarkably little talent for the Fine Arts." Their desire is to create a new form of architecture devoid of any traditional inspiration, one which is essentially practical and suitable for its purpose. In other words they design the plan according to the requirements of the building on a purely constructional basis, and consider the result will produce its own beauty.

Lack of capital is another determining factor in this new form of architecture. Reinforced concrete has replaced stone and granite and everything is being designed and carried out with the greatest economy and simplicity. Russia prides itself in being a nation of workers and considers that its factories and business buildings should look like "work shops" and not like the mansions and palaces of an aristocracy. While the need for economy is evident in all modern Russian buildings, it is commendable that the new Government has not allowed the ancient buildings to fall into decay. Domed palaces and minarets have been painted and regilded. Mansions, now the headquarters of Government departments or of bakeries and other commercial industries, have been redecorated as originally designed. Churches of artistic merit have been repaired, and theatres, the pride of the people, receive particular attention.

Construction is of reinforced concrete throughout, painted in revolutionary red and grey. Walls are reduced to a minimum sufficient only for constructional purposes, while enormous glass areas are introduced to give the maximum window space to the workers. Flat roofs and balconies for the recreation of the workers are also considered essential. These new conditions produce their own problems in a country where the temperature is often 30° F below zero and the snow-fall great. To overcome the cold in winter elaborate heating systems have to be introduced. The windows are covered with a network of heating pipes placed behind the glazing bars, while double glazing is provided for all windows to keep out the cold. The greatest problem is that of the flat roof, as during winter the roof with its parapet walls forms a tank for the snow, with the resultant danger from leakages and burst pipes when thaw sets in. There are various methods of roof construction but the best is that in which a double concrete slab is used with an air space between.

Russia is still in a state of transition. Lack of materials and skilled craftsmen makes it difficult for their advanced dreamers and architects to carry out their conceptions. Nitski, one of the ablest Bolshevik art critics, has said that the dreams of Lenin could not be realized for at least 100 years. Some of the most recent buildings carried out in the modern manner are: the Centrosoyus warehouse; the new Telephone building; the Telegraph building and the Gostorg State building. (T. S. T.)

BIBLIOGRAPHY.—W. Souslow, *Monuments de l'ancienne architecture russe*, 2 vols. (St. Petersburg, 1895–1901); L. Hautecoeur, *L'architecture classique à Saint Petersbourg à la fin du XVIII. siècle* (Paris, 1912); R. H. Newmarch, *The Russian Arts* (New York, 1916); A. Eliasberg, *Russische Baukunst* (München, 1922); W. H. Ward, "Russian Architecture," in *Journal of the Royal Institute of British Architects*, ser. 3, vol. xxix, pp. 261–268 (London, 1922); G. K. Lukomski, *Alt-Russland, Architektur und Kunstgewerke* (München, 1923); *The Russian Art Exhibition*, foreword by C. Brinton, introduction and catalogue by I. Grabar (New York, 1924) and *Die Freskomalersi der Dimitry Kathedrale in Wladimir* (Berlin, 1925).

RUSSIAN ART. A comprehensive essay on the art of Russia implies a survey of the art of many races, beginning from remote antiquity. This article, therefore, deals with those artistic activities that have been manifested in Russia proper since her appearance as an organised and independent state under St. Vladimir (972–1015).

Premongolian and Mongolian Period.—As with their religion, the Russians took their art from Byzantium and up to the 14th century they preserved in their icons all the austerity and simplicity of design and also the economy of colouring of the Byzantine frescoes of the 11th and 12th centuries. The centres of activity during this period were at Kiev, Novgorod and Suzdal, and in all probability a great number of artists were Greeks. A very fine example from this period is the Odiguitry Madonna (12th century) in the Riabushinsky collection at Moscow.

Novgorod School.—The 14th century marks the beginning of a new style and icon-painting at that time flourished in Novgorod. The new elements may be due to a fresh influx of Greek and perhaps Serbian painters, for there are certain characteristics in the Russian icons and frescos of this period which are common to the 14th century frescos both at Mistra (Greece) and in Serbia. However, in such works as the "Ascension" (1363) at Volotovo there is a sense for line and a simplicity of rendering not present in the Greek and Serbian frescos. In this work and also in the St. Theodore Stratilatos (1370) and the "Nativity" in the same monastery, can be clearly discerned all the great qualities which distinguish the Novgorod school in the following century. At the end of the 14th century (1378–1405) a Greek painter referred to by Russian chroniclers as "Philosopher Theophanos the Greek" did works in various churches and monasteries in Moscow and Novgorod.

The golden age of Russian art, the 15th century, is marked by so much grace that some scholars attempt to ascribe it to Italian influence. The chief means by which this elegance is obtained is continuity of outline of the design and either rhythmical linear repetition or symmetrical linear opposition of the movement, imposed on the central figure by the artist's interpretation of the action in the subject. The colouring too shows improvement. Instead of slightly tinted drawings as were the earlier icons, we have icons with clear and harmonious colouring distributed in flat surfaces and emphasised by lines marking the light. The most accomplished master of this period—and indeed in the whole history of Russian art—is Andrea Rublyov (1370–1430), probably a pupil of "Philosopher Theophanos the Greek," one of whose very few preserved works is the Holy Trinity (1408) in the Troitza Cathedral of the Troitza-Sergios monastery near Moscow (even the authenticity of this example is doubted by Kandakov). Another master whose name is frequently mentioned in old records together with Rublyov is Dionysios who worked at the Theraponte monastery. Some fine examples of the icons from this period are in the collections of B. E. Chanenko at Kiev and E. S. Ostruchov and S. P. Riabushinsky at Moscow.

Moscow and Stroganovsky Schools.—After the inclusion by Ivan the Terrible of Novgorod province into the Russian Empire the centre of artistic activity shifts to the capital of the new Empire, Moscow. Design in icons loses simplicity and the figures lose their dignified proportions. Colouring becomes dull and practically identical in all icons, and even their sizes tend towards standardisation. The Byzantine architectural motives in the backgrounds of icons are supplanted by Russian ones, and even the type of faces bears a strong national character. In short, the Moscow school abandoned the high standards of its predecessor and came into closer touch with national life. Gradually icon-painting turned into more a manufacture of devotional objects than art. Meanwhile between the end of the 16th and the beginning of the 17th century sprung up the Stroganovsky school which combined to some extent some of the elements of both its predecessors. The craftsmanship is certainly of a very high grade, but the harshness of design, the somewhat exotic brilliance of colour, the lack of relationship between the national architectural forms in the background and the semi-Byzantine figures, the insistence on detail and finally—especially so in the later stages—the presence of undigested Western influence makes this school very inferior to the Novgorod school. However, it found great favour among the upper classes and became the most appreciated school in Russia. A great number of icons from this school are preserved; an inferior example is hung at the National Gallery. The best known masters from this school are Istoma and Nikiphor Savin, Procopy Tchirin, Ivan Prokopiev and Spiridion Timoviev.

The efforts of Peter the Great to introduce Western civilisation into Russia gradually brought to an end an art which had flourished for over six centuries and Western influence became paramount. Among the first artists of the new era are S. Ushakov, Th. Abrosimov, Ivan Bezmin and Saltanov.

THE NEW ERA

The 18th and the first half of the 19th centuries form an epoch of foreigners in Russia. Just as in the beginnings of Russian religious art the Byzantine artists were predominant, so now Italian, French, Dutch and German artists were working for the Russian court and were laying the foundations of Russian secular painting. Among the great number of foreign painters were four English artists, Walker, Atkinson, Miles and Richard Brompton. While foreign artists were well treated, the conditions under which most of the native artists worked were lamentable. The land owners were closely imitating the Court and had their own architects and painters. These were conscripted from their serfs and remained serfs. It was not unusual for an artist to be flogged because his master was not satisfied with his work. The artist had also to perform other duties, such as valeting, kitchen work, farm work, etc. In spite of this, native artists quickly attained the standards of their European teachers, but strictly speaking, we must acknowledge that Russian art as such was dead and that since the beginning of the 18th century art in Russia was nothing more than a minor branch of European art. Thus we have the various European schools, *e.g.*, Classical, Romantic, Realistic. The most prominent artists of the Classical school are Akimov, Ugrumov, Egorov and Shebuev. Among the Romantics are Kiprensky, Tropinin, Brullov, Prince Gagarin, Alexander Ivanov, Vasnetzov and Vrubel, and among the Realistics are Venetzianov, Vereshchagin, and Repine. The best known landscape painters are Lebedev, Ayvazovsky, Levitan and Syerov. Naturally, as soon as modern art arose in Europe, Russia followed suit. The most important modern artists are V. Kandinsky, Roerich, Larionov, Gontsharova, Chagal, Ostrumova, Punin, Iacovlev and Anrep.

Sculpture.—Sculpture never flourished in Russia owing to the fact that the Orthodox Church does not allow sculpture in churches. There are very few examples of ancient carving extant. Probably the best that can be seen is at Yuryev Polsky on St. George's Cathedral. Among modern sculptors the best-known are Prince Troubetskoy, Orlov, Archipenko, Lipshitz, and Zadkin.

Minor Arts.—Among the lesser arts silver-work was turned out for centuries at Novgorod and Tula. From the 18th century onwards there has been a flourishing porcelain industry in many places in Russia, the most important factories being the Imperial Factory, Garder and Popov. (*See* RUSSIAN ARCHITECTURE.)

BIBLIOGRAPHY.—N. P. Kondakov, *The Russian Icon*, 1927. A БЕНУА: Исторія Русской Живописи въ XIX вѣкѣ, 1901–02.

(S. Ph.)

RUSSIAN LANGUAGE. Together with the closely related White Russian (Byelorussian) and Ukrainian (*q.v.*), Russian belongs to the eastern branch of the Slavonic languages. The term "Great Russian," still sometimes used for "Russian" even in Soviet scholarship, is incorrect, because it perpetuates the erroneous view that the other eastern Slavonic languages are dialects of Russian.

The main phonetic features of Russian, historically considered, are as follows:

1. Common Slavonic (C.S.) *ŭ* and *ĭ* have disappeared as such. If the syllable in which they occurred was stressed, C.S. *ŭ* and *ĭ* have been replaced in Russian by *o* and *e* respectively, but these vowels sometimes appear here sporadically (*e.g.*, ogon' <C.S. *ogni*; *cf.* Lat. *ignis*). Where, however, *ŭ* and *ĭ* occurred in unstressed position, the former has disappeared and the latter has left a trace of itself in the palatal quality of the preceding consonant (*cf.* C.S. *sŭnŭ*, "sleep," *dĭnĭ*, "day" with R. *son, den'*).

2. C.S. *y* has survived, as in White Russian (W.R.); Ukrainian (Ukr.) and Polish *y* is not made so far back in the mouth.

3. C.S. *or, *ol, *er, *el* before a consonant are eked out in Russian with a vowel placed after them, by which, *e.g.*, C.S. *gordŭ*, "town," and *golva*, "head," have become R. *gorod* and *golova*. This phenomenon is called pleophony (*polnoglasije*) and takes the form of paired vowels flanking the "liquid" consonants, in pointed contrast with the Old Bulgarian monosyllables in *gradŭ* and *glava*.

4. C.S. *ǫ* and *ę* (like French *on* and *in*) become *u* and *ja* (*cf.* C.S. *pǫti*, "road," *pęti*, "five," with R. *put', pjat'*).

5. C.S. *tj, *dj* gave R. *č, ž* (*cf.* C.S. *světja*, "candle," *medja*, "boundary," with R. *sveča, meža*), and C.S. *pj, *bj, *vj, *mj* gave R. *pl', bl', vl', ml'* (*e.g.*, R. *zemlja*, "land"). Before C.S. front vowels *i, ĭ, e, ę, ě*, consonants were affected, the tongue being raised when making them in anticipation of the palatalizing vowel. Later what amounted to a new *j* developed in R., as *ĭ* became practically *j*, and *e* and *ě* came to sound like *je* and *ę* like *ja* at the beginning of a word. But the new *j* never converted a preceding dental consonant into a palatalized sibilant or affricate, though it had this effect in White Russian and Polish. The result of all this is that almost every consonant in Russian can be pronounced "hard" or "soft," a distinction which it is very difficult for many foreigners to make, as they tend to pronounce *j* after the unpalatalized consonant.

6. A specially Russian point is that *je* and *ju* beginning a word appear as *o* and *u* respectively (*cf.* C.S. *jezero*, "lake," *jutro*, "morning," with R. *ozero, utro*).

7. Russian has lost the distinctions of quantity which survive, *e.g.*, in Czech, Slovak, Slovene and Serbo-Croatian. The stress is extremely irregular, as it may fall differently in the paradigm of the same noun or in different persons of the same tense. Moreover it is an expiratory stress, so strong that the unstressed syllables may have dulled (centralized) vowels.

All these phonetic peculiarities distinguish Russian as far back as it can be traced. In the earliest documents it appears with an apparatus of grammatical forms little different from that ascribed to Common Slavonic. The history of the language is not so much that of phonetic change as of morphological simplification and syntactic development. The tracing of this process is rendered difficult by the circumstance that a form of Church Slavonic was the ecclesiastical and literary language until the 17th century, and although the Old Church Slavonic texts suffer modifications, producing the still extant Russian recension of Church Slavonic, the Russian forms appear in them at first only by accident. Early Russian is better represented in additions made by the scribe, as in the colophon of the Ostromir Gospels (1056–57), the oldest dated ecclesiastical manuscript of Russian recension. In a certain number of secular documents dating from the 11th century onward Russian forms definitely predominate, but the subject matter is too limited to offer much useful material.

The effect of the church language (Church Slavonic) on Russian has been very strong, comparable in some measure with that of Latin on French or English. Church Slavonic forms of words and suffixes, betrayed by their phonetic peculiarities, have in some instances ousted the native forms, while in others the two sets of forms coexist; the Church Slavonic form generally has the more dignified or metaphorical, the Russian the simpler and more direct sense; even some of the grammatical terminations (*e.g.*, present participle active, certain forms of the adjective, etc.) are Church Slavonic; but speakers are quite unconscious of using anything that is not Russian, and not till the 18th century did even grammarians understand the difference. Less important elements have been the Tatar, which gave the names of oriental objects, including weapons, jewels, stuffs and garments, as well as certain terms concerned with government, and the Polish, which during the 17th century supplied many words needed to express European things and ideas. In the 18th century such borrowings were made from Latin and from almost all the principal west European languages; viz., in Peter I's time mostly from German and Dutch (English supplied some nautical terms), in Catherine II's rather from French, which had become the language of the aristocracy. During the first quarter of the 19th century modern Russian found itself and discarded superfluous Church Slavonic and European borrowings alike. Since then fresh loan words have been taken mainly from the international quasi-Greek terminology, though, like German, Russian sometimes prefers analogous compounds made from its own roots.

Literary Russian as used by educated persons is the central Russian dialect of the Moscow area, modified to some extent by local peculiarities wherever it is spoken. It is still a markedly inflected language, comparable in this respect rather with Latin and Greek than with the languages of western Europe, though during historic times it has lost many of the grammatical forms, whose full development can be studied best in Old Church Slavonic and whose presence can be asserted in the scanty remains of Old Russian. This process has relieved the language of the dual number, except in certain survivals; of the vocative case (some ecclesiastical forms excepted) and of many distinctions in declension, especially in the plural and in the oblique cases of the simple and the more cumbrous forms of the compound adjective; and of the supine, the imperfect, the aorist and the conditional (now indicated by a particle). But this simplification still leaves it with six cases (nominative, accusative, genitive, dative, instrumental and locative), three genders, three substantival declensions (*-a, -o, -i* and traces of *-u*, and consonantal stems), a special pronominal declension with many peculiarities, an adjective which takes its place between them, and a system of numerals in which a compromise between grammar and logic has multiplied difficulties. The forms of the verbs are easier, as only the present indicative has three persons, the imperative has only the second, and the past is, in origin, a participle which, having discarded its copula, distinguishes only gender and number. The infinitive and four participles offer no special difficulty, but the gerundives, or verbal adverbs, derived from the old masculine nominative singular, are rather troublesome. The curious mechanism of aspect by which these few verbal forms express most of our tenses and other shades of meaning of which even English is incapable is briefly explained under SLAVONIC LANGUAGES. On the whole the syntax is simple in the hands of the unpretentious writer, the complicated periods which imitation of Latin and German once brought into fashion having given place to shorter sentences on the French and English model.

Russian dialects fall into three main divisions, which do not greatly differ from one another, Russian being a fairly uniform language when the vast extent over which it is spoken is considered. These dialect groups are the northern or *o* group, the southern or *a* group and a central group which combines features of the other two. The line between the marginal dialects runs roughly east-southeast from Pskov to the Sura and then southward to Astrakhan. The northern group is the most conservative and pronounces very nearly according to the spelling, unaccented *o* remaining *o*, but *o* in general tends to *u*, while *e* before hard consonants is apt to be *jo* and before soft consonants *i*. The southern part of this group—dialects of the Vladimir-Volga type—is alone free from a further peculiarity, viz., a tendency to mix up *c* and *č* (*cokan'je*), which can be traced in the ancient documents of Novgorod, and especially Pskov, and has spread with the Novgorod colonists across the whole of northern Russia to the Urals and to Siberia. These colonial dialects have adopted many words from the Uralian-speaking natives. The southern or *a* group of dialects pronounces unaccented *o* and *e* as *a* and *ja* respectively; with this goes a tendency to pronounce *g* as *h* and to mix up *ŭ* and *v*. The central dialect of Moscow type, which is the foundation of the literary language, covers a very small area, but political causes have made it the language of the governing classes and hence of literature. It is a transitional dialect with a southern vowel system and the northern pronunciation of *g* as in Eng. "go."

The other east Slavonic languages may now be considered as divergent developments of their common recorded ancestor, usually but ambiguously designated "Old Russian" and more properly "Old East Slavonic." White Russian, being nearer to Russian, will be characterized here. For Ukrainian, see UKRAINIAN LANGUAGE.

White Russian.—This language, now sometimes called Byelorussian, has its source in the mediaeval Slavonic dialects spoken in the upper basins of the Western Dvina and the Dnieper. Some of its present characteristics are especially marked in secular manuscripts of the early 13th century, others appeared after the Mongol (Tatar) invasion of eastern Europe, which destroyed the polity of Kiev and exposed White Russian territory to annexation by the feudal power of Lithuania. The absorption of Lithuania by Poland in the 16th century resulted in the replacement of White Russian, the official language of Lithuania, by Polish. After the 18th-century partitions of Poland the White Russian territories were reunited with Russia, and this led to the emergence of White Russian in its modern form. Literary White Russian is based on one of the central dialects and shows considerable Polish influence in its vocabulary. Nevertheless, its essential difference from Russian derives mainly from a divergent regional development.

Phonetically White Russian differs from Russian in the following particulars; viz., the pronunciation of *c'/dz'* for *t'/d'* (*cf. spac'*, "to sleep," with R. *spat'*); hard *č* for soft *č'* (*cf. čytac'*, "to read," with R. *čitat'*); hardened labials finally and before *j*, and hard *r* in all positions (*cf. holub*, "pigeon," *simja*, "family," *car*, "emperor," with R. *golub'*, *sem'ja*, *car'*); long soft affricates (*cf. suddzja*, "judge," *placcje*, "dress," with R. *sud'ja*, *plat'je*); *w* for *v* and *l* finally and before consonants (*cf. chlew*, "byre," *mjow*, "he swept," *prawda*, "truth," *vowk*, "wolf," with R. *chlev*, *mjol*, *pravda*, *volk*); *i/y* for *e/o* under certain conditions (*cf. pi*, "drink," *zly*, "evil," with R. *pej*, *zloj*). The alternation of *h/k/ch* with the sibilants *z/c/s* in declension leads to complications which have been removed in Russian by analogy (*cf. naha*, "leg," dative singular *nazje*, with R. *noga, noge*). In other respects there has been simplification in White Russian; for example, the plurals *i/y* appear in nouns of all categories (*cf. horody*, "towns," *kani*, "horses," *dzvjery*, "doors," *vokny*, "windows," with R. *goroda, koni, dveri, okna*). White Russian syntax is characterized by the use of plural numerals with *dva*, "two" (*cf. dva kani*, "two horses," with R. *dva konja*), the interrogative particle *ci* (*cf. Pol. czy*, Ukr. *čy*) and the avoidance of participial adjectives (*cf. čalavjek jaki čytaje*, "the reading man," with R. *čitajuščij čelovek*).

BIBLIOGRAPHY.—*Russian*: Phonetics: M. V. Trofimov and D. Jones, *Pronunciation of Russian* (Cambridge, New York, 1923); S. C. Boyanus and N. B. Jopson, *Spoken Russian* (London, 1939); S. C. Boyanus, *Russian Pronunciation and Russian Phonetic Reader*, 2 vol. (London, 1955); G. Vinokur, *Russkoje sceničeskoje proiznošenije* (Moscow, 1948); R. I. Avanesov, *Russkoje literaturnoje proiznošenije*, 2nd ed. (Moscow, 1954). Descriptive and Historical Grammars: G. Vinokur, *Russkij jazyk: Istoričeskij očerk* (Moscow, 1945); V. V. Vinogradov, *Russkij jazyk* (Moscow, Leningrad, 1947); L. A. Bulakhovsky, *Kurs russkogo literaturnogo jazyka*, 3rd ed. (Kiev, 1949); W. J. Entwistle and W. A. Morison, *Russian and the Slavonic Languages* (London, New York, 1949); A. Mazon, *Grammaire de la langue russe*, 3rd ed. (Paris, 1949); V. V. Vinogradov (ed.), *Grammatika russkogo jazyka*, 2 vol. (Moscow, 1952–54); W. K. Matthews, *Structure and Development of Russian* (Cambridge, 1953); P. S. Kuznetsov, *Istoričeskaja grammatika russkogo jazyka* (Moscow, 1953). Dialectology: P. S. Kuznetsov, *Russkaja dialektologija* (Moscow, 1951). Dictionaries: I. I. Sreznevsky, *Materialy dlja slovarja drevnerusskogo jazyka*, 3 vol. (St. Petersburg, 1893–1912); D. N. Ushakov and B. M. Volin, *Tolkovyj slovar' russkogo jazyka* (Moscow, 1935–40); M. Vasmer, *Russisches etymologisches Wörterbuch*, vol. i (Heidelberg, 1953); S. I. Ozhegov, *Slovar' russkogo jazyka* (Moscow, 1952); A. I. Smirnitsky, *Russko-anglijskij slovar'* (Moscow, 1952).

White Russian: Descriptive and Historical Grammars: Y. F. Karsky, *Byelorussy*, 2 vol. (Warsaw, 1903–12); C. S. Stang, *Die weissrussische Kanzleisprache des Grossfürstentums Litauen* (Oslo, 1935); **T. P.**

Lomtyov, *Bjelorusskij jazyk* (Moscow, 1951); J. Šerech, *Problems in the Formation of Belorussian* (New York, 1953); N. I. Hursky, *Bjelaruska mova*, vol. i (Minsk, 1954). Dictionary: M. Baykow and S. Nyekrashevich, *Bjelaruska-rasijski slownik* (Moscow, 1926); Y. Kolas, K. Krapiva and P. Hlebka, *Russko-Belorusskij slovar'* (Moscow, 1953).

(N. B. J.; W. K. M.)

RUSSIAN LITERATURE. The natural divisions in the history of Russian literature are formed by the two great landmarks of the reforms of Peter I and the effects of the Soviet Revolution. There are thus three main periods, though these inevitably overlap. They are: old Russian, from the conversion to Christianity of St. Vladimir in 988 to the foundation of Peter the Great's new capital in 1703; modern Russian, from 1703 to the October Revolution of 1917; and the postrevolutionary literature of the U.S.S.R. For historical reasons, including particularly the relative isolation of Russia from western Europe until the 16th century, the middle ages lasted for Russian literature till Peter's time (so that the old Russian period might almost as well be called mediaeval), and many of those features which are commonly associated under the term Renaissance do not begin to appear in Russia till the 17th century. The Russian language, too, largely because of the prolongation in it of Church Slavonic elements, did not assume its modern character till well on in the 18th century. The fundamental changes in mental climate wrought by the October Revolution are in themselves sufficient to explain the beginning of a third literary period with that event.

OLD RUSSIAN LITERATURE (988–1703)

Historically this may be subdivided conveniently into four main epochs: (1) Kievan, with Kiev in the Ukraine as its cultural centre, from the earliest documents of the 11th century to the Mongol conquest in 1240; (2) regional, during which a number of cultural centres such as Novgorod, Pskov and Tver were variously dominant, to the end of the Tatar suzerainty in 1480; (3) Muscovite, in which the Moscow grand dukes became tsars of a strong centralized Russian state which caused Moscow to become the vital literary centre, to the beginning of the "time of troubles" with the death of Ivan the Terrible's son Theodore I in 1598; and (4) transitional, in which the first marked contacts with and influences from the west prepared the way for the beginnings of modern Russian literature, from the end of the "time of troubles" with the accession of Tsar Michael Romanov in 1613 to the beginnings of St. Petersburg in 1703.

Kievan Period (988–1240).—In the days of its greatness, Kiev had a heterogeneous culture, intellectually and aesthetically advanced and powerful. It drew its inspiration from Byzantine Christianity, but was from the outset modified and vitalized by native Slavonic impulses. At the same time it had real contacts with western Europe, and yet had already assimilated something from the culture of contiguous and often closely associated Asian peoples. It had too something of that special quality which runs all through Russian literature expressed by the Russian word *narodnost* (roughly to be translated as "peopleness"), an element which makes a literature retain some intimate and vital relationship to people and soil despite foreign influences and urban sophistication. Kiev of the late 10th century was a peak of European culture, sharing the most valuable developments of east and west, of Byzantine and Latin civilization.

As a result of the Mongol devastations of the 13th century, much was lost and much preserved only in manuscripts of the 16th century. There were the usual types of early Christian religious literature—lives of saints, homilies, books of instruction. There were, too, the expected kind of translated works from Byzantine Greek. But there were also creative writings which, while employing the artificial Church Slavonic of the old Rus, show genuinely literary qualities as well as throw light on the life of the times. Such were the chronicles, for example *The Tale of Bygone Times* (*Povest vremennykh let*) with its account of the beginnings of Rus; and the *Instruction* (*Pouchenie*) of Vladimir Monomakh in which the early 12th-century revered ruler of Kiev sets down his wisdom and practical experience. *The Discourse on Law and Grace* (*Slovo o zakone i blagodati*) by the metropolitan Ilarion shows intellectual ability as well as rhetorical skill. The probably 12th-century adaptation of the Byzantine romantic tale of *Digenis Akritas* (*Devgenievo Deyanie*) reveals marked native folk elements which give it something of the air of a Russian heroic prose epic.

Though these short, balladlike heroic pieces in unrhymed verse for singing by trained minstrels have not survived in manuscripts of earlier than the 17th century, this most important type of poetry of oral tradition evidently arose in the Kievan epoch. Much of its subject matter concerns the doings of the Kiev princes and their noble retainers, treated in a truly heroic yet natural style, in which the work of court poets has been handed down in the mouths of the people. Some of these *byliny* or pieces of the olden days (more traditionally termed *stariny* till the folklorists coined *byliny* in 1830) were copied down for the first time by the Englishman Richard James early in the 17th century in a manuscript preserved in the Bodleian library at Oxford. They are the finest representatives of Russian oral poetry, and this tradition of an oral poetry independent of books has lasted into the 20th century, in which pieces of the *bylina* type continue to be composed and recited on contemporary happenings in parts of northern Russia. Those fairy folktales and collections of vivid proverbs which are a marked feature of Russian popular literature throughout its history also began to appear in the Kievan age.

But the supreme literary achievement of the Kiev period was the heroic poem in rhythmic epic prose known as *The Lay of Igor's Campaign* (*Slovo o polku Igoreve*), composed, very soon after the events it makes so memorable, to celebrate the glories of a tragic expedition made by Prince Igor of Novgorod-Seversk against the Polovtsy (Cumans, or Kipchak Turks) in 1185. This poem survived in an early 16th-century manuscript discovered in 1795 by Count Aleksey Musin-Pushkin and published in 1800, but it perished in the Moscow fire of 1812. It is the one old Russian work that clearly merits a place among the world's masterpieces. Its heroic spirit harmonizes perfectly with the sheer poetic beauty of its language and with its blending of Christian and pagan feeling.[1]

Regional Period (1240–1480).—The fall of the Kievan state and the Tatar conquest of so much of Russia led naturally to the regionalization of culture, and the Eurasian cultural atmosphere was not propitious to literature in general. Much the same chronicles and lives of saints and sermons continued to be produced as in the previous age, with many translations of well-known European works of edification and adventure; but the isolation, not only from western Europe but even from Byzantium, was unfavourable to literary progress, and the output of original writing was small. Much of this latter was of the quality of the *Petition of Daniel the Captive* (*Molenie Daniila Zatochnika*), in which an unknown exile begs aid and patronage from the prince of Pereyaslavl in a fantastic medley of varied learning and rhetoric while voicing a practical complaint against the boyars; interesting to social historians, it scarcely reaches the level of literature. To Suzdal belongs the stirring and warlike *Life of Prince Alexander Nevsky*, with its forceful account of the famous victory of 1242 on the ice of Lake Peipus over the Teutonic Knights. Each centre had its regional chronicle, and there was a good deal of narrative and lament over the Mongol wars. Quite entertaining is the curious and imaginative *Tale of the Indian Empire* (*Skazanye ob indiiskom tsarstve*) with its picture of a mighty Christian Indian ruler, Ivan, who goes into battle with vast armies led by a huge wooden crucifix and vaguely suggests Prester John.

But there are two works of the 15th century which are, in different ways, on a more strictly literary plane: the *Zadonshchina* or *Deeds Across the Don* of the early part of the century, and the *Travels Beyond the Three Seas* (*Khozhdenie za tri morya*) of Afanasy Nikitin. The *Zadonshchina* celebrates the glorious victory of Dimitri (Demetrius) Donskoy of Moscow over the khan Mamai on Kulikovo plain (1380); it has heroic vigour of a somewhat highly wrought kind. The travel narrative of Nikitin, a merchant of Tver, on the other hand, is colloquial and simple, without the

usual Church Slavonic adornments though often introducing oriental words for effect. He describes his own journey for trading purposes to Persia and India which lasted for nearly six years (1466–72), giving a vivid and naïve picture of his life in India especially. Nikitin's *Travels* is the first European account of India.

Muscovite Period (1480–1598).—The 16th century was especially a period of the written expression of the organization of the Muscovite state as it steadily and consciously consolidated itself. The discovery that Moscow was a "third Rome" at its beginning was followed by the production of numerous and often effective encyclopaedic works aimed at a combined religious and secular teaching which would form the kind of society desired by Moscow. Ivan the Terrible, himself no mean polemical letter writer, took a hand in setting out his own kind of political philosophy. His chief epistolary opponent, Andrey Kurbsky, a descendant of Kievan princes, defended the rights of the oppressed nobility with even greater literary skill. Ivan's principal literary apologist, Ivan Peresvetov, with his western political training, produced a remarkable kind of allegorical historical defense of Ivan's terror in his *Tale of Sultan Mahomet* (*Skazanie o Magmete Saltane*), in which the cruel severities of the Ottoman conqueror of Constantinople are lauded as an implied justification of the tsar's conduct. Books such as the *Hundred Chapters* (*Sto glav*), which sets out a kind of *disciplina clericalis* by ecclesiastical conciliar authority, and still more the *Ordering of the Household* (*Domostroy*), are valuable as social documents throwing often clear light on modes and manners which remained the Orthodox Russian way of life for centuries.

This period also marked the beginnings of that kind of western contact which later was to change the whole pattern of Russian literature. Queen Elizabeth I had many dealings with Tsar Ivan which went beyond the mere opening up of active trading. Printing began in Moscow in 1564, though it was little used save for religious, legal and didactic books till the time of Peter the Great. A new impetus was given to the study of learning and theology by the coming of Greek scholars and accomplished men of letters such as Maxim the Greek. There was some interest in literary or rhetorical style stimulated by contacts with Poles.

But native Russian features began at this time also to grow into new life. This is indicated, for instance, by the composition of historical pieces of the *bylina* type on the events of the time. Heroic pieces were written in poetic prose in honour of Ivan the Terrible's conquests; at least one such work, the *Story Concerning the Empire of Kazan* (*Istorya o kazanskom tsarstve*), contains passages of poetic quality reminiscent of ballad or *bylina*.

Transitional Period (1613–1703).—The literary tendencies begun in the 16th century became increasingly powerful in the 17th. As the century advanced, it became ever more clearly an age of transition, though Peter's reforms greatly hurried and enforced developments which otherwise would have been much slower. Especially notable was the development of prose in secular directions such as satire, romance (though mostly only through translations) and the use occasionally of spoken Russian side by side with Church Slavonic. There were significant developments too in poetic style and metre through Polish and Ukrainian influences. But most marked of all was the increasing multiplying of western literary contacts of all kinds, though the tangible results of these were for long not visible.

The "time of troubles" which filled the period between what have been termed the Muscovite and transitional periods (1598–1613) showed many conflicting tendencies. It was rich in popular literary expressions (including *byliny*) of the miseries of the times, but its chief significance lay in the greatly increased foreign influences which it let into Russia. Ivan the Terrible had often encouraged foreigners; but Boris Godunov (1598–1605) went much farther at times, and the Polish rule in Moscow which followed his reign brought in a whole host of Latin western influences from Poland and from the Ukraine, which was then part of Poland. Kiev, too, was once more becoming a source of literary influence which, as in its ancient glory, blended Latin with Byzantine culture. This Ukrainian, hence partly Latin, influence was greatly reinforced when in 1654 much of the Ukraine was united with

[1] In his book *Le Slovo d'Igor* (Paris, 1940) André Mazon, professor at the Collège de France and director of the Institut d'Études Slaves of Paris, considered that the *Slovo* was a forgery and that Musin-Pushkin produced it. Roman Jakobson defended the authenticity of the *Slovo* in the composite volume edited by H. Grégoire, *La Geste du Prince Igor* (New York, 1948).

Russia. It was thus that Simeon Polotsky came to bring his syllabic metre (an entire innovation) from the then recently Polish Kiev to Moscow, and though this was not in the long run the most suitable metre for Russian poets, its introduction undoubtedly served as a stimulus.

It was toward the close of this traditional period that the crude beginnings of a Russian theatre appeared, under the influence of the learned Simeon Polotsky and of Johann Gottfried Grigory (Gregori), a German Lutheran pastor in Moscow. Polotsky introduced didactic drama of the Renaissance grammar-school type, and Grigory inspired the production of biblical narrative and of a morality play on Adam and Eve in a manner reminiscent of English "comedies" in which serious and edifying matter is made to alternate with the buffoonery and clowning of fictitious characters interpolated from low life. The first wooden theatre was built in 1672, but it served merely the court circle of Tsar Alexius. Polotsky's play on the *Prodigal Son,* with its humane and dignified speeches, has a good deal of vitality. But the treatment of *Judith* from the scriptural story is a mixture of exaggeratedly rhetorical declamation with crude comic relief from such characters as a frightened soldier of Holofernes and Judith's maidservant. Theatre proper had to wait for Peter I.

The outstanding achievement of this period was in Russian prose, in the vivid and masterly use for the first time of colloquial Russian as distinct from Church Slavonic in the pioneering *Life of the Archpriest Avvakum* written by himself (*Zhitie Protopopa Avvakuma*) in 1672–73. Avvakum (a form of Habbakuk) was the fanatical but inspiring leader of the Old Believers, who opposed all the major reforms of the patriarch Nikon and all the modern changes which they foreshadowed in the days of Tsar Alexius. Combining intense spiritual pride with the fiercest realism in style, he sought to bring the church and its people back to the ancient traditional piety. In a life of suffering and material hardship which his rebelliousness against the church and state brought upon him, culminating in his being burned at the stake, he exalted with a vivid fury of plain speaking all that the reforms were, as he thought, seeking to obliterate in the loved ancient ways of "Holy Russia." Keeping the Church Slavonic for scriptural citation and formal compliment, he wrote the details of his life in a dynamic colloquial Russian of the people he loved which hitherto had been unknown (except for occasional passages) in any educated writing. As he says of the *Life:*

And if it be plainly told, do not, for God's sake, condemn our plain speech; for I love my natural Russian, and am not accustomed to ornament my talk with the poetry of philosophers; for God does not hearken to fine language, but looks to the matter in hand.

Polemical political and religious writing had been developed in the previous century, but the naturalness and air of spontaneity of Avvakum's descriptions of Russian daily life, in language which springs from a natural genius, make the *Life* a landmark in the history of Russian as well as its leading literary masterpiece of the 17th century.

Avvakum's *Life* was the first Russian autobiography, and indeed the 17th century was essentially a time of first products in new ways of writing, a time of experimental preparation. Rhyme first came to be used (apparently through the influence of the Polish-dominated Ukraine) at its beginning, and the efforts of Polotsky and his disciples combined rhyme with a syllabic pattern with feminine endings as in Polish, in a way which, though not destined to flourish among the best Russian poets, yet did much to prepare the way for more truly Russian creative metres. Satires and moral fables in prose, too, distinctly foreshadowed Radishchev and Krylov, in such pieces as *The Tale of the Trial by Judge Shemyak* (*Povest o Shemyakinom sude*) and *The Tale of the Cock and the Fox* (*Povest o kure i lisitse*), which are both versions of traditional legendary and folk material retold with Russian 17th-century life in view. Avvakum, with his vivid blend of iconoclasm and conservatism, is perhaps the most typical as well as the most important figure of this transitional period.

In an appraisal of the whole extent of old Russian literature in its four periods, it can be realized that literary output throughout was continuous, though varying much in value. From a

strictly literary point of view only a few masterpieces stand out: the *Slovo,* the *Travels* of Nikitin, the writings of Kurbsky and of Peresvetov, Avvakum's *Life* and the best of the *byliny.*

MODERN RUSSIAN LITERATURE (1703–1917)

With the building of St. Petersburg and the strongly conscious and determined beginning of the process of assimilation into Russian literature of all the knowledge and potentialities of western Europe which this "window into Europe" symbolized, modern Russian literature is usually held to begin. The flood of foreign influences which consciously were sought by the authorities and men of letters alike in the 18th century was more definitely formative than the sporadic western influences of the 17th; and, equally, the national consciousness seen in the writings of Avvakum and others of his time was something far less "literary" than the deliberate seeking to make the Russian language a great literary vehicle, which was characteristic of Lomonosov a century later. It is also true that western contacts were beginning to be noticeable as early as the reign of Ivan the Terrible; and, indeed, even under the Tatar yoke Italian merchants formed a slender cultural bridge between Russia and the west. Some again would call the modern Russian period by some such name as the "St. Petersburg age," in view of the central influence of Russia's modern capital and the fact that Moscow once again became the metropolis after the October Revolution when all are agreed that a new period must be taken as beginning. The pioneers of modern Russian in the 18th century, Lomonosov and Karamzin, were conscious and deliberately formative artists, whereas Avvakum, who did so much for Russian as a vivid vehicle for realism and controversy and thus prepared the ground for the modern period, was not consciously concerned with literature at all. He was, in a sense, a gifted barbarian with a dynamic power of language. There was plenty of native virility renascent in the 17th century; and it has been proposed by a Soviet writer to begin the contemporary period with the new consolidation of the Russian state and the resurgence of patriotism after the "time of troubles" with the accession of Tsar Michael Romanov in 1613. But, as has been shown, the 17th century is best regarded as an epoch of transition which prepared the way for modern Russian literature rather than began it.

It was in the 18th century that the chief literary genres, already experimentally or crudely handled in the previous century, first took on shapes that can be recognized as modern. Polotsky and others had combined rhyme with syllabic verse in the preceding epoch, but it was Vasily Tredyakovsky (1703–69) who first proposed the replacing of the syllabic metres imitated from Poland and France by those tonic and accentual measures which have been the accepted mediums of all Russian poetry (except the *byliny,* which retained the intonation of the people) ever since. Polotsky and the German Grigory had made beginnings with artificial and foreign-type plays, but it was Aleksander Sumarokov (1718–77) and Denis I. Fonvizin (1745–92) who first made plays that had some claim to be accounted literature. Tsar Alexius had a little wooden theatre built for the court circle, but it was not till 1756 that Russia had its first regular theatre, with Sumarokov as director. Avvakum and others had written keenly satirical prose, but it was not till the reign of Catherine II (1762–96) that literary satire made its appearance in the periodicals edited by Nikolai I. Novikov (1744–1816) and in Aleksander N. Radishchev's (1749–1801) powerful social satire of the *Journey From Petersburg to Moscow* (*Puteshestvye iz Peterburga v Moskvu*) which was published in 1790 (and burned by the hangman in the same year). There had been much translating of western romances, and popular fiction of the chapbook variety in the 17th century; but Karamzin's sentimental tale *Poor Liza* (*Bednaya Liza*), which was the first that can be called something like a novel proper, did not appear until 1792. Avvakum had appealed for natural colloquial Russian as against pomposity and Church Slavonic for secular writing; it was Lomonosov who wrote the first *Russian Grammar* (1757), and discussed the question of forming truly Russian literary styles suited to various and differing literary compositions.

Inevitably, as modern and more complicated times are approached, the attempt to divide and classify Russian literary epochs becomes more difficult and less effective, and there is far more continuity and overlapping than before. The 19th century stands out as Russia's great classical period of literature. It is primarily the work of this century (with a little in the 20th) that has caused Russian literature to be recognized as among the greatest. It seems best therefore to divide the modern Russian period into two parts: the 18th century, which was especially a time of the deliberate cultivation and imitation of the classicism of the French and those they influenced most; and the 19th century and first years of the 20th, in which Russia produced its greatest creative literature. It was the age of the great Russian classics of literature. Krylov's *Fables* did not appear in volume form until 1809, and he is the first, chronologically, of the Russian classics; so that 1809 is a convenient year to mark the line between the period of classicism, as the 18th century may be termed, and the period of the classics.

Period of Classicism (1703–1809).—This was the period of constructive foreign influence, of literary imitation of French and other foreign models, and latterly to some extent of that assimilation of foreign types which was to lead to the full and creative self-realization of Russian literature in the 19th century. Peter I was mainly utilitarian in his reforms, but inevitably the spate of translating and importation of foreign techniques and the sending of Russians abroad for study opened the way to the influences of the west, and especially of the literature of France. Antiokh Kantemir (*see* CANTEMIR) (1708–44), a Rumanian by birth, an aristocratic and leading poet in the earlier part of the century, was a deliberate imitator of French models. Saturated with classical and French literature, he wrote the best of the poems of the fashionable French type, combining rhyme with syllabic metre, though he sympathized with the reform of Lomonosov which a little later was to make Russian poetry adopt the more natural method of tonic accent. So great became the French influence in fashionable culture that French continued to be the language of fashion among the upper classes till far into the next century. But, in addition to the German influence that was to be expected, English literature also had an important role in this period. Pope was translated and strongly admired, the periodical essayists Joseph Addison and Richard Steele were followed by Moscow works imitative of the *Spectator*, and Laurence Sterne's *Sentimental Journey* and the cult of "sensibility" found favour, as did Samuel Richardson's *Pamela*, which was not without its influence on Karamzin's *Poor Liza*. Shakespeare's *Hamlet* was adapted in French classical style, and the social satirical comedies of Fonvizin owed something also to English Restoration comedy as well as to Molière. The influence of classical Greek and Latin, which had begun with Polotsky in the previous century, now became potent, and was so well assimilated that it brought to birth the best work of the greatest Russian poet of the 18th century, G. R. Derzhavin (*q.v.*; 1743–1816). His best poems show solemn baroque splendour blended with some simple realism. He was far more of a poet proper than Lomonosov, whose reforms he followed.

From the point of view of literary history, however, the greatest names of this epoch are Lomonosov and Karamzin, though neither is of such intrinsic literary quality as Derzhavin. Mikhail V. Lomonosov (*q.v.*; 1711–65) absorbed all the then obtainable knowledge and became poet, grammarian, scientist, literary critic and reformer, all in a comparatively short life. His *Russian Grammar* was a landmark in the development of the language and in the criticism of style; his poetry gave effect lastingly to the metrical reform of Tredyakovsky; his heroic poem *Peter the Great* is a fine piece of rhetoric no longer read; his eulogy of the Russian language (in his *Grammar*) is characteristic of the man and shows the literary breadth of his approach, as compared with, say, the simple praise of Avvakum cited above. Lomonosov wrote:

The Ruler of the Holy Roman Empire, Charles V, used to say that Spanish was fitted for speech with God, French with friends, German with enemies, and Italian with women. But if he had known Russian, he would certainly have added that it was fitted for speech with all of these. For he would have found in it the magnificence of Spanish, the vivacity of French, the vigour of German, the tenderness of Italian and moreover the copiousness and forceful succinctness of expression characteristic of Greek and Latin.

Nikolai M. Karamzin (*q.v.*; 1766–1826), the other important figure of the period (whose work overflowed into the 19th century in which he achieved his greatest fame as the first scholarly writer of a history of Russia), carried on the task of literary and social periodical editing begun by Novikov and Radishchev. Alive to every classical and foreign influence, he marks something like the beginning of the Romantic movement in Russia, but also significantly carried a stage farther the reforms in Russian literary style planned by Lomonosov. Besides his *Poor Liza*, he scored something like a triumph with his *Letters of a Russian Traveller* (*Pisma russkago puteshestvennika*) in 1790, in which Sterne's *Sentimental Journey* is imitated but in an attractive and quite Russian manner.

The period of classicism was a time of artificial and imitative literary development, but beside the following of everything French by men of letters there was at the same time a growing pride in things Russian which found expression in the frequent satire on bogus French behaviour in the comedies of Fonvizin. Under the guidance of Lomonosov and later of Karamzin, prose developed a freer and more natural variety of styles and liberated itself from most of its remaining traces of Church Slavonic. Poetry, by the close of the period, was ready for the "Golden Age" which was to follow. A beginning had been made with social comedy and less successfully with tragedy, and a national theatre had been established. Comic opera too made a notable start with Aleksander O. Ablesimov (1742–83), whose opera *The Miller, Wizard, Quack and Matchmaker* (*Melnik, koldun, obmanshchik i svat*) was written in 1779. Satire, especially under the influence of the French Encyclopaedists, Voltaire and Rousseau, had established itself, and in the hands of Radishchev terrified the formerly liberal Catherine II into sending its author to Siberia for his violent exposure of serfdom and autocracy. (Radishchev was sentenced to death in 1790, but the sentence was commuted to ten years' deportation.) The influence of Shakespeare, which later was to become so effective, began in this epoch. Karamzin's translation of *Julius Caesar* (1787) marked its beginning, though it was not until 1806 that an authentic translation (Vasily Velyaminov's *Othello*) was acted in St. Petersburg freed from the French classical adjustments which had become the rule.

The 18th century was indeed Russia's great formative period in literature. It was also the time when Russian literary figures such as Derzhavin and Karamzin became known in Europe generally. It was a time in which Russia responded, though only through a small educated class, to every literary movement abroad; but, save for a few outstanding poems such as some of Derzhavin's odes, it was not a great creative period.

Period of the Classics (1809–1917).—This period is characterized by the growth of that typically modern Russian class, the intelligentsia (the word seems to have been first used by the Poles and then taken over by the Russians). After Pushkin, the literary lead seemed to be passing from the hereditary upper class to this new intelligentsia, which perhaps had found its beginnings as a literary force with Novikov, who is often said also to have first made for literary journalism a reading public in the 18th century. In the age of Pushkin, poetry was at its very greatest. Later in the 19th century prose, in the form of the novel especially, was Russia's special contribution to world literature. At the close of the epoch, beginning with the 1890s, there was something like a rebirth of poetry under the inspiration of the French Symbolists and their followers. Though they were far from numerous, the epoch had its great dramatists in Griboyedov, Gogol, Ostrovsky and Chekhov. Indeed all the principal forms of literature became of European importance.

Poetry.—At the beginning of this "Pushkin's Golden Age," the conflict between the conservatives of letters (led by Adm. Aleksander Shishkov, 1754–1841) and the Romantic westernizers who followed Karamzin was at its height; into this, Krylov had entered with satiric force by mocking at the critical Slavophils in some of his fables, such as *Parnassus*. Yet I. A. Krylov (*q.v.*; 1768–1844) was a lover of the virtues of Russian peasant life. He began by adapting some of La Fontaine's *Fables*, but even in these he had added to the French originals a peculiar folk quality which

BY COURTESY OF (10) GEORGE H. DORAN, DOUBLEDAY, DORAN AND CO.; PHOTOGRAPHS, (2, 4) F. BRUCKMANN, (5, 6, 8) RISCHGITZ, (7) PHOTOGRAPHISCHE GESELLSCHAFT, (9) JAMES'S PRESS AGENCY, (11) KEYSTONE VIEW CO., (12) UNDERWOOD AND UNDERWOOD

REPRESENTATIVE RUSSIAN WRITERS, 18TH–20TH CENTURIES

1. Mikhail Lomonósov (c. 1711–65)
2. Ivan Krylov (1768–1844)
3. Mikhail Lermontov (1814–41)
4. Alexander Pushkin (1799–1837)
5. Nikolai Gogol (1809–52)
6. Theodore Dostoievsky (1821–81)
7. Nikolai Nekrasov (1821–77)
8. Ivan Turgenev (1818–83)
9. Leo Tolstoy (1828–1910)
10. Anton Chekhov (1860–1904)
11. Maxim Gorki (Alexey Peshkov, 1868–1936)
12. Dmitri Merezhkovsky (1865–1941)

was to become one of the chief delights of Krylov's *Fables* (*Basni*). He had the gift to exploit to the full the realist possibilities of blending the technique of traditional fabulists (he had had several Russian predecessors in the 18th century) with something of that rich fairy tale folk element which is especially characteristic of Russia. Much of the charmingly natural and freshly childlike wisdom and wit of the *Fables* has passed into proverbial speech, and children have never ceased to memorize and enjoy them. Historically, the *Fables* are important as in some sense anticipating that blending of Europe with the Russia of its own people which was to be the glory of Pushkin.

A considerable poet was V. A. Zhukovsky (*q.v.*; 1783–1852). In addition to writing romantic poems and imitations of older ballads, he translated in verse from German and English especially, as well as from Homer. His version of Gray's "Elegy Written in a Country Churchyard," published first in 1802 in Karamzin's literary periodical *Vestnik Evropy* (*Messenger of Europe*), is a magnificent poem and perhaps comes nearer to conveying the qualities of its original than any other known translation.

Though the long struggle between Slavophils and westernizers was to continue indefinitely in political and international matters, the best of the two points of view, so far as the literary language was concerned, were superbly and finally reconciled in Aleksander Pushkin (*q.v.*; 1799–1837). His early love for the French Encyclopaedists, for French classical drama as well as for Shakespeare and Byron, shared his heart with the native linguistic vitality and folk wisdom he had learned from his peasant nurse. In his *Evgheny Oneghin* he makes Tatyana, the girl who had lived only in a country house, confess: "I did not read our journals, I knew Russian badly, and I expressed myself with difficulty in my own native language." Such was the "Frenchifying" of the upper classes. Yet Pushkin made the Russian language do everything with assured inspiration and naturalness, both in prose and verse. In his short and tragic life he showed the "myriad-mindedness" which has been attributed to Shakespeare, and the Greek economy of words and lyric restraint of a truly great poet. His best lyrics are unequalled in their kind since the ancient Hellenes; yet his prose shows almost as much mastery, and he never loses the power of structural beauty. His heroic social long poem of contemporary Russian life, *Evgheny Oneghin* (1823–31), has all the virtues of Byron's *Don Juan* but lacks its unevenness and many lapses of style. His narrative poems, such as *Mazepa* and *The Caucasian Captive* (*Kavkasky plennik*), far outdo Byron in poetic quality of the same kind. His prose tales, such as *The Captain's Daughter* (*Kapitanskaya dochka*), are a landmark in the art of Russian prose. They have become the subjects for all kinds of artistic performance. His verse play *Boris Godunov*, which is markedly influenced by *Hamlet*, has much Shakespearean quality. Pushkin is at once the most Russian of modern poets and the most European, the simplest and the most moving, the most natural and the most artistic. His influence as the supreme Russian classic has remained and widened with time.

At this time St. Petersburg was a veritable "nest of singing birds," among them Evgheny Baratynsky (1800–44) (*see* BARA-TYNSKI, YEVGENIY ABRAMOVICH), the metaphysical lyric poet especially liked by Pushkin; Nikolai Yazykov (1803–46), the master of startlingly vivid rhythmic and visual effects; and, above all, Mikhail Lermontov (*q.v.*; 1814–1841). Like Pushkin, Lermontov wrote narrative prose, notably his *A Hero of Our Time* (*Gheroy nashego vremeni*), published in 1840, which is one of the most vivid psychological studies of a frustrated "superfluous man" ever written. Its hero, Pechorin, like Pushkin's Oneghin, owes something to Byron as well as to the poet's own violent life, but Lermontov never reached anything like that spiritual harmony which at his greatest moments one perceives in Pushkin. His narrative poem *Demon* has never lost its appeal because of the wonderfully musical quality of its verse and the descriptions of that magical Georgian scenery which has inspired Russian poets from Pushkin to Pasternak.

After the middle of the 19th century, poetry, though continuing even more plentifully, generally ceased to be original or creative till it was revitalized by the Symbolist movement and kindred trends

toward the close of the century. Yet it may be said that a simple and profound realism, the outstanding gift of Russian poetry to the world, went on putting forth new growths; and always while Russian soil was watered by western movements—*i.e.*, Romanticism, the work of Edgar Allan Poe (who has been a markedly potent influence) or Symbolism—the resulting poetic plants have been essentially Russian. It is particularly in this last respect that the 19th century contrasts with the mainly imitative poetic qualities of the 18th.

One new type which flowered in this era, though first discovered in the 18th century, was the literary folk song or *pesnya*, which has affinities with the *bylina* and the ballad, yet is sweeter and more profoundly musical. Aleksey V. Koltsov (1808–42) was the first master of this art of Russian song, and he is the nearest thing to Burns of his country. Lermontov's "Cossack Cradle Song," with the exquisite, untranslatable, onomatopoeic refrain *bayushki bayu*, is perhaps the most widely known of this kind. The most representative poet of the century, and probably the greatest after Pushkin, was Fyodor Tyutchev (1803–73), whose lyrics are among the most beautiful. It is characteristic of the upper classes of the time to which Tyutchev belonged that all his nonpoetical writings, often brilliant and critical, were in French. But the intelligentsia had become too interested in social problems to produce works of pure poetry, or they sought to build a Slavophil poetic philosophy as did Aleksey Khomyakov (1804–60) and Ivan Aksakov (1823–86) (*see* AKSAKOV, SERGEI TIMOFEYEVICH). And from the middle of the century poetry began to produce "realism" and "naturalism" in the form of descriptions of the lives of the peasants and passionate pleas in verse for their betterment. Tyutchev, however, with outstanding originality, produced his "Dream at Sea" (*Son na more*), which has something of the weird, profoundly fantastic qualities of Coleridge's "Ancient Mariner."

Of the "poetic realists," the best in literary quality was Count Aleksey Konstantinovich Tolstoy (*q.v.*; 1817–75); the most moving Ivan Nikitin (1824–61), in such poems of the people's lives as his "Kulak"; but the most truly creative and original was Nikolai A. Nekrasov (*q.v.*; 1821–77), who combined real *narodnost* with vigour and vividness in descriptions of the lives of the Russian people. His greatest long poem, *Who gets the Good Life in Russia?* (*Komu na Rusi zhit khorosho*), with its folk-song style, its truly Russian humour and its varied descriptions of Russian types met on a journey through the country in search of the man who gets the "good life," has been loosely compared with Chaucer's *Canterbury Tales*. His realistic idealization of the Russian peasant woman, *Red-nose Frost* (*Moroz krasny nos*), and his *Pedlars* (*Korobeyniki*) are unsurpassed for poetic realism; and he was a master of the literary folk song. Count Aleksey Tolstoy, besides his poems of realism, wrote well in many other genres, including the ballad, as evidenced by his haunting "Prince Mikhaylo Repnin" which describes the slaying in a moment of temporary fury of a faithful prince by his master Tsar Ivan the Terrible. M. E. Saltykov (*q.v.*; 1826–89), a prominent satirist, also belongs to this generation of writers.

In poetry, the conflict between westernizers and Slavophils was to some extent paralleled in the latter half of the century by one between aesthetes or "art for art's sake" poets and those who sought to make their work have primary social relevance. Of these aesthetes, or poets in the stricter sense, the greatest was A. A. Fet or Foeth (*q.v.*; 1820–92). His conservative ways of thought and his following of the poet's craft, often far away from the lives of the people, produced an excellence of form and sometimes a serene tranquillity which offended many of the revolutionary intelligentsia. Yet he could write love lyrics at times as moving as those of Tyutchev. Even in the period of poetic decline, when Fet was long silenced by adverse criticism, the song held its own; so that a now almost forgotten poet like Dimitry N. Sadovnikov (1846–83) could write the balladlike poem on the 18th-century Cossack rebel "Stenka Razin" which has never ceased to be overwhelmingly popular and to be sung in Russia among all types of people.

During this century much of the poetry appeared first in literary periodicals or miscellanies, such as the famous *Sovremennik* (the

Contemporary), first edited by Pushkin and later resuscitated by Nekrasov. This method of publication enabled some of the more philosophical poetry to appear. There was a strong tendency to express philosophic doubts and beliefs in verse. Tyutchev's nature poems are at times a reminder of Lucretius, and Khomyakov was often more a philosophic theologian than a poet. Beside the personal lyric of love and subjective emotion there thus developed types of short poems of philosophic meditation called *dumy*. This poetry of thought was a parallel to the realistic poetry of life.

In the last decade of the century there began something like a renaissance in Russian poetry with the coming of the Symbolists, followed by minor movements such as the Imaginist, Acmeist and Futurist. With these searchings for a new poetry and the resultant creative experiments came many poets who lived on into the 20th century; and some of those who soon followed, such as Boris Pasternak and Vyacheslav Ivanov, continued to write long after the results of the October Revolution had become settled. Indeed the period between the accession of Tsar Nicholas II in 1894 and the revolution of 1917 was one of a creative strength and variety comparable in several respects with the Golden Age. This poetic renaissance continued to show outstanding results well into the postrevolutionary period.

The decline to mere popular versifying of sentimental nostalgia or the like, represented by successful poets such as Semen Nadson (1862–87) and Aleksey Apukhtin (1841–93), was relieved in the years before this revival by only two things: first, the humorous and nonsense verse inaugurated by Count Aleksey Tolstoy with the creation of his imaginary comic literary author Kuzma Prutkov, followed by the brilliant occasional light versifying of Soloviev; and, second, some reflective or philosophical religious poetry of which the mystical poems of Soloviev were again the best exemplars. In this time of weakened poetic creativeness and lowered intellectual vitality which was to herald the renaissance, Vladimir Soloviev (*q.v.;* 1853–1900), as thinker, literary humorist and poet, was the most permanently important Russian writer. It was to some extent the force of his Neoplatonic visionary poetry which gave tone and vitality to the Symbolists, notably Blok, who now suddenly gave a new life to Russian poetry. Philosophers were turning in dissatisfaction from materialism and artists from mere imitation to the recovery of past values of sheer beauty and at the same time the freeing of the artist to be frankly modern. In poetry, whose revival was closely linked with that of painting, the Symbolist movement, led by Konstantin (Constantine) Balmont (1867–1943) and Valery Bryusov (1873–1924) (*qq.v.*), sought to use all that seemed best in the French Symbolists and visionary or fantastic English poets to find a new technique and a new meaning and aim for Russian poetry. Balmont's first poems and Bryusov's pioneer collection *The Russian Symbolists* both appeared in 1894; there followed a series of outstanding poets and poetic impulses which in some measure retained their vitality for some time after the October Revolution, both in Russia and among poets in exile.

But the greatest Russian poet of this Symbolist renaissance was undoubtedly Aleksander (Alexander) Blok (*q.v.;* 1880–1921). His mystical experiences carried him at his best into a poetry in which inspiration and form fused in a way unmatched since the days of Tyutchev. His poem "The Twelve," which symbolically celebrates in the guise of vivid realism the first flush of the 1917 Revolution, somehow combines rhythmical genius with the language of the people in a realistic picture of revolutionary soldiers who yet have symbolic significance related to a mystical vision. This truly great poem was written in 1918, and with it the period of modern Russian prerevolutionary poetry may be said to close.

One of the poets who began work at this time, at first as a Futurist, was Vladimir Mayakovsky (1893–1930), who was to become the idol of the Communist Revolution and its official poetic exponent. Another, perhaps the most profound and intellectually and spiritually developed of the Symbolists, was Vyacheslav Ivanov (1866–1949), who continued to write in Rome (though some of his best work remained unpublished till after his death). But Boris Pasternak (1890–   ) began as a Futurist, absorbed all that was best in the various movements, and had produced outstanding

poetry by the time the Revolution began. Alone among the greater poets he remained in Russia, though after 1932 his published work was largely restricted to translations. With Pasternak, as with Anna Akhmatova, who also remained in Russia, there is an overlap between the prerevolutionary and the postrevolutionary periods.

Prose.—The period under review, which had begun with Krylov, included Pushkin and Tyutchev and ended with Blok, could not but be reckoned a great poetical age. But it was also the great age of the Russian novel. Partly because of the relative untranslatability of poetry and the far greater effectiveness and accessibility of translated novels, it is inevitable that to the world in general the period is primarily that of the great Russian novelists. Moreover the influence of novelists whose work has had world significance, such as Gogol, Turghenyev, Tolstoy, Dostoyevsky and Gorky, has been an intellectual and spiritual force in European literature in a way that that of even the greatest of poets could never be. At the same time a period which produced political, social and philosophical thinkers writing in prose, such as Vissarion Belinsky (*q.v.;* 1811–48), Aleksander (Alexander) Herzen (*q.v.;* 1812–70), Khomyakov, Dmitri Merezhkovsky (*q.v.;* 1865–1941), Ivan Bunin (*q.v.;* 1870–1953), who in 1933 was awarded the Nobel prize for literature, Leonid Andreyev (*q.v.;* 1871–1919) and Mikhail Artsybashev (1878–1927) (*see* ARTSIBASHEV, MIKHAIL PETROVICH), could not but be one in which Russian literature in a wider sense became an outstanding influence in the development of world thought. Whereas, however, the work of intellectual journalists and political thinkers belongs rather to the history of thought than to that of literature proper, this period is rightly regarded as that in which the Russian realist novel flourished and became a world force. Many writers, such as Turghenyev and Merezhkovsky, wrote verse as well as prose; and indeed it was not uncommon for writers to try their hands at all types of literature and journalism before finding their true *métier*. But the fact remains that in this period Russia in several respects led the world in the novel, despite phases of relative decline such as the wave of pessimism and reaction which followed the assassination of Tsar Alexander II in 1881.

This was also the great age of the Russian short story. Both the poets Pushkin and Lermontov had written masterly tales which might well be regarded as short novels, respectively in *The Captain's Daughter* and *A Hero of Our Time* (this latter consisting of five tales or episodes all interconnected to produce an unforgettable picture of Pechorin who is one of the great Russian psychological masterpieces). This was in 1840. Within little more than two years Nikolai Gogol (*q.v.;* 1809–52) had published his *Dead Souls* (*Mertviya dushi*), the first and only complete part of his long satirical prose epic (*poema* as he called it). This set of caricatures of Russian provincial types, reminding the reader in some ways of both Dickens and Ben Jonson, together with Gogol's short stories, made him the first Russian prose writer to have a delighted and influenced public outside his own country. In 1857 Ivan Goncharov (*q.v.;* 1812–91) published his *Oblomov*, which is a study of a type of the "superfluous man" of a declining gentry class, whose devastating realism blended with imaginative sympathy has caused the Russian language to adopt the word *oblomovshchina* to connote this group of immediately recognizable qualities.

In the development of the novel and of its influence outside Russia, Ivan Turghenyev (1818–83) (*see* TURGENEV, IVAN SERGEYEVICH) stands apart for his unique sense of form and construction, somewhat French in quality, combining a genuine "Russianness" with a European appeal in his characterization and descriptions. His group of tales *A Sportsman's Sketches* (1852) was followed by *A Nest of Gentlefolk* (1858) and by *Fathers and Sons* (1862), in which the classical nihilist hero Bazarov makes his appearance. He continued to write outstanding novels and to produce short stories and plays. Absence of a sense of form and construction is characteristic of most Russian novels, so that Turghenyev is in a special sense classical.

Tolstoy and Dostoyevsky, however, are by far the most valued and influential novelists of their period. Each has been a dynamic force in the history of thought as well as in literature of world-wide significance. Count Lyev Nikolayevich Tolstoy (*q.v.*; 1828–1910) completed his two great novels *War and Peace* and *Anna Karenina*, respectively, in 1869 and 1877. *War and Peace* combines the highest art with social realism and a philosophy of history in a way which has made it the world's masterpiece of its kind; *Anna Karenina*, less vast in size, is found by many to be even more readable if less profound. Tolstoy's *Diaries* and his *Confession* enable the reader to follow the development of his innermost mind. Fyodor Dostoyevsky (1821–81) (*see* DOSTOIEVSKI, THEODORE [FYODOR] MIKHAYLOVICH) was the master of the compelling presentation of psychological—often psychopathic—types, who could "get inside" the human mind in its moments of crisis as no other novelist has done. He was a Slavophil, as contrasted with Turghenyev who was for long the literary leader of the westernizers. He was a religious thinker and prophet, while Turghenyev studied social types and problems without plumbing their philosophic implications. Dostoyevsky's greatest novels were *Crime and Punishment* (1866), *The Idiot* (completed 1869), *The Possessed* (*Byesy*) (1871) and *The Brothers Karamazov* (1880).

Anton Chekhov (*q.v.*; 1860–1904) is perhaps to be regarded as a master of short stories and a dramatist rather than a novelist. His pictures of Russian life combine a meticulous exactness with an art which conceals the labour of the task. Some have even thought that his work as an influence, both within and outside Russia, has been as important as that of Tolstoy and Dostoyevsky.

Maxim Gorky (*q.v.*; 1868–1936) is a short-story writer, novelist and dramatist who, like Boris Pasternak in poetry, bridges the October Revolution, though, unlike Pasternak, he became in his later years the recognized literary leader of the Soviet Union. His descriptions of the very lowest and most suffering human beings, and his immense vitality and confidence in the ultimate triumph of revolutionary Socialism made him the pioneer of that "Socialist Realism" which has been the aim of all officially acceptable Soviet literature. But his literary gifts in themselves were not enough to give him a high place and influence abroad. A natural bolshevik, he yet did much to maintain artistic standards and to encourage genuine literature after the Revolution. His *Creatures Who Have Been Human* (*Byvshiye Lyudi*; 1897), *Twenty-Six Men and a Girl* (1899) and *Mother* (1907) are among his most impressive nondramatic works. They bring the Russian peasant and industrial worker to life in a way previously unparalleled. His autobiographical works, beginning with *Childhood* (1913), along with *Mother*, formed the material for most effective films after the Revolution. (*See also* NOVEL: *The European Novel: Russia*.)

Drama.—The literary drama proper begins with the one great play of Aleksander (Alexander) Griboyedov (*q.v.*; 1795–1829), whose *The Mischief of Being Clever* (*Gore ot uma*) became public in 1825. It is a Molièresque comedy in a rhymed irregular metre reminiscent of that of some of Krylov's *Fables*, and while brilliantly witty in dialogue, it is also lively in its characterization. It has become almost a collection of sources for quotations. Several novelists were also playwrights, but the only great novelist (apart from Gogol) who also did outstanding work for the stage was Turghenyev, whose *A Month in the Country* (1850) has rightly achieved European popularity in translation as an example of psychological insight controlled by a sense of form and subtle comic play of personalities. But till the Moscow Art theatre which he did so much to inspire brought Chekhov to the fore, the theatre was dominated by Aleksander (Alexander) Ostrovsky (*q.v.*; 1823–86), who wrote many successful plays, mostly in prose, satirizing the middle classes and the still unwesternized merchants, in such vividly realistic if less well-formed plays as *The Bankrupt* (1850) and *The Poor Bride* (1852). Gogol's one brilliant dramatic masterpiece, *The Government Inspector* (*Revizor*), stands quite by itself in its appeal alike to Russia and Europe. It shows the best qualities of his *Dead Souls* dramatized, and, along with certain of Chekhov's plays, has retained universal popularity.

Chekhov's *The Seagull* (*Chayka*) was triumphantly acted under the great Stanislavsky at the then new Moscow Art theatre in 1898, and there followed under the same production in quick succession *Uncle Vanya*, *The Three Sisters* and *The Cherry Orchard*. Though the meaning of Chekhov's plays is often in dispute, their profound and subtle reality and theatrical craftsmanship never are. With Chekhov's death in 1904 the great age of the Russian drama came to an end, though the theatre continued to grow in popularity and plays to be written successfully. (*See also* DRAMA: *Russian Drama*.)

POSTREVOLUTIONARY LITERATURE

A good deal of writing which carried on existing trends went on for some time in Russia after the Revolution, though some distinguished writers, such as Vyacheslav Ivanov, continued only as *emigrés*. Some outstanding authors, such as Maxim Gorky and Vladimir Mayakovsky, wrote to aid the Soviet regime, while others, such as Boris Pasternak and Anna Akhmatova, either sought to retain their artistic integrity by developing their personal qualities in comparative isolation from state "Socialist Realism" or ceased to produce almost entirely. But the dissolution of the Russian Association of Proletarian Writers (R.A.P.P.) in 1932, and the formation of the state-controlled Union of Soviet Writers in 1934, followed by the death of Gorky in 1936, with the rigorous subordination of art to the needs of Marxism-Leninism under Stalin, made for uniformity and creative sterility. In general it may be said that all forms of literature after Gorky's death tended to be primarily subordinated to the needs of the Soviet state for reconstruction, patriotism and the "struggle for peace," and most of even the more impressive works deliberately served these ends.

Mayakovsky had a vigour and command of proletarian language combined with real poetic sensitiveness which Pasternak was among the first to recognize. But the tension between his unconscious artistic self and his need to support the Revolution as a kind of poet laureate of bolshevism finally led to his suicide. Somewhat similarly ended the young peasant lyric imaginist Yesenin and the *emigrée* poetess Marina Tsvetayeva (1892–1941). Anna Akhmatova, whose intense and profound lyrics of love and personal feeling were outstanding in the early days of the Revolution, afterward wrote only rarely for publication; and indeed subjective lyric poetry was strongly deprecated in Russia till the needs of the "Great Patriotic War" of 1941–45 brought back the lyric and song—at least in popular form, with such graceful and often moving poems as the war songs of Konstantin Simonov (1915–). Simonov illustrates, along with Ilya Ehrenburg (1891–), the really talented poet and man of letters who has turned his pen to whatever the needs of the state happened to be—novels, plays, films, poems or essays came with equal competence from their hands, though neither ever showed clear creative genius.

In the novel, the best work has continued with developments of the historical romance, which had first come to Russia through the influence of Scott and had found its earliest masterpiece in Pushkin's *The Captain's Daughter*. Mikhail Sholokhov (1905–) and Aleksey Nikolayevich Tolstoy (1882–1945) wrote historical novels of real merit in their respective masterpieces, *And Quiet Flows the Don* (*Tikhy Don*) and *Peter the First*. There were scarcely any plays of genius, yet often quite effective political dramas, such as Gorky's *Yegor Bulichev* against bourgeois capitalism and Simonov's *The Russian Question* (*Russky vopros*) against U.S. capitalist newspapers. Novelists and playwrights and poets sought to express the new Soviet hero of factory and collective farm. But one valuable feature of Soviet literary practice was its keen encouragement of poetry for the people, not merely in the writing of verses to stimulate the masses, but in the deliberate and highly successful popularization of the Russian classics. Pushkin and Chekhov found noble and scholarly editions but also cheap reprints which were bought by the million; and factory workers listened to university teachers on the literature of the Golden Age. Folklore was encouraged too, and it is to be remembered that the Russians had never lost that popular receptiveness of poetry which has almost disappeared from western Europe.

Boris Pasternak at mid-century remained the greatest and at once the most truly European and truly Russian of living poets. He excelled in a subtly fantastic poetic prose in his *Tales* (*Rasskazy*) and in the autobiographic fragment of his *Safe Conduct* (*Okhrannaya Gramota*) with its moving account of the discovery of the suicide of Mayakovsky, but perhaps even more in the analytical psychological insight into a young girl's mind seen in his *The Childhood of Lyuvers*. As a poet, despite some eccentricities of vocabulary caused by his early association with the Futurists and his intense seeking after the right tone of music (he was the son of a painter and a musician), he carried on the traditions of Pushkin and Lermontov in original imaginative ways and covered all the assimilated European movements. He has been compared in varying ways with T. S. Eliot, with John Donne and with R. M. Rilke, but he is in fact *sui generis*. As a translator, he did the best versions of some of Shakespeare's plays in Russian, as well as of *Faust*. Though he may miss some of the humour of Shakespeare, in tragic passages he makes the reader or audience feel that here (in *Hamlet* for instance) a great poet is rendering great poetry. Pasternak wrote a small amount of war poetry in which he simply shared the patriotism of the hour, and his little volume of 1945, *Earth's Spaciousness* (*Zemnoy prostor*), shows his simpler manner at its best.

The Soviet government greatly encouraged the study of the art of translation, and others, such as Samuil Marshak (1887–   ), translated foreign poetry with a poet's inner exactness, as may be seen in Marshak's versions of *English Songs and Ballads*, his Shakespeare's *Sonnets* and his Burns. Marshak, like Pasternak, also did well in some of his prose, notably in children's fairy tales. Soviet Russian literature by the 1950s had become very consciously national, with deliberate searching after the literary expression of the mind of the people in *narodnost* and often markedly isolationist tendencies. Its greatest writers were not representative, nor had the quantity of literature of permanent artistic merit been great. Yet it had been regaining some of the old Russian virtues after a time of sheer didacticism, and a renascence of creative work did not seem impossible. In 1943 Pasternak wrote:

> To dreamer and to midnight wanderer
> Moscow is dearer than the whole wide world:
> There he's at home, and at the primal source
> Of all with which the century shall flower.

BIBLIOGRAPHY.—(A selection limited to works available in English.) *General Works:* A. Brueckner, *A Literary History of Russia* (London, 1908); M. Baring, *Landmarks in Russian Literature* (London, 1910); P. Kropotkin, *Ideals and Realities in Russian Literature,* 2nd ed. (London, 1916); J. Lavrin, *Russian Literature* (London, 1927); P. N. Miliukov, *Outlines of Russian Culture* (Philadelphia, 1942); D. S. Mirsky, *A History of Russian Literature* (New York, London, 1949); M. Slonim, *The Epic of Russian Literature* (New York, 1949); T. G. Masaryk, *The Spirit of Russia,* rev. ed. (London, 1955). *Old Russian Literature:* I. Hapgood, *The Epic Songs of Russia* (New York, 1886); S. H. Cross, *The Russian Primary Chronicle* (Cambridge, Mass., 1930); N. K. Chadwick, *Russian Heroic Poetry* (Cambridge, 1932); N. K. Gudzy, *History of Early Russian Literature* (New York, 1949); W. J. Entwistle, *European Balladry,* rev. ed. (London, 1955). *Modern Russian Literature:* L. Wiener, *Anthology of Russian Literature,* two parts (London, 1902–03); N. Jarintzov, *Russian Poets and Poems* (London, 1917); D. S. Mirsky, *Contemporary Russian Literature* (New York, 1926); G. R. Noyes, *Masterpieces of the Russian Drama* (New York, 1933); G. Shelley, *Modern Poems from Russia* (London, 1942); E. J. Simmons, *An Outline of Modern Russian Literature* (Ithaca, 1943); M. Slonim, *Modern Russian Literature* (New York, 1953). *Soviet Russian Literature:* L. Wiener, *The Contemporary Drama of Russia* (Boston, 1924); J. McLeod, *The New Soviet Theatre* (London, 1943); G. Reavey, *Soviet Literature Today* (London, 1946); G. Struve, *Soviet Russian Literature* (London, 1951). *Anthologies of Soviet Literature:* G. Z. Patrick, *Popular Poetry in Soviet Russia* (Berkeley, 1929); E. Lyons, *Six Soviet Plays* (Boston, 1934); G. Reavey and M. Slonim, *Soviet Literature: An Anthology* (London, 1939); I. Montague and H. Marshall, *Soviet Short Stories* (London, 1942); B. G. Guerney, *A Treasury of Russian Literature* (New York, 1943); A. Yarmolinsky, *A Treasury of Russian Verse* (New York, 1949). *Miscellaneous:* E. J. Simmons, *English Literature and Culture in Russia* (Harvard, 1935); L. Strakhovsky, *Craftsmen of the Word: Three Poets of Modern Russia* (Cambridge, Mass., 1949); H. Gifford, *The Hero of His Time: A Theme in Russian Literature* (London, 1950). (C. L. W.)

RUSSIAN SOVIET FEDERATED SOCIALIST REPUBLIC is the official name of Russia proper and of the largest member of the Union of Soviet Socialist Republics, extending from the Finnish frontier and the Baltic to the Bering sea and the Sea of Okhotsk. Originally this was the name of the whole state until it was officially changed on the basis of the agreement of Dec. 30, 1922, for the formation of the U.S.S.R. Thereafter its area changed many times. In 1923 it covered about 7,945,900 sq.mi. or 94.6% of the whole. Later it was successively reduced by the creation of the Uzbek and Turkmen republics in 1924, of the Tajik republic in 1929 and of the Kazakh and Kirghiz republics in 1936. On the eve of World War II the R.S.F.S.R. had an estimated area of 6,374,700 sq.mi. (*i.e.*, 77.3% of the U.S.S.R.); about 24% of the R.S.F.S.R. was then in Europe and the rest in Asia.

The total population of the R.S.F.S.R. was 93,457,996 in Dec. 1926 and 109,278,614 in Jan. 1939. The number of Russians in the R.S.F.S.R. revealed by these two censuses rose from 77,791,124 (52.9% of the total) to 99,019,929 (58.3% of the total). In 1926 the R.S.F.S.R. included 72,848,280 Russians who formed 78% of its total population; no similar data were published for 1939.

The annexations of 1939–45 and certain changes in the administrative divisions within the U.S.S.R. caused new variations in the area of the R.S.F.S.R. In 1940 it was further reduced when the Karelian A.S.S.R., with the area ceded by Finland, became the Karelo-Finnish S.S.R. In 1944 the Tannu Tuva People's Republic, formerly part of China, was included in the R.S.F.S.R. In 1945 the northern part of East Prussia, southern Sakhalin and the Kurile Islands were added to the R.S.F.S.R., while in 1946, when the Karachay Autonomous Region and the Chechen-Ingush A.S.S.R. were suppressed, parts of them were included in Georgia; finally, in 1954, the Crimea was "ceded" by Russia to the Ukraine. At that time the total area of the R.S.F.S.R. was estimated at 6,523,500 sq.mi., or 76% of the U.S.S.R. In Dec. 1953 a new region (*oblast*), Magadan, was formed from part of the Khabarovsk territory (*krai*); in Jan. 1954 five new regions (Arzamas, Balashov, Byelgorod, Lipetsk and Kamensk) were formed in European Russia by revising the boundaries of the existing ones. At that time the R.S.F.S.R. comprised 13 self-governing towns, 53 regions, 6 territories, 12 autonomous republics and 6 autonomous regions.

In Feb. 1951, at the so-called republican legislative election, the R.S.F.S.R. elected 763 deputies to its supreme soviet, while at the Feb. 1955 election the number of deputies increased to 784. As the R.S.F.S.R. elected one deputy per 150,000 inhabitants, the latter number suggested a total population of 117,600,000.

Moscow was the capital of both the U.S.S.R. and the R.S.F.S.R. It was also the seat of two governments, the Soviet and the Russian. Many ministries existed in duplicate, one being Soviet and one Russian. There were, however, no Russian ministries of foreign affairs, of defense, of internal affairs or of state security. Although the Russians constituted only slightly more than half the total population of the U.S.S.R., their strength within the Communist party of the Soviet Union was about three-quarters. (K. Sм.)

RUSSIAN THISTLE, a common name applied especially to *Salsola kali* var. *tenuifolia,* a close relative of *Salsola kali,* the saltwort, which is also known as Russian thistle. Both plants are annuals of the goosefoot family, introduced from Eurasia, and are widespread along railway rights of way and in prairies and plains regions of the United States, forming bushy annuals that break off in the autumn to form tumbleweeds that may be carried long distances by wind, dropping seeds as they go. With good tillage and short rotations, however, they cause little damage in field crops.

(J. M. Bl.)

RUSSKY, NIKOLAI (1854–1918), Russian general, was educated at the infantry military school in St. Petersburg, graduated from the academy of the general staff in 1881, and by 1896 had reached general's rank. During the war with Japan (1904–05) he was the head of the staff of the 2nd army, and planned the offensive carried out by General Grippenberg which led to the prematurely abandoned offensive of Sandepu. In 1914 he commanded the 3rd army, which attacked in Galicia and advanced to Lvov (Lemberg), through which it passed in the further advance to the San-Dniester line. The dramatic entry of the 3rd army into Lvov created for General Russky a prestige out of proportion to the real importance of his success. In Oct. 1914 he was appointed commander in chief of the northwestern and afterward of the northern armies. He continued to hold the command in spite of ill health, and it was at his headquarters that the final scenes of Nicholas II's reign and his abdication took place in March 1917. Soon after the Revolution General Russky retired, and in 1918 he was reported killed by the Bolsheviks.

RUSSO-JAPANESE WAR (1904–05). The seizure by Russia of the Chinese fortress of Port Arthur, which it had a few years previously, in concert with other powers, compelled Japan to relinquish, was from the Russian point of view the logical outcome of its eastward expansion and its need for an ice-free harbour on the Pacific. The extension of the Trans-Siberian railway through Manchuria to Port Arthur and a large measure of influence in Manchuria followed equally naturally. But the whole course of this expansion had been watched with suspicion by Japan, from the time of the Sakhalin incident of 1875—when the island power, then barely emerging from the feudal age, had to cede its half of the island to Russia—to the Shimonoseki treaty of 1895, when the powers compelled it to forego the profits of its victory over China. The subsequent occupation of Port Arthur and other Chinese harbours by European powers, and the evident intention of consolidating Russian influence in Manchuria, were again and again the subject of Japanese representations at St. Petersburg (Leningrad), and these representations became more vigorous when, in 1903, Russia seemed to be about to extend its Manchurian policy into Korea. No less than ten draft treaties were discussed in vain between Aug. 1903 and Feb. 1904, and finally negotiations were broken off on Feb. 5.[1] By the fourth negotiation Japan had decided to use force, and its military and naval preparations kept pace with its diplomacy.

This was in fact an eventuality which had been foreseen and on which the naval and military policy of Japan had been based for ten years. It, too, had its projects of expansion and hegemony, and by the Chino-Japanese War it had gained a start over its rival. The reply of the western powers was first to compel the victor to maintain the territorial integrity of China, and then within two years to establish itself in Chinese harbours. From that moment Japanese policy was directed toward establishing its own hegemony and meeting the advance of Russia with a *fait accompli*. But its armaments were not then adequate to give effect to a strong-handed policy, so that for some years thereafter the government had both to impose heavy burdens on the people and to pursue a foreign policy of marking time, and endured the fiercest criticism on both counts, for the idea of war with Russia was as popular as the taxes necessary to that object were detested. But as the army and the navy grew year by year, the tone of Japanese policy became firmer. In 1902 its position was strengthened by the alliance with England; in 1903 its army, though in the event it proved almost too small, was considered by the military authorities as sufficiently large and well prepared, and the arguments of the Japanese diplomatists stiffened with menaces. Russia, on the other hand, was divided in policy and consequently in military intentions and preparations. In some quarters the force of the new Japanese army was well understood, and the estimates of the balance of military power formed by the Russian minister of war, Alexei Kuropatkin, coincided so remarkably with the facts that at the end of the summer of 1903 he saw that the moment had come when the preponderance was on the side of the Japanese. He therefore proposed to abandon Russian projects in southern Manchuria and the Port Arthur region and to restore Port Arthur to China in return for considerable concessions on the side of Vladivostok.

His plan was accepted, but "a lateral influence suddenly made itself felt, and the completely unexpected result was war." Large commercial interests were in fact involved in the forward policy, "the period of heavy capital expenditure was over, that of profits about to commence," and the power and intentions of Japan were ignored or misunderstood. Thus Russia entered upon the war unprepared in a military sense. To the guards and patrols of the Manchurian railway and the garrisons of Port Arthur and Vladivostok, 80,000 in all, Japan could, in consequence of her recruiting law of 1896, oppose a first-line army of about 270,000 trained men. Behind these, however, there were scarcely 200,000 trained men of the older classes, and at the other end of the long Trans-Siberian railway Russia had almost limitless resources.[2] The

strategical problem for Japan was how to strike a blow sufficiently decisive to secure its object before the then insignificant forces of the East Siberian army were augmented to the point of being unassailable. It turned, therefore, principally upon the efficiency of the Trans-Siberian railway and in calculating this the Japanese made a serious underestimate. In consequence, far from applying the "universal service" principle to its full extent, they trained only one-fifth of the annual contingent of men found fit for service. The quality of the army, thus composed of picked men (a point which is often forgotten), approximated to that of a professional force; but this policy had the result that, since there was no adequate second-line army, parts of the first-line had to be reserved, instead of being employed at the front. And when for want of these active troops the first great victory proved indecisive, half-trained elements had to be sent to the front in considerable numbers—indeed, the ration strength of the army was actually trebled.

Objects of Japanese Attack.—The aim of the war, "limited" in so far that the Japanese never deluded themselves with dreams of attacking Russia at home, was to win such victories as would establish the integrity of Japan itself and place its hegemony in the far east beyond challenge. Now the integrity of Japan was worth little if the Russians could hope ultimately to invade it in superior force, and since Port Arthur was the station of the fleet that might convoy an invasion, as well as the symbol of the longed-for hegemony, the fortress was necessarily the army's first objective, a convincing Sedan was the next. For the navy, which had materially only a narrow margin of superiority over the Russian Pacific squadron, the object was to keep the two halves of that squadron at Port Arthur and Vladivostok respectively separate and to destroy them in detail. But in February weather these objects could not be pursued simultaneously. Prior to the breakup of the ice, the army could disembark only at Chemulpo, far from the objective, or at Dalny under the very eyes of its defenders. The army could therefore, for the moment, occupy only Korea and try to draw upon itself hostile forces that would otherwise be available to assist Port Arthur when the land attack opened. For the navy, instant action was imperative.

On Feb. 8, the main battle fleet, commanded by Vice-Adm. Heihachiro Togo, was on the way to Port Arthur. During the night his torpedo boats surprised the Russian squadron in the harbour and inflicted serious losses, and later in the day the battleships engaged the coast batteries. Repulsed in this attempt, the Japanese established a stringent blockade, which tried the endurance of the ships and the men to the utmost. From time to time the torpedo craft tried to run in past the batteries, attempts were made to block the harbour entrance by sinking vessels in the fairway and free and deadly use was made by both sides of submarine mines. Though not destroyed, the Port Arthur squadron was paralyzed by the instantaneous assertion of naval superiority.

Alexeiev and Makárov.—Adm. Evgeni Alexeiev, the tsar's viceroy in the far east and the evil genius of the war, was at Port Arthur and forbade the navy to take the risks of proceeding to sea.[3] For a time, when, in place of Admiral Starck (who was held responsible for the surprise of February), Adm. Stepan Makárov, an officer of European reputation, commanded the fleet, this lethargy was shaken off. The new commander took his ships to sea every day. But his energetic leadership was soon ended by a tragedy. A field of electromechanical mines was laid by the Japanese in the night of April 12–13, and on the following day the Japanese cruisers stood inshore to tempt the enemy on to the mine field. Makárov, however, crossed it without accident, and pursued the cruisers until Togo's battle fleet appeared, whereupon he went about and steamed for port. In doing so he recrossed the mine field, and this time the mines were effectual. The flagship "Petropavlovsk" was struck and went down with the admiral and 600 men, and another battleship was seriously injured. Then the advocates of passivity regained the upper hand and kept the squadron in the harbour, and henceforward for many months the Japanese navy lay unchallenged off Port Arthur, engaging in minor oper-

---

[1] Belated declarations of war appeared on Feb. 10.
[2] The total Russian army on a peace footing was almost 1,000,000 strong.

[3] A vivid picture of the state of affairs in the navy at this period is given in Semenov's *Rasplata* (Eng. trans.).

ations, covering the transport of troops to the mainland, and watching for the moment when the advance of the army should force the Russian fleet to come out. Meantime seven Japanese cruisers under Vice-Admiral Kaimamura went in search of the Russian Vladivostok squadron; this, however, evaded them for some months, and inflicted some damage on the Japanese mercantile marine and transports.

Landing of Japanese 1st Army.—The Japanese had not waited to gain command of the sea before beginning the sea transport of that part of their troops allotted to Korea. The roads of that country were so poor that the landing had to be made not on the straits of Tsushima, but as far north as possible. Chemulpho, nearer by 50m. to Port Arthur than to Japan, was selected. On the first day of hostilities Rear-Admiral Uriu disembarked troops at Chemulpho under the eyes of the Russian cruiser "Variag," and next day he attacked and destroyed the "Variag" and some smaller war-vessels in the harbour, and the rest of the 1st Army (Gen. Kuroki) was gradually brought over during February and March in spite of an unbeaten and, under Makárov's régime, an enterprising hostile navy. But owing to the thaw and the subsequent break-up of the miserable Korean roads, six weeks passed before the columns of the army (Guard, 2nd and 12th Divisions), strung out along the "Mandarin road" to a total depth of six days' march, closed upon the head at Wiju, the frontier town on the Yalu. Opposite to them they found a large Russian force of all arms.

The Russian commanders, at this stage at least, had not and could not have any definite objective. Both by sea and by land their policy was to mass their resources, repulsing meantime the attacks of the Japanese with as much damage to the enemy and as little to themselves as possible. Their strategy was to gain time without immobilizing themselves so far that the Japanese could impose a decisive action at the moment that suited them best. Both by sea and by land such strategy was an exceedingly difficult game to play. But afloat, had Makárov survived, it would have been played to the end, and Togo's fleet would have been steadily used up. One day, indeed (May 15), two of Japan's largest battleships, the "Hatsuse" and the "Yashima," came in contact with free mines and were sunk. One of them went to the bottom with 500 souls. But the admiral was not on board. The Russian sailors said, when Makárov's fate was made known, "It is not the loss of a battleship. The Japanese are welcome to two of them. It is *he*." Not only the skill, but the force of character required for playing with fire was wanting to Makárov's successors.

Plans of Kuropatkin.—It was much the same on land. Kuropatkin, who had taken command of the army, saw from the first that he would have to gain three months, and disposed his forces as they came on the scene, unit by unit, in perfect accord with the necessities of the case. His expressed intention was to fight no battle until superiority in numbers was on his side. He could have gained his respite by concentrating at Harbin or even at Moukden or at Liao-Yang. But he had to reckon with the fleet[1] at Port Arthur. He knew that the defences of that place were defective, and that if the fleet were destroyed whilst that of Togo kept the sea there would be no Russian offensive. He therefore chose Liao-Yang as the point of concentration, and having thus to gain time by force instead of by distance he pushed out a strong covering detachment towards the Yalu. But little by little he succumbed to his *milieu*, the atmosphere of false confidence and passivity created around him by Alexeiev. After he had minutely arranged the eastern detachment in a series of rearguard positions, so that each fraction of it could contribute a little to the game of delaying the enemy before retiring on the positions next in rear, the commander of the detachment, Zasulich, told him that "it was not the custom of a knight of the Order of St. George to retreat," and Kuropatkin did not use his authority to recall the general, who, whether competent or not, obviously misunderstood his mission. Thus, whilst the detachment was still disposed as a series of rearguards, the foremost fractions of it stood to fight on the Yalu, against odds of four to one.

[1]Not, as is often assumed, the fortress itself.

Battle of the Yalu.—The Japanese 1st Army was carefully concealed about Wiju until it was ready to strike. Determined that in this first battle against a white nation they would show their mettle, the Japanese lavished both time and forethought on the minutest preparations. Forethought was still busy when, in accordance with instructions from Tokio, Kuroki on April 30 ordered the attack to begin at daybreak on May 1. For several miles above Antung the rivers Yalu and Aiho are parallel and connected by numerous channels. The majority of the islands thus formed were held and had been bridged by the Japanese. The points of passage were commanded by high ground a little farther up where the valleys definitely diverge, and beyond the flank of the ill-concealed positions of the defence. The first task of the right division (12th) was to cross the upper Yalu and seize this. To the Guard and 2nd Divisions was assigned the frontal attack on the Chiuliencheng position, where the Russians had about one-half of their forces under Maj.-Gen. Kashtalinski. On April 30, Inouye's 12th Division accomplished its task of clearing the high ground up to the Aiho. The Russians, though well aware that the force in their front was an army, neither retired nor concentrated. Zasulich's mediaeval generalship had been modified so far that he intended to retreat when he had taught the Japanese a lesson, and therefore Kuropatkin's original arrangements were not sensibly modified. So it came about that the combined attack of the 2nd and Guard Divisions against the front, and Inouye on the left flank and rear, found Kashtalinski without support. After a rather ineffective artillery bombardment the Japanese advanced in full force, without hesitation or finesse, and plunging into the river stormed forward under a heavy fire. A few moments afterwards Zasulich ordered the retreat. But the pressure was far too close now. Broken up by superior numbers the Russian line parted into groups, each of which, after resisting bravely for a time, was driven back. Then the frontal attack stopped and both divisions abandoned themselves to the intoxication of victory. Meanwhile, the right attack (12th Division) encountering no very serious resistance, crossed the Aiho and began to move on the left rear of the Russians. On the side of the defence, each colonel had been left to retire as best he could, and thus certain fractions of the retreating Russians encountered Inouye's advancing troops and were destroyed after a most gallant resistance. The rearguard itself, at Hamatan, was almost entirely sacrificed, owing to the wrong direction taken in retreating by its left flankguard. Fresh attempts were made by subordinates to form rearguards, but Zasulich made no stand even at Fêng-hwang-chêng, and the Japanese occupied that town unopposed on May 5. The Japanese losses were 1,100 out of over 40,000 present, the Russian (chiefly in the retreat) at least 2,500 out of some 7,000 engaged.

The Yalu, like Valmy, was a moment in the world's history. It mattered little that the Russians had escaped or that they had been in inferior numbers. The serious fact was that they had been beaten.

Distribution of Russian Forces.—The general distribution of the Russian forces was now as follows: The main army under Kuropatkin was forming, by successive brigades, in two groups— 1st Siberian Corps (Stakelberg), Niu-chwang and Kaiping; 2nd Siberian Corps, Liao-Yang. Zasulich (3rd Corps and various other units) had still 21,000. In the Port Arthur "fortified rayon," under Lieut.-Gen. Stössel (4th Corps), were 27,000 men, and Gen. Linievich around Vladivostok had 23,000. These are, however, paper strengths only, and the actual number for duty cannot have been higher than 110,000 in all. The Trans-Siberian railway was the only line of communication with Europe and western Siberia, and its calculated output of men was 40,000 a month in the summer. In October 1904, therefore, supposing the Japanese to have used part of their forces against Port Arthur, and setting this off against the absence of Linievich and Stössel, Kuropatkin could expect to have a sufficient superiority in numbers to take the offensive. His policy was still, "No battle before we are in superior force."

Landing of Japanese 2nd Army.—For the moment it was equally Japan's interest to mark time in Manchuria. Still intent upon the Russian Port Arthur squadron, she had embarked her

2nd Army (Gen. Oku, 1st, 3rd, 4th and 5th Divisions) during April, and sent it to Chinampo whence, as soon as the ice melted and Kuroki's victory cleared the air, it sailed to the selected landing-place near Pitszewo. Here, under the protection of a continuous chain of war-vessels between the Elliot islands and the mainland, Oku began to disembark on May 5. But the difficulties of the coast were such that it took three weeks to disembark the whole and to extend across the peninsula to Port Adams. Oku then, leaving the 5th Division behind, moved down with the rest towards Kinchow, and after storming that place found himself face to face with a position of enormous strength, Nanshan hill, at the narrowest part of the peninsula, where part of a Russian division (3,000 only out of 12,000 were actually engaged) had fortified itself with extreme care. On May 26 took place the battle of Nanshan. The Japanese attack was convergent, but there was no room for envelopment; the Russian position moreover was "all-round" and presented no flanks, and except for the enfilade fire of the Japanese and Russian gunboats in the shallow bays on either side the battle was locally at every point a frontal attack and defence. The first rush of the assailants carried them up to the wire and other obstacles, but they were for many hours unable to advance a step farther. But the resolute Oku attacked time after time, and at last the 4th Division, on his right, assisted by its gunboats, forced its way into the Russian position. The Russians had just begun to retreat, in accordance with orders from higher authorities. But it was a second undeniable victory. It was, moreover, a preface to those furious assaults on Port Arthur which, because they were the expression of a need that every soldier felt, and not merely of a tactical method, transcend all cool-blooded criticism. The Japanese losses were 4,500 out of 30,000 engaged, or 15%, that of the Russians fully half of the 3,000 engaged. The victors captured many guns, but were too exhausted to pursue the Russians, whose retirement was not made in the best order.

The transports were now conveying the 6th and 11th Divisions to Pitszewo; these were to form the 3rd Army (Nogi) for operations against Port Arthur. Oku exchanged his 1st Division for the 6th. The 2nd Army then turned northward (3rd, 4th, 5th and 6th Divisions). The 10th Division, forming the nucleus of the 4th Army, had begun to land at Takusham on May 19. The 2nd and 4th Armies were the left wing of a widespread converging movement on Liao-Yang. Oku had the greatest distance to march, Kuroki the smallest. The latter therefore had to stand fast in the face of the Russian eastern detachment, which was three days' march at most from Fêng-hwang-chêng and could be supported in three more days by Kuropatkin's main body, whereas the pressure of Oku's advance would not begin to be felt by the Russian southern detachment until the twelfth day at earliest. It was necessary therefore for the first objective to make a slight concession to the second. Oku had to start at the earliest possible moment, even though operations against Port Arthur were thereby delayed for a week or two. In fact, Oku's march began on June 13, Kuroki's on June 24; the moves of the intermediate forces at various dates within this time.

Meanwhile Kuropatkin, assembling the main army week by week, was in a difficult position. His policy of gaining time had received a severe blow in the failure of his executive officer to realize it, and that officer, though his unpursued troops quickly regained their *moral*, had himself completely lost confidence. On the news of the battle (coupled with that of a fresh army appearing on the Korean coast)[1], Kuropatkin instantly sent off part of his embryo central mass to bar the mountain passes of Fenshuiling and Motienling against the imagined relentless pursuit of the victors, and prepared to shift his centre of concentration back to Moukden. The subsidiary protective forces on either flank of Zasulich had promptly abandoned their look-out positions and fallen back to join him. But the commander-in-chief, soon realizing that the Japanese were not pursuing, reasserted himself, sent the protective troops back to their posts, and cancelled all orders for the evacuation of Liao-Yang. From this time forward Kuro-

[1] This was the 2nd Army, waiting in the port of Chinampo for the moment to sail for Pitszewo.

patkin allowed his subordinates little or no initiative. A few days later, Zasulich's persistent requests to be allowed to retreat and the still uncertain movements of the 2nd Army induced him once more to prepare a concentration on Moukden. But on May 6 he learned that the Japanese 1st Army had again halted at Fêng-hwang-chêng and that the 2nd Army was disembarking at Pitszewo, and he resumed (though less confidently) his original idea. The eastern protective detachment, now strengthened and placed under the orders of Count Keller, was disposed with a view to countering any advance on Liao-Yang from the east by a combination of manoeuvre and fighting.

Alexeiev and Kuropatkin.—It was at this moment of doubt that Alexeiev, leaving Port Arthur just in time and profoundly impressed with the precarious state of affairs in the fleet and the fortress, gave the order, as commander-in-chief by land and sea, for an "active" policy (May 19). Kuropatkin, thus required to abandon his own plan, had only to choose between attacking the 1st Army and turning upon Oku. He did not yield at once; a second letter from the viceroy, the news of Nanshan, and above all a signed order from the tsar himself, "Inform General Kuropatkin that I impose upon him all the responsibility for the fate of Port Arthur," were needed to induce him to execute a scheme which in his heart he knew to be perilous. The path of duty for a general saddled with a plan which he disapproves is not easily discoverable. Napoleon in like case refused, at the risk of enforced resignation, and so did Moreau; the generality of lesser men have obeyed.

Stakelberg's 1st Siberian Corps was therefore reinforced towards the end of May up to a strength of above 35,000. But it remained a detachment only. The Liao-Yang central mass was still held in hand, for the landing of the 4th Army—really only a division at present—at Takushan and the wrong placing of another Japanese division supposed to be with Kuroki (really intended for Nogi) had aroused Kuropatkin's fears for the holding capacity of Keller's detachment. Moreover, disliking the whole enterprise, he was most unwilling to use up his army in it. The Russians, then, at the beginning of June, were divided into three groups, the southern, or offensive group (35,000), in the triangle Neuchwang-Haicheng-Kaiping; the eastern or defensive group (30,000), the main body of it guarding the passes right and left of the Wiju-Liao-Yang road, the left (Cossacks) in the roadless hills of the upper Aiho and Yalu valleys; the right (Mishchenko's Cossacks and infantry supports) guarding Fenshuiling pass and the road from Takushan; the reserve (42,000) with Kuropatkin at Liao-Yang; the "Ussuri Army" about Vladivostok; and Stössel's two divisions in the Kwantung peninsula.

On the other side the 1st Army was at Fêng-hwang-chêng with one brigade detached on the roads on either hand, the left being therefore in front of the Takushan division and facing the Fenshuiling. Oku's 2nd Army (four divisions or 60,000 combatants) was about Port Adams. This last was the objective of the attack of Stakelberg's 35,000. Kuropatkin's orders to his subordinate were a compromise between his own plan and Alexeiev's. Stakelberg was to crush by a rapid and energetic advance the covering forces of the enemy met with, and his object was "the capture of the Nanshan position and thereafter an advance on Port Arthur." Yet another object was given him, to "relieve the pressure on Port Arthur by drawing upon himself the bulk of the enemy's forces," and he was not to allow himself to be drawn into a decisive action against superior numbers. Lastly, on June 7, while Stakelberg was proceeding southward on his ill-defined errand, Kuropatkin, imposed upon by the advance of the Takushan column to Siu-yen, forbade him to concentrate to the front, only removing the veto when he learned that the 4th Army had halted and entrenched at Siu-yen.

Battle of Telissu.—On the 14th, all his arrangements for supply and transport being at last complete, Oku moved north. Although he was still short of part of the 6th Division, he was in superior force. He had, moreover, the perfectly definite purpose of fighting his way north, and at Telissu or Wafangkou on June 14, as he expected, he came upon Stakelberg's detachment in an entrenched position. On the 14th and 15th, attacking sharply on the Russian front and lapping round both its flanks, Oku won an important and handsome victory, at a cost of 1,200 men out of 35,000 engaged, while the Russians, with a loss of at least 3,600 out of about 25,000 engaged, retired in disorder. Thus swiftly and disastrously ended the southern expedition. Meantime, except for the movement on Siu-yen already mentioned[1], and various reconnaissances in force by Keller's main body and by Rennenkampf's Cossacks farther inland, all was quiet along the Motienling front. Kuroki entrenched himself carefully about Fêng-hwang-chêng, intending, if attacked by the Russian main army, to defend to the last extremity the ground and the prestige gained on May 1.

From this point to the culmination of the advance at Liao-Yang, the situation of the Japanese closely resembles that of the Prussians in 1866. Haicheng represents Münchengrätz, Liao-Yang Gitschin, and the passes east of Liao-Yang Nachod and Trautenau. The concentration of the various Japanese armies on one battlefield was to be made, not along the circumference of the long arc they occupied, but towards the centre. Similarly, Kuropatkin was in the position of Benedek. He possessed the interior lines and the central reserve which enables interior lines to be utilized, and a stroke of good fortune prolonged the period in which he could command the situation, for on June 23 an unexpected sortie of the Russian Port Arthur squadron paralysed the Japanese land offensive. In the squadron were seen the battleships damaged in the February attacks, and the balance of force was now against Togo, who had lost the "Yashima" and the "Hatsuse." The squadron nevertheless, tamely returned to harbour, Togo resumed the blockade and Nogi began his advance from Nanshan, but the 2nd and 4th Armies came to a standstill at once (naval escort for their seaborne supplies being no longer available), and the 1st Army, whose turn to advance had just arrived, only pushed ahead a few miles to cover a larger supply area. On July 1 the Vladivostok squadron appeared in the Tsushima straits, and then vanished to an unknown destination, and whether this intensified the anxiety of the Japanese or not, it is the fact that the 2nd Army halted for 11 days at Kaiping, bringing the next on its right, 4th Army, to a standstill likewise. Its next advance brought it to the fortified position of Tashichiao, where Kuropatkin had, by drawing heavily upon his central reserve and even on the eastern detachment, massed about two army corps.

Tashichiao.—On the 24th Oku attacked, but the Russian general, Zarubayev, handled his troops very skilfully, and the Japanese were repulsed with a loss of 1,200 men. Zarubayev, who had used only about half his forces in the battle, nevertheless retired in the night, fearing to be cut off by a descent of the approaching 4th Army on Haicheng, and well content to have broken the spell of defeat. Oku renewed the attack next day, but found only a rearguard in front of him, and without following up the retiring Russians he again halted for six days before proceeding to Haicheng to effect a junction with the 4th Army (Nozu), which meantime had won a number of minor actions and forced the passage of the mountains at Fenshuiling South[2].

The 1st Army, after its long halt at Fêng-hwang-chêng, which was employed in minutely organizing the supply service—a task of exceptional difficulty in these roadless mountains—reopened the campaign on June 24, but only tentatively on account of the discouraging news from Port Arthur. A tremendous rainstorm imposed further delays, for the coolies and the native transport that had been laboriously collected scattered in all directions. The Motieniing pass, however, had been seized without difficulty, and Keller's power of counter-attack had been reduced to nothing by the dispatch of most of his forces to the concentration at Tashichiao. But Oku's 2nd Army was now at a standstill at Kaiping, and until he was further advanced the 1st Army could not press forward. The captured passes were therefore fortified (as Fêng-

[1]The occupation of Siu-yen was chiefly the work of the brigade pushed out to his left by Kuroki. Only a portion of the 10th Division from Takushan helped to drive away Mishchenko's Cossacks.
[2]The 5th Division of the 2nd Army had been sent to join the 10th as the latter approached Hsimucheng. The Guard brigade of Kuroki's army which had served with Nozu in the advance had now returned to Fêng-hwang chêng.

hwang-chêng had been) for passive resistance. This, and the movements of the 4th Army, which had set its face towards Haicheng and no longer seemed to be part of a threat on Liao-Yang, led to the idea being entertained at Kuropatkin's headquarters that the centre of gravity was shifting to the south. To clear up the situation Keller's force was augmented and ordered to attack Kuroki. It was repulsed with a loss of nearly 1,000 men in the action at the Motienling (July 17), but it was at least ascertained that considerable forces were still on the Japanese right, and upon the arrival of a fresh army corps from Europe, Kuropatkin announced his intention of attacking Kuroki. And in effect he succeeded in concentrating the equivalent of an army corps, in addition to Keller's force, opposite to Kuroki's right. But having secured this advantage he stood still for five days, and Kuroki had ample time to make his arrangements. The Japanese general occupied some 20m. of front in two halves, separated by 6m. of impassable mountain, and knowing well the danger of a "cordon" defensive, he met the crisis in another and a bolder fashion. Calling in the brigade detached to the assistance of Nozu as well as all other available fractions of his scattered army, he himself attacked on July 31 all along the line. It was little more than an assertion of his will to conquer, but it was effectual. On his left wing the attacks of the Guard and 2nd Divisions (action of Yang-tzu-ling) on the Russian front and flank failed—the frontal attack because of the resolute defence, the flank attack from sheer fatigue of the troops. Count Keller was killed in the defence. Meantime on the Japanese right the 12th Division attacked the large bodies of troops that Kuropatkin had massed (Yu-shu-ling) equally in vain. But one marked success was achieved by the Japanese. The Russian 35th and 36th Regiments (10th European Corps) were caught between two advancing columns, and, thanks to the initiative of one of the column leaders, Okasaki, destroyed. At night, discouraged on each wing by the fall of Count Keller and the fate of the 35th and 36th, the whole Russian force retired on Anping, with a loss of 2,400 to the Japanese 1,000 men.

Russian Retirement on Liao-Yang.—This was the only manifestation of the offensive spirit on Kuropatkin's part during the six months of marking time. It was for defence, sometimes partial and elastic, sometimes rigid and "at-all-costs," that he had made his dispositions throughout. His policy now was to retire on Liao-Yang as slowly as possible and to defend himself in a series of concentric prepared positions. In his orders for the battle around his stronghold there is no word of counter-attack, and his central mass, the special weapon of the commander-in-chief, he gave over to Bilderling and to Zarubayev to strengthen the defence in their respective sections or posted for the protection of his line of retreat. Nevertheless he had every intention of delivering a heavy and decisive counterstroke when the right moment should come, and meantime his defensive tactics would certainly have full play on this prearranged battlefield with its elaborate redoubts, bomb-proofs and obstacles, and its garrison of a strength obviously equal (and in reality superior) to that of the assailants. The Japanese, too, had effected their object, and as they converged on their objective the inner flanks of the three armies had connected and the supreme commander Marshal Oyama had taken command of the whole. But instead of boldly pushing out the 1st Army to such a distance that it could manoeuvre, as Moltke did in 1866 and 1870, he attached it to the general line of battle. It was not in two or three powerful groups but in one long chain of seven deployed divisions that the advance was made.

Battle of Liao-Yang.—On Aug. 25 the 2nd and 4th Armies from Haicheng and the 1st Army from the Yin-tsu-ling and Yu-shu-ling began the last stage of their convergent advance. The Russian first position extended in a semicircle from Anshantien (on the Liao-Yang-Hai-cheng railway) into the hills at Anping, and thence to the Taitse river above Liao-Yang; both sides had mixed detachments farther out on the flanks. The first step in the Japanese plan was the advance of Kuroki's army to Anping. Throughout the 25th, night of the 25th-26th, and the 26th of August, Kuroki advanced, fighting heavily all along the line, until on the night of the 26th the defenders gave up the contested ground at Anping. Hitherto there had only been skirmishing on a large scale on the side of Hai-cheng. Kuropatkin having already drawn in his line of defence on the south side towards Liao-Yang, the 2nd and 4th Japanese Armies delivered what was practically a blow in the air. But on the 27th there was a marked change in the Japanese plan. The right of the 1st Army, when about to continue the advance west on Liao-Yang, was diverted northward by Oyama's orders and ordered to prepare to cross the Taitszeho. The retirement of the Russian southern force into its entrenchments emboldened the Japanese commander-in-chief to imitate Moltke's method to the full. On the 28th, however, the 1st Army made scarcely any progress. The right (12th) division reached the upper Taitszeho, but the divisions that were to come up on its left were held fast by their opponents. The 29th was an uneventful day, on which both sides prepared for the next phase.

The Russians' semicircle, now contracted, rested on the Taitszeho above and below the town, and their forces were massed most closely on either side of the "Mandarin" road that the 1st Army had followed. Opposite this portion of the line was the Guard and the 4th Army. Oku was astride the railway, Kuroki extending towards his proposed crossing-points just beyond Kuropatkin's extreme left (the latter was behind the river). On the 30th the attack was renewed. The Guard, the 4th Army and the 2nd Army were completely repulsed.

On the night of the 30th the first Japanese troops crossed the Taitszeho near Lien-Tao-Wun, and during the 31st three brigades were deployed north of Kwan-tun, facing west. The Russian left wing observed the movement all day, and within its limited local resources made dispositions to meet it. Kuropatkin's opportunity was now come. The remainder of the Japanese 2nd Division was following the 12th, leaving a nine-mile gap between Kuroki and Nozu, as well as the river. It was not into this gap, but upon the isolated divisions of the 1st Army that the Russian general proposed to launch his counterstroke. Reorganizing his southern defences on a shorter front, so as to regain possession of the reserves he had so liberally given away to his subordinates, he began to collect large bodies of troops opposite Kuroki, while Stakelberg and Zarubayev, before withdrawing silently into the lines or rather the fortress of Liao-Yang, again repulsed Oku's determined attacks on the south side. But it was not in confidence of victory that Kuropatkin began the execution of the new plan—rather as a desperate expedient to avoid being cut off by the 1st Army, whose strength he greatly overestimated

On the morning of Sept. 1—the anniversary of Sedan, as the Japanese officers told their men—Oyama, whose intentions the active Kuroki had somewhat outrun, delivered a last attack with the 2nd and 4th Armies and the Guard on the south front, in the hope of keeping the main body of the Russians occupied and so assisting Kuroki, but the assailants encountered no resistance, Zarubayev having already retired into the fortress. North of the Taitszeho the crisis was approaching. Kuroki's left, near the river, vigorously attacked a hill called Manjuyama which formed part of the line of defence of the 17th Corps from Europe. But the right of the 1st Army (12th Division) was threatened by the gathering storm of the counterstroke from the side of Yentai mines, and had it not been that the resolute Okasaki continued the attack on Manjuyama alone the Japanese offensive would have come to a standstill. Manjuyama, thanks to the courage of the army commander and of a single brigadier, was at last carried after nightfall, and the dislodged Russians made two counter-attacks in the dark before they would acknowledge themselves beaten Next morning, when Kuroki (who had conceived the mistaken idea of a general retreat of the Russians on Mukden) was preparing to pursue, the storm broke. Kuropatkin had drawn together seven divisions on the left rear of the 17th Corps, the strength of the whole being about 90,000. On the extreme left was Orlov's brigade of all arms at Yentai mines, then came the 1st Siberian Corps (Stakelberg), the 10th Corps, and finally the 17th. But Orlov, perplexed by conflicting instructions and caught in an unfavourable situation by a brigade of the 12th Division which was executing the proposed "pursuit," gave way—part of his force in actual rout—and the cavalry that was with him was driven back by the Kobi (reserve army) brigade of the Guard. The fugitives

of Orlov's command disordered the on-coming corps of Stakelberg, and the outer flank of the great counterstroke that was to have rolled up Kuroki's thin line came to an entire standstill. Meantime the 10th Corps furiously attacked Okasaki on the Manjuyama, and though its first assault drove in a portion of Okasaki's line, a second and a third, made in the night, failed to shake the constancy of the 15th Brigade Misunderstandings and movements at cross-purposes multiplied on the Russian side, and at midnight Kuropatkin at last obtained information of events on the side of Yentai mines. This was to the effect that Orlov was routed, Stakelberg's command much shaken, and at the same time Zarubayev in Liao-Yang, upon whom Oku and Nozu had pressed a last furious attack, reported that he had only a handful of troops still in reserve. Then Kuropatkin's resolution collapsed, although about three divisions were still intact, and he gave the order to retreat on Mukden.

Russian Retreat on Mukden.—Thus the Japanese had won their great victory with inferior forces, thanks "in the first instance to the defeat of Gen. Orlov. But at least as large a share in the ruin of the Russian operations must be attributed to the steadfast gallantry of the 15th Brigade on Manjuyama." The losses of the Japanese totalled 23,000, those of the Russians 19,000. Coming, as it did, at a moment when the first attacks on Port Arthur had been repulsed with heavy losses, this successful climax of the four months' campaign more than restored the balance. But it was not the expected Sedan. Had the two divisions still kept in Japan been present Kuroki would have had the balance of force on his side, the Russian retreat would have been confused, if not actually a rout, and the war might have been ended on Japan's own terms. As it was, Kuropatkin drew off the whole of his forces in safety, sharply repulsing an attempt at pursuit made by part of the 12th Division on Sept. 4. The railway still delivered 30,000 men a month at Mukden, and Japan had for a time outrun her resources. At St. Petersburg the talk was not of peace but of victory, and after a period of reorganization the Russians advanced afresh to a new trial of strength. But the remainder of the Manchurian campaign proved little more than a series of violent and resultless encounters of huge armies—armies far larger than those which had fought out the real struggle for supremacy at Liao-Yang.

Naval Actions.—At this time the siege of Port Arthur had progressed only so far that the besiegers were able to realize the difficulties before them. Their exertions and sacrifices were not crowned with success until the year had run its full course, and meantime the repeated frustration of their hopes had a moral reaction on the main struggle in Manchuria, apart from keeping one of their armies away from the decisive theatre. At sea, however, the Japanese navy scored two important successes. After months of blockade and minor fighting, the Russian Port Arthur squadron had been brought to action on Aug 10. Admiral Vitheft, Makárov's successor, had put to sea shortly after the appearance of the 3rd Army on the land front of Port Arthur. The battle opened about noon, 20m. south of the harbour; the forces engaged on each side varied somewhat, but Togo finally had a superiority. As the Russians became gradually weaker, the Japanese closed in to within 3m. range, and Prince Ukhtomsky (who succeeded to the command on Vitheft being killed) gave up the struggle at nightfall. The Russians scattered, some vessels heading southward, the majority with the admiral making for Port Arthur, whence they did not again emerge. All the rest were either forced into neutral ports (where they were interned) or destroyed, among the latter being the third-class cruiser "Novik," which had already earned a brilliant reputation for daring, and now steamed half round Japan before she was brought to action and run ashore. The victors blockaded Port Arthur, until near the close of the siege when, after going ashore and examining the remnant of the Russian fleet from 203-Metre hill, Togo concluded that it would be safe to return to Japan and give his ships a complete refit. Kaimura's squadrons, after various adventures, at last succeeded on Aug. 14 in engaging and defeating the Russian Vladivostok squadron (Admiral Jessen). Thus the Russian flag disappeared from the Pacific, and thenceforward only the Baltic fleet could hope seriously to challenge the supremacy of the Japanese navy.

The remainder of the war on land, although it included two battles on a large scale and numerous minor operations, was principally a test of endurance. After Liao-Yang there were no widely extended operations, the area of conflict being confined to the plain of the coast side of the Hun-ho and the fringe of the mountains. Japan had partially accomplished her task, but had employed all her trained men in this partial accomplishment. It was questionable, even in Oct. 1904, whether she could endure the drain of men and money if it were prolonged much further. On the other hand, in Russia opposition to the war, which had never been popular, gradually became the central feature of a widespread movement against irresponsible government. Thus, while the armies in Manchuria faced one another with every appearance of confidence, behind them the situation was exceedingly grave for both parties. A state of equilibrium was established, only momentarily disturbed by Kuropatkin's offensive on the Sha-ho in October, and by the Sandepu incident in the winter, until at last Oyama fought a battle on a grand scale and won it. Even then, however, the results fell far short of anticipation, and the armies settled down into equilibrium again.

Battle of the Sha-ho.—After the battle of Liao-Yang Kuropatkin reverted for a moment to the plan of a concentration to the rear at Tieling. Politically, however, it was important to hold Mukden, the Manchurian capital, and as the Japanese, as on previous occasions, reorganized instead of pursuing, he decided to stand his ground, a resolution which had an excellent effect on his army. Moreover, growing in strength day by day, and aware that the Japanese had outrun their powers, he resolved, in spite of the despondency of many of his senior officers, to take the offensive. He disposed of about 200,000 men, the Japanese had about 170,000. The latter lay entrenched north of Liao-Yang, from a point 9m. west of the railway, through Yentai station and Yentai mines, to the hills farther east. There had been a good deal of rain, and the ground was heavy. Kuropatkin's intention was to work round the Japanese right on the hills with his eastern wing (Stakelberg), to move his western wing (Bilderling) slowly southwards, entrenching each strip of ground gained, and finally with the centre—i.e., Bilderling's left— and Stakelberg, to envelop and crush the 1st Army, which formed the Japanese right, keeping the 4th Army (Nozu) and the 2nd Army (Oku) fixed by means of Bilderling's main body. The manoeuvre began on Oct. 5, and by the evening of the 10th, after four days of advanced-guard fighting, Stakelberg was in his assigned position in the mountainous country, facing west towards Liao-Yang, with his left on the Taitzeho. The advance of Bilderling, however, necessarily methodical and slow in any case, had taken more time than was anticipated. Still, Bilderling crossed the Sha-ho and made some progress towards Yentai, and the demonstration was so far effectual that Kuroki's warnings were almost disregarded by the Japanese headquarters. The commander of the 1st Army, however, took his measures well, and Stakelberg found the greatest trouble in deploying his forces for action in this difficult country. Oyama became convinced of the truth on the 9th and 10th, and prepared a great counterattack. Kuroki, with only a portion of the 1st Army, was left to defend at least 15m. of front, and the entire 2nd and 4th Armies and the general reserves were to be thrown upon Bilderling. On the 11th the real battle opened. Kuroki displayed the greatest skill, but he was of course pressed back by the four-to-one superiority of the Russians. Still the result of Stakelberg's attack, for which he was unable to deploy his whole force, was disappointing, but the main Japanese attack on Bilderling was not much more satisfactory, for the Russians had entrenched every step of their previous advance and fought splendidly. The Russian commander-in-chief states in his work on the war that Bilderling became engaged à fond instead of gradually withdrawing as Kuropatkin intended, and at any rate it is unquestioned that in consequence of the serious position of affairs on the western wing, not only did Stakelberg use his reserves to support Bilderling, when the 12th Division of Kuroki's army was almost at its last gasp and must have yielded to fresh

pressure, but Kuropatkin himself suspended the general offensive on Oct. 13. In the fighting of Oct. 13–16 the Russians gradually gave back as far as the line of Sha-ho, the Japanese following until the armies faced roughly north and south on parallel fronts. The fighting, irregular but severe, continued. Kuropatkin was so far averse to retreat that he ordered a new offensive, which had fair success on the 16th–17th. Kuropatkin wished to continue the offensive, but his corps commanders offered so much opposition to a further offensive that he at last gave up the idea. The positions of the rival armies from Oct. 18, the close of the battle of the Sha-ho, to Jan. 26, 1905, the opening of the battle of Sandepu (Heikoutai)—a period almost entirely devoid of incident—may be described by the old-fashioned term "winter quarters."

In Jan. 1905 the Russians, 300,000 strong, were now organized in three armies, commanded by Generals Linievich, Grippenberg and Kaulbars; the total strength of the Japanese 1st, 2nd and 4th Armies and reserve was estimated by the Russians at 220,000. Towards the end of January Kuropatkin took the offensive. He wished to inflict a severe blow before the enemy could be reinforced by the late besiegers of Port Arthur, and sent Grippenberg with seven divisions against Oku's two on the Japanese left. The battle of Sandepu (Heikoutai), fought in a terrible snowstorm on Jan. 26 and 27, 1905, came near to being a great Russian victory. But after two days' severe fighting, although Grippenberg had not been checked, Kuropatkin, in face of a counterattack by Oyama, decided to abandon the attempt.

Battle of Mukden.—Both sides stood fast in the old positions up to the verge of the last and greatest battle. Kuropatkin was reinforced, and appointed Kaulbars to succeed Grippenberg and Bilderling to the command of the 3rd Army vacated by Kaulbars. On the other hand, Nogi's 3rd Army, released by the fall of Port Arthur, was brought up on the Japanese left, and a new army under Kawamura (5th), formed of one of the Port Arthur and two reserve divisions, was working from the upper Yalu through the mountains towards the Russian left rear. The Russian line covering Mukden was 47m. long, the armies from right to left being 2nd (Kaulbars), 3rd (Bilderling) and 1st (Linievich); a general reserve was at Mukden. On the other side from left to right, on a line 40m. long, were Oku (2nd Army), Nozu (4th), Kuroki (1st) and Kawamura (5th), the general reserve in rear of the centre at Yentai and the 3rd Army in rear of Oku. Each side had about 310,000 men present. The entire front of both armies was heavily entrenched. The Russians had another offensive in contemplation when the Japanese forestalled them by advancing on Feb. 21. The 5th Army gradually drove in Kuropatkin's small detachments in the mountains, and came up in line with Kuroki, threatening to envelop the Russian left. The events on this side and misleading information induced Kuropatkin to pay particular attention to his left. The Japanese 1st and 5th Armies were now engaged (Feb. 25), and elsewhere all was quiet. But on the 27th the fighting spread to the centre, and Nogi (originally behind Oku) was on the march to envelop the Russian right. He was held under observation throughout by Russian cavalry, but it seems that little attention was paid to their reports by Kuropatkin, who was still occupied with Kuroki and Kawamura, and even denuded his right of its reserves to reinforce his left. With a battle-front exceeding two days' marches the wrong distribution of reserves by both sides was a grave misfortune. Kuropatkin was at last convinced, on Feb. 28, of the danger from the west, and did all in his power to form a solid line of defence on the west side of Mukden. Nogi's first attack (March 1–2) had not much success, and a heavy counterstroke was delivered on the 2nd. Fighting for localities and alterations in the interior distribution of the opposing forces occupied much time, and by the 3rd, though the battle had become severe, Kuropatkin had merely drawn in his right and right centre (now facing west and south-west respectively) a little nearer Mukden. His centre on the Sha-ho held firm, Kuroki and Kawamura made but slight progress against his left in the mountains. Nogi and Oyama were equally impressed with the strength of the new (west) Russian front, and, like Grant at Petersburg in 1864, extended farther and farther to the outer flank, the Russians following suit. The Japanese marshal now sent up his army reserve, which had been kept far to the rear at Yentai, to help Nogi. It was not before the evening of March 6 that it came up with the 3rd Army and was placed in position opposite the centre of the Russian west front. On the rest of the line severe local fighting had continued, but the Russian positions were quite unshaken and Kuropatkin's reserves—which would have been invaluable in backing up the counter-attack of March 2—had belatedly returned to face Nogi. He had organized another counterstroke for the 6th, to be led by Kaulbars, but this collapsed unexpectedly after a brief but severe fight.

Russian Retreat on Tieling.—Kuropatkin now decided to draw in his centre and left towards Mukden. On the 7th, the various columns executed their movement to the Hun-ho with complete success, thanks to good staff work. The Japanese followed up only slowly. Nogi and Kaulbars stood fast, facing each other on the west front; after the arrival of the general reserve, Nogi was able to prolong his line to the north and eventually to bend it inwards towards the Russian line of retreat. On the 8th the fighting between Nogi and Kaulbars was very severe, and Kuropatkin now made up his mind to retreat towards Tieling. On the 9th, by Oyama's orders, Nogi extended northward instead of further swinging in south-eastward, Oku now occupied all the original line of the 3rd Army, Nozu alone was left on the south front, and Kuroki and Kawamura began to engage Linievich seriously. But Nogi had not yet reached the Mukden-Tieling railway when, on the night of the 9th, every preparation having been made, Kuropatkin's retreat began. On the 10th, covered by Kaulbars, who held off Nogi, and by strong rearguards at and east of Mukden, the movement continued, and though confusion was prevalent and the rearguards suffered very heavily, the Russians managed to draw off in safety to the northward. On the evening of the 10th, after all their long and hardly contested enveloping marches, Nogi's left and Kawamura's right met north of Mukden. The circle was complete, but there were no Russians in the centre, and a map of the positions of the Japanese on the evening of the 10th shows the 17 divisions thoroughly mixed up and pointing in every direction but that of the enemy. Thus the further pursuit of the Russians could be undertaken only after an interval of reorganization by the northernmost troops of the 5th and 3rd Armies. But the material loss inflicted on the Russians was far heavier than it had ever been before. It is generally estimated that the Russian losses were no less than 97,000, and the Japanese between 40,000 and 50,000. Japan had had to put forth her supreme effort for the battle, while of Russia's whole strength not one-tenth had been used. But Russia's strength in Europe, with but one line whereby it could be brought to bear in the Far East, was immaterial, and on the theatre of war a quarter of the Russian field forces had been killed, wounded or taken.

Rozhestvenski's Voyage.—It remains to narrate briefly the tragic career of the Russian Baltic fleet. Leaving Libau on Oct. 13–15, 1904, the fleet steamed down the North sea, expecting every night to be attacked by torpedo-boats. On the 21st, in their excitement, they opened fire on a fleet of British trawlers on the Dogger Bank (q.v.), and several fishermen were killed. This incident provoked the wildest indignation, and threatened for some days to bring Russia into conflict with England. A British fleet "shadowed" Rozhestvenski for some time, but eventually the Russians were allowed to proceed. On reaching Madagascar, Rozhestvenski heard of the fall of Port Arthur, and the question of returning to Russia arose. But a reinforcement under Rear-Admiral Nebogatov was despatched from the Baltic via Suez early in March 1905, and the armada proceeded by the Straits of Malacca, Nebogatov joining at Kamranh bay in Cochin China. The united fleet was formidable rather in number than in quality; the battleships were of very unequal value, and the faster vessels were tied to the movements of many "lame ducks." Rozhestvenski had, moreover, numerous store-ships, colliers, etc. Nevertheless, the Japanese viewed his approach with considerable anxiety, and braced themselves for a final struggle. Of the vari-

ous courses open to him, Togo prudently chose that of awaiting Rozhestvenski in home waters. The Russians left Kamranh on May 14, and for a time disappeared into the Pacific. It was assumed that they were making for Vladivostok either via Tsushima strait or by the Pacific. Rozhestvenski chose the former course, and on May 27 the fleets met near Tsushima. By superior speed and handling the Japanese gained an increasing advantage, and by the following day the whole Russian fleet, with few exceptions, had been captured or sunk. (*See* TSUSHIMA for battle.)

The Peace of Portsmouth.—After the disasters of Mukden and Tsushima, and being threatened with internal disorder in European Russia, the tsar, early in June, accepted the mediation of the president of the United States, and *pourparlers* were set on foot. The war, meanwhile, drifted on through May, June and July. Linievich, who succeeded Kuropatkin shortly after the battle of Mukden, retired slowly northward, reorganizing his forces and receiving fresh reinforcements from Europe. A Japanese expedition occupied Sakhalin (July 8–30), and another, under General Hasegawa, advanced through Korea towards Vladivostok. But the fighting was desultory. The peace negotiations were opened at Portsmouth (N.H.), on Aug. 9, and by the end of the month the belligerents had agreed as to the main points at issue—that Russia should cede the half of Sakhalin, annexed in 1875, surrender her lease of the Kwantung peninsula and Port Arthur, evacuate Manchuria, and recognize Japan's sphere of influence in Korea. The treaty of peace was signed on Sept. 5, 1905.

BIBLIOGRAPHY.—Among the first-hand narratives the most important are: Ian Hamilton, *A Staff Officer's Scrap Book;* and the *British Officers' Reports,* War Office, 1908. Also *Reports of Military Observers,* General Staff U.S.A.; Major v. Tettau's *18 Monate beim Heere Russlands;* von Schwarz, *Zehn Monate beim Heere Kuropatkins,* and Kuropatkin's own work (part of which has been translated into English). Of detailed military histories the principal are the semi-official series of narratives and monographs produced by the Austrian military journal "Streffleur" (*Einzelschriften über den russ.-japanischen Krieg*); the volumes of lectures delivered at the Russian staff college after the war, French translation (*Conférences sur la guerre russo-japonaise faites à l'Académie Nicolas*); British official *History of the Russo-Japanese War;* German official *Russisch-japanischer Krieg* (Eng. trans. by K. von Donat); Löffler, *Der russisch-japanische Krieg* (Leipzig, 1907; French trans.); L. Gianni Trapani, *La Guerra russo-giapponese* (1908); E. Bujac, *La Guerre russo-japonaise* (1909). Of critical studies one of the most important is Culmann, *Étude sur les caractères généraux de la guerre en extrème-orient* (1909). One naval narrative of absorbing interest has appeared, Semenov's *Rasplata* (Eng. trans.).

RUSSO-POLISH CAMPAIGN.

This campaign, of 1920, which resulted in the defeat and rout of the Soviet Army when it was within sight of the Polish capital, is full of dramatic incident. Organization of command, staff and administration was lacking on both sides, but above all it was the want of a proper system of supply which accounted for the sudden collapse of troops engaged in a victorious advance. The thinly populated territory lying between the Niemen in the north and the Dniester in the south was incapable of supporting large bodies of troops, and as both sides attempted to live on the country during their advances the failure of their operations followed quickly each success.

Cause of the War.—During the course of 1919 and early 1920, the Soviet Government had succeeded in clearing their territory of the White Russian armies under Kolchak, Denikin and Yudenich. They were thus at liberty to examine the situation on their frontiers. With such a mixture of races living side by side in the disputed regions no delimitation of frontier would have suited all parties, and in the absence of authority to enforce a decision, trouble quickly arose between the Soviet and the newly formed Polish State. Poland was determined to maintain her new liberty and had called up fresh levies to support the various legions which had been repatriated from the fronts upon which they had been fighting in the World War. The Soviet began to concentrate their troops towards the west. Inflammatory speeches in Moscow and a fierce propaganda amongst the Polish working people brought Polish public opinion to a fever heat. From seven divisions in January the Soviet had, by March, increased the number of their troops facing the Poles to 20 divisions, with three cavalry divisions. Poland decided that she could not wait quietly for the inevitable Soviet attack by which she would certainly be destroyed, and that she must act at once.

Polish Offensive.—Strategically, the territory in dispute may be divided into two separate areas: White Russia in the north and Volhynia and Podolia in the south. The marshes of the Pripet divide one area from the other. Acting in collusion with Petlura, the Hetman of the Ukraine, who had promised to raise his country against the Soviet, the Poles advanced in April as far as Kiev. By the beginning of May the Polish-Soviet front ran from Dvinsk in the north along the course of the Dnieper to Kiev and thence to the Dniester near Kamenets. No sooner were the Poles established in Kiev than the Soviet northern army began to advance. The Poles were able to transfer troops from the south and counter-attacked the Soviet forces which had already penetrated as far west as Lida and Baranoicze. By the end of May the line held at the beginning of the month had been restored. Operations had been most ably carried out by the Polish minister of war, Gen. Sosnkowski, but there were indications that the Soviet were transferring more and more troops to the west and that a renewal of their attacks might be expected.

At the beginning of June, in the southern area there appeared a new Soviet cavalry leader, Budenny, who completely altered the situation. Budenny had been a non-commissioned officer in the old Russian Army and soon proved himself a man of action. Within a month he had driven back the Poles a distance of 200m. until their line in the south ran just east of Pinsk and Równe (Rovno) to the junction of the Dniester and Siret (Sereth).

Russian Success.—Fighting in the northern area continued intermittently during the month of June, preventing the Poles from transferring troops to the hard-pressed south. Despite the operations in the south it was clear that the main Soviet attack was coming in the north. On July 4 the whole fell. The whole Polish line gave way. Wilno (Vilna) and Minsk were lost in the first week. Grodno fell on July 20 and Bialystok on July 25. By the end of July the Soviet advance guards had reached the Bug. In 25 days the Poles had lost 300m. of territory. The main cause of the collapse was their failure to constitute reserves. In their desire to protect their new territory they had been led into a linear defence on a front of nearly 800m., where they were strong nowhere.

Disposition of Troops.—The Polish situation was now critical. With the help of the French military mission, under Gen. Weygand, a plan for a great counter-attack was evolved on Aug. 6. The situation of the opposing sides on that date was as follows:—

Soviet: (1) Northern group. Four armies—4th, 15th, 3rd and 16th, with a cavalry corps on the extreme north aiming to outflank the Polish left.

(2) Southern group. Two armies—12th and 14th with Budenny's cavalry, along a line from Kowel through Brody to Tarnupol. The men of the Soviet army were unfed and worn out with a month's marching.

Poles: (1) A Northern group formed of units which had been retreating for over a month, strengthened by reinforcements thrown in hastily as they came up. Much material had been lost and the men were tired and hungry, but the approach to the line of the Vistula was beginning to simplify the supply of food and munitions.

(2) Southern group. Three armies—6th, 3rd and 4th—facing the Soviet southern group. Here pressure from the enemy had been by no means so severe as in the north and many of the divisions still retained their original fighting value.

Polish Plan of Attack.—The Polish plan was to withdraw all but a minimum of force from the southern area and to attack the Soviet northern group with the greatest possible strength. The operation bears a close resemblance to Ludendorff's manoeuvre at Tannenberg. In many respects the situation was similar. The Russians were advancing in two main groups divided by the Pripet marshes instead of the Masurian lakes. Here the Soviet southern group was advancing slowly like Rennenkampf's army in 1914. The situation would become critical as

soon as the two Soviet groups converged upon the Polish Army. No time was to be lost. Would the commander of the Soviet armies in the south allow himself to be deceived in the same manner as Rennenkampf?

On August 6 orders for the following fresh groupings were issued from Polish headquarters:—

(1) Three armies—2nd, 1st and 5th—under Gen. Joseph Haller, were to withdraw slowly to the line of the Vistula from Dęblin to Modlin, with the 5th Army pushed well forward on the left to prevent any outflanking of the Polish left between Warsaw and the East Prussian frontier.

(2) Two armies, 3rd and 4th—were to concentrate behind the Wieprz between Chelm and Dęblin, ready to strike due north; the advance of these two armies to commence on Aug. 16.

(3) One army, 6th—would withdraw as necessity arose in the direction of Lemberg, tempting the Soviet southern group away from the critical point in the north.

By Aug. 12 all the armies, with the exception of the two on each flank, had reached their assigned positions without incident. In the south the 3rd had found the 12th Soviet army advancing and had been forced to throw out a detachment on its right flank to cover its concentration. It had been delayed in consequence. In the north, the 5th had been driven back by overwhelming strength and had been unable to prevent the enemy outflanking movement.

Enthusiasm in the Polish army had risen surprisingly in the days since the momentous decision to attack had been taken. The chief of the Polish State, Marshal Pilsudski, had himself taken command of the 3rd and 4th Armies. With the help of Weygand and his staff the service of supply had been restored. New bodies of reinforcements were moved forward from the depôts in Western Poland and the depleted units began to raise their heads again. National optimism returned. The enemy in the south made no determined move and appeared to have no inkling of what was afoot. Every hour that he delayed meant more chance of success for the Polish plan.

Polish Advance.—Gen. Sikorski's 5th Army in the north was the first to move. The Soviet movement round his left had assumed alarming proportions and had to be stopped. On Aug. 14 he pressed forward from his defensive position at Modlin and at once encountered the Soviet 15th Army advancing to the attack. Sikorski persisted in his attacks all through Aug. 15 and 16, his men fighting with determination. Not even the appearance of elements of the Soviet 4th Army in his left rear turned him from his purpose. Throwing out covering detachments to watch his rear, he attacked again on Aug. 17. His determination reaped its reward, for the enemy gave way in front of him, their retreat rapidly developing into a rout.

In the south Pilsudski's armies made good progress. The blow against the left of the Soviet 16th Army came as a complete surprise and they offered little resistance. During Aug. 16 and 17 the Poles covered over 50 miles. By Aug. 18 the 3rd Soviet Army, which lay between the 15th destroyed by Sikorski, and the 16th broken by Pilsudski, turned also in hopeless confusion.

On the extreme Soviet right their 4th Army, containing some of the picked Communist regiments, together with the cavalry corps, had reached the Vistula between Torun and Plock in their great turning movement when Sikorski suddenly advanced. Had they advanced resolutely even then, all might have been well, but they hesitated and were lost. Their half-hearted attacks against Sikorski's left had little effect. It was not till Aug. 20 that the order for a general retreat reached them. On Aug. 22, at Mława, and Aug. 23 at Chorzele they were successful in cutting themselves a passage, but on Aug. 24 at Kovno they ran up against Pilsudski's 4th Army blocking the way. Almost without making an effort to attack they passed ignominiously over the East Prussian border to internment.

The pace of the Polish pursuit was remarkable. From Aug. 16 to Aug. 25 the advanced units of the 2nd army had covered 200m. as the crow flies. The 4th Army averaged 25m. a day in their advance. The service of supply was left far behind. The troops existed as they could upon the exhausted country. Luckily the Soviet resistance was so completely broken that there was no further fear of counter-attack and the Polish units had ample time in which to reorganize.

Conclusion.—The results of the battle of Warsaw, as it has been named, are only exceeded by those of Tannenberg. The Poles captured 70,000 prisoners, 200 guns and 1,000 machine-guns. From 50,000 to 100,000 Soviet troops passed over into East Prussia. The victory of the Poles was due to the adoption of a determined offensive based upon a sound plan. The raising of the *morale* of the beaten troops by the Polish authorities, roused to enthusiasm themselves by the inspiring presence of Gen. Weygand, is little short of miraculous. The crisis of the battle was undoubtedly Aug. 15–16, when Sikorski's 5th army cleared its front. If it was Pilsudski's force which completed the Soviet defeat, it was undoubtedly the magnificent fighting of Sikorski and his men which made victory possible.

BIBLIOGRAPHY.—H. Fenner, *Die Rote Armee, 1920* (1920); S. Szpotsanski, *La Pologne nouvelle et Pilsudski* (1920); M. Pernot, *L'épreuve de la Pologne* (1921). (W. E. I.)

RUSSO-TURKISH WARS. The Greek insurrection in 1824 gave England, France and Russia occasion to press demands upon Turkey, which the Porte refused to accede to, rejecting besides the London Protocol of July 1827. Hostilities broke out in Oct. 1827, when the allied fleet under Admiral Codrington defeated the Turkish flotilla off Navarino. This victory greatly facilitated the eventual Russian operations against Turkey as the Russian army supported and provisioned by her own fleet could march along the coast by the shortest road to Adrianople and thence towards the Turkish capital.

Towards the end of April 1828 the Russian army consisting of three army corps stood between the Pruth-Dniester 69,000 strong, war having been formally declared on April 28. Turkey, whose army was being reorganized at the time, decided to resist the enemy in the quadrilateral, Ruschuk, Silistria, Varna and Shumla, for which purpose she assembled about 80,000 men. One corps of the invading army invested Braila, which was captured on June 17; another Russian corps crossed at the mouth of the Danube on June 11, while a third drove back the garrisons of Ruschuk and Widdin into these fortresses from which they had emerged. The first two Russian corps now advanced on Shumen but finding the Turks to be stronger than they supposed, they fell back on Yenibazar. A Russian force was thrown forward towards Varna but only on the arrival of the Russian guard corps could the idea be entertained of investing it. The siege began on Sept. 10 and a month later Varna surrendered. The Russians owing to numerical weakness retired into winter quarters in Moldavia and Wallachia, leaving two corps in the vicinity of Varna, Pravodi and Bazardjik. The fortress of Silistria was still in Turkish hands and it now became on the resumption of hostilities the principal Russian objective. Sizopol at the entrance to the harbour of Burgas was captured providing the Russians with a base for their operations south of the Danube. Silistria being invested fell on June 29. Meanwhile Reschid Pasha advanced from Shumla against Pravodi hoping to recapture Varna but was beaten off. General Diebitch, who had replaced Wittgenstein as Russian commander-in-chief, defeated Reschid Pasha at Tcherkovna on June 11. Diebitch now decided to advance south of the Balkans. Reschid attempted to hinder his march but was vanquished at Sliven on Aug. 12. Adrianople was entered Aug. 20, but as Diebitch had only 15,000 men and pestilence was ravaging his ranks he deemed it wiser to conclude a treaty in September before Turkey became aware of the state of his army. Success crowned the Russian arms in Asia, Paskevitch gaining two important victories on June 1 and 2 at Erivan, his advance coming to a close by terms of the treaty arranged in Europe. A conference held in London proclaimed the independence of Greece, Russia receiving the islands at the mouth of the Danube, while Moldavia and Wallachia were to be no longer provinces of Turkey, but only under her protectorate.

The War of 1877–78.—The oppression of the Christian subjects of the Sultan had made hostilities in 1877 between Turkey and Russia inevitable. After the Crimean War Turkey promised to grant reforms, thereby bettering the treatment of the Christian population, but the following years brought no material change. In 1875 an insurrection broke out in Hercegovina and Montenegro, to be followed by Serbia openly taking up arms against Turkey. Russia, whose sympathies by reason of race and religion, were wholly on the side of the Slavs, could not remain a silent onlooker of the events in the Balkans. Russian volunteers flocked in great numbers to join the Serbians and General Chernyaeff was entrusted with their command. Disparity of numbers however, went against the Serbians, the Turks gaining several successes, which culminated in their victory at Djunis on Oct. 29, 1876. Alexander II. then stepped forward and insisted on hostilities ceasing, to which Turkey hurriedly assented. A conference now assembled at Constantinople, but after months of deliberation, it failed to come to an agreement, Turkey taking advantage of the divergent views of the Great Powers. She became as time progressed less willing to make concessions. To prepare for all eventualities and to bring greater weight to her influence at the conference Russia mobilized six army corps in Nov. They consisted of the VII., VIII., IX., X., XI. and XII., corps and were concentrated on the southern frontier, on the Rumanian borders. Mobilization arrangements were not worked effectively nor the deployment of the forces. It must be borne in mind that conscription had been only enforced in Jan. 1874 and there was consequently a lack of well trained officers and reserves. Another great obstacle that hindered Russia from dealing a quick blow at Turkey was the lack of a fleet in the Black sea, though this restriction was removed in 1871. Knowing the unprepared state of the forces several experts, among them General Todleben, the world famous defender of Sevastopol in the Crimean War (*q.v.*), were opposed to Russia undertaking an active campaign, but the Pan-Slav movement which was general in Russia, forced the Tsar to declare war April 24. Having underrated her foe Russia began hostilities with insufficient forces, sending 257,000 men into Rumania and 70,000 each to the Caucasus and to the Austrian frontier. The Grand Duke Nicholas, the Tsar's brother, was in command of the forces and orders were instantly given to cross the Rumanian frontier; this state having proclaimed her independence of Turkey afforded every facility to the Russians to move their army to the Danube. Early in June the Russian army was assembled around Bucharest; it consisted of the VIII., IX. and XII. corps, with detachments thrown forward to the Danube. The XI. corps was guarding the region from the river Argis to the river Yalomniza, further east towards the Pruth stood the XIV. corps while the XIII. was expected by the middle of June and the IV. a month later. The Russian army was armed indifferently and tactically was ill trained, which was due to the men being unused to handling their new weapons. The Russian forces in the middle of June which intended crossing the Danube numbered 257,000 men, but one must deduct those guarding the railway line through Rumania.

The Turks numbered 135,000 men north of the Balkans who were distributed in the following manner: 80,000 in the quadrilateral, 23,000 around Vidin, 10,000 in Nicopol, 8,000 in Dobrudja, 3,000 in Tirnovo, 4,000 in Sistovo, 2,000 at Lom Palanka and 5,000 at Rahoff. Forty thousand men were grouped around Adrianople and Constantinople and some 80,000 in Bosnia, Montenegro and Epirus. The Turks besides disposed of another 120,000 men in Asia Minor.

Political and military reasons forced Turkey to remain on the defensive while Russia was bent on the swiftest possible offensive—bordering on rashness. Rumania having allowed the Russians to traverse her territory greatly aided their initial concentration towards the Danube. She was even prepared in the middle of June to join the Russians against the Turks with her force of 32,000 infantry and 5,000 cavalry, but the Russians, feeling certain of an easy victory, declined her proffered help. Two months later they were only too glad to avail themselves of this assistance which would have been of inestimable value in their first operations south of the Danube. To cross this river was their primary object, but this was impeded by the Turkish flotilla which patrolled the Danube and prevented them bridging it. The Russians by means of steam launches, batteries, mines and torpedoes drove the Turkish ironclads into Sulina harbour, one being destroyed, while the smaller vessels were obliged to seek refuge in Silistria and Ruschuk. Mines were laid across the Danube, bridging now being made possible. Hearing of the hostile approach, Abdul Kerim, the Turkish leader, decided not to make a resolute defence against the enemy crossing the Danube, but to attack him, when advancing to besiege Ruschuk and Shumla. The distribution of the Turkish troops remained little changed by the middle of June; the detachments guarding the Danube were generally too weak to offer any serious resistance to the invader.

The Russians began crossing the river in boats at Zimniza early on June 23 and the following day the VIII. corps was across, standing on the southern bank of the Danube. The same day a bridge 1,300 yards long was begun to be constructed at Nicopol, which was ready by July 1, a second one being ready by Aug. 1. The other Russian corps, the XII. and XIII., commanded by the Tsarevitch, having crossed the Danube moved to the Lom and Yantra facing Ruschuk with the object of laying siege to it while the IX. corps made for Nicopol. Gourko's advance guard entered Tirnova July 7, the VIII. corps following it five days later. The Grand Duke Nicholas wished to cross the Balkans with two corps while guarding his right flank with the IX. corps, and watching Ruschuk fortress with the XII. and XIII. corps, but Alexander II. would not sanction this, rightly considering this plan too risky. Gourko left Tirnova July 12 hearing the Shipka Pass was defended by only 3,000 men. He made for the Hainkioi Pass intending to turn the Shipka Pass (q.v.), while a Russian detachment attacked the Pass from the north. Gourko having been delayed 24 hours, was repulsed by the Turks when attacking the Pass; the same fate befell the Russians advancing north of Shipka. Nevertheless next day Gourko again pressed forward, when the Turks offered to negotiate terms of capitulation. While they were being drawn up the Turks evacuated all their positions and retreated to Philipopolis. Gourko's capture of Shipka gave the advantage to the Russians for a short time only, though he hastened to put it in a state of defence and it remained in their hands up to the end of the war. Alarmed by the incursion of the Russians, the Turks recalled Suleiman Pasha from Montenegro with his army 30,000 strong and having transported it by sea to the mouth of Maritza pushed it forward without delay on July 23 between Hermanli and Karabunar. After several engagements against greatly superior forces Gourko received orders Aug. 5 from the Headquarters to return north of the Balkans. The passes being deemed of great importance the Russians decided to defend them with the 9th Division, 4th Rifle Brigade and a Bulgarian contingent.

Meanwhile Nicopol fell July 17, the IX corps capturing 8,000 men and it now received orders to advance to Plevna. General Krudener, its commander, detached one division under Schilder-Schuldner, which without any preliminary reconnaissance attacked the Turks July 20, only to be thrown back with heavy losses by Osman Pasha's much superior force, which had marched from Vidin unperceived by the Russians. Though the Rumanians had warned them of the hostile approach no serious attention was given by the Russian military authorities, for which they had to pay dearly. But even now the Russians thought this to be a momentary check and gave orders to make a fresh effort to capture Plevna, for which purpose they detailed 40,000 men. Osman Pasha had meanwhile entrenched himself round Plevna and had occupied Lovcha on the 26th, thereby securing the direct road to Sofia. The second attempt to capture the town, July 31, failed as the first and the Russians at last began to realize that their forces were inadequate to vanquish the enemy. The Tsar, by an Imperial Ukaze called up the Guard and Grenadier Corps, 24th and 26th Infantry Divisions, also the 2nd and 3rd Infantry Divisions with the 3rd Rifle Brigade which had already left Moscow for Bulgaria. Valuable assistance was also forthcoming from the Rumanian forces, which now joined the Russians. The Russian plan of campaign, which was faulty to a degree, now became absolutely impossible, there being no longer any question

of moving south of the Balkans, whilst Osman from Plevna might threaten not only their right flank, but the bridges across the Danube. Every effort was to be made to vanquish the Turkish force defending Plevna, now greatly strengthened by field works.

At the end of July, Abdul Kerim, the Turkish commander-in-chief was superseded by Mohammed Ali, who decided to attack the Russian forces under the Tsarevitch (XI., XII. and XIII. corps) on the river Lom. Mohammed Ali had two army corps for his offensive, not to mention five divisions at Shumla and two at Ruschuk, but he carried out his movement with little skill, sending his left wing against the Russians standing on the Yantra, which brought about two engagements at Ayazla on Aug. 22 and 23. The Russians retreated slightly, and a week later the XIII. corps was attacked at Karahassankioi, but no serious result was gained by this move. On Sept. 5, another engagement occurred, but though the Russians retired across the Lom the Turks were unable to march further west. The intended plan to unite the forces of Mohammed Ali with those of Suleiman at Trnova failed, his advance producing no effect on the Russian forces assembled around Plevna, which were by that time considerably reinforced (two Russian and three Rumanian infantry divisions, together with a Russian rifle brigade). On the Rumanians joining the Russians, it was agreed that Prince Charles of Rumania should be in nominal command of the forces grouped around Plevna, which were now known as the Western army. But the authority vested in Prince Charles was small, as the Commander-in-Chief, the Grand Duke Nicholas, was living in the vicinity, not to mention the Tsar himself and General Milutin, the War Minister. By this time the Russians had mobilized a huge army.

Meantime Suleiman Pasha was ordered to join Osman, but he was instructed firstly to capture the Shipka Pass which he attempted to do Aug. 21. Severe fighting took place for several days, but Radetsky, being reinforced, maintained his position, beating off every hostile attack. Suleiman in five days having lost 10,000 men, a quarter of his effective strength, decided to fall back on Kazanlik, leaving detachments by the pass. Hearing that Suleiman had been forced to give up momentarily the attempt to capture the Shipka Pass, the Russians began to fear that he might endeavour, by using the Rosalita and Trojan Passes, not only to turn the Shipka Pass, but by moving via Lovcha to get into communication with Osman Pasha, who might at any moment make for Tirnova. For this purpose Prince Imeretinsky was ordered to drive a Turkish detachment from Lovcha, which he forced to retire into Plevna. Leaving a brigade to guard the town, Imeretinsky fell back on Bogot. The Allies now decided to assault Plevna again, for which purpose they assembled about 100,000 men. Three Rumanian divisions were to advance from Grivitza, four Russian from Radishevo, and a division, having a brigade in reserve under Skobeleff, facing the Green Hills. A long artillery preparation took place Sept. 7–11, but the allies failed to make any proper reconnaissance, for which they had to pay a severe penalty, thousands of lives being sacrificed in vain. They advanced on the 11th, but failed to break the Turkish circle of defence. The Rumanians captured a redoubt at Grivitza, but were held up at Radishevo; Skobeleff on his part established himself on the Green Hills, but was thrown back the next day by Osman Pasha, who used his reserves for the counter attack. A serious crisis now arose among the Allies and a council of war was held. Many of the members, including Milutin, the War minister, urged that the army should recross the Danube and renew the advance the following spring with increased forces. This opinion was over-ruled, the Tsar showing great determination, and it was decided to invest Plevna, entrusting all operations to General Todleben, the heroic defender of Sevastopol during the Crimean War. With his arrival, the Russians gained confidence and renewed energy, one and all feeling they were at last being led by a masterly head, that chaos was replaced by order. The Guard Corps, on arriving from Russia, was sent to cut the Turkish communications and the enemy was driven out of Gorni Dubniak and Telish by General Gourko, Plevna being thus cut off from the outer world. In the middle of Nov. the Russians stood as follows: 12 divisions around Plevna, 6 on the Lom; 3 by the Shipka Pass;

2½ on the Plevna-Orhanie road.

Suleiman, now commanding the main Turkish army, took the offensive, crossed the Lom and attacked the Russians at Mechka and Tristenik Nov. 19 and 26, but both times sustained a repulse. Vessil Pasha, who now in place of Suleiman stood facing the Shipka Pass, had been considerably weakened through sending reinforcements to aid Mohammed Ali near Sofia, and he could only muster 20,000 men. Meanwhile Gourko, hearing of Mohammed's preparations to relieve Plevna, urged that the Russians should advance boldly on Sofia, thereby depriving the enemy of the initiative. This plan being agreed to, Gourko, at the head of 30,000 men, drove the Turks out of Entropol, forcing Mohammed to retreat to Araba Konak Nov. 23. Gourko disposed of too small a force to be able to pursue the enemy, and so took up a position near Orhanie. Meantime in Plevna Osman's provisions were getting shorter every day, and ultimately he attempted a sortie, hoping to cut his way through Berkovitza to Sofia. After several hours severe fighting, however, Osman was convinced of the impossibility of breaking through, and surrendered with his whole army, about 40,000 men, on Dec. 10.

The Russians now decided to move on Sofia, cross the Balkans, relieve Shipka from the south and attack Vessil Pasha, the Tsarevitch with his 70,000 men being left to guard the communications. Gourko on Dec. 25 advanced with 5½ divisions against the Turks but on reaching Toshkesen he found that the Turks had already retreated. The Russians, after occupying Sofia, followed the enemy, who was making for Tatar Bazardjik. There Suleiman assumed command, having collected a force 50,000 strong, including reinforcements from Shumen. Radetsky began his attack on Jan. 5 at Shipka, being aided by two columns coming on his left and right; the western, Skobeleff with 17,000; the eastern, Prince Imeretinsky with 19,000 men. The Prince's advance was held up, while Skobeleff, delayed, came on the scene only the following day, when they together captured the Turkish entrenched camp two miles south of the Pass, forcing Vessil Pasha to capitulate with 36,000 men. Suleiman, on hearing of Vessil Pasha's surrender, made for Philipopolis, Gourko following in direct pursuit, while Radetsky cut off his retreat from Adrianople, entering the town with his advanced guard on Jan. 19. After several minor actions near the town Suleiman retreated to the south over the Rhodope Mountains direct to the coast reaching Enos on Jan. 28. His forces were then shipped to Constantinople. The Russians advanced rapidly towards the Turkish capital, reaching the Chataldja lines on Jan. 30. Next day an armistice was concluded, the terms being greatly modified at the Berlin conference which took place the following July, when Russia was deprived of many important concessions, which greatly irritated both the nation and the army. Bulgaria now became an independent principality, while Eastern Roumelia was to be under the protectorate of Turkey.

While these events were taking place in Europe military operations were simultaneously being carried on in the Caucasus. The Grand Duke Michael, the Tsar's brother, commanded the Russian forces which were 65,000 strong. The Turks numbered 70,000 men under Mukhtar Pasha. The same mistake was committed in the Caucasus as had been done in Europe—the Russian army finding itself too weak was obliged to await reinforcements, which arrived by the end of August when they began their advance. The first serious battle occurred on Oct. 15, at Aladja Dagh, when the Turks were defeated, a part of their forces hurriedly making for Kars, which was an important fortress, while the other portion fled to Erzerum. Kars was now invested. A month later on Nov. 18, the Russians stormed and captured it. This was a brilliant feat of arms, perhaps the finest Russian exploit throughout this war. Their communications now being assured, the Russians moved rapidly towards Erzeroum, but the severe winter weather and the strength of the fortifications prevented them capturing it as quickly as they had hoped. When the armistice was concluded Erzeroum was still holding out, but the Turks were now forced to evacuate it under the terms of the armistice. The Russo-Turkish War amply proved the truth of the military maxim that to wage war with insufficient forces is

highly risky. The Russians were many times on the brink of disaster, which would most certainly have occurred had they been faced by abler Turkish leaders and more efficiently trained troops. (A. SMI.)

RUST, RICHARD SUTTON (1815–1906), U.S. clergyman and educator, was born in Ipswich, Mass., on Sept. 12, 1815, the son of a shoemaker. In 1841 he was graduated from Wesleyan university, Middletown, Conn. Ordained an elder in the Methodist Episcopal church in 1846, Rust was president of Wilberforce university, Wilberforce, O., a school for Negroes, 1858–62. For many years he was active in the Freedmen's Aid Society of the Methodist Episcopal church, which he helped to organize in 1866. In 1880 he published *The Freedmen's Aid Society of the Methodist Episcopal Church.* He died June 17, 1906.

RUST, a term usually applied to the reddish deposit formed on iron and having the approximate chemical composition $2Fe_2O_3,3H_2O$. (*See also* CORROSION AND OXIDATION OF METALS.)

RUSTICATION, in architecture, a form of masonry in which the stones have their edges cut back to a careful plane surface, but with the central portion of the stone face either left rough or projecting markedly. (*See* DRAFTED MASONRY.) Rusticated masonry is found in the platform of the tomb of Cyrus at Pasargadae in Persia (560 B.C.) and is common in certain types of Greek and Hellenistic work such as retaining walls and the like. It was similarly used for terrace and retaining walls by the Romans, who also realized its decorative value and employed it not only for such utilitarian works as the Pont du Gard at Nîmes, France and the aqueduct at Segovia, Spain (*c.* 109), but also decoratively as in the Porta Maggiore at Rome (time of Claudius), where the rustication is very rough, and the walls of the temple of Augustus at Vienne, France (*c.* 41), in which the rustication is carefully finished, the faces of the stone cut to a plane and the edges very delicately sunk.

The early Renaissance architects developed this tradition still further, and in the 15th century palaces in Florence used it with magnificent effect. Thus in the Pitti palace, by Brunelleschi (1458), the Riccardi, by Michelozzo (1444–52), and the Strozzi, by Benedetto da Maiano (1489), the carefully studied rustication forms the chief element in the design, and in the Rucellai, from designs by Alberti (1446–51), the wall surfaces between the pilasters are delicately rusticated. During the Baroque period rustication assumed great importance in garden and villa design and all sorts of fantastic surfaces were employed on the projecting portions of the stones, such as vermiculated work, in which the surface is covered with wavy and serpentine sinkages like worm-eaten wood, or treated with vertical dripping forms like lime deposits from dripping water. Sometimes the stones had sides bevelled and brought to a point or ridge in the centre.

The use of rustication was introduced into England by Inigo Jones, as in the gate of the Botanic Gardens at Oxford (1632), and became a dominant feature in much English Renaissance work. In American colonial work this influence is seen in the occasional shaping of outside sheathing boards to imitate rusticated masonry, as in portions of the Morris-Jumel house in New York (1765). Quoins (q.v.), or corner blocks are, in many styles, rusticated, where the face of the wall is left smooth.

RUTABAGA: *see* TURNIP.

RUTACEAE, a family of dicotyledonous plants, mostly shrubs and trees, comprising about 144 genera and 1,600 species found in temperate and tropical regions, and especially abundant in Australia and South Africa. *Ruta graveolens* is rue (*q.v.*). *Citrus* includes the grapefruit, orange, lemon (*qq.v.*), etc. *Chloroxylon swietenia* is satinwood (*q.v.*). *Ptelea trifoliata* is the shrubby trefoil or wafer ash; *Zanthoxylum americanum* is the prickly ash (*q.v.*). *See* A. Engler, "Rutaceae," in Engler and Prantl, *Die Natürlichen Pflanzenfamilien* 19a:187–357, fig. 89–164 (1931).

RUTBA WELLS, a post and watering place in the Syrian desert, in 33° N. and 40° E. The post, which is the headquarters of part of the desert police is the most westerly occupied place in Iraq. Westward from this point L. H. D. Buxton found considerable traces in the desert of palaeolithic remains.

See L. H. D. Buxton, *Antiquaries Journal* (1926).

RUTEBEUF or RUSTEBUEF (*fl.* 1245–1285), French *trouvère*, was born in the first half of the 13th century. His name is nowhere mentioned by his contemporaries. He frequently plays in his verse on the word Rutebeuf, which was probably a pseudonym. Some of his poems have autobiographical value. In *Le Mariage de Rutebeuf* he says that on Jan. 2, 1261, he married a woman old and ugly, with neither dowry nor amiability. In the *Complainte de Rutebeuf* he details a series of misfortunes which have reduced him to abject destitution. In these circumstances he addresses himself to Alphonse, comte de Poitiers, brother of Louis IX, for relief. His distress could not be due to lack of patrons, for his metrical life of Saint Elizabeth of Hungary was written by request of Erard de Valéry, who wished to present it to Isabel, queen of Navarre; and he wrote elegies on the deaths of Anceau de l'Isle Adam, the third of the name, who died about 1251, Eude, comte de Nevers (d. 1267), Thibaut V of Navarre (d. 1270) and Alphonse, comte de Poitiers (d. 1271), which were probably paid for by the families of the personages celebrated. In the *Pauvreté de Rutebeuf* he addresses Louis IX himself.

The piece which is most obviously intended for popular recitation is the *Dit de l'Herberie*, a dramatic monologue in prose and verse supposed to be delivered by a quack doctor. Rutebeuf was also a master in the verse *conte*, and the five of his *fabliaux* that have come down to us are gay and amusing. The adventures of *Frère Denyse le cordelier*, and of *"la dame qui alla trois fois autour du moûtier,"* find a place in the *Cent Nouvelles nouvelles*.

Rutebeuf's serious work as a satirist probably dates from about 1260. His chief topics are the iniquities of the friars, and the defense of the secular clergy of the university of Paris against their encroachments; and he delivered a series of eloquent and insistent poems (1262, 1263, 1268, 1274) exhorting princes and people to take part in the crusades. He was a redoubtable champion of the university of Paris in its quarrel with the religious orders, and he boldly defended Guillaume de Saint-Amour when he was driven into exile. The libels, indecent songs and rhymes condemned by the pope to be burned together with the *Périls des derniers temps* attributed to Saint-Amour, were probably the work of Rutebeuf. The satire of *Renart le Bestourné*, which borrows from the Reynard cycle little but the names under which the characters are disguised, was directed, according to Paulin Paris, against Philip the Bold. To his later years belong his religious poems, and also the *Voie de Paradis*, the description of a dream, in the manner of the *Roman de la Rose*.

The best work of Rutebeuf is to be found in his satires and verse *contes*. A miracle play of his, *Le Miracle de Théophile*, is one of the earliest dramatic pieces extant in French.

BIBLIOGRAPHY.—The *Oeuvres* of Rutebeuf were edited by Achille Jubinal in 1839 (new edition, 1874); a more critical edition is by Dr. Adolf Kressner (*Rustebuef's Gedichte*; Wolfenbüttel, 1885). *See also* the article by Paulin Paris in *Hist. litt. de la France* (1842), vol. xx, pp. 719–783, and *Rutebeuf* (1891), by M. Léon Clédat, in the *Grands Écrivains français* Series.

RUTGERS UNIVERSITY, the state university of New Jersey, has its main campuses in New Brunswick, N.J., with major centres in Newark and Camden. It offers undergraduate and graduate instruction for both men and women.

The university dates from Nov. 10, 1766, when Queen's college was chartered as the eighth college in the American Colonies. It owed its founding largely to the zeal for religion and education of Dutch settlers of the reformed Protestant faith who saw the need of an institution of higher learning that might provide training for candidates for the ministry. The New Brunswick Theological seminary was affiliated with the college until 1856. Classes began in 1771 in New Brunswick, but during the American Revolution the small student body was forced to evacuate the city and meet elsewhere. In 1809 Queen's building, a splendid example of Georgian Colonial architecture designed by John McComb, was erected and for several decades housed all the college work. It became the main administration building of the university.

In 1825 the name of the institution was changed to Rutgers college in honour of Col. Henry Rutgers, a leading churchman and philanthropist of New York city. In 1864 the state legislature designated the newly organized Rutgers Scientific school to be "The State College for the Benefit of Agriculture and the Mechanic Arts," and in 1917 the land-grant units were declared to be the state university of New Jersey. Rutgers is the only land-grant college with a colonial charter. In 1880 the New Jersey Agricultural Experiment station was located at the college farm.

The New Jersey College for Women was created in 1918 by the trustees of Rutgers as an integral part of the university but with a separate campus in New Brunswick. The name "Rutgers University" was adopted in 1924, although the corporate title remained "The Trustees of Rutgers College in New Jersey." Divisions, with the dates of their founding or their association with the university, are: the college of arts and sciences (1766), the college of engineering (1864), the college of agriculture (1864), the school of education (1923), the university extension division (1925), the college of pharmacy (Newark, 1927), the graduate faculty (1932), University college (1934), the Newark Colleges of Arts and Sciences (Newark, 1946), the school of business administration (1946), the school of law (Newark and Camden, 1946, 1949), the institute of microbiology (1949), and the College of South Jersey (Camden, 1950).

Rutgers university was designated by legislation effective July 1, 1945, as the state university of New Jersey "to be utilized as an instrumentality of the State for providing public higher education" on a contractual basis, and the state board of education was given "visitorial general powers of supervision and control" over the university. Management of the institution was vested in a board of trustees of 58 members, 16 of whom would represent the state, seven the alumni and one the State Federation of Women's Clubs. Thirty-four "charter trustees" are elected for life terms by the board.

About 50 courses of study leading to the degrees of bachelor of arts, bachelor of letters, bachelor of science and bachelor of laws were established. Graduate instruction leading to the degrees of master of arts, master of science, master of laws, master of education, doctor of education and doctor of philosophy is also offered.

In 1940–41, prior to the incorporation of the Newark colleges into the university, the enrolment of full-time graduate and undergraduate students was about 3,200. This figure expanded to more than 9,000 in the post-World War II years and then declined slightly to approximately 8,000 by 1950–51. In the latter year there were also about 19,000 part-time students enrolled mainly in the extension divisions.

Rutgers university's physical plant was valued in the early 1950s in excess of $60,000,000 and it comprised more than 50 major structures and more than 3,000 ac. of land. In 1950–51 its endowment was $6,754,000 and its total budget was $14,000,000, 35% of which was met by state appropriations. The Rutgers University libraries contained more than 500,000 catalogued volumes.   (R. P. McC.)

RUTH, GEORGE HERMAN (BABE) (1895–1948), U.S. baseball player, was born at Baltimore, Md., on Feb. 6, 1895. He spent a considerable part of his boyhood in the St. Mary's Industrial school in Baltimore as (by his own account) an incorrigible.

On Feb. 27, 1914, he joined the Baltimore Orioles of the International baseball league and later that year was sold to the Boston Red Sox, with whom he played through the 1918 season as a pitcher, his record including three world series victories. In the 1919 season, performing mostly as an outfielder, Ruth set a new big-league home-run record by hitting 29.

In 1920 Ruth was sold to the New York Yankees and in that season set a new record by hitting 54 home runs. In the winter of 1920–21 the scandal of the 1919 world series became public with the revelation that certain Chicago White Sox players had colluded with gamblers, agreeing to lose the series. Baseball observers called this the greatest crisis in the U.S. national game and credited Ruth's sensational play in 1921, including a new record of 59 home runs, with reviving interest in the sport. He was voted the most valuable player in the American league in 1923.

During his major league career Ruth broke more than 50 records, setting a new record for home runs in one season by hitting 60 in 1927. He led the American league in home runs for 12 years; he hit at least 50 home runs in four separate seasons and 40 in 11 seasons. He played in ten world series—three with Boston and seven with New York. His high earnings and congenial nature tempted Ruth periodically into waywardness, and he was suspended for 30 days of the 1922 baseball season by Baseball Commissioner K. M. Landis for an unauthorized barnstorming tour. In 1925 he was fined $5,000 by Yankee Manager Miller Huggins for "misconduct off the ball field."

Ruth quit the Yankees after the 1934 season, played for a part of a season with the Boston Braves in 1935 and became a coach of the Brooklyn Dodgers in 1938, after which his formal baseball career ended. Throughout World War II he lent himself to patriotic promotions, and he appeared in a motion picture on the life of his teammate, Lou Gehrig. He acted as consultant on the motion picture on his own life. Ruth died in New York city on Aug. 16, 1948. (*See* BASEBALL, Plate I, fig. 3, and Plate II, fig. 1.)

RUTH, BOOK OF, in the Old Testament. The story of Ruth, the Moabitess, great-grandmother of David, is one of the Old Testament Hagiographa (*see* BIBLE: *Old Testament: Canon*). On the other hand, it follows Judges in the Septuagint, the Vulgate and the English version. But although a *late* rearrangement might transfer Ruth from the Hagiographa to the historical books, and place it between Judges and Samuel, no motive can be suggested for the opposite change, unless it had been placed in the last part of the Jewish canon after the second (with the historical books) had been definitely closed. Moreover, the book is untouched by the "prophetic" or "Deuteronomic" editing, which helped to give the "Former Prophets" (Joshua–Kings) their present shape after the fall of the kingdom of Judah. Nor has the narrative any affinity with the view that the history of Israel was a series of examples of divine justice and mercy in the successive rebellions and repentances of the people of God. Finally, if the book had been known when Joshua–Kings was edited it could hardly have been excluded, since David's ancestry (iv, 17, 18–22) was of greater interest than that of Saul (given in 1 Sam. ix, 1), whereas the old history names no ancestor of David beyond his father Jesse.

Date.—The book of Ruth deals with a distant past (Ruth i, 1), and delights in depicting details of antique life and obsolete usages (iv, 7). It views the stormy period before the kingship through the softening atmosphere of time, in contrast to the harsher colours of the old narratives of the book of Judges. It has been argued that, as the author seems to take no offence at the marriage of Israelites with Moabite women, he must have lived before the time of Ezra and Nehemiah (Ezra ix; Neh. xiii); but the same argument would prove that the book of Esther was written before Ezra. The very designation of a period of Hebrew history as "the days of the judges" is based on the exilic "Deuteronomic" parts of the book of Judges (ii, 16 *sqq.*), and although the language sometimes recalls the narratives in Samuel and Kings, it can be assumed, either that the book is the work of a late author acquainted with the earlier literature, or that an old narrative was rewritten. The fact that the language is in contrast to that of Chronicles, Ezra, Nehemiah, etc., has no force since writings evidently more or less contemporary did not necessarily share the same characteristics (observe, for example, the prose parts of Job).

Purpose.—Like the stories appended to Judges, the book of Ruth connects itself with Bethlehem, the birthplace of David. Some connection between Bethlehem and Moab has been found in 1 Chron. iv, 22 (where the Targum and rabbinical exegesis discover references to the story of Ruth), and is explicitly suggested by the isolated 1 Sam. xxii, 3 *seq.*, which knows of some relationship between Moab and David. Next, the writer claims the sympathy of his readers for Ruth, upon whose Moabite origin he insists, and this is noteworthy in view of the aversion with which intermarriage was regarded at a certain period (Deut. xxiii, 3; Neh. xiii; Ezra ix *seq.*). The independent evidence for the present late form of the book has led many scholars to the conclusion that it was directed against the drastic steps associated with the reforms of Ezra and Nehemiah, which, as is known, were not everywhere acceptable. Thus, not only have we a beautiful portrait of a woman of Moabite origin, but she becomes the ancestress of David himself; and in the days of these measures the simple story would raise the question whether the exclusiveness of Judaism was being carried too far.

BIBLIOGRAPHY.—*See* S. R. Driver, *Lit. of the Old. Text.*; C. F. Kent, *Beginnings of Heb. Hist.* p. 310 *seq.*; Cannon, *Theology* vol. xvi, pp. 310–319, all of whom favour a pre-exilic origin. W. Robertson Smith's art. in the *Ency. Brit.* 9th and 11th ed. (portions of which are here retained) was revised and supplemented by T. K. Cheyne in *Ency. Bib.*
(S. A. C.)

RUTHENIA (Ukr. CARPATHO-UKRAINE; Hung. RUTENFÖLD; Czech SUBCARPATHIAN RUTHENIA), a region lying southwest of the central Carpathian mountains; bounded W. by Slovakia, S.W. by Hungary, S. by Rumania and N.E. and N. by the western (formerly Polish) Ukraine. Much of the country is mountainous, deeply dissected by incised valleys which often open into broad, fertile basins in their upper courses. The southern edge of the highland is heavily forested with beech on its lower levels and conifers on the higher. But the plain, largely the drainage basin of the upper Tisza and its tributaries, is the important region. Sheltered from the cold winds of the north and northeast, it receives the full benefit of the moist southwesterly currents and the climate is ideal for cereal cultivation.

Before World War I Ruthenia had been a much neglected part of Upper Hungary. Agricultural methods were primitive and insufficient to assure an adequate standard of living to the population which in its large majority was Ruthenian, a Slavonic people closely related to the Ukrainians. Industrial activity was very small, illiteracy widespread, and the Ruthenian peasants without any initiative as a result of centuries of servitude.

The peace treaty of Trianon (June 4, 1920) brought the country under Czechoslovak administration. The Czechs founded a large number of schools with Ruthenian as the language of instruction, combatted illiteracy and the low state of public health, and helped to modernize the economic life. The area of the province was 4,886 sq.mi.; the population in 1930 was 725,357, including 450,925 Ruthenians (62%), 115,805 Magyars (16%), 95,008 Jews, 34,511 Czechs and Slovaks and 13,804 Germans. With regard to religion 49.5% belonged to the Greek Catholic Church and 15.4% to the Greek Orthodox Church. Uzhgorod, the capital, had 26,669 inhabitants in 1930 and 32,250 in 1941.

Following the Munich agreement of Sept. 29, 1938 (*i.e.*, the first partition of Czechoslovakia), the Prague government appointed on Oct. 9 an autonomous Ruthenian government headed by Father Augustin Voloshyn. By their Vienna award, on Nov. 2, 1938, Germany and Italy forced Ruthenia to cede to Hungary the southern districts including the capital city of Uzhgorod (Ungvar); 606 sq.mi. in all. Voloshyn moved the capital of the remaining part to Khust. On March 14, 1939, at the time of the second partition of Czechoslovakia, Voloshyn proclaimed the independence of his country, which was renamed Carpatho-Ukraine. Independence lasted one day before the Germans authorized occupation and annexation by Hungary.

When Czechoslovakia was restored in its pre-1938 frontiers after World War II, the Soviet government obtained from the Czechoslovak government the cession of Ruthenia. A formal treaty to this effect was signed in Moscow on June 29, 1945, Ruthenia becoming the Transcarpathian oblast of the Ukrainian S.S.R. On March 9, 1946, its Greek Catholic population was forced to abandon its faith and join the Greek Orthodox Church.

The area of the Transcarpathian oblast is 4,916 sq.mi.; population (1947 est.) 900,000. Chief towns: Uzhgorod (cap.), Mukachevo, Khust, Beregovo and Vinogradov (formerly Sevluysh).

See Michael Winch, *Republic for a Day* (London, 1939); Oscar Jaszi, "The Problem of Sub-Carpathian Ruthenia," in R. J. Kerner, ed., *Czechoslovakia; Twenty Years of Independence* (Berkeley, 1940; London, 1941).
(H. Ko.; X.)

RUTHENIANS, a name also applied to those Ukrainians, or Little Russians, who were formerly Austrian subjects. The name is simply a Latinized form of "Russian," the terms "Red Russian," etc., being due to false derivations. When, however, the early Ruthene states lost their independence, the term "Russia" was monopolized by the Muscovite state which, anxious to deny to the Ruthenes a national individuality, gave them the name of

"Little Russians." The Ruthenes themselves adopted the distinguishing title of "Ukrainians," i.e., inhabitants of the Turko-Tatar frontier in S. Russia. The name Ruthene survived among the subjects of Poland and Lithuania, and later, Austria. The Ruthenians are thus neither more nor less than Ukrainians, and their linguistic and ethnographical features are described under that head. Yet they can be distinguished from the Ukrainians of Russia, both by their separate history (see POLAND, GALICIA) and by their religion. After Galicia and Volhynia came under Polish and Lithuanian rule in the 14th century, their upper classes were soon assimilated into the conquering nations, whose language and Catholic faith they adopted. The peasants sank into a state of great degeneracy, which was largely due to the decadence of their own Orthodox priests; recognizing which, they themselves proposed union with Rome. This was proclaimed by the Pope and accepted by the Ruthenes at the Union of Brest-Litovsk, Oct. 6–10, 1596. Under this new "Uniate Church," the Ruthenes retained their Slavonic liturgy and most of the outward forms of the Greek Orthodox Church, while acknowledging the spiritual supremacy of the Pope. Although the two liturgies were nominally entitled to equal treatment in Poland, actually the Uniate was always treated as inferior, and its adherents sank into a lamentable state of ignorance and poverty, due partly to the exactions of their feudal masters, partly to national oppression, partly to their portentous capacity for consuming fiery liquor, their habit of keeping the holidays of both Julian and Gregorian calendars (in 1860 16 districts in Galicia kept 160–200 days annually as holidays) and their superstitions (in 1807 a current method of exorcising cattle plague was to place the carcasses of the stricken animals in the wells, pastures and stables of uninfected districts).

On the partition of Poland, a number of Ruthenes passed back under Russian rule. Many of them were quickly reconverted to the orthodox faith, and every effort was made to Russify them. The orthodox propaganda was extended to Galicia (see PAN-SLAVISM) but the results were more sensational than practical. The Russian Government systematically discouraged Ruthenian nationalism until after the revolution of 1905, when some relaxation was made in the oppressive regulations. Similar efforts were made by the Poles of Galicia, and winked at by the Austrian Government, but here something was done for the Ruthenes. A metropolitan bishopric was founded at Lemberg in 1806, and suffragates added at Przemysl and Stanislaw. In 1877 a Ruthenian chair was established at Lemberg University, but Austria never granted a separate Ruthenian university, in spite of agitation.

After the war the largest body of Ruthenes, those in East Galicia, claimed the right of self-determination, but their short-lived state was soon absorbed in Poland (see GALICIA). The Ruthenes in the N.E. Carpathians were attributed to Czecho-slovakia, special guarantees being laid down for their national autonomy. They were formed into the province of Sub-Carpathian Russia (see CZECHOSLOVAKIA). The Ruthenes of Bessarabia and the Bukovina came under Rumanian rule (where the state religion was orthodox), with the protection of the Rumanian Minorities treaty.

The population of Transcarpathian Oblast, formerly known as Ruthenia (q.v.) and bounded on the northwest by Poland, west by Czechoslovakia, south by Rumania and southwest by Hungary, was estimated at 900,000 in 1947. The 5,000-mi. region had been controlled briefly by Czechoslovakia during World War II before it was seceded to the Soviet Union in Sept. 1945. It became an administrative unit of the Ukrainian S.S.R. See UKRAINE, POLAND, RUSSIA, etc.

See also the publications of the League for Ukrainian National Independence (Geneva 1919–22).   (C. A. M.)

RUTHENIUM, (symbol Ru, atomic number 44, atomic weight 101.7, stable isotopes 102, 104, 101, 99, 100, 96, 98), a metal, member of the platinum group.

Ruthenium, the last member of the platinum family to be discovered, was definitely established as a new element by C. Claus in 1845. A previous announcement by G. Osann in 1828 of a new element of the platinum group, the discovery of which was never confirmed, had suggested the name ruthenium from Ruthenia, Little Russia. Claus retained the name.

Ruthenium, like osmium, forms a tetroxide RuO_4, less stable than OsO_4 but which can likewise be distilled from aqueous solution. The tendency to form the tetroxide is far less strong than it is with osmium and the solutions of ruthenium are consequently easier to handle.

In analytical procedures osmium and ruthenium may be distilled together or, by changing the conditions of the solution, the two may be separated. Osmium is best distilled from a solution containing nitric acid, while ruthenium is best distilled from a solution of its sulphate in sulphuric acid to which sodium bromate is added.

Ruthenium and osmium form a natural alloy with iridium and it is from this portion of crude platinum, insoluble in aqua regia, that they are obtained. They are brought into soluble form, Na_2RuO_4 and Na_2OsO_4, by fusing the crude material with an alkaline oxidizing flux. It is customary to remove osmium first by distilling from the solution acidified with nitric acid, and then to distil the ruthenium tetroxide after making the solution alkaline again and saturating it with chlorine. In preparing pure ruthenium the metal, isolated by distillation as the tetroxide, is absorbed in hydrochloric acid diluted with four volumes of water. After removing excess acid by evaporation on a steam bath, ammonium chloride is added to precipitate a salt, probably $(NH_4)_2[RuCl_5OH]$ or $(NH_4)_2[RuCl_6]$. Reduction of the salt in hydrogen gives metallic ruthenium. If the absorbent solution is treated with nitric acid, the salt obtained will be $(NH_4)_2[RuCl_5NO]$.

The behaviour of the nitrosochloride on hydrolysis differs markedly from that of $(NH_4)_2[RuCl_5OH]$ or $(NH_4)_2[RuCl_6]$. The tightly bound nitroso group prevents the precipitation of a hydrated oxide so that one is able to separate the ruthenium contained in the two types of compounds.

Considerable confusion existed from the time the discoverer C. Claus, in 1845, prepared two chloro salts of ruthenium to which he assigned the formulas K_2RuCl_5 and K_2RuCl_6. Later it was shown that the supposed K_2RuCl_6 was a nitroso salt, K_2RuCl_5NO. The first salt has, since the time of Claus, passed for K_2RuCl_5, which was considered a pentachlororuthenite. Efforts to oxidize this salt to K_2RuCl_6 have been of no avail. In 1904 James Lewis Howe described a monohydrate of K_2RuCl_5 which differed markedly from the former salt in properties, especially in stability toward hydrolysis and in being converted into K_2RuCl_6 by the action of chlorine. It was formed from the earlier K_2RuCl_6 by boiling with dilute alcohol in acid solution and was called an aquo salt. The corresponding rubidium and cesium salts were also prepared, as well as similar salts with bromine in the place of chlorine. It was thought that there might be an instance of isomerism between these two series of pentachlororuthenites.

The explanation of this anomaly depended upon ascertaining the state of valency of the ruthenium in the two types of compounds and in determining the composition of the salts, particularly with respect to water. Raymond Charonnat in 1925 suggested that the true formula for the ordinary pentachlororuthenite is $K_2[RuCl_5OH]$, basing his view on the action of this salt on potassium iodide, and on the formation of the aquo salt by the action of hydrochloric acid on the oxalato compound $K_3[Ru(C_2O_4)_3]$. Howe concluded, in 1927, that no isomerism exists and that the explanation lies in the fact that Claus's K_2RuCl_5 is in reality $K_2[RuCl_5OH]$, in which the ruthenium is quadrivalent and that the aquo salt $K_2RuCl_5.H_2O$ is $K_2[RuCl_5H_2O]$, in which the ruthenium is tervalent.

In reducing solutions with zinc, hydrogen sulfide and other agents, a conspicuous blue colour is formed. Claus had regarded the colour as that of bivalent ruthenium. In 1927 Heinrich Remy and T. Wagner considered it to be that of univalent ruthenium and based their opinion on its being formed when the valency of the ruthenium in K_2RuCl_5 was reduced two units, as measured by the action of sodium amalgam. E. Zintl and P. Zaimis also assumed the presence of univalent ruthenium in the blue solution, basing their view on the potentiometric titration of $RuCl_3$ with chromous or titanous sulphate where with one equivalent they obtained a pale yellow solution, while with the next drop the blue colour began to appear.

Ruthenium sulphate, $Ru(SO_4)_2$, is formed when ruthenium tetroxide is dissolved in sulphuric acid and the resulting orange-yellow solution is evaporated. Hydrogen sulphide does not produce the blue reaction obtained with a solution of the chloride.

Ruthenium shows its relationship to iron through the cyano and nitroso complexes, as exemplified by $K_4[Ru(CN)_6]$ and $K_4[Fe(CN)_6]$ and by $K_2[Ru(CN)_5NO]$ and $K_2[Fe(CN)_5NO]$.

Ruthenium is rarely used in the elemental form. As a hardening constituent it is alloyed with platinum and with palladium. Platinum alloyed with 5% of its weight of ruthenium is equivalent in hardness to platinum with 10% of iridium. For this reason ruthenium-platinum alloys became popular as alternatives to iridioplatinum in the manufacture of jewellery. Ruthenium, usually in conjunction with rhodium, is used as a hardener for palladium intended for jewellery. It is also used in making hard alloys for tipping fountain pens and phonograph needles. (See PLATINUM; PLATINUM METALS.)

(R. GT.)

RUTHERFORD, ERNEST, 1ST BARON RUTHERFORD OF NELSON (1871–1937), British physicist, was born at Nelson, New Zealand on Aug. 30, 1871. Rutherford received his secondary training at Nelson college and, on graduation in 1889, gained a scholarship at the University of New Zealand. By 1893 he had taken his M.A. degree with a double first in mathematics and physical science.

In 1895 Rutherford won an 1851 exhibition scholarship which took him to Cambridge university. At the Cavendish laboratory his ability was recognized at once by J. J. Thomson. His earliest research there was a detector for electromagnetic waves, its essential feature being a small magnetizing coil containing a tiny bundle of magnetized iron wire. Rutherford's second piece of work, done jointly with Thomson, dealt with the temporary conduction in gases which results from ionization produced by X-rays.

In 1897 Rutherford worked with Thomson upon the mobility of ions and related topics, but especially upon the negative ions emitted when ultra-violet light falls upon a clean metal surface. The discovery of Becquerel rays and radium had aroused his curiosity as to just what kind of ions are emitted by radium. At this juncture, Rutherford accepted a call to McGill university in Canada. On reaching the Macdonald laboratory there, in the autumn of 1898, he at once set to work on the radiation from radium, and discovered in 1899 that it is quite complex, consisting first of all of easily absorbed rays—rays which are stopped by a few centimetres of air. These he called alpha-rays. Besides these, he found uranium giving a far more penetrating radiation, able to pass through a sheet of aluminum several millimetres thick. These he named beta-rays, and they proved to be high-speed electrons.

Rutherford's next work at Montreal was done jointly with R. B. Owens. It was a study of thorium emanation which led to the discovery of a new noble gas, later known as thoron. After Frederick Soddy came to McGill university in 1900, he and Rutherford created the modern theory of radioactivity, excellently set forth in Rutherford's *Radioactive Substances and their Radiations*.

In 1909 he accepted an invitation to succeed Sir Arthur Schuster in the Langworthy professorship at Manchester university. It was about this time that he and J. T. Royds proved that alpha-particles consist of helium atoms. The Nobel prize was presented to Rutherford on Dec. 11, 1908, some two years before he began thinking about the scattering of alpha-rays and the nature of a nucleus which could produce such scattering—his nuclear theory—the greatest of all his contributions to physics. In 1912 Niels Bohr came to work in the Manchester laboratory, and it was here that Bohr adapted the nuclear structure of Rutherford to the quantum theory of Max Planck and thus obtained an atomic structure which satisfied the experimental findings of J. R. Rydberg and other spectroscopists. About this time H. G. Moseley got in touch with Rutherford and worked with him during the year 1913. Moseley bombarded the atoms of various elements with cathode rays and proved that the inner structures of these atoms (with the positive charge on the Rutherford nucleus) respond in a group of lines which characterize the elements much as the natural numbers might do, so that each element can be assigned its atomic number. The importance of this discovery lies in the fact that the properties of an element are defined by its atomic number.

In 1919, Rutherford was invited to succeed J. J. Thomson in the Cavendish chair at Cambridge. Honours now came in rapid succession. Rutherford had been knighted in 1914. The Copley medal of the Royal society was bestowed on him in 1922; the presidency of the British Association for the Advancement of Science in 1923, to be followed, two years later, by the presidency of the Royal society. In 1931, he was created 1st Baron Rutherford of Nelson. He died Oct. 19, 1937.

BIBLIOGRAPHY.—E. R. Rutherford, J. Chadwick and C. Ellis, *Radiations from Radioactive Substances* (1930) is a book so thoroughly documented that it serves every need in the way of a chronological list of Rutherford's published papers. (H. Cw.)

RUTHERFORD, MARK, the pen name of William Hale White (1829–1913), English author, born at Bedford, Eng. His father, William White, a member of the nonconformist community of the Bunyan meeting, moved to London, where he was well known as a doorkeeper of the house of commons; he wrote sketches of parliamentary life for the *Illustrated Times*, papers afterward collected by his son as *The Inner Life of the House of Commons* (1897). The son was educated at Cheshunt and New College for the Congregational ministry, but the development of his views prevented his following that career, and he became a clerk in the admiralty.

He had already served an apprenticeship to journalism before he made his name as a novelist by the three books "edited by Reuben Shapcott," *The Autobiography of Mark Rutherford* (1881), *Mark Rutherford's Deliverance* (1885), and *The Revolution in Tanner's Lane* (1887). Under his own name he translated Spinoza's *Ethics* (1883, new ed. 1894). Later books are *Miriam's Schooling, and other Papers* (1890), *Catherine Furze,* 2 vol. (1893), *Clara Hopgood* (1896), *Pages from a Journal, with other Papers* (1900), *John Bunyan* (1905), *More Pages from a Journal* (1910) and *Last Pages* (1915) which was edited by his wife. Though for a long time little appreciated by the public, his novels—particularly the earlier ones—have a power and style which must always give his works a place of their own in the literary history of their time. He died at Groombridge, Sussex, on March 14, 1913.

See A. E. Taylor, "The Novels of Mark Rutherford" in *Essays and Studies* by members of the English association (1913–14).

RUTHERFORD, a borough of Bergen county, New Jersey, U.S., on the Erie railroad, midway between Jersey City and Paterson. Pop. (1950) 17,411; in 1940, 15,466 by federal census. The combined population of Rutherford and the adjoining borough of East Rutherford (7,438 in 1950 and 7,268 in 1940) was 24,849 in 1950. Both boroughs are primarily residential communities, with little manufacturing.

RUTHERGLEN (locally pronounced *Rŭglen*), royal and large burgh of Lanarkshire, Scotland. Pop. (1951) 24,225. Area 1.6 sq.mi. It is situated on left bank of the Clyde, 2½ mi. by the Scottish region railway S.E. of Glasgow, with the east of which it is connected by a bridge. The parish church stands near the spire of the ancient church where, according to tradition, the treaty was made in 1297 with Edward I, by which Sir John Menteith undertook to betray Wallace to the English. The industries include collieries, chemical works, dye works, paper mills, chair making, tube making, pottery, rope- and twine-works.

Rutherglen was erected into a royal burgh by David I in 1126. It then included a portion of Glasgow, but in 1226 the boundaries were rectified so as to exclude the whole of the city, and Rutherglen has continued to resist incorporation with Glasgow. In early times it had a castle, which was taken by Robert Bruce from the English in 1313. It was kept in good repair until after the battle of Langside (1568), when it was burned by order of the regent Moray. In 1679 the Covenanters published their "Declaration and Testimony" at Rutherglen prior to the battles of Drumclog and Bothwell Brig (1679).

RUTHIN, market town and municipal borough, Denbigh parliamentary division, Denbighshire, Wales, 215 mi. N.W. of London by Western region railway. Pop. (1951) 3,599. Area 3.2 sq.mi. Ruthin (*Rhudd ddin,* red fortress) stands on a hill above the river Clwyd. Apart from legends of Arthur, the first fact of note is its connection with the Grey de Ruthyn family (1282). Owen Glendower attacked the castle in 1400; it was later sold to Henry VII; and Elizabeth gave it to the earl of Warwick. In 1646 it was dismantled by the Parliamentarians but later a new castle was built on the site. The church of St. Peter has nearly 500 panels of carved oak. The incumbent is known as the warden.

RUTHVEN (riv'en), name of a noble Scottish family tracing descent from a certain Thor, who settled in Scotland during the reign of David I. In 1488 one of its members, Sir William Ruthven (d. 1528), was created a lord of parliament as Lord Ruthven. Patrick, 3rd Lord Ruthven (c. 1520–1566), played an important part in the political intrigues of the 16th century as a strong Protestant and a supporter of the lords of the congregation. He favoured the marriage of Mary with Darnley, and was the leader of the band which murdered Rizzio. This event was followed by his flight into England, where he died. Ruthven wrote for Queen Elizabeth a *Relation* of the murder, which is preserved in manuscripts in the British museum.

A descendant of the 1st Lord Ruthven in a collateral line, also named Patrick Ruthven (c. 1573–1651), distinguished himself in the service of Sweden, which he entered about 1606. After leaving the Swedish service he was employed by Charles I. in Scotland. He defended Edinburgh castle for the king in 1640, and when the Civil War broke out he joined Charles at Shrewsbury. He led the left wing at the battle of Edgehill, and after this engagement was appointed general-in-chief of the Royalist army. For his services he was created Lord Ruthven of Ettrick in 1639, earl of Forth in 1642 and earl of Brentford in 1644. The earl compelled Essex to surrender Lostwithiel, and was wounded at both battles of Newbury. In 1644 he was superseded in his command by Prince Rupert. After visiting Sweden on a mission for Charles II., Brentford died at Dundee on Feb. 2, 1651. He left no sons and his titles became extinct.

Patrick, 3rd Lord Ruthven, was succeeded as 4th lord by his son William (c. 1541–1584), who like his father was prominent in the political intrigues of the period and was also concerned in the Rizzio murder. In 1582 he devised the plot to seize King James VI., known as the raid of Ruthven, and he was the last-known custodian of the famous silver casket containing the letters alleged to have been written by Mary, queen of Scots, to Bothwell. In 1581 he was created earl of Gowrie, but all his honours were forfeited when he was attainted and executed in May 1584. (See GOWRIE, 3RD EARL OF.)

In 1853 the barony descended to Mary Elizabeth Thornton (c. 1784–1864), the wife of Walter Hore (d. 1878). She and her husband took the name of Hore-Ruthven, borne by later barons.

See the *Ruthven Correspondence*, edited with introduction by the Rev. W. D. Macray (1868); J. H. Round, "The Barony of Ruthven of Freeland" in Joseph Foster's *Collectanea Genealogica* (1881–85); and Sir R. Douglas, *The Peerage of Scotland* (new ed. by Sir J. B. Paul).

RUTILE, the most abundant of the three native forms of titanium dioxide, TiO_2; the others being anatase and brookite (*qq.v.*). Like anatase, it crystallizes in the tetragonal system, but with different angles and cleavages, it being crystallographically related to cassiterite, with which it is isomorphous The crystals resemble cassiterite in their prismatic habit and terminal pyramid planes and also in the twinning; the prism planes are striated vertically. Acicular crystals are sometimes twinned together to form reticulated skeletal plates to which the name "sagenite" (Gr. σαγήνη a net), is applied. At the same time, the colour is usually reddish-brown, though yellowish in the very fine needles, and black in the ferruginous varieties ("nigrine" and "ilmenorutile"); the streak is pale brown. The name rutile, given by A. G. Werner in 1803, refers to the colour (Lat. *rutilus*, red). Crystals are transparent to opaque, and have a brilliant metallic-adamantine lustre. The hardness is 6·5; specific gravity 4·2, ranging up to 5·2 in varieties containing 10% of ferric oxide.

Rutile occurs as a primary constituent in eruptive rocks, but more frequently in schistose rocks. As delicate acicular crystals it is often enclosed in mica and quartz; in mica (*q.v.*) it gives rise to the phenomenon of asterism; and clear transparent quartz (rock-crystal) enclosing rutile is often cut as a gem under the name of "Venus' hair stone" (Pliny's *Veneris crinis*). As a secondary mineral rutile in the form of minute needles is of wide distribution in various sedimentary rocks, especially clays and slates. As rounded grains it is often met with in auriferous sands and gravels. The mineral has little economic value; it has been used for imparting a yellow colour to glass and porcelain, and for this purpose is mined at Risör and other places in Norway.

(L. J. S.)

RUTILIUS CLAUDIUS NAMATIANUS, Roman poet, flourished at the beginning of the 5th century A.D. He was the author of a Latin poem, *De Reditu Suo*, in elegiac metre, describing a coast voyage from Rome to Gaul in A.D. 416. The literary excellence of the work, and the flashes of light which it throws across a momentous but dark epoch of history, combine to give it exceptional importance among the relics of late Roman literature. The poem was in two books; the exordium of the first and the greater part of the second have been lost. What remains consists of about seven hundred lines.

The author is a native of S. Gaul (Toulouse or perhaps Poitiers), and belonged, like Sidonius, to one of the great governing families of the Gaulish provinces. His father was an imperial official with a distinguished career, and Rutilius himself was secretary of State and *praefectus urbi*. After reaching manhood, he passed through the tempestuous period between the death of Theodosius (395) and the fall of the usurper Attalus, which occurred near the date when his poem was written. Undoubtedly the sympathies of Rutilius were with those who during this period dissented from and, when they could, opposed the general tendencies of the imperial policy. We know from himself that he was the intimate of those who belonged to the circle of the great orator Symmachus—men who scouted Stilicho's compact with the Goths, and led the Roman senate to support the pretenders Eugenius and Attalus in the vain hope of reinstating the gods whom Julian had failed to save.

Perhaps the most interesting lines in the whole poem are those in which Rutilius assails the memory of "dire Stilicho," as he names him. Stilicho, "fearing to suffer all that had caused himself to be feared," planted the cruel Goths, his "skin-clad" minions in the very sanctuary of the empire. May Nero rest from all the torments of the damned, that they may seize on Stilicho; for Nero smote his own mother, but Stilicho the mother of the world!

We shall not err in supposing that we have here (what we find nowhere else) an authentic expression of the feeling entertained by a majority of the Roman senate concerning Stilicho. He had but imitated the policy of Theodosius with regard to the barbarians; but even that great emperor had met with passive opposition from the old Roman families. It is noteworthy that Rutilius speaks of the crime of Stilicho in terms far different from those used by Orosius and the historians of the lower empire. They believed that Stilicho was plotting to make his son emperor, and that he called in the Goths in order to climb higher. Rutilius holds that he used the barbarians merely to save himself from impending ruin. The Christian historians assert that Stilicho designed to restore paganism. To Rutilius he is the most uncompromising foe of paganism.

With regard to the form of the poem, Rutilius handles the elegiac couplet with great metrical purity and freedom, and betrays many signs of long study in the elegiac poetry of the Augustan era. The Latin is unusually clean for the times, and is generally fairly classical both in vocabulary and construction. The taste of Rutilius, too, is comparatively pure. It is common to call Claudian the last of the Roman poets. That title might fairly be claimed for Rutilius, unless it be reserved for Merobaudes. At any rate, in passing from Rutilius to Sidonius no reader can fail to feel that he has left the region of Latin poetry for the region of Latin verse.

BIBLIOGRAPHY.—All existing mss. of Rutilius are later than 1494, and are copies from a lost copy of an ancient ms. once at the monastery of Bobio, which disappeared about 1700. The *editio princeps* is that by J. B. Pius (Bologna, 1520), and the principal editions since have been those by Barth (1623), P. Burman (1731, in his edition of the minor Latin poets), Wernsdorf (1778, part of a similar collection), Zumpt (1840), and the critical edition by Lucian Müller (Teubner, Leipzig, 1870), and another by Vessereau (1904); also an annotated edition by Keene, with a translation by G. F. Savage-Armstrong (1906). Müller writes the poet's name as Claudius Rutilius Namatianus, instead of the usual Rutilius Claudius Namatianus; but if the identification of the poet's father with the Claudius mentioned in the Theodosian Code (2, 4, 5) be correct, Müller is probably wrong. Rutilius receives more or less attention from all writers on the history or literature of the times, but a lucid chapter in Beugnot, *Histoire de la destruction du Paganisme en Occident* (1835), may be especially mentioned, and one in Pichon's *Derniers écrivains profanes* (1906). See also O. Schissel von Fleschenberg, *Rutilius Namatianus* (Vienna and Leipzig, 1920).

(J. S. R.)

RUTLAND, EARLS AND DUKES OF. The 1st earl of Rutland was Edward Plantagenet (1373–1415), son of Edmund, duke of York, and grandson of King Edward III. In 1390 he was created earl of Rutland, but was to hold the title only during the lifetime of his father, on whose death in 1402 the earldom accordingly became extinct, the earl then becoming duke of York. The title earl of Rutland seems to have been assumed subsequently by different members of the house of York, though it does not appear that any of them had a legal right to it. One of these was the 1st earl's nephew, Richard Plantagenet, duke of York, father of King Edward IV. Richard's daughter Anne married for her second husband Sir Thomas St. Leger, and their daughter Anne married George Manners, 12th Baron Ros, or Roos (d. 1513). Their son, Thomas Manners (d. 1543), was therefore great-grandson of Richard Plantagenet, who had styled himself earl of Rutland among other titles. In 1525 Thomas Manners was created earl of Rutland, and his descendants have held this title to the present day.

Thomas was a favourite of Henry VIII., who conferred on him many offices and extensive grants of land, including Belvoir Castle, in Leicestershire, which became henceforth the chief residence of his family. He was succeeded in the earldom by his son Henry (c. 1516–1563); and his second son, Sir John Manners, acquired Haddon Hall, Derbyshire, by his marriage with Dorothy, daughter of Sir George Vernon, called "the king of the Peak." Henry, the 2nd earl, was an admiral of the fleet in the reign of Queen Mary, and later enjoyed the favour of Queen Elizabeth.

John, 9th earl (1638–1711), a partisan of the Revolution of 1688, received the Princess Anne at Belvoir Castle on her flight from London; after the accession of Anne to the throne she created him marquess of Granby and duke of Rutland in 1703. The 1st duke was three times married; the divorce in 1670, while he was still known as Lord Ros, of his first wife, Anne, daughter of the marquess of Dorchester, was a very celebrated legal case, being the first instance of divorce *a vinculo* by act of parliament, a divorce *a mensa et thoro* having previously been granted by the ecclesiastical courts. His grandson John, the 3rd duke (1696–1779), was the father of John Manners, marquess of Granby (*q.v.*), a distinguished soldier, whose son Charles, 4th duke of Rutland (1754–1787), succeeded his grandfather. When marquess of Granby he represented Cambridge university in the House of Commons, and hotly opposed the policy that led to war with the American colonies. He helped to procure the entrance of the younger Pitt to the House of Commons, and remained through life Pitt's intimate friend. After succeeding to the dukedom in 1779, he sat in the cabinets of Shelburne and of Pitt, and became lord lieutenant of Ireland in 1784.

He was one of the earliest to advocate a legislative union between Ireland and Great Britain, which he recommended in a letter to Pitt in June 1784. The poet Crabbe was for some time private chaplain to the duke at Belvoir. His wife, Mary Isabella (1756–1831), "the beautiful duchess," whose portrait was four times painted by Sir Joshua Reynolds, was a daughter of the 4th duke of Beaufort. His eldest son, John Henry, 5th duke (1778–1857), was "the duke" in Disraeli's *Coningsby;* the latter's two sons, who succeeded in turn to the dukedom, the marquess of Granby and Lord John Manners, figuring in the same novel as "the marquis of Beaumanoir" and "Lord Henry Sidney" respectively. The 7th duke is noticed separately.

RUTLAND, JOHN JAMES ROBERT MANNERS, 7TH DUKE OF (1818–1906), English statesman, was born at Belvoir Castle on Dec. 13, 1818, the younger son of the 5th duke of Rutland by Lady Elizabeth Howard, daughter of the 5th earl of Carlisle. Lord John Manners, as he then was, was educated at Eton and Trinity College, Cambridge. In 1841 he was returned for Newark in the Tory interest, along with W. E. Gladstone, and sat for that borough until 1847. Subsequently he sat for Colchester, 1850–57; for North Leicestershire, 1857–85; and for East Leicestershire from 1885 until in 1888 he took his seat in the House of Lords upon succeeding to the dukedom.

In 1841 Manners definitely associated himself with the "Young England" party, under the leadership of Disraeli. This party sought to extinguish the predominance of the middle-class *bourgeoisie,* and to re-create the political prestige of the aristocracy by resolutely proving its capacity to ameliorate the social, intellectual, and material condition of the peasantry and the labouring classes. Manners made an extensive tour of inspection in the industrial parts of N. England, in the course of which he and his friend Smythe expounded their views with a brilliancy which frequently extorted compliments from the leaders of the Manchester school. In 1843 he supported Lord Grey's motion for an

inquiry into the condition of England, the serious disaffection of the working classes of the north being a subject to which he was constantly drawing the attention of parliament. Among other measures that he urged were the disestablishment of the Irish Church, the modification of the Mortmain Acts, and the resumption of regular diplomatic relations with the Vatican. In the same year he issued in pamphlet form a strong *Plea for National Holydays.* In 1844 Lord John vigorously supported the Ten-hours Bill, which, though strongly opposed by Bright, Cobden, and other members of the Manchester school, was passed in May 1847.

Manners figured as "Lord Henry Sidney" in Disraeli's *Coningsby,* and not a few of his ideas are represented as those of Egremont in *Sybil* and Waldershare in *Endymion.* But the disruption of the Young England party was already impending. Lord John's support to Peel's decision to increase the Maynooth grant in 1845 led to a difference with Disraeli. Divergences of opinion with regard to Newman's secession from the English Church produced further defections in the ranks, and the rupture was completed by Smythe acquiescing in Peel's conversion to Free Trade. Lord John produced another volume of verse, known as *English Ballads,* chiefly patriotic and historical, in 1850. During the three short administrations of Lord Derby (1851, 1858 and 1866) he sat in the cabinet as first commissioner of the office of works. On the return of the Conservatives to power in 1874 he became postmaster-general in Disraeli's administration, and was made G.C.B. on his retirement in 1880. He was again postmaster-general in Lord Salisbury's administration, 1885–86, and was head of the department when sixpenny telegrams were introduced. Finally, in the Conservative government of 1886–92 he was chancellor of the duchy of Lancaster. He had succeeded to the dukedom of Rutland in March 1888, upon the death of his elder brother. He died on Aug. 4, 1906 at Belvoir Castle.

RUTLAND, a midland county of England, bounded north and east by Lincolnshire, north and west by Leicestershire, and southeast by Northamptonshire. It is the smallest geographical county in England, having an area of 152 sq.mi. Rutland is a fertile county of rolling upland, rising to about 600 ft. on the Leicestershire border. On the western side the villages, built of local ironstone, are a golden colour. In the limestone areas, chiefly on the eastern side, gray stone walls and buildings are typical. The western portion is formed of the Jurassic beds, including Lias, inferior oolites and great oolites, which form the high ground. They dip gently to the east and are interrupted in places by faults, as in the Welland valley between Ketton and Duddington which is crossed by the Seaton viaduct ($\frac{3}{4}$-mi. long and 70-ft. high). The Lower Lias occupies but a small part in the extreme northwest. The Middle Lias includes ferruginous limestone (marlstone) yielding iron in workable quantities and forming the productive soil of the vale of Catmose. The Upper Lias forms the steep slopes below the oolitic scarps, and furnishes materials for bricks and tiles. Rutland's two chief rivers, the Gwash and the Chater, flow roughly parallel from west to east into the Welland, which forms the county's southern boundary.

History.—Ancient stone implements have been found in the Oakham district and along the Gwash river and small late Bronze Age hoards. At the time of the Roman invasion, this region was inhabited by a scanty population of the Coritani tribe. This is inferred by the absence of finds, although Ermine street passes through its eastern portion. Rutland was forested in pre-Norman days and only a few early settlements occurred, which were found on the belt of Northampton sands at its junction with the Lias clays, where dry sites could be found near springs, with pastures on the clay beds. These sites were occupied by a tribe of the Angli in the 6th and 7th centuries, and the whole region was absorbed subsequently in the kingdom of Mercia.

Although mentioned by name in the will of Edward the Confessor, who bequeathed it to his queen Edith for life with remainder to Westminster abbey, Rutland did not rank as a county at the time of the Domesday survey in which the term Rutland is applied only to that portion assessed under Nottinghamshire, while the southeast portion of the modern county is surveyed under Northamptonshire, where it appears as the wapentake of Wiceslea,

Rutland is first mentioned as a distinct county under the administration of a separate sheriff in the pipe roll of 1159, but as late as the 14th century it is designated "Rutland Soke," and the connection with Nottinghamshire, was maintained up to the reign of Henry III, when the sheriff of Nottingham was by statute appointed also escheator in Rutland. Rutland was included in the diocese of Lincoln, and in 1291 it became a new rural deanery within the archdeaconry of Northampton; but on the elevation of Peterborough to an episcopal see by Henry VIII in 1541, the archdeaconry of Northampton with the deanery of Rutland was placed within the newly founded archdeaconry of Oakham.

The Norman Walkelin de Ferrers was connected with this county, and founded Oakham castle in the 12th century. One of the minor battles in the Wars of the Roses was fought (1470) north of Empingham on a site afterward known as hose coat field. Essendine was granted in 1545 to Richard Cecil of Burleigh, and the title of baron of Essenden bestowed on his grandson is retained by the earls of Salisbury. Burley-on-the-hill was the seat of George Villiers, duke of Buckingham, who there entertained James I. The present house was built by the earl of Winchelsea and Nottingham between 1694 and 1702 after the original had been burned down by the Parliament forces in 1645.

The county returned two members to parliament from 1295 until 1885, when the number was reduced to one. With part of the Kesteven division of Lincolnshire it forms the county constituency of Rutland and Stamford.

Agriculture and Trade.—Rutland has always been mainly an agricultural county. The Domesday survey mentions numerous mills in Rutland, and a fishery at Ayston rendered 325 eels. In the 14th century the county exported wool. Stilton cheese has long been made in Leyfield forest and the vale of Catmose, and limestone is quarried in many parts of the county. The development of the economic resources of Rutland was helped by the extension of the Melton Mowbray canal to Oakham, completed in 1803, now disused.

In the east and southeast districts of Rutland the soil is light and shallow, while in other districts it is a fertile loam, and in the vale of Catmose the soil is either clay or loam or a mixture of the two. The east part of the county is chiefly under tillage and the west in grass. The chief crops are barley, wheat, oats, turnips and other roots. Many sheep (Leicesters and Southdowns) and cattle (mainly Shorthorns) are reared. Large quantities of cheese are manufactured and sold as Stilton. Agriculture is practically the only industry of importance, but there is some quarrying and bootmaking. The region producing iron is continued from Northampton into Rutland, and the working of the iron ore forms one of the industries of the county. The limestone quarries at Clipsham and Ketton have been worked since the 13th century. Clipsham stone has been used for many important buildings including cathedrals, Oxford colleges, and the house of commons after it was bombed in World War II; for the Cambridge colleges Ketton stone was largely used. Portland cement has been made at Ketton since 1928.

Population and Administration.—The area of the administrative county is 152 sq.mi., with a population (1951) of 20,537. The county contains five hundreds. Oakham (q.v.) is the county town and the only urban district. There are three rural districts: Ketton, Oakham and Uppingham (q.v.). The county is in the Midland circuit, and assizes are held at Oakham. It has one court of quarter sessions, and is not divided for petty sessional purposes.

BIBLIOGRAPHY.—James Wright, *History and Antiquities of the County of Rutland* (London, 1684); T. Blore, *History and Antiquities of the County of Rutland*, vol. i, pt. 2 (containing the East hundred and including the hundred of Casterton Parva; Stamford, 1811); C. G. Smith, *A Translation of that portion of Domesday Book which relates to Lincolnshire and Rutland* (London, 1870).

RUTLAND, a city of Vermont, U.S., the county seat of Rutland county; on Otter creek, 95 mi. N.E. of Albany (New York). It is on federal highways 4 and 7 and is served by the Delaware and Hudson and the Rutland railways. Pop. (1950) 17,659; 1940 federal census 17,082. Rutland has a beautiful site, 561 ft. above sea level, encircled by the Green mountains. Twenty peaks can be seen from the city hall, and there are 20 lakes within

20 mi. The famous Rutland marble (used for the memorial in Arlington National cemetery and for many public buildings) is quarried in West Rutland and in Proctor (6 mi. N.W.) where there is a large marble display. Some of the underground quarries are 300 ft. below the surface. The manufacturing industries of the city include marble and monument works, and factories making stoneworking machinery, maple-sugar products and utensils and scales. Rutland was settled in 1770, and from 1784 to 1804 was one of the capitals of Vermont. The capitol (1784) is the second oldest building in the state. The village was incorporated in 1847, and in 1892 a part of the town (including the village) was chartered as a city. Plymouth, a village 30 mi. S.E. of Rutland, was the birthplace of Calvin Coolidge.

RUTLEDGE, JOHN (1739–1800), U.S. jurist and statesman, was born in Charleston, S.C. After studying law in England he returned to Charleston where he began to practise in 1761. He was a delegate to the Stamp Act congress in 1765 and to the Continental Congress in 1774–1777 and 1782–1783. He served as chairman of the committee which framed the state constitution of 1776 and as the first president or governor of South Carolina from 1776 to 1778 and again from 1779 to 1782. In 1787, having attained "distinguished rank among the American worthies," he was sent to the Constitutional Convention as one of South Carolina's representatives. There he championed the cause of slavery, urged the assumption of state debts by the national government and argued in favour of dividing society into classes as a basis for representation and requiring high property qualifications for officeholding. Having secured safeguards for slavery in the constitution, he took a strong nationalistic position, recommending as chairman of the committee of detail the granting to the national government of indefinite powers of legislation for the purpose of promoting the general welfare. He was associate justice of the U.S. Supreme Court in 1789–1791, and chief justice of the supreme court of South Carolina in 1791–95. Nominated chief justice of the U.S. Supreme Court in 1795, he failed to win confirmation by the senate. He died in Charleston on July 18, 1800.

(JN. C. M.)

His brother, EDWARD RUTLEDGE (1749–1800), a signatory of the Declaration of Independence, was born in Charleston on Nov. 23, 1749. He studied law in his brother's office, and in London in 1769–73, and practised in Charleston. He served in the Continental Congress in 1774–77, and was sent with John Adams and Benjamin Franklin to confer on terms of peace with Lord Howe on Staten Island in Sept. 1776. As captain of artillery and as lieutenant colonel he served against the British in South Carolina. He was a member of the State legislature from 1782 to 1798, and in 1791 drafted the act which abolished primogeniture in South Carolina. From 1798 until his death Jan. 23, 1800, he was governor of South Carolina.

RUTULI, a people of ancient Italy inhabiting Ardea and the district round it on the coast of Latium, at no very great distance from Aricia, and just west of the territory of the Volsci. They are ranked by the form of their name with the Siculi and Appuli (Apuli), probably also with the Itali, whose real Italic name would probably have been Vituli (*see* ITALY). This suggests that they belong to a fairly early stratum of the Indo-European population of Italy.

RUVIGNY, HENRI DE MASSUE, MARQUIS DE, afterward EARL OF GALWAY (1648–1720), was born in Paris on April 9, 1648, the son of the 1st Marquis de Ruvigny. He saw service under Turenne, who thought very highly of him. He had English connections, and was selected in 1678 by Louis XIV to carry out the secret negotiations for a compact with Charles II, a mission which he executed with great skill. Succeeding his father as "general of the Huguenots," he refused Louis's offer, at the revocation of the Edict of Nantes, to retain him in that office, and in 1690, having gone into exile with his fellow Huguenots, he entered the service of William III of England as a major-general, forfeiting thereby his French estates. In July 1691 he distinguished himself at the battle of Aughrim, and in 1692 he was for a time commander-in-chief in Ireland. He was created Viscount Galway and Baron Portarlington, and received a large grant of forfeited estates in Ireland.

In 1693 Ruvigny fought at Neerwinden and was wounded, and in 1694, with the rank of lieutenant-general, he was sent to command a force in English pay which was to assist the duke of Savoy against the French, and at the same time to relieve the distressed Vaudois. But in 1695 the duke changed sides, the Italian peninsula was neutralized, and Galway's force was withdrawn to the Netherlands. From 1697 to 1701, a critical period of Irish history, the Earl of Galway (he was advanced to that rank in 1697) was practically in control of Irish affairs as lord justice of Ireland. After some years spent in retirement, he was appointed in 1704 to command the allied forces in Portugal, a post which he sustained with honour and success until the battle of Almanza in 1707, in which Galway, in spite of care and skill on his own part, was decisively defeated. But he scraped together a fresh army, and, although infirm, served in one more campaign. His last service was rendered in 1715, when he was sent as one of the lords justices to Ireland during the Jacobite insurrection. He died on Sept. 3, 1720.

RUVO DI PUGLIA, a town and episcopal see of Bari, Apulia, Italy, 21 mi. W. of the city of Bari by tramway, 853 ft. above sea-level. Pop. (1936) 24,748 (town), 25,452 (commune). The cathedral, a splendid basilica with a very lofty nave and two aisles, has three apses, a square campanile and a rich façade with three portals. It belongs to the early 13th century. The interior has a fine triforium. Ruvo occupies the site of the ancient Rubi.

RUWENZORI, also known as Runsoro or Kokora, a mountain range of Central Africa, 65 m. long and with a maximum breadth of 30 m., trending a little east of north, lying just north of the equator between lakes Edward and Albert. The range falls steeply on the west to the central African rift-valley traversed by the Semliki, the western head-stream of the Nile, while on the east the fall is somewhat more gradual towards the western Uganda uplands. The upper parts are separated by fairly low passes into six groups of snowy summits, lying a little west of the central line, rising in each case above 15,000 ft. and reaching, in the culminating point of the western group (Mount Stanley), about 16,800 ft.

The origin of the range seems connected with that of the rift-valley on the west. Ruwenzori is a fault block of the Archaean floor of the continent, bounded east and west by lines of fracture, and having a general dip from west to east. A further upheaval produced an ellipsoidal anticline, causing the strata to dip outwards at a high angle. Traces of volcanic action are almost non-existent. Composed in its outer parts of Archaean gneisses and mica-schists offering no great resistance to denudation, in its centre the range consists of much more refractory rocks (amphibolites, diorites, diabases, etc.), to which fact, coupled with the existence of vertical fractures, the persistence and separation of the higher summits is probably due. The snow-clad area does not now extend more than ten miles in any direction; the snow-line is 13,450 ft. but there is evidence of a former extension to as low as 4,600 ft.

The upper region is almost entirely enveloped by day in thick cloud, which descends on the east to about 9,000 ft., and lower still on the west. As a result, the climate is excessively humid, the northern slopes having a rainfall of 200 inches a year giving extremely damp conditions on the mountain. The rivers are raging torrents and have cut deep valleys between the outer spurs. From the innermost recesses between Mounts Stanley, Speke and Baker, the main branches of the Mobuku descend to the east, while the four principal streams on the west unite to form the Butagu, the drainage on both sides ultimately finding its way to the Semliki, either directly or through lakes George and Edward.

The vegetation displays well-marked zones, varying with the altitude; but owing to the lower level to which the cloud descends on the west the limits of the several zones reach a lower level on the west than on the east. They have been defined as follows by Mr. R. B. Woosnam (1907), as follows, the figures in brackets being the upper limit on the east side:—grass (6,500 ft.), forest (8,500), bamboos (10,000), tree heaths (12,500) and lobelias and senecios (14,500), above which is the summit region of snow and bare rock. The boundaries between the zones merely indicate the levels between which the respective forms are specially characteristic. The forest zone is the best marked, but on the west it merges in part with the low-lying forest of the Semliki valley. Mosses, hepaticae and lichens are prevalent in several of the zones, while bogs, vaccinium and other low-growing plants, are common above the forest zone. Helichrysums are abundant in the zone immediately below the snow. The larger mammals are found chiefly on the lower slopes, but bushbuck, pigs, leopards, monkeys, a hyrax and a serval cat occur at higher altitudes. The birds include kites, buzzards, ravens, sun-birds, touracos, a large swift, and various warblers and other small kinds. The upper limit of human settlement, with cultivation of colocasia and beans, has been placed at 6,700 ft.

In modern times the existence of a snowy range in this part of Africa was first made known by Sir Henry Stanley during the Emin Pasha relief expedition of 1887–89. Stanley named the main mass Ruwenzori, and outlying eastern peaks he called Mt. Gordon Bennett, Mt. Lawson, Mt. Edwin Arnold, etc.—the last named lying north-east of Lake George. Subsequently Stanley's own name was given to the chief summit. One of Stanley's officers, Lieut. Stairs, ascended the western slopes to over 10,000 ft. in 1889, and partial ascents were afterwards made by Dr. Stuhlmann, Mr. Scott-Elliot, Mr. J. E. S. Moore, Sir Harry Johnston, Mr. Douglas Freshfield, and others. Early in 1906 some of the secondary ridges above the snow-line were scaled by Messrs. Grauer, Tegart and Maddox, and by Dr. Wollaston and other members of the British Museum expedition, while later in the year the duke of Abruzzi led a well-equipped expedition to the upper parts of the range and ascended all the principal snow-clad peaks. The expedition produced for the first time a detailed map of the upper region, and threw much light on the geology and natural history of the range.

BIBLIOGRAPHY.—Sir H. M. Stanley, *In Darkest Africa* (London, 1890); G. F. Scott-Elliot, *A Naturalist in Mid-Africa* (London, 1896); J. E. S. Moore, "Tanganyika," etc., *Geog. Jnl.* (January 1901); *To the Mountains of the Moon* (London, 1901); Sir H. H. Johnston, *The Uganda Protectorate* (London, 1902); The Duke of the Abruzzi, in *Geog. Jnl.* (February 1907); R. B. Woosnam, *ibid.* (December 1907); F. de Filippi, *Ruwenzori* (London, 1908), the general account of the Abruzzi expedition, and *Il Ruwenzori, Parte scientifica* (2 vols., Milan, 1909); A. R. F. Wollaston, *From Ruwenzori to the Congo* (London, 1908); R. G. T. Bright, "The Uganda-Congo Boundary," *Geog. Jnl.* (1909); J. W. Gregory, *The Rift Valleys and Geology of East Africa* (1921).

RUYSBROEK or **RUYSBROECK, JAN VAN** (1293–1381), Dutch mystic, was born at Ruysbroek, near Brussels, in 1293. In 1317 he was ordained priest and became vicar of St. Gudule, Brussels. When 60 years of age he withdrew with a few companions to the monastery of Groenendael, near Waterloo, giving himself to meditation and mystical writing, and to a full share of the practical tasks of the society. He was known as the "Ecstatic Teacher," and formed a link between the Friends of God and the Brothers of the Common Life, sects which helped to bring about the Reformation. Ruysbroek insisted that "the soul finds God in its own depths," and noted three stages of progress in what he called "the spiritual ladder" of Christian attainment: (1) the active life, (2) the inward life, (3) the contemplative life. He did not teach the fusion of the self in God, but held that at the summit of the ascent the soul still preserves its identity. His works, of which the most important were *De vera contemplatione* and *De septem gradibus amoris*, were published in 1848 at Hanover; also *Reflections from the Mirror of a Mystic* (1906) and *Die Zierde der geistlichen Hochzeit* (1901).

BIBLIOGRAPHY.—A new edition of his works, *Alle de werken van J. van Ruysbroec de Wonderbare, etc.*, was published at Bussum in 1912 *seq.* A translation of his works into French was begun by the Benedictines of St. Paul de Wisques in 1920 *seq.* The following single works have been translated: *The Book of the Twelve Béguines* (1913); *The Adornment of the Spiritual Marriage*, etc., trans. by C. A. Wynschenk, ed. with introd. and notes by E. Underhill (1916). *See also* R. M. Jones, *Studies in Mystical Religion*, pp. 308–14 (1909); M. Maeterlinck, *Ruysbroek and the Mystics, with selections from The Adornment of the Spiritual Marriage* (trans. by J. T. Stoddart, 1894); V. Scully, *A Mediaeval Mystic* (1910); E. Underhill, *Ruys-*

broeck (1915); Wautier d'Aygalliers, *Ruysbroeck l'admirable* (1923, Eng. trans. 1925).

RUYSDAEL (or RUISDAEL), JACOB VAN (*c.* 1628–1682), the most celebrated of the Dutch landscapists, was born at Haarlem. It is not known where he studied. His father, Isaak, was a framemaker, who also painted and it is suggested that Jacob studied first under him and that he was then under his uncle Solomon Ruisdael (*c.* 1600–1670) an able landscapist. The influence of Cornelisy Vroom, another Haarlem landscapist, has also been traced in his early work; other authorities make him the pupil of Albert van Everdingen. The earliest date that appears on his paintings and etchings is 1646. Two years later he was admitted a member of the gild of St. Luke in Haarlem; in 1659 he obtained the freedom of the city of Amsterdam, and in 1668 his name appears there as a witness to the marriage of Hobbema. During his lifetime his works were little appreciated, and he seems to have suffered from poverty. In 1681 the sect of the Mennonites obtained his admission into the almshouse of the town, where he died on March 14, 1682.

The works of Ruysdael may be studied in the Louvre and the National Gallery, London, and in the collections at The Hague, Amsterdam, Berlin, and Dresden and Leningrad. His favourite subjects are simple woodland scenes, similar to those of Van Everdingen and Hobbema. He is especially noted as a painter of trees, and his rendering of foliage is characterized by the greatest spirit and precision. His views of distant cities, such as that of Haarlem in the possession of the marquess of Bute, and that of Katwijk in the Glasgow Corporation galleries, clearly indicate the influence of Rembrandt. He frequently paints coast-scenes and sea-pieces, but it is in his rendering of lonely forest glades (such as "The Pool in the Wood" at Leningrad) that we find him at his best. The subjects of certain of his mountain scenes seem to be taken from Norway, and have led to the supposition that he had travelled in that country. We have, however, no record of such a journey, and the works in question are probably merely adaptations from the landscapes of Van Everdingen, whose manner he copied at one period. Otto Beit owns a magnificent view of the "Castle of Bentheim" (1653) from which it may be concluded that his wanderings extended to Germany, where he may have made studies for the waterfalls and torrents which appear in many of his pictures. Only a single architectural subject from his brush is known—an admirable interior of the New Church, Amsterdam, in the possession of the marquess of Bute. The prevailing hue of his landscapes is a full rich green, which, however, has darkened with time, while a clear grey tone is characteristic of his sea-pieces. The art of Ruysdael, while it shows little of the scientific knowledge of later landscapists, is sensitive and poetic in sentiment, and direct and skilful in technique. Figures are sparingly introduced into his compositions, and are believed to be from the brush of Adrian Vandevelde, Philip Wouwerman, Nikolaas Berchem, Eglon van der Neer, Ostade and Jan Lingelbach.

Unlike the other great Dutch landscape painters, Ruysdael did not aim at a pictorial record of particular scenes, but he carefully thought out and arranged his compositions. He particularly excels in the painting of cloudy skies which are spanned dome-like over the landscape. A romantic and sometimes deeply poetic sentiment is expressed in his work, as in "The Jewish Burial Ground" at Dresden which is regarded as one of the greatest landscapes ever painted. The "Cornfield" and the "Travellers," etchings, are also significant expressions of landscape art.

See Hofstede de Groot, *Catalogue of Dutch Painters* (1912).

RYAN, JOHN DENIS (1864–1933), American capitalist, was born at Hancock, Mich., on Oct. 10, 1864. In 1889 he went to Denver, where he was employed as a salesman of lubricating oils. In 1901 he secured an interest in a bank at Butte. In 1904 he was made manager of the Amalgamated Copper Company in Montana, becoming president in 1908. He had been elected president of the Anaconda Copper Mining Company in 1905, and after the merging of the Amalgamated interests in the Anaconda in 1910 he continued as president of the latter until 1918. He developed large water powers in Montana, and in 1913 electrified the rail-

way between Butte and Anaconda (100m.), the success of which led to a wide expansion of railway electrification. During 1917–18 Ryan was an executive of the American Red Cross. He was appointed, in April 1918, head of the aircraft board of the committee of national defence, and in August was appointed second assistant secretary of war and director of air service of the U.S. Army, which position he resigned in November. In 1919 he was elected chairman of the Anaconda Copper Mining Company.

RYAZAN, a region of the Russian S.F.S.R., surrounded by those of Moscow, Ivanovo, Gorky, Penza, Tambov and Tula, and not coinciding with the pre-1917 province of the same name. Area 19,613 sq.mi. Pop. (1939) 2,265,873, mainly Great Russians, with some Tatars, Poles and Jews in the towns. The province is drained by the Oka and its tributaries, the Pronya and Pra, and small lakes are numerous in the wide depression of the Oka. Forests cover about one-fifth of the area, conifers, especially pines, prevailing in the more forested north, and deciduous forest with birch, ash and oak appearing in scattered patches in the south. North of the Oka is gray forest soil of little value for agriculture, but south of that river the fertile black earth of the steppe begins. The climate is extreme, average February temperature 3.2° F., July 67° F., rainfall 16 to 18 in. per annum.

Industries.—The region is essentially agricultural, except for a coal mining belt extending along the railway west from Ryazhsk. Dairying is not much developed, as the land is not suitable for pasture, but grain growing gives a good guarantee for the peasant and the villages are large, averaging 534 inhabitants. There are some collective agricultural artels. The chief crops are rye (50%), oats (19%), millet (11.2%) and potatoes (10%). Buckwheat, grass, hemp and sunflower seed are sown. Orchard fruits, especially apples, and cucumbers, cabbages, onions and other vegetables are cultivated in the valley of the Oka. Sheep, working and milch cattle, horses, pigs and a few goats are bred.

Koustar (peasant) textile industries are widespread, as is the making of leather and felt footwear, and the district was once famous for its lacemaking and leather embroidery. The northern region has small industries of this type, including the making of wooden vessels, sledges and boats, the preparation of pitch and tar and basketwork from the reeds in the marshy northern areas which occupy 6% of the region. The electric plant of Ryazan works on peat fuel from these bog areas, and also on the local coal. Marshy areas near the Oka river have been successfully drained and are now pasture lands.

There is a comparatively good railway net and 57% of the rivers are available for steam navigation: a good deal of transit trade goes on throughout the region.

RYAZAN, chief town of the above region, situated on the elevated right bank of the Trubezh, a mile above its confluence with the Oka in 54° 40′ N., 39° 43′ E. Pop. (1939) 95,358. A wide prairie dotted with large villages, the bottom of a former lake, spreads out from the base of the crag on which Ryazan stands, and actually has the aspect of an immense lake when it is inundated in the spring. The town manufactures agricultural machinery, boots, shoes and leather goods, and bricks, and has a distilling industry. It is an important trading centre, on a navigable river, with four railways radiating from it and a good main road linking it with Moscow. The Krestovozdvizhensk church contains tombs of the princes of the 15th and 16th centuries.

The capital of Ryazan principality was Ryazan—now Old Ryazan, a village close to Spask, also on the Oka. It is mentioned in annals as early as 1097, but continued to be the chief town of the principality only until the 14th century. In the 11th century one of the Kiev princes founded, on the banks of a small lake, a fort which received the name of Pereyaslav-Ryazanskiy. In 1294 (or in 1335) the bishop of Murom, compelled to leave his own town, settled in Pereyaslav-Ryazanskiy. The princes of Ryazan followed his example, and by and by completely abandoned the old republican town of Ryazan. In 1300 a congress of Russian princes was held there, and in the following year the town was taken by the Moscow prince. It continued, however, to be the residence of the Ryazan princes until 1517.

RYAZHSK, a town and railway junction in Ryazan region, Russian S.F.S.R., S. of Ryazan, in 53° 42′ N., 40° 3′ E., on the Khupta river. Pop. 16,164. It is a grain collecting centre with an elevator, and manufactures *makhorka* tobacco and spirits.

RYBINSK, a town in Yaroslavl region, Russian S.F.S.R., in 58° 3′ N., 38° 47′ E., on the navigable Volga, opposite the mouth of the Sheksna, which connects the Volga system with Lake Ladoga. Pop. (1939) 139,011. There goods are transhipped from the large Volga boats to the smaller ones of the Marii system linking with Leningrad. There are shipyards, wiredrawing mills, nail, metal and match factories, flour mills, leather works and a brewery.

2. A small settlement of Asiatic Russia on a left bank tributary of the Irtysh in 56° 5′ N., 72° 30′ E.

3. A small town of Asiatic Russia south of the trans-Siberian railway, lying between Krasnoyarsk and Kansk, in 55° 55′ N., 94° .55′ E.

RYDBERG, ABRAHAM VIKTOR (1828–1895), Swedish author and publicist, was born in Jönköping on Dec. 18, 1828. In 1855 he joined the staff of the *Göteborgs Handels-och sjöfart-stidning*, in which his romances successively appeared; he was editorially connected with it until 1876. *The Freebooter on the Baltic* (1857) and *The Last of the Athenians* (1859) gave Rydberg a place in the front rank of contemporary novelists. It was a surprise to his admirers to see him presently turn to theology, but with *The Bible's Teaching about Christ* (1862), in which the aspects of modern Biblical criticism were first placed before Swedish readers, he enjoyed a vast success. He was not elected to the Swedish Academy until 1877, when he had long been the first living author of Sweden. *Roman Days* is a series of archaeological essays on Italy (1876). He collected his poems in 1882; his version of *Faust* dates from 1876. In 1884 he was appointed professor of ecclesiastical history at Stockholm. He died, after a short illness, on Sept. 22, 1895. Rydberg was an idealist of the Romantic type which Sweden had known for three-quarters of a century; he was the last of that race, and, as a writer, perhaps the greatest.

See C. Warburg, *Victor Rydberg, hans levnad och diktning* (1913); L. Lundh, *Viktor Rydberg* (Stockholm, 1918); V. Svanberg, *Rydbergs Singoalla* (Uppsala, 1923).

RYDBERG, PER AXEL (1860–1931), American botanist, was born at Odh, Sweden, on July 6, 1860. He graduated at the gymnasium in Skara, in 1881, and soon after went to the United States, where he continued further study at the University of Nebraska (B.S., 1891; M.S., 1895) and at Columbia (Ph.D., 1898). In the period 1884–98 he also taught natural sciences in several Swedish-American institutions, and during summers in 1891–96 he was field agent for the divisions of botany and agrostology of the U.S. department of agriculture. In 1899 he was made curator at the New York Botanical garden. He made extensive taxonomic studies of the seed plants of the Great Plains and the Rocky mountain region.

He published *Catalogue of the Flora of Montana and the Yellowstone National Park* (1900), *Flora of Colorado* (1906), *Flora of the Rocky Mountains and Adjacent Plains* (1917; 2nd ed., 1922). He also wrote monographs on Saxifragaceae, Rosaceae, Carduaceae and other plant groups, and various contributions to botanical journals.

RYDE, a municipal borough and watering place in the Isle of Wight, Eng., 4½ mi. S.W. of Portsmouth across the Solent. Pop. (1951) 20,105. Area 12.3 sq.mi. On rising ground on the northeast coast, overlooking Spithead, Ryde has woods reaching to the water's edge and miles of golden sands. It is built on the site of a village called La Rye or La Riche, which was destroyed by the French in the reign of Edward II. At the close of the 18th century it was a small fishing hamlet, but it rapidly grew as a watering place and catering for tourists became its chief industry with agriculture second in importance. The ancient Ryde carnival is held annually in September. The town was incorporated in 1868. Ryde is connected by boat with Portsmouth. The principal buildings are All Saints church, the market house and town hall, the Royal Victoria Yacht club, the pavilion, the Royal Isle of Wight infirmary and the Commodore theatre.

RYDER, ALBERT PINKHAM (1847–1917), U.S. painter, was born at New Bedford, Mass., March 19, 1847. About 1868 the family settled in New York city, where Albert briefly studied painting. He first exhibited at the National Academy of Design in 1873, but most of his exhibited work was shown at the Society of American Artists, of which he was a founding member. In 1882 he travelled in Europe, but paintings in the art galleries interested him little. He was an imaginative solitary; his life work of about 150 pictures was produced slowly. By 1900 his powers were impaired and he injured some earlier paintings with misjudged reworkings; thus he unconsciously prepared the way for the many forged examples that appeared. After a critical illness, friends took him to their home at Elmhurst, L.I., where he died March 28, 1917. Major works such as "Siegfried" and "The Race Track" are in public collections in Washington, D.C., and Cleveland, O. Extraordinary colourfulness triumphs over technical imperfections, and his themes range from an idyllic pastoralism through intensifying romanticism to an epic splendor.

See Frederic Fairchild Sherman, *Albert Pinkham Ryder* (New York, 1920). (VL. B.)

RYE, a municipal borough and market town in the Rye parliamentary division of East Sussex, Eng., 11 mi. N.E. from Hastings by road. Pop. (1951) 4,509. Area 1.6 sq.mi. Rye is a picturesque market town, built up a hill by the Rother river, with cobbled streets and timber-framed and Georgian houses. Ypres tower (12th century), which stands on the cliff, was its only defense until Edward III walled the town, but Landgate (1329), one of the three original entrance gates, is all that remains of the 14th century fortifications. The Norman to Perpendicular church of St. Mary has a notable quarter-boy 16th-century clock and in the churchyard is a Georgian reservoir. Other interesting buildings are the old grammar school (1636), the town hall (1742), the old hospital, the Mermaid inn (c. 1420) and the Flushing inn which contains a mural dated 1547.

As part of the manor of Rameslie, Rye was granted by Edward the Confessor to the monks of Fécamp by whom it was retained until resumed by Henry III in 1247. The town became a full member of the Cinque Ports c. 1350 when, with Winchelsea, the other "ancient town," it was added to the confederation. It was then a flourishing port but declined in the late 14th century, partly recovered its prosperity with the decay of Winchelsea in the 15th and 16th centuries and then sank again when the sedimentation and consequent receding of the sea, which had been going on slowly since the 14th century, made the use of the harbour impracticable. By the mid-20th century the Rother's mouth was 2 mi. from the town. Rye was twice burned down by the French, in 1377 and 1448. The town was incorporated in 1289 and was granted a three days' fair. Twice-weekly markets had been held before 1405 when the Friday market was changed to Saturday. The market now serves a wide agricultural area. Industries include light engineering, dry cleaning and the tourist trade.

RYE, a city of Westchester county, New York, U.S., on Long Island sound, 24 mi. N.E. of New York city; served by the New York, New Haven and Hartford and electric railways. Pop. 11,721, 1950 federal census. It is a residential city with several yacht and country clubs and a number of 18th-century houses. The municipal hall is an old inn (Haviland) where Washington and Lafayette were entertained. "Kirby's tide-mill," built before the Revolution, still stands. Rye was the home of John Jay, and his grave is there in the family burying ground. At Rye beach there is a seaside playground of 214 ac. owned and operated by the county. The village was incorporated in 1904, the city in 1942.

RYE, known botanically as *Secale cereale*, is used extensively for food and feed in certain world areas though it is less important than other cereal grain crops. While generally distributed over the world, it is of major importance only on the sandy, poorer and more arid soils of the northern hemisphere.

The spike of the rye plant resembles wheat in having alternately ranked spikelets attached to a zigzag rachis, forming a fairly dense head or "ear." Spikelets are composed of two thin, narrow glumes that subtend two or more florets which, in turn, are enclosed by a lemma and palea. The lemmas taper into awns that are about 2 to 4 cm. long. Each floret contains three stamens and a pistil which, after pollination, develops into a one-seeded fruit that is partly exposed. Threshing free, the fruit is known as a caryopsis and is called the kernel or grain. Grain colour varies, but grayish-green and light brown predominate, while some are almost white. The pericarp sometimes ruptures over the germ. Sterile florets occur to the extent of 25% to 30%, thereby reducing production. Cross-pollination occurs almost completely because the flowers are largely self-sterile. The first foliage leaf is reddish or purplish tinged. Other leaves are long, narrow and thin with a short ligule and a moderate-sized auricle at the juncture of the blade and sheath. The leaf sheaths have a bluish-green bloom. The height and number of culms depend upon growth conditions.

Rye has the tallest and strongest straw of all of the small grain crops. The straw may attain a height of 7 to 8 ft. on fertile soils, but is usually 5 ft. or less. This tall straw makes harvesting difficult. There are numerous fibrous roots and they penetrate downward more deeply than do other small grains.

Rye probably originated in southwestern Asia, like several other important genera such as *Triticum*, *Avena* and *Hordeum*. The progenitor of *Secale cereale* is not known with certainty, though some think that a brittle rachis type is the probable ancestor. There are annual and perennial species that have the brittle rachis. Early cultivation was likely in western Asia, followed by westward migration across the Balkan peninsula and over Europe.

No trace of cultivated rye has been found in early Egyptian monuments, and likewise no reference to this crop is found in ancient writings. However, the name occurs in northern European languages and this suggests early cultivation in this area.

Only one species of cultivated rye is recognized, *Secale cereale*, although several other species have been found growing wild. Rye has 14 somatic chromosomes and there is no evidence of a polyploid series except for artificially produced tetraploids with 28 chromosomes. Most rye is grown as a fall-sown annual, though a small amount is spring-sown with spring instead of winter varieties.

The greatest production of rye occurs in the temperate and cool regions of the world; it grows also where altitudes are high. It has the greatest winter hardiness of all small grains, and its culture extends to the more northerly parts of North America and as far north as the Arctic circle of Europe and Asia. The type of soil has an important influence on geographic distribution. Rye is frequently grown where other crops fail because of low fertility. Most production is from the poorer nonchernozem soils of Europe and the U.S.S.R., and sandier and poorer soils of North America. Soil requirements are modest—even more so than for oats. Rye will produce well on fertile soils, but these types of soils are reserved for growing other crops.

Rye culture follows the conventional methods used for other small grains. Seed may be drilled or sown broadcast at the rate of about six pecks per acre. Rye is not used to any great extent as a nurse crop in establishing forage crops. It is frequently rotated with other crops, although sometimes grown continuously. Seeding is usually in early fall, with ripening sooner than other small grains, or about a week earlier than winter wheat. Harvesting is done mostly in June and July in the northern hemisphere.

The two main uses of rye grain are breadmaking and livestock feed. In making rye bread, various proportions of wheat flour may be used because the gluten of rye is less elastic than that of wheat. Rye stands next to wheat in use for milling and baking of loaf bread; the bread made from it is darker in colour and usually heavier than wheat bread. It is frequently referred to as black bread in Soviet and central European areas, where considerable quantities are consumed. Rye bread is of relatively minor importance in the U.S. except where there are concentrations of racial groups that consume large quantities of this bread.

Livestock feed is one of the main uses of the rye crop. For most classes of livestock it is usually fed in a mixture. It has less fats than has wheat, about the same protein content and compares favourably with wheat and corn for carbohydrates. Vitamin B$_1$ content is slightly lower than in barley and wheat and much lower than in oats. Rye is used also in the making of alcoholic beverages.

Rye straw is fibrous and tough and used less for feed than for litter or bedding. The straw is used for mattresses and thatching in certain areas of the world, and also in the manufacture of hats and paper.

Rye has considerable use for fall and spring cattle grazing. As a spring pasture it is available before permanent pastures have made sufficient growth for livestock use. The leaves are high in vitamin A content. In warmer areas the grain is used for fall grazing and cover cropping. It is also used as a green manure crop, being plowed under in the spring and followed by a crop of greater economic value.

Ergot is a disease condition that follows when the young kernel is penetrated by the fungus *Claviceps purpurea*. This results in purplish-black ergot bodies called sclerotia. They contain pharmaceutical compounds such as ergosterol, ergotoxine, ergotamine, ergonovine, ergoclavine, etc.

Although other diseases, including snow mould, attack rye, most of them cause only minor yield reduction. There are several leaf and stem diseases, such as leaf and stem rust, stalk and head smut, scald and blotch, and some root rots. On the whole, if ergot is omitted, disease losses in rye are less than in other small grains.

Improvement of the rye plant by breeding is difficult because of the high degree of self-sterility. Most improvement has been accomplished by mass selection rather than the pure line method of breeding. Varieties are genetically impure because of cross-pollination. Moderately self-fertile inbred lines can be perpetuated without difficulty. Hybrid vigour with greater productivity than open-pollinated varieties results when selected inbred lines are properly mated. No method has been found to utilize this biologic principle commercially.

Since rye is thrifty and winter-hardy it has been hybridized with wheat, resulting in winter-hardy selections with the appearance and quality of wheat. However, commercial production of varieties from wheat-rye hybrid origin is rather small. Hybrids with other genera have been made.

During the 1940s tetraploids (28 somatic chromosomes) in rye were produced by several scientists. One tetraploid called Tetra Petkus gained some prominence in the early 1950s; it is stiff-strawed, leafy and late in maturity. Kernels are large, weighing 1½ to 2 times as much as common rye. Limited tests indicate Tetra Petkus flour will bake satisfactorily. Reduced yield may result if the tetraploids are sown close to the common varieties because cross-pollinated flowers do not produce seed.

In North America the following varieties of common rye are used commercially: Dakold, Emerald, Pierre, Imperial, Caribou, Antelope, Adams, Rosen, Balbo and Abruzzi. Some exceptional characteristics are the winter hardiness of Dakold and the white kernels of Adams. Most of these varieties have come from stocks of European and Russian origin.

In other countries some important varieties are: Petkus, Kings II, Steel, Star, Ensi, Toivo, Borris Pearl and Vjatka.

Production and Trade.—World production of rye averages about 1,500,000,000 to 1,700,000,000 bu. annually. Of the total, Russian and European production ordinarily account for more than 90%. The U.S.S.R. produces 50% to 60% of the world supply. Before World War II other important growers were Germany and Poland. European countries producing considerable rye are France, the Netherlands, Spain and Austria. The yields are close to 12 bu. per acre except for western Europe and Canada. The frequent low yield is partly due to the fact that rye is grown on poorer soils. European production in the early 1950s was about the same as pre-World War II, but with less acreage. Russian acreage increased 20% with little total production increase. In the same period Canadian acreage and production increased, while the U.S. acreage and production dropped to about one-third. The leading states for production in the U.S. are North Dakota, South Dakota, Minnesota and Nebraska.

Trade in rye has been more limited than with other grains. Seasonal production influences trade between countries. The U.S.S.R., Canada, Turkey and Argentina usually export rye while Germany, Finland, Austria and Norway import much more than they export. The United States has been a large exporter, but in the 1950s began to import modest quantities.   (H. L. Ss.)

RYE GRASS, the common name given to species of the genus *Lolium*, comprising a few annual or perennial Eurasian grasses. Two species are of agricultural importance in the United States,

English or perennial rye grass (*L. perenne*) and Italian rye grass (*L. multiflorum*). Both are used to some extent for meadow, pasture and lawn, especially the latter where a vigorous early growth is desired. Another species (*L. temulentum*), commonly known as darnel and occasionally found in waste places, is supposed to be the tares of the Bible. It is a weed possessing poisonous properties, probably owing to a fungus in the grains. (J. M. BL.)

RYKOV, ALEKSEY IVANOVICH (1881–1938), Russian politician, was born at Saratov, on Feb. 13, 1881, the son of a peasant. At 18 he was a member of the Russian Social Democratic Workers' party (R.S.D.R.P.), visited Nicolai Lenin at Geneva in 1902, and returned to Russia as a revolutionary propagandist in various industrial districts. He was many times arrested and deported, but each time escaped. He attended the 3rd congress of the R.S.D.R.P. (London, 1905) and was elected a member of its central committee. He took part in the 1905 revolution and again was in London as a delegate to the 5th congress (1907). He lived for some time in Paris (1910–11), later returning to Russia. In 1913 he was exiled to Narym, western Siberia; in 1915 he escaped, was recaptured and sent back to Narym where he remained until the March 1917 revolution.

Rykov took an active part in the Nov. 1917 revolution and became people's commissar of the interior in the first Communist government headed by Lenin. In 1918 he became chairman of the Supreme Economic council, in 1923 was elected to the Politburo, and in Jan. 1924, after Lenin's death, was appointed chairman of the council of people's commissars. When Joseph Stalin started his fight against L. D. Trotsky, Rykov sided against the latter believing that by so doing he was working for peace, although he had no illusions about Stalin's thirst for dictatorial power. Later Rykov's influence waned and in 1930 he was succeeded by V. M. Molotov as chairman of the council of people's commissars. In 1931 Rykov became people's commissar for communications but on Sept. 29, 1936, was dismissed from this post and on March 17, 1937, expelled from the All-Union Communist party for his allegedly "treacherous anti-party activity." On March 13, 1938, with N. I. Bukharin, G. G. Yagoda and other "right-wing deviationists," he was sentenced to death and shot the next day.

See A. I. Rykov, *Statii i ryechi* (Articles and Speeches), 4 vol. (Moscow, 1926–28); A. Lomov, *A. I. Rykov* (Moscow, 1926).

RYLANDS, JOHN (1801–1888), English manufacturer and merchant, was born at St. Helens, Lancashire, on Feb. 7, 1801, and was educated at the grammar school in that town. In 1819 he, his elder brothers and his father, a manufacturer of cotton goods, founded the firm of Rylands and Sons, cotton goods and linen manufacturers, at Wigan. The business rapidly increased, dye-works and bleach-works were added, and the discovery of coal under some of the firm's property added materially to its wealth. In 1825 the partners became merchants as well as manufacturers, and subsequently acquired spinning mills at Bolton and elsewhere. In 1847, his father being dead and his brothers having retired, John Rylands assumed entire control of the business, which in 1873 was turned into a limited liability company. John Rylands was a benefactor to various charities, and was one of the original financiers of the Manchester Ship canal. He died at Stretford on Dec. 11, 1888. A permanent memorial, the John Rylands Library, was erected by his widow in Manchester in 1899.

RYLANDS, SIR (WILLIAM) PETER (1868–1948), English industrialist, was born on Oct. 23, 1868, and educated at Charterhouse and at Trinity college, Cambridge. He studied law and was called to the bar in 1894, but four years later became managing director of Rylands Brothers. In 1900 he was made president of the Iron and Steel Wire Manufacturers association, retaining this post for almost a half century. After World War I he became president of the Federation of British Industries (1919–21), the Iron and Steel institute (1926–27) and the National Federation of Iron and Steel Manufacturers (1930). In 1935–36 he was high sheriff of Cheshire.

He was knighted in 1921, created baronet in 1939 and was a commander of the Royal Order of Vasa. He died at Thelwall, Cheshire, England on Oct. 22, 1948.

RYMER, THOMAS (1641–1713), English historiographer royal, was the younger son of Ralph Rymer, lord of the manor of Brafferton in Yorkshire, executed for his share in the "Presbyterian rising" of 1663. Thomas was probably born at Yafforth Hall early in 1641, and was educated at a private school kept at Danby-Wiske by Thomas Smelt, a noted Royalist, and at Sidney Sussex college, Cambridge. He left the university without taking a degree. On May 2, 1666, he became a member of Gray's Inn, and was called to the bar on June 16, 1673. Rymer executed translations, wrote plays, prefaces and complimentary pieces. In 1692 Rymer became historiographer royal.

Within eight months of his official appointment Rymer was directed (Aug. 26, 1693) to carry out that great national undertaking with which his name will always be honourably connected, and of which there is reason to believe that Lords Somers and Halifax were the original promoters. The *Codex Juris Gentium Diplomaticus* (1693) of Leibniz was taken by the editor as the model of the *Foedera*. The plan was to publish all records of alliances and other transactions in which England was concerned with foreign powers from 1101 to the time of publication, limiting the collection to original documents in the royal archives and the great national libraries. Unfortunately, this was not uniformly carried out, and the work contains some extracts from printed chronicles. From 1694 Rymer corresponded with Leibniz, by whom he was greatly influenced with respect to the plan and formation of the *Foedera*. While collecting materials, Rymer unwisely engraved a spurious charter of King Malcolm, acknowledging that Scotland was held in homage from Edward the Confessor. When this came to be known the Scottish antiquaries were extremely indignant, and a controversy arose, the documents in which are now rare and valuable.

At last, on Nov. 20, 1704, was issued the first folio volume of the *Foedera, Conventiones, Litterae et cujuscumque generis Acta Publica inter reges Angliae et alios quosvis imperatores, reges, etc., ab A.D. 1101 ad nostra usque tempora habita aut tractata*. The publication proceeded with rapidity, and 15 volumes were brought out in nine years. Rymer died after the appearance of the last volume, but he had prepared materials for carrying the work down to the end of the reign of James I. These were placed in the hands of Robert Sanderson, his assistant, who produced the remaining five volumes (1715–17 and 1726–35).

Rymer died at Arundel Street, Strand, on Dec. 14, 1713, and was buried in the church of St. Clement Danes. His will was dated July 10, 1713.

In 1810 the Record Commissioners authorized Dr. Adam Clarke to prepare a new and improved edition of the *Foedera*. Six parts, large folio, edited by Clarke, Caley and Holbrooke, were published between 1816 and 1830. Considerable additions were made, but the editing was performed in so unsatisfactory a manner that the publication was suspended in the middle of printing a seventh part. The latter portion, bringing the work down to 1383, was ultimately issued in 1869. A general introduction to the *Foedera* was issued by the Record Commission in 1817, 4to.

The best account of Rymer is to be found in the prefaces to Sir T. D. Hardy's *Syllabus* (1869–85, 3 vols. 8vo).

RYNCHOPIDAE: see SKIMMER.

RYOT or **RAYAT**, properly a subject, then a tenant of the soil (from the Arabic *ra'a*, "to pasture"). The word is used throughout India for the general body of cultivators; but it has a special meaning in different provinces. The *ryotwari* tenure is one of the two main revenue systems in India. Where the land revenue is imposed on an individual or community owning an estate, and occupying a position analogous to that of a landlord, the assessment is known as *zamindari*; and where the land revenue is imposed on individuals who are the actual occupants, the assessment is known as *ryotwari*. (*See* ZAMINDAR.)

RYSWICK, TREATY OF, the treaty of peace which in 1697 ended the war which had begun in 1689 between France on the one side and the Empire, England, Spain and Holland on the other (*see* GRAND ALLIANCE, WAR OF THE). The treaty was signed by all the Powers concerned except the Empire on Sept. 20, 1697, a treaty being concluded between France and the Emperor on Oct. 30.

The basis of the peace was that all towns and districts seized since the treaty of Nijmwegen in 1679 should be restored. Thus France surrendered Freiburg, Breisach and Philippsburg to Germany, although she kept Strasbourg. On the other hand, she regained Pondicherry and Nova Scotia, while Spain recovered Catalonia, and the barrier fortresses of Mons, Luxemburg and Courtrai. The duchy of Lorraine, which for many years had been in the possession of France, was restored to Leopold Joseph, a son of duke Charles V., and the Dutch were to be allowed to garrison some of the chief fortresses in the Netherlands, including Namur and Ypres. Louis undertook to recognize William as king of England, and promised to give no further assistance to James II.; he abandoned his interference in the electorate of Cologne and also the claim which he had put forward to some of the lands of the Rhenish palatinate.

See C. W. von Koch and F. Scholl, *Histoire abrégée des traités de paix* (1817–18); A. Moetjens, *Actes et mémoires de la paix de Ryswick* (The Hague, 1725); A. Legrelle, *Notes et documents sur la paix de Ryswick* (Lille, 1894); H. Vast, *Les Grands Traités du règne de Louis XIV.* (1893–99).

RYŪKYŪ ARCHIPELAGO (called also LUCHU), a long chain of islands forming Okinawa prefecture of Japan, stretching from a point 80 mi. S. of Kyushu to a point 73 mi. from the N.E. coast of Formosa, and lying between 24° and 30° N. and 123° and 130° E. Japanese cartographers reckon the Luchu islands as 55, having a total coastline of 768 mi., an area of 935 sq.mi., and a population (1940) of 574,579. They divide them into three main groups, of which the northern is called Oshima-shoto; the central, Okinawa-gunto; and the southern, Sakishima-retto. The terms *shoto, gunto* and *retto* signify "archipelago," "cluster of islands" and "string of islands" respectively. The last-named group is subdivided into Miyako-gunto and Yayeyama-gunto.

Almost at the extreme north of the chain are two islands with active volcanoes; Nakano-shima (3,485 ft.) and Suwanose-shima (2,697 ft.), but the remaining members of the group give no volcanic indications, and the only other mountain of any size is Yuwan-dake (2,299 ft.) in Amami-Oshima. The capital is Shuri in Okinawa, with a picturesque castle. The more modern town of Nafa, on the same island, possesses the principal harbour and has considerable trade.

Though so close to the tropics, the islands cannot be said to present tropical features: the bamboo is rare; there is no high grass or tangled undergrowth; open plains are numerous; the trees are not crowded together; lakes are wanting; the rivers are insignificant; and an unusual aspect is imparted to the scenery by numerous coral crags. The temperature in Nafa ranges from a mean of 82° F in July to 60° in January.

The fauna includes wild boars and deer, rats and bats. Excellent small ponies are kept, together with cattle, pigs and goats. The majority of the islands are infested with venomous snakes called *habu* (*Trimeresurus*), which attain a length of 6 to 7 ft. and a diameter of from 2½ to 3 in. Their bite generally causes speedy death, and in the island of Amami-Oshima they claim many victims every year. The most important cultivated plant is the sugar-cane, which provides the principal staple of trade.

Luchu is noted for the production of particularly durable vermilion-coloured lacquer, which is much esteemed for table utensils in Japan. The islands also manufacture fabrics.

People.—Although the upper classes in Luchu and Japan closely resemble each other, there are palpable differences between the lower classes, the Luchuans being shorter and better proportioned than the Japanese; having higher foreheads, eyes not so deeply set, faces less flattened, arched and thick eyebrows, better noses, less marked cheek-bones and much greater hairiness. The last characteristic has been attributed to the presence of Ainu blood, and has suggested a theory that when the Japanese race entered south-western Japan from Korea, they drove the Ainu northwards and southwards, one portion of the latter finding their way to Luchu, the other to Yezo. Women of the upper class never appear in public in Luchu, and are not even alluded to in conversation,

but women of the lower orders go about freely with uncovered faces. The Luchu costume resembles that of Japan. The chief staple of the people's diet is the sweet potato, and pork is the principal luxury. An ancient law, still in force, requires each family to keep four pigs. In times of scarcity a species of sago (obtained from the *Cycas revoluta*) is eaten.

History.—Tinsunshi, "Grandson of Heaven," is the mythical founder of the Luchu monarchy. Towards the close of the 12th century his descendants were driven from the throne, but the old national party soon found a victorious leader in Shunten, son of Tametomo, a member of the famous Minamoto family, who, having been expelled from Japan, had come to Luchu and married there. The introduction of the arts of reading and writing are assigned to Shunten's reign. Chinese invasions of Luchu may be traced back to A.D. 605, but they did not result in annexation; and it was in 1372 that China first obtained from the Luchuans recognition of supremacy. Luchuan relations with Japan had long been friendly, but at the end of the 16th century the king refused Japan assistance against Korea, and in 1609 the prince of Satsuma invaded the islands with 3,000 men, took the capital by storm, captured the king and carried him off to Kagoshima. A few years later he was restored to his throne on condition of acknowledging Japanese suzerainty and paying tribute. The Luchuans nevertheless continued to pay tribute to China also.

The Chinese government, however, though taking a benevolent interest in the welfare of the islanders, never attempted to bring them under military sway. The incongruity of this state of affairs did not force itself upon Japan's attention so long as her own empire was divided into a number of semi-independent principalities. But in 1879 the Japanese government, treating Luchu as an integral part of the mikado's dominions, dethroned its prince, pensioned him as the other feudal chiefs had been pensioned, and converted Luchu into a prefecture under the name of Okinawa. China remonstrating, a conference was held in Peking, when plenipotentiaries of the two empires signed an agreement to the effect that the archipelago should be divided equally between the claimants. The Chinese government, however, refused to ratify this compromise, and the Japanese continued their measures for the effective administration of all the islands. Ultimately (1895) Formosa also came into Japan's possession, and her title to the whole chain of islands ceased to be disputed.

BIBLIOGRAPHY.—See Basil Hall, *Account of a Voyage of Discovery to the West Coast of Corea and the Great Loo-choo Island* (London, 1818); Comm. M. C. Perry, *Narrative of the Expedition of an American Squadron to the China Seas and Japan, 1852–1854* (Washington, 1856); B. H. Chamberlain, "The Luchu Islands and their Inhabitants," in the *Geographical Journal*, vol. v. (1895); "Contributions to a Bibliography of Luchu," in *Trans. Asiatic Soc. Japan*, xxiv. (1896); C. S. Leavenworth, "History of the Loo-choo Islands," *Journ. China Br. Royal Asiatic Soc.* xxxvi. (1905); and *see* the *Transactions of the Asiatic Society of Japan* (annual).

RZESZÓW, a town of Poland, in the province of Lwow, situated on the river Wislok, half-way between Lwow and Cracow. Pop. (1931), 27,499. It was founded by Casimir the Great and became the seat of a great family, taking their name from the town and dying out in 1583. The old church shows traces of the original structure built by King Casimir in the 14th century. Ordinarily it is a prosperous town in an agricultural and pastoral district. It was captured by Germany in Sept. 1939.

RZHEV or RZHOV, a town in the Kalinin region of the Russian S.F.S.R., in 56° 20′ N., 34° 19′ E., lying on both sides of the Volga river, here 350 ft. wide, and navigable for steamers. It is a centre for four branch railway lines and a telegraph line, and has a radio station. Pop. (1939) 54,081, mainly employed in sawmilling, leather work, oil pressing, silk spinning, distilling, brewing and the making of machinery. In the 12th century it was part of the principality of Smolensk, which from 1225 was a dependency of Novgorod. In the 15th century the parts of the town on the left and right banks of the river were governed separately under the rule of independent princes.

THIS letter corresponds to the Semitic W (*sin*). The Greek treatment of the sibilants that occur in the Semitic alphabet is somewhat complicated. Semitic ⫫ (*samech*) appears in Greek as Ξ (*ksi*) with the value in early times of *ss*, later and more generally of *x* or *ks*. The name *samech*, however, which through its Aramaean form became in Greek *sigma*, was applied to the letter Ϟ which corresponded to Semitic W (*sin*) and stood for *s*. In certain Greek alphabets the letter was called by the name *san*. Semitic *ssade* appears in the early alphabets of Thera and Corinth in the form M representing *s*. These alphabets have no *sigma*, while those that have *sigma* do not have M.

Greek forms of the letter were Ϟ, Ϛ, Ϛ, ϟ, ϟ. The rounded form appears in the Chalcidic alphabet and from this it was taken

NAME OF FORM	APPROX-IMATE DATE	FORM OF LETTER
PHOENICIAN	B.C. 1,200	W
CRETAN	1,100-900	?Ϟ
THERAEAN	700-600	?Ϟ
ARCHAIC LATIN	700-500	Ϟ
ATTIC	600	Ϟ ϟ
CORINTHIAN	600	?Ϟ
CHALCIDIAN	600	Ϟ
IONIC	403	Ϟ ϟ
ROMAN COLONIAL	PRE-CLASSICAL AND CLASSICAL TIMES	Ϟ Ϛ Ϛ S
URBAN ROMAN		S
FALISCAN		Ϟ S
OSCAN		Ϟ ϟ
UMBRIAN		S
CLASSICAL LATIN AND ONWARDS		S

THE DEVELOPMENT OF THE LETTER "S" FROM THE PHOENICIAN, THROUGH THE CLASSICAL, DOWN TO MODERN TIMES

into Latin. Etruscan had no rounded form, but it appears in Umbrian and Faliscan. In Latin cursive writing of the 6th century the form was Ⅴ, and from this descended the Irish and Saxon forms Γ. The Carolingian form on the other hand was extended above the line instead of below, *e.g.*, ſ. In England in the 17th century the form was ſ and this is occasionally still seen in handwriting when followed by another *s*. The form ß also

occurs, the left hand oblique stroke being really part of a ligature with a preceding letter.

The letter represents an unvoiced fricative. This has become voiced in English when intervocalic (e.g., *houses, nose*). In most other positions it remains unvoiced (e.g., *sing, save, stamp, speak, aspect*). When doubled the letter represents the unvoiced sound in all positions (e.g., *grasses, miss, assess*). (B. F. C. A.)

SAADIA, BEN JOSEPH (892–942): *see* SEADIAH.

SAALE, a river of Germany, a tributary of the Elbe, 226 m. long, rises between Bayreuth and Hof in the Fichtelgebirge. It joins the Elbe just above Barby. It is navigable from Naumburg, 100 m., with the help of sluices, and is connected with the Elster near Leipzig by a canal. Its chief affluents are the Elster, Regnitz and Orla (right), and the Ilm, Unstrut, Salza, Wipper and Bode (left). Its upper course is rapid. It is sometimes called the Thuringian or Saxon Saale, to distinguish it from another Saale (70 m. long), a right-bank tributary of the Main.

SAALFELD, a town of Germany, in the *Land* of Thuringia, situated on the left bank of the Saale, 24 m. S. of Weimar and 77 S.W. of Leipzig by rail. Pop. (1939) 23,325. Saalfeld grew up around the abbey founded in 1075 by Anno, archbishop of Cologne, and the palace built up by the emperor Frederick I. In 1389 it was purchased by the landgrave of Thuringia, and with this district it formed part of Saxony. In 1680 it became the capital of a separate duchy, but in 1699 it was united with Saxe-Coburg, passing to Saxe-Meiningen in 1826. One of the most ancient towns in Thuringia, Saalfeld is still partly surrounded by old walls and bastions, and contains some interesting mediaeval buildings, among them a palace, built in 1679 on the site of the Benedictine abbey of St. Peter, which was destroyed during the Peasants' War; the Gothic church of St. John, dating from the beginning of the 13th century; the Gothic town hall, completed in 1537; the Kitzerstein, a palace standing on an eminence above the river, probably first erected by the German king Henry I., although the present building is not older than the 16th century; and the ruin of the Hoher Schwarm, called later the Sorbenburg, said to have been erected in the 7th century. Saalfeld has a number of prosperous industries, and there are ochre and iron mines in the neighbourhood.

SAAR, a right-bank tributary of the Moselle river. It rises in the Donon, an eminence of the Vosges, and flows generally northward through the Saar coalfield to its junction with the Moselle at Konz. The principal towns on the Saar are Saarguemines, Saarbrücken, Saarlouis (Saarlautern) and Saarburg. The river is navigable up to Saarguemines, a distance of 75 mi., where there is connection with the Rhine-Marne canal.

SAARBRÜCKEN, a town in the Saarland (*q.v.*), on the Saar, 49 mi. by rail N.E. of Metz. Pop. (1950) 105,391. Saarbrücken owes its name to a bridge which existed in Roman times. Its early lords were the bishops of Metz, the counts of the lower Saargau, and the counts of the Ardennes. From 1381 to 1793 it belonged to the counts of Nassau-Saarbrücken, and then, after having been in the possession of France from 1801 to 1815, it passed to Prussia. St. Johann, Malstatt-Burbach and Saarbrücken were united in 1909. The trade of Saarbrücken is chiefly connected with coal, iron and glass. The coal fields extend more than 70 sq.mi. Saarbrücken was heavily bombed during World War II.

SAARBURG, in Alsace-Lorraine: see SARREBOURG.

SAAREMAA (formerly ÖSEL), an island of Estonia, lying in the Baltic sea across the mouth of the Gulf of Riga. Pop. (1934) 55,851. It has a length of 45 mi., and an area of 1,010 sq.mi. The chief town, Arensburg, on the south coast, is a place of 4,339 inhabitants (1938), with summer sea bathing and mud baths. In 1227 Ösel was conquered by the Knights of the Sword, and was governed by its own bishops till 1561 when it passed into the hands of the Danes. By them it was surrendered to the Swedes in 1645. Along with Livonia, it was united to Russia in 1721, passing to Estonia in 1918. In 1940 soviet Russia took possession, and Germany conquered it in 1941.

SAARGEMUND: see SARREGUEMINES.

SAARLAND, an industrial and mining region on the Franco-German frontier, north of Lorraine, near the iron ore of Briey. Area 991 sq.mi.; pop. (1939) 863,726 (est. pop. 1949, 926,000). Chief town, Saarbrücken, pop. (1939) 135,080 (est. pop. 1950, 105,391). The basic industry is coal, good for industrial purposes and gas production and moderate for coke.

The Saar is largely dependent on imports for certain commodities (including food supplies). Bombing during World War II destroyed 76,000 buildings.

History.—For more than a millennium the inhabitants of France and Germany struggled for the zone to which the Saar belongs. The treaty of Versailles (*q.v.*) stipulated that as compensation for the destruction of the coal mines in northern France, and as part payment toward the reparation due from Germany, the latter had to cede to France the Saar coal mines. Germany had to renounce the government of the Saar territory in favour of the League of Nations, in the capacity as trustee. At the end of 15 yr. a plebiscite was to be held and the inhabitants were to indicate the sovereignty under which they desired to be placed. In the event of a union of the territory with Germany, France's rights of ownership in the mines were to be repurchased by Germany at a price payable in gold, to be fixed by three experts. Some stipulations of the treaty were designed to guarantee France complete freedom in working the mines, while others attempted to assure the rights and welfare of the population. The Saarlanders retained, for example, their local assemblies, religious liberties, schools, language and nationality. A local *gendarmerie* was to maintain order. The territory was to be subjected to the French customs regime; but certain receipts from customs duties were to be included in the local budget. A governing commission was to consist of five members chosen by the council of the League and was to include one citizen of France, one native of the Saar (non-French) and three members belonging to three countries other than France and Germany. Though in some respects an executive body, this commission had broad legislative powers. It had merely to hear an electoral assembly before introducing a new tax measure; the opinion of the representatives was not binding. In making the Saar government an object of international responsibility annexationist tendencies had been checked.

From 1918–23 the Saar, nevertheless, was an object of French expansionism. French troops occupied the territory even until 1927; and this meant at times the existence of French courts-martial besides the neutral court that the treaty established. On June 1, 1923, French money was declared sole legal tender and 60% of the heavy industry of the country passed into the hands of French capitalists. In the spring of 1923, all Saar miners downed tools for 100 days and the French chairman of the governing commission, Victor Rault, issued a decree which considered any criticism of the Versailles treaty as a misdemeanour.

Between 1923 and 1933 the Saarlanders enjoyed peace, because after the occupation of the Ruhr French imperialism retreated.

Rault's administration was gradually replaced by that of more impartial officials who adopted a conciliatory policy. The naturally somewhat unsympathetic attitude of the Saarlanders toward the imposed governing body did not prevent the latter from caring for the inhabitants' welfare.

In the years 1933–35 the plebiscite dominated the life of the Saarland. The liberty front—German exiles, Saar socialists, Communists, unionists, Catholics, Jews and Francophiles—defended the Saar against annexation by imperialistic Germany, which was favoured by the German front led by the National Socialists. Hitlerite methods influenced the vote which was held on Jan. 13, 1935, and it does not seem impossible that the ballot itself was manipulated. Nearly 98% of all qualified voters appeared at the polls, an unprecedented showing, although the weather was bad and about 135,000 voters cast their ballots in a location other than the one in which they were living. During the 18 hours in which the ballots were stored, National Socialists had access to them. This fact was concealed by the official reports, which also overlooked discrepancies in the returns. Ninety and three-tenths per cent declared for union with Germany, 8.8% for continued autonomy under the League and 0.4% for French annexation. On March 1, 1935, the Saar territory was handed over to the third reich.

In 1945 the Saar was occupied by Allied troops. In 1947 the representative Saar assembly, against the pro-German Communists, adopted a constitution which made the (somewhat enlarged) Saarland an autonomous state under French protection and within France's economy. In 1950 France was given a lease on the mines by a Franco-Saar convention.

BIBLIOGRAPHY.—Ernest Babelon, *Sarrelouis et Sarrebrück* (Paris, 1918); Robert Capot-Rey, *La Région industrielle sarroise* (Nancy, 1934); Margaret Lambert, *The Saar* (London, 1934); Hermann Overbeck and Georg Wilhelm Sante, *Saar-Atlas* (Gotha, 1934); Sarah Wambaugh, *The Saar Plebiscite* (1940); Helmut Hirsch, *The Saar Territory* (dissertation, Univ. of Chicago, 1945); *Materialien zur Saarfrage*, 5 vol. (Stuttgart, 1949). (H. HH.)

SAARLOUIS, a town in the Saarland (*q.v.*), situated on the left bank of the Saar and on the railway from Saarbrücken to Trier, 40 mi. south of the latter. Pop. (1939) 33,356. Saarlouis was founded in 1681 by Louis XIV of France, and was fortified by Vauban in 1680–85. By the peace of Paris, in 1815, it was ceded to the Allies and by them was made over to Prussia. Marshal Ney was born there. It contains a town hall in which are hung Gobelins, the gift of Louis XIV. There are coal mines in the vicinity, and the town has foundries and large manufactures. During the national socialist regime the city was named Saarlautern.

SAAVEDRA FAJARDO, DIEGO DE (1584–1648), Spanish diplomatist and man of letters, showed himself master of an excellent prose style in his *Idea de un príncipe político cristiano* (1640), of which there is an English translation by Astry (1700). His most interesting work is the *República literaria*, published in 1655 as the *Juicio de Artes y Sciencas* under the name of Claudio Antonio de Cabrera.

SABAC, a town in Serbia, Yugoslavia. Pop. (1931) 12,563, many of whom are Jews. It is a busy river port on the Sava, exporting cereals, prunes, cattle and pigs, with a large weekly market for livestock, cheeses and grain. It is the seat of a bishop, a prefecture and a tribunal. The fortress was built by Mohammed II in 1470 to facilitate incursions into Slavonia. In the Austro-Turkish wars of 1788–91 the Serbs captured the town, and in the first Serbo-Turkish rising, Kara George, in 1806, defeated the Turks at Mishar, near Sabac. In World War I the Serbs took the town and drove the Austrians back across the Sava. Germans occupied the town in World War II.

SABADELL, a town of northeastern Spain, in the province of Barcelona; on the river Ripoll and on the Barcelona-Saragossa railway. Pop. (1940) 45,931 (mun., 47,831). Cloth, linen, paper, flour and brandy are manufactured, and there are iron foundries and sawmills. About half the inhabitants are employed in the textile factories. Sabadell is said to be the Roman *Sebendunum*, but in Spanish annals it is not noticed until the 13th century.

SABAEANS. This name is used loosely for the ancient dwellers in southwest Arabia, in the parts now called Yemen, Hadhramaut and Asir. Strictly it belongs to one tribe and one state only. The chief source of information about these peoples is their inscriptions, found in their own land and elsewhere; other sources are the Greek geographers, Babylonian and Ethiopic inscriptions, the Bible and the record of Aelius Gallus' expedition. The Arab tradition is not of much value and only for the latest period of the history.

History.—The land produced spices and incense and was a stage on the trade road from India, the Malay archipelago and Africa. At an early date men from Arabia migrated to Abyssinia. The oldest State in Yemen of which anything is known was Ma'īn or Ma'ān, the Minaeans of the Greeks. Its chief towns, Karnawu, Kaminahu and Yathil (the modern Barākish) lay in the southern Jōf, about 120km. N.N.E. of Sanaa. Though the names of 20 kings are known the history of Ma'īn cannot be written. Relations with Hadramaut were friendly, indeed they "almost suggest a personal union," and there was a colony or outpost at Ma'īn Muṣrān (now El 'Ola) to guard the trade road to Egypt and Palestine. Later the State of Katabān began to encroach on Minaean territory, and after fighting with and becoming a vassal or ally of Saba, it joined with that State in destroying Ma'īn about 700 B.C. Taking all things into account, the extent of the State, the number of kings, the highly developed script and language, the beginning of the Minaean kingdom cannot be put later than about 1500 B.C. The Sabaeans are mentioned in a Minaean inscription as nomads who raided the caravan road to El 'Ola. This suggests that they may have migrated south to Yemen and founded the kingdom of Saba which bears their name. Perhaps the queen of Sheba lived in the north of Arabia though she has been decorated with the wealth of the kingdom in Yemen. Marib, 100km. east of Sanaa was its capital. An inscription of Sargon (c. 715 B.C.) refers to It'i-amara the Sabaean, and one of Sennacherib (c. 685 B.C.) to Ka-ri-bi-lu, king of Saba'i. More than once the second successor of a Yt' 'Mr was a Krb'l. Most probably the pair referred to by the Assyrian kings was Yt' 'mr'Byn, who completed the Marib dam, so famous in Arab story, and defeated Ma'īn, killing 45,000 of its inhabitants, and his grandson Krb'l Wtr, who finished the overthrow of Ma'īn and pacified the country. Sennacherib speaks of receiving a present from Saba; even court flattery did not dare to call it tribute. About the same time Ausan, which had been a vassal of Katabān, was crushed along with its ally and neighbour Datinat.

Krb'l Wtr was one of the last of a line of rulers who bore the title Mkrb. It was used also by the earlier lords of Katabān. Not long after, the title of king was adopted by the ruler of Saba and used till 115 B.C. This period is marked by the rise of noble clans and ended with the incorporation of Katabān after war both civil and foreign. At home the Hamdān clan tried for the throne and Himyar appears for the first time among the external enemies with Gedarot which had taken the place of the older Ausan. This year 115 is the first of an era by which some of the later monuments are dated. Now began a serious attack on the trade supremacy of the Sabaeans. The Nabataeans fixed themselves across the trade road to Syria and from Egypt as a base Rome tried to control the sea traffic, besides sending Gallus to attack by land. The royal title now became king of Saba and Du Raidān. About A.D. 300 Hadramaut was conquered and the style became king of Saba, Du Raidān, Hadramaut and Yamnat. This change coincided with a slackening of the Roman effort to control the eastern trade. In the middle of the century Abyssinia conquered the land but already in A.D. 375 there was a native king again. His immediate successor adopted the Jewish religion, a mark of an anti-Roman policy, and in A.D. 525 Du Nuwās, the last Jewish king, was killed and an Abyssinian governor ruled the land. The failure of the dam at Marib was at once an effect and a cause of the national decay. In A.D. 579 Persia conquered the country and in A.D. 628 the governor turned Muslim and submitted to the prophet. Katabān was ruled at first by Mkrb and then by kings who may have been foreigners. The capital Tmna lay some 110km. S.E. of Marib. The capital of Hadramaut was Šabwat, the Sabota of the ancients.

Government and Social Conditions.—The States were built up of tribes mostly held together by local ties not by blood bonds. A tribe contained an aristocracy, tenant vassals, resident aliens and serfs. The name Katabān stood for the kingdom and for the tribes composing it; all were children of the god 'Amm. In Saba the tribe of that name stood apart from the others and held a commanding position in the kingdom. The common phrase is "Saba and the tribes." Saba alone is the child of 'lmkh. Later it was put on a level with the other tribes, and was merged in the militia. The king, tribal aristocrats and the temples were the great landholders. Under the form of government in Katabān (probably much the same in the other States) the king was helped and to some extent controlled by a council of elders, though general policy was decided by the assembly of the tribes. In this the serfs had of course no place. At a later time in Saba the government became feudal; no longer did the tribal assembly decide the allocation of the land, the king granted fiefs. The change may have been helped by the example of the temples, where the retainers had to obey the orders of the god whose land they tilled. The offices of Mkrb and king were hereditary and the latter seems often to have associated his son with himself. The land paid three taxes which are never mentioned separately. The amount paid is not known but it was assessed while the crops were standing. Taxes were paid to the temples also; the tithe is named. Public works were done by forced labour. No list of customs, duties or tolls has been found. In early times the title Kbr is given to the chief of a tribe or clan, the governor of a town or district, the chief of the king's serfs and the head of a college of officials; thus there were many offices with one name. Down to the latest times a Kbr was the eponym after whom the year was named. Kyl is first heard of as the name of a leading section of a tribe in the territory of the god Ta'lab Riyam. The ancestors of a petty king are also called Kyl. So it is probable that he was part of the tribal organisation and took the place of the Kbr. The Kyn was an administrative officer to serve princes, temples or cities. One was a priest. The name suggests that he was not a part of the tribal organisation.

Trade and the Arts.—Monuments of the south Arabians have been found in Kuweit and Mesopotamia; a coffin of a dealer in spices was found in Egypt and an altar with a bi-lingual dedication to Wadd in Delos. Spices and incense were the chief exports and re-exports. The road from Hadramaut ran through the capitals of the other three States, so it is not surprising that one tried to make itself supreme. The returning caravans certainly brought back female slaves for the temple service; women from Gaza and Yathrib (Medina) are mentioned. The production of incense was in the hands of the nobles, 3,000 families Pliny says, and was surrounded with various tabus, besides a tithe paid to the temple at Šabwat. Great care was given to irrigation and the terracing of the hills into fields. The people were fine masons and stonecutters. The dam at Marib is now in much the same condition as when Hamdani (A.D. 848) saw it. The buildings were made of stone so carefully dressed that often the joints are scarcely visible; the stones are held together by leaden dowels and pillars are strengthened by mortise and tenon joints. Big buildings were often elaborately decorated and several forms of pillars and capitals were in use. The Arab tales of lofty houses with windows of translucent stone are not much exaggerated. The pointed arch was known. Many of the old cisterns are still in use. Many of the inscriptions are beautiful and testify to the skill of the stone-cutters, who were successful with the figures of animals and conventional foliage in low relief. Figures in the round were less good and in statues of men the body is usually a mere block while the face is wooden and expressionless and often out of proportion. Stone pots and jars for household use are simple but neat and well shaped. Most of the metal work that survives is figures of animals and tablets with inscriptions. The figures are generally crude. One can never be sure that the jewellery, pottery and similar small articles really belong to the land and the period. The best things suggest foreign influence or even origin. At first the coins followed Athenian models and the workmanship is very good in some. Later they degenerated till the owl looks like a jar with two round handles. Curiously the standard is Babylonian. The latest coins are weak imitations of Roman coins.

Inscriptions and Language.—The inscriptions are all on stone or metal. Words are separated by a divider and the letters are never joined. In early times the characters are angular but later the corners are rounded and curves appear. The alphabet is connected with the Phoenician; some of the letters are exactly alike, some look as if they had been purposely altered by those who understood the art of carving in stone, and some not found in Phoenician are formed by differentiation from those that are. Short inscriptions have been found in Mesopotamia in which Sabaean letters are combined with others resembling the Phoenician and Greek forms. It is not certain whether this is an early form of the alphabet or merely a freak. There are 29 letters, the 28 of Arabic and the second form of s which is found in Hebrew. The language is classified with Abyssinian as south Semitic and is split into several dialects which differ in grammatical forms and vocabulary. In Ma'in and Ḳatabān s is used in the pronoun of the third person and in the causative form of the verb where Sabaean has h. Hadramaut has forms which are phonetically later than the other dialects. The vowels are not indicated so the pronunciation of all words is a matter of guesswork. The writing is usually from right to left but some of the oldest inscriptions read alternately from right to left and from left to right. This is occasionally found in later ones but then for special reasons. Presumably there was a literature but it has disappeared. Sabaean inscriptions have been found in Abyssinia and the Ethiopic alphabet is derived from the south Arabian. Inscriptions in various alphabets derived from the Sabaean are found in different parts of Arabia as far north as Damascus and testify to the widespread influence of the south Arabian kingdoms. Many of the south Arabian inscriptions are hard to interpret and the sense highly problematical.

Religion.—Over 100 gods and many temples are named but next to nothing is known about them. Certain deities are common to the whole land. Šams, the sun, is feminine and perhaps all goddesses are forms of it. 'Aṭṭar, the star Venus, is masculine but corresponds philologically with the Babylonian Ishtar and the Canaanite Ashtoreth. The moon, Waraḫ, Šahr or Sīn, occurs occasionally and Il or Ilan is the name of a god as well as a common noun. Each country had its own god; Ma'in had Wadd, Ḳatabān had 'Amm, Saba had Ilmukah and the clan of Hamdān had Ta'lab Riyam. Perhaps these tribal gods are all forms of the moon. There are indications that the moon, sun and Venus formed a divine family. Others are Anbai, Ḍu Samawi, the enigmatic Nakraḥ and Atirat (the Hebrew Ashera). Other divine names are clearly descriptive; Hawbas "the drier" is the moon according to Hamdāni, Kahil "the old," Sa'd "luck" the giver of good fortune and Ḥukm "judgment" the judge. At times kings seem to have been worshipped (after death?). Springs and water courses were inhabited by spirits. The bull, the bull's horns and the crescent were symbols of the moon and a disc stood for both the sun and Venus. Often one cannot decide which of the two is meant. The people were the offspring and the king the firstborn of the god, so the formula runs "god, king and people." There were no images of the gods. To obtain success in one's undertakings it was the custom to dedicate to the god a statue of oneself in stone or figures of men or animals in gold (? gilt). Sacrifices and incense were offered to them. The names for altar and sacrifice are the common Semitic terms, and the altar of incense has among other names that of *miḳtār* as in Hebrew. A variety of spices (the wealth of the land) are named on these altars, as rand, ladanum, costus, tarum, frankincense and others not yet interpreted. Pilgrimages were made at certain seasons and the pilgrim month was named Ḍu Ḥijjatan or Ḍu Maḥajjat. There are many names for the months, some of which refer to agriculture. The name for priest is r-š-w (which may mean giver) and in the El 'Ola texts comes the word l-w-', both masculine and feminine, which looks very like Levite. In later times the name Rahmān for God suggests Jewish influence. Christianity was introduced into South Arabia but it was not favoured because of its association with Abyssinia and the famous church in Sanaa was looked on as a sign of foreign domination. The massacre of Christians in Nejran had political causes as well as religious.

The ruins of the temple at Marib are an open space surrounded by an elliptical wall with the main door at one end of the shorter axis and a smaller at one end of the longer axis. Columns flanked the main door. Outside are several groups of pillars and a set of four may have held a canopy over a throne. The temple at Sirwaḥ is an oblong building with two sets of pillars inside it. One set held up the roof of the sanctuary and the other surrounded a light well. Another at Yeha in Abyssinia is an oblong building with the door at one end. It seems to have been of three stories.   (A. S. T.)

SABAKI, a river, 400 mi. long, in Kenya Colony, Africa, which enters the Indian ocean north of Malinda. As the Athi, it rises north of Nairobi, flows across the Kapoté and Athi plains,

and turns south under the Yatta ridge. Navigation is interrupted by the Lugard falls, 100 mi. from its mouth.

SABANG, a port situated on the island of Pulu Weh, about 20 mi. N. of Kota Raja, the capital of Achin (Atjeh), in north Sumatra, Indonesia, 308 mi. from Penang (from which it lies due west), 608 mi. from Singapore and 1,100 mi. from Batavia. Pop. 8,706.

Sabang is the first port of call in the Malay archipelago for vessels proceeding from Europe eastward, being the westernmost point at the entrance to the Straits of Malacca. The harbour, built in 1887, principally as a coaling station, is sheltered from the heavy swell of the Indian ocean and strong winds by mountains and high stretches of coast line.

SABARKANTHA, a district of Bombay state, republic of India, which includes some areas of the old Sabarkantha agency. Area of the district, 2,447 sq.mi.; pop. (1951), 684,017.

The Sabarkantha Agency, a subagency of the Western India States agency, was set up in 1934 by the combination of the former Banas Kantha and Mahi Kantha agencies, with headquarters at Sadra. The agency comprised 46 petty states, 13 talukas (subdivisions under hereditary landowners) and a number of other estates grouped into 9 thanas (police divisions); the agency occupied a large tract in northwestern Gujarat and five detached areas to the southeast; total area 5,408 sq.mi.; pop. (1941) 457,813. All the Sabarkantha states, etc., were merged into Bombay in 1948.

SABATIER, LOUIS AUGUSTE (1839–1901), French Protestant theologian, was born at Vallon (Ardèche), in the Cévennes, on Oct. 22, 1839, and was educated at the Protestant theological faculty of Montauban and the universities of Tübingen and Heidelberg. After four years' work as a pastor he became professor of reformed dogmatics at Strasbourg. In 1886 he became a teacher in the newly founded religious science department of the École des Hautes Études of the Sorbonne. He died April 12, 1901.

Among his chief works were *The Apostle Paul,* 3rd ed. (1896); *Mémoire sur la notion hébraïque de l'Esprit* (1879); *Les Origines littéraires de l'Apocalypse* (1888); *The Vitality of Christian Dogmas and their Power of Evolution* (1890); *Religion and Modern Culture* (1897); *Historical Evolution of the Doctrine of the Atonement* (1903); *Outlines of a Philosophy of Religion* (1897); and his posthumous *Religions of Authority and the Religion of the Spirit* (1904).

SABATIER, PAUL (1858–1928), French historian, the younger brother of Louis Auguste Sabatier (*q.v.*), was born at Chabrillanoux, in the Cévennes, on Aug. 3, 1858. He studied at the faculty of theology in Paris, and in 1885 became vicar of St. Nicholas, Strasbourg, from which he was expelled on declining the German government's offer of preferment which was conditional on his becoming a German subject. He was then appointed pastor of St. Cierge, but being compelled by ill health to give up his cure, he devoted himself to historical research. The appearance of his *Life of St. Francis,* in 1893, made his name, and his reputation was enhanced by the publication of *Collection d'études et de documents,* in 1898. In 1902 Sabatier founded the International Society of Franciscan Studies, and soon after he organized at Assisi *La Refezione Scolastica* for feeding needy children, in support of which he delivered a brilliant lecture on Modernism in France at London (1905). In 1919 Sabatier became professor of Protestant theology at Strasbourg, which post he held until his death in March 1928.

SABATIER, PAUL (1854–1941), French organic chemist, was born at Carcassonne, Nov. 5, 1854. He studied under Marcellin P. E. Berthelot at the Collège de France, taking his doctor's degree in 1880. After a year at Bordeaux, he moved to the University of Toulouse in 1882.

Sabatier's researches in catalytic organic synthesis, and particularly his discovery of the catalytic activity of finely divided nickel in hydrogenation-dehydrogenation reactions, won for him half the Nobel prize for 1912. His discoveries formed the bases of the margarine, oil hydrogenation and synthetic methanol industries, as well as of numerous laboratory syntheses.

Sabatier explored nearly the whole field of catalytic syntheses in organic chemistry. He personally investigated several hundred hydrogenation and dehydrogenation reactions, showing that several other metals besides nickel possess catalytic activity, though in smaller degree. He also studied catalytic hydration and dehydration, examining carefully both the feasibility of specific reactions and the general activity of the various catalysts.

Sabatier's great discovery was made in 1897 when he and his pupil J. B. Senderens passed ethylene over hot nickel, in an effort to prepare a nickel compound of ethylene. They believed that since carbon monoxide, which has unsaturated valences, combines with nickel to form a carbonyl, then ethylene, too, which is also an unsaturated compound, might form an analogous compound with nickel. Actually, they obtained much carbon, indicating decomposition of the ethylene, and some ethane. Concluding that the ethane could have come only from undecomposed ethylene which had been reduced by hydrogen formed from the ethylene which had decomposed, they tried passing a mixture of hydrogen and ethylene over the nickel, and immediately obtained a smooth reduction.

Sabatier remained at the University of Toulouse until his retirement in 1930, though he had been invited to succeed Henri Moissan (q.v.) at the University of Paris. He died Aug. 14, 1941.

For biographical details see H. S. Taylor, *Journal American Chemical Society,* vol. 66 p. 1615 (1944); H. Vincent, *Comptes rendus de l'Academie des Sciences,* vol. 213, p. 281 (1941). (P. O.)

SABAZIUS, a Phrygian or Thracian deity, frequently identified with Dionysus, sometimes (but less frequently) with Zeus. His worship was closely connected with that of Cybele and Attis and was chthonian and mystic in character. It reached Greece in the 5th century B.C. A few passages state that the Jews worshipped him (confusion with Heb. *sabaōth?*) see Val. Max. I., 3, 2. The true etymology of the name is unknown. Whether he was the same as Sozon, a marine deity of Southern Asia Minor, is doubtful. His image and name are often found on "votive hands," a kind of talisman adorned with emblems, the nature of which is obscure. His ritual and mysteries (*Sacra Savadia*) gained a firm footing in Rome during the 2nd century A.D.

See Eisele in Roscher's *Lexikon, s.v.* (bibl.).

SABBATAI SEBI (1626–1676), Jewish mystic, who claimed to be the Messiah, was born in Smyrna, of Spanish descent. As a lad he was attracted by the mysticism of Luria (q.v.), which impelled him to adopt the ascetic life. He passed his days and nights in a condition of ecstasy. He began to dream of the fulfilment of Messianic hopes, being supported in his vision by the outbreak of English Millenarianism. Christian visionaries fixed the year 1666 for the millennium. Sabbatai's father (Mordecai) was the Smyrna agent for an English house, and often heard of the expectations of the English Fifth Monarchy men. In 1648 (the year which Kabbalists had calculated as the year of salvation) Sabbatai proclaimed himself Messiah, and in Constantinople came across a man, who pretended that he had been warned by a prophetic voice that Sabbatai was indeed the long-awaited Redeemer. At first his adherents were a small circle of devotees who kept their faith a secret. He charmed men by his sweet singing of Psalms, and children were always fascinated by him. He journeyed to Jerusalem, where a local pasha was opposing the Jews, and Sabbatai secured help for them from Cairo. At Cairo Sabbatai married, and secured the support of Raphael Halebi. With a retinue of believers, a charming wife and considerable funds, Sabbatai returned in triumph to the Holy Land. Nathan of Gaza assumed the rôle of Elijah, the Messiah's forerunner, proclaimed the coming restoration of Israel and the salvation of the world through the bloodless victory of Sabbatai "riding on a lion with a seven-headed dragon in his jaws" (Graetz). Again 1666 was given as the apocalyptic year.

Threatened with excommunication by the Rabbis of Jerusalem, Sabbatai returned to Smyrna (autumn of 1665). Here he was received with wild enthusiasm. From the Levant the Sabbataean movement spread to Venice, Amsterdam, Hamburg and London. Sabbatai no longer doubted the reality of his mission. Day by day he was hailed from all the world as king of the Jews. At the beginning of the fateful year 1666 Sabbatai went (or was summoned) to Constantinople. Here he was arrested, but reports of miracles continued, and many of the Turks were inclined to become converts. Soon he was transferred to Abydos. In September Sabbatai was brought before the Sultan, and he had not the courage to refuse to accept Islam. The Messianic imposture ended in the apostacy of Sabbatai. In 1676 he died in obscurity in Albania. A sect of Sabbataeans—the Dormeh of Salonica—survived him and for many years the controversy for and against his claims left an echo in Jewish life.

See Graetz, *History of the Jews,* vol. v. ch. iv. 1. Zangwill has a brilliant sketch of Sabbatai's career in his *Dreamers of the Ghetto.*

SABBATH, the seventh and especially sacred day of the week among the Jews.

Observance.—How tenaciously the Jews held to the observance of the Sabbath may be seen from the fact that on this account the Romans found themselves compelled to exempt them from military service. The rules of the Scribes enumerated thirty-nine main kinds of work forbidden on the Sabbath, and each of these prohibitions gave rise to new subtleties. When the disciples of Jesus plucked ears of corn on the Sabbath they had, according to the Rabbinical views, violated the third of the thirty-nine rules, which forbade harvesting; and in healing the sick Jesus himself broke the rule that a sick man should not receive medical aid unless his life was in danger. In fact, as Jesus put it, the Rabbinical theory seemed to be that the Sabbath was not made for man but man for the Sabbath, the observance of which was so much an end in itself that the rules prescribed for it did not require to be justified by appeal to any larger principle of religion or humanity. The precepts of the law were valuable in the eyes of the Scribes because they were the seal of Jewish particularism, the barrier erected between the world at large and the exclusive community of Yahweh's grace. The ideal at which these rules aimed was absolute rest on the Sabbath from everything that could be called work; and even the exercise of those offices of humanity which the strictest Christian Sabbatarians regard as service to God, and therefore as specially appropriate to his day, was looked on as work. To save life was allowed; danger to life "superseded the Sabbath." The positive duties of its observance were to wear one's best clothes, eat, drink and be glad (justified from Isaiah lviii. 13). A more directly religious element, it is true, was introduced by the practice of attending the synagogue service, but even this service was regarded as a meeting for instruction in the law rather than as an act of worship.

Attitude of Jesus and Early Christian Church.—The general position which Jesus takes up, that "the Sabbath is made for man and not man for the Sabbath," is only a special application of the wider principle that the law is not an end in itself but a help towards the realization in life of the great ideal of love to God and man, which is the sum of all true religion. But Jesus further maintains that this view of the law as a whole, and the interpretation of the Sabbath law which it involves, can be historically justified from the Old Testament. In this connection He introduces two of the main methods to which historical criticism of the Old Testament has recurred in modern times: He appeals to the oldest history rather than to the Pentateuchal code as proving that the later conception of the law was unknown in ancient times (Matthew xii. 3 *seq.*), and to the exceptions to the Sabbath law which the Scribes themselves allowed in the interests of worship (v. 5) or humanity (v. 11), as showing that the Sabbath must originally have been devoted to purposes of worship and humanity, and was not always the purposeless arbitrary thing which the Scribes made it to be. Modern criticism of the history of Sabbath observance among the Hebrews has done little more than follow out these arguments in detail, and show that the result is in agreement with what is known as to the dates of the several component parts of the Pentateuch.

In the early Christian church Jewish Christians continued to keep the Sabbath, like other points of the old law. Eusebius records that the Ebionites observed both the Sabbath and the Lord's day, the weekly celebration of the resurrection. This practice obtained to some extent in wider circles, for the *Apostolical Constitutions* recommend that the Sabbath shall be kept as a memorial feast of the creation, as well as the Lord's day as a memorial of the resurrection. The festal character of the Sabbath was long recognized in a modified form in the Eastern church by a prohibition of fasting on that day, which was also a point in the Jewish Sabbath law. On the other hand Paul from the first days of Gentile Christianity, laid it down definitely that the Jewish Sabbath was not binding on Christians. Controversy with Judaizers led in process of time to direct condemnation of those who still kept the Jewish day (*e.g.*, Co. of Laodicea, A.D. 363). For discussion of the difficult problem when and how the Christian Sunday superseded and took on some characteristics of the Jewish Sabbath *see* SUNDAY. (W. R. S.; S. A. C.)

Origin.—What was the origin of the Sabbath? What part did it play in the life of the Israelite nation before the exile? To these questions confident answers have been given, but the material upon which we can base our conclusions is not sufficiently extensive or clear to warrant dogmatism. It is a noteworthy fact that there is no evidence of Sabbath observance in the patriarchal period: there is, indeed, very little material that can be reckoned as pre-exilic.

There are four passages which seem to point to the conclusion that in the earlier times a close connection existed between the Sabbath and the new-moon festival. In 2 Kings iv. 23 the Shunammite's husband asks, when she proposes to visit the prophet, "Wherefore wilt thou go to him to-day? it is neither new moon nor sabbath." Among the religious observances which Isaiah names as offensive to Yahweh he links together (i. 13) "new moon and sabbath." In Hosea ii. 11 Yahweh says of Israel "I will cause all her mirth to cease, her feasts, her new moons, her sabbaths, and all her solemn assemblies." Amos (viii. 5) denounces the traders who say "When will the new moon be gone, that we may sell corn? and the sabbath, that we may set forth wheat?" The reference in Hosea would make it probable that the Sabbath was a season of festal joy, and that in Amos makes it clear that there was at any rate some cessation of ordinary business activities on that day. By inference this latter conclusion may be deduced from the passage in Kings. The question of the Shunammite's husband suggests that the ass for which she had asked in order to make her journey would have been available, even in harvest time, had the day been a new moon or a Sabbath: the inference surely is that on those days the work of harvesting stood still, so that the beasts would not be required for labour on the farm. This combination of new moon and Sabbath suggested to Meinhold (*Sabbat und Woche im Alten Testament*, 1905) that originally the Sabbath must have been the day of the full moon. This theory is very plausible, though Meinhold's endeavour to explain how the full moon feast came to be transformed into the regular seventh day Sabbath of abstinence is not convincing. Kittel has attacked the fundamental hypothesis on which the theory rests. He contends that the existence of a full moon feast in ancient Israel is nowhere demonstrable, and points out that while the new moon festival has maintained itself in later Judaism there is no survival of a full moon festival. This last argument, however, might easily be countered, for if it be a fact that the full moon festival was converted into the weekly Sabbath the disappearance of the former would be amply accounted for.

Meinhold regards the Decalogue as dating, at the earliest, from the exile, and rejects decidedly the idea that before the exile the Hebrews had a seven day week running throughout the year. Many critics, however, tend distinctly towards the belief that the Decalogue in some simple form may very well go back to the time of Moses. The story of the manna in Exodus xvi. in its original form may represent Moses as the discoverer of the Sabbath; and if so, this would be evidence that in certain streams of tradition Moses was regarded as the sponsor in Israel of the Sabbath. If the kernel of the commandments be accepted as Mosaic the institution of the Sabbath goes back to the very beginnings of the history of Israel. In the decalogue of Exodus xx. 3–17 the command "remember the sabbath day" follows immediately upon the commandments which are concerned with Yahweh and Yahweh's name. This shows how great must have been the importance of the Sabbath, and suggests that it was regarded as in an especial sense Yahweh's day, a fact for which the Old Testament offers abundant confirmation. The emphasis on the Sabbath in this form of the Decalogue is the more noteworthy

in view of the fact that it ignores all the other feasts and rites. It is highly probable, considering the close association between Yahweh and the Sabbath, that the celebration of the latter as a festival goes back to the time when Yahweh first became the national deity. This does not, of course, conflict with the theory that it was connected also with the changes of the moon, which, indeed, seems to be the most probable hypothesis. Whether originally it was the day of the full moon only, or whether the half-moon days were also Sabbaths, it is difficult to say.

It has been objected that a regular rest day like the Sabbath could be celebrated only by a settled agricultural people. Apart from the fact that the ancestors of the Israelite nation were not all nomads it may be urged that even the life of the desert was much more artificial than we have been accustomed to suppose. The wandering herdsmen have many trades. Some of them breed cattle. Slaves and artisans have always been known in the desert. At the oases corn and fruit are cultivated. And peoples in a comparatively primitive state of culture observe rest-days, though these are not as a rule periodic, and are not necessarily consecrated to a particular deity or employed for religious purposes. Hutton Webster (*Rest Days*, 1911), regards the restrictions which characterize them as being in the nature of tabus. Such days are observed at critical seasons, among which are the changes of the moon. He instances in particular the custom of Hawaii, according to which on a strict tabu day there must be no fire or light, and general gloom and silence prevail. No canoes may be launched, no one may bathe, or even be seen out of doors unless his presence is required at the temple. The old Hawaiian system included a remarkable approximation to the institution of a weekly Sabbath. In each lunar month four periods were tabu, the 3rd to the 6th nights, the time of the full moon, including the 14th and 15th nights, the 24th and 25th nights, and the 27th and 28th nights. On the other hand among some peoples such seasons of abstinence developed into joyous festivals and holidays. "Among many peoples in the lower culture," says Hutton Webster, "the time of the new moon and full moon, much less commonly each half moon, is a season of restriction and abstinence." Such days may be dedicated to a god, or may simply be regarded as unlucky days.

A theory that the Jewish Sabbath, name and institution alike, is derived from Babylonian sources was propounded by Friedrich Delitzsch (*Babel and Bible*) and has been widely accepted. To quote Delitzsch, "Since the Babylonians also had a Sabbath (*shabattu*) on which, for the purpose of conciliating the gods, there was a festival—that is to say, no work was to be done—and since the 7th, 14th, 21st and 28th days of the month are marked on a calendar of sacrifices and festivals dug up in Babylonia as days on which 'the shepherd of the great nations' (*i.e.*, the king) shall eat no roast flesh, shall not change his dress, shall not offer sacrifice, as days on which the king shall not mount the chariot, or pronounce judgment, the magus shall not prophesy, even the physician shall not lay his hand upon the sick, in short, as days which are not suitable for any affair, it is scarcely possible for us to doubt that we owe the blessings decreed in the Sabbath or Sunday day of rest in the last resort to that ancient and civilized race on the Euphrates and Tigris."

The evidence adduced by Delitzsch, plausible as it seems, is not however, conclusive. The inscription he quotes—which, though it comes from the "library" of Asurbanipal, is evidently of Babylonian origin—refers only to a particular month, the intercalary Elul, and it is not shown that these special days occurred in the other months. Further, the prohibitions apply only to particular persons such as the king and the physician. It should be noted, too, that the calendar specifies in addition to the 7th, 14th, 21st and 28th days also the 19th as an "evil day" on which the restrictions apply. It is explained that the 19th is the 49th day from the beginning of the preceding month, that is, the end of the seventh week from that starting-point. But even if this explanation is correct the fact would remain that the day of restriction occurs oftener than at the end of each week. In order to discover whether there is evidence of a general restriction of business in Babylonia on particular days C. H. W. Johns (*Ency. Brit.* 11th ed. vol. xxiii. 961 *seq.*) analyzed a great many business contracts, classifying them according to the day of the week on which they were dated. The result showed that on all these "evil days" business was carried on, though, if the documents may be taken as fairly representative, there was a marked diminution of business on the 19th day of the month. During the First Dynasty of Babylon, and in the seventh century B.C., all these days show a falling off in the number of trading transactions. But, on the other hand, during the Kassite period trade went on much as usual on all days, including even the 19th day of the month. In any case these "evil days" seem different from the early Hebrew Sabbath; the latter was just the day when the Shunammite woman might actually have been expected to go on a journey, whereas the former were just the days when the king might not ride in his chariot.

It is true that the Babylonians had a day called *shabattum* or *shapattum*. This seems, however, to be distinct from the days of restriction dealt with in the calendar tablet. In a syllabary *shapattum* is equated to *um nuḫ libbi*, that is, "day of the rest of the heart." It has been urged that here is a proof that the Babylonians had a Sabbath which, like that of the Hebrews, was a rest day. But it is clear from the Babylonian penitential psalms that the real meaning of the words is "day when the heart (of the gods) is propitiated." A tablet discovered by Pinches shows that the *shapattum* was the 15th day of the month. A passage in the astronomical poem of the Babylonian epic *Enuma elish* quite clearly shows that the *shapattum* is the day of the full moon. The verb *shapatu* is elsewhere explained as equivalent to the verb *gamaru*, meaning "to be complete, full." None of the attempted etymologies for Sabbath from the Hebrew is successful, probably for the reason that the word is older than the Hebrew language. It is not unreasonable to suppose that both *shapattum* and *sabbath* are descended from a word belonging to the older tongue from which both the Babylonian language and the Hebrew developed, and that its prime meaning is "full moon day." This would confirm Meinhold's theory that among the Hebrews the Sabbath was originally the full moon day. But the fact that the name is derived from a common source, and that the day itself among both peoples is originally the day of the full moon, must not blind us to the truth that the Babylonians had no real equivalent to the Jewish Sabbath at regular seven-day intervals. Had there been any great likeness between the ways in which the *shapattum* and the Sabbath were celebrated the latter could hardly have been insisted on as a distinctive mark of the Jews.

Sabbatical Year.—An ancient Hebrew law enjoined that in every seventh year the land should lie fallow (Exodus xxiii. 11); vineyard and olive garden, too, are to remain uncultivated. Whatever may be produced under these conditions is to be for the poor and the wild beasts. It is extremely unlikely that this was meant to apply to all cultivated land in the same year. If any attempt were made to carry out this injunction the Sabbatical year must have varied from plot to plot. The later Law of Holiness does, however, prescribe one definite year for all land. According to Josephus the Sabbatical year was a close time for warlike operations. From the same authority we learn that the Jews requested Alexander to remit tribute during the Sabbatical year, and that Tacitus complained that the Jews devoted every seventh year to idleness. Similar is the rule that there should be release of debtors from their debts in each seventh year.

The term has been adopted in universities for a period of freedom from academic duties every seventh year.

BIBLIOGRAPHY.—*See,* besides the literature already cited, Hehn, *Siebenzahl u. Sabbat bei den Babyloniern u. im Alten Testament* (1907); "Sabbath" in *E.R.E.* and Wardle, *Israel and Babylon,* pp. 236 *sqq.* (W. L. W.)

SABBATION or SAMBATYON, a river (1) natural and (2) supernatural. (1) The Targum pseudo-Jonathan to Exod. xxxiv., 10 states that the Ten Tribes were exiled beyond the Sambatyon: this is repeated in Gen. Rabba lxxiii.: Num. Rab. xvi. and Yalqūt Genesis 984. This is therefore a river in Media, identified by Ramban (Deut. xxxii., 26) with the Gozan (II Kings xvii., 6) and a natural stream. Fuenn (*Pirḥe Çafōn* ii., 133) identifies this with the Zab in Adiabene which Xenophon calls Sabatos and which

became corrupted to Sabbation. This river must be sharply distinguished from that mentioned by Josephus (*War,* vii., v., 1) who makes Titus on his return from the destruction of Jerusalem pass, near Beirut, a river which, flowing only on one day in seven, is called after the Sabbath. It will be noted that this river is in Palestine, not in Media and that it is periodic.

(2) With Pliny (*Hist. Nat.* xxxi., 2) two supernatural elements enter the story. First the river rests one day in seven instead of flowing on that day and secondly that day is the Sabbath. A variant of the miracle occurs in Gen. Rabba xi. In the 9th century the mysterious Eldad the Danite carried the wonder still further. In his chronicle the river is waterless but full of sand and stones which roll with a great noise during the week-days but rest on the Sabbath. Th. Noeldeke (*Beiträge zur Gesch. d. Alexanderromans,* 48) traces the Sambatyon in the Alexander legend. The river of sand (*Wadi ar-Raml*) is mentioned by Kazwini (*Cosmography* ed. Wüstenfeld, ii., 17) and by Mas'udi. Benjamin of Tudela mentions the ten tribes and the Gozan river but he ascribes no miraculous properties to it, save that David Alroy crossed it on his mantle. In the 17th century the miracles have increased. Travellers from India relate that the sand or water is curative of leprosy. Menasseh ben Israel states that the sand, if kept in a bottle moves about during the week but rests on Sabbath. It has been suggested that the sand element in the story is to be explained by a confusion of a Hebrew name נהר חל (*Nehar Ḥōl*) which could mean either "weekday river" or "river of sand."

See *Jew. Enc. s.v.* and A. Neubauer, *Jew. Quart. Rev. I.,* "Where are the Ten Tribes?"

SABELLIC (from Latin *Sabellus,* Samnite) has often been used of a minor group of the Italic dialects, namely the pre-Latin dialects of the Paeligni, Marrucini and Vestini (better called North Oscan), of the Volsci, and of the Marsi, Aequi, Sabini and other central Italian tribes (conveniently called Latinian); these dialects are all closely related to Oscan (*q.v.*). The same name, or sometimes Old Sabellic, is also used, but inaccurately, to describe two small but distinct groups of inscriptions from various sites near the east coast of central Italy (1) from Novilara and Fano (near Pesaro); (2) from Belmonte Piceno, Cupra Marittima, Castignano, Bellante, Grecchio and Superequo. These may be better designated, by "East Italic."

The second group, not more recent in date than the 6th century B.C., are doubtless the oldest written documents known from Italian soil. The lines of writing run alternately left to right and right to left, the positions of the letters being both reversed and inverted in the lines written right to left. Their alphabet is clearly of the same Chalcid-Etruscan origin as that of all the other alphabets of ancient Italy (except the Greek and Phoenician), but shows some peculiarities which suggest direct Greek influence; the language, still untranslated, will probably prove to be an Indo-European (two I.-E. stems, *pater* father, *mater* mother have been identified) and ancient Illyrian dialect (*meitime* is an Illyrian name). For it is known from the elder Pliny (*N.H.* 3, 110, *cf.* 113), from the Iguvine tables (*iapuzkum* Iapydian, *i.e.,* belonging to the Illyrian Iapydes), and from archaeological evidence, that there were Illyrian settlers in or near that district, the ancient Picenum, where these inscriptions were discovered.

But the documents of the Novilara group are later in date, distinct in alphabet—this is perhaps of Etruscan origin, but shows certain resemblances both to the Umbrian and to the Oscan alphabets—and probably also in dialect. The suggestion that the dialect, however, is allied to Etruscan itself, is quite unsupported by the evidence; the decorative *motifs,* for example the spiral, which appear on all three of the inscriptions of this group, point rather to the opposite coast of the Adriatic, where similar *motifs* occur, especially round Nesazio, on contemporary monuments; and there is nothing in the word-forms of these documents which may not be Indo-European, while the characteristic Etruscan syncope and elision (at least in the writing) are entirely lacking.

BIBLIOGRAPHY.—R. von Planta, *Grammatik der oskisch-umbrischen Dialekte,* vol. ii., pp. 551 *sqq.,* 664 *sqq.* (1897); two new inscriptions discovered since 1897 were reported in *Rendiconti d. R. Acc. dei*

Lincei, ser. 5, vol. xvii (1908), pp. 681 *sqq.*, and *Notizie degli Scavi*, 1903, pp. 101 *sqq. See* also G. Herbig in M. Ebert's *Real-lexikon der Vorgeschichte, s.vv.* Novilara, Vorsabeller (1927–; bibl.), and R. S. Conway in *Cambridge Ancient History* vol. iv. (1926) p. 445. The inscriptions have been edited anew by J. Whatmough, *Prae-Italic Dialects of Italy: Part II.* (in the press, bibl.), Nos. 342–355.
(J. WH.)

SABELLIUS (*fl.* 230), early Christian presbyter and theologian, was of Libyan origin, and came from the Pentapolis to Rome early in the 3rd century. He became the leader of the strict Modalists (who regarded the Father and the Son as two aspects of the same subject) whom Calixtus had excommunicated along with their most zealous opponent Hippolytus. His party continued to subsist in Rome for a considerable time, and withstood Calixtus as an unscrupulous apostate. In the West, however, the influence of Sabellius seems never to have been important; in the East, on the other hand, after the middle of the 3rd century his doctrine found much acceptance, first in the Pentapolis and afterwards in other provinces. It was violently controverted by the bishops, notably by Dionysius of Alexandria, and the development in the East of the philosophical doctrine of the Trinity after Origen (from 260 to 320) was very powerfully influenced by the opposition to Sabellianism.

Sabellian Doctrine.—The Sabellian doctrine itself, however, during the decades above mentioned underwent many changes in the East and received a philosophical dress. In the 4th century this and the allied doctrine of Marcellus of Ancyra were frequently confounded, so that it is exceedingly difficult to arrive at a clear account of it in its genuine form. Sabellianism, in fact, became a collective name for all those Unitarian doctrines in which the divine nature of Christ was acknowledged. The teaching of Sabellius himself was very closely allied to the older Modalism ("Patripassianism") of Noetus and Praxeas, but was distinguished from it by its more careful theological elaboration and by the account it took of the Holy Spirit. His central proposition was to the effect that Father, Son and Holy Spirit are the same person, three names thus being attached to one and the same being. What weighed most with Sabellius was the monotheistic interest.

Sabellius further maintained that God is not at one and the same time Father, Son and Spirit, but, on the contrary, has been active in three apparently consecutive manifestations or energies—first in the πρόσωπον of the Father as Creator and Lawgiver, then in the πρόσωπον of the Son as Redeemer, and lastly in the πρόσωπον of the Spirit as the Giver of Life. It is by this doctrine of the succession of the πρόσωπα that Sabellius is distinguished from the older Modalists. In particular it is significant, in conjunction with the reference to the Holy Spirit, that Sabellius regards the Father also as merely a form of manifestation of the one God—in other words, has formally put Him in a position of complete equality with the other Persons. This view prepares the way for Augustine's doctrine of the Trinity. Sabellius himself appears to have made use of Stoical formulas (πλατύνεσθαι συστέλλεσθαι), but he chiefly relied upon Scripture, especially such passages as Deut. vi. 4; Exod. xx. 3; Isa. xliv. 6; John x. 38. Of his later history nothing is known; his followers died out in the course of the 4th century.

The sources of our knowledge of Sabellianism are Hippolytus (*Philos*, bk. ix.), Epiphanius (*Haer.* lxii.) and Dionys. Alex. (*Epp.*); also various passages in Athanasius and the other fathers of the 4th century. For modern discussions of the subject *see* Schleiermacher (*Theol. Ztschr.* 1822, Hft. 3); Lange (*Ztschr. f. hist. Theol.* 1832, ii. 2); Döllinger (*Hippolyt u. Kallist.* 1853); Zahn (*Marcell v. Ancyra*, 1867); R. L. Ottley, *The Doctrine of the Incarnation* (1896); various histories of Dogma, and Harnack (*s.v.* "Monarchianismus," in Herzog-Hauck, *Realencyk. für prot. Theol. und Kirche*, xiii. 303). (A. HA.)

SĀBIANS. The Ṣābians (*aṣ-Ṣābi'ūn*) who are first mentioned in the Koran (ii. 59, v. 73, xxii. 17) were a semi-Christian sect of Babylonia, the Elkesaites, closely resembling the Mandaeans or so-called "Christians of St. John the Baptist," but not identical with them. How Mohammed understood the term "Ṣābians" is uncertain, but he mentions them together with the Jews and Christians. The older Mohammedan theologians were agreed that they possessed a written revelation and were entitled accordingly to enjoy a toleration not granted to mere heathen. Curiously enough, the name "Ṣābian" was used by the Meccan idolaters to denote Mohammed himself and his Muslim converts, apparently on account of the frequent ceremonial ablutions which formed a striking feature of the new religion.

From these true Ṣābians the pseudo-Ṣābians of Ḥarrān (*Carrhae*) in Mesopotamia must be carefully distinguished. In A.D. 830 the Caliph Ma'mūn, while marching against the Byzantines, received a deputation of the inhabitants of Ḥarrān. Astonished by the sight of their long hair and extraordinary costume, he inquired what religion they professed, and getting no satisfactory answer threatened to exterminate them, unless by the time of his return from the war they should have embraced either Islam or one of the creeds tolerated in the Koran. Consequently, acting on the advice of a Mohammedan jurist, the Ḥarrānians declared themselves to be "Ṣābians," a name which shielded them from persecution in virtue of its Koranic authority and was so vague that it enabled them to maintain their ancient beliefs undisturbed. There is no doubt as to the general nature of the religious beliefs and practices which they sought to mask. Since the epoch of Alexander the Great Ḥarrān had been a famous centre of pagan and Hellenistic culture; its people were Syrian heathens, star-worshippers versed in astrology and magic. In their temples the planetary powers were propitiated by bloodofferings, and it is probable that human victims were occasionally sacrificed even as late as the 9th century of our era. The more enlightened Ḥarrānians, however, adopted a religious philosophy strongly tinged with Neoplatonic and Christian elements. They produced a brilliant succession of eminent scholars and scientists who transmitted to the Muslims the results of Babylonian civilization and Greek learning, and their influence at the court of Baghdad secured more or less toleration for Ṣābianism, although in the reign of Harūn al-Rashīd the Ḥarrānians had already found it necessary to establish a fund by means of which the conscientious scruples of Muslim officials might be overcome. Accounts of these false Ṣābians reached the West through Maimonides, and then through Arabic sources, long before it was understood that the name in this application was only a disguise.

See also "Nouveaux documents pour l'étude de la religion des Harraniens," by Dozy and De Goeje, in the *Actes* of the sixth Oriental congress, ii. 281 f. (1885); and Chwolsohn, *Sabier und der Sabismus* (1856).

SABICU WOOD is the produce of a large leguminous tree, *Lysiloma latisiliqua*, a native of Cuba, Haiti and the Bahamas. The wood has a rich mahogany colour; it is exceedingly heavy, hard and durable.

SABINE, SIR EDWARD (1788–1883), English astronomer and geodesist, was born in Dublin on Oct. 14, 1788, and was educated at the Royal Military Academy, Woolwich. He was appointed astronomer of the expeditions commanded by Ross and Parry in search of the North-West Passage in 1818 and 1819. Then he went to Spitzbergen and the tropical coasts of Africa and America, where he conducted pendulum experiments for determining the figure of the earth. In 1821 he conducted experiments on the length of the seconds pendulum in London and Paris, his results appearing in *Philosophical Transactions*, 1828. The greater part of his life was devoted to researches on terrestrial magnetism. The establishment of magnetic observatories in various parts of British territory all over the globe was accomplished mainly on his representations. He discovered (1852) a connection between the periodic variation of sunspots and magnetic disturbances on the earth.

Sabine was president of the Royal Society from 1861–1871; received the Copley medal of that society in 1821 and the Royal medal in 1849; and was made K.C.B. in 1869. He died at East Sheen, Surrey, on June 26, 1883.

SABINI. This was an ancient tribe of Italy which was more closely in touch with the Romans from the earliest recorded period than any other Italic people. They dwelt in the mountainous country east of the Tiber, and north of the districts inhabited by the Latins and the Aequians in the heart of the Central Apennines. Their boundary, between the southern portion of the Umbrians on the north-west, and of the Picentines on the north-east, was probably not very closely determined. The traditions connect them closely with the beginning of Rome, and with a large number of its early institutions, such as the worship of Jupiter, Mars, and Quirinus, and the patrician form of marriage (*confarreatio*).

Of their language as distinct from that of the Latins no articulate memorial has survived, but we have a large number of single words attributed to them by Latin writers, among which such forms as (1) *fircus*, Lat. *hircus*; (2) *ausum*, Lat. *aurum*; (3) *novensiles*, Lat. *novensides* ("gods of the nine seats"); (4) the river name *Farfarus*, beside pure Lat. *Fabaris* (Servius, *ad Aen.* vii. 715); and (5) the traditional name of the Sabine king, *Numa Pompilius* (contrasted with Lat. *Quinctilius*), indicate clearly certain peculiarities in Sabine phonology: namely, (1) the representation of the Indo-European palatal aspirate *gh* by *f* instead of Lat. *h*; (2) the retention of *s* between vowels; (3) the change of medial and initial *d* to *l*; (4) the retention of medial *f* which became in Latin *b* or *d*; and (5) the change of Ind.-Eur. *q* to *p*. The tradition (*e.g.*, Paul *ex Fest.* 327 M.) that the Sabines were the parent stock of the Samnites is directly confirmed by the name which the Samnites apparently used for themselves, which, with a Latinized ending, would be *Safini* (*see* SAMNITES and the other articles there cited, dealing with the minor Samnite tribes).

To determine the ethnological relation of these tribes, whom we may call "Safine," to the people of Rome on the one hand, and the earlier stratum or strata of population in Italy on the other, linguistic and archaeological material must be examined. Archaeological evidence connects the Sabines with the patricians of Rome, (*see* ROME, *Ancient History*). What language did the Sabines speak? Was it most nearly akin to Latin or to Oscan or again to Umbrian and Volscian? Festus, though he continually cites the *Lingua Osca,* never spoke of *Lingua Sabina,* but simply of Sabini, and the same is practically true of Varro, who never refers to the language of the Sabines as a living speech, though he does imply (v. 66 and 74) that the dialect used in the district differed somewhat from urban Latin. The speech therefore of the Sabines by Varro's time had become too Latinized to give us more than scanty indications of what it had once been. The language of the Samnites was that which was now known by the name of Oscan.

It appears that in, say, the 7th century, B.C., the Safines spoke a language not differing in any important particulars from that of the Samnites, generally known as Oscan; and that when this warlike tribe combined with the people of the Latian plain to found or fortify or enlarge the city of Rome, and at the end of the 6th century to drive out from it the Etruscans, who had in that century become its masters, they imposed upon the new community many of their own usages, especially within the sphere of politics, but in the end adopted the language of Latium henceforth known as *lingua Latina*.

See R. S. Conway, *Italic Dialects* p. 351 (Cambridge, 1897). For the history of the Sabine district *see* Mommsen, *C.I.L.* ix. p. 396; and Beloch, "Der italische Bund unter römischer Hegemonie" (Leipzig, 1880) and "La Conquista Romana della regione Sabina," in the *Rivista di storia antica* ix. p. 269 (1905).

SABINIANUS, pope from 604 to 606, the successor of St. Gregory the Great.

SABLE, the name of a small quadruped, closely akin to the martens, and known by the zoological name of *Martes zibellina*. It is a native of Siberia and famous for its fur. The name appears to be Slavonic in origin, whence it has been adapted into various languages. The Eng. and Med. Lat. *sabellum* are from the O.Fr. *sable* or *saible* (*see* MARTEN and FUR). "Sable" in English is a rhetorical or poetical synonym for "black." This comes from its usage in heraldry (first in French) for the colour equivalent to black.

SABLE ANTELOPE, a large and handsome South African antelope (*Hippotragus niger*), exhibiting the rare feature of blackness or dark colour in both sexes. The sable and the roan antelope (*H. equinus*) belong to a genus nearly related to the oryxes (*q.v.*), but distinguished by the stout, thickly ringed horns (present in both sexes) rising vertically from a ridge over the eyes at an obtuse angle to the plane of the lower part of the face, and then sweeping backwards in a bold curve. The muzzle is hairy; there is no gland below the eye; the tail is long and tufted. Sable antelopes are among the handsomest of South African antelopes, and are endowed with great speed and staying power. They are commonly met with in herds including from 10 to 20 individuals. Forest-clad highlands are their favourite resorts. The roan antelope is a larger animal, with shorter horns, strawberry-roan in colour in both sexes.

SABLE ISLAND, an island of Nova Scotia, Canada, 110 m S.E. of Cape Canso, in 43° 56′ N. and 60° W. It is composed of shifting sand, and is about 20 m. in length by 1 m. in breadth, rising in places to a height of 85 feet. In the interior is a lake about 10 m. in length. At either end dangerous sandbars run out about 17 m. into the ocean. It has long been known as "the graveyard of the Atlantic"; over 200 known wrecks have been catalogued, and those unrecorded are believed greatly to exceed this number. The coast is without a harbour and liable to fogs and storms; irregular ocean currents of great strength sweep round it, and its colour makes it indistinguishable until close at hand. Since 1873 an efficient lighthouse system and life-saving station has been maintained by the Canadian Government, and the danger has been much lessened. Since 1904 it has been connected with the mainland by wireless telegraphy. Sable Island is the home of the Ipswich sparrow (*Passerculus princeps*).

Sable Island was known to the early navigators as Santa Cruz. *See* G. A. England, *Isles of Romance* (1929); Harold St. John, "Sable Island," with history, zoology and botany, *Boston Soc. Nat. Hist.,* vol. 36, no. 1 (1917).

SABORAIM: *see* GAON.

SABOTAGE, systematic working in such a manner as to delay production, or to injure the quality of the product, a policy sometimes advocated, especially by syndicalists, either to remedy a particular grievance or as part of a general revolutionary program. Sabotage of this kind may conveniently be discussed under two headings:

(1) Exceedingly slow work. This may be either ca' canny (*q.v.*), deliberately slow work, whose extreme form is the "stay-in strike" when the workers enter the factory but do no work at all, or it may take the form of elaborately careful work. Apart from the "stay-in strike," or "sit-down" in the U.S., the only generally effective use of this kind of sabotage has been "working to rule" by railwaymen. The procedure consists in following exactly the rule books, which, if rigorously applied, forthwith disorganize the service, as they generally contain items either obsolete or merely entered for formal purposes of record. An example of the former is the British regulation that every ticket must always be examined on both sides, the latter the Italian regulation that a driver must satisfy himself that he crosses all bridges at or about a certain speed, both of which items have been used for "working to rule" strikes. The first disorganizes the "City rush," the second the long-distance expresses.

(2) Injury to product or other obstruction. The anarchist "propaganda by deed" (*i.e.* assassination of oppressors: *see* ANARCHISM) is not strictly included in this, though in polemical writers the two types of action are often confused. The commonest form is destruction of machinery, but the doing of very bad work, deliberately designed to break down, is also frequent. Destruction of the tools of blacklegs is an allied form of sabotage (it was common in Sheffield in the '60s under the name of "rattening"); and, like sabotage in general, is only common when peaceful picketing is forbidden.

Sabotage as a policy has been advocated by the French trade unions and the (mainly American) Industrial Workers of the World. In both cases the reason given is that the workers are engaged in a class struggle in which the capitalist class shrinks from no methods however brutal, and that the workers cannot afford to abstain from any weapon for sentimental reasons. Its chief advocates, the French *syndicats* and the I.W.W., emerged from the war of 1914–18 and the ensuing crisis much weakened, and the Russian Revolution of Nov. 1917 had injured the general case for sabotage.

Sabotage is also, of course, a weapon commonly employed in

war time, or even in peace, against the essential industries of a hostile power. It may be the results of spy action (probably uncommon) or due to the action of nationally oppressed workers. It is commonly supposed that the Czech workers employed in the arsenals took effective and extensive sabotage action after the invasion by Germany in March 1939. But facts about such sabotage are naturally unobtainable, it being to the interest of both sides to conceal them.

See Georges Sorel, *Reflexions sur la violence* (1910); E. Pataud and E. Pouget, *Comment nous ferons la Revolution* (Eng. tr. 1913); E. Pouget, *Le sabotage* (1910); and DIRECT ACTION and INDUSTRIAL WORKERS OF THE WORLD; SYNDICALISM; TRADE UNIONS.

(R. W. P.)

SABRATHA, an ancient city of Africa Proconsularis (Tripolis), founded in the 7th–6th century B.C. by Tyrian settlers as a factory on the shore of a flat and inhospitable coast, mod. Sabratha Vulpia, 48 mi. W. of Tripoli by rail. Towards the end of the 2nd century A.D. its prosperity began to increase: Antoninus Pius built two temples; the tribunal before which Apuleius (*q.v.*) was tried met here, and under Commodus the Sabratenses had a *statio* (or office) at Ostia (*q.v.*). Towards the end of the 4th century there occurred fiscal exactions, religious disputes and attempts at invasion by the tribes of the interior (the most destructive being that of the Austuriani in A.D. 363), after which, as inscriptions show, the buildings of Sabratha, and notably the baths, were rebuilt. The Vandals themselves, who only occupied Tripolitania in A.D. 455, were defeated by a native rebellion, and after the destruction of their power by the Byzantines the very natives who had invited the aid of the latter rose against them also. During the years of peace following 548 new fortifications were made. Justinian's death, in 565, brought a renewal of the native risings. The Arabs took Tripoli in 643, and Sabratha was surprised in the night and sacked. Excavations have revealed the east gate of the Roman walls, while Byzantine fortifications surround the western portion of the city, where are situated the forum, the *curia* or council hall, a temple of Jupiter (of whom a fine bust was found), and another temple (perhaps the Capitolium), both of the time of Antoninus Pius, two Christian basilicas (one, erected by Justinian, with fine mosaics) and a baptistery. The theatre and the amphitheatre, fairly well preserved and recently carefully restored, lie farther away, near the quarries. The streets are wide and well laid, and the houses are numerous and closely built, without courtyards. There were no less than 12 fountains, supplied by an aqueduct. The Roman harbour was constructed by joining the rocks with masses of concrete, so as to form two moles with a narrow entrance between them; while along the shore were cisterns and storehouses.

SABRE FENCING. The ancient cut and thrust weapon was the backsword beloved of the Elizabethans and known as the "Englishman's traditional weapon." Its traditions were continued by the heavy cavalry sabre mainly handled from the wrist and characterized by wide circular movements—moulinets—with parries made by countercuts. Toward the end of the 19th century, the Italians introduced the light fencing sabre which is now universally used. The Italian sabre school was predominant from the late 19th century, but in the mid-1920s the Hungarians revolutionized the technique of sabre fencing, and their method proved superior to the more classical Italian style in all major international competitions after 1928.

FIG. 1.—THE SABRE GRIP

The sabre has a flattened V-shaped blade with a blunted cutting edge; the last third of the blade is flattened with the end turned over and of sufficient width not to penetrate the mesh of the mask. It has a half circular guard designed to protect the fingers against cuts. Hits may be made with the whole of the front edge or the last third of the back edge (cuts) as well as with the point. In a bout hits are only valid if they arrive with point or edge on the head, arms or trunk above a horizontal line drawn between the tops of the folds formed by the thighs and the trunk of the fencer when in the on guard position. The field of play at sabre is a strip 78 ft. 9 in. (24 m.) long and 6 ft. 7 in. (2 m.) wide.

In the Italian school the stance and the third position when on

guard combined with classical movements have a marked similarity to foil fencing. Hits are, as it were, carried on to the target with the wrist and forearm acting in one piece with the blade. In the Hungarian school, hits and blade movements are controlled by finger play, the wrist remains flexible, the stance is shorter than at

FIG. 2.—FRONT AND PROFILE VIEWS OF THE PARRY OF THE FIRST

foil, and the normal on guard position is the "offensive-defensive" medium guard with the hand placed in low-third.

Sabre fencing is governed by similar conventions as those for foil (*see* FOIL FENCING). These are briefly the limited target, the rule that all hits made directly off the target stop the phrase (the sequence of fencing actions exchanged between two fencers) and

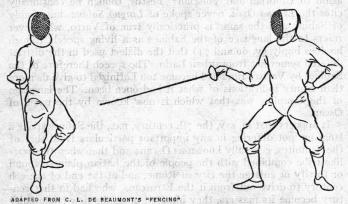

FIG. 3.—THE PARRY OF THE SECOND

annul all subsequent hits, and the observance of the fencing phrase by both fencers in that all correctly executed attacks must be parried or completely avoided, and the phrase must be followed through. The use of point and edge gives a special variety to sabre play, and the advantage of the attack over the defense is especially marked with this weapon. Balance and mobility, timing

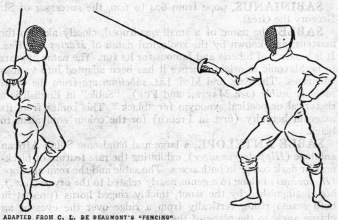

FIG. 4.—THE PARRY OF THE THIRD

and an exact sense of distance, opportunism and a judicious exploitation of the *flèche* (running) attack are characteristics of modern sabre fencing. Stop and time hits with point or edge are much in evidence. Indeed the inclusion of the sword arm in the target necessitates constant vigilance against stop cuts, and normally the fencers remain out of distance to land a hit simply with a lunge.

To hold the sabre the ball of the thumb is placed on the back of the handle (the side farthest from the guard), and the handle is gripped between the thumb and the second phalanx of the index finger with its first phalanx resting on the inside face of the handle; the remaining fingers are wrapped around the handle which lies along the fleshy base of the fingers clear of the palm. The sabre is manipulated by the thumb and forefinger in a similar man-

FIG. 5.—THE PARRY OF THE FOURTH

ner to the foil except that the movements of pulling, pushing and rolling (finger play) are assisted at sabre by the little finger.

In the on guard position the sword hand is in the low-third position level with the right hip, the wrist is bent so that the sabre is almost vertical with the blade in a central position diagonally across the body. This is known as the "offensive-defensive" position. The trunk is kept rather more upright than at foil, the legs are less bent, and the head is held higher to keep it out of distance.

The cardinal rule is "sabre in hand." This means the complete control of the weapon by fingers and wrist with the arm and shoulder as relaxed and supple as possible. This achieves lightness

FIG. 6—THE PARRY OF THE FIFTH

and elasticity in blade control which enables the edge to be checked at any desired point when effecting a parry or landing a hit on the target. Hits with the point are made as at foil but usually with the hand in supination. Cuts are delivered horizontally with the hand in pronation to the sword arm, flank and right cheek; vertically with the hand in half-supination to the head and by a circular motion of the arm while rotating the hand to three-quarter supination to the left cheek and chest.

While there are a wide variety of attacks with point or edge, the vulnerability of almost any movement to a stop hit necessitates

the restriction of the game to simple attacks or the use of the least number of feints required to achieve the desired aim. For the same reason, preparations of attack are mostly confined to actions on the blade and gaining and breaking ground, and the *flèche* at-

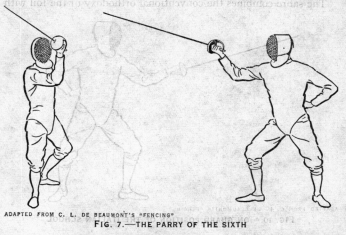

FIG. 7.—THE PARRY OF THE SIXTH

tack is particularly effective. On the other hand, the predilection for the stop hit can be countered by second intention attacks. Countertime or second-intention is the action of drawing the opponent's stop hit, parrying it and riposting. Parries are made by placing the defender's blade across the path of the cut so that if

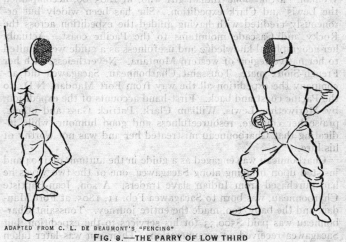

FIG. 8.—THE PARRY OF LOW THIRD

the attack is forced on it finishes on the defender's guard. Counter (or circular) parries are mainly used for defense against attacks with the point or when at close quarters. There are six parries and one supplementary parry of low third (*see* figures). At sabre defense is based on the parries forming two triangles. The

FIG. 9.—ON GUARD POSITION OF THE HUNGARIAN SCHOOL

parries of first, second and fifth constitute the first triangle and deal more particularly with perpendicular cuts. The second triangle comprising the parries of third, fourth and fifth is used mainly against lateral cuts or attacks with the point.

The sabre combines the conventional orthodoxy of the foil with

ADAPTED FROM C. L. DE BEAUMONT'S "FENCING"
FIG. 10.—ON GUARD POSITION OF THE ITALIAN SCHOOL

the opportunism of the épée. Sabre play requires rather more athletic qualities than the other two weapons, and modern sabre is based on subtlety of conception, variation of cadence and speed of execution.   (C.-L. DE B.)

SACAGAWEA or SACAJAWEA (1790?–1884?), the "Bird Woman," a Shoshone Indian girl who, in 1805–06, accompanied the Lewis and Clark expedition. She has been widely but erroneously credited with having guided the expedition across the Rocky and Cascade mountains to the Pacific coast. Actually her geographical knowledge and usefulness as a guide were limited to her native region of western Montana. Nevertheless, with her French-Sioux mate, Toussaint Charbonneau, Sacagawea did accompany the expedition all the way from Fort Mandan, N.D., to the Pacific coast and back. First-hand accounts of the expedition, by Meriwether Lewis, William Clark, Patrick Gass and others, praise her courage, resourcefulness and good humour, while indicating that Charbonneau mistreated her and was not worthy of his hire.

Charbonneau was engaged as a guide in the autumn of 1804 and insisted upon bringing along Sacagawea, one of the two wives he had purchased from Indian slave traders. A son, Jean-Baptiste Charbonneau, was born to Sacagawea Feb. 11, 1805, at Fort Mandan, and the baby, too, made the entire journey. Toussaint Charbonneau was paid $500.33 for his services to the expedition, but Sacagawea received no remuneration. Their son was later taken to St. Louis, Mo., where Clark sponsored his education. The later history of the "Bird Woman" is obscure. An old Indian woman, who called herself Sacagawea and displayed a remarkably intimate and accurate knowledge of the Lewis and Clark expedition, died in Dakota territory in 1884.

See John Bakeless, *Lewis and Clark, Partners in Discovery* (New York, 1947); Charles Morrow Wilson, *Meriwether Lewis of Lewis and Clark* (New York, 1934).

SACCHARIN is a name applied to several organic substances. These comprise (1) derivatives of toluene and (2) derivatives of certain naturally occurring sugars, including milk sugar.

The commonly known saccharin of commerce is derived from toluene. Commercial saccharin is marketed as insoluble saccharin—the imide of ortho-sulphobenzoic acid—and as soluble saccharin—the sodium salt of the acid. Pharmaceutical manufacturers who compound saccharin for consumer use commonly tablet saccharin into tiny pellets containing $\frac{1}{4}$, $\frac{1}{2}$ or 1 gr. of U.S.P. saccharin. The pellets may contain the saccharin as the soluble sodium salt or in the acid form combined with sodium bicarbonate which converts the acid to the sodium salt upon dissolving.

Commercial saccharin is a sweetening agent; it possesses no food value at all. The sweetening power of the commercial powder is estimated at 425 times the sweetening power of ordinary sugar; the commercial crystals, which contain some water of crys-

tallization, are estimated to have a sweetening power 375 times that of sugar. A $\frac{1}{4}$ gr. pellet has roughly the same sweetening power as a level teaspoon of sugar.

Saccharin, scientifically referred to as ortho-benzoicsulphimide, was discovered by Ira Remsen and C. Fahlberg in 1879 in the course of investigations at the Johns Hopkins university on the oxidation o-toluene-sulphonamide. Fahlberg noticed an unaccountable sweet taste to his food and found that this sweetness was present on his hands and arms, despite his having washed thoroughly after leaving the laboratory. Checking over his laboratory apparatus by taste tests, Fahlberg was led to the discovery of the source of this sweetness—saccharin.

Saccharin (1) is a white powder, mildly acidic, and forms neutral salts. It is relatively insoluble in water, chloroform and ether. The melting point of the commercial product is approximately 226° C.

$$\text{I} \qquad \qquad \text{II}$$

Much of the saccharin in commercial use is the white crystalline sodium salt (II). The sodium salt or soluble saccharin normally contains two molecules of water, and the crystals are readily soluble in water. The crystals may be of very small particle size or they may be of a size resembling granulated sugar. Crystalline sodium saccharin is efflorescent, so for easier handling, commercial sodium saccharin may be partially dehydrated, leaving less than one molecule of water in the compound. The partially dried sodium saccharin does not change weight so easily on exposure to the air. In this form it is termed powdered soluble saccharin.

Saccharin is made by treating toluene with chlorosulphonic acid. The reaction produces ortho- and para-toluene sulphonylchlorides. The two products are separated and the ortho-toluene sulphonylchloride is treated with ammonia to form the amide. The amide is then oxidized to saccharin.

Saccharin is used all over the world as a sweetener. It cannot be considered as a substitute for sugar, since it offers no nourishment. However, saccharin is used as part of the diets of people who must avoid excessive sugar intake, such as diabetics. It is also used in the preparation of dietetic foods, dentifrices, mouthwashes, cosmetics and for sweetening tobacco and medicinal preparations, particularly where the presence of sugar might lead to spoilage by fermentation or mould growth. Saccharin is not metabolized; it is excreted unchanged from the body in the urine.

In a number of countries the use of saccharin in food products is discouraged or even prohibited. Prohibition of the use of saccharin is not based on any harmfulness in the substance, but rather because of its lack of food value, persons using saccharin-sweetened foods might be unaware that they were depriving themselves of sugar which might be needed for its high food value.

An authoritative report by C. A. Herter and O. Folin entitled *Influence of Saccharin on the Nutrition and Health of Man*, published by the U.S. department of agriculture in 1911, was studied and reported on in 1912 by a referee board of consulting scientific experts: Ira Remsen, Russell H. Chittenden, John H. Long and A. E. Taylor. After thorough consideration of facts contained in the report, the board concluded that ingestion of saccharin in quantities up to .3 g. per day is without deleterious or poisonous action and is not injurious to health.

Saccharins derived from sugars are lactones of saccharinic acids. When either dextrin or laevulose is boiled with lime, a lactone of the formula $CH_2OH.CH.CH(OH).C(OH).CH_3$ is obtained. It

$$\begin{array}{c} | \qquad\qquad | \\ O\text{——}CO \end{array}$$

crystallizes in prisms soluble in hot water and possesses a bitter taste.

Isosaccharin and metasaccharin, melting points 95° C. and 142° C. respectively, are formed by the action of lime on milk sugar. The sugar derived saccharins are of little commercial importance.

BIBLIOGRAPHY.—T. E. Thorpe, *Dictionary of Applied Chemistry*, vol. vi (1926); O. Beyer, *Über die Kontrolle und Herstellung von Saccharin* (Zurich, 1918); F. Ullman, *Enzyklopädie der technischen Chemie*, vol. 2 (Berlin, 1915); Christian A. Herter and Otto Folin, *Influence of Saccharin on the Nutrition and Health of Man* (1911); O. Garth Fitzhugh, Arthur A. Nelson and John P. Frawley, "A Comparison of the Chronic Toxicities of Synthetic Sweetening Agents," *Journal of the American Pharmaceutical Association*, scientific edition, vol. xl, no. 11 (Nov. 1951). (F. D. SH.)

SACCHETTI, FRANCO (*c.* 1330–*c.* 1400), Italian poet and novelist, was a member of the noble and ancient Florentine family of the Sacchetti (comp. Dante, *Par.*, c. xvi).

While still a young man he achieved repute as a poet, and he appears to have travelled on affairs of more or less importance as far as Genoa, Milan and "Ischiavonia." When a sentence of banishment was passed upon the rest of the house of Sacchetti by the Florentine authorities in 1380, it appears that Franco was expressly exempted, *per esser tanto uomo buono*, and in 1383 he was one of the "eight," discharging the office of prior for the months of March and April.

In 1385 he was chosen ambassador to Genoa, but he preferred to go as podesta to Bibbiena in Casentino. In 1392 he was podesta at San Miniato, and in 1396 he held a similar office at Faenza. In 1398 he received from his fellow citizens the post of captain of their then province of Romagna, having his residence at Portico.

Sacchetti left a considerable number of *sonnetti, canzoni, ballate, madrigali*, etc. His *Novelle*, based on real incidents of Tuscan life, are valuable for the light they throw on the manners of that age.

See N. Sapegno, *Il Trecento* (Milan, 1934).

SACCHI, ANDREA (1599–1661), Italian painter, was the chief representative of the classical current in Roman mid-17th century painting (Nicolas Poussin, being a Frenchman, belonging in a sense apart) and as such he stood in opposition to the full Baroque. He was born at Nettuno, 30 mi. south of Rome, but trained under Francesco Albani at Bologna. After returning to Rome in 1621 he worked there till his death (June 21, 1661), except for short visits to north Italy after 1635 and to Paris in 1640.

His Bolognese training gave him an initial bias toward classicism and a taste for colour. But the direct influence of Raphael is already added to these qualities in the "Miracle of St. Gregory" of 1625–27 (chapter house, St. Peter's). This work brought Sacchi to the notice of the Sacchetti family, who employed him, with Pietro da Cortona, in the decoration of their villa at Castel Fusano in 1627–29. Both artists were next taken on by Cardinal Antonio Barberini to decorate the Barberini palace in Rome, and it was then that the classical and Baroque currents became separated. Sacchi's ceiling fresco, "The Allegory of Divine Wisdom" (1629–33), is a grave, static work, markedly Raphaelesque in conception and containing relatively few figures, in contrast with Pietro da Cortona's full Baroque "Triumph of Divine Providence" in an adjoining room. Sacchi's two altarpieces in Sta. Maria della Concezione, Rome (1631–38), are likewise distinguished by their classicism from the other pictures in the church.

His most important work after the "Divine Wisdom" is the series of eight canvases illustrating the life of St. John the Baptist in the cupola of S. Giovanni in Fonte, Rome (1639–45). He painted a few portraits but concentrated mainly on religious works.

See Hans Posse, *Der Römische Maler Andrea Sacchi* (Leipzig, 1925). (M. W. L. K.)

SACCO-VANZETTI CASE, THE, a murder trial in Massachusetts, extending over seven years, 1920–27, and resulting in the execution of the defendants, Nicola Sacco and Bartolomeo Vanzetti. The trial resulted from the murder in South Braintree, Mass., on April 15, 1920, of F. A. Parmenter, paymaster of a shoe factory, and Alessandro Berardelli, the guard accompanying him, in order to secure the payroll they were carrying. On May 5 Sacco and Vanzetti, two Italians who had immigrated to the United States in 1908, one a shoe worker and the other a fish pedlar, were arrested for the crime. On May 31, 1921, they were brought to trial before Judge Webster Thayer of the Massachusetts superior court and, on July 14, were both found guilty by verdict of the jury. The verdict was disputed by Socialists and

other radicals on the ground that the men had not received a fair trial because of their radical affiliations. Motion for a new trial, on grounds that the identification was not complete, failed. Further motions for a new trial were made from time to time but also failed on grounds that the evidence submitted did not justify it. On Nov. 18, 1925, the confession of Celestino Madeiros that he had participated in the crime, and that neither Sacco nor Vanzetti was present, added a new complication.

Motion for a retrial on the basis of this confession was also denied by Judge Thayer who claimed that Madeiros, already sentenced to execution for another crime, was motivated in assuming the guilt in the hope that the giving of testimony would delay his own death. A motion of appeal to the state supreme court failed, the court taking the position that the trial judge had the final power to determine the matter of retrial on grounds of additional evidence. On April 9, 1927, Judge Thayer sentenced the two defendants to the electric chair.

It was at this point that the storm of protest broke loose. Newspapers in both Europe and America gave large amounts of space to the proceedings, mass meetings were held, and the officials connected with the case were flooded with petitions mingled with threats. The defense carried the case to Gov. A. T. Fuller, holder of the power of clemency, who in addition to a personal investigation appointed Pres. A. Lawrence Lowell of Harvard university, Pres. Samuel W. Stratton of the Massachusetts Institute of Technology and Robert Grant, a former judge, to investigate the case independently.

On Aug. 3, Governor Fuller announced that he had found against the plea, and that his advisory committee had also come to the conclusion that a new trial was not warranted. Successive stays postponed the execution while further vain appeals were made to Judge Thayer, to the supreme judicial court, and finally to members of the U.S. supreme court, the attorney-general and the president. During the days following Governor Fuller's denial of clemency, demonstrations were made in many cities in America and abroad, bombs were set off in New York city and Philadelphia, Pa., and guards were set up against other threats of violence.

The two men were executed on Aug. 23, 1927, both maintaining their innocence.

BIBLIOGRAPHY.—N. D. Baker *et al.* (eds.), *The Sacco-Vanzetti Case: a Transcript of the Record of the Trial* (New York, 1928); F. Frankfurter, *The Case of Sacco and Vanzetti* (Boston, 1927), and *The Outlook*, vol. cl, pp. 1,053 ff. (1928).

SACHAU, CARL EDUARD (1845–1930), German scholar, was born on July 20, 1845 at Neumünster in Holstein. In 1869 he was appointed professor of Semitic languages at the University of Vienna, and in 1876 professor of oriental languages at Berlin, where he became director of the school of oriental languages.

In 1879–80 he travelled extensively in Syria and Mesopotamia, and in 1897–98 in Babylonia and Assyria. He wrote *Syrisch-römisches Rechtsbuch aus dem 5. Jahrhundert* (1890); *Reise in Syrien und Mesopotamien* (1883); *Neuarabische Volkslieder aus Mesopotamien* (1889); *Katalog persischer Handschriften* (1889); *Muhammedanisches Erbrecht von Zansibar und Ost-Afrika* (1894); *Am Euphrat und Tigris* (1900); *Syrische Rechtsbücher* (1907–14).

For a complete bibliography of the works of Sachau, *see* S. Weil, *Die Festschrift zu Ehren Ed. Sachaus* (1915).

SACHEVERELL, HENRY (1674–1724), English ecclesiastic, was the son of Joshua Sacheverell, rector of St. Peter's, Marlborough. He was adopted by his godfather, Edward Hearst, and his wife; was sent to Magdalen college, Oxford, in 1689; was demy of his college from 1689 to 1701 and fellow from 1701 to 1713. Sacheverell took his B.A. in 1693, and became M.A. in 1695 and D.D. in 1708. His first preferment was the small vicarage of Cannock in Staffordshire; and in 1705 he was elected to the chaplaincy of St. Saviour's, Southwark. He had already shown himself a strong, indeed a violent, high churchman by his sermons and pamphlets. In 1709 he gained notoriety by his famous sermons attacking the Whig ministers on the charge of neglecting to watch over the interests of the church. These sermons were delivered, one in Derby on Aug. 15, the other in St. Paul's cathedral on Nov. 5; and both, in excessively violent language, especially aimed at the treasurer, the earl of Godolphin. They were immediately printed and made the preacher the idol of the Tory party.

The attention of the house of commons was drawn to the two sermons by John Dolben in Dec. 1709, and they were denounced as "malicious, scandalous and seditious libels." The ministry, then slowly but surely losing the support of the country, were divided as to the wisdom of impeaching Sacheverell. Sir John Somers was against it; but the earl of Sunderland and Godolphin urged the necessity of a prosecution, and gained the day. The trial lasted from Feb. 27 to March 23, 1710, and the verdict was that Sacheverell should be suspended for three years from preaching and that the two sermons should be burned at the Royal Exchange. The trial hastened the downfall of the ministry, Godolphin being dismissed in August and the other ministers in September. Immediately on the expiration of his sentence (April 13, 1713), Sacheverell was presented by the queen to the valuable rectory of St. Andrew's, Holborn, by the new Tory ministry. He died at the Grove, Highgate, on June 5, 1724. (*See* also ENGLISH HISTORY.)

BIBLIOGRAPHY.—G. M. Trevelyan, *England under Queen Anne*, vol. iii, chap. iii (London, 1930–34); Falconer Madan, *A Bibliography of Dr. H. Sacheverell* (Oxford, 1884).

SACHEVERELL, WILLIAM (1638–1691), English statesman, son of Henry Sacheverell, a country gentleman, entered parliament in 1670 for Derbyshire. He was an opponent of the court policy, especially of the secret treaty with France. In 1678 he was one of the most active investigators of the "Popish Plot," and one of the managers of the impeachment of the five Catholic peers. He also served as a manager in the impeachment of Danby. He made the first suggestion of the Exclusion Bill on Nov. 4, 1678, in a debate raised by Lord Russell with the object of removing the duke from the King's Council. He vigorously promoted the bill in the House of Commons and opposed granting supplies till it should pass.

At the general election following the death of Charles II. in 1685 Sacheverell lost his seat, but he was an active member of the convention parliament. He died on Oct. 9, 1691. In the judgment of Speaker Onslow, Sacheverell was the "ablest parliament man" of the reign of Charles II. He was one of the earliest of English parliamentary orators; his speeches greatly impressed his contemporaries, and in a later generation, as Macaulay observes, they were "a favourite theme of old men who lived to see the conflicts of Walpole and Pulteney."

BIBLIOGRAPHY.—Many of Sacheverell's speeches are reported in Anchitell Grey's *Debates of the House of Commons, 1667–1694* (10 vols., London, 1769). *See* also Sir George Sitwell, *The First Whig* (Scarborough, 1894).

SACHS, HANS (1494–1576), German poet and dramatist, was born at Nuremberg on Nov. 5, 1494. His father was a tailor, and he himself was trained to the calling of a shoemaker. Before this, however, he received a good education at the Latin school of Nuremberg. In 1509 he began his apprenticeship, and was initiated into the art of the Meistersingers by a weaver, Leonhard Nunnenpeck. In 1511 he set out on his *Wanderjahre*, and worked at his craft in many towns, including Regensburg, Passau, Salzburg, Munich, Osnabrück, Lübeck and Leipzig. In 1516 he returned to Nuremberg, where he remained during the rest of his life, working steadily at his handiwork and devoting his leisure time to literature. In 1517 he became master of his gild and in 1519 married. Sachs became an ardent adherent of Luther, and in 1523 wrote in Luther's honour the poem beginning *Die wittenbergisch Nachtigall, Die man jetzt höret überall*, and four dialogues in prose, in which his warm sympathy with the reformer is tempered by counsels of moderation. The town council of Nuremberg then forbade him to publish any more *Büchlein oder Reimen*. Before long, however, the council itself declared for the Reformation. Sachs died on Jan. 19, 1576.

By the year 1567 Sachs had composed, according to his own account, 4,275 *Meisterlieder*, 1,700 tales and fables in verse, and 208 dramas, which filled no fewer than 34 large manuscript volumes; and this was not all, for he continued writing until 1573. The *Meisterlieder* were not printed, being intended solely for the use of the Nuremberg Meistersinger school, of which Sachs was the leading spirit. His fame rests mainly on the *Spruchgedichte*, which include his dramatic writings. His "tragedies" and "comedies" are, however, little more than stories told in dialogue, and divided at convenient pauses into a varying number of acts. The subjects are drawn from the Bible, the classics, the Italian novelists and elsewhere. He succeeds best in the short anecdotal *Fastnachtsspiel* or Shrovetide play, where characterization and humorous situation are of more importance than dramatic form or construction. Farces like *Der fahrende Schüler im Paradies* (1550), *Das Wildbad* (1550), *Das heiss Eisen* (1551), *Der Bauer im Fegefeuer* (1552), are inimitable in their way, and have even been played with success on the modern stage.

Hans Sachs himself made a beginning to an edition of his collected writings by publishing three large folio volumes (1558–61); after his death two other volumes appeared (1578, 1579). A critical edition has been published by the Stuttgart *Literarischer Verein*, edited by A. von Keller and E. Goetze (23 vols., 1870–96); *Sämtliche Fastnachtsspiele*, ed. by E. Goetze (7 vols., 1880–87); *Sämtliche Fabeln und Schwänke*, by the same (3 vols., 1893). There are also editions of selected writings by J. Tittmann (3 vols., 1870–71; new ed., 1883–85) and B. Arnold (2 vols., 1885). *See* E. K. J. Lützelberger, *Hans Sachs* (1876); C. Schweitzer, *Étude sur la vie et les oeuvres de Hans Sachs* (1887); K. Drescher, *Hans Sachs Studien* (1890, 1891); E. Goetze, *Hans Sachs* (1891); A. L. Stiefel, *Hans Sachs-Forschungen* (1894); R. Genée, *Hans Sachs und seine Zeit* (1894; 2nd ed., 1902); E. Geiger, *Hans Sachs als Dichter in seinen Fastnachtsspielen* (1904).

SACHS, JULIUS VON (1832–1897), German botanist, was born at Breslau on Oct. 2, 1832. On leaving school in 1851 he became assistant to the physiologist J. E. Purkinje at Prague. In 1856 he graduated as doctor of philosophy, and established himself as *Privatdozent* for plant physiology in the university of Prague. In 1859 he was appointed physiological assistant to the Agricultural Academy of Tharandt in Saxony; and in 1861 he went to the Agricultural Academy at Poppelsdorf, near Bonn, where he remained until 1867, when he was nominated professor of botany in the university of Freiburg-im-Breisgau. In 1868 he accepted the chair of botany in the university of Würzburg, which he continued to occupy until his death on May 29, 1897.

Sachs was especially associated with the development of plant physiology which marked the latter half of the 19th century, though he contributed to every branch of botany. His earlier papers, in botanical journals and publications of learned societies, are of interest. Prominent among them is the series of "Keimungsgeschichten," which laid the foundation of our knowledge of microchemical methods, and the morphological and physiological details of germination. Then there is his resuscitation of the method of "water-culture," and its application to problems of nutrition; and further, his discovery that the starch-grains to be found in chloroplastids are the first visible product of their assimilatory activity. His later papers were published in the three volumes of the *Arbeiten des botanischen Instituts in Würzburg* (1871–88). Among these are his investigation of the periodicity of growth in length; his researches on heliotropism and geotropism, in which he introduced the "clinostat"; his work on the structure and arrangement of cells in growing-points; the evidence upon which he based his "imbibition-theory" of the transpiration-current; his studies of the assimilatory activity of the green leaf; and other papers.

Sachs' works are: *Handbuch der Experimentalphysiologie der Pflanzen* (1865; French edition, 1868); *Lehrbuch der Botanik* (1868, Eng. ed. 1875 and 1882), a comprehensive work, giving a summary of the botanical science of the period, including the results of original investigations; *Vorlesungen über Pflanzenphysiologie* (1st ed., 1882; 2nd ed., 1887; Eng. ed., Oxford, 1887); *Geschichte der Botanik* (1875, Eng. ed. 1890).

A full account of Sachs' life and work was given by E. C. Pringsheim, *Julius Sachs* (1932); *see* also *Flora*, lxxxiii (1897); *Allg. Deutsch. Biogr.*, liii (1907); *Proc. Roy. Soc.*, lxii (1897); *Naturwiss. Rundschau* (Braunschweig, 1898).

SACHS, MICHAEL (1808–1864), German Rabbi, one of the first of Jewish graduates of the modern universities, was appointed Rabbi in Prague in 1836, and in Berlin in 1844. He took the conservative side against the Reform agitation, and retired from the Rabbinate rather than acquiesce in the use of the organ in the synagogue. Sachs co-operated with Zunz in a new translation of the Bible. He is best remembered for his work on Hebrew poetry, *Religiöse Poesie der Juden in Spanien* (1845).

SACKBUT, Shakbusshe, Sagbut, Draw or Drawing Trumpet, the earliest form of slide trumpet, derived from the Roman buccina, which afterwards developed into the trombone. As soon as the effect of the slide in lengthening the main tube and therefore proportionally deepening the pitch of the instrument was understood, and its capabilities had been realized, the development of a family of powerful tenor and bass instruments followed as a matter of course. The transformation of the busine (*buccina*) into the sackbut involved two or three processes, the addition of the slide being accomplished in at least two stages, the extending portion of the tube being at first straight and later bent or folded to make the instrument less unwieldy. (*See* also Trombone, Trumpet and Buccina.)

SACKETS HARBOR, a village in Jefferson county, New York, U.S.A., at the eastern end of Lake Ontario, on the south shore of Black River bay, about 1 mi. from its mouth, and about 10 mi. W. by S. of Watertown. Pop. (1940) 1,962; (1950) 1,247. Sackets Harbor is served by the New York Central railway. It is built on low land, around a small, nearly enclosed harbour, the northern shore of which is formed by Navy Point, a narrow tongue of land extending about ¼ mi. nearly due eastward from the mainland. In the military cemetery is the grave of Gen. Zebulon M. Pike (*q.v.*), killed at York (Toronto) on April 27, 1813.

The first settlement was made in 1801 by Augustus Sacket and the village was incorporated in 1814. In the war of 1812 Sackets Harbor, important strategic point for the Americans, was the base for naval operations on the Great Lakes. In July 1812 it was attacked by a Canadian provincial squadron and again in May 1813, by a British squadron under Commander Yeo and troops under General Sir George Prevost, on both occasions unsuccessfully. For many years it boasted the world's smallest navy yard, under four acres. It continues to be occupied by Naval Reserves. For several years the property was in charge of the ship keeper's widow and thus was commanded by a woman. The first steamship on the Great Lakes was launched at Sackets Harbor in 1817. Von Schultz and 700 men sailed from the port in Nov. 1838, to invade Canada, were captured near Prescott and Von Schultz was executed at Kingston after the trial.

See A. T. Mahan, *Sea-Power in its Relation to the War of 1812* (Boston, 1905); and W. Kingsford, *The History of Canada*, vol. viii. (Toronto, 1895).

SACKING AND SACK MANUFACTURE. Sacking is a heavy closely-woven fabric, originally made of flax, but now almost exclusively made of jute or of hemp. The more expensive kinds, such as are used for coal sacks for government and other vessels, are made of hemp, but the jute fibre is extensively used for the same purpose, and almost entirely for coal sacks for local house supplies. The same type of fabric is used for wool sacks, cement bags, ore bags, pea sacks and for any heavy substance; it is also made up into a special form of bag for packing cops and rolls of jute and flax yarns for delivery from spinners to manufacturers. Proper sacking is essentially a twilled fabric, in which the number of warp threads per inch greatly exceeds the number per inch of weft. The illustration shows a typical kind of three-leaf twill, double warp sacking. All three-leaf twill sack-

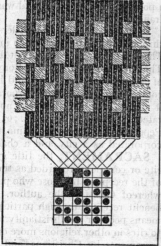

WEAVE AND CLOTH PLANS
Bottom; black squares show unit weave, black circles show three repeats of unit weave: top; plan of 8 units of the weave structure of cloth showing 12 double threads of warp and 6 picks of weft

ings are double in the warp, but four-leaf sackings are usually single; special kinds may be double in the warp. In all cases the warp is comparatively thin, say 6lb. to 8lb. per spyndle, whereas the weft is thick and single from 16lb. to 48lb. per spyndle. Cloths are usually 27in. wide, but other widths are made.

The lower part of the illustration shows four repeats of the three-leaf twill, while the lines drawn to the plan of the fabric show that each line of the design is reproduced in the cloth by two warp threads. Large quantities of cotton sacks are made for flour, sugar and similar produce; these sacks are usually plain cloth, some woven circular in the loom, others made from the piece.

Large quantities of seamless bags or sacks for light substances are woven in the loom, but these are almost invariably made with what is termed the double plain weave; *i.e.*, the cloth, although circular except at the end, is perfectly plain on both sides, and similar in structure to, but wider than hose-pipe (*q.v.*). Circular bags have been made both with three-leaf and four-leaf twills, but it is found much more convenient and economical to make the cloth for these kinds, and in most cases, for all other types, in the piece, and then to make it up into sacks by one or other of the many types of sewing machines. The pieces are first cut up into definite lengths by special machinery, which may be perfectly automatic or semi-automatic—usually the latter, as many thicknesses may be cut at the same time, each of the exact length. The lengths of cloth are then separately doubled up, the sides sewn by special sewing machines.

The chief centres for jute bags are Dundee and Calcutta, all varieties of sacks and bags being made in and around the former city. For paper sacks *see* Paper and Paper Manufacture.

See T. Woodhouse, *The Finishing of Jute and Linen Fabrics* (1928).

SACKVILLE, GEORGE, 1st Viscount (1716–1785), generally remembered as Lord George Sackville or Lord George Germain, third son of Lionel Cranfield Sackville, 1st duke of Dorset, was born on Jan. 26, 1716. Educated at Westminster School and Trinity College, Dublin, he was gazetted captain in 1737, and saw active service in the German campaign. Wounded in the charge of Cumberland's infantry column at Fontenoy, he was taken to the tent of King Louis XV. to have his wound dressed, and was soon released. He received rapid military promotion, and was gazetted major-general in 1755 and lieutenant-general in 1757. Meanwhile he filled the offices of first secretary to his father, the lord-lieutenant of Ireland, and Irish secretary of war, and sat in each of the two Houses of Commons at Westminster and Dublin. In 1758, under the duke of Marlborough, he shared in the ineffective raid on Cancale Bay, and the troops, after a short sojourn in the Isle of Wight, were sent to join the allied army of Duke Ferdinand of Brunswick in Germany. Marlborough died shortly after they landed, and Sackville succeeded him as commander-in-chief of the British contingent. His haughty and domineering temper estranged him both from his second-in-command, Lord Granby, and the commander-in-chief, Prince Ferdinand. This culminated on the day of Minden (August 1, 1758). The British infantry, aided by some of the Hanoverians, had won a brilliant success, and every man in the army looked to the British cavalry to charge and to make it a decisive victory. But Sackville, in spite of repeated orders from Prince Ferdinand, sullenly refused to allow Granby's squadrons to advance. The crisis passed, and the victory remained an indecisive success. A court-martial in 1760 pronounced him guilty of disobedience, and adjudged him "unfit to serve his Majesty in any military capacity whatsoever." In 1763 his name was restored to the list of the Privy Council. In 1769 he allied himself with Lord North. To this period belong the famous Junius Letters, with the authorship of which Sackville was erroneously credited. In 1770, under the terms of a will, he assumed the name of Germain. In 1775, having meantime taken an active part in politics, he became secretary of state for the colonies in the North cabinet, and he was practically the director of the war for the suppression of the revolt in the American colonies. Germain and the North cabinet misunderstood the situation and there was constant friction with the generals and the army in the theatre of war. Nevertheless he received a peerage. He died at Stoneland Lodge (Buckhurst Park) Sussex, on Aug. 26, 1785.

SACKVILLE, THOMAS, 1ST EARL OF DORSET (d. 1608), English statesman and poet, son of Sir Richard Sackville, was born at Buckhurst, Sussex, between 1527 and 1536. He was called to the bar at the Inner Temple. He married Cecily, daughter of Sir John Baker of Sissinghurst, Kent. In 1558 he entered parliament as member for Westmorland, in 1559 he sat for East Grinstead, Sussex, and in 1563–67 for Aylesbury, Buckinghamshire.

During a visit to the continent in 1565 he was imprisoned at Rome for a rash declaration of Protestant opinions. The news of his father's death on April 21, 1566, recalled him to England. On his return he was knighted in the presence of Queen Elizabeth I, receiving at the same time the title of baron of Buckhurst.

He was sent on missions to France in 1568 and again in 1571, when he congratulated Charles IX on his marriage with Elizabeth of Austria. He also took part in the negotiations for the projected marriage of Elizabeth to the duke of Anjou. In 1571 he was created M.A. at Cambridge. In 1572 he was one of the peers who tried Thomas Howard, duke of Norfolk, and in 1586, after he had become a privy councillor, he was selected to convey the sentence of death to Mary queen of Scots.

He was sent in 1587 as ambassador to The Hague but failed to carry out his difficult mission to the queen's satisfaction and was recalled in disgrace. He was, however, liked and trusted by the Dutch and there was talk of sending him there again in 1589–90. This project fell through, but in 1598 he negotiated a new treaty with the states general.

He was elected chancellor of the University of Oxford in 1591, and in 1599 succeeded Lord Burghley as lord high treasurer. In 1601 as high steward he pronounced sentence on Essex. James I confirmed him in the office of lord treasurer. He was created earl of Dorset in 1604, and died suddenly at the council table on April 19, 1608.

Sackville's eldest son, Robert, the 2nd earl (1561–1609), was a member of parliament and a man of great learning. Two other sons were William (c. 1568–91), a soldier killed in the service of Henry IV of France, and Thomas (1571–1646), also a soldier.

Sackville is remembered, not only by his distinguished political career, but by his share in two works, each of which was, in its way, a new departure in English literature. To the second edition (1563) of William Baldwin's *Myrroure for Magistrates,* Sackville contributed the *Complaint* of Henry Stafford, duke of Buckingham, to which he prefixed an *Induction.* This induction was arbitrarily transposed (1610) to the beginning of the collection by a later editor, Richard Niccols, a proceeding which led to the attribution of the general design to Sackville. The originators were certainly Baldwin and his "printer" who designed the *Myrroure* as a continuation of John Lydgate's *Fall of Princes* in the form of laments of the ghosts of great men written by various hands. Fragments of the earliest edition entitled *A Memoriall of such princes as . . . have been unfortunate . . .* are sometimes found bound up with Lydgate's book.

Sackville's *Induction* opens with a description of the oncoming of winter. The poet meets Sorrow, who offers to lead him to the infernal regions that he may see the sad estate of those ruined by their ambition, and thus learn the transient character of earthly joy. At the approaches of Hell he sees a group of terrible abstractions, Remorse of Conscience, Dread, Misery, Revenge, Care, etc., each vividly described. The last of these is War, on whose shield he sees depicted the great battles of antiquity. Finally, penetrating to the realm of Pluto, he is surrounded by the shades, of whom the duke of Buckingham is the first to advance, thus introducing the *Complaint.*

Sackville's models were Gavin Douglas and Virgil. The dignity and artistic quality of the narrative of the fall of Buckingham make the work one of the most important between the *Canterbury Tales* and the *Faerie Queene.*

Sackville has also the credit of being part author with Thomas Norton of the first legitimate tragedy in English. This was *Gorboduc* or *Ferrex and Porrex,* which was "furniture of part of the grand Christmasse in the Inner Temple" in 1560 and was later shown before the queen at Whitehall by "the Gentlemen of Thynner Temple" on Jan. 18, 1562 (*cf.* Sir E. K. Chambers, *The Eliza-*

bethan Stage, iii, 457, Oxford, 1923).

The story is taken from book ii, chap. xvi, of Geoffrey of Monmouth's history. It was first printed (1565) in an unauthorized edition as *The Tragedie of Gorboduc* "where of three Actes were wrytten by Thomas Nortone, and the two laste by Thomas Sackuyle." Another, undated, edition, *The Tragidie of Ferrex and Porrex,* appeared about 1570–71. The tragedies of Seneca were now being translated, and the play is conceived on Senecan lines. The paucity of action is eked out by a dumb show to precede each act, and the place of the chorus is supplied by four "ancient and sage men of Britain." In the variety of incident, however, the authors departed from the classical model. The play is in blank verse, and is the first example of the application of Henry Howard, earl of Surrey's innovation to drama.

Jasper Heywood in the poetical address prefixed to his translation of Seneca's *Thyestes* alludes to "Sackvylde's Sonnets, sweetly sauste," but only one, prefixed to Sir T. Hoby's translation of Baldassare Castiglione's *Courtier,* survived. According to Archbishop George Abbot (*A Sermon preached at Westminster,* 1608), Queen Elizabeth I shared the general high opinion of Sackville's merits as a writer.

The best edition of *Mirror for Magistrates* is that of Lily B. Campbell, edited from original texts in the Huntington library (Cambridge, New York, 1938). *See also* her *Parts added to the Mirror for Magistrates* (Cambridge, New York, 1946); *Gorboduc* in J. W. Cunliffe (ed.), *Early English Classical Tragedies* (Oxford, 1912); *Cambridge History of English Literature,* iii; C. S. Lewis, *English Literature in the 16th Century Excluding Drama* (Oxford, 1954).

SACO, a city of York county, Me., U.S., on the Saco river and the Atlantic ocean, opposite Biddeford and 14 mi. S.W. of Portland. It is on federal highway 1 and is served by the Boston and Maine railroad. The population was (1950) 10,324; (1940) 8,631 by federal census.

There is abundant water power, and the city has cotton mills and various other factories. Thornton academy was founded there in 1811.

The adjoining town of Old Orchard Beach, with one of the finest beaches on the coast (a wide crescent 10 mi. long), has long been a popular summer resort and was a starting point for several early transatlantic flights.

Saco was founded by settlers from Plymouth colony in 1629 through a grant of land which included the present site of the city. The first permanent settlement, however, is recorded as 1623, when Thomas Lewis and Richard Bonython arrived. It was made a part of Massachusetts in 1653 and became represented in the general court in 1659. It was incorporated as Biddeford in 1718. Later it was divided, and that part north of the Saco river was incorporated as Pepperellboro in 1763 in memory of Gen. Sir William Pepperell. In 1805 the name was changed to Saco. It was incorporated as a city and a charter was adopted in 1867.

SACRAMENT, the title given by Christians to an external rite or ceremony regarded as the instrument, or at least a symbol, of the reception by those who participate in it of a spiritual benefit whereof Christ is the author. As the conception of a spiritual benefit received through participation in an external rite is by no means peculiar to Christianity, the expression is often applied also to rites in other religions more or less analogous to those designated sacraments by Christians, and sometimes to any instance of the use of material objects as instruments whereby spiritual benefits may be conveyed or appropriated, even although no religious doctrine or ritual be associated with such conveyance or appropriation.

The present article, however, will be mainly concerned with the Christian conception of a sacrament, and rather with the content and significance of that conception than with its history.

In the *Sentences* of Peter Lombard, bishop of Paris 1159–60, which served for centuries as the theological textbook of western Christendom, *sacramentum* in the most general use of the word is defined (5 *Sent.* dist. 1 B. following Augustine *Ep.* 138 § 8, *signa quae, cum ad res divinas pertinent, sacramenta appellantur*) as *sacrae rei signum;* and, more precisely, as *invisibilis gratiae visibilis forma;* but in its strictest acceptation, wherein it is applicable only to certain Christian rites, as *quod ita signum est gratiae Dei et invisibilis gratiae forma ut ipsius imaginem gerat et causa existat*—an outward and visible sign of an inward divine grace, which it both aptly represents (as immersion in baptismal water represents cleansing from sin, or eating and drinking eucharistic bread and wine the maintenance and strengthening of spiritual life) and also actually imparts to the recipient.

The word *sacramentum* is used in classical Latin literature of the pledge deposited in a temple by the parties to a lawsuit, and also of the soldier's oath of allegiance to his commander; and neither of the senses has been without influence on its employment by Christian theologians. But the far less restricted sense given to it by the Latin-speaking Fathers and their choice of it to render the Greek μυστήριον point to its having had a more general signification, corresponding to its etymology, such as is suggested by St. Thomas Aquinas when he says that that may be called *sacramentum* whereby anything is made sacred (*sacratur*) as that whereby anything is adorned (*ornatur*) is called *ornamentum* (in 4 *Sent.* i. 1; *cf. Summ. Theol.* q.u. lx. art. 1: *Sacramentum dicitur a sacrando, sicut medicamentum a medicando*). Thus, behind the conception of a sacrament lies the notion, common to all peoples, of a "sacred" sphere or world, distinct from, but in close contact with, that of everyday life, so that particular persons, things, places and times can, by recognized methods of "consecration" or "desecration," be removed from one to the other.

The word μυστήριον, employed by the Greek-speaking Church, was associated with the same notion, being the regular designation of religious ceremonies of initiation. These ceremonies distinguished the initiated from those not counted worthy of such translation from the sphere of ordinary life to communion with denizens of a higher world, and suggested the *secrecy* with which "sacred" rites were invested, in order to secure their performance from the intrusion of profane or unconsecrated persons or things. In the New Testament μυστήριον is almost exclusively used of the divine secrets (*e.g.*, of God's purpose to include all nations in the covenant made by him at first with Israel alone) which are described as now at length divulged to the world by the preaching of Christ's apostles. It is not applied to the solemn rites of initiation and communion which were nevertheless already regarded as "means of grace," and came, with the spread of Christianity in the Graeco-Roman world, to be treated as corresponding in the new faith to the ceremonies there denoted by the name, in which Christians from Justin onwards, were accustomed to see a diabolical travesty of the Christian "sacraments." Nor for a long time was the word *sacramentum,* by which the earliest Latin translators of the Scriptures rendered μυστήριον limited to those outward "means of grace" to which it came eventually to be appropriated; and, even after it had been thus appropriated, it was only gradually that among a host of ceremonies and things used in ceremonies, all supposed to convey divine grace in some manner or degree, a certain number were definitely acknowledged as properly entitled to the name of sacraments.

THE SEVEN SACRAMENTS

Seven rites were recognized in the west, from Peter Lombard onwards, as sacraments in the strict sense: Baptism, Confirmation, the Eucharist, Penance, Extreme Unction, Orders and Marriage; the Councils of Trent and of the Vatican endorsed this list which has also been adopted by the orthodox Church of the east. The Churches of the Reformation, on the other hand, acknowledged only baptism and the eucharist, to which indeed a certain preeminence was universally allowed, as entitled to be called sacraments in the proper sense; mainly on the ground that these alone could be proved from Scripture to have been instituted by Christ himself as external ceremonies effecting, or at least attesting and sealing, the conveyance of an inward spiritual grace to worshippers qualified to receive it by faith in the promise expressly associated with its performance by its divine Founder. In demanding that a sacrament in the proper sense must be able to claim institution by Christ the Reformers did not differ from the Roman Church. But they refused to accept inferences from the words of Scripture, though supported by ecclesiastical tradition, as evidence of such institution equivalent to the direct commands to be found for baptism in Matt. xxviii. and for the eucharist especially in 1 Cor. xi.

The Scriptural texts alleged to suggest a like institution for the other rites recognized by the Roman Church as sacraments seemed to them either to be inapplicable to them or else to make no such provision for a particular outward symbol of the promised grace as was necessary to constitute a "sacrament," while the traditional rendering of μυστήριον by *sacramentum* in the application of the word to marriage in Eph. v. 32 could hardly be said to warrant the interpretation of the word there, as intended in a very specialized sense otherwise unknown to the New Testament. Where, however, there was, as with baptism and the eucharist, express scriptural authority for the institution by Christ of an outward and visible sign of an inward spiritual grace, of the bestowal whereof it was to be, to a believer in his promise, at least the assurance, if not the instrument, there the Protestant as well as the Catholic, recognized a genuine sacrament.

There was, however, an important point of difference between them, in respect of such ceremonies as they agreed in regarding as "sacraments." The former denied, and the latter affirmed that they confer grace *ex opere operato.* This phrase seems to have been originally intended to express the belief that sacraments do not depend for their efficacy on the moral character or even on the private beliefs of the individual minister; that where an otherwise qualified person, though wicked or unbelieving, yet intending "to do what the Church does," observes the appointed forms, the recipient need not be afraid that the promised grace is not received; the human minister being no more than an instrument in the hand of the true Giver, Christ Himself. This the Churches of the Reformation for the most part did not deny; the view of Wyclif that only one himself in a state of grace could administer a valid sacrament obtained little acceptance. But the Reformers objected to the phrase *ex opere operato,* which was solemnly reaffirmed against their objections by the Council of Trent. It seemed to them inconsistent with the supreme place assigned in their theology to faith as the sole means of justification. Catholics did not indeed deny that the absence of personal faith in a recipient in whom it could be present (as it could not be, for example, in infants brought to baptism) would present an impediment to this profiting by the grace offered in a sacrament, and on their side, Protestants, in allowing infant baptism, were constrained to admit that the requisite faith was not necessarily that of the individual recipient, but might be that of his parents or of the Church.

Nevertheless, the difference between Catholic and Protestant in that the one laid stress upon the necessity to salvation of sacraments where they could be had, and the other on the indispensableness of faith, which could justify without sacraments, while without it sacraments could not justify, profoundly affected their respective attitudes towards an institution which the Protestant as little intended to disparage as the Catholic. In respect of the eucharist, whereas Luther, Calvin, and the Reformers generally had hoped, by abolishing celebrations at which the priest alone communicated, to restore the primitive frequency of communions, the actual result of the changes introduced by them was to deprive that service in any form of the central place in the public worship of the Church which it had held from the very beginnings of Christianity. Catholics on the other hand were driven by the necessity of maintaining the efficacy of sacraments *ex opere operato* into placing and encouraging a reliance on sacraments which exposed them to the charge of allowing their religion to degenerate in practice into magic.

SYMBOLISM

It cannot be denied that the use of sacraments presents a certain resemblance to some kinds of magic. There is in both the employment of material objects and of bodily gestures in conjunction with a particular form of words to produce effects which, apart from such conjunction, they could not have accomplished. But sacraments resemble far more closely facts of human life which no one would think of describing as magical in any disparaging sense; such as the operation of words, spoken or written, in creating states of feeling, inspiring action, or revealing personality. Here the necessity of intelligent acceptance by those affected of the conventional meaning of the sounds or words employed, the limitation of the effect produced to a certain social context, and the quality (not merely physical, but intellectual or spiritual) of the result obtained distinguish verbal communication (though, as certainly not fully explicable on the principles recognized in the natural sciences, it may fairly be called *mysterious*) from what is usually meant by *magic*. And in these respects, sacraments must be classed with verbal communication. No Christian theologian would allow that these are effective altogether outside of the context of that agreement as to the meaning of the signs and formulas used which exists among Christians, or for the production of merely physical effects according to any law which, like those called "natural," operates irrespectively of the consciousness of those in whose bodies they are produced.

Attempts to treat sacraments as thus effective for "magical" purposes have not been unknown; but they have always been denounced by ecclesiastical authority and regarded as wrong and profane. Without entering into details as to charges of the magical use of sacraments made by theological opponents against particular groups of Christians, it may be observed, in reference to one of special historical importance that, while it is quite arguable that to use the eucharist as a focus of adoring devotion apart from communion is an unwarrantable departure from its original intention, both parties to the controversy here indicated would agree in disapproving as illegitimate any use of it for purposes really other than that or those (whatever it or they may be) for the sake of which it was originally instituted.

Wherever sacraments are used at all (and few Christian denominations have, like the Society of Friends, abandoned the use even of the two which undoubtedly date back to New Testament times), although there may be no crude abuse of them for confessedly magical purposes, quite other than those which the Church holds them to be intended to secure, it is possible to assimilate them to magical performances, by losing sight of their function as vehicles for communicating to individuals a life essentially social and, like all social life, requiring a conventional or ceremonial mode of expression, and of the essentially ethical character of the life which they are thus designed to communicate. The use of material objects or of bodily gestures in the communication of spiritual grace is not alien to the religion of the New Testament, but it is never there taken out of the context of a moral and social life in the imparting and maintaining of which the whole purpose of such use of objects and gestures consists. It is in a firm grasp of the *social* character of sacraments and of the *moral* quality of the life which they are designed to serve as instruments in communicating that the true safeguard against the very real danger of a degeneration of sacramentalism into magic-mongering should be sought rather than in the elimination of sacramentalism from religion, with the whole history of which it is intimately bound up, and by which, as has been well said, "the higher gifts are made accessible to persons of all stages of culture."

"The principle that spiritual values and forces are mediated through material processes," the same writer observes, "runs through nature as a whole." The very production of a new personality is only possible through "a material process the most liable . . . to carnal misuse." "Truth, beauty, goodness . . . . become effective only through material forms." There are "natural sacraments"—the kiss, the handshake, the flag—outside of religion. The admittedly important part which these and their like play in our common social life the sacraments play in religion; and in Christianity in particular, "we are bidden to act as sons of God and sharers in Christ, knowing by an outward sign that we are so. Our reliance is to be on the word and act of God, while the joy of responsive emotion comes and goes." (Gore, *The Holy Spirit and the Church*, pp. 24, 146, 148.)

To the value of sacramentalism to human life Goethe (*Wahrheit u. Dichtung, Th.* ii., B. 7) and Comte, who devised an elaborate system of symbolic rites for his new Religion of Humanity, may be cited as witnesses. That in the early stages of civilization the magical and the sacramental are not easily discriminated is no more than may be said of the magical and the religious in general, or indeed of the magical and the scientific. Primitive magic owes its disappearance at a higher level of culture to its confusion (arising at first from lack of experience, afterwards from the persistence of uncriticized tradition) of different kinds of causation; the supposition, for instance, that the utterance of a name may affect an animal, thing, or unconscious person as it may a person who hears himself called; or that the moral healing of a soul may be effected by external actions without a change in the direction of the will. We still know too little about the interaction of mind and body to despise our ancestors or undeveloped contemporaries for making mistakes in this department, which it has taken centuries of progress, religious and scientific, to render us inexcusable in making. But neither need these ancient errors, even though they may, here as elsewhere, have left traces of themselves, interesting to the archaeologist in conventions and customs which have survived the false beliefs in which they originated, be supposed to render trivial or illusory the higher activities and experiences in connection with which these traces are retained.

THE ARGUMENT OF CONTINUITY

But while we may speak of "natural sacraments" the word is strictly appropriate only where a distinction is drawn between the everyday world and a "sacred" world transcending this, although not necessarily separated from it in space or time. Where the use of the term is extended to the communication of spiritual illumination or power through material symbols apart from religion, we have to do either with a metaphor or, more usually, with a conviction that what is experienced in religion may be employed as a key to the true or ultimate nature of the world as a whole, including those features of it which are revealed to us in that part of our experience which is not in itself specifically religious. For Christians the "sacred" sphere is that which is directly related to Christ, and accordingly nothing can be properly called a "sacrament" which cannot claim authorization by Christ as a vehicle of Divine grace. While a statement in the Bible was taken as, by its presence there, guaranteed to be, when rightly understood, free from error, the undoubted occurrence in Scripture of direct statements that Christ instituted baptism and the eucharist was sufficient to establish their claim. Critical study of the Bible has here, however, altered the situation. Few scholars would now be prepared to regard Matt. xxviii. 19, and 1 Cor. xi. 23 *sqq.* as putting it beyond doubt that the historical Jesus actually prescribed the permanent observance of these rites by his followers. Thus the old question as to the number of sacraments cannot be argued on the old grounds, but rather on that of the continuity between any rite now in use and a rite observed in the primitive Christian community from which the New Testament proceeded; and of the degree in which that community regarded it as intimately bound up with that fellowship with the crucified and risen Saviour which this community existed to offer to all who would join themselves with it.

That baptism and the eucharist were regarded as very intimately bound up with it is certain. Converts were always initiated by a ceremonial washing in Christ's name; such a washing, symbolical of cleansing from sin, being (whether or no actually practised or enjoined by Jesus) familiar to Jews as used in the admission of proselytes and specially associated with Christ's own baptism by John the Baptist, whose mission Christians believed to have been preparatory to their Master's. From the first the followers of Jesus continued the custom, which had plainly been characteristic of his daily intercourse with his disciples, of the solemn blessing and breaking of bread at their social meals; a custom invested with specially solemn associations by the circumstances of His last supper whereat he was believed to have used words identifying the bread and cup shared among his companions with his own body and blood, which were so soon after to be broken and shed upon the cross.

The credentials of the other rites acknowledged by many Christians as sacraments were more doubtful. A laying on of hands symbolical of the gift of the Spirit seems usually from the beginning to have formed part of the initiatory rite, though sometimes detached from the baptism proper; but no tradition connected it with any injunction of Jesus; the gift imparted was associated in the New Testament with extraordinary manifestations not destined to be permanent; of the anointing which later became the chief feature of "confirmation" Scripture says nothing. Jesus had been wont to forgive sins, and sins were believed to be washed away in baptism; but no ceremony or fixed formula is recorded to have been used by Jesus in this connection; only gradually was it realized that sin after baptism would be a normal feature of the Christian's life; nor can scriptural authority be claimed for the system of penitential discipline which was gradually developed in the Church. The unction of the sick mentioned in James was not, like the later rite which appealed to its precedent, intended to be "extreme"; its primary purpose was not the imparting of a spiritual gift, but bodily healing, which alone is mentioned as the object of unction in the only scriptural passage (Mark vi, 13) which appears to represent it as performed by Christ's direction. The setting apart of office-bearers in the Christian community by laying on of hands is certainly apostolical; but this symbolic mode of appointment is nowhere stated in Scripture to have been used or enjoined by Jesus himself. Lastly, the only claim of the immemorial and universal institution of marriage to be a "sacrament of the new law" appears, as said above, to be the incidental observation of St. Paul (doubtless suggested by the prophetic use of it as a symbol of the bond between Yahweh and Israel) that it is a "great mystery" or "sacrament" as representing the union of Christ with his Church. But though only certain rites may be reckoned as sacraments in a prerogative sense, the whole system through which individual members of a religious group are placed, through symbols, conventionally recognized therein as instruments of its communication, in contact with the spiritual life which gives unity to the group may be regarded as sacramental. In Christianity—and the associations of the word "sacrament" are Christian—this is the divine life historically manifested in the person and work of Jesus Christ and believed to be continued in the community which, as inspired by His Spirit, may be called His "mystical body." Here those rites, the continuous experience of grace received through which throughout the history of the community attest the unbroken presence therein of the same source of spiritual life are entitled to the name of sacraments. It is clear that only where there exists faith in the reality of this divine life and in the organic relation of the community thereto, can any significance or efficacy be attributed to these; but also that such faith can only be other than an illusion if this life and this relation are in fact real. (*See also* BAPTISM, EUCHARIST.)

BIBLIOGRAPHY.—Peter Lombard, *Sententiae*, book iv; St. Thomas Aquinas, *Summa Theologica*, part 3; *Concilii Tridentini Canones et Decreta; Sylloge Confessionum sub tempus reformandae Ecclesiae editarum* (Oxford, 1827); Calvin, *Institutes*, book iv; Harnack, *Dogmengeschichte; cf.* the articles on *Sacraments* in Hastings' *Encyclopaedia of Religion and Ethics* and the bibliographies. (C. C. J. W.)

SACRAMENTALS, in the Roman Catholic Church, signs of ecclesiastical institution which differ from sacraments in that they do not give grace of themselves, but only prepare men to receive more worthily the grace of the sacraments. Typical sacramentals are the sign of the cross, holy water, blessed candles, ashes, palms, crucifixes and rosaries. Their special effect derives from the power of the church's prayer. It is conditioned in the concrete by the dispositions of the user. (Cf. *Codex Iuris Canonicis*, cc. 1144 ff.)

SACRAMENTARIANS, the name given to those who during the Reformation controversies not only denied the Roman Catholic doctrine of "transubstantiation," but also the Lutheran "consubstantiation." They admitted a spiritual presence of Christ which the devout soul can receive and enjoy, but denied any physical or corporeal presence. Finally accepting the Confession of Augsburg, they were merged in the general body of Lutherans; with the exception of the Swiss followers of Huldreich Zwingli, whose position was incorporated in the Helvetic Confession. It is a curious inversion of terms that in recent years has led to the name Sacramentarians being applied to those who hold a high or extreme view of the efficacy of the sacraments.

SACRAMENTO, the capital city of California, U.S., and the county seat of Sacramento county, is located at the confluence of the American and Sacramento rivers midway between the Sierra Nevada range and the Pacific ocean. It is on the hub of federal highways 40, 50 and 99, and major routes of the state highway system. It has a municipal airport and several private airports and is served by transcontinental and other air lines serving the Pacific coast area. Railroads serving Sacramento are the Southern Pacific, Western Pacific, Sacramento Northern and Central California Traction company. Facilities are available for the handling of freight traffic from the San Francisco bay area via the Sacramento river to Sacramento. Under construction at mid-20th century was the port of Sacramento, to provide a deepwater port for ocean-going vessels.

The population of Sacramento was 135,761 in 1950, 105,958 in 1940 and 93,750 in 1930. The city occupies 16.7 sq.mi. and is about 30 ft. above sea level. The mean annual temperature is 60° F., and the mean annual rainfall is 18.02 in. The state capitol (built 1860-69 with later addition) stands in a park of 40 ac. (owned by the state) in the heart of the city. A mile east of the capitol (in another state-owned park) is old Fort Sutter, restored and maintained by the state as a historic museum. Within the city limits are the state fairgrounds of 210 ac. The city park system covers 1,337 ac.; a municipal vacation camp is maintained in the mountains; the municipal auditorium (completed 1927) seats 5,000, and the athletic stadium (1928) 25,000. Zoning ordinances are in effect, and a city-planning board was created in 1926. The public-school system provides instruction from the kindergarten through the ninth grade. The Sacramento Junior college and the Sacramento State college provide instruction at the college level. At Davis, 14 mi. W. of Sacramento, is the college of agriculture of the University of California. The State library (427,197 vol.) has a fine law department and the most complete collection in existence on the history of California, and the Crocker art gallery houses one of the largest and most valuable collections in the west. In 1921 the city adopted a council-manager form of government. The assessed valuation of property in 1950 was $190,859,400.

Industries and Commerce.—Sacramento is an important distributing centre and the trading area of 17 counties, a highly productive agricultural, mining and lumbering region. The immediate vicinity produces pears, peaches, plums, apricots, oranges, olives, cherries, strawberries, asparagus, celery, spinach, almonds and Tokay grapes, and harvests some fruit or vegetable every month in the year. Canning and preserving is the city's chief industry. The railroad shops employ more than 6,000 men.

Among the other major industries are can-manufacturing plants, meat-packing plants, rice and flour mills, olive-pickling plants, bean and rice cleaners and polishers, brick and pottery works, box factories and an almond-shelling plant.

History.—On Aug. 12, 1839, Capt. John Augustus Sutter (1803–80), a Swiss army officer, with three companions, landed at the confluence of the American and the Sacramento rivers, coming by rowboat from the port of San Francisco, then known as Yerba Buena. With the help of a few Indians they built an adobe house, roofed with tules, fortified it and surrounded it with a protecting adobe wall. Sutter had obtained from Gov. Juan Alvarado a grant of 11 square leagues of land. Settlers came, whom he welcomed, and his hospitality and prosperity made "Fort Sutter" famous. Situated as it was on the main line of overland travel, it soon became the greatest trading post in the west. Captain Sutter employed several hundred men, had 13,000 head of stock on his ranges, a vast acreage of wheat and a large mercantile business. In 1847 he sent James W. Marshall to find a good site for a new sawmill. A spot was selected on the south fork of the American river, 35 mi. N.E. of the fort at Coloma, and work had begun on the mill when, on Jan. 24, 1848, Marshall picked up in the millrace the first gold nugget found in California. The discovery of gold on his own land by his own man was, ironically, the cause of Sutter's ruin, for his men deserted him, the newcomers pillaged his property and he died in the east a poor man; but it was the foundation of the city's development and of the rapid settlement of the whole state. The site of the present city was surveyed in 1848 and the name Sacramento (already in common use) was adopted. The first sale of town lots was held in Jan. 1849. The federal census reported a population of 6,820 in 1850, and the city was incorporated in that year. For some time conditions were chaotic, as in most new mining towns. Trouble with "squatters" almost led to local war in 1850. In 1849 the city offered $1,000,000 for the honour of being the state capital. The legislature met there in 1852, and in 1854 it was chosen as the permanent seat of government. Three times between 1849 and 1853, and again in 1862, the city suffered from devastating floods, and in 1852 two-thirds of it was destroyed by fire. Further danger from flood has been averted by strong levees and by filling in the low land along the river. By 1856 the Sacramento Valley railroad (the first steam railway in California, built to accommodate the business developed in the gold mines) was completed to Folsom, 23 mi. N.E. of Sacramento. Its chief engineer, Theodore D. Judah, took plans for a feasible route across the mountains to the capitalists in San Francisco and was laughed at as a dreamer. In Sacramento, however, he found four merchants (Leland Stanford, Mark Hopkins, Charles Crocker and Collis P. Huntington) who pledged their personal fortunes to secure the undertaking of the enterprise, and on Feb. 22, 1863, in Sacramento, the construction of the Central Pacific railroad across the Sierras was begun. On May 10, 1869, at Promontory Point, Utah, Stanford drove the golden spike that united the section of road built from the west with the section built from the east, and later in the month the first through train from the Atlantic coast reached the city. Through the rest of the 19th century the growth of Sacramento was steady and gradual, and in 1900 the population was 29,282.

Subsequently, accompanying the increasing productivity of its tributary territory (largely because of irrigation and completion of the great levee system), there was a rapid commercial and industrial expansion.

Between 1900 and 1920 the population considerably more than doubled.

Between 1939 and 1949 postal receipts increased 211%; bank debits 361%; and building permits 261%.

SACRARIUM, a term used in classical Latin for the place where sacred things were kept in a temple or private house. In mediaeval ecclesiology the term is used in various senses; e.g., choir or chancel of a church (usually called sanctuary or presbytery), tabernacle, sacristy, etc.

SACRED HEART. Devotion to the Sacred Heart of Jesus is a cult peculiar to the modern Roman Catholic Church. The principal object of this devotion is the Saviour Himself. Saint Marguerite Marie Alacoque (q.v.), assisted by her director, the Venerable Claude de la Colombière, S.J. (1641–82), spread the devotion. This devotion was strongly opposed by the Jansenists, who claimed that the Heart of Christ was being adored as separate from the rest of His Being. Some of those within the church, led by the Jansenists, also opposed the devotion. The Jansenist synod of Pistoia, assembled by Scipio de Ricci, bishop of Pistoia (1780–91), which formulated this objection against the devotion, was condemned by Pope Pius VII in the Bull *Auctorem Fidei*, Aug. 28, 1794. In May 1805, De Ricci submitted to the papal condemnation of the synod. In 1856 Pius IX introduced the feast into the general calendar of the Roman Catholic Church, fixing the Friday after the Octave of Corpus Christi for its celebration. The Beatification of Blessed M.M. Alacoque in 1864 gave a new impetus to the devotion.

BIBLIOGRAPHY.—See N. Nilles, S.J., *De rationibus festorum SS. Cordis Jesu*, etc., 5th ed. (Innsbruck, 1885); E. Letierce, S.J., *Étude sur le Sacré Coeur et la visitation* (Paris, 1890). These two works contain bibliographical lists. J. Dalgairns, *The Devotions to the Sacred Heart of Jesus* (1853); H. E. Manning, *The Glories of the Sacred Heart* (London, 1876); J. Rix, *Cultus SS. Cordis Jesu et purissimi Cordis B. Virginis Mariae*, 3rd ed. (Freiburg im Breisgau, 1905); and *The Catholic Encyclopedia*, art. "Heart of Jesus, Devotion to the"; *Dictionnaire de Théologie Cath.*, Tom. III, col. 271-351.

SACRIFICE, the ritual destruction of an object, or, more commonly, the slaughter of a victim by effusion of blood, suffo-cation, fire or other means (from Lat. *sacrificium*; *sacer*, holy, and *facere*, to make). While the Hebrew for sacrifice, זבח, makes the killing of the victim the central feature, the Latin word brings out sacralization (see TABU) as an essential element in many cases. The sacrifice of desacralization is also found; hence MM. Hubert and Mauss describe a sacrifice as "a religious act, which, by the consecration of a victim, modifies the moral state of the sacrificer or of certain material objects which he has in view"; *i.e.*, it either confers sanctity or removes it and its analogue, impurity. It is, in fact, "a procedure whereby communication is established between the sacred and profane spheres by a victim, that is to say by an object destroyed in the course of the ceremony."

Principles of Classification.—It is possible to classify sacrifices according to (1) the occasion of the rite, (2) the end to be achieved, (3) the material object to be effected or (4) the form of the rite. (1) The division into periodical and occasional is important in Hindu and other higher religions; the former class is obligatory, the latter facultative. In less developed creeds the difference tends to remain in the background; but where sacrifices are found, solemn annual rites, communal, purificatory or expiatory, are celebrated, and are obligatory. (2) The end to be achieved is sometimes sacralization, sometimes desacralization. In the former case the sacrificer is raised to a higher level; he enters into closer communion with the gods. In the latter either some material object, not necessarily animate, is deprived of a portion of its sanctity and made fit for human use, or the sacrificer himself loses a portion of his sanctity or impurity. In the sacrifice of sacralization the sanctity passes from the victim to the object; in that of desacralization, from the object to the victim. (3) Sacrifices may be classified into (a) subjective or personal, where the sacrificer himself gains or loses sanctity or impurity; (b) objective, where the current of *mana* (see TABU) is directed upon some other person or object, and only a secondary effect is produced on the sacrificer himself.

Ritual.—The necessary elements of a Hindu sacrifice are: (1) the *sacrificer*, who provides the victim, and is affected, directly or indirectly, by the sacrifice; he may or may not be identical with (2) the *officiant*, who performs the rite; we have further (3) the *place*, (4) the *instruments* of sacrifice and (5) the *victim*; where the sacrificer enjoys only the secondary results, the direct influence of the sacrifice is directed toward (6) the *object*; finally, we may distinguish (7) three *moments of the rite* —(a) the *entry*, (b) the *slaughter*, (c) the *exit*.

Sacralization and desacralization, sometimes performed by means of subsidiary sacrifices, were the essential elements of the preparation for sacrifice and the subsequent lustration. In developed forms, such as the offering of *soma*, they assumed a great importance; (1) the sacrificer had to pass from the world of man into a world of the gods; consequently he was separated from the common herd of mankind and purified; he underwent ceremonies emblematic of rebirth and was then subject to numberless taboos imposed for the purpose of maintaining his ceremonial purity. In like manner (2) the officiant prepared himself for his task; but in his case the natural sanctity of the priest relieved him of the necessity of undergoing all that the common man had to pass through; in fact, this was one of the causes which brought him into existence, the other being the need of a functionary familiar with the ritual, who would avoid disastrous errors of procedure, destructive of the efficacy of the sacrifice. (3) Where there was an appointed place of sacrifice there was no need of preparation of a place of sacrifice. (4) The necessary rites included (a) the establishment of the fires, friction being the only permitted method of kindling, (b) the tracing on the ground of the *vedi*, or magical circle, to destroy impurities, (c) the digging of the hole which constituted the real altar, (d) the preparation of the post which represented the sacrificer and to which the victim was tied, and other minor details. (5) The victim might be naturally sacred or might have to undergo sanctification. In the former case (a) individual animals might be distinguished by certain marks, or, (b) the whole species might be allied to the god. In the latter case the victim had to be without blemish; (c) the age, colour or sex of the victim might differ according to the purpose of the sacrifice. It reached a degree of sanctity when only the priest might touch it. Finally, the priest made three turns round it with a lighted torch in his hand, which finally separated it from the world and fitted it for its high purpose. The sacrificer had to remain in contact with the victim, either personally, or, to avoid ritual perils, by the intermediary of the priest. After excuses made to the animal or to the species in general, the victim was placed in position, and silence observed by all who were present. The cord was drawn tight and the victim ceased to breathe; its spirit passed into the world of the gods. It remained to dispose of the corpse. After a rite intended to secure its perfect ceremonial purity, a part of the victim was removed, held over the fire and finally cast into it. The remainder, divided into portions, was cooked; a certain number of these portions fell to the sacrificer, after an invocation, which made them sacred by calling the deity to descend into the offering and thus sanctify the sacrificer. (6) Then followed the rites of desacralization. Finally the priest, the sacrificer, and his wife performed a lustration and the ceremonies were at an end.

With present knowledge the problem of the original form of sacrifice, if there be a single primary form, is insoluble. It is impossible to give a general survey of the purposes of sacrifice; they are too numerous, and it is rare to find any but mixed forms.

Cathartic Sacrifice.—In primitive cults the distinction between sacred and unclean is not well defined (see TABU); consequently we find two types of cathartic sacrifice—(i.) one to cleanse of impurity and make fit for common use, (ii.) the other to rid of sanctity and in like manner render suitable for human use or intercourse.

(i.) The best example of the first class is the scapegoat, where a more concrete idea of expulsion of evil (see DEMONOLOGY, EXORCISM) is present among primitive peoples, such as the Australians.

(ii.) As an example of the second class may be taken the sacrifice of the bull to Rudra, which exemplifies the concentration of holiness in a single animal as representative of its species (see ANIMAL WORSHIP).

Communal Sacrifice.—The common meal is not a primitive rite of adoption. The custom of eating the body of the victim does not necessarily spring from any idea of communion with the god; it may also arise from a desire to incorporate the sanctity which has been imparted to it—an idea on a level with many other food customs (see COUVADE), and based on the idea that eating anything causes its qualities to pass into the eater. Where the victim is an animal specially associated with a god (the most conspicuous case is perhaps that of the corn spirit), it may be granted that the god is eaten; but precisely in these cases there is no custom of giving a portion of the victim to the god.

Deificatory Sacrifice.—The object of certain sacrifices is to provide a tutelary deity of a house, town or frontier. (a) In many countries, those who die a violent death are held to haunt the place where they met their fate; consequently, when a town is built living men are interred beneath the ramparts and the pillars of the gates. (b) In parts of North America the *nagual* or *manitu* animal, of which the Indian dreams during the initiation fast and which is to be his tutelary spirit, is killed with certain rites. (c) Human representatives of the corn or vegetation spirits are killed; in these, as in other cases of the sacrifice of the man-god, the killing of the old god is at the same time the making of a new god. (d) Suicide is treated as a means of raising a human being to the rank of a god. (e) Gods may be sacrificed (in theriomorphic form) to themselves as a means of renewing the life of the god. (f) The method of creating a fetish (see FETISHISM) on the Congo resembles deificatory sacrifice: but here there is no actual slaughter of a human being; magical means are alone relied upon.

Honorific Sacrifices.—Sacrifices tend to be interpreted as gifts to the god. Man seeks to influence his fellow men in various ways, and it is quite natural to find the same ideas in the sphere of religion. Food is often given to a god because he is be-

lieved to take pleasure in eating; the germ of this idea may have been to nourish the divine life. With the spiritualization of the god, comes a refinement of the tastes attributed to him, and the finer parts of the sacrifice, finally it may be only its savour, are alone regarded as acceptable offerings. Just as attendants are provided for the dead, so the god receives sacrifices intended to put slaves at his disposal. The gift theory of sacrifice is closely associated with that of the god as the ruler or king to whom man brings a tribute, just as he had to appear before his earthly king bearing gifts in his hands. The honorific sacrifice is essentially a propitiation but must be distinguished from the *piaculum* (see below).

Mortuary Sacrifice.—Sacrifices, especially of human beings, are offered immediately after a death or at a longer interval. Their object may be (a) to provide a guide to the other world; (b) to provide the dead with servants or a retinue suitable to his rank; (c) to send messengers to keep the dead informed of the things of this world; (d) to strengthen the dead by the blood or life of a living being, in the same way that food is offered to them or blood rituals enjoined on mourners.

Piacular Sacrifice.—Whereas the god receives a gift in the honorific sacrifice, he demands a life in the piacular. The essential feature of the *piaculum* is that it is an expiation for wrong-doing, and the victim is often human.

Human Sacrifice.—If tradition is any guide, human sacrifice seems in many important areas to be of secondary character; in spite of the great development of the rite among the Aztecs, tradition says that it was unknown till 200 years before the conquest; in Polynesia human sacrifices seem to be comparatively modern; and in India they appear to have been rare among the Vedic peoples. On the whole, human sacrifice is far commoner among the semi-civilized and barbarous races than in still lower stages of culture. In Australia, however, where sacrifice of the ordinary type is unknown, the ritual killing of a child is practised in connection with the initiation of a magician.

Among the forms of human sacrifice must be reckoned religious suicide, mainly found in India but not unknown in Africa and other parts of the world.

Sacrifice in Greece and Rome.—Both on the mainland of Greece and in the Greek colonies human sacrifice was practised, usually as a means towards expulsion of evil. (See GREEK RELIGION.)

At Rome the scapegoat did not suffer death; but in the Saturnalia a human victim seems to have been slain till the 4th century A.D. Many forms of animal sacrifice were found. (See ROMAN RELIGION.)

Sacrifice in Egypt.—Of Egyptian ritual little is known. (See EGYPT: *Religion*.)

Sacrifice in India.—Among human sacrifices may be mentioned the *suttee*, or custom of immolating a widow on the funeral pyre of the husband, and the Khond sacrifice of the Meriah, who was either purchased or the son of a victim father. Some days before the sacrifice, the victim, who was often kept in captivity for long periods, was devoted and his sanctity was increased; finally he was put to death by strangulation or pressure. The remains were dismembered and distributed among the fields, excepting the portion offered to the earth goddess, which was buried.

Sacrifice in Africa.—Especially in West Africa, many forms of sacrifice are found. Three main forms of human sacrifice existed: (1) the scapegoat; (2) the messenger; and (3) the expiation; but combinations were not infrequent. On the Congo, if a man committed a murder, the community voted whether he should die or be expelled; if the latter, a victim was killed, of which all partook; this is not a *piaculum* for re-establishment of the tribal bond, for the criminal is driven out of the community.

Sacrifice in America.—The Pawnees had an elaborate ritual, in which a human victim was sacrificed to the Morning Star; the blood of the victims was sprinkled on the fields, and the details of the rite are not unlike those of the Khond custom. The Iroquois sacrifice of the white dog bore in later times the character of a scapegoat festival. In Mexico human sacrifices were very common, the number being estimated at 20,000 a year.

BIBLIOGRAPHY.—H. Hubert and M. Mauss in *Année sociologique*, ii.; J. G. Frazer, *Golden Bough*, ii., iii.; W. R. Smith, *Religion of Semites*; E. B. Taylor, *Primitive Culture*; Ed. Westermarck, *Origin of Moral Ideas* (esp. vol. i. for Human Sacrifice). For Greece and Rome *see* L. Farnell, *Cults of the Greek States*, especially i. 56, 88 *seq.*; W. W. Fowler, *Festivals*; and Pauly, *Realencyklopädie, s.v.* "Sacrifice." The sections of the article "Sacrifice" in *Encyclopaedia of Religion and Ethics* contain references to bibliography and details of importance.

THE IDEA OF SACRIFICE IN THE CHRISTIAN CHURCH

There can be no doubt that the idea of sacrifice occupied an important place in early Christianity. It had been a fundamental element of both Jewish and Gentile religions, and Christianity tended rather to absorb and modify such elements than to abolish them. To a great extent the idea had been modified already. Among the Jews the preaching of the prophets had been a constant protest against the grosser forms of sacrifice, and there are indications that when Christianity arose bloody sacrifices were already beginning to fall into disuse; a saying which was attributed by the Ebionites to Christ repeats this protest in a strong form, "I have come to abolish the sacrifices; and if ye do not cease from sacrificing the wrath of God will not cease from you" (Epiph. xxx. 16). Among the Greeks the philosophers had come to use both argument and ridicule against the idea that the offering of material things could be needed by or acceptable to the Maker of them all. Among both Jews and Greeks the earlier forms of the idea had been rationalized into the belief that the most appropriate offering to God is that of a pure and penitent heart, and that the vocal expression of contrition in prayer or of gratitude in praise is also acceptable.

The best instances of these ideas in the Old Testament are in Psalms l. and li., and in Greek literature the striking words which Porphyry quotes from an earlier writer, "We ought, then, having been united and made like to God, to offer our own conduct as a holy sacrifice to Him, the same being also a hymn and our salvation in passionless excellence of soul" (Euseb. *Dem. Ev.*, 3). The ideas are also found both in the New Testament and in early Christian literature: "Let us offer up a sacrifice of praise to God continually, that is, the fruit of lips which make confession to His name" (Heb. xiii. 15); "That prayers and thanksgivings, made by worthy persons, are the only perfect and acceptable sacrifices I also admit" (Just. Mart. *Trypho*, c. 117); "We honour God in prayer, and offer this as the best and holiest sacrifice with righteousness to the righteous Word" (Clem. Alex. *Strom.*, vii. 6).

But among the Jews two other forms of the idea expressed themselves in usages which have been perpetuated in Christianity, and one of which has had a singular importance for the Christian world. The one form, which probably arose from the conception of Yahweh as in an especial sense the protector of the poor, was that gifts to God may properly be bestowed on the needy, and that consequently alms have the virtue of a sacrifice. Biblical instances of this idea are—"He who doeth alms is offering a sacrifice of praise" (Ecclus. xxxii. 2); "To do good and to communicate forget not, for with such sacrifices God is well pleased" (Heb. xiii. 16); so the offerings sent by the Philippians to Paul when a prisoner at Rome are "an odour of a sweet smell, a sacrifice acceptable, well pleasing to God" (Phil. iv. 18). The other form, which was probably a relic of the conception of Yahweh as the author of natural fertility, was that part of the fruits of the earth should be offered to God in acknowledgment of His bounty, and that what was so offered was especially blessed and brought a blessing upon both those who offered it and those who afterwards partook of it. The persistence of this form of the idea of sacrifice constitutes so marked a feature of the history of Christianity as to require a detailed account of it.

Meals as Thank-offerings.—In the first instance it is probable that among Christians, as among Jews, every meal, and especially every social meal, was regarded as being in some sense a thank-offering. Thanksgiving, blessing and offering were co-ordinate terms. Hence the Talmudic rule, "A man shall not taste anything before blessing it" (*Tosephta Berachoth*, c. 4), and hence St.

Paul's words, "He that eateth, eateth unto the Lord, for he giveth God thanks" (Rom. xiv. 6; *cf.* 1 Tim. iv. 4). But the most important offering was the solemn oblation in the assembly on the Lord's day.

The points in relation to this offering which are clearly demonstrable from the Christian writers of the first two centuries, but which subsequent theories have tended to confuse, are these. (1) It was regarded as a true offering or sacrifice; for in the *Teaching of the Twelve Apostles*, in Justin Martyr and in Irenaeus it is designated by each of the terms which are used to designate sacrifices in the Old Testament. (2) It was primarily an offering of the fruits of the earth to the Creator; this is clear from both Justin Martyr and Irenaeus, the latter of whom not only explicitly states that such oblations are continued among Christians, but also meets the current objection to them by arguing that they are offered to God not as though He needed anything but to show the gratitude of the offerer (Iren. iv. 17, 18). (3) It was offered as a thanksgiving partly for creation and preservation and partly for redemption: the latter is the special purpose mentioned (*e.g.*) in the *Teaching of the Twelve Apostles*; the former is that upon which Irenaeus chiefly dwells; both are mentioned together in Justin Martyr (*Trypho*, c. 41). (4) Those who offered it were required to be not only baptized Christians but also "in love and charity one with another"; there is an indication of this latter requirement in the Sermon on the Mount (Matt. v. 23, 24, where the word translated "gift" is the usual lxx. word for a sacrificial offering, and is so used elsewhere in the same Gospel, viz. Matt. viii. 4, xxiii. 19), and still more explicitly in the *Teaching*, c. 14, "Let not any one who has a dispute with his fellow come together with you (*i.e.* on the Lord's day) until they have been reconciled, that your sacrifice be not defiled." This brotherly unity was symbolized by the kiss of peace. (5) It was offered in the assembly by the hands of the president; this is stated by Justin Martyr (*Apol.* i. 65, 67), and implied by Clement of Rome (*Ep.* i. 44, 4).

Sacred Meals.—Combined with this sacrifice of the fruits of the earth to the Creator in memory of creation and redemption, and probably always immediately following it, was the sacred meal at which part of the offerings was eaten. Such a sacred meal had always, or almost always, formed part of the rites of sacrifice. There was the idea that what had been solemnly offered to God was especially hallowed by Him, and that the partaking of it united the partakers in a special bond both to Him, and to one another. In the case of the bread and wine of the Christian sacrifice, it was believed that, after having been offered and blessed, they became to those who partook of them the body and blood of Christ. This "communion of the body and blood of Christ," which in early writings is clearly distinguished from the thank-offering which preceded it, and which furnished the materials for it, gradually came to supersede the thank-offering in importance, and to exercise a reflex influence upon it. In the time of Cyprian, though not before, we begin to find the idea that the body and blood of Christ were not merely partaken of by the worshippers but also offered in sacrifice, and that the Eucharist was not so much a thank-offering for creation and redemption as a repetition or a showing forth anew of the self-sacrifice of Christ.

This idea is repeated in Ambrose and Augustine, and has since been a dominant idea of both Eastern and Western Christendom. But, though dominant, it has not been universal, nor did it become dominant until several centuries after its first promulgation. The history of it has yet to be written. For, in spite of the important controversies to which it has given birth, no one has taken the pains to distinguish between (i.) the theories which have been from time to time put forth by eminent writers, and which, though they have in some cases ultimately won a general acceptance, have for a long period remained as merely individual opinions, and (ii.) the current beliefs of the great body of Christians which are expressed in recognized formularies. A catena of opinions may be produced in favour of almost any theory; but formularies express the collective or average belief of any given period, and changes in them are a sure indication that there has been a general change in ideas.

It is clear from the evidence of the early Western liturgies that, for at least six centuries, the primitive conception of the nature of the Christian sacrifice remained. There is a clear distinction between the sacrifice and the communion which followed it, and that which is offered consists of the fruits of the earth and not of the body and blood of Christ. Other ideas no doubt attached themselves to the primitive conception, of which there is no certain evidence in primitive times, *e.g.* the idea of the propitiatory character of the offering, but these ideas rather confirm than disprove the persistence of those primitive conceptions themselves. All Eastern liturgies, in their present form, are of later date than the surviving fragments of the earlier Western liturgies, and cannot form the basis of so sure an induction; but they entirely confirm the conclusions to which the Western liturgies lead.

In the course of the 8th and 9th centuries, by the operation of causes which have not yet been fully investigated, the theory which is first found in Cyprian became the dominant belief of Western Christendom. The central point of the sacrificial idea was shifted from the offering of the fruits of the earth to the offering of the body and blood of Christ. The change is marked in the rituals by the duplication of the liturgical forms. The prayers of intercession and oblation, which in earlier times are found only in connection with the former offering, are repeated in the course of the same service in connection with the latter. The designations and epithets which are in earlier times applied to the fruits of the earth are applied to the body and blood. From that time until the Reformation the Christian sacrifice was all but universally regarded as the offering of the body and blood of Christ. The innumerable theories which were framed as to the precise nature of the offering and as to the precise change in the elements all implied that conception of it. It still remains as the accepted doctrine of the Church of Rome. For, although the council of Trent recognized fully the distinction which has been mentioned above between the Eucharist and the sacrifice of the mass, and treated of them in separate sessions (the former in Session xiii., the latter in Session xxii.), it continued the mediaeval theory of the nature of the latter.

The reaction against the mediaeval theory at the time of the Reformation took the form of a return to what had no doubt been an early belief,—the idea that the Christian sacrifice consists in the offering of a pure heart and of vocal thanksgiving. Luther at one period (in his treatise *De captivitate Babylonica*) maintained, though not on historical grounds, that the offering of the oblations of the people was the real origin of the conception of the sacrifice of the Mass; but he directed all the force of his vehement polemic against the idea that any other sacrifice could be efficacious besides the sacrifice of Christ. In the majority of Protestant communities the idea of a sacrifice has almost lapsed. That which among Catholics is most commonly regarded in its aspect as an offering and spoken of as the "mass" is usually regarded in its aspect as a participation in the symbols of Christ's death and spoken of as the "communion." But it may be inferred from the considerable progress of the Anglo-Catholic revival in most English-speaking countries that the idea of sacrifice has not yet ceased to be an important element in the general conception of religion.

See J. H. Srawley and H. Watt, art. "Eucharist" in Hastings, *Encyclopaedia of Religion and Ethics*, vol. v.; R. A. S. Macalister, art. "Sacrifice (Semitic)," *ibid.* vol. ix., p. 31; M. Gaster, art. "Sacrifice, Jewish," *ibid.* p. 24; G. F. Moore, art. "Sacrifice" in the *Encyclopaedia Biblica;* W. R. Smith, *Religion of the Semites* (1889; reprint of 2nd ed., 1907); J. G. Frazer, *The Golden Bough*, pt. vi., "The Scapegoat," and *Folklore in the Old Testament*.

SACRILEGE, the violation or profanation of sacred things. The word comes from the Lat. *sacrilegium,* which originally meant merely the theft of sacred things, although already in Cicero's time it had grown to include in popular speech any insult or injury to them.

In primitive religions inclusive of almost every serious offence even in fields now regarded as merely social or political, its scope is gradually lessened to a single part of one section of ecclesiastical criminology, following inversely the development of the idea of holiness from the concrete to the abstract, from fetishism to mysticism. The primitive defence against sacrilege lay directly in the nature of sacred things, those that held a curse for any violation or profanation (*see* TABU). Early criminal law brought a measure of physical sanction into consideration. The Levitical code exacted of the offender reparation for the damage with the addition of one-fifth of the amount, and an expiatory sacrifice (Lev. v. 15, 16). The tragic story of the stoning of Achan, who stole some of the spoils of Jericho which Joshua had consecrated to the treasury of Yahweh, is one of the most graphic details of Old Testament history (*cf.* Joshua vii. 20–25).

No religion was more prodigal in rules to safeguard that which was holy or consecrated than the Jewish, especially in its temple laws; violation of them often led to mob violence as well as divine chastisement. The temple rules do not apply to synagogues, however, and unseemly conduct in them is liable only to civil action.

While the Roman cults were amply protected by tabus, there was no comprehensive term in Roman law for religious violations and profanations in general. *Sacrilegium* was narrowly construed as the theft of sacred things from a sacred place. According to Ulpian the punishment for *sacrilegium* varied according to the position and standing of the culprit and the circumstances under which the crime was committed. For the lower classes it was crucifixion, burning or the wild beasts. The latter penalty was also attached to theft of sacred things by night, but stealing by day from a temple objects of little value brought only sentence to the mines. People of higher rank were deported. During classical times the law kept to the narrow meaning of *sacrilegium,* but in popular usage it had grown to mean about the same as the English word. Traces of this usage are frequent in Augustan writers. The early church Fathers use the word most frequently in the restricted sense, although an effort has been made to read the wider meaning in Tertullian. But by the middle of the 4th century the narrower meaning had disappeared. In Ambrose, Augustine and Leo I., *sacrilegium* means sacrilege. The wider meaning had invaded the law as well. Mommsen was of the opinion that *sacrilegium* had no settled meaning in the laws of the 4th century. But it was rather that an enlarged application of the idea of sacredness made the crime of sacrilege in the sense of *violatio sacri* a more general one. This was partly due to the influence of Christianity, which sought to include as objects of sacrilege all forms of church property, rather than merely those things consecrated in pagan cults, partly to the efforts of the later emperors to surround themselves and everything emanating from them with highest sanctions. In the Theodosian Code the various crimes which are accounted sacrilege include—apostasy, heresy, schism, Judaism, paganism, attempts against the immunity of churches and clergy or privileges of church courts, the desecration of sacraments, etc., and even Sunday. Along with these crimes against religion went treason to the emperor, offences against the laws, especially counterfeiting, defraudation in taxes, seizure of confiscated property, evil conduct of imperial officers, etc. There is no formal definition of sacrilege in the code of Justinian but the conception remains as wide.

The penitentials (*q.v.*), or early collections of disciplinary canons, gave much attention to sacrilege. The Frankish synods emphasize the crime of seizing church property of every kind, including the vast estates so envied by the lay nobility. The worst sacrilege of all, defiling the Host, is mentioned frequently, and generally brought the death penalty accompanied by the cruellest and most ignominious tortures. The period of the Reformation naturally increased the commonness of the crime. Under the emperor Charles V. the penalty for stealing the Host was the stake; that for other crimes was graded accordingly. In France, in 1561, under Charles IX., it was forbidden under penalty of death to demolish crosses and images and to commit other acts of scandal and impious sedition. In the declaration of 1682, Louis XIV. decreed the same penalty for sacrilege joined to superstition and impiety, and in the somewhat belated religious persecution of the duke of Bourbon in 1724 those convicted of larceny in churches, together with their accomplices, were condemned, the men to the galleys for life or for a term of years, the women to be branded with the letter V and imprisoned for life, or for a term. The trial of La Barre in 1766 at Abbeville is the most famous sacrilege case in modern times. Convicted of wearing his hat while a religious procession was passing—as well as of blasphemy—he was accused as well of having mutilated a crucifix standing on the town bridge. Declared guilty, after torture, he was sentenced to have his tongue cut out, to be beheaded and the body to be burned, a sentence which was confirmed by the parlement of Paris and the bigoted king Louis XV. In the midst of the French Revolution respect for *civic* festivals was sternly enacted, but sacrilege was an almost daily matter of state policy. In 1825 the reactionary parlement once more brought back the middle ages, by decreeing the death penalty for public profanation, the execution to be preceded by the *amende honorable* before the church doors. "Theft sacrilege" was treated in a separate series of equally savage clauses. This ferocious legislation was expressly and summarily abrogated in 1830.

English Law.—In English law, sacrilege is the breaking into a place of worship and stealing therefrom. At common law benefit of clergy was denied to robbers of churches. A statute of 1553 made the breaking or defacing of an altar, crucifix or cross in any church, chapel or churchyard punishable with three months' imprisonment on conviction before two justices, the imprisonment to be continued unless the offender entered into surety for good behaviour at quarter sessions. The tendency of the later law has been to put the offence of sacrilege in the same position as if the offence had not been committed in a sacred building. Thus breaking into a place of worship at night, says Coke, is burglary, for the church is the mansion house of Almighty God. The Larceny Act of 1861 punishes the breaking into, or out of, a place of divine worship in the same way as burglary, and the theft of things sacred in the same way as larceny. Now by the Malicious Damage Act 1861 the unlawful and malicious destroying or damaging any picture, statue, monument or other memorial of the dead, painted glass or other monument or work of art, in any church, chapel, meeting-place or other place of divine worship, is a misdemeanour punishable by imprisonment.

SACRISTY, in ecclesiastical architecture, the room or hall in a church wherein are kept the vestments and utensils (*sacra*) used in the services and celebrations.

SADDLE, a seat, usually of leather, fixed by girths to the back of a horse for riding; also a padded cushion for the back of a draught horse, fastened by girths and crupper; to it are attached the supports for the shafts, and rings for the reins. (*See* SADDLERY AND HARNESS.) The word is also applied to many objects resembling a saddle in shape or function, such as a block to support a spar in a ship, or in machinery to support a rod.

In architecture, a saddle is a piece of wood, metal, marble, etc., at the bottom of a door opening. It is usually raised slightly above the floor on either side, and is used not only to cover the space or joint between the flooring of two adjacent rooms or spaces, but also to raise the bottom of the door sufficiently to clear carpets, rugs, etc. The word saddle is usually restricted to such a member in interior doorways; sill (*q.v.*) is used similarly in the case of exterior doorways. The term is also applied to a saddle-shaped stone used as a coping.

SADDLE IN ARCHITECTURE: (LEFT) IN DOOR OPENING, (RIGHT) STONE COPING

Saddle bars are small, horizontal bars of iron or bronze running across a stained glass window, and fastened to the stone or frame on each side, not only bracing the window structure, but forming a rigid basis to which the leading of the stained glass can be attached.

SADDLERY AND HARNESS. These two terms embrace the equipment for the horse when used for riding or driving. "Harness" was originally a general term for equipment, *e.g.*, the body armour of a soldier. It is now usually confined to the work and driving horse's equipment, "saddle and bridle" being applied to that of the riding horse.

Saddlery is principally a leather trade, and the craft has been established in England as a separate trade since the 13th century, when the London Saddlers' Company received its charter from Edward I. There is evidence also of its early prosperity at Birmingham; the principal seat of the British harness and saddlery trade is now at Walsall. Saddlers' ironmongery embraces the making of buckles, rings, chains, stirrups, spurs, bits, hames.

The "bridle" is the combination of straps, bits, rings, chains and buckles which fits on the horse's head. The headstall consists of the headpiece passing behind the ears and joining the head-band over the forehead; the cheek-straps run down the sides of the head to the bit to which they are fastened; in the "blind" type of driving bridle the "blinkers," rectangular or round leather flaps which prevent the horse from seeing anything except what lies in front, are attached to the cheek-straps; the nose-band passes round the front of the nose just above the nostrils; and the throat-latch extends from the top of the cheek-straps underneath the head. The "martingale," an attachment sometimes used on riding horses, passes between the horse's forelegs, with one end fastened to the saddle girth and the other to the bridle. It keeps the horse from throwing up his head. The bit is the metal contrivance inserted in the mouth to which the reins are attached. There are innumerable patterns of bits, but they may be roughly divided into the straight bar, "snaffle" and "curb." The "snaffle" for the riding horse generally has a smooth, jointed steel mouthpiece, with straight cheek-bars, the rings for the reins and cheek-pieces of the headstall being fixed in the bars at the junction with the mouthpiece. A severer snaffle has the mouthpiece twisted and fluted. The bars prevent the horse's pulling the bit through its mouth. The snaffle without bars is generally termed a "bridoon." The commonest form of bit used in driving is the double-ring snaffle, in which the rings work one within the other, the headstall straps fastening to one and the reins to the other, or, if the horse is driven on the double ring, the reins are buckled to both rings. The curb-bit (Fr. *courbe*, Lat. *curvus*, bent, crooked) is one to which a curb-chain or strap is generally attached, fastened to hooks on the upper ends of the cheek-bars of the bit and passing under the horse's lower jaw in the chin groove. The reins are attached to rings at the lower ends of the cheek-bars, the leverage thus pressing the curb-chain against the jaw. The mouthpiece of the curb-bit is unjointed and commonly has in the centre a "port," *i.e.* a raised curve allowing liberty for the tongue and bringing the pressure on the base of the horse's jaw. The curb-bit and the bridoon can be used together with separate headstalls and reins, and there are many combination bits.

Saddles.—The riding saddle is composed of the "tree," the framework, the parts of which are the pommel or head, the projection which fits over the withers, and the side bars which curve round into the cantle or hind-bow. The tree in the best saddles is made of beechwood split with the grain; thin canvas is glued over the wood to prevent splitting, and iron or steel plates then riveted on the head and on the cantle. Linen webs are fastened lengthwise and across, over which is nailed canvas and serge between which the padding is stuffed. To the tree are fastened the stirrup-bars. The leather covering of the tree should be of pig-skin; cheap saddles are made of sheep-skin stamped to imitate pig-skin. The various parts of the man's saddle are the seat, the skirt, *i.e.*, the fold or pad of leather on either side of the head, and the hanging flaps; knee-rolls are not used as much as they were, except where roughly broken-in horses are ridden. The saddle is cut straight over the withers with a square-ended cantle, as in the hunting saddle, or cut back over the withers with a round-ended cantle, as in the polo saddle. The saddles in use on the continent of Europe still retain the high pommel and cantle and heavy knee-rolls discarded by riders trained in the British school and the hunting-field. The saddles of the East and of the Arabs keep their primitive shape, and they are really seats *in* which rather than *on* which the rider sits. The Mexican saddle, with its silver adornments and embossed leather, is a characteristic type. It has a very high padded pommel and a round-headed projecting cantle.

Harness.—Space forbids the discussion of the varieties of harness for the pair-horse carriage, the four-horse coach, the farm wagon, etc., or the different kinds of ornamentation that are or have been lavished upon it. The leather collar, heavily padded, passes over the head and rests firmly on the shoulders; the hames, linked pieces of metal, fit tightly round it and are fastened at the top and bottom by the hame-straps; they bear the traces, or straps which pass along the horse's sides and the shafts, and are attached to the whiffletree. Where the collar is dispensed with, the traces are attached to a breast-strap against which the horse works. This breast harness is much used for the lightly harnessed American trotting horses, and for military draught horses. The saddle pad is a narrow leather cushion resting on the back and girthed under the belly and held in position by the back-band and crupper, a loop strap passing under the tail. The saddle supports the shafts by straps fitted with shaft loop-holes. The reins pass from the bit through "terrets" or rings on the hames and pad. The harness on the horse's hind-quarters consists of the breeching, passing round behind the horse and helping in backing and stopping the vehicle and the hip-strap fastened to the breeching and passing over the hind-quarters. The bearing rein, or check-rein, when used as a support to the head, or as help to the paces, consists of a separate bridoon-bit with the reins passing through rings on the throat-band and thence slipped over a hook on the pad.

Historical Sketch.—Questions as to the epoch in the history of mankind when the horse was first trained for draught and riding are for archaeologists and anthropologists to discuss (*see* Horse: *Origin and History*). With the domestication of the horse came the development of the bit; first a halter of hide bound the muzzle, then a thong slipped into the mouth, finally replaced by wood or bone. Stone age objects have been found in lake-dwellings, such as that at Robenhausen, near Zürich, which may have been bits; one is slightly curved, with two knobs grooved at either end for the reins. Bits from the bronze age and the iron age can be seen in most museums showing that the forms have changed little. In the late iron age burial of a Gaulish chief with his chariot at Somme-Bionne were two horses' bits of the jointed snaffle type.

In ancient Greece and Rome the bit and bridle were used during historic times, and allusions to riding without them refer to exhibitions of horsemanship. On Trajan's column the Numidians ride without bridles or bits, and various North African tribes trained their horses to obey their voice alone (*cf.* Claudian, *Epig.* i. 10, of the Gaulish *essedarii*, driving without bridle and reins). The *locus classicus* for the bridling and saddling of the Greek horse is Xenophon, Περὶ ἱππικῆς. The Greek name for the bridle bit and reins collectively is χαλινός (Lat. *frenum*), the bit proper στόμιον; in Lat. *frenum* is also used of the bit itself. The headstall (κορυφαία) and cheek-straps (παρήϊα) were richly decorated. In Homer (*Il.* iv. 142) the latter are ornamented with ivory plates stained with purple, and such have been found on the site of Troy (Schliemann, *Ilios*, 476, 631). The head-band also bore a crest (λόφος, *crista*), and in front the ἄμπυξ (*frontale*) might be extended down the face to serve as a defence, as in the mediaeval *chaufrein*. This frontal was a special subject of decoration. Of the two principal types of ancient bits, the unjointed and the jointed mouthpiece, the latter is the most common form. There are also other forms of bits; those with sharp points were called *lupata* (Virg. *Georg.* iii. 208). There is a Greek bit in the British Museum with revolving disks, a device which occurs in mediaeval bits, to give the horse something to keep turning in his mouth. The curb was also used: Xenophon distinguishes between the snaffle (λεῖος χαλινός) and the curb. The curb-strap or chain was termed ὑποχαλινίδια or ψάλιον, which, however, may mean a muzzle. A bronze bit found at Pompeii has a twisted and jointed metal mouthpiece and a plain curved bar acting as a curb-strap. The cheek-bars of the bit take a variety of forms: straight bars, circles with rays, square or oblong plaques, triangles and the swan-necked or S-shaped type are all found. In medieval times complicated and severe bits were used, and heavy bits with cruel mouthpieces and long elaborately curved cheek-bars are still used by Arabs and the riders of Central and South America.

The saddle was not used in Egypt; the Assyrian monuments show decorated saddle-cloths rather than the saddle. The harness of the chariots of Egypt and Assyria are also illustrated on the monuments (*see* especially Sir J. G. Wilkinson, *Manners and Customs of the Ancient Egyptians* revised ed. 1878). The ancient Greeks rode bare-backed as in the Panathenaic frieze of the Parthenon or used a saddle-cloth (ἐφίππιον, Lat. *ephippium*; *sella* as applied to a saddle is quite late). Even the saddle-cloth does not appear to have been in use till the 5th century. A 6th-century vase, found at Daphnae, Lower Egypt (Flinders-Petrie and Murray, *Tanis*, 1888, ii. Pl. xxix.), shows a woman riding astride on a cloth, with fully developed headstall and powerful bit. A black-figured sarcophagus, now in the British Museum, from Clazomenae, shows a long pointed *ephippium* with a chest-strap. These indicate Asiatic influence, for Daphnae was an Ionian and Carian settlement of the 7th century B.C. In Xenophon (*l.c.*) we find that the saddle-cloth had been adopted by the Athenian cavalry, and from his advice as to the seat to be adopted pads or rolls seem to have been added. There were no stirrups (till the time of the emperor Maurice, A.D. 602), and the rider mounted at a vault or by blocks; mounting by the spear used as a vaulting pole was also practised as an athletic feat. On a funeral monument of the time of Nero in the museum at Mainz is the figure of a horseman on a saddle-cloth with something resembling the pommel and cantle of a saddle, but the first saddle proper is found in the so-called column of Theodosius at Constantinople (usually ascribed to the end of the 4th century A.D., though it may be more than 100 years earlier), where two figures are riding on high-peaked saddles resting on embroidered saddle-cloths. In mediaeval times the saddle was much like that of the Oriental saddle of to-day with high peaks before and behind. In the military saddle of the 14th and 15th century the high front parts of the saddle were armoured and extended to protect the legs of the rider. The jousting saddle (*cf.* the example in the Tower of London) becomes almost a box into which the rider is fixed; the high cantle fits round the rider's loins and when charging he lifted himself into practically a standing position in the stirrups. The saddle for use on the road or hunting was much like the Arab saddle of to-day, and similar forms are in use in Europe and elsewhere where the British saddle has not been adopted. Women rode astride or on a pillion behind a male rider. The side-saddle is said to date from the end of the 12th century. For the harness of the ancient draught horse *see* Chariot.

(C. We.)

See J. C. Ginzrot, *Wagen und Fahrwerke der Griechen und Römer* (1817); C. Berjeau, *The Horses of Antiquity, Middle Ages and Renaissance* (1864); J. Philipson, *Harness* (1882); B. Tozer, *The Horse in History* (1908). *See also* Horse; Driving; Horsemanship and Riding.

SADDUCEES, the name of a party which was opposed to the Pharisees down to the destruction of Jerusalem in A.D. 70. The Sadducees have been represented, not so much an organized party, as the lax and wordly-minded aristocrats, who were primarily interested in maintaining their own privileged position; who favoured Greco-Roman culture. Their attitude towards religious questions was purely negative; indeed, they were not a religious party at all. This view, championed by G. Hölscher, is not supported by the early sources. Both in Josephus and the N.T. Sadduceeism is represented as associated with certain definite religious positions; they represented the conservative tendency in matters of religion.

The most probable explanation of the name Sadducees is that proposed by A. Geiger, viz., that it is equivalent to "Zadokites," *i.e.*, "the adherents of the Sons of Zadok." The latter were a priestly family who claimed descent from Zadok, who was head of the priesthood in the days of Solomon (*cf.* 1 Kings i. 34; and ii. 35); Ezekiel (xliv. 10–15) selected this family as worthy of being invested with the control of the Temple; and in fact members of this family formed the Temple hierarchy down to the time of Ben Sira (*cf.* Sirach. li. 12, Hebrew text). Later this priestly line became tainted with Hellenism, and ultimately the high priesthood was usurped by others. After the disappearance of the legitimate high priest of the house of Zadok the title "Zadokites" may well have been assumed by conservative elements in the priesthood, to preserve the earlier traditions of their order.

Unfortunately, we possess no statement from the Sadducean side of their beliefs and principles, unless the "Zadokite" work discovered by Schechter represents, as is possible, the views of a section of the party. There are many controversial references in the Rabbinical literature to the Sadducees on points connected with the interpretation of the law. The main principle that divided the two parties was concerned with the written Torah (the Pentateuch). The supremacy of the law was common ground to both parties, but whereas the Pharisees assigned to the oral tradition a place of authority side by side with the written law, and determining its interpretation, the Sadducees refused to accept any ordinance as binding, unless it was based directly on the written word. The rest of Scripture (the Prophets and the Hagiographa) they regarded as mere Kabbalah "tradition." The Pharisaic device of harmonizing apparent contradictions between the Law and the Prophets by exegetical expedients was not accepted by the Sadducees, who refused to sanction doctrines and practices which could not be based on the written law. Thus the doctrine of a Davidic Messiah was rejected because it was considered that the prophetic teaching on this subject was in conflict with the *Torah*.

R. Leszynsky suggests that the Sadducees, or a section of them, accepted the hope of a priestly Messiah (*cf.* Ex. xix. 6), from which passage it might be inferred that a priestly line was destined to possess the Kingdom. There was also the example of the Priest King Melchizedek, which might easily suggest "Zadok King," or "Sadducean King." According to Acts xxiii. 8, the Sadducees denied the existence of angels and spirits, as well as the doctrine of the resurrection. This probably means that they did not accept the fully developed angelology of later times, while in the latter case the point of controversy was not whether the resurrection was true, but whether it could be proved from the Pentateuch. Another interesting point of difference is concerned with the date of Pentecost. The Sadducean hierarchy had its stronghold in the Temple, and it was only during the last 10 or 20 years of the Temple's existence that the Pharisees finally got control. With the destruction of the Temple in A.D. 70 their power as an organized party disappeared.

See R. Leszynsky, *Die Sadduzäer*, (1912); Art. "Sadducees," *E.R.E.* where further literature is cited. *Cf.* also Burkitt "Jesus and the 'Pharisees'" in *J. Th. S.* xxviii., 392–397.   (G. H. B.)

SADE, DONATIEN ALPHONSE FRANÇOIS, Count [usually called the MARQUIS DE SADE] (1740–1814), French writer, was born in Paris on June 2, 1740. He entered the light horse at fourteen and saw considerable military service before returning to Paris in 1766. Here his vicious practices became notorious, and in 1772 he was condemned to death at Aix for an unnatural offence, and for poisoning. He fled to Italy, but in 1777 he was arrested in Paris, removed to Aix for trial, and there found guilty. In 1778 he escaped from prison, but was soon re-arrested and finally committed to the Bastille. Here he began to write plays and obscene novels. In 1789 he was removed to the Charenton Lunatic Asylum, but was discharged in 1790, only to be recommitted as incurable in 1803. He died there on Dec. 2, 1814. Among his works, all of the type indicated, were *Justine* (1791), *Juliette* (1792), *Philosophie dans le boudoir* (1793) and *Les Crimes de l'amour* (1800). The word Sadism is derived from his name.

See C. R. Dawes, *The Marquis de Sade: his Life and Works* (1927).

SÁ DE MIRANDA, FRANCISCO DE (1485?–1558), Portuguese poet, was the son of a canon of Coimbra belonging to the ancient and noble family of Sá. He probably made his first studies of Greek, Latin and philosophy in one of the colleges of the Old City, and in 1505 went to Lisbon university. He seems to have resided for the most part in the capital down to 1521, dividing his time between the palace and the university, in the latter of which he had taken the degree of doctor of law by 1516.

In the middle of July 1520 he set out across Spain for Italy, and spent the years 1521 to 1525 abroad, visiting Milan, Venice, Florence, Rome, Naples and Sicily "with leisure and curiosity." He enjoyed intimacy with Giovanni Ruccellai, Lattanzio Tolomei and Sannazaro; he saluted the illustrious Vittoria Colonna, a distant connection of his family, and in her house he probably talked with Bembo and Ariosto, and perhaps met Machiavelli and Guicciardini. He brought home with him (*ca.* 1525) the sonnet and canzone of Petrarch, the tercet of Dante, the *ottava rima* of Ariosto, the eclogue in the manner of Sannazaro and Italian hendecasyllabic verse. He did not, however, abandon the short national metre, but carried it to perfection in his *Cartas*.

His *Os Estrangeiros*, produced in 1527–28, was the first Portuguese prose comedy, as his *Cleopatra* (*c.* 1550) is recognised to be the first Portuguese classical tragedy. In 1528 Miranda made his first real attempt to introduce the new forms of verse by writing in Spanish a canzon entitled *Fabula do Mondego*, and in 1530–32 he followed it up with the eclogue *Aleixo*.

The year 1532 had marked his passage from the active to the contemplative life, and the eclogue *Basto*, in the form of a pastoral dialogue written in *redondilhas*, opened his new manner. It has a pronounced personal note, and its episodes are described in a genuinely popular tone. The same epoch saw the composition of his *Cartas* or sententious letters in *quintilhas* which, with *Basto* and his satires, make up the most original, if not the most valuable, portion of his legacy. A more lyrical vein is apparent in the *quintilhas* of *A. Egipciaca Santa Maria*. In 1538 he wrote his second classical prose comedy *Os Vilhalpandos*, which was played before the Cardinal Infant Henry. He died on March 15, 1558.

Sá de Miranda led the way in a revolution in literature, and especially in poetry, which under his influence became higher in aim, purer in tone and broader in sympathy. He introduced the Renaissance into Portugal and at the same time made an austere stand against materialism. Some of his sonnets are admirable, and display a grave tenderness of feeling, a refinement of thought and a simplicity of expression which give them a high value. He wrote much and successfully in Castilian, several of his best eclogues being in that language.

Sá de Miranda's works were first published in 1595, but the admirable critical edition of Madame Michäelis de Vasconcellos (Halle, 1885) containing life, notes and glossary, supersedes all others. His plays can best be read in the 1784 edition of the collected works, *A. Egipciaca Santa Maria* was edited by T. Braga (Oporto, 1913). *See* Sousa Viterbo, *Estudos sobre Sá de Miranda* (3 parts, Coimbra, 1895–96); Decio Carneiro, *Sá de Miranda e a sua obra* (Lisbon, 1895); Theophilo Braga, *Sá de Miranda* (Oporto, 1896); C. Michäelis de Vasconcellos, *Novos estudos sobre Sá de Miranda* in vol. v. (1912) of the *Boletim da Segunda Classe* of the Lisbon Academy of Sciences.

SA'DĪ (*c.* 1184–1291), MUSLIH-UDDĪN, or more correctly MUSHARRIF-UDDĪN B. MUSLIH-UDDĪN, the greatest didactic poet and the most popular writer of Persia, was born about 1184 (A.H. 580) in Shiraz. His early youth was spent in study at the Nizāmiyya in Baghdād and he returned to Isfahan just at the time of the inroads of the Mongols, when the atābeg Sa'd (in whose honour Sa'dī took his pen name) had been deposed by the victorious Khwarizm ruler of Ghiyāss-uddīn (1226). Distressed by the misfortune of his patron and disgusted with the miserable condition of Persia, Sa'dī quitted Shīrāz and entered upon the second period of his life—that of his wanderings (1226–1256).

He proceeded via Balkh, Ghaznī and the Punjab to Gujarāt, on the western coast of which he visited the famous shrine of Sīva in Somnath. After a prolonged stay in Delhi, where he learned Hindūstānī, he sailed for Yemen. Overcome with grief at the loss of a beloved child (when he had married is not known), he undertook an expedition into Abyssinia and a pilgrimage to Mecca and Medina. From there he directed his steps toward Syria and lived as a renowned sheikh for a considerable time in Damascus, which he had once already visited. There and in Baalbek he added to his literary renown that of a first-rate pulpit orator. Weary of Damascus, he withdrew into the desert near Jerusalem and led a solitary wandering life, till one day he was taken captive by a troop of Frankish soldiers, brought to Tripoli, and condemned to forced labour in the trenches of the fortress. After enduring countless hardships, he was eventually rescued by a rich friend in Aleppo, who paid his ransom, and gave him his daughter in marriage. But Sa'dī, unable to live with his quarrelsome wife, set out on fresh travels, first to North Africa and then through the length and breadth of Asia Minor and the adjoining countries. Not until he had passed his 70th year did he return to Shiraz (about 1256; A.H. 653). Finding the place of his birth tranquil and prosperous under the wise rule of Abūbakr b. Sa'd, the son of his old patron (1226–1260; A.H. 623–658), the aged poet took up his permanent abode, interrupted only by repeated pilgrimages to Mecca, and devoted the remainder of his life to Ṣūfic contemplation and poetical composition. He died at Shiraz in 1292 (A.H. 691) according to Hamdallāh Mustaufī (who wrote only 40 years later), or in Dec. 1291 (A.H. 690), at the age of 110 lunar years.

His *Būstān* or "Fruit garden" (1257) and *Gulistān* or "Rosegarden" (1258), both dedicated to the reigning atābeg Abū Bekr, acquired great popularity in both the east and the west, owing to their easy, varied style and their happy *bons mots*. But Sa'dī's *Dīwān*, or collection of lyrical poetry, far surpasses the *Būstān* and *Gulistān*, at any rate in quantity, and perhaps in quality. Minor works are the Arabic *qaṣīdas*, the first of which laments the destruction of the Arabian caliphate by the Mongols in 1258 (A.H. 656); the Persian *qaṣīdas*, partly panegyrical, partly didactical; the *marāthī*, or elegies, beginning with one on the death of Abū Bekr and ending with one on the defeat and demise of the last caliph, Mosta'sim; the *mulamma'āt*, or poems with alternate Persian and Arabic verses of a rather artificial character; the *tarjī'āt*, or refrain-poems; the *ghazals*, or odes; the *ṣāhibiyyah* and *muḳaṭṭa'āt*, or moral aphorisms and epigrams; the *rubā'iyyāt*, or quatrains; and the *mufradāt*, or distichs. Sa'dī's lyrical poems possess neither the easy grace and melodious charm of Hāfiz's songs nor the overpowering grandeur of Jelālud-dīn Rūmī's divine hymns, but they are nevertheless full of deep pathos and show a fearless love of truth.

The first who collected and arranged his works was 'Alī b. Ahmad b. Bīsutūn (1326–1334; A.H. 726–734). The most exact information about Sa'dī's life and works is found in the introduction to W. Bacher's *Sa'dī's Aphorismen und Sinngedichte (Ṣāhibiyyah)* (Strassburg, 1879; a complete metrical translation of the epigrammatic poems), and in the same author's "Sa'dī Studien," in *Zeitschrift der morgenländischen Gesellschaft*, xxx, pp. 81–106; *see also* H. Ethé in W. Geiger's *Grundriss der iranischen Philologie*, ii, pp. 292–296, with full bibliography; and E. G. Browne, *Literary History of Persia*, pp. 525–539. Sa'dī's *Kulliyyāt* or complete works have been edited by Harrington (Calcutta, 1791–1795) with an English translation of some of the prose treatises and of Daulat Shah's notice on the poet, of which a German version is found in Graf's *Rosengarten* (Leipzig, 1846 p. 229 ff.); for the numerous lithographed editions, *see* Rieu's *Pers. Cat. of the Brit. Mus.* ii, p. 596. The *Būstān* has been printed in Calcutta (1810 and 1828), as well as in Lahore, Cawnpore, Tabriz, etc., a critical edition with Persian commentary was published by K. H. Graf at Vienna in 1850 (German metrical translations by the same, Jena 1850, and by Schlechta-Wssehrd, Vienna, 1852); English prose translations by H. W. Clarke (1879); and Ziauddin Gulam Moheiddin (Bombay, 1889); verse by G. S. Davie (1882); French translation by Barbier de Meynard (1880). The best editions of the *Gulistān* are by A. Sprenger (Calcutta, 1851) and by Platts (London, 1874); the best translations into English by Eastwick (1852) and by Platts (1873), the first four *bābs* in prose and verse by Sir Edwin Arnold (1899); into French by Defrémery (1858); into German by Graf (1846); *see also* S. Robinson's *Persian Poetry for English Readers* (1883), pp. 245–366.

SADIYA, the extreme northeast frontier station of British India, headquarters of the Sadiya Frontier Tract of Assam. Pop. (1941) 2,056. It stands high on a grassy plain, nearly surrounded by forest-clad mountains, on the right bank of what is locally (but erroneously) considered the main stream of the Brahmaputra. A railway on the opposite bank connects with the Assam-Bengal line. There is a bazaar, to which the hillmen beyond the frontier—Mishmis, Abors and Khamtis—bring down rubber, wax, ivory and musk, to barter for cotton cloth and salt.

The Sadiya Frontier Tract covers an area of 35,307 sq.mi. extending to Tibet on the north and east and to Burma on the south and southeast, but only 3,309 sq.mi. are under regular administration.

SADLER, MICHAEL THOMAS (1780–1835), English social reformer and economist was born at Snelston, Derbyshire, on Jan. 3, 1780. Entering business in Leeds in 1800, he took an active part in politics, devoting himself particularly to the administration of the poor law. In 1829 he was elected M.P. for Newark and thenceforward, until he was deprived of his seat, he was the leader of factory reform in parliament. He died in Belfast July 29, 1835.

SADLER (or **SADLEIR**), **SIR RALPH** (1507–1587), English statesman, the son of Henry Sadler, steward of the manor of Cilney, near Great Hadham, Hertfordshire, was born at Hackney, Middlesex, in 1507. While a child he was placed in the family of Thomas Cromwell, afterward earl of Essex, whose secretary he eventually became. Sadler held many positions under Henry VIII, but he is best known for his employment under Elizabeth I in connection with the affair of Mary, Queen of Scots. Elizabeth sent him (1559) to Scotland, ostensibly to settle the border disputes, but in reality to secure a union with the Protestant party there, and he helped to arrange the treaty of Leith, July 6, 1560.

In 1568 Sadler was appointed chancellor of the duchy of Lancaster, and in the same year was one of the English commis-

sioners employed in treating on the matters arising from the flight of the Queen of Scots. From this time he seems to have been continually engaged as a discreet and trusty servant in connection with Mary's captivity, and was frequently sent with messages to her. On Aug. 25, 1584, when, owing to the imputations made by his countess, George 6th earl of Shrewsbury resigned his guardianship of the queen, Sadler succeeded him. In September Mary was removed from Sheffield to Wingfield and early in 1585 to Tutbury.

In April, Sadler, after numerous petitions on his part, was permitted to resign his distasteful charge. On March 30, 1587, Sadler died at Standon, and was buried there. His letters on Scottish affairs are most interesting.

BIBLIOGRAPHY.—*Letters and Negotiations of Sir Ralph Sadler* (Edinburgh, 1720); *The State Papers and Letters of Sir R. Sadler*, ed. by Arthur Clifford, with a memoir by Sir Walter Scott, 3 vol. (Edinburgh, 1809).

SADO, a Japanese island in the Niigata prefecture, lying 32 mi. W. of Niigata (*q.v.*), in 38° N., 138° 30′ E. It has a circumference of 130 mi., an area of 331 sq.mi. and a population (1950) of 125,597. The port is Ebisa, on the east coast; and at a distance of 16½ mi., near the west coast, is the town of Aikawa, having in its vicinity gold and silver mines, for which Sado is famous.

SADOWA, a village of Bohemia, 4 mi. N.W. of Königgrätz. Sadowa, with the small adjoining wood, was one of the principal Prussian positions in the decisive battle of July 3, 1866, now usually called Königgrätz (*see* SEVEN WEEKS' WAR).

SAFED KOH, in many respects the most remarkable range of mountains on the northwest frontier of India, extending like a 14,000 ft. wall, straight and rigid, towering above all surrounding hills, from the mass of mountains which overlook Kabul on the southeast to the frontiers of India, and preserving a strike which —being more or less perpendicular to the border line—is in strange contrast to the usual frontier conformation. The highest peak, Sikaram, is 15,600 ft. above sea level, and yet it is not a conspicuous point on this unusually straight-backed range. Geographically the Safed Koh is not an isolated range, for there is no break in the continuity of water divide which connects it with the great Shandur offshoot of the Hindu Kush except the narrow trough of the Kabul river, which cuts a deep waterway across where it makes its way from Dakka into the Peshawar plains.

The same name is often used for the mountain range north of the Hari Rud river in its upper course.

SAFES, STRONG ROOMS AND VAULTS. Although boxes provided with locks or coffers must have followed closely on the development of locks (*q.v.*) and been in use in ancient Egypt, no examples remain of earlier date than the middle ages. The earliest examples extant were constructed of hard wood banded with hammered iron, and subsequent development took place rather on artistic than on practical lines up to the time of the introduction of boxes entirely of iron. On the continent of Europe the iron box was developed to a very high standard of artistic beauty and craftsmanship, but with no real increase of security. Several specimens of these coffers supposed to be of 17th-century workmanship are preserved in the museum at Marlborough house.

Milner's Work.—Up to that time no attempt had been made to make coffers fireproof, for though a patent for fireproofing had been taken out in 1801 by Richard Scott, it does not appear to have been used. In 1834, however, a patent was obtained by William Marr for the application of nonconducting linings, followed about four years later by a similar patent in the name of Charles Chubb. The foundation, however, of the modern safe industry was laid by Thomas Milner, originally a tinsmith of Sheffield, who after a few years' business in Manchester established, in 1830, works at Liverpool for the manufacture of tin-plate and sheet iron boxes and who later made plate iron chests or coffers and, probably the earliest, safes about the year 1846.

Chatwood's Patent, 1860.—Concurrently with the increase of strength in safes and probably with the increased value of articles preserved in safes, the skill of the professional thief had also increased, and this went on for some years until the Cornhill burglary of 1865 called general attention to the question. In 1860 a patent was taken out by Samuel Chatwood for a safe constructed of an outer and inner body with the intervening space filled with ferro-manganese or spiegeleisen in a molten state, the total thickness being 2 in.

It is about this period (1860–1870), perhaps the most important in the history of safes, that the opening of safes by wedges seems to have become prominent. The effect of wedges was to bend out the side of the safe sufficiently to allow of the insertion of a crowbar between the body and the edge of the door, and various devices were adopted by different makers with the object of resisting this mode of attack.

To prevent safes from being opened by the drilling of one or two small holes in such positions as to destroy the security of the lock itself, advantage was taken of the improvements in the manufacture of high carbon steel, and even in what is to-day called the "fire-proof" safe a plate of steel which offers considerable resistance to drilling is placed between the outer door plate and the lock.

About 1888 the "solid" safe was introduced. In this the top, bottom and two sides of the safe, together with the flanges at the back only or at both back and front, are bent from a single steel plate. This construction, with solid corners, only became practicable in consequence of the great improvements which had been made in the quality of steel plates.

The Modern Safe.—The requirements of a modern safe may be briefly summarized as follows:

For fire resisting safes, the safe body must be constructed of steel plate of sufficient thickness, this varying with the dimensions of the safe, to withstand the effect of a fall from an upper floor in the event of a fire and to resist the crushing effect of falling masonry, displaced girders, etc., as safes are frequently buried by falling debris in the ruins of office buildings. The crucial test of the fire resisting capacity of a safe is fully applied under these conditions, *i.e.*, when buried under a red hot mass of ruins, often for a period of several days, before it can be dug out and removed from the collapsed building. The "proofing" of the safe must be of sufficient quantity, packed around the whole area of the body and door to preserve the heat resistance over a long period, otherwise when this reserve is exhausted the safe would become a slow oven and its contents charred and completely destroyed.

Safes which are intended to resist burglars, as well as fire, must be made with greater constructional strength successfully to resist brute force and destructive violence. In addition, they need to be formed from such a combination of metals and alloys as will withstand all forms of cutting and piercing tools and appliances, in addition to the oxy-acetylene cutting blowpipe. This appliance, which is now in wide industrial use, will cut through practically all known steels, so that modern safe makers have had to resort to the metallurgist for the production of ferrous alloys which possess the power to resist the cutting effect of the gas flame, and are impervious to all drilling methods. The more successful of these alloys, although they can be heated by the gas flame to their melting point, cannot be cut, like steel, by the application of a stream of pure oxygen when their melting temperature has been reached.

It is essential that the walls and doors of such safes should be of considerable thickness, as mass is of great importance in providing resistance to the blow-pipe method of attack. The doors of such safes must be closely and accurately fitted to the opening in the safe body and secured in the closed position by a number of suitable moving bolts operated by an external handle. The actual shape of the bolts is not of vital importance, provided they are of sufficient strength and rigidity to resist all forces that can be brought to bear against them in an effort to force the door away from the safe body. The majority of safe manufacturers use bolts formed from either round or flat section steel bars, but others are of special shape and design.

In America, fire-resisting safes usually are not made burglarproof; the highest standard of requirement being 20 minutes' protection against amateur attack through the door. Burglarproof alloy steel chests are however frequently fitted into fire-

resisting safes. Most important are the locks used to control its operation. To provide the maximum amount of security and lengthen the period of resistance that a safe will offer to forcible entry, more than one lock should be employed and the locks need to be made as large as possible to increase the amount of material which has to be removed to expose the lock. It is also advisable to provide the lock with more than one moving bolt to engage with the bolting mechanism, as it is this moving lock bolt which prevents the bolt action being operated and the bolts retracted into the door.

When gunpowder was the only explosive available, it was possible to construct safe locks to resist its use, but with present day high power explosives other methods must be employed. In good quality safes these take the form of independent bolting actions which are brought into active operation only by the actual force of an explosive, when used to destroy the working lock; the effect of such an explosion being to substitute the dogging action of the special device for that of the lock which it was sought to destroy. To prevent the insertion of explosives in the keyholes it is the practice with work intended for bankers' use to provide a shutter, either in the form of a rotating disc or a sliding bar built into the door, to close the entrance to the locks after the keys have been used, the shutter action being in turn locked by a dial on the face of the door. In some instances, keyless combination locks only are used to control the bolting mechanism, but these locks are not in general use or favour in Great Britain, although their use is practically universal in the United States.

Time locks with two, three or four chronometer movements are frequently employed to control the hours for opening safes and vault doors. These locks are fitted in addition to either the key or dial operated locks, and are intended to prevent the door being opened at any other than the official times.

Strong-rooms and Vaults.—For the purpose of providing security for deeds, papers and books against the risk of fire, rooms are built either of brick or concrete, according to the conditions existing on the site and the amount to be expended on the construction, the thickness of the walls varying from 14 inches to 18 inches if built in brick, and from 8 to 14 inches in concrete. Bank vaults and strong-rooms for the custody of securities, cash, etc., are now mainly constructed of reinforced concrete or with a combination of brick and concrete, the thickness of the walls varying with their importance and the ground space available. Generally speaking, reinforced concrete walls can be built of less thickness than brickwork to provide equivalent security against penetration, but in all important vaults and strong-rooms it is advisable to reinforce the walls, roof and floor with linings of steel and flame resisting alloy, forming a self-contained safe inside the concrete shell.

The most effective method of employing steel to reinforce the concrete construction is to use it in the form of plates attached to the inner face of the walls by rag bolts or other suitable connections. The steel then has the protection of the full thickness of the concrete and itself prevents the breaking away of the inner face of the concrete in large sections into the void forming the strong-room, whereas if the steel reinforcement is distributed throughout the concrete walling in the form of bars or mesh work, it can be quickly and easily cut through with the blow-pipe.

In the design of strong-rooms and vaults, the formation of the roof and floor is frequently of more importance than that of the walls, the latter are usually subject to inspection (unless the room is built against an exterior or party wall, which should be avoided if possible), whereas the floor is liable to attack by means of tunnelling which can be carried out without any indication being given until the actual breaking through of the floor of the room. The highest degree of security is obtained when the vault is built as an island with an inspection or patrol passage entirely surrounding it, the floor of the vault being laid on sleeper walls providing for full visibility below the floor level, with suitable lamps and switches for illumination.

Electrical devices are frequently installed to give an alarm in the event of a burglarious attempt upon strong-rooms, either

BY COURTESY OF (1, 3, 5, 9) HOBBS, HART AND COMPANY, LTD., (2, 4, 6, 8) THE MOSLER SAFE COMPANY, (7, 10) THE NATIONAL CITY BANK OF NEW YORK

VARIOUS TYPES OF SAFES, STRONG ROOMS AND VAULTS

1. Closed vault door, English type. Only one combination lock used in this type of door

2. A strong room with the cash or security vault door open, showing complicated mechanism that operates bolts

3. English type of strong room door standing open. Seven large bolts seen in front

4. A circular vault door used almost exclusively for safety deposit vaults. It has two combination locks and one four-movement time lock

5. English type door to vault or strong room. Equipped with four separate combination locks (each combination is known to but one man, thus four men are needed to open this type of door)

6. Safety deposit vault of a large bank, showing thousands of small safe deposit boxes that are rented by the year

7. Barred entrance to a safety deposit vault. Customer must first gain entrance through outer gate before entering vault

8. Steel filing safe equipped with safe-deposit boxes, an armoured steel chest with steel circular door, and filing units. Designed especially for hotels, clubs, lodges, etc.

9. A complete burglar's outfit for opening safes and strong rooms from a photograph taken by the British police after the set had been abandoned by the foiled owners. Acetylene gas containers, hose, torch, bits, drills, levers, chisels and other instruments are shown

10. Safe deposit boxes of the larger types in a vault. Such types are used largely by bond, brokerage and insurance companies

upon the main structure or the door. In no case should they be regarded as a primary means of defense, for they may be put out of action through failure of an essential feature or neglect of maintenance and inspection duties.

A new type of bank vault that is said to be virtually immune to burglar attack through the use of copper in construction has been recently announced by the Copper and Brass Research association in the U.S. It is said that a burglar would require about six hours of uninterrupted effort with the oxy-acetylene torch to penetrate a modern vault door 20 in. thick, containing a 12 in. plate of pure copper. The high resistance of copper to torch attack is explained by the fact that this metal is a rapid conductor of heat, in contrast with other metals of low heat conductivity heretofore used in vault construction. A torch capable of developing a heat between 5,000° F. and 6,000° F. will penetrate the first few inches of a copper plate in a comparatively short time. However, the flame loses its efficiency as the copper conducts the heat rapidly away before the entire body of the metal can be raised to a fusing point, and the torch becomes ineffective.

The ductility of the metal makes it unsuited for successful attack with explosives.

SAFETY GLASS: *see* GLASS, SAFETY.

SAFETY LAMP. Toward the end of the 18th century mine explosions became increasingly common, and efforts were made to devise means of lighting which would be safe in the presence of gas. The explosive nature of a cloud of fine coal dust was not then recognized, and explosions were attributed wholly to gas. The explosions usually originated at the flame of a tallow candle. W. Reid Clanny invented a form of lamp in 1813 in which the external air was blown by bellows through a small cistern of water and the products of combustion forced through a similar water seal. George Stephenson, who was experimenting with lamps for underground use in 1815, concluded that "if a lamp could be made to contain the burnt air above the flame, and permit the firedamp to come in below in small quantity to be burnt as it came in, the burnt air would prevent the passing of the explosion upwards and the velocity of the current from below would also prevent its passing downwards." Though neither type of lamp was satisfactory, some of Clanny and Stephenson's ideas were incorporated in the Davy lamp as the latter was developed and improved. In Aug. 1815, the Sunderland Society of the Prevention of Accidents in Mines interested Sir Humphry Davy in the problem of mine explosion, and by the end of that year the first Davy lamp (*q.v.*) was ready for testing. It had a qualified success, but improvements were rapidly made to the original design and the type was accepted in all coal fields.

Great Britain.—In any mine comprised within the Coal Mines act of 1911, no lamp or light other than a locked safety lamp may be used in any seam in which the air current in the return airway from any ventilating district is normally found to contain more than 0.5% of inflammable gas; and wherever safety lamps are required by the act or by regulations under that act the type must be approved by the secretary of state. The safety lamps in use in the coal mines of Great Britain can be divided into two broad classes; viz., flame safety lamps and electric safety lamps. Flame safety lamps must be provided with double gauzes or some arrangement serving the same purpose.

Gauzes must be rigid in construction and made from suitable material. In lamps fitted with a metal chimney and only one gauze protecting the air outlets, the gauze must be made of wire of not less than 28 standard wire gauge with 28 meshes to the linear inch. In lamps provided with two gauzes, one or both of the gauzes may be made of wire of 26 or 27 standard wire gauge with 20 meshes to the linear inch. The lamp must be so constructed that the parts cannot be put together without the gauze; and it must be provided with an efficient locking device. Lamp glasses must be made of heat-resisting glass capable of withstanding sudden cooling from 212° F. to 60° F. In an electric lamp no liquid must be able to escape from the battery when it is turned upside down. The switch and other contacts must be in flame-tight enclosures. There are two types of electric lamp, the hand lamp and the cap lamp (in which the bulb and reflector are carried on the wearer's head and the battery strapped to his body).

The flame safety lamp serves moreover to ascertain the presence of inflammable gas, for when it is placed in an atmosphere containing firedamp the flame elongates, and if the gas is present in considerable quantity the lamp is filled with blue flame. For testing the presence of gas the flame of the lamp is lowered until the yellow part is at a minimum, when the gas will be discernible as a small blue cap to the flame. The size of cap and the percentage of gas present in the air have been correlated, and as little as 1.5% of firedamp in the air current can be detected.

The detector used with an electrical motor must be of the automatic type which gives visible warning of the presence of a gas-air mixture without manual manipulation. In other places the ordinary flame safety lamp suffices.

In addition to portable lamps, fixed lighting can be used on main roads or defined traffic centres. (J. A. S. R.)

United States.—The flame safety lamp, except for a few cases, had become by mid-20th century primarily a gas testing instrument and was not depended upon for illumination. U.S. usage, based on federal and state laws, recommended that a minimum of two flame safety lamps in good operating condition be available at all mines for testing the presence of methane or oxygen deficiency. U.S. specifications required that each lamp be equipped with double steel or brass gauzes constructed of wire between 29 and 27 American wire gauge (0.0113 to 0.014 in. in diameter), with mesh openings from 28 to 30 per lineal inch. There should be a shield or bonnet so constructed as to prevent injury to the gauzes and shield the gauzes from strong air currents. Lamp locks should be of the magnetic type and the relighting device simple and safe to use in the presence of explosive gas.

Portable electric lamps in the U.S. are chiefly the cap variety using either a caustic or acid electrolite solution. In addition, the permissible flashlight, a hand-held dry cell battery type, was tested and found safe to use under specified conditions.

Methane detectors, electrically operated, are used for special surveys or checks of return air courses, and methane alarms may be used under dangerous fluctuating conditions.

SAFETY RAZOR: *see* RAZOR.

SAFETY VALVE is a valve which lifts at a predetermined pressure and prevents the accumulation of a dangerous pressure in a steam boiler. The resistance to pressure is provided by a weight or by springs, the use of the latter being obligatory if the boiler is not a stationary one. The lever valve (*see* drawing) is loaded with a weight at the end, to keep the valve shut. A casing

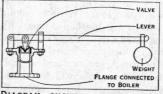

DIAGRAM SHOWING WORKING OF SAFETY VALVE ON STEAM BOILER

with lock may be fitted over to prevent tampering by an unauthorized person. Many boilers carry two safety valves as a precaution, one being locked up. Marine boiler valves are of the direct spring-loaded type, the spring encircling the valve spindle. The pop valve blows off sharply with a pop, and is used for yacht and launch boilers. The valve closes again quickly when the pressure has been slightly reduced.

SAFFARIDS, a Persian dynasty of the 9th century, founded about 866 by Yakub ibn Laith al-Saffar ("the coppersmith"), who gained the command of a body of local troops and took control of his native province of Seistan. He soon added Herat, Fars, Balkh and Tabaristan to his possessions, overthrew the Tahirid governors of Khurasan, and, though still nominally dependent on the caliphs of Baghdad, established a dynasty in Seistan (*see* CALIPHATE: *The Abbasid Caliphs;* and PERSIA: *History*). In 900 Yakub's successor was defeated by the Samanids (*q.v.*), and few of the later Saffarids had any wide authority.

See T. Nöldeke, *Sketches from Eastern History,* tr. by J. S. Black (London, 1892).

SAFFI: *see* SAFI.

SAFFLOWER or BASTARD SAFFRON (*Carthamus tinctorius*), a plant of the family Compositae; its flowers form the basis of the safflower dye of commerce. The plant is a native of the East Indies, but is cultivated in Egypt and to some extent in southern Europe. To obtain the dyeing principle (carthamin, $C_{14}H_{14}O_7$) the flowers are first washed to free them from a soluble yellow colouring matter they contain; they are then dried and powdered, and digested in an alkaline solution in which pieces of clean white cotton are immersed. The alkaline solution having been neutralized with weak acetic acid, the cotton is removed and washed in another alkaline solution. When this second solution is neutralized with acid, carthamin in a pure condition is precipitated as a dark red powder. It forms a brilliant but fugitive scarlet dye for silk, but its principal use is in the preparation of toilet rouge, for which it is mixed with powdered talc.

SAFFRON, a product manufactured from the dried stigmas and part of the style of the saffron crocus, a cultivated form of *Crocus sativus;* some of the wild forms are also employed. The purple flower, which blooms late in autumn, is very similar to that of the common spring crocus, and the stigmas, which protrude from the perianth, are of a characteristic orange-red colour; the fruit is rarely formed. The Egyptians, though acquainted with the bastard safflower (*Carthamus tinctorius*), often used to adulterate saffron, do not seem to have possessed the true saffron; but it is named in Canticles iv, 14 among other sweet-smelling herbs. It is also mentioned by Homer and Hippocrates.

Saffron has long been cultivated in Iran and Kashmir, and is supposed to have been introduced into China by the Mongol invasion. It is mentioned in the Chinese materia medica (*Pun tsaou,* 1552–78). The chief seat of cultivation in early times, however, was the town of Corycus (modern Korghoz) in Cilicia. According to Hehn, the town derived its name from the crocus; Reymond, on the other hand, with more probability, held that the name of the drug arose from that of the town. It was cultivated by the Arabs in Spain about 961, and is mentioned in an English leechbook of the 10th century, but seems to have disappeared from western Europe until reintroduced by the crusaders. According to Hakluyt, it was brought into England from Tripoli by a pilgrim, who hid a stolen corm in the hollow of his staff. It was especially cultivated near Histon in Cambridgeshire and in Essex at Saffron Walden, its cultivators being called "crokers."

Saffron was used as an ingredient in many of the complicated medicines of early times; that it was very largely used in cookery is evidenced by many writers; the Chinese used to employ it largely, and the Iranians and Spaniards still mix it with their rice. As a perfume it was strewn in Greek halls, courts and theatres, and in the Roman baths. The streets of Rome were sprinkled with saffron when Nero made his entry into the city.

It was, however, mainly used as a dye. It was a royal colour in early Greek times, though afterward, perhaps from its abundant use in the baths and as a scented salve, it was especially appropriated by the hetairae. Saffron is chiefly cultivated in Spain, France, Sicily, on the lower spurs of the Apennines and in Iran and Kashmir. It occurs in the form of *cake saffron,* which consists of the stigmas and part of the style which have been "sweated" and pressed together into a cake, and also as *hay saffron,* which consists of the dried stigmas alone.

SAFFRON WALDEN, a market town and municipal borough in the Saffron Walden parliamentary division of Essex, Eng., 43½ mi. N.N.E. from London by the Eastern Region railway. Pop. (1951) 6,825. Area, 11.7 sq.mi. Of the old castle, dating probably from the 12th century, the keep and a few other portions still remain. Near it is a series of curious circular excavations in the chalk, called the Maze, of unknown date or purpose. The earthworks west and south of the town are of great extent; a large Saxon burial ground was there. The church of St. Mary the Virgin contains the tomb of Lord Audley, chancellor to Henry VIII. The town has a museum with good archaeological and natural history collections. In the neighbourhood is the fine mansion of Audley End, built by Thomas, 1st earl of Suffolk, in 1603 on the ruins of the abbey, converted in 1190 from a Benedictine priory founded by Goeffrey de Mandeville in 1136.

Saffron Walden (*Waledana*) was almost certainly fortified by the Britons, and probably by some earlier people. The town corporation grew out of the Guild of the Holy Trinity, which was incorporated under Henry VIII, the lord of the town, in 1514. It was dissolved under Edward VI, and a charter was obtained appointing a treasurer and chamberlain and 24 assistants, who, with the commonalty, formed the corporation. In 1694 William and Mary made Walden a free borough. The culture of saffron was the most characteristic industry at Walden from the reign of Edward III until its gradual extinction about 1768. Carnation growing is now important.

SAFFRON WOOD or Saffronhout (*Elaeodendron croceum*), a South African tree belonging to the staff-tree family (Celastraceae) and yielding valuable timber. The genus *Elaeo-*dendron contains about 30 species, confined to the tropics and subtropics.

SAFI or Asfi, a seaport on the west coast of Morocco, in 32° 20′ N., 9° 12′ W., 106 mi. W.N.W. of Marrakesh. The old town, built on the rapid slope of a plateau toward the sea, is surrounded by crenellated ramparts dominated by an old Portuguese citadel, the Kechla. Safi is the chief town of the *contrôle civil* of Adba-Ahmar and the nearest port to Marrakesh. Trade reached 102,000,000 fr. in 1938 (imports 25,000,000, exports 77,000,000).

The population was (1936) 25,159, including 23,328 natives and 1,831 Europeans; (1944) 35,574, including 32,710 natives and 2,864 Europeans; (1947) 50,800.

In the early 1940s Safi became the second port of Morocco. The port was deepened, permitting eight ocean steamers to dock at one time. A rail line was built to the port from the Kowibgha phosphate deposits, which became the most important item of export.

The town was the site of one of the U.S. landings on Nov. 8, 1942, and for many months of the North African campaign was an important port for the landing of war supplies.

SAGA. The word saga is used in Icelandic for any kind of narrative, written or oral, whether anecdote, story or history. But in English, as in other languages in which it has been borrowed, this word has a narrower sense and is applied to biographies written in Iceland, or occasionally in Norway, during the middle ages. The sagas are thus a branch of literature distinct from annals and summaries of history, many of which were also written in Iceland during the 12th and 13th centuries. Several classes of sagas are distinguished.

Kings' sagas are the oldest class. The heroes described in them were rulers of Norway and of dependencies of Norway who lived between the 9th and 13th centuries. The oldest of the kings' sagas now known is the so-called *First Saga of St. Olaf,* which is a life of St. Olaf, king of Norway (d. 1030), and was written about 1180. It survives only in fragments, but these are sufficient to show its form and style. In form it closely resembled the popular lives of European saints, many of which had been translated into Icelandic in the 12th century. The style was halting and unpractised. The sources were, for the most part, oral. They consisted partly of popular tales about miracles worked through Olaf's agency and partly of verses composed in honour of Olaf during his lifetime and handed down orally. In these verses the battles and great achievements of Olaf were commemorated and they provided an outline of his career, giving the saga its chief value as history. This *First Saga* was used as a source, directly or indirectly, by authors who wrote later lives of Olaf. The most important of these later lives was written by Snorri Sturluson (1179–1241), who incorporated it in his *Heimskringla* (Orb of the World), which is a collection of biographies of rulers of Norway from the 9th century to the 12th.

Sagas of several other Norse rulers were written late in the 12th century and early in the 13th. They included sagas about Olaf Tryggvason (d. 1000), about Haakon the Good (d. *c.* 963), and about the earls of the Orkney Islands. The *Morkinskinna* (Rotten Skin) was written about 1220 and contains detailed sagas about kings who ruled Norway after the death of St. Olaf.

During the 13th and 14th centuries these early kings' sagas were often revised and combined with other works. The greatest of these compilations is the *Book of Flatey,* a magnificent manuscript written about 1390, which contains lives of the Norse kings combined with those of Icelandic heroes.

Icelanders' Sagas.—The terms "Icelanders' sagas" (Icelandic: *Íslendinga sögur*) and "family sagas" are applied to biographies of heroes who are supposed to have lived in Iceland in the 10th and 11th centuries. Many of these heroes had visited the British Isles and lands as distant as Greece and Russia; some had emigrated to Greenland and others were said to have landed on Wineland the Good, as the Icelanders called the American continent.

The oldest of the Icelanders' sagas were written in the first years of the 13th century and were strongly influenced by the kings' sagas in structure, style and material. The sources were many and varied, and included summaries of history and genealogies written in Iceland early in the 12th century, popular tales and poems preserved orally.

The value of Icelanders' sagas as history is difficult to assess. For a time they were accepted as trustworthy records, but it became widely agreed that they are, in the first place, works of art based upon historical and pseudohistorical sources. Such questions cannot, however, be discussed in general terms, for the aims and sources of the author of every saga must be considered separately.

Among the oldest of the Icelanders' sagas may be mentioned the *Fóstbrœðra Saga* (Saga of the Foster-brothers), a great part of which is placed in the wastes of Greenland. *Hallfreðar Saga* (Saga of Hallfred) is the tale of the favourite poet of King Olaf Tryggvason. The *Kormáks Saga* (Saga of Kormák) and the *Bjarnar Saga Hítdœlakappa* (Saga of Björn) are early love stories.

These early Icelanders' sagas are somewhat primitive, but the art of saga writing developed rapidly during the 13th century, reaching its zenith soon after the middle of that century. The most perfect saga of this class in structure is the *Laxdœla Saga* (Saga of the Men of Laxárdal), a story in which women, love and romance play an unusually great part. The *Gísla Saga* (Saga of Gísli) belongs to the same period and is the story of an upright man, outlawed and unjustly persecuted. The *Grettis Saga* (Saga of Grettir the Strong), written rather later, is also an adventurous story of outlawry. Undoubtedly, the greatest of all sagas is the *Njáls Saga* (Saga of Burnt Njáll), written toward the end of the 13th century. There is no more moving tragedy in early Germanic literature and it is among the greatest prose narratives of the world.

Few of the Icelanders' sagas can be assigned to authors whose names are known. An exception is the *Egils Saga* (Saga of Egill), the story of the viking poet of the 10th century. It has lately been shown that this saga was probably written by Snorri Sturluson.

Bishops' Sagas.—At the beginning of the 13th century several sagas were written about bishops of the two Icelandic sees, Skálaholt and Hólar. These included sagas about Thorlák (d. 1193) and Páll (d. 1211), bishops of Skálaholt, and about Jón, bishop of Hólar (d. 1121). Later bishops' sagas were those about Bishop Árni of Skálaholt (d. 1298) and Bishop Laurentius of Hólar (d. 1331).

Sagas of Later Times.—Numerous sagas were written about lay chieftains who lived in Iceland during the 12th and 13th centuries. Most of these were combined at the end of the 13th century in the *Sturlunga Saga* (Saga of the Sturlungar). The largest section of this compilation is the *Íslendinga Saga* (Saga of the Icelanders), a history of the Icelanders beginning with the year 1183 and covering a great part of the 13th century. The author of the *Íslendinga Saga* was Sturla Thórdarson (1214–84), nephew of Snorri Sturluson.

Heroic Sagas.—The term "Heroic sagas" (Icelandic: *Fornaldar sögur*) is applied to sagas about heroes of Scandinavia and continental Germania who lived before Iceland was peopled. The *Ynglinga Saga* (Saga of the Ynglingar) contains legends of the early kings of the Swedes and was written by Snorri Sturluson as an introduction to the *Heimskringla*. The *Skjöldunga Saga* (Saga of the Skjöldungar) was also written early in the 13th century and contained legendary tales about kings of the Danes.

Most sagas of this class date from the late 13th and 14th centuries. Their sources were often ancient heroic poems, such as those preserved in the *Poetic Edda* (see EDDA). One of the best known is the *Völsunga Saga* (Saga of the Völsungs), which contains a prose version of the legends of Sigurd and Brunhild. The *Hrólfs Saga* (Saga of Hrólf Kraka) is also based partly on heroic poetry, and contains interesting legends about the Danes. The *Heiðreks Saga* (Saga of Heiðrek) consists of numerous stories of devious origin, some of them about battles between Goths and Huns in the dark ages. Fantastic as they are, some of these heroic sagas preserve memories of historical events which would otherwise have been forgotten.

Romantic Sagas.—These are prose narratives based upon foreign romances. Many of them were written in Norway under the patronage of King Haakon Haakonarson (1217–63). They were later transcribed in Iceland and revised. They gained wide popularity and gave rise to original compositions in similar style. One of the best known, and perhaps the oldest, of the romantic sagas is the *Tristrams Saga* (Saga of Tristram), written in Norway in 1226, and based upon a French poem of the 12th century.

The *Karlamagnús Saga* (Saga of Charles the Great) contains prose versions of a number of French poems about Charles and his champions, including the *Chanson de Roland* (Song of Roland). Most of the romantic sagas are post-classical, dating from the 14th and later centuries.

(See ICELANDIC LITERATURE.)

BIBLIOGRAPHY.—H. Koht, *The Old Norse Sagas* (1931); B. S. (Phillpotts) Newall, *Edda and Saga* (London, 1931); M. Schlauch, *Romance in Iceland* (London, 1934); G. Turville-Petre, *Origins of Icelandic Literature* (Oxford, 1953).   (G. T.-P.)

SAGAING, a district and division of Burma, lying to the west of Mandalay on both sides of the Irrawaddy. The district has an area of 1,878 sq.mi.; pop. (1941) 387,270, showing an increase of 51,305 in the decade. The chief crops are sesame, millet, rice, peas, wheat and cotton. It lies in the heart of the dry belt, and the rainfall ranges from about 25 to 35 in. In the hot season the maximum shade temperature rises to a little more than 100° F. The lowest readings in the cold season average about 56° F.

Sagaing, the headquarters town, is opposite Ava, a few miles below Mandalay; pop. (1931) 14,127. It was formerly a capital of Burma. The Ava bridge (3,940 ft.), completed in 1934, with its western end at Sagaing, carries the Mandalay-Myitkyina railway and also road traffic. The steamers of the Irrawaddy Flotilla company call daily.

The Sagaing division includes the districts of Upper and Lower Chindwin, Shwebo, Sagaing, Katha, Bhamo, Myitkyina and Naga Hills.

SAGALLO, a small settlement on the north shore of the Gulf of Tajura, French Somaliland. In Jan. 1889 Sagallo was occupied by a Cossack chief named Achinov, who was accompanied by about 200 people, and the archimandrite Païsi, who had been entrusted by the metropolitan of Novgorod with an evangelistic mission to the Abyssinian church; while Achinov stated that he had a commission from the Negus for the purchase of arms and ammunition.

The presence of Achinov at Sagallo was regarded by the French government as an invasion of French territorial rights. The Russian foreign office having disavowed (Feb. 7) any connection with Achinov, instructions were sent from Paris to secure the removal of the Cossacks. On Feb. 17 French warships appeared off the port, and after an ultimatum which had no effect the fort was bombarded, and seven persons killed. The Cossacks then surrendered and were deported to Suez, whence they returned to Russia. Achinov was interned by the Russian government until Oct. 1889. In 1891 he returned to Abyssinia. Païsi was promoted by his ecclesiastical superiors. In Paris the incident caused great excitement among the Russophils, and the consequent demonstrations led to the suppression of the League of Patriots and the prosecution of Paul Déroulède.

See Vicomte de Constantin, *L'Archimandrite Païsi et l'ataman Achinoff* (1891).

SAGAN (ZAGAN), formerly a town in Lower Silesia, Ger., and after 1945 in Zielona Gora province, western Poland, on the Bobr, or Bobrawa, river, a tributary of the Oder, 60 mi. S.S.E. of Frankfort-on-Oder and 102 mi. S.E. of Berlin by the direct main line of railway to Breslau. The population was 4,359 in 1946 and 23,341 in 1939.

The mediate principality of Sagan, forming a portion of the Prussian governmental district of Liegnitz, was formed in 1397 out of a portion of the duchy of Glogau. One of its most famous possessors was Wallenstein.

In modern times the town was still partly surrounded by its old fortifications and numerous mediaeval houses survived. The palace of the dukes of Sagan was built there. During World War II Sagan suffered extensive damage. Industries include cloth weaving and wool spinning.

SAGASTA, PRÁXEDES MATEO (1827–1903), Spanish statesman, born July 21, 1827, at Torrecilla de Cameros, in the province of Logroño. From the first he displayed Liberal inclinations. He entered the Cortes in 1854 as a Progressist deputy for Zamora. Exiled after O'Donnell's *coup d'état* (1856), he returned to sit in the Cortes 1859–63. Exiled again after conspiring with Prim and the Progressists against Isabella, he took part in the rising at Cadiz which culminated in the revolution of Sept. 1868, was minister several times under Serrano and then under King Amadeo, 1868–72. Sagasta headed the most conservative groups of the revolutionary politicians against Ruiz Zorrilla and against the Federal republic in 1873; and in 1874 he vainly attempted to crush the Carlists and to check the Alphonsist military conspiracy that overthrew Serrano (Dec. 1874). After the restoration of the Bourbons, Sagasta was premier in 1885–90 and again in 1892–95.

His attempt to conciliate both the Cubans and the United States by a tardy offer of colonial home rule, the recall of Weyler, and other concessions, did not avert the disastrous war with the United States, and his party was defeated (March, 1899). A trimmer *par excellence*, abler in opposition than in office, Sagasta returned with the Liberals to power in March 1901; in Dec. 1902 he was defeated on a vote of censure and resigned office, dying at Madrid on Jan. 15, 1903.

SAGE, MARGARET OLIVIA SLOCUM (1828–1918), American philanthropist, was born at Syracuse, N.Y., Sept. 8, 1828. She was educated at the Troy, N.Y., Female Seminary, afterwards known as the Emma Willard School. She married Russell Sage in 1869. Knowing her business ability and her interest in charity, her husband left her at his death over $64,000,-000 without restriction. In 1907 the Russell Sage Foundation was incorporated for the "improvement of social and living conditions of the United States of America." To it Mrs. Sage gave $10,000,-000. In 1912 Mrs. Sage bought Marsh island, off the coast of Louisiana, and later turned it over to the State as a permanent refuge for birds. She died in New York city Nov. 4, 1918. By her will she left $36,000,000 to be divided into 52 parts and distributed to various public institutions. It is estimated that during her life she made public gifts to the amount of $40,000,000.

SAGE, RUSSELL (1816–1906), American financier, was born in Oneida county (N.Y.), on Aug. 4, 1816. He had a part interest in 1837–39 in a retail grocery in Troy, and in a wholesale store there in 1839–57. He was an alderman of Troy in 1841–48 and treasurer of Rensselaer county in 1845–49. In 1853–57 he was a Whig representative in Congress. He became an associate of Jay Gould in the development and sale of railways; and in 1863 removed to New York city, where, besides speculating in railway stocks, he became a money-lender and a dealer in "puts" and "calls" and "privileges," and in 1874 bought a seat in the New York Stock Exchange. Sage died in New York on July 22, 1906. His wife, Margaret Olivia Slocum, inherited his fortune, and gave liberal benefactions to different institutions. *See* RUSSELL SAGE FOUNDATION; SAGE, MARGARET OLIVIA SLOCUM.

SAGE-BRUSH, the name given to various shrubby species of *Artemisia* (*q.v.*) native to plains and mountain slopes of western North America. The common sage-brush (*A. tridentata*) is a much-branched shrub, usually 3 ft. to 6 ft., but sometimes 12 ft. high, with silvery-grey, bitter-aromatic foliage, the small, wedge-shaped leaves mostly with three teeth at the outer end. This shrub is very abundant on semi-arid plains, mainly between 1,500 ft. and 6,000 ft. altitude, where it is often a conspicuous and characteristic feature of the vegetation. It occurs from Montana and western Nebraska to British Columbia and California, growing usually on fertile soil.

SAGE HEN or **SAGE-GROUSE** (*Centrocercus urophasianus*), a long-tailed North American grouse. The male is 26 to 30 in. long; breeds in the sage-brush plains from Saskatchewan to Utah and California, feeding on grasshoppers and the leaves and buds of the sage-brush.

SAGINAW, a city of Michigan, U.S., 85 mi. N.W. of Detroit, on the Saginaw river, 15 mi. from its entrance into Saginaw bay (Lake Huron); a port of entry and the county seat of Saginaw county. It is on federal highways 10 and 23, and is served by the Grand Trunk, the New York Central and the Chesapeake and Ohio railways and by Capital Airlines. Pop. (1950) 92,918. The city lies on both banks of the river, on level ground at an altitude of 581 ft. The area is 17 sq.mi. A council-manager form of government was adopted in 1936. There are 200 oil wells in the near vicinity, and the region raises large crops of sugar beets, grain, beans and other vegetables. Saginaw is the metropolis of a wide area, and has a large wholesale and distributing trade. Its manufacturing industries ordinarily employ 25,000 workers. Among the more important are foundries, machine shops and plants making auto parts, rules, sugar, furniture, baking equipment, seed cleaners, caskets, farm and dairy equipment, paper products, truck bodies, graphite products and boilers. Of interest to visitors are the federal building with its French Renaissance type of architecture and the Romanesque Hoyt library; the Schuch hotel with its collections of Indian relics and early Americana; Ojibway Island and Hoyt park. A Veterans Administration hospital was completed in 1950. In 1822 Saginaw City was founded on the west bank of the river, and in 1849 East Saginaw was laid out and financed by eastern capitalists. The two cities were chartered separately in 1859, and were consolidated in 1890. The lumber industry was at its height about 1880–90.

SAGITTARIUS ("the Archer"), in astronomy, the 9th sign of the zodiac denoted by the symbol ♐ an arrow or dart. The Greeks represented this constellation as a centaur in the act of shooting an arrow, and professed it to be Crotus, son of Eupheme, the nurse of the Muses. On account of its southern declination the constellation is not well seen in the latitude of Great Britain; but it is one of the most interesting regions of the sky. A very bright arm of the Milky Way passes through it, and another part of the constellation is occupied by remarkable dark obscuring patches of nebulae. It contains the Trifid nebula and the Omega nebula, both fine examples of bright diffuse nebulae. Cepheid variables and globular clusters seem to congregate in this region, and it is now known that the centre of our galactic system lies in this direction, at a distance of the order of 30,000 light-years from the sun.

SAGO, a food-starch prepared from a deposit in the trunk of several palms, the principal source being the sago palms (*Metroxylon rumphii* and *M. sagu*), a native of the East Indian archipelago, the sago forests being especially extensive in the island of Ceram. The trees flourish only in low marshy situations, seldom attaining a height of 30 ft., with a thick-set trunk. They attain maturity and produce an inflorescence (flower spike) at the age of 15 years, when the enormous pith of the stem is gorged with starch. If the fruit is allowed to form and ripen, the whole of this starchy core material passes into the developing fruits, leaving the stem a mere hollow shell; and the tree after ripening its fruit dies. Accordingly the palms are cut down directly the inflorescence appears, the stems divided into sections and split up, and the starchy pith extracted and grated to a powder. The powder is then kneaded with water over a strainer, through which the starch passes, leaving the woody fibre behind. The starch settles in the bottom of a trough, in which it is floated, and after one or two washings is fit for use by the natives for cakes and soups. That intended for exportation is mixed into a paste with water and rubbed through sieves into small grains, from the size of a coriander seed and larger, whence it is known according to size as pearl sago, bullet sago, etc. A large proportion of the sago imported into Europe comes from Borneo, and the increasing demand has led to a large extension of sago-palm planting. Sago is also obtained from various other East Indian palms such as the Gomuti palm (*Arenga pinnata*), the Kittul palm (*Caryota urens*), the cabbage palm (*Corypha umbraculifera*), besides *Corypha utan*, *Raphia flabelliformis* and *Phoenix farinifera*, also from *Mauritia flexuosa* and *Guilielma gasipaes*, two South American species. It is also obtained from the pith of species of *Cycas*.

SAGUARO: *see* SUWARRO.

SAGUENAY, a river of Quebec province, Canada, flowing into the St. Lawrence 120 m. north-east of Quebec. It drains Lake St. John, from which it issues by two channels, La Grande and La Petite Décharge. It is a source of hydroelectric power, owing to its fall of 314 ft. in its descent to sea level, and the reduction of aluminum from its ores is carried on at the town of Arvida. From Chicoutimi the river is navigable by small steamers, and from Ha Ha bay to the mouth by vessels of the largest size. It is indeed rather a fjord than a river, containing neither rock nor shoal, and having at its mouth a depth of some 600 ft. greater than that of the St. Lawrence. Its width varies from three-quarters of a mile to two miles, and the waters are blackened by the shadow of treeless cliffs, more than 1,000 ft. in height, separated here and there by narrow wooded valleys, and culminating in Capes Trinity and Eternity, 1,600 and 1,800 ft. in height. Tadoussac, at its mouth, is the oldest European trading post in Canada.

Lake St. John is a shallow basin, 26 mi. by 20, with an area of 365 sq.mi. It receives the waters of the Ashuapmuchuan, often spoken of as the upper course of the Saguenay, the Mistassini, the Peribonka and various other important streams. In it is found the *ouananiche,* or land-locked salmon, which attains a weight of about 6 lb.

SAGUNTO, formerly Murviedro, a Spanish town 18 mi. north of Valencia on the Valencia-Barcelona coast railway. Pop. (1950) 26,932 (mun.). The well-preserved Roman theatre looks across the Huerta de Valencia to the Mediterranean. Sagunto is the ancient Saguntum, an ancient Greek or Greek-Iberian town, founded by colonists from Zacynthus (whence its name). About the year 228 B.C. the Romans, disquieted by the enormous growth of Carthaginian power in Spain, concluded an alliance with Saguntum and further required the Carthaginian general, Hasdrubal, not to pass the Ebro. These conditions were observed until 219 when Hannibal judged it safe to begin the war by attacking Saguntum. Confident in Roman protection, the town made a desperate resistance for eight months, at the end of which it was taken by storm. Rome complained to Carthage, requiring the surrender of Hannibal and the members of the council present with him; the council, though doubtful of the wisdom of Hannibal's action, naturally refused, and the second Punic War began. Saguntum never recovered its old importance, and in 138 B.C. was definitely eclipsed by the foundation of Valentia by D. Iunius Brutus, and its population by Lusitanian war-captives who were given the Latin franchise.

SAHAPTIN, a large American Indian linguistic stock, spoken in what is now southeastern Washington, west central Idaho, part of eastern Oregon and north-central California. The four major divisions, all mutually unintelligible, were: northern Sahaptin, spoken by the Yakima, Klikitat, Kittitas, Wanapam, Tenino, Umatilla and Walula tribes; Nez Percé; Cayuse-Molala; and Klamath-Modoc. Cayuse-Molala was formerly called Waiilatpuan and considered a separate stock. Similarly, Klamath-Modoc was separated under the name Lutuamian. Further studies have shown these to be merely divergent branches of Sahaptin.

Earlier the spelling Shahaptian was sometimes used; also, the name occasionally was employed as a designation for the Nez Percé tribe.

See Melville Jacobs, "A Sketch of Northern Sahaptin Grammar" in *University of Washington Publications in Anthropology,* vol. 4, no. 2 (1931). (V. F. R.)

SAHARA, from the Arabic word *sahrá* (wilderness), is the great desert of north Africa, the world's largest desert. It stretches right across Africa from the Atlantic coast through Egypt to the Red sea, beyond which the desert continues into Arabia and Iran. Around its edges there are transitional areas where rainfall is greater and true desert conditions gradually disappear, so that nowhere has it precise boundaries. Its greatest west-east extension exceeds 3,000 mi., and it is seldom less than 1,000 mi. wide. Its total area, perhaps 3,500,000 sq.mi., occupies between a quarter and a third of the African continent. Despite the physical unity of the whole area it includes numerous political divisions, by far the largest part being French.

Geographical Divisions.—The Saharan plateau has an average elevation of 1,000 ft. and is not uniform in character. Across it runs a high central ridge of varying width, including the high mountains of Ahaggar and Tibesti. Geographically five main subdivisions may be recognized, a central area, surrounded by north-

ern, western, southern and eastern areas (*see* map).

The western or Atlantic Sahara is of monotonous relief, generally below 1,500 ft. and with large portions less than 600 ft. above sea level. The central Sahara extending from Mauritania eastward is made up of the Chech Erg, the great Tanezrouft, the Ahaggar massif (with its associated plateaus of Ahenet, Mouydir and the Tasili des Ajjer) and the Fezzan. The Ahaggar is formed of Archaean and Palaeozoic rocks and reaches 9,840 ft. in the peak of Tahat which is sometimes snow-capped. The northern Sahara consists of the Great Western Erg and the Great Eastern Erg, the oasis country of Touat and Gourara, and the Hammada el-Homra to the east. A depression along the south side of the Saharan Atlas is marked in the west by the Oued Draa and to the east by a line of chotts (salt lakes), of which the Chott Djerid, in southern Tunisia, is the largest. Near Biskra these chotts are lower than sea level, and the Gulf of Gabès (Qabes), an arm of the Mediterranean sea, represents a now submerged portion of the depression. The southern Sahara merges gradually on its southern sides into the semidesert areas of the interior of French West Africa. It extends from the mountains of Mauritania through the Adrar des Iforas and the Aïr massif, to the massifs of Tibesti and Ennedi. The highest points in Tibesti, Emi Koussi and Mt. Tousside, an extinct volcano, reach 11,201 and 10,712 ft. respectively. The eastern Sahara extends from the Mediterranean coast to the latitude of Khartoum. In the west is the Libyan desert of uniform relief, with large parts in the north only 600 ft. above sea level; near the coast is the Jebel el Akhdar range, but otherwise this area consists of 500,000 sq.mi. of almost level dunes and sandy wastes, over which no routes pass except those going by way of the Kufra oases. In Egypt the desert is known as the Western desert. Between the Nile and the Red sea is the Arabian (or Eastern) desert in Egypt and the Nubian desert in the northeast of the Sudan.

Geology, Structure and Physiographical Evolution.—Though much work remains to be done, the main features of geology and structure are now fairly well understood. The oldest rocks, of Archaean and Pre-Cambrian Age, were folded and denuded to form the Saharan platform, upon which later deposits have been laid. There have been numerous dislocations, the more marked of which have been accompanied by volcanic activity; several of the highest peaks in the central Sahara are the remains of extinct volcanoes of Tertiary and Quaternary Age. Elsewhere vertical movements of the land have caused the renewal of erosion which has resulted in the cutting of deep valleys and gorges, such as those of the Tasili des Ajjer. During Cretaceous and later times much of the Sahara was submerged, and extensive areas are covered by sandstones, notably the Nubian sandstone of Cretaceous Age, and by limestones laid down in areas of the sea. There are also large basins now occupied by sediments of continental origin deposited by wind or in shallow fresh or saline waters. The horizontally bedded Cretaceous and other rocks form plains, plateaus and escarpments that are dissected by former river valleys and are in striking contrast to the volcanic topography of other areas. The Sahara as a whole is quite distinct from the Atlas mountains of French North Africa which belong, tectonically, to Europe.

The theory of a marine origin for the vast quantities of sand in the Sahara has been disproved, since the sand is of Quaternary, or, at the oldest, Pleistocene, Age and there is no evidence of any marine transgression since pre-Tertiary times. During the Quaternary Ice Age in Europe, the Sahara's climate must have been wetter, so that erosion took place as in other moist temperate or subtropical regions, and there was a proper system of rivers. The vegetation may have been grass with trees. With the retreat of the ice sheets from Europe, vegetation disappeared and arid conditions were established, so that the soil was dried out and became subject to large-scale wind erosion.

Three main types of surface and scenery are commonly recognized today—the erg, the reg and the hammada. The erg is the desert of shifting sand dunes, which lie in the bottom of the great basins where the ancient rivers piled up most alluvium; the Great Western and Eastern Ergs, between Béni-Abbès and Ghadames, are the most difficult of all Saharan areas and are the parts most carefully avoided by modern trans-Saharan routes. The Libyan desert also constitutes an extensive area of unmitigated sandy waste. The reg desert consists of wind-scoured plains strewn with pebbles, boulders and gravels. The hammada are rocky plateaus with bare rock outcrops and are often cut by deeply eroded valleys and gorges; they are common around the Ahaggar and Tibesti and, at lower altitudes, in the western Sahara.

Climate.—Climate is the fundamental basis for the definition of the Saharan region which consists of those areas with rainfall of less than 10 in. a year in the northern districts (south of the Atlas mountains) and 15 in. in the south (in about the latitude of Timbuktu and Agadès, where evaporation is much greater). The limits of the true desert, with perhaps less than five inches of rainfall a year, are rather narrower. The whole area is marked by a general lack of rainfall with great variations from year to year and a tendency for such rain as falls to come in sudden storms at very irregular intervals. Adrar has recorded 3.7 in. in a few hours and Aïn Sefra 3 in. in two days. El-Goléa had only one fall of rain in seven years and Tidikelt only one in ten years. The total rainfall recorded at In Salah in four years amounted to only 0.4 in. Absolute desert occurs in the extensive flat areas of the Tanezrouft or "land of thirst," to the west of the Ahaggar.

The Sahara is one of the hottest, if not the hottest, regions of the world, mean annual temperatures exceeding 80° F. over a high proportion of it and, in parts, 85° F. June, July and August are especially hot months. Shade recordings of 136.4° F. have been reported from Azizia in Tripolitania, and the surface of the ground may sometimes exceed 170° F. There are, however, great differences between day and night temperatures, sometimes as much as 50°–60°, so that while the desert may be a furnace at midday, there is a rapid loss of heat from the ground after sunset, and the nights are usually cool and refreshing. The sky is generally cloudless, and the relative humidity very low, sometimes less than 10%. The most common winds are the northeast trades, though in the western Sahara winds often blow from the west.

In recent years meteorological stations have been established at various points on the edge of the Sahara and after 1932 regular observations were made at the Jules Carde observatory at Tamanrasset (Fort Laperrine) in the Ahaggar mountains, 4,429 ft. above sea level. Figures for this station are given in the table to illustrate some climatic variations of the Sahara.

Vegetation.—Areas from which all plant life is absent form only a small part of the Sahara: the Tanezrouft, for example, and the Hammada of Tinghert, south of Ghadames. Sand deserts are not, however, the most barren parts of the Sahara; mobile dunes can carry little plant life, but the vegetation of the sandy stretches in the basins of the great rivers of Quaternary times can draw on some of the most copious underground water reserves.

Nevertheless plant life is usually poorly developed. It consists of two very distinct types: the permanent, such as betoum (Atlantic turpentine tree, *Pistacia atlantica*) and acacia trees, and thorny shrubs like tamarisks and jujubes; and the ephemeral—delicate herbs whose seeds germinate immediately after rain, grow rapidly, flower for a brief period, set fruits and seeds and then die. This ephemeral vegetation is widely known by the inhabitants of the desert as *acheb*.

The natural vegetation of the oases was probably the oleander with tamarisks. Among introduced plants the date palm is of outstanding importance. Its fruits provide food for local consumption and for trade, and the crushed seeds food for camels.

Fauna.—Domesticated animals have been introduced to all the oases, principally camels, sheep and goats, but the wild fauna of the desert is, like the vegetation, highly specialized. Gazelles, desert antelopes and wild goats are common on the northern and southern edges of the desert; jackal, fox and badger also occur. Bustards are found on the south side of the Saharan Atlas; ostriches are much more scarce than formerly. Horned vipers, scorpions and lizards are common, as are locusts, flies and ticks. The Egyptian monitor (*Varanus niloticus*), looking like a small crocodile, survives in certain areas such as in the tributaries of the Igharghar.

Peoples and Settlements.—Settlement was undoubtedly widespread when the desert area was wetter and better-covered with vegetation. There is evidence of Neolithic and Palaeolithic culture, and rock drawings have been found showing animals that no longer live in the Sahara. Within historic times it is suggested that there may have been drastic changes, because of the Roman military settlements established in places which are now desert or semidesert. But their decline may perhaps have been caused as much by the neglect of the water supply and irrigation systems as by climatic changes. In some cases colonies have been reestablished during the 20th century, especially by the French, on the sites of these abandoned settlements.

The first inhabitants were probably Negroes, who retreated in the face of the advancing Berbers with their swift-moving camels (*méharis*). After the death of Mohammed the Berbers were pushed back by the Arabs who also used camels and who made Islam a unifying element throughout the Sahara. Arabic became the chief language, though Berber pockets survived, chiefly in upland areas in the central Sahara. Slavery was introduced and remained a lucrative trade long into the 20th century. From the mixture of Negro, Berber and Arab there emerged the three great ethnic groups of today: the Tuareg, the Tibbu (Tebu) and the Moors (*qq.v.*).

The Tuareg are camel nomads living in the central parts of the desert. There are several confederations; in the north the Ajjer, the Tasili and the Ahaggar and in the south the Iforas of the Adrar, the Ioulemedden of the middle Niger and the Kel Oui and Kel Gress of the Aïr. They are known as the "people of the veil," because all male Tuareg wear a *litham*, or veil, which they lift only in order to eat. The society is matriarchal, and the women enjoy a degree of liberty unknown elsewhere among Moslem peoples.

The Tibbu of the eastern Sahara closely resemble the Tuareg but have mixed greatly with negroid peoples. They are light or dark bronze in colour and are probably of Hamitic stock. Their language closely resembles Kanuri, spoken in Kanem and in Bornu in northeastern Nigeria.

The Moors or *Beidan* (or whites, as compared with the black peoples of the Sudan) live in the western Sahara. They are mostly nomads, a mixture of Berber and Arab, with the Berber element predominant. Unlike the Tuareg they have been completely Islamized and are a very cultured people.

Other smaller groups include the Chaanba, who are Arabic-speaking nomads and the traditional enemies of the Tuareg, and the Mozabites, a group of heretical Moslems who settled in the Mzab, and whose commercial wisdom has given them an importance out of all proportion to their numbers. In the oases Negroes are still the most numerous. They are the descendants of the original inhabitants and of slaves introduced later. Three classes are recognized: the free men, the proprietors; the Haratin, the tradesmen; and the Negroes or slaves.

Of greater significance than differences of race or language is the distinction between nomadic and sedentary peoples. Pastoral nomads are most numerous on the edges of the desert and around the mountainous areas. The poorer the desert, the more scattered the population. Though the nomads depend most upon their camels, sheep and goats are more numerous; the range of grazing is determined by the availability of fodder and drink-

Seasonal Climatic Variations as Observed at Tamanrasset

	Jan.	Feb.	March	April	May	June	July	Aug.	Sept.	Oct.	Nov.	Dec.	Year
Mean temperature (° F.)	54	58	64	72	78	83	84	83	79	74	65	58	71 (mean)
Mean daily maximum temperature (° F.)	67	72	79	86	92	95	96	95	91	86	79	71	84 (mean)
Mean daily minimum temperature (° F.)	40	43	49	58	64	70	72	71	67	60	51	44	57 (mean)
Mean rainfall (in.)	0.3	0.0	0.0	0.2	0.5	0.2	0.1	0.4	0.1	0.1	0.0	0.0	1.9 (total)
Mean number of rain days	1	0.4	0.4	0.7	2	3	2	3	3	0.5	0.6	0.5	17 (total)
Relative humidity (%)	31	25	23	20	24	21	23	25	24	26	28	31	25 (mean)
Absolute temperatures, maximum (° F.)	79	82	90	96	98	101	99	100	97	91	86	81	101
Absolute temperatures, minimum (° F.)	20	25	32	42	45	59	62	62	56	47	36	27	20

PRINCIPAL GEOGRAPHICAL SUBDIVISIONS OF THE SAHARA

ing water. The Regibat of the Spanish Sahara will migrate 400 mi. to the Chech Erg in search of water for their camels. With the pacification of many areas, razzias or raids by nomads on oasis cultivators are less common than formerly.

The sedentary peoples account for about two-thirds of the total population of the desert. They live in the oases and cultivate with the aid of irrigation. Methods of irrigation include springs, wells, shadoofs, *foggaras* and artesian wells. The shadoof consists of a beam, pivoted between uprights, bearing a weight at one end and a bucket at the other. *Foggaras* are man-made subterranean channels, dug not quite horizontally to tap underground water which is led to the oasis by gravity and supplies a limited but regular amount; they are especially common in Touat and Gourara. Artesian wells are most used around Ouargla (Wargla) and in the Oued Rir, south of the Chott Melrir, where there are more than 1,000 wells supplying 69,000 gal. a minute and irrigating 1,750,000 palms. Unfortunately the withdrawal of these quantities of water has caused a drop in the water table, but measures have now been taken to overcome this drawback. In all Saharan oases the date is the chief tree and the main source of food. In its shade are grown citrus fruits, figs, peaches, apricots, vegetables and cereals such as wheat, barley and millets.

Commerce and Communications.—Saharan commerce is of two types: the supplying of wheat, barley, wool and manufactured goods to the desert peoples in exchange for dates; and the long-established trans-Saharan trade, always the monopoly of the nomads. Salt and ivory were carried across the desert in very early times, and salt is still an important product, especially from Taoudéni and Bilma. In 1950 the Sahara produced more than 14,000 tons of salt, the equivalent of more than 100,000 camel loads which move in huge caravans on *azalaïs*, particularly on the salt route from Taoudéni to Timbuktu. Many other caravan routes remain important despite the introduction of new methods of communication. They include those from Tripoli to Ghat and to Murzuk, Bilma and Lake Chad; from Ouargla to In Salah, Tamanrasset, Zinder and northern Nigeria; from Colomb-Béchar to Tessalit and the upper Niger valley; and from southern Morocco through Atar to Nioro or Senegal. In the eastern Sahara the routes centre on the oases of Faya (Largeau) and Kufra and also link Egypt westward and southwestward with the desert. Camel traffic is important in the market centres such as Biskra, Ghardaïa and Agadès on the desert edge.

Certain routes are commonly used by motor vehicles. Regular though infrequent buses use two roads—one crossing the Tanezrouft to Gao and Niamey in six days and the other passing through the Ahaggar to Agadès and Zinder. Railways reach to the edge of the Sahara from the north, west and south but do not penetrate far. There have been many proposals for a trans-Saharan railway. The most advanced, from Colomb-Béchar via the Tanezrouft to Gao on the Niger, has stopped 60 mi. south of Colomb-Béchar because of the high cost of construction and the economic uncertainty of the scheme. Numerous air routes between Europe and tropical and southern Africa cross the desert using airports on the fringes, as those at Tripoli and Kano.

Political Divisions.—Most of the western and central areas of the Sahara are under French administration. Following the French occupation of Algiers in 1830 they advanced gradually southward. Control of the line of the northern Saharan oases was established when Laghouat and Ghardaïa, in the Mzab valley, were occupied in 1852 and Touggourt (Tuggart) and Ouargla in 1854. Dreams of a vast empire in the northern half of Africa were entertained, as the French also penetrated inland in west and equatorial Africa and established the protectorate of Tunisia in 1881. As early as 1879 plans for a trans-Saharan railway were being discussed, while official missions, notably that of Fernand Foureau and A. F. J. Lamy from 1898 to 1900, helped to establish French claims in the Sahara. These were further recognized by the Anglo-French agreements of 1890, 1898 and 1904, by which various boundaries were fixed and many of the existing political divisions established. The French portions of the Sahara consisted, in 1955, of the Territoires du Sud of Algeria (comprising the four territories of Aïn-Sefra, Ghardaïa, Touggourt and the Saharan oases); the southern parts of the protectorates of Morocco and Tunisia; the interior districts of the Federation of French West Africa (chiefly Mauritania, French Sudan and the Niger colony); and the Chad territory of French Equatorial Africa.

The Spanish Sahara, known as Rio de Oro, is on the Atlantic coast. In the eastern parts of the Sahara are Libya, the territory of which formed an Italian colony from 1912 until World War II, after which it was placed partly under British and partly under French trusteeship until 1951, when it became an independent state—the United Kingdom of Libya—made up of the three provinces of Tripolitania, Cyrenaica and the Fezzan; the independent state of Egypt; and the Sudan, until 1954 the condominium of the Anglo-Egyptian Sudan.

Exploration.—The Egyptians penetrated the Libyan and Nubian deserts in places, and the Carthaginians and Phoenicians knew parts of the northern Sahara and Rio de Oro on the west coast. Roman Africa extended up the Nile to the Second Cataract (Wadi Halfa), but the attempt to discover the sources of the Nile in A.D. 66 did not extend beyond the swamps of the Bahr el Jebel. The Mohammedan conquest of North Africa largely eliminated European influence in the Sahara, although Jewish and Genoese merchants acquired considerable knowledge of the desert during mediaeval times.

The real opening up of the Sahara took place during the 19th century. In 1819 Joseph Ritchie and G. F. Lyon went from Tripoli to Murzuk and into the Fezzan. In 1822 D. Denham, H. Clapperton and W. Oudney crossed the desert from Tripoli and were the first Europeans to see Lake Chad. Maj. A. Gordon Laing went from Tripoli to Timbuktu in 1825 but was murdered on his return journey. In 1827 and 1828 René Caillié, disguised as an Arab, travelled from Sierra Leone to Timbuktu, where he explored the middle Niger valley and then crossed the Sahara to Morocco.

The first scientific expedition was that of Heinrich Barth, who travelled extensively between Tripoli and Lake Chad from 1850 to 1855. G. Rohlfs explored parts of the western Sahara between 1862 and 1867 and later travelled from Tripoli to Siwa and Alexandria. In 1878 he attempted to reach Wadai but penetrated only as far as the Kufra oases. Henri Duveyrier explored the Ghat-Murzuk route between 1859 and 1861 and revealed many facts about the Tuareg. Several explorers were murdered, including Eugène Joubert and R. Dourneaux-Dupéré at Ghadames, on their way to Timbuktu from Algeria (1874); Erwin von Bary travelling from Tripoli to Timbuktu through Aïr (1877); and Col. Paul Flatters, who was killed by the Tuareg in 1881 while making a survey for a proposed French trans-Saharan railway. Timbuktu was reached from Morocco in 1881 by H. Oskar Lenz.

In the last decade of the 19th century, and following the Anglo-French agreement of 1890, the desert was conquered by the French, and since then many of its unknown regions have been explored. Especially important was the mission of F. Foureau and A. F. J. Lamy of 1898–1900, which crossed the desert from Biskra via Agadès and Zinder to Lake Chad, where contact was made with parties led by O. Meynier from the Niger and E. Gentil from the Congo. The military conquest followed in succeeding years. Gen. M. J. F. H. Laperrine was given command of the northern oases and concentrated on making the routes safe from Tuareg raids. He defeated the Ahaggar Tuareg at Tit in 1902 and secured their complete submission by 1905. He then turned his attention to the Tuareg of the Tasili des Ajjer, who were supported by the Senussi of Tripolitania, who themselves were helped by the Turks. He was succeeded by another brilliant soldier, Captain Charlet, but was recalled in World War I to deal with numerous revolts, during which the monk C. E. de Foucauld, one of the Tuareg's best friends, was murdered. Laperrine himself was killed during a flight to survey the possibilities of air services between North and West Africa. Comdr. Jean Tilho carried out military operations against the Senussi of Tibesti and explored Borku, Ennedi and Tibesti, returning in 1917 through Wadai and Darfur. Many French and other travellers and scientists have added greatly to the knowledge of the Sahara in the 20th century. These include E. Arnaud, M. Cortier, E. F. Gautier, R. Chudeau, W. J. Harding King, H. Vischer, A. M. Hassanein Bey, A. Buchanan and F. J. Rennell Rodd. By 1955 it was doubtful if any more discoveries of first magnitude would be made, though large areas remained unexplored.

BIBLIOGRAPHY.—E. Arnaud, *Mission Arnaud-Cortier. Nos confins sahariens* (Paris, 1908); A. Bernard, *Afrique septentrionale et occidentale* in *Géographie Universelle,* ed. by L. Gallois and P. Vidal de La Blache, vol. xi, part 2 (Paris, 1939); E. W. Bovill, *Caravans of the Old Sahara* (London, New York, 1933), "The Sahara," *Antiquity,* 3:414–23 (Gloucester, 1929); A. Buchanan, *Sahara* (London, New York, 1926); R. Capot-Rey, *Le Sahara français* (Paris, 1953); T. F. Chipp, "The Vegetation of the Central Sahara," *Geog. Jour.,* 76 (London, 1930); G. Danielli, "The Italian Colonies," *Geog. R.,* 19:404–19 (New York, 1929); J. Despois, "Types of Native Life in Tripolitania," *ibid.,* 35:352–67 (New York, 1945); J. Dubief, *Essai sur l'hydrologie superficielle du Sahara* (Algiers, 1953); E. F. Gautier and R. Chudeau, *Missions au Sahara,* 2 vol., (i) E. F. Gautier, "Sahara algerien," (ii) R. Chudeau, "Sahara soudanais," (Paris, 1908, 1909); E. F. Gautier, *Le Sahara* (Paris, 1923); J. Gottman, "New Facts and Some Reflections on the Sahara," *Geog. R.* 32:659–63 (New York, 1942); M. Hachisuka (ed.), *Le Sahara* (New York, 1932 *et seq.*), vol. 1 including C. E. P. Brooks, "Le climat du Sahara et de l'Arabie" and P. A. Buxton, "Les Conditions de la vie animale dans les déserts"; A. M. Hassanein Bey, *The Lost Oases* (London, New York, 1925); W. J. Harding King, *A Search for the Masked Tawareks* (London, 1903); T. Monod, "Travels in the Western Sahara, 1934–35," *Geog. Jour.,* 87 (London, 1936) and "New Journey to the Western Sahara, 1935–36," *ibid.,* 89 (1937); N. Pearn and W. Donkin, "A Camel Journey From Tugust to Kano," *ibid.,* 83 (London, 1934); R. Perret, "Le climat du Sahara," *Annales de Géographie,* 44:162–86 (Paris, 1935); F. J. Rennell Rodd, *People of the Veil* (London, 1926); H. Schiffers, "Wasserhaushalt und Probleme der Wassernutzung in der Sahara," *Erdkunde,* 5:51–60 (Bonn, 1951); E. P. Stebbing, "The Encroaching Sahara: the Threat to the West African Colonies," *Geog. Jour.,* 85:506–519 (London, 1935); B. E. Thomas, "Modern Trans-Saharan Routes," *Geog. R.,* 42:267–82 (New York, 1952); C. Vélain, "Etat actuel de nos connaissances sur la géographie et la géologie du Sahara d'après les explorations les plus récents," *Revue de Géographie,* 1:447–517 (Paris, 1906–07); H. Vischer, *Across the Sahara From Tripoli to Bornu* (London, 1910).

(R. W. SL.)

SAHARANPUR, a city and district of the republic of India, in the Meerut division of Uttar Pradesh. The city, situated on a stream called the Damaula Nadi, is about 95 mi. north-northeast of Delhi. Pop. (1951) 148,435. It is an important railway junction, and there are railway workshops and a large woodcarving industry.

The DISTRICT OF SAHARANPUR has an area of 2,126 sq.mi. It forms the most northerly portion of the doab, or alluvial tableland, between the Ganges and Jumna rivers. The population in 1951 was 1,353,636. The district contains the towns of Roorkee and Hardwar (*qq.v.*).

SAHOS or SHOHOS, Africans of Hamitic stock living to the west of Massawa. Probably akin to the Gallas and Afars, they are mostly Mohammedans, a few being Christians.

SAID HALIM, PRINCE (1863–1921), Turkish statesman, the son of Halim Pasha and the grandson of Mohammed Ali, the founder of the last Egyptian dynasty, was born in Cairo and was educated in Turkey, completing his studies in Geneva, Switz. Exiled because of his sympathy with the Young Turkish movement, he affiliated himself to the Committee of Union and Progress in Paris, Fr. After the revolution of July 1908 he returned to Constantinople and was nominated senator. At various times from 1908 to 1918 he was president of the council of state, minister for foreign affairs and general secretary to the Union and Progress party. On June 17, 1913, he became grand vizier, in which capacity he endeavoured to settle the questions of Armenian reforms, Mosul oil and the participation of English, French and Russian capital in the Baghdad railway. He also endeavoured to establish close relations with Greece. Said Halim favoured a Turko-German alliance but sought to keep Turkey neutral in World War I. On its entry into the war he tendered his resignation, which was refused, and he remained in office until Feb. 1917. After the armistice of Mudros, Oct. 31, 1918, Said Halim was imprisoned by the British in Malta. Released in 1921, he was assassinated in Rome, It.,

on Dec. 6, 1921.

SAID PASHA, MOHAMMED (d. 1928), Egyptian statesman, succeeded Boutros Pasha as prime minister of Egypt in 1910. He held office for four difficult years, in which he succeeded in carrying out various administrative reforms and an extension of provincial government. In May 1919 he formed a nonpolitical ministry in the heat of the revolutionary movement but in November resigned with his cabinet. He was minister of education in Saad Zaghlul's cabinet (1924) and acting prime minister during Zaghlul's absence in Europe. He resigned in Oct. 1924, and presently resigned his membership of the Wafd party. Said Pasha died on July 20, 1928.

SAIGA (*Saiga tatarica*), a desert-dwelling antelope inhabiting the Khirghiz steppe. A century ago it extended as far west as Poland. During the later Tertiary period the saiga was widely distributed in Europe and Alaska.

SAIGO TAKAMORI (1832–1877), also known as Saigo the Elder or the Great Saigo. A leader of the Satsuma clan in the island of Kyushu, Japan, he took a prominent part in the overthrow of the Tokugawa shogunate and the restoration of power to the emperor in 1868.

He represented his clan in the government subsequently formed but broke with his colleagues in 1873 because of a dispute about policy toward Korea. Retiring to Satsuma he founded a college, and many young men gathered round him. In 1877 he led the famous Satsuma rebellion against the imperial regime but was defeated in the ensuing campaign; severely wounded at the final battle of Kagoshima he died by the sword of one of his own officers, rather than fall into enemy hands. In later years he became a national hero and the bronze statue of him in Ueno park, Tokyo, is one of the city's best-known monuments. (F. S. G. P.)

SAIGON, capital of the former colony of Cochin-China and after World War II of Vietnam, is on the right bank of the Saigon river. Pop. (1936) 111,000. The town is enclosed by the Saigon river, the Arroyo Chinoise and Arroyo de l'Avalanche except on the southwest, where it adjoins the twin city of Cholon (*q.v.*). Double rows of trees along fine boulevards, with public gardens, cafés and other French features, made it the "Little Paris of the east." Before the French conquest, Saigon, then known as Gai-dinh-thanh, was the capital of Lower Cochin-China, which consisted of the six southern provinces of the Annamese empire, and constituted a viceroyalty under the government of a *kinhluoc.* The French captured it in 1859, and it was part of the territory ceded in 1862. During the Indochinese War of 1946–54, the city was a centre for refugees.

SAILCLOTH AND SAILMAKING. Sailcloth, now more commonly called canvas (*q.v.*) or, in the United States, duck, is usually a double warp, single weft fabric of the same structure as bagging (*see* BAGGING AND BAGS) and tarpaulin, although it is sometimes made with single threads of warp. Hemp and ramie are used in the manufacture of this cloth, but flax and cotton are the chief fibres employed. Many of the sails of fishing smacks and similar vessels are made entirely of cotton—the fabric sometimes retaining its natural colour, but more often dyed or stained tan. Since most of the larger vessels are now driven by steam or oil, the quantity of cloth used for sails is comparatively small. A large quantity of cloth, however, is used on steamships for covers, and for coal bags, sailcloth buckets, etc. The very best kind of sailcloth is made from long flax, as this fibre has flexibility, lightness and strength combined. The number of threads per inch of warp varies from 14 double threads to 48 double threads, and from 12 to 36 shots per inch of weft, while the usual widths are 18, 24, 30 and 36 in. Cotton canvas has for its limits about 26 to 54 threads of warp per inch, and 15 to 46 shots per inch; the warp yarn for cottons may be 2, 3 or several ply.

Sailmaking.—This is a very ancient industry, but is naturally much less important than it was before the introduction of steamships. The operations of the sailmaker may be stated as follows. The dimensions of mast and yards and sail plan being supplied, the master sailmaker is enabled to determine the dimensions of each sail—after due allowance for stretching—in terms of cloths and depth in yards—if a square sail, the number of cloths in the head, number in the foot and the depth in yards; if a fore-

and-aft sail (triangular), the number of cloths in the foot and the depth in yards of the luff or stay and of leech or after-leech; if a fore-and-aft sail (trapezium form), the number of cloths in the head, number in foot and the depth of mast or luff and of after-leech. These particulars obtained, there is got out what is technically termed a "casting," which simply means the shape, length, etc., of each individual cloth in the sail. These figures are given to the cutter, who proceeds to cut out the sail cloth by cloth in consecutive order, numbering them 1, 2, 3, 4, etc.; the series of cloths thus cut out are handed over to the workman, who joins them together by carefully made double flat seams, sewn with twine specially prepared for the purpose, with about 120 stitches in a yard. In the heavy sails the seam is about 1½in. in width, and in the British navy stuck or stitched in the middle of the seam to give additional strength; the seams in the lighter sails are about 1in. wide. The whole of the cloths are then brought together, and spread out, and the tabling (or hemming, so to say) is turned in and finished off with about 72 stitches to a yard. Strengthening pieces or "linings" are affixed where considered necessary, in courses and top-sails such pieces as reef-bands, middle-bands, foot-bands, leech-linings, bunt-line cloths; in top-sails (only) a top-lining or brim; in other and lighter sails such pieces as mast-lining clew and head, tack and corner pieces; holes, such as head, reef, stay (luff), mast, cringle, bunt-line, etc., are also made where required, a grommet of line of suitable size being worked in them to prevent their being cut through. The next thing to be done is to secure the edges of the sail. Bolt-rope, a comparatively soft rope made from the finer hemp yarn (Italian) is used for this purpose; in the British navy it ranges from 1in. (increasing in size by quarter inches) up to 8in. inclusive; it is then neatly sewn on with roping twine specially prepared, the needle and twine passing between and clear of every two strands of the rope in roping.

Where slack sail has to be taken in, it is the practice to leave it to the judgment of the sail-maker; but where possible it is better to set up the rope by means of a tackle to a strain approximate to what it will have to bear when in use, and whilst on the stretch mark it off in yards, as also the edge of the sail in yards, so that by bringing the marks together in roping the sail will stand flat. In the British navy the largest size of rope sewn on to a sail is six inches; sizes above this are used for foot and clew ropes of top-sails and courses, being first wormed, parcelled (that is, wound round with strips of worn canvas), tarred and served over with spun yarn; the foot of the sail is then secured to it by being marled in. Where two sizes of bolt-rope used in roping a sail have to be connected, it is effected by a tapered splice. Cringles (similar to the handle of a maund) formed by a strand of bolt-rope, mostly having a galvanized iron thimble in them as a protection, are then stuck where necessary, as at the corners, sides or leeches, mast or luff; they are required either for making stationary or hauling "taut" by tackle or otherwise certain parts of the sail when in use. Fore-and-aft sails, such as spankers, gaff-sails and storm try-sails, are reduced in size by reef-points made of stout line (four to 20 lb.), crow-footed in the middle, a hole being pierced through every seam; one-half of the point is passed through and the crowfoot sewn firmly to the sail; the number of reefs depends upon the size of the sail, and the reefs are placed parallel to the foot. (T. W.)

UNITED STATES

Sailcloth or canvas is better known by the American trade as numbered duck. England manufactures a great deal from flax, while the U.S. mostly uses cotton. It is a plain woven fabric of heavy construction which varies with its use and is usually of plied warp and filling yarns (although in some cases the warp yarn may be single and drawn two ends per dent). Duck is used for many purposes including sails, tents, tarpaulin, bags, awnings, fire hose, wearing apparel such as overalls, hunting coats, belts, etc. The number of warp ends per inch vary from 26 to 48 and may be 2 to 5 ply and from 16 to 34 filling picks per inch 2 to 8 ply.

Specifications adopted by the Cotton Duck Association specify that duck shall be made of cotton, free from waste and thoroughly cleaned, evenly woven, free from all sizing and free from an excessive number of avoidable imperfections in manufacture. Duck is numbered as follows: No. 1 duck is 22 in. wide and weighs 18 oz. per linear yard and is taken as the basis. For each ounce under 18 the number is increased by one which would make a 17 oz. duck #2, 16 oz. #3 and so on up to #12 which weighs 7 ounces. Duck heavier than 18 oz. per yard is numbered by ciphers, a cipher being added for each ounce increase in weight. Thus 1/0=19 oz. duck; 2/0=20 oz. duck. Duck is made as heavy as 20/0 which would weigh 38 oz. per yard. However, duck above 2/0 is very seldom used.

The numbering of duck conforms in England and the United States in number only. English specifications are based on a 24 in. fabric and on two ply yarn warp and filling for all numbers, while in the United States 22 in. is the standard width and designates that each number shall be more than two ply and varies with the number and the weight per running yard for specified widths in exact proportion. Thus a 24 in. duck would weigh $\frac{1}{11}$ more than the standard 22 in. goods, while 11 in. duck would weigh one-half as much as the standard width. Duck is made in widths from 14 to 120 in., but the most common widths are 22, 28 and 36 in., and have standard lengths of 110 to 120 yd. differing from the English requirements of 40 yd. lengths. Duck in the U.S. is known as hard, medium or soft texture. Hard duck is made from 2/0–#12, and medium texture 2/0–#6.

The English specifications for a #1 duck specifies it should weigh 18.8 oz. per yard, 24 in. wide, be delivered in a 39 yd. bolt, to weigh 46 lb. containing 26 lb. of warp, 660 double ends (approximately 28 ends per inch) and 20 lb. of filling, breaking 340 lb. in the warp and 480 lb. in the filling, using the Avery method of breaking a 24×1 in. test strip. Comparing this with the U.S. Government specification a #1 duck should weigh 18 oz. per linear yard, 22 in. wide, have as a minimum 26 ends and 19 picks per inch of 5 ply warp and filling, and specified widths should weigh in proportion to the 22 in. standard (that is, #1 duck 24 in. wide should weigh 19.6 oz. per yard). The fabric when tested by the 1×1×3 in. grab method, should break 440 lb. in the warp and 370 lb. in the filling. The difference in breaking strength is partially due to the method employed, therefore no comparison can be made. (R. T. F.)

SAILING: see RIGGING; YACHTING; etc.

SAINFOIN (*Onobrychis viciaefolia*) is a low-growing perennial plant of the pea family (Leguminosae), with a woody rootstock, whence proceed the stems, which are covered with fine hairs and bear numerous long pinnate leaves, the segments of which are elliptic. The flowers are borne in close pyramidal or cylindrical clusters on the end of long stalks. Each flower is about half an inch in length with lanceolate calyx-teeth shorter than the corolla, which latter is pink, with darker stripes of the same colour. The pods or legumes are flattened, wrinkled, somewhat sickle-shaped and crested, and contain a single olive-brown seed. In Great Britain the plant is a native of the calcareous districts of the southern counties. It is native through central Europe and Siberia and is sparingly naturalized in the eastern United States.

SAINT. The articles on the different Saints are to be found in their proper alphabetical places, followed not preceded by the word saint, as Peter, Saint; Patrick, Saint; etc.

The term was originally applied, *e.g.* in the New Testament and also in the most ancient monuments of Christian thought, to all believers. In ancient inscriptions it often means those souls who are enjoying eternal happiness, or the martyrs. For a long time, too, *sanctus* was an official title, particularly reserved for bishops (v. *Analecta Bollandiana*, xviii. 410–411). It was not till almost the 6th century that the word became a title of honour specially given to the dead whose cult was publicly celebrated in the churches. It was to the martyrs that the Church first began to pay special honour. We find traces of this in the 2nd half of the 2nd century, in the *Martyrium Polycarpi* (xviii. 3) in connection with a meeting to celebrate the anniversary of the martyr's death. Another passage in the same document (xvii. 3) shows clearly that this was not an innovation, but a custom already established among the Christians. It does not follow that it was henceforth universal. The Church of Rome does not seem to have inscribed in its calendar its martyrs of an earlier date than the 3rd century. The essential form of the cult of the martyrs was that of the honours paid to the illustrious dead; and these honours were officially paid by the community. Each church first confined itself to celebrating its own martyrs; but it was not long before it became customary to celebrate the anniversaries of martyrs of other churches. Finally the famous ascetics began to share in the honours paid to the martyrs.

The cult of the saints early met with opposition, in answer to which the Church Fathers had to defend its lawfulness and explain its nature. The Church of Smyrna had early to explain its position in this matter with regard to St. Polycarp: "We worship Christ, as the Son of God; as to the martyrs, we love them as the disciples and imitators of the Lord" (*Martyrium Polycarpi*, xvii. 3). St. Cyril of Alexandria defends the worship of the martyrs against Julian, St. Asterius and Theodoret against the pagans in general, and they all lay emphasis on the fact that the saints are not looked upon as gods by the Christians, and that the honours paid to them are of quite a different kind from the adoration reserved to God alone. St. Jerome argued against Vigilantius with his accustomed vehemence, and especially meets the objection based on the resemblance between these rites and those of the pagans. But it is above all St. Augustine who in his refutation of Faustus, as well as in his sermons and elsewhere, clearly defined the true character of the honours paid to the saints: "Non eis templa, non eis altaria, non sacrificia exhibemus. Non eis sacerdotes offerunt, absit, Deo praestantur. Etiam apud memorias sanctorum martyrum cum offerimus, nonne Deo offerimus? . . . Quando audisti dici apud memoriam sancti Theogenis: offero tibi, sancte Theogenis, aut offero tibi Petre, aut offero tibi Paule?" (*Sermo*, 273, 7; cf. *Contra Faustum*, xx. 21). The undoubted abuses which grew up, especially during the middle ages, raised up, at the time of the Reformation, fresh adversaries of the cult of the saints. The council of Trent, while reproving all superstitious practices in the invocation of the saints, the veneration of relics and the use of images, expresses as follows the doctrine of the Roman Church: "That the saints who reign with Christ offer to God their prayers for men; that it is good and useful to invoke them by supplication and to have recourse to their aid and assistance in order to obtain from God His benefits through His Son our Saviour Jesus Christ, who alone is our Saviour and Redeemer."

BIBLIOGRAPHY.—*See* H. Thurston, art. "Saints and Martyrs, Christian" in Hastings, *Encyclopaedia of Religion and Ethics*, xi. 51 ff.; L. Duchesne, *Origines du culte chrétien*, 6th ed. (1925).

ST. AFFRIQUE, a town of France, in the department of Aveyron, on the Sorgues, 68 mi. N.N.W. of Beziers on the railway to Clermont Ferrand. Pop. (1936) 5,179. St. Affrique grew up in the 6th century around the tomb of St. Africain, bishop of Comminges. An old bridge over the Sorgues and some megaliths in the neighbourhood, especially the dolmen at Tiergues, are notable.

ST. ALBANS, EARLS OF. The English title of earl of St. Albans was first borne by Richard Bourke, or de Burgh, 4th earl of Clanricarde (d. 1635), who was made earl of St. Albans in 1628.

The second creation of an earl of St. Albans was in 1660, when Henry, Baron Jermyn, was made an earl under this title. *See* below.

ST. ALBANS, CHARLES BEAUCLERK, 1ST DUKE OF, *cr.* 1684 (1670–1726), a natural son of Charles II. by Nell Gwynne. Born in London on May 8, 1670, Charles was made Baron Hedington and earl of Burford in Dec. 1676. He took service with the emperor Leopold I., being present at the siege of Belgrade in 1688. After the battle of Landen in 1693, William III. made him captain of the gentlemen pensioners, and four years later gentleman of the bedchamber. His Whig sentiments prevented his advancement under Anne, but he was restored to favour at the accession of George I. He died at Bath on May 10, 1726. His wife Diana, daughter and heiress of Aubrey de Vere, last earl of Oxford, was a well-known beauty, who became lady of the bedchamber to Caroline, princess of Wales, and survived until Jan. 15, 1742.

ST. ALBANS, HENRY JERMYN, EARL OF (*c.* 1604–1684), son of Sir Thomas Jermyn of Rushbroke, Suffolk, was vice chamberlain and then master of the horse to Queen Henrietta Maria. He accompanied Henrietta Maria in 1644 to France, where he continued to act as her secretary. In the same year he was made governor of Jersey, and conceived the idea of ceding the Channel Islands to France as the price of French aid to Charles against the parliament. When Charles II. went to Breda, Jermyn remained in Paris with Henrietta Maria, who persuaded her son to create him earl of St. Albans in 1660. Gossip even asserted a secret marriage between the queen and Jermyn. At the Restoration St. Albans received various appointments, and he contributed to the close secret understanding between Charles II. and Louis XIV., taking part in the preliminaries of the Treaty of Dover in 1669. In 1664 he obtained a grant of land in London near St. James's Palace, where Jermyn street preserves the memory of his name, and where he built the St. Albans' market on a site afterwards cleared for the construction of Regent street and Waterloo place. The earl, who was a friend and patron of Abraham Cowley, died in January 1684.

ST. ALBANS, a city, municipal borough, and market town in the St. Albans parliamentary division of Hertfordshire, England, on the L.M.S. and L.N.E. railways, 20 mi. northwest of London. Pop. (est. 1938) 36,200. Area 8 sq.mi. St. Albans became the seat of a bishop in 1877, the diocese covering most of Hertfordshire and Bedfordshire, with very small portions of Buckinghamshire, Cambridgeshire and Middlesex. The great cathedral, or abbey church, is finely situated on the steep hill above the small river Ver.

History.—Shortly after the martyrdom of St. Alban, probably in 303, a church was built on the spot, and in 793 Offa, king of Mercia, who professed to have discovered the relics of the martyr, founded in his honour a monastery for Benedictines, which became one of the richest and most important houses of that order in the kingdom. The abbots, Ealdred and Ealmer, at the close of the 10th century began to break up the ruins of the old Roman city of Verulamium for materials to construct a new abbey church; but its erection was delayed till the time of William the Conqueror, when Paul of Caen, a relative of Archbishop Lanfranc, was in 1077 appointed abbot. The church was built on the model of St. Stephen's, Caen, but on a larger scale. It was consecrated in 1115, but had been finished some years before. Of the original Norman church the principal portions now remaining are the eastern bays of the nave, the tower and the transepts, but the main outlines of the building are still those planned by Paul. It is thus one of the most important specimens of Norman architecture in England, with the special characteristic that, owing to the use of the flat broad Roman tile, the Norman portions are peculiarly bare and stern.

About 1155 Robert de Gorham repaired and beautified the early shrine and rebuilt the chapter-house and part of the cloister; but nothing of his work now remains except part of a very beautiful doorway discovered in recent times. About 1200 Abbot John de Cella pulled down the west front and portions of the north and south aisles. He began the erection of the west front in a new and enriched form, and his work was continued by his successor William de Trumpyngtone in a plainer manner. In 1257 the eastern portion was pulled down, and between the middle of the 13th and the beginning of the 14th century a sanctuary, ante-chapel and lady chapel were added, all remarkably fine specimens of the architecture of the period. In 1323 two great columns on the south side suddenly fell, and this necessitated the rebuilding of five bays of the south aisle and the Norman cloisters. Various incongruous additions were made during the Perpendicular period, and much damage was also done during the dissolution of the abbeys to the finer work in the interior. Structural dangers gave rise to an extensive restoration and partial rebuilding, begun under the direction of Sir Gilbert Scott, and completed in 1894 by Lord Grimthorpe, some of whose work was, and remains, the subject of much adverse criticism. The abbey's extreme length outside is 550 ft., which is exceeded by Winchester by 6 ft. The nave (292 ft.) is the longest Gothic nave in the world and exceeds that of Winchester by about 20 ft. The length of the transepts is 175 ft. inside. The monastic buildings have all disappeared except the great gateway.

St. Michael's church (within the site of Verulamium) and St. Stephen's were originally constructed in the 10th century. Considerable portions of the Norman buildings remain. The former contains the tomb of Lord Chancellor Bacon. The restored clockhouse in the market place was built by one of the abbots in the reign of Henry VIII.

To the southwest of St. Albans stood the ancient Verulamium (q.v.), one of the oldest towns in Britain, on Watling street. The corporation bought the site (104 ac.) in 1929 and a museum was built. The ruins served as a quarry not only to the builders of the abbey, but also for the other churches and the monastic buildings of St. Albans, and Roman bricks are found even in the fabric of the churches of neighbouring villages, as at Sandridge, 2½ mi. northeast. After being burned by Boadicea (A.D. 61), Verulamium revived, and its church was famous early in the 8th century. The Saxon royal residence of Kingsbury is variously assigned to the 6th and 8th centuries. In the 9th and 10th centuries the abbots enlarged the town, which was confirmed to them as a borough by Henry II. In 1253 a charter gave borough jurisdiction to the goodmen of St. Albans; and there were several succeeding charters. In 1877 St. Albans became a city. The famous "model" parliament of 1295 was held at St. Albans. Two burgesses were returned to the parliament of 1306–07, but after 1336 such right fell into abeyance until its resumption in 1553. Its abolition, because of bribery, took place in 1852.

During Wat Tyler's insurrection the monastery was besieged by the townspeople, many of whom were executed in consequence. At St. Albans the Lancastrians were defeated on May 21, 1455, their leader, the duke of Somerset, being killed and Henry VI taken prisoner; here, too, Queen Margaret defeated the earl of Warwick on Feb. 17, 1461. During the civil wars the town was garrisoned for the parliament. One of the earliest printing presses in the kingdom was set up in the abbey, and a number of books were printed there in the late 15th century.

Battle of St. Albans, May 22, 1455. The first battle in the Wars of the Roses wherein the smaller Lancastrian force was defeated by the Yorkists and King Henry VI taken prisoner. A subsequent battle at the same place on Feb. 17, 1461, ended in the Lancastrians defeating Warwick and regaining possession of King Henry VI's person. *See* ROSES, WARS OF THE.

See *Victoria County History, Herts,* vol. ii.; Peter Newcome, *The History of the Abbey of St. Albans* (London, 1793); and *Chronica monasterii S. Albani,* ed. by H. T. Riley for "Rolls" series (1863–76).

SAINT ALBANS, a city of northwestern Vermont, U.S.A., a port of entry and county seat of Franklin county; 3 mi. from Lake Champlain (St. Albans bay) and 17 mi. from the Canadian border. It is on federal highway 7, and is served by the Central Vermont railway. Pop. (1950) 8,552. The city is 385 ft. above the level of the lake and is surrounded by hills with fine views of the Green mountains, Lake Champlain and the Adirondacks beyond.

St. Albans bay is a famous fishing ground. The city is a summer resort and touring centre; headquarters of the railway, which employs some 500 persons in its offices and shops, and of various activities of the federal government; and an important shipping point for maple sugar and dairy products, variegated marble and other products of the region and its factories. It is the headquarters of the customs district of Vermont. The first settlement was made in 1774.

The town was organized in 1788, incorporated in 1859 and chartered as a city in 1897. It has a mayor-city council form of government. On Oct. 19, 1864, it was raided from Canada by a party of Confederate soldiers (not in uniform), who looted three banks and wounded several citizens. They escaped to Canada, where the leader and 12 others were arrested, but not deprived of the $208,-000 they had taken. Later $88,000 of this was refunded by the Canadian government. In 1866 and 1870 the Fenians made St. Albans a base for attacks on Canada, and U.S. troops were sent there to preserve neutrality.

ST. ALDWYN, MICHAEL EDWARD HICKS BEACH, 1ST EARL (1837–1916), English statesman, son of Sir Michael Hicks Beach, 8th Bart., whom he succeeded in 1854, was born in London on Oct. 23, 1837, and was educated at Eton and Christ Church, Oxford. He entered parliament as Conservative M.P. for East Gloucestershire in 1864, and held various offices between 1868 and 1880. In 1885 he was elected for West Bristol, and the Conservative party having returned to power, became chancellor of the exchequer and leader of the house of commons. After Gladstone's brief Home Rule ministry in 1886 he entered Lord Salisbury's next cabinet again as Irish secretary, making way for Lord Randolph Churchill as leader of the house; but his eyesight compelled him to resign in 1887 and meanwhile Goschen replaced Lord Randolph as chancellor of the exchequer. From 1888 to 1892 Sir Michael Hicks Beach returned to active work as president of the board of trade, and in 1895—Goschen being transferred to the admiralty—he again became chancellor of the exchequer. In 1899 he lowered the fixed charge for the national debt from 25 to 23 millions—a reduction imperatively required, apart from other reasons, by the difficulties found in redeeming consols at their then inflated price. When compelled to find means for financing the war in South Africa, he insisted on combining the raising of loans with the imposition of fresh taxation; and besides raising the income tax each year, up to 1s. 3d. in 1902, he introduced taxes on sugar and exported coal (1901), and in 1902 proposed the reimposition of the registration duty on corn and flour which had been abolished in 1869 by Lowe. On Lord Salisbury's retirement in 1902 Sir Michael Hicks Beach also left the government.

He accepted the chairmanship of the Royal Commission on Ritualistic Practices in the Church, and he did valuable work as an arbitrator; he was a firm advocate of free trade and by his campaign against Joseph Chamberlain's protectionist programme did much to prevent Balfour from committing his party to that policy.

When Balfour resigned in 1905 he was raised to the peerage as Viscount St. Aldwyn (1906), and was created an earl in 1915. He died in London on April 30, 1916.

ST. AMAND-LES-EAUX, a town of northern France, in the department of Nord, at the junction of the Elnon with the Scarpe, 22 mi. S.E. of Lille by rail. Pop. (1946) 14,218. St. Amand owes its name to St. Amand, bishop of Tongres, who founded a monastery here in the 7th century. The abbey was laid waste by the Normans in 882 and by the count of Hainaut in 1340.

The town was captured by Mary of Burgundy in 1477, by the count of Ligne, Charles V's lieutenant, in 1521, and finally in 1667 by the French. The town has mineral waters and mud baths. The discovery of statues and coins in the mud shows that these must have been used during the Roman period.

ST. AMAND-MONT-ROND, a town of central France, capital of an arrondissement in the department of Cher, 39 mi. S.E. of Bourges on the railway to Montluçon. Pop. (1946) 10,990. The town grew up round a monastery founded by St. Amand, a follower of St. Columban, in the 7th century.

SAINT-AMANT, MARC ANTOINE DE GERARD, SIEUR DE (1594–1661), French poet, was born near Rouen in the year 1594, the son of a merchant. He obtained a patent of nobility, and attached himself to different great noblemen—the duc de Retz and the comte d'Harcourt among others. He saw military service and sojourned at different times in Italy, in England —a sojourn which provoked from him a violent poetical attack on the country, *Albion* (1643)—in Poland, where he held a court appointment for two years, and elsewhere. Saint-Amant's later years were spent in France; and he died at Paris on Dec. 29, 1661. Saint-Amant has left a not inconsiderable body of poetry. His *Albion* and *Rome ridicule* set the fashion of the burlesque poem, a form in which he was excelled by his follower Paul Scarron. In his later years he devoted himself to serious subjects and produced an epic, *Moïse sauvé* (1653). His best work consists of Bacchanalian songs, his *Débauche* being one of the most remarkable convivial poems of its kind,

The standard edition is that in the *Bibliothèque Elzévirienne*, by M. C. L. Livet (2 vols., 1855).

SAINT ANDRÉ, ANDRÉ JEANBON (1749–1813),

French revolutionary, was born at Montauban (Tarn-et-Garonne) on Feb. 25, 1749. In July 1793 he became president of the Convention, entered the Committee of Public Safety and was sent on mission to the Armies of the East. On Sept. 20, 1793, he obtained a vote of one hundred million francs for constructing vessels, and reorganized the military harbours of Brest and Cherbourg. After a mission in the south (July 1794–March 1795) in which he showed great moderation, he was arrested on May 28, 1795, but was released by the amnesty of the year IV. He was then appointed consul at Algiers and Smyrna (1798), imprisoned by the Turks for three years, and subsequently became prefect of the department of Mont-Tonnerre (1801) and commissary-general of the three departments on the left bank of the Rhine. He died at Mainz on Dec. 10, 1813.

See Lévy-Schneider, *Le Conventionnel Jeanbon St. André* (1901).

ST. ANDREWS,

city, royal burgh, university town and seaport of Fifeshire, Scotland. Pop. (1938) 8,383. It is situated on a bay of the North Sea, 12½ mi. S.E. of Dundee by the L.N.E.R., *via* Leuchars junction. It occupies a plateau of sandstone rock about 50 ft. high, on the north breaking off in precipitous cliffs. The Eden enters St. Andrews bay N.W. of the golf links, which rank amongst the finest in the world. The Royal and Ancient Golf club, founded in 1754, is the legislative authority of the game. There is a marine biological station. The city was never surrounded by walls, and of its ancient gates the West Port only remains. The Martyrs' memorial, erected to the honour of martyrs of the Reformation epoch, stands at the west end of the Scores on a cliff overlooking the sea.

The cathedral originated partly in the priory of Canons Regular founded by Bishop Robert (1122–1159). At the end of the 17th century some of the priory buildings were still entire and considerable remains of others existed, but nearly all traces have now disappeared except portions of the wall and the archways. The wall is about three-quarters of a mile long, and bears turrets at intervals.

The cathedral was founded by Bishop Arnold (1159–1162), to supply more ample accommodation than was afforded by the church of St. Regulus. The principal portions extant, partly Norman and partly Early English, are the east and west gables and part of the nave and the south transept. The plan of the cathedral is marked out on the turf.

The castle, on a rocky promontory, is supposed to have been erected by Bishop Roger about the beginning of the 13th century as an episcopal residence, and was strongly fortified. It was destroyed, but rebuilt towards the close of the century. There remains a portion of the south wall enclosing a square tower, the "bottle dungeon" below the northwest tower, the kitchen tower and a subterranean passage. The grounds have been laid out as a public garden.

The town church, formerly the church of the Holy Trinity, was originally founded in 1112 by Bishop Turgot, but was rebuilt about 1800 with the exception of the square tower and spire, and was splendidly restored in 1907–09, the original lines being followed as closely as possible. In this church John Knox first preached in public, and in it, on June 4, 1559, he delivered the famous sermon which led to the stripping of the cathedral and the destruction of the monastic buildings. The church contains a monument to James Sharp, archbishop of St. Andrews (assassinated 1679). In South street is the ruin of the north transept of the chapel of the Blackfriars' monastery founded by Bishop Wishart in 1274; but the Observantine monastery, founded about 1450 by Bishop Kennedy, has disappeared, except the well.

The university of St. Andrews, the oldest in Scotland, owed its origin to a society formed in 1410 by Lawrence of Lindores, abbot of Scone, and others. A charter was issued in 1411 by Bishop Henry Wardlaw (d. 1440), and six bulls were obtained from Benedict XIII in 1413 confirming the charter and constituting the society a university. The lectures were delivered in various parts of the town until 1430, when Wardlaw allowed the lecturers the use of a building called the Paedagogium, or St. John's. St.

Salvator's college was founded and richly endowed by Bishop Kennedy in 1456; seven years later it was granted the power to confer degrees in theology and philosophy, and by the end of the century was regarded as a constituent part of the university. In 1512 St. Leonard's college was founded, and the original Paedagogium nominally changed into a college, with the parish church of St. Michael of Tarvet annexed to it; but its actual erection into a college did not take place until 1537, when it was dedicated to the Blessed Virgin Mary of the Assumption. The outline of the ancient structure is preserved, but its general character has been much altered by various restorations. It forms two sides of a quadrangle. The University library, which includes the older college libraries, was founded before the middle of the 17th century and rebuilt in 1764. The lower hall in the older part of the building was used at times as a provincial meeting-place for the Scottish parliament. When the constitution of the colleges was remodelled in 1579 St. Mary's was set apart for theology; and in 1747 the colleges of St. Salvator and St. Leonard were formed into the United college. The buildings of St. Leonard's are now occupied as a school for girls. The college chapel is in ruins. The United college occupies the site of St. Salvator's college, but the old buildings have been removed, with the exception of the college chapel, now used as the university chapel and the parish church of St. Leonard's, a fine Gothic structure, containing an elaborate tomb of Bishop Kennedy and Knox's pulpit; the entrance gateway, with a square clock tower; and the janitor's house with some classrooms above. Younger hall is used for university functions. University college, Dundee, founded in 1881, was in 1897 affiliated to the university of St. Andrews. The Advanced Medical School of St. Andrews (1898) and the Dental school (1914) are in Dundee. In 1892 provision was made within the university for the instruction of women.

St. Andrews was probably the site of a Pictish stronghold, and tradition declares that Kenneth, the patron saint of Kennoway, established a Culdee monastery here in the 6th century. The foundations of the little church dedicated to the Virgin were discovered on the Kirkheugh in 1860. Another Culdee church of St. Mary on the Rock is supposed to have stood on the Lady's Craig, now covered by the sea. At that period the name of the place was Kilrymont (Gaelic, "The church of the king's mount") or Muckross. St. Andrews is said to have been made a bishopric in the 9th century, and when the Pictish and Scottish churches were united in 908, the primacy was transferred to it from Dunkeld, its bishops being thereafter known as bishops of Alban. It became an archbishopric during the primacy of Patrick Graham (1466–1478). The town was created a royal burgh in 1124. In the 16th century St. Andrews was one of the most important ports north of the Forth, but it fell into decay after the Civil War.

SAINT ARNAUD, JACQUES LEROY DE (1801–

1854), marshal of France, was born at Paris on Aug. 20, 1801. He entered the army in 1817, retired from the service in 1827, and re-entered it at thirty as a sub-lieutenant. He took part in the suppression of the Vendée émeute, and was for a time on General (Marshal) Bugeaud's staff. But his debts and the scandals of his private life compelled him to go to Algeria as a captain in the Foreign Legion. In 1848 he was placed at the head of a brigade during the revolution in Paris. On his return to Africa, it is said because Louis Napoleon considered him suitable to be the military head of a *coup d'état*, an expedition was made into Little Kabylia, in which St. Arnaud provided his superiors with the pretext for bringing him home as a general of division (July 1851). He succeeded Marshal Magnan as minister of war and superintended the military operations of the *coup d'état* of the 2nd of December (1851) which placed Napoleon III. on the throne. A year later he was made marshal of France and a senator, remaining at the head of the war office till 1854, when he set out to command the French in the Crimea, his British colleague being Lord Raglan. He died on board ship on Sept. 29, 1854, shortly after commanding at the battle of the Alma. His body was conveyed to France and buried in the Invalides.

See *Lettres du Maréchal de Saint Arnaud* (Paris, 1855: 2nd edition with memoir by Sainte-Beuve, 1858).

ST. ASAPH, a cathedral village-city of Flintshire, north Wales, on the Rhyl-Denbigh branch of the L.M.S. about 6 mi. from each of these towns. Pop. (1951) 9,860. Its Welsh name, Llanelwy, is derived from the Elwy, between which stream and the Clwyd it stands. Asaph, to whom the cathedral (the smallest in Great Britain, excluding converted parish churches) is dedicated, was bishop here in the 6th century. The small, irregularly built town has also a parish church, remains of a Perpendicular chapel near Ffynnon Fair (St. Mary's Well) and almshouses founded in 1678 by Bishop Barrow. The hill on which St. Asaph stands is Bryn Paulin, with early associations. The early cathedral, of wood, was burned by the English in 1247 and 1282, and that built by Bishop Anian in the 13th century (Decorated) was mostly destroyed during the raids of Owen Glendower (c. 1402). Bishop Redman's building (c. 1480) was completed by the erection of the choir about 1770. Further restoration took place in the 19th century. The church is plain, cruciform, chiefly Decorated but partly Early English, with a square tower; it has a library of nearly 2,000 volumes (some rare). In 1920 the then bishop of St. Asaph was enthroned in his cathedral as the first archbishop of the disestablished church in Wales.

SAINT AUGUSTINE, a city of northeastern Florida, U.S.A., on the coast, 38 mi. S.E. of Jacksonville; a port of entry and the county seat of St. Johns county. It is on federal highway 1 and the East Coast Inland waterway, and is served by the Florida East Coast railway.

The population in 1950 was 13,555; and in 1940 it was 12,090. The population is frequently doubled during tourist seasons.

The city occupies a narrow peninsula formed by the Matanzas and San Sebastian rivers, and is separated from the ocean by the northern end of Anastasia Island (½ mi. wide), where is located one of the world's best bathing beaches. It is the oldest city in the United States.

Many old houses remain, including the oldest house in the United States.

Castillo de San Marcos (once called Ft. Marion), oldest standing fortification in the United States, is a well preserved specimen of Spanish architecture, built of coquina, begun about 1638 and finished in 1756. The old arsenal reconstructed in 1835 by the United States became state headquarters of the national guard. A

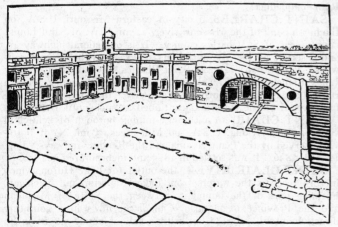

BY COURTESY OF THE ST. AUGUSTINE CHAMBER OF COMMERCE
COURTYARD OF THE CASTILLO DE SAN MARCOS, SHOWING THE INCLINED ARCH BUILT BY THE SPANIARDS FOR THE TRANSPORTATION OF CANNON FROM THE PLAZA TO THE TERREPLEIN. THE STEPS ARE MODERN

wall and moat formerly ran across the peninsula at the northern edge of the city, and the city gate which was in this wall still stands, a picturesque ruin, at the end of St. George street. The Roman Catholic church was built in 1791. The post office was the Spanish government building; the public library and the historical society both occupy buildings of historic interest. There is a beautiful modern church (Presbyterian) built in 1890 by Henry M. Flagler as a memorial to his daughter. St. Augustine is both a winter and a summer resort. The general offices and shops of the railway are there. In 1915 the city adopted a commission-manager form of government.

On St. Augustine's day (Aug. 28), 1565, Pedro Menéndez de Avilés sighted this coast, and on Sept. 6 he landed with his band of colonists and began to fortify the peninsula. In 1586 Sir Francis Drake captured the fort and burned the town, and in 1665 it was pillaged by Capt. John Davis, an English freebooter. Conflicts with the English settlements in South Carolina and Georgia were frequent after 1681. When Florida was ceded to England in 1763 most of the Spanish population of St. Augustine went to Cuba; when in 1783 it came again under Spanish rule, most of the English left for the Carolinas, Georgia, or the West Indies; and when in 1821 it passed to the United States, the Spanish inhabitants remained. On Jan. 7, 1861, three days before Florida passed her Ordinance of Secession, a State force compelled the small garrison to evacuate the fort, but on March 11, 1862, it was retaken without bloodshed, and was then held by the Federals until the close of the war.

ST. AUSTELL, market town, urban district, Penryn and Falmouth parliamentary division, Cornwall, England, 14 mi. N.E. of Truro, on G.W. railway. Pop. (1951) 23,655. Area 28.7 sq.mi. To the north the high ground on which St. Austell stands culminates in Hensbarrow Downs (1,026 ft.). Holy Trinity church is Perpendicular, with Decorated chancel, richly ornamented. The town is the centre of the china clay (kaolin) district, and some 3,000 persons are ordinarily employed in the industry, exports being mainly to the Potteries and Lancashire. Nearby is Menacuddle Well, a good example of an Early English baptistery.

ST. BARTHOLOMEW or **ST. BARTHELEMY,** French West Indian island, 17° 55′ N. and 63° 60′ W., about 130 mi. N.W. of Guadeloupe, of which it is a dependency. The horns of an irregular crescent enclose the bay of St. Jean, pointing north; the surface culminates in a central limestone hill 1,003 ft. high. It is 9 sq.mi. in area, and timberless. Gustavia, on the southwest coast has a small but safe harbour. Lorient is the only other town. The inhabitants, mainly of French and Negro descent, are English-speaking, and numbered 2,331 in 1946. St. Bartholomew was occupied by France in 1648 and ceded to Sweden in 1784. In 1877 it was again acquired by France at the cost of £11,000.

ST. BARTHOLOMEW, MASSACRE OF. This was the name given to the massacre of the Huguenots, which began in Paris on St. Bartholomew's Day, Aug. 24, 1572. The initiative for the crime rests with Catherine de' Medici. Disquieted by the growing influence of Admiral Coligny, who against her wishes was endeavouring to draw Charles IX. into a war with Spain, she resolved to have him assassinated. The attempt failed, however, and Catherine then determined to massacre all the Huguenot leaders.

After holding a council with the Catholic leaders, including the Duke of Anjou, Henry of Guise, the Marshal de Tavannes, the Duke of Nevers, and René de Birague, the keeper of the seals, she persuaded the king that the massacre was a measure of public safety, and on the evening of Aug. 23 succeeded in wringing authorization from him.

The massacre began on Sunday at daybreak, and continued in Paris till Sept. 17. Once let loose, it was impossible to restrain the populace. From Paris the massacre spread to the provinces till Oct. 3. The Duc de Longueville in Picardy, Chabot-Charny (son of Admiral Chabot) at Dijon, the Comte de Matignon (1525–97) in Normandy and other provincial governors refused to authorize the massacres. François Hotman estimates the number killed in the whole of France at 50,000. Catherine de' Medici received the congratulations of all the Catholic powers, and Pope Gregory XIII. commanded bonfires to be lighted and a medal to be struck.

See H. Mariéjol, "La Réforme et la Ligue" (1904), in vol. vi. of the *Histoire de France,* by E. Lavisse, which contains a complete bibliography of the subject.

ST. BENOÎT-SUR-LOIRE, a village of France, in the department of Loiret, on the Loire, 22 mi. E.S.E. of Orléans. Pop. (1946) 508. St. Benoît has a huge basilica, only survival of a 7th century monastery to which the relics of St. Benedict were brought from Monte Cassino. In the crypt is a modern shrine containing the remains of St. Benedict, which still attract many pilgrims. The establishment was very important during the middle ages, owing partly to its school. In 1562 it was pillaged by the Protestants and, though the buildings were restored by Richelieu, the abbey declined. The basilica (1025–1218) has a narthex of two stories and two sets of transepts, surmounted by a square central tower.

SAINT BERNARD, a city of Hamilton county, Ohio, U.S., 15 mi. N.E. of Cincinnati; served by several railways for freight. Pop. (1950) 7,066; (1940) 7,387; (1930) 7,487 by federal census. It is a residential suburb of Cincinnati, and has various manufacturing industries.

ST. BERNARD PASSES, two passes across the main chain of the Alps, both traversed by motor roads. The Great St. Bernard (8,094 ft.) leads (53 mi.) from Martigny (anc. *Octodurus*) in the Rhone valley (Switzerland) to Aosta (anc. *Augusta Praetoria*) in Italy. It was known in Roman times. The hospice on the pass was founded (or perhaps refounded) by St. Bernard of Menthon (d. about 1081), and since the 12th or early 13th century has been in charge of a community of Austin canons, the mother-house being at Martigny. In former days the servants of the canons, and the famous dogs, saved many lives, especially of Italian workmen. In May 1800 Napoleon led his army over the pass, which was then traversed by a bridle road only. The Little St. Bernard (7,178 ft.) also was known in Roman times, and the hospice refounded by St. Bernard of Menthon, though it is now in charge of the military and religious order of SS. Maurice and Lazarus. The pass leads (39 mi.) from Bourg St. Maurice in the Isère valley (Savoie) to Aosta, but is much less frequented by travellers than its neighbour opposite.

There is no certain mention of the road over the pass of the Great St. Bernard (*Alpis Poenina, Poeninus Mons*) before 57 B.C. when Julius Caesar sent Servius Galba over it. Even in Strabo's time it was impassable for wheeled traffic; we find that Augusta Praetoria originally had but two gates, one opening towards the Little St. Bernard (*Alpis Graia*), the other towards Eporedia (Ivrea), but none towards the Alpis Poenina. The military arrangement of the German provinces rendered the construction of the road necessary, and it is mentioned as existing in A.D. 69. Remains of it cut in the rock, some 12½ ft. in width, still exist near the lake at the top of the pass. On the plain at the top of the pass is the temple of Jupiter Poeninus (Penninus), remains of which were excavated in 1890–1893, though objects connected with it had long ago been found. The oldest of the votive-tablets which can be dated belongs to the time of Tiberius, and the temple may be attributed to the beginning of the empire; objects, however, of the first Iron age (4th or 5th century B.C.) were also found and many Gaulish coins. Other buildings, probably belonging to the post station at the top of the pass, were also discovered. Many of the objects found then and in previous years, including many votive-tablets, are in the museum at the hospice of the Great St. Bernard.

The Little St. Bernard was known to the Romans as Alpis Graia. It derived its name from the legend that Hercules, returning from Spain with the oxen of Geryon, crossed the Alps by this route, though the legend rather suits the route through the Maritime Alps. According to some modern scholars, Hannibal passed this way over the Alps (see HANNIBAL, and Partsch in Pauly-Wissowa, *Realencyklopädie* i., 1604). In any case it was the principal pass over the Alps into Gallia Comata until the pass of the Alpis Cottia (Mont Genèvre) was opened by Cn. Pompeius in 75 B.C., and became the principal route, though the road was only completed under Augustus by Cottius in 3 B.C. Various remains of the road are visible, and those of a building (possibly a temple of Jupiter) have been found on the summit of the pass.

See *Notizie degli scavi* (1883), 7 (1894), 46; and C. Promis, *Antichità di Aosta* (Turin, 1862), 115 *sqq.*

ST. BERTRAND-DE-COMMINGES, a village of S.W. France at the foot of the Pyrenees in the department of Haute-Garonne, about 70 mi. S.W. of Toulouse by rail and road. St. Bertrand-de-Comminges (*Lugdunum Convenarum*) was founded in 72 B.C. and by the end of the 5th century became the seat of a bishopric suppressed at the Revolution. The town was destroyed

towards the end of the 6th century by Guntrum, king of Burgundy. St. Bertrand stands about 1 mi. from the left bank of the Garonne on the slopes of an isolated hill crowned by its celebrated cathedral of Notre Dame. The façade of the church with its square tower and the first bay with its aisles are Romanesque, and belong to an 11th century church begun by Bishop Bertrand, afterward canonized. Pop. (1946) 243.

ST. BRIEUC, a town of western France, capital of the department of Côtes-du-Nord, 63 mi. N.W. of Rennes by the railway to Brest. Pop. (1946) 36,674. St. Brieuc owes its origin and its name to the missionary St. Briocus, who came from Wales in the 5th century, and whose tomb afterward attracted crowds of pilgrims. The place was defended in 1375 by Olivier de Clisson against the duke of Brittany, and later attacked by the same Clisson in 1394, the cathedral suffering greatly in both sieges. In 1592 the town was pillaged by the Spaniards, in 1601 ravaged by the plague, and in 1628 surrounded by walls of which no traces remain. Between 1602 and 1768 the states of Brittany several times met at St. Brieuc. It stands 290 ft. above the sea, between 1 and 2 mi. from the English channel and less than a mile from the right bank of the Gouët, at the mouth of which is its seaport, Le Légué. St. Brieuc is the seat of a bishopric in the province of Rennes, and has a 13th-century cathedral, partially rebuilt in the 18th, and afterward restored.

ST. CATHARINES, a city of Ontario, Canada, and the capital of Lincoln county, on the Welland canal and the Canadian National and Niagara, St. Catharines and Toronto electric railways, 35 mi. S. of Toronto. Pop. (1951) 37,984. It is the centre of the Niagara fruit belt. Chief industries include wineries, paper and textile mills, automotive parts and mining machinery plants. It is the site of the annual Royal Canadian Henley regatta and Ontario's largest outdoor horseshow.

ST. CHAMOND, a manufacturing town of east-central France, in the department of Loire, 7½ mi. E.N.E. of St. Etienne, on the railway from St. Etienne to Lyons. Pop. (1946) 14,820. St. Chamond, founded in the 7th century by St. Ennemond or Chamond, archbishop of Lyons, became the chief town of the Jarret, a little principality formed by the valley of the Gier. Silk-milling was introduced in the town in the middle of the 16th century by Gayotti, a native of Bologna. There are remains of a Roman aqueduct.

SAINT CHARLES, a city of eastern Missouri, U.S.A., on the north bank of the Missouri river, 22 mi. N.W. of Saint Louis; county seat of St. Charles county. It is on federal highway 40, and is served by the Missouri-Kansas-Texas and the Wabash railways. Pop. (1950) 14,314. Saint Charles was settled in 1769 by Louis Blanchette, a Frenchman, and later came under Spanish rule. In 1849 it was incorporated as a city. In 1820 it became the first capital of the state and continued as such until 1826.

SAINT CLAIR, an anthracite-mining borough of Schuylkill county, Pennsylvania, U.S.A., on Mill creek, 3 mi. N. of Pottsville; served by the Pennsylvania and the Reading railways. Pop. (1950) 5,856. It was settled in 1825 and incorporated in 1850.

SAINT CLAIR RIVER, the outlet for Lake Huron, which in turn receives the waters from Lakes Superior and Michigan. Forming part of the boundary between the State of Michigan and the Province of Ontario, Canada, it flows in a southerly direction into Lake St. Clair with a fall of about 5.8 ft. in 40 miles. The river discharges through seven mouths, the one known as the south channel being used for deep-draught vessels, while several of the other channels are used for small craft. The south channel was improved by the dredging of separate channels for up-bound and down-bound traffic, extending from deep water in the river into Lake St. Clair.

In 1937 a project, not including compensating works, improving the north channel outlet and adding to the width and depth of the southeast bend was completed. The U.S. congress authorized the widening of the channel at the southeast bend to 700 ft. in March 1945 and further improvements in both sections were authorized in July 1946. The river water level fluctuates with the levels of the lakes above and below. From about the year 1910 on, the difference between the highest and lowest monthly mean levels during the navigation season has been about 4 ft. Occasional fluctuations due to winds of high velocity may be 3.5 ft. in six hours. Near the head of the river are the cities of Port Huron, Mich., and Sarnia, Ont., both of which handle some water-borne commerce but the great bulk of the traffic moves through the river without intermediate stop. This traffic is composed principally of iron ore, grain and limestone down-bound and coal up-bound.

BIBLIOGRAPHY.—Annual Report of the chief of engineers, Government Printing Office (1928); *House Document* No. 253 of the 70th Congress, 1st Session, Government Printing Office (1928); *Transportation on the Great Lakes*, Government Printing Office (1926); Bulletin No. 37, *Survey of Northern and North-western Lake*, U.S. Lake Survey, Detroit (April 1928). (E. JA.; X.)

ST. CLAUDE, a town of eastern France, capital of an arrondissement in the department of Jura, 42 mi. S.S.E. of Lons-le-Saunier by rail. Pop. (1946) 10,749. The town is situated 1,300 ft. above sea level at the western base of Mont Bayard, among the heights of the eastern Jura at the confluence of the Bienne and the Tacon. The cathedral of St. Pierre, once the abbey-church, dates from the 14th to the 18th centuries.

ST. CLOUD, a town of northern France, in the department of Seine-et-Oise, on the left bank of the Seine, 2 mi. W. of the fortifications of Paris by road. Pop. (1946) 17,614. The town is named after Clodoald or Cloud, grandson of Clovis, whose tomb was discovered in a crypt near the present church. He had granted the domain to the bishops of Paris, who possessed it as a fief till the 18th century. At St. Cloud Henry III and the king of Navarre (Henry IV) established their camp during the league for the siege of Paris and there the former was assassinated. The castle, at that time a plain country house belonging to Pierre de Gondi, archbishop of Paris, was acquired in 1658 by the duke of Orleans, who built the palace which perished in 1870. It was at St. Cloud that Bonaparte executed the coup d'état of the 18th Brumaire (1799); after he became emperor the palace was his favourite residence, and there he celebrated his marriage with Marie Louise. In 1815 it was the scene of the signing of the capitulation of Paris. Seized by the Prussians at the beginning of the investment of Paris in 1870, St. Cloud was sacked during the siege. St. Cloud, built on a hill slope overlooking the river, the Bois de Boulogne and Paris, is one of the favourite resorts of the Parisians. Every September, at the time of the pilgrimage of St. Cloud, a fair lasting four weeks is held in the park, which is famous for its beauty. Within its precincts are situated the national Sèvres porcelain manufactory.

ST. CLOUD, a city in central Minnesota, U.S., on the Mississippi river, 70 mi. N.W. of Minneapolis, in the counties of Benton, Sherburne and Stearns, and county seat of the latter. It is on federal highways 10 and 52, is served by the Great Northern and Northern Pacific railways, and by air and bus. Pop. (1950) 28,410. The city ranks first in the nation in the production of coloured granite and second in the production and processing of all types of granite. A large car manufacturing shop of the Great Northern railway is located there. Other important industries include an optical works and factories for the production of floor-sanding machines, refrigerators, boats, playground equipment, brooms, airline tanks, neon signs, frost shields and many other products. The processing of dairy products is of major importance. Among the city's many institutions are the Minnesota State reformatory, the U.S. veterans hospital, Saint Cloud Orphanage, Saint Raphael's and Saint Joseph's homes for the aged, and a state teachers college, Saint John's university for men and Saint Benedict's college for women are within a few miles of the city. St. Cloud was settled in 1852, platted in 1854, incorporated as a village in 1868 and chartered as a city in 1889. In 1912 it adopted a commission-council form of government. Before the days of the railroads it was the terminus of the Hudson's Bay company for unloading the furs brought down from the Red river valley in wooden oxcarts.

ST. CROIX or **SANTA CRUZ,** the largest of the West Indian islands purchased from Denmark by the United States in 1917. It lies 65 mi. S.E. of Puerto Rico, in 17° 40′ N. and 64° 14′ W., is 22 mi. long, varies in breadth from 1 mi. to 6 mi. and has an area of 82 sq.mi. Pop. 12,103 (1950). Hills parallel with the

western coast culminate in Mount Eagle (1,164 ft.). The narrower part is also hilly, but the south shore has marshy tracts with brackish lagoons. Sugar is the staple product, but other crops are being encouraged. The capital, picturesque Christiansted (pop. 4,112) is situated at the head of an inlet on the north shore, but its harbour is largely choked with mud. The only other town, Frederiksted (pop. 1,961) stands on an open roadstead on the west coast. The climate is healthful, with a mean annual temperature of 74° F. and an average annual rainfall of 45.7 in.

St. Croix was discovered in 1493 by Columbus, and owned in turn by Dutch, English and Spanish. In 1651 it was taken by France, and was given to the Knights of Malta in 1653. Denmark purchased it in 1733. Slavery was abolished in 1848 after a violent insurrection. *See* ST. THOMAS; VIRGIN ISLANDS.

See annual *Reports* of the governor of the Virgin islands.

ST. CYR-L'ÉCOLE, a town of France in the department of Seine-et-Oise, 3 mi. W. of Versailles at the end of the old park of Louis XIV. Pop. (1946) 4,458. Its importance is due to the famous military school (*école spéciale militaire*) in which officers for the cavalry and infantry are trained, established in 1808 in a convent where Racine's *Esther* and *Athalie* were first acted. The convent was suppressed at the Revolution.

ST. DAVID'S (TYDDEWI), a cathedral village-city of Pembrokeshire, Wales, situated near the sea to the south-east of St. David's head, the most westerly promontory of south Wales. Pop. (1931) 1,580. St. David's is 10 mi. from Netterson G.W.R. station, and about 16 mi. S.W. from Fishguard. The little town, locally known as "the city," stands in a lofty position near the cathedral close, and consists of five streets focusing on the square, called Cross Keys, the ancient market place still possessing its market cross (restored 1873). The origin of the fine little cathedral and its village "city" in an area so remote under modern conditions is of special interest. North-west Pembrokeshire, like most western promontories of Britain, France and Spain, is remarkably rich in old stone monuments (menhirs, dolmens and stone circles), a fact pointing in all probability to its being on the coastwise and transpeninsular route frequented by prehistoric traders from the Mediterranean to Ireland. (*See* PEMBROKESHIRE.)

The little boats of old were driven hither and thither at the mercy of wind and tide, so the coastland of St. David's head became dotted with alternative landing places, *e.g.*, Porth y Rhaw, St. Non's Bay, Porth Clais, Porth Stinian, Whitesand Bay, which seem to have made the neighbourhood important in pre-Christian times, as one may judge from folk tradition, monuments on the headland, etc.

The pre-Christian tradition was continued by the Celtic saints moving between Ireland and Wales. In early mediaeval days the same route grew important, as pilgrims moved to and from the shrine of St. Iago da Compostella in north-west Spain. (*See* Hartwell Jones, "Celtic Britain and the Pilgrim Movement," *Y Cymmrodor* 1912.) The little landing places on the shore now had Christian chapels, where prayers were possibly said for safe voyages. The most important ruins at present are those of St. Justinian. At a focus behind a group of these small ports, in the quiet sheltered, well-watered valley of the Alun, the fine cathedral of SS. David and Andrew was built, and on the high ground around, as if sheltering it still further, the "village-city" grew. Throughout the middle ages the cathedral was the centre of pilgrimage and the mediaeval roads (often marked by sacred wells) may be traced across Pembrokeshire focusing on St. David's. Two pilgrimages to St. David's were popularly thought to equal one to Rome itself. The early holders of the see ventured, while the central government was weak, to exercise metropolitan rights over much of south Wales, but the increasing power of the Norman penetration reached St. David's and Anselm's forcible appointment of Bernard—a Norman monk—to be bishop in 1115 made St. David's a suffragan see of Canterbury. A conciliatory step, it would appear, was the canonization of David about 1120. Gerald de Barri (Giraldus Cambrensis) strove vainly to regain the ancient power of St. David's from 1199–1203.

The cathedral church is partly built of a beautiful purple-hued sandstone, quarried locally. Its proportions are: length (exclusive of the Trinity and Lady chapels) 254½ ft.; breadth of nave and aisles, 51⅓ ft.; breadth of transepts, including tower, 116 ft.; and height of central tower, 116 feet. The earliest and main portion of the existing fabric was erected under Bishop Peter de Leia (1176–98) in the transitional Norman-English style. Bishop David Martin (1296–1328) built the Lady chapel; Bishop Henry de Gower (1328–47) made many additions in the Decorated style, including the stone rood screen and southern porch; and Bishop Edward Vaughan (1509–22) erected the Trinity chapel between the choir and Lady chapel. The cathedral suffered severely during the changes brought about by the Reformation and at the hands of Bishop William Barlow (1536–48) and again during the civil wars of the 17th century. Subsequent restorations took place. The interior of the nave, separated by six wide bays from the aisles, is imposing with its triforium and clerestory. It has an elaborate roof of Irish oak, the gift of Treasurer Owen Pole (c. 1500). The nave is divided from the choir by Bishop Gower's fine stone screen, while the choir contains the richly carved stalls erected by Bishop Tully (1460–81), the episcopal throne, and an oaken screen that serves to separate choir and presbytery. Bishop Vaughan's chapel contains fine Tudor fanvaulting, and the Lady chapel decorated sedilia. To the north of the cathedral is the ruined shell of the beautiful chapel with an adjoining tower, forming part of the college of St. Mary, founded by John of Gaunt and Bishop Adam Houghton in 1377. On the west bank of the Alun stand the ruins of the episcopal palace erected by Bishop Gower (c. 1342). The palace was built for residential purposes rather than for defense and occupies three sides of a quadrangle 120 ft. square, and, though roofless and deserted for nearly three centuries, retains most of its principal features. The great hall, 96 ft. by 33 ft., possesses a traceried wheel window; the chief portal is still imposing; and the chapel retains its curious bell turret; while the peculiar but graceful arcaded parapet of the roof extends intact throughout the whole length of the building. Partially dismantled by Bishop Barlow (c. 1540) the half-ruined palace was occasionally occupied by succeeding bishops prior to the civil wars. The Close contains the deanery and other residences of the cathedral clergy, mostly occupying the sites of ancient buildings. It formerly owned four gateways, of which the South or Tower gate alone remains.

ST. DENIS, a suburb 5½ mi. north of Notre Dame de Paris, capital of an arrondissement in the department of Seine. Pop. (1946) 69,939. St. Denis, an important junction on the northern railway, stands in a plain on the right bank of the Seine, which is here joined by the canal of St. Denis. It has numerous metallurgical works, where railway material, naval engines and the like are constructed, distilleries of spirits, glassworks, potteries and manufactories of drugs, chemical products, oils, nickel plate and pianos. The name and fame of the town are derived from the abbey founded by Dagobert I on the spot where St. Denis, the apostle of Paris, was interred.

St. Denis, the ancient *Catulliacum*, was a town of no pretensions till the foundation of its abbey, which became one of the most powerful in France. The rebuilding of the church, begun in the 12th century by Suger, was completed in the 13th century. Among the many domains of the abbey was the French Vexin. It was held during the later middle ages by the French kings and vassals of the abbey, and to this fact is due their adoption of the oriflamme or red banner of St. Denis as the royal standard. Louis XIV reduced the abbey to the rank of a priory; and at the Revolution it was suppressed, the tombs being violated and the church sacked (1793). Louis XVIII caused all the articles belonging to St. Denis to be brought back to their original site, and added numerous other monuments from the suppressed abbeys. But it was not until after 1848 that, under the direction of Viollet-le-Duc, the basilica recovered its original appearance. St. Denis which was the key of Paris on the north, was more than once pillaged in the Hundred Years' War, suffering especially in 1358 and 1406. A sanguinary battle, in which the Catholic leader Constable Anne de Montmorency found victory and death, was fought between Huguenots and Catholics in the neighbourhood

on Nov. 10, 1567.

The church exhibits the transition from the Romanesque to the Gothic style. The west front was built between 1137 and 1140. The right-hand tower is almost pure Romanesque; that on the left was Gothic, but its spire was struck by lightning in 1837. The porch formed by the first three bays contains some remains of the bascilica of Pippin the Short and Charlemagne, by whom the church was rebuilt. The nave proper (235 ft. long and 57 wide) has seven bays, and dates, as well as most of the choir and transepts, from the reign of St. Louis. The secondary apse (*rond-point*) and its semicircular chapels (consecrated in 1144) are considered as the first perfected attempt at Gothic. The transepts have fine façades, the north of the 12th, the south of the 13th century, each with two unfinished towers; if the plan had been fully carried out there would have been six towers beside a central spire in lead. The church contains a series of tombs of the kings and princes of the royal houses of France. The most remarkable are those of Louis XII and Anne of Brittany, executed from 1516 to 1532; of Henry II and Catherine de' Medici, a masterpiece by Germain Pilon (1564–1583); of Louis of Orleans and Valentine of Milan, from the old church of the Celestines at Paris (1502–1515); of Francis I and Claude of France, one of the most splendid tombs of the Renaissance, executed under the direction of Philibert Delorme (1550–1560); and that of Dagobert, which, though considerably dilapidated, ranks as one of the most curious of mediaeval (13th-century) works of art. In the apse some stained glass of the time of Suger remains.

The crypt dates partly from the 10th or 11th century. In the centre is the vault where the coffin of the king used to lie until, to make room for that of his successor, it was removed to its final resting place. It is at present occupied by the coffin of Louis XVIII, the last sovereign whose body was borne to St. Denis. Besides fine statues, the crypt contains the Bourbon vault, in which among other coffins are deposited the remains of Louis XVI and Marie Antoinette.

See F. de Guilhermy, *Monographie de l'église royale de St. Denis* (Paris, 1848).

ST. DIÉ, a town of eastern France, capital of an arrondissement in the department of Vosges, 38 mi. N.E. of Épinal by rail. Pop. (1940) 15,637. St. Dié (*Deodatum, Theodata, S. Deodati Fanum*) grew up round a monastery founded in the 7th century by St. Deodatus of Nevers, who retired to this place. In the 10th century the community became a chapter of canons. Among the privileges enjoyed by them was that of coining money. Though they co-operated in building the town walls, the canons and the dukes of Lorraine soon became rivals for the authority over St. Dié. The institution of a town council in 1628, and the establishment in 1777 of a bishopric which appropriated part of their spiritual jurisdiction, greatly diminished the influence of the canons; and with the Revolution they were swept away. During the wars of the 15th, 16th and 17th centuries the town was repeatedly sacked. It was also partially destroyed by fire in 1065, 1155, 1554, and 1757. St. Dié is on the Meurthe in a basin surrounded by well-wooded hills. The cathedral has a Romanesque nave (12th century) and a Gothic choir; the portal of red stone dates from the 18th century. A fine cloister (13th century), containing a stone pulpit, communicates with the Petite-Église or Notre-Dame, 12th-century Romanesque. St. Dié is the seat of a bishop and of a sub-prefect.

ST. DIZIER, a town of northeastern France, in the department of Haute-Marne, 45 mi. N.N.W. of Chaumont by rail, on the Marne and the Haute-Marne canal. Pop. (1940) 19,532. It is an important centre of the iron trade. It dates from the 3rd century, when the relics of Bishop St. Didier were brought there.

ST. DUNSTAN'S. St. Dunstan's is a charity for the treatment, training and lifelong aftercare of men and women blinded on war service. It was founded in 1915 by Sir Arthur Pearson, himself blind during the last ten years of his life. The work began in a house called "St. Dunstan's" in Regent's park, London. Its purpose then was the care of British soldiers, sailors and airmen blinded in or as a result of, World War I, of whom there were

STE. ANNE DE BEAUPRÉ—SAINTE-BEUVE

to include men and women of the services subsidiary to the armed
forces, and to policemen, firemen, members of the merchant navy
and fishing fleet, and all personnel of the civil defense, nursing
and medical services who might be blinded on duty. On the
death of Sir Arthur Pearson, Lady (Arthur) Pearson, occupied
the office of president of the organization, and in 1947 Sir Neville
Pearson, their only son, took her place. The chairman of the council was Sir Ian Fraser, an officer blinded in 1916.

On completion of treatment, patients are transferred to the
training centre for one to two years. The centre is residential
and there is no charge for board, lodging, education or training
in any of the regular occupations or professions, or special courses.
St. Dunstan's also provides all necessary apparatus, books and
equipment and makes grants for special needs, children's maintenance and education, etc. Early weeks are spent learning typewriting, braille reading, games and pastimes, learning to look after
daily needs, walking alone, etc. Training for a career then follows. Subjects studied include public affairs, the law, the church,
physiotherapy, telephone operating, public and commercial administration, shopkeeping, factory work including machine mind-
ing, lecturing, journalism and a variety of handicrafts. The
St. Dunstaner then returns to his own home. Thenceforward, until the end of his life, he remains under the organization's care.

St. Dunstan's is associated with the Scottish National Institution for the War-Blinded (Newington house, Edinburgh) in caring for war-blinded Scotsmen. St. Dunstan's, with Newington
house, is recognized by the government departments concerned as
the official centre for the training, re-education, settlement and
aftercare of blinded service men and women, and has branches and
affiliations throughout the commonwealth and empire. St. Dunstan's receives no state aid, but has considerable endowments and
is supported by voluntary contributions. The administrative offices are at 191, Marylebone road, London, N.W. 1.   (I. Fr.)

STE. ANNE DE BEAUPRÉ, pop. (1951) 1,827, a village
of Montmorency county, Quebec, Canada, at the junction of the
Ste. Anne river with the St. Lawrence, and on the Canadian National railway system 21 mi. northeast of the city of Quebec. It
stands in a rolling agricultural country, with hills in the background; and near by on the Ste. Anne river, are beautiful falls
and excellent fishing. Ste. Anne is a notable Roman Catholic
place of pilgrimage; annual pilgrimages are made from all over
Canada and the United States to see Ste. Anne's shrine and to participate in special religious services. Among the sights of interest
is a huge panoramic painting of the "Day of Crucifixion" on a
canvas 45 ft. high and 360 ft. in circumference. Ste. Anne is the
headquarters of the French-Canadian Redemptorists and the seat
of their college.

SAINTE-BEUVE, CHARLES AUGUSTIN (1804–
1869), French critic, was born at Boulogne-sur-Mer on Dec. 23,
1804. He was a posthumous child. His father, a native of Picardy,
and controller of town-dues at Boulogne, was a man of literary
tastes; his mother was half English, her father, a mariner of
Boulogne, having married an Englishwoman. Charles Augustin
was sent to a boarding school in Paris to attend the classes of
the Collège Charlemagne, and then of the Collège Bourbon. He
then studied medicine, but after four years abandoned it to join
the staff of the new Liberal newspaper, *The Globe,* in which he
published the excellent articles on the French poetry of the 16th
century afterwards separately published as *Tableau historique et
critique de la poésie française au XVIᵉ siècle* (2nd ed., 1842).
In 1829 he made his first venture as a poet with the *Vie, poésies, et
pensées de Joseph Delorme.* His own name did not appear; but
Joseph Delorme, that "Werther in the shape of Jacobin and
medical student," as Guizot called him, was the Sainte-Beuve of
those days himself. In 1830 came his second volume of poems,
the *Consolations.* But the critic in him grew to prevail more and
more and pushed out the poet. Sainte-Beuve was at this time a
devoted Catholic and a little later for a very short period a
disciple of Lamennais. But he gradually separated from his
Catholic friends, and at the same time a coldness grew up between
him and Victor Hugo, whose warm friendship he had won by an

early article on *Odes et Ballades.* He became the lover of Madame
Hugo, and a definite separation between the former friends ensued
in 1834. In 1831 the *Revue des deux mondes* was founded, and
from the first Sainte-Beuve was one of the most active and important contributors. He brought out his novel of *Volupté* in 1834,
his third and last volume of poetry, the *Pensées d'août,* in 1837.
He had long meditated work on Port-Royal, which took shape in
a series of lectures delivered at Lausanne in 1838. The book
occupied him at intervals until 1848—*Port Royal* (5 vols. 1840–
48; 5th ed., 1888–91).

In 1840 Victor Cousin, then minister of public instruction,
appointed him one of the keepers of the Mazarin library, an
appointment which gave him rooms at the library, and a competence, and leisure for study. With a Greek teacher, M.
Pantasides, he read and re-read the Greek poets. Articles on
Homer, Theocritus, Apollonius of Rhodes, and Meleager in the
Revue des deux mondes were fruits of his new Greek studies.
But in general his subjects were taken from the great literature of his own country. Seven volumes of *Portraits,* contributed to the *Revue de Paris* and the *Revue des deux mondes,*
exhibit his work in the years from 1832 to 1848, a work constantly increasing in range and value. In 1844 he was elected to
the French Academy as successor to Casimir Delavigne, and was
received there at the beginning of 1845 by Victor Hugo.

In March 1848 was published an account of secret-service
money distributed in the late reign, and Sainte-Beuve was put
down as having received the sum of one hundred francs. The
sum appears to have been in reality paid for alterations to a
smoky chimney in the library, but Sainte-Beuve was annoyed at
the imputation and resigned his chair. He lectured for a time at
Liége, but returned to Paris within a year. Dr. Véron, the editor
of the *Constitutionnel,* proposed to him that he should supply that
newspaper with a literary article for every Monday; and thus
the famous *Causeries du lundi* were started. Sainte-Beuve now
lived in the small house in the Rue Montparnasse (No. 11), which
he occupied for the remainder of his life, and where in 1850 his
mother, from whom he seems to have inherited his good sense,
tact and finesse, died at the age of eighty-six. For three years
he continued writing every Monday for the *Constitutionnel;* then
he passed, with a similar engagement, to the *Moniteur.* In 1857
his Monday articles began to be published in volumes, and by 1862
formed a collection in 15 volumes; they afterwards were resumed
under the title of *Nouveaux lundis,* which now make a collection
of 13 volumes more.

In 1854 he was nominated to the chair of Latin poetry at the
college of France. He was rudely interrupted by the students,
and resigned; he was then appointed lecturer on French literature
at the École Normale Supérieure. Here he lectured for four
years. During this period his contributions to the *Moniteur* were
intermittent. He now returned to a regular Monday article for
the *Constitutionnel.*

The Empire was tardy in acknowledging his merits, and it was
not until 1865 that he received the senatorship with its income
sufficient to make him independent, and his health was failing
him. He could seldom attend the meetings of the senate; the part
he took there, however, on two famous occasions—when the nomination of Ernest Renan to the college of France came under discussion in 1867, and the law on the press in the year following—
offended the majority in that conservative assembly and delighted
those who "belonged," to use his own phrase, "to the diocese of
free thought." He gave further pleasure in this diocese by leaving
the *Moniteur* at the beginning of 1869, and contributing to a
Liberal journal, the *Temps.* This defection finally alienated him
from the Bonapartists, and lost him the friendship of the Princess
Mathilde. His literary activity suffered little abatement, but pain
made him at last unable to sit to write; he could only stand or lie.
He died in his house in the Rue Montparnasse on Oct. 13, 1869.

The root of Sainte-Beuve's criticism is his single-hearted devotion to truth. What he called "fictions" in literature, in politics,
in religion, were not allowed to influence him. Some one had
talked on his being tenacious of a certain set of literary opinions.
"I hold very little," he answers, "to literary opinions; literary

opinions occupy very little place in my life and in my thoughts. What does occupy me seriously is life itself and the object of it." "I am accustomed incessantly to call my judgments in question anew, and to re-cast my opinions the moment I suspect them to be without validity." "What I have wished" (in *Port-Royal*) "is to say not a word more than I thought, to stop even a little short of what I believed in certain cases, in order that my words might acquire more weight as historical testimony." To all exaggeration and untruth, from whatever side it proceeded, he had an antipathy. "I turn my back upon the Michelets and Quinets, but I cannot hold out my hand to the Veuillots."

But Sainte-Beuve could not have been the great critic he was had he not had, at the service of this his love of truth and measure, the conscientious industry of a Benedictine. "I never have a holiday. On Monday towards noon I lift up my head, and breathe for about an hour; after that the wicket shuts again and I am in my prison cell for seven days." The *Causeries* were at this price. They came once a week, and to write one of them as he wrote it was indeed a week's work.

To mental independence, industry, measure and lucidity, his criticism adds the merit of happy temper and disposition. Sainte-Beuve has more, as a critic, than the external politeness which once at any rate distinguished his countrymen; he has a personal charm of manner due to a sweet and humane temper. He complained of *un peu de dureté*, "a certain dose of hardness," in the new generation of writers. The personality of an author had a peculiar importance for him; the poetical side of his subjects, however latent it might be, always attracted him and he always sought to extricate it. This was because he had the instincts of the true poetic nature. As a guide to bring us to a knowledge of the great personalities in French literature he is unrivalled.

BIBLIOGRAPHY.—See his "Ma Biographie" in *Nouveaux lundis*, xiii, *Lettres à la princesse* (1873); *Correspondance* (1877–78) and *Nouvelle Correspondance* (1880); the Vicomte d'Haussonville's *Sainte-Beuve* (1875); Scherer, *Études critiques sur la littérature contemporaine*, iv (1863–95); G. Michaut, *Sainte-Beuve avant les Lundis* (1903); L. F. Choisy, *Sainte-Beuve, L'Homme et le poète* (1921); G. Michaut, *Sainte-Beuve* (1921); L. F. Mott, *Sainte-Beuve* (1925).

SAINTE-CLAIRE DEVILLE, ÉTIENNE HENRI (1818–1881), French chemist, was born on March 11, 1818, in the island of St. Thomas, West Indies, where his father was French consul. In 1844, having graduated as doctor of medicine and doctor of science, he was appointed to organize the new faculty of science at Besançon, where he acted as dean and professor of chemistry from 1845 to 1851. He succeeded A. J. Balard at the École Normale, Paris, in 1851, and in 1859 became professor at the Sorbonne in place of J. B. A. Dumas (*q.v.*). He died at Boulogne-sur-Seine on July 1, 1881.

He began his experimental work in 1841 with investigations of oil of turpentine and tolu balsam, in the course of which he discovered toluene (*q.v.*). His most important work was in inorganic and thermal chemistry. In 1849 he discovered nitrogen pentoxide, the first of the so-called anhydrides of the monobasic acids to be isolated. In 1855 he devised a method by which aluminum (*q.v.*) could be prepared on a large scale by the aid of sodium, the manufacture of which he also developed. His best known contribution to chemistry is his work on the phenomena of reversible reactions (*see* REACTION KINETICS).

ST. ELMO'S FIRE, the glow accompanying the brushlike discharges of atmospheric electricity which usually appears as a tip of light on the extremities of pointed objects such as church towers or the masts of ships during stormy weather. It is commonly accompanied by a crackling or fizzing noise.

St. Elmo's fire, or corona discharge, is commonly observed on the periphery of propellers, along the wing tips, windshield and nose of aircraft flying in dry snow, ice crystals, or in the vicinity of thunderstorms. The discharge may be sufficiently strong to cause a noisy disturbance in the radio, called static, which may obliterate all other signals. The corona discharge from an aircraft may initiate a lightning discharge which, striking the aeroplane, may cause small structural damage, impair the radio or temporarily blind the pilot. Various flight procedures, in addition to mechanical and electrical devices designed to reduce the charge accumu-

lation, are utilized as safeguards in preventing or minimizing discharges. The name St. Elmo is an Italian corruption, through *Sant' Ermo*, of St. Erasmus, the patron saint of Mediterranean sailors, who regard St. Elmo's fire as the visible sign of his guardianship.

See Hazlitt's edition of Brand's and Ellis's *Antiquities* (1905), *s.v.* "Castor and Pollux." (E. J. MR.)

STE.-MARIE-AUX-MINES or MARKIRCH, a town of France in the department of Haut-Rhin intersected by the Lièpvrette, an affluent of the Rhine. Pop. (1946) 6,217. The once productive silver, copper and lead mines of the neighbourhood were worked from the 9th till the 19th century. The main industries of the place are weaving and dyeing. The river was at one time the boundary between the German and French languages; the German-speaking inhabitants on the right bank were Protestants and subject to the counts of Rappoltstein, while the French inhabitants were Roman Catholics and under the rule of the dukes of Lorraine.

ST. EMILION, a town of southwestern France, in the department of Gironde, $2\frac{1}{2}$ mi. from the right bank of the Dordogne and 27 mi. E.N.E. of Bordeaux by rail. Pop. (1946) 766. The town derived its name from a hermit who lived there in the 7th and 8th centuries. The town has remains of ramparts of the 12th and 13th centuries. The parish, once collegiate church, dates from the 12th and 13th centuries. A Gothic cloister adjoins the church. A belfry (12th, 13th and 15th centuries) commanding the town is built on the terrace, beneath which are hollowed in the rock the oratory and hermitage of St. Emilion, and adjoining them a large ancient monolithic church. Remains of a monastery of the Cordeliers (15th and 17th centuries) and of a building (13th century) known as the Palais Cardinal, are also to be seen. St. Emilion is celebrated for its wines.

SAINTE-PALAYE, JEAN BAPTISTE LA CURNE (or LACURNE) **DE** (1697–1781), French scholar, was born at Auxerre on June 6, 1697. His father, Edme, had been gentleman of the bedchamber to the duke of Orleans, brother of Louis XIV, a position which descended to his son. In 1724 he had been elected an associate of the Académie des Inscriptions et Belles-Lettres, and from this time he devoted himself exclusively to the work of this society. He began a series of studies on the chroniclers of the middle ages for the *Historiens des Gaules et de la France* (edited by Dom Bouquet): Raoul Glaber, Helgaud, the *Gesta* of Louis VII, the chronicle of Morigny, Rigord and his continuator, William le Breton, the monk of St. Denis, Jean de Venette, Froissart and the Jouvencel. His *Glossaire de la langue française* was ready in 1756, but remained in manuscript for more than a century. He died on March 1, 1781.

See the biography of La Curne, with a list of his published works and those in manuscript, at the beginning of the tenth and last volume of the *Dictionnaire historique de l'ancien langage françois, ou glossaire de la langue françoise depuis son origine jusqu'au siècle de Louis XIV*, published by Louis Favre (1875–82).

SAINTES, a town of western France, capital of an arrondissement in the department of Charente-Maritime, 47 mi. S.E. of La Rochelle by the railway from Nantes to Bordeaux. Pop. (1946) 23,441. Saintes (*Mediolanum* or *Mediolanium*), the capital of the Santones, was a flourishing town before Caesar's conquest of Gaul; in the middle ages it was capital of the Saintonge. Christianity was introduced by St. Eutropius, its first bishop, in the middle of the 3rd century. Charlemagne rebuilt its cathedral. The Normans burned the town in 845 and 854. Richard Coeur de Lion was besieged and captured there by his father Henry II. In 1242 St. Louis defeated the English there, but the town was not permanently recovered from the English until the reign of Charles V. It has Roman remains, of which the best preserved is the arch of Germanicus, dating from the reign of Tiberius. This formerly stood on a Roman bridge destroyed in 1843, when it was removed and reconstructed on the right bank of the river. Ruins of baths and of an amphitheatre are also to be seen. The large amphitheatre dates probably from the close of the 1st or beginning of the 2nd century and was capable of holding 20,000 spectators. Saintes was a bishop's see till 1790; the cathedral of St. Peter, built in the early 12th century, was rebuilt in the 15th century and again after it had been almost destroyed by the Huguenots in 1568. It has a 15th century tower. The church of St. Eutropius (6th century, rebuilt in the 11th having had its nave destroyed in the Wars of Religion) stands above a large, well-lighted crypt adorned with richly sculptured capitals and containing the tomb of St. Eutropius (4th or 5th century). The fine stone spire dates from the 15th century. Notre-Dame (11th and 12th centuries) has a noble clock tower and is now desecrated. The old *hôtel de ville* (16th and 18th centuries) contains a library. Small vessels ascend the river as far as Saintes, which carries on trade in grain, brandy and wine, has iron foundries and railway works and manufactures earthenware and tiles.

ST. ÉTIENNE, an industrial town of east-central France, capital of the department of Loire, 310 mi. S.S.E. of Paris and 36 mi. S.S.W. of Lyons by rail. Pop. (1946) 177,966. At the close of the 12th century St. Étienne was a parish of the Pays de Gier belonging to the abbey of Valbenoîte. By the middle of the 14th century the coal trade was developing, and in the early 15th century Charles VII allowed the town to build fortifications. The manufacture of firearms for the state was begun at St. Étienne under Francis I and was put under the surveillance of state inspectors early in the 18th century. The manufacture grew rapidly. The first railways opened in France were the line between St. Étienne and Andrézieux on the Loire in 1828 and that between St. Étienne and Lyons in 1831. In 1856 St. Étienne became the administrative centre of the department.

St. Étienne stands on the Furens, which flows through it from southeast to northwest, partly underground, and is important for the silk manufacture. The town is the seat of a prefect, of tribunals of first instance and of commerce, of a chamber of commerce and of a board of trade-arbitrators and has schools of mining, chemistry and dyeing, etc.

The town owes its importance chiefly to the coal basin which extends between Firminy and Rive-de-Gier over an area 20 mi. long by 5 mi. wide and is second only to those of Nord and Pas-de-Calais in France. The mineral is of two kinds—smelting coal, said to be the best in France, and gas coal. There are manufactures of ribbons, trimmings and other goods made from silk and mixtures of cotton and silk. This industry dates from the early 17th century and is carried on chiefly in small factories (electricity supplying the motive power). The attendant industry of dyeing is carried on on a large scale. The manufacture of steel and iron and of heavy iron goods such as armour-plating is important. Firearms are manufactured at the national factory under the direction of artillery officers. Private firms make both military rifles and sporting-guns, revolvers, etc. Other industries are the manufacture of elastic fabrics, glass, cartridges, liqueurs, hemp cables, etc. Weaving machinery, cycles, automobiles and agricultural implements are also made.

ST. EUSTATIUS and **SABA,** two Netherlands West Indian islands located respectively 9 mi. and 16 mi. N.W. of St. Kitts. Politically, they are part of the colony of Curacao (*q.v.*). St. Eustatius (area: 7 sq.mi.; pop. 1950, 955) is composed of volcanic hills and intervening valleys. There is an open roadstead off Oranjestad on the west. Saba (5 sq.mi.; pop. 1950, 1,110) is a volcanic cone rising 2,851 ft. from the sea. Its town, Bottom, can be approached from the shore 800 ft. below only by steps in solid rock known as "the Ladder." Some of the best boats in the Caribbean are built there; the wood is imported and the vessels, when completed, are lowered over the face of the cliffs. Many men from both islands are employed as seamen on ships elsewhere, so that women predominate by 50% in Saba and more than 20% in St. Eustatius. Remittances home are an important factor in the islands' economy. (L. W. Be.)

SAINT-ÉVREMOND, CHARLES DE MARGUETEL DE SAINT-DENIS, Seigneur de (1610–1703), was born at Saint-Denis-le-Guast, near Coutances, on April 1, 1610. He served through a great part of the Thirty Years' War, distinguishing himself at the siege of Landrecies (1637), when he was made captain. During his campaigns he studied the works of Montaigne and the Spanish and Italian languages. In 1639 he met Gassendi in Paris, and became one of his disciples. He was present at Rocroy,

at Nordlingen and at Lerida. For a time he was personally attached to Condé, but offended him by a satirical remark and was deprived of his command in the prince's guards in 1648.

During the Fronde, Saint-Évremond was a steady royalist. The duke of Candale (of whom he has left a very severe portrait) gave him a command in Guienne, and Saint-Évremond, who had reached the grade of *maréchal de camp,* is said to have saved 50,000 livres in less than three years. He was one of the numerous victims involved in the fall of Fouquet. His letter to Marshal Créqui on the peace of the Pyrenees, which is said to have been discovered by Colbert's agents at the seizure of Fouquet's papers, seems a very inadequate cause for his disgrace. Saint-Évremond fled to Holland and to England, where he was kindly received by Charles II and was pensioned. After James II's flight to France Saint-Évremond was invited to return, but he declined. Hortense Mancini, the most attractive of Mazarin's attractive group of nieces, came to England in 1670, and set up a *salon* for love-making, gambling and witty conversation, and here Saint-Évremond was for many years at home. He died on Sept. 29, 1703, and was buried in Westminster abbey.

Saint-Évremond empowered Des Maizeaux to publish his works after his death, and they were published in London (2 vols., 1705), and often reprinted. His masterpiece in irony is the so-called *Conversation du maréchal d'Hocquincourt avec le père Canaye* (the latter a Jesuit and Saint-Évremond's master at school).

His *Oeuvres mêlées,* edited from the MSS. by Silvestre and Des Maizeaux, were printed by Jacob Tonson (London, 1705, 2 vols.; 2nd ed., 3 vols., 1709), with a notice by Des Maizeaux. His correspondence with Ninon de Lenclos, whose fast friend he was, was published in 1752; *La Comédie des académistes*, written in 1643, was printed in 1650. Modern editions of his works are by Hippeau (Paris, 1852), C. Giraud (Paris, 1865), and a selection (1881) with a notice by M. de Lescure.

ST. GALL, a canton in northeast Switzerland, bordered by the principality of Liechtenstein and by Vorarlberg (Austria). It entirely surrounds the canton of Appenzell, which formerly belonged to the abbots of St. Gall. Five other cantons lie along its north, west and south borders.

Its area is 777.2 sq.mi., of which about 88% are reckoned "productive," forests covering about 165 sq.mi. and vineyards only about 1 sq.mi. The altitude above sea level varies from 1,309 ft. (the Lake of Constance) to 10,667 ft. (the Ringelspitz) in the extreme south. There are nearly 3 sq.mi. of glaciers but slightly over one-quarter of the unproductive area consists of lakes, including portions of the Lake of Constance, of the Wallensee, and of the Lake of Zürich, together with several small lakes wholly within its limits. The canton is mountainous in the south near its borders with the Grisons and Glarus, but towards Thurgau the surface is characterized by hummocky hill country. Considerable low-lying alluvial plains occur along the courses of the Linth and Rhine, particularly in those sections of the rivers which form, in part, its frontiers on the east and southwest. Within the canton, the most important streams are the upper River Thur and the lower and middle portions of its principal tributary, the Sitter. It has ports on the Lake of Constance (Rorschach) and of Zürich (Rapperswil), while Weesen is the chief town on the Wallensee. Probably the most fashionable watering place is Ragatz, receiving the hot mineral waters (95° F.) of Pfäfers by means of a 3 mi. conduit. The main railway lines from Zürich past Sargans for Coire, and from Sargans past Rorschach for Constance skirt its borders, while the capital is on the direct railway line from Zürich past Wil to Rorschach, and communicates by rail with Appenzell and with towns in the Toggenburg (*q.v.*). In 1930 the population of the canton was 286,362 of whom 279,230 were German-speaking, 4,989 Italian-speaking and 993 French-speaking, while there were 170,445 Catholics, 114,545 Protestants and 704 Jews; in 1950 the population was 309,106. The capital of the canton is St. Gall, population (1950) 68,011; the other most populous places (1950 census) are Rorschach (pop. 11,325), Altstätten (pop. 8,603), Gossau (pop. 8,316) and Wattwil (6,336). In the southern and more Alpine portion of the canton the inhabitants mainly follow pastoral pursuits, while in the central and northern regions agriculture is frequently combined with manufactures.

The canton is one of the most industrial in Switzerland. Cotton spinning is widely spread, though the characteristic industry is the manufacture of muslin, embroidery and lace, chiefly at the capital and at Altstätten; the value of the embroidery and lace exported from the canton, though fluctuating, normally amounts to about one-seventh of the total export trade of Switzerland. Ores of iron and of manganese are raised in the Gonzen mine near Sargans. The canton is divided into 14 administrative districts, which comprise 91 communes.

The existing constitution dates from 1890. The legislature (*Grossrat*) of 174 deputies is elected on the principle of proportional representation. Each commune of 1,500 Swiss inhabitants or less has a right to one member, and as many more as the divisor 1,500 justifies. Members hold office for three years. The seven members of the executive (*Regierungsrat*) also hold office for three years and are elected by the combined communes. The two members of the federal *Ständerat* are named by the legislature, while the 13 members of the federal *Nationalrat* have, since 1911, been elected by a scheme of proportional representation, using the popular vote. The right of "facultative referendum" and of "initiative" as to legislative projects has, since 1875 and 1890 respectively, belonged to any 4,000 electors, but in case of "initiative" in constitutional matters (1861) 10,000 must sign the demand. The canton of St. Gall, a great part of which formerly belonged to the abbots of St. Gall, is one of the later political units, having been formed in 1803, from numerous districts, some of which, *e.g.*, Gaster, Uznach and Gams, had been controlled by the adjacent and older cantons since the 15th century.

ST. GALLEN (Fr. **ST. GALL**), capital of the Swiss canton of that name, is situated in the upland valley of the Steinach, 2,195 ft. above sea-level. Its population is almost all German-speaking, while the Protestants and Catholics each comprise about half the population, with a small number of Jews. In 1920 the population was 70,437; in 1930 63,947, and in 1941 62,360, a decrease due partly to World Wars I and II.

St. Gallen owes its origin to St. Gall, an Irish hermit, who in 614, built his cell in the forest which then covered the site, and lived there till his death in 640. About the middle of the 8th century the collection of hermits' dwellings was transformed into a regularly organized Benedictine monastery. For the next three centuries this was one of the chief seats of learning and education in Europe. About 954 the monastery and its buildings were surrounded by walls as a protection against the Saracens, and this was the origin of the town.

In 1311 St. Gallen became a free imperial city, and about 1353 the gilds, headed by that of the cloth-weavers, obtained the control of the civic government, while in 1415 it bought its liberty from the German king Sigismund. This growing independence did not please the abbots, who had been made princes of the Empire in 1204, and there followed a long struggle between them and their rebellious subjects of St. Gallen and Appenzell. In 1411 the Appenzellers became "allies" of the Swiss confederation, as did the town of St. Gallen a few months later, this connection becoming an "everlasting" alliance in 1454, while in 1457 the town was finally freed from the abbot. After further conflicts, the abbot in 1490 concluded an alliance with the Swiss which reduced his position almost to that of a "subject district." The townsmen adopted the Reformation in 1524, and this new cause of difference further envenomed their relations with the abbots. Both abbot and town were admitted regularly to the Swiss diet, but neither succeeded in its attempts to be received a full member of the Confederation. In 1798 and finally in 1805 the abbey was secularized, while out of part of its dominions and those of the town the canton Säntis (now St. Gall) was formed, with St. Gallen as capital.

St. Gallen is by rail 9 m. S.W. of Rorschach, its port on the lake of Constance, and 53 m. E. of Zürich. The older or central portion of the town retains the air of a small rural capital, but the newer quarters present the aspect of a modern commercial centre. Its chief building is the abbey church of the celebrated old monastery (dating in its present form from 1756–1765). It has been a cathedral church (Catholic) since 1846. The famous library is housed in the former palace of the abbot, and is one of the most renowned in Europe by reason of its rich treasures of early mss. and printed books. Other portions of the monastic buildings are used as the offices of the cantonal authorities, and contain the extensive archives both of this monastery and of that of Pfäfers.

See *Dict. geogr. de la Suisse*, vol. iv. (1906).

SAINT-GAUDENS, AUGUSTUS (1848–1907), American sculptor, was born in Dublin, Ireland, on March 1, 1848, the son of a French father, a shoemaker by trade, and an Irish mother, and was taken to America in infancy. He was apprenticed to a cameo-cutter, studying in the schools of Cooper Union (1861) and the National Academy of Design, New York (1865–1866). His earliest work in sculpture, made upon the eve of his departure, in 1868, for Paris, was a bronze bust of his father, Bernard P. E. Saint-Gaudens. After some delay he was admitted as a pupil of Jouffroy in l'École des Beaux-Arts, and two years later, with his fellow-student Mercié, he went to Italy, where he remained three years. While in Rome he executed his statues "Hiawatha" and "Silence." Returning in 1873 to New York he made, the following year, an admirable bust of the statesman, William M. Evarts, and was commissioned by John La Farge to execute a relief of adoring angels for St. Thomas' Episcopal Church, New York, a work which immediately won the esteem of his brother artists. The church was destroyed by fire a few years later. His statue of Admiral Farragut, Madison Square, New York, was ordered in 1876, exhibited at the Paris salon of 1880 and unveiled in 1881. It was received with enthusiasm and from its first appearance Saint-Gaudens was recognized as a new leader in his art. To this period also belong the "Randall" of the "Sailors' Snug Harbour," Staten Island, and the beautiful caryatides for the Vanderbilt fireplace, preserved in the Metropolitan Museum.

At all times throughout his life the sculptor found diversion from more serious tasks in modelling portraits of friends in low relief. Among these we may note the medallions and placques of Bastien-Lepage and Dr. Henry Shiff (1880); Homer Saint-Gaudens and the children of Prescott Hall Butler (1881); Mrs. Stanford White (1884); Robert Louis Stevenson (1887); William M. Chase and the children of Jacob H. Schiff (1888); Kenyon Cox (1889), etc. Yet another form of sculpture was developed in his high-reliefs of Dr. Henry Bellows (1885) and Dr. McCosh (1889); and the lovely "Amor Caritas," which, with variations, long occupied his mind. His noble statue of Lincoln was unveiled in 1887 in Lincoln park, Chicago, and was at once accepted as the country's ideal. In Springfield, Mass., his unique "Deacon Chapin," known as "The Puritan," appeared also in 1887. The Adams memorial (1891) in Rock Creek cemetery, Washington, D.C., is considered by many to be Saint-Gaudens' greatest work; indeed not a few rate it as America's highest artistic achievement. The mysterious draped figure with shadowed face is often called "Grief," but the sculptor had no such intention; "Peace" or "Nirvana" better convey the meaning. The Garfield memorial in Fairmount park, Philadelphia, was completed in 1895. The Shaw memorial in Boston, a monument to Robert G. Shaw, colonel of a negro regiment in the Civil War, was begun in 1884 and occupied the master intermittently for more than 12 years, being dedicated in 1897. It is a large relief in bronze, measuring some 15 by 11 ft., and containing many marching soldiers, led by their young officer on horseback. The year 1897 saw likewise the completion of the "Logan" on a fiery steed, in Grant park, Chicago.

Another famous equestrian statue is the "General Sherman" which was begun in 1892 and dedicated in 1903. Standing at the entrance of Central park at 59th Street and Fifth Avenue, New York, this golden group of the mounted commander led by a beautiful winged "Victory" is one of the most impressive of the city's monuments. The "Sherman" was shown with other works of Saint-Gaudens at the Paris Exposition of 1900, receiving there the highest honours. The sculptor was made an officer of the Legion of Honour and corresponding member of the Institute of

France. A bronze copy of his "Amor Caritas" was purchased by the French Government. Other important works are the Peter Cooper memorial, New York; the "Parnell," in Dublin; the Phillips Brooks monument in Boston and a fine seated figure of Lincoln, recently erected on Chicago's lake front. Saint-Gaudens died at Cornish, N.H., on Aug. 3, 1907. He is rightly regarded as America's greatest sculptor and his work continues to exert a powerful and beneficent influence in the United States. In 1877 he married Augusta F. Homer and left a son, Homer Saint-Gaudens, now director of fine arts of the Carnegie Institute, Pittsburgh, Pa. His brother Louis (1854–1913) also a sculptor, assisted Augustus Saint-Gaudens in some of his creations.

See Royal Cortissoz, *Augustus Saint-Gaudens* (1907); Lorado Taft, *History of American Sculpture* (1903) and *Modern Tendencies in Sculpture* (1921); Kenyon Cox, *Old Masters and New* (1905); C. Lewis Hind, *Augustus Saint-Gaudens* (1908); Homer Saint-Gaudens, *The Reminiscences of Augustus Saint-Gaudens* (1913).   (L. T.)

ST. GAUDENS, a town of France, capital of an arrondissement in the department of Haute-Garonne, 1 m. from the river Garonne, 57 mi. S.S.W. of Toulouse on the railway to Tarbes. Pop. (1936) 4,684. St. Gaudens derives its name from a martyr of the 5th century, at whose tomb a college of canons was established. It was important as a capital of the Nébouzan, as the residence of the bishops of Comminges and for its cloth industry. The church, once collegiate, dates chiefly from the 11th and 12th centuries, but the main entrance is flamboyant Gothic.

SAINT-GERMAIN, Comte de (*c.* 1710–*c.* 1780) called *der Wundermann*, a celebrated adventurer. Of his parentage and place of birth nothing is definitely known; the common version is that he was a Portuguese Jew. He knew nearly all the European languages, and spoke German, English, Italian, French (with a Piedmontese accent), Portuguese and Spanish. Grimm affirms him to have been the man of the best parts he had ever known. He was a musical composer and a capable violinist. His knowledge of history was comprehensive, and his accomplishments as a chemist, on which be based his reputation, were in many ways real and considerable. He pretended to have a secret for removing flaws from diamonds, and to be able to transmute metals. The most remarkable of his professed discoveries was of a liquid which could prolong life, and by which he asserted he had himself lived 2,000 years.

Saint-Germain is mentioned in a letter of Horace Walpole's as being in London about 1743, and as being arrested as a Jacobite spy and released. Walpole says: "He is called an Italian, a Spaniard, a Pole; a somebody that married a great fortune in Mexico and ran away with her jewels to Constantinople; a priest, a fiddler, a vast nobleman." At the French court, where he appeared about 1748, he exercised for a time extraordinary influence and was employed on secret missions by Louis XV.; but, having interfered in the dispute between Austria and France, he was compelled in June 1760, on account of the hostility of the duke of Choiseul, to remove to England. He appears to have resided in London for one or two years, but was at St. Petersburg in 1762, and is asserted to have played an important part in connexion with the conspiracy against the emperor Peter III. in July of that year, a plot which placed Catherine II. on the Russian throne. He then went to Germany, where, according to the *Mémoires authentiques* of Cagliostro, he was the founder of freemasonry, and initiated Cagliostro into that rite. He was again in Paris from 1770 to 1774, and after frequenting several of the German courts he took up his residence in Schleswig-Holstein, where he and the Landgrave Charles of Hesse pursued together the study of the "secret" sciences. He died at Schleswig in or about 1780–1785, although he is said to have been seen in Paris in 1789.

Andrew Lang in his *Historical Mysteries* (1904) discusses the career of Saint-Germain, and cites the various authorities for it. Saint-Germain figures prominently in the correspondence of Grimm and of Voltaire. See also Oettinger, *Graf Saint-German* (1846); F. Bülau, *Geheime Geschichten und räthselhafte Menschen*, Band i. (1850–60); Lascelles Wraxall, *Remarkable Adventures* (1863); and U. Birch in the *Nineteenth Century* (January 1908).

SAINT-GERMAIN, CLAUDE LOUIS, Comte de (1707–1778), French general, was born on April 15, 1707, at the Château of Vertamboz. He entered the army, but left France, apparently on account of a duel, and fought in the armies of the elector palatine and the elector of Bavaria. Then, after a brief service under Frederick the Great of Prussia, he joined Marshal Saxe in the Netherlands, and was created a field-marshal of the French army. On the outbreak of the Seven Years' War (1756) he was appointed lieutenant-general, but he fell a victim to court intrigues and professional jealousy. He resigned his commission in 1760 and accepted an appointment as field-marshal from Frederick V. of Denmark, being charged in 1762 with the reorganization of the Danish army. On the death of Frederick in 1766 he returned to France, bought a small estate in Alsace near Lauterbach, and devoted his time to religion and farming. In October 1775 he was appointed minister of war by Louis XVI., but his efforts to effect economies and to introduce Prussian discipline in the French army brought on such opposition that he resigned in September 1777. He died in his apartment at the arsenal on Jan. 15, 1778.

ST. GERMAIN, TREATY OF (*see* also VERSAILLES, TRIANON, and NEUILLY, TREATIES OF). Austria and Hungary had up to 1918 formed a diplomatic unit, but in Oct. 1918 they were virtually two separate states. The Armistice of Nov. 4 still recognized Austria-Hungary as a diplomatic unit, but Austria was proclaimed a Republic Nov. 12, as was Hungary Nov. 16. The Armistice concluded by the Powers direct with Hungary (Nov. 13) recognized that Power's *de facto* independence of Austria.

All the Powers, except the United States, early asserted that the "Fourteen Points," etc., did not apply to the settlements with Austria and Hungary. In Jan. 1919 it was known that even Wilson favoured including in Italy part of the Slovene population of Istria and Carniola, and would make Italy further concessions. On April 14 he agreed to grant Italy the Tirol south of the Brenner Pass, with about 250,000 Germans, as well as the Trentino, as already agreed by France and Great Britain. It was known also that the Czechoslovak State would include over 3,000,000 Germans. Austria was to be reduced to some two-thirds of her German-speaking territories. In mid-April the French Prime Minister Clemenceau obtained from the Allies the further important decision to prohibit union between Austria and Germany without the unanimous consent of the Council of the League. This was embodied in the draft treaty with Germany of May 6, and formed article 80 of the Treaty of Versailles of June 28, appearing as article 88 of the Treaty of St. Germain, and article 72 of the Treaty of Neuilly.

On May 2 the Austrian delegation was invited to Paris. On June 2 they were presented with a very imperfect draft treaty, followed by a more detailed one on July 20. Austria made great protests, turning mainly on two points. She asserted the applicability of the "Fourteen Points" to her case, and her right therefore to retain all her German subjects. President Wilson alone was willing to extend the application of the "Fourteen Points" to Austria; the treaty assigned 3,500,000 Germans to Czechoslovakia, about 250,000 to Italy. The other main point of dispute was how far Austria must accept the responsibilities of old Austria-Hungary. The Allies finally decided that the Austrian Republic was not a new State but an old one lopped off certain outlying provinces and endowed with a new government. The Allies recognized this government *de facto* by accepting their credentials on May 22 and *de jure* on Sept. 10, by signing the treaty with them at St. Germain-en-Laye. It came into force on July 16 1920.

Part I. The Covenant, and Part XIII. Labour, are as in the Treaty of Versailles.

Part II. of the Austrian Treaty details the borders of the new Austrian State.

Part III. Political Clauses for Europe.—This deals with technical details such as the financial obligations of the former Austrian empire affecting Italy, Yugoslavia, Czechoslovakia and Rumania. Articles 49–50 arranged for a plebiscite in two areas of the Klagenfurt basin. This plebiscite, taken in 1920, went in Austria's favour. West Hungary, with about 333,000 souls, was transferred from Hungary to Austria but ultimately, in 1921, without its chief town (*see* BURGENLAND). Further clauses in Part III dealt with the protection of racial and religious minorities. Article No. 88 prohibits Austria from alienating her independence (*i.e.*, joining Germany) otherwise than with the consent of the Council of the League of Nations.

Part IV. Austrian Interests Outside Europe.—As in the Treaty of Versailles this part provides for a total renunciation of state properties immovable and movable outside Europe, and also of treaties, capitulations, concessions, etc., in the following countries: Morocco, Egypt, Siam and China.

Part V. Military, Naval and Air Clauses followed the general lines of the similar clauses in the Treaty of Versailles but showed somewhat more consideration to Austria. A long-service voluntary force not exceeding 30,000 was allowed. The manufacture of arms, etc., was confined to a single factory (article 132). The naval clauses were very drastic; the whole Austro-Hungarian navy was broken up or distributed among the Allies, Austria only retaining four patrol boats on her inland waters. The air clauses were as in the German treaty.

Part VI. Prisoners of War and Graves, *Part XI.* Aerial Navigation, were as in the German Treaty, with a few very small alterations.

Part VII. Penalties provided for the trial before Allied military tribunals of Austrian offenders against the laws and customs of war. This provision was not executed.

Part VIII. Reparations; *Part IX.* Financial Clauses; *Part X.* Economic Clauses.—By article 177 Austria accepted responsibility for herself and her Allies for causing loss and damage to the Allied (Entente) governments by the war. The rest of the "Reparation Chapter" followed the corresponding section in the German treaty. No lump sum was fixed, but discretion was, in effect, given to the Reparation commission to fix it. Austria handed over her whole commercial fleet and much livestock to the Allies. Czechoslovakia, Yugoslavia, Poland and Rumania had, however, to contribute to expenses incurred by the Allies in liberating their territory from Austria. The financial clauses involved many complex questions as to the allocation of pre-war debt and the distribution of war debts. All these provisions were somewhat relaxed by the Supreme council on March 17, 1921, and the process was completed by Austria placing her finances under control of the league in Sept. 1922 (*see* AUSTRIA).

Part XII. Ports, waterways and railways, merely stressed some points in the corresponding section of the German treaty.

See *Treaty Series*, No. II (Cmd. 400 of 1919); also H. W. V. Temperley (ed.), *A History of the Peace Conference of Paris;* vol. iv. and v. (Institute of International Affairs, London, 1921).

ST. GERMAIN-EN-LAYE, a town of northern France, in the department of Seine-et-Oise, 13 mi. W.N.W. of Paris by rail. Pop. (1946) 22,013. Built on a hill on the left bank of the Seine and on the edge of a forest 10,000 to 11,000 ac. in extent, St. Germain has a bracing climate, which makes it a summer residence for Parisians. A monastery in honour of St. Germain, bishop of Paris, was built in the forest of Laye by King Robert. Louis VI built a castle close by. Burned by the English, rebuilt by Louis IX, and again by Charles V, this castle was completed by Francis I. A new castle was begun by Henry II and completed by Henry IV; it was subsequently demolished, except the so-called Henry IV pavilion. The old castle has been restored. James II of England died at St. Germain.

ST. GERMANS, a village in the Bodmin parliamentary division of Cornwall, Eng., on the St. Germans or Lynher creek, 22 mi. E.S.E. of Bodmin by road. Pop. (1951) 2,084. It is an agricultural district with market gardens and quarries and is also a holiday centre. St. Germanus, bishop of Auxerre in France, founded a monastery there in the 5th century and before 931 it was the seat of the Cornish bishopric founded by Athelstan. The see was transferred to Creditou in *c.* 1043 and to Exeter *c.* 1050. In the 12th century a priory of Augustinian canons was established at St. Germans, and the present church of St. Germanus, consecrated in 1261, was built. Mostly the original Norman, it has Early English, Perpendicular and Decorated additions and the east

window is by E. Burne Jones. After the suppression of the monasteries the crown retained the borough until 1610. Elizabeth I created it a parliamentary borough and from 1563 until 1832 it returned two members. In the villages of the district, Callington was granted a market in 1267 and the pannier market still exists; Cotehele house, above the Tamar near Calstock, is a beautiful Tudor house (1485–1539) formerly the seat of the Edgcumbe family and given to the National trust in 1947; St. Germans has a row of six gabled almshouses, probably 17th-century work.

ST. GILLES, a town of southern France, in the department of Gard, on the canal from the Rhone to Cette, 12½ mi. S.S.E. of Nîmes by road. Pop. (1946) 4,473. In the middle ages St. Gilles, the ancient *Vallis Flaviana,* was the seat of an abbey founded in the 7th century by St. Aegidius (St. Gilles). It acquired wealth and power under the counts of Toulouse, who added to their title that of counts of St. Gilles. The church was founded 1116. The lower part of the Romanesque front (12th century) has three bays decorated with columns and bas-reliefs. There is a 12th century crypt. St. Gilles was the seat of the first grand priory of the Knights Hospitallers in Europe (12th century) and was their place of embarkation for the east. In 1226 the countship of St. Gilles was united to the crown. In 1562 the Protestants ravaged the abbey, which they occupied till 1622, and in 1774 it was suppressed. The town has an important trade in wines.

ST. GOTTHARD PASS, an important motor and railway route from northern Europe to Italy. It takes its name from St. Gotthard, bishop of Hildesheim (d. 1038), but does not seem to be mentioned before the early 13th century perhaps because the access to it lies through two very narrow Alpine valleys much exposed to avalanches. The hospice on the summit is first mentioned in 1331, and from 1683 onward was in charge of two Capuchin friars. But in 1775 the buildings near it were damaged by an avalanche, while in 1799–1800 everything was destroyed by the French soldiery. Rebuilt in 1834, the hospice was burnt in March 1905. The mule path (dating from about 1293) across the pass served for many centuries. The carriage road was only constructed between 1820 and 1830. Beneath the pass is the St. Gotthard tunnel (pierced in 1872–1880, 9¼ mi. in length, and attaining a height of 3,786 ft.), through which runs the railway (opened in 1882) from Lucerne to Milan (175½ mi.). The railway runs first along the northern and eastern shores of Lake Lucerne, from Lucerne to Flüelen (32¼ mi.), and then up the Reuss valley past Altdorf and Wassen, near which is the first of the famous spiral tunnels, to Göschenen (56 mi. from Lucerne). Here the line enters the tunnel and gains, at Airolo, the valley of

A SECTION OF THE ST. GOTTHARD PASS IN THE FREMOLA VALLEY

the Ticino or the Val Leventina, which it descends, through several spiral tunnels, till at Biasca (38 mi. from Göschenen) it reaches more level ground. Thence it runs past Bellinzona to Lugano (30½ mi. from Biasca) and reaches Italian territory at Chiasso, 35 mi. from Milan. The railway is now the property of the Swiss Government.

ST. HELENA, an island and British colony in the South Atlantic, 15° 55′ 26″ S., 5° 42′ 30″ W. (Ladder Hill observatory). Area 47.3 sq.mi., extreme length, southwest to northeast, 10½ mi., extreme breadth 6½ mi. The island is wholly of volcanic origin, the activity being long extinct, while subaerial denudation has greatly modified it and marine erosion has formed perpendicular cliffs 450 to 2,000 ft. high on the east, north and west sides. Its principal feature, a semicircular ridge of mountains, with the culminating summit of Diana's peak (2,704 ft.), is the northern rim of a great crater; the southern rim having been breached hypothetically forms the centre of the ring. From the crater wall outward water-cut gorges stretch in all directions, widening as they approach the sea into valleys, some of which are 1,000 ft. deep. These valleys contain small streams. Springs of pure water are abundant. Along the enclosing hillsides caves have been formed by the washing out of the softer rocks. The lavas are basalts, andesites, trachytes and phonolites; there is much volcanic ash, tuff, scoriae, etc., and conspicuous features are formed by rocks, representing a late period of activity. Such features are Ass's Ears, Lot and Lot's Wife and the Chimney. There are several subsidiary craters. The only practicable landing place is on the leeward side at St. James's bay. From the head of the bay a narrow valley extends for 1½ mi. The greatest extent of level ground is in the northeast of the island, where are the Deadwood and Longwood plains, more than 1,700 ft. above the sea.

Although the island is within the tropics, its climate is healthful and temperate. This is due to the southeast tradewind and to the effect of the cold waters of the South Atlantic current. The temperature varies on the sea level from 68° to 90° F. in summer and 57° to 84° in winter. The higher regions are about 10° cooler. The rainfall varies considerably.

Flora and Fauna.—St. Helena has three vegetation zones: (1) the coast zone, extending inland for 1 mi. to 1½ mi., now "dry, barren, soilless, lichen-coated, and rocky," with little save prickly pears, wire grass and *Mesembryanthemum;* (2) the middle zone (400–1,800 ft.), extending about ¾ mi. inland, with shallower valleys and grassier slopes—the English broom and gorse, brambles, willows, poplars and Scotch pines being the prevailing forms; and (3) the central zone, about 3 mi. long and 2 mi. wide, the home, for the most part, of the indigenous vegetation. Many of the endemic species have become extinct, but by 1955 some of the rarer ones were protected. The indigenous vegetation shows affinities with that of Africa, and its exotic appearance gives the island almost the aspect of a botanic garden; for example, the oak, thoroughly naturalized, grows next to the bamboo and banana. Common trees include the endemic cabbage tree (*Senecio*), the cedar and the eucalyptus. The New Zealand flax (*Phormium*) was introduced from that country with great commercial success, and encouragement has been given by the government to the cultivation of lily bulbs (*Lilium longiflorum*).

Besides domestic animals the only land mammals are rabbits, rats and mice, the rats being especially abundant. The only endemic land bird is a small plover called the wirebird, *Charadrius sanctae-helenae*. Introduced birds now common on the island include the avadavat, Java sparrow, cardinal, ground dove, partridge (the Indian *chukar*), ring-necked pheasant and guinea fowl. Among sea birds are the sooty tern, white-winged tern and noddy. There are no freshwater fish but of 65 species of seafish caught 17 are peculiar to St. Helena; economically the more important kinds are gurnard, eel, cod, mackerel, tunny, bullseye, cavalley, flounder, hogfish, mullet and skulpin.

History.—The island was discovered on May 21, 1502, by the Portuguese João de Nova Castella, on his voyage home from India, and by him named St. Helena. The Portuguese found it uninhabited, imported livestock, fruit trees and vegetables, built a chapel and one or two houses and left their sick there to be taken home, if recovered, by the next ship, but they formed no permanent settlement. Its first known permanent resident was Fernando Lopez, a Portuguese in India, who had turned traitor, and had been mutilated by order of Alphonso d'Albuquerque. He preferred being marooned to returning to Portugal in his maimed condition, and was landed at St. Helena in 1513, with three or four Negro slaves. By royal command he visited Portugal some time later, but returned to St. Helena, where he died in 1546. In 1584 two Japanese ambassadors to Rome landed at the island. The first Englishman known to have visited it was Thomas Cavendish, who touched

there in June 1588 during his voyage around the world. Another English seaman, Captain Kendall, visited St. Helena in 1591, and in 1593 Sir James Lancaster stopped at the island on his way home from the east. In 1603 the same commander again visited St. Helena on his return from the first voyage equipped by the East India company. The Portuguese had by this time given up calling at the island, which appears to have been occupied by the Dutch about 1645. The Dutch occupation was temporary and ceased in 1651, the year before they founded Cape Town. The (British) East India company appropriated the island immediately after the departure of the Dutch, and in 1659 they dispatched a small force of troops and others under John Dutton to form a settlement. The company was confirmed in possession by a clause in their charter of 1661. The fort built by the company was named after the duke of York (James II).

On New Year's day, 1673, the Dutch succeeded in capturing St. Helena, but they were ejected the following May 5 by Sir Richard Munden. By a new charter granted in Dec. 1673 the East India company were declared "the true and absolute lords and proprietors of the island." Thereafter St. Helena was in the undisturbed possession of Great Britain, though in 1706 two ships anchored off Jamestown were carried off by the French. In 1673 the inhabitants had numbered about 1,000, of whom nearly half were Negro slaves. In 1810 the company began to bring in Chinese from their factory at Canton. During the company's rule the island prospered; homeward-bound vessels, numbering hundreds in a year, anchored in the roadstead and stayed for considerable periods refitting and revictualling. Large sums of money were thus expended in the island, where wealthy merchants and officials had their residence. The plantations were worked by slaves, who were subjected to very barbarous laws until 1792, when a new code of regulations ensured their humane treatment and prohibited the importation of any new slaves. Later it was enacted that all children of slaves born on or after Christmas day 1818 should be free, and between 1826 and 1836 all slaves were set at liberty.

Among the governors appointed by the company to rule at St. Helena was one of the Huguenot refugees, Capt. Stephen Poirier (1697–1707), who attempted unsuccessfully to introduce the cultivation of the vine. A later governor (1741–42) was Robert Jenkins (*q.v.*) of "Jenkins' ear" fame. William Dampier visited the island in 1691 and 1701; Halley's mount commemorates the visit paid by the astronomer Edmund Halley in 1676–78.

In 1815 the British government selected St. Helena as the place of detention of Napoleon Bonaparte. He was brought to the island in October of that year and lodged at Longwood, where he died in May 1821. During this period the island was strongly garrisoned by regular troops, and the governor, Sir Hudson Lowe, was nominated by the crown. After Napoleon's death the East India company resumed full control of St. Helena until April 22, 1834, on which date it was, in virtue of an act passed in 1833, vested in the crown. As a port of call the island continued to enjoy a fair measure of prosperity until about 1870.

Afterward the great decrease in the number of vessels visiting Jamestown deprived the islanders of their principal means of subsistence. When steamers began to be substituted for sailing vessels and when the Suez canal was opened (1869) fewer ships passed the island and fewer still found it necessary to call. The withdrawal in 1906 of the small garrison, hitherto maintained by the imperial government, was another cause of depression, but during World War I the island was again garrisoned. During the South African War (1899–1902) some thousands of prisoners were detained at St. Helena, which has also served as the place of exile of several Zulu chiefs, an ex-sultan of Zanzibar and others. In 1922 Ascension Island (*q.v.*), up to that time under the care of the British admiralty, was made a dependency of St. Helena. Similarly, Tristan da Cunha (*q.v.*) and the associated islands of Nightingale, Inaccessible and Gough, became dependencies of St. Helena in 1938. The island was of strategic importance in the naval operations of World War II.

Population.—When discovered the island was uninhabited. The majority of the population are of mixed European (British, Dutch, Portuguese), East Indian and African descent. The origi-

nal European settlement was made by John Dutton with a few soldiers and followers sent in 1659 by the (British) East India company to annex the island. Subsequently more soldiers and settlers
were sent from England, and their numbers were augmented by
members of the crews of ships returning to Europe from the east.
From 1840 onward for a considerable period there was an influx
of freed slaves of West African origin. The estimated population
of the colony proper in 1953 was 4,895, of whom about one-third
live at Jamestown, the port and capital. Longwood, where Napoleon died in 1821, is 3½ mi. E. of Jamestown. Most of the population is Anglican in religion. St. Helena is the seat of an Anglican bishopric (within the province of South Africa) established
in 1859. Ascension and Tristan da Cunha are in the diocese.

Education is compulsory and is provided free for all children
between the ages of 5 and 15 years. There were 11 primary schools
and 1 secondary school in 1953, and the total number of pupils
was 1,223.

Letters patent of 1939 provide for an executive council consisting of the government secretary and the colonial treasurer
ex officio and such other nominated members as may be approved;
and for an advisory council consisting of six persons not holding
any office under the crown, two nominees of the friendly societies
and one representing the phormium flax industry. The governor
makes ordinances, as there is no legislative council, but power is
reserved to the sovereign in council to legislate by order. The governor also acts as chief justice.

Economy.—Less than a third of the area of the island is suitable for farming. The principal crops are phormium flax and
potatoes. Cattle and sheep are raised—but there is no outside
market—and lace making is carried on. Local trade received a
severe blow when, with completion of the Suez canal, ships en
route from Europe to the orient ceased to call at the island. The
principal exports are phormium fibre, tow rope and twine, and
small quantities of wool and lily bulbs are sold. St. Helena's ten-
year development program (revised 1951) was financed entirely
from an allocation of £200,000 under the Colonial Development
and Welfare act of 1945. The only banking institution is the government savings bank. Bank of England notes and the coinage
of the United Kingdom are legal tender, but South African currency also circulates and is acceptable. The colony's revenue in
1952 was £127,536 and the expenditure £142,022. There is an
insular mail steamship service to England and to South Africa, and
direct cable communication with Cape Town and Porthcurno, Eng.
(for London).

BIBLIOGRAPHY.—*A St. Helena Bibliography* (London, 1937); N.
Young, *Napoleon in Exile: St. Helena, 1815–1821,* 2 vol. (London,
1915); G. B. Johnson, *St. Helena: Human Geography* (London, 1930);
Sir A. Kitson *et al., Geological Notes on St. Helena* (London, 1931); O.
Aubry, *St. Helena* (London, Philadelphia, 1937); P. Gosse, *St. Helena,
1502–1938* (London, 1938); *Colonial Report on St. Helena* (H.M.S.O.,
London, annual).   (G. A. J.; X.)

ST. HELENS, a municipal, county and parliamentary borough,
Lancashire, England, 12 mi. E.N.E. by road of Liverpool. Pop.
(1951) 110,260. Area 12.4 sq.mi. The town's modern development began with the opening of coal mines in the 17th century
and was furthered when glass works were started in 1773. It is one
of the world's biggest glass-making centres, employing nearly 20,-
000 workers in the 1950s. The industry is based on field sand
found in southwest Lancashire. Other important manufactures include patent medicines, iron and brass foundries, pottery and textiles. There is a trading estate at Parr. St. Mary's church (rebuilt after a fire in 1916) occupies the site of "Sainct Elyn's
Chapell" after which the town is named. The Gamble institute
houses a technical school and a public library. The town was
incorporated in 1868; became a parliamentary borough in 1885 (returning one member) and a county borough in 1888.

ST. HELIER, capital of Jersey, Channel Islands. About 1150
an abbey was built on an islet in St. Aubin's bay and dedicated to
St. Helier, a legendary hermit said to have been martyred on a
neighbouring rock. The monks acquired land on the main island
opposite and opened a market, around which shops and taverns
sprang up. When the court began to meet there on market days,
further houses were built. What had been a tiny fishing hamlet

became a town, but quite a small one. In 1685 it had only 210
houses.

Its more rapid growth began in the 18th century with the building of the harbour, followed by an inrush of French aristocrats
fleeing from the Revolution. Then in modern times came a great
invasion of Englishmen fleeing from income tax. It became a
busy commercial centre, which by 1951 had 25,360 residents.

In the Royal square, the former market place, where in 1781
the battle of Jersey was fought and the last French invasion defeated, stand the Town church (mainly 14th and 15th century), the
Royal court (built 1865), the public library (1886) and the States'
chamber (1887), while Fort Regent (1815) frowns down from
the hill above. On another hill Victoria college (1852), a public
school with 330 boys, commemorates a visit of Queen Victoria.

The abbey fell into ruins after the Reformation and was replaced
in Elizabeth's reign by Elizabeth castle. Its first governor was
Sir Walter Raleigh. There Charles II took refuge twice during
the civil wars. (*See also* CHANNEL ISLANDS and JERSEY.)
                                                          (G. R. B.)

BIBLIOGRAPHY.—G. R. Balleine, *The Bailiwick of Jersey* (London,
1951); E. T. Nicolle, *The Town of St. Helier* (Jersey, 1931); N. V. L.
Rybot, *The Islet of St. Helier and Elizabeth Castle* (Jersey, 1951).

ST. HUBERT, a small town of Belgium in the province of
Luxembourg and in the heart of the Ardennes. Pop. (1939) 3,025.
Its abbey church contains the shrine of St. Hubert, and has an
annual pilgrimage. According to tradition the church and a monastery attached to it were founded in the 7th century by Plectrude,
wife of Pippin of Herstal. The second church was built in the
12th century, but burned in the 16th century. The present building has been restored in modern times and presents no special
feature. The spot where St. Hubert is supposed to have met the
stag with the crucifix between its antlers is about 5 mi. from the
town. St. Hubert is the patron saint of huntsmen.

ST. HYACINTHE, a city and port of entry of Quebec,
Canada, and capital of St. Hyacinthe county, 50 mi. E.N.E. of
Montreal, on the Yamaska river and on the Canadian National
railway. Pop. (1951) 20,236. It is the seat of a Roman Catholic
bishop and contains a classical college, a technical school, a dairy
school, two monasteries and several other educational and charitable institutions. Manufactures include organs, leather, shoes, silks,
furniture, woollens and mill machinery. The city is a distributing
centre for the surrounding district.

ST. IMIER, a town in the west of the canton of Berne, Switz.,
on the railway from Biel to La-Chaux-de-Fonds. It lies at the
foot of Mont Soleil (4,240 ft.), which is ascended by a funicular
railway. It is the centre of the watchmaking industry, a health
resort, and a place for winter sports. The inhabitants, (1950)
5,972, are French-speaking and generally Protestant.

SAINTINE, JOSEPH XAVIER (1798–1865), French
novelist and dramatist, whose real surname was BONIFACE, was
born in Paris on July 10, 1798. In 1823 he produced a volume of
poetry in the manner of the Romanticists, entitled *Poèmes, odes, et
épitres.* In 1836 appeared *Picciola,* the story of the comte de
Charney, a political prisoner in Piedmont, whose reason was saved
by his cult of a tiny flower growing between the paving stones of
his prison yard. This story is a masterpiece of the sentimental
kind and has been translated into many European languages.
Saintine also wrote a great number of plays.

Saintine died on Jan. 21, 1865.

ST. IVES, a municipal borough and fishing port in the St.
Ives parliamentary division of Cornwall, Eng., 20 mi. N.E. of
Land's End and 8 mi. N. by E. of Penzance by road. Pop. (1951)
9,051. Area 6.7 sq.mi. It lies on the north coast, its little harbour
sheltered from the Atlantic by The Island, a strip of land running
out to a granite knoll. The picturesque old town, with its winding
streets and colour-washed stone cottages housing fishermen and
artists, with their boats, clusters along this strip and round the
harbour; the ground rises steeply behind, and to the southeast a
modern residential quarter extends around the sandy bay for about
2½ mi. to Carbis Bay. Fishing and tin-mining were important until the late 19th century when pilchards ceased to visit the waters
and many miners emigrated. The beautiful sandy beaches and

the mild climate inspired the inhabitants to make St. Ives a holiday centre, and this trade has superseded the others.

The name St. Ives commemorates St. Eia, a 5th-century woman missionary who, according to tradition, floated over from Ireland on a leaf (coracle) and was later martyred. The present church of St. Ia is of the 15th century with a noble tower. Perkin Warbeck was proclaimed King Richard IV when he anchored in St. Ives bay in 1497. In 1639 a charter of incorporation was granted with provision for four fairs annually, two weekly markets and a grammar school, but as the town declared for parliament in the Civil War its charter was withdrawn by Charles II. The present charter was granted in 1690. The guildhall was completed in 1940.

ST. IVES, a market town and municipal borough in Huntingdonshire, England, mainly on the left bank of the Ouse, 6 mi. E. of Huntingdon. Pop. (1951) 3,078. Area 3.6 sq.mi. The river is crossed by a 15th-century bridge with a chapel over the centre pier that was restored in 1689. The church of All Saints is Perpendicular, with earlier portions and a rebuilt spire. Oliver Cromwell lived in Old Slepe hall (demolished 1848) for five years, and his statue stands in the market place, the centre of the town. St. Ives was noted for its eight-day fair beginning on Monday in Easter week, granted to the abbot of Ramsey by Henry I. In the reign of Henry III merchants from Flanders came to the fair, which had become so important that the king granted it to be continued beyond the eight days if the abbot agreed to pay a fee of £50 yearly for the extra days. The fair, with a market on Monday granted to the abbot in 1286, survives and was purchased by the town in 1874, the year of incorporation, from the duke of Manchester. The markets, extremely important to St. Ives as an agricultural centre, were substantially altered to give greater facilities for auction sales. The Norris library and museum, opened in 1933, is mainly devoted to books and collections relating to the county.

ST. JEAN-D'ANGÉLY, a town of western France, in the department of Charente-Maritime, 33 mi. E. of Rochefort by rail. Pop. (1946) 6,606. St. Jean is named after the neighbouring forest of Angéry (*Angeriacum*). Pippin I of Aquitaine in the 9th century established there a Benedictine monastery, afterward reputed to possess the head of John the Baptist. This relic attracted hosts of pilgrims; a town grew up, took the name of St. Jean-d'Angeri, afterward d'Angély, was fortified in 1131, and in 1204 received a charter from Philip Augustus. The possession of the place was disputed between French and English in the Hundred Years' War, and between Catholics and Protestants at a later date. Louis XIII took it from the Protestants in 1621 and changed its name to Bourg-Louis. St. Jean lies on the right bank of the Boutonne, which is navigable for small vessels.

ST. JEAN-DE-LUZ, a coast town of southwestern France, in the department of Basses-Pyrenees, at the mouth of the Nivelle, 14 mi. S.W. of Bayonne on a branch of the Southern railway. Pop. (1946) 10,234. From the 14th to the 17th century St. Jean-de-Luz enjoyed a prosperity due to its mariners and fishermen. Its vessels were the first to set out for Newfoundland in 1520. In 1558, the Spaniards attacked and burned the town. In 1627, however, it was able to equip 80 vessels, which succeeded in saving the island of Ré from the duke of Buckingham. In 1660 the treaty of the Pyrenees was signed at St. Jean-de-Luz. At that time the population numbered 15,000. The cession of Newfoundland to England in 1713, the loss of Canada, and the silting-up of the harbour contributed to the decline of the town's maritime trade. St. Jean-de-Luz is situated in the Basque country on the bay of St. Jean-de-Luz, the entrance to which is protected by breakwaters and moles. It has a 13th-century church, the chief features of which are the galleries in the nave, which, by the Basque custom, are reserved for men.

ST. JOHN, OLIVER (c. 1598–1673), English statesman and judge, was the son of Oliver St. John of Cayshoe, Bedfordshire, and great-grandson of the first Lord St. John of Bletso. He was educated at Queens' college, Cambridge, and was called to the bar in 1626. He got into trouble with the court over a seditious publication and became closely associated with the future parliamentary leaders. He was employed as a lawyer by the earl of Bedford and was a member of the Providence Island company with the earl of

Warwick, Lord Saye and John Pym. In 1637, as counsel for John Hampden, he made a notable speech defending Hampden's refusal to pay ship money. In 1638 he married, as his second wife, Elizabeth Cromwell, a cousin of Oliver Cromwell, to whom his first wife also had been distantly related. The marriage led to an intimate friendship with Cromwell. St. John was member for Totnes in both the short and the long parliament, where he acted in close alliance with Bedford, Hampden and Pym and led the attack on ship money (*q.v.*). In 1641, with a view of securing his support, the king appointed St. John solicitor general. Nonetheless he took an active part in promoting the impeachment and attainder of the earl of Strafford and in preparing other bills brought forward by the popular party in the commons.

During the civil war St. John gradually became a recognized leader of the Independents and in the quarrel between the parliament and the army in 1647 he sided with the latter. Throughout he enjoyed Cromwell's confidence.

In 1648 St. John was appointed chief justice of the common pleas. He refused to act as one of the commissioners for the trial of Charles I. In 1651 he went to The Hague on an unsuccessful mission to negotiate a union between England and the Netherlands. In the same year he was sent with other commissioners to settle the government of Scotland and to prepare the way for its union with England. Otherwise, during the Commonwealth and Protectorate he largely confined himself to his judicial duties, having no great sympathy for the new order. After the Restoration he published an account of his past conduct (*The Case of Oliver St. John*, 1660), which saved him from any more severe vengeance than exclusion from public office. He retired to his house in Northamptonshire till 1662, when he went to live abroad. He died on Dec. 31, 1673.

SAINT JOHN, the capital of St. John county, New Brunswick, Canada, in 45° 14′ N., and 66° 3′ W., 481 mi. from Montreal. Pop. (1951) 50,779. It is situated at the mouth of the St. John river on a rocky peninsula. With it are incorporated the neighbouring towns of Carleton and Portland.

Saint John was visited in 1604 by the Sieur de Monts (1560–c. 1630) and his lieutenant Champlain, but it was not until 1635 that Charles de la Tour (d. 1666) established a trading post, called Fort St. Jean (*see* Parkman, *The Old Régime in Canada*), which existed under French rule until 1758, when it passed into the hands of Britain. In 1783 a body of United Empire Loyalists landed at Saint John and established a city, called Parr Town until 1785 when it was incorporated with Conway (Carleton), under royal charter, as the city of Saint John. It soon became and remained the largest town in the province, but for military reasons was not chosen as the capital. (*See* FREDERICTON.) Its growth was checked by several destructive fires, especially that of June 1877. It was rebuilt of stone and brick.

The river enters the harbour through a rocky gorge, which is passable by ships during each ebb and flow of the tide. Saint John is the Atlantic terminus of the Canadian Pacific railway and one of the termini of the Canadian National railways, and joins with Halifax in being one of the chief winter ports of Canada. The harbour is deep, sheltered, free from ice and always accessible, with 32 ft. of water at low tide and 58 to 60 ft. at high tide. It is the distributing centre for a large district, ricn in agricultural produce and lumber. It also has an important fishery trade. There are textile works and engineering shops. Among the exports are timber, pulp, fish, cattle, apples, dairy produce, metal manufactures and motorcars. The industries include a structural steel plant with two dry docks, each 1,150 ft. long. Saint John has a municipal airport for both land and sea planes and air service connecting with Trans-Canada at Moncton.

ST. JOHN, one of the Virgin Islands of the United States, formerly the Danish West Indies. It lies 4 mi. E. of St. Thomas and is 10 mi. long and 2½ mi. wide; area, 19 sq.mi. It is a mass of rugged mountains, the highest of which is Camel mountain (1,270 ft.). Although one of the best watered and most fertile of the Virgin group, it has little commerce. It is a free port, and possesses in Coral bay the best harbour of refuge in the Antilles. The village of Cruz Bay lies on the northern coast. Pop. (1950) 749.

ST. JOHN, a river of New Brunswick, Canada, rising in two branches, one in the state of Maine, U.S., and the other in the province of Quebec. The U.S. branch, known as the Walloostook, flows northeast to the New Brunswick frontier, where it turns southeast and for 80 mi. forms the international boundary. A little above Grand Falls the St. John enters Canada and flows through New Brunswick into the Bay of Fundy at St. John. Its total length is 399 mi. It is navigable for large steamers as far as Fredericton (86 mi.), and in spring and early summer for smaller vessels to Grand Falls (220 mi.), where a series of falls and rapids form a descent of 70 to 80 ft. Above the falls it is navigable for 65 mi. It drains an area of 26,000 sq.mi., of which half is in New Brunswick, and receives numerous tributaries, of which the chief are the Aroostook, Allagash, Madawaska (draining Lake Temiscouata in Quebec), Tobique and Nashwaak.

ST. JOHN OF JERUSALEM, KNIGHTS OF THE ORDER OF THE HOSPITAL OF, known also later as the KNIGHTS OF RHODES and the SOVEREIGN ORDER OF THE KNIGHTS OF MALTA. The history of this order divides itself naturally into four periods: (1) from its foundation in Jerusalem during the first crusade to its expulsion from the Holy Land after the fall of the Latin kingdom in 1291; (2) from 1309–1310, when the order was established in Rhodes, to its expulsion from the island in 1522; (3) from 1529 to 1798, during which its headquarters were in Malta; and (4) its modern development, as reconstituted after its virtual destruction in 1798.

Early Development.—Ever since Jerusalem became a centre of Christian pilgrimage, a hospital or hospice for pilgrims had existed there; and early in the 11th century one of these was restored, served by Benedictines and later dedicated to St. John the Baptist. When, in 1099, the crusaders surrounded the Holy City, the head of this hospital was a certain Gerard (*q.v.*) who is said to have assisted them during the siege. After the capture of the city he used his popularity to enlarge and reconstitute the hospital and adopted for his order the Augustinian rule. Donations and privileges were thereafter showered upon the new establishment in both Syria and Europe. In 1113 Pope Paschal II took the order and its possessions under his immediate protection (bull of Feb. 15 to Gerard), his act being confirmed in 1119 by Calixtus II and subsequently by other popes. Gerard was indeed, as Pope Paschal called him, the institutor of the order, if not its founder. It retained, however, during his lifetime its purely eleemosynary character. The armed defense of pilgrims may have been part of its functions, but its organization as an aggressive military force was the work of Raymond du Puy who succeeded as grand master on the death of Gerard (Sept. 3, 1120). The statesmanlike qualities of Raymond rendered his long mastership epoch-making for the order; and from 1137, when the knights accepted custody of the newly fortified castle of Bait Jibrin, they took a regular part in the wars of the Cross. During the second crusade Raymond was present at the council of the leaders held at Acre in 1148, which resulted in the ill-fated expedition against Damascus. The failure at Damascus was repaired five years later by the capture of Ascalon (Aug. 1153), in which the grand master and his knights had a conspicuous share.

Meanwhile, in addition to its ever-growing wealth, the order had received from successive popes privileges which rendered it, like the companion order of the Temple, increasingly independent of and obnoxious to the secular clergy. During the 30 years of Raymond's rule the hospital, which Gerard had instituted to meet a local need, had become universal, and establishments were formed east and west. After Oct. 1158, when his presence is attested at Verona, this master builder of the order disappears from history; he died some time between this date and 1160 when the name of another grand master, Gilbert d'Assailly, appears.

Organization of the Order.—The rule of the hospital, as formulated by Raymond du Puy, was based upon that of the Augustinian canons (*q.v.*). Its further developments, of which only the salient characteristics can be mentioned here, were closely analogous to those of the Templars (*q.v.*), whose statutes regulating the life of the brethren, the terms of admission to the order, the maintenance of discipline and the scale of punishments, cul-

minating in expulsion are, *mutatis mutandis,* closely paralleled by those of the Hospitallers.

Within the order were the three classes of knights, chaplains and serving brothers. The dominant class was that of the knights, in whose hands lay all power within the order. At its head was the master who held office for life. His powers were limited only by the statutes and customs and by the chapter general which, however, was only an occasional body summoned by himself. He was assisted in the exercise of his authority by the great officers of the order—prior, preceptor, marshal, hospitaller, drapier and treasurer—to whom were added, shortly after 1300, the turcopolier and admiral. The unit of provincial administration was the priory (England constituted one, while in Italy there were seven), and within each of these there were a number of commanderies (there were 36 in England at the end of the middle ages). As the order increased in size, the brethren came to be grouped in nations or tongues, and in the 14th century the division of the order into its seven tongues (Provence, Auvergne, France, Italy, Spain, England, Germany) was a recognized feature of its constitution. One of the great officers was placed at the head of each tongue; priories and commanderies were reserved for the brethren of the tongue concerned, and disputes were settled within the assembly of the tongue. From the later middle ages the Hospitallers were rather a federation of national societies than a united cosmopolitan order.

In two important respects the knights of St. John differed from the Templars. The latter were a purely military organization; the Hospitallers, on the other hand, were at the outset preponderatingly a nursing brotherhood, and though this character was subordinated during their later period of military importance, it never disappeared. It continued to be a rule of the order that in its establishments it was for the sick to give orders, for the brethren to obey. The chapters were largely occupied with the building, furnishing and improvement of hospitals, to which were attached learned physicians and surgeons who had the privilege of eating with the knights. The revenues of particular properties were charged with providing luxuries (*e.g.,* white bread) for the patients, and the various provinces of the order with the duty of forwarding blankets, clothes, wine and food for their use. The Hospitallers, moreover, encouraged the affiliation of women to their order, which the monastic and purely military rule of the Templars sternly forbade.

The Knights in Syria.—As the wealth and military resources of the orders grew, so did their influence in the affairs of the Latin states. The military feudal class among the Syrian Franks had never been sufficiently numerous to ensure effective settlement, and it was continuously impoverished by a variety of causes. As a result the orders acquired castles which lay magnates could no longer afford to maintain, and with the buildings the knights secured the appurtenances—lands and rights over tenants. The Hospitallers acquired Bait Jibrin in 1137, Krak (Crac) des Chevaliers and an extensive border area to the north and east in 1142, Arca and Jebel Akkar in 1170, Chastel Ruge in 1177 and Margat, which later became the headquarters of the order, in 1186. To this extent the military orders were replacing the feudal aristocracy as landlords. It was a change in the balance of power which weakened the monarchy of Jerusalem, for the orders were not bound to the king by the same ties of allegiance as were the feudatories.

The role which the orders were enabled to play in the affairs of the kingdom was reflected in events. The Templars refused to take part in invasions of Egypt led by King Amalric I, but the Hospitallers encouraged the project, supplied the king with an important contingent of his army and bargained with him for the price of that support almost as an independent power. In the problems of regency and succession which followed the death of Amalric in 1174, the masters of the military orders emerged as figures of the first importance, and when Baldwin V died in 1185 all the castles of the kingdom were given into their custody.

These problems weakened the kingdom at a time when Saladin's power was advancing and prepared the way for the disasters of 1187: the annihilation of the Christian army at Hattin and the loss of Jerusalem (*see* CRUSADES). The Hospitallers played a full part in the vain military effort to avert these defeats. After Hattin, Saladin spared the lives of nearly all his prisoners except the Templars and Hospitallers whom he massacred in cold blood. This uncharacteristic act is a measure of the respect in which the knights were held by the Moslems. The Hospitallers were again prominent in the ensuing third crusade and especially distinguished themselves in King Richard of England's victory at Arsuf (1191). During the following decade there was a steady development of the property and privileges of the order.

During the 13th century the Latin states in Syria were less securely established than they had been during the 12th century: the settlement grew progressively weaker until, with the loss of Acre in 1291, it was finally extinguished. The authority of the monarchy was compromised by the succession of women and by the civil war provoked by the conduct of the emperor Frederick II in Syria and Cyprus, and was never subsequently resurrected. The way was left clear for certain groups, such as baronial families, Italian merchant communities and the military orders, to follow their particular interests unchecked by higher authority.

In this way the Hospitallers played a part in weakening Latin Syria. They were engaged in frequent disputes with diocesans and with the Templars. From 1199, in opposition to the Templars, they supported an Armenian claimant to the principality of Antioch and were not reconciled to its prince Bohemund IV until 1231. They held aloof from the efforts of Frederick II to recover Jerusalem. In 1240–41 they and the Templars gave differing advice to the crusaders Thibaut IV of Champagne and Richard of Cornwall in their efforts to negotiate a truce with the Moslems. The two orders again took different sides in the war between the Venetians and Genoese which devastated Acre between 1256 and 1258. In 1236 it had come to the attention of Pope Gregory IX that, in pursuance of their own private quarrels, the knights were contemplating alliance with the sect of the Assassins, and he sternly rebuked them both on this account and because of their backsliding from the ideals of their order (*see* his letters translated in E. J. King's *The Knights Hospitallers in the Holy Land*, pp. 234–236).

It must be emphasized that in these respects the knights were no worse than their contemporaries in Syria and that there is another side to the picture. The order was to the fore in all the major attacks made on the Moslems during the 13th century. It played a distinguished part in the invasions of Egypt by the forces of the fifth crusade in 1218–21 and by those of St. Louis in 1249–50. It joined the expeditions led by Andrew II of Hungary (1217) and by Thibaut of Champagne (1239). It maintained the great strongholds of Krak and Margat, which up to their loss (1271 and 1285 respectively) continued to serve as bulwarks against Moslem attack and as bases from which Christian raids were organized. The order accepted the custody of the exposed city of Ascalon in 1243 and that of the fortified monastery on Mount Thabor in 1257. At all times it spared neither men nor resources to hold the Moslems at bay.

In the years 1258–60 there were signs of the military orders composing their differences, but it was already too late. In 1260 Bibars, the Mameluke sultan of Egypt, was already free from the Tatar threat, and in 1265 he began the series of conquests which culminated in the fall of Acre in 1291 and in the expulsion of the Franks from Syria. The headquarters of the order were moved to Cyprus. Under a great master Guillaume de Villaret, the order was drastically reformed by a series of statutes between 1301 and 1304. In 1308 a new chapter in its history began when the knights conquered Rhodes from the Byzantines: the order was to rule that island as a sovereign power for more than two centuries.

The Knights in Rhodes.—The character and aims of the order were profoundly affected by their newly acquired sovereignty. The Hospitallers ruled an island too narrow to monopolize their energies but occupying a position of vast commercial and strategic importance. Close to the Anatolian mainland, commanding the outlet of the archipelago and lying in the direct trade route between Europe and the east, Rhodes had become the chief distributing point in the lively commerce which, in spite of papal objections, Christian traders maintained with the Moslem states; the

Hospitallers were thus divided between their duty as sovereign, which was to watch over the interests of their subjects, and their duty as Christian warriors, which was to combat the infidel. In view of the fact that the crusading spirit was everywhere declining, it is not surprising that their policy was henceforth directed less by religious than by political and commercial considerations. Not that they altogether neglected their duty as protectors of the Cross: they became a naval power and maintained a fleet of galleys until the loss of Malta; their consuls in Egypt and Jerusalem watched over the interests of pilgrims; their hospitals were still maintained for the service of the sick and the destitute. But, side by side with this, secularization proceeded apace; even toward the infidel the attitude of the knights was necessarily influenced by the fact that their supplies of provisions were mainly drawn from the Moslem mainland. By the 15th century their crusading spirit had grown so weak that they even attempted to negotiate a commercial treaty with the Ottoman sultan; the project broke down on the refusal of the knights to accept the sultan's suzerainty.

Throughout its occupation of Rhodes, the hospital was always ready to give all possible support to any major attack on the Moslems. In 1344 its galleys took part in the conquest of Smyrna, a town which the knights continued to hold until 1402. They contributed to the force that Peter I of Cyprus led to the temporary capture of Alexandria in 1365. A contingent was at the disaster of Nicopolis in 1396. They showed courage and great military skill in defending Rhodes. In 1440 and 1444 they repelled attacks launched from Egypt. In 1480 the garrison, commanded by the grand master Pierre d'Aubusson, held at bay an Ottoman fleet and army. A still greater attack was mounted in 1522 by Suleiman the Magnificent. Reinforcements failed, the Christian powers sent no assistance, and in the next year the knights capitulated, withdrawing with all the honours of war to Crete. Their occupation of Rhodes had postponed for about two centuries the appearance of the Ottomans as a first-rate naval power in the Mediterranean, a debt which Europe never sufficiently acknowledged. When the emperor Charles V received news of the final siege he exclaimed: "Nothing in the world has been so well lost as Rhodes!" But he would give no help in the plans for its recovery, but instead he gave to the hospital the island of Malta and the fortress of Tripoli.

The Knights in Malta.—The settlement of the Hospitallers in Malta was contemporaneous with the Reformation, which profoundly affected the order. In England the refusal of the grand prior and knights to acknowledge the royal supremacy led to the confiscation of their estates by Henry VIII, and though not formally suppressed, the English organization practically ceased to exist. The knights of Malta, as they came to be known, nonetheless continued their vigorous warfare. In 1550 they defeated the redoubtable corsair Dragut, but in 1551 their position in Tripoli, always precarious, became untenable and they capitulated to the Turks and concentrated their forces in Malta. On May 18, 1565, the Ottoman fleet appeared off the island and one of the most famous sieges in history began. It was ultimately raised in September on the appearance of a large relieving force dispatched by the Spanish viceroy of Sicily, after 25,000 of the enemy had fallen. The memory of the grand master Jean Parisot de la Vallette, the hero of the siege, who died in 1568, is preserved in the city of Valletta which was built on the site of the struggle.

In 1571 the knights shared in the victory of Lepanto. This crowning success, however, was followed during the 17th century by a long period of depression due to internal dissensions and culminating during the Thirty Years' War, the position of the order being seriously affected by the terms of the peace of Westphalia (1648). The character of the order at this date became more exclusively aristocratic, and its wealth, partly acquired by commerce and partly derived from the contributions of the commanderies scattered throughout Europe, was enormous. The wonderful fortifications, planned by French architects and improved by every grand master in turn, the magnificent churches, chapels, *auberges* and the great library founded in 1650 were the outward and visible signs of the growth of a corresponding luxury in the private life of the order. Nevertheless, under Ramon Perellos

(1697–1720) and Antonio Manoel de Vilhena (1722–36), the knights restored their prestige in the Mediterranean by victories over the Turks. In 1741 Emmanuele Pinto, a man of strong character, became grand master. He expelled the Jesuits, resisted papal encroachments on his authority and, refusing to summon the general chapter, ruled as a despot. Emanuel, prince de Rohan (d. 1797), who was elected grand master in succession to Francisco Jimenes de Texada in 1775, made serious efforts to revive the old spirit of the order. The last great expedition of the Maltese galleys was worthy of its noblest traditions: they were sent to carry supplies for the sufferers from the great earthquake that destroyed Messina in 1783. They had long ceased to be effective fighting ships and survived mainly as gorgeous state barges in which the knights sailed on ceremonial pleasure trips.

The French Revolution was fatal to the order. Rohan made no secret of his sympathy with the losing cause in France, and Malta became a refuge-place for the *émigrés*. In 1792 the vast possessions of the order in France were confiscated; six years later the Directory resolved on the forcible seizure of Malta itself. When Napoleon occupied the island on his way to Egypt in 1798 the grand master Ferdinand von Hompesch organized no resistance, and the knights' long rule of the island came to an end. With this the history of the order of St. John practically ends.

The Order in Modern Times.—After their expulsion from Malta, the knights ceased to be a territorial power and lost their *raison d'être* as a military order. After 1814 Malta was retained by the British, and subsequent French expansion into North Africa extinguished the Barbary corsairs. But the order continued to exist, although much reduced in size, and to fulfil the original purpose of its founder. Since its first beginnings it had never ceased to serve the poor and sick, and from the early 19th century the order, in all its forms, has continued to discharge this Christian work in accordance with its own splendid tradition.

After establishing itself temporarily, first at Catania and then at Ferrara, the order moved to Rome in 1834, where its headquarters remained. The pope, as first superior of the order, appointed a grand master in 1801, but between 1805 and 1879 appointed only lieutenant masters. But the renown gained by the order in the relief of suffering was such that in 1879 the pope re-established the mastership. The third of the restored line, Prince Ludovico Chigi della Rovere Albani, died in 1951. The order, organized into the Italian and German tongues, still retained certain diplomatic privileges and at mid-20th century had accredited representatives with five governments, including that of Spain.

In addition, there remained two orders of St. John of Jerusalem of Protestant origin. During the Reformation in Germany the master and knights of Brandenburg adopted the new religion. They remained divided from the main order, but joined with it again in 1763. This bailiwick of Brandenburg was suppressed in 1810, but it was restored by the king of Prussia 43 years later. It was not recognized by the order in Rome, but continued as an independent Protestant body. It supports a number of hospitals in Germany and in many respects provided a model for the second Protestant order, that in England.

The grand priory of England, like other religious orders in that country, came to an end as a result of the religious settlement of Henry VIII and Elizabeth I. The grand masters in Malta continued to appoint titular grand priors of England, but the order had neither roots nor property there. Its restoration in the 19th century was due to the initiative taken by the French knights, whose organization was temporarily revived between 1814 and 1848. The Greek War of Independence raised hopes that the order might regain Rhodes; English support was needed, and as a means to this end the French worked for the revival of the English priory, so that in 1831 Sir Robert Peat became prior of the Venerable Tongue of England. The English knights hoped to become a Protestant branch of the main order, but the lieutenant masters in Rome ruled that Protestants could not be admitted, and in 1858 the English knights proclaimed themselves an independent order. By its constitution of 1871 (which subsequently was little amended) it became the Order of St. John of Jerusalem in Eng-

land under the headship of its own prior. Between 1861 and 1888 that office was held by William Drogo Montagu, seventh duke of Manchester, and during that period the philanthropic work of the order assumed the modern forms: the life saving medal was instituted in 1874; the opthalmic hospital was founded in Jerusalem in 1882; and the St. John's Ambulance brigade followed in 1888, growing from an association which the order had founded ten years earlier. Also in 1874, the order acquired the site and remains of the priory at Clerkenwell which had been the headquarters of the Hospitallers in England from the 1140s until 1559. It became an imperial order, incorporated by royal charter as the Order of the Hospital of St. John of Jerusalem in the British realm. The reigning monarch is its sovereign head, and it has subordinate commanderies in certain of the dominions. From 1888 the prince of Wales (after 1901 King Edward VII) was its grand prior, until in 1910 that office was assumed by Arthur duke of Connaught.

The British order added to its lustre by outstanding work in the medical field in World Wars I and II.

BIBLIOGRAPHY.—For further study the work of J. Delaville le Roulx is essential; his great edition of the *Cartulaire général des Hospitaliers de Saint-Jean de Jérusalem, 1100–1310*, 4 vol. (Paris, 1894–1904) is of fundamental importance, and his *Les Hospitaliers en Terre Sainte et à Chypre, 1100–1310* (Paris, 1904) is based on his own study of the cartulary. *See* also his *Les Hospitaliers à Rhodes jusq'à la mort de Philibert de Nailhac, 1310–1421* (Paris, 1913). Among the best works in English are J. M. Kemble's introduction to *The Knights Hospitallers in England*, Camden Soc. (London, 1857); W. Porter, *History of the Knights of Malta*, 2 vol. (London, 1853; 2nd ed., 1883); and E. J. King, *The Knights Hospitallers in the Holy Land* (London, 1931) and *The Knights of St. John in the British Empire* (London, 1934). (R. C. SMA.; X.)

ST. JOHNS (ST. JEAN), a city and port of entry of Quebec, Canada, and capital of St. Johns county, 27 mi. S.E. of Montreal by rail, on the Richelieu river and at the head of the Chambly canal. Pop. (1951), 19,305. A large export trade in lumber, grain and farm produce is carried on, and its mills and factories produce flour, silk, pottery, hats, etc. Three railways, the Canadian National, Canadian Pacific and Central Vermont, enter St. Johns. On the opposite bank of the river is the flourishing town of St. Jean d'Iberville (usually known simply as Iberville), connected with St. Johns by several bridges.

ST. JOHN'S, the capital of Newfoundland, a province of Canada, on the east coast of the island, in the peninsula of Avalon, in 47° 33′ 54″ N. and 52° 40′ 18″ W. It is the most easterly city of the American continent. Pop. (1951) 52,873, mostly of Irish descent and Roman Catholics. It stands on rising ground on the north side of a landlocked harbour, which opens suddenly in the lofty coast. The entrance, known as The Narrows, guarded by Signal hill (520 ft.) and South Side hill (620 ft.), is about 1,400 ft. wide, narrowing to 600 ft. between Pancake and Chain rocks. At the termination of the Narrows the harbour trends suddenly to the west, thus completely shutting out the ocean swell. The port has sufficient water for vessels of 30 ft. draught. There is good wharf accommodation, with a graving and a floating dock.

St. John's was first settled by Devonshire fishermen early in the 16th century. It was twice sacked by the French, and captured by them in the Seven Years' War (1762), but recaptured in the same year, and remained in British possession. Both in the American Revolution and the War of 1812 it was the headquarters of the British fleet. The old city, built entirely of wood, was twice destroyed by fire (1816–1817 and 1846). Half of it was again swept away in 1892, but new and more substantial buildings were erected, notably the Anglican and Roman Catholic cathedrals. Education is in the hands of the various religious bodies. St. John's practically monopolizes the commerce of the island, being the centre of the cod, seal and whale fisheries. The chief industries are connected with the outfitting of the fishing vessels, or with the disposal and processing of their catch. Although nearly all the commerce of the island is sea-borne a narrow-gauge railway (operated by the Canadian National system) runs from St. John's to Port aux Basques on the southwest corner of the island, from whence a railway ferry connects with Sydney, N.S. St. John's is also on Trans-Canada Air Lines flights. The city imports iron, coal, cattle and general produce, and exports fish, oil, wood pulp and paper.

SAINT JOHNSBURY, a town of northeastern Vermont, U.S., the county seat of Caledonia county, and a village of the same name; 37 mi. E.N.E. of Montpelier, on the Passumpsic river and federal highways 2 and 5. It is served by the Canadian Pacific, the Maine Central and the St. Johnsbury and Lamoille County railways. Pop. (1950) 7,370; (1940) 7,437. It is the home of the Fairbanks platform scale, invented there in 1830 by Thaddeus Fairbanks and manufactured there from 1837, and of the largest maple-sugar plant in the country. The town was settled in 1786 by Jonathan Arnold, and was named after Hector St. John de Crèvecoeur, author of *Letters from an American Farmer* (1782). The village was incorporated in 1853. In 1923 the town adopted a city-manager government.

ST. JOHN'S WORT, the general name for species of *Hypericum* (family Hypericaceae), especially *H. perforatum,* small shrubby plants with slender stems, sessile opposite leaves which are often dotted with pellucid glands, and showy yellow flowers. *H. androsaemum* is tutsan (Fr. *tout saine*), so called from its healing properties. *H. calycinum* (Rose of Sharon), a creeping plant with large almost solitary flowers 3 to 4 in. across, is a plant of southeast Europe which has become naturalized in Great Britain in various places in hedges and thickets. The genus comprises about 250 species of herbs or undershrubs, native mostly to temperate and subtropical regions. About 30 species, chiefly herbaceous, are found in North America, widely distributed across the continent but most numerous in the eastern states and adjacent Canada. Many species are cultivated.

ST. JOSEPH, a city of southwestern Michigan, U.S., on Lake Michigan, at the mouth of the St. Joseph river and immediately west of Benton Harbor; a port of entry and the county seat of Berrien county. It is on federal highways 12, 31 and 33, and is served by the New York Central, the Chesapeake and Ohio and the South Shore Electric railways, and by motorbus lines.

The population was 10,223 in 1950 and 8,963 in 1940 by the federal census. St. Joseph and Benton Harbor, connected by a wide thoroughfare and a ship canal, are practically one community, with a combined population estimated at 35,000, which is doubled in summer by visitors. The surrounding country is the famous Michigan fruit belt. The traffic of the harbour in 1949 amounted to 372,747 tons.

St. Joseph has a variety of industries employing more than 6,000 persons. Principal manufactured products are washing machines, castings, industrial rubber goods, paper boxes, pistons and piston pins, printing products and hosiery.

In 1679 La Salle built Ft. Miami on or near the site of St. Joseph. The present city was settled in 1829, incorporated as a village in 1836 and chartered as a city in 1891.

ST. JOSEPH, a city of northwestern Missouri, U.S., on the east bank of the Missouri river, 55 mi. N.W. of Kansas City; a port of entry and the county seat of Buchanan county. It is on federal highways 36, 59, 71, 169 and 275; and is served by the Burlington Route, the Chicago Great Western, the Missouri Pacific, the Rock Island, the Santa Fe and the Union Pacific railways, and by Mid-Continent Airlines. Pop. (1950) 78,588; (1940) 75,711. The city covers 15 sq.mi. on bluffs above the river, graded down considerably in the business and eastern residential section. There are numerous public and parochial schools, churches, hotels with 2,200 guest rooms, and hospitals. Just east of the city is a state hospital for the insane (1874). The leading industries are livestock feeding and meat packing, grain production and milling; the principal products are paper tablets, flour and mixed feeds, cereals, pharmaceuticals, beer, garments, candy, jewellery, mattresses, dairy products, caskets, cabinets, brick, livestock serum, Christmas decorations and artificial trees, structural steel, tile, cinder blocks, tents, chemicals, vinegar, millinery, caps, hats, textiles, canned foods, wire rope, fabricated houses, plastic signs, fluorescent fixtures and battery cables. The daily *St. Joseph News-Press* was established in 1903 by a merger of the *Daily News* and *Evening Press.*

In 1826 Joseph Robidoux, a French Canadian, established an Indian trading post there, known as Blacksnake Hills. After the "Platte Purchase" in 1836 other settlers came in, and in 1843 Robidoux laid out a town, which he named in honour of his patron saint. It became the county seat in 1846 and in 1851 was chartered as a city. It developed early into an important trading centre, and was a busy outfitting point during the years of heavy travel by prospectors and other emigrants to the Rocky mountains and the Pacific coast. On April 3, 1860, the first rider of the "Pony Express" galloped out of St. Joseph (the eastern terminus of the service during the 18 months of its operation), and a year later Lincoln's inaugural address was carried through to Sacramento (nearly 2,000 mi.) in 7 days and 17 hours. During the Civil War St. Joseph was held continuously by the Unionists, but local sentiment was bitterly divided. After the war a period of rapid development set in, which increased the population from 8,932 in 1860 to 19,565 in 1870, and to 77,403 in 1910.

SAINT-JUST, ANTOINE LOUIS LÉON DE RICHEBOURG DE (1767–1794), French revolutionary leader, was born at Decize in the Nivernais on Aug. 25, 1767. At the outbreak of the Revolution he was elected an officer in the National Guard of the Aisne. He assumed a stoical demeanour united to a tyrannical policy. He entered into correspondence with Robespierre, who, flattered by his worship, admitted him to his friendship. Thus supported, Saint-Just became deputy to the National Convention, where he made his first speech on the condemnation of Louis XVI—gloomy, fanatical, remorseless in tone—on Nov. 13, 1792. In the convention, in the Jacobin club, and among the populace he was dubbed the "St. John of the Messiah of the People." In the name of the Committee of Public Safety he drew up reports to the convention upon the absorbing themes of the overthrow of the party of the Gironde (report of July 8, 1793), of the Hébertists, and finally, of that denunciation of Danton which consigned him and his followers to the guillotine. Camille Desmoulins said of Saint-Just—the youth with the beautiful countenance and the long fair locks—"He carries his head like a Holy Sacrament." "And I," savagely replied Saint-Just, "will make him carry his like a Saint Denis." The threat was not vain: Desmoulins accompanied Danton to the scaffold.

Saint-Just proposed that the National Convention should, through its committees, direct all military movements and all branches of the government (report of Oct. 10, 1793). This was agreed to, and Saint-Just was despatched to Strasbourg to superintend the military operations. It was suspected that the enemy without was being aided by treason within. Saint-Just "organized the Terror," and soon the heads of all suspects sent to Paris were falling under the guillotine. But there were no executions at Strasbourg, and Saint-Just repressed the excesses of J. G. Schneider, who, acting as public prosecutor to the revolutionary tribunal of the Lower Rhine, had ruthlessly applied the Terror in Alsace. Schneider was sent to Paris and guillotined. The conspiracy was defeated, the frontier was delivered and Germany invaded. On his return Saint-Just was made president of the convention. Later, with the army of the north, he placed before the generals the dilemma of victory over the enemies of France or trial by the dreaded Revolutionary tribunal; and before the eyes of the army he organized a force charged with the slaughter of those who should seek refuge by flight. He succeeded again, and Belgium was gained for France (May, 1794).

Meanwhile affairs in Paris looked gloomier than ever, and Robespierre recalled Saint-Just to the capital. Saint-Just proposed a dictatorship. At the famous sitting of the 9th Thermidor, he presented as the report of the committees of General Security and Public Safety a document expressing his own views, a sight of which had been refused to the other members of committee the previous evening. Then the storm broke. He was interrupted, and the sitting ended with an order for Robespierre's arrest, which entailed that of Saint-Just. On the following day, July 28, 1794, 22 men, nearly all young, were guillotined. Saint-Just maintained his proud self-possession to the last.

See *Oeuvres de Saint-Just, précédées d'une notice historique sur sa vie* (1833–34); E. Fleury, *Études révolutionnaires* (2 vol., 1851), with which *cf.* articles by Sainte-Beuve (*Causeries du lundi,* vol. v), Cuvillier-Fleury (*Portraits politiques et révolutionnaires*); E. Hamel, *Histoire de Saint-Just* (1859), which brought a fine to the publishers for outrage on public decency; F. A. Aulard, *Les Orateurs de la Législative et de la Convention* (2nd ed., 1905); M. Lenéru, *Saint-Just* (1922). The *Oeuvres complètes de Saint-Just* were edited with notes by C. Vellay (1908).

ST. JUST (St. Just in Penwith), a market town of Cornwall, England, 7 mi. W. of Penzance. Pop. of urban district (1951) 4,122. Area 12 sq.mi. The town lies in a wild district 1 mi. inland from Cape Cornwall, which is 4 mi. N. of Land's End.

ST. KILDA (Gaelic *Hirta*, "the western land"), largest of a small group of about sixteen islets of the Outer Hebrides, Inverness-shire, Scotland. It is included in the civil parish of Harris, and is situated 40 mi. W. of North Uist. It measures 3 mi. from E. to W. and 2 mi. from N. to S. Except at the landing place on the southeast, the cliffs rise sheer out of deep water, and on the northeast side the highest eminence in the island, Conagher, forms a precipice 1,220 ft. high. The inhabitants, an industrious Gaelic-speaking community who numbered 36 in 1930, were that year evacuated at their own request and were settled mainly in Morvern parish, Co. Argyll. The island is practically cut off from the world for eight months of the year. It has been in the possession of the Macleods for hundreds of years except for the period 1779–1871.

ST. KITTS or **ST. CHRISTOPHER,** an island in the British West Indies, forming, with Nevis and Anguilla, one of the presidencies in the colony of the Leeward Islands. It is a long oval with a narrow neck of land projecting from the southeastern end; total length 23 mi., area 68 sq.mi. Mountains traverse the central part from northwest to southeast, the highest being Mount Misery (3,711 ft.). The island is well watered, fertile and healthy, and its climate is cool and dry (temperature between 78° and 85° F.; average annual rainfall 38 in.). The rim of land formed by the skirts of the mountains, and the valley of Basseterre are cultivable. The higher slopes of the hills afford pasturage; the summits are crowned with dense woods. Sugar is the chief product and export, followed by sea-island cotton. Primary education is free and compulsory. In 1950 there were 17 government and 2 subsidized private primary schools and three government-aided secondary schools. Basseterre (pop. 12,194), on the southwest coast, is the island's port as well as capital of the presidency. St. Kitts was discovered in 1493 by Columbus but was not occupied until 1623, when Thomas Warner made the first English settlement in the West Indies there. It was seized by the French three times between 1666 and 1782 and held for short periods, but remained British from 1783.

The island had a population of 29,818 by the 1946 census, mostly Negro. (L. W. Be.)

SAINT-LAMBERT, JEAN FRANÇOIS DE (1716–1803), French poet, was born at Nancy on Dec. 26, 1716. He entered the army and, when Stanislaus Leszczynski was established in 1737 as duke of Lorraine, he became an official at his court at Lunéville. He left the army after the Hanoverian campaign of 1756–57, and devoted himself to literature, producing a volume of descriptive verse, *Les Saisons* (1769), now never read, many articles for the *Encyclopédie,* and some miscellaneous works. He was admitted to the Academy in 1770. His fame, however, comes chiefly from his amours. He was already high in the favour of the marquise de Boufflers, Stanislaus's mistress, whom he addressed in his verses as *Doris* and *Thémire*, when Voltaire in 1748 came to Lunéville with the marquise du Châtelet. Her infatuation for him and its fatal termination are known to all readers of the life of Voltaire. His subsequent liaison with Madame d'Houdetot, Rousseau's Sophie, proved permanent. He published in 1798 the *Principe des moeurs chez toutes les nations ou catéchisme universel,* and published his *Oeuvres philosophiques* two years before his death on Feb. 9, 1803. Madame d'Houdetot survived until Jan. 28, 1813.

See G. Maugras, *La Cour de Lunéville* (1904) and *La Marquise de Boufflers* (1907); also the literature dealing with Rousseau and Voltaire.

ST. LAURENT, LOUIS STEPHEN (1882–   ), Canadian statesman, born on Feb. 1, 1882, at Compton, Que., studied at St. Charles college, Sherbrooke, and Laval university, Quebec, Que. Called to the bar at Quebec in 1905, he practised law until Dec. 10, 1941, when he entered federal politics as minister of justice and attorney general. He was later secretary of state for external affairs, and on Nov. 15, 1948, became the 17th prime minister of Canada.

St. Laurent was first elected to parliament as Liberal member for Quebec East on Feb. 9, 1942, and was returned in the 1945 and 1949 elections.

ST. LAWRENCE. The river St. Lawrence, in North America, with the five fresh-water inland seas (*see* GREAT LAKES), Superior, Michigan, Huron, Erie and Ontario, forms one of the great river systems of the world, having a length of 1,900 mi. from the source of the river St. Louis (which rises near the source of the Mississippi and falls into the head of Lake Superior) to Cape Gaspé, where it empties into the Gulf of St. Lawrence. The river is here considered as rising at the foot of Lake Ontario, where the name St. Lawrence is first applied to it.

The river, to the point where it crosses 45° N. in its northeasterly course, forms the boundary line between the state of New York and the province of Ontario; thence to the sea it is wholly within Canadian territory, running through the province of Quebec. At Point des Monts, 260 mi. below Quebec, it is 26 mi. wide, and where it finally merges into the Gulf of St. Lawrence, 150 mi. farther on, it is 90 mi. wide, this stretch being broken by the large island of Anticosti, lying in the mouth. The character of the river banks varies with the geological formations through which it runs. Passing over the Archaean rocks of the Laurentian from Kingston to Brockville the shores are very irregular, and the river is broken up by protrusions of granite and gneiss into a large number of picturesque islands, "The Thousand Islands," frequented as a summer resort. From Brockville to Montreal the river runs through flat-bedded Cambro-Silurian limestones, with rapids at several points, which are run by light-draught passenger boats. For the up trip the rapids are avoided by canalization. From Montreal to Three Rivers the course is through an alluvial plain overlying the limestones, the river at one point expanding into Lake St. Peter, 20 mi. long by 10 mi. wide, with a practically uniform depth of 10 ft. Below Three Rivers the banks grow gradually higher until, after passing Quebec through a cleft in slate rocks of Cambrian age, the river widens, washing the feet of the Laurentian mountains on its north shore; while a more moderately hilly country, terminating in the Shickshock mountains of the Gaspé Peninsula, skirts its south shore.

From Kingston, at the head of the river, to Montreal (170 mi.), navigation is limited to vessels of 14 ft. draught. From Montreal to Quebec (160 mi.), a ship channel has been dredged to a depth of 30 ft.; below Quebec the river is navigable by vessels of any draught. The locks of the present canals are 45 ft. wide, with an available depth of 14 ft. and a minimum length of 270 ft.; but plans are under consideration for a new ship canal allowing vessels of 25 or 30 ft. draught to enter Lake Ontario, from which the new Welland canal of the same depth leads to the Upper Lakes.

In the stretch between Montreal and Quebec the ship channel is a national work, and improvements have been undertaken to secure everywhere a minimum depth of 30 ft. and a width of 450 ft. The river from Kingston to the sea is well supplied with aids to navigation. In the dredged portions lights are arranged in pairs of leading lights on foundations sufficiently high and solid to resist the pressure of ice movement, and there is an elaborate system of fog alarms, lighted and other buoys, as well as telegraphic, wireless and telephonic communication, storm signal, weather and ice-reporting stations and a lifesaving service.

Montreal, at the head of ocean navigation, the largest city in Canada, is an important distributing centre for all points in western Canada, and enjoys an extensive shipping trade with the United Kingdom. Quebec is the summer port used by the largest steamers in the Canadian trade. There are numerous flourishing towns on the river, from Kingston, a grain transferring port, to the sea. Large quantities of lumber are handled at mills along the river.

A natural highway between all points west of the Maritime Provinces and Europe, the St. Lawrence permits ocean traffic to penetrate 1,000 m. into the heart of the country. It is, moreover, the shortest freight route from the Great Lakes to Europe. From Buffalo to Liverpool via New York involves rail or barge canal transport of 496 m. and an ocean voyage of 3,034 nautical miles. Via Montreal there is a 14-ft. transport of 348 m. and river and ocean voyage of 2,772 nautical miles. From Quebec to Liverpool by Cape Race is 2,801 nautical miles, while the route by Belle Isle, more nearly a great circle course, usually taken between July and October, is only 2,633 nautical miles. On the other hand the St. Lawrence is not open in winter and the average time between the arrival of the first vessel at Montreal from sea and the departure of the last ocean vessel is seven months. From Kingston to Quebec the river freezes every winter, except at points where the current is rapid. Below Quebec, although there is border ice, the river never freezes. Efforts have been made to lengthen the season of navigation by using specially constructed steamers to break the ice; and it is claimed that the season of navigation could be materially lengthened, and winter floods prevented by keeping the river open to Montreal. Winter ferries are maintained at Quebec, between Prince Edward island and Nova Scotia, and between Newfoundland and Sydney, Cape Breton.

The river above tide water is not subject to excessive flooding, the maximum rise in the spring and early summer months, chiefly from northern tributaries from the Ottawa eastward, being 10 feet. The Great Lakes serve as impounding reservoirs for the gradual distribution of all overflows in the west. At Montreal, soon after the river freezes, there is a local rise of about 10 ft. in the level in the harbour, caused by restriction of the channel by anchor ice; and in the spring when the volume is augmented, this obstruction leads to a further rise. To prevent flooding of the lower parts of the city a dike was built in 1887 along the river front, which prevented a serious flooding in 1899.

Tides enter the Gulf of St. Lawrence from the Atlantic chiefly through Cabot strait (between Cape Breton and Newfoundland), which is 75 m. wide and 250 fathoms deep. The tide entering through Belle Isle strait, 10 m. wide and 30 fathoms deep, is comparatively little felt. The greatest range is attained in Northumberland strait and in Chaleur bay, where it amounts to 10 feet. At the entrance to the estuary at Anticosti it has again the oceanic range of about 6 ft., and proceeds up the estuary with an ever-increasing range, which attains its maximum of 19 ft. at the lower end of Orleans island, 650 m. from the ocean at Cabot strait. At Quebec, 30 m. farther up, the range is nearly as great; but at 40 m. above Quebec it is largely cut off by the Richelieu Rapids, and finally ceases to be felt at Three Rivers, at the lower end of Lake St. Peter, 760 m. from the ocean.

The St. Lawrence provides ample water-power, which is being increasingly used, and from Lake Superior to the gulf there are numerous points on its tributaries where power has been developed.

Nearly all the rivers flowing into the St. Lawrence below Quebec are stocked with salmon. In the salt water of the gulf and lower river, mackerel, cod, herring, smelt, sea-trout, striped bass and other fish are caught for market.

The St. Lawrence is spanned by the following railway bridges: (1) A truss bridge near Cornwall. (2) A truss bridge with a swing at Coteau Landing. (3) A cantilever bridge at Caughnawaga. (4) The Victoria Jubilee bridge, 6,592 ft. long by 67 ft. wide, with 25 spans, double railway and trolley tracks, driveways and sidewalks. (5) A cantilever bridge, having a central span of 1,800 ft., crosses the river at a point 7 m. above Quebec. The southern half of the superstructure, while in course of erection in August 1907, fell, killing 78 men, and necessitating a serious delay in the completion of the work.

Discovery of St. Lawrence.—The St. Lawrence was discovered by Jacques Cartier, commissioned by the king of France to explore and trade on the American coast. Cartier entered the strait of Belle Isle in 1534; but Breton fishermen had previously resorted there in summer and penetrated as far as Brest, 11 leagues west of Blanc Sablon, the dividing line between Quebec

and Labrador. Cartier circled the gulf, but missed the entrance to the river. On his second voyage in 1536 he named a bay on the north shore of the gulf, which he entered on Aug. 10, the feast of St. Lawrence, *Baye Sainct Laurens*, and the name gradually extended over the whole river, though Cartier himself always wrote of the River of Canada. Early in September, he reached "Canada," now Quebec, and on Oct. 2 reached Hochelaga, now Montreal. No permanent settlement was then made. The first, Tadousac, at the mouth of the Saguenay, was established by Champlain in 1603, and Quebec was settled by him in 1608. Between that time and 1616 Champlain explored the whole river system as far west as Lake Huron, reaching it by way of the Ottawa river, and taking possession of the country in the name of the king of France. It became British by the treaty of Paris, in 1763.

See S. E. Dawson, *The St. Lawrence, its Basin and Border Lands* (New York, 1905) (historical); *St. Lawrence Pilot* (7th ed., Hydrographic Office, Admiralty, London, 1906); *Sailing Directions for the St. Lawrence River to Montreal* (United States Hydrographic Office publication, No. 108 D, Washington, 1907); *Annual Reports* of the Canadian Departments of Marine and Fisheries, Public Works, and Railways and Canals, Ottawa; *Transactions* (Royal Society, Canada, 1898–99), vol. iv. sec. iii.; T. C. Keefer on "Ice Floods and Winter Navigation of the St. Lawrence," *Transactions* (Canadian Society of Civil Engineers, Presidential Address of W. P. Anderson, on improvements to navigation on St. Lawrence, 1904). (W. P. A.)

ST. LEGER, SIR ANTHONY (*c.* 1496–1559), lord deputy of Ireland, eldest son of Ralph St. Leger, a gentleman of Kent, was educated abroad and at Cambridge. He quickly gained the favour of Henry VIII., and was appointed in 1537 president of a commission for inquiring into the condition of Ireland. In 1540 he was appointed lord deputy of Ireland. His first task was to repress disorder, and he at once proceeded with severity against the Kavanaghs, permitting them, however, to retain their lands, on their accepting feudal tenure on the English model. By a similar policy he exacted obedience from the O'Mores, the O'Tooles and the O'Conors in Leix and Offaly; and having conciliated the O'Briens in the west and the earl of Desmond in the south, the lord deputy carried an act in the Irish parliament in Dublin conferring the title of king of Ireland on Henry VIII. and his heirs. Conn O'Neill, who in the north had remained sullenly hostile, was brought to submission by vigorous measures. For the most part, however, St. Leger's policy was one of moderation and conciliation—rather more so, indeed, than Henry VIII. approved. St. Leger's personal influence was proved by an outbreak of disturbance when he visited England in 1544, and the prompt restoration of order on his return some months later. St. Leger retained his office under Edward VI., and again effectually quelled attempts at rebellion by the O'Conors and O'Byrnes. From 1548 to 1550 he was in England. He was recalled from Ireland in 1551. Under Mary he was again lord deputy from 1553 to 1556, when he was recalled on a charge of falsifying accounts. He died (March 16, 1559) before the investigation was completed.

His great-grandson, Sir William St. Leger, took part in "the flight of the earls" (*see* O'Neill) in 1607, and spent several years abroad. Having received a pardon from James I. and large grants of land in Ireland, he was appointed president of Munster by Charles I. in 1627. He supported Strafford, actively assisting in raising and drilling the Irish levies destined for the royalist service. In the great rebellion of 1641 he executed martial law in his province with the greatest severity, hanging large numbers of rebels, often without much proof of guilt. He was still struggling with the insurrection when he died at Cork on July 2, 1642.

A biography of Sir Anthony St. Leger will be found in *Athenae Cantabrigienses*, by C. H. Cooper and T. Cooper (Cambridge, 1858); see also *Calendar of State Papers relating to Ireland, Hen. VIII.–Eliz.*; *Calendar of Letters and Papers of the Reign of Henry VIII.*; *Calendar of State Papers (Domestic Series), Edward VI.–James I.*; *Calendar of Carew MSS.*; J. O'Donovan's edition of *Annals of Ireland by the Four Masters* (7 vols., Dublin, 1851); Richard Bagwell, *Ireland under the Tudors* (3 vols., London, 1885–90); J. A. Froude, *History of England* (12 vols., London, 1856–70). For Sir William St. Leger, see *Strafford's Letters and Despatches* (2 vols., London, 1739); Thomas Carte, *History of the Life of James, Duke of Ormonde* (6 vols., Oxford, 1851); *History of the Irish Confederation and the War in Ireland,* edited by Sir J. T. Gilbert (Dublin, 1882-91).

ST. LEONARDS, EDWARD BURTENSHAW SUGDEN, 1st Baron (1781-1875), lord chancellor of Great Britain, was the son of a hairdresser of Duke street, Westminster, and was born on Feb. 12, 1781. After practising for some years as a conveyancer, he was called to the bar at Lincoln's Inn in 1807, having already published his well-known treatise on the *Law of Vendors and Purchasers* (14th ed., 1862). His parliamentary career was noticeable for his opposition to the Reform bill of 1832. He was appointed solicitor general in 1829, was lord chancellor of Ireland in 1834 and again from 1841 to 1846.

Under Lord Derby's first administration in 1852 he became lord chancellor and was raised to the peerage as Lord St. Leonards. In this position he devoted himself with energy and vigour to the reform of the law; in 1855 he was offered the great seal again, but had to refuse. He died at Boyle farm, Thames Ditton, on Jan. 20, 1875.

Lord St. Leonards was the author of various important legal publications, many of which have passed through several editions. *See* J. R. Atlay, *Lives of the Victorian Chancellors,* vol. ii.

ST. LIZIER-DE-COUSERANS, a village of southwestern France in the department of Ariège on the right bank of the Salat, 1 mi. N.N.W. of St. Girons. Pop. (1946) 1,008. St. Lizier, in ancient times one of the 12 cities of Novempopulania under the name of *Lugdunum Consoranorum,* was later capital of the Couserans and seat of a bishopric (suppressed at the Revolution) to the holders of which the town belonged. It has a cathedral of the 12th and 14th centuries with a fine Romanesque cloister, and also remains of Roman ramparts. The old episcopal palace (17th century) and the adjoining church (14th and 17th centuries), once the cathedral with its fine chapter hall (12th century), remain. The Salat is crossed by a bridge of the 12th or 13th century.

ST. LÔ, a town of northwestern France, capital of the department of Manche, 47½ mi. W. by S. of Caen by rail. Pop. (1946) 5,659. St. Lô, called *Briovera* in the Gallo-Roman period, owes its present name to St. Lô (Laudus), bishop of Coutances (d. 568). In the middle ages St. Lô became an important fortress and a centre for the weaving industry. In 1574 the town, which had embraced Calvinism, was stormed by the Catholics and many of its inhabitants massacred. In 1800 it was made capital of its department in place of Coutances.

In the *hôtel de ville* is the "Torigni marble," the pedestal of an ancient statue, the inscriptions on which relate chiefly to the annual assemblies of the Gallic deputies held at Lyons under the Romans.

ST. LOUIS, the chief city of Missouri, U.S., is situated in a central position in the Mississippi drainage system, on the west bank of the river, about 20 mi. below its confluence with the Missouri, 200 mi. above the influx of the Ohio and about 1,270 mi. above the Gulf of Mexico. Area 61.37 sq.mi.; pop. (1950) 856,-623; (1940) 816,048; (1930) 821,960; (1920) 772,897; (1910) 687,029; (1900) 575,238; (1890) 451,770 by the federal census. In 1940, 9.8% were foreign-born and 13.4% nonwhite.

Physical Features.—The city spreads along the river front for about 19 mi. and westward about 7 mi. Near the river the land rises rapidly for about one-third of a mile and then gradually, the uplands in the western part of the city being about 300 ft. above high-water mark. The river front and railroad routes have been the principal determining factors in the situation of industrial areas.

History.—In 1763 Gilbert Antoine de St. Maxent and Pierre Laclede Liguest, merchants of New Orleans, organized a firm which obtained from the French director-general of Louisiana the exclusive right to trade with the Missouri river Indians and with those west of the Mississippi above the Missouri. On Feb. 15, 1764, a party of workmen headed by Auguste Chouteau landed at the site previously selected by Laclede for his trading post and on the following day began work.

In addition to Laclede's original party, settlers came from Cahokia; others who desired to escape from English rule in the Illinois country came, and at the end of the first year 40 families

were living at St. Louis. The town was named by Laclede in honour of Louis XV, but for many years it was locally known as Laclede's village, and as Paincourt. Within its borders and in the general neighbourhood were several mounds erected by a prehistoric people.

In 1765, when the British military took possession of the Illinois country east of the Mississippi, Louis St. Ange de Bellerive, the French commandant, retired with his soldiers to St. Louis, and continued to rule over that part which had been ceded to Spain in 1762, but over which Spain had not asserted her authority. St. Ange was left in control by the Spanish until Feb. 7, 1770, when he was superseded by Don Pedro Piernas, the first Spanish lieutenant governor of Upper Louisiana.

In 1772 the village had a population of 399 whites and 198 slaves. During the administration of St. Ange only one street had a name, the Rue Royale, which now bears the prosaic name of Main street. Later the road which ran to the Bonhomme settlement (Walnut street) was known as the Rue Bonhomme; Market street was the Rue de la Tour; Second street, Rue de l'Eglise.

Modern Third street ran along rising ground in the rear of the village; there the barns were located and it was known as the Rue des Granges. West and northwest of the village lay the common fields, a fenced area in which each settler could, by permission, secure a lot for tillage. To the south and southwest the settlers enclosed a large tract for common pasturage and wood supply.

Excepting the Spanish officials, soldiers and a few traders, the inhabitants were French, and all were Roman Catholics. Families intermarried to such an extent that it is said that at the time of the transfer to the United States, two-thirds of the inhabitants were related. The traders carried on an extensive traffic with the Indian tribes along the Mississippi and Missouri rivers, and monopolized the trade with the Osage. Several large fortunes were made in furs and many families of St. Louis trace their ancestry back to the French fur traders of Spanish days.

The great market was New Orleans; thither the inhabitants shipped their surplus flour and packs of furs. Of the early traders the most prominent were the Chouteaus, Auguste and Pierre, who for many years enjoyed a monopoly of the Osage trade and built up a substantial fortune.

In May 1780 a force of British regulars and Indians descended on the city, but the Spanish soldiery and the settlers beat off the invaders. In 1803 about half of the inhabitants of Upper Louisiana were Americans, but few became residents of St. Louis. Under Spanish rule the town grew slowly and at the close of the regime contained only 180 houses, most of which were scattered along two streets which ran parallel with the river.

On March 9, 1804, Carlos Dehault DeLassus, the Spanish lieutenant governor, formally delivered Upper Louisiana to Capt. Amos Stoddard of the United States army, who had been authorized to act as agent and commissioner of the French republic; and on March 10 Stoddard took possession of Upper Louisiana for the United States. In 1804 congress created the district of Louisiana and placed it under the jurisdiction of the officers of Indiana territory. St. Louis became the governmental headquarters for the district. In 1805 the district of Louisiana was cut off from the jurisdiction of Indiana and made into the territory of Louisiana. St. Louis was again chosen as the seat of government. In 1812 the territory of Missouri was created, with St. Louis still the territorial capital.

In 1808 the town of St. Louis was created as a result of a petition of about 160 inhabitants, but it was not until 1809 that St. Louis was legally incorporated as a town by the court of common pleas. In 1808 the *Louisiana Gazette* was established, this being the first newspaper west of the Mississippi river. The publication of the territorial laws in 1808 marked the appearance of the first book to be printed in what is now the state of Missouri. By 1815 the population probably did not exceed 2,600. Not until 1819 were primitive fire engines supplied by private subscription. In 1821, at the time of the admission of Missouri to the union, there were 621 buildings and a population of 5,600. In 1822 the state legislature incorporated St. Louis as a city.

During the territorial period the composition of the population had undergone a distinct change. The French element, although still socially and financially prominent, was being engulfed by people from Virginia and Kentucky, but there was also a sprinkling of New Englanders and the Irish were numerous enough in 1819 to form a Hibernian Benevolent society.

The fur trade continued to be a principal source of wealth. Up to 1809, with the exception of the original firm of Maxent, Laclede and Company, and the later Clamorgan company, the trade had been largely a matter of individual enterprise, aided occasionally by special concessions such as the Chouteau monopoly of the Osage trade.

But in 1807 Manuel Lisa ascended the Missouri river and built a post at the mouth of the Big Horn and, in 1809, formed the St. Louis Missouri Fur company. A rival organization headed by William H. Ashley in 1822 founded a company which later became known as the Rocky Mountain Fur company; the American Fur company, of which John Jacob Astor was the principal figure, established an office in St. Louis in 1822 and soon became the dominant factor in the fur trade. Astor retired in 1834 and the western department of the company was sold to Pratte, Chouteau and Company.

This organization continued to control most of the western fur trade until 1860. St. Louis was also the outfitting place for much of the trade with the North Mexican provinces.

After 1812 St. Louis attracted many settlers including a large foreign element, which, in the 1820s and 1830s was predominantly German. The failure of the reform movement of 1848 brought another tide of German migration. In 1840 the population was 16,469; after that the growth was rapid, the population in 1850 being 77,860 and ten years later 160,773. In 1817 steamboats began to operate to St. Louis, in 1832, 80 steamboats arrived; in 1838, 154, and in 1845, 213. In 1854 St. Louis ranked third in enrolled tonnage among U.S. cities. After that the river traffic increased tremendously; in 1860 5,178 vessels arrived at St. Louis and 5,218 departed, the total tonnage for the year being 844,039.

In the 1830s St. Louis, like other towns in the west, became interested in the development of railroads. The Pacific Railroad company, the parent of the Missouri Pacific, was organized in 1850; the line was begun in 1851, and the first 40 mi. were opened to Franklin (Pacific), Mo., two years later. In 1856 it reached Jefferson City, and Sedalia in 1861. A southwestern branch of the Missouri Pacific was opened to Rolla in 1861. The St. Louis and Iron Mountain railway, incorporated in 1851, was opened from St. Louis to Pilot Knob, Mo., in 1858. The St. Louis, Kansas City and Northern railway was completed as far as Macon, Mo., in 1859. Thus before the Civil War St. Louis became the terminal for four western railroads. The Ohio and Mississippi railroad, to Cincinnati, was completed in 1857; it connected with the Baltimore and Ohio railroad, thus giving St. Louis rail access to the Atlantic coast.

By 1860 the city extended for about six and one-half miles along the river front and reached westward between three and four miles. Most of the houses were built of brick, as were many of the sidewalks. Soft coal was used as fuel, frequently creating a pall of smoke. Missouri was a slave state, but only 1,500 slaves were owned in St. Louis and most of these were in domestic service. The Germans and the newcomers from the north were abolitionists. Many of the businessmen, regardless of their views on the slavery question, were opposed to secession. They feared that a break in the union would be injurious to business, and felt that it was vital to St. Louis to have the Mississippi river under the control of the United States.

Soon after Abraham Lincoln's election it became evident that Gov. Claiborne Jackson was a secessionist and intended to take the state out of the union. He was backed by a secessionist legislature. The state government authorized the election of delegates to assemble in convention to consider the question of the secession of Missouri. The delegates concluded that there was no adequate cause for Missouri to dissolve her connection with the union.

The next step of the unionists was to prevent the St. Louis arsenal from falling into the hands of the secessionists. Capt. Nathaniel Lyon, with the assistance of the "Wide Awakes," who had been transformed into military companies known as "home guards," succeeded in protecting the arsenal and in shipping most of its guns to Illinois. The governor then authorized the assembly of militia near St. Louis. A camp, named after the governor, was laid out on the western outskirt of the city. Lyon and Francis Blair believed that the purpose of the establishment of Camp Jackson was the seizure of the city. On May 10, 1861, Lyon sent three columns of home guards to capture the camp. The force was overwhelming and Frost, the commander, surrendered without a struggle.

An unfortunate outbreak of violence occurred while the prisoners were under guard and about 25 people, several of them civilians, were killed or wounded. For 48 hours the citizens were in a state of panic, but when no other acts of violence occurred, the excitement subsided, and those who had fled returned to their homes.

After the Camp Jackson episode the wavering took a firm stand on one side or the other. But it soon became evident that the city was overwhelmingly unionist in sentiment. Lynch's "slave pen," a place where adult slaves had been sold at auction, was closed, and the slave pen where children were sold was soon transformed into a military prison. Eminent citizens hoped that the warring factions in the state might be brought into agreement by a conference of the leaders. On June 11 Governor Jackson and Gen. Sterling Price met Blair and Lyon in a conference at the Planters' hotel, but no agreement was reached. The governor hastened to Jefferson City, issued a call for 50,000 troops and then evacuated the capital.

Throughout the Civil War St. Louis remained a unionist stronghold. There Gen. John C. Frémont, in command of the western department, established his headquarters, and from there Gen. Henry Halleck directed movements in the Mississippi valley. Thousands of troops were encamped in and about the city. For many months St. Louis was under martial law; thousands of prisoners of war, and about 40,000 refugees were cared for during the war. St. Louis was the headquarters of the Western Sanitary commission which had charge of much of the war relief work.

Cultural Development.—For a quarter of a century after the Civil War the city was the centre of a remarkable philosophic and cultural movement. Its inspirer was Henry Conrad Brokmeyer (1828–1906), who later became prominent in state politics and was lieutenant governor of Missouri in 1876–80. Brokmeyer, a Prussian from Minden, arrived at St. Louis in 1856. He attracted William T. Harris, a brilliant graduate of Yale university, who taught in the St. Louis schools during 1858–67 and was superintendent of schools during 1867–80.

Brokmeyer and Harris gathered about them a group of idealistic thinkers and formed a philosophical society which became the sponsor of *The Journal of Speculative Philosophy* (1867–93), the first periodical of the sort in English. For many years Harris, its editor, was the foremost exponent of Hegelian philosophy in the United States.

Economic Progress.—After the Civil War St. Louis grew with unusual rapidity; by 1870 the population was 310,864. In ten years it had almost doubled; St. Louis had become the principal distribution point for the Mississippi valley. But it soon found its supremacy challenged by Chicago, when the railroads made Chicago the terminal for lines to the Pacific coast. After 1870 the Mississippi and Ohio rivers gradually lost their importance as highways and the railroads became the great carriers of interstate commerce.

After 1870 the history of St. Louis was mainly economic. It retained its prominence as a wholesale centre and also became one of the great manufacturing cities in the world.

Louisiana Purchase Exposition.—In 1898 a site on the western outskirts of the city was selected for an exposition to celebrate the 100th anniversary of the purchase of Louisiana from France. The grounds covered 1,240 ac., of which 250 were under roof. The total cost, apart from individual exhibitions, was about $42,500,000, of which the national government contributed $5,000,000 and the city and citizens of St. Louis $10,-000,000. The exposition was opened to the public in 1904. During the seven months of its existence, 12,804,616 paid admissions were collected, and total admissions were 19,694,855. Two permanent buildings remained from it, the Jefferson memorial, the home of the Missouri Historical society, and the Art building.

Later Developments.—In 1933 the city determined to turn its central river front district into a national park, at a cost of $30,000,000. The federal government agreed to put up three-fourths of the money and the city one-fourth. By 1941 the 40-block site had been cleared. The normal Republican city was ruled by a Democratic administration (for the first time in 24 years) from 1933 to 1941, when a Republican mayor was heavily victorious again. In the municipal elections of April 1949 the Democrats won control of the city government from the Republicans who had been in control since 1941.

City Zones.—From 1840 to 1880 the river front was the busiest part of the city. Along the central part for 3.7 mi. stretches the levee. When the railroads took the place of the river as the principal means of transportation, the importance of the levee declined. River traffic, however, underwent some revival with the establishment by the government of a line of steel barges between St. Louis and New Orleans.

Beginning at Fourth street and extending west to 14th on high ground between Market street and Delmar boulevard is the sky-scraper business district. The largest retail establishments, several of them department stores, are on Olive street and Washington avenue. In this district are commercial hotels, theatres, clubs, office buildings, wholesale houses and factories. The downtown district extends westward. In 1923 a bond issue of $87,352,500 for public improvements was voted, including $6,000,000 for a memorial plaza and building, $5,000,000 for a municipal auditorium and $4,000,000 for a new courthouse. The plaza extends from Market street to Olive street and from 12th to 15th streets making a remarkable civic centre. At the south end are the city hall, municipal courts and auditorium; at the north the public library. Facing 12th between Market and Chestnut streets is the courthouse.

Adjacent to the downtown retail district on every side are wholesale and jobbing houses, warehouses and factories. Here are most of the plants which produce shoes and shoemaking machinery, garments, drugs and medicines. To the west of the downtown district, spreading out like a fan and extending as far as Grand avenue, was the finest residential district in the 1870s. A $2,600,000 plaza, with a $60,000 Carl Milles fountain, was built opposite Union station.

Olive, Market, Delmar (once Morgan street) and other thoroughfares were widened. A depressed superhighway, completed in 1937, traverses the city from east to west.

Industrial Development.—St. Louis is a leading U.S. industrial area. Its advantageous position near the sources of supply of raw materials, the proximity of a vast, thickly populated area and of the soft-coal fields of Illinois, railroad and highway facilities and electric power make it a natural centre for large industrial plants, and for jobbing and wholesale houses. There were 2,960 factories employing 244,516 people in 1947 in the St. Louis industrial area. Leading industries are assembling and manufacturing automobiles, shoes, drugs, chemicals, beer, electric goods, tobacco, brick, terra-cotta and other clay products, railway and street cars, stoves, ranges and furnaces, steel and lead, hardware, various kinds of machinery, clothing, boxes and woodenware products. St. Louis is one of the largest centres of shoe manufacture in the United States. It is one of the largest of all markets for furs, hides, wool, horses and mules, grain, dry goods, millinery and men's hats. It is a centre for the manufacture of poultry and livestock feed and of meat packing. The total value of factory products in 1947 in the city's industrial area was $1,296,471,000.

The metropolitan district in 1950 had a population of 1,673,-467, and the outlying regions were growing more rapidly than the city proper. Metropolitan St. Louis is a rapidly expanding industrial unit, but the outlying communities oppose enlarging the city boundary. The principal industrial areas followed naturally the lines of transportation; hence industry and warehousing gravitated early to the river front where rail as well as water transport was convenient. (The decline of the river steamboat was to cause many old buildings of the levee district to lose value and to bring about the razing of 40 blocks.)

Other manufacturing areas grew up along the railroads branching through the city. St. Louis is strategically located with respect to transportation. Thirteen major railroads converge there, six major air lines use the municipal airport, numerous truck lines provide service and the navigable water system connects with all of the principal mid-continent cities.

St. Louis is also a wholesale centre, with its preferential trade territory being 14 states in the middle west. The United States census of distribution credited it with $3,047,000,000 of wholesale business of all types in 1948. Total retail sales of stores in St. Louis city were estimated at $978,300,000 in 1949. Adjacent to the industrial sections are densely populated tenement districts where most of the unskilled foreign-born and Negro labourers live. The industrial area includes several cities on the Illinois side, such as East St. Louis, National City, Madison and Granite City.

South of East St. Louis is the Cahokia power plant, which supplies power to many St. Louis industrial plants.

The Eads bridge, the first across the Mississippi at St. Louis, was completed in 1874, but was not successful until 1889, when the Terminal Railroad association was formed. In 1951 it controlled 368 mi. of track, the Eads and Merchant's bridges and the Union station, and had 137 switching locomotives (82 diesel and 55 steam). The McKinley bridge, built by the Illinois Traction company, is independent. In 1918 the St. Louis Municipal (or free) bridge was completed; it was later named the Douglas MacArthur bridge.

Other bridges spanning the Mississippi at or near St. Louis are: East St. Louis Veterans Memorial, Chain of Rocks, Jefferson Barracks and Lewis and Clark.

Education.—The first permanent kindergarten and kindergarten training school in connection with public schools in the United States were established in St. Louis in 1873. The city in 1951 maintained the Harris Teachers and junior college for white students, the Stowe Teachers and junior college for Negro students, 7 high schools for white and 2 for Negro children, 2 technical high schools, 7 evening schools, 106 elementary schools for white and 37 for Negro children, a division of audiovisual education, an FM radio station, and a large stadium for high school athletics. The registration in the high schools for 1949–50 was 18,473; in the technical high schools, 4,060; in the elementary schools, 72,625; and in the evening schools in the adult education program, 3,659 (average nightly attendance). There were 5,008 employees in the public schools, 3,764 of whom were in the department of instruction. The day schools cost the city $18,974,-729 for the year 1949–50. The Roman Catholic Church maintained 22 high schools with an enrolment of 7,654, and 76 elementary schools with an enrolment of 28,838. The Lutheran Church (Missouri synod) maintained in 1950 1 high school and 21 elementary schools. In or near St. Louis there are a number of excellent private schools. The National Council of Christians and Jews instigated a new approach in education in St. Louis, as elsewhere, through its program in intergroup relations carried through the American Council on Education.

Washington university and St. Louis university are the most important institutions of higher learning. The former (1853) is made up of the college of liberal arts, the schools of engineering, architecture, business and public administration, social work, law, medicine, dentistry, nursing and fine arts, the Henry Shaw school of botany, the university college, the summer school, the graduate school of arts and sciences and the Sever institute of technology. Most of the buildings are in the Tudor-Gothic style of architecture. The faculty in 1950–51 numbered 1,411 and the students 12,048. Endowment in 1950–51 was $30,244,000. The institution is nonsectarian. St. Louis university was founded by a Catholic bishop as St. Louis academy in 1818, renamed St. Louis

THE DOWNTOWN DISTRICT OF ST. LOUIS

General air view showing the Mississippi river in the upper right hand corner. The two large buildings in the lower centre are the Civil Courts building and the Federal building

PLATE II ST. LOUIS

BY COURTESY OF THE ST. LOUIS CHAMBER OF COMMERCE

PUBLIC BUILDINGS OF ST. LOUIS

1. Civil Courts building. Plaza Commission, architects
2. Federal building (U.S. court and customs house). Mauran, Russell, Crowell, and Mullgardt, architects
3. Federal Reserve Bank building. Mauran, Russell, Crowell, and Mull-

gardt, architects
4. Municipal auditorium, facing the Memorial plaza. The building has an opera house with a seating capacity of 3,500 persons and an arena seating 12,500 persons. The Plaza Commission, consisting of members of seven firms of architects, designed the building

college in 1820 and incorporated as St. Louis university in 1832. A Jesuit institution, it was the first university west of the Mississippi river to receive a charter. The university is composed of the college of arts and sciences, the schools of divinity, medicine, dentistry, law, commerce and finance, and nursing, the graduate school, the college of philosophy and letters, the institute of technology and the Parks college of aeronautical technology. In addition St. Louis university is affiliated with six corporate colleges, some located in St. Louis county. The faculty in 1950–51 numbered 1,285 and the students 8,943, both exclusive of the corporate colleges. The endowment in 1950–51 was $4,052,066.

Other institutions of higher learning in St. Louis or its suburbs are the St. Louis Roman Catholic Theological seminary (Kenrick seminary) (Roman Catholic, 1818), St. Stanislaus seminary (Roman Catholic, 1823), Lindenwood college, St. Charles (1827), Shurtleff college, Alton, Ill. (1827), McKendree college, Lebanon, Ill. (1828), Monticello college, Godfrey, Ill. (1835), Concordia Theological seminary (Lutheran Church-Missouri synod, 1839), Eden Theological seminary (German Evangelical Synod of North America, 1850), Principia college, Elsah, Ill. (1898), and Jefferson college (1940).

Libraries and Museums.—In addition to the libraries of Washington and St. Louis universities, there are the public library (1,026,529 vol., 929,835 pamphlets and 27,673 maps) with a circulation close to 2,000,000, 20 branches in its own or other buildings and 2 bookmobiles; the Mercantile library (191,290 vol. and pamphlets); the Missouri Historical society, housed in the Jefferson memorial in Forest park, with a collection of about 80,000 vol. and pamphlets, and about 1,000,000 manuscripts pertaining primarily to the history of the Mississippi valley. The society also maintains an archaeological and historical museum and houses the Charles Lindbergh trophies and medals.

An association of music lovers maintains a symphony orchestra. In Forest park is the open-air municipal theatre, which seats 10,000. The City Art museum in Forest park houses a valuable collection of paintings, statuary, tapestries and other works of art.

The Artists' guild offers prizes to encourage artists and gives frequent art exhibits.

Hospitals.—The chief hospitals are the Barnard Free Skin and Cancer, Barnes, Jewish, St. Louis Children's, St. Luke's, St. Mary's, the Shriners' (for crippled children), Evangelical Deaconess, De Paul, Missouri Baptist, St. John's, St. Louis City, Homer G. Phillips, Bliss Psychopathic, Robert Koch, McMillan, St. Louis Maternity, Firmin Desloge, Lutheran, Missouri Pacific, Frisco Employee's, Bethesda and Veterans' Administration.

Newspapers; Water Supply.—The chief newspapers are the *Post-Dispatch* and the *Globe-Democrat*. Foreign language newspapers include weeklies in Jewish, Italian, German, Hungarian, Bohemian and Polish.

The waterworks are near Chain of Rocks park in the extreme northern part of the city, where large settling basins and a filtering plant are located. The Mississippi is the source of supply. After 1923 additional waterworks were built at Howard's Bend on the Missouri river about 30 mi. above its mouth, with a reservoir at Olivette.

Parks and Public Buildings.—The most notable park is Forest park (1,380 ac.), portions of which have been left wild. The western part was used for the Louisiana Purchase exposition of 1904. In the park are the City Art museum, Jefferson memorial, field house, municipal theatre, two public golf links, tennis courts, baseball and soccer fields and zoological gardens. Other large parks are Tower Grove (277 ac.), Carondelet (180 ac.), O'Fallon (159 ac.), Fairground (131.46 ac.) and Tilles (58 ac.).

The Missouri Botanical garden (125 ac.), one of the finest in the United States, was a gift to the city from Henry Shaw (1800–89), who also endowed the botanical school of Washington university. The city maintains 69 parks covering about 3,000 ac. and 44 playgrounds for children.

Of historical interest are the Old Cathedral (Catholic) and the old courthouse, the latter being the scene of the Dred Scott trial. The most imposing public buildings are the city hall, courthouse,

public library, municipal auditorium, Union station, federal building, art museum and Jefferson memorial. Churches include the Roman Catholic cathedral, the Westminster Presbyterian, Christ Church cathedral (Episcopalian), Second Baptist, St. John's Methodist Episcopal, First Church of Christ Scientist and Temple Israel.

Government.—In 1840 a police force composed of a captain, three lieutenants and 28 privates was organized. In 1841 the boundaries were enlarged and the city was divided into five wards. In 1842 voting by ballot was introduced, and an engineering department composed of the city engineer, street commissioner and superintendent of the waterworks was established. A health department was created in 1843. The following year the taxpaying qualification for voters was removed. In 1859 an amendment to the charter provided that the city council was to be a one-chamber body called the common council and composed of 20 members, two from each of the wards. In 1861 the legislature established the metropolitan police of St. Louis, and placed it under the control of a board of police commissioners appointed by the governor. The mayor was an ex-officio member of the board. The police department was then made independent of city government. In 1866 the council was again made bicameral. In 1871 the number of wards was increased to at least 12.

Up to 1876 St. Louis and St. Louis county were a judicial unit, and jointly controlled the courthouse, jail, insane asylum and poor farm. By an act of the state legislature in 1875 provision was made for the separation of the city and county, for the city to extend its boundaries and for a new charter. In 1876 the provisions were carried into effect. The courthouse, jail, insane asylum and poor farm became the property of the city and the old county debt became a city obligation. Under the charter of 1876 the city was divided into 28 wards. The mayor was to hold office for four years and was given extensive power of appointment. The municipal assembly was bicameral, being composed of a council of 13 and a house of delegates composed of one member from each ward. The mayor appointed a board of public improvements composed of the street, sewer, water, harbour and wharf and park commissioners. Each commissioner was head of a department. The charter also provided for a health department, for an elective school board of 28 members, one from each ward, for a board of assessors and a board of equalization.

In 1914 a new charter went into force. Under this charter the mayor holds office for four years and is given large powers of appointment and supervision. The board of aldermen is made up of a president and 28 aldermen, who hold office for four years. The board is a legislative body and has large powers, especially over money bills. The mayor appoints the members of the board of public service; this is composed of the president of the board and directors of public utilities, of streets and sewers, of public welfare and of public safety. Each is the head of a department. The department of finance is headed by a comptroller; the law department is headed by the city counsellor. The charter provides for two city courts, for a board of standardization, a board of estimate and apportionment and a city plan commission. One of the reasons for the adoption of a new charter was the desire to safeguard the city against the machinations of politicians and political rings. To effect this, provisions were introduced for the recall of officials, for the initiation of legislation by petitions signed by 5% of the voters and for the referendum upon ordinances if called for by 2% of the registered voters.

BIBLIOGRAPHY.—L. U. Reavis, *Saint Louis: the Future Great City of the World* (1879); W. Hyde and H. L. Conard, *Encyclopaedia of the History of St. Louis* (1899); M. S. Snow (ed.), *History of the Development of Missouri and Particularly of St. Louis*, 2 vol. (1908); W. B. Stevens, *St. Louis, the Fourth City* (1909); I. H. Lionberger, *The Annals of St. Louis* (1929); Merchants Exchange of St. Louis, *Annual Statements of the Trade and Commerce of St. Louis* (1865–1927); J. T. Scharf, *History of Saint Louis City and County* (1883); Louis Houck, *A History of Missouri* (1908), *The Spanish Regime in Missouri* (1909); F. L. Billon, *Annals of St. Louis* (1886–88); Auguste Chouteau, *Chouteau's Journal of the Founding of St. Louis* (1911); Charles E. Peterson, *Colonial St. Louis* (1949); St. Louis Chamber of Commerce, *St. Louis Facts* (1950), *St. Louis as It Is Today* (1950); F. L. Billon, *An-*

nals of St. Louis . . . under the French and Spanish Dominations (1886), Annals of St. Louis in its Territorial Days from 1804 to 1821 (1888); F. C. Shoemaker, Missouri and Missourians, vol. 1, 2 (1943); E. H. Shepard, Early History of St. Louis and Missouri from its First Exploration by White Men in 1673 to 1843 (1870).   (R. P. Br.)

SAINT LOUIS, administrative seat of the French subcolonies Senegal (q.v.) and Mauritania, first capital (1895–1902) of French West Africa (q.v.), a considerable regional market, and the onetime French West African port for overseas and Senegal river trade.

Located at the point where the Senegal reaches a dune-covered sand bar, behind which it flows 12 mi. before entering the sea, it is near the climatic division between Sahara and Sudan. Its original site, and present commercial core and locale of the Senegalese government, is a bar-shaped island 1¼ mi. long. This is connected by two short bridges with native fishermen's quarters and the Mauritanian government offices on the main sand bar, and by a bridge 2,132 ft. long, with a suburb at the mainland terminal of the railroad to Dakar (q.v.), 168 mi. south. The total population (1936 census) was 33,100; (1938) 35,929 including 1,000 Europeans.

Vessels drawing up to 10 ft. can cross the bar and navigate the river during the rains (July-September inclusive), but water traffic has been supplanted by rails. Founded in 1659 by Dieppe merchants, Saint Louis is the oldest colonial establishment in Africa belonging to France. After 1854 it became the base of military expeditions leading to the formation of French West Africa. Made one of the two original communes in Senegal in 1872, its citizens may vote for a representative in the French chamber of deputies. Institutions include a secondary school on the model of a French lycée, a school for sons of Moslem chiefs (specializing in administration, law and accounting), and a hospital.

See R. Rousseau, "Le site et les origines de Saint-Louis," La Géographie 44 (1925).   (D. Wh.)

ST. LOUIS-SAN FRANCISCO RAILWAY COMPANY, popularly known as "The Frisco," was incorporated on Aug. 28, 1916, as successor to a company formed in 1876, having for its purpose the construction of a railroad from St. Louis, Mo., to the Pacific coast. This original plan, however, did not fully materialize. The present railroad comprises a total of 5,175 mi. of road, extending from St. Louis and Kansas City, Mo., through Missouri, Kansas, Oklahoma, Arkansas into Texas, and crossing the Mississippi river at Memphis, Tenn., it passes through Tennessee, Mississippi, Alabama and Florida to the port of Pensacola on the Gulf of Mexico. The railway serves a rapidly developing section of the United States. The more important industries in the territory are iron and steel and other manufactures in St. Louis and Kansas City, Mo., Memphis, Tenn. and Birmingham, Ala.; the mid-continent oil fields; coal mining; lead and zinc mining; livestock raising; grain and cotton growing; and fruit and dairying in the great Ozark region.

(J. M. Ku.; X.)

ST. LUCIA, the largest of the British Windward Islands, West Indies, in 13° 54′ N. and 60° 59′ W., 24 mi. S. of Martinique and 21 mi. N.E. of St. Vincent. Area 233 sq.mi., length 27 mi., maximum breadth 14 mi.; circumference 150 mi. It is considered one of the loveliest of the West Indian islands. It is a mass of mountains, rising steeply from the water, their summits bathed in perpetual mist. The highest of these is Morne Gimie (3,145 ft.), but the Pitons (2,619 ft. and 2,461 ft.) are the chief natural feature—two immense pyramids of rock rising abruptly from the sea with their slopes, inclined at a 60° angle, clothed on three sides with dense verdure. Near Petit Piton is Soufrière, a low-lying volcanic crater. The boiling sulphur springs which give Soufrière its name are at Ventine, 2½ mi. S.E. of the town of Soufrière. Rainfall averages 91 in. a year, the temperature averages 80° F.

History.—St. Lucia was discovered by Columbus in 1502 and named after the saint on whose day it was sighted. The Dutch are said to have built a fort there, but the first attempt to settle was made by Englishmen in 1605. Carib resistance compelled its abandonment. From this time until the island became definitely a British possession in 1814 it was the scene of fiercely recurring

struggles between England and France; and 13 British regiments gained the right to inscribe the name St. Lucia on their colours. In the first half of the 17th century it was included in royal grants made by the kings of England and France; but English settlers were long deterred by the unlucky reputation which St. Lucia gained after a second disastrous attempt at colonization in 1638, frustrated by sickness and native hostility. The French were more successful, sending settlers from Martinique in 1650, by whom a treaty was made with the Caribs ten years later. England defeated the French shortly afterward, and regained the island, but it was restored by the peace of Breda in 1667.

Another British settlement under a grant of 1722 was frustrated by France. In 1748 the two nations agreed to regard St. Lucia as neutral. In 1762 it was captured by Rodney and Monckton, only to be given up once more by the treaty of Paris. In 1778 it again surrendered to the British, who used its harbours as a naval base; and it was from Gros Islet bay that Rodney sailed before his famous victory over de Grasse in April 1782. Between 1782 and 1803 the possession of St. Lucia passed six times between England and France, England having to suppress a vigorous revolutionist part, aided by insurgent slaves, before gaining possession in 1803, confirmed by a final cession in 1814. From this time the island was administered as a crown colony—under Barbados from 1838 to 1885.

Representative government was obtained by the constitution of 1924 which introduced an elective element into the legislative council, and the constitution of 1936 provided for an unofficial majority in the council.

French influence on the development of St. Lucia has been very great, and is illustrated by the preponderance of the Roman Catholic Church and the survival of a French patois. In the years following 1763 French planters came from St. Vincent and Grenada and formed cotton and sugar plantations. In 1772 the population was said to number 15,000, mostly slaves. In 1834, when the slaves were emancipated there were in St. Lucia more than 13,000 Negro slaves, 2,600 free Negroes and 2,300 whites. Prosperity was greatly retarded by the frequent wars, by epidemics of cholera and smallpox and by the decline of the sugar-cane industry. Improvement came with the increase of banana and cocoa cultivation, and resuscitation of sugar-cane cultivation.

The excellent landlocked harbour of Castries, one of the best in the West Indies, gives St. Lucia great strategic importance. In 1940, as part of its "destroyer-bases" agreement with Great Britain, the United States acquired on 99-yr. lease a naval and air base on Gros Islet bay, 4 mi. from Castries, along with other facilities. These were all relinquished by 1949, but the United States retained the right to re-establish them in the event of war or grave emergency.

Population and Economic Conditions.—The population of St. Lucia was estimated at 79,500 in 1950. Castries (pop. 7,056), the capital, on the N.W. coast, was almost completely destroyed by fire in June 1948, but rebuilding on a carefully planned basis began shortly thereafter. The bulk of the inhabitants of the island are Negroes and mulattoes; the rest are whites or of East Indian extraction. A French patois is generally spoken by most, gradually being supplanted by English. The government subsidizes primary education through grants-in-aid to the island's denominational primary schools (principally Roman Catholic) and two secondary schools.

Government is under an appointed administrator (subordinate to the governor of the Windward Islands, of which colony St. Lucia forms part). The legislative council is partly appointed, partly elected.

The colony's essentially agricultural economy is dominated by sugar raising. In 1950 St. Lucia produced 10,441 tons of sugar. Although much of the land is held in large estates, there were more than 4,000 individual proprietors in 1949. Fishing is carried on extensively for the local market and provided full-time employment for 1,750 persons in 1949. In addition to sugar and sugar products, copra and coconuts, cacao, bananas and lime products are exported to non-West Indian areas. There is also a flourishing charcoal trade with Barbados. In 1950 exports totalled £309,071 in value; imports, principally flour, rice and other foodstuffs and a wide variety of manufactured goods, were valued at £1,093,372.

External communication is by steamer service which is irregular but fairly frequent, and by air. St. Lucia enjoys better air service than any other of the British West Indian islands except Jamaica and Trinidad.

BIBLIOGRAPHY.—A. E. Aspinall, *A Pocket Guide to the West Indies* (1940); R. R. Platt *et al.*, *European Possessions in the Caribbean Area* (1941); *West Indies Year Book* (annual); Colonial Office, *Colonial Annual Reports.*   (L. W. Be.)

ST. MAIXENT (L'École), a town of western France, in the department of Deux Sèvres, on the Sèvre Niortaise, 15 mi. N.E. of Niort by rail. Pop. (1946) 5,440. The fine abbey church, built from the 12th to the 15th century, was in great part destroyed by the Protestants in the 16th century and rebuilt from 1670 to 1682 in flamboyant Gothic. There is a Romanesque nave and a lofty 15th century tower over the west front. The crypt contains the tomb of St. Maxentius, second abbot of the monastery, which was founded about 460. The prosperity of the town was at its height after the promulgation of the edict of Nantes, when it numbered 12,000 inhabitants.

ST. MALO, a seaport of western France, capital of an arrondissement in the department of Ille-et-Vilaine, 51 mi. N.N.W. of Rennes by rail. Pop. (1946) 11,311.

In the 6th century the island on which St. Malo stands was the retreat of Abbot Aaron, who gave asylum in his monastery to Malo (Maclovius or Malovius), a Cambrian priest, who afterwards became bishop of Aleth (now St. Servan); the see was transferred to St. Malo only in the 12th century. In the 17th century the maritime power of St. Malo attained some importance. In Nov. 1693 and July 1695 the English vainly bombarded it. The St. Malo shipowners financed the Rio de Janeiro expedition of Duguay-Trouin in 1711 and also lent the king large sums for carrying on the war of the Spanish Succession. In June 1758 the English inflicted great loss on the royal shipping in the harbour of St. Servan, but another expedition in the following September received a complete check. In 1778 and during the wars of the Empire the St. Malo privateers resumed their activity. In 1789 St. Servan was separated from St. Malo, and in 1801 St. Malo lost its bishopric.

St. Malo is situated on the English channel on the right bank of the estuary of the Rance at its mouth. It is a garrison town surrounded by ramparts which include portions dating from the 14th, 15th and 16th centuries but as a whole were rebuilt at the end of the 17th century and restored in the 19th century. The most important of the gates are that of St. Vincent and the Grande Porte, defended by two massive 15th-century towers. The granite island on which St. Malo stands communicates with the mainland on the northeast by a causeway known as the "Sillon" (furrow), commanded by the old 14th and 15th century castle, flanked with four towers, one of which, the great keep, is an older and loftier structure. In the sea round about lie other granite rocks, which have been turned to account in the defenses of the coast. The rocks and beach are continually changing their appearance, owing to the violence of the tides; spring tides sometimes rise 50 ft. above low-water level, and the sea sometimes washes over the ramparts. The harbour of St. Malo lies south of the town in the creek separating it from the neighbouring town of St. Servan. Including the contiguous and connected basins belonging to St. Servan, it comprises an outer basin, a tidal harbour, two wet-docks and an inner reservoir, affording a total length of quayage of over 2 mi. The wet-docks have a minimum depth of 13 to 15 ft. on sill, but the tidal harbour is dry at low water. The great bulk of trade is with England, the exports comprising large quantities of fruit, dairy produce, early potatoes and other vegetables and slate. The principal imports consist of coal and timber. The Southern railway maintains a regular service of steamers between Southampton and St. Malo. The port carries on shipbuilding and equips a fleet for the Newfoundland cod-fisheries. The industries also include iron- and copper-founding and the manufacture of portable forges and other iron goods and rope. The town is the seat of a sub-prefect and has a tribunal of commerce.

St. Malo is largely frequented for sea-bathing, but not so much as Dinard, on the opposite side of the Rance. The town presents a tortuous maze of narrow streets and small squares lined with high and sometimes quaint buildings. Above all rises the stone spire (1859) of the cathedral, a building begun in the 12th century but added to and rebuilt at several subsequent periods.

SAINT-MARC GIRARDIN (1801–1873), French politician and man of letters, whose real name was MARC GIRARDIN, was born in Paris on Feb. 22, 1801. After a brilliant university career in Paris he began in 1828 to contribute to the *Journal des Débats,* on the staff of which he remained for nearly half a century. At the accession of Louis Philippe he was appointed professor of history at the Sorbonne and master of requests in the Conseil d'État. Soon afterwards he exchanged his chair of history for one of poetry, continuing to contribute political articles to the *Débats* and sitting as deputy in the chamber from 1835 to 1848. He was charged in 1833 with a mission to study German methods of education and issued a report advocating the necessity of newer methods and of technical instruction. In 1844 he was elected a member of the academy. During the revolution of Feb. 1848 Girardin was for a moment a minister, but after the establishment of the republic he was not re-elected deputy. After the war of 1870–71 he was returned to the Bordeaux assembly by his old department—the Haute Vienne. His Orleanist tendencies and his objections to the republic were strong, and though he at first supported Thiers, he afterwards became a leader of the opposition to the president. He died on April 1, 1873, at Morsang-sur-Seine, before Thiers was actually driven from power.

His chief work is his *Cours de littérature dramatique* (1843–63), a series of lectures better described by its second title, *De l'usage des passions dans le drame.*

See Hatzfield and Meunier, *Les Critiques littéraires du XIXe siècle* (1894).

SAINT-MARTIN, LOUIS CLAUDE DE (1743–1803), French philosopher, known as "le philosophe inconnu," the name under which his works were published, was born at Amboise on Jan. 18, 1743. While in garrison at Bordeaux he came under the influence of Martinez de Pasquales, who taught a species of mysticism drawn from cabbalistic sources and endeavoured to found a secret cult with magical or theurgical rites. In 1771 Saint-Martin left the army to become a preacher of mysticism, first in Paris, and then in England, Italy, Switzerland and the French provinces. At Strasbourg in 1788 he met Charlotte de Boecklin, who introduced him to the writings of Jacob Boehme and inspired in him a semi-romantic attachment. He was brought up a strict Catholic and always remained attached to the church, although his first work, *Of Errors and Truth,* was placed upon the Index. He died at Aunay, near Paris, on Oct. 23, 1803.

His chief works are a translation of the works of Boehme; *Lettre à un ami sur la Révolution Française; Eclair sur l'association humaine; De l'esprit des choses; Ministère de l'homme-esprit.* Other treatises appeared in his *Oeuvres posthumes* (1807). Saint-Martin's ideal society was "a natural and spiritual theocracy," in which God would raise up men of mark, who would regard themselves strictly as "divine commissioners" to guide the people.

See A. J. Matter, *Saint-Martin, le philosophe inconnu* (1862); A. Franck, *La Philosophie mystique en France à la fin du dix-huitième siècle* (1866); A. E. Waite, *The Life of Louis Claude de Saint-Martin* (1901). There are English translations of *The Ministry of Man the Spirit* (1864) and of *Select Correspondence* (1863) by E. B. Penny.

ST. MARTIN, an island in the West Indies, about 5 mi. S. of the British island of Anguilla in 18° N. and 63° W. It is 37 sq.mi. in area and nearly triangular in form, composed of conical hills, culminating in Paradise peak (1,024 ft.). It is the only island in the Antilles owned by two European powers; 20 sq.mi. in the N., belonging to France, form a dependency of Guadeloupe, while the rest, belonging to Holland, is a dependency of Curaçao. Sugar, formerly its staple, has been succeeded by salt. The chief town of the French area is Marigot, a free port on the W. coast; of the Dutch, Philipsburg, on the S. St. Martin was first occupied by French freebooters in 1638, but ten years later the division between France and Holland was peaceably made. The inhabitants, mostly English-speaking Negroes, numbered in 1946, 6,786 in the French part, and in the Dutch (1947) 1,697.

ST. MARYLEBONE: see MARYLEBONE, ST.

SAINT MARYS, a city of Auglaize county, Ohio, U.S.A., on the Saint Marys river, 85 mi. W.N.W. of Columbus. It is served by the New York Central and the Nickel Plate railways. Population was 6,211 in 1950, 5,532 in 1940 and 5,433 in 1930 by the federal census. It is in the gas and oil region of the state, and has various manufacturing industries. A mile west is Lake Saint Marys (17,600 ac.), constructed as a reservoir to supply the Miami and Erie canal (abandoned about 1900), and now developed as a pleasure resort.

Saint Marys is on the site of a Shawnee village, where James Girty (captured in Pennsylvania when a boy of 13 by a French and Indian force and adopted by the Shawnees) established a trading post in 1782. For this reason the place was for some years called Girty's Town. Ft. Saint Marys was built in 1784 or 1785 by Gen. Wayne; Ft. Barbee in 1812 by Col. Joshua Barbee at the instance of Gen. Harrison. The town was laid out in 1823 and became a city in 1903.

SAINT MARYS, a borough of Elk county, Pennsylvania, U.S.A., on Elk creek and federal highway 120, at an altitude of 1,700 ft.; served by the Pennsylvania railway. The population of the borough was 7,852 in 1950; and 7,653 in 1940 by federal census. The borough was incorporated in 1848.

ST. MAWES, village in parish of St. Just-in-Roseland, Cornwall, England, on an arm of Falmouth harbour. Pop. of parish (1931) 970. There is a considerable fishing industry. The harbour is guarded by a large circular castle dating from the time of Henry VIII. St. Mawes was a borough, 1562–1835.

ST. MICHAEL'S (*São Miguel*), the largest island in the Portuguese archipelago of the Azores. Pop. (1940), 148,018; area, 288 sq.mi. See AZORES.

ST. MICHAEL'S MOUNT, a lofty pyramidal island, exhibiting a curious combination of slate and granite, rising 400 yd. from the shore of Mount's bay, Cornwall, England. It is united with Marazion by a natural causeway passable only at low tide. If its questionable identity with the Mictis of Timaeus and the Ictis of Diodorus Siculus be allowed, St. Michael's Mount is one of the most historic spots in the west of England. It was possibly held by a religious body in the Confessor's time and given by Robert, count of Mortain, to Mount St. Michael, of which Norman abbey it continued to be a priory until the dissolution of the alien houses by Henry V, when it was given to the abbess and Convent of Syon. It was a resort of pilgrims, encouraged by Pope Gregory (11th century). The Mount was captured by Henry Pomeroy in the reign of Richard I. John de Vere, earl of Oxford, seized it and held it against the king's troops in 1473. Perkin Warbeck occupied it in 1497. Humphry Arundell, governor of St. Michael's Mount, led the rebellion of 1549. During the reign of Queen Elizabeth it was given to Robert, earl of Salisbury, by whose son it was sold to Sir Francis Basset, whose brother, Sir Arthur Basset, held it against the parliament until July 1646. It was sold in 1659 to Colonel John St. Aubyn and is now the property of his descendant Lord St. Levan, who has a residence in the castle. The chapel is extra-diocesan. Many relics are preserved in the castle. The chapel of St. Michael, a beautiful 15th century building, has an embattled tower. The harbour, widened in 1823 to allow vessels of 500 tons to enter, has a pier dating from the 15th century. Pop. (1931) 71.

ST. MIHIEL, a town of northeastern France, in the department of Meuse, on the right bank of the Meuse and the Canal de l'Est, 23 mi. S. by E. of Verdun by rail. Pop. (1946) 4,335. St. Mihiel is famous for its Benedictine abbey of St. Michael, founded in 709. The abbey buildings (occupied by the municipal offices) date from the end of the 17th century and the beginning of the 18th century, and the church from the 17th century. The church of St. Étienne, chiefly in the flamboyant Gothic style, contains a magnificent Holy Sepulchre by Ligier Richier. St. Mihiel formerly possessed fortifications and two castles, destroyed in 1635.

Battle of St. Mihiel, 1918.—In his first conference with the commander-in-chief of the French armies, Gen. Pershing visualized the reduction of the St. Mihiel salient as the first U.S. operation in World War I. In accordance with studies made at his headquarters in Sept. 1917, he planned that the decisive U.S. effort would be against the German railroad system north and east of the Meuse river and the ore deposits in the vicinity of Metz and Longwy, with the elimination of the St. Mihiel salient as a necessary preliminary. Though early American control of the Woevre sector was agreed (May 19, 1918) the demands for American troops to assist the Allies in meeting the Germans elsewhere limited further steps along these lines to the creation of supply installations. At Bombon, on July 24, the commanders-in-chief, having determined to maintain the offensive, accepted Gen. Pershing's proposal that his army should undertake to reduce the St. Mihiel salient before the autumn rains began about the middle of September. This operation harmonized with the Château Thierry offensive and the British and French attacks against the Amiens and Ypres-Lys salients, made in order to free strategic railroads, preparatory to more extended operations. The counter-offensives against the Marne and Amiens saliens in July and Aug. had gained such advantages that it was apparent the emergency which justified the dispersion of American divisions had passed. On Aug. 9, final decision was given for the immediate assembly of the American army for an attack against the St. Mihiel salient.

The American troops in France—at this time over 1,200,000—were sufficient for the offensive, but they were dispersed along the front from Switzerland to the Channel. While the I Army Headquarters, two corps and corps troops and seven divisions were operating in the Marne offensive, other American divisions were holding sectors in the Vosges and Lorraine and several were training as reserves behind the British front. To assemble these combat and service troops into an army and undertake a major operation within the short period available and with the staffs so recently organized was an extremely difficult task. Deficiencies in artillery, aviation and special troops, caused by shipment of an undue proportion of infantry and machine guns to assist the Allies, were largely met by the French. While the I American army was given a distinct and independent mission, Gen. Pershing suggested, as expedient, that it should function under the nominal direction of Gen. Pétain, the French commander-in-chief, in order to assure co-ordination on the part of the French armies adjacent to the I army and to provide French units needed at the outset for supply services. To all intents and purposes the I army was entirely independent of French command, as all plans were prepared and all movements and operations ordered by the commander of the I army. The initial battle plan approved by Marshal Foch by Aug. 17, contemplated as an ultimate objective the general line: Marieulles (east of the Moselle), the heights south of Gorzé, Mars la Tour, Etain and the employment of 25 divisions under Gen. Pershing's personal direction. In furtherance of this plan, the scattered divisions, corps and service troops were first gathered in areas about Chaumont and Neufchâteau and then, beginning Aug. 28, the army advanced to its battle position.

The I American army took command of the front from Port-Sur-Seille (east of the Moselle) to Watronville (north of Les Eparges) from the II and VIII French Armies on Aug. 30. On this day, at I American Army headquarters (Ligny-en-Barrois), Marshal Foch discussed with Gen. Pershing a general plan for future operations and proposed employing American divisions under French command in the Champagne and Meuse-Argonne regions with a material reduction of the St. Mihiel forces in order to make available American troops for these new operations. Gen. Pershing could not accept such plans as they would require the immediate separation of the recently formed I American army into several groups delaying further the formation of a distinct American army. Moreover, an enormous amount of preparations had already been made in supplies and munitions and in construction of roads, railroads, regulating stations and other installations for the supply of the army on a particular front. While willing to accept the employment of the American army as a unit where desired, Gen. Pershing would not entertain proposals for its disruption. At a later conference on Sept. 2, the employment of the American army as a unit was conceded and a decision reached to the effect that after reducing the St. Mihiel salient, the I American army would attack by Sept. 25 between the Meuse river and Argonne forest (*see* MEUSE-ARGONNE OPERATION). As a result of the decisions, the depth of the St. Mihiel operation was limited to the line Vigneulles, Thiaucourt, Regnieville. The number of divisions to be used was reduced and the time shortened. There were 15 American divisions (each equal in size to 2 French divisions) and 4 French divisions available, 6 of which would be in reserve. Furthermore, 2 army corps headquarters and corps troops, practically all army artillery and aviation and the 1st, 2nd and 4th divisions, the first 2 destined for a leading part in the St. Mihiel attack, were all due to be withdrawn and started for the Meuse-Argonne by the fourth day of the battle.

The salient had been held by the Germans since Sept. 1914. It covered the most sensitive section of the enemy's position on the western front; *i.e.*, the Mézières-Sedan-Metz railroad and the Briey Iron Basin; it threatened the entire region between Verdun and Nancy and interrupted the main railroad line from Paris to the east. Its primary strength lay in the natural defensive features of the terrain itself. The western face of the salient extended along the rugged, heavily-wooded eastern heights of the Meuse; the southern face followed the heights of the Meuse for 5 mi. to the east and then crossed the plain of the Woevre, including within the German lines the detached heights of Louvemont and Mont Sec, which dominated the plain and afforded the enemy unusual facilities for observation. The enemy had reinforced the positions by every artificial means during a period of four years. Having concentrated by night movements over 600,000 men on the battlefield, the troops of the I army were deployed in attack positions on the night of Sept. 11. On the south face of the salient was the I corps (4 divisions in line) extending from the Moselle westward. On its left was the IV corps (3 divisions in line) with left facing Mont Sec. These 2 corps were to deliver the main attack, the advance pivoting on the centre of the I corps. The left of the IV corps was to advance toward the heart of the salient where contact would be made with the V corps from the west. On the western face of the salient lay the V corps (3 divisions in line) extended from Mouilly via Les Eparges to Watronville. While the centre division made a deep advance to gain contact with the IV corps on the south, the rest of the corps was to limit its advance while covering the flanks of the centre division. Between the IV and V corps around the apex of the salient, the II French corps (3 divisions in line) covering 24 mi., had the mission of attacking to hold the enemy in the salient. American artillery and aviation were greatly augmented by French artillery and aviation and assisted indirectly by the British independent air force located south of Nancy. The heavy artillery could reach the railroads entering Metz.

Gen. Foch's Army Detachment C held the salient on Sept. 12 with 8 divisions in line and 3 divisions in immediate reserve. While the Germans had an inkling of a possible American attack as early as Sept. 1, the magnitude and imminence were not suspected. An American ruse at Belfort, which comprised extensive preparation for an attack in that region, proved misleading to the enemy. A decision having been made to withdraw in face of a serious attack at St. Mihiel, preparations for a deliberate and methodical withdrawal were under way, some dismounted batteries having been displaced, when the Americans launched their attack at dawn on Sept. 12. After four hours' violent artillery preparation, accompanied by small tanks, the I and IV corps advanced. The infantry of the V corps attacked at 8 A.M. The operation was carried out with precision. Just after daylight of the 13th, elements of the IV and V corps joined at Vigneulles, 11 mi. N.E. of St. Mihiel. The enemy was overwhelmed, and all objectives were reached on the afternoon of Sept. 13. During the 14th and 15th, while the two German counterattacks were repulsed by the I corps, the Americans advanced along the Moselle to the line Jaulny-Pagny-sur-Moselle. On Sept. 14–16, local operations continued, American patrols advancing to Dampvitoux, eastern edge of Etang de Lachaussee, Jonville and Fresnes-en-Woevre. The swiftness with which the operation was carried out enabled the Americans to smother the opposition to such an extent that they suffered less than 7,500 casualties during the actual period of the advance. During the battle the Germans engaged four new divisions and drew into local reserve several other divisions.

The Americans captured nearly 16,000 prisoners (over 4,000 in the salient proper), 443 guns and large stores of material and supplies. The moral result of the victory was striking. An American army had suddenly appeared and crushed the enemy in one of his strongest positions. No form of propaganda could overcome the depressing effect on the enemy of this demonstration of ability to organize a large American force in so short a time and drive it successfully through its defenses. The strength of the I American army in the battle totalled over 500,000 Americans and 100,000 French, approximately 2,900 cannons, 400 tanks and 1,000 aeroplanes.　　　　　(H. A. DR.; J. J. P.)

ST. MORITZ, loftiest (6,037 ft.) and most populous village of the Upper Engadine in the Swiss canton of the Grisons. Pop. (1941) 2,305; about half were German-speaking, the rest chiefly Romansch and Italian. About half were Protestant and half Roman Catholic. It is built above the north shore of the lake of the same name, and is 56 mi. from Coire by the Albula railway. The village is about 1 mi. north of the baths, an electric tramway connecting the two. Both are ordinarily frequented by foreign visitors. The baths (chalybeate, sparkling with free carbonic acid) were already well-known in the 16th century.

ST. NAZAIRE, a town of France, capital of an arrondissement in the department of Loire-Inférieure, 40 mi. W.N.W. of Nantes by rail and 29 mi. by river. Pop. (1936) 38,627. According to remains discovered, St. Nazaire seems to occupy the site of the ancient *Corbilo*, placed by Strabo among the more important maritime towns of Gaul. At the close of the 4th century the site of Corbilo was occupied by Saxons, and, their conversion to Christianity being effected one or two hundred years later by St. Felix of Nantes, the place took the name of St. Nazaire. Under the Second Empire it was chosen as the site of the new harbour for Nantes, because the ascent of the Loire was becoming difficult. St. Nazaire, on the Loire at its mouth, is a modern town. It possesses a granite dolmen 10 ft. by 5 ft. resting horizontally on two other stones. The harbour, accessible to largest ships, is separated from the estuary by a narrow strip of land and comprises an outer harbour and entrance, two floating docks, three graving docks and the extensive shipbuilding yards of the Loire Co. and of the General Transatlantic Co. whose steamers connect St. Nazaire with Mexico, the Antilles and the Isthmus of Panama. Ships for the navy and the mercantile marine are built, and there are important steelworks, blast furnaces, forges and steam sawmills.

The town is the seat of a sub-prefect and has a board of trade-arbitrators, a chamber of commerce and a tribunal of commerce.

ST. NEOTS (pronounced St. Neets), a market town in Huntingdonshire, England, on the right bank of the Ouse, 51½ mi. N. of London by the L.N.E.R. Pop. of urban district (1938) 4,087. Area 2.2 sq.mi. A stone bridge, built in 1589 from the ruins of a former priory, here crosses the river and connects the county with Bedfordshire.

St. Mary's church is a fine Perpendicular building of the later 15th century, with original oak roof.

ST. NICOLAS, town, province of East Flanders, Belgium, 12 mi. southwest of Antwerp, a railway junction on the Antwerp-Ghent line, with linen manufactories of its own, and the central market of Waes; formerly barren and bleak downs, it is now highly productive. Pop. (est. 1939) 42,190.

ST. NICOLAS or ST. NICOLAS DU PORT, a town of northeastern France, in the department of Meurthe-et-Moselle, on the left bank of the Meurthe, 8 mi. S.E. of Nancy by rail. Pop. (1936) 5,078. The town has a fine Gothic church (15th and 16th century), possessing a finger joint of St. Nicolas, formerly the object of pilgrimages which were themselves the origin of well-known fairs. The fairs declined after 1635, when the Swedes sacked the town. Important saltworkings are nearby.

ST. OMER, a town and fortress of northern France, capital of an arrondissement in the department of Pas-de-Calais, 42 mi. W.N.W. of Lille on the railway to Calais. Pop. (1946) 18,106.

Omer, bishop of Thérouanne, in the 7th century established the monastery of St. Bertin, from which that of Notre-Dame was an offshoot. In the 9th century the village which grew up round the monasteries was named St. Omer. In 1559 St. Omer became a bishopric and Notre-Dame was raised to the rank of cathedral. The town and monastery were surrounded by walls by 980. Situated on the borders of frequently disputed territories, St. Omer long continued subject to siege and military disaster. In 1071 Philip I and Count Arnulf III of Flanders were defeated at St. Omer by Robert the Frisian. In 1127 the town received a communal charter from William Clito, count of Flanders. In 1493 it came to the Low Countries as part of the Spanish dominion. In 1677, after 17 days' siege, Louis XIV forced the town to capitulate; and the peace of Nijmwegen permanently confirmed the conquest. In 1711 St. Omer, on the verge of surrendering to Prince Eugene and the duke of Marlborough owing to famine, was saved by the daring of Jacqueline Robin, who brought provisions into the place. St. Omer ceased to be a bishopric in 1801.

At St. Omer begins the canalized portion of the Aa, which reaches the sea at Gravelines, and under its walls connects with the Neuffossé canal, which ends at the Lys. There are two harbours outside and one within the city. The old cathedral belongs almost entirely to the 13th, 14th and 15th centuries. A heavy square tower finished in 1499 surmounts the west portal. The church contains interesting paintings, a colossal statue of Christ seated between the Virgin and St. John (13th century, originally belonging to the cathedral of Thérouanne) and the cenotaph of St. Omer (13th century). The richly decorated chapel in the transept contains a wooden figure of the Virgin (12th century), the object of pilgrimages. Some arches and a lofty tower are all that remain of the abbey church of St. Bertin. St. Sepulchre (14th century) has a beautiful stone spire and stained-glass windows. There is a fine collection of records in the town hall, which was built of the materials of the abbey of St. Bertin. There are several houses of the 16th and 17th centuries; of the latter the finest is the Hôtel Colbert, once the royal lodging. St. Omer is the seat of a sub-prefect, of a court of assizes, of a tribunal of commerce, of a chamber of commerce, and of a board of trade arbitrators. It was the British headquarters during part of World War I. The industries include the manufacture of linen goods, sugar, soap, tobacco pipes and mustard, the distilling of oil and liqueurs, dyeing, salt-refining, malting and brewing.

The suburb of Haut Pont to the north of St. Omer is inhabited by a special stock, which has remained faithful to the Flemish tongue, its original costume and its peculiar customs, and is distinguished by honesty and industry. The ground which these people cultivate has been reclaimed from the marsh, and the *lègres* (*i.e.*, the square blocks of land) communicate with each other only by boats floated on the ditches and canals that divide them. At the end of the marsh, on the borders of the forest of Clairmarais, are the ruins of the abbey founded in 1140 by Thierry d'Alsace, to which Thomas Becket betook himself in 1165.

SAINTONGE, one of the old provinces of France, of which Saintes (*q.v.*) was the capital, was bounded on the north-west by Aunis, on the north-east by Poitou, on the east by Angoumois, on the south by Guyenne, and on the west by Guyenne and the Atlantic. It now forms a small portion of the department of Charente and the greater part of that of Charente Inférieure. Originally occupied by the Gaulish *Santones,* whose name it preserves, the district subsequently formed part of Aquitania Secunda. It formed the bishopric of Saintes and was divided into two *pagi: Santonicus* (whence Saintonge) and *Alienensis* (Aunis). Divided between the kings of England and France in 1259 it was wholly ceded to the king of England in 1360, but reconquered by Du Guesclin in 1371. Up to 1789 it was in the same *gouvernement* with Angoumois, but for judicial purposes Saintonge was under the parlement of Bordeaux and Angoumois under that of Paris.

See D. Massiou, *Histoire politique, civile et religieuse de la Saintonge*

et de l'Aunis, 6 vol. (1836–39; 2nd ed., 1846); P. D. Rainguet, *Biographie saintongeaise* (1852). *See* also the publications of the *Société des archives hist. de la Saintonge et de l'Aunis* (1874 seq.).

ST. PANCRAS, a metropolitan borough of London, England, bounded east by Islington, southeast by Finsbury, south by Holborn and west by St. Marylebone and Hampstead, and extending north to the boundary of the county of London. Pop. (1951) 138,377. Area 4.2 sq.mi. In the centre of the borough are Camden Town and Kentish Town and the three great railway termini of Euston, St. Pancras and King's Cross, with their extensive goods depots and adjacent hotels. To the south of this lies the residential district of Bloomsbury (part of which is in Holborn), one mainly of university buildings and private hotels, and with several fine squares. North of the railway stations are residential districts near Hampstead heath and Regent's park, including Gospel Oak and part of Highgate.

There are considerable open spaces, the largest of which are Waterlow park, parts of Regent's park and of Primrose hill, Parliament Hill fields (bought for the public in 1886) and Kenwood (purchased in 1919). The last contains Kenwood house, bequeathed to the public by Lord Iveagh (d. 1927) together with its noted collection of pictures.

A thoroughfare, called successively Tottenham Court road, Hampstead road, Camden High street, Kentish Town road, and Highgate road, runs from south to north; Euston road crosses it in the south, and Camden road and Chalk Farm road branch from it at Camden Town. The old parish church of St. Pancras in the Fields, near Pancras road, has lost its ancient character as a result of reconstruction, though it retains several early monuments. The new parish church of St. Pancras is in Woburn place. University college (a part of London university), Gower street, was founded in 1826 and provides education in all branches common to universities excepting theology. With the department of medicine is connected the University College hospital (1833) opposite the college. There are several other hospitals: among them the Royal Free hospital (Gray's Inn road), the London Skin hospital (Fitzroy square) and the Elizabeth Garrett Anderson Hospital for Women (Euston road). The site of the Foundling hospital (*q.v.*), in the old Lamb's Conduit fields, has been transformed into a permanent open-air study and play centre for children through a fund initiated for the purpose by Lord Rothermere. Other institutions are the British Medical association in Tavistock square (1925), the Royal Veterinary college and the North Western polytechnic (1929). The Mary Ward (formerly Passmore Edwards) settlement, first named for its principal benefactor, was founded largely through the instrumentality of Mrs. Humphry Ward. In Euston road are the British headquarters of the Society of Friends, the new buildings of which were completed in 1926. Park Village East and Park Village West, at the north end of Albany street and separated by the canal, were built by John Nash.

St. Pancras with Holborn returns two members to parliament, for St. Pancras North, and Holborn and St. Pancras South. Many of the inhabitants are employed in work connected with the railways. There are also cigarette, furniture and piano-making industries.

St. Pancras is mentioned in Domesday as belonging to the chapter of St. Paul's cathedral, in which body the lordship of the manors of Cantelows (Kentish Town) and Totenhall (Tottenham Court) was invested. Camden Town takes its name from Baron Camden (d. 1794), lord chancellor under George III. King's Cross was so called from a statue of George IV, erected in 1830 and greatly ridiculed and removed in 1845, but an earlier name, Battle Bridge, is traditionally derived from the stand of Queen Boadicea against the Romans, or from one of Alfred's contests with the Danes.

SAINT PAUL, the capital city of Minnesota, U.S.A., a port of entry, the judicial seat of Ramsey county, and federal headquarters for the state; 2 mi. below the head of navigation on the Mississippi river and 1,836 mi. from its mouth. It is on federal highways 10, 12, 52 and 61; and is served by the Burlington Route, the Chicago Great Western, the Chicago, Milwaukee, St. Paul and Pacific, the Chicago, St. Paul, Minneapolis and Omaha, the Great Northern, the Minneapolis and St. Louis, the Northern Pacific, the Rock Island, the Soo Line and electric interurban railways, a terminal switching and belt line, motor coach and truck lines. Air service is supplied by Capital, Mid-Continent, Northwest and Western air lines.

The population was 271,606 in 1930, of whom 44,143 were foreign-born white (largely from the Scandinavian countries, Germany and Canada); 1950 federal census 309,474. The Twin

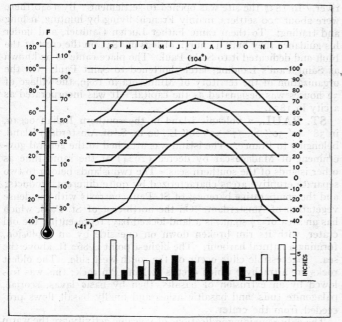

WEATHER GRAPH OF SAINT PAUL. THE THERMOMETER INDICATES THE ANNUAL MEAN TEMPERATURE; THE MIDDLE CURVE SHOWS THE MONTHLY MEAN TEMPERATURE; THE CURVES ABOVE AND BELOW, THE HIGHEST AND LOWEST EVER RECORDED. THE COLUMNS INDICATE THE NORMAL MONTHLY PRECIPITATION: (BLACK) TOTAL PRECIPITATION (INCLUDING MELTED SNOW); (WHITE) SNOWFALL

Cities (Saint Paul and Minneapolis) and their immediate suburbs constitute a great urban community of about 1,107,000.

Transportation Facilities.—Saint Paul is picturesquely located on a series of benches or terraces of irregular breadth and height, reaching a maximum of 266 ft. above the level of the river and merging in an elevated rolling plateau. It occupies 55.44 sq.mi., mostly on the north (or "east") bank of the Mississippi, but including an area in a bend of the river on the south side, opposite the heart of the business district. Six highway bridges and several used by railways cross the river within the city limits, connecting the main part of the city with the "west" side, and connecting Saint Paul with Minneapolis. Because of the irregular nature of the terrain and the numerous railways entering the city, there are 67 other bridges spanning railroad tracks and valleys. Saint Paul is indeed "the port of entry to the great northwest." The nine railway systems have an aggregate mileage of 59,250 mi., one-fourth of the total railway mileage of the United States. They enter the city along the foot of the bluffs, or through a narrow valley giving access to the highlands back of the city. All use the Union depot, completed in 1926 at a cost of $15,000,-000. A switching and interchange railway, serving all the lines, handles 775,000 cars in a year.

After a long period during which the river, originally the principal artery of commerce, had scarcely been used, regular barge service on the upper Mississippi was again inaugurated (by the Inland Waterways corporation) in the summer of 1927. Shipments in and out of the port of Saint Paul in 1949 totalled 1,300,-821 tons. There are three municipal terminals for handling general cargo, grain, coal and ore and passenger service. Many motor truck lines and numerous bus lines operate in and out of the city in all directions.

On the south bank of the river, opposite the river terminal and little more than a mile from the courthouse, the principal rail-

way freight terminals and the bus depot, is the municipal airport (375.6 ac.).

The city is the northwestern headquarters for the U.S. railway mail service and U.S. district engineer.

Buildings and Parks.—Dominating the view as the city is approached from the south and the east is the sky line of the loop section with the state capitol in the background. Prominent in this sky line is the new city hall and courthouse. Costing $4,-000,000, this structure departs from the typical monumental public building and places full emphasis upon the utilization of space, and it depends for beauty upon its simplicity of lines, mass and shadows, rather than upon columns and ornaments; and secondly, on the works of art contained in it and the excellence of the interior finish.

The state capitol stands on high ground north of the business district, where it commands a view of the entire city. Designed by Cass Gilbert, Saint Paul architect, this structure of Minnesota granite and white Georgia marble, with massive central dome, was completed in 1905 at a cost of $4,500,000. Included in the state building group are the state office building and the State Historical society building. Other prominent buildings are the federal building and the municipal auditorium, which seats more than 12,000 in the main arena and in addition has a theatre section, numerous smaller halls, conference rooms and exhibit areas. The residential sections of the city, mostly on high ground, are beautiful with trees, shrubbery and wide lawns. The most noted street, Summit avenue, 200 ft. wide, winds for part of its length along the edge of the bluff, commanding fine views of the river gorge and the lower terraces of the city. Adjoining the city on the southwest is the Fort Snelling military reservation of 2,000 ac. The picturesque original fort, built in 1822, still stands high on the bluff. The city's park system covers 2,207 ac. including nine large parks (up to 600 ac.) connected by drives and river boulevards and 80 smaller triangles and monument sites. Harriet Island, opposite the business section of the city, has been made a pleasure ground. Three of the parks contain large lakes and golf courses, and there are 53 lakes in the county. Indian Mounds park (named from the Sioux burial mounds which it encloses) on Dayton's bluff commands a magnificent view of the Mississippi. Next to it are the grounds of the state fish hatchery, one of the best equipped in the country.

On the northern edge of the city, bounded by it on three sides, are the 260-ac. grounds and beautiful buildings (owned by the state) of the Minnesota Agricultural society, the scene of the annual state fair, the largest one in the United States, with an attendance in 1950 of 905,563.

Schools and Churches.—In the northwestern corner of the city, adjoining the fair grounds, is the farm campus (419 ac.) of the state university, where the schools of agriculture and the main agricultural experiment station are located. Saint Paul is the seat also of Macalester college (Presbyterian, founded in 1885); Hamline university (Methodist, chartered 1854); the College of St. Thomas (Roman Catholic, 1885); the College of St. Catherine (Roman Catholic, 1905); Bethel college and seminary (Baptist); Luther Theological seminary; and St. Paul theological seminary (Roman Catholic); the St. Paul College of Law; and a number of secondary and special training schools under various auspices, including one for the training of laboratory technicians. The public schools are housed in 73 buildings, most of them modern in construction. The system includes eight athletic fields and 52 playgrounds. The public library occupies an entire block. In one wing is the valuable Hill reference library, maintained by the heirs of James J. Hill, and part of his famous gallery of paintings, which included the best collection of the Barbizon school in America. The law library of the state is housed in the capitol, and the collection of the Minnesota Historical society has a fine building of its own. Two daily newspapers are published. The *Pioneer-Press*, established in 1853, is one of the oldest newspapers in the northwest.

Saint Paul is the see of a Roman Catholic archdiocese. The Cathedral of Saint Paul is one of the notable ecclesiastical structures of the country.

There are 281 churches, representing all the principal faiths and denominations. The charitable agencies which depend for support on voluntary contributions are financed through a joint annual campaign, which raises about $1,500,000. The community chest and several of the larger philanthropic agencies are housed in a central administration building provided by the Amherst H. Wilder charity, a trust fund of about $3,800,000, established in 1910 for the benefit of the poor of the city.

Government.—Saint Paul operates under a charter adopted in 1912 and effective Jan. 1, 1914, establishing a commission form of government. Elections are held biennially. The voters elect a mayor, a comptroller and six councilmen or commissioners; three justices of the peace, two municipal judges and four constables. The mayor assigns each commissioner to one of the six departments of government (public safety, public works, public utilities, parks and public buildings, finance, and libraries, auditorium and museums) as its administrative head. Saint Paul's public schools are administered by a school board of seven members, authorized by city charter amendment in 1950. Fiscal powers relating to tax levy and budget control are retained by city council and comptroller under basic charter provisions. The mayor is ex-officio president of the council and has the veto power over its acts, but they may be passed over his veto by four votes. The comptroller is also the civil service commissioner. A city planning board was created in 1918. In 1922 it submitted a general city plan, and in 1924 a zoning ordinance was adopted. Saint Paul has a low death rate, a low infant mortality, high level literacy, a high percentage in school attendance, high percentage of home ownership and an index figure for cost of living below the average. The valuation of taxable property for 1950 was $533,034,198.

Trade and Manufactures.—Saint Paul, near the head of navigation on the Mississippi river, became the railroad centre of the northwest in the days when the river was the principal artery of transportation. Because of these transportation advantages, it also became the distributing centre of the northwest. Today the wholesalers and jobbers distribute food, dry goods, clothing, general merchandise, hardware, petroleum products, printing specialties and farm implements nationally and internationally. The South Saint Paul (adjacent to Saint Paul) livestock market has grown so that it is second only to Chicago in the receipt and slaughter of livestock.

Poultry, dairy and food products from the surrounding agricultural area are also processed in large quantities. Printing and publishing is one of the major industries of Saint Paul. Among the firms in this field are the world's largest publishers of law books and the largest producers of calendars and advertising specialties in the United States. Automobiles and accessories, wearing apparel and furs, foundries and machine shops are also important in the industrial life of the city. Saint Paul supplies the world with the familiar cellulose tapes and produces abrasives and other products. More than 800 manufacturers in the Saint Paul industrial area make about $600,000,000 worth of products annually. The city has an important agricultural industry in the production of mushrooms, which are raised in large quantities in the caves in the sandstone bluffs on the west side of the river. The caves are also used to age cheese, most of which is a Roquefort type developed at the University of Minnesota farm school and called "Minnesota blue." Saint Paul has 18 banks, with total resources of $541,819,228 in 1950. Debits to individual accounts in that year amounted to $5,601,766,572. The federal land bank and the federal intermediate credit bank for the northwest are both located in Saint Paul.

History.—The site of Saint Paul was known to the Indians as *Innijiska*, the White Rock. It was occasionally used as a camping place, but it was not until about 1800 that an Indian village was established there. The first white visitor of record was the Jesuit missionary, Father Louis Hennepin, in 1680, but probably the traders Pierre Radisson and Médart, sieur de Groseilliers, were there in 1658. Robert, sieur de la Salle, mentions the locality in a letter written in 1682. In 1766 Jonathan Carver (*q.v.*) of Massachusetts made an adventurous journey by way of Mackinac across Wisconsin and into Minnesota, and his heirs claimed the entire site of Saint Paul and much adjacent territory on the ground of an alleged grant made to him by the Indians. In 1805 Lieut. Zebulon M. Pike, sent by Thomas Jefferson to take possession of the region, bought most of the ground now occupied by the city, as well as the Fort Snelling reservation, from the Sioux for 60 gal. of whiskey and a few presents, to which congress later added $2,000 in cash. In 1823 the first steamboat made its way up the river. In 1837 the site was opened to settlement. By 1840 there were about 200 settlers, mainly French, living by hunting, fishing and trading. To them came Father Lucien Gaultier, and under his guidance they built a church of logs in 1841 on the crest of the bluff and dedicated it to Saint Paul. The place came to be known as Saint Paul's Landing, later shortened to Saint Paul. On the organization of the territory of Minnesota in 1849, the village of 32 houses was designated as the capital. It was incorporated as a city in 1854.

ST. PAUL, a volcanic island in the southern Indian ocean, in 38° 42′ 50″ S., 77° 32′ 29″ E., 60 m. S. of Amsterdam island, belonging to France. The island was attached to the general government of Madagascar by decree (1924) at the same time as other islands of the southern seas. The two islands belong to two separate eruptive areas characterized by quite different products; and the comparative bareness of St. Paul contrasts with the dense vegetation of Amsterdam. On the north-east of St. Paul, which has an area of $2\frac{3}{4}$ sq.m., is a land-locked bay, representing the old crater, with its rim broken down on one side by an explosion, forming a natural harbour. The highest point is 862 ft. above the sea. Inaccessible cliffs occur on the south-west side. The oldest rocks are a trachyte which occurs at Nine Pin rock; this was followed by an extrusion of basalts, then by basic lavas, scoriae, palagonite tuffs, and basaltic ashes and finally basalt flows proceeded from the crater.

The only remaining indications of volcanic activity are the warm springs and emanations of carbon dioxide. The island is uninhabited but the waters are well stocked with fish.

SAINTPAULIA: *see* AFRICAN VIOLET.

ST. PAUL'S ROCKS, a number of islets in the Atlantic, nearly 1° N. of the equator and 540 mi. from South America, in 29° 15′ W. The whole space occupied does not exceed 1,400 ft. in length by about half as much in breadth. Besides sea-fowl the only land creatures are insects and spiders. Fish are abundant, seven species being collected by the "Challenger." Darwin considered the rocks not of volcanic origin; later investigators maintain that they probably are eruptive.

ST. PETER, a city of Minnesota, U.S.A., on the west bank of the Minnesota river, 75 mi. S.W. of Minneapolis; county seat of Nicollet county. It is served by the Chicago and North Western and the Chicago, St. Paul, Minneapolis and Omaha railways, and by bus lines. Pop. (1950) 7,754. St. Peter is an important grain, livestock, dairying, limestone and lumber market, and is the seat of a state hospital for the insane and of Gustavus Adolphus college (Swedish Evangelical Lutheran, 1862). The city was founded about 1852, incorporated as a village in 1865, and chartered as a city in 1891. In 1857 a bill making it the state capital passed the legislature, but was not signed by the governor.

ST. PETER PORT, the chief town of Guernsey, one of the Channel Islands. Pop. (1951) 16,799. It lies on a steep slope above its harbour, on the east coast of the island. The harbour is enclosed by breakwaters, the southernmost of which connects with the shore and continues beyond an islet on which stands Castle Cornet (12th century). A sea wall extends more than a mile towards the port of St. Sampson. To the south of the town is Fort George. The old boundaries of the town are marked by five stones. St. Peter's, the town church, standing low by the side of the quay, dates from various periods, with possible remnants of Norman walls, and has fine details of the 14th and 15th centuries. The Elizabeth college for boys was founded by Queen Elizabeth I. Hauteville house, the residence of Victor Hugo from 1856 to 1870, is preserved as he left it, and the authorities of the city of Paris are now its trustees. Among other works which he produced in this island fastness was *Les Travailleurs de la Mer* (1863), unsurpassed even among the works of its author for splendour of imagination and for pathos.

The original harbour was built under King Edward I, if not earlier; it was added to under Queen Elizabeth I and outside this harbour lay a roadstead, landward of the islet of Castle Cornet. Most of this roadstead was enclosed by breakwaters in the mid-19th century, and the large harbour thus formed has had its quayage increased by the completion in 1930 of a jetty projecting out into the pool. A large export trade in fruit, vegetables and flowers is carried on, and it is a popular port for visiting yachts from England and continental Europe. (B. C. DE G.)

ST. PETERSBURG: see LENINGRAD.

SAINT PETERSBURG, a city of Pinellas county, Fla., U.S., on the west coast, 20 mi. S.W. of Tampa; served by the Atlantic Coast Line and the Seaboard Air Line railways, by National, Delta and Eastern airlines and by Cuban and South American air freight lines. The city covers 58.1 sq.mi. on the southern tip of Pinellas peninsula; it is bordered on the west and south by the Gulf of Mexico and on the east and northeast by Tampa bay. The 7-mi. Gandy bridge connects St. Petersburg with Tampa, 20 mi. across the bay. Three causeways across Boca Ciega bay on the west connect the city with the Gulf Beach keys along the Gulf of Mexico; a 13-mi. lower bay bridge to Bradenton and Key West was under construction in 1951. The city has 33 mi. of water front, a municipal airport, solarium, swimming pools and 6 mi. of water-front park with piers and marina. Assessed valuation in 1950 was $164,982,627; the form of government is commission-manager. Apartments and numerous guest homes care for a tourist industry of 500,000 annually. The setting is subtropical, the climate mild and equable. Beginning in 1910, a local newspaper has given away its entire edition on any day in which the sun has not shown at press time (2 P.M.), an average of four times a year. St. Petersburg is a spring training baseball centre. The commerce of its international airport (Pinellas county) in 1949 amounted to 7,080,546 lb. of air freight, third largest in poundage in the U.S., and included fish, fruit, winter vegetables, flowers and bulbs, cattle, furniture, drugs, jewellery and automobiles transshipped to foreign countries. St. Petersburg was platted in 1885, became a town in 1887 and was incorporated as a city in 1903. In 1950 it had 402 manufacturing firms employing 4,000 persons with an industrial pay roll in excess of $7,000,000. The population in 1950 was 96,738.

SAINT-PIERRE, BERNARDIN DE (1737–1814), French man of letters, was born at Havre on Jan. 19, 1737. He was educated at Caen and at Rouen, and became an engineer. According to his own account he served in the army, taking part in the Hesse campaign of 1760, but was dismissed for insubordination, and, after quarrelling with his family, was in some difficulty. He appeared at Malta, St. Petersburg, Warsaw, Dresden, Berlin, holding brief commissions as an engineer and rejoicing in romantic adventures. He came back to Paris in 1765 poorer than he set out. He came into possession of a small sum at his father's death, and in 1768 he set out for the Isle of France (Mauritius) with a government commission, and remained there three years, returning home in 1771. On his return from Mauritius he was introduced to D'Alembert and his friends, but he was most attracted to J. J. Rousseau, of whom in his last years he saw much, and on whom he formed both his character and his style. His *Voyage à l'Île de France* (2 vols., 1773) gained him a reputation as a champion of innocence and religion, and in consequence, through the exertions of the bishop of Aix, a pension of 1,000 livres a year. The *Études de la nature* (3 vols., 1784) was an attempt to prove the existence of God from the wonders of nature.

His masterpiece, *Paul et Virginie*, appeared in 1787 in a supplementary volume of the *Études*, and his second great success, much less sentimental and showing not a little humour, the *Chaumière indienne*, not till 1790. In 1792 he married a very young girl, Félicité Didot, who brought him a considerable dowry. For a short time in 1792 he was superintendent of the Jardin des Plantes, and on the suppression of the office received a pension of 3,000 livres. In 1795 he became a member of the Institute. After his first wife's death he married in 1800, when he was sixty-three, another young girl, Désirée Pelleport, and is said to have been very happy with her. On Jan. 21, 1814 he died at his house at Eragny, near Pontoise.

Paul et Virginie has been pronounced gaudy in style and unhealthy in tone. Bernardin's merit lies in his breaking away from the arid vocabulary which more than a century of classical writing had brought upon France, in his genuine preference for the beauties of nature, and in his attempt to describe them faithfully. After Rousseau, and even more than Rousseau, Bernardin was in French literature the apostle of the return to nature, though both in him and his immediate follower Chateaubriand there is still much mannerism and unreality.

Aimé Martin, disciple of Bernardin and the second husband of his second wife, published a complete edition of his works in 18 volumes (1818–20), afterwards increased by seven volumes of correspondence and memoirs (1826). *Paul et Virginie*, the *Chaumière indienne*, etc. have often been separately reprinted. See also Arvède Barin's *Bernardin de Saint Pierre* (1891).

SAINT-PIERRE, CHARLES IRÉNÉE CASTEL, ABBÉ DE (1658–1743), French writer, was born at the Château de Saint-Pierre l'Église near Cherbourg on Feb. 18, 1658. His father was *bailli* of the Cotentin, and Saint-Pierre was educated by the Jesuits. In Paris he frequented the salons of Madame de la Fayette and of the marquise de Lambert. He was presented to the abbacy of Tiron, and was elected to the Academy in 1695. In the same year he gained a footing at court as almoner to Madame. But in 1718, in consequence of the political offence given by his *Discours sur la polysynodie*, he was expelled from the Academy. He died in Paris on April 29, 1743.

Saint-Pierre's works are almost entirely occupied with an acute criticism of politics, law and social institutions. They had a great influence on Rousseau, who left elaborate examinations of some of them, and reproduced not a few of their ideas in his own work. His *Projet de paix perpétuelle*, which was destined to exercise considerable influence on the development of the various schemes for securing universal peace which culminated in the Holy Alliance, was published in 1713 at Utrecht, where he was acting as secretary to the French plenipotentiary, the Abbé de Polignac. His works were published at Amsterdam in 1738–40 and his *Annales politiques* in London in 1757. A discussion of his principles, with a view to securing a just estimation of the high value of his political and economic ideas, is given by S. Siégler Pascal in *Un Contemporain égaré au XVIIIe siècle. Les Projets de l'abbé de Saint-Pierre, 1658–1743* (Paris, 1900).

ST. PIERRE and MIQUELON, the largest islands of two small groups 10 mi. off the south coast of Newfoundland; united area about 93 sq.mi. Both islands are rugged masses of granite, with a few small streams and lakes, a thin covering of soil and scanty vegetation. Area of St. Pierre group, 10 sq.mi.; Miquelon group, 83 sq.mi. The population of the two islands in 1950 was 4,606, the capital city of St. Pierre having 3,997 people.

The islands were occupied by the French in 1604 and fortified in 1696. In 1702 they were captured by the British and held till 1763, when they were given back to France as a fishing station. They are thus the sole remnant of the French colonies in North America. Taken by the English in 1778, restored to France in 1783, again captured and depopulated by the English in 1793, recovered by France in 1802 and lost in 1803, the islands have remained in undisputed French possession since 1814 (treaty of Paris). Their importance is due to their proximity to the Grand Banks. Primary education is free, with two schools for boys and three for girls, besides private schools.

Fishing activities of the archipelago have been limited to coastal fishing in dories. Salted and dried cod is exported to the Antilles, but production is not sufficient for the economy of the islands. Thanks to a substantial subsidy from France, however, a company was formed in 1951 to produce frozen fish fillets and by-products of fish.

St. Pierre also has a fur industry (fox and mink). The pelts, which are shipped to the markets of the world, are of good quality.

Communication between St. Pierre and Canada is maintained by a French vessel, property of the government. This boat transports passengers, mail and freight on the St. Pierre-Halifax line during the winter and on the St. Pierre-Sydney line during the summer. Non-scheduled air transport is furnished by a Canadian company, Maritime Central Airways. A small steamer with accommodation for passengers and freight provides transportation between the islands of St. Pierre and Miquelon. Administration of the islands and public services is carried out by a governor, assisted by a private council. In 1946 a general council, composed of 14 members elected by universal franchise, assumed a large part in the administration of this territory. It acquired power particularly over the local budget and the fixing of customs, tariffs and all other taxes. The territory of St. Pierre and Miquelon is represented in the French parliament by a member in the national assembly and by a senator in the council of the republic. It elects, as well, a representative to *l'assemblée de l'union française*.

See Henrique, *Les Colonies françaises*, t. ii (Paris, 1889); Levasseur, *La France*, t. ii (Paris, 1893); *L'Année coloniale*, yearly from 1899. (C. CY.)

ST. POL, COUNTS OF. The countship of St. Pol-sur-Ternoise owed its importance to its position between the countship of Flanders and the lands of the Capetian kings of France. It appears at the beginning of the 11th century bounded by the Aa, the Lys and the Canche. The *castrum* of St. Pol, built c. 1023 near Ternoise, commanded the crossroads to Thérouanne, Béthune and Arras. Formerly vassals of the count of Flanders through the count of Boulogne, the Candavènes, who formed the first dynasty of St. Pol (1025–1205), were able to resist Flemish domination, particularly in the time of Hugh II (1081–1126), relying instead on the Capetians. The same policy prevailed under the two following dynasties, to which the county, now owing allegiance to the counts of Artois, successively fell in female succession; viz., the house of Châtillon (1205–1371), particularly devoted to Philip the Fair in his struggle against Guy of Dampierre (*see* also BLOIS, COUNTSHIP OF), and the house of Luxembourg-Ligny (1371–1482), one of the last members of which, Louis, constable of France was beheaded in 1475 on the order of Louis XI. The French kingdom thus became possessed of the county, which passed to the house of Bourbon-Vendôme, then to that of Orléans-Longueville.

See P. Feuchère, "Les Origines du Comté de St. Pol," *Revue du Nord* (Lille, 1952).   (MI. M.)

ST. POL-DE-LÉON, a town of N.W. France, in the department of Finistère, about 1 mi. from the shore of the English channel, and 13½ mi. N. of Morlaix by the railway to Roscoff. Pop. (1946) 5,812. In the 6th century a Welsh monk, Paul, became bishop of the small town of Léon, and lord of the domain in its vicinity, which passed to his successors and was increased by them. St. Pol-de-Léon is a quaint town with several old houses. The cathedral (13th and 14th centuries) is largely in the Gothic style. The west front has a projecting portico and two towers with granite spires. Within the church there are beautifully carved stalls of the 16th century, a wooden shrine containing the bell of St. Pol-de-Léon, said to cure headache and diseases of the ear, and a huge baptismal font, popularly regarded as the stone coffin of Conan Meriadec, king of the Bretons. Notre Dame du Kreizker is mainly late 14th century. Fishing is carried on.

ST. PÖLTEN, an old town and bishopric in Lower Austria, annexed by Germany in 1938, on the left bank of the Traisen.

Inhabited since the Roman period, the modern town grew up around an abbey founded there in the 9th century and dedicated to St. Hippolytus, whose name in corrupted form was adopted for the town. St. Pölten is an important railway junction and has a considerable development of industries, notably cotton-spinning and the manufacture of iron and hardware. In addition, several religious institutions have grown up around the old abbey church. Pop. (1934), 36,619; (1939) 45,037.

SAINT PRIEST, EMMANUEL LOUIS MARIE GUIGNARD, VICOMTE DE (1789–1881), French politician, third son of the following, took part in the invasion of France in 1814. At the Restoration he was in the service of the duke of Angoulême, and during the Hundred Days tried to raise Dauphiné in the royal cause. He served in Spain in 1823, and after two years at Berlin became French ambassador at Madrid, where he negotiated in 1828 the settlement of the Spanish debt. After the July revolution Frederick VII. made him a grandee of Spain with the title of duke of Almazan. He arranged the escapade of the duchess of Berry in Provence in 1832, and was imprisoned for 10 months. He arranged an asylum in Austria for the duchess, and returned to Paris, where he was a leader of legitimist society until his death at Saint Priest, near Lyon on Feb. 26, 1881.

SAINT PRIEST, FRANÇOIS EMMANUEL GUIGNARD, CHEVALIER, then COMTE DE (1735–1821), French statesman, was born at Grenoble on March 12, 1735. He entered the army at the age of fifteen, leaving it in 1763 with the grade of colonel. After four years as representative of the court of France at Lisbon, he went to Constantinople, where he remained, with a short interval, until 1785, and married Wilhelmina von Ludolf, daughter of the Neapolitan ambassador. After a few months at the Hague, he joined Necker's ministry as minister without portfolio, and in Necker's second cabinet held office as minister of the interior until Dec. 1790. In 1795 he joined the comte de Provence at Verona as minister of the household. He followed the exiled court to Blankenburg and Mittau, retiring in 1808 to Switzerland.

He wrote *Mémoires sur l'ambassade de France en Turquie et le commerce des français dans le Levant* (ed. C. Schefer, 1877); and *Examen des assemblées provinciales* (1787).

ST. PRIVAT, a village of Lorraine, 7 mi. N.W. of Metz. The village and the slopes to the west played a great part in the battle of Gravelotte (Aug. 18, 1870). (*See* METZ and FRANCO-GERMAN WAR.)

At St. Privat occurred the famous repulse of the Prussian Guard by Marshal Canrobert's corps.

ST. QUENTIN, a manufacturing town of northern France, capital of an arrondissement in the department of Aisne, 32 mi. N.N.W. of Laon by rail. Pop. (1946) 48,556. St. Quentin (anc. *Augusta Veromanduorum*) stood at the meeting-place of five military roads. In the 3rd century it was the scene of the martyrdom of Gaius Quintinus. The date of the foundation of the bishopric is uncertain, but about 532 it was transferred to Noyon. Towards the middle of the 7th century St. Eloi (Eligius), bishop of Noyon, established a collegiate chapter at St. Quentin's tomb, which became a famous place of pilgrimage. The importance of the town was increased during the middle ages by the rise of its cloth manufacture. The town was surrounded by walls in 883. It became under Pippin, grandson of Charlemagne, one of the principal domains of the counts of Vermandois, and in 1080 received from Count Herbert IV a charter which was extended in 1103. From 1420 to 1471 St. Quentin was occupied by the Burgundians. In 1557 it was taken by the Spaniards (*see* below). Two years later the town was restored to the French, and in 1560 it was assigned as the dowry of Mary Stuart. During the Franco-Prussian War St. Quentin repulsed the German attacks of Oct. 8, 1870; and in January 1871 it was the centre of the great battle fought by General Faidherbe. In World War I St. Quentin was held by the Germans from the end of Aug. 1914 to Oct. 1, 1918.

The town stands on the right bank of the Somme, at its junction with the St. Quentin canal (which unites the Somme with the Scheldt) and the Crozat canal (which unites it with the Oise). The collegiate church of St. Quentin, a fine Gothic building of the 12th, 13th, 14th and 15th centuries, damaged during World War I, was reopened in 1920. It has no west façade but terminates at that end in a tower and portal of Romanesque architecture; it has double transepts. The choir (13th century) has remains of a choir screen of the 14th century. Under the choir is a crypt of the 11th century, containing the tombs of St. Quentin (Quintin) and his fellow-martyrs Victoricus and Gentianus. The hôtel-de-ville of St. Quentin (only slightly damaged) is a Gothic building of the 14th, 15th and 16th centuries, with a flamboyant façade, adorned with curious sculptures. St. Quentin is the seat of a sub-prefect, of a tribunal of commerce, of a board of trade-arbitrators, and a chamber of commerce. The town has recovered its industrial activity and is the centre of a district which manufactures cotton and woollen fabrics. St. Quentin produces chiefly window-curtains and carries on the spinning and preliminary processes and the bleaching and finishing. Other industries are the making of embroideries by machinery and by hand, and the manufacture of iron goods, machinery and chemical products. Trade is in grain, flax, cotton and wool.

1. Battle of 1557.—An army of Spaniards under Emmanuel Philibert of Savoy, invading France from the Meuse, joined an allied contingent of English troops under the walls of St. Quentin, which was then closely besieged. Admiral Coligny threw himself into the town, and the old Constable Montmorency prepared to relieve it. On St. Lawrence's Day, Aug. 10, the relieving column reached the town without difficulty, but time was wasted in drawing off the garrison, for the pontoons intended to bridge the canal had marched at the tail of the column, and when brought up were mismanaged. The besiegers, recovering from their surprise, formed the plan of cutting off the retreat of the relieving army. Montmorency had thrown out the necessary protective posts, but at the point which the besiegers chose for their passage the post was composed of poor troops, who fled at the first shot. Thus, while the constable was busy with his boats, the Spanish army filed across the Bridge of Rouvroy, some distance above the town, with impunity, and Montmorency, in the hope of executing his mission without fighting, refused to allow the cavalry under the duc de Nevers to charge them, and miscalculated his time of freedom. The Spaniards, enormously superior in force, cut off and destroyed the French gendarmerie who formed the vanguard of the column, and then headed off the slow-moving infantry south of Essigny-le-

Grand. Around the 10,000 French gathered some 40,000 assailants with forty-two guns. The cannon thinned their ranks, and at last the cavalry broke in and slaughtered them. Yet Coligny gallantly held St. Quentin for seventeen days longer, Nevers rallied the remnant of the army and, garrisoning Péronne, Ham and other strong places, entrenched himself in front of Compiègne, and the allies, disheartened by a war of sieges and skirmishes, came to a standstill. Soon afterwards Philip, jealous of the renown of his generals and unwilling to waste his highly trained soldados in ineffective fighting, ordered the army to retreat (Oct. 17), disbanded the temporary regiments and dispersed the permanent corps in winter quarters.

2. **The Battle of 1871.**—This was fought between the German I. Army under General von Goeben and the French commanded by General Faidherbe. The latter concentrated about St. Quentin on Jan. 18, and took up a defensive position on both sides of the Somme Canal. The Germans, though inferior in numbers, were greatly superior in discipline and training, and Goeben boldly decided to attack both wings of the French together on the 19th. The attack took the customary enveloping form. After several hours' fighting it was brought to a standstill, but Goeben, using his reserves in masterly fashion, drove a wedge into the centre of the French line between the canal and the railway, and followed this up with another blow on the other bank of the canal, along the Ham road. This was the signal for a decisive attack by the whole of the left wing of the Germans, but the French offered strenuous resistance, and it was not until four o'clock that Faidherbe made up his mind to retreat. By skilful dispositions and orderly movement most of his infantry and all but six of his guns were brought off safely, but a portion of the army was cut off by the victorious left wing of the Germans, and the defeat, the last act in a long-drawn-out struggle, was sufficiently decisive to deny to the defenders any hope of taking the field again without an interval of rest and reorganization. Ten days later the general armistice was signed. (*See* further FRANCO-GERMAN WAR.)

ST. QUENTIN, BATTLE OF, 1918. This is the name commonly given to the first phase of the great offensive of the Germans in 1918, by which they hoped to gain a military decision before the inflow of American reinforcements, the exhaustion of their food supplies under the stranglehold of the British Navy, and the obvious weakening of their allies could definitely turn the scales against them. The strategic conditions under which the offensive of March 21, 1918, was launched on the front north and south of St. Quentin are recounted under WORLD WAR I, and succeeding phases in LYS, BATTLE OF THE; CHEMIN DES DAMES, BATTLE OF THE, 1918; and MARNE, SECOND BATTLE OF THE.

At 4.30 A.M. on March 21, 1918, the sudden crash of some 6,000 German guns heralded the breaking of a storm which, in grandeur of scale, of awe and of destruction, surpassed any other in World War I. By nightfall a German flood had inundated forty miles of the British front; a week later it had reached a depth of nearly forty miles, and was almost lapping the outskirts of Amiens, and in the ensuing weeks the Allied cause itself was almost submerged. These weeks rank with that of the Marne in 1914 as the two gravest crises of World War I. In them Germany came desperately near to regaining that lost chance, and best chance, of victory, which she had forfeited in early September, 1914. Why, when the Allies had made so little visible impression on the German front in two years of constant offensive, were the Germans able to tear a huge hole in the Allied front within a few days? Why, as this breach so far exceeded in size the dream-aims of its Allied forerunners, did it fail to obtain any decisive results? In seeking the answer to these "whys" lies the prime historical interest of the battle of St. Quentin, 1918.

The Opposing Forces.—Between Nov. 1, 1917 and March 21, 1918, the German divisions on the western front were increased from 146 to 192, troops being withdrawn from Russia, Galicia, Italy and the East. By these means the German armies in the West were reinforced by no less than 18,492 officers and 553,794 other ranks. Finally it was decided to make available 62 divisions for the main attack. These troops were systematically trained in new tactics of mobile warfare behind the front, while

every effort was made to conceal the actual area of attack, which extended from near Lens in the north to a little south of La Fère.

The opposing line on this front was held, except for a few miles in the north, by the III. (Byng) and V. (Gough) British Armies respectively. The front of the III. Army extended from just south of the village of Gavrelle to half a mile north of Gouzeaucourt (26½ m.), and on March 21 was held by 10 divi-

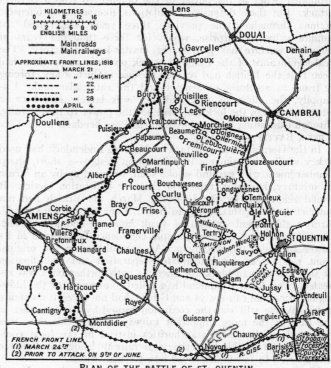

PLAN OF THE BATTLE OF ST. QUENTIN

sions in line and seven in reserve. The V. Army front (42 m.), extended on a recent relief of the French (*see* WORLD WAR I), ran from the right of the III. Army to the village of Barisis, a little south of the river Oise, between the forests of Coucy and St. Gobain. On this extended front there were 11 divisions in line and three in reserve.

German Plan.—The attack was to be carried out by four armies:— (a) XVII. Army (Below), comprising 17 divisions, was to attack on the frontage Gavrelle-Moeuvres. (b) II. Army (Marwitz), comprising 18 divisions, was to attack from Moeuvres to Pontru (north of St. Quentin). (c) XVIII. Army (Hutier), comprising 24 divisions was to attack from Pontru to Vendeuil (south of St. Quentin). (d) VII. Army (Gayl) was to demonstrate with three divisions against La Fère.

The motive of this plan, devised by Ludendorff, now the directing brain of the German war-machine, was that the main strength of the German effort should be exerted north of the Somme—with the aim of driving the British Army back towards the coast and of cutting it off from the French—while the Somme and the XVIII. Army guarded the Germans' southern flank. This plan was radically changed in execution because Ludendorff gained rapid success where he desired it little and failed to gain success where he wanted it most.

To mystify the enemy as to the frontage selected for the main attack, subsidiary operations were prepared all along the Allied front, in Flanders, Champagne and the Argonne. From March 14 onwards the crown prince's army group was to bombard the enemy's headquarters on his front and make a show of bringing up reinforcements, and Gallwitz's army group was to carry out an attack on Verdun up to the point of engaging his infantry. The forming up for deployment of the attacking armies was begun on March 10, the divisions being organized in groups normally in a depth of three lines. The first or assault line was made the strongest, and was moved close up to the front on March 20. The second line of divisions was some three to five km. in rear, and the third seven to ten km. behind the second line; the third line was to be held in reserve under the higher command, and was only to be used as the operations developed.

The Prelude.—On the British side, while the seriousness of the menace was appreciated, there was an apparently well-grounded belief in the power of the defence to stop a German attack. But these defensive calculations, like so many offensive actions throughout the previous three years, underrated the infinite value of surprise, which for three thousand years of recorded warfare has proved the master-key to victory. The real significance of the Cambrai attack on Nov. 20 previous had been that the British had revived the use of such a key, forging it from an amalgam of armour and the caterpillar tank. Unhappily, the effect of this tank key was largely lost because when inserted in the lock they had not the power to turn it fully, through exhausting their strength in the Passchendaele mud. (*See* YPRES, BATTLES OF, 1917.)

In the German counter-attack of Nov. 30 Ludendorff had used a key similar in principle if different in design—a short, sharp bombardment with gas and smoke shell, followed up by an inrush of infantry, specially trained in the new infiltration tactics. It would seem that by the following March the British had not sufficiently taken this lesson to heart. For, just as were the V. Army's subsequent excuses of weak numbers and a long line, the command had expressed ample confidence beforehand in its power to resist the onslaught. As a result, when the original front was forced, an inadequate preparation and co-ordination of the measures to block the enemy's path further back was revealed. The Army Command had failed to arrange for the blowing up of certain causeways and G.H.Q. had not given it a definite order. Worse still was the confusion caused by the fact that in the case of the more important railway bridges, this duty was entrusted to the railway authorities instead of the local commanders, and in this way the vital railway bridge at Peronne was allowed to fall undestroyed into German hands.

If this was good luck for the Germans, their thorough and skilful preparations for the initial assault had earned them success—although here again fortune favoured them. Ludendorff's solution for breaking the deadlock was a compound of wider frontages of attack, new infantry tactics, and, above all, for surprise, a lavish use of gas in a brief but intense artillery bombardment. For it, masses of artillery were brought up close to the front line in concealment, and against the V. Army front opened fire without preliminary ranging. This was to be followed by the infiltration of many dispersed little groups of automatic rifles and machine-guns. But the effect of the gas-gained surprise was immensely increased by nature, which in the early hours of March 21 provided a thick mist, which cloaked the infiltrating assailants as much as it masked the defending machine-guns. Without this aid it is questionable how far the German tactical surprise would have succeeded, and in this lay the essential inferiority of the German method of surprise, which still depended on unarmoured infantry, compared with the British surprise at Cambrai, and later, on Aug. 8, 1918, which was achieved by armoured machines.

The Attack, March 21.—While the bombardment, with a lavish mixture of gas and smoke shell, opened at 4.30 A.M. the German infantry attack did not begin until 9.40 A.M., when a general move forward was made under the cover of a creeping barrage, supplemented by low-flying aircraft. The British outpost zone was overrun almost everywhere by midday, but this was inevitable, and had been foreseen. But the northern attack met such stubborn resistance against the right of Byng's III. Army that it had not seriously penetrated the main battle zone even by the night of the 22nd, and, despite putting in successive reinforcements, the capture of Vaulx-Vraucourt was then the high-water mark of its progress. On most parts of Gough's V. Army front the battle-zone resistance was just as firm, but the flood found a way through on the 21st near La Fère, on the extreme right, at Essigny and Ronssoy. The resistance of the

21st Division at Epéhy for a time checked this last breach from spreading northward, but it began to crumble so deeply that the neighbouring sectors were affected. Southward, near St. Quentin, the line sagged still more deeply, and on the night of the 22nd Gough felt compelled to order a general retirement to the line of the Somme.

On the 23rd Ludendorff gave the XVIII. Army, his left or southern wing, a limited permission to exploit this opportunity along the line of least resistance. But for several days he still pinned his faith and reserve strength to his right wing, despite the relatively small progress of his XVII. Army in the north and by the enforced postponement of its intended supplementary attack towards Arras, where Byng had anticipated the blow by a partial withdrawal. When the postponed blow was attempted on the 28th it collapsed under a storm of fire from the expectant defence. No fog came to the German aid. At last Ludendorff threw his weight into the push along the Somme westward, although he still held his left wing in a tight rein. But by that time the new surge towards Amiens was almost as stagnant, its impetus slackening far less because of the resistance than because of the exhaustion of the German troops and the difficulty of supply in so rapid and deep an advance. This was accentuated because their route had taken them across the desert formed by the old battlefields of 1916. On March 30 and April 4 they made fresh attempts, but the effect was and could only be local. For the resistance in the south had been given time, and relief from pressure, to harden into a crust which the belated intervention of fresh German reserves could not break.

On April 4 the great battle to all intents and purposes came to an end. The initial success had been great; since March 21 from a base of 74 m. a penetration of no less than 38 m. had been effected; the ground lost in 1916 and abandoned in 1917 had been more than made good, and vast quantities of stores as well as 90,000 prisoners and 1,200 guns had been captured. The British Armies had been seriously defeated, and 20 French divisions had been drawn into the battle; yet, in spite of the fact that 90 German divisions had been engaged, neither the transition to a war of movement nor the separation of the British and French forces had been achieved.

Conclusion.—The supreme features of this great offensive are, first, the immensity of its outward results compared with any previous offensive in the west; second, its ineffectiveness to attain decisive results. For the first it would be both unjust and untrue to blame the defending troops. They achieved miracles of heroic endurance, and the prolonged resistance in most of the battle zone is the proof. The real cause of the subsequently rapid flowback lay in the frequent breakdown of control and communication. During three years of trench warfare the British had built up an elaborate and complex system, largely dependent on the telephone, and when the static suddenly became fluid they paid the inevitable penalty of violating those fundamental axioms of war—simplicity and flexibility.

On the German side, Arras was the actual rock on which their plan broke, and by which their advance was diverted into less profitable channels. It is possible that military conservatism cost them dear. For Colonel Bruchmüller, the famous artillery battle-piece "producer," brought from the eastern front for this offensive, has revealed that while Hutier's army carried out his surprise bombardment designs, Below's in the north clung to their old-fashioned methods, refusing to dispense with preliminary ranging. But if Hutier scored at the outset, his onrush slackened as his supplies and reinforcements failed with the distance covered, and when due tribute has been paid to the sturdy resistance, the German advance is seen really to have beaten itself.

(B. H. L. H.)

ST. RÉMY (-DE-PROVENCE), a town of southeastern France in the department of Bouches-du-Rhône, 15 mi. N.E. of Arles by road. Pop. (1936) 3,625. It lies to the north of the range of hills named the Alpines or Alpilles in a valley of olive trees. The church has a 14th-century spire. About a mile to the south are Gallo-Roman relics of the ancient Glanum, destroyed about 480, including a triumphal arch and a fine three-storied mausoleum. Near by is the old priory of St. Paul-de-Mausole with a Romanesque church and cloister.

ST. RIQUIER, a town of northern France, in the department of Somme, 8 mi. N.E. of Abbeville by rail. Pop. (1936) 1,313. St. Riquier (originally *Centula*) was famous for its abbey, founded about 625 by Riquier (*Richarnis*), son of the governor of the town. It was enriched by King Dagobert and prospered under the abbacy of Angilbert, son-in-law of Charlemagne. The fine Flamboyant church of the 15th and 16th centuries has a richly sculptured west front. The treasury, among other valuable relics, possesses a copper cross said to be the work of St. Eloi (Eligius). In 1544 the town was burned by the English, an event which marks the beginning of its decline.

SAINTS, BATTLE OF THE. This battle was fought between the fleets of England and France in the channel between the islands of Dominica and Guadeloupe on April 12, 1782. It takes its name from the Saints Is. in the channel. The French had 35 battleships under the Comte de Grasse based on Martinique, and their object was to give the British fleet the slip, and capture Jamaica. The British fleet of 36 ships was based on St. Lucia and was under Rodney.

The British Admiral kept close watch on the French movements. When, therefore, on April 8, the signal came that the French were out, the British were immediately after them on a northerly course. At dawn on April 9 the British van, under Hood, was close to de Grasse, who was forced to order his store-ships to make for Guadeloupe, sending two of his battleships to protect them. Hood was soon in action with the French rear, and his position was awkward in that he only, of the English, had made the Saints passage, the centre and rear being becalmed under the lee of Dominica. De Grasse was thus in a position to attack him with all his force, but he merely cannonaded his enemy from a distance. The British van suffered enough to make it necessary subsequently for it to change places with the rear, under Drake, but the arrival of Rodney caused de Grasse to withdraw, and the French battleship *Cato* was put out of action.

During the ensuing night and day the French gained somewhat and seemed likely to get clear away, but on the night of the 10th two battleships, the *Jason* and the *Zélé*, collided and the former was so seriously injured that de Grasse had to part with her. It would have been better for him had he dispensed with the *Zélé* also, for on the 11th she fell far behind the rest of the fleet, and it became clear that she would fall a victim to the British unless de Grasse turned to help her. This he did; and thus a general action was joined on April 12, the French by then having only 30 effective ships. The two fleets approached one another on opposite courses with the wind from the east; the British were sailing roughly north and the French south, the latter being the nearer to the wind. The fight began early, and by 10 o'clock the moment for the British to get on the same course as the French had arrived.

Rodney, however, never issued orders to this effect for, at this juncture, the wind shifted four points to the south. This meant that gaps appeared in the French line, and, more important, the English could turn to starboard and sail through them. Rodney and his flag-captain, Sir Charles Douglas, both grasped the possibilities of the situation, and the former decided to risk it. There were no signals for the movement so, relying on the force of example, Rodney took his flagship, the *Formidable*, stationed in the centre, through a convenient gap in the rear of the French centre. He was followed by the five ships immediately astern, all raking the French as they passed. A similar movement took place in the rear. Captain Affleck, in the *Bedford*, passing through the head of the same French squadron, was followed by Hood with the entire British rear. The French were thus broken into three bodies, de Grasse, in the *Ville de Paris*, with other ships of the centre being isolated between the two points of intersection, and, after a gallant defence, captured.

Rodney's officers blamed him for not putting up a more energetic pursuit, but he preferred to make sure of cutting the enemy off from their base. Actually the bad morale of the French, and the complete scattering of their fleet, rendered either alternative nugatory.

BIBLIOGRAPHY.—G. B. Mundy, *Life of Rodney* (1830); D. Hannay, *Letters of Hood* (1895); J. K. Laughton, *Letters of Lord Barham*, vol. i. & ii. (1907–10); Geoffrey Callender, *Sea Kings of Britain* (1917); W. M. James, *"The British Navy in Adversity"* (1926).

(G. A. R. C.; J. G. B.)

SAINT-SAËNS, CHARLES CAMILLE (1835–1921), French composer, was born in Paris on Oct. 3, 1835. For a short time he studied composition under Halévy, and in 1852, and again in 1864, competed without success for the Grand Prix de Rome. In 1853, when only eighteen, he was appointed organist at the Church of St. Merry, and from 1861 to 1877 was organist at the Madeleine, in succession to Lefébure-Wély. In 1867 his cantata "Les Noces de Prométhée" won a prize at the International Exhibition of that year but his first operas *La Princesse jaune* (1872) and *Le Timbre d'argent* (1877) had no great success. It was with his brilliantly effective "symphonic poems" *Le Rouet d'Omphale*, *La Danse Macabre*, *Phaéton* and *La Jeunesse d'Hercule* that he first attracted general attention as a composer, though his powers as a pianist had been recognised from the first. His success as a dramatic composer was however not long delayed.

Through the influence of Liszt, his Biblical opera *Samson et Dalila* was brought out at Weimar in 1877 when its merits were immediately recognised, though it was not until 1890 that it was first heard in France, namely at Rouen. This work, generally accepted as his operatic masterpiece, had been begun as far back as 1869, and an act had been heard at one of Colonne's concerts in 1875. The following year it was given in Paris at the Eden Theatre, and finally in 1892 it was produced at the Grand Opera, where it has remained ever since, one of the most attractive works of the *répertoire*. Its Biblical subject prevented its performance in London until 1909, when it was given at Covent Garden with great success. None of his works is better calculated to exemplify the dual tendencies of his style. The first act, with its somewhat formal choruses, suggests the influence of Bach and Handel, and is treated rather in the manner of an oratorio. The more dramatic portions of the opera are not uninfluenced by Meyerbeer, while in the Dalila music there are occasional suggestions of Gounod. But though Saint-Saëns was an eclectic he put the stamp of his own individuality on every scene of the opera.

After the production of *Samson et Dalila* Saint-Saëns stood at the parting of the ways and compromised to some extent between the traditional style of the French school and the newer Wagnerian methods. As the result none of his later operas—*Etienne Marcel* (Lyons, 1879), *Henry VIII.* (Grand Opéra, 1883), *Proserpine* (Opéra-Comique, 1887), *Ascanio* (Grand Opéra, 1890), *Phryné* (Opéra-Comique, 1893), *Las Barbares* (Grand Opéra, 1901) achieved anything like the success of *Samson et Dalila*. But Saint-Saëns by no means confined his attentions to the stage, his compositions including examples in almost every department of the art. Among these may be mentioned the oratorios and cantatas *Oratorio de Noël*, *Les Noces de Prométhée*, *Le Déluge*, *La Lyre et la Harpe*; three symphonies; the four symphonic poems previously named; five pianoforte concertos; three violin concertos; the ballet *Zavotte*; many chamber works; a Mass and a Requiem, besides a quantity of piano and organ music, and many songs. His literary works in turn include *Harmonie et mélodie*, *Portraits et souvenirs*, and *Problèmes et mystères*, besides a volume of poems, *Rimes familières*. He died in Algiers on Dec. 16, 1921.

SAINTSBURY, GEORGE EDWARD BATEMAN (1845–1933), English man of letters, was born at Southampton on Oct. 23, 1845. He was educated at King's college school, London, and at Merton college, Oxford (B.A. 1868), and spent six years in Guernsey as senior classical master of Elizabeth college (1868–74). From 1874 to 1876 he was headmaster of the Elgin educational institute. He began his literary career in 1875 as a critic for the *Academy*, and for ten years was actively engaged in journalism, becoming an important member of the staff of the *Saturday Review*. From 1895 to 1915 he was professor of rhetoric and English literature at Edinburgh university. Saintsbury's work bears the mark of his vast range of reading. Among the most important of his many works are his *Short History of French Literature* (1882; 6th ed., Oxford, 1901); *A Short History of*

English Literature (1898; 3rd ed., 1903); an edition of the *Minor Caroline Poets* (3 vols., 1905–21); *A History of Criticism* (3 vols., 1900–04); *A History of English Prosody* (3 vols., 1906–21); *The History of English Criticism* (1911); and *A History of the French Novel* (1917–19).

ST. SERVAN, a town of western France, in the department of Ille-et-Vilaine, on right bank of the Rance, south of St. Malo, from which it is separated by the Anse des Sablons, a creek 1 mi. wide. Pop. (1936) 10,986. The "Cité" occupies the site of the city of Aleth, which at the close of the Roman empire supplanted Corseul as the capital of the Curiosolites. Aleth was not Christianized till the 6th century, when St. Malo became its first bishop. At the Revolution St. Servan became a separate commune from St. Malo. North of the town is a wet dock, forming part of the harbour of St. Malo. The dock is used chiefly by coasting and fishing vessels, a fleet starting annually for the Newfoundland codfisheries.

SAINT-SIMON, CLAUDE HENRI DE ROUVROY, COMTE DE (1760–1825), French socialist, was born in Paris on Oct. 17, 1760. He fought in the War of American Independence, was imprisoned in the Luxembourg during the Terror, and, on his release, amassed a small fortune by land speculation. He was also the originator of schemes to unite the Atlantic and Pacific by a canal, and to construct a waterway from Madrid to the sea. He continued his experiments throughout his life with the result that he was completely impoverished, and for some years before his death he was obliged to work nine hours a day to earn £40 a year. In 1823 he attempted suicide. He died two years later, on May 19, at Paris. Although a prolific writer his work attracted little attention while he lived and it was only after his death that his influence became considerable.

As a thinker Saint-Simon was deficient in system, clearness and consecutive strength; but his influence on modern thought is undeniable, both as the historic founder of French socialism and as suggesting much of what was afterwards elaborated into Comtism. Apart from the details of his socialistic teaching, his main ideas are simple, and are at once a reaction against the French Revolution and the militarism of Napoleon. So far was he from advocating fresh social revolt that he appealed to Louis XVIII. to inaugurate the new order of things. In opposition, however, to the feudal and military system, he advocated an arrangement by which the industrial chiefs should control society. In place of the mediaeval church the spiritual direction of society should fall to the men of science. What Saint-Simon desired, therefore, was an industrialist state directed by modern science in which universal association should suppress war, and society should be organized for productive labour by the most capable men. The social aim is to produce things useful to life.

Although the contrast between labour and capital is not emphasised by Saint-Simon, the cause of the poor is discussed, and in his greatest work, *The New Christianity,* it takes the form of a religion. It was this development of his teaching that occasioned his final quarrel with Comte. Previous to the publication of the *Nouveau Christianisme,* Saint-Simon had not concerned himself with theology; but here, beginning with a belief in God he endeavours to resolve Christianity into its essential elements and finally propounds this precept—"The whole of society ought to strive towards the amelioration of the moral and physical existence of the poorest class; society ought to organize itself in the way best adapted for attaining this end." This principle became the watchword of the entire school of Saint-Simon.

Of the disciples who propagated his doctrines the most important were Olinde Rodrigues, and Barthélemy Prosper Enfantin (*q.v.*), who together had received Saint-Simon's last instructions. Their first step was to establish a journal, *Le Producteur,* but it was discontinued in 1826. The sect, however, had begun to grow, and before the end of 1828, had meetings not only in Paris but in many provincial towns. An important departure was made in 1828 by Amand Bazard, who gave a "complete exposition of the Saint-Simonian faith" in a long course of lectures at Paris, which were well attended. His *Exposition de la doctrine de St. Simon* (2 vols., 1828–1830), which is by far the best account of it, won

more adherents. The second volume was chiefly by Enfantin, who along with Bazard stood at the head of the society, but who was superior in metaphysical power, and was prone to push his deductions to extremities. The revolution of July (1830) brought a new freedom to the socialist reformers. A proclamation was issued demanding the community of goods, the abolition of the right of inheritance, and the enfranchisement of women. Early next year the school obtained possession of the *Globe* through Pierre Leroux (*q.v.*), who had joined the school, which now numbered some of the ablest and most promising young men of France.

The members formed themselves into an association arranged in three grades, and constituting a society or family, which lived out of a common purse in the Rue Monsigny. Before long, however, the sect was split by dissensions between Bazard, a man of logical and solid temperament, and Enfantin, who desired to establish a fantastic sacerdotalism with lax notions as to the relation of the sexes. After a time Bazard seceded, together with many of the strongest supporters of the school. A series of extravagant entertainments given by the society during the winter of 1832 reduced its financial resources and discredited it in character. They finally removed to Ménilmontant, to a property of Enfantin, where they lived in a communistic society, distinguished by a peculiar dress. Shortly after the chiefs were tried and condemned for proceedings prejudicial to the social order; and the sect was broken up (1832).

Saint-Simonism.—In the doctrine of the followers of Saint-Simon we find a great advance on the confused views of the master. In the philosophy of history they recognize epochs of two kinds, the critical or negative and the organic or constructive. The former, in which philosophy is the dominating force, is characterized by war, egotism and anarchy; the latter, which is controlled by religion, is marked by the spirit of obedience, devotion and association. The two spirits of antagonism and association are the social principles whose prevalence determines the character of an epoch. The spirit of association, which tends more and more to prevail over its opponent, is to be the keynote of the social development of the future. Under the present system the industrial chief exploits the proletariat, the members of which, though nominally free, must accept his terms under pain of starvation. The only remedy for this is the abolition of the law of inheritance, and the union of all the instruments of labour in a social fund, which shall be exploited by association. Society thus becomes sole proprietor, intrusting to social groups and social functionaries the management of the various properties. The right of succession is transferred from the family to the state.

The school of Saint-Simon insists strongly on the claims of merit; they advocate a social hierarchy in which each man shall be placed according to his capacity and rewarded according to his works. This is, indeed, a most special and pronounced feature of the Saint-Simon socialism, whose theory of government is a kind of spiritual or scientific autocracy, degenerating into the fantastic sacerdotalism of Enfantin. With regard to the family and the relation of the sexes the school of Saint-Simon advocated the complete emancipation of woman and her entire equality with man. The "social individual" is man and woman, who are associated in the exercise of the triple function of religion, the state and the family. In its official declarations the school maintained the sanctity of the Christian law of marriage. Connected with these doctrines was their famous theory of the "rehabilitation of the flesh," deduced from the philosophic theory of the school, which was a species of Pantheism, though they repudiated the name. On this theory they rejected the dualism so much emphasized by Catholic Christianity in its penances and mortifications, and held that the body should be restored to its due place of honour.

An excellent edition of the works of Saint-Simon and Enfantin was published by the survivors of the sect (47 vols., Paris, 1865–78). Of his other works the most important are, *Lettres d'un habitant de Genève* (1802); *Du Système Industriel* (1821); *Catéchisme des Industriels* (1823–24); *Nouveau Christianisme* (1825). *See also* Georges Weill, *Un Précurseur du socialisme, Saint-Simon et son oeuvre* (Paris, 1894), and a history of the *École Saint-Simonienne,* by the same author

(1896); G. Dumas, *Psychologie de deux messies positivistes St. Simon et Comte* (1905); G. Brunet, *Mysticisme social de Saint-Simon* (1925); E. N. Butler, *The St-Simonian Religion in Germany* (1926); and M. Leroy, *Vie véritable de Saint-Simon* (1925).

SAINT-SIMON, LOUIS DE ROUVROY, Duc de (1675-1755), French soldier, diplomatist and writer of memoirs, was born at Versailles on Jan. 16, 1675. The peerage granted to his father, Claude de St. Simon, is the central fact in his history. The boy had for godfather and godmother Louis XIV. and the queen. After some tuition by the Jesuits (especially by Sanadon, the editor of Horace), he joined the *mousquetaires gris* in 1692. He was present at the siege of Namur, and the battle of Neerwinden. At this time he chose to begin the crusade of his life by instigating, if not bringing, an action on the part of the peers of France against Luxembourg, his victorious general, on a point of precedence. He fought, however, another campaign or two (not under Luxembourg), and in 1695 married Gabrielle de Durfort, daughter of the maréchal de Lorges, under whom he latterly served. He seems to have regarded her with respect and affection; and she sometimes succeeded in modifying his aristocratic ideas. But as he did not receive the promotion he desired he flung up his commission in 1702. Louis took a dislike to him, and it was with difficulty that he was able to keep a footing at court. He was, however, intensely interested in all the transactions of Versailles, and by dint of a most heterogeneous collection of instruments, ranging from dukes to servants, he managed to obtain the extraordinary secret information which he has handed down.

His own part appears to have been entirely subordinate. He was appointed ambassador to Rome in 1705, but the appointment was cancelled before he started. At last he attached himself to the duke of Orleans and, though this was hardly likely to conciliate Louis's goodwill to him, it gave him at least the status of belonging to a definite party, and it eventually placed him in the position of tried friend to the acting chief of the state. He was able, moreover, to combine attachment to the duke of Burgundy with that to the duke of Orleans. Both attachments were no doubt all the more sincere because of his undying hatred to "the bastards," that is to say, the illegitimate sons of Louis XIV. It does not appear that this hatred was founded on moral reasons or on any real fear that these bastards would be intruded into the succession. The true cause of his wrath was that they had precedence of the peers.

The death of Louis seemed to give Saint-Simon a chance of realizing his hopes. The duke of Orleans was at once acknowledged regent, and Saint-Simon was of the council of regency. But he had little real influence with the regent. In 1721 he was appointed ambassador to Spain to arrange for the marriage (not destined to take place) of Louis XV. and the infanta. His own account of the cessation of his intimacy with Orleans and Dubois, the latter of whom had never been his friend, is, like his own account of some other events of his life, obscure. But there can be little doubt that he was practically ousted by the favourite. He survived for more than thirty years; but little is known of his life. His wife died in 1743, his eldest son a little later; he had other family troubles, and he was loaded with debt. When he died, at Paris on March 2, 1755, he had almost entirely outlived his own generation, and the prosperity of his house.

Saint-Simon was an indefatigable writer, and he began very early to set down in black and white all the gossip he collected, all his interminable legal disputes of precedence, and a vast mass of unclassified and almost unclassifiable matter. Most of his manuscripts came into the possession of the government, and it was long before their contents were published in anything like fulness. Saint-Simon, though careless and sometimes even ungrammatical, ranks among the most striking memoir-writers of France, the country richest in memoirs of any in the world. He has been compared to Tacitus, and for once the comparison is just. In the midst of his enormous mass of writing, phrases scarcely inferior to the Roman's occur frequently, and here and there are passages of sustained description equal, for intense concentration of light and life, to those of Tacitus or of any other historian. As may be expected from the vast extent of his work, it is in the highest degree unequal. But he is at the same time not a writer who can be "sampled" easily, inasmuch as his most characteristic phrases sometimes occur in the midst of long stretches of quite uninteresting matter. The interest of the *Memoirs,* independent of the large addition of positive knowledge which they make, is one of constant surprise at the novel and adroit use of word and phrase. Some of Macaulay's most brilliant portraits and sketches of incident are adapted and sometimes almost literally translated from Saint-Simon.

The first edition of Saint-Simon (some scattered pieces may have been printed before) appeared in 1788. It was a mere selection in three volumes and was much cut down before it was allowed to appear. Next year four more volumes made their appearance, and in 1791 a new edition, still further increased. The whole, or rather not the whole, was printed in 1829–1830 and reprinted some ten years later. The real creator of Saint-Simon, as far as a full and exact text is concerned, was M. Chéruel, whose edition in 20 volumes dates from 1856, and was reissued again revised in 1872. The standard edition is that edited by A. de Boislisle for the *Grands Ecrivains de la France* Series. For criticism on Saint-Simon there is nothing better than Sainte-Beuve's two sketches in the 3rd and 15th volumes of the *Causeries du lundi.* The latter was written to accompany M. Chéruel's first edition. In English by far the most accurate treatment is in a Lothian prize essay by E. Cannan (Oxford and London, 1885).

ST. THOMAS, a city and port of entry of Ontario, Can., capital of Elgin county, on Kettle creek, 18 mi. S. of London and 8 mi. N. of Lake Erie. Pop. (1951) 17,942. It is an important station on the Canadian National, New York Central, London & Port Stanley, Chesapeake and Ohio, Wabash, and Canadian Pacific railways. A collegiate institute and Alma Ladies' college are located there. The New York Central railway shops and car-wheel foundry, flour, flax and planing mills, shoe and knitted-goods factories are among the chief industries.

ST. THOMAS (São Tomé), a volcanic island in the Gulf of Guinea immediately north of the equator (0° 23′ N.) and in 6° 40′ E. With the island of Principe (Prince's island, *see* below), and the small territory of Sarame around the fortress of São João Batista of Ajudá, on the coast of Dahomey, it forms the Portuguese province of S. Tomé and Principe. From the Gabun, the nearest point of the mainland of Africa, St. Thomas is distant 166 m., and from Cameroon 297 m. The length of the island is 32 m., the breadth W. to E. 21 m.; the area 400 sq.m.

From the coast the land rises towards lofty mountains (St. Thomas over 7,000 ft.). Malaria is common in the lower regions, but the unhealthiness of the island is largely due to the absence of hygienic precautions and to alcoholism. Conditions are now being improved. Manufacture of brandy ceased at the end of 1929. During the dry season (June to September) the temperature ranges in the lower parts between 66.2° and 80.6° F, and in the higher parts between 57.2° and 68°; in the rainy season it ranges between 69.8° and 89.6° in the lower parts, and between 64.4° and 80.6° in the higher parts. On Coffee mount (2,265 ft.) the mean of ten years was 68.9°, the maximum 90.5° and the minimum 47.3°. The heat is tempered by the equatorial ocean current. The rainfall is very heavy save on the north coast, but has steadily decreased of recent years, simultaneously with disafforestation.

Communications.—There are 200 kilometres of good motor roads, and 500 km. of Decauville line are in use. A State railway of 19 km. runs from S. Tomé to Vila da Trindade and the Milagrosa plantation; 45 km. more are being laid. S. Tomé and Principe are connected with Europe by cable. S. Tomé has a wireless station communicating directly with Cape Verde, Angola, etc. Telephone lines link the capital with the principal settlements and plantations. Two Portuguese and one German steamship line maintain a monthly service, and other ships call frequently.

Agriculture and Trade.—The soil is extremely fertile, and three-fifths of the island is covered with forest. Among the products are oranges, lemons, figs, mangroves, and, in the lower districts, the vine, pineapple, guava and banana. The first object of cultivation was sugar, and to this the island owed its prosperity in the 16th century. Sugar has been displaced by coffee, and, principally, cocoa, introduced in 1795 and 1822 respectively. The cocoa zone lies between 650 and 2,000 ft. above the sea. Fourfifths of the total production of the island is cocoa. In 1907 the export of cocoa (including that from Principe) was over 24,000 tons, about a sixth of the world's supply. In 1912 it had risen to 35,706 tons, the Province then ranking as the second producing country in the world. 125,000 acres are under cocoa. In 1906 and 1918 plant diseases gave much trouble. These are now controlled; but labour difficulties and, especially, the severe competition of the west coast of Africa, particularly Nigeria, have caused a great diminution, production being now 15,000 tons.

Vanilla and cinchona bark both succeed well, the latter at altitudes of from 1,800 to 3,300 ft. In 1905, 125 tons of bark were exported. Production has since diminished. Rubber, cinnamon, camphor and the kola-nut are grown. Coffee, of splendid quality, reached its maximum production in 1902, when S. Tomé produced 1,769,959 kg. and Principe 247 kg. Products of the oil-palm in 1921 were 2,808,664 kg.

The chief exports in 1925, in order of their importance, were (in kilos): cocoa 20,861,000; coconut 3,338,000; coffee 171,953; and cinchona 70,807. In the same year imports (in tons) were, in order of importance: maize 2,635; rice 2,069; dried fish 1,830; and beans 1,674. In 1927 the chief exports from S. Tomé were (in kilos): cocoa, 15,767,156, valued at $76,755,155.00; and coconut, 2,997,316, valued at $4,419,045.25. From Principe: cocoa 1,000,692, value $5,355,171.53; and coconut, 395,480, value $588,476.56. Imports in 1925 (both islands) were valued at $31,195,326.00 (£1-$97.382), and exports at $68,513,874.00, a favourable balance of £383,218 ($ here means escudos, not dollars).

For 1926–27, the budget was balanced at revenue 10,213,658 escudos, and expenditure 9,173,658 escudos ordinary and 1,040,000 extraordinary. A new customs tariff protects Portuguese products, especially beer, cement (1,000 tons used annually), wines and distilled liquors.

Population.—At the last census, the inhabitants of S. Tomé were returned at 57,382, of whom 26,537 were natives, 29,894 imported labourers and 951 were classed as Europeans. The inhabitants, apart from the Europeans, consist (i.) of descendants of the original settlers, who were convicts from Portugal, slaves and others from Brazil, and negroes from the Gabun and other parts of the Guinea coast. They are known as "natives" and use a Negro-Portuguese "lingua de S. Tomé." (ii.) On the south-west coast are Angolares—some 3,000 in number—descendants of 200 Angola slaves wrecked at Sete Pedras in 1544. They retain their Bunda speech and customs, and are expert fishermen and canoemen. (iii.) Contract labourers from Cape Verde, Kabinda, etc., and Angola. These form the bulk of the population. In 1891, before the great development of the cocoa industry, the population was only 22,000. According to Aug. Chevalier (in *Occidente*, May 20, 1910), the population of St. Thomas and Principe combined in Dec. 1909 was 68,221, the "natives" being given at over 23,000.

St. Thomas, capital and chief port of the province, residence of the governor and of the Curador (the legal guardian of the serviçaes, *i.e.*, labourers), is situated on Chaves bay on the north-east coast. It is the starting point of a railway 9 m. long, which connects with the Decauville railways on the cocoa estates. Material has been acquired for the installation of a water supply; and plans are being made to supply the town and plantations with electricity produced by water power from the Contador river.

History.—St. Thomas was discovered in 1470 by the Portuguese navigators João de Santarem and Pedro de Escobar, who in the beginning of the following year discovered Annobon ("Good Year"). They found St. Thomas uninhabited. The first attempts at colonization were João de Paiva's in 1485; but nothing permanent was accomplished till 1493, when a body of criminals and of young Jews were sent to the island, and the present capital was founded by Alvaro de Carminha, in about 1500.

In the middle of the 16th century there were over 80 sugar mills on the island, which then had a population of 50,000; but in 1567 the settlement was attacked by the French, and in 1574 the Angolares began raids which only ended with their subjugation in 1693. In 1595 there was a slave revolt; and from 1641 to 1644 the Dutch, who had plundered the capital in 1600, held possession of the island. The French did great damage in 1709; the sugar trade had passed to Brazil and internal anarchy reduced St.

Thomas to a deplorable state. It was not until the later half of the 19th century that prosperity began to return.

The greatly increased demand for cocoa which arose in the last decade of the century led to the establishment of many additional plantations. Planters, however, were handicapped by the scarcity of labour. The difficulty was met by the recruitment of indentured natives from Angola, as many as 6,000 being brought over in one year. The mortality among these labourers was great, but they were well treated on the plantations. No provision was, however, made for their repatriation, while the great majority were brought by force from remote parts of central Africa and had no idea of the character of the agreement into which they were compelled to enter. The system was denounced in both Portugal and Great Britain as indistinguishable from slavery, though slavery had been abolished in Portuguese dominions in 1878. In March 1909 certain firms, British and German, as the result of investigations made in Angola and St. Thomas, refused any longer to import cocoa from St. Thomas or Principe islands unless the recruitment of labourers for the plantations was made voluntary. Representations to Portugal were made by the British government, and the Lisbon authorities stopped recruitment entirely from July 1909 to February 1910, when it was resumed under new regulations. British consular agents were stationed in Angola and St. Thomas to watch the working of these regulations. As one means of obviating the difficulties encountered in Angola the recruitment of labourers from Mozambique was begun in 1908, the men going out on a yearly contract.

The plantations are now well equipped and administered, with good houses and good labourers' quarters. There is an excellent medical service, government doctors visit all labour centres weekly, and there are special health regulations for the plantations. The labourers are well fed. In S. Tomé, mortality among negro labourers on plantations, in 1923–27, was 27·6 per 1,000, including infant mortality and accidents in work, as against a total mortality for the Province of 40 per 1,000. In 1927, 4,900 labourers, recruited in Angola, entered the colony. Many were repatriated to Angola, Mozambique and Cape Verde, after finishing their contracts. The number of labourers at the end of the year was 3,000 more than at the beginning. Recruiting is from Angola, Cape Verde and Mozambique. Labourers are contracted in their country of origin, in the presence of the authorities, for two or three years. On termination of their contracts, they are repatriated, unless they wish to re-engage. They are fed, lodged and clothed by the employers. Generally half of their earnings is treated as deferred pay, and paid on their return home, in the country of origin. Fulfilment of contracts is supervised by a State department, with a branch in Principe.

BIBLIOGRAPHY.—B. S. G. Lisboa, *S. Thomé* (1908); W. A. Cadbury, *Labour in Portuguese West Africa* (2nd ed., London, 1910); *A ilha de S. Thomé* (Lisbon, 1907); *The Boa Entrada Plantations* (Edinburgh, 1907); and British Consular Reports. See also A. Negreiros, *Historia ethnographica da Ilha de S. Thomé* (Lisbon, 1895) and *Île de San Thomé* (Paris, 1901); C. Gravier "Mission scientifique à l'île de San Thomé" *Nouv. Arch. Miss. Scient. t. xv.* (Paris, 1907); A. Pinto de Miranda Guedes, "Viação em S. Thomé," *B. S. G. Lisboa* (1902); also *Boletim da Agencia Geral das Colonias* (Lisbon, monthly); and *Monografia das Colonias Portuguezas* (Agencia Geral das Colonias, Lisbon). (H. Bp.)

ST. THOMAS, an island in the West Indies and the most important, commercially, of the Virgin island group purchased by the United States from Denmark in 1917. Charlotte Amalie, the principal port and harbour of the Virgin islands, is situated near the middle of the southern coast of the island.

St. Thomas lies in 18° 20′ N. and 64° 55′ W., 40 mi. east of Puerto Rico, 1,442 mi. south, 20° E. from New York city and 1,020 mi. from the Panama canal. It is 12 mi. long, varies in width from 1 mi. to 3 mi. and has an area of 32 sq.mi., or 20,480 acres. It is of volcanic origin. The main ridge, peaks of a submerged range, extends east and west the length of the island. Its hills are steep and rocky and sparsely covered with vegetation, the original timber having been cut away for lumber and charcoal. Two summits, Crown mountain and Signal hill, rise above 1,500 feet. Many of the spurs of the ridge slope down to the shore and form protected bays where the buccaneers of the 17th and 18th centuries found refuge. The climate is salubrious, particularly during the first quarter of the year when the trade winds blow. The mean temperature is 78° F., the thermometer rarely falling below 64° and rarely rising above 91°. The average rainfall is 38·23 in.; the driest weather is in March and the rainy season in October and November. Drinking water is stored in cisterns because of the dearth of wells.

After the abolition of slavery in 1848, agriculture became decadent. By 1917 the population was only 10,191 and it was 9,834 in 1930. By 1940, however, there were 11,265 inhabitants. The population in 1950 was 13,811, federal census. Destruction of the once profitable rum export trade as a result of United States prohibition of liquor contributed heavily to economic decline. From 1926 to 1933 the annual federal government contribution to the municipal treasury of St. Thomas and St. John averaged around $100,000, but gradual improvement was made after 1931. By 1950 the federal contribution had increased to $279,000. Improved hotels and a stimulation of the tourist trade, along with governmental encouragement of small landholdings, were important among the economic developments. Most of the island's agricultural and dairy produce is for local consumption and ship supplies. Native handicraft work and rum distilleries provide the chief direct exports.

St. Thomas Island was discovered and named by Christopher Columbus on his second voyage in 1493. The first colony was planted in 1657 by the Dutch who soon after abandoned it and migrated to New Amsterdam (New York). The Danes arrived and took formal possession in 1666, but their first colony also failed. The Danish West India company dispatched an expedition under Governor Jorgen Iversen which landed in St. Thomas harbour on May 25, 1672, and effected a permanent settlement. Later Huguenot refugees from St. Kitts were granted asylum.

In 1755 the king of Denmark acquired the company's rights and made the harbour a free port. The island was temporarily seized by England in 1801–02, and again held by her in 1807–15, but was restored to and held by Denmark until 1917, when it was sold to the United States.

The chief value of the island is the harbour of Charlotte Amalie, one of the best in the Antilles, important as a United States naval base. It is perfectly landlocked, with a bottlenecked entrance, and has a deserved reputation for refuge. It commands the gateway to the Caribbean through the Virgin passage and is a port of call for passenger steamers from New York and European ports bound for the Panama canal and Central America via the Lesser Antilles. There are ample coaling facilities, oil reservoirs, shipyards and machine shops, floating docks and wharves with electric cranes.

Charlotte Amalie, pop. 11,463 (known as St. Thomas city from 1917 to 1932), the seat of government of the Virgin Islands, lies on three low spurs of the island ridge, dubbed "Foretop, Maintop and Mizzentop." A single level street parallel to the water front forms a common base for three cone-shaped clusters of white dwellings on the green background of the ridges. Government hill is one of the attractive residential sections, the location affording constant enjoyment of the breezes and panorama. English is the prevailing language, but Danish, Dutch, French and Spanish are also common. For general government, see VIRGIN ISLANDS.

See *West Indies Yearbook* (London and Montreal, annual), and *Annual Reports* of the governor of the Virgin islands. (M. F. DE C.)

ST. TROND, town, province of Limburg, Belg., 18 mi. northwest of Liège in an important strategic position near the frontier. Pop. (1947 census) 79,020.

ST. VINCENT, JOHN JERVIS, EARL OF (1735–1823), British admiral, was the second son of Swynfen Jervis, solicitor to the admiralty, and treasurer of Greenwich hospital. He was born at Meaford, Staffordshire, on Jan. 9, 1735, and entered the navy on Jan. 4, 1749. He became lieutenant on Feb. 19, 1755, and served in that rank till 1759, taking part in the conquest of Quebec. He was made commander of the "Scorpion" sloop in 1759, and post-captain in 1760. During the peace he commanded the "Alarm" (32) in the Mediterranean, and when he was put on half pay he travelled in Europe, taking professional notes everywhere. While the War of American Independence lasted, he commanded the "Fourroyant" (80) in the Channel, taking part in the battle of Ushant (1778) (*see* KEPPEL, AUGUSTUS) and in the various reliefs of Gibraltar. His most signal service was the capture (April 19, 1782) of the French "Pégase" (74) after a long chase. In 1783 he entered parliament as member for Launceston, and in the general election of 1784 as member for Yarmouth. In politics he was a strong Whig. On Sept. 24, 1787, he attained flag rank, and was promoted vice-admiral in 1793. From 1793 till 1795 he was in the West Indies co-operating with the army in the conquest of the French islands. On his return he was promoted admiral. In November 1795 he took command in the Mediterranean, where he maintained the blockade of Toulon, and aided the allies of Great Britain in Italy.

But in 1796 the occupation of Italy by the French armies closed all the ports to his ships, and Malta was not yet in the possession of Great Britain. Then the addition of the Spanish fleet to the French altered the balance of strength in the Mediterranean. The Spaniards were very inefficient, and Jervis would have held his ground, if one of his subordinates had not taken the extraordinary course of returning to England, because he thought that the dangerous state of the country required that all its forces should be concentrated at home. He was therefore obliged to act on the instructions sent to him and to retire to the Atlantic, withdrawing the garrisons from Corsica and other places. His headquarters were now on the coast of Portugal, and his chief duty was to watch the Spanish fleet at Cadiz. On Feb. 14, 1797, he gained a most complete victory against heavy odds. (*See* ST. VINCENT, BATTLE OF.) The determination to fight, and the admirable discipline of his squadron, which was very largely the fruit of his own care in preparation, supply the best proof that he was a commander of a high order. For this victory, which came at a very critical time, he was made an earl and was granted a pension of £3,000. His qualities as a disciplinarian were soon to be put to a severe test. In 1797 the grievances of the sailors, which were of old standing, and had led to many mutinies of single ships, came to a head in the great general mutinies at Spithead and the Nore. Similar movements took place on the coast of Ireland and at the Cape of Good Hope. (*See* NAVY AND NAVIES: *History*.) The spirit spread to the fleet under St. Vincent, and there was an undoubted danger that some outbreak would take place in his command. The peril was averted by his foresight and severity. He had always taken great care of the health of his men, and was as strict with the officers as with sailors. It must in justice be added that he was peculiarly fitted for the work. He carried his strictness with his officers to an extent which aroused the actual hatred of many among them, and exasperated Sir John Orde (1751–1824) into challenging him to fight a duel. Yet he cannot be denied the honour of having raised the discipline of the navy to a higher level than it had reached before; he was always ready to promote good officers, and the efficiency of the squadron with which Nelson won the battle of the Nile was largely due to him. His health broke down under the strain of long cruising, and in June 1799 he resigned his command.

When St. Vincent's health was restored in the following year he took the command of the Channel fleet, into which he introduced his own rigid system of discipline to the bitter anger of the captains. But his method was fully justified by the fact that he was able to maintain the blockade of Brest for 121 days with his fleet. In 1801 he became first lord and held the office till Pitt returned to power in 1803. His administration is famous in the history of the navy, for he now applied himself to the very necessary task of reforming the corruptions of the dockyards. Naturally he was fiercely attacked in and out of parliament. His peremptory character led him to do the right thing with the maximum of dictation at Whitehall as on the quarter-deck of his flagship. He also gave an opening to his critics by devoting himself so wholly to the reform of the dockyards that he neglected the preparation of the fleet for war. He would not recognize the possibility that the peace of Amiens would not last. Pitt made himself the mouthpiece of St. Vincent's enemies, mainly because he considered him as a dangerous member of the party which was weakening the position of England in the face of Napoleon. When Pitt's second ministry was formed in 1803, St. Vincent refused to take the command of the Channel fleet at his request. After Pitt's death he resumed the duty with the temporary rank of admiral of the fleet in 1806, but held it only till the following year. After 1810 he retired to his house at Rochetts in Essex. The rank of admiral of the fleet was conferred on him in 1821 on the coronation of George IV., and he died on March 14, 1823. Lord St. Vincent married his cousin Martha Parker, who died childless in 1816. There is a monument to him in St. Paul's Cathedral, and portraits of him at different periods of his life are numerous. The earldom granted to Jervis became extinct on his death, but a viscounty, created for him in 1801, passed by special remainder to Edward Jervis Ricketts (1767–1857), the second son of his sister Mary who had married William Henry Ricketts, of Longwood, Hampshire. The 2nd viscount took the name of Jervis, and the title is still held by his descendants.   (D. H.)

The *Life* by J. S. Tucker (2 vols.), whose father had been the admiral's secretary (marred by excessive eulogy). *See* W. N. Anson, *Life of John Jervis, Admiral Lord St. Vincent* (1913); also W. L. Clowes, *The Royal Navy* . . . vol. iv. The life by Captain Brenton is rather inaccurate. The *Naval Career of Admiral John Markham* contains an account of the reforms in the navy. His administrations produced a swarm of pamphlets. Many mentions of him will be found in the correspondence of Nelson.

ST. VINCENT, a British island in the Windward group of the West Indies, lying about 13° 9′ N, 61° 14′ W, south of St. Lucia and west of Barbados. The island is about 18 mi. long, with a maximum width of 11 mi., and has an area of 133 sq.mi. Beautiful, thickly wooded volcanic hills form its backbone, with picturesque valleys intermingled. The highest summit is the volcano Soufrière (3,822 ft.) in the north. Two eruptions of Soufrière, in 1821 and in 1902, were especially disastrous, the latter devastating some of the most fertile parts of the island. The climate is fairly healthful and in winter very pleasant, but hurricanes are not infrequent. Two (in 1780 and in 1898) were especially destructive of both life and property. Rainfall averages 101.32 in. annually; the normal temperature range is from 66° to 88° F.

The colony of St. Vincent includes most of the Grenadines (q.v.) (area: 17 sq.mi.; 1946 pop. 4,479) and is part of the loosely federated Windward Islands colony. It has a common governor and shares some judicial institutions with the other Windward colonies, but has its own separate partly-appointed, partly-elected legislative body. Kingstown (1946 pop. 4,833), on the southwestern coast, is the capital as well as the chief port. The colony's population (1949 est. 66,170) is nearly 75% of Negro descent. Only 2½% is white; the remainder of mixed or East Indian blood. A very few are of almost pure Carib stock. Primary education, free but not compulsory, is provided by 16 government and 22 government-subsidized schools (1949). There are two government secondary schools.

St. Vincent is predominantly agricultural and has a virtual monopoly of the world market for arrowroot, its principal crop. Sugar was formerly the colony's economic backbone but, in contrast with most of the other West Indian islands, became relatively unimportant, with an annual output of 2,000 to 2,500 tons. A distinctive and fancy quality molasses is produced. Sea Island cotton and peanuts and some coconuts, sweet potatoes and cassava are grown. The principal trade is with the United Kingdom, Canada, and the United States.

St. Vincent was discovered by Christopher Columbus on Jan. 22 (St. Vincent's day) 1498. Its Carib inhabitants, however, were left almost undisturbed for more than a century. In 1627 Charles I of England granted the island to the earl of Carlisle, but no effective occupation was made. In 1672 it was regranted to Lord Willoughby. Meanwhile, French and Dutch as well as English settlements were attempted, with the French dominant until the Seven Years' War, when Gen. Robert Monckton occupied it (1762). The treaty of Paris confirmed British possession, and settlement proceeded despite Carib refusal to accept British sovereignty. After some fighting in 1773, a treaty was concluded with the Caribs, who were granted lands in the north as a reserve. In 1779 the island was seized by the French, but was restored to Britain in 1783. In 1795 the Caribs rose, assisted by French from Martinique, and were finally subdued the following year. Most of

them were then deported to the Bay Islands (off Honduras). Emancipation of Negro slaves in 1834 was disastrous for the island's economy. In 1848 Portuguese labourers were introduced, followed by East Indians in 1861.

See Colonial Office, *Colonial Annual Reports.*   (L. W. Be.)

ST. VINCENT, BATTLE OF, fought on the 14th of February 1797, between the British and Spanish fleets, the most famous and important of many encounters which have taken place at the same spot. The battle first revealed the full capacity of Nelson, which was well known in the navy, to all his countrymen. In 1796 the Spanish government had made the disastrous alliance with the French republic, which reduced its country to the level of a pawn in the game against England. The Spanish fleet, which was in a complete state of neglect, was forced to sea. It consisted of 27 sail of the line under the command of Don José de Córdoba—fine ships, but manned in haste by drafts of soldiers, and of landsmen forced on board by the press. Even the flagships had only about eighty sailors each in their crews. Cordoba was drifting about with his unmanageable ships in two confused divisions separated from one another, in light winds from the west and west-south-west, at a distance of from 25 to 30 m. S.W. of the Cape. While in this position he was sighted by Sir John Jervis, of whose nearness to himself he was ignorant, and who had sailed from Lisbon to attack him with only 15 sail of the line. Jervis did not hesitate to give battle. Six Spanish ships were to the south of him, separated by a long interval from the others which were to the south-west. The British squadron was formed into a single line ahead, and was steered to pass between the two divisions of the Spaniards. The six vessels were thus cut off. A feeble attempt was made by them to molest the British, but being now to leeward as Jervis passed to the west of them, and being unable to face the rapid and well directed fire to which they were exposed, they sheered off. One only ran down the British line, and passing to the stern of the last ship succeeded in joining the bulk of her fleet to windward. As the British line passed through the gap between the Spanish divisions ships were tacked in succession to meet the windward portion of the enemy. If this movement had been carried out fully, all the British ships would have gone through the gap and the Spaniards to windward would have been able to steer unimpeded to the north, and perhaps to avoid being brought to a close general action. Their chance of escape was baffled by the independence and promptitude of Nelson. His ship, the "Captain" (74), was the third from the end of the British line. Without waiting for orders he made a sweep to the west and threw himself across the bows of the Spaniards. His movement was seen and approved by Jervis, who then ordered the other ships in his rear to follow Nelson's example. The British force was thrown bodily on the enemy. As the Spanish crews were too utterly unpractised to handle their ships, and could not carry out the orders of their officers which they did not understand, their ships were soon driven into a herd, and fell on board of one another. Their incompetence as gunners enabled the "Captain" to assail their flagship, the huge "Santissima Trinidad" (130), with comparative impunity. The "San Josef" (112), and the "San Nicolas" (80), which fell aboard of one another, were both carried by boarding by the "Captain." Four Spanish ships, the "Salvador del Mundo" and "San Josef" (112), the "San Nicolas" (80), and the "San Isidro" (74), were taken. The "Santissima Trinidad" is said to have struck, but she was not taken possession of. By about half-past three the Spaniards were fairly beaten. More prizes might have been taken, but Sir John Jervis put a stop to the action to secure the four which had surrendered. The Spaniards were allowed to retreat to Cadiz. Sir John Jervis was made Earl St. Vincent (q.v.) for his victory. The battle, which revealed the worthlessness of the Spanish navy, relieved the British government from a load of anxiety, and may be said to have marked the complete predominance of its fleet on the sea.   (D. H.)

AUTHORITIES.—A very interesting account of the battle of Cape St. Vincent, *A Narrative of the Proceedings of the British Fleet, etc.* (London, 1797), illustrated by plans, was published immediately afterwards by Colonel Drinkwater Bethune, author of the *History of the Siege of*

Gibraltar, who was an eyewitness from the "Lively" frigate. *See also* James's *Naval History* (London, 1837); Captain Mahan, *The Influence of Sea Power on the French Revolution and Empire* (London, 1892); Professor Goeffrey Callender, *The Naval Side of British History* (1924).

ST. VITUS' DANCE (Chorea Minor; Sydenham's Chorea) is a name commonly applied to the neurological manifestations of rheumatic infection. The disease is characterized by irregular, involuntary and purposeless movements of muscle groups. These movements are most obvious in the extremities and face, but are present in the trunk and may involve muscles of phonation and swallowing. While the names are derived from descriptive terms applied to epidemics of dancing mania in the 14th, 15th and 16th centuries, common usage of the term chorea condones its retention. The name St. Vitus' dance originated in the fact that sufferers from the mania were wont to resort to the chapels of St. Vitus (more than one in Swabia, Ger.), the saint being believed to possess the power of cure.

Chorea is chiefly a disease of childhood, occurring most frequently between the ages of 5 and 15 years and much more frequently in females. It may occur in young adults and is an infrequent complication of pregnancy, when it is especially severe. Chorea has a close association with rheumatic fever and may be considered a peculiar manifestation of this disease. Episodes of chorea commonly occur in children who have had rheumatic fever. Patients with chorea who have evidence of systemic infection as indicated by fever, increase of white blood cells or of the sedimentation rate of red blood cells, have rheumatic heart disease as frequently as do those who have rheumatic fever. However, if these indications of systemic infection are absent, heart disease is uncommon, and if it does occur it is especially apt to be gradual stenosis of the mitral valve. Some effort has been made to separate rheumatic chorea from chorea of psychogenic origin on the basis of laboratory findings, but this differentiation is difficult to substantiate.

While emotional crises and anxiety may appear to be intimately related to the onset of chorea, they are a manifestation of the disease and do not precipitate it. Facial grimaces, tics and habit spasms are frequently confused with chorea, but these repetitive movements are quite different from the inco-ordinated purposeless movements of the disease. These movements, which are typical and recognizable, are usually preceded by or appear with, evidence of irritability and emotional instability, chiefly episodes of crying initiated by trivial incidents.

The symptoms vary in severity. They may be mild or completely incapacitating. They are often first considered as awkwardness. Inability to hold objects or to write properly and difficulty in walking are frequent. Vague identification of deterioration in ability to perform customary tasks is soon replaced by recognition of gross twitching of muscle groups, most easily observed in the extremities. The movements are more marked on one side but are present on both.

While there is debate concerning the pathological changes in the central nervous system, there is considerable evidence that both the emotional manifestations and the typical movements are related to changes in the cerebral cortex.

Attacks of chorea tend to be self-limited although the duration is several weeks. Recurrence is frequent. Recovery is hastened by rest in bed in a pleasant sympathetic environment, and patients improve quickly in hospitals or convalescent sanitaria. Sedation with phenobarbitol is especially helpful, and administration of salicylates is often advisable. (D. E. C.)

SAINT-WANDRILLE, a village of northwestern France, in the department of Seine-Inférieure, 28 mi. west-northwest of Rouen by rail. Pop. (1946) 227.

Saint-Wandrille is celebrated for the ruins of its Benedictine abbey. The abbey was founded in the 7th century by St. Wandrille. In the 13th century it was burned down, and the rebuilding was not completed until the 16th century. Later it was practically destroyed by the Huguenots and was again restored. The demolition of the church was begun at the time of the Revolution. The abbey church belongs to the 13th and 14th centuries; portions of the nave walls supported by flying buttresses are standing, and

the windows and vaulting of the side aisles are in fair preservation. There is a cloister, from which a Renaissance door opens into the refectory, containing a richly ornamented *lavabo.* The refectory has graceful windows.

SAIONJI, KIMMOCHI, Prince (1849–1940), Japanese statesman, was born in Oct. 1849, at Kyoto. When less than 20 years of age, he took part in the councils which led to the Restoration, and at 19 was commander in chief of an imperial army. In 1881 he commenced his official career, and in the following year accompanied Hirobumi Ito to Europe and the United States to investigate the parliamentary system. In 1885 Saionji was appointed minister to Austria; three years later he became vice-president of the house of peers and was raised to the privy council in 1894. In the same year he received the portfolio of education in the second Ito cabinet.

In July 1903 Saionji became the leader of the Seiyu-Kai and in 1906 prime minister; he was again premier from 1911 to 1912. In 1919 he represented Japan as chief envoy at the peace conference and in 1920 he was made prince. He was famous as Emperor Hirohito's chief adviser and as the last of Emperor Meiji's Genro (elder statesmen).

Saionji died Nov. 24, 1940.

SAIS (Egyptian *Sai*), an ancient city of the Egyptian Delta, lying westward of the Thermuthiac or Sebennytic branch of the Nile. It was the capital of the 5th nome of Lower Egypt and must have been important from remote times. In the 8th century B.C. Sais held the hegemony of the Western Delta, while Bubastite families ruled in the east and the kings of Ethiopia in Upper Egypt. At the time when invasions by the Assyrians drove out the Ethiopian Taracus again and again, the chief of the 20 princes to whom Esarhaddon and Assur-bani-pal successively entrusted the government was Niku, king of Sais and Memphis. His son Psammetichus (*q.v.*) was the founder of the 26th dynasty. Although the main seat of government was at Memphis, Sais remained the royal residence throughout this flourishing dynasty.

Neit, the goddess of Sais, was identified with Athena, and Osiris was worshipped there in a great festival.

The brick enclosure wall of the temple is still plainly visible near the little village of Sa-el-hagar (Sa of stone) on the east bank of the Rosetta branch; otherwise only crude brick ruins and rubbish heaps remain on the site, but a few relics conveyed to Alexandria and Europe in the Roman age have come down to our day, notably the inscribed statue of a priest of Neit who was high in favour with Psammetichus III, Cambyses and Darius. Bronze figures of deities are now the most interesting objects to be found at Sa-el-hagar.

SAISSET, BERNARD (d. *c.* 1314), French bishop, was abbot of Saint Antonin de Pamiers in 1268. Boniface VIII, detaching the city of Pamiers from the diocese of Toulouse in 1295, made it the seat of a new bishopric and appointed Saisset to the see. Of a headstrong temperament, Saisset as abbot brought to an end (1297) the struggle with the counts of Foix, begun two centuries before, for the lordship of the city of Pamiers, which had been shared between the counts and abbots by the feudal contract of *pariage.* As an ardent Languedocian he hated the French and opposed Philip IV. But when he tried to organize a general rising of the south, he was denounced to the king, perhaps by his old enemies the count of Foix and the bishop of Toulouse. Philip IV charged Richard Leneveu, archdeacon of Auge in the diocese of Lisieux, and Jean de Picquigni, vidame of Amiens, to make an investigation, which lasted several months.

Saisset was on the point of escaping to Rome when the vidame of Amiens surprised him by night in his episcopal palace. He was brought to Senlis and on Oct. 24, 1301, appeared before Philip and his court. He was charged with high treason, and Philip tried to obtain from the pope the canonical degradation of Saisset. Boniface VIII, who had supported Saisset against the count of Foix (when Saisset was a legate), ordered the king in Dec. 1301 to free the bishop, in order that he might go to Rome to justify himself. At the same time disagreement between Boniface and Philip became more acute, and in the process Saisset was forgotten. He had been turned over in Feb. 1302 into the keeping of Jacques des Normands, the papal legate, and was ordered to leave the kingdom at once.

Saisset lived at Rome until after the incident at Anagni. In 1308 the king pardoned him and restored him to his see. He died, still bishop of Pamiers, about 1314.

BIBLIOGRAPHY.—J. M. Vidal, *Bernard Saisset, évêque de Pamiers* (Toulouse, 1926); Georges Digard, *Philippe le Bel et le Saint Siège de 1285 à 1304,* 2 vol. (Paris, Liège, 1936); C. de Vic and J. J. Vaissete, *Histoire générale de Languedoc,* new ed. (Toulouse, 1872–1905).

SAISSET, ÉMILE EDMOND (1814–1863), French philosopher, born at Montpellier, Fr., on Sept. 16, 1814, studied philosophy in the school of Victor Cousin and carried on his eclectic tradition.

He was professor of philosophy at Caen, at the École Normale in Paris and later at the Sorbonne.

His works include *Discours de la philosophie de Leibnitz* (1857); *Précurseurs et disciples de Descartes* (1862); and *Critique et histoire de la philosophie* (1865).

Saisset died in Paris on Dec. 17, 1863.

SAITO, MAKOTO, VISCOUNT (1858–1936), Japanese sailor and administrator, was born a commoner at Iwate Ken. He joined the navy in 1873, and was rapidly promoted, being gazetted commander in 1897. The discipline of the Japanese navy, strict as it was, still left something to be desired, and when he became captain in 1898 Saito declared his intention of revising some of the existing regulations and enforcing a stricter observance of others. In the same year he was appointed vice-minister of the navy under Admiral Count Yamamoto. Two years later he was gazetted rear admiral in recognition of his valuable services in the development of the navy along western lines. He was promoted to vice-admiral in 1904 and became admiral in 1912. He received several decorations for his services in the Russo-Japanese war, where he profited by his experience as naval aide-de-camp to the emperor in the Chino-Japanese conflict. He was minister for the navy in 1913 and 1914.

After the upheaval of the Koreans in 1919 under the rule of Marshal Hasegawa, Baron Saito was appointed governor general of Korea. His chief concern was education, and the number of schools there was greatly increased.

He was created baron in 1907, and was raised to the rank of viscount in 1925. He was appointed chief delegate to the naval disarmament conference at Geneva in 1927 and resigned his governor-generalship soon after.

In Feb. 1936 Saito was assassinated.

SAKA or SHAKA, the name of various tribes which invaded India from central Asia. More accurately, it denotes the tribe which invaded India 140–130 B.C. They are the Sacae of classical authors and the Se of the Chinese, representing an original Sek or Sōk. The Chinese state that they were a pastoral people in the neighbourhood of the modern Kashgar.

About 160 B.C. the Saka were driven southward by the advance of the Yue-Chi (*q.v.*) from the east. One portion appears to have settled in western Afghanistan, hence called Sakasthana, in modern Persian Seistan. The other section occupied the Punjab and possessed themselves of Sind, Gujarat and Malwa. The rulers of these provinces bore the title of satrap (*kshatrapa* or *chhatrapa*) and were apparently subordinate to a king who ruled over the valley of Kabul and the Punjab. In 57 B.C. the Sakas were attacked simultaneously by Parthians from the west and by the Malava clans from the east and their power was destroyed.

BIBLIOGRAPHY.—P. Gardner, *Coins of the Greek and Scythic Kings of India* (London, 1886); O. Franke, *Beiträge aus chinesischen Quellen zur Kenntnis der Turkvölker und Skythen Zentralasiens* (Berlin, 1904); Vincent Smith, *Early History of India,* revised by S. M. Edwardes (Oxford, 1924); F. W. Thomas, "Sakastana," *Journal of the Royal Asiatic Society* (London, 1906).

SAKAI, the name offensively used by Malays for the Senoi.

SAKÉ is the national beverage of Japan. In nature it stands midway between beer and wine. It is made chiefly from rice by fermentation with the mould Aspergillus oryzae. Saké contains from 12% to 15% of alcohol and about 3% of solid matter (extractives), 0.3% of lactic acid, a small quantity of volatile acid,

0.5% of sugar and 0.8% of glycerin. Saké is a yellowish-white liquid, its flavour somewhat resembling that of madeira or sherry. (*See* WINE.)

SAKHALIN, an elongated, mountainous island, approximately 24,560 sq.mi. in area, located off the Pacific coast of the U.S.S.R. Irregularly shaped, Sakhalin varies in width from 17 to 140 mi. (between 141° 49′ E. and 144° 45′ E.) and extends over 580 mi. from Cape Yelizaveta in the south (45° 54′ N.) to Cape Kril'on (Crillon) in the north (54° 25′ N.). Between the island and the Asian mainland is the Tatar strait, an arm of the Sea of Japan, which in its narrowest section, called Nevelskoi (Nevel'skogo) strait (about 4 mi. wide), freezes in winter. The north and east coasts are washed by the cold waters of the Sea of Okhotsk. La Pérouse strait separates Sakhalin from Japanese Hokkaido, 25 mi. to the south.

Physical Features.—Mountains parallel much of the east and west coasts. The rugged, western Kamyshevy range, though rising scarcely above 4,000 ft., is the longest and most formidable of the island's ranges. In its southern extension, south of the 49th parallel, the range actually forms the spine of the island. Along the east coast, the mountains are more rounded and less extensive, terminating on the south in the Terpeniya peninsula; yet they contain the highest peaks on the island (Mt. Lopatina, 5,278 ft., and Mt. Nevelskoi, 4,585 ft.).

North of 51° N., the elevation of the island becomes lower and the uplands yield to unattractive lowlands. Enclosed by the coastal ranges is a central valley, from 3 to 19 mi. wide, drained northeastward to Okhotsk sea by the Tym river and southward to the Gulf of Terpeniya by the Poronai river. A narrow watershed separates the headwaters of the rivers, while sand bars and lagoons clutter the estuaries. Rapids impede the upper course of the Tym, but the Poronai, in which salmon and other fish abound, is navigable for small craft for about 30 mi. There are other shorter rivers on the island, including the Susunai in the extreme south, and numerous lakes.

Climate.—Sakhalin has a severe climate. Winter temperatures, lower than might be suggested by latitude (*i.e.,* from Odessa to Tula), result from the cold winds which sweep in from the north over Okhotsk sea. The January mean ranges from 17° F. in the south to —10° F. in the north. The summers are cool, but thermally less varied than are the winters. Mean July temperatures of 60° F.–64° F. prevail throughout the Tym-Poronai valley. The relative warmth of the Kuro Shiwo current ameliorates the climate of the west coast, while the Okhotsk current chills the east. Dampness and fog are characteristic of the coasts. Off the north coast drift ice may appear as late as July. The vegetation period varies from 97 days in the north to 167 in the extreme south. Much of the 20 in. (and more) annual precipitation occurs in summer and autumn, occasionally resulting in destructive floods. Snow falls from October to May, persisting on the mountain slopes until August.

Soils and Vegetation.—Basically, the soils of the island consist of infertile podsols, with barren tundra common throughout the northern lowland and on the higher uplands. However, the alluvial soils of the valleys are fertile, support luxurious meadows and, in the southern half of the island where a more favourable climate prevails, permit the growing of foodstuffs. Taiga (coniferous) forest covers most of Sakhalin, with spruce and fir dominant. In the protected valleys may be found Manchurian deciduous species, while bamboo grows along the west coast. Fur-bearing animals are abundant in the forest and there are a great variety of birds.

History.—Although the island was first visited by Japanese, Russian and Dutch navigators (1630–49), it remained for the Japanese in 1805–08 to prove that Sakhalin was not a projection of the mainland but an island. Japanese fishing stations appeared along the southwest coast, but little settlement occurred. However, a growing interest in the island on the part of both the Japanese and Russian governments led, in 1855, to the establishment of a joint condominium. Twenty years of competition resulted in the treaty of St. Petersburg, 1875, in which Japan relinquished its claims to Sakhalin in exchange for the Kurile Islands to the east.

Under complete Russian sovereignty, Sakhalin served for many years as a penal colony.

The treaty of Portsmouth, 1905, which ended the Russo-Japanese War, divided the island at the 50th parallel, establishing Japanese dominion over the southern half, called Karafuto. The Russian inhabitants withdrew northward, and their numbers declined from 40,000 to about 6,000 by World War I. As a result of rapid Japanese immigration, the population of Karafuto grew to more than 68,000 by 1917. Between 1920 and 1924, Japan occupied the Russian half of the island, but with the establishment of Soviet power in the far east it was forced to withdraw, retaining important mining concessions in the north.

Upon the collapse of Japan at the end of World War II, Soviet troops entered Karafuto and most of the 400,000 Japanese inhabitants were subsequently evacuated to Japan proper. In Jan. 1947, Sakhalin, together with the Kurile Islands, became a separate *oblast* of the U.S.S.R., with Yuzhno-Sakhalinsk (Toyohara) in the Susunai valley as the capital.

Population.—From a pre-World War II population of 120,000, the Russian population was estimated to have more than doubled by the mid-1950s. A small group of native peoples, numbering several thousand, still inhabited the island, divided primarily into two main ethnic groups: the Tungus-Manchurian, including the Tungus proper and the Goldi (Nanais) in the interior; and the Palaeo-Asiatics, including the Ainus in the south and the Gilyaks (Nivkhis) near the coasts.

Resources and Industry.—The wealth of the island lies in its minerals, fisheries and lumber and paper products. Petroleum, the existence of which was first officially reported in 1894, is the most important resource. Okha and Ekhabi, near the northeast coast, are the main fields. Contributing about 3% to the total Soviet oil production, they are the major source of supply for the entire Soviet far east. Refineries are located at Okha, as well as at Port Moskal'vo, a deep-water port on the Gulf of Sakhalin. A pipeline links the refineries to Nikolayevsk on the mainland near the mouth of the Amur river. Sakhalin's coal deposits, the reserves of which are reputed to be about 4,500,000,000 tons, are mainly lignite. Principal mining centres are located along the west coast near Aleksandrovsk and Uglegorsk.

The commercial fisheries are well-developed as the result of Japanese enterprise prior to World War II. Fishing, both maritime and inland, is a common occupation of the inhabitants, with fish a major item of diet. Small fishing villages, many of which possess canneries and other facilities for handling the catch, dot the south and west coasts. The lumber and paper industries are also concentrated in the south, primarily at Tomari, Kholmsk and Nevel'sk.

Agriculture, confined to the southern half of the island, is relatively unimportant. With a cultivated area of about 75,000 ac., the main crops are grains, vegetables, potatoes and sugar beets, etc. Livestock raising and dairying, based on the lush natural meadows in the valleys, have considerable potential.

Transportation.—Roads are virtually nonexistent and, save for a short line between Okha and Port Moskal'vo, the railroads are all in the southern half of the island, of prewar Japanese construction. Regular steamer connection exists between Aleksandrovsk and Nikolayevsk in the navigation season, from mid-May to Nov. 1.

See L. S. Berg, *Geographical Zones of the Soviet Union*, vol. ii, pp. 465-474 (Moscow, 1952); *Geographical Atlas for Teachers of Middle School*, pp. 134, 150 (Moscow, 1954). (D. Jn.)

SAKI, the name of a group of tropical American monkeys. The sakis form the genus *Pithecia*, which also includes the Uakaris (*q.v.*). They are characterized by their long, bushy and non-prehensile tails, distinct whiskers and beard, and the elongated hair on the crown of the head, which may either radiate from a point in the centre, or be divided by a median parting. They are very delicate animals and normally silent (*see* PRIMATES).

SAKTISM. The worship of *Sakti*, or female energy, is believed to be derived from lower cults prevalent in northeast Bengal and Assam. The principal Sakti shrine is situated at Kamakshya (? the fulfilment of lust) on the summit of a hill

two miles west of Gauhati. In Indian speculation the male principle is often regarded as quiescent, while the female principle is active and creative, a view which it may be noted is found in the physiological ideas of the Ba Ila, who hold that the male element is an inert creature but upon the female depend all the generative functions (*Ila-speaking Peoples*, 1920, vol. i. p. 227). A close connection exists with Tantrism, the ritual for which includes the *pancamakara*, the five elements, beginning with *m, madya, mâmsa, matsya, mudrâ, maithuna* (wine, meat, fish, parched grain, copulation). Apart from this, caste restrictions are minimized, girl widows may remarry, women are honoured.

The most popular Sakti worship relates to Durga and Kali and there is ample evidence that human sacrifice is in theory an essential element of the ritual.

See Sir C. Eliot, *Hinduism and Buddhism* (1922).

SAL (*Shorea robusta*), a valuable timber tree the wood of which resembles teak. Large forests of sal occur in India, where the tree is widely planted and officially protected. The genus *Shorea* (family Dipterocarpaceae) contains about 90 species found in India, Ceylon and thence eastward to the Philippines.

SALA, GEORGE AUGUSTUS HENRY (1828–1895), English journalist, was born in London, on Nov. 24, 1828. He was educated in Paris and London. In his earlier years he did odd jobs in scene-painting and book illustration. He wrote articles and stories for Charles Dickens in *Household Words* and *All the Year Round,* and in 1856 Dickens sent him to Russia as a special correspondent. Sala engaged in many journalistic enterprises, but he is best known for his journalism on the *Daily Telegraph,* with which he became connected in 1857. For that paper he did his most characteristic work, whether as a foreign correspondent in all parts of the world, or as a writer of leaders or special articles. In 1892, when his reputation was at its height, he started a weekly paper called *Sala's Journal*, but it was a disastrous failure; and in 1895 he had to sell his library of 13,000 volumes. Lord Rosebery gave him a civil list pension of £100 a year. He died at Brighton on Dec. 8, 1895.

See *The Life and Adventures of George Augustus Sala, written by himself* (2 vols., 1895).

SALAD, a preparation of fresh or cooked vegetables or other ingredients, eaten cold, and served with a dressing of which oil, vinegar and salt are essential ingredients. The word comes from Med. Lat. *salata,* salted, pickled, *salare,* to sprinkle with *salt.*

Salads are prepared from raw green leaves and stems such as lettuces, watercress and endive, but many varieties are also made from fresh fruits and cold cooked vegetables. Cold fish, poultry, game, meat and eggs, may likewise be included.

The preparation of lettuce, endive, watercress, small cress and corn salad needs care. For salad green leaves are best when young and should be gathered early before the sun is up and kept in a cool place until needed. Soaking in cold water for ½ hour before use makes them crisp. Each leaf should be separated and washed thoroughly. Watercress needs special care in cleansing, and small cress should have the black seed cases removed and should be kept in small bunches. After cleansing, the plants should be well drained in a salad basket, on a cloth on a sieve, or in a colander, or they can be shaken lightly in a cloth. The leaves may well be broken with the fingers or cut with a fruit knife; a steel knife must never be used or both colour and flavour will be spoilt. Chives, radishes, tomatoes and celery, cabbage, cucumbers and onion are in this class, as they are used raw. Chives may be chopped or whole; radishes cut in slices or whole; celery used in pieces or shredded, when it curls and makes a pretty garnish; tomatoes cut in slices or quarters; cucumbers in slices, cubes or shreds, cabbage shredded, green peppers shredded; chopped or sliced canned pimento is much used, as cubes or shredded.

Among fruits used for salads are bananas cut in slices, apples cut in cubes, oranges in slices or in natural divisions, pineapples and pears in cubes, cherries and plums, stoned, whole or in halves, grapefruit in sections, kumquats whole and shredded, grapes (seeded). Cold cooked vegetables useful in salads are also numerous, *e.g.,* peas, beans, carrots, turnips, potatoes, artichokes, beetroot and cauliflower buds, asparagus tips, brussels sprouts, spinach or other greens, okra, whole boiled onions. Care must be taken when cooking these, as if overcooked they will break up and become too soft; they may be cut in cubes, shreds or slices. Occasionally raw grated carrot is used.

Salad Dressings.—(1) The simple French dressing of oil and vinegar, seasoned with pepper, salt, mustard and sugar. This may be further flavoured with chopped tarragon, chervil, parsley, shalot, onion or chives. This dressing is used for green salads and for fruit and vegetable salads when served with poultry and cold meats. Cubes of apple with a French dressing are delicious with cold meat. Use at least twice as much oil as vinegar, seasoning to taste. Mix all in a basin and pour over the salad, mixing thoroughly; or mix from the oil and vinegar cruets directly on to the prepared salad, pouring the oil over the leaves first, for the vinegar is apt to make them flabby and it runs off them, whereas the oil coats them and then holds the vinegar; mix thoroughly.

(2) Mayonnaise (see also SAUCE). This dressing is used when a salad is to be served as a separate course, e.g., salmon mayonnaise, and for the more elaborate salads.

Garnishes.—Hard-boiled egg in slices or yolk of egg rubbed through a wire sieve and the white chopped, the two being placed in alternate groups; beetroot in fancy shapes, cucumber crimped and cut in slices, celery shredded and made to curl by keeping in cold water 30 minutes before use, the small heart of a lettuce, bunches of mustard and cress.

For fruit salad, a syrup flavoured with lemon, liqueurs or wine is made, and to this fruits of all descriptions are added.

(E. G. C.)

SALADE, SALLET or SALET, a headpiece introduced in the early 15th century replacing the heavy helmet. Its essential features were its smooth rounded surface, like an inverted bowl, and its long projecting neck guard. Usually there was no movable vizor, but the front fixed part covered most of the face, a slit being left for the eyes. (See HELMET.)

SALADIN (Arab. *Salah ud-Din,* "Honour of the Faith") (1138–1193), first Ayyubite sultan of Egypt, was born at Tekrit in 1138. The brilliance of his career was made possible only by the condition of the east in the 12th century. Such authority as remained to the orthodox caliph of Baghdad (see CALIPHATE) or to the heretical Fatimites (q.v.) of Cairo was exercised by their viziers. The Seljuk empire had, after 1104, been divided and subdivided among Turkish atabegs. The Latin kingdom of Jerusalem had existed since 1098 only because it was a united force in the midst of disintegration. Gradually, however, Christian enthusiasm had aroused a counter enthusiasm among the Moslems. Zengi, atabeg of Mosul, had inaugurated the sacred war by his campaigns in Syria (1135–46). Nureddin, his son, had continued his work by further conquests in Syria and Damascus, by the organization of his conquered lands and by "publishing everywhere the Holy War."

The opportunity of Saladin lay therefore in the fact that his lifetime covers the period when there was a conscious demand for political union in the defense of the Mohammedan faith. By race Saladin was a Kurd of Armenia. His father, Ayyub (Job), and his uncle Shirguh, sons of a certain Shadhy of Ajdanakan near Dawin, were both generals in Zengi's army. In 1139 Ayyub received Baalbek from Zengi, in 1146 he moved, on Zengi's death, to the court of Damascus. In 1154 his influence secured Damascus to Nureddin and he was made governor. Saladin was therefore educated in the most famous centre of Moslem learning, and represented the best traditions of Moslem culture.

His career falls into three parts: the conquest of Egypt, 1164–74, the annexation of Syria and Mesopotamia, 1174–86; and lastly the destruction of the Latin kingdom and subsequent campaigns against the Christians, 1187–92. The conquest of Egypt was essential to Nureddin. It was a menace to his empire on the south, the occasional ally of the Franks and the home of the unorthodox caliphs. His pretext was the plea of an exiled vizier, and Shirguh was ordered to Egypt in 1164, taking Saladin as his lieutenant. The Christians under King Amalric I of Jerusalem immediately intervened; and the four expeditions which ensued in 1164, 1167,

1168 and 1169 were duels between Christians and Saracens. They resulted in heavy Christian losses, the death of Shirguh and the appointment of Saladin as vizier with the title of al-Malik al-Nasir. His relations toward the Fatimite caliph were marked by extraordinary tact, and on his death in 1171 Saladin was powerful enough to substitute the name of the orthodox caliph in all Egyptian mosques. The Mohammedan religion was thus united against Christianity. To Nureddin he was invariably submissive, but from the vigour which he employed in adding to the fortifications of Cairo and the haste with which he retreated from an attack on Montréal (1171) and Krak (Kerak, 1173) it is clear that he feared his lord's jealousy.

In 1174 Nureddin died, and the period of Saladin's conquests in Syria began. Nureddin's vassals rebelled against his youthful heir, as-Salih, and Saladin came north, nominally to his assistance. In 1174 he entered Damascus, Emesa and Hamah; in 1175 Baalbek and the towns round Aleppo.

The next step was political independence. He suppressed the name of as-Salih in prayers and on the coinage and was formally recognized by the caliph in 1175. In 1176 he defeated an invasion by Saif ud-Din of Mosul and reached an agreement with as-Salih and also with the Assassins. In 1177 he returned by Damascus to Cairo, which he enriched with colleges, a citadel and an aqueduct. From 1177 to 1180 he made war on the Christians from Egypt, and in 1180 he imposed terms of peace on the sultan of Konia. From 1181 to 1183 he was chiefly occupied in Syria. In 1183 he induced the atabeg Imad ud-Din to exchange Aleppo for the insignificant Sinjar and in 1186 he received the homage of the atabeg of Mosul. The last independent vassal was thus subdued and the Latin kingdom enclosed on every side by a hostile empire.

In 1187 a four years' truce was broken by the brilliant brigand Raynald of Châtillon, and thus began Saladin's third period of conquest. In May a small body of Templars and Hospitallers was cut to pieces at Tiberias, and on July 4 Saladin inflicted a crushing defeat upon the united Christian army at Hittin. He then over-ran Palestine, on Sept. 20 besieged Jerusalem and on Oct. 2, after chivalrous clemency to the Christian inhabitants, crowned his victories by entering and purifying the Holy City. In the kingdom only Tyre was left to the Christians. Probably Saladin made his worst strategical error in neglecting to conquer it before winter. The Christians had thus a stronghold whence their remnant marched to attack Acre in June 1189. Saladin immediately surrounded the Christian army and began the famous siege.

Saladin's lack of a fleet enabled the Christians to receive reinforcements and thus to recover from defeat by land. On June 8, 1191, Richard of England arrived, and on July 12 Acre capitulated without Saladin's permission. Richard followed up his victory by an admirably ordered march down the coast to Jaffa and a great victory at Arsuf (q.v.).

During 1191 and 1192 there were four small campaigns in southern Palestine when Richard circled round Beitnuba and Ascalon with Jerusalem as objective. In Jan. 1192 he acknowledged his impotence by renouncing Jerusalem to fortify Ascalon. Negotiations for peace accompanied these demonstrations, which showed that Saladin was master of the situation. Though in July Richard secured two brilliant victories at Jaffa, the treaty made on Sept. 2 was a triumph for Saladin. Only the coast line was left to the Latin kingdom, with a free passage to Jerusalem; and Ascalon was demolished. The union of the Mohammedan east had beyond question dealt the death blow to the Latin kingdom. Richard returned to Europe, and Saladin returned to Damascus, where on March 4, 1193, after a few days' illness, he died. He was buried in Damascus and mourned by the whole east. (See CRUSADES.)

The character of Saladin and of his work is singularly vivid. In many ways he was a typical Mohammedan, fiercely hostile toward the unbelievers who had occupied Syria, though tolerant to his own Christian subjects, intensely devout and regular in prayers and fasting. He showed the pride of race in the declaration that "God reserved this triumph for the Ayyubites before all others." His generosity and hospitality were proved in his gifts to Richard and his treatment of captives. He had the oriental's power of endurance, alternating with violent and emotional courage. Other virtues were all his own, his extreme gentleness, his love for children, his flawless honesty, his invariable kindliness, his chivalry to women and the weak. Above all he typifies the Mohammedan's utter self-surrender to a sacred cause. His achievements were the inevitable expression of his character. He was not a statesman, for he left no constitution or code to the east; his empire was divided among his relatives on his death. As a strategist, though of great ability, he cannot be compared to Richard. As a general, he never organized an army. "My troops will do nothing," he confessed, "save when I ride at their head and review them." He is famous in eastern history as the conqueror who stemmed the tide of western conquest on the east and turned it definitely from east to west, as the hero who momentarily united the unruly east and as the saint who realized in his personality the highest virtues and ideals of Mohammedanism.

BIBLIOGRAPHY.—The contemporary Arabian authorities are Saladin's secretary Imad ud-Din and his army judge Beha ud-Din. The latter is translated in J. F. Michaud's *Recueil des historiens des Croisades* (Paris, 1876), together with the general history of Ibn Athir (1160–1233), the eulogist of the atabegs of Mosul but the unwilling admirer of Saladin, and parts of the general history of Abulfeda. The autobiography of the poet Usama ibn Munkidh (1095–1188), edited by H. Derenbourg (Paris, 1886), gives an invaluable picture of eastern life. Later Arabian authorities are Ibn Khallikan (1211–82) and Abu Shama (born 1267). Of Christian authorities the following are important: the history of William of Tyre (1137–85); the *Itinerarium peregrinorum,* probably the Latin version of the *Carmen Ambrosii* (ed. by W. Stubbs, "Rolls" series, London, 1864); and the *Chronique d'outremer,* or the French translation of William of Tyre's history and its continuation by Ernoul, the squire of Balian, seigneur of Ibelin (1228). The best modern authority is Stanley Lane-Poole's *Saladin* ("Heroes of the Nations" series, London, 1903). *See* also the bibliography to CRUSADES.
(W. F. K.; X.)

SALAMANCA, a frontier province of western Spain, formed in 1833 out of the southern part of the ancient kingdom of León, and bounded north by Zamora and Valladolid, east by Ávila, south by Cáceres and west by Portugal. Pop. (1950) 410,929; area, 4,758 sq.mi. Salamanca belongs almost entirely to the basin of the Duero (Portuguese *Douro, q.v.*), its principal rivers being the Tormes, which after a course of 135 mi. flows into the Duero; the Yeltes and the Agueda, also tributaries of the Duero; and the Alagon, an affluent of the Tagus. The southern border is partly defined along the crests of the Gredos and Gata ranges, but the highest point is La Alberca (5,692 ft.) in the Sierra de Peña de Francia, a little farther north. Forests of oak, pine, beech and chestnut cover a wide area in the south and southwest. Of the 50 Spanish provinces only Badajoz, Cáceres and Teruel have a larger number of livestock. Gold is found in the streams, and iron, lead, copper, zinc, coal and rock crystal in the hills, but the mines are only partially developed. The capital, Salamanca (*q.v.*) and Ciudad Rodrigo (*q.v.*) and Béjar (10,474) are the chief towns. The railways from Zamora, Medina, Plasencia and Peñaranda converge upon the capital, whence two lines go westward into Portugal—one via Barca d'Alva to Oporto, the other via Villar Formoso to Guarda. The province was occupied by nationalist troops shortly after the outbreak of the civil war of 1936–39.

SALAMANCA, the capital of the Spanish province of Salamanca (anc. *Salmantica* or *Elmantica*), on the right bank of the river Tormes, 2,648 ft. above sea level and 172 mi. by rail N.W. of Madrid. Pop. (1950) 79,600 (mun., 79,789).

The town was of importance as early as 222 B.C., when it was captured by Hannibal from the Vettones; and it afterward became under the Romans the ninth station on the Via Lata from Merida to Saragossa. It passed successively under the rule of the Goths and the Moors, till the latter were finally driven out about 1055. About 1100 many foreign settlers were induced by Alphonso VI to establish themselves in the district, and the city was enlarged by Count Raymond of Burgundy. The *Fuero de Salamanca,* a celebrated code of civil law, probably dates from about 1200. Thenceforward, until the second half of the 16th century, the prosperity of the university rendered the city one of the most important in Spain.

Salamanca is the centre of a network of railways which radiate north to Zamora, northeast to Medina, east to Peñaranda,

south to Plasencia, west-southwest to Guarda in Portugal and west to Oporto in Portugal. The river is here crossed by a bridge 500 ft. long built on 26 arches, 15 of which are of Roman origin, while the remainder date from the 16th century. The city is still much the same in outward appearance as when its tortuous streets were thronged with students. The university was naturally the chief source of wealth to the town, the population of which in the 16th century numbered 50,000, nearly 8,000 of whom were students. Its decay of course reacted on the townsfolk, but it fortunately also arrested the process of modernization. The ravages of war alone have wrought serious damage, for the French in their defensive operations in 1811–12 almost destroyed the western quarter. Salamanca was again the scene of bitter fighting between nationalist and loyalist troops during the civil war of 1936–39. The magnificent Plaza Mayor, built by Andres Garcia de Quiñones at the beginning of the 18th century, and capable of holding 20,000 people to witness a bullfight, is one of the finest squares in Europe. It is surrounded by an arcade of 90 arches on Corinthian columns, one side of the square being occupied by the municipal buildings.

The University.—Salamanca is still rich in educational establishments. It still keeps up its university, with the separate faculties of letters, philosophy, sciences, law and medicine; its university and provincial public library, with many thousand volumes and manuscripts; its Irish college, provincial institute, superior normal school, ecclesiastical seminary (founded in 1778), economic and other learned societies, and very many charitable foundations. The city still has its 25 parishes, 25 colleges, and as many more or less ruined convents, and 10 yet flourishing religious houses. The university, the oldest in the peninsula, was founded about 1230 by Alphonso IX of León, and refounded in 1242 by St. Ferdinand of Castile. Under the patronage of the learned Alphonso X its wealth and reputation greatly increased (1252–82), and its schools of canon law and civil law attracted students even from Paris and Bologna. In the 15th and 16th centuries it was renowned throughout Europe. Here Christopher Columbus lectured on his discoveries, and here the Copernican system was taught long before it had won general acceptance. But soon after 1550 a period of decline set in.

Principal Buildings.—The old cathedral is a cruciform building of the 12th century, begun by Bishop Jeronimo, the confessor of the Cid (*q.v.*). Its style of architecture is that Late Romanesque which prevailed in the south of France, but the builder showed much originality in the construction of the dome, which covers the crossing of the nave and transepts. The inner dome is made to spring, not from immediately above the arches, but from a higher stage of a double arcade pierced with windows. The thrust of the vaulting is borne by four massive pinnacles, and over the inner dome is an outer pointed one covered with tiles. The Capilla de Talavera is used as a chapel for service according to the Mozarabic rite, which is celebrated there six times a year. On the north of and adjoining the old church stands the new cathedral, built from designs by Juan Gil de Ontañon. Though begun in 1509 the work of construction made little progress until 1513, when it was entrusted to Ontañon under Bishop Francisco de Bobadilla; though not finished till 1734, it is a notable example of the late Gothic and Plateresque styles. Its length is 340 ft. and its breadth 160 ft. The treasury is very rich, and among other articles possesses a custodia which is a masterpiece of goldsmith's work, and a bronze crucifix of undoubted authenticity, which was borne before the Cid in battle.

Of the university buildings the façade of the library is a peculiarly rich example of late 15th-century Gothic. The cloisters are light and elegant; the grand staircase ascending from them has a fine balustrade of foliage and figures. The Colegio de Nobles Irlandeses was built in 1521 from designs by Pedro de Ibarra. The double arcaded cloister is a fine piece of work of the best period of the Renaissance. The Jesuit college is an immense and ugly Renaissance building begun in 1614 by Juan Gomez de Mora. The Colegio Viejo, also called San Bartolome, was rebuilt in the 18th century, and serves as the governor's palace. The Dominican convent of San Esteban shows a mixture of styles from the 13th century onward. The church is Gothic with a Plateresque façade of great lightness and delicacy. The convent of the Augustinas Recoletas, begun by G. Fontana in 1616, is in better taste than any other Renaissance building in the city. The church is rich in marble fittings and contains several fine pictures of the Neapolitan school, especially the Conception by J. Ribera (1588–1656) over the altar. The convent of the Espiritu Santo has a good door by A. Berruguete (c. 1480–1561). Many of the private houses are untouched examples of the domestic architecture of the times in which they were built.

See B. Dorado, *Compendio histórico de la ciudad de Salamanca* (Salamanca, 1863); M. Villar y Macias, *Historia de Salamanca* (3 vols., Salamanca, 1887); H. Rashdall, *Universities of Europe in the Middle Ages*, vol. ii, pt. I (London, 1895); E. Esperabé, *Historia pragmática e interna de la Universidad de Salamanca* (2 vols. Salamanca, 1914–17). (X.)

Battle of Salamanca, 1812. (For the operations which preceded this battle see PENINSULAR WAR.)—On July 22, 1812, the Allied army under Wellington (about 46,000 with 60 guns) was drawn up south of Salamanca, the left resting on the river Tormes, with a division under Pakenham on the north bank of Cabrerizos. Wellington's object was to cover Salamanca and guard his communications through Ciudad Rodrigo with Portugal. The French under Marshal Marmont (about 42,000 with 70 guns) were collecting toward Wellington's right, stretching southward from Calvariza de Ariba. The country generally is undulating.

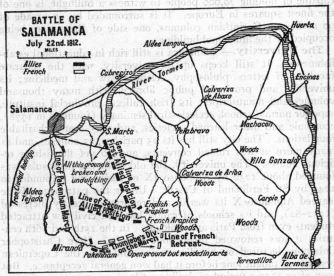

Until the morning of the battle it had been uncertain whether Marmont wished to reach Salamanca by the right or left bank of the Tormes, or to gain the Ciudad Rodrigo road, but Wellington now felt that the latter was his real objective. At daylight there was a rush by both armies for the two commanding hills of the Arapiles; the Allies gained the northern (since termed the "English"), and the French the southern (since termed the "French") Arapiles. While Marmont was closing up his forces, a complete change of position was carried out by Wellington. Pakenham was directed to march through Salamanca, crossing the Tormes, and move under cover to a wood near Aldea Tejada, while Wellington took up a line under cover of a ridge between Arapiles and Aldea Tejada. By noon his old right had become his left, and he was nearer to the Ciudad Rodrigo road, flanking Marmont should he move toward it.

It was not Wellington's wish (*Despatches*, July 21, 1812) to fight a battle "unless under very advantageous circumstances." He knew that large reinforcements were nearing the French, and, having determined to fall back toward Portugal, he began to pass his baggage along the Ciudad Rodrigo road. Marmont, about 2 P.M., seeing the dust of his baggage column, ignorant of his true position, and anxious to intercept his retreat, ordered two divisions under Maucune to push westward, while he himself attacked Arapiles. Maucune moved off, flanked by some cavalry and 50 guns, leaving a gap between him and the rest of the French. Wellington instantly took advantage of this. Directing Pakenham to attack the head of the leading French division, and a Portuguese brigade (Pack) to occupy the enemy by assaulting the south (or French) Arapiles, he prepared to bear down in strength upon Maucune's right flank. The French attack upon Arapiles was after hard fighting repulsed; and, at about 5 P.M., Maucune's force, when in confusion from the fierce attack of Pakenham and Wellington in front and flank and suffering severely, was suddenly trampled down "with a terrible clamour and disturbance" (Napier) by an irresistible charge of cavalry under Sir Stapleton Cotton. This counterstroke decided the battle, Marmont's left wing was being completely broken. The French made a gallant but fruitless effort to retrieve the day, and repulsed Pack's attack upon the French Arapiles; but, as the light waned, Clausel, Marmont being wounded, drew off the French army toward Alba de Tormes and retired to Valladolid. Both armies lost heavily, the Allies about 6,000, the French some 15,000 men, 12 guns, 2 eagles and several standards. The rout would have been even more thorough had not the castle and ford at Alba de Tormes been evacu-

ated by its Spanish garrison without Wellington's knowledge. Salamanca was a brilliant victory, and followed by the capture of Madrid, it severely shook the French domination in Spain. (C. W. Ro.)

SALAMANCA, a city of Cattaraugus county, New York, U.S.A., 63 mi. S. by E. of Buffalo, on both sides of the Allegheny river. It is on federal highway 219 and state highways 17 and 18. It is served by the Erie, the Baltimore and Ohio and the Pennsylvania railways and by interurban trolleys and motorbus lines. Pop. 1950, 8,850. Salamanca is on both sides of the river, at an altitude of 1,390 ft., with wooded hills on the horizon. It lies in the Allegany Indian Reservation, and all land is held under a 99-year lease, authorized by congress in 1892. It is within a few miles of the Allegany State park of 65,000 ac.

Industries consist of railroad shops and terminals, furniture factories, tannery, plastic moulding, worsted yarns, print rolls, last blocks and milk-gathering plants. It was first settled in 1855 and called Hemlock. It was later named after a Spanish banker who was a large stockholder in the first railroad built in the county in 1862.

SALAMANDER, properly the term for the tailed amphibians constituting the order Caudata. The group includes eight families of very diverse form, the majority of which are exclusively North American. See AMPHIBIA.

In Europe the term may refer principally to the genus *Salamandra*, which is restricted to the western parts of the Palaearctic region. The fire salamander, *S. salamandra*, is the well-known black and yellow creature inhabiting central Europe and northwest Africa, and southwest Asia; the black salamander, *S. atra*, is restricted to the Alps. These salamanders, far from being able to withstand the action of fire, as was believed by the ancients, are found only in damp places. They often emerge in great numbers in misty weather or after thunderstorms. Although harmless to man, the large glands on their smooth, shiny bodies secrete a milky poison, which protects them from many enemies. The bright coloration of *S. salamandra* may therefore have a warning function.

THE EUROPEAN FIRE SALAMANDER, AFTER BREHM

The two well-known European species pair on land, the male clasping the female at the arms, and the impregnation is internal. Long after pairing the female gives birth to living young. *S. salamandra*, which lives at low altitudes (up to 3,000 ft.), deposits her young, 10 to 50 in number, in the water, in springs or cool rivulets. These young at birth are similar to small newt larvae, and provided with external gills. *S. atra*, on the other hand, inhabits more hilly regions, up to 9,000 ft. Such altitudes not being, as a rule, suitable for larval life in the water, the young are retained in the uterus until after metamorphosis. Only two young, rarely three or four, are born, and may measure as much as 50 mm. at birth, the mother measuring only 120. The fertilized eggs are large and numerous, as in *S. salamandra*, but only one develops in each uterus, the embryo being nourished on the other eggs, the embryos of which break down into a soupy "vitelline mass." The embryo passes through three stages——(1) still enclosed within the egg membrane and living on its own yolk; (2) free, within the vitelline mass, which is swallowed by the mouth; (3) there is no more vitelline mass, but the embryo develops long external gills, which serve for a nutritive exchange through the maternal uterus, these gills functioning in the same way as the chorionic villi of the mammalian embryo's placenta. Embryos, in the second stage, if artificially released from the uterus, are able to live in water, but the uterine gills soon wither and are shed and are replaced by other gills similar to those in the larva of *S. salamandra*. In *S. salamandra* without access to water, the development of the embryos becomes closely similar to that of *S. atra*.

BIBLIOGRAPHY.—H. Gadow, "Amphibia and Reptiles" (*Cambridge Nat. Hist.*); E. R. Dunn, *Salamanders of the family Plethodontidae* (1926); E. Schwalbe, *Zeitschr. für Biol.* (1896 and 1897); G. K. Noble, *Biology of the Amphibia* (1931). (K. P. S.)

SALAMIS, an island of Greece in the Saronic Gulf of the Aegean Sea, extending along the coasts of Attica and Megaris, and enclosing the Bay of Eleusis between two narrow straits on the W. and S. Its area is 36 sq.m., its greatest length in any direction 10 m.; its extremely irregular shape gives rise to the modern popular name Κουλλοῦρι, i.e., baker's crescent. In Homer Salamis was the home of the Aeginetan prince Telamon and his sons Ajax and Teucer, and this tradition is confirmed by the position of the ancient capital of the island opposite Aegina. It subsequently passed into the hands of the Megarians, but was wrested from them about 600 B.C. by the Athenians under Solon (*q.v.*) and definitely awarded to Athens by Sparta's arbitration. Though Attic tradition claimed Salamis as an ancient possession the island was not strictly Athenian territory; a 6th-century inscription shows that it was treated either as a cleruchy or as a privileged foreign dependency. The town of Salamis was removed to an inlet of the east coast opposite Attica. In 480 Salamis became the base of the allied Greek fleet after the retreat from Artemisium, while the Persians took their station along the Attic coast off Phalerum. Through the stratagem of the Athenian Themistocles the Greeks were enclosed in the straits by the enemy, who had wheeled by night across the entrance of the east channel and detached a squadron to block the west outlet. The Greeks had thus no resource but to fight, while the Persians could not utilize their superior numbers, and as they advanced into the narrow neck of the east strait were thrown into confusion. The allies, among whom the Athenians and Aeginetans were conspicuous, seized this opportunity to make a vigorous attack which probably broke the enemy's line. After waging a losing fight for several hours the Persians retreated with a loss of 200 sail and of an entire corps landed on the islet of Psyttaleia in the channel; the Greeks lost only 40 ships out of more than 300. During the Peloponnesian War Salamis served as a repository for the country stock of Attica. About 350 Salamis obtained the right of issuing copper coins. In 318 Cassander placed in it a Macedonian garrison which was finally withdrawn through the advocacy of the Achaean statesman Aratus (232). The Athenians thereupon supplanted the inhabitants by a cleruchy of their own citizens. By the 2nd century A.D. the settlement had fallen into decay. In modern times Salamis, which is chiefly peopled by Albanians, has regained importance through the transference of the naval arsenal to Ambelaki near the site of the ancient capital. Excavations in this region have revealed large numbers of late Mycenaean tombs.

AUTHORITIES.—Strabo, pp. 383, 393–394; Pausanias i. 35–36; Plutarch, *Solon,* 8–10; Aeschylus, *Persae,* 337–471; Herodotus viii. 40–95; Diodorus xi. 15–19; Plutarch, *Themistocles,* 11–15; W. Goodwin, *Papers of the American School of Classical Studies at Athens,* I. p. 237 ff. (Boston, 1885); G. B. Grundy, *Great Persian War* (London, 1901), ch. ix.; B. V. Head, *Historia numorum* (Oxford, 1887), pp. 328–329; A. Wilhelm in *Athenische Mitteilungen* (1898), pp. 466–486; W. Judeich, *ibid.* (1899), pp. 321–338; C. Horner, *Quaestiones Salaminiae* (Basle, 1901); H. Raase, *Die Schlacht bei Salamis* (Rostock, 1904); R. W. Macan, Appendix to *Herodotus vii.–ix.* (London, 1908); J. Beloch in *Klio* (1908). (M. C.)

SALAMIS, the principal city of ancient Cyprus, situated on the east coast north of the river Pedias (Pediaeus). It had a good harbour, well situated for commerce with Phoenicia, Egypt and Cilicia, which was replaced in mediaeval times by Famagusta

(*q.v.*), and is wholly silted now. Its trade was mainly in corn, wine and oil from the midland plain, and in salt from the neighbouring lagoons. Traditionally, Salamis was founded after the Trojan War (c. 1180 B.C.) by Teucer from the island Salamis, off Attica, but there was a Mycenaean colony somewhat earlier.

A king Kisu of Silna (Salamis) is mentioned in a list of tributaries of Assur-bani-pal of Assyria in 668 B.C., and Assyrian influence is seen in terra-cotta figures from a shrine excavated in 1890–1891. Salamis seems to have been the principal Hellenic power in the island. The revolts against Persia in 500 B.C., 386–380 B.C. and 352 B.C. were led respectively by its kings Onesilas, Evagoras (*q.v.*) and Pnytagoras. In 306 B.C. Demetrius Poliorcetes won a great naval victory here over Ptolemy I. of Egypt. Under Egyptian and Roman administration Salamis flourished greatly, though the seat of government was at New Paphos (*see* PAPHOS). But it was greatly damaged in the Jewish revolt of A.D. 116–117; suffered repeatedly from earthquakes, and was wholly rebuilt by Constantius II. (A.D. 337–361) under the name Constantia. There was a large Jewish colony, and a Christian community was founded by Paul and Barnabas in A.D. 45–46. Barnabas was himself a Cypriote, and his reputed tomb, discovered in A.D. 477, is still shown near the monastery of Ail Barnába. St. Epiphanius was archbishop A.D. 367–402. The Greek city was destroyed by the Arabs under the Caliph Moawiya in 647; Christian survivors migrated to the neighbouring Ammochostos (*see* FAMAGUSTA).

See W. H. Engel, *Kypros* (Berlin, 1841; classical allusions); J. A. R. Munro and H. A. Tubbs, *Journ. Hellenic Studies,* xii. 59 ff., 298 ff. (site and monuments); British Museum, *Excavations in Cyprus* (London, 1899; Mycenaean tombs); G. F. Hill, *Brit. Mus. Cat. Coins of Cyprus* (London, 1904; coins); J. L. Myres, *Archaeologia,* lxvi. 159–178 ("Prison of St. Catharine"); E. Oberhummer in Pauly-Wissowa (*s.v.*). (J. L. MY.)

SAL AMMONIAC or **AMMONIUM CHLORIDE,** the earliest known salt of ammonia (*q.v.*), was formerly much used in dyeing and metallurgic operations.

The name *Hammoniacus sal* (from ἄμμος sand) occurs in Pliny, who relates that it was applied to a kind of fossil salt found below the sand, in a district of Cyrenaica. The general opinion is, that the sal ammoniac of the ancients was the same as that of the moderns; but the imperfect description of Pliny is far from being conclusive. The native sal ammoniac of Bucharia, described by Model and Karsten, and analysed by M. H. Klaproth, has no resemblance to the salt described by Pliny. The same remark applies to the sal ammoniac of volcanoes. Dioscorides, in mentioning sal ammoniac, makes use of a phrase quite irreconcilable with the description of Pliny, and applicable rather to rocksalt than to our sal ammoniac. Sal ammoniac, he says, is peculiarly prized if it can be easily split into rectangular fragments. Finally, we have no proof whatever that sal ammoniac occurs near the temple of Jupiter Ammon, or in any part of Cyrenaica, so it is improbable that the name is derived from Ammon, and it seems that the term sal ammoniac was applied as indefinitely by the ancients as most of their other chemical terms. In any case there can be no doubt that it was well known to the alchemists as early as the 13th century.

Egypt is the country where sal ammoniac was first manufactured, and thence Europe for many years was supplied with it. This commerce was first carried on by the Venetians, and afterwards by the Dutch. In 1716 C. J. Geoffroy read a paper to the French Academy, showing that sal ammoniac must be formed by sublimation; but his opinion was opposed so violently by W. Homberg and N. Lemery, that the paper was not printed. In 1719 D. Lemaire, the French consul at Cairo, sent the Academy an account of the mode of manufacturing sal ammoniac in Egypt. The salt, it appeared, was obtained by simple sublimation from soot. In the year 1760 Linnaeus communicated to the Royal Society a correct detail of the whole process, which he had received from Dr. F. Hasselquist, who had travelled in that country as a naturalist. The dung of black cattle, horses, sheep, goats, etc., which contains sal ammoniac ready formed, is collected during the first four months of the year, when the animals feed on the spring grass, a kind of clover. It is dried, and sold to the common people as fuel. The soot from this fuel is carefully collected and sold to the sal ammoniac makers, who work only during the months of March and April, for it is only at that season of the year that the dung is fit for their purpose.

The composition of this salt (NH_4Cl) seems to have been first discovered by J. P. Tournefort in 1700. The experiments of C. J. Geoffroy in 1716 and 1723 were still more decisive, and those of H. L. Duhamel de Monceau, in 1735, left no doubt upon the subject. Thomson first deduced its composition synthetically from his observation that when hydrochloric acid gas and ammonia gas are brought in contact with each other, they always combine in equal volumes.

The first attempt to manufacture sal ammoniac in Europe was made, about the beginning of the 18th century, by Goodwin, a London chemist, who appears to have used the mother lye of common salt and putrid urine as ingredients. The first successful manufacture of sal ammoniac in Great Britain was established in Edinburgh about the year 1760. It was first manufactured in France about the same time by A. Baumé. It is now obtained from the ammoniacal liquor of gas works by distilling the liquor with milk of lime and passing the ammonia so obtained into hydrochloric acid. The solution of ammonium chloride so obtained is evaporated and the crude ammonium chloride purified by sublimation.

The salt volatilizes (mostly in the form of a mixed vapour of the two components, which reunite on cooling), and condenses in the dome in the form of a characteristically fibrous and tough crust.

Sal ammoniac (ammonium chloride, British and United States pharmacopoeiae) as used in medicine is a white crystalline odourless powder having a saline taste. It is soluble in 3 parts of cold water and in 50 parts of 90% alcohol. It is incompatible with carbonates of the alkalis. Ammonium chloride has a different action and therapeutic use from the rest of the ammonium salts. It possesses only slight influence over the heart and respiration, but it has a specific effect on mucous membranes as the elimination of the drug takes place largely through the lungs, where it aids in loosening bronchial secretions. This action renders it of the utmost value in bronchitis and pneumonia with associated bronchitis.

The drug may be given in a mixture with glycerine or liquorice to cover the disagreeable taste or it may be used in a spray by means of an atomizer.

Though ammonium chloride has irritant properties which may disorder the stomach, yet if its mucous membrane be depressed and atonic the drug may improve its condition, and it has been used with success in gastric and intestinal catarrhs of a subacute type and is given before meals in painful dyspepsia due to hyperacidity.

The drug is also an intestinal and hepatic stimulant and a feeble diuretic and diaphoretic, and has been considered a specific in some forms of neuralgia.

See AMMONIA.

SALANDRA, ANTONIO (1853–1931), Italian statesman, was born at Troia, Puglia, in 1853. He first entered parliament as member for Lucera, and from the beginning of his political career was a Liberal of the right wing. When Sidney Sonnino became treasury minister in the Crispi cabinet of 1893, Salandra was chosen under-secretary in that department. He was minister of finance in the first Sonnino cabinet of 1906 and treasury minister in the second (1909–10). When, in March 1914, Giolitti resigned, Salandra was called upon to form the new cabinet, and in June he had to face a revolutionary outbreak in the Marches and Romagna.

Salandra was premier on the outbreak of World War I, and it was the Salandra cabinet which took the momentous decision of proclaiming Italy's neutrality, in spite of the existence of the Triple Alliance, because Austria-Hungary had violated art. 7 of the Triple Alliance by declaring war on Serbia without a previous agreement with Italy.

In May 1915 Salandra assumed the still greater responsibility of bringing Italy into the war on the side of the Allies. On resigning office in June 1916, in consequence of the Austrian offensive in the Trentino, he continued to support both the Boselli and the Orlando cabinets. During the disturbed period from 1919 to 1922 Salandra upheld the principles of orthodox Liberalism, and opposed the policy of the various cabinets who truckled to the extremists. He succeeded Tittoni as Italian delegate on the League of Nations Council and Assembly, and represented the Italian thesis in the Italo-Greek conflict arising from the massacre of the Tellini mission in Epirus in Aug. 1923. The Fascist movement was supported from the first by Salandra, but he did not join the Fascist party, and when he felt that Fascism was incompatible with the old Liberal tradition, especially after Mussolini's speech of Jan. 3, 1925, he withdrew his support, without, however, abandoning the Chamber. Subsequently his opposition became considerably attenuated, and in 1928 on the proposal of Mussolini, he was created a senator. Salandra died Dec. 19, 1931.

SALARIA, VIA, an ancient highroad of Italy which ran from Rome by Reate and Asculum to Castrum Truentinum (Porto d'Ascoli) on the Adriatic coast, a distance of 151 mi. Its first portion was the route by which the Sabines came to fetch salt from the marshes at the mouth of the Tiber. Considerable remains of its course through the Apennines survive.

SALAR JUNG, SIR (1829–1883), Indian statesman of Hyderabad, born in 1829, descendant of a family of officials under the Adil Shahi kings of Bijapur, then under the Delhi emperors and lastly under the nizams. Sir Salar Jung's personal name was Mir Turab Ali. He succeeded his uncle Suraju 'l-Mulk as prime minister of Hyderabad in 1853. Salar Jung disciplined Arab mercenaries, the more valuable part of the nizam's army, and employed them against the rapacious nobles and bands of robbers who had annihilated the trade of the country. He then constituted courts of justice at Hyderabad, organized the police force, constructed and repaired irrigation works and established schools. On the outbreak of the mutiny he supported the British, and although unable to hinder an attack on the residency, he warned the British minister that it was in contemplation. The attack was repulsed; the Hyderabad contingent remained loyal, and their loyalty served to ensure the tranquillity of the Deccan. Salar Jung took advantage of the preoccupation of the British government with the mutiny to push his reforms more boldly, and when the Calcutta authorities were again at liberty to consider the condition of affairs his work had been carried far toward completion. During the lifetime of the nizam Afzulu'd-dowla, Salar Jung was considerably hampered by his master's jealous supervision. When Mir Mahbub Ali, however, succeeded his father in 1869, Salar Jung, at the instance of the British government, was associated in the regency with the principal noble of the state, the Shamsu 'l-Umara or Amir Kabir, and enjoyed an increased authority. In 1876 he visited England, unsuccessfully attempting to obtain the restoration of Berar. He died at Hyderabad on Feb. 8, 1883.

SALAYAR (Dutch SALAJAR), a group of islands between 5° 36′ and 7° 25′ S. and 119° 50′ and 121° 30′ E., Celebes, Indonesia, including Tambalongang, Pulasi and Bahuluwang. The main island, Salayar, is more than 50 mi. long and 8 mi. at its widest point; area, 248 sq.mi. The strata of the island are sedimentary rocks; except in the north and northwest it is covered by fertile soil. Pop. (1930) 76,501, mainly a mixture of Macassars, Buginese and natives of Luvu and Buton, Salayar being one of the most thickly populated parts of the division of Celebes. Trepang, tortoise shell, copra, coconut oil and salt are exported. The islands were occupied by Japan, 1942–45.

SALDANHA BAY, an inlet on the southwestern coast of South Africa, 63 mi. by sea north by west of Cape Town, forming a landlocked harbour. The northern part of the inlet is known as Hoetjes bay. From Kalabas Kraal on the Cape Town-Clanwilliam railway, a narrow gauge line was built via Hopefield to Hoetjes bay—126 mi. from Cape Town. It was used as a naval base during World War II. Saldanha bay was named after Antonio de Saldanha, captain in Albuquerque's fleet which visited south Africa in 1503.

SALDERN, FRIEDRICH CHRISTOPH VON (1719–1785), Prussian soldier and military writer, entered the army in

1735, and was transferred to the Guards in 1739. As one of Frederick's aides-de-camp he was the first to discover the approach of Neipperg's Austrians at Mollwitz. He commanded a guard battalion at Leuthen, again distinguished himself at Hochkirch and was promoted major-general. In 1760 at Liegnitz Frederick gave him four hours in which to collect, arrange and despatch the spoils of the battle, 6,000 prisoners, 100 wagons, 82 guns and 5,000 muskets. His complete success made him a marked man even in Frederick's army. At Torgau, Saldern and Möllendorf (*q.v.*) with their brigades converted a lost battle into a great victory by their desperate assault on the Siptitz heights. The manoeuvring skill, as well as the iron resolution, of the attack, has excited the wonder of modern critics, and after Torgau Saldern was accounted the "completest general of infantry alive" (Carlyle). In the following winter, however, being ordered by Frederick to sack Hubertusburg, Saldern refused on the ground of conscience. Nothing was left for him but to retire, but after the peace the general was at once made inspector of the troops at Magdeburg. In 1766 he became lieutenant-general. Saldern was a pedant of the most pronounced type. In one of his works he discussed at great length the question between 76 and 75 paces to the minute as the proper cadence of infantry. "Saldern-tactics" contributed powerfully to the disaster of Jena in 1806. His works included *Taktik der Infanterie* (Dresden, 1784) and *Taktische Grundsätze* (Dresden, 1786), and were the basis of the British "Dundas" drill-book.

See Küster, *Charakterzüge des Generalleutnants von Saldern* (1792).

SALE, GEORGE (*c.* 1697–1736), English Orientalist, was the son of a London merchant. In 1720 he was admitted a student of the Inner Temple, but subsequently practised as a solicitor. Having studied Arabic for some time in England, he became, in 1726, one of the correctors of the Arabic version of the New Testament, begun in 1720 by the Society for Promoting Christian Knowledge, and subsequently took the principal part in the work. He made an extremely paraphrastic, but, for his time, admirable English translation of the Koran (1734 and often reprinted), and had a European reputation as an Orientalist. He died on Nov. 13, 1736.

SALE, SIR ROBERT HENRY (1782–1845), British soldier, entered the 36th Foot in 1795, and went to India in 1798, as a lieutenant of the 12th Foot. He served in the operations against Tippoo Sahib, against the raja of Travancore (1808–09) and in the expedition to Mauritius (1810). After some years he became major in the 13th, with which regiment he was for the rest of his life associated. In the Burmese War he led the 13th in all the actions up to the capture of Rangoon, in one of which he killed the enemy's leader in single combat. In the concluding operations of the war, being now lieutenant-colonel, he commanded a brigade, and at Malown (1826) he was severely wounded. In 1838, on the outbreak of the Afghan War, Sale was assigned to the command of the 1st Bengal brigade of the army assembling on the Indus. His column arrived at Kandahar in April 1839, and in May it occupied the Herat plain. The Kandahar force next set out on its march to Kabul, and a month later Ghazni was stormed, Sale in person leading the storming column and distinguishing himself in single combat. The place was well provisioned, and on its supplies the army finished its march to Kabul easily. He was left, as second-in-command, with the army of occupation, and in the interval between the two wars conducted several small campaigns ending with the action of Parwan which led directly to the surrender of Dost Mohammed.

By this time the army had settled down to the quiet life of cantonments, and Lady Sale and her daughter came to Kabul. But the policy of the Indian Government in stopping the subsidy to the frontier tribes roused them into hostility, and Sale's brigade received orders to clear the line of communication to Peshawar. After severe fighting Sale entered Jalalabad on Nov. 12, 1841. Ten days previously he had received news of the murder of Sir Alexander Burnes, along with orders to return with all speed to Kabul. These orders he, for various reasons, decided to ignore; suppressing his personal desire to return to protect his wife and family, he gave orders to push on, and on occupying Jalalabad at once set about making the old and half-ruined fortress fit to stand

a siege. There followed a close and severe investment. At last Pollock and the relieving army appeared, only to find that the garrison had on April 7, 1842, relieved itself by a brilliant and completely successful attack on Akbar's lines. Pollock and Sale after a time took the offensive, and after the victory of Haft Kotal, Sale's division encamped at Kabul again.

At the end of the war Sale received the thanks of parliament. In 1845, as quartermaster-general to Sir H. Gough's army, Sale again took the field. At Moodkee (Mudki) he was wounded and he died on Dec. 21, 1845. His wife was among Akbar's captives. Among the few possessions she was able to keep from Afghan plunderers was her diary (*Journal of the Disasters in Afghanistan,* London, 1843).

See Gleig, *Sale's Brigade in Afghanistan* (London, 1846); Kaye, *Lives of Indian Officers* (London, 1867); W. Sale, *Defence of Jellalabad* (London, 1846); Regimental History of the 13th Light Infantry.

SALE, a municipal borough in the Altrincham and Sale parliamentary division, Cheshire, Eng., 5 mi. S.W. of Manchester. Pop. (1951) 43,168. Area 5.7 sq.mi. In 1930 the urban districts of Sale and Ashton-upon-Mersey were amalgamated. The borough, created in 1935, is mainly residential but market gardening to supply Manchester is extensive. The Mersey river separates Sale from Manchester, Salford and Stretford. The Bridgewater canal passes through the town.

SALÉ (SLĀ), a seaport on the Atlantic coast of Morocco, on the north side of the Bu Ragreg, opposite Rabat (*q.v.*). Salé, inhabited by a native bourgeoisie, has many Moslem sanctuaries, mosques, *zaouïas, medersas* and tombs of saints. In the middle ages, it was the most important merchant port and entrepôt of the west coast. In the 17th century it became an independent republic, a great centre of corsairs. Various French and English expeditions tried, without much success, to put an end to it. Pop. (1944) 53,819, including 2,868 Europeans, 3,173 Jews, 47,778 natives.

SALE CITY, the first city to be proclaimed in Gippsland province in the county of Tanjil, Victoria, Austr., on the Thomson river, 127½ mi. by rail E.S.E. of Melbourne. Pop. (1953) 6,300. It is an important administrative and educational centre situated in a rich agricultural (dairying and mixed farming) irrigation district. Sale City is the seat of the Anglican bishop of Gippsland and also of the Roman Catholic bishop of Sale. The climate is temperate; the average annual rainfall is 24 in.

SALEM, a city and district of Madras state, republic of India. The city is on both banks of the Tirumanimuttar river, 3 mi. from a station on the Southern railway, 206 mi. S.W. of Madras city. Pop. (1951) 202,335. There is a considerable weaving industry. Its situation in a green valley between the Shevaroy and Jarugumalai hills is picturesque.

The DISTRICT OF SALEM has an area of 7,063 sq.mi. Except toward the south it is hilly, with extensive plains lying between the several ranges. It consists of three distinct tracts, formerly known as the Talaghat, the Baramahal and the Balaghat. The Talaghat is situated below the Eastern Ghats on the level of the Carnatic generally; the Baramahal includes the whole face of the Ghats and a wide area of country at their base; and the Balaghat is situated above the Ghats on the tableland of Mysore.

The western part of the district is mountainous. Among the chief ranges are the Shevaroys, the Kalrayans, the Melagiris, the Kollimalais, the Pachamalais and the Yelagiris. The population in 1951 was 3,371,769. The principal crops are millets, rice, pulses, mangoes and oilseeds. Coffee is grown on the Shevaroy hills. The chief irrigation work is the Barur tank system. The Southern railway runs through the district, with two narrow-gauge branches. The chief industry is cotton weaving, and magnesite and steatite are worked, and there are iron and steel works. The district was acquired partly by the treaty of peace with Tippoo Sultan in 1792 and partly by the partition treaty of Mysore in 1799.

SALEM, a city of Massachusetts, U.S.A., on the coast, 15 mi. N.E. of Boston; a port of entry, one of the county seats of Essex county and a city of great historic interest. It is served by the Boston and Maine railroad.

Pop. (1950) 41,880; (1940) 41,213 by federal census. The city's area of 8.2 sq.mi. comprises a peninsula projecting toward the northeast between Marblehead and Beverly, Winter Island (connected with the neck of the peninsula by a causeway) and some territory on the mainland.

The commerce of Salem's harbour is largely from coal and oil. Its manufactures include chemicals, cotton goods, shoes, leather, candy, valves, mattresses, incandescent bulbs, fluorescent tubes and radio tubes. Salem is the seat of a state teachers college (1854).

The assessed valuation of property for 1940 was $53,975,000.

Salem is one of the oldest cities in New England and has preserved an unusual number of historic and literary landmarks. In the centre of the city is the common (8 ac.). On a bluff projecting into South river is the old Burying point, set aside in 1637, with stones dating back to 1673; and in Broad street is another old burial ground, laid out in 1655. The famous India (or Crowninshield's) wharf became a coal pocket. The custom house (described by Nathaniel Hawthorne in the introduction to *The Scarlet Letter*) was built in 1818–19; the oldest of the three courthouses, which has great monolithic Corinthian columns, in 1839–41; the city hall, in 1837.

There are many old dwellings built by shipowners before the Revolution. Many are of the gambrel type, and they are rich in beautiful doorways, doorheads and other fine architectural details. The Salem Maritime national historic site comprises Derby wharf, the customhouse and three other buildings. Among the houses of special interest are the birthplace of Nathaniel Hawthorne (built before 1692); the "house of the seven gables," in use as a social settlement; the "witch house," where Jonathan Corwin is said to have held preliminary examinations in the witchcraft trials. The Essex institute (1848) and the Peabody museum (in the East Indian Marine hall, built in 1824) contain rich collections relating to colonial life.

Salem was founded in 1626 by Roger Conant (1593–1679) as a commercial venture, partly agricultural and partly to provide a wintering-place for the Banks fishermen. The name was probably chosen in allusion to Psalm lxxvi, 2. In 1628 a patent for the territory was granted by the New England council to the Dorchester Company, which promptly sent out a small colony under John Endecott as governor. This patent was superseded in 1629 by the charter for the Colony of Massachusetts Bay. Endecott continued as governor until the arrival (1630) of John Winthrop, who soon moved the seat of government to Charlestown and then to Boston. In 1629 the first Congregational Church in America was organized in Salem, and Roger Williams (*q.v.*) was one of its first pastors. In 1686 the people of Salem, guarding against the danger of being dispossessed by a new charter, secured a deed to their land from the Indians for £20. Salem village (then part of Salem, but now in Danvers) was the centre of the witchcraft delusion of 1692. Beginning with accusations by ten young girls that Tituba, the West Indian slave of the Rev. Samuel Parris, and two old women had bewitched them, the hysteria spread rapidly, and within four months hundreds were arrested and tried, 19 hanged, and one pressed to death for refusing to plead. The reaction came quickly, and in May 1693 Governor Phelps ordered the release of all prisoners held on the charge of witchcraft. Salem was an important port after 1670, especially in the India trade, and Salem privateers were conspicuous in the Seven Years' War, during the Revolution (when 158 of them took 445 prizes), and in the War of 1812. The first provincial assembly of Massachusetts met in Salem in 1774. On Feb. 20, 1775, at the North bridge, the first armed resistance of the Revolution was offered by the men of the town to royal troops sent to search for hidden cannon. Marblehead was set off from Salem in 1649, Beverly in 1668 and Danvers in 1752. Salem was chartered as a city in 1836. It was the birthplace of Nathaniel Hawthorne, William H. Prescott, Nathaniel Bowditch, Jones Very and William Wetmore Story.

SALEM, a city of southwestern New Jersey, U.S., the county seat of Salem county; 38 mi. S.W. of Philadelphia, on the Salem river, 2 mi. from its confluence with the Delaware. It is served by the Pennsylvania-Reading Seashore railroad and motorbus lines. The vicinity abounds in small river craft for pleasure. Pop. (1950) 9,050; (1940) 8,618. It is the trade centre for a rich agricultural region and has important manufactures, including floor coverings, canned food, canning machinery and glass. The public library was established in 1804; the county offices occupy the old Johnson house, built in 1804; and in the Friends' burial ground (set aside in 1676) is an oak tree 88 ft. high, with a spread of $\frac{1}{4}$ ac., a survivor of the original forest. In Finn's Point national cemetery, 4 mi. N. of Salem, are buried about 2,460 Confederate soldiers, who died while prisoners of war at Ft. Delaware, on an island in the Delaware river near the mouth of the Salem. Salem is the oldest permanent English settlement along the Delaware. It was founded in 1675 by John Fenwicke, an English Quaker, who bought from the Indians the land now embraced in Salem and Cumberland counties, and selected the site of the present city for his settlement, naming it Salem because of its peaceful aspect. In 1682 he submitted to the authority of the proprietors of West Jersey. Salem was incorporated as a town in 1695 and as a city in 1858.

SALEM, a city of Columbiana county, Ohio, U.S., 67 mi. S.E. of Cleveland; served by the Pennsylvania railway. The population was 12,754 in 1950 and was 12,301 in 1940 by the federal census.

Salem is in a fertile agricultural region, where coal and natural gas are plentiful, and has important manufactures (including pumps, furnaces, machinery, bathroom fixtures, chinaware, automobile bodies and various other articles). Salem was settled by Friends in 1806, incorporated as a town in 1830, as a village in 1852 and as a city in 1887. It was a "station" on the underground railroad and the headquarters of the Western Anti-Slavery society, which published there *The Anti-Slavery Bugle*.

SALEM, the capital city of Oregon, U.S., and county seat of Marion county; on the Willamette river, 51 mi. S.S.W. of Portland. It is on federal highway 99E and is served by the Southern Pacific and the Oregon Electric railways and by motor coach lines. Pop. (1950) 43,140; 1940 federal census 30,908. In the heart of the Willamette valley, Salem is surrounded by rich farm land producing fruits, berries, nuts, hops, mint, mushrooms and seed; it is the only region in the United States where long-fibre flax is raised. Manufacturing industries include fruit, berry and vegetable canneries, a paper mill, large sawmills, also sash and door factories, woollen mills, ironworks and two linen mills. All but two of the state institutions are in or near the city, and at Chemawa, 5 mi. N., is a government school for Indians. On an 18-ac. campus in the heart of the city is Willamette university (Methodist Episcopal; 1842), an outgrowth of the mission work of the Methodist Episcopal church begun in the vicinity by Jason Lee in 1834. Around the mission and the school grew up a settlement which in 1853 was chartered as a city and in 1860 became the capital of the state.

SALEM, a town of southwestern Virginia, U.S., the county seat of Roanoke county; on the Roanoke river and federal highway 11, 6 mi. W. of Roanoke. It is served by the Norfolk and Western and the Virginian railways. Pop. 6,823 in 1950 and 5,737 in 1940 by the federal census. Salem lies about 1,000 ft. above sea level, in the beautiful region between the Blue Ridge and the Allegheny mountains. It is the seat of Roanoke college, coeducational (Lutheran; 1842), and of two orphanages (Baptist and Lutheran) and has a variety of manufacturing plants. The town was laid out in 1802, incorporated in 1806 and became the county seat in 1838. Since 1922 Salem has had a council-manager form of government.

SALE OF GOODS. The law of sale is usually treated as a branch of the law of contract, because sale is effected by contract. Thus Pothier entitles his classical treatise on the subject, *Traité du contrat de vente*. But a completed contract of sale is something more. It is a contract plus a transfer of property. By an agreement to sell a *ius in personam* is created; by a sale of *ius in rem* is transferred. The essence of sale is the transfer of property for a price. If there be no agreement for a price, express or implied, the transaction is of the nature of a gift. So, too, if commodity be exchanged for commodity, the transaction is called barter (*q.v.*) and not sale, and the rules relating to sales do not apply in their entirety. Again, a contract of sale must contemplate an absolute transfer of the property in the thing sold or agreed to be sold. A mortgage may be in the form of a conditional sale, but English law regards the substance and not the form of the transaction. If in substance the object of the transaction is to secure the repayment of a debt, and not to transfer the absolute property in the thing sold, the law at once annexes to the transaction the complex consequences which attach to a mortgage. So, too, it is not always easy to distinguish a contract for the sale of an article from a contract for the supply of work and materials. If a man orders a set of false teeth from a dentist the contract is one of sale, but if he employs a dentist to stop one of his teeth with gold the contract is for the supply of work and materials. The distinction is of practical importance, because very different rules of law apply to the two classes of contract. The property which may be the subject of sale may be either movable or immovable, tangible or intangible. The present article relates only to the sale of goods—that is to say, tangible movable property.

The Code of 1893.—In 1847, when Justice Story wrote his work on the sale of personal property, the law of sale was still in process of development. Many rules were still unsettled, especially the rules relating to implied conditions and warranties. But for several years the main principles have been well settled. In 1891 the subject seemed ripe for codification, and Lord Herschell introduced a codifying bill which two years later passed into law as the Sale of Goods Act, 1893.

Sale is a consensual contract. The parties to the contract may supplement it with any stipulations or conditions they may see fit to agree to. The code in no wise seeks to fetter this discretion. It lays down a few positive rules—such, for instance, as that which reproduces the 17th section of the Statute of Frauds. But the main object of the act is to provide clear rules for those cases where the parties have either formed no intention or have failed to express it. When parties enter into a contract they contemplate its smooth performance, and they seldom provide for contingencies which may interrupt that performance—such as the insolvency of the buyer or the destruction of the thing sold before it is delivered. It is the province of the code to provide for these contingencies, leaving the parties free to modify by express stipulation the provisions imparted by law. When the code was in contemplation the case of Scotland gave rise to difficulty. Scottish law varies widely from English. To speak broadly, the Scottish law of sale differs from the English by adhering to the rules of Roman law, while the English common law has worked out rules of its own. The Codifying bill of 1891 applied only to England, but on the advice of Lord Watson it was extended to Scotland. As the English and Irish laws of sale were the same, the case of Ireland gave rise to no difficulty, and the act now applies to the whole of Great Britain. As regards England and Ireland, very little change in the law has been effected. As regards Scotland, the process of assimilation has been carried further, but this has not been completed. In a few cases the Scottish rule has been saved or re-enacted, in a few other cases it has been modified, while on other points, where the laws were dissimilar, the English rules have been adopted.

The act is divided into six parts, the first dealing with the formation of the contract. The 1st section, which may be regarded as the keystone of the act, is in the following terms: "A contract of sale of goods is a contract whereby the seller transfers or agrees to transfer the property in goods to the buyer for a money consideration called the price. A contract of sale may be absolute or conditional. When under a contract of sale the property in the goods is transferred from the seller to the buyer the contract is called a 'sale,' but when the transfer of the property in the goods is to take place at a future time or subject to some condition thereafter to be fulfilled the contract is called an 'agreement to sell.' An agreement to sell becomes a sale when the time elapses or the conditions are fulfilled subject to which the property in the goods is to be transferred." This section clearly enunciates the consensual nature of the contract, and this is confirmed by sec. 55, which provides that "where any right, duty or liability would arise under a contract of sale by impli-

cation of law," it may be negatived or varied by express agreement, or by the course of dealing between the parties, or by usage, if the usage be such as to bind both parties to the contract. The next question is who can sell and buy. The act is framed on the plan that if the law of contract were codified, this act would form a chapter in the code. The question of capacity is therefore referred to the general law, but a special provision is inserted (sec. 2) relating to the supply of necessaries to infants and other persons who are incompetent to contract. Though an infant cannot contract he must live, and he can only get goods by paying for them. The law, therefore, provides that he is liable to pay a reasonable price for necessaries supplied to him, and it defines necessaries as "goods suitable to the condition in life of such minor or other person, and to his actual requirements at the time of the sale and delivery."

The 4th section of the act reproduces the famous 17th section of the Statute of Frauds, which was an act "for the prevention of frauds and perjuries." The object of that statute was to prevent people from setting up bogus contracts of sale by requiring material evidence of the contract. The section provides that "a contract for the sale of any goods of the value of £10 or upwards shall not be enforceable by action unless the buyer shall accept part of the goods so sold, and actually receive the same, or give something in earnest to bind the contract, or in part payment, or unless some note or memorandum in writing of the contract be made and signed by the party to be charged, or his agent in that behalf." It is a much-disputed question whether this enactment has brought about good or harm. It has defeated many an honest claim, though it may have prevented many a dishonest one from being put forward. When judges and juries have been satisfied of the *bona fides* of a contract which does not appear to satisfy the statute, they have done their best to get round it. Every expression in the section has been the subject of numerous judicial decisions, which run into almost impossible refinements, and illustrate the maxim that hard cases make bad law. It is to be noted that Scotland is excluded from the operation of sec. 4. The Statute of Frauds has never been applied to Scotland, and Scotsmen appear never to have felt the want of it.

As regards the subject-matter of the contract, the act provides that it may consist either of existing goods or "future goods"—that is to say, goods to be manufactured or acquired by the seller after the making of the contract (sec. 5). Suppose that a man goes into a gunsmith's shop and says, "This gun suits me, and if you will make or get me another like it I will buy the pair." This is a good contract, and no question as to its validity would be likely to occur to the lay mind. But lawyers have seriously raised the question, whether there could be a valid contract of sale when the subject-matter of the contract was not in existence at the time when the contract was made. The price is an essential element in a contract of sale. It may be either fixed by the contract itself, or left to be determined in some manner thereby agreed upon, *e.g.*, by the award of a third party. But there are many cases in which the parties intend to effect a sale, and yet say nothing about the price. Suppose that a man goes into an hotel and orders dinner without asking the price. How is it to be fixed? The law steps in and says that, in the absence of any agreement, a reasonable price must be paid (sec. 8). This prevents extortion on the part of the seller, and unreasonableness or fraud on the part of the buyer.

Warranty.—The next question dealt with is the difficult one of conditions and warranties (secs. 10 and 11). The parties may insert what stipulations they like in a contract of sale, but the law has to interpret them. The term "warranty" has a peculiar and technical meaning in the law of sale. It denotes a stipulation which the law regards as collateral to the main purpose of the contract. A breach, therefore, does not entitle the buyer to reject the goods, but only to claim damages. Suppose that a man buys a particular horse, which is warranted quiet to ride and drive. If the horse turns out to be vicious, the buyer's only remedy is to claim damages, unless he has expressly reserved a right to return it. But if, instead of buying a particular horse, a man applies to a dealer to supply him with a quiet horse, and the dealer supplies him with a vicious one, the stipulation is a condition. The buyer can either return the horse, or keep it and claim damages. Of course the right of rejection must be exercised within a reasonable time. In Scotland no distinction has been drawn between conditions and warranties, and the act preserves the Scottish rule by providing that, in Scotland, "failure by the seller to perform any material part of a contract of sale" entitles the buyer either to reject the goods within a reasonable time after delivery, or to retain them and claim compensation (sec. 11 [2]). In England it is a very common trick for the buyer to keep the goods, and then set up in reduction of the price that they are of inferior quality to what was ordered. To discourage this practice in Scotland the act provides that, in that country, the court may require the buyer who alleges a breach of contract to bring the agreed price into court pending a decision of the case (sec. 59). It seems a pity that this sensible rule was not extended to England.

In early English law *caveat emptor* was the general rule, and it was one well suited to primitive times. Men either bought their goods in the open market-place, or from their neighbours, and buyer and seller contracted on a footing of equality. Now the complexity of modern commerce, the division of labour and the increase of technical skill, have altogether altered the state of affairs. The buyer is more and more driven to rely on the honesty, skill and judgment of the seller or manufacturer. Modern law has recognized this, and protects the buyer by implying various conditions and warranties in contracts of sale, which may be summarized as follows: First, there is an implied undertaking on the part of the seller that he has a right to sell the goods (sec. 12). Secondly, if goods be ordered by description, they must correspond with that description (sec. 13). Thirdly, there is the case of manufacturers or sellers who deal in particular classes of goods. They naturally have better means of judging of their merchandise than the outside public, and the buyer is entitled within limits to rely on their skill or judgment. A tea merchant or grocer knows more about tea than his customers can, and so does a gunsmith about guns. In such cases, if the buyer makes known to the seller the particular purpose for which the goods are required, there is an implied condition that the goods are reasonably fit for it, and if no particular purpose be indicated there is an implied condition that the goods supplied are of merchantable quality (sec. 14). Fourthly, in the case of a sale by sample, there is "an implied condition that the bulk shall correspond with the sample in quality," and that the buyer shall have a reasonable opportunity of comparing the bulk with the sample (sec. 15).

Effects of Contract.—The main object of sale is the transfer of ownership from seller to buyer, and it is often both a difficult and an important matter to determine the precise moment at which the change of ownership is effected. According to Roman law, which is still the foundation of most European systems, the property in a thing sold did not pass until delivery to the buyer. English law has adopted the principle that the property passes at such time as the parties intend it to pass. Express stipulations as to the time when the property is to pass are very rare. The intention of the parties has to be gathered from their conduct. A long train of judicial decisions has worked out a series of rules for determining the presumed intention of the parties, and these rules are embodied in secs. 16 to 20 of the act. The first rule is a negative one. In the case of unascertained goods, *i.e.*, goods defined by description only, and not specifically identified, "no property in the goods is transferred to the buyer unless and until the goods are ascertained." If a man orders ten tons of scrap iron from a dealer, it is obvious that the dealer can fulfil his contract by delivering any ten tons of scrap that he may select, and that until the ten tons have been set apart, no question of change of ownership can arise. But when a specific article is bought, or when goods ordered by description are appropriated to the contract, the passing of the property is a question of intention. Delivery to the buyer is strong evidence of intention to change the ownership, but it is not conclusive. Goods may be delivered to the buyer on approval, or for sale or return. Delivery to a carrier for the buyer operates in the main as a delivery to the buyer, but the seller may deliver to the carrier, and yet reserve to himself a right of disposal. On the other hand, when there is a sale of a specific article, which is in a fit state for delivery, the property in the article *prima facie* passes at once, even though delivery be delayed. When the contract is for the sale of unascertained goods, which are ordered by description, the property in the goods passes to the buyer, when, with the express or implied consent of the parties, goods of the required description are "unconditionally appropriated to the contract." It is perhaps to be regretted that the codifying act did not adopt the test of delivery, but it was thought better to adhere to the familiar phraseology of the cases. Section 20 deals with the transfer of risk from seller to buyer, and lays down the *prima facie* rule that "the goods remain at the seller's risk until the property therein is transferred to the buyer, but when the property therein is transferred to the buyer, the goods are at the buyer's risk whether delivery has been made or not." *Res perit domino* is therefore the maxim of English, as well as of Roman law.

Title.—In the vast majority of cases people only sell what they have a right to sell, but the law has to make provision for cases where a man sells goods which he is not entitled to sell. An agent may misconceive or exceed his authority. Stolen goods may be passed from buyer to buyer. Then comes the question, Which of two innocent parties is to suffer? Is the original owner to be permanently deprived of his property, or is the loss to fall on the innocent purchaser? Roman law threw the loss on the buyer, *Nemo plus iuris in alium transferre potest quam ipse habet.* French law, in deference to modern commerce, protects the innocent purchaser and throws the loss on the original owner. "En fait de meubles, possession vaut titre" (*Code civil*, art. 1,599). English law is a compromise between these opposing theories. It adopts the Roman rule as its guiding principle, but qualifies it with certain exceptions, which cover perhaps the majority of the actual cases which occur (secs. 21 to 26). In the first place, the provisions of the Factors Act, 1889 (extended to Scotland by 53 and 54 Vict. c. 40), are preserved. That act validates sales and other dispositions of goods by mercantile agents acting within the apparent scope of their authority, and also protects innocent purchasers who obtain goods from sellers left in possession, or from intending buyers who have got possession of the goods while negotiations are pending. In most cases a contract induced by fraud is voidable only, and not void, and the act provides, accordingly, that a voidable contract of sale shall not be voided to the prejudice of an innocent purchaser. The ancient privilege of market overt (*i.e.*, "open market") is preserved intact (sec. 22). The section does not apply to Scotland, nor to the law relating to the sale of horses which is contained in two old statutes, 2 and 3 Phil. and Mar. c. 7, and 31 Eliz. c. 12. The minute regulations of those statutes are never complied with, so their practical effect is to take horses out of the category of things which can be sold in market overt. The privilege of market overt applies only to markets by prescription, and does not attach to newly-created markets. The operation of the custom is therefore fitful and capricious. For example, every shop in the City of London is within the custom, but the custom does not extend to the greater London outside. If then a man buys a stolen watch in Fleet street, he may get a good title to it, but he cannot do so if he buys it a few doors off in the Strand. There is, however, a qualification of the rights acquired by purchase even in market overt. When goods have been stolen and the thief is prosecuted to conviction, the property in the goods thereupon revests in the original owner, and he is entitled to get them back either by a summary order of the convicting court or by action. This rule dates back to the statute 21 Hen. VIII. c. 11. It was probably intended rather to encourage prosecutions in the interests of public justice than to protect people whose goods were stolen.

Having dealt with the effects of sale, first, as between seller and buyer, and, secondly, as between the buyer and third parties, the act proceeds to determine what, in the absence of convention, are the reciprocal rights and duties of the parties in the performance of their contract (secs. 27 to 37). "It is the duty of the seller to deliver the goods and of the buyer to accept and pay for them in accordance with the terms of the contract of sale" (sec. 27). In ordinary cases the seller's duty to deliver the goods is satisfied if he puts them at the disposal of the buyer at the place of sale. The normal contract of sale is represented by a cash sale in a shop. The buyer pays the price and takes away the goods "Unless otherwise agreed, delivery of the goods and payment of the price are concurrent conditions" (sec. 27). But agreement, express or implied, may create infinite variations on the normal contract. It is to be noted that when goods are sent to the buyer which he is entitled to reject, and does reject, he is not bound to send them back to the seller. It is sufficient if he intimate to the seller his refusal to accept them (sec. 36).

Remedies of Buyer and Seller.—The ultimate sanction of a contract is the legal remedy for its breach. Seller and buyer have each their appropriate remedies. If the property in the goods has passed to the buyer, or if, under the contract, "the price is payable on a day certain irrespective of delivery," the seller's remedy for breach of the contract is an action for the price (sec. 49). In other cases his remedy is an action for damages for non-acceptance. In the case of ordinary goods of commerce the measure of damages is the difference between the contract price and the market or current price at the time when the goods ought to have been accepted. The convenient market-price rule is subordinate to the general principle that "the measure of damages is the estimated loss directly and naturally resulting in the ordinary course of events from the buyer's breach of contract" (sec. 56). Similar considerations apply to the buyer's right of action for non-delivery of the goods (sec. 51). In exceptional circumstances the remedy of specific performance is available to the buyer (sec. 52). Thus the court might order the specific delivery of an autograph letter of an otherwise unrecorded signatory of the Declaration of Independence. The seller's rights are further protected by the rules as to lien and stoppage *in transitu* (secs. 38 to 48).

The sixth and last part of the act is supplemental, and is mainly concerned with drafting explanations, but sec. 58 contains some rules for regulating sales by auction. The practice known as a "knock-out" has since been struck at by the Auctions (Bidding Agreements) Act, 1927, by which it is declared illegal and punishable.

The act of 1893 has been adopted in substance by very many of the colonial possessions, and has been followed in the main by the American Sales Act (U.S.A.). (M. D. C.)

C.I.F. Contracts.—These are in a class by themselves. The law governing them is mostly of recent growth and, nearly all of it, case law. They are contracts for the sale of sea-borne goods where the price quoted covers cost, insurance and freight. Hence the name. But the distinguishing characteristic of these sales is this: Performance is effected by tender of the documents in place of the delivery of the actual goods. Indeed, in the business world they are often referred to as sales of documents. By their means the goods are often sold many times over while still afloat; even though the ship be sunk or the goods perish no loss need fall upon the buyer, because he is protected under the policy of insurance effected on the goods or the bill of lading under which they are carried.

The documents are naturally the focus of attention. The seller must tender to the buyer the invoice, the bill of lading and the policy of insurance. On this point the requirements of the English courts are strict. By bill of lading is meant a bill or document attesting that the goods have been loaded on board, not that a shipping company is under contract to carry the goods on a named or subsequent ship. In the United States the practice may be different and the courts there may recognize "received for shipment" bills of lading and similar documents which circulate freely enough in the commercial world. Similarly with the policy of insurance. English law requires the tender of a policy. In the United States certificates of insurance and even more informal

records of the contract of insurance are in recognized use. In this respect perhaps English law lags a little behind commercial practice, for certainly these certificates are a great convenience and by special agreement can be regularly employed. But in criticizing the law as it stands it must not be forgotten that other interests besides those of buyer and seller are affected; the banker and underwriter have to be taken into account. The banker for his part has up till now resolutely set his face against the so-called "bill of lading" which gives no certain information as to the whereabouts of the goods.

When the documents are tendered the buyer must be ready and willing to pay the price. He is not entitled to withhold payment until he has had an opportunity of examining the goods. The term "net cash" in a c.i.f. contract means cash against documents. The property passes, if any one general rule can be laid down on the subject, when the documents are tendered. But on this as on other aspects of the sale there is a growing body of law to which it is very difficult to do justice in a general statement. Some of the topics are not altogether free from difficulty. Moreover, though it is a form of contract in use the world over, the law governing it is by no means as uniform as could be wished. Accordingly it has been suggested, though the suggestion has a greater measure of support on the Continent where it originated than in either England or the United States, that attempts should be made to secure uniformity along the lines of the York-Antwerp rules. More doubtless will be heard of the proposal as time goes on. (H. Got.)

UNITED STATES

The English law, as stated above, gives even in its details a picture of the American law. There is, to be sure, no market overt in the United States; and the American Factors' Acts are not only less broad in scope than the English, but, even with their narrower scope, are found only in a handful of States. Their policy should be compared with that of the statutes requiring filing or recording of chattel mortgages (*see* BILL OF SALE) and of conditional sales (*see* INSTALMENT PURCHASE). Where found, they commonly permit a consignee of goods, whose business also includes selling on his own account, to make an effective pledge of his principal's goods to secure his own debt; but the American law extends such powers to the "intending purchaser" who has secured possession only in a few specific cases, such as (in many States) instalment purchase. It should also be noted that the rule that risk follows title has an exception where title is withheld—as in the instalment purchase—only for securing payment of the price.

The chief divergence of American sales law from that described above has to do with warranties; *i.e.*, the nature of the seller's obligation with reference to the kind and quality of goods sold. The facts which will place some obligation on the seller with reference to quality are substantially the same in both countries. But in the United States, if the seller has undertaken any obligation in this respect, the buyer will, in the majority of States, be entitled not only to damages (the English "warranty") but also (at his election) to return the goods and recover the price (the English "condition"). This rule as indicated, is not universal. The American common law was in some conflict and confusion on the point, and the Uniform Sales Act, incorporating the view just stated, has not been adopted as yet (1928) in 20 of the States.

The long controversy over the buyer's power to return defective goods indicates the extent to which the law of warranty has been a creature of mercantile law, designated to settle disputes about goods between merchants. Of recent years, however, the law of warranty has been put to another striking social use: that of allocating the risks incident, in a highly industrialized society, to the unavoidable use of goods manufactured by persons with whom the user has no direct contact, who may be a "corporation" located in a distant place, whose methods the user has neither skill nor opportunity to know—but whose efficiency he is forced by the nature of the market to rely upon. Injury in those cases results from a tack or a piece of glass concealed in cake or a can of beans, from the explosion of an automatic water-heater, or from the breaking of an automobile wheel. In such cases return of the goods is not in question, but only the allocation of the damage suffered. The device of an action for negligence has recently been extended for this purpose; but it seems to be limited to personal injury, as opposed to property damage; and it is obviously ineffective in the many States in which the burden rests on the injured plaintiff of proving the manufacturer negligent in regard to the particular defective article. There is some tendency to shift the burden to the manufacturer where the article is one, which, if negligently made, would be dangerous; i.e., to make an injury due to defect raise a presumption of negligence in manufacture. Under this rule the remedy "for negligence" is effective—so effective indeed, as apparently to have given rise to a considerable volume of fraudulent claims. The remedy in negligence, too, may well be extended to any injured purchaser.

But the remedy for the same injury by way of the law of warranty seems in almost all States to be limited to the specific purchaser against his specific seller; it has been held to extend neither to his wife, his child, his employee nor his guest. Nor, under most decisions, will it run against the manufacturer if the plaintiff bought the article not directly from him, but from an intervening dealer. On the other hand, wherever remedy in warranty is available, it requires no proof of negligence at all: the seller is held to guarantee against dangerous defects in the article. It is clear the situation is one in which the courts are groping toward satisfying a definite social need, and yet one in which the traditional legal devices are only with delay and distortion capable of being made to fill the need.

Documents of Title.—One feature of American law in which wide changes have been worked in recent years requires mention. The old rule that no man might convey goods which he did not own imposes on buyers either a noticeable risk (of having any goods which have been improperly sold to them recovered by their true owners) or a degree of investigation incompatible with rapid turnover. Especially dangerous and impracticable is this in the case of bankers advancing money on the security of goods in warehouse or in transit; a banker's margin of profit is too low to make losses readily compensable, and enquiry into title is in general outside his competence. A practice therefore grew up, in the case of goods in warehouse, of accepting the warehouseman's receipt for the goods, if fair on its face, as full evidence of title to the goods, and of dealing with the receipt as with the goods themselves. The same practice has developed, even earlier, with reference to bills of lading, i.e., carriers' receipts for goods entrusted to their care.

This mercantile custom has now received full warrant at law, in America, in all 28 States which have adopted the Uniform Sales Act (beginning in 1906); also, as to warehouse receipts, in the 48 States which have enacted the Uniform Warehouse Receipts Act (beginning in 1906); in more than half the States, as to bills of lading, and in all bills of lading arising out of interstate shipments, by the adoption of the Uniform Bills of Lading Act by Congress and many State legislatures (beginning in 1909). Sharp distinction is taken under these acts between straight or *non-negotiable* documents, which do not contain a promise to deliver to the *order* of named person, and which can transfer only such rights as the transferor possesses; and on the other hand, *order* or negotiable documents, which do carry a promise to deliver to the order of a named person, and which in general carry to a *bona fide* purchaser (or pledgee) for value all the rights apparent on their face, even though the transferor may have lacked such rights. The English law is to the same effect, and even expressly extends the same rules to policies of marine insurance drawn in proper form. All the American uniform acts named above are the work of Prof. Samuel Williston, whose credit in this connection is as great as that of Chalmers in England, and whose text on sales (see *The Law of Sales*, 2nd ed., 1924) promises to remain for a generation the authoritative work on the subject.

(K. N. L.)

BIBLIOGRAPHY.—C. Blackburn, *A Treatise on the Effect of Contract of Sale* (1845, 3rd ed. by W. R. Norman and L. C. Thomas, 1910); J. Bedarride, *Des achats et ventes* (1862), in *Droit Commercial*, 17 vol. (1854-64); J. P. Benjamin, *Sale of Personal Property* (1868,

6th ed. by W. C. A. Ker, 1920); W. W. Story, *A Treatise on the Sale of Personal Property* (4th ed. by E. H. Bennett, Boston, Mass., 1871); R. Campbell, *The Law relating to the Sale of Goods and Commercial Agency* (2nd ed. 1891); J. B. Moyle, *Contract of Sale in the Civil Law* (1892); Sir M. D. E. S. Chalmers, *Sale of Goods Act* (1894, 10th ed. 1924); R. Brown, *Notes and Commentaries on the Sale of Goods Act, 1893*, etc. (1895); E. J. Schuster, *Principles of German Civil Law* (1907); S. Williston, *Law Governing Sales of Goods at Common Law* (2nd ed., 1924); A. R. Kennedy, *Contracts of Sale on C.I.F. Terms* (1924); H. Goitein, *C.I.F. Contracts* (2nd ed. 1926).

SALEP, a drug extensively used in oriental countries as a nervine restorative and fattener, and also much prescribed in paralytic affections. It is not used in European medicine. It consists of the tuberous roots of various species of *Orchis* and *Eulophia*, which are decorticated, washed, heated until horny in appearance, and then dried. Its most important constituent is a mucilaginous substance which it yields with cold water to the extent of 48%.

SALERNO (known in Roman and mediaeval times as Salernum), a small seaport, archiepiscopal see and capital of a province of the same name, about 30 mi. S.E. of Naples, Italy, finely situated at the foot of an amphitheatre of hills. Pop. (1936) 41,925 (town), 67,009 (commune). The modern town is of little commercial importance, but as a sea base and communications centre was bombed by the Allies in World War II.

The site was of some strategic significance under the Roman Republic and Empire, but the town was of only secondary importance until mediaeval times. It was dismantled by Charlemagne in the 9th century. Later it became the fortified capital of an independent principality and the rival of Benevento. During the 9th and 10th centuries it was frequently attacked by the Saracens. It was taken in 1076 by the Normans under Robert Guiscard. In 1194 it was sacked by Henry VI., and its development ceased. Salerno revived somewhat in the early 13th century, under Frederick II. (1194-1250), but soon fell into decay. The historic interest of Salerno centres round its medical school, the foundation of which is ascribed to the legendary "four masters"—a Latin, a Greek, a Jew and a Saracen. The legend represents the syncretic cultural influences under which the school arose. In the 10th and 11th centuries the place was a health resort. Under Norman rule the medical element became organized and was profoundly influenced by the work of Constantine the African (d. 1087, q.v.), secretary to Robert Guiscard who translated medical works from Arabic into Latin. A contemporary who translated medical works from Greek was Alfanus, archbishop of Salerno. A Jewish element was early in evidence. Under Frederick II. lectures in Hebrew were given at Naples, and one of the most important Latin translators from the Arabic, the Jew, Faraj ben Salim (d. c. 1290), worked at Salerno. The decline of the school dates from 1224, when Frederick II. instituted a university at Naples. The very well known doggerel Latin verses on the preservation of health, known as the *Regimen Sanitatis Salerni*, have been translated into almost every European language. They are addressed to an apocryphal "King of England," usually supposed to be Robert of Normandy, but there is no doubt that the verses are mostly of the 14th century. They are probably, in the main, the work of Arnald of Villanova (1235-1313).

The school is regarded as the earliest university in Europe. It became, in the later middle ages, a place of bogus degrees but survived till 1811, when it was closed by Napoleon.

BIBLIOGRAPHY.—F. Hartmann, *Die Literatur von Früh- und Hochsalerno* (Leipzig, 1919), and C. Singer, *Essays on the History of Medicine, presented to K. Sudhoff* (Oxford, 1924), contain bibliographies. The legends of Salerno are disposed of by C. Singer in *From Magic to Science* (1928), and the Arabic and Hebrew Salernitan relationships are discussed by him in *The Legacy of Israel* (Oxford, 1927). The work of Alphanus is printed by C. Burkhard, *Nemesii Episcopi Premnon Physcon . . . Alfano Salerni in Latinum translatum* (Leipzig, 1917). The records of the University of Salerno are collected by H. Rashdall, *The Universities of the Middle Ages*, 3 vols. (Oxford, 1895). An important document, recording the physicians at Salerno, is C. A. Garufi, *Necrologio del Liber Confratum di S. Matteo di Salerno* (1922), discussed by P. Capparoni, *Magistri Salernitani noudum cogniti* (London, 1921). The last edition of the *Scola Salernitana* is by F. R. Packard and F. H. Garrison, *The School of*

Salernum Regimen Sanitatis Salernitanum (1920). (C. Sı.; X.)

SALESBURY or SALISBURY, WILLIAM (*c.* 1520–*c.* 1584), Welsh scholar, was a native of Denbighshire, being the son of Foulke Salesbury, who belonged to a family said to be descended from a certain Adam of Salzburg, a member of the ducal house of Bavaria, who came to England in the 12th century. Salesbury was educated at Oxford, where he accepted the Protestant faith, but he passed most of his life at Llanrwst, working at his literary undertakings. The greatest Welsh scholar of his time, Salesbury was acquainted with nine languages, including Latin, Greek and Hebrew, and was learned in philology and botany. He died about 1584. About 1546 he edited a collection of Welsh proverbs (*Oll synwyr pen kembero*), probably the first book printed in Welsh, and in 1547 his *Dictionary in Englyshe and Welshe* was published (facsimile edition, 1877). In 1563 the English parliament ordered the Welsh bishops to arrange for the translation of the Scriptures and the Book of Common Prayer into Welsh. The New Testament was assigned to Salesbury, who had previously translated parts of it. He received assistance from Richard Davies, bishop of St. Davids, and also from Thomas Huet, or Hewett (d. 1591), but he himself did the greater part of the work. The translation was made from the Greek, but Latin versions were consulted, and in Oct. 1567 the New Testament was published in Welsh for the first time. This translation never became very popular, but it served as the basis for the new one made by Bishop William Morgan (*c.* 1547–1604).

Salesbury and Davies continued to work together, translating various writings into Welsh, until about 1576 when the literary partnership was broken. After this event, Salesbury, although continuing his studies, produced nothing of importance.

SALESMANSHIP. Like other skills, salesmanship is based on a body of knowledge that approaches a science; but a mere knowledge of the principles involved is not sufficient to make a person a good salesman. He must be able to apply these principles with an efficiency gained only by practice. Certain native abilities are helpful, but most of the needed skills can be acquired by any normal person willing to study and practise diligently.

The salesman is a concomitant of the industrial era wherein most goods are manufactured for exchange rather than for use by the maker. The maker himself employs salesmen to sell his product to the middleman, the middleman uses salesmen to sell to other middlemen or to consumers, while some manufacturers sell directly to the final buyers. The production of goods on a large scale usually involves the problem of finding buyers for those goods, because it is cheaper for the salesman to contact several buyers than for each of those buyers to contact several manufacturers. Thus the salesman performs an economic function, imparting to the product time utility, place utility or possession utility. The buyer is willing to pay for these utilities for the same reason that he pays for the form utility imparted by the manufacturers.

In addition the salesman often brings to his customer a fund of helpful suggestions relating to the use of his product or its resale at a profit, thereby still further meriting the payment he receives for his work. With this recognition of the importance of the salesman's work came a marked improvement in his economic and social status.

There are many types of selling and just as many types of salesmen, each of which should be fitted by endowment and training for his particular task. This need for varied abilities makes it possible for nearly anyone to find some sort of congenial sales work. At one extreme is the sales engineer who requires considerable academic training before he receives his specialized education from the company whose product and services he sells. This man must be intelligent and possess a better-than-average personality. At the other extreme may be classed the clerk in a chain store whose duties embrace little more than making change and wrapping parcels. Little education or product knowledge is demanded, and personality traits are not of so great importance.

Between these extremes are found salesmen and saleswomen whose jobs vary widely as to type of employer (manufacturer, wholesaler, retailer), type of product sold (tangible or intangible, specialty or staple), complexity (some jobs are simple while others involve the performance of many functions), personality preferred (some selling demands aggressiveness while other sales jobs are best handled by persons of the type termed by psychologists as "submissive"), repetitive or pioneering (some salesmen call on the same customers at frequent intervals while others are always calling on new prospective buyers), seeking out customers (retail store salesmen wait for customers to walk in while insurance salesmen must seek out their customers), physical vigour required (some selling work is light and easy while other jobs demand great strength and stamina), general difficulty (the greater the difficulties to be surmounted, the higher the rewards to the salesman who can surmount them).

Most salesmen work as part of an organization, not as individual entrepreneurs. This is true whether they work for a manufacturer, wholesaler, retailer or as a door-to-door salesman. An organization implies management of the individuals in that organization, and the head of the sales organization or department is usually called the sales manager.

In a large manufacturing establishment this department may embrace hundreds or even thousands of individuals, and it is divided and subdivided by geographical divisions, by products sold, by type of prospects called on, or by the functions performed by the salesmen. Over each division of the organization is placed a minor sales manager responsible for sales in his jurisdiction and responsible to the man immediately above him in the chain of command.

The management of a sales organization is subject to the same principles that govern management anywhere. Management is management, but the methods used by the sales manager will vary with the manager himself and with the type of salesmen under him. Here are the same extremes as those seen in the political world—the extreme of dictatorship on the one hand and, on the other, a considerable degree of democracy marked by a two-way flow of ideas between the sales manager and salesmen and by a large amount of self-management exercised by the salesmen. The higher the type of salesman involved, the greater the degree of self-government granted him; the lower type of salesman requires more detailed supervision.

The sales manager gives careful attention to such problems as analysis of the market, estimating potential sales, fixing quotas for each territory and salesman, analysis of the product sold, determination of marketing policies, selection of salesmen, their training, assignment to proper duties, their supervision in the field, analysis of their jobs, methods of compensation, stimulation to optimum effort, adequate reports from salesmen, conferences with individual salesmen or with groups varying in size up to a general convention, pensions and retirement programs, and dealings with unions in which his salesmen may hold membership.

In selecting new salesmen the sales manager employs personal interviews, credentials and references, and various psychological tests to determine aptitudes, attitudes and pertinent personality traits. Such tests may forecast with accuracy the testee's probable success, but they have not supplanted the judgment of the manager, based on personal appraisal of the applicant.

After the new salesman is hired, he is usually put through a course of training that may vary from a few days to a couple of years in length, depending on the complexity of the product or service to be sold and on the difficulties in selling it. This training may be accomplished through classroom instruction; trips through or actual work in the factory; accompanying experienced salesmen and watching them operate; coaching in the field by persons trained for such work; or correspondence courses in which the young salesman must study printed lessons and pass examinations on them. Careful training greatly increases the productiveness of salesmen.

Assignment of salesmen to various duties is based on an analysis of the jobs to determine precisely each salesman's duties. A proper job analysis enables the sales manager to choose for each job a man who, as nearly as possible, will fit that job. The result is happier, more efficient salesmen, and a lower rate of turnover in the sales force.

Most salesmen, like other workers, require some supervision. This may be done in large organizations by men whose status is similar to that of factory foremen, each of whom supervises the work of a group of salesmen. In retail stores the department head or proprietor does this.

Salesmen are paid in a wide variety of ways ranging from a straight time wage or salary to a straight commission on volume of sales. In choosing or devising a method of compensation the sales manager seeks one that will accomplish these objectives: attract the type of salesman he wants, keep him working happily, pay him for doing what the sales manager wants him to do, offer him an incentive to put forth his best efforts, and not be too complicated to understand or too costly to operate. The time wage gives the sales manager the greatest degree of control; the commission offers the strongest selling incentive to the salesman. A combination is often worked out to afford the salesman some feeling of security based on a fixed salary or drawing account on which he can depend even when his sales fall below normal. To this may be added payments or bonuses based on volume of sales, number of new customers, collections made by salesmen, opening of new accounts, etc. Some companies have tried profit-sharing plans for paying their salesmen, but these are hard to compute and the salesman is likely to feel that profits depend too much on others' efforts. Above all, any system of compensation must appeal to the salesman as being equitable.

To stimulate salesmen to greater effort, resort may be had to contests, with attractive prizes for the winning salesmen. Bulletins and house organs are also used to develop and maintain enthusiasm. Salesmen are usually expected to make daily reports on their activities, these reports being used by the sales manager as a basis for determining policies and helping the salesmen who need help.

Unions among salesmen are relatively rare in the United States, although in some fields the movement had made progress by mid-20th century. Pensions likewise gained in popularity, although many salesmen feel quite competent to make their own provisions against old age.

In learning to be a salesman, a person must master three areas of knowledge. He must learn all he can about the product or service he is to sell; he must study himself and strive to develop a good selling personality; and he must study prospective buyers or prospects so that he may learn what objectives each is seeking and what desires each is trying to satisfy. Only when he has learned this can the salesman intelligently and helpfully demonstrate how his proposition will meet those needs.

The salesman thus becomes a practical psychologist, specializing in motivation. He learns to recognize such buying motives as greed, the urge to feel important, love of family, physical comfort or pleasure, knowledge, imitation, romance, health, caution, love of beauty, and the desire for security. He adapts his presentation to the individual prospect, making it appeal to whichever buying motives dominate that prospect at that time.

To make a sale, the salesman must carry the prospect through five mental stages, viz., attention to the salesman and his proposition, interest in that proposition, desire to possess it, confidence that it will be as represented by the salesman, and finally, action or the decision to buy.

To accomplish this, the salesman himself must often take certain definite steps. The first may be to locate his prospect, a task of vital importance to many specialty salesmen, although one seldom performed by the store salesman. To discover logical prospects the salesman functions as a detective, utilizing many sources of information.

His next step is termed the preapproach or the gathering of information about the prospect—information pertinent to his task. This will include, among other items, the question of which buying motives are most likely to appeal to the prospect; but it embraces also such matters as ability to buy, actual need for the proposition, hobbies, preferences and prejudices in many lines. The preapproach continues even after the salesman and prospect face each other.

Perhaps the next step is the winning of the interview or a chance to tell his story—sometimes a challenging sales project in itself.

Then comes the actual demonstration of his proposition, which is a dual task—to awaken in the prospect's mind a feeling of need and to show how the salesman's proposition meets that need. He utilizes logical reasoning and emotional appeals, usually relying more heavily on the latter; he listens attentively at proper times and displays tact in other ways; he avoids argument; he speaks the prospect's language; he dramatizes his points; he follows a more or less standardized sales talk to insure its completeness and effectiveness; he treats competition firmly but fairly; he meets a variety of objections and questions raised by the prospect, being careful to give them due weight and to avoid becoming involved in a debate; he takes the prospect through the successive mental stages of buying, making certain that he has taken each step before urging him to take the next one.

Finally, the salesman attempts to gain the buying decision or to close the sale. If he is a skilled salesman he has injected into his canvass a number of intimations that the prospect has decided to buy, such suggestions being known as "trial closes." The prospect's reaction informs the salesman as to whether he can safely proceed with the real closing effort. Also, he watches the prospect closely to detect signs of rising interest.

In closing, most salesmen use such proved techniques as obtaining a series of affirmative replies to various questions that lead or add up to the final decision; getting a decision on a minor point as size of order, date of delivery, terms, or colour desired; summarizing the talking points previously made; simply asking for the order. He strives to avoid creating an atmosphere of tension. Rather, he seeks to convey the impression that consummating a sale is nothing out of the ordinary for either buyer or salesman. He makes the final decision seem like merely one more in a series of decisions.

After he obtains the order, the salesman strives to take his departure with dignity and poise, leaving the door open for future sales. And finally, he will follow through on the sale to assure himself that the buyer is thoroughly pleased with his purchase. The truly professional salesman always remembers that his ultimate success depends upon the service he renders the buyer.

BIBLIOGRAPHY.—J. C. Aspley, *Sales Managers Handbook* (1950); N. A. Brisco, Griffith and Robinson, *Store Salesmanship,* 3rd ed. (1947); B. R. Canfield, *Salesmanship Practices and Problems* (1950); K. C. Ingram, *Winning Your Way with People* (1949); P. W. Ivey, *Successful Salesmanship* (1947); F. M. Jones, *Principles of Retailing* (1949); H. H. Maynard and H. C. Nolen, *Sales Management,* revised ed. (1950); C. B. Roth, *The Handbook of Selling* (1947); F. A. Russell and F. H. Beach, *Textbook of Salesmanship,* 4th ed. (1949); H. R. Tosdal, *Introduction to Sales Management,* 3rd ed. (1950).　　(F. A. R.)

SALES TAXES. Sales, excise and commodity taxes refer to taxes levied upon sellers of designated goods and services. When the classes of commodities are defined in tax legislation by broad classes and the tax base is the money value of the things sold, the tax is called a sales tax.

Usually sales taxes are levied upon manufacturers, wholesalers or retailers. When sales taxes are levied upon the services sold by workers, they are very close to income taxes restricted to wages and salaries.

Commodity taxes in one form or another are found in every country, and their use dates back to antiquity. Many small countries employ import duties in place of internal sales taxes because of the administrative convenience of the concentration of goods at ports-of-entry. These duties play much the same role as do internal sales taxes in larger countries. Manufacture sales taxes are limited to countries with important fabricating industries. Canada first imposed such a tax in 1920 and continued it with many modifications.

The federal government of the United States has never levied a tax officially described as a sales tax, but it has levied an assortment of commodity taxes both at the manufacture and the retail levels. Retail sales taxes, widely used by American states, were introduced during the 1930s under the pressure of dwindling revenues from other sources, and they became a main revenue source for many states. This type of taxation spread to local governments also. In California, all major cities and many minor ones have retail sales taxes.

Great Britain introduced the misnamed "purchase tax" in 1940 as a war measure with differential and high rates, exceeding 100% in some instances. The purpose was to curtail the production of luxury items, permitting an increase in the output of utility items. This wholesale sales tax was continued into the postwar era with a downward modification of rates.

Sales taxes are commonly believed to fall upon consumers by raising the prices paid for taxed items. Sellers who are legally responsible for the tax are, according to this view, simply collectors of the tax from consumers. It is this belief that provides the basis for the claim that sales taxes are regressive, when the burden of the tax is compared with income size. Other explanations have been suggested.

According to some authorities, sales taxes are only partly shifted to buyers; a portion of the taxes rests upon sellers by reducing their money incomes. The degree of shifting to buyers depends upon the character of the market, whether competitive or monopolistic, the nature of the demand for each commodity, and the cost conditions surrounding its production.

Some experts regard sales taxes as falling upon sellers and their suppliers by reducing their money incomes. Such taxes are looked upon as similar to nonsystematic income taxes without exemptions. Buyers pay higher prices for taxed items but pay less for other commodities, suggesting that as a group they do not bear sales or commodity taxes. The legislative assumption that consumers pay such taxes in their entirety receives only modest support among economists.

BIBLIOGRAPHY.—John F. Due, *The General Manufacturers' Sales Tax in Canada* (Toronto, 1952), and *Government Finance,* ch. 15–18 (Homewood, Ill., 1954); Ursula K. Hicks, *Public Finance,* ch. 5, 9, 10 (London, 1947); Earl R. Rolph, *The Theory of Fiscal Economics,* ch. 6, 7 (Berkeley, Calif., 1954). (E. R. R.)

SALFORD, a city and a municipal, county and parliamentary borough, Lancashire, Eng., 2 mi. W. of Manchester. Pop. (1951) 178,194. Area 8.1 sq.mi. The parliamentary borough returns two members, for Salford East and Salford West. Salford is a quarter sessions borough.

The borough, composed of three townships identical with the ancient manors of Salford, Pendleton and Broughton, is for the most part separated from Manchester by the river Irwell. The main railway station is Exchange station which is connected with Victoria station, Manchester, by one of the longest railway platforms in the world. Salford town hall was built in 1825 and Pendleton town hall in 1866. St. John's Roman Catholic cathedral was opened in 1848. Peel park, formerly Lark hill but renamed after Sir Robert Peel, contains the art gallery and museum and the Royal Technical college (1896). In Bhuile Hall park is the natural history museum.

The only old building remaining in Salford is Ordsall hall, the ancient seat of the Radcliffe family, which dates from 1350. Kersall cell, the site of a 12th-century Cluniac monastery, was the birthplace of John Byrom (1692–1763). James Joule, the physicist, (1818–89) was born in Salford.

The Flemish weavers settled first in Salford in about 1360, and from that date it has been one of the foremost cotton towns. To the opening of the Manchester ship canal (*q.v.*) in 1894 is due its great commercial importance, for it contains the largest docks on this canal. Raw cotton is imported and among many exports are manufactured cotton and woollen goods, machinery and locomotives. Salford is an important centre for importing timber and also a great distributing centre. It has more than 1,000 factories which include cotton spinning, bleaching and dyeing, brewing, the making of rubber goods and waterproofed fabrics, paper mills and engineering.

Neolithic implements, British urns and Roman coins have been found within the borough. Domesday Book mentions the Great Hundred of Salford (of which Manchester formed a part) as held by Edward the Confessor and covering some 400 sq.mi. At the Conquest it was part of the domain granted to Roger le Poitevin. In 1228 Henry III granted the town an annual fair and market

and a weekly market; in 1825 George IV granted two annual fairs and a weekly market. When the corporation bought the market rights they built a new market, on the site of the old cattle market, which was opened in 1939.

In 1230 Ranulf de Blundeville, earl of Chester, granted a charter constituting Salford a free borough and it was administered according to this charter until 1791. In 1267 Salford was granted by Henry III, with all the crown demesne, to his son Emund, earl of Lancaster.

When the house of Lancaster succeeded to the throne their Lancashire possessions were kept separate and Salford remained part of the duchy of Lancaster thereafter. The borough was incorporated as a municipal borough in 1844; Broughton and Pendleton were amalgamated with it in 1853; in 1888 it became a county borough. It was raised to the status of a city in 1926.

SALICACEAE, a family of dioecious trees or shrubs consisting of two genera, the flowers borne in characteristic catkins. The family is essentially characteristic of the north temperate zone of both hemispheres, but *Salix* also extends into the arctic and tropical regions.

Populus, known as poplar (*q.v.*), conservatively estimated to have about 18 species in 1900, had more than 100 additional species proposed in the succeeding half century. *Salix,* known as willow (*q.v.*), has in excess of 1,000 described species, but many of these are probably only forms or varieties and others are hybrids. (*See* also OSIER.) (E. D. ML.)

SALICETI, ANTOINE CHRISTOPHE (1757–1809), French revolutionary, was born at Saliceto, Corsica, on Aug. 26, 1757.

After studying law in Tuscany, he became an *avocat* at the upper council of Bastia and was elected deputy of the third estate to the French states-general in 1789. Later he was elected as deputy to the Convention and voted for the death of Louis XVI. He was sent to Corsica on a mission to oppose counterrevolutionary intrigues, but the success of his adversaries compelled him to withdraw to Provence, where he took part in repressing revolts at Marseilles and Toulon. On that mission he met and helped his compatriot Napoleon Bonaparte.

His friendship with Robespierre led to his denunciation on 9 Thermidor year II, but he was saved by the amnesty of Brumaire year IV.

Saliceti subsequently organized the army of Italy and the two departments into which Corsica had been divided, was deputy to the Council of the Five Hundred and accepted various offices under the consulate and the empire, being minister of police and of war at Naples under Joseph Bonaparte (1806–09).

He died at Naples on Dec. 23, 1809.

SALICIN (SALICINUM), the bitter principle of willow bark, $C_{13}H_{18}O_7$, found in most species of *Salix* and *Populus.*

Salicin is prepared from a decoction of the bark by first precipitating the tannin by milk of lime, then evaporating the filtrate to a soft extract and dissolving out the salicin by alcohol. As met with in commerce it is usually in the form of glossy white scales or needles.

Salicin is neutral, bitter, odourless, unaltered by exposure to the air, soluble in about 30 parts of water and 80 parts of alcohol at the ordinary temperature, and in 0.7 of boiling water or in 2 parts of boiling alcohol, and more freely in alkaline liquids. It is also soluble in acetic acid without alteration, but is insoluble in chloroform and benzol.

Salicin is used in medicine for the same purposes as salicylic acid (*q.v.*), but is much less effective.

SALIC LAW and other Frankish laws. The Salic law is one of those early mediaeval Frankish laws which, with other early Germanic laws, are known collectively as *leges germanorum.* It originated with the Salian Franks. The Salic law has come down in numerous manuscripts. The most ancient form, represented by Latin manuscript no. 4404 in the Bibliothèque Nationale, consists of 65 chapters. The second form has the same 65 chapters, but contains interpolated provisions. The third text consists of 99 chapters. The fourth version, as amended by Charlemagne, consists of 70 chapters with the Latinity corrected and without the glosses. The last version, published by B. J. Herold at Basel in 1557 is founded on the second recension.

The law is a compilation, the various chapters were composed at different periods, and we do not possess the original form of the compilation. Even the most ancient text, that in 65 chapters, contains passages which a comparison with the later texts shows to be interpolations. The scale of judicial fines is given in the *denarius* ("which makes so many *solidi*"), and it is known that the monetary system of the *solidus* did not appear until the Merovingian period. Even in its earliest form the law contains no trace of paganism—a significant fact when we consider how closely law and religion are related in their origins. The Romans are clearly indicated in the law as subjects, but as not yet forming part of the army, which consists solely of the *antrustions, i.e.,* Frankish warriors of the king's bodyguard. As yet the law is not impregnated with the Christian spirit; this absence of both Christian and Pagan elements is due to the fact that many of the Franks were still heathens, although their king had been converted to Christianity. (For contrary opinion *see* Franz Beyerle in the *Zeitschrift der Savigny-Stiftung*, xliv, 216 *seq.*) Christian enactments were introduced gradually into the later versions. Finally, we find capitularies of the kings immediately following Clovis being gradually incorporated in the text of the law—*e.g.,* the *Pactum pro tenore pacis* of Childebert I and Clotaire I (511–558), and the *Edictum Chilperici* (561–584), chapter iii of which cites and emends the Salic law.

The law as originally compiled underwent modifications of varying importance before it took the form known to us in Latin ms. No. 4404, to which the edict of Childebert I and Clotaire I is already appended. Finally, Charlemagne, who took a keen interest in the ancient documents, had the law emended, the operation consisting in eliminating the Malberg glosses, which were no longer intelligible, correcting the Latinity of the ancient text, omitting a certain number of interpolated chapters, and adding others which had obtained general sanction.

The Salic law is not a political law; it is in no way concerned with the succession to the throne of France, and it is absolutely false to suppose that it was the Salic law that was invoked in 1316 and 1322 to exclude the daughters of Louis X and Philip V from the succession to the throne. The Salic law is pre-eminently a penal code, which shows the amount of fines for various offenses and crimes, and contains, besides, some civil law enactments, such as the famous chapter on succession to private property (de alode), which declares that daughters cannot inherit land.

Of the numerous editions of the Salic law only the principal ones can be mentioned: J. M. Pardessus, *Loi salique* (Paris, 1843), 8 texts; A. Holder, *Lex Salica* (1879 *seq.*), reproductions of all the mss. with all the abbreviations; H. Geffcken, *Lex Salica* (Leipzig, 1898), the text in 65 chapters, with commentary paragraph by paragraph, and appendix of *additamenta:* and the edition undertaken by Bruno Krusch for the *Mon. Germ. hist.* For further information *see* E. Mayer-Homberg, *Die fränkischen Volksrechte und das Reichsrecht* (1912); Cl. v. Schwerin, in the *Neues Archiv*, xl, 581 *seq.;* Bruno Krusch, in the *Neues Archiv*, xl, 497 *seq.*, and in the *Nachrichten der Gesellschaft der Wissenschaften zu Göttingen* (1916), 683 *seq.;* E. Heymann and others, in the *Neues Archiv*, xli, 375 *seq.*, 419 *seq.;* Franz Beyerle, in the *Zeitschrift der Savigny-Stiftung*, xliv, 216 *seq.*

The *Lex Ripuaria* was the law of the Ripuarian Franks, whose centre was Cologne. We have no ancient mss. of the law of the Ripuarians; the 35 mss. we possess, as well as those now lost which served as the basis of the old editions, do not go back beyond the time of Charlemagne.

On analysis, the law of the Ripuarians, which contains 89 chapters, falls into three heterogeneous divisions. Chapters i–xxviii consist of a scale of compositions; but, although the fines are calculated, not on the unit of 15 *solidi*, as in the Salic law, but on that of 18 *solidi*, it is clear that this part is already influenced by the Salic law. Chapters xxix–lxiv are taken directly from the Salic law; the provisions follow the same arrangement; the unit of the compositions is 15 *solidi;* but capitularies are interpolated relating to the affranchisement and sale of immovable property. Chapters lxv–lxxxix consist of provisions of various kinds, some taken from lost capitularies and from the Salic law, and others of unknown origin.

There is an edition of the text of the Ripuarian law in *Mon. Ger. hist. Leges* (1883), v. 185 *seq.* by R. Sohm, who also brought out a separate edition in 1885 for the use of schools. For further information *see* the prefaces to Sohm's editions; H. Brunner, *Deutsche Rechtsgeschichte* (2nd ed., Leipzig, 1906), I, 442; Bruno Krusch, *Die Lex Bajuvariorum, mit zwei Anhängen: Lex Alamannorum und Lex*

Ribuaria (1924) 333 *seq.* and *Neue Forschungen über die drei oberdeutschen Leges: Bajuvariorum, Alamannorum, Ribuariorum* (1927) 142 *seq.;* Franz Beyerle, in the *Zeitschrift der Savigny-Stiftung*, xlviii, 264 *seq.*

Lastly, we possess a judicial text in 48 paragraphs, which bears the title of *Notitia vel commemoratio de illa ewa (law), quae se ad Amorem habet.* This was in use in the district along the Yssel formerly called Hamalant. The name Hamalant is unquestionably derived from the Frankish tribe of the Chamavi, and the document is often called *Lex Francorum Chamavorum.*

There is an edition of this text by R. Sohm in *Mon. Germ. hist. Leges*, v. 269, and another appended to the same writer's school edition of the *Lex Ribuaria. See* also Fustel de Coulanges, *Nouvelles Recherches sur quelques problèmes d'histoire* (1891).

(C. Pf.; K. A. Eck.)

SALICYLIC ACID, employed in many medicinal preparations and in food preservation because of its powerful antiseptic properties, is *ortho*-hydroxybenzoic acid, $HO.C_6H_4.CO_2H$. It also finds considerable use in the manufacture of dyestuffs. (*See* Dyes, Synthetic.) It crystallizes from hot water in prismatic needles melting at 156°–159° C., and when carefully heated it sublimes without decomposition, this sublimation being sometimes applied as a method of purification. Salicylic acid and salicylaldehyde occur in the oils from various species of *Spiraea*, whereas methyl salicylate, a colourless oil boiling at 222° C., is the main constituent of oil of wintergreen from *Gaultheria procumbens* and *G. fragrantissima.* Salicylic acid was first obtained by R. Piria (1838) on treating salicylaldehyde with potassium hydroxide and until 1874 was mainly obtained by the hydrolysis of methyl salicylate.

It is now manufactured from phenol (*q.v.*) by processes based on H. Kolbe's celebrated synthesis of the acid discovered in 1859, and on R. Schmidt's improvement whereby sodium phenoxide (or phenolate), $C_6H_5.ONa$, is converted into sodium phenylcarbonate, $C_6H_5O.CO_2Na$, and the latter salt heated under pressure until transformed completely into sodium salicylate, $HO.C_6H_4.CO_2Na$.

Preparation.—Pure phenol is converted by concentrated aqueous sodium hydroxide into sodium phenoxide and this salt is dried carefully and pulverized in a strong steel vessel (autoclave) capable of withstanding considerable pressure. The anhydrous sodium phenoxide powder is then saturated under pressure (100 lb. per square inch) with carbon dioxide and heated in the autoclave at 120°–140° C. The resulting sodium salicylate is dissolved in water, decolorized with stannous salts or with zinc and charcoal and then acidified with mineral acid, when salicylic acid is precipitated, collected and washed with cold water.

For dye making, the precipitated acid is sufficiently pure, but for preservative and medicinal purposes further purification is effected either by distillation in superheated steam or by sublimation.

Since salicylic acid is 35 times more soluble in hot than in cold water (100 parts of water at 15° C. dissolve 0.225 part of salicylic acid), it may be readily crystallized from this solvent or from alcohol in which it dissolves more freely (1 part in 2.5 parts of 90% alcohol).

Salicylic acid in aqueous solution develops a violet coloration with ferric chloride, and with bromine water it gives tribromophenol bromide, $C_6H_2Br_3.OBr$. Sodium in boiling amyl alcohol reduces it to *n*-pimelic acid, $CO_2H.[CH_2]_5.CO_2H$. When heated at 195°–220° C., it decomposes, yielding phenol and carbon dioxide, but also giving phenyl salicylate, $HO.C_6H_4.CO_2.C_6H_5$ (salol). This drug, also prepared by the action at 125° C. of phosphorus oxychloride or carbonyl chloride on a mixture of sodium phenoxide and salicylate, crystallizes from alcohol in rhombic plates melting at 42° C. and it boils at 172° C.,/12 mm. Acetylsalicylic acid (*see* Aspirin), prepared by the action of acetyl chloride on salicylic acid or its sodium salt, crystallizes in colourless needles and melts at 132° C. (with decomposition).

Applications of Salicylic Acid and Salicylates.—Salicylic acid has a strong inhibitory influence on the growth of microorganisms, and retards the action of unorganized ferments and of the ferments of alcoholic and acetic fermentations. It has a widespread employment as a preservative of foods and beverages in concentrations of 0.5–6 parts per 1,000. It is thus used in jams and other fruit preparations, in glues and albuminoid substances, and also in milk, beer and wine. The use of salicylic acid as a food preservative was, however, condemned by a commission of the U.S. government in 1904.

Applied externally as an antiseptic and antipruritic to wounds and parasitic skin diseases, salicylic acid is less irritating than phenol, but may in strong solution have a destructive action on the horny layer of the epidermis. It is employed to remove corns and warts and in the treatment of lupus. It is a constituent of dental preparations and mouth washes.

For internal use, salicylic acid has been almost completely replaced by its sodium salt (sodii salicylas, official dose o.6 to 2.09 g.) and its acetyl derivative (aspirin), which are less irritant to the mucous membrane of the stomach.

Methyl salicylate is now made synthetically from salicylic acid and methyl alcohol. It is used as a flavour for foods, beverages, tooth paste, etc.

Salicylic acid is the basis of numerous drugs and therapeutic agents, and in addition to the above-mentioned there are also salipyrin, salophen, diuretin and many others.

The greater proportion of salicylic acid is, however, employed in the manufacture of such azo-dyes as alizarin yellow (khaki yellow), chrysamine, anthracene brown, cloth brown, cotton yellow, diamine yellow N, anthracene yellow, etc. Large quantities serve for the preparation of 5-aminosalicylic acid which is an intermediate in the production of the important wool dye, diamond black.

BIBLIOGRAPHY.—For preparation and chemical properties: T. E. Thorpe, *Dictionary of Applied Chemistry*, vol. 1–10 (1937–50); F. Ullmann, *Enzyklopädie der technischen Chemie*, 2nd ed. (1928). For application in medicine and therapeutics: W. H. Martindale and W. Westcott, *Extra Pharmacopoeia*, vol. 1, 19th ed. (1928–29).

(G. T. M.)

SALIDA, a city of Chaffee county, Colo., U.S., on the Arkansas river, federal highways 50 and 285, and the Rio Grande railroad, 140 mi. S.W. of Denver. The population was 4,516 in 1950 and was 4,969 in 1940 by federal census.

The city lies at an altitude of 7,050 ft. in a basin almost surrounded by mountains rising to heights of more than 14,000 ft. It is headquarters for the San Isabel National forest. There is some granite quarried in the county, and a granite shed is in Salida, where there are also repair shops for the railroad, a creosoting plant, a coal-screening plant, large stockyards and a large rainbow trout commercial fish hatchery.

Salida (so-called because the city stands at the outlet of the upper Arkansas basin) was settled and incorporated in 1880, when the Rio Grande railroad began service to the community.

SALIERI, ANTONIO (1750–1825), Italian composer, was born at Legnano, It., on Aug. 19, 1750. In 1766 he was taken to Vienna, Aus., by F. L. Gassmann, who introduced him to the emperor Joseph. His first opera, *Le Donne letterate*, was produced at the Burg-Theater in 1770. Others followed in rapid succession, and his *Armida* (1771) was a triumphant success. On Gassmann's death in 1774, he became Kapellmeister and, on the death of Bonno in 1788, Hofkapellmeister. He held his offices for 50 years, though he made frequent visits to Italy and Paris, and composed music for many European theatres. His chef-d'oeuvre was *Tarare*, later called *Axur, re d'Ormus* (1787), a work which was preferred by the Viennese public to Wolfgang Mozart's *Don Giovanni*. His last opera was *Die Neger*, produced in 1804. After this he devoted himself to the composition of church music, for which he had a very decided talent. Salieri lived on friendly terms with F. J. Haydn, but was a bitter enemy to Mozart, though the wild suggestion that he actually poisoned him (albeit made the basis of Nicolas Rimsky-Korsakov's *Mozart and Salieri*) has long been scouted. He retired from office on his full salary in 1824, and died at Vienna on May 7, 1825.

Salieri gave lessons in composition to M. Cherubini and to Ludwig van Beethoven, who dedicated to him his three sonatas for pianoforte and violin, op. 12.

See also Albert von Hermann, *Antonio Salieri, eine Studie* (1897); J. F. Edler von Mosel, *Über das Leben und die Werke des Antonio Salieri* (Vienna, 1827).

SALII ("dancers"). An ancient priesthood at Rome, consisting of two colleges, each of 12 members, the Salii Palatini and the Salii Collini or Agonenses, connected respectively with the worship of Mars on the Palatine and the Quirinus on the *collis Quirinalis*. They wore armour of an ancient pattern, probably the old war dress of the Italians, and in particular, carried shields called *ancilia*, shaped somewhat like the figure 8. These they carried in procession on certain days of the year, in March (Mars's month) and October (end of the campaigning season under early conditions), singing a very ancient hymn or hymns (*axamenta*, in honour of all the gods, and separate hymns to single deities, called by their names). They were assisted by women similarly dressed and called *saliae virgines*; these were hired for the occasion in historical times. The whole performance was accompanied with dancing.

All this suggests a war dance, and can easily be paralleled from the customs of uncivilized peoples. But the matter is complicated by a statement of Johannes Lydus, a late and untrustworthy author, that on March 15 a man clad in goatskins and called Mamurius was driven out with rods. This person Lydus identifies with Mamurius Veturius, said to have been the smith who made the *ancilia* after a pattern fallen from heaven. (*See* Joannes Lydus, *De Mensibus*, p. 105, 19 Wünsch.) But the name may mean "old Mars," hence it has been plausibly conjectured that the ritual is at least in part connected with vegetation, the "old Mars" or worn-out spirit of fertility being yearly driven away. As, however, we have no proof that the Salii were connected with this ceremony, it is open to us to suppose, with Georg Wissowa, that it is a mere coincidence of date, and that the name of the skin-clad figure was a popular one only, made up from the unintelligible words *mamuri veturi* in the Saliar hymn.

The balance of evidence certainly is in favour of supposing the ritual of the Salii to have been purely war magic, in its origin at least. There were also Salii at Tibur, of whom nothing is known (Servius on *Aen*, viii, 285).

BIBLIOGRAPHY.—W. Warde Fowler, *Roman Festivals of the Period of the Republic* (1908); Georg Wissowa, *Religion und Kultus der Römer* in J. von Müller's *Handbuch der klassischen Ultertumswissenschaft*, 2nd ed. (1912); Sir J. G. Frazer, *Golden Bough*, vol. ix, 3rd ed., 229 ff. (bibl.).

SALINA, a city near the centre of Kansas, U.S., on the Smoky Hill river and federal highways 40 and 81; the county seat of Saline county. It is served by the Missouri Pacific, the Rock Island, the Santa Fe and the Union Pacific railways. Pop. (1950) 26,141; 21,073 in 1940 by the federal census. It is the seat of Kansas Wesleyan university (Methodist Episcopal; established 1886) and Marymount college (Catholic, for girls).

The city operates under a commission-manager form of government. It has a city plan, zoning regulations, parks, a municipal band and swimming pool, and an assessed valuation (1950) of $32,500,000.

Salina has a large wholesale and retail trade and varied manufactures. The annual volume of wholesale and retail trade is about $100,000,000. Flour milling is the chief industry. The city was founded in 1858 and chartered in 1870. The first railway (the Union Pacific) came through in 1867. The first flour mill (still in operation and using the original water turbines) was built in 1868.

SALINA CRUZ, southernmost port of Mexico on the Pacific coast in the state of Oaxaca at the southern terminus of the transisthmian railway across Tehuantepec. The population in 1940 was 4,614. In the north-western part of the bay, Salina Cruz lies at the mouth of the Tehuantepec river, and is divided into a free port and a fiscal port. Opened for business in 1907, its costly artificial harbour decayed and silted after the opening of the Panama Canal cut off its traffic. It was reopened in 1936 after extensive dredging.

Lying in a hot, semiarid area, Salina Cruz is chiefly a transshipment point for petroleum products from Minatitlan on the north to supply the western parts of Mexico. It also exports coffee from Chiapas to the United States. (HD. C.)

SALINAS, a city of western California, U.S., 9 mi. from Monterey bay, in the Salinas River valley, between the Gabilan and the Santa Lucia mountains; the county seat of Monterey county. It is on federal highway 101 and is served by the Southern Pacific railway. Pop. 13,895 in 1950 and 11,586 in 1940 by federal census. The Salinas valley is one of the richest agricultural regions in the United States, producing especially lettuce, broccoli, celery, artichokes, sugar beets, dry beans, bulbs and seeds.

The California rodeo is held there annually. Four miles from Salinas is Ft. Ord. Salinas was settled in 1858; became the county seat in 1872, in place of Monterey; and was incorporated as a city in 1874.

SALISBURY, JAMES EDWARD HUBERT GASCOYNE-CECIL, 4TH MARQUESS OF (1861–1947), British politician, eldest son of the 3rd marquis (*see* SALISBURY, ROBERT A. T. G.-C.), was educated at Eton and University college, Oxford. He entered parliament in 1885 and succeeded to the peerage in 1903. He served in the South African War, and on his return entered the ministry, joining the cabinet in 1903. In the crisis over the Parliament bill he threw in his lot with the "Die-hards." He did not join either coalition government during World War I, but was critical of both, taking an independent line. He gradually came to assume the informal leadership of the conservative opposition first in the house of lords, and afterward in the party generally. In a speech on Oct. 16, 1922, he categorically demanded the freedom of the party. Three days later the policy was accepted at the Carlton Club meeting. He was lord president in the council in Bonar Law's cabinet and in Stanley Baldwin's first cabinet. In Baldwin's second cabinet he was lord privy seal, and from Curzon's death in 1925 until 1929 was leader of the house of lords. He was created K.G. in 1917. He died on April 4, 1947.

SALISBURY, ROBERT ARTHUR TALBOT GASCOYNE-CECIL, 3RD MARQUIS OF (1830–1903), British statesman, second son of James, 2nd marquis, by his first wife, Frances Mary Gascoyne, was born at Hatfield on Feb. 3, 1830. Lord Robert Cecil, as he then was, was educated at Eton and Christ Church, Oxford. His health was delicate and after leaving Oxford, he spent nearly two years at sea on a voyage round the world, visiting Cape Colony, Australia, Tasmania and New Zealand. On his return home he stood for parliament and on Aug. 22, 1853, was returned unopposed as member for the borough of Stamford in Lincolnshire. In the same year he was elected to a fellowship of All Souls.

He married in July 1857, the eldest daughter of Sir Edward Hall Alderson, Baron of the Court of Exchequer, a man of notable parts who at Cambridge had earned the rare distinction of being both Senior Wrangler, Senior Classic and Smith's Prizeman. His daughter inherited his abilities but there was very little money, and to add to his income Lord Robert joined the staff of the *Saturday Review* which had been lately founded by his brother-in-law, Mr. Alexander Beresford-Hope, this being, so far as is known, his only contribution to pure journalism. Most of his writing was done for the *Quarterly Review,* whose articles were then exclusively anonymous. The literary quality and vigorous lucidity of his style secured him a welcome in its pages, and of the 24 numbers which appeared between the years 1860 and 1866 there were only three which did not contain an article from his pen. Six of these have since been republished in volume form —three of them biographical essays on Pitt and Castlereagh and three dealing with foreign questions. These were uncompromisingly denunciatory of Lord John Russell's policy and to the study required for an effective presentation of his case may probably be traced his first knowledge of and interest in foreign affairs.

In the House of Commons.—Speeches on the same subjects, and notably one or two in 1864 on the abandonment of Denmark at the time of Germany's annexation of Schleswig-Holstein, placed him for the first time by general consent in the front rank of parliamentary debaters. When Lord Russell's Government was defeated over Mr. Gladstone's Reform bill in 1866, it was a foregone conclusion that he should be among those invited to join Lord Derby's cabinet. His eldest brother had died in 1865 and it was as Lord Cranborne that, in July 1866, he took office as secretary of State for India.

He only held it for seven months. The story of that ministry is well known. In the summer of 1866 the Tory party, assisted by a secession of anti-democratic Liberals, defeated Mr. Gladstone's Reform bill as tending dangerously in the direction of household suffrage. In the summer of 1867, the same party passed a Reform bill which established household suffrage. Lord Cranborne, with two other members of the Cabinet, Lord Carnarvon and General Peel, resigned on Feb. 9, two days before the bill's introduction. The breach was embittered by the tactics which the two leaders employed towards their junior colleagues. They kept them in the dark till within a week or two of the bill's production; offered reassurance in the shape of counter-checks and limitations which were changed with every meeting of the cabinet —and were in fact all abandoned in the course of the bill's passage through parliament—and allowed them no opportunity for considered argument. Their belief that there had been a deliberate attempt to hustle them into a consent which it was known that they would not have given freely, estranged them personally from Disraeli for many years afterwards. When the parliamentary fight was over Lord Cranborne accepted the constitutional change as an accomplished fact which it behoved every good citizen to make the best of, and it was the offence against public morality of which he held his party and its leaders to have been guilty that became the theme of an article called "The Conservative Surrender" which appeared that October in the *Quarterly Review.* Its quality and its easily divined authorship procured it a sensational reception. Seven editions of the number which contained it had to be issued in order to meet the demand for it.

On April 12, 1868, his father died and his House of Commons career came to an end. During the six years which followed (1868–1874), Lord Salisbury joined actively from below the gangway in the warfare which his late colleagues waged against Mr. Gladstone's legislation. In 1870 he was chosen chancellor of Oxford university in succession to Lord Derby,—an indication of the reputation which his attitude in '67 had won for him among the more serious representatives of the party outside Parliament. It was a distinction which he always peculiarly prized. When, after the defeat of the Liberals in 1874, Disraeli undertook the formation of his second ministry, almost his first step was to invite the return of this alienated colleague. Under actual conditions there could be no risk of a repetition of his earlier experience, and after a few days of painful hesitation, he accepted. On Feb. 17 he resumed control of the Government of India where a disastrous famine claimed all his energies. By a curious chance a similar visitation had synchronised with his previous brief tenure of office, and he had left behind him a high reputation for success in dealing with it.

The first two years of this ministry were uneventful—except in connection with an ecclesiastical measure—the Public Worship Act, introduced in 1874 by Archbishop Tait. Lord Salisbury and his chief took opposite sides upon it, and the momentary clashing of their swords in debate excited some quite unfounded anticipations of ministerial rupture. But in 1876 a crisis arose in the southeast of Europe, one of whose incidental results was to fix permanently Lord Salisbury's destiny in public life.

The Eastern Question.—Two or three of the European provinces of the Turkish Empire had revolted against its misgovernment; there had been a voluminous interchange of notes and protocols among the signatory Powers of the Treaty of Paris; the already autonomous principality of Serbia had taken up arms in support of its co-religionists, and finally the Russian tsar had mobilised his army and declared that, if the rest of Europe did not act, he would. A conference of the Great Powers had thereupon been called to meet at Constantinople in December, to draw up a scheme of reforms and, by securing the Porte's acceptance of it, avert the threatened war.

The repercussion of these events in England had been peculiarly characterized. The insurrection in Bulgaria had been suppressed by Turkish irregular troops with incidents of great savagery. Misled by the optimism of the British embassy at Constantinople, the prime minister—now become Lord Beaconsfield—had poured scorn upon the first newspaper reports of these outrages, and in the impassioned agitation which Gladstone initiated on the subject throughout the country, the Tory Government became an object for almost equal denunciation with the Turkish sultan. Salisbury resented the agitation, but was himself admittedly sympathetic with the cause of the insurgent Christians and had privately urged his colleagues to dissociate England once and for all from the incriminated cause of Turkish ineptitude. His views were known or divined and when Beaconsfield invited him to serve as plenipotentiary to the Constantinople Conference, the appointment helped to quiet the prevailing excitement and was received with general acclamation. At first all went smoothly at the Conference; there was no difficulty in obtaining unanimous agreement among the Christian Powers as to the reforms to be recommended. But there success stopped. The Turkish envoys rejected all proposals, and were deaf to every argument. Salisbury would have tried that of force, but his colleagues refused, and on Jan. 20, 1877, the conference broke up and Russia was left to carry out her originally proclaimed purpose.

She declared war on April 24. Throughout the remainder of that year counsels in the British cabinet were divided. The prime minister and Cairns advocated present intervention; Salisbury and Carnarvon opposed a resolute veto to any action which the Turks could construe into acquiescence in their defiance of Europe; and Derby, the foreign secretary, supported them with impartial loyalty. Agreement between the warring groups was obtained for a declaration of neutrality, balanced by a warning addressed to Russia that no attempt on Constantinople itself would be tolerated.

The change of issues foreshadowed in this document materialised in the new year and with it a change in cabinet grouping. The Turkish defence, at first resolute and successful, suddenly collapsed and when the Russian troops in rapid advance appeared upon the threshold of the forbidden city Lord Salisbury was foremost in urging that men-of-war should be sent up to the Bosphorus for its protection. On this decision being taken (Jan. 23), Derby and Carnarvon resigned, though the former was subsequently persuaded to withdraw his resignation.

An armistice was agreed upon and a treaty of peace, negotiated between the two belligerents, was signed at San Stefano on March 3. It provided for a huge Slav State under Russian protection stretching right across the Balkans and completely isolating Constantinople. Russia announced that at the approaching conference of the Signatory Powers required under treaty law to legalize the settlement she would admit discussion on those parts only of the new treaty which were "of European interest." The other Powers hesitated to enforce their rights but England declared that unless the treaty were submitted in its entirety she must decline to participate in the congress; Russia again refused, the summoning of the congress was indefinitely postponed, and when the British cabinet met on March 27 it was to face an imminent probability of war. They called out the Reserves and telegraphed orders for a contingent of Indian troops to be at once embarked for the Mediterranean. Lord Derby resigned the same evening and Lord Salisbury, who had taken a leading part in these decisions, was appointed foreign secretary the following day.

He signalized his accession to control by a despatch whose contents were telegraphed on April 1 to every capital and which became famous as the Salisbury Circular. Its object was to show that the Treaty of San Stefano, by reducing the Turkish Empire to vassalage, would constitute a greater menace to the interests of other Powers than would have arisen from its frank dismemberment in Russia's favour. It was by the treaty as a whole that this result would be achieved and it was as a whole therefore that it must be submitted to the judgment of Europe. This document, by the lucidity of its style and argument, the impression of resolution which it conveyed and the subtly indirect appeals which it contained to the interests or sentiments of the different neutral nations, effected an immediate revolution in the international position. Hesitation disappeared; the rest of Europe ranged itself on the side of the British contention and Russia could do no other than submit.

But danger was not over with the removal of obstacles to the

meeting of the Powers. In present conditions a failure of agreement at the Congress itself must precipitate a general war and Salisbury refused to risk that possibility. He entered into private communication with Russia and satisfied himself that the provisions which either side regarded as vital were capable of adjustment. On May 31st a secret agreement was signed between him and the Russian ambassador binding both Powers not to push dispute on these provisions to the point of rupture at the Congress. Russia's price for this adjustment was her retention of her Asiatic conquests, and to counteract the effect of these Salisbury co-incidentally arranged a convention with Turkey. Under this, in consideration of her ceding Cyprus to England and entering into an engagement of administrative reform in Asia Minor, England guaranteed her Asiatic frontier against further aggression.

These preparations having been effected, the Congress, summoned by Prince Bismarck, met at Berlin on June 13. Lord Beaconsfield and Lord Salisbury attended it, and a month later a treaty was signed there by the seven great Powers. It secured all the objects for which England had contended, and when the two plenipotentiaries returned to London Beaconsfield was able to announce that they had brought back "Peace with Honour."

In Opposition.—At the general election of 1880, the Conservative party was heavily defeated. Lord Beaconsfield died the following spring, and Lord Salisbury succeeded him as leader in the House of Lords, sharing with Sir Stafford Northcote in the leadership of the party as a whole. During this period of opposition and in the election campaign which closed it, he spoke continually on public platforms and developed gifts for attracting and holding mass meetings of working men which hitherto had had little opportunity for display.

In home affairs his attitude was distinguished alike from that of the Tory Democrats of that day and that of the more old-fashioned Toryism. He made no attempt, like the former, to clothe his views in radical or democratic phraseology, but on the other hand he was disdainful of privilege and frankly indifferent to tradition. That the confidence begotten of economic stability and respect for individual rights was of supreme importance to the class whose welfare depends on full and well-paid employment; that theorists and phrasemakers are the enemy, always and everywhere; above all, that unity and mutual trust are the indispensable foundation for all moral and all material welfare in a nation,—were the recurrent texts from which he spoke. But he demurred to the title of Conservative: "There is much . . . which it is highly undesirable to conserve." He identified himself strongly with the movement for housing reform and in speaking to a bill promoted by a Royal Commission of which he had been a member, he shocked the rigid individualists of his own and the opposite party by his warm advocacy of State expenditure in dealing with the evils of overcrowding.

In 1884 Gladstone introduced a bill for enfranchising two million agricultural voters and divorced it from the large re-arrangement of seats which such an unequally distributed addition to the electorate would require. Salisbury saw in this procedure an intention of manipulating the constituencies in a party sense and invited the House of Lords to compel an appeal to the country on the question by refusing to pass one bill without the other. They did so and a tempestuous campaign of protest against their action followed. It was responded to by a similar campaign in their favour, in which Salisbury took a prominent part. The recurrent climax of his speeches was a challenge to the Government to dissolve parliament and so obtain the verdict of the electors on the issue. Through the Queen's mediation the controversy was closed by Gladstone's giving the required guarantee of impartiality in the Redistribution bill by inviting Salisbury and Sir Stafford Northcote to assist in drawing it up.

On June 8, 1885, the Liberals, disorganized by Sudanese disaster, allowed their Government to be defeated on a Budget vote and Mr. Gladstone resigned. The passage of the Franchise Act had made a dissolution impossible until the new registers were completed in November, and there were patent reasons why Salisbury, whom the Queen summoned, should refuse to take office. It would lose for his party all the advantage of attack in the approaching elections, and it would place on it the invidious responsibility of governing Ireland without the Crimes act, whose necessity it had urged and which was due to expire that summer. But the state of affairs abroad which the Queen revealed to him decided Salisbury upon acceptance. England was at that moment without friends or authority in Europe; perennial antagonists—Russia and Austria—France and Germany—had been negotiating reconciliation at her expense; if present conditions were suffered to continue it seemed to him that any catastrophe was possible. He kissed hands as prime minister and foreign secretary on June 24.

First Ministry.—His tenure of office this time was too short for the testing of any policy, but he achieved one sensational success. That September, the southern Bulgarians, who had been left under Turkish rule by the Treaty of Berlin, revolted and proclaimed union with their northern brethren. These and their Prince, Alexander of Battenberg, had in the intervening seven years quarrelled hopelessly with their Russian patron and Russia was now foremost in vindication of the treaty and insistence upon an immediate reversal of the achieved union. A conference of the Powers was called and the rest of the Continent rallied to the Russian demand. Salisbury alone refused. Now that the union had become an accomplished fact, he declared, the Bulgarians would never willingly surrender it and to force surrender, as the Imperial Governments proposed, by means of a Turkish military "execution," was unthinkable. For weeks he was argued with, pressed, objurgated for stultifying the united authority of Europe. He refused to give in and on Nov. 25 the conference broke up. Meanwhile Serbia, outraged at the accretion of territory illicitly secured by her neighbour, had invaded Bulgaria. Her unexpected and crushing defeat by Prince Alexander converted the great Powers to a depressed recognition of the facts upon which Salisbury had insisted. In December he was appealed to for help in discovering some face-saving compromise and the sultan was induced to come to a direct agreement with Prince Alexander, in which the union was recognized. The Treaty Powers had only to acquiesce, while the continental press turned round and congratulated the British minister upon the prescience and firmness which had saved Europe from a disastrous blunder.

Before this settlement was finally consummated Salisbury had left office. The general election in November had resulted in giving the Irish party the casting vote in the House of Commons. In December Gladstone had announced his adhesion to Home Rule and Salisbury's ministry was defeated on an amendment to the address on Jan. 26, 1886. Gladstone introduced his Home Rule bill which, with the assistance of 90 dissident Liberals, was rejected, on June 8. Parliament was dissolved; the Unionists gained a decisive victory though not one giving a majority to the Conservatives independently of their allies. On July 20, the Queen sent for Salisbury who, with her leave, pressed Hartington to take the premiership in his stead. But the Liberal-Unionist chief refused, promising independent support, and Lord Salisbury formed his second Government which remained in power for six years,—1886–92.

Government of 1886–92.—The worst difficulty which it had to encounter was at starting. Lord Randolph Churchill, who was the second man in the ministry and leader in the House of Commons, found himself unable to work with his colleagues, and resigned at the end of the year. The most popular platform speaker in the party, he was at that time without a rival on his own front bench, and the break up of the Government was anticipated. Salisbury again offered to widen its support by retiring in Hartington's favour, and Hartington again refused. But he advised his lieutenant, Goschen, to join the cabinet, which in the end suffered no permanent injury by Lord Randolph's defection. Salisbury, who at the outset had surrendered the foreign office to Lord Iddesleigh, now resumed its direction (Jan. 1887).

England was no longer in the position of dangerous isolation which she had occupied when he took office in 1885. The initiatory approaches which he had then made to the German chancellor had re-established friendly relations between them, and his successful obstinacy about Bulgaria had presented England to Europe as a power that had to be reckoned with. In '86, circum-

stances all combined to draw her towards the grouping of Central European Powers,—Germany, Austria and Italy as against the Russo-French combination. Russia had been alienated by her resistance to the coercion of Bulgaria, while across the Channel France's growing resentment at her continued presence in Egypt had operated in the same direction. But in 1887 there was an interval of hesitation. Salisbury was repelled by the German chancellor's methods. Throughout the preceding autumn and winter he had been ceaselessly resisting the chancellor's efforts to induce an Anglo-Russian war and so shift the Bulgarian quarrel from Austrian to English shoulders. The menacing pressure with which the chancellor visited any crossing of his wishes by a friendly Power had been a constant source of irritation. Salisbury's wish for a wider choice in friendships expressed itself that spring in a new departure in Egyptian policy. He offered to Turkey—as the suzerain power—an engagement to evacuate Egypt in three years if the conditions for her security permitted and with a right of re-entry reserved. After prolonged negotiation the sultan agreed to sign a convention to that effect (May 22, 1887). But France rejected the proffered compromise with indignation, and under threats of violence from her and Russia the sultan withdrew his consent, and refused ratification. The attempt, though it failed in its main object in a reconciliation with France, was not fruitless. It freed England from further solicitations and intrigues on the score of Egypt. She had made her offer and it had been rejected. Thenceforward, as Lord Salisbury soon made abundantly clear, she would consult only her own judgment as to the period of her occupation.

But France's inveteracy was decisive in determining England's continental friendships for the next ten years. Lord Salisbury declined to give them the character of alliances. In response to insistent requests from the Austrian and Italian Governments, backed by a private letter of strong appeal from the German chancellor (Nov. 22), he that autumn signed an engagement (the Tripartite Agreement, Dec. 10, 1887), to join with them in resisting any future coercion of Turkey on the part of Russia. The chancellor's letter hinted at a more general and binding adhesion to the Triple Alliance and it was followed by other suggestions to the same effect. These were ignored or evaded and more definite proposals met with more definite refusals. In the spring of 1887, Italy had asked for a defensive alliance specifically directed against France and in Jan. 1889 Germany invited a similar compact. Salisbury's answer on both occasions was that an undertaking to fight on an unarrived issue was contrary to the traditions of English policy and was impossible for a Constitutional Government.

To maintain this refusal of the only thing that constituted an alliance in Continental eyes without falling into the pit of national isolation was a difficult problem for diplomacy. Salisbury's large success in solving it during the period of his ministry was due in the main to his avoidance of exaggerated claims and his readiness not only to acquiesce in but actively to assist those of other countries wherever they were in any way admissible. Thus the detachment which must otherwise have become a source of jealousy and suspicion was, time and again, presented in a guise attractive to the needs of other nations. England never occupied a position of greater authority in Europe than during this time, and after Bismarck's retirement in 1890 Salisbury's became the dominating figure among European statesmen.

The white invasion of Africa which signalized that decade afforded opportunity for a marked display of his capacity for international co-operation. It was a movement unique in history for the rapidity, and, it may be added, the human benefit of its achievement. But behind the inrush of explorers, missionaries and traders of all nations, had now come their Governments, whose claims—undefined and illimitable—were, by the end of the eighties, advancing to inevitable conflict. England, whether by earlier occupation or the present activity of her adventurers, was a competitor in every region, north, south, east and west, and Lord Salisbury accepted the initiative to bring order out of chaos which was thus marked out for him. He engaged in negotiations, delimitations, arbitrations, and struck the best bargains he could for his own clients compatible with an instructed sympathy with their rivals' requirements. With an eye for a future still eight years distant he averted encroachment upon the Nile valley up to the river's source, though no Englishman had as yet set foot south of Wady Halfa, and placated French enmity beforehand by a large complaisance in the west and north-west of the continent. He reasoned suavely with Italy's aspirations and sharply with Portugal's baseless obstruction to the northward advance of Cecil Rhodes' South Africans; and when England's and Germany's irreducible requirements proved incompatible, threw Heligoland into the scales in security of a peaceful settlement (June 1890). When he left office the main outlines of actual occupation and prospective "spheres of influence" had been drawn without the serious chilling of a single international relationship.

The elections of 1892 resulted in a victory for the Liberal party though with a small and unharmonious majority. Gladstone passed a bill for Home Rule and one for Welsh Disestablishment through the House of Commons in successive sessions, but the evident want of enthusiasm in the country for either measure encouraged Salisbury, in accordance with the principle on which he acted in this connection, to invite their rejection by the House of Lords. The place of the Lords in the Constitution was to secure an appeal to the electorate but they could only wisely assert it against the House of Commons when there were sound reasons to believe that the electorate agreed with them. On this occasion his judgment proved amply justified. Parliament was dissolved in '95 and the verdict of the constituencies ratified the Lords' action by a substantial majority. Lord Salisbury again became prime minister and foreign secretary while the Liberal Unionist leaders established the fusion of the two sections of the party by joining his cabinet.

Third Ministry.—This was in many ways the least satisfactory of Lord Salisbury's four tenures of the foreign office. Since he was last in office the German emperor had quarrelled with England over Far East politics, and never afterwards paid more than lip service to the old friendship. The breach with France was not yet healed, and, though Lord Salisbury's personal authority remained and the influence of his initiative, England was isolated in European sympathy throughout this period. He found diplomacy once more absorbed in the Near East problem as the result of a peculiarly atrocious outbreak of Turkish cruelty and misgovernment in Armenia. After failing in a private proposal to Germany to join in some drastic enterprise—its details are not known—for the dismemberment or subjugation of Turkey, he appealed in 1896 to the Christian Powers as a whole to take combined action for enforcing reform on the Porte. They agreed and accepted his initiative. The "Concert of Europe" succeeded both in this matter and in a subsequent crisis in Crete, in averting the ever-present danger of a breach in the "armed truce" on the continent. But as regarded the lot of the unhappy Armenians it proved a sore disappointment to its author—Russia, who, in the strange whirligig of time, had become the champion of Turkish independences, vetoing, with German support, any form of coercion at Constantinople.

In the summer of 1895 a long-drawn-out frontier dispute between British Guiana and Venezuela achieved sudden importance through the action of the American Government which, with a view to hastening a conclusion, addressed a singularly discourteous despatch to that of England, claiming rights of dictation rather than intervention. Lord Salisbury, after some delay, replied with a reasoned demurrer to such a development of the Monroe doctrine. President Cleveland responded in a fierce speech, foreshadowing ultimatums, and was applauded by his public in a wild outbreak of anglo-phobic jingoism. Lord Salisbury declined the quarrel and some months later, when feelings had cooled, tacitly conceded America's claim to intervene and agreed to defer the whole question to neutral arbitration, whose verdict substantially conceded the British case. (Oct. 1899.)

In the winter of '97-98 a stir of anger was roused in England by Russia's illegal seizure from China of two ports—Port Arthur and Talienwan—which were supposed to secure domination over Pekin, and Lord Salisbury was much censured for passing the

aggression by with no more than a diplomatic protest. Events elsewhere called urgently for complaisance. The culminating crisis of the long quarrel with France over Egypt was imminent and Lord Salisbury held that its peaceful issue would depend on her finding no militant encouragement from sympathetic outsiders when the moment came. Colonel Marchand had been for more than three years making his way through the forests of Central Africa with instructions to assert a French claim upon the upper waters of the Nile before England had established an effective occupation there. He succeeded in fact in arriving that July at Fashoda a few weeks before General Kitchener reached it, steaming hurriedly up the river from the battle of Omdurman. But the news of the planting of the French flag and that of its removal reached Paris concurrently and with it a telegram from Lord Salisbury announcing the British occupation of the post and warning the French Government and people in the clearest terms that no compromise on England's claim upon the Nile valley was possible. Popular passion, dangerously excited for a few days, was thus compelled in the first moment of its ebullition to face the gravity of the decision to be taken and in the end it suffered its Government, discouragingly advised thereto by its Russian ally, to follow counsels of peace. The episode thus safely passed through proved, in spite of the resentment which it aroused at the time, the close of the quarrel that had so long kept the two nations apart. The resentment was artificially prolonged by the general unpopularity in which England was submerged through the South African war the following year, but when in 1901 that had passed by, the way was left open for the automatic operation of the forces which three years later resulted in the Entente.

The successful conduct of this crisis was Lord Salisbury's last diplomatic achievement of any note. He surrendered the foreign office in Nov. 1900, and the prime ministership in July 1902—only deferring this final retirement to avoid the embarrassment of a change before peace had been concluded in South Africa. He died a year later on Aug. 22, 1903.

Science was his main interest outside his profession and he was also widely read in history and theology. He was a strong churchman and a devout Christian, his religious faith constituting the fundamental inspiration of his life.   (G. Ce.)

See *Speeches of the Marquis of Salisbury*, ed. H. W. Lucy, with short biography (1885) and Lord Salisbury's *Essays*, 2 vol. (1905); also F. S. Pulling, *Life and Speeches of the Marquis of Salisbury* (1885); S. H. Jeyes, *Life and Times of the Marquis of Salisbury*, 4 vol. (1895–96); G. G. Cecil, *Life of Robert, Marquis of Salisbury* (1921).

SALISBURY, ROBERT CECIL, 1ST EARL OF SALISBURY (1563–1612), English secretary of state and lord high treasurer, was born on June 1, 1563, the only surviving son of Lord Burghley by his second wife, Mildred, daughter of Sir Anthony Cooke, tutor to Edward VI, and sister to Sir Francis Bacon's mother. (*See* BACON, FRANCIS.) Robert Cecil was educated at home, probably by his learned mother, and at St. John's college, Cambridge, for an unknown period around 1581. He was given his M.A. in 1605, although he had been lord steward of the university from 1591 and lord chancellor from 1600 until his death. He was admitted to Gray's Inn in 1580, but how long he studied law is not recorded. Probably to broaden his education he visited France in 1584, and accompanied Lord Derby to the Spanish Netherlands in 1588. He was married on Aug. 31, 1589, to Elizabeth Brooke, daughter of Lord Cobham. After Sir Francis Walsingham's death in 1590, Cecil gradually took over the work of the secretaryship of state, although not formally appointed to that office until July 5, 1596. He had been knighted and sworn of the privy council in 1591. He was elected to parliament for Westminster in 1584 and 1586, and for Hertfordshire in 1588, 1592, 1597 and 1601, and was the official exponent of government policy in the house of commons from 1593 until 1603, when he was created Baron Cecil of Essendine, and then in the upper house. Early in 1598 he headed a mission to Henry IV of France to try to prevent the inclusion of anything prejudicial to the English or Dutch in the treaty of Vervins between France and Spain. After his father's death in 1598 he became and remained the chief minister of the crown until his own death. His chief rival for the favour of Elizabeth I was the earl of Essex. He had already had a tussle with the earl over the appointment of the attorney general in 1594 when his candidate, Sir Edward Coke, was preferred to Bacon, whom Essex supported. When in 1601 Essex was on trial for rebellion he alleged that Cecil had once said that only the Spanish infanta had any claim to succeed Elizabeth. Cecil's denial was supported by the witness Essex named. The incident had an important bearing upon his future because he could now disprove the false rumours which had reached James VI of Scotland that the secretary was hostile to his claims to the English throne. Cecil entered into a secret correspondence with the king and gave him the excellent advice not to plague Elizabeth formally to recognize him as her successor, but to be careful to cultivate her good will. As Cecil expected, James succeeded Elizabeth unopposed, and retained her secretary of state as his chief minister. Sir Walter Raleigh, dismissed as captain of the Guard, listened to plotters who proposed to force the king to relax the penal laws against Catholics. Raleigh was also accused of a conspiracy, on behalf of Arabella Stuart, a cousin of James and next to him in the line of succession, on whose behalf Spanish assistance was being sought, and was tried and condemned to death, but his sentence was commuted to imprisonment in the Tower. Cecil was held responsible for Raleigh's prolonged incarceration, but as it continued for four years after his death he was probably not blameworthy. He was one of the chief examiners of the conspirators in the Gunpowder plot to blow up the two houses of parliament, but the suggestion that he fabricated it in order to enhance his position has been decisively refuted. He was a persecutor of those Catholics who upheld the papal claims to depose heretical monarchs and release subjects from their allegiance. The test of loyalty for Catholics in the oath of 1606 was willingness or refusal to denounce those claims. His tract entitled *An Answere to Certain Scandalous Papers* (1606), denied that he intended to exterminate all English Catholics. A Calvinist in doctrine but not in church organization he felt that the "turbulent humours" of the Puritans necessitated their coercion. He was not, like his master, an enthusiastic advocate of the union of England and Scotland, but he supported the plantation of Ulster and accepted the barony of Clogher in Tyrone, Ireland, of 12,500 ac. He did not actively participate in the formation of the Virginia company.

In 1604 Cecil was created Viscount Cranborne and the next year earl of Salisbury. In 1608 he became lord treasurer, and found that the king was £1,000,000 in debt. By new impositions on merchandise and other measures he reduced the debt to £300,000 but could not balance expenditures and revenue. He failed, however, to persuade parliament to accept the Great Contract of 1610, by which the revenue would have been increased by £200,000 minus about £100,000 received from various feudal dues which would be abandoned. He was equally unsuccessful in curbing James's extravagances. In foreign affairs he negotiated peace with Spain in 1604, but sympathized with the Dutch in their war of independence. When the 12 years' truce was arranged in 1609, England joined France in guaranteeing the Dutch against any infringement of it by Spain. He did not agree with the king's dreams of preventing wars by marriage alliances between the Catholic and Protestant powers. One of his last services was the betrothal of the Princess Elizabeth to Frederick of the Palatinate.

Salisbury died on May 24, 1612, worn out by his ministerial labours. James gave him the nickname of "little beagle" because of his diminutive body. It is uncertain whether he ever occupied the new house he built at Hatfield, an estate he acquired by exchanging it with James for Theobalds. He was a good administrator but not a great statesman because of his lack of originality. He perceived that the revenue of the crown was inadequate and that parliament should supply the deficit, but failed to see that frequent applications to parliament must inevitably change its relations to the monarchy. He tried to prolong the Elizabethan system after it had outgrown its usefulness but cannot be held responsible for James's attempts to magnify the royal prerogative.

BIBLIOGRAPHY.—Many sources for Salisbury's career are of a general nature and should be sought in the *Bibliography of British History,* the Tudor period (1932), ed. by Conyers Read, and the Stuart period (1928), ed. by Godfrey Davies. The papers at Hatfield have been calendared to 1606 (XVIII [1940]) by the Hist. MSS. Comm. Other letters are in *Correspondence of King James VI of Scotland with Sir Robert Cecil,* ed. by John Bruce (1861); and *The Secret Correspondence of Sir Robert Cecil with James I,* ed. by Lord Hailes (1766); *Illustrations of British History,* ed. by Edmund Lodge (1838); and Ralph Winwood, *Memorials of Affairs of State,* ed. Edmund Sawyer (1725). The Winwood papers are described in Hist. MSS. Comm. Buccleuch MSS. i (1899). A small tract entitled *The State and Dignitie of a Secretarie of Estates Place* (1642) is ascribed to Salisbury. It is reprinted in *Harleian Miscellany* (1808-13) v. The only modern biography is by Algernon Cecil, *A Life of Robert Cecil, First Earl of Salisbury* (1915). John Gerard's charges in *What Was the Gunpowder Plot?* are refuted in S. R. Gardiner's *What Gunpowder Plot Was,* both 1897.
(G. Ds.)

SALISBURY, ROLLIN D. (1858-1922), U.S. geologist, was born at Spring Prairie, Wis., Aug. 17, 1858, graduated from Beloit College in 1881, and later spent a year in graduate study at the University of Heidelberg, Ger. He taught successively at Beloit college, at the University of Wisconsin, and, from 1892 at the new University of Chicago. From 1899 till his death on Aug. 15, 1922, he was dean of Chicago's Ogden Graduate School of Science. From 1903 to 1919 he was head of the new department of geography, building up probably the strongest department in that field in the country, although his own teaching remained largely in geology. On the retirement of T. C. Chamberlin in 1919, he became head of the department of geology.

Salisbury's chief researches were in glacial geology. His early studies made famous the "driftless area" of the upper Mississippi valley. In 1895, as a member of the Peary Relief expedition, he studied glaciers in Greenland. His most systematic field work was on the Pleistocene formations of New Jersey. In 1904-06 appeared the three volumes of *Geology,* written jointly with T. C. Chamberlin, which was for many years the standard U.S. textbook of geology. Later he wrote a succession of textbooks on college geology, physiography and geography. (R. T. Cn.)

SALISBURY, THOMAS DE MONTACUTE, 4TH EARL OF (1388-1428), was son of John, the third earl, who was executed in 1400 as a supporter of Richard II. Thomas was granted part of his father's estates and summoned to parliament in 1409, though not fully restored till 1421. He was present throughout the campaign of Agincourt in 1415, and at the naval engagement before Harfleur in 1416, and in 1417-18. During the spring of 1419 he held an independent command, capturing Fécamp, Honfleur and other towns, was appointed lieutenant-general of Normandy, and created earl of Perche. In 1420 he was in chief command in Maine, and defeated the Maréchal de Rieux near Le Mans. When Henry V went home next year Salisbury remained in France as the chief lieutenant of Thomas, duke of Clarence. The duke, through his own rashness, was defeated at Baugé on March 21, 1421. Salisbury came up with the archers too late to retrieve the day, but recovered the bodies of the dead, and by a skilful retreat averted further disaster. He soon gathered a fresh force, and in June was able to report to the king "this part of your land stood in good plight never so well as now." (*Foedera,* x. 131.) Salisbury's success in Maine marked him out as John of Bedford's chief lieutenant in the war after Henry's death. In 1423 he was appointed governor of Champagne, and by his dash and vigour secured one of the chief victories of the war at Crevant on July 30. Subsequent operations completed the conquest of Champagne, and left Salisbury free to join Bedford at Verneuil. There his "judgment and valour" won the day. During the next three years Salisbury was employed on the Norman border and in Maine. After a year's visit to England he returned to the chief command in the field in July, 1428. Against the judgment of Bedford he determined to make Orleans his principal objective, and began the siege on Oct. 12; whilst surveying the city from a window in Tourelles he was wounded by a cannon-shot, and died on Nov. 3, 1428. Salisbury was the most skilful soldier on the English side after the death of Henry V. He was a patron of John Lydgate, who presented to him his book *The Pilgrim* (now Harley ms. 4826, with a miniature of Salisbury, engraved in Strutt's *Regal Antiquities*). By his first wife Eleanor Holand, daughter of Thomas, earl of Kent, Salisbury had an only daughter Alice, in her own right countess of Salisbury, who married Richard

Neville, and was mother of Warwick the King-maker. His second wife, Alice, was granddaughter of Geoffrey Chaucer, and after his death married William de la Pole, duke of Suffolk.

The chief accounts of Salisbury's campaigns are to be found in the *Gesta Henrici Quinti,* edited by B. Williams for the Eng. Hist. Soc. (London, 1850) in the *Vita Henrici Quinti* (erroneously attributed to Thomas of Elmham), edited by T. Hearne (Oxford, 1727); the *Chronique* of E. de Monstrelet, edited by L. D. d'Arcq (Paris, 1857–1862); the *Chroniques* of Jehan de Waurin, edited by W. and E. L. C. P. Hardy (London, 1864–1891); and the *Chronique de la Pucelle* of G. Cousinot, edited by Vallet de Viriville (Paris, 1859). For modern accounts *see* Sir J. H. Ramsay, *Lancaster and York* (Oxford, 1892); and C. Oman, *Political History of England,* 1377–1485 (London, 1906).

(C. L. K.)

SALISBURY, WILLIAM LONGSWORD (or **LONGESPÉE**), 3RD EARL OF (d. 1226), was an illegitimate son of Henry II, who granted him the estates of Appleby, Lincolnshire (1188). In 1198 he received from Richard I the hand of Isabella, or Ela (d. 1261), daughter and heiress of William, earl of Salisbury, and was granted this title with the lands of the earldom. He was received with favour by King John, who appointed him sheriff of Wiltshire in 1200, and subsequently gave him many important military and diplomatic posts, thus retaining his allegiance during the period of excommunication. In 1213 Salisbury was sent in command of a fleet to attack Philip of France, and, by his successful action at Damme, he foiled the projected invasion of England; but in the following year he was captured by the French and was only exchanged after prolonged negotiations. On his return to England he supported John in opposition to the baronial party, but feeling that the king's cause was hopeless, he surrendered to Louis on his arrival in England.

After the death of John, however, Salisbury deserted the French side in 1217, supported Herbert de Burgh and the young king, Henry III, and was appointed sheriff of Lincoln. It is asserted by Matthew Parker that he took part in the siege of Damietta (1219), but the evidence in support of this is scanty. It is known, however, that he supported the excommunication of William of Aumâle in 1221; that he assisted in the war on the Welsh marches (1224); and that in 1225 he accompanied the expedition to Gascony. On the return voyage he was wrecked on the isle of Ré, and the hardships which he suffered probably hastened his death, which occurred on March 7, 1226, at Salisbury.

SALISBURY, a city and municipal borough, and the county town of Wiltshire, England, 23 mi. W. of Winchester, with stations on the Southern and Great Western railways. Pop. (1931) 26,456; (est. 1938) 28,260. Area 4.4 sq.mi. The city lies in the valley at the junction of the rivers Avon, Wylye, Nadder and Bourne. The cathedral stands out above the city, which is partly laid out in squares called the "Chequers." To the north rises the bare upland of Salisbury plain. The neighbourhood of Salisbury was one of the most important areas in prehistoric England. It seems to have been a meeting place of early cultures, *e.g.,* of the people who made beakers and the people who built megaliths; 6 mi. N. is Stonehenge (*q.v.*). The Blackmore museum in the city has exhibits of almost every age from the neighbourhood. Most intimately associated, however, with the origins of Salisbury is the great prehistoric fortress of Old Sarum. It is about 2 mi. N. of the present city. The great mound has a fosse and earthwork, while the summit is hollowed out like a crater and its rim surmounted by a rampart. It was an important site in Romano-British times and especially in the period immediately preceding the arrival of the Romans. It was known to the Romans as *Sorbiodunum.* In 552 it was taken by Cenric, who named it *Searesbyrig* ("dry town") and it became the home of the kings of Wessex. Alfred strengthened the castle, and it was selected by Edgar as a place of national assembly to devise means of checking the Danes. About 1075 Old Sarum became the seat of a bishopric. Osmund, the second bishop, compiled a missal which forms the groundwork of the celebrated "Sarum Use." The "Sarum Breviary" was printed at Venice in 1483, and upon this, the most widely prevalent of English liturgies, the prayer books of Edward VI were mainly based. Osmund also built a cathedral, in the form of a plain cross. The garrison and priests, confined within a small space, were at perpetual feud; and after a licence

had been granted by Pope Honorius III, it was decided to move down into the fertile Avon valley. In 1102 Bishop Roger Poore obtained a comprehensive charter from Henry I. With the building of New Sarum in the 13th century and the transference to it of the see, Old Sarum lapsed to the crown. By the 16th century it was in ruins, and in 1608 it was ordered that the town walls should be demolished.

The new city, under the name of New Sarum (New Saresbury, Salisbury) immediately began to spring up close around the cathedral. A charter of Henry III creating it a free city in 1227 recites the removal from Old Sarum, the king's ratification and his laying the foundation stone of the church. In 1611 the city obtained a charter of incorporation from James I under the title of "mayor and commonalty" of the city of New Sarum.

The cathedral church of St. Mary is a beautiful example of Early English architecture, begun and completed, save its spire and a few details, within one brief period (1220–1266). There is a tradition that Elias de Derham, canon of the cathedral (d. 1245), was the principal architect. The building is 473 ft. in extreme length, the length of the nave being 229 ft. 6 in., the choir 151 ft., and the lady chapel 68 ft. 6 in. The width of the nave is 82 ft. and the height 84 ft. The spire, the highest in England, measures 404 ft. (For plan, *see* GOTHIC ARCHITECTURE: *Gothic Architecture in England.*) The cathedral consists of a nave of ten bays, with aisles and a lofty north porch, main transepts with eastern aisles, choir with aisles, lesser transepts, presbytery and lady chapel. The two upper stories of the tower and the spire above are early Decorated. The west front, the last portion of the original building completed, bears in its rich ornamentation signs of the transition to the Decorated style. The perfect uniformity of the building is no less remarkable within than without. The frequent use of Purbeck marble for shafts contrasts with the delicate gray freestone which is the principal building material. An unhappy restoration of the cathedral (1782–1791) destroyed many magnificent stained-glass windows which had escaped the Reformation, and also removed two Perpendicular chapels and the detached belfry which stood to the northwest of the cathedral. The lady chapel is the earliest part of the original building. The cloisters, south of the church, were built directly after its completion. The fine octagonal chapter-house is of the time of Edward I with a series of contemporary sculptures. The library contains many valuable mss. and ancient printed books. The diocese covers all Dorsetshire, except four parishes, the greater part of Wiltshire, and eight parishes in whole or in part in Southampton, two each in Berkshire and Devonshire and one in Somersetshire. There are three ancient parish churches: St. Martin's, with square tower and spire, and possessing a Norman font and Early English portions in the choir; St. Thomas's (of Canterbury), founded in 1240 as a chapel to the cathedral, and rebuilt in the 15th century; and St. Edmund's, founded as the collegiate church of secular canons in 1268, but later rebuilt in the Perpendicular period. The residence of the college of secular priests is occupied by the ecclesiastical college of St. Edmund's, founded in 1873. St. John's chapel, founded by Bishop Robert Bingham in the 13th century, is occupied by a dwelling house. There is a chapel attached to the St. Nicholas hospital. The poultry cross, or high cross, an open hexagon with six arches and a central pillar, was erected by Lord Montacute before 1335. Among remaining specimens of ancient domestic architecture are the banquet hall of John Halle, wool merchant, built about 1470 and since 1930 used as a cinema; and Audley house (16th century), repaired in 1881 as a diocesan church house. Salisbury returned two members to parliament until 1885 when the number was reduced to one. Since 1918 it has been in the Salisbury division of the county.

SALISBURY, capital of Southern Rhodesia, Africa. Pop. (1936) 32,846, including 11,392 whites and 20,177 natives. Altitude 4,865 ft. It was founded in 1890, is well laid out, has good shops, and an excellent water supply. The distance by rail to Capetown is 1,659 mi., and to Beira 374 mi. It is the centre of a gold-producing area.

SALISBURY, a city of southeastern Maryland, U.S.A., at the head of navigation on the Wicomico river; the county seat of Wicomico county. It is on federal highways 13 and 50 and is served by the Pennsylvania and (for freight) the Baltimore and Eastern railways.

Pop. (1950) 15,141; in 1940 it was 13,313. It is the wholesale distributing centre for the "eastern shore" of Maryland south of Delaware.

Salisbury was founded in 1732, organized as a town in 1812, incorporated in 1854 and chartered as a city in 1880.

Lumber, building materials, leather goods and wearing apparel are manufactured there. Agricultural products include cantaloupes, strawberries and cucumbers. There are also nurseries and sea food and meat packing plants. In 1925 the State Teacher's College of Salisbury was established.

SALISBURY, a city of North Carolina, U.S., the county seat of Rowan county; 120 mi. W.S.W. of Raleigh, near the Yadkin river. It is on federal highways 29, 52 and 70, and is served by the Southern and the Yadkin railways.

Pop. (1950) 20,102; in 1940, 19,037 by federal census. It is an industrial and commercial centre in the rich Piedmont section of the state, and is the seat of Catawba college (Reformed church; opened in 1851 at Newton and moved to Salisbury in 1923) and Livingstone college for Negroes (1882). The community has cotton mills, car shops and various other manufacturing plants. It is the site of a veterans administration neuropsychiatric hospital.

There are granite quarries and iron deposits in the vicinity. The city operates under a council-manager form of government. Salisbury was incorporated as a town in 1755, and as a city in 1770. During the Civil War it was the seat of a Confederate military prison. On April 12, 1865, a cavalry engagement near by resulted in the capture of 1,364 Confederate soldiers. There is a national cemetery there, containing 12,186 graves.

SALISH. This tribe, popularly known as Flathead, has given name to the Salishan family of Indians, all speaking cognate dialects, in British Columbia and north-western United States. None of the Salishan tribes were agricultural or matrilineal; those on the coast practised potlatch festivals, accumulated wealth, held slaves and lived in plank houses like the other coastal tribes of the area. Inland, arts and customs were simpler. The principal groups or tribes are: 1, Interior Salish, comprising the Shuswap, Lillooet, Thompson or Ntlakyapamuk, Okanagan in British Columbia, and the Flathead or Salish proper, Kalispel, Coeur d'Alêne, Spokane, Methow in the United States; 2, Coast Salish, in order from north to south: Bellacoola of Dean's inlet, Comox, Cowichan of Vancouver island, Nanaimo, Squawmish, Lummi, Snohomish, Snoqualmie (Seattle), Puyallup, Nisquallie, Cowlitz, Skokomish, Songish, Clallam of Strait of Juan de Fuca, Quinault, Chehalis, and, south of Columbia river, Tillamook called also Nehalim.

In 1909 the total population was 18,600, somewhat more than half being respectively in the interior and in Canada. The original number was perhaps three times as great.

SALITE (from Sala, Sweden, its original locality), a variety of monoclinic pyroxene (q.v.).

SALIVAN, a group of tribes of South American Indians, usually regarded as constituting an independent linguistic stock. The Salivas, from whom the stock gets its name, lived originally along the western side of the Orinoco and for some distance west along its tributaries, from above the mouth of the Vichada to the Sinaruco.

They were a peaceful, docile folk, who, being attacked by the Caribs in the latter part of the 17th century, withdrew westward up the Meta and Vichada toward their heads. In the main a hunting and fishing people, they had no maize and but little manioc.

Like some of the neighbouring groups, they were accustomed to exhume the bones of the dead after a year or so, burn and reduce them to powder and then drink this, mixed with their fermented beer.

See J. Cassani, *Historia de la provincia de la compañia de Jesús del Nuevo Reino de Granada* (Madrid, 1741).

SALLUST [GAIUS SALLUSTIUS CRISPUS] (86–34 B.C.), Roman historian, belonging to a well-known plebeian family, was born at Amiternum in the country of the Sabines. After an ill-spent youth he entered public life, and was elected tribune of the people in 52. From the first he was a decided partisan of Caesar, to whom he owed such political advancement as he attained. In 50 he was removed from the senate by the censor Appius Claudius Pulcher, restored in 49 and became quaestor. In 46 he was praetor, and accompanied Caesar in his African campaign, which ended in the decisive defeat of the remains of the Pompeian party at Thapsus. He was then made governor of Numidia, where he was oppressive and extortionate. On his return to Rome he purchased and laid out in great splendour the famous gardens on the Quirinal known as the *Horti Sallustiani*. He now retired from public life.

His account of the Catiline conspiracy (*De coniuratione Catilinae* or *Bellum Catilinarium*) and of the Jugurthine War (*Bellum Jugurthinum*) have come down to us complete, together with fragments of his larger and most important work (*Historiae*), a history of Rome from 78–67, intended as a continuation of L. Cornelius Sisenna's work. In the *Catiline Conspiracy* Sallust adopts the usually accepted view of Catiline, and describes him as the deliberate foe of law, order and morality, without attempting to give any adequate explanation of his views and intentions. Catiline, it must be remembered, had supported the party of Sulla, to which Sallust was opposed. He is careful to clear Caesar of complicity and on the whole he is not unfair towards Cicero.

His *Jugurthine War*, again, though a valuable and interesting monograph, is not a satisfactory performance. Here, as in the *Catiline*, he dwells upon the feebleness of the senate and aristocracy, too often in a tiresome, moralizing vein, but as a military history the work is unsatisfactory in the matter of geographical and chronological details, though vivid in its depiction of character and scenery. The extant fragments of the *Histories* (some discovered in 1886) are enough to show the political partisan, who took a keen pleasure in describing the reaction against the dictator's policy and legislation after his death. Two letters (*Duae epistolae de republica ordinanda*), and an attack upon Cicero (*Invectiva* or *Declamatio in Ciceronem*), frequently attributed to Sallust, are probably the work of a rhetorician of the first century A.D., also the author of a counter-invective by Cicero.

Editions and translations in various languages are numerous. Editio princeps (1470); (text and notes) F. Jacobs, H. Wirz (1894); G. Long, revised by J. G. Frazer, with chief fragments of *Histories* (1884); English translation by A. W. Pollard (1882); (text and tr.) J. C. Rolfe (Loeb library, 1921). There are many separate editions of the *Catilina* and *Jugurtha*, chiefly for school use. The fragments have been edited by F. Kritz (1853) and B. Maurenbrecher (1891–93); and there is an Italian translation (with notes) of the supposititious letters by G. Vittori (1897).

SALMASIUS, CLAUDIUS, the Latinized name of CLAUDE SAUMAISE (1588–1653), French classical scholar, born at Semur-en-Auxois in Burgundy on April 15, 1588. He was educated at Paris and Heidelberg, where he went over to Protestantism. In 1609 he brought out an edition of Florus. He then returned to Burgundy, and qualified for the succession to his father's post, which he eventually lost on account of his religion. In 1620 he published Casaubon's notes on the *Augustan History*, with copious additions of his own. In 1623 he married Anne Mercier, a Protestant lady of a distinguished family. In 1629 Salmasius produced his *magnum opus* as a critic, his commentary on Solinus's *Polyhistor*, or rather on Pliny, to whom Solinus is indebted for the most important part of his work. Salmasius learned Arabic to qualify himself for the botanical part of his task. In 1631 he went as professor to Leiden, where he composed for Frederick of Nassau his *De Re Militari Romanorum*, not published till 1657. He was persistently attacked by a clique led by Daniel Heinsius. His *De primatu Papae* (1645) excited a warm controversy in France.

In November 1649 appeared his *Defensio regia pro Carolo I*. It does not appear who influenced him to write it but Charles II. defrayed the expense of printing, and presented the author with £100. The first edition was anonymous, but the author was universally known. This celebrated work, in our day principally famous for the reply it provoked from Milton (1651) even in its own time added little to the reputation of the author. His reply to Milton, which he left unfinished at his death, and which was published by his son in 1660, is insipid as well as abusive. Salmasius died on Sept. 3, 1653.

As a commentator and critic, Salmasius is entitled to high rank. His notes on the *Augustan History* and Solinus display not only massive erudition but massive good sense as well; his perception of the meaning of his author is commonly very acute, and his emendations are frequently felicitous.

The life of Salmasius was written by Philibert de la Mare, but never printed; it was used by Papillon, whose account of Salmasius in his *Bibliothèque des auteurs de Bourgogne* (Dijon, 1745), is by far the best extant, and contains an exhaustive list of his works, both printed and in ms. There is an *éloge* by A. Clément prefixed to his edition of Salmasius' *Letters* (Leiden, 1656), and another by C. B. Morisot, in his own *Letters* (Dijon, 1656). *See also* E. Haag, *La France protestante* (ix, 149–173); and, for the *Defensio regia*, D. Masson's *Life of Milton.*

SALMERÓN, NICOLÁS (1838–1908), Spanish statesman, born at Alhama la Seca, Almeria, April 10, 1838. Professor of literature and philosophy at Madrid, he co-operated with Castelar on *La Democracia* and in 1865 was a member of the directing committee of the Republican party. Imprisoned as a suspect in 1867, he was elected to the Cortes in 1871 and on the resignation of Amadeo (Feb. 11, 1873) was naturally marked out to be the leader of the party which sought to establish a republic in Spain. He succeeded Pí y Margall in the presidency of the republic on July 18, 1873, but resigned (Sept. 7), when he found that the generals insisted on executing rebels taken in arms. His successor, Castelar, was compelled to restore order by drastic means. Salmerón took part in the attack made on him in the Cortes on Jan. 3, 1874, and went into exile until recalled by Sagasta in 1881. In 1886 he was elected to the Cortes as Progressive deputy for Madrid. He died at Pau, Sept. 21, 1908.

SALMON, THOMAS WILLIAM (1876–1927), U.S. physician and psychiatrist, was born in Lansingburg, N.Y., on Jan. 6, 1876. He was educated in the public schools and at the Lansingburg academy. In 1899 he took his degree in medicine at the Albany Medical college and then entered private practice for a short time. Two years later he was appointed to the Willard State hospital where he made one of the earliest studies of the role of humans as disease carriers. In 1903 he was commissioned in the U.S. public health service. There he developed an interest in the medical problems of some maritime patients. As a result, he suggested and provided the plans for a hospital ship for deep sea fishermen which later materialized to excellent advantage. In 1905 he was asked to undertake an assignment in conjunction with the immigration office at Ellis Island. New York state authorities had become alarmed at the prevalence of foreign born among patients admitted to state hospitals, and plans were made for more careful scrutiny of immigrants on their arrival. Under Salmon's direction, a psychiatric service was incorporated into the regular medical department at Ellis Island which proved invaluable in weeding out the insane and defective and provided a more humane and scientific reception of helpless immigrants. By this time, his publications on the subject were well known and respected and when the federal immigration law was in process of revision, his aid was requested at congressional hearings. Much of his advice was incorporated into the new law. In 1915 he resigned from the public health service to become medical director of the newly formed National Committee for Public Hygiene. In this capacity, he gave practical guidance toward the extension of hygiene knowledge and the applications of psychiatry to public welfare. The second most outstanding achievement of his career was his role in establishing neuropsychiatric services for the armed forces during World War I. For this and related activities, he was awarded the D.S.M. After the war, he provided plans for model hospitals to care for mentally disabled veterans. In 1921 he resigned from the national committee to become professor of psychiatry at Columbia university, where he virtually established that field of study on an independent basis. Salmon edited the volume on neuropsychiatry in the *Medical History of the World War.* He died on Aug. 13, 1927.

SALMON AND SALMONIDAE. The family Salmonidae, as understood in modern ichthyology, consists of three principal groups of fishes, which will be referred to here as the salmon, the trouts and the chars. Formerly the lake herrings or ciscoes and the whitefishes, also, were included. However, the last mentioned groups, having larger scales and a skull that differs in structure, now are generally assigned to a separate family called Coregonidae.

The Salmonidae have robust, somewhat-rounded, muscular bodies. The skeleton is bony, and the fins have soft rays only. The lower pair of fins, the ventrals, are attached to the abdomen, far behind the upper pair, the pectoral fins. A fleshy fin, without rays, is situated on the back behind the larger dorsal fin, and the caudal fin usually is more or less concave or forked. The entire body, exclusive of the head, is covered with small smooth-edged scales, of which more than a hundred are present along the middle of the side.

These fishes are more or less midway in zoological classification between the sharks with their primitive cartilaginous skeleton and the higher fishes such as the basses and cods with a complex bony frame. In colour the Salmonidae are greatly specialized, however, since many of them rival the most brilliant productions of the tropical seas.

Nearly all the members of the family live in the northern part of the northern hemisphere and are largely restricted to coastwise waters, neighbouring islands and the inland waters of North America, Europe and Asia. Only a few have spread naturally beyond this range, as in the Atlas Mountains of northern Africa. However, several species have been widely distributed and have become well established far beyond their natural range by the help of man.

Virtually all Salmonidae make some sort of migration to spawn. Those that live habitually in fresh water may ascend the stream they occupy only a short distance; inhabitants of lakes migrate somewhat farther as they ascend the streams; while those species that live chiefly in the sea make long migrations, to and in fresh-water rivers, some of which are exceedingly great as shown subsequently. Salmonidae are carnivorous, and normally feed on live bait. Fish, crustaceans and many insects are included in the diet.

The Salmon (genus *Oncorhynchus*).—The name, salmon, when used herein as a group name is restricted to the several species of the Pacific belonging to the genus *Oncorhynchus*. This is done, notwithstanding that the name salmon no doubt was used for the anadromous species of the genus *Salmo* long before it came into use for the members of the genus *Oncorhynchus*. This procedure seems necessary because no other common English name is available for *Oncorhynchus*, whereas most of the species of the genus *Salmo* have long been known as trout. Therefore, the common Atlantic salmon, and its relatives, will be discussed in this article under the general group name, "trouts."

The salmon, as defined in the preceding paragraph, differ externally from the trouts and chars in the size of the anal fin. In the salmon this fin is longer than it is high and has 13 or more developed rays, whereas in the trouts and chars it is higher than it is long and has fewer than 12 developed rays.

Five commercially important species of salmon of the genus *Oncorhynchus* occur on the Pacific coast of the United States and northward to Alaska, and to northern Asia, with a few more that are restricted to Japan and vicinity. These fishes are the source of the large annual pack of canned salmon shipped to virtually all parts of the world, and constituting a familiar article of diet to many millions of people. The catch for the United States, Canada and Alaska ran up to the impressive total of approximately 825,-145,000 lb. in 1941. Of this amount the United States contributed about 86,455,700 lb., Canada 193,664,200 lb. and Alaska 545,024,-370 lb.

Of the five important species of salmon, the Chinook or king salmon, *Oncorhynchus tschawytscha*, grows the largest, occasionally attaining a weight of 70 to 100 lb., though the average weight probably does not exceed 20 lb. However, only about 5.5% of the total catch for the United States, Canada and Alaska for 1941 consisted of this species, the smallest amount yielded by any one species.

The chum or dog salmon, *Oncorhynchus keta,* although much smaller than the king salmon, generally weighing only about 7–10 lb., contributed about 18% to the catch of 1941. The silver salmon, *Oncorhynchus kisutch,* attaining an average weight of about 5 to 8 lb., furnished about 21%; the sockeye or blueback, *Oncorhynchus nerka,* which also reaches a weight of about 5 to 8 lb., yielded about 26% and the pink or humpback salmon, *Oncorhynchus gorbuscha,* averaging only about 3–5 lb. in weight, furnished about 29% of the 1941 catch. Therefore, the smallest of the five species exceeded every other species in the quantity supplied.

It is evident from the foregoing statistics that by far the greater part of the catch of salmon came from Alaska in 1941, as has been the case for many years. The catch in the United States has declined more or less gradually. For example, in 1928 it amounted to 131,792,900 lb., in 1934 to 106,691,900 lb. and in 1941 to 86,455,700 lb. Assuming that the efforts devoted to fishing remained about equal, the decline is impressive. The depletion is not so great as it is for the Atlantic salmon, *Salmo salar,* on the coast of the United States, as will be shown subsequently. Yet it is evident that the decline is serious. How to overcome the obstacles occasioned by industrial developments, especially the high dams built across salmon streams, awaits a satisfactory solution.

The salmon as well as some of the trouts, are anadromous. That is, they migrate from the sea to fresh-water streams to spawn. Some of the species ascend streams to their headwaters, whereas others spawn in the lower stretches of rivers. The king salmon goes to the headwaters. It has been found in the upper Yukon river, 3,000 mi. or so from the sea. The pink salmon, on the other hand, commonly spawns only a few miles above salt water.

The fish come in from the sea in fine condition. Upon entering fresh water they cease feeding, and sometimes they wear themselves out completely trying to reach proper places to deposit their eggs. They will ascend rapids and falls, often jumping vertically several times their own length in passing difficult places. By the time they have spawned they often are terribly emaciated, and have broken and ragged fins. However, whether worn out or still in fair condition the fish die after spawning. It is not known that a salmon has lived to spawn more than once.

When the fish reach the spawning ground, which it is believed is more or less in the selfsame spot where these mature males and females themselves were hatched, the female with body, tail and fins prepares a trough-shaped depression in gravel or sand. The eggs are deposited in the "nest" thus prepared, and are fertilized at the same time by the male. Upon completion of this process the female covers the eggs with the excavated or other material, which is the final act in the life cycle. She, as well as the male, now appear to have lost interest in life. They drift downstream more or less with the current, and as already indicated they soon die.

The relatively large eggs, $\frac{1}{4}$ in. or more in diameter, may hatch in 60 days, though the incubation period may be prolonged several days by a drop in the temperature of a degree or two and shortened several days by a similar increase in temperature.

The newly hatched fish with their tremendously large yolk sac are quite helpless. They remain hidden among pebbles on the spawning ground until the yolk is absorbed. At that stage in life the young fish begin to swim about and to seek food. After remaining in fresh water from a few months to perhaps a year or more they descend the streams and enter salt water. When once in salt water the fish grow rapidly.

Sometime between the ages of two to seven years the fish have matured. Sexual products have developed, and the urge to spawn causes them to re-enter the fresh-water streams they descended to fulfil their final mission in life, in the same vicinity where their ancestors completed their life cycle.

The Trouts (genus *Salmo*).—The trouts are among the most difficult fishes to classify. Indeed, scarcely two ichthyologists agree as to the number of species that should be recognized. What one authority regards a valid species another may recognize as only subspecifically distinct, or only as a variety or race. The reasons for the confusion are the irregularities in the anatomical structures, the great variation in colour and the confusing irregularities in habits. Regardless of these difficulties, some generally accepted species exist, but a reasonable and logical interpretation of the group as a whole is missing. The problem may now be virtually impossible of satisfactory solution, because of the near extinction of certain forms of restricted distribution. Furthermore, through fish culture seemingly fertile hybrids have been produced, and various forms have been distributed and have become intermixed with native species.

The Atlantic salmon, *Salmo salar,* is one of the well-known and generally recognized species of the genus. It occurs on both sides of the North Atlantic and ranges well within the Arctic circle. In Europe it occurs as far south as the Bay of Biscay, and in North America to Cape Cod and formerly to the Hudson river. It has many near relatives that live habitually in fresh-water lakes and streams.

Salmo salar has been greatly reduced in abundance in some parts of its range. In New England it may be listed among the "vanishing animals." This depletion is in part the result of overfishing, but the construction of dams across rivers without providing "fish ladders," and the pollution of streams have constituted a far greater menace. Whether the streams formerly occupied can again be made suitable and the fish restored is an unsolved problem. Neither is it known whether the fish can be brought back in commercial numbers in those rivers that are still frequented to a limited extent.

The life history of *Salmo salar* is better known than that of any other species of the family, and therefore is described herein in some detail. In general, it is similar to that of the Pacific salmon. It also ascends rivers to spawn, but unlike the Pacific salmon it does not habitually die after spawning. To the contrary, an Atlantic salmon may live to spawn three or four times. The migration upstream starts in the autumn and occurs from October to February. *Salmo salar,* like the Pacific salmon, does not feed while in fresh water en route to its spawning ground. In the meantime the sexual products are developed at the expense of the other tissues. This causes the flesh, which was red and fat when the fish left the sea, to become pale and watery. In the breeding male the jaws become prolonged during migration; the lower one becomes curved upward, or even acquires a hook, and the teeth grow large. The silvery colour becomes replaced by a dull gray in the female, while the male acquires irregular dark and reddish spots on the body.

The eggs, as in the Pacific salmon, are deposited in shallow excavations made in sand or gravel by the female and covered by her after spawning is finished. The eggs are 6 or 7 mm., or fully $\frac{1}{4}$ in. in diameter, and incubation extends over a period of about 5 months.

The newly hatched fish is 15–18 mm., or about $\frac{3}{4}$ in. long. It is quite helpless at first and lies hidden among the pebbles until the big yolk sac it retains at hatching is absorbed. When the yolk is all gone the fish is an inch or more long. It then swims actively and begins its search for food. The little fish, known as a "parr," soon becomes brilliant in colour, and has 10 or 11 dark cross bars, alternating with bright red spots.

The parr live in fresh water a variable length of time, according to the locality and factors not well understood. Most of the fish migrate to the sea principally in the spring and early summer, at the age of two years, when they have attained a length of about six inches. However, some linger in fresh water, especially in northern localities, three, four, five or even six years.

When the young fish approach tidewater they lose the bars and spots, and become silvery for their sojourn in the sea. These fish, now known as "smolts," stay in or near the mouths of rivers and in estuaries for some time, although by fall they have disappeared. Little is known of their movements during the first winter in the sea. It is certain, however, that they grow rapidly on the abundant diet in the ocean, for when they reappear on the coast the following spring they are 16 in. and more in length, and weigh 1½–7 lb. or, rarely, even more. The fish, now known as "grilse," are distinguishable from older fish by the slenderer body, smaller head, more deeply forked caudal and by the more numerous spots on the body, which at this stage in life are bluish rather than black.

A few individuals, especially males, may spawn during the grilse stage, but the great majority remain in the sea. Many fish spawn after living in the ocean two years, while others do not make a return migration for three, four or even five years. As it is improbable that any Atlantic salmon lives more than eight or nine years, it follows that the individuals that spawn three or four times, as stated elsewhere, are the ones that reproduce early in life, and not the ones that remain at sea four or five years and spawn for the first time at the age of about six or seven years.

A tremendously large size for a trout is attained by the Atlantic salmon. An individual weighing 83 lb. has been reported from England. None even approaching such a weight has been found in America where a 50-lb. fish is a rarity. Large individuals are not necessarily very old, as they probably are fish that remained on rich feeding grounds in the sea without spawning. As the fish while en route to the spawning grounds do not feed, they become emaciated, and growth is greatly retarded. In general, the individuals that begin spawning early in life and spawn every year do not grow large, whereas those that spawn for the first time late in life, and perhaps spawn only once, reach a large size.

Landlocked Salmon (*Salmo sp.*).—It already has been stated that the Atlantic salmon has many near relatives that habitually live in fresh water. The nearest of all are the landlocked forms. The lake dwellers received this name from the belief long held that their ancestors, *Salmo salar,* in some way became shut off from the sea and were obliged to remain in fresh water. It seems more probable in the light of present knowledge that some young *Salmo salar* found certain lakes, which they reached while migrating toward the sea, a sufficiently agreeable substitute for the ocean to remain there voluntarily and permanently. Thus, landlocked salmon seems to be a misnomer, and "lake salmon" has been suggested as a substitute.

Under the influence of the new environment in the lakes the progeny in the course of time diverged sufficiently from the parent stock, *Salmo salar,* to become recognized as distinct species. In fact, several species have been named, but in this case as in others general agreement as to their validity is lacking. Therefore, no attempt to list the species herein has been made.

Colonies of landlocked salmon exist in New England, eastern Canada and in Europe. While these fish spend most of their lives in lakes, they retain the migratory instinct of their ancestors and ascend rivers to spawn. In general, landlocked salmon run smaller than the Atlantic salmon, though individuals weighing 20 lb. and more have been reported. They are protected and reserved for sport, only, in the United States.

Numerous other species of *Salmo* occur in the fresh waters of North America, and of Europe, and a few are found in the mountains of northern Africa. The fresh-water trouts are especially difficult to classify. Among them are the brown trout, *Salmo trutta,* and the Loch Laven trout, *Salmo levensis,* of Europe, which have long been subjects of fish culture and have been widely distributed artificially.

In western North America there are numerous closely related species of *Salmo,* which J. O. Snyder regarded as belonging to two main groups. These he called "rainbow series" and the "cut-throat series." The same investigator, after many years of study, came to the conclusion that the steelhead trout, long held to be a distinct species somewhat intermediate of the rainbow and cut-throat trouts, is not entitled to specific rank. Professor Snyder said, "A steelhead is a sea migrant of the particular species inhabiting the stream, and in our waters (California) it may be either a cut-throat steelhead or a rainbow steelhead, and there is no occasion to apply a Linnaean binomial name to a steelhead as such." (John O. Snyder, "The Trouts of California," *Calif. Fish and Game,* vol. 26, no. 2, April 1940, Dept. Nat. Resources, State of California.)

The steelhead trout offers another illustration of the extreme difficulties met in classifying trouts. It is also an illustration of the diversity of habits, since it shows that some rainbow and cut-throat trouts retain the migratory instinct of distant ancestors and continue to migrate to the sea, whereas others remain in fresh water throughout life.

The rainbow and cut-throat trouts are extensively cultivated in America, where they also are protected and reserved for sport. There are many records of rainbow and cut-throat trouts weighing 20 lb. and more, but the average size is much smaller.

Chars (genus *Salvelinus*).—Many species of char occur in Europe and the cold regions of the north, the range extending far into the Arctic circle. Some of the species continue to live in salt water, like all the ancestors of the living species no doubt did. However, others have become chiefly or wholly restricted to fresh water. Certain species that live in fresh water in the southern part of their range throughout life will enter salt water if they inhabit streams adjacent to cold seas. *Salvelinus fontinalis,* known in the United States as the "eastern brook trout," for example, ranges southward into Georgia, but it enters the sea only from Cape Cod northward. Even there only a part of the population of any one river "run down" to the sea. The ones that enter salt water are called "sea trout." These fish are not to be confused, however, with the sea trout of the southern shores of the U.S. which are not Salmonidae, but are members of the croaker family, Sciaenidae.

The chars, that is, the species of the genus *Salvelinus,* generally are distinguishable from the trouts of the genus *Salmo* by the smaller scales, which are so minute as to be hardly visible in some species, and usually they may also be distinguished by the colour, since the chars have reddish spots, whereas the trouts have dark ones. However, for certain identification it is necessary to examine the teeth on the roof of the mouth. In *Salvelinus* teeth are present in a group on the anterior part of the vomer only, whereas in *Salmo* the teeth extend back on the vomer in a double zigzag series.

The chars generally are valued as food and game fishes. Thus, the eastern brook trout in America is extensively cultivated, and has been distributed by man far beyond its natural range, and is protected as a game fish. However, there is a disliked member, the "Dolly Varden trout," *Salvelinus malma,* which occurs in the Pacific coast states of the U.S. and ranges northward to Alaska, Kamchatka, U.S.S.R., and to Japan. The Dolly Varden is highly predatory, destructive of salmon eggs and young salmon and is not regarded as a good game fish.

Chars generally do not run large in size, often attaining a length of only about 10-12 in., though some individuals of those species that run down to the sea may attain a length of about 24 in.

The Great Lakes Trout (*Cristivomer namaycush*).—This fish, as its name indicates, lives in the Great Lakes of North America, and in other deep lakes northward and beyond to the Arctic circle. It does not belong to one of the major groups of Salmonidae named at the beginning of this article, though its relationship is with the trouts, genus *Salmo.* It is readily distinguished, however, as it lacks bright colours, and has pale yellow or grayish spots rather than dark ones. Further, its tail is more deeply forked. Although it does not belong to one of the major groups of Salmonidae, it is important enough to require at least brief mention. It is among the largest of the entire family. A maximum weight of 100 lb. has been reported. Certainly a weight of 50 to 80 lb. is occasionally attained, though the average weight of the fish that reach the markets is less than 10 lb. While the Great Lakes trout is chiefly a commercial fish, it is also a game fish of importance. The annual catch for the Great Lakes is around 10,000,000 lb. (S. F. Hd.)

BIBLIOGRAPHY.—See *Salmon and Trout Magazine* (London) and papers by C. H. Gilbert and others in *Bull. U.S. Fisheries Bureau;* W. L. Calderwood, *The Life of the Salmon* (1907); J. A. Hutton, *Salmon Scales* (1909) and *Salmon Scale Examination* (1910); D. S. Jordan and B. W. Evermann, *Fishes of North America* (1896–1900) and *American Food and Game Fishes* (1904); D. S. Jordan and K. Oshimo, "Salmo formosanus," *Proc. Acad. Nat. Sci. Philadelphia* (1919); P. D. Malloch, *The Life History of Salmon, Sea Trout, etc.* (1910); C. T. Regan, *British Freshwater Fishes* (1911); "Systematic Arrangement of Salmonidae," *Ann. Mag. Nat. Hist.* (1914); J. O.

Snyder, "The Trouts of California," *Calif. Fish and Game* (1940); W. C. Kendall, "The Fishes of New England; The Salmon Family; pt. 2, The Salmons," *Memoirs, Monographs on the Nat. Hist. of New England.*

SALMON-BERRY (*Rubus spectabilis*), a vigorous North American shrub of the raspberry genus, native from California to Alaska and eastward to Idaho, bearing rose-coloured flowers and large salmon-coloured edible berries. The name is applied also to the thimble-berry (*R. parviflorus*), of similar range but extending farther eastward, with white flowers and red scarcely edible fruit.

SALMONEUS, in Greek mythology, son of Aeolus (king of Magnesia, in Thessaly, looked upon as the mythic ancestor of the Aeolian race), grandson of Hellen and brother of Sisyphus. He removed to Elis, where he built the town of Salmone, and became ruler of the country. His subjects were ordered to worship him under the name of Zeus; he built a bridge of bronze, over which he drove at full speed in his chariot to imitate thunder, the effect being heightened by dried skins and cauldrons trailing behind, while torches were thrown into the air to represent lightning. At last Zeus smote him with his thunderbolt, and destroyed the town (Apollodorus i, 89; Hyginus, *Fab.*, 60, 61; Strabo viii, p. 356; Manilius, *Astronom.*, 5, 91; Virgil, *Aen.*, vi, 585). This is a confused recollection of some old rite of weather magic. At Crannon in Thessaly there was a bronze chariot, which in time of drought was shaken and prayers offered for rain (Antigonus of Carystus, *Historiae mirabiles*, 15).

Frazer, *Golden Bough*, see index s.v.; another interpretation in S. Reinach, *Cultes, Mythes et Religions*, II, 160.

SALOME, the name of one of the women present at the crucifixion of Jesus (Mk. xv, 40) and at the sepulchre (xvi, 1). The name is derived from Heb. *shālōm*, "peace." Comparison with Matt. xxvii, 56, suggests that she was the wife of Zebedee. The name was borne by some of the Herod family also, notably by the daughter of Herodias by her first husband, the disinherited Herod Philip. She is probably the "damsel" (whose name is not given) mentioned in connection with the death of John the Baptist (Matt. xiv, 3–6; Mk. vi, 17–22). She afterward married her uncle, Herod Philip the Tetrarch. The reading in Mk. vi, 22 adopted by Hort, however, assumes that the girl dancer was Herod Antipas' own daughter, also called Herodias.

See Josephus, *Ant.* XVIII v, 4; *Jewish War*, I, xxx, 7; Justin, *Dial.* 49; Schürer, *The Jewish People in the Time of Jesus Christ.*

SALOMON, ALICE (1872–1948), German social worker and educator, was born in Berlin, of Jewish parentage, in 1872. She was one of the first women granted a Ph.D. degree from the University of Berlin (1906), where her doctoral thesis concerned the inequality of pay between men and women doing equivalent work. Although she attended a general university, her experience there convinced her that training for social work ought properly to be received in special schools. She originated the first regular training course in this field (1899), which grew into the first German social work school, and was president of the school until her retirement in 1925. She was also president of the Federation of German Schools for Social Work and thus trained and influenced the next generation of social workers. Throughout this period, she was active in international feminist work and studied social conditions outside Germany.

During World War I, she organized the German women's voluntary work. After 1918, she remained aloof from political activities, convinced that social workers served their community best if unaffiliated. In 1932 she received a medal for special service to the state, by unanimous consent of the Prussian cabinet. At the same time, the University of Berlin gave her an honorary M.D. degree, and the social work school founded by her was renamed the Alice Salomon school. In 1937 she was exiled from nazi Germany and went to the U.S., where she continued her work as a lecturer. She died Aug. 30, 1948, in New York city.

SALOMON, HAYM (1740–1785), early American financier and patriot of Jewish-Portuguese origin, was born in Lissa, Poland in 1740. He went to America following some revolutionary activities in defense of Polish liberty.

When he arrived in New York, he established himself as a commission merchant, and his personality and keen discernment soon made him a successful financier. During the American Revolutionary War, Salomon was with the patriotic party known as "Sons of Liberty." Within a short time he was made financial agent of the French government, for which services he accepted no commission. His ability and patriotic activities brought him to the attention of Robert Morris, who assigned him to the office of the superintendent of finance, where he handled all the bills of exchange.

Among his many other contributions to the colonies, Salomon subscribed heavily to government loans, endorsed notes, gave generously to soldiers and statesmen, and equipped several military units with his own money. He was made interpreter during the war, and was permitted to go into the British lines, but on two occasions was thrown into prison. He escaped, but suffered ill health from exposure, which later led to his death.

While living in Philadelphia (1778–85), Salomon initiated a measure in behalf of Jewry in the state of Pennsylvania which later resulted in more liberal conditions of employment for them. At that time, persons seeking to qualify for civic employment in Pennsylvania were required to take an oath affirming their belief in the New as well as the Old Testaments. Salomon presented a petition to the Council of Censors on Dec. 23, 1783, in which he requested the removal of this condition, so that public service might not be closed to orthodox Jews. Later, the constitution of the state was so amended.

Salomon died in Philadelphia, Pa., on Jan. 6, 1785.

BIBLIOGRAPHY.—Patriotic Foundation of Chicago, *The Story of the George Washington-Robert Morris-Haym Salomon Monument* (1942); Charles Edward Russell, *Haym Salomon and the Revolution* (1930); Howard Melvin Fast, *Haym Salomon, Son of Liberty* (1941).

SALON (-de-Provence), a town of southeastern France, in the department of Bouches-du-Rhône, 40 mi. N.N.W. of Marseilles by rail. Pop. (1936) 9,047. Salon is situated on the eastern border of the plain of Crau and on the irrigation canal of Craponne. The church of St. Laurent is 14th century, and the church of St. Michel (12th century) has a fine Romanesque portal. The central part of the town preserves a gateway of the 15th century and the remains of fortifications. There are remains of Roman walls near Salon, and in the *hôtel-de-ville* (17th century) there is a milestone of the 4th century.

The town carries on trade in olive oil and soap. Olives are grown in the district, and there is a trade in them.

SALONIKA (sah-lŏn-ē'ka̤, popularly să-lŏn'ĭ-ka̤) or THESSALONIKE, as the name was officially fixed in August 1937, the capital of Greek Macedonia, and one of the principal seaports of southeastern Europe. Pop. (1928, last census before World War II) 236,524, including some 50,000 Sephardic Jews, whose ancestors fled thither in the 16th century from Spain and Portugal: their language is a corrupt form of Spanish, called Ladino (*i.e.*, Latin).

Salonika lies on the west side of the Chalcidic peninsula, at the head of the Gulf of Salonika (*Sinus Thermaicus*), on a fine bay whose southern edge is formed by the Kalamara heights, while its northern and western side is the broad alluvial plain produced by the Vardar and Vistritza rivers.

Antiquities.—The Via Egnatia of the Romans (Grand Rue du Vardar) traverses the city from east to west, between the Vardar gate and the Kalamara gate. Excavations there have revealed the Hellenistic *agora* near the present prefecture. Two Roman triumphal arches used to span the Via Egnatia. The arch near the Vardar gate—a massive stone structure probably erected towards the end of the 1st century A.D., was destroyed in 1867 to furnish material for repairing the city walls; an imperfect inscription from it is preserved in the British museum. The other arch, assigned to the reign of Galerius (A.D. 305–311), is built of brick and partly faced with sculptured marble.

The ecclesiastical architecture of Salonika was once remarkable for its specimens of early Christian (Byzantine) origin and style, with well-preserved mural decorations. St. Sophia (Aya Sofia), formerly the cathedral, probably erected in the 6th century by Justinian's architect Anthemius, was converted into a mosque in 1589. The nave, forming a Greek cross, is surmounted by a hemispherical dome covered with a rich mosaic representing the Ascension. St. Demetrius, which was probably older than the time of Justinian, consisted of a long nave and two side aisles, each terminating eastward in an atrium the full height of the nave, in a style not known to occur in any other church. This church was destroyed by the great fire of 1917. It is partly repaired but mainly ruinous. St. George's, conjecturally assigned to the reign of Constantine (d. 337), is circular in plan, measuring internally 80 ft. in diameter. The external wall is 18 ft. thick, and at the angles of an inscribed octagon are chapels formed in the thickness of the wall, and roofed with wagon-headed vaults visible on the exterior; the eastern chapel, however, is enlarged and developed into a bema and apse projecting beyond the circle, and the western and southern chapels constitute the two entrances of the building. The dome is covered throughout its entire surface of 800 sq. yd. with what is the largest work in ancient mosaic still extant, representing a series of fourteen saints standing in the act of adoration in front of temples and colonnades. The Eski Juma, or Old Mosque, is another interesting basilica, evidently later than Constantine, with side aisles and an apse without side chapels.

Salonika is the see of an Orthodox Greek archbishop. Each religious community has its own schools and places of worship, among the most important being the Jewish high-school, the Jesuit college, a high-school founded in 1860 and supported by the Jewish Mission of the Established Church of Scotland, a German school, dating from 1887, and a college for boys and a secondary school for girls, both managed by the French *Mission Laïque* and subsidized after 1905 by the French government.

Railways, Harbour and Commerce.—Salonika is the principal Aegean seaport of the Balkan Peninsula, the centre of the import trade of all Macedonia, and the natural port of shipment for the products of an even larger area. It is the terminus of four railways. One line goes north to Nish in Serbia, where it meets the main line (Paris–Vienna–Constantinople) of the Oriental railways; another, after following the same route as far as Usküb in Macedonia, branches off to Mitrovitza in Albania. A third line extends westward from Salonika to Monastir. A fourth, the Constantinople junction railway to Constantinople, was partly dismantled and put out of use in 1921, but re-organized later. It now runs via Séres and Kavalla and joins the main line at Kuleli Burgas.

The new harbour, which was opened to navigation in Dec. 1901, allows the direct transhipment of all merchandise whatever may be the direction of the wind, which was previously apt to render shipping operations difficult. The harbour works consist of a breakwater 1,835 ft. long, with 28 ft. of water on its landward side for a width of 492 ft. Opposite the breakwater is a quay 1,475 ft. long, which was widened in 1903–07 to a breadth of 306 ft.; at each end of the quay a pier 656 ft. long projects into the sea. Between the extremities of these two piers and those of the breakwater are the two entrances to the harbour. Salonika exports grain, flour, bran, silk cocoons, chrome, manganese, iron, hides and skins, cattle and sheep, wool, eggs, opium, tobacco and fennel. Other industries are cotton-spinning, brewing, tanning, iron-founding, and the manufacture of bricks, tiles, soap, flour, ironmongery and ice. The spirit called mastic or raki is largely produced.

Province of Macedonia, of which Salonika is the capital, is rich in minerals, including chrome, manganese, zinc, antimony, iron, argentiferous lead, arsenic and lignite, but some of these are unworked. The chief agricultural products are grain, rice, beans, cotton, opium and poppy seed, sesame, fennel, red pepper; there is also some trade in timber, live stock, skins, furs, wool and silk cocoons. Apart from the industries carried on in the capital, there are manufactures of wine, liqueurs, sesame oil, cloth, macaroni and soap. The principal towns, Séres, Vodena and Kavalla, are described in separate articles; Tikvesh is the centre of an agricultural region, Karaferia a manufacturing town, and Drama one of the centres of tobacco cultivation. The total population of Macedonia is in the neighbourhood of 1,500,000. This total includes the large number of refugees who were settled here after 1922. The Greeks form about 90% of the population; there are no Muslims except those of Albanian origin. Bulgarians number about 77,000, being about 5% of the total.

History.—Thessalonica was built on the site of the older Greek city of Therma, so called in allusion to the hot-springs of the neighbourhood. It was founded in 315 B.C. by Cassander, who gave it the name of his wife, a sister of Alexander the Great. It was a military and commercial station on a main line of communication between Rome and the East, and had reached its zenith before the seat of empire was transferred to Constantinople. It became famous in connection with the early history of Christianity through the two epistles addressed by St. Paul to the community which he founded here; and in the later defence of the ancient civilization against the barbarian inroads it played a considerable part. In A.D. 390, 7,000 citizens who had been guilty of insurrection were massacred in the hippodrome by command of Theodosius. Constantine repaired the port, and probably enriched the town with some of its buildings. During the iconoclastic reigns of terror it stood on the defensive, and succeeded in saving the artistic treasures of its churches: in the 9th century Joseph, one of its bishops, died in chains for his defence of image-worship. In the 7th century the Macedonian Slavs strove, but failed, to capture the city. It was the attempt made to transfer the whole Bulgarian trade to Thessalonica that in the close of the 9th century caused the invasion of the empire by Simeon of Bulgaria. In 904 the Saracens from the Cyrenaica took the place by storm, and the inhabitants to the number of 22,000 were sold as slaves throughout the countries of the Mediterranean. In 1185 the Normans of Sicily took Thessalonica after a ten days' siege, and perpetrated endless barbarities, of which Eustathius, then bishop of the see, has left an account. In 1204 Baldwin, conqueror of Constantinople, conferred the kingdom of Thessalonica on Boniface, marquis of Montferrat; but in 1222 Theodore, despot of Epirus, one of the natural enemies of the new kingdom, took the city and had himself crowned there by the patriarch of Macedonian Bulgaria. On the death of Demetrius, who had been supported in his endeavour to recover his father's throne by Pope Honorius III., the empty title of king of Salonika was adopted by several claimants. In 1266 the house of Burgundy received a grant of the titular kingdom from Baldwin II. when he was titular emperor, and it was sold by Eudes IV. to Philip of Tarentum, titular emperor of Romania, in 1320. The Venetians to whom the city was transferred by one of the Palaeologi, were in power when Murad II. appeared and on May 1st, 1430, in spite of the desperate resistance of the inhabitants, took the city, which had thrice previously been in the hands of the Turks. They cut to pieces the body of St. Demetrius, the patron saint of Salonika, who had been the Roman proconsul of Greece under Maximian and was martyred in A.D. 306. In 1876 the French and German consuls at Salonika were murdered by the Turkish populace. On Sept. 4, 1890, more than 2,000 houses were destroyed by fire in the south-eastern quarters of the city. During the early years of the 20th century Salonika was the headquarters of the Committee of Union and Progress, the central organization of the Young Turkey Party, which carried out the constitutional revolution of 1908. Before this event the weakness of Turkey had encouraged the belief that Salonika would ultimately pass under the control of Austria-Hungary or one of the Balkan States, and this belief gave rise to many political intrigues which helped to delay the solution of the Macedonian Question.

When the first Balkan War broke out in 1912, Salonika surrendered to the Greeks on the festival of its patron, St. Demetrios, Nov. 8, after 482 years of Turkish occupation. King George I. proceeded to what was now the second largest city of his kingdom, but was assassinated there on March 18, 1913, by a Greek, named Schinasi.

The Treaty of London of May 30, 1913, assigned Salonika to Greece, and the battle of Kilkis in the second Balkan War of that year prevented the Bulgarians from approaching it. Salonika was becoming more and more Hellenized when World War I brought it into prominence as the base of the Allied operations in the Near East. (*See* Salonika Campaigns 1915–18.)

In 1916 a Venizelist revolution against King Constantine broke out there, and on Oct. 9 E. Venizelos arrived and formed a provisional government, which the Allies recognized, and to which Lord Granville was accredited as British representative. This government declared war on Nov. 23 against Bulgaria and Germany. On Aug. 18, 1917, a great fire destroyed a large part of the city, including the church of St. Demetrius. After the war an arrangement was made by which Yugoslavia should have a "Serbian Zone" in the harbour. After the proclamation of the Greek republic, Salonika often had a decisive voice in politics, and the large immigration of Greek refugees from Asia Minor further Hellenized the country round it. Salonika again figured prominently in World War II.

German forces driving southward from Bulgaria captured the city April 9, 1941, only three days after their initial assault on Greece. By so doing they cut off all Thrace from the rest of Greece and split Macedonia in two.

See General Sarrail, *Mon Commandement en Orient, 1916–18* (1920); P. Risal, *La Ville Convoitée, Salonique* (1914); *Greek Refugee Settlement* (League of Nations, Geneva, 1926).

SALONIKA CAMPAIGNS 1915–18. Under the heading Serbian Campaigns the collapse and subjugation of Serbia in 1915 is related in this work. The present article describes the campaigns in Salonika which formed the sequel to this Allied disaster.

I. OBJECTS OF THE EXPEDITION

Although undertaken for political objects—to bring relief to a hard-pressed ally and to check the influence of Germany in the Balkans—the Salonika campaigns were ultimately crowned by the first decisive military success of the World War. For on the Macedonian front the continent-wide trench barriers of the Central Powers were first breached beyond repair, and there too was knocked away the first national prop—Bulgaria—of the Germanic alliance. To disentangle cause from effect is difficult where moral, military and economic threads are so closely interwoven as in the years 1914–18, yet the fact at least stands out that the overthrow of Bulgaria began the series of national capitulations which ended with that of Germany on Nov. 11, 1918.

If Salonika was for several years an unproductive field of military effort, an infringement of the law of economy of force, which in some measure justified the German gibe that it was their largest concentration camp—"an enemy army, prisoner of itself" —the historian, when weighing his verdict, must throw the counterpoise of 1918 into the scales. And not this only, for it must be remembered that the Allied occupation of the Salonika front made possible the rebuilding of the Serbian army—from the ragged and disorganized survivors of the 1915 winter retreat through Albania to the well-equipped and irresistible force which broke through the Vardar front in Sept. 1918. On the credit side also must be set the fact that the Salonika expedition prevented the danger that Greece might become a submarine base for the Central Powers, one which would have lain in deadly proximity to the British artery of communication with the East via the Suez Canal. And again, that the Allied force contained the bulk of the Bulgarian army—although it is perhaps doubtful whether these would have placed their services at Germany's disposal for any front more remote from their homeland.

Although the Salonika expedition was the immediate outcome of the Serbian débâcle of Sept.–Oct. 1915, the idea had an earlier origin. For Salonika was not only the one feasible channel of Allied communication with and supply to Serbia, but that front offered a possible strategic flank for attack once the trench line on the western front had been welded into a seemingly impenetrable barrier. As far back as 1914, British and French naval missions, with guns, had been sent to support the Serbians, and they had also been supplied with munitions by the Salonika route. The question, too, had been mooted of a larger employment of military force in that theatre, but British commitments at Gallipoli led to this project being shelved—until the Bulgarian mobilization for war on the side of the Central Powers.

Throughout the summer of 1915 the two warring coalitions had been bidding for intervention on the part of the Bulgarians, and in this diplomatic bargaining the Entente suffered a moral and a material handicap—the first, their obvious failure at the Dardanelles; the second, Serbia's reluctance to concede any part of Bulgarian Macedonia, which she had seized as her share of the spoils of the second Balkan war of 1913. As this was the one prize on which the Bulgarians had set their heart, and as Austria had nothing to deter her from offering territory that belonged to her enemy—Serbia—the Entente offers failed to attract Bulgaria. Her intervention on the opposite side meant that free communication could be easily established between Germany and Turkey, and as a consequence that the Entente forces on the Gallipoli peninsula were imminently menaced.

II. THE RETREAT TO SALONIKA

Faced with this critical situation, the French and British Governments decided, albeit tardily, to succour Serbia with an expeditionary force.

In this the French Government took the lead and nominated as commander Gen. Sarrail, the former chief of the III. Army in the Verdun sector. Sarrail's political activities had earned him the distrust of the military authorities; but the same factor, through his influence with the parties of the Left, made it difficult to ignore him completely. His removal by Joffre from the III. Army command placed the Government in a temporary dilemma, and they eagerly seized the opportunity of placating Sarrail and his political supporters by appointing him to a conveniently distant theatre of war.

While the constitution of Sarrail's force was still under discussion, the Bulgarian mobilization on Sept. 22 forced the hands of the Entente Governments. A hurried order was sent for the dispatch to Salonika of contingents from Gallipoli, preliminary to the arrival of reinforcements from France. Preceded by staff officers, the British 10th and French 156th Divs. began to disembark at Salonika on Oct. 5, and they were followed by the French 57th Division. On the same day, however, the Greek promise of aid to Serbia, made by M. Venizelos, was repudiated by King Constantine, and the Venizelist Government fell—to be replaced by that of M. Zaimis, which took neutrality as its keynote. This reacted at once not only on the Franco-British plan but on their operations. The Greek officials, civil and military, at Salonika did their best, or worst, to obstruct the disembarkation of the Allied contingents.

To increase the confusion, the intended concentration point was several times changed by successive orders from Paris until, on Sarrail's arrival on Oct. 12, he decided, in view of his slender resources and the doubtful attitude of the Greek army in his rear, to concentrate no further forward than the Demir Qapu (Demir Kapija) defile. The limited object was to protect the railway and to ease the pressure on the Serbian forces to the north by repelling a Bulgarian advance from Strumitsa (Strumica)—which would sever that line and so the Serbian line of retreat. Meanwhile, the British troops under Gen. Mahon began moving up to Doiran, in echelon behind the right of the French.

On Oct. 14 the vanguard of the French troops came into action at Strumitsa station (in Serbia), driving back a Bulgarian reconnaissance, and on Oct. 17, in response to Serbian urgings, a brigade was sent forward beyond the Demir Qapu defile as far as Krivolak. Reinforced by the arrival of the French 122nd Div. Sarrail began, on Nov. 3, an offensive northward to facilitate the Serbian retreat. But the seizure of the Babuna pass by the Bulgarians closed the channel of southward retreat for the main Serbian army, and finally shattered the hope that the Serbians might fall back on the relieving force, as was the advice of their allies.

Sarrail was thus faced with a difficult problem. On the one hand the gallant French efforts to break through toward the Babuna had failed and they were forced on the defensive, and, on the other, he received news of the Serbian decision to retreat westward through Albania toward the Adriatic. With his small force thus isolated he took the only possible decision—to fall

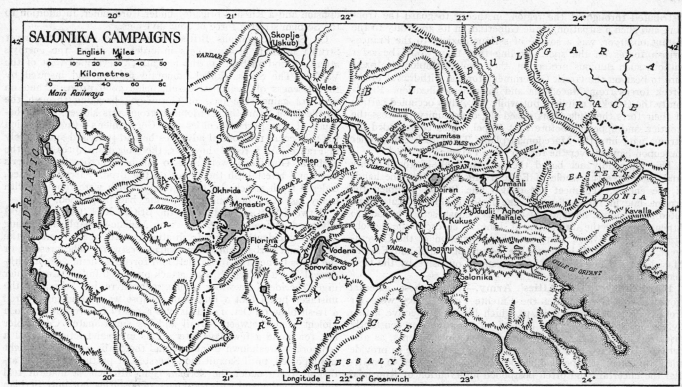

SALONIKA CAMPAIGNS

English Miles

Kilometres

Main Railways

back towards Salonika. This decision raised further problems. Were they to hold on there, or evacuate Greek soil altogether? With the disappearance of Serbia beneath the enemy flood, the Entente Powers could no longer claim that they were at Salonika merely to use a line of communication to which Serbia was by treaty entitled. The other justification, that they had come at the request of the Greek Government was now nullified by the downfall of Venizelos. Considerations of prestige and their desire to use Salonika as a base for diplomatic operations in the Balkans led the Entente Governments to remain, but without any clear policy as to the future.

Even with the decision to retreat taken, the Franco-British forces were not "out of the wood." The withdrawal had to be made down a single-track railway, through a country without roads—converted by the autumn rains into a swamp—and in face of a pursuing enemy. The retreat was made by echelons, in four stages, and only by a narrow margin did the French frustrate Bulgarian efforts to outflank and cut their retreat, first at the Demir Qapu defile, and again at Strumitsa station. The British, too, on the right were heavily attacked, and any weakening of their line at this critical juncture might have been fatal to the extrication of the Allied forces from the noose into which they had been pushed.

Fortunately, once the Greek frontier was regained the pursuit halted—mainly because the Germans were reluctant to undertake further commitments in the Balkans to the detriment of their strength in other theatres. Falkenhayn held that the Macedonian operations should be left to the Bulgarians, but this policy overlooked the fact that the Greeks, however friendly to the Germans, would have resented any invasion of their territory by the Bulgarians. Thus by Dec. 12 the retreating forces were safely out of reach of their pursuers, facing them across the frontier. After pausing for a few days on a line stretching roughly from Sorovičevo to Lake Doiran, the withdrawal was resumed, and by Dec. 18 the forces of Sarrail and Mahon were back in the vicinity of Salonika. Covering this base an entrenched line was constructed, on an 80m. arc stretching from the mouth of the Vardar through Doganji to the Gulf of Orfano, and occupied early in the new year.

Allied Reinforcements.—The delay in the expected en-

emy offensive enabled the Entente force to receive reinforcements, not only French and British but Serbian, for the remnant of their army, after resting and being re-equipped at Corfu, was brought round to Salonika. From April onwards the stream steadily swelled until by July their strength on the Salonika front reached a total of 152,000, divided into three armies of two divisions each. The French had four divisions. The British had been raised to five divisions (10th, 22nd, 26th, 27th, 28th), and later a sixth (60th), organized in two army corps; in May Lieut.-Gen. G. F. (later Sir George) Milne took over command as general officer commanding the British Salonika Force. The total allied force was thus a little over 300,000 men. Opposing it early in 1916 were the Bulgarian I. and II. Armies and the German XI. Army—a total of some 280,000 men—aligned on a front from Lake Okhrida on the west to the point where the Struma enters Bulgaria on the east. But from March onwards the drain on the German forces at Verdun led Falkenhayn to withdraw the German troops, all but one division; by 1918 the XI. Army, though German in name and in staff, contained only one complete German battalion.

On the Entente side the reaction of Verdun took the form of orders from Joffre to Sarrail to pin down the enemy on his front, in order if possible to prevent Falkenhayn drawing upon the forces there. Accordingly the French moved out west of the Vardar towards Vodena and the British advanced north to Kukus. This advance, although it lengthened the front to be defended and the lines of communication, was of essential value for the security of the Allied force, for the entrenched position at Salonika itself was dominated from the mountains east of the town, and might become untenable if these heights were occupied by the enemy. But in how small degree the Allied advance fixed the Germans can be gauged from the previous paragraph, and Sarrail, who had been placed under Joffre's supreme command in Dec., received instructions not only to operate with greatly increased vigor on the Salonika front but also to prepare and organize a definite offensive to be launched simultaneously with the anticipated entry of Rumania into the war.

Meantime the situation was complicated by a Greek incident; until 1918 politics were to play a larger part in the Salonika theatre than war. The neutral Greek forces, five corps, were distributed throughout the region, in theory to guard the frontier; and such a situation, while Gilbertian in its absurdity to the distant observer, was a source of serious anxiety to the Franco-British forces on the spot. Feeling that they would be safer without such dubious protection, they brought diplomatic pressure to bear on the Greek Government for the withdrawal of the Greek forces from Macedonia and their demobilization. Reluctantly the Greeks complied, but while the Allies occupied certain of their forts the Bulgarians seized the opportunity to cross the frontier, and appeared before Fort Rupel, which commanded the Struma gate into the Macedonian plain. The Greek commander thereupon handed over the fort to them (May 26).

This unfriendly act bared the eastern flank of the Entente army, and gave the whole of Eastern Macedonia into the hands of the enemy. To meet the danger the British occupied the Struma line in force. Further, the Entente Governments instituted an economic blockade of the Greek coast, sent a brigade to Athens, and by the ultimatum of June 21 enforced the demobilization of the Greek army and the resignation of the Government. As it proved, however, the seizure of Rupel and Eastern Macedonia did not develop into a general offensive by the German-Bulgarian forces.

Handicaps of the Allies' Army.—While these external troubles with Greece beset the Entente Powers, they were far from the sum of the handicaps which hindered effective action by the Salonika force. The idea of an offensive was constantly discussed between the French and British Governments, as also between Joffre and Sarrail; but, apart from reluctance to provide adequate forces, it depended on too many contingencies, in particular the uncertain and often postponed intervention of Rumania. Furthermore the internal troubles of the Salonika force were notorious. Sarrail had the title of "Commander-in-chief of the Allied Armies in the Orient," and with him Cordonnier commanded the French forces; but his status was a nebulous one. Not only was the British commander to all intents independent, but also the Italian—a detachment arrived from Italy in Aug. 1916.

Apart from the defect that Sarrail's orders were issued from French headquarters without consultation with the other Allied Powers, Sarrail's own personality was not such as to weld this loose understanding into an effective co-operation. In a heterogeneous force, composed of French, British, Italians, Serbians and Russians, it was hardly a recommendation that the chief commander should be known not to have the confidence of his own supreme command, and that even the suspicion should exist that he was conducting operations with one eye on the political game at home. The British, by polite but firm insistence on their independence, maintained tranquil relations; wrangles and disputes between the other Allied commands were continual, and the majority were unfortunately attributable to the policy or tactlessness of Sarrail.

While the Allied leaders were debating ways and means, the opposing armies moved, on Aug. 17, to forestall and dislocate the Allied offensive, which they judged would synchronize with Rumania's intervention. The Bulgarians made their effort on the two wings. The eastern wing from Rupel drove back the French cavalry on the east of the Struma and pressed down towards its mouth. But they dissipated their force by detaching part to seize the coastal strip of Kavalla, and the stout resistance of the British prevented them forcing the river line. On the western wing the position was more critical, for the Bulgarian advance from the Monastir area drove the Serbs out of Florina and reached Lake Ostrovo before they were ultimately held.

III. THE FIRST AND SECOND ALLIED OFFENSIVES

These reverses caused a further change in Sarrail's plan for the Allied offensive; the forces east of the Vardar were merely to contain the enemy, while those west of the Vardar carried out the offensive. Thus to all intents it became no more than a counter-offensive to restore the impaired situation in this sector. To release additional French troops the British extended their line west from Doiran to the Vardar; Sarrail was thus enabled to form an offensive group (of 2½ French divisions, one Serbian

division and a Russian brigade) under Cordonnier, in addition to the Serbian striking force of four divisions.

On Sept. 10 various British detachments crossed the river Struma in raids at six points in order to divert the enemy's attention, and on Sept. 11 the real attack developed west of the Vardar. The Serbs, skilled mountain fighters and inspired by the closeness of their native soil, made good progress, and on Sept. 14 gained the pass of Gorničeyo, breaking through the hostile front. But the Cordonnier group was slower, partly because of transport difficulties and Cordonnier's own inclination for the secure methodical advances he had practised successively in France. As a result, however, the Bulgarians, broken by the Serbs at Gorničeyo, were able to fall back across Cordonnier's front and re-establish their lines on the Brod. Sarrail, incensed, ordered fresh attacks by both groups, which were repulsed with heavy loss—as Cordonnier, protesting, had prophesied.

Between Sept. 30 and Oct. 8 the British XVI. Corps (Briggs) advanced its front to the line Agho Mahale-Ormanli, as a fixing move, coincidently with a fresh attack on the main front by the French and Serbs from Kaimakčalan westward. The pressure of the Serbs turned the Bulgar left and forced a further slight withdrawal, but a Franco-Russian attack on Oct. 6 failed. Cordonnier urged the idea of a wider turning manoeuvre, but Sarrail, in the mistaken belief that a Bulgarian collapse was imminent, ordered a fresh blow on Oct. 14. This was a costly failure and led to a violent scene between Sarrail and his subordinate. Cordonnier left for home a few days later. This internal friction caused a temporary breakdown of action, and the Serbs were left to fight unsupported, until Sarrail took the step of putting the whole attacking force under the Serbian Gen. Michich—a man of real military genius and with the knack of inspiring not only Serbian but other national forces.

Michich attacked in the Crna bend on Nov. 12 while, to aid this offensive, Milne's troops made local attacks and raids as a diversion on the Struma. Despite rain and snow the Serbs pressed on, turning successive positions, with the French, Russians and an Italian brigade on their left. Monastir was outflanked and on Nov. 19 was found evacuated—the first important Serbian town to be regained. For a moment there was a real opportunity of exploitation, as the Bulgarians were in full retreat towards Prilep; but the immediate attacking forces were tired and hungry, and Sarrail suspended the advance—to the annoyance of the Serbs, who, in default of receiving fresh reserves, tried to press on unsupported until exhaustion stopped them.

By this time the Rumanian collapse, under pressure of the convergent German and Bulgarian attacks, was clear, and on Dec. 11 Sarrail received instructions to consolidate a defensive line embracing as much of the regained territory as possible. This line stretched from Lake Prespa—just north of Monastir—north slopes of Kaimakčalan—to the Vardar, and thence by Doiran to the Struma and down to the sea. Its worst feature was that the commanding heights were held almost everywhere by the enemy. This front was to remain practically unchanged until Sept. 1918.

Reorganization.—Apart from the incident of a threatening Greek concentration in Thessaly—settled by a fresh ultimatum—the winter months of 1916–17 passed quickly, and the opportunity was taken to reorganize and regroup the forces. From the Gulf of Orfani to the Vardar the front was held solidly by the British, owing to Milne's insistence, but on the rest of the front Sarrail followed his usual plan of interspersing detachments of the various nationalities—presumably on the principle "*divide et impera.*" Whatever its personal advantages it was hardly conducive to prompt and effective action. Reinforcements had now brought the French up to a strength of eight divisions, while there were six Serbian and 1½ Italian divisions—making with the British 21½ divisions, plus two Russian brigades. The total Allied strength was approximately 600,000, while the Greek National Defence, or Venizelist army, was in process of formation. This concentration afforded adequate reserves for a resolute offensive in the spring.

Confronting the Allies were still the nominal German XI.

Army, and Bulgarian I. and II. Armies, comprising the equivalent of one German and 13 Bulgarian divisions,[1] of which practically half faced the British. Apart from the II. Army, these forces were under a German Commander-in-chief, Gen. Von Scholtz. On their side no large move was considered, partly because the Bulgarians had already achieved their principal territorial aims, and merely desired to hold tight, while the Germans were satisfied with immobilizing so large an Allied force at no expenditure to themselves.

For the 1917 campaign Sarrail's scheme was for a preliminary flanking move on the extreme west, between Lakes Okhrida and Prespa, to shake the enemy's hold in the Monastir area; following this was to be the main fixing attack by the British on the Doiran front; then the French, Russians and Italians in the south-west of the Crna bend were to advance; and finally the Serbs were to strike the decisive blow to the west again.

The preliminary move began on March 12 and was soon suspended, achieving little apart from a creditable French local success on a spur west of Monastir. Then came the British turn —to attack the key position formed by the Dub and lesser ridges which commanded the passage between Lake Doiran and the Vardar. Milne had rejected an alternative proposal of Sarrail's that he should attack to gain Seres, which while attractive as a political advertisement had no military value, and being dominated by the hills behind would have been difficult to hold. After a two days' artillery preparation, in vile weather, the British infantry advanced to the assault, on a two-division front (22nd and 26th), at 9.45 P.M. on April 24, the late hour being to gain surprise and protection. On the left the enemy's first position was gained and held, but in the centre and right the difficulties of the Jumeaux ravine and the strength of the resistance foiled the attackers.

Worst of all, their sacrifice was in vain and their "fixing" rôle rendered abortive because the attack west of the Vardar was postponed by Sarrail, ostensibly for climatic reasons. Not until May 9 did the other attacks develop. Sarrail had rejected the Italian proposal for a flanking manoeuvre, in preference for a frontal blow, and this, made by the French and Italians, was a costly failure. The Serbian attack was even less effectual, in fact hardly developed, partly owing to internal political troubles then rife and partly to their want of confidence in the higher direction and in the genuineness of its intention to support their efforts. Once more the British, on the night of May 8, had delivered a fixing attack, and once more their heavy sacrifice had been purposeless. The offensive was definitely closed down by Sarrail on May 24.

The Bulgarians, content with the prestige of this successful repulse, attempted no counter-stroke, and as the Allied forces were neither in the mood nor the condition for further efforts, the front relapsed into stagnation for the rest of the year. The only minor incidents were a successful local advance in Sept. by the French on the extreme left, west of Lake Okhrida, and Milne's withdrawal of his right from the marshy valley to the foot-hills west of the Struma, a precaution to lessen the danger of malaria and dysentery. The focus of interest again became political—common action was taken to settle the simmering menace and intrigues of Greece. In June, Allied troops invaded Thessaly, but the abdication of King Constantine was forced without fighting, and the Venizelist Government returned to power. The consequent reinforcement of the Allies by the Greek army came as a prospective counterpoise to the contemplated withdrawal of two British divisions in Sept. for the projected offensive in Palestine.

Sarrail Superseded.—At the end of 1917 the new Clemenceau ministry recalled Sarrail, in response to the renewed requests of the British and Italian Governments, which were supported by Foch. His successor was Gen. Guillaumat, who had distinguished himself as an army commander on the Verdun front. His first aim was to restore confidence and cohesion in the Allied forces at Salonika, while hastening the reorganization

[1] A Bulgarian division had almost twice the infantry strength of a French or German division.

and training of the Greek army. His second, to think out and prepare the plan for a fresh offensive, adopting in its main outlines one which Gen. Michich had suggested in 1916. But to obtain the sanction of the Allied Governments was more difficult, obsessed as they were with the threatened German offensive in France, and in any case dubious of the effectiveness of any major operation in Macedonia. While biding his time, however, Guillaumat seized the opportunity to "blood" his new Greek troops in an ably planned *coup de main* against the Srka di Legen ridge. Supported by a powerful concentration of French artillery it was completely successful, and Guillaumat withdrew the attackers into reserve before any possible counterstroke might dilute the moral tonic. On the main front there were no other incidents of note between Jan. and Sept. 1918; but away on the Adriatic coast, in Albania, Ferrero's Italian XVI. Corps, aided by a French division, advanced in July from the Viosa to the line of the Semeni and Devol rivers; an Austrian counter-offensive late in Aug. regained most of the lost ground.

In July also, Gen. Guillaumat, his task of reorganization completed, was summoned back to France, to be entrusted with the defence of the capital in view of the critical situation caused by the German offensives. A man who put first not his own interests, nor even those of France, but his duty to the Allied forces as a whole, his military ability had won the respect, as his character had won the esteem, of the multifarious contingents. He was succeeded by Gen. Franchet d'Esperey, who, if perhaps not possessing the exceptional tact and supra-national outlook of Guillaumat, was yet an able strategist, and well able to maintain allied co-operation. He adopted and put the finishing touches to Guillaumat's offensive plan, while the latter utilized his position at the centre of policy to gain sanction for its execution. Winning over M. Clemenceau, he then went to London and Rome on the same mission, and at last on Sept. 11 Franchet d'Esperey was authorized to attack—if there was still little confidence in its success.

IV. THE DEFEAT OF BULGARIA

The military situation on the eve of the offensive was numerically little changed. The Bulgarians had a ration strength of some 700,000 and a rifle strength of 200,000—divided into the same three armies. The Allies had a ration strength of about 574,000 and a rifle strength of 157,000, although against the inferiority of numbers they could put a slight preponderance in artillery and a heavy one in aircraft. But the real defect on the enemy's side was the first underlying war-weariness of the Bulgarians and their dissatisfaction with their German directors; and secondly the divided command by which the so-called German XI. Army and the Bulgarian I. Army—from Doiran westwards— were under Von Scholtz, while the Bulgarian II. Army and the coastal detachments were under the Bulgarian commander-in-chief, Gen. Gekoff.

For the new offensive Franchet d'Esperey's plan was first to strike a concentrated blow with a Franco-Serb group under Michich on a narrow front of seven miles along the Sokol-Dobro Polje range, aiming at a tactical break-through and a subsequent expansion of the breach to gain and clear the triangle formed by the Crna and the Vardar. This would menace the enemy's communications on both flanks, and the offensive would then be taken up in turn by the other forces along the front. The initial objectives were relatively modest, for the possibility of a strategic break-through, ending in the overthrow of the enemy armies, was no more than an idea in the commander's mind.

The immense difficulties of the terrain and the scantiness of reserves made even this limited aim far from certain of success. But Franchet d'Esperey's plan, made possible by the wholehearted co-operation of the other Allied commanders, was an admirable fulfilment of the principle of concentration. On the vital sector six Serbian and two French divisions with 600 guns— more than a third of the total artillery strength in Macedonia— were concentrated against one Bulgarian division, and to do this the other sectors were almost stripped of their artillery.

The offensive began on Sept. 1, as the British 27th Div. made a feint attack in the Vardar valley to divert the enemy's attention, and on the night of Sept. 14 a heavy bombardment was begun on the real front of attack. Next morning at 5:30 A.M. the French divisions assaulted and after hard fighting gained the Dobro Polje ridge, the Sokol also falling by the evening—opening a path for the Serbian divisions of the I Army, hitherto in reserve, to be pushed through. At the same time the Serbian II Army advanced to the attack. By nightfall on Sept. 16 a penetration of 5 mi. had been made.

The Serbian troops now wonderfully inspired by success and the sight of their homeland swept forward with such *élan* that by the night of Sept. 17 they were 20 mi. forward, and the breach had been expanded to 25 mi. by Greek and French divisions on the flank. After the initial clash resistance was feeble, partly because the mountains hampered the lateral movement of reserves. By Sept. 19 the left wing of the attackers had reached across the Crna, while the right wing was rolling up the front eastward toward the Vardar, and between the two wings the Serbian cavalry had penetrated to Kavadarci in the apex of the Crna-Vardar triangle. Meanwhile on Sept. 18 Milne's troops attacked on the whole front from the Vardar to Lake Doiran in order to prevent the Bulgarians withdrawing troops to dam the breach west of the Vardar. Facing the British were the pick of the Bulgarian troops and also the strongest fortified positions, so that although they penetrated the enemy's lines along most of the front, it was little wonder that lack of reserves and artillery compelled them to yield up the larger part of their gains. But they had fulfilled their mission of pinning down the enemy including the reserves during these critical days, Sept. 18 and 19, and by Sept. 21 the whole of the enemy's front west of the Vardar had collapsed under the convergent pressure of the exploiting Serbs and of the French on their flanks.

By the afternoon of the same day the collapse had extended to the Doiran-Vardar front, and the British aeroplanes spread considerable havoc among the troops of the Bulgarian VI Army falling back through the narrow Kosturino pass. Similarly, on the extreme west, facing Prilep, the Italians joined in the advance. From now on the advance became a strategic pursuit, now fast, now slow, in which successive rear-guard resistances of the enemy were outflanked. On Sept. 23 the Serbian spearhead reached Gradsko, and Veles three days later. Seizing their opportunity, a French cavalry brigade under Gen. Jouinot-Gambetta made a dash for Skoplje (Usküb), and seized this vital centre of communications, the key to the whole front, on Sept. 29. This definitely separated the XI Army from the remainder of the Bulgarian forces, forcing them on divergent lines of retreat. To the southeast the British had already invaded Bulgaria itself, taking Strumica on Sept. 26. That night a Bulgarian staff officer arrived at British headquarters to ask for an armistice, and three days later the Bulgarians capitulated, accepting the Allied terms unreservedly. The first national prop of the Central Alliance had fallen. While the reoccupation of Serbia proceeded rapidly, a mixed striking force was rapidly organized under Milne's command to advance through Thrace on Constantinople, and had pressed as far as the Maritsa, seizing the bridgeheads, when Turkey—its force in Syria already annihilated by Allenby—surrendered on Oct. 30. (*See* WORLD WAR I: *Bibliography*.)

BIBLIOGRAPHY.—M. P. E. Sarrail, *Mon Commandement en Orient* (1920); Mackensen, *Von Bukarest bis Salonika* (Berlin, 1920); Reichsarchin Einzelschriften, *Der Endkampf in Mazedonien* (Berlin, 1921); L. Villari, *The Macedonian Campaign* (1922); Landfried, *Der Endkampf in Mazedonien 1918* (Berlin, 1923); Feyler, *Campagne en Macédoine 1917–18* (Paris, 1926). (B. H. L. H.)

SALSETTE (or SASHTI; *i.e.*, "sixty-six villages"), a large island north of Bombay city. Its area (246 sq.mi.) was distributed in April 1950 between Greater Bombay and Thana district (within which the whole island formerly lay). It is connected with Bombay Island and also with the mainland by bridge and causeway. In various parts of the island are ruins of Portuguese churches, convents and villas, and at Kanheri are 109 Buddhist cave shrines dating from the end of the 2nd century A.D. Salsette is crossed by the Central and Western railways, and the island is encircled by a motor road. The island was taken from the Portuguese by the

Marathas in 1739 and from them by the British in 1774; it was formally annexed by the East India company in 1782. There is another Salsette in the Portuguese settlement of Goa.

SALSIFY or SALSAFY, *Tragopogon porrifolius*, sometimes called oyster plant or vegetable oyster, a hardy biennial with long, cylindrical, fleshy, esculent roots, which, when properly cooked, are extremely delicate and wholesome; it occurs in meadows and pastures in the Mediterranean region and in Britain is confined to the south of England, but is not native. The leaves are linear-lanceolate. The second season a handsome purplish flower is borne atop a stalk 2–4 ft. high; the mature seed head appears much like that of an enlarged dandelion. Salsify requires a free, rich, deep soil, which should be trenched in autumn, the manure used being placed at two spades' depth from the surface. The first crop should be sown in March and the main crop in April, in rows a foot from each other, the plants being afterward thinned to 8 in. apart. In November the whitish roots should be taken up and stored in sand for immediate use, others being secured in a similar way during intervals of mild weather. Salsify is widely naturalized as a wayside weed in the United States and Canada. In the United States, salsify is widely grown in home gardens but is of little importance as a market vegetable. It is sown about the average date of last frost in the spring, in rows about $1\frac{1}{2}$ ft. apart and thinned to 3–4 in. apart. It requires the entire growing season to develop. Roots may be harvested and stored in a moist cellar or dug as needed through the winter. The roots are not damaged by freezing of the soil but must not be allowed to freeze after harvest. (V. R. B.)

SALSOMAGGIORE, a town of Emilia, Italy, in the province of Parma, 6 mi. southwest of Fidentia by steam tramway. Pop. (1951) 16,961, commune. It is a popular watering place. The water is strongly saline and is also used for inhalation. The wells are, some of them, over 2,000 ft. deep and yield illuminating gas and oil as well as water.

SALT, SIR TITUS, BART., 1869 (1803–1876), English manufacturer, was born on Sept. 20, 1803, at Morley, Yorkshire. His success in introducing the coarse Russian wool (*donskoi*) into English worsted manufacture, due to special machinery of his own devising, gave his firm a great impetus. In 1836 he solved the difficulties of working alpaca (*q.v.*) wool, created an enormous industry in the production of the staple goods for which that name was retained and became one of the richest manufacturers in Bradford. In 1853 he opened, a few miles out of the city on the Aire, the extensive works and model manufacturing town of Saltaire. He died on Sept. 20, 1876.

SALT. In chemistry the term salt is applied generically to any compound formed by substituting the hydrogen of an acid by a metal or a group of elements acting as a metal. (*See* ACIDS AND BASES.) Common salt, or, simply, salt, is the name given to the varied natural and industrial forms of sodium chloride, NaCl. Pure sodium chloride may be made by passing dry hydrogen chloride gas into a saturated solution of the salt whereupon the purified salt is deposited as a colourless crystalline powder. It crystallizes in the cubic system, usually as cubes (*see* below under *Rock Salt*). The melting point is 804° C., which is a bright red heat. Vaporization begins near this temperature. It dissolves easily in cold water and a little more readily in hot water; 100 parts by weight of water dissolve 35.87 parts of salt at 20° C., 39.18 parts at 100° C. and 39.8 parts at 109.7° C., the boiling point of the saturated solution. If a saturated solution in water be cooled to −10° C. a crystalline hydrate, $NaCl.2H_2O$, separates. (*See* HYDRATE.) Solution of salt in water is accompanied by reduction of temperature: 36 parts of salt in dissolving in 100 parts of water at 12.6° C. will lower the temperature to 10.1° C. If the same proportion of salt and snow be intimately mixed the temperature falls to −21.3° C.

Salt occurs in the sea, in natural brines and in the crystalline form, as rock salt. Its most abundant source is the ocean. Assuming that each gallon of sea water contains 0.2547 lb. of salt, and allowing an average density of 2.24 for rock salt, it has been computed that if dried up the entire ocean would yield no less than 4,500,000 cubic miles of rock salt or about $14\frac{1}{2}$ times the bulk of the entire continent of Europe above high-water mark. Natural brines having commercial importance are those of Austria; France; Germany; of Kharaghoda and Kuda in India; of Michigan, New York state, Ohio, Pennsylvania, West Virginia and the salt lake of Utah in the United States; and of the Dead sea. In Great Britain salt brines are met with in Cheshire, Worcestershire, Lancashire and Yorkshire, and have been found by deep boring in Derbyshire, Staffordshire and Midlothian. Salt in brines is nearly always accompanied by the chlorides and sulphates of potassium, calcium and magnesium; in many cases carbonates and the valuable element bromine are present. Sea water contains on the average about 3.33% of solids, but the concentration of salts varies from about 2.9% in the polar seas to 3.55% and upward at the equator. Enclosed seas such as the Mediterranean and Red seas contain a higher proportion of salt than the open ocean at the same latitude (*See* OCEAN AND OCEANOGRAPHY.) From Dittmar's analyses of sea water taken during the "Challenger" expedition, the average composition of the solids in sea water may be considered to be: sodium chloride 2.60%, magnesium chloride 0.31%, magnesium sulphate 0.22%, calcium sulphate 0.12%, potassium chloride 0.07% and magnesium bromide 0.007%. The mixed salt obtained by evaporation of sea water has, however, the following composition irrespective of the source of the sea water: sodium chloride 77.82%, magnesium chloride 9.44%, magnesium sulphate 6.57%, calcium sulphate 3.44%, potassium chloride 2.11%, magnesium bromide 0.22% and some calcium carbonate.

Natural Brines.—The Dead sea, which covers an area of about 340 sq. mi., contains approximately 11,600,000,000 tons of salt, and the River Jordan, which contains only 35 parts of salt per 100,000 of water, adds each year 850,000 tons of salt to this total. The composition of Dead sea water is given in the following table (although the salts exist as ions in solution and are so analyzed; it is customary to express the analyses in terms of compounds):

Dead Sea Waters	Surface water	Deep water (250 ft.)
Specific gravity	1.1651	1.2356
Sodium chloride	6.11%	7.20%
Potassium chloride	0.85%	1.25%
Magnesium bromide	0.38%	0.61%
Magnesium chloride	9.46%	13.73%
Calcium chloride	2.63%	3.82%
Calcium sulphate	0.11%	0.05%
Total solids	19.54%	26.66%

The concentration of salts in the Dead sea increases to a depth of about 250 feet, after which it remains practically constant. At this depth and below it is a concentrated solution, which, indeed, is supersaturated when pumped up, for a slight deposition of salt takes place owing to diminished pressure. Noteworthy features of Dead sea water are its relative freedom from sulphates and the high proportions of potassium and bromine. These facts, coupled with the circumstance that atmospheric conditions in Palestine are favourable to solar evaporation for about eight months of the year, indicate that the production of salt, potassium and even bromine is feasible in the Dead sea area, the process as regards salt and potash being similar to that described below under *Manufacture*. The brines at Kharaghoda resemble sea water in the character of their dissolved salts, but are much more concentrated and in some cases practically saturated as shown by analysis no. 2.

Kharaghoda Brines	1	2
Specific gravity	1.134	1.220
Sodium chloride	13.15%	14.52%
Potassium chloride	0.29%	0.78%
Magnesium bromide	0.05%	0.15%
Magnesium chloride	2.05%	9.48%
Magnesium sulphate	1.19%	0.85%
Calcium sulphate	0.33%	0.33%
Calcium carbonate	0.01%	0.02%
Total solids	17.07%	26.13%

The following table gives the composition of some concentrated natural brines used for the production of salt in various countries.

Concentrated Natural Brine	Droitwich	Winsford	Syracuse, N.Y.	St. Charles, Mich.	Artern, Saxony	Friedrichshall, Württemberg
	%	%	%	%	%	%
Sodium chloride	24.97	25.46	21.71	22.84	25.27	25.49
Sodium sulphate	0.26	..	..	..	..	..
Potassium chloride	..	..	..	..	0.12	..
Potassium sulphate	..	..	..	..	0.29	..
Magnesium bromide	..	..	..	0.26	..	..
Magnesium chloride	0.05	0.21	0.14	4.03	0.42	0.01
Calcium sulphate	0.37	0.45	0.50	0.20	0.40	0.44
Calcium chloride	..	..	0.19	0.77	..	..
Total solids	25.65	26.11	22.54	28.10	26.50	25.54

Certain natural brines occurring in England and the United States are of interest, not only from the economic point of view, but also because they contain salts not usually found in brines, such as the chlorides of barium and strontium; when salt is produced from such brines special methods of manufacture are adopted. In Great Britain these brines were found at great depth in boreholes in Derbyshire, Staffordshire and Midlothian during the search for petroleum wells. In the U.S. they occur in the Ohio valley district of West Virginia and in Ohio, at depths ranging from 1,100 ft. to 1,600 ft.

	Renishaw, Derbyshire	West Calder, Scotland	Pomeroy, Ohio	Malden, W. Virginia
Depth (feet)	3,198	3,910		
Specific gravity	1.127	1.063	1.075	1.063
Sodium chloride	10.28%	6.26%	7.92%	6.01%
Potassium chloride	0.03%	0.04%	0.04%	0.06%
Magnesium bromide	0.11%	0.07%		
Magnesium chloride	0.84%	0.55%	0.57%	0.50%
Calcium chloride	4.23%	1.34%	1.36%	1.49%
Strontium chloride	0.12%	0.16%	0.03%	0.02%
Barium chloride	0.14%	0.07%	0.04%	0.07%
Total solids	15.75%	8.49%	9.96%	8.15%

It has been suggested that those brines which are characterized by the absence of carbonates and sulphates have been produced by a natural process akin to the "Permutit" process for softening water.
(J. J. F.; A. G. F.; X.)

ROCK SALT

Rock salt is crystalline halitè (sodium chloride) occurring in the form of rock masses and beds. It has a wide geographic distribution and occurs abundantly in rocks of all ages. Because of its great solubility in water it occurs under extremely thick cover in humid regions, but lies close to the surface in arid regions.

All important rock-salt deposits originated from the evaporation of sea water at some time during the geologic past. Some 77% of the mineral matter in normal sea water is sodium chloride. Upon evaporation of about nine-tenths of the volume of sea water, rock salt is precipitated. The precipitation of rock salt overlaps the precipitation of calcium sulphate (gypsum and anhydrite) on the one hand and potassium and magnesium salts on the other. Thus these compounds commonly occur with rock salt. Deposits are found in beds from a few feet to many hundreds of feet thick. In age these beds are distributed through much of geologic time from the Cambrian through the Mesozoic.

Since it is necessary to evaporate a large quantity of sea water to deposit a small amount of salt, it is thought that many extremely thick rock-salt beds were deposited in partly enclosed arms of the seas in which evaporation was greater than inflow of fresher water. The supply of water was continually renewed by inflowing currents while a barrier on the sea floor at the entrance to the basin prevented the outflow of the concentrated saline water so that the salts were deposited in thick beds on the basin floor.

Such bedded salt deposits occur in the lower Cambrian of the Punjab Salt range in Pakistan and in Iran, but are little exploited. The Silurian and Devonian rocks of the northeastern United States and Ontario in Canada contain important rock-salt deposits which are extensively worked for industrial and domestic use. The Carboniferous of Nova Scotia contains extensive rock-salt deposits which are utilized in eastern Canada and northeastern United

States. The Pennsylvanian (Carboniferous) of Colorado and Utah contains large amounts of unexploited rock salt.

The rocks of Permian age contain some of the largest rock-salt deposits in the world. The most important are the Zechstein deposits of Germany, long exploited not only for their common salt but for their potassium content. The salt deposits of the sub-Carpathian region extending from Poland through Hungary and Rumania may be of this age. In the Donetz basin and the Volga region of European U.S.S.R. are extremely important deposits of Permian rock salt. In the United States enormous thicknesses of rock salt underlie much of the Permian basin extending from Kansas to western Texas.

The Triassic of England contains important rock-salt deposits which have been worked for many years. In the Tyrol the Triassic strata also contain important salt deposits. In the province of Szechwan, China, rock salt occurs in beds of Triassic age and has been exploited through salt wells for more than 2,000 years.

Another type of rock-salt deposit which is economically important is the salt dome. This deposit has been forced up by earth pressure from great depths in the form of plugs of roughly circular shape a few yards to a mile across. The domes appear to be a development of folding, in which the salt is forced up through other rocks, because of its great plasticity under high pressure, from depths as great as 20,000 ft. Such salt domes are abundant along the Gulf coast of southern United States and extend into the east Texas basin and northern Louisiana. Many domes occur at shallow depths and are extensively mined to supply the southern United States. Similar domes in the sub-Carpathian region of Europe have been worked since ancient times. The north German plain has many domes, extensively worked, which are thought to have originated below 6,000 feet.

Rock salt may be exploited by usual mining methods. Another method of exploitation is by drilling wells into the salt strata, pumping water down them to dissolve the salt and treating the returning brine in a manner similar to the treatment of natural brines. It is difficult to arrive at any estimate of the relative importance of rock-salt production as compared with production of other types of salt since most available statistics make no distinction between natural and artificial brines. However, practically all important salt production for industrial uses is from rock salt deposits. The United States and Europe are leaders in exploitation of rock salt deposits. However, South American countries rapidly developed their deposits, with Brazil ranking as the largest producer outside United States and Europe. (J. M. Hs.)

Manufacture.—At one time almost all of the salt used in commerce was produced from the evaporation of sea water, and sea salt still is a staple commodity in many maritime countries, especially where the climate is dry and the summer of long duration. At mid-20th century, commercial salt was manufactured (1) from rock salt and (2) from sea water and other natural and artificial brines. Most of the artificial brines are obtained by pumping water into wells drilled into underground salt beds and pumping up the solution which results when this water dissolves salt from the deposit. In addition to the ordinary uses of crystalline salts, much is used directly in the form of brine in industrial countries.

Manufacture from Rock Salt.—The beds of rock salt are mined or quarried by the usual excavation methods, depending upon the depths and thicknesses of the deposits and upon local conditions. In some cases the mined rock salt is dissolved and salt manufactured by treatment of the brine as described below. This treatment affords opportunities for purification of the salt. Where the rock salt is of high degree of purity, as in the United States and in Galicia, the salt is ground, sieved and marketed with no further treatment. The mined salt in large lumps is first crushed, then more finely ground and screened to separate the various size grades; the oversize material going back to the mill and the acceptable sizes being packed for market, usually by bagging. A disadvantage of such salt is the tendency to revert to hard masses in storage. In Germany rock salt is treated in similar fashion, except that the larger fragments of impurities such as anhydrite and gypsum are hand picked from the coarsely crushed rock salt. Less pure German rock salt is purified by fusion, either alone or with sodium carbonate and silica or with chalk and saltpetre (sodium nitrate). In some cases, the fused mass is "blown" with air to burn away carbonaceous material, leaving a clear melt which crystallizes on cooling. After separation from the slag by concussion, the salt is ground and sieved. Alternately, an impure salt is leached with a saturated solution of pure salt in dilute hydrochloric acid whereby impurities such as gypsum, magnesium salts and iron oxide are dissolved. The treated salt is filtered, washed with a saturated solution of pure salt, dried, ground and graded for market.

Manufacture from Brines.—When an aqueous solution of several salts is evaporated, the salts separate, each as it reaches its point of saturation in the solution. The solubilities of the salts in the complex solution will, in general, be similar to but not the same as the solubilities for the same salts in water. In the case of sea water and many brines the order of deposition is calcium carbonate, calcium sulphate, sodium chloride, magnesium sulphate, carnallite (potassium magnesium chloride) and magnesium chloride. These salts are not, however, deposited within sharply defined limits of concentration. As each salt reaches its own point of saturation it deposits along with all the other salts which have reached their own saturation points. Therefore each salt deposited is contaminated by some of the other salts and by the residual brine. Further, the relative solubilities are altered by temperature and hence in solar evaporation the difference in temperature between day and night and also the seasonal temperature changes affect the character of the salt deposited. The art of the salt maker is to produce grades of salt suitable for the particular use to which it is to be put.

Salt is produced by solar evaporation from sea water in France, Portugal, Spain, Italy, India, the U.S.S.R. and the United States—in fact, in nearly all maritime countries. The processes generally adopted are similar in principle, although details of evaporating pans and of manufacturing plants vary with local conditions. A preliminary concentration is usually carried out by allowing the brine to flow through a series of channels to concentration ponds constructed of wood, puddled clay or concrete. The areas of the ponds vary from 280 sq. ft. to 50 ac. in different countries. The solution is concentrated first to a specific gravity of about 1.21. At this stage, suspended impurities (sand and clay) and the less soluble salts (calcium carbonate or chalk and calcium sulphate) are removed. The clear concentrated brine is now run successively into a series of crystallizing pans, usually three, where the salt is deposited. The total area of the crystallizing pans is approximately one-tenth of that of the evaporating pans. In the first crystallizing pan the brine is concentrated to a specific gravity of 1.25 and here the best grade of salt is produced. The specific gravity of the mother liquor increases slowly during crystallization of the salt because of the increasing concentration of the other salts. The mother liquor reaches a specific gravity of 1.26 in the second pan where a second grade of salt is obtained. In the third pan a specific gravity of 1.275 is obtained and here the lowest grade of salt is deposited. The final mother liquor, termed "bitterns," is used in some countries (e.g., France, India and the United States) for the manufacture of potash, bromine, Epsom salts (magnesium sulphate) and magnesium chloride.

The salt in each crystallizing pan is raked into rows and allowed to drain for several days, is then collected into heaps, drained again, lifted from the pans and finally dried. As a tax is levied on salt (by weight) in most European countries, it is obviously an advantage to trade in the dried material. The salt from the first pan is frequently used locally as table salt, that from the second pan may go into the chemical industry and that from the third pan is used for pickling fish, refrigeration and other purposes. Typical compositions of the salts thus produced are given in the following table:

	Grade I	Grade II	Grade III
	%	%	%
Sodium chloride	96.0	95.0	91.0
Calcium sulphate	1.0	0.9	0.4
Magnesium sulphate	0.2	0.5	0.4
Magnesium chloride	0.2	0.5	1.2
Insoluble matter	—	trace	0.8
Water (moisture)	2.6	3.1	6.2
	100.0	100.0	100.0

In England, Germany, most of the eastern part of the United States and other places where it is impractical to manufacture salt by means of solar heat, the brines are concentrated and evaporated by artificial heat. Formerly the brine was concentrated in open pans over fire. More recently steam-jacketed vessels were used, but now the largest part of the salt produced in the colder countries is manufactured in multiple-effect vacuum evaporators and an important quantity is made in open crystallizers or grainers which produce a type of crystal preferred for use in some of the food industries. The brine, natural or artificial, is first pumped into settling tanks, where calcium and magnesium compounds may be removed by chemical treatment, usually lime and sodium hydroxide are used. After settling and filtration, the brine is delivered to the grainer, which is a long open trough with steam coils. The brine is fed into the grainer at approximately the same rate as that at which evaporation is taking place and at a temperature only slightly below that of the brine in the grainer. The residue of brine or bitterns, may be removed daily or less often or may be withdrawn continuously. The evaporation occurs at the surface of the liquid and the crystals originate there. They remain at the surface, held up by the surface tension of the brine. The crystal grows at the top edges, becoming a small inverted hollow pyramid or hopper. Eventually the hopper sinks and ceases to grow. When the crystals are recovered the salt is largely in the form of flakes, whence the name "flake salt." When multiple-effect evaporators are used, the vacuum in each vessel is adjusted so that the vapour from the first vessel is sufficiently hot to boil the brine in the second; the vapour from the second supplying the heat to operate the third vessel or effect. The brine is usually sent through the stages or effects in succession, although in the case of salt manufacture, fresh brine may be fed to each stage if desired. In a triple-effect system, vacuums of 15 in., 25 in. and 27 in. of mercury have been found efficient. With open pans, one ton of coal will produce about two to two and one-half tons of salt whereas it will yield five to six tons of salt with an efficient triple-effect plant.

In France and Germany weak brines which could not profitably be used for saltmaking with the aid of artificial heat are first concentrated by a natural process. The brine is pumped to the top of a towerlike structure of scaffolding enclosing brush wood and is distributed by means of a spray over the top of the brushwood. Exposure to the air as the brine trickles down rapidly concentrates it and the process is continued until the brine is sufficiently strong to be used in ordinary concentration pans.

The brines at Pomeroy, O., containing notable quantities of the salt barium chloride, were formerly concentrated in steam-jacketed vessels without treatment to remove this salt, but it is now customary to remove barium by addition of "salt cake" (crude sodium sulphate) followed by sedimentation or filtration or both to separate the precipitated barium sulphate. By this procedure barium chloride content of the salt is reduced to negligible quantities.

Saltmaking and salt mining seem to be healthful occupations, occasional slight soreness of the eyes being the only ailment; whereas exposure to the atmosphere about open grainers seems to confer some degree of immunity against colds, rheumatism, neuralgia and similar troubles.

Uses.—The best-known use of sodium chloride is as table salt. For this service, a fine-grained salt of high purity is used. To ensure that it will remain free-flowing when exposed to the atmosphere, small quantities of sodium carbonate or trisodium phosphate sufficient to combine with such hygroscopic impurities as calcium and magnesium chlorides are added. Usually potassium iodide is added in small quantity to overcome any possible iodine deficiency of the consumer. Common salt used for various manufacturing purposes may be coarser in grain than table salt. Salt is used universally as a condiment and preservative. It is employed in meat packing and fish curing, in the dairy and pickle industries, for salting cattle and curing hides and as a brine for refrigeration. It is indispensable to the manufacture of sodium carbonate (washing soda), sodium bicarbonate (baking soda), sodium hydroxide (caustic soda), hydrochloric acid, bleaching powder, chlorine and many other heavy and fine chemicals. The glass and soap industries are dependent upon it and it is used also in the glaze and enamel trades. As a flux, it enters into metallurgical processes and has been used in the manufacture of cement to aid in the recovery of potash as a by-product.

The grading of salt is complex and varies in different countries. In the United States, the main grades are: dry solar fine-milled, dry solar kiln-dried, granulated, "southern granulated," high-grade, high-grade granulated, packer's, medium, special medium, rock (of various grades), table and kosher. These grade names refer to purity, method of manufacture and grain size; and while they are generally descriptive, they cannot always be taken literally.

The production of salt is one of the world's most widely distributed mineral industries. Outputs of salt vary with the population and industrial activity of the country in question. Heavily populated countries like India and China require the major part of their production for food uses only; the United States on the other hand requires several times as much salt for industrial purposes as is consumed in food. A great many countries contribute to total world production of salt; but the output of the United States far exceeds all others, amounting at mid-century to approximately 14,600,000 short tons annually. Other leading salt producing countries and their approximate annual output in short tons at mid-century were, United Kingdom (3,297,000), China (2,267,000), India (2,215,000), France (1,700,000), Germany (1,500,000) and Italy (709,000). (R. H. Rn.)

Ancient History and Religious Symbolism.—Salt must have been quite unattainable to primitive man in many parts of the world. Thus the *Odyssey* (xi, 122 *et seq.*) speaks of inlanders who did not know the sea and used no salt with their food. In some parts of America, and even of India (among the Todas), salt was first introduced by Europeans; and there are still parts of central Africa where its use is a luxury confined to the rich. Indeed, where men live mainly on milk and flesh, consuming the latter raw or roasted, so that its salts are not lost, it is not necessary to add sodium chloride, and thus we understand how the Numidian nomads in the time of Sallust and the Bedouins of Hadramut at the present day never eat salt with their food. On the other hand, a cereal or vegetable diet calls for a supplement of salt, and so does boiled meat.

The habitual use of salt is intimately connected with the advance from nomadic to agricultural life; *i.e.*, with precisely that step in civilization which had most influence on the cults of almost all ancient nations. The gods were worshipped as the givers of the kindly fruits of the earth, and, as all over the world "bread and salt" go together in common use and common phrase, salt was habitually associated with offerings, at least with all offerings which consisted in whole or in part of cereal elements. This practice obtained among the Greeks and Romans and among the Semitic peoples (Lev. ii, 13).

As covenants were ordinarily made over a sacrificial meal, in which salt was a necessary element, the expression "a covenant of salt" (Numb. xviii, 19) is easily understood; it is probable, moreover, that the preservative qualities of salt made it a peculiarly fitting symbol of an enduring compact, and influenced the choice of this particular element of the covenant meal as that which sealed an obligation to fidelity. Hence the Greek phrase ἅλας καὶ τράπεζαν παραβαίνειν, the Arab phrase "there is salt between us," the expression "to eat the salt of the palace" (Ezra iv, 14, R.V.) and the modern Persian phrase *namak harâm*, "untrue to salt" (*i.e.*, disloyal or ungrateful) and many others.

Salt and incense, the chief economic and religious necessaries of the ancient world, play a great part in all that we know of the ancient highways of commerce. Thus one of the oldest roads in Italy is the *Via Salaria*, by which the produce of the salt pans of Ostia was carried into the Sabine country. Herodotus' account of the caravan route uniting the salt oases of the Libyan desert (iv, 181 *et seq.*) makes it plain that this was mainly a salt road, and to the present day the caravan trade of the Sahara is largely in salt. The salt of Palmyra was an important element in the vast trade between the Syrian ports and the Persian gulf (*see* PALMYRA), and long after the glory of the great merchant city was past "the salt of Tadmor" retained its reputation (Mas'ūdi viii, 398). In like manner the ancient trade between the Aegean and the coasts of southern Russia was largely dependent on the salt pans at the mouth of the Dnieper and on the salt fish brought from this district (Herod. iv, 53; Dio Chrys. p. 437). The vast salt mines of northern India were worked before the time of Alexander (Strabo v, 2, 6; xv, 1, 30). The economic importance of salt is further indicated by the prevalence down to the present day of salt taxes or of government monopolies. In oriental systems of taxation high imposts on salt are seldom lacking and are often carried out oppressively with the result that the article is apt to reach the consumer in an impure state largely mixed with earth. "The salt which has lost its savour" (Matt. v, 13) is simply the earthy residuum of such an impure salt after the sodium chloride has been washed out.

Cakes of salt have been used as money; *e.g.*, in Abyssinia and elsewhere in Africa, and in Tibet and adjoining parts. (*See* the testimony of Marco Polo and Sir Henry Yule's note on analogous customs down to our own time, in his translation of Polo ii, 48 *et seq.* The same work gives interesting details as to the importance of salt in the financial system of the Mongol emperors, ii, 200 *et seq.*).

In the Roman army an allowance of salt was made to officers and men, from which in imperial times this *salarium* was converted into an allowance of money for salt. (X.)

BIBLIOGRAPHY.—W. C. Phalen, "Technology of Salt Making in the United States," U.S. Bureau of Mines Bulletin no. 146 (1917), and "Salt Resources of the United States," U.S. Geological Survey Bulletin no. 669 (1919); R. L. Sherlock, *Rock-Salt and Brine*, vol. xviii of the *Memoirs* of the Geological Survey of the U.K. (1921); D. K. Tressler *et al.*, *Marine Products of Commerce* (1923), U.S. Bureau of Mines, *Information Circular 7062* (1939); U.S. Bureau of Mines, *Minerals Yearbook* (1932, 1934, 1939); C. D. Looker, "Salt as a Chemical Raw Material," *Chemical Industry*, vol. 49 (1941); U.S. Bureau of Standards, *Simplified Practice Recommendation R70-42* (1942); F. Kutnewsky, "Salt of the Earth," *Compressed Air Magazine*, vol. 47 (1942); W. T. Read, *Industrial Chemistry*, 3rd ed. (1944); E. R. Riegel, *Industrial Chemistry*, 5th ed. (1950). (R. H. Rn.)

SALTA, a northwestern province of Argentina. An official decree of Sept. 23, 1943, awarded to Salta the departments of San Antonio de los Cobres and Pastos Grandes, both in the former territory of Los Andes. The province is bounded on the west by Chile. Area, after these boundary changes, 59,759 sq.mi.; pop. (1914 census) 140,927, (1947 est.) 288,205. In terms of its present boundaries the western part of the province lies in the Andean highlands and is characterized by lofty chains of mountains (sierras) and high, intermont basins or *salares*. The sandy and rock-strewn volcanic soils support a sparse cover of stunted plants and hard grasses. The climate is arid and cold, although extreme diurnal variations in temperature are common. Streams are numerous but small, and nearly all drain into the *salares,* where their waters are rapidly evaporated. In the valleys of the central and eastern parts of the province the vegetation is exuberant, with thick forests of valuable woods. The eastern plain is well watered and hot, with precipitation and temperatures decreasing westward with increasing altitudes. The capital of the province is Salta (*q.v.*).

The chief rail communications of the province are provided by the Belgrans railway, with connections to all of the principal parts of Argentina and to Bolivia, and across the Andes to Antofagasta, Chile. The excellent natural forage in the province has long made livestock raising a lucrative enterprise. Since colonial times Salta has supplied the markets of northern Chile with cattle, formerly driven on the hoof across the Andes, and when prices are sufficiently high to offset transportation costs, the animals are in demand in the markets of the east coast. Sheep raising is also important. Although a great variety of crops is planted, tobacco (considered the best in the country) and sugar cane lead in commercial importance. The province also produces appreciable quantities of timber and minerals, and ordinarily ranks third among the Argentine states in the production of petroleum. Other minerals include gold, silver, copper, marble and lead.

(R. W. Rd.; X.)

SALTA, a city of Argentina and capital of a province of the same name, in the picturesque and historic valley of Lerma, 1,007 mi. by rail N.N.W. of Buenos Aires. Population (1947 est.) 60,-000. Salta was founded in 1582 (under the name of San Felipe de Lerma) by Hernando de Lerma, governor of Tucumán. In 1813, during the War of Independence, the Spanish forces under General Pio Tristán, after suffering a decisive defeat at Salta, were obliged to capitulate to Gen. Manuel Belgrano. Salta, 3,895 ft. above sea level, is the centre of a rich mineral and timber region. Mean monthly temperatures range from 53° F. in June to 72° F. in January; average annual rainfall is 28 in., with a distinct dry season from May to October.

A colonial city that has preserved and perpetuated colonial architecture and traditions, Salta holds many attractions for tourists and offers exceptional hotel accommodations and travel facilities.

SALTASH, municipal borough, Bodmin parliamentary division, Cornwall, Eng., 5 mi N.W. of Plymouth, on the Western region railway. Pop. (1951) 7,924. Area 9.8 sq.mi. It is on the wooded shore of the Tamar estuary, on the lower part of which lies the port and naval station of Plymouth. Local communications are maintained by river steamers. At Saltash the Royal Albert bridge (1857–59) carries the railway across the estuary. The church of St. Nicholas and St. Faith has an early Norman tower. The church of St. Stephen retains its ornate Norman font.

Saltash (Esse, 1297; Ash, 1302; Assheburgh, 1392) belonged to the manor of Trematon and at the Domesday survey was held by Reginald de Valletort. Reginald's descendant and namesake granted a charter to Saltash about 1190. This charter was confirmed in the fifth year of Richard II. Roger de Valletort gave the borough of Saltash to the earl of Cornwall. Thenceforth the earls and subsequently the dukes of Cornwall were the lords of Saltash. The privilege of parliamentary representation was conferred by Edward VI. In 1584 Queen Elizabeth I granted a charter of incorporation to Saltash. This was superseded by another in 1683 but the modern charter was adopted in 1886. In 1832 Saltash was deprived of its two members.

SALT-BUSH, the name given especially in Australia to plants of the genus *Atriplex* (family Chenopodiaceae), which inhabit arid saline soils, notably to *A. halimoides* and *A. nummularia,* which are cultivated for forage. *A. semibaccata,* also native to Australia, is grown as a forage plant in California, where it is known as Australian salt-bush. (*See* GREASEWOOD.)

SALT DOMES. Generically the term salt dome is used commonly to include all salt structure; *i.e.,* any anticlinal type structure containing a core of rock salt which has been formed in part or whole by the growth of the core. Specifically the term should be restricted to the special and perhaps mature type of salt structure having a circular or quasicircular plane section, such as the piercement domes of the Texas-Louisiana coastal plain.

When a block of strata including a bed of rock salt (the mother bed) is subjected to any of the geologic forces which normally produce folding or faulting, the resulting structures are likely to be sharper and substantially different from those formed under similar conditions with salt absent. Rock salt is plastic and will flow under sufficient pressure differentials. It is also generally of lower specific gravity than the strata with which it is associated (the country rock), particularly at depth, and thus is relatively buoyant. Under great enough pressure differentials the salt will flow in the folded beds and the structure of the overlying strata will be accentuated over that of the underlying strata. Furthermore, any structural disturbance of the originally level-lying, salt-

containing formations, or even erosional redistributions of their overburden, is likely to result in disturbance of isostatic equilibrium. Under great enough inequality of load the salt may even breach the overlying beds, thus forming a piercement structure or dome, the diapir fold of Mrazec. In form and mechanics of formation the specific salt dome much resembles a volcanic plug, the salt occupying the position and being structurally almost the functional equivalent of the igneous magma. The salt core, once isostatic equilibrium has been sufficiently disturbed, becomes the active structure-building element. We are dealing with the intrusion of a magma, if one may borrow the word, of sedimentary and evaporite origin. The analogy is valid since salt has been known to form even horizontal intrusions or sills. Aside from the intrusion of igneous rocks the only other geologic processes which resemble genetically the formation of salt structures are the formation of structures by the flow of highly plastic clays or shales. Examples of such structures are formed by the *argille scagliose* of Italy, the *pug* of New Zealand or of mixtures of highly plastic clays and shales with gypsum and perhaps salt such as occur in the Lower Fars of southwestern Iran.

Origin.—The origin of salt structures has long been the subject of speculation, often of great controversy, and is covered by voluminous literature. The German and Rumanian structures were first studied in detail. European geologists early formulated the theory, which came to be generally accepted, that the structures are formed by the flow of originally bedded salt under pressure. Students of American domes were slow to recognize the genetic kinship with European structures. The first vague speculations regarded the domes as having been Cretaceous outliers in Tertiary seas. Robert T. Hill, in the early part of the 20th century, considered that the salt and cap-rock cores of the domes were precipitated from solution by circulating waters. This theory, elaborated and modified by N. M. Fenneman and Gilbert D. Harris, suggested that the little understood force supposed to be exerted by growing crystals was sufficient to account for the uplift of the overlying and contiguous sedimentary rocks. For a time it received wide acceptance. Volcanic forces were suggested from time to time either to explain uplift, provide a source for the solutions or, through heat, to account for the plasticity of the salt. Later, U.S. geologists came to accept generally the theory of intrusive origin.

Formation.—There are at least three distinct positive and important steps in the formation of salt structure: (1) the deposition of a series of sedimentary rocks, including the mother bed of salt and overlying sediments; (2) the initiation of salt flow through the subjection of the mother bed of salt to sufficient pressure differentials. E. De Golyer and others believed that the initial flow is practically always the result of folding or faulting and that it is rarely, if ever, the result of isostatic adjustment; (3) flow of salt. This must continue to the extent necessary to satisfy the pressure differentials established by folding or unequal loading. The salt flow of many structures may be caused entirely by forces established by compressive folding. De Golyer believed, however, that in most domes the quantitatively important flow is the result of isostatic adjustment. A flow of the lighter plastic salt results from the pressure on the mother bed of the heavier sediments overlying the flanks of the structure.

Once the original condition of equilibrium, which should exist in a flat-lying series of bedded rocks, has been disturbed by folding or faulting or once a salt structure has started to grow as a result of compressive forces, new stresses upon the mother salt become effective as a result of differential loading. Since salt is lighter generally than the sediments with which it is associated, particularly at depth, such differential loading stresses become effective in minute degree even with the smallest disturbance of the bed of mother salt, always assuming no disturbance of surface conditions, either by erosion or deposition. With substantial disturbance of the original equilibrium in the mother salt either through folding, faulting, tilting or flow of salt, such stresses alone may become of sufficient magnitude to cause the flow of the salt to continue. If we assume the simple case of a salt anticline caused by compressive folding and buried under thousands of feet of younger sediments with low resistance texture, such as probably occur in the North German plain and in the Gulf coastal plain of the United States, it is probable that the extra loading will cause the salt to breach the crest of its anticline and flow upward, assuming a tubelike form as a matter of least skin friction. As a unit volume of salt displaces a unit volume of the heavier overlying sediments, the difference between the load on the mother salt and the overburden on the upward-flowing salt (the compelling stress) should increase, and growth should continue at an accelerated rate until the mother bed of salt is exhausted, cut off by the formation of a rim syncline or until a condition of equilibrium in load is approached. Growth may stop before the salt reaches the surface, as in most Texas and Louisiana domes; it may continue until it reaches the surface and is removed by erosion, as in many Rumanian structures, or it may form great mountains with salt glaciers flowing down their sides, as in the Iranian deserts. Most salt domes are believed to root deeply; *e.g.*, those of Iran and Texas-Louisiana at 20,000–25,000 ft. Flow induced by differential loading is believed to be the chief reason for their continued growth. De Golyer believes, however, that growth is seldom if ever initiated by such forces. It is noteworthy that, even with the almost perfectly fluid system of L. L. Nettleton's striking device for demonstrating mechanically the effectiveness of such forces in dome formation, it was necessary to apply an outside force to destroy the normal condition of equilibrium and thus initiate the flow of the lighter fluid into the overlying heavier one.

Cap Rock.—A salt structure may or may not include cap rock, the *gypshut* of the Germans. It is a phenomenon best developed or best known and studied in the Texas-Louisiana domes, where the cap rock was explored for oil and sulphur. It consists usually of a tip or thimble of anhydrite over and in direct contact with the generally flat top of the salt core. The anhydrite cap grades upward by alteration into the gypsum cap which is generally overlain by a limestone or calcite cap. The thickness of the entire cap rock when present varies from a few feet or inches to a thickness of 1,000 ft. or more, as in the sulphur and Lake Calcasieu domes of Louisiana. Cap rock often contains other sulphates, sulphites and carbonates but in minor amounts. It also includes, rarely, blocks of limestone, shale and sandstones, apparently plucked from the formations through which the plug has passed. Sulphur is of common occurrence in the limestone and gypsum cap rocks.

The principal theories of origin of cap rock are: (1) that it is a shield of anhydrite, primarily a part of the normal salt series, carried upward to its present position by the growth of the core and that the limestone and gypsum caps result from alteration of the anhydrite; (2) the more generally accepted theory that the anhydrite, known to occur disseminated through the salt, freed through solution of the salt by circulating water, has been concentrated at the periphery of the salt core, has been compacted or recrystallized into massive anhydrite and may or may not have been altered into gypsum, limestone, sulphur, etc. Schistose structure is of common occurrence in the anhydrite cap. Cap rock is also of common occurrence in the German and Isthmus of Tehuantepec structures but is rarely found in the Iranian, Rumanian and Colorado-Utah structures. Most European students adhere to the theory of residual origin.

Distribution.—Salt structures and salt domes, formerly regarded as unusual, with continued prospecting and study are known to be of fairly common occurrence. There are three and possibly four regions of salt basins in the North American continent where these structures are known to occur. The best explored region is that of coastal Texas, Louisiana and Mississippi, an area extending northward to include the so-called interior domes of northeast Texas, northwest Louisiana and continuing into Arkansas. This area may extend southward into northeastern Mexico. There is also a salt-structure basin in the northern coastal plain of the Isthmus of Tehuantepec, states of Veracruz and Tabasco, Mexico. Another notable occurrence is the group of bold structures of the Paradox basin of southeastern Utah and southwestern Colorado. There appears to be a salt dome at Malagash, N.S.

In South America salt domes or structures are known only in the highlands near Bogotá, Colombia, and in the Amazon region of Peru.

The best-known European occurrences are in the Hanover district and its extensions, the Magdeburg-Halberstadt basin, the eastern part of the north German plain and adjoining areas in the Netherlands and throughout most of Denmark. They are also known in Spain and in southern France. Numerous salt structures occur in Rumania, along the outer margins of the Carpathian arc and in the Transylvanian basin. Salt structures are of abundant occurrence in the Emba basin, just northeast of the Caspian sea. They have been found also in the Ukraine, and salt occurrences in arctic Siberia appear to be of salt-dome type.

The faulted anticlines of the Kohat region of Pakistan may be salt structures and possibly the Punjab Salt range is the result, in some part at least, of the flowage of salt.

Salt structures are also known to occur in Algeria and Tunisia, northern Africa, near the Dead sea in Palestine and along the Gulf of Suez in Egypt.

The most spectacular known occurrence of salt domes is that of southwestern Iran, extending through the many islands of the southern half of the Persian gulf to the margins of the Arabian peninsula. In most of the known domes of this arid region the salt core comes to the surface. This may result in any type of topographic expression from a deep hollow where the salt has been dissolved away and where the more resistant country rocks still form a rim several thousand feet high to that of a simple, bold circular hill of salt standing 1,000 ft. or so above the surrounding plain. A number of the domes have glacierlike plumes of salt extending down for three or four miles from the outcrop of the core. Salt domes occur also on the Iranian plateau and at least one dome occurs in southern Iraq, near the Kuwait border. There is also a group of little and vaguely known salt structures in the Hadramut of Arabia and there are believed to be salt structures within the southern end of the Red sea graben.

Many important mineral deposits occur in salt structures or salt domes. The limestone cap rock or the limestone brought to the surface by the formation of the structure has been burned for lime at many places, and common salt is mined from the cores of many of the structures. Beds of potassium are mined from the salt complex of many of the German domes, and the extremely important sulphur deposits of the Texas and Louisiana coastal plain are found in the cap rock of salt domes. The oil deposits of the same region, of the Isthmus of Tehuantepec region of Mexico, of the outer Carpathian arc and the Transylvanian basin of Rumania, of the north German coastal plain, extending into the Netherlands, and of the Emba basin in the U.S.S.R. are found in traps resulting from the formation of salt structures or salt domes. Some of the oil is found in cap rock where present but most of it comes from overlying sands arched into simple or faulted anticlines by the intrusion of the salt nucleus and in sands tilted by the intrusion of the salt core and dipping away from it.

(E. L. DE.)

SALTILLO, capital city of the Mexican state of Coahuila. Pop. (est. 1950) 70,000; altitude 5,244 ft. Served by National Railways of Mexico, Saltillo is linked by highways to Eagle Pass, Tex. (286 mi.) via the steel and coal centres of Monclova and Sabinas, and to the other branches of the Pan-American highway passing southward through Montrrey and Torrón.

Saltillo is at the northern edge of the great central plateau of Mexico. Its cool, dry, healthful climate made it a summer resort, with facilities for golfing, hunting and swimming. Founded in 1586, Saltillo retains few of its colonial buildings beyond an impressive cathedral and is chiefly significant as an active commercial and manufacturing centre and communications hub. It has an annual fair of importance and manufactures cotton and woollen fabrics, knitted goods and flour. Its blankets or serapes have for centuries been considered among Mexico's finest and many are collector's items. Coal seams near by are exploited on a small scale, though the chief reserves lie in the Sabinas basin and are estimated at perhaps 850,000,000 metric tons. (HD. C.)

SALT LAKE CITY, the capital city of Utah, U.S., and

the county seat of Salt Lake county, on the Jordan river, 11 mi. E. of Great Salt lake, at the foot of the Wasatch mountains, about equally distant from Denver, Colo., Los Angeles and San Francisco, Calif., and Spokane, Wash. It is on federal highways 40, 50 and 91; has a modern municipal airport and is the concentration and distribution point for air mail between the Pacific coast and the east; and is served by the Denver and Rio Grande Western, the Union Pacific, the Western Pacific and several electric railways, and by commercial airlines. The population was 182,121 in 1950; it was 149,934 in 1940; and in 1930 it was 140,267.

Physical Aspect and Buildings.—Salt Lake City is the largest city between the Rockies and the coast, and is the headquarters of the Church of Jesus Christ of Latter-Day Saints (Mormons), by whom it was founded and who are still the largest single element in the population. It has an area of 53.87 sq.mi., an altitude of 4,255 ft., and is almost surrounded by mountain peaks, some of which reach a height of 12,000 ft. The site was chosen by Brigham Young (q.v.), and the basic plan of the city was determined by the original survey under his direction, which laid it out in ten-acre blocks, separated by streets 132 ft. wide. In one of these blocks (Temple square, originally the centre of the community) stand the great Mormon temple which no "gentile" may enter, built of gray granite (1853–93) with walls six feet thick and six spires, the highest (220 ft.) surmounted by a copper statue of the angel Moroni; the tabernacle (a low building seating 10,000, with a turtle-shaped aluminum-covered roof unsupported by pillars or beams) where recitals are given daily on the magnificent organ (11,000 pipes); the assembly hall, also of granite, seating 2,500; a bureau of information and a museum of pioneer relics; the first house built in Utah (enclosed in a protecting shelter); monuments to Joseph Smith and his brother Hyrum; and a monument to the sea gulls which at a critical hour of the early colony's history saved the crops and other vegetation from destruction by grasshoppers. In the adjoining block are the administration building of the church; the Genealogical Society building; Eagle gate, formerly the entrance to Brigham Young's estate; the Beehive house and the Lion house, two of his residences. The state capitol (a fine colonnaded building of marble and Utah granite, completed in 1916) stands half a mile northeast of Temple square, at the head of State street (a long, straight thoroughfare) on an eminence commanding the entire valley and backed by the mountains.

East of it is Memory grove, a park created in honour of the veterans of World War I, at the entrance to City Creek canyon. On the east edge of the city is the campus of the University of Utah (established by the provisional government of the state of Deseret, 1850).

Beyond the university is Fort Douglas, an installation utilized mostly for the civilian components of the armed forces (army and air national guard, reserve components of army, navy and marine corps, and R.O.T.C. instructor personnel. During World War II it was headquarters for the 9th service command. At the entrance to Emigration canyon, east of the military reservation, is a point (marked by This Is The Place monument) where Brigham Young looked down over the valley and said he recognized the site that had been shown to him in a vision.

The state prison is located at the point of the mountain, south of the city, in Salt Lake county. Saltair, 15 mi. W. of the city, is a popular pleasure resort on the lake (in which it is impossible to sink, on account of the large amount [about 27%] of salt in the water).

Churches and Schools.—Of the 152 churches, about 60% are Mormon chapels, and the rest (including a Roman Catholic cathedral) represent most of the faiths and denominations commonly found in U.S. cities. The public-school system comprises 32 elementary, nine junior high and three senior high schools, and a part-time school for boys and girls who go to work before the age of 18. There are several private schools; Westminster college (Presbyterian, established 1875); and various hospitals and charitable institutions. Interest in music, the dance and the drama was fostered from the beginning by Brigham Young. The Tabernacle choir (500 voices) is one of the best choruses in the United States, and the Salt Lake theatre (one of the foremost in

design and appointments when it was built in 1862) had a brilliant history. Salt Lake City ranked second among the large cities of the country in the proportion of children and young people attending school and in literacy.

The general death rate and the infant mortality are among the lowest in the country. In 1911 the city adopted a commission form of government. The assessed valuation of Salt Lake county property for 1950 was $233,607,780.

Commerce and Industry.—Salt Lake City is the commercial, financial and industrial centre of the state of Utah and of a large additional part of the intermountain territory. It is the seat of the fourth branch (established 1918) of the Federal Reserve Bank of San Francisco, serving 31 counties in Idaho and four in Nevada besides the entire state of Utah. Debits to accounts in the local banking institutions amounted in 1949 to $2,700,003,055. Manufacturing expanded rapidly during World War II. Many national firms established branch factories or distributing offices there, to supply the natural trade territory of the city (500,000 sq.mi.), and many local industries have extended their markets to cover the country. Among the leading industries are slaughtering and meat packing, printing and publishing, the refining of oil, the smelting of silver, lead and copper, and the manufacture of beet sugar, candy, flour and radio equipment.

Receipts at the stockyards totalled 1,493,374 head in 1949, of which the local packing plants used 245,688 head. There is an oil refinery with a capacity of 25,000 bbl. of crude per day, producing all types of petroleum products. The suburb of Murray, 7 mi. S. (population in 1950, 9,006), is a great smelting centre.

History.—The history of Salt Lake City is bound up with that of the Mormons and the state (see UTAH). On July 22, 1847, an advance party of Mormons, led by Orson Pratt and Erastus Snow, in search of a place where they might "colonize in peace and safety," entered the Salt Lake valley. On July 24, Brigham Young arrived and approved the site, and on July 28 he chose the spot for the temple. Ploughing and planting were begun forthwith; the hard sun-baked earth was flooded by building a dam in City Creek canyon; and an irrigation system was devised. The city was named the City of the Great Salt Lake, and was so called until 1868. Before the end of 1847 the main body of the people arrived. A theocratic government was set up, with a bishop in charge of each of the 19 wards into which the community was divided. The settlers were U.S. citizens squatting on foreign soil, for the region at that time belonged to Mexico, and they were practically beyond the reach of any civil government, as their leaders had desired. This isolation was of brief duration. The treaty of Guadalupe-Hidalgo, at the close of the Mexican War, transferred the region to the United States, and after the discovery of gold in California, the city was overrun with caravans of treasure seekers. Many of the colonists deserted to join the stream of prospectors, notwithstanding the attitude of their leader, who opposed the exploitation of mineral wealth (even in Utah) and whose ideal was a community of farmers, merchants and manufacturers. Those who stayed at home grew rich as outfitters.

There was a considerable immigration from Europe in the early years, especially from England, where the Mormon missions were very successful. By 1850 the city had a population of 6,000.

Salt Lake City was chartered in 1851 by the territorial legislature of Utah. After the Civil War the non-Mormon population steadily increased, and there was a long period of conflict between the opposing elements, as well as officially between the Mormon church and the U.S. government over the practice of polygamy and other matters of dispute (see LATTER-DAY SAINTS), all of which happily is now long past.

SALTO, third city of Uruguay and capital of a department of the same name. Pop. (1950 est.) 48,000. It lies on the Uruguay river opposite the Argentine town of Concordia, 365 mi. by rail from Montevideo and 221 mi. by water from Buenos Aires.

The province of Salto covers 4,866 sq.mi., with a pop. of 99,754 (1941 est.) or 20.5 per square mile, slightly less than the average for the country, which was (1941) 30.3. It is a rolling prairie land, devoted very largely to the raising of high-grade cattle with some farms and vineyards about the principal towns.

SALTON SEA or SALTON SINK, a depression in the Imperial Valley, Calif., whose water surface is 248.7 ft. below sea level. Its drainage area of about 7,500 sq.mi. is mainly desert land and consequently the sink used normally to be dry, though at times the rate of inflow exceeded that of evaporation sufficiently to form a temporary lake. In 1905 during the construction of irrigation works in the valley, the Colorado river left its channel and flooded the sink to a maximum depth of 79 ft. with a surface area of about 330,000 ac. When the river was finally brought back to its proper course the water in the sink began to subside. After 1920 this tendency ceased, and, fed chiefly by the irrigation ditches of the region, the sea became fairly constant at a level of about 37 ft. at its deepest point.

SALTPETRE: see NITRIC ACID AND NITRATES.

SALT RANGE, a hill system in the West Punjab and North-West Frontier Province of Pakistan, deriving its name from its extensive deposits of rock salt. The range commences in Jhelum district, in the lofty hill of Chel (3,701 ft.), on the right bank of the river Jhelum, traverses Shahpur district, crosses the Indus in Mianwali district, thence a southern branch forms the boundary between Bannu and Dera Ismail Khan until it finally merges in the Waziristan system of mountains. The Salt range contains the great mines of Mayo, Warcha and Kalabagh, which supply the wants of all northern India and Pakistan. Coal of an inferior quality is also found.

SALTYKOV, MICHAEL EVGRAFOVICH (1826–1889), Russian satirist who wrote under the pseudonym of Nicolay Evgrafovich Stchedrin, was born in the province of Tula, Jan. 15 (27), 1826. In 1848 he published *Zaputennoye Dyelo* ("A Complicated Affair"), which led to his banishment to Vyatka, where he spent eight years as a minor government official. The clever picture of Russian provincial officials in his *Gubernskie Otcherki* ("Provincial Sketches") resulted from this experience. After an interval given to writing he was appointed deputy governor, first of Ryazan and then of Tver. On his return to St. Petersburg in 1864 he was appointed president of the local boards of taxation successively at Penza, Tula and Ryazan. In 1868 he finally left the civil service. His principal works are: *Poshekhonskaya Starina* ("The Old Times of Poshekhona"), *Istoria odnavo Goroda* ("The History of a Town"); *A Satirical History of Russia*; *Messieurs et Mesdames Pompadours;* and *Messieurs Golovloff.* He died in St. Petersburg on April 30 (May 12), 1889.

SALUS, an ancient Roman goddess of safety (from defeat, etc.). In 302 B.C. a temple on the Quirinal was dedicated to Salus (Livy x, 1), Salus being identified with Hygieia (*q.v.*). See Wissowa, *Relig. u. Kultus*, p. 131.

SALUTATIONS or GREETINGS, the customary forms of kindly or respectful address, especially on meeting or parting or on occasions of ceremonious approach. Etymologically *salutation* (Lat. *salutatio*, "wishing health") refers only to words spoken.

Embraces.—Forms of salutation frequent among savages and barbarians may persist almost unchanged in civilized custom. The habit of affectionate clasping or embracing is seen at the meetings of the Andaman islanders and Australian blacks, or where the Fuegians in friendly salute hug "like the grip of a bear." This natural gesture appears in old Semitic and Aryan custom.

Rubbing Noses.—The salute by smelling or sniffing (often called by travellers "rubbing noses") belongs to Polynesians, Malays, Burmese and other Indo-Chinese, Mongols, etc., extending thence eastward to the Eskimo and westward to Lapland.

Kissing.—The kiss, the salute by tasting, appears constantly in Semitic and Aryan antiquity. Herodotus describes the Persians of his time as kissing one another—if equals on the mouth, if one was somewhat inferior on the cheek (Herod. i, 134). In Greece, in the classic period, it became customary to kiss the hand, breast or knee of a superior. In Rome the kisses of inferiors became a burdensome civility (Martial xii, 59). The early Christians made it the sign of fellowship: "greet all the brethren with an holy kiss." Of more ceremonial form is the kiss of peace given to the newly baptized and in the celebration of the Eucharist, which is retained by the Greek church. After a time, by ecclesiastical regulations, men were only allowed to kiss men, and women women, and eventually in the Roman Catholic Church the ceremonial kiss at the communion was only exchanged by the ministers, a relic or cross called an *osculatorium* or *pax* being carried to the people to be kissed. While the kiss has thus been adopted as a religious rite, its original social use has continued. Among men, however, it has become less effusive. Court ceremonial keeps up the kiss on the cheek between sovereigns and the kissing of the hand by subjects. When these osculations cease to be performed they are still talked to by way of politeness: Austrians say, *"Küss d' Hand!"* and Spaniards, *"Beso a Vd. las manos!"* ("I kiss your hand!") Strokings, pattings and other caresses have been turned to use as salutations.

Weeping.—Weeping for joy is sometimes affected as a salutation. Highly ceremonious weeping is performed by several rude races when, meeting after absence, they renew the lamentations over those friends who have died in the meantime. Among the Australian natives, the male nearest of kin presses his breast to the newcomer's, and the nearest female relative, with piteous lamentations, embraces his knees with one arm, while with the other she scratches her face till the blood drops. Obviously this is mourning. So, too, the New Zealand *tangi* is performed at the reception of a distinguished visitor, whether he has really dead friends to mourn or not. Weeping, as A. R. Brown has shown, is for the Andamanese a rite for the revival of sentiments that have lain dormant, the renewal of interrupted social relations and for the recognition of a change in personal relations.

Cowering.—Cowering or crouching is a natural gesture of fear or inability to resist. Its extreme form is lying prostrate, face to the ground. In barbaric society, as soon as distinctions are marked between master and slave, chief and commoner, these tokens of submission become salutations. The sculptures of Egypt and Assyria show the lowly prostrations of the ancient east, while in Dahomey or Siam subjects crawl before the king. A later stage is to suggest, but not actually perform, the prostration, as the Arab bends his hand to the ground and puts it to his lips or forehead, or the Tongan would touch the sole of a chief's foot, thus symbolically placing himself under his feet.

Kneeling.—Kneeling prevails in the middle stages of culture, as in the ceremonial of China; Hebrew custom sets it rather apart as an act of homage to a deity; mediaeval Europe distinguishes between kneeling in worship on both knees and on one knee only in homage.

Bowing.—Bowing, as a salute of reverence, appears in its extreme in oriental custom, as among the ancient Israelites: "bowed himself to the ground seven times." The Chinese according to the degree of respect implied bow kneeling or standing. The bowing salutation, varying in Europe from something less than the Eastern salaam down to the slightest inclination of the head, is given mutually. Uncovering is a common mode of salutation, originally a sign of disarming or defencelessness or destitution in the presence of a superior. Taking off the hat by men has for ages been the accepted mode in the western world. Some eastern nations are apt to see disrespect in baring the head, but insist on the feet being uncovered. Europeans have been called on to conform to a native custom by taking off their shoes to enter the royal presence. In Burma it is respectful to squat in the presence of a superior; elsewhere the inferior should stand.

Handshaking.—Grasping hands appears in antiquity as a legal act symbolic of the parties joining in compact, peace or friendship. In marriage, the hand grasp was part of the ancient Hindu ceremony, as was the "dextrarum iunctio" in Rome, which passed on into the Christian rite and became a mere salutation.

Words of Greeting.—As to words of salutation, even among the lower races certain ordinary phrases have passed into formal greetings. Many formulas express difference of rank and consequent respect, as where the Basuto salute their chiefs with *"Tama sevata!"* (*i.e.*, "Greeting, wild beast!"). Congo negroes returning from a journey salute their wives with an affectionate

"*Okowe!*" but they, meekly kneeling round him, may not repeat the word, but must say "*Ka! ka!*" Among cultured nations, salutations are apt to be expressions of peace and goodwill. Such formulas run on from age to age, and the latter may be traced on to the Muslim greeting, "*Salām 'alaikum!*" ("The peace be on you"), to which the reply is "*Wa-'alaikum as-salām!*" ("And on you be the peace," *sc.* "of God!"). This greeting is a password among fellow believers, for it may not be used by or to an infidel. The Babylonian form, "O king, live for ever!" (Dan. iii, 9), represents a series of phrases, which continue still in the "*Vivat rex!*" ("Long live the king!"). The Greeks said, "Be joyful!" both at meeting and parting. The Romans applied "*Salve!*" ("Be in health!") especially at meeting, and "*Vale!*" ("Be well!") at parting. In the modern civilized world, everywhere, the old inquiry after health appears, the "How do you do?" becoming so formal as often to be said on both sides, without either waiting for an answer. Hardly less wide in range is the set of phrases "Good day!" "Good night!" etc., varying according to the hour and translated into every language of Christendom. Among other European phrases, some correspond to our "Welcome!" and "Farewell!" while the religious element is exemplified by our "Good-bye!" ("God be with you!") and French "*Adieu!*" Such half-meaningless forms of salutation serve the purpose of keeping up social intercourse.

SALUZZO, a city and episcopal see of Piedmont, It., in the province of Cuneo, 42 mi. S. of Turin by rail, 1,296 ft. above sea level. Pop. (1936) 10,443, town; 15,938, commune. The upper town preserves some part of the fortifications which protected it when, previous to the plague of 1630, the city had about 30,000 inhabitants. The old castle of the marquises of Saluzzo (the line runs 1142–1548) now serves as a prison. Besides the Gothic cathedral (1480–1511), with the tombs of the marquises, the churches of San Giovanni (formerly San Domenico), San Bernardo and the Casa Cavazza, now the municipal museum, are noteworthy. Railways run to Cuneo and Airasca (the latter on the Turin-Pinerolo line).

Henry IV restored the marquisate to Charles Emmanuel I of Savoy at the peace of Lyons in 1601.

SALVADOR, EL (sometimes incorrectly called San Salvador from its capital city), the smallest and most densely populated republic of Central America and probably the most intensively cultivated country in Latin America. It is bounded on the north and east by Honduras, on the south by the Pacific ocean and on the west and northwest by Guatemala. It is the only republic of Central America which has no Atlantic seaboard. The republic is 140 mi. long from east to west and 60 mi. wide; its greatest length is about 160 mi. Its area is 13,176 sq.mi. (34,126 sq.km.).

Physical Features.—The chief physical features of El Salvador are the two mountain chains, largely independent of the central Cordillera of Central America, which cross the country and the rich river valleys (chiefly that of the Río Lempa). The mountains are accented by a series of volcanic cones, some of ancient and some of recent origin, which cross the country from east to west. Most of the area of the country is comprised in the plateau, about 2,000 ft. high, between the mountain chains, the region in which the coffee of El Salvador is cultivated, and in which are situated the volcanoes. The Río Lempa rises in Guatemala, crosses a corner of Honduras, and entering El Salvador near Citala, flows east, forming its famously rich and beautiful valley, turns south at the base of the volcano Siguatepeque and enters the Pacific at 80° 40′ W. The Lempa is the only river of importance, and although it can be navigated for portions of its course, is little used. The Río San Miguel drains the country between the Bay of Fonseca and the Lempa valley. The volcanoes are clustered into more or less well-defined groups, and in some of these, beautiful crater lakes are found; the largest of these, Lake Ilopango, has been used as a landing place for seaplanes. The most important volcanic groups are, from west to east: the Izalco group, including Izalco (thrown up in 1770), Marcelino, Santa Ana (8,300 ft.), Naranjos, Águila, San Juan de Dios, Apaneca, Tamajaso and Lagunita; the San Salvador group, 30 mi. east, the

chief cone of which is San Salvador; Cojutepeque to the northeast; the San Vicente group farther east, marked by San Vicente volcano and Lake Ilopango; and the San Miguel group, to the southeast, including notable landmarks like San Miguel (7,120 ft.), Chinameca, Buenapa, Usulatán, Tecapa and Taburete. Two other volcanoes, Cacaguateque and Sociedad, in the northeastern portion of the country, lie in the Cordillera and are not to be taken as part of the El Salvador groups proper. Many of these volcanoes are in eruption, and San Miguel has had violent outbursts in recent years.

Climate.—Because El Salvador is locked in as it is by the Cordillera which marks its boundaries with Guatemala and Honduras, it has an almost temperate climate on the tableland and along the mountain slopes, which are intensively cultivated for coffee, often to the very summits of the hills or volcanoes. The lowland is often hot and sultry when the winds are not blowing. The recognized seasons are the wet and the dry, the wet season, from May to October, being confusingly called "winter" in El Salvador, the dry season, from November to April, "summer." Winds and thunderstorms mark the middle of the wet season, in July and August, and in September and October the rains are almost continuous, but moderate. Following the August storms, there is a brief dry spell, the "dog days," *veranillo* or "little summer," when crops are planted and preparations made for obtaining the greatest productivity from the soil. In the earlier days, there was a tradition that no revolution could be fought during the *veranillo,* as both armies insisted on returning home to attend to their planting. For general geology *see* CENTRAL AMERICA: *Geology.*

History.—El Salvador was conquered by Pedro de Alvarado, Cortes' lieutenant, who invaded the present republic in 1524 and early the next year met and defeated the Indians and captured their capital, Cuscatlán, placing the rule of the new region under the captain generalcy of Guatemala. El Salvador declared its independence from Spain with the other countries of Central America on Sept 15, 1821, and its history was that of Central America during the early period. Its independent career was marked by numerous revolutions and wars against other Central American countries. Through World War I, apparently following Mexico's example, El Salvador remained neutral, and later requested the United States to explain a reference in the Versailles treaty to the Monroe Doctrine.

What was hailed as El Salvador's first free election in almost 20 years was held in Jan. 1931 when Arturo Araujo was chosen president. Economic distress, however, combined with the general surge of reform spirit throughout Latin America, led in December to the government's overthrow and the elevation of Gen. Maximiliano Hernández Martínez to the presidency. Although the United States and a number of other American republics at first refused to recognize the Hernández Martínez regime, the general remained in power for more than a decade, and until 1944 Salvadoran politics were meaningful only as they related to his essentially authoritarian government.

General Hernández Martínez was at length deposed in 1944. The disorders were precipitated in February, when the subservient national assembly voted to extend the general's presidential term until Dec. 31, 1949. This action brought a storm of protest, and on April 2, 1944, an abortive rebellion was launched by Arturo Romero and Gen. Tito Calvo. Once the ill-fated uprising was suppressed, President Hernández Martínez ordered the execution of General Calvo and other army officers who had been involved in the affair. The executions gave rise to renewed protests. On May 5 the university students organized a demonstration which, joined by other elements of the population, became an effective general strike by May 8, when Hernández Martínez, pointing out that it was impossible to "shoot everybody," at length resigned from the presidency and went into exile.

Salvadoran politics, however, remained turbulent and unstable. Gen. Andrés I. Menéndez succeeded Hernández Martínez as president, but Menéndez himself was overthrown five months later in a military uprising successfully led by Col. Osmín Aguirre y Salinas. The Aguirre coup served primarily to complicate the situation; his political opponents coalesced around the leadership of former supreme court chieftain Miguel Tomás Molina, who established a government-in-exile in Honduras. The two rival regimes co-existed until March 1, 1945, when Gen. Salvador Castañeda Castro was inaugurated as president and the government-in-exile was abandoned.

Castañeda Castro had been the only candidate in a presidential election held under outgoing President Aguirre's direction on Jan. 14-16. Installed in the presidency, Castañeda Castro sponsored the writing of the constitution of 1945. In 1948, he attempted to extend his term of office. This move produced a military uprising against him, and he was deposed on Dec. 14. The revolutionists formed a governing junta composed of three army officers and two civilians. This group provided for a presidential election to be held in 1950, at which time Lieut. Col. Oscar Osorio, one of the members of the junta, emerged as president. A new constitution was proclaimed later that year.

Population.—According to the 1950 census of the Americas, El Salvador had a population of 1,855,917. A large proportion of the people live on farms, and the number of landowners includes a large percentage of small landowners; these small farmers raise coffee and sugar which is milled in larger properties or *centrals,* which buy the crop or prepare it for the market on a percentage basis. The chief cities are San Salvador, the capital, 161,951; Santa Ana, 51,702; Nueva San Salvador (Santa Tecla), 18,313; San Miguel, 26,702; Sonsonate, 17,949; Cojutepeque, 10,015; Ahuachapán, 10,294; San Vicente, 10,950. The principal ports are Acajutla (2,018) and La Unión (7,890).

The people of El Salvador are made up of white, chiefly Spanish, stock (about 10%); mixed blood, Spanish and Indian (about 50%) and Indian (40%). There are very few Negroes. The rulers are chiefly of the white group, and this strain is jealously guarded; the large coffee planters are whites of Spanish colonial origin, there being some foreigners. The Indians of El Salvador constitute an important element of the population, being industrious, efficient and commanding, as a class, higher wages on the plantations than the mixed bloods of similar social groups; Indian villages are still largely segregated by their own choice, but they have their own little coffee farms and work at wages, with their families, for the white owners of the larger estates.

Government.—The constitution adopted in 1950 provided for division of the government into executive, legislative and judicial branches. The legislative body is a unicameral congress which meets in regular session twice a year. Voting is obligatory for every male citizen of 18 years or over, but this provision is not enforced. The president is elected by popular vote for a term of four years, and is ineligible to succeed himself. In the event of death, disability or removal of the president, an *ad interim* president is elected by the cabinet, chief justice and congress. A new election must then he held within six months, and the new president's four-year term begins the following Jan. 1. The president has a cabinet, the members of which may attend sessions of congress and answer questions submitted them there. The judiciary is composed of a supreme court, two courts of third instance and several of first and second instance. The supreme court is made up of a chief justice and six judges from the court of third instance.

Defense.—The defensive forces consist of the permanent army, limited to 3,000 men, a militia and a national guard.

Education and Religion.—In 1945 there were 1,519 primary schools with 3,701 teachers and 100,000 students, 50 secondary schools with 6,982 students, and one university with 835 students. Provision was made in the 1947 budget for the expenditure of the equivalent of about $8,000,000 U.S. for educational purposes. The Roman Catholic religion prevails, although there is freedom of worship. The church is headed by an archbishop at San Salvador and bishops at Santa Ana and San Miguel.

Industry and Agriculture.—El Salvador is chiefly an agricultural state and produces coffee, sugar and specialities in quantities which make it an important factor, in proportion to its size, in world markets. Coffee is the chief crop, production amounting to 89,605 metric tons in 1950 and providing more than 80% of the export value. Sugar is ordinarily second in production. Maize, which is shipped to neighbouring Central American countries, including Costa Rica and Nicaragua, is third. Beans are a similar food crop, and some wheat is also exported. Of the specialities, balsam of Peru and indigo are the chief, and both are important. Balsam (*q.v.*), a healing drug, is produced solely in El Salvador, the nisnomer coming down from early Spanish days, when Peru was best known.

There is some mining, about 200 mining establishments being listed as in operation; gold production in 1949 was 28,103 troy ounces; silver, 447,851 troy ounces.

Commerce and Trade.—With 80% to 90% of all exports made up by coffee, El Salvador's prosperity is dependent upon the size of her coffee crop and the world price. Before World War II the heavy overproduction of this commodity had affected the country's economy. Nevertheless, in terms of U.S. dollars, the value of foreign trade increased. Exports in 1950 totalled $69,-502,000 and imports $47,231,000. About three-quarters of the trade is ordinarily with the United States.

Communications.—The interior is well supplied with railways and with highways. The El Salvador railway was opened in 1882, and the International railways finished their line to La Unión in 1922 and connected up with the Guatemala line in 1929. There is also a short railway from San Salvador to Acajutla, on the Pacific coast.

El Salvador was perhaps the most active of all Central American countries in constructing its portion of the Inter-American highway, completing its portion in the early 1940s. In 1950 the total highway mileage was 1,693, of which 934 mi. were all-weather roads.

Finance.—The monetary unit is the colón, stabilized at 40 cents U.S. The public debt on Dec. 31, 1950, was $10,381,805, all external. Ordinary government expenditure in 1950 was $35,395,-579; ordinary revenue, $35,347,019. The 1951 budget was estimated to balance at approximately $44,000,000.

BIBLIOGRAPHY.—Department of Overseas Trade, *Reports* (London, annual); Foreign Policy Association, *Reports* (Semimonthly); P. F. Martin, *Salvador of the Twentieth Century* (1911).

(L. W. Be.; G. I. B.)

SALVADOR or BAHIA, the oldest city of Brazil, for 250 years the capital of the country and now the capital of the state of Bahia, was founded by Thomé de Souza in 1549. Lat. 13° S. and long. 30° 31′ W. Pop. (1950) 395,993. A picturesque and bluff-formed peninsula extending southward, ranging from slightly above sea level to 250 ft., separates Todos os Santos bay, a deep body of water 25 mi. long and 20 mi. wide, from the Atlantic ocean. Salvador is situated on the inner side of the peninsula, facing west.

The mean temperature is 78° F. and the annual rainfall is 52 in. Having outgrown its original bay-level site, the city today extends well over higher levels. Lower and upper sections are connected by elevators and by graded and winding roads. Narrow streets, principally old business structures and some residences, warehouses, commercial activity, new docks and shipping services typify the lower city. On upper levels there are new parks, modern streets and boulevards, fine residences, flower gardens, modern shops, hotels, schools, theatres, churches. Electric car lines radiate to suburbs. A railway to Joazeiro, 350 mi., connects with steamer service on the São Francisco river; also there is rail connection to Lençois, Toca da Onça and the state of Sergipe, all of which provide outlets for agricultural products via Salvador. During the period 1900 to 1920 and again from 1940 to the census of 1950 the population of Salvador showed a substantial increase of about 30%. Most marked advances of later years were the extension of paved streets, modern business houses, further extension of electricity for domestic purposes and numerous civic improvements. Cia Brasileira de Energia operates streetcars, telephones and power services. Port improvements were begun as early as 1909, but made only fair progress. Ships dock (instead of anchoring in the bay) and cargo is efficiently transferred to and from ships. There are numerous extensive warehouses and mechanical energy is replacing physical labour in handling cargo. Exports from the port include cacao, hides, tobacco, coffee, sugar, rubber, diamonds, castor oil beans and hard woods. The total of exports for the years 1947 to 1949 amounted to an average of 218,000 metric tons annually. Manufactured goods imported during the same period of years ranged from 167,800 to 217,000 tons per year. A considerable number of industrial plants are engaged in manufacture of less complicated commodities. The Brazilian government maintains a dockyard at Salvador; a second one is operated by a British corporation. There is a coaling station with Welsh and other fuels on hand. Smaller vessels are built here and ship repairing occupies the attention of skilled mechanics and many labourers. The good financial condition of the state of Bahia reacted favourably on the city's progress.

Salvador is an important refining centre of petroleum, considerable amounts of oil having been discovered in the neighbourhood of the city. (R. D'E.)

SALVAGE, includes a service rendered voluntarily by a person by saving life or property from peril, and also the reward for such service and in certain cases the thing saved, as from fire on land. Usually the word is employed in reference to salvage at sea, which has two divisions: (1) civil salvage, (2) military salvage.

Civil Salvage.—This is defined in English law as such a service as may become the ground of a reward in an admiralty court, and arises from the preservation of life or property from dangers of the sea. The jurisdiction to give it is an admiralty jurisdiction. But the right to reward was recognized in the courts of common law before the admiralty court became, as it now is, a part of the High Court of Justice, *e.g.*, by enforcing a possessory lien of the salvor over the salved property. The origin of the rule has been traced to the doctrine of Roman law that "spontaneous services" in the protection of lives and property should be rewarded. But that doctrine has not found a place in English law, except as part of the maritime law administered in the court of admiralty. Thus services on land, as in rescuing lives or houses or goods from fire, do not entitle the person rendering those services to reward, unless he has acted under some contract or employment. But at sea or in a harbour or dock the right to reward springs from the service itself if it has been rendered to a ship, or her passengers, crew or cargo, or to property which has been thrown or washed out of her.

The right to salvage for saving lives from ships is the creation of modern statutes. Formerly the admiralty court treated the fact that lives had been saved as enhancing the merit of a salvage of property by the same salvors, where the two could be connected; and so indirectly gave life salvage. And this is still the position in cases where the Merchant Shipping Act of 1894 does not apply. This act (s. 544) applies to all cases in which the "services are rendered wholly or in part within British waters in saving life from any British or foreign vessel, or elsewhere in saving life from any British vessel." Also (s. 545) it can be applied, by Order in Council, to life salvage from ships of any foreign country whose Government "is willing that salvage should be awarded by British courts for services rendered in saving life from ships belonging to that country where the ship is beyond the limits of British jurisdiction." By s. 544 life salvage is made payable "by the owner of the vessel, cargo or apparel saved"; and is to be paid in priority to all other claims for salvage. Where the value of the vessel, cargo and apparel saved is insufficient to pay the life salvage, the Board of Trade may in their discretion make up the deficiency, in whole or in part, out of the Mercantile Marine Fund. The effect of the act is to impose a common responsibility upon the owners of ship and cargo to the extent of their property saved. Whatever is saved becomes a fund out of which life salvors may be rewarded, and to which they are entitled in priority to other salvors. By the Maritime Convention Act 1911 a master who does not render assistance to any person in danger of being lost at sea is guilty of a misdemeanour.

This limitation of the reward to the amount of the property salved also applies in the case of salvage of property. The ordinary remedy of the salvor is against the property itself by proceedings *in rem,* to enforce the maritime lien given him by the law upon that property. This enables him to arrest the property, if within the jurisdiction, into whose hands soever it may have come; and, if necessary, the court will order a sale, and payment of his claim out of the proceeds. The salvor has also a remedy *in personam* against the owners or others interested in the property saved; but it seems that this right depends upon property having been saved, and having come to the owner's hands. The amount which can be awarded is limited by the value of that property.

In order to create a right to salvage lives or property saved must have been in danger—either in immediate peril, or in a position of "difficulty and reasonable apprehension." Danger to the salvor is not essential, though it enhances his claim to reward. Again, the service must have helped towards saving the lives or property. Ineffectual efforts, however strenuous and meritorious, do not give rise to a claim. But the service need not be completely successful. If it has contributed to an ultimate rescue it will be rewarded, though that may have been accomplished by others. And as we have seen, there must have been ultimate success. Some of the property involved in the adventure must have been saved. And its value, or the fund realized by its sale, limits the total of the awards to all the salvors. Cases, of course, occur in which services at sea are employed by ships in danger: as where a steamer with a broken propeller shaft employs another steamer to tow her; or where a vessel which has lost her anchors employs another to procure anchors for her from shore. In such cases the conditions of reward above set out may not apply. Reward may be payable, notwithstanding entire failure or success, by the express or implied terms of the employment. But such a reward is not truly "salvage."

Services that are rendered in the performance of a duty do not bestow a claim to salvage. Thus the crew cannot (while still the crew) be salvors of the ship or cargo; nor can the passengers, unless they have voluntarily stayed on the ship for the purpose of saving her. Nor can a pilot employed as such be salvor, unless he has boarded a vessel in such exceptional circumstances that his doing so for pilotage fees could not reasonably be expected; or unless the circumstances of the service, entered upon as pilotage, have so changed as to alter its character. Again, the owners and crew of a tug employed to tow a ship cannot claim salvage for rescuing her from danger which may arise during towage, unless circumstances have supervened which were not contemplated, and are such as to require extraordinary aid from the tug, or to expose her to extraordinary risk. Officers and crew of a ship of the royal navy may, with consent of the Admiralty, recover salvage when they have rendered services outside the protection which their ship ought to afford. No claim, however, can be made in respect of the ship herself, except she be specially equipped with salvage plant.

The reward depends first, on the degree of the danger to the property salved, on its value, and on the effect of the services rendered; next, on the risks run by the salvors, the length and severity of their efforts, the enterprise and skill displayed, and on the value and efficiency of the vessel or apparatus they have used, and the risks to which they have exposed her. Negligent or improper conduct of the salvors will cause a diminution or total disallowance of the award.

In apportioning the award given for a salvage service among the owners, master and crew of the vessel by means of which it has been rendered, the special circumstances of each case have to be considered. In nearly all cases a large portion goes to the owners, and as in recent times the value and efficiency of ships (especially of steamships) have increased, so the proportion of the whole usually awarded to the owners has also increased. In an ordinary case of salvage by a steamship towing a distressed ship into safety, the share of the owners has often been about three-fourths; of the remainder the master usually gets about one-third, and the officers and crew divide the rest in proportion to their ratings. But where the salving ship has sustained special damage in the service, or her owners have been put to loss by it, that is taken into consideration. On the other hand, where special personal services have been rendered by members of the crew they are specially rewarded.

An agreement as to the salvage to be paid is sometimes made at the time the assistance is given. When made fairly the court will act upon it, though it may turn out to be a bad bargain for one or other of the parties. But if the facts were not correctly apprehended by one or both, or if the position was one of such difficulty that those salved had no real option as to accepting the salvor's terms, the court will set the agreement aside.

The award of salvage is generally made in one sum against ship, freight and cargo; and those interests contribute to the amount in proportion to the value saved. Each is liable to the salvors for his own share, and for no more. If, however, the shipowner pays the cargo's share, he has a lien upon it for the amount.   (T. G. C.)

Military Salvage.—This is such a service as may become ground for a reward in a prize court for the rescue of property from the enemy in time of war. It involves the determination of two questions: first, whether the property is to be restored to its original owner or condemned as prize to the recaptor; and second, what amount of salvage, if any, is to accompany restitution. The first question depends upon the law of nations, which may be taken to be that where a ship has been carried by an enemy *infra praesidia,* and especially after a sentence of condemnation, the title of the original owner is divested, and does not revest upon recapture by third parties. In such a case, therefore, *iure gentium* restitution cannot be claimed. The municipal law of civilized countries, however, does not encourage subjects to "make reprisals upon one another," and laws are generally found, as in England, which as between subjects of that particular State provide for restitution irrespective of any change in the title to the subject matter which may have occurred. But (speaking henceforth of England) in cases which do not fall strictly within these acts, the old maritime law, which was in unison with the general law of nations, is applied by the courts. Moreover, the English Prize Acts do not apply to foreign owners of recaptured prizes, and therefore no award can be made against them unless in accordance with the law of nations. In practice the courts have acted upon the "rule of reciprocity" where recaptures have been made of the property of formal allies, dealing with them as the allied State would have dealt with English property. If a neutral vessel is recaptured restitution is always ordered, unless the vessel is in peril of condemnation or destruction. An exception to the rule of restitution as between British subjects is made in the case of a British ship which has been "set forth as a ship of war" by the captor, and subsequently retaken by a British ship. Such a ship is not liable to restoration, but is the prize of the recaptor. This exception, the object of which is to encourage the capture of armed ships, dates from 1793, previous acts having provided for restitution upon payment of a moiety as salvage. The condition of setting forth as a ship of war is satisfied, where under a fair semblance of authority, which is not disproved, the ship "has been used in the operations of war, and constituted a part of the naval force of the enemy."

The right to salvage and the amount which will be allowed are also questions of the *ius gentium,* though usually governed by municipal law. In England the first statutory recognition of the right occurs in 1648, when an act of the Commonwealth provided that British vessels captured by an enemy and retaken by British ships shall be restored upon payment of one-eighth of the value of the property in lieu of salvage, or one-half in the case of a prize "set forth as a ship of war." Since the first act, and down to the act of 1805 inclusive, a distinction has always been drawn between a recapture effected by one of the royal ships of war and a recapture by a privateer or other vessel. In the former case the allowance has always been one-eighth, in the latter it varied, but was usually one-sixth. In the act of 1692 a clause gave salvage to a privateer, rising in amount from one-eighth to one-half according to the number of hours the prize had been in the enemy's possession, but this clause has disappeared since 1756. There is no provision in the present act for the payment of salvage, except in case of recapture by one of His Majesty's ships, but it seems beyond question that recaptors are entitled at law to salvage, although they may hold no commission

from the Crown. Similarly, salvage is awarded in the case of recapture from pirates or from a mutinous crew. In the case of royal ships the act of 1864 allows one-eighth salvage, which in cases of "special difficulty or danger" the court may increase to an amount not exceeding a quarter.   (M. Bт.)

UNITED STATES

Mariners are not under any legal obligation to render salvage services to *property* in peril at sea. Salvage awards are granted by the maritime law in order to encourage them to undertake the peril and responsibility of performing such services. However, the duty of master mariners to render assistance to every *person* in peril at sea has been laid down by statute in the leading maritime countries (see Salvage Act of Aug. 1, 1912, c. 268, s. 2; *Comp. Stat.* s. 7,991). Under American law, failure of a master of a vessel to fulfil this duty renders him liable to a penalty not exceeding $1,000, or imprisonment not exceeding two years, or both. The reward for life salvage is not so definitely provided for in American law as in England. By the Act of Aug. 1, 1912 (c. 268, s. 3; *Comp. Stat.* s. 7,992), salvors of human life may recover an award for such service only where a salvage award is made with respect to a salved vessel, her cargo and accessories. Salvors of life receive no award unless property is saved. A private vessel may take off the crew and passengers of a sinking liner, but unless some property is saved, no claim for salvage award will lie. But the property saved need not be saved by the salvors of human life. And if any property is saved, it matters not by whom, the salvage award on that property which, as will be hereafter remarked, usually does not exceed half of its salved value, is the fund from which the award for life salvage must be drawn (*The Admiral Evans,* 286 Fed. Rep. 442). It is provided by statute that with the exception of ships of war, or vessels appropriated exclusively to public service, salvors of human life who have taken part in the services are entitled to a fair share of the remuneration awarded to the salvors of the vessel, her cargo and accessories (Salvage Act of Aug. 1, 1912, c. 268, s. 3; *Comp. Stat.* s. 7,992).

The Government may claim salvage for services rendered by its public vessels. By the Act of July 1, 1918 (Stat. L. 40, p. 705, c. 114), the secretary of the navy is authorized to cause vessels under his control, adapted to the purpose, to afford salvage service to private or public vessels in distress, and to determine and collect reasonable compensation therefor when such salvage service is rendered by a vessel especially equipped for the purpose, or by a tug. The implication which might be drawn from the statute that, where the service is rendered by a public vessel not specially equipped for salvage service, such as a man-of-war or a transport, the Government may not demand and collect a salvage award, has been rejected by the courts. The Government has sued for and been allowed salvage award for salvage services rendered to a British merchant vessel by a merchant vessel owned by the U.S. Shipping Board and operated as a munitions ship for Government account (*The Impoco,* 287 Fed. 400). In the case of salvage services rendered by any merchant vessel owned or operated by the United States or the U.S. Emergency Fleet Corporation (now U.S. Merchant Fleet Corporation), it is provided by s. 10 of the Act of March 9, 1920 (Suits in Admiralty Act c. 95; *Comp. Stat.* s. 1,251), that the United States and the crew of any such vessel shall have the right to collect and sue for salvage services rendered, and any moneys recovered therefrom by the United States for its own benefit, shall be paid into the U.S. Treasury, to the credit of the department of the Government, or of the U.S. Shipping Board, or of the Emergency (Merchant) Fleet Corporation having control of the possession or operation of the vessel.

Salvage Award.—By statute, the master and crew of the salving vessel, in rendering services to another vessel of common ownership, are entitled to salvage award (Salvage Act of Aug. 1, 1912, c. 268, s. 1; *Comp. Stat.* s. 7,990). In the absence of request by the distressed vessel, salvage services, to merit an award, must be rendered directly to the salved property. It has been held that where a dry-dock is on fire and tugs extinguish the flames, if a vessel in the dry-dock does not request such services and has other means of protecting itself, no salvage award may be claimed from it. The services were rendered directly to the dry-dock and perhaps incidentally benefited the vessel lying in it, but no salvage award may be claimed from the vessel (*Merritt and Chapman D. & W. Co. v. United States* [*The Leviathan*], 274 U.S. 611). So, also, where vessels are moored alongside a river quay, services rendered by tugs in extinguishing a fire on one of the vessels do not give rise to a salvage claim against the vessels near by, unless the vessels against which the claim is made requested the salvors to perform the services (*The City of Atlanta*, 56 Fed. 252). In the same circumstances, however, if the salvors devote their attention to the other vessels and tow them away from the burning vessel, then salvage award may be claimed from them. It is not essential that there should be direct contact between the structure, gear or personnel of the salving vessel and the vessel saved. A word of warning to a vessel heading for a shoal, which enables her to avoid destruction, is a salvage service (*South American S.S. Co. v. Atlantic Towing Co.*, 22 F. [2d] 16). Likewise, a vessel which stands by another in distress, even though she does nothing else, is entitled to salvage award (*The Sapinero*, 5 F. [2d] 56; *The Manchester Brigade*, 276 Fed. 410).

It often happens that while the services are rendered under the apprehension of grave peril, the result shows that the vessel was not in danger at all or at least not to the extent anticipated. In such case it has been held that it is the apprehended danger which fixes the value of the services and controls the amount of the award. The owner of the salved property will not be heard to argue that subsequent developments showed that the salvage was unnecessary or that the risks taken by the salvors were less in fact than they appeared at the time the services were rendered (*The Lowther Castle*, 195 Fed. 604). But see *The Sapinero*, 5 F. (2d) 56, holding that the master of the distressed ship exaggerated the plight of his vessel. Apparently it is the peril reasonably apprehended which controls.

Success is of the essence of a salvage service. But if a salvor undertakes a salvage service and is ready and able to carry it to completion, he cannot be summarily dismissed on the arrival of other assistance and thus deprived of salvage award. If a salvor is dismissed after he has contributed to the ultimate success of the operation and is ready and able to continue, he is entitled to share in the salvage award. Cases frequently arise where salvors are relieved by other vessels belonging to the same ownership as that of the distressed vessel. It has been held that the first salvors are entitled to share in the salvage award (*The Annie Lord*, 251 Fed. 157; *The Manchester Brigade*, 276 Fed. 410). However, a salved vessel need not retain incompetent salvors and is free to obtain whatever assistance is available. Whether or not the first set of salvors are entitled to share in the award depends on what they did and what they were able to do (*The Santa Rosa*, 295 Fed. 350).

Claims for Salvage.—In making demands for salvage, and in exacting security under process *in rem* against the salved property, salvors must be careful not to be exorbitant in their demands. The amount of salvage award is entirely discretionary with the court. A grasping attitude on the part of salvors will often work against their claim for salvage. Indeed it may cause the court to dismiss their claim entirely where their conduct is of such character as to destroy whatever merit there may have been in the service (*The Gypsy Queen*, 284 Fed. 607). The salved interests must also show the proper attitude. Owners of salved ships should make reasonable offers of award, or else the court may penalize them for putting the salvors to the expense of litigation (*The Western Star*, 157 Fed. 489). Interest on the amount of the award may be allowed, in the discretion of the court (*The Naiwa*, 3 F. [2d] 381).

Where salvors are negligent in the performance of the service, or in care of the property after deliverance from the peril, the owner of the salved property may urge the fact against them in reduction of salvage award or as a complete defence to the claim (*The Henry Steers, Jr.*, 110 Fed. 578; *The Bremen*, 111 Fed.

228; *The Ragnarok*, 158 Fed. 694; *Albury* v. *Cargo Ex. Lugano*, 215 Fed. 963; *The F. Q. Barstow*, 257 Fed. 395).

Salvage awards, in the view of the United States maritime law, while having as their purpose the encouragement of salvage service, must be fixed in such amounts as not to deprive the owner of the property saved of all benefit of the service.

Amount of Award.—This depends, in each case, on the facts. The courts frequently advert to awards made in similar cases, but precedents serve only as a guide. They have no controlling force (*The Buckhannon*, 284 Fed. 917). The appellate courts will not disturb the award made by the trial judge unless there appears to be such a clear abuse of discretion as to amount to an error of law (*The Bay of Naples*, 48 Fed. 737; *The Kia Ora*, 352 Fed. 507; *The Naiwa*, 3 F. [2d] 381; *The Santa Rosa*, 5 F. [2d] 478; *The Zaca*, 7 F. [2d] 69). A classic definition of the elements to be considered by a court in fixing salvage award was given by the U.S. Supreme Court in *The Blackwall*, 10 Wall. 1, 14:—

"(1.) The labour expended by the salvors in rendering the salvage service. (2.) The promptitude, skill, and energy displayed in rendering the service and saving the property. (3.) The value of the property employed by the salvors in rendering the service, and the danger to which such property was exposed. (4.) The risk incurred by the salvors in securing the property from the impending peril. (5.) The value of the property saved. (6.) The degree of danger from which the property was rescued."

It is, therefore, apparent that the amount of award in the various classes of salvage can not be readily classified because of the highly variable factors which enter into them. The following cases, grouped according to the nature of the service, will give some idea of the amounts of salvage awards. Towage on high seas: *The Varzin*, 180 Fed. 892; *The Melderskin*, 249 Fed. 776; *The Western Pride*, 274 Fed. 920; *The Katrina Luckenbach*, 61 Ct. Cls. 632. Releasing stranded vessels: *The St. Paul*, 82 Fed. 104; *The Kia Ora*, 352 Fed. 507; *The Santa Rosa*, 295 Fed. 350. Extinguishing fire on vessels: *The F. Q. Barstow*, 257 Fed. 793; *The Huttonwood*, 262 Fed. 452; *The Zaca*, 7 F. (2d) 69; *The Florence Luckenbach*, 9 F. (2d) 1,008. Towing vessels away from burning vessels or pier: *The Geo. W. Elzey*, 250 Fed. 602; *The West Mount*, 277 Fed. 168; *The Thorwald Halvorsen*, 281 Fed. 506; *The Magnetic*, 293 Fed. 94; *The Santa Barbara*, 299 Fed. 152.

Where the salved vessel has been abandoned by her master and crew and is therefore derelict, the salvage awards run much higher than otherwise. The ancient rule was that the salvage award amounted to a moiety of the salved value. While this rule is no longer regarded as controlling, there are a few cases of derelict salvage awards which even exceed 50% (*The Edwards*, 12 Fed. 508; *The Flower City*, 16 Fed. 866; *The Bay of Naples*, 48 Fed. 737; *The Myrtle Tunnel*, 146 Fed. 324; *The Flora Rodgers*, 152 Fed. 286).

Division of Award.—The division of salvage award between the owner of the salving vessel and the master, officers and crew is subject to the circumstances of each case. Where a vessel is towed from her position of distress at sea to a port of refuge, or where a stranded vessel is released, the salvage award is often divided four-fifths to the shipowner and one-fifth to the crew. In cases of towage on the high seas, where the salving crew has incurred considerable peril, the crew's share may run much higher. An exceptional case arose when the "Katrina Luckenbach," steaming in convoy from Gibraltar to Hampton Roads in Aug. 1918, broke down at sea. The "Gaelic Prince," of the same convoy, took the "Katrina Luckenbach" in tow and brought her 1,356 m. to Hampton Roads, through an area in which German submarines were operating. Great risk was incurred by the master and crew of the "Gaelic Prince," because by taking the "Katrina Luckenbach" in tow their vessel became vulnerable to attack by a submarine. The court, in rendering a salvage award to the "Gaelic Prince" of $93,000 in addition to the salvor's expenses, allowed two-thirds of it to the master, officers and crew (*Prince Line Ltd.* v. *The United States*, 61 Ct. Cls. 632). In cases of salvage services rendered to burning vessels, whether at sea or in port, the crew's share is usually from about one-quarter to one-third, because of the personal risk involved. It may be more in cases of specific heroism. It should be borne in mind, however, that the facts of each case control the amount of salvage award and the share of it to be given to the officers and crew of the salving vessel. The services rendered by the personnel are considered by the court in fixing their share of the salvage award. Following this principle, if the facts show that the crew did nothing more than attend to their ordinary routine duties at sea, as in the case of towage of a vessel on a calm sea, the court may exclude the crew entirely from the award, particularly where both vessels are owned by the same interests (*The Lewis Bros.*, 287 Fed. 143; *The Lake Elmont*, 1924 A.M.C. 711). The crew's fund is usually pro-rated according to the monthly wages, the master's share figured on double his monthly wages.

Settlement Agreement.—The seaman is specially protected by law from those who would deprive him by agreement of his right to salvage award. He is the ward of the admiralty, and in order to protect him from those who would cause him to discount his rights in salvage, it has been provided by statute that every stipulation by which any seaman consents to abandon any right which he may have or obtain in the nature of salvage shall be wholly inoperative (*U.S. Rev. Stat.* 4,535; *Comp. Stat.* s. 8,324). However, it has been intimated in an *obiter dictum* that a settlement made with the seaman after the performance of the salvage service would be valid where the shipowner has acted in good faith (*Rivers* v. *Lockwood*, 239 Fed. 380).

Salvage awards are frequently agreed on by the parties without the need of litigation, and the shipowner commonly conducts the negotiations. If a suit proves necessary to collect the award, the shipowner has the right to sue on behalf of the crew (*Castner, Curran and Bullitt* v. *United States*, 5 F. [2nd] 214). The shipowner, however, has not any authority to bind the crew by any arrangement which he may make with the salved interests. Indeed, if the settlement which the shipowner agrees to accept is not commensurate with the services rendered, the crew may maintain direct action against the salved interests for their proper share of salvage award. The arrangements made by their shipowner are not a bar to their recovery (*Bergher* v. *General Petroleum Co.*, 242 Fed. 967). The common practice in salvage settlements without litigation is that the salved interests, in paying the entire award to the owner of the salving ship, demand and receive an agreement of indemnity by which the owner of the salving vessel agrees to hold harmless the salved interests from any future claims which may be made by the crew in respect of the salvage services. Thus the owner of the salving vessel takes upon himself the responsibility for the salvage settlement and assumes the obligation of making good to his own crew any deficiency of salvage award which any court in the future may allow to the seamen in addition to their share of the award fixed by the settlement. It is generally considered that any payment which the seaman receives, whether in consideration of the surrender of his salvage rights, or in the distribution of a settlement fund received by his shipowner, is deemed a payment *pro tanto* on account of any salvage award to which the seaman may be entitled (*The Edward Lee*, Fed. Cas. No. 4,292; *The Adirondack*, 5 Fed. 214; *Baker Salvage Co.* v. *The Taylor Dickson*, 40 Fed. 261; *Rivers* v. *Lockwood*, 239 Fed. 380). See also SALVAGING. (E. S. M.)

BIBLIOGRAPHY.—C. Abbott, *A Treatise of the Law Relative to Merchant Ships and Seamen*, 14th ed. (1901); Sir W. R. Kennedy, *A Treatise on the Law of Civil Salvage*, 2nd ed. (1907); E. S. Roscoe, *On the Admiralty Jurisdiction and Practice*, 4th ed. (1920); T. G. Carver, *Treatise on the Law Relating to Carriage of Goods by Sea*, 7th ed. (1925).

SALVAGE CORPS. Salvage corps are bodies of men specially trained and equipped for emergency fire salvage work. In Great Britain, some salvage work is undertaken by local authority fire brigades, but there are special salvage corps in London, Liverpool and Glasgow maintained and administered by insurance companies. Typical of these corps and the largest of them is the London Salvage corps, a force of men specializing in emergency fire salvage work. It attends fires for the purpose of reducing as far as possible damage resulting directly and indirectly from fire and fire-fighting operations.

The corps is maintained and administered by fire insurance offices in the London area and was formed in 1866 when the insurance companies, which had for the previous 150 years or so maintained the public fire service for the London area, decided they could no longer continue to meet this responsibility. Following the passing of the Metropolitan Fire Brigade act, 1865, the companies handed over their fire stations, appliances and personnel to the metropolitan board of works, the local authority in London at that time, but decided to establish and maintain the salvage corps for the purpose of continuing the salvage work and other duties on behalf of the companies which had hitherto been carried out by the insurance fire brigades.

The corps maintains three stations and has nine motor tenders and three portable pumps. It works in close co-operation with the nine fire brigades in the greater London area and receives by direct telephone line from the London fire brigade notification of every fire call, within a minute of its being received by that brigade, excepting those known to be in respect of chimney fires, motor vehicles on highways, burning rubbish or other incidents at which salvage work is clearly unnecessary. From the other fire brigades in the area it receives early notification of fires at which salvage work may be practicable.

An immediate turnout is made to all calls in the central London area and also to special risks such as docks, departmental stores and large warehouses beyond this area; in the case of other fires in the outer districts it is the general practice to wait for details from the fire brigade of the nature of the fire, the property involved and the method of extinction being employed. As most first attendance fire engines are fitted with radio transmitters, this information is usually obtained within a very few minutes of the receipt of the fire call. The corps attend more than 2,000 calls annually.

Salvagemen wear a traditional type of fire helmet, long waterproof coats, rubber thigh boots, and belts with axes and handlamps, and the salvage tenders of the corps look very much like fire brigade engines, in that they are painted red and have loud ringing bells and twin amber flashing lights to facilitate progress through traffic en route to fires.

The equipment used includes waterproof sheets of various sizes up to 18 ft. square and telescopic stanchions for slinging the sheets; metal trays for collecting dripping water; axes, augers, crowbars, hammers, lock wrenches, padlock removers, saws, spanners, valve keys and other tools of various kinds; brooms, squeegees, mops, scoops and buckets; sawdust "dollies" for damming doorways, etc., and bags of sawdust; drain guards and drain rods; lamps of various kinds; ladders; electric generators, fans, diffusers and lighting equipment; pickaxes, shovels and road wedges; chamois leathers, cleaning rags and dusters; deodorizing equipment; oil, oiling brushes and oil sprayers; heavy tarpaulins, tubular steel scaffolding, corrugated iron, roofing felt, nails and padlocks; asbestos, leather and rubber gloves; cordage and clasp knives; paraffin heaters; lifting tackle; spare sprinkler heads; debris baskets, packing cases, metal drums, sack hooks and sack trucks.

While fire-fighting operations are in progress, the work of the corps includes moving and covering contents with waterproof sheets; diverting water by means of sheets slung from fixtures in walls or on specially designed stanchions; picking up carpets and other contents; clearing water off floors by means of brooms, squeegees and scoops; damming off doorways and floor openings; opening up drains and keeping them clear, within and outside the premises (this is often of considerable importance in basements and in connection with neighbouring property); pumping out basements and elevator wells which have become flooded; ventilating, when the state of the fire permits, to clear smoke, heat and steam; deodorizing premises and stock affected by smoke; and protecting any neighbouring property which is exposed; *i.e.*, where there are broken windows or other uncovered openings, or outside stock. It is not usual to remove contents from premises which are on fire but this is sometimes necessary in buildings or parts of buildings which are likely to be completely involved.

After the fire has been brought under control and the protective measures have been completed, the nature of the work changes.

Passages are cut through debris to facilitate drainage; wet floors are covered with sawdust, and, as soon as water ceases to drip through the floors and ceilings, the salvage covers are removed to assist drying out. Dangerous building features of a minor nature —broken and loose slates, glass and plaster—are removed and the buildings are made as weatherproof as possible by covering windows and roofs with heavy tarpaulins or roofing felt. If the roof has sustained structural damage, temporary repairs are effected by the use of tubular scaffolding.

Prompt attention is given to the treatment of contents. Where possible, heating apparatus is put into operation and the corps makes use of a number of its portable heaters. Machinery and other metal contents, such as stocks of tools, machine parts, metal fittings, hinges, nails and screws are dried and oiled to prevent rusting; and furniture is leathered and dried, to prevent staining and more serious damage. Considerable damage is often prevented by examining the stock and removing wet packing; this is particularly necessary, for instance, for such things as fabrics and leather goods, which are liable to stain, and cutlery, which may rust. In severe fires, the stock which is not too severely damaged may be removed to temporary or alternative storage. It sometimes happens that articles of special value, such as jewellery, are lost in fires and a careful search is made by screening all the debris, often with considerable success.

The corps also reinstates sprinkler systems which have been in use. Where premises cannot be made secure or left in the custody of an authorized person, a member of the corps remains on duty.

As well as doing salvage work at fires, the corps also attends premises where there are sprinkler leakages, burst pipes, overflowing tanks and the like and carries out work very similar to much which is undertaken at fires.

Such salvage work is of value to insurance companies and underwriters and also to property owners and occupiers, because in addition to minimizing the physical and monetary loss caused by fires and similar disasters it enables business to be resumed and homes to be reoccupied much more quickly than would otherwise be the case. (A. S. Pn.)

SALVAGING. Salvage work, or the raising and recovery of sunken ships and cargoes, has always had a fascination, probably, first, for the reason that little is known of the subject by the public, and, second, because the spirit of adventure appeals to us still, although possibly in a modified degree compared with that which sent our forefathers out to search for hidden treasures in far-off lands.

Salvage engineering has always been confined to a small number of the engineering profession, although it is a highly technical business, where skill, experience and determination are pitted against wind and sea. It necessitates trained men and special appliances and is a work that must be carried on night and day whenever the elements permit.

Marine salvage may be divided under a few principal headings:

1. The raising of vessels sunk in deep water by means of pontoons, etc.

2. Raising by the application of compressed air to expel the water.

3. Refloating of ships stranded on rocks or sand where the bottom is damaged and temporary repairs have to be made by divers, and where pumping plant of different descriptions is used to free the vessel of water.

4. Uprighting of capsized vessels, etc.

Salvage Plant.—The salvage ship is one of the most important factors in salvage operations, and, though generally a small vessel, she carries a very complicated equipment of appliances for use in the work, with a view to rendering her as independent as possible of assistance from ashore and enabling her to make repairs, etc., in out-of-the-way places where it would be difficult to obtain other assistance.

As an example, a typical modern type is composite built (170 ft. long by 30 ft. wide), is fitted with triple expansion engines and has a speed of 14 knots. She accommodates about 80 officers and men, consisting of engineers, artisans, divers, motor engineers, electrical engineers and others. Her equipment consists of portable pump-

ing plant of 5,000 tons per hour which can be transferred to the wrecked vessel, portable oil-driven air compressors, portable electric lighting plant and electric submersible pumps which work under water.

At the mastheads the vessel has powerful electric arc lamps of 5,000 candlepower with sufficient length of watertight cables to allow their being placed on the wrecked ship and operated by the salvage ship's dynamos; also searchlights, submarine arc and incandescent lamps for the divers and submarine oxyacetylene burning plant for cutting plates under water, as well as a complete equipment of submarine pneumatic drilling machines up to three inches in diameter, pneumatic hammers, rock-boring drills and submarine photographic apparatus. She is fitted with long-range wireless telegraphy. Being constructed of wood, she is able to remain alongside a damaged ship in rough weather.

At one time steam pumps were entirely used in salvage operations, and were supplied with portable boilers so that they might be placed on board a wreck. They performed excellent service, generally under most difficult conditions. To place such heavy gear on board a wrecked ship from a salvage craft rolling alongside on a winter night required a large amount of skill and care. When placed in position they had to be connected to the portable boilers, and steam had to be raised before they were available for pumping. It was also necessary to place a supply of coal on board if the ship's bunkers were not available, and this supply was often washed away. Steam pumps were retained on board the salvage ship, since they could perform work that certain later types of pumping plants could not do; for instance, sand, coal, grain and even copper and iron ore could be discharged by them from under water.

The internal-combustion engine (q.v.) went a great way toward revolutionizing salvage pumping plant. It was much lighter than the steam pump, required no boiler, and the fuel could be carried to the wreck in barrels or drums in an ordinary ship's lifeboat. Further, when not required for work it could be stopped and started again in a few minutes, while steam has always to be kept on the portable boilers of the steam pumps. The advantages of the oil motor-driven centrifugal pump will be obvious; it is just as efficient for pumping water as the steam pump, saves in cost of running, takes up less stowage space and uses paraffin or gasoline as fuel, which can generally be obtained without difficulty. The sizes in general use are 12 in. and 6 in.

Electrically driven submersible pumping machinery was tried under all conditions and found more efficient than any of the older

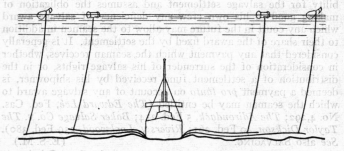

FIG. 1.—DIAGRAM OF NINE-INCH STEEL LIFTING WIRES IN POSITION UNDER A WRECK WITH THEIR FREE ENDS BUOYED

The wires are made fast to lifting ships at low tide so that when the tide rises, the wreck is lifted off the bottom

types. It can be placed aboard in boats and driven from the dynamos of the salvage ship lying off the wreck. There is no necessity to secure it, as it works practically without vibration and can be used from the derricks and lowered down into the water. Its great advantage is that while the ordinary salvage pump has a lifting capacity of only 30 ft., the submersible pump is able to raise the water to a height of 80 ft.; no priming is necessary, and no particular attention need be paid to the discharge hose as far as making it air and watertight. Earlier electric salvage pumps that were tried were fitted with watertight cases and proved entirely unsuccessful for this particular kind of work. In the submersible pump, water is allowed free access to the electrical parts.

Lifting Operations.—With this somewhat brief description of salvage plant used, the particulars of actual salvage operations will be explained, commencing with the raising of sunken vessels from deep water by means of lifting barges dependent on the rise and fall of tide.

The method of procedure is to place lifting vessels of sufficient buoyancy over the wreck and pass a number of nine-inch steel wire ropes under the vessel, bringing the ends of the wires up and making them fast to the lifting ships at low water; then as the tide rises, if the calculations have been correct, the vessel is raised from the bottom the height of the rise of tide, and carried into shallower water where the wreck is grounded; the operations are continued each tide until her decks are above water (*see* figs. 1 and 2). The

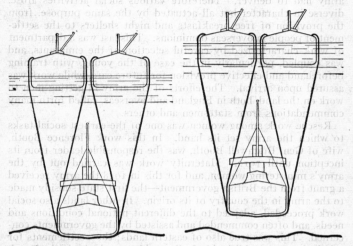

FIG. 2.—ON THE LEFT, THE LIFTING WIRES HAVE BEEN MADE FAST TO LIFTING LIGHTERS; ON THE RIGHT, THE WRECK IS CLEAR OF THE BOTTOM, AT HIGH WATER. IT IS THEN TOWED TO SHALLOWER DEPTHS AND THE OPERATION REPEATED

fractures are then patched by the divers, salvage pumps are installed and the vessel is pumped out and floated. The dimensions of lifting vessels that have been employed in a large number of cases are: length 165 ft., breadth 36 ft. and lifting capacity 1,500 tons maximum.

One of the principal difficulties with this method is the placing of the heavy wire cables under the bottom of the wreck, especially if she has sunk in sand, mud or clay. If she is not too deeply embedded this is generally accomplished by towing them under, with two vessels, one on each side, having the ends of the cables attached to them. Where this is found not to be possible, because the wreck has become too deeply embedded, a system of hydraulic boring at high pressure is used.

In cases where there is little or no rise of tide, submersible pontoons are used. These are really steel cylinders with a lifting capacity ranging from 50 tons each to 250 tons or more. They are divided into three watertight compartments and fitted with low-pressure air connections for expelling the water and with high-pressure air for opening the valves. The ends of the cylinders used at the lifting of H.M.S. "Gladiator" were dome-shaped and covered with collision mats to protect them against chafing. Strong channel bars were riveted around the pontoons at intervals to carry the wire cables, and the whole of the cylinders between the channel bars were covered with three-inch fir planking for protection against obstructions when lifting. Double six-inch special extra-flexible wire ropes were fitted in the required position around the pontoons, and to these were attached plate shackles to which the nine-inch lifting wires were fastened. In this case the pontoons were used to make the vessel upright, as she lay over on her beam ends at an angle of 113°.

The nine-inch wire cables were swept under the wreck and the outside ends attached to the pontoons. These were filled with water and sunk alongside the ship; the other ends of the wires

were then hove in as tightly as possible and made fast to massive steel bollards fastened to the upper side of the ship. The cylinders or pontoons were then emptied of water by means of compressed air and the vessel was uprighted, assistance being also given by compressed air and pumping from some of the sound compartments.

In this case pontoons were used only on one side. In order to raise a vessel that is sunk and lying upright on the bottom, two sets of cylinders are necessary; the plan of lifting is as follows:

A sufficient number of nine-inch wire cables are placed under the ship, the pontoons are attached to the ends of the wires on one side of the ship and filled with water, and by heaving in on the opposite cables they are hauled down into the required positions alongside the wreck. Hydraulic gripping machines of a special form are attached to the pontoons on the other side of the wreck, and the wire cables are roved through these hydraulic grips. When everything is ready, the pontoons are filled and allowed to slide down the wire cables to the bottom. The grips are then closed from the surface vessel and compressed air is pumped down to all the pontoons, which expels the water; if sufficient buoyancy has been given by the pontoons, the vessel is brought to the surface.

In the method of lifting by compressed air, all openings are closed by the divers and compressed air is pumped down to connections made to all the different compartments from air compressors of the salvage ships. The water is then expelled through the fractures and the vessel rises to the surface. This method entails a very large amount of diving work, as funnels, etc., have to be cut away and the openings closed and made airtight. Decks have to be strongly shored up and supported.

The conditions of stranding are varied. Assume a large vessel stranded on a rocky bottom on an exposed coast, sustaining such damage that all compartments are filled with water and the vessel appears at first sight to be a hopeless wreck. A diver's survey of the position is made as soon as possible, and at the same time a careful survey is made of all compartments to ascertain whether the water falls in each at the same rate as the tide. Some compartments will generally be found to be holding water; that is to say, the tide does not ebb and flow in them as it does outside. The amount of pumping plant required can thus be gauged easily for compartments under these conditions. When the tide ebbs and flows as it does outside, considerable damage to the outer bottom is indicated, which necessitates extra pumping plant and the patching of the fractures by divers.
                                                                                                (F. Y.)

SALVARSAN or "606," the trade name of dihydrochloride of dioxy-diamino-arsenobenzene, a remedy for syphilis, invented by Paul Ehrlich and introduced to the public in 1910. It is a yellow powder which is prepared for injection into a vein by a rather complicated process. A little later Ehrlich invented a modification, "914" or neosalvarsan, which was much easier to use; and preparations of this type became those most commonly employed until the advent of mapharsen and the antibiotics. Of rather another order were silver salvarsan and neosilver salvarsan, in which the action of arsenic is assisted by that of silver. There was a fairly large variety of arsenobenzene preparations made by different firms. They were sold in Great Britain only after satisfaction of government tests of toxicity and therapeutic activity applied to each batch. In the United States the arsenobenzene preparations became known as arsphenamines. A moderate dose of an arsenobenzene preparation usually caused the germs of syphilis to disappear from the secretions of open sores within a day, and a rapid amelioration of symptoms followed, but it was necessary to treat for 1½ to 2 years or more and to use also either the older remedy, mercury, or the newer one, bismuth.

The arsenobenzene preparations were not tolerated equally well by all patients. In a minute percentage of cases they could cause death by damaging the small vessels of the brain or the kidneys. Other toxic effects were jaundice and an inflammation of the skin (either of which might be fatal) and a variety of minor troubles. Serious effects from arsenobenzene injections were, however, far too rare to counteract their very great advantages. One of the most important of these was the rapidity with which patients were rendered noninfectious. (*See* also VENEREAL DISEASES.)

(L. W. H.; X.)

SALVATION ARMY, a religious philanthropic organization founded by William Booth (*q.v.*), who in 1865 began to hold meetings for preaching in the streets in London and in tents, music halls, theatres and elsewhere.

In 1878 the mission, which had spread beyond London, was reorganized on a quasi-military basis, and the title of the Salvation Army was definitely adopted in June of that year, with William Booth as "general" of the whole body. The spiritual operations of the army rapidly expanded, in spite of much disorderly opposition in some places. In doctrine, the army is in harmony with the main principles of the evangelical bodies, "as embodied in the three creeds of the Church." Its preaching is practical and direct, asseverating the reality of sin and redemption, and the supreme duty of self-sacrifice for the sake of the salvation of others.

Organization.—The army was organized under the general for the time being, who issued all orders and regulations. Large powers devolved upon other officers, such as the chief of the staff, the foreign secretary and the chancellor, who directed affairs from the international headquarters in London. The system of government was autocratic, "unquestioning obedience" being required throughout all ranks. The army was divided, usually in harmony with national boundaries, into territories, each under a territorial commander, with headquarters in the capital of the country. The territories were generally divided into divisions, which included a number of corps, each supporting its own captain and lieutenant. The soldiers or members were drawn from all classes of the community. The property of the army in the United Kingdom was held by the general for the time being, for the benefit of the army exclusively, he being constituted the sole trustee of the property, in the disposal of which and in the appointment of his successor he was placed under the government of a deed poll, executed by Booth while the body was still known as the Christian Mission and enrolled in the court of chancery in Aug. 1878. In other countries various modifications were necessary, but the general's ultimate control was practically assured.

The announcement of the founder's death was accompanied by the intimation that his eldest son, William Bramwell Booth (*q.v.*), formerly his chief of staff, had become the new general. Under the deed poll of 1878, each general appointed his successor under seal, but the name of the person so chosen was not divulged until the proper time. At an international staff council in 1904 a supplementary deed poll was adopted, the principal object of which was to set up machinery for removing from the position any general who proved to be unworthy of confidence and also for the selection of a general by a high council of the army called into being for this purpose, in the event of the position becoming vacant through failure to appoint or other cause. In Jan. 1929 the high council voted to remove General Booth on the ground of incapacity, but Booth carried the issue to the courts. The court decided that the removal was illegal because no hearing had been given the general or his representatives before the vote was taken. On Feb. 13 after such a hearing a second vote had the same result as the first, and the council proceeded to elect Edward J. Higgins, formerly chief of staff, as the new general. Booth intended to continue the fight, but he died in June. In Sept. 1934 Comdr. Evangeline Booth, the founder's daughter, and leader of the army in the U.S., was elected to succeed General Higgins, and assumed command in November.

Extension.—In many quarters it was feared that after the withdrawal of the forceful and picturesque personality who had dominated Salvation Army affairs for a generation, and had raised up a world-wide following from what was originally a despised and derided local effort in the slums of London, the army would decline. World Wars I and II also were a menace to all international organizations. These fears, however, proved to be groundless. The number of adherents steadily increased, and the "field" occupied grew greatly in extent.

New organizations were called into existence, especially for influencing and instructing the young of both sexes. Careful provision was made to ensure a constant replenishment of officers

by means of colleges for the training of cadets. Each year young men and women are trained for army work, to which they have to devote the whole of their time. Congresses on national and international lines are held frequently for the instruction and encouragement of officers; and constantly increasing use is made of the printing press.

Social Work.—The social work, which received its first great impetus in 1890 with the publication of *In Darkest England and the Way Out,* by William Booth, became not only more extensive but more varied in character. This work from the first was regarded by the army leaders as an organized warfare against social evils in order to clear the way for evangelization.

It was realized that the physical and environmental condition of many of the people, especially in great cities, made it extremely difficult for them to apprehend the spiritual message which the army had to deliver. Therefore various social activities arose, diverse in character but all actuated by the same purpose, from the provision of free breakfasts and night shelters to the settlement of people in overseas dominions. This last was a department of work characterized by careful selection of the emigrants, and was coupled, particularly in the case of the young, with training beforehand and effective provision for future care, while work was assured upon arrival. The efforts of the army in getting men to work on the land, both in England and overseas, called forth many commendations from statesmen and others.

Rescue work among women was one of the earliest social tasks to which the army set its hand. In this work Florence Booth, wife of Gen. Bramwell Booth, was the responsible leader from its inception until 1912. Maternity work was carried out by the army's ministering women, and for this in 1918 the army received a grant from the British government—the first state subsidy made to the army in the country of its origin. In other lands also social work proceeded, adapted to the different national conditions and needs, and often commended and assisted by the governments concerned. This was true also of eastern lands; thus, settlements for criminals were established in India, and leper colonies in the Dutch Indies.

Spiritual Character of the Work.—The army maintained its original character as a body of spiritual witness and aggressive evangelism. In theory and creed it is at one in almost every respect with orthodox evangelical belief, but its methods—its realistic presentation of religion, and its use of various constraining means to bring people to salvation—distinguish it from other religious bodies. It continues to lay the greatest emphasis upon the need for conversion, preceded by penitence, and followed by growth in holiness. The people gathered into its ranks are cared for by its officers and trained in a real separation from the world and devotion to Christ. They are set to work immediately with a definite objective, their zeal is employed in the winning of others, and public testimony is required from them, however unlearned or backward in religious experience they may be.

A large place in the army's endeavours is given to music. In every country the band—usually a brass band—is a feature of army work. The strains of such a band, reaching farther than the human voice, draw numbers within earshot of the army's message who would otherwise not be attracted. The army also made use of improvisations of various kinds, not only because in this way public attention is more likely to be caught, but because these methods prevent the officers from falling into the conventional and the ordinary.

The army exacts a high standard of behaviour from its adherents. In the series of *Orders and Regulations* for officers and for the rank and file, definite guidance is given even in the smaller matters of everyday conduct. Officers accept a relative poverty, being content to receive sufficient for their simple needs. There are contributory funds from which they receive allowances on retirement, and from which provision is made for widows and orphans. Marriages are solemnized "under the flag," and children of members are dedicated to become soldiers or officers in the "war." Officers wear a regulation uniform, which it is not permissible for the individual to vary. The uniform is regarded as a means of confessing to the world the fact of separation and consecration, as opening the way to many opportunities of usefulness which would not otherwise appear, and as making possible instant recognition and fellowship among Salvationists themselves. One of the great principles of the army, firmly adhered to, is that women have absolute parity of privilege, position and dignity.

Salvation Army funds are raised from the voluntary offerings of the corps, from open-air and other collections, from the profits on publications and general trading, and from friends interested in evangelical and charitable work. The financial statements of the various funds are annually published, certified by public accountants.

Reports and statistics of the spiritual and social operations of the army are given in the annual *Salvation Army Year Book* and in the *War Cry* and other publications issued at headquarters (Queen Victoria street, London, E. C. 4).

George Lyndon Carpenter was elected general in 1939, Albert Orsborn succeeded him in 1946 and in 1954 he retired and Wilfred Kitching became the seventh general.

The army had corps and outposts in 85 countries and territories throughout the world in 1954. Its 17,002 corps included 26,775 commissioned officers, 104,778 local officers (laymen) and thousands of soldiers and adherents.

BIBLIOGRAPHY.—William Booth, *Orders and Regulations for Field Officers* (London, 1886), *Orders and Regulations for Soldiers*, rev. ed. (London, 1927), *In Darkest England and the Way Out* (London, 1890), *A Talk With W. E. Gladstone at His Own Fireside About the Salvation Army* (London, 1897); Bramwell Booth, *Servants of All* (London, 1899), *Echoes and Memories* (London, 1925); R. T. Booth, *Salvation Soldiery* (London, 1882); F. St. G. de L. Booth-Tucker, *The Life of Catherine Booth*, 2 vol. (London, 1893); G. S. Railton, *Heathen England and What to Do for It* (London, 1877), *Twenty-one Years' the Salvation Army* (London, 1890); A. White, *Truth About the Salvation Army* (London, 1892), *The Great Idea* (London, 1909); T. F. G. Coates, *The Prophet of the Poor: The Life Story of General Booth* (London, 1905); H. Begbie, *Broken Earthenware* (London, 1909) and *Life of General William Booth*, 2 vol. (London, New York, 1920); F. E. Booth, *Powers of Salvation Army Officers* (London, 1923), *Extracts From General Booth's Journal, 1921–22* (London, 1925); St. John Ervine, *God's Soldier: General William Booth*, 2 vol. (London and Toronto, 1934; New York, 1935); J. Manson, *The Salvation Army and the Public*, 2nd ed. (London, 1908). (X.)

THE UNITED STATES

The Salvation Army began its operations officially in March 1880 in the United States, the first country to which evangelists were sent from England. A family of converts had gone to Philadelphia in 1879 and started evangelical services. At their request Gen. William Booth sent Commissioner George Scott Railton and seven women assistants as pioneer officers. The original staff soon found it impossible to cope with the success attending their efforts, and more help was sent from England. The U.S., however, soon began to produce its own officers, a development which grew through the years until by the 1950s four training colleges were devoted exclusively to maintaining the requisite supply of officers. These send out annually into the field young men and women as officer reinforcements, in addition to providing help for the missionary countries of the world.

After having served in England and as national leader in Canada, Evangeline Booth, daughter of the founder, William Booth, became national commander for the U.S. in 1904. For 30 years she continued to direct Salvation Army work, much progress being made in the extension of welfare services. During World War I specialized services organized for the nation at war endeared the organization to the U.S. public, and Evangeline Booth was awarded the distinguished service medal.

Commander Booth was succeeded by Commissioner E. J. Parker when she was elected general in 1934 and became international leader of the organization. Commissioner Donald McMillan became national commander in 1953.

Again in World War II the services of the Salvation Army, which became a participant in the United Service organizations (U.S.O.), were helpful in maintaining morale among the fighting forces, and during the Korean war this service was continued.

Activities of the Salvation Army in the U.S. include sheltering, evangelistic meetings, rehabilitation centres, care for the unmarried mother and her child, children's homes, clinics, family welfare, aid to prisoners and their families, free employment bureaus, search for missing relatives, camps and summer outings for women and children, and social and religious instruction.

In 1952 the army held 91,854 meetings on street corners in the U.S. In its social service program 35,992 patients were treated in 8 clinics and dispensaries; 1,349 missing persons were located; 34 maternity homes and hospitals for unwed mothers cared for 9,384 women and children; and 16,874 mothers and children were sent to summer camps. A total of 108 men's social service centres provided shelter and work for 32,610 men.

In the field of prison work, 8,449 prisoners were assisted on discharge and given employment in 1952; 1,988 prisoners were paroled in care of the Salvation Army.

During 1953 emergency service was rendered by the Salvation Army in connection with the tornadoes at Waco (Tex.), Flint (Mich.), and Worcester (Mass.), and in other areas where emergencies of disastrous proportion took place. (Do. McM.)

SALVEMINI, GAETANO (1873–), Italian historian, was born in Molfetta in Sept. 1873. In 1902 he became professor of mediaeval and modern history at Messina university. He then went to Pisa university and in 1917 was appointed to the chair of history at Florence university. Historical works by Salvemini included *Magnati e popolani nel commune di Firenze dal 1280 al 1295* (1899), *La Rivoluzione francese 1789–92* (1906), *Mazzini* (1905) and *L'Italia e gl'Imperi Centrali dal 1871 al 1915*. He edited the Liberal newspaper *L'Unità* (1911–21).

Before World War I he vigorously criticized the Socialists for halfhearted social work and attacked Giovanni Giolitti's electoral methods. During the war he was a leading advocate of Italian diplomatic moderation. He was a member of the Italian parliament, 1919–21.

After the fascists captured power, however, his political activity was made impossible, and, being suspect, he was in constant personal danger. In June 1925 he was arrested in Rome and taken to Florence, where he was charged on the hearsay evidence of a printer with complicity in the production of an antifascist newspaper, *Non-Mollare*. His case was postponed till July 1925, when he was provisionally released. In Oct. 1925 he left the country, going to London and later to the United States. In 1940 he became a naturalized citizen of the U.S. He was appointed in 1934 Lauro de Bosis lecturer in history of Italian civilization at Harvard university, Cambridge, Mass., a post he held until he became professor emeritus in 1948.

His later works included *The Fascist Dictatorship in Italy* (1927), *What To Do With Italy* (1943), *Historian and Scientist* (1939) and *Prelude to World War Two* (1949).

SALVI, NICOLA (NICCOLÒ) (1697–1751), Italian sculptor, born in 1697 in Rome, began in the studio of the painter Niccolò Ricciolini and subsequently studied architecture under Antonio Canevari. In 1732 he competed unsuccessfully for the façade of S. Giovanni in Laterano, Rome, but in the same year his project for the Trevi fountain was chosen in preference to those of a great number of competitors. This is the work on which Salvi's reputation rests. Most of his energy was absorbed by it. He was responsible not only for the over-all design but also for the details of the decoration and the program of the statuary. After Salvi's death Giuseppe Pannini finished the fountain in 1762, somewhat altering the original scheme. The idea of combining palace front and fountain was derived from a project by Pietro da Cortona, but the grand pageantry of the central triumphal arch with its mythological and allegorical figures, of the natural rock formations and of the gushing water was Salvi's. This queen of fountains is the swan song of the Roman Baroque era.

Salvi also executed minor works in churches and has the doubtful merit (with Luigi Vanvitelli) of having enlarged G. L. Bernini's Palazzo Odescalchi. He died in 1751. (RF. W.)

SALVIA, a large genus belonging to the family Labiatae (*q.v.*), containing about 550 species in the temperate and warmer regions of both hemispheres. The name is derived from the Latin *salvo*, from the healing properties of the garden sage, *S. officinalis*, which has been known for at least three centuries and which has been cultivated in kitchen gardens for the grayish-green wrinkled leaves that are commonly used in flavouring meats. *S. verbenaca* is found in Great Britain in dry pastures and waste places, as is also *S. pratensis*.

Many native species of *Salvia* occur in western North America, especially in California, where 15 species are found. Among these are *S. carduacea* (thistle sage), cultivated for its thistlelike, white-woolly foliage and blue flowers; *S. columbariae* and related, mostly Mexican, species are the source of chia.

Some Californian sages are important bee plants, among them the black sage (*S. mellifera*) and the bigflower sage (*S. grandiflora*).

Some of the salvias are among the most showy of soft-wooded plants, the blossoms being of a bright glowing scarlet. A useful species is *S. splendens*, a Brazilian shrub, commonly called scarlet sage. Treated as a tender annual, it is one of the most popular bedding plants in American gardens.

There are other very ornamental species of easy growth, increased by cuttings in spring, and succeeding well in ordinary rich loamy soil.

SALVIAN, a Christian writer of the 5th century, was born probably at Cologne (*De gub. Dei*, vi, 8, 13) some time between 400 and 405. He was educated at the school of Trèves and seems to have been brought up as a Christian. His writings show legal knowledge.

He married Palladia, the daughter of heathen parents, Hypatius and Quieta, whose displeasure he incurred by persuading his wife to retire with him to a distant monastery, which was almost certainly that founded by St. Honoratus at Lerins.

It was presumably at Lerins that Salvian made the acquaintance of Honoratus (d. 429), Hilary of Arles (d. 449) and Eucherius of Lyons (d. 449). That he was a friend of the former and wrote an account of his life is learned from Hilary (*Vita Hon.*, ap. Migne, l, 1260).

To Eucherius' two sons, Salonius and Veranus, he acted as tutor in consort with Vincent of Lerins. Salvian continued his friendly intercourse with both father and sons long after the latter had left his care; it was to Salonius (then a bishop) that he wrote his explanatory letter just after the publication of his treatise *Ad ecclesiam;* and to the same prelate a few years later he dedicated his great work, the *De gubernatione Dei*. Salvian spent the last years of his life at Marseilles (Gennadius, ap. Migne, lviii, 1099). It has been conjectured that Salvian paid a visit to Carthage, but this is a mere inference based on the minute details he gives of the state of this city just before its fall (*De gub.*, vii, viii). He seems to have been still living at Marseilles when Gennadius wrote under the papacy of Gelasius (492–496).

Of Salvian's writings there are extant *De gubernatione Dei* (more correctly *De praesenti judicio*) and *Ad ecclesiam*, and a series of nine letters. The *De gubernatione*, Salvian's greatest work, was written between 439 and 450; it furnishes a valuable if prejudiced description of life in 5th-century Gaul. Salvian deals with the same problem that had moved the eloquence of Augustine and Orosius. Why were these miseries falling on the empire? Could it be, as the pagans said, because the age had forsaken its old gods? or as the semipagan creed of some Christians taught, that God did not constantly overrule the world he had created (i, 1)? He concludes that the misery of the Roman world is all attributable to the neglect of God's commandments and the terrible sins of every class of society. It is difficult to credit the universal wickedness adduced by Salvian, especially in face of the contemporary testimony of Symmachus, Ausonius and Sidonius. Salvian was a 5th-century socialist of the most extreme type, and a zealous ascetic who exaggerated, albeit unconsciously, the faults that he desired to eradicate.

The *Ad ecclesiam* was first printed in Sichard's *Antidoton* (Basel, 1528), the *De gubernatione* by Brassican (Basel, 1530). Salvian's works are reprinted (after Baluze) in Migne's *Cursus patrologiae*, ser. lat. vol. liii. For bibliography, *see* T. G. Schoenemann's *Bibliotheca patrum* (ii, 823), and the prefaces to the editions of C. Halm (*Monum. Germ.*, 1877) and F. Pauly (Vienna, *Corp. scr. eccl. Lat.*, 1883). *See* also S. Dill, *Roman Society in the Last Century of the Western Empire*, new ed. (1906).

SALVINI, TOMMASO (1829–1915), Italian actor, was born at Milan on Jan. 1, 1829. His father and mother were both actors, and Salvini first appeared when he was barely 14 years of age as Pasquino in Goldoni's *Donne curiose*. In 1847 he joined the company of Adelaide Ristori, and with her he played the title role in Alfieri's *Oreste* at the Teatro Valle in Rome. He fought in the cause of Italian independence in 1849; otherwise his life was an unbroken series of successes in his art. He acted frequently in England and made five visits to America, his first in 1873 and his last in 1889. In 1886 he played there Othello to the Iago of Edwin Booth.

Apart from Othello, which he played for the first time at Vicenza in June 1856, his most famous impersonations included Conrad in Paolo Giacometti's *La Morte civile*, Egisto in Alfieri's *Merope*, Saul in Alfieri's *Saul*, Paolo in Silvio Pellico's *Francesca da Rimini*, Oedipus in Nicolini's play of that name, and Macbeth and King Lear.

Salvini retired from the stage in 1890, but in Jan. 1902 he took part in the celebration in Rome of Adelaide Ristori's 80th birthday.

See his *Ricordi, anedotti ed impressioni* (Milan, 1895); *Leaves From the Autobiography of Tommaso Salvini* (London, 1893); G. Piccini, *Vita aneddotica di Tommaso Salvini* (Florence, 1908).

SALVINIA, a small genus of fern allies belonging to the Salviniaceae family of the class Filicinae, or true ferns, and consisting of small floating aquatic plants that are widely distributed in tropical regions. One species (*S. rotundifolia*), of a total of about ten species, is commonly grown in aquariums and has escaped to ponds and marshes in parts of southern United States.

(J. M. BL.)

SALWEEN, a district in the Tenasserim division of Burma. Area, 2,582 sq.mi. Pop. (1941) 56,878, of whom more than 50,000 were aboriginal tribesmen (mostly Karens and some Shans). Almost the whole district is a maze of mountains intersected by deep ravines, the only level land of any considerable extent being found in the valley of the Yunzalin, while the country is covered with dense forest, of which portions are reserved. The district is drained by three principal rivers, the Salween, Yunzalin and Bilin, fed by mountain torrents. The Yunzalin, which rises in the extreme north, is navigable with some difficulty in the dry season as far as Papun; the Bilin is not navigable within the limits of the district except by small boats and rafts. The district headquarters are at Papun. The rainfall is heavy. A considerable trade is carried on with Siam by bridle paths across the mountains.

SALWEEN, a river of Tibet, China (Yunnan) and Burma. This river, called Nam Kong by the Shans, Thanlwin by the Burmese, Lu Kiang, Nu Kiang or Lu Tzu Kiang by the Chinese, is the longest river in Burma and one of the wildest and most picturesque streams in the world. It rises in Tibet south of the Kuen-lun, and is thus a much longer river than the Irrawaddy. From the time it leaves Tibet it has a very narrow basin, and for long stretches has no other affluents than the mountain torrents from the hills, which rise from 3,000 to 5,000 or 6,000 ft. above the level of the river bed. In the dry season the banks are alternate stretches of blinding white, fine sand, and a chaos of huge boulders, masses and slabs of rock, with here and there, usually where a tributary enters, long stretches of shingle. In the rains all these disappear, and the water laps against forest trees and the abrupt slope of the hills. The average difference between high and low water level of the Salween throughout the Shan states is between 50 and 60 ft., and in some places it is as much as 90.

There are many rapids, caused by reefs of rock running across the bed, or by a sudden fall of from one to several feet, which produce very rough water below the swift glide; but the most dangerous places for navigation are where a point juts out into the stream, and the current, thrown back, causes a violent double backwater. Nevertheless, long stretches of the river, extending to scores of miles, are habitually navigated by native boats. The current is extremely variable, from ½ m.p.h. to ten knots. Launches ply regularly from Moulmein to the mouth of the Yunzalin, in lower Burma. The worst part of the whole Salween, so far as is known, is the gorge between the mouth of the Yunzalīn and Kyaukhnyat. It is quite certain that steam launches could ply over very long sections of the river above that, perhaps as far as the Kaw ferry, or even the Kunlong ferry. In British territory, however, there are very few settlements on the river itself, and frequently the ferry villages are built 1,000 ft. above the river.

The Chinese believe the Salween valley to be deadly to all strangers, but it is in Chinese territory—particularly in the Lu Kiang, or Möng Hkö state—that there is the largest population on the river until Lower Burma is reached. A description of the Salween resolves itself into a list of the ferries at which it can be crossed, for no one marches up the river. The river is bridged by the Chinese on the main route from Tēng Yüeh (Momien) and Bhamo to Tali-fu. Native boats can ply from Kyodan S., and light draught steamers ascend as far as Shwegūn, 63 m. from Moulmein.

The Salween enters the sea in the Gulf of Martaban by two mouths, one to the north and one to the south of Bilugyun island. The southern mouth is the more important, and is the one by which ocean-going craft approach the port of Moulmein. The Salween cuts the British Shan States nearly in half, and is a very formidable natural obstacle. It seems probable, however, that long stretches of it can be opened to trade. It is certainly no less navigable than the Middle Mekong or the Yangtsze-kiang above I-chang.

SALYES (Gr. Σάλυες; also SALLYES, SALYI, SALLUVII), a people occupying the plain south of the Druentia (Durance) between the Rhone and the Alps. According to Strabo (iv. p. 203) the older Greeks called them Ligyes, and their territory *Ligustikē*. In 154 B.C. the inhabitants of Massalia, who had been connected with the Romans by ties of friendship since the second Punic war, appealed for aid against the Oxybii and Decietes (or Deciates). These people, called by Livy (*Epit.* 47) "transalpine Ligurians," were perhaps two smaller tribes included under the general name of Salyes. They were defeated by Quintus Opimius. In 125–124 B.C. hostilities broke out between the Romans and the Salyes from the same cause. Gaius Sextius Calvinus (123–122 B.C.), subdued the Salyes, destroyed their chief town, and founded near its ruins the colony of Aquae Sextiae (Aix). Part of their territory was handed over to Massaliots. From this time the Salyes practically disappear from history.

For ancient authorities *see* A. Holder, *Altceltischer Sprachschatz*, ii. (1904).

SALZA, HERMANN VON (c. 1170–1239), master of the Teutonic Order, and councillor of the emperor Frederick II., entered the Teutonic Order in early life, became very intimate with Frederick II., took part in the expedition to Damietta in 1221, and accompanied the emperor on the crusade of 1228. About 1210 he was appointed master of the Teutonic Order, and in 1226 received the province of Kulm from Conrad I., duke of Masovia, in return for help against the Prussians. In 1230 the conquest of Prussia was begun by the Order, although not under his immediate leadership. In 1225 he reconciled Valdemar II., king of Denmark, with Henry I., count of Schwerin, and thus won again the land on the right bank of the Elbe for the Empire, and the recognition of imperial superiority over Denmark. Trusted by Pope Gregory IX. and the emperor alike, he brought about the treaty of San Germano between them in 1230, was the only witness when they met in conference at Anagni in the same year, and it was he who, in 1235, induced Frederick's son, Henry, to submit to his father. He died on March 19, 1239 at Barletta in Apulia, and was buried there in the chapel of his Order.

See A. Koch, *Hermann von Salza, Meister des deutschen Ordens* (Leipzig, 1885).

SALZBRUNN, a watering-place in the Prussian province of Silesia, Germany, at the foot of the Riesengebirge, 30 mi. S.W. of Breslau, by rail to Waldenburg. Pop. (1933) 13,761. It consists of Ober-, Neu- and Nieder-Salzbrunn, and manufactures glass, wire goods and yarn. Its alkalo-saline springs were known as early as 1316. Gerhart Hauptmann was born there in 1862.

SALZBURG, a province of Austria, seized by Germany in March 1938, covers an area of 2,762 sq.mi. It includes from south to north parts of the following lithological belts of the Alps, the crystalline, the slate and schist, the limestone High Alps, and the *flysch* zones. The first named extends from the glacier-capped Hohe Tauern and southern slopes of the Niedere Tauern to the line of the Pinzgau eastward to the Mandling pass. This is a region much dissected by tributaries of the Salzach and characterised by forestry and pastoral pursuits. The most important valley is that of the Gastein leading to a col between the Hohe and Niedere Tauern ranges and followed by a railway to Carinthia. North of this belt is a wedge-shaped mass of slates and schist, with softer outlines and lower forested heights, which is in turn replaced by the lake-strewn plateau of Dachstein limestone, split into several detached blocks, *e.g.*, the eastern end of the Kitzbühl Alps, the Salzburg Alps (Birnhorn, 8,637 ft.), the Reiteralpe and the glacier-capped Schönfeldspitze mass (8,708 ft.). Part of the Dachstein group also belongs to Salzburg. Drainage is effected mainly by the Salzach which in its upper course follows a west-east marshy valley (Pinzgau) along the foot of the Hohe Tauern, at the junction of crystallines and slates, to Schwarzach St. Veit, where it takes a transverse course through a wider and more fertile valley (Ponzgau), breaking through a narrow pass between the Hagengebirge and the Tennegebirge and reaching the foreland at Salzburg; the upper waters of the Enns and Mur take the drainage of the eastern half of the Niedere Tauern. Salzburg is noted for its numerous beautiful lakes and the many magnificent falls on its rivers, *e.g.*, the four Krimmler falls, together 2,085 ft. high, the most important falls in the Eastern Alps and the Tauern fall (660 ft.).

The enclosed basins of the higher mountain districts experience very hard winters and settlement in them is thin and confined to the sunny slopes and alluvial fans. About 16% of the total area is unproductive and of the remainder some 11% is given over to crops and 10% to meadows. Forestry and pastoral activities, aided by a wealth of Alpine pasture (some 30% of the area) are most important. Mineral resources include: salt at Hallein, copper near Bischofshofen, iron-ore at Werfen, marble (Adnet) and small quantities of gold, silver and arsenic. The absence of coal is compensated by the rich stores of water, from which electrical power is developed at Lend Gastein, Bärenwerk, etc., yet industry is only moderately progressive. Catering for visitors to the spas, scenic resorts · and centres for winter-sports is the most remunerative industry. Apart from Salzburg (*q.v.*), the capital, the population of 267,440 (1939) is rurally distributed, mainly along the valleys and chief lines of traffic, and no other town reaches 10,000 inhabitants. The people are of German stock and mainly Roman Catholic in religion, with a high standard of education. In 1938 Salzburg was made a German *gau*.

See F. Martin, *Kunstgeschichte von Salzburg* (Vienna, 1924) and E. Spengler, *Geologischer Führer durch die Salzburger Alpen und das Salzkammergut* (Berlin, 1924); E. Kriechbaum, *Salzburg und das Oberdonauland* (Berlin, 1938).

SALZBURG, the capital of the province of Salzburg, Austria, seized by Germany in March 1938, lies on both banks of the Salzach where this river leaves its narrow valley through the limestone Alps and enters the Alpine foreland.

The situation is important economically and strategically, for here several types of physical region, with differing agricultural possibilities, meet and the Orient route from Germany through Munich joins the Orient route from France through Switzerland and branches along the Salzach valley and through the Hohe Tauern to Carinthia and Italy. The site has been occupied since pre-Roman time, the original settlement being replaced by a Roman trading town (*Juvavum*) which was sacked by the barbarians (477). The modern city grew up around the monastery and bishopric founded here about 700 by St. Rupert of Worms, who preached Christianity in the district at the invitation of its ruler Duke Theodo of Bavaria, and its history from that time is closely bound up with that of the see. The present name, due to the local abundance of salt, appears first in 816 by which time it had been raised to an archbishopric. Its archbishops gained in temporal power and dignity and were made imperial princes by Rudolf of Hapsburg in 1278.

Relations between the ecclesiastical rulers on the one hand and the nobles and people on the other were always difficult, *e.g.*, during the Peasants' War of 1525–26, quelled with the aid of the Swabian League, and contributing to a reaction against the church when Salzburg became a stronghold of resistance to the Reformation. Persecution was rife and Protestant citizens were driven from the town. Nevertheless, the movement grew and in 1731–32, aided by the intervention of Frederick William I. of Prussia, 30,000 people sold their possessions and left the see, 6,000 of them leaving the capital. By the peace of Lunéville (1802) the see was secularized and given to the archduke of Austria. Following the peace of Pressburg (1805) it fell to Austria but four years later passed to Bavaria, returning to Austria in 1816 with the exception of a small portion on the left bank of the Salzach. In 1849 it became a crownland, several of its districts being transferred to Tirol, and remained so until 1918, when it became part of the Austrian republic. With the rest of Austria it was annexed to Germany by Hitler in March 1938.

Its ecclesiastical buildings include 8 convents and 25 churches, the majority interesting from their antiquity, architecture or associations. Of these, the 17th century cathedral, one of the largest and most perfect specimens of the Renaissance style in the Germanic countries, is on the model of St. Peter's at Rome. Though situated in the old town it is bounded on three sides by open squares, which permit its beauties to be appreciated. Other buildings of note are the old and new residences of the archbishops, the latter occupied by government offices, the present palace, the 15th century town-hall and the Mozart house and museum. The only relic of the university (1623–1810) is a theological seminary. By the suppression of its university Salzburg has been prevented from making that contribution to Austrian culture that its importance as an administrative and spiritual centre leads one to expect.

Salzburg has had a heavy seasonal tourist traffic, favoured by a healthy climate, delightful scenic surroundings and excellent music.

Its manufactures include brewing, book-binding, musical instruments and marble wares and light iron goods.

Pop. (1939) of the *Reichsgau* of Salzburg was 267,440; and of the town, 79,264.

SALZGITTER, a town in the province of Niedersachsen, Germany, on the Mittelland canal and the Hildesheim-Börssum railway, 12 mi. S.W. of Brunswick. Pop. (1939) 11,661. It was formerly only a small town, known chiefly for its salt baths; however, after 1937 it was enlarged into a model housing settlement as the residence for workers in the newly created Hermann Göring Coal and Iron works factories nearby. Coal and coke for smelting ore was brought cheaply and easily from the Ruhr by the Mittelland canal, opened in 1937.

SALZKAMMERGUT is a mountainous district of Austria forming the drainage area of the Traun and its tributaries above Gmunden. Originally its name (literally "salt-exchequer property") and its economic importance were derived from the valuable salt deposits, worked from prehistoric times at Hallstätt and Aussee, but although these are still valuable the region is rapidly developing as a health and tourist resort. Belonging to the eastern Alps it contains the Dachstein group (Dachstein, 9,830 ft.) with the most easterly glaciers of the Alps, the Totes Gebirge (Grosser Priel, 8,248 ft.), the Höllengebirge (Höllenkogel, 6,109 ft.), the Ischler and Sensen groups. Among its lakes are Traun, Hallstätt, St. Wolfgang and Atter, largest in Austria (18 sq.mi., 1,527 ft. above sea-level, 560 ft. deep), each over-shadowed by forested heights. The district embraced parts of the Austrian provinces of Styria, Salzburg and Upper Austria, and the occupations of its population, apart from those suggested above, are cattle-rearing, forestry and the development of electricity. The towns are small, along the valleys and lake shores. Among them Gmunden (*q.v.*) is the chief, while Hallstätt is famous for its museum of local finds illustrative of the cultural period to which it gave its name. Germany annexed the district in 1938.

SAMAIN, ALBERT VICTOR (1858–1900), French poet, was born at Lille on April 4, 1858. He was educated at the lycée of that town, and on leaving it entered a bank as a clerk. He enjoyed no literary associations, and his talent developed slowly

in solitude. About 1884 Samain went to Paris, having obtained a clerkship in the Préfecture de la Seine, which he held for most of his life. His earliest volume of poems, *Au Jardin de l'infante*, led to the sudden recognition of his talent, and to applause from critics of widely different schools. In 1897 this book was reprinted in a more popular form, with the addition of a section entitled *L'Urne penchée*. Samain's second volume, *Aux flancs du vase,* appeared in 1898. His health began to fail and he withdrew to the country, where he died, in the neighbourhood of the village of Magny-les-Hameaux, on Aug. 18, 1900. A third volume of his poems, *Le Chariot d'or,* appeared after his death, with a lyrical drama, *Polyphème* (1901), which was produced at the Théâtre de l'Oeuvre in 1904. Samain's natural life was patiently spent in squalid conditions; he escaped from them into an imaginative world of the most exquisite refinement.

See also R. Doumic, "Trois Poètes," in the *Revue des deux mondes* (Oct. 1900); L. Bocquet, *Albert Samain, sa vie, son oeuvre* (1905); and E. W. Gosse, *French Profiles* (1905); F. Gohin, *L'Oeuvre poétique d'Albert Samain, 1858–1900* (1919); G. Bonneau, *A. Samain, poète Symboliste* (1925).

SAMANA RANGE, mountain ridge in the Kohat district of the North-West Frontier Province of Pakistan, commanding the south boundary of Tirah. The ridge lies between the Khanki valley on the north and the Miranzai valley on the south, and extends for some 30 mi. W. from Hangu to the Samana Suk. It is some 6,000 to 7,000 ft. high. Beyond the Samana Suk lies the pass, known as the Chagru Kotal, across which the Tirah Expedition marched in 1897. On the opposite hill on the other side of this road is the famous position of Dargai (*see* TIRAH: *Campaign*). After the Miranzai Expedition of 1891 this range was occupied by British troops and eleven posts were established along its crest, the two chief posts being Fort Lockhart and Fort Gulistan. In 1897 all the forts on the Samana were attacked by the Orakzais, and this and the Afridi attack on the Khyber pass were the two chief causes of the Tirah Expedition. When Lord Curzon reorganized the frontier in 1900, British garrisons were withdrawn from most of the Samana forts, which were later held by a corps of tribal police 450 strong, called the Samana Rifles.

SAMANIDS, the first great native dynasty which arose in Persia after the Arab conquest. In the 8th century Saman, a Persian noble of Balkh, who was a close friend of the Arab governor of Khurasan, Asad ibn 'Abdullah, was converted from Zoroastrianism to Islam. His son Asad, named after Asad ibn 'Abdullah, had four sons who rendered distinguished service to the caliph al-Ma'mun. In return they all received provinces: Nuh obtained Samarkand; Ahmad, Ferghana; Yahya, Shash; and Ilyas, Herat. In 875 Ahmad's son Nasr was recognized by the caliph al-Mu'tamid as governor of Transoxiana. He was succeeded in 892 by his brother Isma'il, who overthrew the Saffarids (*q.v.*) in Khurasan and the Zaidites of Tabaristan and thus, though remaining nominally a provincial governor under the caliph of Baghdad, established an almost independent rule over Transoxiana and eastern Persia, with Bukhara as his capital.

The descendants and successors of Isma'il, almost all renowned for the impulse that they gave both to the patriotic feelings and the national poetry of modern Persia (*see* PERSIAN LITERATURE), were Ahmad ibn Isma'il (907–914); Nasr II, ibn Ahmad, the patron and friend of the great poet Rudagi (914–943); Nuh I, ibn Nasr (943–954); 'Abd ul-Malik I, ibn Nuh (954–961); Mansur I, ibn Nuh, whose vizier Bal'ami translated Tabari's universal history into Persian (961–976); Nuh II, ibn Mansur, whose court poet Dakiki began the Shahnama (976–997); Mansur II, ibn Nuh (997–999); and 'Abd ul-Malik II, ibn Nuh (999). Under their government, which was organized on a loosely centralized feudal system, the provinces of Transoxiana and Khurasan attained a high degree of prosperity. The expansion of their industry and commerce is attested by the use of Samanid silver dirhems as currency all over the north of Asia, and they have been found in great numbers in Pomerania, Sweden and Norway, brought by Russian traders. The later interruption of the northern trade routes was a factor in weakening the dynasty; and it succumbed eventually to the internal feuds and rivalries of the nobles and to the pressure of the rising Turkish powers in central

Asia and Afghanistan.

Under Mansur I a Turkish slave, Alptagin, formerly commander of 'Abd ul-Malik's guard at Bukhara, had to flee for refuge to the mountainous regions of Ghazni, where he established a semi-independent rule, to which, after his death in 977, his son-in-law Sabuktagin, likewise a former Turkish slave, succeeded. Nuh II, in order to retain at least a nominal sway over those Afghan territories, confirmed him in his position and invested Sabuktagin's son Mahmud with the governorship of Khurasan, in reward for the help they had given him in his struggles with a confederation of disaffected nobles under the leadership of Fa'ik. During this conflict, the greater part of Transoxiana was occupied by the Turkish Kara-khanids, whose chief, Boghra Khan, occupied Bukhara for a short time in 992. Sabuktagin died in the same year as Nuh II (997); and Mahmud (see MAHMUD OF GHAZNI), confronted with an internal contest against his own brother Isma'il, had to withdraw for a short time from Khurasan. This interval sufficed for Fa'ik, supported by a Kara-khanid force under the Ilek khan Nasr I, to concentrate power in his own hands and to involve Mansur II in a conflict with Mahmud. After the deposition of Mansur, who was suspected of intending to come to an agreement with Mahmud, the latter took possession of Khurasan. A few months later, the Ilek khan Nasr marched on Bukhara and carried 'Abd ul-Malik and his relatives into captivity. The last prince of the Samanid house, Muntasir, a bold warrior and a poet of no mean talent, carried on guerrilla warfare for some years against both Mahmud and the Kara-khanids, till he was assassinated in 1005. (See CALIPHATE and PERSIA: History.)

See W. Barthold, *Turkestan Down to the Mongol Invasion* (London, 1928); S. Lane-Poole, *Muhammadan Dynasties* (Westminster, 1894).

SAMANIEGO, FELIX MARIA DE (1745–1801), Spanish fabulist. His *Fábulas en verso castellano* (1781–84), imitations or translations for the most part of Phaedrus, La Fontaine and Gay, are excellent of their kind.

SAMARA (now KUIBYSHEV), a region of the Russian S.F.S.R., lying east of the Volga river, except for the territory enclosed in the great Volga loop, and south of the Tatar A.S.S.R. Its southern boundary lies between the Great Irgiz and the railway from Saratov to Uralsk, and runs parallel to the latter to the boundary of the Kazakstan S.S.R., on the Obschiy Syrt plateau. Chkalov region and the Bashkir A.S.S.R. lie to the east.

South of the Volga loop (Samarskaya Luka) is a low flat steppe recently emerged from the post-Pliocene Aral-Caspian basin, while from the Samara river to the Sok are Permian formations. The region is a transition area between the black earth and the salt steppe types of soil. The most fertile black earth, with a humus content of 18%, lies to the northeast of the region in the lyesso-steppe area—*i.e.*, steppe with patches of forest, here mainly oak. Between the Samara river and the Moksha, except for a patch north and south along the eastern part of the latter stream, the black earth is of poorer humus content, of a sandy type, and patches of salted soil appear, especially near the Volga. South of the Great Irgiz river the soil is salt steppe, and there are salt marshes. South of the Samara river there is no forest, but the land in the loop and to the north of it is forested, and there is a patch of forest on the north bank, west of Buzuluk.

The region is undergoing a process of rapid desiccation. It has an arid climate, the rainfall varying from 8 to 16 in. per annum, mostly falling in spring and summer in heavy showers, so that the runoff is excessive and only the surface becomes saturated. The prevailing winds are from the northeast, dry and strong, and blowing with great violence in winter, so that snow does not lie and the ground is exposed to severe winter frost. The average July temperature at Kuibyshev is 70.4° F. and January 9.3° F. An added disadvantage is the liability to years of excessive drought such as 1911 and 1921. Winter lasts for five months and rain falls on an average of 95 days per annum, 34 of which are in June–August. Thunderstorms are frequent in June and July and, if accompanied by dry hail, may ruin the crops.

Diminution in the spring rainfall causes the disastrous famines to which the region is subject. Of the inhabitants, 90% are occupied in agriculture, depending on the crops for sustenance and for purchase of necessities. Bad harvests, therefore, such as those of 1911 and 1921, bring disaster. In 1921 great numbers died of starvation and starvation diseases and others fled from the region, many to perish on the road. Bands of starving children, whose parents had succumbed first in their efforts to feed the children, penetrated even as far as the Caucasus. Livestock diminished, and when the weakened survivors of the terrible period faced the next year there was a shortage of everything, from seeds and instruments to working cattle.

The area subsequently revived to an extraordinary degree, an evidence of the fertility of its famous black soil. Attention had been concentrated on the drought problem and the need for more intensive agriculture in Samara as early as 1864, and some efforts were made to improve the type of cultivation. Further evidence of the crisis of extensive agriculture in the region is the great variation in the harvest. In 1911 there was not enough to satisfy local needs, in 1913 a surplus of 110,000,000 poods (3,972,430,-000 lb.). Six experimental stations were established to study local problems, Besenchuk, Buguruslan, Alekseyev, Bugulma, Buzuluk, and one connected with the Kuibyshev agricultural school at Kinel. In 1927 collective farming became the foundation of agricultural policy. Mechanized agriculture achieved considerable success in its struggle with drought.

The main lines along which attempts are being made to improve agriculture and lessen the chances of famine in the district are the increasing practice of irrigation; a wider range of variety in crops, and especially the sowing of grasses and lucerne, in which respect Kuibyshev stands first in the regions of the famine area; the preservation of what forest is left, and the planting of more trees, in view of their protective value in a windswept region, and their influence on moisture conditions in the soil; the greater extension of stock raising, in view of the increasing importance of meat, dairy products, fats and wool for the growing industrial regions. Though many experiments have been made, no kind of winter corn able to withstand the severe conditions has yet been discovered, but more drought resisting varieties of hard wheat, which commands a better market than soft wheat, have been introduced.

About 90% of Kuibyshev region is favourable for vegetation, and of this about two-thirds is ploughed land, about one-tenth is forest and scrub, and the rest is pasture, meadowland or garden. In the stock-raising areas, cattle, sheep and pigs are at pre-1914 level, but horses are still much below that level. Cattle plague often devastates the herds. A few dairy artels have been established. Bee-keeping and poultry raising are subsidiary occupations. The manufactures in the region are entirely dependent on local products and include flour milling, distilling, starch manufacture, tobacco making, confectionery, woollen goods, leather and matches. Most of them are of the small scale, peasant type. Two sugar factories were working before 1914, and there is one factory producing agricultural machinery.

The population (1939) was 2,767,562 of which 1,994,409 was rural and 773,153 urban. The population consists mainly of Great Russians, with Mordvas, Chuvashes, Tatars and Bashkirs. The ethnographic variety is great, and the colonies of Poles, Mennonites from Danzig, and Circassians settled there in 1847–59 by the government added to it. Difficulties of overcoming illiteracy under these conditions are great. Area of the region is 33,-475 sq.mi. The Volga is the great artery of commerce, but its tributaries are shallow and not suitable for navigation, with the exception of the Great Irgiz up to Kushum. Kuibyshev is linked by rail with Moscow on the west, and with Ufa and Chkalov on the east, while a branch line reaches the Sok river. Roads are poor, there are few bridges, and transport difficulties hamper development. The chief towns are Kuibyshev (see SAMARA), Pugachevsk, Buzuluk (qq.v.), and Buguruslan.

See P. A. Preobrazhenskiy *The Restoration of Agriculture in the Famine Area of Russia* (1922, in English); *Colonisation of the Samara Region* (1923, in Russian); M. M. Dubenskiy, *The Central Volga Region* (1927, in Russian).

SAMARA (now KUIBYSHEV), a town of the Russian S.F.S.R. in the region of Kuibyshev, in 53° 11′ N., 50° 9′ E., on the left bank of the Volga loop, at the junction of the Samara river. Pop. (1939) 390,267. It is a fine river port, and acts as an entrepôt for goods brought by rail and transhipped, or vice versa. Its industries include the making of machinery, distilling, brewing, matchmaking, sawmilling, leatherwork and flour milling. There are municipal electricity, water and canal and tram services. Near the town is a *kumiss* or fermented mare's milk sanatorium. Samara was built in 1586 to secure communication between the recently conquered principalities of Kazan and Astrakhan. Later discontent among the serfs led to a rising in the district in 1774 and the town was the centre for its leader, Pugachev. In 1670 it had been captured by the rebel Stenka Razin. Its importance as a trading centre dates from the end of the 18th century, when colonization spread eastward. In 1918 the Russian state gold treasure was transferred from Kazan to Samara, under the charge of employees of the tsarist government, but when the military situation became critical it was removed under an escort of Czech soldiers.

SAMARIA, ancient city of Palestine in the tribe of Ephraim, 6 mi. N. of Shechem (Nablus). The site, an isolated hill in the centre of Palestine, is one of great natural strength. Sebastiyeh, a village of 600 inhabitants, occupies part of the area of the royal city; its houses are mostly built with ancient materials.

History.—Omri, king of Israel, bought the hill from its owner, Shemer, for two talents of silver, and erected a city which he made his capital (I Kings xvi, 24). The evidence of the excavations establishes that the site was unoccupied prior to the time of Omri (10th century B.C.). Ahab occupied the city, built a temple and remodelled Omri's palace, which was further extended later and probably by Jeroboam II. Ben-hadad II of Syria in the days of Elijah and Elisha, after having been repulsed from its walls (I Kings xx, 34) returned to besiege it and bring it to dire straits through famine (II Kings vi, vii). Shalmaneser IV laid siege to it for three years (724–22 B.C.), but died during its progress. The operation was completed by Sargon, who deported its inhabitants and substituted for them a new body of settlers from Cutha, according to Jewish tradition, the ancestors of the Samaritans. Alexander the Great conquered it in 331 B.C., as did also later Ptolemy Lagos and Antiochus Poliorcetes. It offered a lively resistance to the fanatical John Hyrcanus. Pompey rebuilt it, and Gabinius restored it. Herod the Great was its chief benefactor. A temple, hippodrome and colonnaded streets were among his endowments; their remains still arrest attention. He made it his capital and it took the name Sebaste (commemorating Augustus). The rise of Nablus (Neapolis), restored by Vespasian, involved the gradual decay of Sebaste. The crusaders built a church on the hill and established a bishopric. The church, like so many others, was later converted into a mosque. Here were shown the tombs of Elisha, Obadiah and John the Baptist.

Archaeology.—From 1908 to 1910 excavations under the auspices of Harvard university were carried out on the site, the results of which were published in 1924. The oldest edifice found on the hill was the palace of Omri, added to and enlarged by Ahab and Jeroboam II. An interesting discovery was that of a number of Hebrew texts traced in ink on tiles in Hebrew writing of a beautiful type belonging to the 9th century B.C. The foundations of a forum, senate house, palace, city gate flanked by two round towers, etc., have been laid bare. The low ground to the northeast was the site of the stadium.

See G. A. Reisner, C. S. Fisher, D. G. Lyon, *Harvard Excavations at Samaria* (1908–10) (1924); R. Dussaud, "Samarie au temps d'Achab," *Syria* 6, 314 *et seq.* (1925).   (E. Ro.)

SAMARITANS, the name given to a peculiar religious community formerly widespread throughout Samaria in Palestine and now represented by a few families at Nablus, near the site of the ancient Shechem. They claim to be descendants of the ten tribes, denying that the latter were ever deported en masse to Assyria, as related in the Old Testament (II Kings xvii, 23). Their religion, they assert, represents the true, unalloyed teaching of Moses, since they accept the Pentateuch alone as holy scripture. This they transmit in an archaic script resembling ancient Phoenician characters and in a text which differs slightly (sometimes only through dogmatic manipulation) from that of the Jews. They identify the "chosen place" of God not, as do the Jews, with Zion, but with Mt. Gerizim, overlooking Shechem. In their version of Deuteronomy xxvii, 4, the altar

of God is enjoined to be erected on that mountain, not on Mt. Ebal, as in the Jewish recension, and a similar injunction is appended to the Ten Commandments, after Exodus xx, 17, and Deuteronomy v, 21. The temple at Jerusalem and the earlier shrine at Shiloh are regarded as apostatic.

The origin of the sect is obscure because the native and the Jewish accounts (in Josephus, *Jewish Antiquities*, xi, 7, 2; c. 8) are alike tendentious, the former deliberately apologetic and the latter deliberately defamatory. Most probably, the inhabitants of Samaria first organized themselves as a schismatic community when the Jews, regarding them as mongrel stock, refused their aid in the building of the Second Temple (Ezra iv, 1–3). The schism seems to have crystallized, however, only about 200 years later, when a rival temple was established, about 332 B.C., on Mt. Gerizim.

In spite of the differences which separated the two communities, their external histories at first ran parallel. Samaritans as well as Jews were deported to Egypt by Ptolemy Lagos, the two parties subsequently continuing their rivalry in Alexandria; while under Antiochus IV Epiphanes they too were compelled to devote their sanctuary to the worship of a heathen god (II Maccabees v, 25; vi, 2). Open hostility would appear to have developed especially when the Hasmonaean state of the Jews embarked upon a policy of expansion, and this reached its climax with the destruction of the Samaritan temple by John Hyrcanus I in 129 B.C. Thereupon the Samaritans found themselves caught between the Jews on the one hand and the Romans on the other. When the Jews were subjugated in 63, Samaria was liberated from Jewish domination and entered briefly upon a new lease of life. The capital city was restored by the Roman governor Gabinius and enjoyed the special favour of Herod, who there celebrated his marriage with Mariamne. On the other hand, the Samaritans supported the Jews in an uprising against Vespasian and paid dearly in a retributive massacre, and like the Jews they were grievously oppressed by Hadrian, who burned their traditional writings. They seem also to have shared in the Jewish dispersion, for in later times we hear of Samaritans and their synagogues in Egypt, in Rome and in other parts of the empire. During the 4th century, however, they enjoyed a brief renascence on their native soil under the leadership of a certain Baba Rabba, who built many synagogues (some of them excavated in the second quarter of the 20th century) in the villages around Shechem. Eventually, hostility to the Christians brought about their final eclipse. In 529 a rigorous edict against them was promulgated by Justinian, and although he subsequently softened its terms, renewed hostility on their part resulted, in 572, in a definitive withdrawal of all their rights and privileges by Justin II.

Under Arab and, later, under Turkish rule, the history of the Samaritans is generally one of constant oppression and subjection, relieved only by occasional bright intervals. Although they are mentioned in later times by such Arab writers as Masudi (943) and Sharastani (d. 1153); by Jewish travellers such as Benjamin of Tudela (1163) and Obadiah Bertinoro (1488 in Egypt), by Jehan de Mandeville (1322), William of Baldensel (1336) and others, little was known of them in Europe until Joseph Scaliger opened communications with them in 1583. In consequence of the interest thus aroused, the traveller Pietro della Valle visited them in 1616 and obtained from them a copy of their Pentateuch, of their ancient Aramaic translation (Targum) of it and of various other writings. At that time they had already quit their colony in Damascus and were beginning also to abandon their other settlements and to concentrate themselves in Nablus. By mid-20th century they lived mainly in a special quarter of that city, about 190 in number, though a few families had migrated to Tel Aviv and Jaffa. Their economic and cultural level is extremely low, and their principal problem is how to perpetuate themselves without infringing the forbidden degrees of marriage.

Religion.—Briefly summarized, the creed of the Samaritans is as follows: (1) God is one, incorporeal and without associate; (2) Moses is the only prophet, a preordained creature *sui generis,* the vessel of the divine "light" and "image" and the intercessor for man on the final Day of Judgment; (3) the Law of Moses, coeval with the world, is the only divine revelation and is immutable; (4) Mt. Gerizim is the chosen place of God, the only centre of worship and the "navel of the earth"; (5) there will be a Day of Requital and Reward, when the dead will emerge from their graves, the righteous to enter paradise, the guilty to roast in eternal fire. The Samaritans divide their history into a period of Divine Pleasure (*Rahuta*), when their temple was standing, and one of Divine Displeasure (*Fanuta*), which has continued ever since it was destroyed. Eventually, 6,000 years after creation, a Restorer (*Taheb*) will arise to ameliorate their fortunes. He will live 110 years.

In religious practice, the Samaritans observe only those laws and institutions that are prescribed in the Pentateuch. They interpret them, however, in a manner divergent from normative Jewish tradition, often agreeing with the Sadducees against the Pharisees and with sectarian Jewish usages later revived by the Qaraites. Passover, for example, begins on the 14th day of that lunar month the beginning of which falls in April (*Abib*; *cf.* Deuteronomy xvi, 1); Pentecost falls always on a Sunday, since the law (Leviticus xxiii, 15) which dates it seven weeks "from the morrow of the sabbath" is taken to refer to the sabbath in the paschal week. They do not wear prayer shawls or phylacteries, interpreting the laws of Numbers xv, 37–41, and Deuteronomy vi, 8, symbolically. The law of levirate marriage (Deuteronomy xxv, 5) is taken to enjoin the marriage of a widow to any near kinsman of her deceased husband, not specifically to his blood brother. The paschal sacrifice is still offered on Mt. Gerizim, and pilgrimages are made thither on each of the seasonal festivals.

The religious direction of the community is vested in a high priest. Formerly he traced his ancestry to Aaron, but in 1623 the Aaronid line died out, and ever since he has been known as the "priest levite," claiming descent from Aaron's uncle Uzziel (Exodus vi, 18).

In Jewish tradition, the Samaritans are styled Cuthaeans, the implication being that they are not genuine Israelites but simply descendants of the foreign colonists from Cutha allegedly imported into Samaria by the Assyrian conqueror when the kingdom of Israel fell in 722 B.C. (II Kings xvii, 24). Various restrictions are imposed on intercourse with them, and intermarriage is forbidden.

Language and Literature.—The Samaritan language is a dialect of Western Aramaic. After the Moslem conquest in 632, however, it was superseded by Arabic for all but liturgical purposes.

During the Hellenistic period, the Samaritans appear to have composed several works, including a translation of their Pentateuch in Greek, but all of these perished except for a few fragments. Of extant writings there is none which can be dated before the 4th century A.D. The Targum or Samaritan-Aramaic version of the Pentateuch was most probably redacted about that time, though it was clearly based on a much older tradition and must have undergone various recensions. It bears a strange similarity in many points to the contemporary Jewish Targum of Onkelos. To the same period belong the liturgical compositions of Amram Darah and Marqah, as well as the latter's midrashic commentary (called "The Book of Wonders") on parts of the Pentateuch, all in Aramaic. The last named is especially valuable not only from the linguistic viewpoint but also because it exemplifies a tradition of exegesis divergent from that of the Jews and because it anticipates several concepts and even idioms found later in the Koran. With the possible exception of one or two hymns there is nothing further until the 11th century, when there appears an Arabic version of the Pentateuch probably composed by Abul-hasan of Tyre and later revised by Abu Said and Abul-barakat. Of the same date (1053) is an anonymous commentary on Genesis, interesting because it quotes from books of the Bible other than the Pentateuch and from the Mishnah. Other mediaeval writings of note are: (1) the *Kafi*, or "Ritual Compendium," by Joseph ben Solomon of Askar, a village near Shechem (1042); (2) the *Masa'il al-Khilaf*, a disquisition on differences between the Samaritans and the Jews, by Munajja ben Sadaqah (c. 1150); and (3) the *Tabakh*, or "Potpourri," a collection of ritualistic and doctrinal discussions by Abul-hasan of Tyre. All these works are in Arabic. To the same period probably belongs also an Aramaic book of biblical legends known as "The Stories (*Asatir*) of Moses," though this would appear to draw upon far older sources. Of Samaritan chronicles, mention may be made especially of the *Taulida*, commenced in 1149 by Eleazar ben Amram and continued in 1334 by Jacob ben Ishmael in Damascus, as well as of the so-called Samaritan Book of Joshua, a record of events from the death of Moses until the 4th century A.D. This work appears to have been compiled from traditional material at some time in the 13th century. An Arabic chronicle by Abul-fath, written in Egypt in 1355, has also survived. There are also several minor theological treatises and a more ambitious work entitled "Way of the Heart" (*Sirr all-Qalb*) by Abraham Qabazi of Damascus (1532), as well as a poetic book of praises in honour of Moses (*Molad Mosheh*) by Qabazi's pupil Ismail ar-Rumaihi (1537). In the 19th century, translations of these works were made from Arabic into Samaritan by the priests Pinehas ben Isaac and Jacob ben Aaron, and such activity was continued later by Abisha ben Pinehas and Ab Hasda (Abul-hasan) ben Jacob.

The principal collections of Samaritan manuscripts are in the British Museum and the Vatican library. Most of the literature remains unedited and untranslated.

BIBLIOGRAPHY.—James A. Montgomery, *The Samaritans* (Philadelphia, 1907); Moses Gaster, *The Samaritans* (London, 1925) and *The Asatir of Moses* (London, 1927). The Pentateuch was edited with critical apparatus by August von Gall (Giessen, 1914–18). A convenient edition of the Targum is that by Adolf Brüll (Frankfurt, 1874–75). For the liturgy, see A. Cowley, *The Samaritan Liturgy* (Oxford, 1909). The best grammar of the Samaritan language is that of J. H. Petermann in the "Porta Linguarum Orientalium Series" (Karlsruhe and Leipzig, 1873). (T. H. G.)

SAMARIUM (symbol Sm, atomic number 62, atomic weight 150.43) is a metallic element belonging to the rare-earth group. The element, as well as the mineral samarskite, is named after the Russian engineer Col. M. Samarski. It has seven natural, stable isotopes: Sm^{144} (3.16%); Sm^{147} (15.07%); Sm^{148} (11.27%); Sm^{149} (13.84%); Sm^{150} (7.47%); Sm^{152} (26.63%); and Sm^{154} (22.53%). One of these, Sm^{147}, is a naturally occurring radioactive isotope; it has a half life of 1.4×10^{11} years and is an α-particle emitter. The element was discovered in 1879 by L. de Boisbaudran and was obtained in the form of very pure compounds by E. Demarcay about 1901. Samarium occurs in many minerals such as monazite, gadolinite, samarskite, etc.; it is also

found among the fission products of uranium, thorium and plutonium.

Formerly it was usually separated from other members of the rare-earth group by the fractional crystallization of the double magnesium nitrate from 50% nitric acid; many other procedures were also used which involved long-continued fractionations. Since 1945, rapid separation has been achieved on adsorption columns. Bands of adsorbed rare earths containing samarium are eluted down an ion-exchange column with a buffered solution of citric acid or ethylenediamine tetra-acetic acid. Very pure samarium can be obtained by this means. The common oxide (Sm_2O_3) has a pale yellow colour and is rapidly soluble in most acids, giving topaz-yellow salts such as samarium sulphate ($Sm_2[SO_4]_3.8H_2O$). The salts are paramagnetic. The metal is a silver colour and oxidizes slowly in air. It melts around 1,052° C. and has a density of 7.54 g. per cubic centimetre. The crystal structure of samarium is rhombohedral, with $a = 8.996$ Å ($Å = 10^{-10}$ m.), $\alpha = 23° 13'$, $Z = 3$. The metal has been prepared by electrolysis of the fused halides and by thermal reduction with some alkaline-earth metals. It is several hundred times as volatile at a given temperature as lanthanum, and the metal can be prepared readily by mixing lanthanum metal with samarium oxide and distilling the samarium metal away in a high vacuum at around 1,400° C.

A divalent oxide (SmO) and a divalent series of compounds exist. Most of these divalent compounds are soluble in water but rapidly bring about its decomposition. It has been found desirable to take advantage of the divalent state in rapidly separating samarium from the other rare earths. J. K. Marsh (1942) found that sodium amalgams will reduce samarium salts. The samarium is subsequently extracted from the amalgam in a fairly pure state by the use of acids, although special procedures have to be followed in order to separate the samarium from europium and ytterbium, which are also reduced. While it readily forms an amalgam with mercury, it is extremely difficult to separate the pure samarium metal from the mercury. The trivalent solutions give a characteristic absorption spectrum and the element has a characteristic spark spectrum. It has found rather limited use in the ceramic industry and as a catalyst for certain organic reactions. One of its isotopes has a high capture cross section for neutrons. Therefore, samarium acts as a powerful poison to some nuclear chain reactions. (*See* RARE EARTHS.) (F. H. SP.)

SAMARKAND, a city of Asiatic U.S.S.R., in 39° 39' N., 66° 56' E., situated in the Uzbek S.S.R. Pop. (1939) 134,346. The city is the ancient Maracanda, the capital of Sogdiana, then the residence of the Moslem Samanid dynasty, and subsequently the capital of the Mongol prince Timur. It was captured by the Russians under General Kaufmann, after a fierce struggle, in 1868 and for a time declined. In 1900 its population was 58,194, but after the foundation of the Uzbek republic in 1924, with Samarkand as its administrative centre, the town grew rapidly; an electric power station was constructed, and there are leather factories, cotton cleaning mills, flour mills, distilleries and pencil and brick factories. It is linked by rail with Chkalov and with the Caspian, and these lines are joined up via Semipalatinsk with the trans-Siberian line.

Samarkand is situated at a height of 2,358 ft. in the fertile loess valley of the Zaraf-shan, at the point where the river issues from the western spurs of the Tien-shan, on a high plain, with the snow-clad Hissar range rising to the south, from which bracing winds blow and make the city more healthful than others in central Asia. Within a journey of a couple of days lie the glacier snouts of the Archa-Maidan, "Place of Junipers."

The Russian part of the town has wide streets lined with poplar, acacia, willow and elm trees, but the Moslem part is an intricate labyrinth of narrow, winding streets. Gardening, the making of pottery and metal goods, and trade in cotton, silk, wheat, rice, horses, asses, fruit and cutlery are among the occupations of the people. The native city, with its maze of yellow houses nestling among the trees, and from which rises the turquoise cupola of the Bibi-Khanum (a college erected in 1388 by a Chinese wife of Timur), centres on the Rigistan, a square around which are three *madrasahs* (Moslem colleges), Ulug-beg, Shir-dar and Tilla-kari, of great architectural symmetry and beauty, decorated with enamelled tiles of various colours. Outside the walls of Samarkand are the Hazret Shah-Zindeh, the summer palace of Timur, on a terrace reached by 40 marble steps, and the grave of Shah-Zindeh (Kasim ibn Abbas), a companion of Timur. The latter was a famous shrine in the 14th century (Ibn Batuta's *Travels*, iii, 52). The Gur Amir, the tomb of Timur, a dome-crowned chapel, has suffered much from time and earthquakes; on its interior walls are turquoise arabesques and inscriptions in gold.

Maracanda was destroyed by Alexander the Great in 329 B.C. and was the scene of the murder of Cleitus. Ruins of its buildings, among which are plain and enamelled tiles and Graeco-Bactrian coins, lie outside Samarkand and are now called Aphrosiab. The city reappears as Samarkand at the time of the Arab conquest, when it was finally reduced by Kotaiba ibn Muslim in A.D. 711-712. Under the Samanids it became a brilliant seat of Arabic civilization and is reported to have been defended by 110,000 men when besieged by Jenghiz Khan in 1221, by whom it was destroyed and pillaged. When Timur (Tamerlane) made it his residence in 1369, its inhabitants numbered 150,000. The magnificent buildings of Timur's successors, which still remain, testify to its former wealth, but by the beginning of the 18th century it was almost uninhabited. It fell under Chinese dominion and subsequently under that of the amir of Bukhara, and finally under that of Russia.

SAMAWA, a town on the Euphrates in 31° N., 45° E., at the junction of the Hindieh and Hilla branches of the Euphrates. The town is on the Baghdad-Basra railway and there is a good clear stretch of river as far as Nasiriyeh 71 m. down stream (up stream the river is practically impassable). It is also situated on the caravan routes to Hilla, Nejef and Basra, in a fertile area and is a centre of trade in local agricultural products, including vegetables, rice and wheat and barley. Like most of the Euphrates towns it is a market for such imported goods as sugar, indigo and coffee and also Manchester goods. A good deal of wool is raised locally and woollen carpets are manufactured in the town. Pop. (estimated) 10,000.

SAMBALPUR, a town and district of British India, in the province of Orissa. The town is on the left bank of the river Mahanadi, and the terminus of a branch of the Bengal-Nagpur railway. Pop. (1931) 15,017. It contains a ruined fort with old temples.

The DISTRICT OF SAMBALPUR has an area of 5,419 sq.mi. and a population (1941) of 1,182,622. The Mahanadi, which is the only important river, divides it into unequal parts. The greater portion is an undulating plain, with ranges of rugged hills, the largest of which is the Bara Pahar, covering an area of 300 sq.m., and attaining at Debrigarh a height of 2,267 ft. The Mahanadi affords means of water communication for 90 m.; its principal tributaries in Sambalpur are the Ib, Kelo and Jhira. To the west of the Mahanadi the district is under close cultivation; to the east the country is broken by hills and a considerable area is under forest. Gold dust and diamonds have been found near Hirakud, at the junction of the Ib and Mahanadi.

Sambalpur lapsed to the British in 1849, and was attached to Bengal until 1862, when it was transferred to the Central Provinces. In 1905 Sambalpur was transferred back again to Bengal, without the subdivisions of Phuljhar and Chandarpur-Padampur. On the outbreak of the Mutiny in 1857 a general rising took place, and it was not until 1864 that tranquillity was restored.

SAMBOURNE, EDWARD LINLEY (1844–1910), English draughtsman, illustrator and designer, was born in London, on Jan. 4, 1844. He was educated at the City of London school, and also received a few months' education at the South Kensington school of art. After a six years' "gentleman apprenticeship" with John Penn and Son, marine engineers, Greenwich, his humorous and fanciful sketches made surreptitiously in the drawing-office of that firm were shown to Mark Lemon, editor of *Punch,* and at once secured him an invitation to draw for that journal. In April 1867 appeared his first sketch, "Pros and Cons," and from that time his work was regularly seen, with rare excep-

tions, in the weekly pages of *Punch*. In 1871 he was called to the *Punch* "table." He drew his first political cartoon, properly so-called, in 1884, and ten years later began regularly to design the weekly second cartoon, following Sir John Tenniel as chief cartoonist in 1901. He died on Aug. 3, 1910.

See M. H. Spielmann, *The History of Punch* (1895).

SAMBUCA, SAMBUTE, SAMBIUT, SAMBUE, SAMBUQUE, an ancient stringed instrument of Asiatic origin generally supposed to be a small triangular harp of shrill tone (Arist. Quint. Meib. ii. p. 101). But there is no certainty on the point and the most widely different characters have been ascribed to the instrument from time to time in the older records. Thus it has been described as a kind of tambourine, as a sort of flute, as a cithara, as another form of the sackbut, and so on.

SAMLAND, a peninsula of Germany, in the province of East Prussia, on the Baltic. It separates the Frisches Haff on the west from the Kurisches Haff on the north-east, and is bounded on the south by the river Pregel and on the east by the Deime. Its shape is oblong; it is 43 m. long, and 18 broad, and has an area of 900 sq.m. The surface is mostly flat, but on the west sand-hills rise to a height of 300 ft. The chief product is amber. The former episcopal see of Samland was founded by Pope Innocent IV. in 1249 and subordinated to the archbishop of Riga. Bishop Georg von Polentz embraced the Reformation in 1523, and in 1525 the district was incorporated with the duchy of Prussia.

SAMNAN: *see* SEMNAN.

SAMNITES, the name given by the Romans to the warlike tribes inhabiting the mountainous centre of the southern half of Italy. The word *Samnites* was not the name, so far as we know, used by the Samnites themselves, which would seem rather to have been (the Oscan form of) the word which in Latin appears as *Sabini* (*see* below). The ending of *Samnites* seems to be connected with the name by which they were known to the Greeks of the Campanian coast. Both from tradition and from surviving inscriptions (*see* OSCAN and R. S. Conway, *Italic Dialects*, pp. 169–206) it is clear that they spoke Oscan; and tradition records that the Samnites were an offshoot of the Sabines (see *e.g.*, Festus, p. 326 Müller). On two inscriptions, of which one is unfortunately incomplete, and the other is the legend on a coin of the Social War, we have the form *Safinim*, which would be in Latin *Sabinium*, and is best regarded as the nominative or accusative singular, neuter or masculine, agreeing with some substantive understood, such as *nummum* (*see* Conway, *ibid.*, pp. 188, 216).

The abundance of the group names ending in the suffix *-no-* in all the Samnite districts classes them unmistakably with the great Safine stock (*see* SABINI). The Samnites are intimately related to the patrician class at Rome (*see* ROME: *Ancient History*).

The longest and most important monument of the Oscan language, as it was spoken by the Samnites (in, probably, the 3rd century B.C.) is the small bronze tablet, engraved on both sides, known as the *Tabula Agnonensis*, found in 1848 at the modern village Agnone, not very far from the site of Bovianum, which was the centre of the northern group of Samnites called *Pentri*. This inscription, now preserved in the British Museum, is carefully engraved in full Oscan alphabet.

The text and commentary will be found in Conway, *op. cit.*, p. 191: it contains a list of deities to whom statues were erected in the precinct sacred to Ceres, or some allied divinity, and on the back a list of deities to whom altars were erected.

See R. S. Conway, *Dialectorum Italicarum exempla selecta,* and C. D. Buck, *Oscan and Umbrian Grammar.*

SAMO, a tall, robust-looking people inhabiting the borders of Upper Volta and the French Sudan. They speak a language, still little known, apparently related to Sia, and live in independent villages, distributed in quarters consisting of flat-roofed houses of mud. Marriage is restricted within the village but must be outside the extended family group. In the case of a divorce the children remain with the father. The family property passes to the brother of the deceased, and personal goods, or individual property, is inherited by the eldest son. The Samo are skilled cultivators, and raise cattle. They are animists and perform seasonal sacrifices and worship sacred animals protecting the villages. The dead are exposed and then buried in special places set apart for (1) old men, (2) young men, (3) old women and (4) young women.

See Tauxier, *Le Noir du Yatenga* (1917).

SAMOA. The Samoan group of islands extends from 13° 26′ to 14° 22′ S. lat. and from 168° 10′ to 172° 48′ W. long., and is about 1,600 mi. E. of New Zealand, 2,700 mi. E. of Australia and 2,200 mi. S. of the Hawaiian Islands. The archipelago is divided administratively into two parts: the six islands east of 171° W. long. constitute American Samoa, a dependency of the U.S., and the nine islands west of the 171° meridian constitute Western Samoa, a trusteeship territory administered by New Zealand. American Samoa consists of the inhabited islands of Tutuila, Tau, Olosega, Ofu and Aunuu and the uninhabited coral atoll Rose Island. Swains Island, 210 mi. N.W. of Tutuila and considered to be outside the Samoan archipelago, was made a part of American Samoa in 1925. Western Samoa consists of the inhabited islands of Upolu, Savaii, Manono and Apolima and the uninhabited islands of Fanuatapu, Namua, Nuutele, Naulua and Nuusafee.

The total area of American Samoa is 76 sq.mi. Tutuila, the largest island of American Samoa, is about 18 mi. long and from 5 to 6 mi. across in the widest part. Western Samoa has a total land area of 1,133 sq.mi. Savaii, the largest island, has an area of about 700 sq.mi. and is 46 mi. long; Upolu has an area of about 400 sq.mi. and is 45 mi. long. The other seven islands of Western Samoa are quite small.

All the Samoan islands, except Nuusafee, are rocky and of volcanic origin. Upolu, Savaii and Tutuila have high inland ridges rising to peaks of 6,094 ft. in Savaii, 3,608 ft. in Upolu and 2,141 ft. in Tutuila. These islands have little level land except along the coast and in the case of Tutuila there is a broad fertile plain in the southwestern part of the island. The soil is alluvial and quite fertile in the valleys. Because of the heavy rainfall, the soil on hillsides is thin and there is no subsoil.

The climate of the islands is tropical but equable for a good portion of the year. The rainfall is heavy and the range in temperatures is small. From May to November strong southeast winds blow and the islands have experienced many severe hurricanes. June and July are the coolest and pleasantest months. The average temperature is 79.3° F. with a mean range from 73.8° to 84.7°. The average yearly rainfall for a period of 41 years has been 193.5 in.

History.—The archipelago was probably discovered by Jacob Roggeveen, a Dutchman, in 1722. The islands were subsequently visited by Louis de Bougainville in 1768, the comte de la Pérouse in 1787, Edwards in 1791 and Otto von Kotzebue in 1824. The first missionaries to go to Samoa were two members of the London Missionary society who established a mission in 1830. Charles Wilkes, a U.S. explorer, surveyed the islands in 1839. Great Britain, the U.S. and Germany appointed representatives on the islands in 1847, 1853 and 1861, respectively.

In Jan. 1878 the U.S. signed a treaty with the then independent Samoan kingdom which gave the U.S. the right to establish a coaling station in the harbour of Pago Pago, best in the archipelago. A trading agreement was also concluded. Germany and Great Britain received similar privileges the following year, but the interests of the three countries were often in conflict. A conference of the three powers, held in Berlin in 1889, concluded a general act providing for the neutrality of the islands and establishing in effect a tripartite protectorate over the islands.

This arrangement did not operate so successfully as planned, and on Nov. 7, 1899, a treaty was concluded between Great Britain, Germany and the U.S. by which the paramount interests of the United States in those Samoan islands east of 171° W. long. were recognized and Germany's interests in the other Samoan islands were similarly recognized. Great Britain withdrew from Samoa altogether in consideration of rights in Tonga and the Solomon Islands. The high chiefs of the islands of Tutuila and Aunuu ceded those islands to the U.S. on April 17, 1900, and the chiefs of Tau, Olosega and Ofu Islands ceded their islands to the U.S. on July 16, 1904. The U.S. congress accepted the islands

under a joint resolution approved Feb. 20, 1929.

Germany controlled Western Samoa until World War I. New Zealand troops occupied the islands on Aug. 30, 1914, and the League of Nations granted New Zealand a mandate over them in 1920. Western Samoa was made a trusteeship territory by the United Nations with New Zealand as the administering authority on Jan. 25, 1947.

Population.—The population of American Samoa totalled 18,937 in 1950 with about four-fifths of the population on the main island of Tutuila. The population of Western Samoa was estimated at 73,000 in 1948. The Samoans are Polynesian and closely akin to the people of Hawaii and the Maoris of New Zealand.

The Samoan language is believed to be the oldest form of Polynesian speech in existence. It is closely related to the Maori, Tahitian, Hawaiian and Tongan languages. Despite the increasing contacts with the western world, Samoan culture is still the dominant influence in the lives of the people. The village, composed of 30 to 40 households, is the basic social and political unit.

Most of the population have become converts to Christianity. In Western Samoa, one-half of the population is affiliated with the London Missionary society. Other major religious affiliations in Samoa are Roman Catholic, Methodist, Mormon and Seventh-Day Adventist.

Government.—*American Samoa.*—American Samoa is an unorganized U.S. possession with a governor appointed by the president of the United States. On Feb. 19, 1900, the islands were placed under the jurisdiction of the navy department, and the governor was a naval officer. Administration was transferred to the jurisdiction of the department of the interior on July 1, 1951.

For purposes of local administration, American Samoa is divided into three administrative districts. Each district has a governor who is appointed by the governor of American Samoa from the ranks of county chiefs. In each village of the district a chief is appointed by the district governor.

As a result of a legislative reorganization in Feb. 1948, the *annual fono,* which met annually or on the call of the governor, was replaced with a bicameral legislature, known as the legislature of American Samoa. The legislature consists of the house of representatives, with 54 members popularly elected for two-year terms, and the house of alii, with 12 members who hold the highest titles in American Samoa. Membership is restricted to permanent residents of the islands and 64 out of 66 members must be natives. The legislature has only advisory powers. The governor also has an advisory council consisting of from five to seven Samoans.

The judiciary consists of a high court presided over by a chief justice and two to four associate judges, six district courts, each of which has one judge, and a village court in each village, presided over by a local magistrate. The seat of government is at Pago Pago on Tutuila.

Western Samoa.—An act of the general assembly of New Zealand, effective March 10, 1948, reorganized the government of Western Samoa. The administration is headed by a high commissioner (formerly the administrator) appointed by the governor-general of New Zealand. He governs with the aid of the council of state, which consists of Samoan leaders. The high commissioner consults the council of state on all proposals for legislation and on matters affecting Samoan customs and welfare.

The legislative assembly (formerly the legislative council) was created, presided over by the high commissioner or his nominee. The assembly consists of the Samoan members of the council of state, 11 additional Samoans who are nominated by a native *fono,* or assembly, no more than 5 elected Europeans and no more than 6 official members, of whom 3 are nominated by the governor-general of New Zealand and 3 by the high commissioner. ·The legislative powers of the assembly are wide, with certain notable exceptions such as laws relating to defense questions and foreign affairs. Village and local affairs are controlled by native village officials nominated by the villagers. The seat of government is at Apia on Upolu.

Education.—Education in American Samoa is compulsory for all children from 7 to 15 years of age, inclusive. Instruction is in English. It was estimated in 1950 that 93% of all persons ten years of age or older were literate. In that year there were 5,093 children enrolled in public and private schools with a total of 161 teachers; about 80% of the enrolment was in public schools. During the fiscal year ending June 30, 1950, about 26% of the expenditures of American Samoa went to public education.

Education in Western Samoa is dependent to a very great extent on the activities of various missions. In 1945 there were 500 schools of all types (of which 387 were missionary schools), with 724 teachers (of which 351 were pastors, 86 natives and 287 Europeans); in 1947 there were 31,391 pupils (of which 20,523 were in missionary schools). Education is not compulsory and there is no age limit on attendance. Instruction in elementary schools is in Samoan while in the more advanced schools it is largely in English. About 8% of Western Samoa's expenditures during the 1947–48 fiscal year went for public education.

Finance.—Total revenues collected in American Samoa during the

1949–50 fiscal year from such sources as per capita taxes, real estate taxes, licence fees and customs duties amounted to $407,713 in addition to a U.S. government appropriation of $55,000; expenditures amounted to $661,143. The Bank of American Samoa, founded in 1914 by the naval government, is the only financial institution in the territory; it had resources of $1,778,914 in Nov. 1947.

Western Samoa became self-supporting in 1931; as of March 31, 1947, the accumulated surplus totalled £417,758. Resources in the 1947–48 fiscal year amounted to about £320,000 and expenditures to about £475,000, necessitating the use of a part of the accumulated surplus and a subsidy of £70,400 from the New Zealand government.

Economy.—The natural resources of Samoa are of little economic consequence. There are no minerals and no timber of sufficient quantity to warrant industrial development for export. Commercial fishing had not been developed at mid-20th century. The main products of American Samoa are copra and native handicraft consisting principally of mats and rugs woven from local grasses. Western Samoa's main products are copra, cocoa beans, dessicated coconut and bananas.

Agriculture is the basis of the Samoan economy. Crops cultivated are corn, beans, peas, watermelons, cucumbers, squash, eggplant, tomatoes, lettuce, radishes, sweet potatoes, breadfruit, papayas, bananas, taro and pineapple. There are also some cattle, and in American Samoa a small dairy industry.

Imports by American Samoa in the 1949–50 fiscal year totalled $886,961; the major imports were preserved meat and textiles. Exports totalled $313,070, two-thirds of which were copra (3,160,000 lbs.). Western Samoa's imports in 1946 amounted to £478,695 and consisted mostly of foodstuffs and textiles; exports totalled £719,050 and consisted mostly of copra, cocoa beans and dessicated coconut.

BIBLIOGRAPHY.—Ernest Beaglehole, *Trusteeship and New Zealand's Pacific Dependencies* (1947); F. J. H. Grattan, *An Introduction to Samoan Culture* (1948); Rupert Emerson *et al.*, *America's Pacfic Dependencies* (1949); U.S. Navy Department, *American Samoa: Information on American Samoa Transmitted by the United States to the Secretary-General of the United Nations Pursuant to Article 73(e) of the Charter* (June 1948–June 1950); United Nations Trusteeship Council, *Report of the UN Visiting Mission to Trust Territories in the Pacific on Western Samoa* (August 15, 1950); United Nations Trusteeship Council, *Report to Trusteeship Council by the UN Mission to Western Samoa* (1948). (S. Nr.)

SÁMOS, an island in the Aegean sea, separated from the mainland of Turkey by a strait of only about a mile in width; about 27 mi. in length, by 14 in greatest breadth; occupied by mountains, of which the highest, Mt. Kerkis, near its western end, is 4,710 ft. high. This range continues from Mt. Mycale on the mainland. Samos was annexed to Greece in 1912. The capital is at Vathy, in a deep bay on the north coast, a quite modern town, well paved and connected by carriage roads with villages round both sides of the bay, and with Tigani on the south coast, the site of the ancient city. A third port, Carlovasi, farther west on the northern coast, serves a separate lowland district. The island is remarkably fertile, and a great portion of it is covered with vineyards. Oil, raisins, silk, cotton and tobacco are also grown, and barges and sailing vessels are built at Tigani, almost wholly from native timber. Cigarette making employs many women and girls, the tobacco coming chiefly from Thrace. The population in 1940 was 69,138. The predominant religion is the Orthodox Greek; the metropolitan district is Samos and Icaria.

History.—At the time of the great migrations, in the 11th century B.C., Samos received an Ionian population mainly from Epidaurus in Argolis. By the 7th century B.C. it had become one of the leading commercial centres of Greece through its position near the Maeander and Caÿster trade-routes from inner Asia Minor. The Samians also traded with the Black sea and with Egypt, and claimed to be the first Greeks to reach the Straits of Gibraltar. Their commerce brought them into close relations with Cyrene, Corinth and Chalcis, but made them bitter rivals of their neighbour, Miletus. The feud involved both cities in the Levantine war (7th century B.C.) when Corinth built triremes for the Samians. The result favoured Miletus, but in the 6th century the insular position of Samos preserved it from mainland aggressions to which Miletus was exposed. About 535 B.C., when its oligarchy was overturned by the tyrant Polycrates (q.v.), Samos reached the height of its prosperity. Its navy "ruled the waves" from its new deep-sea harbour, and blockaded the mainland subjects of Persia; the tunnelled aqueduct (still open) secured copious water, and the great Temple of Hera was built. Polycrates first intrigued, and then quarrelled, with the Persian governor of Lydia,

and after his death by treachery, Darius conquered Samos and partly depopulated it. It had regained much when, in 499, it joined the general revolt of the Ionians against Persia; but owing to jealousy of Miletus, part of its contingent, at the decisive battle of Lade (494), deserted. In 479, however, following Xerxes' defeats in Greece, Samos betrayed the Persian fleet to the Greeks at Mycale. In the Delian League the Samians held special privilege and remained loyal to Athens until 440, when a dispute with Miletus, which the Athenians had decided against them, provoked them to secede. With a fleet of 60 ships they held their own for some time against a large Athenian fleet led by Pericles himself, but after a siege, capitulated and were degraded to a tributary rank. Towards the end of the Peloponnesian war, when Miletus became a Spartan naval base, Samos appears as one of the most loyal dependencies of Athens; and a temporary home of the Athenian democracy during the revolution of the Four Hundred at Athens (411 B.C.), and in the last stage of the war, it was rewarded with the Athenian franchise. This friendly attitude towards Athens was accompanied by the establishment of democracy. After the downfall of Athens, Samos was besieged by Lysander and again placed under an oligarchy. In 394, when the Spartan navy withdrew, the island declared its independence and re-established a democracy, but by the Peace of Antalcidas (387) it fell under Persian dominion. Recovered by the Athenians in 366, after a siege, it received a body of military settlers. After 322, when Athens was again deprived of Samos, its fate is obscure. For some time (about 275–270 B.C.) it served as a base for the Egyptian fleet, at other periods it recognized the overlordship of Syria; in 189 B.C. it was transferred by the Romans to the kings of Pergamum. Enrolled from 133 in the Roman province of Asia, it revolted to Aristonicus (132) and Mithridates (88), and forfeited its autonomy, but recovered it between the reigns of Augustus and Vespasian, and remained prosperous. Under Byzantine rule Samos became the head of the Aegean *theme* (military district). After the 13th century it passed through much the same changes as Chios (q.v.), and became the property of the Genoese firm of Giustiniani (1346–1566). At the Turkish conquest it was severely depopulated, and provided with new settlers, partly Albanians.

During the Greek War of Independence Samos bore a conspicuous part, and it was in the strait between the island and Mt. Mycale that Canaris blew up a Turkish frigate, in the presence of the army assembled for invasion. The enterprise was abandoned and Samos held its own to the end of the war. On the conclusion of peace the island was, indeed, again handed over to the Turks, but since 1835 held an exceptionally advantageous position, being in fact self-governed, though tributary to the Turkish empire, and ruled by a Greek governor nominated by the Porte, who had the title of "Prince of Samos," and was supported and controlled by a Greek council and assembly. The prosperity of the island bore witness to the wisdom of this arrangement, but did not prevent annexation to Greece when the political situation allowed it.

The ancient capital was on the south coast, at the modern Tigani, directly opposite to the promontory of Mycale. A natural cove, dominated by a low hill, has been converted by ancient and modern breakwaters into a safe port for small vessels. Behind the modern town rises a steep enclosing ridge, Astypalaea, crowned by Polycrates' wall, and perforated by his aqueduct. From this city a road led about 4m. W. to the Temple of Hera, whose site, close to the shore, is still marked by a single column, which has given to the neighbouring headland the name of Capo Colonna. Though so little remains standing, German excavators have revealed its massive foundations.

The modern capital of the island was, until recently, at Khora, about 2m. from the sea and from Tigani, but in the 19th century the capital was transferred to Vathy, on the north coast.

Samos was the birthplace of Pythagoras (q.v.), the philosopher, whose name and figure are found on coins of the city in imperial times. It also produced a school of sculptors beginning with Rhoecus and Theodorus, who are said to have invented the art of casting statues in bronze. Rhoecus was also the architect of the Temple of Hera. Another famous Samian sculptor was Pythagoras, who migrated to Rhegium. The vases of Samos are among the most characteristic Ionian pottery in the 6th century. The name Samian ware, often given to a kind of red pottery found in Roman settlements, has no scientific value; it is derived from a passage in Pliny, *N.H.* xxxv. 160 *sqq.*

See Herodotus, especially book iii.; Thucydides, especially books i. and viii.; Xenophon, *Hellenica*, books i. ii.; Strabo, xiv. pp. 636–639; L. E. Hicks and G. F. Hill, *Greek Historical Inscriptions* (1901), No. 81; B. V. Head, *Historia Numorum* (1887), pp. 515–518; Panofka, *Res Samiorum* (1822); Curtius, *Urkunden zur Geschichte von Samos* (Wesel, 1873); H. F. Tozer, *Islands of the Aegean* (1890); J. Boehlau, *Aus ionischen und italischen Nekropolen,* Pauly Wissowa, *s.v.*

SAMOSATA (Sumeisat, modern Samsat), a city on the right bank of the upper Euphrates on the borders of Mesopotamia and Armenia in 37° 30′ N., 38° 30′ E. Samosata is an important crossing place of the river close to the point where it enters the plain. It forms one of the series of border forts, of which Edessa (*q.v.*) was the most important, which had a stormy history in relation to the frontier defence of Upper Mesopotamia. It had an additional importance as forming a point at which the crossing of the river could be made. Although it is uncertain whether it was ever on the Persian royal road, there was a bridge at this point in Strabo's time, when the city is described as being strongly fortified and the centre of a small but very fertile district. From this point caravan routes diverge to Diarbekr in the north, and downstream to Urfah (Edessa) but it lies off the main route.

The fortunes of Samosata followed those of the great empires at whose boundaries it stood. It appears originally to have been a Hittite city, and it was incorporated in the Assyrian empire in 708 B.C. Later it passed into the hands of the successors of Alexander, and became the capital of Commagene. In A.D. 72 it became a Roman province. In later times it passed through a series of changes, losing its status as the capital city of a district under Constantine, and in the tenth century becoming temporarily a *theme,* or administrative military district of the Byzantine Empire. It is said in the thirteenth century to have been an Armenian settlement, but today it is mainly occupied by Kurds.

SAMOTHRACE (mod. Gr. *Samothraki,* Turk. *Semadrek*), an island in the north of the Aegean Sea, nearly opposite the mouth of the Hebrus (Maritza) north of Imbros and north-east of Lemnos. It has a population of 3,866, nearly all Greek. Though of small extent it is, next to Mount Athos, by far the most conspicuous natural feature in this part of the Aegean (5,240 ft.). In *Iliad* xiii. 12, the poet represents Poseidon using its summit to survey the plain of Troy. This mountainous character and the absence of harbours precluded political importance, while permitting the survival of the archaic worship of the CABEIRI (*q.v.*) which Herodotus (ii. 51) and others attributed to "Pelasgian" aborigines. Probably on account of its sacred character the island always enjoyed autonomy, even in the time of Pliny.

The "Victory of Samothrace," set up by Demetrius Poliorcetes *c.* 305 B.C., was discovered in the island in 1863, and is now in the Louvre. The ancient city was situated at Palaeopoli below the modern village on the N. side of the island close to the sea; with considerable remains of ancient walls, in Cyclopean style, of the sanctuary of the Cabeiri, and of other edifices of Ptolemaic and later date. A considerable sponge fishery is carried on. On the N. coast are much-frequented hot sulphur springs.

Samothrace was occupied by Germany in World War II.

SAMOVAR [Russ. *samovarŭ*], an urn for making tea after the Russian fashion; it is usually of copper, and is kept boiling by a tube filled with live charcoal passing through the centre. The word is usually taken in Russia to mean "self-boiler" (*samŭ,* self, and *baritī,* boil), but it is more probably an adaptation of a Tatar word *sanabar,* a tea-urn.

SAMOYEDES, a Neo-Siberian tribe, spread in small groups from the Altai mountains down the basins of the Ob and Yenisei, and along the shores of the Arctic ocean from the mouth of the latter river to the White sea, subdivided into three main groups: (*a*) The Yuraks in the coast-region from the Yenisei to the White sea; (*b*) the Tavghi Samoyedes, between the Yenisei and the Khatanga; (*c*) the Ostiak Samoyedes, intermingled with Os-

tiaks, in the forest regions of Tobolsk and Yeniseisk.

The Samoyedes, who now maintain themselves by hunting and fishing on the lower Ob, are partly mixed in the S. with Ostiaks. Clothed in skins, they make use of implements in bone and stone, eat carnivorous animals—the wolf included—and cherish superstitions regarding the teeth of the bear. Their huts are erected with stone; their graves are mere boxes left in the tundra. Death is ascribed to an evil female spirit. Personal belongings are buried with the dead. The religion is fetishism mixed with Shamanism, the shaman (*tadji-bei*) being a representative of the great divinity, Nim. Women become Shamans.

Of the S. Samoyedes, who are completely Tatarized, the Beltirs live by agriculture and cattle-breeding in the Abakan steppe. They profess Christianity, and speak a language closely resembling that of the Sagai Tatars. The Kaibals, or Koibals, can hardly be distinguished from the Minusinsk Tatars and support themselves by rearing cattle. Castrén considers that three of their stems are of Ostiak origin, the remainder being Samoyedic. The Kamasins, in the Kansk district of Yeniseisk, are either herdsmen or agriculturists. They speak a language with an admixture of Tatar words, and some of their stems contain a large Tatar element. The interesting nomadic tribe of Karagasses, in the Sayan mountains, is disappearing; the few representatives are rapidly losing their anthropological features, their Turkish language and their distinctive dress. The Motors are now little more than a memory. One portion of the tribe emigrated to China and was there exterminated; the remainder have disappeared among the Tuba Tatars and the Soyotes. The Samoyedes on the Ob in Tomsk may number about 7,000.

See M. A. Castrén *Grammatik der samoyedischen Sprachen* (1854); *Dictionary* (1855); *Ethnologische Vorlesungen über die altaischen Völker* (1857); *Versuch einer koibalischen und karagassischen Sprachlehre* (1857); also A. Middendorf, *Reise in den äussersten Norden und Osten Sibiriens* (1875) and M. A. Czaplicka, *Aboriginal Siberia* (1914).

SAMPAN, the name of the typical light boat of far Eastern rivers and coastal waters; it is usually propelled by a single scull over the stern, and the centre and after part is covered by an awning or screen of matting. The word is said to be Chinese, *san,* thin, and *pan,* board. Others take it to be of Malay origin.

SAMPLE, a small portion of merchandise taken from the whole to serve as a specimen or evidence of the whole; hence a pattern or model. (*See* SALE OF GOODS.)

SAMPLER, a model or pattern to be copied, particularly a small rectangular piece of embroidery worked on canvas or other material as a pattern or example of a beginner's skill in needlework, as a means of teaching the stitches. Down to comparatively recent times every little girl worked her "sampler," and examples of 17th century work are still found and have become the object of the collector's search. *See* ill. on p. 924. They usually contained the alphabet, the worker's name, the date and Bible texts, verses, mottoes, the whole surrounded with some conventional design. The earliest sampler in existence is dated 1643 and is in the Victoria and Albert museum, South Kensington.

See M. B. Huish, *Samplers and Tapestry Embroideries* (1900).

SAMPSON, WILLIAM THOMAS (1840–1902), American naval commander, was born at Palmyra, N.Y., on Feb. 9, 1840, and graduated at the head of his class from the U.S. Naval academy in 1861. In this year he was promoted to master, and in the following year was made lieutenant. He was executive officer in the "Patapsco" when she was blown up in Charleston harbour in Jan. 1865. He served on distant stations and (1868–71 and 1876–78) at the Naval academy, and became lieutenant-commander in 1866 and commander in 1874. He was a member of the International Prime Meridian and Time Conference in 1884, and of the board of fortifications in 1885–1886; was superintendent of the Naval academy from 1886 to 1890; and was promoted to captain and served as delegate at the International Maritime Conference at Washington in 1889. He was chief of the Bureau of Ordnance in 1893–97. About 95% of the guns employed in the Spanish-American War were made under his superintendence. His influence was felt decisively in the distribution of guns and armour, and in the training of the personnel of the navy. He

BY COURTESY OF THE METROPOLITAN MUSEUM OF ART

A SAMPLER OF 1747, FROM THE FISHBACK COLLECTION

superintended the gunnery training and prepared a new drill-book for the fleet. In Feb. 1898, Sampson, then a captain, was president of the board of inquiry as to the cause of destruction of the "Maine." At the outbreak of the war with Spain he was placed in charge of the North Atlantic Squadron, and conducted the blockade of Cuba. When it was known that Admiral Cervera, with a Spanish fleet, had left the Cape Verde islands, Sampson withdrew a force from the blockade to cruise in the Windward Passage, and made an attack upon the forts at San Juan, Porto Rico. After his return to the coast of Cuba he conducted the blockade of Santiago, and the ships under his command destroyed the Spanish vessels when they issued from the harbour of Santiago and attempted to escape. (*See* SPANISH-AMERICAN WAR OF 1898.) Sampson himself was not actually present at the battle, having started for Siboney just before it began to confer with Gen. Shafter, commanding the land forces. He reached the scene of battle as the last Spanish vessel surrendered, and the engagement was fought in accordance with his instructions. He was promoted to commodore in 1898, to rear-admiral on March 3, 1899, and was made commandant of the Boston (Charlestown) navy yard in October of the same year. He died in Washington, D.C., on May 6, 1902.

See W. A. M. Goode, *With Sampson Through the War* (1899); A. T. Mahan, "Sampson's Naval Career," *McClure's Magazine,* vol. xix. (1902); James Parker, *Rear Admirals Schley, Sampson and Cervera* (1910).

SAMSHUI ("Three Waters"), former treaty port in the province of Kwangtung, South China, in latitude 23° 5′ N. and longitude 112° 49′ E., about 25 miles due west of Canton. It commands an important position at the junction of the Si Kiang (West river) and Pei Kiang (North river) and lies at the apex of the deltaic network of river channels which lead to the Canton river or directly to the sea by the Si Kiang.

Samshui is thus favourably situated for the collection and distribution of trade commodities, but after the port was opened to

foreign trade in 1897 it did not grow to any considerable extent, largely owing to the proximity of Canton. Its trade was based on the large junk and launch traffic of the delta region. The export trade through the port was largely from Wuchow and Nanning higher up the Si Kiang.

The boycott of Hong Kong in 1925–26 affected the foreign trade of Samshui considerably.

After the outbreak of the Chinese-Japanese war in 1937 the trade of the port increased until the end of 1938, when the Japanese occupied the Canton delta.

The customs revenue figures for these years were as follows:

1936— $77,908 (U.S.)
1937—$518,344 (U.S.)
1938—$437,787 (U.S.)

The town established railway connection with Canton in 1904; its estimated Chinese population in 1931 was 9,160.

SAMSON, whose deeds are recorded in Judges xiv.–xvi., was a hero of early Hebrew folk-tales. He belonged to the tribe of Dan, and was renowned for his exploits against the Philistines. The narratives are marked by a grim and boisterous humour, and are so little concerned with religion that they may almost be called pagan. But, though they contribute little towards the understanding of Hebrew religion, they add much to our knowledge of early customs, and throw light on Philistine civilization. Their account of the relationships between Hebrews and Philistines, too, is of some historical worth. (*See* PHILISTINES.)

It has often been noted that there are points of resemblance between the story of Samson and the myths of Gilgamesh, Melkart, and Hercules; but, while the kinship must be admitted, Samson is much more human than his counterparts in pagan myth and legend, and is probably to be regarded as a historical person. The story contains many features drawn from solar mythology. The name Samson is a derivative, of uncertain meaning, from the Hebrew word Sun—*shemesh*. It is noteworthy that a shrine of the Sun, Beth-Shemesh, stood in the neighbourhood of Samson's home. Long hair, in which according to the story lay the secret of his strength, is a familiar feature of solar heroes, as a symbol of the sun's rays. His exploit with the gates of Gaza may be connected with the myth which represents the sun as passing through a double-gated door on the eastern horizon. It has, indeed, been argued that the entire Samson story is a solar myth; but it is apparently much more highly probable that in this case the story of a popular hero has been expanded and decorated by mythological motifs.

Why does a story so lacking in religious interest appear in the book, and why is an almost pagan character like Samson reckoned among the saviours of Israel, when the story itself does not record any deliverance of the people from Philistine oppression? There is some evidence that the story was not included in an earlier form of Judges, and that a later editor was constrained by its popularity to insert it. The account of Samson's birth—suspiciously reminiscent of an incident in the history of Gideon—and dedication as a Nazirite, Judges xiii., is an editorial attempt to fit for more respectable company the boisterous, sensual Samson of the folk-tales, who wears his Nazirite costume with some obvious difficulty, and is moved far more by his own erratic impulses than by the spirit of Yahweh. S. A. Cook, comparing Judges xiii. with vi. 11–24, suggests that Samson may have been regarded as the founder of a local Manahathite cult.

See Burney, *Judges,* pp. 335–408, A. S. Palmer, *The Samson-Saga, and its place in comparative Religion;* S. A. Cook, *Journ. of Theol. Stud.* 1927, pp. 372 *sqq.*   (W. L. W.)

SAMSONOV, ALEXANDER (1859–1914), Russian general, passed through the cavalry school in St. Petersburg, and served in the war with Turkey in 1877–78. On passing out of the academy of the general staff in 1884 he was appointed on the general staff. He was commandant of the cavalry school at Elisavetgrad (1896–1904), and in 1902 was promoted to the rank of general. In the war with Japan (1904–05) he commanded the Ussuri mounted brigade and the Siberian Cossack division. In 1909 he was made ataman of the Don Cossacks, and became governor-general and commander of troops in Turkestan. In Aug.

1914 he was appointed commander of the 2nd army, concentrated on the Narev. The desire to take pressure off France at the earliest possible moment led the Russian supreme command to give an order for an advance into eastern Prussia in spite of Samsonov's report that his army was not ready for an advance. As a result of the absence of support from Rennenkampf's 1st army Samsonov's army was destroyed in the battle of Tannenberg (Aug. 26–29). Convinced that the battle was hopelessly lost, he ordered his staff to extricate themselves from the German ring, and shot himself in a wood.

SAMSUN (anc. *Amisus*), the chief town of the Samsun vilayet in Asiatic Turkey, situated on the south coast of the Black sea between the deltas of the Kizil and Yeshil Irmaks. Pop. (1950) 43,937. It is connected by metalled roads with Sivas and Kaisarieh, and by sea with Istanbul. Samsun is a thriving town and the outlet for the trade of the Sivas vilayet. Steamers lie about 1 mi. from the shore in an open roadstead, and in winter landing is sometimes impossible. Its district is one of the principal sources of Turkish tobacco, a whole variety of which is known as "Samsun." Samsun exports cereals, tobacco and wool. Amisus, which stood on a promontory about 1½ mi. N.W. of Samsun, was, next to Sinope, the most flourishing of the Greek settlements on the Euxine, and under the kings of Pontus it was a rich trading town. By the 1st century A.D. it had displaced Sinope as the north port of the great trade route from central Asia, and later it was one of the chief towns of the Comneni of Trebizond.

SAMUCAN, a group of tribes of South American Indians, constituting an independent linguistic stock, so called from the Samucos, one of its best-known tribes. The area occupied by this stock lies on the borders of the Bolivian Chaco, roughly between 19° 30′ and 21° S. lat. and from slightly west of the Paraguay river westward to near the Parapiti. Living in a subdesert area, the Samucan tribes are mainly a seminomadic hunting folk of peaceful and friendly character and simple culture. They wear little or no clothing, and construct flimsy and temporary huts of mats. They have no canoes, but are excellent swimmers. The spear, club and a very long bow are their weapons. Their social organization is of the simplest. Their religious ceremonies are marked by elaborate masked dances.

See G. Boggiani, *I Ciamacoco* (*Atti Soc. Romana Antropologia*, vol. ii); J. Cardus, *Las Missiones Franciscanas . . . de la Republica de Bolivia* (1886).

SAMUEL, a prophet who played an important part in the establishment of the Hebrew kingdom under Saul, and became naturally the hero of numerous legends, some of which are found interspersed among narratives of greater historical value in the early part of 1 Samuel. This mixture of legend with history tends to obscure the facts, and the difficulties of recovering the true story are aggravated because we find two absolutely contradictory representations of his attitude toward the idea of monarchy. According to one of these, after a severe defeat inflicted upon Israel by the Philistines, involving the temporary loss of the ark (1 Samuel, iv), Samuel, acting in the tradition of the judges, summons "all Israel" to Mizpah (vii), performs rites of purification, and offers sacrifice to Yahweh. The Philistines are subdued by the miraculous intervention of Yahweh, and Israel recovers its lost territory. Samuel thereafter rules as a theocratic judge. His sons, whom he would make his successors, are corrupt, and the people demand a king, like those of the surrounding nations, to rule them. Despite the solemn warnings of Samuel as to the arrogant oppression of kings the people are insistent, and, by Yahweh's instruction, Samuel concedes their demand, choosing, by sacred lot, Saul (x, 17–24). The same adverse attitude toward the institution of monarchy is even more emphatically expressed in the long farewell address of abdication made by Samuel (xii). Quite different is the view we find in 1 Sam. ix–x, 16. Here Samuel is a local seer of so little renown that his fame is unknown to Saul, who, seeking some lost asses, is advised by a servant to consult him. Samuel receives the divine command to annoint Saul as king, which, seemingly, he does with unqualified enthusiasm. It is obvious that of the two representations the latter will be nearer the truth; had Samuel been really a theocratic judge tradition would hardly have dwarfed him to the grade of a local

seer, whereas the contrary proceeding is quite natural. Further, the strong antimonarchical ideas are surely the product of a later age, when the nation had experienced the exactions and follies of subsequent kings, whom they came to look upon as responsible for the national misfortunes (viii, 7; x, 19; xii, 12).

What, then, is the nucleus of important fact in these traditions? It is probable that the birthplace of Samuel was Ramah, and that —though the story of his dedication to the service of the sanctuary at Shiloh is idyll rather than history—he was a priestly seer who came into prominence during the dark days of Philistine oppression. The strong tradition as to his being the "king-maker" must rest on some historic basis; and, though later tradition has exalted Samuel at the expense of Saul, we may believe that he played an important part in the installation of Israel's first king. Though Samuel's denunciations of the monarchical idea are but the reflections of the views of a later age, they seem to have a point of contact with the history, for it is probable that the breach between Samuel and Saul in connection with Agag, 1 Samuel xv, was only the culmination of earlier divergences. Late tradition emphasizes this by its representation of Samuel as anointing David to replace Saul. (*See* SAMUEL, BOOKS OF.) (W. L. W.)

SAMUEL, HERBERT SAMUEL, 1ST VISCOUNT (1870–), British politician, was born at Liverpool on Nov. 6, 1870. He was educated at University College school, London, and at Balliol college, Oxford. In 1895 and 1900 he unsuccessfully contested South Oxfordshire as a Liberal, and in 1902 was elected for the Cleveland division of Yorkshire. He entered Sir Henry Campbell-Bannerman's government in 1905 as parliamentary undersecretary to the home office. In 1908 he was sworn into the privy council. From 1909 to 1910 he was chancellor of the duchy of Lancaster, with a seat in the cabinet, and in 1910 became postmaster general. He held this office until 1914, and then became for a year president of the Local Government board. From 1915 to 1916 he was again postmaster general and chancellor of the duchy of Lancaster, and in 1916 became home secretary. He acted as chairman of the select committee on national expenditure (1917–18), and in 1919 was special commissioner to Belgium. He was high commissioner to Palestine, 1920 until Aug. 1925, when he was made chairman of the royal commission appointed to inquire into conditions in the coal industry. In 1926 he was created G.C.B. He was chairman, Liberal party organization, 1927–29; home secretary, national government, 1931; resigned in 1932; he went into opposition in 1933. In 1937 he was created a viscount. He became leader of the Liberal party in the house of lords in 1944. Samuel wrote *Memoirs* (1945) and *Essays in Physics* (1950).

SAMUEL, BOOKS OF, two books of the Old Testament, which in the Jewish canon are ranked among the Former Prophets (Joshua–Kings) in contrast to the Latter Prophets (Isaiah–Malachi).

Contents.—The books of Judges, Samuel and Kings are made up of a series of extracts from various sources, and freely handled by copyists down to a late date, as is shown by the numerous and often important variations between the Hebrew text and the Greek version (Septuagint). The main redaction of Judges and Kings was made under the influence of the ideas which characterize Deuteronomy, that is, after the reforms ascribed to Josiah (2 Kings, xxiii); but in Samuel the "Deuteronomic" hand is much less prominent and the chronological system which runs through Judges and Kings occurs only occasionally.

The book of Samuel completes the history of the "Judges" of Israel (11th century B.C.), and begins by relating the events which led to the institution of the monarchy under Saul, the part played by Samuel being especially prominent (1 Sam. i–xiv). The interest is then transferred to David, the founder of the Judaean dynasty, and his early life is narrated with great wealth of detail. As Saul loses the divine favour, David's position advances, until, after the death of Saul and the overthrow of Israel, he gains the allegiance of a disorganized people (1 Sam. xv–2 Sam. iv), and Jerusalem becomes the centre of his empire (v–viii)—c. 1000 B.C. A more connected narrative is now given of the history of David (ix–xx), which is separated from the account of his death and Solomon's accession (1 Ki. i., ii.) by an appendix of miscellaneous contents (xxi.–xxiv.).

Samuel and Saul.—The introductory account (i.–iv. 1*a*) of the birth, dedication and calling of the young prophet Samuel is a valuable picture of religious life at the sanctuary at Shiloh. It is connected by the prophecy of the punishment of the house of Eli (iii. 11 *sqq.*) with the defeat of the Israelites by the Philistines at Ebenezer near Aphek, the loss of the ark (iv. 1*b*–22), and its subsequent fortunes (v.–vii. 1). A Philistine oppression of 20 years ends when Samuel, here the recognized "judge" of Israel, gains a great victory at Ebenezer near Mizpah (vii.). But the deliverance of Israel from the Philistines is also ascribed to Saul (xiv.); there is no room for both in the history of the prophet (*see* vii. 14), and it is now generally recognized that two conflicting representations have been combined: (*a*) vii., viii., x. 17–24, xii., (*b*) ix. 1–x. 16, xiii., xiv. (*See* further SAMUEL, SAUL.) The account of Eli, Shiloh and the ark (i.–iii.) is a natural prelude to iv.–vii., where, however, we lose sight of Samuel and the prophecy. The punishment of Eli and his sons (iv.) becomes a passing interest. The sequel of the defeat in iv. is not stated, although other allusions to the fall of Shiloh (Jer. vii. 12–15, xxvi. 6, 9, Ps. lxxviii. 60 *sqq.*), and the subsequent reappearance of the priestly family at Nob (xxi. *seq.*) suggest that a fuller account of the events must have been extant. A narrative of Eli and the priesthood of Shiloh has probably been used to form an introduction to Samuel's victory (vii.), and it has been supplemented partly by the account of the early life of the future prophet and judge (note the present abrupt introduction of Eli in i. 3) and partly by narratives of the history of the ark (v. *seq.*). The section was handled at a relatively late period. This is clear from the presence of the Deuteronomic prophecy in ii. 27–36, which hints at the rise of the Zadokite priests of Jerusalem. Also, Hannah's psalm (ii. 1–10)—the prototype of the "Magnificat"—is a post-exilic passage, "probably composed in celebration of some national success" (Driver); its present suitability rests upon the interpretation of verse 5.

Saul.—Saul's reign is introduced in xiii. 1, where a blank has been left for his age at accession (some mss. insert "30"); the duration of his reign is also textually uncertain. The formula is parallel to that in 2 Sam. ii. 10 *seq.*, v. 4 *seq.*, and frequently in the Book of Kings, with the additional feature that the age at accession, there usually confined to the Judaean kings, is here given for the Israelite Saul and his son Ishbosheth (*i.e.*, Ishbaal). The summary in xiv. 47 *sqq.* is immediately followed by a reference to the continuous Philistine warfare (v. 52, contrast vii. 13) which forms an introduction to the life of David. But the summary gives a picture of Saul's ability and position which differs so markedly from the subsequent more extensive narratives of David's history that its genuineness has sometimes been questioned; nevertheless, it is substantiated by the old poem quoted from the Book of Jashar in 2 Sam. i. 17–27, and a fundamental divergence in the traditions may be assumed. Similarly in 2 Sam. ii. 8–10*a*, the length of Ishbaal's reign conflicts with the history of David (ii. 11 and iv. 1–v. 3), and the reorganization of (north) Israel with the aid of Abner does not accord with other traditions, which represent David as the deliverer of (all?) Israel from the Philistine yoke (iii. 18, xix. 9). But ii. 8–10*a*, in common with 1 Sam. xiii. 1, xiv. 47–51 (*cf.*, also the introduction in 1 Sam. vii. 2 and the conclusion vii. 15–17), are of a literary character different from the detailed narratives; the redactional or annalistic style is noticeable, and they contain features characteristic of the annals which form the framework of Kings. In Kings the Israelite and Judaean records are kept carefully separate and the independent standpoint of each is at once obvious. Here, however, much complication arises from the combination of traditions of distinct origin, independent records of Saul having been revised or supplemented by writers whose interest lay in David.

David.—The stories of the relations between the founders of the respective monarchies of Israel and of Judah reflect the popular interest in DAVID (*q.v.*). Apart from the more detailed and continuous history, there are miscellaneous passages in 2

Sam. v.–viii., with an introduction (v. 1–3), and a concluding chapter rounding off David's reign (viii.). A similar collection in xxi.–xxiv. severs the closely-knit sequence of narratives in ix.–xx. (the "Court history of David") from David's death in 1 Ki. i.–ii. Their contents range over all periods, from the Amalekite war (viii. 12, *cf.* 1 Sam. xxx.) to David's "last words" (xxiii. 1; but *see* 1 Kings i. 1 and ii. 1). In particular they narrate the capture of Jerusalem from the Jebusites (v. 6–10) and other fights in that district as far as Gezer (*vv.* 17–25), the purchase of land from a Jebusite for the erection of an altar (xxiv.; *see* 1 Chron. xxi.–xxii. 1, 2 Chron. iii. 1), and the pacification of the Gibeonites (xxi. 1–14). The last two inter-related narratives are severed by the no less inter-related material in xxi. 15 *sqq.*, xxiii. 8 *sq.* (connected with the conflicts in ch. v.); and these in turn are now separated by the psalm in xxii. (Ps. xviii.) and by David's "last words." The repetition of the list of officials in viii. 15–18 and xx. 23–26 is attributed by several authorities (after Budde) to the later insertion of ix.–xx. 22. On this view, the two groups v.–viii., xxi.–xxiv. were once contiguous—though not necessarily in their *present* form or order.

The compiler of 2 Sam. v.–viii. has placed *after* the capture of Jerusalem (v. 6 *sqq.*) the conflict with the Philistines (v. 17 *sqq.*), where the "hold" is not Zion but some place of retreat, perhaps Adullam (*cf.* xxiii. 14). Similarly, the conflicts in xxi. 15 *sqq.*, xxiii. 8 *sqq.*, which are located around Gath, Lehi (so read xxiii. 11), Pas-dammim (so v. 9; *see* 1 Chron. xi. 13), Bethlehem, and the valley of Rephaim, should also precede the occupation of Jerusalem and the subsequent partition of territory among David's sons and others (*e.g.*, xiii. 23, near Bethel). These passages combine to furnish a representation of the events leading to the capture of the capital which is distinct from and now superseded by the detailed narratives in ii. 12–iv. Here, Ishbaal is east of the Jordan, David's men are engaged in fighting Benjamin and Israel—even at Gibeon (about 6 m. N.W. of Jerusalem), the interest of the history is in David's former relations with Israel at Saul's court, and he is regarded as the future deliverer of the oppressed people. The fragments preserved in 2 Sam. v.–viii., xxi.–xxiv. throw another light upon David's relations to Saul's family (xxi. 1–14, contrast ix.); and the stories of heroic conflicts with giant-like figures of Gath, etc. (xxiii. 9 *seq.*, 18, *cf.* 1 Chron. xi. 11, 20) find no place by the side of the more detailed records of his sojourn under the protection of a king of Gath, one of a confederation of Philistine cities (1 Sam. xxvii., xxix.). It is possible that popular stories of the conquest of the earlier inhabitants have been applied to the PHILISTINES (*q.v.*); their general character associates them with the legends of the "sons of Anak," who enter into Judaean (perhaps originally Calebite) tradition elsewhere (Num. xiii. 22, 28), and who according to one group of traditions occupied all the hill-country from Hebron northwards (Josh. xi. 21 *sqq.*, xv. 14).

Saul and David.—The accounts of David's conflicts with giant heroes and of the conquest of Jerusalem and its district belong to Judaean traditions which have been almost superseded by other traditions of the rise of the Hebrew monarchy and by popular narratives of early relations between the Judaean David and the (north) Israelite king and people. The emphasis (in 1 Sam.) upon the rejection of Saul, his enmity towards David, the latter's chivalry, and his friendship for Jonathan, partly account for the present literary intricacies. On quite general grounds, divine traditions of distinct origin (Calebite or Jerahmeelite; indigenous Judaean; North Israelite or Benjamite) are to be expected in a work now in post-exilic form. Moreover, the late genealogy of Saul in 1 Chron. viii. 29 *sqq.*, ix. 35 *sqq.*, is evidence of a keen interest in the Saulidae in post-exilic times. David's history is handled independently of Saul in 1 Sam. xxv.; and the narrative, now editorially connected with the context (v. 1, *see* xxviii. 3; and v. 44, *see* 2 Sam. iii. 15), gives a valuable picture of his life in the south of Palestine, with which we may compare his relations with south Judaean cities in xxx. 26–31. (The chapter with the prophecy of Abigail may be of Calebite origin.) His flight northwards to the Philistine king of Gath (xxvii.) is hardly connected with the preceding situations in xxiv. 17–22, xxv., or xxvi. 21–25, or with his previous slaughter of Philistines at Keilah (xxiii. 1–15). His earlier successes over them are ignored in xxix. 5, although the couplet there quoted now finds its only explanation in xviii. 7 after the death of Goliath and the defeat of the Philistines. These traditions of the relations between Judah and the Philistines (cf. xxvii. 5 seq.) are distinct from the popular stories of giants of Gath, and now form part of the joint history of David and Saul.

The independent narrative of Saul's fate represents one of the disastrous attacks which recur in earlier and later history of the north (xxviii.-4, xxix.). The geographical data are confused by the stories of David (see 1 Sam. xxviii. 4, xxix. 1), and while the "Philistines" march north to Jezreel to deliver their attack, David's presence is not discovered until Aphek is reached (xxix.). His journey is the opportunity for an Amalekite raid (xxx. cf. xxvii. 8 seq.), and a defeat of Amalek by David proves more successful than that which led to Saul's rejection (xv. 20 seq. 26–28). Similarly, Saul's disaster leaves Israel again in the hands of the "Philistines" (xxxi. 7, cf. xiii. 6 seq.), and it is for David to save the people of Israel out of their hands (2 Sam. iii. 18, cf. 1 Sam. ix. 16); so, also, David's wars (2 Sam. viii.) bear a certain resemblance to those of Saul (1 Sam. xiv. 47). The sequel to the joint history has another version of Saul's death (2 Sam. i. 6–10, 13–16), and an Amalekite is the offender; contrast his death in i. 15 seq. with iv. 10 seq. The chapter explains the transference of the royal insignia from Israel to Judah. Here is quoted (from the "Book of Jashar") the old poetical lament over the death of the valiant friends Saul and Jonathan, describing their successful warlike career, the wealth they brought the people, and the vivid sense of national misfortune (i. 19–27). It is utilized for the history of David, to whom it is attributed.

In general, it appears that those narratives wherein the histories of Saul and David are combined—very much in favour of the latter—were originally distinct from those where (a) Saul's figure is more in accord with the old poem from the Book of Jashar, and (b) where David's victories over prehistoric giants and his warlike movements to Jerusalem pave the way for the foundation—from a particular Judaean standpoint—of his remarkably long dynasty, for the literary problem of 1 and 2 Samuel is that of the writing of the history of the early monarchy and how it came to be formed.

BIBLIOGRAPHY.—See further the (German) commentaries of Löhr (1894), Nowack, Budde (1902) and Caspari (1926); H. P. Smith in the Internat. Crit. Comm. (1899) with his O.T. History (pp. 107–155), and A. R. S. Kennedy, Cent. Bible (1905); articles by Stenning in Hastings' Dict. and Stade in Ency. Bib. For the text see especially Wellhausen's model commentary (1871); Driver, Text of Samuel (1913); Budde in Haupt's Sacred Books of the O.T. (1894); Dhorme, Livres de Samuel (1910). For the psychological character of the several narratives see Gressmann's Schriften d. A.T. in Auswahl (Göttingen).
(S. A. C.)

SAMUEL OF NEHARDEA, usually called MAR SAMUEL or YARḤINAI (c. 165–c. 257), Babylonian Rabbi, was born in Nehardea in Babylonia and died there c. 257. He is associated with the fame of his great contemporary Rab ('Abba 'Arika q.v.). Besides his mastery in the traditional Law, Samuel was famed for his scientific attainments. He was one of the first to compile a Calendar of the Jewish year, thus preparing the way for the fixation of the festivals by means of scientific calculations. But Samuel's fame rests on the service which he rendered in adapting the life of the Jews of the diaspora to the law of the land. "The law of the State is binding law," was the principle which Samuel enunciated. When the king of Persia, Shapur, captured Mazaca-Caesarea, the Cappadocian capital, Samuel refused to mourn for the 12,000 Jews who lost their lives in its defence.

See Graetz, History of the Jews (English translation), vol. ii. ch. xix.
(I. A.)

SAN, BATTLES OF THE: see DUNAJEC-SAN, BATTLES OF THE; VISTULA-SAN, BATTLES OF THE.

SANA (Arabic Ṣan'ā'), a town of Yemen, southwestern Arabia, situated in 15° 22' N. and 44° 10' E. It is placed in a broad depression, running locally nearly north and south, on the lofty uptilted western edge of the great Arabian land block. It is 7,500 ft. above sea level and is connected with its chief port,

Hodeida (q.v.), on the Red sea, by a road which crosses the Qarn al-Wa'l pass (9,300 ft.), 25 mi. W. of the city, and then follows the plateau steps down to the coast. The population of Sana is estimated at 50,000.

Early traditions of ancient Sana connect it with the old kingdom of Himyar. Its early name was Azāl, possibly associated with Uzal of Gen. x, 27. A Syriac writer of the 6th century mentions a Himyarite nation of Auzalites. Its later name, signifying "fortified," is associated with the Abyssinian conquerors of Yemen. Sana was the capital of the Abyssinian, Abraha (A.D. 525), who built there the famous church (al-qalīs) which was destroyed two centuries later by order of the caliph Mansur (Azraqi, p. 91). Its later history has been a record of desert raids interspersed with periods of prosperity. After the withdrawal of the Turks (1918), Sana became the capital of the imam of Yemen proper.

The town consists of three parts: (1) the Medina, the old city, now the Arab quarter, on the east, containing the principal mosques. Here also, at its southeast corner, is the citadel al-Qasr. On the crest of Jabal Nukum (2,000 ft. above the valley) are the ruins of the old fort of al-Birash, and the Mutawakkil, formerly containing the palace of the imams, covering its western face; (2) the Bir 'Azab, west of the city, the residential area; and (3), on the extreme west, the Qā' al-Yahūd, or Jewish quarter. The city, with the Qasr and Mutawakkil, is surrounded by a lofty and thick wall. The Bir 'Azab and Qā' al-Yahūd are enclosed in a similar wall, but of more recent construction, connected with that of the city by the Mutawakkil, the whole forming a rough figure eight, some 2½ mi. long from east to west and ¾ mi. in breadth. The walls are pierced by eight gates. The city itself has narrow, paved streets, with massive flat-roofed houses of several stories. The Jami' Masjid, or principal mosque, with a model of the Ka'ba at Mecca in the centre, stands on the site of the Christian church built by Abraha (see above). Among the other mosques, of which there are 48 in all, that of Salah-al-Din is one of the finest. Ruins alone remain of the Qasr Ghumdan and other ancient buildings whose splendours were sung by the poets of the early days of Islam.

The neighbourhood of Sana suffers from a lack of water, but, in places where this is brought from the hill streams on the west, fields of barley and alfalfa (lucerne) and market gardens are seen, particularly at Raudha, a suburb 6 mi. N. of the town, and in the deep gorges of the Wadi Dhahr and Wadi Hadda, the terraced orchards of which are celebrated for their fine fruit trees. The water supply of the town is derived from numerous wells and from the Ghail Aswad, a small canal.

SANĀ'Ī, the common name of ABULMAJD MAJDŪD B. ADAM, the earliest among the great Ṣūfic poets of Persia, was a native of Ghazni (in Afghanistan). He flourished in the reigns of the Ghaznevid sultāns Ibrāhīm (1059–1099, 451–492 A.H.), his son Mas'ūd (1099–1114) and his grandson Bahrām (1118–1152). He composed chiefly qaṣīdas in honour of his sovereign Ibrāhīm and the great men of the realm, but the ridicule of a half-mad jester is said to have caused him to abandon the career of a court panegyrist and to devote his poetical abilities to higher subjects. For forty years he led a life of retirement and poverty, in which he wrote his great double-rhymed poem on ethics, which served as model to the masterpieces of Farīd-uddīn 'Attār and Jelāl ud-dīn Rūmī, the Ḥadīqat ul-ḥaqīqat, or "Garden of Truth" (also called Alkitāb alfakhrī). Sanā'ī wrote, besides the Ḥadīqat and the Ṭarīq-i-taḥqīq, several other Ṣūfic mathnawīs of similar purport: for instance, the Sair ul'ibād ilā'ma'ād, or "Man's Journey towards the Other World" (also called Kunūz-urrumūz, "The Treasures of Mysteries"); the 'Ishqnāma, or "Book of Love"; the 'Aqlnāma or "Book of Intellect"; the Kārnāma, or "Record of Stirring Deeds," etc.; and an extensive dīwān or collection of lyrical poetry. He died in 1150.

See Abdullatīf al-'Abbāsi's commentary (completed 1632 and preserved in a somewhat abridged form in several copies of the India Office Library); on the poet's life and works, Ouseley, Biogr. Notices, 184–187; Rieu's and Flügel's Catalogues, etc.; E. G. Browne, Literary History of Persia (1906), ii. 317–322; H. Ethé in W. Geiger's Grundriss der iranischen Philologie, ii. 282–284.

SAN ANGELO, a city of southwest Texas, U.S., 217 mi. N.W. of San Antonio, on federal highway 87, at an altitude of 1,847 ft.; county seat of Tom Green county. It is served by the Gulf, Colorado and Santa Fe and the Panhandle and Santa Fe railways.

Pop. (1950) 51,889; (1940) 25,802 by the federal census. It is an important wool and mohair market; has a large jobbing business and various manufacturing industries; and is the trade centre for a wide stock-raising and farming territory. Tom Green county has 200 mi. of spring-fed running streams and a large state and a large federal fish hatchery. San Angelo has an air force basic flying field. In 1915 the city adopted a commission-manager form of government.

Old Fort Concho, a post on the transcontinental mail-stage route, is still standing.

SAN ANTONIO, a city of Texas, U.S., and county seat of Bexar county; 80 mi. S.S.W. of Austin, on the San Antonio river at the mouth of the San Pedro. It is on federal highways 81, 87, 90, 181 and 281; has a municipal airport used by several air lines; and is served by the Missouri-Kansas-Texas, the Missouri Pacific and the Southern Pacific railways (with two direct lines to the deepwater port of Corpus Christi, 150 mi. S.S.E.) and by motor-bus lines in all directions. Pop. (1950) 406,811; (1940) 253,854 by the federal census.

San Antonio is surrounded by rich agricultural regions and there are still largely undeveloped, producing oil fields. It is the financial and commercial centre of a wide area; headquarters of the principal customs district on the Mexican border and has a foreign trade zone located at the municipal airport, the first such zone established inland. It is the seat of the largest military establishment of the United States government; one of the most picturesque and historically interesting of American cities; and a winter resort. The San Antonio, San Pedro and Acequia rivers together provide 30 mi. of winding waterways within the city limits, spanned by hundreds of bridges. The city consists of 69.4 sq.mi.

In the downtown section is the historic Alamo, the chapel of the Franciscan mission San Antonio de Valero (founded 1718), which since 1883 has been maintained by the state as a public monument and museum. Facing the Military plaza, where executions took place under Spanish and Mexican rule, is the former Governor's palace (1749), and south and west of the plaza lies the picturesque Mexican quarter.

The Veramendi palace, where Col. B. R. Milam was killed (Dec. 5, 1835) by a sharpshooter, is near by. Above and around the quaint old buildings rise the tall hotels and business structures of the modern city.

South of the city are four Franciscan missions: La Purisima Concepción de Acuna (founded in eastern Texas in 1716, and moved to San Antonio in 1731); San José de Aguayo (1720–31), one of the largest and most beautiful of the missions in America, with an exquisitely carved stone window; San Juan de Capistrano (1731); and San Francisco de la Espada (founded in eastern Texas in 1690 and moved to San Antonio in 1731). The city's drives are shaded by palms, live oaks and pecan trees. Its 56 public parks and plazas cover more than 2,000 ac. and provide facilities for polo, golf, rifle practice, swimming, tennis and other outdoor sports.

The water supply (purchased by the city from a private corporation in 1924 for $7,000,000) comes from more than 30 artesian wells, with a daily capacity of more than 120,000,000 gal. In the southern suburbs are two artesian wells, with a daily flow of 800,000 gal. of hot sulphur water, used for the treatment of rheumatism and skin diseases.

Near one of these wells is the Southwestern State Hospital for the Insane (1892).

The establishment of the United States armed forces at San Antonio includes Fort Sam Houston on Government hill, headquarters of the 4th army; three aviation fields and two flying schools, one of which is Randolph field, "the West Point of the air"; Kelly Air Force base, Lackland Air Force base, Brooks Air Force base and Brooke Army Medical centre. The military pay-roll expenditures amounted to more than $130,000,000 annually at mid-20th century. The anniversary of the battle of San Jacinto (April 21) is celebrated regularly by a week-long fiesta; and in February each year the Texas open golf tourney and a polo tourney are held. San Antonio has 75 public and 52 private schools, including Our Lady of the Lake college (1896) conducted by the Sisters of Divine Providence; 265 churches; and a number of charitable institutions. It is the see of Protestant Episcopal and Roman Catholic bishops.

The city operates under a commission form of government, adopted in 1914. The assessed valuation of property for 1949 was $415,249,350.

The area of the trade territory of San Antonio is greater than the combined area of several eastern states. The customs district of San Antonio has considerable commerce (largely exports) with Mexico. The city has about 720 wholesale houses, and its manufacturing establishments had an output in 1949 valued at $130,000,000. The principal manufactures are iron and steel, textiles, cigars, leather goods, clothing and soap. The oil fields in the vicinity have developed rapidly since the first one at Somerset (18 mi. S.) was opened in 1919. Bank clearings were $3,665,-359,463 in 1949.

San Antonio was important as the capital of Texas under Spanish and Mexican rule, and its history is closely bound up with that of the state (*see* TEXAS).

SAN ANTONIO DE LOS BAÑOS, a small town in Havana province, Cuba, about 23 mi. (by rail) S.W. of Havana. Pop. (1943) 16,512. San Antonio de los Baños is served by the western branch of the United Railways of Havana. It is on the banks of the Ariguanabo river, which drains a lake of the same name, and is itself one of the many "disappearing rivers" of the island; it becomes lost in a cave near San Antonio. The town has mineral springs and baths and is a summer resort. The tobacco of the Vuelta Abajo lands around the city is famous. The pueblo arose in the middle of the 18th century as a camp for convicts from Mexico. It became a villa in 1794.

Early in the 19th century refugees from Santo Domingo settled there and founded coffee estates that gave the place great prosperity for some years. Subsequently the cultivation of tobacco and development of the textile industry renewed its prosperity.

SANATRUCES (*Sinatruces*, Pers. *Sanatruk*), Parthian king. In the troublous times after the death of Mithradates II (*c.* 88 B.C.) he was made king by the Sacaraucae, a Mongolian tribe which had invaded Iran in 76 B.C. He was 80 years old and reigned 7 years; his successor was his son Phraates III. (Lucian, *Macrob.* 15; Phlegon, fr. 12 *ap.* Phot. cod. 97; Appian, *Mithr.* 104: Dio Cass. xxxvi, 45).

SANAVIRONAN, a small group of tribes of South American Indians, supposed, on meagre evidence, to constitute an independent linguistic stock. The Sanavironas, from whom the stock is named, and their relatives the Comechingones, lived in the Sierra de Cordoba, in the province of that name in Argentina. Only brief references to them are made by the early writers, and they are now extinct. They were said to have worn long tunics and mantles of wool and to have had some copper ornaments. They were remarkable in that they lived in semisubterranean houses, each containing several families. They were agricultural and used irrigation.

BIBLIOGRAPHY.—E. Boman, *Antiquités de la Region Andine de la République Argentine,* etc. (Paris, 1908); P. Cabrera, *Cordoba del Tucumán prehispaña y porto-historica* (Cordoba, Sept.–Oct. 1931).

SAN BENITO, a city of Cameron county, Tex., U.S., in the rich valley of the lower Rio Grande, 20 mi. N.W. of Brownsville; on federal highways 83 and 281 and served by the Missouri Pacific railway lines. Pop. (1950) 13,264; (1940) 9,501 by the federal census. It is the trade centre of an irrigated region, which produces fruit, vegetables and cotton to the value of $9,000,000 annually.

The city was founded in 1908, incorporated in 1910.

SAN BERNARDINO, a city of southern California, U.S., 60 mi. E. of Los Angeles, at the entrance to the Cajon pass from the north and the San Gorgonio pass from the east, 1,050 ft. above sea level; the county seat of San Bernardino county. It is on federal highways 66 and 99, and is served by the Santa Fe, the Southern Pacific, the Union Pacific and by motor coach and truck lines in every direction. Pop. (1950) 63,058. The city is surrounded by the orange groves, vineyards, orchards and fields of the fertile San Bernardino valley, and has for background the San Bernardino mountain range, with Mt. San Bernardino (11,600 ft.) only 20 mi. E. It is a division terminal of the Santa Fe railroad, which maintains extensive repair shops there and employs altogether more than 2,500 persons in the city. Other leading industries are the manufacture of steel, iron and steel castings, aeroplanes, lumber and meat products, ice and refrigerators. Norton Air Force Base is there.

In 1810, on the feast day of San Bernardino of Siena, a party of missionaries, soldiers and Indians from the San Gabriel Mission, under the leadership of Father Dumetz, came into the San Bernardino valley to establish a station for travellers between the Mission and the Sierras to the north, and built a chapel on a site now within the southern boundary of the city. In 1851 a colony of Mormons (about 500) came from Salt Lake, laid out a city, and did much to develop the agricultural possibilities of the valley. The county was organized in 1853, with its seat at San Bernardino, which was incorporated as a town in 1854. It was chartered as a city in 1864 and again in 1905. The Southern Pacific in 1876, and the Santa Fe in 1885, connected it first with the ocean and then with the east, and by 1900 the population had grown to 6,150.

SAN BLAS, a tribe of Indians, also known as the Cuna-Cuna or Tule, who live on the north coast of Panama between San Blas point and Port Obaldia. Although in contact with Europeans since the 16th century they have maintained racial purity and independence by vigorous opposition to foreign settlement. Their language is a Chibchan dialect, and their culture also shows South American origin. Reports of white Indians among this tribe have arisen from pronounced cases of hereditary albinism.

See H. W. Krieger, "Material culture of . . . South-eastern Panama" *U.S. National Museum, Bulletin 134* (1926).

SAN CARLOS, a municipality (with administrative centre and 17 *barrios* or districts) and port of the province of Negros Occidental, of the island of Negros, Philippine Islands. Pop. (1939), 69,990; 60 were white. San Carlos is a point of export for sugar, which is extensively produced in the surrounding region. The vernacular is a dialect of Bisayan. Of the inhabitants aged 6 to 19 inclusive, 13.5% attended school in 1939, and 22.2% of the population 10 years old and over was literate. The number of parcels of land declared for taxation in 1938 was 1,840.

SAN CARLOS, a municipality (with administrative centre and 51 *barrios* or districts) of the province of Pangasinan, Luzon, Philippine Islands, on the railway running from Manila to Dagupan. Pop. (1939) 47,334, of whom 23,093 were males and there were no whites. It is in the midst of a fertile agricultural region. The buri palm fibre is used for making the native helmet (salacot). The town has brickyards, pottery factories and trade of importance. The Pangasinan language is the vernacular. Of the inhabitants aged 6 to 19 inclusive, 33.5% attended school in 1939, while 50.1% of the population 10 years old and over was literate. (C. S. L.)

SANCERRE, a town of central France, in the department of Cher, 34 mi. N.E. of Bourges by rail. Pop. (1946) 1,803. Sancerre, which gives its name to the small wine-growing district of Sancerrois, stands on an isolated vine-clad hill (1,000 ft.) about 1 mi. from the left bank of the Loire. A cylindrical keep of the 15th century is the only relic of an ancient stronghold of the counts of Sancerre. From 1037 to 1152 the title of count of Sancerre was held by the counts of Champagne; from the latter year till 1640 it had its own counts, descended from Theobald IV of Champagne.

SANCHI, a small village in Central India, famous as the site of what are almost certainly the oldest buildings in India now standing. They are Buddhist topes (Pali. *thūpa*; Sanskrit, *stūpa*), that is, memorial mounds, standing on the level top of a small sandstone hill about 300 ft. high on the left bank of the river Betwa. The number of topes on this and the adjoining hills is

considerable. On the Sānchi hill itself are only ten, but one of these is by far the most important and imposing of all. It is a solid dome of stone, about 103 ft. in diameter, and now about 42 ft. high. It must formerly have been much higher, the top having

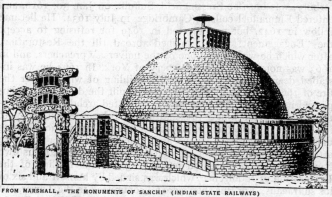

FROM MARSHALL, "THE MONUMENTS OF SANCHI" (INDIAN STATE RAILWAYS)
A STŪPA AT SANCHI, INDIA, AN EXAMPLE OF BUDDHIST ARCHITECTURE, SHOWING THE SACRED UMBRELLA ON THE DOME

originally formed a terrace, 34 ft. in diameter, on which stood lofty columns. Round the base is a flagged pathway surrounded by a stone railing and entered at the four points of the compass by gateways some 18 ft. high. Both gateways and railing are elaborately covered with bas-reliefs and inscriptions. The latter give the names of the donors of particular portions of the architectural ornamentation, and most of them are written in the

FROM MARSHALL, "THE MONUMENTS OF SANCHI" (INDIAN STATE RAILWAYS)
GUPTA TEMPLE, SANCHI, INDIA; BUILT ABOUT A.D. 300–500
This Buddhist shrine is an example of Indian "Renaissance" architecture

characters used before and after the time of Asoka in the middle of the 3rd century B.C. The monuments are Buddhist, the bas-reliefs illustrate passages in the Buddhist writings, and the inscriptions make use of Buddhist technical terms.

SANCHUNIATHON, an ancient Phoenician sage, who belongs more to legend than to history. He is said to have flourished "even before the Trojan times." Philo Herennius of Byblus claimed to have translated his writings from the Phoenician originals. According to Philo, Sanchuniathon derived the sacred lore from the mystic inscriptions on the Ἀμμουνεῖς (probably *hammānim*, "sun pillars," *cf.* Is. xxvii. 9, etc.) which stood in the Phoenician temples. That any writings of Sanchuniathon ever existed it is impossible to say. Philo conjured with a venerable name to gain credit for his narrative.

See Eusebius, *Praep. Ev.* i. 9 (Müller, *Fragm. hist. Graec.* iii. pp. 563 *seq.*).

SAN CRISTÓBAL (formerly called SAN CRISTÓBAL DE LOS LLANOS, CIUDAD DE LAS CASAS and CIUDAD REAL), a town of Mexico, in the State of Chiapas, on a level tableland about 6,700 ft. above sea level and 48 mi. E.N.E. of Tuxtla Gutiérrez. Population 11,768. The surrounding country is fertile and healthful and is populated chiefly with Indians. San Cristóbal was founded in 1528 on the site of an Indian village, and afterwards was famous as the residence of Las Casas, bishop of Chiapas. It was the capital of Chiapas until near the end of the 19th century.

SANCROFT, WILLIAM (1616–1693), archbishop of Canterbury, was born at Fressingfield, Suffolk, on Jan. 30, 1616, and entered Emmanuel college, Cambridge, in July 1634. He became fellow in 1642, but was ejected in 1649 for refusing to accept the "Engagement." He remained abroad till the Restoration, after which he was chosen one of the university preachers, and in 1663 was nominated to the deanery of York. In 1664 he was installed dean of St. Paul's, to the rebuilding of which, after the fire of 1666, he gave £1,400. He also rebuilt the deanery, and improved its revenue. In 1668 he was admitted archdeacon of Canterbury upon the king's presentation, but he resigned the post in 1670. In 1677, being now prolocutor of the Convocation, he was unexpectedly advanced to the archbishopric of Canterbury. He attended Charles II. upon his deathbed. He wrote with his own hand the petition presented in 1687 against the reading of the Declaration of Indulgence, which was signed by himself and six of his suffragans. For this they were all committed to the Tower, but were acquitted. Upon the withdrawal of James II. he concurred with the Lords in a declaration to the prince of Orange for a free parliament, and due indulgence to the Protestant dissenters. But, when that prince and his consort were declared king and queen, he refused to take the oath to them, and was accordingly suspended and deprived. From Aug. 5, 1691, till his death on Nov. 24, 1693, he retired to his native place.

He published *Fur praedestinatus* (1651), *Modern Politics* (1652), and *Three Sermons* (1694). *Nineteen Familiar Letters to Mr. North* (afterwards Sir Henry North) appeared in 1757. *See* G. O'Oyly, *Life of Sancroft* (2 vols., 1821); A. Strickland, *Lives of the Seven Bishops* (1866).

SANCTIONS AND GUARANTEES in international law correspond to the means adopted in national law to enforce legal decisions. During the years which followed the World War it became increasingly apparent that the most important and the most enduring of European political problems was that known as the problem of "security" (*q.v.*).

As a deduction from the new conception of security the word "sanctions" began to replace in the language of diplomacy the word "alliance." Security was now to be sought not in limited agreements between small groups of states to fight together whenever any of them should, for whatever cause, be involved in international conflict, but in common agreements among a greater or smaller number of states to act together when—and only when—the established rights of one of them had been violated by force. Security, therefore, must be found in "sanctions" against the wrongdoer. For some time indeed, the word "guarantees" was used instead of, or on an equal footing with, the word "sanctions," but gradually the use of the word "guarantee" disappeared and the word "sanctions" took its place.

The discussions which occurred after the war soon showed that there were two ways by which Governments believed the result in view could be achieved; first, by creating a general system embracing all the States throughout the world; and second, by creating limited arrangements applying to a certain number of States situated in geographical proximity to each other and bound together by common bonds of material interest.

Article 16 of the Covenant.—It was by the general method that the first step was made towards the organization of a true system of international sanctions. This first step consisted in the adoption of the Covenant of the League of Nations, Article 16 of which imposes obligations upon every member of the League to adopt common coercive measures, including especially a financial and economic boycott, against states which, in violation of the undertakings of the Covenant, resort to war. But unfortunately Article 16 contained ambiguities which seriously diminished the confidence of Governments in its efficiency. It was not, therefore, generally regarded as by itself creating a sufficiently sound system of sanctions to solve the problem of security. For that reason the Temporary Mixed Commission set up by the Council of the League of Nations prepared in 1923 the draft treaty of mutual guarantee (or assistance), on the basis of which was prepared the

Geneva Protocol of 1924. Both instruments were founded on the clear acceptance by all signatory states of obligations to co-operate by military or other necessary means against an aggressor.

Regional Guarantees.—The second method received its first application in the Anglo-American-French guarantee treaties drawn up in 1919 at Paris. These treaties failed to secure ratification, and were replaced by the Franco-Belgian, Franco-Polish and other similar treaties of alliance. The Little Entente was another example of the same method. But it was recognized even by the authors of these treaties that although they were subject to the Covenant of the League they were, nevertheless, liable to degenerate into alliances of the old sort, and that therefore they would be dangerous unless they were effectively controlled by the League. The Temporary Mixed Commission above mentioned in its draft treaty of mutual assistance for the first time combined the two methods into one coherent system. The Protocol similarly recognized the utility of special treaties in support of general sanctions, but on condition that such special treaties could only be applied *after* it had been recognized by some impartial arbitrator that aggression had taken place. After the failure of the combination method of the Geneva Protocol, a return was made in the Locarno Agreements to the method of partial treaties. These agreements, however, in no way resembled an old-time alliance; the concern of their authors was plainly to create one more stable element in a new system of general international sanctions against aggression. (*See* LEAGUE OF NATIONS and bibliography thereto and INTERNATIONAL LAW, PUBLIC.) (P. J. N.-B.)

On Oct. 9, 1935, the League Assembly, with Austria and Hungary dissenting, declared that Italy had resorted to war contrary to Article XII of the Covenant. Fifty member states pledged to apply collective sanctions against Italy and, in due course, these countries adopted an arms embargo. A financial embargo was added by 48 states, a boycott of imports from Italy by 47 states, a ban on certain exports to Italy by 47 states, and a pact of mutual support by 34 states. The U.S., acting independently, applied an embargo to both belligerents. League sanctions did not include oil and, as limited, they failed to arrest Italy's invasion of Ethiopia. In June 1936, sanctions were abandoned and an endeavour by France to apply sanctions to Germany when it marched troops into the Rhineland did not materialize.

BIBLIOGRAPHY.—*International Sanctions; A Report by a Group of Members of the Royal Institute of International Affairs* (1938); Royal Institute of International Affairs, *Sanctions* (London, 1935); P. S. Wild, *Sanctions and Treaty Enforcement* (1934).

SANCTI SPÍRITUS, an old Cuban city in Las Villas province, is on a sandy plain in an angle of the Yayabo river, which winds through the city. Pop. (1943), 28,262. It is connected by railway with Zaza del Medio, on the main railway line of the island, and with its port, Tunas de Zaza, 30 mi. (by rail) to the south. Sancti Spíritus was one of the seven cities founded by Diego Velásquez. Its settlement was ordered in 1514 and accomplished in 1516. The present city is about two miles from the original site (Pueblo Viejo). In 1518, as a result of the war of the Comunidades of Castille, a mimic war broke out in Sancti Spíritus among its two score villagers. The place was sacked by French and English corsairs in 1719. Sancti Spíritus grew rapidly in the second quarter of the 20th century in consequence of the expansion of the hide and dairy industries. (C. E. Mc.)

SANCTORIUS (the Latin form of SANTORIO SANTORIO) (1561–1636), professor at Padua and colleague of Galileo, owes his medical fame to his demonstration that loss by "insensible perspiration" exceeds all other bodily excretions combined. Being inspired by the devices of Galileo, he invented a thermometer and an apparatus for measuring the pulse, and also a trocar and a cannula. His chief works are the *De Medicina Statica* (1614) and a commentary on the *Canon* of Avicenna.

SANCTUARY, a sacred or consecrated place, particularly one affording refuge, protection or right of asylum. The word is also applied to the privilege itself, the right of safe refuge, and even to places of refuge for animals, such as a "bird sanctuary." In Egyptian, Greek or Roman temples it was applied to the *cella* in which stood the statue of the god, and the Latin word for altar, *ara,* was used for protection as well. In Roman Catholic usage sanctuary is sometimes applied to the whole church, as a consecrated building, but is generally limited to the choir. The idea that such places afforded refuge to criminals or refugees is founded upon the primitive and universal belief in the contagion of holiness. Hence it was sacrilege to remove the man who had gained the holy precincts; he was henceforth invested with a part of the sacredness of the place, and was inviolable so long as he remained there. The story of the death of Demosthenes (*q.v.*) is a famous instance. Not all Greek and Roman temples, however, had the right of sanctuary. But where it existed, the action of the Roman civil law was suspended, and in imperial times the statues and pictures of the emperors were a protection against pursuit. Roman law did not recognize the use of Christian sanctuaries until toward the end of the 4th century, but the growing recognition of the office of bishop as intercessor helped much to develop it. In 399 the right of Christian sanctuary was finally and definitely recognized, and in 419 the privilege was extended in the western empire to 50 paces from the church door. In 431, by an edict of Theodosius and Valentinian it was extended to include the church court-yard and whatever stood therein, in order to provide some other place than the church for the fugitives to eat and sleep. Justinian in a Novel of the year 535 limited the privilege to those not guilty of the grosser crimes. In the new Germanic kingdoms, while violent molestation of the right of sanctuary was forbidden, the fugitive was given up after an oath had been taken not to put him to death. This legislation was copied by the Church at the council of Orleans in 511; the penalty of penance was added, and the whole decree backed by the threat of excommunication. Thus it passed into Gratian's Decretum, but historians like Gregory of Tours have many tales to tell showing how frequently it was violated.

The earliest extant mention of the right of sanctuary in England is contained in the code of laws issued by the Anglo-Saxon king Aethelberht in A.D. 600. By these he who infringed the church's privilege was to pay twice the fine attaching to an ordinary breach of the peace. Crosses inscribed with the word "Sanctuarium," were common on the highways, serving probably as sign-posts to guide fugitives to neighbouring sanctuaries. The canon law allowed the protection of sanctuary to those guilty of crimes of violence for a limited time only, in order that some compensation (*wergild*) should be made, or to check blood-vengeance. The procedure, upon seeking sanctuary, was regulated in the minutest detail. The fugitive had to make confession of his crime to one of the clergy, to surrender his arms, swear to observe the rules and regulations of the religious houses, pay an admission fee, give, under oath, fullest details of his crime (the instrument used, the name of the victim, etc.), and at Durham he had to toll a special bell as a formal signal that he prayed sanctuary, and put on a gown of black cloth on the left shoulder of which was embroidered a St. Cuthbert's cross. The protection afforded by a sanctuary at common law was this: a person accused of felony might fly for safeguard of his life to sanctuary, and there, within 40 days, go, clothed in sack-cloth, before the coroner, confess the felony and take an oath of *abjuration of the realm,* whereby he undertook to quit the kingdom, and not return without the king's leave. Upon confession he was, *ipso facto,* convicted of the felony, suffered attainder of blood and forfeited all his goods, but had time allowed him to fulfil his oath. The abjurer started forth on his journey, armed only with a wooden cross, bareheaded and clothed in a long white robe, which made him conspicuous among mediaeval wayfarers. He had to keep to the king's highway, was not allowed to remain more than two nights in any one place, and must make his way to the coast quickly. The time allowed for his journey was not long. In Edward III.'s reign only nine days were given an abjurer to walk from Yorkshire to Dover.

Under the Norman kings there appear to have been two kinds of sanctuary; one *general,* which belonged to every church, and another *peculiar,* which had its force in a grant by charter from the king. This latter type could not be claimed by prescription, and had to be supported by usage within legal memory. General sanctuaries protected only those guilty of felonies, while those

by special grant gave immunity even to those accused of high or petty treason, not for a time only but apparently for life. Of chartered sanctuaries there were at least 22: Abingdon, Armathwaite, Beaulieu, Battle Abbey, Beverley, Colchester, Derby, Durham, Dover, Hexham, Lancaster, St. Mary le Bow (London), St. Martin's le Grand (London), Merton Priory, Northampton, Norwich, Ripon, Ramsey, Wells, Westminster, Winchester, York. At the Reformation general and peculiar sanctuaries both suffered drastic curtailment of their privileges, but the great chartered ones suffered most. By the reforming act of 1540 Henry VIII. established seven cities as peculiar sanctuaries. These were Wells, Westminster, Northampton, Manchester (afterwards transferred to Chester), York, Derby and Launceston. By an act of James I. (1623), sanctuary, as far as crime was concerned, was abolished throughout the kingdom. The privilege lingered on for civil processes in certain districts which had been the site of former sanctuaries and which became the haunts of criminals who there resisted arrest—a notable example being that known as Whitefriars between Fleet Street and the Thames, east of the Temple. This locality was nicknamed Alsatia (the name first occurs in Shadwell's plays in Charles II.'s reign), and there criminals were able to a large extent to defy the law, arrests only being possible under writs of the lord chief justice. So flagrant became the abuses that in 1697 the "Escape from Prison Act," finally abolished all such alleged privileges. A further amending act of 1723 completed the work of destruction. The privileged places named in the two acts were the Minories, Salisbury Court, Whitefriars, Fulwood's Rents, Mitre Court, Baldwin's Gardens, The Savoy, The Clink, Deadman's Place, Montague Close, The Mint and Stepney.

In Scotland the most famous sanctuaries were those attaching to the Church of Wedale, now Stow, near Galashiels, and that of Lesmahagow, Lanark. All religious sanctuaries were abolished in the northern kingdom at the Reformation. But the debtor found sanctuary from "diligence" in Holyrood House and its precincts until late in the 17th century. This sanctuary did not protect criminals, or even all debtors, *e.g.,* not crown debtors or fraudulent bankrupts; and it was possible to execute a *meditatio fugae* warrant within the sanctuary. The abolition of imprisonment for debt in 1881 practically abolished this privilege of sanctuary.

A presumptive right of sanctuary attached to the royal palaces, and arrests could not be made there. In Anglo-Saxon times the king's peace extended to the palace and 3,000 paces around it: it extended to the king himself beyond the precincts. At the present day members of parliament cannot be served with writs or arrested within the precincts of the houses of parliament, which extend to the railings of Palace yard. During the Irish agitation of the 'eighties Parnell and others of the Irish members avoided arrest for some little while by living in the house and never passing outside the gates of the yard. The houses of ambassadors were in the past quasi-sanctuaries. This was a natural corollary of their diplomatic immunities (*see* DIPLOMACY).

In Europe, generally, the right of sanctuary survived under restrictions down to the end of the 18th century. In Germany the more serious crimes of violence were always excepted. Highwaymen, robbers, traitors and habitual criminals could not claim church protection. In 1418 sanctuary was further regulated by a bull of Martin V. and in 1504 by another of Julius II. In a modified form the German *Asylrecht* lasted to modern times, not being finally abolished till about 1780. In France *le droit d'asile* existed throughout the middle ages, but was much limited by an edict of Francis I. in 1539. It was entirely abolished at the Revolution.

BIBLIOGRAPHY.—Samuel Pegge, "Sketch of History of Asylum or Sanctuary," Soc. of Antiq. of London, *Archaeologia* viii. 1–44 (1787); Henri Wallon, *Droit d'asile* (1837); Aug. von Bulmerincq, *Das Asylrecht* (Dorpat, 1853); A. P. Stanley, *Memorials of Westminster Abbey* (1882); Bissel, *The Law of Asylum in Israel* (1884); J. C. Cox, *The Sanctuaries and Sanctuary Seekers of Medieval England* (1911); J. Groll, *Die Elemente des Kirchlichen Freiungsrechtes* (1911).

SAND, GEORGE (1804–1876), the pseudonym of Madame Amandine Lucile Aurore Dudevant, *née* Dupin.

George Sand was the daughter of Maurice Dupin, a retired lieutenant, and of Sophie Delaborde, the daughter of a Paris bird-fancier. Their ill-assorted marriage took place only a month before the birth of the child (July 1, 1804; at Paris). Her paternal grandfather was M. Dupin de Francueil, a farmer-general of the revenue, who married the widow of Count Horn, a natural son of Louis XV., she in her turn being the natural daughter of Maurice de Saxe, the most famous of the many illegitimate children of Augustus the Strong, by Marie Rinteau ("Mlle. de Verrières"). George Sand, who was a firm believer in the doctrine of heredity, devotes a whole volume of her autobiography (*Histoire de ma vie*, 1857 seq.) to the elaboration of this strange pedigree. She boasts of the royal blood which ran through her veins, but she is no less frank in declaring that she is *vilaine et très vilaine*, a daughter of the people who shares by birth their instincts and sympathies. Her birth itself was romantic. Her father died when she was a small child, and her mother, after a struggle, abandoned Aurore to the care of her grandmother, Madame Dupin de Francueil, who was a survival of the ancien régime.

Her childhood was spent at Nohant, near La Châtre in Berry, Madame Dupin's country house. Here she imbibed the passionate love of country scenes and country life which neither absence, politics nor dissipation could uproot; here she learnt to understand the ways and thoughts of the peasants, and laid up that rich store of scenes and characters which a marvellously retentive memory enabled her to draw upon at will. Next to the grandmother, the most important person in the household at Nohant was Deschatres. He was an ex-abbé who had shown his devotion to his mistress when her life was threatened during the Revolution, and henceforward was installed at Nohant as factotum. He was maire of the village, tutor to Aurore's half-brother, and undertook the education of the girl. At odd hours of lessons she picked up a smattering of Latin, music and natural science, but most days were holidays and spent in country rambles and games with village children.

From the free out-door life at Nohant she passed at thirteen to the convent of the English Augustinians at Paris, where for the first two years she never went outside the walls. Nothing better shows the plasticity of her character than the ease with which she adapted herself to this sudden change. One day in the convent chapel she underwent conversion in the mystical sense. There is no doubt of the sincerity of her narrative, or even the permanence of her religious feelings under all her many phases of faith and aberrations of conduct.

Again in 1820 Aurore exchanged the restraint of a convent for freedom, being recalled to Nohant by Mme. de Francueil, who had no intention of letting her granddaughter grow up a *dévote*. She rode across country with her brother, she went out shooting with Deschatres, she sat by the cottage doors on the long summer evenings and heard the flax-dressers tell their tales of witches and warlocks. She was a considerable linguist and knew English, Italian and some Latin, though she never tackled Greek. She read widely though unsystematically, studying philosophy in Aristotle, Leibnitz, Locke and Condillac, and feeding her imagination with *René* and *Childe Harold*. Her confessor lent her the *Génie du Christianisme*, and to this book she ascribes the first change in her religious views.

On her grandmother's death she married on Dec. 11, 1822, Casimir Dudevant, natural son of Baron Dudevant. He seems then to have been neither better nor worse than the Berrichon squires around him, and the first years of her married life, during which her son Maurice and her daughter Solange were born, except for lovers' quarrels, were passed in peace and quietness, though signs were not wanting of the coming storm. Among these must be mentioned her friendship with Aurélien de Sèze, advocate-general at Bourdeau, which her husband resented. So long as the conventions were preserved she endured her life, but when her husband took to drinking and made love to the maids under her eyes she resolved to break a yoke that had grown intolerable. She then discovered a paper docketed "Not to be opened till after my death," which was nothing but a railing accusation against herself. She at once quitted Nohant, taking with her Solange, and in 1831 an amicable separation was agreed upon, by which her whole estate was surrendered to the husband with the stipulation that she should receive, in return for this

relinquishment on her part, an allowance of £120 a year.

Aurore Dudevant had regained her liberty, and made no secret of her intention to use it to the full. She endeavoured unsuccessfully to eke out her irregularly paid allowance by various expedients, and lived in a garret. She found a friend in Delatouche, the editor of *Figaro*. He was a native of Berry, like herself, a stern but kindly taskmaster who taught her the trade of journalism. On the staff of *Figaro* was another compatriot, Jules Sandeau, a clever and attractive young lawyer. Articles written in common soon led to a complete literary partnership, and in 1831 there appeared in the *Revue de Paris* a joint novel entitled *Prima Donna* and signed Jules Sand. Shortly after this was published in book form with the same signature a second novel, *Rose et Blanche*. The sequel to this literary alliance is best recounted in George Sand's own words: "I resisted him for three months but then yielded; I lived in my own apartment in an unconventional style." Her first independent novel, *Indiana* (1832), was written at the instigation of Delatouche, and the world-famous pseudonym George (originally Georges) Sand was adopted as a compromise between herself and her partner. The one wished to throw *Indiana* into the common stock, the other refused to lend his name, or even part of his name, to a work in which he had had no share. The novel was received with instant acclamation. *Indiana* is a direct transcript of the author's personal experiences (the disagreeable husband is M. Dudevant to the life), and an exposition of her theory of sexual relations which is founded thereon. To many critics it seemed that she had said her whole say and that nothing but replicas could follow. *Valentine*, which was published in the same year, indicated that it was but the first chapter in a life of endless adventures, and that the imagination which turned the crude facts into poetry, and the fancy which played about them like a rainbow, were inexhaustible.

Her liaison with Jules Sandeau, which lasted more than a year, was abruptly terminated by the discovery in their apartment on an unexpected return from Nohant of *une blanchisseuse quelconque*. For a short while she was broken hearted:—"My heart is a cemetery!" she wrote to Sainte-Beuve. "A necropolis," was the comment of her discarded lover when years later the remark was repeated to him.

Her third novel, *Lélia* (1833), is in the same vein, a stronger and more outspoken diatribe against society and the marriage law. Lélia is a female Manfred, and Dumas had some reason to complain that George Sand was giving them "du lord Byron au kilo." But a new chapter in her life was now to open. In her despair she turned for comfort and counsel to Sainte-Beuve, now constituted her regular father confessor. He recommended new friendships, but she found Dumas "trop commis-voyageur," Jouffroy too serenely virtuous and Musset "trop dandy." Mérimée was tried for a week, but the cool cynic and the perfervid apostle of women's rights proved mutually repulsive. Alfred de Musset was introduced, and the two natures leapt together.

The Musset Episode.—Towards the end of 1833 George Sand, after winning the reluctant consent of Musset's mother, set out in the poet's company for Italy, and in January 1834 the pair reached Venice, staying first at the Hôtel Danieli and then in lodgings. At first it was a veritable honeymoon; conversation never flagged and either found in the other his soul's complement. But there is a limit to love-making, and George Sand, always practical, set to work to provide the means of living. Musset, though he depended on her exertions, was first bored and then irritated at the sight of this *terrible vache à écrire*, whose pen was going for eight hours a day, and sought diversion in the cafés and other less reputable resorts of pleasure. The consequence was a nervous illness, through which George Sand nursed him with tenderness and care. But she made love at the same time to a young Venetian doctor whom she had called in, by name Pagello. The two found their way eventually to Paris, leaving Musset in Italy, deeply wounded in his affections, but, to do him justice, taking all the blame for the rupture on himself. George Sand soon tired of her new love, and even before she had given him his congé was dying to be on again with the old. She cut off her hair and sent it to Musset as a token of penitence, but Musset, though he still flirted with her, never quite forgave her infidelity and refused to admit her to his deathbed. Among the mass of *romans à clef* and pamphlets which the adventure produced, two only have any literary importance, Musset's *Confessions d'un enfant du siècle* and George Sand's *Elle et lui*. In the former woman appears as the serpent whose trail is over all; in the latter, written twenty-five years after the event, she is the guardian angel abused and maltreated by men. *Lui et elle*, the rejoinder of the poet's brother Paul de Musset, was even more a travesty of the facts with no redeeming graces of style.

It remains to trace the influence, direct or indirect, of the poet on the novelist. *Jacques* was the first outcome of the journey to Italy, and in precision and splendour of style it marks a distinct progress. In *Les Lettres d'un voyageur*, which ran in the *Revue des deux mondes* between 1834 and 1836, we have not only impressions of travel, but the direct impressions of men and things not distorted by the exigencies of a novel. The Everard of the *Lettres* introduces us to a new and for the time a dominant influence on the life and writings. Michel de Bourges was the counsel whose eloquent pleadings brought the suit for a judicial separation to a successful issue in 1836. Unlike her former lovers, he was a man of masterful will, a philosopher who carried her intellect by storm before he laid siege to her heart. He preached republicanism to her by the hour, and even locked her up in her bedroom to reflect on his sermons. She was but half converted, and fled before long from a republic in which art and poetry had no place. Other celebrities who figure in the *Lettres* under a transparent disguise are Liszt and Mme. d'Agoult (known to literature as Daniel Stern), whom she met in Switzerland and entertained for some months at Nohant. Liszt, in after years when they had drifted apart, wrote of her: "George Sand catches her butterfly and tames it in her cage by feeding it on flowers and nectar—this is the love period. Then she sticks her pin into it when it struggles—that is the congé and it always comes from her. Afterwards she vivisects it, stuffs it, and adds it to her collection of heroes for novels." There is some truth in the satire, but it wholly misrepresents her rupture with Chopin.

Liaison with Chopin.—It was doubtless a revulsion of feeling against the doctrinaires, especially the strong influence of Lamennais and P. Leroux, and in particular against the puritanic reign of Michel that made her turn to Chopin. She found the *maestro* towards the end of 1837 dispirited by a temporary eclipse of popularity and in the first stage of his fatal malady, and carried him off to winter with her in the south. How she roughed it on an island unknown to tourists is told in *Un hiver à Majorque* (1842), a book of travel that may take rank with Heine's *Reisebilder*. In nearly all George Sand's loves there was a strong strain of motherly feeling. Chopin was first petted by her like a spoilt darling and then nursed for years like a sick child. In the end Chopin remonstrated with her for refusing to receive her ne'er do well son-in-law, Clésinger, at Nohant, and when she resented his interference, he left her in anger.

Meanwhile, during this, her second period, George Sand allowed herself to be the mouthpiece of others—"un écho qui embellissait la voix," as Delatouche expressed it. *Spiridion* (1838) and *Les Sept cordes de la lyre* (1840) are mystic echoes of Lamennais. *Le Compagnon du tour de France* (1841), *Les Maîtres mosaïstes* and *Le Meunier d'Angibault* (1845), *Le Péché de M. Antoine* (1847) are all socialistic novels. George Sand had adopted her socialism from Pierre Leroux, and many works of this period are inspired by his humanitarianism. *Consuelo* (1842–1844) and its sequel *La Comtesse de Rudolstadt* (1843–1845) are *fantaisies à la Chopin*, though the stage on which they are played is the Venice of Musset. Chopin is the Prince Karol of *Lucrezia Floriani* (1847), a self-portraiture unabashed as the *Tagebuch einer Verlorenen* and innocent as *Paul et Virginie*.

George Sand wrote with the rapidity of Walter Scott and the regularity of Anthony Trollope. For years her custom was to retire to her desk at 10 P.M. and not to rise from it till 5 A.M. She wrote *à la diable*, starting with some central thesis to set forth or some problem to investigate, but with no predetermined plot or plan of action. Round this nucleus her characters (too

often mere puppets) grouped themselves, and the story gradually crystallized. This unmethodical method produces in her longer and more ambitious novels, in *Consuelo* for instance and its continuation, a tangled wilderness, the clue to which is lost or forgotten; but in her novelettes, when there is no change of scenery and the characters are few and simple, it results in the perfection of artistic writing, "an art that nature makes."

The Pastoral Novels.—From novels of revolt and tendency novels George Sand turned at last to simple stories of rustic life, the genuine pastoral. It is here that she shows her true originality and by these she will chiefly live. George Sand by her birth and bringing-up was half a peasant herself, in M. Faguet's phrase, "un paysan qui savait parler." She had got to know the heart of the peasant—his superstitions, his suspiciousness and low cunning, no less than his shrewdness, his sturdy independence and his strong domestic attachments. *Jeanne* (1844) begins the series which has been happily called the Bucolics of France. To paint a Joan of Arc who lives and dies inglorious is the theme she sets herself, and through most of the novel it is perfectly executed. The last chapters when Jeanne appears as the Velida of Mont Barbot and the Grande Pastoure are a falling off and a survival of the romanticism of her second manner. *La Mare au diable* (1846) is a clear-cut gem, perfect as a work of Greek art. *François le champi* and *La Petite Fadette* are of no less exquisite workmanship. *Les Maîtres sonneurs* (1853) brings the series of village novels to a close, but as closely akin to them must be mentioned the *Contes d'une grande-mère*, delightful fairy tales of the Talking Oak, Wings of Courage and Queen Coax, told to her grandchildren in the last years of her life.

The revolution of 1848 arrested for a while her novelistic activities. She composed manifestos for her friends, addressed letters to the people, and even started a newspaper. But her political ardour was short-lived; she cared little about forms of government, and, when the days of June dashed to the ground her hopes of social regeneration, she returned to her quiet country ways and her true vocation as an interpreter of nature, a spiritualizer of the commonest sights of earth and the homeliest household affections. In 1849 she writes from Berry to a political friend: "You thought that I was drinking blood from the skulls of aristocrats. No, I am studying Virgil and learning Latin!" In her latest works she went back to her earlier themes of romantic and unchartered love, but the scene is shifted from Berry, which she felt she had exhausted, to other provinces of France, and instead of passionate manifestos we have a gallery of *genre* pictures treated in the spirit of *François le champi*. "Vous faites," she said to her friend Honoré de Balzac, "la comédie humaine; et moi, c'est l'églogue humaine que j'ai voulu faire."

George Sand was as fond of acting as Goethe, and like him began with a puppet stage, succeeded by amateur theatricals, the chief entertainment provided for her guests at Nohant. Undaunted by many failures, she dramatized several of her novels with moderate success—*François le champi*, played at the Odéon in 1849, and *Les Beaux Messieurs de Bois-Doré* (1862) were the best; *Claudie*, produced in 1851, is a charming pastoral play, and *Le Marquis de Villemer* (1864) (in which she was helped by Dumas fils) was a genuine triumph. Her statue by Clésinger was placed in the foyer of the Théâtre Français in 1877.

George Sand died at Nohant on the 8th of June 1876. To a youth and womanhood of storm and stress had succeeded an old age of serene activity and then of calm decay. Her nights were spent in writing, which seemed in her case a relaxation from the real business of the day, playing with her grandchildren, gardening, conversing with her visitors—it might be Balzac or Dumas, or Octave Feuillet or Matthew Arnold—or writing long letters to Sainte-Beuve and Flaubert. "Calme, toujours plus de calme," was her last prayer, and her dying words, "Ne détruisez pas la verdure."

BIBLIOGRAPHY.—The collected edition of George Sand's works was published in Paris (1862–83) in 96 volumes, with supplement 109 volumes; the *Histoire de ma vie* appeared in 20 volumes in 1854-55. The *Étude bibliographique sur les œuvres de George Sand* by the vicomte de Spoelberch de Lovenjoul (Brussels, 1868) gives the most complete bibliography. Of Vladimir Karenin's (pseudonym of

Mme. Komarova) *George Sand*, the most complete life, the first two volumes (1899–1901) carry the life down to 1839. There is much new material in *George Sand et sa fille*, by S. Rocheblave (1905), *Correspondance de G. Sand et d'Alfred de Musset* (Brussels, 1904), *Correspondance entre George Sand et Gustave Flaubert* (1904), and *Lettres à Alfred de Musset et à Sainte-Beuve* (1897). E. M. Caro's *George Sand* (1887) is rather a critique than a life. *See* studies by Sainte-Beuve in the *Causeries du lundi* and in *Portraits contemporains;* Jules Lemaître in *Les Contemporains*, vol. iv.; E. Faguet, *XIXe Siècle;* F. W. H. Myers, *Essays Ancient and Modern* (1883); Henry James in *North American Review* (April 1902); Matthew Arnold, *Mixed Essays* (1879). *See* also René Doumic's *George Sand* (1909), which has been translated into English by Alys Hallard as *George Sand: Some Aspects of her Life and Writings* (1910); C. Maurras, *Les Amants de Venise; George Sand et Musset* (1916); L. Vincent, *George Sand et le Berry* (2 vols. 1919); E. A. A. L. Seillière, *George Sand* (1920); E. W. Schermerhorn, *The Seven Strings of the Lyre. The Life of George Sand* (1804–76) (1928); and Eng. trans., by M. J. Howe, of her *Journal Intime* as *The Intimate Journal of George Sand* (1929).

SAND. The products of rocks and minerals broken down by natural or artificial agencies are gravels, sands, silts and clays. In the U.S. the term sand is applied to particles $\frac{1}{16}$ to 2 mm. diameter, and in Europe to those from .02 to 2 mm. diameter. Although most of the rock-making minerals occurring on the earth's crust are found in sands, only a limited number are met with at all frequently. For several reasons quartz is by far the commonest ingredient; it is abundant in rocks, is comparatively hard and has practically no cleavage so that it is not readily worn down to a fine state. Moreover it is nearly insoluble in water and does not decompose. In certain localities feldspar, calcareous material, iron ores and volcanic glass, among other substances, have been found to be dominant constituents of sand. Most quartzose sands contain a small quantity of feldspar. Small plates of white mica, which, though soft and very fissile, decompose slowly, are often present. In addition, all sands contain small quantities of "heavy" rock-forming minerals among which may be garnet, tourmaline, zircon, rutile, topaz, pyroxenes, amphiboles, iron ores, etc.

In certain shore and river sands these heavier constituents become concentrated as a result of current action and the removal of the lighter constituents. Economically valuable deposits may then be yielded. Such are the sands worked for diamonds and other gem stones, those bearing gold, platinum, tin, monazite and other ores. The greensands, widely distributed over the floor of the ocean and found in ancient strata on the continents, owe their colour to the presence of glauconite, a potash-bearing mineral. These sands are used for water softening and for land dressing, and attempts have been made to extract potash from them.

In the pottery, glassmaking and silicate (water glass) industries very pure quartzose sands are used in large quantities as a source of silica. Similar sands are required for lining the hearths of acid-steel furnaces and for foundry mixtures. Moulding sands, that is, the sands utilized in foundries for making the moulds in which metal is cast, usually have a clayey bond uniting the grains of quartz. Because of the hardness and poor cleavage of quartz, sands are used extensively as abrasives. Garnet sands, although of more restricted occurrence, are similarly used. Ordinary sands find a multitude of other uses, among which may be mentioned the preparation of mortar, cement and concrete. They are frequently sources of water supply. (P. G. H. B.; X.)

SANDALWOOD, a fragrant wood obtained from various trees of the natural order Santalaceae, and principally from *Santalum album*, a native of India. The use of sandalwood dates as far back at least as the 5th century B.C. It is still extensively used in India and China, wherever Buddhism prevails, being employed in funeral rites and religious ceremonies. In India it is used in the manufacture of boxes, fans and other ornamental articles of inlaid work. The oil, obtained by distilling the wood in chips, is used as a perfume, few native Indian attars or essential oils being free from admixture with it. As a powder or paste the wood is employed in the pigments used by the Brahmans for their distinguishing caste-marks.

Red sandalwood is the product of a small leguminous tree, *Pterocarpus santalinus*, native of S. India, Ceylon and the Philippine Islands. A fresh surface of the wood has a rich deep red colour, which on exposure, however, assumes a dark brownish tint; its principal application is in wool-dyeing. Several other species of *Pterocarpus*, notably *P. indicus*, contain the same dyeing principle and can be used as substitutes for red sandalwood. The barwood and camwood of the Guinea Coast of Africa, from *Baphia nitida* or an allied species, called *santal rouge d'Afrique* by the French, are also closely allied to the red sandalwood of Oriental countries.

As a substitute for copaiba (*q.v.*), sandalwood oil, distilled from the wood of *Santalum album*, is pleasanter to take, but it is less efficient and more expensive.

SANDARAC, in mineralogy realgar or native arsenic disulphide, but generally a resinous exudation obtained from the small coniferous tree *Tetraclinis articulata*, native of the northwest regions of Africa, and especially the Atlas mountains. The resin, a natural exudation on the stems, comes into commerce as small round balls or elongated tears, transparent, and having a delicate yellow tinge. It is used as a varnish and as incense, and by the Arabs medicinally as a remedy for diarrhoea. An analogous resin is procured in China from *Callitris sinensis*, and in southern Australia, under the name of pine gum, from various species of Callitris. (F. L. A.)

SANDAWE, less correctly Sandawi, a small tribe of about 15,000 persons living in the Kondoa-Irangi district of Tanganyika Territory, Africa, between the rivers Bubu and Mponde. Attention was drawn to their language by the late Dr. Oskar Baumann, who visited their country in 1892, and was able to collect some specimens, being especially struck by the remarkable fact of its containing clicks (*q.v.*), which had up to that time only been observed in the Hottentot and Bushman languages of South Africa, and in those adjacent Bantu languages which had borrowed them. It was investigated at a later date by E. Nigmann (1909) and, more scientifically, by Dr. Otto Dempwolff (1916). The only English writer who has treated the subject in any detail is F. J. Bagshawe, Political Officer at Mbulu, who was in close contact with these people from 1917 to 1923.

It has been assumed, though without sufficient reason, that all languages containing clicks must be related to each other, and that there can be no possible relationship between a click-language and one where clicks are absent. That this position, however, is by no means generally accepted, appears from the disputes which have arisen over the question whether the Hottentot and the Bushman groups (neither consisting of a single language) have a common origin, or are entirely distinct. (*See* AFRICA: *Anthropology and Ethnology;* BUSHMAN LANGUAGES.)

The three clicks found in Sandawe seem to be identical with three of the Nama clicks—those which have been adopted into Zulu and are represented in the current orthography by *c* (dental), *q* (cerebral or "retroflex") and *x* (lateral). The last-named is not produced in quite the same way as by the Nama, but, as observed by Dr. Dempwolff, the sound is exactly the same. Both Nigmann and Bagshawe have noticed the fact that the Sandawe clicks form a distinct syllable, at any rate in some cases (it is not clear from the latter's account whether the rule is invariable), whereas in Zulu they form an integral part of a syllable, the pronunciation of which constitutes one of the greatest difficulties to a European learner.

The word-stress appears to be extremely variable and is often the only distinction between words of similar form, but different meaning (*e.g.*, *nóa* "elephant" and *noá* "claw"). Intonation ("tone") is also, as in the Hottentot and Bushman languages, a very important feature: *tsa* with a high tone means "pot," with a low tone "tear." Both these points await fuller investigation.

A large proportion of the Sandawe vocabulary can be correlated with Nama words, and a less amount with other Hamitic languages, such as Tatoga, Iraku and even Somali. But this is an unsatisfactory basis for deducing relationship, otherwise Sandawe might be claimed as a Bantu language, since Dr. Dempwolff gives a longer list of words which can be identified as Bantu (obviously borrowed from Swahili, Gogo, Hehe, Irangi, etc.), than of those which he has traced to Nama. A far more trustworthy criterion is to be found in the grammatical framework of the language and here there is little room for doubt. Sandawe possesses grammatical gender, suffixes to denote the plural, case-endings for nouns (an "instrumental case" is almost identical, both in form and meaning with that found in Nama), and other features in common with Nama and also, to a less extent, with other Hamitic languages. One peculiarity, the use of a different form for a verb in singular and plural (*e.g., tha* "he runs," *giribe* "they run"), is neither Hamitic, Bantu nor Sudanic. The order of words in a simple sentence (subject, object, verb: "he cattle herds," instead of "he herds cattle") and the position of the genitive (possessor preceding the thing possessed: *Humbu tse,* "ox's head," not, as in Bantu, "head of ox") are the same as in Nama, but differ from the normal Hamitic type. In both cases there would appear to be sufficient reasons for the difference.

Professor Alfredo Trombetti is inclined to think that the Sandawe are, of all existing peoples, those most nearly related to the Hottentots.

BIBLIOGRAPHY.—F. J. Bagshawe, "The Peoples of the Happy Valley," in *Journal of the African Society,* vol. xxiv. (1924-25), Nos. 93, 95, 96; Oskar Baumann, *Durch Masailand zur Nilquelle* (Berlin, 1894); E. Nigmann, "Versuch eines Wörterbuchs für Kissandaui," *Mitteilungen des Seminars für orientalische Sprachen,* vol. xii. (Berlin, 1909); Alfredo Trombetti, *La Lingua degli Ottentotti e la Lingua dei Wa-Sandawi* (Bologna, 1910); Dr. Otto Dempwolff, *Die Sandawe. Linguistisches und ethnographisches Material aus Deutsch-Ostafrika* (Hamburg, 1916).
(A. WE.)

SANDAY, WILLIAM (1843–1920), English theological scholar, was born at Holme Pierrepont, Notts., on Aug. 1, 1843, the son of William Sanday, sheep and cattle breeder. Educated at Repton and Balliol College, Oxford, he became a scholar of Corpus Christi in 1863. He was a fellow and lecturer at Trinity in 1866, and was ordained in 1867. In 1876 after holding various college livings, he was appointed principal of Hatfield Hall, Durham. In 1882 he was appointed Ireland professor of exegesis at Oxford, and in 1895 Lady Margaret professor of divinity and canon of Christ Church, positions which he held until 1919. He died at Oxford on Sept. 16, 1920. Sanday was one of the pioneers in introducing to English students the mass of work done by Continental scholars in biblical criticism. An example of the admirable work he accomplished in this direction is his *Life of Christ in Recent Research* (1907).

His chief works are *The Authorship and Historical Character of the Fourth Gospel* (1872); *The Gospels in the Second Century* (1876); *The Oracles of God* (1891); *The Early History and Origin of the Doctrine of Biblical Inspiration* (1893); *Commentary on the Epistle to the Romans* (with Dr. Headlam, 1895); *Outlines of the Life of Christ* (1905, a republication of an article in Hastings' *Dictionary of the Bible*); *Christologies, Ancient and Modern* (1910) and *Personality in Christ and in Ourselves* (1911); *Bishop Gore's Challenge to Criticism* (1914); *New Testament Background* (1918).

SAND-BLASTING AND SHOT PEENING. Sand-blast is a method of cleaning or marking surfaces by the discharge of sand, steel shot or grit through a nozzle at high velocity by means of compressed air. The abrasive action can be effected on internal parts without difficulty. Concisely, the applications of the process may be summarized as follows: cleaning sand from castings, with or without a view to painting or enameling, or annealing; cleaning scale from stampings for similar reasons; cleaning partly-finished products, as sheets, tubes, strips, sometimes for subsequent electric or gas welding, or motorcar and cycle parts, etc., and numerous fittings, prior to tinning, galvanizing or plating; cleaning tire moulds, printers' lithographic sheets, pottery ware after firing, iron and stone buildings and painted or rusty ironwork, hardened tools to enable cracks to be detected; sharpening and dressing files; matting ebonite articles to improve insulation and appearance; frosting, badging and marking glassware of all kinds.

Small apparatus for marking and engraving glass is worked with a hand bellows, but in larger outfits a power-driven compressor is employed. Pressures range from about 15 lb. to 80 lb. per square inch. Fine sand is selected for glass decoration and coarse sand or flint for uses where much is lost through no collecting apparatus being installed. For most metal work chilled round or crushed iron shot is best, as it lasts a much longer time

than sand or flint before going into useless dust. The outfits are constructed in many ways, some having a flexible hose carrying the blast nozzle, and the operator wears a safety breathing helmet and plays the nozzle on the work. Another way is to have a metal cabinet with window through which the operator looks while he turns the object about under the fixed sand jet nozzle; rubber gauntlets are worn, passed through arm holes in the

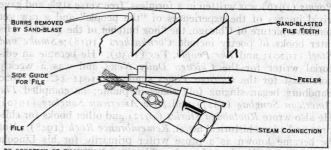

BY COURTESY OF TILIGHMAN'S PATENT STEAM SAND BLAST CO.

SAND BLAST SHOWING JET DRIVING A STREAM OF SAND AND WATER AGAINST THE TEETH OF A NEWLY-CUT FILE

door. Castings are dealt with on machines, including the tumbling barrel, which constantly turns the castings over to expose all the surfaces to the action of the jet led through one or both ends. The rotary table cleaner carries the castings past a rubber curtain into a chamber containing one or more jets, and then out again. The reciprocating table design conveys large or long castings through the blast chamber, out to the other side, on which they are turned over and returned through by the table. In the Mathewson file-sharpening system a stream of very fine sand and water (in effect a liquid grindstone) is driven against the teeth by a steam jet. The backs of the teeth are thus ground off; newly-cut files have the burr driven away, much improving the cutting power, and worn files are freshened up practically as new. The sketch shows the apparatus on which the file is laid and moved to and fro by hand until found to be quite sharp.

"Gunite" is a process similar to sand-blasting by which a concrete mortar can be applied with an air gun to steel surfaces or to wood forms which may then be removed. The surface is often wrapped with wire mesh which becomes imbedded in the finished concrete surface. This process is much used for fireproofing or corrosion-proofing structural steel but it has also been used to produce canal linings, tanks, etc.

Shot Peening is a process by which the surface of a steel part of an automobile or other device that must undergo repeated stress and strain is blasted with round shot of steel, glass or other hard smooth material. The purpose is to prevent cracking during the normal service life of the structural piece. This process first came into use for automobile parts but its success brought it into widespread usefulness. It had long been observed that automotive parts which proved adequately strong under the usual static tests would crack through when placed under severe road tests or regular service. These cracks, known as fatigue cracks are well understood. They are microscopic cracks that start in an area of tension and slowly work their way through the part under repeated stress. It was known that such cracks did not start in areas that were compressed or under compressive stress. The success of shot peening in stopping the development of such cracks is due to the fact that a shot-peened surface is permanently deformed by thousands of tiny blows and it therefore retains a residual compressive stress which is usually larger than any applied tensile stress. Hence, at the surface where fatigue cracks usually start there is a compressive stress at all times which greatly inhibits the start of microscopic cracks. The beating and cooling of welded parts produces contraction stresses of both tensile and compressive nature. If the tensile contraction or cooling stresses are at the surface, fatigue cracking is a potential danger, but this danger may be greatly mitigated by shot peening the surfaces of the part after welding.
(L. E. G.)

SANDBURG, CARL (1878–   ), U.S. author, was born Jan. 6, 1878, at Galesburg, Ill. The son of a poor immigrant, he travelled west at the age of 17 and worked in Kansas as a farm hand and dishwasher. He served in the army in Puerto Rico during the Spanish-American War and in 1902 was graduated from Lombard college at Galesburg. Sandburg was secretary to the mayor of Milwaukee, 1910–12, and in 1913 was associate editor of *System* magazine in Chicago. In 1914 he won the *Poetry* magazine's Levinson prize for his poem *Chicago*. His *Chicago Poems* (1916) was written in a formless, free verse style and gave vivid images of the experiences of "the people" and a raw yet sensitive picture of Chicago, the "hog butcher of the world." His later books of poetry include *Cornhuskers* (1918); *Smoke and Steel* (1920); and *The People, Yes* (1936). He became an editorial writer for the *Chicago Daily News* and was a weekly columnist for the *Chicago Times* syndicate, 1941–45. In 1920 Sandburg began singing folk songs in public; he compiled *The American Songbag* (1927) and *New American Songbag* (1950). He also wrote *Rootabaga Stories* (1922) and other books for children and a long historical novel, *Remembrance Rock* (1948). But he became known as a prose writer primarily for his Lincoln biographies. *Abraham Lincoln—The Prairie Years* (1926) was widely acclaimed, and he won a Pulitzer prize for *Abraham Lincoln—The War Years,* 4 vol. (1939). In 1951 he won the Pulitzer prize for *Complete Poems* (1950).

SANDEAU, LÉONARD SYLVAIN JULIEN (JULES) (1811–1883), French novelist, was born at Aubusson, Fr., on Feb. 19, 1811. Sent to Paris to study law, he spent much of his time with unruly students. In 1831 he and Amandine Lucile Aurore Dudevant (George Sand) were living in Paris. The intimacy did not last long, but it produced *Rose et Blanche* (1831), a novel written in common under the name Jules Sand, from which George Sand took the idea of her famous pseudonym.

Sandeau continued for nearly 50 years to produce novels and to collaborate in plays. His works include *Marianna* (1839), in which he drew a portrait of George Sand; *Le Docteur Herbeau* (1841); *Catherine* (1845); and *Mademoiselle de la Seiglière* (1848), a picture of society under Louis Philippe, dramatized in 1851. *Le Gendre de M. Poirier* (1854) was one of several plays he wrote with Émile Augier.

Sandeau was made conservateur of the Mazarin library in 1853, elected to the French academy in 1858 and the next year appointed librarian of St. Cloud.

He died in Paris on April 24, 1883.

SAND-EEL, or SAND-LANCE. The fishes known under these names form a small family (Ammodytidae). Their body is of an elongate-cylindrical shape, with the head terminating in a long conical snout, the projecting lower jaw forming the pointed end. A low dorsal fin occupies nearly the whole length of the back, and a long anal fin commences immediately behind the vent, which is placed about midway between the head and caudal fin. The tail is forked and the pectorals are short. The absence of ventral fins indicates the burrowing habits of these fishes. In the Japanese *Bleekeria* small jugular ventral fins are present. The scales, when present, are small; but generally the development of scales has only proceeded to the formation of oblique folds of the integument. The dentition is quite rudimentary.

Sand-eels are small littoral marine fishes, only one species attaining a length of 18 in. (*Ammodytes lanceolatus*). They live in shoals at various depths on a sandy bottom, and bury themselves in the sand on the slightest alarm. Sand-eels destroy a great quantity of fry and other small creatures, such as the lancelet (*Amphioxus*), which lives in similar localities. They are excellent eating, and are much sought after for bait. The eggs of sand-eels are small, heavier than sea-water and slightly adhesive; they are scattered among the grains of sand in which the fishes live.

Sand-eels are common in the north Atlantic; a species scarcely distinct from the European common sand-lance occurs on the Pacific side of North America, another on the east coast of South Africa. On the British coast three species are found.

SANDEFJORD, the oldest and most famous spa in Norway, on the coast, 86 mi. S.S.W. of Oslo by the Skien railway. Pop. (1946) 5,803. The springs are sulphurous, saline and chalybeate. Specimens of *jaettegryder* or giant's cauldrons may be seen at Gaardaasen and Vindalsbugt, some upwards of 23 ft. in depth.

SANDEMAN, SIR ROBERT GROVES (1835–1892), Indian officer and administrator, was the son of General Robert Turnbull Sandeman, and was born on Feb. 25, 1835. He was educated at Perth and St. Andrews university, and joined the 33rd Bengal Infantry in 1856. In 1857, he took part in the final capture of Lucknow as adjutant of the 11th Bengal Lancers. After the suppression of the Mutiny he was appointed to the Punjab Commission by Sir John Lawrence. In 1866 he was appointed district officer of Dera Ghazi Khan, and there first showed his capacity in dealing with the Baluch tribes. He was the first to break through the close-border system of Lord Lawrence, by extending British influence to the independent tribes beyond the border. In his hands this policy worked admirably, owing to his tact in managing the tribesmen and his genius for control. In 1876 he negotiated the treaty with the khan of Kalat, which subsequently governed the relations between Kalat and the Indian government; and in 1877 he was made agent to the governor-general in Baluchistan, an office which he held till his death. During the second Afghan war in 1878 his influence over the tribesmen was of the utmost importance, since it enabled him to keep intact the line of communications with Kandahar, and to control the tribes after the British disaster at Maiwand. For these services he was made K.C.S.I. in 1879. In 1889 he occupied the Zhob valley, a strategic advantage which opened the Gomal Pass through the Waziri country to caravan traffic. He died at Bela, the capital of Las Bela state, on Jan. 29, 1892.

See T. H. Thornton, *Sir Robert Sandeman* (1895); and R. I. Bruce, *The Forward Policy* (1900).

SANDERS, NICHOLAS (c. 1530–1581), Roman Catholic agent and historian, born about 1530 at Charlwood, Surrey, was a son of William Sanders, once sheriff of Surrey, who was descended from the Sanders of Sanderstead. Educated at Winchester and New College, Oxford, he was elected fellow in 1548 and graduated B.C.L. in 1551. Soon after Elizabeth's accession he went to Rome where he was befriended by Pole's confidant, Cardinal Morone; he also owed much to the generosity of Sir Francis Englefield (q.v.). He was ordained priest at Rome, and was, even before the end of 1550, mentioned as a likely candidate for the cardinal's hat. For the next few years he was employed by Cardinal Hosius, the learned Polish prelate, in his efforts to check the spread of heresy in Poland, Lithuania and Prussia. In 1565 like many other English exiles, he made his headquarters at Louvain, and after a visit to the Imperial Diet at Augsburg in 1566, he threw himself into the literary controversy between Bishop Jewel (see JEWEL, JOHN) and Harding.

His expectations of the cardinalate were disappointed by Pius V's death in 1572, and Sanders spent the next few years at Madrid trying to embroil Philip II, who gave him a pension of 300 ducats, in open war with Elizabeth. Sanders found his opportunity in 1579, when a force of Spaniards and Italians was despatched to Smerwick to assist James Fitzmaurice and his Geraldines in stirring up an Irish rebellion. The Spaniards were, however, annihilated by Lord Grey in 1580, and after nearly two years of wandering in Irish woods and bogs Sanders died of cold and starvation in the spring of 1581.

The writings of Sanders have been the basis of all Roman Catholic histories of the English Reformation. The most important was his *De Origine ac Progressu schismatis Anglicani*, which was continued after 1558 by Edward Rishton, and printed at Cologne in 1585; it has been often re-edited and translated, the best English edition being that by David Lewis (London, 1877).

See Lewis's *Introduction* (1877); *Calendars of Irish, Foreign and Spanish State Papers, and of the Carew MSS.;* Knox's *Letters of Cardinal Allen;* T. F. Kirby's *Winchester Scholars;* R. Bagwell's *Ireland under the Tudors;* A. O. Meyer's *England und die katholische Kirche unter Königin Elisabeth* (1910); the *Catholic Encyclopaedia;* and T. G. Law in *Dict. Nat. Biogr.* i, 259–261 with bibl.; T. M. Veech, *Dr. Nicolas Sanders and the English Reformation 1530–1581* (Louvain, 1935).

SAND FLY, any of the blood-sucking biting midges belonging to the family Ceratopogonidae of the order Diptera (q.v.). They belong to the genera *Culicoides, Lasiohelia* and *Leptoconops* and attack man and warm-blooded animals most viciously. All are small, under 3 mm., and generally grayish or brownish in colour, but a few are yellow; the wings are covered with tiny hairs forming a weak pattern; the strong veins are in front, the other veins weak. Because of their minute size and difficulty of seeing them when they bite they are called "no-see-ums" in parts of North America; also "punkies." The larvae are aquatic, live in the tide zone of sandy beaches, in decaying vegetation, tree holes and mud. The adults are crepuscular and nocturnal but bite viciously on dark days; they are so fragile that they remain in hiding with even a moderate breeze, but may form large swarms in the lee of buildings and enter houses through mosquito screens. Many seashore areas are made extremely uncomfortable by them. Species of *Culicoides* are vectors in Africa and tropical America of the filarial worms, *Acanthocheilonema perstans* and *Mansonella ozzardi*, but these are nonpathogenic in man. There are 33 species of *Culicoides* in the British Isles. The name sand fly is also applied to species of *Simulium* in some parts of the world.   (C. H. CN.)

SAND-FLY FEVER (Flebotomus fever, pappataci fever) is an acute, infectious, febrile disease caused by a specific filterable virus and producing temporary incapacitation. It is transmitted by the female sand fly, *Flebotomus papatasii*, and is prevalent in the moist subtropical countries of the eastern hemisphere lying between 20° and 45° N. lat., particularly around the Mediterranean sea, in the middle east and parts of India. It breaks out in epidemic form during the summer season following the breeding of this species of fly, but between epidemics the reservoir is unknown and there is no conclusive evidence that the virus is congenitally transmitted in the insect host. The sand fly becomes infected from biting infected persons when the virus is circulating in the patient's blood, not more than 48 hours before the clinical onset and no more than the first 24 hours thereafter. The virus then requires seven to ten days incubation, after which the sand fly remains infected for life.

Pathogenesis and Symptomatology.—Man becomes infected from the bites of infected sand flies. Using human adults of both sexes and different racial groups as volunteers, A. B. Sabin, C. B. Philip and J. R. Paul (1944) obtained 95% infection following skin exposure to infected *Flebotomus papatasii*. The virus multiplies and becomes widely disseminated throughout the body, and within two and one-half to five days after exposure there is suddenly a feeling of lassitude, abdominal distress and dizziness, followed within one day by a chilly sensation and a rapid rise in temperature during the next 24 to 48 hours to 102°–104.5° F. (38.8°–40.3° C.). As in dengue (*q.v.*) there are typically severe frontal headache and postorbital pain, intense muscular and joint pains, likewise a flushed appearance of the face, but no true rash or subsequent desquamation. During the first day of fever there is an accelerated pulse. Usually after two days the temperature slowly returns to normal; only rarely is there a second episode of fever. Following the febrile period there is great fatigue and weakness, accompanied by slow pulse and frequently subnormal blood pressure. Convalescence may require only a few days or several weeks.

Prognosis is always favourable in sand-fly fever. The average case is considerably less severe than in dengue. Diagnosis is based on the clinical manifestations, the geographical area in which the disease occurs, the prevalence of *Flebotomus papatasii* and the epidemic development of the disease. More specifically, although there is no change in the total number of white blood corpuscles, there is an increase in the proportion of immature neutrophilic forms (*e.g.*, a marked shift to the left in the Schilling count). Treatment is entirely symptomatic.

Prevention.—Sand flies breed in vegetation within a few hundred feet of human habitations. These breeding places are difficult to discover, hence larvicidal control is impractical. The blood-sucking females feed only from sunset to sunrise and only at ground level, so that sleeping quarters above the ground floor provide moderately good protection. Ordinary mosquito netting and screening are useless, since the unfed female flies can pass through 18-mesh squares. Insect repellents such as dimethyl phthalate, dibutyl phthalate and benzyl benzoate, when applied to exposed skin, will keep sand flies away for a few hours, but the use of DDT-pyrethrum sprays on verandas, on screens, around doors and windows and within habitations will readily kill all adult sand flies which alight on the sprayed surfaces. With this procedure an epidemic can be rapidly terminated.

BIBLIOGRAPHY.—C. Birt, "Phlebotomus Fever in Malta and Crete," *Jour. Roy. Army Med. Corps,* vol. 14, pp. 236–258 (1910); C. Birt, "Sandfly Fever in India," *ibid.*, vol. 15, pp. 140–147 (1910); R. Doerr, K. Franz and S. Taussig, "Das Pappataciefieber, ein epidemisches Dreitage-Fieber im adriatischen Kustengebiete Oesterreich-Ungarns," *Wien. klin. Wochenschr.*, vol. 22, p. 609 (1909); M. Hertig, *Ann. Rept. Gorgas Memorial Lab.*, 1945, pp. 14–17 (1946); A. B. Sabin, C. B. Philip and J. R. Paul, "Phlebotomus (Pappataci or Sandfly) Fever: A Disease of Military Importance," *J.A.M.A.*, vol. 125, pp. 603–606, 693–699 (1944); H. E. Whittingham and A. F. Rook, "Observations on the Life History and Bionomics of *Phlebotomus papatasii*," *Brit. Med. Jour.*, part 2, p. 1,144 (1923).   (E. C. F.)

SANDFORD, JOHN DE (d. 1294), archbishop of Dublin, was probably an illegitimate son of the baronial leader, Gilbert Basset (d. 1241), or of his brother Fulk Basset, bishop of London from 1241 until his death in 1259. John first appears as an official of Henry III in Ireland and of Edward I in both England and Ireland; he was appointed dean of St. Patrick's, Dublin, in 1275. In 1284 he was chosen archbishop of Dublin in succession to John of Darlington; some, however, objected to this choice and Sandford resigned his claim; but was elected a second time while he was in Rome, and returning to Ireland was allowed to take up the office. In 1288, during a time of great confusion, the archbishop acted as governor of Ireland. In 1290 he resigned and returned to England. Sandford served Edward I in the great case over the succession to the Scottish throne in 1292 and also as an envoy to the German king, Adolph of Nassau, and the princes of the empire. On his return from Germany he died at Yarmouth on Oct. 2, 1294.

Sandford's elder brother, FULK (d. 1271), was also archbishop of Dublin. He is called Fulk de Sandford and also Fulk Basset because of his relationship to the Bassets. Having been archdeacon of Middlesex and treasurer and chancellor of St. Paul's cathedral, London, he was appointed archbishop of Dublin by Pope Alexander IV in 1256.

He took a slight part in the government of Ireland under Henry III and died at Finglas, near Dublin, on May 4, 1271.

SAND GROUSE, the name applied to birds resembling grouse (*q.v.*) in certain features but more closely related to the pigeons. They inhabit desert regions. They comprise the family Pteroclidae. A common form is Pallas's sand grouse (*Syrrhaptes paradoxus*), of central Asia which occasionally invades Europe in large flocks. The nest is on the ground and contains four inconspicuous eggs. The wings are long. The birds' plumage is adapted to the colour of the desert. Sand grouse supply their young with water by soaking the breast feathers in water, which the little birds drink (*see* P. A. Buxton, *Animal Life in Deserts,* New York, 1923). Fossil species occur in the Miocene formation.   (K. P. S.)

SANDHURST, a large village in the Wokingham parliamentary division of Berkshire, Eng., 9 mi. N. of Aldershot. Pop. (1951) 5,244. Between the village and the town of Camberley, in wooded grounds with a lake and playing fields, lies the Royal Military academy, Sandhurst, where most of the potential regular officers for the British army undergo a course of general and military education as officer cadets. The present R.M.A. is heir to the functions performed up to 1939 by both the Royal Military academy at Woolwich and the Royal Military college at Sandhurst. The R.M.C. was established by royal warrant in 1802 at Great Marlow, largely as a result of the efforts of Col. J. G. Le Marchant and Gen. Francis Jarry, an exiled French officer, who had organized a training school for officers at High Wycombe three years earlier. The move to Sandhurst took place in 1812 when the "Old Building" there was completed. The college at first included a senior department for the training of staff officers, but in 1858 this was made entirely separate and in 1862 was transferred to the present staff college building in the same grounds. In 1911 a new building was added to accommodate the increasing numbers of cadets. After World War I, during which it was for a time reduced to four months, the length of the course was fixed at 18 months and officers were trained for commissions in all branches of the British and Indian armies except the artillery, engineers and signals which were separately provided for at Woolwich. In order to educate and train all regular army officers on a common basis it was planned to amalgamate the R.M.A. and the R.M.C. at Sandhurst in 1940. World War II intervened and Sandhurst became temporarily the location of an O.C.T.U. (Officer Cadet Training unit), but in Jan. 1947 the present academy came into being.

Most cadets enter the academy at 18½–19½ years after passing the competitive army entrance examination and doing a short period of army training as other ranks. Others are selected while doing national service and, if not up to the educational standard required, go to a special company attached to Sandhurst for a preliminary course. Another source of cadets is the college established by the war office at Welbeck abbey in 1953 for boys of about 16½ who intend to obtain commissions in technical arms.

The academy has a major general as commandant and is organized into three colleges, each of four companies, with training and administrative staff. There are also more than 70 civilian lecturers in the four departments of mathematics, science, modern subjects and languages, headed by a director of studies responsible to the commandant. Some cadets are prepared with a view to taking the mechanical sciences tripos at Cambridge university or the degree course at the military college of science, others for the army interpretership examination. Atomic physics and the problems of government, especially within the Commonwealth, are studied. The military courses includes history, organization and administration, military law, tactics, drill, signals and weapon training. In addition to the usual games and societies, mountaineering, exploration and ocean sailing are officially sponsored in order to encourage the development of leadership qualities.

At the end of the course commissions are allotted in the arms of the service according to existing vacancies. First choice of regiment is usually given to those high up in the order of merit, which is determined by a formula which combines educational achievement with an assessment of personal qualities. Each term the Queen's medal is awarded to the first cadet in this order and the Sword of Honour to the cadet considered by the commandant to be the best of the term. Much of the organization of daily routine is left to the senior cadets from whom under officers are selected in each company. Cadets at Sandhurst receive the pay of their rank during their previous service in the army. The course in military subjects is common to candidates for commissions in all arms: appropriate specialist training is provided for each officer immediately after commissioning.

In 1955 between 800 and 900 cadets were generally undergoing training at the same time: about one-tenth were from commonwealth and other overseas territories. Pakistan, Ceylon, the Gold Coast, Nigeria, Malaya, Fiji, Burma, the Arab countries and Thailand are regularly represented. (W. F. G.)

SAN DIEGO, a Pacific coast city of California, U.S., situated 16 mi. N. of the Mexican border; a port of entry and county seat of San Diego county. It is on federal highways 80, 101 and 395 and is served by the San Diego and Arizona Eastern and the Santa Fe railways, by American, United and Western air lines and by bus lines and coastal, intercoastal and foreign steamship lines. A municipal airport (Lindbergh field), lying along San Diego bay and within five minutes' drive of the city business centre, accommodates both land and sea planes, and there are several commercial and governmental airports.

The population of San Diego was 334,387 in 1950 and 203,341 in 1940 by federal census.

City land area is 98.98 sq.mi. and it extends back 13.8 mi. at its extreme width. The climate is equable, with mean average temperature of 61° F. and average annual precipitation (falling chiefly in winter) of ten inches. San Diego bay is a 14-mi.-long landlocked crescent-shaped basin separated from the ocean by a low, narrow sandspit extending northwest from the mainland below the city and expanding at its northwestern extremity to include the city of Coronado and the U.S. naval air station (North Island). San Diego's business district has many tall and massive stores, office buildings and hotels.

In the city's centre lies Balboa park (1,400 ac.), the site of the Panama-California exposition of 1915–16 and the California Pacific International exposition of 1935–36. The park contains a natural history museum, a museum of man, a fine arts gallery, botanical and zoological gardens and a contiguous stadium seating 30,000, occupying a natural amphitheatre. Near the northern extremity of the city, on the ocean north of La Jolla, is Scripps Institution of Oceanography (part of the University of California). The city contains the second largest state college, San Diego State college. San Diego public schools, under the supervision of a five-member board of education, spent $13,449,214 during 1948–49, or an average of $228.44 per pupil based on an average daily attendance of 45,828.

In 1931 the city adopted a council-manager form of government. Assessed valuation of property in 1950 was $311,586,940; bank debits totalled $3,103,075,285. Total new construction activity for the decade 1941–50 was approximately $281,700,000. After World War II four major freeways to the city's outlying districts were built—Cabrillo, Mission Valley, Wabash and Montgomery. Water problems are solved by importation of Colorado river water, which is supplemented by collection of local runoff in eight near-by reservoirs.

San Diego offers many recreational opportunities. Water sports —speedboating, aquaplaning, yachting, swimming and rowing— may be enjoyed on its bays, harbour and beaches, while on land numerous sporting activities are available to resident and tourist alike. The $23,000,000 Mission Bay development was begun in 1945 to provide a 4,000-ac. marine and recreation park and a San Diego river flood-control channel.

Two near-by race tracks, Del Mar Turf club and Agua Caliente track, provide horse-racing fans enjoyment the year round. The city is the home of many flying and gliding clubs and a centre for deep-sea and fresh-water fishing. Another tourist attraction is Cabrillo National monument on Point Loma. Tourist trade netted the area $54,000,000 in 1949.

The roomy (22 sq.mi.) and accessible natural harbour is the first port of call for vessels operating through the Panama canal. A channel with an average width of 2,000 ft. and a minimum depth of 36 ft. was provided by government and municipal improvements. Terminal facilities include 57,210 ft. of berthing space, excluding government-owned wharves. From 1911 when the tidelands were ceded to the city by the state, to 1950 about $14,000,000 was invested by San Diego in building and maintaining the port. Cargo handled in the 1949–50 fiscal year was 1,282,585 tons valued at $77,090,980. Fishing is another important industry, with the local fishing fleet employing about 3,300 fishermen and 2,500 cannery workers (1951). An estimated 108,379 tons of fish valued at $14,631,165 entered the port in the year 1949–50, and value of the tuna pack alone was $58,000,000.

Aviation is one of San Diego's chief industries, with large and important factories in the area. Total factory pay rolls to an estimated 25,000 workers in all industries amounted to $78,700,-000 in 1949. Navy civilian and active duty personnel pay rolls were about $97,000,000 for the same period. Approximately 445 industrial and manufacturing establishments produced goods valued at about $275,000,000 (1950) and total pay rolls in San Diego, including civilian, military and governmental workers, approximated $420,000,000. Total employment as of Oct. 1950 was 167,300 and unemployment 8,500 in the area. Of the total employment figure 41,500 were engaged in trade, 35,300 in service, 30,150 in manufacturing, 23,650 in government, 11,800 in construction, 8,700 in transportation, communications and utilities and 7,550 in agriculture.

San Diego is the headquarters of the 11th naval district and site of one of the largest and most diversified operational bases in the world. Major naval activities of the area include a naval station, air station, amphibious base, training centre, auxiliary air station, electronics laboratory, supply depot, fleet sonar school and marine corps recruit depot. Many world records in aviation were established by the army and navy at San Diego, and it was the scene of such feats as the first controlled glider flight (1883), the first photographs from the air (1911), the first night flying, the first refuelling in flight and the first seaplane flight.

San Diego bay was discovered in 1542 by navigator Juan Rodríguez Cabrillo, in the service of Spain, and was named in 1602 by Spanish explorer Sebastián Vizcaíno. At Old Town, north of the city centre, the first European settlement in Upper California was made in 1769. On July 16 Father Junipero Serra founded the mission of San Diego de Alcala (the first of the California chain of Franciscan missions) and shortly thereafter a military presidio was established. The mission was moved in 1774 to a site 8 mi. from the centre of the modern city, where it still stands in a good state of restoration.

San Diego began the revolt against Governor Victoria in 1831, but in 1836 was intensely loyal to Mexican authority, in opposition to Gov. Juan Bautista Alvarado and the northern towns. It was made a port of entry in 1828, and in 1840 had a population of 140. In July 1846 it was occupied by U.S. forces under Gen. John C. Frémont. In 1850 the city was incorporated, but as it did not grow it lost its charter in 1852. In 1867 there were only a dozen inhabitants. Then a pioneer builder, A. E. Horton (d. 1909), laid out a new city 3 mi. below the old site. By 1870 it had a population of 2,300, and in that year a military reservation was established on Point Loma. In 1871 work started on the Santa Fe railroad; in 1872 the new city was incorporated; and in 1874 it was made a port of entry. The boom was ended by the depression of 1873–76, but development was resumed when the railroad reached the city in 1884. By 1890 the population had grown to 16,159, and the city's growth thereafter was rapid. (D. C. Cr.)

SAND LILY (*Leucocrinum montanum*), a North American plant of the lily family (Liliaceae, *q.v.*), native to plains and mountain valleys from South Dakota and Nebraska west to the Pacific coast. It is a small stemless perennial with long, narrow, grasslike leaves tufted on a short rootstock from which rise also the nearly stalkless, pure white, fragrant, slender-tubed, lilylike flowers, about 2 in. long and ½ in. across. The sand lily, often called star lily, is a conspicuous early spring flower in many parts of its range. (*See* Soap Plants.)

SANDOMIERZ, a small town of Poland in the province of Kielce, 140 mi. S.S.E. of Warsaw by river and on the left bank of the Vistula, opposite the confluence of the San. It is one of the oldest towns of Poland, being mentioned as early as 1079; from 1139 to 1332 it was the chief town of the principality of the same name. In 1240 and in 1259 it was burned by the Mongols. In 1429 it was the seat of a congress for the establishment of peace with Lithuania, and in 1570 the "Consensus Sandomiriensis" was held there for uniting the Lutherans, Calvinists and Moravian Brethren. Subsequent wars, and especially the Swedish (*e.g.*, in 1655), ruined the town. There in 1702 the Polish supporters of Augustus of Saxony banded together against Charles XII of Sweden. The beautiful cathedral was built between 1120 and 1191; it was rebuilt in stone in 1360, and is one of the oldest monuments of Polish architecture. Two of the churches are fine relics of the 13th century. The castle, built by Casimir III (14th century), still exists. The city gives title to an episcopal see (Roman Catholic). It was occupied by Germany in 1939 and returned to Poland in 1945. Pop. (1946) 8,357.

SANDOWAY, a town and district in the Arakan division of the Union of Burma. The town (pop. 1931, 4,070) is an ancient one and is said to have once been the capital of Arakan. The district has an area of 4,157 sq.mi.; pop. (1941) 139,747. The country is mountainous. Some peaks in the north attain 4,000 ft. and more. The chief pass is the Taungup crossed by a cart track leading from the village of Taungup to Prome on the Irrawaddy. The streams are mountain torrents to within a few miles of the coast; the mouth of the Gwa forms a good anchorage for vessels of from 9- to 10-ft. draught. The hills are clad with evergreen forest or useless bamboo brake on their lower slopes; by evergreen oak forests on the higher parts. Only small areas of the district are available for cultivation and except for a few acres of tobacco nearly all the cultivation is rice. Sandoway was ceded to the British, with the rest of Arakan (*q.v.*) by the treaty of Yandabo in 1826. It became part of the independent Union of Burma on Jan. 4, 1948.

SANDOWN, watering place, forming with Shanklin, an urban district, Isle of Wight, Eng., 6½ mi. S. of Ryde by rail. Pop. (1931) 6,302. It is on the southeast coast of the island, with a wide sandy shore. Pop., urban district (est. 1938), 10,930. Area 5.5 sq.mi.

SANDPAPER, an abrasive material prepared by coating stout paper with glue and sifting fine sand over its surface before the glue sets. Sandcloth is prepared in the same way. It is widely used for smoothing the surface of wood, for rubbing down paint and other purposes. (*See also* Emery; Glass-paper.)

SANDPIPER, the name given to all the smaller limicoline birds which are not plovers (*q.v.*), snipe (*q.v.*) or phalaropes (*q.v.*). The greenshank (*q.v.*) and the redshank (*q.v.*) are also related to the common sandpiper or summer snipe (*Tringa hypoleucus*). This little bird is a summer visitor to northern Europe and Asia. In the British Isles it arrives in May. It frequents clear streams, beside which it nests on the ground. There are four eggs, protectively coloured, as is also the case with the young. It winters in India, Australia and the Cape. In America it is replaced by *Actitis macularius*, the peetweet or spotted sandpiper, having similar habits. The green sandpiper (*T. ochropus*) is unique among the group, except for the North American solitary sandpiper (*Calidris solitarius*), in using the old nests of other birds wherein to lay eggs. Another European species is the wood sandpiper (*T. glareola*), like the last very dark in colour.

Other forms include the knot (*q.v.*), the dunlin (*q.v.*), the sanderling (*Calidris arenaria*), which lacks the hind toe, the purple sandpiper (*C. striata*) and the little, Temminck's and American stints (*T. minuta, T. temmincki* and *Pisobia minutilla*). The American stint, often called the least sandpiper, is darker and ranges from the arctic to Brazil. Bonaparte's sandpiper (*P. fuscicollis*), distinguished by its white tail coverts, is a common American form. It is called the white-rumped sandpiper.

The semipalmated sandpiper (*Ereunetes pusillus*) has partially webbed feet; it is a small form, breeding in arctic America. The buff-breasted sandpiper (*Tryngites subruficollis*) is common in the Mississippi valley in autumn and breeds in Alaska and Keewatin, wintering in Argentina and Uruguay.

SANDRINGHAM, a village in Norfolk, Eng., 3 mi. from the Wash and 2½ from Wolferton on the Eastern Region railway. Pop. (1931) 648. Sandringham house, a country seat of the king, was acquired by King Edward VII in 1863. The estate, of 15,578 ac., includes a park of 200 ac. The church of St. Mary Magdalene contains memorials of the royal family.

SAND SPRINGS, a city of Tulsa county, Okla., U.S., on the Arkansas river and federal highway 64, 8 mi. W. of Tulsa; served by the Missouri-Kansas-Texas and the Sand Springs railways. The population was 6,982 in 1950 and was 6,137 in 1940 by the federal census. It has important manufacturing industries, especially glassworks, cotton mills, chemical plants and smelters. The town was founded in 1911 and in 1918 it was chartered as a city.

SANDSTONE is a consolidated rock built up dominantly of grains of sand (*q.v.*) held together by a cementing substance. Sandstones are composed mainly of quartz, but may vary in composition in the same manner as sands. By increase in the size of their constituents they pass into conglomerates (*q.v.*) and by decrease into arenaceous shales and clay rocks. When the grains of sand are angular, the rock is termed a grit.

The minerals of sandstones are the same as those of sands. Quartz is the commonest; with it often occurs a certain amount of feldspar (as in the rock arkose) and frequently white mica. The flakes of mica may often be seen lying on the bedding planes and may give the sandstone a fissile character (*e.g.*, paving stone) of much value in quarrying. The cementing material is often fine chalcedonic silica, or it may be secondary quartz, when a quartzite-like rock is produced. Calcareous material (calcite), glauconite, iron oxides, carbonaceous matter and other substances also act as cements and give the sandstones characteristic colours. Glauconitic sandstones are greenish, ferruginous sandstones, red, brown and yellow or gray. When the cementing substance is clay, the rock is often of white or gray colour and firmly compacted.

Pure sandstones may contain as much as 99% of silica. If relatively soft they are crushed to sand for commercial purposes. If firmly cemented they are utilized, on account of the resistance of silica to heat, for the manufacture of silica bricks, furnace linings, hearths, etc. Of this character is the well-known rock "ganister" worked in the districts of Sheffield, South Wales, etc. Less pure, but firmly-cemented siliceous sandstones are used for the making of grindstones and millstones. Similar rocks, as well as calcareous, dolomitic (see DOLOMITE) and ferruginous sandstones are extensively worked as building-stones, mostly by quarries but sometimes by mines. As sandstones are always porous, they do not take a good polish, and are not used as ornamental stones, but this property makes them valuable storage basins and sources of water (e.g., the Trias of the Midlands). (P. G. H. B.)

SANDUSKY, a city of northern Ohio, U.S., a port of entry and the county seat of Erie co.; on Sandusky bay (an arm of Lake Erie), 56 mi. S.W. of Cleveland. It is served by the Baltimore and Ohio, the Big Four, the New York Central, the Nickel Plate and the Pennsylvania railways and by lake steamers. Pop. 1950 by federal census, 29,375. It has an extensive lake trade, the largest fresh-water fishing industry in the country and many diversified manufacturing industries. The traffic of the harbour in 1949 was 14,000,000 tons. The aggregate factory output in 1949 was valued at $60,000,000. Among the leading industries are the manufacture of crayons, radios, steel foundry products, ball bearings, paper-shipping cases and packing material. The city is built on a fine limestone ledge, and there are extensive deposits of marl, sand, gravel and clay in the vicinity. Just south of Sandusky is the Ohio Soldiers and Sailors home. From Put-in-Bay (an island about 12 mi. N.W. of Sandusky) Commodore Oliver Hazard Perry and his fleet sailed out on the morning of Sept. 10, 1813, for the battle of Lake Erie. English traders visited the site of Sandusky as early as 1749, and by 1763 a fort had been erected, which was burned by the Wyandot Indians on May 16 of that year, during the Pontiac uprising. Permanent settlement began in 1817, and in 1845 Sandusky was chartered as a city. In 1916 it adopted a commission-manager form of government.

SAND VERBENA (Abronia), a large genus of plants of the four-o'clock family (Nyctaginaceae), allied to the Mirabilis of the gardens, comprising about 50 species, native chiefly to dry sandy soils in western North America. They are low, often prostrate annuals or biennials, with opposite, entire, thick, sometimes viscid leaves; showy, red, yellow or white, usually fragrant flowers, clustered in stalked heads encircled at the base by bracts, and a broadly-winged fruiting achene enclosing a single shining seed. The white sand verbena (A. fragrans), with very numerous fragrant flowers, occurs from Iowa to Idaho and south to Texas and Mexico. The yellow sand verbena (A. latifolia) and the pink sand verbena (A. umbellata), found along the seashore from southern California to British Columbia, are grown as ornamentals in borders and rockeries. Various species bloom in immense profusion in deserts during the short rainy season.

SANDWICH, EDWARD MONTAGU or MOUNTAGU, 1ST EARL OF (1625–1672), English admiral, was born on July 27, 1625, son of Sir Sidney Montagu (d. 1644) of Hinchinbrooke, who was a brother of Sir Henry Montagu, 1st earl of Manchester, and of Edward Montagu, 1st Lord Montagu of Boughton. He joined the parliamentary party at the outbreak of the Civil War. In 1643 he raised a regiment, and he fought at Marston Moor, Naseby and at the siege of Bristol. Though one of Oliver Cromwell's intimate friends and M.P. for Huntingdonshire, 1645–48, he took little part in public affairs until 1653, when he was appointed a member of the council of state. In 1656 he was made a general at sea, his colleague being Robert Blake. He took part in the covering operations against Dunkirk in 1657 and was chosen a member of Cromwell's house of lords in the same year. In 1659 he was sent by Richard Cromwell with a fleet to arrange a peace between Sweden and Denmark. After the fall of Richard he resigned his command and assisted in the restoration of Charles II. Again general at sea early in 1660, Montagu carried the fleet over to the side of the exiled king, and was entrusted with the duty of fetching Charles from the Netherlands. He was then made a knight of the Garter,

and in July 1660 was created earl of Sandwich.

During the war with the Dutch in 1664–65 Lord Sandwich commanded a squadron under the duke of York and distinguished himself in the battle off Lowestoft on June 3, 1665. When the duke retired later in the same year he became commander in chief. Trouble arose over certain valuable Dutch prizes which he had taken, and Lord Sandwich was dismissed from his command, but as a solatium was sent to Madrid as ambassador extraordinary. He arranged a treaty with Spain and mediated a treaty between Spain and Portugal (Feb. 1668). In 1670 he was appointed president of the council of trade and plantations. When the third Dutch war broke out in 1672 Lord Sandwich again commanded a squadron under the duke of York and during the fight in Solebay (Southwold bay) on May 28, 1672, his ship, the "Royal James," after having taken a conspicuous part in the action, caught fire and was blown up. The earl's body was found some days later and was buried in Westminster Abbey.

Lord Sandwich claimed to have a certain knowledge of science, and his translation of a Spanish work on the Art of Metals appeared in 1674. He is mentioned frequently in the Diary of his kinsman, Samuel Pepys. See also F. R. Harris, Life of Edward Montague, 2 vol. (London, 1912).

SANDWICH, JOHN MONTAGU, 4TH EARL OF (1718–1792), was born on Nov. 3, 1718, and succeeded his grandfather, Edward, the 3rd earl, in the earldom in 1729. Educated at Eton and at Trinity college, Cambridge, he spent some time in travelling, and on his return to England in 1739 he took his seat in the house of lords as a follower of the duke of Bedford. He was a commissioner of the admiralty, plenipotentiary to the congress at Breda (1746), first lord of the admiralty (1748), and in 1753 a principal secretary of state. He took a leading part in the prosecution of John Wilkes. He had been associated with Wilkes in the notorious fraternity of Medmenham, and his attitude now in turning against the former companion of his pleasures made him very unpopular, and, from a line in the Beggar's Opera, he was known henceforward as "Jemmy Twitcher." He was postmaster general in 1768, secretary of state in 1770, and again first lord of the admiralty from 1771 to 1782. For corruption and incapacity Sandwich's administration is unique in the history of the British navy. He died on April 30, 1792.

The Sandwich Islands (see HAWAII) were named after him by Captain Cook. His Voyage round the Mediterranean in the Years 1738 and 1739 was published posthumously in 1799, with a flattering memoir by J. Cooke; the Life, Adventures, Intrigues and Amours of the celebrated Jemmy Twitcher (1770), which is extremely rare, tells a very different tale. See also the various collections of letters, memoirs and papers of the time, including Horace Walpole's Letters and Memoirs and the Bedford Correspondence.

SANDWICH, a market town and municipal borough in the Dover parliamentary division of Kent, Eng., 12 mi. E. of Canterbury on the Stour river. Pop. (1951) 4,140. Area 3.3 sq.mi. One of the original Cinque Ports, and second in precedence to Hastings, it is now 2 mi. from the sea. In the line of the old defensive ramparts, now marked by a public walk, the Fisher gate (dating from 1384, restored 1954) is the only gateway remaining, the other three —Newgate, Sandown and Canterbury gates—having been pulled down in the 18th century; the Barbican was built in 1539 as one of a chain of blockhouses along the coast. In the twisting streets of Sandwich are timber-framed houses, and others built by the Flemings; e.g., White Friars on the site of a 13th-century Carmelite priory; three ancient hospitals—St. Bartholomew's (probably founded 1217), just outside the town, with a fine Early English chapel, St. Thomas' dating from 1392 and rebuilt in 1864, and St. John's; three old churches—St. Clement's (the parish church since 1948) which dates from the 12th century and has a beautiful Norman tower, St. Mary the Virgin which stands on the site of a 7th-century monastery, but is not now in regular use, and St. Peter's, of various dates from the 12th century, where the curfew is still rung at 8 p.m. on the tenor bell and which is now the chapel of Sir Roger Manwood's grammar school (1563). The school's present buildings were put up in 1895 and the old house, Manwood court (1564), is now a private house. The guildhall, a 16th-century building, is still in use.

Rutupiae (Richborough, q.v.), 1¼ mi. N. of Sandwich, was established as a Roman town in A.D. 43 and was the centre of administration and one of the main entries from the continent. Sandwich was called Lundenvic by the Saxons and later became Sandwic; it was a borough by prescription before 1226, when the record of mayors begins. The governing charter until 1835 was that granted by Charles II in 1684. For many centuries the naval headquarters, the port for the wool trade and chief port of embarkation for the European continent, Sandwich lost its importance in the 16th century when the harbour became silted up. The town flourished again when the Flemish refugees were given permission by Elizabeth I to live there; during the Napoleonic Wars; during World War I; and in World War II when it was extensively used for the construction of Mulberry harbour. The chief industries are agriculture, and the manufacture of antibiotics, rubber products, shuttlecocks, textiles and welding equipment. It is also a holiday town with fine golf links and sands at Sandwich bay.

SANDYS (Săndz), **SIR EDWIN** (1561–1629), British statesman and a founder of the colony of Virginia, was the second son of Edwin Sandys, archbishop of York, and his wife Cecily Wilford. He was born in Worcestershire on Dec. 9, 1561. He was educated at Merchant Taylors' school and at Corpus Christi college, Oxford, and, though he never took orders, became a prebendary of York. He retained his prebend until 1599. He was entered in the Middle Temple in 1589. From the year 1593 till 1599 he travelled abroad. When in Venice he became closely connected with Fra Paolo Sarpi, who helped him in the composition of the treatise on the religious state of Europe, known as the *Europae speculum*. In 1605 this treatise was printed from a stolen copy under the title, *A Relation of the State of Religion in Europe*. Sandys procured the suppression of this edition, but the book was reprinted at the Hague in 1629. He was member for Andover in 1586 and for Plympton in 1589. On James I's accession Sandys was knighted. He sat in the king's first parliament as member for Stockbridge. He assailed the great monopolies, and he endeavoured to secure to all prisoners the right of employing counsel. He had been connected with the East India company before 1614, and took an active part in its affairs till 1629. His most memorable services were, however, rendered to the (London) Virginia company, to which he became treasurer in 1619. He sat in later parliaments as member for Sandwich in 1621, for Kent in 1624, and for Penrhyn in 1625. He died in Oct. 1629.

See Alex. Brown's *Genesis of the United States* (London, 1890).

SANDYS, GEORGE (1578–1644), English traveller, colonist and poet, the seventh and youngest son of Edwin Sandys, archbishop of York, was born on March 2, 1578. He studied at St. Mary hall, Oxford, but took no degree. In 1610 he set out on a journey which he described in *A Relation of a Journey begun An. Dom. 1610, in Four Books* (published in 1615 and dedicated, like all Sandys' works, to Charles I). He visited Italy, Constantinople, Egypt, Palestine and Cyprus and his observations on geography and ethnology made his work a valuable source book to Sir Francis Bacon, John Milton and Sir Thomas Browne. He took a great interest in the early colonization of America and in 1621 became colonial treasurer of the Virginia company and sailed for Virginia with Sir Francis Wyat, the new governor, who had married his niece. In 1624, when Virginia became a crown colony, he was created a member of the council. He returned to England about 1631.

He had published a translation of part of Ovid's *Metamorphoses* in 1621; he completed this in 1626, and later added to it a translation of book I of the *Aeneid* (1632). On this rests his claim to be considered, by John Dryden, as "the best versifier of the former age." As a translator, he aimed at the closest possible rendering of the Latin text, and this led him to perform a remarkable feat of compression—his translation of the *Metamorphoses* occupies exactly the same number of lines as the original. His greatest importance was in the development of the closed, antithetically balanced couplet, which was later brought to perfection by Dryden and Alexander Pope, both of whom read Sandys' translation of Ovid in boyhood. Also interesting was his use of a compressed, Latinate poetic diction; he was one of the first, and certainly the most influential, of the poets who adopted Latin syntax, chose Latin verbs rather than compound English ones, and, above all, used English words in their original Latin sense for the sake of brevity and wit. Many of the words of this type associated traditionally with Milton's style are borrowed from Sandys. The *Metamorphoses* is also of interest as the chief source of John Keats' knowledge of classical fable.

His other works include *A Paraphrase upon the Psalmes of David, etc.* (1636); *A Paraphrase upon the Divine Poems* (1638); and a translation of *Christ's Passion* from the Latin of Hugo Grotius (1640). His *Poetical Works* were edited in two volumes, with a memoir, by Richard Hooper (London, 1872).

See B. Penrose, *Urbane Travellers, 1591–1635* (Philadelphia, 1942); and, for an account of his influence on poetic diction, G. Tillotson, *On the Poetry of Pope*, 2nd ed. (London, 1951).

SAN FERNANDO, a seaport of southern Spain, in the province of Cadiz, on the Isla de León, a rocky island among the salt marshes which line the southern shore of Cadiz bay. Pop. (1950) 41,196 (mun.). San Fernando was probably a Carthaginian settlement. On a hill to the south stood a temple dedicated to the Tyrian Hercules; to the east is a Roman bridge, rebuilt in the 15th century after partial demolition by the Moors. The arsenal was founded in 1790. During the Peninsular War the cortes met at San Fernando (1810), but the present name of the town dates only from 1813; it was previously known as Isla de León. San Fernando is one of the three principal naval ports of Spain. The town is connected with Cadiz (4½ mi. N.W.) by a railway, and there is an electric tramway from the arsenal (in the suburb of La Carraca) to Cadiz. In the neighbourhood salt is largely produced and stone is quarried; the manufactures include spirits, beer, leather, esparto fabrics, soap, hats, sails and ropes; and there is a large iron-foundry. Nationalists occupied San Fernando early in the civil war of 1936–39.

SAN FERNANDO (DE LA UNION), a municipality, capital and port of the mountainous province of La Union, Luzon, Philippine Islands, on the west coast, 208 mi. from Manila. Pop. (1948) 28,742. A good road connects it with Bauang, whence there is railway connection with Manila. Tobacco is produced in the surrounding region and is shipped from the port in considerable quantities. Other agricultural products are palay (rice), abacá (Manila hemp), maize (corn), sugar and coconuts. Ilocano is the vernacular. Of the inhabitants aged 6 to 19 inclusive, 46.4% in 1939 attended school, and 60.2% of the population 10 years old and over was literate. (C. S. L.)

SAN FERNANDO (DE PAMPANGA), a municipality (with 32 *barrios* or districts) and capital of the province of Pampanga, Luzon, Philippine Islands, on the Manila-Dagupan railway, in the southeast part of the province. Pop. (1948) 39,549. It is the centre of a fertile agricultural region and has a trade of considerable importance. The vernacular is Pampango. Of the inhabitants aged 6 to 19 inclusive, 40.3% were reported in 1939 as attending school, while 64% of the population 10 years old and over was reported as literate.

SANFORD, a city in central Florida, U.S., the county seat of Seminole county; on Lake Monroe (the head of navigation on the St. Johns river) about midway (by rail) between Jacksonville and Tampa. It is on federal highways 17 and 92, and is served by the Atlantic Coast Line railroad and river transportation.

Pop. (1950) 11,935; (1940) 10,217 by federal census. The city lies around a wide curve in the lake shore and has several small lakes within its limits. Sanford is a winter resort, with several hotels and provision for all the sports and pleasures compatible with the climate. In 1920 it adopted a commission-manager form of government, and development came under the supervision of a city planning and zoning commission established in 1923. It is the centre of a subirrigated region devoted chiefly to the growing of celery and other truck crops. Sanford is a division point on the railroad; and has precooling plants, a large icing station and several manufacturing industries.

The city was founded about 1871 by Gen. Henry S. Sanford and was incorporated in 1877. In 1887 it suffered from a disastrous fire. The first citrus nurseries in Florida were planted there and Sanford became the chief centre of the production and shipping of oranges. The "great freeze" of 1895 wiped out this industry. Later, however, the cultivation of citrus fruits was revived.

SAN FRANCISCO, premier port and financial centre of the Pacific coast, is centrally located on the coast of California in 37° 47′ 22.55″ N. lat. and 122° 25′ 40.76″ W. long. It is situated on a peninsula bounded on the west by the Pacific ocean, north and east by San Francisco bay and south by the wooded hills and fertile valleys of San Mateo county. The highest elevation is 938 ft. San Francisco bay is one of the finest and safest landlocked harbours in the world, which partially accounts for the city's importance as a port. Entrance from the Pacific to the bay is through the Golden Gate, a channel having a depth of 63 fathoms and a width of 1⅛ mi. The city covers 44.6 sq.mi. and is built to an appreciable extent on hills—Telegraph, Russian, Nob, Rincon, Bernal heights, Potrero, Larsen peak, Twin peaks, Mt. Davidson (933.6 ft.), Mt. Olympus, Buena Vista, Lone mountain and Lincoln park. Romantic and cosmopolitan in character, San Francisco holds a lure peculiar to few cities of the world. Population (1950) 760,753; (1940) 634,536; (1930) 634,394; (1910) 416,912.

San Francisco bay contains several picturesque islands, while a number of large cities line the lateral side of the bay. Yerba Buena and Treasure Islands are about half way between San Francisco and Oakland. Yerba Buena is used as a naval station and training school. Treasure Island, site of the Golden Gate International exposition of 1939–40, is used as a naval receiving station. Alcatraz Island stands high above the water and is surmounted by a great military prison, topped by a lighthouse 214 ft. high. Angel Island lies to the north of Alcatraz. Upon it is located Ft. McDowell, the United States quarantine and immigrant station. During World War I the island was used as a training and internment camp.

Belvedere Island is an exclusive residential and yachting territory and lies to the northwest of Angel Island. San Francisco and 11 other contiguous cities account for 1,521,923 persons or one half of the total population of the San Francisco bay region (1950 U.S. census).

The construction of two mammoth bridges has expedited travel over the bay remarkably. The first, the San Francisco-Oakland Bay bridge extending 8½ mi. across the bay, was opened on

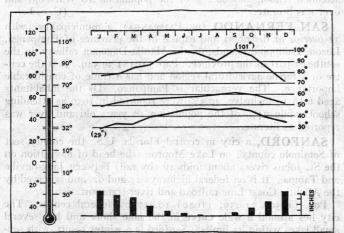

WEATHER GRAPH OF SAN FRANCISCO. THE THERMOMETER INDICATES THE ANNUAL MEAN TEMPERATURE. THE MIDDLE CURVE SHOWS THE MONTHLY MEAN TEMPERATURE. THE CURVES ABOVE AND BELOW THE HIGHEST AND LOWEST EVER RECORDED. THE COLUMNS INDICATE THE NORMAL MONTHLY PRECIPITATION

Nov. 12, 1936. It is the longest bridge in the world over navigable water and was erected at a cost of $77,200,000, to be liquidated by tolls. The second bridge spans the famous Golden Gate with a central suspension section of 4,200 ft. It was erected at a cost of $35,000,000 and was opened to the public on May 28, 1937.

The climate is practically free from extremes, with a uniform relative humidity and an abundance of sunshine. Rainfall constituted the entire precipitation over a period of 50 years, with

one or two extreme exceptions when a very light snowfall was recorded. Long records show heaviest rainfall from November through March, ranging from two to five inches for a single month. Between April and October the rainfall averages less than 0.3 in. per month, with only a trace in July and August. Long records of the U.S. weather bureau show: temperature, mean maximum 62.6°, mean minimum 50.2° and monthly mean 56.1°; relative humidity 69%; total precipitation 22.02 in.; average hourly wind velocity 9.2 m.p.h., prevailing direction, west; sunshine 65% of possible, with 167 all-clear days. Hours of fog over San Francisco bay average 153 per year.

Government.—San Francisco has a consolidated city and county government, with legislative powers vested in a board of supervisors of 11 members, 5 being elected every two years for four-year terms. The mayor, treasurer, assessor, city attorney, public defender, district attorney, sheriff and superior and municipal court judges are elected by the people and serve terms of four years. The chief administrative officer is appointed by the mayor but thereafter has permanent tenure. The controller, appointed by the mayor, subject to confirmation by the supervisors, also has permanent tenure. The mayor appoints members of and supervises police, fire, civil service, public utilities, park and recreation, welfare, library and city planning boards or commissions, and may remove his appointees except civil service, public utilities and welfare commissioners. The mayor also has a power of veto over legislation. The San Francisco Unified school district and the city and county have coterminous boundaries. Members of the board of education are nominated by the mayor and passed on by the voters.

San Francisco's five charters were granted respectively in 1850, 1856, 1861, 1898 and 1932. Initiative and referendum clauses were first embraced in the 1898 charter.

Outstanding are the many public buildings, street improvements, parks and other achievements. The fire and police departments were established on a sound base. The police department in 1950 employed 1,771 and the fire department 1,734. The water system is municipally operated. The average daily water demand on the system is 83,300,000 gal. The city also possesses extensively developed power resources.

History.—In his search for Monterey, Don Gaspar de Portola, governor of Lower California, left San Diego in July 1769 and some months later members of his little band discovered San Francisco bay and the tip of the peninsula whereon the city is situated. From that time until California became a part of the United States, San Francisco became an objective of international strategy.

In 1775, Don Manuel Ayala sailed through the Golden Gate in the "San Carlos," a packet of the Spanish royal navy. It was the first ship to gain entrance to the bay from the Pacific ocean. While the Spaniards won the credit of the discovery, the English, years before, narrowly missed gaining possession of the bay and the surrounding territory as well, for in 1579 Sir Francis Drake, the English explorer, sailed within a few miles of the "Golden Gate" and came to anchor in a little cove a few miles north, in what is known as Drake's bay.

In 1776 a land expedition commanded by Col. Juan Bautista de Anza arrived on the peninsula and established the Presidio and the Misión Dolores. The following year (1777) Padre Junípero Serra, father of the California missions, arrived. With the establishment of the Presidio, and the subsequent establishment of the *pueblo* of Yerba Buena, began the San Francisco of the present. From 1776 until 1806 the inhabitants, soldiers and missionaries led a quiet, happy existence, occupying themselves with building the mission and the presidio, and doing only work enough to get the necessaries of life. For excitement they had their Spanish *fiestas*, cockfights and rodeos, while from time to time sailors, adventurers and visiting ranchers added a novelty. Trading in hides and tallow constituted the principal business of the period, though wines and brandies made by the missionaries were exchanged for ship's goods of varied assortment. Fur trading was also beginning to take on a commercial aspect. Eventually, this proved to be the principal business of the community.

In 1806 Russia made an attempt through Nicolai Rezanov (*q.v.*) to establish a settlement and lay claim to some territory in the name of the tsar.

They were unsuccessful, but a Russian colony was eventually planted at Ft. Ross, less than 100 mi. north of San Francisco, which was intended to serve as a supply station and vegetable farm for the Russian possessions in Alaska. The outpost was established in March 1811 and a stockade was built on Bodega bay. It became the headquarters for Russian traders and trappers of seal and sea otter. Until they abandoned it in 1841, their growing inroads toward the San Francisco bay area were a source of irritation to the provincial authorities.

With the exception of a few quarrels between Mexicans and foreign colonists, as the Americans and other nationalities were called, all was tranquil until war was declared by the United States on Mexico on May 13, 1846. There was great excitement in San Francisco some weeks later when the news arrived. On July 9, 1848, Capt. John B. Montgomery of the U.S. navy, arrived with the sloop-of-war "Portsmouth" and raised the U.S. flag on the plaza, known now as Portsmouth plaza, claiming the territory for the United States. The community continued under the name of Yerba Buena until 1847 when it was changed to San Francisco. At this time there were some 200 buildings and 800 inhabitants in the village.

The discovery of gold at Coloma in Jan. 1848 was not taken seriously in San Francisco, and it was not until April of that year that the settlement became infected with the "gold bug." Then every one with an outfit stampeded for the mountains in search of gold. Then a city of tents and shanties arose; gambling was rife and prices extraordinary.

During the early '50s San Francisco experienced its darkest days. Crime was rampant, while the city government was too inefficient or too indifferent to suppress it. Bancroft, in his *History of California*, states that up to 1854 there were 4,200 homicides and 1,200 suicides, while the records of the next few years following show many deaths by violence, the high mark being reached in 1855 with 585.

In 1851 the Vigilance committee was formed and freed the city of most of the lawless element, either by hanging or driving them from the town. It was necessary for the committee to come together again in 1856, when for a second time it succeeded in restoring order in the community. Altogether more than 8,000 reputable citizens served on the two committees.

With the decline of gold production between 1855 and 1860, San Francisco came into its own as the Pacific coast's main port, and through world trade the city grew substantially and conservatively. This reign of conservatism, however, was interrupted by the unparalleled development of the Nevada silver mines and the city again experienced days similar to those of '49. There was a long period of frenzied speculation during which huge fortunes were won and lost within a few minutes. Panic gripped the people and only the financially strong survived. Many descendants of the successful financial giants of the silver period reside in San Francisco and have so handled their heritage that they are numbered among California's wealthiest and most influential citizens.

At the outbreak of the Civil War San Francisco showed evidence of being strongly pro-Union although thousands of arms were shipped in, to Southern sympathizers, for the purpose of winning Californians over to their cause or to encourage them to launch an independent republic. Nothing came of this venture and San Francisco remained, with California, a Union stronghold. The famed Pony Express, established in 1860, for a short time gave San Francisco quick mail and express communication with the interior of the country. The city's isolation, however, was not permanently removed until the first transcontinental railway was opened in 1869. The railway to Los Angeles was completed in 1876, thereby giving San Francisco connections with the east and south. (*See* below for an account of the earthquake and fire of 1906.)

Industries and Commerce.—California department of employment figures for 1947 showed that in San Francisco there were 2,315 manufacturing establishments, 71,013 wage earners and $242,120,000 in annual wages. According to the federal census for 1947, there was $410,326,000 value added by manufacture. In the six-county bay area there were 3,671 establishments, 131,161 wage earners making $393,346,000, $1,049,490,000 value added by manufacture.

The ten manufacturing groups reported with the highest value added by manufacture in San Francisco in the 1947 U.S. census, as shown in the accompanying table, amounted to $358,659,000 out of a total value added by manufacture for all products of $410,326,000.

Food and kindred products	$122,446,000
Printing and publishing	71,380,000
Apparel and related products	35,815,000
Fabricated metal products	35,508,000
Chemicals and allied products	28,764,000
Machinery, except electrical	23,728,000
Furniture and fixtures	14,547,000
Paper and allied products	10,189,000
Electrical machinery	8,320,000
Miscellaneous manufacturing	7,962,000

The sales of San Francisco firms selling at wholesale, in 1948 federal census, amounted to $4,020,854,000 or $2,643,240,000 above the 1939 total. Trade at retail in San Francisco of 23,863 licenced retail outlets, as reported in 1949 by the state board of equalization, was $1,274,357,000. The annual pay roll amounted to $175,268,000. In addition to the retail trade in San Francisco there were 6,558 service establishments reporting in 1947, with annual receipts of $187,890,000. These establishments reported 47,859 employees and an annual pay roll of $128,328,000.

San Francisco's business extends to all parts of the world; in the confines of the immediate trade area are a number of cities and towns, the greater number of which border on the bay. In the west bay section, on the San Francisco peninsula, the outstanding communities are San Francisco, Burlingame, San Mateo, Redwood City, Palo Alto and San Jose. North of San Francisco on the Marin peninsula are the towns of San Rafael, Sausalito, Mill Valley and San Anselmo.

In the east bay region are Oakland, Alameda, Berkeley, Richmond and San Leandro.

These sections form a central unit and comprise the immediate all-year market.

Transportation and Distribution.—Converging in San Francisco are 7 major transcontinental rail routes and numerous local routes; 68 regularly scheduled shipping services plus 105 other lines calling irregularly, and 15 bulk carrier fleets including tankers; more than 40 common carrier truck lines and hundreds of others offering nonscheduled services; and 4 transcontinental bus routes.

The San Francisco bay area ranked sixth (1947) in tonnage of water-borne commerce of all U.S. ports, with an 18,000,000-ton lead over any other Pacific coast port. San Francisco is the focal point of two bridges, the San Francisco-Oakland Bay bridge, a link in both federal highways 40 and 50, and the Golden Gate bridge, a link in federal highway 101.

Three modern air terminals in the bay area are within 30 min. of the heart of San Francisco. The enlarged municipal airport is the focal point of transcontinental and north-south services by transport planes. In 1950 there were five scheduled domestic air carriers and scheduled overseas services to the Hawaiian Islands, the orient and Australia.

The bay area is 450 sq.mi. The harbour has 18 mi. of berthing space, including 43 modern piers equipped with complete facilities. The harbour is controlled by a board of state harbour commissioners appointed by the governor.

In 1949, 3,731 ships with a registered tonnage of 18,189,385 arrived, and 3,726 ships with a tonnage of 18,146,704 departed. San Francisco's exports in 1949 were valued at $311,469,972; imports, $212,614,866.

The ten largest export classifications are vegetable products, edible, inedible and beverages; machinery and vehicles; textiles; nonmetallic minerals; chemicals; animals and animal products, edible and inedible; metals; wood and paper.

The principal imports are raw silk, coffee, sugar, copra, coconut oil, burlap, newsprint and tea. The 1948 report of the army chief engineer shows the relative tonnages of the water-borne commerce of San Francisco bay as follows: total (long tons) 29,042,655; foreign 2,885,902; coastwise 19,225,593; internal and intraport 7,676,571.

Rail traffic in San Francisco totalled 167,822 cars in 1949. San Francisco airport traffic in 1949 totalled 78,332 planes, 1,038,962 passengers, 14,956,009 lb. air mail and 6,935,745 lb. air express.

Finance.—The Federal Reserve bank of San Francisco is the headquarters of the 12th federal reserve district, which ranked third among the 12 districts with the volume of business during 1949, measured by bank debits totalling $115,375,573,000. The San Francisco stock exchange (nation's second largest regional security market) transactions during 1949 reached a market value of $145,591,885. There is also the San Francisco mining exchange.

There were 18 banks in San Francisco in 1950, several with branches. A few operated branch systems throughout the state. Thirteen banks were under state supervision—six commercial; two commercial and savings; two commercial, savings and trust; one savings; two savings and trust; and one title insurance company operating trust departments. There were five national banks.

San Francisco bank clearings in 1949 totalled $19,512,000,000 and ranked fifth in the nation, and bank debits totalled $28,032,-353,000. San Francisco's 18 banks reported as of Dec. 31, 1949, total deposits of $8,795,095,670, of which $4,048,466,479 were time and $4,746,629,191 demand. Total resources amounted to $9,452,612,874.

Since there is no state property tax, the only levy in San Francisco is the combined city and county tax. The tax rate for the fiscal year 1949–50 was $5.66 on $100 assessed valuation. Revenues receivable during the 1949–50 fiscal year were estimated at $133,320,341, of which $60,647,398 was from taxes on property assessed by city and county and the state board of equalization.

Education.—San Francisco's institutions of learning include the affiliated colleges of the University of California, San Francisco State college, the University of San Francisco, City College of San Francisco and numerous law and medical schools. Eight miles across the bay from San Francisco, at Berkeley, is the University of California, one of the largest in the United States; while at Palo Alto is Leland Stanford Jr. university (q.v.). Near Oakland is St. Mary's college, and in the hills of Oakland is Mills college, an institution for women.

During the school year ended June 1950 San Francisco public day schools had an enrolment of 184,285—9,419 in kindergartens, 40,529 in elementary schools, 12,402 in junior and junior-senior high schools and 15,323 in high schools. At the same time there were thousands in special schools, 91,609 adults in evening schools and 11,015 in junior colleges. There were 3,279 teachers. The average daily attendance was 79,289 in public schools. The operating cost per average daily attendance in 1949 was $278.39. The value of the school property was $52,362,854.

Public schools were listed as follows: 78 kindergartens, 81 elementary and grammar; 10 junior high schools; 9 senior high schools; 3 adult evening schools; 1 continuation school; 5 adult day schools and 1 junior college.

Public Buildings and Parks.—The group of buildings in the civic centre consists of the city hall, Exposition auditorium which has a seating capacity of 12,000 in the main auditorium, San Francisco public library, the state building, an opera house and other buildings, and a federal office building. A mint building was finished early in 1937.

California palace of the Legion of Honor, in Lincoln park overlooking the Golden Gate, is a replica of the palace of the Legion of Honor in Paris.

In Golden Gate park are the De Young Memorial museum, Academy of Sciences, Steinhart aquarium and the Museum of Anthropology. Near the Presidio is the San Francisco museum of art. At Kearny and Washington streets is the Hall of Justice, containing police courts and the criminal department of the superior court. Other buildings are the old United States

mint, built in 1874; the post office; the customs house and the United States appraiser's buildings; and the Ferry building, built by the state in 1896, which is 659 ft. long and 156 ft. wide, containing many state offices.

San Francisco is noted for its parks. There are 54 parks and 94 recreational units, with a total acreage of 4,635.37. In addition to the municipal parks, the several government reservations, the largest of which is the Presidio comprising 1,542 ac., all go toward augmenting the aggregate area of the city parks. All of San Francisco's parks are "man-made."

The Golden Gate park, a well-known playground, comprises 1,017 ac. and is about 3 mi. long and ½ mi. wide, extending from Stanyan street on the east to the Pacific ocean on the west, and lies in the midst of San Francisco's residential districts. In the park are many museums and monuments, an aviary, aquarium, music temple, stadium, tennis courts, baseball and football grounds, bridle paths, an athletic field and running track, paddocks and children's playgrounds. Improved driveways in the park exceed 25 mi. in length. At the western end of the park is to be seen the sloop "Gjoa," the only vessel that ever navigated the northwest passage; it was given to San Francisco by its owner, Capt. Roald Amundsen.

Streets and Boulevards.—San Francisco's street system was begun in 1835 when Calle de la Fundación or Foundation street was laid out. The first survey, made in 1839, covered what is now the financial and retail sections of the city. Other streets and avenues were gradually added until 1845 when Jasper O'Farrell made a second survey. This system applied the "checkerboard layout," with Market street the main artery and division point.

The streets north of Market run north and south and east and west; the streets south run parallel to Market street and at right angles. The Market street slant is about southwest and northeast. Among the scenic boulevards are the Marina, Twin Peaks, Market street extension, Lincoln, Embarcadero and Great Highway paralleling the ocean.

San Francisco's Chinatown comprises an area paralleling Grant Ave. between Bush St. and Columbus Ave. The "town" is hedged in by the financial, hotel and apartment house districts and a part of North Beach or "Latin Quarter."

A chamber of commerce study indicated that in 1949 there were 20,000 Chinese residents in San Francisco, most of whom resided in Chinatown.

Fires, Earthquake and Reconstruction.—Seven times San Francisco has been swept by disastrous fires. The first fire of note occurred on Dec. 24, 1849, and was followed in quick succession by others on May 4, 1850; June 14, 1850; Sept. 17, 1850; May 4, 1851, and June 22, 1851. In 1906 came the greatest conflagration experienced on the western coast.

Following the earthquake which occurred early on the morning of April 18, 1906, flames swept through the city creating havoc, especially in the central business and residential sections. Thousands of buildings, hundreds of lives and approximately $350,000,000 were the losses sustained. An area of 497 city blocks, or 4 sq.mi., was devastated. According to official records 28,188 buildings valued at $105,000,000 were destroyed. The value of the contents of the structures wiped out was impossible to estimate. Insurance companies and San Francisco financial houses estimate the insurance paid at $300,000,000, though many companies failed in the attempt to meet their obligations, while others repudiated them. Aid in the form of money to the sum of $10,000,000 was contributed by American, European and Asiatic communities, while additional millions in food and clothing were rushed to the stricken city, whose inhabitants slept in the remaining houses, parks and the streets for weeks. The flames were subdued by the generous use of dynamite, with the result that many expensive buildings were sacrificed to "back-fire" to save other sections of the city. While San Francisco had experienced earthquake disturbances in 1868, 1898 and 1900, that of 1906 was the most violent.

Within a remarkably short time San Francisco began the struggle to rehabilitate itself. Owing to the courage and energy of the people, within a year following the catastrophe the city was taking on a somewhat normal appearance. The new structures were planned along more costly and substantial lines. With the aid of San Francisco banks and the money received from insurance companies, the city went forward step by step and a beautiful San Francisco once more arose from the debris and ashes.

(R. B. Kr.; W. Bn.)

SANGER, JOHN (1816–1889), English circus proprietor, was born at Chew Magna, Somerset, in 1816, the son of an old sailor who had turned showman. In 1845 he started with his brother George a conjuring exhibition at Birmingham. The venture was successful, and the brothers, who had been interested spectators of the equestrian performances at Astley's amphitheatre, London, then started touring the country with a circus entertainment consisting of a horse and pony and three or four human performers. Eventually John and George Sanger became lessees of the Agricultural hall, London, and there produced a large number of elaborate spectacles. In 1871 the Sangers leased Astley's where they gave an equestrian pantomime every winter, touring in the summer with a large circus. Subsequently the partnership was dissolved, each brother producing his own show. John Sanger died while touring, at Ipswich on Aug. 22, 1889, the business being continued by his son.

SANGERHAUSEN, a town in the Prussian province of Saxony, Germany, near the south base of the Harz mountains, 30 mi. W. of Halle. Pop. (1939) 12,653. Sangerhausen is mentioned in a document of 991 as appertaining to the estates of the emperor.

By marriage it passed to the landgrave of Thuringia, it fell in 1249 to Meissen, and in 1291 to Brandenburg. In 1372 it passed to Saxony and formed a portion of that territory until 1815 when it was united with Prussia.

SAN GERMÁN, a town in the southwestern part of Puerto Rico, about 5 mi. from the Mona channel on the west and the Caribbean sea in the south.

The population of the town by the census of 1950 was 8,872, and of the municipal district, 29,553.

The original settlement was founded in 1512 by Diego, a son of Columbus. The modern town of San Germán was founded in 1573, after the old San Germán was destroyed by French pirates. For many years San Germán was the seat of government of the western district.

The Porta Coeli convent, one of the oldest buildings of the Spanish settlement in the West Indies, was built in 1538. The Puerto Rican Polytechnic institute, offering undergraduate studies, is located at San Germán. (J. L.-Ee.)

SANGIHE (SANGIR) AND TALAUT ISLANDS, a group of islands off the northeast coast of Celebes, Netherlands Indies. Area, 808 sq.mi.; population (1930) 158,729, including 93 Europeans and 2,814 Chinese.

The Sangihe Islands continue the northeastern extension of Celebes toward Mindanao, in the Philippines, and are set upon a long, narrow ridge, along a volcanic band, with very deep water on either side.

Although fringed with recent coral formation, they are distinctly volcanic, with active volcanoes, Mount Awu, on Sangihe Island, having experienced recent severe eruptions, while earthquakes also have occurred. Sangihe, Siau and Tagulanda are the chief islands, and Talisse and Banka (Banka lies off the east coast of Sumatra) are between Tagulanda and the mainland of Celebes.

Banka gives its name to Banka passage, the channel by which entry is obtained from Celebes sea to the Molucca passage. Sangihe is 27 mi. long, and from 9 to 17 in width, is mountainous in the north, elevation decreasing considerably in the south, and has a coast which is generally steep. It has an average rainfall of 195 in., and, with Siau, has an exceptionally fertile volcanic soil with extensive cultivation of nutmegs, coco-nuts and Manila hemp. Taruna, on the west coast, is the capital, where a *contrôleur* resides who is in charge of all of the islands. It, and Peta, on the east coast, are regular ports of call; also Hulu, the capital and port of Siau, and Tagulandang, and Talisse, on the islands of that name. Tagulandang has two mountains of 2,500

ft., sloping from east to west, and Ruang, a small island west of Tagulandang, has an active volcano.

The people of Sangihe and Siau are closely related to the people of Minahasa and of portions of the Philippine Islands, with fair complexion, high nose and stiff, short black hair. They were formerly terrorized by the dreaded pirates of Sulu (islands off the S.E. coast of Mindanao, in the Philippines). But later, under direct Dutch rule, the Sangihe and Siau islanders progressed wonderfully, under the peaceful regime of Dutch rule, like their near relatives the Minahasese, and like these also, they became mostly Christians. Society is based on the matriarchal system, and the people, who speak a language of their own, live by agriculture and fishing and trading in wood, copra and nutmegs. The very fine and white Manila hemp they grow is practically only for domestic consumption, and its weaving is the most important industry. The Talaut, or Talaud, Islands consist of a group lying northeast of Sangihe, the chief of which is Karakelang, 39 mi. long and 15 wide, in the north. Heights of 2,300 ft. are said to exist in the southern part. The coast is steep, except on the south shore, which is fringed by a wide reef. Some tiny islands known as the Nanusa Islands lie northeast of Karakelang, and vessels run regularly to these, and to Beo, the capital of Karakelang, and of the group, where a *gezaghebber* resides, also to Lirung, the port and capital of a long island lying close to and southeast of Karakelang. The Sangihe and Talaut Islands were incorporated under the direct rule of the Dutch governor of Ternate as far back as 1677. Later they were attached to the residency of Manado; in 1942, during World War II, they passed under Japanese military control. (E. E. L.; X.)

SAN GIMIGNANO a town of Tuscany, Italy, in the province of Siena, 24 mi. N.W. of Siena, at an elevation of 1,089 ft. Pop. (1936) 3,426 (town); 11,270 (commune). Being surrounded by its ancient walls, and retaining 13 out of its original 72 towers, it is, with its predominantly Gothic architecture, a thoroughly mediaeval town in appearance. In the Palazzo Comunale (1288-1323) is a fresco by Lippo Memmi of the Madonna enthroned (1317), copied from the "Majestas" at Siena. The Collegiata (the former cathedral) of the 12th century was enlarged after 1466 by Giuliano da Maiano, whose brother Benedetto carved the altar and ciborium in the chapel of S. Fina. The beautiful frescoes with scenes from her life (she was a local saint who died at the age of 15 in 1253) are the earliest work of Domenico Ghirlandajo (1475). The cathedral contains other 14th-century and early Renaissance paintings, including New Testament scenes by Barna da Siena (1380) and some fine choir stalls. S. Agostino (1280–1298) contains a famous series of frescoes by Benozzo Gozzoli, with scenes from the life of St. Augustine (1463-1467). The town was independent in the 13th century, but in 1353, owing to the dissensions of the Salvucci (Ghibellines) and Ardinghelli (Guelphs), it fell into the hands of Florence.

See R. Pantini, *San Gimignano e Certaldo* (Bergamo, 1905).

SAN GIULIANO, ANTONINO PATERNO-CASTELLI, Marquis di (1852–1914), Italian statesman, was born at Catania on Dec. 10, 1852, a member of a noble Sicilian family. After graduating in law at the University of Catania he became, in 1879, mayor of his native city, and in 1882 was elected to parliament. When in 1892 Signor Giolitti became premier, San Giuliano was selected as undersecretary for agriculture, while in the second Pelloux ministry (1899–1900) he held the portfolio of posts and telegraphs. Having been defeated at the election of 1904, he was nominated senator. When in Dec. 1905 Signor Fortis became prime minister he was appointed minister for foreign affairs, and on the fall of the cabinet early in 1906 he was appointed ambassador in London, where he remained until 1910. From London he was transferred to Paris, but he soon returned to the Consulta as foreign minister in the Luzzatti cabinet (1910–1911), and continued at the same post in Signor Giolitti's administration. San Giuliano was an ardent believer in the Triple Alliance but having retained his portfolio under Salandra, after Giolitti's resignation in March 1914, he carried out with complete loyalty the policy of neutrality adopted by Italy on the outbreak of World War I. He died in Rome on Oct. 16, 1914.

SANGLI, formerly a princely state composed of scattered territories (total area 1,146 sq.mi.; pop., 1941, 293,381) in the Deccan Kolhapur agency; merged into Bombay province on March 8, 1948. Sangli town (pop., 1951, 50,287), on the Southern railway 11 mi. from Miraj junction, is now the headquarters of Satara South district, Bombay state, republic of India. It is known for the manufacture of brass and copper vessels and has a textile mill. Willingdon college and the New Engineering college are institutions of Poona university.

SANHEDRIN: *see* SYNEDRIUM.

SANITATION: *see* HYGIENE.

SANITATION OF BUILDINGS. To preserve the health of the occupiers of a building, it is imperative that all polluted water and solid organic refuse be removed from the premises at frequent intervals. Where the buildings are in a town it is usual for the local authority to remove the solid dry refuse by carting, but where a public water supply is available, liquid wastes are flushed away through a system of pipes. These comprise waste pipes to carry washing water, soil pipes to carry human excreta and rainwater pipes. If such pipes pass under the grounds of the premises they are termed drains and usually discharge eventually into sewers or into cesspools or septic tanks.

Drains.—Outside drains are usually composed of glazed stoneware or vitrified earthenware pipes, 2 ft. long, not often larger than 4 in. diameter for branches and 6 in. diameter for the main drain. All drains inside a building, whether under- or aboveground, are usually of iron pipe. If the pipes are cast iron the joints are caulked with oakum and molten lead. If of wrought iron or steel they are screw joints. All drains that carry solids should be provided with accessible clean-out caps, which can be readily unscrewed for the admission of cleaning rods, to remove obstructions which may choke the drains. It is good practice to have a clean-out cap or plug at each change in direction of a drain pipe. The drains must be run straight between these clean-out points.

Soil Pipes.—In British plumbing practice these are not disconnected where they are jointed to the drains, but waste pipes and rainwater pipes discharge into or onto gulley traps at the base of the wall. Each house should have its own system of drains, separated from the sewer by a disconnecting chamber or manhole. The chamber is usually placed near the boundary of the property so as to prevent, as far as possible, the entry of sewer gas into the house drainage system. The intercepting trap is shaped so as to allow of removing obstructions on the outer side of the trap, and it is preferable for the manhole cover to be sealed. If the chamber is in an isolated position, the cover, which should be of cast iron, may be provided with a grating to afford means of ventilation, otherwise the chamber is fitted with a ventilating pipe to form a fresh-air inlet, and this is carried up well above ground level to some position where an accidental emission of drain gas would not cause a nuisance. Any such chamber should be built of the best bricks or cement concrete, suitably provided with curved channels for the branch connections. Such channels may be formed in the concrete or composed of half-round glazed pipes. Where inspection at bends is required, or where branches meet, but where it is considered to be too expensive or unnecessary to build a chamber, a shaft of 6-in. pipes is sometimes substituted, the whole being carefully jointed and supported by concrete. Since complete access to the drain is then impossible, the inspection will be confined to locating the position of a blockage or leakage to any particular length of pipes. When there is any possibility of the drains being flooded by the sewer, special interception traps are used in which a floating ball seals the inlet, and prevents the reversal of the flow. No traps using hinged valves or other mechanical contrivances should be allowed.

In American plumbing practice all soil and waste stacks are usually installed within the buildings to prevent them from becoming frozen. These stacks generally are connected at their base to a system of iron main drain and branch drains in the basement, either at the basement ceiling or under the basement floor. In some cities, it is compulsory to have a main drain-trap with a fresh air inlet pipe located at the point where the main house-drain leaves the building to disconnect the house from street sewer gas,

and to insure a proper ventilation of the house drainage system.

In other sections of the United States, however, the main drain-trap and fresh air inlet are not permitted. In such places the house-drain runs directly to the sewer, cesspool, or septic tanks, without the intervention of a main or intercepting trap.

The gradients of the drains are usually arranged as to not only ensure the system being self-cleansing, but also so that they do not discharge their contents at such a rate that the solids are left behind to putrify on the sides of the channels. It is usual to fix the velocity at about 3 feet per second for these purposes.

Advantage may be taken of an inspection chamber or shaft to provide ventilation to the drains. All connections between branches and the main drain are made by specially designed pipes provided with junctions.

Drain Tests.—Drain testing is undertaken for two reasons:— (a) to ensure that the system of a new house is satisfactory before the dwelling is inhabited, (b) to locate defects in systems already in use. The testing in each case differs somewhat as it is considered that new drains should be able to pass severer tests than those which have been in use some years. New drains are, therefore, usually subjected to the "water test" in which any length of the drain is first closed at the lower end by some form of plug or stopper, and the drain is then filled with water so as to give a maximum head of pressure of not more than about 6 feet. The stopper is fitted with an expanding rubber ring, and constructed in some cases so that the air can escape, and the required head may be obtained by adding vertical lengths of 1 inch diameter pipe to a similar plug at the upper end of the pipe line. A slight diminution in the head may be observed at the commencement of the test, due to absorption by the joints and possibly by the pipes, but this will soon cease, and no further drop should occur for a period of an hour. The pipe trenches should all be left open until the tests have been made, the inspector being thus able to locate any fault if indicated by a fall in water level. For drains already in use it is customary to use the "smoke test." For this machines are used which generate smoke and then, by means of fans or pistons, pump it into the branch or main drain. Compressed air tests are also used, any leakage being shown on the gauge attached to the pump. Smoke "rockets" have been advocated in the past, but the amount of smoke generated is small and the effect is local. Smell tests, using peppermint, calcium carbide, etc., have also been used, but the difficulty in locating the leakage of a smell, and the great difficulty in preventing the chemical getting on the hands or clothes, has made this test almost obsolete. If smoke is used it is generated in a receiver connected to the fan or pump on one side and to a hose on the other, and is formed by the burning of oily waste, or any substance which will give off a dense cloud.

Obstructions in drains are usually removed by rods which can be jointed together to form any length, and occasionally fitted with brushes or scrapers.

Traps.—In British plumbing practice all parts of the drainage system, when there is any possibility of drain air entering the house, are disconnected by traps, the only exception being the soil pipe, which is connected to the drain by a bend. Such traps are placed either on the drainage system itself, or under each of the house plumbing fixtures and the "Seal" should always be about 2 in. to avoid the effect of evaporation. Gulley-traps are installed to disconnect roof-leaders and sink waste-pipes from the drainage system. For sink wastes the liquid has to pass along an open channel outside the building for a length of at least 18 in. before entering the trap. It is intended to so prevent grease entering the drain by causing it to cool and solidify and remain either in the channel or the trap.

FIG. 1.—RAINWATER GULLEY

Grease traps are frequently specially provided where large quantities of grease may be expected, as from the cooking departments of hotels and clubs. The hot liquid enters near the base of the apparatus and leaves at the same level, and the grease rises to the surface where it cools and solidifies. The water area is made as large as practicable and a wire basket or galvanized iron tray is provided to remove the grease, which operation should be frequently carried out.

Another type of grease trap operates by means of a syphon, the grease on the water surface being broken up by a flush, but it is generally found unsatisfactory. Traps are always placed under all sanitary fittings and are of the P or S type.

In American plumbing practice every plumbing fixture including baths, shower receptors, water closets, urinals, lavatories, or wash basins, sinks, laundry tubs, floor-drains, area-drains, roof

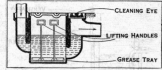

FIG. 2.—GREASE TRAP

CLEANING EYE
LIFTING HANDLES
GREASE TRAY

water-leaders and every fixture or fitting that discharges into a house drainage system must be properly and effectively trapped as close to the fixture or fitting as conditions will permit. These traps are of a variety of forms such as P. S. bottles, pot or drum, etc. All have water seals. Some are provided with check valves to prevent a back-flow of sewage through them. None, however, are permitted which depend upon mechanical contrivances as a substitute for a water seal. The water seal may, however, be augmented by a float, a check valve or other contrivance which will automatically close against back pressure. This protects the house against a backing-up of sewage as from a choked or flooded street sewer.

All fixture traps within a building must be protected against loss of seal by syphonage or air compression. The seal must remain intact to prevent sewer gas from entering the building through the traps. This trap protection is accomplished by the installation of special arrangements of vent piping which opens to the outer air and maintains the air pressure back of the trap seals practically at atmosphere.

Antisyphonage.—Since every sanitary fixture in a building must be trapped, possibilities might arise in which the seals of such traps would be broken by either increase or decrease of the air pressure unless provided against. Such cases would occur where a range of fixtures were connected to one soil or waste pipe and hence an antisyphonage or vent pipe is always provided. If no ventilating branches were provided it might be possible for a fitting on an upper floor to syphon out the water in the trap of the fittings below by reducing the air pressure in the branch. Unsealing could also happen through the discharge of the upper fitting compressing the air in a branch below and so forcing the seal of a trap below. While such possibilities are not nowadays considered of such importance as formerly, the antisyphonage pipes are always fitted, as they form a convenient method of ventilating the branches. Each antisyphonage pipe connects the head of the trap to a ventilating stack which may be carried up above the eaves of the house, or may be connected into the soil pipe above the highest branch. Such soil pipe has,

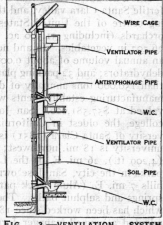

FIG. 3.—VENTILATION SYSTEM FROM LAVATORIES

WIRE CAGE
VENTILATOR PIPE
ANTISYPHONAGE PIPE
W.C.
VENTILATOR PIPE
SOIL PIPE
W.C.

in any case, to be continued full bore either well above the eaves, or to such a position that the gases let free cannot cause a nuisance or enter the house by means of chimneys, skylights, windows or other openings. The open ends of soil pipes, and any other pipes used as ventilators, are best covered by a wire cage to prevent their being used by birds for nesting purposes.

Water Closets.—Of the sanitary fittings or fixtures usually found in buildings, the water closet is of the most importance. The "wash-down" and syphon closets are now practically the standard types, being simple, self-cleansing, reasonably quiet and

having no moving parts. They may either stand on the floor or be supported by brackets.

The "valve" closet is the most modern adaptation of the now obsolete "pan" closet. It has the disadvantage of possessing many moving parts, and requires careful setting and use. It can, however, be quite a successful and hygienic apparatus but is usually expensive.

All closet basins are now made of the plainest and simplest design possible and are usually of white glazed stoneware. All sharp bends or angles are carefully avoided, and no part of the apparatus is allowed to be concealed by woodwork or ornamental finish. The flushing is arranged to not only throw a strong rush of water into the trap, but a portion of the flush is passed round the hollow rim to cleanse the sides of the basin.

Flushing Cisterns.—In Great Britain these are always specified to be of the "waste-water-prevention" type as the Water

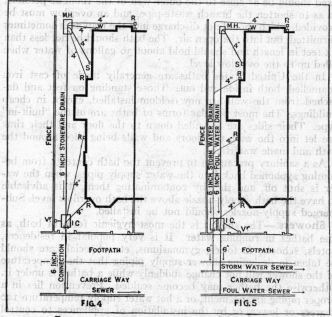

FIG. 4.—COMBINED SYSTEM OF HOUSE DRAINING
FIG. 5.—SEPARATE SYSTEM OF HOUSE DRAINAGE

Companies insist that their discharge shall be limited to a specified amount at each use. Two gallons is usually allowed, but three would be better, and unfortunately as little as one and a half gallons is often found. The cistern should be placed not less than five feet above the fitting flushed and connected to the latter by a $1\frac{1}{2}$ inch diameter pipe, so as to give a good rush of water. An overflow must be placed below the inlet and should discharge direct into the open air, so as to give warning of irregular working of the valve. Similar cisterns are also made to discharge automatically at chosen intervals and so flush such fittings as ranges of urinals and closets. It is compulsory for such cisterns, whether automatic or otherwise, to be fitted to all apparatus receiving human excreta, so that there shall be no possibility of contamination of the rest of the water in the building. As regards the regulations in force for house drainage, reference should be made to the local by-laws, as these vary in detail in the different towns.

In the United States the water closets in general use in residences are flushed by "low-drain" tanks usually of vitreous china. The flush connection is generally about 2 in. diameter and short. The tank is supplied with water through a ball cash and a $\frac{1}{2}$ in. supply pipe. The flushing appliance generally is either in the form of a syphon within the tank or a hollow flush valve usually of rubber. Each tank is provided with an overflow to the closet bowl, and a re-fill tube, which re-establishes the seal in the closet-trap after the flush has stopped and while the tank is being re-filled by the ball cock. Tank closets are generally installed in residences and other buildings where the water supply pipes are comparatively small in diameter.

Direct Flush Valves.—In large buildings such as hotels, office buildings, etc., where the water supply pipes are comparatively large, the water closets are flushed directly from the water supply pipes through slow-closing flush valves. These may be regulated to any length of flush desired. When the closet is properly flushed the valve shuts automatically. It is a mistake to install these valves when the supply pipes are too small or the pressure too low. The pipes should be larger than one inch and the pressure greater than 20 lb. per square inch behind the valve.

Baths.—In Great Britain baths are now usually made of enamelled cast iron or glazed stoneware, but copper and zinc have occasionally been used. The two latter, however, require the support of framing, which is usually of wood, a material which is unsuitable for the hot, moist atmosphere of a bathroom. Cast iron baths may be provided with feet, but the stoneware type generally rest direct on the floor. The end at which the taps and outlet are fixed should be as close to the outer wall of the room as possible, so as to shorten the branch waste-pipe, and an overflow must be provided, which should not discharge into the trap as is sometimes permitted, but into the open air. The bath should be not less than six feet in length and should hold about 30 gallons of water when filled up to the overflow level.

In the United States baths are generally made of cast iron enamelled, both inside and out. Those standing on feet and detached from the wall are now seldom installed, except in cheap buildings. The most popular forms of baths are of the "built-in" type. Their sides are extended down to the floor and their rims are let into the wall, the floors and walls being tiled around the bath and made watertight.

As a sanitary precaution to prevent the bath contents from becoming syphoned back into the water supply pipes, when the water is shut off, and thereby contaminating them, it is advisable to have the bath supply-nozzle above the bath overflow level. Submerged supply-nozzles should not be installed.

Showers.—The shower is the most hygienic form of bath, as one bathes in running water. It is very popular in residences, hotels, schools, factories, gymnasiums, etc. Special care should be taken in designing shower supply piping that the temperature of the shower will not change suddenly while a bather is under it. Otherwise the bather may become scalded. Prevention lies in a proper piping arrangement, or a hot water supply temperature 120 degrees or lower, or by the installation of appliances to control automatically the shower temperature. A shower may be arranged over a bath, or over a floor receptor furnished with a floor drain. The control valves should be located so that they may be reached from outside the shower. Shower bathing has become so popular in America that many of the leading hotels are now equipped with one shower in each room, in addition to the regular plunge baths.

Urinals.—In Great Britain these fittings are not usually provided in private houses but are necessary in such places as hotels and clubs. They should be simple in design and provided with an automatic flushing cistern. They are usually about 4 feet high, are made of glazed porcelain and in as few parts as possible, and flushed by pipes or sprays at the back. The old types with straight sides and back and made of slate or cast iron cannot be kept clean and are to be considered obsolete. The liquids are removed by an open channel to a trapped gulley close to the outside wall. The liquid is then removed by a pipe similar to a soil pipe which is not trapped at ground level.

In the United States there is quite a variety of urinals in use in hotels, clubs and public buildings. Usually they are made of vitreous china and are attached to the wall or stand on the floor. Some are flushed from overhead tanks with chain-pull, or by timed automatic-flush. Others are equipped with direct flush valves which close slowly and automatically, being adjusted to a suitable time and volume of flush. Several makes are provided with local ventilation attachments to which vent pipes may be connected to remove offensive odors and prevent them from diffusing throughout the toilet rooms.

Lavatories.—In America the lavatories, or wash basins, are practically all made of vitreous china. Some are attached to the walls by brackets. Others are supported on legs or china pedestals.

To permit of washing in running water, if desired, the hot and cold supplies should connect into a nozzle arranged at a suitable height over the lavatory slab. The waste outlet is preferably of the "pop-up" type, the plug being operated by a knob or handle over the lavatory slab. Every lavatory should have an overflow connection and be separately trapped close to the bowl. The fixture should have no woodwork enclosing any part. It should all be open with access for keeping it clean.

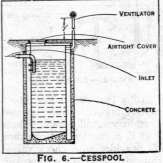

FIG. 6.—CESSPOOL

Kitchen Sinks.—These are made of enamelled cast iron, vitreous china or glazed porcelain and are set on legs, their backs being secured to the wall. There is a great variety of forms on the American market. The latest and best are one-piece fixtures with sink, drain boards, backs and apron all in one casting. The sink supply should be in the form of a combination faucet which permits the user to regulate the temperature of the water drawn. Sinks in some residences are provided with an electric dish washer compartment. Some are made in combination with a laundry tub. Some of the latest combinations comprise a sink in the middle, an electric dish washer at one end, and an electric clothes washer at the other end, all three compartments discharging their wastes through the trap under the sink.

Where much greasy dishwater will pass through a sink trap, the trap should be of a type especially designed to intercept the grease. This prevents the grease from getting into and clogging the house drains. The best type of grease trap for placing under a sink has its body in the form of a cold water jacket. Cold water to the plumbing fixtures passes through the grease trap jacket and so chills the grease in the sink waste water much more effectively than the air, or earth-cooled grease trap. (G. S. Co.; T. N. T.)

SAN JOSE, a city of California, U.S., 50 mi. S.E. of San Francisco and 7 mi. S.E. of the southern end of San Francisco bay; the county seat of Santa Clara county. It is served by the Southern Pacific, the Western Pacific and by numerous motor-coach and truck lines. The population was 95,280 in 1950 and was 68,457 in 1940 by the federal census.

It is a delightful residential city in the heart of the beautiful and fertile Santa Clara valley, and the largest fruit-canning and packing centre of the United States. The county has 95,468 ac. in orchards (including 51,590 ac. of prunes), 1,503 in berries and 26,707 in vegetables. In and near the city are 44 canneries with an annual volume of about 9,000,000 cases; also evaporators and dehydrators; and 32 packing plants, which produce a total of more than 150,000 tons annually of dried fruit. The output of all the manufacturing establishments within the city limits in 1947 was valued at $57,581,000. San Jose is the seat of San Jose State college, the oldest in California (established 1862). The University of Santa Clara (1851) is in an adjoining suburb; Stanford university is 18 mi. northwest; and on the top of Mt. Hamilton (4,209 ft.), 26 mi. E., is the Lick observatory. Besides several parks in the city, San Jose owns a tract of 716 ac. in the foothills 7 mi. E. (Alum Rock park) which contains many mineral springs and sulphur baths. The New Almaden quicksilver mine, which has been worked since 1824, is 14 mi. S. In 1916 the city adopted a council-manager form of government. The assessed valuation for 1949 was $108,995,540. Bank clearings in that year totalled $561,186,111. Near San Jose is Moffett field, base of the United States military air transport service, and the Ames Aeronautical Research laboratory of the national advisory committee on aeronautics. Also in this area is the world's largest cement plant.

The Pueblo de San José de Guadalupe, the first Spanish pueblo in California, was founded on Nov. 29, 1777, primarily to promote agriculture, so that the country need not be dependent on Mexico for provisions. Father Junípero Serra had already (Jan. 18, 1777) established the Mission of Santa Clara de Asís in the vicinity.

Plants, seeds and cuttings were supplied to the mission and to the settlers. In March 1846 Gen. J. C. Frémont, with a party of 62, visited the valley, and in July the town was occupied by Capt. Fallon and the U.S. flag was raised over it. The first state legislature convened in San Jose on Dec. 15, 1849, and this was the seat of government until May 1, 1851. The city was incorporated in 1850 and reincorporated in 1865. By 1870 the population was 9,089. After the secularization of the church properties in 1834 the mission orchards and gardens were neglected, and the Santa Clara valley was given over largely to cattle and horse ranges. The foundation of the fruit industry on a commercial scale is credited to Louis Pellier, who in 1856 brought a number of prune cuttings from his home near Agen.

SAN JOSÉ or **SAN JOSÉ DE COSTA RICA,** the capital of the republic of Costa Rica and of the department of San José; in the central plateau of the country, 3,868 ft. above sea level, and on the transcontinental railway from the Pacific port of Puntarenas to the Atlantic port of Limón. Pop. (1950) 86,718. San José is an episcopal see, the most populous city in Costa Rica and the centre of a rich agricultural region; its climate is temperate, its water supply pure and abundant. The city was founded in 1738, and became the capital in 1823. It is thoroughly modern in appearance, with well-paved streets lighted by electricity; its houses are one- or two-storied to minimize the danger from earthquake. The suburbs consist chiefly of cane huts, tenanted by Indians and mestizos. The larger of two public gardens, the Morazán park, contains a representative collection of the Costa Rican flora. The principal buildings are the cathedral, founded in the 18th century but restored after 1870, the hospital, government offices, institutes of law and medicine and of physical geography, training school for teachers, national bank, museum, library and barracks. The staple trade of San José is in coffee. (*See also* COSTA RICA.)

SAN JUAN, an Andean province of Argentina, bounded north and east by La Rioja, south by San Luis and Mendoza and west by Chile, from which it is separated by the Andean cordilleras. Area 33,257 sq.mi.; pop. (1947 estimate) 258,778. It is roughly mountainous, and belongs to the closed drainage basin of western Argentina, centring in the province of Mendoza. It is traversed by several rivers, fed by the melting snows of the Andes and discharging into the swamps and lagoons in the southeastern part of the province, the largest of which is the Huanacache lagoon. The largest of these rivers are the Bermejo, Jachal or Zonión and San Juan. They are all used for irrigation. The climate is extremely hot and dry in summer, but the winter temperature is mild and pleasant. Agriculture is the principal occupation of its inhabitants, though the soil is generally sterile and the rainfall uncertain and very light. Cereals are grown in some localities, and fruits and wine grapes of excellent quality are cultivated under irrigation on a large scale.

The province contains gold, silver, copper, iron, lead, coal and salt. Pastoral interests are largely in feeding cattle for the Chilean markets, for which large areas of alfalfa are grown in the irrigated valleys of the Andes. Rail communication is provided by the Belgrano and the San Martín railways.

The capital of the province is San Juan (estimated population, 1943, 80,000), in a great bend of the San Juan river, 97 mi. N. of Mendoza and about 750 mi. from Buenos Aires by rail. The city was founded in 1562 by Juan Jufré, a companion of Pedro del Castillo, the founder of Mendoza, and was the capital of the province after 1820. The original settlement, named San Juan de la Frontera and now referred to as Pueblo Viejo, 4 mi. N., was abandoned in 1593 because of frequent inundations. The present town is about 2,165 ft. above sea level and is defended from inundations by an embankment called the Murallón. The city has suffered severely from political disorders, and in 1894 was nearly destroyed by an earthquake. But with the possible exception of the earthquake of March 20, 1861, which completely destroyed the city of Mendoza, Argentina never suffered a greater disaster than the earthquake that occurred in San Juan province on Jan. 15, 1944. Whatever the intensity of the shock may have been elsewhere in the province, the worst damage and greatest

loss of lives were sustained by the city of San Juan. More than 90% of the buildings, including the cathedral, the government house, municipal building, churches, schools, hospitals, railway station and historical monuments, were either destroyed or damaged beyond repair, and the toll of lives was numbered in the thousands. (R. W. RD.; X.)

SAN JUAN, the capital of Puerto Rico and its oldest, largest and most important city. Its population according to the census of 1950 was 367,846 (actually 223,949 on that date, but in 1951 the capital city absorbed the neighbouring municipality of Río Piedras, which in 1950 had a population of 132,369). In 1940 the population of San Juan was 169,247. In its growth, the city also absorbed Santurce, Condado, Miramar and other suburban districts.

BY COURTESY OF THE U.S. BUREAU OF INSULAR AFFAIRS

THE GOVERNOR'S PALACE, SAN JUAN

The city's harbour is a large and almost landlocked bay with a rather narrow entrance from the Atlantic.

San Juan owes its foundation to the noted explorer and colonizer, Juan Ponce de León. This leader accompanied Columbus on his second voyage, when he discovered Puerto Rico, in 1493. Afterward, in 1508, Ponce de León was sent on an exploring expedition to the island, and then for the first time saw the bay on which San Juan is situated and called it "Puerto Rico," or Rich Port. After reporting his discoveries he was again sent to the island to effect a settlement, and did so near the modern site of the city.

The first settlement, known as Caparra, was on the mainland, because of its greater safety from enemies approaching from the sea. Soon, however, that site was abandoned, and the modern one was selected. Substantial buildings, forts and fortifications were built during the following years. The city was completely surrounded by a massive wall, with moats and gates and bridges which made San Juan a typical walled city of the Spanish type. On a high bluff overlooking and commanding the entrance to the harbour Morro Castle was built for the protection of the harbour and city against the numerous fleets of the enemies of Spain. Along the harbour walls were other fortifications, and on the ocean front, besides Morro Castle, the great fortress of San Cristóbal, the Escambrón, the Princesa and other batteries were built.

Streets and Buildings.—The city is of the Spanish type, with narrow streets and numerous and rather low buildings, with balconies. Among the notable modern buildings are the marble capitol, of classic type, completed in 1928; the Condado-Vanderbilt and the Caribe Hilton hotels; the Federal building, housing the post office, the U.S. court and other federal offices; the U.S. customs house; the University of Puerto Rico; the Puerto Rico casino; the Atheneum; the Y.M.C.A. building; the Carnegie library; the Central High school building; the Professional building; and many others. The city retains many of its ancient characteristics, however.

There are many buildings of historic interest. Besides the old castles, El Morro and San Cristóbal, are the Casa Blanca, built for the son of Ponce de León, and the cathedral, which contains his tomb. La Fortaleza, the governor's residence and offices, was commenced and partially built in 1533, only 40 years after Columbus' discovery of the island. It was also called in Spanish times the Palace of Santa Catalina.

Commerce.—The harbour is one of the best and most commodious in the West Indies. Several passenger steamers are in regular service between San Juan and New York city. Steamers from France and Spain visit the island. Freight lines connect the city and nearly all southern and eastern ports of the U.S., and regular service is maintained with other West Indian islands. Passenger and freight service is also maintained with South American ports. The number of vessels entering and clearing San Juan is nearly 3,000 annually.

Air transportation is of great importance to Puerto Rico, which is located midway between North and South America. The city of San Juan links three continents, the Antilles and the Virgin Islands, and serves as a port of entry to the French, British and Dutch West Indies. Sugar, coffee, tobacco and fruits are the principal products exported, while the principal imports are lumber, iron and steel, machinery, automobiles and trucks, flour, rice and other food products. The city is a distributing point for the West Indies of many important manufactured products.

(H. M. T.; J. L.-EE.)

SAN JUAN or HARO ISLANDS, an archipelago (San Juan, Orcas, Shaw, López, Blakely, Cypress, etc.) lying between Vancouver island and the mainland of North America. These islands were for many years the subject of dispute between the British and the U.S. Governments, and were finally assigned to the latter country by the arbitration of the emperor of Germany (on Oct. 21, 1872). Geographically, the cluster certainly belongs to the mainland, from which it is separated by Rosario Strait, generally much under 50 fathoms in depth, while Haro Strait, separating it from Vancouver island, has depths ranging from 100 to 190 fathoms. In 1873 the islands, formerly considered part of Whatcom county, Wash., were made the separate county of San Juan. Of the total area of 200 sq.m., about 60 are in San Juan, 60 in Orcas and 30 in López.

See *Papers relating to the Treaty of Washington*, vol. v. (1872), and the map in *Petermann's Mitteilungen* (1873).

SANKARAN NAIR, SIR CHETTUR (1857–1934), Indian jurist and politician, was born in the Malabar country on July 11, 1857, and educated for a legal career. Enrolled as a vakil of the Madras high court, he was appointed in 1899 government pleader and public prosecutor in Madras. In 1907 he was appointed advocate general, being the first Indian to hold the post in the province. In the following year he was made puisne judge of the Madras high court. He was by this time well known as a strong social reformer, a supporter of the Indian National Congress (being president of the 13th meeting, held at Amraoti in 1897), as a publicist and as founder and editor of the *Madras Review* and *The Madras Law Journal*. He was for many years a member of the Madras legislature. One of the first Indians and the first Madrasi to become a member of the Government of India he was selected for the education portfolio in 1915, but resigned in July 1919, on the ground that martial law was being continued in the Punjab too long after the disturbances had ceased. Taking a favourable view of the Montagu-Chelmsford reforms, he was appointed to the India Council in London in January 1920, but resigned to take office in the Indore State in November 1921. A vigorous condemnation of the non-cooperation movement entitled *Gandhi and Anarchy* (1922) contained references to the Punjab troubles, which led Sir Michael O'Dwyer, late lieutenant-governor of the Punjab, to bring a successful libel action against the author in London in the summer of 1924. Elected a member of the Council of State of India in 1925 Nair continued to pursue an independent line, and when that house decided in 1928 to co-operate with the Statutory commission under Sir John Simon, the viceroy appointed him chairman of the all-India committee to sit with the commission, comprising members of both houses of the legislature. (F. H. BR.)

SANKEY, JOHN SANKEY, 1ST VISCOUNT, OF MORETON (1866–1948), British lawyer, was born on Oct. 26, 1866. Educated at Lancing and at Jesus college, Oxford, he was called to the bar at the Middle Temple in 1892. He took silk in 1909 and from that time advanced rapidly in his profession. He became a judge in the King's Bench division in 1914 and a lord justice of appeal in 1928.

Sankey was chairman of the royal commission on the coal industry in 1919. In 1929 he was raised to the peerage and appointed lord chancellor. He was created a viscount in 1932 and retired in June 1935. He died Feb. 6, 1948.

SÂNKHYA or SAMKHYA, the oldest system of Indian philosophy, its founder, Kapila, having been born at Kapilavastu, probably a century before Buddha's birth. For the system *see*

SANSKRIT LANGUAGE AND LITERATURE: *Philosophical Systems.*

SAN LEANDRO, a city of Alameda county, California, U.S.A., adjoining Oakland. It is served by the Southern Pacific and the Western Pacific railways. Pop. (1950) 27,498. San Leandro produces air conditioning and mechanical draft equipment, aircraft supplies, automobiles and automobile parts, calculating machines, farm equipment, metal stampings and spring and wire products. San Leandro was settled in 1836 and incorporated in 1872.

SAN LUCAR (SANLÚCAR DE BARRAMEDA), a fortified seaport of southern Spain, in the province of Cádiz; 27 mi. by sea from Cádiz, on the left bank of the Guadalquivir estuary, and on the Puerto de Santa Maria-San Lucar and Jerez de la Frontera-Bonanza railways. Pop. (1940), 28,446 (mun., 32,848). Inscriptions and ruins prove that San Lucar and Bonanza were Roman settlements, though the original names are unknown. San Lucar was captured from the Moors in 1264, after an occupation lasting more than five and a half centuries. After 1492 it became an important centre of trade with America. From this port Columbus sailed across the Atlantic in 1498, and Magellan started in 1519 to circumnavigate the world. The 14th-century church and the palace of the dukes of Medina Sidonia contain many valuable pictures. The hospital of St. George was established by Henry VIII of England. The Guadalquivir estuary is deep and sheltered. Bonanza, 2 mi. by rail up the river, and on the same bank, is the headquarters of the shipping and fishing trades. It is named after a chapel dedicated here by the South American Company of Seville to the Virgin of Fair Weather (*Virgen de la Bonanza*). The fisheries and agricultural trade of San Lucar are considerable; there are flour mills in the town.

SAN LUIS, one of the three Argentine provinces forming the region of *Cuyo*, an Araucanian word meaning "land of sand." Area, 29,632 sq.mi.; pop. (1914 census) 116,266 (1947 est.) 164,-379. Although the province is in the Andean plain, much of its surface is broken by chains of mountains, the largest of which is the Sierra de San Luis. Except in the west, where temperatures are excessively high, the climate is warm and dry. In the moister regions forests are extensive and provide an important source of wealth, as do also the mineral resources (copper, iron, wolfram, gold, silver, mica and lead). There are relatively few rivers, the principal ones being the Desaguadero, Quinto, Conlara and San Luis. The economy is based chiefly on mining, lumbering, agriculture and stock raising, the emphasis with respect to the latter two categories being placed on cattle, sheep, cereals and fruits. The capital is San Luis, pop. (1941 est.) 30,021, founded in 1596 by Martín de Loyola, governor of the captaincy general of Chile. Mercedes, the largest city in the province, has an estimated population of 37,666. Both cities have rail connections with Buenos Aires and with Santiago, Chile, across the Andes, and are on the Santiago-Buenos Aires link of the Pan American highway.

(R. W. RD.; X.)

SAN LUIS OBISPO, a city of California, U.S.A., 8 mi. from the ocean and 190 mi. N.W. of Los Angeles; county seat of San Luis Obispo county. It is on federal highway 101 and the Pacific Coast and the Southern Pacific railways. Pop. (1950) 14,162. Its harbour (Port San Luis, on the bay 9 mi. S.W. of the city) is an important oil port. The city was founded by Father Junípero Serra, who built there his fifth mission, now used as a parish church. The California State Polytechnic college is there.

SAN LUIS POTOSÍ, a central state of Mexico, bounded north by Coahuila, east by Nuevo León, Tamaulipas and Veracruz, south by Hidalgo, Querétaro and Guanajuato, and west by Zacatecas. Area, 24,411 sq.mi. Pop. (1950) 855,336. The state belongs wholly to the high plateau region, with the exception of a small area in the southeast angle, where the tableland breaks down into the tropical valley of the Pánuco. The surface is comparatively level, with some low mountainous wooded ridges. The mean elevation is about 6,000 ft., ensuring a temperate climate. The rainfall is light and uncertain and the state is poorly provided with rivers. The soil is fertile and in favourable seasons large crops of wheat, Indian corn, beans and cotton are grown on the uplands. In the low tropical valleys, sugar, coffee,

THE TOWN OF SAN MARINO, CAPITAL OF THE REPUBLIC

San Marino, founded probably in the 4th century, is situated on the slopes of the mountain whose steep sides and crags constitute in great part the territory of the Republic. It has three citadels, all overlooking Rimini (Italy) and the Adriatic. The turreted building on the left is the Parliament house

PLATE II

SAN MARINO

1. Winding street in the Borgo or Lower Town of San Marino
2. The militia of San Marino

3. Buildings in the Borgo

tobacco, peppers and fruit are staple products. Stock raising is an important industry and hides, tallow and wool are exported. Fine cabinet and construction woods are also exported to a limited extent. San Luis Potosí ranks among the leading mining states of Mexico. The Catorce district has some of the richest silver mines in the country. Other well-known silver mining districts are Peñón Blanco, Ramos and Guadalcázar. The development of Guadalcázar dates from 1620 and its ores yield gold, copper, zinc and bismuth, as well as silver. In the Ramos district, Cocinera lode is said to have had a total yield of more than $60,000,000. Railway facilities are provided by the Mexican National lines. The capital is San Luis Potosí, and other towns, with populations as of 1940, are: Matehuala (16,548), a mining town 20 mi. E. by W. of Catorce, with which it is connected by a branch railway; Catorce (7,000 in 1910 and only 753 in 1940), an important mining town 110 mi. N. (direct) of San Luis Potosí (capital) and 8 mi. from its railway station on the Mexican National; at an elevation of 8,780 ft., Santa María de Río (2,816), 37 mi. S.E. of the capital; Venado (2,011), 45 mi. N. of the capital; Ríoverde (8,503), an agricultural centre with a national agriculture experiment station in its vicinity; Soledad Díez Gutiérrez (2,227), near the capital.

SAN LUIS POTOSÍ, a city of Mexico and capital of a state of the same name, near the head of the valley of the Río Verde (a tributary of the Pánuco), 215 mi. N.W. of Mexico City. Pop. (1950) 156,324. The city is served by the Mexican National railways. The altitude of the city, 6,168 ft. above sea level, gives it a cool temperate climate, though the sun temperatures are high.

Notable buildings are the cathedral and government palace fronting on the Plaza Mayor, the latter conspicuous for its façade of rose-coloured stone; the churches of El Carmen, San Francisco and Guadalupe; the La Paz theatre, mint, penitentiary and the Instituto Científico, in which law, medicine and science are taught. San Luis Potosí is an important railway and distributing centre, with a considerable trade in cattle, tallow, wool, hides and minerals. Its proximity to the port of Tampico, with which it was connected by railway in 1885, greatly increased its commercial importance, though in earlier days it was also one of the principal centres of the diligence and pack-train traffic of this part of Mexico. The city has cotton and woollen factories, and large smelting works. Ores and crude metals from adjacent states are brought there for smelting and refining.

San Luis Potosí was founded in 1586. It was the centre of colonial administration and played a very important part in the civil wars and political disorders following Mexican independence. It was the seat of the Mexican government of Benito Juárez in 1863. Imprisoned there by Porfirio Díaz in June 1910, Francisco I. Madero drew up his famous "Plan of San Luis Potosí" (Oct. 7) which launched the Mexican Revolution on Nov. 20, 1910.

SAN MARCOS, a city of south central Texas, U.S., on federal highway 81, 30 mi. S. of Austin; county seat of Hays county. It is served by the Missouri-Kansas-Texas and the Missouri Pacific railways. Pop. (1950) 9,980; 6,006 in 1940 by the federal census. It is the seat of the Southwest Texas State Teachers college and San Marcos academy. San Marcos is a centre of hybrid corn and cotton breeding farms and livestock marketing. Industrial development includes nonferrous metal die-casting, ceramic products, feed dehydrating, meat processing and wool scouring for processing into consumer goods. San Marcos was founded in 1848 and was chartered as a city in 1877.

SAN MARINO, a republic in northern Italy, 14 mi. S.W. of Rimini by road. It is the smallest republic in the world (38 sq.mi. in area). The population in 1950 was 12,780. Most of the republic falls within the diocese of Montefeltro, a small portion within that of Rimini.

The council consists of 60 members and is elected by proportional representation from single party lists. Its functions are deliberative and legislative, while a council of 12 exercises the executive functions of government. The peaceful revolution of March 25, 1906, restored the original system of election to the council (which had become a close corporation, renewed by co-option) by the *Arengo*, or assembly of heads of families, one-third

of the council being henceforth renewable every three years. In 1909 the household suffrage was replaced by universal male suffrage, but women have never yet been enfranchised. The election of the two *capitani reggenti* takes place every six months. They enter into office on April 1 and Oct. 1 with much traditional pomp and preside over the two councils; but the real governmental power is in the hands of two secretaries of state.

The available armed forces of the republic form a total of about 1,200 men, all citizens able to bear arms being technically obliged to do so from the age of 16 to 60 years. Italian money is current.

The republic entered into treaty relations with Italy in 1862; and a considerable part of its revenue is drawn from the Italian government in exchange for an acknowledgment of the Italian state monopolies in tobacco, playing cards, etc. Only in 1922 did San Marino find it necessary to introduce an income tax. No longer are titles conferred for a consideration, but a fruitful source of revenue is found in the frequent change of postage stamps (first issued in 1877). In addition, a casino was licensed in 1949, but strong Italian pressure led to its closure in 1951. The chief exports, besides postage stamps, are stone from Monte Titano—the legendary founder of San Marino was a Dalmatian stone cutter—and the strong wine grown on this volcanic soil.

After the destruction of the San Marino-Rimini railway in World War II, San Marino was linked to the outside world only by a bus service.

Antiquities.—The old church is first mentioned in 951. There are traces of three different *enceintes* of the 14th, 15th and 16th centuries. The principal church (Pieve), in classical style, dates from 1826-38 and contains the body of St. Marinus. The museum contains among other curiosities the banner of Garibaldi's "Italic Legion" which sought refuge at San Marino in 1849. The archives were rearranged and described by C. Malagola. The arms of the republic are three peaks, each crowned with a tower.

History.—According to tradition, the republic was founded by Marinus, a native of Arbe, probably after the middle of the 4th century. The *Castellum Sancti Marini* is mentioned in 755; the oldest document in the republican archives mentions the abbot of San Marino in 885. The republic, as a rule, avoided the faction fights of the middle ages but joined the Ghibellines and was interdicted by the pope in 1247-49. After this it was protected by the Montefeltro family (later dukes of Urbino) and the papacy and successfully resisted the attempts of Sigismondo Malatesta against its liberty. It fell into the hands of Caesar Borgia in 1503 but soon regained its freedom. Other attacks failed, but civil discords in the meantime increased. Its independence was recognized in 1631 by the papacy. In 1739 Cardinal Alberoni attempted to deprive it of its independence, but this was restored in 1740 and was respected by Napoleon.

In World War II San Marino remained neutral, but suffered a severe bombing raid and other infringements of its neutrality. In contrast with Italy, after the overthrow of the Fascists in 1945, the republic was governed by a "popular front" coalition of Liberals, Radicals, Socialists and Communists, while the Christian Democrat party provided the opposition. The control of profits and the establishment of social services were the main items of the government's policy.

BIBLIOGRAPHY.—M. Delfico, *Memorie storiche della Repubblica di S. Marino,* 4th ed. (Naples, 1865); J. T. Bent, *A Freak of Freedom, or the Republic of San Marino* (London, 1879); C. Malagola, *L'Archivio Governativo della Repubblica di San Marino* (Bologna, 1891); C. Ricci, *La Repubblica di San Marino* (Bergamo, 1903); *Verbale dell' Arringo Generale dei Capi-Famiglia tenutosi il giorno di Domenica, 25 Marzo, 1906* (S. Marino, 1906); Marino Fattori, *Ricordi storici della Repubblica di S. Marino,* 6th ed. by O. Fattori (Foligno, 1912); *Verbale del Consiglio Grande e Generale della Seduta, 18 Settembre, 1920* (S. Marino, 1920); W. Miller, "Democracy at San Marino," *History,* vol. vii (London, April 1922); Ente Nazionale Industrie Turistiche, *La Repubblica di San Marino* (Rome, 1933); E. Armstrong, *Italian Studies* (1934).

SAN MARTÍN, JOSÉ DE (1778–1850), South American soldier and statesman, was born at Yapeyú, on the river Uruguay, on Feb. 25, 1778. He was educated in Madrid for a military career and served against the Moors and in the struggle against Napoleon. In 1812 he offered his services to the Government of

Buenos Aires in its war for independence. Early in 1814 he was placed in command of the revolutionary army operating against the Spaniards in upper Peru, but soon resigned his command, realizing that the permanent success of the revolutionary movement depended upon the expulsion of the Spaniards from Chile, and also from their stronghold in Peru. To carry out this purpose, he enlisted the co-operation of the government of Buenos Aires, and, assisted by Bernardo O'Higgins, raised and equipped at Mendoza, a well-trained army of Argentines and Chileans for the invasion of Chile. In Jan. 1817, he suddenly carried his army (3,000 infantry, 1,000 cavalry and baggage) across the Andes through the Uspallata pass, outgeneraled the Spanish commanders and routed a large part of their forces at Chacabuco, on Feb. 12, 1817. Northern Chile, including Santiago, the capital of the country, being now freed of the Spanish, he turned the government over to O'Higgins, and set about the reconquest of the south, which he effected in the decisive victory of Maipú (April 5, 1818), thus completely establishing the independence of Chile.

With half of his program accomplished, he laid his plans for the attack upon Peru. He not only reorganized the army, but with the aid of Lord Cochrane constructed a fleet to operate simultaneously with it. In July 1821, the Spaniards evacuated Lima before the combined forces of the army and navy, and retired to the mountains. San Martín entered the city, proclaimed the independence of Peru, and assumed the reins of government under the title of protector. His position, however, was not yet secure. He was threatened by royalist operations in the interior, by jealousy among the patriots and by the rivalry of Bolívar, whose victories in Colombia and Ecuador had carried him southward to the northern borders of Peru. The great Colombian's ambition could brook no rival, and on Sept. 20, 1822, San Martín, having paved the way for the conclusive victories of Junín (1824) and Ayacucho (1824), resigned his authority and retired from the country. Finding it impossible to live a peaceful private life in South America, he withdrew as an exile to Europe. There he lived in poverty until his death at Boulogne on Aug. 17, 1850, from time to time vainly offering his services to the distracted nations he had helped to found.

San Martín did more than any other man for the cause of independence in the Argentine, Chile and Peru. He was an able soldier and a clear-sighted and vigorous statesman.

See W. S. Robertson, *Rise of the Spanish Republics* (1918); Anna Schoelkopf, *Don José de San Martín, 1778-1850, A Study of His Career* (1924); and B. Moses, *The Intellectual Background of the Revolution in South America, 1810-1824* (1926).   (W. B. P.)

SAN MARTÍN, a department of Peru, has an area of 17,450 sq.mi., and a population (1950) of 141,730. It includes mountainous areas and the valley of the Huallaga river, a tributary of the Marañón and the Amazon. It is bounded on the north and east by the department of Loreto, from which it was formed in 1906, south by Huánuco, and west by the departments of Libertad and Amazonas. The capital is Moyobamba (pop., 1950, 9,202), situated on the Mayo river, a tributary of the Huallaga. The principal trade outlet is through Yurimaguas (Loreto), a port on the Huallaga, to Iquitos about 500 mi. distant. A highway through the department was under construction in the early 1950s.   (L. W. Be.)

SAN MATEO, a city of San Mateo county, California, U.S.A., on the west side of San Francisco bay, 19 mi. S. of San Francisco. It has a commercial airport and is served by the Southern Pacific railway and by bus lines. Pop. (1950) 41,782. The city operates under a city-manager form of government.

SANMICHELE, MICHELE (1484-1559), Italian architect, was born in San Michele near Verona. He was a pupil of his father Giovanni and his uncle Bartolommeo, both architects at Verona, and went at an early age to Rome to study classic sculpture and architecture. Among his first works are the duomo of Montefiascone, the church of San Domenico at Orvieto, several palaces and a fine tomb in S. Domenico. He was also employed by the signoria of Venice as a military architect. One of Sanmichele's most graceful designs is the Cappella de' Peregrini in the church of S. Bernardino at Verona. He built a number of fine palaces at Verona, including those of Canossa, Bevilacqua and Pompei, as well as the graceful Ponte Nuovo. In 1527 Sanmichele began to transform the fortifications of Verona according to the newer system of corner bastions which he did much to advance. His last work (1559) was the round church of the Madonna di Campagna, 1½ mi. from Verona. He also wrote a work on classic architecture, *I Cinque Ordini dell' architettura*, printed at Verona in 1735.

See Ronzani and Luciolli, *Fabbriche . . . di M. Sanmichele* (Venice, 1832); and Selva, *Elogio di Sanmichele* (Rome, 1814).

SAN MIGUEL, the capital of the department of San Miguel, El Salvador; 80 mi. E. by S. of San Salvador, near the right bank of the Río Grande, and at the foot of the volcano of San Miguel or Jucuapa (7,120 ft.). Population (1950) 26,831.

San Miguel is an important city, on the main line of the International railways of Central America. It possesses several handsome churches, municipal buildings, law courts and two well-equipped hospitals.

Near it are the ruins of an ancient Indian town. San Miguel has a flourishing trade in coffee, cotton, sisal, grain, cattle and indigo. Its port is La Unión (q.v.).

San Miguel was founded in 1530 by Spanish settlers and became a city in 1586.

SAN MIGUEL, a municipality (with administrative centre and 18 *barrios* or districts) of the province of Bulacan, Luzon, Philippine Islands, about 40 mi. N. of Manila on the Manila-Dagupan railway. Pop. (1939), 26,759 of whom 13,505 were males and 5 were white. The fertile surrounding region produces abundant crops of palay (rice). Maize (corn) and sugar are also produced. Cattle breeding and fish breeding are extensively carried on, and the municipality is noted for the manufacture of hats and silk textiles, furniture, and alcohol from the nipa palm. There is much weaving and tanning. Sibul springs, about 8 mi. N.E., is a health resort. Tagalog is the vernacular. Of the inhabitants of San Miguel aged 6 to 19 inclusive, 32.3% attended school in 1939, while 64.2% of the population 10 years old and over was literate.

SAN MINIATO, a town and episcopal see of Tuscany, Italy, in the province of Pisa, 26 mi. W. by S. of Florence by the railway to Pisa, 512 ft. above sea level, on a hill 2 mi. S. of the railway. Pop. (1936) 3,082 (town); 21,463 (commune). Its cathedral was remodelled in 1489 and has a façade decorated with disks of majolica. It manufactures glass, olive oil, leather and hats and has a castle of Frederick II, the residence of the imperial governors of Tuscany from 1226 to 1286, and from them bears the name of San Miniato al Tedesco.

SAN NICOLÁS DE LOS ARROYOS, a town and river port of Argentina, in the province of Buenos Aires, on the west bank of the Paraná, 150 mi. by rail N.W. of the city of Buenos Aires. Population (1940 est.) 39,959. It is a flourishing commercial town and a port of call both for river and ocean-going steamers of medium tonnage. It is a rail station on the main line from Buenos Aires to Rosario and north and is also the terminus of a branch line running from Pergamino. It exports wheat, flour, wool and meat. The town is the judicial centre for the northern district of Buenos Aires. San Nicolás was founded in 1749 by José de Aguilar on lands given for that purpose by his wife (*née* Ugarte). Its growth was slow until near the end of the 19th century.

SANOCRYSIN. A proprietary gold preparation (gold and sodium thiosulphate) which is of proved value in the treatment of certain skin diseases and of doubtful value in rheumatoid arthritis and tuberculosis. Incautious use may lead to widespread toxic manifestations including skin rashes, gastrointestinal upsets and blood changes.

SAN PABLO, a municipality of the province of Laguna, Luzon, Philippine islands, about 9 mi. S. of Laguna de Bay, and about 35 mi. S.S.E. of Manila. Pop. (1939) 46,311 (a gain of 14,912 since 1918) of whom 22,952 were males and 32 were white. It has railway connections with Manila by way of Malvar, in the province of Batangas. Coconut palms grow in great abundance, and copra is the chief product. Abacá and rice are also grown. The language spoken is Tagalog.   (C. S. L.)

SANQUHAR, a royal and small burgh of Dumfriesshire, Scotland. Pop. (1951) 3,356. It is situated on the Nith, 26 mi. N.W. of Dumfries by the L.M.S. railway. It became a burgh of barony in 1484 and a royal burgh in 1596, and was the scene of the exhibition of the Covenanters' Declaration, attached to the market cross in 1680 by Richard Cameron and in 1685 by James Renwick. The town is a popular summer resort and the principal coal mart in the county. Industries include iron, brick and spade works. There are cattle and sheep fairs, and an agricultural show is held every May. Sanquhar castle, on a hill overlooking the Nith, once belonged to the Crichtons, but is now a ruin, though considerably restored.

SAN RAFAEL, a beautiful residential city of California, U.S.A., 10 mi. N. of San Francisco, on San Pablo straits, at the foot of Mount Tamalpais; the county seat of Marin county. It is served by the Northwestern Pacific railroad and interurban bus lines. Pop., 1950, federal census, 13,830; in 1940, 8,573. There are private schools and the Dominican College of San Rafael (established in 1850, at Monterey). A Franciscan mission was established there in 1817 and around it a settlement grew up. The original mission has been completely destroyed, but a replica was built on the site. The city was incorporated in 1874.

SAN REMO, a seaport of Liguria, Italy, in the province of Imperia, on the Riviera di Ponente, 9¾ mi. E. of Ventimiglia by rail, and 84 mi. S.W. of Genoa. Pop. (1936) 23,963 (town); 31,769 (commune). Climbing the slope of a steep hill it looks south over a small bay, and, protected towards the north by hills rising gradually from 500 to 8,000 ft., it is in climate one of the most favoured places on the whole coast, which accounts for its reputation as a winter resort. The older town, with its narrow steep streets and lofty sombre houses protected against earthquakes by arches connecting them, contrasts with the new visitors' town, containing all the public buildings, which has grown up at the foot of the hill. The small harbour is sheltered by its sickle-shaped mole, 1,300 ft. long. Besides the Romanesque cathedral of San Siro, the white-domed church of the Madonna della Costa, at the top of the old town, may be mentioned. The Emperor Frederick's residence at San Remo in 1887–1888 greatly increased its repute as a winter resort. Flowers, especially roses and carnations, are extensively grown for export, and olives, lemons and palms are also cultivated.

SAN REMO, CONFERENCE OF (April 19–26, 1920). This conference was preceded by a meeting of the Supreme Allied Council (Mr. Lloyd George, M. Millerand, and Sig. Nitti) from Feb. 12 to 23 in London, where the main lines of the future Treaty of Sèvres (*see* SÈVRES, TREATY OF) with Turkey were laid down, and the draft treaty with Hungary and the Fiume question were discussed. At San Remo itself, where the three statesmen above mentioned were joined by representatives of Greece, Belgium and Japan, the Turkish Treaty was the first and principal business dealt with, and the framework of the Sèvres Treaty was there constructed. The mandates for Syria, Palestine and 'Iraq were assigned to France and Great Britain respectively, and an Anglo-French oil agreement was negotiated which covered Rumania and the French and British non-self-governing colonies as well as the Middle East. The most controversial question dealt with, as between the Allies, was that of the maximum strength of the German army—both its total and the number of troops allowed in the neutral zone skirting the area under Allied occupation. On account of the Kapp *Putsch* and other internal disorders the German Government asked the conference to permit the increase of the German army to twice the strength allowed by the Versailles Treaty. This request was refused and Germany charged with default in respect both of reparations and disarmament. At the same time the German Government was informed of the intention of the Allies to invite them to a direct conference. (*See* SPA, CONFERENCE OF.)

SAN SALVADOR, the capital of the republic of El Salvador; situated in the valley of Las Hamacas, on the river Asalguate, at an altitude of 2,115 ft., and 30 mi. inland from the Pacific. Pop. (1950) 160,380.

San Salvador is connected by rail with La Unión on the Pacific and with all of the chief cities of El Salvador, and by the through line of the International Railways of Central America and the National Railways of Mexico with Guatemala, Mexico and the United States; also with the Pacific port of Acajutla by the older El Salvador railway. It is connected with the port of La Libertad by highway.

In addition to the government offices, its buildings include a handsome university, a modest cathedral, a national theatre, an academy of science and literature, a chamber of commerce, an astronomical observatory and a number of hospitals and charitable institutions. There are two large parks and an excellent botanical garden.

In the Plaza Morazán, the largest of many shaded squares, is a bronze and marble monument to the last president of united Central America, from whom the plaza takes its name. San Salvador is the only city in the republic which has important manufactures; these include the production of soap, silk goods, cotton cloth, cigars, flour and spirits. Beyond these activities, there had been little industrial development by the 1950s.

The city has an abundant water supply. It was founded by Don Jorge de Alvarado in 1528, at a spot near the present site, to which it was transferred in 1539.

Except for the year 1839–40 San Salvador was the capital of the republic from 1834 on. It was temporarily ruined by earthquakes in 1854 and 1873.

SANS-CULOTTES, the term originally given during the early years of the French Revolution to the ill-clad and ill-equipped volunteers of the Revolutionary army, and later applied generally to the ultra-democrats of the Revolution. They were for the most part men of the poorer classes, or leaders of the populace, but during the Terror public functionaries and persons of good education styled themselves *citoyens sans-culottes* ("citizens without knee-breeches"). The distinctive costume of the typical sans-culotte was the *pantalon* (long trousers)—in place of the *culottes* worn by the upper classes—the *carmagnole* (short-skirted coat), the red cap of liberty and *sabots* (wooden shoes). The influence of the sans-culottes ceased with the reaction that followed the fall of Robespierre (July 1794), and the name itself was proscribed. In the Republican Calendar the complementary days at the end of the year were at first called *Sans-culottides;* this name was, however, suppressed by the Convention when the constitution of the year III (1795) was adopted, that of *jours complémentaires* being substituted.

SAN SEBASTIAN (Basque *Iruchulo,* and officially Guipúzcoa), a seaport and capital of the Spanish province of Guipúzcoa, on the Bay of Biscay, and on the Northern railway from Madrid to France. Pop. (1950) 100,000 (mun., 113,776). The city became the summer residence of the court in 1886. It occupies a narrow sandy peninsula, which terminates on the northern or seaward side in a lofty mass of sandstone, Monte Urgull; it is flanked on the east by the estuary of the river Urumea, on the west by the broad bay of La Concha. The old town, rebuilt after the fire of 1813, lies partly at the foot of Monte Urgull, partly on its lower slopes. Until 1863 it was enclosed by walls and ramparts, and a strong fort, the Castillo de la Mola, still crowns the heights of Urgull. The Alameda separates the old town from the new and gardens and villas now extend right up Monte Igueldo. The bay of La Concha has a broad sandy shore. There are saw and flour mills, and manufactures of preserves, soap, candles, glass and paper, especially in the busy suburb that has sprung up on the right bank of the Urumea. The fisheries are important. Vessels of 12 ft. draught can nearly always enter both dock and harbour. Larger vessels anchor south-east of Santa Clara Island. Nationalist forces captured San Sebastian during the civil war of 1936–39.

SAN SEVERINO (anc. *Septempeda*), a town and episcopal see of the Marches, Italy, in the province of Macerata, from which it is 18 mi. W. by S. by rail. Pop. (1936) 3,975 (town); 16,141 (commune). The lower town is situated 781 ft. above sea-level, and contains the new cathedral of S. Agostina, with a fine altar-piece by Pinturicchio (1489). S. Lorenzo in Doliolo and S. Domenico are both Romanesque churches. The Palazzo

Comunale has some interesting pictures by artists of the Marches. Lorenzo and Giacomo Salimbeni da San Severino, who painted an important series of frescoes in the oratory of S. Giovanni Battista at Urbino in 1416, were natives of the town. So was Lorenzo di Alessandro, of the end of the 15th century, whose pictures are mainly to be found in the Marches. The old cathedral of S. Severino is in the upper town (1,129 ft. above sea-level); it contains frescoes by the two Salimbeni, and very fine choir stalls (1483–1513). The ancient Septempeda lay 1 m. below the modern town, on the branch road which ran from Nuceria Camellaria, on the Via Flaminia.

SAN SEVERO, a city in Apulia, Italy, in the province of Foggia, from which it is 17 mi. N.N.W. by rail. Pop. (1936) 37,159 (town), 37,702 (commune). It lies at the foot of the spurs of Monte Gargano, 292 ft. above sea-level. It is the see of a bishop (since 1580), and has some remains of its old fortifications. San Severo dates from the middle ages. It was laid in ruins by Frederick II. In 1799 the town was almost entirely destroyed by the French. In 1627, 1828 and 1851 the town suffered from earthquakes. It is surrounded by fertile vineyards and oliveyards.

SANSKRIT LANGUAGE AND LITERATURE. The most important branch of the Indo-European family of languages in Asia is Aryan or Indo-Iranian, with two main divisions: Iranian and Indo-Aryan. Languages belonging to the latter are spoken to-day by 250 million people in India, where they are the dominant languages except in the south, in Ceylon and the Maldive Islands, and throughout western Asia and Europe by colonies of Gypsies (see ROMANY LANGUAGE). As languages of administration they spread at one time far into central Asia, where now is Chinese Turkestan; and as vehicles of Buddhism they have influenced through translation the whole of central and eastern Asia; Hindu civilization carried their vocabulary into the East Indies and the Malay peninsula. The oldest documents of Indo-Aryan are composed in Sanskrit. These are the Vedic texts. Their exact date is unknown, but it is probable that the oldest of them belong to the latter half of the second millennium B.C. They were probably composed before the Aryans had learned the use of writing; but being religious texts which it was essential to preserve unchanged they were handed down by an oral tradition which by various controls was made exceedingly exact. Even at the time of entry into India there must have been some dialectical differences in the language as spoken by the various invading tribes; with their further extension into India itself these differences became accentuated. The language of the Vedic texts shows a certain mixture, but is in the main founded upon the dialect of the north-west of India. With the advance of Aryan culture into the Punjab and the Gangetic plain the eastern dialects gained in importance; and this eastern influence, discernible in the earliest texts, constantly gains ground.

The most archaic of these texts is the Rig-veda, a collection of liturgical hymns; this is followed by the Atharva-veda, consisting chiefly of magical formulas, of prayers, curses and incantations. Considerably later come the first compositions in prose, commentaries on the Veda and philosophical treatises termed Brāhmaṇas and Upanishads. Although originally preserved as a religious language, Sanskrit was finally used for secular purposes. The earliest inscription in Sanskrit dates from 150 A.D., but it became the regular language of official inscriptions only in the 4th century A.D. But long before that the grammarians (of whom the most celebrated was Pāṇini in the 4th century B.C.) had fixed it as a learned language to which alone a strict interpretation confines the name Sanskrit, "the perfected," but which may conveniently be termed Classical Sanskrit as opposed to the Vedic or older form. As a literary language it is still cultivated; and a vast literature—philosophical, narrative, lyrical, dramatic, technical—has been written in it. Standing, in form at least, between the later Vedic and the Classical, but more nearly approaching the latter, is the language of the two great epics, the Mahābhārata and the Rāmāyaṇa, in which the influence of the spoken language can clearly be seen. For in the meantime the spoken dialects continued to develop. Some of these, such as Pali and the Prakrits (qq.v.), were in turn crystallized and used as religious languages

by new sects as well as for secular purposes before Sanskrit was so employed. From these vernaculars are eventually derived the modern Indo-Aryan languages. Sanskrit, the literary language, although preserving the sound-system of Vedic practically unchanged, did not escape the influence of its descendants. The grammar was considerably changed, chiefly in a simplifying and normalizing direction; meanings of words were altered and de-

VOWELS			CONSONANTS				
Initial.	**Medial.**	**Equivalent.**		**Equivalent.**			**Equivalent.**
अ	—	a	क	k	GUTTURALS	प	p
अ			ख	kh		फ	ph
आ	T	ā	ग	g		ब	b
			घ	gh		भ	bh
			ङ	ṅ		म	m
इ	f	i	च	c	PALATALS	य	y
ई		ī	छ	ch		र	r
उ		u	ज	j		ल	l
ऊ		ū	झ	jh	or झ	व	v
ऋ		ṛ (or ṛ̣)	ञ	ñ			
ॠ		ṝ (or ṝ̣)	ट	ṭ	CEREBRALS	श	ś (or ç)
ऌ		ḷ (or ḷ̣)	ठ	ṭh		ष	ṣ
			ड	ḍ		स	s
			ढ	ḍh		ह	h
ए		e	ण	ṇ			
ऐ		ai	त	t	DENTALS	ः	ḥ (Visarga)
ओ		o	थ	th			
औ		au	द	d		ं	ṁ (or ṃ)(Anusvāra)
			ध	dh			
			न	n			

FROM MACDONELL, "SANSKRIT GRAMMAR FOR STUDENTS" (CLARENDON PRESS)

veloped, and vast quantities of new words were gradually absorbed after being given a Sanskrit form. On the other hand Sanskrit has continued to influence the spoken languages.

Sounds.—The sound-system of Sanskrit consisted of: (a) Fourteen vowels, viz.: Twelve simple vowels: a, ā, i, ī, u, ū, ṛ, ṝ, ṛ, ḷ, (ḹ), ē, ō . Two diphthongs: ai, au.

(b) Thirty-six consonants, viz.: Five series of stops and nasals: guttural: k, kh, g, gh, ṅ; palatal: c, ch, j, jh, ñ; cerebral: ṭ, ṭh, ḍ, ḍh, ṇ; dental: t, th, d, dh, n; labial: p, ph, b, bh, m. Four semi-vowels: y, r, l, v. Three sibilants: palatal ś, cerebral ṣ, dental s. Two aspirates: voiced h, unvoiced ḥ (visarga). A nasal with loose closure of the lips ṁ (anusvāra), and another nasal m̐ (anunāsika) which probably was a simple nasalization of the vowel rather than a consonant proper.

Vowels.—The vowel-system was inherited practically unchanged from the common Indo-Iranian period, the only specific Sanskrit development being the change of the Indo-Iranian short diphthongs *ai, *au (=Avestic aē, ao) to ē, ō (still classed as diphthongs by Indian grammarians) and of the long diphthongs *āi, *āu to ai, au. Thus to Avestic daēvo haomo uxδāiš gāuš Sanskrit corresponds with dēváḥ sómaḥ ukthāih gáuḥ. The comparative simplicity of the vowel-system and the great predominance of the vowels a and ā were due to the fact that in the Indo-Iranian period four distinct Indo-European sounds—e, o, a, ṇ (ṅ, ṇ̃, ṃ)—had coalesced in the one sound a (similarly ē, ō, ā had all become ā). The only trace left of the earlier differentiation was the fact that an original guttural before ă representing older ĕ had become a palatal: thus we have sácatē, "follows," from *sekʷetai (Greek hépetai, Latin sequitur), but sákṣat, "he shall follow" beside Gk. hépsetai. Similarly the 12 I.E. diphthongs—ei, oi, ai, eu, *ou, au, ēi, ōi, āi, ēu, ōu, āu*—were merged in four Skt. sounds *ē, ō, ai, au*. In this way the vowel alternation (especially between *e* and *o*), a characteristic feature of Indo-European, was largely lost. Nevertheless, where the word contained a sonant the alternation, although diminished in scope, was still discernible: *e.g.*, I.E. *ei: oi: i* became Skt. *ē: i* (*e.g.*, Gk. *leípei: loipós: élipe*=Skt. *rēcati: rēkaḥ: aricat*), I.E. *e, o: ē, ō* became Skt. *a: ā*. The correspondences thus resulting—*a: ā; i: ē: ai; u: ō: au; ṛ: ar: ār*—being associated with particular grammatical formations were still further developed in Sanskrit into a system, which, early recognized by the Indian grammarians, was used by them in their description of the formation of the language.

Consonants.—The consonant-system has remained much truer to the original Indo-European. It is characterized by the rarity of spirants and by the opposition of unaspirated and aspirated stops (both surd and voiced) in each series. In preserving the voiced aspirate stops unchanged, Sanskrit and its descendants (for most of the modern Indo-Aryan languages still possess these sounds) are unique among the Indo-European languages, in which these sounds either became surd aspirates and later spirants (as in Greek and Latin) or lost their aspiration (as in Iranian, Balto-Slavonic, Armenian, Albanian, Germanic, Celtic). Thus to Greek *phérō*, Latin *fero*, Eng. *bear*, Sanskrit corresponds with *bhárāmi*, to Gk. *éthēke*, Lat. *fēcit*, Eng. *deed* with *ádhāt*.

Some consonants were restricted in their use: *ñ* appeared only before or after palatals, *ṅ* only finally or before gutturals (and where a guttural had subsequently disappeared), *ṇ* only between vowels and semivowels or before cerebral stops, *ḥ* only finally or before sibilants and surd gutturals or labials, *ṁ* only finally or before consonants. Neither aspirate nor *h* nor *ś* ended a word. At the end of a sentence only the following consonants were used: *k, ṭ, t, p, ṅ, n, m, ḥ*.

Of the palatals *ch* appears as a single consonant only initially: elsewhere it is always doubled unless preceded by another consonant, for it corresponds to the Indo-European group *sk₁*: *e.g.*, *chindánti* "they cut"=Latin *scindunt*, *gácchāmi* "I go"=Greek *báskō*, *vānchā* "wish." *Germ. Wunsch*. *j* represents two I.E. sounds (1) palatal *g₁* (=Gk. *g*, Avestic *z*): *jánaḥ* "birth"=Av, *zanō*, Gk. *génos*, Lat. *genus*; (2) velar *gw* before an original *ĕ* or *ĭ* (=Av. *j*): *jīváḥ* "alive"= Av. *jīvō*, Lat. *vivos, cf.* Gk. *bíos*, Eng. *quick, jh* does not belong to the Indo-European part of the vocabulary, but appears only in onomatopoeic and borrowed words, or in words taken from the vernacular in which the frequent Sanskrit groups *dhy* and *hy* became (*j*)*jh*.

Of the sibilants *ś* corresponds to I.E. palatal *k₁*: in this Sanskrit agrees with the other eastern I.E. languages (Balto-Slavonic, Albanian, Armenian, Iranian) which have an *s* or *sh* sound as opposed to the *k* (*h* in Germanic) of the western languages: *e.g.*, *śatám* "100"=Av. *satem*, Lithuanian *šimtas*, but Gk. *he-katón*, Lat. *centum*, Eng. *hundred*. Before the surd dentals this *ś* became *s*: *viśáti* "enters," *viṣṭáḥ* "entered." But *ṣ* also corresponds to I.E. *s* when preceded by *i, u, r* or *k*, agreeing in this with Iranian and partly with Armenian and Balto-Slavonic. The chief innovation in the consonant-system is the introduction of the third series, the cerebrals or linguals (better termed retroflex). The dentals were formed by the tip of the tongue striking the roots of the teeth, the cerebrals by the tip of the tongue, bent backwards, striking further back on the palate. In the oldest Sanskrit they are derived from the dentals when immediately preceded by *ṣ* or **z* (which subsequently disappeared): thus **diśtas* (=Lat. *dictus*) became **diṣtas* and then *diṣṭáḥ*; **mizdham* (=Gk. *misthós*) became **miẓḍham* and then *mīḍhám*. Later also under the influence of a preceding *r* or *ṛ* dentals became cerebrals: such words are loans from the popular dialect, but they begin to appear in the literary language even as early as the Rigveda: thus *víkataḥ* "monstrous" is derived from *víkṛtaḥ* "strange." Some words, however, contain cerebrals which cannot be explained as derived from dentals in either of these ways. It is probable that these sounds were characteristic of both the families of languages, Muṇḍā and Dravidian, which the Aryan speakers of Sanskrit found in possession of India; and the appearance of them in Sanskrit and its descendants (and in a few of the adjoining Iranian

languages such as Baluchi and Pashto) can scarcely be unconnected with this fact.

The Indian grammarians emphasized the difference in the pronunciation of consonants according as they came at the beginning, in the middle or at the end of a word or before other consonants. These differences, though slight, have ended in transforming the whole Sanskrit consonant-system in its descendants, the modern Indo-Aryan languages. Final consonants were pronounced without being fully exploded: in the spoken languages these final consonants had disappeared before the middle of the 3rd century B.C. A similar pronunciation is assigned to consonants before stops: in the spoken languages these were early assimilated (*e.g.*, *suptáḥ* became *suttō*). *y* and *v* were pronounced more strongly initially than intervocalically: in the modern languages initial *y–* has remained or become *j*, but intervocalic *–y–* has been lost. [This contrast is observable even in the dialect of the Rigveda. For in the phonetically weak position of the termination and in certain accessory words intervocalic *–dh–* has lost its occlusion and become *–h–*: *ihí* "go"=Greek *íthi*, *śēmahē* "we lie"=Gk. *keímetha*. Further in all words intervocalic *–ḍ–* has become *–ḷ–*, although other more easterly dialects still preserve it (through whose influence it was afterwards re-established in Classical Sanskrit: thus Classical *nīḍaḥ* "nest" (from **nizḍa-*) is *nīḷáḥ* in Vedic.]

Accent.—Our knowledge of the accent of Sanskrit words is derived from its marking in the more important Vedic texts and from the statements of grammarians. It was predominantly a musical or tonic, not a stress, accent. Three different types are generally distinguished, the *udātta* "raised," *anudātta* "unraised" and *svarita* the rising-falling accent following the *udātta*. Generally the position of the *udātta* agrees, as far as can be ascertained by comparison, with that of the chief word accent of Indo-European. The rhythm of Sanskrit was purely quantitative; in verse metre depended only on the number and the length of the syllables composing a line, and was entirely independent of accent. In this respect, the Yashts of Avestan literature are similar.

GRAMMAR

Nouns.—Sanskrit makes a perfect distinction between nouns (including adjectives, pronouns and indeclinables) and verbs. The declension of nouns comprises three numbers—singular, dual and plural; and eight cases, viz., nominative, accusative, instrumental, dative, ablative, genitive, locative, vocative. In the majority of declensions ablative and genitive are not distinguished in the singular, nor dative and ablative in the plural, while the dual universally has only three separate forms,—(1) nom.-acc.-voc., (2) inst.-dat.-abl., (3) gen.-loc. These confusions were inherited from Indo-European, but the tendency to confuse still further the forms and functions of the cases continued within Sanskrit itself, the genitive especially enlarging its sphere at the expense of other cases. This process, continued in the spoken languages down to the present day, has resulted in a noun declension, which for the most part consists of two cases only—(1) a direct case founded on the Sanskrit nominative and accusative; (2) an oblique case founded on the Sanskrit genitive or, perhaps, in some forms, the dative. Among the numbers the dual by itself was reserved to express natural pairs (such as *akṣī* "the eyes," *karṇáu* "the ears"), or any two objects or persons already referred to or present in the mind of the speaker or hearer; otherwise the use of the word for "two" itself was required.

Although the idea of case was in the main expressed by the termination (as, *e.g.*, the nominative by *–s* in *dēvás*=Latin *deus*, the accusative by *–m* in *dēvám*=*deum*), it was sometimes accompanied by change in the pre-terminational element, and was connected with a shift of accent:

	Skt.	Greek	Skt.	Greek	Skt.	Greek
nom.	*pát*	*pós* (Doric)	*dyáuḥ*	*Zeús*	*pitá*	*patḗr*
acc.	*pádam*	*póda*	*dyám*	*Zēn-a*	*pitáram*	*patéra*
gen.	*padáḥ*	*podós*	*diváḥ*	*Diós*	*pitúḥ*	*cf. patrós*
dat.	*padḗ*	*cf. podí*	*divḗ*	*cf. Dií*	*pitrḗ*	*cf. patrí*
loc.	*padí*	*podí*	*dyávi*	Lat. *Jove*	*pitári*	
voc.			*dyáuḥ*	*Zeú*	*pitar*	*páter*

There was, however, one important class of stems, namely masc.

and neut. in −*a* and fem. in −*ā* (corresponding to the −*o* and −*ā* stems of Greek and Latin), in which the accent was fixed either on the stem or on the termination throughout the paradigm without any change in the form of the stem, of the type *áśvaḥ* =Gk. *híppos,* Lat. *equos.* There had, moreover, been a tendency in the pre-Sanskrit period to fix the form even of the variable stems, especially those consisting only of a root: thus the long vowel was generalized in *vāc–* "voice" (nom. *vák*):

	Skt.	Latin	Avestic	Greek
acc.	*vācam*	*vōcem*	*vācim*	
gen.	*vācáḥ*	*vōcis*	*vacō*	*opós*

But in the process of normalization the vowel declension (and especially with the stems in −*a* −*ā*) was predominant, and even in Sanskrit itself there was a considerable transference of consonant-stems and root-stems to this declension: *e.g., páda-* "foot," *dvára-* "door," *dánta-* "tooth" replaced *pād- pad-, dant- dat-, dvār- dur-.* This proceeded apace in the spoken tongue, for the declension of the modern languages rests exclusively on vowel-stems and of these chiefly on the −*a* −*ā* stems.

As in Indo-European, the pronominal declension differed from the nominal, that of the personal pronouns radically, that of the demonstratives and others to a varying degree. In the personal pronoun each number had a different root (*t*[*u*]*vám* "thou," *yūyám* "you"), while that of the first person had different roots also for the nominative and the oblique cases (*ahám* "I," *mǎm* "me," *vayám* "we," *asmǎn* "us"). The tendency of the two declensions, the nominal and the pronominal, to influence each other is observable: *e.g.,* the nominal ending of the neuter sing. nom. and acc. −*m* as in *kím* "what?" (=Lat. *quid*) replaced the −*d* or −*t* still found in other pronouns (*tát* "that"=Lat. *is-tud*). In the spoken language this mutual influence continued to react until practically all distinction between the two types of declension was lost. Perhaps the most satisfactory explanation of the various elements that stand between Indo-European demonstrative pronouns and their case endings is to be found in Hittite where the original pronominal stems were appended to the sentence connective (Skt. "tasmin"=Hit. "ta [sentence connective] + smi [pronoun]"; Sk. "tas"=Hit. "ta+as"), etc.

Numerals.—The numeral-system, built upon a decimal basis, is that of Indo-European. There are separate names for the numbers up to 10; from 11 to 19 compounds of the units with the word for 10 partly correspond with those of Greek and Latin: *e.g., d*(u)*vádaśa* "12"=Gk. *dṓdeka,* Lat. *duōdecim.* Above that the tens (20, 30, etc.) were in origin probably compounds expressing a number of tens, and the intermediate numbers were formed by compounds of the units with these: *e.g., páñca* "5" (Gk. *pénte,* Lat. *quīnque*), *pañcāśát* "50" (*cf.* Gk. *pentḗkonta,* Lat. *quīnquāginta*), *páñcapañcāśat* "55." There are separate words for 100 and 1000. The special word for 100,000 (*lakṣaḥ,* whence modern *lākh*) is post-vedic. The numerals from 1 to 19 are adjectives; the rest are substantives.

Gender.—Traces of the distinction of gender between animate (=masculine and feminine) and inanimate (=neuter) are seen in the use of the neut. *udakám* "water as a medium of floating, etc.," and the fem. *ápaḥ* "water as personified as sentient beings." But for the most part in Sanskrit gender is grammatical and largely independent of nature, except that male and female living beings are usually (though not always) respectively masculine or feminine. There were three genders—masculine, feminine and neuter. The neuter was distinguished by its termination (or lack of termination) in the nominative and accusative, and by the fact that the form of the accusative was the same as that of the nominative. But the masculine and feminine substantives were primarily distinguished only by the form of an adjective, if there were one, in agreement with them (as often, *e.g.,* in French or German). But there was a tendency to reserve certain types of stem for one or other gender. Thus the −*a* stems in Sanskrit are reserved only for masculine and neuter nouns (although in Greek they may still be feminine, *e.g., hē híppos* "the mare"); and the −*ā* stems are mostly feminine. In the older language the −*i* stems might be masculine or feminine; in the later language they are

almost all feminine. Similarly even in Classical Sanskrit −*i* stems are either masculine or feminine; but in the spoken language there was a growing tendency to confine them to feminine: thus words of this declension which are masculine in Sanskrit become feminines in the modern languages: *agníḥ* m. "fire" (=Lat. *ignis*) becomes Hindi *āg* f.

Verbs.—In the Vedic language the verbal system is of considerable complexity. A verb might have various stems, viz. present (sometimes more than one), aorist (three in number, root, *e.g., ásthām*=Gk. *éstēn,* strong, *e.g., aricam*=Gk. *élipon,* sigmatic, *e.g., araikṣam*=Gk. *éleipsa*); perfect (characterized by reduplication and peculiar terminations); future (rare in the old language). The significance of the stems lay in the mode of action they expressed. Very generally speaking, the present indicated continuous action, the aorist momentary action, the perfect a state resulting from past action. The various present stems indicated various types of present-stem action, such as intensive, repetitive, inchoative, causative, desiderative, etc. Each of the first three stems had five moods—indicative expressing fact, injunctive and subjunctive expressing will and futurity, optative expressing wish, imperative expressing command. In the indicative of the present, perfect and future stems there were two tenses, present and past; the aorist stem was in the indicative confined to the past tense. Each tense had three persons and three numbers—singular, dual and plural. Finally each tense could be conjugated in two voices with different terminations—active and middle. Among the parts of the infinite verb there was connected with each stem a participle which could be either active or middle, present, past, or perfect, and independent of tense stems a past participle, one or more infinitives (for the most part case-forms of verbal nouns), a gerundive (=future passive participle) and an indeclinable participle or gerund. The total number of possible forms belonging to any one verb is thus very great.

The idea of time was expressed in the indicative primarily by the termination: the primary endings expressing present and future time, the secondary endings past (and also, to some extent, future) time. Past time was usually still further defined by the prefixing of a particle, *a* or *ā*, before the verb (corresponding to the Greek and Armenian augment), *e.g., dádhāmi* "I place," *ádadhām* "I placed"=Gk. *títhēmi, étithēn.* The active voice indicated that the action performed had reference to some person or thing other than the doer, the middle that the action had reference to the doer in some way or other: *e.g.,* active *taṇḍulǎn nēnēkti* "he washes the rice" (French *il lave*), middle *pāṇi nēniktē* "he washes his hands" (*il se lave les mains*). As in Greek, the middle could also be used to express passive sense, but this use was later confined to the perfect and especially the aorist stems, while a special present stem (characterized by the suffix −*yá-* with middle terminations) was used for the present passive: *e.g., labhatē* "he takes," *labhyatē* "is taken." The expression of person was inherent in the verbal form, and pronouns were used only when emphasis was desired. As with the nouns, there were two types of stems—the athematic with variable accent and variable stem form to which the terminations were directly attached (type *ás-ti* "he is"=Gk. *esti,* Lat. *est*), the thematic with invariable accent and stem between which and the termination the vowel *a* was inserted (type *váh-a-ti*=Lat. *veh-i-t*). There was a growing tendency for verbs to be brought into this class from the other, since its conjugation was the more normal; thus *yunák-ti* (3rd plur. *yuñj-ánti*) "joins," contrasted with the already thematic Lat. *jung-i-t,* became later *yuñj-a-ti* (3rd plur. *yuñj-a-nti*). This type almost alone survives in the modern languages.

This verbal system was greatly simplified in Classical Sanskrit. The injunctive mood almost, and the subjunctive entirely, disappeared or were incorporated in the imperative. The aorist and perfect stems remained only in the indicative, and the aorist participle disappeared. The infinitive was reduced to one form only (the accusative of a noun in −*tu*-, corresponding in form to the Latin supine, *e.g., jñātum* "to know"=[*g*]*nōtum*), and the absolutive to two, one for simple, one for compound verbs. This left the present stem predominant; and though the aorist and the perfect survived in the indicative, their meaning was scarcely, if at all, to be distinguished from that of the past tense of the present stem (*i.e.*, the imperfect). Finally even in Sanskrit itself the imperfect tended to be replaced by the past participle used as a finite verb. Among the spoken languages in some areas the aorist seems to have been developed further as a past tense, but as a whole the verb of the modern languages possesses a present system based on the Sanskrit present stem and a past system based on the Sanskrit past participle.

Syntax.—In its main lines the syntax of Sanskrit is Indo-European, and the primary uses of its cases, moods and tenses can be paralleled from other Indo-European languages. Its most peculiar development was in the region of composition. Compounds, usually of not more than two members, are common in the Vedic texts. Even in the Epic their extension is considerable, and compounds consisting of three or four separate members are not rare. In the later, more artificial, language compounds may be met with which extend over a page or more.

Vocabulary.—Sanskrit shows a constant change and development of vocabulary. Part of this is in the natural evolution of already existing material. The main constituent of the vocabulary of Vedic Sanskrit is Indo-European, but even here there are some words which are not Indo-European. One source of such words is undoubtedly the languages which the Aryans found in India; and recently J. Przyluski has demonstrated that some (such as *bāṇáḥ* "arrow," *mayūraḥ* "peacock," *karpāsam* "cotton") were received from *Muṇḍā* or Austro-Asiatic languages. Another source for new words was found in the spoken Aryan languages: words taken from these were given a Sanskrit form. In this way even original Sanskrit words returned under a new form: we have already seen how *vikrita-*, having in the spoken language become *vikaṭa-*, was readopted in that form in the literary tongue, and retained side by side with *vikrita-*.

BIBLIOGRAPHY.—Grammar, Elementary: E. D. Perry, *Sanskrit Primer* (1901); C. R. Lanman, *Sanskrit Reader* (1912); A. A. Macdonell, *Sanskrit Grammar for Beginners* (1927), *Vedic Reader* (1917), *Vedic Grammar for Students* (1916). Advanced: W. D. Whitney, *Sanskrit Grammar* (1889); A. A. Macdonell, *Vedic Grammar* (1910). Dictionaries: M. Monier-Williams, *Sanskrit-English Dictionary* (1899), and the smaller dictionaries of C. Capeller (1891) and A. A. Macdonell (1924).   (R. L. T.)

LITERATURE

The history of Sanskrit literature like the political history of ancient India suffers from the total want of anything like a fixed chronology. In its vast range there is scarcely a work of importance the date of which can be fixed with absolute certainty. The original composition of most Sanskrit works can indeed be confidently assigned to certain general periods but as to many of them, there is reason to doubt whether they have come down to us in their original shape.

The history of Sanskrit literature readily divides itself into two main periods—the Vedic and the classical. These periods partly overlap, and some of the later Vedic works are included in that period on account of their subject matter, and archaic style, rather than for any claim to a higher antiquity than some of the oldest works of classical Sanskrit. The first period may be put at 1500–200 B.C. and the second 500 B.C.–A.D. 1000.

THE VEDIC PERIOD

Saṃhitās.—The term *veda, i.e.* (sacred) "knowledge," "lore"—embraces a body of writings the origin of which is ascribed to divine revelation (*śruti,* literally "hearing"), and which forms the foundation of the Brāhmanical system of religious belief. This sacred canon is divided into three or (according to a later scheme) four co-ordinate collections, likewise called Veda: (1) the *Rig-veda,* or lore of praise (or hymns); (2) the *Sāma-veda,* or lore of tunes (or chants); (3) the *Yajur-veda,* or lore of prayer (or sacrificial formulas); and (4) the *Atharva-veda,* or lore of the Atharvans. Each of these four Vedas is a collection (*saṃhitā*) of sacred, mostly poetical, texts of a devotional nature, called *mantra.* This entire body of texts (and particularly the first three collections) is also known as the *trayī vidyā,* or threefold wisdom, of hymn (*rich*), tune or chant (*sāman*), and prayer (*yajus*)—the fourth Veda, when included, being classed together with the Rik.

Classes of Priests.—The Brāhmanical religion finds its practical expression chiefly in sacrificial performances. The Vedic sacrifice requires for its proper performance the attendance of four officiating priests, each of whom is assisted by one or more (usually three) subordinate priests, viz.: (1) the *Hotar* (or *hotri, i.e.,* either "sacrificer," or "invoker"), whose chief business is to invoke the gods, in prayers or hymns; (2) the *Udgātar* (udgātri), or chorister, who has to perform chants (*stotra*) in connection with the hotar's invocations; (3) the *Adhvaryu,* or offering priest *par excellence,* who performs all the material duties of the sacrifice, such as the kindling of the fires; (4) the *Brahman,* or chief "priest," who superintends the performance and rectifies any mistakes that may be committed. The Sāmaveda and Yajurveda form special song and prayer books, arranged for the practical use of the udgātar and adhvaryu respectively; while the Rik-saṃhitā, though not arranged for any such practical purpose, contains the entire body of sacred lyrics whence the hotar draws the material for his recitations. The brahman had no special textbook assigned to him, but was expected to be familiar with all the Saṃhitās as well as with the practical details of the sacrificial performance. (*See* BRAHMAN and BRĀHMAṆA.)

Brāhmaṇas.—The several Saṃhitās have attached to them certain theological prose works, called *Brāhmaṇa,* which also form part of the canon. Their object is to explain the relationship of the Vedic texts to the now very elaborate sacrificial ceremonial and to explain their mystic import. (*See* BRĀHMAṆA.)

Āraṇyakas and Upanishads.—Closely connected with the Brāhmaṇas are two classes of treatises called *Āraṇyaka* and *Upanishad.* The Āraṇyakas, *i.e.,* works "relating to the forest," intended to be read or expounded by anchorites in the quiet of the forest, resemble the Brāhmaṇas, which they supplement by dealing with special points of ritual. The Upanishads are of a more mystical nature, and form the first attempts at a systematic treatment of metaphysical questions. From their pantheistic views later developed the Vedānta philosophy. The Upanishads have to be assigned to very different periods of Sanskrit literature. The oldest treatises of this kind are doubtless those which form part of the Saṃhitās, Brāhmaṇas and Āraṇyakas of the three older Vedas.

Different Recensions.—As the sacred texts were not committed to writing till a much later period, but were handed down orally in the Brāhmaṇical schools, it was inevitable that local differences of reading should spring up, which in course of time gave rise to a number of independent versions. Such different text-recensions, called *śākhā* (*i.e.,* branch), were at one time very numerous, but only a limited number have survived. As regards the Saṃhitās, the poetical form of the hymns, as well as the concise style of the sacrificial formulas, rendered these texts less liable to change.

Vedāṅgas.—Besides the purely ceremonial matter, the Brāhmaṇas also contained a considerable amount of matter bearing on the correct interpretation of the Vedic texts; and, indeed, the sacred obligation incumbent on the Brāhmans of handing down correctly the letter and sense of those texts necessarily involved a good deal of serious grammatical and etymological study in the Brāhmaṇical schools. These literary pursuits resulted in the accumulation of much learned material, which it became desirable to throw into a systematic form. These practical requirements were met by a class of treatises, grouped under six different heads or subjects, called *Vedāṅgas, i.e.,* members, or limbs, of the (body of the) Veda. In their present form these works represent a rather advanced stage of scientific development. Though a few of them are composed in metrical form—the majority belong to a class of writings called *sūtra, i.e.,* "string," consisting of strings of rules in the shape of tersely expressed aphorisms, intended to be committed to memory.

Sūtras.—The Sūtras form a connecting link between the Vedic and the classical periods of literature. These treatises are included among the Vedic writings, and in point of language may be considered as the latest products of the Vedic age, but they are no longer *śruti* or revelation. They are of human, not of divine, origin. The Sūtras are regarded nevertheless as works of great authority, second only to that of the revealed Scriptures;

in contrast to the latter they are called *smriti*, or tradition.

The six branches of Vedic science, included under the term Vedānga, are as follows:—

1. *Śikshā*, or Phonetics.—In addition to a small treatise ascribed to the great grammarian Pāṇini, the *Pāṇinīya śikshā*, there are usually included under this head certain works, called *Prātiśākhya*, i.e., "belonging to a certain *śākhā* or recension," which deal minutely with the phonetic peculiarities of the several Saṃhitās, and are of great importance for Vedic textual criticism.

2. *Chhandas*, or Metre.—Tradition makes the *Chhandaḥ-sūtra* of Piṅgala the starting-point of prosody. The Vedic metres, however, occupy but a small part of this treatise; they are particularly dealt with in the Nidāna-sūtra of the Sāmaveda, and in a chapter of the Rik-prātiśakhya. For later profane prosody, on the other hand, Piṅgala's treatise is valuable.

3. *Vyākaraṇa*, or Grammar.—Pāṇini's famous grammar is said to be *the* Vedānga; but it marks the culminating point of grammatical research rather than the beginning, and treats chiefly of the post-Vedic language.

4. *Nirukta*, or Etymology.—Yāska's *Nirukta* deals entirely with Vedic etymology and exegesis. It consists, in the first place, of strings of words in three chapters: (1) synonymous words; (2) such as are purely or chiefly Vedic; and (3) names of deities. These lists are followed by Yāska's commentary, interspersed with numerous illustrations. Yāska quotes the works of several predecessors but his is by several centuries the oldest surviving work of its kind. The above four studies deal with the correct understanding of texts, the next two with rites and their proper seasons.

5. *Jyotisha*, or Astronomy.—The metrical treatise which has come down to us in two different recensions under the title of Jyotisha, ascribed to one Lagadha, or Lagata, seems to be the oldest existing systematic treatise on astronomical subjects.

6. *Kalpa*, or Ceremonial.—Sacrificial practice gave rise to a large number of systematic sūtra-manuals for the several classes of priests. The most important of these works have come down to us, and they occupy by far the most prominent place among the literary productions of the sūtra-period. The Kalpa-sūtras, or rules of ceremonial, are of two kinds: (1) the *Śrauta-sūtras*, which are based on the śruti, and teach the performance of the great sacrifices, requiring three sacrificial fires; and (2) the *Smārta-sūtras*, or rules based on the smṛiti or tradition. The latter class again includes two kinds of treatises: (1) the *Grihya-sūtras*, or domestic rules, treating of ordinary family rites, such as marriage, birth, name-giving, etc., connected with simple offerings in the domestic fire; and (2) the *Sāmayāchārika-* (or *Dharma-*) *sūtras*, which treat of customs and temporal duties, and are supposed to have formed the chief sources of the later law-books.

THE FOUR VEDAS

After this brief characterization of the various branches of Vedic literature, we proceed to take a rapid survey of the several Vedic collections.

Rigveda.—The *Rigveda-saṃhitā* has come down to us in the recension of the Śākala school, which shows that it consists of 1,028 hymns, including eleven so-called *Vālakhilyas*, probably of later date. The hymns are composed in a great variety of metres, and consist, on an average, of rather more than 10 verses each, or about 10,600 verses altogether. This body of sacred lyrics has been subdivided by ancient authorities in a twofold way, viz. either from a purely artificial point of view, into eight *ashtakas* of about equal length, or, on a more natural principle, based on the origin of the hymns, and invariably adopted by European scholars, into ten books, or *maṇḍalas*, of unequal length. Tradition has handed down the names of the reputed authors, or rather inspired "seers" (*rishi*), of most hymns. These indications have enabled scholars to form some idea as to the probable way in which the Rik-saṃhitā originated, though much still remains to be cleared up by future research.

Maṇḍalas ii.–vii. are evidently arranged on a uniform plan. Each of them is ascribed to a different family of rishis, whence they are usually called the six "family-books": ii., the Gritsa-madas; iii., the Viśvāmitras or Kuśikas; iv., the Vāmadevyas; v., the Atris; vi., the Bharadvājas; and vii., the Vasishṭhas. Further, each of these books begins with the hymns addressed to Agni, the god of fire, which are followed by those to Indra, whereupon follow those addressed to minor deities—the Viśve Devāh ("all-gods"), the Maruts (storm-gods), etc. Again, the hymns addressed to each deity are arranged in a descending order, according to the number of verses of which they consist.

Maṇḍala i., the longest in the whole Saṃhitā, contains 191 hymns, ascribed, with the exception of a few isolated ones, to sixteen poets of different families, and consisting of one larger (50 hymns) and nine shorter collections. Here again the hymns of each author are arranged on precisely the same principle as the "family-books." Maṇḍalas viii. and ix., on the other hand, have a special character of their own. To the Sāmaveda, these two maṇḍalas have contributed a much larger proportion of verses than any of the others. The hymns of the eighth book are ascribed to a number of different rishis, mostly belonging to the Kāṇva family. The chief peculiarity of this maṇḍala, however, consists in the strophic character of its composition and the numerous repetitions throughout it. It is closely connected with the first half of the first maṇḍala and they were evidently added as beginning and end to the collected ii.–vii. The ninth maṇḍala consists entirely of hymns (114) addressed to *Soma*, the deified juice of the so-called "moon-plant" (*Sarcostemma viminale*, or *Asclepias acida*), and ascribed to poets of different families. They are called *pavamānī*, "purificational," because they were to be recited by the hotar while the juice expressed from the soma plants was clarifying. The hymns are by poets of the same families as ii.–vii. and it is evident that when these hymns were collected the soma hymns were taken out and put into a single collection. There are also a few soma hymns in the later books (i., viii., x.).

Maṇḍala x. contains the same number of hymns (191) as the first, which it nearly equals in actual length. In the latter half of the book the hymns are clearly arranged according to the number of verses, in decreasing order—occasional exceptions to this rule being easily adjusted by the removal of a few apparently added verses. This maṇḍala came into existence after the other nine were in their present form, a fact of which there is abundant evidence. It shows considerable uniformity and is all older than the latest insertions in other books of the former collectors.

It is usual to call the Rik-saṃhitā (as well as the Atharvan) an historical collection, as compared with the two Saṃhitās put together for purely ritualistic purposes. And indeed, although the Rigveda itself, in its oldest form, may have been intended as a common prayer-book, for the whole of the Brāhmaṇical community, it is certain that in the stage in which it has been finally handed down it includes a certain portion of hymn material (and even some secular poetry) which could never have been used for purposes of religious service. It may, therefore, be assumed that the Rik-saṃhitā contains all of the nature of popular lyrics that was accessible to the collectors, or seemed to them worthy of being preserved. The question as to the exact period when the hymns were collected cannot be answered with any approach to accuracy. For many reasons, however, which cannot be detailed here, scholars have come to fix on the year 1000 B.C. as an approximate date for the collection of the Vedic hymns. From that time every means that human ingenuity could suggest was adopted to secure the sacred texts against the risks connected with oral transmission. But, as there is abundant evidence to show that even then not only had the text of the hymns suffered corruption, but their language had become antiquated to a considerable extent, and was only partly understood, the period during which the great mass of the hymns were actually composed must have lain considerably farther back, and may very likely have extended over the earlier half of the second millenary, or from about 2000 to 1500 B.C.

As regards the people which raised for itself this imposing monument, the hymns exhibit it as settled in the regions watered by the mighty Sindhu (Indus), with its eastern and western tributaries, the land of the five rivers (Panj-āb) thus forming the central home of the Vedic people. But, while its advanced guard has already debouched upon the plains of the upper Gaṅgā and Yamunā, those who bring up the rear are still found loitering far behind in the narrow glens of the Kubhā (Cabul) and Gomatī (Gomal). Scattered over this tract of land, in hamlets and villages, the Vedic Āryas are leading chiefly the life of herdsmen and husbandmen. The numerous clans and tribes, ruled over by chiefs and kings, have still constantly to vindicate their right to the land but lately wrung from an inferior race of darker hue. Not infrequently, too, the light-coloured Āryas wage internecine war with one another—as when the Bharatas, with allied tribes of the Panjāb, goaded on by the royal sage Viśvāmitra, invade the country of the Tṛitsu king Sudās, to be defeated in the "ten kings' battle," through the inspired power of the priestly singer Vasishṭha. The priestly office has already become one of high social importance by the side of the political rulers, and to a large extent an hereditary profession; though it does not yet present the baneful features of an exclusive caste.

The religious belief of the people consists in a system of natural symbolism, a worship of the elementary forces of nature, regarded as beings endowed with reason and power superior to those of man. In giving utterance to this simple belief, the priestly spokesman has, however, frequently worked into it his own speculative and mystic notions. Indra, the stout-hearted ruler of the cloud-region, receives by far the largest share of the devout attentions of the Vedic singer. His ever-renewed battle with the malicious demons of darkness and drought, for the recovery of the heavenly light and the rain-spending cows of the sky, forms an inexhaustible theme of spirited song. Next to him, in the affections of the people, stands Agni (*ignis*), the god of fire, invoked as the genial inmate of the Aryan household, and as the bearer of oblations, and mediator between gods and men. Indra and Agni are thus, as it were, the divine representatives of the king (or chief) and the priest of the Aryan community; and if, in the arrangement of the Saṃhitā, the Brāhmanical collectors gave precedence to Agni, it was but one of many avowals of their own hierarchical pretensions. Hence also the hymns to Indra are mostly followed, in the family collections, by those addressed to the Viśve Devāḥ (the "all-gods") or to the Maruts, the warlike storm-gods and faithful companions of Indra, as the divine impersonations of the Aryan freemen, the *viś* or clan. But, while Indra and Agni are undoubtedly the favourite figures of the Vedic pantheon, there is reason to believe that these gods had but lately supplanted another group of deities who play a less prominent part in the hymns, viz., Father Heaven (Dyaus Pitar, Ζεὺς πατήρ, Jupiter); Varuna (probably οὐρανός), the all-embracing (esp. nocturnal) heavens; Mitra (Zend. Mithra), the genial light of day; and Savitar, the quickener, and Sūrya (ἥλιος), the vivifying sun.

Brāhmaṇas of Rigveda.—Of the Brāhmaṇas that were handed down in the schools of the *Bahvrichas* (*i.e.*, "possessed of many verses"), as the followers of the Rigveda are called, two have come down to us, viz. those of the Aitareyins and the Kaushītakins. The *Aitareya-brāhmaṇa* and the *Kaushītaki-* (or *Śāṅkhāyana-*) *brāhmaṇa* evidently have for their groundwork the same stock of traditional exegetic matter. They differ, however, considerably in their arrangement of this matter. There is also a certain amount of material peculiar to each of them. The Kaushītaka is, upon the whole, far more concise in its style and more systematic in its arrangement—features which would lead one to infer that it is probably the more modern work of the two. While the Aitareya deals almost exclusively with the Soma sacrifice, the Kaushītaka first treats of the several kinds of *haviryajña*, or offerings of rice, milk and ghee, and then of the Soma sacrifice. Sāyaṇa, in the introduction to his commentary on the work, ascribes the Aitareya to the sage Mahidāsa Aitareya (*i.e.*, son of Itarā), also mentioned elsewhere as a philosopher; and it seems likely enough that this person arranged the Brāhmaṇa and founded the school of the Aitareyins. Regarding the authorship of the sister work we have no definite statement. Probably it is what one of the manuscripts calls it—the Brāhmaṇa of Śāṅkhāyana (composed) in accordance with the views of Kaushītaki.

Each of these two Brāhmaṇas is supplemented by a "forest-book," or Āraṇyaka. The *Aitareyāraṇyaka* is not a uniform production. It consists of five books (*āraṇyaka*), three of which, the first and the last two, are of a liturgical nature, treating of the ceremony called *mahāvrata*, or great vow. The last of these books, composed in sūtra form, is, however, doubtless of later origin. The second and third books are purely speculative, and are also styled the *Bahvricha-brāhmaṇa-upanishad*. Again, the last four chapters of the second book are usually singled out as the *Aitareya-upanishad*, ascribed, like its Brāhmaṇa (and the first book), to Mahidāsa Aitareya; and the third book is also referred to as the *Saṃhitā-upanishad*. As regards the *Kaushītaki-āraṇyaka*, this work consists of fifteen adhyāyas, the first two (treating of the mahāvrata ceremony) and the seventh and eighth of which correspond to the first, fifth, and third books of the Aitareyāraṇyaka respectively, whilst the four adhyāyas usually inserted between them constitute the highly interesting *Kaushītaki-* (*brāhmaṇa-*) *upanishad*, of which we possess two different recensions. The remaining portions (9–15) of the Āraṇyaka treat of the vital airs, the internal Agnihotra, ending with the vaṃśa, or succession of teachers. Of *Kalpa-sūtras*, or manuals of sacrificial ceremonial, composed for the use of the hotar priest, two different sets are in existence, the *Āśvalāyana-* and the *Śāṅkhāyana-sūtra*. Each of these works follows one of the two Brāhmaṇas of the Rik as its chief authority: the Aitareya and Kaushītaka respectively. Both consist of a *Śrauta-* and a *Grihya-sūtra*. Āśvalāyana seems to have lived about the same time as Pāṇini (? *c.* 400 B.C.)—his own teacher, Śaunaka, who completed the Rik-prātiśākhya, being probably intermediate between the great grammarian and Yāska, the author of the Nirukta. Śaunaka himself is said to have been the author of a *Śrauta-sūtra* (which was, however, more of the nature of a Brāhmaṇa) and to have destroyed it on seeing his pupil's work. A *Grihya-sūtra* is still quoted under his name by later writers. The *Āśvalāyana Śrauta-sūtra* consists of twelve, the *Grihya* of four, adhyāyas.

Regarding Śāṅkhāyana still less is known; but he, too, was doubtless a comparatively modern writer, who, like Āśvalāyana, founded a new school of ritualists. Hence the Kaushītaki-brāhmaṇa, adopted (and perhaps improved) by him, also goes under his name, just as the Aitareya is sometimes called Āśvalāyana-Brāhmaṇa. The Śāṅkhāyana Śrauta-sūtra consists of eighteen adhyāyas. The last two chapters of the work are, however, a later addition, while the two preceding chapters, on the contrary, present a comparatively archaic, brāhmaṇa-like appearance. The Grihya-sūtra consists of six chapters, the last two of which are likewise later appendages. The *Sāmbavya Grihya-sūtra*, of which a single ms. is at present known, seems to be closely connected with the preceding work. Professor Bühler also refers to the Rigveda the *Vāsishṭha-dharmaśāstra*, composed of mixed sūtras and couplets.

A few works remain to be noticed, bearing chiefly on the textual form and traditionary records of the Rik-saṃhitā. The Prātiśākhyas have already been referred to as the chief repositories of śikshā or Vedic phonetics. Among these works the *Rik-prātiśākhya* occupies the first place. The original composition of this important work is ascribed to the same Śākalya from whom the vulgate recension of the (Śākala) Saṃhitā takes its name. He is also said to be the author of the existing *Pada-pāṭha* (*i.e.*, the text-form in which each word is given unconnected with those that precede and follow it).

Sāmaveda.—The term *sāman*, of uncertain derivation, denotes a solemn tune or melody to be sung or chanted to a *rich* or verse. The set chants (*stotra*) of the Soma sacrifice are as a rule performed in triplets, either actually consisting of three different verses, or of two verses which, by the repetition of certain parts, are made, as it were, to form three. The three verses are usually chanted to the same tune; but in certain cases two verses sung to the same tune had a different *sāman* enclosed between them. One and the same *sāman* or tune may thus be sung to many different verses; but, as in teaching and practising the tunes the same verse was invariably used for a certain tune, the term *sāman*, as well as the special technical names of *sāmans*, are not infrequently applied to the verses themselves with which they were ordinarily connected.

In accordance with the distinction between *rich* or text and *sāman* or tune, the sāman-hymnal consists of two parts: the *Sāma-veda-saṃhitā*, or collection of texts (*rich*) used for making up sāman-hymns, and the *Gāna*, or tune-books, song-books. The textual matter of the Saṃhitā consists of somewhat under 1600 different verses, selected from the Rik-saṃhitā, with the exception of some seventy-five verses, some of which have been taken from Khila hymns, whilst others which also occur in the Atharvan or Yajurveda, as well as such not otherwise found, may perhaps have formed part of some other recension of the Rik. The *Sāma-veda-saṃhitā* is divided into two chief parts, the *pūrva-* (first) and the *uttara-* (second) *ārchika*. The second part contains the texts of the sāman-hymns, arranged in the order in which they are actually required for the *stotras* or chants of the various Soma sacrifices. The first part, on the other hand, contains the body of tune-verses, or verses used for practising the several sāmans or tunes upon—the tunes themselves being given in the *Grāma-geya-gāna* (*i.e.*, songs to be sung in the village), the tune-book specially belonging to the Pūrvārchika.

Sāmaveda-brāhmaṇas.—The title of *Brāhmaṇa* is bestowed by the Chhandogas, or followers of the Sāmaveda, on a considerable number of treatises. The majority of the Sāmaveda-brāhmaṇas present, however, none of the characteristic features of other works of that class; but they are rather of the nature of sūtras and kindred treatises, with which they probably belong to the same period of literature. Moreover, the contents of these works —as might indeed be expected from the nature of the duties of the priests for whom they were intended—are of an extremely arid and technical character, though they all are doubtless of some importance, either for the textual criticism of the Saṃhitā or on account of the legendary and other information they supply.

If the Sāmaveda has thus its ample share of Brāhmaṇa-literature, though in part of a somewhat questionable character, it is not less richly supplied with sūtra-treatises, or works on exegesis, some of which probably belong to the oldest works of that class.

Yajurveda.—This, the sacrificial Veda of the Adhvaryu priests, divides itself into an older and a younger branch, or, as they are usually called, the Black (*krishna*) and the White (*śukla*) Yajurveda. Tradition ascribes the foundation of the Yajurveda to the sage Vaiśampāyana. Of his disciples three are specially named, viz.: Katha, Kalāpin and Yāska Paiṅgi, the last of whom again is stated to have communicated the sacrificial science to Tittiri. We have three old collections of Yajus-texts, viz. the *Kāṭhaka,* the *Kālāpaka* or *Maitrāyaṇi Samhitā,* and the *Taittirīya-saṃhitā*. The *Kāṭhaka* and *Kālāpaka* are frequently mentioned together; and the author of the "great commentary" on Pāṇini once remarks that these works were taught in every village. From the *Kaṭhas* and *Kālāpas* proper schools seem early to have branched off, each with their own recensions of the text. As regards the Taittirīya-saṃhitā, that collection, too, in course of time gave rise to a number of different schools, the text handed down being that of the Āpastambas.

The four collections of old Yajus texts, so far known to us, while differing more or less considerably in arrangement and verbal points, have the main mass of their textual matter in common. This common matter consists of both sacrificial prayers (*yajus*) in verse and prose, and exegetic or illustrative prose portions (*brāhmaṇa*). A prominent feature of the old Yajus texts, as compared with the other Vedas, is the constant intermixture of textual and exegetic portions. The Charakas and Taittirīyas thus do not recognize the distinction between Saṃhitā and Brāhmaṇa in the sense of two separate collections of texts, but they have only a Saṃhitā, or collection, which includes likewise the exegetic or Brāhmaṇa portions. The Taittirīyas seem at last to have been impressed with their want of a separate Brāhmaṇa and to have set about supplying the deficiency in rather an awkward fashion: instead of separating from each other the textual and exegetic portions of their Saṃhitā, they merely added to the latter a supplement (in three books), which shows the same mixed condition, and applied to it the title of *Taittirīya-brāhmaṇa*.

The *Maitrāyaṇī Saṃhitā*, the identity of which with the original Kālāpaka has been proved pretty conclusively by Dr. L. v. Schröder, who attributes the change of name of the Kālāpa-Maitrāyaṇīyas to Buddhist influences, consists of four books, attached to which is the *Maitri-* (or *Maitrāyaṇī*) *upanishad*. The *Kāṭhaka*, on the other hand, consists of five parts, the last two of which, however, are perhaps later additions, containing merely the prayers of the hotar priest, and those used at the horse-sacrifice. There is, moreover, the beautiful *Kaṭha-* or *Kāṭhaka-upanishad*, which is also, and more usually, ascribed to the Atharvaveda, and from which Sānkhya-Yoga ideas may have developed.

Samhitā of the White Yajurveda.—The defective arrangement of the Yajus texts was at last remedied by a different school of Adhvaryus, the Vājasaneyins. The reputed originator of this school and its text-recension is Yājñavalkya Vājasaneya (son of Vājasani). The result of the rearrangement of the texts was a collection of sacrificial mantras, the *Vājasaneyi-saṃhitā*, and a Brāhmaṇa, the *Śatapatha*. On account of the greater lucidity of this arrangement, the Vājasaneyins called their texts the White (or clear) Yajurveda—the name of Black (or obscure) Yajus being for opposite reasons applied to the Charaka texts. Both the Saṃhitā and Brāhmaṇa of the Vājasaneyins have come down to us in two different recensions, viz., those of the *Mādhyandina* and *Kāṇva* schools. In several points of difference the Kāṇva recension agrees with the practice of the Rik-saṃhitā, and there probably was some connection between the Yajus school of Kāṇvas and the famous family of ṛishis of that name to which the eighth maṇḍala of the Rik is attributed.

The *Vājasaneyi-saṃhitā* consists of forty adhyāyas, the first eighteen of which contain the formulas of the ordinary sacrifices. The last fifteen (or even twenty-two) adhyāyas are doubtless a later addition. The last adhyāya is commonly known under the title of *Vājasaneyi-saṃhitā* (or *Iśāvāsya-*) *upanishad*. Its object seems to be to point out the fruitlessness of mere works, and to insist on the necessity of man's acquiring a knowledge of the supreme spirit.

The last book is of the Upanishad order, and bears the special title of *Brihad-* (great) *āraṇyaka;* its last six chapters are the *Brihadāraṇyaka-upanishad,* the most important of all Upanishads. As regards the age of the Śatapatha, the probability is that the main body of the work is considerably older than the time of Pāṇini, but that some of its latter parts were considered by Pāṇini's critic Kātyāyana to be of about the same age as, or not much older than, Pāṇini.

The consolidation of the Brāhmanical hierarchy and the institution of a common system of ritual worship, which called forth the liturgical Vedic collections, were doubtless consummated in the so-called Madhya-deśa, or "midland," lying between the Sarasvatī and the confluence of the Yamunā and Gaṅgā; and more especially in its western part, the Kuru–kshetra, or land of the Kurus, with the adjoining territory of the Pañchālas, between the Yamunā and Gaṅgā. From thence the original schools of Vaidik ritualism gradually extended their sphere over the adjacent parts. The Charakas seem for a long time to have held sway in the western and north-western regions; while the Taittirīyas in course of time spread over the whole of the peninsula south of the Narmadā (Nerbudda), where their ritual has remained pre-eminently the object of study till comparatively recent times. The Vājasaneyins, on the other hand, having first gained a footing in the lands on the lower Ganges, chiefly, it would seem, through the patronage of King Janaka of Videha, thence gradually worked their way westwards, and eventually succeeded in superseding the older schools north of the Vindhya.

Atharvaveda.—The Artharvan was the latest of Vedic collections to be recognized as part of the sacred canon. That it is also the youngest Veda is proved by its language, which in vocabulary and grammar marks an intermediate stage between the main body of the Rik and the Brāhmaṇa period. In regard also to the nature of its contents, and the spirit which pervades them, this Vedic collection occupies a position apart from the others. Whilst the older Vedas seem clearly to reflect the recognized religious notions and practices of the upper classes of the Āryan tribes, as jealously watched over by a priesthood deeply interested in the undiminished maintenance of the traditional observances, the fourth Veda, on the other hand, deals mainly with all manner of superstitious practices such as have at all times found a fertile soil in the lower strata of primitive and less advanced peoples, and are even apt, below the surface, to maintain their tenacious hold on the popular mind in comparatively civilized communities. Although the constant intermingling with the aboriginal tribes may well be believed to have exercised a deteriorating influence on the Vedic people in this respect, it can scarcely be doubted that superstitious practices of the kind revealed by the Atharvan and the tenth book of the Rik must at all times have been present among the Āryan people, and that they only came to the surface when they received the stamp of recognized forms of popular belief by the admission of these collections of spells and incantations into the sacred canon. If in this phase of superstitious belief the old gods still find a place, their character has visibly changed so as to be more in accordance with those mystic rites and magic performances and the part they are called upon to play in them, as the promoters of the votary's cabalistic practices and the averters of the malicious designs of mortal enemies and the demoniac influences to which he would ascribe his fears and failures as well as his bodily ailments. The fourth Veda may thus be said to supplement in a remarkable manner the picture of the domestic life of the Vedic Āryan as presented in the Grihya-sūtras or house-rules; for while these deal only with the orderly aspects of the daily duties and periodic observances in the life of the respectable householder, the Atharvaveda allows us a deep insight into "the obscurer relations and emotions of human life"; and, it may with truth be said that "the literary diligence of the Hindus has in this instance preserved a document of priceless value for the institutional history of early India as well as for the ethnological history of the human race" (M. Bloomfield). It is worthy of note that the Atharvaveda is practically unknown in the south of India.

This body of spells and hymns is traditionally associated with two old mythic priestly families, the Atharvans and Aṅgiras, their names, in the plural, serving either singly or combined (Atharvāṅgirasas) as the oldest appellation of the collection. The two families or classes of priests are by tradition connected with the service of the sacred fire; but whilst the Atharvans seem to have devoted themselves to the auspicious aspects of the fire-cult and the performance of propitiatory rites, the Aṅgiras, on the other hand, are represented as having been mainly engaged in the uncanny practices of sorcery and exorcism. The current text of the Atharva-saṃhitā—apparently the recension of the Śaunaka school—consists of some 750 different pieces, about five-sixths of which is in various metres, the remaining portion being in prose. The whole mass is divided into twenty books. The principle of distribution is for the most part a merely formal one, in books i.-xiii. pieces of the same or about the same number of verses being placed together in the same book. The next five books, xiv.-xviii., have each its own special subject: xiv. treats of marriage and sexual union; xv., in prose, of the Vrātya, or religious vagrant; xvi. consists chiefly of prose formulas of conjuration; xvii. of a lengthy mystic hymn; and xviii. contains all that relates to death and funeral rites. Of the last two books no account is taken in the Atharva-prātiśākhya, and they indeed stand clearly in the relation of supplements to the original collection. The nineteenth book evidently was the result of a subsequent gleaning of pieces similar to those of the earlier books, which had probably escaped the collectors' attention; while the last book, consisting almost entirely of hymns to Indra taken from the Rik-saṃhitā, is nothing more than a liturgical manual of recitations and chants required at the Soma sacrifice; its only original portion being the ten so-called *kuntāpa* hymns (127–136), consisting partly of laudatory recitals of generous patrons of sacrificial priests and partly of riddles and didactic subjects.

The Atharvan has come down to us in a much less satisfactory state of preservation than any of the other Saṃhitās. The discovery in Kashmir of a second recension of the Atharva-saṃhitā, contained in a single birch-bark ms., written in the Śāradā character, has provided further material for its study. This new recension, ascribed to the Paippalāda school, consists likewise of twenty books (*kāṇḍa*), but in textual matter and arrangement it differs very much from the current text. While lacking much of the latter the new version offers a good deal of fresh matter, amounting to about one-sixth of the whole. From the Mahā-bhāshya and other works quoting as the beginning of the Atharva-saṃhitā a verse that coincides with the first verse of the sixth hymn of the current text, it has long been known that at least one other recension must have existed; but the first leaf of the Kashmir ms. having been lost, it cannot be determined whether the new recension (as seems all but certain) corresponds to the one referred to in those works.

Atharvaveda-brāhmaṇa.—The only Brāhmaṇa of the Atharvan, the *Gopatha-brāhmaṇa*, is one of the most modern and least important works of its class. It consists of two parts, the first of which contains cosmogonic speculations, interspersed with legends, mostly adapted from other Brāhmaṇas, and general instructions on religious duties and observances; while the second part treats, in a very desultory manner, of various points of the sacrificial ceremonial.

Atharvaveda-sūtras.—The Kalpa-sūtras belonging to this Veda comprise both a manual of śrauta rites, the *Vaitāna-sūtra*, and a manual of domestic rites, the *Kauśika-sūtra*. The teacher Kauśika is repeatedly referred to in the work on points of ceremonial doctrine. The last sūtra-work to be noticed in connection with this Veda is the *Śaunakīyā Chaturādhyāyikā*, being a Prātiśākhya of the Atharva-saṃhitā, so called from its consisting of four lectures (adhyāya). Although Śaunaka can hardly be credited with being the actual author of the work, considering that his opinion is rejected in the only rule where his name appears, there is no reason to doubt that it chiefly embodies the phonetic theories of that teacher, which were afterwards perfected by members of his school. Whether this Śaunaka is identical with the writer of that name to whom the final redaction of the Śākalaprātiśākhya of the Rik is ascribed is not known.

Upanishads.—Another class of writings traditionally connected with the Atharvaveda are the numerous *Upanishads* which do not specially attach themselves to one or other of the Saṃhitās or Brāhmaṇas of the other Vedas. The Ātharvana-upanishads, mostly composed in ślokas, may be roughly divided into two classes: those of a purely speculative or general pantheistic character, treating chiefly of the nature of the supreme spirit, and the means of attaining to union therewith, and those of a sectarian tendency. Of the former category, a limited number—such as the Praśna, Muṇḍaka and Māṇḍūkya-upanishads—have probably to be assigned to the later period of Vedic literature; whilst the others presuppose more or less distinctly the existence of some fully developed system of philosophy, especially the Vedānta or the Yoga. The sectarian Upanishads, on the other hand—identifying the supreme spirit either with one of the forms of Vishṇu (such as the Nārāyaṇa, Nṛisiṃha-tāpanīya, Rāma-tāpanīya, Gopāla-tāpanīya Upanishads), or with Śiva (e.g., the Rudra-upanishad), or with some other deity—belong to post-Vedic times.

THE CLASSICAL PERIOD

The Classical Literature of India is almost entirely a product of artificial growth, in the sense that its vehicle was not the language of the general body of the people, but of a small and educated class. It would scarcely be possible, even approximately, to fix the time when the literary idiom ceased to be understood by the common people. We only know that in the 3rd century B.C. there existed several dialects in different parts of northern India which differed considerably from the Sanskrit; and Buddhist tradition states that Gautama Śākyamuni himself, in the 6th century B.C., used the local dialect of Magadha (Behar) in preaching his new doctrine. Not unlikely, indeed, popular dialects, differing perhaps but slightly from one another, may have existed as early as the time of the Vedic hymns, when the Indo-Aryans, divided into clans and tribes, occupied the Land of the Seven Rivers; but such dialects must have sprung up after the extension of the Aryan sway and language over the whole breadth of northern India. But there is no reason why, even with the existence of local dialects, the literary language should not have kept in touch with the people in India, as elsewhere, save for the fact that from a certain time that language remained altogether stationary, allowing the vernacular dialects more and more to diverge from it. Although linguistic research had been successfully carried on in India for centuries, the actual grammatical fixation of Sanskrit seems to have taken place about contemporaneously with the first spread of Buddhism; and indeed that popular religious movement undoubtedly exercised a powerful influence on the linguistic development of India.

Epic Poems.—The Hindus, like the Greeks, possess two great national epics, the *Mahābhārata* and the *Rāmāyaṇa*. The *Mahābhārata*, *i.e.*, "the great (poem or tale) of the Bhāratas," is not so much a uniform epic poem as a great collection of poetry, consisting of a mass of legendary and didactic matter, worked into and round a central heroic narrative. The authorship of this work is aptly attributed to Vyāsa, "the arranger," the personification of Indian recension. Only the bare outline of the leading story can here be given.

At Hastināpura (sixty miles from the modern Delhi) in the Bharata country Dhritarāshtra, the elder of the princes, being blind, was passed over for his brother Pāṇḍu on the death of their father. On the death of Pāṇḍu, however, Dhritarāshtra assumed the government, assisted by his uncle Bhīshma, the Nestor of the poem. Pāṇḍu had five sons, Yudhishthira, Bhīma and Arjuna, by his chief wife Kūntī, and the twins Nakula and Sahadeva by his wife Mādrī. From their great-grandfather Kuru both families are called *Kauravas;* but for distinction that name is more usually applied to the sons of Dhritarāshtra, while their cousins, as the younger line, are named, after their father, *Pāṇḍavas*. The Pāṇḍavas were brought up at their uncle's court like his own sons. The rivalry and varying fortunes of these two houses form the main plot of the great epic. The Pāṇḍu princes soon proved themselves greatly superior to their cousins; and Yudhishthira, the eldest of them all, was to be appointed heir-apparent. But they had to leave the country to escape the plots of their jealous cousins. In their exile Draupadī, daughter of King Drupada of Panchāla, won by Arjuna in open contest, became the wife of the five brothers. At the contest they met their cousin, nephew of their mother Kuntī, the famous Yādava prince Krishṇa of Dvārakā, who ever afterwards remained their faithful friend and confidential adviser. Dhritarāshtra now divided the kingdom between the two houses; whereupon the Pāṇḍavas built for themselves the city of Indraprastha (on the site of the modern Delhi). After a time of great prosperity, Yudhishthira, in a game of dice, lost everything to Duryodhana, when it was settled that the Pāṇḍavas should retire to the forest for twelve years, but should afterwards be restored to their kingdom if they succeeded in passing an additional year in disguise. During their forest-life they met with many adventures, among which may be mentioned their encounter with King Jayadratha of Chedi, who had carried off Draupadī from their hermitage. After the twelfth year has expired they leave the forest, and, assuming various disguises, take service at the court of King Virāta of Matsya. Here all goes well for a time till the queen's brother Kīchaka, a great warrior and commander of the royal forces, falls in love with Draupadī, and is slain by Bhīma. The Kauravas, profiting by Kīchaka's death, now invade the Matsyan kingdom, when the Pāṇḍavas side with King Virāta, and there ensues, on the field of Kurukshetra, during eighteen days, a series of fierce battles, ending in the annihilation of the Kauravas; only the Pāṇḍavas, Arjuna and his charioteer Krishṇa survived on the victorious side. Yudhishthira now at last becomes yuva-rāja, and eventually king—Dhritarāshtra having resigned and retired with his wife and Kuntī to the forest, where they soon after perish in a conflagration. Learning also of the death of Krishṇa, Yudhishthira himself at last becomes tired of life and resigns his crown; and the five princes, with their faithful wife, and a dog that joins them, set out for Mount Meru, to seek admission to Indra's heaven. On the way one by one drops off, till Yudhishthira alone, with the dog, reaches the gate of heaven; but, the dog being refused admittance, the king declines entering without it, when the dog turns out to be no other than the god of Justice himself, having assumed that form to test Yudhishthira's constancy. But, finding neither his wife nor his brothers in heaven, and being told that they are in the nether world to expiate their sins, the king insists on sharing their fate, when this, too, proves a trial, and they are all reunited to enjoy perpetual bliss.

The complete work consists of upwards of 100,000 couplets—its contents thus being nearly eight times the bulk of the *Iliad* and *Odyssey* combined. It is divided into eighteen books, with a supplement, entitled Harivaṃśa, or genealogy of the god Hari (Krishṇa-Vishṇu). The portion relating to the feud of the rival houses constitutes somewhere between a fourth and a fifth of the work; and it is by no means improbable that this portion once formed a separate poem, called the *Bhārata*. While some of the episodes are so loosely connected with the story as to be readily severed from it, others are so closely interwoven with it that their removal would seriously injure the very texture of the work. This, however, only shows that the original poem must have undergone some kind of revision, or perhaps repeated revisions. That such has indeed taken place, at the hand of Brāhmans, for sectarian and caste purposes, cannot be doubted. According to Lassen's opinion, which has been very generally accepted by scholars, the main story of the poem would be based on historical events: on a destructive war waged between the two neighbouring peoples of the Kurus and Panchālas, who occupied the western and eastern parts of the Madhyadeśa (or "middle land" between the Ganges and Jumna) respectively, and ending in the overthrow of the Kuru dynasty. On the original accounts of these events—perhaps handed down in the form of lays or sagas—the Pāṇḍava element would subsequently have been grafted as calculated to promote the class interests of the Brāhmanical revisers.

Date of the Epic.—The earliest direct information regarding the existence of epic poetry in India is in a passage of Dion Chrysostom (*c.* A.D. 80)—"even among the Indians, they say, Homer's poetry is sung, having been translated by them into their own dialect and tongue." It is generally agreed that this does not imply an Indian translation of Homer but means that the Indians had similar works. Whence Dion derived his information is not known; but as many leading names of the Mahābhārata and even the name of the poem itself are mentioned in Pāṇini's grammatical rules, not only must the Bhārata legend have been current in his time (? *c.* 400 B.C.), but most probably it was at the time of Patañjali, the author of the "great commentary" on Pāṇini (*c.* 150 B.C.). It cannot, however, be doubted that long before that time heroic song had been diligently cultivated in India at the courts of princes and among Kshatriyas, the knightly order, generally. In the *Mahābhārata* itself the transmission of epic legend is in some way connected with the Sūtas, a social class which, in the caste-system, is defined as resulting from the union of Kshatriya men with Brāhmaṇa women, and which supplied the office of charioteers and heralds, as well as (along with the Māgadhas) that of professional minstrels. Be this as it may, there is reason to believe that, as Hellas had her ἀοιδοί who sang the κλέα ἀνδρῶν, and Iceland her skalds who recited favourite sagas, so India had from olden times her professional bards, who delighted to sing the praises of kings and inspire the knights with warlike feelings. If in this way a stock of heroic poetry had gradually accumulated which reflected an earlier state of society and manners, we can well understand why, after the Brāhmanical order of things had been definitely established, the priests should have deemed it desirable to subject these traditional memorials of Kshatriya chivalry and prestige to their own censorship, and adapt them to their own canons of religious and civil law. Such a revision would doubtless require considerable skill and tact; and if in the present version of the work much remains that seems contrary to the Brāhmanical code and pretensions—*e.g.*, the polyandric union of Draupadī and the Pāṇḍu princes—the reason probably is that such features were too firmly rooted in the popular tradition to be readily eliminated; and all the revisers could do was to explain them away as best they could. Thus Draupadī's abnormal position is actually accounted for in five different ways, one of these representing it as an act of duty and filial obedience on the part of Arjuna who, on bringing home his fair prize and announcing it to his mother, is told by her, before seeing what it is, to share it with his brothers. The epic in time became a great treatise on duty (*dharma*) inculcating the divine origin of Brāhman institutions, the caste system and the superiority of the priestly caste not only over the people but over kings. From inscriptions we know that by the end of the 5th century A.D. the Mahābhārata was appealed to as an authority on matters of law, and that its extent was practically what it now is, including its supplement, the Harivaṃśa. Indeed, everything seems to point to the probability of the work having been complete by about A.D. 200. But, whilst Bhārata and Kuru heroic lays may, and probably do, go back to a much earlier age, it seems hardly possible to assume that the Pāṇḍava epic in its present form can have been composed before the Greek invasion of India, or about 300 B.C. Moreover, it is by no means impossible that the epic narrative was originally composed—as some other portions of the works are—in prose, either continuous or mixed with snatches of verse. The leading position occupied in the existing epic by Krishna (whence it is actually called *kārshṇa-veda*, or the veda of Krishna), and the Vaishṇava spirit pervading it, make it very probable that it assumed its final form under the influence of the Bhāgavata sect with whom Vāsudeva (Krishna), originally apparently a venerated local hero, came to be regarded as a veritable god, and incarnation of Vishṇu. Its culminating point this sectarian feature attains in the *Bhagavat-gītā* (*i.e.*, the upanishad), "sung by the holy one"—the famous theosophic episode, in which Krishna, in lofty and highly poetic language, expounds the doctrine of faith (*bhakti*) and claims adoration as the incarnation of the supreme spirit. Of the purely legendary matter incorporated with the leading story of the poem, not a little, doubtless, is at least as old as the latter itself. Some of these episodes—especially the well-known story of Nala and Damayantī, and the touching legend of Sāvitrī—themselves form epic gems of high poetic value.

The Rāmāyaṇa, *i.e.*, poem "relating to Rāma," is ascribed to the poet Vālmīki; and, allowance being made for some later additions, the poem indeed presents the appearance of being the work of an individual genius. In its present form it consists of some 24,000 ślokas, or 48,000 lines of sixteen syllables, divided into seven books.

(I.) King Daśaratha of Kośala, reigning at Ayodhyā (Oudh), has four sons borne him by three wives, viz., Rāma, Bharata and the twins Lakshmaṇa and Śatrughna. Rāma wins for a wife Sītā, daughter of Janaka, king of Videha. (II.) On his return to Ayodhyā he is to be appointed heir-apparent; but Bharata's mother persuades the king now to grant her a long promised boon and insists on his banishing his eldest son for fourteen years, and appointing her son instead. Separation from his favourite son soon breaks the king's heart, whereupon the ministers call on Bharata to assume the reins of government. He refuses, however, and, betaking himself to Rāma's retreat on the Chitrakūṭa mountain (in Bundelkhund), implores him to return; but, unable to shake Rāma's resolve to complete his term of exile, he consents to take charge of the kingdom in the meantime. (III.) After a ten years' happy residence in the forest, Rāvaṇa, the demon-king of Ceylon, carries off Sītā to his capital Laṅkā while her two protectors are away in pursuit of a golden deer sent to mislead them. While she resolutely rejects the Rākshasa's addresses, Rāma sets out with his brother to her rescue. (IV.) After numerous adventures they enter into an alliance with Sugrīva, king of the monkeys; and, with the assistance of the monkey-general Hanumān, and Rāvaṇa's own brother Vibhīshaṇa, they prepare to assault Laṅkā. (V.) The monkeys, tearing up rocks and trees, construct a passage across the straits—the so-called Adam's Bridge, still designated Rāma's Bridge in India. (VI.) Rāma crosses with his allies, slays the demon and captures the stronghold; Sītā successfully undergoes an ordeal by fire to clear herself of the suspicion of infidelity; they return to Ayodhyā, where, after a triumphal entry, Rāma is installed. (VII.) Rāma, how-

ever, seeing that the people are not yet satisfied of Sītā's purity, resolves to put her away; whereupon, in the forest, she falls in with Vālmīki himself, and at his hermitage gives birth to two sons. While growing up there, they are taught by the sage the use of the bow, as well as the Vedas, and the Rāmāyaṇa as far as the capture of Laṅkā and the royal entry into Ayodhyā. Ultimately Rāma discovers and recognizes them by their wonderful deeds and their likeness to himself, and takes his wife and sons back with him.

The first and last books are later additions by which the poem has been turned to the glory of Vishṇu. In these two books Rāma has become deified and identified with the god Vishṇu, whilst in the body of the poem his character is simply that of a perfect man and model hero. The background of the epic is a purely mythological one—Rāma representing the god Indra, and Sītā—in accordance with the meaning of the name—the personified "Furrow," as which she is already invoked in the *Rigveda*, and hence is a tutelary spirit of the tilled earth, wedded to Indra, the Jupiter Pluvius. Rāvaṇa would correspond to the demon Vritra of the *Rigveda*.

One version of the same story, with, however, many important variations of details, forms an episode of the *Mahābhārata*, the *Rāmopākhyāna*, the relation of which to Vālmīki's work is still a matter of uncertainty. In respect of both versification and diction the Rāmāyaṇa is of a distinctly more refined character than the larger poem; and, indeed, Vālmīki is seen already to cultivate some of that artistic style of poetry which was carried to excess in the later artificial poems (Kāvyas), whence the title of *ādi-kavi*, or first poet, is commonly applied to him. The *Rāmāyaṇa* itself contains a prophecy like that of Horace's to the effect that it will always live on the lips of men, and it has been more than fulfilled. No story in India has attained such popularity. It has been translated into many vernaculars and through the version of Tulsi Das has exerted a tremendous influence on the spiritual life of India. To characterize the Indian epics in a single word: though often disfigured by fancies and exaggerations, they are yet noble works, abounding in passages of remarkable descriptive power, intense pathos, and high poetic grace and beauty; and while, as works of art, they are far inferior to the Greek epics, in some respects they appeal far more strongly to the romantic mind of Europe, namely, by their loving appreciation of natural beauty, their exquisite delineation of womanly love and devotion, and their tender sentiment of mercy and forgiveness.

Purāṇas and Tantras.—The *Purāṇas* are partly legendary, partly speculative histories of the universe, compiled for the purpose of promoting some special, locally prevalent form of Brāhmanical belief. They deal with cosmogony, stories of gods, sages and heroes, Vishṇu's avatars, the solar and lunar lines of kings and other pseudo-historical matter. They are sometimes styled a fifth Veda, and may indeed in a certain sense be looked upon as the scriptures of Brāhmanical India. The term *purāṇa*, signifying "old," applied originally to prehistoric, especially cosmogonic, legends, and then to collections of ancient traditions generally. They are popular encyclopaedias of useful knowledge mostly with a Vaishṇava tendency. They are connected in subject matter with the *Mahābhārata* and have some relationship to the law books and go back to a common source.

They are almost entirely composed in the epic couplet, and indeed in much the same easy flowing style as the epic poems, to which they are, however, as a rule greatly inferior in poetic value.

According to the traditional classification of these works, there are said to be eighteen (*Mahā-*, or great) *Purāṇas*, and as many *Upa-purāṇas*, or subordinate Purāṇas. The former are by some authorities divided into three groups of six, according as one or other of the three primary qualities of external existence—goodness, darkness (ignorance), and passion—is supposed to prevail in them, viz. the *Vishṇu, Nāradīya, Bhāgavata, Garuḍa, Padma, Varāha*—*Matsya, Kūrma, Liṅga, Śiva, Skanda, Agni*—*Brahmāṇḍa, Brahmavaivarta, Mārkaṇḍeya, Bhavishya, Vāmana* and *Brahma-Purāṇas*. The eighteen principal Purāṇas are said to consist of together 400,000 couplets. In northern India the Vaishṇava Purāṇas, especially the *Bhāgavata* and *Vishṇu*, are by far the most popular. The former is held in the highest estimation, and, especially through the vernacular versions of its tenth book, treating of the story of Kṛishṇa, has powerfully influenced the religious belief of India.

From the little we know regarding the Upa-purāṇas, their character does not seem to differ very much from that of the principal sectarian Purāṇas. Besides these two classes of works there is a large number of so-called *Sthala-purāṇas*, or chronicles recounting the history and merits of some holy "place" or shrine, where their recitation usually forms an important part of the daily service.

The *Tantras* have to be considered as partly a collateral and partly a later development of the sectarian Purāṇas; though, unlike these, they can hardly lay claim to any intrinsic poetic value. These works are looked upon as their sacred writings by the numerous *Śāktas*, or worshippers of the female energy (*śakti*) of some god, especially the wife of Śiva, in one of her many forms (Pārvatī, Devī, Kālī, Bhavānī, Durgā). This worship of a female representation of the divine power appears already in some of the Purāṇas; but in the Tantras it assumes quite a peculiar character, being largely intermixed with magic performances and mystic rites, partly, indeed, of a grossly immoral nature. (*See* HINDU-ISM.) *See* the series of Tantric works edited by A. Avalon.

Artificial Epics and Romances.—About the beginning of the Christian era a new class of epic poems begins to make its appearance, differing widely in character from those that had preceded it. These later productions are of a decidedly artificial character, and must necessarily have been beyond the reach of any but the highly cultivated. They are, on the whole, singularly deficient in incident and invention, their subject matter being almost entirely derived from the old epics. Nevertheless, these works are by no means devoid of merit and interest; and a number of them display considerable descriptive power and a wealth of genuine poetic sentiment. The simple heroic couplet has been largely discarded for various more or less elaborate metres; and in accordance with this change of form the diction becomes gradually more complicated.

The generic appellation of such works is *kāvya*, which, meaning "poem," or the work of an individual poet (*kavi*), is, as we have seen, already applied to the *Rāmāyaṇa*. Six poems of this kind are singled out by native rhetoricians as standard works, under the title of *Mahākāvya*, or great poems. Two of these are ascribed to the famous dramatist Kālidāsa, the most prominent figure of this period of Indian literature and truly a master of the poetic art. In a comparatively modern couplet he is represented as having been one of nine literary "gems" at the court of a king Vikramāditya. Whether this name refers to Chandragupta II. Vikramāditya or not, Kālidāsa must have flourished about this time, *c*. A.D. 400. Of the principal poets of this class, whose works have come down to us, he appears to be one of the earliest; but there can be little doubt that he was preceded in this as in other departments of poetic composition by many lesser lights, eclipsed by the sun of his fame, and forgotten. Thus the *Buddhacharita*, a Sanskrit poem on the life of the reformer, which was translated into Chinese about A.D. 420, and the author of which, Aśvaghosha, is placed by Buddhist tradition as early as the time of Kanishka (who began to reign in A.D. 78), calls itself, not without reason, a "mahākāvya"; and the panegyrics contained in some of the inscriptions of the 4th century likewise display, both in verse and ornate prose, many of the characteristic features of the kāvya style of composition.

Of the six universally recognized "great poems" here enumerated, the first two, and doubtless the two finest, are those attributed to Kālidāsa. (1) The *Raghuvaṃśa*, or "race of Raghu," celebrates the ancestry and deeds of Rāma. The work, consisting of nineteen cantos, is manifestly incomplete; but hitherto no copy has been discovered of the six additional cantos which are supposed to have completed it. (2) The *Kumāra-sambhava*, or "the birth of (the war-god) Kumāra" (or Skanda), the son of Śiva and Pārvatī, consists of seventeen cantos, the last ten of which are looked upon as spurious by some scholars, mainly on account of their erotic character, not a strong argument. There is no reason to doubt that the eighth canto is by Kālidāsa but he cannot have

written much of the other nine. (3) The *Kirātārjunīya*, or combat between the Pāṇḍava prince Arjuna and the god Śiva, in the guise of a Kirāta or wild mountaineer, is a poem in eighteen cantos, by Bhāravi, who is mentioned together with Kālidāsa in an inscription dated A.D. 634. (4) The *Śiśupāla-badha*, or slaying of Śiśupāla, who, being a prince of Chedi, reviled Kṛishṇa, who had carried off his intended wife, and was killed by him at the inauguration sacrifice of Yudhishthira, is a poem consisting of twenty cantos, attributed to Māgha (ninth cent.), whence it is also called *Māghakāvya*. (5) The *Rāvaṇabadha*, or "slaying of Rāvaṇa," more commonly called *Bhaṭṭikāvya*, was composed for the practical purpose of illustrating the less common grammatical forms and the figures of rhetoric and poetry. Bhaṭṭi, apparently the author's name, is usually identified with the well-known grammarian Bhartṛihari, whose death Professor M. Müller, from a Chinese statement, fixes at A.D. 650, while others make him Bhartṛihari's son. (6) The *Naishadhīya*, or *Naishadha-charita*, the life of Nala, king of Nishadha, is ascribed to Śrī-Harsha (son of Hīra), who is supposed to have lived in the latter part of the 12th century. The *Nalodaya* deals with the same subject but the author's main object is to show his skill in tricks of style and metre. The long lost and recently discovered *Janakī-harana of Kumāradāsa* (eighth cent.) takes its subject (the rape of Sītā) from the *Rāmāyaṇa* strongly imitative of Kālidāsa; it is, however, the work of a poet of no mean ability. The stanzas of the *Rāghavapāṇḍavīya* are so ambiguously worded that the poem may be interpreted as relating to the leading story of either the *Rāmāyaṇa* or the *Mahābhārata*. Less ambitious in composition, though styling itself a mahākāvya, is the *Vikramāṅka-devacharita*, a panegyric written about A.D. 1085 by the Kashmir poet Bilhaṇa, in honour of his patron the Chālukya king Vikramāditya of Kalyāṇa, regarding the history of whose dynasty it supplies some valuable information.

In this place may also be mentioned, as composed in accordance with the Hindu poetic canon, Kalhaṇa's *Rājataraṅgiṇī* (*c*. A.D. 1150) or "river of kings," being a chronicle of the kings of Kashmir, and the only important historical work in the Sanskrit language, although even here considerable allowance has to be made for poetic licence and fancy.

Under the general term "kāvya" Indian critics include, however, not only compositions in verse, but also certain kinds of prose works composed in choice diction richly embellished with flowers of rhetoric. The feature generally regarded by writers on poetics as the chief mark of excellence in this ornate prose style is the frequency and length of its compounds; whilst for metrical compositions the use of long compounds is expressly discouraged by some schools of rhetoric.

The Drama.—The Hindus ascribe the origin of dramatic representation to the sage Bharata (the word in Sanskrit means also "actor"). We know that treatises on the dramatic art existed at the time of Pāṇini, as he mentions two authors of *Naṭa-sūtras*, or "rules for actors," Śilālin and Kṛiśāśva. Now the words *naṭa* and *nāṭya*—as well as *nāṭaka*, the common term for "drama"—being derived (like the modern vernacular "Nautch"=*nṛitya*) from the root *naṭ* (*nṛit*) "to dance," seem to point to a pantomimic or choral origin of the dramatic art. Fortunately, however, Patañjali, in his "great commentary," speaks of the actor as singing, and of people going "to hear the actor." Nay, he even mentions two subjects, taken from the cycle of Vishṇu legends: the slaying of Kaṃsa (by Krishṇa) and the binding of Bali (by Vishṇu)—which were represented on the stage both by mimic action and declamation. Judging from these allusions, theatrical entertainments in those days seem to have been very much on a level with the old religious spectacles or mysteries of Europe. It is not, however, till some centuries later that we meet with the first real dramas, which mark at the same time the very culminating point of Indian dramatic composition. Although we know the names of at least five predecessors of Kālidāsa, nothing but a few quotations from them have been preserved.

The long disputed possibility of Greek influence on the Sanskrit drama is not now maintained, although there are some superficial points of resemblance. The Hindu dramatist has little regard for the "unities" of the classical stage, though he is hardly ever guilty of extravagance in his disregard of them. Unlike the Greek dramatic theory, it is an invariable rule of Indian dramaturgy, that every play, however much of the tragic element it may contain, must have a happy ending. A death never takes place on the stage, nor is anything indecorous allowed. The dialogue is invariably carried on in prose plentifully interspersed with those neatly turned lyrical stanzas in which the Indian poet delights to depict some aspect of nature, or some temporary physical or mental condition. The outstanding feature of the Hindu play, however, is the mixed nature of its language. While the hero and leading male characters speak Sanskrit, women and inferior male characters use various Prākrit dialects. As regards these dialectic varieties, it can hardly be doubted that at the time when they were first employed in this way they were local vernacular dialects; but in the course of the development of the scenic art they became permanently fixed for special dramatic purposes, just as the Sanskrit had, long before that time, become fixed for general literary purposes. Thus it would happen that these Prākrit dialects, having once become stationary, were soon left behind by the spoken vernaculars, until the difference between them was as great as between the Sanskrit and the Prākrits.

The *Mrichchhakatikā*, or "little clay cart," has been considered earliest of the existing dramas because of a certain clumsiness of construction, but probably does not antedate the sixth century. According to several stanzas in the prologue, the play was composed by a king Śūdraka, but it is probably the work of a poet patronized by him. Chārudatta, a Brāhman merchant, reduced to poverty, and Vasantasenā, an accomplished courtezan, meet and fall in love with each other. This forms the main plot, which is interwoven with a political underplot, resulting in a change of dynasty. The connection between the two plots is effected by means of the king's rascally brother-in-law, who pursues Vasantasenā with his addresses, as well as by the part of the rebel cowherd Āryaka, who, having escaped from prison, finds shelter in the hero's house. The wicked prince, on being rejected, strangles Vasantasenā, and accuses Chārudatta of having murdered her; but, just as the latter is about to be executed, his lady love appears again on the scene. Meanwhile Āryaka has succeeded in deposing the king, and, having himself mounted the throne of Ujjain, he raises Vasantasenā to the position of an honest woman, to enable her to become the wife of Chārudatta. The play is one of the longest, consisting of not less than ten acts, some of which, however, are very short. The interest of the action is, on the whole, well sustained; and, altogether, the piece presents a vivid picture of the social manners of the time, whilst the author shows himself imbued with a keen sense of humour, and a master in the delineation of character.

Kālidāsa.—In Kālidāsa the dramatic art attained its highest point of perfection. From this accomplished poet we have three well-constructed plays, abounding in stanzas of exquisite tenderness and fine descriptive passages: the two well-known mytho-pastoral dramas, *Śakuntalā* in seven and *Vikramorvaśī* in five acts, and a piece of court intrigue, distinctly inferior to the other two, entitled *Mālavikāgnimitra* in five acts. The plot of the last named is as follows: King Agnimitra, who has two wives, falls in love with Mālavikā, maid to the first queen. His wives endeavour to frustrate their affection for each other, but in the end Mālavikā turns out to be a princess by birth, and is accepted by the queens as their sister.

Śrī Harshadeva.—Śrī-Harshadeva—identical with the king (Śilāditya) Harshavardhana of Kānyakubja (Kanauj) mentioned above, who ruled in the first half of the 7th century—has three plays attributed to him; they are probably only dedicated to him by poets patronized by him. This at least commentators state to have been the case as regards the *Ratnāvalī*, the authorship of which they assign to Bāna. Indeed, had they been the king's own productions, one might have expected the Chinese pilgrims (especially I-tsing, who saw one of the plays performed) to mention the fact. The *Ratnāvalī*, "the pearl necklace," is a graceful comedy of domestic manners, with well-drawn characters. Ratnāvalī, a Ceylon princess, is sent by her father to the court of King Udayana of Vatsa to become his second wife. She suffers shipwreck, but is rescued and received into Udayana's palace under the name of Sāgarikā, as one of Queen Vāsavadattā's attendants. The king falls in love with her, and the queen tries to keep them apart, but, on learning the maiden's origin, she becomes reconciled, and recognizes her as a "sister." Very similar in construction, but inferior, is the *Priyadarśikā*, in four acts, having for its plot another amour of the same king. The scene of the third play, the *Nāgānanda*, or "joy of the serpents" (in five acts), on the other hand, is laid in semi-divine regions. In spite of its shortcomings of construction the *Nāgānanda* is a play of considerable merit, the characters being drawn with a sure hand, and the humour is by no means despicable.

Bhavabhūti, a Brāhman of Vidarbha, passed his literary life chiefly at the court of Yaśovarman of Kanauj (*c.* A.D. 700). Bhavabhūti was the author of three plays, two of which, the *Mahāvīracharita* ("life of the great hero") and the *Uttararāmacharita* with very little action ("later life of Rāma"), in seven acts each, form together a dramatized version of the story of the *Rāmāyaṇa*. The third, the *Mālatīmādhava*, is a domestic drama in ten acts, representing the fortunes of Mādhava and Mālatī, the son and daughter of two ministers of neighbouring kings, who from childhood have been destined for each other, but, by the resolution of the maiden's royal master to marry her to an old and ugly favourite of his, are for a while threatened with permanent separation. The action of the play is full of life, and abounds in stirring, though sometimes improbable, incidents. The poet is considered by native critics to be not only not inferior to Kālidāsa, but even to have surpassed him in his *Uttararāmacharita*.

Minor Dramatists.—Bhaṭṭa Nārāyaṇa, the author of the *Veṇīsaṃhāra* ("the binding up of the braid of hair," based on an incident in the Mahābhārata), is known to have been alive in A.D. 840. The piece is composed in a style similar to that of Bhavabhūti's plays, but is inferior to them in dramatic construction and poetic merit, though valued by critics for its strict adherence to the rules of the dramatic theory, and popular in India, owing to its partiality for the cult of Krishṇa. The *Hanuman-nāṭaka* is a dramatized version of the story of Rāma, interspersed with numerous purely descriptive poetic passages. Contrary to the general practice, Sanskrit alone is employed in it. The play is attributed to Dāmodara Miśra (11th cent.), but gives the impression of being the production of different hands. Bhāsa is traditionally one of the great dramatists of India, a predecessor of Kālidāsa, but nothing of his has survived.

The *Mudrārākshasa*, or "Rākshasa (the minister) with the signet," is unique in being a drama of political intrigue, partly based on historical events, the plot turning on the reconciliation of Rākshasa, the minister of the murdered king Nanda, with the hostile party, consisting of Prince Chandragupta (the Greek Sandrocottus, 315–291 B.C.), who succeeded Nanda, and his minister Chāṇakya. The plot is developed with considerable dramatic skill, in vigorous, if not particularly elegant, language. The play was composed by Viśākhadatta, not much later than A.D. 860.

The *Prabodha-chandrodaya*, or "the moon-rise of intelligence," composed by Krishṇamiśra about the 12th century, is an allegorical play, in six acts, the *dramatis personae* of which consist entirely of abstract ideas and symbolical figures divided into two conflicting hosts; it is full of vigour, however. It depicts the struggle between the wicked king Error and the good king Reason.

Lyrical, Descriptive and Didactic Poetry.—Allusion has already been made to the marked predilection of the mediaeval Indian poet for depicting in a single stanza some peculiar physical or mental situation. The profane lyrical poetry consists chiefly of such little poetic pictures, which form a prominent feature of dramatic compositions. Numerous poets and poetesses are only known to us through such detached stanzas, preserved in native anthologies or manuals of rhetoric, and enshrining a vast amount of descriptive and contemplative poetry. An excellent specimen of a longer poem, of a partly descriptive, partly erotic character, is Kālidāsa's *Meghadūta*, or "cloud messenger," in which a banished yaksha (demi-god) sends a love-message across India to his wife in the Himālaya, and describes, in verse-pictures of the stately mandākrāntā metre the various places over which the messenger, a cloud, will have to sail in his airy voyage. Another much-admired descriptive poem by Kālidāsa is the *Ritu-saṃhāra*, or "collection of the seasons," in which the attractive features of the six seasons are successively set forth.

As regards religious lyrics, the fruit of sectarian fervour, a large collection of hymns and detached stanzas, extolling some special deity, might be made from Purāṇas and other works. Of independent productions of this kind only a few of the more important can be mentioned here. Śankara Āchārya, the great Vedāntist, who seems to have flourished about A.D. 800, is credited with several devotional poems, especially the *Ānanda-laharī*, or "wave of joy," a hymn of 103 stanzas, in praise of the goddess Pārvatī. The *Sūrya-śataka*, or century of stanzas in praise of Sūrya, the sun, is ascribed to Mayūra, the contemporary (and, according to a tradition, the father-in-law) of Bāṇa (in the early part of the 7th century). The latter poet himself composed the *Chaṇḍikāstotra*, a hymn of 102 stanzas, extolling Śiva's consort. The *Khaṇḍapraśasti*, a poem celebrating the ten avatāras of Vishṇu, is ascribed to no other than Hanumān, the monkey general, himself. Jayadeva's beautiful poem *Gītagovinda*, which, like most productions concerning Kṛishṇa, is of a very sensuous character, is a religious drama.

Didactic Poetry.—The particular branch of didactic poetry in which India is especially rich is that of moral maxims, expressed in single stanzas or couplets, and forming the chief vehicle of the *Nīti-śāstra* or ethic science. Excellent collections of such aphorisms have been published—in Sanskrit and German by Böhtlingk, and in English by John Muir. Probably the oldest original collection of this kind is that ascribed to Chāṇakya, but really much later.

Fables and Narratives.—For purposes of popular instruction stanzas of an ethical import were early worked up with existing prose fables and popular stories. A collection of this kind, a mirror for princes, was translated into Pahlavī in the reign of the Persian king Khusru Anushirvan, A.D. 531–579; but neither this translation nor the original is any longer extant. A Syriac translation, however, made from the Pahlavī in the same century, under the title of "Qualilag and Dimnag"—from the Sanskrit "Karataka and Damanaka," two jackals who play an important part as the lion's counsellors—has been discovered and published. The Sanskrit original, which probably consisted of fourteen chapters, was afterwards recast—the result being the *Panchatantra*, or "five books" (or headings), of which several recensions exist. A popular but late summary of this work, in four books, the *Hitopadeśa*, or "Salutary Counsel," has been shown by Peterson to have been composed by one Nārāyaṇa. Other highly popular collections of stories and fairy tales, interspersed with sententious verses, are: the *Vetālapanchaviṃśati*, or "twenty-five (stories) of the Vetāla" (the original of the Baitāl Pachīsī), older than the 11th century, since both Kshemendra and Somadeva have used it; and the *Śuka-saptati*, or "seventy (stories related) by the parrot," the author and age of which are unknown.

SCIENTIFIC AND TECHNICAL LITERATURE

Law (*Dharma*).—Among the technical treatises of the later Vedic period, certain portions of the Kalpa-sūtras, or manuals of ceremonial, peculiar to particular schools, are the earliest attempts at a systematic treatment of law subjects. These are the *Dharma-sūtras*, or "rules of (religious) law." The Dharmasūtras consist chiefly of strings of terse rules, containing the essentials of the science, and intended to be committed to memory, and to be expounded orally by the teacher—thus forming, as it were, epitomes of class lectures. These rules are interspersed with stanzas or "gāthās," in various metres, either composed by the author himself or quoted from elsewhere, which generally give the substance of the preceding rules. One can well understand why such couplets should gradually have become more popular, and should ultimately have led to the appearance of works entirely composed in verse. Such metrical law-books did spring up

in large numbers, not all at once, but over a long period of time. These works are the metrical *Dharma-śāstras*, or, as they are usually called, the *Smriti*, "recollection, tradition,"—a term which, as we have seen, belonged to the whole body of Sūtras (as opposed to the *Śruti*, or revelation), but which has become the almost exclusive title of the versified institutes of law (and the few Dharmasūtras still extant). Of metrical Smritis about forty are known to exist, but their total number probably amounted to at least double that figure.

Manu.—With the exception of a few of these works—such as the *Agni-*, *Yama-* and *Vishṇu-Smritis*—which are ascribed to the respective gods, the authorship of the Smritis is attributed to old rishis, such as Atri, Kāṇva, Vyāsa, Śāṇḍilya, Bharadvāja. It is, however, extremely doubtful whether, as a rule, there really existed a traditional connection between these works and their alleged authors or schools named after them. The idea, which early suggested itself to Sanskrit scholars, that Smritis which passed by the names of old Vedic teachers and their schools might simply be metrical recasts of the Dharma- (or Grihya-) sūtras of these schools, was a very natural one, and, indeed, is still a very probable one, though the loss of the original Sūtras makes it difficult to prove. One could, however, scarcely account for the disappearance of the Dharmasūtras of some of the most important schools except on the ground that they were given up in favour of other works; and it is not very likely that this should have been done, unless there was some guarantee that the new works, upon the whole, embodied the doctrines of the old authorities of the respective schools. Thus, as regards the most important of the Smritis, the *Mānava-Dharmaśāstra*, there exist both a Śrauta- and a Grihya-sūtra of the Mānava school of the Black Yajus, but no such Dharmasūtra has hitherto been discovered, although the former existence of such a work has been made all but certain by Professor Bühler's discovery of quotations from a *Mānavam*, consisting partly of prose rules, and partly of couplets, some of which occur literally in the Manusmriti, whilst others have been slightly altered there to suit later doctrines, or have been changed from the original trishtubh into the epic metre. The idea of an old lawgiver Manu Svāyambhuva—"sprung from the self-existent (svayam-bhū)" god Brahman (m.)—reaches far back into Vedic antiquity: he is mentioned as such in early texts; and in Yāska's *Nirukta* a śloka occurs, giving his opinion on a point of inheritance. But whether or not the Mānava-Dharmasūtra embodied what were supposed to be the authoritative precepts of this sage on questions of sacred law we do not know; nor can it as yet be shown that the Manusmriti, which seems itself to have undergone considerable modifications, is the lineal descendant of that Dharmasūtra.

The Mānava Dharmaśāstra consists of twelve books, the first and last of which, treating of creation, transmigration and final beatitude, are, however, generally regarded as later additions. In them the legendary sage Bhrigu, here called a Mānava, is introduced as Manu's disciple, through whom the great teacher has his work promulgated. Except in these two books the work shows no special relation to Manu, for, though he is occasionally referred to in it, the same is done in other Smritis. The oldest existing commentary on the *Mānava-Dharmaśāstra* is by Medhātithi, who is usually supposed to have lived in the 10th century. The most esteemed of the commentaries is that of Kullūka Bhaṭṭa, composed at Benares in the 15th century.

Yājñavalkya.—Next in importance among Smritis ranks the *Yājñavalkya Dharmaśāstra*. Based on the Manusmriti, it represents a more advanced stage of legal theory and definition than that work. Yājñavalkya, as we have seen, is looked upon as the founder of the Vājasaneyins or White Yajus, and the author of the Śatapatha-brāhmaṇa. The work bears some resemblance to the *Pāraskara-grihyasūtra* of the *white Yajur Veda* but a connection between it and the *Mānava-grihyasūtra* seems, however, likewise evident. As in the case of Manu, ślokas are quoted in various works from a *Brihat-* and a *Vriddha- Yājñavalkya*. The Yājñavalkya-smriti consists of three books, corresponding to the three great divisions of the Indian theory of law: *āchāra*, rule of conduct (social and caste duties); *vyavahāra*, civil and criminal law; and *prāyaśchitta*, penance or expiation.

Nāradasmriti.—The *Nāradīya-Dharmaśāstra*, or *Nāraḍas-mriti*, is a more practical work; indeed, it is probably the most systematic and businesslike of all the Smritis. It does not concern itself with religious and moral precepts, but is strictly confined to law.

Whether any of the Dharmaśāstras were ever used in India as actual "codes of law" for the practical administration of justice is doubtful. No doubt these works were held to be of the highest authority as laying down the principles of religious and civil duty; but it was not so much any single text as the whole body of the Smriti that was looked upon as the embodiment of the divine law. Hence, the moment the actual work of codification begins in the 11th century, we find the jurists engaged in practically showing how the Smritis confirm and supplement each other, and in reconciling seeming contradictions between them. This new phase of Indian jurisprudence begins with Vijñāneśvara's *Mitākṣharā*, which, although primarily a commentary on Yājñavalkya, is so rich in original matter and illustrations from other Smritis that it is far more adapted to serve as a code of law than the work it professes to explain. This treatise is held in high esteem all over India, with the exception of the Bengal or Gaurīya school of law, which recognizes as its chief authority the digest of its founder, Jīmūtavāhana, especially the chapter on succession, entitled *Dāyabhāga*. Based on the Mitākṣharā are the *Smritichandrikā*, a work of great common sense, written by Devānḍa Bhaṭṭa, in the 13th century, and highly esteemed in Southern India; and the *Vīramitrodaya*, a compilation consisting of two chapters, on āchāra and vyavahāra, made in the first half of the 17th century by Mitramiśra, for Rājā Vīrasiṃha, or Bīrsinh Deo of Orchhā, who murdered Abul Fazl, the minister of the emperor Akbar, and author of the *Āīn-i Akbarī*. There is no need here to enumerate any more of the vast number of treatises on special points of law, the more important of which will be found mentioned in English digests of Hindu law.

Philosophy.—The contemplative Indian mind shows at all times a strong disposition for metaphysical speculation. In the old religious lyrics this may be detected from the very first. Not to speak of the abstract nature of some even of the oldest Vedic deities, this propensity betrays itself in a certain mystic symbolism, tending to refine and spiritualize the original purely physical character and activity of some of the more prominent gods, and to impart a deep and subtle import to the rites of the sacrifice. The primitive worship of more or less isolated elemental forces and phenomena had evidently ceased to satisfy the religious wants of the more thoughtful minds. Various syncretist tendencies show the drift of religious thought towards some kind of unity and of the divine powers, be it in the direction of the pantheistic idea, or in that of an organized polytheism, or even towards monotheism. In the latter age of the hymns the pantheistic idea is rapidly gaining ground, and finds vent in various cosmogonic speculations; and in the Brāhmaṇa period we see it fully developed. The fundamental conception of this doctrine finds its expression in the two synonymous terms *brāhman* (neutr.), probably originally "mystic effusion, devotional utterance," then "holy impulse," and *ātman* (masc.), "breath, self, soul."

The recognition of the essential sameness of the individual souls, emanating all alike (whether really or imaginarily) from the ultimate spiritual essence (*parama-brahman*) "as sparks issue from the fire," and destined to return thither, involved some important problems. Considering the infinite diversity of individual souls of the animal and vegetable world, exhibiting various degrees of perfection, is it conceivable that each of them is the immediate efflux of the Supreme Being, the All-perfect, and that each, from the lowest to the highest, could re-unite therewith directly at the close of its mundane existence? The difficulty implied in the latter question was at first met by the assumption of an intermediate state of expiation and purification, a kind of purgatory; but the whole problem found at last a more comprehensive solution in the doctrine of transmigration (*saṃsāra*). This doctrine not found in the *Rigveda* was probably aboriginal and adopted by the Aryan invaders. The notion of *saṃsāra* has become an axiom, a universally conceded principle of Indian philo-

sophy. Thus the latter has never quite risen to the heights of pure thought; its object is indeed *jijñāsa*, the search for saving knowledge; but it is an inquiry (*mīmāṃsā*) into the nature of things undertaken not solely for the attainment of the truth, but with a view to a specific object—the discontinuance of *saṃsāra*, the cessation of mundane existence after the present life. The task of the philosopher is to discover the means of attaining *moksha*, "release" from the bondage of material existence, and union with the Supreme Self—in fact, salvation. Desire is due to ignorance or wrong knowledge of the true nature of things and is the cause of transmigration. The purpose of each philosophical school is to attain true and saving knowledge. Intense self-contemplation being the only way of attaining the all-important knowledge, this doctrine left little or no room for those mediatorial offices of the priest, so indispensable in ceremonial worship; and indeed we actually read of Brāhman sages resorting to Kshatriya princes (in the Upanishads) to hear them expound the true doctrine of salvation. But, in spite of their anti-hierarchical tendency, these speculations continued to gain ground; and in the end the body of treatises propounding the pantheistic doctrine, the Upanishads, were admitted into the sacred canon, as appendages to the ceremonial writings, the Brāhmaṇas. The Upanishads thus form literally "the end of the Veda," the *Vedānta*; but their adherents claim this title for their doctrines in a metaphorical rather than in a material sense, as "the ultimate aim and consummation of the Veda."

In later times the radical distinction between these speculative appendages and the bulk of the Vedic writings was strongly accentuated in a new classification of the sacred scriptures. According to this scheme they were supposed to consist of two great divisions—the *Karma-kāṇḍa*, "the work-section," or practical ceremonial (exoteric) part, consisting of the Saṃhitās and Brāhmaṇas (including the ritual portions of the Āraṇyakas), and the *Jñānakāṇḍa*, "the knowledge-section," or speculative (esoteric) part. These two divisions are also called respectively the *Pūrva-* ("former") and *Uttara-* ("latter," or higher) *kāṇḍa*; and when the speculative tenets of the Upanishads came to be formulated into a regular system it was deemed desirable that there should also be a special system corresponding to the older and larger portion of the Vedic writings. Thus arose the two systems—the *Pūrva-* (or *Karma-*) *mīmāṃsā*, or "prior (practical) speculation," and the *Uttara-* (or *Brāhma-*) *mīmāṃsā*, or higher inquiry (into the nature of the godhead), usually called the Vedānta philosophy.

Philosophical Systems.—It is not yet possible to determine, even approximately, the time when the so-called *Darśanas* (literally "demonstrations"), or systems of philosophy which subsequently arose, were first formulated. And, though they have certainly developed from the tenets enunciated in the Upanishads, there is some doubt as to the exact order in which these systems succeeded each other. Of all the systems the Vedānta has indeed remained most closely in touch with the speculations of the Upanishads, which it has further developed and systematized. The authoritative expositions of the systems have, however, apparently passed through several redactions; and, in their present form, these sūtra-works evidently belong to a comparatively recent period, none of them being probably older than the early centuries of our era. By far the ablest general review of the philosophical systems (except the Vedānta) produced by a native scholar is the *Sarva-darśana-saṅgraha* ("summary of all the Darśanas"), composed in the 14th century, from a Vedāntist point of view, by the great exegete Mādhava Āchārya.

Among the different systems, six are generally recognized as orthodox, as being (either wholly or for the most part) consistent with the Vedic religion—two and two of which are again more closely related to each other than to the rest, viz.:

(1) *Pūrva-mīmāṃsā* (*Mīmāṃsā*), and (2) *Uttara-mīmāṃsā* (*Vedānta*);

(3) *Sānkhya*, and (4) *Yoga*;

(5) *Nyāya*, and (6) *Vaiśeshika*.

Mīmāṃsā.—1. The (*Pūrva-*) *Mīmāṃsā* (First Inquiry) is not a system of philosophy in the proper sense of the word, but rather a system of dogmatic criticism and scriptural interpretation. It maintains the eternal existence of the Veda, the different parts of which are minutely classified. Its principal object, however, is to ascertain the religious (chiefly ceremonial) duties enjoined in the Veda, and to show how these duties must be performed, and what are the special merits and rewards attaching to them. Hence arises the necessity of determining the principles for rightly interpreting the Vedic texts, as also of what forms its only claim to being classed among speculative systems, namely, a philosophical examination of the means of, and the proper method for, arriving at accurate knowledge. The foundation of this school, as well as the composition of the Sūtras or aphorisms, the *Mīmāṃsā-darśana*, which constitute its chief doctrinal authority, is ascribed to Jaimini. The Sūtras were commented on by Śabara Svāmin in his *Bhāshya;* and further annotations (*Tantra-vārttika* and *Śloka-vārttika*) thereon were supplied by the great theologian Kumārila Bhaṭṭa (about A.D. 700). The most approved general introduction to the study of the Mīmāṃsā is the metrical *Jaiminīya-Nyāya mālāvistara*, with a prose commentary, both by Mādhava Āchārya.

Vedānta.—2. The *Vedānta* philosophy or *Uttara-mīmāṃsā* (Second Inquiry) in the comparatively primitive form in which it presents itself in most of the older Upanishads, constitutes the earliest phase of sustained metaphysical speculation. In its essential features it remains to this day the prevalent belief of Indian thinkers, and enters largely into the religious life and convictions of the people. It is an idealistic monism, which derives the universe from an ultimate conscious spiritual principle, the one and only existent from eternity—the *Ātman*, the Self, or the *Purusha*, the Person, the *Brahman*. It is this primordial essence or Self that pervades all things, and gives life and light to them, "without being sullied by the visible outward impurities or the miseries of the world, being itself apart"—and into which all things will, through knowledge, ultimately resolve themselves. "The wise who perceive him as being within their own Self, to them belongs eternal peace, not to others." But, while the commentators never hesitate to interpret the Upanishads as being in perfect agreement with the Vedāntic system, as elaborated in later times, there is often considerable difficulty in accepting their explanations. In these treatises only the leading features of the pantheistic theory find utterance, generally in vague and mystic, though often in singularly powerful and poetical language, from which it is not always possible to extract the author's real idea on fundamental points, such as the relation between the Supreme Spirit and the phenomenal world—whether the latter was actually evolved from the former by a power inherent in him, or whether the process is altogether a fiction, an illusion of the individual self.

The foundation of the Vedānta system, as "the completion of the Veda," is naturally ascribed to Vyāsa, the mythic arranger of the Vedas, who is said to be identical with Bādarāyaṇa the reputed author of the *Brahmā-* (or *Śārīraka-*) *sūtra*, the authoritative, though highly obscure, summary of the system. The most distinguished interpreter of these aphorisms is the famous Malabar theologian Śankara Āchārya, who also commented on the principal Upanishads and the Bhagavadgītā, and is said to have spent the greater part of his life in wandering all over India, as far as Kashmir, and engaging in disputations with teachers—whether of the Śaiva, or Vaishnava, or less orthodox persuasions—with the view of rooting out heresy and re-establishing the doctrine of the Upanishads. In Śankara's philosophy the theory that the material world has no real existence, but is a mere illusion of the individual soul wrapt in ignorance,—that, therefore, it has only a practical or conventional (*vyāvahārika*) but not a transcendental or true (*pāramārthika*) reality,—is strictly enforced. In accordance with this distinction, a higher (*parā*) and a lower (*aparā*) form of knowledge is recognized; the former being concerned with the Brahman (n.), whilst the latter deals with the personal Brahmā, the Īśvara, or lord and creator, who, however, is a mere illusory form of the divine spirit, resulting from ignorance of the human soul. To the question why the Supreme Self (or rather his fictitious development, the Highest Lord) should have sent forth this phantasmagory this great thinker (with the author of the Sūtras) can return no better answer than that it must have been done for sport (*līlā*), without any special motive—since to ascribe such a motive to the

Supreme Lord would be limiting his self-sufficiency—and that the process of creation has been going on from all eternity. Śankara's *Śārīraka-mīmāṃsā-bhāshya* has given rise to a large number of exegetic treatises, of which Vāchaspati-miśra's exposition, entitled *Bhāmatī*, is the most esteemed. Of numerous other commentaries on the Brahma-sūtras, the *Śrī-bhāshya*, by Rāmānuja, the founder of the Śrī-Vaishnava sect, is the most noteworthy. This religious teacher, who flourished in the first half of the 12th century, caused a schism in the Vedānta school. Instead of adhering to Śankara's orthodox *advaita*, or non-duality, doctrine, he interpreted the obscure Sūtras in accordance with his theory of *viśishṭādvaita, i.e.,* non-duality of the (two) distinct (principles), or, as it is more commonly explained, non-duality of that which is qualified (by attributes). According to this theory the Brahman is neither devoid of form and quality, nor is it all things; but it is endowed with all good qualities, and matter is distinct from it; whilst bodies consist of souls (*chit*) and matter (*achit*); and God is the soul. On the religious side, Rāmānuja adopts the tenets of the ancient Vishnuite Pāñcharātra sect, and, identifying the Brahman with Vishnu, combines with his theory the ordinary Vaishnava doctrine of periodical descents (*avatāra*) of the deity, in various forms, for the benefit of creatures; and allowing considerable play to the doctrine that faith (*bhakti*), not knowledge (*vidyā*), is the means of final emancipation. This phase of Indian religious belief, which has attached itself to the Vedānta theory more closely than to any other, makes its appearance very prominently in the *Bhagavadgītā*, the episode of the *Mahābhārata*, already referred to—where, however, it attaches itself to Sānkhya-yoga rather than to Vedānta tenets—and is even more fully developed in some of the Purāṇas, especially the Bhāgavata. Its highest phase of development this doctrine probably reached in the Vaishnava sect founded, towards the end of the 15th century, by Chaitanya, whose followers subsequently grafted the Vedānta speculations on his doctrine. In opposition both to Śankara's theory of absolute unity, and to Rāmānuja's doctrine of qualified unity—though leaning more towards the latter—Mādhva Āchārya, or Pūrṇaprajña (A.D. 1197–1276), started his *dvaita*, or duality doctrine, according to which there is a difference between God and the human soul (*jīva*), as well as between God and nature; whilst the individual souls, which are innumerable, eternal, and indestructible, are likewise different from one another; but, though distinct, are yet united with God, like tree and sap, in an indissoluble union. This doctrine also identifies the Brahman with Vishnu, by the side of whom, likewise infinite, is the goddess Lakshmī, as Prakṛiti (nature), from whom inert matter (*jaḍa*) derives its energy. Here also *bhakti*, devotion to God, is the saving element. A popular summary of the Vedānta doctrine is the *Vedānta-sāra* by Sadānanda, which has been frequently printed and translated.

Sānkhya.—The *Sānkhya* system seems to derive its name from its systematic enumeration (*sankhyā*) of the twenty-five principles (*tattva*) it recognizes—consisting of twenty-four material and an independent immaterial principle. In opposition to the Vedānta school, which maintains the eternal coexistence of a spiritual principle of reality and an unspiritual principle of unreality, the Sānkhya assumes the eternal coexistence of a material first cause, which it calls either *mūla-Prakṛiti* (fem.), "prime Originant" (matter), or *Pradhāna*, "the principal" cause, and a plurality of individual souls, *Purusha*, which continually interact on one another. The system recognizes no intelligent creator (such as the *Īśvara*, or demiurgus, of the Vedānta)—whence it is called *nirīśvara*, godless; but it conceives the Material First Cause, itself unintelligent, to have become developed, by a gradual process of evolution, into all the actual forms of the phenomenal universe, excepting the souls. Its first emanation is *buddhi*, intelligence; whence springs *ahamkāra*, consciousness; thence the subtle elements of material forms, namely, five elementary particles (*tanmātra*) and eleven organs of sense; and finally, from the elementary particles, five elements. The souls have from all eternity been connected with matter,—having in the first place become invested with a subtle frame (*linga-*, or *sūkshma-, śarīra*), consisting of seventeen principles, namely, intelligence, consciousness, elementary particles, and organs of sense and action, including mind. To account for the spontaneous development of matter, the system assumes the latter to consist of three constituents (*guṇa*) which are possessed of different qualities, viz. *sattva*, of pleasing qualities, such as "goodness," lightness, luminosity; *rajas*, of pain-giving qualities, such as "force," passion, activity; and *tamas*, of deadening qualities, such as "darkness," rigidity, dullness, and which, if not in a state of equipoise, cause unrest and development. Through all this course of development, the soul itself remains perfectly detached, its sole properties being those of purity and intelligence, and the functions usually regarded as "psychic" being due to the mechanical processes of the internal organs themselves evolved out of inanimate matter. Invested with its subtle frame, which accompanies it through the cycle of transmigration, the soul, for the sake of fruition, connects itself ever anew with matter, thus, as it were, creating for itself ever new forms of material existence; and it is only on attaining perfect knowledge, which reveals the absolute distinction between soul and matter, that the Purusha is liberated from the miseries of Saṃsāra, and continues to exist in a state of absolute consciousness and detachment from matter. The existence of God, on the other hand, is denied by this theory, or rather considered as incapable of proof; the existence of evil and misery, for one thing, being thought incompatible with the notion of a divine creator and ruler of the world.

The reputed originator of this school is the sage Kapila, to whom tradition ascribes the composition of the fundamental text-book, the *Sānkhya-sūtra*, or *Sānkhya-pravachana*, as well as the *Tattva-samāsa*, a mere catalogue of the principles but these are comparatively modern. Probably the oldest existing work is Īśvarakrishṇa's excellent *Sānkhya-kārikā*, which gives, in the narrow compass of sixty-nine ślokas, a lucid and complete sketch of the system.

Yoga.—The *Yoga* system is a branch of the preceding school, holding the same opinions on most points treated in common in their Sūtras, with the exception of one important point, the existence of God. To the twenty-five principles (*tattva*) of the Nirīśvara Sānkhya, the last of which was the *Purusha*, the Yoga adds, as the twenty-sixth, the *Nirguṇa Purusha*, or Self devoid of qualities, the Supreme God of the system. Hence the Yoga is called the *Seśvara* (theistical) *Sānkhya*. But over and above the purely speculative part of its doctrine, which it has adopted from the sister school, the theistic Sānkhya has developed a complete system of mortification of the senses—by means of prolonged apathy and abstraction, protracted rigidity of posture, and similar practices—many of which are already alluded to in the Upanishads—with the view of attaining complete concentration (*yoga*) on, and an ecstatic vision of, the Deity, and the acquisition of miraculous powers. It is from this portion of the system that the school derives the name by which it is more generally known.

Nyāya and Vaiśeshika.—The *Nyāya* and *Vaiśeshika* (the latter the older) are separate branches of one and the same school, which supplement each other and the doctrines of which have virtually become amalgamated into a single system of philosophy. The term Nyāya (*ni-āya*, "in-going," entering), though properly meaning "analytical investigation," as applied to philosophical inquiry generally, has come to be taken more commonly in the narrower sense of "logic," because this school has entered more thoroughly than any other into the laws and processes of thought, and has worked out a formal system of reasoning which forms the Hindu standard of logic.

The followers of these schools generally recognize six categories (*padārtha*): substance (*dravya*), quality (*guṇa*), action (*karma*), generality (*sāmānya*), particularity (*viśesha*), intimate relation (*samavāya*) to which was added a seventh, non-existence (*abhāva*). Substances forming the substrata of qualities and actions are of two kinds: eternal (without a cause), namely, space, time, ether, soul and the atoms of mind, earth, water, fire and air; and non-eternal, comprising all compounds, or the things we perceive, and which must have a cause of their existence.

Causality is of three kinds: that of intimate relation (material cause); that of non-intimate relation (between parts of a compound); and instrumental causality (effecting the union of component parts). Material things are thus composed of atoms (*aṇu*), *i.e.*, ultimate simple substances, or units of space, eternal, unchangeable and without dimension, characterized only by "particularity (*viśesha*)." It is from this predication of ultimate "particulars" that the Vaiśeshikas, the originators of the atomistic doctrine, derive their name. The Nyāya draws a clear line between matter and spirit, and has worked out a careful and ingenious system of psychology. It distinguishes between individual or living souls (*jīvātman*), which are numerous, infinite and eternal, and the Supreme Soul (*Paramātman*), which is one only, the seat of eternal knowledge, and the maker and ruler (*Īśvara*) of all things. It is by his will and agency that the unconscious living souls (soul-atoms, in fact) enter into union with the (material) atoms of mind, etc., and thus partake of the pleasures and sufferings of mundane existence.

The original collection of *Nyāya-sūtras* is ascribed to Gautama, and that of the *Vaiśeshika-sūtras* to Kaṇāda. The etymological meaning of the latter name seems to be "atom eater," whence in works of hostile critics the synonymous terms *Kaṇa-bhuj* or *Kaṇa-bhaksha* are sometimes derisively applied to him, doubtless in allusion to his theory of atoms.

Heretical Systems.—As regards the different heretical systems of Hindu philosophy, there is no occasion, in a sketch of Sanskrit literature, to enter into the tenets of the two great anti-Brāhmanical sects, the Jainas and Buddhists. Among the minor systems may be mentioned the following:

The *Chārvākas* are an ancient sect of undisguised materialists, who deny the existence of the soul, and consider the human person (*purusha*) to be an organic body endowed with sensibility and with thought, resulting from a modification of the component material elements, but their authoritative text-book, the *Bārhaspatya-sūtra*, is only known so far from a few quotations in polemics against the school. The sect was anti-Brāhmanical and such moral teaching as it taught was pure hedonism.

The *Pāñcharātras*, or *Bhāgavatas*, are an early Vaishnava sect, in which the doctrine of faith, already alluded to, is strongly developed. Hence their tenets are defended by Rāmānuja, though they are partly condemned as heretical in the Brahma-sūtras.

The *Pāśupatas*, one of several Śaiva (Māheśvara) sects, hold the Supreme Being (*Īśvara*), whom they identify with Śiva (as *paśu-pati*, or "lord of beasts"), to be the creator and ruler of the world, but not its material cause. With the Sānkhyas they admit the notion of a plastic material cause, the *Pradhāna*; while they follow Patañjali in maintaining the existence of a Supreme God.

Grammar (Vyākaraṇa).—*Pāṇini.* Linguistic inquiry, phonetic as well as grammatical, was early resorted to both for the purpose of elucidating the meaning of the Veda and with the view of settling its textual form. The particular work which came ultimately to be looked upon as the "vedānga" representative of grammatical science, and has ever since remained the standard authority on Sanskrit grammar in India, is Pāṇini's *Ashṭādhyāyī*, so called from its "consisting of eight lectures (*adhyāya*)," of four *pādas* each. For a comprehensive grasp of linguistic facts, and a penetrating insight into the structure of the vernacular language, this work stands probably unrivalled in the literature of any nation—though few other languages, it is true, afford such facilities as the Sanskrit for a scientific analysis. Pāṇini's system of arrangement differs entirely from that usually adopted in our grammars, namely, according to the parts of speech. As the work is composed in aphorisms intended to be learnt by heart, economy of memory-matter was the author's paramount consideration. His object was chiefly attained by the grouping together of all cases exhibiting the same phonetic or formative feature, no matter whether or not they belonged to the same part of speech. For this purpose he also makes use of a highly artificial and ingenious system of algebraic symbols, consisting of technical letters (*anubandha*), used chiefly with suffixes and indicative of the changes which the roots or stems have to undergo in word-formation. The date of

Pāṇini has been the subject of much discussion but may be safely put at about 400 B.C.

Pāṇini mentions some sixty-four predecessors which shows that this study had undergone a long process of development. Perhaps the most important of his predecessors was Sākaṭāyana, also mentioned by Yāska—the author of the Nirukta, who is likewise supposed to have preceded Pāṇini—as the only grammarian (vaiyākaraṇa) who held with the etymologists (nairukta) that all nouns are derived from verbal roots.

Pāṇini's Sūtras continued for ages after to form the centre of grammatical activity. But, as his own work had superseded those of his predecessors, so many of the scholars who devoted themselves to the task of perfecting his system have sunk into oblivion.

Kātyāyana.—The earliest of his successors whose work has come down to us (though perhaps not in a separate form) is Kātyāyana, the author of a large collection of concise critical notes, called *Vārttika,* intended to supplement and correct the Sūtras, or give them greater precision.

Patañjali.—Kātyāyana was followed by Patañjali, the author of the (Vyākaraṇa-) *Mahā-bhāshya,* or Great Commentary, who flourished about 150 B.C. For the great variety of information it incidentally supplies regarding the literature and manners of the period, this is, from an historical and antiquarian point of view, one of the most important works of the classical Sanskrit literature. The Mahābhāshya is not a continuous commentary on Pāṇini's grammar, but a collection of the critical comments or *kārikās* on 1,713 of the 4,000 rules of Pāṇini. Patañjali is also called Gonardīya perhaps meaning "a native of Gonarda," a place, probably identical with Goṇḍa, a town some 20 m. northwest of Oudh—and Goṇikāputra, or son of Goṇika.

Lexicography.—Sanskrit dictionaries (*kośa*), invariably composed in verse, are either homonymous or synonymous, or partly the one and partly the other. There are occasional attempts at alphabetical order in the former but not in the latter. There are many intended for the use of poets and are collections of rare words and synonyms, rather than lexicons of the language. The great dictionary is the famous *Amara-kośa* ("immortal treasury") by Amarasiṃha, who probably lived early in the 6th century. This dictionary consists of a synonymous and a short homonymous part; whilst in the former the words are distributed in sections according to subjects, such as heaven and the gods, time and seasons, etc.; in the latter they are arranged according to their final letter, without regard to the number of syllables.

Prosody (Chhandas).—The oldest treatises on prosody have already been referred to in the account of the technical branches of the later Vedic literature. Among more modern treatises the most important is the *Mrita-sanjīvanī,* a commentary on Piṅgala's Sūtra, by Halāyudha (perhaps identical with the author of the glossary above referred to). Sanskrit prosody, which is probably not surpassed by any other either in variety of metre or in harmoniousness of rhythm, recognizes two classes of metres, namely, such as consist of a certain number of syllables of fixed quantity, and such as are regulated by groups of breves or metrical instants, this latter class being again of two kinds, according as it is or is not bound by a fixed order of feet.

Music (Saṅgīta).—The musical art has been practised in India from early times. The theoretic treatises on profane music now extant are, however, quite modern productions. The two most highly esteemed works are the *Saṅgīta-ratnākara* ("jewel-mine of music"), by Śārngadeva, and the *Saṅgīta-darpaṇa* ("mirror of music"), by Dāmodara. Each of these works consists of seven chapters, treating respectively of—(1) sound and musical notes (*svara*); (2) melodies (*rāga*); (3) music in connection with the human voice (*prakīrṇaka*); (4) musical compositions (*prabandha*); (5) time and measure (*tāla*); (6) musical instruments and instrumental music (*vādya*); (7) dancing and acting (*nṛtta* or *nṛtya*).

Rhetoric (Alaṅkāra-śāstra).—Treatises on the theory of literary composition are very numerous. Indeed, a subject of this description—involving such nice distinctions as regards the various kinds of poetic composition, the particular subjects and

characters adapted for them, and the different sentiments or mental conditions capable of being both depicted and called forth by them—could not but be congenial to the Indian mind. The *Nātya Śāstra* of Bharata is possibly as early as the sixth century. Not much later is the *Kāvyādarśa,* or "mirror of poetry," by Daṇḍin, the author of the novel *Daśakumāracharita.* The work consists of three chapters, treating—(1) of two different local styles (*rīti*) of poetry, the Gauḍī or eastern and the Vaidarbhī or southern (to which later critics add four others, the Pāñchālī, Māgadhī, Lāṭī, and Āvantikā); (2) of the graces and ornaments of style, as tropes, figures, similes; (3) of alliteration, literary puzzles and twelve kinds of faults to be avoided in composing poems. Other important works are the *Kāvyālaṅkāra,* by the Kashmirian Rudraṭa (9th century), the *Daśarūpa,* or "ten kinds of drama," by Dhanaṃjaya (10th century), the *Sarasvatī-kaṇṭhābharaṇa,* "the neck-ornament of Sarasvatī (the goddess of eloquence)," a treatise, in five chapters, on poetics generally (11th century), the *Kāvya-prakāśa,* "the lustre of poetry," (12th century) by Mammaṭa, a Kashmirian, and the late but important *Sāhitya-darpaṇa* (c. A.D. 1450).

Medicine (Āyur-veda, Vaidya-śāstra).—Though the early cultivation of the healing art is amply attested by frequent allusions in the Vedic writings, it was doubtless not till a much later period that the medical practice advanced beyond a certain degree of empirical skill and pharmaceutic routine. From the simultaneous mention of the three humours (wind, bile, phlegm) in a *vārttika* to Pāṇini (v. 1, 38), some kind of humoral pathology would, however, seem to have been prevalent among Indian physicians several centuries before our era. The oldest existing work is supposed to be the *Charaka-saṃhitā,* a bulky cyclopaedia in ślokas, mixed with prose sections, which consists of eight chapters, and was probably composed for the most part in the early centuries of our era. Whether the Chinese tradition which makes Charaka the court physician of King Kanishka (c. A.D. 100) rests on fact is uncertain. Of equal authority, but doubtless somewhat more modern, is the *Suśruta* (-*saṃhitā*), which Suśruta is said to have received from Dhanvantari, the Indian Aesculapius, whose name, however, appears also among the "nine gems." It consists of six chapters, and is likewise composed in mixed verse and prose—the greater simplicity of arrangement, as well as some slight attention paid in it to surgery, betokening an advance upon Charaka. Both works are, however, characterized by great prolixity, and contain much matter which has little connection with medicine.

Astronomy and Mathematics.—Early Indian astronomical knowledge is summed up in the *Jyotisha Vedānga* (ed. Weber, 1862). A more scientific era is marked by the appearance of the five original Siddhāntas (partly extant in revised redactions and in quotations), the very names of two of which suggest Western influence, namely, the *Paitāmaha-, Sūrya-, Vasishtha-, Romaka-* (i.e., Roman) and *Pauliśa-siddhāntas.* Based on these are the works of the most distinguished Indian astronomers, namely, Āryabhaṭa, probably born in 476; Varāha-mihira, probably 505–587; Brahmagupta, who completed his *Brahma-sphuta-siddhānta* in 628; Bhaṭṭa Utpala (10th century), distinguished especially as commentator of Varāha-mihira; and Bhāscara Āchārya, who, born in 1114, finished his great course of astronomy, the *Siddhānta-śiromaṇi,* in 1150.

In the works of several of these writers, from Āryabhaṭa onwards, special attention is paid to mathematical (especially arithmetical and algebraic) computations. The question whether Āryabhaṭa was acquainted with the researches of the Greek algebraist Diophantus (c. A.D. 360) remains still unsettled, but, even if this was the case, algebraic science seems to have been carried by him beyond the point attained by the Greeks.

BIBLIOGRAPHY.—Lassen, *Indische Altertumskunde,* 4 vols. (1842); A. A. Macdonell, *India's Past* (1927); L. D. Barnett, *Antiquities of India* (1913); J. G. Bühler (ed.), *Grundriss d. Indo-Arischen Philologie* 1896 ff.; J. Muir, *Original Sanskrit Texts,* 5 vols. (1889); F. Max Müller, *Ancient Sanskrit Literature;* L. von Schroeder, *India's Literature and Culture* (1888); A. A. Macdonell, *Sanskrit Literature* (1909); A. B. Keith, *Classical Sanskrit Literature* (1927), *History of Sanskrit Literature* (1928); M. Winternitz, *Geschichte d. Indischen Litteratur* (1905–20); A. Kaegi, *Rig-Veda* (1886); A. A. Macdonell and A. B. Keith, *Vedic Index,* 2 vols. (1912); R. H. T. Griffith, *Translation of the Rig-Veda,* 2 vols. (1896–97); A. B. Keith, *Religion and Philosophy of the Veda,* 2 vols. (1925); H. Oldenberg, *Die Religion des Vedas* (1896); P. Deussen, *Philosophie des Vedas* (1896), *Die Philosophie der Upanishads* (1899, Eng. trans. 1906), *Sechzig Upanishads* (1897); A. Holtzmann, *Das Mahābhārata,* 4 vols. (1892–95); Translations of the Mahābhārata by P. C. Roy (1883–94) and by M. N. Dutt (5 vols.

1896); W. Hopkins, *The Great Epic of India* (1902); H. Jacobi, *Das Rāmāyana* (1893); Baumgartner, *Das Rāmāyana* (1896); M. N. Dutt, *Translation of the Rāmāyana* (1896); F. E. Pargiter, *The Dynasties of the Kali Age* (1913); J. G. Bühler, *Die indischen Inschriften und das Alter der indischen Kunstpoesie* (1890); A. Hillebrandt, *Kālidāsa* (1912); H. H. Wilson, *Specimens of the Theatre of the Hindus*, 2 vols. (1871); Sylvain Lévi, *Le Théâtre Indien* (1890); A. B. Keith, *The Sanskrit Drama* (1926); J. Hertel, *Das Panchatantra* (1912); F. Max Müller, *Six Systems of Indian Philosophy* (1889); A. Garbe, *Philosophy of Ancient India* (1897), *Sānkhya Philosophie* (1894); P. Deussen, *System des Vedanta* (1893); Lanman, *W. D. Whitney's Atharva veda Samhita*, 2 vols. (1905); R. E. Hume, *The Thirteen Principal Upanishads* (1934); F. Edgerton, *The Panchatantra Reconstructed*, 2 vols. (1924); H. Oldenberg, *The Grihya-Sutras*, vols. 29 and 30 of the *Sacred Books of the East* edited by Max Müller (1886); M. Bloomfield, *Hymns of the Atharvaveda* (1897) vol. 42 of *Sacred Books of the East*; W. Caland, *Altindisches Zauber Ritual* (1900); W. Caland, *Das Vaitānasutra des Atharvaveda* (1910).

(H. J. E.; J. Al.)

SANSON, CHARLES HENRI

(b. 1739), public executioner of Paris from 1788 to 1795, was great-grandson of Charles Sanson, who had received in 1688 the office of *exécuteur des hautes oeuvres de Paris*, which became hereditary in his family. Sanson's brothers exercised the same trade in other towns. In the last days of 1789 Gorsas in the *Courrier de Paris* accused Sanson of harbouring a Royalist press in his house. Sanson was brought to trial, but acquitted, and Gorsas withdrew the accusation. After the execution of Louis XVI., a statement by Sanson was inserted in the *Thermomètre politique* (13th February 1793) in contradiction of the false statements made in respect of the king's behaviour when confronted with death. He surrendered his office in 1795 to his son Henri, who had been his deputy for some time, and held his father's office till his death in 1840. There is no record of the elder Sanson's death. Henri's son Clément Henri was the last of the family to hold the office.

The romantic tales told of C. H. Sanson have their origin in the apocryphal *Mémoires pour servir à l'histoire de la Révolution Française par Sanson* (2 vols., 1829). Other *Mémoires of Sanson*, edited by A. Grégoire (ps. for V. Lombard) in 1830, and by M. d'Olbreuze (6 vols., 1862–63) are equally fictitious. The few facts definitely ascertainable are collected by G. Lenôtre in *La Guillotine pendant la Révolution* (1893).

SANSOVINO, ANDREA CONTUCCI DEL MONTE

(1460–1529), Florentine sculptor and architect, was the son of a shepherd, Niccolo di Domenico Contucci, and was born at Monte Sansovino near Arezzo, whence he took his name. He was a pupil of Antonio Pollaiuolo, and at first worked in the style of 15th-century Florence. Early works are: the terra-cotta altarpiece in Santa Chiara at Monte Sansovino, and the marble reliefs of the "Annunciation," the "Coronation of the Virgin," a "Pietà," the "Last Supper," and various statuettes in the Corbinelli chapel of S. Spirito at Florence. In 1490 he was invited to Portugal by King John II. and some pieces of sculpture by him still exist in the monastic church of Coimbra. These early reliefs show strongly the influence of Donatello. The beginning of a more pagan style is shown in the statues of "St. John baptizing Christ" over the east door of the Florentine baptistery. This group was, however, finished by the weaker hand of Vincenzo Danti. In 1502 he executed the marble font at Volterra, with good reliefs of the "Four Virtues" and the "Baptism of Christ." The statues of the Virgin and John the Baptist in the cathedral of Genoa were completed in 1503. His earliest work in Rome is probably the monument of Pietro da Vicenza (1504), in the church of Ara Coeli. The monuments of Cardinal Ascanio Maria Sforza and of the bishop Hieronimus Bassus for the church of S. Maria del Popolo are among his most important works. In 1512, Sansovino executed a group of the "Madonna and Child with St. Anne," now over one of the side altars in the church of S. Agostino. From 1513 to 1528 he was at Loreto, where he cased the outside of the Santa Casa in white marble, covered with reliefs and statuettes in niches between engaged columns; the greater part of his sculpture was executed by his assistants, and though the general effect is rich and magnificent, the individual pieces are both dull and feeble, the greater part of the work being executed by his assistants. The earlier reliefs, executed by Sansovino himself, are interesting. Jacopo Sansovino was his best pupil.

SANSOVINO, JACOPO

(1486–1570), Italian sculptor and architect, was born at Caprese near Florence, his family name being Tatti. He became a pupil of Andrea Sansovino, from whom he received his name. In 1503 he accompanied Giuliano di Sangallo to Rome, devoting himself there to the study of the antique. Julius II. employed him to restore damaged statues, and he made a copy of the Laocoön group, which was afterwards cast in bronze. In 1511 he returned to Florence, and began the statue of St. James the Elder, which is now in a niche in one of the great piers of the Duomo. He carved a nude figure of "Bacchus and Pan," now in the Bargello. Soon afterwards Jacopo returned to Rome, and designed for his fellow-citizens the church of S. Giovanni dei Fiorentini, carried out by Antonio Sangallo the younger. A marble group of the "Madonna and Child," now in S. Agostino, was his next important work. In 1527 Jacopo fled from the sack of Rome to Venice, where he remained the rest of his life. He had charge of the public buildings adjacent to the Piazza di S. Marco, with the exception of the Doge's Palace. His most important works of sculpture at Venice are the colossal statues of "Neptune" and "Mars" on the grand staircase of the ducal palace; the bronze doors of the sacristy of St. Mark, cast in 1556 and the series of six bronze reliefs round the choir of the same church. In 1565 he completed a small bronze gate with a graceful relief of "Christ surrounded by Angels"; this gate shuts off the altar of the Reserved Host in the choir of St. Mark's. He made the monument of the Doge Francesco Venier, who died in 1556.

Jacopo's chief claim to distinction rests upon the numerous fine Venetian buildings which he designed, such as the public library, the mint and the Palazzo Corner della Cà Grande and the Palazzo Manin on the grand canal; also the graceful Loggetta of the Campanile di San Marco with the bronze statues of Peace, Mercury, Apollo and Pallas. Among his ecclesiastical works the chief were the choir of S. Fantino, the church of S. Martino and the façades of S. Maria Mater Domini and of the Scuola di S. Giorgio dei Schiavoni.

In 1545 the roof of the public library, which he was then constructing, fell in; on this account he was imprisoned and fined. However, he was soon set at liberty, and in 1548 he was restored to his post. He died on Nov. 27, 1570. Sansovino's architectural works have much beauty of proportion and grace of ornament, a little marred in some cases by an excess of sculptured decoration, though the carving itself is always beautiful, both in design and execution. He used the classic orders with great freedom and tasteful invention, and was instrumental in introducing the High Renaissance into Venice. He was much assisted by Alessandro Vittoria (1524–1608).

See Vasari, *Vite* (ed. Milanesi); T. Temanza, *Vita di J. Sansovino* (Venice, 1752); L. Pittoni, *J. Sansovino* (Venice, 1909).

SAN STEFANO, TREATY OF,

a treaty signed between Russia and Turkey on March 3, 1878, concluding the Russo-Turkish War. It created a very great vassal principality of Bulgaria, enlarged Serbia, and increased Montenegro to three times its size. The independence of all three States was recognized by the Porte. Russia obtained the Dobrudja, Ardahan, Kars, Bayazid and Batum, and the demolition of all the Danube fortresses. Improved conditions were promised the Armenian Christians; the autonomy of Bosnia-Hercegovina was to be admitted. But the treaty was viewed with concern by other countries.

In effect this treaty would have disintegrated the Turkish empire. The additional power falling to Russia directly and indirectly would have been tremendous. In the Balkans themselves there were protests from the Armenians and Greeks who, especially, would be sufferers in the rearrangement of territories, and from all the inhabitants of the different ceded provinces. Great Britain was especially opposed to the treaty because of the almost certainty that the Big Bulgaria would prove to be entirely under Russian influence. Austria also saw her Balkan interests threatened, and it was Austria who first demanded that the whole matter should be discussed by a European congress. The consequence was the meeting of the Congress of Berlin (*q.v.*), June 13–July 13, 1878, which entirely redrafted the Treaty of San

Stefano. (*See* also Eastern Question.)

SANTA ANA, the capital of the department of Santa Ana, El Salvador, 50 mi. by rail N.W. of San Salvador. Population (1950), 51,676. It is situated about 2,100 ft. above sea level, in a valley surrounded by high mountains, which are covered by coffee and sugar plantations and woods.

Cigars, pottery, starch, spirits, sugar and various textiles are manufactured, and the export trade in coffee and sugar has developed rapidly since the opening in 1900 of a railway to San Salvador and the Pacific port of Acajutla.

SANTA ANA, a city of southern California, U.S., 35 mi. S.E. of Los Angeles and 10 mi. from the ocean on the west and the Santa Ana mountains on the east; the county seat of Orange county. It is served by the Pacific Electric, the Santa Fe and the Southern Pacific railways, and by motor-coach lines. Pop. (1950) 45,534; (1940) 31,921, by federal census. It is the commercial centre of the rich Santa Ana valley (producing especially oranges, avocados, dairy products and beans) and the neighbouring oil fields; and has numerous factories making a variety of products, including aircraft parts, glass, beet sugar, farm machinery, woollen goods, tiles, pumps, perfumes, preserved fruits, tools and citrus products. There are many fruit-packing plants and canneries in and about the city. Santa Ana was platted in 1869 and incorporated in 1888. In 1900 the population was 4,933, and it increased more than ninefold in the next 50 years.

SANTA ANNA, ANTONIO LOPEZ DE (1795–1876), Mexican revolutionist, dictator, president and soldier, was born in Jalapa, Vera Cruz, on Feb. 21, 1795. Entering the Spanish colonial army as cadet in 1810, he served against the revolutionists in Tamaulipas, Tex., and Vera Cruz until March 29, 1821, when he declared in favour of the *Plan de Iguala*. This revolution resulted in Mexican independence and the empire of A. de Itúrbide. Santa Anna advanced rapidly under the empire until Itúrbide attempted to remove him from Vera Cruz. He pronounced opportunely for a republic and the subsequent revolution led to the downfall of Itúrbide. Santa Anna was sent to San Luis Potosí, where he failed in another attempt at revolution, was recalled, and next sent to Yucatán, where he spent about a year as governor and military commander, returning to Mexico in 1825 and in 1827 to civil and military command in Vera Cruz. He subverted the election of 1828 by a revolution in favour of V. Guerrero, who became president. He defeated an ill-advised attempt of the Spaniards to recapture Mexico in 1829 and, resigning his commands, retired to his hacienda, Manga de Clavo, where, except for a futile effort to sustain Guerrero, he was quiescent until 1832, when he headed a revolution which made M. G. Pedraza president. In 1833 Santa Anna became president, an office that, alternating with various substitutes, he occupied until his defeat and capture by the Texans at San Jacinto, April 21, 1836. He returned to Mexico in 1837, retiring to his hacienda until called to command forces against the French. He lost a leg in action against them at Vera Cruz. Santa Anna was president ad interim for a few weeks in 1839 and in 1841 again seized the office by revolution. He was captured by the counterrevolutionists in 1845 and was exiled. He retired to Havana, Cuba, but returned to Mexico the following year upon the outbreak of war with the U.S. He was offered the presidency but, preferring to lead in the field, commanded the Mexicans in the battles of Angostura and Cerro Gordo and minor engagements. Early in 1847 he also assumed the presidency but, after his final defeats in the siege of Mexico City, retired to exile in Jamaica, from which, in 1850, he moved to New Granada. Recalled by the conservatives, he resumed the presidency for the fifth and last time on April 29, 1853. He became supreme dictator but was again exiled Aug. 11, 1855. He twice attempted to return to Mexico, but was turned back by the French in 1864 and by U.S. naval forces in 1867. As a result of amnesty, he returned to Mexico in 1874 and, poor, broken and blind, died June 20, 1876. Santa Anna was unscrupulous, immoral and of no fixed principles, but he was energetic and of a magnetic personality. He fancied himself a western Napoleon and was the chief contributor to the disturbed condition of Mexico for 30 years. He fostered a tradition of success not entirely justified by facts and in time of national crisis his turbulent countrymen again and again turned to him as the one possible leader.

See Cambas, *Gobernantes de Mejico;* Wharton, *El Presidente.*

SANTA BARBARA, a municipality (with administrative centre and 70 *barrios* or districts) of the province of Iloilo, island of Panay, Republic of the Philippines, on the Jalaur river, a few miles north of Iloilo (the provincial capital), on the Iloilo-Capiz railway. Pop. (1939) 35,406 (a gain of 6,939 since 1918), of whom 17,415 were males and none was white. The chief agricultural products are sugar, maize (corn), palay (rice), cacao, coconuts and tobacco. Cattle raising and textile weaving are also carried on. The vernacular is Panay-Bisayan. Of the inhabitants aged 6 to 19 inclusive, 42.2% were reported in 1939 as attending school, while 57.6% of the population ten years old and over was reported as literate.

SANTA BARBARA, a city of southwestern California, U.S., on the Pacific ocean, 90 mi. above Los Angeles; the county seat of Santa Barbara county. It is on federal highway 101 and is served by the Southern Pacific railway, United Air Lines and motorbus lines. Pop. (1950) 44,764; (1940) 34,958, by federal census. The city lies around a crescent beach, on the southern slope of the Santa Ynez mountains. The beauty of the situation, the ideal climate throughout the year, the luxuriant semitropical vegetation, the historic interest and the picturesque modern architecture combine to make it one of the most delightful resorts of the state. A modified Spanish type of architecture generally prevails. Old Mission Santa Barbara, established by Father Junípero Serra in 1786, is the largest and best preserved of the California missions, and is now the Franciscan headquarters for the Pacific coast. The University of California (Santa Barbara) has a fine location overlooking the ocean. A fiesta, "Old Spanish days," is held in August every year. In the Painted cave, 13 mi. distant, are fine rock paintings generally attributed to prehistoric Indians. This region produces a great variety of fruits, nuts and vegetables, including about half the entire commercial crop of lima beans grown in the United States. There are high-gravity oil fields near by. A Spanish presidio was established there in 1782, four years before the mission. Santa Barbara took part in the revolution of 1829, and in the following sectional struggles inclined to the side of Monterey and the north. It was occupied by the Americans in Aug. 1846; then by the Californians in October; again by the U.S. forces on Nov. 27, 1846. In 1850 it was incorporated as a city. The railroad reached it in 1887. On June 29, 1925, a disastrous earthquake visited it, but the city was rapidly rebuilt.

SANTA CATALINA, an island in the Pacific ocean, one of the Santa Barbara group, about 50 mi. S. of the centre of Los Angeles, Calif., and 30 mi. by steamer from Wilmington (Los Angeles harbour). A part of the state of California and Los Angeles county, it comprises 76 sq.mi. and is 22 mi. long and 8 mi. wide at its greatest width. Spurs and canyons which radiate from the main mountain ridges running the length of the island form numerous picturesque bay openings and coves. Highest point is Mt. Orizaba (2,109 ft.). Santa Catalina attracts several hundred thousand tourists each year. Most famous attraction is the undersea gardens off the southern coast, where luxuriant marine vegetation and many varieties of fish are seen from glass-bottomed boats. Also well known is the Catalina Bird park. The Gulf of Santa Catalina and the San Pedro channel, which separate the island from the mainland, are noted as a game-fishing ground, yielding tuna, marlin and broadbill swordfish, white sea bass, rock bass and yellowtail. The climate is dry and sunny; the temperature averages about 10° warmer than the southern California coastal areas in winter, and 10° cooler in summer.

Santa Catalina was discovered in 1542 by Juan Rodriguez Cabrillo, Portuguese navigator in the service of Spain. Sebastian Vizcaino, also sailing under the flag of Spain, rediscovered the island in 1602 on the eve of the feast of St. Catherine and named it Santa Catalina in honour of the saint. It became part of the Republic of Mexico in 1822, and became part of California with the signing of the Guadalupe-Hidalgo treaty, ending the California-Mexican War in 1848. The principal city is Avalon (pop., 1950, 1,498).

SANTA CATARINA, a maritime state of southern Brazil, bounded north by Paraná, east by the Atlantic, south by Rio Grande do Sul and west by the Argentine territory of Misiones (*q.v.*). It has an area of 36,235 sq.mi. and the population in 1950 was 1,578,159.

The Serra do Mar rises not far from the coast and leaves only a narrow coast zone; the plateau above is much broken with irregular ranges of mountains. The coast region, which is interrupted by swamps and lagoons, is hot, humid and densely forested; the plateau is less densely wooded, temperate, and its fertile plains or open *campos* are devoted in large part to stock raising.

The drainage of the western and southern parts of the state is westward to the Uruguay, the rivers being tributaries of the Uruguay, which forms the southern boundary. A number of prosperous areas settled by Germans—the largest and best known including Blumenau, Dona Francisca, Joinvile, Itajaí, Brusque, Dom Pedro and São Bento—are devoted chiefly to agriculture. There is not so much cultivation on a large scale as in São Paulo and the northern provinces. Coffee is produced to a limited extent, as are also Indian corn, beans, onions, fruit and mandioca. A prominent industry is the gathering and preparation of *mate* or Paraguayan tea (*Ilex paraguayensis*), which is an article of export.

The mineral resources include coal, iron, silver, gold and petroleum; the first alone is mined. A railway, the Dona Teresa Cristina, runs from Laguna, at the mouth of a lagoon of that name on the southern coast, northward to the port of Imbituba, as also westward up the valley of the Rio Tubarão to the coalfields of that name (69 mi.) and southward to Araranguá. Another, a branch of the São Paulo-Rio Grande, runs from São Francisco do Sul inland to União da Vitória on the main line which crosses the western part of this state. Another short line connects Blumenau with Trombudo.

The capital of the state is Florianópolis (*q.v.*), also called Santa Catarina; other towns (the population given being that of the municipal district in 1950) are Blumenau (48,581), Lages (78,300), Laguna (38,966), Joinvile (44,368), Itajaí (51,976), Brusque (32,614), São José (22,899), opposite Florianópolis, Araranguá (38,808), Tubarão (67,643), and São Francisco (20,159), a good port in the northern part of the state.

SANTA CLARA or VILLA-CLARA, the capital of Las Villas province, Cuba, about 185 mi. (by rail) E.S.E. of Havana. Pop. (1943) 53,981. It is situated near the centre of the island, on a plateau, between two small streams, and is served by three railway lines and the Central highway. The streets are straight and wide, and there are many fine buildings. The oldest church is of the latter part of the 18th century. The city is surrounded by fertile plains, which are cultivated in cane or devoted to grazing. Santa Clara was founded in 1689 by a band of families from Remedios.

SANTA CLARA, a town of Santa Clara county, California, U.S., adjoining San Jose on the northwest. It is served by the Southern Pacific railway and by motor coach, air and truck lines. Pop. (1950) 11,702; in 1940, 6,650. It has immense fruit canneries and green-fruit and dried-fruit packing plants and other large and diversified manufacturing industries. It is the seat of the Mission of Santa Clara de Asis, founded by Father Junípero Serra in 1777, and of the University of Santa Clara (Roman Catholic), established in 1851.

SANTA CRUZ, ÁLVARO DE BAZAN, 1ST MARQUIS OF (1526–1588), Spanish admiral, born at Granada on Dec. 12, 1526, of an ancient family. In 1564 he aided in the capture of Velez de Gomera, was appointed in 1568 to command the galleys of Naples and was thus brought into close relations with Don John of Austria during the formation of the Holy League (1570). In the operations at Lepanto (Oct. 7, 1571) Bazan was always in favour of the more energetic course: his prompt action averted disaster when the allied line was broken. He accompanied Don John at the taking of Tunis (1572). When Philip II of Spain enforced his claim as heir to the crown of Portugal (1580–81), Santa Cruz held a naval command. In 1583 he was sent against the prior of Crato, an illegitimate representative of the Portuguese royal family, who with his friends held the island possessions of Portugal in the Atlantic. His victory off Terceira decided the struggle in favour of Spain. A zealous advocate of war against England, he made to Philip, on Aug. 9, 1583, the first definite suggestion of the Armada. The King's political and financial embarrassments caused many delays, and Santa Cruz, who was to have commanded, was hindered from acting with effect. He was at Lisbon without the means of fitting out his fleet when Drake burned the Spanish ships at Cadiz (1587). Santa Cruz's independence of judgment finally offended the king and he was held responsible for failures and delays. He died on Feb. 9, 1588, at Lisbon. He was the designer of the great galleons which were employed to carry the trade between Cadiz and Vera Cruz in Mexico.

See C. Fernández Duro, *La Armada Invencible,* 2 vol. (1884–85); A. Altolaguirre y Duvale, *Don Alvaro de Bazán . . . estudio histórico-biográfico* (1888); W. Stirling Maxwell, *Don John of Austria . . .* 2 vol. (1883).

SANTA CRUZ, an eastern department of Bolivia, bounded north by El Beni, east by Brazil, south by Paraguay and Chuquisaca and west by Chuquisaca and Cochabamba. Area 143,918 sq.mi. Pop. (1947 est.) 393,000. It is only partly explored. It consists of a great plain extending east from the base of the Andes to the frontiers of Brazil and Paraguay, broken by occasional isolated hills, and in the northeast by a detached group of low sierras known collectively as the Chiquitos, which belong to the Brazilian highlands rather than to the Andes. On the western side of the department is an upland zone belonging to the eastern slope of the Andes, and there the Bolivian settlements are chiefly concentrated. The great plains, whose general elevation is about 900 ft. above the sea, are so level that the drainage does not carry off the water in the rainy season, and immense areas are flooded for months at a time. Extensive areas are permanently swampy. There are forests in the north and west, but the larger part of the department consists of open grassy plains, suitable for grazing. There are two river systems, one belonging to the Amazon and the other to the Plata basins. The first includes the Guapay or Río Grande, Piray or Sara, Yapacani and Maracó, upper tributaries of the Mamoré, and the San Miguel, Blanco, Baures and Paragua tributaries of the Guaporé—both draining the western and northern parts of the department. In the extreme east a few streams flow eastward into the Paraguay, the largest of which is the Otuquis; their channels are partly hidden in swamps and lagoons. The climate of the plains is hot; nevertheless, on the Andean slopes the temperature is more agreeable. Products of the western districts are sugar, rum, cacao, rice, cotton, coffee and maize. Rubber and medicinal products are also exported. The Guapay is navigable for small boats in high water, and also the lower courses of the other rivers named.

The principal markets for Santa Cruz products are in the Bolivian cities of the Andes. No railway leads to the capital, Santa Cruz; and the principal means of communication is by air.

The only large town of the department is Santa Cruz (pop., 1946 est., 33,000), on the Piray, a tributary of the Mamoré, 1,450 ft. above sea level. It is situated on a lower terrace of the Andean slope in a highly fertile district, devoted to growing sugar cane and stock raising. It is a dusty, straggling, frontier town with a population consisting chiefly of whites. There are flour mills, sugar mills, distilleries, tanneries and leather manufactories. The original site of Santa Cruz de la Sierra was in the uplands, but it was removed to its present site about 1590, the phrase "de la Sierra" being kept until early in the 20th century.

SANTA CRUZ, a municipality (with administrative centre and 21 *barrios* or districts), capital of the province of Laguna, Luzon, Republic of the Philippines, on the southeast shore of Laguna de Bay, about 35 mi. southeast of Manila, with which it has railway connection. Pop. (1939) 17,649 (a gain of 3,493 since 1918), of whom 8,912 were males and 5 were white. Santa Cruz is a sugar centre and has a number of sugar mills and other manufactures. Other important products are palay (rice) and maize (corn). Tagalog is the vernacular. Of the inhabitants aged 6 to 19 inclusive, 40.4% were reported in 1939 as attending school, while 73% of the population 10 years old and over was reported as literate. The number of parcels of private land declared for taxation in 1938 was 3,936, and the number of owners was 2,974.

(C. S. L.)

SANTA CRUZ, a city of California, U.S., on the northern headland of Monterey bay, 80 mi. S. of San Francisco; the county seat of Santa Cruz county. It is served by the Southern Pacific railway.

The population in 1950 was 21,970; (1940) 16,896; (1930) 14,395, by the federal census.

From a curving beach the city slopes up to the foothills

of the Santa Cruz mountains, in surroundings of great natural beauty. The mountains are covered with one of the noblest redwood forests of the state. Among the Santa Cruz bigtrees, 6 mi. from the heart of the city, are some 65 ft. in circumference and 300 ft. high. The State Redwood park is 23 mi. north. Poultry, bulbs (especially narcissus, freesia and gladiolus), berries, cherries, grapes, other fruits and vegetables, are the principal products of the region. Loganberries were originated there; strawberries are picked nine months of the year; and the strip of land along the coast from Santa Cruz to San Francisco produces most of the artichokes grown in the United States. The city has a considerable fishing industry. Principal industrial products are clothing, canned goods, leather, cement, crates and boxes, lumber, limestone, sand, rock and gravel, furniture, paint, mattresses and water heaters. The city owns the long wharf, which extends out 2,600 ft. into deep water. A Franciscan mission (no longer in existence) was established there in 1791, and the Pueblo of Branciforte (never very important) was founded near by in 1797. In July 1846 the U.S. flag was raised over the town, and in 1876 it was chartered as a city.

SANTA CRUZ DE TENERIFE, a seaport and the capital of Tenerife and of the Canary Islands; in 28° 28′ N. and 16° 15′ W., on the east coast. Pop. (1950) 75,000 (mun., 102,437). Santa Cruz occupies a small plain which is bounded by rugged volcanic rocks, and seamed by watercourses which are dry almost throughout the year.

Scarcely any vegetation, except cactuses and euphorbias, is to be seen in the neighbourhood.

Almost the entire town was rebuilt in the 19th century, when its population more than trebled. There are many good public buildings, including a school of navigation, technical institute, library, natural history museum and hospital. An aqueduct 5 mi. long brings pure water from the mountains of the interior. Dromedaries from the adjacent islands of Lanzarote and Fuerteventura are used to convey merchandise and in agriculture. The town was bombarded by the British fleet under Robert Blake in 1657, and by Horatio Nelson, who lost his arm during the attack, in 1797. Some British flags lost on that occasion hang in one of the churches.

Santa Cruz is an important coaling station and commercial centre. (*See* CANARY ISLANDS.)

SANTA FÉ, a central province of Argentina, bounded north by the Chaco territory, east by Corrientes and Entre Ríos, south by Buenos Aires, and west by Córdoba and Santiago del Estero. Population (1914 census) 502,452, (1947 est.) 1,695,383; area, 51,354 sq.mi. The two largest cities in the province are Santa Fé, the capital, and Rosario, the second largest city in Argentina.

For the most part the province belongs to the great pampa region of Argentina and has no wooded lands in the south except along the river courses. In the north there are extensive forests of commercially valuable woods, interspersed with grassy *campos.* The surface is a level alluvial plain, and the soils are among the most productive in the country. The climate is healthful and moderate, with mean annual temperatures ranging from 63° F. in the south to 68° F. in the north. Rainfall varies from 28 in. to 35 in. per year, and is more abundant in the littoral region than in the interior.

The leading crops are flax, corn, alfalfa and wheat, together with smaller but significant acreages of oats, rye and barley. In the northern part of the province peanuts, tobacco, sugar cane and cotton are grown. Although agriculture provides the principal source of wealth, the livestock industry is developed extensively and the province is often ranked as the second largest producer of cattle in Argentina. In addition to beef and dairy cattle, large numbers of sheep and hogs are raised. The principal industries of the province are based on dairy and forest products; several large companies are engaged in the exploitation of *quebracho,* in addition to which there are several large sugar refineries, flour mills, breweries and distilleries. Rail, highway, water and air communications are highly developed, and the province is surpassed in its economic position within the country only by the province of Buenos Aires.   (R. W. RD.; X.)

SANTA FÉ, a city of Argentina and capital of the province of that name, on the Santa Fé channel of the Paraná near the mouth of the Salado, about 310 mi. N.W. of Buenos Aires. Pop. (1947 est.) 152,000. It is built on a sandy plain a little above the river level. It is regularly laid out and contains a cathedral, bishop's palace, Jesuits' college and church dating from 1660, a university, the cabildo or town hall facing on the principal square and provincial government buildings. It serves as headquarters of the Santa Fé railway. The town is less modern in appearance than Rosario, and has a number of old residences and educational and charitable institutions. It is a port of call for small river steamers and is in ferry communication with Paraná on the opposite bank of the river. Its shipping port for larger steamers was at Colastiné, until 1911, when the modern port of Santa Fé was opened, with large docks capable of accommodating ocean-going vessels. Santa Fé has railway communications with Rosario, Córdoba, Tucumán and the frontier of the Chaco.

Santa Fé was founded by Juan de Garay in 1573.

SANTA FE, capital of New Mexico, U.S., in the northern part of the state, on the Rio Santa Fe; county seat of Santa Fe county and oldest seat of government in the United States. It is on federal highways 64, 84, 85 and 285, is connected by bus with the Santa Fe railway at Lamy (18 mi. S.), and is served by American, United and Trans World air lines. Pop. (1950) 27,998. It lies 7,000 ft. high, at the foot of the Sangre de Cristo range. The climate is dry, sunny and invigorating, with an average annual rainfall of 14.49 in. and an average monthly mean temperature ranging from 28.8° F. in January to 69° F. in July. The original Spanish plaza is still the heart of the city. Located there is the old governor's palace, built in 1610, occupied continuously until 1909 by the Spanish, Indian, Mexican and U.S. governors of New Mexico and now housing the collections of the Historical Society of New Mexico and the exhibits of the Museum of New Mexico and the School of American Research.

The Art gallery of the Museum of New Mexico is an example of the "Santa Fe" architecture (reproducing in a blend the façades of six early New Mexico missions), where members of the Santa Fe and Taos "art colonies" exhibit their work before sending it east. Near the plaza is the chapel of San Miguel (early 17th century), and "the old house" of Indian construction, possibly antedating the Spanish occupation. St. Francis cathedral dates from 1869 and occupies the site of a church built in 1622. In the northeastern part of the city are the ruins of Fort Marcy, built by General Kearny in 1846. A stone in the plaza marks the end of the old Santa Fe Trail. The modern structures are mainly in the distinctive "Santa Fe" type of architecture, developed (largely since 1910, through the efforts of a small group of persons connected with the School of American Research and the State Museum) by combining features from the terraced dwellings of the Pueblo Indians, the crumbling Franciscan missions, and the *haciendas* of Spaniard and Mexican. The Pecos Division of the Santa Fe National Forest lies 5 mi. east of the city. Farther away, at distances ranging from 9 to 75 mi., are the Indian pueblos of Tesuque, San Juan, Santa Clara, San Ildefonso (home of Maria, the pottery maker), and Taos (one of the few remaining pueblos where the Indians still live in terraced houses); Chimayo, a Spanish plaza, where pilgrims come to be healed at the Santuario, and where blankets are woven on looms 100 years old; the Puyé cliff dwellings and those of Rito de los Frijoles; the Pecos River canyon, the hot springs of Ojo Caliente, the petrified forest near Cerrillos, and the turquoise mines near Bonanza.

Santa Fe was the site of prehistoric Indian pueblos, of which few remains above ground were left when the Spaniards came. The Villa Real de la Santa Fe de San Francisco was founded in 1610, during the administration of Don Pedro de Peralta, and the building of the presidio was begun at the same time. By 1630 there was a population of 250 Spaniards, 700 Indians and 50 half-breeds. In 1680, the Pueblo Indians drove out their conquerors (*see* NEW MEXICO) and enjoyed independence until Diego de Vargas quietly secured their submission again in 1692. Minor revolts took place in 1694 and 1696. Since 1712 an annual fiesta has been held in commemoration of the reconquest of 1692. During the 18th century a considerable trade in sheep, wool, pelts and wines developed, chiefly with Chihuahua and the Indians of the plains. Later, Santa Fe became the centre of an extensive commerce with the United States, carried on at first by pack animals, and from 1822 by wagon trains over the old Santa Fe Trail from Independence and Kansas City. In the later years of Spanish rule a number of American citizens were imprisoned in the dungeons of the governor's palace, charged with entering the province for trade and commerce, among whom were Maj. Zebulon M. Pike (1807), Auguste Pierre Chouteau and Joseph de Mun (1817) and David Meriwether (later a governor of New Mexico) in 1819. On Aug. 18, 1846, the city was occupied by an American force under Gen. S. W. Kearny. A few months later the Mexicans assassinated the new governor, Charles Bent, and other Americans, but the revolt was quickly suppressed. In 1847 an English newspaper was established (the first in New Mexico) and in 1848 an English school was opened. At the outbreak of the Civil War the officers at Fort Marcy sympathized with the Southern cause. In 1862 the city was taken by Gen. H. H. Sibley, and for two weeks the flag of the Confederacy floated over the governor's palace. The first railway reached the city in 1880.

SANTAL, an aboriginal tribe of Bihar, which gives its name to the Santal Parganas district (q.v.). In 1941 the Santals numbered 829,025. They are short and dark skinned, with broad noses, thick and everted lips, coarse and occasionally curly (but not woolly) hair, and prominent cheekbones. They are good cultivators and cattle breeders and are also skilful hunters. They have an elaborate tribal structure, with 12 exogamous clans; their villages are well-built and clean, and each has its cadre of village officials and each pargana or group of villages its chiefs, who are assisted or controlled by a council. The Santals' religion is animistic. They practise both fraternal polyandry and sororal polygamy. Santali is a dialect of the Munda language Kherwari.

See C. H. Bompas, *Folklore of the Santal Parganas* (London, 1909); A. Campbell and R. M. McPhail, *A Santali-English Dictionary,* 2 vol. (Pokhuria, 1933).

SANTALACEAE, the sandalwood family, dicotyledonous, semiparasitic shrubs, trees and herbs of tropical and temperate regions. There are 30 genera and about 400 species. *Santalum album* is the true sandalwood (q.v.). The bastard toadflax (*Thesium humifusum*), an herbaceous root parasite with green leaves, native to Great Britain, belongs to this family. To it belong the North American species of *Comandra*, likewise called bastard toadflax and sometimes parasitic, and also the oil nut or buffalo nut (*Pyrularia pubera*), of the Appalachian region.

See R. Pilger, "Santalaceae," Engler and Prantl, *Die Natürlichen Pflanzenfamilien* 16b: 52–97, fig. 27–47. (1935).

SANTAL PARGANAS, a district of the Bhagalpur division of Bihar, Republic of India. Area 5,480 sq.mi. Pop. (1951) 2,322,092. In the east a sharply defined belt of hills stretches for about 100 mi.; west of this a rolling tract of long ridges with intervening depressions covers about 2,500 sq.mi., while there is a narrow strip of alluvial country about 120 mi. long, lying for the most part along the loop line of the Eastern railway running roughly parallel to the Ganges in the north and east of the district. The principal range in the east is that of the Rajmahal hills, which cover about 2,000 sq.mi.; they nowhere exceed 2,000 ft. The alluvial tract has the damp heat and moist soil of the lower Ganges basin, while the undulating and hilly portions are swept by the hot westerly winds of Bihar and are very cool in the winter. Coal is worked in the small Jaintia field. Pakaur is the chief centre of the shellac-making industry.

The early history of British administration is a record of the measures taken to pacify and civilize the Paharias of the Rajmahal hills, who under Mohammedan rule had been turbulent robbers and marauders. The Santals, who numbered 829,025 in 1941 began to migrate there from Chota Nagpur and the adjoining districts in the late 18th century. The oppression of landlords, the exactions of Hindu moneylenders and the consequent loss of land caused a rebellion (the Santal War) in 1855–56. This led to the establishment of a form of administration congenial to the immigrants; and a land settlement was afterward carried out on conditions favourable to the cultivators. The Daman-i-Koh, mean-

ing "the skirts of the hills," a government estate of 1,356 sq.mi., was established as a reserve for them and other aboriginals, such as the Paharias. The district is traversed by both the loop line and the chord line (running parallel to the southwest border) of the Eastern railway. It contains the old Mohammedan city of Rajmahal and the modern commercial mart of Sahibganj (pop. 1941, 20,742), both on the Ganges; and the Hindu place of pilgrimage of Deoghar (Deogarh) (pop. 1941, 19,792). The administrative headquarters are at Dumka, or Naya Dumka (pop., 1941, 10,811).

See W. B. Oldham, *Santal Parganas Manual* (Calcutta, 1898); F. B. Bradley-Birt, *The Story of an Indian Upland* (London, 1905).

SANTA MARIA (DA BOCCA DO MONTE), an inland town of Brazil, in Rio Grande do Sul, 162 mi. by rail west of Margem do Taquarí, the railway terminus for Pôrto Alegre, about 80 mi. by water northwest of that city. The population in 1950 was 45,907 for the city and the *município* 84,274. Santa Maria, which lies 382 ft. above the sea, is the commercial centre of a rich district on the slopes of short mountain ranges, one of which, the Serra do Pinhal, forms the water parting between the eastern and western river systems of the state. The town derives its chief importance as the junction of the railway from Pôrto Alegre and the Brazilian railway from São Paulo to the Uruguay border.

SANTA MARTA, a city and port of Colombia and the capital of the department of Magdalena, on a small bay 40 mi. E.N.E. of the mouth of the Magdalena river. Pop. (1947) 43,950. It is built partly on the beach and partly on the slopes of the Sierra Nevada de Santa Marta toward the southeast. Though small, the harbour is one of the best and safest on the coast, as no river flows into it to fill its anchorage with silt. The city is an episcopal see and has a cathedral. A 176 mi. railway runs southward to Fundación. Ciénaga (on the large lagoon of Ciénaga) connects with steamers running to Barranquilla (50 mi. farther).

Santa Marta was founded by Rodrigo de Bástidas in 1525, and became an important port and centre of trade during the Spanish colonial era. It was also a base of operations in the exploration and conquest of the interior.

SANTA MAURA (LEUCADIA, LEUCAS, LEVKAS) (Λευκάδα, ancient Λευκάς), one of the Ionian Islands (20 mi. N. to S., 5–8 mi. E. to W.; area 169 sq.mi.; population (1951) 37,752), off the coast of Acarnania (Greece), S. of the entrance to the Gulf of Arta. It is a rugged mass of limestone and bituminous shales (partly Tertiary), rising to 2,000 and 3,000 ft. with limited areas of level ground. The grain crop suffices only for a few months' local consumption; but much olive oil is produced. The vineyards (in the west especially) yield red wine (bought mainly by Rouen, Cette, Trieste and Venice); the currant, introduced about 1859, has come to be the principal source of wealth; and cotton, flax, tobacco and valonia are grown. The salt trade, formerly of importance, has suffered from customs regulations. The chief town, Amaxichi (more usually Santa Maura, after the neighbouring fort), is at the northeast end opposite the lagoon. In the southwest is the village of Vasiliki, whence the currant crop is exported.

Cyclopean and polygonal walls at Kaligoni (south of Amaxichi) probably mark the ancient acropolis of Neritus (or Nericus), and the later Corinthian settlement of Leucas. From this point a Roman bridge seems to have crossed to the mainland. Between the town and Fort Santa Maura extends a Turkish aqueduct partly destroyed with the town by the earthquake of 1825. Forts Alexander and Constantine commanding the bridge are relics of the Russian occupation; the other forts are of Turko-Venetian origin. The magnificent cliff, 2,000 ft. high, at Cape Ducato at the S. end of the island, still bears the ruined temple of Apollo Leucatas (hence the modern name). At the annual festival of Apollo a criminal was obliged to plunge from the summit into the sea, where, however, an effort was made to pick him up; and it was by the same leap that Sappho and Artemisia, daughter of Lygdamis, are said to have ended their lives.

A theory has been proposed by Professor Dörpfeld that Leucas is the island described in the *Odyssey* under the name of Ithaca; arguing that the Homeric description of the island and its position, and also the identification of such sites as the palace of

Odysseus, the harbour of Phorcys, the grotto of the Nymphs and the island Asteris, where the suitors lay in wait for Telemachus, suit Leucas better than does the island called Ithaca (*q.v.*).

The strait separating it from the mainland is liable to silt. In 1903, however, a canal was completed 50 ft. broad and 17 ft. deep. The island was occupied by axis troops in 1941.

See Corfu; also P. Goessler, *Leukas-Ithaka* (Stuttgart, 1904); W. Dörpfeld, *Alt-Ithaka*, 2 vols. (Stuttgart, 1927).

SANTA MONICA, a city of Los Angeles county, California, U.S.A., on the Pacific ocean, 16 mi. W. of Los Angeles. It is on federal highways 66 and 101A and is served by the Union Pacific, the Santa Fe and the Southern Pacific railways and by bus lines. Population in 1950 was 71,595 and in 1940 it was 53,500 by the federal census. It is primarily a year-round seaside resort, beautifully situated on the Palisades, facing broad Santa Monica bay, and protected by mountains on the north. The elaborate and varied recreation facilities include a municipal fishing pier. Santa Monica was incorporated in 1886 and chartered as a city in 1907. It has the great Douglas Aircraft plant, Cloverfield airport and numerous beach and aquatic attractions. In 1947 the city adopted a council-manager form of government.

SANTANDER, a maritime province of northern Spain, bounded north by the Bay of Biscay, east by the province of Biscay, south by Burgos and Palencia, and west by Leon and Oviedo. Pop. (1950) 400,088, area 2,108 sq.mi. Santander was part of the Roman province of Cantabria, which, after passing under the empire of the Goths, became the principality of Asturias (*q.v.*). The portion called Asturia de Santa Juliana, or Santillana, was included in the kingdom of Old Castile, and, on the subdivision of the old provinces of Spain in 1833, became the province of Santander. The province is traversed from east to west by the Cantabrian Mountains (*q.v.*), which in the Picos de Europa reach a height of over 8,600 ft., and send off numerous branches to the sea. The province is traversed from north to south by the railway and high road from Santander by Palencia to Madrid; the highest point on the railway (Venta de Pazozal) is 3,229 ft. above the sea. Other railways connect Santander with Bilbao on the east and with Cabezona de la Sal on the west. The province saw some of the heaviest fighting of the civil war of 1936–39; it was occupied by nationalists in 1937.

SANTANDER, the capital of the Spanish province of Santander, seat of a bishop and one of chief seaports of Spain; 316 mi. by rail N. of Madrid, on the Bay of Santander, an inlet of the Bay of Biscay. Pop. (1950) 85,000 (mun., 102,510). It is on the inside of a rocky peninsula, Cabo Mayor, which shelters a harbour from 2 to 3 mi. wide and 4 mi. long. Santander is divided into an upper and a lower town. The Muelle is officially named Paseo de Pereda, in honour of the great novelist. The harbour was improved after 1850. In the civil war of 1936–39 Santander was attacked by Nationalist columns from Biscay, Soncillo and Navarre, well-supplied with tanks. It fell Aug. 16, 1937.

SANTAREM, a city of Brazil in the state of Pará, on the right bank of the Tapajoz, near its entrance into the Amazon. Population (1950) town 14,604 and *município* 61,611. It is one of the most important towns and distributing centres of the Amazon between Belém and Manaus and is a port of call for all river steamers and a station on the Amazon cable line. Santarém is 435 mi. from Belém (by air) and is served regularly by Panair do Brasil. Seen from the river the town is attractive in appearance and consists of a European (white) and an Indian quarter, the latter of palm-thatched huts. Ruins remain of a fort built in colonial times to protect the population against hostile Indians. Its principal public buildings are a municipal hall and tribunal, a large municipal warehouse, a market, theatre and two churches. The productions of the neighbourhood are cacao, Brazil nuts, rubber, tobacco, sugar cane and cattle; and the rivers furnish an abundance of fish, which are cured here at the season of low water, when turtle eggs are also gathered upstream for the manufacture of oil and "butter." The Tapajoz is navigable for steamers to the rapids, 170 mi. above Santarém, and for small boats nearly to Diamantino, Mato Grosso, and a considerable trade comes from

Mato Grosso and the settlements along its banks. Santarém was founded by a Jesuit missionary in 1661 as an Indian *aldeia*, and became a city in 1848.

SANTAREM, a city on the right bank of the river Tagus, 51 mi. by rail N.E. of Lisbon, Portugal. Pop. (1940) 11,785. The older part contains the ruined castle of Alcaçova, famous in the middle ages as a royal residence. Below is Ribeira de Santarem, a comparatively modern river-port, and on the opposite bank is Almeirim, a village which was also a royal residence until 1755, when it was almost entirely destroyed by earthquake. Santarem has some trade in fish and agricultural produce, including wine and olive oil. Its chief buildings are an ecclesiastical seminary; the late Gothic church of the Convento da Graça, which contains the tomb of Pedro Alvares Cabral, the first Portuguese to visit South America (1502); the Igreja do Milagro, an early Renaissance church; and the church of Santa Iría (St. Irene), from which the name of the city is derived. There is a fine bridge.

Santarem is the Roman *Scallabis*, renamed *Praesidium Iulium* by Julius Caesar. From its position in the Tagus valley it became an important fortress during the wars between the Moors, Portuguese and Spaniards. Alphonso VI. of Castile first took it from the Moors in 1093, but it was recaptured and occupied by them until 1147, when Alphonso I. of Portugal recovered it. The Almohades endeavoured to win it back in 1184, but were defeated. The Miguelites were defeated here in 1834 (*see* Portugal: *History*).

The administrative district of Santarem coincides with the eastern part of the ancient province of Estremadura (*q.v.*); population (1950) 458,658; area 2,583 sq.mi.

SANTAROSA, ANNIBALE SANTORRE DI ROSSI DE POMAROLO, Count of (1783–1825), Piedmontese insurgent, and leader in the revival (Risorgimento) of Italy, was born at Savigliano, near Coni, on Nov. 18, 1783. He was the son of a general officer in the Sardinian army who was killed at the battle of Mondovi in 1796. Santarosa entered the service of Napoleon during the annexation of Piedmont to France, and was sub-prefect of Spezia from 1812 to 1814. After the restoration of the king of Sardinia in 1814, he continued in the public service. When in 1821 the Austrian army was moved south to coerce the Neapolitans, Santarosa conspired to obtain the intervention of the Piedmontese in favour of the Neapolitans by an attack on the Austrian lines of communication. The conspirators sought the co-operation of the prince of Carignano, afterwards King Charles Albert. On March 6, 1821, Santarosa and three associates had an interview with the prince, and on the 10th they carried out the military "pronunciamiento" which proclaimed the Spanish Constitution. The movement had no real popular support, and very soon collapsed. Santarosa was arrested, but escaped, and fled to France, living for a time in Paris under the name of Conti. Here he wrote in French and published in 1822 his *La révolution piémontaise*, which attracted the notice of Victor Cousin, by whom he was finally concealed. He was imprisoned and expelled from Paris. He passed over to England, where he found refuge in London with Ugo Foscolo. He accompanied his countryman Giacinto Collegno to Greece in Nov. 1824. He was killed when the Egyptian troops attacked the island of Sphacteria, near Navarino, on May 8, 1825.

See Atto Vannucci, *I Martiri della libertà italiana* (Milan, 1877), and vol. ix. of the series called *I Contemporanei italiani* (Turin), in which there is a life by Angelo de Gubernatis. Santarosa's correspondence was edited by Bianchi, *Lettere di Santorre Santarosa* (Turin, 1877). A personal description by Victor Cousin will be found in the *Revue des deux mondes* for March 1, 1840.

SANTA ROSA, a city of California, U.S., 52 mi. N. by W. of San Francisco, in a broad valley of the Coast ranges, at an altitude of 150 ft.; the county seat of Sonoma county. It is served by the Northwestern Pacific railway, Southwest Airways, and by motor-stage and truck lines.

Population (1950) was 17,902; 1940 federal census 12,605. It is the trading centre and shipping point for a wide area, producing large quantities of poultry, eggs, cheese, butter, prunes, grapes, berries, hops, wool and other agricultural products. Because of the favourable conditions of climate and soil which it presented for horticultural experiments, Luther Burbank in 1875 chose Santa

Rosa for his home.

The city has varied manufacturing industries, supplying local needs and utilizing local products. Santa Rosa was settled about 1838 and incorporated in 1853.

In 1854 it replaced Sonoma as the county seat and in 1867 it was chartered as a city. It suffered severely in the earthquake of April 18, 1906. Since 1920 it has had a council-manager form of government.

SANTA TECLA, Salvador: *see* NUEVA SAN SALVADOR.

SANTAYANA, GEORGE (1863–1952), U.S. philosopher and poet, was born at Madrid, Dec. 16, 1863. At the age of nine he was taken to the United States.

He received the degree of B.A. from Harvard university in 1886, and served there, first as instructor, and then as professor of philosophy, from 1889 to 1912. For a long time his attachment to literature competed with "the love of wisdom."

In 1894 he published *Sonnets and Other Poems;* at later intervals he issued small volumes of classically compact and severely beautiful poetry, warmed with the restrained emotionalism of a Spaniard and an aristocrat and coloured with the peculiar melancholy of one who envied the consolations of "that splendid error [religion] which conforms better to the impulses of the soul" than life itself can do.

His first essay in philosophy was *The Sense of Beauty* (1896), which even the matter-of-fact Hugo Münsterberg rated as the best American contribution to aesthetics; five years later appeared *Interpretations of Poetry and Religion;* then for seven years he worked on *The Life of Reason.*

These five volumes, *Reason in Common Sense, Reason in Society, Reason in Religion, Reason in Art,* and *Reason in Science,* at once lifted Santayana to fame.

In 1912 he abandoned his position at Harvard and went to live in Europe. For many years he wandered from country to country, adding industriously to his philosophical product and reputation. Early during World War II, he settled in Rome at the convent of the Little Company of Mary. In 1923 he issued *Scepticism and Animal Faith,* as an introduction to "one more system of philosophy"; and in 1927 he published *The Realm of Essence,* first of four volumes on *Realms of Being.* These later works have given form and completeness to a world view which, in the *Life of Reason,* modestly announced itself as merely a contemporary application of Aristotle's thought. Epistemologically, Santayana's position is that idealism is true, but irrelevant and useless. Certainly the only reality is experience; and the "realm of essence" means the colours, forms, tastes, odours, pressures and temperatures which sensation gives, and the ideas, words, images and other interpretative representations which thought weaves around these essential experiences of the flesh. Our belief that these perceptions, by and large, fairly report the "external world" (the "realm of matter") is a form of "animal faith," a rough hypothesis which has the sufficient sanction of pragmatic use, and embodies the concordant element in the experience of all normal men.

Consequently we may accept as real what the senses report, and in every case this is matter. "In natural philosophy I am a decided materialist—apparently the only one living." Matter is far more complex in its structure, and far subtler in its possibilities, than we supposed; and to Santayana there is nothing strained in viewing thought as a function quite as natural and corporeal as digestion, and as transitory. "I believe there is nothing immortal. . . . No doubt the spirit and energy of the world is what is acting in us, as the sea is what rises in every little wave; but it passes through us; and cry out as we may, it will move on. Our privilege is to have perceived it as it moved." Mechanism is universal, and prevails even in the inmost recesses of the soul. Consciousness has no causal efficacy; it may see, and enjoy or deplore, the operations of life, but it cannot further or impede them in any way. Despite this materialism and scepticism, Santayana discussed the problems and ideals of religion with the sympathy of a poet and the tolerance of a sage. "Religion is human experience interpreted by human imagination. . . . Matters of religion should never be matters of controversy. . . . We

seek rather to honour the piety and understand the poetry embodied in these fables."

In ethics Santayana cleaves to Aristotle: "In Aristotle the conception of human nature is perfectly sound: everything ideal has a natural basis, and everything natural an ideal fulfilment. His ethics, when thoroughly digested and weighed, will seem perfectly final." A rational morality, based upon secular education and intelligence, would serve for a society of philosophers; but for the majority of mankind morality will have to retain its emotional basis in natural affection and the social training of the home. So too with government: we must put up with the second best, which so admirably accords with our own quality. Democracy has many faults, but it has the great virtue of providing a more equal opportunity than other forms of government to talent and genius of whatever origin and rank. Perhaps in the distant future men will be sufficiently intelligent to combine aristocracy with democracy, giving the franchise to all, but limiting office to the fit. Till then we must suffer fools gladly.

WRITINGS.—*Sonnets and Other Poems* (1894); *The Sense of Beauty* (1896); *Lucifer, a Theological Tragedy* (1899); *Interpretations of Poetry and Religion* (1900); *The Hermit of Carmel, and Other Poems* (1901); *The Life of Reason, or the Phases of Human Progress* (1905–06); *Three Philosophical Poets* (Lucretius, Dante and Goethe) (1910); *Winds of Doctrine* (1913); *Character and Opinion in the United States* (1920); *Egotism in German Philosophy* (1916; rev. ed. 1940); *Poems* (1923); *Scepticism and Animal Faith* (1923); *Soliloquies in England* (1925); *Dialogues in Limbo* (1925); *Platonism and the Spiritual Life* (1927); *Realms of Being,* 4 vol. (1927–40); *The Last Puritan,* a novel (1936); *Obiter Scripta* (1936); *Persons and Places,* 2 vol. (1944–45); *Dominations and Powers* (1951). (W. Du.; X.)

SANTIAGO, a province in the northern part of central Chile, bounded northwest by Valparaíso, north by Aconcagua, east by Argentina, south by O'Higgins, southwest by Colchagua, and west by the Pacific. Area, 6,559 sq.mi.; population (1950), 1,933,445, of whom 1,200,754 lived in the urban area of the national capital. Physiographically the province is divided into three longitudinal zones: the coastal mountains and valleys, the central valley, and the western watershed of the Andes. Climatically the greater part of the province has a Mediterranean type characterized by mild, rainy winters and warm to hot, dry summers. Winter precipitation in the Andes is principally in the form of snow, the meltwaters from which feed the perennial streams (tributaries of the Río Maipó) that are vitally important to the agricultural economy of the central valley during the long period of summer drought. The natural vegetation, similar to Mediterranean *maquis* (California *chaparral*), has been largely cleared from the lands suited to agriculture and grazing; the most conspicuous trees in the valley lands, found principally along irrigation canals and roads, are eucalyptus and Lombardy poplars, both of which are exotic. Under irrigation the fertile alluvial soils of the central valley are highly productive, large areas being planted in wheat, barley, corn, alfalfa, potatoes, legumes, grapes, figs, olives and a great variety of other temperate and subtropical fruits, cereals and vegetables. In addition to its leading agricultural position, Santiago ranks high in the production of cattle and other livestock. Although most of the land is still held in large *haciendas* or *fundos,* the need for increased agricultural production to feed the large urban population of Santiago is gradually resulting in the subdivision of lands, especially in the vicinity of the capital.

SANTIAGO or SANTIAGO DE CHILE, a city of Chile, capital of the republic and of a province of the same name, on the Mapocho river, a small tributary of the Maipó or Maipú, 115 mi. southeast of Valparaíso by rail, in 33° 26′ 42″ S., 70° 40′ 36″ W. Population (1950 est.) 1,200,754. The city is built on a wide, beautiful plain about 1,860 ft. above sea level, between the main range of the Andes and the less elevated heights of Cuesta del Prado. In the centre of the city rises the rocky hill of Santa Lucía, once forming its citadel, but now converted into a pleasure-ground, with winding walks, picturesque views, theatres, restaurants and monuments. Immediately north-northwest and northeast are other hills, known as Colina, Renca and San Cristóbal, and overshadowing all are the snow-clad Andean peaks of La Chapa and Los Amarillos, visible from all parts of the city. The

Mapocho, once the cause of destructive inundations (especially in 1609 and 1783), was enclosed with solid embankments during the administration of Ambrosio O'Higgins, and is crossed by several handsome bridges; the oldest (1767–79) of these has 11 arches.

Santiago is laid out with great regularity, and its comparatively broad straight streets form parallelograms and enclose several handsome public squares, the Plaza de Armas, Plaza Constitución and others. It has all the characteristics of a modern capital: fine public buildings and private residences, broad avenues, well-paved and well-lighted streets and modern conveniences of every sort. There are many modern skyscrapers and apartment houses, particularly along the Avenida Bernardo O'Higgins, the main thoroughfare. The electric tramway and lighting company, which before World War I had been in German hands, was reorganized as a Chilean enterprise. It constructed hydroelectric projects at Santiago in 1921, and secured the contract for supplying power to the railway from Santiago to Valparaíso after its electrification, as well as for lighting the city and running its tramcars. In 1924 the government granted a concession to a local firm for the construction of an underground way through the centre of the city (5½ mi. long, 33 ft. below the surface). Water is brought in through two aqueducts, one 5 mi. long (1865), and the other from Laguna Negra 33 mi. away.

There is a railway communicating with Valparaíso, with Los Andes and the international tunnel, and with the provincial capitals of the south and the north.

Manufacturing industries play an important role in Santiago, constituting more than 50% of the country's total. Among the leading industries are breweries, flour-mills, foundries, machine-shops, woodworking plants, tanneries, knitting-mills, soap factories, factories for making shoes, hats, umbrellas and articles of clothing.

The cathedral, facing on the Plaza de Armas, was erected originally in 1619 by Pedro de Valdivia. It was rebuilt by García Hurtado de Mendoza, destroyed by the earthquake of 1647, and was rebuilt on a new plan subsequent to 1748. It is 351 ft. long and 92 ft. wide, has only one tower and is not striking in appearance. Its interior decorations, however, are rich and in good taste.

Among the other ecclesiastical buildings are the church of San Augustín, erected in 1595 by Cristóbal de Vera, and in modern times adorned with a pillared portico; the church of San Francisco (the oldest in Santiago); La Merced and Santo Domingo, dating

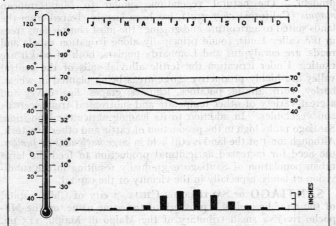

WEATHER GRAPH OF SANTIAGO. THE THERMOMETER INDICATES THE ANNUAL MEAN TEMPERATURE. THE CURVE SHOWS THE MONTHLY MEAN TEMPERATURE, AND THE COLUMNS, THE NORMAL MONTHLY PRECIPITATION

from the 18th century; the church of the Reformed Dominicans, rich in monolithic marble columns; the Carmen Alto, or church of the Carmelite nunnery, a small Gothic structure; the Augustine nunnery, founded by Bishop Medellín in 1576; the episcopal palace; and the chapel erected in 1852 to the memory of Pedro de Valdivia, next to the house in which he is reputed to have lived.

There are two cemeteries—one exclusively Roman Catholic and the other secularized. Mural interment is the custom in Santiago.

Among the secular buildings the more noteworthy are the capitol with its rows of massive columns and its beautiful gardens; the Moneda, or executive residence, which contains the offices of the cabinet ministers also; the civic centre; the courts, or palace of justice; the post office and telegraph department; the exposition palace in the Quinta Normal, which houses the national museum; the University of Chile, dating from 1842; the national library; the national conservatory of music; the astronomical observatory; the national institute; the mint; and a municipal theatre. There are also a military school and a number of charitable institutions.

The old Universidad de San Felipe, founded in 1747, was closed in 1839, and was succeeded three years later by the present national university.

Facing the capitol, which includes the two halls of congress, is a small park and commemorative shaft, marking the spot where stood the Jesuits' church which was burned down on the night of Dec. 8, 1868, and with it "2,000 victims, more or less," chiefly women.

Santiago was founded in 1541 by Pedro de Valdivia, who was engaged in the conquest of Chile, and it received the title of Santiago del Nuevo Estremo. It has suffered from earthquakes and from political disorder. After the defeat of the royalists at Chacabuco (Feb. 12, 1817), it was occupied by the revolutionary forces under Gen. José de San Martín. Though the scene of many revolutionary outbreaks, it has never been subjected to a regular siege.

The fifth international conference of American states was held in Santiago in 1923, and the third Pan American Highway congress convened there in 1939.

The province of Santiago, bounded N. by Aconcagua, E. by Argentina, S. by O'Higgins and Colchagua and W. by the Pacific and Valparaíso, has an area of 6,559 sq.mi. and a population (1940 census) of 1,261,717. It embraces part of the "Valle de Chile," celebrated for its fertility and fine climate.

SANTIAGO DE COMPOSTELA or **SANTIAGO,** a city of northwest Spain, in the province of Corunna; at the northern terminus of a railway from Tuy, near the confluence of the Sar and Sarela rivers, and 32 mi. S.W. of the city of Corunna. Pop. (1940) 30,127 (mun., 49,191). The Galician region, of which the city is the centre, is composed of hills which have been strongly folded and faulted and where in consequence metal veins occur. In the ages when metal began to be known in the west people from the Mediterranean moved along the coasts of western Europe, and with these movements was associated the cult of the megaliths. In those days navigation was precarious and sailors made for one of a number of small ports which had a common focus inland. Santiago was probably a focus for the numerous ports on the Galician rias. (Cf. Canterbury and St. David's.) At Padron, one of the ports of Santiago, there are two great stones called *Barca* and *Patron* (the ship and the skipper). The tradition of the sanctity of the old stone monuments lingered for centuries and the legend arose that St. James the Apostle had, after his martyrdom in Palestine, been borne hither for burial and that the body was brought ashore at Padron.

After the Moorish conquest the northwest corner was the only part of Spain that retained its independence and it was the region from which the reconquest of Spain for Christendom was begun. This produced a great enthusiasm for the Christian religion, an enthusiasm fanned by the reputed discovery of the bones of St. James at Compostela. A church was built over the relics and a bishopric transferred thither. The city thus became a centre for pilgrims and when the royal family of Castile became connected by marriage with that of Burgundy, which was associated with the Cluniac monks, the site gained an international significance. The road (*route de S. Jacques*) of the pilgrims became famous and many of the great romances of the middle ages developed from the tales told by the pilgrims to while away the tedium of the long journey to this remote corner of Spain. (Cf. the *Canterbury Tales.*) There were also many pilgrims from those western fringes of Europe, which had been connected with Galicia ages before in the early days of metal. The city was formerly the capital of Galicia, and is still the seat of a university and of an archbishopric, which long disputed the claim of Toledo to the primacy of all Spain. Its chief industries, apart from agriculture, are brewing, distillation of spirits, and the manufacture of linen, paper, soap, chocolate and matches. The city has also been long celebrated for its silversmiths' work.

In 1078 the erection of the present cathedral was begun and it was consecrated in 1211. It is a cruciform Romanesque building. The Puerta Santa is kept closed, except in jubilee years, when it is opened by the archbishop. Perhaps the chief beauty of the cathedral is the Portico de la Gloria, behind the western classic portal. It is a work of the 12th century, and probably the utmost development of which round-arched Gothic is capable. The shafts, tympana, and archivolts of the three doorways which open on to the nave and aisles are a mass of strong sculpture.

The Hospicio de los Reyes, on the north of the Plaza Mayor, for the reception of pilgrims, was begun in 1504 by Enrique de Egas under Ferdinand and Isabella.

SANTIAGO DE CUBA, a city and seaport of Cuba, on the southern coast of the eastern end of the island, capital of the province of Oriente, and next to Havana the most important city of the republic. Population of the city (1943) 118,266 and of the *municipio* 120,577. It is connected by the Cuba railway with Havana, 540 mi. to the W.N.W.; short railways extend into the interior through gaps in the mountains northward; and there are steamer connections with other Cuban ports and with New York and Europe.

Santiago is situated about 6 mi. inland on a magnificent land-locked bay (6 mi. long and 3 mi. wide), connected with the Caribbean sea by a long, narrow, winding channel with rocky escarpment walls, in places less than 200 yd. apart. The largest vessels have ready entrance to the harbour but direct access to the wharves is impossible for those of more than moderate draught (about 14 ft.). Smith key, an island used as a watering place, divides it into an outer and an inner basin. To the east of the sea portal stand the Morro, a picturesque fort (built 1633 *seq.*), on a jutting point 200 ft. above the water, and the Estrella; and to the west the Socapa. West of the harbour are low hills, to the east precipitous cliffs, and north and northeast, below the superb background of the Sierra Maestra, is an amphitheatre of hills, over which the city straggles in tortuous streets. The houses are mostly of one story. In the cathedral, Diego Velázquez (*c.* 1460–1524), conqueror of Cuba, was buried. It has suffered much from earthquakes and has been extensively repaired. Probably the oldest building in Cuba is the convent of San Francisco (a church since the secularization of the religious orders in 1841), which dates in part from the first half of the 16th century. Great improvements have been made in the city since the end of colonial rule, especially as regards the streets, the water supply and other public works and sanitation. On a hill overlooking the city is a beautiful schoolhouse of native limestone, erected by the American military government as a model for the rest of the island. Santiago is the hottest city of Cuba (mean temperature in winter about 82° F., in summer about 88°), owing mainly to the mountains that shut off the breezes from the east. There is superb mountain scenery on the roads to El Caney and San Luis in the thickly populated valley of the Cauto. In the barren mountainous country surrounding the city are valuable mines of iron, copper and manganese. On these the prosperity of the province largely depends. There are also foundries, soapworks, tanyards and cigar factories. The city has an important trade with the interior, with other Cuban ports, and to a less extent with New York and European ports. Mineral ores, tobacco and cigars, coffee, cacao, sugar, rum and cabinetwoods are the main articles of export.

History.—Santiago is less important politically under the republic than it was when Cuba was a Spanish dependency. The place was founded in 1514 by Diego Velázquez, and the capital of the island was removed thither from Baracoa. Its splendid bay, and easy communication with the capital of Santo Domingo, then the seat of government of the Indies, determined its original importance. From Santiago in 1518–19 departed the historic expeditions of Juan de Grijalva, Hernan Cortes and Pánfilo de Narváez. Cortes was the first mayor of Santiago. So important already was the city that its *ayuntamiento* had the powers of a Spanish city of the second class. In 1522 it received the arms and title of *ciudad*, and its church was made the cathedral of the island. But before 1550 the drain of military expeditions to the continent, the quarrels of civil, military and ecclesiastical powers, and of citizens, and the emigration of colonists to the Main produced a gradual decline. In 1589 Havana became the capital. Santiago was occupied and plundered by French corsairs in 1553, and again by a British military force from Jamaica in 1662. The capture of that island had caused an immigration of Spanish refugees to Santiago that greatly increased its importance; and the illicit trade to the same island—mainly in hides and cattle—that flourished from this time onward was a main prop of prosperity. From 1607 to 1826 the island was divided into two departments, with Santiago as the capital of the eastern department. After 1826 Santiago was simply the capital of a province. In July 1741 a British squadron from Jamaica under Adm. Edward Vernon and Gen. Thomas Wentworth landed at Guantánamo and during four months operated unsuccessfully against Santiago. The climate made great ravages among the British, who lost perhaps 2,000 out of 5,000 men. The bishopric became an archbishopric in 1788, when a suffragan bishopric was established at Havana. After the cession of Santo Domingo to France, and after the French evacuation of that island, thousands of refugees settled in and about Santiago. They founded coffee and sugar plantations and gave a great impulse to trade. There were destructive earthquakes in 1675, 1679, 1766 and 1852. In the 19th century some striking historical events are associated with Santiago, including the Virginius affair of 1873. The most notable military and naval events (in Cuba) of the Spanish-American War (*q.v.*) of 1898 took place at and near Santiago. Monuments commemorate the actions at El Caney and San Juan hill. The city's learned societies flourished independently of those of the capital, and in 1949 its university was granted official recognition equal to that of Havana.

SANTIAGO DE LAS VEGAS, an inland city of Havana province, Cuba, south of Havana. Pop. (1943) 9,385; (*municipio*, 25,201). Tobacco is the principal industry. An agricultural experiment station is maintained there by the Cuban government. The town dates from 1688, when a church was built for a colony of tobacco cultivators of the neighbourhood.

SANTIAGO DEL ESTERO, a province of Argentina, bounded north by Salta and the Chaco territory, east by the Chaco and Santa Fé, south by Córdoba, and west by Catamarca, Tucumán and Salta. Area 52,222 sq.mi.; pop. (1914) 261,678; (1947) 469,377. With the exception of the Sierra de Guasayán in the west and the Sumampa and Ambargasta hills in the south, the surface is a vast plain, more than two-thirds of which is covered with a great variety of commercially valuable trees. There are extensive swamps along the river courses and large saline areas, especially in the southwest. The most important rivers are the Salado and the Dulce, between which lie the most fertile lands in the province. The climate is extremely hot in the summer, the maximum temperature being as high as 118° F.; frosts occur occasionally in the winter. There is an average annual rainfall of from 20 in. to 25 in., most of which falls in summer.

Although the forests provide the principal source of wealth, agriculture and stock raising are also important. The principal crops are wheat, alfalfa, linseed, corn and cotton, in addition to which a wide variety of fruits is raised.

The province is traversed by several railway lines which afford connection with all parts of Argentina, and with Bolivia and Chile.

The provincial capital, SANTIAGO DEL ESTERO, is on the right bank of the Río Dulce, 630 mi. N.W. of Buenos Aires, with which it is connected by rail. Population (1941 est.) 58,925. The city stands on a level open plain, 520 ft. above sea level, and in the vicinity of large swamps (*esteros*) bordering the Río Dulce, from which its name is derived. There are a number of interesting old buildings in the city—a government house, several churches, a Jesuit college, a Franciscan convent and a girls' orphanage. The city was founded in 1553 by Francisco de

Aguirre and was the first capital of the province of Tucumán, the earliest settled of the La Plata provinces. (R. W. Rᴅ.; X.)

SANTI QUARANTA, a seaport of Albania, on the Bay of Butrinto, and opposite the island of Corfu (Corcyra). Pop. before the Italian occupation of 1939, about 5,000, of whom 75% were Orthodox and the remainder Moslems.

In the neighbourhood are the ruins of the ancient Buthrotum, traditionally founded by Helenus, son of Priam (*see* Virgil, *Aen.* iii, 291 *et seq.*). In the 1st century B.C. Buthrotum became a Roman colony on the main highway between Dyrrachium (Durazzo) and Apollonia. The modern city belonged to the Venetians from the 14th century till 1797 when it was captured by Ali Pasha of Janina. In 1939 the Italians renamed the town Porto Edda, after Mussolini's daughter. It was captured by the Greeks Dec. 6, 1940, and held until Germany's Balkan invasion in April 1941.

SANTO DOMINGO (officially known as the Dominican Republic) occupies the eastern two-thirds of the island of Hispaniola and has an area of about 19,129 sq.mi. Its population by the census of 1950 was 2,121,000. There are several hundred Spanish and a few other European families living in the country but the mass of the population is Afro-American. Spanish is the universal language and the cultural heritage is that of Spain.

The Dominican Republic is very mountainous (*see* HAITI). Extending northwest to southeast and almost in the centre of the country is the great Cordillera Central whose highest elevation exceeds 10,000 ft. and whose maximum width is 80 mi. This great mountain mass is largely unoccupied and is heavily forested. It receives an abundant rainfall and is the chief drainage divide of the country. The mountains and valleys north of this central core are well watered as a rule and support nearly two-thirds of the population. Sugar, cacao, tobacco and coffee are the chief money crops, but as elsewhere in the republic, most of the land is held by small farmers and utilized for sustenance crops. This section contains the famous Vega Real of early Spanish days. South of the Cordillera Central much of the land is arid, necessitating extensive irrigation. A thriving sugar industry is found east and west of Ciudad Trujillo. Mineral developments of some promise include iron, bauxite and gypsum. There are a number of good harbours in the republic. Docks are in operation at Ciudad Trujillo, Puerto Plata, La Romana, San Pedro de Macorís and Barahona. At the other ports lighters must be used.

History.—The area now occupied by the Dominican Republic along with the portion now included in the Republic of Haiti was held by Spain as the colony of Hispaniola until the Treaty of Ryswick in 1697. After that date the Haitian portion was ceded to France and the Dominican portion remained under Spanish dominion and became known as Santo Domingo, after the patron saint of Columbus' father. At the end of the 18th century the Spanish control was lost and the entire island came under the French. When the French lost control of the colony in the early part of the 19th century, the empires of Toussaint L'Ouverture and Jean Jacques Dessalines for a time united the entire island under one government, independent of all European powers. During the second decade of the 19th century, Spain again asserted its dominion over the eastern end of the island but was forced out by a revolution in 1821. A republic was proclaimed under the guidance of Colombia. The following year, Pres. Jean Pierre Boyer of Haiti invaded the country and again united the island under one flag. In 1844, the year following Boyer's downfall, the Dominican Republic was founded and since that date two political entities have been maintained. The presidency of the new republic alternated, with one exception, between Buenaventura Báez and Pedro Santana until in 1861 when Spain, on the invitation of Santana, again annexed the country. Dissatisfaction with Spanish rule brought revolution and the Spanish withdrew for the last time in 1865. Four years later, when Báez was again president, a treaty was negotiated by Gen. O. E. Babcock, U.S., for the annexation of the Dominican Republic to the United States. This treaty was ratified by the Dominican senate but was rejected by the United States. With the exception of the rule of Ulíses Heureaux, 1882–99, presidents followed each

other in rapid succession and an unstable condition prevailed. An unusually violent revolution broke out following the election of Eladio Victoria in Feb. 1912 and the United States sent a mediatory commission which helped to effect a temporary agreement. Victoria resigned and the popular Archbishop Adolfo A. Nouel was elected president. He proved a poor executive and Bordas Valdes became provisional president. Revolution again became active and a second commission was sent from the United States. Bordas resigned and Báez became provisional president on Aug. 27, 1914. Juan Isidro Jiménez took office as president in December of the same year. He was deposed in April 1916 by Desiderio Arias, the secretary of war, who assumed power. On May 5, U.S. forces were landed, Henríquez y Carvajal was then appointed as provisional president. More trouble followed and the United States felt compelled to intervene formally, establishing, on Nov. 29, 1916, the Military Government of the United States in Santo Domingo. As the occupation was not undertaken with the object of destroying the sovereignty of the Dominican Republic, arrangements were made for the withdrawal of U.S. forces as soon as conditions warranted. The military governor sailed on Oct. 24, 1922, when a satisfactory provisional government had been set up.

On June 26, 1924, the Dominican Republic ratified the treaty proposed by the United States and on July 12 the last of the U.S. forces were withdrawn. Horacio Vásquez was at the same time inaugurated as president for four years, a term which was subsequently extended by constitutional amendment to six years. In the last year of his administration (Feb. 1930), Vásquez was suddenly expelled from office by a revolution and after a brief period under Provisional Pres. Ureña, Gen. Leonidas Trujillo became president.

In the following two decades, Gen. Trujillo, either as president or as military chief at the side of the president selected by him, carried out a program of thoroughgoing economic and political consolidation. Relations with the neighbouring republic of Haiti were initially hostile, with much border warfare, but tended to improve in the period after 1940. Relations with the Venezuelan regime of Acción Democrática (1945–48) were equally hostile, as well as with the administrations of Ramón Grau San Martín and Prío Socarrás in Cuba. A program of road building and the improvement of water supplies, irrigation, hospital and school construction was consistently carried out. A central bank was set up (1949–50), the foreign debt paid off, the internal debt reduced (to $21,761,000 by June 30, 1951) and the budget maintained in balance (revenue in 1950, for example, totalled $96,-590,000 and expenditures $90,881,000; the 1951 budget was estimated to balance at $74,606,000). When Trujillo took the presidency, the national income was equivalent to $30,000,000; in 1951 it exceeded $300,000,000.

Government, Education, Finance.—A representative government is established under the constitution. All males over 18 years of age are qualified to vote. The administration is in the hands of three co-ordinate powers: the executive, the legislative and the judicial. The chief executive is the president. Prior to the constitution of June 13, 1924, he was elected by indirect vote for six years and was not eligible for re-election to a second successive term. At that time the term was reduced to four years and election was made by direct vote. The office of vice-president was created for the first time. The president cannot be re-elected to the presidency nor elected to the vice-presidency for the constitutional period following. He is assisted by a cabinet consisting of the secretaries of the seven departments: interior and police, foreign affairs, treasury and commerce, war and navy, justice and public instruction, agriculture and immigration, promotion and communications. There are 12 provinces, each of which elects by direct popular vote, for four periods, one senator and two members to the chamber of deputies. Each province has an appointed governor and is divided into communes, with necessary local officials. The supreme court is composed of a chief justice and six justices. Courts of appeal are located in two or three of the larger centres. A court of first instance is located in each province and in each commune there is at least one local court. The Policía Nacional Dominicana (Guardia) has the double function of police and army.

This organization was trained by and largely modelled after the U.S. marine corps.

Primary education is free and, in theory, compulsory. It is supported by local communities with national participation in the cost. Secondary schools and the university are supported by the national government. The state contributes to the support of the Catholic Church; other religious bodies are free to organize and maintain congregations.

The peso is at par with the U.S. dollar. External debt had all been paid off by 1952, except a few thousand dollars' worth of bonds for which the fiscal agents held the funds to pay them when presented.

Production and Trade.—Agriculture provides the principal source of wealth. Sugar, produced on property exploited by foreign capital, in the main, is the foremost product (a record total of 587,343 short tons, plus 25,813,275 gal. of blackstrap molasses was produced in 1950–51). It has gone to Great Britain traditionally, but an increasing proportion enters the world market. Coffee (326,899 bags of 132 lb. each in the 1950–51 season) and cacao (34,000 short tons) encountered steady and dependable demand after 1937; tobacco (24,200 short tons) and bananas are other but relatively minor sources of trade. Some mineral developments began to give promising signs in the late 1940s.

The rapid expansion of export trade brought its total value for 1951 to more than $108,000,000 while the value of imports exceeded $48,000,000. Leading customers are the United States (44% of the total in 1950) and the United Kingdom (42%). Principal suppliers are the United States (73% in 1950), the Netherlands Antilles (5%) and the United Kingdom and West Germany (each 2%). The chief ports are Ciudad Trujillo, San Pedro de Macorís and La Romana.

The public railroad mileage of the republic at mid-20th century was about 170, and in addition there were about 650 mi. of industrial narrow-gauge lines operated mostly by the sugar companies. There were about 500 mi. of improved highway connecting Ciudad Trujillo with northern points and with the Republic of Haiti. Foreign shipping facilities and foreign air line connections were tending to increase.

BIBLIOGRAPHY.—R. S. Platt, *Latin America, Countrysides and United Regions* (1943); G. A. Mejía, *Historia de Santo Domingo*, 4 vol. to 1528 (Ciudad Trujillo, 1949–51); S. Welles, *Naboth's Vineyard; the Dominican Republic, 1844–1924*, 2 vol. (1928); C. C. Tansill, *United States and Santo Domingo, 1798–1873* (1938); A. F. MacDonald, *Latin American Politics and Government* (1949); J. F. Bannon and P. M. Dunne, *Latin America* (1948); C. L. Jones, *The Caribbean Since 1900* (1936); D. G. Munro, *Latin American Republics* (1942); Brookings Institution, *Refugee Settlement in the Dominican Republic* (1942). (R. B. H.; C. E. Mc.)

SANTORIN (corruption of St. Irene) or THERA, a volcanic island in the Aegean sea, the southernmost of the Sporades. Officially it is a province in the Greek department of the Cyclades (*q.v.*), divided into 9 communes.

In shape Santorin forms a crescent and encloses a bay on the north, east and south; on the western side lies the smaller island of Therasia. The encircling wall thus formed, elliptical, and 18 mi. round its inner rim, is broken in two places—toward the northwest by a strait a mile in breadth, where the water is not less than 1,100 ft. deep, and southwest by an aperture about 3 mi. wide, shallow, with Aspronisi (White Island) in the middle. From the bay, cliffs rise perpendicularly to as much as 1,000 ft.; but toward the open sea, both in Santorin and Therasia, the ground slopes and has been converted into broad level terraces of tufaceous agglomerate, which though bare and ashen, produce the famous Santorin wine. The tufa itself is exported as cement especially for house-roofs.

Toward the southeast, the limestone peak of Mount Elias (1,856 ft.) existed before the volcano was formed. In the middle of the bay lie three small volcanic islands, Palaea- Mikra- and Nea-Kaümene (Old, Little and New Burnt islands). The highest, Nea-Kaümene, was thrown up in 1707 and 1866 to 351 ft. above the sea.

Because of the depth at the foot of the cliff there is no anchorage, and vessels have to be moored to the shore, except at one point in the neighbourhood of the modern town, where there is a patch of shallow bottom. The cliffs show horizontal bands of black lava, white and yellow tufa, and other volcanic strata, red, purple, brown and green, with but little herbage. The modern town of Thera (or Phera, as it is commonly pronounced) is built at the edge of these cliffs, overlooking the bay at a height of 900 ft.

The foundations of the houses and in some cases their sides, are excavated in the tufa, so that they are hardly traceable except by their chimneys. Because of the absence of timber—for, except the fig, cactus and palm, there are hardly any trees on the island—they are roofed with barrel vaults. Both wood and occasionally water are imported from neighbouring islands, for there are no wells, and the rain water, collected in cisterns, sometimes fails.

The next largest village, Apanomeria ("Upper Part"), near the north entrance, is crowded together in a whitewashed mass above the reddest rocks in the island.

Geology.—Most geologists agree that the whole of the bay was once covered by a single volcanic cone, represented by the outward slope of Santorin and Therasia, with its crater at the Kaümene Islands; and that the bay results from explosion and subsidence.

The Kaümene Islands arose subsequently, and Palaea-Kaümene is considered to be prehistoric. Principal eruptions in historic times were those of 196 B.C. (Strabo 57), when flames arose from the water between Thera and Therasia for four days and an island appeared; of A.D. 726, when again an island was thrown up; of 1570, when Mikra-Kaümene arose; of 1650, which destroyed many lives by noxious exhalations, and ended in the upheaval of an island in the sea to the northeast of Santorin, which is now a reef below sea level; that of 1707, when Nea-Kaümene arose; and that of 1866, when Nea-Kaümene was extended toward the south and enlarged threefold.

In the southern parts both of Santorin and Therasia prehistoric dwellings were found at some height above the sea, and there was evidence that these date from a period antecedent to the formation of the bay. This was demonstrated by their position underneath the layer of tufa which covers the islands and by these layers of tufa being broken off precipitously, in the same way as the lava rocks, a fact which could only be explained by the supposition that they all fell in together.

The foundations of the dwellings rested not on the tufa but on the lava below it; and here and there between the stones, branches of wild olive were found, according to a mode of building that still prevailed in the island in modern times in order to resist the shocks of earthquakes.

Few implements of metal were found. Vases of imported Cretan ware date this settlement to the middle Minoan period, and connect the volcanic explosion with the earthquake which wrecked the first palace at Cnossus.

In Greek legend the island of Thera originated from a clod of earth presented to the Argonauts by Triton (Apoll. Rhod., *Argonaut*, iv, 1551 *et seq.*, 1731 *et seq.*). A colony was left there by Cadmus (Herod., iv, 147.). Subsequently a colony from Sparta, including Minyan refugees from Lemnos, was brought by Theras, who gave the island his own name, in place of Calliste. But the chief event in Thera's history was the planting of its famous colony of Cyrene on the north coast of Africa by Battus in 631 B.C., in accordance with a command of the Delphic oracle. Thera, as a member of the league of the Cyclades, was from 308 to 145 B.C. under the protectorate of the Ptolemies.

The ancient capital occupied a site on the eastern coast now called Mesavouno, between Mount Elias and the sea. It has been excavated since 1895 by Baron Hiller von Gärtringen. There are extensive cemeteries; a Heroum of Artemidorus; an Agora; a Royal Portico; a temple of Dionysus and the Ptolemies, later dedicated to the Caesars; the Ptolemaic barracks and a gymnasium. The main street has narrow lanes to right and left; one leads to the sanctuary of the Egyptian gods. Near the street there is a small theatre, beneath the seats of which is a cistern into which rain water drains from the auditorium: water was evidently scarce then as now. Farther southeast are the temples of Ptolemy Euergetes III, and of Apollo Carneius; finally, where the rocks fall precipitously, a gymnasium of the Ephebi. Numerous rock-carvings and inscriptions have been discovered, as well as statues and vases. Near the west foot of Mount Elias is the temple of Thea Basileia, perfect even to the roof, now dedicated to St. Nicolas Marmorites.

Tournefort mentions that in his time nine or ten chapels were dedicated to St. Irene, the patron saint of the place; the name Santorin was given after the fourth crusade, when the island formed a portion of the duchy of the archipelago.

BIBLIOGRAPHY.—L. Ross, *Inselreisen*, vol. i (Stuttgart, 1840); C. Bursian, *Geographie von Griechenland,* vol. ii (Leipzig, 1872); F. Fouqué, *Santorin et ses éruptions* (1879); Neumann and Partsch, *Physicalische Geographie von Griechenland* (Breslau, 1885); J. Th. Bent, *The Cyclades* (1885); H. F. Tozer, *The Islands of the Aegean* (1890); Hiller von Gärtringen, *Thera* (Berlin, 1899 *et seq.*); Baedeker's *Greece*, 3rd Eng. ed. (1905).

SANTOS, a city and seaport of Brazil, in the state of São Paulo, about 200 mi. S.W. of Rio de Janeiro, and 49 mi. by rail S.E. of São Paulo city. Population (1950) 206,920. Santos covers an alluvial plain on the inner side of an island (São Vicente) formed by an inland tidal channel sometimes called the Santos river. The commercial part of the city is some miles from the mouth of the channel, but the residential sections extend across the plain and line the beach facing the sea. The city is only a few feet above sea level, the island is swampy and deep, cement-lined channels drain the city. The Santos river is free from obstructions and in front of the city widens into a bay deep enough for the largest vessels. The water front, once beds of mud and slime, the source of many epidemics of fever, was faced by a wall of stone and cement. The quay is about 3 mi. long and can accommodate 50 steamers at one time; belt conveyors operated by steam load several thousand bags of coffee per hour. Many warehouses are splendidly equipped with machinery which replaces manual labour. The British-built but government-owned railway to São Paulo ("heart of coffee-land"), 49 mi. distant, transports the bulk of coffee of that region to Santos, making the line the best paying railway in South America. A paved highway from São Paulo to Santos was completed by the state government in 1919. Another, and wider, road was opened to traffic in 1947.

Santos has passed Rio de Janeiro in the amount of its exports and is now the world's greatest coffee port, shipping annually from 8,000,000 to 13,000,000 bags. The annual imports have increased in 20 years from 1,653,450 to 2,693,194 metric tons. About 3,000 ships visit the port yearly, the busiest season being from August to January. The other exports include cotton, sugar, rice, rum, fruit, hides and manufactured goods. Bananas are grown in the vicinity for the River Plate markets.

An annual rainfall of about 77 in. and a mean temperature of 69° F., combined formerly to create unhealthful conditions, but the building of a series of drainage canals, extension of modern sanitation, paving of streets, construction of better houses and port improvements were largely responsible for the change to a healthful city. A suburban seaside resort, Guarujá draws many visitors from inland parts of Brazil.

The first settlement on the São Paulo coast was that of São Vicente in 1532, about 6 mi. S. of Santos on the same island. Other settlements soon followed, among them that of Santos in 1543-46, and later on the small fort at the entrance to its harbour, which was used for protection against Indian raids from the north. São Vicente did not prosper, and was succeeded (1681) by São Paulo as the capital and by Santos as the seaport of the colony. It was captured by the English privateer, Thomas Cavendish, in 1591, when São Vicente was burned.

SANTOS-DUMONT, ALBERTO (1873-1932), Brazilian aeronaut, was born at São Paulo, Brazil, on July 20, 1873. In 1897 he made his first balloon ascent from Paris. In 1898 he began to construct dirigible airships, and after many failures built one which, on Oct. 19, 1901, won the Deutsch prize and a prize from the Brazilian government for the first flight in a given time from Saint Cloud to the Eiffel tower. In 1903 he erected at Neuilly the first airship station. There he kept his fleet of dirigibles and travelled in them about the streets of Paris between

the houses.

In 1905 Santos-Dumont turned his attention to heavier-than-air machines, and after experiment with a vertical-propeller model, he built in 1906 a machine on the principle of the box kite, and with it won the Deutsch-Archdeacon prize in October, while in November he flew 220 m. in 21 sec. In 1909 he produced his famous "demoiselle" or "grasshopper" monoplane, the forerunner of the modern light plane. On Dec. 3, 1928, after many years of residence in France, he returned to Brazil. On his arrival the government declared a half-holiday in his honour.

Santos-Dumont wrote *My Airships: A Story of My Life* (1904).

SANUTO or **SANUDO, MARINO,** the younger (1466-1533), Venetian historian, son of the senator, Leonardo Sanuto, was born on May 22, 1466. Marino Sanuto was elected a member of the Maggior Consiglio when only 20 years old, and became a senator in 1498. He collected a fine library, which was rich in mss. and chronicles both Venetian and foreign, including the famous Altino chronicle, the basis of early Venetian history.

His chief works are: *Itinerario in terra ferma* (ed. Rawdon Brown, 1847); *I commentarii della guerra di Ferrara,* an account of the war between the Venetians and Ercole d'Este (Venice, 1829); *La Spedizione di Carlo VIII* (MS. in the Louvre); *Le Vite dei Dogi,* vol. xxii of Muratori's *Rerum Italicarum Scriptores* (1733). The *Diarii,* his most important work, which cover the period from Jan. 1, 1496, to Sept. 1533, were edited by various scholars and published at Venice (58 vol., 1879-1903). Owing to the relations of the Venetian republic with the whole of Europe and the east it is practically a universal chronicle.

BIBLIOGRAPHY.—M. Rawdon Brown, *Ragguagli sulla vita e sulle opere di Marino Sanuto,* 3 vol. (Venice, 1837-38); G. Tiraboschi, *Storia della Letteratura Italiana,* vol. vi; R. Fulin, *Marin Sanudo* (Turin, 1880); Ricotti, *I Diarii di Marin Sanudo* (Turin, 1880); G. de Leva, *Marin Sanudo* (Venice, 1888).

SAN VICENTE, the capital of the department of San Vicente, El Salvador; 30 mi. E. of San Salvador, on the river Acahuapa, a left-hand tributary of the Lempa. Pop. (1950) 10,945. San Vicente is situated in a volcanic region abounding in hot springs and geysers. The volcano of San Vicente, the highest in the department, reaches an altitude of more than 7,000 ft. There are indigo and tobacco plantations. Shoes, hats, cloth, silk, spirits and cigars are manufactured. San Vicente was founded in 1634 on the site of Tehuacan, an ancient Indian city. For one year (1839-40) it was the capital of the republic.

SÃO FRANCISCO, a river of eastern Brazil rising in the southwest part of the state of Minas Gerais, about 20° 30′ S., 46° 40′ W., near the narrow valley of the Rio Grande, a tributary of Paraná, and within 240 mi. of the coast west of Rio de Janeiro. It flows in a general north-northeast direction across the great central plateau of Brazil to about lat. 9° 30′ S., long. 42° W., where it turns northeast and then southeast in a great bend, entering the Atlantic in lat. 10° 29′ S. It has a total length of 1,800 mi. and a fall of 2,700-2,800 ft. It is navigable from the Atlantic to Piranhas (148 mi.) and is nearly 1 mi. wide at Penedo, 22 mi. from the sea. Above Piranhas, about 193 mi. from its mouth, are the falls of Paulo Afonso, where the river plunges through a narrow gorge—in one place only 51 ft. wide— and over three successive falls, altogether 265 ft. The obstructed part of the river is about 190 mi. long, and consists of a series of rapids above the falls and a deep canyon with whirlpools for some distance below. The Brazilian government has built a railway around these falls from Piranhas (151 ft. elevation) to Jatobá (978 ft.) with an extension of 71 mi.

Above Jatobá there is another series of rapids, called the Sobradinho, nearly 90 mi. above the lower rapids, which are navigable at high water, and above these an unobstructed channel for light-draught river boats up to Pirapora, a little above the mouth of the Rio das Velhas, a distance of 984 mi. There the river runs through a barren, semiarid region, sparsely settled. The rapids of Pirapora are 17 mi. above the mouth of the Rio das Velhas, and this point, the head of navigation on the river, and 1,742 ft. above sea level, is the objective-point of the Central do Brasil railway, the purpose being to create by rail and river a central route from Rio de Janeiro to the northern ports of Salvador and Recife.

The principal tributaries of the São Francisco are: on the

right, the Pará, Paraopeba, Velhas and Verde-Grande; on the left, the Indayá, Abaeté, Paracatú, Urucuya, Carinhanha, Corrente and Grande. Several of these tributaries are navigable for long distances by small boats—the aggregate being a little more than 1,000 mi. Some authorities give the aggregate navigable channels of the São Francisco as 4,350 mi. The upper valley of the São Francisco is partly forested, has a temperate climate, with a mean annual temperature of 85° F. and a rainfall of 1,637 mm. The rainy season is from December to March, but on the lower river there are sometimes droughts covering several years.

An admirable description of this great river is given by Richard Burton in *The Highlands of Brazil* (1869), and a more technical description by E. Liais in *Hydrographie du Haut San-Francisco et du Rio das Velhas* (Rio de Janeiro, 1865).

SÃO LEOPOLDO, a city of the state of Rio Grande do Sul, Brazil, on the left bank of the Rio dos Sinos, 20½ mi. by rail north of Pôrto Alegre. It is the chief town of a *município* (commune) of the same name, having an area of 340 sq.mi. and inhabited chiefly by German colonists. Population (1950) of the *município*, 76,251. São Leopoldo has river and railway communication with Pôrto Alegre and railway connection with Santa Maria. It is a prosperous industrial town, with broad straight streets, substantial buildings and good schools. Among the articles which it manufactures are matches, hats, boots and shoes, soap, liqueurs and artificial drinks, leather and leatherwork and earthenware. In the surrounding districts cattle and hogs are raised, and jerked beef, hides, pork, lard, potatoes, beans, *farinha de mandioca* (cassava flour), Indian corn, tobacco and a great variety of vegetables and fruits are produced.

The city was originally a German colony founded by the emperor Pedro I in 1824 and established at a place known as the Feitoria Real de Cânhamo (Royal flax factory).

SÃO LUIS or in full, SÃO LUÍS DO MARANHÃO, a seaport of northern Brazil, capital of the state of Maranhão, on the west side of an island of the same name, in lat. 2° 30′ S., long. 44° 17′ W. of Greenwich, about 300 mi. E.S.E. of Belém (Para). Population of the *município* (1950) 121,917. An important part of the population is made up of the planters of the state, who live in town and leave their estates to the care of overseers. The island of Maranhão lies off the mouths of the rivers Mearim and Itapecurú, between the Bay of São Marcos on the west and the Bay of São José on the east, and is separated from the mainland by a small channel called the *Canal do Mosquito*. It is irregular in outline, its greatest length from northeast to southwest being 34 mi., and its greatest breadth 19 mi. Its surface is broken by a number of low hills and short valleys. The city is built upon a tongue of land between two small estuaries, Anil and Bacanga, which unite and open upon the Bay of São Marcos. It covers two low hills and the intervening valley, the transverse streets sloping sharply to the estuary on either side. These slopes make it difficult to use vehicles in the streets, but they afford a natural surface drainage which makes São Luís cleaner and more healthful than are usually the coast towns of tropical Brazil. The buildings are of the old Portuguese type, with massive walls of broken stone and mortar, having an outside finish of plaster or glazed tiles and roofs of red tiles. The principal public buildings are the cathedral, a large and severely plain structure, the Episcopal palace, the Carmelite church, the Government palace, town hall, customhouse, hospital and a number of asylums, convents and charitable schools. There are schools of law, pharmacy, agriculture and arts. Exports are mainly babassu nuts and cotton. Communication with the mainland is carried on by means of small steamers, and by a railway which crosses the eastern part of the state to Senador Furtado on the Parnaíba river opposite Teresina.

São Luís was founded in 1612 by La Rivardière, a French officer commissioned by Henry IV to establish a colony in this vicinity. The French colony was expelled in 1615 by the Portuguese, who, in turn, surrendered to the Dutch in 1641. In 1644 the Dutch abandoned the island, when the Portuguese resumed possession and held the city to the end of their colonial rule in Brazil. The city became the seat of a bishopric in 1679.

SAÔNE, a river of east France, 301 mi. long, rising in the Faucilles mountains (Vosges), 15 mi. S.W. of Épinal at a height of 1,300 ft. and uniting with the Rhône at Lyons. The name is derived from *Sauconna*, a 4th-century name. Rising in the Vosges Hercynian massif, it meanders in the wide depression on Jurassic and Tertiary rocks between the Plateau of Langres, the Côte d'Or and the mountains of Charolais and Beaujolais on the west, and the western slopes of the Vosges and Jura and the plain of Bresse and the plateau of Dombes on the east. Near Allerey the Saône unites with the Doubs (left), which rivals it in volume and exceeds it in length at this point. At Chalon-sur-Saône it turns south, and passes Mâcon. Below Tréveux its valley narrows, winds past the Mont d'Or group and joins the Rhone at Lyons. The Saône is canalized from Corre to Lyons, a distance of 233 mi., the normal depth of water being 6½ ft. At Corre (confluence with the Coney) it connects with the Eastern canal, at Heuilley (below Gray) with the Saône-Marne canal, at St. Symphorien (above St. Jean-de-Losne) with the Rhône-Rhine canal, and at St. Jean-de-Losne with the canal de Bourgogne and at Chalon with the Canal du Centre. (*See* RHÔNE.)

SAÔNE-ET-LOIRE, a department of east-central France formed from the districts of Autunois, Brionnais, Chalonnais, Charollais and Mâconnais, previously belonging to Burgundy. It is bounded north by the department of Côte d'Or, east by that of Jura, southeast by Rhône and Loire, south by Rhône and Loire, west by Allier and Nièvre. Pop. (1946) 506,749. Area, 3,331 sq.mi. The department extends down into the valley of the Loire on the west and into that of the Saône on the east, both with Pliocene deposits, from a high, but discontinuous, central north-to-south axis, stretching from the Côte d'Or (Jurassic) to the Beaujolais (largely granitic). The chief break in the highlands is used by the railway through the Charollais from Dijon through Beaune to Digoin on the Loire, and by the canal from Châlon-sur-Saône to Dijon. On the east the department extends beyond the Saône to include a large part of the region of Bresse which focuses chiefly on Châlon. The heights of the Morvan (2,959 ft. in the department) rise on the northwestern border.

The average temperature at Mâcon (52° or 53° F.), the most temperate spot in the department, is slightly higher than at Paris, the winter being colder and the summer hotter. At the same town the yearly rainfall is about 33 in., but both the rigour of the climate and the amount of rain increases in the hilly districts.

Agriculture prospers in Saône-et-Loire. Wheat, oats and maize are the chief cereals; potatoes, clover and other fodder, and mangold-wurzels are important, and beets, hemp, colza and rape are also grown. Excellent pasture is found in the valleys of the Saône and other rivers. The vine, one of the principal resources of the department, is cultivated chiefly in the neighbourhood of Châlon and Mâcon. Of the wines of Mâconnais, the vintage of Thorins is in high repute. The white Charollais oxen are one of the finest French breeds; horses, pigs and sheep are reared, and poultry farming is a thriving occupation in the Bresse. The industrial importance of the department is great, chiefly owing to its coal and iron mines; the chief coal mines are those near Creusot, Autun and Chapelle-sous-Dun. A pit at Épinac is more than 2,600 ft. in depth. Iron is mined at Mazenay and Change, and manganese is found at Romanèche and there are quarries of various kinds. There are well-known warm mineral springs containing chloride of sodium and iron at Bourbon-Lancy. The iron and engineering works of Schneider and Company at Le Creusot are the largest in France. The department also has many distilleries, potteries, porcelain works (Digoin and Charolles), tile works, oil works and glass factories, and manufactures leather goods, esparto goods, sugar and fecula. Its commerce between the north and the midi is facilitated by navigable streams—the Loire, Saône, Doubs and Seille—the Canal du Centre, which joins Chalon-sur-Saône with Digoin on the Loire, and the canal from Roanne to Digoin and the lateral Loire canal, both following the main river valley. The chief railway of the department is the P.L.M.

Saône-et-Loire forms the diocese of Autun; it is part of the district of the 8th army corps (Bourges); its educational centre is Lyons and its court of appeal that of Dijon. It is divided into

5 arrondissements—Mâcon, Louhans, Chalon-sur-Saône, Autun, Charolles—51 cantons, and 590 communes. Mâcon, Chalon-sur-Saône, Autun, Le Creusot, Cluny, Montceau-Les-Mines, Louhans, Charolles (*qq.v.*), Tournus and Paray-le-Monial are the chief towns in the department. St. Marcellès-Châlon has a Romanesque church, once attached to an abbey where Peter Abélard died; Anzy has a Romanesque church and other remains of an important monastery; Sully has a château of the 16th century; and Semur-en-Brionnais and Varennes-l'Arconce fine Romanesque churches. Prehistoric remains of the Old Stone Age have been found at Solutré near Mâcon, and have given the name Solutrian to a period of prehistoric time.

SÃO PAULO, a state of Brazil extending from 19° 54′ to 25° 15′ S. lat. and bounded north by Mato Grosso and Minas Gerais, east by Minas Gerais, Rio de Janeiro and the Atlantic, south by the Atlantic and Paraná and west by Paraná and Mato Grosso. Pop. (1950) 9,242,610; area 95,459 sq.mi. The state has a coast 373 mi. long, skirted closely by the Serra do Mar, below which is a narrow coastal zone broken by lagoons, tidal channels and mountain spurs. Above is an extensive plateau, 1,500 to 3,000 ft. above sea level. Isolated ranges of low elevation break the surface in places, but in general the state may be described as a tableland with an undulating surface sloping westward to the Paraná. The extreme eastern part, however, has an eastward slope and belongs to the Paraíba basin. The state is traversed by a number of large rivers, tributaries of the Paraná, the largest of which are the Rio Grande, Peixe, Tieté, Aguapeí, Tigre and Paranapanema. The eastern slopes of the Serra do Mar are well wooded but there are wide grassy plains (*campos*) on the plateau. A large part of western São Paulo is still unsettled. The coastal zone has a hot climate, and it also has a heavy rainfall. On the plateau the rainfall is sufficiently abundant, but the air is drier and more bracing, the sun temperature being high and the nights cool. The open country is singularly healthful, but the river lowlands are generally not so.

The great industries are agricultural, and the most conspicuous is coffee production. São Paulo produces more than one-half the total Brazilian crop and its one great port, Santos, is the largest coffee-shipping port in the world. The *terra roxa* (red earth) lands of the central and northern parts of the state are peculiarly favourable. This soil is ferruginous, pasty and free from stone, and it covers the higher surface of the plateau with a thick layer. The best plantations are on the high divides between the river courses, and not in their eroded valleys.

The other agricultural products of the state include sugar, cotton, rice, tobacco, Indian corn, beans, mandioca, bananas and other fruits, and many of the vegetables of the temperate zone. Cereals can be grown, but climatic conditions have been considered unfavourable. Sugar cane was the first exotic to be cultivated in São Paulo, and was its principal product in colonial times. Cotton was largely produced, especially during the American Civil War. The industry nearly disappeared, but now is again improving because of the demand for fibre by the national cotton factories. The cultivation of rice also is increasing, under the stimulus of protective duties. Although São Paulo is not classed as a pastoral region, the state possesses large herds of cattle, which are being improved by the importation of purebred stock from Europe. Butter and cheese are produced to a limited extent, and the supply of fresh milk to the cities is attracting some attention. Attention is also given, to a limited extent, to the breeding of horses and mules. The most general and profitable of the animal industries is the breeding of swine, which thrive remarkably on the plateau. The state has an excellent agricultural school and experiment station at Piracicaba, and there is also a zootechnic station near the capital.

The principal manufactures are cotton and woollen textiles, jute bagging, *aramina* fabrics, furniture, iron and bronze, coffee machinery and agricultural implements, artificial liquors and food products. Steam power is generally used, though both electric and hydraulic power are employed. The iron mines and works at Ipanema, near Sorocaba, a government enterprise, are one of the oldest industries of the state, dating back to the first quarter of the 19th century.

São Paulo is well provided with railways, which include the pioneer line from Santos to Jundiaí (formerly owned by the British but taken over by the state government) which has a double track from Santos to the city of São Paulo, the Paulista lines which are a continuation of the Santos-Jundiaí line into the interior, the Mogiana lines running northward from Campinas through rich coffee districts to Uberaba in Minas Gerais and into Goiás. The São Paulo branch of the Central do Brasil line which passes through the eastern part of the state and provides communication with the national capital, the São Paulo and Rio Grande which crosses the states of Paraná, Santa Catarina and Rio Grande and connects with the railways of Uruguay, and the line from São Paulo to Puerto Esperança. The ports of the state are Santos, which is visited by large steamers in the foreign trade, and Cananéia, Iguape, São Sebastião and Ubatuba which are engaged in the coasting trade only. Cananéia and Iguape are chiefly known for the rice grown in their vicinity.

The capital of the state is São Paulo (*q.v.*) and its principal port and second city in importance is Santos (*q.v.*). The chief cities and towns, with populations in 1950 are as follows, the enumeration being for municipalities or parishes, including large rural areas and sometimes including separate villages: Campinas (*q.v.*); Guaratinguetá (37,404), on the Paraíba, 120 mi. E.N.E. of São Paulo; Piracicaba (88,855), 85 mi. N.W. of São Paulo; Limeira (46,822), in a fertile thickly-settled district; Rio Claro (47,698), 135 mi. N.W. of Santos, on a branch of the Paulista railway, in a fertile coffee-producing region, 2,030 ft. above the sea; Taubaté (53,759), one of the oldest cities of the state, on the Paraíba 80 mi. E.N.E. of the capital, in a rich agricultural district, with works for refining oil from the petroleum-bearing shales which are in the vicinity; Bragança (52,177), 50 mi. N. of São Paulo in a fertile country partly devoted to sugar production and stock; São José dos Campos (45,258); Tieté (18,073) on the Tieté river northwest of São Paulo; Pindamonhagaba (29,286), on the Paraíba river and Central do Brasil railway 105 mi. N.E. of São Paulo in a long settled district, 1,770 ft. above the sea, producing coffee, sugar, rice, Indian corn, beans, rum and cattle; Sorocaba (94,868; city 69,631), a prosperous manufacturing and commercial town on the Rio Sorocaba and Sorocabana railway, 50 mi. W. of São Paulo; Itu, or Ytú (31,295), about 70 mi. W.N.W. of São Paulo on the Tieté river and Ituana railway, with water power derived from the Salto (falls) do Itú, and with important manufactures; São Carlos (48,750); Casa Branca (21,662), in the northern coffee region; Paraíbuna (16,919); Pirassununga (26,413); Batatais (21,827); Franca (55,023); Jacareí (27,850); Botucatú (41,868); Jundiaí (69,879), 86 mi. N. of Santos, an important manufacturing town and railway junction, 2,320 ft. above sea level; Ribeirão Preto (91,374; city 65,081), 197 mi. N. of Campinas on the Mogiana railway in a fertile coffee-producing region; Iguape (15,541), a port on the southern coast of the state, on a tidewater channel of sufficient depth for coastwise steamers, with exports of rice and timber; Lorena (25,141), 130 mi. N.E. of São Paulo, beautifully situated, 1,760 ft. above the sea, a station on the Central do Brasil railway, and the junction of a branch railway to the Campos do Jordão where the national government has established a military sanatorium because of its dry, bracing climate.

São Paulo was settled in 1532 by the Portuguese under Martim Afonso de Souza, who established a colony near Santos, at São Vicente, now an unimportant village. It was originally called the *capitania* of São Vicente (organized 1534) and covered the whole of southern Brazil from Rio de Janeiro south. After the suppression of the captaincy grants, parts of this enormous territory were cut off from time to time to form other captaincies, from which developed the present states of Rio de Janeiro, Minas Gerais, Mato Grosso, Paraná, Santa Catarina and Rio Grande do Sul. In 1681 São Paulo succeeded São Vicente as the capital of the captaincy. (R. D'E.)

SÃO PAULO, a city of Brazil, capital of a state of the same name, largest industrial center of the nation and seat of a bishopric, on the Tieté river 49 mi. by rail N.W. of the port of Santos and 308 mi. by rail S.W. of Rio de Janeiro. City population in 1950 was 2,227,512. São Paulo is connected by rail with Santos, its port, with Rio de Janeiro and with other inland cities. In great part the city occupies an elevated open stretch of tableland commanding extensive views of the surrounding country; and a small part of it is in the low alluvial land bordering the Tieté. The upper part has several slight elevations forming healthful residential districts. The city is just within the tropics, but its elevation (2,500 ft. above the sea) gives it a temperate climate, bracing in the cool season and yet with high sun temperatures in summer. The city is singularly healthful.

In the mid-19th century it was still a small colonial village; 100 years later it was the third town in South America. In 1945,

12,838 building licences for new homes and apartment houses were issued. Originally, the city derived its wealth from coffee and cotton-growing in the rich red soil section of the state. The construction in near-by Cubatão of a power plant with a capacity of more than 500,000 h.p. enabled the city to become one of the largest industrial centres in Latin America. In 1950 there were 353,530 industrial workers in the city out of a total of 610,109 of all plants in the state (which, in turn, had 35% of the industrial population of all Brazil). The busy centre of the city, called "Triangle," with its skyscrapers and continuous activity, is the most characteristic part of São Paulo. There are fine avenues, imposing buildings, including the state university, the Pacaembú stadium (capacity, 70,000), the Jockey Club course and pleasant residential districts such as Jardim America and Avenida Paulista. The Butantan institute, a research centre for the study of snakes and the production of antitoxins and antivenins, is unique of its kind. The museum and monument of Ipiranga commemorates the national declaration of independence in 1822. The city, which has a large Italian population, was founded by the Jesuits under Manuel de Nobrega (in 1554) as an Indian settlement and at first bore the name of Piratininga. In 1681 it succeeded São Vicente as the capital of the captaincy. (R. D'E.)

SÃO SALVADOR, Brazil: see SALVADOR.

SAPAJOU, an alternative name for the American capuchin monkeys (q.v.), comprising the genus *Cebus*. (See also PRIMATES.)

SAPAN or SAPPAN WOOD, a soluble red dyewood (Malay *sapang*), from a tree belonging to the leguminous genus *Caesalpinia* (*C. sappan*), a native of tropical Asia and the Indian archipelago. The wood is somewhat lighter in colour than Brazil wood and its other allies, but the same tinctorial principle, brazilin, appears to be common to all.

SAPARUA, the name of the chief island, and capital, of the Uliassers, a group of islands lying east of the island of Amboina, in the Moluccas. Japan occupied Saparua in 1942.

SAPINDACEAE, a large family of dicotyledonous plants, with about 150 genera and 2,000 species, chiefly tropical, consisting of trees, shrubs and vines. The leaves are mostly alternate and compound, occasionally simple, while the flowers, mostly small, are irregular or unsymmetrical, mostly polygamo-dioecius, the fruits various. Important fruit trees include the litchi (q.v.) (*Litchi chinensis*), of China, longan (*Euphoria longana*) of China and India, the rambutan (*Nephelium lappaceum*) and palusan (*Nephelium mutabile*) of the Indo-Malayan region, the akee (q.v.) (*Blighia sapida*) of Africa, and others. The seeds of *Schleichera oleosa* yield macassar oil, while the aril surrounding the seeds is edible. Other species yield important timbers, and the bark of still others is rich in saponin. The varnish tree (*Koelreuteria*) is widely cultivated in Europe and North America as an ornamental.

See L. Radlkofer, "Sapindaceae," *Pflanzenreich* 98 (iv, 165): 1–1539, fig. 1–45 (1931–33).

SAPONINS AND SAPOGENINS. Saponins are water-soluble plant substances characterized by special properties, namely, the ability to lower the surface tension of water and hence to cause foaming, the ability to destroy red blood corpuscles (haemolysis) and the ability to kill fish, all at relatively low concentrations. They probably are present in all plants, having been identified in more than 75 families and more than 500 species. They may be distributed throughout the plant or occur in high concentration in one part of the plant; e.g., the root or bulb, leaves, bark, flowers, fruit flesh or seeds. Their function in the plant is not known. Some appear to serve as a storage form of carbohydrate (q.v.) in the plant, whereas others seem to be waste products of plant metabolism.

Common names for plants containing high concentrations of saponins are soap root, soap wort, soap bark, soap plant and amole. These names are indicative of their use as cleansing agents by peoples throughout the world since ancient times. They do not form a scum in hard water, and even in comparatively modern times were preferred to soap for laundering fine fabrics, such as silk shawls. They formerly were used as foaming agents in foam-type fire extinguishers and as wetting agents in agricultural sprays, but were displaced for these purposes by the less expensive synthetic detergents and wetting agents. Saponin solutions are used in photographic emulsions to permit even spreading on the base, and in multilayered coatings to permit spreading and adhesion of successive layers.

Aborigines throughout all parts of the world have used saponins for catching fish. A quantity of a plant having a high saponin content was crushed and stirred into a pool. After a short time the fish rose to the surface and were taken easily.

It is estimated that from 300 to 400 species of plants were used for this purpose. As early as the 13th century, in order to prevent extermination of the fish, laws were passed forbidding the use of fish poisons. Saponins cause death in fish probably by disabling the breathing mechanism of the gills. Although saponins are haemolytic and toxic to warm-blooded animals when injected into the blood stream, they are not absorbed from the intestines. Hence fish killed by saponins can be eaten with safety. The non-toxicity to man on ingestion is evident when one considers that the foaming properties of certain beverages, such as root beer, result from the presence of saponins.

Chemically the saponins belong to a large class of substances known as glycosides (see GLUCOSIDES, NATURAL). When a water solution of a saponin is heated in the presence of a strong acid, the saponin molecule is split into fragments with the addition of the elements of one molecule of water at every point at which scission takes place (hydrolysis). The products are a molecule of sapogenin and several molecules of one or more kinds of sugar (see CARBOHYDRATES). For example, in the hydrolysis of digitonin, one of three different saponins isolated from foxglove leaves, each molecule combines with five molecules of water to yield one molecule of a sapogenin, called digitogenin, one molecule of xylose and four molecules of galactose.

Because several different saponins may occur in the same plant, and because the saponins are amorphous and not readily crystallized, it has been difficult to isolate them in a pure state, and at mid-20th century relatively little work had been done on the chemistry of the saponins themselves. The sapogenins, on the other hand, are crystalline compounds that are purified readily, and a large amount of work had been expended in attempts to determine the way in which the constituent atoms are linked together. It was found that the sapogenins thus far isolated belong to two main types. One type contains 27 carbon atoms with varying numbers of hydrogen and oxygen atoms. They have at least one alcoholic function (hydroxyl group), and contain a carbon framework like that present in the animal and plant alcohols known as sterols. Hence they are called steroid sapogenins. The saponins from foxglove leaves, sarsaparilla root, yucca and agave, belong to this class. Some steroid sapogenins, such as diosgenin prepared commercially from a Mexican yam, have become valuable raw materials for the synthesis of the female hormone, progesterone, and the adrenal cortical hormone, cortisone.

The second type of sapogenin contains 30 carbon atoms, along with varying amounts of hydrogen and oxygen. They are called triterpene sapogenins because there are three times as many carbon atoms in the molecule as in a terpene molecule (see TERPENES). Like the steroid sapogenins, they contain at least one alcoholic function (hydroxyl group), but in addition they contain an acid function (carboxyl group) and sometimes are called acid sapogenins. Saponins yielding triterpene sapogenins appear to be more widely distributed than those yielding steroid sapogenins. Moreover, the same triterpene sapogenin may occur free, as well as combined with sugars as a saponin. Oleanolic acid can be obtained by hydrolysis of saponins present in guaiac bark, sugar beets or calendula flowers. It also occurs free in clove buds, in the waxy coatings of olive and mistletoe leaves and in grape skins.

A further point of interest is that the triterpene alcohols, which occur in plant resins, are related closely in structure to the triterpene sapogenins. By replacing the acid function, COOH, of oleanolic acid by the group CH₃, a compound is obtained which is identical with beta-amyrin, a triterpene alcohol isolated from Manila elemi and other resins. (C. R. N.)

SAPOTACEAE, a family of tropical dicotyledonous plants, most of which are trees with leathery leaves. There are 35 genera and about 600 species, many of which are of economic importance as sources of gutta percha (q.v.), balata, shea butter, ironwood, etc. *Chrysophyllum cainito* is the West Indian star apple. *Mimusops huberi* is the Brazilian milk tree. *Achras zapota* of tropical America, cultivated in all tropical countries, yields the excellent fruit known as the sapodilla or naseberry, and the important chicle (*q.v.*), the basis of much chewing gum. *Lucuma nervosa* is the egg-fruit or canistel, of South America, now naturalized in Florida and the West Indies. The important commercial product gutta percha is chiefly derived from various species of *Palaquium* and *Payena* growing in the Malay peninsula and archipelago.

SAPPHIC METRE, certain forms of quantitative verse, named after their supposed originator, the Aeolic poetess Sappho (*cf.* ALCAICS). For two of her famous metres *see* CHORIAMBIC VERSE. Characteristic of all these metres is the emergence of a choriambus (- ⌣ ⌣ -), or perhaps a dactyl (- ⌣ ⌣), in the midst of what appears to be a series of feet of other lengths, especially trochees (- ⌣) (*q.v.*). The best-known employment of lines of this sort is in the Sapphic stanza, three Sapphic hendecasyllables followed by an Adonic, thus:

> iam sătis terris nivis ătque dirae
>
> grandinis misit păter et rubenti
>
> dextĕra sacras iaculatus arces
>
> terruit urbem.

This is used occasionally in Latin by Catullus, frequently by Horace, who introduced some small modifications (fourth syllable always long, fifth syllable almost always the end of a word), and by later writers; in the Middle Ages it was much used for hymns, notably by Gregory the Great.

In modern languages, the Sapphic stanza has been imitated, sometimes with fair success, as by Swinburne:

> Heard the flying feet of the Loves behind her
> Make a sudden thunder upon the waters,
> As the thunder flung from the strong unclosing
> Wings of a great wind.

But it remains an exotic, not well suited to our methods of versification.

SAPPHIRE, a blue transparent variety of corundum (*q.v.*), or native alumina, much valued as a gem-stone. It is essentially the same mineral as ruby, from which it differs chiefly in colour which, normally, varies from palest blue to deep indigo, the most esteemed tint being that of the blue cornflower. Many crystals are parti-coloured, but by skilful cutting, the deep-coloured portion may be caused to colour the entire gem. As the sapphire crystallizes in the rhombohedral system it is dichroic, but in pale stones this character may not be well marked. In a deep-coloured stone the colour may be resolved, by the dichroscope, into an ultramarine blue and a bluish or yellowish green. In blue tourmaline and in iolite—stones sometimes mistaken for sapphire—the dichroism is much more distinct. The blue of sapphire has been referred to the presence of oxides of chromium, iron or titanium, whilst an organic origin has also been suggested. On exposure to high temperature, sapphires usually lose colour, but, unlike rubies, do not regain it on cooling. A. Verneuil succeeded in imparting a sapphire-blue colour to artificial alumina by addition of 1·5% of magnetic oxide of iron and 0·5% of titanic acid (*Comptes rendus*, Jan. 17, 1910). According to F. Bordas, sapphire exposed to the action of radium changes to green and then to yellow.

Under artificial illumination many sapphires appear dark and inky, and in some cases the blue changes to a violet. In spite of its hardness, which slightly exceeds that of ruby, it has been sometimes engraved as a gem.

Sapphires occur, with many other gem-stones, as pebbles or rolled crystals in the alluvial deposits of sand and gravel of Ceylon, the gem-gravel being known locally as *illam*. The principal localities are Ratnapura, Rakwana and Matara. Some of the slightly-cloudy Ceylon sapphires, usually greyish-blue, display when cut with a convex face a chatoyant luminosity, sometimes forming a luminous star of six rays, or "star-sapphires".

The asterism seems due to the presence of microscopic tubular cavities, or to enclosure of crystalline minerals, arranged in a definite system. In 1875 sapphires were discovered in deposits of clay and sand in Battambang (Siam), where they have been worked on a considerable scale; they occur also with rubies in the provinces of Chantabun and Krat. Many of the Siamese

sapphires are very dark, some being so deeply tinted as to appear almost black by reflected light. In Upper Burma sapphires occur in association with rubies, but are much less important (*see* RUBY), and they are also found in the Zanskar range, Kashmir, especially near the village of Soomjam, associated with tourmaline. Madagascar yields sapphires as rolled crystals generally of very deep colour. They are widely distributed through the gold-bearing drifts of Victoria, New South Wales and Queensland, but the blue of the Australian stones is usually dark, and it is notable that green tints are not infrequent. The Anakie sapphire-fields of Queensland are situated to the west of Emerald and east of the Drummond Range. Coarse sapphire is found in many parts of the United States, and the mineral occurs of gem quality in North Carolina and Montana. The great corundum deposits of Corundum Hill, Macon county, N.C., have yielded good sapphires, and they are found also at Cowee Creek in the same county. In Montana, sapphires were found in washing for gold in 1865, and have been worked on a large scale. The rolled crystals of sapphire occur, with garnet and other minerals, in glacial deposits, and have probably been derived from dikes of igneous rocks, like andesite and lamprophyre. They display much variety of colour, and exhibit peculiar brilliancy when cut, but are often of pale tints. The principal localities are at Missouri Bar, Ruby Bar and other places near Helena, where they were first worked, and also at Yogo Gulch, near Utica. The Helena crystals are of tabular habit, being composed of the basal pinacoid with a very short hexagonal prism, whilst at Yogo Gulch many of the crystals affect a rhombohedral habit. The Montana sapphires and the matrix have been described by Dr. G. F. Kunz, Professor L. V. Pirsson and Dr. J. H. Pratt (*Amer. Jour. Sc.*, ser. 4 vol. iv., 1897). The sapphire occurs also in Europe, being found in the Iserweise of Bohemia and in the basalt of the Rhine valley, Le-Puy-en-Velay in France, and in tholeiite intrusions in the island of Mull, but the European stones have no interest as gems.

SAPPHO (or as she calls herself PSAPPHO), the greatest poetess of Greece, was a native of Lesbos. In spite of her fame almost every detail in her history is doubtful. Only a few of the many and often conflicting statements made about her by ancient authors can be checked by her own writings. It would seem probable that she came of an aristocratic Mytilenean family (another account connects her with Eresus) and was born round about 600 B.C., so that she was contemporary with Pittacus and with the poet Alcaeus, with whom she may have exchanged verses. No less than eight versions of her father's name are recorded by Suïdas, of which Scamandronymus, the form given by Herodotus (ii. 135), may be taken as the most acceptable. Her mother is said to have been named Cleïs, and if the fragment *inc. lib.*, 17 is rightly ascribed, the statement is supported by the fact that her daughter also was a Cleïs. There is more certainty about her brothers, or at any rate about two of the three, Charaxus and Larichus. She speaks of Larichus as being cupbearer, a position filled by youths of good family, and Charaxus (though not mentioned by name in the extant remains) is evidently the "brother" referred to in ᾱ 3. We learn from Herodotus and others that he sailed to Egypt and bought out a courtesan, Rhodopis or Doricha, for which Sappho attacked him. ᾱ 3 seems to be a prayer for his safe return from overseas and a reconciliation with his sister and ᾱ4b perhaps contained a prayer that Doricha may not entangle him again. The poetess's family is of less interest than the pupils, friends and rivals with whom we meet repeatedly in the fragments of the poems, with their references on the one hand to Atthis, once loved but now estranged, Anactoria, gone far away, Dica, "lovelier than soft Gyriuno," on the other to Andromeda, who stole Atthis away, Gorgo and others. In ᾱ11 there seems to be a hint of some enmity towards the house of Penthilus, with which Pittacus was connected by marriage, but it happens most frequently that where we have names the thought cannot be followed far, and that in the longer pieces, where affection is most touchingly, or distaste most cuttingly expressed, no names have survived. Apart from the relations just referred to we know next to nothing of the life of Sappho. She is said to have been banished, like other aristocrats, and to have gone to Sicily, but this flight has left no trace in the remains unless the reference to Aphrodite of Panormus in $\overline{\alpha}7$ $App.$ be such. As for the story of her passion for Phaon and her leap from the Leucadian rock, it bears every sign of being pure fiction. There are two references to the advance of old age; we cannot tell whether her own or another's. Of the end of her life we know nothing at all.

Sappho's poems are said by Tullius Laurea to have been arranged in nine books. Suidas says there were nine books of lyrical poems, but epigrams, elegeia, etc., besides. The author of P. Oxy, 1800, also counts a separate book of elegeia, but his figure for the books of lyrical poems is lost. From the fragments we know of only eight books of lyrical poems. It appears that these books were, as far as possible, arranged according to metre (Bk. 1, for instance, containing only pieces in the so-called Sapphic stanza, and so on), but in the case of one book (the Epithalamia, perhaps Bk. 8) according to subject. The language seems to be no literary dialect, but the ordinary speech used by the contemporaries of the poetess, and so to differ in a greater or less degree from almost all the other Greek poetry that has come down to us. The conjunction of extreme simplicity of language with intensity of emotion, from which the poetry derives its peculiar effect, as well as the perfection of the form, has hitherto completely baffled translators, Swinburne among the rest.

Until comparatively recent times the poetry of Sappho survived only in the quotations made by ancient authors. The number of the fragments thus preserved was not inconsiderable, but their text was often seriously depraved, and, with two exceptions—the complete or nearly complete poems cited by Dionysius of Halicarnassus "Longinus"—their extent was insignificant. Within the last 50 years, however, there have been recovered from the soil of Egypt papyrus rolls and vellum codices, written at dates ranging from the 2nd to the 6th or 7th centuries A.D., which contain authentic texts of Sappho, terribly mutilated indeed, but remarkable for the integrity of their tradition. These remains are now preserved in Oxford, Berlin, London, Florence, Halle and Graz, and photographic facsimiles of parts of them may be seen in the publications of the Egyptian Exploration Society, the Berlin academy, the Società Italiana and the Graeca Halensis. Of the older editors, who were concerned only with the quotations, none but Bergk need be mentioned (*Poetae lyricae graecae*, 4th ed., Leipzig, 1882). Those who have done most for the editing and interpretation of the book texts are Professors W. Schubart and U. von Wilamowitz Moellendorff in Germany and A. S. Hunt in England. The only complete collection of all the known material is in Σαπφοῦς μέλη (Oxford, 1925), by E. Lobel, but a reference may be made to Diehl's *Anthologia Lyrica*, iv. (Leipzig, 1923), though the text is uncritical and much of the illustrative material irrelevant. In the introductions to Σαπφοῦς μέλη and its companion volume Ἀλκαίου μέλη (Oxford, 1927), will be found an attempt to establish the proper method of constituting the text. There is an article on Sappho by W. Aly in Pauly-Wissowa, *Realencyklopädie*, which collects the material for the life work of the poetess, but its conclusions should be treated with caution.

BIBLIOGRAPHY.—J. A. Symonds, *Studies of the Greek Poets* (3 vols., 1873–76, new ed. 1921); H. W. Smyth, *Greek Melic Poets* (1900); P. Brandt, *Sappho* (Leipsic, 1905); B. Steiner, *Sappho* (1907); *Sappho: Life and Work* (1910); J. M. F. Bascoul, *La chaste Sappho de Lesbos et le mouvement féministe à Athènes au 4ème siècle av. J.-C.* (1911), and *La chaste Sappho et Stesichore* (1913); M. M. Patrick, *Sappho and the Island of Lesbos* (1912); J. M. Edmonds, *Sappho in the added light of the new fragments* (1912); U. von Wilamowitz-Moellendorff, *Sappho und Simonides* (1913); E. M. Cox, *Sappho and the Sapphic Metre in English, with bibliographical notes* (1916). Text, J. M. Edmonds, *Lyra-Graeca* (3 vols., 1922–27). (E. Ll.)

SAPPORO, the official capital of Hokkaido, Japan, situated in 43° 4′ N. and 141° 21′ E. Pop. (1950) 313,850. It was chosen in 1870, and owed its prosperity at the outset chiefly to public institutions established in connection with the colonization bureau.

Sapporo has a university which pays special attention to agricultural science, a museum, sawmills, flour mills, breweries and hemp and flax factories.

SAPROPEL is an unconsolidated sedimentary deposit rich in bituminous substances. It is distinguished from peat in being rich in fatty and waxy substances and poor in cellulosic material. The term was first used by H. Potonié in 1904. When consolidated into rock, sapropel becomes oil shale, bituminous shale or boghead coal. The principal components are certain types of algae which are rich in fats and waxes. Minor constituents are mineral grains and decomposed fragments of spores, fungi, bacteria and nonvascular plants. The organic materials accumulate in water under reducing conditions, mostly in fresh water.

See David White, *Treatise on Sedimentation* (1932). (P. D. T.)

SAPROPHYTES, the name given in botany to plants which grow upon decaying organic matter, the products of the decay of which they absorb. Many fungi (*q.v.*) are saprophytic, as are some orchids (*q.v.*) and other flowering plants.

SAPRU, SIR TEJ BAHADUR (1875–1949), Indian jurist and politician, was a Kashmiri Brahmin born on Dec. 8, 1875. He was a successful advocate of the high court of Allahabad from 1896; a member of the United Provinces legislative council (1913–16); and a member of the imperial legislative council (1916–20). In 1919–20 he was president of the United Provinces Liberal league. In Dec. 1920 he was appointed law member of the governor general's executive council, but resigned to resume his practice in February 1923. Later in the year he was a representative of India at the imperial conference in London. A man of great gifts of expression, he had a leading share in the drafting of the Nehru report of the so-called All-Parties conference formulating a scheme of dominion self-government for India approved at a conference held at Lucknow in August 1928. He was active in the promotion of education. He died Jan. 20, 1949, in Allahabad.

(F. H. BR.; X.)

SAPSUCKER, the name given to American woodpeckers of the genus *Sphyrapicus*; there are three North American species—*S. varius,* the yellow-bellied sapsucker of eastern U.S.; *S. ruber,* the red-breasted sapsucker, and *S. thyroideus,* the Williamson sapsucker, the two latter inhabiting the western mountain ranges of Canada and the U.S.

All species have a habit of girdling trees with rows of holes. *S. ruber* has a dull red head and breast; this tint is confined to the head and (in the males) throat in *S. varius,* and to the throat alone in the male *S. thyroideus,* which has a bright yellow belly.

SAPULPA, a city of northeastern Oklahoma, U.S., on federal highways 66 and 75; the county seat of Creek county. It is served by the Frisco and the Tulsa-Sapulpa Union railways.

The population was 13,031 in 1950 and 12,249 in 1940 by federal census. It is in one of the principal oil and gas producing areas of the Mid-Continent field. The city was founded in 1888 and incorporated in 1898. In 1922 it adopted a commission-manager form of government.

SARABAND, a slow dance, generally believed to have originated in Spain in the earlier half of the 16th century. The most probable account of the word is that the dance was named after Zarabanda, a celebrated dancer of Seville. Its music is in triple time, generally with three minims in the bar. Many examples occur in the Suites and Partitas of Handel and J. S. Bach.

SARACENS, the current designation among the Christians in the middle ages for their Muslim enemies, especially for the Muslims in Europe. In earlier times the name *Saraceni* was applied by Greeks and Romans to the nomad Arabs of the Syro-Arabian desert who harassed the frontier of the empire. Σαρακηνή, being a district in the Sinaitic peninsula (Ptolemy v. 16).

SARAGOSSA (*Zaragoza*), an inland province of northern Spain, one of the three into which Aragon was divided in 1833; bounded on the north by Logroño and Navarre, north-east and east by Huesca, south-east by Lérida and Tarragona, south by Teruel and Guadalajara and west by Soria. Pop. (1950) 616,881; area, 6,608 sq.mi. Saragossa belongs wholly to the basin of the Ebro (*q.v.*). The main valley is bounded on the south-west by the Sierra de Moncayo (with the highest elevation 7,707 ft.).

Saragossa is traversed by the Ebro Valley Railway, which connects Miranda with Lérida, Barcelona and Tarragona, and has a branch to Huesca; it also communicates via Calatayud with

Madrid and Sagunto; and there are local lines to Cariñena (south-west from Saragossa) and to Tarazona and Borja (near the right bank of the Ebro). The only towns with over 5,000 inhabitants (pop. 1940) are Saragossa (205,833) (*q.v.*); Calatayud (15,116) (*q.v.*); Tarazona (10,375), an episcopal see, with a curious 13th-century cathedral; Caspe (7,343); Egea (7,398); Tauste (5,814); Épila (5,096); and Alagón (6,130). (On the inhabitants and history of this region, *see* ARAGON.)

SARAGOSSA, the capital of the Spanish province of Saragossa and formerly of the kingdom of Aragon, seat of an archbishop, of a court of appeal, and of the captain general of Aragon; on the right bank of the river Ebro, 212 mi. by rail N.E. of Madrid. Pop. (1940) 205,833 (mun., 238,601). Saragossa (Celtiberian, *Salduba*) was made a colony by Augustus at the close of the Celtiberian War (25 B.C.), and renamed *Caesarea Augusta* or *Caesaraugusta*, from which "Saragossa" is derived. Under the Romans it was the chief commercial and military station in the Ebro valley, and the seat of one of the four *conventus juridici* (assizes) of Hither Spain.

Saragossa was captured in 452 by the Suebi, and in 476 by the Visigoths, whose rule lasted until the Moorish conquest in 712, and under whom Saragossa was the first city to abandon the Arian heresy. In 777 its Moorish ruler, the viceroy of Barcelona, appealed to Charlemagne for aid against the powerful caliph of Cordova, Abd-ar-Rahman I. Charlemagne besieged the Cordovan army in *Sarkosta*, as the city was then called; but a rebellion of his Saxon subjects compelled him to withdraw his army. The Moors were finally expelled by Alphonso I of Aragon in 1118, after a siege lasting nine months. As the capital of Aragon, Saragossa prospered greatly until the second half of the 15th century, when the court was transferred to Castile.

In 1710 the allied British and Austrian armies defeated the forces of Philip V at Saragossa in the war of the Spanish Succession.

It was in the Peninsular War (*q.v.*) that the city reached the zenith of its fame. An ill-armed body of citizens, led by José de Palafox y Melzi (*see* PALAFOX), held the hastily-entrenched city against Marshal Lefebvre from June 15 to Aug. 15, 1808. The siege was then raised in consequence of the reverse suffered by the French at Bailén (*q.v.*), but it was renewed on Dec. 20 and on the 27th of January the invaders entered the city. Even then they encountered a desperate resistance, and it was not until Feb. 20 that the defenders were compelled to capitulate. Thousands of people perished in the city, largely through famine and disease. Among the defenders was the famous "Maid of Saragossa," Maria Agustín, whose exploits were described by Byron in *Childe Harold* (1, 55 *sqq.*). During the civil war of 1936–39, Saragossa was captured by the Nationalists.

Saragossa is an important railway junction; it is connected by main lines with Valladolid, Madrid and Valencia in the west and south, and by the Ebro Valley railway with Catalonia and the Basque provinces; also with France, via the Somport tunnel and with the northern districts of Aragon and Cariñena on the southwest. The city is built in highly cultivated land, irrigated by a multitude of streams which distribute the waters of the Imperial canal, and surrounded by an arid plain exposed to the sweep of violent gales which blow down, hot in summer and icy in winter.

One of its two stone bridges, the seven-arched Puente de Piedra, dates from 1447; there is also an iron bridge for the railway to Pamplona. The two most important buildings of Saragossa are its cathedrals, to each of which the chapter is attached for six months in the year. La Seo ("The See") is the older of the two, dating chiefly from the 14th century; its prevailing style is Gothic, but the oldest portion, the lower walls of the apse, is Byzantine.

The Iglesia Metropolitana del Pilar is the larger building, dating only from the latter half of the 17th century; it was built after designs by Herrera el Mozo, and owes its name to one of the most venerated objects in Spain, the "pillar" of jaspar on which the Virgin is said to have alighted when she manifested herself to St. James as he passed through Saragossa. The university was founded in 1474.

SARAGOSSA, COUNCILS OF (*Concilia Caesaraugustana*). In or about 380 a council of Spanish and Aquitanian bishops adopted at Saragossa eight canons bearing more or less directly on the prevalent heresy of Priscillianism (*see* PRISCILLIAN).

A second council, held in 592, solved practical problems incident to the recent conversion of the West Goths from Arianism to orthodox Christianity.

The third council, in 691, issued five canons on discipline. In 1318 a provincial synod proclaimed the elevation of Saragossa to the rank of an archbishopric; and from Sept. 1565 to Feb. 1566 a similar synod made known the decrees of Trent.

SARAJEVO, capital of the Bosnian People's Republic, Yugoslavia. Pop. (census 1931) 78,173, (1948) 118,806, chiefly Serbs and Croats. It lies in a fine situation in a valley 1,800 ft. above sea level.

Though it is still half oriental and wholly beautiful with its hundred mosques, its ancient Turkish bazaar, picturesque wooden houses and cypress groves, it was largely rebuilt after western fashion in 1878. Sarajevo is the seat of a Roman Catholic bishop, an Orthodox metropolitan and the highest Moslem religious authority in Yugoslavia. Notable in the town are the *Begava Djamia* (Džamia), or mosque of Husref Bey, founded in 1465 and among the three most beautiful mosques in Europe, the Roman Catholic and Orthodox cathedrals, the hospitals, the town hall, the museum and the university, founded in 1946. Near the bazaar is the oldest church in Bosnia, containing a 14th-century picture of the Virgin. The industries include potteries, silk and flour mills, a sugar beet factory, timber and, under state control, a brewery, tobacco, embroidery and carpet factories. Weaving on hand looms is an important industry.

Founded in 1262 by the Hungarian general Cotroman, under the name of Bosnavar or Vrhbosna, Sarajevo was enlarged two centuries later, and takes its name from the palace (Turkish, *serai*) which he founded. During the wars between Turkey and Austria, its ownership was often contested; and it fell before King Matthias I of Hungary in 1480, and before Prince Eugene of Savoy in 1697. Destructive fires laid it waste in 1480, 1644, 1656, 1687 and 1789.

Sarajevo was chosen as the seat of Turkish government in 1850 instead of Travnik. In 1878 it became the seat of the Austro-Hungarian administration of Bosnia-Hercegovina and subsequently of the Bosnian diet. Under Austrian rule it was largely modernized, but the schools established also served as a focus of Serb nationalist feeling.

Students at Sarajevo perpetrated the murder of the archduke Francis Ferdinand (*q.v.*) which led to World War I. As the archduke motored from manoeuvres to a gala lunch in the city a bomb was thrown unsuccessfully in the suburbs. The fatal shots were fired as the archduke's car reversed out of a narrow street leading off the quays, opposite the chief bridge. (*See* also DIMITRIEVIĆ DRAGUTIN; JOVANOVIĆ, LJUBA.) In Nov. 1918 the diet at Sarajevo proclaimed union with Yugoslavia.

In World War II, during part of which it was nominally included in the kingdom of Croatia, Sarajevo suffered considerable damage from Allied bombing. In 1944 it was reincorporated into Yugoslavia.

SARAN, a district in the Tirhut division of Bihar, Republic of India. Area, 2,669 sq.mi. Pop. (1951) 3,155,144. It is a vast alluvial plain with a general inclination toward the southeast, as indicated by the flow of the rivers in that direction. The principal rivers, besides the Ganges, are the Gandak and Gogra, which are navigable throughout the year. The district has long been noted for its high state of cultivation and dense population. It yields large crops of rice, besides other cereals, pulses, oil seeds, poppy and sugar cane.

The indigo industry, formerly of the first importance, declined, and sugar refining in great part took its place. The production of saltpetre is an industry of some importance. Saran is exposed to drought and flood.

It suffered from famines in 1874 and 1897, and from floods in 1921, when 20 in. of rain fell in a single night.

A scheme for irrigation from the Gandak river, started in 1878, proved a failure, and the canals were long closed to irrigation. But a Gandak valley project was made a part of India's five-year plan of 1951. At Manjhi there are the remains of a fort, with ramparts still 30 ft. high, which date back to about the 6th century A.D. The administrative headquarters were established at Chapra pop. (1951) 64,309.

SARANAC LAKE, a village of northeastern New York, U.S., in the Adirondack mountains, near Lower Saranac lake, on the boundary line between Essex and Franklin counties; served by the New York Central railway and air line. Pop. (1950) 6,913; (1940) 7,138 by federal census. It is a summer and a winter resort, for both health and pleasure. Near the village, at an altitude of 1,650 ft., is the Trudeau sanatorium, founded in 1884 as the Adirondack Cottage sanatorium by Edward L. Trudeau (1848–1915), the first semicharitable institution in the U.S. for the open-air treatment of early tuberculosis. Trudeau, attacked by tuberculosis soon after beginning medical practice in New York city in 1872, had gone to the Adirondacks to die in a place he loved, but before the first winter was over was surprised to find his health greatly improved. He stayed on, making Saranac Lake his home for the remaining 40 years of his life, and out of his personal experience developed a method of treatment which had a wide influence. The sanatorium grew to a small village in itself, and Saranac Lake became a resort for private patients. Robert Louis Stevenson spent the winter of 1887–88 at Saranac Lake. In 1894 Trudeau established the Saranac laboratory for research in tuberculosis (the first of its kind in the U.S.) and after his death an endowment was raised for it (under the name of the Trudeau foundation) as a memorial to him. In 1916 the Trudeau School of Tuberculosis was opened (also the first institution of its kind) to give specialized instruction in the diagnosis and treatment of the disease to practising physicians. The village of Saranac Lake was incorporated in 1892. Other institutions in the vicinity are the New York State Ray Brook sanatorium, Stony Wold sanatorium, Sanatorium Gabriels and Will Rogers International Variety clubs. Paul Smith's college (forestry and hotel management) is located there.

SARAPUL, a town of European U.S.S.R., in the Udmurt A.S.S.R. on the river Kama, in 56° 32′ N., 53° 45′ E. Population, 24,959. It is the centre for an agricultural district, and has oil-pressing, rope-making, brewing and leather industries. Like other towns in the Udmurt A.S.S.R., it depends on Asiatic Russia for a market for its manufactured products.

SARASATE Y NAVASCUES, PABLO MARTIN MELITON DE (1844–1908), Spanish violinist, was born at Pamplona on March 10, 1844. At the age of 12 he began to study under Jean Alard at the Paris conservatoire. His first public appearance as a concert violinist was in 1860. He paid the first of many visits to London, where he enjoyed great popularity, in 1861, and in the course of his career he visited all other parts of Europe and also both North and South America. He was one of the first and most fascinating violinists of modern times, his playing being remarkable equally for purity and sweetness of tone, and for facility of execution. He died at Biarritz, Fr., on Sept. 20, 1908.

SARASIN or SARRAZIN, **JEAN FRANÇOIS** (1614–1654), French author, son of Roger Sarasin, treasurer-general at Caen, was born at Hermanville near Caen. He was on terms of intimate friendship with Paul Scarron, with whom he exchanged verses, with Gilles Ménage, and with Paul Pellisson. In 1639 he supported Georges de Scudéry in his attack on Pierre Corneille with a *Discours de la tragédie.* He accompanied Léon Bouthillier, comte de Chavigny, secretary of state for foreign affairs, on various diplomatic errands until 1643–44. He joined in the pamphlet war against Pierre de Montmaur, against whom he directed his satire, *Bellum parasiticum* (1644). He was accused of writing satires on Jules Mazarin, and for a short time gave up the practice of verse. In 1648 he entered the household of Armand de Bourbon, prince de Conti, whose marriage with Mazarin's niece he helped to negotiate. He died at Pézénas, on Dec. 5, 1654. The most considerable of his poems were the epic fragments of *Rollon con-*

quérant and *La guerre espagnole,* with *Dulot vaincu* and the *Pompe funèbre* in honour of Vincent Voiture. As a poet he was overrated, but he wrote excellent pieces of prose narration, the *Histoire du siége de Dunkerque* (1649) and the unfinished *Conspiration de Walstein* (1651).

His *Oeuvres* appeared in 1656, *Nouvelles Oeuvres* (2 vol.) in 1674. His *Poésies* were edited in 1877 by Octave Uzanne with an introductory note. A new edition of his *Oeuvres* was published in 1926 by Paul Festugières. Much of his correspondence is preserved in the library of the Arsenal, Paris. *See* Albert Mennung's *Jean François Sarasins Leben und Werke* (2 vol., Halle, 1902–04).

SARASOTA, a city on the west coast of Florida, U.S., 53 mi. S. of Tampa; the county seat of Sarasota county and one of the most charming resorts of the state. It is on federal highway 41 and the Tamiami trail; has a municipal airport, a deep-water harbour and municipal docks; and is served by the Atlantic Coast Line and the Seaboard Air Line railways. Pop. 18,896 in 1950 and 11,141 in 1940 by the federal census.

The city lies on the east shore of Sarasota bay, connected by causeways with long palm-studded keys to the west (St. Armands, Longboat, Lido and Siesta). The assessed valuation in 1949–50 was $50,385,890. Sarasota was founded in the early '80s by a Scotch syndicate of which Sir John Gillespie was president. In 1885 his son, J. Hamilton Gillespie, laid out there the first golf course in the U.S.

SARASWATI, a river in the Punjab frequently mentioned in the *Rig-Veda.* Its meaning, "abounding in pools," suggests that it was at that early period a larger river than now. It is lost in the desert sands toward Rājpūtāna. Corresponding phonetically to the Iranian *Haraqaiti* (the modern Helmand), the name may have been applied to the Indus by the invading Aryans before they reached the eastern Punjab, but it soon ceased to refer to that river. As the Sarsūti, its present name, it joins the Ghaggar, the dry bed of the Hakra, the lost river of the Indian desert which can still be traced to its junction with the Indus. With the Drishadwati the Saraswati formed the west boundary of Brahmavarta, and was the holy stream of Vedic India. As "fluent" it became the personified goddess of eloquence, learning and wisdom, wife of Manu, mother of the *Vedas,* and a daughter of Brahman. From her the Sarsūt Brahmans (*q.v.*) claim their name. Another Saraswati, in Guzerāt, also loses itself in the sand.

See A. A. Macdonell and A. B. Keith, *Vedic Index* (1912); A. A. Macdonell, *Vedic Mythology* (Strassburg, 1897); and E. W. Hopkins, *Epic Mythology,* (Strassburg, 1915).

SARATOGA, BATTLES OF. The plan of campaign for the British in America in 1777 sought to isolate New England by occupying the Hudson valley. Gen. John Burgoyne, the author of the plan, coming down from Canada via Lakes Champlain and George, was to meet Viscount Howe, marching up from New York, at Albany. A third, but much smaller force, under Barry St. Leger, was to advance from Oswego down the Mohawk valley and join the other two columns. The plan failed because Howe, the British commander-in-chief, marched on Philadelphia, George Germaine, Viscount Sackville, the secretary of state, having failed to give him definite instructions. Burgoyne, with about 8,000 men, including seven regiments of British regulars and 3,000 Germans, reached Ticonderoga (July 1), which was evacuated by its weak garrison (July 6). He reassembled his army after the pursuit at Skenesborough and marched through the woods and swamps to Fort Edward, which was evacuated by the American commander Maj. Gen. Philip Schuyler, who retreated across the Hudson to Stillwater, 30 mi. above Albany (July 31). The march was most laborious, involving the construction of 40 bridges, and necessitated a long halt at Fort Edward. Burgoyne should have taken his army back to Ticonderoga, and transferred it to Fort George, where a direct road led to Fort Edward. Had he taken this route, he might have reached Albany by the 16th.

A German detachment, on the advice of "Colonel" Skene, who was also responsible for the recent march, was sent to Bennington to seize horses and supplies, but was surrounded and almost annihilated by the Green Mountain militia, under John Stark (Aug. 16). Burgoyne now became uneasy; he had left nearly 1,000 men to garrison Ticonderoga; he had heard from Howe of his intention to invade Pennsylvania; and St. Leger was held up before Fort Stanwix (actually St. Leger retreated Aug. 22). But he considered himself bound by his orders to press on to Albany. Having collected 30 days' rations, he crossed the Hudson (Sept. 13) and encamped near Saratoga. The Englishman, Gates, who had displaced Schuyler in command (Aug. 19), was encamped 4 m. away, on Bemis's Heights, with 12,000 men and was daily receiving reinforcements. Burgoyne advanced to the attack (Sept. 19). But Arnold came out with 3,000 men to meet him at Freeman's Farm. After 4 hours' fierce fighting Arnold retired, and Burgoyne encamped on the battlefield, but he had lost over 500 men, including a large number of officers, victims of Morgan's sharpshooters. Burgoyne heard (Sept. 21) from Clinton, who had been left in command at New York, that he was about to make a diversion up the Hudson. He sent a despatch to Clinton (Sept. 27) asking for orders. The answer was never received. Clinton started with a small force (Oct. 3) and captured two forts on the west bank, but he never had any intention of penetrating to Albany.

Burgoyne had now under 5,000 "effectives" left, and his supplies were running short. He reckoned that they might last till the 20th. He led out 1,500 men on reconnaissance (Oct. 7), but the Americans made a fierce counter-attack, and led by Arnold, inflicted a severe defeat upon the British army. Next day Burgoyne began his retreat, but Gates, with 20,000 men, surrounded him at Saratoga. Burgoyne opened negotiations on the 14th and the Convention of Saratoga was signed (Oct. 17), Burgoyne insisting that it was not a capitulation, and finding a precedent in the Seven Years' War.

See F. J. Hudleston, *Gentleman Johnny Burgoyne* (1928).

SARATOGA SPRINGS, a city of Saratoga county, New York, U.S.A., 30 mi. N. of Albany and 12 mi. W. of the Hudson river; served by the Boston and Maine and the Delaware and Hudson railways. Pop. (1950) 15,434; (1940) 13,705. The city is in a region of great historic interest, and has been famous for its medicinal mineral springs since colonial days. It is a pleasure resort in summer, a health resort at all seasons, and is the seat of Skidmore college for women (1911).

Adjoining the city is "Yaddo," the beautiful estate of Katrina Trask (Mrs. George Foster Peabody), which after her death in 1922 was made a summer retreat for a limited number of painters, writers and other creative artists. Saratoga lake (6 mi. long) is 3 mi. S.E. of the city. The August races of the Saratoga Association for the Improvement of the Breed of Horses (organized 1863) draw a brilliant attendance. Among the long established hotels is the Grand Union (400 rooms). The Convention hall seats 3,000. The 122 springs (heavily charged with carbonic acid gas and containing in varying proportions bicarbonates of lime, sodium, magnesium, chloride of sodium and other minerals) are in a reservation of 1,100 ac., owned and controlled by the State. The State bath houses have a capacity of about 5,000 treatments daily, and the bottling plant can fill 6,000,000 pint bottles in a year. The therapeutic value of the springs was known to the Indians, and the Saratoga country was a favourite summer camping ground of the Iroquois. It became a theatre of hostilities between the French and English colonists and their Indian allies. In 1693 a French expedition was checked in a sharp conflict near Mt. McGregor by an English and colonial force. In 1745 the settlement on the Hudson directly east of the present city of Saratoga Springs (called Saratoga at first, later Old Saratoga and now Schuylerville) was attacked by French and Indians, who massacred many of its inhabitants. The battles of Saratoga (*q.v.*) in the Revolutionary War were fought at Bemis Heights, 12 m. S.E. of Saratoga Springs. Most of the battlefield has been acquired by the State of New York, and Congress in 1926 authorized making it a national military park. The first white man known to have benefited from the Saratoga waters was Sir William Johnson, whose Indian friends carried him to the springs in 1767. A log house for the lodging of visitors was built in 1771; in 1783 Gen. Philip Schuyler and his family camped at the springs through the summer; in 1791 Gideon Putnam bought a large tract of land and put up the first inn; and in 1793 Dr. Valentine Seaman published a book about the waters which spread the knowledge of their curative properties.

Other hotels (large barn-like wooden structures) were built early in the 19th century, and by 1820 the Springs had become a popular resort. The Civil War brought depression, and cut off the patronage from the South; but soon afterwards, with the establishment of the races and the rebuilding of the United States hotel, it again became popular, and in the 1870's and '80s was one of the most fashionable watering-places of America ("the Queen of Spas"). Commercial exploitation of the springs (bottling the water and liquefying the carbonic acid gas) diminished their flow until they almost disappeared, and the resort was again depressed until the State intervened, first prohibiting the pumping and later acquiring the property (1909) and placing it in charge of the conservation commission (1916). Under State management the flow and mineral strength of the springs have been restored, and the patronage has increased tenfold in a decade. Saratoga Springs was incorporated as a village in 1826 and as a city in 1915.

SARATOV, a region of the Russian S.F.S.R., much smaller than the former Saratov province, lying on the right bank of the Volga river, with Penza on the north, Tambov on the west, Stalingrad on the south, and the German Volga Autonomous republic and Kuibyshev on the east. Its area is 31,815 sq.mi. and its pop. (1939) 1,798,805 (urban 665,763; rural 1,133,042). A small portion of it, the Novo-Uzensk district, lies east of the German Volga republic. The region occupies the eastern part of the great central plateau of Russia, which slopes gently to the south until it merges imperceptibly into the steppe region; its eastern slope, deeply cut into by ravines, falls abruptly to the Volga. The higher parts range from 700 to 900 ft. above the sea, while the Volga flows at an elevation of 20 ft. only at Khvalynsk in the north, and thus the river banks have a hilly appearance.

Every geological formation from the Carboniferous to the Miocene is represented, though the older formations are concealed under Cretaceous deposits of fossiliferous marls, flint-bearing clays and iron-bearing sandstones. The boulder clay of the Finland and Olonets ice sheets penetrates into the east of the region, and loess and other post-glacial deposits are found in the southeast. Iron ore is abundant and chalk, lime and white pottery clay are obtained in some parts.

The region is comparatively well drained; the upper course of the Sura, a tributary of the Volga, lies in the north, and the upper Medvedyitsa and Khoper flow south and drain into the Don. They are navigable in spite of their shallows, and ready-made boats are brought in pieces from the Volga, and put together on their shores. The forest has almost disappeared; houses are made of clay and dung is used for fuel.

The climate is severe and continental, with a recorded range of temperature of 119° F. in some parts; at Saratov the average January temperature is 12.4° F., the average July temperature 71.5° F. The Volga at Saratov is frozen for 162 days in the year. Rainfall is scanty and irregular, varying between 8 and 16 in. in normal years and much less in drought years, the rain falling mainly in spring and early summer. The region is arid and rapid desiccation is progressing. In the north and west are sandy black-earth soils, interspersed with dark gray forest lands and gray wooded clays (Volsk, Khvalynsk, the northern part of Petrovsk). In Petrovsk, Serdobsk, Atkarsk and Balashov counties are clayey black earths, while Balashov contains a strip of rich black earth with a high humus content, although even here there are patches of salt land and salt marshes.

The yield of the soil in Saratov region has become stabilized at a low level because, although the soil contains about 6–10% of humus, its friability disappears after a few years of persistent planting with cereals. The great variability of crop yield, sometimes so low as to reduce the district to starvation (*e.g.*, in 1921), and the appearance of salting indicate the need for more intensive methods of agriculture. Attempts are being made to increase the friability of the soil, to put large areas under grass for several years, and to introduce plough culture and better types of crop rotation, with less fallow, and to introduce the sowing of the more drought resisting types of grain. Marmots, mice and insects are great pests to agriculture. Experimental stations have been established at eight points and the agronomical faculty of the University of Saratov has an experimental institute. In the Novo-Uzensk district east of the German Volga republic the soil and drought problem is even more acute; here are light brown and brown clayey soils, with some chestnut brown soil and sands and salty areas. In good years crops are successful, in drought years famine is severe. For 50 years the peasants there have been practising a form of irrigation and plans have been made for lagoon irrigation of an extensive area above the town of Novo-Uzensk and near the settlement of Alexandrov-Gai, utilizing the waters of the Great Uzen.

Winter rye is the main crop, summer wheat, millet, oats and sunflower seed come next and potatoes are increasingly grown. Barley forms a very small percentage of the harvest. The region was slow in recovering from the terrible years of 1917-21.

There is a fair amount of stock raising in the district; sheep and working cattle occupy the first place, and horses and pigs are also bred, but on the whole this is a diminishing industry. Cucumbers, melons, watermelons, and vegetables are grown around Saratov, Volsk, Atkarsk and Kamyshin, and in the Novo-Uzensk district. Beetroot cultivation is increasing.

Poultry raising of an export character is carried on, but dairy produce is not much developed. Fishing and the preparation of caviare are important at Kamyshin. A more intensive development of cattle breeding for meat and dairy purposes would lead to greater development of local production of bran and cattle foods, with a probable development of the bacon industry in dependence on by-products from the dairying industry. Flour milling is the main industry, oil pressing from oleaginous seeds is an export industry and there is some tobacco manufacture. There are metalworks dependent on the local iron, and a shale-using electric plant at Saratov. The shale is obtained from the Kashpir beds near Syzran and is brought cheaply by water.

The railway net includes the line from Tambov to Kamyshin, with a branch linking with Penza, a line from Tambov to Saratov, one from Volsk on the Volga going through Petrovsk and Atkarsk to Balanda, part of the Penza-Syzran line, and the branch from the Volga through Novo-Uzensk to Alexandrov-Gai. The region is thus better supplied than the Kuibyshev region and has a good deal of transit trade between shipping and railway lines.

The rate of literacy is considerably higher than in the Kuibyshev region, though it is low among women. Saratov university helps to spread a higher standard of culture in the district. The chief towns are Saratov, Kuznetsk (*qq.v.*), Balachov and Volsk; the remaining centres have fewer than 20,000 inhabitants.

The district of Saratov has been inhabited since at least the Neolithic period. The inhabitants of a later epoch left numerous bronze remains in their *kurgans* (burial mounds) but their ethnological position is still uncertain. In the 8th and 9th centuries the seminomad Burtases peopled the territory and recognized the authority of the Khazar princes.

SARATOV, a city of the Russian S.F.S.R., in the oblast of Saratov, in 51° 35′ N., 46° 1′ E., on the Volga river, and on the plateau slopes near that river. Landslips from the Sokolov hill (560 ft.) often occur. Two ravines divide the city into three parts. The streets are wide and regular, with broad squares, and there are some fine buildings. Pop. (1939) 375,860.

Industries developed in Saratov include iron smelting, ship-building, the making of nails and bolts, sawmilling, flour milling and railway repair shops. A large combine harvester plant was established there.

The shallowness of the Volga river opposite the city and the immense shoals along its right bank proved drawbacks, but Saratov became a river port of some importance. Linked by rail with other shipping points, it built up an extensive collecting and entrepôt trade. The importance of Saratov, a major transfer centre for petroleum, was increased after World War II, a pipe line to Moscow for the transportation of gas being completed in 1946. During the war Saratov had been expanded in order to exploit the sources of the natural gas which had been discovered.

A university was established there in 1919, and there are institutes and other educational institutions, and various museums.

Saratov was the capital of the Saratov government until 1928 and of the Lower Volga territory from that date until 1934. It came under the control of the Russian S.F.S.R. in 1943.

Saratov was founded at the end of the 16th century, 7 mi. above the modern site, to which it was removed about 1605. Sary-tau or Yellow mountain on which it stands has been inhabited from remote antiquity.

SARAWAK, a British crown colony on the northwest coast of Borneo lying between lat. 0° 50′ and 5° N. and long. 109° 36′ and 115° 40′ E. Area *c.* 47,000 sq.mi. (about the size of England). Pop. (1947) 546,385. It has a coastline of about 450 mi. on the China sea and is bounded on the northeast by British North Borneo and on the southeast by Indonesian Borneo.

Climate and Physical Features.—The climate is tropical but not unhealthy. The thermometer rarely rises above 90° F. and often falls to 70° F. at night. The heat is usually tempered by a breeze but humidity is generally high. The annual rainfall varies between 100 and 200 in. There are no marked seasonal changes but there is more rain from October to March than in the other six months. The alluvial coastal plain varies from 5 to 50 mi. in width. The rest of the country consists of forest-covered hills and mountains, a long irregular range forming the spine of the island of Borneo with peaks up to 5,000 and 6,000 ft. These are mostly of sandstone but there are extrusions of limestone forming sheer cliffs and pinnacles. There are many fine rivers, chief among them being the Rejang, Baram, Limbang and Batang Lupar. All of these are navigable; the first-named by ocean-going ships for a distance of 170 mi. (For flora and fauna, *see* BORNEO.)

Ethnology.—The main indigenous groups are the Iban (Sea-Dayak), Malay, Melanau, Land-Dayak, and the miscellaneous group of tribes known as Kayans, Kenyahs, Kelabits, Muruts and others. The Malays are Mohammedans, the others pagans (animist) except where converted to Christianity. Nonindigenous peoples are Europeans, Chinese, Javanese and Indians. The 1947 census disclosed that Europeans formed 0.1% of the total, Malays 17.9% and Chinese 26.6%. Chinese were formerly encouraged to settle but immigration has in recent years been severely restricted.

Administration.—The governor is assisted by an executive council. The legislative body is a council known as the *Council Negri*. Both these councils contain unofficial as well as official members and consist of persons of all races living in the territory. Administration is conducted by a civil service composed of British and of native officers. The higher posts in the service are at present mainly held by British officials but promotion is open to all.

Local government has been established in most parts of the country. This is in the hands of local authorities in the rural areas and municipal boards in the towns. All local government bodies have their own treasuries, their revenue consisting of rates levied by the authority supplemented by grants from the central government.

The judicial system comprises a supreme court, circuit courts and magistrates courts administering the ordinary law of the territory, and native courts which apply the native or customary law in appropriate cases.

The governor of Sarawak is also the high commissioner for the state of Brunei, a Malay state under British protection and ruled by a Malay sultan, the land boundaries of which march with those of Sarawak.

History.—Sarawak was known to the explorers and map makers of the 16th century, but its history as a state begins with the arrival of James Brooke (*q.v.*) in 1840. Then part of the sultanate of Brunei, the country was in rebellion against the rapacity of the sultan's officials. Brooke restored order, and a year later was publicly installed at Kuching as rajah of the territory then known as Sarawak which extended from Cape Datu to the Samarahan river, an area of about 7,000 sq.mi.

The rajah immediately began to introduce the elements of good government. He abolished slavery, suppressed head-hunting, and, with the help of a young naval officer who afterward became Admiral Sir Henry Keppel, expelled pirates from the Saribas and Batang Lupar rivers. Accretions of territory took place from time to time throughout the 19th century, generally because the native peoples preferred the reasonably good government of Rajah Brooke to the oppression of the Malay nobles, and the country finally attained its present size in 1905.

James Brooke, who had been created a K.C.B. in 1863, was succeeded in 1868 by his nephew Sir Charles Johnson Brooke (1828–1917). In 1888 a treaty was concluded which placed the state under British protection and in return gave the United Kingdom the right to control its foreign relations while leaving the internal administration of the country entirely in the hands of the rajah. The rajah's title was formally recognized by Edward VII in 1904. The third rajah, Sir Charles Vyner Brooke, G.C.M.G. (1874–), succeeded his father in 1917.

In 1941 to mark the centenary of Brooke rule a proposal for a new constitution with a representative legislature was proclaimed, but the Japanese invasion intervened. Such was the disruption, misery and ruin caused by three and a half years of Japanese occupation that the rajah decided, with the consent of his council, to cede the country to the British crown; and on July 1, 1946, the cession was accepted. The first governor of the new colony, Sir Charles Arden Clarke, was appointed in Oct. 1946.

Social Services.—Primary education is gradually being brought within the reach of all, though the difficulty of the terrain and scattered population make the process a slow one. Teachers are trained at a college in Kuching. Post-primary education is provided on a small scale by one government and a few mission schools. In 1952 there were 41 government schools, 94 run by local authorities, 71 mission schools and 226 Chinese schools. Medical and health services are made available by the government by means of hospitals and dispensaries, many of the latter being mobile and consisting of powered boats operating on the rivers and streams.

The Red Cross society has a branch in Sarawak, and institutions for the care of special sections of the community include a boys' home for juvenile delinquents, a leper settlement, a mental hospital and homes for the aged and destitute at Sibu and Kuching. The Boy Scout and Girl Guide associations find supporters among young people of all races.

Trade and Industry.—The chief exports are mineral oil, rubber, sago flour, pepper, cutch (a tanning extract) and timber. Gold is mined in small quantities and coal of good quality has been found but is somewhat inaccessible. There are several minor industries. Some 13,000 sq.mi. of land are in cultivation, including about 11,000 under rice. Fishing and fish curing are the means of livelihood of many Malays and Chinese.

Imports in 1952 were valued at $382,946,000 and exports at $438,563,000.

Government revenue (1951) totalled $47,349,000 and expenditure $22,517,000. Local currency is the Malayan dollar valued at 32.67 cents U.S. and at 2s. 4d. in sterling in 1952.

Towns.—The chief towns are Kuching (pop. 38,000), the capital, having a large Chinese trading community, the main government offices, Anglican and Roman Catholic cathedrals, museum, wharves, warehouses and dockyard; Sibu (pop. c. 10,000); and Miri (9,000), the centre of the Sarawak oil fields. Other administrative centres with settlements of a few thousand persons are Simanggang, Sarikei, Binatang, Mukah, Bintulu and Limbang.

Communications.—Internal communication is chiefly by water, there being no extensive road system and no railways. There are some 450 mi. of roads in and around the towns and a trunk road from Kuching to Simanggang was under construction in 1953. There is a modern airfield near Kuching and there are landing grounds in a few other places. A regular air service and good steamship services operate between Sarawak, Singapore and North Borneo.

There are exterior wireless links, and an extensive system of wireless telegraph stations throughout the territory.

(C. W. Da.)

SARCOPHAGUS, the name given to a coffin in stone, which on account of its caustic qualities, according to Pliny (H.N. xxxvi. 27), consumed the body in 40 days (Gr. σαρκοφάγος, literally "flesh-eating," from σάρξ, flesh, φαγεῖν, to eat); also by the Greeks to a sepulchral chest, in stone or other material, which was more or less enriched with ornament and sculpture. One of the finest examples known is the sarcophagus of Tutankhamun (c.

AN ETRUSCAN TERRA COTTA URN OF THE THIRD CENTURY, B.C., IN THE FORM OF A SARCOPHAGUS

1550 B.C.) made of granite and ornamented with angels with outspread wings. Of later date are the green porphyry sarcophagus and the terra-cotta sarcophagus from Clazomenae; both of these date from the early 6th century B.C., and are in the British Museum. The finest Greek examples are those found at Sidon in 1887 by Hamdy Bey, which are now in the Imperial Museum at Constantinople. (See GREEK ART.) Of Etruscan sarcophagi there are numerous examples in terracotta; occasionally they are miniature representations of temples, and are sometimes in the form of a couch on which rest figures of the deceased; one of these is in the British Museum. The earliest Roman sarcophagus is that of Scipio in the Vatican (3rd century B.C.), carved in peperino stone.

Of later Roman sarcophagi, there is an immense series enriched with figures in high relief, of which the chief are the Niobid example in the Lateran, the Lycomedes sarcophagus in the Capitol, the Penthesilea sarcophagus in the Vatican, and the immense sarcophagus representing a battle between the Romans and the barbarians, in the Museo delle Terme. In later Roman work there was a great decadence in the sculpture, so that in the following centuries recourse was had to the red Egyptian porphyry, of which the sarcophagi of Constantia (A.D. 355) and of the empress Helena (A.D. 589), both in the Vatican, are fine examples. Later, during the Byzantine period, there is a large series, either in museums or in the cloisters of the Italian churches. They are generally decorated with a series of niches with figures in them, divided by small attached shafts with semicircular or sloping covers carved with religious emblems, one of the best examples

THE FRONT OF A SMALL ROMAN SARCOPHAGUS, OF THE THIRD CENTURY B.C., DEPICTING THE FOUR SEASONS

being the sarcophagus of Sta. Barbara, dating from the beginning of the 6th century, at Ravenna, where there are many others.

SARDANAPALUS, SARDANAPALLUS or SARDANAPALOS, according to Greek fable, the last great king of Assyria, was undoubtedly Assur-bani-pal (q.v.). The Greeks took him to be the most effeminate of a line of effeminate princes, but adequate evidence from Assyria proves him to have been quite the opposite. Greek legend has Sardanapalus, frightened by a siege, burning himself and his wives to death in his palace. This was actually the fate into which the mighty Assur-bani-pal frightened his rebellious half-brother, Shamash-shumukin, in the siege of Babylon in 648 B.C.

SARDICA, COUNCIL OF, an ecclesiastical council convened in 343 by the emperors Constantius and Constans, to attempt a settlement of the Arian controversies, which were then at their height. Of the 170 bishops assembled, about 90 (principally from the West) were Athanasians, while on the other side were 80 Eusebians from the east. The anticipated agreement, however, was not attained; and the result of the council was simply to embitter the relations between the two great religious parties, and those between the western and eastern halves of the empire. For as Athanasius and Marcellus of Ancyra appeared on the scene, and the western bishops declined to exclude them, the Eusebian bishops of the east absolutely refused to take part, and contented themselves with formulating a written protest addressed to numerous foreign prelates.

Especial importance attaches to this council through the fact that Canons 3–5 invest the Roman bishop with a prerogative which became of great historical importance, as the first legal recognition of his jurisdiction over other sees and the basis for the further development of his primacy.

The canons are printed in C. Mirbt, *Quellen zur Geschichte des Papsttums* (1901), p. 46 f.; Hefele, *Conciliengeschichte,* ed. 2, i, 533 *et seq.*

SARDINE, the young of the pilchard (*q.v.*), and also used for other related small herrings when similarly preserved in oil.

SARDINIA (Ital. *Sardegna*), the second largest island in the Mediterranean, 9,187 sq.mi. in area. Politically it is part of Italy. It lies only $7\frac{1}{2}$ mi. south of the French island of Corsica, from which it is separated by the Strait of Bonifacio. Terranova Pausania (or Olbia) at the northeast end of Sardinia is 145 mi. southwest of Civitavecchia, on the Italian mainland.

Physical Features.—Sardinia differs from the mainland and from Sicily in being geologically a much older country with large expanses of old primary rocks. With Corsica it forms part of a range of mountains rising over 13,000 ft. from the flat floor of the sea. Sardinia is a mountainous island, but there are no clearly defined mountain ranges and no permanent snow or glaciers. It consists largely of a patchwork of rolling plateaus, which do not break down into fertile hills, as is so often the case on the mainland of Italy; except for a few small coastal areas, there is only one plain, the Campidano, which stretches for 60 mi. from Cagliari in the south to Oristano in the west.

The mountains of the eastern half of the island are largely granite. In the northeast, in the Gallura district, which is entirely composed of granite, the highest point is Monte Limbara (4,393 ft.) southwest of Terranova; farther south the Gennargentu chain rises to 6,616 ft. in the twin summits of Bruncu Spinta and Punta la Marmora. The northwestern part of Sardinia, Nurra, is volcanic, as are the mountains south of it which come close to the west coast; the highest point is Monte Ferru (3,448 ft.). The southwestern groups of Iglesiente and Sulcis contain the two chief mining districts of the island: Sarrabus in the southeast is a domelike granite region, largely uninhabited and partly covered with trees.

There are only two rivers of any size, the Tirso (94 mi.), which drains most of the middle of the island to the Gulf of Oristano on the west coast, and the Coghinas (65 mi.) which flows through a narrow valley to the north coast. Even they are practically dry by the end of summer.

Climate.—The main causes of Sardinia's poverty and backwardness have been summer drought and violent winds, especially the northwesterly *maestrale* and the hot moist *scirocco*. The January and July mean temperatures at Sassari in the north (735 ft.) are 47.3° F. and 75.6° F., and at Cagliari in the south (246 ft.) 48.9° and 76.6°. Rainfall reaches 40 in. only in the mountains of Gennargentu and north of Iglesias and is less than 25 in. on all the lower ground. At Cagliari it is only about 19 in. It practically all occurs in late autumn and spring.   (M. M. C.)

Flora and Fauna.—There are about 1,950 species of vascular plant mostly of the Mediterranean type (*Silene, Dianthus, Genista, Cistus,* etc.) though about 40 seem to have migrated from the steppes of northern Africa in Pliocene times and about 60 show links with Africa and Sicily. The flora is more nearly Corsican than Sicilian. The woody vegetation of lowland and hill (up to 2,900 ft.) consists mainly of evergreen shrubs, the forests having been destroyed by man, leaving, in the dry uncultivated parts, macchia containing mastic, strawberry tree, myrtle, tree heath, etc. In

the south a tree spurge, *Euphorbia dendroides,* and in the Nurra the dwarf palm, form part of the macchia. Rock heaths with *Helichrysum, Genista,* etc., occur here and there among the scrub.

In the montane region (above 2,900 ft.) the trees and shrubs are mostly deciduous. Sweet chestnuts and oaks form most of the forests, though the chestnuts are limited in distribution. The commonest of the three oaks is the holm oak which forms extensive forests in the southwestern and southeastern (*e.g.* Sarrabus) hills and is accompanied in the higher places by the peony, *Paeonia officinalis* and sometimes by tree heath. The cork oak grows specially in the north, in the Gallura area and in the mountains from Mt. Nieddu and Mt. Leruo to opposite Nuoro where the holm oak begins. The sessile oak, adapted to the higher mountains and mostly avoiding the limestones, forms forests chiefly round the Gennargentu massif and Mt. Santa Vittoria, also in the Catena del Marghine. There are alpine mats with thyme, thrift, etc., among the highest peaks.

The wild sheep *Ovis musimon,* known in Sardinia in classical times, is now found nowhere else but Sardinia and Corsica and is there protected. There are also special varieties of red deer, wild boar, hare and rodents, a Sardinian weasel (*Mustela boccaniela*) and a wild cat (*Felis ocreata*). The domestic donkeys are very small. Unexpectedly there are no bears, wolves, otters, squirrels or moles; no Italian sparrows or magpies. The Sardinian partridge (*Alectoris barbara*), unknown anywhere else in Europe but found in Tunisia, Algeria and Morocco, is also protected in the nature reserve at Golfo Aranci. There is a variety of trout like that in Algeria, Asia Minor and Persia. No poisonous or smooth snakes or slow worms are found but one lizard, *Lacerta fitzingeri,* one newt, *Molge rusconii* (a north African form) and one toad, *Bufo viridis.* Many of the 100 species of beetles are endemic and at least 12 species of butterflies and moths and two genera of land and fresh-water snails are found nowhere else.   (X.)

ARCHAEOLOGY AND HISTORY

Prehistoric and Pre-Roman Civilizations.—The earliest evidence of human occupation in Sardinia dates from the time when metal was coming into use in the western Mediterranean. Although some stations (*e.g.,* Macomer in central Sardinia) have yielded lithic industries without metal, a pure Neolithic phase is not so far distinguishable from the Chalcolithic stage. The first habitations were perhaps cave dwellings (*e.g.,* San Bartolomeo and other grottoes near Cagliari and in western Sardinia), but it was not long before the Proto-Sardinians began to live a farming life in hut villages. Cult places in caves (San Michele near Ozieri) and religious monuments (a square platform built of large stones at Monte d'Accoddi, northwest of Sassari) are known. The dead were buried in artificial grottoes, which show an antechamber and one or more cells, generally rectangular in plan, sometimes with pillars and roughly carved symbols or figures. These tombs are called by the Sardinians *domus de gianas* ("witches' houses") and form more or less extensive cemeteries, the best known of which was excavated at Anghelu Ruju near Alghero. Cist graves in stone circles were found in northern Sardinia (Arzachena), and a few small dolmens still existing in the island must go back to the same period. Menhirs are not infrequent and may be related to sanctuaries and burial places. A good idea of the material civilization and common life is furnished by the funerary equipment at Anghelu Ruju, which includes flint blades, stone axes, maceheads, arrowheads, copper daggers and implements, personal ornaments. Stone "idols" are also present and may be interpreted as attendants of the dead. They show the female form in a quite schematic rendering which recalls similar although not identical figures from the Aegean. Pottery comprises undecorated, impressed and incised wares, differing in shape and ornament, among which curvilinear and "spiral-ribbon" patterns are frequent. The typical bell beakers demonstrate a direct link with the Spanish beaker culture.

This Sardinian Copper Age was still flourishing in the first half of the second millennium B.C., and was apparently influenced and transformed very slowly by the impulse of the Bronze Age civilizations which were already ancient in the near east. Minoan and Mycenaean influence was not as direct as in Sicily, but commercial intercourse with Crete may be proved from the beginning of the Late Minoan period, toward 1500 B.C. (copper pig-ingots with linear A signs found at Serra Ilixi). In any case the breaking of a real Bronze Age culture in Sardinia cannot be perceived till near the end of the second millennium, and in spite of the oriental influence its substantial local ancestry seems indisputable. Its peak is not to be dated earlier than the 8th or 7th century B.C., that is to say in the period of historical Phoenician and Greek colonization in the western Mediterranean. And it survived in more or less degenerate forms down to the Carthaginian and Roman conquest of the island.

Since the Proto-Sardinians did not know of any system of writing, native historical records are not available. The Greek sources adumbrate a kind of fabulous golden age in Sardinia before the arrival of the Carthaginian invaders, with intensive cultivation and building. In fact, the monuments suggest a period of cultural flowering and prosperity which may hardly be noticed in any later phase of the history of the island. About 1,000 stone towers, the so-called nuraghi (sing. nuraghe), are still a peculiar feature of the Sardinian landscape. They belong to the Sardinian Bronze Age civilization, which is therefore called nuraghi culture by scholars. These towers are in the shape of a truncated cone and built of large stones laid in more or less regular courses; they contain superposed round chambers capped by tall pointed corbelled roofs and connected with a winding staircase. Such a tower is nothing more than the chief element of complex buildings comprising bastions and turrets with corridors, round chambers and cisterns; e.g. those excavated at Abbasanta (the so-called Nuraghe Losa), at Torralba, and at Barumini. The nuraghi are sometimes interlinked in defensive systems (e.g. Giara di Gèsturi). But in many cases fortified villages of partially stone-built round huts appear in close connection with the nuraghi, which may therefore be considered as residential castles of chieftains including storerooms, foundries and even places for religious use. Other isolated buildings are in the form of rectangular temples (Serra Orrios), monumental wells (Sàrdara, Serri, Ballao) and fountains (Lomarzu). The graves show a development of earlier local types. The subterranean chamber tombs become bigger, imitating more closely the internal structure of civil habitations. On the other hand grandiose megalithic grave monuments are encountered, deriving from simpler dolmen-corridors or cists, with a rectangular cell covered by a corbelled roof and with a panelled portal slab in the centre of an exedra façade,—the so-called "giants' tombs." Objects for everyday life and for religion, yielded copiously by the dwellings and sanctuaries or found in hoards, include bronze implements and weapons, ornaments, decorated and coarse pottery. However, there is a kind of production which calls for special attention, namely the bronze votive statuettes portraying men, chiefly warriors, women, animals, more infrequently mythological beings and small models of ships or buildings.

The race which built the nuraghi was probably a definite ethnical unity, having its roots in the first prehistoric population of the island. In as far as Sardinian place names produce evidence for a knowledge of the lost language of the Proto-Sardinians, these appear to be of Palaeo-Mediterranean origin with some Iberian affinities. Perhaps Ligurian elements settled on the northern coasts, but there is no doubt that no Indo-European invasion reached the island before the Roman conquest. Classical authors mention some names of native peoples; e.g., the *Ioleis* or *Ilienses*. Archaeological evidence from the nuraghi culture suggests a strongly organized power of tribal states. The working of metal from the local mines may be reckoned to have been the chief source of wealth. However, the presence of Phoenician trade settlements along the Sardinian coasts since the 8th century B.C. must have vigorously contributed to Proto-Sardinian prosperity.

The Phoenician shippers and traders, driven westward in search of metal, included the mining zone of Sardinia in their system of commercial routes and founded trading posts, which became the important towns of Caralis (Cagliari), Nora, Bithia, Sulci, Tharros, Cornus. Attempts at colonization by the Greeks (Olbia in northwestern Sardinia) were unsuccessful because of the jealous opposition of the Phoenicians. After Carthage had attained leadership over the western Phoenicians, the struggle for supremacy in the west caused a more direct control to be exercised over the colonists on the island. After a long period of peaceful coexistence with the indigenous peoples, the Carthaginians began, about 500 B.C., the military conquest of the most productive parts of Sardinia. This drove the proudest of the Proto-Sardinians to a fierce life in a reduced mountain zone, a development that left a noticeable mark upon the character of the later Sardinians. The thriving Phoenician and Carthaginian civilization, with its orientalizing and half-grecizing elements, is copiously documented by the finds of cemeteries, as at Tharros, Sulci and Cagliari, and by the religious and civil monuments of Nora and Cagliari.

Roman Period.—During the first Punic War the Romans tried to take Sardinia. However, not earlier than the end of the war, in 238 B.C., they took advantage of a revolt of Carthaginian mercenaries to demand the surrender of the island. The native tribes opposed the Romans, but were conquered after several bloody campaigns; the island became a province under the government of a praetor or propraetor, to whose jurisdiction Corsica was added soon afterward. A rebellion in 215 B.C., fostered by the Carthaginians, was quelled by T. Manlius Torquatus. After this the island began to furnish considerable supplies of corn; it was treated as a conquered country, not containing a single free city, and the inhabitants were obliged to pay a tithe in corn and a further money contribution. There were saltworks as early as about 150 B.C. There were two insurrections of the mountain tribes, in 181 and in 114 B.C., but even in the time of Strabo there was considerable brigandage.

In the division of provinces made by Augustus, Sardinia and Corsica fell to the share of the senate, but in A.D. 6, Augustus, because of the frequent disturbances, took them over and placed them under a praefectus. In A.D. 67 Nero restored Sardinia to the senate (but not Corsica) in exchange for Achaea, and the former was then governed by a *legatus pro praetore;* but Vespasian took it over again before A.D. 78, and placed it under an imperial procurator as praefectus. It returned to the senate, not before A.D. 83 but certainly before the reign of M. Aurelius, when we find it governed by a proconsul, as it was under Commodus; the latter, or perhaps Septimius Severus, took it over again and placed it under a procurator as praefectus once more. A bronze tablet discovered in 1866 near the village of Esterzili is inscribed with a decree of the time of Otho with regard to the boundaries of three tribes, the Gallienses, Patulienses and Campani, who inhabited the eastern part of the island. Caralis was the only city with Roman civic rights in Sardinia in Pliny's time (when it received the privilege is unknown). A Roman colony had been founded at Turris Libisonis (Porto Torres) and others, later on, at Usellis and Cornus. We hear little of the island under the empire, except as a granary and as remarkable for its unhealthiness and the audacity of its brigands. It was often used as a place of exile. (MA. P.)

Vandal and Byzantine Rule.—After they had crossed over into Africa from Spain in 429 the Vandals occupied Sardinia in 456 and held it till its conquest in 534 by the Byzantines under Duke Cyril. Apart from an attempt to retake the island made in 468 by Marcellinus under the emperors Leo I (of the east) and Anthemius (of the west), the Vandal rule was pacific. It allowed of a period of cultural revival, largely motivated by the enforced residence for about 20 years at Cagliari of 120 North African bishops, who had been banished by King Thrasamund. Among the exiled bishops were St. Fulgentius and the bishop of Hippo, who had brought with him the relics of St. Augustine, which were recovered in 720 by the Lombard king Liutprand and taken to Pavia.

The "African" cultural renaissance in Sardinia is testified by the remains of the monastery built by Fulgentius near the basilica of S. Saturnino, Cagliari, as well as by the code of St. Hilary in the capitular library of St. Peter, Rome, and in the Laudian manuscripts of the Bodleian library, Oxford.

Under the Eastern Roman empire Sardinia was one of the seven provinces of the prefecture of Africa of the praetorium. It was under a *praeses* for civil affairs and a *dux* for military. In the

8th century the two posts were held successively by the same person. In 552–553 the island was occupied by the Goths under Totila, but after the end of Gothic rule in Italy, Sardinia long remained under the Eastern empire. Letters from Gregory the Great written at the end of the 6th century denounce Byzantine misgovernment and give evidence of pressure being exercised by the Lombards on the Sardinian coast. A Greek inscription found at Portotorres in 1927 shows that this pressure persisted in the early 8th century, when the first Arab attempts to conquer the island (711) were made. These vain attempts were repeated throughout the 8th century and, with greater persistence, in the 9th, when the Arabs sought to take advantage of the extreme difficulty of communication between Byzantium and the island resulting from their capture of Sicily in 827–31. The defense was entrusted to, and stubbornly prosecuted by, the islanders themselves, probably under local leaders, and an autonomous government was set up, at first *de facto* and later *de jure*, when the island was divided into four districts (*giudicati*). Einhard records that in 815 the Sardinians sent ambassadors to the emperor Louis the Pious to seek an alliance against the common enemy. In 851 Pope Leo IV requested the Sardinians to send forces to garrison Rome against the Arabs.

The Giudicati and Italian Influence.—The four Sardinian *giudicati* of Cagliari, Arborea, Torres and Gallura appear clearly defined territorially and politically only in the 11th century, after the defeat in Sardinian waters in 1016 of the Arab chief Mugajd by combined Sardinian, Pisan and Genoese forces. From that time Sardinia became a field for expansion for these republics, as well as for Marseilles and Gaeta, and was opened to the monastic immigration encouraged by the Roman see, which now claimed sovereignty over the island. Of the many competitors for its exploitation, Pisa and Genoa were the most successful and, through alliances with the *giudici*, secured politico—mercantile zones of influence—Pisa mostly in the north and west, Genoa in the south and east. Pisa got for her own archbishop the right to the apostolic legation and the primacy of Sardinia and Corsica. Subsequently Genoa, to counteract its rival, subsidized Barisone I, *giudice* of Arborea, to enable him to acquire for himself the investiture of the whole *Regnum Sardiniae*. This attempt failed, Barisone was arrested for bankruptcy and the *regnum* was granted to Pisa by Frederick Barbarossa. The peace of 1169 brought about a temporary truce between the two republics, soon broken by dissensions among the *giudici*, who sought help and protection now from one of the two city-states, now from the other. The *giudicato* of Cagliari passed through marriage to Pisan families (Massa, Visconti, Donoratico) and finally to the same republic that provided the capital with the notable fortifications that still stand. The *giudicato* of Torres passed from the protection of Pisa to that of Genoa until the marriage of Adelasia, heiress of Gallura and Logudoro, *en seconde noce* to Enzio of Hohenstaufen, natural son of Frederick II. Enzio took the title *rex Sardiniae* but, as he was imprisoned by the Bolognese in 1249, his rule was carried on by vicars. With the battle of Meloria (1284) the influence of Pisa was limited to the districts of Cagliari and Gallura; Genoa controlled the other districts, also through its noble families (Spinola, Malaspina, Doria). Throughout the 11th, 12th and 13th centuries, however, Pisan influence predominated, in the arts almost exclusively, as shown by the many churches built at this time, especially the basilicas of S. Gavino, Portotorres, and Sta. Maria, Ardara. Important documents on the economic life of the period survive in the *condaghe* or patrimonial registers of ecclesiastics, drawn up in the vernacular, with annotations concerning income and expenditure and property titles.

Aragonese Domination.—In 1297 Boniface VIII granted to James II of Aragon the *Regnum Sardiniae et Corsicae*, but Sardinia was effectually conquered by the Aragonese only in 1326, with the help of the *giudicato* of Arborea, which, however, kept its independence and defended itself strenuously against the same Aragonese throughout the 14th century. A war that broke out about 1350 between the *giudice* Mariano IV and King Peter IV of Aragon was won by the latter, who, at the first extraordinary meeting of parliament received from Mariano an oath of fealty (1355).

A few years later war was started again by Mariano and carried on heroically by his daughter, Eleonora of Arborea, who signed a new peace treaty with King John I of Aragon (1386). After the death of Eleonora (1404) the *giudicato* was reduced to a fief of Aragon (1410) and, after a last vain attempt at insurrection had been suppressed at the battle of Macomer (1478), brought wholly under the Aragonese crown. Under Aragonese rule, and then under that of Spain, the feudal regime was restored: the administration was unified and placed under a viceroy residing at Cagliari. A Sardinian parliament with three branches (*stamenti*)—military, ecclesiastical and royal—was set up. Despite the provisions extended by Alphonso V of Aragon to the whole island for the observance of the code of rights promulgated by Mariano IV of Arborea and perfected by Eleonora (1392)—the *Carta de Logu* (university library, Cagliari)—the island's economy, flourishing under the *giudici*, declined. The population, oppressed by taxation, decreased and the island fell into a state of lethargy.   (R. Du.)

Modern History.—Sardinia remained a Spanish province until the War of the Spanish Succession. In 1708 Cagliari was bombarded by an English fleet and on its capitulation the island became Austrian. The supreme council of the island was immediately transferred from Madrid to Vienna and Austria was confirmed in possession by the Treaty of Utretcht in 1713. Cardinal Giulio Alberoni, Philip V's minister, hoped to make Sardinia a jumping-off point for the recapture of Spain's former Italian possessions, and in 1717 he dispatched a squadron from Barcelona which recaptured the island. The victory was, however, short-lived. In 1720 by the Treaty of London the Quadruple Alliance united Sicily to Naples under Austrian rule and compensated Victor Amadeus II of Savoy for his loss of Sicily by making him king of Sardinia.

The house of Savoy took an interest in their new kingdom and sought to establish their authority over the feudal nobles and over the church. In 1726 Pope Benedict XIII confirmed the king in the right of presentation to bishoprics and yielded the papal prerogative of investiture to the crown. Throughout the 18th century efforts were made to improve the social and economic conditions of Sardinia: schools in Italian were started in order to link the island more closely with the mainland, empty lands were repopulated with Piedmontese, Ligurians and Corsicans, agriculture was encouraged, the salt pans improved, and some revival of old industries and the introduction of new ones were attempted. In 1793 the French attacked Sardinia and bombarded Cagliari, but were repelled by the islanders. The *stamenti* then presented a memorandum to the king asking for a measure of local autonomy and the opening of all posts, except that of viceroy, to all citizens. Their request was rejected but the movement which it represented found support in a popular revolt rising out of the economic discontent of the people. The revolt lasted for about two years, but faded out on the flight to France of the popular leader, Gian Maria Angioj. In 1799 Charles Emmanuel IV took refuge in Sardinia after his expulsion from Piedmont by the French. His successor Victor Emmanuel lived in Cagliari from 1806 till 1814, when he left his brother Charles Felix there as viceroy. During the next two years Charles Felix embarked on various reforms affecting agriculture, taxation, public health and the administration of justice, but it was Charles Albert who took real account of Sardinia's needs. In 1835 he abolished feudal rights, and, though in practice some continued to exist, the ensuing division of seignorial lands among private owners and communes formed the basis of the 19th and 20th century agrarian economy of Sardinia. Charles Albert sought to improve administration and finance, to reform the army, to establish charitable institutions, to improve schools, to open up roads, to improve communications with Genoa and Turin, and in general to spread the language and culture of the mainland. In 1847, at the request of the *stamenti*, Sardinia was united to the other provinces of Piedmont with the same standing in the kingdom; this position was confirmed by the *statuto* of 1848 and Sardinians sat in the Piedmontese parliament. The islanders played an active part in the Italian struggle for unity and independence, and from 1861 Sardinia formed a part of the kingdom of Italy.

On the outbreak of war between Italy and the Allies in 1940 Sardinia had a garrison of between 200,000 and 250,000, including the 9th German motorized division. The island's airfields were used as bases for attack in the Mediterranean. In 1943 Allied air attacks on the island began and increased in intensity as the time for the invasion of Sicily drew near. The Germans had increased the number of air squadrons in Sardinia, but in July Allied air attacks made many airfields unusable. The Allies had expected that a serious attack might have to be made on Sardinia, but early in Oct. 1943 Winston Churchill noted that on Sept. 19 it had fallen as a mere incident in the Italian campaign. It was occupied by a small number of Allied troops, some anti-Fascist exiles returned, and in a short time life had returned more or less to normal.

THE PEOPLE

The census of Nov. 1951 showed that Sardinia had a population of 1,273,850, an increase of 23% on the figure for 1936 (Italy 11.9%). The density of population is 136 per sq.mi. (Italy 412.6); in the northeast province of Nuoro it is only 93.5. Apart from the small mountain region of the Valle d'Aosta (75.5 per sq.mi.), the low regional figure was equalled only in the Trentino-Alto Adige. As in Sicily, the vast majority of the people live in compact villages and small towns, mostly in settlements containing 1,000–2,000 people; there are few towns of any size, only one, Cagliari, with more than 100,000 inhabitants.

The birth rate fell from 28.3 per 1,000 in 1936 to 25.7 in 1952 (Italy 18.0), the death rate also fell from 14 to 9, so that the natural increase in 1952 was 16.7 (Italy 7.9). The rate of infant mortality fell to 69 per 1,000 live births in 1951, a great improvement on 89 in 1936 but still very high compared with rates of 41 in Tuscany and 45 in Emilia-Romagna. It was estimated that before the systematic attack on the anopheles mosquito made by British, U.S. and Italian experts in 1947–48 more than 190,000 people were seriously affected by malaria and that 2,000,000 working days were lost annually through the disease. By 1952 there were scarcely any new cases and the number of recrudescent cases was very small. But tuberculosis remained a scourge; in 1952 the death rate was 782 per 1,000,000 of the population, the only region with a higher rate being Trentino-Alto Adige with 849 (Italy 613). The high incidence of infant mortality and of tuberculosis and other diseases like trachoma is undoubtedly connected with poverty and with the unhygienic living conditions which are particularly bad in the remote rural settlements.

Government.—Sardinia is one of the five regions on which a special form of local self-government was conferred by the Italian constitution of 1948 (*see* also SICILY: *Government*); the regional statute was adopted by an Italian constitutional law in Feb. 1948. Some measure of local self-government existed after the late summer of 1943, when Sardinia was occupied by the Allies, mainly because the island was cut off from the mainland of Italy and to a great extent left to its own resources. A sense of the need to establish definite contact led the Italian government in March 1944 to appoint a high commissioner for the island, as had been done in Sicily in January, and regional autonomy was granted to Sardinia by an amendment to the Sicilian statute of May 15, 1946.

As in Sicily, the administration of Sardinia was put in the hands of the president of the region, the elected regional assembly, and the *giunta*, the executive committee of the assembly, the state retaining control of justice, communications and the armed forces. But the assembly's legislative powers are less extensive than those of the Sicilian assembly. The Sardinian assembly was not given authority to legislate on educational matters, it can only "adapt the provisions of the national laws to its particular needs" in every grade of education, nor has it exclusive power, like the Sicilian assembly, to legislate on all questions concerning agriculture, land reclamation, industry and commerce. In fact, in view of the extreme poverty of Sardinia and of the great need for agrarian reform (*see* below), it was very important that the statute contained a special provision for the drawing up of a plan by the state and the region together for the economic and social reconstruction of Sardinia. The important executive function of maintaining public order was not (as it was in Sicily) conferred by the statute on the president and the *giunta*. The Italian government may delegate to the region the right to safeguard public order, in which case this function will be exercised by the president within the limits of directions laid down by the national government.

The president is elected by the assembly from among its members, represents the region, promulgates its laws and together with the *giunta* constitutes the government. He has the right to attend meetings of the Italian council of ministers and to speak though not to vote when Sardinian affairs are discussed, but he does not, like the Sicilian president, hold the rank of minister.

The financial provisions of the statute are framed with regard to the island's poverty. In addition to the proceeds of local taxation, to be raised in conformity with national principles, Sardinia receives a definite proportion of certain state taxes; *e.g.*, nine-tenths of the taxes of lands and buildings in the region and of the taxes on state monopolies. The region also receives rents paid for hydroelectric concessions, and the state has undertaken to make special grants for particular projects of public works and land improvement.

The first regional assembly was elected in May 1949. There are three provinces, Cagliari, Nuoro and Sassari.

ECONOMIC CONDITIONS

Agriculture.—More than half the employed population of Sardinia is engaged in agriculture, and most of the total area of the island is covered by agricultural and forest land. In general, the agrarian economy has remained unchanged for centuries; a certain amount of cereals is grown, but the chief source of livelihood is livestock. Arable farming is regarded mainly as an adjunct to pastoral, and the land is often only plowed to improve the grazing; tree culture (chiefly vines and olives) is confined to a few limited coastal zones and to the areas lying immediately round the centres of habitation. In 1952 48% of the agricultural and forest land was rough permanent pasture (Italy 14.4%), 27.8% arable (Italy 47.3%) and only 3.5% under tree crops (Italy 8.8%). Even in the naturally fertile Campidano most of the land is divided between permanent grazing and arable alternating with grazing.

More than half the farms are 3 ha. (7½ ac.) or less, more than a quarter under 1 ha., and they often lie far from the towns and villages in which 92% of the people live. The consequent difficulty of farming the land well is aggravated by these small farms, being broken up into numerous tiny strips often lying several miles apart and interspersed with bits of other properties. Large estates are few in number and consist mainly of rough pasture and forest. In 1939 only 4.3% of the agricultural income of Sardinia came from estates with an income of over 80,000 lire. Agriculture is dominated by the pathological splitting up of property, by extreme poverty of mobile capital and by very limited investment in farming. There is practically no mechanized cultivation and primitive methods of shallow plowing are still practised; a wooden plow pulled by an ox can still be seen working alongside an iron plow drawn by a horse.

The higher regions produce cork trees, oaks, pines, acacias and sweet chestnuts, but there are only a few remote places where these trees have survived in any numbers the depredations of 19th century speculators and the attacks of the huge herds of sheep and goats. Some effort was made in the 1930s to increase the forest area, chiefly with holm-oak coppices, but reafforestation is made difficult by drought and wind, and the planting of young trees gave way to the slower process of seeding. The most important non-forest tree is the olive. The climate is suited to olive trees, which grow at altitudes up to 2,300 ft., and even a little higher in sheltered valleys, and produce good quality oil particularly in the northwest.

Crops.—Little more wheat is grown than is needed for home consumption, and it is mostly hard wheat which can stand the long dry summers. The yield is low, 9.8 quintals (1 quintal = approx. 225 lb.) per hectare in 1952 (average 16.8 for Italy, 31.3 for Lombardy), and could be raised not only by the use of selected seed, chemical fertilizers and machinery, but by improving the milling which in some districts is still done with grindstones turned by donkeys. Barley does well, and some is grown for fodder, but its yield is also low. Vines can be grown at altitudes up to 3,000 ft., but most vineyards are on the edge of the lowlands. Output is small (616,000 hl. in 1952) partly because most of the wines produced have poor keeping qualities, partly because of the lack of storage cellars.

Livestock.—The principal source of wealth is livestock, sheep and goats; Sardinia has more of both than any other region, and nearly a quarter of all the sheep and goats of Italy. The number of cattle compares reasonably well with the average for Italy, the ratio to the population in 1952 being 16.5% compared with 18.4% for Italy. Cattle are mainly bred for work; the local crossbreeds, Sardo-Modicana and Bruno-Sardo, give poor yields of milk but are good workers. Sheep produce the milk from which large quantities of cheese are made and exported to North America and France as well as to the Italian mainland. Mutton is less important, but Sardinian lamb is in demand on the mainland. The wool is coarse in quality, but makes a strong cloth impervious to wet.

Land Reform.—In 1940 the Italian government had plans for land reclamation covering about one-third of the island's total area; work had been carried out on a small scheme involving about 54,000 ha. mostly in the marshy Campidano, which was known as one of the plague spots of Italy. The new agricultural settlements of Mussolinia (now Arborea) and Terralba were established and mixed farming on north Italian lines was carried on by settlers from north Italy on farms of 20 ha. each. By 1948 good results were being obtained. The wheat yield averaged 15 quintals per hectare compared with Sardinia's average of 8 or 9 quintals, the breed of cattle had improved and from vines grown on the surrounding hills good wines were being produced and exported. Italian agricultural experts knew, however, that not only would the Italian state have to finance any plan of reform, but skilful persuasion would be needed to overcome the obstinate refusal of Sardinian farmers to accept suggestions from outside, particularly if it involved reduction in the size of their flocks and herds and a change from extensive to intensive farming.

Fisheries.—Tunny fishing is of some importance, but is not carried on by Sardinians, who have no liking for the sea, but by Sicilians.

Industry.—The mining industry of Sardinia is of great antiquity: there are workings dating from the Bronze Age, and mining was carried on later by the Phoenicians, the Romans and by the Pisans in the middle ages. The most important minerals now mined are zinc and lead of which Sardinia supplies about 80% and 93% respectively of Italy's production, but antimony, copper, iron, manganese, molybdenum, nickel, cobalt and tin are also mined in small quantities. The chief lead and zinc mines are in Iglesiente in the southwest, and much of the smelting is done in the island. There are two coal fields, one in Sulcis in the southwest, around Carbonia, where about 1,000,000 tons of coal of poor quality with a high sulphur content are mined annually. The other field in Seui, near Tortoli on the east side of Sardinia, produces better quality coal, but only about 50,000 tons a year. After Italy lost the Istrian coal fields to Yugoslavia under the 1947 treaty, Sardinia produced most of Italy's coal, but the quality is too poor for it to be much used in industry. The granite of Sardinia is used locally and exported. The salt pans at Cagliari and Carloforte are important.

Communications and Ports.—Sardinia is reasonably well-served by railways. State railway lines of normal gauge connect Terranova with Cagliari, with Porto Torres and Sassari via Chilivani, and with Iglesias via Decimomannu. Narrow-gauge lines run from Tortoli and Sorgoni to Cagliari, from Nuoro via Macomer to Bosa and via Ozieri to Chilivani, and from Palau to Sassari and Alghero, and there are also private lines connected with the mines. There are four main north-south roads and four east-west.

There are few seaports, but some of them have excellent natural harbours. The three chief commercial ports are Cagliari, Terranova Pausania and Porto Torres. Cagliari's harbour is entirely artificial, and the port owes most of its importance to the proximity of the lead and zinc industry and to the export of salt. Terranova handles the bulk of the mail and passenger traffic with Italy. Porto Torres, which lies at the western end of the north coast on the gulf of Asinara, is the port of export for Sassari, the second town in Sardinia, and for iron ore from the mines in Nurra. At the northeast end of Sardinia a group of islands shelter the naval station of La Maddalena, on the south coast of the island of the same name and connected by a causeway with the island of Caprera, famous as the home of Giuseppe Garibaldi. (M. M. C.)

BIBLIOGRAPHY.—C. Zervos, *La Civilization de la Sardaigne* (Paris, 1954; London, 1955); G. Pinza, "Monumenti primitive della Sardegna," in *Monumenti Antichi dei Lincei*, IX (Rome, 1901); T. E. Peet, *The Stone and Bronze Ages in Italy and Sicily* (Oxford, 1909), pp. 143 ff., 225 ff.; D. Mackenzie in *Papers of the British School in Rome*, v (Rome, 1910), pp. 89 ff., and *ibid.*, vi (Rome, 1913), pp. 127 ff.; F. von Duhn and G. Herbig in *Reallexikon der Vorgeschichte*, M. W. L. F. Ebert (ed.) (Berlin, 1924 ff.), s.v. "Italien: Sardinien, Sarden"; A. Taramelli in *Il Convegno Archeologico in Sardegna* (Reggio Emilia, 1929) and *Enciclopedia Italiana*, vol. xxx (Rome, 1936), s.v. "Sardegna"; C. Bellieni, *La Sardegna e i Sardi nella civiltà del mondo antico*, 2 vol. (Cagliari, 1931); J. Whatmough, *The Foundations of Roman Italy* (London, 1929) pp. 367 ff.; E. Pais, *Storia della Sardegna e della Corsica durante il dominio romano*, 2 vol. (Rome, 1923); M. Pallottino, *La Sardegna Nuragica* (Rome, 1950); R. Besta, *La Sardegna medioevale* (Rome, 1908–09); R. Delogu, *L'Architettura del Medioevo in Sardegna* (Rome, 1953); *Studi Etruschi*, periodical (Florence); *Studi Sardi*, periodical (Cagliari).

SARDIS, more correctly SARDES (αἰΣάρδεις), the capital of the ancient kingdom of Lydia, the seat of a *conventus* under the Roman Empire, and the metropolis of the province Lydia in later Roman and Byzantine times, was situated in the middle Hermus valley, at the foot of Mt. Tmolus, a steep and lofty spur of which formed the citadel. It was about 2½ mi. south of the Hermus. The earliest reference to Sardis is in Alcman (Bergk, *Fr.* 24, *c.* 650 B.C.); in the *Iliad* the name Hydē seems to be given to the city of the Maeonian (*i.e.*, Lydian) chiefs, and in later times, Hydē was said to be the older name of Sardis, or the name of its citadel. It is, however, more probable that Sardis was not the original capital of the Maeonians, but that it became so amid the changes which produced the powerful Lydian empire of the 8th century B.C. The city was captured by the Cimmerians in the 7th century, by the Persians and by the Athenians in the 6th, and by Antiochus the Great at the end of the 3rd century. Once at least, under the emperor Tiberius, in A.D. 17, it was destroyed by an earthquake; but it was always rebuilt, and was one of the great cities of Asia Minor till the later Byzantine period. As one of the Seven Churches of Asia, it was addressed by the author of the Apocalypse in terms which seem to imply that its population was notoriously soft and faint-hearted. Its importance was due, first to its military strength, secondly to its situation on an important highway leading from the interior to the Aegean coast, and thirdly to its commanding the wide and fertile plain of the Hermus.

The early Lydian kingdom was far advanced in the industrial arts (*see* LYDIA), and Sardis was the chief seat of its manufactures. The most important of these trades was the manufacture and dyeing of delicate woollen stuffs and carpets.

In the Hellenistic and Roman periods Sardis was eclipsed by Pergamum (the Attalid capital), by Ephesus (the capital of the province of Asia) and probably also by Smyrna. After Constantinople became the capital of the east a new road system grew up connecting the provinces with the capital. Sardis then lay rather apart from the great lines of communication and lost some of its importance. It still, however, retained its titular supremacy and continued to be the seat of the metropolitan bishop of the province of Lydia, formed in A.D. 295. It is enumerated as third, after Ephesus and Smyrna, in the list of cities of the Thracesian *thema* given by Constantine Porphyrogenitus in the 10th century; but in the actual history of the next four centuries it plays a part very inferior to Magnesia ad Sipylum and Philadelphia (*see* ALA-SHEHR), which have retained their pre-eminence in the district. The Hermus valley began to suffer from the inroads of the Seljuk Turks about the end of the 11th century; but the successes of the Greek general Philocales in 1118 relieved the district for the time, and the ability of the Comneni, together with the gradual decay of the Seljuk power, retained it in the Byzantine dominions. The country round Sardis was frequently ravaged both by Christians and by Turks during the 13th century. Soon after 1301 the Seljuk amirs overran the whole of the Hermus and Cayster valleys, and a fort on the citadel of Sardis was handed over to them by treaty in 1306. Finally in 1390 Philadelphia, which had for some time been an independent Christian city, surrendered to Sultan Bayezid's mixed army of Ottoman Turks and Byzantine Christians, and the Seljuk power in the Hermus valley was merged in the Ottoman empire. The latest reference to the city of Sardis relates its capture (and probable destruction) by Timur in 1402. Its site is now practically deserted.

The ruins of Sardis, so far as they are now visible, are chiefly of the Roman time; but though few ancient sites offered better hope of results, the necessity for heavy initial expenditure was a deterrent (e.g., to H. Schliemann). On the banks of the Pactolus two columns of a great Ionic temple, now known to be that of Cybele-Artemis were still standing. More than one attempt to excavate this temple, the last by G. Dennis in 1882, was made and prematurely brought to an end by lack of funds. In 1910–1914 and also in 1922, the temple site and part of the necropolis were studied by H. C. Butler and others, of the American Society for the Excavation of Sardis.

See reports in *Am. Journal of Archaeology*, 1911–27, and the volumes of *Sardis*, especially I. and II. (H. C. Butler) on the history of the excavations down to 1914, and VI. pts. 1–2 (E. Littmann-W. H. Buckler) on the Lydian inscriptions; results and bibliography in Pauly-Wissowa *R. Enc.* XIII. 2123 f. (Bürchner-Deeters-J. Keil); for the city's history in early Christian times, W. M. Ramsay, *Letters to the Seven Churches* (1904), V. Schultze, *Altchristliche Städte* II. 2,145 f. (1926).

SARDOU, VICTORIEN (1831–1908), French dramatist, was born in Paris on Sept. 5, 1831. The Sardous were settled at Le Cannet, a village near Cannes, where they owned an estate, planted with olive trees. A night's frost killed all the trees and the family was ruined. Victorien's father, Antoine Léandre Sardou, came to Paris, and earned his living in a succession of employments. Victorien had to make his way as best he could. A play of his, *La Taverne des étudiants*, produced at the Odéon on April 1, 1854, was withdrawn after five nights. Many disappointments followed; some plays were rejected, others were accepted and not performed.

Sardou was now in actual want, and his misfortunes culminated in an attack of typhoid fever. He was dying in his garret, surrounded with his rejected manuscripts. A lady named Mlle. de Brécourt nursed him back to health, and introduced him to Mlle. Déjazet. Then fortune began to smile on the author. It is true that *Candide*, the first play he wrote for Mlle. Déjazet, was stopped by the censor, but *Les Premières Armes de Figaro, Monsieur Garat,* and *Les Prés Saint Gervais*, produced almost in succession, had a splendid run, and *Les Pattes de mouche* (1860: afterwards anglicized as *A Scrap of Paper*) obtained a similar success at the Gymnase. *Fédora* (1882) was written expressly for Sarah Bernhardt, as were many of his later plays. He soon ranked with Augier and Dumas. He ridiculed the vulgar and selfish middle-class person in *Nos Intimes* (1861: anglicized as *Peril*), the gay old bachelors in *Les Vieux Garçons* (1865), the modern Tartufes in *Séraphine* (1868), the rural element in *Nos Bons Villageois* (1866), old-fashioned customs and antiquated political beliefs in *Les Ganaches* (1862), the revolutionary spirit and those who thrive on it in *Rabagas* (1872) and *Le Roi Carotte* (1872), and the then threatened divorce laws in *Divorçons* (1880).

He struck a new vein by introducing a strong historic element in some of his dramatic romances. Thus he borrowed *Théodora* (1884) from Byzantine annals, *La Haine* (1874) from Italian chronicles, *La Duchesse d' Athènes* from the forgotten records of mediaeval Greece. *Patrie* (1869) is founded on the rising of the Dutch *gueux* at the end of the 16th century. The scene of *La Sorcière* (1904) was laid in Spain in the 16th century. The French Revolution furnished him with three plays, *Les Merveilleuses, Thermidor* (1891) and *Robespierre* (1902). The last named was written expressly for Sir Henry Irving, and produced at the Lyceum theatre, as was *Dante* (1903). The imperial epoch was revived in *La Tosca* (1887) and *Madame Sans Gêne* (1893). Later plays were *La Piste* (1905) and *Le Drame des poisons* (1907).

Sardou married his benefactress, Mlle. de Brécourt, but eight years later he became a widower, and soon after the revolution of 1870 was married again, to Mlle. Soulié. He was elected to the French Academy in 1878. He died at Paris on Nov. 8, 1908.

See L. Lacour, *Trois théâtres* (1880); Brander Matthews, *French Dramatists* (New York, 1881); R. Doumic, *Écrivains d'aujourd'hui* (Paris, 1895); F. Sarcey, *Quarante ans de théâtre* (vol. vi., 1901).

SARGASSO SEA, a tract of the North Atlantic ocean covered with floating seaweed (*Sargassum*, originally named *sargaço* by the Portuguese). This tract is bounded approximately by 25° and 31° N. and by 40° and 70° W., but its extent and density are influenced by winds and ocean currents. The weed, known as Gulf Weed (*Sargassum Bacciferum*), belongs to the brown algae (*q.v.*), and is easily recognized by small berry-like bladders. The floating masses are believed to be replenished by additional supplies torn from the coasts to the south-west and carried by currents to the great whirl of the Sargasso sea. The weed supports a considerable amount of somewhat low forms of animal life of a type always more characteristic of the littoral zone than of the open ocean. The Sargasso sea was first reported by Columbus, who on his initial "West Indies" voyage was involved in it for several days. The widely credited story of ships becoming embedded in the weed beyond possibility of escape was disproved by the "Michael Sars" expedition (1910).

SARGENT, JOHN SINGER (1856–1925), Anglo-American painter. For 40 years before his death John Singer Sargent was too towering a personality for his contemporaries to judge either him or his work in true perspective. A tall commanding presence, with a small head well set on broad shoulders, with large, somewhat prominent grey eyes, kindly in expression though nothing escaped them, with a close-cut beard at a time when nine men out of 10 were clean-shaven, he made an instant impression upon those who came into contact with him. During the last years of his life, with his great size, his dark hair and beard turned silver-white, his florid complexion, and an air about him of singular freshness and calm, he had a look as of some serene and beneficent Jove.

That he was a great artist is universally acknowledged, but that he was a great man his life attested—in its austerity, its generous highmindedness, its breadth of vision, and above all in its independence of praise, fame or wealth.

Essentially a cosmopolitan, he was of American descent. His father, Dr. Fitzwilliam Sargent, was born in Gloucester, Massachusetts, where his ancestors, emigrating from Gloucester, England, settled before 1650. For his medical training Fitzwilliam Sargent went to Philadelphia, and married Miss Mary Newbold Singer, a member of an old Philadelphia family. In 1854 the young couple went for change of air and scene to Europe, with no premonition that this journey would result in their permanent establishment abroad. Two years later, on Jan. 12, 1856, in Florence, at the Casa Arretini, on the Lungarno Guicciardini, their son, John Singer Sargent, was born. He showed his special aptitudes from his earliest childhood, which was spent at Nice, in Rome, in Dresden, with periodical returns to Florence. Whenever possible he took drawing lessons of a desultory kind, interrupted by the exigencies of schooling and a life of constant travel. His mother, who all her life loved to sketch in water-colours, recognised and encouraged his unusual gifts.

His own awakening to the enchantment of being able to express his delight in the visual world came to him, he once mentioned, at Mürren, in the summers of 1868 to 1870. His early drawings were carefully painstaking efforts to show every variation in rock forms, or in the verdure that sprang from their crevices. In 1873 he won a prize for drawing at the Accademia in Florence.

In 1876 he paid the first of many visits to America, but before the short interruption of this trip he had begun his artistic education in earnest, having entered the studio of Carolus-Duran, in Paris, in 1874, at the age of eighteen.

A fellow student described him as a tall, slenderly built, rather silent youth, with a friendly, somewhat shy manner, who could, on occasions, in spite of his diffidence, express himself with startling decision. His industry was no less remarkable than his youthful strength which was not unduly taxed by the strain of attending the classes not only at Duran's studio, but the Beaux Arts and evening life classes as well.

Contrary to many published recollections, Sargent himself declared, perhaps with characteristic modesty, that he was by no means a brilliant pupil, and that he only acquired his amazing technical skill by continued concentrated effort. What he did recognise, with instant appreciation and lifelong acknowledgment, was the scientific precision of the method taught by Carolus Duran, who had based his theories on a close study of Franz Hals and Velasquez. John Sargent, not without struggle, made this technique his own, and it gave him, at the start, the assured mastery of his materials.

His first picture, exhibited in the Salon of 1878, won an honourable mention. It was called "En route pour la Pêche," and is now in the Corcoran Gallery at Washington. In the next year's Salon he showed the portrait of his master, which he had painted in 1877, at the age of 21, and which was instantly acclaimed as of extraordinary promise. Shortly after, emancipated from schools, he made a pilgrimage to Spain, which he had already visited as a boy, and the studies done in the Prado Gallery, which, after his death, were sold at Christie's at such phenomenal prices, were painted on this occasion.

Immediately after his return to Paris he painted the beautiful canvases "El Jaleo" (Salon 1882), now at Fenway Court, Boston, and "The Children of E. D. Boit" (Salon 1883), now in the Boston Fine Arts Museum. Of "The Lady of the Rose" (Miss Burkhardt), which was shown in 1881 and gained a second class medal, Henry James wrote that it was the work of "a talent which on the very threshold of its career has nothing more to learn." This was a phrase, for to the end of his days Sargent remained the student, making even briefer the span between brain and hand, between conception and achievement; yet these early canvases are remarkably mature, with a beauty of surface texture he rarely excelled, and with the atmospheric "quality" he had learned from Velasquez. He had the special readiness of genius to absorb great traditions, to take valuable hints from every source, and incorporate them into his own work with the freshness and vigour of a deeply original mind.

From the outset commissions came to him unsought. He had to knock at no doors; but it was not till the Salon of 1884, when he showed the portrait of Madame Gautreau (Metropolitan Museum of New York), that the painter awoke to find himself famous—or infamous. Madame Gautreau was the friend of Gambetta, acclaimed by the Republican party, and Sargent was accused of having purposely done a caricature. The journalists outdid each other in senseless abuse.

This experience, with its astounding unreason, probably laid the foundation for his almost incredible independence of critical comment. Irritated by adulation, detesting every form of publicity, he could never be induced, unless it was forced upon him, to read any criticism of his own work, appreciative or the reverse.

So furious and so prolonged was the outcry in the French Press that finally, in a fit of disgust, Sargent left Paris and moved to London. His first studio was in Kensington, but in 1885 he had already settled at 33 Tite Street, Chelsea. In 1901 he bought the adjacent house (No. 31), and a door was cut through between the two studios. Here he lived and worked till his death on April 15, 1925.

Into these 40 years of his London domicile was crowded the experience of a dozen ordinary lifetimes. His first exhibited study of childhood: "Carnation, Lily, Lily, Rose," was bought in 1887, by the Chantrey bequest, for the Tate Gallery. A few years later the Luxembourg acquired the picture of the Spanish dancer "Carmencita," painted 1890, shown at the Royal Academy 1891. In spite of adverse criticism, it was not long before he was in great demand as a portrait painter, and the unflagging zeal of his industry kept pace with every triumph of public recognition. He numbered among his sitters princes and princesses, musicians, actors, teachers, writers, statesmen and diplomats. Many of his distinguished models he painted in their habit as they lived. The great groups of "The Duke of Marlborough and his Family" (1905), the "Ladies Acheson," (1902), the "Daughters of the

Hon. Percy Wyndham" (1900), the "Misses Hunter" (1902), etc., and a noble series of single portraits, notably those of the Duke and Duchess of Connaught (1908), the Duke (1901) and Duchess of Portland (1902), Lord Russell of Killowen (1900); of Francis Penrose, Esq. (1898), and of innumerable beautiful women: The Duchess of Sutherland (1904), the Countess of Warwick (1904), Lady Agnew (1893), Lady (Ian) Hamilton (1896), Mrs. Hammersley (1893), increased his every-growing prestige.

In 1894 he was elected an associate, in 1897 to full membership of the Royal Academy, and at the exhibitions at Burlington House his portraits were the centre of interest and of controversy. It became a high distinction to be painted by him, and hundreds clamoured for the honour in vain. Universities offered him degrees, he had as many medals as a war veteran. Quite unmoved by all this acclamation, he retained the serene simplicity of manner that made him so exceptional and so distinguished a figure.

In the sense of being generally understood John Sargent was never a popular painter. Painting is the most outspoken of the arts, but its language is not easy to read. Its apparent simplicity and the directness of its appeal to the eyes are misleading, and in the case of pictures so incisive and brilliant, so uncompromising in their truth, so unerring and authoritative in their presentation of character, it was no wonder that they awakened as much resentment as admiration. There are mysteries of light, as well as of darkness, and the secrets of this accomplishment were no less inscrutable, became actually more tantalising, because the method of expression was so frank, and looked so amazingly easy to imitate. And he was imitated, inevitably, but in no single instance with any distinction. Referred to as a psychologist or a satirist, he was frequently accused of deliberately accentuating the less pleasing qualities in his sitters—a foolish legend he dismissed with a shrug of his shoulders. "I chronicle," he once said, "I do not judge." Though his outlook on life was essentially indulgent, his sense of humour was irrepressible, and the unerring rectitude of his realism struck at a deep-rooted human weakness—a preference to be seen not as we are but as we should like to be.

In that its conclusions are so little deliberate painting differs from literature. John Sargent did not sum up his characters, he painted what he saw; but he caught, subconsciously perhaps, each fugitive betrayal of a passing thought, a restless movement, a smile or a glance. This subtle power of definition has been, in all ages, the peculiar gift of great portrait painters.

In recalling the astonishing variety and scope of his work, it may be assumed that he was almost indifferent to the form in which he was called upon to portray the modern spirit. His only prayer must have been that that spirit should not be utterly commonplace. For dullness he had no talent, even his magic touch failed to enliven it. Before the strange, the unexpected, the bizarre, his resource and his freshness were unfailing. No happy invention was permitted to degenerate into a formula. He never repeated himself. For the extremes of youth and of age he had undeniable tenderness; with incredible delicacy he portrayed the flower-like freshness of one, and if he did not disguise in the other the hint of decrepitude it was generally illumined by more than a suggestion of wisdom and dignity.

At the very height of his fame, in 1910, he decided to give up the painting of portraits. He had grown tired of the tyranny of sitters, and had begun to lose interest in his work. This decision, so typical of his artistic integrity, he lived up to. Only in exceptional instances was he afterwards induced to break his rule, and then never for considerations of money. Though he lived on a generous scale, he was never a wealthy man. Always ready to give a helping hand to a student, or to a brother artist, he was at once too busy and too impatient of all forms of implied superiority ever to want to teach. Deliberately then, perhaps, he set his face against the scattering of his energies over too wide a field. An omnivorous reader and a passionate musician, an excellent host and a most entertaining guest, his rare leisure was all too adequately filled.

In a holiday spirit he began to play with water-colour (in which medium he had made his earliest efforts at painting) and the result of his first summer of freedom may be seen in the sparkling brilliance, the irresistible gaiety of the 80 sketches bought *en bloc* by the Brooklyn Fine Arts Museum. His disciplined hand had acquired an almost miraculous lightness and certainty of touch.

But a heavier task had already for years been engaging his energies, and the last 20 years of his life were given more and more to the magnificent series of decorations which illustrate the range of his great gifts. It was said of his "History of Religion," begun in 1890 and not completed till 1916 (the subject for the great Hall in the Boston Public Library known as Sargent Hall), that his work here was not only a monument to the picturesque possibilities of his colossal subject, but to the sheer erudition of the painter. This task took him on several journeys to Egypt, Palestine, etc., as well as for a few months almost every year to America, where he had a studio in Boston, in the Columbus Avenue Building; and he had also another studio in London, for these huge decorations, at The Avenue Studios, 75 Fulham Road.

In 1914, at the outset of the War, he was on holiday in Austria, and he witnessed with horror the disintegration of the Europe he had known. He gave without stint; and when the opportunity offered went to the front to record his impressions at first hand. In his famous war picture "Gassed" (London War Museum) he testified to his deep admiration for the invincible pluck of the British soldier. In the background, through the waning light of the late afternoon, we see the ground carpeted by writhing figures; while a tragic procession of wounded men, blinded by gas, staggers towards the dressing station.

The quieter life in London suited Sargent's temperament better than the more lavish social exactions of Boston. In London finally he was to know an honour no living painter had hitherto experienced. The magnificent series of portraits, bequeathed to the nation by Asher Wertheimer, were hung in the National Gallery. A wing in the Tate Gallery, the gift of Sir Joseph Duveen, now houses these, and such other works by Sargent as are already in national possession—the portraits of Lord Ribblesdale (1902), of Coventry Patmore (1895), of Henry James (1914), Octavia Hill (1899), of Ellen Terry as Lady Macbeth (1899), and many others. Sargent is represented in the principal galleries of the world, but the Metropolitan in New York, and the Boston Fine Arts Museum, are particularly rich in fine examples. The decorations for the Boston Library, for the Boston Fine Arts Museum, for the Harvard Memorial Chapel, absorbed him till, fortunate to the end, death overtook him in his sleep, in his 70th year, with no evident diminution of his forces, no weakening of his physical or mental energy.

In looking back over his immense achievement, his extraordinary vitality strikes one first. His slightest sketch pulsates with life. The beautiful suavity of his style, acquired through the iron discipline of years, never sacrificed its spontaneity. He shirked no labour, and knew no greater joy in life than this concentration on work provided him. He would paint a head twenty times over in order to establish an appearance of fluency and ease. His insight into character went far beyond ordinary perception either of artists or of laymen; at its best it became a miracle of intuition as of skill in its rendition.

What he lacked entirely may be called, for lack of a better term, the feminine touch. Beauty or charm that were not in direct relation with his subject he could not entertain. This severity was his strength in contradistinction to the weakness of much of the art of the period which perpetuated the worship of purely irrelevant sweetness.

Taken as a whole his portraits, drawn from every class of society, in their great number and variety, in the boldness, the wit, the keen incisiveness and the distinction of their presentation, must come to be considered an epitome of the age he lived in—of its stateliness and splendour, of its elegance and grace, of its pretentiousness and its vulgarity. The human panorama, in its every manifestation, he found endlessly diverting and delineating it as he did with uncompromising directness, his work, in its unflinching yet happy realism, bears the very stamp of truth.

Mr. Sargent had never married. He had been a devoted son and brother, and was survived by his two sisters, Emily Sargent and Mrs. Francis Ormond. His body was interred at Brookwood cemetery. Memorial services were held at Westminster abbey, at the request of the Royal academy, and a replica in bronze of the Crucifixion, with a memorial tablet, has been placed in the Crypt of St. Paul's cathedral.   (J. HN.)

SARGON, more correctly SARRU-KINU ("the legitimate king"), an Assyrian general who, on the death of Shalmaneser IV, during the siege of Samaria, seized the crown on the 12th of Tebet 722 B.C. He claimed to be the descendant of the early kings, and accordingly assumed the name of a famous king of Babylonia who had reigned about 2,000 years before him. His first achievement was the capture of Samaria, 27,200 of its inhabitants being carried into captivity. Meanwhile Babylon had revolted under a Chaldaean prince, Merodach-baladan, who maintained his power there for 12 years. In 720 B.C. Yahu-bihdi of Hamath led Arpad, Damascus and Palestine into revolt: this was suppressed, and the Philistines and Egyptians were defeated at Raphia (mod. er-Rafa). In 719 B.C. Sargon defeated the Minni to the east of Armenia, and in 717 overthrew the combined forces of the Hittites and Moschi (Old Testament Meshech). The Hittite city of Carchemish was placed under an Assyrian governor, and its trade passed into Assyrian hands.

The following year Sargon was attacked by a great confederacy of the northern nations—Ararat, the Moschi, Tibareni, etc.—and in the course of the campaign he marched into the land of the Medes in the direction of the Caspian. In 715 B.C. the Minni were defeated, and one of their chiefs, Dāyuku or Daiukku (Deioces), transported to Hamath. In 714 B.C. the army of Rusas of Ararat was annihilated, and a year later five Median chiefs, including Arbaku (Arbaces) became tributary. Cilicia and the Tibareni also submitted as well as the city of Malatia, eastern Cappadocia being annexed to the Assyrian empire. A league was formed between Merodach-baladan and the princes of the west, but before the confederates could move, an Assyrian army was sent against Ashdod, and Edom, Moab and Judah submitted to Sargon, who was free to turn his attention to Babylonia, and Merodach-baladan was driven from Babylon, where Sargon was crowned king. Shortly after this Sargon sent a statue of himself to Cyprus and annexed the kingdom of Commagene. He was murdered in 705 B.C., probably in the palace he had built at Dur-Sargina, now Khorsabad, which was excavated by P. E. Botta.

BIBLIOGRAPHY.—F. Thureau-Dangin, *Huitième Campagne de Sargon* (714 B.C.) (1912); A. T. Olmstead, *History of Assyria* (1923), 206–208; Sydney Smith, *Cambridge Ancient History*, vol. iii (1925), 43–60. For Sargon the Ancient, founder of the Accadian Empire, *see* S. Langdon, *Cambridge Ancient History*, vol. i (1923), 402–408.

SARI BAIR, BATTLE OF, 1915: *see* DARDANELLES CAMPAIGN.

SARIPUL or SIRIPUL, a town and khanate of Afghanistan. The town lies 100 mi. S.W. of Balkh; estimated pop. 18,000. Two-thirds of the people are Uzbegs and the rest Hazaras. The khanate, which lies between Balkh and Maimana, was allotted to the Afghans by the Anglo-Russian boundary agreement of 1873.

SARI QAMISH, BATTLE OF, 1914. This battle in Dec. 1914, between the Russians and the Turks in the Caucasus, is described under CAUCASUS, CAMPAIGN IN THE. It arose out of Enver Pasha's rash project for a wide enveloping manoeuvre in midwinter, and although almost carried to success by the astonishing fortitude of the Turkish troops, ended in a disaster which almost annihilated the Turkish 3rd army.

SARK (SERCQ), one of the smaller Channel Islands, lying 7 mi. east of Guernsey, is 3 mi. long and 1½ mi. in extreme breadth. Area 2 sq.mi.; pop. (1951) 563. It is divided into Great Sark (the more northerly) and Little Sark, connected by the Coupée, an isthmus more than 100 yd. long but only 6 ft. wide, with precipices going down 300 ft. on each side to the sea. The coastal scenery is of considerable beauty. Creux, the harbour of Sark, on the east side, communicates with the interior solely by two tunnels, one dating from 1588, the other from 1868. There is another harbour (opened 1949) at La Masseline. The island is highest (375 ft.) about the centre of Great Sark, where stand the church, a few dwellings and a mill. Groups of houses at La Ville,

Valette, Collinette, Dixcart and in Little Sark, suggest much earlier settlements. About the 6th century the Celtic saint, St. Magloire, founded a monastery there. There is little record of permanent settlement until the 16th century, when Elizabeth I granted the island as a manor to Helier de Carteret who, as its first seigneur, repeopled the island, dividing the land among 40 farmers. De Carteret set up a scheme of government—partly manorial, partly parochial—which still prevails; the lordship of the island is still in the hands of a hereditary seigneur (or dame in the event of female inheritance). The island is included in the bailiwick of Guernsey, but has a court of justice of its own. There is also a court of chief pleas, whose members are the holders of the 40 original properties, and whose president is the seneschal, the principal government officer and judge of the island, appointed by the seigneur. Farming, fishing and the tourist trade are the chief occupations.

(B. C. DE G.)

SARMATAE or **SAUROMATAE** (the second form is mostly used by the earlier Greek writers, the other by the later Greeks and the Romans), a people whom Herodotus (iv. 21, 117) puts on the eastern boundary of Scythia (*q.v.*) beyond the Tanais (*Don*). He says expressly that they were not pure Scythians, but, being descended from young Scythian men and Amazons (iv. 110-117), spoke an impure dialect and allowed their women to take part in war and to enjoy much freedom. Hippocrates classes them as Scythian. From this we may infer that they spoke a language cognate with the Scythic. The greater part of the barbarian names occurring in the inscriptions of Olbia, Tanais, and Panticapaeum are supposed to be Sarmatian, and as they have been well explained from the Iranian language now spoken by the Ossetes of the Caucasus, these are supposed to be the representatives of the Sarmatae and can be shown to have a direct connection with the Alani (*q.v.*), one of their tribes. By the 3rd century B.C. the Sarmatae appear to have supplanted the Scyths proper in the plains of south Russia, where they remained dominant until the Gothic and Hunnish invasions. Their chief divisions were the Rhoxolani (*q.v.*), the Iazyges (*q.v.*), with whom the Romans had to deal on the Danube and Theiss, and the Alani. M. I. Rostovtzev has put serious difficulties in the way of the assumption that Sauromatae and Sarmatae were actually the same people; *see* his *Iranians and Greeks in S. Russia* (1922), and *Skifiya i Bospor* (1925).

SARMIENTO, DOMINGO FAUSTINO (1811-1888), Argentine educator, author, journalist and president of the republic, was born in San Juan de la Frontera on Feb. 14, 1811. He had little formal education and at an early age, because of his political opinions, took refuge in Chile, where he earned a precarious livelihood. In 1836 he returned to San Juan and was imprisoned for propaganda, but escaped to Chile in 1839 and engaged in journalism, editing *El Mercurio* of Valparaiso and founding *El Nacional* in Santiago. In 1841 he went back to Argentina to join the resistance to the dictator Rosas, but perceiving it to be useless, returned to Chile, where he added politics to journalism, founded the first Chilean normal school, was a member of the faculty of the university and waged violent polemics in behalf of liberal government and public instruction. His interest in public education was intense and in 1846 led him to make a several years' visit to Europe, Africa and the United States to study educational methods. In 1852 Gen. Urquiza's rebellion against Rosas drew him once more to Argentina and on Feb. 3, 1852, he assisted in overthrowing the dictator at the battle of Monte Caseros. Unwilling, however, to acknowledge Urquiza's political domination, he withdrew to Chile, but in 1856 reappeared in Buenos Aires, thrust himself into the journalistic arena and commenced a farsighted campaign for public education. Elected governor of San Juan in 1862, while representing Buenos Aires in the national senate, he surrendered this position in 1864 to become minister to Chile and Peru and, in 1865, to the United States. While there he was elected president of Argentina for the term Oct. 12, 1868, to Oct. 12, 1874. As president he maintained political, economic and social stability, successfully terminated the War of the Triple Alliance against Paraguay (1865-70) and completely reorganized and amplified the national system of public instruction. Soon after he retired from the presidency he was re-elected to the senate and then appointed director of education in the province of Buenos Aires. He continued to maintain an aggressive journalistic stand on all debatable questions. In 1878 he became editor of *El Nacional;* was appointed minister of the interior in President Avellaneda's government in 1879 and in 1881 was made national superintendent of schools, in which capacity he was able to carry to its logical conclusion much of his long campaign for universal education. He died in Asunción, Paraguay, on Sept. 11, 1888. In the first instance an educator, Sarmiento achieved fame also as an author. His complete works fill 52 volumes, and *Facundo ó la civilización y la barbarie* (1845), a portrait of Argentina in the epoch of Rosas, is the best known work in Argentina's literature and has been frequently translated. Notable also are: *Recuerdos de provincias* (Santiago de Chile, 1850), *Viajes* (Santiago, 1849), *Vida de Lincoln* (New York, 1866), *Las escuelas: base de la prosperidad y de la república en los Estados Unidos* (New York, 1866).

(W. B. P.)

See J. G. Guerra, *Sarmiento su vida y sus obras* (Santiago de Chile, 1901); J. P. Paz Soldan, *Domingo Faustino Sarmiento* (Buenos Aires, 1911); A. Coester, *The Literary History of Spanish America* (New York, 1916); R. Blanco-Fombona, *Grandes escritores de América* (Madrid, 1917); *Enciclopedia Universal Ilustrada* (Madrid, 1927).

SARNATH, 4 mi. from Benares city, in India, is the scene of the richest of the recent archaeological discoveries in the United Provinces. It was known to occupy the place of the Deer Park, where Gautama Buddha first launched his reforming faith and preached the "eight-fold path"; but except for a vast dismantled stupa, there was, at the beginning of this century, little indication of its buried treasures. The Chinese pilgrim, Hiuen Tsang, in the 7th century, had visited the Deer Park, and described a monastery for 1,500 monks, a stupa, and in front of it a memorial pillar which Asoka had built, 70 feet high and polished like a mirror. In 1904, with Lord Curzon's encouragement, the ruins of Sarnath were opened, and the work of excavation went on for years. Asoka's monumental column is broken and fallen, though its surface retains its polish. A museum houses the finds of diggers.

SARNEN, the capital of the western half (or Obwalden) of the Swiss canton of Unterwalden. It stands 1,558 ft. above sea-level, at the north end of the lake of Sarnen (3 sq.mi. in extent), and is 4½ mi. by rail from Alpnachstad, its port on the lake of Lucerne. Pop. (1950), 6,199. In the archives is preserved the famous ms. the *White Book of Sarnen*, which contains one of the earliest known versions of the Tell legend. (*See* TELL, WILLIAM.)

SARNIA, a city and port of entry, Ontario, Can., capital of Lambton county, 55 mi. N.E. of Detroit, Mich., on the left bank of the river St. Clair at the foot of Lake Huron. Pop. (1951) 34,697. It is on the Canadian National and the Chesapeake and Ohio railways, and is an important transshipping point for Great Lakes steamers carrying lumber, grain, coal and package freight. It contains a large oil refinery which handles the greater part of the product of the Ontario oil region, and is headquarters of the massive government-owned Polymer corporation engaged in the production of synthetic rubber. The Canadian National railway crosses the river at this point by the St. Clair tunnel, 6,025 ft. long or, including the approaches, 2¼ mi., which connects with the U.S. city of Port Huron, Mich.; motor traffic uses the Blue Water bridge.

SARNO (anc. *Sarnus*), a town of Campania, Italy, in the province of Salerno, 15 mi. N.E. from that city and 30 mi. E. of Naples by the main railway. Pop. (1951) 26,290 (commune). It lies at the foot of the Apennines, 92 ft. above sea-level, near the sources of the Sarno (anc. *Sarnus*), a stream connected by canal with Pompeii and the sea. Teias was defeated here by Narses in A.D. 552. Sarno has the ruins of a mediaeval castle, which belonged to Count Francesco Coppola, who took an important part in the conspiracy of the barons against Ferdinand of Aragon in 1485. Walter of Brienne is buried in the ancient church of S. Maria della Foce rebuilt in 1701. The travertine which forms round the springs of the Sarno was used even at Pompeii as building material.

SARONNO, a town of Lombardy, Italy, in the province of Milan, from which city it is distant 13 mi. N.N.W. by rail. Pop.

(1936), 15,782 (town); 29,017 (commune). The pilgrimage church of the Madonna dei Miracoli, begun in 1498 by Vincenzo dell' Orto, has a dome of rich architecture; the campanile dates from 1516. Internally it is decorated with fine frescoes by Gaudenzio Ferrari, representing a concert of angels, while those in the choir are by Bernardino Luini and are among his finest works. The place is well known for its gingerbread (*amaretti*) and is also a manufacturing town.

SARPEDON, in Greek legend, son of Zeus and Laodameia, Lycian prince and hero of the Trojan war. He fought on the side of the Trojans and was slain by Patroclus. Apollo rescued his body and, by the command of Zeus, handed it over to Sleep and Death, by whom it was conveyed for burial to Lycia, where a sanctuary (Sarpedoneum) was erected in his honour. In later tradition, Sarpedon was the son of Zeus and Europa and the brother of Minos. Having been expelled from Crete by the latter, he and his comrades sailed for Asia, where he finally became king of Lycia.

　　See Homer, *Iliad*, v. 479, xii. 292, 419–683; Apollodorus iii. 3 ff.

SARPI, PAOLO (1552–1623), Venetian patriot, scholar and church reformer, was born at Venice, on Aug. 14, 1552. Against the wish of his relatives, he entered the order of the Servi di Maria, a minor Augustinian congregation of Florentine origin, at the age of thirteen. He assumed the name of Paolo, by which, with the epithet *Servita*, he was always known to his contemporaries. In 1570 he sustained no fewer than three hundred and eighteen theses at a disputation in Mantua, with such applause that the duke made him court theologian. Sarpi spent four years at Mantua, applying himself to mathematics and the Oriental languages. After leaving Mantua, he repaired to Milan, where he enjoyed the protection of Cardinal Borromeo, but was soon transferred by his superiors to Venice, as professor of philosophy at the Servite convent. In 1579 he was sent to Rome on business connected with the reform of his order, which occupied him several years, and brought him into intimate relations with three successive popes, as well as the grand inquisitor and other persons of influence. He returned to Venice in 1588, and passed the next seventeen years in study, occasionally interrupted by the part he was compelled to take in the internal disputes of his community. He was twice recommended for preferment to a bishopric, but the pope refused his sanction in each case. Sarpi, therefore, continued to occupy himself with mathematics, metaphysics and anatomy. The only certain physiological discovery which can be safely attributed to him is that of the contractility of the iris. It must be remembered, however, that his treatises on scientific subjects are lost, and only known from imperfect abstracts.

In the dispute which arose between Paul V. (*q.v.*) and Venice on the extent of the papal jurisdiction in the Venetian State, Sarpi prepared on behalf of the republic a memoir, pointing out that the threatened censures might be met in two ways—*de facto*, by prohibiting their publication, and *de jure*, by an appeal to a general council. The document was received with universal applause, and Sarpi was immediately made canonist and theological counsellor to the republic. In the following April Paul excommunicated the Venetians and sought to lay their dominions under an interdict. Sarpi now republished the anti-papal opinions of the famous canonist Gerson. In an anonymous tract published shortly afterwards (*Risposta di un Dottore in Teologia*) he laid down principles which struck at the very root of the pope's authority in secular things. This book was promptly put upon the *Index*, and the republication of Gerson was attacked by Bellarmine with a severity which obliged Sarpi to reply in an *Apologia*. The *Considerazioni sulle censure* and the *Trattato dell' interdetto*, the latter partly prepared under his direction by other theologians, speedily followed. Numerous other pamphlets appeared, inspired or controlled by Sarpi, who had received the further appointment of censor over all that should be written at Venice in defence of the republic. The Venetian clergy, a few religious orders excepted, disregarded the interdict, and discharged their functions as usual. The Catholic powers refused to be drawn into the quarrel. At length (April 1607) a compromise was arranged through the mediation of the king of France. which. while salving over the

pope's dignity, conceded the points at issue.

The republic rewarded Sarpi by making him state counsellor in jurisprudence, and giving him access to the state archives. On Oct. 5 he was attacked by a band of assassins and left for dead, but the wounds were not mortal. The bravos found a refuge in the papal territories. "Agnosco stylum Curiae Romanae," Sarpi himself pleasantly said, when his surgeon commented upon the ragged and inartistic character of the wounds.

The remainder of Sarpi's life was spent peacefully in his cloister, though plots against him continued to be formed, and he occasionally spoke of taking refuge in England. In 1615 a dispute between the Venetian government and the Inquisition respecting the prohibition of a book led him to write on the history and procedure of the Venetian Inquisition; and in 1619 his chief literary work, the *History of the Council of Trent*, was printed at London under the name of Pietro Soave Polano, an anagram of Paolo Sarpi Veneto. Sarpi never acknowledged his authorship. He survived the publication four years, dying on Jan. 15, 1623. His posthumous *History of the Interdict* was printed at Venice the year after his death, with the disguised imprint of Lyons.

Great light has been thrown upon Sarpi's real belief and the motives of his conduct by the letters of Christoph von Dohna, envoy of Christian, prince of Anhalt, to Venice, published by Moritz Ritter in the *Briefe und Acten zur Geschichte des dreissigjährigen Krieges*, vol. ii. (Munich, 1874). These letters seem to show that Sarpi was a patriot first and a religious reformer afterwards. His scientific attainments must have been great; and, though Sarpi did not, as has been asserted, invent the telescope, he immediately turned it to practical account by constructing a map of the moon.

Sarpi's life was written by his enthusiastic disciple, Father Fulgenzio Micanzio, whose work is meagre and uncritical. Bianchi-Giovini's biography (1836) is greatly marred by digressions, and is inferior in some respects to that by Arabella Georgina Campbell (1869), which is enriched by numerous references to MSS. unknown to Bianchi-Giovini. T. A. Trollope's *Paul the Pope and Paul the Friar* (1861) is in the main a mere abstract of Bianchi-Giovini, but adds a spirited account of the conclave of Paul V. The incidents of the Venetian dispute from day to day are related in the contemporary diaries published by Enrico Cornet (Vienna, 1859). Giusto Fontanini's *Storia arcana della vita di Pietro Sarpi* (1863), a bitter libel, is nevertheless important for the letters of Sarpi it contains, as Griselini's *Memorie e aneddote* (1760) is from the author's access to Sarpi's unpublished writings, afterwards unfortunately destroyed by fire. Foscarini's *History of Venetian Literature* is important on the same account. Sarpi's memoirs on state affairs remain in the Venetian archives. Portions of his correspondence have been printed at various times, and inedited letters from him are of frequent occurrence in public libraries. The King's library in the British Museum has a valuable collection of tracts in the Interdict controversy, formed by Consul Smith.

[In addition to the above works *see* Balan, *Fra Paolo Sarpi* (Venice, 1887) and Pascolato, *Fra Paolo Sarpi* (Milan, 1893). Some hitherto unpublished letters of Sarpi were edited by Karl Benrath and published, under the title *Paolo Sarpi. Neue Briefe, 1608–16* (at Leipzig in 1909).]

(R. G.)

SARPSBORG, a seaport and manufacturing town of Norway, in Smaalenene *amt* (county), 68 m. S.S.E. of Oslo on the Gothenburg railway. Pop. (1930) 12,401. It became important through the utilization of the falls in the river Glommen for driving sawmills and generating electric power. The Sarpsfos is a majestic fall, descending 74 ft. with a width of 120 ft., and providing 50,000 h.p. for factories for calcium carbide (used for manufacturing acetylene gas), paper, cellulose, zinc, wood pulp and aluminium; and spinning and weaving mills. The port is at Sannesund; its quays can be reached by vessels drawing 20 feet. The town was founded in the 11th century, and destroyed by the Swedes in 1567. The existing town dates from 1839.

SARRACENIA or **SIDE-SADDLE FLOWER:** *see* PITCHER PLANTS.

SARRAIL, MAURICE PAUL EMMANUEL (1856–1929), French soldier, was born at Carcassonne (Aude) on April 6, 1856. He graduated from the St. Cyr Military academy in 1877, and after a series of promotions was appointed in 1907 director of infantry at the war office. In 1911 he was promoted general of division and on Nov. 1, 1913, was given command of the 8th army corps, being later (April 24, 1914) transferred to the 6th corps which he commanded on the outbreak of World

War I. On Sept. 2, 1914, after leading the 6th corps with credit at the battle of the Frontiers, he succeeded Ruffey as commander of the 3rd army which played a brilliant part during the retreat to the Marne. During the trench warfare operations of 1914–15 he was less successful, however, and he was transferred to the chief command of the French army of the east. He became commander in chief of the Allied forces on that front (*see* SALONIKA CAMPAIGNS 1915–18). After the war of 1914–18 he devoted himself to politics and stood, unsuccessfully, as radical deputy for Paris. He was, in Jan. 1925, appointed high commissioner in Syria. His administration was severely criticized; during the rebellion which broke out among the Jebel Druses he bombarded the native quarter of Damascus. In Oct. 1925, as a result of the report by General Dupont, he was relieved of his post. He died on March 23, 1929.

See P. Coblentz, *The Silence of Sarrail* (London, 1930).

SARRAUT, ALBERT PIERRE (1872–   ), French politician, was born at Bordeaux, graduated in law, and became *conseiller-général* of the canton of Lezignan. He attached himself to the radical-socialist group, and worked on the *Dépêche de Toulouse,* of which his brother, Maurice Sarraut, was one of the editors. He was poet and author as well as journalist. In 1909 he was made under secretary at the war ministry in the first Briand cabinet. In 1911 he was appointed to succeed Klobukowski as governor general of Indo-China. On the outbreak of war in 1914 he returned to France, and became minister of public instruction; later he served in the 30th infantry regiment, and then became again governor general of Indo-China. He was wounded at Hanoi (Tonkin) by a shot fired by a discharged official. In 1922 he became minister for the colonies in the Poincaré government, and in that capacity drew up an important scheme for the develop-

ment of each of the units of the French colonial empire. He was sent in 1925 to Angora as French ambassador for a short time. In 1926 he was elected senator. He held office under Poincaré, 1927–28, and Herriot, 1932; and was premier from Oct. to Nov. 1933. In 1934 he was minister of the interior in the Doumergue government. He was premier from January to June 1936 when he had to face the crisis caused by the German reoccupation of the Rhineland. From June 1937 he held various ministerial posts in successive governments until June 1940. Deported to Germany during World War II, Sarraut was liberated in 1945.

SARRAZIN, JACQUES (1588–1660), French painter, born at Noyon in 1588. He went to Rome where he obtained employment from Cardinal Aldobrandini at Frascati, where he won the friendship of Domenichino, with whom he afterward worked on the high altar of St. Andrea della Valle. He decorated the great portal and the dome of the western façade of the interior court of the Louvre. Sarrazin died on Dec. 3, 1660.

SARREBOURG, a town of France, in the department of Moselle, 44 mi. northwest from Strasbourg. Pop. (1946) 8,667. It has been identified with the Pons Saravi of the Romans; it belonged to the bishops of Metz and the dukes of Lorraine.

SARREGUEMINES (SAARGEMÜND), a town of France, in the department of Moselle at the confluence of the Blies and the Saar, 40 mi. E. of Metz, 60 mi. N.W. of Strasbourg by rail. Pop. (1946) 13,375. Sarreguemines, originally a Roman settlement, obtained civic rights early in the 13th century. In 1297 it was ceded by the count of Saarbrücken to the duke of Lorraine, and passed with Lorraine in 1766 to France, being transferred to Germany in 1871 and to France in 1919. It makes faience, plush, velvet, porcelain and earthenware.

END OF VOLUME NINETEEN

PRINTED IN THE U. S. A. BY R. R. DONNELLEY & SONS CO.